# Summa Theologica

# Summa Theologica

## ST. THOMAS AQUINAS

COYOTE CANYON PRESS
2018

Published by Coyote Canyon Press 2018

Claremont, California



Complete American Edition

Translated by Fathers of the English Dominican Province

Summa Theologica, Part I ("Prima Pars")

Summa Theologica, Part I-II ("Pars Prima Secundae")

Summa Theologica, Part II-II "(Secunda Secundae")

Summa Theologica, Part III ("Tertia Pars")

Cover design and drawing of Thomas Aquinas
by Thomas Fasano



ISBN 978-1-7321903-2-0
Printed in the United States of America

# Table of Contents

# SUMMA THEOLOGICA PART I ("Prima Pars")

## PROLOGUE

Because the Master of Catholic Truth ought not only to teach the proficient, but also to instruct beginners (according to the Apostle: As Unto Little Ones in Christ, I Gave You Milk to Drink, Not Meat— 1 Cor. iii. 1, 2)—we purpose in this book to treat of whatever belongs to the Christian Religion, in such a way as may tend to the instruction of beginners. We have considered that students in this Science have not seldom been hampered by what they have found written by other authors, partly on account of the multiplication of useless questions, articles, and arguments; partly also because those things that are needful for them to know are not taught according to the order of the subject-matter, but according as the plan of the book might require, or the occasion of the argument offer; partly, too, because frequent repetition brought weariness and confusion to the minds of the readers.

Endeavoring to avoid these and other like faults, we shall try, by God's help, to set forth whatever is included in this Sacred Science as briefly and clearly as the matter itself may allow.

SUMMA THEOLOGICA

## QUESTION 1

THE NATURE AND EXTENT OF SACRED DOCTRINE (in Ten Articles)

To place our purpose within proper limits, we first endeavor to investigate the nature and extent of this sacred doctrine. Concerning this there are ten points of inquiry:

(1) Whether it is necessary?

(2) Whether it is a science?

(3) Whether it is one or many?

(4) Whether it is speculative or practical?

(5) How it is compared with other sciences?

(6) Whether it is the same as wisdom?

(7) Whether God is its subject-matter?

(8) Whether it is a matter of argument?

(9) Whether it rightly employs metaphors and similes?

(10) Whether the Sacred Scripture of this doctrine may be expounded in different senses?

FIRST ARTICLE [I, Q. 1, Art. 1]

Whether, besides Philosophy, any Further Doctrine Is Required?

Objection 1: It seems that, besides philosophical science, we have no need of any further knowledge. For man should not seek to know what is above reason: "Seek not the things that are too high for thee" (Ecclus. 3:22). But whatever is not above reason is fully treated of in philosophical science. Therefore any other knowledge besides philosophical science is superfluous.

Obj. 2: Further, knowledge can be concerned only with being, for nothing can be known, save what is true; and all that is, is true. But everything that is, is treated of in philosophical science—even God Himself; so that there is a part of philosophy called theology, or the divine science, as Aristotle has proved (Metaph. vi). Therefore, besides philosophical science, there is no need of any further knowledge.

*On the contrary,* It is written (2 Tim. 3:16): "All Scripture inspired of God is profitable to teach, to reprove, to correct, to instruct in justice." Now Scripture, inspired of God, is no part of philosophical science, which has been built up by human reason. Therefore it is useful that besides philosophical science, there should be other knowledge, i.e. inspired of God.

*I answer that,* It was necessary for man's salvation that there should be a knowledge revealed by God besides philosophical science built up by human reason. Firstly, indeed, because man is directed to God, as to an end that surpasses the grasp of his reason: "The eye hath not seen, O God, besides Thee, what things Thou hast prepared for them that wait for Thee" (Isa. 66:4). But the end must first be known by men who are to direct their thoughts and actions to the end. Hence it was necessary for the salvation of man that certain truths which exceed human reason should be made known to him by divine revelation. Even as regards those truths about God which human reason could have discovered, it was necessary that man should be taught by a divine revelation; because the truth about God such as reason could discover, would only be known by a few, and that after a long time, and with the admixture of many errors. Whereas man's whole salvation, which is in God, depends upon the knowledge of this truth. Therefore, in order that the salvation of men might be brought about more fitly and more surely, it was necessary that they should be taught divine truths by divine revelation. It was therefore necessary that besides philosophical science built up by reason, there should be a sacred science learned through revelation.

Reply Obj. 1: Although those things which are beyond man's knowledge may not be sought for by man through his reason, nevertheless, once they are revealed by God, they must be accepted by faith. Hence the sacred text continues, "For many things are shown to thee above the understanding of man" (Ecclus. 3:25). And in this, the sacred science consists.

Reply Obj. 2: Sciences are differentiated according to the various means through which knowledge is obtained. For the astronomer and the physicist both may prove the same conclusion: that the earth, for instance, is round: the astronomer by means of mathematics (i.e. abstracting from matter), but the physicist by means of matter itself. Hence there is no reason why those things which may be learned from philosophical science, so far as they can be known by natural reason, may not also be taught us by another science so far as they fall within revelation. Hence theology included in sacred doctrine differs in kind from that theology which is part of philosophy.

SECOND ARTICLE [I, Q. 1, Art. 2]

Whether Sacred Doctrine Is a Science?

Objection 1: It seems that sacred doctrine is not a science. For every science proceeds from self-evident principles. But sacred doctrine proceeds from articles of faith which are not self-evident, since their truth is not admitted by all: "For all men have not faith" (2 Thess. 3:2). Therefore sacred doctrine is not a science.

Obj. 2: Further, no science deals with individual facts. But this sacred science treats of individual facts, such as the deeds of Abraham, Isaac and Jacob and such like. Therefore sacred doctrine is not a science.

*On the contrary,* Augustine says (De Trin. xiv, 1) "to this science alone belongs that whereby saving faith is begotten, nourished, protected and strengthened." But this can be said of no science except sacred doctrine. Therefore sacred doctrine is a science.

*I answer that,* Sacred doctrine is a science. We must bear in mind that there are two kinds of sciences. There are some which proceed from a principle known by the natural light of intelligence, such as arithmetic and geometry and the like. There are some which proceed from principles known by the light of a higher science: thus the science of perspective proceeds from principles established by geometry, and music from principles established by arithmetic. So it is that sacred doctrine is a science because it proceeds from principles established by the light of a higher science, namely, the science of God and the blessed. Hence, just as the musician accepts on authority the principles taught him by the mathematician, so sacred science is established on principles revealed by God.

Reply Obj. 1: The principles of any science are either in themselves self-evident, or reducible to the conclusions of a higher science; and such, as we have said, are the principles of sacred doctrine.

Reply Obj. 2: Individual facts are treated of in sacred doctrine, not because it is concerned with them principally, but they are introduced rather both as examples to be followed in our lives (as in moral sciences) and in order to establish the authority of those men through whom the divine revelation, on which this sacred scripture or doctrine is based, has come down to us.

THIRD ARTICLE [I, Q. 1, Art. 3]

Whether Sacred Doctrine Is One Science?

Objection 1: It seems that sacred doctrine is not one science; for according to the Philosopher (Poster. i) "that science is one which treats only of one class of subjects." But the creator and the creature, both of whom are treated of in sacred doctrine, cannot be grouped together under one class of subjects. Therefore sacred doctrine is not one science.

Obj. 2: Further, in sacred doctrine we treat of angels, corporeal creatures and human morality. But these belong to separate philosophical sciences. Therefore sacred doctrine cannot be one science.

*On the contrary,* Holy Scripture speaks of it as one science: "Wisdom gave him the knowledge [scientiam] of holy things" (Wis. 10:10).

*I answer that,* Sacred doctrine is one science. The unity of a faculty or habit is to be gauged by its object, not indeed, in its material aspect, but as regards the precise formality under which it is an object. For example, man, ass, stone agree in the one precise formality of being colored; and color is the formal object of sight. Therefore, because Sacred Scripture considers things precisely under the formality of being divinely revealed, whatever has been divinely revealed possesses the one precise formality of the object of this science; and therefore is included under sacred doctrine as under one science.

Reply Obj. 1: Sacred doctrine does not treat of God and creatures equally, but of God primarily, and of creatures only so far as they are referable to God as their beginning or end. Hence the unity of this science is not impaired.

Reply Obj. 2: Nothing prevents inferior faculties or habits from being differentiated by something which falls under a higher faculty or habit as well; because the higher faculty or habit regards the object in its more universal formality, as the object of the *common sense* is whatever affects the senses, including, therefore, whatever is visible or audible. Hence the *common sense,* although one faculty, extends to all the objects of the five senses. Similarly, objects which are the subject-matter of different philosophical sciences can yet be treated of by this one single sacred science under one aspect precisely so far as they can be included in revelation. So that in this way, sacred doctrine bears, as it were, the stamp of the divine science which is one and simple, yet extends to everything.

FOURTH ARTICLE [I, Q. 1, Art. 4]

Whether Sacred Doctrine Is a Practical Science?

Objection 1: It seems that sacred doctrine is a practical science; for a practical science is that which ends in action according to the Philosopher (Metaph. ii). But sacred doctrine is ordained to action: "Be ye doers of the word, and not hearers only" (James 1:22). Therefore sacred doctrine is a practical science.

Obj. 2: Further, sacred doctrine is divided into the Old and the New Law. But law implies a moral science which is a practical science. Therefore sacred doctrine is a practical science.

*On the contrary,* Every practical science is concerned with human operations; as moral science is concerned with human acts, and architecture with buildings. But sacred doctrine is chiefly concerned with God, whose handiwork is especially man. Therefore it is not a practical but a speculative science.

*I answer that,* Sacred doctrine, being one, extends to things which belong to different philosophical sciences because it considers in each the same formal aspect, namely, so far as they can be known through divine revelation. Hence, although among the philosophical sciences one is speculative and another practical, nevertheless sacred doctrine includes both; as God, by one and the same science, knows both Himself and His works. Still, it is speculative rather than practical because it is more concerned with divine things than with human acts; though it does treat even of these latter, inasmuch as man is ordained by them to the perfect knowledge of God in which consists eternal bliss. This is a sufficient answer to the Objections.

FIFTH ARTICLE [I, Q. 1, Art. 5]

Whether Sacred Doctrine Is Nobler than Other Sciences?

Objection 1: It seems that sacred doctrine is not nobler than other sciences; for the nobility of a science depends on the certitude it establishes. But other sciences, the principles of which cannot be doubted, seem to be more certain than sacred doctrine; for its principles—namely, articles of faith—can be doubted. Therefore other sciences seem to be nobler.

Obj. 2: Further, it is the sign of a lower science to depend upon a higher; as music depends on arithmetic. But sacred doctrine does in a sense depend upon philosophical sciences; for Jerome observes, in his Epistle to Magnus, that "the ancient doctors so enriched their books with the ideas and phrases of the philosophers, that thou knowest not what more to admire in them, their profane erudition or their scriptural learning." Therefore sacred doctrine is inferior to other sciences.

*On the contrary,* Other sciences are called the handmaidens of this one: "Wisdom sent her maids to invite to the tower" (Prov. 9:3).

*I answer that,* Since this science is partly speculative and partly practical, it transcends all others speculative and practical. Now one speculative science is said to be nobler than another, either by reason of its greater certitude, or by reason of the higher worth of its subject-matter. In both these respects this science surpasses other speculative sciences; in point of greater certitude, because other sciences derive their certitude from the natural light of human reason, which can err; whereas this derives its certitude from the light of divine knowledge, which cannot be misled: in point of the higher worth of its subject-matter because this science treats chiefly of those things which by their sublimity transcend human reason; while other sciences consider only those things which are within reason's grasp. Of the practical sciences, that one is nobler which is ordained to a further purpose, as political science is nobler than military science; for the good of the army is directed to the good of the State. But the purpose of this science, in so far as it is practical, is eternal bliss; to which as to an ultimate end the purposes of every practical science are directed. Hence it is clear that from every standpoint, it is nobler than other sciences.

Reply Obj. 1: It may well happen that what is in itself the more certain may seem to us the less certain on account of the weakness of our intelligence, "which is dazzled by the clearest objects of nature; as the owl is dazzled by the light of the sun" (Metaph. ii, lect. i). Hence the fact that some happen to doubt about articles of faith is not due to the uncertain nature of the truths, but to the weakness of human intelligence; yet the slenderest knowledge that may be obtained of the highest things is more desirable than the most certain knowledge obtained of lesser things, as is said in *de Animalibus* xi.

Reply Obj. 2: This science can in a sense depend upon the philosophical sciences, not as though it stood in need of them, but only in order to make its teaching clearer. For it accepts its principles not from other sciences, but immediately from God, by revelation. Therefore it does not depend upon other sciences as upon the higher, but makes use of them as of the lesser, and as handmaidens: even so the master sciences make use of the sciences that supply their materials, as political of military science. That it thus uses them is not due to its own defect or insufficiency, but to the defect of our intelligence, which is more easily led by what is known through natural reason (from which proceed the other sciences) to that which is above reason, such as are the teachings of this science.

SIXTH ARTICLE [I, Q. 1, Art. 6]

Whether This Doctrine Is the Same as Wisdom?

Objection 1: It seems that this doctrine is not the same as wisdom. For no doctrine which borrows its principles is worthy of the name of wisdom; seeing that the wise man directs, and is not directed (Metaph. i). But this doctrine borrows its principles. Therefore this science is not wisdom.

Obj. 2: Further, it is a part of wisdom to prove the principles of other sciences. Hence it is called the chief of sciences, as is clear in Ethic. vi. But this doctrine does not prove the principles of other sciences. Therefore it is not the same as wisdom.

Obj. 3: Further, this doctrine is acquired by study, whereas wisdom is acquired by God's inspiration; so that it is numbered among the gifts of the Holy Spirit (Isa. 11:2). Therefore this doctrine is not the same as wisdom.

*On the contrary,* It is written (Deut. 4:6): "This is your wisdom and understanding in the sight of nations."

*I answer that,* This doctrine is wisdom above all human wisdom; not merely in any one order, but absolutely. For since it is the part of a wise man to arrange and to judge, and since lesser matters should be judged in the light of some higher principle, he is said to be wise in any one order who considers the highest principle in that order: thus in the order of building, he who plans the form of the house is called wise and architect, in opposition to the inferior laborers who trim the wood and make ready the stones: "As a wise architect, I have laid the foundation" (1 Cor. 3:10). Again, in the order of all human life, the prudent man is called wise, inasmuch as he directs his acts to a fitting end: "Wisdom is prudence to a man" (Prov. 10: 23). Therefore he who considers absolutely the highest cause of the whole universe, namely God, is most of all called wise. Hence wisdom is said to be the knowledge of divine things, as Augustine says (De Trin. xii, 14). But sacred doctrine essentially treats of God viewed as the highest cause—not only so far as He can be known through creatures just as philosophers knew Him—"That which is known of God is manifest in them" (Rom. 1:19)—but also as far as He is known to Himself alone and revealed to others. Hence sacred doctrine is especially called wisdom.

Reply Obj. 1: Sacred doctrine derives its principles not from any human knowledge, but from the divine knowledge, through which, as through the highest wisdom, all our knowledge is set in order.

Reply Obj. 2: The principles of other sciences either are evident and cannot be proved, or are proved by natural reason through some other science. But the knowledge proper to this science comes through revelation and not through natural reason. Therefore it has no concern to prove the principles of other sciences, but only to judge of them. Whatsoever is found in other sciences contrary to any truth of this science must be condemned as false: "Destroying counsels and every height that exalteth itself against the knowledge of God" (2 Cor. 10:4, 5).

Reply Obj. 3: Since judgment appertains to wisdom, the twofold manner of judging produces a twofold wisdom. A man may judge in one way by inclination, as whoever has the habit of a virtue judges rightly of what concerns that virtue by his very inclination towards it. Hence it is the virtuous man, as we read, who is the measure and rule of human acts. In another way, by knowledge, just as a man learned in moral science might be able to judge rightly about virtuous acts, though he had not the virtue. The first manner of judging divine things belongs to that wisdom which is set down among the gifts of the Holy Ghost: "The spiritual man judgeth all things" (1 Cor. 2:15). And Dionysius says (Div. Nom. ii): "Hierotheus is taught not by mere learning, but by experience of divine things." The second manner of judging belongs to this doctrine which is acquired by study, though its principles are obtained by revelation.

SEVENTH ARTICLE [I, Q. 1, Art. 7]

Whether God Is the Object of This Science?

Objection 1: It seems that God is not the object of this science. For in every science, the nature of its object is presupposed. But this science cannot presuppose the essence of God, for Damascene says (De Fide Orth. i, iv): "It is impossible to define the essence of God." Therefore God is not the object of this science.

Obj. 2: Further, whatever conclusions are reached in any science must be comprehended under the object of the science. But in Holy Writ we reach conclusions not only concerning God, but concerning many other things, such as creatures and human morality. Therefore God is not the object of this science.

*On the contrary,* The object of the science is that of which it principally treats. But in this science, the treatment is mainly about God; for it is called theology, as treating of God. Therefore God is the object of this science.

*I answer that,* God is the object of this science. The relation between a science and its object is the same as that between a habit or faculty and its object. Now properly speaking, the object of a faculty or habit is the thing under the aspect of which all things are referred to that faculty or habit, as man and stone are referred to the faculty of sight in that they are colored. Hence colored things are the proper objects of sight. But in sacred science, all things are treated of under the aspect of God: either because they are God Himself or because they refer to God as their beginning and end. Hence it follows that God is in very truth the object of this science. This is clear also from the principles of this science, namely, the articles of faith, for faith is about God. The object of the principles and of the whole science must be the same, since the whole science is contained virtually in its principles. Some, however, looking to what is treated of in this science, and not to the aspect under which it is treated, have asserted the object of this science to be something other than God—that is, either things and signs; or the works of salvation; or the whole Christ, as the head and members. Of all these things, in truth, we treat in this science, but so far as they have reference to God.

Reply Obj. 1: Although we cannot know in what consists the essence of God, nevertheless in this science we make use of His effects, either of nature or of grace, in place of a definition, in regard to whatever is treated of in this science concerning God; even as in some philosophical sciences we demonstrate something about a cause from its effect, by taking the effect in place of a definition of the cause.

Reply Obj. 2: Whatever other conclusions are reached in this sacred science are comprehended under God, not as parts or species or accidents but as in some way related to Him.

EIGHTH ARTICLE [I, Q. 1, Art. 8]

Whether Sacred Doctrine is a Matter of Argument?

Objection 1: It seems this doctrine is not a matter of argument. For Ambrose says (De Fide 1): "Put arguments aside where faith is sought." But in this doctrine, faith especially is sought: "But these things are written that you may believe" (John 20:31). Therefore sacred doctrine is not a matter of argument.

Obj. 2: Further, if it is a matter of argument, the argument is either from authority or from reason. If it is from authority, it seems unbefitting its dignity, for the proof from authority is the weakest form of proof. But if it is from reason, this is unbefitting its end, because, according to Gregory (Hom. 26), "faith has no merit in those things of which human reason brings its own experience." Therefore sacred doctrine is not a matter of argument.

*On the contrary,* The Scripture says that a bishop should "embrace that faithful word which is according to doctrine, that he may be able to exhort in sound doctrine and to convince the gainsayers" (Titus 1:9).

*I answer that,* As other sciences do not argue in proof of their principles, but argue from their principles to demonstrate other truths in these sciences: so this doctrine does not argue in proof of its principles, which are the articles of faith, but from them it goes on to prove something else; as the Apostle from the resurrection of Christ argues in proof of the general resurrection (1 Cor. 15). However, it is to be borne in mind, in regard to the philosophical sciences, that the inferior sciences neither prove their principles nor dispute with those who deny them, but leave this to a higher science; whereas the highest of them, viz. metaphysics, can dispute with one who denies its principles, if only the opponent will make some concession; but if he concede nothing, it can have no dispute with him, though it can answer his objections. Hence Sacred Scripture, since it has no science above itself, can dispute with one who denies its principles only if the opponent admits some at least of the truths obtained through divine revelation; thus we can argue with heretics from texts in Holy Writ, and against those who deny one article of faith, we can argue from another. If our opponent believes nothing of divine revelation, there is no longer any means of proving the articles of faith by reasoning, but only of answering his objections—if he has any—against faith. Since faith rests upon infallible truth, and since the contrary of a truth can never be demonstrated, it is clear that the arguments brought against faith cannot be demonstrations, but are difficulties that can be answered.

Reply Obj. 1: Although arguments from human reason cannot avail to prove what must be received on faith, nevertheless, this doctrine argues from articles of faith to other truths.

Reply Obj. 2: This doctrine is especially based upon arguments from authority, inasmuch as its principles are obtained by revelation: thus we ought to believe on the authority of those to whom the revelation has been made. Nor does this take away from the dignity of this doctrine, for although the argument from authority based on human reason is the weakest, yet the argument from authority based on divine revelation is the strongest. But sacred doctrine makes use even of human reason, not, indeed, to prove faith (for thereby the merit of faith would come to an end), but to make clear other things that are put forward in this doctrine. Since therefore grace does not destroy nature but perfects it, natural reason should minister to faith as the natural bent of the will ministers to charity. Hence the Apostle says: "Bringing into captivity every understanding unto the obedience of Christ" (2 Cor. 10:5). Hence sacred doctrine makes use also of the authority of philosophers in those questions in which they were able to know the truth by natural reason, as Paul quotes a saying of Aratus: "As some also of your own poets said: For we are also His offspring" (Acts 17:28). Nevertheless, sacred doctrine makes use of these authorities as extrinsic and probable arguments; but properly uses the authority of the canonical Scriptures as an incontrovertible proof, and the authority of the doctors of the Church as one that may properly be used, yet merely as probable. For our faith rests upon the revelation made to the apostles and prophets who wrote the canonical books, and not on the revelations (if any such there are) made to other doctors. Hence Augustine says (Epis. ad Hieron. xix, 1): "Only those books of Scripture which are called canonical have I learned to hold in such honor as to believe their authors have not erred in any way in writing them. But other authors I so read as not to deem everything in their works to be true, merely on account of their having so thought and written, whatever may have been their holiness and learning."

NINTH ARTICLE [I, Q. 1, Art. 9]

Whether Holy Scripture Should Use Metaphors?

Objection 1: It seems that Holy Scripture should not use metaphors. For that which is proper to the lowest science seems not to befit this science, which holds the highest place of all. But to proceed by the aid of various similitudes and figures is proper to poetry, the least of all the sciences. Therefore it is not fitting that this science should make use of such similitudes.

Obj. 2: Further, this doctrine seems to be intended to make truth clear. Hence a reward is held out to those who manifest it: "They that explain me shall have life everlasting" (Ecclus. 24:31). But by such similitudes truth is obscured. Therefore, to put forward divine truths by likening them to corporeal things does not befit this science.

Obj. 3: Further, the higher creatures are, the nearer they approach to the divine likeness. If therefore any creature be taken to represent God, this representation ought chiefly to be taken from the higher creatures, and not from the lower; yet this is often found in Scriptures.

*On the contrary,* It is written (Osee 12:10): "I have multiplied visions, and I have used similitudes by the ministry of the prophets." But to put forward anything by means of similitudes is to use metaphors. Therefore this sacred science may use metaphors.

*I answer that,* It is befitting Holy Writ to put forward divine and spiritual truths by means of comparisons with material things. For God provides for everything according to the capacity of its nature. Now it is natural to man to attain to intellectual truths through sensible objects, because all our knowledge originates from sense. Hence in Holy Writ, spiritual truths are fittingly taught under the likeness of material things. This is what Dionysius says (Coel. Hier. i): "We cannot be enlightened by the divine rays except they be hidden within the covering of many sacred veils." It is also befitting Holy Writ, which is proposed to all without distinction of persons—"To the wise and to the unwise I am a debtor" (Rom. 1:14)—that spiritual truths be expounded by means of figures taken from corporeal things, in order that thereby even the simple who are unable by themselves to grasp intellectual things may be able to understand it.

Reply Obj. 1: Poetry makes use of metaphors to produce a representation, for it is natural to man to be pleased with representations. But sacred doctrine makes use of metaphors as both necessary and useful.

Reply Obj. 2: The ray of divine revelation is not extinguished by the sensible imagery wherewith it is veiled, as Dionysius says (Coel. Hier. i); and its truth so far remains that it does not allow the minds of those to whom the revelation has been made, to rest in the metaphors, but raises them to the knowledge of truths; and through those to whom the revelation has been made others also may receive instruction in these matters. Hence those things that are taught metaphorically in one part of Scripture, in other parts are taught more openly. The very hiding of truth in figures is useful for the exercise of thoughtful minds and as a defense against the ridicule of the impious, according to the words "Give not that which is holy to dogs" (Matt. 7:6).

Reply Obj. 3: As Dionysius says, (Coel. Hier. i) it is more fitting that divine truths should be expounded under the figure of less noble than of nobler bodies, and this for three reasons. Firstly, because thereby men's minds are the better preserved from error. For then it is clear that these things are not literal descriptions of divine truths, which might have been open to doubt had they been expressed under the figure of nobler bodies, especially for those who could think of nothing nobler than bodies. Secondly, because this is more befitting the knowledge of God that we have in this life. For what He is not is clearer to us than what He is. Therefore similitudes drawn from things farthest away from God form within us a truer estimate that God is above whatsoever we may say or think of Him. Thirdly, because thereby divine truths are the better hidden from the unworthy.

TENTH ARTICLE [I, Q. 1, Art. 10]

Whether in Holy Scripture a Word may have Several Senses?

Objection 1: It seems that in Holy Writ a word cannot have several senses, historical or literal, allegorical, tropological or moral, and anagogical. For many different senses in one text produce confusion and deception and destroy all force of argument. Hence no argument, but only fallacies, can be deduced from a multiplicity of propositions. But Holy Writ ought to be able to state the truth without any fallacy. Therefore in it there cannot be several senses to a word.

Obj. 2: Further, Augustine says (De util. cred. iii) that "the Old Testament has a fourfold division as to history, etiology, analogy and allegory." Now these four seem altogether different from the four divisions mentioned in the first objection. Therefore it does not seem fitting to explain the same word of Holy Writ according to the four different senses mentioned above.

Obj. 3: Further, besides these senses, there is the parabolical, which is not one of these four.

*On the contrary,* Gregory says (Moral. xx, 1): "Holy Writ by the manner of its speech transcends every science, because in one and the same sentence, while it describes a fact, it reveals a mystery."

*I answer that,* The author of Holy Writ is God, in whose power it is to signify His meaning, not by words only (as man also can do), but also by things themselves. So, whereas in every other science things are signified by words, this science has the property, that the things signified by the words have themselves also a signification. Therefore that first signification whereby words signify things belongs to the first sense, the historical or literal. That signification whereby things signified by words have themselves also a signification is called the spiritual sense, which is based on the literal, and presupposes it. Now this spiritual sense has a threefold division. For as the Apostle says (Heb. 10:1) the Old Law is a figure of the New Law, and Dionysius says (Coel. Hier. i) "the New Law itself is a figure of future glory." Again, in the New Law, whatever our Head has done is a type of what we ought to do. Therefore, so far as the things of the Old Law signify the things of the New Law, there is the allegorical sense; so far as the things done in Christ, or so far as the things which signify Christ, are types of what we ought to do, there is the moral sense. But so far as they signify what relates to eternal glory, there is the anagogical sense. Since the literal sense is that which the author intends, and since the author of Holy Writ is God, Who by one act comprehends all things by His intellect, it is not unfitting, as Augustine says (Confess. xii), if, even according to the literal sense, one word in Holy Writ should have several senses.

Reply Obj. 1: The multiplicity of these senses does not produce equivocation or any other kind of multiplicity, seeing that these senses are not multiplied because one word signifies several things, but because the things signified by the words can be themselves types of other things. Thus in Holy Writ no confusion results, for all the senses are founded on one—the literal—from which alone can any argument be drawn, and not from those intended in allegory, as Augustine says (Epis. 48). Nevertheless, nothing of Holy Scripture perishes on account of this, since nothing necessary to faith is contained under the spiritual sense which is not elsewhere put forward by the Scripture in its literal sense.

Reply Obj. 2: These three—history, etiology, analogy—are grouped under the literal sense. For it is called history, as Augustine expounds (Epis. 48), whenever anything is simply related; it is called etiology when its cause is assigned, as when Our Lord gave the reason why Moses allowed the putting away of wives—namely, on account of the hardness of men's hearts; it is called analogy whenever the truth of one text of Scripture is shown not to contradict the truth of another. Of these four, allegory alone stands for the three spiritual senses. Thus Hugh of St. Victor (Sacram. iv, 4 Prolog.) includes the anagogical under the allegorical sense, laying down three senses only—the historical, the allegorical, and the tropological.

Reply Obj. 3: The parabolical sense is contained in the literal, for by words things are signified properly and figuratively. Nor is the figure itself, but that which is figured, the literal sense. When Scripture speaks of God's arm, the literal sense is not that God has such a member, but only what is signified by this member, namely operative power. Hence it is plain that nothing false can ever underlie the literal sense of Holy Writ.

## QUESTION 2

THE EXISTENCE OF GOD (In Three Articles)

Because the chief aim of sacred doctrine is to teach the knowledge of God, not only as He is in Himself, but also as He is the beginning of things and their last end, and especially of rational creatures, as is clear from what has been already said, therefore, in our endeavor to expound this science, we shall treat:

(1) Of God;

(2) Of the rational creature's advance towards God;

(3) Of Christ, Who as man, is our way to God.

In treating of God there will be a threefold division, for we shall consider:

(1) Whatever concerns the Divine Essence;

(2) Whatever concerns the distinctions of Persons;

(3) Whatever concerns the procession of creatures from Him.

Concerning the Divine Essence, we must consider:

(1) Whether God exists?

(2) The manner of His existence, or, rather, what is *not* the manner of His existence;

(3) Whatever concerns His operations—namely, His knowledge, will, power.

Concerning the first, there are three points of inquiry:

(1) Whether the proposition "God exists" is self-evident?

(2) Whether it is demonstrable?

(3) Whether God exists?

FIRST ARTICLE [I, Q. 2, Art. 1]

Whether the Existence of God Is Self-Evident?

Objection 1: It seems that the existence of God is self-evident. Now those things are said to be self-evident to us the knowledge of which is naturally implanted in us, as we can see in regard to first principles. But as Damascene says (De Fide Orth. i, 1,3), "the knowledge of God is naturally implanted in all." Therefore the existence of God is self-evident.

Obj. 2: Further, those things are said to be self-evident which are known as soon as the terms are known, which the Philosopher (1 Poster. iii) says is true of the first principles of demonstration. Thus, when the nature of a whole and of a part is known, it is at once recognized that every whole is greater than its part. But as soon as the signification of the word "God" is understood, it is at once seen that God exists. For by this word is signified that thing than which nothing greater can be conceived. But that which exists actually and mentally is greater than that which exists only mentally. Therefore, since as soon as the word "God" is understood it exists mentally, it also follows that it exists actually. Therefore the proposition "God exists" is self-evident.

Obj. 3: Further, the existence of truth is self-evident. For whoever denies the existence of truth grants that truth does not exist: and, if truth does not exist, then the proposition "Truth does not exist" is true: and if there is anything true, there must be truth. But God is truth itself: "I am the way, the truth, and the life" (John 14:6) Therefore "God exists" is self-evident.

*On the contrary,* No one can mentally admit the opposite of what is self-evident; as the Philosopher (Metaph. iv, lect. vi) states concerning the first principles of demonstration. But the opposite of the proposition "God is" can be mentally admitted: "The fool said in his heart, There is no God" (Ps. 52:1). Therefore, that God exists is not self-evident.

*I answer that,* A thing can be self-evident in either of two ways: on the one hand, self-evident in itself, though not to us; on the other, self-evident in itself, and to us. A proposition is self-evident because the predicate is included in the essence of the subject, as "Man is an animal," for animal is contained in the essence of man. If, therefore the essence of the predicate and subject be known to all, the proposition will be self-evident to all; as is clear with regard to the first principles of demonstration, the terms of which are common things that no one is ignorant of, such as being and non-being, whole and part, and such like. If, however, there are some to whom the essence of the predicate and subject is unknown, the proposition will be self-evident in itself, but not to those who do not know the meaning of the predicate and subject of the proposition. Therefore, it happens, as Boethius says (Hebdom., the title of which is: "Whether all that is, is good"), "that there are some mental concepts self-evident only to the learned, as that incorporeal substances are not in space." Therefore I say that this proposition, "God exists," of itself is self-evident, for the predicate is the same as the subject, because God is His own existence as will be hereafter shown (Q. 3, Art. 4). Now because we do not know the essence of God, the proposition is not self-evident to us; but needs to be demonstrated by things that are more known to us, though less known in their nature—namely, by effects.

Reply Obj. 1: To know that God exists in a general and confused way is implanted in us by nature, inasmuch as God is man's beatitude. For man naturally desires happiness, and what is naturally desired by man must be naturally known to him. This, however, is not to know absolutely that God exists; just as to know that someone is approaching is not the same as to know that Peter is approaching, even though it is Peter who is approaching; for many there are who imagine that man's perfect good which is happiness, consists in riches, and others in pleasures, and others in something else.

Reply Obj. 2: Perhaps not everyone who hears this word "God" understands it to signify something than which nothing greater can be thought, seeing that some have believed God to be a body. Yet, granted that everyone understands that by this word "God" is signified something than which nothing greater can be thought, nevertheless, it does not therefore follow that he understands that what the word signifies exists actually, but only that it exists mentally. Nor can it be argued that it actually exists, unless it be admitted that there actually exists something than which nothing greater can be thought; and this precisely is not admitted by those who hold that God does not exist.

Reply Obj. 3: The existence of truth in general is self-evident but the existence of a Primal Truth is not self-evident to us.

SECOND ARTICLE [I, Q. 2, Art. 2]

Whether It Can Be Demonstrated That God Exists?

Objection 1: It seems that the existence of God cannot be demonstrated. For it is an article of faith that God exists. But what is of faith cannot be demonstrated, because a demonstration produces scientific knowledge; whereas faith is of the unseen (Heb. 11:1). Therefore it cannot be demonstrated that God exists.

Obj. 2: Further, the essence is the middle term of demonstration. But we cannot know in what God's essence consists, but solely in what it does not consist; as Damascene says (De Fide Orth. i, 4). Therefore we cannot demonstrate that God exists.

Obj. 3: Further, if the existence of God were demonstrated, this could only be from His effects. But His effects are not proportionate to Him, since He is infinite and His effects are finite; and between the finite and infinite there is no proportion. Therefore, since a cause cannot be demonstrated by an effect not proportionate to it, it seems that the existence of God cannot be demonstrated.

*On the contrary,* The Apostle says: "The invisible things of Him are clearly seen, being understood by the things that are made" (Rom. 1:20). But this would not be unless the existence of God could be demonstrated through the things that are made; for the first thing we must know of anything is whether it exists.

*I answer that,* Demonstration can be made in two ways: One is through the cause, and is called *a priori,* and this is to argue from what is prior absolutely. The other is through the effect, and is called a demonstration *a posteriori*; this is to argue from what is prior relatively only to us. When an effect is better known to us than its cause, from the effect we proceed to the knowledge of the cause. And from every effect the existence of its proper cause can be demonstrated, so long as its effects are better known to us; because since every effect depends upon its cause, if the effect exists, the cause must pre-exist. Hence the existence of God, in so far as it is not self-evident to us, can be demonstrated from those of His effects which are known to us.

Reply Obj. 1: The existence of God and other like truths about God, which can be known by natural reason, are not articles of faith, but are preambles to the articles; for faith presupposes natural knowledge, even as grace presupposes nature, and perfection supposes something that can be perfected. Nevertheless, there is nothing to prevent a man, who cannot grasp a proof, accepting, as a matter of faith, something which in itself is capable of being scientifically known and demonstrated.

Reply Obj. 2: When the existence of a cause is demonstrated from an effect, this effect takes the place of the definition of the cause in proof of the cause's existence. This is especially the case in regard to God, because, in order to prove the existence of anything, it is necessary to accept as a middle term the meaning of the word, and not its essence, for the question of its essence follows on the question of its existence. Now the names given to God are derived from His effects; consequently, in demonstrating the existence of God from His effects, we may take for the middle term the meaning of the word "God".

Reply Obj. 3: From effects not proportionate to the cause no perfect knowledge of that cause can be obtained. Yet from every effect the existence of the cause can be clearly demonstrated, and so we can demonstrate the existence of God from His effects; though from them we cannot perfectly know God as He is in His essence.

THIRD ARTICLE [I, Q. 2, Art. 3]

Whether God Exists?

Objection 1: It seems that God does not exist; because if one of two contraries be infinite, the other would be altogether destroyed. But the word "God" means that He is infinite goodness. If, therefore, God existed, there would be no evil discoverable; but there is evil in the world. Therefore God does not exist.

Obj. 2: Further, it is superfluous to suppose that what can be accounted for by a few principles has been produced by many. But it seems that everything we see in the world can be accounted for by other principles, supposing God did not exist. For all natural things can be reduced to one principle which is nature; and all voluntary things can be reduced to one principle which is human reason, or will. Therefore there is no need to suppose God's existence.

*On the contrary,* It is said in the person of God: "I am Who am." (Ex. 3:14)

*I answer that,* The existence of God can be proved in five ways.

The first and more manifest way is the argument from motion. It is certain, and evident to our senses, that in the world some things are in motion. Now whatever is in motion is put in motion by another, for nothing can be in motion except it is in potentiality to that towards which it is in motion; whereas a thing moves inasmuch as it is in act. For motion is nothing else than the reduction of something from potentiality to actuality. But nothing can be reduced from potentiality to actuality, except by something in a state of actuality. Thus that which is actually hot, as fire, makes wood, which is potentially hot, to be actually hot, and thereby moves and changes it. Now it is not possible that the same thing should be at once in actuality and potentiality in the same respect, but only in different respects. For what is actually hot cannot simultaneously be potentially hot; but it is simultaneously potentially cold. It is therefore impossible that in the same respect and in the same way a thing should be both mover and moved, i.e. that it should move itself. Therefore, whatever is in motion must be put in motion by another. If that by which it is put in motion be itself put in motion, then this also must needs be put in motion by another, and that by another again. But this cannot go on to infinity, because then there would be no first mover, and, consequently, no other mover; seeing that subsequent movers move only inasmuch as they are put in motion by the first mover; as the staff moves only because it is put in motion by the hand. Therefore it is necessary to arrive at a first mover, put in motion by no other; and this everyone understands to be God.

The second way is from the nature of the efficient cause. In the world of sense we find there is an order of efficient causes. There is no case known (neither is it, indeed, possible) in which a thing is found to be the efficient cause of itself; for so it would be prior to itself, which is impossible. Now in efficient causes it is not possible to go on to infinity, because in all efficient causes following in order, the first is the cause of the intermediate cause, and the intermediate is the cause of the ultimate cause, whether the intermediate cause be several, or only one. Now to take away the cause is to take away the effect. Therefore, if there be no first cause among efficient causes, there will be no ultimate, nor any intermediate cause. But if in efficient causes it is possible to go on to infinity, there will be no first efficient cause, neither will there be an ultimate effect, nor any intermediate efficient causes; all of which is plainly false. Therefore it is necessary to admit a first efficient cause, to which everyone gives the name of God.

The third way is taken from possibility and necessity, and runs thus. We find in nature things that are possible to be and not to be, since they are found to be generated, and to corrupt, and consequently, they are possible to be and not to be. But it is impossible for these always to exist, for that which is possible not to be at some time is not. Therefore, if everything is possible not to be, then at one time there could have been nothing in existence. Now if this were true, even now there would be nothing in existence, because that which does not exist only begins to exist by something already existing. Therefore, if at one time nothing was in existence, it would have been impossible for anything to have begun to exist; and thus even now nothing would be in existence—which is absurd. Therefore, not all beings are merely possible, but there must exist something the existence of which is necessary. But every necessary thing either has its necessity caused by another, or not. Now it is impossible to go on to infinity in necessary things which have their necessity caused by another, as has been already proved in regard to efficient causes. Therefore we cannot but postulate the existence of some being having of itself its own necessity, and not receiving it from another, but rather causing in others their necessity. This all men speak of as God.

The fourth way is taken from the gradation to be found in things. Among beings there are some more and some less good, true, noble and the like. But *more* and less are predicated of different things, according as they resemble in their different ways something which is the maximum, as a thing is said to be hotter according as it more nearly resembles that which is hottest; so that there is something which is truest, something best, something noblest and, consequently, something which is uttermost being; for those things that are greatest in truth are greatest in being, as it is written in *Metaph.* ii. Now the maximum in any genus is the cause of all in that genus; as fire, which is the maximum heat, is the cause of all hot things. Therefore there must also be something which is to all beings the cause of their being, goodness, and every other perfection; and this we call God.

The fifth way is taken from the governance of the world. We see that things which lack intelligence, such as natural bodies, act for an end, and this is evident from their acting always, or nearly always, in the same way, so as to obtain the best result. Hence it is plain that not fortuitously, but designedly, do they achieve their end. Now whatever lacks intelligence cannot move towards an end, unless it be directed by some being endowed with knowledge and intelligence; as the arrow is shot to its mark by the archer. Therefore some intelligent being exists by whom all natural things are directed to their end; and this being we call God.

Reply Obj. 1: As Augustine says (Enchiridion xi): "Since God is the highest good, He would not allow any evil to exist in His works, unless His omnipotence and goodness were such as to bring good even out of evil." This is part of the infinite goodness of God, that He should allow evil to exist, and out of it produce good.

Reply Obj. 2: Since nature works for a determinate end under the direction of a higher agent, whatever is done by nature must needs be traced back to God, as to its first cause. So also whatever is done voluntarily must also be traced back to some higher cause other than human reason or will, since these can change or fail; for all things that are changeable and capable of defect must be traced back to an immovable and self-necessary first principle, as was shown in the body of the Article.

## QUESTION 3

OF THE SIMPLICITY OF GOD (In Eight Articles)

When the existence of a thing has been ascertained there remains the further question of the manner of its existence, in order that we may know its essence. Now, because we cannot know what God is, but rather what He is not, we have no means for considering how God is, but rather how He is not.

Therefore, we must consider:

(1) How He is not;

(2) How He is known by us;

(3) How He is named.

Now it can be shown how God is not, by denying Him whatever is opposed to the idea of Him, viz. composition, motion, and the like. Therefore

(1) we must discuss His simplicity, whereby we deny composition in Him; and because whatever is simple in material things is imperfect and a part of something else, we shall discuss (2) His perfection; (3) His infinity; (4) His immutability; (5) His unity.

Concerning His simplicity, there are eight points of inquiry:

(1) Whether God is a body?

(2) Whether He is composed of matter and form?

(3) Whether in Him there is composition of quiddity, essence or nature, and subject?

(4) Whether He is composed of essence and existence?

(5) Whether He is composed of genus and difference?

(6) Whether He is composed of subject and accident?

(7) Whether He is in any way composite, or wholly simple?

(8) Whether He enters into composition with other things?

FIRST ARTICLE [I, Q. 3, Art. 1]

Whether God Is a Body?

Objection 1: It seems that God is a body. For a body is that which has the three dimensions. But Holy Scripture attributes the three dimensions to God, for it is written: "He is higher than Heaven, and what wilt thou do? He is deeper than Hell, and how wilt thou know? The measure of Him is longer than the earth and broader than the sea" (Job 11:8, 9). Therefore God is a body.

Obj. 2: Further, everything that has figure is a body, since figure is a quality of quantity. But God seems to have figure, for it is written: "Let us make man to our image and likeness" (Gen. 1:26). Now a figure is called an image, according to the text: "Who being the brightness of His glory and the figure," i.e. the image, "of His substance" (Heb. 1:3). Therefore God is a body.

Obj. 3: Further, whatever has corporeal parts is a body. Now Scripture attributes corporeal parts to God. "Hast thou an arm like God?" (Job 40:4); and "The eyes of the Lord are upon the just" (Ps. 33:16); and "The right hand of the Lord hath wrought strength" (Ps. 117:16). Therefore God is a body.

Obj. 4: Further, posture belongs only to bodies. But something which supposes posture is said of God in the Scriptures: "I saw the Lord sitting" (Isa. 6:1), and "He standeth up to judge" (Isa. 3:13). Therefore God is a body.

Obj. 5: Further, only bodies or things corporeal can be a local term *wherefrom* or whereto. But in the Scriptures God is spoken of as a local term whereto, according to the words, "Come ye to Him and be enlightened" (Ps. 33:6), and as a term *wherefrom* : "All they that depart from Thee shall be written in the earth" (Jer. 17:13). Therefore God is a body.

*On the contrary,* It is written in the Gospel of St. John (John 4:24): "God is a spirit."

*I answer that,* It is absolutely true that God is not a body; and this can be shown in three ways. First, because no body is in motion unless it be put in motion, as is evident from induction. Now it has been already proved (Q. 2, A. 3), that God is the First Mover, and is Himself unmoved. Therefore it is clear that God is not a body. Secondly, because the first being must of necessity be in act, and in no way in potentiality. For although in any single thing that passes from potentiality to actuality, the potentiality is prior in time to the actuality; nevertheless, absolutely speaking, actuality is prior to potentiality; for whatever is in potentiality can be reduced into actuality only by some being in actuality. Now it has been already proved that God is the First Being. It is therefore impossible that in God there should be any potentiality. But every body is in potentiality because the continuous, as such, is divisible to infinity; it is therefore impossible that God should be a body. Thirdly, because God is the most noble of beings. Now it is impossible for a body to be the most noble of beings; for a body must be either animate or inanimate; and an animate body is manifestly nobler than any inanimate body. But an animate body is not animate precisely as body; otherwise all bodies would be animate. Therefore its animation depends upon some other thing, as our body depends for its animation on the soul. Hence that by which a body becomes animated must be nobler than the body. Therefore it is impossible that God should be a body.

Reply Obj. 1: As we have said above (Q. 1, A. 9), Holy Writ puts before us spiritual and divine things under the comparison of corporeal things. Hence, when it attributes to God the three dimensions under the comparison of corporeal quantity, it implies His virtual quantity; thus, by depth, it signifies His power of knowing hidden things; by height, the transcendence of His excelling power; by length, the duration of His existence; by breadth, His act of love for all. Or, as says Dionysius (Div. Nom. ix), by the depth of God is meant the incomprehensibility of His essence; by length, the procession of His all-pervading power; by breadth, His overspreading all things, inasmuch as all things lie under His protection.

Reply Obj. 2: Man is said to be after the image of God, not as regards his body, but as regards that whereby he excels other animals. Hence, when it is said, "Let us make man to our image and likeness", it is added, "And let him have dominion over the fishes of the sea" (Gen. 1:26). Now man excels all animals by his reason and intelligence; hence it is according to his intelligence and reason, which are incorporeal, that man is said to be according to the image of God.

Reply Obj. 3: Corporeal parts are attributed to God in Scripture on account of His actions, and this is owing to a certain parallel. For instance the act of the eye is to see; hence the eye attributed to God signifies His power of seeing intellectually, not sensibly; and so on with the other parts.

Reply Obj. 4: Whatever pertains to posture, also, is only attributed to God by some sort of parallel. He is spoken of as sitting, on account of His unchangeableness and dominion; and as standing, on account of His power of overcoming whatever withstands Him.

Reply Obj. 5: We draw near to God by no corporeal steps, since He is everywhere, but by the affections of our soul, and by the actions of that same soul do we withdraw from Him; thus, to draw near to or to withdraw signifies merely spiritual actions based on the metaphor of local motion.

SECOND ARTICLE [I, Q. 3, Art. 2]

Whether God Is Composed of Matter and Form?

Objection 1: It seems that God is composed of matter and form. For whatever has a soul is composed of matter and form; since the soul is the form of the body. But Scripture attributes a soul to God; for it is mentioned in Hebrews (Heb. 10:38), where God says: "But My just man liveth by faith; but if he withdraw himself, he shall not please My soul." Therefore God is composed of matter and form.

Obj. 2: Further, anger, joy and the like are passions of the composite. But these are attributed to God in Scripture: "The Lord was exceeding angry with His people" (Ps. 105:40). Therefore God is composed of matter and form.

Obj. 3: Further, matter is the principle of individualization. But God seems to be individual, for He cannot be predicated of many. Therefore He is composed of matter and form.

*On the contrary,* Whatever is composed of matter and form is a body; for dimensive quantity is the first property of matter. But God is not a body as proved in the preceding Article; therefore He is not composed of matter and form.

*I answer that,* It is impossible that matter should exist in God. First, because matter is in potentiality. But we have shown (Q. 2, A. 3) that God is pure act, without any potentiality. Hence it is impossible that God should be composed of matter and form. Secondly, because everything composed of matter and form owes its perfection and goodness to its form; therefore its goodness is participated, inasmuch as matter participates the form. Now the first good and the best—viz. God—is not a participated good, because the essential good is prior to the participated good. Hence it is impossible that God should be composed of matter and form. Thirdly, because every agent acts by its form; hence the manner in which it has its form is the manner in which it is an agent. Therefore whatever is primarily and essentially an agent must be primarily and essentially form. Now God is the first agent, since He is the first efficient cause. He is therefore of His essence a form; and not composed of matter and form.

Reply Obj. 1: A soul is attributed to God because His acts resemble the acts of a soul; for, that we will anything, is due to our soul. Hence what is pleasing to His will is said to be pleasing to His soul.

Reply Obj. 2: Anger and the like are attributed to God on account of a similitude of effect. Thus, because to punish is properly the act of an angry man, God's punishment is metaphorically spoken of as His anger.

Reply Obj. 3: Forms which can be received in matter are individualized by matter, which cannot be in another as in a subject since it is the first underlying subject; although form of itself, unless something else prevents it, can be received by many. But that form which cannot be received in matter, but is self-subsisting, is individualized precisely because it cannot be received in a subject; and such a form is God. Hence it does not follow that matter exists in God.

THIRD ARTICLE [I, Q. 3, Art. 3]

Whether God is the Same as His Essence or Nature?

Objection 1: It seems that God is not the same as His essence or nature. For nothing can be in itself. But the substance or nature of God—i.e. the Godhead—is said to be in God. Therefore it seems that God is not the same as His essence or nature.

Obj. 2: Further, the effect is assimilated to its cause; for every agent produces its like. But in created things the *suppositum* is not identical with its nature; for a man is not the same as his humanity. Therefore God is not the same as His Godhead.

*On the contrary,* It is said of God that He is life itself, and not only that He is a living thing: "I am the way, the truth, and the life" (John 14:6). Now the relation between Godhead and God is the same as the relation between life and a living thing. Therefore God is His very Godhead.

*I answer that,* God is the same as His essence or nature. To understand this, it must be noted that in things composed of matter and form, the nature or essence must differ from the *suppositum,* because the essence or nature connotes only what is included in the definition of the species; as, humanity connotes all that is included in the definition of man, for it is by this that man is man, and it is this that humanity signifies, that, namely, whereby man is man. Now individual matter, with all the individualizing accidents, is not included in the definition of the species. For this particular flesh, these bones, this blackness or whiteness, etc., are not included in the definition of a man. Therefore this flesh, these bones, and the accidental qualities distinguishing this particular matter, are not included in humanity; and yet they are included in the thing which is man. Hence the thing which is a man has something more in it than has humanity. Consequently humanity and a man are not wholly identical; but humanity is taken to mean the formal part of a man, because the principles whereby a thing is defined are regarded as the formal constituent in regard to the individualizing matter. On the other hand, in things not composed of matter and form, in which individualization is not due to individual matter—that is to say, to *this* matter—the very forms being individualized of themselves—it is necessary the forms themselves should be subsisting *supposita.* Therefore *suppositum* and nature in them are identified. Since God then is not composed of matter and form, He must be His own Godhead, His own Life, and whatever else is thus predicated of Him.

Reply Obj. 1: We can speak of simple things only as though they were like the composite things from which we derive our knowledge. Therefore in speaking of God, we use concrete nouns to signify His subsistence, because with us only those things subsist which are composite; and we use abstract nouns to signify His simplicity. In saying therefore that Godhead, or life, or the like are in God, we indicate the composite way in which our intellect understands, but not that there is any composition in God.

Reply Obj. 2: The effects of God do not imitate Him perfectly, but only as far as they are able; and the imitation is here defective, precisely because what is simple and one, can only be represented by divers things; consequently, composition is accidental to them, and therefore, in them *suppositum* is not the same as nature.

FOURTH ARTICLE [I, Q. 3, Art. 4]

Whether Essence and Existence Are the Same in God?

Objection 1: It seems that essence and existence are not the same in God. For if it be so, then the divine being has nothing added to it. Now being to which no addition is made is universal being which is predicated of all things. Therefore it follows that God is being in general which can be predicated of everything. But this is false: "For men gave the incommunicable name to stones and wood" (Wis. 14:21). Therefore God's existence is not His essence.

Obj. 2: Further, we can know *whether* God exists as said above (Q. 2, A. 2); but we cannot know what He is. Therefore God's existence is not the same as His essence—that is, as His quiddity or nature.

*On the contrary,* Hilary says (Trin. vii): "In God existence is not an accidental quality, but subsisting truth." Therefore what subsists in God is His existence.

*I answer that,* God is not only His own essence, as shown in the preceding article, but also His own existence. This may be shown in several ways. First, whatever a thing has besides its essence must be caused either by the constituent principles of that essence (like a property that necessarily accompanies the species—as the faculty of laughing is proper to a man—and is caused by the constituent principles of the species), or by some exterior agent—as heat is caused in water by fire. Therefore, if the existence of a thing differs from its essence, this existence must be caused either by some exterior agent or by its essential principles. Now it is impossible for a thing's existence to be caused by its essential constituent principles, for nothing can be the sufficient cause of its own existence, if its existence is caused. Therefore that thing, whose existence differs from its essence, must have its existence caused by another. But this cannot be true of God; because we call God the first efficient cause. Therefore it is impossible that in God His existence should differ from His essence. Secondly, existence is that which makes every form or nature actual; for goodness and humanity are spoken of as actual, only because they are spoken of as existing. Therefore existence must be compared to essence, if the latter is a distinct reality, as actuality to potentiality. Therefore, since in God there is no potentiality, as shown above (A. 1), it follows that in Him essence does not differ from existence. Therefore His essence is His existence. Thirdly, because, just as that which has fire, but is not itself fire, is on fire by participation; so that which has existence but is not existence, is a being by participation. But God is His own essence, as shown above (A. 3); if, therefore, He is not His own existence He will be not essential, but participated being. He will not therefore be the first being—which is absurd. Therefore God is His own existence, and not merely His own essence.

Reply Obj. 1: A thing that has nothing added to it can be of two kinds. Either its essence precludes any addition; thus, for example, it is of the essence of an irrational animal to be without reason. Or we may understand a thing to have nothing added to it, inasmuch as its essence does not require that anything should be added to it; thus the genus animal is without reason, because it is not of the essence of animal in general to have reason; but neither is it to lack reason. And so the divine being has nothing added to it in the first sense; whereas universal being has nothing added to it in the second sense.

Reply Obj. 2: "To be" can mean either of two things. It may mean the act of essence, or it may mean the composition of a proposition effected by the mind in joining a predicate to a subject. Taking "to be" in the first sense, we cannot understand God's existence nor His essence; but only in the second sense. We know that this proposition which we form about God when we say "God is," is true; and this we know from His effects (Q. 2, A. 2).

FIFTH ARTICLE [I, Q. 3, Art. 5]

Whether God Is Contained in a Genus?

Objection 1: It seems that God is contained in a genus. For a substance is a being that subsists of itself. But this is especially true of God. Therefore God is in a genus of substance.

Obj. 2: Further, nothing can be measured save by something of its own genus; as length is measured by length and numbers by number. But God is the measure of all substances, as the Commentator shows (Metaph. x). Therefore God is in the genus of substance.

*On the contrary,* In the mind, genus is prior to what it contains. But nothing is prior to God either really or mentally. Therefore God is not in any genus.

*I answer that,* A thing can be in a genus in two ways; either absolutely and properly, as a species contained under a genus; or as being reducible to it, as principles and privations. For example, a point and unity are reduced to the genus of quantity, as its principles; while blindness and all other privations are reduced to the genus of habit. But in neither way is God in a genus. That He cannot be a species of any genus may be shown in three ways. First, because a species is constituted of genus and difference. Now that from which the difference constituting the species is derived, is always related to that from which the genus is derived, as actuality is related to potentiality. For animal is derived from sensitive nature, by concretion as it were, for that is animal, which has a sensitive nature. Rational being, on the other hand, is derived from intellectual nature, because that is rational, which has an intellectual nature, and intelligence is compared to sense, as actuality is to potentiality. The same argument holds good in other things. Hence since in God actuality is not added to potentiality, it is impossible that He should be in any genus as a species. Secondly, since the existence of God is His essence, if God were in any genus, He would be the genus *being,* because, since genus is predicated as an essential it refers to the essence of a thing. But the Philosopher has shown (Metaph. iii) that being cannot be a genus, for every genus has differences distinct from its generic essence. Now no difference can exist distinct from being; for non-being cannot be a difference. It follows then that God is not in a genus. Thirdly, because all in one genus agree in the quiddity or essence of the genus which is predicated of them as an essential, but they differ in their existence. For the existence of man and of horse is not the same; as also of this man and that man: thus in every member of a genus, existence and quiddity—i.e. essence—must differ. But in God they do not differ, as shown in the preceding article. Therefore it is plain that God is not in a genus as if He were a species. From this it is also plain that He has no genus nor difference, nor can there be any definition of Him; nor, save through His effects, a demonstration of Him: for a definition is from genus and difference; and the mean of a demonstration is a definition. That God is not in a genus, as reducible to it as its principle, is clear from this, that a principle reducible to any genus does not extend beyond that genus; as, a point is the principle of continuous quantity alone; and unity, of discontinuous quantity. But God is the principle of all being. Therefore He is not contained in any genus as its principle.

Reply Obj. 1: The word substance signifies not only what exists of itself—for existence cannot of itself be a genus, as shown in the body of the article; but, it also signifies an essence that has the property of existing in this way—namely, of existing of itself; this existence, however, is not its essence. Thus it is clear that God is not in the genus of substance.

Reply Obj. 2: This objection turns upon proportionate measure which must be homogeneous with what is measured. Now, God is not a measure proportionate to anything. Still, He is called the measure of all things, in the sense that everything has being only according as it resembles Him.

SIXTH ARTICLE [I, Q. 3, Art. 6]

Whether in God There Are Any Accidents?

Objection 1: It seems that there are accidents in God. For substance cannot be an accident, as Aristotle says (Phys. i). Therefore that which is an accident in one, cannot, in another, be a substance. Thus it is proved that heat cannot be the substantial form of fire, because it is an accident in other things. But wisdom, virtue, and the like, which are accidents in us, are attributes of God. Therefore in God there are accidents.

Obj. 2: Further, in every genus there is a first principle. But there are many genera of accidents. If, therefore, the primal members of these genera are not in God, there will be many primal beings other than God—which is absurd.

*On the contrary,* Every accident is in a subject. But God cannot be a subject, for "no simple form can be a subject", as Boethius says (De Trin.). Therefore in God there cannot be any accident.

*I answer that,* From all we have said, it is clear there can be no accident in God. First, because a subject is compared to its accidents as potentiality to actuality; for a subject is in some sense made actual by its accidents. But there can be no potentiality in God, as was shown (Q. 2, A. 3). Secondly, because God is His own existence; and as Boethius says (Hebdom.), although every essence may have something superadded to it, this cannot apply to absolute being: thus a heated substance can have something extraneous to heat added to it, as whiteness, nevertheless absolute heat can have nothing else than heat. Thirdly, because what is essential is prior to what is accidental. Whence as God is absolute primal being, there can be in Him nothing accidental. Neither can He have any essential accidents (as the capability of laughing is an essential accident of man), because such accidents are caused by the constituent principles of the subject. Now there can be nothing caused in God, since He is the first cause. Hence it follows that there is no accident in God.

Reply Obj. 1: Virtue and wisdom are not predicated of God and of us univocally. Hence it does not follow that there are accidents in God as there are in us.

Reply Obj. 2: Since substance is prior to its accidents, the principles of accidents are reducible to the principles of the substance as to that which is prior; although God is not first as if contained in the genus of substance; yet He is first in respect to all being, outside of every genus.

SEVENTH ARTICLE [I, Q. 3, Art. 7]

Whether God Is Altogether Simple?

Objection 1: It seems that God is not altogether simple. For whatever is from God must imitate Him. Thus from the first being are all beings; and from the first good is all good. But in the things which God has made, nothing is altogether simple. Therefore neither is God altogether simple.

Obj. 2: Further, whatever is best must be attributed to God. But with us that which is composite is better than that which is simple; thus, chemical compounds are better than simple elements, and animals than the parts that compose them. Therefore it cannot be said that God is altogether simple.

*On the contrary,* Augustine says (De Trin. iv, 6,7): "God is truly and absolutely simple."

*I answer that,* The absolute simplicity of God may be shown in many ways. First, from the previous articles of this question. For there is neither composition of quantitative parts in God, since He is not a body; nor composition of matter and form; nor does His nature differ from His *suppositum* ; nor His essence from His existence; neither is there in Him composition of genus and difference, nor of subject and accident. Therefore, it is clear that God is nowise composite, but is altogether simple. Secondly, because every composite is posterior to its component parts, and is dependent on them; but God is the first being, as shown above (Q. 2, A. 3). Thirdly, because every composite has a cause, for things in themselves different cannot unite unless something causes them to unite. But God is uncaused, as shown above (Q. 2, A. 3), since He is the first efficient cause. Fourthly, because in every composite there must be potentiality and actuality; but this does not apply to God; for either one of the parts actuates another, or at least all the parts are potential to the whole. Fifthly, because nothing composite can be predicated of any single one of its parts. And this is evident in a whole made up of dissimilar parts; for no part of a man is a man, nor any of the parts of the foot, a foot. But in wholes made up of similar parts, although something which is predicated of the whole may be predicated of a part (as a part of the air is air, and a part of water, water), nevertheless certain things are predicable of the whole which cannot be predicated of any of the parts; for instance, if the whole volume of water is two cubits, no part of it can be two cubits. Thus in every composite there is something which is not it itself. But, even if this could be said of whatever has a form, viz. that it has something which is not it itself, as in a white object there is something which does not belong to the essence of white; nevertheless in the form itself, there is nothing besides itself. And so, since God is absolute form, or rather absolute being, He can be in no way composite. Hilary implies this argument, when he says (De Trin. vii): "God, Who is strength, is not made up of things that are weak; nor is He Who is light, composed of things that are dim."

Reply Obj. 1: Whatever is from God imitates Him, as caused things imitate the first cause. But it is of the essence of a thing to be in some sort composite; because at least its existence differs from its essence, as will be shown hereafter, (Q. 4, A. 3).

Reply Obj. 2: With us composite things are better than simple things, because the perfections of created goodness cannot be found in one simple thing, but in many things. But the perfection of divine goodness is found in one simple thing (QQ. 4, A. 1, and 6, A. 2).

EIGHTH ARTICLE [I, Q. 3, Art. 8]

Whether God Enters into the Composition of Other Things?

Objection 1: It seems that God enters into the composition of other things, for Dionysius says (Coel. Hier. iv): "The being of all things is that which is above being—the Godhead." But the being of all things enters into the composition of everything. Therefore God enters into the composition of other things.

Obj. 2: Further, God is a form; for Augustine says (De Verb. Dom. [Serm. xxxviii]) that, "the word of God, which is God, is an uncreated form." But a form is part of a compound. Therefore God is part of some compound.

Obj. 3: Further, whatever things exist, in no way differing from each other, are the same. But God and primary matter exist, and in no way differ from each other. Therefore they are absolutely the same. But primary matter enters into the composition things. Therefore also does God. Proof of the minor—whatever things differ, they differ by some differences, and therefore must be composite. But God and primary matter are altogether simple. Therefore they nowise differ from each other.

*On the contrary,* Dionysius says (Div. Nom. ii): "There can be no touching Him," i.e. God, "nor any other union with Him by mingling part with part."

Further, the first cause rules all things without commingling with them, as the Philosopher says (De Causis).

*I answer that,* On this point there have been three errors. Some have affirmed that God is the world-soul, as is clear from Augustine (De Civ. Dei vii, 6). This is practically the same as the opinion of those who assert that God is the soul of the highest heaven. Again, others have said that God is the formal principle of all things; and this was the theory of the Almaricians. The third error is that of David of Dinant, who most absurdly taught that God was primary matter. Now all these contain manifest untruth; since it is not possible for God to enter into the composition of anything, either as a formal or a material principle. First, because God is the first efficient cause. Now the efficient cause is not identical numerically with the form of the thing caused, but only specifically: for man begets man. But primary matter can be neither numerically nor specifically identical with an efficient cause; for the former is merely potential, while the latter is actual. Secondly, because, since God is the first efficient cause, to act belongs to Him primarily and essentially. But that which enters into composition with anything does not act primarily and essentially, but rather the composite so acts; for the hand does not act, but the man by his hand; and, fire warms by its heat. Hence God cannot be part of a compound. Thirdly, because no part of a compound can be absolutely primal among beings—not even matter, nor form, though they are the primal parts of every compound. For matter is merely potential; and potentiality is absolutely posterior to actuality, as is clear from the foregoing (Q. 3, A. 1): while a form which is part of a compound is a participated form; and as that which participates is posterior to that which is essential, so likewise is that which is participated; as fire in ignited objects is posterior to fire that is essentially such. Now it has been proved that God is absolutely primal being (Q. 2, A. 3).

Reply Obj. 1: The Godhead is called the being of all things, as their efficient and exemplar cause, but not as being their essence.

Reply Obj. 2: The Word is an exemplar form; but not a form that is part of a compound.

Reply Obj. 3: Simple things do not differ by added differences—for this is the property of compounds. Thus man and horse differ by their differences, rational and irrational; which differences, however, do not differ from each other by other differences. Hence, to be quite accurate, it is better to say that they are, not different, but diverse. Hence, according to the Philosopher (Metaph. x), "things which are diverse are absolutely distinct, but things which are different differ by something." Therefore, strictly speaking, primary matter and God do not differ, but are by their very being, diverse. Hence it does not follow they are the same.

## QUESTION 4

THE PERFECTION OF GOD (In Three Articles)

Having considered the divine simplicity, we treat next of God's perfection. Now because everything in so far as it is perfect is called good, we shall speak first of the divine perfection; secondly of the divine goodness.

Concerning the first there are three points of inquiry:

(1) Whether God is perfect?

(2) Whether God is perfect universally, as having in Himself the perfections of all things?

(3) Whether creatures can be said to be like God?

FIRST ARTICLE [I, Q. 4, Art. 1]

Whether God is Perfect?

Objection 1: It seems that perfection does not belong to God. For we say a thing is perfect if it is completely made. But it does not befit God to be made. Therefore He is not perfect.

Obj. 2: Further, God is the first beginning of things. But the beginnings of things seem to be imperfect, as seed is the beginning of animal and vegetable life. Therefore God is imperfect.

Obj. 3: Further, as shown above (Q. 3, A. 4), God's essence is existence. But existence seems most imperfect, since it is most universal and receptive of all modification. Therefore God is imperfect.

*On the contrary,* It is written: "Be you perfect as also your heavenly Father is perfect" (Matt. 5:48).

*I answer that,* As the Philosopher relates (Metaph. xii), some ancient philosophers, namely, the Pythagoreans and Leucippus, did not predicate "best" and "most perfect" of the first principle. The reason was that the ancient philosophers considered only a material principle; and a material principle is most imperfect. For since matter as such is merely potential, the first material principle must be simply potential, and thus most imperfect. Now God is the first principle, not material, but in the order of efficient cause, which must be most perfect. For just as matter, as such, is merely potential, an agent, as such, is in the state of actuality. Hence, the first active principle must needs be most actual, and therefore most perfect; for a thing is perfect in proportion to its state of actuality, because we call that perfect which lacks nothing of the mode of its perfection.

Reply Obj. 1: As Gregory says (Moral. v, 26,29): "Though our lips can only stammer, we yet chant the high things of God." For that which is not made is improperly called perfect. Nevertheless because created things are then called perfect, when from potentiality they are brought into actuality, this word "perfect" signifies whatever is not wanting in actuality, whether this be by way of perfection or not.

Reply Obj. 2: The material principle which with us is found to be imperfect, cannot be absolutely primal; but must be preceded by something perfect. For seed, though it be the principle of animal life reproduced through seed, has previous to it, the animal or plant from which is came. Because, previous to that which is potential, must be that which is actual; since a potential being can only be reduced into act by some being already actual.

Reply Obj. 3: Existence is the most perfect of all things, for it is compared to all things as that by which they are made actual; for nothing has actuality except so far as it exists. Hence existence is that which actuates all things, even their forms. Therefore it is not compared to other things as the receiver is to the received; but rather as the received to the receiver. When therefore I speak of the existence of man, or horse, or anything else, existence is considered a formal principle, and as something received; and not as that which exists.

SECOND ARTICLE [I, Q. 4, Art. 2]

Whether the Perfections of All Things Are in God?

Objection 1: It seems that the perfections of all things are not in God. For God is simple, as shown above (Q. 3, A. 7); whereas the perfections of things are many and diverse. Therefore the perfections of all things are not in God.

Obj. 2: Further, opposites cannot coexist. Now the perfections of things are opposed to each other, for each thing is perfected by its specific difference. But the differences by which genera are divided, and species constituted, are opposed to each other. Therefore because opposites cannot coexist in the same subject, it seems that the perfections of all things are not in God.

Obj. 3: Further, a living thing is more perfect than what merely exists; and an intelligent thing than what merely lives. Therefore life is more perfect than existence; and knowledge than life. But the essence of God is existence itself. Therefore He has not the perfections of life, and knowledge, and other similar perfections.

*On the contrary,* Dionysius says (Div. Nom. v) that "God in His one existence prepossesses all things."

*I answer that,* All created perfections are in God. Hence He is spoken of as universally perfect, because He lacks not (says the Commentator, *Metaph.* v) any excellence which may be found in any genus. This may be seen from two considerations. First, because whatever perfection exists in an effect must be found in the effective cause: either in the same formality, if it is a univocal agent—as when man reproduces man; or in a more eminent degree, if it is an equivocal agent—thus in the sun is the likeness of whatever is generated by the sun's power. Now it is plain that the effect pre-exists virtually in the efficient cause: and although to pre-exist in the potentiality of a material cause is to pre-exist in a more imperfect way, since matter as such is imperfect, and an agent as such is perfect; still to pre-exist virtually in the efficient cause is to pre-exist not in a more imperfect, but in a more perfect way. Since therefore God is the first effective cause of things, the perfections of all things must pre-exist in God in a more eminent way. Dionysius implies the same line of argument by saying of God (Div. Nom. v): "It is not that He is this and not that, but that He is all, as the cause of all." Secondly, from what has been already proved, God is existence itself, of itself subsistent (Q. 3, A. 4). Consequently, He must contain within Himself the whole perfection of being. For it is clear that if some hot thing has not the whole perfection of heat, this is because heat is not participated in its full perfection; but if this heat were self-subsisting, nothing of the virtue of heat would be wanting to it. Since therefore God is subsisting being itself, nothing of the perfection of being can be wanting to Him. Now all created perfections are included in the perfection of being; for things are perfect, precisely so far as they have being after some fashion. It follows therefore that the perfection of no one thing is wanting to God. This line of argument, too, is implied by Dionysius (Div. Nom. v), when he says that, "God exists not in any single mode, but embraces all being within Himself, absolutely, without limitation, uniformly;" and afterwards he adds that, "He is the very existence to subsisting things."

Reply Obj. 1: Even as the sun (as Dionysius remarks, (Div. Nom. v)), while remaining one and shining uniformly, contains within itself first and uniformly the substances of sensible things, and many and diverse qualities; *a fortiori* should all things in a kind of natural unity pre-exist in the cause of all things; and thus things diverse and in themselves opposed to each other, pre-exist in God as one, without injury to His simplicity. This suffices for the Reply to the Second Objection.

Reply Obj. 3: The same Dionysius says (Div. Nom. v) that, although existence is more perfect than life, and life than wisdom, if they are considered as distinguished in idea; nevertheless, a living thing is more perfect than what merely exists, because living things also exist and intelligent things both exist and live. Although therefore existence does not include life and wisdom, because that which participates in existence need not participate in every mode of existence; nevertheless God's existence includes in itself life and wisdom, because nothing of the perfection of being can be wanting to Him who is subsisting being itself.

THIRD ARTICLE [I, Q. 4, Art. 3]

Whether Any Creature Can Be Like God?

Objection 1: It seems that no creature can be like God. For it is written (Ps. 85:8): "There is none among the gods like unto Thee, O Lord." But of all creatures the most excellent are those which are called by participation gods. Therefore still less can other creatures be said to be like God.

Obj. 2: Further, likeness implies comparison. But there can be no comparison between things in a different genus. Therefore neither can there be any likeness. Thus we do not say that sweetness is like whiteness. But no creature is in the same genus as God: since God is no genus, as shown above (Q. 3, A. 5). Therefore no creature is like God.

Obj. 3: Further, we speak of those things as like which agree in form. But nothing can agree with God in form; for, save in God alone, essence and existence differ. Therefore no creature can be like to God.

Obj. 4: Further, among like things there is mutual likeness; for like is like to like. If therefore any creature is like God, God will be like some creature, which is against what is said by Isaias: "To whom have you likened God?" (Isa. 40:18).

*On the contrary,* It is written: "Let us make man to our image and likeness" (Gen. 1:26), and: "When He shall appear we shall be like to Him" (1 John 3:2).

*I answer that,* Since likeness is based upon agreement or communication in form, it varies according to the many modes of communication in form. Some things are said to be like, which communicate in the same form according to the same formality, and according to the same mode; and these are said to be not merely like, but equal in their likeness; as two things equally white are said to be alike in whiteness; and this is the most perfect likeness. In another way, we speak of things as alike which communicate in form according to the same formality, though not according to the same measure, but according to more or less, as something less white is said to be like another thing more white; and this is imperfect likeness. In a third way some things are said to be alike which communicate in the same form, but not according to the same formality; as we see in non-univocal agents. For since every agent reproduces itself so far as it is an agent, and everything acts according to the manner of its form, the effect must in some way resemble the form of the agent. If therefore the agent is contained in the same species as its effect, there will be a likeness in form between that which makes and that which is made, according to the same formality of the species; as man reproduces man. If, however, the agent and its effect are not contained in the same species, there will be a likeness, but not according to the formality of the same species; as things generated by the sun's heat may be in some sort spoken of as like the sun, not as though they received the form of the sun in its specific likeness, but in its generic likeness. Therefore if there is an agent not contained in any genus, its effect will still more distantly reproduce the form of the agent, not, that is, so as to participate in the likeness of the agent's form according to the same specific or generic formality, but only according to some sort of analogy; as existence is common to all. In this way all created things, so far as they are beings, are like God as the first and universal principle of all being.

Reply Obj. 1: As Dionysius says (Div. Nom. ix), when Holy Writ declares that nothing is like God, it does not mean to deny all likeness to Him. For, "the same things can be like and unlike to God: like, according as they imitate Him, as far as He, Who is not perfectly imitable, can be imitated; unlike according as they fall short of their cause," not merely in intensity and remission, as that which is less white falls short of that which is more white; but because they are not in agreement, specifically or generically.

Reply Obj. 2: God is not related to creatures as though belonging to a different genus, but as transcending every genus, and as the principle of all genera.

Reply Obj. 3: Likeness of creatures to God is not affirmed on account of agreement in form according to the formality of the same genus or species, but solely according to analogy, inasmuch as God is essential being, whereas other things are beings by participation.

Reply Obj. 4: Although it may be admitted that creatures are in some sort like God, it must nowise be admitted that God is like creatures; because, as Dionysius says (Div. Nom. ix): "A mutual likeness may be found between things of the same order, but not between a cause and that which is caused." For, we say that a statue is like a man, but not conversely; so also a creature can be spoken of as in some sort like God; but not that God is like a creature.

## QUESTION 5

OF GOODNESS IN GENERAL (In Six Articles)

We next consider goodness: First, goodness in general. Secondly, the goodness of God.

Under the first head there are six points of inquiry:

(1) Whether goodness and being are the same really?

(2) Granted that they differ only in idea, which is prior in thought?

(3) Granted that being is prior, whether every being is good?

(4) To what cause should goodness be reduced?

(5) Whether goodness consists in mode, species, and order?

(6) Whether goodness is divided into the virtuous, the useful, and the pleasant?

FIRST ARTICLE [I, Q. 5, Art. 1]

Whether Goodness Differs Really from Being?

Objection 1: It seems that goodness differs really from being. For Boethius says (De Hebdom.): "I perceive that in nature the fact that things are good is one thing: that they are is another." Therefore goodness and being really differ.

Obj. 2: Further, nothing can be its own form. "But that is called good which has the form of being," according to the commentary on *De Causis.* Therefore goodness differs really from being.

Obj. 3: Further, goodness can be more or less. But being cannot be more or less. Therefore goodness differs really from being.

*On the contrary,* Augustine says (De Doctr. Christ. i, 42) that, "inasmuch as we exist we are good."

*I answer that,* Goodness and being are really the same, and differ only in idea; which is clear from the following argument. The essence of goodness consists in this, that it is in some way desirable. Hence the Philosopher says (Ethic. i): "Goodness is what all desire." Now it is clear that a thing is desirable only in so far as it is perfect; for all desire their own perfection. But everything is perfect so far as it is actual. Therefore it is clear that a thing is perfect so far as it exists; for it is existence that makes all things actual, as is clear from the foregoing (Q. 3, A. 4; Q. 4, A. 1). Hence it is clear that goodness and being are the same really. But goodness presents the aspect of desirableness, which being does not present.

Reply Obj. 1: Although goodness and being are the same really, nevertheless since they differ in thought, they are not predicated of a thing absolutely in the same way. Since being properly signifies that something actually is, and actuality properly correlates to potentiality; a thing is, in consequence, said simply to have being, accordingly as it is primarily distinguished from that which is only in potentiality; and this is precisely each thing's substantial being. Hence by its substantial being, everything is said to have being simply; but by any further actuality it is said to have being relatively. Thus to be white implies relative being, for to be white does not take a thing out of simply potential being; because only a thing that actually has being can receive this mode of being. But goodness signifies perfection which is desirable; and consequently of ultimate perfection. Hence that which has ultimate perfection is said to be simply good; but that which has not the ultimate perfection it ought to have (although, in so far as it is at all actual, it has some perfection), is not said to be perfect simply nor good simply, but only relatively. In this way, therefore, viewed in its primal (i.e. substantial) being a thing is said to be simply, and to be good relatively (i.e. in so far as it has being) but viewed in its complete actuality, a thing is said to be relatively, and to be good simply. Hence the saying of Boethius (De Hebdom.), "I perceive that in nature the fact that things are good is one thing; that they are is another," is to be referred to a thing's goodness simply, and having being simply. Because, regarded in its primal actuality, a thing simply exists; and regarded in its complete actuality, it is good simply—in such sort that even in its primal actuality, it is in some sort good, and even in its complete actuality, it in some sort has being.

Reply Obj. 2: Goodness is a form so far as absolute goodness signifies complete actuality.

Reply Obj. 3: Again, goodness is spoken of as more or less according to a thing's superadded actuality, for example, as to knowledge or virtue.

SECOND ARTICLE [I, Q. 5, Art. 2]

Whether Goodness Is Prior in Idea to Being?

Objection 1: It seems that goodness is prior in idea to being. For names are arranged according to the arrangement of the things signified by the names. But Dionysius (Div. Nom. iii) assigned the first place, amongst the other names of God, to His goodness rather than to His being. Therefore in idea goodness is prior to being.

Obj. 2: Further, that which is the more extensive is prior in idea. But goodness is more extensive than being, because, as Dionysius notes (Div. Nom. v), "goodness extends to things both existing and non-existing; whereas existence extends to existing things alone." Therefore goodness is in idea prior to being.

Obj. 3: Further, what is the more universal is prior in idea. But goodness seems to be more universal than being, since goodness has the aspect of desirable; whereas to some non-existence is desirable; for it is said of Judas: "It were better for him, if that man had not been born" (Matt. 26:24). Therefore in idea goodness is prior to being.

Obj. 4: Further, not only is existence desirable, but life, knowledge, and many other things besides. Thus it seems that existence is a particular appetible, and goodness a universal appetible. Therefore, absolutely, goodness is prior in idea to being.

*On the contrary,* It is said by Aristotle (De Causis) that "the first of created things is being."

*I answer that,* In idea being is prior to goodness. For the meaning signified by the name of a thing is that which the mind conceives of the thing and intends by the word that stands for it. Therefore, that is prior in idea, which is first conceived by the intellect. Now the first thing conceived by the intellect is being; because everything is knowable only inasmuch as it is in actuality. Hence, being is the proper object of the intellect, and is primarily intelligible; as sound is that which is primarily audible. Therefore in idea being is prior to goodness.

Reply Obj. 1: Dionysius discusses the Divine Names (Div. Nom. i, iii) as implying some causal relation in God; for we name God, as he says, from creatures, as a cause from its effects. But goodness, since it has the aspect of desirable, implies the idea of a final cause, the causality of which is first among causes, since an agent does not act except for some end; and by an agent matter is moved to its form. Hence the end is called the cause of causes. Thus goodness, as a cause, is prior to being, as is the end to the form. Therefore among the names signifying the divine causality, goodness precedes being. Again, according to the Platonists, who, through not distinguishing primary matter from privation, said that matter was non-being, goodness is more extensively participated than being; for primary matter participates in goodness as tending to it, for all seek their like; but it does not participate in being, since it is presumed to be non-being. Therefore Dionysius says that "goodness extends to non-existence" (Div. Nom. v).

Reply Obj. 2: The same solution is applied to this objection. Or it may be said that goodness extends to existing and non-existing things, not so far as it can be predicated of them, but so far as it can cause them—if, indeed, by non-existence we understand not simply those things which do not exist, but those which are potential, and not actual. For goodness has the aspect of the end, in which not only actual things find their completion, but also towards which tend even those things which are not actual, but merely potential. Now being implies the habitude of a formal cause only, either inherent or exemplar; and its causality does not extend save to those things which are actual.

Reply Obj. 3: Non-being is desirable, not of itself, but only relatively—i.e. inasmuch as the removal of an evil, which can only be removed by non-being, is desirable. Now the removal of an evil cannot be desirable, except so far as this evil deprives a thing of some being. Therefore being is desirable of itself; and non-being only relatively, inasmuch as one seeks some mode of being of which one cannot bear to be deprived; thus even non-being can be spoken of as relatively good.

Reply Obj. 4: Life, wisdom, and the like, are desirable only so far as they are actual. Hence, in each one of them some sort of being is desired. And thus nothing can be desired except being; and consequently nothing is good except being.

THIRD ARTICLE [I, Q. 5, Art. 3]

Whether Every Being Is Good?

Objection 1: It seems that not every being is good. For goodness is something superadded to being, as is clear from A. 1. But whatever is added to being limits it; as substance, quantity, quality, etc. Therefore goodness limits being. Therefore not every being is good.

Obj. 2: Further, no evil is good: "Woe to you that call evil good and good evil" (Isa. 5:20). But some things are called evil. Therefore not every being is good.

Obj. 3: Further, goodness implies desirability. Now primary matter does not imply desirability, but rather that which desires. Therefore primary matter does not contain the formality of goodness. Therefore not every being is good.

Obj. 4: Further, the Philosopher notes (Metaph. iii) that "in mathematics goodness does not exist." But mathematics are entities; otherwise there would be no science of mathematics. Therefore not every being is good.

*On the contrary,* Every being that is not God is God's creature. Now every creature of God is good (1 Tim. 4:4): and God is the greatest good. Therefore every being is good.

*I answer that,* Every being, as being, is good. For all being, as being, has actuality and is in some way perfect; since every act implies some sort of perfection; and perfection implies desirability and goodness, as is clear from A. 1. Hence it follows that every being as such is good.

Reply Obj. 1: Substance, quantity, quality, and everything included in them, limit being by applying it to some essence or nature. Now in this sense, goodness does not add anything to being beyond the aspect of desirability and perfection, which is also proper to being, whatever kind of nature it may be. Hence goodness does not limit being.

Reply Obj. 2: No being can be spoken of as evil, formally as being, but only so far as it lacks being. Thus a man is said to be evil, because he lacks some virtue; and an eye is said to be evil, because it lacks the power to see well.

Reply Obj. 3: As primary matter has only potential being, so it is only potentially good. Although, according to the Platonists, primary matter may be said to be a non-being on account of the privation attaching to it, nevertheless, it does participate to a certain extent in goodness, viz. by its relation to, or aptitude for, goodness. Consequently, to be desirable is not its property, but to desire.

Reply Obj. 4: Mathematical entities do not subsist as realities; because they would be in some sort good if they subsisted; but they have only logical existence, inasmuch as they are abstracted from motion and matter; thus they cannot have the aspect of an end, which itself has the aspect of moving another. Nor is it repugnant that there should be in some logical entity neither goodness nor form of goodness; since the idea of being is prior to the idea of goodness, as was said in the preceding article.

FOURTH ARTICLE [I, Q. 5, Art. 4]

Whether Goodness Has the Aspect of a Final Cause?

Objection 1: It seems that goodness has not the aspect of a final cause, but rather of the other causes. For, as Dionysius says (Div. Nom. iv), "Goodness is praised as beauty." But beauty has the aspect of a formal cause. Therefore goodness has the aspect of a formal cause.

Obj. 2: Further, goodness is self-diffusive; for Dionysius says (Div. Nom. iv) that goodness is that whereby all things subsist, and are. But to be self-giving implies the aspect of an efficient cause. Therefore goodness has the aspect of an efficient cause.

Obj. 3: Further, Augustine says (De Doctr. Christ. i, 31) that "we exist because God is good." But we owe our existence to God as the efficient cause. Therefore goodness implies the aspect of an efficient cause.

*On the contrary,* The Philosopher says (Phys. ii) that "that is to be considered as the end and the good of other things, for the sake of which something is." Therefore goodness has the aspect of a final cause.

*I answer that,* Since goodness is that which all things desire, and since this has the aspect of an end, it is clear that goodness implies the aspect of an end. Nevertheless, the idea of goodness presupposes the idea of an efficient cause, and also of a formal cause. For we see that what is first in causing, is last in the thing caused. Fire, e.g. heats first of all before it reproduces the form of fire; though the heat in the fire follows from its substantial form. Now in causing, goodness and the end come first, both of which move the agent to act; secondly, the action of the agent moving to the form; thirdly, comes the form. Hence in that which is caused the converse ought to take place, so that there should be first, the form whereby it is a being; secondly, we consider in it its effective power, whereby it is perfect in being, for a thing is perfect when it can reproduce its like, as the Philosopher says (Meteor. iv); thirdly, there follows the formality of goodness which is the basic principle of its perfection.

Reply Obj. 1: Beauty and goodness in a thing are identical fundamentally; for they are based upon the same thing, namely, the form; and consequently goodness is praised as beauty. But they differ logically, for goodness properly relates to the appetite (goodness being what all things desire); and therefore it has the aspect of an end (the appetite being a kind of movement towards a thing). On the other hand, beauty relates to the cognitive faculty; for beautiful things are those which please when seen. Hence beauty consists in due proportion; for the senses delight in things duly proportioned, as in what is after their own kind—because even sense is a sort of reason, just as is every cognitive faculty. Now since knowledge is by assimilation, and similarity relates to form, beauty properly belongs to the nature of a formal cause.

Reply Obj. 2: Goodness is described as self-diffusive in the sense that an end is said to move.

Reply Obj. 3: He who has a will is said to be good, so far as he has a good will; because it is by our will that we employ whatever powers we may have. Hence a man is said to be good, not by his good understanding; but by his good will. Now the will relates to the end as to its proper object. Thus the saying, "we exist because God is good" has reference to the final cause.

FIFTH ARTICLE [I, Q. 5, Art. 5]

Whether the Essence of Goodness Consists in Mode, Species and Order?

Objection 1: It seems that the essence of goodness does not consist in mode, species and order. For goodness and being differ logically. But mode, species and order seem to belong to the nature of being, for it is written: "Thou hast ordered all things in measure, and number, and weight" (Wis. 11:21). And to these three can be reduced species, mode and order, as Augustine says (Gen. ad lit. iv, 3): "Measure fixes the mode of everything, number gives it its species, and weight gives it rest and stability." Therefore the essence of goodness does not consist in mode, species and order.

Obj. 2: Further, mode, species and order are themselves good. Therefore if the essence of goodness consists in mode, species and order, then every mode must have its own mode, species and order. The same would be the case with species and order in endless succession.

Obj. 3: Further, evil is the privation of mode, species and order. But evil is not the total absence of goodness. Therefore the essence of goodness does not consist in mode, species and order.

Obj. 4: Further, that wherein consists the essence of goodness cannot be spoken of as evil. Yet we can speak of an evil mode, species and order. Therefore the essence of goodness does not consist in mode, species and order.

Obj. 5: Further, mode, species and order are caused by weight, number and measure, as appears from the quotation from Augustine. But not every good thing has weight, number and measure; for Ambrose says (Hexam. i, 9): "It is of the nature of light not to have been created in number, weight and measure." Therefore the essence of goodness does not consist in mode, species and order.

*On the contrary,* Augustine says (De Nat. Boni. iii): "These three—mode, species and order—as common good things, are in everything God has made; thus, where these three abound the things are very good; where they are less, the things are less good; where they do not exist at all, there can be nothing good." But this would not be unless the essence of goodness consisted in them. Therefore the essence of goodness consists in mode, species and order.

*I answer that,* Everything is said to be good so far as it is perfect; for in that way only is it desirable (as shown above, AA. 1, 3). Now a thing is said to be perfect if it lacks nothing according to the mode of its perfection. But since everything is what it is by its form (and since the form presupposes certain things, and from the form certain things necessarily follow), in order for a thing to be perfect and good it must have a form, together with all that precedes and follows upon that form. Now the form presupposes determination or commensuration of its principles, whether material or efficient, and this is signified by the mode: hence it is said that the measure marks the mode. But the form itself is signified by the species; for everything is placed in its species by its form. Hence the number is said to give the species, for definitions signifying species are like numbers, according to the Philosopher (Metaph. x); for as a unit added to, or taken from a number, changes its species, so a difference added to, or taken from a definition, changes its species. Further, upon the form follows an inclination to the end, or to an action, or something of the sort; for everything, in so far as it is in act, acts and tends towards that which is in accordance with its form; and this belongs to weight and order. Hence the essence of goodness, so far as it consists in perfection, consists also in mode, species and order.

Reply Obj. 1: These three only follow upon being, so far as it is perfect, and according to this perfection is it good.

Reply Obj. 2: Mode, species and order are said to be good, and to be beings, not as though they themselves were subsistences, but because it is through them that other things are both beings and good. Hence they have no need of other things whereby they are good: for they are spoken of as good, not as though formally constituted so by something else, but as formally constituting others good: thus whiteness is not said to be a being as though it were by anything else; but because, by it, something else has accidental being, as an object that is white.

Reply Obj. 3: Every being is due to some form. Hence, according to every being of a thing is its mode, species, order. Thus, a man has a mode, species and order as he is white, virtuous, learned and so on; according to everything predicated of him. But evil deprives a thing of some sort of being, as blindness deprives us of that being which is sight; yet it does not destroy every mode, species and order, but only such as follow upon the being of sight.

Reply Obj. 4: Augustine says (De Nat. Boni. xxiii), "Every mode, as mode, is good" (and the same can be said of species and order). "But an evil mode, species and order are so called as being less than they ought to be, or as not belonging to that which they ought to belong. Therefore they are called evil, because they are out of place and incongruous."

Reply Obj. 5: The nature of light is spoken of as being without number, weight and measure, not absolutely, but in comparison with corporeal things, because the power of light extends to all corporeal things; inasmuch as it is an active quality of the first body that causes change, i.e. the heavens.

SIXTH ARTICLE [I, Q. 5, Art. 6]

Whether Goodness Is Rightly Divided into the Virtuous*, the Useful and the Pleasant? [*"Bonum honestum" is the virtuous good considered as fitting. Cf. II-II, Q. 141, A. 3; Q. 145.]

Objection 1: It seems that goodness is not rightly divided into the virtuous, the useful and the pleasant. For goodness is divided by the ten predicaments, as the Philosopher says (Ethic. i). But the virtuous, the useful and the pleasant can be found under one predicament. Therefore goodness is not rightly divided by them.

Obj. 2: Further, every division is made by opposites. But these three do not seem to be opposites; for the virtuous is pleasing, and no wickedness is useful; whereas this ought to be the case if the division were made by opposites, for then the virtuous and the useful would be opposed; and Tully speaks of this (De Offic. ii). Therefore this division is incorrect.

Obj. 3: Further, where one thing is on account of another, there is only one thing. But the useful is not goodness, except so far as it is pleasing and virtuous. Therefore the useful ought not to divided against the pleasant and the virtuous.

*On the contrary,* Ambrose makes use of this division of goodness (De Offic. i, 9)

*I answer that,* This division properly concerns human goodness. But if we consider the nature of goodness from a higher and more universal point of view, we shall find that this division properly concerns goodness as such. For everything is good so far as it is desirable, and is a term of the movement of the appetite; the term of whose movement can be seen from a consideration of the movement of a natural body. Now the movement of a natural body is terminated by the end absolutely; and relatively by the means through which it comes to the end, where the movement ceases; so a thing is called a term of movement, so far as it terminates any part of that movement. Now the ultimate term of movement can be taken in two ways, either as the thing itself towards which it tends, e.g. a place or form; or a state of rest in that thing. Thus, in the movement of the appetite, the thing desired that terminates the movement of the appetite relatively, as a means by which something tends towards another, is called the useful; but that sought after as the last thing absolutely terminating the movement of the appetite, as a thing towards which for its own sake the appetite tends, is called the virtuous; for the virtuous is that which is desired for its own sake; but that which terminates the movement of the appetite in the form of rest in the thing desired, is called the pleasant.

Reply Obj. 1: Goodness, so far as it is identical with being, is divided by the ten predicaments. But this division belongs to it according to its proper formality.

Reply Obj. 2: This division is not by opposite things; but by opposite aspects. Now those things are called pleasing which have no other formality under which they are desirable except the pleasant, being sometimes hurtful and contrary to virtue. Whereas the useful applies to such as have nothing desirable in themselves, but are desired only as helpful to something further, as the taking of bitter medicine; while the virtuous is predicated of such as are desirable in themselves.

Reply Obj. 3: Goodness is not divided into these three as something univocal to be predicated equally of them all; but as something analogical to be predicated of them according to priority and posteriority. Hence it is predicated chiefly of the virtuous; then of the pleasant; and lastly of the useful.

# QUESTION 6

THE GOODNESS OF GOD (In Four Articles)

We next consider the goodness of God; under which head there are four points of inquiry:

(1) Whether goodness belongs to God?

(2) Whether God is the supreme good?

(3) Whether He alone is essentially good?

(4) Whether all things are good by the divine goodness?

FIRST ARTICLE [I, Q. 6, Art. 1]

Whether God is good?

Objection 1: It seems that to be good does not belong to God. For goodness consists in mode, species and order. But these do not seem to belong to God; since God is immense and is not ordered to anything else. Therefore to be good does not belong to God.

Obj. 2: Further, the good is what all things desire. But all things do not desire God, because all things do not know Him; and nothing is desired unless it is known. Therefore to be good does not belong to God.

*On the contrary,* It is written (Lam. 3:25): "The Lord is good to them that hope in Him, to the soul that seeketh Him."

*I answer that,* To be good belongs pre-eminently to God. For a thing is good according to its desirableness. Now everything seeks after its own perfection; and the perfection and form of an effect consist in a certain likeness to the agent, since every agent makes its like; and hence the agent itself is desirable and has the nature of good. For the very thing which is desirable in it is the participation of its likeness. Therefore, since God is the first effective cause of all things, it is manifest that the aspect of good and of desirableness belong to Him; and hence Dionysius (Div. Nom. iv) attributes good to God as to the first efficient cause, saying that, God is called good "as by Whom all things subsist."

Reply Obj. 1: To have mode, species and order belongs to the essence of caused good; but good is in God as in its cause, and hence it belongs to Him to impose mode, species and order on others; wherefore these three things are in God as in their cause.

Reply Obj. 2: All things, by desiring their own perfection, desire God Himself, inasmuch as the perfections of all things are so many similitudes of the divine being; as appears from what is said above (Q. 4, A. 3). And so of those things which desire God, some know Him as He is Himself, and this is proper to the rational creature; others know some participation of His goodness, and this belongs also to sensible knowledge; others have a natural desire without knowledge, as being directed to their ends by a higher intelligence.

SECOND ARTICLE [I, Q. 6, Art. 2]

Whether God Is the Supreme Good?

Objection 1: It seems that God is not the supreme good. For the supreme good adds something to good; otherwise it would belong to every good. But everything which is an addition to anything else is a compound thing: therefore the supreme good is a compound. But God is supremely simple; as was shown above (Q. 3, A. 7). Therefore God is not the supreme good.

Obj. 2: Further, "Good is what all desire," as the Philosopher says (Ethic. i, 1). Now what all desire is nothing but God, Who is the end of all things: therefore there is no other good but God. This appears also from what is said (Luke 18:19): "None is good but God alone." But we use the word supreme in comparison with others, as e.g. supreme heat is used in comparison with all other heats. Therefore God cannot be called the supreme good.

Obj. 3: Further, supreme implies comparison. But things not in the same genus are not comparable; as, sweetness is not properly greater or less than a line. Therefore, since God is not in the same genus as other good things, as appears above (QQ. 3, A. 5; 4, A. 3) it seems that God cannot be called the supreme good in relation to others.

*On the contrary,* Augustine says (De Trin. ii) that, the Trinity of the divine persons is "the supreme good, discerned by purified minds."

*I answer that,* God is the supreme good simply, and not only as existing in any genus or order of things. For good is attributed to God, as was said in the preceding article, inasmuch as all desired perfections flow from Him as from the first cause. They do not, however, flow from Him as from a univocal agent, as shown above (Q. 4, A. 2); but as from an agent which does not agree with its effects either in species or genus. Now the likeness of an effect in the univocal cause is found uniformly; but in the equivocal cause it is found more excellently, as, heat is in the sun more excellently than it is in fire. Therefore as good is in God as in the first, but not the univocal, cause of all things, it must be in Him in a most excellent way; and therefore He is called the supreme good.

Reply Obj. 1: The supreme good does not add to good any absolute thing, but only a relation. Now a relation of God to creatures, is not a reality in God, but in the creature; for it is in God in our idea only: as, what is knowable is so called with relation to knowledge, not that it depends on knowledge, but because knowledge depends on it. Thus it is not necessary that there should be composition in the supreme good, but only that other things are deficient in comparison with it.

Reply Obj. 2: When we say that good is what all desire, it is not to be understood that every kind of good thing is desired by all; but that whatever is desired has the nature of good. And when it is said, "None is good but God alone," this is to be understood of essential goodness, as will be explained in the next article.

Reply Obj. 3: Things not of the same genus are in no way comparable to each other if indeed they are in different genera. Now we say that God is not in the same genus with other good things; not that He is any other genus, but that He is outside genus, and is the principle of every genus; and thus He is compared to others by excess, and it is this kind of comparison the supreme good implies.

THIRD ARTICLE [I, Q. 6, Art. 3]

Whether to Be Essentially Good Belongs to God Alone?

Objection 1: It seems that to be essentially good does not belong to God alone. For as *one* is convertible with being, so is good; as we said above (Q. 5, A. 1). But every being is one essentially, as appears from the Philosopher (Metaph. iv); therefore every being is good essentially.

Obj. 2: Further, if good is what all things desire, since being itself is desired by all, then the being of each thing is its good. But everything is a being essentially; therefore every being is good essentially.

Obj. 3: Further, everything is good by its own goodness. Therefore if there is anything which is not good essentially, it is necessary to say that its goodness is not its own essence. Therefore its goodness, since it is a being, must be good; and if it is good by some other goodness, the same question applies to that goodness also; therefore we must either proceed to infinity, or come to some goodness which is not good by any other goodness. Therefore the first supposition holds good. Therefore everything is good essentially.

*On the contrary,* Boethius says (De Hebdom.), that "all things but God are good by participation." Therefore they are not good essentially.

*I answer that,* God alone is good essentially. For everything is called good according to its perfection. Now perfection of a thing is threefold: first, according to the constitution of its own being; secondly, in respect of any accidents being added as necessary for its perfect operation; thirdly, perfection consists in the attaining to something else as the end. Thus, for instance, the first perfection of fire consists in its existence, which it has through its own substantial form; its secondary perfection consists in heat, lightness and dryness, and the like; its third perfection is to rest in its own place. This triple perfection belongs to no creature by its own essence; it belongs to God only, in Whom alone essence is existence; in Whom there are no accidents; since whatever belongs to others accidentally belongs to Him essentially; as, to be powerful, wise and the like, as appears from what is stated above (Q. 3, A. 6); and He is not directed to anything else as to an end, but is Himself the last end of all things. Hence it is manifest that God alone has every kind of perfection by His own essence; therefore He Himself alone is good essentially.

Reply Obj. 1: "One" does not include the idea of perfection, but only of indivision, which belongs to everything according to its own essence. Now the essences of simple things are undivided both actually and potentially, but the essences of compounds are undivided only actually; and therefore everything must be one essentially, but not good essentially, as was shown above.

Reply Obj. 2: Although everything is good in that it has being, yet the essence of a creature is not very being; and therefore it does not follow that a creature is good essentially.

Reply Obj. 3: The goodness of a creature is not its very essence, but something superadded; it is either its existence, or some added perfection, or the order to its end. Still, the goodness itself thus added is good, just as it is being. But for this reason is it called being because by it something has being, not because it itself has being through something else: hence for this reason is it called good because by it something is good, and not because it itself has some other goodness whereby it is good.

FOURTH ARTICLE [I, Q. 6, Art. 4]

Whether All Things Are Good by the Divine Goodness?

Objection 1: It seems that all things are good by the divine goodness. For Augustine says (De Trin. viii), "This and that are good; take away this and that, and see good itself if thou canst; and so thou shalt see God, good not by any other good, but the good of every good." But everything is good by its own good; therefore everything is good by that very good which is God.

Obj. 2: Further, as Boethius says (De Hebdom.), all things are called good, accordingly as they are directed to God, and this is by reason of the divine goodness; therefore all things are good by the divine goodness.

*On the contrary,* All things are good, inasmuch as they have being. But they are not called beings through the divine being, but through their own being; therefore all things are not good by the divine goodness, but by their own goodness.

*I answer that,* As regards relative things, we must admit extrinsic denomination; as, a thing is denominated "placed" from "place," and "measured" from "measure." But as regards absolute things opinions differ. Plato held the existence of separate ideas (Q. 84, A. 4) of all things, and that individuals were denominated by them as participating in the separate ideas; for instance, that Socrates is called man according to the separate idea of man. Now just as he laid down separate ideas of man and horse which he called absolute man and absolute horse, so likewise he laid down separate ideas of "being" and of "one," and these he called absolute being and absolute oneness; and by participation of these, everything was called "being" or "one"; and what was thus absolute being and absolute one, he said was the supreme good. And because good is convertible with being, as one is also; he called God the absolute good, from whom all things are called good by way of participation.

Although this opinion appears to be unreasonable in affirming separate ideas of natural things as subsisting of themselves—as Aristotle argues in many ways—still, it is absolutely true that there is first something which is essentially being and essentially good, which we call God, as appears from what is shown above (Q. 2, A. 3), and Aristotle agrees with this. Hence from the first being, essentially such, and good, everything can be called good and a being, inasmuch as it participates in it by way of a certain assimilation which is far removed and defective; as appears from the above (Q. 4, A. 3).

Everything is therefore called good from the divine goodness, as from the first exemplary effective and final principle of all goodness. Nevertheless, everything is called good by reason of the similitude of the divine goodness belonging to it, which is formally its own goodness, whereby it is denominated good. And so of all things there is one goodness, and yet many goodnesses.

This is a sufficient Reply to the Objections.

# QUESTION 7

THE INFINITY OF GOD (In Four Articles)

After considering the divine perfection we must consider the divine infinity, and God's existence in things: for God is everywhere, and in all things, inasmuch as He is boundless and infinite.

Concerning the first, there are four points of inquiry:

(1) Whether God is infinite?

(2) Whether anything besides Him is infinite in essence?

(3) Whether anything can be infinitude in magnitude?

(4) Whether an infinite multitude can exist?

FIRST ARTICLE [I, Q. 7, Art. 1]

Whether God Is Infinite?

Objection 1: It seems that God is not infinite. For everything infinite is imperfect, as the Philosopher says; because it has parts and matter, as is said in Phys. iii. But God is most perfect; therefore He is not infinite.

Obj. 2: Further, according to the Philosopher (Phys. i), finite and infinite belong to quantity. But there is no quantity in God, for He is not a body, as was shown above (Q. 3, A. 1). Therefore it does not belong to Him to be infinite.

Obj. 3: Further, what is here in such a way as not to be elsewhere, is finite according to place. Therefore that which is a thing in such a way as not to be another thing, is finite according to substance. But God is this, and not another; for He is not a stone or wood. Therefore God is not infinite in substance.

*On the contrary,* Damascene says (De Fide Orth. i, 4) that "God is infinite and eternal, and boundless."

*I answer that,* All the ancient philosophers attribute infinitude to the first principle, as is said (Phys. iii), and with reason; for they considered that things flow forth infinitely from the first principle. But because some erred concerning the nature of the first principle, as a consequence they erred also concerning its infinity; forasmuch as they asserted that matter was the first principle; consequently they attributed to the first principle a material infinity to the effect that some infinite body was the first principle of things.

We must consider therefore that a thing is called infinite because it is not finite. Now matter is in a way made finite by form, and the form by matter. Matter indeed is made finite by form, inasmuch as matter, before it receives its form, is in potentiality to many forms; but on receiving a form, it is terminated by that one. Again, form is made finite by matter, inasmuch as form, considered in itself, is common to many; but when received in matter, the form is determined to this one particular thing. Now matter is perfected by the form by which it is made finite; therefore infinite as attributed to matter, has the nature of something imperfect; for it is as it were formless matter. On the other hand, form is not made perfect by matter, but rather is contracted by matter; and hence the infinite, regarded on the part of the form not determined by matter, has the nature of something perfect. Now being is the most formal of all things, as appears from what is shown above (Q. 4, A. 1, Obj. 3). Since therefore the divine being is not a being received in anything, but He is His own subsistent being as was shown above (Q. 3, A. 4), it is clear that God Himself is infinite and perfect.

From this appears the Reply to the First Objection.

Reply Obj. 2: Quantity is terminated by its form, which can be seen in the fact that a figure which consists in quantity terminated, is a kind of quantitative form. Hence the infinite of quantity is the infinite of matter; such a kind of infinite cannot be attributed to God; as was said above, in this article.

Reply Obj. 3: The fact that the being of God is self-subsisting, not received in any other, and is thus called infinite, shows Him to be distinguished from all other beings, and all others to be apart from Him. Even so, were there such a thing as a self-subsisting whiteness, the very fact that it did not exist in anything else, would make it distinct from every other whiteness existing in a subject.

SECOND ARTICLE [I, Q. 7, Art. 2]

Whether Anything but God Can Be Essentially Infinite?

Objection 1: It seems that something else besides God can be essentially infinite. For the power of anything is proportioned to its essence. Now if the essence of God is infinite, His power must also be infinite. Therefore He can produce an infinite effect, since the extent of a power is known by its effect.

Obj. 2: Further, whatever has infinite power, has an infinite essence. Now the created intellect has an infinite power; for it apprehends the universal, which can extend itself to an infinitude of singular things. Therefore every created intellectual substance is infinite.

Obj. 3: Further, primary matter is something other than God, as was shown above (Q. 3, A. 8). But primary matter is infinite. Therefore something besides God can be infinite.

*On the contrary,* The infinite cannot have a beginning, as said in Phys. iii. But everything outside God is from God as from its first principle. Therefore besides God nothing can be infinite.

*I answer that,* Things other than God can be relatively infinite, but not absolutely infinite. For with regard to infinite as applied to matter, it is manifest that everything actually existing possesses a form; and thus its matter is determined by form. But because matter, considered as existing under some substantial form, remains in potentiality to many accidental forms, which is absolutely finite can be relatively infinite; as, for example, wood is finite according to its own form, but still it is relatively infinite, inasmuch as it is in potentiality to an infinite number of shapes. But if we speak of the infinite in reference to form, it is manifest that those things, the forms of which are in matter, are absolutely finite, and in no way infinite. If, however, any created forms are not received into matter, but are self-subsisting, as some think is the case with angels, these will be relatively infinite, inasmuch as such kinds of forms are not terminated, nor contracted by any matter. But because a created form thus subsisting has being, and yet is not its own being, it follows that its being is received and contracted to a determinate nature. Hence it cannot be absolutely infinite.

Reply Obj. 1: It is against the nature of a made thing for its essence to be its existence; because subsisting being is not a created being; hence it is against the nature of a made thing to be absolutely infinite. Therefore, as God, although He has infinite power, cannot make a thing to be not made (for this would imply that two contradictories are true at the same time), so likewise He cannot make anything to be absolutely infinite.

Reply Obj. 2: The fact that the power of the intellect extends itself in a way to infinite things, is because the intellect is a form not in matter, but either wholly separated from matter, as is the angelic substance, or at least an intellectual power, which is not the act of any organ, in the intellectual soul joined to a body.

Reply Obj. 3: Primary matter does not exist by itself in nature, since it is not actually being, but potentially only; hence it is something concreated rather than created. Nevertheless, primary matter even as a potentiality is not absolutely infinite, but relatively, because its potentiality extends only to natural forms.

THIRD ARTICLE [I, Q. 7, Art. 3]

Whether an Actually Infinite Magnitude Can Exist?

Objection 1: It seems that there can be something actually infinite in magnitude. For in mathematics there is no error, since "there is no lie in things abstract," as the Philosopher says (Phys. ii). But mathematics uses the infinite in magnitude; thus, the geometrician in his demonstrations says, "Let this line be infinite." Therefore it is not impossible for a thing to be infinite in magnitude.

Obj. 2: Further, what is not against the nature of anything, can agree with it. Now to be infinite is not against the nature of magnitude; but rather both the finite and the infinite seem to be properties of quantity. Therefore it is not impossible for some magnitude to be infinite.

Obj. 3: Further, magnitude is infinitely divisible, for the continuous is defined that which is infinitely divisible, as is clear from Phys. iii. But contraries are concerned about one and the same thing. Since therefore addition is opposed to division, and increase opposed to diminution, it appears that magnitude can be increased to infinity. Therefore it is possible for magnitude to be infinite.

Obj. 4: Further, movement and time have quantity and continuity derived from the magnitude over which movement passes, as is said in Phys. iv. But it is not against the nature of time and movement to be infinite, since every determinate indivisible in time and circular movement is both a beginning and an end. Therefore neither is it against the nature of magnitude to be infinite.

*On the contrary,* Every body has a surface. But every body which has a surface is finite; because surface is the term of a finite body. Therefore all bodies are finite. The same applies both to surface and to a line. Therefore nothing is infinite in magnitude.

*I answer that,* It is one thing to be infinite in essence, and another to be infinite in magnitude. For granted that a body exists infinite in magnitude, as fire or air, yet this could not be infinite in essence, because its essence would be terminated in a species by its form, and confined to individuality by matter. And so assuming from these premises that no creature is infinite in essence, it still remains to inquire whether any creature can be infinite in magnitude.

We must therefore observe that a body, which is a complete magnitude, can be considered in two ways; mathematically, in respect to its quantity only; and naturally, as regards its matter and form.

Now it is manifest that a natural body cannot be actually infinite. For every natural body has some determined substantial form. Since therefore the accidents follow upon the substantial form, it is necessary that determinate accidents should follow upon a determinate form; and among these accidents is quantity. So every natural body has a greater or smaller determinate quantity. Hence it is impossible for a natural body to be infinite. The same appears from movement; because every natural body has some natural movement; whereas an infinite body could not have any natural movement; neither direct, because nothing moves naturally by a direct movement unless it is out of its place; and this could not happen to an infinite body, for it would occupy every place, and thus every place would be indifferently its own place. Neither could it move circularly; forasmuch as circular motion requires that one part of the body is necessarily transferred to a place occupied by another part, and this could not happen as regards an infinite circular body: for if two lines be drawn from the centre, the farther they extend from the centre, the farther they are from each other; therefore, if a body were infinite, the lines would be infinitely distant from each other; and thus one could never occupy the place belonging to any other.

The same applies to a mathematical body. For if we imagine a mathematical body actually existing, we must imagine it under some form, because nothing is actual except by its form; hence, since the form of quantity as such is figure, such a body must have some figure, and so would be finite; for figure is confined by a term or boundary.

Reply Obj. 1: A geometrician does not need to assume a line actually infinite, but takes some actually finite line, from which he subtracts whatever he finds necessary; which line he calls infinite.

Reply Obj. 2: Although the infinite is not against the nature of magnitude in general, still it is against the nature of any species of it; thus, for instance, it is against the nature of a bicubical or tricubical magnitude, whether circular or triangular, and so on. Now what is not possible in any species cannot exist in the genus; hence there cannot be any infinite magnitude, since no species of magnitude is infinite.

Reply Obj. 3: The infinite in quantity, as was shown above, belongs to matter. Now by division of the whole we approach to matter, forasmuch as parts have the aspect of matter; but by addition we approach to the whole which has the aspect of a form. Therefore the infinite is not in the addition of magnitude, but only in division.

Reply Obj. 4: Movement and time are whole, not actually but successively; hence they have potentiality mixed with actuality. But magnitude is an actual whole; therefore the infinite in quantity refers to matter, and does not agree with the totality of magnitude; yet it agrees with the totality of time and movement: for it is proper to matter to be in potentiality.

FOURTH ARTICLE [I, Q. 7, Art. 4]

Whether an Infinite Multitude Can Exist?

Objection 1: It seems that an actually infinite multitude is possible. For it is not impossible for a potentiality to be made actual. But number can be multiplied to infinity. Therefore it is possible for an infinite multitude actually to exist.

Obj. 2: Further, it is possible for any individual of any species to be made actual. But the species of figures are infinite. Therefore an infinite number of actual figures is possible.

Obj. 3: Further, things not opposed to each other do not obstruct each other. But supposing a multitude of things to exist, there can still be many others not opposed to them. Therefore it is not impossible for others also to coexist with them, and so on to infinitude; therefore an actual infinite number of things is possible.

*On the contrary,* It is written, "Thou hast ordered all things in measure, and number, and weight" (Wis. 11:21).

*I answer that,* A twofold opinion exists on this subject. Some, as Avicenna and Algazel, said that it was impossible for an actually infinite multitude to exist absolutely; but that an accidentally infinite multitude was not impossible. A multitude is said to be infinite absolutely, when an infinite multitude is necessary that something may exist. Now this is impossible; because it would entail something dependent on an infinity for its existence; and hence its generation could never come to be, because it is impossible to pass through an infinite medium.

A multitude is said to be accidentally infinite when its existence as such is not necessary, but accidental. This can be shown, for example, in the work of a carpenter requiring a certain absolute multitude; namely, art in the soul, the movement of the hand, and a hammer; and supposing that such things were infinitely multiplied, the carpentering work would never be finished, forasmuch as it would depend on an infinite number of causes. But the multitude of hammers, inasmuch as one may be broken and another used, is an accidental multitude; for it happens by accident that many hammers are used, and it matters little whether one or two, or many are used, or an infinite number, if the work is carried on for an infinite time. In this way they said that there can be an accidentally infinite multitude.

This, however, is impossible; since every kind of multitude must belong to a species of multitude. Now the species of multitude are to be reckoned by the species of numbers. But no species of number is infinite; for every number is multitude measured by one. Hence it is impossible for there to be an actually infinite multitude, either absolute or accidental. Likewise multitude in nature is created; and everything created is comprehended under some clear intention of the Creator; for no agent acts aimlessly. Hence everything created must be comprehended in a certain number. Therefore it is impossible for an actually infinite multitude to exist, even accidentally. But a potentially infinite multitude is possible; because the increase of multitude follows upon the division of magnitude; since the more a thing is divided, the greater number of things result. Hence, as the infinite is to be found potentially in the division of the continuous, because we thus approach matter, as was shown in the preceding article, by the same rule, the infinite can be also found potentially in the addition of multitude.

Reply Obj. 1: Every potentiality is made actual according to its mode of being; for instance, a day is reduced to act successively, and not all at once. Likewise the infinite in multitude is reduced to act successively, and not all at once; because every multitude can be succeeded by another multitude to infinity.

Reply Obj. 2: Species of figures are infinite by infinitude of number. Now there are various species of figures, such as trilateral, quadrilateral and so on; and as an infinitely numerable multitude is not all at once reduced to act, so neither is the multitude of figures.

Reply Obj. 3: Although the supposition of some things does not preclude the supposition of others, still the supposition of an infinite number is opposed to any single species of multitude. Hence it is not possible for an actually infinite multitude to exist.

## QUESTION 8

THE EXISTENCE OF GOD IN THINGS (In Four Articles)

Since it evidently belongs to the infinite to be present everywhere, and in all things, we now consider whether this belongs to God; and concerning this there arise four points of inquiry:

(1) Whether God is in all things?

(2) Whether God is everywhere?

(3) Whether God is everywhere by essence, power, and presence?

(4) Whether to be everywhere belongs to God alone?

FIRST ARTICLE [I, Q. 8, Art. 1]

Whether God Is in All Things?

Objection 1: It seems that God is not in all things. For what is above all things is not in all things. But God is above all, according to the Psalm (Ps. 112:4), "The Lord is high above all nations," etc. Therefore God is not in all things.

Obj. 2: Further, what is in anything is thereby contained. Now God is not contained by things, but rather does He contain them. Therefore God is not in things but things are rather in Him. Hence Augustine says (Octog. Tri. Quaest. qu. 20), that "in Him things are, rather than He is in any place."

Obj. 3: Further, the more powerful an agent is, the more extended is its action. But God is the most powerful of all agents. Therefore His action can extend to things which are far removed from Him; nor is it necessary that He should be in all things.

Obj. 4: Further, the demons are beings. But God is not in the demons; for there is no fellowship between light and darkness (2 Cor. 6:14). Therefore God is not in all things.

*On the contrary,* A thing is wherever it operates. But God operates in all things, according to Isa. 26:12, "Lord ... Thou hast wrought all our works in [Vulg.: 'for'] us." Therefore God is in all things.

*I answer that,* God is in all things; not, indeed, as part of their essence, nor as an accident, but as an agent is present to that upon which it works. For an agent must be joined to that wherein it acts immediately and touch it by its power; hence it is proved in Phys. vii that the thing moved and the mover must be joined together. Now since God is very being by His own essence, created being must be His proper effect; as to ignite is the proper effect of fire. Now God causes this effect in things not only when they first begin to be, but as long as they are preserved in being; as light is caused in the air by the sun as long as the air remains illuminated. Therefore as long as a thing has being, God must be present to it, according to its mode of being. But being is innermost in each thing and most fundamentally inherent in all things since it is formal in respect of everything found in a thing, as was shown above (Q. 7, A. 1). Hence it must be that God is in all things, and innermostly.

Reply Obj. 1: God is above all things by the excellence of His nature; nevertheless, He is in all things as the cause of the being of all things; as was shown above in this article.

Reply Obj. 2: Although corporeal things are said to be in another as in that which contains them, nevertheless, spiritual things contain those things in which they are; as the soul contains the body. Hence also God is in things containing them; nevertheless, by a certain similitude to corporeal things, it is said that all things are in God; inasmuch as they are contained by Him.

Reply Obj. 3: No action of an agent, however powerful it may be, acts at a distance, except through a medium. But it belongs to the great power of God that He acts immediately in all things. Hence nothing is distant from Him, as if it could be without God in itself. But things are said to be distant from God by the unlikeness to Him in nature or grace; as also He is above all by the excellence of His own nature.

Reply Obj. 4: In the demons there is their nature which is from God, and also the deformity of sin which is not from Him; therefore, it is not to be absolutely conceded that God is in the demons, except with the addition, "inasmuch as they are beings." But in things not deformed in their nature, we must say absolutely that God is.

SECOND ARTICLE [I, Q. 8, Art. 2]

Whether God Is Everywhere?

Objection 1: It seems that God is not everywhere. For to be everywhere means to be in every place. But to be in every place does not belong to God, to Whom it does not belong to be in place at all; for "incorporeal things," as Boethius says (De Hebdom.), "are not in a place." Therefore God is not everywhere.

Obj. 2: Further, the relation of time to succession is the same as the relation of place to permanence. But one indivisible part of action or movement cannot exist in different times; therefore neither can one indivisible part in the genus of permanent things be in every place. Now the divine being is not successive but permanent. Therefore God is not in many places; and thus He is not everywhere.

Obj. 3: Further, what is wholly in any one place is not in part elsewhere. But if God is in any one place He is all there; for He has no parts. No part of Him then is elsewhere; and therefore God is not everywhere.

*On the contrary,* It is written, "I fill heaven and earth." (Jer. 23:24).

*I answer that,* Since place is a thing, to be in place can be understood in a twofold sense; either by way of other things—i.e. as one thing is said to be in another no matter how; and thus the accidents of a place are in place; or by a way proper to place; and thus things placed are in a place. Now in both these senses, in some way God is in every place; and this is to be everywhere. First, as He is in all things giving them being, power and operation; so He is in every place as giving it existence and locative power. Again, things placed are in place, inasmuch as they fill place; and God fills every place; not, indeed, like a body, for a body is said to fill place inasmuch as it excludes the co-presence of another body; whereas by God being in a place, others are not thereby excluded from it; indeed, by the very fact that He gives being to the things that fill every place, He Himself fills every place.

Reply Obj. 1: Incorporeal things are in place not by contact of dimensive quantity, as bodies are but by contact of power.

Reply Obj. 2: The indivisible is twofold. One is the term of the continuous; as a point in permanent things, and as a moment in succession; and this kind of the indivisible in permanent things, forasmuch as it has a determinate site, cannot be in many parts of place, or in many places; likewise the indivisible of action or movement, forasmuch as it has a determinate order in movement or action, cannot be in many parts of time. Another kind of the indivisible is outside of the whole genus of the continuous; and in this way incorporeal substances, like God, angel and soul, are called indivisible.

Such a kind of indivisible does not belong to the continuous, as a part of it, but as touching it by its power; hence, according as its power can extend itself to one or to many, to a small thing, or to a great one, in this way it is in one or in many places, and in a small or large place.

Reply Obj. 3: A whole is so called with reference to its parts. Now part is twofold: viz. a part of the essence, as the form and the matter are called parts of the composite, while genus and difference are called parts of species. There is also part of quantity into which any quantity is divided. What therefore is whole in any place by totality of quantity, cannot be outside of that place, because the quantity of anything placed is commensurate to the quantity of the place; and hence there is no totality of quantity without totality of place. But totality of essence is not commensurate to the totality of place. Hence it is not necessary for that which is whole by totality of essence in a thing, not to be at all outside of it. This appears also in accidental forms which have accidental quantity; as an example, whiteness is whole in each part of the surface if we speak of its totality of essence; because according to the perfect idea of its species it is found to exist in every part of the surface. But if its totality be considered according to quantity which it has accidentally, then it is not whole in every part of the surface. On the other hand, incorporeal substances have no totality either of themselves or accidentally, except in reference to the perfect idea of their essence. Hence, as the soul is whole in every part of the body, so is God whole in all things and in each one.

THIRD ARTICLE [I, Q. 8, Art. 3]

Whether God Is Everywhere by Essence, Presence and Power?

Objection 1: It seems that the mode of God's existence in all things is not properly described by way of essence, presence and power. For what is by essence in anything, is in it essentially. But God is not essentially in things; for He does not belong to the essence of anything. Therefore it ought not to be said that God is in things by essence, presence and power.

Obj. 2: Further, to be present in anything means not to be absent from it. Now this is the meaning of God being in things by His essence, that He is not absent from anything. Therefore the presence of God in all things by essence and presence means the same thing. Therefore it is superfluous to say that God is present in things by His essence, presence and power.

Obj. 3: Further, as God by His power is the principle of all things, so He is the same likewise by His knowledge and will. But it is not said that He is in things by knowledge and will. Therefore neither is He present by His power.

Obj. 4: Further, as grace is a perfection added to the substance of a thing, so many other perfections are likewise added. Therefore if God is said to be in certain persons in a special way by grace, it seems that according to every perfection there ought to be a special mode of God's existence in things.

*On the contrary,* A gloss on the Canticle of Canticles (5) says that, "God by a common mode is in all things by His presence, power and substance; still He is said to be present more familiarly in some by grace." [*The quotation is from St. Gregory, (Hom. viii in Ezech.)].

*I answer that,* God is said to be in a thing in two ways; in one way after the manner of an efficient cause; and thus He is in all things created by Him; in another way he is in things as the object of operation is in the operator; and this is proper to the operations of the soul, according as the thing known is in the one who knows; and the thing desired in the one desiring. In this second way God is especially in the rational creature which knows and loves Him actually or habitually. And because the rational creature possesses this prerogative by grace, as will be shown later (Q. 12). He is said to be thus in the saints by grace.

But how He is in other things created by Him, may be considered from human affairs. A king, for example, is said to be in the whole kingdom by his power, although he is not everywhere present. Again a thing is said to be by its presence in other things which are subject to its inspection; as things in a house are said to be present to anyone, who nevertheless may not be in substance in every part of the house. Lastly, a thing is said to be by way of substance or essence in that place in which its substance may be. Now there were some (the Manichees) who said that spiritual and incorporeal things were subject to the divine power; but that visible and corporeal things were subject to the power of a contrary principle. Therefore against these it is necessary to say that God is in all things by His power.

But others, though they believed that all things were subject to the divine power, still did not allow that divine providence extended to these inferior bodies, and in the person of these it is said, "He walketh about the poles of the heavens; and He doth not consider our things [*Vulg.: 'He doth not consider ... and He walketh,' etc.]" (Job 22:14). Against these it is necessary to say that God is in all things by His presence.

Further, others said that, although all things are subject to God's providence, still all things are not immediately created by God; but that He immediately created the first creatures, and these created the others. Against these it is necessary to say that He is in all things by His essence.

Therefore, God is in all things by His power, inasmuch as all things are subject to His power; He is by His presence in all things, as all things are bare and open to His eyes; He is in all things by His essence, inasmuch as He is present to all as the cause of their being.

Reply Obj. 1: God is said to be in all things by essence, not indeed by the essence of the things themselves, as if He were of their essence; but by His own essence; because His substance is present to all things as the cause of their being.

Reply Obj. 2: A thing can be said to be present to another, when in its sight, though the thing may be distant in substance, as was shown in this article; and therefore two modes of presence are necessary; viz. by essence and by presence.

Reply Obj. 3: Knowledge and will require that the thing known should be in the one who knows, and the thing willed in the one who wills. Hence by knowledge and will things are more truly in God than God in things. But power is the principle of acting on another; hence by power the agent is related and applied to an external thing; thus by power an agent may be said to be present to another.

Reply Obj. 4: No other perfection, except grace, added to substance, renders God present in anything as the object known and loved; therefore only grace constitutes a special mode of God's existence in things. There is, however, another special mode of God's existence in man by union, which will be treated of in its own place (Part III).

FOURTH ARTICLE [I, Q. 8, Art. 4]

Whether to Be Everywhere Belongs to God Alone?

Objection 1: It seems that to be everywhere does not belong to God alone. For the universal, according to the Philosopher (Poster. i), is everywhere, and always; primary matter also, since it is in all bodies, is everywhere. But neither of these is God, as appears from what is said above (Q. 3). Therefore to be everywhere does not belong to God alone.

Obj. 2: Further, number is in things numbered. But the whole universe is constituted in number, as appears from the Book of Wisdom (Wis. 11:21). Therefore there is some number which is in the whole universe, and is thus everywhere.

Obj. 3: Further, the universe is a kind of "whole perfect body" (Coel. et Mund. i). But the whole universe is everywhere, because there is no place outside it. Therefore to be everywhere does not belong to God alone.

Obj. 4: Further, if any body were infinite, no place would exist outside of it, and so it would be everywhere. Therefore to be everywhere does not appear to belong to God alone.

Obj. 5: Further, the soul, as Augustine says (De Trin. vi, 6), is "whole in the whole body, and whole in every one of its parts." Therefore if there was only one animal in the world, its soul would be everywhere; and thus to be everywhere does not belong to God alone.

Obj. 6: Further, as Augustine says (Ep. 137), "The soul feels where it sees, and lives where it feels, and is where it lives." But the soul sees as it were everywhere: for in a succession of glances it comprehends the entire space of the heavens in its sight. Therefore the soul is everywhere.

*On the contrary,* Ambrose says (De Spir. Sanct. i, 7): "Who dares to call the Holy Ghost a creature, Who in all things, and everywhere, and always is, which assuredly belongs to the divinity alone?"

*I answer that,* To be everywhere primarily and absolutely, is proper to God. Now to be everywhere primarily is said of that which in its whole self is everywhere; for if a thing were everywhere according to its parts in different places, it would not be primarily everywhere, forasmuch as what belongs to anything according to part does not belong to it primarily; thus if a man has white teeth, whiteness belongs primarily not to the man but to his teeth. But a thing is everywhere absolutely when it does not belong to it to be everywhere accidentally, that is, merely on some supposition; as a grain of millet would be everywhere, supposing that no other body existed. It belongs therefore to a thing to be everywhere absolutely when, on any supposition, it must be everywhere; and this properly belongs to God alone. For whatever number of places be supposed, even if an infinite number be supposed besides what already exist, it would be necessary that God should be in all of them; for nothing can exist except by Him. Therefore to be everywhere primarily and absolutely belongs to God and is proper to Him: because whatever number of places be supposed to exist, God must be in all of them, not as to a part of Him, but as to His very self.

Reply Obj. 1: The universal, and also primary matter are indeed everywhere; but not according to the same mode of existence.

Reply Obj. 2: Number, since it is an accident, does not, of itself, exist in place, but accidentally; neither is the whole but only part of it in each of the things numbered; hence it does not follow that it is primarily and absolutely everywhere.

Reply Obj. 3: The whole body of the universe is everywhere, but not primarily; forasmuch as it is not wholly in each place, but according to its parts; nor again is it everywhere absolutely, because, supposing that other places existed besides itself, it would not be in them.

Reply Obj. 4: If an infinite body existed, it would be everywhere; but according to its parts.

Reply Obj. 5: Were there one animal only, its soul would be everywhere primarily indeed, but only accidentally.

Reply Obj. 6: When it is said that the soul sees anywhere, this can be taken in two senses. In one sense the adverb "anywhere" determines the act of seeing on the part of the object; and in this sense it is true that while it sees the heavens, it sees in the heavens; and in the same way it feels in the heavens; but it does not follow that it lives or exists in the heavens, because to live and to exist do not import an act passing to an exterior object. In another sense it can be understood according as the adverb determines the act of the seer, as proceeding from the seer; and thus it is true that where the soul feels and sees, there it is, and there it lives according to this mode of speaking; and thus it does not follow that it is everywhere.

## QUESTION 9

THE IMMUTABILITY OF GOD (In Two Articles)

We next consider God's immutability, and His eternity following on His immutability. On the immutability of God there are two points of inquiry:

(1) Whether God is altogether immutable?

(2) Whether to be immutable belongs to God alone?

FIRST ARTICLE [I, Q. 9, Art. 1]

Whether God is altogether immutable?

Objection 1: It seems that God is not altogether immutable. For whatever moves itself is in some way mutable. But, as Augustine says (Gen. ad lit, viii, 20), "The Creator Spirit moves Himself neither by time, nor by place." Therefore God is in some way mutable.

Obj. 2: Further, it is said of Wisdom, that "it is more mobile than all things active [Vulg. 'mobilior']" (Wis. 7:24). But God is wisdom itself; therefore God is movable.

Obj. 3: Further, to approach and to recede signify movement. But these are said of God in Scripture, "Draw nigh to God and He will draw nigh to you" (James 4:8). Therefore God is mutable.

*On the contrary,* It is written, "I am the Lord, and I change not" (Malachi 3:6).

*I answer that,* From what precedes, it is shown that God is altogether immutable. First, because it was shown above that there is some first being, whom we call God; and that this first being must be pure act, without the admixture of any potentiality, for the reason that, absolutely, potentiality is posterior to act. Now everything which is in any way changed, is in some way in potentiality. Hence it is evident that it is impossible for God to be in any way changeable. Secondly, because everything which is moved, remains as it was in part, and passes away in part; as what is moved from whiteness to blackness, remains the same as to substance; thus in everything which is moved, there is some kind of composition to be found. But it has been shown above (Q. 3, A. 7) that in God there is no composition, for He is altogether simple. Hence it is manifest that God cannot be moved. Thirdly, because everything which is moved acquires something by its movement, and attains to what it had not attained previously. But since God is infinite, comprehending in Himself all the plenitude of perfection of all being, He cannot acquire anything new, nor extend Himself to anything whereto He was not extended previously. Hence movement in no way belongs to Him. So, some of the ancients, constrained, as it were, by the truth, decided that the first principle was immovable.

Reply Obj. 1: Augustine there speaks in a similar way to Plato, who said that the first mover moves Himself; calling every operation a movement, even as the acts of understanding, and willing, and loving, are called movements. Therefore because God understands and loves Himself, in that respect they said that God moves Himself, not, however, as movement and change belong to a thing existing in potentiality, as we now speak of change and movement.

Reply Obj. 2: Wisdom is called mobile by way of similitude, according as it diffuses its likeness even to the outermost of things; for nothing can exist which does not proceed from the divine wisdom by way of some kind of imitation, as from the first effective and formal principle; as also works of art proceed from the wisdom of the artist. And so in the same way, inasmuch as the similitude of the divine wisdom proceeds in degrees from the highest things, which participate more fully of its likeness, to the lowest things which participate of it in a lesser degree, there is said to be a kind of procession and movement of the divine wisdom to things; as when we say that the sun proceeds to the earth, inasmuch as the ray of light touches the earth. In this way Dionysius (Coel. Hier. i) expounds the matter, that every procession of the divine manifestation comes to us from the movement of the Father of light.

Reply Obj. 3: These things are said of God in Scripture metaphorically. For as the sun is said to enter a house, or to go out, according as its rays reach the house, so God is said to approach to us, or to recede from us, when we receive the influx of His goodness, or decline from Him.

SECOND ARTICLE [I. Q. 9, Art. 2]

Whether to Be Immutable Belongs to God Alone?

Objection 1: It seems that to be immutable does not belong to God alone. For the Philosopher says (Metaph. ii) that "matter is in everything which is moved." But, according to some, certain created substances, as angels and souls, have not matter. Therefore to be immutable does not belong to God alone.

Obj. 2: Further, everything in motion moves to some end. What therefore has already attained its ultimate end, is not in motion. But some creatures have already attained to their ultimate end; as all the blessed in heaven. Therefore some creatures are immovable.

Obj. 3: Further, everything which is mutable is variable. But forms are invariable; for it is said (Sex Princip. i) that "form is essence consisting of the simple and invariable." Therefore it does not belong to God alone to be immutable.

*On the contrary,* Augustine says (De Nat. Boni. i), "God alone is immutable; and whatever things He has made, being from nothing, are mutable."

*I answer that,* God alone is altogether immutable; whereas every creature is in some way mutable. Be it known therefore that a mutable thing can be called so in two ways: by a power in itself; and by a power possessed by another. For all creatures before they existed, were possible, not by any created power, since no creature is eternal, but by the divine power alone, inasmuch as God could produce them into existence. Thus, as the production of a thing into existence depends on the will of God, so likewise it depends on His will that things should be preserved; for He does not preserve them otherwise than by ever giving them existence; hence if He took away His action from them, all things would be reduced to nothing, as appears from Augustine (Gen. ad lit. iv, 12). Therefore as it was in the Creator's power to produce them before they existed in themselves, so likewise it is in the Creator's power when they exist in themselves to bring them to nothing. In this way therefore, by the power of another—namely, of God—they are mutable, inasmuch as they are producible from nothing by Him, and are by Him reducible from existence to non-existence.

If, however, a thing is called mutable by a power in itself, thus also in some manner every creature is mutable. For every creature has a twofold power, active and passive; and I call that power passive which enables anything to attain its perfection either in being, or in attaining to its end. Now if the mutability of a thing be considered according to its power for being, in that way all creatures are not mutable, but those only in which what is potential in them is consistent with non-being. Hence, in the inferior bodies there is mutability both as regards substantial being, inasmuch as their matter can exist with privation of their substantial form, and also as regards their accidental being, supposing the subject to coexist with privation of accident; as, for example, this subject *man* can exist with *not-whiteness* and can therefore be changed from white to not-white. But supposing the accident to be such as to follow on the essential principles of the subject, then the privation of such an accident cannot coexist with the subject. Hence the subject cannot be changed as regards that kind of accident; as, for example, snow cannot be made black. Now in the celestial bodies matter is not consistent with privation of form, because the form perfects the whole potentiality of the matter; therefore these bodies are not mutable as to substantial being, but only as to locality, because the subject is consistent with privation of this or that place. On the other hand incorporeal substances, being subsistent forms which, although with respect to their own existence are as potentiality to act, are not consistent with the privation of this act; forasmuch as existence is consequent upon form, and nothing corrupts except it lose its form. Hence in the form itself there is no power to non-existence; and so these kinds of substances are immutable and invariable as regards their existence. Wherefore Dionysius says (Div. Nom. iv) that "intellectual created substances are pure from generation and from every variation, as also are incorporeal and immaterial substances." Still, there remains in them a twofold mutability: one as regards their potentiality to their end; and in that way there is in them a mutability according to choice from good to evil, as Damascene says (De Fide ii, 3,4); the other as regards place, inasmuch as by their finite power they attain to certain fresh places—which cannot be said of God, who by His infinity fills all places, as was shown above (Q. 8, A. 2).

Thus in every creature there is a potentiality to change either as regards substantial being as in the case of things corruptible; or as regards locality only, as in the case of the celestial bodies; or as regards the order to their end, and the application of their powers to divers objects, as in the case with the angels; and universally all creatures generally are mutable by the power of the Creator, in Whose power is their existence and non-existence. Hence since God is in none of these ways mutable, it belongs to Him alone to be altogether immutable.

Reply Obj. 1: This objection proceeds from mutability as regards substantial or accidental being; for philosophers treated of such movement.

Reply Obj. 2: The good angels, besides their natural endowment of immutability of being, have also immutability of election by divine power; nevertheless there remains in them mutability as regards place.

Reply Obj. 3: Forms are called invariable, forasmuch as they cannot be subjects of variation; but they are subject to variation because by them their subject is variable. Hence it is clear that they vary in so far as they are; for they are not called beings as though they were the subject of being, but because through them something has being.

## QUESTION 10

THE ETERNITY OF GOD (In Six Articles)

We must now consider the eternity of God, concerning which arise six points of inquiry:

(1) What is eternity?

(2) Whether God is eternal?

(3) Whether to be eternal belongs to God alone?

(4) Whether eternity differs from time?

(5) The difference of aeviternity and of time.

(6) Whether there is only one aeviternity, as there is one time, and one eternity?

FIRST ARTICLE [I, Q. 10, Art. 1]

Whether This Is a Good Definition of Eternity, "The Simultaneously- Whole and Perfect Possession of Interminable Life"?

Objection 1: It seems that the definition of eternity given by Boethius (De Consol. v) is not a good one: "Eternity is the simultaneously-whole and perfect possession of interminable life." For the word "interminable" is a negative one. But negation only belongs to what is defective, and this does not belong to eternity. Therefore in the definition of eternity the word "interminable" ought not to be found.

Obj. 2: Further, eternity signifies a certain kind of duration. But duration regards existence rather than life. Therefore the word "life" ought not to come into the definition of eternity; but rather the word "existence."

Obj. 3: Further, a whole is what has parts. But this is alien to eternity which is simple. Therefore it is improperly said to be "whole."

Obj. 4: Many days cannot occur together, nor can many times exist all at once. But in eternity, days and times are in the plural, for it is said, "His going forth is from the beginning, from the days of eternity" (Micah 5:2); and also it is said, "According to the revelation of the mystery hidden from eternity" (Rom. 16:25). Therefore eternity is not omni-simultaneous.

Obj. 5: Further, the whole and the perfect are the same thing. Supposing, therefore, that it is "whole," it is superfluously described as "perfect."

Obj. 6: Further, duration does not imply "possession." But eternity is a kind of duration. Therefore eternity is not possession.

*I answer that,* As we attain to the knowledge of simple things by way of compound things, so must we reach to the knowledge of eternity by means of time, which is nothing but the numbering of movement by *before* and after. For since succession occurs in every movement, and one part comes after another, the fact that we reckon before and after in movement, makes us apprehend time, which is nothing else but the measure of before and after in movement. Now in a thing bereft of movement, which is always the same, there is no before or after. As therefore the idea of time consists in the numbering of before and after in movement; so likewise in the apprehension of the uniformity of what is outside of movement, consists the idea of eternity.

Further, those things are said to be measured by time which have a beginning and an end in time, because in everything which is moved there is a beginning, and there is an end. But as whatever is wholly immutable can have no succession, so it has no beginning, and no end.

Thus eternity is known from two sources: first, because what is eternal is interminable—that is, has no beginning nor end (that is, no term either way); secondly, because eternity has no succession, being simultaneously whole.

Reply Obj. 1: Simple things are usually defined by way of negation; as "a point is that which has no parts." Yet this is not to be taken as if the negation belonged to their essence, but because our intellect which first apprehends compound things, cannot attain to the knowledge of simple things except by removing the opposite.

Reply Obj. 2: What is truly eternal, is not only being, but also living; and life extends to operation, which is not true of being. Now the protraction of duration seems to belong to operation rather than to being; hence time is the numbering of movement.

Reply Obj. 3: Eternity is called whole, not because it has parts, but because it is wanting in nothing.

Reply Obj. 4: As God, although incorporeal, is named in Scripture metaphorically by corporeal names, so eternity though simultaneously whole, is called by names implying time and succession.

Reply Obj. 5: Two things are to be considered in time: time itself, which is successive; and the "now" of time, which is imperfect. Hence the expression "simultaneously-whole" is used to remove the idea of time, and the word "perfect" is used to exclude the "now" of time.

Reply Obj. 6: Whatever is possessed, is held firmly and quietly; therefore to designate the immutability and permanence of eternity, we use the word "possession."

SECOND ARTICLE [I, Q. 10, Art. 2]

Whether God is Eternal?

Objection 1: It seems that God is not eternal. For nothing made can be predicated of God; for Boethius says (De Trin. iv) that, "The now that flows away makes time, the now that stands still makes eternity;" and Augustine says (Octog. Tri. Quaest. qu. 28) "that God is the author of eternity." Therefore God is not eternal.

Obj. 2: Further, what is before eternity, and after eternity, is not measured by eternity. But, as Aristotle says (De Causis), "God is before eternity and He is after eternity": for it is written that "the Lord shall reign for eternity, and beyond [*Douay: 'for ever and ever']" (Ex. 15:18). Therefore to be eternal does not belong to God.

Obj. 3: Further, eternity is a kind of measure. But to be measured belongs not to God. Therefore it does not belong to Him to be eternal.

Obj. 4: Further, in eternity, there is no present, past or future, since it is simultaneously whole; as was said in the preceding article. But words denoting present, past and future time are applied to God in Scripture. Therefore God is not eternal.

*On the contrary,* Athanasius says in his Creed: "The Father is eternal, the Son is eternal, the Holy Ghost is eternal."

*I answer that,* The idea of eternity follows immutability, as the idea of time follows movement, as appears from the preceding article. Hence, as God is supremely immutable, it supremely belongs to Him to be eternal. Nor is He eternal only; but He is His own eternity; whereas, no other being is its own duration, as no other is its own being. Now God is His own uniform being; and hence as He is His own essence, so He is His own eternity.

Reply Obj. 1: The "now" that stands still, is said to make eternity according to our apprehension. As the apprehension of time is caused in us by the fact that we apprehend the flow of the "now," so the apprehension of eternity is caused in us by our apprehending the "now" standing still. When Augustine says that "God is the author of eternity," this is to be understood of participated eternity. For God communicates His eternity to some in the same way as He communicates His immutability.

Reply Obj. 2: From this appears the answer to the Second Objection. For God is said to be before eternity, according as it is shared by immaterial substances. Hence, also, in the same book, it is said that "intelligence is equal to eternity." In the words of Exodus, "The Lord shall reign for eternity, and beyond," eternity stands for age, as another rendering has it. Thus it is said that the Lord will reign beyond eternity, inasmuch as He endures beyond every age, i.e. beyond every kind of duration. For age is nothing more than the period of each thing, as is said in the book *De Coelo* i. Or to reign beyond eternity can be taken to mean that if any other thing were conceived to exist for ever, as the movement of the heavens according to some philosophers, then God would still reign beyond, inasmuch as His reign is simultaneously whole.

Reply Obj. 3: Eternity is nothing else but God Himself. Hence God is not called eternal, as if He were in any way measured; but the idea of measurement is there taken according to the apprehension of our mind alone.

Reply Obj. 4: Words denoting different times are applied to God, because His eternity includes all times; not as if He Himself were altered through present, past and future.

THIRD ARTICLE [I, Q. 10, Art. 3]

Whether to Be Eternal Belongs to God Alone?

Objection 1: It seems that it does not belong to God alone to be eternal. For it is written that "those who instruct many to justice," shall be "as stars unto perpetual eternities [*Douay: 'for all eternity']" (Dan. 12:3). Now if God alone were eternal, there could not be many eternities. Therefore God alone is not the only eternal.

Obj. 2: Further, it is written "Depart, ye cursed into eternal [Douay: 'everlasting'] fire" (Matt. 25:41). Therefore God is not the only eternal.

Obj. 3: Further, every necessary thing is eternal. But there are many necessary things; as, for instance, all principles of demonstration and all demonstrative propositions. Therefore God is not the only eternal.

*On the contrary,* Jerome says (Ep. ad Damasum, xv) that "God is the only one who has no beginning." Now whatever has a beginning, is not eternal. Therefore God is the only one eternal.

*I answer that,* Eternity truly and properly so called is in God alone, because eternity follows on immutability; as appears from the first article. But God alone is altogether immutable, as was shown above (Q. 9, A. 1). Accordingly, however, as some receive immutability from Him, they share in His eternity. Thus some receive immutability from God in the way of never ceasing to exist; in that sense it is said of the earth, "it standeth for ever" (Eccl. 1:4). Again, some things are called eternal in Scripture because of the length of their duration, although they are in nature corruptible; thus (Ps. 75:5) the hills are called "eternal" and we read "of the fruits of the eternal hills." (Deut. 33:15). Some again, share more fully than others in the nature of eternity, inasmuch as they possess unchangeableness either in being or further still in operation; like the angels, and the blessed, who enjoy the Word, because "as regards that vision of the Word, no changing thoughts exist in the Saints," as Augustine says (De Trin. xv). Hence those who see God are said to have eternal life; according to that text, "This is eternal life, that they may know Thee the only true God," etc. (John 17:3).

Reply Obj. 1: There are said to be many eternities, accordingly as many share in eternity, by the contemplation of God.

Reply Obj. 2: The fire of hell is called eternal, only because it never ends. Still, there is change in the pains of the lost, according to the words "To extreme heat they will pass from snowy waters" (Job 24:19). Hence in hell true eternity does not exist, but rather time; according to the text of the Psalm "Their time will be for ever" (Ps. 80:16).

Reply Obj. 3: Necessary means a certain mode of truth; and truth, according to the Philosopher (Metaph. vi), is in the mind. Therefore in this sense the true and necessary are eternal, because they are in the eternal mind, which is the divine intellect alone; hence it does not follow that anything beside God is eternal.

FOURTH ARTICLE [I. Q. 10, Art. 4]

Whether Eternity Differs from Time?

Objection 1: It seems that eternity does not differ from time. For two measures of duration cannot exist together, unless one is part of the other; for instance two days or two hours cannot be together; nevertheless, we may say that a day or an hour are together, considering hour as part of a day. But eternity and time occur together, each of which imports a certain measure of duration. Since therefore eternity is not a part of time, forasmuch as eternity exceeds time, and includes it, it seems that time is a part of eternity, and is not a different thing from eternity.

Obj. 2: Further, according to the Philosopher (Phys. iv), the "now" of time remains the same in the whole of time. But the nature of eternity seems to be that it is the same indivisible thing in the whole space of time. Therefore eternity is the "now" of time. But the "now" of time is not substantially different from time. Therefore eternity is not substantially different from time.

Obj. 3: Further, as the measure of the first movement is the measure of every movement, as said in Phys. iv, it thus appears that the measure of the first being is that of every being. But eternity is the measure of the first being—that is, of the divine being. Therefore eternity is the measure of every being. But the being of things corruptible is measured by time. Time therefore is either eternity or is a part of eternity.

*On the contrary,* Eternity is simultaneously whole. But time has a "before" and an "after." Therefore time and eternity are not the same thing.

*I answer that,* It is manifest that time and eternity are not the same. Some have founded this difference on the fact that eternity has neither beginning nor an end; whereas time has a beginning and an end. This, however, makes a merely accidental, and not an absolute difference because, granted that time always was and always will be, according to the idea of those who think the movement of the heavens goes on for ever, there would yet remain a difference between eternity and time, as Boethius says (De Consol. v), arising from the fact that eternity is simultaneously whole; which cannot be applied to time: for eternity is the measure of a permanent being; while time is a measure of movement. Supposing, however, that the aforesaid difference be considered on the part of the things measured, and not as regards the measures, then there is some reason for it, inasmuch as that alone is measured by time which has beginning and end in time. Hence, if the movement of the heavens lasted always, time would not be of its measure as regards the whole of its duration, since the infinite is not measurable; but it would be the measure of that part of its revolution which has beginning and end in time.

Another reason for the same can be taken from these measures in themselves, if we consider the end and the beginning as potentialities; because, granted also that time always goes on, yet it is possible to note in time both the beginning and the end, by considering its parts: thus we speak of the beginning and the end of a day or of a year; which cannot be applied to eternity. Still these differences follow upon the essential and primary differences, that eternity is simultaneously whole, but that time is not so.

Reply Obj. 1: Such a reason would be a valid one if time and eternity were the same kind of measure; but this is seen not to be the case when we consider those things of which the respective measures are time and eternity.

Reply Obj. 2: The "now" of time is the same as regards its subject in the whole course of time, but it differs in aspect; for inasmuch as time corresponds to movement, its "now" corresponds to what is movable; and the thing movable has the same one subject in all time, but differs in aspect a being here and there; and such alteration is movement. Likewise the flow of the "now" as alternating in aspect is time. But eternity remains the same according to both subject and aspect; and hence eternity is not the same as the "now" of time.

Reply Obj. 3: As eternity is the proper measure of permanent being, so time is the proper measure of movement; and hence, according as any being recedes from permanence of being, and is subject to change, it recedes from eternity, and is subject to time. Therefore the being of things corruptible, because it is changeable, is not measured by eternity, but by time; for time measures not only things actually changed, but also things changeable; hence it not only measures movement but it also measures repose, which belongs to whatever is naturally movable, but is not actually in motion.

FIFTH ARTICLE [I, Q. 10, Art. 5]

The Difference of Aeviternity and Time

Objection 1: It seems that aeviternity is the same as time. For Augustine says (Gen. ad lit. viii, 20, 22, 23), that "God moves the spiritual through time." But aeviternity is said to be the measure of spiritual substances. Therefore time is the same as aeviternity.

Obj. 2: Further, it is essential to time to have "before" and "after"; but it is essential to eternity to be simultaneously whole, as was shown above in the first article. Now aeviternity is not eternity; for it is written (Ecclus. 1:1) that eternal "Wisdom is before age." Therefore it is not simultaneously whole but has "before" and "after"; and thus it is the same as time.

Obj. 3: Further, if there is no "before" and "after" in aeviternity, it follows that in aeviternal things there is no difference between being, having been, or going to be. Since then it is impossible for aeviternal things not to have been, it follows that it is impossible for them not to be in the future; which is false, since God can reduce them to nothing.

Obj. 4: Further, since the duration of aeviternal things is infinite as to subsequent duration, if aeviternity is simultaneously whole, it follows that some creature is actually infinite; which is impossible. Therefore aeviternity does not differ from time.

*On the contrary,* Boethius says (De Consol. iii) "Who commandest time to be separate from aeviternity."

*I answer that,* Aeviternity differs from time, and from eternity, as the mean between them both. This difference is explained by some to consist in the fact that eternity has neither beginning nor end, aeviternity, a beginning but no end, and time both beginning and end. This difference, however, is but an accidental one, as was shown above, in the preceding article; because even if aeviternal things had always been, and would always be, as some think, and even if they might sometimes fail to be, which is possible to God to allow; even granted this, aeviternity would still be distinguished from eternity, and from time.

Others assign the difference between these three to consist in the fact that eternity has no "before" and "after"; but that time has both, together with innovation and veteration; and that aeviternity has "before" and "after" without innovation and veteration. This theory, however, involves a contradiction; which manifestly appears if innovation and veteration be referred to the measure itself. For since "before" and "after" of duration cannot exist together, if aeviternity has "before" and "after," it must follow that with the receding of the first part of aeviternity, the after part of aeviternity must newly appear; and thus innovation would occur in aeviternity itself, as it does in time. And if they be referred to the things measured, even then an incongruity would follow. For a thing which exists in time grows old with time, because it has a changeable existence, and from the changeableness of a thing measured, there follows "before" and "after" in the measure, as is clear from *Physic.* iv. Therefore the fact that an aeviternal thing is neither inveterate, nor subject to innovation, comes from its changelessness; and consequently its measure does not contain "before" and "after." We say then that since eternity is the measure of a permanent being, in so far as anything recedes from permanence of being, it recedes from eternity. Now some things recede from permanence of being, so that their being is subject to change, or consists in change; and these things are measured by time, as are all movements, and also the being of all things corruptible. But others recede less from permanence of being, forasmuch as their being neither consists in change, nor is the subject of change; nevertheless they have change annexed to them either actually or potentially. This appears in the heavenly bodies, the substantial being of which is unchangeable; and yet with unchangeable being they have changeableness of place. The same applies to the angels, who have an unchangeable being as regards their nature with changeableness as regards choice; moreover they have changeableness of intelligence, of affections and of places in their own degree. Therefore these are measured by aeviternity which is a mean between eternity and time. But the being that is measured by eternity is not changeable, nor is it annexed to change. In this way time has "before" and "after"; aeviternity in itself has no "before" and "after," which can, however, be annexed to it; while eternity has neither "before" nor "after," nor is it compatible with such at all.

Reply Obj. 1: Spiritual creatures as regards successive affections and intelligences are measured by time. Hence also Augustine says (Gen. ad lit. viii, 20, 22, 23) that to be moved through time, is to be moved by affections. But as regards their nature they are measured by aeviternity; whereas as regards the vision of glory, they have a share of eternity.

Reply Obj. 2: Aeviternity is simultaneously whole; yet it is not eternity, because "before" and "after" are compatible with it.

Reply Obj. 3: In the very being of an angel considered absolutely, there is no difference of past and future, but only as regards accidental change. Now to say that an angel was, or is, or will be, is to be taken in a different sense according to the acceptation of our intellect, which apprehends the angelic existence by comparison with different parts of time. But when we say that an angel is, or was, we suppose something, which being supposed, its opposite is not subject to the divine power. Whereas when we say he will be, we do not as yet suppose anything. Hence, since the existence and non-existence of an angel considered absolutely is subject to the divine power, God can make the existence of an angel not future; but He cannot cause him not to be while he is, or not to have been, after he has been.

Reply Obj. 4: The duration of aeviternity is infinite, forasmuch as it is not finished by time. Hence, there is no incongruity in saying that a creature is infinite, inasmuch as it is not ended by any other creature.

SIXTH ARTICLE [I. Q. 10, Art. 6]

Whether There Is Only One Aeviternity?

Objection 1: It seems that there is not only one aeviternity; for it is written in the apocryphal books of Esdras: "Majesty and power of ages are with Thee, O Lord."

Obj. 2: Further, different genera have different measures. But some aeviternal things belong to the corporeal genus, as the heavenly bodies; and others are spiritual substances, as are the angels. Therefore there is not only one aeviternity.

Obj. 3: Further, since aeviternity is a term of duration, where there is one aeviternity, there is also one duration. But not all aeviternal things have one duration, for some begin to exist after others; as appears in the case especially of human souls. Therefore there is not only one aeviternity.

Obj. 4: Further, things not dependent on each other do not seem to have one measure of duration; for there appears to be one time for all temporal things; since the first movement, measured by time, is in some way the cause of all movement. But aeviternal things do not depend on each other, for one angel is not the cause of another angel. Therefore there is not only one aeviternity.

*On the contrary,* Aeviternity is a more simple thing than time, and is nearer to eternity. But time is one only. Therefore much more is aeviternity one only.

*I answer that,* A twofold opinion exists on this subject. Some say there is only one aeviternity; others that there are many aeviternities. Which of these is true, may be considered from the cause why time is one; for we can rise from corporeal things to the knowledge of spiritual things.

Now some say that there is only one time for temporal things, forasmuch as one number exists for all things numbered; as time is a number, according to the Philosopher (Physic. iv). This, however, is not a sufficient reason; because time is not a number abstracted from the thing numbered, but existing in the thing numbered; otherwise it would not be continuous; for ten ells of cloth are continuous not by reason of the number, but by reason of the thing numbered. Now number as it exists in the thing numbered, is not the same for all; but it is different for different things. Hence, others assert that the unity of eternity as the principle of all duration is the cause of the unity of time. Thus all durations are one in that view, in the light of their principle, but are many in the light of the diversity of things receiving duration from the influx of the first principle. On the other hand others assign primary matter as the cause why time is one; as it is the first subject of movement, the measure of which is time. Neither of these reasons, however, is sufficient; forasmuch as things which are one in principle, or in subject, especially if distant, are not one absolutely, but accidentally. Therefore the true reason why time is one, is to be found in the oneness of the first movement by which, since it is most simple, all other movements are measured. Therefore time is referred to that movement, not only as a measure is to the thing measured, but also as accident is to subject; and thus receives unity from it. Whereas to other movements it is compared only as the measure is to the thing measured. Hence it is not multiplied by their multitude, because by one separate measure many things can be measured.

This being established, we must observe that a twofold opinion existed concerning spiritual substances. Some said that all proceeded from God in a certain equality, as Origen said (Peri Archon. i); or at least many of them, as some others thought. Others said that all spiritual substances proceeded from God in a certain degree and order; and Dionysius (Coel. Hier. x) seems to have thought so, when he said that among spiritual substances there are the first, the middle and the last; even in one order of angels. Now according to the first opinion, it must be said that there are many aeviternities as there are many aeviternal things of first degree. But according to the second opinion, it would be necessary to say that there is one aeviternity only; because since each thing is measured by the most simple element of its genus, it must be that the existence of all aeviternal things should be measured by the existence of the first aeviternal thing, which is all the more simple the nearer it is to the first. Wherefore because the second opinion is truer, as will be shown later (Q. 47, A. 2); we concede at present that there is only one aeviternity.

Reply Obj. 1: Aeviternity is sometimes taken for age, that is, a space of a thing's duration; and thus we say many aeviternities when we mean ages.

Reply Obj. 2: Although the heavenly bodies and spiritual things differ in the genus of their nature, still they agree in having a changeless being, and are thus measured by aeviternity.

Reply Obj. 3: All temporal things did not begin together; nevertheless there is one time for all of them, by reason of the first measured by time; and thus all aeviternal things have one aeviternity by reason of the first, though all did not begin together.

Reply Obj. 4: For things to be measured by one, it is not necessary that the one should be the cause of all, but that it be more simple than the rest.

# QUESTION 11

THE UNITY OF GOD (In Four Articles)

After the foregoing, we consider the divine unity; concerning which there are four points of inquiry:

(1) Whether "one" adds anything to "being"?

(2) Whether "one" and "many" are opposed to each other?

(3) Whether God is one?

(4) Whether He is in the highest degree one?

FIRST ARTICLE [I, Q. 11, Art. 1]

Whether "One" Adds Anything to "Being"?

Objection 1: It seems that "one" adds something to "being." For everything is in a determinate genus by addition to being, which penetrates all *genera.* But "one" is a determinate genus, for it is the principle of number, which is a species of quantity. Therefore "one" adds something to "being."

Obj. 2: Further, what divides a thing common to all, is an addition to it. But "being" is divided by "one" and by "many." Therefore "one" is an addition to "being."

Obj. 3: Further, if "one" is not an addition to "being," "one" and "being" must have the same meaning. But it would be nugatory to call "being" by the name of "being"; therefore it would be equally so to call being "one." Now this is false. Therefore "one" is an addition to "being."

*On the contrary,* Dionysius says (Div. Nom. 5, ult.): "Nothing which exists is not in some way one," which would be false if "one" were an addition to "being," in the sense of limiting it. Therefore "one" is not an addition to "being."

*I answer that,* "One" does not add any reality to "being"; but is only a negation of division; for "one" means undivided "being." This is the very reason why "one" is the same as "being." Now every being is either simple or compound. But what is simple is undivided, both actually and potentially. Whereas what is compound, has not being whilst its parts are divided, but after they make up and compose it. Hence it is manifest that the being of anything consists in undivision; and hence it is that everything guards its unity as it guards its being.

Reply Obj. 1: Some, thinking that the "one" convertible with "being" is the same as the "one" which is the principle of number, were divided into contrary opinions. Pythagoras and Plato, seeing that the "one" convertible with "being" did not add any reality to "being," but signified the substance of "being" as undivided, thought that the same applied to the "one" which is the principle of number. And because number is composed of unities, they thought that numbers were the substances of all things. Avicenna, however, *on the contrary,* considering that "one" which is the principle of number, added a reality to the substance of "being" (otherwise number made of unities would not be a species of quantity), thought that the "one" convertible with "being" added a reality to the substance of beings; as "white" to "man." This, however, is manifestly false, inasmuch as each thing is "one" by its substance. For if a thing were "one" by anything else but by its substance, since this again would be "one," supposing it were again "one" by another thing, we should be driven on to infinity. Hence we must adhere to the former statement; therefore we must say that the "one" which is convertible with "being," does not add a reality to being; but that the "one" which is the principle of number, does add a reality to "being," belonging to the genus of quantity.

Reply Obj. 2: There is nothing to prevent a thing which in one way is divided, from being another way undivided; as what is divided in number, may be undivided in species; thus it may be that a thing is in one way "one," and in another way "many." Still, if it is absolutely undivided, either because it is so according to what belongs to its essence, though it may be divided as regards what is outside its essence, as what is one in subject may have many accidents; or because it is undivided actually, and divided potentially, as what is "one" in the whole, and is "many" in parts; in such a case a thing will be "one" absolutely and "many" accidentally. On the other hand, if it be undivided accidentally, and divided absolutely, as if it were divided in essence and undivided in idea or in principle or cause, it will be "many" absolutely and "one" accidentally; as what are "many" in number and "one" in species or "one" in principle. Hence in that way, being is divided by "one" and by "many"; as it were by "one" absolutely and by "many" accidentally. For multitude itself would not be contained under "being," unless it were in some way contained under "one." Thus Dionysius says (Div. Nom., cap. ult.) that "there is no kind of multitude that is not in a way one. But what are many in their parts, are one in their whole; and what are many in accidents, are one in subject; and what are many in number, are one in species; and what are many in species, are one in genus; and what are many in processions, are one in principle."

Reply Obj. 3: It does not follow that it is nugatory to say "being" is "one"; forasmuch as "one" adds an idea to "being."

SECOND ARTICLE [I, Q. 11, Art. 2]

Whether "One" and "Many" Are Opposed to Each Other?

Objection 1: It seems that "one" and "many" are not mutually opposed. For no opposite thing is predicated of its opposite. But every *multitude* is in a certain way one, as appears from the preceding article. Therefore "one" is not opposed to "multitude."

Obj. 2: Further, no opposite thing is constituted by its opposite. But *multitude* is constituted by one. Therefore it is not opposed to "multitude."

Obj. 3: Further, "one" is opposed to "one." But the idea of "few" is opposed to "many." Therefore "one" is not opposed to "many."

Obj. 4: Further, if "one" is opposed to "multitude," it is opposed as the undivided is to the divided; and is thus opposed to it as privation is to habit. But this appears to be incongruous; because it would follow that "one" comes after "multitude," and is defined by it; whereas, *on the contrary,* "multitude" is defined by "one." Hence there would be a vicious circle in the definition; which is inadmissible. Therefore "one" and "many" are not opposed.

*On the contrary,* Things which are opposed in idea, are themselves opposed to each other. But the idea of "one" consists in indivisibility; and the idea of "multitude" contains division. Therefore "one" and "many" are opposed to each other.

*I answer that,* "One" is opposed to "many," but in various ways. The *one* which is the principle of number is opposed to multitude which is number, as the measure is to the thing measured. For "one" implies the idea of a primary measure; and number is *multitude* measured by *one,* as is clear from Metaph. x. But the one which is convertible with *being* is opposed to multitude by way of privation; as the undivided is to the thing divided.

Reply Obj. 1: No privation entirely takes away the being of a thing, inasmuch as privation means "negation in the subject," according to the Philosopher (Categor. viii). Nevertheless every privation takes away some being; and so in being, by reason of its universality, the privation of being has its foundation in being; which is not the case in privations of special forms, as of sight, or of whiteness and the like. And what applies to being applies also to one and to good, which are convertible with being, for the privation of good is founded in some good; likewise the removal of unity is founded in some one thing. Hence it happens that multitude is some one thing; and evil is some good thing, and non-being is some kind of being. Nevertheless, opposite is not predicated of opposite; forasmuch as one is absolute, and the other is relative; for what is relative being (as a potentiality) is non-being absolutely, i.e. actually; or what is absolute being in the genus of substance is non-being relatively as regards some accidental being. In the same way, what is relatively good is absolutely bad, or vice versa; likewise what is absolutely *one* is relatively many, and vice versa.

Reply Obj. 2: A *whole* is twofold. In one sense it is homogeneous, composed of like parts; in another sense it is heterogeneous, composed of dissimilar parts. Now in every homogeneous whole, the whole is made up of parts having the form of the whole; as, for instance, every part of water is water; and such is the constitution of a continuous thing made up of its parts. In every heterogeneous whole, however, every part is wanting in the form belonging to the whole; as, for instance, no part of a house is a house, nor is any part of a man a man. Now multitude is such a kind of a whole. Therefore inasmuch as its part has not the form of the multitude, the latter is composed of unities, as a house is composed of not houses; not, indeed, as if unities constituted multitude so far as they are undivided, in which way they are opposed to multitude; but so far as they have being, as also the parts of a house make up the house by the fact that they are beings, not by the fact that they are not houses.

Reply Obj. 3: "Many" is taken in two ways: absolutely, and in that sense it is opposed to "one"; in another way as importing some kind of excess, in which sense it is opposed to "few"; hence in the first sense two are many but not in the second sense.

Reply Obj. 4: "One" is opposed to "many" privatively, inasmuch as the idea of "many" involves division. Hence division must be prior to unity, not absolutely in itself, but according to our way of apprehension. For we apprehend simple things by compound things; and hence we define a point to be, "what has no part," or "the beginning of a line." "Multitude" also, in idea, follows on "one"; because we do not understand divided things to convey the idea of multitude except by the fact that we attribute unity to every part. Hence "one" is placed in the definition of "multitude"; but "multitude" is not placed in the definition of "one." But division comes to be understood from the very negation of being: so what first comes to mind is being; secondly, that this being is not that being, and thus we apprehend division as a consequence; thirdly, comes the notion of one; fourthly, the notion of multitude.

THIRD ARTICLE [I, Q. 11, Art. 3]

Whether God Is One?

Objection 1: It seems that God is not one. For it is written "For there be many gods and many lords" (1 Cor. 8:5).

Obj. 2: Further, "One," as the principle of number, cannot be predicated of God, since quantity is not predicated of God; likewise, neither can "one" which is convertible with "being" be predicated of God, because it imports privation, and every privation is an imperfection, which cannot apply to God. Therefore God is not one.

*On the contrary,* It is written "Hear, O Israel, the Lord our God is one Lord" (Deut. 6:4).

*I answer that,* It can be shown from these three sources that God is one. First from His simplicity. For it is manifest that the reason why any singular thing is "this particular thing" is because it cannot be communicated to many: since that whereby Socrates is a man, can be communicated to many; whereas, what makes him this particular man, is only communicable to one. Therefore, if Socrates were a man by what makes him to be this particular man, as there cannot be many Socrates, so there could not in that way be many men. Now this belongs to God alone; for God Himself is His own nature, as was shown above (Q. 3, A. 3). Therefore, in the very same way God is God, and He is this God. Impossible is it therefore that many Gods should exist.

Secondly, this is proved from the infinity of His perfection. For it was shown above (Q. 4, A. 2) that God comprehends in Himself the whole perfection of being. If then many gods existed, they would necessarily differ from each other. Something therefore would belong to one which did not belong to another. And if this were a privation, one of them would not be absolutely perfect; but if a perfection, one of them would be without it. So it is impossible for many gods to exist. Hence also the ancient philosophers, constrained as it were by truth, when they asserted an infinite principle, asserted likewise that there was only one such principle.

Thirdly, this is shown from the unity of the world. For all things that exist are seen to be ordered to each other since some serve others. But things that are diverse do not harmonize in the same order, unless they are ordered thereto by one. For many are reduced into one order by one better than by many: because one is the *per se* cause of one, and many are only the accidental cause of one, inasmuch as they are in some way one. Since therefore what is first is most perfect, and is so *per se* and not accidentally, it must be that the first which reduces all into one order should be only one. And this one is God.

Reply Obj. 1: Gods are called many by the error of some who worshipped many deities, thinking as they did that the planets and other stars were gods, and also the separate parts of the world. Hence the Apostle adds: "Our God is one," etc.

Reply Obj. 2: "One" which is the principle of number is not predicated of God, but only of material things. For "one" the principle of number belongs to the genus of mathematics, which are material in being, and abstracted from matter only in idea. But "one" which is convertible with being is a metaphysical entity and does not depend on matter in its being. And although in God there is no privation, still, according to the mode of our apprehension, He is known to us by way only of privation and remotion. Thus there is no reason why a certain kind of privation should not be predicated of God; for instance, that He is incorporeal and infinite; and in the same way it is said of God that He is one.

FOURTH ARTICLE [I, Q. 11, Art. 4]

Whether God Is Supremely One?

Objection 1: It seems that God is not supremely *one.* For "one" is so called from the privation of division. But privation cannot be greater or less. Therefore God is not more "one" than other things which are called "one."

Obj. 2: Further, nothing seems to be more indivisible than what is actually and potentially indivisible; such as a point and unity. But a thing is said to be more "one" according as it is indivisible. Therefore God is not more *one* than unity is *one* and a point is one.

Obj. 3: Further, what is essentially good is supremely good. Therefore what is essentially *one* is supremely one. But every being is essentially one, as the Philosopher says (Metaph. iv). Therefore every being is supremely one; and therefore God is not *one* more than any other being is one.

*On the contrary,* Bernard says (De Consid. v): "Among all things called one, the unity of the Divine Trinity holds the first place."

*I answer that,* Since one is an undivided being, if anything is supremely *one* it must be supremely being, and supremely undivided. Now both of these belong to God. For He is supremely being, inasmuch as His being is not determined by any nature to which it is adjoined; since He is being itself, subsistent, absolutely undetermined. But He is supremely undivided inasmuch as He is divided neither actually nor potentially, by any mode of division; since He is altogether simple, as was shown above (Q. 3, A. 7). Hence it is manifest that God is *one* in the supreme degree.

Reply Obj. 1: Although privation considered in itself is not susceptive of more or less, still according as its opposite is subject to more or less, privation also can be considered itself in the light of more and less. Therefore according as a thing is more divided, or is divisible, either less or not at all, in the degree it is called more, or less, or supremely, *one.*

Reply Obj. 2: A point and unity which is the principle of number, are not supremely being, inasmuch as they have being only in some subject. Hence neither of them can be supremely *one.* For as a subject cannot be supremely one, because of the difference within it of accident and subject, so neither can an accident.

Reply Obj. 3: Although every being is *one* by its substance, still every such substance is not equally the cause of unity; for the substance of some things is compound and of others simple.

## QUESTION 12

HOW GOD IS KNOWN BY US (In Thirteen Articles)

As hitherto we have considered God as He is in Himself, we now go on to consider in what manner He is in the knowledge of creatures; concerning which there are thirteen points of inquiry:

(1) Whether any created intellect can see the essence of God?

(2) Whether the essence of God is seen by the intellect through any created image?

(3) Whether the essence of God can be seen by the corporeal eye?

(4) Whether any created intellectual substance is sufficient by its own natural powers to see the essence of God?

(5) Whether the created intellect needs any created light in order to see the essence of God?

(6) Whether of those who see God, one sees Him more perfectly than another?

(7) Whether any created intellect can comprehend the essence of God?

(8) Whether the created intellect seeing the essence of God, knows all things in it?

(9) Whether what is there known is known by any similitudes?

(10) Whether the created intellect knows at once what it sees in God?

(11) Whether in the state of this life any man can see the essence of God?

(12) Whether by natural reason we can know God in this life?

(13) Whether there is in this life any knowledge of God through grace above the knowledge of natural reason?

FIRST ARTICLE [I, Q. 12, Art. 1]

Whether Any Created Intellect Can See the Essence of God?

Objection 1: It seems that no created intellect can see the essence of God. For Chrysostom (Hom. xiv. in Joan.) commenting on John 1:18, "No man hath seen God at any time," says: "Not prophets only, but neither angels nor archangels have seen God. For how can a creature see what is increatable?" Dionysius also says (Div. Nom. i), speaking of God: "Neither is there sense, nor image, nor opinion, nor reason, nor knowledge of Him."

Obj. 2: Further, everything infinite, as such, is unknown. But God is infinite, as was shown above (Q. 7, A. 1). Therefore in Himself He is unknown.

Obj. 3: Further, the created intellect knows only existing things. For what falls first under the apprehension of the intellect is being. Now God is not something existing; but He is rather super-existence, as Dionysius says (Div. Nom. iv). Therefore God is not intelligible; but above all intellect.

Obj. 4: Further, there must be some proportion between the knower and the known, since the known is the perfection of the knower. But no proportion exists between the created intellect and

God; for there is an infinite distance between them. Therefore the created intellect cannot see the essence of God.

*On the contrary,* It is written: "We shall see Him as He is" (1 John 2:2).

*I answer that,* Since everything is knowable according as it is actual, God, Who is pure act without any admixture of potentiality, is in Himself supremely knowable. But what is supremely knowable in itself, may not be knowable to a particular intellect, on account of the excess of the intelligible object above the intellect; as, for example, the sun, which is supremely visible, cannot be seen by the bat by reason of its excess of light.

Therefore some who considered this, held that no created intellect can see the essence of God. This opinion, however, is not tenable. For as the ultimate beatitude of man consists in the use of his highest function, which is the operation of his intellect; if we suppose that the created intellect could never see God, it would either never attain to beatitude, or its beatitude would consist in something else beside God; which is opposed to faith. For the ultimate perfection of the rational creature is to be found in that which is the principle of its being; since a thing is perfect so far as it attains to its principle. Further the same opinion is also against reason. For there resides in every man a natural desire to know the cause of any effect which he sees; and thence arises wonder in men. But if the intellect of the rational creature could not reach so far as to the first cause of things, the natural desire would remain void.

Hence it must be absolutely granted that the blessed see the essence of God.

Reply Obj. 1: Both of these authorities speak of the vision of comprehension. Hence Dionysius premises immediately before the words cited, "He is universally to all incomprehensible," etc. Chrysostom likewise after the words quoted says: "He says this of the most certain vision of the Father, which is such a perfect consideration and comprehension as the Father has of the Son."

Reply Obj. 2: The infinity of matter not made perfect by form, is unknown in itself, because all knowledge comes by the form; whereas the infinity of the form not limited by matter, is in itself supremely known. God is Infinite in this way, and not in the first way: as appears from what was said above (Q. 7, A. 1).

Reply Obj. 3: God is not said to be not existing as if He did not exist at all, but because He exists above all that exists; inasmuch as He is His own existence. Hence it does not follow that He cannot be known at all, but that He exceeds every kind of knowledge; which means that He is not comprehended.

Reply Obj. 4: Proportion is twofold. In one sense it means a certain relation of one quantity to another, according as double, treble and equal are species of proportion. In another sense every relation of one thing to another is called proportion. And in this sense there can be a proportion of the creature to God, inasmuch as it is related to Him as the effect of its cause, and as potentiality to its act; and in this way the created intellect can be proportioned to know God.

SECOND ARTICLE [I, Q. 12, Art. 2]

Whether the Essence of God Is Seen by the Created Intellect Through an Image?

Objection 1: It seems that the essence of God is seen through an image by the created intellect. For it is written: "We know that when He shall appear, we shall be like to Him, and [Vulg.: 'because'] we shall see Him as He is" (1 John 3:2).

Obj. 2: Further, Augustine says (De Trin. v): "When we know God, some likeness of God is made in us."

Obj. 3: Further, the intellect in act is the actual intelligible; as sense in act is the actual sensible. But this comes about inasmuch as sense is informed with the likeness of the sensible object, and the intellect with the likeness of the thing understood. Therefore, if God is seen by the created intellect in act, it must be that He is seen by some similitude.

*On the contrary,* Augustine says (De Trin. xv) that when the Apostle says, "We see through a glass and in an enigma [*Douay: 'in a dark manner']," "by the terms 'glass' and 'enigma' certain similitudes are signified by him, which are accommodated to the vision of God." But to see the essence of God is not an enigmatic nor a speculative vision, but is, *on the contrary,* of an opposite kind. Therefore the divine essence is not seen through a similitude.

*I answer that,* Two things are required both for sensible and for intellectual vision—viz. power of sight, and union of the thing seen with the sight. For vision is made actual only when the thing seen is in a certain way in the seer. Now in corporeal things it is clear that the thing seen cannot be by its essence in the seer, but only by its likeness; as the similitude of a stone is in the eye, whereby the vision is made actual; whereas the substance of the stone is not there. But if the principle of the visual power and the thing seen were one and the same thing, it would necessarily follow that the seer would receive both the visual power and the form whereby it sees, from that one same thing.

Now it is manifest both that God is the author of the intellectual power, and that He can be seen by the intellect. And since the intellective power of the creature is not the essence of God, it follows that it is some kind of participated likeness of Him who is the first intellect. Hence also the intellectual power of the creature is called an intelligible light, as it were, derived from the first light, whether this be understood of the natural power, or of some perfection superadded of grace or of glory. Therefore, in order to see God, there must be some similitude of God on the part of the visual faculty, whereby the intellect is made capable of seeing God. But on the part of the object seen, which must necessarily be united to the seer, the essence of God cannot be seen by any created similitude. First, because as Dionysius says (Div. Nom. i), "by the similitudes of the inferior order of things, the superior can in no way be known;" as by the likeness of a body the essence of an incorporeal thing cannot be known. Much less therefore can the essence of God be seen by any created likeness whatever. Secondly, because the essence of God is His own very existence, as was shown above (Q. 3, A. 4), which cannot be said of any created form; and so no created form can be the similitude representing the essence of God to the seer. Thirdly, because the divine essence is uncircumscribed, and contains in itself super-eminently whatever can be signified or understood by the created intellect. Now this cannot in any way be represented by any created likeness; for every created form is determined according to some aspect of wisdom, or of power, or of being itself, or of some like thing. Hence to say that God is seen by some similitude, is to say that the divine essence is not seen at all; which is false.

Therefore it must be said that to see the essence of God, there is required some similitude in the visual faculty, namely, the light of glory strengthening the intellect to see God, which is spoken of in the Psalm (35:10), "In Thy light we shall see light." The essence of God, however, cannot be seen by any created similitude representing the divine essence itself as it really is.

Reply Obj. 1: That authority speaks of the similitude which is caused by participation of the light of glory.

Reply Obj. 2: Augustine speaks of the knowledge of God here on earth.

Reply Obj. 3: The divine essence is existence itself. Hence as other intelligible forms which are not their own existence are united to the intellect by means of some entity, whereby the intellect itself is informed, and made in act; so the divine essence is united to the created intellect, as the object actually understood, making the intellect in act by and of itself.

THIRD ARTICLE [I, Q. 12, Art. 3]

Whether the Essence of God Can Be Seen with the Bodily Eye?

Objection 1: It seems that the essence of God can be seen by the corporeal eye. For it is written (Job 19:26): "In my flesh I shall see … God," and (Job 42:5), "With the hearing of the ear I have heard Thee, but now my eye seeth Thee."

Obj. 2: Further, Augustine says (De Civ. Dei xxix, 29): "Those eyes" (namely the glorified) "will therefore have a greater power of sight, not so much to see more keenly, as some report of the sight of serpents or of eagles (for whatever acuteness of vision is possessed by these creatures, they can see only corporeal things) but to see even incorporeal things." Now whoever can see incorporeal things, can be raised up to see God. Therefore the glorified eye can see God.

Obj. 3: Further, God can be seen by man through a vision of the imagination. For it is written: "I saw the Lord sitting upon a throne," etc. (Isa. 6:1). But an imaginary vision originates from sense; for the imagination is moved by sense to act. Therefore God can be seen by a vision of sense.

*On the contrary,* Augustine says (De Vid. Deum, Ep. cxlvii): "No one has ever seen God either in this life, as He is, nor in the angelic life, as visible things are seen by corporeal vision."

*I answer that,* It is impossible for God to be seen by the sense of sight, or by any other sense, or faculty of the sensitive power. For every such kind of power is the act of a corporeal organ, as will be shown later (Q. 78). Now act is proportional to the nature which possesses it. Hence no power of that kind can go beyond corporeal things. For God is incorporeal, as was shown above (Q. 3, A. 1). Hence He cannot be seen by the sense or the imagination, but only by the intellect.

Reply Obj. 1: The words, "In my flesh I shall see God my Saviour," do not mean that God will be seen with the eye of the flesh, but that man existing in the flesh after the resurrection will see God. Likewise the words, "Now my eye seeth Thee," are to be understood of the mind's eye, as the Apostle says: "May He give unto you the spirit of wisdom … in the knowledge of Him, that the eyes of your heart" may be "enlightened" (Eph. 1:17, 18).

Reply Obj. 2: Augustine speaks as one inquiring, and conditionally. This appears from what he says previously: "Therefore they will have an altogether different power (viz. the glorified eyes), if they shall see that incorporeal nature;" and afterwards he explains this, saying: "It is very credible, that we shall so see the mundane bodies of the new heaven and the new earth, as to see most clearly God everywhere present, governing all corporeal things, not as we now see the invisible things of God as understood by what is made; but as when we see men among whom we live, living and exercising the functions of human life, we do not believe they live, but see it." Hence it is evident how the glorified eyes will see God, as now our eyes see the life of another. But life is not seen with the corporeal eye, as a thing in itself visible, but as the indirect object of the sense; which indeed is not known by sense, but at once, together with sense, by some other cognitive power. But that the divine presence is known by the intellect immediately on the sight of, and through, corporeal things, happens from two causes—viz. from the perspicuity of the intellect, and from the refulgence of the divine glory infused into the body after its renovation.

Reply Obj. 3: The essence of God is not seen in a vision of the imagination; but the imagination receives some form representing God according to some mode of similitude; as in the divine Scripture divine things are metaphorically described by means of sensible things.

FOURTH ARTICLE [I, Q. 12, Art. 4]

Whether Any Created Intellect by Its Natural Powers Can See the Divine Essence?

Objection 1: It seems that a created intellect can see the Divine essence by its own natural power. For Dionysius says (Div. Nom. iv): "An angel is a pure mirror, most clear, receiving, if it is right to say so, the whole beauty of God." But if a reflection is seen, the original thing is seen. Therefore since an angel by his natural power understands himself, it seems that by his own natural power he understands the Divine essence.

Obj. 2: Further, what is supremely visible, is made less visible to us by reason of our defective corporeal or intellectual sight. But the angelic intellect has no such defect. Therefore, since God is supremely intelligible in Himself, it seems that in like manner He is supremely so to an angel. Therefore, if he can understand other intelligible things by his own natural power, much more can he understand God.

Obj. 3: Further, corporeal sense cannot be raised up to understand incorporeal substance, which is above its nature. Therefore if to see the essence of God is above the nature of every created intellect, it follows that no created intellect can reach up to see the essence of God at all. But this is false, as appears from what is said above (A. 1). Therefore it seems that it is natural for a created intellect to see the Divine essence.

*On the contrary,* It is written: "The grace of God is life everlasting" (Rom. 6:23). But life everlasting consists in the vision of the Divine essence, according to the words: "This is eternal life, that they may know Thee the only true God," etc. (John 17:3). Therefore to see the essence of God is possible to the created intellect by grace, and not by nature.

*I answer that,* It is impossible for any created intellect to see the essence of God by its own natural power. For knowledge is regulated according as the thing known is in the knower. But the thing known is in the knower according to the mode of the knower. Hence the knowledge of every knower is ruled according to its own nature. If therefore the mode of anything's being exceeds the mode of the knower, it must result that the knowledge of the object is above the nature of the knower. Now the mode of being of things is manifold. For some things have being only in this one individual matter; as all bodies. But others are subsisting natures, not residing in matter at all, which, however, are not their own existence, but receive it; and these are the incorporeal beings, called angels. But to God alone does it belong to be His own subsistent being. Therefore what exists only in individual matter we know naturally, forasmuch as our soul, whereby we know, is the form of certain matter. Now our soul possesses two cognitive powers; one is the act of a corporeal organ, which naturally knows things existing in individual matter; hence sense knows only the singular. But there is another kind of cognitive power in the soul, called the intellect; and this is not the act of any corporeal organ. Wherefore the intellect naturally knows natures which exist only in individual matter; not as they are in such individual matter, but according as they are abstracted therefrom by the considering act of the intellect; hence it follows that through the intellect we can understand these objects as universal; and this is beyond the power of the sense. Now the angelic intellect naturally knows natures that are not in matter; but this is beyond the power of the intellect of our soul in the state of its present life, united as it is to the body. It follows therefore that to know self-subsistent being is natural to the divine intellect alone; and this is beyond the natural power of any created intellect; for no creature is its own existence, forasmuch as its existence is participated. Therefore the created intellect cannot see the essence of God, unless God by His grace unites Himself to the created intellect, as an object made intelligible to it.

Reply Obj. 1: This mode of knowing God is natural to an angel—namely, to know Him by His own likeness refulgent in the angel himself. But to know God by any created similitude is not to know the essence of God, as was shown above (A. 2). Hence it does not follow that an angel can know the essence of God by his own power.

Reply Obj. 2: The angelic intellect is not defective, if defect be taken to mean privation, as if it were without anything which it ought to have. But if the defect be taken negatively, in that sense every creature is defective, when compared with God; forasmuch as it does not possess the excellence which is in God.

Reply Obj. 3: The sense of sight, as being altogether material, cannot be raised up to immateriality. But our intellect, or the angelic intellect, inasmuch as it is elevated above matter in its own nature, can be raised up above its own nature to a higher level by grace. The proof is, that sight cannot in any way know abstractedly what it knows concretely; for in no way can it perceive a nature except as this one particular nature; whereas our intellect is able to consider abstractedly what it knows concretely. Now although it knows things which have a form residing in matter, still it resolves the composite into both of these elements; and it considers the form separately by itself. Likewise, also, the intellect of an angel, although it naturally knows the concrete in any nature, still it is able to separate that existence by its intellect; since it knows that the thing itself is one thing, and its existence is another. Since therefore the created intellect is naturally capable of apprehending the concrete form, and the concrete being abstractedly, by way of a kind of resolution of parts; it can by grace be raised up to know separate subsisting substance, and separate subsisting existence.

FIFTH ARTICLE [I, Q. 12, Art. 5]

Whether the Created Intellect Needs Any Created Light in Order to See the Essence of God?

Objection 1: It seems that the created intellect does not need any created light in order to see the essence of God. For what is of itself lucid in sensible things does not require any other light in order to be seen. Therefore the same applies to intelligible things. Now God is intelligible light. Therefore He is not seen by means of any created light.

Obj. 2: Further, if God is seen through a medium, He is not seen in His essence. But if seen by any created light, He is seen through a medium. Therefore He is not seen in His essence.

Obj. 3: Further, what is created can be natural to some creature. Therefore if the essence of God is seen through any created light, such a light can be made natural to some other creature; and thus, that creature would not need any other light to see God; which is impossible. Therefore it is not necessary that every creature should require a superadded light in order to see the essence of God.

*On the contrary,* It is written: "In Thy light we shall see light" (Ps. 35:10).

*I answer that,* Everything which is raised up to what exceeds its nature, must be prepared by some disposition above its nature; as, for example, if air is to receive the form of fire, it must be prepared by some disposition for such a form. But when any created intellect sees the essence of God, the essence of God itself becomes the intelligible form of the intellect. Hence it is necessary that some supernatural disposition should be added to the intellect in order that it may be raised up to such a great and sublime height. Now since the natural power of the created intellect does not avail to enable it to see the essence of God, as was shown in the preceding article, it is necessary that the power of understanding should be added by divine grace. Now this increase of the intellectual powers is called the illumination of the intellect, as we also call the intelligible object itself by the name of light of illumination. And this is the light spoken of in the Apocalypse (Apoc. 21:23): "The glory of God hath enlightened it"—viz. the society of the blessed who see God. By this light the blessed are made "deiform"—i.e. like to God, according to the saying: "When He shall appear we shall be like to Him, and [Vulg.: 'because'] we shall see Him as He is" (1 John 2:2).

Reply Obj. 1: The created light is necessary to see the essence of God, not in order to make the essence of God intelligible, which is of itself intelligible, but in order to enable the intellect to understand in the same way as a habit makes a power abler to act. Even so corporeal light is necessary as regards external sight, inasmuch as it makes the medium actually transparent, and susceptible of color.

Reply Obj. 2: This light is required to see the divine essence, not as a similitude in which God is seen, but as a perfection of the intellect, strengthening it to see God. Therefore it may be said that this light is to be described not as a medium in which God is seen, but as one by which He is seen; and such a medium does not take away the immediate vision of God.

Reply Obj. 3: The disposition to the form of fire can be natural only to the subject of that form. Hence the light of glory cannot be natural to a creature unless the creature has a divine nature; which is impossible. But by this light the rational creature is made deiform, as is said in this article.

SIXTH ARTICLE [I. Q. 12, Art. 6]

Whether of Those Who See the Essence of God, One Sees More Perfectly Than Another?

Objection 1: It seems that of those who see the essence of God, one does not see more perfectly than another. For it is written (1 John 3:2): "We shall see Him as He is." But He is only in one way. Therefore He will be seen by all in one way only; and therefore He will not be seen more perfectly by one and less perfectly by another.

Obj. 2: Further, Augustine says (Octog. Tri. Quaest. qu. xxxii): "One person cannot see one and the same thing more perfectly than another." But all who see the essence of God, understand the Divine essence, for God is seen by the intellect and not by sense, as was shown above (A. 3). Therefore of those who see the divine essence, one does not see more clearly than another.

Obj. 3: Further, That anything be seen more perfectly than another can happen in two ways: either on the part of the visible object, or on the part of the visual power of the seer. On the part of the object, it may so happen because the object is received more perfectly in the seer, that is, according to the greater perfection of the similitude; but this does not apply to the present question, for God is present to the intellect seeing Him not by way of similitude, but by His essence. It follows then that if one sees Him more perfectly than another, this happens according to the difference of the intellectual power; thus it follows too that the one whose intellectual power is higher, will see Him the more clearly; and this is incongruous; since equality with angels is promised to men as their beatitude.

*On the contrary,* Eternal life consists in the vision of God, according to John 17:3: "This is eternal life, that they may know Thee the only true God," etc. Therefore if all saw the essence of God equally in eternal life, all would be equal; the contrary to which is declared by the Apostle: "Star differs from star in glory" (1 Cor. 15:41).

*I answer that,* Of those who see the essence of God, one sees Him more perfectly than another. This, indeed, does not take place as if one had a more perfect similitude of God than another, since that vision will not spring from any similitude; but it will take place because one intellect will have a greater power or faculty to see God than another. The faculty of seeing God, however, does not belong to the created intellect naturally, but is given to it by the light of glory, which establishes the intellect in a kind of "deiformity," as appears from what is said above, in the preceding article.

Hence the intellect which has more of the light of glory will see God the more perfectly; and he will have a fuller participation of the light of glory who has more charity; because where there is the greater charity, there is the more desire; and desire in a certain degree makes the one desiring apt and prepared to receive the object desired. Hence he who possesses the more charity, will see God the more perfectly, and will be the more beatified.

Reply Obj. 1: In the words, "We shall see Him as He is," the conjunction "as" determines the mode of vision on the part of the object seen, so that the meaning is, we shall see Him to be as He is, because we shall see His existence, which is His essence. But it does not determine the mode of vision on the part of the one seeing; as if the meaning was that the mode of seeing God will be as perfect as is the perfect mode of God's existence.

Thus appears the answer to the Second Objection. For when it is said that one intellect does not understand one and the same thing better than another, this would be true if referred to the mode of the thing understood, for whoever understands it otherwise than it really is, does not truly understand it, but not if referred to the mode of understanding, for the understanding of one is more perfect than the understanding of another.

Reply Obj. 3: The diversity of seeing will not arise on the part of the object seen, for the same object will be presented to all—viz. the essence of God; nor will it arise from the diverse participation of the object seen by different similitudes; but it will arise on the part of the diverse faculty of the intellect, not, indeed, the natural faculty, but the glorified faculty.

SEVENTH ARTICLE [I, Q. 12, Art. 7]

Whether Those Who See the Essence of God Comprehend Him?

Objection 1: It seems that those who see the divine essence, comprehend God. For the Apostle says (Phil. 3:12): "But I follow after, if I may by any means comprehend [Douay: 'apprehend']." But the Apostle did not follow in vain; for he said (1 Cor. 9:26): "I ... so run, not as at an uncertainty." Therefore he comprehended; and in the same way, others also, whom he invites to do the same, saying: "So run that you may comprehend."

Obj. 2: Further, Augustine says (De Vid. Deum, Ep. cxlvii): "That is comprehended which is so seen as a whole, that nothing of it is hidden from the seer." But if God is seen in His essence, He is seen whole, and nothing of Him is hidden from the seer, since God is simple. Therefore whoever sees His essence, comprehends Him.

Obj. 3: Further, if we say that He is seen as a "whole," but not "wholly," it may be contrarily urged that "wholly" refers either to the mode of the seer, or to the mode of the thing seen. But he who sees the essence of God, sees Him wholly, if the mode of the thing seen is considered; forasmuch as he sees Him as He is; also, likewise, he sees Him wholly if the mode of the seer is meant, forasmuch as the intellect will with its full power see the Divine essence. Therefore all who see the essence of God see Him wholly; therefore they comprehend Him.

*On the contrary,* It is written: "O most mighty, great, and powerful, the Lord of hosts is Thy Name. Great in counsel, and incomprehensible in thought" (Jer. 32:18,19). Therefore He cannot be comprehended.

*I answer that,* It is impossible for any created intellect to comprehend God; yet "for the mind to attain to God in some degree is great beatitude," as Augustine says (De Verb. Dom., Serm. xxxviii).

In proof of this we must consider that what is comprehended is perfectly known; and that is perfectly known which is known so far as it can be known. Thus, if anything which is capable of scientific demonstration is held only by an opinion resting on a probably proof, it is not comprehended; as, for instance, if anyone knows by scientific demonstration that a triangle has three angles equal to two right angles, he comprehends that truth; whereas if anyone accepts it as a probable opinion because wise men or most men teach it, he cannot be said to comprehend the thing itself, because he does not attain to that perfect mode of knowledge of which it is intrinsically capable. But no created intellect can attain to that perfect mode of the knowledge of the Divine intellect whereof it is intrinsically capable. Which thus appears—Everything is knowable according to its actuality. But God, whose being is infinite, as was shown above (Q. 7), is infinitely knowable. Now no created intellect can know God infinitely. For the created intellect knows the Divine essence more or less perfectly in proportion as it receives a greater or lesser light of glory. Since therefore the created light of glory received into any created intellect cannot be infinite, it is clearly impossible for any created intellect to know God in an infinite degree. Hence it is impossible that it should comprehend God.

Reply Obj. 1: "Comprehension" is twofold: in one sense it is taken strictly and properly, according as something is included in the one comprehending; and thus in no way is God comprehended either by intellect, or in any other way; forasmuch as He is infinite and cannot be included in any finite being; so that no finite being can contain Him infinitely, in the degree of His own infinity. In this sense we now take comprehension. But in another sense "comprehension" is taken more largely as opposed to "non-attainment"; for he who attains to anyone is said to comprehend him when he attains to him. And in this sense God is comprehended by the blessed, according to the words, "I held him, and I will not let him go" (Cant. 3:4); in this sense also are to be understood the words quoted from the Apostle concerning comprehension. And in this way "comprehension" is one of the three prerogatives of the soul, responding to hope, as vision responds to faith, and fruition responds to charity. For even among ourselves not everything seen is held or possessed, forasmuch as things either appear sometimes afar off, or they are not in our power of attainment. Neither, again, do we always enjoy what we possess; either because we find no pleasure in them, or because such things are not the ultimate end of our desire, so as to satisfy and quell it. But the blessed possess these three things in God; because they see Him, and in seeing Him, possess Him as present, having the power to see Him always; and possessing Him, they enjoy Him as the ultimate fulfilment of desire.

Reply Obj. 2: God is called incomprehensible not because anything of Him is not seen; but because He is not seen as perfectly as He is capable of being seen; thus when any demonstrable proposition is known by probable reason only, it does not follow that any part of it is unknown, either the subject, or the predicate, or the composition; but that it is not as perfectly known as it is capable of being known. Hence Augustine, in his definition of comprehension, says the whole is comprehended when it is seen in such a way that nothing of it is hidden from the seer, or when its boundaries can be completely viewed or traced; for the boundaries of a thing are said to be completely surveyed when the end of the knowledge of it is attained.

Reply Obj. 3: The word "wholly" denotes a mode of the object; not that the whole object does not come under knowledge, but that the mode of the object is not the mode of the one who knows. Therefore he who sees God's essence, sees in Him that He exists infinitely, and is infinitely knowable; nevertheless, this infinite mode does not extend to enable the knower to know infinitely; thus, for instance, a person can have a probable opinion that a proposition is demonstrable, although he himself does not know it as demonstrated.

EIGHTH ARTICLE [I, Q. 12, Art. 8]

Whether Those Who See the Essence of God See All in God?

Objection 1: It seems that those who see the essence of God see all things in God. For Gregory says (Dialog. iv): "What do they not see, who see Him Who sees all things?" But God sees all things. Therefore those who see God see all things.

Obj. 2: Further, whoever sees a mirror, sees what is reflected in the mirror. But all actual or possible things shine forth in God as in a mirror; for He knows all things in Himself. Therefore whoever sees God, sees all actual things in Him, and also all possible things.

Obj. 3: Further, whoever understands the greater, can understand the least, as is said in *De Anima* iii. But all that God does, or can do, are less than His essence. Therefore whoever understands God, can understand all that God does, or can do.

Obj. 4: Further, the rational creature naturally desires to know all things. Therefore if in seeing God it does not know all things, its natural desire will not rest satisfied; thus, in seeing God it will not be fully happy; which is incongruous. Therefore he who sees God knows all things.

*On the contrary,* The angels see the essence of God; and yet do not know all things. For as Dionysius says (Coel. Hier. vii), "the inferior angels are cleansed from ignorance by the superior angels." Also they are ignorant of future contingent things, and of secret thoughts; for this knowledge belongs to God alone. Therefore whosoever sees the essence of God, does not know all things.

*I answer that,* The created intellect, in seeing the divine essence, does not see in it all that God does or can do. For it is manifest that things are seen in God as they are in Him. But all other things are in God as effects are in the power of their cause. Therefore all things are seen in God as an effect is seen in its cause. Now it is clear that the more perfectly a cause is seen, the more of its effects can be seen in it. For whoever has a lofty understanding, as soon as one demonstrative principle is put before him can gather the knowledge of many conclusions; but this is beyond one of a weaker intellect, for he needs things to be explained to him separately. And so an intellect can know all the effects of a cause and the reasons for those effects in the cause itself, if it comprehends the cause wholly. Now no created intellect can comprehend God wholly, as shown above (A. 7). Therefore no created intellect in seeing God can know all that God does or can do, for this would be to comprehend His power; but of what God does or can do any intellect can know the more, the more perfectly it sees God.

Reply Obj. 1: Gregory speaks as regards the object being sufficient, namely, God, who in Himself sufficiently contains and shows forth all things; but it does not follow that whoever sees God knows all things, for he does not perfectly comprehend Him.

Reply Obj. 2: It is not necessary that whoever sees a mirror should see all that is in the mirror, unless his glance comprehends the mirror itself.

Reply Obj. 3: Although it is more to see God than to see all things else, still it is a greater thing to see Him so that all things are known in Him, than to see Him in such a way that not all things, but the fewer or the more, are known in Him. For it has been shown in this article that the more things are known in God according as He is seen more or less perfectly.

Reply Obj. 4: The natural desire of the rational creature is to know everything that belongs to the perfection of the intellect, namely, the species and the genera of things and their types, and these everyone who sees the Divine essence will see in God. But to know other singulars, their thoughts and their deeds does not belong to the perfection of the created intellect nor does its natural desire go out to these things; neither, again, does it desire to know things that exist not as yet, but which God can call into being. Yet if God alone were seen, Who is the fount and principle of all being and of all truth, He would so fill the natural desire of knowledge that nothing else would be desired, and the seer would be completely beatified. Hence Augustine says (Confess. v): "Unhappy the man who knoweth all these" (i.e. all creatures) "and knoweth not Thee! but happy whoso knoweth Thee although he know not these. And whoso knoweth both Thee and them is not the happier for them, but for Thee alone."

NINTH ARTICLE [I, Q. 12, Art. 9]

Whether What Is Seen in God by Those Who See the Divine Essence, Is Seen Through Any Similitude?

Objection 1: It seems that what is seen in God by those who see the Divine essence, is seen by means of some similitude. For every kind of knowledge comes about by the knower being assimilated to the object known. For thus the intellect in act becomes the actual intelligible, and the sense in act becomes the actual sensible, inasmuch as it is informed by a similitude of the object, as the eye by the similitude of color. Therefore if the intellect of one who sees the Divine essence understands any creatures in God, it must be informed by their similitudes.

Obj. 2: Further, what we have seen, we keep in memory. But Paul, seeing the essence of God whilst in ecstasy, when he had ceased to see the Divine essence, as Augustine says (Gen. ad lit. ii, 28,34), remembered many of the things he had seen in the rapture; hence he said: "I have heard secret words which it is not granted to man to utter" (2 Cor. 12:4). Therefore it must be said that certain similitudes of what he remembered, remained in his mind; and in the same way, when he actually saw the essence of God, he had certain similitudes or ideas of what he actually saw in it.

*On the contrary,* A mirror and what is in it are seen by means of one likeness. But all things are seen in God as in an intelligible mirror. Therefore if God Himself is not seen by any similitude but by His own essence, neither are the things seen in Him seen by any similitudes or ideas.

*I answer that,* Those who see the divine essence see what they see in God not by any likeness, but by the divine essence itself united to their intellect. For each thing is known in so far as its likeness is in the one who knows. Now this takes place in two ways. For as things which are like one and the same thing are like to each other, the cognitive faculty can be assimilated to any knowable object in two ways. In one way it is assimilated by the object itself, when it is directly informed by a similitude, and then the object is known in itself. In another way when informed by a similitude which resembles the object; and in this way, the knowledge is not of the thing in itself, but of the thing in its likeness. For the knowledge of a man in himself differs from the knowledge of him in his image. Hence to know things thus by their likeness in the one who knows, is to know them in themselves or in their own nature; whereas to know them by their similitudes pre-existing in God, is to see them in God. Now there is a difference between these two kinds of knowledge. Hence, according to the knowledge whereby things are known by those who see the essence of God, they are seen in God Himself not by any other similitudes but by the Divine essence alone present to the intellect; by which also God Himself is seen.

Reply Obj. 1: The created intellect of one who sees God is assimilated to what is seen in God, inasmuch as it is united to the Divine essence, in which the similitudes of all things pre-exist.

Reply Obj. 2: Some of the cognitive faculties form other images from those first conceived; thus the imagination from the preconceived images of a mountain and of gold can form the likeness of a golden mountain; and the intellect, from the preconceived ideas of genus and difference, forms the idea of species; in like manner from the similitude of an image we can form in our minds the similitude of the original of the image. Thus Paul, or any other person who sees God, by the very vision of the divine essence, can form in himself the similitudes of what is seen in the divine essence, which remained in Paul even when he had ceased to see the essence of God. Still this kind of vision whereby things are seen by this likeness thus conceived, is not the same as that whereby things are seen in God.

TENTH ARTICLE [I, Q. 12, Art. 10]

Whether Those Who See the Essence of God See All They See in It at the Same Time?

Objection 1: It seems that those who see the essence of God do not see all they see in Him at one and the same time. For according to the Philosopher (Topic. ii): "It may happen that many things are known, but only one is understood." But what is seen in God, is understood; for God is seen by the intellect. Therefore those who see God do not see all in Him at the same time.

Obj. 2: Further, Augustine says (Gen. ad lit. viii, 22, 23), "God moves the spiritual creature according to time"—i.e. by intelligence and affection. But the spiritual creature is the angel who sees God. Therefore those who see God understand and are affected successively; for time means succession.

*On the contrary,* Augustine says (De Trin. xvi): "Our thoughts will not be unstable, going to and fro from one thing to another; but we shall see all we know at one glance."

*I answer that,* What is seen in the Word is seen not successively, but at the same time. In proof whereof, we ourselves cannot know many things all at once, forasmuch as understand many things by means of many ideas. But our intellect cannot be actually informed by many diverse ideas at the same time, so as to understand by them; as one body cannot bear different shapes simultaneously. Hence, when many things can be understood by one idea, they are understood at the same time; as the parts of a whole are understood successively, and not all at the same time, if each one is understood by its own idea; whereas if all are understood under the one idea of the whole, they are understood simultaneously. Now it was shown above that things seen in God, are not seen singly by their own similitude; but all are seen by the one essence of God. Hence they are seen simultaneously, and not successively.

Reply Obj. 1: We understand one thing only when we understand by one idea; but many things understood by one idea are understood simultaneously, as in the idea of a man we understand "animal" and "rational"; and in the idea of a house we understand the wall and the roof.

Reply Obj. 2: As regards their natural knowledge, whereby they know things by diverse ideas given them, the angels do not know all things simultaneously, and thus they are moved in the act of understanding according to time; but as regards what they see in God, they see all at the same time.

ELEVENTH ARTICLE [I, Q. 12, Art. 11]

Whether Anyone in This Life Can See the Essence of God?

Objection 1: It seems that one can in this life see the Divine essence. For Jacob said: "I have seen God face to face" (Gen. 32:30). But to see Him face to face is to see His essence, as appears from the words: "We see now in a glass and in a dark manner, but then face to face" (1 Cor. 13:12).

Obj. 2: Further, the Lord said to Moses: "I speak to him mouth to mouth, and plainly, and not by riddles and figures doth he see the Lord" (Num. 12:8); but this is to see God in His essence. Therefore it is possible to see the essence of God in this life.

Obj. 3: Further, that wherein we know all other things, and whereby we judge of other things, is known in itself to us. But even now we know all things in God; for Augustine says (Confess. viii): "If we both see that what you say is true, and we both see that what I say is true; where, I ask, do we see this? neither I in thee, nor thou in me; but both of us in the very incommutable truth itself above our minds." He also says (De Vera Relig. xxx) that, "We judge of all things according to the divine truth"; and (De Trin. xii) that, "it is the duty of reason to judge of these corporeal things according to the incorporeal and eternal ideas; which unless they were above the mind could not be incommutable." Therefore even in this life we see God Himself.

Obj. 4: Further, according to Augustine (Gen. ad lit. xii, 24, 25), those things that are in the soul by their essence are seen by intellectual vision. But intellectual vision is of intelligible things, not by similitudes, but by their very essences, as he also says (Gen. ad lit. xiii, 24, 25). Therefore since God is in our soul by His essence, it follows that He is seen by us in His essence.

*On the contrary,* It is written, "Man shall not see Me, and live" (Ex. 32:20), and a gloss upon this says, "In this mortal life God can be seen by certain images, but not by the likeness itself of His own nature."

*I answer that,* God cannot be seen in His essence by a mere human being, except he be separated from this mortal life. The reason is because, as was said above (A. 4), the mode of knowledge follows the mode of the nature of the knower. But our soul, as long as we live in this life, has its being in corporeal matter; hence naturally it knows only what has a form in matter, or what can be known by such a form. Now it is evident that the Divine essence cannot be known through the nature of material things. For it was shown above (AA. 2, 9) that the knowledge of God by means of any created similitude is not the vision of His essence. Hence it is impossible for the soul of man in this life to see the essence of God. This can be seen in the fact that the more our soul is abstracted from corporeal things, the more it is capable of receiving abstract intelligible things. Hence in dreams and alienations of the bodily senses divine revelations and foresight of future events are perceived the more clearly. It is not possible, therefore, that the soul in this mortal life should be raised up to the supreme of intelligible objects, i.e. to the divine essence.

Reply Obj. 1: According to Dionysius (Coel. Hier. iv) a man is said in the Scriptures to see God in the sense that certain figures are formed in the senses or imagination, according to some similitude representing in part the divinity. So when Jacob says, "I have seen God face to face," this does not mean the Divine essence, but some figure representing God. And this is to be referred to some high mode of prophecy, so that God seems to speak, though in an imaginary vision; as will later be explained (II-II, Q. 174) in treating of the degrees of prophecy. We may also say that Jacob spoke thus to designate some exalted intellectual contemplation, above the ordinary state.

Reply Obj. 2: As God works miracles in corporeal things, so also He does supernatural wonders above the common order, raising the minds of some living in the flesh beyond the use of sense, even up to the vision of His own essence; as Augustine says (Gen. ad lit. xii, 26, 27, 28) of Moses, the teacher of the Jews; and of Paul, the teacher of the Gentiles. This will be treated more fully in the question of rapture (II-II, Q. 175).

Reply Obj. 3: All things are said to be seen in God and all things are judged in Him, because by the participation of His light, we know and judge all things; for the light of natural reason itself is a participation of the divine light; as likewise we are said to see and judge of sensible things in the sun, i.e., by the sun's light. Hence Augustine says (Soliloq. i, 8), "The lessons of instruction can only be seen as it were by their own sun," namely God. As therefore in order to see a sensible object, it is not necessary to see the substance of the sun, so in like manner to see any intelligible object, it is not necessary to see the essence of God.

Reply Obj. 4: Intellectual vision is of the things which are in the soul by their essence, as intelligible things are in the intellect. And thus God is in the souls of the blessed; not thus is He in our soul, but by presence, essence and power.

TWELFTH ARTICLE [I, Q. 12, Art. 12]

Whether God Can Be Known in This Life by Natural Reason?

Objection 1: It seems that by natural reason we cannot know God in this life. For Boethius says (De Consol. v) that "reason does not grasp simple form." But God is a supremely simple form, as was shown above (Q. 3, A. 7). Therefore natural reason cannot attain to know Him.

Obj. 2: Further, the soul understands nothing by natural reason without the use of the imagination. But we cannot have an imagination of God, Who is incorporeal. Therefore we cannot know God by natural knowledge.

Obj. 3: Further, the knowledge of natural reason belongs to both good and evil, inasmuch as they have a common nature. But the knowledge of God belongs only to the good; for Augustine says (De Trin. i): "The weak eye of the human mind is not fixed on that excellent light unless purified by the justice of faith." Therefore God cannot be known by natural reason.

*On the contrary,* It is written (Rom. 1:19), "That which is known of God," namely, what can be known of God by natural reason, "is manifest in them."

*I answer that,* Our natural knowledge begins from sense. Hence our natural knowledge can go as far as it can be led by sensible things. But our mind cannot be led by sense so far as to see the essence of God; because the sensible effects of God do not equal the power of God as their cause. Hence from the knowledge of sensible things the whole power of God cannot be known; nor therefore can His essence be seen. But because they are His effects and depend on their cause, we can be led from them so far as to know of God "whether He exists," and to know of Him what must necessarily belong to Him, as the first cause of all things, exceeding all things caused by Him.

Hence we know that His relationship with creatures so far as to be the cause of them all; also that creatures differ from Him, inasmuch as He is not in any way part of what is caused by Him; and that creatures are not removed from Him by reason of any defect on His part, but because He superexceeds them all.

Reply Obj. 1: Reason cannot reach up to simple form, so as to know "what it is"; but it can know "whether it is."

Reply Obj. 2: God is known by natural knowledge through the images of His effects.

Reply Obj. 3: As the knowledge of God's essence is by grace, it belongs only to the good; but the knowledge of Him by natural reason can belong to both good and bad; and hence Augustine says (Retract. i), retracting what he had said before: "I do not approve what I said in prayer, 'God who willest that only the pure should know truth.' For it can be answered that many who are not pure can know many truths," i.e. by natural reason.

THIRTEENTH ARTICLE [I, Q. 12, Art. 13]

Whether by Grace a Higher Knowledge of God Can Be Obtained Than by Natural Reason?

Objection 1: It seems that by grace a higher knowledge of God is not obtained than by natural reason. For Dionysius says (De Mystica Theol. i) that whoever is the more united to God in this life, is united to Him as to one entirely unknown. He says the same of Moses, who nevertheless obtained a certain excellence by the knowledge conferred by grace. But to be united to God while ignoring of Him "what He is," comes about also by natural reason. Therefore God is not more known to us by grace than by natural reason.

Obj. 2: Further, we can acquire the knowledge of divine things by natural reason only through the imagination; and the same applies to the knowledge given by grace. For Dionysius says (Coel. Hier. i) that "it is impossible for the divine ray to shine upon us except as screened round about by the many colored sacred veils." Therefore we cannot know God more fully by grace than by natural reason.

Obj. 3: Further, our intellect adheres to God by grace of faith. But faith does not seem to be knowledge; for Gregory says (Hom. xxvi in Ev.) that "things not seen are the objects of faith, and not of knowledge." Therefore there is not given to us a more excellent knowledge of God by grace.

*On the contrary,* The Apostle says that "God hath revealed to us His spirit," what "none of the princes of this world knew" (1 Cor. 2:10), namely, the philosophers, as the gloss expounds.

*I answer that,* We have a more perfect knowledge of God by grace than by natural reason. Which is proved thus. The knowledge which we have by natural reason contains two things: images derived from the sensible objects; and the natural intelligible light, enabling us to abstract from them intelligible conceptions.

Now in both of these, human knowledge is assisted by the revelation of grace. For the intellect's natural light is strengthened by the infusion of gratuitous light; and sometimes also the images in the human imagination are divinely formed, so as to express divine things better than those do which we receive from sensible objects, as appears in prophetic visions; while sometimes sensible things, or even voices, are divinely formed to express some divine meaning; as in the Baptism, the Holy Ghost was seen in the shape of a dove, and the voice of the Father was heard, "This is My beloved Son" (Matt. 3:17).

Reply Obj. 1: Although by the revelation of grace in this life we cannot know of God "what He is," and thus are united to Him as to one unknown; still we know Him more fully according as many and more excellent of His effects are demonstrated to us, and according as we attribute to Him some things known by divine revelation, to which natural reason cannot reach, as, for instance, that God is Three and One.

Reply Obj. 2: From the images either received from sense in the natural order, or divinely formed in the imagination, we have so much the more excellent intellectual knowledge, the stronger the intelligible light is in man; and thus through the revelation given by the images a fuller knowledge is received by the infusion of the divine light.

Reply Obj. 3: Faith is a kind of knowledge, inasmuch as the intellect is determined by faith to some knowable object. But this determination to one object does not proceed from the vision of the believer, but from the vision of Him who is believed. Thus as far as faith falls short of vision, it falls short of the knowledge which belongs to science, for science determines the intellect to one object by the vision and understanding of first principles.

# QUESTION 13

THE NAMES OF GOD (In Twelve Articles)

After the consideration of those things which belong to the divine knowledge, we now proceed to the consideration of the divine names. For everything is named by us according to our knowledge of it.

Under this head, there are twelve points for inquiry:

(1) Whether God can be named by us?

(2) Whether any names applied to God are predicated of Him substantially?

(3) Whether any names applied to God are said of Him literally, or are all to be taken metaphorically?

(4) Whether any names applied to God are synonymous?

(5) Whether some names are applied to God and to creatures univocally or equivocally?

(6) Whether, supposing they are applied analogically, they are applied first to God or to creatures?

(7) Whether any names are applicable to God from time?

(8) Whether this name "God" is a name of nature, or of the operation?

(9) Whether this name "God" is a communicable name?

(10) Whether it is taken univocally or equivocally as signifying God, by nature, by participation, and by opinion?

(11) Whether this name, "Who is," is the supremely appropriate name of God?

(12) Whether affirmative propositions can be formed about God?

FIRST ARTICLE [I, Q. 13, Art. 1]

Whether a Name Can Be Given to God?

Objection 1: It seems that no name can be given to God. For Dionysius says (Div. Nom. i) that, "Of Him there is neither name, nor can one be found of Him;" and it is written: "What is His name, and what is the name of His Son, if thou knowest?" (Prov. 30:4).

Obj. 2: Further, every name is either abstract or concrete. But concrete names do not belong to God, since He is simple, nor do abstract names belong to Him, forasmuch as they do not signify any perfect subsisting thing. Therefore no name can be said of God.

Obj. 3: Further, nouns are taken to signify substance with quality; verbs and participles signify substance with time; pronouns the same with demonstration or relation. But none of these can be applied to God, for He has no quality, nor accident, nor time; moreover, He cannot be felt, so as to be pointed out; nor can He be described by relation, inasmuch as relations serve to recall a thing mentioned before by nouns, participles, or demonstrative pronouns. Therefore God cannot in any way be named by us.

*On the contrary,* It is written (Ex. 15:3): "The Lord is a man of war, Almighty is His name."

*I answer that,* Since according to the Philosopher (Peri Herm. i), words are signs of ideas, and ideas the similitude of things, it is evident that words relate to the meaning of things signified through the medium of the intellectual conception. It follows therefore that we can give a name to anything in as far as we can understand it. Now it was shown above (Q. 12, AA. 11, 12) that in this life we cannot see the essence of God; but we know God from creatures as their principle, and also by way of excellence and remotion. In this way therefore He can be named by us from creatures, yet not so that the name which signifies Him expresses the divine essence in itself. Thus the name "man" expresses the essence of man in himself, since it signifies the definition of man by manifesting his essence; for the idea expressed by the name is the definition.

Reply Obj. 1: The reason why God has no name, or is said to be above being named, is because His essence is above all that we understand about God, and signify in word.

Reply Obj. 2: Because we know and name God from creatures, the names we attribute to God signify what belongs to material creatures, of which the knowledge is natural to us. And because in creatures of this kind what is perfect and subsistent is compound; whereas their form is not a complete subsisting thing, but rather is that whereby a thing is; hence it follows that all names used by us to signify a complete subsisting thing must have a concrete meaning as applicable to compound things; whereas names given to signify simple forms, signify a thing not as subsisting, but as that whereby a thing is; as, for instance, whiteness signifies that whereby a thing is white. And as God is simple, and subsisting, we attribute to Him abstract names to signify His simplicity, and concrete names to signify His substance and perfection, although both these kinds of names fail to express His mode of being, forasmuch as our intellect does not know Him in this life as He is.

Reply Obj. 3: To signify substance with quality is to signify the *suppositum* with a nature or determined form in which it subsists. Hence, as some things are said of God in a concrete sense, to signify His subsistence and perfection, so likewise nouns are applied to God signifying substance with quality. Further, verbs and participles which signify time, are applied to Him because His eternity includes all time. For as we can apprehend and signify simple subsistences only by way of compound things, so we can understand and express simple eternity only by way of temporal things, because our intellect has a natural affinity to compound and temporal things. But demonstrative pronouns are applied to God as describing what is understood, not what is sensed. For we can only describe Him as far as we understand Him. Thus, according as nouns, participles and demonstrative pronouns are applicable to God, so far can He be signified by relative pronouns.

SECOND ARTICLE [I, Q. 13, Art. 2]

Whether Any Name Can Be Applied to God Substantially?

Objection 1: It seems that no name can be applied to God substantially. For Damascene says (De Fide Orth. i, 9): "Everything said of God signifies not His substance, but rather shows forth what He is not; or expresses some relation, or something following from His nature or operation."

Obj. 2: Further, Dionysius says (Div. Nom. i): "You will find a chorus of holy doctors addressed to the end of distinguishing clearly and praiseworthily the divine processions in the denomination of God." Thus the names applied by the holy doctors in praising God are distinguished according to the divine processions themselves. But what expresses the procession of anything, does not signify its essence. Therefore the names applied to God are not said of Him substantially.

Obj. 3: Further, a thing is named by us according as we understand it. But God is not understood by us in this life in His substance. Therefore neither is any name we can use applied substantially to God.

*On the contrary,* Augustine says (De Trin. vi): "The being of God is the being strong, or the being wise, or whatever else we may say of that simplicity whereby His substance is signified." Therefore all names of this kind signify the divine substance.

*I answer that,* Negative names applied to God, or signifying His relation to creatures manifestly do not at all signify His substance, but rather express the distance of the creature from Him, or His relation to something else, or rather, the relation of creatures to Himself.

But as regards absolute and affirmative names of God, as "good," "wise," and the like, various and many opinions have been given. For some have said that all such names, although they are applied to God affirmatively, nevertheless have been brought into use more to express some remotion from God, rather than to express anything that exists positively in Him. Hence they assert that when we say that God lives, we mean that God is not like an inanimate thing; and the same in like manner applies to other names; and this was taught by Rabbi Moses. Others say that these names applied to God signify His relationship towards creatures: thus in the words, "God is good," we mean, God is the cause of goodness in things; and the same rule applies to other names.

Both of these opinions, however, seem to be untrue for three reasons. First because in neither of them can a reason be assigned why some names more than others are applied to God. For He is assuredly the cause of bodies in the same way as He is the cause of good things; therefore if the words "God is good," signified no more than, "God is the cause of good things," it might in like manner be said that God is a body, inasmuch as He is the cause of bodies. So also to say that He is a body implies that He is not a mere potentiality, as is primary matter. Secondly, because it would follow that all names applied to God would be said of Him by way of being taken in a secondary sense, as healthy is secondarily said of medicine, forasmuch as it signifies only the cause of the health in the animal which primarily is called healthy. Thirdly, because this is against the intention of those who speak of God. For in saying that God lives, they assuredly mean more than to say the He is the cause of our life, or that He differs from inanimate bodies.

Therefore we must hold a different doctrine—viz. that these names signify the divine substance, and are predicated substantially of God, although they fall short of a full representation of Him. Which is proved thus. For these names express God, so far as our intellects know Him. Now since our intellect knows God from creatures, it knows Him as far as creatures represent Him. Now it is shown above (Q. 4, A. 2) that God prepossesses in Himself all the perfections of creatures, being Himself simply and universally perfect. Hence every creature represents Him, and is like Him so far as it possesses some perfection; yet it represents Him not as something of the same species or genus, but as the excelling principle of whose form the effects fall short, although they derive some kind of likeness thereto, even as the forms of inferior bodies represent the power of the sun. This was explained above (Q. 4, A. 3), in treating of the divine perfection. Therefore the aforesaid names signify the divine substance, but in an imperfect manner, even as creatures represent it imperfectly. So when we say, "God is good," the meaning is not, "God is the cause of goodness," or "God is not evil"; but the meaning is, "Whatever good we attribute to creatures, pre-exists in God," and in a more excellent and higher way. Hence it does not follow that God is good, because He causes goodness; but rather, *on the contrary,* He causes goodness in things because He is good; according to what Augustine says (De Doctr. Christ. i, 32), "Because He is good, we are."

Reply Obj. 1: Damascene says that these names do not signify what God is, forasmuch as by none of these names is perfectly expressed what He is; but each one signifies Him in an imperfect manner, even as creatures represent Him imperfectly.

Reply Obj. 2: In the significance of names, that from which the name is derived is different sometimes from what it is intended to signify, as for instance, this name "stone" [lapis] is imposed from the fact that it hurts the foot [loedit pedem], but it is not imposed to signify that which hurts the foot, but rather to signify a certain kind of body; otherwise everything that hurts the foot would be a stone [*This refers to the Latin etymology of the word *lapis,* which has no place in English]. So we must say that these kinds of divine names are imposed from the divine processions; for as according to the diverse processions of their perfections, creatures are the representations of God, although in an imperfect manner; so likewise our intellect knows and names God according to each kind of procession; but nevertheless these names are not imposed to signify the procession themselves, as if when we say "God lives," the sense were, "life proceeds from Him"; but to signify the principle itself of things, in so far as life pre-exists in Him, although it pre-exists in Him in a more eminent way than can be understood or signified.

Reply Obj. 3: We cannot know the essence of God in this life, as He really is in Himself; but we know Him accordingly as He is represented in the perfections of creatures; and thus the names imposed by us signify Him in that manner only.

THIRD ARTICLE [I, Q. 13, Art. 3]

Whether Any Name Can Be Applied to God in Its Literal Sense?

Objection 1: It seems that no name is applied literally to God. For all names which we apply to God are taken from creatures; as was explained above (A. 1). But the names of creatures are applied to God metaphorically, as when we say, God is a stone, or a lion, or the like. Therefore names are applied to God in a metaphorical sense.

Obj. 2: Further, no name can be applied literally to anything if it should be withheld from it rather than given to it. But all such names as "good," "wise," and the like are more truly withheld from God than given to Him; as appears from Dionysius says (Coel. Hier. ii). Therefore none of these names belong to God in their literal sense.

Obj. 3: Further, corporeal names are applied to God in a metaphorical sense only; since He is incorporeal. But all such names imply some kind of corporeal condition; for their meaning is bound up with time and composition and like corporeal conditions. Therefore all these names are applied to God in a metaphorical sense.

*On the contrary,* Ambrose says (De Fide ii), "Some names there are which express evidently the property of the divinity, and some which express the clear truth of the divine majesty, but others there are which are applied to God metaphorically by way of similitude." Therefore not all names are applied to God in a metaphorical sense, but there are some which are said of Him in their literal sense.

*I answer that,* According to the preceding article, our knowledge of God is derived from the perfections which flow from Him to creatures, which perfections are in God in a more eminent way than in creatures. Now our intellect apprehends them as they are in creatures, and as it apprehends them it signifies them by names. Therefore as to the names applied to God—viz. the perfections which they signify, such as goodness, life and the like, and their mode of signification. As regards what is signified by these names, they belong properly to God, and more properly than they belong to creatures, and are applied primarily to Him. But as regards their mode of signification, they do not properly and strictly apply to God; for their mode of signification applies to creatures.

Reply Obj. 1: There are some names which signify these perfections flowing from God to creatures in such a way that the imperfect way in which creatures receive the divine perfection is part of the very signification of the name itself as "stone" signifies a material being, and names of this kind can be applied to God only in a metaphorical sense. Other names, however, express these perfections absolutely, without any such mode of participation being part of their signification as the words "being," "good," "living," and the like, and such names can be literally applied to God.

Reply Obj. 2: Such names as these, as Dionysius shows, are denied of God for the reason that what the name signifies does not belong to Him in the ordinary sense of its signification, but in a more eminent way. Hence Dionysius says also that God is above all substance and all life.

Reply Obj. 3: These names which are applied to God literally imply corporeal conditions not in the thing signified, but as regards their mode of signification; whereas those which are applied to God metaphorically imply and mean a corporeal condition in the thing signified.

FOURTH ARTICLE [I, Q. 13, Art. 4]

Whether Names Applied to God Are Synonymous?

Objection 1: It seems that these names applied to God are synonymous names. For synonymous names are those which mean exactly the same. But these names applied to God mean entirely the same thing in God; for the goodness of God is His essence, and likewise it is His wisdom. Therefore these names are entirely synonymous.

Obj. 2: Further, if it be said these names signify one and the same thing in reality, but differ in idea, it can be objected that an idea to which no reality corresponds is a vain notion. Therefore if these ideas are many, and the thing is one, it seems also that all these ideas are vain notions.

Obj. 3: Further, a thing which is one in reality and in idea, is more one than what is one in reality and many in idea. But God is supremely one. Therefore it seems that He is not one in reality and many in idea; and thus the names applied to God do not signify different ideas; and thus they are synonymous.

*On the contrary,* All synonyms united with each other are redundant, as when we say, "vesture clothing." Therefore if all names applied to God are synonymous, we cannot properly say "good God" or the like, and yet it is written, "O most mighty, great and powerful, the Lord of hosts is Thy name" (Jer. 32:18).

*I answer that,* These names spoken of God are not synonymous. This would be easy to understand, if we said that these names are used to remove, or to express the relation of cause to creatures; for thus it would follow that there are different ideas as regards the diverse things denied of God, or as regards diverse effects connoted. But even according to what was said above (A. 2), that these names signify the divine substance, although in an imperfect manner, it is also clear from what has been said (AA. 1, 2) that they have diverse meanings. For the idea signified by the name is the conception in the intellect of the thing signified by the name. But our intellect, since it knows God from creatures, in order to understand God, forms conceptions proportional to the perfections flowing from God to creatures, which perfections pre-exist in God unitedly and simply, whereas in creatures they are received and divided and multiplied. As therefore, to the different perfections of creatures, there corresponds one simple principle represented by different perfections of creatures in a various and manifold manner, so also to the various and multiplied conceptions of our intellect, there corresponds one altogether simple principle, according to these conceptions, imperfectly understood. Therefore although the names applied to God signify one thing, still because they signify that under many and different aspects, they are not synonymous.

Thus appears the solution of the First Objection, since synonymous terms signify one thing under one aspect; for words which signify different aspects of one thing, do not signify primarily and absolutely one thing; because the term only signifies the thing through the medium of the intellectual conception, as was said above.

Reply Obj. 2: The many aspects of these names are not empty and vain, for there corresponds to all of them one simple reality represented by them in a manifold and imperfect manner.

Reply Obj. 3: The perfect unity of God requires that what are manifold and divided in others should exist in Him simply and unitedly. Thus it comes about that He is one in reality, and yet multiple in idea, because our intellect apprehends Him in a manifold manner, as things represent Him.

FIFTH ARTICLE [I, Q. 13, Art. 5]

Whether What Is Said of God and of Creatures Is Univocally Predicated of Them?

Objection 1: It seems that the things attributed to God and creatures are univocal. For every equivocal term is reduced to the univocal, as many are reduced to one; for if the name "dog" be said equivocally of the barking dog, and of the dogfish, it must be said of some univocally—viz. of all barking dogs; otherwise we proceed to infinitude. Now there are some univocal agents which agree with their effects in name and definition, as man generates man; and there are some agents which are equivocal, as the sun which causes heat, although the sun is hot only in an equivocal sense. Therefore it seems that the first agent to which all other agents are reduced, is an univocal agent: and thus what is said of God and creatures, is predicated univocally.

Obj. 2: Further, there is no similitude among equivocal things. Therefore as creatures have a certain likeness to God, according to the word of Genesis (Gen. 1:26), "Let us make man to our image and likeness," it seems that something can be said of God and creatures univocally.

Obj. 3: Further, measure is homogeneous with the thing measured. But God is the first measure of all beings. Therefore God is homogeneous with creatures; and thus a word may be applied univocally to God and to creatures.

*On the contrary,* whatever is predicated of various things under the same name but not in the same sense, is predicated equivocally. But no name belongs to God in the same sense that it belongs to creatures; for instance, wisdom in creatures is a quality, but not in God. Now a different genus changes an essence, since the genus is part of the definition; and the same applies to other things. Therefore whatever is said of God and of creatures is predicated equivocally.

Further, God is more distant from creatures than any creatures are from each other. But the distance of some creatures makes any univocal predication of them impossible, as in the case of those things which are not in the same genus. Therefore much less can anything be predicated univocally of God and creatures; and so only equivocal predication can be applied to them.

*I answer that,* Univocal predication is impossible between God and creatures. The reason of this is that every effect which is not an adequate result of the power of the efficient cause, receives the similitude of the agent not in its full degree, but in a measure that falls short, so that what is divided and multiplied in the effects resides in the agent simply, and in the same manner; as for example the sun by exercise of its one power produces manifold and various forms in all inferior things. In the same way, as said in the preceding article, all perfections existing in creatures divided and multiplied, pre-exist in God unitedly. Thus when any term expressing perfection is applied to a creature, it signifies that perfection distinct in idea from other perfections; as, for instance, by the term "wise" applied to man, we signify some perfection distinct from a man's essence, and distinct from his power and existence, and from all similar things; whereas when we apply to it God, we do not mean to signify anything distinct from His essence, or power, or existence. Thus also this term "wise" applied to man in some degree circumscribes and comprehends the thing signified; whereas this is not the case when it is applied to God; but it leaves the thing signified as incomprehended, and as exceeding the signification of the name. Hence it is evident that this term "wise" is not applied in the same way to God and to man. The same rule applies to other terms. Hence no name is predicated univocally of God and of creatures.

Neither, on the other hand, are names applied to God and creatures in a purely equivocal sense, as some have said. Because if that were so, it follows that from creatures nothing could be known or demonstrated about God at all; for the reasoning would always be exposed to the fallacy of equivocation. Such a view is against the philosophers, who proved many things about God, and also against what the Apostle says: "The invisible things of God are clearly seen being understood by the things that are made" (Rom. 1:20). Therefore it must be said that these names are said of God and creatures in an analogous sense, i.e. according to proportion.

Now names are thus used in two ways: either according as many things are proportionate to one, thus for example "healthy" predicated of medicine and urine in relation and in proportion to health of a body, of which the former is the sign and the latter the cause: or according as one thing is proportionate to another, thus "healthy" is said of medicine and animal, since medicine is the cause of health in the animal body. And in this way some things are said of God and creatures analogically, and not in a purely equivocal nor in a purely univocal sense. For we can name God only from creatures (A. 1). Thus whatever is said of God and creatures, is said according to the relation of a creature to God as its principle and cause, wherein all perfections of things pre-exist excellently. Now this mode of community of idea is a mean between pure equivocation and simple univocation. For in analogies the idea is not, as it is in univocals, one and the same, yet it is not totally diverse as in equivocals; but a term which is thus used in a multiple sense signifies various proportions to some one thing; thus "healthy" applied to urine signifies the sign of animal health, and applied to medicine signifies the cause of the same health.

Reply Obj. 1: Although equivocal predications must be reduced to univocal, still in actions, the non-univocal agent must precede the univocal agent. For the non-univocal agent is the universal cause of the whole species, as for instance the sun is the cause of the generation of all men; whereas the univocal agent is not the universal efficient cause of the whole species (otherwise it would be the cause of itself, since it is contained in the species), but is a particular cause of this individual which it places under the species by way of participation. Therefore the universal cause of the whole species is not an univocal agent; and the universal cause comes before the particular cause. But this universal agent, whilst it is not univocal, nevertheless is not altogether equivocal, otherwise it could not produce its own likeness, but rather it is to be called an analogical agent, as all univocal predications are reduced to one first non-univocal analogical predication, which is being.

Reply Obj. 2: The likeness of the creature to God is imperfect, for it does not represent one and the same generic thing (Q. 4, A. 3).

Reply Obj. 3: God is not the measure proportioned to things measured; hence it is not necessary that God and creatures should be in the same genus.

The arguments adduced in the contrary sense prove indeed that these names are not predicated univocally of God and creatures; yet they do not prove that they are predicated equivocally.

SIXTH ARTICLE [I, Q. 13, Art. 6]

Whether Names Predicated of God Are Predicated Primarily of Creatures?

Objection 1: It seems that names are predicated

primarily of creatures rather than of God. For we name anything accordingly as we know it, since "names", as the Philosopher says, "are signs of ideas." But we know creatures before we know God. Therefore the names imposed by us are predicated primarily of creatures rather than of God.

Obj. 2: Further, Dionysius says (Div. Nom. i): "We name God from creatures." But names transferred from creatures to God, are said primarily of creatures rather than of God, as "lion," "stone," and the like. Therefore all names applied to God and creatures are applied primarily to creatures rather than to God.

Obj. 3: Further, all names equally applied to God and creatures, are applied to God as the cause of all creatures, as Dionysius says (De Mystica Theol.). But what is applied to anything through its cause, is applied to it secondarily, for "healthy" is primarily predicated of animal rather than of medicine, which is the cause of health. Therefore these names are said primarily of creatures rather than of God.

*On the contrary,* It is written, "I bow my knees to the Father, of our Lord Jesus Christ, of Whom all paternity in heaven and earth is named" (Eph. 3:14,15); and the same applies to the other names applied to God and creatures. Therefore these names are applied primarily to God rather than to creatures.

*I answer that,* In names predicated of many in an analogical sense, all are predicated because they have reference to some one thing; and this one thing must be placed in the definition of them all. And since that expressed by the name is the definition, as the Philosopher says (Metaph. iv), such a name must be applied primarily to that which is put in the definition of such other things, and secondarily to these others according as they approach more or less to that first. Thus, for instance, "healthy" applied to animals comes into the definition of "healthy" applied to medicine, which is called healthy as being the cause of health in the animal; and also into the definition of "healthy" which is applied to urine, which is called healthy in so far as it is the sign of the animal's health. Thus all names applied metaphorically to God, are applied to creatures primarily rather than to God, because when said of God they mean only similitudes to such creatures. For as "smiling" applied to a field means only that the field in the beauty of its flowering is like the beauty of the human smile by proportionate likeness, so the name of "lion" applied to God means only that God manifests strength in His works, as a lion in his. Thus it is clear that applied to God the signification of names can be defined only from what is said of creatures. But to other names not applied to God in a metaphorical sense, the same rule would apply if they were spoken of God as the cause only, as some have supposed. For when it is said, "God is good," it would then only mean "God is the cause of the creature's goodness"; thus the term good applied to God would included in its meaning the creature's goodness. Hence "good" would apply primarily to creatures rather than to God. But as was shown above (A. 2), these names are applied to God not as the cause only, but also essentially. For the words, "God is good," or "wise," signify not only that He is the cause of wisdom or goodness, but that these exist in Him in a more excellent way. Hence as regards what the name signifies, these names are applied primarily to God rather than to creatures, because these perfections flow from God to creatures; but as regards the imposition of the names, they are primarily applied by us to creatures which we know first. Hence they have a mode of signification which belongs to creatures, as said above (A. 3).

Reply Obj. 1: This objection refers to the imposition of the name.

Reply Obj. 2: The same rule does not apply to metaphorical and to other names, as said above.

Reply Obj. 3: This objection would be valid if these names were applied to God only as cause, and not also essentially, for instance as "healthy" is applied to medicine.

SEVENTH ARTICLE [I, Q. 13, Art. 7]

Whether Names Which Imply Relation to Creatures Are Predicated of God Temporally?

Objection 1: It seems that names which imply relation to creatures are not predicated of God temporally. For all such names signify the divine substance, as is universally held. Hence also Ambrose says (De Fide i) that this name "Lord" is the name of power, which is the divine substance; and "Creator" signifies the action of God, which is His essence. Now the divine substance is not temporal, but eternal. Therefore these names are not applied to God temporally, but eternally.

Obj. 2: Further, that to which something applies temporally can be described as made; for what is white temporally is made white. But to make does not apply to God. Therefore nothing can be predicated of God temporally.

Obj. 3: Further, if any names are applied to God temporally as implying relation to creatures, the same rule holds good of all things that imply relation to creatures. But some names are spoken of God implying relation of God to creatures from eternity; for from eternity He knew and loved the creature, according to the word: "I have loved thee with an everlasting love" (Jer. 31:3). Therefore also other names implying relation to creatures, as "Lord" and "Creator," are applied to God from eternity.

Obj. 4: Further, names of this kind signify relation. Therefore that relation must be something in God, or in the creature only. But it cannot be that it is something in the creature only, for in that case God would be called "Lord" from the opposite relation which is in creatures; and nothing is named from its opposite. Therefore the relation must be something in God also. But nothing temporal can be in God, for He is above time. Therefore these names are not applied to God temporally.

Obj. 5: Further, a thing is called relative from relation; for instance lord from lordship, as white from whiteness. Therefore if the relation of lordship is not really in God, but only in idea, it follows that God is not really Lord, which is plainly false.

Obj. 6: Further, in relative things which are not simultaneous in nature, one can exist without the other; as a thing knowable can exist without the knowledge of it, as the Philosopher says (Praedic. v). But relative things which are said of God and creatures are not simultaneous in nature. Therefore a relation can be predicated of God to the creature even without the existence of the creature; and thus these names "Lord" and "Creator" are predicated of God from eternity, and not temporally.

*On the contrary,* Augustine says (De Trin. v) that this relative appellation "Lord" is applied to God temporally.

*I answer that,* The names which import relation to creatures are applied to God temporally, and not from eternity.

To see this we must learn that some have said that relation is not a reality, but only an idea. But this is plainly seen to be false from the very fact that things themselves have a mutual natural order and habitude. Nevertheless it is necessary to know that since relation has two extremes, it happens in three ways that a relation is real or logical. Sometimes from both extremes it is an idea only, as when mutual order or habitude can only go between things in the apprehension of reason; as when we say a thing "the same as itself." For reason apprehending one thing twice regards it as two; thus it apprehends a certain habitude of a thing to itself. And the same applies to relations between *being* and non-being formed by reason, apprehending *non-being* as an extreme. The same is true of relations that follow upon an act of reason, as genus and species, and the like.

Now there are other relations which are realities as regards both extremes, as when for instance a habitude exists between two things according to some reality that belongs to both; as is clear of all relations, consequent upon quantity; as great and small, double and half, and the like; for quantity exists in both extremes: and the same applies to relations consequent upon action and passion, as motive power and the movable thing, father and son, and the like.

Again, sometimes a relation in one extreme may be a reality, while in the other extreme it is an idea only; and this happens whenever two extremes are not of one order; as sense and science refer respectively to sensible things and to intellectual things; which, inasmuch as they are realities existing in nature, are outside the order of sensible and intellectual existence. Therefore in science and in sense a real relation exists, because they are ordered either to the knowledge or to the sensible perception of things; whereas the things looked at in themselves are outside this order, and hence in them there is no real relation to science and sense, but only in idea, inasmuch as the intellect apprehends them as terms of the relations of science and sense. Hence the Philosopher says (Metaph. v) that they are called relative, not forasmuch as they are related to other things, but as others are related to them. Likewise for instance, "on the right" is not applied to a column, unless it stands as regards an animal on the right side; which relation is not really in the column, but in the animal.

Since therefore God is outside the whole order of creation, and all creatures are ordered to Him, and not conversely, it is manifest that creatures are really related to God Himself; whereas in God there is no real relation to creatures, but a relation only in idea, inasmuch as creatures are referred to Him. Thus there is nothing to prevent these names which import relation to the creature from being predicated of God temporally, not by reason of any change in Him, but by reason of the change of the creature; as a column is on the right of an animal, without change in itself, but by change in the animal.

Reply Obj. 1: Some relative names are imposed to signify the relative habitudes themselves, as "master" and "servant," "father," and "son," and the like, and these relatives are called predicamental [secundum esse]. But others are imposed to signify the things from which ensue certain habitudes, as the mover and the thing moved, the head and the thing that has a head, and the like: and these relatives are called transcendental [secundum dici]. Thus, there is the same two-fold difference in divine names. For some signify the habitude itself to the creature, as "Lord," and these do not signify the divine substance directly, but indirectly, in so far as they presuppose the divine substance; as dominion presupposes power, which is the divine substance. Others signify the divine essence directly, and consequently the corresponding habitudes, as "Saviour," "Creator," and suchlike; and these signify the action of God, which is His essence. Yet both names are said of God temporarily so far as they imply a habitude either principally or consequently, but not as signifying the essence, either directly or indirectly.

Reply Obj. 2: As relations applied to God temporally are only in God in our idea, so, "to become" or "to be made" are applied to God only in idea, with no change in Him, as for instance when we say, "Lord, Thou art become [Douay: 'hast been'] our refuge" (Ps. 89:1).

Reply Obj. 3: The operation of the intellect and the will is in the operator, therefore names signifying relations following upon the action of the intellect or will, are applied to God from eternity; whereas those following upon the actions proceeding according to our mode of thinking to external effects are applied to God temporally, as "Saviour," "Creator," and the like.

Reply Obj. 4: Relations signified by these names which are applied to God temporally, are in God only in idea; but the opposite relations in creatures are real. Nor is it incongruous that God should be denominated from relations really existing in the thing, yet so that the opposite relations in God should also be understood by us at the same time; in the sense that God is spoken of relatively to the creature, inasmuch as the creature is related to Him: thus the Philosopher says (Metaph. v) that the object is said to be knowable relatively because knowledge relates to it.

Reply Obj. 5: Since God is related to the creature for the reason that the creature is related to Him: and since the relation of subjection is real in the creature, it follows that God is Lord not in idea only, but in reality; for He is called Lord according to the manner in which the creature is subject to Him.

Reply Obj. 6: To know whether relations are simultaneous by nature or otherwise, it is not necessary [to consider the order] of things to which they belong but the meaning of the relations themselves. For if one in its idea includes another, and vice versa, then they are simultaneous by nature: as double and half, father and son, and the like. But if one in its idea includes another, and not vice versa, they are not simultaneous by nature. This applies to science and its object; for the object knowable is considered as a potentiality, and the science as a habit, or as an act. Hence the knowable object in its mode of signification exists before science, but if the same object is considered in act, then it is simultaneous with science in act; for the object known is nothing as such unless it is known. Thus, though God is prior to the creature, still because the signification of Lord includes the idea of a servant and vice versa, these two relative terms, "Lord" and "servant," are simultaneous by nature. Hence, God was not "Lord" until He had a creature subject to Himself.

EIGHTH ARTICLE [I, Q. 13, Art. 8]

Whether This Name "God" Is a Name of the Nature?

Objection 1: It seems that this name, "God," is not a name of the nature. For Damascene says (De Fide Orth. 1) that "God ( *Theos* ) is so called from *theein* which means to take care of, and to cherish all things; or from *aithein* that is, to burn, for our God is a fire consuming all malice; or from *theasthai,* which means to consider all things." But all these names belong to operation. Therefore this name "God" signifies His operation and not His nature.

Obj. 2: Further, a thing is named by us as we know it. But the divine nature is unknown to us. Therefore this name "God" does not signify the divine nature.

*On the contrary,* Ambrose says (De Fide i) that "God" is a name of the nature.

*I answer that,* Whence a name is imposed, and what the name signifies are not always the same thing. For as we know substance from its properties and operations, so we name substance sometimes for its operation, or its property; e.g. we name the substance of a stone from its act, as for instance that it hurts the foot [loedit pedem]; but still this name is not meant to signify the particular action, but the stone's substance. The things, on the other hand, known to us in themselves, such as heat, cold, whiteness and the like, are not named from other things. Hence as regards such things the meaning of the name and its source are the same.

Because therefore God is not known to us in His nature, but is made known to us from His operations or effects, we name Him from these, as said in A. 1; hence this name "God" is a name of operation so far as relates to the source of its meaning. For this name is imposed from His universal providence over all things; since all who speak of God intend to name God as exercising providence over all; hence Dionysius says (Div. Nom. ii), "The Deity watches over all with perfect providence and goodness." But taken from this operation, this name "God" is imposed to signify the divine nature.

Reply Obj. 1: All that Damascene says refers to providence; which is the source of the signification of the name "God."

Reply Obj. 2: We can name a thing according to the knowledge we have of its nature from its properties and effects. Hence because we can know what stone is in itself from its property, this name "stone" signifies the nature of the stone itself; for it signifies the definition of stone, by which we know what it is, for the idea which the name signifies is the definition, as is said in *Metaph.* iv. Now from the divine effects we cannot know the divine nature in itself, so as to know what it is; but only by way of eminence, and by way of causality, and of negation as stated above (Q. 12, A. 12). Thus the name "God" signifies the divine nature, for this name was imposed to signify something existing above all things, the principle of all things and removed from all things; for those who name God intend to signify all this.

NINTH ARTICLE [I, Q. 13, Art. 9]

Whether This Name "God" Is Communicable?

Objection 1: It seems that this name "God" is communicable. For whosoever shares in the thing signified by a name shares in the name itself. But this name "God" signifies the divine nature, which is communicable to others, according to the words, "He hath given us great [Vulg.: 'most great'] and precious promises, that by these we [Vulg.: 'ye'] may be made partakers of the divine nature" (2 Pet. 1:4). Therefore this name "God" can be communicated to others.

Obj. 2: Further, only proper names are not communicable. Now this name "God" is not a proper, but an appellative noun; which appears from the fact that it has a plural, according to the text, "I have said, You are gods" (Ps. 81:6). Therefore this name "God" is communicable.

Obj. 3: Further, this name "God" comes from operation, as explained. But other names given to God from His operations or effects are communicable; as "good," "wise," and the like. Therefore this name "God" is communicable.

*On the contrary,* It is written: "They gave the incommunicable name to wood and stones" (Wis. 14:21), in reference to the divine name. Therefore this name "God" is incommunicable.

*I answer that,* A name is communicable in two ways: properly, and by similitude. It is properly communicable in the sense that its whole signification can be given to many; by similitude it is communicable according to some part of the signification of the name. For instance this name "lion" is properly communicable to all things of the same nature as "lion"; by similitude it is communicable to those who participate in the nature of a lion, as for instance by courage, or strength, and those who thus participate are called lions metaphorically. To know, however, what names are properly communicable, we must consider that every form existing in the singular subject, by which it is individualized, is common to many either in reality, or in idea; as human nature is common to many in reality, and in idea; whereas the nature of the sun is not common to many in reality, but only in idea; for the nature of the sun can be understood as existing in many subjects; and the reason is because the mind understands the nature of every species by abstraction from the singular. Hence to be in one singular subject or in many is outside the idea of the nature of the species. So, given the idea of a species, it can be understood as existing in many. But the singular, from the fact that it is singular, is divided off from all others. Hence every name imposed to signify any singular thing is incommunicable both in reality and idea; for the plurality of this individual thing cannot be; nor can it be conceived in idea. Hence no name signifying any individual thing is properly communicable to many, but only by way of similitude; as for instance a person can be called "Achilles" metaphorically, forasmuch as he may possess something of the properties of Achilles, such as strength. On the other hand, forms which are individualized not by any *suppositum,* but by and of themselves, as being subsisting forms, if understood as they are in themselves, could not be communicable either in reality or in idea; but only perhaps by way of similitude, as was said of individuals. Forasmuch as we are unable to understand simple self-subsisting forms as they really are, we understand them as compound things having forms in matter; therefore, as was said in the first article, we give them concrete names signifying a nature existing in some *suppositum.* Hence, so far as concerns images, the same rules apply to names we impose to signify the nature of compound things as to names given to us to signify simple subsisting natures.

Since, then, this name "God" is given to signify the divine nature as stated above (A. 8), and since the divine nature cannot be multiplied as shown above (Q. 11, A. 3), it follows that this name "God" is incommunicable in reality, but communicable in opinion; just in the same way as this name "sun" would be communicable according to the opinion of those who say there are many suns. Therefore, it is written: "You served them who by nature are not gods," (Gal. 4:8), and a gloss adds, "Gods not in nature, but in human opinion." Nevertheless this name "God" is communicable, not in its whole signification, but in some part of it by way of similitude; so that those are called gods who share in divinity by likeness, according to the text, "I have said, You are gods" (Ps. 81:6).

But if any name were given to signify God not as to His nature but as to His *suppositum,* accordingly as He is considered as "this something," that name would be absolutely incommunicable; as, for instance, perhaps the Tetragrammaton among the Hebrew; and this is like giving a name to the sun as signifying this individual thing.

Reply Obj. 1: The divine nature is only communicable according to the participation of some similitude.

Reply Obj. 2: This name "God" is an appellative name, and not a proper name, for it signifies the divine nature in the possessor; although God Himself in reality is neither universal nor particular. For names do not follow upon the mode of being in things, but upon the mode of being as it is in our mind. And yet it is incommunicable according to the truth of the thing, as was said above concerning the name "sun."

Reply Obj. 3: These names "good," "wise," and the like, are imposed from the perfections proceeding from God to creatures; but they do not signify the divine nature, but rather signify the perfections themselves absolutely; and therefore they are in truth communicable to many. But this name "God" is given to God from His own proper operation, which we experience continually, to signify the divine nature.

TENTH ARTICLE [I, Q. 13, Art. 10]

Whether This Name "God" Is Applied to God Univocally by Nature, by Participation, and According to Opinion?

Objection 1: It seems that this name "God" is applied to God univocally by nature, by participation, and according to opinion. For where a diverse signification exists, there is no contradiction of affirmation and negation; for equivocation prevents contradiction. But a Catholic who says: "An idol is not God," contradicts a pagan who says: "An idol is God." Therefore "God" in both senses is spoken of univocally.

Obj. 2: Further, as an idol is God in opinion, and not in truth, so the enjoyment of carnal pleasures is called happiness in opinion, and not in truth. But this name "beatitude" is applied univocally to this supposed happiness, and also to true happiness. Therefore also this name "God" is applied univocally to the true God, and to God also in opinion.

Obj. 3: Further, names are called univocal because they contain one idea. Now when a Catholic says: "There is one God," he understands by the name God an omnipotent being, and one venerated above all; while the heathen understands the same when he says: "An idol is God." Therefore this name "God" is applied univocally to both.

*On the contrary,* The idea in the intellect is the likeness of what is in the thing as is said in Peri Herm. i. But the word "animal" applied to a true animal, and to a picture of one, is equivocal. Therefore this name "God" applied to the true God and to God in opinion is applied equivocally.

Further, No one can signify what he does not know. But the heathen does not know the divine nature. So when he says an idol is God, he does not signify the true Deity. On the other hand, a Catholic signifies the true Deity when he says that there is one God. Therefore this name "God" is not applied univocally, but equivocally to the true God, and to God according to opinion.

*I answer that,* This name "God" in the three aforesaid significations is taken neither univocally nor equivocally, but analogically. This is apparent from this reason: Univocal terms mean absolutely the same thing, but equivocal terms absolutely different; whereas in analogical terms a word taken in one signification must be placed in the definition of the same word taken in other senses; as, for instance, "being" which is applied to "substance" is placed in the definition of being as applied to "accident"; and "healthy" applied to animal is placed in the definition of healthy as applied to urine and medicine. For urine is the sign of health in the animal, and medicine is the cause of health.

The same applies to the question at issue. For this name "God," as signifying the true God, includes the idea of God when it is used to denote God in opinion, or participation. For when we name anyone god by participation, we understand by the name of god some likeness of the true God. Likewise, when we call an idol god, by this name god we understand and signify something which men think is God; thus it is manifest that the name has different meanings, but that one of them is comprised in the other significations. Hence it is manifestly said analogically.

Reply Obj. 1: The multiplication of names does not depend on the predication of the name, but on the signification: for this name "man," of whomsoever it is predicated, whether truly or falsely, is predicated in one sense. But it would be multiplied if by the name "man" we meant to signify different things; for instance, if one meant to signify by this name "man" what man really is, and another meant to signify by the same name a stone, or something else. Hence it is evident that a Catholic saying that an idol is not God contradicts the pagan asserting that it is God; because each of them uses this name "God" to signify the true God. For when the pagan says an idol is God, he does not use this name as meaning God in opinion, for he would then speak the truth, as also Catholics sometimes use the name in that sense, as in the Psalm, "All the gods of the Gentiles are demons" (Ps. 95:5).

The same remark applies to the Second and Third Objections. For these reasons proceed from the different predication of the name, and not from its various significations.

Reply Obj. 4 ["*On the contrary,*" par. 1]: The term "animal" applied to a true and a pictured animal is not purely equivocal; for the Philosopher takes equivocal names in a large sense, including analogous names; because also being, which is predicated analogically, is sometimes said to be predicated equivocally of different predicaments.

Reply Obj. 5 ["*On the contrary,*" par. 2] : Neither a Catholic nor a pagan knows the very nature of God as it is in itself; but each one knows it according to some idea of causality, or excellence, or remotion (Q. 12, A. 12). So a pagan can take this name "God" in the same way when he says an idol is God, as the Catholic does in saying an idol is not God. But if anyone should be quite ignorant of God altogether, he could not even name Him, unless, perhaps, as we use names the meaning of which we know not.

ELEVENTH ARTICLE [I, Q. 13, Art. 11]

Whether This Name, HE WHO IS, Is the Most Proper Name of God?

Objection 1: It seems that this name HE WHO IS is not the most proper name of God. For this name "God" is an incommunicable name. But this name HE WHO IS, is not an incommunicable name. Therefore this name HE WHO IS is not the most proper name of God.

Obj. 2: Further, Dionysius says (Div. Nom. iii) that "the name of good excellently manifests all the processions of God." But it especially belongs to God to be the universal principle of all things. Therefore this name "good" is supremely proper to God, and not this name HE WHO IS.

Obj. 3: Further, every divine name seems to imply relation to creatures, for God is known to us only through creatures. But this name HE WHO IS imports no relation to creatures. Therefore this name HE WHO IS is not the most applicable to God.

*On the contrary,* It is written that when Moses asked, "If they should say to me, What is His name? what shall I say to them?" The Lord answered him, "Thus shalt thou say to them, HE WHO IS hath sent me to you" (Ex. 3:13, 14). Therefore this name HE WHO IS most properly belongs to God.

*I answer that,* This name HE WHO IS is most properly applied to God, for three reasons:

First, because of its signification. For it does not signify form, but simply existence itself. Hence since the existence of God is His essence itself, which can be said of no other (Q. 3, A. 4), it is clear that among other names this one specially denominates God, for everything is denominated by its form.

Secondly, on account of its universality. For all other names are either less universal, or, if convertible with it, add something above it at least in idea; hence in a certain way they inform and determine it. Now our intellect cannot know the essence of God itself in this life, as it is in itself, but whatever mode it applies in determining what it understands about God, it falls short of the mode of what God is in Himself. Therefore the less determinate the names are, and the more universal and absolute they are, the more properly they are applied to God. Hence Damascene says (De Fide Orth. i) that, "HE WHO IS, is the principal of all names applied to God; for comprehending all in itself, it contains existence itself as an infinite and indeterminate sea of substance." Now by any other name some mode of substance is determined, whereas this name HE WHO IS, determines no mode of being, but is indeterminate to all; and therefore it denominates the "infinite ocean of substance."

Thirdly, from its consignification, for it signifies present existence; and this above all properly applies to God, whose existence knows not past or future, as Augustine says (De Trin. v).

Reply Obj. 1: This name HE WHO IS is the name of God more properly than this name "God," as regards its source, namely, existence; and as regards the mode of signification and consignification, as said above. But as regards the object intended by the name, this name "God" is more proper, as it is imposed to signify the divine nature; and still more proper is the Tetragrammaton, imposed to signify the substance of God itself, incommunicable and, if one may so speak, singular.

Reply Obj. 2: This name "good" is the principal name of God in so far as He is a cause, but not absolutely; for existence considered absolutely comes before the idea of cause.

Reply Obj. 3: It is not necessary that all the divine names should import relation to creatures, but it suffices that they be imposed from some perfections flowing from God to creatures. Among these the first is existence, from which comes this name, HE WHO IS.

TWELFTH ARTICLE [I, Q. 13, Art. 12]

Whether Affirmative Propositions Can Be Formed About God?

Objection 1: It seems that affirmative propositions cannot be formed about God. For Dionysius says (Coel. Hier. ii) that "negations about God are true; but affirmations are vague."

Obj. 2: Further, Boethius says (De Trin. ii) that "a simple form cannot be a subject." But God is the most absolutely simple form, as shown (Q. 3): therefore He cannot be a subject. But everything about which an affirmative proposition is made is taken as a subject. Therefore an affirmative proposition cannot be formed about God.

Obj. 3: Further, every intellect is false which understands a thing otherwise than as it is. But God has existence without any composition as shown above (Q. 3, A. 7). Therefore since every affirmative intellect understands something as compound, it follows that a true affirmative proposition about God cannot be made.

*On the contrary,* What is of faith cannot be false. But some affirmative propositions are of faith; as that God is Three and One; and that He is omnipotent. Therefore true affirmative propositions can be formed about God.

*I answer that,* True affirmative propositions can be formed about God. To prove this we must know that in every true affirmative proposition the predicate and the subject signify in some way the same thing in reality, and different things in idea. And this appears to be the case both in propositions which have an accidental predicate, and in those which have an essential predicate. For it is manifest that "man" and "white" are the same in subject, and different in idea; for the idea of man is one thing, and that of whiteness is another. The same applies when I say, "man is an animal"; since the same thing which is man is truly animal; for in the same *suppositum* there is sensible nature by reason of which he is called animal, and the rational nature by reason of which he is called man; hence here again predicate and subject are the same as to *suppositum,* but different as to idea. But in propositions where one same thing is predicated of itself, the same rule in some way applies, inasmuch as the intellect draws to the *suppositum* what it places in the subject; and what it places in the predicate it draws to the nature of the form existing in the *suppositum* ; according to the saying that "predicates are to be taken formally, and subjects materially." To this diversity in idea corresponds the plurality of predicate and subject, while the intellect signifies the identity of the thing by the composition itself.

God, however, as considered in Himself, is altogether one and simple, yet our intellect knows Him by different conceptions because it cannot see Him as He is in Himself. Nevertheless, although it understands Him under different conceptions, it knows that one and the same simple object corresponds to its conceptions. Therefore the plurality of predicate and subject represents the plurality of idea; and the intellect represents the unity by composition.

Reply Obj. 1: Dionysius says that the affirmations about God are vague or, according to another translation, "incongruous," inasmuch as no name can be applied to God according to its mode of signification.

Reply Obj. 2: Our intellect cannot comprehend simple subsisting forms, as they really are in themselves; but it apprehends them as compound things in which there is something taken as subject and something that is inherent. Therefore it apprehends the simple form as a subject, and attributes something else to it.

Reply Obj. 3: This proposition, "The intellect understanding anything otherwise than it is, is false," can be taken in two senses, accordingly as this adverb "otherwise" determines the word "understanding" on the part of the thing understood, or on the part of the one who understands. Taken as referring to the thing understood, the proposition is true, and the meaning is: Any intellect which understands that the thing is otherwise than it is, is false. But this does not hold in the present case; because our intellect, when forming a proposition about God, does not affirm that He is composite, but that He is simple. But taken as referring to the one who understands, the proposition is false. For the mode of the intellect in understanding is different from the mode of the thing in its essence. Since it is clear that our intellect understands material things below itself in an immaterial manner; not that it understands them to be immaterial things; but its manner of understanding is immaterial. Likewise, when it understands simple things above itself, it understands them according to its own mode, which is in a composite manner; yet not so as to understand them to be composite things. And thus our intellect is not false in forming composition in its ideas concerning God.

## QUESTION 14

OF GOD'S KNOWLEDGE (In Sixteen Articles)

Having considered what belongs to the divine substance, we have now to treat of God's operation. And since one kind of operation is immanent, and another kind of operation proceeds to the exterior effect, we treat first of knowledge and of will (for understanding abides in the intelligent agent, and will is in the one who wills); and afterwards of the power of God, the principle of the divine operation as proceeding to the exterior effect. Now because to understand is a kind of life, after treating of the divine knowledge, we consider the divine life. And as knowledge concerns truth, we consider truth and falsehood. Further, as everything known is in the knower, and the types of things as existing in the knowledge of God are called ideas, to the consideration of knowledge will be added the treatment of ideas.

Concerning knowledge, there are sixteen points for inquiry:

(1) Whether there is knowledge in God?

(2) Whether God understands Himself?

(3) Whether He comprehends Himself?

(4) Whether His understanding is His substance?

(5) Whether He understands other things besides Himself?

(6) Whether He has a proper knowledge of them?

(7) Whether the knowledge of God is discursive?

(8) Whether the knowledge of God is the cause of things?

(9) Whether God has knowledge of non-existing things?

(10) Whether He has knowledge of evil?

(11) Whether He has knowledge of individual things?

(12) Whether He knows the infinite?

(13) Whether He knows future contingent things?

(14) Whether He knows enunciable things?

(15) Whether the knowledge of God is variable?

(16) Whether God has speculative or practical knowledge of things?

FIRST ARTICLE [I, Q. 14, Art. 1]

Whether There Is Knowledge [*Scientia] in God?

Objection 1: It seems that in God there is not knowledge. For knowledge is a habit; and habit does not belong to God, since it is the mean between potentiality and act. Therefore knowledge is not in God.

Obj. 2: Further, since science is about conclusions, it is a kind of knowledge caused by something else which is the knowledge of principles. But nothing is caused in God; therefore science is not in God.

Obj. 3: Further, all knowledge is universal, or particular. But in God there is no universal or particular (Q. 3, A. 5). Therefore in God there is not knowledge.

*On the contrary,* The Apostle says, "O the depth of the riches of the wisdom and of the knowledge of God" (Rom. 11:33).

*I answer that,* In God there exists the most perfect knowledge. To prove this, we must note that intelligent beings are distinguished from non-intelligent beings in that the latter possess only their own form; whereas the intelligent being is naturally adapted to have also the form of some other thing; for the idea of the thing known is in the knower. Hence it is manifest that the nature of a non-intelligent being is more contracted and limited; whereas the nature of intelligent beings has a greater amplitude and extension; therefore the Philosopher says (De Anima iii) that "the soul is in a sense all things." Now the contraction of the form comes from the matter. Hence, as we have said above (Q. 7, A. 1) forms according as they are the more immaterial, approach more nearly to a kind of infinity. Therefore it is clear that the immateriality of a thing is the reason why it is cognitive; and according to the mode of immateriality is the mode of knowledge. Hence it is said in *De Anima* ii that plants do not know, because they are wholly material. But sense is cognitive because it can receive images free from matter, and the intellect is still further cognitive, because it is more separated from matter and unmixed, as said in *De Anima* iii. Since therefore God is in the highest degree of immateriality as stated above (Q. 7, A. 1), it follows that He occupies the highest place in knowledge.

Reply Obj. 1: Because perfections flowing from God to creatures exist in a higher state in God Himself (Q. 4, A. 2), whenever a name taken from any created perfection is attributed to God, it must be separated in its signification from anything that belongs to that imperfect mode proper to creatures. Hence knowledge is not a quality of God, nor a habit; but substance and pure act.

Reply Obj. 2: Whatever is divided and multiplied in creatures exists in God simply and unitedly (Q. 13, A. 4). Now man has different kinds of knowledge, according to the different objects of His knowledge. He has *intelligence* as regards the knowledge of principles; he has *science* as regards knowledge of conclusions; he has wisdom, according as he knows the highest cause; he has *counsel* or *prudence,* according as he knows what is to be done. But God knows all these by one simple act of knowledge, as will be shown (A. 7). Hence the simple knowledge of God can be named by all these names; in such a way, however, that there must be removed from each of them, so far as they enter into divine predication, everything that savors of imperfection; and everything that expresses perfection is to be retained in them. Hence it is said, "With Him is wisdom and strength, He hath counsel and understanding" (Job 12:13).

Reply Obj. 3: Knowledge is according to the mode of the one who knows; for the thing known is in the knower according to the mode of the knower. Now since the mode of the divine essence is higher than that of creatures, divine knowledge does not exist in God after the mode of created knowledge, so as to be universal or particular, or habitual, or potential, or existing according to any such mode.

SECOND ARTICLE [I, Q. 14, Art. 2]

Whether God Understands Himself?

Objection 1: It seems that God does not understand Himself. For it is said by the Philosopher (De Causis), "Every knower who knows his own essence, returns completely to his own essence." But God does not go out from His own essence, nor is He moved at all; thus He cannot return to His own essence. Therefore He does not know His own essence.

Obj. 2: Further, to understand is a kind of passion and movement, as the Philosopher says (De Anima iii); and knowledge also is a kind of assimilation to the object known; and the thing known is the perfection of the knower. But nothing is moved, or suffers, or is made perfect by itself, "nor," as Hilary says (De Trin. iii), "is a thing its own likeness." Therefore God does not understand Himself.

Obj. 3: Further, we are like to God chiefly in our intellect, because we are the image of God in our mind, as Augustine says (Gen. ad lit. vi). But our intellect understands itself, only as it understands other things, as is said in *De Anima* iii. Therefore God understands Himself only so far perchance as He understands other things.

*On the contrary,* It is written: "The things that are of God no man knoweth, but the Spirit of God" (1 Cor. 2:11).

*I answer that,* God understands Himself through Himself. In proof whereof it must be known that although in operations which pass to an external effect, the object of the operation, which is taken as the term, exists outside the operator; nevertheless in operations that remain in the operator, the object signified as the term of operation, resides in the operator; and accordingly as it is in the operator, the operation is actual. Hence the Philosopher says (De Anima iii) that "the sensible in act is sense in act, and the intelligible in act is intellect in act." For the reason why we actually feel or know a thing is because our intellect or sense is actually informed by the sensible or intelligible species. And because of this only, it follows that sense or intellect is distinct from the sensible or intelligible object, since both are in potentiality.

Since therefore God has nothing in Him of potentiality, but is pure act, His intellect and its object are altogether the same; so that He neither is without the intelligible species, as is the case with our intellect when it understands potentially; nor does the intelligible species differ from the substance of the divine intellect, as it differs in our intellect when it understands actually; but the intelligible species itself is the divine intellect itself, and thus God understands Himself through Himself.

Reply Obj. 1: Return to its own essence means only that a thing subsists in itself. Inasmuch as the form perfects the matter by giving it existence, it is in a certain way diffused in it; and it returns to itself inasmuch as it has existence in itself. Therefore those cognitive faculties which are not subsisting, but are the acts of organs, do not know themselves, as in the case of each of the senses; whereas those cognitive faculties which are subsisting, know themselves; hence it is said in *De Causis* that, "whoever knows his essence returns to it." Now it supremely belongs to God to be self-subsisting. Hence according to this mode of speaking, He supremely returns to His own essence, and knows Himself.

Reply Obj. 2: Movement and passion are taken equivocally, according as to understand is described as a kind of movement or passion, as stated in *De Anima* iii. For to understand is not a movement that is an act of something imperfect passing from one to another, but it is an act, existing in the agent itself, of something perfect. Likewise that the intellect is perfected by the intelligible object, i.e. is assimilated to it, this belongs to an intellect which is sometimes in potentiality; because the fact of its being in a state of potentiality makes it differ from the intelligible object and assimilates it thereto through the intelligible species, which is the likeness of the thing understood, and makes it to be perfected thereby, as potentiality is perfected by act. On the other hand, the divine intellect, which is no way in potentiality, is not perfected by the intelligible object, nor is it assimilated thereto, but is its own perfection, and its own intelligible object.

Reply Obj. 3: Existence in nature does not belong to primary matter, which is a potentiality, unless it is reduced to act by a form. Now our passive intellect has the same relation to intelligible objects as primary matter has to natural things; for it is in potentiality as regards intelligible objects, just as primary matter is to natural things. Hence our passive intellect can be exercised concerning intelligible objects only so far as it is perfected by the intelligible species of something; and in that way it understands itself by an intelligible species, as it understands other things: for it is manifest that by knowing the intelligible object it understands also its own act of understanding, and by this act knows the intellectual faculty. But God is a pure act in the order of existence, as also in the order of intelligible objects; therefore He understands Himself through Himself.

THIRD ARTICLE [I, Q. 14, Art. 3]

Whether God Comprehends Himself?

Objection 1: It seems that God does not comprehend Himself. For Augustine says (Octog. Tri. Quaest. xv), that "whatever comprehends itself is finite as regards itself." But God is in all ways infinite. Therefore He does not comprehend Himself.

Obj. 2: If it is said that God is infinite to us, and finite to Himself, it can be urged to the contrary, that everything in God is truer than it is in us. If therefore God is finite to Himself, but infinite to us, then God is more truly finite than infinite; which is against what was laid down above (Q. 7, A. 1). Therefore God does not comprehend Himself.

*On the contrary,* Augustine says (Octog. Tri. Quaest. xv), that "Everything that understands itself, comprehends itself." But God understands Himself. Therefore He comprehends Himself.

*I answer that,* God perfectly comprehends Himself, as can be thus proved. A thing is said to be comprehended when the end of the knowledge of it is attained, and this is accomplished when it is known as perfectly as it is knowable; as, for instance, a demonstrable proposition is comprehended when known by demonstration, not, however, when it is known by some probable reason. Now it is manifest that God knows Himself as perfectly as He is perfectly knowable. For everything is knowable according to the mode of its own actuality; since a thing is not known according as it is in potentiality, but in so far as it is in actuality, as said in *Metaph.* ix. Now the power of God in knowing is as great as His actuality in existing; because it is from the fact that He is in act and free from all matter and potentiality, that God is cognitive, as shown above (AA. 1, 2). Whence it is manifest that He knows Himself as much as He is knowable; and for that reason He perfectly comprehends Himself.

Reply Obj. 1: The strict meaning of "comprehension" signifies that one thing holds and includes another; and in this sense everything comprehended is finite, as also is everything included in another. But God is not said to be comprehended by Himself in this sense, as if His intellect were a faculty apart from Himself, and as if it held and included Himself; for these modes of speaking are to be taken by way of negation. But as God is said to be in Himself, forasmuch as He is not contained by anything outside of Himself; so He is said to be comprehended by Himself, forasmuch as nothing in Himself is hidden from Himself. For Augustine says (De Vid. Deum. ep. cxii), "The whole is comprehended when seen, if it is seen in such a way that nothing of it is hidden from the seer."

Reply Obj. 2: When it is said, "God is finite to Himself," this is to be understood according to a certain similitude of proportion, because He has the same relation in not exceeding His intellect, as anything finite has in not exceeding finite intellect. But God is not to be called finite to Himself in this sense, as if He understood Himself to be something finite.

FOURTH ARTICLE [I, Q. 14, Art. 4]

Whether the Act of God's Intellect Is His Substance?

Objection 1: It seems that the act of God's intellect is not His substance. For to understand is an operation. But an operation signifies something proceeding from the operator. Therefore the act of God's intellect is not His substance.

Obj. 2: Further, to understand one's act of understanding, is to understand something that is neither great nor chiefly understood, but secondary and accessory. If therefore God be his own act of understanding, His act of understanding will be as when we understand our act of understanding: and thus God's act of understanding will not be something great.

Obj. 3: Further, every act of understanding means understanding something. When therefore God understands Himself, if He Himself is not distinct from this act of understanding, He understands that He understands Himself; and so on to infinity. Therefore the act of God's intellect is not His substance.

*On the contrary,* Augustine says (De Trin. vii), "In God to be is the same as to be wise." But to be wise is the same thing as to understand. Therefore in God to be is the same thing as to understand. But God's existence is His substance, as shown above (Q. 3, A. 4). Therefore the act of God's intellect is His substance.

*I answer that,* It must be said that the act of God's intellect is His substance. For if His act of understanding were other than His substance, then something else, as the Philosopher says (Metaph. xii), would be the act and perfection of the divine substance, to which the divine substance would be related, as potentiality is to act, which is altogether impossible; because the act of understanding is the perfection and act of the one understanding. Let us now consider how this is. As was laid down above (A. 2), to understand is not an act passing to anything extrinsic; for it remains in the operator as his own act and perfection; as existence is the perfection of the one existing: just as existence follows on the form, so in like manner to understand follows on the intelligible species. Now in God there is no form which is something other than His existence, as shown above (Q. 3). Hence as His essence itself is also His intelligible species, it necessarily follows that His act of understanding must be His essence and His existence.

Thus it follows from all the foregoing that in God, intellect, and the object understood, and the intelligible species, and His act of understanding are entirely one and the same. Hence when God is said to be understanding, no kind of multiplicity is attached to His substance.

Reply Obj. 1: To understand is not an operation proceeding out of the operator, but remaining in him.

Reply Obj. 2: When that act of understanding which is not subsistent is understood, something not great is understood; as when we understand our act of understanding; and so this cannot be likened to the act of the divine understanding which is subsistent.

Thus appears the Reply to the Third Objection. For the act of divine understanding subsists in itself, and belongs to its very self and is not another's; hence it need not proceed to infinity.

FIFTH ARTICLE [I, Q. 14, Art. 5]

Whether God Knows Things Other Than Himself?

Objection 1: It seems that God does not know things besides Himself. For all other things but God are outside of God. But Augustine says (Octog. Tri. Quaest. qu. xlvi) that "God does not behold anything out of Himself." Therefore He does not know things other than Himself.

Obj. 2: Further, the object understood is the perfection of the one who understands. If therefore God understands other things besides Himself, something else will be the perfection of God, and will be nobler than He; which is impossible.

Obj. 3: Further, the act of understanding is specified by the intelligible object, as is every other act from its own object. Hence the intellectual act is so much the nobler, the nobler the object understood. But God is His own intellectual act. If therefore God understands anything other than Himself, then God Himself is specified by something else than Himself; which cannot be. Therefore He does not understand things other than Himself.

*On the contrary,* It is written: "All things are naked and open to His eyes" (Heb. 4:13).

*I answer that,* God necessarily knows things other than Himself. For it is manifest that He perfectly understands Himself; otherwise His existence would not be perfect, since His existence is His act of understanding. Now if anything is perfectly known, it follows of necessity that its power is perfectly known. But the power of anything can be perfectly known only by knowing to what its power extends. Since therefore the divine power extends to other things by the very fact that it is the first effective cause of all things, as is clear from the aforesaid (Q. 2, A. 3), God must necessarily know things other than Himself. And this appears still more plainly if we add that the very existence of the first effective cause—viz. God—is His own act of understanding. Hence whatever effects pre-exist in God, as in the first cause, must be in His act of understanding, and all things must be in Him according to an intelligible mode: for everything which is in another, is in it according to the mode of that in which it is.

Now in order to know how God knows things other than Himself, we must consider that a thing is known in two ways: in itself, and in another. A thing is known in itself when it is known by the proper species adequate to the knowable object; as when the eye sees a man through the image of a man. A thing is seen in another through the image of that which contains it; as when a part is seen in the whole by the image of the whole; or when a man is seen in a mirror by the image in the mirror, or by any other mode by which one thing is seen in another.

So we say that God sees Himself in Himself, because He sees Himself through His essence; and He sees other things not in themselves, but in Himself; inasmuch as His essence contains the similitude of things other than Himself.

Reply Obj. 1: The passage of Augustine in which it is said that God "sees nothing outside Himself" is not to be taken in such a way, as if God saw nothing outside Himself, but in the sense that what is outside Himself He does not see except in Himself, as above explained.

Reply Obj. 2: The object understood is a perfection of the one understanding not by its substance, but by its image, according to which it is in the intellect, as its form and perfection, as is said in *De Anima* iii. For "a stone is not in the soul, but its image." Now those things which are other than God are understood by God, inasmuch as the essence of God contains their images as above explained; hence it does not follow that there is any perfection in the divine intellect other than the divine essence.

Reply Obj. 3: The intellectual act is not specified by what is understood in another, but by the principal object understood in which other things are understood. For the intellectual act is specified by its object, inasmuch as the intelligible form is the principle of the intellectual operation: since every operation is specified by the form which is its principle of operation; as heating by heat. Hence the intellectual operation is specified by that intelligible form which makes the intellect in act. And this is the image of the principal thing understood, which in God is nothing but His own essence in which all images of things are comprehended. Hence it does not follow that the divine intellectual act, or rather God Himself, is specified by anything else than the divine essence itself.

SIXTH ARTICLE [I, Q. 14, Art. 6]

Whether God Knows Things Other Than Himself by Proper Knowledge?

Objection 1: It seems that God does not know things other than Himself by proper knowledge. For, as was shown (A. 5), God knows things other than Himself, according as they are in Himself. But other things are in Him as in their common and universal cause, and are known by God as in their first and universal cause. This is to know them by general, and not by proper knowledge. Therefore God knows things besides Himself by general, and not by proper knowledge.

Obj. 2: Further, the created essence is as distant from the divine essence, as the divine essence is distant from the created essence. But the divine essence cannot be known by the created essence, as said above (Q. 12, A. 2). Therefore neither can the created essence be known by the divine essence. Thus as God knows only by His essence, it follows that He does not know what the creature is in its essence, so as to know "what it is," which is to have proper knowledge of it.

Obj. 3: Further, proper knowledge of a thing can come only through its proper ratio [i.e., concept]. But as God knows all things by His essence, it seems that He does not know each thing by its proper ratio; for one thing cannot be the proper ratio of many and diverse things. Therefore God has not a proper knowledge of things, but a general knowledge; for to know things otherwise than by their proper ratio is to have only a common and general knowledge of them.

*On the contrary,* To have a proper knowledge of things is to know them not only in general, but as they are distinct from each other. Now God knows things in that manner. Hence it is written that He reaches "even to the division of the soul and the spirit, of the joints also and the marrow, and is a discerner of thoughts and intents of the heart; neither is there any creature invisible in His sight" (Heb. 4:12,13).

*I answer that,* Some have erred on this point, saying that God knows things other than Himself only in general, that is, only as beings. For as fire, if it knew itself as the principle of heat, would know the nature of heat, and all things else in so far as they are hot; so God, through knowing Himself as the principle of being, knows the nature of being, and all other things in so far as they are beings.

But this cannot be. For to know a thing in general and not in particular, is to have an imperfect knowledge. Hence our intellect, when it is reduced from potentiality to act, acquires first a universal and confused knowledge of things, before it knows them in particular; as proceeding from the imperfect to the perfect, as is clear from *Phys.* i. If therefore the knowledge of God regarding things other than Himself is only universal and not special, it would follow that His understanding would not be absolutely perfect; therefore neither would His being be perfect; and this is against what was said above (Q. 4, A. 1). We must therefore hold that God knows things other than Himself with a proper knowledge; not only in so far as being is common to them, but in so far as one is distinguished from the other. In proof thereof we may observe that some wishing to show that God knows many things by one, bring forward some examples, as, for instance, that if the centre knew itself, it would know all lines that proceed from the centre; or if light knew itself, it would know all colors.

Now these examples although they are similar in part, namely, as regards universal causality, nevertheless they fail in this respect, that multitude and diversity are caused by the one universal principle, not as regards that which is the principle of distinction, but only as regards that in which they communicate. For the diversity of colors is not caused by the light only, but by the different disposition of the diaphanous medium which receives it; and likewise, the diversity of the lines is caused by their different position. Hence it is that this kind of diversity and multitude cannot be known in its principle by proper knowledge, but only in a general way. In God, however, it is otherwise. For it was shown above (Q. 4, A. 2) that whatever perfection exists in any creature, wholly pre-exists and is contained in God in an excelling manner. Now not only what is common to creatures—viz. being—belongs to their perfection, but also what makes them distinguished from each other; as living and understanding, and the like, whereby living beings are distinguished from the non-living, and the intelligent from the non-intelligent. Likewise every form whereby each thing is constituted in its own species, is a perfection; and thus all things pre-exist in God, not only as regards what is common to all, but also as regards what distinguishes one thing from another. And therefore as God contains all perfections in Himself, the essence of God is compared to all other essences of things, not as the common to the proper, as unity is to numbers, or as the centre (of a circle) to the (radiating) lines; but as perfect acts to imperfect; as if I were to compare man to animal; or six, a perfect number, to the imperfect numbers contained under it. Now it is manifest that by a perfect act imperfect acts can be known not only in general, but also by proper knowledge; thus, for example, whoever knows a man, knows an animal by proper knowledge; and whoever knows the number six, knows the number three also by proper knowledge.

As therefore the essence of God contains in itself all the perfection contained in the essence of any other being, and far more, God can know in Himself all of them with proper knowledge. For the nature proper to each thing consists in some degree of participation in the divine perfection. Now God could not be said to know Himself perfectly unless He knew all the ways in which His own perfection can be shared by others. Neither could He know the very nature of being perfectly, unless He knew all modes of being. Hence it is manifest that God knows all things with proper knowledge, in their distinction from each other.

Reply Obj. 1: So to know a thing as it is in the knower, may be understood in two ways. In one way this adverb "so" imports the mode of knowledge on the part of the thing known; and in that sense it is false. For the knower does not always know the object known according to the existence it has in the knower; since the eye does not know a stone according to the existence it has in the eye; but by the image of the stone which is in the eye, the eye knows the stone according to its existence outside the eye. And if any knower has a knowledge of the object known according to the (mode of) existence it has in the knower, the knower nevertheless knows it according to its (mode of) existence outside the knower; thus the intellect knows a stone according to the intelligible existence it has in the intellect, inasmuch as it knows that it understands; while nevertheless it knows what a stone is in its own nature. If however the adverb 'so' be understood to import the mode (of knowledge) on the part of the knower, in that sense it is true that only the knower has knowledge of the object known as it is in the knower; for the more perfectly the thing known is in the knower, the more perfect is the mode of knowledge.

We must say therefore that God not only knows that all things are in Himself; but by the fact that they are in Him, He knows them in their own nature and all the more perfectly, the more perfectly each one is in Him.

Reply Obj. 2: The created essence is compared to the essence of God as the imperfect to the perfect act. Therefore the created essence cannot sufficiently lead us to the knowledge of the divine essence, but rather the converse.

Reply Obj. 3: The same thing cannot be taken in an equal manner as the ratio of different things. But the divine essence excels all creatures. Hence it can be taken as the proper ratio of each thing according to the diverse ways in which diverse creatures participate in, and imitate it.

SEVENTH ARTICLE [I, Q. 14, Art. 7]

Whether the Knowledge of God Is Discursive?

Objection 1: It seems that the knowledge of God is discursive. For the knowledge of God is not habitual knowledge, but actual knowledge. Now the Philosopher says (Topic. ii): "The habit of knowledge may regard many things at once; but actual understanding regards only one thing at a time." Therefore as God knows many things, Himself and others, as shown above (AA. 2, 5), it seems that He does not understand all at once, but discourses from one to another.

Obj. 2: Further, discursive knowledge is to know the effect through its cause. But God knows things through Himself; as an effect (is known) through its cause. Therefore His knowledge is discursive.

Obj. 3: Further, God knows each creature more perfectly than we know it. But we know the effects in their created causes; and thus we go discursively from causes to things caused. Therefore it seems that the same applies to God.

*On the contrary,* Augustine says (De Trin. xv), "God does not see all things in their particularity or separately, as if He saw alternately here and there; but He sees all things together at once."

*I answer that,* In the divine knowledge there is no discursion; the proof of which is as follows. In our knowledge there is a twofold discursion: one is according to succession only, as when we have actually understood anything, we turn ourselves to understand something else; while the other mode of discursion is according to causality, as when through principles we arrive at the knowledge of conclusions. The first kind of discursion cannot belong to God. For many things, which we understand in succession if each is considered in itself, we understand simultaneously if we see them in some one thing; if, for instance, we understand the parts in the whole, or see different things in a mirror. Now God sees all things in one (thing), which is Himself. Therefore God sees all things together, and not successively. Likewise the second mode of discursion cannot be applied to God. First, because this second mode of discursion presupposes the first mode; for whosoever proceeds from principles to conclusions does not consider both at once; secondly, because to discourse thus is to proceed from the known to the unknown. Hence it is manifest that when the first is known, the second is still unknown; and thus the second is known not in the first, but from the first. Now the term of discursive reasoning is attained when the second is seen in the first, by resolving the effects into their causes; and then the discursion ceases. Hence as God sees His effects in Himself as their cause, His knowledge is not discursive.

Reply Obj. 1: Although there is only one act of understanding in itself, nevertheless many things may be understood in one (medium), as shown above.

Reply Obj. 2: God does not know by their cause, known, as it were previously, effects unknown; but He knows the effects in the cause; and hence His knowledge is not discursive, as was shown above.

Reply Obj. 3: God sees the effects of created causes in the causes themselves, much better than we can; but still not in such a manner that the knowledge of the effects is caused in Him by the knowledge of the created causes, as is the case with us; and hence His knowledge is not discursive.

EIGHTH ARTICLE [I, Q. 14, Art. 8]

Whether the Knowledge of God Is the Cause of Things?

Objection 1: It seems that the knowledge of God is not the cause of things. For Origen says, on Rom. 8:30, "Whom He called, them He also justified," etc.: "A thing will happen not because God knows it as future; but because it is future, it is on that account known by God, before it exists."

Obj. 2: Further, given the cause, the effect follows. But the knowledge of God is eternal. Therefore if the knowledge of God is the cause of things created, it seems that creatures are eternal.

Obj. 3: Further, "The thing known is prior to knowledge, and is its measure," as the Philosopher says (Metaph. x). But what is posterior and measured cannot be a cause. Therefore the knowledge of God is not the cause of things.

*On the contrary,* Augustine says (De Trin. xv), "Not because they are, does God know all creatures spiritual and temporal, but because He knows them, therefore they are."

*I answer that,* The knowledge of God is the cause of things. For the knowledge of God is to all creatures what the knowledge of the artificer is to things made by his art. Now the knowledge of the artificer is the cause of the things made by his art from the fact that the artificer works by his intellect. Hence the form of the intellect must be the principle of action; as heat is the principle of heating. Nevertheless, we must observe that a natural form, being a form that remains in that to which it gives existence, denotes a principle of action according only as it has an inclination to an effect; and likewise, the intelligible form does not denote a principle of action in so far as it resides in the one who understands unless there is added to it the inclination to an effect, which inclination is through the will. For since the intelligible form has a relation to opposite things (inasmuch as the same knowledge relates to opposites), it would not produce a determinate effect unless it were determined to one thing by the appetite, as the Philosopher says (Metaph. ix). Now it is manifest that God causes things by His intellect, since His being is His act of understanding; and hence His knowledge must be the cause of things, in so far as His will is joined to it. Hence the knowledge of God as the cause of things is usually called the "knowledge of approbation."

Reply Obj. 1: Origen spoke in reference to that aspect of knowledge to which the idea of causality does not belong unless the will is joined to it, as is said above.

But when he says the reason why God foreknows some things is because they are future, this must be understood according to the cause of consequence, and not according to the cause of essence. For if things are in the future, it follows that God knows them; but not that the futurity of things is the cause why God knows them.

Reply Obj. 2: The knowledge of God is the cause of things according as things are in His knowledge. Now that things should be eternal was not in the knowledge of God; hence although the knowledge of God is eternal, it does not follow that creatures are eternal.

Reply Obj. 3: Natural things are midway between the knowledge of God and our knowledge: for we receive knowledge from natural things, of which God is the cause by His knowledge. Hence, as the natural objects of knowledge are prior to our knowledge, and are its measure, so, the knowledge of God is prior to natural things, and is the measure of them; as, for instance, a house is midway between the knowledge of the builder who made it, and the knowledge of the one who gathers his knowledge of the house from the house already built.

NINTH ARTICLE [I, Q. 14, Art. 9]

Whether God Has Knowledge of Things That Are Not?

Objection 1: It seems that God has not knowledge of things that are not. For the knowledge of God is of true things. But "truth" and "being" are convertible terms. Therefore the knowledge of God is not of things that are not.

Obj. 2: Further, knowledge requires likeness between the knower and the thing known. But those things that are not cannot have any likeness to God, Who is very being. Therefore what is not, cannot be known by God.

Obj. 3: Further, the knowledge of God is the cause of what is known by Him. But it is not the cause of things that are not, because a thing that is not, has no cause. Therefore God has no knowledge of things that are not.

*On the contrary,* The Apostle says: "Who ... calleth those things that are not as those that are" (Rom. 4:17).

*I answer that,* God knows all things whatsoever that in any way are. Now it is possible that things that are not absolutely, should be in a certain sense. For things absolutely are which are actual; whereas things which are not actual, are in the power either of God Himself or of a creature, whether in active power, or passive; whether in power of thought or of imagination, or of any other manner of meaning whatsoever. Whatever therefore can be made, or thought, or said by the creature, as also whatever He Himself can do, all are known to God, although they are not actual. And in so far it can be said that He has knowledge even of things that are not.

Now a certain difference is to be noted in the consideration of those things that are not actual. For though some of them may not be in act now, still they were, or they will be; and God is said to know all these with the knowledge of vision: for since God's act of understanding, which is His being, is measured by eternity; and since eternity is without succession, comprehending all time, the present glance of God extends over all time, and to all things which exist in any time, as to objects present to Him. But there are other things in God's power, or the creature's, which nevertheless are not, nor will be, nor were; and as regards these He is said to have knowledge, not of vision, but of simple intelligence. This is so called because the things we see around us have distinct being outside the seer.

Reply Obj. 1: Those things that are not actual are true in so far as they are in potentiality; for it is true that they are in potentiality; and as such they are known by God.

Reply Obj. 2: Since God is very being everything is, in so far as it participates in the likeness of God; as everything is hot in so far as it participates in heat. So, things in potentiality are known by God, although they are not in act.

Reply Obj. 3: The knowledge of God, joined to His will is the cause of things. Hence it is not necessary that what ever God knows, is, or was, or will be; but only is this necessary as regards what He wills to be, or permits to be. Further, it is in the knowledge of God not that they be, but that they be possible.

TENTH ARTICLE [I, Q. 14, Art. 10]

Whether God Knows Evil Things?

Objection 1: It seems that God does not know evil things. For the Philosopher (De Anima iii) says that the intellect which is not in potentiality does not know privation. But "evil is the privation of good," as Augustine says (Confess. iii, 7). Therefore, as the intellect of God is never in potentiality, but is always in act, as is clear from the foregoing (A. 2), it seems that God does not know evil things.

Obj. 2: Further, all knowledge is either the cause of the thing known, or is caused by it. But the knowledge of God is not the cause of evil, nor is it caused by evil. Therefore God does not know evil things.

Obj. 3: Further, everything known is known either by its likeness, or by its opposite. But whatever God knows, He knows through His essence, as is clear from the foregoing (A. 5). Now the divine essence neither is the likeness of evil, nor is evil contrary to it; for to the divine essence there is no contrary, as Augustine says (De Civ. Dei xii). Therefore God does not know evil things.

Obj. 4: Further, what is known through another and not through itself, is imperfectly known. But evil is not known by God; for the thing known must be in the knower. Therefore if evil is known through another, namely, through good, it would be known by Him imperfectly; which cannot be, for the knowledge of God is not imperfect. Therefore God does not know evil things.

*On the contrary,* It is written (Prov. 15:11), "Hell and destruction are before God [Vulg: 'the Lord']."

*I answer that,* Whoever knows a thing perfectly, must know all that can be accidental to it. Now there are some good things to which corruption by evil may be accidental. Hence God would not know good things perfectly, unless He also knew evil things. Now a thing is knowable in the degree in which it is; hence since this is the essence of evil that it is the privation of good, by the fact that God knows good things, He knows evil things also; as by light is known darkness. Hence Dionysius says (Div. Nom. vii): "God through Himself receives the vision of darkness, not otherwise seeing darkness except through light."

Reply Obj. 1: The saying of the Philosopher must be understood as meaning that the intellect which is not in potentiality, does not know privation by privation existing in it; and this agrees with what he said previously, that a point and every indivisible thing are known by privation of division. This is because simple and indivisible forms are in our intellect not actually, but only potentially; for were they actually in our intellect, they would not be known by privation. It is thus that simple things are known by separate substances. God therefore knows evil, not by privation existing in Himself, but by the opposite good.

Reply Obj. 2: The knowledge of God is not the cause of evil; but is the cause of the good whereby evil is known.

Reply Obj. 3: Although evil is not opposed to the divine essence, which is not corruptible by evil; it is opposed to the effects of God, which He knows by His essence; and knowing them, He knows the opposite evils.

Reply Obj. 4: To know a thing by something else only, belongs to imperfect knowledge, if that thing is of itself knowable; but evil is not of itself knowable, forasmuch as the very nature of evil means the privation of good; therefore evil can neither be defined nor known except by good.

ELEVENTH ARTICLE [I, Q. 14, Art. 11]

Whether God Knows Singular Things?

Objection 1: It seems that God does not know singular things. For the divine intellect is more immaterial than the human intellect. Now the human intellect by reason of its immateriality does not know singular things; but as the Philosopher says (De Anima ii), "reason has to do with universals, sense with singular things." Therefore God does not know singular things.

Obj. 2: Further, in us those faculties alone know the singular, which receive the species not abstracted from material conditions. But in God things are in the highest degree abstracted from all materiality. Therefore God does not know singular things.

Obj. 3: Further, all knowledge comes about through the medium of some likeness. But the likeness of singular things in so far as they are singular, does not seem to be in God; for the principle of singularity is matter, which, since it is in potentiality only, is altogether unlike God, Who is pure act. Therefore God cannot know singular things.

*On the contrary,* It is written (Prov. 16:2), "All the ways of a man are open to His eyes."

*I answer that,* God knows singular things. For all perfections found in creatures pre-exist in God in a higher way, as is clear from the foregoing (Q. 4, A. 2). Now to know singular things is part of our perfection. Hence God must know singular things. Even the Philosopher considers it incongruous that anything known by us should be unknown to God; and thus against Empedocles he argues (De Anima i and *Metaph.* iii) that God would be most ignorant if He did not know discord. Now the perfections which are divided among inferior beings, exist simply and unitedly in God; hence, although by one faculty we know the universal and immaterial, and by another we know singular and material things, nevertheless God knows both by His simple intellect.

Now some, wishing to show how this can be, said that God knows singular things by universal causes. For nothing exists in any singular thing, that does not arise from some universal cause. They give the example of an astrologer who knows all the universal movements of the heavens, and can thence foretell all eclipses that are to come. This, however, is not enough; for singular things from universal causes attain to certain forms and powers which, however they may be joined together, are not individualized except by individual matter. Hence he who knows Socrates because he is white, or because he is the son of Sophroniscus, or because of something of that kind, would not know him in so far as he is this particular man. Hence according to the aforesaid mode, God would not know singular things in their singularity.

On the other hand, others have said that God knows singular things by the application of universal causes to particular effects. But this will not hold; forasmuch as no one can apply a thing to another unless he first knows that thing; hence the said application cannot be the reason of knowing the particular, for it presupposes the knowledge of singular things.

Therefore it must be said otherwise, that, since God is the cause of things by His knowledge, as stated above (A. 8), His knowledge extends as far as His causality extends. Hence as the active power of God extends not only to forms, which are the source of universality, but also to matter, as we shall prove further on (Q. 44, A. 2), the knowledge of God must extend to singular things, which are individualized by matter. For since He knows things other than Himself by His essence, as being the likeness of things, or as their active principle, His essence must be the sufficing principle of knowing all things made by Him, not only in the universal, but also in the singular. The same would apply to the knowledge of the artificer, if it were productive of the whole thing, and not only of the form.

Reply Obj. 1: Our intellect abstracts the intelligible species from the individualizing principles; hence the intelligible species in our intellect cannot be the likeness of the individual principles; and on that account our intellect does not know the singular. But the intelligible species in the divine intellect, which is the essence of God, is immaterial not by abstraction, but of itself, being the principle of all the principles which enter into the composition of things, whether principles of the species or principles of the individual; hence by it God knows not only universal, but also singular things.

Reply Obj. 2: Although as regards the species in the divine intellect its being has no material conditions like the images received in the imagination and sense, yet its power extends to both immaterial and material things.

Reply Obj. 3: Although matter as regards its potentiality recedes from likeness to God, yet, even in so far as it has being in this wise, it retains a certain likeness to the divine being.

TWELFTH ARTICLE [I, Q. 14, Art. 12]

Whether God Can Know Infinite Things?

Objection 1: It seems that God cannot know infinite things. For the infinite, as such, is unknown; since the infinite is that which, "to those who measure it, leaves always something more to be measured," as the Philosopher says (Phys. iii). Moreover, Augustine says (De Civ. Dei xii) that "whatever is comprehended by knowledge, is bounded by the comprehension of the knower." Now infinite things have no boundary. Therefore they cannot be comprehended by the knowledge of God.

Obj. 2: Further, if we say that things infinite in themselves are finite in God's knowledge, against this it may be urged that the essence of the infinite is that it is untraversable, and the finite that it is traversable, as said in *Phys.* iii. But the infinite is not traversable either by the finite or by the infinite, as is proved in Phys. vi. Therefore the infinite cannot be bounded by the finite, nor even by the infinite; and so the infinite cannot be finite in God's knowledge, which is infinite.

Obj. 3: Further, the knowledge of God is the measure of what is known. But it is contrary to the essence of the infinite that it be measured. Therefore infinite things cannot be known by God.

*On the contrary,* Augustine says (De Civ. Dei xii), "Although we cannot number the infinite, nevertheless it can be comprehended by Him whose knowledge has no bounds."

*I answer that,* Since God knows not only things actual but also things possible to Himself or to created things, as shown above (A. 9), and as these must be infinite, it must be held that He knows infinite things. Although the knowledge of vision which has relation only to things that are, or will be, or were, is not of infinite things, as some say, for we do not say that the world is eternal, nor that generation and movement will go on for ever, so that individuals be infinitely multiplied; yet, if we consider more attentively, we must hold that God knows infinite things even by the knowledge of vision. For God knows even the thoughts and affections of hearts, which will be multiplied to infinity as rational creatures go on for ever.

The reason of this is to be found in the fact that the knowledge of every knower is measured by the mode of the form which is the principle of knowledge. For the sensible image in sense is the likeness of only one individual thing, and can give the knowledge of only one individual. But the intelligible species of our intellect is the likeness of the thing as regards its specific nature, which is participable by infinite particulars; hence our intellect by the intelligible species of man in a certain way knows infinite men; not however as distinguished from each other, but as communicating in the nature of the species; and the reason is because the intelligible species of our intellect is the likeness of man not as to the individual principles, but as to the principles of the species. On the other hand, the divine essence, whereby the divine intellect understands, is a sufficing likeness of all things that are, or can be, not only as regards the universal principles, but also as regards the principles proper to each one, as shown above. Hence it follows that the knowledge of God extends to infinite things, even as distinct from each other.

Reply Obj. 1: The idea of the infinite pertains to quantity, as the Philosopher says (Phys. i). But the idea of quantity implies the order of parts. Therefore to know the infinite according to the mode of the infinite is to know part after part; and in this way the infinite cannot be known; for whatever quantity of parts be taken, there will always remain something else outside. But God does not know the infinite or infinite things, as if He enumerated part after part; since He knows all things simultaneously, and not successively, as said above (A. 7). Hence there is nothing to prevent Him from knowing infinite things.

Reply Obj. 2: Transition imports a certain succession of parts; and hence it is that the infinite cannot be traversed by the finite, nor by the infinite. But equality suffices for comprehension, because that is said to be comprehended which has nothing outside the comprehender. Hence it is not against the idea of the infinite to be comprehended by the infinite. And so, what is infinite in itself can be called finite to the knowledge of God as comprehended; but not as if it were traversable.

Reply Obj. 3: The knowledge of God is the measure of things, not quantitatively, for the infinite is not subject to this kind of measure; but it is the measure of the essence and truth of things. For everything has truth of nature according to the degree in which it imitates the knowledge of God, as the thing made by art agrees with the art. Granted, however, an actually infinite number of things, for instance, an infinitude of men, or an infinitude in continuous quantity, as an infinitude of air, as some of the ancients held; yet it is manifest that these would have a determinate and finite being, because their being would be limited to some determinate nature. Hence they would be measurable as regards the knowledge of God.

THIRTEENTH ARTICLE [I, Q. 14, Art. 13]

Whether the Knowledge of God Is of Future Contingent Things?

Objection 1: It seems that the knowledge of God is not of future contingent things. For from a necessary cause proceeds a necessary effect. But the knowledge of God is the cause of things known, as said above (A. 8). Since therefore that knowledge is necessary, what He knows must also be necessary. Therefore the knowledge of God is not of contingent things.

Obj. 2: Further, every conditional proposition of which the antecedent is absolutely necessary must have an absolutely necessary consequent. For the antecedent is to the consequent as principles are to the conclusion: and from necessary principles only a necessary conclusion can follow, as is proved in *Poster.* i. But this is a true conditional proposition, "If God knew that this thing will be, it will be," for the knowledge of God is only of true things. Now the antecedent conditional of this is absolutely necessary, because it is eternal, and because it is signified as past. Therefore the consequent is also absolutely necessary. Therefore whatever God knows, is necessary; and so the knowledge of God is not of contingent things.

Obj. 3: Further, everything known by God must necessarily be, because even what we ourselves know, must necessarily be; and, of course, the knowledge of God is much more certain than ours. But no future contingent things must necessarily be. Therefore no contingent future thing is known by God.

*On the contrary,* It is written (Ps. 32:15), "He Who hath made the hearts of every one of them; Who understandeth all their works," i.e. of men. Now the works of men are contingent, being subject to free will. Therefore God knows future contingent things.

*I answer that,* Since as was shown above (A. 9), God knows all things; not only things actual but also things possible to Him and creature; and since some of these are future contingent to us, it follows that God knows future contingent things.

In evidence of this, we must consider that a contingent thing can be considered in two ways; first, in itself, in so far as it is now in act: and in this sense it is not considered as future, but as present; neither is it considered as contingent (as having reference) to one of two terms, but as determined to one; and on account of this it can be infallibly the object of certain knowledge, for instance to the sense of sight, as when I see that Socrates is sitting down. In another way a contingent thing can be considered as it is in its cause; and in this way it is considered as future, and as a contingent thing not yet determined to one; forasmuch as a contingent cause has relation to opposite things: and in this sense a contingent thing is not subject to any certain knowledge. Hence, whoever knows a contingent effect in its cause only, has merely a conjectural knowledge of it. Now God knows all contingent things not only as they are in their causes, but also as each one of them is actually in itself. And although contingent things become actual successively, nevertheless God knows contingent things not successively, as they are in their own being, as we do but simultaneously. The reason is because His knowledge is measured by eternity, as is also His being; and eternity being simultaneously whole comprises all time, as said above (Q. 10, A. 2). Hence all things that are in time are present to God from eternity, not only because He has the types of things present within Him, as some say; but because His glance is carried from eternity over all things as they are in their presentiality. Hence it is manifest that contingent things are infallibly known by God, inasmuch as they are subject to the divine sight in their presentiality; yet they are future contingent things in relation to their own causes.

Reply Obj. 1: Although the supreme cause is necessary, the effect may be contingent by reason of the proximate contingent cause; just as the germination of a plant is contingent by reason of the proximate contingent cause, although the movement of the sun which is the first cause, is necessary. So likewise things known by God are contingent on account of their proximate causes, while the knowledge of God, which is the first cause, is necessary.

Reply Obj. 2: Some say that this antecedent, "God knew this contingent to be future," is not necessary, but contingent; because, although it is past, still it imports relation to the future. This however does not remove necessity from it; for whatever has had relation to the future, must have had it, although the future sometimes does not follow. On the other hand some say that this antecedent is contingent, because it is a compound of necessary and contingent; as this saying is contingent, "Socrates is a white man." But this also is to no purpose; for when we say, "God knew this contingent to be future," contingent is used here only as the matter of the word, and not as the chief part of the proposition. Hence its contingency or necessity has no reference to the necessity or contingency of the proposition, or to its being true or false. For it may be just as true that I said a man is an ass, as that I said Socrates runs, or God is: and the same applies to necessary and contingent. Hence it must be said that this antecedent is absolutely necessary. Nor does it follow, as some say, that the consequent is absolutely necessary, because the antecedent is the remote cause of the consequent, which is contingent by reason of the proximate cause. But this is to no purpose. For the conditional would be false were its antecedent the remote necessary cause, and the consequent a contingent effect; as, for example, if I said, "if the sun moves, the grass will grow."

Therefore we must reply otherwise; that when the antecedent contains anything belonging to an act of the soul, the consequent must be taken not as it is in itself, but as it is in the soul: for the existence of a thing in itself is different from the existence of a thing in the soul. For example, when I say, "What the soul understands is immaterial," this is to be understood that it is immaterial as it is in the intellect, not as it is in itself. Likewise if I say, "If God knew anything, it will be," the consequent must be understood as it is subject to the divine knowledge, i.e. as it is in its presentiality. And thus it is necessary, as also is the antecedent: "For everything that is, while it is, must be necessarily be," as the Philosopher says in *Peri Herm.* i.

Reply Obj. 3: Things reduced to act in time, as known by us successively in time, but by God (are known) in eternity, which is above time. Whence to us they cannot be certain, forasmuch as we know future contingent things as such; but (they are certain) to God alone, whose understanding is in eternity above time. Just as he who goes along the road, does not see those who come after him; whereas he who sees the whole road from a height, sees at once all travelling by the way. Hence what is known by us must be necessary, even as it is in itself; for what is future contingent in itself, cannot be known by us. Whereas what is known by God must be necessary according to the mode in which they are subject to the divine knowledge, as already stated, but not absolutely as considered in their own causes. Hence also this proposition, "Everything known by God must necessarily be," is usually distinguished; for this may refer to the thing, or to the saying. If it refers to the thing, it is divided and false; for the sense is, "Everything which God knows is necessary." If understood of the saying, it is composite and true; for the sense is, "This proposition, 'that which is known by God is' is necessary."

Now some urge an objection and say that this distinction holds good with regard to forms that are separable from the subject; thus if I said, "It is possible for a white thing to be black," it is false as applied to the saying, and true as applied to the thing: for a thing which is white, can become black; whereas this saying, "a white thing is black" can never be true. But in forms that are inseparable from the subject, this distinction does not hold, for instance, if I said, "A black crow can be white"; for in both senses it is false. Now to be known by God is inseparable from the thing; for what is known by God cannot be known. This objection, however, would hold if these words "that which is known" implied any disposition inherent to the subject; but since they import an act of the knower, something can be attributed to the thing known, in itself (even if it always be known), which is not attributed to it in so far as it stands under actual knowledge; thus material existence is attributed to a stone in itself, which is not attributed to it inasmuch as it is known.

FOURTEENTH ARTICLE [I, Q. 14, Art. 14]

Whether God Knows Enunciable Things?

Objection 1: It seems that God does not know enunciable things. For to know enunciable things belongs to our intellect as it composes and divides. But in the divine intellect, there is no composition. Therefore God does not know enunciable things.

Obj. 2: Further, every kind of knowledge is made through some likeness. But in God there is no likeness of enunciable things, since He is altogether simple. Therefore God does not know enunciable things.

*On the contrary,* It is written: "The Lord knoweth the thoughts of men" (Ps. 93:11). But enunciable things are contained in the thoughts of men. Therefore God knows enunciable things.

*I answer that,* Since it is in the power of our intellect to form enunciations, and since God knows whatever is in His own power or in that of creatures, as said above (A. 9), it follows of necessity that God knows all enunciations that can be formed.

Now just as He knows material things immaterially, and composite things simply, so likewise He knows enunciable things not after the manner of enunciable things, as if in His intellect there were composition or division of enunciations; for He knows each thing by simple intelligence, by understanding the essence of each thing; as if we by the very fact that we understand what man is, were to understand all that can be predicated of man. This, however, does not happen in our intellect, which discourses from one thing to another, forasmuch as the intelligible species represents one thing in such a way as not to represent another. Hence when we understand what man is, we do not forthwith understand other things which belong to him, but we understand them one by one, according to a certain succession. On this account the things we understand as separated, we must reduce to one by way of composition or division, by forming an enunciation. Now the species of the divine intellect, which is God's essence, suffices to represent all things. Hence by understanding His essence, God knows the essences of all things, and also whatever can be accidental to them.

Reply Obj. 1: This objection would avail if God knew enunciable things after the manner of enunciable things.

Reply Obj. 2: Enunciatory composition signifies some existence of a thing; and thus God by His existence, which is His essence, is the similitude of all those things which are signified by enunciation.

FIFTEENTH ARTICLE [I, Q. 14, Art. 15]

Whether the Knowledge of God Is Variable?

Objection 1: It seems that the knowledge of God is variable. For knowledge is related to what is knowable. But whatever imports relation to the creature is applied to God from time, and varies according to the variation of creatures. Therefore the knowledge of God is variable according to the variation of creatures.

Obj. 2: Further, whatever God can make, He can know. But God can make more than He does. Therefore He can know more than He knows. Thus His knowledge can vary according to increase and diminution.

Obj. 3: Further, God knew that Christ would be born. But He does not know now that Christ will be born; because Christ is not to be born in the future. Therefore God does not know everything He once knew; and thus the knowledge of God is variable.

*On the contrary,* It is said, that in God "there is no change nor shadow of alteration" (James 1:17).

*I answer that,* Since the knowledge of God is His substance, as is clear from the foregoing (A. 4), just as His substance is altogether immutable, as shown above (Q. 9, A. 1), so His knowledge likewise must be altogether invariable.

Reply Obj. 1: "Lord", "Creator" and the like, import relations to creatures in so far as they are in themselves. But the knowledge of God imports relation to creatures in so far as they are in God; because everything is actually understood according as it is in the one who understands. Now created things are in God in an invariable manner; while they exist variably in themselves. We may also say that "Lord", "Creator" and the like, import the relations consequent upon the acts which are understood as terminating in the creatures themselves, as they are in themselves; and thus these relations are attributed to God variously, according to the variation of creatures. But "knowledge" and "love," and the like, import relations consequent upon the acts which are understood to be in God; and therefore these are predicated of God in an invariable manner.

Reply Obj. 2: God knows also what He can make,

and does not make. Hence from the fact that He can make more than He makes, it does not follow that He can know more than He knows, unless this be referred to the knowledge of vision, according to which He is said to know those things which are in act in some period of time. But from the fact that He knows some things might be which are not, or that some things might not be which are, it does not follow that His knowledge is variable, but rather that He knows the variability of things. If, however, anything existed which God did not previously know, and afterwards knew, then His knowledge would be variable. But this could not be; for whatever is, or can be in any period of time, is known by God in His eternity. Therefore from the fact that a thing exists in some period of time, it follows that it is known by God from eternity. Therefore it cannot be granted that God can know more than He knows; because such a proposition implies that first of all He did not know, and then afterwards knew.

Reply Obj. 3: The ancient Nominalists said that it was the same thing to say "Christ is born" and "will be born" and "was born"; because the same thing is signified by these three—viz. the nativity of Christ. Therefore it follows, they said, that whatever God knew, He knows; because now He knows that Christ is born, which means the same thing as that Christ will be born. This opinion, however, is false; both because the diversity in the parts of a sentence causes a diversity of enunciations; and because it would follow that a proposition which is true once would be always true; which is contrary to what the Philosopher lays down (Categor. iii) when he says that this sentence, "Socrates sits," is true when he is sitting, and false when he rises up. Therefore, it must be conceded that this proposition is not true, "Whatever God knew He knows," if referred to enunciable propositions. But because of this, it does not follow that the knowledge of God is variable. For as it is without variation in the divine knowledge that God knows one and the same thing sometime to be, and sometime not to be, so it is without variation in the divine knowledge that God knows an enunciable proposition is sometime true, and sometime false. The knowledge of God, however, would be variable if He knew enunciable things by way of enunciation, by composition and division, as occurs in our intellect. Hence our knowledge varies either as regards truth and falsity, for example, if when either as regards truth and falsity, for example, if when a thing suffers change we retained the same opinion about it; or as regards diverse opinions, as if we first thought that anyone was sitting, and afterwards thought that he was not sitting; neither of which can be in God.

SIXTEENTH ARTICLE [I, Q. 14, Art. 16]

Whether God Has a Speculative Knowledge of Things?

Objection 1: It seems that God has not a speculative knowledge of things. For the knowledge of God is the cause of things, as shown above (A. 8). But speculative knowledge is not the cause of the things known. Therefore the knowledge of God is not speculative.

Obj. 2: Further, speculative knowledge comes by abstraction from things; which does not belong to the divine knowledge. Therefore the knowledge of God is not speculative.

*On the contrary,* Whatever is the more excellent must be attributed to God. But speculative knowledge is more excellent than practical knowledge, as the Philosopher says in the beginning of Metaphysics. Therefore God has a speculative knowledge of things.

*I answer that,* Some knowledge is speculative only; some is practical only; and some is partly speculative and partly practical. In proof whereof it must be observed that knowledge can be called speculative in three ways: first, on the part of the things known, which are not operable by the knower; such is the knowledge of man about natural or divine thing[s]. Secondly, as regards the manner of knowing—as, for instance, if a builder consider a house by defining and dividing, and considering what belongs to it in general: for this is to consider operable things in a speculative manner, and not as practically operable; for operable means the application of form to matter, and not the resolution of the composite into its universal formal principles. Thirdly, as regards the end; "for the practical intellect differs in its end from the speculative," as the Philosopher says (De Anima iii). For the practical intellect is ordered to the end of the operation; whereas the end of the speculative intellect is the consideration of truth. Hence if a builder should consider how a house can be made, not ordering this to the end of operation, but only to know (how to do it), this would be only a speculative considerations as regards the end, although it concerns an operable thing. Therefore knowledge which is speculative by reason of the thing itself known, is merely speculative. But that which is speculative either in its mode or as to its end is partly speculative and partly practical: and when it is ordained to an operative end it is simply practical.

In accordance with this, therefore, it must be said that God has of Himself a speculative knowledge only; for He Himself is not operable. But of all other things He has both speculative and practical knowledge. He has speculative knowledge as regards the mode; for whatever we know speculatively in things by defining and dividing, God knows all this much more perfectly.

Now of things which He can make, but does not make at any time, He has not a practical knowledge, according as knowledge is called practical from the end. But He has a practical knowledge of what He makes in some period of time. And, as regards evil things, although they are not operable by Him, yet they fall under His practical knowledge, like good things, inasmuch as He permits, or impedes, or directs them; as also sicknesses fall under the practical knowledge of the physician, inasmuch as he cures them by his art.

Reply Obj. 1: The knowledge of God is the cause, not indeed of Himself, but of other things. He is actually the cause of some, that is, of things that come to be in some period of time; and He is virtually the cause of others, that is, of things which He can make, and which nevertheless are never made.

Reply Obj. 2: The fact that knowledge is derived from things known does not essentially belong to speculative knowledge, but only accidentally in so far as it is human.

In answer to what is objected *on the contrary,* we must say that perfect knowledge of operable things is obtainable only if they are known in so far as they are operable. Therefore, since the knowledge of God is in every way perfect, He must know what is operable by Him, formally as such, and not only in so far as they are speculative. Nevertheless this does not impair the nobility of His speculative knowledge, forasmuch as He sees all things other than Himself in Himself, and He knows Himself speculatively; and so in the speculative knowledge of Himself, he possesses both speculative and practical knowledge of all other things.

## QUESTION 15

OF IDEAS (In Three Articles)

After considering the knowledge of God, it remains to consider ideas. And about this there are three points of inquiry:

(1) Whether there are ideas?

(2) Whether they are many, or one only?

(3) Whether there are ideas of all things known by God?

FIRST ARTICLE [I, Q. 15, Art. 1]

Whether There Are Ideas?

Objection 1: It seems that there are no ideas. For Dionysius says (Div. Nom. vii), that God does not know things by ideas. But ideas are for nothing else except that things may be known through them. Therefore there are no ideas.

Obj. 2: Further, God knows all things in Himself, as has been already said (Q. 14, A. 5). But He does not know Himself through an idea; neither therefore other things.

Obj. 3: Further, an idea is considered to be the principle of knowledge and action. But the divine essence is a sufficient principle of knowing and effecting all things. It is not therefore necessary to suppose ideas.

*On the contrary,* Augustine says (Octog. Tri. Quaest. qu. xlvi), "Such is the power inherent in ideas, that no one can be wise unless they are understood."

*I answer that,* It is necessary to suppose ideas in the divine mind. For the Greek word *Idea* is in Latin Forma. Hence by ideas are understood the forms of things, existing apart from the things themselves. Now the form of anything existing apart from the thing itself can be for one of two ends: either to be the type of that of which it is called the form, or to be the principle of the knowledge of that thing, inasmuch as the forms of things knowable are said to be in him who knows them. In either case we must suppose ideas, as is clear for the following reason:

In all things not generated by chance, the form must be the end of any generation whatsoever. But an agent does not act on account of the form, except in so far as the likeness of the form is in the agent, as may happen in two ways. For in some agents the form of the thing to be made pre-exists according to its natural being, as in those that act by their nature; as a man generates a man, or fire generates fire. Whereas in other agents (the form of the thing to be made pre-exists) according to intelligible being, as in those that act by the intellect; and thus the likeness of a house pre-exists in the mind of the builder. And this may be called the idea of the house, since the builder intends to build his house like to the form conceived in his mind. As then the world was not made by chance, but by God acting by His intellect, as will appear later (Q. 46, A. 1), there must exist in the divine mind a form to the likeness of which the world was made. And in this the notion of an idea consists.

Reply Obj. 1: God does not understand things according to an idea existing outside Himself. Thus Aristotle (Metaph. ix) rejects the opinion of Plato, who held that ideas existed of themselves, and not in the intellect.

Reply Obj. 2: Although God knows Himself and all else by His own essence, yet His essence is the operative principle of all things, except of Himself. It has therefore the nature of an idea with respect to other things; though not with respect to Himself.

Reply Obj. 3: God is the similitude of all things according to His essence; therefore an idea in God is identical with His essence.

SECOND ARTICLE [I, Q. 15, Art. 2]

Whether Ideas Are Many?

Objection 1: It seems that ideas are not many. For an idea in God is His essence. But God's essence is one only. Therefore there is only one idea.

Obj. 2: Further, as the idea is the principle of knowing and operating, so are art and wisdom. But in God there are not several arts or wisdoms. Therefore in Him there is no plurality of ideas.

Obj. 3: Further, if it be said that ideas are multiplied according to their relations to different creatures, it may be argued on the contrary that the plurality of ideas is eternal. If, then, ideas are many, but creatures temporal, then the temporal must be the cause of the eternal.

Obj. 4: Further, these relations are either real in

creatures only, or in God also. If in creatures only, since creatures are not from eternity, the plurality of ideas cannot be from eternity, if ideas are multiplied only according to these relations. But if they are real in God, it follows that there is a real plurality in God other than the plurality of Persons: and this is against the teaching of Damascene (De Fide Orth. i, 10), who says, in God all things are one, except "ingenerability, generation, and procession." Ideas therefore are not many.

*On the contrary,* Augustine says (Octog. Tri. Quaest. qu. xlvi), "Ideas are certain principal forms, or permanent and immutable types of things, they themselves not being formed. Thus they are eternal, and existing always in the same manner, as being contained in the divine intelligence. Whilst, however, they themselves neither come into being nor decay, yet we say that in accordance with them everything is formed that can rise or decay, and all that actually does so."

*I answer that,* It must necessarily be held that ideas are many. In proof of which it is to be considered that in every effect the ultimate end is the proper intention of the principal agent, as the order of an army (is the proper intention) of the general. Now the highest good existing in things is the good of the order of the universe, as the Philosopher clearly teaches in *Metaph.* xii. Therefore the order of the universe is properly intended by God, and is not the accidental result of a succession of agents, as has been supposed by those who have taught that God created only the first creature, and that this creature created the second creature, and so on, until this great multitude of beings was produced. According to this opinion God would have the idea of the first created thing alone; whereas, if the order itself of the universe was created by Him immediately, and intended by Him, He must have the idea of the order of the universe. Now there cannot be an idea of any whole, unless particular ideas are had of those parts of which the whole is made; just as a builder cannot conceive the idea of a house unless he has the idea of each of its parts. So, then, it must needs be that in the divine mind there are the proper ideas of all things. Hence Augustine says (Octog. Tri. Quaest. qu. xlvi), "that each thing was created by God according to the idea proper to it," from which it follows that in the divine mind ideas are many. Now it can easily be seen how this is not repugnant to the simplicity of God, if we consider that the idea of a work is in the mind of the operator as that which is understood, and not as the image whereby he understands, which is a form that makes the intellect in act. For the form of the house in the mind of the builder, is something understood by him, to the likeness of which he forms the house in matter. Now, it is not repugnant to the simplicity of the divine mind that it understand many things; though it would be repugnant to its simplicity were His understanding to be formed by a plurality of images. Hence many ideas exist in the divine mind, as things understood by it; as can be proved thus. Inasmuch as He knows His own essence perfectly, He knows it according to every mode in which it can be known. Now it can be known not only as it is in itself, but as it can be participated in by creatures according to some degree of likeness. But every creature has its own proper species, according to which it participates in some degree in likeness to the divine essence. So far, therefore, as God knows His essence as capable of such imitation by any creature, He knows it as the particular type and idea of that creature; and in like manner as regards other creatures. So it is clear that God understands many particular types of things and these are many ideas.

Reply Obj. 1: The divine essence is not called an idea in so far as it is that essence, but only in so far as it is the likeness or type of this or that thing. Hence ideas are said to be many, inasmuch as many types are understood through the self-same essence.

Reply Obj. 2: By wisdom and art we signify that by which God understands; but an idea, that which God understands. For God by one understands many things, and that not only according to what they are in themselves, but also according as they are understood, and this is to understand the several types of things. In the same way, an architect is said to understand a house, when he understands the form of the house in matter. But if he understands the form of a house, as devised by himself, from the fact that he understands that he understands it, he thereby understands the type or idea of the house. Now not only does God understand many things by His essence, but He also understands that He understands many things by His essence. And this means that He understands the several types of things; or that many ideas are in His intellect as understood by Him.

Reply Obj. 3: Such relations, whereby ideas are multiplied, are caused not by the things themselves, but by the divine intellect comparing its own essence with these things.

Reply Obj. 4: Relations multiplying ideas do not exist in created things, but in God. Yet they are not real relations, such as those whereby the Persons are distinguished, but relations understood by God.

THIRD ARTICLE [I, Q. 15, Art. 3]

Whether There Are Ideas of All Things That God Knows?

Objection 1: It seems that there are not ideas in God of all things that He knows. For the idea of evil is not in God; since it would follow that evil was in Him. But evil things are known by God. Therefore there are not ideas of all things that God knows.

Obj. 2: Further, God knows things that neither are, nor will be, nor have been, as has been said above (A. 9). But of such things there are no ideas, since, as Dionysius says (Div. Nom. v): "Acts of the divine will are the determining and effective types of things." Therefore there are not in God ideas of all things known by Him.

Obj. 3: Further, God knows primary matter, of which there can be no idea, since it has no form. Hence the same conclusion.

Obj. 4: Further, it is certain that God knows not only species, but also genera, singulars, and accidents. But there are not ideas of these, according to Plato's teaching, who first taught ideas, as Augustine says (Octog. Tri. Quaest. qu. xlvi). Therefore there are not ideas in God of all things known by Him.

*On the contrary,* Ideas are types existing in the divine mind, as is clear from Augustine (Octog. Tri. Quaest. qu. xlvi). But God has the proper types of all things that He knows; and therefore He has ideas of all things known by Him.

*I answer that,* As ideas, according to Plato, are principles of the knowledge of things and of their generation, an idea has this twofold office, as it exists in the mind of God. So far as the idea is the principle of the making of things, it may be called an "exemplar," and belongs to practical knowledge. But so far as it is a principle of knowledge, it is properly called a "type," and may belong to speculative knowledge also. As an exemplar, therefore, it has respect to everything made by God in any period of time; whereas as a principle of knowledge it has respect to all things known by God, even though they never come to be in time; and to all things that He knows according to their proper type, in so far as they are known by Him in a speculative manner.

Reply Obj. 1: Evil is known by God not through its own type, but through the type of good. Evil, therefore, has no idea in God, neither in so far as an idea is an "exemplar" nor as a "type."

Reply Obj. 2: God has no practical knowledge, except virtually, of things which neither are, nor will be, nor have been. Hence, with respect to these there is no idea in God in so far as idea signifies an "exemplar" but only in so far as it denotes a "type."

Reply Obj. 3: Plato is said by some to have considered matter as not created; and therefore he postulated not an idea of matter but a concause with matter. Since, however, we hold matter to be created by God, though not apart from form, matter has its idea in God; but not apart from the idea of the composite; for matter in itself can neither exist, nor be known.

Reply Obj. 4: Genus can have no idea apart from the idea of species, in so far as idea denotes an "exemplar"; for genus cannot exist except in some species. The same is the case with those accidents that inseparably accompany their subject; for these come into being along with their subject. But accidents which supervene to the subject, have their special idea. For an architect produces through the form of the house all the accidents that originally accompany it; whereas those that are superadded to the house when completed, such as painting, or any other such thing, are produced through some other form. Now individual things, according to Plato, have no other idea than that of species; both because particular things are individualized by matter, which, as some say, he held to be uncreated and the concause with the idea; and because the intention of nature regards the species, and produces individuals only that in them the species may be preserved. However, divine providence extends not merely to species; but to individuals as will be shown later (Q. 22, A. 3).

## QUESTION 16

OF TRUTH (In Eight Articles)

Since knowledge is of things that are true, after the consideration of the knowledge of God, we must inquire concerning truth. About this there are eight points of inquiry:

(1) Whether truth resides in the thing, or only in the intellect?

(2) Whether it resides only in the intellect composing and dividing?

(3) On the comparison of the true to being.

(4) On the comparison of the true to the good.

(5) Whether God is truth?

(6) Whether all things are true by one truth, or by many?

(7) On the eternity of truth.

(8) On the unchangeableness of truth.

FIRST ARTICLE [I, Q. 16, Art. 1]

Whether Truth Resides Only in the Intellect?

Objection 1: It seems that truth does not reside only in the intellect, but rather in things. For Augustine (Soliloq. ii, 5) condemns this definition of truth, "That is true which is seen"; since it would follow that stones hidden in the bosom of the earth would not be true stones, as they are not seen. He also condemns the following, "That is true which is as it appears to the knower, who is willing and able to know," for hence it would follow that nothing would be true, unless someone could know it. Therefore he defines truth thus: "That is true which is." It seems, then, that truth resides in things, and not in the intellect.

Obj. 2: Further, whatever is true, is true by reason of truth. If, then, truth is only in the intellect, nothing will be true except in so far as it is understood. But this is the error of the ancient philosophers, who said that whatever seems to be true is so. Consequently mutual contradictories seem to be true as seen by different persons at the same time.

Obj. 3: Further, "that, on account of which a thing is so, is itself more so," as is evident from the Philosopher (Poster. i). But it is from the fact that a thing is or is not, that our thought or word is true or false, as the Philosopher teaches (Praedicam. iii). Therefore truth resides rather in things than in the intellect.

*On the contrary,* The Philosopher says (Metaph. vi), " The true and the false reside not in things, but in the intellect."

*I answer that,* As the good denotes that towards which the appetite tends, so the true denotes that towards which the intellect tends. Now there is this difference between the appetite and the intellect, or any knowledge whatsoever, that knowledge is according as the thing known is in the knower, whilst appetite is according as the desirer tends towards the thing desired. Thus the term of the appetite, namely good, is in the object desirable, and the term of the intellect, namely true, is in the intellect itself. Now as good exists in a thing so far as that thing is related to the appetite—and hence the aspect of goodness passes on from the desirable thing to the appetite, in so far as the appetite is called good if its object is good; so, since the true is in the intellect in so far as it is conformed to the object understood, the aspect of the true must needs pass from the intellect to the object understood, so that also the thing understood is said to be true in so far as it has some relation to the intellect. Now a thing understood may be in relation to an intellect either essentially or accidentally. It is related essentially to an intellect on which it depends as regards its essence; but accidentally to an intellect by which it is knowable; even as we may say that a house is related essentially to the intellect of the architect, but accidentally to the intellect upon which it does not depend.

Now we do not judge of a thing by what is in it accidentally, but by what is in it essentially. Hence, everything is said to be true absolutely, in so far as it is related to the intellect from which it depends; and thus it is that artificial things are said to be true as being related to our intellect. For a house is said to be true that expresses the likeness of the form in the architect's mind; and words are said to be true so far as they are the signs of truth in the intellect. In the same way natural things are said to be true in so far as they express the likeness of the species that are in the divine mind. For a stone is called true, which possesses the nature proper to a stone, according to the preconception in the divine intellect. Thus, then, truth resides primarily in the intellect, and secondarily in things according as they are related to the intellect as their principle. Consequently there are various definitions of truth. Augustine says (De Vera Relig. xxxvi), "Truth is that whereby is made manifest that which is;" and Hilary says (De Trin. v) that "Truth makes being clear and evident" and this pertains to truth according as it is in the intellect. As to the truth of things in so far as they are related to the intellect, we have Augustine's definition (De Vera Relig. xxxvi), "Truth is a supreme likeness without any unlikeness to a principle": also Anselm's definition (De Verit. xii), "Truth is rightness, perceptible by the mind alone"; for that is right which is in accordance with the principle; also Avicenna's definition (Metaph. viii, 6), "The truth of each thing is a property of the essence which is immutably attached to it." The definition that "Truth is the equation of thought and thing" is applicable to it under either aspect.

Reply Obj. 1: Augustine is speaking about the truth of things, and excludes from the notion of this truth, relation to our intellect; for what is accidental is excluded from every definition.

Reply Obj. 2: The ancient philosophers held that the species of natural things did not proceed from any intellect, but were produced by chance. But as they saw that truth implies relation to intellect, they were compelled to base the truth of things on their relation to our intellect. From this, conclusions result that are inadmissible, and which the Philosopher refutes (Metaph. iv). Such, however, do not follow, if we say that the truth of things consists in their relation to the divine intellect.

Reply Obj. 3: Although the truth of our intellect is caused by the thing, yet it is not necessary that truth should be there primarily, any more than that health should be primarily in medicine, rather than in the animal: for the virtue of medicine, and not its health, is the cause of health, for here the agent is not univocal. In the same way, the being of the thing, not its truth, is the cause of truth in the intellect. Hence the Philosopher says that a thought or a word is true "from the fact that a thing is, not because a thing is true."

SECOND ARTICLE [I, Q. 16, Art. 2]

Whether Truth Resides Only in the Intellect Composing and Dividing?

Objection 1: It seems that truth does not reside only in the intellect composing and dividing. For the Philosopher says (De Anima iii) that as the senses are always true as regards their proper sensible objects, so is the intellect as regards "what a thing is." Now composition and division are neither in the senses nor in the intellect knowing "what a thing is." Therefore truth does not reside only in the intellect composing and dividing.

Obj. 2: Further, Isaac says in his book *On Definitions* that truth is the equation of thought and thing. Now just as the intellect with regard to complex things can be equated to things, so also with regard to simple things; and this is true also of sense apprehending a thing as it is. Therefore truth does not reside only in the intellect composing and dividing.

*On the contrary,* the Philosopher says (Metaph. vi) that with regard to simple things and "what a thing is," truth is "found neither in the intellect nor in things."

*I answer that,* As stated before, truth resides, in its primary aspect, in the intellect. Now since everything is true according as it has the form proper to its nature, the intellect, in so far as it is knowing, must be true, so far as it has the likeness of the thing known, this being its form, as knowing. For this reason truth is defined by the conformity of intellect and thing; and hence to know this conformity is to know truth. But in no way can sense know this. For although sight has the likeness of a visible thing, yet it does not know the comparison which exists between the thing seen and that which itself apprehends concerning it. But the intellect can know its own conformity with the intelligible thing; yet it does not apprehend it by knowing of a thing "what a thing is." When, however, it judges that a thing corresponds to the form which it apprehends about that thing, then first it knows and expresses truth. This it does by composing and dividing: for in every proposition it either applies to, or removes from the thing signified by the subject, some form signified by the predicate: and this clearly shows that the sense is true of any thing, as is also the intellect, when it knows "what a thing is"; but it does not thereby know or affirm truth. This is in like manner the case with complex or non-complex words. Truth therefore may be in the senses, or in the intellect knowing "what a thing is," as in anything that is true; yet not as the thing known in the knower, which is implied by the word "truth"; for the perfection of the intellect is truth as known. Therefore, properly speaking, truth resides in the intellect composing and dividing; and not in the senses; nor in the intellect knowing "what a thing is."

And thus the Objections given are solved.

THIRD ARTICLE [I, Q. 16, Art. 3]

Whether the True and Being Are Convertible Terms?

Objection 1: It seems that the true and being are not convertible terms. For the true resides properly in the intellect, as stated (A. 1); but being is properly in things. Therefore they are not convertible.

Obj. 2: Further, that which extends to being and not-being is not convertible with being. But the true extends to being and not-being; for it is true that what is, is; and that what is not, is not. Therefore the true and being are not convertible.

Obj. 3: Further, things which stand to each other in order of priority and posteriority seem not to be convertible. But the true appears to be prior to being; for being is not understood except under the aspect of the true. Therefore it seems they are not convertible.

*On the contrary,* the Philosopher says (Metaph. ii) that there is the same disposition of things in being and in truth.

*I answer that,* As good has the nature of what is desirable, so truth is related to knowledge. Now everything, in as far as it has being, so far is it knowable. Wherefore it is said in *De Anima* iii that "the soul is in some manner all things," through the senses and the intellect. And therefore, as good is convertible with being, so is the true. But as good adds to being the notion of desirable, so the true adds relation to the intellect.

Reply Obj. 1: The true resides in things and in the intellect, as said before (A. 1). But the true that is in things is convertible with being as to substance; while the true that is in the intellect is convertible with being, as the manifestation with the manifested; for this belongs to the nature of truth, as has been said already (A. 1). It may, however, be said that being also is in things and in the intellect, as is the true; although truth is primarily in the intellect, while being is primarily in things; and this is so because truth and being differ in idea.

Reply Obj. 2: Not-being has nothing in itself whereby it can be known; yet it is known in so far as the intellect renders it knowable. Hence the true is based on being, inasmuch as not-being is a kind of logical being, apprehended, that is, by reason.

Reply Obj. 3: When it is said that being cannot be apprehended except under the notion of the true, this can be understood in two ways. In the one way so as to mean that being is not apprehended, unless the idea of the true follows apprehension of being; and this is true. In the other way, so as to mean that being cannot be apprehended unless the idea of the true be apprehended also; and this is false. But the true cannot be apprehended unless the idea of being be apprehended also; since being is included in the idea of the true. The case is the same if we compare the intelligible object with being. For being cannot be understood, unless being is intelligible. Yet being can be understood while its intelligibility is not understood. Similarly, being when understood is true, yet the true is not understood by understanding being.

FOURTH ARTICLE [I, Q. 16, Art. 4]

Whether Good Is Logically Prior to the True?

Objection 1: It seems that good is logically prior to the true. For what is more universal is logically prior, as is evident from *Phys.* i. But the good is more universal than the true, since the true is a kind of good, namely, of the intellect. Therefore the good is logically prior to the true.

Obj. 2: Further, good is in things, but the true in the intellect composing and dividing as said above (A. 2). But that which is in things is prior to that which is in the intellect. Therefore good is logically prior to the true.

Obj. 3: Further, truth is a species of virtue, as is clear from *Ethic.* iv. But virtue is included under good; since, as Augustine says (De Lib. Arbit. ii, 19), it is a good quality of the mind. Therefore the good is prior to the true.

*On the contrary,* What is in more things is prior logically. But the true is in some things wherein good is not, as, for instance, in mathematics. Therefore the true is prior to good.

*I answer that,* Although the good and the true are convertible with being, as to suppositum, yet they differ logically. And in this manner the true, speaking absolutely, is prior to good, as appears from two reasons. First, because the true is more closely related to being than is good. For the true regards being itself simply and immediately; while the nature of good follows being in so far as being is in some way perfect; for thus it is desirable. Secondly, it is evident from the fact that knowledge naturally precedes appetite. Hence, since the true regards knowledge, but the good regards the appetite, the true must be prior in idea to the good.

Reply Obj. 1: The will and the intellect mutually include one another: for the intellect understands the will, and the will wills the intellect to understand. So then, among things directed to the object of the will, are comprised also those that belong to the intellect; and conversely. Whence in the order of things desirable, good stands as the universal, and the true as the particular; whereas in the order of intelligible things the converse is the case. From the fact, then, that the true is a kind of good, it follows that the good is prior in the order of things desirable; but not that it is prior absolutely.

Reply Obj. 2: A thing is prior logically in so far as it is prior to the intellect. Now the intellect apprehends primarily being itself; secondly, it apprehends that it understands being; and thirdly, it apprehends that it desires being. Hence the idea of being is first, that of truth second, and the idea of good third, though good is in things.

Reply Obj. 3: The virtue which is called "truth" is not truth in general, but a certain kind of truth according to which man shows himself in deed and word as he really is. But truth as applied to "life" is used in a particular sense, inasmuch as a man fulfills in his life that to which he is ordained by the divine intellect, as it has been said that truth exists in other things (A. 1). Whereas the truth of "justice" is found in man as he fulfills his duty to his neighbor, as ordained by law. Hence we cannot argue from these particular truths to truth in general.

FIFTH ARTICLE [I, Q. 16, Art. 5]

Whether God Is Truth?

Objection 1: It seems that God is not truth. For truth consists in the intellect composing and dividing. But in God there is not composition and division. Therefore in Him there is not truth.

Obj. 2: Further, truth, according to Augustine (De Vera Relig. xxxvi) is a "likeness to the principle." But in God there is no likeness to a principle. Therefore in God there is not truth.

Obj. 3: Further, whatever is said of God, is said of Him as of the first cause of all things; thus the being of God is the cause of all being; and His goodness the cause of all good. If therefore there is truth in God, all truth will be from Him. But it is true that someone sins. Therefore this will be from God; which is evidently false.

*On the contrary,* Our Lord says, "I am the Way, the Truth, and the Life" (John 14:6).

*I answer that,* As said above (A. 1), truth is found in the intellect according as it apprehends a thing as it is; and in things according as they have being conformable to an intellect. This is to the greatest degree found in God. For His being is not only conformed to His intellect, but it is the very act of His intellect; and His act of understanding is the measure and cause of every other being and of every other intellect, and He Himself is His own existence and act of understanding. Whence it follows not only that truth is in Him, but that He is truth itself, and the sovereign and first truth.

Reply Obj. 1: Although in the divine intellect there is neither composition nor division, yet in His simple act of intelligence He judges of all things and knows all things complex; and thus there is truth in His intellect.

Reply Obj. 2: The truth of our intellect is according to its conformity with its principle, that is to say, to the things from which it receives knowledge. The truth also of things is according to their conformity with their principle, namely, the divine intellect. Now this cannot be said, properly speaking, of divine truth; unless perhaps in so far as truth is appropriated to the Son, Who has a principle. But if we speak of divine truth in its essence, we cannot understand this unless the affirmative must be resolved into the negative, as when one says: "the Father is of Himself, because He is not from another." Similarly, the divine truth can be called a "likeness to the principle," inasmuch as His existence is not dissimilar to His intellect.

Reply Obj. 3: Not-being and privation have no truth of themselves, but only in the apprehension of the intellect. Now all apprehension of the intellect is from God. Hence all the truth that exists in the statement—"that a person commits fornication is true"—is entirely from God. But to argue, "Therefore that this person fornicates is from God", is a fallacy of Accident.

SIXTH ARTICLE [I, Q. 16, Art. 6]

Whether There Is Only One Truth, According to Which All Things Are True?

Objection 1: It seems that there is only one truth, according to which all things are true. For according to Augustine (De Trin. xv, 1), "nothing is greater than the mind of man, except God." Now truth is greater than the mind of man; otherwise the mind would be the judge of truth: whereas in fact it judges all things according to truth, and not according to its own measure. Therefore God alone is truth. Therefore there is no other truth but God.

Obj. 2: Further, Anselm says (De Verit. xiv), that, "as is the relation of time to temporal things, so is that of truth to true things." But there is only one time for all temporal things. Therefore there is only one truth, by which all things are true.

*On the contrary,* it is written (Ps. 11:2), "Truths are decayed from among the children of men."

*I answer that,* In one sense truth, whereby all things are true, is one, and in another sense it is not. In proof of which we must consider that when anything is predicated of many things univocally, it is found in each of them according to its proper nature; as animal is found in each species of animal. But when anything is predicated of many things analogically, it is found in only one of them according to its proper nature, and from this one the rest are denominated. So healthiness is predicated of animal, of urine, and of medicine, not that health is only in the animal; but from the health of the animal, medicine is called healthy, in so far as it is the cause of health, and urine is called healthy, in so far as it indicates health. And although health is neither in medicine nor in urine, yet in either there is something whereby the one causes, and the other indicates health. Now we have said (A. 1) that truth resides primarily in the intellect; and secondarily in things, according as they are related to the divine intellect. If therefore we speak of truth, as it exists in the intellect, according to its proper nature, then are there many truths in many created intellects; and even in one and the same intellect, according to the number of things known. Whence a gloss on Ps. 11:2, "Truths are decayed from among the children of men," says: "As from one man's face many likenesses are reflected in a mirror, so many truths are reflected from the one divine truth." But if we speak of truth as it is in things, then all things are true by one primary truth; to which each one is assimilated according to its own entity. And thus, although the essences or forms of things are many, yet the truth of the divine intellect is one, in conformity to which all things are said to be true.

Reply Obj. 1: The soul does not judge of things according to any kind of truth, but according to the primary truth, inasmuch as it is reflected in the soul, as in a mirror, by reason of the first principles of the understanding. It follows, therefore, that the primary truth is greater than the soul. And yet, even created truth, which resides in our intellect, is greater than the soul, not simply, but in a certain degree, in so far as it is its perfection; even as science may be said to be greater than the soul. Yet it is true that nothing subsisting is greater than the rational soul, except God.

Reply Obj. 2: The saying of Anselm is correct in so far as things are said to be true by their relation to the divine intellect.

SEVENTH ARTICLE [I, Q. 16, Art. 7]

Whether Created Truth Is Eternal?

Objection 1: It seems that created truth is eternal. For Augustine says (De Lib. Arbit. ii, 8) "Nothing is more eternal than the nature of a circle, and that two added to three make five." But the truth of these is a created truth. Therefore created truth is eternal.

Obj. 2: Further, that which is always, is eternal. But universals are always and everywhere; therefore they are eternal. So therefore is truth, which is the most universal.

Obj. 3: Further, it was always true that what is true in the present was to be in the future. But as the truth of a proposition regarding the present is a created truth, so is that of a proposition regarding the future. Therefore some created truth is eternal.

Obj. 4: Further, all that is without beginning and end is eternal. But the truth of enunciables is without beginning and end; for if their truth had a beginning, since it was not before, it was true that truth was not, and true, of course, by reason of truth; so that truth was before it began to be. Similarly, if it be asserted that truth has an end, it follows that it is after it has ceased to be, for it will still be true that truth is not. Therefore truth is eternal.

*On the contrary,* God alone is eternal, as laid down before (Q. 10, Art. 3).

*I answer that,* The truth of enunciations is no other than the truth of the intellect. For an enunciation resides in the intellect, and in speech. Now according as it is in the intellect it has truth of itself: but according as it is in speech, it is called enunciable truth, according as it signifies some truth of the intellect, not on account of any truth residing in the enunciation, as though in a subject. Thus urine is called healthy, not from any health within it but from the health of an animal which it indicates. In like manner it has been already said that things are called true from the truth of the intellect. Hence, if no intellect were eternal, no truth would be eternal. Now because only the divine intellect is eternal, in it alone truth has eternity. Nor does it follow from this that anything else but God is eternal; since the truth of the divine intellect is God Himself, as shown already (A. 5).

Reply Obj. 1: The nature of a circle, and the fact that two and three make five, have eternity in the mind of God.

Reply Obj. 2: That something is always and everywhere, can be understood in two ways. In one way, as having in itself the power of extension to all time and to all places, as it belongs to God to be everywhere and always. In the other way as not having in itself determination to any place or time, as primary matter is said to be one, not because it has one form, but by the absence of all distinguishing form. In this manner all universals are said to be everywhere and always, in so far as universals are independent of place and time. It does not, however, follow from this that they are eternal, except in an intellect, if one exists that is eternal.

Reply Obj. 3: That which now is, was future, before it (actually) was; because it was in its cause that it would be. Hence, if the cause were removed, that thing's coming to be was not future. But the first cause is alone eternal. Hence it does not follow that it was always true that what now is would be, except in so far as its future being was in the sempiternal cause; and God alone is such a cause.

Reply Obj. 4: Because our intellect is not eternal, neither is the truth of enunciable propositions which are formed by us, eternal, but it had a beginning in time. Now before such truth existed, it was not true to say that such a truth did exist, except by reason of the divine intellect, wherein alone truth is eternal. But it is true now to say that that truth did not then exist: and this is true only by reason of the truth that is now in our intellect; and not by reason of any truth in the things. For this is truth concerning not-being; and not-being has not truth of itself, but only so far as our intellect apprehends it. Hence it is true to say that truth did not exist, in so far as we apprehend its not-being as preceding its being.

EIGHTH ARTICLE [I, Q. 16, Art. 8]

Whether Truth Is Immutable?

Objection 1: It seems that truth is immutable. For Augustine says (De Lib. Arbit. ii, 12), that "Truth and mind do not rank as equals, otherwise truth would be mutable, as the mind is."

Obj. 2: Further, what remains after every change is immutable; as primary matter is unbegotten and incorruptible, since it remains after all generation and corruption. But truth remains after all change; for after every change it is true to say that a thing is, or is not. Therefore truth is immutable.

Obj. 3: Further, if the truth of an enunciation changes, it changes mostly with the changing of the thing. But it does not thus change. For truth, according to Anselm (De Verit. viii), "is a certain rightness" in so far as a thing answers to that which is in the divine mind concerning it. But this proposition that "Socrates sits", receives from the divine mind the signification that Socrates does sit; and it has the same signification even though he does not sit. Therefore the truth of the proposition in no way changes.

Obj. 4: Further, where there is the same cause, there is the same effect. But the same thing is the cause of the truth of the three propositions, "Socrates sits, will sit, sat." Therefore the truth of each is the same. But one or other of these must be the true one. Therefore the truth of these propositions remains immutable; and for the same reason that of any other.

*On the contrary,* It is written (Ps. 11:2), "Truths are decayed from among the children of men."

*I answer that,* Truth, properly speaking, resides only in the intellect, as said before (A. 1); but things are called true in virtue of the truth residing in an intellect. Hence the mutability of truth must be regarded from the point of view of the intellect, the truth of which consists in its conformity to the thing understood. Now this conformity may vary in two ways, even as any other likeness, through change in one of the two extremes. Hence in one way truth varies on the part of the intellect, from the fact that a change of opinion occurs about a thing which in itself has not changed, and in another way, when the thing is changed, but not the opinion; and in either way there can be a change from true to false. If, then, there is an intellect wherein there can be no alternation of opinions, and the knowledge of which nothing can escape, in this is immutable truth. Now such is the divine intellect, as is clear from what has been said before (Q. 14, A. 15). Hence the truth of the divine intellect is immutable. But the truth of our intellect is mutable; not because it is itself the subject of change, but in so far as our intellect changes from truth to falsity, for thus forms may be called mutable. Whereas the truth of the divine intellect is that according to which natural things are said to be true, and this is altogether immutable.

Reply Obj. 1: Augustine is speaking of divine truth.

Reply Obj. 2: The true and being are convertible terms. Hence just as being is not generated nor corrupted of itself, but accidentally, in so far as this being or that is corrupted or generated, as is said in *Phys.* i, so does truth change, not so as that no truth remains, but because that truth does not remain which was before.

Reply Obj. 3: A proposition not only has truth, as other things are said to have it, in so far, that is, as they correspond to that which is the design of the divine intellect concerning them; but it is said to have truth in a special way, in so far as it indicates the truth of the intellect, which consists in the conformity of the intellect with a thing. When this disappears, the truth of an opinion changes, and consequently the truth of the proposition. So therefore this proposition, "Socrates sits," is true, as long as he is sitting, both with the truth of the thing, in so far as the expression is significative, and with the truth of signification, in so far as it signifies a true opinion. When Socrates rises, the first truth remains, but the second is changed.

Reply Obj. 4: The sitting of Socrates, which is the cause of the truth of the proposition, "Socrates sits," has not the same meaning when Socrates sits, after he sits, and before he sits. Hence the truth which results, varies, and is variously signified by these propositions concerning present, past, or future. Thus it does not follow, though one of the three propositions is true, that the same truth remains invariable.

## QUESTION 17

CONCERNING FALSITY (In Four Articles)

We next consider falsity. About this four points of inquiry arise:

(1) Whether falsity exists in things?

(2) Whether it exists in the sense?

(3) Whether it exists in the intellect?

(4) Concerning the opposition of the true and the false.

FIRST ARTICLE [I, Q. 17, Art. 1]

Whether Falsity Exists in Things?

Objection 1: It appears that falsity does not exist in things. For Augustine says (Soliloq. ii, 8), "If the true is that which is, it will be concluded that the false exists nowhere; whatever reason may appear to the contrary."

Obj. 2: Further, false is derived from *fallere* (to deceive). But things do not deceive; for, as Augustine says (De Vera Relig. 33), they show nothing but their own species. Therefore the false is not found in things.

Obj. 3: Further, the true is said to exist in things by conformity to the divine intellect, as stated above (Q. 16). But everything, in so far as it exists, imitates God. Therefore everything is true without admixture of falsity; and thus nothing is false.

*On the contrary,* Augustine says (De Vera Relig. 34): "Every body is a true body and a false unity: for it imitates unity without being unity." But everything imitates the divine unity yet falls short of it. Therefore in all things falsity exists.

*I answer that,* Since true and false are opposed, and since opposites stand in relation to the same thing, we must needs seek falsity, where primarily we find truth; that is to say, in the intellect. Now, in things, neither truth nor falsity exists, except in relation to the intellect. And since every thing is denominated simply by what belongs to it *per se,* but is denominated relatively by what belongs to it accidentally; a thing indeed may be called false simply when compared with the intellect on which it depends, and to which it is compared *per se* but may be called false relatively as directed to another intellect, to which it is compared accidentally. Now natural things depend on the divine intellect, as artificial things on the human. Wherefore artificial things are said to be false simply and in themselves, in so far as they fall short of the form of the art; whence a craftsman is said to produce a false work, if it falls short of the proper operation of his art.

In things that depend on God, falseness cannot be found, in so far as they are compared with the divine intellect; since whatever takes place in things proceeds from the ordinance of that intellect, unless perhaps in the case of voluntary agents only, who have it in their power to withdraw themselves from what is so ordained; wherein consists the evil of sin. Thus sins themselves are called untruths and lies in the Scriptures, according to the words of the text, "Why do you love vanity, and seek after lying?" (Ps. 4:3): as on the other hand virtuous deeds are called the "truth of life" as being obedient to the order of the divine intellect. Thus it is said, "He that doth truth, cometh to the light" (John 3:21).

But in relation to our intellect, natural things which are compared thereto accidentally, can be called false; not simply, but relatively; and that in two ways. In one way according to the thing signified, and thus a thing is said to be false as being signified or represented by word or thought that is false. In this respect anything can be said to be false as regards any quality not possessed by it; as if we should say that a diameter is a false commensurable thing, as the Philosopher says (Metaph. v, 34). So, too, Augustine says (Soliloq. ii, 10): "The true tragedian is a false Hector": even as, *on the contrary,* anything can be called true, in regard to that which is becoming to it. In another way a thing can be called false, by way of cause—and thus a thing is said to be false that naturally begets a false opinion. And whereas it is innate in us to judge things by external appearances, since our knowledge takes its rise from sense, which principally and naturally deals with external accidents, therefore those external accidents, which resemble things other than themselves, are said to be false with respect to those things; thus gall is falsely honey; and tin, false gold. Regarding this, Augustine says (Soliloq. ii, 6): "We call those things false that appear to our apprehension like the true:" and the Philosopher says (Metaph. v, 34): "Things are called false that are naturally apt to appear such as they are not, or what they are not." In this way a man is called false as delighting in false opinions or words, and not because he can invent them; for in this way many wise and learned persons might be called false, as stated in *Metaph.* v, 34.

Reply Obj. 1: A thing compared with the intellect is said to be true in respect to what it is; and false in respect to what it is not. Hence, "The true tragedian is a false Hector," as stated in Soliloq. ii, 6. As, therefore, in things that are is found a certain non-being, so in things that are is found a degree of falseness.

Reply Obj. 2: Things do not deceive by their own nature, but by accident. For they give occasion to falsity, by the likeness they bear to things which they actually are not.

Reply Obj. 3: Things are said to be false, not as compared with the divine intellect, in which case they would be false simply, but as compared with our intellect; and thus they are false only relatively.

To the argument which is urged *on the contrary,* likeness or defective representation does not involve the idea of falsity except in so far as it gives occasion to false opinion. Hence a thing is not always said to be false, because it resembles another thing; but only when the resemblance is such as naturally to produce a false opinion, not in any one case, but in the majority of instances.

SECOND ARTICLE [I, Q. 17, Art. 2]

Whether There Is Falsity in the Senses?

Objection 1: It seems that falsity is not in the senses. For Augustine says (De Vera Relig. 33): "If all the bodily senses report as they are affected, I do not know what more we can require from them." Thus it seems that we are not deceived by the senses; and therefore that falsity is not in them.

Obj. 2: Further, the Philosopher says (Metaph. iv, 24) that falsity is not proper to the senses, but to the imagination.

Obj. 3: Further, in non-complex things there is neither true nor false, but in complex things only. But affirmation and negation do not belong to the senses. Therefore in the senses there is no falsity.

*On the contrary,* Augustine says (Soliloq. ii, 6), "It appears that the senses entrap us into error by their deceptive similitudes."

*I answer that,* Falsity is not to be sought in the senses except as truth is in them. Now truth is not in them in such a way as that the senses know truth, but in so far as they apprehend sensible things truly, as said above (Q. 16, A. 2), and this takes place through the senses apprehending things as they are, and hence it happens that falsity exists in the senses through their apprehending or judging things to be otherwise than they really are.

The knowledge of things by the senses is in proportion to the existence of their likeness in the senses; and the likeness of a thing can exist in the senses in three ways. In the first way, primarily and of its own nature, as in sight there is the likeness of colors, and of other sensible objects proper to it. Secondly, of its own nature, though not primarily; as in sight there is the likeness of shape, size, and of other sensible objects common to more than one sense. Thirdly, neither primarily nor of its own nature, but accidentally, as in sight, there is the likeness of a man, not as man, but in so far as it is accidental to the colored object to be a man.

Sense, then, has no false knowledge about its proper objects, except accidentally and rarely, and then, because of the unsound organ it does not receive the sensible form rightly; just as other passive subjects because of their indisposition receive defectively the impressions of the agent. Hence, for instance, it happens that on account of an unhealthy tongue sweet seems bitter to a sick person. But as to common objects of sense, and accidental objects, even a rightly disposed sense may have a false judgment, because it is referred to them not directly, but accidentally, or as a consequence of being directed to other things.

Reply Obj. 1: The affection of sense is its sensation itself. Hence, from the fact that sense reports as it is affected, it follows that we are not deceived in the judgment by which we judge that we experience sensation. Since, however, sense is sometimes affected erroneously of that object, it follows that it sometimes reports erroneously of that object; and thus we are deceived by sense about the object, but not about the fact of sensation.

Reply Obj. 2: Falsity is said not to be proper to sense, since sense is not deceived as to its proper object. Hence in another translation it is said more plainly, "Sense, about its proper object, is never false." Falsity is attributed to the imagination, as it represents the likeness of something even in its absence. Hence, when anyone perceives the likeness of a thing as if it were the thing itself, falsity results from such an apprehension; and for this reason the Philosopher says (Metaph. v, 34) that shadows, pictures, and dreams are said to be false inasmuch as they convey the likeness of things that are not present in substance.

Reply Obj. 3: This argument proves that the false is not in the sense, as in that which knows the true and the false.

THIRD ARTICLE [I, Q. 17, Art. 3]

Whether Falsity Is in the Intellect?

Objection 1: It seems that falsity is not in the intellect. For Augustine says (Qq. lxxxiii, 32), "Everyone who is deceived, understands not that in which he is deceived." But falsity is said to exist in any knowledge in so far as we are deceived therein. Therefore falsity does not exist in the intellect.

Obj. 2: Further, the Philosopher says (De Anima iii, 51) that the intellect is always right. Therefore there is no falsity in the intellect.

*On the contrary,* It is said in De Anima iii, 21, 22 that "where there is composition of objects understood, there is truth and falsehood." But such composition is in the intellect. Therefore truth and falsehood exist in the intellect.

*I answer that,* Just as a thing has being by its proper form, so the knowing faculty has knowledge by the likeness of the thing known. Hence, as natural things cannot fall short of the being that belongs to them by their form, but may fall short of accidental or consequent qualities, even as a man may fail to possess two feet, but not fail to be a man; so the faculty of knowing cannot fail in knowledge of the thing with the likeness of which it is informed; but may fail with regard to something consequent upon that form, or accidental thereto. For it has been said (A. 2) that sight is not deceived in its proper sensible, but about common sensibles that are consequent to that object; or about accidental objects of sense. Now as the sense is directly informed by the likeness of its proper object, so is the intellect by the likeness of the essence of a thing. Hence the intellect is not deceived about the essence of a thing, as neither the sense about its proper object. But in affirming and denying, the intellect may be deceived, by attributing to the thing of which it understands the essence, something which is not consequent upon it, or is opposed to it. For the intellect is in the same position as regards judging of such things, as sense is as to judging of common, or accidental, sensible objects. There is, however, this difference, as before mentioned regarding truth (Q. 16, A. 2), that falsity can exist in the intellect not only because the knowledge of the intellect is false, but because the intellect is conscious of that knowledge, as it is conscious of truth; whereas in sense falsity does not exist as known, as stated above (A. 2).

But because falsity of the intellect is concerned essentially only with the composition of the intellect, falsity occurs also accidentally in that operation of the intellect whereby it knows the essence of a thing, in so far as composition of the intellect is mixed up in it. This can take place in two ways. In one way, by the intellect applying to one thing the definition proper to another; as that of a circle to a man. Wherefore the definition of one thing is false of another. In another way, by composing a definition of parts which are mutually exclusive. For thus the definition is not only false of the thing, but false in itself. A definition such as "a reasonable four-footed animal" would be of this kind, and the intellect false in making it; for such a statement as "some reasonable animals are four-footed" is false in itself. For this reason the intellect cannot be false in its knowledge of simple essences; but it is either true, or it understands nothing at all.

Reply Obj. 1: Because the essence of a thing is the proper object of the intellect, we are properly said to understand a thing when we reduce it to its essence, and judge of it thereby; as takes place in demonstrations, in which there is no falsity. In this sense Augustine's words must be understood, "that he who is deceived, understands not that wherein he is deceived;" and not in the sense that no one is ever deceived in any operation of the intellect.

Reply Obj. 2: The intellect is always right as regards first principles; since it is not deceived about them for the same reason that it is not deceived about what a thing is. For self-known principles are such as are known as soon as the terms are understood, from the fact that the predicate is contained in the definition of the subject.

FOURTH ARTICLE [I, Q. 17, Art. 4]

Whether True and False Are Contraries?

Objection 1: It seems that true and false are not contraries. For true and false are opposed, as that which is to that which is not; for "truth," as Augustine says (Soliloq. ii, 5), "is that which is." But that which is and that which is not are not opposed as contraries. Therefore true and false are not contrary things.

Obj. 2: Further, one of two contraries is not in the other. But falsity is in truth, because, as Augustine says, (Soliloq. ii, 10), "A tragedian would not be a false Hector, if he were not a true tragedian." Therefore true and false are not contraries.

Obj. 3: Further, in God there is no contrariety, for "nothing is contrary to the Divine Substance," as Augustine says (De Civ. Dei xii, 2). But falsity is opposed to God, for an idol is called in Scripture a lie, "They have laid hold on lying" (Jer. 8:5), that is to say, "an idol," as a gloss says. Therefore false and true are not contraries.

*On the contrary,* The Philosopher says (Peri Herm. ii), that a false opinion is contrary to a true one.

*I answer that,* True and false are opposed as contraries, and not, as some have said, as affirmation and negation. In proof of which it must be considered that negation neither asserts anything nor determines any subject, and can therefore be said of being as of not-being, for instance not-seeing or not-sitting. But privation asserts nothing, whereas it determines its subject, for it is "negation in a subject," as stated in *Metaph.* iv, 4: v. 27; for blindness is not said except of one whose nature it is to see. Contraries, however, both assert something and determine the subject, for blackness is a species of color. Falsity asserts something, for a thing is false, as the Philosopher says (Metaph. iv, 27), inasmuch as something is said or seems to be something that it is not, or not to be what it really is. For as truth implies an adequate apprehension of a thing, so falsity implies the contrary. Hence it is clear that true and false are contraries.

Reply Obj. 1: What is in things is the truth of the thing; but what is apprehended, is the truth of the intellect, wherein truth primarily resides. Hence the false is that which is not as apprehended. To apprehend being, and not-being, implies contrariety; for, as the Philosopher proves (Peri Herm. ii), the contrary of this statement "God is good," is, "God is not good."

Reply Obj. 2: Falsity is not founded in the truth which is contrary to it, just as evil is not founded in the good which is contrary to it, but in that which is its proper subject. This happens in either, because true and good are universals, and convertible with being. Hence, as every privation is founded in a subject, that is a being, so every evil is founded in some good, and every falsity in some truth.

Reply Obj. 3: Because contraries, and opposites by way of privation, are by nature about one and the same thing, therefore there is nothing contrary to God, considered in Himself, either with respect to His goodness or His truth, for in His intellect there can be nothing false. But in our apprehension of Him contraries exist, for the false opinion concerning Him is contrary to the true. So idols are called lies, opposed to the divine truth, inasmuch as the false opinion concerning them is contrary to the true opinion of the divine unity.

## QUESTION 18

THE LIFE OF GOD (In Four Articles)

Since to understand belongs to living beings, after considering the divine knowledge and intellect, we must consider the divine life. About this, four points of inquiry arise:

(1) To whom does it belong to live?

(2) What is life?

(3) Whether life is properly attributed to God?

(4) Whether all things in God are life?

FIRST ARTICLE [I, Q. 18, Art. 1]

Whether to Live Belongs to All Natural Things?

Objection 1: It seems that to live belongs to all natural things. For the Philosopher says (Phys. viii, 1) that "Movement is like a kind of life possessed by all things existing in nature." But all natural things participate in movement. Therefore all natural things partake of life.

Obj. 2: Further, plants are said to live, inasmuch as they have in themselves a principle of movement of growth and decay. But local movement is naturally more perfect than, and prior to, movement of growth and decay, as the Philosopher shows (Phys. viii, 56, 57). Since then, all natural bodies have in themselves some principle of local movement, it seems that all natural bodies live.

Obj. 3: Further, amongst natural bodies the elements are the less perfect. Yet life is attributed to them, for we speak of "living waters." Much more, therefore, have other natural bodies life.

*On the contrary,* Dionysius says (Div. Nom. vi, 1) that "The last echo of life is heard in the plants," whereby it is inferred that their life is life in its lowest degree. But inanimate bodies are inferior to plants. Therefore they have not life.

*I answer that,* We can gather to what things life belongs, and to what it does not, from such things as manifestly possess life. Now life manifestly belongs to animals, for it said in *De Vegetab.* i [*De Plantis i, 1] that in animals life is manifest. We must, therefore, distinguish living from lifeless things, by comparing them to that by reason of which animals are said to live: and this it is in which life is manifested first and remains last. We say then that an animal begins to live when it begins to move of itself: and as long as such movement appears in it, so long as it is considered to be alive. When it no longer has any movement of itself, but is only moved by another power, then its life is said to fail, and the animal to be dead. Whereby it is clear that those things are properly called living that move themselves by some kind of movement, whether it be movement properly so called, as the act of an imperfect being, i.e. of a thing in potentiality, is called movement; or movement in a more general sense, as when said of the act of a perfect thing, as understanding and feeling are called movement. Accordingly all things are said to be alive that determine themselves to movement or operation of any kind: whereas those things that cannot by their nature do so, cannot be called living, unless by a similitude.

Reply Obj. 1: These words of the Philosopher may be understood either of the first movement, namely, that of the celestial bodies, or of the movement in its general sense. In either way is movement called the life, as it were, of natural bodies, speaking by a similitude, and not attributing it to them as their property. The movement of the heavens is in the universe of corporeal natures as the movement of the heart, whereby life is preserved, is in animals. Similarly also every natural movement in respect to natural things has a certain similitude to the operations of life. Hence, if the whole corporeal universe were one animal, so that its movement came from an "intrinsic moving force," as some in fact have held, in that case movement would really be the life of all natural bodies.

Reply Obj. 2: To bodies, whether heavy or light, movement does not belong, except in so far as they are displaced from their natural conditions, and are out of their proper place; for when they are in the place that is proper and natural to them, then they are at rest. Plants and other living things move with vital movement, in accordance with the disposition of their nature, but not by approaching thereto, or by receding from it, for in so far as they recede from such movement, so far do they recede from their natural disposition. Heavy and light bodies are moved by an extrinsic force, either generating them and giving them form, or removing obstacles from their way. They do not therefore move themselves, as do living bodies.

Reply Obj. 3: Waters are called living that have a continuous current: for standing waters, that are not connected with a continually flowing source, are called dead, as in cisterns and ponds. This is merely a similitude, inasmuch as the movement they are seen to possess makes them look as if they were alive. Yet this is not life in them in its real sense, since this movement of theirs is not from themselves but from the cause that generates them. The same is the case with the movement of other heavy and light bodies.

SECOND ARTICLE [I, Q. 18, Art. 2]

Whether Life Is an Operation?

Objection 1: It seems that life is an operation. For nothing is divided except into parts of the same genus. But life is divided by certain operations, as is clear from the Philosopher (De Anima ii, 13), who distinguishes four kinds of life, namely, nourishment, sensation, local movement and understanding. Therefore life is an operation.

Obj. 2: Further, the active life is said to be different from the contemplative. But the contemplative is only distinguished from the active by certain operations. Therefore life is an operation.

Obj. 3: Further, to know God is an operation. But this is life, as is clear from the words of John 18:3, "Now this is eternal life, that they may know Thee, the only true God." Therefore life is an operation.

*On the contrary,* The Philosopher says (De Anima ii, 37), "In living things, to live is to be."

*I answer that,* As is clear from what has been said (Q. 17, A. 3), our intellect, which takes cognizance of the essence of a thing as its proper object, gains knowledge from sense, of which the proper objects are external accidents. Hence from external appearances we come to the knowledge of the essence of things. And because we name a thing in accordance with our knowledge of it, as is clear from what has already been said (Q. 13, A. 1), so from external properties names are often imposed to signify essences. Hence such names are sometimes taken strictly to denote the essence itself, the signification of which is their principal object; but sometimes, and less strictly, to denote the properties by reason of which they are imposed. And so we see that the word "body" is used to denote a genus of substances from the fact of their possessing three dimensions: and is sometimes taken to denote the dimensions themselves; in which sense body is said to be a species of quantity. The same must be said of life. The name is given from a certain external appearance, namely, self-movement, yet not precisely to signify this, but rather a substance to which self-movement and the application of itself to any kind of operation, belong naturally. To live, accordingly, is nothing else than to exist in this or that nature; and life signifies this, though in the abstract, just as the word "running" denotes "to run" in the abstract.

Hence "living" is not an accidental but an essential predicate. Sometimes, however, life is used less properly for the operations from which its name is taken, and thus the Philosopher says (Ethic. ix, 9) that to live is principally to sense or to understand.

Reply Obj. 1: The Philosopher here takes "to live" to mean an operation of life. Or it would be better to say that sensation and intelligence and the like, are sometimes taken for the operations, sometimes for the existence itself of the operator. For he says (Ethic. ix, 9) that to live is to sense or to understand—in other words, to have a nature capable of sensation or understanding. Thus, then, he distinguishes life by the four operations mentioned. For in this lower world there are four kinds of living things. It is the nature of some to be capable of nothing more than taking nourishment, and, as a consequence, of growing and generating. Others are able, in addition, to sense, as we see in the case of shellfish and other animals without movement. Others have the further power of moving from place to place, as perfect animals, such as quadrupeds, and birds, and so on. Others, as man, have the still higher faculty of understanding.

Reply Obj. 2: By vital operations are meant those whose principles are within the operator, and in virtue of which the operator produces such operations of itself. It happens that there exist in men not merely such natural principles of certain operations as are their natural powers, but something over and above these, such as habits inclining them like a second nature to particular kinds of operations, so that the operations become sources of pleasure. Thus, as by a similitude, any kind of work in which a man takes delight, so that his bent is towards it, his time spent in it, and his whole life ordered with a view to it, is said to be the life of that man. Hence some are said to lead a life of self-indulgence, others a life of virtue. In this way the contemplative life is distinguished from the active, and thus to know God is said to be life eternal.

Wherefore the Reply to the Third Objection is clear.

THIRD ARTICLE [I, Q. 18, Art. 3]

Whether Life Is Properly Attributed to God?

Objection 1: It seems that life is not properly attributed to God. For things are said to live inasmuch as they move themselves, as previously stated (A. 2). But movement does not belong to God. Neither therefore does life.

Obj. 2: Further, in all living things we must needs suppose some principle of life. Hence it is said by the Philosopher (De Anima ii, 4) that "the soul is the cause and principle of the living body." But God has no principle. Therefore life cannot be attributed to Him.

Obj. 3: Further, the principle of life in the living things that exist among us is the vegetative soul. But this exists only in corporeal things. Therefore life cannot be attributed to incorporeal things.

*On the contrary,* It is said (Ps. 83:3): "My heart and my flesh have rejoiced in the living God."

*I answer that,* Life is in the highest degree properly in God. In proof of which it must be considered that since a thing is said to live in so far as it operates of itself and not as moved by another, the more perfectly this power is found in anything, the more perfect is the life of that thing. In things that move and are moved, a threefold order is found. In the first place, the end moves the agent: and the principal agent is that which acts through its form, and sometimes it does so through some instrument that acts by virtue not of its own form, but of the principal agent, and does no more than execute the action. Accordingly there are things that move themselves, not in respect of any form or end naturally inherent in them, but only in respect of the executing of the movement; the form by which they act, and the end of the action being alike determined for them by their nature. Of this kind are plants, which move themselves according to their inherent nature, with regard only to executing the movements of growth and decay.

Other things have self-movement in a higher degree, that is, not only with regard to executing the movement, but even as regards to the form, the principle of movement, which form they acquire of themselves. Of this kind are animals, in which the principle of movement is not a naturally implanted form; but one received through sense. Hence the more perfect is their sense, the more perfect is their power of self-movement. Such as have only the sense of touch, as shellfish, move only with the motion of expansion and contraction; and thus their movement hardly exceeds that of plants. Whereas such as have the sensitive power in perfection, so as to recognize not only connection and touch, but also objects apart from themselves, can move themselves to a distance by progressive movement. Yet although animals of the latter kind receive through sense the form that is the principle of their movement, nevertheless they cannot of themselves propose to themselves the end of their operation, or movement; for this has been implanted in them by nature; and by natural instinct they are moved to any action through the form apprehended by sense. Hence such animals as move themselves in respect to an end they themselves propose are superior to these. This can only be done by reason and intellect; whose province it is to know the proportion between the end and the means to that end, and duly coordinate them. Hence a more perfect degree of life is that of intelligent beings; for their power of self-movement is more perfect. This is shown by the fact that in one and the same man the intellectual faculty moves the sensitive powers; and these by their command move the organs of movement. Thus in the arts we see that the art of using a ship, i.e. the art of navigation, rules the art of ship-designing; and this in its turn rules the art that is only concerned with preparing the material for the ship.

But although our intellect moves itself to some things, yet others are supplied by nature, as are first principles, which it cannot doubt; and the last end, which it cannot but will. Hence, although with respect to some things it moves itself, yet with regard to other things it must be moved by another. Wherefore that being whose act of understanding is its very nature, and which, in what it naturally possesses, is not determined by another, must have life in the most perfect degree. Such is God; and hence in Him principally is life. From this the Philosopher concludes (Metaph. xii, 51), after showing God to be intelligent, that God has life most perfect and eternal, since His intellect is most perfect and always in act.

Reply Obj. 1: As stated in *Metaph.* ix, 16, action is twofold. Actions of one kind pass out to external matter, as to heat or to cut; whilst actions of the other kind remain in the agent, as to understand, to sense and to will. The difference between them is this, that the former action is the perfection not of the agent that moves, but of the thing moved; whereas the latter action is the perfection of the agent. Hence, because movement is an act of the thing in movement, the latter action, in so far as it is the act of the operator, is called its movement, by this similitude, that as movement is an act of the thing moved, so an act of this kind is the act of the agent, although movement is an act of the imperfect, that is, of what is in potentiality; while this kind of act is an act of the perfect, that is to say, of what is in act as stated in *De Anima* iii, 28. In the sense, therefore, in which understanding is movement, that which understands itself is said to move itself. It is in this sense that Plato also taught that God moves Himself; not in the sense in which movement is an act of the imperfect.

Reply Obj. 2: As God is His own very existence and understanding, so is He His own life; and therefore He so lives that He has no principle of life.

Reply Obj. 3: Life in this lower world is bestowed on a corruptible nature, that needs generation to preserve the species, and nourishment to preserve the individual. For this reason life is not found here below apart from a vegetative soul: but this does not hold good with incorruptible natures.

FOURTH ARTICLE [I, Q. 18, Art. 4]

Whether All Things Are Life in God?

Objection 1: It seems that not all things are life in God. For it is said (Acts 17:28), "In Him we live, and move, and be." But not all things in God are movement. Therefore not all things are life in Him.

Obj. 2: Further, all things are in God as their first model. But things modelled ought to conform to the model. Since, then, not all things have life in themselves, it seems that not all things are life in God.

Obj. 3: Further, as Augustine says (De Vera Relig. 29), a living substance is better than a substance that does not live. If, therefore, things which in themselves have not life, are life in God, it seems that things exist more truly in God than themselves. But this appears to be false; since in themselves they exist actually, but in God potentially.

Obj. 4: Further, just as good things and things made in time are known by God, so are bad things, and things that God can make, but that never will be made. If, therefore, all things are life in God, inasmuch as known by Him, it seems that even bad things and things that will never be made are life in God, as known by Him, and this appears inadmissible.

*On the contrary,* (John 1:3, 4), it is said, "What was made, in Him was life." But all things were made, except God. Therefore all things are life in God.

*I answer that,* In God to live is to understand, as before stated (A. 3). In God intellect, the thing understood, and the act of understanding, are one and the same. Hence whatever is in God as understood is the very living or life of God. Now, wherefore, since all things that have been made by God are in Him as things understood, it follows that all things in Him are the divine life itself.

Reply Obj. 1: Creatures are said to be in God in a twofold sense. In one way, so far are they are held together and preserved by the divine power; even as we say that things that are in our power are in us. And creatures are thus said to be in God, even as they exist in their own natures. In this sense we must understand the words of the Apostle when he says, "In Him we live, move, and be"; since our being, living, and moving are themselves caused by God. In another sense things are said to be in God, as in Him who knows them, in which sense they are in God through their proper ideas, which in God are not distinct from the divine essence. Hence things as they are in God are the divine essence. And since the divine essence is life and not movement, it follows that things existing in God in this manner are not movement, but life.

Reply Obj. 2: The thing modelled must be like the model according to the form, not the mode of being. For sometimes the form has being of another kind in the model from that which it has in the thing modelled. Thus the form of a house has in the mind of the architect immaterial and intelligible being; but in the house that exists outside his mind, material and sensible being. Hence the ideas of things, though not existing in themselves, are life in the divine mind, as having a divine existence in that mind.

Reply Obj. 3: If form only, and not matter, belonged to natural things, then in all respects natural things would exist more truly in the divine mind, by the ideas of them, than in themselves. For which reason, in fact, Plato held that the *separate* man was the true man; and that man as he exists in matter, is man only by participation. But since matter enters into the being of natural things, we must say that those things have simply being in the divine mind more truly than in themselves, because in that mind they have an uncreated being, but in themselves a created being: whereas this particular being, a man, or horse, for example, has this being more truly in its own nature than in the divine mind, because it belongs to human nature to be material, which, as existing in the divine mind, it is not. Even so a house has nobler being in the architect's mind than in matter; yet a material house is called a house more truly than the one which exists in the mind; since the former is actual, the latter only potential.

Reply Obj. 4: Although bad things are in God's knowledge, as being comprised under that knowledge, yet they are not in God as created by Him, or preserved by Him, or as having their type in Him. They are known by God through the types of good things. Hence it cannot be said that bad things are life in God. Those things that are not in time may be called life in God in so far as life means understanding only, and inasmuch as they are understood by God; but not in so far as life implies a principle of operation.

## QUESTION 19

THE WILL OF GOD (In Twelve Articles)

After considering the things belonging to the divine knowledge, we consider what belongs to the divine will. The first consideration is about the divine will itself; the second about what belongs strictly to His will; the third about what belongs to the intellect in relation to His will. About His will itself there are twelve points of inquiry:

(1) Whether there is will in God?

(2) Whether God wills things apart from Himself?

(3) Whether whatever God wills, He wills necessarily?

(4) Whether the will of God is the cause of things?

(5) Whether any cause can be assigned to the divine will?

(6) Whether the divine will is always fulfilled?

(7) Whether the will of God is mutable?

(8) Whether the will of God imposes necessity on the things willed?

(9) Whether there is in God the will of evil?

(10) Whether God has free will?

(11) Whether the will of expression is distinguished in God?

(12) Whether five expressions of will are rightly assigned to the divine will?

FIRST ARTICLE [I, Q. 19, Art. 1]

Whether There Is Will in God?

Objection 1: It seems that there is not will in God. For the object of will is the end and the good. But we cannot assign to God any end. Therefore there is not will in God.

Obj. 2: Further, will is a kind of appetite. But appetite, as it is directed to things not possessed, implies imperfection, which cannot be imputed to God. Therefore there is not will in God.

Obj. 3: Further, according to the Philosopher (De Anima iii, 54), the will moves, and is moved. But God is the first cause of movement, and Himself is unmoved, as proved in Phys. viii, 49. Therefore there is not will in God.

*On the contrary,* The Apostle says (Rom. 12:2): "That you may prove what is the will of God."

*I answer that,* There is will in God, as there is intellect: since will follows upon intellect. For as natural things have actual existence by their form, so the intellect is actually intelligent by its intelligible form. Now everything has this aptitude towards its natural form, that when it has it not, it tends towards it; and when it has it, it is at rest therein. It is the same with every natural perfection, which is a natural good. This aptitude to good in things without knowledge is called natural appetite. Whence also intellectual natures have a like aptitude as apprehended through its intelligible form; so as to rest therein when possessed, and when not possessed to seek to possess it, both of which pertain to the will. Hence in every intellectual being there is will, just as in every sensible being there is animal appetite. And so there must be will in God, since there is intellect in Him. And as His intellect is His own existence, so is His will.

Reply Obj. 1: Although nothing apart from God is His end, yet He Himself is the end with respect to all things made by Him. And this by His essence, for by His essence He is good, as shown above (Q. 6, A. 3): for the end has the aspect of good.

Reply Obj. 2: Will in us belongs to the appetitive part, which, although named from appetite, has not for its only act the seeking what it does not possess; but also the loving and the delighting in what it does possess. In this respect will is said to be in God, as having always good which is its object, since, as already said, it is not distinct from His essence.

Reply Obj. 3: A will of which the principal object is a good outside itself, must be moved by another; but the object of the divine will is His goodness, which is His essence. Hence, since the will of God is His essence, it is not moved by another than itself, but by itself alone, in the same sense as understanding and willing are said to be movement. This is what Plato meant when he said that the first mover moves itself.

SECOND ARTICLE [I, Q. 19, Art. 2]

Whether God Wills Things Apart from Himself?

Objection 1: It seems that God does not will things apart from Himself. For the divine will is the divine existence. But God is not other than Himself. Therefore He does not will things other than Himself.

Obj. 2: Further, the willed moves the willer, as the appetible the appetite, as stated in *De Anima* iii, 54. If, therefore, God wills anything apart from Himself, His will must be moved by another; which is impossible.

Obj. 3: Further, if what is willed suffices the willer, he seeks nothing beyond it. But His own goodness suffices God, and completely satisfies His will. Therefore God does not will anything apart from Himself.

Obj. 4: Further, acts of will are multiplied in proportion to the number of their objects. If, therefore, God wills Himself and things apart from Himself, it follows that the act of His will is manifold, and consequently His existence, which is His will. But this is impossible. Therefore God does not will things apart from Himself.

*On the contrary,* The Apostle says (1 Thess. 4:3): "This is the will of God, your sanctification."

*I answer that,* God wills not only Himself, but other things apart from Himself. This is clear from the comparison which we made above (A. 1). For natural things have a natural inclination not only towards their own proper good, to acquire it if not possessed, and, if possessed, to rest therein; but also to spread abroad their own good amongst others, so far as possible. Hence we see that every agent, in so far as it is perfect and in act, produces its like. It pertains, therefore, to the nature of the will to communicate as far as possible to others the good possessed; and especially does this pertain to the divine will, from which all perfection is derived in some kind of likeness. Hence, if natural things, in so far as they are perfect, communicate their good to others, much more does it appertain to the divine will to communicate by likeness its own good to others as much as possible. Thus, then, He wills both Himself to be, and other things to be; but Himself as the end, and other things as ordained to that end; inasmuch as it befits the divine goodness that other things should be partakers therein.

Reply Obj. 1: The divine will is God's own existence essentially, yet they differ in aspect, according to the different ways of understanding them and expressing them, as is clear from what has already been said (Q. 13, A. 4). For when we say that God exists, no relation to any other object is implied, as we do imply when we say that God wills. Therefore, although He is not anything apart from Himself, yet He does will things apart from Himself.

Reply Obj. 2: In things willed for the sake of the end, the whole reason for our being moved is the end, and this it is that moves the will, as most clearly appears in things willed only for the sake of the end. He who wills to take a bitter draught, in doing so wills nothing else than health; and this alone moves his will. It is different with one who takes a draught that is pleasant, which anyone may will to do, not only for the sake of health, but also for its own sake. Hence, although God wills things apart from Himself only for the sake of the end, which is His own goodness, it does not follow that anything else moves His will, except His goodness. So, as He understands things apart from Himself by understanding His own essence, so He wills things apart from Himself by willing His own goodness.

Reply Obj. 3: From the fact that His own goodness suffices the divine will, it does not follow that it wills nothing apart from itself, but rather that it wills nothing except by reason of its goodness. Thus, too, the divine intellect, though its perfection consists in its very knowledge of the divine essence, yet in that essence knows other things.

Reply Obj. 4: As the divine intellect is one, as seeing the many only in the one, in the same way the divine will is one and simple, as willing the many only through the one, that is, through its own goodness.

THIRD ARTICLE [I, Q. 19, Art. 3]

Whether Whatever God Wills He Wills Necessarily?

Objection 1: It seems that whatever God wills He wills necessarily. For everything eternal is necessary. But whatever God wills, He wills from eternity, for otherwise His will would be mutable. Therefore whatever He wills, He wills necessarily.

Obj. 2: Further, God wills things apart from Himself, inasmuch as He wills His own goodness. Now God wills His own goodness necessarily. Therefore He wills things apart from Himself necessarily.

Obj. 3: Further, whatever belongs to the nature of God is necessary, for God is of Himself necessary being, and the principle of all necessity, as above shown (Q. 2, A. 3). But it belongs to His nature to will whatever He wills; since in God there can be nothing over and above His nature as stated in *Metaph.* v, 6. Therefore whatever He wills, He wills necessarily.

Obj. 4: Further, being that is not necessary, and being that is possible not to be, are one and the same thing. If, therefore, God does not necessarily will a thing that He wills, it is possible for Him not to will it, and therefore possible for Him to will what He does not will. And so the divine will is contingent upon one or the other of two things, and imperfect, since everything contingent is imperfect and mutable.

Obj. 5: Further, on the part of that which is indifferent to one or the other of two things, no action results unless it is inclined to one or the other by some other power, as the Commentator [*Averroes] says in Phys. ii. If, then, the Will of God is indifferent with regard to anything, it follows that His determination to act comes from another; and thus He has some cause prior to Himself.

Obj. 6: Further, whatever God knows, He knows necessarily. But as the divine knowledge is His essence, so is the divine will. Therefore whatever God wills, He wills necessarily.

*On the contrary,* The Apostle says (Eph. 1:11): "Who worketh all things according to the counsel of His will." Now, what we work according to the counsel of the will, we do not will necessarily. Therefore God does not will necessarily whatever He wills.

*I answer that,* There are two ways in which a thing is said to be necessary, namely, absolutely, and by supposition. We judge a thing to be absolutely necessary from the relation of the terms, as when the predicate forms part of the definition of the subject: thus it is absolutely necessary that man is an animal. It is the same when the subject forms part of the notion of the predicate; thus it is absolutely necessary that a number must be odd or even. In this way it is not necessary that Socrates sits: wherefore it is not necessary absolutely, though it may be so by supposition; for, granted that he is sitting, he must necessarily sit, as long as he is sitting. Accordingly as to things willed by God, we must observe that He wills something of absolute necessity: but this is not true of all that He wills. For the divine will has a necessary relation to the divine goodness, since that is its proper object. Hence God wills His own goodness necessarily, even as we will our own happiness necessarily, and as any other faculty has necessary relation to its proper and principal object, for instance the sight to color, since it tends to it by its own nature. But God wills things apart from Himself in so far as they are ordered to His own goodness as their end. Now in willing an end we do not necessarily will things that conduce to it, unless they are such that the end cannot be attained without them; as, we will to take food to preserve life, or to take ship in order to cross the sea. But we do not necessarily will things without which the end is attainable, such as a horse for a journey which we can take on foot, for we can make the journey without one. The same applies to other means. Hence, since the goodness of God is perfect, and can exist without other things inasmuch as no perfection can accrue to Him from them, it follows that His willing things apart from Himself is not absolutely necessary. Yet it can be necessary by supposition, for supposing that He wills a thing, then He is unable not to will it, as His will cannot change.

Reply Obj. 1: From the fact that God wills from eternity whatever He wills, it does not follow that He wills it necessarily; except by supposition.

Reply Obj. 2: Although God necessarily wills His own goodness, He does not necessarily will things willed on account of His goodness; for it can exist without other things.

Reply Obj. 3: It is not natural to God to will any of those other things that He does not will necessarily; and yet it is not unnatural or contrary to His nature, but voluntary.

Reply Obj. 4: Sometimes a necessary cause has a non-necessary relation to an effect; owing to a deficiency in the effect, and not in the cause. Even so, the sun's power has a non-necessary relation to some contingent events on this earth, owing to a defect not in the solar power, but in the effect that proceeds not necessarily from the cause. In the same way, that God does not necessarily will some of the things that He wills, does not result from defect in the divine will, but from a defect belonging to the nature of the thing willed, namely, that the perfect goodness of God can be without it; and such defect accompanies all created good.

Reply Obj. 5: A naturally contingent cause must be determined to act by some external power. The divine will, which by its nature is necessary, determines itself to will things to which it has no necessary relation.

Reply Obj. 6: As the divine essence is necessary of itself, so is the divine will and the divine knowledge; but the divine knowledge has a necessary relation to the thing known; not the divine will to the thing willed. The reason for this is that knowledge is of things as they exist in the knower; but the will is directed to things as they exist in themselves. Since then all other things have necessary existence inasmuch as they exist in God; but no absolute necessity so as to be necessary in themselves, in so far as they exist in themselves; it follows that God knows necessarily whatever He wills, but does not will necessarily whatever He wills.

FOURTH ARTICLE [I, Q. 19, Art. 4]

Whether the Will of God Is the Cause of Things?

Objection 1: It seems that the will of God is not the cause of things. For Dionysius says (Div. Nom. iv, 1): "As our sun, not by reason nor by pre-election, but by its very being, enlightens all things that can participate in its light, so the divine good by its very essence pours the rays of goodness upon everything that exists." But every voluntary agent acts by reason and pre-election. Therefore God does not act by will; and so His will is not the cause of things.

Obj. 2: Further, The first in any order is that

which is essentially so, thus in the order of burning things, that comes first which is fire by its essence. But God is the first agent. Therefore He acts by His essence; and that is His nature. He acts then by nature, and not by will. Therefore the divine will is not the cause of things.

Obj. 3: Further, Whatever is the cause of anything, through being *such* a thing, is the cause by nature, and not by will. For fire is the cause of heat, as being itself hot; whereas an architect is the cause of a house, because he wills to build it. Now Augustine says (De Doctr. Christ. i, 32), "Because God is good, we exist." Therefore God is the cause of things by His nature, and not by His will.

Obj. 4: Further, Of one thing there is one cause. But the [cause of] created things is the knowledge of God, as said before (Q. 14, A. 8). Therefore the will of God cannot be considered the cause of things.

*On the contrary,* It is said (Wis. 11:26), "How could anything endure, if Thou wouldst not?"

*I answer that,* We must hold that the will of God is the cause of things; and that He acts by the will, and not, as some have supposed, by a necessity of His nature.

This can be shown in three ways: First, from the order itself of active causes. Since both intellect and nature act for an end, as proved in *Phys.* ii, 49, the natural agent must have the end and the necessary means predetermined for it by some higher intellect; as the end and definite movement is predetermined for the arrow by the archer. Hence the intellectual and voluntary agent must precede the agent that acts by nature. Hence, since God is first in the order of agents, He must act by intellect and will.

This is shown, secondly, from the character of a natural agent, of which the property is to produce one and the same effect; for nature operates in one and the same way unless it be prevented. This is because the nature of the act is according to the nature of the agent; and hence as long as it has that nature, its acts will be in accordance with that nature; for every natural agent has a determinate being. Since, then, the Divine Being is undetermined, and contains in Himself the full perfection of being, it cannot be that He acts by a necessity of His nature, unless He were to cause something undetermined and indefinite in being: and that this is impossible has been already shown (Q. 7, A. 2). He does not, therefore, act by a necessity of His nature, but determined effects proceed from His own infinite perfection according to the determination of His will and intellect.

Thirdly, it is shown by the relation of effects to their cause. For effects proceed from the agent that causes them, in so far as they pre-exist in the agent; since every agent produces its like. Now effects pre-exist in their cause after the mode of the cause. Wherefore since the Divine Being is His own intellect, effects pre-exist in Him after the mode of intellect, and therefore proceed from Him after the same mode. Consequently, they proceed from Him after the mode of will, for His inclination to put in act what His intellect has conceived appertains to the will. Therefore the will of God is the cause of things.

Reply Obj. 1: Dionysius in these words does not intend to exclude election from God absolutely; but only in a certain sense, in so far, that is, as He communicates His goodness not merely to certain things, but to all; and as election implies a certain distinction.

Reply Obj. 2: Because the essence of God is His intellect and will, from the fact of His acting by His essence, it follows that He acts after the mode of intellect and will.

Reply Obj. 3: Good is the object of the will. The words, therefore, "Because God is good, we exist," are true inasmuch as His goodness is the reason of His willing all other things, as said before (A. 2, ad 2).

Reply Obj. 4: Even in us the cause of one and the same effect is knowledge as directing it, whereby the form of the work is conceived, and will as commanding it, since the form as it is in the intellect only is not determined to exist or not to exist in the effect, except by the will. Hence, the speculative intellect has nothing to say to operation. But the power is cause, as executing the effect, since it denotes the immediate principle of operation. But in God all these things are one.

FIFTH ARTICLE [I, Q. 19, Art. 5]

Whether Any Cause Can Be Assigned to the Divine Will?

Objection 1: It seems that some cause can be assigned to the divine will. For Augustine says (Qq. lxxxiii, 46): "Who would venture to say that God made all things irrationally?" But to a voluntary agent, what is the reason of operating, is the cause of willing. Therefore the will of God has some cause.

Obj. 2: Further, in things made by one who wills to make them, and whose will is influenced by no cause, there can be no cause assigned except by the will of him who wills. But the will of God is the cause of all things, as has been already shown (A. 4). If, then, there is no cause of His will, we cannot seek in any natural things any cause, except the divine will alone. Thus all science would be in vain, since science seeks to assign causes to effects. This seems inadmissible, and therefore we must assign some cause to the divine will.

Obj. 3: Further, what is done by the willer, on account of no cause, depends simply on his will. If, therefore, the will of God has no cause, it follows that all things made depend simply on His will, and have no other cause. But this also is not admissible.

*On the contrary,* Augustine says (Qq. lxxxiii, 28): "Every efficient cause is greater than the thing effected." But nothing is greater than the will of God. We must not then seek for a cause of it.

*I answer that,* In no wise has the will of God a cause. In proof of which we must consider that, since the will follows from the intellect, there is cause of the will in the person who wills, in the same way as there is a cause of the understanding, in the person that understands. The case with the understanding is this: that if the premiss and its conclusion are understood separately from each other, the understanding the premiss is the cause that the conclusion is known. If the understanding perceive the conclusion in the premiss itself, apprehending both the one and the other at the same glance, in this case the knowing of the conclusion would not be caused by understanding the premisses, since a thing cannot be its own cause; and yet, it would be true that the thinker would understand the premisses to be the cause of the conclusion. It is the same with the will, with respect to which the end stands in the same relation to the means to the end, as do the premisses to the conclusion with regard to the understanding.

Hence, if anyone in one act wills an end, and in another act the means to that end, his willing the end will be the cause of his willing the means. This cannot be the case if in one act he wills both end and means; for a thing cannot be its own cause. Yet it will be true to say that he wills to order to the end the means to the end. Now as God by one act understands all things in His essence, so by one act He wills all things in His goodness. Hence, as in God to understand the cause is not the cause of His understanding the effect, for He understands the effect in the cause, so, in Him, to will an end is not the cause of His willing the means, yet He wills the ordering of the means to the end. Therefore, He wills this to be as means to that; but does not will this on account of that.

Reply Obj. 1: The will of God is reasonable, not because anything is to God a cause of willing, but in so far as He wills one thing to be on account of another.

Reply Obj. 2: Since God wills effects to proceed from definite causes, for the preservation of order in the universe, it is not unreasonable to seek for causes secondary to the divine will. It would, however, be unreasonable to do so, if such were considered as primary, and not as dependent on the will of God. In this sense Augustine says (De Trin. iii, 2): "Philosophers in their vanity have thought fit to attribute contingent effects to other causes, being utterly unable to perceive the cause that is shown above all others, the will of God."

Reply Obj. 3: Since God wills effects to come from causes, all effects that presuppose some other effect do not depend solely on the will of God, but on something else besides: but the first effect depends on the divine will alone. Thus, for example, we may say that God willed man to have hands to serve his intellect by their work, and intellect, that he might be man; and willed him to be man that he might enjoy Him, or for the completion of the universe. But this cannot be reduced to other created secondary ends. Hence such things depend on the simple will of God; but the others on the order of other causes.

SIXTH ARTICLE [I, Q. 19, Art. 6]

Whether the Will of God Is Always Fulfilled?

Objection 1: It seems that the will of God is not always fulfilled. For the Apostle says (1 Tim. 2:4): "God will have all men to be saved, and to come to the knowledge of the truth." But this does not happen. Therefore the will of God is not always fulfilled.

Obj. 2: Further, as is the relation of knowledge to truth, so is that of the will to good. Now God knows all truth. Therefore He wills all good. But not all good actually exists; for much more good might exist. Therefore the will of God is not always fulfilled.

Obj. 3: Further, since the will of God is the first cause, it does not exclude intermediate causes. But the effect of a first cause may be hindered by a defect of a secondary cause; as the effect of the motive power may be hindered by the weakness of the limb. Therefore the effect of the divine will may be hindered by a defect of the secondary causes. The will of God, therefore, is not always fulfilled.

*On the contrary,* It is said (Ps. 113:11): "God hath done all things, whatsoever He would."

*I answer that,* The will of God must needs always be fulfilled. In proof of which we must consider that since an effect is conformed to the agent according to its form, the rule is the same with active causes as with formal causes. The rule in forms is this: that although a thing may fall short of any particular form, it cannot fall short of the universal form. For though a thing may fail to be, for example, a man or a living being, yet it cannot fail to be a being. Hence the same must happen in active causes. Something may fall outside the order of any particular active cause, but not outside the order of the universal cause; under which all particular causes are included: and if any particular cause fails of its effect, this is because of the hindrance of some other particular cause, which is included in the order of the universal cause. Therefore an effect cannot possibly escape the order of the universal cause. Even in corporeal things this is clearly seen. For it may happen that a star is hindered from producing its effects; yet whatever effect does result, in corporeal things, from this hindrance of a corporeal cause, must be referred through intermediate causes to the universal influence of the first heaven. Since, then, the will of God is the universal cause of all things, it is impossible that the divine will should not produce its effect. Hence that which seems to depart from the divine will in one order, returns into it in another order; as does the sinner, who by sin falls away from the divine will as much as lies in him, yet falls back into the order of that will, when by its justice he is punished.

Reply Obj. 1: The words of the Apostle, "God will have all men to be saved," etc. can be understood in three ways. First, by a restricted application, in which case they would mean, as Augustine says (De praed. sanct. i, 8: Enchiridion 103), "God wills all men to be saved that are saved, not because there is no man whom He does not wish saved, but because there is no man saved whose salvation He does not will." Secondly, they can be understood as applying to every class of individuals, not to every individual of each class; in which case they mean that God wills some men of every class and condition to be saved, males and females, Jews and Gentiles, great and small, but not all of every condition. Thirdly, according to Damascene (De Fide Orth. ii, 29), they are understood of the antecedent will of God; not of the consequent will. This distinction must not be taken as applying to the divine will itself, in which there is nothing antecedent nor consequent, but to the things willed.

To understand this we must consider that everything, in so far as it is good, is willed by God. A thing taken in its primary sense, and absolutely considered, may be good or evil, and yet when some additional circumstances are taken into account, by a consequent consideration may be changed into the contrary. Thus that a man should live is good; and that a man should be killed is evil, absolutely considered. But if in a particular case we add that a man is a murderer or dangerous to society, to kill him is a good; that he live is an evil. Hence it may be said of a just judge, that antecedently he wills all men to live; but consequently wills the murderer to be hanged. In the same way God antecedently wills all men to be saved, but consequently wills some to be damned, as His justice exacts. Nor do we will simply, what we will antecedently, but rather we will it in a qualified manner; for the will is directed to things as they are in themselves, and in themselves they exist under particular qualifications. Hence we will a thing simply inasmuch as we will it when all particular circumstances are considered; and this is what is meant by willing consequently. Thus it may be said that a just judge wills simply the hanging of a murderer, but in a qualified manner he would will him to live, to wit, inasmuch as he is a man. Such a qualified will may be called a willingness rather than an absolute will. Thus it is clear that whatever God simply wills takes place; although what He wills antecedently may not take place.

Reply Obj. 2: An act of the cognitive faculty is according as the thing known is in the knower; while an act of the appetite faculty is directed to things as they exist in themselves. But all that can have the nature of being and truth virtually exists in God, though it does not all exist in created things. Therefore God knows all truth; but does not will all good, except in so far as He wills Himself, in Whom all good virtually exists.

Reply Obj. 3: A first cause can be hindered in its effect by deficiency in the secondary cause, when it is not the universal first cause, including within itself all causes; for then the effect could in no way escape its order. And thus it is with the will of God, as said above.

SEVENTH ARTICLE [I, Q. 19, Art. 7]

Whether the Will of God Is Changeable?

Objection 1: It seems that the will of God is changeable. For the Lord says (Gen. 6:7): "It repenteth Me that I have made man." But whoever repents of what he has done, has a changeable will. Therefore God has a changeable will.

Obj. 2: Further, it is said in the person of the Lord: "I will speak against a nation and against a kingdom, to root out, and to pull down, and to destroy it; but if that nation shall repent of its evil, I also will repent of the evil that I have thought to do to them" (Jer. 18:7, 8). Therefore God has a changeable will.

Obj. 3: Further, whatever God does, He does voluntarily. But God does not always do the same thing, for at one time He ordered the law to be observed, and at another time forbade it. Therefore He has a changeable will.

Obj. 4: Further, God does not will of necessity what He wills, as said before (A. 3). Therefore He can both will and not will the same thing. But whatever can incline to either of two opposites, is changeable substantially; and that which can exist in a place or not in that place, is changeable locally. Therefore God is changeable as regards His will.

*On the contrary,* It is said: "God is not as a man, that He should lie, nor as the son of man, that He should be changed" (Num. 23:19).

*I answer that,* The will of God is entirely unchangeable. On this point we must consider that to change the will is one thing; to will that certain things should be changed is another. It is possible to will a thing to be done now, and its contrary afterwards; and yet for the will to remain permanently the same: whereas the will would be changed, if one should begin to will what before he had not willed; or cease to will what he had willed before. This cannot happen, unless we presuppose change either in the knowledge or in the disposition of the substance of the willer. For since the will regards good, a man may in two ways begin to will a thing. In one way when that thing begins to be good for him, and this does not take place without a change in him. Thus when the cold weather begins, it becomes good to sit by the fire; though it was not so before. In another way when he knows for the first time that a thing is good for him, though he did not know it before; hence we take counsel in order to know what is good for us. Now it has already been shown that both the substance of God and His knowledge are entirely unchangeable (QQ. 9, A. 1; 14, A. 15). Therefore His will must be entirely unchangeable.

Reply Obj. 1: These words of the Lord are to be understood metaphorically, and according to the likeness of our nature. For when we repent, we destroy what we have made; although we may even do so without change of will; as, when a man wills to make a thing, at the same time intending to destroy it later. Therefore God is said to have repented, by way of comparison with our mode of acting, in so far as by the deluge He destroyed from the face of the earth man whom He had made.

Reply Obj. 2: The will of God, as it is the first and universal cause, does not exclude intermediate causes that have power to produce certain effects. Since however all intermediate causes are inferior in power to the first cause, there are many things in the divine power, knowledge and will that are not included in the order of inferior causes. Thus in the case of the raising of Lazarus, one who looked only on inferior causes might have said: "Lazarus will not rise again," but looking at the divine first cause might have said: "Lazarus will rise again." And God wills both: that is, that in the order of the inferior cause a thing shall happen; but that in the order of the higher cause it shall not happen; or He may will conversely. We may say, then, that God sometimes declares that a thing shall happen according as it falls under the order of inferior causes, as of nature, or merit, which yet does not happen as not being in the designs of the divine and higher cause. Thus He foretold to Ezechias: "Take order with thy house, for thou shalt die, and not live" (Isa. 38:1). Yet this did not take place, since from eternity it was otherwise disposed in the divine knowledge and will, which is unchangeable. Hence Gregory says (Moral. xvi, 5): "The sentence of God changes, but not His counsel"—that is to say, the counsel of His will. When therefore He says, "I also will repent," His words must be understood metaphorically. For men seem to repent, when they do not fulfill what they have threatened.

Reply Obj. 3: It does not follow from this argument that God has a will that changes, but that He sometimes wills that things should change.

Reply Obj. 4: Although God's willing a thing is not by absolute necessity, yet it is necessary by supposition, on account of the unchangeableness of the divine will, as has been said above (A. 3).

EIGHTH ARTICLE [I, Q. 19, Art. 8]

Whether the Will of God Imposes Necessity on the Things Willed?

Objection 1: It seems that the will of God imposes necessity on the things willed. For Augustine says (Enchiridion 103): "No one is saved, except whom God has willed to be saved. He must therefore be asked to will it; for if He wills it, it must necessarily be."

Obj. 2: Further, every cause that cannot be hindered, produces its effect necessarily, because, as the Philosopher says (Phys. ii, 84) "Nature always works in the same way, if there is nothing to hinder it." But the will of God cannot be hindered. For the Apostle says (Rom. 9:19): "Who resisteth His will?" Therefore the will of God imposes necessity on the things willed.

Obj. 3: Further, whatever is necessary by its antecedent cause is necessary absolutely; it is thus necessary that animals should die, being compounded of contrary elements. Now things created by God are related to the divine will as to an antecedent cause, whereby they have necessity. For the conditional statement is true that if God wills a thing, it comes to pass; and every true conditional statement is necessary. It follows therefore that all that God wills is necessary absolutely.

*On the contrary,* All good things that exist God wills to be. If therefore His will imposes necessity on things willed, it follows that all good happens of necessity; and thus there is an end of free will, counsel, and all other such things.

*I answer that,* The divine will imposes necessity on some things willed but not on all. The reason of this some have chosen to assign to intermediate causes, holding that what God produces by necessary causes is necessary; and what He produces by contingent causes contingent.

This does not seem to be a sufficient explanation, for two reasons. First, because the effect of a first cause is contingent on account of the secondary cause, from the fact that the effect of the first cause is hindered by deficiency in the second cause, as the sun's power is hindered by a defect in the plant. But no defect of a secondary cause can hinder God's will from producing its effect. Secondly, because if the distinction between the contingent and the necessary is to be referred only to secondary causes, this must be independent of the divine intention and will; which is inadmissible. It is better therefore to say that this happens on account of the efficacy of the divine will. For when a cause is efficacious to act, the effect follows upon the cause, not only as to the thing done, but also as to its manner of being done or of being. Thus from defect of active power in the seed it may happen that a child is born unlike its father in accidental points, that belong to its manner of being. Since then the divine will is perfectly efficacious, it follows not only that things are done, which God wills to be done, but also that they are done in the way that He wills. Now God wills some things to be done necessarily, some contingently, to the right ordering of things, for the building up of the universe. Therefore to some effects He has attached necessary causes, that cannot fail; but to others defectible and contingent causes, from which arise contingent effects. Hence it is not because the proximate causes are contingent that the effects willed by God happen contingently, but because God prepared contingent causes for them, it being His will that they should happen contingently.

Reply Obj. 1: By the words of Augustine we must understand a necessity in things willed by God that is not absolute, but conditional. For the conditional statement that if God wills a thing it must necessarily be, is necessarily true.

Reply Obj. 2: From the very fact that nothing resists the divine will, it follows that not only those things happen that God wills to happen, but that they happen necessarily or contingently according to His will.

Reply Obj. 3: Consequents have necessity from their antecedents according to the mode of the antecedents. Hence things effected by the divine will have that kind of necessity that God wills them to have, either absolute or conditional. Not all things, therefore, are absolute necessities.

NINTH ARTICLE [I, Q. 19, Art. 8]

Whether God Wills Evils?

Objection 1: It seems that God wills evils. For every good that exists, God wills. But it is a good that evil should exist. For Augustine says (Enchiridion 95): "Although evil in so far as it is evil is not a good, yet it is good that not only good things should exist, but also evil things." Therefore God wills evil things.

Obj. 2: Further, Dionysius says (Div. Nom. iv, 23): "Evil would conduce to the perfection of everything," i.e. the universe. And Augustine says (Enchiridion 10, 11): "Out of all things is built up the admirable beauty of the universe, wherein even that which is called evil, properly ordered and disposed, commends the good more evidently in that good is more pleasing and praiseworthy when contrasted with evil." But God wills all that appertains to the perfection and beauty of the universe, for this is what God desires above all things in His creatures. Therefore God wills evil.

Obj. 3: Further, that evil should exist, and should not exist, are contradictory opposites. But God does not will that evil should not exist; otherwise, since various evils do exist, God's will would not always be fulfilled. Therefore God wills that evil should exist.

*On the contrary,* Augustine says (Qq. 83,3): "No wise man is the cause of another man becoming worse. Now God surpasses all men in wisdom. Much less therefore is God the cause of man becoming worse; and when He is said to be the cause of a thing, He is said to will it." Therefore it is not by God's will that man becomes worse. Now it is clear that every evil makes a thing worse. Therefore God wills not evil things.

*I answer that,* Since the ratio of good is the ratio of appetibility, as said before (Q. 5, A. 1), and since evil is opposed to good, it is impossible that any evil, as such, should be sought for by the appetite, either natural, or animal, or by the intellectual appetite which is the will. Nevertheless evil may be sought accidentally, so far as it accompanies a good, as appears in each of the appetites. For a natural agent intends not privation or corruption, but the form to which is annexed the privation of some other form, and the generation of one thing, which implies the corruption of another. Also when a lion kills a stag, his object is food, to obtain which the killing of the animal is only the means. Similarly the fornicator has merely pleasure for his object, and the deformity of sin is only an accompaniment. Now the evil that accompanies one good, is the privation of another good. Never therefore would evil be sought after, not even accidentally, unless the good that accompanies the evil were more desired than the good of which the evil is the privation. Now God wills no good more than He wills His own goodness; yet He wills one good more than another. Hence He in no way wills the evil of sin, which is the privation of right order towards the divine good. The evil of natural defect, or of punishment, He does will, by willing the good to which such evils are attached. Thus in willing justice He wills punishment; and in willing the preservation of the natural order, He wills some things to be naturally corrupted.

Reply Obj. 1: Some have said that although God does not will evil, yet He wills that evil should be or be done, because, although evil is not a good, yet it is good that evil should be or be done. This they said because things evil in themselves are ordered to some good end; and this order they thought was expressed in the words "that evil should be or be done." This, however, is not correct; since evil is not of itself ordered to good, but accidentally. For it is beside the intention of the sinner, that any good should follow from his sin; as it was beside the intention of tyrants that the patience of the martyrs should shine forth from all their persecutions. It cannot therefore be said that such an ordering to good is implied in the statement that it is a good thing that evil should be or be done, since nothing is judged of by that which appertains to it accidentally, but by that which belongs to it essentially.

Reply Obj. 2: Evil does not operate towards the perfection and beauty of the universe, except accidentally, as said above (ad 1). Therefore Dionysius in saying that "evil would conduce to the perfection of the universe," draws a conclusion by reduction to an absurdity.

Reply Obj. 3: The statements that evil exists, and that evil exists not, are opposed as contradictories; yet the statements that anyone wills evil to exist and that he wills it not to be, are not so opposed; since either is affirmative. God therefore neither wills evil to be done, nor wills it not to be done, but wills to permit evil to be done; and this is a good.

TENTH ARTICLE [I, Q. 19, Art. 10]

Whether God Has Free-Will?

Objection 1: It seems that God has not free-will. For Jerome says, in a homily on the prodigal son [*Ep. 146, ad Damas.]; "God alone is He who is not liable to sin, nor can be liable: all others, as having free-will, can be inclined to either side."

Obj. 2: Further, free-will is the faculty of the reason and will, by which good and evil are chosen. But God does not will evil, as has been said (A. 9). Therefore there is not free-will in God.

*On the contrary,* Ambrose says (De Fide ii, 3): "The Holy Spirit divideth unto each one as He will, namely, according to the free choice of the will, not in obedience to necessity."

*I answer that,* We have free-will with respect to what we will not of necessity, nor by natural instinct. For our will to be happy does not appertain to free-will, but to natural instinct. Hence other animals, that are moved to act by natural instinct, are not said to be moved by free-will. Since then God necessarily wills His own goodness, but other things not necessarily, as shown above (A. 3), He has free will with respect to what He does not necessarily will.

Reply Obj. 1: Jerome seems to deny free-will to God not simply, but only as regards the inclination to sin.

Reply Obj. 2: Since the evil of sin consists in turning away from the divine goodness, by which God wills all things, as above shown, it is manifestly impossible for Him to will the evil of sin; yet He can make choice of one of two opposites, inasmuch as He can will a thing to be, or not to be. In the same way we ourselves, without sin, can will to sit down, and not will to sit down.

ELEVENTH ARTICLE [I, Q. 19, Art. 11]

Whether the Will of Expression Is to Be Distinguished in God?

Objection 1: It seems that the will of expression is not to be distinguished in God. For as the will of God is the cause of things, so is His wisdom. But no expressions are assigned to the divine wisdom. Therefore no expressions ought to be assigned to the divine will.

Obj. 2: Further, every expression that is not in agreement with the mind of him who expresses himself, is false. If therefore the expressions assigned to the divine will are not in agreement with that will, they are false. But if they do agree, they are superfluous. No expressions therefore must be assigned to the divine will.

*On the contrary,* The will of God is one, since it is the very essence of God. Yet sometimes it is spoken of as many, as in the words of Ps. 110:2: "Great are the works of the Lord, sought out according to all His wills." Therefore sometimes the sign must be taken for the will.

*I answer that,* Some things are said of God in their strict sense; others by metaphor, as appears from what has been said before (Q. 13, A. 3). When certain human passions are predicated of the Godhead metaphorically, this is done because of a likeness in the effect. Hence a thing that is in us a sign of some passion, is signified metaphorically in God under the name of that passion. Thus with us it is usual for an angry man to punish, so that punishment becomes an expression of anger. Therefore punishment itself is signified by the word anger, when anger is attributed to God. In the same way, what is usually with us an expression of will, is sometimes metaphorically called will in God; just as when anyone lays down a precept, it is a sign that he wishes that precept obeyed. Hence a divine precept is sometimes called by metaphor the will of God, as in the words: "Thy will be done on earth, as it is in heaven" (Matt. 6:10). There is, however, this difference between will and anger, that anger is never attributed to God properly, since in its primary meaning it includes passion; whereas will is attributed to Him properly. Therefore in God there are distinguished will in its proper sense, and will as attributed to Him by metaphor. Will in its proper sense is called the will of good pleasure; and will metaphorically taken is the will of expression, inasmuch as the sign itself of will is called will.

Reply Obj. 1: Knowledge is not the cause of a thing being done, unless through the will. For we do not put into act what we know, unless we will to do so. Accordingly expression is not attributed to knowledge, but to will.

Reply Obj. 2: Expressions of will are called divine wills, not as being signs that God wills anything; but because what in us is the usual expression of our will, is called the divine will in God. Thus punishment is not a sign that there is anger in God; but it is called anger in Him, from the fact that it is an expression of anger in ourselves.

TWELFTH ARTICLE [I, Q. 19, Art. 12]

Whether Five Expressions of Will Are Rightly Assigned to the Divine Will?

Objection 1: It seems that five expressions of will—namely, prohibition, precept, counsel, operation, and permission—are not rightly assigned to the divine will. For the same things that God bids us do by His precept or counsel, these He sometimes operates in us, and the same things that He prohibits, these He sometimes permits. They ought not therefore to be enumerated as distinct.

Obj. 2: Further, God works nothing unless He wills it, as the Scripture says (Wis. 11:26). But the will of expression is distinct from the will of good pleasure. Therefore operation ought not to be comprehended in the will of expression.

Obj. 3: Further, operation and permission appertain to all creatures in common, since God works in them all, and permits some action in them all. But precept, counsel, and prohibition belong to rational creatures only. Therefore they do not come rightly under one division, not being of one order.

Obj. 4: Further, evil happens in more ways than good, since "good happens in one way, but evil in all kinds of ways," as declared by the Philosopher (Ethic. ii, 6), and Dionysius (Div. Nom. iv, 22). It is not right therefore to assign one expression only in the case of evil—namely, prohibition—and two—namely, counsel and precept—in the case of good.

*I answer that,* By these signs we name the expression of will by which we are accustomed to show that we will something. A man may show that he wills something, either by himself or by means of another. He may show it by himself, by doing something either directly, or indirectly and accidentally. He shows it directly when he works in his own person; in that way the expression of his will is his own working. He shows it indirectly, by not hindering the doing of a thing; for what removes an impediment is called an accidental mover. In this respect the expression is called permission. He declares his will by means of another when he orders another to perform a work, either by insisting upon it as necessary by precept, and by prohibiting its contrary; or by persuasion, which is a part of counsel. Since in these ways the will of man makes itself known, the same five are sometimes denominated with regard to the divine will, as the expression of that will. That precept, counsel, and prohibition are called the will of God is clear from the words of Matt. 6:10: "Thy will be done on earth as it is in heaven." That permission and operation are called the will of God is clear from Augustine (Enchiridion 95), who says: "Nothing is done, unless the Almighty wills it to be done, either by permitting it, or by actually doing it."

Or it may be said that permission and operation refer to present time, permission being with respect to evil, operation with regard to good. Whilst as to future time, prohibition is in respect to evil, precept to good that is necessary and counsel to good that is of supererogation.

Reply Obj. 1: There is nothing to prevent anyone declaring his will about the same matter in different ways; thus we find many words that mean the same thing. Hence there is no reason why the same thing should not be the subject of precept, operation, and counsel; or of prohibition or permission.

Reply Obj. 2: As God may by metaphor be said to will what by His will, properly speaking, He wills not; so He may by metaphor be said to will what He does, properly speaking, will. Hence there is nothing to prevent the same thing being the object of the will of good pleasure, and of the will of expression. But operation is always the same as the will of good pleasure; while precept and counsel are not; both because the former regards the present, and the two latter the future; and because the former is of itself the effect of the will; the latter its effect as fulfilled by means of another.

Reply Obj. 3: Rational creatures are masters of their own acts; and for this reason certain special expressions of the divine will are assigned to their acts, inasmuch as God ordains rational creatures to act voluntarily and of themselves. Other creatures act only as moved by the divine operation; therefore only operation and permission are concerned with these.

Reply Obj. 4: All evil of sin, though happening in many ways, agrees in being out of harmony with the divine will. Hence with regard to evil, only one expression is assigned, that of prohibition. On the other hand, good stands in various relations to the divine goodness, since there are good deeds without which we cannot attain to the fruition of that goodness, and these are the subject of precept; and there are others by which we attain to it more perfectly, and these are the subject of counsel. Or it may be said that counsel is not only concerned with the obtaining of greater good; but also with the avoiding of lesser evils.

## QUESTION 20

GOD'S LOVE (In Four Articles)

We next consider those things that pertain absolutely to the will of God. In the appetitive part of the soul there are found in ourselves both the passions of the soul, as joy, love, and the like; and the habits of the moral virtues, as justice, fortitude and the like. Hence we shall first consider the love of God, and secondly His justice and mercy. About the first there are four points of inquiry:

(1) Whether love exists in God?

(2) Whether He loves all things?

(3) Whether He loves one thing more than another?

(4) Whether He loves more the better things?

FIRST ARTICLE [I, Q. 20, Art. 1]

Whether Love Exists in God?

Objection 1: It seems that love does not exist in God. For in God there are no passions. Now love is a passion. Therefore love is not in God.

Obj. 2: Further, love, anger, sorrow and the like, are mutually divided against one another. But sorrow and anger are not attributed to God, unless by metaphor. Therefore neither is love attributed to Him.

Obj. 3: Further, Dionysius says (Div. Nom. iv): "Love is a uniting and binding force." But this cannot take place in God, since He is simple. Therefore love does not exist in God.

*On the contrary,* It is written: "God is love" (John 4:16).

*I answer that,* We must needs assert that in God there is love: because love is the first movement of the will and of every appetitive faculty. For since the acts of the will and of every appetitive faculty tend towards good and evil, as to their proper objects: and since good is essentially and especially the object of the will and the appetite, whereas evil is only the object secondarily and indirectly, as opposed to good; it follows that the acts of the will and appetite that regard good must naturally be prior to those that regard evil; thus, for instance, joy is prior to sorrow, love to hate: because what exists of itself is always prior to that which exists through another. Again, the more universal is naturally prior to what is less so. Hence the intellect is first directed to universal truth; and in the second place to particular and special truths. Now there are certain acts of the will and appetite that regard good under some special condition, as joy and delight regard good present and possessed; whereas desire and hope regard good not as yet possessed. Love, however, regards good universally, whether possessed or not. Hence love is naturally the first act of the will and appetite; for which reason all the other appetite movements presuppose love, as their root and origin. For nobody desires anything nor rejoices in anything, except as a good that is loved: nor is anything an object of hate except as opposed to the object of love. Similarly, it is clear that sorrow, and other things like to it, must be referred to love as to their first principle. Hence, in whomsoever there is will and appetite, there must also be love: since if the first is wanting, all that follows is also wanting. Now it has been shown that will is in God (Q. 19, A. 1), and hence we must attribute love to Him.

Reply Obj. 1: The cognitive faculty does not move except through the medium of the appetitive: and just as in ourselves the universal reason moves through the medium of the particular reason, as stated in *De Anima* iii, 58, 75, so in ourselves the intellectual appetite, or the will as it is called, moves through the medium of the sensitive appetite. Hence, in us the sensitive appetite is the proximate motive-force of our bodies. Some bodily change therefore always accompanies an act of the sensitive appetite, and this change affects especially the heart, which, as the Philosopher says (De part. animal. iii, 4), is the first principle of movement in animals. Therefore acts of the sensitive appetite, inasmuch as they have annexed to them some bodily change, are called passions; whereas acts of the will are not so called. Love, therefore, and joy and delight are passions; in so far as they denote acts of the intellective appetite, they are not passions. It is in this latter sense that they are in God. Hence the Philosopher says (Ethic. vii): "God rejoices by an operation that is one and simple," and for the same reason He loves without passion.

Reply Obj. 2: In the passions of the sensitive appetite there may be distinguished a certain material element—namely, the bodily change—and a certain formal element, which is on the part of the appetite. Thus in anger, as the Philosopher says (De Anima iii, 15, 63, 64), the material element is the kindling of the blood about the heart; but the formal, the appetite for revenge. Again, as regards the formal element of certain passions a certain imperfection is implied, as in desire, which is of the good we have not, and in sorrow, which is about the evil we have. This applies also to anger, which supposes sorrow. Certain other passions, however, as love and joy, imply no imperfection. Since therefore none of these can be attributed to God on their material side, as has been said (ad 1); neither can those that even on their formal side imply imperfection be attributed to Him; except metaphorically, and from likeness of effects, as already show (Q. 3, A. 2, ad 2; Q. 19, A. 11). Whereas, those that do not imply imperfection, such as love and joy, can be properly predicated of God, though without attributing passion to Him, as said before (Q. 19, A. 11).

Reply Obj. 3: An act of love always tends towards two things; to the good that one wills, and to the person for whom one wills it: since to love a person is to wish that person good. Hence, inasmuch as we love ourselves, we wish ourselves good; and, so far as possible, union with that good. So love is called the unitive force, even in God, yet without implying composition; for the good that He wills for Himself, is no other than Himself, Who is good by His essence, as above shown (Q. 6, AA. 1, 3). And by the fact that anyone loves another, he wills good to that other. Thus he puts the other, as it were, in the place of himself; and regards the good done to him as done to himself. So far love is a binding force, since it aggregates another to ourselves, and refers his good to our own. And then again the divine love is a binding force, inasmuch as God wills good to others; yet it implies no composition in God.

SECOND ARTICLE [I, Q. 20, Art. 2]

Whether God Loves All Things?

Objection 1: It seems that God does not love all things. For according to Dionysius (Div. Nom. iv, 1), love places the lover outside himself, and causes him to pass, as it were, into the object of his love. But it is not admissible to say that God is placed outside of Himself, and passes into other things. Therefore it is inadmissible to say that God loves things other than Himself.

Obj. 2: Further, the love of God is eternal. But things apart from God are not from eternity; except in God. Therefore God does not love anything, except as it exists in Himself. But as existing in Him, it is no other than Himself. Therefore God does not love things other than Himself.

Obj. 3: Further, love is twofold—the love, namely, of desire, and the love of friendship. Now God does not love irrational creatures with the love of desire, since He needs no creature outside Himself. Nor with the love of friendship; since there can be no friendship with irrational creatures, as the Philosopher shows (Ethic. viii, 2). Therefore God does not love all things.

Obj. 4: Further, it is written (Ps. 5:7): "Thou hatest all the workers of iniquity." Now nothing is at the same time hated and loved. Therefore God does not love all things.

*On the contrary,* It is said (Wis. 11:25): "Thou lovest all things that are, and hatest none of the things which Thou hast made."

*I answer that,* God loves all existing things. For all existing things, in so far as they exist, are good, since the existence of a thing is itself a good; and likewise, whatever perfection it possesses. Now it has been shown above (Q. 19, A. 4) that God's will is the cause of all things. It must needs be, therefore, that a thing has existence, or any kind of good, only inasmuch as it is willed by God. To every existing thing, then, God wills some good. Hence, since to love anything is nothing else than to will good to that thing, it is manifest that God loves everything that exists. Yet not as we love. Because since our will is not the cause of the goodness of things, but is moved by it as by its object, our love, whereby we will good to anything, is not the cause of its goodness; but conversely its goodness, whether real or imaginary, calls forth our love, by which we will that it should preserve the good it has, and receive besides the good it has not, and to this end we direct our actions: whereas the love of God infuses and creates goodness.

Reply Obj. 1: A lover is placed outside himself, and made to pass into the object of his love, inasmuch as he wills good to the beloved; and works for that good by his providence even as he works for his own. Hence Dionysius says (Div. Nom. iv, 1): "On behalf of the truth we must make bold to say even this, that He Himself, the cause of all things, by His abounding love and goodness, is placed outside Himself by His providence for all existing things."

Reply Obj. 2: Although creatures have not existed from eternity, except in God, yet because they have been in Him from eternity, God has known them eternally in their proper natures; and for that reason has loved them, even as we, by the images of things within us, know things existing in themselves.

Reply Obj. 3: Friendship cannot exist except towards rational creatures, who are capable of returning love, and communicating one with another in the various works of life, and who may fare well or ill, according to the changes of fortune and happiness; even as to them is benevolence properly speaking exercised. But irrational creatures cannot attain to loving God, nor to any share in the intellectual and beatific life that He lives. Strictly speaking, therefore, God does not love irrational creatures with the love of friendship; but as it were with the love of desire, in so far as He orders them to rational creatures, and even to Himself. Yet this is not because He stands in need of them; but only on account of His goodness, and of the services they render to us. For we can desire a thing for others as well as for ourselves.

Reply Obj. 4: Nothing prevents one and the same thing being loved under one aspect, while it is hated under another. God loves sinners in so far as they are existing natures; for they have existence and have it from Him. In so far as they are sinners, they have not existence at all, but fall short of it; and this in them is not from God. Hence under this aspect, they are hated by Him.

THIRD ARTICLE [I, Q. 20, Art. 3]

Whether God Loves All Things Equally?

Objection 1: It seems that God loves all things equally. For it is said: "He hath equally care of all" (Wis. 6:8). But God's providence over things comes from the love wherewith He loves them. Therefore He loves all things equally.

Obj. 2: Further, the love of God is His essence. But God's essence does not admit of degree; neither therefore does His love. He does not therefore love some things more than others.

Obj. 3: Further, as God's love extends to created things, so do His knowledge and will extend. But God is not said to know some things more than others; nor will one thing more than another. Neither therefore does He love some things more than others.

*On the contrary,* Augustine says (Tract. in Joan. cx): "God loves all things that He has made, and amongst them rational creatures more, and of these especially those who are members of His only-begotten Son Himself."

*I answer that,* Since to love a thing is to will it good, in a twofold way anything may be loved more, or less. In one way on the part of the act of the will itself, which is more or less intense. In this way God does not love some things more than others, because He loves all things by an act of the will that is one, simple, and always the same. In another way on the part of the good itself that a person wills for the beloved. In this way we are said to love that one more than another, for whom we will a greater good, though our will is not more intense. In this way we must needs say that God loves some things more than others. For since God's love is the cause of goodness in things, as has been said (A. 2), no one thing would be better than another, if God did not will greater good for one than for another.

Reply Obj. 1: God is said to have equally care of all, not because by His care He deals out equal good to all, but because He administers all things with a like wisdom and goodness.

Reply Obj. 2: This argument is based on the intensity of love on the part of the act of the will, which is the divine essence. But the good that God wills for His creatures, is not the divine essence. Therefore there is no reason why it may not vary in degree.

Reply Obj. 3: To understand and to will denote the act alone, and do not include in their meaning objects from the diversity of which God may be said to know or will more or less, as has been said with respect to God's love.

FOURTH ARTICLE [I, Q. 20, Art. 4]

Whether God Always Loves More the Better Things?

Objection 1: It seems that God does not always love more the better things. For it is manifest that Christ is better than the whole human race, being God and man. But God loved the human race more than He loved Christ; for it is said: "He spared not His own Son, but delivered Him up for us all" (Rom. 8:32). Therefore God does not always love more the better things.

Obj. 2: Further, an angel is better than a man. Hence it is said of man: "Thou hast made him a little less than the angels" (Ps. 8:6). But God loved men more than He loved the angels, for it is said: "Nowhere doth He take hold of the angels, but of the seed of Abraham He taketh hold" (Heb. 2:16). Therefore God does not always love more the better things.

Obj. 3: Further, Peter was better than John, since he loved Christ more. Hence the Lord, knowing this to be true, asked Peter, saying: "Simon, son of John, lovest thou Me more than these?" Yet Christ loved John more than He loved Peter. For as Augustine says, commenting on the words, "Simon, son of John, lovest thou Me?": "By this very mark is John distinguished from the other disciples, not that He loved him only, but that He loved him more than the rest." Therefore God does not always love more the better things.

Obj. 4: Further, the innocent man is better than the repentant, since repentance is, as Jerome says (Cap. 3 in Isa.), "a second plank after shipwreck." But God loves the penitent more than the innocent; since He rejoices over him the more. For it is said: "I say to you that there shall be joy in heaven upon the one sinner that doth penance, more than upon ninety-nine just who need not penance" (Luke 15:7). Therefore God does not always love more the better things.

Obj. 5: Further, the just man who is foreknown is better than the predestined sinner. Now God loves more the predestined sinner, since He wills for him a greater good, life eternal. Therefore God does not always love more the better things.

*On the contrary,* Everything loves what is like it, as appears from (Ecclus. 13:19): "Every beast loveth its like." Now the better a thing is, the more like is it to God. Therefore the better things are more loved by God.

*I answer that,* It must needs be, according to what has been said before, that God loves more the better things. For it has been shown (AA. 2, 3), that God's loving one thing more than another is nothing else than His willing for that thing a greater good: because God's will is the cause of goodness in things; and the reason why some things are better than others, is that God wills for them a greater good. Hence it follows that He loves more the better things.

Reply Obj. 1: God loves Christ not only more than He loves the whole human race, but more than He loves the entire created universe: because He willed for Him the greater good in giving Him "a name that is above all names," in so far as He was true God. Nor did anything of His excellence diminish when God delivered Him up to death for the salvation of the human race; rather did He become thereby a glorious conqueror: "The government was placed upon His shoulder," according to Isa. 9:6.

Reply Obj. 2: God loves the human nature assumed by the Word of God in the person of Christ more than He loves all the angels; for that nature is better, especially on the ground of the union with the Godhead. But speaking of human nature in general, and comparing it with the angelic, the two are found equal, in the order of grace and of glory: since according to Rev 21:17, the measure of a man and of an angel is the same. Yet so that, in this respect, some angels are found nobler than some men, and some men nobler than some angels. But as to natural condition an angel is better than a man. God therefore did not assume human nature because He loved man, absolutely speaking, more; but because the needs of man were greater; just as the master of a house may give some costly delicacy to a sick servant, that he does not give to his own son in sound health.

Reply Obj. 3: This doubt concerning Peter and John has been solved in various ways. Augustine interprets it mystically, and says that the active life, signified by Peter, loves God more than the contemplative signified by John, because the former is more conscious of the miseries of this present life, and therefore the more ardently desires to be freed from them, and depart to God. God, he says, loves more the contemplative life, since He preserves it longer. For it does not end, as the active life does, with the life of the body.

Some say that Peter loved Christ more in His members, and therefore was loved more by Christ also, for which reason He gave him the care of the Church; but that John loved Christ more in Himself, and so was loved more by Him; on which account Christ commended His mother to his care. Others say that it is uncertain which of them loved Christ more with the love of charity, and uncertain also which of them God loved more and ordained to a greater degree of glory in eternal life. Peter is said to have loved more, in regard to a certain promptness and fervor; but John to have been more loved, with respect to certain marks of familiarity which Christ showed to him rather than to others, on account of his youth and purity. While others say that Christ loved Peter more, from his more excellent gift of charity; but John more, from his gifts of intellect. Hence, absolutely speaking, Peter was the better and more beloved; but, in a certain sense, John was the better, and was loved the more. However, it may seem presumptuous to pass judgment on these matters; since "the Lord" and no other "is the weigher of spirits" (Prov. 16:2).

Reply Obj. 4: The penitent and the innocent are related as exceeding and exceeded. For whether innocent or penitent, those are the better and better loved who have most grace. Other things being equal, innocence is the nobler thing and the more beloved. God is said to rejoice more over the penitent than over the innocent, because often penitents rise from sin more cautious, humble, and fervent. Hence Gregory commenting on these words (Hom. 34 in Ev.) says that, "In battle the general loves the soldier who after flight returns and bravely pursues the enemy, more than him who has never fled, but has never done a brave deed."

Or it may be answered that gifts of grace, equal in themselves, are more as conferred on the penitent, who deserved punishment, than as conferred on the innocent, to whom no punishment was due; just as a hundred pounds [marcoe] are a greater gift to a poor man than to a king.

Reply Obj. 5: Since God's will is the cause of goodness in things, the goodness of one who is loved by God is to be reckoned according to the time when some good is to be given to him by divine goodness. According therefore to the time, when there is to be given by the divine will to the predestined sinner a greater good, the sinner is better; although according to some other time he is the worse; because even according to some time he is neither good nor bad.

# QUESTION 21

THE JUSTICE AND MERCY OF GOD (In Four Articles)

After considering the divine love, we must treat of God's justice and mercy. Under this head there are four points of inquiry:

(1) Whether there is justice in God?

(2) Whether His justice can be called truth?

(3) Whether there is mercy in God?

(4) Whether in every work of God there are justice and mercy?

FIRST ARTICLE [I, Q. 21, Art. 1]

Whether There Is Justice in God?

Objection 1: It seems that there is not justice in God. For justice is divided against temperance. But temperance does not exist in God: neither therefore does justice.

Obj. 2: Further, he who does whatsoever he wills and pleases does not work according to justice. But, as the Apostle says: "God worketh all things according to the counsel of His will" (Eph. 1:11). Therefore justice cannot be attributed to Him.

Obj. 3: Further, the act of justice is to pay what is due. But God is no man's debtor. Therefore justice does not belong to God.

Obj. 4: Further, whatever is in God, is His essence. But justice cannot belong to this. For Boethius says (De Hebdom.): "Good regards the essence; justice the act." Therefore justice does not belong to God.

*On the contrary,* It is said (Ps. 10:8): "The Lord is just, and hath loved justice."

*I answer that,* There are two kinds of justice. The one consists in mutual giving and receiving, as in buying and selling, and other kinds of intercourse and exchange. This the Philosopher (Ethic. v, 4) calls commutative justice, that directs exchange and intercourse of business. This does not belong to God, since, as the Apostle says: "Who hath first given to Him, and recompense shall be made him?" (Rom. 11:35). The other consists in distribution, and is called distributive justice; whereby a ruler or a steward gives to each what his rank deserves. As then the proper order displayed in ruling a family or any kind of multitude evinces justice of this kind in the ruler, so the order of the universe, which is seen both in effects of nature and in effects of will, shows forth the justice of God. Hence Dionysius says (Div. Nom. viii, 4): "We must needs see that God is truly just, in seeing how He gives to all existing things what is proper to the condition of each; and preserves the nature of each in the order and with the powers that properly belong to it."

Reply Obj. 1: Certain of the moral virtues are concerned with the passions, as temperance with concupiscence, fortitude with fear and daring, meekness with anger. Such virtues as these can only metaphorically be attributed to God; since, as stated above (Q. 20, A. 1), in God there are no passions; nor a sensitive appetite, which is, as the Philosopher says (Ethic. iii, 10), the subject of those virtues. On the other hand, certain moral virtues are concerned with works of giving and expending; such as justice, liberality, and magnificence; and these reside not in the sensitive faculty, but in the will. Hence, there is nothing to prevent our attributing these virtues to God; although not in civil matters, but in such acts as are not unbecoming to Him. For, as the Philosopher says (Ethic. x, 8), it would be absurd to praise God for His political virtues.

Reply Obj. 2: Since good as perceived by intellect is the object of the will, it is impossible for God to will anything but what His wisdom approves. This is, as it were, His law of justice, in accordance with which His will is right and just. Hence, what He does according to His will He does justly: as we do justly what we do according to law. But whereas law comes to us from some higher power, God is a law unto Himself.

Reply Obj. 3: To each one is due what is his own. Now that which is directed to a man is said to be his own. Thus the master owns the servant, and not conversely, for that is free which is its own cause. In the word debt, therefore, is implied a certain exigence or necessity of the thing to which it is directed. Now a twofold order has to be considered in things: the one, whereby one created thing is directed to another, as the parts of the whole, accident to substance, and all things whatsoever to their end; the other, whereby all created things are ordered to God. Thus in the divine operations debt may be regarded in two ways, as due either to God, or to creatures, and in either way God pays what is due. It is due to God that there should be fulfilled in creatures what His will and wisdom require, and what manifests His goodness. In this respect, God's justice regards what befits Him; inasmuch as He renders to Himself what is due to Himself. It is also due to a created thing that it should possess what is ordered to it; thus it is due to man to have hands, and that other animals should serve him. Thus also God exercises justice, when He gives to each thing what is due to it by its nature and condition. This debt however is derived from the former; since what is due to each thing is due to it as ordered to it according to the divine wisdom. And although God in this way pays each thing its due, yet He Himself is not the debtor, since He is not directed to other things, but rather other things to Him. Justice, therefore, in God is sometimes spoken of as the fitting accompaniment of His goodness; sometimes as the reward of merit. Anselm touches on either view where he says (Prosolog. 10): "When Thou dost punish the wicked, it is just, since it agrees with their deserts; and when Thou dost spare the wicked, it is also just; since it befits Thy goodness."

Reply Obj. 4: Although justice regards act, this does not prevent its being the essence of God; since even that which is of the essence of a thing may be the principle of action. But good does not always regard act; since a thing is called good not merely with respect to act, but also as regards perfection in its essence. For this reason it is said (De Hebdom.) that the good is related to the just, as the general to the special.

SECOND ARTICLE [I, Q. 21, Art. 2]

Whether the Justice of God Is Truth?

Objection 1: It seems that the justice of God is not truth. For justice resides in the will; since, as Anselm says (Dial. Verit. 13), it is a rectitude of the will, whereas truth resides in the intellect, as the Philosopher says (Metaph. vi; Ethic. vi, 2,6). Therefore justice does not appertain to truth.

Obj. 2: Further, according to the Philosopher (Ethic. iv, 7), truth is a virtue distinct from justice. Truth therefore does not appertain to the idea of justice.

*On the contrary,* it is said (Ps. 84:11): "Mercy and truth have met each other": where truth stands for justice.

*I answer that,* Truth consists in the equation of mind and thing, as said above (Q. 16, A. 1). Now the mind, that is the cause of the thing, is related to it as its rule and measure; whereas the converse is the case with the mind that receives its knowledge from things. When therefore things are the measure and rule of the mind, truth consists in the equation of the mind to the thing, as happens in ourselves. For according as a thing is, or is not, our thoughts or our words about it are true or false. But when the mind is the rule or measure of things, truth consists in the equation of the thing to the mind; just as the work of an artist is said to be true, when it is in accordance with his art.

Now as works of art are related to art, so are works of justice related to the law with which they accord. Therefore God's justice, which establishes things in the order conformable to the rule of His wisdom, which is the law of His justice, is suitably called truth. Thus we also in human affairs speak of the truth of justice.

Reply Obj. 1: Justice, as to the law that governs, resides in the reason or intellect; but as to the command whereby our actions are governed according to the law, it resides in the will.

Reply Obj. 2: The truth of which the Philosopher is speaking in this passage, is that virtue whereby a man shows himself in word and deed such as he really is. Thus it consists in the conformity of the sign with the thing signified; and not in that of the effect with its cause and rule: as has been said regarding the truth of justice.

THIRD ARTICLE [I, Q. 21, Art. 3]

Whether Mercy Can Be Attributed to God?

Objection 1: It seems that mercy cannot be attributed to God. For mercy is a kind of sorrow, as Damascene says (De Fide Orth. ii, 14). But there is no sorrow in God; and therefore there is no mercy in Him.

Obj. 2: Further, mercy is a relaxation of justice. But God cannot remit what appertains to His justice. For it is said (2 Tim. 2:13): "If we believe not, He continueth faithful: He cannot deny Himself." But He would deny Himself, as a gloss says, if He should deny His words. Therefore mercy is not becoming to God.

*On the contrary,* it is said (Ps. 110:4): "He is a merciful and gracious Lord."

*I answer that,* Mercy is especially to be attributed to God, as seen in its effect, but not as an affection of passion. In proof of which it must be considered that a person is said to be merciful [misericors], as being, so to speak, sorrowful at heart [miserum cor]; being affected with sorrow at the misery of another as though it were his own. Hence it follows that he endeavors to dispel the misery of this other, as if it were his; and this is the effect of mercy. To sorrow, therefore, over the misery of others belongs not to God; but it does most properly belong to Him to dispel that misery, whatever be the defect we call by that name. Now defects are not removed, except by the perfection of some kind of goodness; and the primary source of goodness is God, as shown above (Q. 6, A. 4). It must, however, be considered that to bestow perfections appertains not only to the divine goodness, but also to His justice, liberality, and mercy; yet under different aspects. The communicating of perfections, absolutely considered, appertains to goodness, as shown above

(Q. 6, AA. 1, 4); in so far as perfections are given to things in proportion, the bestowal of them belongs to justice, as has been already said (A. 1); in so far as God does not bestow them for His own use, but only on account of His goodness, it belongs to liberality; in so far as perfections given to things by God expel defects, it belongs to mercy.

Reply Obj. 1: This argument is based on mercy, regarded as an affection of passion.

Reply Obj. 2: God acts mercifully, not indeed by going against His justice, but by doing something more than justice; thus a man who pays another two hundred pieces of money, though owing him only one hundred, does nothing against justice, but acts liberally or mercifully. The case is the same with one who pardons an offence committed against him, for in remitting it he may be said to bestow a gift. Hence the Apostle calls remission a forgiving: "Forgive one another, as Christ has forgiven you" (Eph. 4:32). Hence it is clear that mercy does not destroy justice, but in a sense is the fulness thereof. And thus it is said: "Mercy exalteth itself above judgement" (James 2:13).

FOURTH ARTICLE [I, Q. 21, Art. 4]

Whether in Every Work of God There Are Mercy and Justice?

Objection 1: It seems that not in every work of God are mercy and justice. For some works of God are attributed to mercy, as the justification of the ungodly; and others to justice, as the damnation of the wicked. Hence it is said: "Judgment without mercy to him that hath not done mercy" (James 2:13). Therefore not in every work of God do mercy and justice appear.

Obj. 2: Further, the Apostle attributes the conversion of the Jews to justice and truth, but that of the Gentiles to mercy (Rom. 15). Therefore not in every work of God are justice and mercy.

Obj. 3: Further, many just persons are afflicted in this world; which is unjust. Therefore not in every work of God are justice and mercy.

Obj. 4: Further, it is the part of justice to pay what is due, but of mercy to relieve misery. Thus both justice and mercy presuppose something in their works: whereas creation presupposes nothing. Therefore in creation neither mercy nor justice is found.

*On the contrary,* It is said (Ps. 24:10): "All the ways of the Lord are mercy and truth."

*I answer that,* Mercy and truth are necessarily found in all God's works, if mercy be taken to mean the removal of any kind of defect. Not every defect, however, can properly be called a misery; but only defect in a rational nature whose lot is to be happy; for misery is opposed to happiness. For this necessity there is a reason, because since a debt paid according to the divine justice is one due either to God, or to some creature, neither the one nor the other can be lacking in any work of God: because God can do nothing that is not in accord with His wisdom and goodness; and it is in this sense, as we have said, that anything is due to God. Likewise, whatever is done by Him in created things, is done according to proper order and proportion wherein consists the idea of justice. Thus justice must exist in all God's works. Now the work of divine justice always presupposes the work of mercy; and is founded thereupon. For nothing is due to creatures, except for something pre-existing in them, or foreknown. Again, if this is due to a creature, it must be due on account of something that precedes. And since we cannot go on to infinity, we must come to something that depends only on the goodness of the divine will—which is the ultimate end. We may say, for instance, that to possess hands is due to man on account of his rational soul; and his rational soul is due to him that he may be man; and his being man is on account of the divine goodness. So in every work of God, viewed at its primary source, there appears mercy. In all that follows, the power of mercy remains, and works indeed with even greater force; as the influence of the first cause is more intense than that of second causes. For this reason does God out of abundance of His goodness bestow upon creatures what is due to them more bountifully than is proportionate to their deserts: since less would suffice for preserving the order of justice than what the divine goodness confers; because between creatures and God's goodness there can be no proportion.

Reply Obj. 1: Certain works are attributed to justice, and certain others to mercy, because in some justice appears more forcibly and in others mercy. Even in the damnation of the reprobate mercy is seen, which, though it does not totally remit, yet somewhat alleviates, in punishing short of what is deserved.

In the justification of the ungodly, justice is seen, when God remits sins on account of love, though He Himself has mercifully infused that love. So we read of Magdalen: "Many sins are forgiven her, because she hath loved much" (Luke 7:47).

Reply Obj. 2: God's justice and mercy appear both in the conversion of the Jews and of the Gentiles. But an aspect of justice appears in the conversion of the Jews which is not seen in the conversion of the Gentiles; inasmuch as the Jews were saved on account of the promises made to the fathers.

Reply Obj. 3: Justice and mercy appear in the punishment of the just in this world, since by afflictions lesser faults are cleansed in them, and they are the more raised up from earthly affections to God. As to this Gregory says (Moral. xxvi, 9): "The evils that press on us in this world force us to go to God."

Reply Obj. 4: Although creation presupposes nothing in the universe; yet it does presuppose something in the knowledge of God. In this way too the idea of justice is preserved in creation; by the production of beings in a manner that accords with the divine wisdom and goodness. And the idea of mercy, also, is preserved in the change of creatures from non-existence to existence.

## QUESTION 22

THE PROVIDENCE OF GOD (In Four Articles)

Having considered all that relates to the will absolutely, we must now proceed to those things which have relation to both the intellect and the will, namely providence, in respect to all created things; predestination and reprobation and all that is connected with these acts in respect especially of man as regards his eternal salvation. For in the science of morals, after the moral virtues themselves, comes the consideration of prudence, to which providence would seem to belong. Concerning God's providence there are four points of inquiry:

(1) Whether providence is suitably assigned to God?

(2) Whether everything comes under divine providence?

(3) Whether divine providence is immediately concerned with all things?

(4) Whether divine providence imposes any necessity upon things foreseen?

FIRST ARTICLE [I, Q. 22, Art. 1]

Whether Providence Can Suitably Be Attributed to God?

Objection 1: It seems that providence is not becoming to God. For providence, according to Tully (De Invent. ii), is a part of prudence. But prudence, since, according to the Philosopher (Ethic. vi, 5, 9, 18), it gives good counsel, cannot belong to God, Who never has any doubt for which He should take counsel. Therefore providence cannot belong to God.

Obj. 2: Further, whatever is in God, is eternal. But providence is not anything eternal, for it is concerned with existing things that are not eternal, according to Damascene (De Fide Orth. ii, 29). Therefore there is no providence in God.

Obj. 3: Further, there is nothing composite in God. But providence seems to be something composite, because it includes both the intellect and the will. Therefore providence is not in God.

*On the contrary,* It is said (Wis. 14:3): "But Thou, Father, governest all things by providence [*Vulg. But 'Thy providence, O Father, governeth it.']."

*I answer that,* It is necessary to attribute providence to God. For all the good that is in created things has been created by God, as was shown above (Q. 6, A. 4). In created things good is found not only as regards their substance, but also as regards their order towards an end and especially their last end, which, as was said above, is the divine goodness (Q. 21, A. 4). This good of order existing in things created, is itself created by God. Since, however, God is the cause of things by His intellect, and thus it behooves that the type of every effect should pre-exist in Him, as is clear from what has gone before (Q. 19, A. 4), it is necessary that the type of the order of things towards their end should pre-exist in the divine mind: and the type of things ordered towards an end is, properly speaking, providence. For it is the chief part of prudence, to which two other parts are directed—namely, remembrance of the past, and understanding of the present; inasmuch as from the remembrance of what is past and the understanding of what is present, we gather how to provide for the future. Now it belongs to prudence, according to the Philosopher (Ethic. vi, 12), to direct other things towards an end whether in regard to oneself—as for instance, a man is said to be prudent, who orders well his acts towards the end of life—or in regard to others subject to him, in a family, city or kingdom; in which sense it is said (Matt. 24:45), "a faithful and wise servant, whom his lord hath appointed over his family." In this way prudence or providence may suitably be attributed to God. For in God Himself there can be nothing ordered towards an end, since He is the last end. This type of order in things towards an end is therefore in God called providence. Whence Boethius says (De Consol. iv, 6) that "Providence is the divine type itself, seated in the Supreme Ruler; which disposeth all things": which disposition may refer either to the type of the order of things towards an end, or to the type of the order of parts in the whole.

Reply Obj. 1: According to the Philosopher (Ethic. vi, 9, 10), "Prudence is what, strictly speaking, commands all that 'ebulia' has rightly counselled and 'synesis' rightly judged" [*Cf. I-II, Q. 57, A. 6]. Whence, though to take counsel may not be fitting to God, from the fact that counsel is an inquiry into matters that are doubtful, nevertheless to give a command as to the ordering of things towards an end, the right reason of which He possesses, does belong to God, according to Ps. 148:6: "He hath made a decree, and it shall not pass away." In this manner both prudence and providence belong to God. Although at the same time it may be said that the very reason of things to be done is called counsel in God; not because of any inquiry necessitated, but from the certitude of the knowledge, to which those who take counsel come by inquiry. Whence it is said: "Who worketh all things according to the counsel of His will" (Eph. 1:11).

Reply Obj. 2: Two things pertain to the care of providence—namely, the "reason of order," which is called providence and disposition; and the execution of order, which is termed government. Of these, the first is eternal, and the second is temporal.

Reply Obj. 3: Providence resides in the intellect; but presupposes the act of willing the end. Nobody gives a precept about things done for an end; unless he will that end. Hence prudence presupposes the moral virtues, by means of which the appetitive faculty is directed towards good, as the Philosopher says. Even if Providence has to do with the divine will and intellect equally, this would not affect the divine simplicity, since in God both the will and intellect are one and the same thing, as we have said above (Q. 19).

SECOND ARTICLE [I, Q. 22, Art. 2]

Whether Everything Is Subject to the Providence of God?

Objection 1: It seems that everything is not subject to divine providence. For nothing foreseen can happen by chance. If then everything was foreseen by God, nothing would happen by chance. And thus hazard and luck would disappear; which is against common opinion.

Obj. 2: Further, a wise provider excludes any defect or evil, as far as he can, from those over whom he has a care. But we see many evils existing. Either, then, God cannot hinder these, and thus is not omnipotent; or else He does not have care for everything.

Obj. 3: Further, whatever happens of necessity does not require providence or prudence. Hence, according to the Philosopher (Ethic. vi, 5, 9, 10, 11): "Prudence is the right reason of things contingent concerning which there is counsel and choice." Since, then, many things happen from necessity, everything cannot be subject to providence.

Obj. 4: Further, whatsoever is left to itself cannot be subject to the providence of a governor. But men are left to themselves by God in accordance with the words: "God made man from the beginning, and left him in the hand of his own counsel" (Ecclus. 15:14). And particularly in reference to the wicked: "I let them go according to the desires of their heart" (Ps. 80:13). Everything, therefore, cannot be subject to divine providence.

Obj. 5: Further, the Apostle says (1 Cor. 9:9): "God doth not care for oxen [*Vulg. 'Doth God take care for oxen?']": and we may say the same of other irrational creatures. Thus everything cannot be under the care of divine providence.

*On the contrary,* It is said of Divine Wisdom: "She reacheth from end to end mightily, and ordereth all things sweetly" (Wis. 8:1).

*I answer that,* Certain persons totally denied the existence of providence, as Democritus and the Epicureans, maintaining that the world was made by chance. Others taught that incorruptible things only were subject to providence and corruptible things not in their individual selves, but only according to their species; for in this respect they are incorruptible. They are represented as saying (Job 22:14): "The clouds are His covert; and He doth not consider our things; and He walketh about the poles of heaven." Rabbi Moses, however, excluded men from the generality of things corruptible, on account of the excellence of the intellect which they possess, but in reference to all else that suffers corruption he adhered to the opinion of the others.

We must say, however, that all things are subject to divine providence, not only in general, but even in their own individual selves. This is made evident thus. For since every agent acts for an end, the ordering of effects towards that end extends as far as the causality of the first agent extends. Whence it happens that in the effects of an agent something takes place which has no reference towards the end, because the effect comes from a cause other than, and outside the intention of the agent. But the causality of God, Who is the first agent, extends to all being, not only as to constituent principles of species, but also as to the individualizing principles; not only of things incorruptible, but also of things corruptible. Hence all things that exist in whatsoever manner are necessarily directed by God towards some end; as the Apostle says: "Those things that are of God are well ordered [*Vulg. 'Those powers that are, are ordained of God': 'Quae autem sunt, a Deo ordinatae sunt.' St. Thomas often quotes this passage, and invariably reads: 'Quae a Deo sunt, ordinata sunt.']" (Rom. 13:1). Since, therefore, as the providence of God is nothing less than the type of the order of things towards an end, as we have said; it necessarily follows that all things, inasmuch as they participate in existence, must likewise be subject to divine providence. It has also been shown (Q. 14, AA. 6, 11) that God knows all things, both universal and particular. And since His knowledge may be compared to the things themselves, as the knowledge of art to the objects of art, all things must of necessity come under His ordering; as all things wrought by art are subject to the ordering of that art.

Reply Obj. 1: There is a difference between universal and particular causes. A thing can escape the order of a particular cause; but not the order of a universal cause. For nothing escapes the order of a particular cause, except through the intervention and hindrance of some other particular cause; as, for instance, wood may be prevented from burning, by the action of water. Since then, all particular causes are included under the universal cause, it could not be that any effect should take place outside the range of that universal cause. So far then as an effect escapes the order of a particular cause, it is said to be casual or fortuitous in respect to that cause; but if we regard the universal cause, outside whose range no effect can happen, it is said to be foreseen. Thus, for instance, the meeting of two servants, although to them it appears a chance circumstance, has been fully foreseen by their master, who has purposely sent them to meet at the one place, in such a way that the one knows not about the other.

Reply Obj. 2: It is otherwise with one who has care of a particular thing, and one whose providence is universal, because a particular provider excludes all defects from what is subject to his care as far as he can; whereas, one who provides universally allows some little defect to remain, lest the good of the whole should be hindered. Hence, corruption and defects in natural things are said to be contrary to some particular nature; yet they are in keeping with the plan of universal nature; inasmuch as the defect in one thing yields to the good of another, or even to the universal good: for the corruption of one is the generation of another, and through this it is that a species is kept in existence. Since God, then, provides universally for all being, it belongs to His providence to permit certain defects in particular effects, that the perfect good of the universe may not be hindered, for if all evil were prevented, much good would be absent from the universe. A lion would cease to live, if there were no slaying of animals; and there would be no patience of martyrs if there were no tyrannical persecution. Thus Augustine says (Enchiridion 2): "Almighty God would in no wise permit evil to exist in His works, unless He were so almighty and so good as to produce good even from evil." It would appear that it was on account of these two arguments to which we have just replied, that some were persuaded to consider corruptible things—e.g. casual and evil things—as removed from the care of divine providence.

Reply Obj. 3: Man is not the author of nature; but he uses natural things in applying art and virtue to his own use. Hence human providence does not reach to that which takes place in nature from necessity; but divine providence extends thus far, since God is the author of nature. Apparently it was this argument that moved those who withdrew the course of nature from the care of divine providence, attributing it rather to the necessity of matter, as Democritus, and others of the ancients.

Reply Obj. 4: When it is said that God left man to himself, this does not mean that man is exempt from divine providence; but merely that he has not a prefixed operating force determined to only the one effect; as in the case of natural things, which are only acted upon as though directed by another towards an end; and do not act of themselves, as if they directed themselves towards an end, like rational creatures, through the possession of free will, by which these are able to take counsel and make a choice. Hence it is significantly said: "In the hand of his own counsel." But since the very act of free will is traced to God as to a cause, it necessarily follows that everything happening from the exercise of free will must be subject to divine providence. For human providence is included under the providence of God, as a particular under a universal cause. God, however, extends His providence over the just in a certain more excellent way than over the wicked; inasmuch as He prevents anything happening which would impede their final salvation. For "to them that love God, all things work together unto good" (Rom. 8:28). But from the fact that He does not restrain the wicked from the evil of sin, He is said to abandon them: not that He altogether withdraws His providence from them; otherwise they would return to nothing, if they were not preserved in existence by His providence. This was the reason that had weight with Tully, who withdrew from the care of divine providence human affairs concerning which we take counsel.

Reply Obj. 5: Since a rational creature has, through its free will, control over its actions, as was said above (Q. 19, A. 10), it is subject to divine providence in an especial manner, so that something is imputed to it as a fault, or as a merit; and there is given it accordingly something by way of punishment or reward. In this way, the Apostle withdraws oxen from the care of God: not, however, that individual irrational creatures escape the care of divine providence; as was the opinion of the Rabbi Moses.

THIRD ARTICLE [I, Q. 22, Art. 3]

Whether God Has Immediate Providence Over Everything?

Objection 1: It seems that God has not immediate providence over all things. For whatever is contained in the notion of dignity, must be attributed to God. But it belongs to the dignity of a king, that he should have ministers; through whose mediation he provides for his subjects. Therefore much less has God Himself immediate providence over all things.

Obj. 2: Further, it belongs to providence to order all things to an end. Now the end of everything is its perfection and its good. But it appertains to every cause to direct its effect to good; wherefore every active cause is a cause of the effect of providence. If therefore God were to have immediate providence over all things, all secondary causes would be withdrawn.

Obj. 3: Further, Augustine says (Enchiridion 17) that, "It is better to be ignorant of some things than to know them, for example, vile things": and the Philosopher says the same (Metaph. xii, 51). But whatever is better must be assigned to God. Therefore He has not immediate providence over bad and vile things.

*On the contrary,* It is said (Job 34:13): "What other hath He appointed over the earth? or whom hath He set over the world which He made?" On which passage Gregory says (Moral. xxiv, 20): "Himself He ruleth the world which He Himself hath made."

*I answer that,* Two things belong to providence—namely, the type of the order of things foreordained towards an end; and the execution of this order, which is called government. As regards the first of these, God has immediate providence over everything, because He has in His intellect the types of everything, even the smallest; and whatsoever causes He assigns to certain effects, He gives them the power to produce those effects. Whence it must be that He has beforehand the type of those effects in His mind. As to the second, there are certain intermediaries of God's providence; for He governs things inferior by superior, not on account of any defect in His power, but by reason of the abundance of His goodness; so that the dignity of causality is imparted even to creatures. Thus Plato's opinion, as narrated by Gregory of Nyssa (De Provid. viii, 3), is exploded. He taught a threefold providence. First, one which belongs to the supreme Deity, Who first and foremost has provision over spiritual things, and thus over the whole world as regards genus, species, and universal causes. The second providence, which is over the individuals of all that can be generated and corrupted, he attributed to the divinities who circulate in the heavens; that is, certain separate substances, which move corporeal things in a circular direction. The third providence, over human affairs, he assigned to demons, whom the Platonic philosophers placed between us and the gods, as Augustine tells us (De Civ. Dei, 1, 2: viii, 14).

Reply Obj. 1: It pertains to a king's dignity to have ministers who execute his providence. But the fact that he has not the plan of those things which are done by them arises from a deficiency in himself. For every operative science is the more perfect, the more it considers the particular things with which its action is concerned.

Reply Obj. 2: God's immediate provision over everything does not exclude the action of secondary causes; which are the executors of His order, as was said above (Q. 19, AA. 5, 8).

Reply Obj. 3: It is better for us not to know low and vile things, because by them we are impeded in our knowledge of what is better and higher; for we cannot understand many things simultaneously; because the thought of evil sometimes perverts the will towards evil. This does not hold with God, Who sees everything simultaneously at one glance, and whose will cannot turn in the direction of evil.

FOURTH ARTICLE [I, Q. 22, Art. 4]

Whether Providence Imposes Any Necessity on Things Foreseen?

Objection 1: It seems that divine providence imposes necessity upon things foreseen. For every effect that has a *per se* cause, either present or past, which it necessarily follows, happens from necessity; as the Philosopher proves (Metaph. vi, 7). But the providence of God, since it is eternal, pre-exists; and the effect flows from it of necessity, for divine providence cannot be frustrated. Therefore divine providence imposes a necessity upon things foreseen.

Obj. 2: Further, every provider makes his work as stable as he can, lest it should fail. But God is most powerful. Therefore He assigns the stability of necessity to things provided.

Obj. 3: Further, Boethius says (De Consol. iv, 6): "Fate from the immutable source of providence binds together human acts and fortunes by the indissoluble connection of causes." It seems therefore that providence imposes necessity upon things foreseen.

*On the contrary,* Dionysius says that (Div. Nom. iv, 23) "to corrupt nature is not the work of providence." But it is in the nature of some things to be contingent. Divine providence does not therefore impose any necessity upon things so as to destroy their contingency.

*I answer that,* Divine providence imposes necessity upon some things; not upon all, as some formerly believed. For to providence it belongs to order things towards an end. Now after the divine goodness, which is an extrinsic end to all things, the principal good in things themselves is the perfection of the universe; which would not be, were not all grades of being found in things. Whence it pertains to divine providence to produce every grade of being. And thus it has prepared for some things necessary causes, so that they happen of necessity; for others contingent causes, that they may happen by contingency, according to the nature of their proximate causes.

Reply Obj. 1: The effect of divine providence is not only that things should happen somehow; but that they should happen either by necessity or by contingency. Therefore whatsoever divine providence ordains to happen infallibly and of necessity happens infallibly and of necessity; and that happens from contingency, which the plan of divine providence conceives to happen from contingency.

Reply Obj. 2: The order of divine providence is unchangeable and certain, so far as all things foreseen happen as they have been foreseen, whether from necessity or from contingency.

Reply Obj. 3: That indissolubility and unchangeableness of which Boethius speaks, pertain to the certainty of providence, which fails not to produce its effect, and that in the way foreseen; but they do not pertain to the necessity of the effects. We must remember that properly speaking "necessary" and "contingent" are consequent upon being, as such. Hence the mode both of necessity and of contingency falls under the foresight of God, who provides universally for all being; not under the foresight of causes that provide only for some particular order of things.

## QUESTION 23

OF PREDESTINATION (In Eight Articles)

After consideration of divine providence, we must treat of predestination and the book of life. Concerning predestination there are eight points of inquiry:

(1) Whether predestination is suitably attributed to God?

(2) What is predestination, and whether it places anything in the predestined?

(3) Whether to God belongs the reprobation of some men?

(4) On the comparison of predestination to election; whether, that is to say, the predestined are chosen?

(5) Whether merits are the cause or reason of predestination, or reprobation, or election?

(6) of the certainty of predestination; whether the predestined will infallibly be saved?

(7) Whether the number of the predestined is certain?

(8) Whether predestination can be furthered by the prayers of the saints?

FIRST ARTICLE [I, Q. 23, Art. 1]

Whether Men Are Predestined by God?

Objection 1: It seems that men are not predestined by God, for Damascene says (De Fide Orth. ii, 30): "It must be borne in mind that God foreknows but does not predetermine everything, since He foreknows all that is in us, but does not predetermine it all." But human merit and demerit are in us, forasmuch as we are the masters of our own acts by free will. All that pertains therefore to merit or demerit is not predestined by God; and thus man's predestination is done away.

Obj. 2: Further, all creatures are directed to their end by divine providence, as was said above (Q. 22, AA. 1, 2). But other creatures are not said to be predestined by God. Therefore neither are men.

Obj. 3: Further, the angels are capable of beatitude, as well as men. But predestination is not suitable to angels, since in them there never was any unhappiness (miseria); for predestination, as Augustine says (De praedest. sanct. 17), is the "purpose to take pity [miserendi]" [*See Q. 22, A. 3]. Therefore men are not predestined.

Obj. 4: Further, the benefits God confers upon men are revealed by the Holy Ghost to holy men according to the saying of the Apostle (1 Cor. 2:12): "Now we have received not the spirit of this world, but the Spirit that is of God: that we may know the things that are given us from God." Therefore if man were predestined by God, since predestination is a benefit from God, his predestination would be made known to each predestined; which is clearly false.

*On the contrary,* It is written (Rom. 8:30): "Whom He predestined, them He also called."

*I answer that,* It is fitting that God should predestine men. For all things are subject to His providence, as was shown above (Q. 22, A. 2). Now it belongs to providence to direct things towards their end, as was also said (Q. 22, AA. 1, 2). The end towards which created things are directed by God is twofold; one which exceeds all proportion and faculty of created nature; and this end is life eternal, that consists in seeing God which is above the nature of every creature, as shown above (Q. 12, A. 4). The other end, however, is proportionate to created nature, to which end created being can attain according to the power of its nature. Now if a thing cannot attain to something by the power of its nature, it must be directed thereto by another; thus, an arrow is directed by the archer towards a mark. Hence, properly speaking, a rational creature, capable of eternal life, is led towards it, directed, as it were, by God. The reason of that direction pre-exists in God; as in Him is the type of the order of all things towards an end, which we proved above to be providence. Now the type in the mind of the doer of something to be done, is a kind of pre-existence in him of the thing to be done. Hence the type of the aforesaid direction of a rational creature towards the end of life eternal is called predestination. For to destine, is to direct or send. Thus it is clear that predestination, as regards its objects, is a part of providence.

Reply Obj. 1: Damascene calls predestination an imposition of necessity, after the manner of natural things which are predetermined towards one end. This is clear from his adding: "He does not will malice, nor does He compel virtue." Whence predestination is not excluded by Him.

Reply Obj. 2: Irrational creatures are not capable of that end which exceeds the faculty of human nature. Whence they cannot be properly said to be predestined; although improperly the term is used in respect of any other end.

Reply Obj. 3: Predestination applies to angels, just as it does to men, although they have never been unhappy. For movement does not take its species from the term *wherefrom* but from the term *whereto.* Because it matters nothing, in respect of the notion of making white, whether he who is made white was before black, yellow or red. Likewise it matters nothing in respect of the notion of predestination whether one is predestined to life eternal from the state of misery or not. Although it may be said that every conferring of good above that which is due pertains to mercy; as was shown previously (Q. 21, AA. 3, 4).

Reply Obj. 4: Even if by a special privilege their predestination were revealed to some, it is not fitting that it should be revealed to everyone; because, if so, those who were not predestined would despair; and security would beget negligence in the predestined.

SECOND ARTICLE [I, Q. 23, Art. 2]

Whether Predestination Places Anything in the Predestined?

Objection 1: It seems that predestination does place something in the predestined. For every action of itself causes passion. If therefore predestination is action in God, predestination must be passion in the predestined.

Obj. 2: Further, Origen says on the text, "He who was predestined," etc. (Rom. 1:4): "Predestination is of one who is not; destination, of one who is." And Augustine says (De Praed. Sanct.): "What is predestination but the destination of one who is?" Therefore predestination is only of one who actually exists; and it thus places something in the predestined.

Obj. 3: Further, preparation is something in the thing prepared. But predestination is the preparation of God's benefits, as Augustine says (De Praed. Sanct. ii, 14). Therefore predestination is something in the predestined.

Obj. 4: Further, nothing temporal enters into the definition of eternity. But grace, which is something temporal, is found in the definition of predestination. For predestination is the preparation of grace in the present; and of glory in the future. Therefore predestination is not anything eternal. So it must needs be that it is in the predestined, and not in God; for whatever is in Him is eternal.

*On the contrary,* Augustine says (De Praed. Sanct. ii, 14) that "predestination is the foreknowledge of God's benefits." But foreknowledge is not in the things foreknown, but in the person who foreknows them. Therefore, predestination is in the one who predestines, and not in the predestined.

*I answer that,* Predestination is not anything in the predestined; but only in the person who predestines. We have said above that predestination is a part of providence. Now providence is not anything in the things provided for; but is a type in the mind of the provider, as was proved above (Q. 22, A. 1). But the execution of providence which is called government, is in a passive way in the thing governed, and in an active way in the governor. Whence it is clear that predestination is a kind of type of the ordering of some persons towards eternal salvation, existing in the divine mind. The execution, however, of this order is in a passive way in the predestined, but actively in God. The execution of predestination is the calling and magnification; according to the Apostle (Rom. 8:30): "Whom He predestined, them He also called and whom He called, them He also magnified [Vulg. 'justified']."

Reply Obj. 1: Actions passing out to external matter imply of themselves passion—for example, the actions of warming and cutting; but not so actions remaining in the agent, as understanding and willing, as said above (Q. 14, A. 2; Q. 18, A. 3, ad 1). Predestination is an action of this latter class. Wherefore, it does not put anything in the predestined. But its execution, which passes out to external things, has an effect in them.

Reply Obj. 2: Destination sometimes denotes a real mission of someone to a given end; thus, destination can only be said of someone actually existing. It is taken, however, in another sense for a mission which a person conceives in the mind; and in this manner we are said to destine a thing which we firmly propose in our mind. In this latter way it is said that Eleazar "determined not to do any unlawful things for the love of life" (2 Macc. 6:20). Thus destination can be of a thing which does not exist. Predestination, however, by reason of the antecedent nature it implies, can be attributed to a thing which does not actually exist; in whatsoever way destination is accepted.

Reply Obj. 3: Preparation is twofold: of the patient in respect to passion and this is in the thing prepared; and of the agent to action, and this is in the agent. Such a preparation is predestination, and as an agent by intellect is said to prepare itself to act, accordingly as it preconceives the idea of what is to be done. Thus, God from all eternity prepared by predestination, conceiving the idea of the order of some towards salvation.

Reply Obj. 4: Grace does not come into the definition of predestination, as something belonging to its essence, but inasmuch as predestination implies a relation to grace, as of cause to effect, and of act to its object. Whence it does not follow that predestination is anything temporal.

THIRD ARTICLE [I, Q. 23, Art. 3]

Whether God Reprobates Any Man?

Objection 1: It seems that God reprobates no man. For nobody reprobates what he loves. But God loves every man, according to (Wis. 11:25): "Thou lovest all things that are, and Thou hatest none of the things Thou hast made." Therefore God reprobates no man.

Obj. 2: Further, if God reprobates any man, it would be necessary for reprobation to have the same relation to the reprobates as predestination has to the predestined. But predestination is the cause of the salvation of the predestined. Therefore reprobation will likewise be the cause of the loss of the reprobate. But this false. For it is said (Osee 13:9): "Destruction is thy own, O Israel; Thy help is only in Me." God does not, then, reprobate any man.

Obj. 3: Further, to no one ought anything be imputed which he cannot avoid. But if God reprobates anyone, that one must perish. For it is said (Eccles. 7:14): "Consider the works of God, that no man can correct whom He hath despised." Therefore it could not be imputed to any man, were he to perish. But this is false. Therefore God does not reprobate anyone.

*On the contrary,* It is said (Malachi 1:2,3): "I have loved Jacob, but have hated Esau."

*I answer that,* God does reprobate some. For it was said above (A. 1) that predestination is a part of providence. To providence, however, it belongs to permit certain defects in those things which are subject to providence, as was said above (Q. 22, A. 2). Thus, as men are ordained to eternal life through the providence of God, it likewise is part of that providence to permit some to fall away from that end; this is called reprobation. Thus, as predestination is a part of providence, in regard to those ordained to eternal salvation, so reprobation is a part of providence in regard to those who turn aside from that end. Hence reprobation implies not only foreknowledge, but also something more, as does providence, as was said above (Q. 22, A. 1). Therefore, as predestination includes the will to confer grace and glory; so also reprobation includes the will to permit a person to fall into sin, and to impose the punishment of damnation on account of that sin.

Reply Obj. 1: God loves all men and all creatures, inasmuch as He wishes them all some good; but He does not wish every good to them all. So far, therefore, as He does not wish this particular good—namely, eternal life—He is said to hate or reprobated them.

Reply Obj. 2: Reprobation differs in its causality from predestination. This latter is the cause both of what is expected in the future life by the predestined—namely, glory—and of what is received in this life—namely, grace. Reprobation, however, is not the cause of what is in the present—namely, sin; but it is the cause of abandonment by God. It is the cause, however, of what is assigned in the future—namely, eternal punishment. But guilt proceeds from the free-will of the person who is reprobated and deserted by grace. In this way, the word of the prophet is true—namely, "Destruction is thy own, O Israel."

Reply Obj. 3: Reprobation by God does not take anything away from the power of the person reprobated. Hence, when it is said that the reprobated cannot obtain grace, this must not be understood as implying absolute impossibility: but only conditional impossibility: as was said above (Q. 19, A. 3), that the predestined must necessarily be saved; yet a conditional necessity, which does not do away with the liberty of choice. Whence, although anyone reprobated by God cannot acquire grace, nevertheless that he falls into this or that particular sin comes from the use of his free-will. Hence it is rightly imputed to him as guilt.

FOURTH ARTICLE [I, Q. 23, Art. 4]

Whether the Predestined Are Chosen by God? [*"Eligantur."]

Objection 1: It seems that the predestined are not chosen by God. For Dionysius says (Div. Nom. iv, 1) that as the corporeal sun sends his rays upon all without selection, so does God His goodness. But the goodness of God is communicated to some in an especial manner through a participation of grace and glory. Therefore God without any selection communicates His grace and glory; and this belongs to predestination.

Obj. 2: Further, election is of things that exist. But predestination from all eternity is also of things which do not exist. Therefore, some are predestined without election.

Obj. 3: Further, election implies some discrimination. Now God "wills all men to be saved" (1 Tim. 2:4). Therefore, predestination which ordains men towards eternal salvation, is without election.

*On the contrary,* It is said (Eph. 1:4): "He chose us in Him before the foundation of the world."

*I answer that,* Predestination presupposes election in the order of reason; and election presupposes love. The reason of this is that predestination, as stated above (A. 1), is a part of providence. Now providence, as also prudence, is the plan existing in the intellect directing the ordering of some things towards an end; as was proved above (Q. 22, A. 2). But nothing is directed towards an end unless the will for that end already exists. Whence the predestination of some to eternal salvation presupposes, in the order of reason, that God wills their salvation; and to this belong both election and love:—love, inasmuch as He wills them this particular good of eternal salvation; since to love is to wish well to anyone, as stated above (Q. 20, AA. 2 ,3):—election, inasmuch as He wills this good to some in preference to others; since He reprobates some, as stated above (A. 3). Election and love, however, are differently ordered in God, and in ourselves: because in us the will in loving does not cause good, but we are incited to love by the good which already exists; and therefore we choose someone to love, and so election in us precedes love. In God, however, it is the reverse. For His will, by which in loving He wishes good to someone, is the cause of that good possessed by some in preference to others. Thus it is clear that love precedes election in the order of reason, and election precedes predestination. Whence all the predestinate are objects of election and love.

Reply Obj. 1: If the communication of the divine goodness in general be considered, God communicates His goodness without election; inasmuch as there is nothing which does not in some way share in His goodness, as we said above (Q. 6, A. 4). But if we consider the communication of this or that particular good, He does not allot it without election; since He gives certain goods to some men, which He does not give to others. Thus in the conferring of grace and glory election is implied.

Reply Obj. 2: When the will of the person choosing is incited to make a choice by the good already pre-existing in the object chosen, the choice must needs be of those things which already exist, as happens in our choice. In God it is otherwise; as was said above (Q. 20, A. 2). Thus, as Augustine says (De Verb. Ap. Serm. 11): "Those are chosen by God, who do not exist; yet He does not err in His choice."

Reply Obj. 3: God wills all men to be saved by His antecedent will, which is to will not simply but relatively; and not by His consequent will, which is to will simply.

FIFTH ARTICLE [I, Q. 23, Art. 5]

Whether the Foreknowledge of Merits Is the Cause of Predestination?

Objection 1: It seems that foreknowledge of merits is the cause of predestination. For the Apostle says (Rom. 8:29): "Whom He foreknew, He also predestined." Again a gloss of Ambrose on Rom. 9:15: "I will have mercy upon whom I will have mercy" says: "I will give mercy to him who, I foresee, will turn to Me with his whole heart." Therefore it seems the foreknowledge of merits is the cause of predestination.

Obj. 2: Further, Divine predestination includes the divine will, which by no means can be irrational; since predestination is "the purpose to have mercy," as Augustine says (De Praed. Sanct. ii, 17). But there can be no other reason for predestination than the foreknowledge of merits. Therefore it must be the cause of reason of predestination.

Obj. 3: Further, "There is no injustice in God" (Rom. 9:14). Now it would seem unjust that unequal things be given to equals. But all men are equal as regards both nature and original sin; and inequality in them arises from the merits or demerits of their actions. Therefore God does not prepare unequal things for men by predestinating and reprobating, unless through the foreknowledge of their merits and demerits.

*On the contrary,* The Apostle says (Titus 3:5): "Not by works of justice which we have done, but according to His mercy He saved us." But as He saved us, so He predestined that we should be saved. Therefore, foreknowledge of merits is not the cause or reason of predestination.

*I answer that,* Since predestination includes will, as was said above (A. 4), the reason of predestination must be sought for in the same way as was the reason of the will of God. Now it was shown above (Q. 19, A. 5), that we cannot assign any cause of the divine will on the part of the act of willing; but a reason can be found on the part of the things willed; inasmuch as God wills one thing on account of something else. Wherefore nobody has been so insane as to say that merit is the cause of divine predestination as regards the act of the predestinator. But this is the question, whether, as regards the effect, predestination has any cause; or what comes to the same thing, whether God pre-ordained that He would give the effect of predestination to anyone on account of any merits.

Accordingly there were some who held that the effect of predestination was pre-ordained for some on account of pre-existing merits in a former life. This was the opinion of Origen, who thought that the souls of men were created in the beginning, and according to the diversity of their works different states were assigned to them in this world when united with the body. The Apostle, however, rebuts this opinion where he says (Rom. 9:11,12): "For when they were not yet born, nor had done any good or evil ... not of works, but of Him that calleth, it was said of her: The elder shall serve the younger."

Others said that pre-existing merits in this life are the reason and cause of the effect of predestination. For the Pelagians taught that the beginning of doing well came from us; and the consummation from God: so that it came about that the effect of predestination was granted to one, and not to another, because the one made a beginning by preparing, whereas the other did not. But against this we have the saying of the Apostle (2 Cor. 3:5), that "we are not sufficient to think anything of ourselves as of ourselves." Now no principle of action can be imagined previous to the act of thinking. Wherefore it cannot be said that anything begun in us can be the reason of the effect of predestination.

And so others said that merits following the effect of predestination are the reason of predestination; giving us to understand that God gives grace to a person, and pre-ordains that He will give it, because He knows beforehand that He will make good use of that grace, as if a king were to give a horse to a soldier because he knows he will make good use of it. But these seem to have drawn a distinction between that which flows from grace, and that which flows from free will, as if the same thing cannot come from both. It is, however, manifest that what is of grace is the effect of predestination; and this cannot be considered as the reason of predestination, since it is contained in the notion of predestination. Therefore, if anything else in us be the reason of predestination, it will outside the effect of predestination. Now there is no distinction between what flows from free will, and what is of predestination; as there is not distinction between what flows from a secondary cause and from a first cause. For the providence of God produces effects through the operation of secondary causes, as was above shown (Q. 22, A. 3). Wherefore, that which flows from free-will is also of predestination. We must say, therefore, that the effect of predestination may be considered in a twofold light—in one way, in particular; and thus there is no reason why one effect of predestination should not be the reason or cause of another; a subsequent effect being the reason of a previous effect, as its final cause; and the previous effect being the reason of the subsequent as its meritorious cause, which is reduced to the disposition of the matter. Thus we might say that God pre-ordained to give glory on account of merit, and that He pre-ordained to give grace to merit glory. In another way, the effect of predestination may be considered in general. Thus, it is impossible that the whole of the effect of predestination in general should have any cause as coming from us; because whatsoever is in man disposing him towards salvation, is all included under the effect of predestination; even the preparation for grace. For neither does this happen otherwise than by divine help, according to the prophet Jeremias (Lam. 5:21): "convert us, O Lord, to Thee, and we shall be converted." Yet predestination has in this way, in regard to its effect, the goodness of God for its reason; towards which the whole effect of predestination is directed as to an end; and from which it proceeds, as from its first moving principle.

Reply Obj. 1: The use of grace foreknown by God is not the cause of conferring grace, except after the manner of a final cause; as was explained above.

Reply Obj. 2: Predestination has its foundation in the goodness of God as regards its effects in general. Considered in its particular effects, however, one effect is the reason of another; as already stated.

Reply Obj. 3: The reason for the predestination of some, and reprobation of others, must be sought for in the goodness of God. Thus He is said to have made all things through His goodness, so that the divine goodness might be represented in things. Now it is necessary that God's goodness, which in itself is one and undivided, should be manifested in many ways in His creation; because creatures in themselves cannot attain to the simplicity of God. Thus it is that for the completion of the universe there are required different grades of being; some of which hold a high and some a low place in the universe. That this multiformity of grades may be preserved in things, God allows some evils, lest many good things should never happen, as was said above (Q. 22, A. 2). Let us then consider the whole of the human race, as we consider the whole universe. God wills to manifest His goodness in men; in respect to those whom He predestines, by means of His mercy, as sparing them; and in respect of others, whom he reprobates, by means of His justice, in punishing them. This is the reason why God elects some and rejects others. To this the Apostle refers, saying (Rom. 9:22, 23): "What if God, willing to show His wrath [that is, the vengeance of His justice], and to make His power known, endured [that is, permitted] with much patience vessels of wrath, fitted for destruction; that He might show the riches of His glory on the vessels of mercy, which He hath prepared unto glory" and (2 Tim. 2:20): "But in a great house there are not only vessels of gold and silver; but also of wood and of earth; and some, indeed, unto honor, but some unto dishonor." Yet why He chooses some for glory, and reprobates others, has no reason, except the divine will. Whence Augustine says (Tract. xxvi. in Joan.): "Why He draws one, and another He draws not, seek not to judge, if thou dost not wish to err." Thus too, in the things of nature, a reason can be assigned, since primary matter is altogether uniform, why one part of it was fashioned by God from the beginning under the form of fire, another under the form of earth, that there might be a diversity of species in things of nature. Yet why this particular part of matter is under this particular form, and that under another, depends upon the simple will of God; as from the simple will of the artificer it depends that this stone is in part of the wall, and that in another; although the plan requires that some stones should be in this place, and some in that place. Neither on this account can there be said to be injustice in God, if He prepares unequal lots for not unequal things. This would be altogether contrary to the notion of justice, if the effect of predestination were granted as a debt, and not gratuitously. In things which are given gratuitously, a person can give more or less, just as he pleases (provided he deprives nobody of his due), without any infringement of justice. This is what the master of the house said: "Take what is thine, and go thy way. Is it not lawful for me to do what I will?" (Matt. 20:14,15).

SIXTH ARTICLE [I, Q. 23, Art. 6]

Whether Predestination Is Certain?

Objection 1: It seems that predestination is not certain. Because on the words "Hold fast that which thou hast, that no one take thy crown," (Rev 3:11), Augustine says (De Corr. et Grat. 15): "Another will not receive, unless this one were to lose it." Hence the crown which is the effect of predestination can be both acquired and lost. Therefore predestination cannot be certain.

Obj. 2: Further, granted what is possible, nothing impossible follows. But it is possible that one predestined—e.g. Peter—may sin and then be killed. But if this were so, it would follow that the effect of predestination would be thwarted. This then, is not impossible. Therefore predestination is not certain.

Obj. 3: Further, whatever God could do in the past, He can do now. But He could have not predestined whom He hath predestined. Therefore now He is able not to predestine him. Therefore predestination is not certain.

*On the contrary,* A gloss on Rom. 8:29: "Whom He foreknew, He also predestinated", says: "Predestination is the foreknowledge and preparation of the benefits of God, by which whosoever are freed will most certainly be freed."

*I answer that,* Predestination most certainly and infallibly takes effect; yet it does not impose any necessity, so that, namely, its effect should take place from necessity. For it was said above (A. 1), that predestination is a part of providence. But not all things subject to providence are necessary; some things happening from contingency, according to the nature of the proximate causes, which divine providence has ordained for such effects. Yet the order of providence is infallible, as was shown above (Q. 22, A. 4). So also the order of predestination is certain; yet free-will is not destroyed; whence the effect of predestination has its contingency. Moreover all that has been said about the divine knowledge and will (Q. 14, A. 13; Q. 19, A. 4) must also be taken into consideration; since they do not destroy contingency in things, although they themselves are most certain and infallible.

Reply Obj. 1: The crown may be said to belong to a person in two ways; first, by God's predestination, and thus no one loses his crown: secondly, by the merit of grace; for what we merit, in a certain way is ours; and thus anyone may lose his crown by mortal sin. Another person receives that crown thus lost, inasmuch as he takes the former's place. For God does not permit some to fall, without raising others; according to Job 34:24: "He shall break in pieces many and innumerable, and make others to stand in their stead." Thus men are substituted in the place of the fallen angels; and the Gentiles in that of the Jews. He who is substituted for another in the state of grace, also receives the crown of the fallen in that in eternal life he will rejoice at the good the other has done, in which life he will rejoice at all good whether done by himself or by others.

Reply Obj. 2: Although it is possible for one who is predestinated considered in himself to die in mortal sin; yet it is not possible, supposed, as in fact it is supposed. that he is predestinated. Whence it does not follow that predestination can fall short of its effect.

Reply Obj. 3: Since predestination includes the divine will as stated above (A. 4): and the fact that God wills any created thing is necessary on the supposition that He so wills, on account of the immutability of the divine will, but is not necessary absolutely; so the same must be said of predestination. Wherefore one ought not to say that God is able not to predestinate one whom He has predestinated, taking it in a composite sense, thought, absolutely speaking, God can predestinate or not. But in this way the certainty of predestination is not destroyed.

SEVENTH ARTICLE [I, Q. 23, Art. 7]

Whether the Number of the Predestined Is Certain?

Objection 1: It seems that the number of the predestined is not certain. For a number to which an addition can be made is not certain. But there can be an addition to the number of the predestined as it seems; for it is written (Deut. 1:11): "The Lord God adds to this number many thousands," and a gloss adds, "fixed by God, who knows those who belong to Him." Therefore the number of the predestined is not certain.

Obj. 2: Further, no reason can be assigned why God pre-ordains to salvation one number of men more than another. But nothing is arranged by God without a reason. Therefore the number to be saved pre-ordained by God cannot be certain.

Obj. 3: Further, the operations of God are more perfect than those of nature. But in the works of nature, good is found in the majority of things; defect and evil in the minority. If, then, the number of the saved were fixed by God at a certain figure, there would be more saved than lost. Yet the contrary follows from Matt. 7:13,14: "For wide is the gate, and broad the way that leadeth to destruction, and many there are who go in thereat. How narrow is the gate, and strait is the way that leadeth to life; and few there are who find it!" Therefore the number of those pre-ordained by God to be saved is not certain.

*On the contrary,* Augustine says (De Corr. et Grat. 13): "The number of the predestined is certain, and can neither be increased nor diminished."

*I answer that,* The number of the predestined is certain. Some have said that it was formally, but not materially certain; as if we were to say that it was certain that a hundred or a thousand would be saved; not however these or those individuals. But this destroys the certainty of predestination; of which we spoke above (A. 6). Therefore we must say that to God the number of the predestined is certain, not only formally, but also materially. It must, however, be observed that the number of the predestined is said to be certain to God, not by reason of His knowledge, because, that is to say, He knows how many will be saved (for in this way the number of drops of rain and the sands of the sea are certain to God); but by reason of His deliberate choice and determination. For the further evidence of which we must remember that every agent intends to make something finite, as is clear from what has been said above when we treated of the infinite (Q. 7, AA. 2 ,3). Now whosoever intends some definite measure in his effect thinks out some definite number in the essential parts, which are by their very nature required for the perfection of the whole. For of those things which are required not principally, but only on account of something else, he does not select any definite number *per se* ; but he accepts and uses them in such numbers as are necessary on account of that other thing. For instance, a builder thinks out the definite measurements of a house, and also the definite number of rooms which he wishes to make in the house; and definite measurements of the walls and roof; he does not, however, select a definite number of stones, but accepts and uses just so many as are sufficient for the required measurements of the wall. So also must we consider concerning God in regard to the whole universe, which is His effect. For He pre-ordained the measurements of the whole of the universe, and what number would befit the essential parts of that universe—that is to say, which have in some way been ordained in perpetuity; how many spheres, how many stars, how many elements, and how many species. Individuals, however, which undergo corruption, are not ordained as it were chiefly for the good of the universe, but in a secondary way, inasmuch as the good of the species is preserved through them. Whence, although God knows the total number of individuals, the number of oxen, flies and such like, is not pre-ordained by God *per se* ; but divine providence produces just so many as are sufficient for the preservation of the species. Now of all creatures the rational creature is chiefly ordained for the good of the universe, being as such incorruptible; more especially those who attain to eternal happiness, since they more immediately reach the ultimate end. Whence the number of the predestined is certain to God; not only by way of knowledge, but also by way of a principal pre-ordination.

It is not exactly the same thing in the case of the number of the reprobate, who would seem to be pre-ordained by God for the good of the elect, in whose regard "all things work together unto good" (Rom. 8:28). Concerning the number of all the predestined, some say that so many men will be saved as angels fell; some, so many as there were angels left; others, as many as the number of angels created by God. It is, however, better to say that, "to God alone is known the number for whom is reserved eternal happiness [*From the 'secret' prayer of the missal, 'pro vivis et defunctis.']"

Reply Obj. 1: These words of Deuteronomy must be taken as applied to those who are marked out by God beforehand in respect to present righteousness. For their number is increased and diminished, but not the number of the predestined.

Reply Obj. 2: The reason of the quantity of any one part must be judged from the proportion of that part of the whole. Thus in God the reason why He has made so many stars, or so many species of things, or predestined so many, is according to the proportion of the principal parts to the good of the whole universe.

Reply Obj. 3: The good that is proportionate to the common state of nature is to be found in the majority; and is wanting in the minority. The good that exceeds the common state of nature is to be found in the minority, and is wanting in the majority. Thus it is clear that the majority of men have a sufficient knowledge for the guidance of life; and those who have not this knowledge are said to be half-witted or foolish; but they who attain to a profound knowledge of things intelligible are a very small minority in respect to the rest. Since their eternal happiness, consisting in the vision of God, exceeds the common state of nature, and especially in so far as this is deprived of grace through the corruption of original sin, those who are saved are in the minority. In this especially, however, appears the mercy of God, that He has chosen some for that salvation, from which very many in accordance with the common course and tendency of nature fall short.

EIGHTH ARTICLE [I, Q. 23, Art. 8]

Whether Predestination Can Be Furthered by the Prayers of the Saints?

Objection 1: It seems that predestination cannot be furthered by the prayers of the saints. For nothing eternal can be preceded by anything temporal; and in consequence nothing temporal can help towards making something else eternal. But predestination is eternal. Therefore, since the prayers of the saints are temporal, they cannot so help as to cause anyone to become predestined. Predestination therefore is not furthered by the prayers of the saints.

Obj. 2: Further, as there is no need of advice except on account of defective knowledge, so there is no need of help except through defective power. But neither of these things can be said of God when He predestines. Whence it is said: "Who hath helped the Spirit of the Lord? [*Vulg.: 'Who hath known the mind of the Lord?'] Or who hath been His counsellor?" (Rom. 11:34). Therefore predestination cannot be furthered by the prayers of the saints.

Obj. 3: Further, if a thing can be helped, it can also be hindered. But predestination cannot be hindered by anything. Therefore it cannot be furthered by anything.

*On the contrary,* It is said that "Isaac besought the Lord for his wife because she was barren; and He heard him and made Rebecca to conceive" (Gen. 25:21). But from that conception Jacob was born, and he was predestined. Now his predestination would not have happened if he had never been born. Therefore predestination can be furthered by the prayers of the saints.

*I answer that,* Concerning this question, there were different errors. Some, regarding the certainty of divine predestination, said that prayers were superfluous, as also anything else done to attain salvation; because whether these things were done or not, the predestined would attain, and the reprobate would not attain, eternal salvation. But against this opinion are all the warnings of Holy Scripture, exhorting us to prayer and other good works.

Others declared that the divine predestination was altered through prayer. This is stated to have the opinion of the Egyptians, who thought that the divine ordination, which they called fate, could be frustrated by certain sacrifices and prayers. Against this also is the authority of Scripture. For it is said: "But the triumpher in Israel will not spare and will not be moved to repentance" (1 Kings 15:29); and that "the gifts and the calling of God are without repentance" (Rom. 11:29).

Wherefore we must say otherwise that in predestination two things are to be considered—namely, the divine ordination; and its effect. As regards the former, in no possible way can predestination be furthered by the prayers of the saints. For it is not due to their prayers that anyone is predestined by God. As regards the latter, predestination is said to be helped by the prayers of the saints, and by other good works; because providence, of which predestination is a part, does not do away with secondary causes but so provides effects, that the order of secondary causes falls also under providence. So, as natural effects are provided by God in such a way that natural causes are directed to bring about those natural effects, without which those effects would not happen; so the salvation of a person is predestined by God in such a way, that whatever helps that person towards salvation falls under the order of predestination; whether it be one's own prayers or those of another; or other good works, and such like, without which one would not attain to salvation. Whence, the predestined must strive after good works and prayer; because through these means predestination is most certainly fulfilled. For this reason it is said: "Labor more that by good works you may make sure your calling and election" (2 Pet. 1:10).

Reply Obj. 1: This argument shows that predestination is not furthered by the prayers of the saints, as regards the preordination.

Reply Obj. 2: One is said to be helped by another in two ways; in one way, inasmuch as he receives power from him: and to be helped thus belongs to the weak; but this cannot be said of God, and thus we are to understand, "Who hath helped the Spirit of the Lord?" In another way one is said to be helped by a person through whom he carries out his work, as a master through a servant. In this way God is helped by us; inasmuch as we execute His orders, according to 1 Cor. 3:9: "We are God's co-adjutors." Nor is this on account of any defect in the power of God, but because He employs intermediary causes, in order that the beauty of order may be preserved in the universe; and also that He may communicate to creatures the dignity of causality.

Reply Obj. 3: Secondary causes cannot escape the order of the first universal cause, as has been said above (Q. 19, A. 6), indeed, they execute that order. And therefore predestination can be furthered by creatures, but it cannot be impeded by them.

## QUESTION 24

THE BOOK OF LIFE (In Three Articles)

We now consider the book of life; concerning which there are three points of inquiry:

(1) What is the book of life?

(2) Of what life is it the book?

(3) Whether anyone can be blotted out of the book of life?

FIRST ARTICLE [I, Q. 24, Art. 1]

Whether the Book of Life Is the Same As Predestination?

Objection 1: It seems that the book of life is not the same thing as predestination. For it is said, "All things are the book of life" (Ecclus. 4:32)—i.e. the Old and New Testament according to a gloss. This, however, is not predestination. Therefore the book of life is not predestination.

Obj. 2: Further, Augustine says (De Civ. Dei xx, 14) that "the book of life is a certain divine energy, by which it happens that to each one his good or evil works are recalled to memory." But divine energy belongs seemingly, not to predestination, but rather to divine power. Therefore the book of life is not the same thing as predestination.

Obj. 3: Further, reprobation is opposed to predestination. So, if the book of life were the same as predestination, there should also be a book of death, as there is a book of life.

*On the contrary,* It is said in a gloss upon Ps. 68:29, "Let them be blotted out of the book of the living," "This book is the knowledge of God, by which He hath predestined to life those whom He foreknew."

*I answer that,* The book of life is in God taken in a metaphorical sense, according to a comparison with human affairs. For it is usual among men that they who are chosen for any office should be inscribed in a book; as, for instance, soldiers, or counsellors, who formerly were called "conscript" fathers. Now it is clear from the preceding (Q. 23, A. 4) that all the predestined are chosen by God to possess eternal life. This conscription, therefore, of the predestined is called the book of life. A thing is said metaphorically to be written upon the mind of anyone when it is firmly held in the memory, according to Prov. 3:3: "Forget not My Law, and let thy heart keep My commandments," and further on, "Write them in the tables of thy heart." For things are written down in material books to help the memory. Whence, the knowledge of God, by which He firmly remembers that He has predestined some to eternal life, is called the book of life. For as the writing in a book is the sign of things to be done, so the knowledge of God is a sign in Him of those who are to be brought to eternal life, according to 2 Tim. 11:19: "The sure foundation of God standeth firm, having this seal; the Lord knoweth who are His."

Reply Obj. 1: The book of life may be understood in two senses. In one sense as the inscription of those who are chosen to life; thus we now speak of the book of life. In another sense the inscription of those things which lead us to life may be called the book of life; and this also is twofold, either as of things to be done; and thus the Old and New Testament are called a book of life; or of things already done, and thus that divine energy by which it happens that to each one his deeds will be recalled to memory, is spoken of as the book of life. Thus that also may be called the book of war, whether it contains the names inscribed of those chosen for military service; or treats of the art of warfare, or relates the deeds of soldiers.

Hence the solution of the Second Objection.

Reply Obj. 3: It is the custom to inscribe, not those who are rejected, but those who are chosen. Whence there is no book of death corresponding to reprobation; as the book of life to predestination.

Reply Obj. 4: Predestination and the book of life are different aspects of the same thing. For this latter implies the knowledge of predestination; as also is made clear from the gloss quoted above.

SECOND ARTICLE [I, Q. 24, Art. 2]

Whether the Book of Life Regards Only the Life of Glory of the Predestined?

Objection 1: It seems that the book of life does not only regard the life of glory of the predestined. For the book of life is the knowledge of life. But God, through His own life, knows all other life. Therefore the book of life is so called in regard to divine life; and not only in regard to the life of the predestined.

Obj. 2: Further, as the life of glory comes from God, so also does the life of nature. Therefore, if the knowledge of the life of glory is called the book of life; so also should the knowledge of the life of nature be so called.

Obj. 3: Further, some are chosen to the life of grace who are not chosen to the life of glory; as it is clear from what is said: "Have not I chosen you twelve, and one of you is a devil?" (John 6:71). But the book of life is the inscription of the divine election, as stated above (A. 1). Therefore it applies also to the life of grace.

*On the contrary,* The book of life is the knowledge of predestination, as stated above (ibid.). But predestination does not regard the life of grace, except so far as it is directed to glory; for those are not predestined who have grace and yet fail to obtain glory. The book of life altogether is only so called in regard to the life of glory.

*I answer that,* The book of life, as stated above (A. 1), implies a conscription or a knowledge of those chosen to life. Now a man is chosen for something which does not belong to him by nature; and again that to which a man is chosen has the aspect of an end. For a soldier is not chosen or inscribed merely to put on armor, but to fight; since this is the proper duty to which military service is directed. But the life of glory is an end exceeding human nature, as said above (Q. 23, A. 1). Wherefore, strictly speaking, the book of life regards the life of glory.

Reply Obj. 1: The divine life, even considered as a life of glory, is natural to God; whence in His regard there is no election, and in consequence no book of life: for we do not say that anyone is chosen to possess the power of sense, or any of those things that are consequent on nature.

From this we gather the Reply to the Second Objection. For there is no election, nor a book of life, as regards the life of nature.

Reply Obj. 3: The life of grace has the aspect, not of an end, but of something directed towards an end. Hence nobody is said to be chosen to the life of grace, except so far as the life of grace is directed to glory. For this reason those who, possessing grace, fail to obtain glory, are not said to be chosen simply, but relatively. Likewise they are not said to be written in the book of life simply, but relatively; that is to say, that it is in the ordination and knowledge of God that they are to have some relation to eternal life, according to their participation in grace.

THIRD ARTICLE [I, Q. 24, Art. 3]

Whether Anyone May Be Blotted Out of the Book of Life?

Objection 1: It seems that no one may be blotted out of the book of life. For Augustine says (De Civ. Dei xx, 15): "God's foreknowledge, which cannot be deceived, is the book of life." But nothing can be taken away from the foreknowledge of God, nor from predestination. Therefore neither can anyone be blotted out from the book of life.

Obj. 2: Further, whatever is in a thing is in it according to the disposition of that thing. But the book of life is something eternal and immutable. Therefore whatsoever is written therein, is there not in a temporary way, but immovably, and indelibly.

Obj. 3: Further, blotting out is the contrary to inscription. But nobody can be written a second time in the book of life. Neither therefore can he be blotted out.

*On the contrary,* It is said, "Let them be blotted out from the book of the living" (Ps. 68:29).

*I answer that,* Some have said that none could be blotted out of the book of life as a matter of fact, but only in the opinion of men. For it is customary in the Scriptures to say that something is done when it becomes known. Thus some are said to be written in the book of life, inasmuch as men think they are written therein, on account of the present righteousness they see in them; but when it becomes evident, either in this world or in the next, that they have fallen from that state of righteousness, they are then said to be blotted out. And thus a gloss explains the passage: "Let them be blotted out of the book of the living." But because not to be blotted out of the book of life is placed among the rewards of the just, according to the text, "He that shall overcome, shall thus be clothed in white garments, and I will not blot his name out of the book of life" (Apoc. 3:5) (and what is promised to holy men, is not merely something in the opinion of men), it can therefore be said that to be blotted out, and not blotted out, of the book of life is not only to be referred to the opinion of man, but to the reality of the fact. For the book of life is the inscription of those ordained to eternal life, to which one is directed from two sources; namely, from predestination, which direction never fails, and from grace; for whoever has grace, by this very fact becomes fitted for eternal life. This direction fails sometimes; because some are directed by possessing grace, to obtain eternal life, yet they fail to obtain it through mortal sin. Therefore those who are ordained to possess eternal life through divine predestination are written down in the book of life simply, because they are written therein to have eternal life in reality; such are never blotted out from the book of life. Those, however, who are ordained to eternal life, not through divine predestination, but through grace, are said to be written in the book of life not simply, but relatively, for they are written therein not to have eternal life in itself, but in its cause only. Yet though these latter can be said to be blotted out of the book of life, this blotting out must not be referred to God, as if God foreknew a thing, and afterwards knew it not; but to the thing known, namely, because God knows one is first ordained to eternal life, and afterwards not ordained when he falls from grace.

Reply Obj. 1: The act of blotting out does not refer to the book of life as regards God's foreknowledge, as if in God there were any change; but as regards things foreknown, which can change.

Reply Obj. 2: Although things are immutably in God, yet in themselves they are subject to change. To this it is that the blotting out of the book of life refers.

Reply Obj. 3: The way in which one is said to be blotted out of the book of life is that in which one is said to be written therein anew; either in the opinion of men, or because he begins again to have relation towards eternal life through grace; which also is included in the knowledge of God, although not anew.

# QUESTION 25

THE POWER OF GOD (In Six Articles)

After considering the divine foreknowledge and will, and other things pertaining thereto, it remains for us to consider the power of God. About this are six points of inquiry:

(1) Whether there is power in God?

(2) Whether His power is infinite?

(3) Whether He is almighty?

(4) Whether He could make the past not to have been?

(5) Whether He could do what He does not, or not do what He does?

(6) Whether what He makes He could make better?

FIRST ARTICLE [I, Q. 25, Art. 1]

Whether There Is Power in God?

Objection 1: It seems that power is not in God. For as primary matter is to power, so God, who is the first agent, is to act. But primary matter, considered in itself, is devoid of all act. Therefore, the first agent—namely, God—is devoid of power.

Obj. 2: Further, according to the Philosopher (Metaph. vi, 19), better than every power is its act. For form is better than matter; and action than active power, since it is its end. But nothing is better than what is in God; because whatsoever is in God, is God, as was shown above (Q. 3, A. 3). Therefore, there is no power in God.

Obj. 3: Further, Power is the principle of operation. But the divine power is God's essence, since there is nothing accidental in God: and of the essence of God there is no principle. Therefore there is no power in God.

Obj. 4: Further, it was shown above (Q. 14, A. 8; Q. 19, A. 4) that God's knowledge and will are the cause of things. But the cause and principle of a thing are identical. We ought not, therefore, to assign power to God; but only knowledge and will.

*On the contrary,* It is said: "Thou art mighty, O Lord, and Thy truth is round about Thee" (Ps. 88:9).

*I answer that,* Power is twofold—namely, passive, which exists not at all in God; and active, which we must assign to Him in the highest degree. For it is manifest that everything, according as it is in act and is perfect, is the active principle of something: whereas everything is passive according as it is deficient and imperfect. Now it was shown above (Q. 3, A. 2; Q. 4, AA. 1, 2), that God is pure act, simply and in all ways perfect, nor in Him does any imperfection find place. Whence it most fittingly belongs to Him to be an active principle, and in no way whatsoever to be passive. On the other hand, the notion of active principle is consistent with active power. For active power is the principle of acting upon something else; whereas passive power is the principle of being acted upon by something else, as the Philosopher says (Metaph. v, 17). It remains, therefore, that in God there is active power in the highest degree.

Reply Obj. 1: Active power is not contrary to act, but is founded upon it, for everything acts according as it is actual: but passive power is contrary to act; for a thing is passive according as it is potential. Whence this potentiality is not in God, but only active power.

Reply Obj. 2: Whenever act is distinct from power, act must be nobler than power. But God's action is not distinct from His power, for both are His divine essence; neither is His existence distinct from His essence. Hence it does not follow that there should be anything in God nobler than His power.

Reply Obj. 3: In creatures, power is the principle not only of action, but likewise of effect. Thus in God the idea of power is retained, inasmuch as it is the principle of an effect; not, however, as it is a principle of action, for this is the divine essence itself; except, perchance, after our manner of understanding, inasmuch as the divine essence, which pre-contains in itself all perfection that exists in created things, can be understood either under the notion of action, or under that of power; as also it is understood under the notion of *suppositum* possessing nature, and under that of nature. Accordingly the notion of power is retained in God in so far as it is the principle of an effect.

Reply Obj. 4: Power is predicated of God not as something really distinct from His knowledge and will, but as differing from them logically; inasmuch as power implies a notion of a principle putting into execution what the will commands, and what knowledge directs, which three things in God are identified. Or we may say, that the knowledge or will of God, according as it is the effective principle, has the notion of power contained in it. Hence the consideration of the knowledge and will of God precedes the consideration of His power, as the cause precedes the operation and effect.

SECOND ARTICLE [I, Q. 25, Art. 2]

Whether the Power of God Is Infinite?

Objection 1: It seems that the power of God is not infinite. For everything that is infinite is imperfect according to the Philosopher (Phys. iii, 6). But the power of God is far from imperfect. Therefore it is not infinite.

Obj. 2: Further, every power is made known by its effect; otherwise it would be ineffectual. If, then, the power of God were infinite, it could produce an infinite effect, but this is impossible.

Obj. 3: Further, the Philosopher proves (Phys. viii, 79) that if the power of any corporeal thing were infinite, it would cause instantaneous movement. God, however, does not cause instantaneous movement, but moves the spiritual creature in time, and the corporeal creature in place and time, as Augustine says (Gen. ad lit. 20, 22, 23). Therefore, His power is not infinite.

*On the contrary,* Hilary says (De Trin. viii), that "God's power is immeasurable. He is the living mighty one." Now everything that is immeasurable is infinite. Therefore the power of God is infinite.

*I answer that,* As stated above (A. 1), active power exists in God according to the measure in which He is actual. Now His existence is infinite, inasmuch as it is not limited by anything that receives it, as is clear from what has been said, when we discussed the infinity of the divine essence (Q. 7, A. 1). Wherefore, it is necessary that the active power in God should be infinite. For in every agent is it found that the more perfectly an agent has the form by which it acts the greater its power to act. For instance, the hotter a thing is, the greater the power has it to give heat; and it would have infinite power to give heat, were its own heat infinite. Whence, since the divine essence, through which God acts, is infinite, as was shown above (Q. 7, A. 1) it follows that His power likewise is infinite.

Reply Obj. 1: The Philosopher is here speaking of an infinity in regard to matter not limited by any form; and such infinity belongs to quantity. But the divine essence is otherwise, as was shown above (Q. 7, A. 1); and consequently so also His power. It does not follow, therefore, that it is imperfect.

Reply Obj. 2: The power of a univocal agent is wholly manifested in its effect. The generative power of man, for example, is not able to do more than beget man. But the power of a non-univocal agent does not wholly manifest itself in the production of its effect: as, for example, the power of the sun does not wholly manifest itself in the production of an animal generated from putrefaction. Now it is clear that God is not a univocal agent. For nothing agrees with Him either in species or in genus, as was shown above (Q. 3, A. 5; Q. 4, A. 3). Whence it follows that His effect is always less than His power. It is not necessary, therefore, that the infinite power of God should be manifested so as to produce an infinite effect. Yet even if it were to produce no effect, the power of God would not be ineffectual; because a thing is ineffectual which is ordained towards an end to which it does not attain. But the power of God is not ordered toward its effect as towards an end; rather, it is the end of the effect produced by it.

Reply Obj. 3: The Philosopher (Phys. viii, 79) proves that if a body had infinite power, it would cause a non-temporal movement. And he shows that the power of the mover of heaven is infinite, because it can move in an infinite time. It remains, therefore, according to his reckoning, that the infinite power of a body, if such existed, would move without time; not, however, the power of an incorporeal mover. The reason of this is that one body moving another is a univocal agent; wherefore it follows that the whole power of the agent is made known in its motion. Since then the greater the power of a moving body, the more quickly does it move; the necessary conclusion is that if its power were infinite, it would move beyond comparison faster, and this is to move without time. An incorporeal mover, however, is not a univocal agent; whence it is not necessary that the whole of its power should be manifested in motion, so as to move without time; and especially since it moves in accordance with the disposition of its will.

THIRD ARTICLE [I, Q. 25, Art. 3]

Whether God Is Omnipotent?

Objection 1: It seems that God is not omnipotent. For movement and passiveness belong to everything. But this is impossible with God, for He is immovable, as was said above (Q. 2, A. 3). Therefore He is not omnipotent.

Obj. 2: Further, sin is an act of some kind. But God cannot sin, nor "deny Himself" as it is said in 2 Tim. 2:13. Therefore He is not omnipotent.

Obj. 3: Further, it is said of God that He manifests His omnipotence "especially by sparing and having mercy" [*Collect, 10th Sunday after Pentecost]. Therefore the greatest act possible to the divine power is to spare and have mercy. There are things much greater, however, than sparing and having mercy; for example, to create another world, and the like. Therefore God is not omnipotent.

Obj. 4: Further, upon the text, "God hath made foolish the wisdom of this world" (1 Cor. 1:20), a gloss says: "God hath made the wisdom of this world foolish [*Vulg.: 'Hath not God,' etc.] by showing those things to be possible which it judges to be impossible." Whence it would seem that nothing is to be judged possible or impossible in reference to inferior causes, as the wisdom of this world judges them; but in reference to the divine power. If God, then, were omnipotent, all things would be possible; nothing, therefore impossible. But if we take away the impossible, then we destroy also the necessary; for what necessarily exists is impossible not to exist. Therefore there would be nothing at all that is necessary in things if God were omnipotent. But this is an impossibility. Therefore God is not omnipotent.

*On the contrary,* It is said: "No word shall be impossible with God" (Luke 1:37).

*I answer that,* All confess that God is omnipotent; but it seems difficult to explain in what His omnipotence precisely consists: for there may be doubt as to the precise meaning of the word 'all' when we say that God can do all things. If, however, we consider the matter aright, since power is said in reference to possible things, this phrase, "God can do all things," is rightly understood to mean that God can do all things that are possible; and for this reason He is said to be omnipotent. Now according to the Philosopher (Metaph. v, 17), a thing is said to be possible in two ways. First in relation to some power, thus whatever is subject to human power is said to be possible to man. Secondly absolutely, on account of the relation in which the very terms stand to each other. Now God cannot be said to be omnipotent through being able to do all things that are possible to created nature; for the divine power extends farther than that. If, however, we were to say that God is omnipotent because He can do all things that are possible to His power, there would be a vicious circle in explaining the nature of His power. For this would be saying nothing else but that God is omnipotent, because He can do all that He is able to do.

It remains therefore, that God is called omnipotent because He can do all things that are possible absolutely; which is the second way of saying a thing is possible. For a thing is said to be possible or impossible absolutely, according to the relation in which the very terms stand to one another, possible if the predicate is not incompatible with the subject, as that Socrates sits; and absolutely impossible when the predicate is altogether incompatible with the subject, as, for instance, that a man is a donkey.

It must, however, be remembered that since every agent produces an effect like itself, to each active power there corresponds a thing possible as its proper object according to the nature of that act on which its active power is founded; for instance, the power of giving warmth is related as to its proper object to the being capable of being warmed. The divine existence, however, upon which the nature of power in God is founded, is infinite, and is not limited to any genus of being; but possesses within itself the perfection of all being. Whence, whatsoever has or can have the nature of being, is numbered among the absolutely possible things, in respect of which God is called omnipotent. Now nothing is opposed to the idea of being except non-being. Therefore, that which implies being and non-being at the same time is repugnant to the idea of an absolutely possible thing, within the scope of the divine omnipotence. For such cannot come under the divine omnipotence, not because of any defect in the power of God, but because it has not the nature of a feasible or possible thing. Therefore, everything that does not imply a contradiction in terms, is numbered amongst those possible things, in respect of which God is called omnipotent: whereas whatever implies contradiction does not come within the scope of divine omnipotence, because it cannot have the aspect of possibility. Hence it is better to say that such things cannot be done, than that God cannot do them. Nor is this contrary to the word of the angel, saying: "No word shall be impossible with God." For whatever implies a contradiction cannot be a word, because no intellect can possibly conceive such a thing.

Reply Obj. 1: God is said to be omnipotent in respect to His active power, not to passive power, as was shown above (A. 1). Whence the fact that He is immovable or impassible is not repugnant to His omnipotence.

Reply Obj. 2: To sin is to fall short of a perfect action; hence to be able to sin is to be able to fall short in action, which is repugnant to omnipotence. Therefore it is that God cannot sin, because of His omnipotence. Nevertheless, the Philosopher says (Topic. iv, 3) that God can deliberately do what is evil. But this must be understood either on a condition, the antecedent of which is impossible—as, for instance, if we were to say that God can do evil things if He will. For there is no reason why a conditional proposition should not be true, though both the antecedent and consequent are impossible: as if one were to say: "If man is a donkey, he has four feet." Or he may be understood to mean that God can do some things which now seem to be evil: which, however, if He did them, would then be good. Or he is, perhaps, speaking after the common manner of the heathen, who thought that men became gods, like Jupiter or Mercury.

Reply Obj. 3: God's omnipotence is particularly shown in sparing and having mercy, because in this is it made manifest that God has supreme power, that He freely forgives sins. For it is not for one who is bound by laws of a superior to forgive sins of his own free will. Or, because by sparing and having mercy upon men, He leads them on to the participation of an infinite good; which is the ultimate effect of the divine power. Or because, as was said above (Q. 21, A. 4), the effect of the divine mercy is the foundation of all the divine works. For nothing is due to anyone, except on account of something already given him gratuitously by God. In this way the divine omnipotence is particularly made manifest, because to it pertains the first foundation of all good things.

Reply Obj. 4: The absolute possible is not so called in reference either to higher causes, or to inferior causes, but in reference to itself. But the possible in reference to some power is named possible in reference to its proximate cause. Hence those things which it belongs to God alone to do immediately—as, for example, to create, to justify, and the like—are said to be possible in reference to a higher cause. Those things, however, which are of such kind as to be done by inferior causes are said to be possible in reference to those inferior causes. For it is according to the condition of the proximate cause that the effect has contingency or necessity, as was shown above (Q. 14, A. 1, ad 2). Thus is it that the wisdom of the world is deemed foolish, because what is impossible to nature, it judges to be impossible to God. So it is clear that the omnipotence of God does not take away from things their impossibility and necessity.

FOURTH ARTICLE [I, Q. 25, Art. 4]

Whether God Can Make the Past Not to Have Been?

Objection 1: It seems that God can make the past not to have been. For what is impossible in itself is much more impossible than that which is only impossible accidentally. But God can do what is impossible in itself, as to give sight to the blind, or to raise the dead. Therefore, and much more can He do what is only impossible accidentally. Now for the past not to have been is impossible accidentally: thus for Socrates not to be running is accidentally impossible, from the fact that his running is a thing of the past. Therefore God can make the past not to have been.

Obj. 2: Further, what God could do, He can do now, since His power is not lessened. But God could have effected, before Socrates ran, that he should not run. Therefore, when he has run, God could effect that he did not run.

Obj. 3: Further, charity is a more excellent virtue than virginity. But God can supply charity that is lost; therefore also lost virginity. Therefore He can so effect that what was corrupt should not have been corrupt.

*On the contrary,* Jerome says (Ep. 22 ad Eustoch.): "Although God can do all things, He cannot make a thing that is corrupt not to have been corrupted." Therefore, for the same reason, He cannot effect that anything else which is past should not have been.

*I answer that,* As was said above (Q. 7, A. 2), there does not fall under the scope of God's omnipotence anything that implies a contradiction. Now that the past should not have been implies a contradiction. For as it implies a contradiction to say that Socrates is sitting, and is not sitting, so does it to say that he sat, and did not sit. But to say that he did sit is to say that it happened in the past. To say that he did not sit, is to say that it did not happen. Whence, that the past should not have been, does not come under the scope of divine power. This is what Augustine means when he says (Contra Faust. xxix, 5): "Whosoever says, If God is almighty, let Him make what is done as if it were not done, does not see that this is to say: If God is almighty let Him effect that what is true, by the very fact that it is true, be false": and the Philosopher says (Ethic. vi, 2): "Of this one thing alone is God deprived—namely, to make undone the things that have been done."

Reply Obj. 1: Although it is impossible accidentally for the past not to have been, if one considers the past thing itself, as, for instance, the running of Socrates; nevertheless, if the past thing is considered as past, that it should not have been is impossible, not only in itself, but absolutely since it implies a contradiction. Thus, it is more impossible than the raising of the dead; in which there is nothing contradictory, because this is reckoned impossible in reference to some power, that is to say, some natural power; for such impossible things do come beneath the scope of divine power.

Reply Obj. 2: As God, in accordance with the perfection of the divine power, can do all things, and yet some things are not subject to His power, because they fall short of being possible; so, also, if we regard the immutability of the divine power, whatever God could do, He can do now. Some things, however, at one time were in the nature of possibility, whilst they were yet to be done, which now fall short of the nature of possibility, when they have been done. So is God said not to be able to do them, because they themselves cannot be done.

Reply Obj. 3: God can remove all corruption of the mind and body from a woman who has fallen; but the fact that she had been corrupt cannot be removed from her; as also is it impossible that the fact of having sinned or having lost charity thereby can be removed from the sinner.

FIFTH ARTICLE [I, Q. 25, Art. 5]

Whether God Can Do What He Does Not?

Objection 1: It seems that God cannot do other than what He does. For God cannot do what He has not foreknown and pre-ordained that He would do. But He neither foreknew nor pre-ordained that He would do anything except what He does. Therefore He cannot do except what He does.

Obj. 2: Further, God can only do what ought to be done and what is right to be done. But God is not bound to do what He does not; nor is it right that He should do what He does not. Therefore He cannot do except what He does.

Obj. 3: Further, God cannot do anything that is not good and befitting creation. But it is not good for creatures nor befitting them to be otherwise than as they are. Therefore God cannot do except what He does.

*On the contrary,* It is said: "Thinkest thou that I cannot ask My Father, and He will give Me presently more than twelve legions of angels?" (Matt. 26:53). But He neither asked for them, nor did His Father show them to refute the Jews. Therefore God can do what He does not.

*I answer that,* In this matter certain persons erred in two ways. Some laid it down that God acts from natural necessity in such way that as from the action of nature nothing else can happen beyond what actually takes place—as, for instance, from the seed of man, a man must come, and from that of an olive, an olive; so from the divine operation there could not result other things, nor another order of things, than that which now is. But we showed above (Q. 19, A. 3) that God does not act from natural necessity, but that His will is the cause of all things; nor is that will naturally and from any necessity determined to those things. Whence in no way at all is the present course of events produced by God from any necessity, so that other things could not happen. Others, however, said that the divine power is restricted to this present course of events through the order of the divine wisdom and justice without which God does nothing. But since the power of God, which is His essence, is nothing else but His wisdom, it can indeed be fittingly said that there is nothing in the divine power which is not in the order of the divine wisdom; for the divine wisdom includes the whole potency of the divine power. Yet the order placed in creation by divine wisdom, in which order the notion of His justice consists, as said above (Q. 21, A. 2), is not so adequate to the divine wisdom that the divine wisdom should be restricted to this present order of things. Now it is clear that the whole idea of order which a wise man puts into things made by him is taken from their end. So, when the end is proportionate to the things made for that end, the wisdom of the maker is restricted to some definite order. But the divine goodness is an end exceeding beyond all proportion things created. Whence the divine wisdom is not so restricted to any particular order that no other course of events could happen. Wherefore we must simply say that God can do other things than those He has done.

Reply Obj. 1: In ourselves, in whom power and essence are distinct from will and intellect, and again intellect from wisdom, and will from justice, there can be something in the power which is not in the just will nor in the wise intellect. But in God, power and essence, will and intellect, wisdom and justice, are one and the same. Whence, there can be nothing in the divine power which cannot also be in His just will or in His wise intellect. Nevertheless, because His will cannot be determined from necessity to this or that order of things, except upon supposition, as was said above (Q. 19, A. 3), neither are the wisdom and justice of God restricted to this present order, as was shown above; so nothing prevents there being something in the divine power which He does not will, and which is not included in the order which He has place in things. Again, because power is considered as executing, the will as commanding, and the intellect and wisdom as directing; what is attributed to His power considered in itself, God is said to be able to do in accordance with His absolute power. Of such a kind is everything which has the nature of being, as was said above (A. 3). What is, however, attributed to the divine power, according as it carries into execution the command of a just will, God is said to be able to do by His ordinary power. In this manner, we must say that God can do other things by His absolute power than those He has foreknown and pre-ordained He would do. But it could not happen that He should do anything which He had not foreknown, and had not pre-ordained that He would do, because His actual doing is subject to His foreknowledge and pre-ordination, though His power, which is His nature, is not so. For God does things because He wills so to do; yet the power to do them does not come from His will, but from His nature.

Reply Obj. 2: God is bound to nobody but Himself. Hence, when it is said that God can only do what He ought, nothing else is meant by this than that God can do nothing but what is befitting to Himself, and just. But these words "befitting" and "just" may be understood in two ways: one, in direct connection with the verb "is"; and thus they would be restricted to the present order of things; and would concern His power. Then what is said in the objection is false; for the sense is that God can do nothing except what is now fitting and just. If, however, they be joined directly with the verb "can" (which has the effect of extending the meaning), and then secondly with "is," the present will be signified, but in a confused and general way. The sentence would then be true in this sense: "God cannot do anything except that which, if He did it, would be suitable and just."

Reply Obj. 3: Although this order of things be restricted to what now exists, the divine power and wisdom are not thus restricted. Whence, although no other order would be suitable and good to the things which now are, yet God can do other things and impose upon them another order.

SIXTH ARTICLE [I, Q. 25, Art. 6]

Whether God Can Do Better Than What He Does?

Objection 1: It seems that God cannot do better than He does. For whatever God does, He does in a most powerful and wise way. But a thing is so much the better done as it is more powerfully and wisely done. Therefore God cannot do anything better than He does.

Obj. 2: Further, Augustine thus argues (Contra Maximin. iii, 8): "If God could, but would not, beget a Son His equal, He would have been envious." For the same reason, if God could have made better things than He has done, but was not willing so to do, He would have been envious. But envy is far removed from God. Therefore God makes everything of the best. He cannot therefore make anything better than He does.

Obj. 3: Further, what is very good and the best of all cannot be bettered; because nothing is better than the best. But as Augustine says (Enchiridion 10), "each thing that God has made is good, and, taken all together they are very good; because in them all consists the wondrous beauty of the universe." Therefore the good in the universe could not be made better by God.

Obj. 4: Further, Christ as man is full of grace and truth, and has the Spirit without measure; and so He cannot be better. Again created happiness is described as the highest good, and thus cannot be better. And the Blessed Virgin Mary is raised above all the choirs of angels, and so cannot be better than she is. God cannot therefore make all things better than He has made them.

*On the contrary,* It is said (Eph. 3:20): "God is able to do all things more abundantly than we desire or understand."

*I answer that,* The goodness of anything is twofold; one, which is of the essence of it—thus, for instance, to be rational pertains to the essence of man. As regards this good, God cannot make a thing better than it is itself; although He can make another thing better than it; even as He cannot make the number four greater than it is; because if it were greater it would no longer be four, but another number. For the addition of a substantial difference in definitions is after the manner of the addition of unity of numbers (Metaph. viii, 10). Another kind of goodness is that which is over and above the essence; thus, the good of a man is to be virtuous or wise. As regards this kind of goodness, God can make better the things He has made. Absolutely speaking, however, God can make something else better than each thing made by Him.

Reply Obj. 1: When it is said that God can make a thing better than He makes it, if "better" is taken substantively, this proposition is true. For He can always make something else better than each individual thing: and He can make the same thing in one way better than it is, and in another way not; as was explained above. If, however, "better" is taken as an adverb, implying the manner of the making; thus God cannot make anything better than He makes it, because He cannot make it from greater wisdom and goodness. But if it implies the manner of the thing done, He can make something better; because He can give to things made by Him a better manner of existence as regards the accidents, although not as regards the substance.

Reply Obj. 2: It is of the nature of a son that he should be equal to his father, when he comes to maturity. But it is not of the nature of anything created, that it should be better than it was made by God. Hence the comparison fails.

Reply Obj. 3: The universe, the present creation being supposed, cannot be better, on account of the most beautiful order given to things by God; in which the good of the universe consists. For if any one thing were bettered, the proportion of order would be destroyed; as if one string were stretched more than it ought to be, the melody of the harp would be destroyed. Yet God could make other things, or add something to the present creation; and then there would be another and a better universe.

Reply Obj. 4: The humanity of Christ, from the fact that it is united to the Godhead; and created happiness from the fact that it is the fruition of God; and the Blessed Virgin from the fact that she is the mother of God; have all a certain infinite dignity from the infinite good, which is God. And on this account there cannot be anything better than these; just as there cannot be anything better than God.

## QUESTION 26

OF THE DIVINE BEATITUDE (In Four Articles)

After considering all that pertains to the unity of the divine essence, we come to treat of the divine beatitude. Concerning this, there are four points of inquiry:

(1) Whether beatitude belongs to God?

(2) In regard to what is God called blessed; does this regard His act of intellect?

(3) Whether He is essentially the beatitude of each of the blessed?

(4) Whether all other beatitude is included in the divine beatitude?

FIRST ARTICLE [I, Q. 26, Art. 1]

Whether Beatitude Belongs to God?

Objection 1: It seems that beatitude does not belong to God. For beatitude according to Boethius (De Consol. iv) "is a state made perfect by the aggregation of all good things." But the aggregation of goods has no place in God; nor has composition. Therefore beatitude does not belong to God.

Obj. 2: Further, beatitude or happiness is the reward of virtue, according to the Philosopher (Ethic. i, 9). But reward does not apply to God; as neither does merit. Therefore neither does beatitude.

*On the contrary,* The Apostle says: "Which in His times He shall show, who is the Blessed and only Almighty, the King of Kings and Lord of Lords." (1 Tim. 6:15).

*I answer that,* Beatitude belongs to God in a very special manner. For nothing else is understood to be meant by the term beatitude than the perfect good of an intellectual nature; which is capable of knowing that it has a sufficiency of the good which it possesses, to which it is competent that good or ill may befall, and which can control its own actions. All of these things belong in a most excellent manner to God, namely, to be perfect, and to possess intelligence. Whence beatitude belongs to God in the highest degree.

Reply Obj. 1: Aggregation of good is in God, after the manner not of composition, but of simplicity; for those things which in creatures is manifold, pre-exist in God, as was said above (Q. 4, A. 2; Q. 13, A. 4), in simplicity and unity.

Reply Obj. 2: It belongs as an accident to beatitude or happiness to be the reward of virtue, so far as anyone attains to beatitude; even as to be the term of generation belongs accidentally to a being, so far as it passes from potentiality to act. As, then, God has being, though not begotten; so He has beatitude, although not acquired by merit.

SECOND ARTICLE [I, Q. 26, Art. 2]

Whether God Is Called Blessed in Respect of His Intellect?

Objection 1: It seems that God is not called blessed in respect to His intellect. For beatitude is the highest good. But good is said to be in God in regard to His essence, because good has reference to being which is according to essence, according to Boethius (De Hebdom.). Therefore beatitude also is said to be in God in regard to His essence, and not to His intellect.

Obj. 2: Further, Beatitude implies the notion of end. Now the end is the object of the will, as also is the good. Therefore beatitude is said to be in God with reference to His will, and not with reference to His intellect.

*On the contrary,* Gregory says (Moral. xxxii, 7): "He is in glory, Who whilst He rejoices in Himself, needs not further praise." To be in glory, however, is the same as to be blessed. Therefore, since we enjoy God in respect to our intellect, because "vision is the whole of the reward," as Augustine says (De Civ. Dei xxii), it would seem that beatitude is said to be in God in respect of His intellect. it would seem that beatitude is said to be in God in respect of His intellect.

*I answer that,* Beatitude, as stated above (A. 1), is the perfect good of an intellectual nature. Thus it is that, as everything desires the perfection of its nature, intellectual nature desires naturally to be happy. Now that which is most perfect in any intellectual nature is the intellectual operation, by which in some sense it grasps everything. Whence the beatitude of every intellectual nature consists in understanding. Now in God, to be and to understand are one and the same thing; differing only in the manner of our understanding them. Beatitude must therefore be assigned to God in respect of His intellect; as also to the blessed, who are called blessed [beati] by reason of the assimilation to His beatitude.

Reply Obj. 1: This argument proves that beatitude belongs to God; not that beatitude pertains essentially to Him under the aspect of His essence; but rather under the aspect of His intellect.

Reply Obj. 2: Since beatitude is a good, it is the object of the will; now the object is understood as prior to the act of a power. Whence in our manner of understanding, divine beatitude precedes the act of the will at rest in it. This cannot be other than the act of the intellect; and thus beatitude is to be found in an act of the intellect.

THIRD ARTICLE [I, Q. 26, Art. 3]

Whether God Is the Beatitude of Each of the Blessed?

Objection 1: It seems that God is the beatitude of each of the blessed. For God is the supreme good, as was said above (Q. 6, AA. 2, 4). But it is quite impossible that there should be many supreme goods, as also is clear from what has been said above (Q. 11, A. 3). Therefore, since it is of the essence of beatitude that it should be the supreme good, it seems that beatitude is nothing else but God Himself.

Obj. 2: Further, beatitude is the last end of the rational nature. But to be the last end of the rational nature belongs only to God. Therefore the beatitude of every blessed is God alone.

*On the contrary,* The beatitude of one is greater than that of another, according to 1 Cor. 15:41: "Star differeth from star in glory." But nothing is greater than God. Therefore beatitude is something different from God.

*I answer that,* The beatitude of an intellectual nature consists in an act of the intellect. In this we may consider two things, namely, the object of the act, which is the thing understood; and the act itself which is to understand. If, then, beatitude be considered on the side of the object, God is the only beatitude; for everyone is blessed from this sole fact, that he understands God, in accordance with the saying of Augustine (Confess. v, 4): "Blessed is he who knoweth Thee, though he know nought else." But as regards the act of understanding, beatitude is a created thing in beatified creatures; but in God, even in this way, it is an uncreated thing.

Reply Obj. 1: Beatitude, as regards its object, is the supreme good absolutely, but as regards its act, in beatified creatures it is their supreme good, not absolutely, but in that kind of goods which a creature can participate.

Reply Obj. 2: End is twofold, namely, *objective* and subjective, as the Philosopher says (Greater Ethics i, 3), namely, the "thing itself" and "its use." Thus to a miser the end is money, and its acquisition. Accordingly God is indeed the last end of a rational creature, as the thing itself; but created beatitude is the end, as the use, or rather fruition, of the thing.

FOURTH ARTICLE [I, Q. 26, Art. 4]

Whether All Other Beatitude Is Included in the Beatitude of God?

Objection 1: It seems that the divine beatitude does not embrace all other beatitudes. For there are some false beatitudes. But nothing false can be in God. Therefore the divine beatitude does not embrace all other beatitudes.

Obj. 2: Further, a certain beatitude, according to some, consists in things corporeal; as in pleasure, riches, and such like. Now none of these have to do with God, since He is incorporeal. Therefore His beatitude does not embrace all other beatitudes.

*On the contrary,* Beatitude is a certain perfection. But the divine perfection embraces all other perfection, as was shown above (Q. 4, A. 2). Therefore the divine beatitude embraces all other beatitudes.

*I answer that,* Whatever is desirable in whatsoever beatitude, whether true or false, pre-exists wholly and in a more eminent degree in the divine beatitude. As to contemplative happiness, God possesses a continual and most certain contemplation of Himself and of all things else; and as to that which is active, He has the governance of the whole universe. As to earthly happiness, which consists in delight, riches, power, dignity, and fame, according to Boethius (De Consol. iii, 10), He possesses joy in Himself and all things else for His delight; instead of riches He has that complete self-sufficiency, which is promised by riches; in place of power, He has omnipotence; for dignities, the government of all things; and in place of fame, He possesses the admiration of all creatures.

Reply Obj. 1: A particular kind of beatitude is false according as it falls short of the idea of true beatitude; and thus it is not in God. But whatever semblance it has, howsoever slight, of beatitude, the whole of it pre-exists in the divine beatitude.

Reply Obj. 2: The good that exists in things corporeal in a corporeal manner, is also in God, but in a spiritual manner.

We have now spoken enough concerning what pertains to the unity of the divine essence.

TREATISE ON THE MOST HOLY TRINITY (QQ. 27-43)

## QUESTION 27

THE PROCESSION OF THE DIVINE PERSONS (In Five Articles)

Having considered what belongs to the unity of the divine essence, it remains to treat of what belongs to the Trinity of the persons in God. And because the divine Persons are distinguished from each other according to the relations of origin, the order of the doctrine leads us to consider firstly, the question of origin or procession; secondly, the relations of origin; thirdly, the persons.

Concerning procession there are five points of inquiry:

(1) Whether there is procession in God?

(2) Whether any procession in God can be called generation?

(3) Whether there can be any other procession in God besides generation?

(4) Whether that other procession can be called generation?

(5) Whether there are more than two processions in God?

FIRST ARTICLE [I, Q. 27, Art. 1]

Whether There Is Procession in God?

Objection 1: It would seem that there cannot be any procession in God. For procession signifies outward movement. But in God there is nothing mobile, nor anything extraneous. Therefore neither is there procession in God.

Obj. 2: Further, everything which proceeds differs from that whence it proceeds. But in God there is no diversity; but supreme simplicity. Therefore in God there is no procession.

Obj. 3: Further, to proceed from another seems to be against the nature of the first principle. But God is the first principle, as shown above (Q. 2, A. 3). Therefore in God there is no procession.

*On the contrary,* Our Lord says, "From God I proceeded" (John 8:42).

*I answer that,* Divine Scripture uses, in relation to God, names which signify procession. This procession has been differently understood. Some have understood it in the sense of an effect, proceeding from its cause; so Arius took it, saying that the Son proceeds from the Father as His primary creature, and that the Holy Ghost proceeds from the Father and the Son as the creature of both. In this sense neither the Son nor the Holy Ghost would be true God: and this is contrary to what is said of the Son, "That ... we may be in His true Son. This is true God" (1 John 5:20). Of the Holy Ghost it is also said, "Know you not that your members are the temple of the Holy Ghost?" (1 Cor. 6:19). Now, to have a temple is God's prerogative. Others take this procession to mean the cause proceeding to the effect, as moving it, or impressing its own likeness on it; in which sense it was understood by Sabellius, who said that God the Father is called Son in assuming flesh from the Virgin, and that the Father also is called Holy Ghost in sanctifying the rational creature, and moving it to life. The words of the Lord contradict such a meaning, when He speaks of Himself, "The Son cannot of Himself do anything" (John 5:19); while many other passages show the same, whereby we know that the Father is not the Son. Careful examination shows that both of these opinions take procession as meaning an outward act; hence neither of them affirms procession as existing in God Himself; whereas, since procession always supposes action, and as there is an outward procession corresponding to the act tending to external matter, so there must be an inward procession corresponding to the act remaining within the agent. This applies most conspicuously to the intellect, the action of which remains in the intelligent agent. For whenever we understand, by the very fact of understanding there proceeds something within us, which is a conception of the object understood, a conception issuing from our intellectual power and proceeding from our knowledge of that object. This conception is signified by the spoken word; and it is called the word of the heart signified by the word of the voice.

As God is above all things, we should understand what is said of God, not according to the mode of the lowest creatures, namely bodies, but from the similitude of the highest creatures, the intellectual substances; while even the similitudes derived from these fall short in the representation of divine objects. Procession, therefore, is not to be understood from what it is in bodies, either according to local movement or by way of a cause proceeding forth to its exterior effect, as, for instance, like heat from the agent to the thing made hot. Rather it is to be understood by way of an intelligible emanation, for example, of the intelligible word which proceeds from the speaker, yet remains in him. In that sense the Catholic Faith understands procession as existing in God.

Reply Obj. 1: This objection comes from the idea of procession in the sense of local motion, or of an action tending to external matter, or to an exterior effect; which kind of procession does not exist in God, as we have explained.

Reply Obj. 2: Whatever proceeds by way of outward procession is necessarily distinct from the source whence it proceeds, whereas, whatever proceeds within by an intelligible procession is not necessarily distinct; indeed, the more perfectly it proceeds, the more closely it is one with the source whence it proceeds. For it is clear that the more a thing is understood, the more closely is the intellectual conception joined and united to the intelligent agent; since the intellect by the very act of understanding is made one with the object understood. Thus, as the divine intelligence is the very supreme perfection of God (Q. 14, A. 2), the divine Word is of necessity perfectly one with the source whence He proceeds, without any kind of diversity.

Reply Obj. 3: To proceed from a principle, so as to be something outside and distinct from that principle, is irreconcilable with the idea of a first principle; whereas an intimate and uniform procession by way of an intelligible act is included in the idea of a first principle. For when we call the builder the principle of the house, in the idea of such a principle is included that of his art; and it would be included in the idea of the first principle were the builder the first principle of the house. God, Who is the first principle of all things, may be compared to things created as the architect is to things designed.

SECOND ARTICLE [I, Q. 27, Art. 2]

Whether Any Procession in God Can Be Called Generation?

Objection 1: It would seem that no procession in God can be called generation. For generation is change from non-existence to existence, and is opposed to corruption; while matter is the subject of both. Nothing of all this belongs to God. Therefore generation cannot exist in God.

Obj. 2: Further, procession exists in God, according to an intelligible mode, as above explained (A. 1). But such a process is not called generation in us; therefore neither is it to be so called in God.

Obj. 3: Further, anything that is generated derives existence from its generator. Therefore such existence is a derived existence. But no derived existence can be a self-subsistence. Therefore, since the divine existence is self-subsisting (Q. 3, A. 4), it follows that no generated existence can be the divine existence. Therefore there is no generation in God.

*On the contrary,* It is said (Ps. 2:7): "This day have I begotten Thee."

*I answer that,* The procession of the Word in God is called generation. In proof whereof we must observe that generation has a twofold meaning: one common to everything subject to generation and corruption; in which sense generation is nothing but change from non-existence to existence. In another sense it is proper and belongs to living things; in which sense it signifies the origin of a living being from a conjoined living principle; and this is properly called birth. Not everything of that kind, however, is called begotten; but, strictly speaking, only what proceeds by way of similitude. Hence a hair has not the aspect of generation and sonship, but only that has which proceeds by way of a similitude. Nor will any likeness suffice; for a worm which is generated from animals has not the aspect of generation and sonship, although it has a generic similitude; for this kind of generation requires that there should be a procession by way of similitude in the same specific nature; as a man proceeds from a man, and a horse from a horse. So in living things, which proceed from potential to actual life, such as men and animals, generation includes both these kinds of generation. But if there is a being whose life does not proceed from potentiality to act, procession (if found in such a being) excludes entirely the first kind of generation; whereas it may have that kind of generation which belongs to living things. So in this manner the procession of the Word in God is generation; for He proceeds by way of intelligible action, which is a vital operation:—from a conjoined principle (as above described):—by way of similitude, inasmuch as the concept of the intellect is a likeness of the object conceived:—and exists in the same nature, because in God the act of understanding and His existence are the same, as shown above (Q. 14, A. 4). Hence the procession of the Word in God is called generation; and the Word Himself proceeding is called the Son.

Reply Obj. 1: This objection is based on the idea of generation in the first sense, importing the issuing forth from potentiality to act; in which sense it is not found in God.

Reply Obj. 2: The act of human understanding in ourselves is not the substance itself of the intellect; hence the word which proceeds within us by intelligible operation is not of the same nature as the source whence it proceeds; so the idea of generation cannot be properly and fully applied to it. But the divine act of intelligence is the very substance itself of the one who understands (Q. 14, A. 4). The Word proceeding therefore proceeds as subsisting in the same nature; and so is properly called begotten, and Son. Hence Scripture employs terms which denote generation of living things in order to signify the procession of the divine Wisdom, namely, conception and birth; as is declared in the person of the divine Wisdom, "The depths were not as yet, and I was already conceived; before the hills, I was brought forth." (Prov. 8:24). In our way of understanding we use the word "conception" in order to signify that in the word of our intellect is found the likeness of the thing understood, although there be no identity of nature.

Reply Obj. 3: Not everything derived from another has existence in another subject; otherwise we could not say that the whole substance of created being comes from God, since there is no subject that could receive the whole substance. So, then, what is generated in God receives its existence from the generator, not as though that existence were received into matter or into a subject (which would conflict with the divine self-subsistence); but when we speak of His existence as received, we mean that He Who proceeds receives divine existence from another; not, however, as if He were other from the divine nature. For in the perfection itself of the divine existence are contained both the Word intelligibly proceeding and the principle of the Word, with whatever belongs to His perfection (Q. 4, A. 2).

THIRD ARTICLE [I, Q. 27, Art. 3]

Whether Any Other Procession Exists in God Besides That of the Word?

Objection 1: It would seem that no other procession exists in God besides the generation of the Word. Because, for whatever reason we admit another procession, we should be led to admit yet another, and so on to infinitude; which cannot be. Therefore we must stop at the first, and hold that there exists only one procession in God.

Obj. 2: Further, every nature possesses but one mode of self-communication; because operations derive unity and diversity from their terms. But procession in God is only by way of communication of the divine nature. Therefore, as there is only one divine nature (Q. 11, A. 4), it follows that only one procession exists in God.

Obj. 3: Further, if any other procession but the intelligible procession of the Word existed in God, it could only be the procession of love, which is by the operation of the will. But such a procession is identified with the intelligible procession of the intellect, inasmuch as the will in God is the same as His intellect (Q. 19, A. 1). Therefore in God there is no other procession but the procession of the Word.

*On the contrary,* The Holy Ghost proceeds from the Father (John 15:26); and He is distinct from the Son, according to the words, "I will ask My Father, and He will give you another Paraclete" (John 14:16). Therefore in God another procession exists besides the procession of the Word.

*I answer that,* There are two processions in God; the procession of the Word, and another.

In evidence whereof we must observe that procession exists in God, only according to an action which does not tend to anything external, but remains in the agent itself. Such an action in an intellectual nature is that of the intellect, and of the will. The procession of the Word is by way of an intelligible operation. The operation of the will within ourselves involves also another procession, that of love, whereby the object loved is in the lover; as, by the conception of the word, the object spoken of or understood is in the intelligent agent. Hence, besides the procession of the Word in God, there exists in Him another procession called the procession of love.

Reply Obj. 1: There is no need to go on to infinitude in the divine processions; for the procession which is accomplished within the agent in an intellectual nature terminates in the procession of the will.

Reply Obj. 2: All that exists in God, is God (Q. 3, AA. 3, 4); whereas the same does not apply to others. Therefore the divine nature is communicated by every procession which is not outward, and this does not apply to other natures.

Reply Obj. 3: Though will and intellect are not diverse in God, nevertheless the nature of will and intellect requires the processions belonging to each of them to exist in a certain order. For the procession of love occurs in due order as regards the procession of the Word; since nothing can be loved by the will unless it is conceived in the intellect. So as there exists a certain order of the Word to the principle whence He proceeds, although in God the substance of the intellect and its concept are the same; so, although in God the will and the intellect are the same, still, inasmuch as love requires by its very nature that it proceed only from the concept of the intellect, there is a distinction of order between the procession of love and the procession of the Word in God.

FOURTH ARTICLE [I, Q. 27, Art. 4]

Whether the Procession of Love in God Is Generation?

Objection 1: It would seem that the procession of love in God is generation. For what proceeds by way of likeness of nature among living things is said to be generated and born. But what proceeds in God by way of love proceeds in the likeness of nature; otherwise it would be extraneous to the divine nature, and would be an external procession. Therefore what proceeds in God by way of love, proceeds as generated and born.

Obj. 2: Further, as similitude is of the nature of the word, so does it belong to love. Hence it is said, that "every beast loves its like" (Ecclus. 13:19). Therefore if the Word is begotten and born by way of likeness, it seems becoming that love should proceed by way of generation.

Obj. 3: Further, what is not in any species is not in the genus. So if there is a procession of love in God, there ought to be some special name besides this common name of procession. But no other name is applicable but generation. Therefore the procession of love in God is generation.

*On the contrary,* Were this true, it would follow that the Holy Ghost Who proceeds as love, would proceed as begotten; which is against the statement of Athanasius: "The Holy Ghost is from the Father and the Son, not made, nor begotten, but proceeding."

*I answer that,* The procession of love in God ought not to be called generation. In evidence whereof we must consider that the intellect and the will differ in this respect, that the intellect is made actual by the object understood residing according to its own likeness in the intellect; whereas the will is made actual, not by any similitude of the object willed within it, but by its having a certain inclination to the thing willed. Thus the procession of the intellect is by way of similitude, and is called generation, because every generator begets its own like; whereas the procession of the will is not by way of similitude, but rather by way of impulse and movement towards an object.

So what proceeds in God by way of love, does not proceed as begotten, or as son, but proceeds rather as spirit; which name expresses a certain vital movement and impulse, accordingly as anyone is described as moved or impelled by love to perform an action.

Reply Obj. 1: All that exists in God is one with the divine nature. Hence the proper notion of this or that procession, by which one procession is distinguished from another, cannot be on the part of this unity: but the proper notion of this or that procession must be taken from the order of one procession to another; which order is derived from the nature of the will and intellect. Hence, each procession in God takes its name from the proper notion of will and intellect; the name being imposed to signify what its nature really is; and so it is that the Person proceeding as love receives the divine nature, but is not said to be born.

Reply Obj. 2: Likeness belongs in a different way to the word and to love. It belongs to the word as being the likeness of the object understood, as the thing generated is the likeness of the generator; but it belongs to love, not as though love itself were a likeness, but because likeness is the principle of loving. Thus it does not follow that love is begotten, but that the one begotten is the principle of love.

Reply Obj. 3: We can name God only from creatures (Q. 13, A. 1). As in creatures generation is the only principle of communication of nature, procession in God has no proper or special name, except that of generation. Hence the procession which is not generation has remained without a special name; but it can be called spiration, as it is the procession of the Spirit.

FIFTH ARTICLE [I, Q. 27, Art. 5]

Whether There Are More Than Two Processions in God?

Objection 1: It would seem that there are more than two processions in God. As knowledge and will are attributed to God, so is power. Therefore, if two processions exist in God, of intellect and will, it seems that there must also be a third procession of power.

Obj. 2: Further, goodness seems to be the greatest principle of procession, since goodness is diffusive of itself. Therefore there must be a procession of goodness in God.

Obj. 3: Further, in God there is greater power of fecundity than in us. But in us there is not only one procession of the word, but there are many: for in us from one word proceeds another; and also from one love proceeds another. Therefore in God there are more than two processions.

*On the contrary,* In God there are not more than two who proceed—the Son and the Holy Ghost. Therefore there are in Him but two processions.

*I answer that,* The divine processions can be derived only from the actions which remain within the agent. In a nature which is intellectual, and in the divine nature these actions are two, the acts of intelligence and of will. The act of sensation, which also appears to be an operation within the agent, takes place outside the intellectual nature, nor can it be reckoned as wholly removed from the sphere of external actions; for the act of sensation is perfected by the action of the sensible object upon sense. It follows that no other procession is possible in God but the procession of the Word, and of Love.

Reply Obj. 1: Power is the principle whereby one thing acts on another. Hence it is that external action points to power. Thus the divine power does not imply the procession of a divine person; but is indicated by the procession therefrom of creatures.

Reply Obj. 2: As Boethius says (De Hebdom.), goodness belongs to the essence and not to the operation, unless considered as the object of the will.

Thus, as the divine processions must be denominated from certain actions; no other processions can be understood in God according to goodness and the like attributes except those of the Word and of love, according as God understands and loves His own essence, truth and goodness.

Reply Obj. 3: As above explained (Q. 14, A. 5; Q. 19, A. 5), God understands all things by one simple act; and by one act also He wills all things. Hence there cannot exist in Him a procession of Word from Word, nor of Love from Love: for there is in Him only one perfect Word, and one perfect Love; thereby being manifested His perfect fecundity.

## QUESTION 28

THE DIVINE RELATIONS (In Four Articles)

The divine relations are next to be considered, in four points of inquiry:

(1) Whether there are real relations in God?

(2) Whether those relations are the divine essence itself, or are extrinsic to it?

(3) Whether in God there can be several relations distinct from each other?

(4) The number of these relations.

FIRST ARTICLE [I, Q. 28, Art. 1]

Whether There Are Real Relations in God?

Objection 1: It would seem that there are no real relations in God. For Boethius says (De Trin. iv), "All possible predicaments used as regards the Godhead refer to the substance; for nothing can be predicated relatively." But whatever really exists in God can be predicated of Him. Therefore no real relation exists in God.

Obj. 2: Further, Boethius says (De Trin. iv) that, "Relation in the Trinity of the Father to the Son, and of both to the Holy Ghost, is the relation of the same to the same." But a relation of this kind is only a logical one; for every real relation requires and implies in reality two terms. Therefore the divine relations are not real relations, but are formed only by the mind.

Obj. 3: Further, the relation of paternity is the relation of a principle. But to say that God is the principle of creatures does not import any real relation, but only a logical one. Therefore paternity in God is not a real relation; while the same applies for the same reason to the other relations in God.

Obj. 4: Further, the divine generation proceeds by way of an intelligible word. But the relations following upon the operation of the intellect are logical relations. Therefore paternity and filiation in God, consequent upon generation, are only logical relations.

*On the contrary,* The Father is denominated only from paternity; and the Son only from filiation. Therefore, if no real paternity or filiation existed in God, it would follow that God is not really Father or Son, but only in our manner of understanding; and this is the Sabellian heresy.

*I answer that,* relations exist in God really; in proof whereof we may consider that in relations alone is found something which is only in the apprehension and not in reality. This is not found in any other genus; forasmuch as other genera, as quantity and quality, in their strict and proper meaning, signify something inherent in a subject. But relation in its own proper meaning signifies only what refers to another. Such regard to another exists sometimes in the nature of things, as in those things which by their own very nature are ordered to each other, and have a mutual inclination; and such relations are necessarily real relations; as in a heavy body is found an inclination and order to the centre; and hence there exists in the heavy body a certain respect in regard to the centre and the same applies to other things. Sometimes, however, this regard to another, signified by relation, is to be found only in the apprehension of reason comparing one thing to another, and this is a logical relation only; as, for instance, when reason compares man to animal as the species to the genus. But when something proceeds from a principle of the same nature, then both the one proceeding and the source of procession, agree in the same order; and then they have real relations to each other. Therefore as the divine processions are in the identity of the same nature, as above explained (Q. 27, AA. 2, 4), these relations, according to the divine processions, are necessarily real relations.

Reply Obj. 1: Relationship is not predicated of God according to its proper and formal meaning, that is to say, in so far as its proper meaning denotes comparison to that in which relation is inherent, but only as denoting regard to another. Nevertheless Boethius did not wish to exclude relation in God; but he wished to show that it was not to be predicated of Him as regards the mode of inherence in Himself in the strict meaning of relation; but rather by way of relation to another.

Reply Obj. 2: The relation signified by the term "the same" is a logical relation only, if in regard to absolutely the same thing; because such a relation can exist only in a certain order observed by reason as regards the order of anything to itself, according to some two aspects thereof. The case is otherwise, however, when things are called the same, not numerically, but generically or specifically. Thus Boethius likens the divine relations to a relation of identity, not in every respect, but only as regards the fact that the substance is not diversified by these relations, as neither is it by relation of identity.

Reply Obj. 3: As the creature proceeds from God in diversity of nature, God is outside the order of the whole creation, nor does any relation to the creature arise from His nature; for He does not produce the creature by necessity of His nature, but by His intellect and will, as is above explained (Q. 14, AA. 3, 4; Q. 19, A. 8). Therefore there is no real relation in God to the creature; whereas in creatures there is a real relation to God; because creatures are contained under the divine order, and their very nature entails dependence on God. On the other hand, the divine processions are in one and the same nature. Hence no parallel exists.

Reply Obj. 4: Relations which result from the mental operation alone in the objects understood are logical relations only, inasmuch as reason observes them as existing between two objects perceived by the mind. Those relations, however, which follow the operation of the intellect, and which exist between the word intellectually proceeding and the source whence it proceeds, are not logical relations only, but are real relations; inasmuch as the intellect and the reason are real things, and are really related to that which proceeds from them intelligibly; as a corporeal thing is related to that which proceeds from it corporeally. Thus paternity and filiation are real relations in God.

SECOND ARTICLE [I, Q. 28, Art. 2]

Whether Relation in God Is the Same As His Essence?

Objection 1: It would seem that the divine relation is not the same as the divine essence. For Augustine says (De Trin. v) that "not all that is said of God is said of His substance, for we say some things relatively, as Father in respect of the Son: but such things do not refer to the substance." Therefore the relation is not the divine essence.

Obj. 2: Further, Augustine says (De Trin. vii) that, "every relative expression is something besides the relation expressed, as master is a man, and slave is a man." Therefore, if relations exist in God, there must be something else besides relation in God. This can only be His essence. Therefore essence differs from relation.

Obj. 3: Further, the essence of relation is the being referred to another, as the Philosopher says (Praedic. v). So if relation is the divine essence, it follows that the divine essence is essentially itself a relation to something else; whereas this is repugnant to the perfection of the divine essence, which is supremely absolute and self-subsisting (Q. 3, A. 4). Therefore relation is not the divine essence.

*On the contrary,* Everything which is not the divine essence is a creature. But relation really belongs to God; and if it is not the divine essence, it is a creature; and it cannot claim the adoration of latria; contrary to what is sung in the Preface: "Let us adore the distinction of the Persons, and the equality of their Majesty."

*I answer that,* It is reported that Gilbert de la Porree erred on this point, but revoked his error later at the council of Rheims. For he said that the divine relations are assistant, or externally affixed.

To perceive the error here expressed, we must consider that in each of the nine genera of accidents there are two points for remark. One is the nature belonging to each one of them considered as an accident; which commonly applies to each of them as inherent in a subject, for the essence of an accident is to inhere. The other point of remark is the proper nature of each one of these genera. In the genera, apart from that of *relation,* as in quantity and quality, even the true idea of the genus itself is derived from a respect to the subject; for quantity is called the measure of substance, and quality is the disposition of substance. But the true idea of relation is not taken from its respect to that in which it is, but from its respect to something outside. So if we consider even in creatures, relations formally as such, in that aspect they are said to be "assistant," and not intrinsically affixed, for, in this way, they signify a respect which affects a thing related and tends from that thing to something else; whereas, if relation is considered as an accident, it inheres in a subject, and has an accidental existence in it. Gilbert de la Porree considered relation in the former mode only.

Now whatever has an accidental existence in creatures, when considered as transferred to God, has a substantial existence; for there is no accident in God; since all in Him is His essence. So, in so far as relation has an accidental existence in creatures, relation really existing in God has the existence of the divine essence in no way distinct therefrom. But in so far as relation implies respect to something else, no respect to the essence is signified, but rather to its opposite term.

Thus it is manifest that relation really existing in God is really the same as His essence and only differs in its mode of intelligibility; as in relation is meant that regard to its opposite which is not expressed in the name of essence. Thus it is clear that in God relation and essence do not differ from each other, but are one and the same.

Reply Obj. 1: These words of Augustine do not imply that paternity or any other relation which is in God is not in its very being the same as the divine essence; but that it is not predicated under the mode of substance, as existing in Him to Whom it is applied; but as a relation. So there are said to be two predicaments only in God, since other predicaments import habitude to that of which they are spoken, both in their generic and in their specific nature; but nothing that exists in God can have any relation to that wherein it exists or of whom it is spoken, except the relation of identity; and this by reason of God's supreme simplicity.

Reply Obj. 2: As the relation which exists in creatures involves not only a regard to another, but also something absolute, so the same applies to God, yet not in the same way. What is contained in the creature above and beyond what is contained in the meaning of relation, is something else besides that relation; whereas in God there is no distinction, but both are one and the same; and this is not perfectly expressed by the word "relation," as if it were comprehended in the ordinary meaning of that term. For it was above explained (Q. 13, A. 2), in treating of the divine names, that more is contained in the perfection of the divine essence than can be signified by any name. Hence it does not follow that there exists in God anything besides relation in reality; but only in the various names imposed by us.

Reply Obj. 3: If the divine perfection contained only what is signified by relative names, it would follow that it is imperfect, being thus related to something else; as in the same way, if nothing more were contained in it than what is signified by the word "wisdom," it would not in that case be a subsistence. But as the perfection of the divine essence is greater than can be included in any name, it does not follow, if a relative term or any other name applied to God signify something imperfect, that the divine essence is in any way imperfect; for the divine essence comprehends within itself the perfection of every genus (Q. 4, A. 2).

THIRD ARTICLE [I, Q. 28, Art. 3]

Whether the Relations in God Are Really Distinguished from Each Other?

Objection 1: It would seem that the divine relations are not really distinguished from each other. For things which are identified with the same, are identified with each other. But every relation in God is really the same as the divine essence. Therefore the relations are not really distinguished from each other.

Obj. 2: Further, as paternity and filiation are by name distinguished from the divine essence, so likewise are goodness and power. But this kind of distinction does not make any real distinction of the divine goodness and power. Therefore neither does it make any real distinction of paternity and filiation.

Obj. 3: Further, in God there is no real distinction but that of origin. But one relation does not seem to arise from another. Therefore the relations are not really distinguished from each other.

*On the contrary,* Boethius says (De Trin.) that in God "the substance contains the unity; and relation multiplies the trinity." Therefore, if the relations were not really distinguished from each other, there would be no real trinity in God, but only an ideal trinity, which is the error of Sabellius.

*I answer that,* The attributing of anything to another involves the attribution likewise of whatever is contained in it. So when "man" is attributed to anyone, a rational nature is likewise attributed to him. The idea of relation, however, necessarily means regard of one to another, according as one is relatively opposed to another. So as in God there is a real relation (A. 1), there must also be a real opposition. The very nature of relative opposition includes distinction. Hence, there must be real distinction in God, not, indeed, according to that which is absolute—namely, essence, wherein there is supreme unity and simplicity—but according to that which is relative.

Reply Obj. 1: According to the Philosopher (Phys. iii), this argument holds, that whatever things are identified with the same thing are identified with each other, if the identity be real and logical; as, for instance, a tunic and a garment; but not if they differ logically. Hence in the same place he says that although action is the same as motion, and likewise passion; still it does not follow that action and passion are the same; because action implies reference as of something "from which" there is motion in the thing moved; whereas passion implies reference as of something "which is from" another. Likewise, although paternity, just as filiation, is really the same as the divine essence; nevertheless these two in their own proper idea and definitions import opposite respects. Hence they are distinguished from each other.

Reply Obj. 2: Power and goodness do not import any opposition in their respective natures; and hence there is no parallel argument.

Reply Obj. 3: Although relations, properly speaking, do not arise or proceed from each other, nevertheless they are considered as opposed according to the procession of one from another.

FOURTH ARTICLE [I, Q. 28, Art. 3]

Whether in God There Are Only Four Real Relations—Paternity, Filiation, Spiration, and Procession?

Objection 1: It would seem that in God there are not only four real relations—paternity, filiation, spiration and procession. For it must be observed that in God there exist the relations of the intelligent agent to the object understood; and of the one willing to the object willed; which are real relations not comprised under those above specified. Therefore there are not only four real relations in God.

Obj. 2: Further, real relations in God are understood as coming from the intelligible procession of the Word. But intelligible relations are infinitely multiplied, as Avicenna says. Therefore in God there exists an infinite series of real relations.

Obj. 3: Further, ideas in God are eternal (Q. 15, A. 1); and are only distinguished from each other by reason of their regard to things, as above stated. Therefore in God there are many more eternal relations.

Obj. 4: Further, equality, and likeness, and identity are relations: and they are in God from eternity. Therefore several more relations are eternal in God than the above named.

Obj. 5: Further, it may also contrariwise be said that there are fewer relations in God than those above named. For, according to the Philosopher (Phys. iii text 24), "It is the same way from Athens to Thebes, as from Thebes to Athens." By the same way of reasoning there is the same relation from the Father to the Son, that of paternity, and from the Son to the Father, that of filiation; and thus there are not four relations in God.

*I answer that,* According to the Philosopher (Metaph. v), every relation is based either on quantity, as double and half; or on action and passion, as the doer and the deed, the father and the son, the master and the servant, and the like. Now as there is no quantity in God, for He is great without quantity, as Augustine says (De Trin. i, 1) it follows that a real relation in God can be based only on action. Such relations are not based on the actions of God according to any extrinsic procession, forasmuch as the relations of God to creatures are not real in Him (Q. 13, A. 7). Hence, it follows that real relations in God can be understood only in regard to those actions according to which there are internal, and not external, processions in God. These processions are two only, as above explained (Q. 27, A. 5), one derived from the action of the intellect, the procession of the Word; and the other from the action of the will, the procession of love. In respect of each of these processions two opposite relations arise; one of which is the relation of the person proceeding from the principle; the other is the relation of the principle Himself. The procession of the Word is called generation in the proper sense of the term, whereby it is applied to living things. Now the relation of the principle of generation in perfect living beings is called paternity; and the relation of the one proceeding from the principle is called filiation. But the procession of Love has no proper name of its own (Q. 27, A. 4); and so neither have the ensuing relations a proper name of their own. The relation of the principle of this procession is called spiration; and the relation of the person proceeding is called procession: although these two names belong to the processions or origins themselves, and not to the relations.

Reply Obj. 1: In those things in which there is a difference between the intellect and its object, and the will and its object, there can be a real relation, both of science to its object, and of the willer to the object willed. In God, however, the intellect and its object are one and the same; because by understanding Himself, God understands all other things; and the same applies to His will and the object that He wills. Hence it follows that in God these kinds of relations are not real; as neither is the relation of a thing to itself. Nevertheless, the relation to the word is a real relation; because the word is understood as proceeding by an intelligible action; and not as a thing understood. For when we understand a stone; that which the intellect conceives from the thing understood, is called the word.

Reply Obj. 2: Intelligible relations in ourselves are infinitely multiplied, because a man understands a stone by one act, and by another act understands that he understands the stone, and again by another, understands that he understands this; thus the acts of understanding are infinitely multiplied, and consequently also the relations understood. This does not apply to God, inasmuch as He understands all things by one act alone.

Reply Obj. 3: Ideal relations exist as understood by God. Hence it does not follow from their plurality that there are many relations in God; but that God knows these many relations.

Reply Obj. 4: Equality and similitude in God are not real relations; but are only logical relations (Q. 42, A. 3, ad 4).

Reply Obj. 5: The way from one term to another and conversely is the same; nevertheless the mutual relations are not the same. Hence, we cannot conclude that the relation of the father to the son is the same as that of the son to the father; but we could conclude this of something absolute, if there were such between them.

# QUESTION 29

THE DIVINE PERSONS (In Four Articles)

Having premised what have appeared necessary notions concerning the processions and the relations, we must now approach the subject of the persons.

First, we shall consider the persons absolutely, and then comparatively as regards each other. We must consider the persons absolutely first in common; and then singly.

The general consideration of the persons seemingly involves four points:

(1) The signification of this word "person";

(2) the number of the persons;

(3) what is involved in the number of persons, or is opposed thereto; as diversity, and similitude, and the like; and

(4) what belongs to our knowledge of the persons.

Four subjects of inquiry are comprised in the first point:

(1) The definition of "person."

(2) The comparison of person to essence, subsistence, and hypostasis.

(3) Whether the name of person is becoming to God?

(4) What does it signify in Him?

FIRST ARTICLE [I, Q. 29, Art. 1]

The Definition of "Person"

Objection 1: It would seem that the definition of person given by Boethius (De Duab. Nat.) is insufficient—that is, "a person is an individual substance of a rational nature." For nothing singular can be subject to definition. But "person" signifies something singular. Therefore person is improperly defined.

Obj. 2: Further, substance as placed above in the definition of person, is either first substance, or second substance. If it is the former, the word "individual" is superfluous, because first substance is individual substance; if it stands for second substance, the word "individual" is false, for there is contradiction of terms; since second substances are the genera or species. Therefore this definition is incorrect.

Obj. 3: Further, an intentional term must not be included in the definition of a thing. For to define a man as "a species of animal" would not be a correct definition; since man is the name of a thing, and species is a name of an intention. Therefore, since person is the name of a thing (for it signifies a substance of a rational nature), the word "individual" which is an intentional name comes improperly into the definition.

Obj. 4: Further, "Nature is the principle of motion and rest, in those things in which it is essentially, and not accidentally," as Aristotle says (Phys. ii). But person exists in things immovable, as in God, and in the angels. Therefore the word "nature" ought not to enter into the definition of person, but the word should rather be "essence."

Obj. 5: Further, the separated soul is an individual substance of the rational nature; but it is not a person. Therefore person is not properly defined as above.

*I answer that,* Although the universal and particular exist in every genus, nevertheless, in a certain special way, the individual belongs to the genus of substance. For substance is individualized by itself; whereas the accidents are individualized by the subject, which is the substance; since this particular whiteness is called "this," because it exists in this particular subject. And so it is reasonable that the individuals of the genus substance should have a special name of their own; for they are called "hypostases," or first substances.

Further still, in a more special and perfect way, the particular and the individual are found in the rational substances which have dominion over their own actions; and which are not only made to act, like others; but which can act of themselves; for actions belong to singulars. Therefore also the individuals of the rational nature have a special name even among other substances; and this name is "person."

Thus the term "individual substance" is placed in the definition of person, as signifying the singular in the genus of substance; and the term "rational nature" is added, as signifying the singular in rational substances.

Reply Obj. 1: Although this or that singular may not be definable, yet what belongs to the general idea of singularity can be defined; and so the Philosopher (De Praedic., cap. De substantia) gives a definition of first substance; and in this way Boethius defines person.

Reply Obj. 2: In the opinion of some, the term "substance" in the definition of person stands for first substance, which is the hypostasis; nor is the term "individual" superfluously added, forasmuch as by the name of hypostasis or first substance the idea of universality and of part is excluded. For we do not say that man in general is an hypostasis, nor that the hand is since it is only a part. But where "individual" is added, the idea of assumptibility is excluded from person; for the human nature in Christ is not a person, since it is assumed by a greater—that is, by the Word of God. It is, however, better to say that substance is here taken in a general sense, as divided into first and second, and when "individual" is added, it is restricted to first substance.

Reply Obj. 3: Substantial differences being unknown to us, or at least unnamed by us, it is sometimes necessary to use accidental differences in the place of substantial; as, for example, we may say that fire is a simple, hot, and dry body: for proper accidents are the effects of substantial forms, and make them known. Likewise, terms expressive of intention can be used in defining realities if used to signify things which are unnamed. And so the term "individual" is placed in the definition of person to signify the mode of subsistence which belongs to particular substances.

Reply Obj. 4: According to the Philosopher (Metaph. v, 5), the word "nature" was first used to signify the generation of living things, which is called nativity. And because this kind of generation comes from an intrinsic principle, this term is extended to signify the intrinsic principle of any kind of movement. In this sense he defines "nature" (Phys. ii, 3). And since this kind of principle is either formal or material, both matter and form are commonly called nature. And as the essence of anything is completed by the form; so the essence of anything, signified by the definition, is commonly called nature. And here nature is taken in that sense. Hence Boethius says (De Duab. Nat.) that, "nature is the specific difference giving its form to each thing," for the specific difference completes the definition, and is derived from the special form of a thing. So in the definition of "person," which means the singular in a determined genus, it is more correct to use the term "nature" than "essence," because the latter is taken from being, which is most common.

Reply Obj. 5: The soul is a part of the human species; and so, although it may exist in a separate state, yet since it ever retains its nature of unibility, it cannot be called an individual substance, which is the hypostasis or first substance, as neither can the hand nor any other part of man; thus neither the definition nor the name of person belongs to it.

SECOND ARTICLE [I, Q. 29, Art. 2]

Whether "Person" Is the Same As Hypostasis, Subsistence, and Essence?

Objection 1: It would seem that "person" is the same as "hypostasis," "subsistence," and "essence." For Boethius says (De Duab. Nat.) that "the Greeks called the individual substance of the rational nature by the name hypostasis." But this with us signifies "person." Therefore "person" is altogether the same as "hypostasis."

Obj. 2: Further, as we say there are three persons in God, so we say there are three subsistences in God; which implies that "person" and "subsistence" have the same meaning. Therefore "person" and "subsistence" mean the same.

Obj. 3: Further, Boethius says (Com. Praed.) that the Greek *ousia,* which means essence, signifies a being composed of matter and form. Now that which is composed of matter and form is the individual substance called "hypostasis" and "person."

Therefore all the aforesaid names seem to have the same meaning.

Obj. 4: *On the contrary,* Boethius says (De Duab. Nat.) that genera and species only subsist; whereas individuals are not only subsistent, but also substand. But subsistences are so called from subsisting, as substance or hypostasis is so called from substanding. Therefore, since genera and species are not hypostases or persons, these are not the same as subsistences.

Obj. 5: Further, Boethius says (Com. Praed.) that matter is called hypostasis, and form is called *ousiosis* —that is, subsistence. But neither form nor matter can be called person. Therefore person differs from the others.

*I answer that,* According to the Philosopher (Metaph. v), substance is twofold. In one sense it means the quiddity of a thing, signified by its definition, and thus we say that the definition means the substance of a thing; in which sense substance is called by the Greeks *ousia,* what we may call "essence." In another sense substance means a subject or *suppositum,* which subsists in the genus of substance. To this, taken in a general sense, can be applied a name expressive of an intention; and thus it is called *suppositum.* It is also called by three names signifying a reality—that is, "a thing of nature," "subsistence," and "hypostasis," according to a threefold consideration of the substance thus named. For, as it exists in itself and not in another, it is called "subsistence"; as we say that those things subsist which exist in themselves, and not in another. As it underlies some common nature, it is called "a thing of nature"; as, for instance, this particular man is a human natural thing. As it underlies the accidents, it is called "hypostasis," or "substance." What these three names signify in common to the whole genus of substances, this name "person" signifies in the genus of rational substances.

Reply Obj. 1: Among the Greeks the term "hypostasis," taken in the strict interpretation of the word, signifies any individual of the genus substance; but in the usual way of speaking, it means the individual of the rational nature, by reason of the excellence of that nature.

Reply Obj. 2: As we say "three persons" plurally in God, and "three subsistences," so the Greeks say "three hypostases." But because the word "substance," which, properly speaking, corresponds in meaning to "hypostasis," is used among us in an equivocal sense, since it sometimes means essence, and sometimes means hypostasis, in order to avoid any occasion of error, it was thought preferable to use "subsistence" for hypostasis, rather than "substance."

Reply Obj. 3: Strictly speaking, the essence is what is expressed by the definition. Now, the definition comprises the principles of the species, but not the individual principles. Hence in things composed of matter and form, the essence signifies not only the form, nor only the matter, but what is composed of matter and the common form, as the principles of the species. But what is composed of this matter and this form has the nature of hypostasis and person. For soul, flesh, and bone belong to the nature of man; whereas this soul, this flesh and this bone belong to the nature of this man. Therefore hypostasis and person add the individual principles to the idea of essence; nor are these identified with the essence in things composed of matter and form, as we said above when treating of divine simplicity (Q. 3, A. 3).

Reply Obj. 4: Boethius says that genera and species subsist, inasmuch as it belongs to some individual things to subsist, from the fact that they belong to genera and species comprised in the predicament of substance, but not because the species and genera themselves subsist; except in the opinion of Plato, who asserted that the species of things subsisted separately from singular things. To substand, however, belongs to the same individual things in relation to the accidents, which are outside the essence of genera and species.

Reply Obj. 5: The individual composed of matter and form substands in relation to accident from the very nature of matter. Hence Boethius says (De Trin.): "A simple form cannot be a subject." Its self-subsistence is derived from the nature of its form, which does not supervene to the things subsisting, but gives actual existence to the matter and makes it subsist as an individual. On this account, therefore, he ascribes hypostasis to matter, and *ousiosis,* or subsistence, to the form, because the matter is the principle of substanding, and form is the principle of subsisting.

THIRD ARTICLE [I, Q. 29, Art. 3]

Whether the Word "Person" Should Be Said of God?

Objection 1: It would seem that the name "person" should not be said of God. For Dionysius says (Div. Nom.): "No one should ever dare to say or think anything of the supersubstantial and hidden Divinity, beyond what has been divinely expressed to us by the oracles." But the name "person" is not expressed to us in the Old or New Testament. Therefore "person" is not to be applied to God.

Obj. 2: Further, Boethius says (De Duab. Nat.): "The word person seems to be taken from those persons who represented men in comedies and tragedies. For person comes from sounding through [personando], since a greater volume of sound is produced through the cavity in the mask. These "persons" or masks the Greeks called *prosopa,* as they were placed on the face and covered the features before the eyes." This, however, can apply to God only in a metaphorical sense. Therefore the word "person" is only applied to God metaphorically.

Obj. 3: Further, every person is a hypostasis. But the word "hypostasis" does not apply to God, since, as Boethius says (De Duab. Nat.), it signifies what is the subject of accidents, which do not exist in God. Jerome also says (Ep. ad Damas.) that, "in this word hypostasis, poison lurks in honey." Therefore the word "person" should not be said of God.

Obj. 4: Further, if a definition is denied of anything, the thing defined is also denied of it. But the definition of "person," as given above, does not apply to God. Both because reason implies a discursive knowledge, which does not apply to God, as we proved above (Q. 14, A. 12); and thus God cannot be said to have "a rational nature." And also because God cannot be called an individual substance, since the principle of individuation is matter; while God is immaterial: nor is He the subject of accidents, so as to be called a substance. Therefore the word "person" ought not to be attributed to God.

*On the contrary,* In the Creed of Athanasius we say: "One is the person of the Father, another of the Son, another of the Holy Ghost."

*I answer that,* "Person" signifies what is most perfect in all nature—that is, a subsistent individual of a rational nature. Hence, since everything that is perfect must be attributed to God, forasmuch as His essence contains every perfection, this name "person" is fittingly applied to God; not, however, as it is applied to creatures, but in a more excellent way; as other names also, which, while giving them to creatures, we attribute to God; as we showed above when treating of the names of God (Q. 13, A. 2).

Reply Obj. 1: Although the word "person" is not found applied to God in Scripture, either in the Old or New Testament, nevertheless what the word signifies is found to be affirmed of God in many places of Scripture; as that He is the supreme self-subsisting being, and the most perfectly intelligent being. If we could speak of God only in the very terms themselves of Scripture, it would follow that no one could speak about God in any but the original language of the Old or New Testament. The urgency of confuting heretics made it necessary to find new words to express the ancient faith about God. Nor is such a kind of novelty to be shunned; since it is by no means profane, for it does not lead us astray from the sense of Scripture. The Apostle warns us to avoid "profane novelties of words" (1 Tim. 6:20).

Reply Obj. 2: Although this name "person" may not belong to God as regards the origin of the term, nevertheless it excellently belongs to God in its objective meaning. For as famous men were represented in comedies and tragedies, the name "person" was given to signify those who held high dignity. Hence, those who held high rank in the Church came to be called "persons." Thence by some the definition of person is given as "hypostasis distinct by reason of dignity." And because subsistence in a rational nature is of high dignity, therefore every individual of the rational nature is called a "person." Now the dignity of the divine nature excels every other dignity; and thus the name "person" pre-eminently belongs to God.

Reply Obj. 3: The word "hypostasis" does not apply to God as regards its source of origin, since He does not underlie accidents; but it applies to Him in its objective sense, for it is imposed to signify the subsistence. Jerome said that "poison lurks in this word," forasmuch as before it was fully understood by the Latins, the heretics used this term to deceive the simple, to make people profess many essences as they profess several hypostases, inasmuch as the word "substance," which corresponds to hypostasis in Greek, is commonly taken amongst us to mean essence.

Reply Obj. 4: It may be said that God has a rational *nature,* if reason be taken to mean, not discursive thought, but in a general sense, an intelligent nature. But God cannot be called an "individual" in the sense that His individuality comes from matter; but only in the sense which implies incommunicability. "Substance" can be applied to God in the sense of signifying self-subsistence. There are some, however, who say that the definition of Boethius, quoted above (A. 1), is not a definition of person in the sense we use when speaking of persons in God. Therefore Richard of St. Victor amends this definition by adding that "Person" in God is "the incommunicable existence of the divine nature."

FOURTH ARTICLE [I, Q. 29, Art. 4]

Whether This Word "Person" Signifies Relation?

Objection 1: It would seem that this word "person," as applied to God, does not signify relation, but substance. For Augustine says (De Trin. vii, 6): "When we speak of the person of the Father, we mean nothing else but the substance of the Father, for person is said in regard to Himself, and not in regard to the Son."

Obj. 2: Further, the interrogation "What?" refers to essence. But, as Augustine says: "When we say there are three who bear witness in heaven, the Father, the Word, and the Holy Ghost, and it is asked, Three what? the answer is, Three persons." Therefore person signifies essence.

Obj. 3: According to the Philosopher (Metaph. iv), the meaning of a word is its definition. But the definition of "person" is this: "The individual substance of the rational nature," as above stated. Therefore "person" signifies substance.

Obj. 4: Further, person in men and angels does not signify relation, but something absolute. Therefore, if in God it signified relation, it would bear an equivocal meaning in God, in man, and in angels.

*On the contrary,* Boethius says (De Trin.) that "every word that refers to the persons signifies relation." But no word belongs to person more strictly than the very word "person" itself. Therefore this word "person" signifies relation.

*I answer that,* A difficulty arises concerning the meaning of this word "person" in God, from the fact that it is predicated plurally of the Three in contrast to the nature of the names belonging to the essence; nor does it in itself refer to another, as do the words which express relation.

Hence some have thought that this word "person" of itself expresses absolutely the divine essence; as this name "God" and this word "Wise"; but that to meet heretical attack, it was ordained by conciliar decree that it was to be taken in a relative sense, and especially in the plural, or with the addition of a distinguishing adjective; as when we say, "Three persons," or, "one is the person of the Father, another of the Son," etc. Used, however, in the singular, it may be either absolute or relative. But this does not seem to be a satisfactory explanation; for, if this word "person," by force of its own signification, expresses the divine essence only, it follows that forasmuch as we speak of "three persons," so far from the heretics being silenced, they had still more reason to argue. Seeing this, others maintained that this word "person" in God signifies both the essence and the relation. Some of these said that it signifies directly the essence, and relation indirectly, forasmuch as "person" means as it were "by itself one" [per se una]; and unity belongs to the essence. And what is "by itself" implies relation indirectly; for the Father is understood to exist "by Himself," as relatively distinct from the Son. Others, however, said, *on the contrary,* that it signifies relation directly; and essence indirectly; forasmuch as in the definition of "person" the term nature is mentioned indirectly; and these come nearer to the truth.

To determine the question, we must consider that something may be included in the meaning of a less common term, which is not included in the more common term; as "rational" is included in the meaning of "man," and not in the meaning of "animal." So that it is one thing to ask the meaning of the word animal, and another to ask its meaning when the animal in question is man. Also, it is one thing to ask the meaning of this word "person" in general; and another to ask the meaning of "person" as applied to God. For "person" in general signifies the individual substance of a rational figure. The individual in itself is undivided, but is distinct from others. Therefore "person" in any nature signifies what is distinct in that nature: thus in human nature it signifies this flesh, these bones, and this soul, which are the individuating principles of a man, and which, though not belonging to "person" in general, nevertheless do belong to the meaning of a particular human person.

Now distinction in God is only by relation of origin, as stated above (Q. 28, AA. 2, 3), while relation in God is not as an accident in a subject, but is the divine essence itself; and so it is subsistent, for the divine essence subsists. Therefore, as the Godhead is God so the divine paternity is God the Father, Who is a divine person. Therefore a divine person signifies a relation as subsisting. And this is to signify relation by way of substance, and such a relation is a hypostasis subsisting in the divine nature, although in truth that which subsists in the divine nature is the divine nature itself. Thus it is true to say that the name "person" signifies relation directly, and the essence indirectly; not, however, the relation as such, but as expressed by way of a hypostasis. So likewise it signifies directly the essence, and indirectly the relation, inasmuch as the essence is the same as the hypostasis: while in God the hypostasis is expressed as distinct by the relation: and thus relation, as such, enters into the notion of the person indirectly. Thus we can say that this signification of the word "person" was not clearly perceived before it was attacked by heretics. Hence, this word "person" was used just as any other absolute term. But afterwards it was applied to express relation, as it lent itself to that signification, so that this word "person" means relation not only by use and custom, according to the first opinion, but also by force of its own proper signification.

Reply Obj. 1: This word "person" is said in respect to itself, not to another; forasmuch as it signifies relation not as such, but by way of a substance—which is a hypostasis. In that sense Augustine says that it signifies the essence, inasmuch as in God essence is the same as the hypostasis, because in God what He is, and whereby He is are the same.

Reply Obj. 2: The term "what" refers sometimes to the nature expressed by the definition, as when we ask; What is man? and we answer: A mortal rational animal. Sometimes it refers to the *suppositum,* as when we ask, What swims in the sea? and answer, A fish. So to those who ask, Three what? we answer, Three persons.

Reply Obj. 3: In God the individual—i.e. distinct and incommunicable substance—includes the idea of relation, as above explained.

Reply Obj. 4: The different sense of the less common term does not produce equivocation in the more common. Although a horse and an ass have their own proper definitions, nevertheless they agree univocally in animal, because the common definition of animal applies to both. So it does not follow that, although relation is contained in the signification of divine person, but not in that of an angelic or of a human person, the word "person" is used in an equivocal sense. Though neither is it applied univocally, since nothing can be said univocally of God and creatures (Q. 13, A. 5).

## QUESTION 30

THE PLURALITY OF PERSONS IN GOD (In Four Articles)

We are now led to consider the plurality of the persons: about which there are four points of inquiry:

(1) Whether there are several persons in God?

(2) How many are they?

(3) What the numeral terms signify in God?

(4) The community of the term "person."

FIRST ARTICLE [I, Q. 30, Art. 1]

Whether There Are Several Persons in God?

Objection 1: It would seem that there are not several persons in God. For person is "the individual substance of a rational nature." If then there are several persons in God, there must be several substances; which appears to be heretical.

Obj. 2: Further, Plurality of absolute properties does not make a distinction of persons, either in God, or in ourselves. Much less therefore is this effected by a plurality of relations. But in God there is no plurality but of relations (Q. 28, A. 3). Therefore there cannot be several persons in God.

Obj. 3: Further, Boethius says of God (De Trin. i), that "this is truly one which has no number." But plurality implies number. Therefore there are not several persons in God.

Obj. 4: Further, where number is, there is whole and part. Thus, if in God there exist a number of persons, there must be whole and part in God; which is inconsistent with the divine simplicity.

*On the contrary,* Athanasius says: "One is the person of the Father, another of the Son, another of the Holy Ghost." Therefore the Father, and the Son, and the Holy Ghost are several persons.

*I answer that,* It follows from what precedes that there are several persons in God. For it was shown above (Q. 29, A. 4) that this word "person" signifies in God a relation as subsisting in the divine nature. It was also established (Q. 28, A. 1) that there are several real relations in God; and hence it follows that there are also several realities subsistent in the divine nature; which means that there are several persons in God.

Reply Obj. 1: The definition of "person" includes "substance," not as meaning the essence, but the *suppositum* which is made clear by the addition of the term "individual." To signify the substance thus understood, the Greeks use the name "hypostasis." So, as we say, "Three persons," they say "Three hypostases." We are not, however, accustomed to say Three substances, lest we be understood to mean three essences or natures, by reason of the equivocal signification of the term.

Reply Obj. 2: The absolute properties in God, such as goodness and wisdom, are not mutually opposed; and hence, neither are they really distinguished from each other. Therefore, although they subsist, nevertheless they are not several subsistent realities—that is, several persons. But the absolute properties in creatures do not subsist, although they are really distinguished from each other, as whiteness and sweetness; on the other hand, the relative properties in God subsist, and are really distinguished from each other (Q. 28, A. 3). Hence the plurality of persons in God.

Reply Obj. 3: The supreme unity and simplicity of God exclude every kind of plurality of absolute things, but not plurality of relations. Because relations are predicated relatively, and thus the relations do not import composition in that of which they are predicated, as Boethius teaches in the same book.

Reply Obj. 4: Number is twofold, simple or absolute, as two and three and four; and number as existing in things numbered, as two men and two horses. So, if number in God is taken absolutely or abstractedly, there is nothing to prevent whole and part from being in Him, and thus number in Him is only in our way of understanding; forasmuch as number regarded apart from things numbered exists only in the intellect. But if number be taken as it is in the things numbered, in that sense as existing in creatures, one is part of two, and two of three, as one man is part of two men, and two of three; but this does not apply to God, because the Father is of the same magnitude as the whole Trinity, as we shall show further on (Q. 42, AA. 1, 4).

SECOND ARTICLE [I, Q. 30, Art. 2]

Whether There Are More Than Three Persons in God?

Objection 1: It would seem that there are more than three persons in God. For the plurality of persons in God arises from the plurality of the relative properties as stated above (A. 1). But there are four relations in God as stated above (Q. 28, A. 4), paternity, filiation, common spiration, and procession. Therefore there are four persons in God.

Obj. 2: The nature of God does not differ from His will more than from His intellect. But in God, one person proceeds from the will, as love; and another proceeds from His nature, as Son. Therefore another proceeds from His intellect, as Word, besides the one Who proceeds from His nature, as Son; thus again it follows that there are not only three persons in God.

Obj. 3: Further, the more perfect a creature is, the more interior operations it has; as a man has understanding and will beyond other animals. But God infinitely excels every creature. Therefore in God not only is there a person proceeding from the will, and another from the intellect, but also in an infinite number of ways. Therefore there are an infinite number of persons in God.

Obj. 4: Further, it is from the infinite goodness of the Father that He communicates Himself infinitely in the production of a divine person. But also in the Holy Ghost is infinite goodness. Therefore the Holy Ghost produces a divine person; and that person another; and so to infinity.

Obj. 5: Further, everything within a determinate number is measured, for number is a measure. But the divine persons are immense, as we say in the Creed of Athanasius: "The Father is immense, the Son is immense, the Holy Ghost is immense." Therefore the persons are not contained within the number three.

*On the contrary,* It is said: "There are three who bear witness in heaven, the Father, the Word, and the Holy Ghost" (1 John 5:7). To those who ask, "Three what?" we answer, with Augustine (De Trin. vii, 4), "Three persons." Therefore there are but three persons in God.

*I answer that,* As was explained above, there can be only three persons in God. For it was shown above that the several persons are the several subsisting relations really distinct from each other. But a real distinction between the divine relations can come only from relative opposition. Therefore two opposite relations must needs refer to two persons: and if any relations are not opposite they must needs belong to the same person. Since then paternity and filiation are opposite relations, they belong necessarily to two persons. Therefore the subsisting paternity is the person of the Father; and the subsisting filiation is the person of the Son. The other two relations are not opposed to each other; therefore these two cannot belong to one person: hence either one of them must belong to both of the aforesaid persons; or one must belong to one person, and the other to the other. Now, procession cannot belong to the Father and the Son, or to either of them; for thus it would follows that the procession of the intellect, which in God is generation, wherefrom paternity and filiation are derived, would issue from the procession of love, whence spiration and procession are derived, if the person generating and the person generated proceeded from the person spirating; and this is against what was laid down above (Q. 27, AA. 3, 4). We must consequently admit that spiration belongs to the person of the Father, and to the person of the Son, forasmuch as it has no relative opposition either to paternity or to filiation; and consequently that procession belongs to the other person who is called the person of the Holy Ghost, who proceeds by way of love, as above explained. Therefore only three persons exist in God, the Father, the Son, and the Holy Ghost.

Reply Obj. 1: Although there are four relations in God, one of them, spiration, is not separated from the person of the Father and of the Son, but belongs to both; thus, although it is a relation, it is not called a property, because it does not belong to only one person; nor is it a personal relation—i.e. constituting a person. The three relations—paternity, filiation, and procession—are called personal properties, constituting as it were the persons; for paternity is the person of the Father, filiation is the person of the Son, procession is the person of the Holy Ghost proceeding.

Reply Obj. 2: That which proceeds by way of intelligence, as word, proceeds according to similitude, as also that which proceeds by way of nature; thus, as above explained (Q. 27, A. 3), the procession of the divine Word is the very same as generation by way of nature. But love, as such, does not proceed as the similitude of that whence it proceeds; although in God love is co-essential as being divine; and therefore the procession of love is not called generation in God.

Reply Obj. 3: As man is more perfect than other animals, he has more intrinsic operations than other animals, because his perfection is something composite. Hence the angels, who are more perfect and more simple, have fewer intrinsic operations than man, for they have no imagination, or feeling, or the like. In God there exists only one real operation—that is, His essence. How there are in Him two processions was above explained (Q. 27, AA. 1, 4).

Reply Obj. 4: This argument would prove if the Holy Ghost possessed another goodness apart from the goodness of the Father; for then if the Father produced a divine person by His goodness, the Holy Ghost also would do so. But the Father and the Holy Ghost have one and the same goodness. Nor is there any distinction between them except by the personal relations. So goodness belongs to the Holy Ghost, as derived from another; and it belongs to the Father, as the principle of its communication to another. The opposition of relation does not allow the relation of the Holy Ghost to be joined with the relation of principle of another divine person; because He Himself proceeds from the other persons who are in God.

Reply Obj. 5: A determinate number, if taken as a simple number, existing in the mind only, is measured by one. But when we speak of a number of things as applied to the persons in God, the notion of measure has no place, because the magnitude of the three persons is the same (Q. 42, AA. 1, 4), and the same is not measured by the same.

THIRD ARTICLE [I, Q. 30, Art. 3]

Whether the Numeral Terms Denote Anything Real in God?

Objection 1: It would seem that the numeral terms denote something real in God. For the divine unity is the divine essence. But every number is unity repeated. Therefore every numeral term in God signifies the essence; and therefore it denotes something real in God.

Obj. 2: Further, whatever is said of God and of creatures, belongs to God in a more eminent manner than to creatures. But the numeral terms denote something real in creatures; therefore much more so in God.

Obj. 3: Further, if the numeral terms do not denote anything real in God, and are introduced simply in a negative and removing sense, as plurality is employed to remove unity, and unity to remove plurality; it follows that a vicious circle results, confusing the mind and obscuring the truth; and this ought not to be. Therefore it must be said that the numeral terms denote something real in God.

*On the contrary,* Hilary says (De Trin. iv): "If we admit companionship"—that is, plurality—"we exclude the idea of oneness and of solitude;" and Ambrose says (De Fide i): "When we say one God, unity excludes plurality of gods, and does not imply quantity in God." Hence we see that these terms are applied to God in order to remove something; and not to denote anything positive.

*I answer that,* The Master (Sent. i, D, 24) considers that the numeral terms do not denote anything positive in God, but have only a negative meaning. Others, however, assert the contrary.

In order to resolve this point, we may observe that all plurality is a consequence of division. Now division is twofold; one is material, and is division of the continuous; from this results number, which is a species of quantity. Number in this sense is found only in material things which have quantity. The other kind of division is called formal, and is effected by opposite or diverse forms; and this kind of division results in a multitude, which does not belong to a genus, but is transcendental in the sense in which being is divided by one and by many. This kind of multitude is found only in immaterial things.

Some, considering only that multitude which is a species of discrete quantity, and seeing that such kind of quantity has no place in God, asserted that the numeral terms do not denote anything real in God, but remove something from Him. Others, considering the same kind of multitude, said that as knowledge exists in God according to the strict sense of the word, but not in the sense of its genus (as in God there is no such thing as a quality), so number exists in God in the proper sense of number, but not in the sense of its genus, which is quantity.

But we say that numeral terms predicated of God are not derived from number, a species of quantity, for in that sense they could bear only a metaphorical sense in God, like other corporeal properties, such as length, breadth, and the like; but that they are taken from multitude in a transcendent sense. Now multitude so understood has relation to the many of which it is predicated, as "one" convertible with "being" is related to being; which kind of oneness does not add anything to being, except a negation of division, as we saw when treating of the divine unity (Q. 11, A. 1); for "one" signifies undivided being. So, of whatever we say "one," we imply its undivided reality: thus, for instance, "one" applied to man signifies the undivided nature or substance of a man. In the same way, when we speak of many things, multitude in this latter sense points to those things as being each undivided in itself.

But number, if taken as a species of quantity, denotes an accident added to being; as also does "one" which is the principle of that number. Therefore the numeral terms in God signify the things of which they are said, and beyond this they add negation only, as stated (Sent. i, D, 24); in which respect the Master was right (Sent. i, D, 24). So when we say, the essence is one, the term "one" signifies the essence undivided; and when we say the person is one, it signifies the person undivided; and when we say the persons are many, we signify those persons, and their individual undividedness; for it is of the very nature of multitude that it should be composed of units.

Reply Obj. 1: One, as it is a transcendental, is wider and more general than substance and relation. And so likewise is multitude; hence in God it may mean both substance and relation, according to the context. Still, the very signification of such names adds a negation of division, beyond substance and relation; as was explained above.

Reply Obj. 2: Multitude, which denotes something real in creatures, is a species of quantity, and cannot be used when speaking of God: unlike transcendental multitude, which adds only indivision to those of which it is predicated. Such a kind of multitude is applicable to God.

Reply Obj. 3: "One" does not exclude multitude, but division, which logically precedes one or multitude. Multitude does not remove unity, but division from each of the individuals which compose the multitude. This was explained when we treated of the divine unity (Q. 11, A. 2).

It must be observed, nevertheless, that the opposite arguments do not sufficiently prove the point advanced. Although the idea of solitude is excluded by plurality, and the plurality of gods by unity, it does not follow that these terms express this signification alone. For blackness is excluded by whiteness; nevertheless, the term whiteness does not signify the mere exclusion of blackness.

FOURTH ARTICLE [I, Q. 30, Art. 4]

Whether This Term "Person" Can Be Common to the Three Persons?

Objection 1: It would seem that this term "person" cannot be common to the three persons. For nothing is common to the three persons but the essence. But this term "person" does not signify the essence directly. Therefore it is not common to all three.

Obj. 2: Further, the common is the opposite to the incommunicable. But the very meaning of person is that it is incommunicable; as appears from the definition given by Richard of St. Victor (Q. 29, A. 3, ad 4). Therefore this term "person" is not common to all the three persons.

Obj. 3: Further, if the name "person" is common to the three, it is common either really, or logically. But it is not so really; otherwise the three persons would be one person; nor again is it so logically; otherwise person would be a universal. But in God there is neither universal nor particular; neither genus nor species, as we proved above (Q. 3, A. 5). Therefore this term 'person' is not common to the three.

*On the contrary,* Augustine says (De Trin. vii, 4) that when we ask, "Three what?" we say, "Three persons," because what a person is, is common to them.

*I answer that,* The very mode of expression itself shows that this term "person" is common to the three when we say "three persons"; for when we say "three men" we show that "man" is common to the three. Now it is clear that this is not community of a real thing, as if one essence were common to the three; otherwise there would be only one person of the three, as also one essence.

What is meant by such a community has been variously determined by those who have examined the subject. Some have called it a community of exclusion, forasmuch as the definition of "person" contains the word "incommunicable." Others thought it to be a community of intention, as the definition of person contains the word "individual"; as we say that to be a species is common to horse and ox. Both of these explanations, however, are excluded by the fact that "person" is not a name of exclusion nor of intention, but the name of a reality. We must therefore resolve that even in human affairs this name "person" is common by a community of idea, not as genus or species, but as a vague individual thing. The names of genera and species, as man or animal, are given to signify the common natures themselves, but not the intentions of those common natures, signified by the terms genus or species. The vague individual thing, as "some man," signifies the common nature with the determinate mode of existence of singular things—that is, something self-subsisting, as distinct from others. But the name of a designated singular thing signifies that which distinguishes the determinate thing; as the name Socrates signifies this flesh and this bone. But there is this difference—that the term "some man" signifies the nature, or the individual on the part of its nature, with the mode of existence of singular things; while this name "person" is not given to signify the individual on the part of the nature, but the subsistent reality in that nature. Now this is common in idea to the divine persons, that each of them subsists distinctly from the others in the divine nature. Thus this name "person" is common in idea to the three divine persons.

Reply Obj. 1: This argument is founded on a real community.

Reply Obj. 2: Although person is incommunicable, yet the mode itself of incommunicable existence can be common to many.

Reply Obj. 3: Although this community is logical and not real, yet it does not follow that in God there is universal or particular, or genus, or species; both because neither in human affairs is the community of person the same as community of genus or species; and because the divine persons have one being; whereas genus and species and every other universal are predicated of many which differ in being.

## QUESTION 31

OF WHAT BELONGS TO THE UNITY OR PLURALITY IN GOD (In Four Articles)

We now consider what belongs to the unity or plurality in God; which gives rise to four points of inquiry:

(1) Concerning the word "Trinity";

(2) Whether we can say that the Son is other than the Father?

(3) Whether an exclusive term, which seems to exclude otherness, can be joined to an essential name in God?

(4) Whether it can be joined to a personal term?

FIRST ARTICLE [I, Q. 31, Art. 1]

Whether There Is Trinity in God?

Objection 1: It would seem there is not trinity in God. For every name in God signifies substance or relation. But this name "Trinity" does not signify the substance; otherwise it would be predicated of each one of the persons: nor does it signify relation; for it does not express a name that refers to another. Therefore the word "Trinity" is not to be applied to God.

Obj. 2: Further, this word "trinity" is a collective term, since it signifies multitude. But such a word does not apply to God; as the unity of a collective name is the least of unities, whereas in God there exists the greatest possible unity. Therefore this word "trinity" does not apply to God.

Obj. 3: Further, every trine is threefold. But in God there is not triplicity; since triplicity is a kind of inequality. Therefore neither is there trinity in God.

Obj. 4: Further, all that exists in God exists in the unity of the divine essence; because God is His own essence. Therefore, if Trinity exists in God, it exists in the unity of the divine essence; and thus in God there would be three essential unities; which is heresy.

Obj. 5: Further, in all that is said of God, the concrete is predicated of the abstract; for Deity is God and paternity is the Father. But the Trinity cannot be called trine; otherwise there would be nine realities in God; which, of course, is erroneous. Therefore the word trinity is not to be applied to God.

*On the contrary,* Athanasius says: "Unity in Trinity; and Trinity in Unity is to be revered."

*I answer that,* The name "Trinity" in God signifies the determinate number of persons. And so the plurality of persons in God requires that we should use the word trinity; because what is indeterminately signified by plurality, is signified by trinity in a determinate manner.

Reply Obj. 1: In its etymological sense, this word "Trinity" seems to signify the one essence of the three persons, according as trinity may mean trine-unity. But in the strict meaning of the term it rather signifies the number of persons of one essence; and on this account we cannot say that the Father is the Trinity, as He is not three persons. Yet it does not mean the relations themselves of the Persons, but rather the number of persons related to each other; and hence it is that the word in itself does not express regard to another.

Reply Obj. 2: Two things are implied in a collective term, plurality of the *supposita,* and a unity of some kind of order. For "people" is a multitude of men comprehended under a certain order. In the first sense, this word "trinity" is like other collective words; but in the second sense it differs from them, because in the divine Trinity not only is there unity of order, but also with this there is unity of essence.

Reply Obj. 3: "Trinity" is taken in an absolute sense; for it signifies the threefold number of persons. "Triplicity" signifies a proportion of inequality; for it is a species of unequal proportion, according to Boethius (Arithm. i, 23). Therefore in God there is not triplicity, but Trinity.

Reply Obj. 4: In the divine Trinity is to be understood both number and the persons numbered. So when we say, "Trinity in Unity," we do not place number in the unity of the essence, as if we meant three times one; but we place the Persons numbered in the unity of nature; as the *supposita* of a nature are said to exist in that nature. On the other hand, we say "Unity in Trinity"; meaning that the nature is in its *supposita.*

Reply Obj. 5: When we say, "Trinity is trine," by reason of the number implied, we signify the multiplication of that number by itself; since the word trine imports a distinction in the *supposita* of which it is spoken. Therefore it cannot be said that the Trinity is trine; otherwise it follows that, if the Trinity be trine, there would be three *supposita* of the Trinity; as when we say, "God is trine," it follows that there are three *supposita* of the Godhead.

SECOND ARTICLE [I, Q. 31, Art. 2]

Whether the Son Is Other Than the Father?

Objection 1: It would seem that the Son is not other than the Father. For "other" is a relative term implying diversity of substance. If, then, the Son is other than the Father, He must be different from the Father; which is contrary to what Augustine says (De Trin. vii), that when we speak of three persons, "we do not mean to imply diversity."

Obj. 2: Further, whosoever are other from one another, differ in some way from one another. Therefore, if the Son is other than the Father, it follows that He differs from the Father; which is against what Ambrose says (De Fide i), that "the Father and the Son are one in Godhead; nor is there any difference in substance between them, nor any diversity."

Obj. 3: Further, the term alien is taken from *alius* (other). But the Son is not alien from the Father, for Hilary says (De Trin. vii) that "in the divine persons there is nothing diverse, nothing alien, nothing separable." Therefore the Son is not other than the Father.

Obj. 4: Further, the terms "other person" and "other thing" [alius et aliud] have the same meaning, differing only in gender. So if the Son is another person from the Father, it follows that the Son is a thing apart from the Father.

*On the contrary,* Augustine [*Fulgentius, De Fide ad Petrum i.] says: "There is one essence of the Father and Son and Holy Ghost, in which the Father is not one thing, the Son another, and the Holy Ghost another; although the Father is one person, the Son another, and the Holy Ghost another."

*I answer that,* Since as Jerome remarks [*In substance, Ep. lvii.], a heresy arises from words wrongly used, when we speak of the Trinity we must proceed with care and with befitting modesty; because, as Augustine says (De Trin. i, 3), "nowhere is error more harmful, the quest more toilsome, the finding more fruitful." Now, in treating of the Trinity, we must beware of two opposite errors, and proceed cautiously between them—namely, the error of Arius, who placed a Trinity of substance with the Trinity of persons; and the error of Sabellius, who placed unity of person with the unity of essence.

Thus, to avoid the error of Arius we must shun the use of the terms diversity and difference in God, lest we take away the unity of essence: we may, however, use the term "distinction" on account of the relative opposition. Hence whenever we find terms of "diversity" or "difference" of Persons used in an authentic work, these terms of "diversity" or "difference" are taken to mean "distinction." But lest the simplicity and singleness of the divine essence be taken away, the terms "separation" and "division," which belong to the parts of a whole, are to be avoided: and lest quality be taken away, we avoid the use of the term "disparity": and lest we remove similitude, we avoid the terms "alien" and "discrepant." For Ambrose says (De Fide i) that "in the Father and the Son there is no discrepancy, but one Godhead": and according to Hilary, as quoted above, "in God there is nothing alien, nothing separable."

To avoid the heresy of Sabellius, we must shun the term "singularity," lest we take away the communicability of the divine essence. Hence Hilary says (De Trin. vii): "It is sacrilege to assert that the Father and the Son are separate in Godhead." We must avoid the adjective "only" (unici) lest we take away the number of persons. Hence Hilary says in the same book: "We exclude from God the idea of singularity or uniqueness." Nevertheless, we say "the only Son," for in God there is no plurality of Sons. Yet, we do not say "the only God," for the Deity is common to several. We avoid the word "confused," lest we take away from the Persons the order of their nature. Hence Ambrose says (De Fide i): "What is one is not confused; and there is no multiplicity where there is no difference." The word "solitary" is also to be avoided, lest we take away the society of the three persons; for, as Hilary says (De Trin. iv), "We confess neither a solitary nor a diverse God."

This word "other" [alius], however, in the masculine sense, means only a distinction of *suppositum* ; and hence we can properly say that "the Son is other than the Father," because He is another *suppositum* of the divine nature, as He is another person and another hypostasis.

Reply Obj. 1: "Other," being like the name of a particular thing, refers to the *suppositum* ; and so, there is sufficient reason for using it, where there is a distinct substance in the sense of hypostasis or person. But diversity requires a distinct substance in the sense of essence. Thus we cannot say that the Son is diverse from the Father, although He is another.

Reply Obj. 2: "Difference" implies distinction of form. There is one form in God, as appears from the text, "Who, when He was in the form of God" (Phil. 2:6). Therefore the term "difference" does not properly apply to God, as appears from the authority quoted. Yet, Damascene (De Fide Orth. i, 5) employs the term "difference" in the divine persons, as meaning that the relative property is signified by way of form. Hence he says that the hypostases do not differ from each other in substance, but according to determinate properties. But "difference" is taken for "distinction," as above stated.

Reply Obj. 3: The term "alien" means what is extraneous and dissimilar; which is not expressed by the term "other" [alius]; and therefore we say that the Son is "other" than the Father, but not that He is anything "alien."

Reply Obj. 4: The neuter gender is formless; whereas the masculine is formed and distinct; and so is the feminine. So the common essence is properly and aptly expressed by the neuter gender, but by the masculine and feminine is expressed the determined subject in the common nature. Hence also in human affairs, if we ask, Who is this man? we answer, Socrates, which is the name of the *suppositum* ; whereas, if we ask, What is he? we reply, A rational and mortal animal. So, because in God distinction is by the persons, and not by the essence, we say that the Father is other than the Son, but not something else; while conversely we say that they are one thing, but not one person.

THIRD ARTICLE [I, Q. 31, Art. 3]

Whether the Exclusive Word "Alone" Should Be Added to the Essential Term in God?

Objection 1: It would seem that the exclusive word "alone" [solus] is not to be added to an essential term in God. For, according to the Philosopher (Elench. ii, 3), "He is alone who is not with another." But God is with the angels and the souls of the saints. Therefore we cannot say that God is alone.

Obj. 2: Further, whatever is joined to the essential term in God can be predicated of every person *per se,* and of all the persons together; for, as we can properly say that God is wise, we can say the Father is a wise God; and the Trinity is a wise God. But Augustine says (De Trin. vi, 9): "We must consider the opinion that the Father is not true God alone." Therefore God cannot be said to be alone.

Obj. 3: Further if this expression "alone" is joined to an essential term, it would be so joined as regards either the personal predicate or the essential predicate. But it cannot be the former, as it is false to say, "God alone is Father," since man also is a father; nor, again, can it be applied as regards the latter, for, if this saying were true, "God alone creates," it would follow that the "Father alone creates," as whatever is said of God can be said of the Father; and it would be false, as the Son also creates. Therefore this expression "alone" cannot be joined to an essential term in God.

*On the contrary,* It is said, "To the King of ages, immortal, invisible, the only God" (1 Tim. 1:17).

*I answer that,* This term "alone" can be taken as a categorematical term, or as a syncategorematical term. A categorematical term is one which ascribes absolutely its meaning to a given *suppositum* ; as, for instance, "white" to man, as when we say a "white man." If the term "alone" is taken in this sense, it cannot in any way be joined to any term in God; for it would mean solitude in the term to which it is joined; and it would follow that God was solitary, against what is above stated (A. 2). A syncategorematical term imports the order of the predicate to the subject; as this expression "every one" or "no one"; and likewise the term "alone," as excluding every other *suppositum* from the predicate. Thus, when we say, "Socrates alone writes," we do not mean that Socrates is solitary, but that he has no companion in writing, though many others may be with him. In this way nothing prevents the term "alone" being joined to any essential term in God, as excluding the predicate from all things but God; as if we said "God alone is eternal," because nothing but God is eternal.

Reply Obj. 1: Although the angels and the souls of the saints are always with God, nevertheless, if plurality of persons did not exist in God, He would be alone or solitary. For solitude is not removed by association with anything that is extraneous in nature; thus anyone is said to be alone in a garden, though many plants and animals are with him in the garden. Likewise, God would be alone or solitary, though angels and men were with Him, supposing that several persons were not within Him. Therefore the society of angels and of souls does not take away absolute solitude from God; much less does it remove respective solitude, in reference to a predicate.

Reply Obj. 2: This expression "alone," properly speaking, does not affect the predicate, which is taken formally, for it refers to the *suppositum,* as excluding any other suppositum from the one which it qualifies. But the adverb "only," being exclusive, can be applied either to subject or predicate. For we can say, "Only Socrates"—that is, no one else—"runs: and Socrates runs only"—that is, he does nothing else. Hence it is not properly said that the Father is God alone, or the Trinity is God alone, unless some implied meaning be assumed in the predicate, as, for instance, "The Trinity is God Who alone is God." In that sense it can be true to say that the Father is that God Who alone is God, if the relative be referred to the predicate, and not to the *suppositum*. So, when Augustine says that the Father is not God alone, but that the Trinity is God alone, he speaks expositively, as he might explain the words, "To the King of ages, invisible, the only God," as applying not to the Father, but to the Trinity alone.

Reply Obj. 3: In both ways can the term "alone" be joined to an essential term. For this proposition, "God alone is Father," can mean two things, because the word "Father" can signify the person of the Father; and then it is true; for no man is that person: or it can signify that relation only; and thus it is false, because the relation of paternity is found also in others, though not in a univocal sense. Likewise it is true to say God alone creates; nor, does it follow, "therefore the Father alone creates," because, as logicians say, an exclusive diction so fixes the term to which it is joined that what is said exclusively of that term cannot be said exclusively of an individual contained in that term: for instance, from the premiss, "Man alone is a mortal rational animal," we cannot conclude, "therefore Socrates alone is such."

FOURTH ARTICLE [I, Q. 31, Art. 4]

Whether an Exclusive Diction Can Be Joined to the Personal Term?

Objection 1: It would seem that an exclusive diction can be joined to the personal term, even though the predicate is common. For our Lord speaking to the Father, said: "That they may know Thee, the only true God" (John 17:3). Therefore the Father alone is true God.

Obj. 2: Further, He said: "No one knows the Son but the Father" (Matt. 11:27); which means that the Father alone knows the Son. But to know the Son is common (to the persons). Therefore the same conclusion follows.

Obj. 3: Further, an exclusive diction does not exclude what enters into the concept of the term to which it is joined. Hence it does not exclude the part, nor the universal; for it does not follow that if we say "Socrates alone is white," that therefore "his hand is not white," or that "man is not white." But one person is in the concept of another; as the Father is in the concept of the Son; and conversely. Therefore, when we say, The Father alone is God, we do not exclude the Son, nor the Holy Ghost; so that such a mode of speaking is true.

Obj. 4: Further, the Church sings: "Thou alone art Most High, O Jesus Christ."

*On the contrary,* This proposition "The Father alone is God" includes two assertions—namely, that the Father is God, and that no other besides the Father is God. But this second proposition is false, for the Son is another from the Father, and He is God. Therefore this is false, The Father alone is God; and the same of the like sayings.

*I answer that,* When we say, "The Father alone is God," such a proposition can be taken in several senses. If "alone" means solitude in the Father, it is false in a categorematical sense; but if taken in a syncategorematical sense it can again be understood in several ways. For if it exclude (all others) from the form of the subject, it is true, the sense being "the Father alone is God"—that is, "He who with no other is the Father, is God." In this way Augustine expounds when he says (De Trin. vi, 6): "We say the Father alone, not because He is separate from the Son, or from the Holy Ghost, but because they are not the Father together with Him." This, however, is not the usual way of speaking, unless we understand another implication, as though we said "He who alone is called the Father is God." But in the strict sense the exclusion affects the predicate. And thus the proposition is false if it excludes another in the masculine sense; but true if it excludes it in the neuter sense; because the Son is another person than the Father, but not another thing; and the same applies to the Holy Ghost. But because this diction "alone," properly speaking, refers to the subject, it tends to exclude another Person rather than other things. Hence such a way of speaking is not to be taken too literally, but it should be piously expounded, whenever we find it in an authentic work.

Reply Obj. 1: When we say, "Thee the only true God," we do not understand it as referring to the person of the Father, but to the whole Trinity, as Augustine expounds (De Trin. vi, 9). Or, if understood of the person of the Father, the other persons are not excluded by reason of the unity of essence; in so far as the word "only" excludes another thing, as above explained.

The same Reply can be given to Obj. 2. For an essential term applied to the Father does not exclude the Son or the Holy Ghost, by reason of the unity of essence. Hence we must understand that in the text quoted the term "no one" [*Nemo = non-homo, i.e. no man] is not the same as "no man," which the word itself would seem to signify (for the person of the Father could not be excepted), but is taken according to the usual way of speaking in a distributive sense, to mean any rational nature.

Reply Obj. 3: The exclusive diction does not exclude what enters into the concept of the term to which it is adjoined, if they do not differ in *suppositum,* as part and universal. But the Son differs in suppositum from the Father; and so there is no parity.

Reply Obj. 4: We do not say absolutely that the Son alone is Most High; but that He alone is Most High "with the Holy Ghost, in the glory of God the Father."

## QUESTION 32

THE KNOWLEDGE OF THE DIVINE PERSONS (In Four Articles)

We proceed to inquire concerning the knowledge of the divine persons; and this involves four points of inquiry:

(1) Whether the divine persons can be known by natural reason?

(2) Whether notions are to be attributed to the divine persons?

(3) The number of the notions?

(4) Whether we may lawfully have various contrary opinions of these notions?

FIRST ARTICLE [I, Q. 32, Art. 1]

Whether the Trinity of the Divine Persons Can Be Known by Natural Reason?

Objection 1: It would seem that the trinity of the divine persons can be known by natural reason. For philosophers came to the knowledge of God not otherwise than by natural reason. Now we find that they said many things about the trinity of persons, for Aristotle says (De Coelo et Mundo i, 2): "Through this number"—namely, three—"we bring ourselves to acknowledge the greatness of one God, surpassing all things created." And Augustine says (Confess. vii, 9): "I have read in their works, not in so many words, but enforced by many and various reasons, that in the beginning was the Word, and the Word was with God, and the Word was God," and so on; in which passage the distinction of persons is laid down. We read, moreover, in a gloss on Rom. 1 and Ex. 8 that the magicians of Pharaoh failed in the third sign—that is, as regards knowledge of a third person—i.e. of the Holy Ghost—and thus it is clear that they knew at least two persons. Likewise Trismegistus says: "The monad begot a monad, and reflected upon itself its own heat." By which words the generation of the Son and procession of the Holy Ghost seem to be indicated. Therefore knowledge of the divine persons can be obtained by natural reason.

Obj. 2: Further, Richard St. Victor says (De Trin. i, 4): "I believe without doubt that probable and even necessary arguments can be found for any explanation of the truth." So even to prove the Trinity some have brought forward a reason from the infinite goodness of God, who communicates Himself infinitely in the procession of the divine persons; while some are moved by the consideration that "no good thing can be joyfully possessed without partnership." Augustine proceeds (De Trin. x, 4; x, 11, 12) to prove the trinity of persons by the procession of the word and of love in our own mind; and we have followed him in this (Q. 27, AA. 1, 3). Therefore the trinity of persons can be known by natural reason.

Obj. 3: Further, it seems to be superfluous to teach what cannot be known by natural reason. But it ought not to be said that the divine tradition of the Trinity is superfluous. Therefore the trinity of persons can be known by natural reason.

*On the contrary,* Hilary says (De Trin. i), "Let no man think to reach the sacred mystery of generation by his own mind." And Ambrose says (De Fide ii, 5), "It is impossible to know the secret of generation. The mind fails, the voice is silent." But the trinity of the divine persons is distinguished by origin of generation and procession (Q. 30, A. 2). Since, therefore, man cannot know, and with his understanding grasp that for which no necessary reason can be given, it follows that the trinity of persons cannot be known by reason.

*I answer that,* It is impossible to attain to the knowledge of the Trinity by natural reason. For, as above explained (Q. 12, AA. 4, 12), man cannot obtain the knowledge of God by natural reason except from creatures. Now creatures lead us to the knowledge of God, as effects do to their cause. Accordingly, by natural reason we can know of God that only which of necessity belongs to Him as the principle of things, and we have cited this fundamental principle in treating of God as above (Q. 12, A. 12). Now, the creative power of God is common to the whole Trinity; and hence it belongs to the unity of the essence, and not to the distinction of the persons. Therefore, by natural reason we can know what belongs to the unity of the essence, but not what belongs to the distinction of the persons. Whoever, then, tries to prove the trinity of persons by natural reason, derogates from faith in two ways. Firstly, as regards the dignity of faith itself, which consists in its being concerned with invisible things, that exceed human reason; wherefore the Apostle says that "faith is of things that appear not" (Heb. 11:1), and the same Apostle says also, "We speak wisdom among the perfect, but not the wisdom of this world, nor of the princes of this world; but we speak the wisdom of God in a mystery which is hidden" (1 Cor. 2:6, 7). Secondly, as regards the utility of drawing others to the faith. For when anyone in the endeavor to prove the faith brings forward reasons which are not cogent, he falls under the ridicule of the unbelievers: since they suppose that we stand upon such reasons, and that we believe on such grounds.

Therefore, we must not attempt to prove what is of faith, except by authority alone, to those who receive the authority; while as regards others it suffices to prove that what faith teaches is not impossible. Hence it is said by Dionysius (Div. Nom. ii): "Whoever wholly resists the word, is far off from our philosophy; whereas if he regards the truth of the word"—i.e. "the sacred word, we too follow this rule."

Reply Obj. 1: The philosophers did not know the mystery of the trinity of the divine persons by its proper attributes, such as paternity, filiation, and procession, according to the Apostle's words, "We speak the wisdom of God which none of the princes of the world"—i.e. the philosophers—"knew" (1 Cor. 2:6). Nevertheless, they knew some of the essential attributes appropriated to the persons, as power to the Father, wisdom to the Son, goodness to the Holy Ghost; as will later on appear. So, when Aristotle said, "By this number," etc., we must not take it as if he affirmed a threefold number in God, but that he wished to say that the ancients used the threefold number in their sacrifices and prayers on account of some perfection residing in the number three. In the Platonic books also we find, "In the beginning was the word," not as meaning the Person begotten in God, but as meaning the ideal type whereby God made all things, and which is appropriated to the Son. And although they knew these were appropriated to the three persons, yet they are said to have failed in the third sign—that is, in the knowledge of the third person, because they deviated from the goodness appropriated to the Holy Ghost, in that knowing God "they did not glorify Him as God" (Rom. 1); or, because the Platonists asserted the existence of one Primal Being whom they also declared to be the father of the universe, they consequently maintained the existence of another substance beneath him, which they called "mind" or the "paternal intellect," containing the idea of all things, as Macrobius relates (Som. Scip. iv). They did not, however, assert the existence of a third separate substance which might correspond to the Holy Ghost. So also we do not assert that the Father and the Son differ in substance, which was the error of Origen and Arius, who in this followed the Platonists. When Trismegistus says, "Monad begot monad," etc., this does not refer to the generation of the Son, or to the procession of the Holy Ghost, but to the production of the world. For one God produced one world by reason of His love for Himself.

Reply Obj. 2: Reason may be employed in two ways to establish a point: firstly, for the purpose of furnishing sufficient proof of some principle, as in natural science, where sufficient proof can be brought to show that the movement of the heavens is always of uniform velocity. Reason is employed in another way, not as furnishing a sufficient proof of a principle, but as confirming an already established principle, by showing the congruity of its results, as in astrology the theory of eccentrics and epicycles is considered as established, because thereby the sensible appearances of the heavenly movements can be explained; not, however, as if this proof were sufficient, forasmuch as some other theory might explain them. In the first way, we can prove that God is one; and the like. In the second way, reasons avail to prove the Trinity; as, when assumed to be true, such reasons confirm it. We must not, however, think that the trinity of persons is adequately proved by such reasons. This becomes evident when we consider each point; for the infinite goodness of God is manifested also in creation, because to produce from nothing is an act of infinite power. For if God communicates Himself by His infinite goodness, it is not necessary that an infinite effect should proceed from God: but that according to its own mode and capacity it should receive the divine goodness. Likewise, when it is said that joyous possession of good requires partnership, this holds in the case of one not having perfect goodness: hence it needs to share some other's good, in order to have the goodness of complete happiness. Nor is the image in our mind an adequate proof in the case of God, forasmuch as the intellect is not in God and ourselves univocally. Hence, Augustine says (Tract. xxvii. in Joan.) that by faith we arrive at knowledge, and not conversely.

Reply Obj. 3: There are two reasons why the knowledge of the divine persons was necessary for us. It was necessary for the right idea of creation. The fact of saying that God made all things by His Word excludes the error of those who say that God produced things by necessity. When we say that in Him there is a procession of love, we show that God produced creatures not because He needed them, nor because of any other extrinsic reason, but on account of the love of His own goodness. So Moses, when he had said, "In the beginning God created heaven and earth," subjoined, "God said, Let there be light," to manifest the divine Word; and then said, "God saw the light that it was good," to show proof of the divine love. The same is also found in the other works of creation. In another way, and chiefly, that we may think rightly concerning the salvation of the human race, accomplished by the Incarnate Son, and by the gift of the Holy Ghost.

SECOND ARTICLE [I, Q. 32, Art. 2]

Whether There Are Notions in God?

Objection 1: It would seem that in God there are no notions. For Dionysius says (Div. Nom. i): "We must not dare to say anything of God but what is taught to us by the Holy Scripture." But Holy Scripture does not say anything concerning notions. Therefore there are none in God.

Obj. 2: Further, all that exists in God concerns the unity of the essence or the trinity of the persons. But the notions do not concern the unity of the essence, nor the trinity of the persons; for neither can what belongs to the essence be predicated of the notions: for instance, we do not say that paternity is wise or creates; nor can what belongs to the persons be so predicated; for example, we do not say that paternity begets, nor that filiation is begotten. Therefore there do not exist notions in God.

Obj. 3: Further, we do not require to presuppose any abstract notions as principles of knowing things which are devoid of composition: for they are known of themselves. But the divine persons are supremely simple. Therefore we are not to suppose any notions in God.

*On the contrary,* Damascene says (De Fide Orth. iii, 5): "We recognize difference of hypostases [i.e. of persons], in the three properties; i.e. in the paternal, the filial, and the processional." Therefore we must admit properties and notions in God.

*I answer that,* Prepositivus, considering the simplicity of the persons, said that in God there were no properties or notions, and wherever there were mentioned, he propounded the abstract for the concrete. For as we are accustomed to say, "I beseech your kindness"—i.e. you who are kind—so when we speak of paternity in God, we mean God the Father.

But, as shown above (Q. 3, A. 3, ad 1), the use of concrete and abstract names in God is not in any way repugnant to the divine simplicity; forasmuch as we always name a thing as we understand it. Now, our intellect cannot attain to the absolute simplicity of the divine essence, considered in itself, and therefore, our human intellect apprehends and names divine things, according to its own mode, that is in so far as they are found in sensible objects, whence its knowledge is derived. In these things we use abstract terms to signify simple forms; and to signify subsistent things we use concrete terms. Hence also we signify divine things, as above stated, by abstract names, to express their simplicity; whereas, to express their subsistence and completeness, we use concrete names.

But not only must essential names be signified in the abstract and in the concrete, as when we say Deity and God; or wisdom and wise; but the same applies to the personal names, so that we may say paternity and Father.

Two chief motives for this can be cited. The first arises from the obstinacy of heretics. For since we confess the Father, the Son, and the Holy Ghost to be one God and three persons, to those who ask: "Whereby are They one God? and whereby are They three persons?" as we answer that They are one in essence or deity; so there must also be some abstract terms whereby we may answer that the persons are distinguished; and these are the properties or notions signified by an abstract term, as paternity and filiation. Therefore the divine essence is signified as "What"; and the person as "Who"; and the property as "Whereby."

The second motive is because one person in God is related to two persons—namely, the person of the Father to the person of the Son and the person of the Holy Ghost. This is not, however, by one relation; otherwise it would follow that the Son also and the Holy Ghost would be related to the Father by one and the same relation. Thus, since relation alone multiplies the Trinity, it would follow that the Son and the Holy Ghost would not be two persons. Nor can it be said with Prepositivus that as God is related in one way to creatures, while creatures are related to Him in divers ways, so the Father is related by one relation to the Son and to the Holy Ghost; whereas these two persons are related to the Father by two relations. For, since the very specific idea of a relation is that it refers to another, it must be said that two relations are not specifically different if but one opposite relation corresponds to them. For the relation of lord and father must differ according to the difference of filiation and servitude. Now, all creatures are related to God as His creatures by one specific relation. But the Son and the Holy Ghost are not related to the Father by one and the same kind of relation. Hence there is no parity.

Further, in God there is no need to admit any real relation to the creature (Q. 28, A. 1, 3); while there is no reason against our admitting in God, many logical relations. But in the Father there must be a real relation to the Son and to the Holy Ghost. Hence, corresponding to the two relations of the Son and of the Holy Ghost, whereby they are related to the Father, we must understand two relations in the Father, whereby He is related to the Son and to the Holy Ghost. Hence, since there is only one Person of the Father, it is necessary that the relations should be separately signified in the abstract; and these are what we mean by properties and notions.

Reply Obj. 1: Although the notions are not mentioned in Holy Scripture, yet the persons are mentioned, comprising the idea of notions, as the abstract is contained in the concrete.

Reply Obj. 2: In God the notions have their significance not after the manner of realities, but by way of certain ideas whereby the persons are known; although in God these notions or relations are real, as stated above (Q. 28, A. 1). Therefore whatever has order to any essential or personal act, cannot be applied to the notions; forasmuch as this is against their mode of signification. Hence we cannot say that paternity begets, or creates, or is wise, or is intelligent. The essentials, however, which are not ordered to any act, but simply remove created conditions from God, can be predicated of the notions; for we can say that paternity is eternal, or immense, or such like. So also on account of the real identity, substantive terms, whether personal or essential, can be predicated of the notions; for we can say that paternity is God, and that paternity is the Father.

Reply Obj. 3: Although the persons are simple, still without prejudice to their simplicity, the proper ideas of the persons can be abstractedly signified, as above explained.

THIRD ARTICLE [I, Q. 32, Art. 3]

Whether There Are Five Notions?

Objection 1: It would seem that there are not five notions. For the notions proper to the persons are the relations whereby they are distinguished from each other. But the relations in God are only four (Q. 28, A. 4). Therefore the notions are only four in number.

Obj. 2: Further, as there is only one essence in God, He is called one God, and because in Him there are three persons, He is called the Trine God. Therefore, if in God there are five notions, He may be called quinary; which cannot be allowed.

Obj. 3: Further, if there are five notions for the three persons in God, there must be in some one person two or more notions, as in the person of the Father there is innascibility and paternity, and common spiration. Either these three notions really differ, or not. If they really differ, it follows that the person of the Father is composed of several things. But if they differ only logically, it follows that one of them can be predicated of another, so that we can say that as the divine goodness is the same as the divine wisdom by reason of the common reality, so common spiration is paternity; which is not to be admitted. Therefore there are not five notions.

Obj. 4: *On the contrary,* It seems that there are more; because as the Father is from no one, and therefrom is derived the notion of innascibility; so from the Holy Ghost no other person proceeds. And in this respect there ought to be a sixth notion.

Obj. 5: Further, as the Father and the Son are the common origin of the Holy Ghost, so it is common to the Son and the Holy Ghost to proceed from the Father. Therefore, as one notion is common to the Father and the Son, so there ought to be one notion common to the Son and to the Holy Ghost.

*I answer that,* A notion is the proper idea whereby we know a divine Person. Now the divine persons are multiplied by reason of their origin: and origin includes the idea of someone from whom another comes, and of someone that comes from another, and by these two modes a person can be known. Therefore the Person of the Father cannot be known by the fact that He is from another; but by the fact that He is from no one; and thus the notion that belongs to Him is called "innascibility." As the source of another, He can be known in two ways, because as the Son is from Him, the Father is known by the notion of "paternity"; and as the Holy Ghost is from Him, He is known by the notion of "common spiration." The Son can be known as begotten by another, and thus He is known by "filiation"; and also by another person proceeding from Him, the Holy Ghost, and thus He is known in the same way as the Father is known, by "common spiration." The Holy Ghost can be known by the fact that He is from another, or from others; thus He is known by "procession"; but not by the fact that another is from Him, as no divine person proceeds from Him.

Therefore, there are Five notions in God: "innascibility," "paternity," "filiation," "common spiration," and "procession." Of these only four are relations, for "innascibility" is not a relation, except by reduction, as will appear later (Q. 33, A. 4, ad 3). Four only are properties. For "common spiration" is not a property; because it belongs to two persons. Three are personal notions—i.e. constituting persons, "paternity," "filiation," and "procession." "Common spiration" and "innascibility" are called notions of Persons, but not personal notions, as we shall explain further on (Q. 40, A. 1, ad 1).

Reply Obj. 1: Besides the four relations, another notion must be admitted, as above explained.

Reply Obj. 2: The divine essence is signified as a reality; and likewise the persons are signified as realities; whereas the notions are signified as ideas notifying the persons. Therefore, although God is one by unity of essence, and trine by trinity of persons, nevertheless He is not quinary by the five notions.

Reply Obj. 3: Since the real plurality in God is founded only on relative opposition, the several properties of one Person, as they are not relatively opposed to each other, do not really differ. Nor again are they predicated of each other, because they are different ideas of the persons; as we do not say that the attribute of power is the attribute of knowledge, although we do say that knowledge is power.

Reply Obj. 4: Since Person implies dignity, as stated above (Q. 19, A. 3), we cannot derive a notion of the Holy Spirit from the fact that no person is from Him. For this does not belong to His dignity, as it belongs to the authority of the Father that He is from no one.

Reply Obj. 5: The Son and the Holy Ghost do not agree in one special mode of existence derived from the Father; as the Father and the Son agree in one special mode of producing the Holy Ghost. But the principle on which a notion is based must be something special; thus no parity of reasoning exists.

FOURTH ARTICLE [I, Q. 32, Art. 4]

Whether It Is Lawful to Have Various Contrary Opinions of Notions?

Objection 1: It would seem that it is not lawful to have various contrary opinions of the notions. For Augustine says (De Trin. i, 3): "No error is more dangerous than any as regards the Trinity": to which mystery the notions assuredly belong. But contrary opinions must be in some way erroneous. Therefore it is not right to have contrary opinions of the notions.

Obj. 2: Further, the persons are known by the notions. But no contrary opinion concerning the persons is to be tolerated. Therefore neither can there be about the notions.

*On the contrary,* The notions are not articles of faith. Therefore different opinions of the notions are permissible.

*I answer that,* Anything is of faith in two ways; directly, where any truth comes to us principally as divinely taught, as the trinity and unity of God, the

Incarnation of the Son, and the like; and concerning these truths a false opinion of itself involves heresy, especially if it be held obstinately. A thing is of faith, indirectly, if the denial of it involves as a consequence something against faith; as for instance if anyone said that Samuel was not the son of Elcana, for it follows that the divine Scripture would be false. Concerning such things anyone may have a false opinion without danger of heresy, before the matter has been considered or settled as involving consequences against faith, and particularly if no obstinacy be shown; whereas when it is manifest, and especially if the Church has decided that consequences follow against faith, then the error cannot be free from heresy. For this reason many things are now considered as heretical which were formerly not so considered, as their consequences are now more manifest.

So we must decide that anyone may entertain contrary opinions about the notions, if he does not mean to uphold anything at variance with faith. If, however, anyone should entertain a false opinion of the notions, knowing or thinking that consequences against the faith would follow, he would lapse into heresy.

By what has been said all the objections may be solved.

## QUESTION 33

OF THE PERSON OF THE FATHER (In Four Articles)

We now consider the persons singly; and first, the Person of the Father, concerning Whom there are four points of inquiry:

(1) Whether the Father is the Principle?

(2) Whether the person of the Father is properly signified by this name "Father"?

(3) Whether "Father" in God is said personally before it is said essentially?

(4) Whether it belongs to the Father alone to be unbegotten?

FIRST ARTICLE [I, Q. 33, Art. 1]

Whether It Belongs to the Father to Be the Principle?

Objection 1: It would seem that the Father cannot be called the principle of the Son, or of the Holy Ghost. For principle and cause are the same, according to the Philosopher (Metaph. iv). But we do not say that the Father is the cause of the Son. Therefore we must not say that He is the principle of the Son.

Obj. 2: Further, a principle is so called in relation to the thing principled. So if the Father is the principle of the Son, it follows that the Son is a person principled, and is therefore created; which appears false.

Obj. 3: Further, the word principle is taken from priority. But in God there is no "before" and "after," as Athanasius says. Therefore in speaking of God we ought not to used the term principle.

*On the contrary,* Augustine says (De Trin. iv, 20), "The Father is the Principle of the whole Deity."

*I answer that,* The word "principle" signifies only that whence another proceeds: since anything whence something proceeds in any way we call a principle; and conversely. As the Father then is the one whence another proceeds, it follows that the Father is a principle.

Reply Obj. 1: The Greeks use the words "cause" and "principle" indifferently, when speaking of God; whereas the Latin Doctors do not use the word "cause," but only "principle." The reason is because "principle" is a wider term than "cause"; as "cause" is more common than "element." For the first term of a thing, as also the first part, is called the principle, but not the cause. Now the wider a term is, the more suitable it is to use as regards God (Q. 13, A. 11), because the more special terms are, the more they determine the mode adapted to the creature. Hence this term "cause" seems to mean diversity of substance, and dependence of one from another; which is not implied in the word "principle." For in all kinds of causes there is always to be found between the cause and the effect a distance of perfection or of power: whereas we use the term "principle" even in things which have no such difference, but have only a certain order to each other; as when we say that a point is the principle of a line; or also when we say that the first part of a line is the principle of a line.

Reply Obj. 2: It is the custom with the Greeks to say that the Son and the Holy Ghost are principled. This is not, however, the custom with our Doctors; because, although we attribute to the Father something of authority by reason of His being the principle, still we do not attribute any kind of subjection or inferiority to the Son, or to the Holy Ghost, to avoid any occasion of error. In this way, Hilary says (De Trin. ix): "By authority of the Giver, the Father is the greater; nevertheless the Son is not less to Whom oneness of nature is give."

Reply Obj. 3: Although this word principle, as regards its derivation, seems to be taken from priority, still it does not signify priority, but origin. For what a term signifies, and the reason why it was imposed, are not the same thing, as stated above (Q. 13, A. 8).

SECOND ARTICLE [I, Q. 33, Art. 2]

Whether This Name "Father" Is Properly the Name of a Divine Person?

Objection 1: It would seem that this name "Father" is not properly the name of a divine person. For the name "Father" signifies relation. Moreover "person" is an individual substance. Therefore this name "Father" is not properly a name signifying a Person.

Obj. 2: Further, a begetter is more common than father; for every father begets; but it is not so conversely. But a more common term is more properly applied to God, as stated above (Q. 13, A. 11). Therefore the more proper name of the divine person is begetter and genitor than Father.

Obj. 3: Further, a metaphorical term cannot be the proper name of anyone. But the word is by us metaphorically called begotten, or offspring; and consequently, he of whom is the word, is metaphorically called father. Therefore the principle of the Word in God is not properly called Father.

Obj. 4: Further, everything which is said properly of God, is said of God first before creatures. But generation appears to apply to creatures before God; because generation seems to be truer when the one who proceeds is distinct from the one whence it proceeds, not only by relation but also by essence. Therefore the name "Father" taken from generation does not seem to be the proper name of any divine person.

*On the contrary,* It is said (Ps. 88:27): "He shall cry out to me: Thou art my Father."

*I answer that,* The proper name of any person signifies that whereby the person is distinguished from all other persons. For as body and soul belong to the nature of man, so to the concept of this particular man belong this particular soul and this particular body; and by these is this particular man distinguished from all other men. Now it is paternity which distinguishes the person of the Father from all other persons. Hence this name "Father," whereby paternity is signified, is the proper name of the person of the Father.

Reply Obj. 1: Among us relation is not a subsisting person. So this name "father" among us does not signify a person, but the relation of a person. In God, however, it is not so, as some wrongly thought; for in God the relation signified by the name "Father" is a subsisting person. Hence, as above explained (Q. 29, A. 4), this name "person" in God signifies a relation subsisting in the divine nature.

Reply Obj. 2: According to the Philosopher (De Anima ii, text 49), a thing is denominated chiefly by its perfection, and by its end. Now generation signifies something in process of being made, whereas paternity signifies the complement of generation; and therefore the name "Father" is more expressive as regards the divine person than genitor or begettor.

Reply Obj. 3: In human nature the word is not a subsistence, and hence is not properly called begotten or son. But the divine Word is something subsistent in the divine nature; and hence He is properly and not metaphorically called Son, and His principle is called Father.

Reply Obj. 4: The terms "generation" and "paternity" like the other terms properly applied to God, are said of God before creatures as regards the thing signified, but not as regards the mode of signification. Hence also the Apostle says, "I bend my knee to the Father of my Lord Jesus Christ, from whom all paternity in heaven and on earth is named" (Eph. 3:14). This is explained thus. It is manifest that generation receives its species from the term which is the form of the thing generated; and the nearer it is to the form of the generator, the truer and more perfect is the generation; as univocal generation is more perfect than non-univocal, for it belongs to the essence of a generator to generate what is like itself in form. Hence the very fact that in the divine generation the form of the Begetter and Begotten is numerically the same, whereas in creatures it is not numerically, but only specifically, the same, shows that generation, and consequently paternity, is applied to God before creatures. Hence the very fact that in God a distinction exists of the Begotten from the Begetter as regards relation only, belongs to the truth of the divine generation and paternity.

THIRD ARTICLE [I, Q. 33, Art. 3]

Whether This Name "Father" Is Applied to God, Firstly As a Personal Name?

Objection 1: It would seem that this name "Father" is not applied to God, firstly as a personal name. For in the intellect the common precedes the particular. But this name "Father" as a personal name, belongs to the person of the Father; and taken in an essential sense it is common to the whole Trinity; for we say "Our Father" to the whole Trinity. Therefore "Father" comes first as an essential name before its personal sense.

Obj. 2: Further, in things of which the concept is the same there is no priority of predication. But paternity and filiation seem to be of the same nature, according as a divine person is Father of the Son, and the whole Trinity is our Father, or the creature's; since, according to Basil (Hom. xv, De Fide), to receive is common to the creature and to the Son. Therefore "Father" in God is not taken as an essential name before it is taken personally.

Obj. 3: Further, it is not possible to compare things which have not a common concept. But the Son is compared to the creature by reason of filiation or generation, according to Col. 1:15: "Who is the image of the invisible God, the first-born of every creature." Therefore paternity taken in a personal sense is not prior to, but has the same concept as, paternity taken essentially.

*On the contrary,* The eternal comes before the temporal. But God is the Father of the Son from eternity; while He is the Father of the creature in time. Therefore paternity in God is taken in a personal sense as regards the Son, before it is so taken as regards the creature.

*I answer that,* A name is applied to that wherein is perfectly contained its whole signification, before it is applied to that which only partially contains it; for the latter bears the name by reason of a kind of similitude to that which answers perfectly to the signification of the name; since all imperfect things are taken from perfect things. Hence this name "lion" is applied first to the animal containing the whole nature of a lion, and which is properly so called, before it is applied to a man who shows something of a lion's nature, as courage, or strength, or the like; and of whom it is said by way of similitude.

Now it is manifest from the foregoing (Q. 27, A. 2; Q. 28, A. 4), that the perfect idea of paternity and filiation is to be found in God the Father, and in God the Son, because one is the nature and glory of the Father and the Son. But in the creature, filiation is found in relation to God, not in a perfect manner, since the Creator and the creature have not the same nature; but by way of a certain likeness, which is the more perfect the nearer we approach to the true idea of filiation. For God is called the Father of some creatures, by reason only of a trace, for instance of irrational creatures, according to Job 38:28: "Who is the father of the rain? or who begot the drops of dew?" Of some, namely, the rational creature (He is the Father), by reason of the likeness of His image, according to Deut. 32:6: "Is He not thy Father, who possessed, and made, and created thee?" And of others He is the Father by similitude of grace, and these are also called adoptive sons, as ordained to the heritage of eternal glory by the gift of grace which they have received, according to Rom. 8:16, 17: "The Spirit Himself gives testimony to our spirit that we are the sons of God; and if sons, heirs also." Lastly, He is the Father of others by similitude of glory, forasmuch as they have obtained possession of the heritage of glory, according to Rom. 5:2: "We glory in the hope of the glory of the sons of God." Therefore it is plain that "paternity" is applied to God first, as importing regard of one Person to another Person, before it imports the regard of God to creatures.

Reply Obj. 1: Common terms taken absolutely, in the order of our intelligence, come before proper terms; because they are included in the understanding of proper terms; but not conversely. For in the concept of the person of the Father, God is understood; but not conversely. But common terms which import relation to the creature come after proper terms which import personal relations; because the person proceeding in God proceeds as the principle of the production of creatures. For as the word conceived in the mind of the artist is first understood to proceed from the artist before the thing designed, which is produced in likeness to the word conceived in the artist's mind; so the Son proceeds from the Father before the creature, to which the name of filiation is applied as it participates in the likeness of the Son, as is clear from the words of Rom. 8:29: "Whom He foreknew and predestined to be made conformable to the image of His Son."

Reply Obj. 2: To "receive" is said to be common to the creature and to the Son not in a univocal sense, but according to a certain remote similitude whereby He is called the First Born of creatures. Hence the authority quoted subjoins: "That He may be the First Born among many brethren," after saying that some were conformed to the image of the Son of God. But the Son of God possesses a position of singularity above others, in having by nature what He receives, as Basil also declares (Hom. xv De Fide); hence He is called the only begotten (John 1:18): "The only begotten Who is in the bosom of the Father, He hath declared unto us."

From this appears the Reply to the Third Objection.

FOURTH ARTICLE [I, Q. 33, Art. 4]

Whether It Is Proper to the Father to Be Unbegotten?

Objection 1: It would seem that it is not proper to the Father to be unbegotten. For every property supposes something in that of which it is the property. But "unbegotten" supposes nothing in the Father; it only removes something. Therefore it does not signify a property of the Father.

Obj. 2: Further, Unbegotten is taken either in a privative, or in a negative sense. If in a negative sense, then whatever is not begotten can be called unbegotten. But the Holy Ghost is not begotten; neither is the divine essence. Therefore to be unbegotten belongs also to the essence; thus it is not proper to the Father. But if it be taken in a privative sense, as every privation signifies imperfection in the thing which is the subject of privation, it follows that the Person of the Father is imperfect; which cannot be.

Obj. 3: Further, in God, "unbegotten" does not signify relation, for it is not used relatively. Therefore it signifies substance; therefore unbegotten and begotten differ in substance. But the Son, Who is begotten, does not differ from the Father in substance. Therefore the Father ought not to be called unbegotten.

Obj. 4: Further, property means what belongs to one alone. Since, then, there are more than one in God proceeding from another, there is nothing to prevent several not receiving their being from another. Therefore the Father is not alone unbegotten.

Obj. 5: Further, as the Father is the principle of the person begotten, so is He of the person proceeding. So if by reason of his opposition to the person begotten, it is proper to the Father to be unbegotten it follows that it is proper to Him also to be unproceeding.

*On the contrary,* Hilary says (De Trin. iv): "One is from one—that is, the Begotten is from the Unbegotten—namely, by the property in each one respectively of innascibility and origin."

*I answer that,* As in creatures there exist a first and a secondary principle, so also in the divine Persons, in Whom there is no before or after, is formed the principle not from a principle, Who is the Father; and the principle from a principle, Who is the Son.

Now in things created a first principle is known in two ways; in one way as the first *principle,* by reason of its having a relation to what proceeds from itself; in another way, inasmuch as it is a *first* principle by reason of its not being from another. Thus therefore the Father is known both by paternity and by common spiration, as regards the persons proceeding from Himself. But as the principle, not from a principle He is known by the fact that He is not from another; and this belongs to the property of innascibility, signified by this word "begotten."

Reply Obj. 1: Some there are who say that innascibility, signified by the word "unbegotten," as a property of the Father, is not a negative term only, but either that it means both these things together—namely, that the Father is from no one, and that He is the principle of others; or that it imports universal authority, or also His plenitude as the source of all. This, however, does not seem true, because thus innascibility would not be a property distinct from paternity and spiration; but would include them as the proper is included in the common. For source and authority signify in God nothing but the principle of origin. We must therefore say with Augustine (De Trin. v, 7) that "unbegotten" imports the negation of passive generation. For he says that "unbegotten" has the same meaning as "not a son." Nor does it follow that "unbegotten" is not the proper notion of the Father; for primary and simple things are notified by negations; as, for instance, a point is defined as what has no part.

Reply Obj. 2: "Unbegotten" is taken sometimes in a negative sense only, and in that sense Jerome says that "the Holy Ghost is unbegotten," that is, He is not begotten. Otherwise "unbegotten" may be taken in a kind of privative sense, but not as implying any imperfection. For privation can be taken in many ways; in one way when a thing has not what is naturally belongs to another, even though it is not of its own nature to have it; as, for instance, if a stone be called a dead thing, as wanting life, which naturally belongs to some other things. In another sense, privation is so called when something has not what naturally belongs to some members of its genus; as for instance when a mole is called blind. In a third sense privation means the absence of what something ought to have; in which sense, privation imports an imperfection. In this sense, "unbegotten" is not attributed to the Father as a privation, but it may be so attributed in the second sense, meaning that a certain person of the divine nature is not begotten, while some person of the same nature is begotten. In this sense the term "unbegotten" can be applied also to the Holy Ghost. Hence to consider it as a term proper to the Father alone, it must be further understood that the name "unbegotten" belongs to a divine person as the principle of another person; so that it be understood to imply negation in the genus of principle taken personally in God. Or that there be understood in the term "unbegotten" that He is not in any way derived from another; and not only that He is not from another by way only of generation. In this sense the term "unbegotten" does not belong at all to the Holy Ghost, Who is from another by procession, as a subsisting person; nor does it belong to the divine essence, of which it may be said that it is in the Son or in the Holy Ghost from another—namely, from the Father.

Reply Obj. 3: According to Damascene (De Fide Orth. ii, 9), "unbegotten" in one sense signifies the same as "uncreated"; and thus it applies to the substance, for thereby does the created substance differ from the uncreated. In another sense it signifies what is not begotten, and in this sense it is a relative term; just as negation is reduced to the genus of affirmation, as "not man" is reduced to the genus of substance, and "not white" to the genus of quality. Hence, since "begotten" implies relation in God, "unbegotten" belongs also to relation. Thus it does not follow that the Father unbegotten is substantially distinguished from the Son begotten; but only by relation; that is, as the relation of Son is denied of the Father.

Reply Obj. 4: In every genus there must be something first; so in the divine nature there must be some one principle which is not from another, and which we call "unbegotten." To admit two innascibles is to suppose the existence of two Gods, and two divine natures. Hence Hilary says (De Synod.): "As there is one God, so there cannot be two innascibles." And this especially because, did two innascibles exist, one would not be from the other, and they would not be distinguished by relative opposition: therefore they would be distinguished from each other by diversity of nature.

Reply Obj. 5: The property of the Father, whereby He is not from another, is more clearly signified by the removal of the nativity of the Son, than by the removal of the procession of the Holy Ghost; both because the procession of the Holy Ghost has no special name, as stated above (Q. 27, A. 4, ad 3), and because also in the order of nature it presupposes the generation of the Son. Hence, it being denied of the Father that He is begotten, although He is the principle of generation, it follows, as a consequence, that He does not proceed by the procession of the Holy Ghost, because the Holy Ghost is not the principle of generation, but proceeds from the person begotten.

## QUESTION 34

OF THE PERSON OF THE SON (In Three Articles)

We next consider the person of the Son. Three

names are attributed to the Son—namely, "Son," "Word," and "Image." The idea of Son is gathered from the idea of Father. Hence it remains for us to consider Word and Image.

Concerning Word there are three points of inquiry:

(1) Whether Word is an essential term in God, or a personal term?

(2) Whether it is the proper name of the Son?

(3) Whether in the name of Word is expressed relation to creatures?

FIRST ARTICLE [I, Q. 34, Art. 1]

Whether Word in God Is a Personal Name?

Objection 1: It would seem that Word in God is not a personal name. For personal names are applied to God in a proper sense, as Father and Son. But Word is applied to God metaphorically, as Origen says on (John 1:1), "In the beginning was the Word." Therefore Word is not a personal name in God.

Obj. 2: Further, according to Augustine (De Trin. ix, 10), "The Word is knowledge with love;" and according to Anselm (Monol. lx), "To speak is to the Supreme Spirit nothing but to see by thought." But knowledge and thought, and sight, are essential terms in God. Therefore Word is not a personal term in God.

Obj. 3: Further, it is essential to word to be spoken. But, according to Anselm (Monol. lix), as the Father is intelligent, the Son is intelligent, and the Holy Ghost is intelligent, so the Father speaks, the Son speaks, and the Holy Ghost speaks; and likewise, each one of them is spoken. Therefore, the name Word is used as an essential term in God, and not in a personal sense.

Obj. 4: Further, no divine person is made. But the Word of God is something made. For it is said, "Fire, hail, snow, ice, the storms which do His Word" (Ps. 148:8). Therefore the Word is not a personal name in God.

*On the contrary,* Augustine says (De Trin. vii, 11): "As the Son is related to the Father, so also is the Word to Him Whose Word He is." But the Son is a personal name, since it is said relatively. Therefore so also is Word.

*I answer that,* The name of Word in God, if taken in its proper sense, is a personal name, and in no way an essential name.

To see how this is true, we must know that our own word taken in its proper sense has a threefold meaning; while in a fourth sense it is taken improperly or figuratively. The clearest and most common sense is when it is said of the word spoken by the voice; and this proceeds from an interior source as regards two things found in the exterior word—that is, the vocal sound itself, and the signification of the sound. For, according to the Philosopher (Peri Herm. i) vocal sound signifies the concept of the intellect. Again the vocal sound proceeds from the signification or the imagination, as stated in *De Anima* ii, text 90. The vocal sound, which has no signification cannot be called a word: wherefore the exterior vocal sound is called a word from the fact the it signifies the interior concept of the mind. Therefore it follows that, first and chiefly, the interior concept of the mind is called a word; secondarily, the vocal sound itself, signifying the interior concept, is so called; and thirdly, the imagination of the vocal sound is called a word. Damascene mentions these three kinds of words (De Fide Orth. i, 17), saying that "word" is called "the natural movement of the intellect, whereby it is moved, and understands, and thinks, as light and splendor;" which is the first kind. "Again," he says, "the word is what is not pronounced by a vocal word, but is uttered in the heart;" which is the third kind. "Again," also, "the word is the angel"—that is, the messenger "of intelligence;" which is the second kind. Word is also used in a fourth way figuratively for that which is signified or effected by a word; thus we are wont to say, "this is the word I have said," or "which the king has commanded," alluding to some deed signified by the word either by way of assertion or of command.

Now word is taken strictly in God, as signifying the concept of the intellect. Hence Augustine says (De Trin. xv, 10): "Whoever can understand the word, not only before it is sounded, but also before thought has clothed it with imaginary sound, can already see some likeness of that Word of Whom it is said: In the beginning was the Word." The concept itself of the heart has of its own nature to proceed from something other than itself—namely, from the knowledge of the one conceiving. Hence "Word," according as we use the term strictly of God, signifies something proceeding from another; which belongs to the nature of personal terms in God, inasmuch as the divine persons are distinguished by origin (Q. 27, AA. 3, 4, 5). Hence the term "Word," according as we use the term strictly of God, is to be taken as said not essentially, but personally.

Reply Obj. 1: The Arians, who sprang from Origen, declared that the Son differed in substance from the Father. Hence, they endeavored to maintain that when the Son of God is called the Word, this is not to be understood in a strict sense; lest the idea of the Word proceeding should compel them to confess that the Son of God is of the same substance as the Father. For the interior word proceeds in such a manner from the one who pronounces it, as to remain within him. But supposing Word to be said metaphorically of God, we must still admit Word in its strict sense. For if a thing be called a word metaphorically, this can only be by reason of some manifestation; either it makes something manifest as a word, or it is manifested by a word. If manifested by a word, there must exist a word whereby it is manifested. If it is called a word because it exteriorly manifests, what it exteriorly manifests cannot be called word except in as far as it signifies the interior concept of the mind, which anyone may also manifest by exterior signs. Therefore, although Word may be sometimes said of God metaphorically, nevertheless we must also admit Word in the proper sense, and which is said personally.

Reply Obj. 2: Nothing belonging to the intellect can be applied to God personally, except word alone; for word alone signifies that which emanates from another. For what the intellect forms in its conception is the word. Now, the intellect itself, according as it is made actual by the intelligible species, is considered absolutely; likewise the act of understanding which is to the actual intellect what existence is to actual being; since the act of understanding does not signify an act going out from the intelligent agent, but an act remaining in the agent. Therefore when we say that word is knowledge, the term knowledge does not mean the act of a knowing intellect, or any one of its habits, but stands for what the intellect conceives by knowing. Hence also Augustine says (De Trin. vii, 1) that the Word is "begotten wisdom;" for it is nothing but the concept of the Wise One; and in the same way It can be called "begotten knowledge." Thus can also be explained how "to speak" is in God "to see by thought," forasmuch as the Word is conceived by the gaze of the divine thought. Still the term "thought" does not properly apply to the Word of God. For Augustine says (De Trin. xv, 16): "Therefore do we speak of the Word of God, and not of the Thought of God, lest we believe that in God there is something unstable, now assuming the form of Word, now putting off that form and remaining latent and as it were formless." For thought consists properly in the search after the truth, and this has no place in God. But when the intellect attains to the form of truth, it does not think, but perfectly contemplates the truth. Hence Anselm (Monol. lx) takes "thought" in an improper sense for "contemplation."

Reply Obj. 3: As, properly speaking, Word in God is said personally, and not essentially, so likewise is to "speak." Hence, as the Word is not common to the Father, Son and Holy Ghost, so it is not true that the Father, Son, and Holy Ghost are one speaker. So Augustine says (De Trin. vii, 1): "He who speaks in that co-eternal Word is understood as not alone in God, but as being with that very Word, without which, forsooth, He would not be speaking." On the other hand, "to be spoken" belongs to each Person, for not only is the word spoken, but also the thing understood or signified by the word. Therefore in this manner to one person alone in God does it belong to be spoken in the same way as a word is spoken; whereas in the way whereby a thing is spoken as being understood in the word, it belongs to each Person to be spoken. For the Father, by understanding Himself, the Son and the Holy Ghost, and all other things comprised in this knowledge, conceives the Word; so that thus the whole Trinity is "spoken" in the Word; and likewise also all creatures: as the intellect of a man by the word he conceives in the act of understanding a stone, speaks a stone. Anselm took the term "speak" improperly for the act of understanding; whereas they really differ from each other; for "to understand" means only the habitude of the intelligent agent to the thing understood, in which habitude no trace of origin is conveyed, but only a certain information of our intellect; forasmuch as our intellect is made actual by the form of the thing understood. In God, however, it means complete identity, because in God the intellect and the thing understood are altogether the same, as was proved above (Q. 14, AA. 4, 5). Whereas to "speak" means chiefly the habitude to the word conceived; for "to speak" is nothing but to utter a word. But by means of the word it imports a habitude to the thing understood which in the word uttered is manifested to the one who understands. Thus, only the Person who utters the Word is "speaker" in God, although each Person understands and is understood, and consequently is spoken by the Word.

Reply Obj. 4: The term "word" is there taken figuratively, as the thing signified or effected by word is called word. For thus creatures are said to do the word of God, as executing any effect, whereto they are ordained from the word conceived of the divine wisdom; as anyone is said to do the word of the king when he does the work to which he is appointed by the king's word.

SECOND ARTICLE [I, Q. 34, Art. 2]

Whether "Word" Is the Son's Proper Name?

Objection 1: It would seem that "Word" is not the proper name of the Son. For the Son is a subsisting person in God. But word does not signify a subsisting thing, as appears in ourselves. Therefore word cannot be the proper name of the person of the Son.

Obj. 2: Further, the word proceeds from the speaker by being uttered. Therefore if the Son is properly the word, He proceeds from the Father, by way only of utterance; which is the heresy of Valentine; as appears from Augustine (De Haeres. xi).

Obj. 3: Further, every proper name of a person signifies some property of that person. Therefore, if the Word is the Son's proper name, it signifies some property of His; and thus there will be several more properties in God than those above mentioned.

Obj. 4: Further, whoever understands conceives a word in the act of understanding. But the Son understands. Therefore some word belongs to the Son; and consequently to be Word is not proper to the Son.

Obj. 5: Further, it is said of the Son (Heb. 1:3): "Bearing all things by the word of His power;" whence Basil infers (Cont. Eunom. v, 11) that the

Holy Ghost is the Son's Word. Therefore to be Word is not proper to the Son.

*On the contrary,* Augustine says (De Trin. vi, 11): "By Word we understand the Son alone."

*I answer that,* "Word," said of God in its proper sense, is used personally, and is the proper name of the person of the Son. For it signifies an emanation of the intellect: and the person Who proceeds in God, by way of emanation of the intellect, is called the Son; and this procession is called generation, as we have shown above (Q. 27, A. 2). Hence it follows that the Son alone is properly called Word in God.

Reply Obj. 1: "To be" and "to understand" are not the same in us. Hence that which in us has intellectual being, does not belong to our nature. But in God "to be" and "to understand" are one and the same: hence the Word of God is not an accident in Him, or an effect of His; but belongs to His very nature. And therefore it must needs be something subsistent; for whatever is in the nature of God subsists; and so Damascene says (De Fide Orth. i, 18) that "the Word of God is substantial and has a hypostatic being; but other words [as our own] are activities if the soul."

Reply Obj. 2: The error of Valentine was condemned, not as the Arians pretended, because he asserted that the Son was born by being uttered, as Hilary relates (De Trin. vi); but on account of the different mode of utterance proposed by its author, as appears from Augustine (De Haeres. xi).

Reply Obj. 3: In the term "Word" the same property is comprised as in the name Son. Hence Augustine says (De Trin. vii, 11): "Word and Son express the same." For the Son's nativity, which is His personal property, is signified by different names, which are attributed to the Son to express His perfection in various ways. To show that He is of the same nature as the Father, He is called the Son; to show that He is co-eternal, He is called the Splendor; to show that He is altogether like, He is called the Image; to show that He is begotten immaterially, He is called the Word. All these truths cannot be expressed by only one name.

Reply Obj. 4: To be intelligent belongs to the Son, in the same way as it belongs to Him to be God, since to understand is said of God essentially, as stated above (Q. 14, AA. 2, 4). Now the Son is God begotten, and not God begetting; and hence He is intelligent, not as producing a Word, but as the Word proceeding; forasmuch as in God the Word proceeding does not differ really from the divine intellect, but is distinguished from the principle of the Word only by relation.

Reply Obj. 5: When it is said of the Son, "Bearing all things by the word of His power"; "word" is taken figuratively for the effect of the Word. Hence a gloss says that "word" is here taken to mean command; inasmuch as by the effect of the power of the Word, things are kept in being, as also by the effect of the power of the Word things are brought into being. Basil speaks widely and figuratively in applying Word to the Holy Ghost; in the sense perhaps that everything that makes a person known may be called his word, and so in that way the Holy Ghost may be called the Son's Word, because He manifests the Son.

THIRD ARTICLE [I, Q. 34, Art. 3]

Whether the Name "Word" Imports Relation to Creatures?

Objection 1: It would seem that the name 'Word' does not import relation to creatures. For every name that connotes some effect in creatures, is said of God essentially. But Word is not said essentially, but personally. Therefore Word does not import relation to creatures.

Obj. 2: Further, whatever imports relation to creatures is said of God in time; as "Lord" and "Creator." But Word is said of God from eternity. Therefore it does not import relation to the creature.

Obj. 3: Further, Word imports relation to the source whence it proceeds. Therefore, if it imports relation to the creature, it follows that the Word proceeds from the creature.

Obj. 4: Further, ideas (in God) are many according to their various relations to creatures. Therefore if Word imports relation to creatures, it follows that in God there is not one Word only, but many.

Obj. 5: Further, if Word imports relation to the creature, this can only be because creatures are known by God. But God does not know beings only; He knows also non-beings. Therefore in the Word are implied relations to non-beings; which appears to be false.

*On the contrary,* Augustine says (QQ. lxxxiii, qu. 63), that "the name Word signifies not only relation to the Father, but also relation to those beings which are made through the Word, by His operative power."

*I answer that,* Word implies relation to creatures. For God by knowing Himself, knows every creature. Now the word conceived in the mind is representative of everything that is actually understood. Hence there are in ourselves different words for the different things which we understand. But because God by one act understands Himself and all things, His one only Word is expressive not only of the Father, but of all creatures.

And as the knowledge of God is only cognitive as regards God, whereas as regards creatures, it is both cognitive and operative, so the Word of God is only expressive of what is in God the Father, but is both expressive and operative of creatures; and therefore it is said (Ps. 32:9): "He spake, and they were made;" because in the Word is implied the operative idea of what God makes.

Reply Obj. 1: The nature is also included indirectly in the name of the person; for person is an individual substance of a rational nature. Therefore the name of a divine person, as regards the personal relation, does not imply relation to the creature, but it is implied in what belongs to the nature. Yet there is nothing to prevent its implying relation to creatures, so far as the essence is included in its meaning: for as it properly belongs to the Son to be the Son, so it properly belongs to Him to be God begotten, or the Creator begotten; and in this way the name Word imports relation to creatures.

Reply Obj. 2: Since the relations result from actions, some names import the relation of God to creatures, which relation follows on the action of God which passes into some exterior effect, as to create and to govern; and the like are applied to God in time. But others import a relation which follows from an action which does not pass into an exterior effect, but abides in the agent—as to know and to will: such are not applied to God in time; and this kind of relation to creatures is implied in the name of the Word. Nor is it true that all names which import the relation of God to creatures are applied to Him in time; but only those names are applied in time which import relation following on the action of God passing into exterior effect.

Reply Obj. 3: Creatures are known to God not by a knowledge derived from the creatures themselves, but by His own essence. Hence it is not necessary that the Word should proceed from creatures, although the Word is expressive of creatures.

Reply Obj. 4: The name of Idea is imposed chiefly to signify relation to creatures; and therefore it is applied in a plural sense to God; and it is not said personally. But the name of Word is imposed chiefly to signify the speaker, and consequently, relation to creatures, inasmuch as God, by understanding Himself, understands every creature; and so there is only one Word in God, and that is a personal one.

Reply Obj. 5: God's knowledge of non-beings and God's Word about non-beings are the same; because the Word of God contains no less than does the knowledge of God, as Augustine says (De Trin. xv, 14). Nevertheless the Word is expressive and operative of beings, but is expressive and manifestive of non-beings.

# QUESTION 35

OF THE IMAGE (In Two Articles)

We next inquire concerning the image: about which there are two points of inquiry:

(1) Whether Image in God is said personally?

(2) Whether this name belongs to the Son alone?

FIRST ARTICLE [I, Q. 35, Art. 1]

Whether Image in God Is Said Personally?

Objection 1: It would seem that image is not said personally of God. For Augustine (Fulgentius, De Fide ad Petrum i) says, "The Godhead of the Holy Trinity and the Image whereunto man is made are one." Therefore Image is said of God essentially, and not personally.

Obj. 2: Further, Hilary says (De Synod.): "An image is a like species of that which it represents." But species or form is said of God essentially. Therefore so also is Image.

Obj. 3: Further, Image is derived from imitation, which implies "before" and "after." But in the divine persons there is no "before" and "after." Therefore Image cannot be a personal name in God.

*On the contrary,* Augustine says (De Trin. vii, 1): "What is more absurd than to say that an image is referred to itself?" Therefore the Image in God is a relation, and is thus a personal name.

*I answer that,* Image includes the idea of similitude. Still, not any kind of similitude suffices for the notion of image, but only similitude of species, or at least of some specific sign. In corporeal things the specific sign consists chiefly in the figure. For we see that the species of different animals are of different figures; but not of different colors. Hence if the color of anything is depicted on a wall, this is not called an image unless the figure is likewise depicted. Further, neither the similitude of species or of figure is enough for an image, which requires also the idea of origin; because, as Augustine says (QQ. lxxxiii, qu. 74): "One egg is not the image of another, because it is not derived from it." Therefore for a true image it is required that one proceeds from another like to it in species, or at least in specific sign. Now whatever imports procession or origin in God, belongs to the persons. Hence the name "Image" is a personal name.

Reply Obj. 1: Image, properly speaking, means whatever proceeds forth in likeness to another. That to the likeness of which anything proceeds, is properly speaking called the exemplar, and is improperly called the image. Nevertheless Augustine (Fulgentius) uses the name of Image in this sense when he says that the divine nature of the Holy Trinity is the Image to whom man was made.

Reply Obj. 2: species, as mentioned by Hilary in the definition of image, means the form derived from one thing to another. In this sense image is said to be the species of anything, as that which is assimilated to anything is called its form, inasmuch as it has a like form.

Reply Obj. 3: Imitation in God does not signify posteriority, but only assimilation.

SECOND ARTICLE [I, Q. 35, Art. 2]

Whether the Name of Image Is Proper to the Son?

Objection 1: It would seem that the name of Image is not proper to the Son; because, as Damascene says (De Fide Orth. i, 18), "The Holy Ghost is the Image of the Son." Therefore Image does not belong to the Son alone.

Obj. 2: Further, similitude in expression belongs to the nature of an image, as Augustine says (QQ. lxxxiii, qu. 74). But this belongs to the Holy Ghost, Who proceeds from another by way of similitude.

Therefore the Holy Ghost is an Image; and so to be Image does not belong to the Son alone.

Obj. 3: Further, man is also called the image of God, according to 1 Cor. 11:7, "The man ought not to cover his head, for he is the image and the glory of God." Therefore Image is not proper to the Son.

*On the contrary,* Augustine says (De Trin. vi, 2): "The Son alone is the Image of the Father."

*I answer that,* The Greek Doctors commonly say that the Holy Ghost is the Image of both the Father and of the Son; but the Latin Doctors attribute the name Image to the Son alone. For it is not found in the canonical Scripture except as applied to the Son; as in the words, "Who is the Image of the invisible God, the firstborn of creatures" (Col. 1:15) and again: "Who being the brightness of His glory, and the figure of His substance." (Heb. 1:3).

Some explain this by the fact that the Son agrees with the Father, not in nature only, but also in the notion of principle: whereas the Holy Ghost agrees neither with the Son, nor with the Father in any notion. This, however, does not seem to suffice. Because as it is not by reason of the relations that we consider either equality or inequality in God, as Augustine says (De Trin. v, 6), so neither (by reason thereof do we consider) that similitude which is essential to image. Hence others say that the Holy Ghost cannot be called the Image of the Son, because there cannot be an image of an image; nor of the Father, because again the image must be immediately related to that which it is the image; and the Holy Ghost is related to the Father through the Son; nor again is He the Image of the Father and the Son, because then there would be one image of two; which is impossible. Hence it follows that the Holy Ghost is in no way an Image. But this is no proof: for the Father and the Son are one principle of the Holy Ghost, as we shall explain further on (Q. 36, A. 4). Hence there is nothing to prevent there being one Image of the Father and of the Son, inasmuch as they are one; since even man is one image of the whole Trinity.

Therefore we must explain the matter otherwise by saying that, as the Holy Ghost, although by His procession He receives the nature of the Father, as the Son also receives it, nevertheless is not said to be "born"; so, although He receives the likeness of the Father, He is not called the Image; because the Son proceeds as word, and it is essential to word to be like species with that whence it proceeds; whereas this does not essentially belong to love, although it may belong to that love which is the Holy Ghost, inasmuch as He is the divine love.

Reply Obj. 1: Damascene and the other Greek Doctors commonly employ the term image as meaning a perfect similitude.

Reply Obj. 2: Although the Holy Ghost is like to the Father and the Son, still it does not follow that He is the Image, as above explained.

Reply Obj. 3: The image of a thing may be found in something in two ways. In one way it is found in something of the same specific nature; as the image of the king is found in his son. In another way it is found in something of a different nature, as the king's image on the coin. In the first sense the Son is the Image of the Father; in the second sense man is called the image of God; and therefore in order to express the imperfect character of the divine image in man, man is not simply called the image, but "to the image," whereby is expressed a certain movement of tendency to perfection. But it cannot be said that the Son of God is "to the image," because He is the perfect Image of the Father.

# QUESTION 36

OF THE PERSON OF THE HOLY GHOST (In Four Articles)

We proceed to treat of what belongs to the person of the Holy Ghost, Who is called not only the Holy Ghost, but also the Love and Gift of God. Concerning the name "Holy Ghost" there are four points of inquiry:

(1) Whether this name, "Holy Ghost," is the proper name of one divine Person?

(2) Whether that divine person Who is called the Holy Ghost, proceeds from the Father and the Son?

(3) Whether He proceeds from the Father through the Son?

(4) Whether the Father and the Son are one principle of the Holy Ghost?

FIRST ARTICLE [I, Q. 36, Art. 1]

Whether This Name "Holy Ghost" Is the Proper Name of One Divine Person?

Objection 1: It would seem that this name, "Holy Ghost," is not the proper name of one divine person. For no name which is common to the three persons is the proper name of any one person. But this name of 'Holy Ghost' [*It should be borne in mind that the word "ghost" is the old English equivalent for the Latin "spiritus,"] whether in the sense of "breath" or "blast," or in the sense of "spirit," as an immaterial substance. Thus, we read in the former sense (Hampole, Psalter x, 7), "The Gost of Storms" [spiritus procellarum], and in the latter "Trubled gost is sacrifice of God" (Prose Psalter, A.D. 1325), and "Oure wrestlynge is ... against the spiritual wicked gostes of the ayre" (More, "Comfort against Tribulation"); and in our modern expression of "giving up the ghost." As applied to God, and not specially to the third Holy Person, we have an example from Maunder, "Jhesu Criste was the worde and the goste of Good." (See Oxford Dictionary).) is common to the three persons; for Hilary (De Trin. viii) shows that the "Spirit of God" sometimes means the Father, as in the words of Isa. 61:1: "The Spirit of the Lord is upon me;" and sometimes the Son, as when the Son says: "In the Spirit of God I cast out devils" (Matt. 12:28), showing that He cast out devils by His own natural power; and that sometimes it means the Holy Ghost, as in the words of Joel 2:28: "I will pour out of My Spirit over all flesh." Therefore this name 'Holy Ghost' is not the proper name of a divine person.

Obj. 2: Further, the names of the divine persons are relative terms, as Boethius says (De Trin.). But this name "Holy Ghost" is not a relative term. Therefore this name is not the proper name of a divine Person.

Obj. 3: Further, because the Son is the name of a divine Person He cannot be called the Son of this or of that. But the spirit is spoken of as of this or that man, as appears in the words, "The Lord said to Moses, I will take of thy spirit and will give to them" (Num. 11:17) and also "The Spirit of Elias rested upon Eliseus" (4 Kings 2:15). Therefore "Holy Ghost" does not seem to be the proper name of a divine Person.

*On the contrary,* It is said (1 John 5:7): "There are three who bear witness in heaven, the Father, the Word, and the Holy Ghost." As Augustine says (De Trin. vii, 4): "When we ask, Three what? we say, Three persons." Therefore the Holy Ghost is the name of a divine person.

*I answer that,* While there are two processions in God, one of these, the procession of love, has no proper name of its own, as stated above (Q. 27, A. 4, ad 3). Hence the relations also which follow from this procession are without a name (Q. 28, A. 4): for which reason the Person proceeding in that manner has not a proper name. But as some names are accommodated by the usual mode of speaking to signify the aforesaid relations, as when we use the names of procession and spiration, which in the strict sense more fittingly signify the notional acts than the relations; so to signify the divine Person, Who proceeds by way of love, this name "Holy Ghost" is by the use of scriptural speech accommodated to Him. The appropriateness of this name may be shown in two ways. Firstly, from the fact that the person who is called "Holy Ghost" has something in common with the other Persons. For, as Augustine says (De Trin. xv, 17; v, 11), "Because the Holy Ghost is common to both, He Himself is called that properly which both are called in common. For the Father also is a spirit, and the Son is a spirit; and the Father is holy, and the Son is holy." Secondly, from the proper signification of the name. For the name spirit in things corporeal seems to signify impulse and motion; for we call the breath and the wind by the term spirit. Now it is a property of love to move and impel the will of the lover towards the object loved. Further, holiness is attributed to whatever is ordered to God. Therefore because the divine person proceeds by way of the love whereby God is loved, that person is most properly named "The Holy Ghost."

Reply Obj. 1: The expression Holy Spirit, if taken as two words, is applicable to the whole Trinity: because by 'spirit' the immateriality of the divine substance is signified; for corporeal spirit is invisible, and has but little matter; hence we apply this term to all immaterial and invisible substances. And by adding the word "holy" we signify the purity of divine goodness. But if Holy Spirit be taken as one word, it is thus that the expression, in the usage of the Church, is accommodated to signify one of the three persons, the one who proceeds by way of love, for the reason above explained.

Reply Obj. 2: Although this name "Holy Ghost" does not indicate a relation, still it takes the place of a relative term, inasmuch as it is accommodated to signify a Person distinct from the others by relation only. Yet this name may be understood as including a relation, if we understand the Holy Spirit as being breathed [spiratus].

Reply Obj. 3: In the name Son we understand that relation only which is of something from a principle, in regard to that principle: but in the name "Father" we understand the relation of principle; and likewise in the name of Spirit inasmuch as it implies a moving power. But to no creature does it belong to be a principle as regards a divine person; but rather the reverse. Therefore we can say "our Father," and "our Spirit"; but we cannot say "our Son."

SECOND ARTICLE [I, Q. 36, Art. 2]

Whether the Holy Ghost Proceeds from the Son?

Objection 1: It would seem that the Holy Ghost does not proceed from the Son. For as Dionysius says (Div. Nom. i): "We must not dare to say anything concerning the substantial Divinity except what has been divinely expressed to us by the sacred oracles." But in the Sacred Scripture we are not told that the Holy Ghost proceeds from the Son; but only that He proceeds from the Father, as appears from John 15:26: "The Spirit of truth, Who proceeds from the Father." Therefore the Holy Ghost does not proceed from the Son.

Obj. 2: Further, In the creed of the council of Constantinople (Can. vii) we read: "We believe in the Holy Ghost, the Lord and Life-giver, who proceeds from the Father; with the Father and the Son to be adored and glorified." Therefore it should not be added in our Creed that the Holy Ghost proceeds from the Son; and those who added such a thing appear to be worthy of anathema.

Obj. 3: Further, Damascene says (De Fide Orth. i): "We say that the Holy Ghost is from the Father, and we name Him the spirit of the Father; but we do not say that the Holy Ghost is from the Son, yet we name Him the Spirit of the Son." Therefore the Holy Ghost does not proceed from the Son.

Obj. 4: Further, Nothing proceeds from that wherein it rests. But the Holy Ghost rests in the Son; for it is said in the legend of St. Andrew: "Peace be to you and to all who believe in the one

God the Father, and in His only Son our Lord Jesus Christ, and in the one Holy Ghost proceeding from the Father, and abiding in the Son." Therefore the Holy Ghost does not proceed from the Son.

Obj. 5: Further, the Son proceeds as the Word. But our breath [spiritus] does not seem to proceed in ourselves from our word. Therefore the Holy Ghost does not proceed from the Son.

Obj. 6: Further, the Holy Ghost proceeds perfectly from the Father. Therefore it is superfluous to say that He proceeds from the Son.

Obj. 7: Further "the actual and the possible do not differ in things perpetual" (Phys. iii, text 32), and much less so in God. But it is possible for the Holy Ghost to be distinguished from the Son, even if He did not proceed from Him. For Anselm says (De Process. Spir. Sancti, ii): "The Son and the Holy Ghost have their Being from the Father; but each in a different way; one by Birth, the other by Procession, so that they are thus distinct from one another." And further on he says: "For even if for no other reason were the Son and the Holy Ghost distinct, this alone would suffice." Therefore the Holy Spirit is distinct from the Son, without proceeding from Him.

*On the contrary,* Athanasius says: "The Holy Ghost is from the Father and the Son; not made, nor created, nor begotten, but proceeding."

*I answer that,* It must be said that the Holy Ghost is from the Son. For if He were not from Him, He could in no wise be personally distinguished from Him; as appears from what has been said above (Q. 28, A. 3; Q. 30, A. 2). For it cannot be said that the divine Persons are distinguished from each other in any absolute sense; for it would follow that there would not be one essence of the three persons: since everything that is spoken of God in an absolute sense, belongs to the unity of essence. Therefore it must be said that the divine persons are distinguished from each other only by the relations. Now the relations cannot distinguish the persons except forasmuch as they are opposite relations; which appears from the fact that the Father has two relations, by one of which He is related to the Son, and by the other to the Holy Ghost; but these are not opposite relations, and therefore they do not make two persons, but belong only to the one person of the Father. If therefore in the Son and the Holy Ghost there were two relations only, whereby each of them were related to the Father, these relations would not be opposite to each other, as neither would be the two relations whereby the Father is related to them. Hence, as the person of the Father is one, it would follow that the person of the Son and of the Holy Ghost would be one, having two relations opposed to the two relations of the Father. But this is heretical since it destroys the Faith in the Trinity. Therefore the Son and the Holy Ghost must be related to each other by opposite relations. Now there cannot be in God any relations opposed to each other, except relations of origin, as proved above (Q. 28, A. 4). And opposite relations of origin are to be understood as of a "principle," and of what is "from the principle." Therefore we must conclude that it is necessary to say that either the Son is from the Holy Ghost; which no one says; or that the Holy Ghost is from the Son, as we confess.

Furthermore, the order of the procession of each one agrees with this conclusion. For it was said above (Q. 27, AA. 2, 4; Q. 28, A. 4), that the Son proceeds by the way of the intellect as Word, and the Holy Ghost by way of the will as Love. Now love must proceed from a word. For we do not love anything unless we apprehend it by a mental conception. Hence also in this way it is manifest that the Holy Ghost proceeds from the Son.

We derive a knowledge of the same truth from the very order of nature itself. For we nowhere find that several things proceed from one without order except in those which differ only by their matter; as for instance one smith produces many knives distinct from each other materially, with no order to each other; whereas in things in which there is not only a material distinction we always find that some order exists in the multitude produced. Hence also in the order of creatures produced, the beauty of the divine wisdom is displayed. So if from the one Person of the Father, two persons proceed, the Son and the Holy Ghost, there must be some order between them. Nor can any other be assigned except the order of their nature, whereby one is from the other. Therefore it cannot be said that the Son and the Holy Ghost proceed from the Father in such a way as that neither of them proceeds from the other, unless we admit in them a material distinction; which is impossible.

Hence also the Greeks themselves recognize that the procession of the Holy Ghost has some order to the Son. For they grant that the Holy Ghost is the Spirit "of the Son"; and that He is from the Father "through the Son." Some of them are said also to concede that "He is from the Son"; or that "He flows from the Son," but not that He proceeds; which seems to come from ignorance or obstinacy. For a just consideration of the truth will convince anyone that the word procession is the one most commonly applied to all that denotes origin of any kind. For we use the term to describe any kind of origin; as when we say that a line proceeds from a point, a ray from the sun, a stream from a source, and likewise in everything else. Hence, granted that the Holy Ghost originates in any way from the Son, we can conclude that the Holy Ghost proceeds from the Son.

Reply Obj. 1: We ought not to say about God anything which is not found in Holy Scripture either explicitly or implicitly. But although we do not find it verbally expressed in Holy Scripture that the Holy Ghost proceeds from the Son, still we do find it in the sense of Scripture, especially where the Son says, speaking of the Holy Ghost, "He will glorify Me, because He shall receive of Mine" (John 16:14). It is also a rule of Holy Scripture that whatever is said of the Father, applies to the Son, although there be added an exclusive term; except only as regards what belongs to the opposite relations, whereby the Father and the Son are distinguished from each other. For when the Lord says, "No one knoweth the Son, but the Father," the idea of the Son knowing Himself is not excluded. So therefore when we say that the Holy Ghost proceeds from the Father, even though it be added that He proceeds from the Father alone, the Son would not thereby be at all excluded; because as regards being the principle of the Holy Ghost, the Father and the Son are not opposed to each other, but only as regards the fact that one is the Father, and the other is the Son.

Reply Obj. 2: In every council of the Church a symbol of faith has been drawn up to meet some prevalent error condemned in the council at that time. Hence subsequent councils are not to be described as making a new symbol of faith; but what was implicitly contained in the first symbol was explained by some addition directed against rising heresies. Hence in the decision of the council of Chalcedon it is declared that those who were congregated together in the council of Constantinople, handed down the doctrine about the Holy Ghost, not implying that there was anything wanting in the doctrine of their predecessors who had gathered together at Nicaea, but explaining what those fathers had understood of the matter. Therefore, because at the time of the ancient councils the error of those who said that the Holy Ghost did not proceed from the Son had not arisen, it was not necessary to make any explicit declaration on that point; whereas, later on, when certain errors rose up, another council [*Council of Rome, under Pope Damasus] assembled in the west, the matter was explicitly defined by the authority of the Roman Pontiff, by whose authority also the ancient councils were summoned and confirmed. Nevertheless the truth was contained implicitly in the belief that the Holy Ghost proceeds from the Father.

Reply Obj. 3: The Nestorians were the first to introduce the error that the Holy Ghost did not proceed from the Son, as appears in a Nestorian creed condemned in the council of Ephesus. This error was embraced by Theodoric the Nestorian, and several others after him, among whom was also Damascene. Hence, in that point his opinion is not to be held. Although, too, it has been asserted by some that while Damascene did not confess that the Holy Ghost was from the Son, neither do those words of his express a denial thereof.

Reply Obj. 4: When the Holy Ghost is said to rest or abide in the Son, it does not mean that He does not proceed from Him; for the Son also is said to abide in the Father, although He proceeds from the Father. Also the Holy Ghost is said to rest in the Son as the love of the lover abides in the beloved; or in reference to the human nature of Christ, by reason of what is written: "On whom thou shalt see the Spirit descending and remaining upon Him, He it is who baptizes" (John 1:33).

Reply Obj. 5: The Word in God is not taken after the similitude of the vocal word, whence the breath [spiritus] does not proceed; for it would then be only metaphorical; but after the similitude of the mental word, whence proceeds love.

Reply Obj. 6: For the reason that the Holy Ghost proceeds from the Father perfectly, not only is it not superfluous to say He proceeds from the Son, but rather it is absolutely necessary. Forasmuch as one power belongs to the Father and the Son; and because whatever is from the Father, must be from the Son unless it be opposed to the property of filiation; for the Son is not from Himself, although He is from the Father.

Reply Obj. 7: The Holy Ghost is distinguished from the Son, inasmuch as the origin of one is distinguished from the origin of the other; but the difference itself of origin comes from the fact that the Son is only from the Father, whereas the Holy Ghost is from the Father and the Son; for otherwise the processions would not be distinguished from each other, as explained above, and in Q. 27.

THIRD ARTICLE [I, Q. 36, Art. 3]

Whether the Holy Ghost Proceeds from the Father Through the Son?

Objection 1: It would seem that the Holy Ghost does not proceed from the Father through the Son. For whatever proceeds from one through another, does not proceed immediately. Therefore, if the Holy Ghost proceeds from the Father through the Son, He does not proceed immediately; which seems to be unfitting.

Obj. 2: Further, if the Holy Ghost proceeds from the Father through the Son, He does not proceed from the Son, except on account of the Father. But "whatever causes a thing to be such is yet more so." Therefore He proceeds more from the Father than from the Son.

Obj. 3: Further, the Son has His being by generation. Therefore if the Holy Ghost is from the Father through the Son, it follows that the Son is first generated and afterwards the Holy Ghost proceeds; and thus the procession of the Holy Ghost is not eternal, which is heretical.

Obj. 4: Further, when anyone acts through another, the same may be said conversely. For as we say that the king acts through the bailiff, so it can be said conversely that the bailiff acts through the king. But we can never say that the Son spirates the Holy Ghost through the Father. Therefore it can never be said that the Father spirates the Holy Ghost through the Son.

*On the contrary,* Hilary says (De Trin. xii): "Keep me, I pray, in this expression of my faith, that I may ever possess the Father—namely Thyself: that I may adore Thy Son together with Thee: and that I may deserve Thy Holy Spirit, who is through Thy Only Begotten."

*I answer that,* Whenever one is said to act through another, this preposition "through" points out, in what is covered by it, some cause or principle of that act. But since action is a mean between the agent and the thing done, sometimes that which is covered by the preposition "through" is the cause of the action, as proceeding from the agent; and in that case it is the cause of why the agent acts, whether it be a final cause or a formal cause, whether it be effective or motive. It is a final cause when we say, for instance, that the artisan works through love of gain. It is a formal cause when we say that he works through his art. It is a motive cause when we say that he works through the command of another. Sometimes, however, that which is covered by this preposition "through" is the cause of the action regarded as terminated in the thing done; as, for instance, when we say, the artisan acts through the mallet, for this does not mean that the mallet is the cause why the artisan acts, but that it is the cause why the thing made proceeds from the artisan, and that it has even this effect from the artisan. This is why it is sometimes said that this preposition "through" sometimes denotes direct authority, as when we say, the king works through the bailiff; and sometimes indirect authority, as when we say, the bailiff works through the king.

Therefore, because the Son receives from the Father that the Holy Ghost proceeds from Him, it can be said that the Father spirates the Holy Ghost through the Son, or that the Holy Ghost proceeds from the Father through the Son, which has the same meaning.

Reply Obj. 1: In every action two things are to be considered, the *suppositum* acting, and the power whereby it acts; as, for instance, fire heats through heat. So if we consider in the Father and the Son the power whereby they spirate the Holy Ghost, there is no mean, for this is one and the same power. But if we consider the persons themselves spirating, then, as the Holy Ghost proceeds both from the Father and from the Son, the Holy Ghost proceeds from the Father immediately, as from Him, and mediately, as from the Son; and thus He is said to proceed from the Father through the Son. So also did Abel proceed immediately from Adam, inasmuch as Adam was his father; and mediately, as Eve was his mother, who proceeded from Adam; although, indeed, this example of a material procession is inept to signify the immaterial procession of the divine persons.

Reply Obj. 2: If the Son received from the Father a numerically distinct power for the spiration of the Holy Ghost, it would follow that He would be a secondary and instrumental cause; and thus the Holy Ghost would proceed more from the Father than from the Son; whereas, *on the contrary,* the same spirative power belongs to the Father and to the Son; and therefore the Holy Ghost proceeds equally from both, although sometimes He is said to proceed principally or properly from the Father, because the Son has this power from the Father.

Reply Obj. 3: As the begetting of the Son is co-eternal with the begetter (and hence the Father does not exist before begetting the Son), so the procession of the Holy Ghost is co-eternal with His principle. Hence, the Son was not begotten before the Holy Ghost proceeded; but each of the operations is eternal.

Reply Obj. 4: When anyone is said to work through anything, the converse proposition is not always true. For we do not say that the mallet works through the carpenter; whereas we can say that the bailiff acts through the king, because it is the bailiff's place to act, since he is master of his own act, but it is not the mallet's place to act, but only to be made to act, and hence it is used only as an instrument. The bailiff is, however, said to act through the king, although this preposition "through" denotes a medium, for the more a *suppositum* is prior in action, so much the more is its power immediate as regards the effect, inasmuch as the power of the first cause joins the second cause to its effect. Hence also first principles are said to be immediate in the demonstrative sciences. Therefore, so far as the bailiff is a medium according to the order of the subject's acting, the king is said to work through the bailiff; but according to the order of powers, the bailiff is said to act through the king, forasmuch as the power of the king gives the bailiff's action its effect. Now there is no order of power between Father and Son, but only order of 'supposita'; and hence we say that the Father spirates through the Son; and not conversely.

FOURTH ARTICLE [I, Q. 36, Art. 4]

Whether the Father and the Son Are One Principle of the Holy Ghost?

Objection 1: It would seem that the Father and the Son are not one principle of the Holy Ghost. For the Holy Ghost does not proceed from the Father and the Son as they are one; not as they are one in nature, for the Holy Ghost would in that way proceed from Himself, as He is one in nature with Them; nor again inasmuch as they are united in any one property, for it is clear that one property cannot belong to two subjects. Therefore the Holy Ghost proceeds from the Father and the Son as distinct from one another. Therefore the Father and the Son are not one principle of the Holy Ghost.

Obj. 2: Further, in this proposition "the Father and the Son are one principle of the Holy Ghost," we do not designate personal unity, because in that case the Father and the Son would be one person; nor again do we designate the unity of property, because if one property were the reason of the Father and the Son being one principle of the Holy Ghost, similarly, on account of His two properties, the Father would be two principles of the Son and of the Holy Ghost, which cannot be admitted. Therefore the Father and the Son are not one principle of the Holy Ghost.

Obj. 3: Further, the Son is not one with the Father more than is the Holy Ghost. But the Holy Ghost and the Father are not one principle as regards any other divine person. Therefore neither are the Father and the Son.

Obj. 4: Further, if the Father and the Son are one principle of the Holy Ghost, this one is either the Father or it is not the Father. But we cannot assert either of these positions because if the one is the Father, it follows that the Son is the Father; and if the one is not the Father, it follows that the Father is not the Father. Therefore we cannot say that the Father and the Son are one principle of the Holy Ghost.

Obj. 5: Further, if the Father and the Son are one principle of the Holy Ghost, it seems necessary to say, conversely, that the one principle of the Holy Ghost is the Father and the Son. But this seems to be false; for this word "principle" stands either for the person of the Father, or for the person of the Son; and in either sense it is false. Therefore this proposition also is false, that the Father and the Son are one principle of the Holy Ghost.

Obj. 6: Further, unity in substance makes identity. So if the Father and the Son are the one principle of the Holy Ghost, it follows that they are the same principle; which is denied by many. Therefore we cannot grant that the Father and the Son are one principle of the Holy Ghost.

Obj. 7: Further, the Father, Son and Holy Ghost are called one Creator, because they are the one principle of the creature. But the Father and the Son are not one, but two Spirators, as many assert; and this agrees also with what Hilary says (De Trin. ii) that "the Holy Ghost is to be confessed as proceeding from Father and Son as authors." Therefore the Father and the Son are not one principle of the Holy Ghost.

*On the contrary,* Augustine says (De Trin. v, 14) that the Father and the Son are not two principles, but one principle of the Holy Ghost.

*I answer that,* The Father and the Son are in everything one, wherever there is no distinction between them of opposite relation. Hence since there is no relative opposition between them as the principle of the Holy Ghost it follows that the Father and the Son are one principle of the Holy Ghost.

Some, however, assert that this proposition is incorrect: "The Father and the Son are one principle of the Holy Ghost," because, they declare, since the word "principle" in the singular number does not signify "person," but "property," it must be taken as an adjective; and forasmuch as an adjective cannot be modified by another adjective, it cannot properly be said that the Father and the Son are one principle of the Holy Ghost unless one be taken as an adverb, so that the meaning should be: They are one principle—that is, in one and the same way. But then it might be equally right to say that the Father is two principles of the Son and of the Holy Ghost—namely, in two ways. Therefore, we must say that, although this word "principle" signifies a property, it does so after the manner of a substantive, as do the words "father" and "son" even in things created. Hence it takes its number from the form it signifies, like other substantives. Therefore, as the Father and the Son are one God, by reason of the unity of the form that is signified by this word "God"; so they are one principle of the Holy Ghost by reason of the unity of the property that is signified in this word "principle."

Reply Obj. 1: If we consider the spirative power, the Holy Ghost proceeds from the Father and the Son as they are one in the spirative power, which in a certain way signifies the nature with the property, as we shall see later (ad 7). Nor is there any reason against one property being in two *supposita* that possess one common nature. But if we consider the *supposita* of the spiration, then we may say that the Holy Ghost proceeds from the Father and the Son, as distinct; for He proceeds from them as the unitive love of both.

Reply Obj. 2: In the proposition "the Father and the Son are one principle of the Holy Ghost," one property is designated which is the form signified by the term. It does not thence follow that by reason of the several properties the Father can be called several principles, for this would imply in Him a plurality of subjects.

Reply Obj. 3: It is not by reason of relative properties that we speak of similitude or dissimilitude in God, but by reason of the essence. Hence, as the Father is not more like to Himself than He is to the Son; so likewise neither is the Son more like to the Father than is the Holy Ghost.

Reply Obj. 4: These two propositions, "The Father and the Son are one principle which is the Father," or, "one principle which is not the Father," are not mutually contradictory; and hence it is not necessary to assert one or other of them. For when we say the Father and the Son are one principle, this word "principle" has not determinate supposition but rather it stands indeterminately for two persons together. Hence there is a fallacy of "figure of speech" as the argument concludes from the indeterminate to the determinate.

Reply Obj. 5: This proposition is also true:—The one principle of the Holy Ghost is the Father and the Son; because the word "principle" does not stand for one person only, but indistinctly for the two persons as above explained.

Reply Obj. 6: There is no reason against saying that the Father and the Son are the same principle, because the word "principle" stands confusedly and indistinctly for the two Persons together.

Reply Obj. 7: Some say that although the Father

and the Son are one principle of the Holy Ghost, there are two spirators, by reason of the distinction of *supposita*, as also there are two spirating, because acts refer to subjects. Yet this does not hold good as to the name "Creator"; because the Holy Ghost proceeds from the Father and the Son as from two distinct persons, as above explained; whereas the creature proceeds from the three persons not as distinct persons, but as united in essence. It seems, however, better to say that because spirating is an adjective, and spirator a substantive, we can say that the Father and the Son are two spirating, by reason of the plurality of the *supposita* but not two spirators by reason of the one spiration. For adjectival words derive their number from the *supposita* but substantives from themselves, according to the form signified. As to what Hilary says, that "the Holy Ghost is from the Father and the Son as His authors," this is to be explained in the sense that the substantive here stands for the adjective.

## QUESTION 37

OF THE NAME OF THE HOLY GHOST—LOVE (In Two Articles)

We now inquire concerning the name "Love," on which arise two points of inquiry:

(1) Whether it is the proper name of the Holy Ghost?

(2) Whether the Father and the Son love each other by the Holy Ghost?

FIRST ARTICLE [I, Q. 37, Art. 2]

Whether "Love" Is the Proper Name of the Holy Ghost?

Objection 1: It would seem that "Love" is not the proper name of the Holy Ghost. For Augustine says (De Trin. xv, 17): "As the Father, Son and Holy Ghost are called Wisdom, and are not three Wisdoms, but one; I know not why the Father, Son and Holy Ghost should not be called Charity, and all together one Charity." But no name which is predicated in the singular of each person and of all together, is a proper name of a person. Therefore this name, "Love," is not the proper name of the Holy Ghost.

Obj. 2: Further, the Holy Ghost is a subsisting person, but love is not used to signify a subsisting person, but rather an action passing from the lover to the beloved. Therefore Love is not the proper name of the Holy Ghost.

Obj. 3: Further, Love is the bond between lovers, for as Dionysius says (Div. Nom. iv): "Love is a unitive force." But a bond is a medium between what it joins together, not something proceeding from them. Therefore, since the Holy Ghost proceeds from the Father and the Son, as was shown above (Q. 36, A. 2), it seems that He is not the Love or bond of the Father and the Son.

Obj. 4: Further, Love belongs to every lover. But the Holy Ghost is a lover: therefore He has love. So if the Holy Ghost is Love, He must be love of love, and spirit from spirit; which is not admissible.

*On the contrary,* Gregory says (Hom. xxx, in Pentecost.): "The Holy Ghost Himself is Love."

*I answer that,* The name Love in God can be taken essentially and personally. If taken personally it is the proper name of the Holy Ghost; as Word is the proper name of the Son.

To see this we must know that since as shown above (Q. 27, AA. 2, 3, 4, 5), there are two processions in God, one by way of the intellect, which is the procession of the Word, and another by way of the will, which is the procession of Love; forasmuch as the former is the more known to us, we have been able to apply more suitable names to express our various considerations as regards that procession, but not as regards the procession of the will. Hence, we are obliged to employ circumlocution as regards the person Who proceeds, and the relations following from this procession which are called "procession" and "spiration," as stated above (Q. 27, A. 4, ad 3), and yet express the origin rather than the relation in the strict sense of the term. Nevertheless we must consider them in respect of each procession simply. For as when a thing is understood by anyone, there results in the one who understands a conception of the object understood, which conception we call word; so when anyone loves an object, a certain impression results, so to speak, of the thing loved in the affection of the lover; by reason of which the object loved is said to be in the lover; as also the thing understood is in the one who understands; so that when anyone understands and loves himself he is in himself, not only by real identity, but also as the object understood is in the one who understands, and the thing loved is in the lover. As regards the intellect, however, words have been found to describe the mutual relation of the one who understands the object understood, as appears in the word "to understand"; and other words are used to express the procession of the intellectual conception—namely, "to speak," and "word." Hence in God, "to understand" is applied only to the essence; because it does not import relation to the Word that proceeds; whereas "Word" is said personally, because it signifies what proceeds; and the term "to speak" is a notional term as importing the relation of the principle of the Word to the Word Himself. On the other hand, on the part of the will, with the exception of the words "dilection" and "love," which express the relation of the lover to the object loved, there are no other terms in use, which express the relation of the impression or affection of the object loved, produced in the lover by fact that he loves—to the principle of that impression, or "vice versa." And therefore, on account of the poverty of our vocabulary, we express these relations by the words "love" and "dilection": just as if we were to call the Word "intelligence conceived," or "wisdom begotten."

It follows that so far as love means only the relation of the lover to the object loved, "love" and "to love" are said of the essence, as "understanding" and "to understand"; but, on the other hand, so far as these words are used to express the relation to its principle, of what proceeds by way of love, and "vice versa," so that by "love" is understood the "love proceeding," and by "to love" is understood "the spiration of the love proceeding," in that sense "love" is the name of the person and "to love" is a notional term, as "to speak" and "to beget."

Reply Obj. 1: Augustine is there speaking of charity as it means the divine essence, as was said above (here and Q. 24, A. 2, ad 4).

Reply Obj. 2: Although to understand, and to will, and to love signify actions passing on to their objects, nevertheless they are actions that remain in the agents, as stated above (Q. 14, A. 4), yet in such a way that in the agent itself they import a certain relation to their object. Hence, love also in ourselves is something that abides in the lover, and the word of the heart is something abiding in the speaker; yet with a relation to the thing expressed by word, or loved. But in God, in whom there is nothing accidental, there is more than this; because both Word and Love are subsistent. Therefore, when we say that the Holy Ghost is the Love of the Father for the Son, or for something else; we do not mean anything that passes into another, but only the relation of love to the beloved; as also in the Word is imported the relation of the Word to the thing expressed by the Word.

Reply Obj. 3: The Holy Ghost is said to be the bond of the Father and Son, inasmuch as He is Love; because, since the Father loves Himself and the Son with one Love, and conversely, there is expressed in the Holy Ghost, as Love, the relation of the Father to the Son, and conversely, as that of the lover to the beloved. But from the fact that the Father and the Son mutually love one another, it necessarily follows that this mutual Love, the Holy Ghost, proceeds from both. As regards origin, therefore, the Holy Ghost is not the medium, but the third person in the Trinity; whereas as regards the aforesaid relation He is the bond between the two persons, as proceeding from both.

Reply Obj. 4: As it does not belong to the Son, though He understands, to produce a word, for it belongs to Him to understand as the word proceeding; so in like manner, although the Holy Ghost loves, taking Love as an essential term, still it does not belong to Him to spirate love, which is to take love as a notional term; because He loves essentially as love proceeding; but not as the one whence love proceeds.

SECOND ARTICLE [I, Q. 37, Art. 2]

Whether the Father and the Son Love Each Other by the Holy Ghost?

Objection 1: It would seem that the Father and the Son do not love each other by the Holy Ghost. For Augustine (De Trin. vii, 1) proves that the Father is not wise by the Wisdom begotten. But as the Son is Wisdom begotten, so the Holy Ghost is the Love proceeding, as explained above (Q. 27, A. 3). Therefore the Father and the Son do not love Themselves by the Love proceeding, which is the Holy Ghost.

Obj. 2: Further, in the proposition, "The Father and the Son love each other by the Holy Ghost," this word "love" is to be taken either essentially or notionally. But it cannot be true if taken essentially, because in the same way we might say that "the Father understands by the Son"; nor, again, if it is taken notionally, for then, in like manner, it might be said that "the Father and the Son spirate by the Holy Ghost," or that "the Father generates by the Son." Therefore in no way is this proposition true: "The Father and the Son love each other by the Holy Ghost."

Obj. 3: Further, by the same love the Father loves the Son, and Himself, and us. But the Father does not love Himself by the Holy Ghost; for no notional act is reflected back on the principle of the act; since it cannot be said that the "Father begets Himself," or that "He spirates Himself." Therefore, neither can it be said that "He loves Himself by the Holy Ghost," if "to love" is taken in a notional sense. Again, the love wherewith He loves us is not the Holy Ghost; because it imports a relation to creatures, and this belongs to the essence. Therefore this also is false: "The Father loves the Son by the Holy Ghost."

*On the contrary,* Augustine says (De Trin. vi, 5): "The Holy Ghost is He whereby the Begotten is loved by the one begetting and loves His Begetter."

*I answer that,* A difficulty about this question is objected to the effect that when we say, "the Father loves the Son by the Holy Ghost," since the ablative is construed as denoting a cause, it seems to mean that the Holy Ghost is the principle of love to the Father and the Son; which cannot be admitted.

In view of this difficulty some have held that it is false, that "the Father and the Son love each other by the Holy Ghost"; and they add that it was retracted by Augustine when he retracted its equivalent to the effect that "the Father is wise by the Wisdom begotten." Others say that the proposition is inaccurate and ought to be expounded, as that "the Father loves the Son by the Holy Ghost"—that is, "by His essential Love," which is appropriated to the Holy Ghost. Others further say that this ablative should be construed as importing a sign, so that it means, "the Holy Ghost is the sign that the Father loves the Son"; inasmuch as the Holy Ghost proceeds from them both, as Love. Others, again, say that this ablative must be construed as importing the relation of formal cause, because the Holy Ghost is the love whereby the Father and the Son formally love each other. Others, again, say that it should be construed as importing the relation of a formal effect; and these approach nearer to the truth.

To make the matter clear, we must consider that since a thing is commonly denominated from its forms, as "white" from whiteness, and "man" from humanity; everything whence anything is denominated, in this particular respect stands to that thing in the relation of form. So when I say, "this man is clothed with a garment," the ablative is to be construed as having relation to the formal cause, although the garment is not the form. Now it may happen that a thing may be denominated from that which proceeds from it, not only as an agent is from its action, but also as from the term itself of the action—that is, the effect, when the effect itself is included in the idea of the action. For we say that fire warms by heating, although heating is not the heat which is the form of the fire, but is an action proceeding from the fire; and we say that a tree flowers with the flower, although the flower is not the tree's form, but is the effect proceeding from the form. In this way, therefore, we must say that since in God "to love" is taken in two ways, essentially and notionally, when it is taken essentially, it means that the Father and the Son love each other not by the Holy Ghost, but by their essence. Hence Augustine says (De Trin. xv, 7): "Who dares to say that the Father loves neither Himself, nor the Son, nor the Holy Ghost, except by the Holy Ghost?" The opinions first quoted are to be taken in this sense. But when the term Love is taken in a notional sense it means nothing else than "to spirate love"; just as to speak is to produce a word, and to flower is to produce flowers. As therefore we say that a tree flowers by its flower, so do we say that the Father, by the Word or the Son, speaks Himself, and His creatures; and that the Father and the Son love each other and us, by the Holy Ghost, or by Love proceeding.

Reply Obj. 1: To be wise or intelligent is taken only essentially in God; therefore we cannot say that "the Father is wise or intelligent by the Son." But to love is taken not only essentially, but also in a notional sense; and in this way, we can say that the Father and the Son love each other by the Holy Ghost, as was above explained.

Reply Obj. 2: When the idea of an action includes a determined effect, the principle of the action may be denominated both from the action, and from the effect; so we can say, for instance, that a tree flowers by its flowering and by its flower. When, however, the idea of an action does not include a determined effect, then in that case, the principle of the action cannot be denominated from the effect, but only from the action. For we do not say that the tree produces the flower by the flower, but by the production of the flower. So when we say, "spirates" or "begets," this imports only a notional act. Hence we cannot say that the Father spirates by the Holy Ghost, or begets by the Son. But we can say that the Father speaks by the Word, as by the Person proceeding, "and speaks by the speaking," as by a notional act; forasmuch as "to speak" imports a determinate person proceeding; since "to speak" means to produce a word. Likewise to love, taken in a notional sense, means to produce love; and so it can be said that the Father loves the Son by the Holy Ghost, as by the person proceeding, and by Love itself as a notional act.

Reply Obj. 3: The Father loves not only the Son, but also Himself and us, by the Holy Ghost; because, as above explained, to love, taken in a notional sense, not only imports the production of a divine person, but also the person produced, by way of love, which has relation to the object loved. Hence, as the Father speaks Himself and every creature by His begotten Word, inasmuch as the Word "begotten" adequately represents the Father and every creature; so He loves Himself and every creature by the Holy Ghost, inasmuch as the Holy Ghost proceeds as the love of the primal goodness whereby the Father loves Himself and every creature. Thus it is evident that relation to the creature is implied both in the Word and in the proceeding Love, as it were in a secondary way, inasmuch as the divine truth and goodness are a principle of understanding and loving all creatures.

## QUESTION 38

OF THE NAME OF THE HOLY GHOST, AS GIFT (In Two Articles)

There now follows the consideration of the Gift; concerning which there are two points of inquiry:

(1) Whether "Gift" can be a personal name?

(2) Whether it is the proper name of the Holy Ghost?

FIRST ARTICLE [I, Q. 38, Art. 1]

Whether "Gift" Is a Personal Name?

Objection 1: It would seem that "Gift" is not a personal name. For every personal name imports a distinction in God. But the name of "Gift" does not import a distinction in God; for Augustine says (De Trin. xv, 19): that "the Holy Ghost is so given as God's Gift, that He also gives Himself as God." Therefore "Gift" is not a personal name.

Obj. 2: Further, no personal name belongs to the divine essence. But the divine essence is the Gift which the Father gives to the Son, as Hilary says (De Trin. ix). Therefore "Gift" is not a personal name.

Obj. 3: Further, according to Damascene (De Fide Orth. iv, 19) there is no subjection nor service in the divine persons. But gift implies a subjection both as regards him to whom it is given, and as regards him by whom it is given. Therefore "Gift" is not a personal name.

Obj. 4: Further, "Gift" imports relation to the creature, and it thus seems to be said of God in time. But personal names are said of God from eternity; as "Father," and "Son." Therefore "Gift" is not a personal name.

*On the contrary,* Augustine says (De Trin. xv, 19): "As the body of flesh is nothing but flesh; so the gift of the Holy Ghost is nothing but the Holy Ghost." But the Holy Ghost is a personal name; so also therefore is "Gift."

*I answer that,* The word "gift" imports an aptitude for being given. And what is given has an aptitude or relation both to the giver and to that to which it is given. For it would not be given by anyone, unless it was his to give; and it is given to someone to be his. Now a divine person is said to belong to another, either by origin, as the Son belongs to the Father; or as possessed by another. But we are said to possess what we can freely use or enjoy as we please: and in this way a divine person cannot be possessed, except by a rational creature united to God. Other creatures can be moved by a divine person, not, however, in such a way as to be able to enjoy the divine person, and to use the effect thereof. The rational creature does sometimes attain thereto; as when it is made partaker of the divine Word and of the Love proceeding, so as freely to know God truly and to love God rightly. Hence the rational creature alone can possess the divine person. Nevertheless in order that it may possess Him in this manner, its own power avails nothing: hence this must be given it from above; for that is said to be given to us which we have from another source. Thus a divine person can "be given," and can be a "gift."

Reply Obj. 1: The name "Gift" imports a personal distinction, in so far as gift imports something belonging to another through its origin. Nevertheless, the Holy Ghost gives Himself, inasmuch as He is His own, and can use or rather enjoy Himself; as also a free man belongs to himself. And as Augustine says (In Joan. Tract. xxix): "What is more yours than yourself?" Or we might say, and more fittingly, that a gift must belong in a way to the giver. But the phrase, "this is this one's," can be understood in several senses. In one way it means identity, as Augustine says (In Joan. Tract. xxix); and in that sense "gift" is the same as "the giver," but not the same as the one to whom it is given. The Holy Ghost gives Himself in that sense. In another sense, a thing is another's as a possession, or as a slave; and in that sense gift is essentially distinct from the giver; and the gift of God so taken is a created thing. In a third sense "this is this one's" through its origin only; and in this sense the Son is the Father's; and the Holy Ghost belongs to both. Therefore, so far as gift in this way signifies the possession of the giver, it is personally distinguished from the giver, and is a personal name.

Reply Obj. 2: The divine essence is the Father's gift in the first sense, as being the Father's by way of identity.

Reply Obj. 3: Gift as a personal name in God does not imply subjection, but only origin, as regards the giver; but as regards the one to whom it is given, it implies a free use, or enjoyment, as above explained.

Reply Obj. 4: Gift is not so called from being actually given, but from its aptitude to be given. Hence the divine person is called Gift from eternity, although He is given in time. Nor does it follow that it is an essential name because it imports relation to the creature; but that it includes something essential in its meaning; as the essence is included in the idea of person, as stated above (Q. 34, A. 3).

SECOND ARTICLE [I, Q. 38, Art. 2]

Whether "Gift" Is the Proper Name of the Holy Ghost?

Objection 1: It would seem that Gift is not the proper name of the Holy Ghost. For the name Gift comes from being given. But, as Isaiah says (9:16): "A Son is given to us." Therefore to be Gift belongs to the Son, as well as to the Holy Ghost.

Obj. 2: Further, every proper name of a person signifies a property. But this word Gift does not signify a property of the Holy Ghost. Therefore Gift is not a proper name of the Holy Ghost.

Obj. 3: Further, the Holy Ghost can be called the spirit of a man, whereas He cannot be called the gift of any man, but "God's Gift" only. Therefore Gift is not the proper name of the Holy Ghost.

*On the contrary,* Augustine says (De Trin. iv, 20): "As 'to be born' is, for the Son, to be from the Father, so, for the Holy Ghost, 'to be the Gift of God' is to proceed from Father and Son." But the Holy Ghost receives His proper name from the fact that He proceeds from Father and Son. Therefore Gift is the proper name of the Holy Ghost.

*I answer that,* Gift, taken personally in God, is the proper name of the Holy Ghost.

In proof of this we must know that a gift is properly an unreturnable giving, as Aristotle says (Topic. iv, 4)—i.e. a thing which is not given with the intention of a return—and it thus contains the idea of a gratuitous donation. Now, the reason of donation being gratuitous is love; since therefore do we give something to anyone gratuitously forasmuch as we wish him well. So what we first give him is the love whereby we wish him well. Hence it is manifest that love has the nature of a first gift, through which all free gifts are given. So since the Holy Ghost proceeds as love, as stated above (Q. 27, A. 4; Q. 37, A. 1), He proceeds as the first gift. Hence Augustine says (De Trin. xv, 24): "By the gift, which is the Holy Ghost, many particular gifts are portioned out to the members of Christ."

Reply Obj. 1: As the Son is properly called the Image because He proceeds by way of a word, whose nature it is to be the similitude of its principle, although the Holy Ghost also is like to the Father; so also, because the Holy Ghost proceeds from the Father as love, He is properly called Gift, although the Son, too, is given. For that the Son is given is from the Father's love, according to the words, "God so loved the world, as to give His only begotten Son" (John 3:16).

Reply Obj. 2: The name Gift involves the idea of belonging to the Giver through its origin; and thus it imports the property of the origin of the Holy Ghost—that is, His procession.

Reply Obj. 3: Before a gift is given, it belongs only to the giver; but when it is given, it is his to whom it is given. Therefore, because "Gift" does not import the actual giving, it cannot be called a gift of man, but the Gift of God giving. When, however, it has been given, then it is the spirit of man, or a gift bestowed on man.

## QUESTION 39

OF THE PERSONS IN RELATION TO THE ESSENCE (In Eight Articles)

Those things considered which belong to the divine persons absolutely, we next treat of what concerns the person in reference to the essence, to the properties, and to the notional acts; and of the comparison of these with each other.

As regards the first of these, there are eight points of inquiry:

(1) Whether the essence in God is the same as the person?

(2) Whether we should say that the three persons are of one essence?

(3) Whether essential names should be predicated of the persons in the plural, or in the singular?

(4) Whether notional adjectives, or verbs, or participles, can be predicated of the essential names taken in a concrete sense?

(5) Whether the same can be predicated of essential names taken in the abstract?

(6) Whether the names of the persons can be predicated of concrete essential names?

(7) Whether essential attributes can be appropriated to the persons?

(8) Which attributes should be appropriated to each person?

FIRST ARTICLE [I, Q. 39, Art. 1]

Whether in God the Essence Is the Same As the Person?

Objection 1: It would seem that in God the essence is not the same as person. For whenever essence is the same as person or *suppositum*, there can be only one *suppositum* of one nature, as is clear in the case of all separate substances. For in those things which are really one and the same, one cannot be multiplied apart from the other. But in God there is one essence and three persons, as is clear from what is above expounded (Q. 28, A. 3; Q. 30, A. 2). Therefore essence is not the same as person.

Obj. 2: Further, simultaneous affirmation and negation of the same things in the same respect cannot be true. But affirmation and negation are true of essence and of person. For person is distinct, whereas essence is not. Therefore person and essence are not the same.

Obj. 3: Further, nothing can be subject to itself. But person is subject to essence; whence it is called *suppositum* or "hypostasis." Therefore person is not the same as essence.

*On the contrary,* Augustine says (De Trin. vi, 7): "When we say the person of the Father we mean nothing else but the substance of the Father."

*I answer that,* The truth of this question is quite clear if we consider the divine simplicity. For it was shown above (Q. 3, A. 3) that the divine simplicity requires that in God essence is the same as *suppositum*, which in intellectual substances is nothing else than person. But a difficulty seems to arise from the fact that while the divine persons are multiplied, the essence nevertheless retains its unity. And because, as Boethius says (De Trin. i), "relation multiplies the Trinity of persons," some have thought that in God essence and person differ, forasmuch as they held the relations to be "adjacent"; considering only in the relations the idea of "reference to another," and not the relations as realities. But as it was shown above (Q. 28, A. 2) in creatures relations are accidental, whereas in God they are the divine essence itself. Thence it follows that in God essence is not really distinct from person; and yet that the persons are really distinguished from each other. For person, as above stated (Q. 29, A. 4), signifies relation as subsisting in the divine nature. But relation as referred to the essence does not differ therefrom really, but only in our way of thinking; while as referred to an opposite relation, it has a real distinction by virtue of that opposition. Thus there are one essence and three persons.

Reply Obj. 1: There cannot be a distinction of *suppositum* in creatures by means of relations, but only by essential principles; because in creatures relations are not subsistent. But in God relations are subsistent, and so by reason of the opposition between them they distinguish the *supposita* ; and yet the essence is not distinguished, because the relations themselves are not distinguished from each other so far as they are identified with the essence.

Reply Obj. 2: As essence and person in God differ in our way of thinking, it follows that something can be denied of the one and affirmed of the other; and therefore, when we suppose the one, we need not suppose the other.

Reply Obj. 3: Divine things are named by us after the way of created things, as above explained (Q. 13, AA. 1, 3). And since created natures are individualized by matter which is the subject of the specific nature, it follows that individuals are called "subjects," *supposita*, or "hypostases." So the divine persons are named *supposita* or "hypostases," but not as if there really existed any real "supposition" or "subjection."

SECOND ARTICLE [I, Q. 39, Art. 2]

Whether It Must Be Said That the Three Persons Are of One Essence?

Objection 1: It would seem not right to say that the three persons are of one essence. For Hilary says (De Synod.) that the Father, Son and Holy Ghost "are indeed three by substance, but one in harmony." But the substance of God is His essence. Therefore the three persons are not of one essence.

Obj. 2: Further, nothing is to be affirmed of God except what can be confirmed by the authority of Holy Writ, as appears from Dionysius (Div. Nom. i). Now Holy Writ never says that the Father, Son and Holy Ghost are of one essence. Therefore this should not be asserted.

Obj. 3: Further, the divine nature is the same as the divine essence. It suffices therefore to say that the three persons are of one nature.

Obj. 4: Further, it is not usual to say that the person is of the essence; but rather that the essence is of the person. Therefore it does not seem fitting to say that the three persons are of one essence.

Obj. 5: Further, Augustine says (De Trin. vii, 6) that we do not say that the three persons are "from one essence [ex una essentia]," lest we should seem to indicate a distinction between the essence and the persons in God. But prepositions which imply transition, denote the oblique case. Therefore it is equally wrong to say that the three persons are "of one essence [unius essentiae]."

Obj. 6: Further, nothing should be said of God which can be occasion of error. Now, to say that the three persons are of one essence or substance, furnishes occasion of error. For, as Hilary says (De Synod.): "One substance predicated of the Father and the Son signifies either one subsistent, with two denominations; or one substance divided into two imperfect substances; or a third prior substance taken and assumed by the other two." Therefore it must not be said that the three persons are of one substance.

*On the contrary,* Augustine says (Contra Maxim. iii) that the word homoousion, which the Council of Nicaea adopted against the Arians, means that the three persons are of one essence.

*I answer that,* As above explained (Q. 13, AA. 1, 2), divine things are named by our intellect, not as they really are in themselves, for in that way it knows them not; but in a way that belongs to things created. And as in the objects of the senses, whence the intellect derives its knowledge, the nature of the species is made individual by the matter, and thus the nature is as the form, and the individual is the *suppositum* of the form; so also in God the essence is taken as the form of the three persons, according to our mode of signification. Now in creatures we say that every form belongs to that whereof it is the form; as the health and beauty of a man belongs to the man. But we do not say of that which has a form, that it belongs to the form, unless some adjective qualifies the form; as when we say: "That woman is of a handsome figure," or: "This man is of perfect virtue." In like manner, as in God the persons are multiplied, and the essence is not multiplied, we speak of one essence of the three persons, and three persons of the one essence, provided that these genitives be understood as designating the form.

Reply Obj. 1: Substance is here taken for the "hypostasis," and not for the essence.

Reply Obj. 2: Although we may not find it declared in Holy Writ in so many words that the three persons are of one essence, nevertheless we find it so stated as regards the meaning; for instance, "I and the Father are one (John 10:30)," and "I am in the Father, and the Father in Me (John 10:38)"; and there are many other texts of the same import.

Reply Obj. 3: Because "nature" designates the principle of action while "essence" comes from being [essendo], things may be said to be of one nature which agree in some action, as all things which give heat; but only those things can be said to be of "one essence" which have one being. So the divine unity is better described by saying that the three persons are "of one essence," than by saying they are "of one nature."

Reply Obj. 4: Form, in the absolute sense, is wont to be designated as belonging to that of which it is the form, as we say "the virtue of Peter." On the other hand, the thing having form is not wont to be designated as belonging to the form except when we wish to qualify or designate the form. In which case two genitives are required, one signifying the form, and the other signifying the determination of the form, as, for instance, when we say, "Peter is of great virtue [magnae virtutis]," or else one genitive must have the force of two, as, for instance, "he is a man of blood"—that is, he is a man who sheds much blood [multi sanguinis]. So, because the divine essence signifies a form as regards the person, it may properly be said that the essence is of the person; but we cannot say the converse, unless we add some term to designate the essence; as, for instance, the Father is a person of the "divine essence"; or, the three persons are "of one essence."

Reply Obj. 5: The preposition "from" or "out of" does not designate the habitude of a formal cause, but rather the habitude of an efficient or material cause; which causes are in all cases distinguished from those things of which they are the causes. For nothing can be its own matter, nor its own active principle. Yet a thing may be its own form, as appears in all immaterial things. So, when we say, "three persons of one essence," taking essence as having the habitude of form, we do not mean that essence is different from person, which we should mean if we said, "three persons from the same essence."

Reply Obj. 6: As Hilary says (De Synod.): "It would be prejudicial to holy things, if we had to do away with them, just because some do not think them holy. So if some misunderstand *homoousion*, what is that to me, if I understand it rightly? ... The oneness of nature does not result from division, or from union or from community of possession, but from one nature being proper to both Father and Son."

THIRD ARTICLE [I, Q. 39, Art. 3]

Whether Essential Names Should Be Predicated in the Singular of the Three Persons?

Objection 1: It would seem that essential names, as the name "God," should not be predicated in the singular of the three persons, but in the plural. For as "man" signifies "one that has humanity," so God signifies "one that has Godhead." But the three persons are three who have Godhead. Therefore the three persons are "three Gods."

Obj. 2: Further, Gen. 1:1, where it is said, "In the beginning God created heaven and earth," the Hebrew original has "Elohim," which may be rendered "Gods" or "Judges": and this word is used on account of the plurality of persons. Therefore the three persons are "several Gods," and not "one" God.

Obj. 3: Further, this word "thing" when it is said absolutely, seems to belong to substance. But it is predicated of the three persons in the plural. For Augustine says (De Doctr. Christ. i, 5): "The things that are the objects of our future glory are the Father, Son and Holy Ghost." Therefore other essential names can be predicated in the plural of the three persons.

Obj. 4: Further, as this word "God" signifies "a being who has Deity," so also this word "person" signifies a being subsisting in an intellectual nature. But we say there are three persons. So for the same reason we can say there are "three Gods."

*On the contrary,* It is said (Deut. 6:4): "Hear, O Israel, the Lord thy God is one God."

*I answer that,* Some essential names signify the essence after the manner of substantives; while others signify it after the manner of adjectives. Those which signify it as substantives are predicated of the three persons in the singular only, and not in the plural. Those which signify the essence as adjectives are predicated of the three persons in the plural. The reason of this is that substantives signify something by way of substance, while adjectives signify something by way of accident, which adheres to a subject. Now just as substance has existence of itself, so also it has of itself unity or multitude; wherefore the singularity or plurality of a substantive name depends upon the form signified by the name. But as accidents have their existence in a subject, so they have unity or plurality from their subject; and therefore the singularity and plurality of adjectives depends upon their *supposita*. In creatures, one form does not exist in several *supposita* except by unity of order, as the form of an ordered multitude. So if the names signifying such a form are substantives, they are predicated of many in the singular, but otherwise if they adjectives. For we say that many men are a college, or an army, or a people; but we say that many men are collegians. Now in God the divine essence is signified by way of a form, as above explained (A. 2), which, indeed, is simple and supremely one, as shown above (Q. 3, A. 7; Q. 11, A. 4). So, names which signify the divine essence in a substantive manner are predicated of the three persons in the singular, and not in the plural. This, then, is the reason why we say that Socrates, Plato and Cicero are "three men"; whereas we do not say the Father, Son and Holy Ghost are "three Gods," but "one God"; forasmuch as in the three *supposita* of human nature there are three humanities, whereas in the three divine Persons there is but one divine essence. On the other hand, the names which signify essence in an adjectival manner are predicated of the three persons plurally, by reason of the plurality of *supposita*. For we say there are three "existent" or three "wise" beings, or three "eternal," "uncreated," and "immense" beings, if these terms are understood in an adjectival sense. But if taken in a substantive sense, we say "one uncreated, immense, eternal being," as Athanasius declares.

Reply Obj. 1: Though the name "God" signifies a being having Godhead, nevertheless the mode of signification is different. For the name "God" is used substantively; whereas "having Godhead" is used adjectively. Consequently, although there are "three having Godhead," it does not follow that there are three Gods.

Reply Obj. 2: Various languages have diverse modes of expression. So as by reason of the plurality of *supposita* the Greeks said "three hypostases," so also in Hebrew "Elohim" is in the plural. We, however, do not apply the plural either to "God" or to "substance," lest plurality be referred to the substance.

Reply Obj. 3: This word "thing" is one of the transcendentals. Whence, so far as it is referred to relation, it is predicated of God in the plural; whereas, so far as it is referred to the substance, it is predicated in the singular. So Augustine says, in the passage quoted, that "the same Trinity is a thing supreme."

Reply Obj. 4: The form signified by the word "person" is not essence or nature, but personality. So, as there are three personalities—that is, three personal properties in the Father, Son and Holy Ghost—it is predicated of the three, not in the singular, but in the plural.

FOURTH ARTICLE [I, Q. 39, Art. 4]

Whether the Concrete Essential Names Can Stand for the Person?

Objection 1: It would seem that the concrete, essential names cannot stand for the person, so that we can truly say "God begot God." For, as the logicians say, "a singular term signifies what it stands for." But this name "God" seems to be a singular term, for it cannot be predicated in the plural, as above explained (A. 3). Therefore, since it signifies the essence, it stands for essence, and not for person.

Obj. 2: Further, a term in the subject is not modified by a term in the predicate, as to its signification; but only as to the sense signified in the predicate. But when I say, "God creates," this name "God" stands for the essence. So when we say "God begot," this term "God" cannot by reason of the notional predicate, stand for person.

Obj. 3: Further, if this be true, "God begot," because the Father generates; for the same reason this is true, "God does not beget," because the Son does not beget. Therefore there is God who begets, and there is God who does not beget; and thus it follows that there are two Gods.

Obj. 4: Further, if "God begot God," He begot either God, that is Himself, or another God. But He did not beget God, that is Himself; for, as Augustine says (De Trin. i, 1), "nothing begets itself." Neither did He beget another God; as there is only one God. Therefore it is false to say, "God begot God."

Obj. 5: Further, if "God begot God," He begot either God who is the Father, or God who is not the Father. If God who is the Father, then God the Father was begotten. If God who is not the Father, then there is a God who is not God the Father: which is false. Therefore it cannot be said that "God begot God."

*On the contrary,* In the Creed it is said, "God of God."

*I answer that,* Some have said that this name "God" and the like, properly according to their nature, stand for the essence, but by reason of some notional adjunct are made to stand for the Person. This opinion apparently arose from considering the divine simplicity, which requires that in God, He "who possesses" and "what is possessed" be the same. So He who possesses Godhead, which is signified by the name God, is the same as Godhead. But when we consider the proper way of expressing ourselves, the mode of signification must be considered no less than the thing signified. Hence as this word "God" signifies the divine essence as in Him Who possesses it, just as the name "man" signifies humanity in a subject, others more truly have said that this word "God," from its mode of signification, can, in its proper sense, stand for person, as does the word "man." So this word "God" sometimes stands for the essence, as when we say "God creates"; because this predicate is attributed to the subject by reason of the form signified—that is, Godhead. But sometimes it stands for the person, either for only one, as when we say, "God begets," or for two, as when we say, "God spirates"; or for three, as when it is said: "To the King of ages, immortal, invisible, the only God," etc. (1 Tim. 1:17).

Reply Obj. 1: Although this name "God" agrees with singular terms as regards the form signified not being multiplied; nevertheless it agrees also with general terms so far as the form signified is to be found in several *supposita*. So it need not always stand for the essence it signifies.

Reply Obj. 2: This holds good against those who say that the word "God" does not naturally stand for person.

Reply Obj. 3: The word "God" stands for the person in a different way from that in which this word "man" does; for since the form signified by this word "man"—that is, humanity—is really divided among its different subjects, it stands of itself for the person, even if there is no adjunct determining it to the person—that is, to a distinct subject. The unity or community of the human nature, however, is not a reality, but is only in the consideration of the mind. Hence this term "man" does not stand for the common nature, unless this is required by some adjunct, as when we say, "man is a species"; whereas the form signified by the name "God"—that is, the divine essence—is really one and common. So of itself it stands for the common nature, but by some adjunct it may be restricted so as to stand for the person. So, when we say, "God generates," by reason of the notional act this name "God" stands for the person of the Father. But when we say, "God does not generate," there is no adjunct to determine this name to the person of the Son, and hence the phrase means that generation is repugnant to the divine nature. If, however, something be added belonging to the person of the Son, this proposition, for instance, "God begotten does not beget," is true. Consequently, it does not follow that there exists a "God generator," and a "God not generator"; unless there be an adjunct pertaining to the persons; as, for instance, if we were to say, "the Father is God the generator" and the "Son is God the non-generator" and so it does not follow that there are many Gods; for the Father and the Son are one God, as was said above (A. 3).

Reply Obj. 4: This is false, "the Father begot God, that is Himself," because the word "Himself," as a reciprocal term, refers to the same *suppositum*. Nor is this contrary to what Augustine says (Ep. lxvi ad Maxim.) that "God the Father begot another self [alterum se]," forasmuch as the word "se" is either in the ablative case, and then it means "He begot another from Himself," or it indicates a single relation, and thus points to identity of nature. This is, however, either a figurative or an emphatic way of speaking, so that it would really mean, "He begot another most like to Himself." Likewise also it is false to say, "He begot another God," because although the Son is another than the Father, as above explained (Q. 31, A. 2), nevertheless it cannot be said that He is "another God"; forasmuch as this adjective "another" would be understood to apply to the substantive God; and thus the meaning would be that there is a distinction of Godhead. Yet this proposition "He begot another God" is tolerated by some, provided that "another" be taken as a substantive, and the word "God" be construed in apposition with it. This, however, is an inexact way of speaking, and to be avoided, for fear of giving occasion to error.

Reply Obj. 5: To say, "God begot God Who is God the Father," is wrong, because since the word "Father" is construed in apposition to "God," the word "God" is restricted to the person of the Father; so that it would mean, "He begot God, Who is Himself the Father"; and then the Father would be spoken of as begotten, which is false. Wherefore the negative of the proposition is true, "He begot God Who is not God the Father." If however, we understand these words not to be in apposition, and require something to be added, then, *on the contrary,* the affirmative proposition is true, and the negative is false; so that the meaning would be, "He begot God Who is God Who is the Father." Such a rendering however appears to be forced, so that it is better to say simply that the affirmative proposition is false, and the negative is true. Yet Prepositivus said that both the negative and affirmative are false, because this relative "Who" in the affirmative proposition can be referred to the *suppositum* ; whereas in the negative it denotes both the thing signified and the *suppositum.* Whence, in the affirmative the sense is that "to be God the Father" is befitting to the person of the Son; and in the negative sense is that "to be God the Father," is to be removed from the Son's divinity as well as from His personality. This, however, appears to be irrational; since, according to the Philosopher (Peri Herm. ii), what is open to affirmation, is open also to negation.

FIFTH ARTICLE [I, Q. 39, Art. 5]

Whether Abstract Essential Names Can Stand for the Person?

Objection 1: It would seem that abstract essential names can stand for the person, so that this proposition is true, "Essence begets essence." For Augustine says (De Trin. vii, i, 2): "The Father and the Son are one Wisdom, because they are one essence; and taken singly Wisdom is from Wisdom, as essence from essence."

Obj. 2: Further, generation or corruption in ourselves implies generation or corruption of what is within us. But the Son is generated. Therefore since the divine essence is in the Son, it seems that the divine essence is generated.

Obj. 3: Further, God and the divine essence are the same, as is clear from what is above explained (Q. 3, A. 3). But, as was shown, it is true to say that "God begets God." Therefore this is also true: "Essence begets essence."

Obj. 4: Further, a predicate can stand for that of which it is predicated. But the Father is the divine essence; therefore essence can stand for the person of the Father. Thus the essence begets.

Obj. 5: Further, the essence is "a thing begetting," because the essence is the Father who is begetting. Therefore if the essence is not begetting, the essence will be "a thing begetting," and "not begetting": which cannot be.

Obj. 6: Further, Augustine says (De Trin. iv, 20): "The Father is the principle of the whole Godhead." But He is principle only by begetting or spirating. Therefore the Father begets or spirates the Godhead.

*On the contrary,* Augustine says (De Trin. i, 1): "Nothing begets itself." But if the essence begets the essence, it begets itself only, since nothing exists in God as distinguished from the divine essence. Therefore the essence does not beget essence.

*I answer that,* Concerning this, the abbot Joachim erred in asserting that as we can say "God begot God," so we can say "Essence begot essence": considering that, by reason of the divine simplicity God is nothing else but the divine essence. In this he was wrong, because if we wish to express ourselves correctly, we must take into account not only the thing which is signified, but also the mode of its signification as above stated (A. 4). Now although "God" is really the same as "Godhead," nevertheless the mode of signification is not in each case the same. For since this word "God" signifies the divine essence in Him that possesses it, from its mode of signification it can of its own nature stand for person. Thus the things which properly belong to the persons, can be predicated of this word, "God," as, for instance, we can say "God is begotten" or is "Begetter," as above explained (A. 4). The word "essence," however, in its mode of signification, cannot stand for Person, because it signifies the essence as an abstract form. Consequently, what properly belongs to the persons whereby they are distinguished from each other, cannot be attributed to the essence. For that would imply distinction in the divine essence, in the same way as there exists distinction in the *supposita.*

Reply Obj. 1: To express unity of essence and of person, the holy Doctors have sometimes expressed themselves with greater emphasis than the strict propriety of terms allows. Whence instead of enlarging upon such expressions we should rather explain them: thus, for instance, abstract names should be explained by concrete names, or even by personal names; as when we find "essence from essence"; or "wisdom from wisdom"; we should take the sense to be, *the Son* who is essence and wisdom, is from the Father who is essence and wisdom. Nevertheless, as regards these abstract names a certain order should be observed, forasmuch as what belongs to action is more nearly allied to the persons because actions belong to *supposita.* So "nature from nature," and "wisdom from wisdom" are less inexact than "essence from essence."

Reply Obj. 2: In creatures the one generated has not the same nature numerically as the generator, but another nature, numerically distinct, which commences to exist in it anew by generation, and ceases to exist by corruption, and so it is generated and corrupted accidentally; whereas God begotten has the same nature numerically as the begetter. So the divine nature in the Son is not begotten either directly or accidentally.

Reply Obj. 3: Although God and the divine essence are really the same, nevertheless, on account of their different mode of signification, we must speak in a different way about each of them.

Reply Obj. 4: The divine essence is predicated of the Father by mode of identity by reason of the divine simplicity; yet it does not follow that it can stand for the Father, its mode of signification being different. This objection would hold good as regards things which are predicated of another as the universal of a particular.

Reply Obj. 5: The difference between substantive and adjectival names consist in this, that the former carry their subject with them, whereas the latter do not, but add the thing signified to the substantive. Whence logicians are wont to say that the substantive is considered in the light of *suppositum,* whereas the adjective indicates something added to the *suppositum.* Therefore substantive personal terms can be predicated of the essence, because they are really the same; nor does it follow that a personal property makes a distinct essence; but it belongs to the *suppositum* implied in the substantive. But notional and personal adjectives cannot be predicated of the essence unless we add some substantive. We cannot say that the "essence is begetting"; yet we can say that the "essence is a thing begetting," or that it is "God begetting," if "thing" and God stand for person, but not if they stand for essence. Consequently there exists no contradiction in saying that "essence is a thing begetting," and "a thing not begetting"; because in the first case "thing" stands for person, and in the second it stands for the essence.

Reply Obj. 6: So far as Godhead is one in several *supposita,* it agrees in a certain degree with the form of a collective term. So when we say, "the Father is the principle of the whole Godhead," the term Godhead can be taken for all the persons together, inasmuch as it is the principle in all the divine persons. Nor does it follow that He is His own principle; as one of the people may be called the ruler of the people without being ruler of himself. We may also say that He is the principle of the whole Godhead; not as generating or spirating it, but as communicating it by generation and spiration.

SIXTH ARTICLE [I, Q. 39, Art. 6]

Whether the Persons Can Be Predicated of the Essential Terms?

Objection 1: It would seem that the persons cannot be predicated of the concrete essential names; so that we can say for instance, "God is three persons"; or "God is the Trinity." For it is false to say, "man is every man," because it cannot be verified as regards any particular subject. For neither Socrates, nor Plato, nor anyone else is every man. In the same way this proposition, "God is the Trinity," cannot be verified of any one of the *supposita* of the divine nature. For the Father is not the Trinity; nor is the Son; nor is the Holy Ghost. So to say, "God is the Trinity," is false.

Obj. 2: Further, the lower is not predicated of the higher except by accidental predication; as when I say, "animal is man"; for it is accidental to animal to be man. But this name "God" as regards the three persons is as a general term to inferior terms, as Damascene says (De Fide Orth. iii, 4). Therefore it seems that the names of the persons cannot be predicated of this name "God," except in an accidental sense.

*On the contrary,* Augustine says, in his sermon on Faith [*Serm. ii, in coena Domini], "We believe that one God is one divinely named Trinity."

*I answer that,* As above explained (A. 5), although adjectival terms, whether personal or notional, cannot be predicated of the essence, nevertheless substantive terms can be so predicated, owing to the real identity of essence and person. The divine essence is not only really the same as one person, but it is really the same as the three persons. Whence, one person, and two, and three, can be predicated of the essence as if we were to say, "The essence is the Father, and the Son, and the Holy Ghost." And because this word "God" can of itself stand for the essence, as above explained (A. 4, ad 3), hence, as it is true to say, "The essence is the three persons"; so likewise it is true to say, "God is the three persons."

Reply Obj. 1: As above explained this term "man" can of itself stand for person, whereas an adjunct is required for it to stand for the universal human nature. So it is false to say, "Man is every man"; because it cannot be verified of any particular human subject. *On the contrary,* this word "God" can of itself be taken for the divine essence. So, although to say of any of the *supposita* of the divine nature, "God is the Trinity," is untrue, nevertheless it is true of the divine essence. This was denied by Porretanus because he did not take note of this distinction.

Reply Obj. 2: When we say, "God," or "the divine essence is the Father," the predication is one of identity, and not of the lower in regard to a higher species: because in God there is no universal and singular. Hence, as this proposition, "The Father is God" is of itself true, so this proposition "God is the Father" is true of itself, and by no means accidentally.

SEVENTH ARTICLE [I, Q. 39, Art. 7]

Whether the Essential Names Should Be Appropriated to the Persons?

Objection 1: It would seem that the essential names should not be appropriated to the persons. For whatever might verge on error in faith should be avoided in the treatment of divine things; for, as Jerome says, "careless words involve risk of heresy" [*In substance Ep. lvii.]. But to appropriate to any one person the names which are common to the three persons, may verge on error in faith; for it may be supposed either that such belong only to the person to whom they are appropriated or that they belong to Him in a fuller degree than to the others. Therefore the essential attributes should not be appropriated to the persons.

Obj. 2: Further, the essential attributes expressed in the abstract signify by mode of form. But one person is not as a form to another; since a form is not distinguished in subject from that of which it is the form. Therefore the essential attributes, especially when expressed in the abstract, are not to be appropriated to the persons.

Obj. 3: Further, property is prior to the appropriated, for property is included in the idea of the appropriated. But the essential attributes, in our way of understanding, are prior to the persons; as what is common is prior to what is proper. Therefore the essential attributes are not to be appropriated to the persons.

*On the contrary,* the Apostle says: "Christ the power of God and the wisdom of God" (1 Cor. 1:24).

*I answer that,* For the manifestation of our faith it is fitting that the essential attributes should be appropriated to the persons. For although the trinity of persons cannot be proved by demonstration, as was above expounded (Q. 32, A. 1), nevertheless it is fitting that it be declared by things which are more known to us. Now the essential attributes of God are more clear to us from the standpoint of reason than the personal properties; because we can derive certain knowledge of the essential attributes from creatures which are sources of knowledge to us, such as we cannot obtain regarding the personal properties, as was above explained (Q. 32, A. 1). As, therefore, we make use of the likeness of the trace or image found in creatures for the manifestation of the divine persons, so also in the same manner do we make use of the essential attributes. And such a manifestation of the divine persons by the use of the essential attributes is called "appropriation."

The divine person can be manifested in a twofold manner by the essential attributes; in one way by similitude, and thus the things which belong to the intellect are appropriated to the Son, Who proceeds by way of intellect, as Word. In another way by dissimilitude; as power is appropriated to the Father, as Augustine says, because fathers by reason of old age are sometimes feeble; lest anything of the kind be imagined of God.

Reply Obj. 1: The essential attributes are not appropriated to the persons as if they exclusively belonged to them; but in order to make the persons manifest by way of similitude, or dissimilitude, as above explained. So, no error in faith can arise, but rather manifestation of the truth.

Reply Obj. 2: If the essential attributes were appropriated to the persons as exclusively belonging to each of them, then it would follow that one person would be as a form as regards another; which Augustine altogether repudiates (De Trin. vi, 2), showing that the Father is wise, not by Wisdom begotten by Him, as though only the Son were Wisdom; so that the Father and the Son together only can be called wise, but not the Father without the Son. But the Son is called the Wisdom of the Father, because He is Wisdom from the Father Who is Wisdom. For each of them is of Himself Wisdom; and both together are one Wisdom. Whence the Father is not wise by the wisdom begotten by Him, but by the wisdom which is His own essence.

Reply Obj. 3: Although the essential attribute is in its proper concept prior to person, according to our way of understanding; nevertheless, so far as it is appropriated, there is nothing to prevent the personal property from being prior to that which is appropriated. Thus color is posterior to body considered as body, but is naturally prior to "white body," considered as white.

EIGHTH ARTICLE [I, Q. 39, Art. 8]

Whether the Essential Attributes Are Appropriated to the Persons in a Fitting Manner by the Holy Doctors?

Objection 1: It would seem that the essential attributes are appropriated to the persons unfittingly by the holy doctors. For Hilary says (De Trin. ii): "Eternity is in the Father, the species in the Image; and use is in the Gift." In which words he designates three names proper to the persons: the name of the "Father," the name "Image" proper to the Son (Q. 35, A. 2), and the name "Bounty" or "Gift," which is proper to the Holy Ghost (Q. 38, A. 2). He also designates three appropriated terms. For he appropriates "eternity" to the Father, species to the Son, and "use" to the Holy Ghost. This he does apparently without reason. For "eternity" imports duration of existence; species, the principle of existence; and 'use' belongs to the operation. But essence and operation are not found to be appropriated to any person. Therefore the above terms are not fittingly appropriated to the persons.

Obj. 2: Further, Augustine says (De Doctr. Christ. i, 5): "Unity is in the Father, equality in the Son, and in the Holy Ghost is the concord of equality and unity." This does not, however, seem fitting; because one person does not receive formal denomination from what is appropriated to another. For the Father is not wise by the wisdom begotten, as above explained (Q. 37, A. 2, ad 1). But, as he subjoins, "All these three are one by the Father; all are equal by the Son, and all united by the Holy Ghost." The above, therefore, are not fittingly appropriated to the Persons.

Obj. 3: Further, according to Augustine, to the Father is attributed "power," to the Son "wisdom," to the Holy Ghost "goodness." Nor does this seem fitting; for "strength" is part of power, whereas strength is found to be appropriated to the Son, according to the text, "Christ the strength [*Douay: power] of God" (1 Cor. 1:24). So it is likewise appropriated to the Holy Ghost, according to the words, "strength [*Douay: virtue] came out from Him and healed all" (Luke 6:19). Therefore power should not be appropriated to the Father.

Obj. 4: Likewise Augustine says (De Trin. vi, 10): "What the Apostle says, "From Him, and by Him, and in Him," is not to be taken in a confused sense." And (Contra Maxim. ii) "'from Him' refers to the Father, 'by Him' to the Son, 'in Him' to the Holy Ghost." This, however, seems to be incorrectly said; for the words "in Him" seem to imply the relation of final cause, which is first among the causes. Therefore this relation of cause should be appropriated to the Father, Who is "the principle from no principle."

Obj. 5: Likewise, Truth is appropriated to the Son, according to John 14:6, "I am the Way, the Truth, and the Life"; and likewise "the book of life," according to Ps. 39:9, "In the beginning of the book it is written of Me," where a gloss observes, "that is, with the Father Who is My head," also this word "Who is"; because on the text of Isaias, "Behold I go to the Gentiles" (65:1), a gloss adds, "The Son speaks Who said to Moses, I am Who am." These appear to belong to the Son, and are not appropriated. For "truth," according to Augustine (De Vera Relig. 36), "is the supreme similitude of the principle without any dissimilitude." So it seems that it properly belongs to the Son, Who has a principle. Also the "book of life" seems proper to the Son, as signifying "a thing from another"; for every book is written by someone. This also, "Who is," appears to be proper to the Son; because if when it was said to Moses, "I am Who am," the Trinity spoke, then Moses could have said, "He Who is Father, Son, and Holy Ghost, and the Holy Ghost sent me to you," so also he could have said further, "He Who is the Father, and the Son, and the Holy Ghost sent me to you," pointing out a certain person. This, however, is false; because no person is Father, Son and Holy Ghost. Therefore it cannot be common to the Trinity, but is proper to the Son.

*I answer that,* Our intellect, which is led to the knowledge of God from creatures, must consider God according to the mode derived from creatures. In considering any creature four points present themselves to us in due order. Firstly, the thing itself taken absolutely is considered as a being. Secondly, it is considered as one. Thirdly, its intrinsic power of operation and causality is considered. The fourth point of consideration embraces its relation to its effects. Hence this fourfold consideration comes to our mind in reference to God.

According to the first point of consideration, whereby we consider God absolutely in His being, the appropriation mentioned by Hilary applies, according to which "eternity" is appropriated to the Father, species to the Son, "use" to the Holy Ghost. For "eternity" as meaning a "being" without a principle, has a likeness to the property of the Father, Who is "a principle without a principle." Species or beauty has a likeness to the property of the Son. For beauty includes three conditions, "integrity" or "perfection," since those things which are impaired are by the very fact ugly; due "proportion" or "harmony"; and lastly, "brightness" or "clarity," whence things are called beautiful which have a bright color.

The first of these has a likeness to the property of the Son, inasmuch as He as Son has in Himself truly and perfectly the nature of the Father. To insinuate this, Augustine says in his explanation (De Trin. vi, 10): "Where—that is, in the Son—there is supreme and primal life," etc.

The second agrees with the Son's property, inasmuch as He is the express Image of the Father. Hence we see that an image is said to be beautiful, if it perfectly represents even an ugly thing. This is indicated by Augustine when he says (De Trin. vi, 10), "Where there exists wondrous proportion and primal equality," etc.

The third agrees with the property of the Son, as the Word, which is the light and splendor of the intellect, as Damascene says (De Fide Orth. iii, 3). Augustine alludes to the same when he says (De Trin. vi, 10): "As the perfect Word, not wanting in anything, and, so to speak, the art of the omnipotent God," etc.

"Use" has a likeness to the property of the Holy Ghost; provided the "use" be taken in a wide sense, as including also the sense of "to enjoy"; according as "to use" is to employ something at the beck of the will, and "to enjoy" means to use joyfully, as Augustine says (De Trin. x, 11). So "use," whereby the Father and the Son enjoy each other, agrees with the property of the Holy Ghost, as Love. This is what Augustine says (De Trin. vi, 10): "That love, that delectation, that felicity or beatitude, is called use by him" (Hilary). But the "use" by which we enjoy God, is likened to the property of the Holy Ghost as the Gift; and Augustine points to this when he says (De Trin. vi, 10): "In the Trinity, the Holy Ghost, the sweetness of the Begettor and the Begotten, pours out upon us mere creatures His immense bounty and wealth." Thus it is clear how "eternity," species, and "use" are attributed or appropriated to the persons, but not essence or operation; because, being common, there is nothing in their concept to liken them to the properties of the Persons.

The second consideration of God regards Him as "one." In that view Augustine (De Doctr. Christ. i,

5) appropriates "unity" to the Father, "equality" to the Son, "concord" or "union" to the Holy Ghost. It is manifest that these three imply unity, but in different ways. For "unity" is said absolutely, as it does not presuppose anything else; and for this reason it is appropriated to the Father, to Whom any other person is not presupposed since He is the "principle without principle." "Equality" implies unity as regards another; for that is equal which has the same quantity as another. So equality is appropriated to the Son, Who is the "principle from a principle." "Union" implies the unity of two; and is therefore appropriated to the Holy Ghost, inasmuch as He proceeds from two. And from this we can understand what Augustine means when he says (De Doctr. Christ. i, 5) that "The Three are one, by reason of the Father; They are equal by reason of the Son; and are united by reason of the Holy Ghost." For it is clear that we trace a thing back to that in which we find it first: just as in this lower world we attribute life to the vegetative soul, because therein we find the first trace of life. Now "unity" is perceived at once in the person of the Father, even if by an impossible hypothesis, the other persons were removed. So the other persons derive their unity from the Father. But if the other persons be removed, we do not find equality in the Father, but we find it as soon as we suppose the Son. So, all are equal by reason of the Son, not as if the Son were the principle of equality in the Father, but that, without the Son equal to the Father, the Father could not be called equal; because His equality is considered firstly in regard to the Son: for that the Holy Ghost is equal to the Father, is also from the Son. Likewise, if the Holy Ghost, Who is the union of the two, be excluded, we cannot understand the oneness of the union between the Father and the Son. So all are connected by reason of the Holy Ghost; because given the Holy Ghost, we find whence the Father and the Son are said to be united.

According to the third consideration, which brings before us the adequate power of God in the sphere of causality, there is said to be a third kind of appropriation, of "power," "wisdom," and "goodness." This kind of appropriation is made both by reason of similitude as regards what exists in the divine persons, and by reason of dissimilitude if we consider what is in creatures. For "power" has the nature of a principle, and so it has a likeness to the heavenly Father, Who is the principle of the whole Godhead. But in an earthly father it is wanting sometimes by reason of old age. "Wisdom" has likeness to the heavenly Son, as the Word, for a word is nothing but the concept of wisdom. In an earthly son this is sometimes absent by reason of lack of years. "Goodness," as the nature and object of love, has likeness to the Holy Ghost; but seems repugnant to the earthly spirit, which often implies a certain violent impulse, according to Isa. 25:4: "The spirit of the strong is as a blast beating on the wall." "Strength" is appropriated to the Son and to the Holy Ghost, not as denoting the power itself of a thing, but as sometimes used to express that which proceeds from power; for instance, we say that the strong work done by an agent is its strength.

According to the fourth consideration, i.e. God's relation to His effects, there arise[s] appropriation of the expression "from Whom, by Whom, and in Whom." For this preposition "from" [ex] sometimes implies a certain relation of the material cause; which has no place in God; and sometimes it expresses the relation of the efficient cause, which can be applied to God by reason of His active power; hence it is appropriated to the Father in the same way as power. The preposition "by" [per] sometimes designates an intermediate cause; thus we may say that a smith works "by" a hammer. Hence the word "by" is not always appropriated to the Son, but belongs to the Son properly and strictly, according to the text, "All things were made by Him" (John 1:3); not that the Son is an instrument, but as "the principle from a principle." Sometimes it designates the habitude of a form "by" which an agent works; thus we say that an artificer works by his art. Hence, as wisdom and art are appropriated to the Son, so also is the expression "by Whom." The preposition "in" strictly denotes the habitude of one containing. Now, God contains things in two ways: in one way by their similitudes; thus things are said to be in God, as existing in His knowledge. In this sense the expression "in Him" should be appropriated to the Son. In another sense things are contained in God forasmuch as He in His goodness preserves and governs them, by guiding them to a fitting end; and in this sense the expression "in Him" is appropriated to the Holy Ghost, as likewise is "goodness." Nor need the habitude of the final cause (though the first of causes) be appropriated to the Father, Who is "the principle without a principle": because the divine persons, of Whom the Father is the principle, do not proceed from Him as towards an end, since each of Them is the last end; but They proceed by a natural procession, which seems more to belong to the nature of a natural power.

Regarding the other points of inquiry, we can say that since "truth" belongs to the intellect, as stated above (Q. 16, A. 1), it is appropriated to the Son, without, however, being a property of His. For truth can be considered as existing in the thought or in the thing itself. Hence, as intellect and thing in their essential meaning, are referred to the essence, and not to the persons, so the same is to be said of truth. The definition quoted from Augustine belongs to truth as appropriated to the Son. The "book of life" directly means knowledge but indirectly it means life. For, as above explained (Q. 24, A. 1), it is God's knowledge regarding those who are to possess eternal life. Consequently, it is appropriated to the Son; although life is appropriated to the Holy Ghost, as implying a certain kind of interior movement, agreeing in that sense with the property of the Holy Ghost as Love. To be written by another is not of the essence of a book considered as such; but this belongs to it only as a work produced. So this does not imply origin; nor is it personal, but an appropriation to a person. The expression "Who is" is appropriated to the person of the Son, not by reason of itself, but by reason of an adjunct, inasmuch as, in God's word to Moses, was prefigured the delivery of the human race accomplished by the Son. Yet, forasmuch as the word "Who" is taken in a relative sense, it may sometimes relate to the person of the Son; and in that sense it would be taken personally; as, for instance, were we to say, "The Son is the begotten 'Who is,'" inasmuch as "God begotten is personal." But taken indefinitely, it is an essential term. And although the pronoun "this" [iste] seems grammatically to point to a particular person, nevertheless everything that we can point to can be grammatically treated as a person, although in its own nature it is not a person; as we may say, "this stone," and "this ass." So, speaking in a grammatical sense, so far as the word "God" signifies and stands for the divine essence, the latter may be designated by the pronoun "this," according to Ex. 15:2: "This is my God, and I will glorify Him."

## QUESTION 40

OF THE PERSONS AS COMPARED TO THE RELATIONS OR PROPERTIES (In Four Articles)

We now consider the persons in connection with the relations, or properties; and there are four points of inquiry:

(1) Whether relation is the same as person?

(2) Whether the relations distinguish and constitute the persons?

(3) Whether mental abstraction of the relations from the persons leaves the hypostases distinct?

(4) Whether the relations, according to our mode of understanding, presuppose the acts of the persons, or contrariwise?

FIRST ARTICLE [I, Q. 40, Art. 1]

Whether Relation Is the Same As Person?

Objection 1: It would seem that in God relation is not the same as person. For when things are identical, if one is multiplied the others are multiplied. But in one person there are several relations; as in the person of the Father there is paternity and common spiration. Again, one relation exists in two person, as common spiration in the Father and in the Son. Therefore relation is not the same as person.

Obj. 2: Further, according to the Philosopher (Phys. iv, text. 24), nothing is contained by itself. But relation is in the person; nor can it be said that this occurs because they are identical, for otherwise relation would be also in the essence. Therefore relation, or property, is not the same as person in God.

Obj. 3: Further, when several things are identical, what is predicated of one is predicated of the others. But all that is predicated of a Person is not predicated of His property. For we say that the Father begets; but not that the paternity is begetting. Therefore property is not the same as person in God.

*On the contrary,* in God "what is" and "whereby it is" are the same, according to Boethius (De Hebdom.). But the Father is Father by paternity. In the same way, the other properties are the same as the persons.

*I answer that,* Different opinions have been held on this point. Some have said that the properties are not the persons, nor in the persons; and these have thought thus owing to the mode of signification of the relations, which do not indeed signify existence "in" something, but rather existence "towards" something. Whence, they styled the relations "assistant," as above explained (Q. 28, A. 2). But since relation, considered as really existing in God, is the divine essence Itself, and the essence is the same as person, as appears from what was said above (Q. 39, A. 1), relation must necessarily be the same as person.

Others, therefore, considering this identity, said that the properties were indeed the persons; but not "in" the persons; for, they said, there are no properties in God except in our way of speaking, as stated above (Q. 32, A. 2). We must, however, say that there are properties in God; as we have shown (Q. 32, A. 2). These are designated by abstract terms, being forms, as it were, of the persons. So, since the nature of a form requires it to be "in" that of which it is the form, we must say that the properties are in the persons, and yet that they are the persons; as we say that the essence is in God, and yet is God.

Reply Obj. 1: Person and property are really the same, but differ in concept. Consequently, it does not follow that if one is multiplied, the other must also be multiplied. We must, however, consider that in God, by reason of the divine simplicity, a twofold real identity exists as regards what in creatures are distinct. For, since the divine simplicity excludes the composition of matter and form, it follows that in God the abstract is the same as the concrete, as "Godhead" and "God." And as the divine simplicity excludes the composition of subject and accident, it follows that whatever is attributed to God, is His essence Itself; and so, wisdom and power are the same in God, because they are both in the divine essence. According to this twofold identity, property in God is the same as person. For personal properties are the same as the persons because the abstract and the concrete are the same in God; since they are the subsisting persons themselves, as paternity is the Father Himself, and filiation is the Son, and procession is the Holy Ghost. But the non-personal properties are the same as the persons according to the other reason of identity, whereby whatever is attributed to God is His own essence. Thus, common spiration is the same as the person of the Father, and the person of the Son; not that it is one self-subsisting person; but that as there is one essence in the two persons, so also there is one property in the two persons, as above explained (Q. 30, A. 2).

Reply Obj. 2: The properties are said to be in the essence, only by mode of identity; but in the persons they exist by mode of identity, not merely in reality, but also in the mode of signification; as the form exists in its subject. Thus the properties determine and distinguish the persons, but not the essence.

Reply Obj. 3: Notional participles and verbs signify the notional acts: and acts belong to a *suppositum*. Now, properties are not designated as supposita, but as forms of supposita. And so their mode of signification is against notional participles and verbs being predicated of the properties.

SECOND ARTICLE [I, Q. 40, Art. 2]

Whether the Persons Are Distinguished by the Relations?

Objection 1: It would seem that the persons are not distinguished by the relations. For simple things are distinct by themselves. But the persons are supremely simple. Therefore they are distinguished by themselves, and not by the relation.

Obj. 2: Further, a form is distinguished only in relation to its genus. For white is distinguished from black only by quality. But "hypostasis" signifies an individual in the genus of substance. Therefore the hypostases cannot be distinguished by relations.

Obj. 3: Further, what is absolute comes before what is relative. But the distinction of the divine persons is the primary distinction. Therefore the divine persons are not distinguished by the relations.

Obj. 4: Further, whatever presupposes distinction cannot be the first principle of distinction. But relation presupposes distinction, which comes into its definition; for a relation is essentially what is towards another. Therefore the first distinctive principle in God cannot be relation.

*On the contrary,* Boethius says (De Trin.): "Relation alone multiplies the Trinity of the divine persons."

*I answer that,* In whatever multitude of things is to be found something common to all, it is necessary to seek out the principle of distinction. So, as the three persons agree in the unity of essence, we must seek to know the principle of distinction whereby they are several. Now, there are two principles of difference between the divine persons, and these are "origin" and "relation." Although these do not really differ, yet they differ in the mode of signification; for "origin" is signified by way of act, as "generation"; and "relation" by way of the form, as "paternity."

Some, then, considering that relation follows upon act, have said that the divine hypostases are distinguished by origin, so that we may say that the Father is distinguished from the Son, inasmuch as the former begets and the latter is begotten. Further, that the relations, or the properties, make known the distinctions of the hypostases or persons as resulting therefrom; as also in creatures the properties manifest the distinctions of individuals, which distinctions are caused by the material principles.

This opinion, however, cannot stand—for two reasons. Firstly, because, in order that two things be understood as distinct, their distinction must be understood as resulting from something intrinsic to both; thus in things created it results from their matter or their form. Now origin of a thing does not designate anything intrinsic, but means the way from something, or to something; as generation signifies the way to a thing generated, and as proceeding from the generator. Hence it is not possible that what is generated and the generator should be distinguished by generation alone; but in the generator and in the thing generated we must presuppose whatever makes them to be distinguished from each other. In a divine person there is nothing to presuppose but essence, and relation or property. Whence, since the persons agree in essence, it only remains to be said that the persons are distinguished from each other by the relations. Secondly: because the distinction of the divine persons is not to be so understood as if what is common to them all is divided, because the common essence remains undivided; but the distinguishing principles themselves must constitute the things which are distinct. Now the relations or the properties distinguish or constitute the hypostases or persons, inasmuch as they are themselves the subsisting persons; as paternity is the Father, and filiation is the Son, because in God the abstract and the concrete do not differ. But it is against the nature of origin that it should constitute hypostasis or person. For origin taken in an active sense signifies proceeding from a subsisting person, so that it presupposes the latter; while in a passive sense origin, as "nativity," signifies the way to a subsisting person, and as not yet constituting the person.

It is therefore better to say that the persons or hypostases are distinguished rather by relations than by origin. For, although in both ways they are distinguished, nevertheless in our mode of understanding they are distinguished chiefly and firstly by relations; whence this name "Father" signifies not only a property, but also the hypostasis; whereas this term "Begetter" or "Begetting" signifies property only; forasmuch as this name "Father" signifies the relation which is distinctive and constitutive of the hypostasis; and this term "Begetter" or "Begotten" signifies the origin which is not distinctive and constitutive of the hypostasis.

Reply Obj. 1: The persons are the subsisting relations themselves. Hence it is not against the simplicity of the divine persons for them to be distinguished by the relations.

Reply Obj. 2: The divine persons are not distinguished as regards being, in which they subsist, nor in anything absolute, but only as regards something relative. Hence relation suffices for their distinction.

Reply Obj. 3: The more prior a distinction is, the nearer it approaches to unity; and so it must be the least possible distinction. So the distinction of the persons must be by that which distinguishes the least possible; and this is by relation.

Reply Obj. 4: Relation presupposes the distinction of the subjects, when it is an accident; but when the relation is subsistent, it does not presuppose, but brings about distinction. For when it is said that relation is by nature to be towards another, the word "another" signifies the correlative which is not prior, but simultaneous in the order of nature.

THIRD ARTICLE [I, Q. 40, Art. 3]

Whether the Hypostases Remain If the Relations Are Mentally Abstracted from the Persons?

Objection 1: It would seem that the hypostases remain if the properties or relations are mentally abstracted from the persons. For that to which something is added, may be understood when the addition is taken away; as man is something added to animal which can be understood if rational be taken away. But person is something added to hypostasis; for person is "a hypostasis distinguished by a property of dignity." Therefore, if a personal property be taken away from a person, the hypostasis remains.

Obj. 2: Further, that the Father is Father, and that He is someone, are not due to the same reason. For as He is the Father by paternity, supposing He is some one by paternity, it would follow that the Son, in Whom there is not paternity, would not be "someone." So when paternity is mentally abstracted from the Father, He still remains "someone"—that is, a hypostasis. Therefore, if property be removed from person, the hypostasis remains.

Obj. 3: Further, Augustine says (De Trin. v, 6): "Unbegotten is not the same as Father; for if the Father had not begotten the Son, nothing would prevent Him being called unbegotten." But if He had not begotten the Son, there would be no paternity in Him. Therefore, if paternity be removed, there still remains the hypostasis of the Father as unbegotten.

*On the contrary,* Hilary says (De Trin. iv): "The Son has nothing else than birth." But He is Son by "birth." Therefore, if filiation be removed, the Son's hypostasis no more remains; and the same holds as regards the other persons.

*I answer that,* Abstraction by the intellect is twofold—when the universal is abstracted from the particular, as animal abstracted from man; and when the form is abstracted from the matter, as the form of a circle is abstracted by the intellect from any sensible matter. The difference between these two abstractions consists in the fact that in the abstraction of the universal from the particular, that from which the abstraction is made does not remain; for when the difference of rationality is removed from man, the man no longer remains in the intellect, but animal alone remains. But in the abstraction of the form from the matter, both the form and the matter remain in the intellect; as, for instance, if we abstract the form of a circle from brass, there remains in our intellect separately the understanding both of a circle, and of brass. Now, although there is no universal nor particular in God, nor form and matter, in reality; nevertheless, as regards the mode of signification there is a certain likeness of these things in God; and thus Damascene says (De Fide Orth. iii, 6) that "substance is common and hypostasis is particular." So, if we speak of the abstraction of the universal from the particular, the common universal essence remains in the intellect if the properties are removed; but not the hypostasis of the Father, which is, as it were, a particular.

But as regards the abstraction of the form from the matter, if the non-personal properties are removed, then the idea of the hypostases and persons remains; as, for instance, if the fact of the Father's being unbegotten or spirating be mentally abstracted from the Father, the Father's hypostasis or person remains.

If, however, the personal property be mentally abstracted, the idea of the hypostasis no longer remains. For the personal properties are not to be understood as added to the divine hypostases, as a form is added to a pre-existing subject: but they carry with them their own *supposita,* inasmuch as they are themselves subsisting persons; thus paternity is the Father Himself. For hypostasis signifies something distinct in God, since hypostasis means an individual substance. So, as relation distinguishes and constitutes the hypostases, as above explained (A. 2), it follows that if the personal relations are mentally abstracted, the hypostases no longer remain. Some, however, think, as above noted, that the divine hypostases are not distinguished by the relations, but only by origin; so that the Father is a hypostasis as not from another, and the Son is a hypostasis as from another by generation. And that the consequent relations which are to be regarded as properties of dignity, constitute the notion of a person, and are thus called "personal properties." Hence, if these relations are mentally abstracted, the hypostasis, but not the persons, remain.

But this is impossible, for two reasons: first, because the relations distinguish and constitute the hypostases, as shown above (A. 2); secondly, because every hypostasis of a rational nature is a person, as appears from the definition of Boethius (De Duab. Nat.) that, "person is the individual substance of a rational nature." Hence, to have hypostasis and not person, it would be necessary to abstract the rationality from the nature, but not the property from the person.

Reply Obj. 1: Person does not add to hypostasis a distinguishing property absolutely, but a distinguishing property of dignity, all of which must be taken as the difference. Now, this distinguishing property is one of dignity precisely because it is understood as subsisting in a rational nature. Hence, if the distinguishing property be removed from the person, the hypostasis no longer remains; whereas it would remain were the rationality of the nature removed; for both person and hypostasis are individual substances. Consequently, in God the distinguishing relation belongs essentially to both.

Reply Obj. 2: By paternity the Father is not only Father, but is a person, and is "someone," or a hypostasis. It does not follow, however, that the Son is not "someone" or a hypostasis; just as it does not follow that He is not a person.

Reply Obj. 3: Augustine does not mean to say that the hypostasis of the Father would remain as unbegotten, if His paternity were removed, as if innascibility constituted and distinguished the hypostasis of the Father; for this would be impossible, since "being unbegotten" says nothing positive and is only a negation, as he himself says. But he speaks in a general sense, forasmuch as not every unbegotten being is the Father. So, if paternity be removed, the hypostasis of the Father does not remain in God, as distinguished from the other persons, but only as distinguished from creatures; as the Jews understand it.

FOURTH ARTICLE [I, Q. 40, Art. 4]

Whether the properties presuppose the notional acts?

Objection 1: It would seem that the notional acts are understood before the properties. For the Master of the Sentences says (Sent. i, D, xxvii) that "the Father always is, because He is ever begetting the Son." So it seems that generation precedes paternity in the order of intelligence.

Obj. 2: Further, in the order of intelligence every relation presupposes that on which it is founded; as equality presupposes quantity. But paternity is a relation founded on the action of generation. Therefore paternity presupposes generation.

Obj. 3: Further, active generation is to paternity as nativity is to filiation. But filiation presupposes nativity; for the Son is so called because He is born. Therefore paternity also presupposes generation.

*On the contrary,* Generation is the operation of the person of the Father. But paternity constitutes the person of the Father. Therefore in the order of intelligence, paternity is prior to generation.

*I answer that,* According to the opinion that the properties do not distinguish and constitute the hypostases in God, but only manifest them as already distinct and constituted, we must absolutely say that the relations in our mode of understanding follow upon the notional acts, so that we can say, without qualifying the phrase, that "because He begets, He is the Father." A distinction, however, is needed if we suppose that the relations distinguish and constitute the divine hypostases. For origin has in God an active and passive signification—active, as generation is attributed to the Father, and spiration, taken for the notional act, is attributed to the Father and the Son; passive, as nativity is attributed to the Son, and procession to the Holy Ghost. For, in the order of intelligence, origin, in the passive sense, simply precedes the personal properties of the person proceeding; because origin, as passively understood, signifies the way to a person constituted by the property. Likewise, origin signified actively is prior in the order of intelligence to the non-personal relation of the person originating; as the notional act of spiration precedes, in the order of intelligence, the unnamed relative property common to the Father and the Son. The personal property of the Father can be considered in a twofold sense: firstly, as a relation; and thus again in the order of intelligence it presupposes the notional act, for relation, as such, is founded upon an act: secondly, according as it constitutes the person; and thus the notional act presupposes the relation, as an action presupposes a person acting.

Reply Obj. 1: When the Master says that "because He begets, He is Father," the term "Father" is taken as meaning relation only, but not as signifying the subsisting person; for then it would be necessary to say conversely that because He is Father He begets.

Reply Obj. 2: This objection avails of paternity as a relation, but not as constituting a person.

Reply Obj. 3: Nativity is the way to the person of the Son; and so, in the order of intelligence, it precedes filiation, even as constituting the person of the Son. But active generation signifies a proceeding from the person of the Father; wherefore it presupposes the personal property of the Father.

# QUESTION 41

OF THE PERSONS IN REFERENCE TO THE NOTIONAL ACTS (In Six Articles)

We now consider the persons in reference to the notional acts, concerning which six points of inquiry arise:

(1) Whether the notional acts are to be attributed to the persons?

(2) Whether these acts are necessary, or voluntary?

(3) Whether as regards these acts, a person proceeds from nothing or from something?

(4) Whether in God there exists a power as regards the notional acts?

(5) What this power means?

(6) Whether several persons can be the term of one notional act?

FIRST ARTICLE [I, Q. 41, Art. 1]

Whether the Notional Acts Are to Be Attributed to the Persons?

Objection 1: It would seem that the notional acts are not to be attributed to the persons. For Boethius says (De Trin.): "Whatever is predicated of God, of whatever genus it be, becomes the divine substance, except what pertains to the relation." But action is one of the ten genera. Therefore any action attributed to God belongs to His essence, and not to a notion.

Obj. 2: Further, Augustine says (De Trin. v, 4,5) that, "everything which is said of God, is said of Him as regards either His substance, or relation." But whatever belongs to the substance is signified by the essential attributes; and whatever belongs to the relations, by the names of the persons, or by the names of the properties. Therefore, in addition to these, notional acts are not to be attributed to the persons.

Obj. 3: Further, the nature of action is of itself to cause passion. But we do not place passions in God. Therefore neither are notional acts to be placed in God.

*On the contrary,* Augustine (Fulgentius, De Fide ad Petrum ii) says: "It is a property of the Father to beget the Son." Therefore notional acts are to be placed in God.

*I answer that,* In the divine persons distinction is founded on origin. But origin can be properly designated only by certain acts. Wherefore, to signify the order of origin in the divine persons, we must attribute notional acts to the persons.

Reply Obj. 1: Every origin is designated by an act. In God there is a twofold order of origin: one, inasmuch as the creature proceeds from Him, and this is common to the three persons; and so those actions which are attributed to God to designate the proceeding of creatures from Him, belong to His essence. Another order of origin in God regards the procession of person from person; wherefore the acts which designate the order of this origin are called notional; because the notions of the persons are the mutual relations of the persons, as is clear from what was above explained (Q. 32, A. 2).

Reply Obj. 2: The notional acts differ from the relations of the persons only in their mode of signification; and in reality are altogether the same. Whence the Master says that "generation and nativity in other words are paternity and filiation" (Sent. i, D, xxvi). To see this, we must consider that the origin of one thing from another is firstly inferred from movement: for that anything be changed from its disposition by movement evidently arises from some cause. Hence action, in its primary sense, means origin of movement; for, as movement derived from another into a mobile object, is called "passion," so the origin of movement itself as beginning from another and terminating in what is moved, is called "action." Hence, if we take away movement, action implies nothing more than order of origin, in so far as action proceeds from some cause or principle to what is from that principle. Consequently, since in God no movement exists, the personal action of the one producing a person is only the habitude of the principle to the person who is from the principle; which habitudes are the relations, or the notions. Nevertheless we cannot speak of divine and intelligible things except after the manner of sensible things, whence we derive our knowledge, and wherein actions and passions, so far as these imply movement, differ from the relations which result from action and passion, and therefore it was necessary to signify the habitudes of the persons separately after the manner of act, and separately after the manner of relations. Thus it is evident that they are really the same, differing only in their mode of signification.

Reply Obj. 3: Action, so far as it means origin of movement, naturally involves passion; but action in that sense is not attributed to God. Whence, passions are attributed to Him only from a grammatical standpoint, and in accordance with our manner of speaking, as we attribute "to beget" with the Father, and to the Son "to be begotten."

SECOND ARTICLE [I, Q. 41, Art. 2]

Whether the Notional Acts Are Voluntary?

Objection 1: It would seem that the notional acts are voluntary. For Hilary says (De Synod.): "Not by natural necessity was the Father led to beget the Son."

Obj. 2: Further, the Apostle says, "He transferred us to the kingdom of the Son of His love" (Col. 1:13). But love belongs to the will. Therefore the Son was begotten of the Father by will.

Obj. 3: Further, nothing is more voluntary than love. But the Holy Ghost proceeds as Love from the Father and the Son. Therefore He proceeds voluntarily.

Obj. 4: Further, the Son proceeds by mode of the intellect, as the Word. But every word proceeds by the will from a speaker. Therefore the Son proceeds from the Father by will, and not by nature.

Obj. 5: Further, what is not voluntary is necessary. Therefore if the Father begot the Son, not by the will, it seems to follow that He begot Him by necessity; and this is against what Augustine says (Ad Orosium qu. vii).

*On the contrary,* Augustine says, in the same book, that, "the Father begot the Son neither by will, nor by necessity."

*I answer that,* When anything is said to be, or to be made by the will, this can be understood in two senses. In one sense, the ablative designates only concomitance, as I can say that I am a man by my will—that is, I will to be a man; and in this way it can be said that the Father begot the Son by will; as also He is God by will, because He wills to be God, and wills to beget the Son. In the other sense, the ablative imports the habitude of a principle as it is said that the workman works by his will, as the will is the principle of his work; and thus in that sense it must be said the God the Father begot the Son, not by His will; but that He produced the creature by His will. Whence in the book *De Synod.*, it is said: "If anyone say that the Son was made by the Will of God, as a creature is said to be made, let him be anathema." The reason of this is that will and nature differ in their manner of causation, in such a way that nature is determined to one, while the will is not determined to one; and this because the effect is assimilated to the form of the agent, whereby the latter acts. Now it is manifest that of one thing there is only one natural form whereby it exists; and hence such as it is itself, such also is its work. But the form whereby the will acts is not only one, but many, according to the number of ideas understood. Hence the quality of the will's action does not depend on the quality of the agent, but on the agent's will and understanding. So the will is the principle of those things which may be this way or that way; whereas of those things which can be only in one way, the principle is nature. What, however, can exist in different ways is far from the divine nature, whereas it belongs to the nature of a created being; because God is of Himself necessary being, whereas a creature is made from nothing. Thus, the Arians, wishing to prove the Son to be a creature, said that the Father begot the Son by will, taking will in the sense of principle. But we, *on the contrary*, must assert that the Father begot the Son, not by will, but by nature. Wherefore Hilary says (De Synod.): "The will of God gave to all creatures their substance: but perfect birth gave the Son a nature derived from a substance impassible and unborn. All things created are such as God willed them to be; but the Son, born of God, subsists in the perfect likeness of God."

Reply Obj. 1: This saying is directed against those who did not admit even the concomitance of the Father's will in the generation of the Son, for they said that the Father begot the Son in such a manner by nature that the will to beget was wanting; just as we ourselves suffer many things against our will from natural necessity—as, for instance, death, old age, and like ills. This appears from what precedes and from what follows as regards the words quoted, for thus we read: "Not against His will, nor as it were, forced, nor as if He were led by natural necessity did the Father beget the Son."

Reply Obj. 2: The Apostle calls Christ the Son of the love of God, inasmuch as He is superabundantly loved by God; not, however, as if love were the principle of the Son's generation.

Reply Obj. 3: The will, as a natural faculty, wills something naturally, as man's will naturally tends to happiness; and likewise God naturally wills and loves Himself; whereas in regard to things other than Himself, the will of God is in a way, undetermined in itself, as above explained (Q. 19, A. 3). Now, the Holy Ghost proceeds as Love, inasmuch as God loves Himself, and hence He proceeds naturally, although He proceeds by mode of will.

Reply Obj. 4: Even as regards the intellectual conceptions of the mind, a return is made to those first principles which are naturally understood. But God naturally understands Himself, and thus the conception of the divine Word is natural.

Reply Obj. 5: A thing is said to be necessary "of itself," and "by reason of another." Taken in the latter sense, it has a twofold meaning: firstly, as an efficient and compelling cause, and thus necessary means what is violent; secondly, it means a final cause, when a thing is said to be necessary as the means to an end, so far as without it the end could not be attained, or, at least, so well attained. In neither of these ways is the divine generation necessary; because God is not the means to an end, nor is He subject to compulsion. But a thing is said to be necessary "of itself" which cannot but be: in this sense it is necessary for God to be; and in the same sense it is necessary that the Father beget the Son.

THIRD ARTICLE [I, Q. 41, Art. 3]

Whether the Notional Acts Proceed from Something?

Objection 1: It would seem that the notional acts do not proceed from anything. For if the Father begets the Son from something, this will be either from Himself or from something else. If from something else, since that whence a thing is generated exists in what is generated, it follows that something different from the Father exists in the Son, and this contradicts what is laid down by Hilary (De Trin. vii) that, "In them nothing diverse or different exists." If the Father begets the Son from Himself, since again that whence a thing is generated, if it be something permanent, receives as predicate the thing generated therefrom just as we say, "The man is white," since the man remains, when not from white he is made white—it follows that either the Father does not remain after the Son is begotten, or that the Father is the Son, which is false. Therefore the Father does not beget the Son from something, but from nothing.

Obj. 2: Further, that whence anything is generated is the principle regarding what is generated. So if the Father generate the Son from His own essence or nature, it follows that the essence or nature of the Father is the principle of the Son. But it is not a material principle, because in God nothing material exists; and therefore it is, as it were, an active principle, as the begetter is the principle of the one begotten. Thus it follows that the essence generates, which was disproved above (Q. 39, A. 5).

Obj. 3: Further, Augustine says (De Trin. vii, 6) that the three persons are not from the same essence; because the essence is not another thing from person. But the person of the Son is not another thing from the Father's essence. Therefore the Son is not from the Father's essence.

Obj. 4: Further, every creature is from nothing. But in Scripture the Son is called a creature; for it is said (Ecclus. 24:5), in the person of the Wisdom begotten,"I came out of the mouth of the Most High, the first-born before all creatures": and further on (Ecclus. 24:14) it is said as uttered by the same Wisdom, "From the beginning, and before the world was I created." Therefore the Son was not begotten from something, but from nothing. Likewise we can object concerning the Holy Ghost, by reason of what is said (Zech. 12:1): "Thus saith the Lord Who stretcheth forth the heavens, and layeth the foundations of the earth, and formeth the spirit of man within him"; and (Amos 4:13) according to another version [*The Septuagint]: "I Who form the earth, and create the spirit."

*On the contrary,* Augustine (Fulgentius, De Fide ad Petrum i, 1) says: "God the Father, of His nature, without beginning, begot the Son equal to Himself."

*I answer that,* The Son was not begotten from nothing, but from the Father's substance. For it was explained above (Q. 27, A. 2; Q. 33, AA. 2 ,3) that paternity, filiation and nativity really and truly exist in God. Now, this is the difference between true "generation," whereby one proceeds from another as a son, and "making," that the maker makes something out of external matter, as a carpenter makes a bench out of wood, whereas a man begets a son from himself. Now, as a created workman makes a thing out of matter, so God makes things out of nothing, as will be shown later on (Q. 45, A. 1), not as if this nothing were a part of the substance of the thing made, but because the whole substance of a thing is produced by Him without anything else whatever presupposed. So, were the Son to proceed from the Father as out of nothing, then the Son would be to the Father what the thing made is to the maker, whereto, as is evident, the name of filiation would not apply except by a kind of similitude. Thus, if the Son of God proceeds from the Father out of nothing, He could not be properly and truly called the Son, whereas the contrary is stated (1 John 5:20): "That we may be in His true Son Jesus Christ." Therefore the true Son of God is not from nothing; nor is He made, but begotten.

That certain creatures made by God out of nothing are called sons of God is to be taken in a metaphorical sense, according to a certain likeness of assimilation to Him Who is the true Son. Whence, as He is the only true and natural Son of God, He is called the "only begotten," according to John 1:18, "The only begotten Son, Who is in the bosom of the Father, He hath declared Him"; and so as others are entitled sons of adoption by their similitude to Him, He is called the "first begotten," according to Rom. 8:29: "Whom He foreknew He also predestinated to be made conformable to the image of His Son, that He might be the first born of many brethren." Therefore the Son of God is begotten of the substance of the Father, but not in the same way as man is born of man; for a part of the human substance in generation passes into the substance of the one begotten, whereas the divine nature cannot be parted; whence it necessarily follows that the Father in begetting the Son does not transmit any part of His nature, but communicates His whole nature to Him, the distinction only of origin remaining as explained above (Q. 40, A. 2).

Reply Obj. 1: When we say that the Son was born of the Father, the preposition "of" designates a consubstantial generating principle, but not a material principle. For that which is produced from matter, is made by a change of form in that whence it is produced. But the divine essence is unchangeable, and is not susceptive of another form.

Reply Obj. 2: When we say the Son is begotten of the essence of the Father, as the Master of the Sentences explains (Sent. i, D, v), this denotes the habitude of a kind of active principle, and as he expounds, "the Son is begotten of the essence of the Father"—that is, of the Father Who is essence; and so Augustine says (De Trin. xv, 13): "When I say of the Father Who is essence, it is the same as if I said more explicitly, of the essence of the Father."

This, however, is not enough to explain the real meaning of the words. For we can say that the creature is from God Who is essence; but not that it is from the essence of God. So we may explain them otherwise, by observing that the preposition "of" [de] always denotes consubstantiality. We do not say that a house is "of" [de] the builder, since he is not the consubstantial cause. We can say, however, that something is "of" another, if this is its consubstantial principle, no matter in what way it is so, whether it be an active principle, as the son is said to be "of" the father, or a material principle, as a knife is "of" iron; or a formal principle, but in those things only in which the forms are subsisting, and not accidental to another, for we can say that an angel is "of" an intellectual nature. In this way, then, we say that the Son is begotten 'of' the essence of the Father, inasmuch as the essence of the Father, communicated by generation, subsists in the Son.

Reply Obj. 3: When we say that the Son is begotten of the essence of the Father, a term is added which saves the distinction. But when we say that the three persons are 'of' the divine essence, there is nothing expressed to warrant the distinction signified by the preposition, so there is no parity of argument.

Reply Obj. 4: When we say "Wisdom was created," this may be understood not of Wisdom which is the Son of God, but of created wisdom given by God to creatures: for it is said, "He created her [namely, Wisdom] in the Holy Ghost, and He poured her out over all His works" (Ecclus. 1:9, 10). Nor is it inconsistent for Scripture in one text to speak of the Wisdom begotten and wisdom created, for wisdom created is a kind of participation of the uncreated Wisdom. The saying may also be referred to the created nature assumed by the Son, so that the sense be, "From the beginning and before the world was I made"—that is, I was foreseen as united to the creature. Or the mention of wisdom as both created and begotten insinuates into our minds the mode of the divine generation; for in generation what is generated receives the nature of the generator and this pertains to perfection; whereas in creation the Creator is not changed, but the creature does not receive the Creator's nature. Thus the Son is called both created and begotten, in order that from the idea of creation the immutability of the Father may be understood, and from generation the unity of nature in the Father and the Son. In this way Hilary expounds the sense of this text of Scripture (De Synod.). The other passages quoted do not refer to the Holy Ghost, but to the created spirit, sometimes called wind, sometimes air, sometimes the breath of man, sometimes also the soul, or any other invisible substance.

FOURTH ARTICLE [I, Q. 41, Art. 4]

Whether in God There Is a Power in Respect of the Notional Acts?

Objection 1: It would seem that in God there is no power in respect of the notional acts. For every kind of power is either active or passive; neither of which can be here applied, there being in God nothing which we call passive power, as above explained (Q. 25, A. 1); nor can active power belong to one person as regards another, since the divine persons were not made, as stated above (A. 3). Therefore in God there is no power in respect of the notional acts.

Obj. 2: Further, the object of power is what is possible. But the divine persons are not regarded as possible, but necessary. Therefore, as regards the notional acts, whereby the divine persons proceed, there cannot be power in God.

Obj. 3: Further, the Son proceeds as the word, which is the concept of the intellect; and the Holy Ghost proceeds as love, which belongs to the will. But in God power exists as regards effects, and not as regards intellect and will, as stated above (Q. 25, A. 1). Therefore, in God power does not exist in reference to the notional acts.

*On the contrary,* Augustine says (Contra Maxim. iii, 1): "If God the Father could not beget a co-equal Son, where is the omnipotence of God the Father?" Power therefore exists in God regarding the notional acts.

*I answer that,* As the notional acts exist in God, so must there be also a power in God regarding these acts; since power only means the principle of act. So, as we understand the Father to be principle of generation; and the Father and the Son to be the principle of spiration, we must attribute the power of generating to the Father, and the power of spiration to the Father and the Son; for the power of generation means that whereby the generator generates. Now every generator generates by something. Therefore in every generator we must suppose the power of generating, and in the spirator the power of spirating.

Reply Obj. 1: As a person, according to notional acts, does not proceed as if made; so the power in God as regards the notional acts has no reference to a person as if made, but only as regards the person as proceeding.

Reply Obj. 2: Possible, as opposed to what is necessary, is a consequence of a passive power, which does not exist in God. Hence, in God there is no such thing as possibility in this sense, but only in the sense of possible as contained in what is necessary; and in this latter sense it can be said that as it is possible for God to be, so also is it possible that the Son should be generated.

Reply Obj. 3: Power signifies a principle: and a principle implies distinction from that of which it is the principle. Now we must observe a double distinction in things said of God: one is a real distinction, the other is a distinction of reason only. By a real distinction, God by His essence is distinct from those things of which He is the principle by creation: just as one person is distinct from the other of which He is principle by a notional act. But in God the distinction of action and agent is one of reason only, otherwise action would be an accident in God. And therefore with regard to those actions in respect of which certain things proceed which are distinct from God, either personally or essentially, we may ascribe power to God in its proper sense of principle. And as we ascribe to God the power of creating, so we may ascribe the power of begetting and of spirating. But "to understand" and "to will" are not such actions as to designate the procession of something distinct from God, either essentially or personally. Wherefore, with regard to these actions we cannot ascribe power to God in its proper sense, but only after our way of understanding and speaking: inasmuch as we designate by different terms the intellect and the act of understanding in God, whereas in God the act of understanding is His very essence which has no principle.

FIFTH ARTICLE [I, Q. 41, Art. 5]

Whether the Power of Begetting Signifies a Relation, and Not the Essence?

Objection 1: It would seem that the power of begetting, or of spirating, signifies the relation and not the essence. For power signifies a principle, as appears from its definition: for active power is the principle of action, as we find in *Metaph.* v, text 17. But in God principle in regard to Person is said notionally. Therefore, in God, power does not signify essence but relation.

Obj. 2: Further, in God, the power to act [posse] and 'to act' are not distinct. But in God, begetting signifies relation. Therefore, the same applies to the power of begetting.

Obj. 3: Further, terms signifying the essence in God, are common to the three persons. But the power of begetting is not common to the three persons, but proper to the Father. Therefore it does not signify the essence.

*On the contrary,* As God has the power to beget the Son, so also He wills to beget Him. But the will to beget signifies the essence. Therefore, also, the power to beget.

*I answer that,* Some have said that the power to beget signifies relation in God. But this is not possible. For in every agent, that is properly called power, by which the agent acts. Now, everything that produces something by its action, produces something like itself, as to the form by which it acts; just as man begotten is like his begetter in his human nature, in virtue of which the father has the power to beget a man. In every begetter, therefore, that is the power of begetting in which the begotten is like the begetter.

Now the Son of God is like the Father, who begets Him, in the divine nature. Wherefore the divine nature in the Father is in Him the power of begetting. And so Hilary says (De Trin. v): "The birth of God cannot but contain that nature from which it proceeded; for He cannot subsist other than God, Who subsists from no other source than God."

We must therefore conclude that the power of begetting signifies principally the divine essence as the Master says (Sent. i, D, vii), and not the relation only. Nor does it signify the essence as identified with the relation, so as to signify both equally. For although paternity is signified as the form of the Father, nevertheless it is a personal property, being in respect to the person of the Father, what the individual form is to the individual creature. Now the individual form in things created constitutes the person begetting, but is not that by which the begetter begets, otherwise Socrates would beget Socrates. So neither can paternity be understood as that by which the Father begets, but as constituting the person of the Father, otherwise the Father would beget the Father. But that by which the Father begets is the divine nature, in which the Son is like to Him. And in this sense Damascene says (De Fide Orth. i, 18) that generation is the "work of nature," not of nature generating, but of nature, as being that by which the generator generates. And therefore the power of begetting signifies the divine nature directly, but the relation indirectly.

Reply Obj. 1: Power does not signify the relation itself of a principle, for thus it would be in the genus of relation; but it signifies that which is a principle; not, indeed, in the sense in which we call the agent a principle, but in the sense of being that by which the agent acts. Now the agent is distinct from that which it makes, and the generator from that which it generates: but that by which the generator generates is common to generated and generator, and so much more perfectly, as the generation is more perfect. Since, therefore, the divine generation is most perfect, that by which the Begetter begets, is common to Begotten and Begetter by a community of identity, and not only of species, as in things created. Therefore, from the fact that we say that the divine essence "is the principle by which the Begetter begets," it does not follow that the divine essence is distinct (from the Begotten): which would follow if we were to say that the divine essence begets.

Reply Obj. 2: As in God, the power of begetting is the same as the act of begetting, so the divine essence is the same in reality as the act of begetting or paternity; although there is a distinction of reason.

Reply Obj. 3: When I speak of the "power of begetting," power is signified directly, generation indirectly: just as if I were to say, the "essence of the Father." Wherefore in respect of the essence, which is signified, the power of begetting is common to the three persons: but in respect of the notion that is connoted, it is proper to the person of the Father.

SIXTH ARTICLE [I, Q. 41, Art. 6]

Whether Several Persons Can Be the Term of One Notional Act?

Objection 1: It would seem that a notional act can be directed to several Persons, so that there may be several Persons begotten or spirated in God. For whoever has the power of begetting can beget. But the Son has the power of begetting. Therefore He can beget. But He cannot beget Himself: therefore He can beget another son. Therefore there can be several Sons in God.

Obj. 2: Further, Augustine says (Contra Maxim. iii, 12): "The Son did not beget a Creator: not that He could not, but that it behoved Him not."

Obj. 3: Further, God the Father has greater power to beget than has a created father. But a man can beget several sons. Therefore God can also: the more so that the power of the Father is not diminished after begetting the Son.

*On the contrary,* In God "that which is possible," and "that which is" do not differ. If, therefore, in God it were possible for there to be several Sons, there would be several Sons. And thus there would be more than three Persons in God; which is heretical.

*I answer that,* As Athanasius says, in God there is only "one Father, one Son, one Holy Ghost." For this four reasons may be given.

The first reason is in regard to the relations by which alone are the Persons distinct. For since the divine Persons are the relations themselves as subsistent, there would not be several Fathers, or several Sons in God, unless there were more than one paternity, or more than one filiation. And this, indeed, would not be possible except owing to a material distinction: since forms of one species are not multiplied except in respect of matter, which is not in God. Wherefore there can be but one subsistent filiation in God: just as there could be but one subsistent whiteness.

The second reason is taken from the manner of the processions. For God understands and wills all things by one simple act. Wherefore there can be but one person proceeding after the manner of word, which person is the Son; and but one person proceeding after the manner of love, which person is the Holy Ghost.

The third reason is taken from the manner in which the persons proceed. For the persons proceed naturally, as we have said (A. 2), and nature is determined to one.

The fourth reason is taken from the perfection of the divine persons. For this reason is the Son perfect, that the entire divine filiation is contained in Him, and that there is but one Son. The argument is similar in regard to the other persons.

Reply Obj. 1: We can grant, without distinction, that the Son has the same power as the Father; but we cannot grant that the Son has the power "generandi" [of begetting] thus taking "generandi" as the gerund of the active verb, so that the sense would be that the Son has the "power to beget." Just as, although Father and Son have the same being, it does not follow that the Son is the Father, by reason of the notional term added. But if the word "generandi" [of being begotten] is taken as the gerundive of the passive verb, the power "generandi" is in the Son—that is, the power of being begotten. The same is to be said if it be taken as the gerundive of an impersonal verb, so that the sense be "the power of generation"—that is, a power by which it is generated by some person.

Reply Obj. 2: Augustine does not mean to say by those words that the Son could beget a Son: but that if He did not, it was not because He could not, as we shall see later on (Q. 42, A. 6, ad 3).

Reply Obj. 3: Divine perfection and the total absence of matter in God require that there cannot be several Sons in God, as we have explained. Wherefore that there are not several Sons is not due to any lack of begetting power in the Father.\

# QUESTION 42

OF EQUALITY AND LIKENESS AMONG THE DIVINE PERSONS (In Six Articles)

We now have to consider the persons as compared to one another: firstly, with regard to equality and likeness; secondly, with regard to mission. Concerning the first there are six points of inquiry.

(1) Whether there is equality among the divine persons?

(2) Whether the person who proceeds is equal to the one from Whom He proceeds in eternity?

(3) Whether there is any order among the divine persons?

(4) Whether the divine persons are equal in greatness?

(5) Whether the one divine person is in another?

(6) Whether they are equal in power?

FIRST ARTICLE [I, Q. 42, Art. 1]

Whether There Is Equality in God?

Objection 1: It would seem that equality is not becoming to the divine persons. For equality is in relation to things which are one in quantity as the Philosopher says (Metaph. v, text 20). But in the divine persons there is no quantity, neither continuous intrinsic quantity, which we call size, nor continuous extrinsic quantity, which we call place and time. Nor can there be equality by reason of discrete quantity, because two persons are more than one. Therefore equality is not becoming to the divine persons.

Obj. 2: Further, the divine persons are of one essence, as we have said (Q. 39, A. 2). Now essence is signified by way of form. But agreement in form makes things to be alike, not to be equal. Therefore, we may speak of likeness in the divine persons, but not of equality.

Obj. 3: Further, things wherein there is to be found equality, are equal to one another, for equality is reciprocal. But the divine persons cannot be said to be equal to one another. For as Augustine says (De Trin. vi, 10): "If an image answers perfectly to that whereof it is the image, it may be said to be equal to it; but that which it represents cannot be said to be equal to the image." But the Son is the image of the Father; and so the Father is not equal to the Son. Therefore equality is not to be found among the divine persons.

Obj. 4: Further, equality is a relation. But no relation is common to the three persons; for the persons are distinct by reason of the relations. Therefore equality is not becoming to the divine persons.

*On the contrary,* Athanasius says that "the three persons are co-eternal and co-equal to one another."

*I answer that,* We must needs admit equality among the divine persons. For, according to the Philosopher (Metaph. x, text 15, 16, 17), equality signifies the negation of greater or less. Now we cannot admit anything greater or less in the divine persons; for as Boethius says (De Trin. i): "They must needs admit a difference [namely, of Godhead] who speak of either increase or decrease, as the Arians do, who sunder the Trinity by distinguishing degrees as of numbers, thus involving a plurality." Now the reason of this is that unequal things cannot have the same quantity. But quantity, in God, is nothing else than His essence. Wherefore it follows, that if there were any inequality in the divine persons, they would not have the same essence; and thus the three persons would not be one God; which is impossible. We must therefore admit equality among the divine persons.

Reply Obj. 1: Quantity is twofold. There is quantity of "bulk" or dimensive quantity, which is to be found only in corporeal things, and has, therefore, no place in God. There is also quantity of "virtue," which is measured according to the perfection of some nature or form: to this sort of quantity we allude when we speak of something as being more, or less, hot; forasmuch as it is more or less, perfect in heat. Now this virtual quantity is measured firstly by its source—that is, by the perfection of that form or nature: such is the greatness of spiritual things, just as we speak of great heat on account of its intensity and perfection. And so Augustine says (De Trin. vi, 18) that "in things which are great, but not in bulk, to be greater is to be better," for the more perfect a thing is the better it is. Secondly, virtual quantity is measured by the effects of the form. Now the first effect of form is being, for everything has being by reason of its form. The second effect is operation, for every agent acts through its form. Consequently virtual quantity is measured both in regard to being and in regard to action: in regard to being, forasmuch as things of a more perfect nature are of longer duration; and in regard to action, forasmuch as things of a more perfect nature are more powerful to act. And so as Augustine (Fulgentius, De Fide ad Petrum i) says: "We understand equality to be in the Father, Son and Holy Ghost, inasmuch as no one of them either precedes in eternity, or excels in greatness, or surpasses in power."

Reply Obj. 2: Where we have equality in respect of virtual quantity, equality includes likeness and something besides, because it excludes excess. For whatever things have a common form may be said to be alike, even if they do not participate in that form equally, just as the air may be said to be like fire in heat; but they cannot be said to be equal if one participates in the form more perfectly than another. And because not only is the same nature in both Father and Son, but also is it in both in perfect equality, therefore we say not only that the Son is like to the Father, in order to exclude the error of Eunomius, but also that He is equal to the Father to exclude the error of Arius.

Reply Obj. 3: Equality and likeness in God may be designated in two ways—namely, by nouns and by verbs. When designated by nouns, equality in the divine persons is mutual, and so is likeness; for the Son is equal and like to the Father, and conversely. This is because the divine essence is not more the Father's than the Son's. Wherefore, just as the Son has the greatness of the Father, and is therefore equal to the Father, so the Father has the greatness of the Son, and is therefore equal to the Son. But in reference to creatures, Dionysius says (Div. Nom. ix): "Equality and likeness are not mutual." For effects are said to be like their causes, inasmuch as they have the form of their causes; but not conversely, for the form is principally in the cause, and secondarily in the effect.

But verbs signify equality with movement. And although movement is not in God, there is something that receives. Since, therefore, the Son receives from the Father, this, namely, that He is equal to the Father, and not conversely, for this reason we say that the Son is equalled to the Father, but not conversely.

Reply Obj. 4: In the divine persons there is nothing for us to consider but the essence which they have in common and the relations in which they are distinct. Now equality implies both—namely, distinction of persons, for nothing can be said to be equal to itself; and unity of essence, since for this reason are the persons equal to one another, that they are of the same greatness and essence. Now it is clear that the relation of a thing to itself is not a real relation. Nor, again, is one relation referred to another by a further relation: for when we say that paternity is opposed to filiation, opposition is not a relation mediating between paternity and filiation. For in both these cases relation would be multiplied indefinitely. Therefore equality and likeness in the divine persons is not a real relation distinct from the personal relations: but in its concept it includes both the relations which distinguish the persons, and the unity of essence. For this reason the Master says (Sent. i, D, xxxi) that in these "it is only the terms that are relative."

SECOND ARTICLE [I, Q. 42, Art. 2]

Whether the Person Proceeding Is Co-eternal with His Principle, As the Son with the Father?

Objection 1: It would seem that the person proceeding is not co-eternal with His principle, as the Son with the Father. For Arius gives twelve modes of generation. The first mode is like the issue of a line from a point; wherein is wanting equality of simplicity. The second is like the emission of rays from the sun; wherein is absent equality of nature. The third is like the mark or impression made by a seal; wherein is wanting consubstantiality and executive power. The fourth is the infusion of a good will from God; wherein also consubstantiality is wanting. The fifth is the emanation of an accident from its subject; but the accident has no subsistence. The sixth is the abstraction of a species from matter, as sense receives the species from the sensible object; wherein is wanting equality of spiritual simplicity. The seventh is the exciting of the will by knowledge, which excitation is merely temporal. The eighth is transformation, as an image is made of brass; which transformation is material. The ninth is motion from a mover; and here again we have effect and cause. The tenth is the taking of species from genera; but this mode has no place in God, for the Father is not predicated of the Son as the genus of a species. The eleventh is the realization of an idea [ideatio], as an external coffer arises from the one in the mind. The twelfth is birth, as a man is begotten of his father; which implies priority and posteriority of time. Thus it is clear that equality of nature or of time is absent in every mode whereby one thing is from another. So if the Son is from the Father, we must say that He is less than the Father, or later than the Father, or both.

Obj. 2: Further, everything that comes from another has a principle. But nothing eternal has a principle. Therefore the Son is not eternal; nor is the Holy Ghost.

Obj. 3: Further, everything which is corrupted ceases to be. Hence everything generated begins to be; for the end of generation is existence. But the Son is generated by the Father. Therefore He begins to exist, and is not co-eternal with the Father.

Obj. 4: Further, if the Son be begotten by the Father, either He is always being begotten, or there is some moment in which He is begotten. If He is always being begotten, since, during the process of generation, a thing must be imperfect, as appears in successive things, which are always in process of becoming, as time and motion, it follows that the Son must be always imperfect, which cannot be admitted. Thus there is a moment to be assigned for the begetting of the Son, and before that moment the Son did not exist.

*On the contrary,* Athanasius declares that "all the three persons are co-eternal with each other."

*I answer that,* We must say that the Son is co-eternal with the Father. In proof of which we must consider that for a thing which proceeds from a principle to be posterior to its principle may be due to two reasons: one on the part of the agent, and the other on the part of the action. On the part of the agent this happens differently as regards free agents and natural agents. In free agents, on account of the choice of time; for as a free agent can choose the form it gives to the effect, as stated above (Q. 41, A. 2), so it can choose the time in which to produce its effect. In natural agents, however, the same happens from the agent not having its perfection of natural power from the very first, but obtaining it after a certain time; as, for instance, a man is not able to generate from the very first. Considered on the part of action, anything derived from a principle cannot exist simultaneously with its principle when the action is successive. So, given that an agent, as soon as it exists, begins to act thus, the effect would not exist in the same instant, but in the instant of the action's termination. Now it is manifest, according to what has been said (Q. 41, A. 2), that the Father does not beget the Son by will, but by nature; and also that the Father's nature was perfect from eternity; and again that the action whereby the Father produces the Son is not successive, because thus the Son would be successively generated, and this generation would be material, and accompanied with movement; which is quite impossible. Therefore we conclude that the Son existed whensoever the Father existed and thus the Son is co-eternal with the Father, and likewise the Holy Ghost is co-eternal with both.

Reply Obj. 1: As Augustine says (De Verbis Domini, Serm. 38), no mode of the procession of any creature perfectly represents the divine generation. Hence we need to gather a likeness of it from many of these modes, so that what is wanting in one may be somewhat supplied from another; and thus it is declared in the council of Ephesus: "Let Splendor tell thee that the co-eternal Son existed always with the Father; let the Word announce the impassibility of His birth; let the name Son insinuate His consubstantiality." Yet, above them all the procession of the word from the intellect represents it more exactly; the intellectual word not being posterior to its source except in an intellect passing from potentiality to act; and this cannot be said of God.

Reply Obj. 2: Eternity excludes the principle of duration, but not the principle of origin.

Reply Obj. 3: Every corruption is a change; and so all that corrupts begins not to exist and ceases to be. The divine generation, however, is not changed, as stated above (Q. 27, A. 2). Hence the Son is ever being begotten, and the Father is always begetting.

Reply Obj. 4: In time there is something indivisible—namely, the instant; and there is something else which endures—namely, time. But in eternity the indivisible "now" stands ever still, as we have said above (Q. 10, A. 2, ad 1; A. 4, ad 2). But the generation of the Son is not in the "now" of time, or in time, but in eternity. And so to express the presentiality and permanence of eternity, we can say that "He is ever being born," as Origen said (Hom. in Joan. i). But as Gregory [*Moral. xxix, 21] and Augustine [*Super Ps. 2:7] said, it is better to say "ever born," so that "ever" may denote the permanence of eternity, and "born" the perfection of the only Begotten. Thus, therefore, neither is the Son imperfect, nor "was there a time when He was not," as Arius said.

THIRD ARTICLE [I, Q. 42, Art. 3]

Whether in the Divine Persons There Exists an Order of Nature?

Objection 1: It would seem that among the divine persons there does not exist an order of nature. For whatever exists in God is the essence, or a person, or a notion. But the order of nature does not signify the essence, nor any of the persons, or notions. Therefore there is no order of nature in God.

Obj. 2: Further, wherever order of nature exists, there one comes before another, at least, according to nature and intellect. But in the divine persons there exists neither priority nor posteriority, as declared by Athanasius. Therefore, in the divine persons there is no order of nature.

Obj. 3: Further, wherever order exists, distinction also exists. But there is no distinction in the divine nature. Therefore it is not subject to order; and order of nature does not exist in it.

Obj. 4: Further, the divine nature is the divine essence. But there is no order of essence in God. Therefore neither is there of nature.

*On the contrary,* Where plurality exists without order, confusion exists. But in the divine persons there is no confusion, as Athanasius says. Therefore in God order exists.

*I answer that,* Order always has reference to some principle. Wherefore since there are many kinds of principle—namely, according to site, as a point; according to intellect, as the principle of demonstration; and according to each individual cause—so are there many kinds of order. Now principle, according to origin, without priority, exists in God as we have stated (Q. 33, A. 1): so there must likewise be order according to origin, without priority; and this is called 'the order of nature': in the words of Augustine (Contra Maxim. iv): "Not whereby one is prior to another, but whereby one is from another."

Reply Obj. 1: The order of nature signifies the notion of origin in general, not a special kind of origin.

Reply Obj. 2: In things created, even when what is derived from a principle is co-equal in duration with its principle, the principle still comes first in the order of nature and reason, if formally considered as principle. If, however, we consider the relations of cause and effect, or of the principle and the thing proceeding therefrom, it is clear that the things so related are simultaneous in the order of nature and reason, inasmuch as the one enters the definition of the other. But in God the relations themselves are the persons subsisting in one nature. So, neither on the part of the nature, nor on the part the relations, can one person be prior to another, not even in the order of nature and reason.

Reply Obj. 3: The order of nature means not the ordering of nature itself, but the existence of order in the divine Persons according to natural origin.

Reply Obj. 4: Nature in a certain way implies the idea of a principle, but essence does not; and so the order of origin is more correctly called the order of nature than the order of essence.

FOURTH ARTICLE [I, Q. 4, Art. 4]

Whether the Son Is Equal to the Father in Greatness?

Objection 1: It would seem that the Son is not equal to the Father in greatness. For He Himself said (John 14:28): "The Father is greater than I"; and the Apostle says (1 Cor. 15:28): "The Son Himself shall be subject to Him that put all things under Him."

Obj. 2: Further, paternity is part of the Father's dignity. But paternity does not belong to the Son. Therefore the Son does not possess all the Father's dignity; and so He is not equal in greatness to the Father.

Obj. 3: Further, wherever there exist a whole and a part, many parts are more than one only, or than fewer parts; as three men are more than two, or than one. But in God a universal whole exists, and a part; for under relation or notion, several notions are included. Therefore, since in the Father there are three notions, while in the Son there are only two, the Son is evidently not equal to the Father.

*On the contrary,* It is said (Phil. 2:6): "He thought it not robbery to be equal with God."

*I answer that,* The Son is necessarily equal to the Father in greatness. For the greatness of God is nothing but the perfection of His nature. Now it belongs to the very nature of paternity and filiation that the Son by generation should attain to the possession of the perfection of the nature which is in the Father, in the same way as it is in the Father Himself. But since in men generation is a certain kind of transmutation of one proceeding from potentiality to act, it follows that a man is not equal at first to the father who begets him, but attains to equality by due growth, unless owing to a defect in the principle of generation it should happen otherwise. From what precedes (Q. 27, A. 2; Q. 33, AA. 2 ,3), it is evident that in God there exist real true paternity and filiation. Nor can we say that the power of generation in the Father was defective, nor that the Son of God arrived at perfection in a successive manner and by change. Therefore we must say that the Son was eternally equal to the Father in greatness. Hence, Hilary says (De Synod. Can. 27): "Remove bodily weakness, remove the beginning of conception, remove pain and all human shortcomings, then every son, by reason of his natural nativity, is the father's equal, because he has a like nature."

Reply Obj. 1: These words are to be understood of Christ's human nature, wherein He is less than the Father, and subject to Him; but in His divine nature He is equal to the Father. This is expressed by Athanasius, "Equal to the Father in His Godhead; less than the Father in humanity": and by Hilary (De Trin. ix): "By the fact of giving, the Father is greater; but He is not less to Whom the same being is given"; and (De Synod.): "The Son subjects Himself by His inborn piety"—that is, by His recognition of paternal authority; whereas "creatures are subject by their created weakness."

Reply Obj. 2: Equality is measured by greatness. In God greatness signifies the perfection of nature, as above explained (A. 1, ad 1), and belongs to the essence. Thus equality and likeness in God have reference to the essence; nor can there be inequality or dissimilitude arising from the distinction of the relations. Wherefore Augustine says (Contra Maxim. iii, 13), "The question of origin is, Who is from whom? but the question of equality is, Of what kind, or how great, is he?" Therefore, paternity is the Father's dignity, as also the Father's essence:

since dignity is something absolute, and pertains to the essence. As, therefore, the same essence, which in the Father is paternity, in the Son is filiation, so the same dignity which, in the Father is paternity, in the Son is filiation. It is thus true to say that the Son possesses whatever dignity the Father has; but we cannot argue—"the Father has paternity, therefore the Son has paternity," for there is a transition from substance to relation. For the Father and the Son have the same essence and dignity, which exist in the Father by the relation of giver, and in the Son by relation of receiver.

Reply Obj. 3: In God relation is not a universal whole, although it is predicated of each of the relations; because all the relations are one in essence and being, which is irreconcilable with the idea of universal, the parts of which are distinguished in being. Person likewise is not a universal term in God as we have seen above (Q. 30, A. 4). Wherefore all the relations together are not greater than only one; nor are all the persons something greater than only one; because the whole perfection of the divine nature exists in each person.

FIFTH ARTICLE [I, Q. 42, Art. 5]

Whether the Son Is in the Father, and Conversely?

Objection 1: It would seem that the Son and the Father are not in each other. For the Philosopher (Phys. iv, text. 23) gives eight modes of one thing existing in another, according to none of which is the Son in the Father, or conversely; as is patent to anyone who examines each mode. Therefore the Son and the Father are not in each other.

Obj. 2: Further, nothing that has come out from another is within. But the Son from eternity came out from the Father, according to Mic. 5:2: "His going forth is from the beginning, from the days of eternity." Therefore the Son is not in the Father.

Obj. 3: Further, one of two opposites cannot be in the other. But the Son and the Father are relatively opposed. Therefore one cannot be in the other.

*On the contrary,* It is said (John 14:10): "I am in the Father, and the Father is in Me."

*I answer that,* There are three points of consideration as regards the Father and the Son; the essence, the relation and the origin; and according to each the Son and the Father are in each other. The Father is in the Son by His essence, forasmuch as the Father is His own essence and communicates His essence to the Son not by any change on His part. Hence it follows that as the Father's essence is in the Son, the Father Himself is in the Son; likewise, since the Son is His own essence, it follows that He Himself is in the Father in Whom is His essence. This is expressed by Hilary (De Trin. v), "The unchangeable God, so to speak, follows His own nature in begetting an unchangeable subsisting God. So we understand the nature of God to subsist in Him, for He is God in God." It is also manifest that as regards the relations, each of two relative opposites is in the concept of the other. Regarding origin also, it is clear that the procession of the intelligible word is not outside the intellect, inasmuch as it remains in the utterer of the word. What also is uttered by the word is therein contained. And the same applies to the Holy Ghost.

Reply Obj. 1: What is contained in creatures does not sufficiently represent what exists in God; so according to none of the modes enumerated by the Philosopher, are the Son and the Father in each other. The mode the most nearly approaching to the reality is to be found in that whereby something exists in its originating principle, except that the unity of essence between the principle and that which proceeds therefrom is wanting in things created.

Reply Obj. 2: The Son's going forth from the Father is by mode of the interior procession whereby the word emerges from the heart and remains therein. Hence this going forth in God is only by the distinction of the relations, not by any kind of essential separation.

Reply Obj. 3: The Father and the Son are relatively opposed, but not essentially; while, as above explained, one relative opposite is in the other.

SIXTH ARTICLE [I, Q. 42, Art. 6]

Whether the Son Is Equal to the Father in Power?

Objection 1: It would seem that the Son is not equal to the Father in power. For it is said (John 5:19): "The Son cannot do anything of Himself but what He seeth the Father doing." But the Father can act of Himself. Therefore the Father's power is greater than the Son's.

Obj. 2: Further, greater is the power of him who commands and teaches than of him who obeys and hears. But the Father commands the Son according to John 14:31: "As the Father gave Me commandment so do I." The Father also teaches the Son: "The Father loveth the Son, and showeth Him all things that Himself doth" (John 5:20). Also, the Son hears: "As I hear, so I judge" (John 5:30). Therefore the Father has greater power than the Son.

Obj. 3: Further, it belongs to the Father's omnipotence to be able to beget a Son equal to Himself. For Augustine says (Contra Maxim. iii, 7), "Were He unable to beget one equal to Himself, where would be the omnipotence of God the Father?" But the Son cannot beget a Son, as proved above (Q. 41, A. 6). Therefore the Son cannot do all that belongs to the Father's omnipotence; and hence He is not equal to Him power.

*On the contrary,* It is said (John 5:19): "Whatsoever things the Father doth, these the Son also doth in like manner."

*I answer that,* The Son is necessarily equal to the Father in power. Power of action is a consequence of perfection in nature. In creatures, for instance, we see that the more perfect the nature, the greater power is there for action. Now it was shown above (A. 4) that the very notion of the divine paternity and filiation requires that the Son should be the Father's equal in greatness—that is, in perfection of nature. Hence it follows that the Son is equal to the Father in power; and the same applies to the Holy Ghost in relation to both.

Reply Obj. 1: The words, "the Son cannot of Himself do anything," do not withdraw from the Son any power possessed by the Father, since it is immediately added, "Whatsoever things the Father doth, the Son doth in like manner"; but their meaning is to show that the Son derives His power from the Father, of Whom He receives His nature. Hence, Hilary says (De Trin. ix), "The unity of the divine nature implies that the Son so acts of Himself [per se], that He does not act by Himself [a se]."

Reply Obj. 2: The Father's "showing" and the Son's "hearing" are to be taken in the sense that the Father communicates knowledge to the Son, as He communicates His essence. The command of the Father can be explained in the same sense, as giving Him from eternity knowledge and will to act, by begetting Him. Or, better still, this may be referred to Christ in His human nature.

Reply Obj. 3: As the same essence is paternity in the Father, and filiation in the Son: so by the same power the Father begets, and the Son is begotten. Hence it is clear that the Son can do whatever the Father can do; yet it does not follow that the Son can beget; for to argue thus would imply transition from substance to relation, for generation signifies a divine relation. So the Son has the same omnipotence as the Father, but with another relation; the Father possessing power as "giving" signified when we say that He is able to beget; while the Son possesses the power of "receiving," signified by saying that He can be begotten.

# QUESTION 43

THE MISSION OF THE DIVINE PERSONS (In Eight Articles)

We next consider the mission of the divine persons, concerning which there are eight points of inquiry:

(1) Whether it is suitable for a divine person to be sent?

(2) Whether mission is eternal, or only temporal?

(3) In what sense a divine person is invisibly sent?

(4) Whether it is fitting that each person be sent?

(5) Whether both the Son and the Holy Ghost are invisibly sent?

(6) To whom the invisible mission is directed?

(7) Of the visible mission.

(8) Whether any person sends Himself visibly or invisibly?

FIRST ARTICLE [I, Q. 43, Art. 1]

Whether a Divine Person Can Be Properly Sent?

Objection 1: It would seem that a divine person cannot be properly sent. For one who is sent is less than the sender. But one divine person is not less than another. Therefore one person is not sent by another.

Obj. 2: Further, what is sent is separated from the sender; hence Jerome says, commenting on Ezech. 16:53: "What is joined and tied in one body cannot be sent." But in the divine persons there is nothing that is separable, as Hilary says (De Trin. vii). Therefore one person is not sent by another.

Obj. 3: Further, whoever is sent, departs from one place and comes anew into another. But this does not apply to a divine person, Who is everywhere. Therefore it is not suitable for a divine person to be sent.

*On the contrary,* It is said (John 8:16): "I am not alone, but I and the Father that sent Me."

*I answer that,* the notion of mission includes two things: the habitude of the one sent to the sender; and that of the one sent to the end whereto he is sent. Anyone being sent implies a certain kind of procession of the one sent from the sender: either according to command, as the master sends the servant; or according to counsel, as an adviser may be said to send the king to battle; or according to origin, as a tree sends forth its flowers. The habitude to the term to which he is sent is also shown, so that in some way he begins to be present there: either because in no way was he present before in the place whereto he is sent, or because he begins to be there in some way in which he was not there hitherto. Thus the mission of a divine person is a fitting thing, as meaning in one way the procession of origin from the sender, and as meaning a new way of existing in another; thus the Son is said to be sent by the Father into the world, inasmuch as He began to exist visibly in the world by taking our nature; whereas "He was" previously "in the world" (John 1:1).

Reply Obj. 1: Mission implies inferiority in the one sent, when it means procession from the sender as principle, by command or counsel; forasmuch as the one commanding is the greater, and the counsellor is the wiser. In God, however, it means only procession of origin, which is according to equality, as explained above (Q. 42, AA. 4, 6).

Reply Obj. 2: What is so sent as to begin to exist where previously it did not exist, is locally moved by being sent; hence it is necessarily separated locally from the sender. This, however, has no place in the mission of a divine person; for the divine person sent neither begins to exist where he did not previously exist, nor ceases to exist where He was. Hence such a mission takes place without a separation, having only distinction of origin.

Reply Obj. 3: This objection rests on the idea of

mission according to local motion, which is not in God.

SECOND ARTICLE [I, Q. 43, Art. 2]

Whether Mission Is Eternal, or Only Temporal?

Objection 1: It would seem that mission can be eternal. For Gregory says (Hom. xxvi, in Ev.), "The Son is sent as He is begotten." But the Son's generation is eternal. Therefore mission is eternal.

Obj. 2: Further, a thing is changed if it becomes something temporally. But a divine person is not changed. Therefore the mission of a divine person is not temporal, but eternal.

Obj. 3: Further, mission implies procession. But the procession of the divine persons is eternal. Therefore mission is also eternal.

*On the contrary,* It is said (Gal. 4:4): "When the fullness of the time was come, God sent His Son."

*I answer that,* A certain difference is to be observed in all the words that express the origin of the divine persons. For some express only relation to the principle, as "procession" and "going forth." Others express the term of procession together with the relation to the principle. Of these some express the eternal term, as "generation" and "spiration"; for generation is the procession of the divine person into the divine nature, and passive spiration is the procession of the subsisting love. Others express the temporal term with the relation to the principle, as "mission" and "giving." For a thing is sent that it may be in something else, and is given that it may be possessed; but that a divine person be possessed by any creature, or exist in it in a new mode, is temporal.

Hence "mission" and "giving" have only a temporal significance in God; but "generation" and "spiration" are exclusively eternal; whereas "procession" and "giving," in God, have both an eternal and a temporal signification: for the Son may proceed eternally as God; but temporally, by becoming man, according to His visible mission, or likewise by dwelling in man according to His invisible mission.

Reply Obj. 1: Gregory speaks of the temporal generation of the Son, not from the Father, but from His mother; or it may be taken to mean that He could be sent because eternally begotten.

Reply Obj. 2: That a divine person may newly exist in anyone, or be possessed by anyone in time, does not come from change of the divine person, but from change in the creature; as God Himself is called Lord temporally by change of the creature.

Reply Obj. 3: Mission signifies not only procession from the principle, but also determines the temporal term of the procession. Hence mission is only temporal. Or we may say that it includes the eternal procession, with the addition of a temporal effect. For the relation of a divine person to His principle must be eternal. Hence the procession may be called a twin procession, eternal and temporal, not that there is a double relation to the principle, but a double term, temporal and eternal.

THIRD ARTICLE [I, Q. 43, Art. 3]

Whether the Invisible Mission of the Divine Person Is Only According to the Gift of Sanctifying Grace?

Objection 1: It would seem that the invisible mission of the divine person is not only according to the gift of sanctifying grace. For the sending of a divine person means that He is given. Hence if the divine person is sent only according to the gift of sanctifying grace, the divine person Himself will not be given, but only His gifts; and this is the error of those who say that the Holy Ghost is not given, but that His gifts are given.

Obj. 2: Further, this preposition, "according to," denotes the habitude of some cause. But the divine person is the cause why the gift of sanctifying grace is possessed, and not conversely, according to Rom. 5:5, "the charity of God is poured forth in our hearts by the Holy Ghost, Who is given to us." Therefore it is improperly said that the divine person is sent according to the gift of sanctifying grace.

Obj. 3: Further, Augustine says (De Trin. iv, 20) that "the Son, when temporally perceived by the mind, is sent." But the Son is known not only by sanctifying grace, but also by gratuitous grace, as by faith and knowledge. Therefore the divine person is not sent only according to the gift of sanctifying grace.

Obj. 4: Further, Rabanus says that the Holy Ghost was given to the apostles for the working of miracles. This, however, is not a gift of sanctifying grace, but a gratuitous grace. Therefore the divine person is not given only according to the gift of sanctifying grace.

*On the contrary,* Augustine says (De Trin. iii, 4) that "the Holy Ghost proceeds temporally for the creature's sanctification." But mission is a temporal procession. Since then the creature's sanctification is by sanctifying grace, it follows that the mission of the divine person is only by sanctifying grace.

*I answer that,* The divine person is fittingly sent in the sense that He exists newly in any one; and He is given as possessed by anyone; and neither of these is otherwise than by sanctifying grace.

For God is in all things by His essence, power and presence, according to His one common mode, as the cause existing in the effects which participate in His goodness. Above and beyond this common mode, however, there is one special mode belonging to the rational nature wherein God is said to be present as the object known is in the knower, and the beloved in the lover. And since the rational creature by its operation of knowledge and love attains to God Himself, according to this special mode God is said not only to exist in the rational creature but also to dwell therein as in His own temple. So no other effect can be put down as the reason why the divine person is in the rational creature in a new mode, except sanctifying grace. Hence, the divine person is sent, and proceeds temporally only according to sanctifying grace.

Again, we are said to possess only what we can freely use or enjoy: and to have the power of enjoying the divine person can only be according to sanctifying grace. And yet the Holy Ghost is possessed by man, and dwells within him, in the very gift itself of sanctifying grace. Hence the Holy Ghost Himself is given and sent.

Reply Obj. 1: By the gift of sanctifying grace the rational creature is perfected so that it can freely use not only the created gift itself, but enjoy also the divine person Himself; and so the invisible mission takes place according to the gift of sanctifying grace; and yet the divine person Himself is given.

Reply Obj. 2: Sanctifying grace disposes the soul to possess the divine person; and this is signified when it is said that the Holy Ghost is given according to the gift of grace. Nevertheless the gift itself of grace is from the Holy Ghost; which is meant by the words, "the charity of God is poured forth in our hearts by the Holy Ghost."

Reply Obj. 3: Although the Son can be known by us according to other effects, yet neither does He dwell in us, nor is He possessed by us according to those effects.

Reply Obj. 4: The working of miracles manifests sanctifying grace as also does the gift of prophecy and any other gratuitous graces. Hence gratuitous grace is called the "manifestation of the Spirit" (1 Cor. 12:7). So the Holy Ghost is said to be given to the apostles for the working of miracles, because sanctifying grace was given to them with the outward sign. Were the sign only of sanctifying grace given to them without the grace itself, it would not be simply said that the Holy Ghost was given, except with some qualifying term; just as we read of certain ones receiving the gift of the spirit of prophecy, or of miracles, as having from the Holy Ghost the power of prophesying or of working miracles.

FOURTH ARTICLE [I, Q. 43, Art. 4]

Whether the Father Can Be Fittingly Sent?

Objection 1: It would seem that it is fitting also that the Father should be sent. For being sent means that the divine person is given. But the Father gives Himself since He can only be possessed by His giving Himself. Therefore it can be said that the Father sends Himself.

Obj. 2: Further, the divine person is sent according to the indwelling of grace. But by grace the whole Trinity dwells in us according to John 14:23: "We will come to him and make Our abode with him." Therefore each one of the divine persons is sent.

Obj. 3: Further, whatever belongs to one person, belongs to them all, except the notions and persons. But mission does not signify any person; nor even a notion, since there are only five notions, as stated above (Q. 32, A. 3). Therefore every divine person can be sent.

*On the contrary,* Augustine says (De Trin. ii, 3), "The Father alone is never described as being sent."

*I answer that,* The very idea of mission means procession from another, and in God it means procession according to origin, as above expounded. Hence, as the Father is not from another, in no way is it fitting for Him to be sent; but this can only belong to the Son and to the Holy Ghost, to Whom it belongs to be from another.

Reply Obj. 1: In the sense of "giving" as a free bestowal of something, the Father gives Himself, as freely bestowing Himself to be enjoyed by the creature. But as implying the authority of the giver as regards what is given, "to be given" only applies in God to the Person Who is from another; and the same as regards "being sent."

Reply Obj. 2: Although the effect of grace is also from the Father, Who dwells in us by grace, just as the Son and the Holy Ghost, still He is not described as being sent, for He is not from another. Thus Augustine says (De Trin. iv, 20) that "The Father, when known by anyone in time, is not said to be sent; for there is no one whence He is, or from whom He proceeds."

Reply Obj. 3: Mission, meaning procession from the sender, includes the signification of a notion, not of a special notion, but in general; thus "to be from another" is common to two of the notions.

FIFTH ARTICLE [I, Q. 43, Art. 5]

Whether It Is Fitting for the Son to Be Sent Invisibly?

Objection 1: It would seem that it is not fitting for the Son to be sent invisibly. For invisible mission of the divine person is according to the gift of grace. But all gifts of grace belong to the Holy Ghost, according to 1 Cor. 12:11: "One and the same Spirit worketh all things." Therefore only the Holy Ghost is sent invisibly.

Obj. 2: Further, the mission of the divine person is according to sanctifying grace. But the gifts belonging to the perfection of the intellect are not gifts of sanctifying grace, since they can be held without the gift of charity, according to 1 Cor. 13:2: "If I should have prophecy, and should know all mysteries, and all knowledge, and if I should have all faith so that I could move mountains, and have not charity, I am nothing." Therefore, since the Son proceeds as the word of the intellect, it seems unfitting for Him to be sent invisibly.

Obj. 3: Further, the mission of the divine person is a procession, as expounded above (AA. 1, 4). But the procession of the Son and of the Holy Ghost differ from each other. Therefore they are distinct missions if both are sent; and then one of them would be superfluous, since one would suffice for the creature's sanctification.

*On the contrary,* It is said of divine Wisdom (Wis. 9:10): "Send her from heaven to Thy Saints, and from the seat of Thy greatness."

*I answer that,* The whole Trinity dwells in the

mind by sanctifying grace, according to John 14:23: "We will come to him, and will make Our abode with him." But that a divine person be sent to anyone by invisible grace signifies both that this person dwells in a new way within him and that He has His origin from another. Hence, since both to the Son and to the Holy Ghost it belongs to dwell in the soul by grace, and to be from another, it therefore belongs to both of them to be invisibly sent. As to the Father, though He dwells in us by grace, still it does not belong to Him to be from another, and consequently He is not sent.

Reply Obj. 1: Although all the gifts, considered as such, are attributed to the Holy Ghost, forasmuch as He is by His nature the first Gift, since He is Love, as stated above (Q. 38, A. 1), some gifts nevertheless, by reason of their own particular nature, are appropriated in a certain way to the Son, those, namely, which belong to the intellect, and in respect of which we speak of the mission of the Son. Hence Augustine says (De Trin. iv, 20) that "The Son is sent to anyone invisibly, whenever He is known and perceived by anyone."

Reply Obj. 2: The soul is made like to God by grace. Hence for a divine person to be sent to anyone by grace, there must needs be a likening of the soul to the divine person Who is sent, by some gift of grace. Because the Holy Ghost is Love, the soul is assimilated to the Holy Ghost by the gift of charity: hence the mission of the Holy Ghost is according to the mode of charity. Whereas the Son is the Word, not any sort of word, but one Who breathes forth Love. Hence Augustine says (De Trin. ix 10): "The Word we speak of is knowledge with love." Thus the Son is sent not in accordance with every and any kind of intellectual perfection, but according to the intellectual illumination, which breaks forth into the affection of love, as is said (John 6:45): "Everyone that hath heard from the Father and hath learned, cometh to Me," and (Ps. 38:4): "In my meditation a fire shall flame forth." Thus Augustine plainly says (De Trin. iv, 20): "The Son is sent, whenever He is known and perceived by anyone." Now perception implies a certain experimental knowledge; and this is properly called wisdom [sapientia], as it were a sweet knowledge [sapida scientia], according to Ecclus. 6:23: "The wisdom of doctrine is according to her name."

Reply Obj. 3: Since mission implies the origin of the person Who is sent, and His indwelling by grace, as above explained (A. 1), if we speak of mission according to origin, in this sense the Son's mission is distinguished from the mission of the Holy Ghost, as generation is distinguished from procession. If we consider mission as regards the effect of grace, in this sense the two missions are united in the root which is grace, but are distinguished in the effects of grace, which consist in the illumination of the intellect and the kindling of the affection. Thus it is manifest that one mission cannot be without the other, because neither takes place without sanctifying grace, nor is one person separated from the other.

SIXTH ARTICLE [I, Q. 43, Art. 6]

Whether the Invisible Mission Is to All Who Participate Grace?

Objection 1: It would seem that the invisible mission is not to all who participate grace. For the Fathers of the Old Testament had their share of grace. Yet to them was made no invisible mission; for it is said (John 7:39): "The Spirit was not yet given, because Jesus was not yet glorified." Therefore the invisible mission is not to all partakers in grace.

Obj. 2: Further, progress in virtue is only by grace. But the invisible mission is not according to progress in virtue; because progress in virtue is continuous, since charity ever increases or decreases; and thus the mission would be continuous. Therefore the invisible mission is not to all who share in grace.

Obj. 3: Further, Christ and the blessed have fullness of grace. But mission is not to them, for mission implies distance, whereas Christ, as man, and all the blessed are perfectly united to God. Therefore the invisible mission is not to all sharers in grace.

Obj. 4: Further, the Sacraments of the New Law contain grace, and it is not said that the invisible mission is sent to them. Therefore the invisible mission is not to all that have grace.

*On the contrary,* According to Augustine (De Trin. iii, 4; xv, 27), the invisible mission is for the creature's sanctification. Now every creature that has grace is sanctified. Therefore the invisible mission is to every such creature.

*I answer that,* As above stated (AA. 3, 4 ,5), mission in its very meaning implies that he who is sent either begins to exist where he was not before, as occurs to creatures; or begins to exist where he was before, but in a new way, in which sense mission is ascribed to the divine persons. Thus, mission as regards the one to whom it is sent implies two things, the indwelling of grace, and a certain renewal by grace. Thus the invisible mission is sent to all in whom are to be found these two conditions.

Reply Obj. 1: The invisible mission was directed to the Old Testament Fathers, as appears from what Augustine says (De Trin. iv, 20), that the invisible mission of the Son "is in man and with men. This was done in former times with the Fathers and the Prophets." Thus the words, "the Spirit was not yet given," are to be applied to that giving accompanied with a visible sign which took place on the day of Pentecost.

Reply Obj. 2: The invisible mission takes place also as regards progress in virtue or increase of grace. Hence Augustine says (De Trin. iv, 20), that "the Son is sent to each one when He is known and perceived by anyone, so far as He can be known and perceived according to the capacity of the soul, whether journeying towards God, or united perfectly to Him." Such invisible mission, however, chiefly occurs as regards anyone's proficiency in the performance of a new act, or in the acquisition of a new state of grace; as, for example, the proficiency in reference to the gift of miracles or of prophecy, or in the fervor of charity leading a man to expose himself to the danger of martyrdom, or to renounce his possessions, or to undertake any arduous work.

Reply Obj. 3: The invisible mission is directed to the blessed at the very beginning of their beatitude. The invisible mission is made to them subsequently, not by "intensity" of grace, but by the further revelation of mysteries; which goes on till the day of judgment. Such an increase is by the "extension" of grace, because it extends to a greater number of objects. To Christ the invisible mission was sent at the first moment of His conception; but not afterwards, since from the beginning of His conception He was filled with all wisdom and grace.

Reply Obj. 4: Grace resides instrumentally in the sacraments of the New Law, as the form of a thing designed resides in the instruments of the art designing, according to a process flowing from the agent to the passive object. But mission is only spoken of as directed to its term. Hence the mission of the divine person is not sent to the sacraments, but to those who receive grace through the sacraments.

SEVENTH ARTICLE [I, Q. 43, Art. 7]

Whether It Is Fitting for the Holy Ghost to Be Sent Visibly?

Objection 1: It would seem that the Holy Ghost is not fittingly sent in a visible manner. For the Son as visibly sent to the world is said to be less than the Father. But the Holy Ghost is never said to be less than the Father. Therefore the Holy Ghost is not fittingly sent in a visible manner.

Obj. 2: Further, the visible mission takes place by way of union to a visible creature, as the Son's mission according to the flesh. But the Holy Ghost did not assume any visible creature; and hence it cannot be said that He exists otherwise in some creatures than in others, unless perhaps as in a sign, as He is also present in the sacraments, and in all the figures of the law. Thus the Holy Ghost is either not sent visibly at all, or His visible mission takes place in all these things.

Obj. 3: Further, every visible creature is an effect showing forth the whole Trinity. Therefore the Holy Ghost is not sent by reason of those visible creatures more than any other person.

Obj. 4: Further, the Son was visibly sent by reason of the noblest kind of creature—namely, the human nature. Therefore if the Holy Ghost is sent visibly, He ought to be sent by reason of rational creatures.

Obj. 5: Further, whatever is done visibly by God is dispensed by the ministry of the angels; as Augustine says (De Trin. iii, 4,5,9). So visible appearances, if there have been any, came by means of the angels. Thus the angels are sent, and not the Holy Ghost.

Obj. 6: Further, the Holy Ghost being sent in a visible manner is only for the purpose of manifesting the invisible mission; as invisible things are made known by the visible. So those to whom the invisible mission was not sent, ought not to receive the visible mission; and to all who received the invisible mission, whether in the New or in the Old Testament, the visible mission ought likewise to be sent; and this is clearly false. Therefore the Holy Ghost is not sent visibly.

*On the contrary,* It is said (Matt. 3:16) that, when our Lord was baptized, the Holy Ghost descended upon Him in the shape of a dove.

*I answer that,* God provides for all things according to the nature of each thing. Now the nature of man requires that he be led to the invisible by visible things, as explained above (Q. 12, A. 12). Wherefore the invisible things of God must be made manifest to man by the things that are visible. As God, therefore, in a certain way has demonstrated Himself and His eternal processions to men by visible creatures, according to certain signs; so was it fitting that the invisible missions also of the divine persons should be made manifest by some visible creatures.

This mode of manifestation applies in different ways to the Son and to the Holy Ghost. For it belongs to the Holy Ghost, Who proceeds as Love, to be the gift of sanctification; to the Son as the principle of the Holy Ghost, it belongs to the author of this sanctification. Thus the Son has been sent visibly as the author of sanctification; the Holy Ghost as the sign of sanctification.

Reply Obj. 1: The Son assumed the visible creature, wherein He appeared, into the unity of His person, so that whatever can be said of that creature can be said of the Son of God; and so, by reason of the nature assumed, the Son is called less than the Father. But the Holy Ghost did not assume the visible creature, in which He appeared, into the unity of His person; so that what is said of it cannot be predicated of Him. Hence He cannot be called less than the Father by reason of any visible creature.

Reply Obj. 2: The visible mission of the Holy Ghost does not apply to the imaginary vision which is that of prophecy; because as Augustine says (De Trin. ii, 6): "The prophetic vision is not displayed to corporeal eyes by corporeal shapes, but is shown in the spirit by the spiritual images of bodies. But whoever saw the dove and the fire, saw them by their eyes. Nor, again, has the Holy Ghost the same relation to these images that the Son has to the rock, because it is said, 'The rock was Christ' (1 Cor. 10:4). For that rock was already created, and after the manner of an action was named Christ, Whom it typified; whereas the dove and the fire suddenly appeared to signify only what was happening. They seem, however, to be like to the flame of the burning bush seen by Moses and to the column which the people followed in the desert, and to the lightning and thunder issuing forth when the law was given on the mountain. For the purpose of the bodily appearances of those things was that they might signify, and then pass away." Thus the visible mission is neither displayed by prophetic vision, which belongs to the imagination, and not to the body, nor by the sacramental signs of the Old and New Testament, wherein certain pre-existing things are employed to signify something. But the Holy Ghost is said to be sent visibly, inasmuch as He showed Himself in certain creatures as in signs especially made for that purpose.

Reply Obj. 3: Although the whole Trinity makes those creatures, still they are made in order to show forth in some special way this or that person. For as the Father, Son and Holy Ghost are signified by diverse names, so also can They each one be signified by different things; although neither separation nor diversity exists amongst Them.

Reply Obj. 4: It was necessary for the Son to be declared as the author of sanctification, as explained above. Thus the visible mission of the Son was necessarily made according to the rational nature to which it belongs to act, and which is capable of sanctification; whereas any other creature could be the sign of sanctification. Nor was such a visible creature, formed for such a purpose, necessarily assumed by the Holy Ghost into the unity of His person, since it was not assumed or used for the purpose of action, but only for the purpose of a sign; and so likewise it was not required to last beyond what its use required.

Reply Obj. 5: Those visible creatures were formed by the ministry of the angels, not to signify the person of an angel, but to signify the Person of the Holy Ghost. Thus, as the Holy Ghost resided in those visible creatures as the one signified in the sign, on that account the Holy Ghost is said to be sent visibly, and not as an angel.

Reply Obj. 6: It is not necessary that the invisible mission should always be made manifest by some visible external sign; but, as is said (1 Cor. 12:7)—"the manifestation of the Spirit is given to every man unto profit"—that is, of the Church. This utility consists in the confirmation and propagation of the faith by such visible signs. This has been done chiefly by Christ and by the apostles, according to Heb. 2:3, "which having begun to be declared by the Lord, was confirmed unto us by them that heard."

Thus in a special sense, a mission of the Holy Ghost was directed to Christ, to the apostles, and to some of the early saints on whom the Church was in a way founded; in such a manner, however, that the visible mission made to Christ should show forth the invisible mission made to Him, not at that particular time, but at the first moment of His conception. The visible mission was directed to Christ at the time of His baptism by the figure of a dove, a fruitful animal, to show forth in Christ the authority of the giver of grace by spiritual regeneration; hence the Father's voice spoke, "This is My beloved Son" (Matt. 3:17), that others might be regenerated to the likeness of the only Begotten. The Transfiguration showed it forth in the appearance of a bright cloud, to show the exuberance of doctrine; and hence it was said, "Hear ye Him" (Matt. 17:5). To the apostles the mission was directed in the form of breathing to show forth the power of their ministry in the dispensation of the sacraments; and hence it was said, "Whose sins you shall forgive, they are forgiven" (John 20:23): and again under the sign of fiery tongues to show forth the office of teaching; whence it is said that, "they began to speak with divers tongues" (Acts 2:4). The visible mission of the Holy Ghost was fittingly not sent to the fathers of the Old Testament, because the visible mission of the Son was to be accomplished before that of the Holy Ghost; since the Holy Ghost manifests the Son, as the Son manifests the Father. Visible apparitions of the divine persons were, however, given to the Fathers of the Old Testament which, indeed, cannot be called visible missions; because, according to Augustine (De Trin. ii, 17), they were not sent to designate the indwelling of the divine person by grace, but for the manifestation of something else.

EIGHTH ARTICLE [I, Q. 43, Art. 8]

Whether a Divine Person Is Sent Only by the Person Whence He Proceeds Eternally?

Objection 1: It would seem that a divine person is sent only by the one whence He proceeds eternally. For as Augustine says (De Trin. iv), "The Father is sent by no one because He is from no one." Therefore if a divine person is sent by another, He must be from that other.

Obj. 2: Further, the sender has authority over the one sent. But there can be no authority as regards a divine person except from origin. Therefore the divine person sent must proceed from the one sending.

Obj. 3: Further, if a divine person can be sent by one whence He does not proceed, then the Holy Ghost may be given by a man, although He proceeds not from him; which is contrary to what Augustine says (De Trin. xv). Therefore the divine person is sent only by the one whence He proceeds.

*On the contrary,* The Son is sent by the Holy Ghost, according to Isa. 48:16, "Now the Lord God hath sent Me and His Spirit." But the Son is not from the Holy Ghost. Therefore a divine person is sent by one from Whom He does not proceed.

*I answer that,* There are different opinions on this point. Some say that the divine person is sent only by the one whence He proceeds eternally; and so, when it is said that the Son of God is sent by the Holy Ghost, this is to be explained as regards His human nature, by reason of which He was sent to preach by the Holy Ghost. Augustine, however, says (De Trin. ii, 5) that the Son is sent by Himself, and by the Holy Ghost; and the Holy Ghost is sent by Himself, and by the Son; so that to be sent in God does not apply to each person, but only to the person proceeding from another, whereas to send belongs to each person.

There is some truth in both of these opinions; because when a person is described as being sent, the person Himself existing from another is designated, with the visible or invisible effect, applicable to the mission of the divine person. Thus if the sender be designated as the principle of the person sent, in this sense not each person sends, but that person only Who is the principle of that person who is sent; and thus the Son is sent only by the Father; and the Holy Ghost by the Father and the Son. If, however, the person sending is understood as the principle of the effect implied in the mission, in that sense the whole Trinity sends the person sent. This reason does not prove that a man can send the Holy Ghost, forasmuch as man cannot cause the effect of grace.

The answers to the objections appear from the above.

TREATISE ON THE CREATION (QQ. 44-49)

# QUESTION 44

THE PROCESSION OF CREATURES FROM GOD, AND OF THE FIRST CAUSE OF ALL THINGS (In Four Articles)

After treating of the procession of the divine persons, we must consider the procession of creatures from God. This consideration will be threefold:

(1) of the production of creatures;

(2) of the distinction between them;

(3) of their preservation and government.

Concerning the first point there are three things to be considered:

(1) the first cause of beings;

(2) the mode of procession of creatures from the first cause;

(3) the principle of the duration of things.

Under the first head there are four points of inquiry:

(1) Whether God is the efficient cause of all beings?

(2) Whether primary matter is created by God, or is an independent coordinate principle with Him?

(3) Whether God is the exemplar cause of beings or whether there are other exemplar causes?

(4) Whether He is the final cause of things?

FIRST ARTICLE [I, Q. 44, Art. 1]

Whether It Is Necessary That Every Being Be Created by God?

Objection 1: It would seem that it is not necessary that every being be created by God. For there is nothing to prevent a thing from being without that which does not belong to its essence, as a man can be found without whiteness. But the relation of the thing caused to its cause does not appear to be essential to beings, for some beings can be understood without it; therefore they can exist without it; and therefore it is possible that some beings should not be created by God.

Obj. 2: Further, a thing requires an efficient cause in order to exist. Therefore whatever cannot but exist does not require an efficient cause. But no necessary thing can not exist, because whatever necessarily exists cannot but exist. Therefore as there are many necessary things in existence, it appears that not all beings are from God.

Obj. 3: Further, whatever things have a cause, can be demonstrated by that cause. But in mathematics demonstration is not made by the efficient cause, as appears from the Philosopher (Metaph. iii, text 3); therefore not all beings are from God as from their efficient cause.

*On the contrary,* It is said (Rom. 11:36): "Of Him, and by Him, and in Him are all things."

*I answer that,* It must be said that every being in any way existing is from God. For whatever is found in anything by participation, must be caused in it by that to which it belongs essentially, as iron becomes ignited by fire. Now it has been shown above (Q. 3, A. 4) when treating of the divine simplicity that God is the essentially self-subsisting Being; and also it was shown (Q. 11, AA. 3, 4) that subsisting being must be one; as, if whiteness were self-subsisting, it would be one, since whiteness is multiplied by its recipients. Therefore all beings apart from God are not their own being, but are beings by participation. Therefore it must be that all things which are diversified by the diverse participation of being, so as to be more or less perfect, are caused by one First Being, Who possesses being most perfectly.

Hence Plato said (Parmen. xxvi) that unity must come before multitude; and Aristotle said (Metaph. ii, text 4) that whatever is greatest in being and greatest in truth, is the cause of every being and of every truth; just as whatever is the greatest in heat is the cause of all heat.

Reply Obj. 1: Though the relation to its cause is not part of the definition of a thing caused, still it follows, as a consequence, on what belongs to its essence; because from the fact that a thing has being by participation, it follows that it is caused. Hence such a being cannot be without being caused, just as man cannot be without having the faculty of laughing. But, since to be caused does not enter into the essence of being as such, therefore is it possible for us to find a being uncaused.

Reply Obj. 2: This objection has led some to say that what is necessary has no cause (Phys. viii, text 46). But this is manifestly false in the demonstrative sciences, where necessary principles are the causes of necessary conclusions. And therefore Aristotle says (Metaph. v, text 6), that there are some necessary things which have a cause of their necessity. But the reason why an efficient cause is required is not merely because the effect is not necessary, but because the effect might not be if the cause were not. For this conditional proposition is true, whether the antecedent and consequent be possible or impossible.

Reply Obj. 3: The science of mathematics treats its object as though it were something abstracted mentally, whereas it is not abstract in reality. Now, it is becoming that everything should have an efficient cause in proportion to its being. And so, although the object of mathematics has an efficient cause, still, its relation to that cause is not the reason why it is brought under the consideration of the mathematician, who therefore does not demonstrate that object from its efficient cause.

SECOND ARTICLE [I, Q. 44, Art. 2]

Whether Primary Matter Is Created by God?

Objection 1: It would seem that primary matter is not created by God. For whatever is made is composed of a subject and of something else (Phys. i, text 62). But primary matter has no subject. Therefore primary matter cannot have been made by God.

Obj. 2: Further, action and passion are opposite members of a division. But as the first active principle is God, so the first passive principle is matter. Therefore God and primary matter are two principles divided against each other, neither of which is from the other.

Obj. 3: Further, every agent produces its like, and thus, since every agent acts in proportion to its actuality, it follows that everything made is in some degree actual. But primary matter is only in potentiality, formally considered in itself. Therefore it is against the nature of primary matter to be a thing made.

*On the contrary,* Augustine says (Confess. xii, 7), Two "things hast Thou made, O Lord; one nigh unto Thyself"—viz. angels—"the other nigh unto nothing"—viz. primary matter.

*I answer that,* The ancient philosophers gradually, and as it were step by step, advanced to the knowledge of truth. At first being of grosser mind, they failed to realize that any beings existed except sensible bodies. And those among them who admitted movement, did not consider it except as regards certain accidents, for instance, in relation to rarefaction and condensation, by union and separation. And supposing as they did that corporeal substance itself was uncreated, they assigned certain causes for these accidental changes, as for instance, affinity, discord, intellect, or something of that kind. An advance was made when they understood that there was a distinction between the substantial form and matter, which latter they imagined to be uncreated, and when they perceived transmutation to take place in bodies in regard to essential forms. Such transmutations they attributed to certain universal causes, such as the oblique circle [*The zodiac, according to Aristotle (De Gener. ii)], or ideas, according to Plato. But we must take into consideration that matter is contracted by its form to a determinate species, as a substance, belonging to a certain species, is contracted by a supervening accident to a determinate mode of being; for instance, man by whiteness. Each of these opinions, therefore, considered "being" under some particular aspect, either as "this" or as "such"; and so they assigned particular efficient causes to things. Then others there were who arose to the consideration of "being," as being, and who assigned a cause to things, not as "these," or as "such," but as "beings."

Therefore whatever is the cause of things considered as beings, must be the cause of things, not only according as they are "such" by accidental forms, nor according as they are "these" by substantial forms, but also according to all that belongs to their being at all in any way. And thus it is necessary to say that also primary matter is created by the universal cause of things.

Reply Obj. 1: The Philosopher (Phys. i, text 62), is speaking of "becoming" in particular—that is, from form to form, either accidental or substantial. But here we are speaking of things according to their emanation from the universal principle of being; from which emanation matter itself is not excluded, although it is excluded from the former mode of being made.

Reply Obj. 2: Passion is an effect of action. Hence it is reasonable that the first passive principle should be the effect of the first active principle, since every imperfect thing is caused by one perfect. For the first principle must be most perfect, as Aristotle says (Metaph. xii, text 40).

Reply Obj. 3: The reason adduced does not show that matter is not created, but that it is not created without form; for though everything created is actual, still it is not pure act. Hence it is necessary that even what is potential in it should be created, if all that belongs to its being is created.

THIRD ARTICLE [I, Q. 44, Art. 3]

Whether the Exemplar Cause Is Anything Besides God?

Objection 1: It would seem that the exemplar cause is something besides God. For the effect is like its exemplar cause. But creatures are far from being like God. Therefore God is not their exemplar cause.

Obj. 2: Further, whatever is by participation is reduced to something self-existing, as a thing ignited is reduced to fire, as stated above (A. 1). But whatever exists in sensible things exists only by participation of some species. This appears from the fact that in all sensible species is found not only what belongs to the species, but also individuating principles added to the principles of the species. Therefore it is necessary to admit self-existing species, as for instance, a *per se* man, and a *per se* horse, and the like, which are called the exemplars. Therefore exemplar causes exist besides God.

Obj. 3: Further, sciences and definitions are concerned with species themselves, but not as these are in particular things, because there is no science or definition of particular things. Therefore there are some beings, which are beings or species not existing in singular things, and these are called exemplars. Therefore the same conclusion follows as above.

Obj. 4: Further, this likewise appears from Dionysius, who says (Div. Nom. v) that self-subsisting being is before self-subsisting life, and before self-subsisting wisdom.

*On the contrary,* The exemplar is the same as the idea. But ideas, according to Augustine (QQ. 83, qu. 46), are "the master forms, which are contained in the divine intelligence." Therefore the exemplars of things are not outside God.

*I answer that,* God is the first exemplar cause of all things. In proof whereof we must consider that if for the production of anything an exemplar is necessary, it is in order that the effect may receive a determinate form. For an artificer produces a determinate form in matter by reason of the exemplar before him, whether it is the exemplar beheld externally, or the exemplar interiorily conceived in the mind. Now it is manifest that things made by nature receive determinate forms. This determination of forms must be reduced to the divine wisdom as its first principle, for divine wisdom devised the order of the universe, which order consists in the variety of things. And therefore we must say that in the divine wisdom are the types of all things, which types we have called ideas—i.e. exemplar forms existing in the divine mind (Q. 15, A. 1). And these ideas, though multiplied by their relations to things, in reality are not apart from the divine essence, according as the likeness to that essence can be shared diversely by different things. In this manner therefore God Himself is the first exemplar of all things. Moreover, in things created one may be called the exemplar of another by the reason of its likeness thereto, either in species, or by the analogy of some kind of imitation.

Reply Obj. 1: Although creatures do not attain to a natural likeness to God according to similitude of species, as a man begotten is like to the man begetting, still they do attain to likeness to Him, forasmuch as they represent the divine idea, as a material house is like to the house in the architect's mind.

Reply Obj. 2: It is of a man's nature to be in matter, and so a man without matter is impossible. Therefore although this particular man is a man by participation of the species, he cannot be reduced to anything self-existing in the same species, but to a superior species, such as separate substances. The same applies to other sensible things.

Reply Obj. 3: Although every science and definition is concerned only with beings, still it is not necessary that a thing should have the same mode in reality as the thought of it has in our understanding. For we abstract universal ideas by force of the active intellect from the particular conditions; but it is not necessary that the universals should exist outside the particulars in order to be their exemplars.

Reply Obj. 4: As Dionysius says (Div. Nom. iv), by "self-existing life and self-existing wisdom" he sometimes denotes God Himself, sometimes the powers given to things themselves; but not any self-subsisting things, as the ancients asserted.

FOURTH ARTICLE [I, Q. 44, Art. 4]

Whether God Is the Final Cause of All Things?

Objection 1: It would seem that God is not the final cause of all things. For to act for an end seems to imply need of the end. But God needs nothing. Therefore it does not become Him to act for an end.

Obj. 2: Further, the end of generation, and the form of the thing generated, and the agent cannot be identical (Phys. ii, text 70), because the end of generation is the form of the thing generated. But God is the first agent producing all things. Therefore He is not the final cause of all things.

Obj. 3: Further, all things desire their end. But all things do not desire God, for all do not even know Him. Therefore God is not the end of all things.

Obj. 4: Further, the final cause is the first of causes. If, therefore, God is the efficient cause and the final cause, it follows that before and after exist in Him; which is impossible.

*On the contrary,* It is said (Prov. 16:4): "The Lord has made all things for Himself."

*I answer that,* Every agent acts for an end: otherwise one thing would not follow more than another from the action of the agent, unless it were by chance. Now the end of the agent and of the patient considered as such is the same, but in a different way respectively. For the impression which the agent intends to produce, and which the patient intends to receive, are one and the same. Some things, however, are both agent and patient at the same time: these are imperfect agents, and to these it belongs to intend, even while acting, the acquisition of something. But it does not belong to the First Agent, Who is agent only, to act for the acquisition of some end; He intends only to communicate His perfection, which is His goodness; while every creature intends to acquire its own perfection, which is the likeness of the divine perfection and goodness. Therefore the divine goodness is the end of all things.

Reply Obj. 1: To act from need belongs only to an imperfect agent, which by its nature is both agent and patient. But this does not belong to God, and therefore He alone is the most perfectly liberal giver, because He does not act for His own profit, but only for His own goodness.

Reply Obj. 2: The form of the thing generated is

not the end of generation, except inasmuch as it is the likeness of the form of the generator, which intends to communicate its own likeness; otherwise the form of the thing generated would be more noble than the generator, since the end is more noble than the means to the end.

Reply Obj. 3: All things desire God as their end, when they desire some good thing, whether this desire be intellectual or sensible, or natural, i.e. without knowledge; because nothing is good and desirable except forasmuch as it participates in the likeness to God.

Reply Obj. 4: Since God is the efficient, the exemplar and the final cause of all things, and since primary matter is from Him, it follows that the first principle of all things is one in reality. But this does not prevent us from mentally considering many things in Him, some of which come into our mind before others.

## QUESTION 45

THE MODE OF EMANATION OF THINGS FROM THE FIRST PRINCIPLE (In Eight Articles)

The next question concerns the mode of the emanation of things from the First Principle, and this is called creation, and includes eight points of inquiry:

(1) What is creation?

(2) Whether God can create anything?

(3) Whether creation is anything in the very nature of things?

(4) To what things it belongs to be created?

(5) Whether it belongs to God alone to create?

(6) Whether creation is common to the whole Trinity, or proper to any one Person?

(7) Whether any trace of the Trinity is to be found in created things?

(8) Whether the work of creation is mingled with the works of nature and of the will?

FIRST ARTICLE [I, Q. 45, Art. 1]

Whether to Create Is to Make Something from Nothing?

Objection 1: It would seem that to create is not to make anything from nothing. For Augustine says (Contra Adv. Leg. et Proph. i): "To make concerns what did not exist at all; but to create is to make something by bringing forth something from what was already."

Obj. 2: Further, the nobility of action and of motion is considered from their terms. Action is therefore nobler from good to good, and from being to being, than from nothing to something. But creation appears to be the most noble action, and first among all actions. Therefore it is not from nothing to something, but rather from being to being.

Obj. 3: Further, the preposition "from" [ex] imports relation of some cause, and especially of the material cause; as when we say that a statue is made from brass. But "nothing" cannot be the matter of being, nor in any way its cause. Therefore to create is not to make something from nothing.

*On the contrary,* On the text of Gen. 1, "In the beginning God created," etc., the gloss has, "To create is to make something from nothing."

*I answer that,* As said above (Q. 44, A. 2), we must consider not only the emanation of a particular being from a particular agent, but also the emanation of all being from the universal cause, which is God; and this emanation we designate by the name of creation. Now what proceeds by particular emanation, is not presupposed to that emanation; as when a man is generated, he was not before, but man is made from "not-man," and white from "not-white." Hence if the emanation of the whole universal being from the first principle be considered, it is impossible that any being should be presupposed before this emanation. For nothing is the same as no being. Therefore as the generation of a man is from the "not-being" which is "not-man," so creation, which is the emanation of all being, is from the "not-being" which is "nothing."

Reply Obj. 1: Augustine uses the word creation in an equivocal sense, according as to be created signifies improvement in things; as when we say that a bishop is created. We do not, however, speak of creation in that way here, but as it is described above.

Reply Obj. 2: Changes receive species and dignity, not from the term *wherefrom,* but from the term whereto. Therefore a change is more perfect and excellent when the term *whereto* of the change is more noble and excellent, although the term *wherefrom,* corresponding to the term *whereto,* may be more imperfect: thus generation is simply nobler and more excellent than alteration, because the substantial form is nobler than the accidental form; and yet the privation of the substantial form, which is the term *wherefrom* in generation, is more imperfect than the contrary, which is the term *wherefrom* in alteration. Similarly creation is more perfect and excellent than generation and alteration, because the term *whereto* is the whole substance of the thing; whereas what is understood as the term *wherefrom* is simply not-being.

Reply Obj. 3: When anything is said to be made from nothing, this preposition "from" [ex] does not signify the material cause, but only order; as when we say, "from morning comes midday"—i.e. after morning is midday. But we must understand that this preposition "from" [ex] can comprise the negation implied when I say the word "nothing," or can be included in it. If taken in the first sense, then we affirm the order by stating the relation between what is now and its previous non-existence. But if the negation includes the preposition, then the order is denied, and the sense is, "It is made from nothing—i.e. it is not made from anything"—as if we were to say, "He speaks of nothing," because he does not speak of anything. And this is verified in both ways, when it is said, that anything is made from nothing. But in the first way this preposition "from" [ex] implies order, as has been said in this reply. In the second sense, it imports the material cause, which is denied.

SECOND ARTICLE [I, Q. 45, Art. 2]

Whether God Can Create Anything?

Objection 1: It would seem that God cannot create anything, because, according to the Philosopher (Phys. i, text 34), the ancient philosophers considered it as a commonly received axiom that "nothing is made from nothing." But the power of God does not extend to the contraries of first principles; as, for instance, that God could make the whole to be less than its part, or that affirmation and negation are both true at the same time. Therefore God cannot make anything from nothing, or create.

Obj. 2: Further, if to create is to make something from nothing, to be created is to be made. But to be made is to be changed. Therefore creation is change. But every change occurs in some subject, as appears by the definition of movement: for movement is the act of what is in potentiality. Therefore it is impossible for anything to be made out of nothing by God.

Obj. 3: Further, what has been made must have at some time been becoming. But it cannot be said that what is created, at the same time, is becoming and has been made, because in permanent things what is becoming, is not, and what has been made, already is: and so it would follow that something would be, and not be, at the same time. Therefore when anything is made, its becoming precedes its having been made. But this is impossible, unless there is a subject in which the becoming is sustained. Therefore it is impossible that anything should be made from nothing.

Obj. 4: Further, infinite distance cannot be crossed. But infinite distance exists between being and nothing. Therefore it does not happen that something is made from nothing.

*On the contrary,* It is said (Gen. 1:1): "In the beginning God created heaven and earth."

*I answer that,* Not only is it [not] impossible that anything should be created by God, but it is necessary to say that all things were created by God, as appears from what has been said (Q. 44, A. 1). For when anyone makes one thing from another, this latter thing from which he makes is presupposed to his action, and is not produced by his action; thus the craftsman works from natural things, as wood or brass, which are caused not by the action of art, but by the action of nature. So also nature itself causes natural things as regards their form, but presupposes matter. If therefore God did only act from something presupposed, it would follow that the thing presupposed would not be caused by Him. Now it has been shown above (Q. 44, AA. 1, 2), that nothing can be, unless it is from God, Who is the universal cause of all being. Hence it is necessary to say that God brings things into being from nothing.

Reply Obj. 1: Ancient philosophers, as is said above (Q. 44, A. 2), considered only the emanation of particular effects from particular causes, which necessarily presuppose something in their action; whence came their common opinion that "nothing is made from nothing." But this has no place in the first emanation from the universal principle of things.

Reply Obj. 2: Creation is not change, except according to a mode of understanding. For change means that the same something should be different now from what it was previously. Sometimes, indeed, the same actual thing is different now from what it was before, as in motion according to quantity, quality and place; but sometimes it is the same being only in potentiality, as in substantial change, the subject of which is matter. But in creation, by which the whole substance of a thing is produced, the same thing can be taken as different now and before only according to our way of understanding, so that a thing is understood as first not existing at all, and afterwards as existing. But as action and passion coincide as to the substance of motion, and differ only according to diverse relations (Phys. iii, text 20, 21), it must follow that when motion is withdrawn, only diverse relations remain in the Creator and in the creature. But because the mode of signification follows the mode of understanding as was said above (Q. 13, A. 1), creation is signified by mode of change; and on this account it is said that to create is to make something from nothing. And yet "to make" and "to be made" are more suitable expressions here than "to change" and "to be changed," because "to make" and "to be made" import a relation of cause to the effect, and of effect to the cause, and imply change only as a consequence.

Reply Obj. 3: In things which are made without movement, to become and to be already made are simultaneous, whether such making is the term of movement, as illumination (for a thing is being illuminated and is illuminated at the same time) or whether it is not the term of movement, as the word is being made in the mind and is made at the same time. In these things what is being made, is; but when we speak of its being made, we mean that it is from another, and was not previously. Hence since creation is without movement, a thing is being created and is already created at the same time.

Reply Obj. 4: This objection proceeds from a false imagination, as if there were an infinite medium between nothing and being; which is plainly false. This false imagination comes from creation being taken to signify a change existing between two forms.

THIRD ARTICLE [I, Q. 45, Art. 3]

Whether Creation Is Anything in the Creature?

Objection 1: It would seem that creation is not anything in the creature. For as creation taken in a passive sense is attributed to the creature, so creation taken in an active sense is attributed to the Creator. But creation taken actively is not anything in the Creator, because otherwise it would follow that in God there would be something temporal. Therefore creation taken passively is not anything in the creature.

Obj. 2: Further, there is no medium between the Creator and the creature. But creation is signified as the medium between them both: since it is not the Creator, as it is not eternal; nor is it the creature, because in that case it would be necessary for the same reason to suppose another creation to create it, and so on to infinity. Therefore creation is not anything in the creature.

Obj. 3: Further, if creation is anything besides the created substance, it must be an accident belonging to it. But every accident is in a subject. Therefore a thing created would be the subject of creation, and so the same thing would be the subject and also the term of creation. This is impossible, because the subject is before the accident, and preserves the accident; while the term is after the action and passion whose term it is, and as soon as it exists, action and passion cease. Therefore creation itself is not any thing.

*On the contrary,* It is greater for a thing to be made according to its entire substance, than to be made according to its substantial or accidental form. But generation taken simply, or relatively, whereby anything is made according to the substantial or the accidental form, is something in the thing generated. Therefore much more is creation, whereby a thing is made according to its whole substance, something in the thing created.

*I answer that,* Creation places something in the thing created according to relation only; because what is created, is not made by movement, or by change. For what is made by movement or by change is made from something pre-existing. And this happens, indeed, in the particular productions of some beings, but cannot happen in the production of all being by the universal cause of all beings, which is God. Hence God by creation produces things without movement. Now when movement is removed from action and passion, only relation remains, as was said above (A. 2, ad 2). Hence creation in the creature is only a certain relation to the Creator as to the principle of its being; even as in passion, which implies movement, is implied a relation to the principle of motion.

Reply Obj. 1: Creation signified actively means the divine action, which is God's essence, with a relation to the creature. But in God relation to the creature is not a real relation, but only a relation of reason; whereas the relation of the creature to God is a real relation, as was said above (Q. 13, A. 7) in treating of the divine names.

Reply Obj. 2: Because creation is signified as a change, as was said above (A. 2, ad 2), and change is a kind of medium between the mover and the moved, therefore also creation is signified as a medium between the Creator and the creature. Nevertheless passive creation is in the creature, and is a creature. Nor is there need of a further creation in its creation; because relations, or their entire nature being referred to something, are not referred by any other relations, but by themselves; as was also shown above (Q. 42, A. 1, ad 4), in treating of the equality of the Persons.

Reply Obj. 3: The creature is the term of creation as signifying a change, but is the subject of creation, taken as a real relation, and is prior to it in being, as the subject is to the accident. Nevertheless creation has a certain aspect of priority on the part of the object to which it is directed, which is the beginning of the creature. Nor is it necessary that as long as the creature is it should be created; because creation imports a relation of the creature to the Creator, with a certain newness or beginning.

FOURTH ARTICLE [I, Q. 45, Art. 4]

Whether to Be Created Belongs to Composite and Subsisting Things?

Objection 1: It would seem that to be created does not belong to composite and subsisting things. For in the book, *De Causis* (prop. iv) it is said, "The first of creatures is being." But the being of a thing created is not subsisting. Therefore creation properly speaking does not belong to subsisting and composite things.

Obj. 2: Further, whatever is created is from nothing. But composite things are not from nothing, but are the result of their own component parts. Therefore composite things are not created.

Obj. 3: Further, what is presupposed in the second emanation is properly produced by the first: as natural generation produces the natural thing, which is presupposed in the operation of art. But the thing supposed in natural generation is matter. Therefore matter, and not the composite, is, properly speaking, that which is created.

*On the contrary,* It is said (Gen. 1:1): "In the beginning God created heaven and earth." But heaven and earth are subsisting composite things. Therefore creation belongs to them.

*I answer that,* To be created is, in a manner, to be made, as was shown above (Q. 44, A. 2, ad 2, 3). Now, to be made is directed to the being of a thing. Hence to be made and to be created properly belong to whatever being belongs; which, indeed, belongs properly to subsisting things, whether they are simple things, as in the case of separate substances, or composite, as in the case of material substances. For being belongs to that which has being—that is, to what subsists in its own being. But forms and accidents and the like are called beings, not as if they themselves were, but because something is by them; as whiteness is called a being, inasmuch as its subject is white by it. Hence, according to the Philosopher (Metaph. vii, text 2) accident is more properly said to be "of a being" than "a being." Therefore, as accidents and forms and the like non-subsisting things are to be said to co-exist rather than to exist, so they ought to be called rather "concreated" than "created" things; whereas, properly speaking, created things are subsisting beings.

Reply Obj. 1: In the proposition "the first of created things is being," the word "being" does not refer to the subject of creation, but to the proper concept of the object of creation. For a created thing is called created because it is a being, not because it is "this" being, since creation is the emanation of all being from the Universal Being, as was said above (A. 1). We use a similar way of speaking when we say that "the first visible thing is color," although, strictly speaking, the thing colored is what is seen.

Reply Obj. 2: Creation does not mean the building up of a composite thing from pre-existing principles; but it means that the "composite" is created so that it is brought into being at the same time with all its principles.

Reply Obj. 3: This reason does not prove that matter alone is created, but that matter does not exist except by creation; for creation is the production of the whole being, and not only matter.

FIFTH ARTICLE [I, Q. 45, Art. 5]

Whether It Belongs to God Alone to Create?

Objection 1: It would seem that it does not belong to God alone to create, because, according to the Philosopher (De Anima ii, text 34), what is perfect can make its own likeness. But immaterial creatures are more perfect than material creatures, which nevertheless can make their own likeness, for fire generates fire, and man begets man. Therefore an immaterial substance can make a substance like to itself. But immaterial substance can be made only by creation, since it has no matter from which to be made. Therefore a creature can create.

Obj. 2: Further, the greater the resistance is on the part of the thing made, so much the greater power is required in the maker. But a "contrary" resists more than "nothing." Therefore it requires more power to make (something) from its contrary, which nevertheless a creature can do, than to make a thing from nothing. Much more therefore can a creature do this.

Obj. 3: Further, the power of the maker is considered according to the measure of what is made. But created being is finite, as we proved above when treating of the infinity of God (Q. 7, AA. 2, 3, 4). Therefore only a finite power is needed to produce a creature by creation. But to have a finite power is not contrary to the nature of a creature. Therefore it is not impossible for a creature to create.

*On the contrary,* Augustine says (De Trin. iii, 8) that neither good nor bad angels can create anything. Much less therefore can any other creatures.

*I answer that,* It sufficiently appears at the first glance, according to what precedes (A. 1), that to create can be the action of God alone. For the more universal effects must be reduced to the more universal and prior causes. Now among all effects the most universal is being itself: and hence it must be the proper effect of the first and most universal cause, and that is God. Hence also it is said (De Causis prop., iii) that "neither intelligence nor the soul gives us being, except inasmuch as it works by divine operation." Now to produce being absolutely, not as this or that being, belongs to creation. Hence it is manifest that creation is the proper act of God alone.

It happens, however, that something participates the proper action of another, not by its own power, but instrumentally, inasmuch as it acts by the power of another; as air can heat and ignite by the power of fire. And so some have supposed that although creation is the proper act of the universal cause, still some inferior cause acting by the power of the first cause, can create. And thus Avicenna asserted that the first separate substance created by God created another after itself, and the substance of the world and its soul; and that the substance of the world creates the matter of inferior bodies. And in the same manner the Master says (Sent. iv, D, 5) that God can communicate to a creature the power of creating, so that the latter can create ministerially, not by its own power.

But such a thing cannot be, because the secondary instrumental cause does not participate the action of the superior cause, except inasmuch as by something proper to itself it acts dispositively to the effect of the principal agent. If therefore it effects nothing, according to what is proper to itself, it is used to no purpose; nor would there be any need of certain instruments for certain actions. Thus we see that a saw, in cutting wood, which it does by the property of its own form, produces the form of a bench, which is the proper effect of the principal agent. Now the proper effect of God creating is what is presupposed to all other effects, and that is absolute being. Hence nothing else can act dispositively and instrumentally to this effect, since creation is not from anything presupposed, which can be disposed by the action of the instrumental agent. So therefore it is impossible for any creature to create, either by its own power or instrumentally—that is, ministerially.

And above all it is absurd to suppose that a body can create, for no body acts except by touching or moving; and thus it requires in its action some pre-existing thing, which can be touched or moved, which is contrary to the very idea of creation.

Reply Obj. 1: A perfect thing participating any nature, makes a likeness to itself, not by absolutely producing that nature, but by applying it to something else. For an individual man cannot be the cause of human nature absolutely, because he would then be the cause of himself; but he is the cause of human nature being in the man begotten; and thus he presupposes in his action a determinate matter whereby he is an individual man. But as an individual man participates human nature, so every created being participates, so to speak, the nature of being; for God alone is His own being, as we have said above (Q. 7, AA. 1, 2). Therefore no created being can produce a being absolutely, except forasmuch as it causes "being" in "this": and so it is necessary to presuppose that whereby a thing is this thing, before the action whereby it makes its own likeness. But in an immaterial substance it is not possible to presuppose anything whereby it is this thing; because it is what it is by its form, whereby it has being, since it is a subsisting form. Therefore an immaterial substance cannot produce another immaterial substance like to itself as regards its being, but only as regards some added perfection; as we may say that a superior angel illuminates an inferior, as Dionysius says (Coel. Hier. iv, x). In this way even in heaven there is paternity, as the Apostle says (Eph. 3:15): "From whom all paternity in heaven and on earth is named." From which evidently appears that no created being can cause anything, unless something is presupposed; which is against the very idea of creation.

Reply Obj. 2: A thing is made from its contrary indirectly (Phys. i, text 43), but directly from the subject which is in potentiality. And so the contrary resists the agent, inasmuch as it impedes the potentiality from the act which the agent intends to induce, as fire intends to reduce the matter of water to an act like to itself, but is impeded by the form and contrary dispositions, whereby the potentiality (of the water) is restrained from being reduced to act; and the more the potentiality is restrained, the more power is required in the agent to reduce the matter to act. Hence a much greater power is required in the agent when no potentiality pre-exists. Thus therefore it appears that it is an act of much greater power to make a thing from nothing, than from its contrary.

Reply Obj. 3: The power of the maker is reckoned not only from the substance of the thing made, but also from the mode of its being made; for a greater heat heats not only more, but quicker. Therefore although to create a finite effect does not show an infinite power, yet to create it from nothing does show an infinite power: which appears from what has been said (ad 2). For if a greater power is required in the agent in proportion to the distance of the potentiality from the act, it follows that the power of that which produces something from no presupposed potentiality is infinite, because there is no proportion between "no potentiality" and the potentiality presupposed by the power of a natural agent, as there is no proportion between "not being" and "being." And because no creature has simply an infinite power, any more than it has an infinite being, as was proved above (Q. 7, A. 2), it follows that no creature can create.

SIXTH ARTICLE [I, Q. 45, Art. 6]

Whether to Create Is Proper to Any Person?

Objection 1: It would seem that to create is proper to some Person. For what comes first is the cause of what is after; and what is perfect is the cause of what is imperfect. But the procession of the divine Person is prior to the procession of the creature: and is more perfect, because the divine Person proceeds in perfect similitude of its principle; whereas the creature proceeds in imperfect similitude. Therefore the processions of the divine Persons are the cause of the processions of things, and so to create belongs to a Person.

Obj. 2: Further, the divine Persons are distinguished from each other only by their processions and relations. Therefore whatever difference is attributed to the divine Persons belongs to them according to the processions and relations of the Persons. But the causation of creatures is diversely attributed to the divine Persons; for in the Creed, to the Father is attributed that "He is the Creator of all things visible and invisible"; to the Son is attributed that by Him "all things were made"; and to the Holy Ghost is attributed that He is "Lord and Life-giver." Therefore the causation of creatures belongs to the Persons according to processions and relations.

Obj. 3: Further, if it be said that the causation of the creature flows from some essential attribute appropriated to some one Person, this does not appear to be sufficient; because every divine effect is caused by every essential attribute—viz. by power, goodness and wisdom—and thus does not belong to one more than to another. Therefore any determinate mode of causation ought not to be attributed to one Person more than to another, unless they are distinguished in creating according to relations and processions.

*On the contrary,* Dionysius says (Div. Nom. ii) that all things caused are the common work of the whole Godhead.

*I answer that,* To create is, properly speaking, to cause or produce the being of things. And as every agent produces its like, the principle of action can be considered from the effect of the action; for it must be fire that generates fire. And therefore to create belongs to God according to His being, that is, His essence, which is common to the three Persons. Hence to create is not proper to any one Person, but is common to the whole Trinity.

Nevertheless the divine Persons, according to the nature of their procession, have a causality respecting the creation of things. For as was said above (Q. 14, A. 8; Q. 19, A. 4), when treating of the knowledge and will of God, God is the cause of things by His intellect and will, just as the craftsman is cause of the things made by his craft. Now the craftsman works through the word conceived in his mind, and through the love of his will regarding some object. Hence also God the Father made the creature through His Word, which is His Son; and through His Love, which is the Holy Ghost. And so the processions of the Persons are the type of the productions of creatures inasmuch as they include the essential attributes, knowledge and will.

Reply Obj. 1: The processions of the divine Persons are the cause of creation, as above explained.

Reply Obj. 2: As the divine nature, although common to the three Persons, still belongs to them in a kind of order, inasmuch as the Son receives the divine nature from the Father, and the Holy Ghost from both: so also likewise the power of creation, whilst common to the three Persons, belongs to them in a kind of order. For the Son receives it from the Father, and the Holy Ghost from both. Hence to be the Creator is attributed to the Father as to Him Who does not receive the power of creation from another. And of the Son it is said (John 1:3), "Through Him all things were made," inasmuch as He has the same power, but from another; for this preposition "through" usually denotes a mediate cause, or "a principle from a principle." But to the Holy Ghost, Who has the same power from both, is attributed that by His sway He governs, and quickens what is created by the Father through the Son. Again, the reason for this particular appropriation may be taken from the common notion of the appropriation of the essential attributes. For, as above stated (Q. 39, A. 8, ad 3), to the Father is appropriated power which is chiefly shown in creation, and therefore it is attributed to Him to be the Creator. To the Son is appropriated wisdom, through which the intellectual agent acts; and therefore it is said: "Through Whom all things were made." And to the Holy Ghost is appropriated goodness, to which belong both government, which brings things to their proper end, and the giving of life—for life consists in a certain interior movement; and the first mover is the end, and goodness.

Reply Obj. 3: Although every effect of God proceeds from each attribute, each effect is reduced to that attribute with which it is naturally connected; thus the order of things is reduced to "wisdom," and the justification of the sinner to "mercy" and "goodness" poured out super-abundantly. But creation, which is the production of the very substance of a thing, is reduced to "power."

SEVENTH ARTICLE [I, Q. 45, Art. 7]

Whether in Creatures Is Necessarily Found a Trace of the Trinity?

Objection 1: It would seem that in creatures there is not necessarily found a trace of the Trinity. For anything can be traced through its traces. But the trinity of persons cannot be traced from the creatures, as was above stated (Q. 32, A. 1). Therefore there is no trace of the Trinity in creatures.

Obj. 2: Further, whatever is in creatures is created. Therefore if the trace of the Trinity is found in creatures according to some of their properties, and if everything created has a trace of the Trinity, it follows that we can find a trace of the Trinity in each of these (properties): and so on to infinitude.

Obj. 3: Further, the effect represents only its own cause. But the causality of creatures belongs to the common nature, and not to the relations whereby the Persons are distinguished and numbered. Therefore in the creature is to be found a trace not of the Trinity but of the unity of essence.

*On the contrary,* Augustine says (De Trin. vi, 10), that "the trace of the Trinity appears in creatures."

*I answer that,* Every effect in some degree represents its cause, but diversely. For some effects represent only the causality of the cause, but not its form; as smoke represents fire. Such a representation is called a "trace": for a trace shows that someone has passed by but not who it is. Other effects represent the cause as regards the similitude of its form, as fire generated represents fire generating; and a statue of Mercury represents Mercury; and this is called the representation of "image." Now the processions of the divine Persons are referred to the acts of intellect and will, as was said above (Q. 27). For the Son proceeds as the word of the intellect; and the Holy Ghost proceeds as love of the will. Therefore in rational creatures, possessing intellect and will, there is found the representation of the Trinity by way of image, inasmuch as there is found in them the word conceived, and the love proceeding.

But in all creatures there is found the trace of the Trinity, inasmuch as in every creature are found some things which are necessarily reduced to the divine Persons as to their cause. For every creature subsists in its own being, and has a form, whereby it is determined to a species, and has relation to something else. Therefore as it is a created substance, it represents the cause and principle; and so in that manner it shows the Person of the Father, Who is the "principle from no principle." According as it has a form and species, it represents the Word as the form of the thing made by art is from the conception of the craftsman. According as it has relation of order, it represents the Holy Ghost, inasmuch as He is love, because the order of the effect to something else is from the will of the Creator. And therefore Augustine says (De Trin. vi 10) that the trace of the Trinity is found in every creature, according "as it is one individual," and according "as it is formed by a species," and according as it "has a certain relation of order." And to these also are reduced those three, "number," "weight," and "measure," mentioned in the Book of Wisdom (9:21). For "measure" refers to the substance of the thing limited by its principles, "number" refers to the species, "weight" refers to the order. And to these three are reduced the other three mentioned by Augustine (De Nat. Boni iii), "mode," species, and "order," and also those he mentions (QQ. 83, qu. 18): "that which exists; whereby it is distinguished; whereby it agrees." For a thing exists by its substance, is distinct by its form, and agrees by its order. Other similar expressions may be easily reduced to the above.

Reply Obj. 1: The representation of the trace is to be referred to the appropriations: in which manner we are able to arrive at a knowledge of the trinity of the divine persons from creatures, as we have said (Q. 32, A. 1).

Reply Obj. 2: A creature properly speaking is a thing self-subsisting; and in such are the three above-mentioned things to be found. Nor is it necessary that these three things should be found in all that exists in the creature; but only to a subsisting being is the trace ascribed in regard to those three things.

Reply Obj. 3: The processions of the persons are also in some way the cause and type of creation; as appears from the above (A. 6).

EIGHTH ARTICLE [I, Q. 45, Art. 8]

Whether Creation Is Mingled with Works of Nature and Art?

Objection 1: It would seem that creation is mingled in works of nature and art. For in every operation of nature and art some form is produced. But it is not produced from anything, since matter has no part in it. Therefore it is produced from nothing; and thus in every operation of nature and art there is creation.

Obj. 2: Further, the effect is not more powerful than its cause. But in natural things the only agent is the accidental form, which is an active or a passive form. Therefore the substantial form is not produced by the operation of nature; and therefore it must be produced by creation.

Obj. 3: Further, in nature like begets like. But some things are found generated in nature by a thing unlike to them; as is evident in animals generated through putrefaction. Therefore the form of these is not from nature, but by creation; and the same reason applies to other things.

Obj. 4: Further, what is not created, is not a creature. If therefore in nature's productions there were not creation, it would follow that nature's productions are not creatures; which is heretical.

*On the contrary,* Augustine (Super Gen. v, 6,14,15) distinguishes the work of propagation, which is a work of nature, from the work of creation.

*I answer that,* The doubt on this subject arises from the forms which, some said, do not come into existence by the action of nature, but previously exist in matter; for they asserted that forms are latent. This arose from ignorance concerning matter, and from not knowing how to distinguish between potentiality and act. For because forms pre-exist in matter, "in potentiality," they asserted that they pre-exist "simply." Others, however, said that the forms were given or caused by a separate agent by way of creation; and accordingly, that to each operation of nature is joined creation. But this opinion arose from ignorance concerning form. For they failed to consider that the form of the natural body is not subsisting, but is that by which a thing is. And therefore, since to be made and to be created belong properly to a subsisting thing alone, as shown above (A. 4), it does not belong to forms to be made or to be created, but to be "concreated." What, indeed, is properly made by the natural agent is the "composite," which is made from matter.

Hence in the works of nature creation does not enter, but is presupposed to the work of nature.

Reply Obj. 1: Forms begin to be actual when the composite things are made, not as though they were made "directly," but only "indirectly."

Reply Obj. 2: The active qualities in nature act by virtue of substantial forms: and therefore the natural agent not only produces its like according to quality, but according to species.

Reply Obj. 3: For the generation of imperfect animals, a universal agent suffices, and this is to be found in the celestial power to which they are assimilated, not in species, but according to a kind of analogy. Nor is it necessary to say that their forms are created by a separate agent. However, for the generation of perfect animals the universal agent does not suffice, but a proper agent is required, in the shape of a univocal generator.

Reply Obj. 4: The operation of nature takes place only on the presupposition of created principles; and thus the products of nature are called creatures.

## QUESTION 46

OF THE BEGINNING OF THE DURATION OF CREATURES (In Three Articles)

Next must be considered the beginning of the duration of creatures, about which there are three points for treatment:

(1) Whether creatures always existed?

(2) Whether that they began to exist is an article of Faith?

(3) How God is said to have created heaven and earth in the beginning?

FIRST ARTICLE [I, Q. 46, Art. 1]

Whether the Universe of Creatures Always Existed?

Objection 1: It would seem that the universe of creatures, called the world, had no beginning, but existed from eternity. For everything which begins to exist, is a possible being before it exists: otherwise it would be impossible for it to exist. If therefore the world began to exist, it was a possible being before it began to exist. But possible being is matter, which is in potentiality to existence, which results from a form, and to non-existence, which results from privation of form. If therefore the world began to exist, matter must have existed before the world. But matter cannot exist without form: while the matter of the world with its form is the world. Therefore the world existed before it began to exist: which is impossible.

Obj. 2: Further, nothing which has power to be always, sometimes is and sometimes is not; because so far as the power of a thing extends so long it exists. But every incorruptible thing has power to be always; for its power does not extend to any determinate time. Therefore no incorruptible thing sometimes is, and sometimes is not: but everything which has a beginning at some time is, and at some time is not; therefore no incorruptible thing begins to exist. But there are many incorruptible things in the world, as the celestial bodies and all intellectual substances. Therefore the world did not begin to exist.

Obj. 3: Further, what is unbegotten has no beginning. But the Philosopher (Phys. i, text 82) proves that matter is unbegotten, and also (De Coelo et Mundo i, text 20) that the heaven is unbegotten. Therefore the universe did not begin to exist.

Obj. 4: Further, a vacuum is where there is not a body, but there might be. But if the world began to exist, there was first no body where the body of the world now is; and yet it could be there, otherwise it would not be there now. Therefore before the world there was a vacuum; which is impossible.

Obj. 5: Further, nothing begins anew to be moved except through either the mover or the thing moved being otherwise than it was before. But what is otherwise now than it was before, is moved. Therefore before every new movement there was a previous movement. Therefore movement always was; and therefore also the thing moved always was, because movement is only in a movable thing.

Obj. 6: Further, every mover is either natural or voluntary. But neither begins to move except by some pre-existing movement. For nature always moves in the same manner: hence unless some change precede either in the nature of the mover, or in the movable thing, there cannot arise from the natural mover a movement which was not there before. And the will, without itself being changed, puts off doing what it proposes to do; but this can be only by some imagined change, at least on the part of time. Thus he who wills to make a house tomorrow, and not today, awaits something which will be tomorrow, but is not today; and at least awaits for today to pass, and for tomorrow to come; and this cannot be without change, because time is the measure of movement. Therefore it remains that before every new movement, there was a previous movement; and so the same conclusion follows as before.

Obj. 7: Further, whatever is always in its beginning, and always in its end, cannot cease and cannot begin; because what begins is not in its end, and what ceases is not in its beginning. But time always is in its beginning and end, because there is no time except "now" which is the end of the past and the beginning of the future. Therefore time cannot begin or end, and consequently neither can movement, the measure of what is time.

Obj. 8: Further, God is before the world either in the order of nature only, or also by duration. If in the order of nature only, therefore, since God is eternal, the world also is eternal. But if God is prior by duration; since what is prior and posterior in duration constitutes time, it follows that time existed before the world, which is impossible.

Obj. 9: Further, if there is a sufficient cause, there is an effect; for a cause to which there is no effect is an imperfect cause, requiring something else to make the effect follow. But God is the sufficient cause of the world; being the final cause, by reason of His goodness, the exemplar cause by reason of His wisdom, and the efficient cause, by reason of His power as appears from the above (Q. 44, AA. 2, 3, 4). Since therefore God is eternal, the world is also eternal.

Obj. 10: Further, eternal action postulates an eternal effect. But the action of God is His substance, which is eternal. Therefore the world is eternal.

*On the contrary,* It is said (John 17:5), "Glorify Me, O Father, with Thyself with the glory which I had before the world was"; and (Prov. 8:22), "The Lord possessed Me in the beginning of His ways, before He made anything from the beginning."

*I answer that,* Nothing except God can be eternal. And this statement is far from impossible to uphold: for it has been shown above (Q. 19, A. 4) that the will of God is the cause of things. Therefore things are necessary, according as it is necessary for God to will them, since the necessity of the effect depends on the necessity of the cause (Metaph. v, text 6). Now it was shown above (Q. 19, A. 3), that, absolutely speaking, it is not necessary that God should will anything except Himself. It is not therefore necessary for God to will that the world should always exist; but the world exists forasmuch as God wills it to exist, since the being of the world depends on the will of God, as on its cause. It is not therefore necessary for the world to be always; and hence it cannot be proved by demonstration.

Nor are Aristotle's reasons (Phys. viii) simply, but relatively, demonstrative—viz. in order to contradict the reasons of some of the ancients who asserted that the world began to exist in some quite impossible manner. This appears in three ways. Firstly, because, both in *Phys.* viii and in De Coelo i, text 101, he premises some opinions, as those of Anaxagoras, Empedocles and Plato, and brings forward reasons to refute them. Secondly, because wherever he speaks of this subject, he quotes the testimony of the ancients, which is not the way of a demonstrator, but of one persuading of what is probable. Thirdly, because he expressly says (Topic. i, 9), that there are dialectical problems, about which we have nothing to say from reason, as, "whether the world is eternal."

Reply Obj. 1: Before the world existed it was possible for the world to be, not, indeed, according to a passive power which is matter, but according to the active power of God; and also, according as a thing is called absolutely possible, not in relation to any power, but from the sole habitude of the terms which are not repugnant to each other; in which sense possible is opposed to impossible, as appears from the Philosopher (Metaph. v, text 17).

Reply Obj. 2: Whatever has power always to be, from the fact of having that power, cannot sometimes be and sometimes not be; but before it received that power, it did not exist.

Hence this reason which is given by Aristotle (De Coelo i, text 120) does not prove simply that incorruptible things never began to exist; but that they did not begin by the natural mode whereby things generated and corruptible begin.

Reply Obj. 3: Aristotle (Phys. i, text 82) proves that matter is unbegotten from the fact that it has not a subject from which to derive its existence; and (De Coelo et Mundo i, text 20) he proves that heaven is ungenerated, forasmuch as it has no contrary from which to be generated. Hence it appears that no conclusion follows either way, except that matter and heaven did not begin by generation, as some said, especially about heaven. But we say that matter and heaven were produced into being by creation, as appears above (Q. 44, A. 1, ad 2).

Reply Obj. 4: The notion of a vacuum is not only "in which is nothing," but also implies a space capable of holding a body and in which there is not a body, as appears from Aristotle (Phys. iv, text 60). Whereas we hold that there was no place or space before the world was.

Reply Obj. 5: The first mover was always in the same state: but the first movable thing was not always so, because it began to be whereas hitherto it was not. This, however, was not through change, but by creation, which is not change, as said above (Q. 45, A. 2, ad 2). Hence it is evident that this reason, which Aristotle gives (Phys. viii), is valid against those who admitted the existence of eternal movable things, but not eternal movement, as appears from the opinions of Anaxagoras and Empedocles. But we hold that from the moment that movable things began to exist movement also existed.

Reply Obj. 6: The first agent is a voluntary agent. And although He had the eternal will to produce some effect, yet He did not produce an eternal effect. Nor is it necessary for some change to be presupposed, not even on account of imaginary time. For we must take into consideration the difference between a particular agent, that presupposes something and produces something else, and the universal agent, who produces the whole. The particular agent produces the form, and presupposes the matter; and hence it is necessary that it introduce the form in due proportion into a suitable matter. Hence it is correct to say that it introduces the form into such matter, and not into another, on account of the different kinds of matter. But it is not correct to say so of God Who produces form and matter together: whereas it is correct to say of Him that He produces matter fitting to the form and to the end. Now, a particular agent presupposes time just as it presupposes matter. Hence it is correctly described as acting in time "after" and not in time "before," according to an imaginary succession of time after time. But the universal agent who produces the thing and time also, is not correctly described as acting now, and not before, according to an imaginary succession of time succeeding time, as if time were presupposed to His action; but He must be considered as giving time to His effect as much as and when He willed, and according to what was fitting to demonstrate His power. For the world leads more evidently to the knowledge of the divine creating power, if it was not always, than if it had always been; since everything which was not always manifestly has a cause; whereas this is not so manifest of what always was.

Reply Obj. 7: As is stated (Phys. iv, text 99), "before" and "after" belong to time, according as they are in movement. Hence beginning and end in time must be taken in the same way as in movement. Now, granted the eternity of movement, it is necessary that any given moment in movement be a beginning and an end of movement; which need not be if movement be a beginning. The same applies to the "now" of time. Thus it appears that the idea of the instant "now," as being always the beginning and end of time, presupposes the eternity of time and movement. Hence Aristotle brings forward this reason (Phys. viii, text 10) against those who asserted the eternity of time, but denied the eternity of movement.

Reply Obj. 8: God is prior to the world by priority of duration. But the word "prior" signifies priority not of time, but of eternity. Or we may say that it signifies the eternity of imaginary time, and not of time really existing; thus, when we say that above heaven there is nothing, the word "above" signifies only an imaginary place, according as it is possible to imagine other dimensions beyond those of the heavenly body.

Reply Obj. 9: As the effect follows from the cause that acts by nature, according to the mode of its form, so likewise it follows from the voluntary agent, according to the form preconceived and determined by the agent, as appears from what was said above (Q. 19, A. 4; Q. 41, A. 2). Therefore, although God was from eternity the sufficient cause of the world, we should not say that the world was produced by Him, except as preordained by His will—that is, that it should have being after not being, in order more manifestly to declare its author.

Reply Obj. 10: Given the action, the effect follows according to the requirement of the form, which is the principle of action. But in agents acting by will, what is conceived and preordained is to be taken as the form, which is the principle of action. Therefore from the eternal action of God an eternal effect did not follow; but such an effect as God willed, an effect, to wit, which has being after not being.

SECOND ARTICLE [I, Q. 46, Art. 2]

Whether It Is an Article of Faith That the World Began?

Objection 1: It would seem that it is not an article of faith but a demonstrable conclusion that the world began. For everything that is made has a beginning of its duration. But it can be proved demonstratively that God is the effective cause of the world; indeed this is asserted by the more approved philosophers. Therefore it can be demonstratively proved that the world began.

Obj. 2: Further, if it is necessary to say that the world was made by God, it must therefore have been made from nothing or from something. But it was not made from something; otherwise the matter of the world would have preceded the world; against which are the arguments of Aristotle (De Coelo i), who held that heaven was ungenerated. Therefore it must be said that the world was made from nothing; and thus it has being after not being. Therefore it must have begun.

Obj. 3: Further, everything which works by intellect works from some principle, as appears in all kinds of craftsmen. But God acts by intellect: therefore His work has a principle. The world, therefore, which is His effect, did not always exist.

Obj. 4: Further, it appears manifestly that certain arts have developed, and certain countries have begun to be inhabited at some fixed time. But this would not be the case if the world had been always. Therefore it is manifest that the world did not always exist.

Obj. 5: Further, it is certain that nothing can be equal to God. But if the world had always been, it would be equal to God in duration. Therefore it is certain that the world did not always exist.

Obj. 6: Further, if the world always was, the consequence is that infinite days preceded this present day. But it is impossible to pass through an infinite medium. Therefore we should never have arrived at this present day; which is manifestly false.

Obj. 7: Further, if the world was eternal, generation also was eternal. Therefore one man was begotten of another in an infinite series. But the father is the efficient cause of the son (Phys. ii, text 5). Therefore in efficient causes there could be an infinite series, which is disproved (Metaph. ii, text 5).

Obj. 8: Further, if the world and generation always were, there have been an infinite number of men. But man's soul is immortal: therefore an infinite number of human souls would actually now exist, which is impossible. Therefore it can be known with certainty that the world began, and not only is it known by faith.

*On the contrary,* The articles of faith cannot be proved demonstratively, because faith is of things "that appear not" (Heb. 11:1). But that God is the Creator of the world: hence that the world began, is an article of faith; for we say, "I believe in one God," etc. And again, Gregory says (Hom. i in Ezech.), that Moses prophesied of the past, saying, "In the beginning God created heaven and earth": in which words the newness of the world is stated. Therefore the newness of the world is known only by revelation; and therefore it cannot be proved demonstratively.

*I answer that,* By faith alone do we hold, and by no demonstration can it be proved, that the world did not always exist, as was said above of the mystery of the Trinity (Q. 32, A. 1). The reason of this is that the newness of the world cannot be demonstrated on the part of the world itself. For the principle of demonstration is the essence of a thing. Now everything according to its species is abstracted from "here" and "now"; whence it is said that universals are everywhere and always. Hence it cannot be demonstrated that man, or heaven, or a stone were not always. Likewise neither can it be demonstrated on the part of the efficient cause, which acts by will. For the will of God cannot be investigated by reason, except as regards those things which God must will of necessity; and what He wills about creatures is not among these, as was said above (Q. 19, A. 3). But the divine will can be manifested by revelation, on which faith rests. Hence that the world began to exist is an object of faith, but not of demonstration or science. And it is useful to consider this, lest anyone, presuming to demonstrate what is of faith, should bring forward reasons that are not cogent, so as to give occasion to unbelievers to laugh, thinking that on such grounds we believe things that are of faith.

Reply Obj. 1: As Augustine says (De Civ. Dei xi, 4), the opinion of philosophers who asserted the eternity of the world was twofold. For some said that the substance of the world was not from God, which is an intolerable error; and therefore it is refuted by proofs that are cogent. Some, however, said that the world was eternal, although made by God. For they hold that the world has a beginning, not of time, but of creation, so that in a certain hardly intelligible way it was always made. "And they try to explain their meaning thus (De Civ. Dei x, 31): for as, if the foot were always in the dust from eternity, there would always be a footprint which without doubt was caused by him who trod on it, so also the world always was, because its Maker always existed." To understand this we must consider that the efficient cause, which acts by motion, of necessity precedes its effect in time; because the effect is only in the end of the action, and every agent must be the principle of action. But if the action is instantaneous and not successive, it is not necessary for the maker to be prior to the thing made in duration as appears in the case of illumination. Hence they say that it does not follow necessarily if God is the active cause of the world, that He should be prior to the world in duration; because creation, by which He produced the world, is not a successive change, as was said above (Q. 45, A. 2).

Reply Obj. 2: Those who would say that the world was eternal, would say that the world was made by God from nothing, not that it was made after nothing, according to what we understand by the word creation, but that it was not made from anything; and so also some of them do not reject the word creation, as appears from Avicenna (Metaph. ix, text 4).

Reply Obj. 3: This is the argument of Anaxagoras (as quoted in Phys. viii, text 15). But it does not lead to a necessary conclusion, except as to that intellect which deliberates in order to find out what should be done, which is like movement. Such is the human intellect, but not the divine intellect (Q. 14, AA. 7, 12).

Reply Obj. 4: Those who hold the eternity of the world hold that some region was changed an infinite number of times, from being uninhabitable to being inhabitable and "vice versa," and likewise they hold that the arts, by reason of various corruptions and accidents, were subject to an infinite variety of advance and decay. Hence Aristotle says (Meteor. i), that it is absurd from such particular changes to hold the opinion of the newness of the whole world.

Reply Obj. 5: Even supposing that the world always was, it would not be equal to God in eternity, as Boethius says (De Consol. v, 6); because the divine Being is all being simultaneously without succession; but with the world it is otherwise.

Reply Obj. 6: Passage is always understood as being from term to term. Whatever bygone day we choose, from it to the present day there is a finite number of days which can be passed through. The objection is founded on the idea that, given two extremes, there is an infinite number of mean terms.

Reply Obj. 7: In efficient causes it is impossible to proceed to infinity *per se* —thus, there cannot be an infinite number of causes that are *per se* required for a certain effect; for instance, that a stone be moved by a stick, the stick by the hand, and so on to infinity. But it is not impossible to proceed to infinity *accidentally* as regards efficient causes; for instance, if all the causes thus infinitely multiplied should have the order of only one cause, their multiplication being accidental, as an artificer acts by means of many hammers accidentally, because one after the other may be broken. It is accidental, therefore, that one particular hammer acts after the action of another; and likewise it is accidental to this particular man as generator to be generated by another man; for he generates as a man, and not as the son of another man. For all men generating hold one grade in efficient causes—viz. the grade of a particular generator. Hence it is not impossible for a man to be generated by man to infinity; but such a thing would be impossible if the generation of this man depended upon this man, and on an elementary body, and on the sun, and so on to infinity.

Reply Obj. 8: Those who hold the eternity of the world evade this reason in many ways. For some do not think it impossible for there to be an actual infinity of souls, as appears from the Metaphysics of Algazel, who says that such a thing is an accidental infinity. But this was disproved above (Q. 7, A. 4). Some say that the soul is corrupted with the body. And some say that of all souls only one will remain. But others, as Augustine says [*Serm. xiv, De Temp. 4, 5; De Haeres., haeres. 46; De Civ. Dei xii. 13], asserted on this account a circuit of souls—viz. that souls separated from their bodies return again thither after a course of time; a fuller consideration of which matters will be given later (Q. 75, A. 2; Q. 118, A. 6). But be it noted that this argument considers only a particular case. Hence one might say that the world was eternal, or at least some creature, as an angel, but not man. But we are considering the question in general, as to whether any creature can exist from eternity.

THIRD ARTICLE [I, Q. 46, Art. 3]

Whether the Creation of Things Was in the Beginning of Time?

Objection 1: It would seem that the creation of things was not in the beginning of time. For whatever is not in time, is not of any part of time. But the creation of things was not in time; for by the creation the substance of things was brought into being; and time does not measure the substance of things, and especially of incorporeal things. Therefore creation was not in the beginning of time.

Obj. 2: Further, the Philosopher proves (Phys. vi, text 40) that everything which is made, was being made; and so to be made implies a "before" and "after." But in the beginning of time, since it is indivisible, there is no "before" and "after." Therefore, since to be created is a kind of "being made," it appears that things were not created in the beginning of time.

Obj. 3: Further, even time itself is created. But time cannot be created in the beginning of time, since time is divisible, and the beginning of time is indivisible. Therefore, the creation of things was not in the beginning of time.

*On the contrary,* It is said (Gen. 1:1): "In the beginning God created heaven and earth."

*I answer that,* The words of Genesis, "In the beginning God created heaven and earth," are expounded in a threefold sense in order to exclude three errors. For some said that the world always was, and that time had no beginning; and to exclude this the words "In the beginning" are expounded—viz. "of time." And some said that there are two principles of creation, one of good things and the other of evil things, against which "In the beginning" is expounded—"in the Son." For as the efficient principle is appropriated to the Father by reason of power, so the exemplar principle is appropriated to the Son by reason of wisdom, in order that, as it is said (Ps. 103:24), "Thou hast made all things in wisdom," it may be understood that God made all things in the beginning—that is, in the Son; according to the word of the Apostle (Col. 1:16), "In Him"—viz. the Son—"were created all things." But others said that corporeal things were created by God through the medium of spiritual creation; and to exclude this it is expounded thus: "In the beginning"—i.e. before all things—"God created heaven and earth." For four things are stated to be created together—viz. the empyrean heaven, corporeal matter, by which is meant the earth, time, and the angelic nature.

Reply Obj. 1: Things are said to be created in the beginning of time, not as if the beginning of time were a measure of creation, but because together with time heaven and earth were created.

Reply Obj. 2: This saying of the Philosopher is understood "of being made" by means of movement, or as the term of movement. Because, since in every movement there is "before" and "after," before any one point in a given movement—that is, whilst anything is in the process of being moved and made, there is a "before" and also an "after," because what is in the beginning of movement or in its term is not in "being moved." But creation is neither movement nor the term of movement, as was said above (Q. 45, AA. 2, 3). Hence a thing is created in such a way that it was not being created before.

Reply Obj. 3: Nothing is made except as it exists. But nothing exists of time except "now." Hence time cannot be made except according to some "now"; not because in the first "now" is time, but because from it time begins.

# QUESTION 47

OF THE DISTINCTION OF THINGS IN GENERAL (In Three Articles)

After considering the production of creatures, we come to the consideration of the distinction of things. This consideration will be threefold—first, of the distinction of things in general; secondly, of the distinction of good and evil; thirdly, of the distinction of the spiritual and corporeal creature.

Under the first head, there are three points of inquiry:

(1) The multitude or distinction of things.

(2) Their inequality.

(3) The unity of the world.

FIRST ARTICLE [I, Q. 47, Art. 1]

Whether the Multitude and Distinction of Things Come from God?

Objection 1: It would seem that the multitude and distinction of things does not come from God. For one naturally always makes one. But God is supremely one, as appears from what precedes (Q. 11, A. 4). Therefore He produces but one effect.

Obj. 2: Further, the representation is assimilated to its exemplar. But God is the exemplar cause of His effect, as was said above (Q. 44, A. 3). Therefore, as God is one, His effect is one only, and not diverse.

Obj. 3: Further, the means are proportional to the end. But the end of the creation is one—viz. the divine goodness, as was shown above (Q. 44, A. 4). Therefore the effect of God is but one.

*On the contrary,* It is said (Gen. 1:4, 7) that God "divided the light from the darkness," and "divided waters from waters." Therefore the distinction and multitude of things is from God.

*I answer that,* The distinction of things has been ascribed to many causes. For some attributed the distinction to matter, either by itself or with the agent. Democritus, for instance, and all the ancient natural philosophers, who admitted no cause but matter, attributed it to matter alone; and in their opinion the distinction of things comes from chance according to the movement of matter. Anaxagoras, however, attributed the distinction and multitude of things to matter and to the agent together; and he said that the intellect distinguishes things by extracting what is mixed up in matter.

But this cannot stand, for two reasons. First, because, as was shown above (Q. 44, A. 2), even matter itself was created by God. Hence we must reduce whatever distinction comes from matter to a higher cause. Secondly, because matter is for the sake of the form, and not the form for the matter, and the distinction of things comes from their proper forms. Therefore the distinction of things is not on account of the matter; but rather, *on the contrary,* created matter is formless, in order that it may be accommodated to different forms.

Others have attributed the distinction of things to secondary agents, as did Avicenna, who said that God by understanding Himself, produced the first intelligence; in which, forasmuch as it was not its own being, there is necessarily composition of potentiality and act, as will appear later (Q. 50, A. 3). And so the first intelligence, inasmuch as it understood the first cause, produced the second intelligence; and in so far as it understood itself as in potentiality it produced the heavenly body, which causes movement, and inasmuch as it understood itself as having actuality it produced the soul of the heavens.

But this opinion cannot stand, for two reasons. First, because it was shown above (Q. 45, A. 5) that to create belongs to God alone, and hence what can be caused only by creation is produced by God alone—viz. all those things which are not subject to generation and corruption. Secondly, because, according to this opinion, the universality of things would not proceed from the intention of the first agent, but from the concurrence of many active causes; and such an effect we can describe only as being produced by chance. Therefore, the perfection of the universe, which consists of the diversity of things, would thus be a thing of chance, which is impossible.

Hence we must say that the distinction and multitude of things come from the intention of the first agent, who is God. For He brought things into being in order that His goodness might be communicated to creatures, and be represented by them; and because His goodness could not be adequately represented by one creature alone, He produced many and diverse creatures, that what was wanting to one in the representation of the divine goodness might be supplied by another. For goodness, which in God is simple and uniform, in creatures is manifold and divided and hence the whole universe together participates the divine goodness more perfectly, and represents it better than any single creature whatever.

And because the divine wisdom is the cause of the distinction of things, therefore Moses said that things are made distinct by the word of God, which is the concept of His wisdom; and this is what we read in Gen. 1:3, 4: "God said: Be light made ... And He divided the light from the darkness."

Reply Obj. 1: The natural agent acts by the form which makes it what it is, and which is only one in one thing; and therefore its effect is one only. But the voluntary agent, such as God is, as was shown above (Q. 19, A. 4), acts by an intellectual form. Since, therefore, it is not against God's unity and simplicity to understand many things, as was shown above (Q. 15, A. 2), it follows that, although He is one, He can make many things.

Reply Obj. 2: This reason would apply to the representation which reflects the exemplar perfectly, and which is multiplied by reason of matter only; hence the uncreated image, which is perfect, is only one. But no creature represents the first exemplar perfectly, which is the divine essence; and, therefore, it can be represented by many things. Still, according as ideas are called exemplars, the plurality of ideas corresponds in the divine mind to the plurality of things.

Reply Obj. 3: In speculative things the medium of demonstration, which demonstrates the conclusion perfectly, is one only; whereas probable means of proof are many. Likewise when operation is concerned, if the means be equal, so to speak, to the end, one only is sufficient. But the creature is not such a means to its end, which is God; and hence the multiplication of creatures is necessary.

SECOND ARTICLE [I, Q. 47, Art. 2]

Whether the Inequality of Things Is from God?

Objection 1: It would seem that the inequality of things is not from God. For it belongs to the best to produce the best. But among things that are best, one is not greater than another. Therefore, it belongs to God, Who is the Best, to make all things equal.

Obj. 2: Further, equality is the effect of unity (Metaph. v, text 20). But God is one. Therefore, He has made all things equal.

Obj. 3: Further, it is the part of justice to give unequal to unequal things. But God is just in all His works. Since, therefore, no inequality of things is presupposed to the operation whereby He gives being to things, it seems that He has made all things equal.

*On the contrary,* It is said (Ecclus. 33:7): "Why does one day excel another, and one light another, and one year another year, one sun another sun? [Vulg.: 'when all come of the sun']. By the knowledge of the Lord they were distinguished."

*I answer that,* When Origen wished to refute those who said that the distinction of things arose from the contrary principles of good and evil, he said that in the beginning all things were created equal by God. For he asserted that God first created only the rational creatures and all equal; and that inequality arose in them from free-will, some being turned to God more and some less, and others turned more and others less away from God. And so those rational creatures which were turned to God by free-will, were promoted to the order of angels according to the diversity of merits. And those who were turned away from God were bound down to bodies according to the diversity of their sin; and he said this was the cause of the creation and diversity of bodies. But according to this opinion, it would follow that the universality of bodily creatures would not be the effect of the goodness of God as communicated to creatures, but it would be for the sake of the punishment of sin, which is contrary to what is said: "God saw all the things that He had made, and they were very good" (Gen. 1:31). And, as Augustine says (De Civ. Dei ii, 3): "What can be more foolish than to say that the divine Architect provided this one sun for the one world, not to be an ornament to its beauty, nor for the benefit of corporeal things, but that it happened through the sin of one soul; so that, if a hundred souls had sinned, there would be a hundred suns in the world?"

Therefore it must be said that as the wisdom of God is the cause of the distinction of things, so the same wisdom is the cause of their inequality. This may be explained as follows. A twofold distinction is found in things; one is a formal distinction as regards things differing specifically; the other is a material distinction as regards things differing numerically only. And as the matter is on account of the form, material distinction exists for the sake of the formal distinction. Hence we see that in incorruptible things there is only one individual of each species, forasmuch as the species is sufficiently preserved in the one; whereas in things generated and corruptible there are many individuals of one species for the preservation of the species. Whence it appears that formal distinction is of greater consequence than material. Now, formal distinction always requires inequality, because as the Philosopher says (Metaph. viii, 10), the forms of things are like numbers in which species vary by addition or subtraction of unity. Hence in natural things species seem to be arranged in degrees; as the mixed things are more perfect than the elements, and plants than minerals, and animals than plants, and men than other animals; and in each of these one species is more perfect than others. Therefore, as the divine wisdom is the cause of the distinction of things for the sake of the perfection of the universe, so it is the cause of inequality. For the universe would not be perfect if only one grade of goodness were found in things.

Reply Obj. 1: It is part of the best agent to produce an effect which is best in its entirety; but this does not mean that He makes every part of the whole the best absolutely, but in proportion to the whole; in the case of an animal, for instance, its goodness would be taken away if every part of it had the dignity of an eye. Thus, therefore, God also made the universe to be best as a whole, according to the mode of a creature; whereas He did not make each single creature best, but one better than another. And therefore we find it said of each creature, "God saw the light that it was good" (Gen. 1:4); and in like manner of each one of the rest. But of all together it is said, "God saw all the things that He had made, and they were very good" (Gen. 1:31).

Reply Obj. 2: The first effect of unity is equality; and then comes multiplicity; and therefore from the Father, to Whom, according to Augustine (De Doctr. Christ. i, 5), is appropriated unity, the Son proceeds to Whom is appropriated equality, and then from Him the creature proceeds, to which belongs inequality; but nevertheless even creatures share in a certain equality—namely, of proportion.

Reply Obj. 3: This is the argument that persuaded Origen: but it holds only as regards the distribution of rewards, the inequality of which is due to unequal merits. But in the constitution of things there is no inequality of parts through any preceding inequality, either of merits or of the disposition of the matter; but inequality comes from the perfection of the whole. This appears also in works done by art; for the roof of a house differs from the foundation, not because it is made of other material; but in order that the house may be made perfect of different parts, the artificer seeks different material; indeed, he would make such material if he could.

THIRD ARTICLE [I, Q. 47, Art. 3]

Whether There Is Only One World?

Objection 1: It would seem that there is not only one world, but many. Because, as Augustine says (QQ. 83, qu. 46), it is unfitting to say that God has created things without a reason. But for the same reason He created one, He could create many, since His power is not limited to the creation of one world; but rather it is infinite, as was shown above (Q. 25, A. 2). Therefore God has produced many worlds.

Obj. 2: Further, nature does what is best and much more does God. But it is better for there to be many worlds than one, because many good things are better than a few. Therefore many worlds have been made by God.

Obj. 3: Further, everything which has a form in matter can be multiplied in number, the species remaining the same, because multiplication in number comes from matter. But the world has a form in matter. Thus as when I say "man" I mean the form, and when I say "this man," I mean the form in matter; so when we say "world," the form is signified, and when we say "this world," the form in the matter is signified. Therefore there is nothing to prevent the existence of many worlds.

*On the contrary,* It is said (John 1:10): "The world was made by Him," where the world is named as one, as if only one existed.

*I answer that,* The very order of things created by God shows the unity of the world. For this world is called one by the unity of order, whereby some things are ordered to others. But whatever things come from God, have relation of order to each other, and to God Himself, as shown above (Q. 11, A. 3; Q. 21, A. 1). Hence it must be that all things should belong to one world. Therefore those only can assert that many worlds exist who do not acknowledge any ordaining wisdom, but rather believe in chance, as Democritus, who said that this world, besides an infinite number of other worlds, was made from a casual concourse of atoms.

Reply Obj. 1: This reason proves that the world is one because all things must be arranged in one order, and to one end. Therefore from the unity of order in things Aristotle infers (Metaph. xii, text 52) the unity of God governing all; and Plato (Tim.), from the unity of the exemplar, proves the unity of the world, as the thing designed.

Reply Obj. 2: No agent intends material plurality as the end forasmuch as material multitude has no certain limit, but of itself tends to infinity, and the infinite is opposed to the notion of end. Now when it is said that many worlds are better than one, this has reference to material order. But the best in this sense is not the intention of the divine agent; forasmuch as for the same reason it might be said that if He had made two worlds, it would be better if He had made three; and so on to infinite.

Reply Obj. 3: The world is composed of the whole of its matter. For it is not possible for there to be another earth than this one, since every earth would naturally be carried to this central one, wherever it was. The same applies to the other bodies which are part of the world.

## QUESTION 48

THE DISTINCTION OF THINGS IN PARTICULAR (In Six Articles)

We must now consider the distinction of things in particular; and firstly the distinction of good and evil; and then the distinction of the spiritual and corporeal creatures.

Concerning the first, we inquire into evil and its cause.

Concerning evil, six points are to be considered:

(1) Whether evil is a nature?

(2) Whether evil is found in things?

(3) Whether good is the subject of evil?

(4) Whether evil totally corrupts good?

(5) The division of evil into pain and fault.

(6) Whether pain, or fault, has more the nature of evil?

FIRST ARTICLE [I, Q. 48, Art. 1]

Whether Evil Is a Nature?

Objection 1: It would seem that evil is a nature. For every genus is a nature. But evil is a genus; for the Philosopher says (Praedic. x) that "good and evil are not in a genus, but are genera of other things." Therefore evil is a nature.

Obj. 2: Further, every difference which constitutes a species is a nature. But evil is a difference constituting a species of morality; for a bad habit differs in species from a good habit, as liberality from illiberality. Therefore evil signifies a nature.

Obj. 3: Further, each extreme of two contraries is a nature. But evil and good are not opposed as privation and habit, but as contraries, as the Philosopher shows (Praedic. x) by the fact that between good and evil there is a medium, and from evil there can be a return to good. Therefore evil signifies a nature.

Obj. 4: Further, what is not, acts not. But evil acts, for it corrupts good. Therefore evil is a being and a nature.

Obj. 5: Further, nothing belongs to the perfection of the universe except what is a being and a nature. But evil belongs to the perfection of the universe of things; for Augustine says (Enchir. 10, 11) that the "admirable beauty of the universe is made up of all things. In which even what is called evil, well ordered and in its place, is the eminent commendation of what is good." Therefore evil is a nature.

*On the contrary,* Dionysius says (Div. Nom. iv), "Evil is neither a being nor a good."

*I answer that,* One opposite is known through the other, as darkness is known through light. Hence also what evil is must be known from the nature of good. Now, we have said above that good is everything appetible; and thus, since every nature desires its own being and its own perfection, it must be said also that the being and the perfection of any nature is good. Hence it cannot be that evil signifies being, or any form or nature. Therefore it must be that by the name of evil is signified the absence of good. And this is what is meant by saying that "evil is neither a being nor a good." For since being, as such, is good, the absence of one implies the absence of the other.

Reply Obj. 1: Aristotle speaks there according to the opinion of Pythagoreans, who thought that evil was a kind of nature; and therefore they asserted the existence of the genus of good and evil. For Aristotle, especially in his logical works, brings forward examples that in his time were probable in the opinion of some philosophers. Or, it may be said that, as the Philosopher says (Metaph. iv, text 6), "the first kind of contrariety is habit and privation," as being verified in all contraries; since one contrary is always imperfect in relation to another, as black in relation to white, and bitter in relation to sweet. And in this way good and evil are said to be genera not simply, but in regard to contraries; because, as every form has the nature of good, so every privation, as such, has the nature of evil.

Reply Obj. 2: Good and evil are not constitutive differences except in morals, which receive their species from the end, which is the object of the will, the source of all morality. And because good has the nature of an end, therefore good and evil are specific differences in moral things; good in itself, but evil as the absence of the due end. Yet neither does the absence of the due end by itself constitute a moral species, except as it is joined to the undue end; just as we do not find the privation of the substantial form in natural things, unless it is joined to another form. Thus, therefore, the evil which is a constitutive difference in morals is a certain good joined to the privation of another good; as the end proposed by the intemperate man is not the privation of the good of reason, but the delight of sense without the order of reason. Hence evil is not a constitutive difference as such, but by reason of the good that is annexed.

Reply Obj. 3: This appears from the above. For the Philosopher speaks there of good and evil in morality. Because in that respect, between good and evil there is a medium, as good is considered as something rightly ordered, and evil as a thing not only out of right order, but also as injurious to another. Hence the Philosopher says (Ethic. iv, i) that a "prodigal man is foolish, but not evil." And from this evil in morality, there may be a return to good, but not from any sort of evil, for from blindness there is no return to sight, although blindness is an evil.

Reply Obj. 4: A thing is said to act in a threefold sense. In one way, formally, as when we say that whiteness makes white; and in that sense evil considered even as a privation is said to corrupt good, forasmuch as it is itself a corruption or privation of good. In another sense a thing is said to act effectively, as when a painter makes a wall white. Thirdly, it is said in the sense of the final cause, as the end is said to effect by moving the efficient cause. But in these two ways evil does not effect anything of itself, that is, as a privation, but by virtue of the good annexed to it. For every action comes from some form; and everything which is desired as an end, is a perfection. And therefore, as Dionysius says (Div. Nom. iv): "Evil does not act, nor is it desired, except by virtue of some good joined to it: while of itself it is nothing definite, and beside the scope of our will and intention."

Reply Obj. 5: As was said above, the parts of the universe are ordered to each other, according as one acts on the other, and according as one is the end and exemplar of the other. But, as was said above, this can only happen to evil as joined to some good. Hence evil neither belongs to the perfection of the universe, nor does it come under the order of the same, except accidentally, that is, by reason of some good joined to it.

SECOND ARTICLE [I, Q. 48, Art. 2]

Whether Evil Is Found in Things?

Objection 1: It would seem that evil is not found in things. For whatever is found in things, is either something, or a privation of something, that is a "not-being." But Dionysius says (Div. Nom. iv) that "evil is distant from existence, and even more distant from non-existence." Therefore evil is not at all found in things.

Obj. 2: Further, "being" and "thing" are convertible. If therefore evil is a being in things, it follows that evil is a thing, which is contrary to what has been said (A. 1).

Obj. 3: Further, "the white unmixed with black is the most white," as the Philosopher says (Topic. iii, 4). Therefore also the good unmixed with evil is the greater good. But God makes always what is best, much more than nature does. Therefore in things made by God there is no evil.

*On the contrary,* On the above assumptions, all prohibitions and penalties would cease, for they exist only for evils.

*I answer that,* As was said above (Q. 47, AA. 1, 2), the perfection of the universe requires that there should be inequality in things, so that every grade of goodness may be realized. Now, one grade of goodness is that of the good which cannot fail. Another grade of goodness is that of the good which can fail in goodness, and this grade is to be found in existence itself; for some things there are which cannot lose their existence as incorruptible things, while some there are which can lose it, as things corruptible.

As, therefore, the perfection of the universe requires that there should be not only beings incorruptible, but also corruptible beings; so the perfection of the universe requires that there should be some which can fail in goodness, and thence it follows that sometimes they do fail. Now it is in this that evil consists, namely, in the fact that a thing fails in goodness. Hence it is clear that evil is found in things, as corruption also is found; for corruption is itself an evil.

Reply Obj. 1: Evil is distant both from simple being and from simple "not-being," because it is neither a habit nor a pure negation, but a privation.

Reply Obj. 2: As the Philosopher says (Metaph. v, text 14), being is twofold. In one way it is considered as signifying the entity of a thing, as divisible by the ten "predicaments"; and in that sense it is convertible with thing, and thus no privation is a being, and neither therefore is evil a being. In another sense being conveys the truth of a proposition which unites together subject and attribute by a copula, notified by this word "is"; and in this sense being is what answers to the question, "Does it exist?" and thus we speak of blindness as being in the eye; or of any other privation. In this way even evil can be called a being. Through ignorance of this distinction some, considering that things may be evil, or that evil is said to be in things, believed that evil was a positive thing in itself.

Reply Obj. 3: God and nature and any other agent make what is best in the whole, but not what is best in every single part, except in order to the whole, as was said above (Q. 47, A. 2). And the whole itself, which is the universe of creatures, is all the better and more perfect if some things in it can fail in goodness, and do sometimes fail, God not preventing this. This happens, firstly, because "it belongs to Providence not to destroy, but to save nature," as Dionysius says (Div. Nom. iv); but it belongs to nature that what may fail should sometimes fail; secondly, because, as Augustine says (Enchir. 11), "God is so powerful that He can even make good out of evil." Hence many good things would be taken away if God permitted no evil to exist; for fire would not be generated if air was not corrupted, nor would the life of a lion be preserved unless the ass were killed. Neither would avenging justice nor the patience of a sufferer be praised if there were no injustice.

THIRD ARTICLE [I, Q. 48, Art. 3]

Whether Evil Is in Good As in Its Subject?

Objection 1: It would seem that evil is not in good as its subject. For good is something that exists. But Dionysius says (Div. Nom. iv, 4) that "evil does not exist, nor is it in that which exists." Therefore, evil is not in good as its subject.

Obj. 2: Further, evil is not a being; whereas good is a being. But "non-being" does not require being as its subject. Therefore, neither does evil require good as its subject.

Obj. 3: Further, one contrary is not the subject of another. But good and evil are contraries. Therefore, evil is not in good as in its subject.

Obj. 4: Further, the subject of whiteness is called white. Therefore also the subject of evil is evil. If, therefore, evil is in good as in its subject, it follows that good is evil, against what is said (Isa. 5:20): "Woe to you who call evil good, and good evil!"

*On the contrary,* Augustine says (Enchiridion 14) that "evil exists only in good."

*I answer that,* As was said above (A. 1), evil imports the absence of good. But not every absence of good is evil. For absence of good can be taken in a privative and in a negative sense. Absence of good, taken negatively, is not evil; otherwise, it would follow that what does not exist is evil, and also that everything would be evil, through not having the good belonging to something else; for instance, a man would be evil who had not the swiftness of the roe, or the strength of a lion. But the absence of good, taken in a privative sense, is an evil; as, for instance, the privation of sight is called blindness.

Now, the subject of privation and of form is one and the same—viz. being in potentiality, whether it be being in absolute potentiality, as primary matter, which is the subject of the substantial form, and of privation of the opposite form; or whether it be being in relative potentiality, and absolute actuality, as in the case of a transparent body, which is the subject both of darkness and light. It is, however, manifest that the form which makes a thing actual is a perfection and a good; and thus every actual being is a good; and likewise every potential being, as such, is a good, as having a relation to good. For as it has being in potentiality, so has it goodness in potentiality. Therefore, the subject of evil is good.

Reply Obj. 1: Dionysius means that evil is not in existing things as a part, or as a natural property of any existing thing.

Reply Obj. 2: "Not-being," understood negatively, does not require a subject; but privation is negation in a subject, as the Philosopher says (Metaph. iv, text 4), and such "not-being" is an evil.

Reply Obj. 3: Evil is not in the good opposed to it as in its subject, but in some other good, for the subject of blindness is not "sight," but "animal." Yet, it appears, as Augustine says (Enchiridion 13), that the rule of dialectics here fails, where it is laid down that contraries cannot exist together. But this is to be taken as referring to good and evil in general, but not in reference to any particular good and evil. For white and black, sweet and bitter, and the like contraries, are only considered as contraries in a special sense, because they exist in some determinate genus; whereas good enters into every genus. Hence one good can coexist with the privation of another good.

Reply Obj. 4: The prophet invokes woe to those who say that good as such is evil. But this does not follow from what is said above, as is clear from the explanation given.

FOURTH ARTICLE [I, Q. 48, Art. 4]

Whether Evil Corrupts the Whole Good?

Objection 1: It would seem that evil corrupts the whole good. For one contrary is wholly corrupted by another. But good and evil are contraries. Therefore evil corrupts the whole good.

Obj. 2: Further, Augustine says (Enchiridion 12) that "evil hurts inasmuch as it takes away good." But good is all of a piece and uniform. Therefore it is wholly taken away by evil.

Obj. 3: Further, evil, as long as it lasts, hurts, and takes away good. But that from which something is always being removed, is at some time consumed, unless it is infinite, which cannot be said of any created good. Therefore evil wholly consumes good.

*On the contrary,* Augustine says (Enchiridion 12) that "evil cannot wholly consume good."

*I answer that,* Evil cannot wholly consume good. To prove this we must consider that good is threefold. One kind of good is wholly destroyed by evil, and this is the good opposed to evil, as light is wholly destroyed by darkness, and sight by blindness. Another kind of good is neither wholly destroyed nor diminished by evil, and that is the good which is the subject of evil; for by darkness the substance of the air is not injured. And there is also a kind of good which is diminished by evil, but is not wholly taken away; and this good is the aptitude of a subject to some actuality.

The diminution, however, of this kind of good is not to be considered by way of subtraction, as diminution in quantity, but rather by way of remission, as diminution in qualities and forms. The remission likewise of this habitude is to be taken as contrary to its intensity. For this kind of aptitude receives its intensity by the dispositions whereby the matter is prepared for actuality; which the more they are multiplied in the subject the more is it fitted to receive its perfection and form; and, *on the contrary,* it receives its remission by contrary dispositions which, the more they are multiplied in the matter, and the more they are intensified, the more is the potentiality remitted as regards the actuality.

Therefore, if contrary dispositions cannot be multiplied and intensified to infinity, but only to a certain limit, neither is the aforesaid aptitude diminished or remitted infinitely, as appears in the active and passive qualities of the elements; for coldness and humidity, whereby the aptitude of matter to the form of fire is diminished or remitted, cannot be infinitely multiplied. But if the contrary dispositions can be infinitely multiplied, the aforesaid aptitude is also infinitely diminished or remitted; yet, nevertheless, it is not wholly taken away, because its root always remains, which is the substance of the subject. Thus, if opaque bodies were interposed to infinity between the sun and the air, the aptitude of the air to light would be infinitely diminished, but still it would never be wholly removed while the air remained, which in its very nature is transparent. Likewise, addition in sin can be made to infinitude, whereby the aptitude of the soul to grace is more and more lessened; and these sins, indeed, are like obstacles interposed between us and God, according to Isa. 59:2: "Our sins have divided between us and God." Yet the aforesaid aptitude of the soul is not wholly taken away, for it belongs to its very nature.

Reply Obj. 1: The good which is opposed to evil is wholly taken away; but other goods are not wholly removed, as said above.

Reply Obj. 2: The aforesaid aptitude is a medium between subject and act. Hence, where it touches act, it is diminished by evil; but where it touches the subject, it remains as it was. Therefore, although good is like to itself, yet, on account of its relation to different things, it is not wholly, but only partially taken away.

Reply Obj. 3: Some, imagining that the diminution of this kind of good is like the diminution of quantity, said that just as the continuous is infinitely divisible, if the division be made in an ever same proportion (for instance, half of half, or a third of a third), so is it in the present case. But this explanation does not avail here. For when in a division we keep the same proportion, we continue to subtract less and less; for half of half is less than half of the whole. But a second sin does not necessarily diminish the above mentioned aptitude less than a preceding sin, but perchance either equally or more.

Therefore it must be said that, although this aptitude is a finite thing, still it may be so diminished infinitely, not *per se,* but accidentally; according as the contrary dispositions are also increased infinitely, as explained above.

FIFTH ARTICLE [I, Q. 48, Art. 5]

Whether Evil Is Adequately Divided into Pain* and Fault?

[*Pain here means "penalty": such was its original signification, being derived from "poena." In this sense we say "Pain of death, Pain of loss, Pain of sense."—Ed.]

Objection 1: It would seem that evil is not adequately divided into pain and fault. For every defect is a kind of evil. But in all creatures there is the defect of not being able to preserve their own existence, which nevertheless is neither a pain nor a fault. Therefore evil is inadequately divided into pain and fault.

Obj. 2: Further, in irrational creatures there is neither fault nor pain; but, nevertheless, they have corruption and defect, which are evils. Therefore not every evil is a pain or a fault.

Obj. 3: Further, temptation is an evil, but it is not a fault; for "temptation which involves no consent, is not a sin, but an occasion for the exercise of virtue," as is said in a gloss on 2 Cor. 12; not is it a pain; because temptation precedes the fault, and the pain follows afterwards. Therefore, evil is not sufficiently divided into pain and fault.

Obj. 4: *On the contrary,* It would seem that this division is superfluous: for, as Augustine says (Enchiridion 12), a thing is evil "because it hurts." But whatever hurts is penal. Therefore every evil comes under pain.

*I answer that,* Evil, as was said above (A. 3), is the privation of good, which chiefly and of itself consists in perfection and act. Act, however, is twofold; first, and second. The first act is the form and integrity of a thing; the second act is its operation. Therefore evil also is twofold. In one way it occurs by the subtraction of the form, or of any part required for the integrity of the thing, as blindness is an evil, as also it is an evil to be wanting in any member of the body. In another way evil exists by the withdrawal of the due operation, either because it does not exist, or because it has not its due mode and order. But because good in itself is the object of the will, evil, which is the privation of good, is found in a special way in rational creatures which have a will. Therefore the evil which comes from the withdrawal of the form and integrity of the thing, has the nature of a pain; and especially so on the supposition that all things are subject to divine providence and justice, as was shown above (Q. 22, A. 2); for it is of the very nature of a pain to be against the will. But the evil which consists in the subtraction of the due operation in voluntary things has the nature of a fault; for this is imputed to anyone as a fault to fail as regards perfect action, of which he is master by the will. Therefore every evil in voluntary things is to be looked upon as a pain or a fault.

Reply Obj. 1: Because evil is the privation of good, and not a mere negation, as was said above (A. 3), therefore not every defect of good is an evil, but the defect of the good which is naturally due. For the want of sight is not an evil in a stone, but it is an evil in an animal; since it is against the nature of a stone to see. So, likewise, it is against the nature of a creature to be preserved in existence by itself, because existence and conservation come from one and the same source. Hence this kind of defect is not an evil as regards a creature.

Reply Obj. 2: Pain and fault do not divide evil absolutely considered, but evil that is found in voluntary things.

Reply Obj. 3: Temptation, as importing provocation to evil, is always an evil of fault in the tempter; but in the one tempted it is not, properly speaking, a fault; unless through the temptation some change is wrought in the one who is tempted; for thus is the action of the agent in the patient. And if the tempted is changed to evil by the tempter he falls into fault.

Reply Obj. 4: In answer to the opposite argument, it must be said that the very nature of pain includes the idea of injury to the agent in himself, whereas the idea of fault includes the idea of injury to the agent in his operation; and thus both are contained in evil, as including the idea of injury.

SIXTH ARTICLE [I, Q. 48, Art. 6]

Whether Pain Has the Nature of Evil More Than Fault Has?

Objection 1: It would seem that pain has more

of evil than fault. For fault is to pain what merit is to reward. But reward has more good than merit, as its end. Therefore pain has more evil in it than fault has.

Obj. 2: Further, that is the greater evil which is opposed to the greater good. But pain, as was said above (A. 5), is opposed to the good of the agent, while fault is opposed to the good of the action. Therefore, since the agent is better than the action, it seems that pain is worse than fault.

Obj. 3: Further, the privation of the end is a pain consisting in forfeiting the vision of God; whereas the evil of fault is privation of the order to the end. Therefore pain is a greater evil than fault.

*On the contrary,* A wise workman chooses a less evil in order to prevent a greater, as the surgeon cuts off a limb to save the whole body. But divine wisdom inflicts pain to prevent fault. Therefore fault is a greater evil than pain.

*I answer that,* Fault has the nature of evil more than pain has; not only more than pain of sense, consisting in the privation of corporeal goods, which kind of pain appeals to most men; but also more than any kind of pain, thus taking pain in its most general meaning, so as to include privation of grace or glory.

There is a twofold reason for this. The first is that one becomes evil by the evil of fault, but not by the evil of pain, as Dionysius says (Div. Nom. iv): "To be punished is not an evil; but it is an evil to be made worthy of punishment." And this because, since good absolutely considered consists in act, and not in potentiality, and the ultimate act is operation, or the use of something possessed, it follows that the absolute good of man consists in good operation, or the good use of something possessed. Now we use all things by the act of the will. Hence from a good will, which makes a man use well what he has, man is called good, and from a bad will he is called bad. For a man who has a bad will can use ill even the good he has, as when a grammarian of his own will speaks incorrectly. Therefore, because the fault itself consists in the disordered act of the will, and the pain consists in the privation of something used by the will, fault has more of evil in it than pain has.

The second reason can be taken from the fact that God is the author of the evil of pain, but not of the evil of fault. And this is because the evil of pain takes away the creature's good, which may be either something created, as sight, destroyed by blindness, or something uncreated, as by being deprived of the vision of God, the creature forfeits its uncreated good. But the evil of fault is properly opposed to uncreated good; for it is opposed to the fulfilment of the divine will, and to divine love, whereby the divine good is loved for itself, and not only as shared by the creature. Therefore it is plain that fault has more evil in it than pain has.

Reply Obj. 1: Although fault results in pain, as merit in reward, yet fault is not intended on account of the pain, as merit is for the reward; but rather, *on the contrary,* pain is brought about so that the fault may be avoided, and thus fault is worse than pain.

Reply Obj. 2: The order of action which is destroyed by fault is the more perfect good of the agent, since it is the second perfection, than the good taken away by pain, which is the first perfection.

Reply Obj. 3: Pain and fault are not to be compared as end and order to the end; because one may be deprived of both of these in some way, both by fault and by pain; by pain, accordingly as a man is removed from the end and from the order to the end; by fault, inasmuch as this privation belongs to the action which is not ordered to its due end.

# QUESTION 49

THE CAUSE OF EVIL (In Three Articles)

We next inquire into the cause of evil. Concerning this there are three points of inquiry:

(1) Whether good can be the cause of evil?

(2) Whether the supreme good, God, is the cause of evil?

(3) Whether there be any supreme evil, which is the first cause of all evils?

FIRST ARTICLE [I, Q. 49, Art. 1]

Whether Good Can Be the Cause of Evil?

Objection 1: It would seem that good cannot be the cause of evil. For it is said (Matt. 7:18): "A good tree cannot bring forth evil fruit."

Obj. 2: Further, one contrary cannot be the cause of another. But evil is the contrary to good. Therefore good cannot be the cause of evil.

Obj. 3: Further, a deficient effect can proceed only from a deficient cause. But evil is a deficient effect. Therefore its cause, if it has one, is deficient. But everything deficient is an evil. Therefore the cause of evil can only be evil.

Obj. 4: Further, Dionysius says (Div. Nom. iv) that evil has no cause. Therefore good is not the cause of evil.

*On the contrary,* Augustine says (Contra Julian. i, 9): "There is no possible source of evil except good."

*I answer that,* It must be said that every evil in some way has a cause. For evil is the absence of the good, which is natural and due to a thing. But that anything fail from its natural and due disposition can come only from some cause drawing it out of its proper disposition. For a heavy thing is not moved upwards except by some impelling force; nor does an agent fail in its action except from some impediment. But only good can be a cause; because nothing can be a cause except inasmuch as it is a being, and every being, as such, is good.

And if we consider the special kinds of causes, we see that the agent, the form, and the end, import some kind of perfection which belongs to the notion of good. Even matter, as a potentiality to good, has the nature of good. Now that good is the cause of evil by way of the material cause was shown above (Q. 48, A. 3). For it was shown that good is the subject of evil. But evil has no formal cause, rather is it a privation of form; likewise, neither has it a final cause, but rather is it a privation of order to the proper end; since not only the end has the nature of good, but also the useful, which is ordered to the end. Evil, however, has a cause by way of an agent, not directly, but accidentally.

In proof of this, we must know that evil is caused in the action otherwise than in the effect. In the action evil is caused by reason of the defect of some principle of action, either of the principal or the instrumental agent; thus the defect in the movement of an animal may happen by reason of the weakness of the motive power, as in the case of children, or by reason only of the ineptitude of the instrument, as in the lame. On the other hand, evil is caused in a thing, but not in the proper effect of the agent, sometimes by the power of the agent, sometimes by reason of a defect, either of the agent or of the matter. It is caused by reason of the power or perfection of the agent when there necessarily follows on the form intended by the agent the privation of another form; as, for instance, when on the form of fire there follows the privation of the form of air or of water. Therefore, as the more perfect the fire is in strength, so much the more perfectly does it impress its own form, so also the more perfectly does it corrupt the contrary. Hence that evil and corruption befall air and water comes from the perfection of the fire: but this is accidental; because fire does not aim at the privation of the form of water, but at the bringing in of its own form, though by doing this it also accidentally causes the other. But if there is a defect in the proper effect of the fire—as, for instance, that it fails to heat—this comes either by defect of the action, which implies the defect of some principle, as was said above, or by the indisposition of the matter, which does not receive the action of the fire, the agent. But this very fact that it is a deficient being is accidental to good to which of itself it belongs to act. Hence it is true that evil in no way has any but an accidental cause; and thus is good the cause of evil.

Reply Obj. 1: As Augustine says (Contra Julian. i): "The Lord calls an evil will the evil tree, and a good will a good tree." Now, a good will does not produce a morally bad act, since it is from the good will itself that a moral act is judged to be good. Nevertheless the movement itself of an evil will is caused by the rational creature, which is good; and thus good is the cause of evil.

Reply Obj. 2: Good does not cause that evil which is contrary to itself, but some other evil: thus the goodness of the fire causes evil to the water, and man, good as to his nature, causes an act morally evil. And, as explained above (Q. 19, A. 9), this is by accident. Moreover, it does happen sometimes that one contrary causes another by accident: for instance, the exterior surrounding cold heats (the body) through the concentration of the inward heat.

Reply Obj. 3: Evil has a deficient cause in voluntary things otherwise than in natural things. For the natural agent produces the same kind of effect as it is itself, unless it is impeded by some exterior thing; and this amounts to some defect belonging to it. Hence evil never follows in the effect, unless some other evil pre-exists in the agent or in the matter, as was said above. But in voluntary things the defect of the action comes from the will actually deficient, inasmuch as it does not actually subject itself to its proper rule. This defect, however, is not a fault, but fault follows upon it from the fact that the will acts with this defect.

Reply Obj. 4: Evil has no direct cause, but only an accidental cause, as was said above.

SECOND ARTICLE [I, Q. 49, Art. 2]

Whether the Supreme Good, God, Is the Cause of Evil?

Objection 1: It would seem that the supreme good, God, is the cause of evil. For it is said (Isa. 45:5,7): "I am the Lord, and there is no other God, forming the light, and creating darkness, making peace, and creating evil." And Amos 3:6, "Shall there be evil in a city, which the Lord hath not done?"

Obj. 2: Further, the effect of the secondary cause is reduced to the first cause. But good is the cause of evil, as was said above (A. 1). Therefore, since God is the cause of every good, as was shown above (Q. 2, A. 3; Q. 6, AA. 1, 4), it follows that also every evil is from God.

Obj. 3: Further, as is said by the Philosopher (Phys. ii, text 30), the cause of both safety and danger of the ship is the same. But God is the cause of the safety of all things. Therefore He is the cause of all perdition and of all evil.

*On the contrary,* Augustine says (QQ. 83, qu. 21), that, "God is not the author of evil because He is not the cause of tending to not-being."

*I answer that,* As appears from what was said (A. 1), the evil which consists in the defect of action is always caused by the defect of the agent. But in God there is no defect, but the highest perfection, as was shown above (Q. 4, A. 1). Hence, the evil which consists in defect of action, or which is caused by defect of the agent, is not reduced to God as to its cause.

But the evil which consists in the corruption of some things is reduced to God as the cause. And this appears as regards both natural things and voluntary things. For it was said (A. 1) that some agent inasmuch as it produces by its power a form to which follows corruption and defect, causes by its power that corruption and defect. But it is manifest that the form which God chiefly intends in things created is the good of the order of the universe. Now, the order of the universe requires, as was said above (Q. 22, A. 2, ad 2; Q. 48, A. 2), that there should be some things that can, and do sometimes, fail. And thus God, by causing in things the good of the order of the universe, consequently and as it were by accident, causes the corruptions of things, according to 1 Kings 2:6: "The Lord killeth and maketh alive." But when we read that "God hath not made death" (Wis. 1:13), the sense is that God does not will death for its own sake. Nevertheless the order of justice belongs to the order of the universe; and this requires that penalty should be dealt out to sinners. And so God is the author of the evil which is penalty, but not of the evil which is fault, by reason of what is said above.

Reply Obj. 1: These passages refer to the evil of penalty, and not to the evil of fault.

Reply Obj. 2: The effect of the deficient secondary cause is reduced to the first non-deficient cause as regards what it has of being and perfection, but not as regards what it has of defect; just as whatever there is of motion in the act of limping is caused by the motive power, whereas what there is of obliqueness in it does not come from the motive power, but from the curvature of the leg. And, likewise, whatever there is of being and action in a bad action, is reduced to God as the cause; whereas whatever defect is in it is not caused by God, but by the deficient secondary cause.

Reply Obj. 3: The sinking of a ship is attributed to the sailor as the cause, from the fact that he does not fulfil what the safety of the ship requires; but God does not fail in doing what is necessary for the safety of all. Hence there is no parity.

THIRD ARTICLE [I, Q. 49, Art. 3]

Whether There Be One Supreme Evil Which Is the Cause of Every Evil?

Objection 1: It would seem that there is one supreme evil which is the cause of every evil. For contrary effects have contrary causes. But contrariety is found in things, according to Ecclus. 33:15: "Good is set against evil, and life against death; so also is the sinner against a just man." Therefore there are many contrary principles, one of good, the other of evil.

Obj. 2: Further, if one contrary is in nature, so is the other. But the supreme good is in nature, and is the cause of every good, as was shown above (Q. 2, A. 3; Q. 6, AA. 2, 4). Therefore, also, there is a supreme evil opposed to it as the cause of every evil.

Obj. 3: Further, as we find good and better things, so we find evil and worse. But good and better are so considered in relation to what is best. Therefore evil and worse are so considered in relation to some supreme evil.

Obj. 4: Further, everything participated is reduced to what is essential. But things which are evil among us are evil not essentially, but by participation. Therefore we must seek for some supreme essential evil, which is the cause of every evil.

Obj. 5: Further, whatever is accidental is reduced to that which is *per se*. But good is the accidental cause of evil. Therefore, we must suppose some supreme evil which is the per se cause of evils. Nor can it be said that evil has no per se cause, but only an accidental cause; for it would then follow that evil would not exist in the many, but only in the few.

Obj. 6: Further, the evil of the effect is reduced to the evil of the cause; because the deficient effect comes from the deficient cause, as was said above (AA. 1, 2). But we cannot proceed to infinity in this matter. Therefore, we must suppose one first evil as the cause of every evil.

*On the contrary,* The supreme good is the cause of every being, as was shown above (Q. 2, A. 3; Q. 6, A. 4). Therefore there cannot be any principle opposed to it as the cause of evils.

*I answer that,* It appears from what precedes that there is no one first principle of evil, as there is one first principle of good.

First, indeed, because the first principle of good is essentially good, as was shown above (Q. 6, AA. 3, 4). But nothing can be essentially bad. For it was shown above that every being, as such, is good (Q. 5, A. 3); and that evil can exist only in good as in its subject (Q. 48, A. 3).

Secondly, because the first principle of good is the highest and perfect good which pre-contains in itself all goodness, as shown above (Q. 6, A. 2). But there cannot be a supreme evil; because, as was shown above (Q. 48, A. 4), although evil always lessens good, yet it never wholly consumes it; and thus, while good ever remains, nothing can be wholly and perfectly bad. Therefore, the Philosopher says (Ethic. iv, 5) that "if the wholly evil could be, it would destroy itself"; because all good being destroyed (which it need be for something to be wholly evil), evil itself would be taken away, since its subject is good.

Thirdly, because the very nature of evil is against the idea of a first principle; both because every evil is caused by good, as was shown above (A. 1), and because evil can be only an accidental cause, and thus it cannot be the first cause, for the accidental cause is subsequent to the direct cause.

Those, however, who upheld two first principles, one good and the other evil, fell into this error from the same cause, whence also arose other strange notions of the ancients; namely, because they failed to consider the universal cause of all being, and considered only the particular causes of particular effects. For on that account, if they found a thing hurtful to something by the power of its own nature, they thought that the very nature of that thing was evil; as, for instance, if one should say that the nature of fire was evil because it burnt the house of a poor man. The judgment, however, of the goodness of anything does not depend upon its order to any particular thing, but rather upon what it is in itself, and on its order to the whole universe, wherein every part has its own perfectly ordered place, as was said above (Q. 47, A. 2, ad 1).

Likewise, because they found two contrary particular causes of two contrary particular effects, they did not know how to reduce these contrary particular causes to the universal common cause; and therefore they extended the contrariety of causes even to the first principles. But since all contraries agree in something common, it is necessary to search for one common cause for them above their own contrary proper causes; as above the contrary qualities of the elements exists the power of a heavenly body; and above all things that exist, no matter how, there exists one first principle of being, as was shown above (Q. 2, A. 3).

Reply Obj. 1: Contraries agree in one genus, and they also agree in the nature of being; and therefore, although they have contrary particular causes, nevertheless we must come at last to one first common cause.

Reply Obj. 2: Privation and habit belong naturally to the same subject. Now the subject of privation is a being in potentiality, as was said above (Q. 48, A. 3). Hence, since evil is privation of good, as appears from what was said above (Q. 48, AA. 1, 2, 3), it is opposed to that good which has some potentiality, but not to the supreme good, who is pure act.

Reply Obj. 3: Increase in intensity is in proportion to the nature of a thing. And as the form is a perfection, so privation removes a perfection. Hence every form, perfection, and good is intensified by approach to the perfect term; but privation and evil by receding from that term. Hence a thing is not said to be evil and worse, by reason of access to the supreme evil, in the same way as it is said to be good and better, by reason of access to the supreme good.

Reply Obj. 4: No being is called evil by participation, but by privation of participation. Hence it is not necessary to reduce it to any essential evil.

Reply Obj. 5: Evil can only have an accidental cause, as was shown above (A. 1). Hence reduction to any 'per se' cause of evil is impossible. And to say that evil is in the greater number is simply false. For things which are generated and corrupted, in which alone can there be natural evil, are the smaller part of the whole universe. And again, in every species the defect of nature is in the smaller number. In man alone does evil appear as in the greater number; because the good of man as regards the senses is not the good of man as man—that is, in regard to reason; and more men seek good in regard to the senses than good according to reason.

Reply Obj. 6: In the causes of evil we do not proceed to infinity, but reduce all evils to some good cause, whence evil follows accidentally.

TREATISE ON THE ANGELS (QQ. 50-64)

# QUESTION 50

OF THE SUBSTANCE OF THE ANGELS ABSOLUTELY CONSIDERED (In Five Articles)

Now we consider the distinction of corporeal and spiritual creatures: firstly, the purely spiritual creature which in Holy Scripture is called angel; secondly, the creature wholly corporeal; thirdly, the composite creature, corporeal and spiritual, which is man.

Concerning the angels, we consider first what belongs to their substance; secondly, what belongs to their intellect; thirdly, what belongs to their will; fourthly, what belongs to their creation.

Their substance we consider absolutely and in relation to corporeal things.

Concerning their substance absolutely considered, there are five points of inquiry:

(1) Whether there is any entirely spiritual creature, altogether incorporeal?

(2) Supposing that an angel is such, we ask whether it is composed of matter and form?

(3) We ask concerning their number.

(4) Of their difference from each other.

(5) Of their immortality or incorruptibility.

FIRST ARTICLE [I, Q. 50, Art. 1]

Whether an Angel Is Altogether Incorporeal?

Objection 1: It would seem that an angel is not entirely incorporeal. For what is incorporeal only as regards ourselves, and not in relation to God, is not absolutely incorporeal. But Damascene says (De Fide Orth. ii) that "an angel is said to be incorporeal and immaterial as regards us; but compared to God it is corporeal and material. Therefore he is not simply incorporeal."

Obj. 2: Further, nothing is moved except a body, as the Philosopher says (Phys. vi, text 32). But Damascene says (De Fide Orth. ii) that "an angel is an ever movable intellectual substance." Therefore an angel is a corporeal substance.

Obj. 3: Further, Ambrose says (De Spir. Sanct. i, 7): "Every creature is limited within its own nature." But to be limited belongs to bodies. Therefore, every creature is corporeal. Now angels are God's creatures, as appears from Ps. 148:2: "Praise ye" the Lord, "all His angels"; and, farther on (verse 4), "For He spoke, and they were made; He commanded, and they were created." Therefore angels are corporeal.

*On the contrary,* It is said (Ps. 103:4): "Who makes His angels spirits."

*I answer that,* There must be some incorporeal creatures. For what is principally intended by God in creatures is good, and this consists in assimilation to God Himself. And the perfect assimilation of an effect to a cause is accomplished when the effect imitates the cause according to that whereby the cause produces the effect; as heat makes heat. Now, God produces the creature by His intellect and will (Q. 14, A. 8; Q. 19, A. 4). Hence the perfection of the universe requires that there should be intellectual creatures. Now intelligence cannot be the action of a body, nor of any corporeal faculty; for every body is limited to "here" and "now." Hence the perfection of the universe requires the existence of an incorporeal creature.

The ancients, however, not properly realizing the force of intelligence, and failing to make a proper distinction between sense and intellect, thought that nothing existed in the world but what could be apprehended by sense and imagination. And because bodies alone fall under imagination, they supposed that no being existed except bodies, as the Philosopher observes (Phys. iv, text 52,57). Thence came the error of the Sadducees, who said there was no spirit (Acts 23:8).

But the very fact that intellect is above sense is a reasonable proof that there are some incorporeal things comprehensible by the intellect alone.

Reply Obj. 1: Incorporeal substances rank between God and corporeal creatures. Now the medium compared to one extreme appears to be the other extreme, as what is tepid compared to heat seems to be cold; and thus it is said that angels, compared to God, are material and corporeal, not, however, as if anything corporeal existed in them.

Reply Obj. 2: Movement is there taken in the sense in which it is applied to intelligence and will. Therefore an angel is called an ever mobile substance, because he is ever actually intelligent, and not as if he were sometimes actually and sometimes potentially, as we are. Hence it is clear that the objection rests on an equivocation.

Reply Obj. 3: To be circumscribed by local limits belongs to bodies only; whereas to be circumscribed by essential limits belongs to all creatures, both corporeal and spiritual. Hence Ambrose says (De Spir. Sanct. i, 7) that "although some things are not contained in corporeal place, still they are none the less circumscribed by their substance."

SECOND ARTICLE [I, Q. 50, Art. 2]

Whether an Angel Is Composed of Matter and Form?

Objection 1: It would seem that an angel is composed of matter and form. For everything which is contained under any genus is composed of the genus, and of the difference which added to the genus makes the species. But the genus comes from the matter, and the difference from the form (Metaph. xiii, text 6). Therefore everything which is in a genus is composed of matter and form. But an angel is in the genus of substance. Therefore he is composed of matter and form.

Obj. 2: Further, wherever the properties of matter exist, there is matter. Now the properties of matter are to receive and to substand; whence Boethius says (De Trin.) that "a simple form cannot be a subject": and the above properties are found in the angel. Therefore an angel is composed of matter and form.

Obj. 3: Further, form is act. So what is form only is pure act. But an angel is not pure act, for this belongs to God alone. Therefore an angel is not form only, but has a form in matter.

Obj. 4: Further, form is properly limited and perfected by matter. So the form which is not in matter is an infinite form. But the form of an angel is not infinite, for every creature is finite. Therefore the form of an angel is in matter.

*On the contrary,* Dionysius says (Div. Nom. iv): "The first creatures are understood to be as immaterial as they are incorporeal."

*I answer that,* Some assert that the angels are composed of matter and form; which opinion Avicebron endeavored to establish in his book of the *Fount of Life.* For he supposes that whatever things are distinguished by the intellect are really distinct. Now as regards incorporeal substance, the intellect apprehends that which distinguishes it from corporeal substance, and that which it has in common with it. Hence he concludes that what distinguishes incorporeal from corporeal substance is a kind of form to it, and whatever is subject to this distinguishing form, as it were something common, is its matter. Therefore, he asserts the universal matter of spiritual and corporeal things is the same; so that it must be understood that the form of incorporeal substance is impressed in the matter of spiritual things, in the same way as the form of quantity is impressed in the matter of corporeal things.

But one glance is enough to show that there cannot be one matter of spiritual and of corporeal things. For it is not possible that a spiritual and a corporeal form should be received into the same part of matter, otherwise one and the same thing would be corporeal and spiritual. Hence it would follow that one part of matter receives the corporeal form, and another receives the spiritual form. Matter, however, is not divisible into parts except as regarded under quantity; and without quantity substance is indivisible, as Aristotle says (Phys. i, text 15). Therefore it would follow that the matter of spiritual things is subject to quantity; which cannot be. Therefore it is impossible that corporeal and spiritual things should have the same matter.

It is, further, impossible for an intellectual substance to have any kind of matter. For the operation belonging to anything is according to the mode of its substance. Now to understand is an altogether immaterial operation, as appears from its object, whence any act receives its species and nature. For a thing is understood according to its degree of immateriality; because forms that exist in matter are individual forms which the intellect cannot apprehend as such. Hence it must be that every individual substance is altogether immaterial.

But things distinguished by the intellect are not necessarily distinguished in reality; because the intellect does not apprehend things according to their mode, but according to its own mode. Hence material things which are below our intellect exist in our intellect in a simpler mode than they exist in themselves. Angelic substances, on the other hand, are above our intellect; and hence our intellect cannot attain to apprehend them, as they are in themselves, but by its own mode, according as it apprehends composite things; and in this way also it apprehends God (Q. 3).

Reply Obj. 1: It is difference which constitutes the species. Now everything is constituted in a species according as it is determined to some special grade of being because "the species of things are like numbers," which differ by addition and subtraction of unity, as the Philosopher says (Metaph. viii, text 10). But in material things there is one thing which determines to a special grade, and that is the form; and another thing which is determined, and this is the matter; and hence from the latter the genus is derived, and from the former the "difference." Whereas in immaterial things there is no separate determinator and thing determined; each thing by its own self holds a determinate grade in being; and therefore in them genus and "difference" are not derived from different things, but from one and the same. Nevertheless, this differs in our mode of conception; for, inasmuch as our intellect considers it as indeterminate, it derives the idea of their genus; and inasmuch as it considers it determinately, it derives the idea of their "difference."

Reply Obj. 2: This reason is given in the book on the Fount of Life, and it would be cogent, supposing that the receptive mode of the intellect and of matter were the same. But this is clearly false. For matter receives the form, that thereby it may be constituted in some species, either of air, or of fire, or of something else. But the intellect does not receive the form in the same way; otherwise the opinion of Empedocles (De Anima i, 5, text 26) would be true, to the effect that we know earth by earth, and fire by fire. But the intelligible form is in the intellect according to the very nature of a form; for as such is it so known by the intellect. Hence such a way of receiving is not that of matter, but of an immaterial substance.

Reply Obj. 3: Although there is no composition of matter and form in an angel, yet there is act and potentiality. And this can be made evident if we consider the nature of material things which contain a twofold composition. The first is that of form and matter, whereby the nature is constituted. Such a composite nature is not its own existence but existence is its act. Hence the nature itself is related to its own existence as potentiality to act. Therefore if there be no matter, and supposing that the form itself subsists without matter, there nevertheless still remains the relation of the form to its very existence, as of potentiality to act. And such a kind of composition is understood to be in the angels; and this is what some say, that an angel is composed of, "whereby he is," and "what is," or "existence," and "what is," as Boethius says. For "what is," is the form itself subsisting; and the existence itself is whereby the substance is; as the running is whereby the runner runs. But in God "existence" and "what is" are not different as was explained above (Q. 3, A. 4). Hence God alone is pure act.

Reply Obj. 4: Every creature is simply finite, inasmuch as its existence is not absolutely subsisting, but is limited to some nature to which it belongs. But there is nothing against a creature being considered relatively infinite. Material creatures are infinite on the part of matter, but finite in their form, which is limited by the matter which receives it. But immaterial created substances are finite in their being; whereas they are infinite in the sense that their forms are not received in anything else; as if we were to say, for example, that whiteness existing separate is infinite as regards the nature of whiteness, forasmuch as it is not contracted to any one subject; while its "being" is finite as determined to some one special nature.

Whence it is said (De Causis, prop. 16) that "intelligence is finite from above," as receiving its being from above itself, and is "infinite from below," as not received in any matter.

THIRD ARTICLE [I, Q. 50, Art. 3]

Whether the Angels Exist in Any Great Number?

Objection 1: It would seem that the angels are not in great numbers. For number is a species of quantity, and follows the division of a continuous body. But this cannot be in the angels, since they are incorporeal, as was shown above (A. 1). Therefore the angels cannot exist in any great number.

Obj. 2: Further, the more a thing approaches to unity, so much the less is it multiplied, as is evident in numbers. But among other created natures the angelic nature approaches nearest to God. Therefore since God is supremely one, it seems that there is the least possible number in the angelic nature.

Obj. 3: Further, the proper effect of the separate substances seems to be the movements of the heavenly bodies. But the movements of the heavenly bodies fall within some small determined number, which we can apprehend. Therefore the angels are not in greater number than the movements of the heavenly bodies.

Obj. 4: Dionysius says (Div. Nom. iv) that "all intelligible and intellectual substances subsist because of the rays of the divine goodness." But a ray is only multiplied according to the different things that receive it. Now it cannot be said that their matter is receptive of an intelligible ray, since intellectual substances are immaterial, as was shown above

(A. 2). Therefore it seems that the multiplication of intellectual substances can only be according to the requirements of the first bodies—that is, of the heavenly ones, so that in some way the shedding form of the aforesaid rays may be terminated in them; and hence the same conclusion is to be drawn as before.

*On the contrary,* It is said (Dan. 7:10): "Thousands of thousands ministered to Him, and ten thousands times a hundred thousand stood before Him."

*I answer that,* There have been various opinions with regard to the number of the separate substances. Plato contended that the separate substances are the species of sensible things; as if we were to maintain that human nature is a separate substance of itself: and according to this view it would have to be maintained that the number of the separate substances is the number of the species of sensible things. Aristotle, however, rejects this view (Metaph. i, text 31) because matter is of the very nature of the species of sensible things. Consequently the separate substances cannot be the exemplar species of these sensible things; but have their own fixed natures, which are higher than the natures of sensible things. Nevertheless Aristotle held (Metaph. xi, text 43) that those more perfect natures bear relation to these sensible things, as that of mover and end; and therefore he strove to find out the number of the separate substances according to the number of the first movements.

But since this appears to militate against the teachings of Sacred Scripture, Rabbi Moses the Jew, wishing to bring both into harmony, held that the angels, in so far as they are styled immaterial substances, are multiplied according to the number of heavenly movements or bodies, as Aristotle held (Metaph. xi, text 43); while he contended that in the Scriptures even men bearing a divine message are styled angels; and again, even the powers of natural things, which manifest God's almighty power. It is, however, quite foreign to the custom of the Scriptures for the powers of irrational things to be designated as angels.

Hence it must be said that the angels, even inasmuch as they are immaterial substances, exist in exceeding great number, far beyond all material multitude. This is what Dionysius says (Coel. Hier. xiv): "There are many blessed armies of the heavenly intelligences, surpassing the weak and limited reckoning of our material numbers." The reason whereof is this, because, since it is the perfection of the universe that God chiefly intends in the creation of things, the more perfect some things are, in so much greater an excess are they created by God. Now, as in bodies such excess is observed in regard to their magnitude, so in things incorporeal is it observed in regard to their multitude. We see, in fact, that incorruptible bodies, exceed corruptible bodies almost incomparably in magnitude; for the entire sphere of things active and passive is something very small in comparison with the heavenly bodies. Hence it is reasonable to conclude that the immaterial substances as it were incomparably exceed material substances as to multitude.

Reply Obj. 1: In the angels number is not that of discrete quantity, brought about by division of what is continuous, but that which is caused by distinction of forms; according as multitude is reckoned among the transcendentals, as was said above (Q. 30, A. 3; Q. 11).

Reply Obj. 2: From the angelic nature being the nighest unto God, it must needs have least of multitude in its composition, but not so as to be found in few subjects.

Reply Obj. 3: This is Aristotle's argument (Metaph. xii, text 44), and it would conclude necessarily if the separate substances were made for corporeal substances. For thus the immaterial substances would exist to no purpose, unless some movement from them were to appear in corporeal things. But it is not true that the immaterial substances exist on account of the corporeal, because the end is nobler than the means to the end. Hence Aristotle says (Metaph. xii, text 44) that this is not a necessary argument, but a probable one. He was forced to make use of this argument, since only through sensible things can we come to know intelligible ones.

Reply Obj. 4: This argument comes from the opinion of such as hold that matter is the cause of the distinction of things; but this was refuted above (Q. 47, A. 1). Accordingly, the multiplication of the angels is not to be taken according to matter, nor according to bodies, but according to the divine wisdom devising the various orders of immaterial substances.

FOURTH ARTICLE [I, Q. 50, Art. 4]

Whether the Angels Differ in Species?

Objection 1: It would seem that the angels do not differ in species. For since the "difference" is nobler than the 'genus,' all things which agree in what is noblest in them, agree likewise in their ultimate constitutive difference; and so they are the same according to species. But all angels agree in what is noblest in them—that is to say, in intellectuality. Therefore all the angels are of one species.

Obj. 2: Further, more and less do not change a species. But the angels seem to differ only from one another according to more and less—namely, as one is simpler than another, and of keener intellect. Therefore the angels do not differ specifically.

Obj. 3: Further, soul and angel are contra-distinguished mutually from each other. But all souls are of the one species. So therefore are the angels.

Obj. 4: Further, the more perfect a thing is in nature, the more ought it to be multiplied. But this would not be so if there were but one individual under one species. Therefore there are many angels of one species.

*On the contrary,* In things of one species there is no such thing as "first" and "second" [prius et posterius], as the Philosopher says (Metaph. iii, text 2). But in the angels even of the one order there are first, middle, and last, as Dionysius says (Hier. Ang. x). Therefore the angels are not of the same species.

*I answer that,* Some have said that all spiritual substances, even souls, are of the one species. Others, again, that all the angels are of the one species, but not souls; while others allege that all the angels of one hierarchy, or even of one order, are of the one species.

But this is impossible. For such things as agree in species but differ in number, agree in form, but are distinguished materially. If, therefore, the angels be not composed of matter and form, as was said above (A. 2), it follows that it is impossible for two angels to be of one species; just as it would be impossible for there to be several whitenesses apart, or several humanities, since whitenesses are not several, except in so far as they are in several substances. And if the angels had matter, not even then could there be several angels of one species. For it would be necessary for matter to be the principle of distinction of one from the other, not, indeed, according to the division of quantity, since they are incorporeal, but according to the diversity of their powers; and such diversity of matter causes diversity not merely of species, but of genus.

Reply Obj. 1: "Difference" is nobler than genus, as the determined is more noble than the undetermined, and the proper than the common, but not as one nature is nobler than another; otherwise it would be necessary that all irrational animals be of the same species; or that there should be in them some form which is higher than the sensible soul. Therefore irrational animals differ in species according to the various determined degrees of sensitive nature; and in like manner all the angels differ in species according to the diverse degrees of intellectual nature.

Reply Obj. 2: More and less change the species, not according as they are caused by the intensity or remissness of one form, but according as they are caused by forms of diverse degrees; for instance, if we say that fire is more perfect than air: and in this way the angels are diversified according to more or less.

Reply Obj. 3: The good of the species preponderates over the good of the individual. Hence it is much better for the species to be multiplied in the angels than for individuals to be multiplied in the one species.

Reply Obj. 4: Numerical multiplication, since it can be drawn out infinitely, is not intended by the agent, but only specific multiplication, as was said above (Q. 47, A. 3). Hence the perfection of the angelic nature calls for the multiplying of species, but not for the multiplying of individuals in one species.

FIFTH ARTICLE [I, Q. 50, Art. 5]

Whether the Angels Are Incorruptible?

Objection 1: It would seem that the angels are not incorruptible; for Damascene, speaking of the angel, says (De Fide Orth. ii, 3) that he is "an intellectual substance, partaking of immortality by favor, and not by nature."

Obj. 2: Further, Plato says in the Timaeus: "O gods of gods, whose maker and father am I: You are indeed my works, dissoluble by nature, yet indissoluble because I so will it." But gods such as these can only be understood to be the angels. Therefore the angels are corruptible by their nature

Obj. 3: Further, according to Gregory (Moral. xvi), "all things would tend towards nothing, unless the hand of the Almighty preserved them." But what can be brought to nothing is corruptible. Therefore, since the angels were made by God, it would appear that they are corruptible of their own nature.

*On the contrary,* Dionysius says (Div. Nom. iv) that the intellectual substances "have unfailing life, being free from all corruption, death, matter, and generation."

*I answer that,* It must necessarily be maintained that the angels are incorruptible of their own nature. The reason for this is, that nothing is corrupted except by its form being separated from the matter. Hence, since an angel is a subsisting form, as is clear from what was said above (A. 2), it is impossible for its substance to be corruptible. For what belongs to anything considered in itself can never be separated from it; but what belongs to a thing, considered in relation to something else, can be separated, when that something else is taken away, in view of which it belonged to it. Roundness can never be taken from the circle, because it belongs to it of itself; but a bronze circle can lose roundness, if the bronze be deprived of its circular shape. Now to be belongs to a form considered in itself; for everything is an actual being according to its form: whereas matter is an actual being by the form. Consequently a subject composed of matter and form ceases to be actually when the form is separated from the matter. But if the form subsists in its own being, as happens in the angels, as was said above (A. 2), it cannot lose its being. Therefore, the angel's immateriality is the cause why it is incorruptible by its own nature.

A token of this incorruptibility can be gathered from its intellectual operation; for since everything acts according as it is actual, the operation of a thing indicates its mode of being. Now the species and nature of the operation is understood from the object. But an intelligible object, being above time, is everlasting. Hence every intellectual substance is incorruptible of its own nature.

Reply Obj. 1: Damascene is dealing with perfect immortality, which includes complete immutability; since "every change is a kind of death," as Augustine says (Contra Maxim. iii). The angels obtain perfect immutability only by favor, as will appear later (Q. 62).

Reply Obj. 2: By the expression 'gods' Plato understands the heavenly bodies, which he supposed to be made up of elements, and therefore dissoluble of their own nature; yet they are for ever preserved in existence by the Divine will.

Reply Obj. 3: As was observed above (Q. 44, A. 1) there is a kind of necessary thing which has a cause of its necessity. Hence it is not repugnant to a necessary or incorruptible being to depend for its existence on another as its cause. Therefore, when it is said that all things, even the angels, would lapse into nothing, unless preserved by God, it is not to be gathered therefrom that there is any principle of corruption in the angels; but that the nature of the angels is dependent upon God as its cause. For a thing is said to be corruptible not merely because God can reduce it to non-existence, by withdrawing His act of preservation; but also because it has some principle of corruption within itself, or some contrariety, or at least the potentiality of matter.

## QUESTION 51

OF THE ANGELS IN COMPARISON WITH BODIES (In Three Articles)

We next inquire about the angels in comparison with corporeal things; and in the first place about their comparison with bodies; secondly, of the angels in comparison with corporeal places; and, thirdly, of their comparison with local movement.

Under the first heading there are three points of inquiry:

(1) Whether angels have bodies naturally united to them?

(2) Whether they assume bodies?

(3) Whether they exercise functions of life in the bodies assumed?

FIRST ARTICLE [I, Q. 51, Art. 1]

Whether the Angels Have Bodies Naturally United to Them?

Objection 1: It would seem that angels have bodies naturally united to them. For Origen says (Peri Archon i): "It is God's attribute alone—that is, it belongs to the Father, the Son, and the Holy Ghost, as a property of nature, that He is understood to exist without any material substance and without any companionship of corporeal addition." Bernard likewise says (Hom. vi. super Cant.): "Let us assign incorporeity to God alone even as we do immortality, whose nature alone, neither for its own sake nor on account of anything else, needs the help of any corporeal organ. But it is clear that every created spirit needs corporeal substance." Augustine also says (Gen. ad lit. iii): "The demons are called animals of the atmosphere because their nature is akin to that of aerial bodies." But the nature of demons and angels is the same. Therefore angels have bodies naturally united to them.

Obj. 2: Further, Gregory (Hom. x in Ev.) calls an angel a rational animal. But every animal is composed of body and soul. Therefore angels have bodies naturally united to them.

Obj. 3: Further, life is more perfect in the angels than in souls. But the soul not only lives, but gives life to the body. Therefore the angels animate bodies which are naturally united to them.

*On the contrary,* Dionysius says (Div. Nom. iv) that "the angels are understood to be incorporeal."

*I answer that,* The angels have not bodies naturally united to them. For whatever belongs to any nature as an accident is not found universally in that nature; thus, for instance, to have wings, because it is not of the essence of an animal, does not belong to every animal. Now since to understand is not the act of a body, nor of any corporeal energy, as will be shown later (Q. 75, A. 2), it follows that to have a body united to it is not of the nature of an intellectual substance, as such; but it is accidental to some intellectual substance on account of something else. Even so it belongs to the human soul to be united to a body, because it is imperfect and exists potentially in the genus of intellectual substances, not having the fulness of knowledge in its own nature, but acquiring it from sensible things through the bodily senses, as will be explained later on (Q. 84, A. 6; Q. 89, A. 1). Now whenever we find something imperfect in any genus we must presuppose something perfect in that genus. Therefore in the intellectual nature there are some perfectly intellectual substances, which do not need to acquire knowledge from sensible things. Consequently not all intellectual substances are united to bodies; but some are quite separated from bodies, and these we call angels.

Reply Obj. 1: As was said above (Q. 50, A. 1) it was the opinion of some that every being is a body; and consequently some seem to have thought that there were no incorporeal substances existing except as united to bodies; so much so that some even held that God was the soul of the world, as Augustine tells us (De Civ. Dei vii). As this is contrary to Catholic Faith, which asserts that God is exalted above all things, according to Ps. 8:2: "Thy magnificence is exalted beyond the heavens"; Origen, while refusing to say such a thing of God, followed the above opinion of others regarding the other substances; being deceived here as he was also in many other points, by following the opinions of the ancient philosophers. Bernard's expression can be explained, that the created spirit needs some bodily instrument, which is not naturally united to it, but assumed for some purpose, as will be explained (A. 2). Augustine speaks, not as asserting the fact, but merely using the opinion of the Platonists, who maintained that there are some aerial animals, which they termed demons.

Reply Obj. 2: Gregory calls the angel a rational animal metaphorically, on account of the likeness to the rational nature.

Reply Obj. 3: To give life effectively is a perfection simply speaking; hence it belongs to God, as is said (1 Kings 2:6): "The Lord killeth, and maketh alive." But to give life formally belongs to a substance which is part of some nature, and which has not within itself the full nature of the species. Hence an intellectual substance which is not united to a body is more perfect than one which is united to a body.

SECOND ARTICLE [I, Q. 51, Art. 2]

Whether Angels Assume Bodies?

Objection 1: It would seem that angels do not assume bodies. For there is nothing superfluous in the work of an angel, as there is nothing of the kind in the work of nature. But it would be superfluous for the angels to assume bodies, because an angel has no need for a body, since his own power exceeds all bodily power. Therefore an angel does not assume a body.

Obj. 2: Further, every assumption is terminated in some union; because to assume implies a taking to oneself [ad se sumere]. But a body is not united to an angel as to a form, as stated (A. 1); while in so far as it is united to the angel as to a mover, it is not said to be assumed, otherwise it would follow that all bodies moved by the angels are assumed by them. Therefore the angels do not assume bodies.

Obj. 3: Further, angels do not assume bodies from the earth or water, or they could not suddenly disappear; nor again from fire, otherwise they would burn whatever things they touched; nor again from air, because air is without shape or color. Therefore the angels do not assume bodies.

*On the contrary,* Augustine says (De Civ. Dei xvi) that angels appeared to Abraham under assumed bodies.

*I answer that,* Some have maintained that the angels never assume bodies, but that all that we read in Scripture of apparitions of angels happened in prophetic vision—that is, according to imagination. But this is contrary to the intent of Scripture; for whatever is beheld in imaginary vision is only in the beholder's imagination, and consequently is not seen by everybody. Yet Divine Scripture from time to time introduces angels so apparent as to be seen commonly by all; just as the angels who appeared to Abraham were seen by him and by his whole family, by Lot, and by the citizens of Sodom; in like manner the angel who appeared to Tobias was seen by all present. From all this it is clearly shown that such apparitions were beheld by bodily vision, whereby the object seen exists outside the person beholding it, and can accordingly be seen by all. Now by such a vision only a body can be beheld. Consequently, since the angels are not bodies, nor have they bodies naturally united with them, as is clear from what has been said (A. 1; Q. 50, A. 1), it follows that they sometimes assume bodies.

Reply Obj. 1: Angels need an assumed body, not for themselves, but on our account; that by conversing familiarly with men they may give evidence of that intellectual companionship which men expect to have with them in the life to come. Moreover that angels assumed bodies under the Old Law was a figurative indication that the Word of God would take a human body; because all the apparitions in the Old Testament were ordained to that one whereby the Son of God appeared in the flesh.

Reply Obj. 2: The body assumed is united to the angel not as its form, nor merely as its mover, but as its mover represented by the assumed movable body. For as in the Sacred Scripture the properties of intelligible things are set forth by the likenesses of things sensible, in the same way by Divine power sensible bodies are so fashioned by angels as fittingly to represent the intelligible properties of an angel. And this is what we mean by an angel assuming a body.

Reply Obj. 3: Although air as long as it is in a state of rarefaction has neither shape nor color, yet when condensed it can both be shaped and colored as appears in the clouds. Even so the angels assume bodies of air, condensing it by the Divine power in so far as is needful for forming the assumed body.

THIRD ARTICLE [I, Q. 51, Art. 3]

Whether the Angels Exercise Functions of Life in the Bodies Assumed?

Objection 1: It would seem that the angels exercise functions of life in assumed bodies. For pretence is unbecoming in angels of truth. But it would be pretence if the body assumed by them, which seems to live and to exercise vital functions, did not possess these functions. Therefore the angels exercise functions of life in the assumed body.

Obj. 2: Further, in the works of the angels there is nothing without a purpose. But eyes, nostrils, and the other instruments of the senses, would be fashioned without a purpose in the body assumed by the angel, if he perceived nothing by their means. Consequently, the angel perceives by the assumed body; and this is the most special function of life.

Obj. 3: Further, to move hither and thither is one of the functions of life, as the Philosopher says (De Anima ii). But the angels are manifestly seen to move in their assumed bodies. For it was said (Gen. 18:16) that "Abraham walked with" the angels, who had appeared to him, "bringing them on the way"; and when Tobias said to the angel (Tob. 5:7, 8): "Knowest thou the way that leadeth to the city of Medes?" he answered: "I know it; and I have often walked through all the ways thereof." Therefore the angels often exercise functions of life in assumed bodies.

Obj. 4: Further, speech is the function of a living subject, for it is produced by the voice, while the voice itself is a sound conveyed from the mouth.

But it is evident from many passages of Sacred Scripture that angels spoke in assumed bodies. Therefore in their assumed bodies they exercise functions of life.

Obj. 5: Further, eating is a purely animal function. Hence the Lord after His Resurrection ate with His disciples in proof of having resumed life (Luke 24). Now when angels appeared in their assumed bodies they ate, and Abraham offered them food, after having previously adored them as God (Gen. 18). Therefore the angels exercise functions of life in assumed bodies.

Obj. 6: Further, to beget offspring is a vital act. But this has befallen the angels in their assumed bodies; for it is related: "After the sons of God went in to the daughters of men, and they brought forth children, these are the mighty men of old, men of renown" (Gen. 6:4). Consequently the angels exercised vital functions in their assumed bodies.

*On the contrary,* The bodies assumed by angels have no life, as was stated in the previous article (ad 3). Therefore they cannot exercise functions of life through assumed bodies.

*I answer that,* Some functions of living subjects have something in common with other operations; just as speech, which is the function of a living creature, agrees with other sounds of inanimate things, in so far as it is sound; and walking agrees with other movements, in so far as it is movement. Consequently vital functions can be performed in assumed bodies by the angels, as to that which is common in such operations; but not as to that which is special to living subjects; because, according to the Philosopher (De Somn. et Vig. i), "that which has the faculty has the action." Hence nothing can have a function of life except what has life, which is the potential principle of such action.

Reply Obj. 1: As it is in no wise contrary to truth for intelligible things to be set forth in Scripture under sensible figures, since it is not said for the purpose of maintaining that intelligible things are sensible, but in order that properties of intelligible things may be understood according to similitude through sensible figures; so it is not contrary to the truth of the holy angels that through their assumed bodies they appear to be living men, although they are really not. For the bodies are assumed merely for this purpose, that the spiritual properties and works of the angels may be manifested by the properties of man and of his works. This could not so fittingly be done if they were to assume true men; because the properties of such men would lead us to men, and not to angels.

Reply Obj. 2: Sensation is entirely a vital function. Consequently it can in no way be said that the angels perceive through the organs of their assumed bodies. Yet such bodies are not fashioned in vain; for they are not fashioned for the purpose of sensation through them, but to this end, that by such bodily organs the spiritual powers of the angels may be made manifest; just as by the eye the power of the angel's knowledge is pointed out, and other powers by the other members, as Dionysius teaches (Coel. Hier.).

Reply Obj. 3: Movement coming from a united mover is a proper function of life; but the bodies assumed by the angels are not thus moved, since the angels are not their forms. Yet the angels are moved accidentally, when such bodies are moved, since they are in them as movers are in the moved; and they are here in such a way as not to be elsewhere, which cannot be said of God. Accordingly, although God is not moved when the things are moved in which He exists, since He is everywhere; yet the angels are moved accidentally according to the movement of the bodies assumed. But they are not moved according to the movement of the heavenly bodies, even though they be in them as the movers in the thing moved, because the heavenly bodies do not change place in their entirety; nor for the spirit which moves the world is there any fixed locality according to any restricted part of the world's substance, which now is in the east, and now in the west, but according to a fixed quarter; because "the moving energy is always in the east," as stated in Phys. viii, text 84.

Reply Obj. 4: Properly speaking, the angels do not talk through their assumed bodies; yet there is a semblance of speech, in so far as they fashion sounds in the air like to human voices.

Reply Obj. 5: Properly speaking, the angels cannot be said to eat, because eating involves the taking of food convertible into the substance of the eater.

Although after the Resurrection food was not converted into the substance of Christ's body, but resolved into pre-existing matter; nevertheless Christ had a body of such a true nature that food could be changed into it; hence it was a true eating. But the food taken by angels was neither changed into the assumed body, nor was the body of such a nature that food could be changed into it; consequently, it was not a true eating, but figurative of spiritual eating. This is what the angel said to Tobias: "When I was with you, I seemed indeed to eat and to drink; but I use an invisible meat and drink" (Tob. 12:19).

Abraham offered them food, deeming them to be men, in whom, nevertheless, he worshipped God, as God is wont to be in the prophets, as Augustine says (De Civ. Dei xvi).

Reply Obj. 6: As Augustine says (De Civ. Dei xv): "Many persons affirm that they have had the experience, or have heard from such as have experienced it, that the Satyrs and Fauns, whom the common folk call incubi, have often presented themselves before women, and have sought and procured intercourse with them. Hence it is folly to deny it. But God's holy angels could not fall in such fashion before the deluge. Hence by the sons of God are to be understood the sons of Seth, who were good; while by the daughters of men the Scripture designates those who sprang from the race of Cain. Nor is it to be wondered at that giants should be born of them; for they were not all giants, albeit there were many more before than after the deluge." Still if some are occasionally begotten from demons, it is not from the seed of such demons, nor from their assumed bodies, but from the seed of men taken for the purpose; as when the demon assumes first the form of a woman, and afterwards of a man; just as they take the seed of other things for other generating purposes, as Augustine says (De Trin. iii), so that the person born is not the child of a demon, but of a man.

# QUESTION 52

OF THE ANGELS IN RELATION TO PLACE (In Three Articles)

We now inquire into the place of the angels. Touching this there are three subjects of inquiry:

(1) Is the angel in a place?

(2) Can he be in several places at once?

(3) Can several angels be in the same place?

FIRST ARTICLE [I, Q. 52, Art. 1]

Whether an Angel Is in a Place?

Objection 1: It would seem that an angel is not in a place. For Boethius says (De Hebdom.): "The common opinion of the learned is that things incorporeal are not in a place." And again, Aristotle observes (Phys. iv, text 48,57) that "it is not everything existing which is in a place, but only a movable body." But an angel is not a body, as was shown above (Q. 50). Therefore an angel is not in a place.

Obj. 2: Further, place is a "quantity having position." But everything which is in a place has some position. Now to have a position cannot befit an angel, since his substance is devoid of quantity, the proper difference of which is to have a position. Therefore an angel is not in a place.

Obj. 3: Further, to be in a place is to be measured and to be contained by such place, as is evident from the Philosopher (Phys. iv, text 14,119). But an angel can neither be measured nor contained by a place, because the container is more formal than the contained; as air with regard to water (Phys. iv, text 35,49). Therefore an angel is not in a place.

*On the contrary,* It is said in the Collect [*Prayer at Compline, Dominican Breviary]: "Let Thy holy angels who dwell herein, keep us in peace."

*I answer that,* It is befitting an angel to be in a place; yet an angel and a body are said to be in a place in quite a different sense. A body is said to be in a place in such a way that it is applied to such place according to the contact of dimensive quantity; but there is no such quantity in the angels, for theirs is a virtual one. Consequently an angel is said to be in a corporeal place by application of the angelic power in any manner whatever to any place.

Accordingly there is no need for saying that an angel can be deemed commensurate with a place, or that he occupies a space in the continuous; for this is proper to a located body which is endowed with dimensive quantity. In similar fashion it is not necessary on this account for the angel to be contained by a place; because an incorporeal substance virtually contains the thing with which it comes into contact, and is not contained by it: for the soul is in the body as containing it, not as contained by it. In the same way an angel is said to be in a place which is corporeal, not as the thing contained, but as somehow containing it.

And hereby we have the answers to the objections.

SECOND ARTICLE [I, Q. 52, Art. 2]

Whether an Angel Can Be in Several Places at Once?

Objection 1: It would seem that an angel can be in several places at once. For an angel is not less endowed with power than the soul. But the soul is in several places at once, for it is entirely in every part of the body, as Augustine says (De Trin. vi). Therefore an angel can be in several places at once.

Obj. 2: Further, an angel is in the body which he assumes; and, since the body which he assumes is continuous, it would appear that he is in every part thereof. But according to the various parts there are various places. Therefore the angel is at one time in various places.

Obj. 3: Further, Damascene says (De Fide Orth. ii) that "where the angel operates, there he is." But occasionally he operates in several places at one time, as is evident from the angel destroying Sodom (Gen. 19:25). Therefore an angel can be in several places at the one time.

*On the contrary,* Damascene says (De Fide Orth. ii) that "while the angels are in heaven, they are not on earth."

*I answer that,* An angel's power and nature are finite, whereas the Divine power and essence, which is the universal cause of all things, is infinite: consequently God through His power touches all things, and is not merely present in some places, but is everywhere. Now since the angel's power is finite, it does not extend to all things, but to one determined thing. For whatever is compared with one power must be compared therewith as one determined thing. Consequently since all being is compared as one thing to God's universal power, so is one particular being compared as one with the angelic power. Hence, since the angel is in a place by the application of his power to the place, it follows that he is not everywhere, nor in several places, but in only one place.

Some, however, have been deceived in this matter. For some who were unable to go beyond the reach of their imaginations supposed the indivisibility of the angel to be like that of a point; consequently they thought that an angel could be only in a place which is a point. But they were manifestly deceived, because a point is something indivisible, yet having its situation; whereas the angel is indivisible, and beyond the genus of quantity and situation. Consequently there is no occasion for determining in his regard one indivisible place as to situation: any place which is either divisible or indivisible, great or small suffices, according as to his own free-will he applies his power to a great or to a small body. So the entire body to which he is applied by his power, corresponds as one place to him.

Neither, if any angel moves the heavens, is it necessary for him to be everywhere. First of all, because his power is applied only to what is first moved by him. Now there is one part of the heavens in which there is movement first of all, namely, the part to the east: hence the Philosopher (Phys. vii, text 84) attributes the power of the heavenly mover to the part which is in the east. Secondly, because philosophers do not hold that one separate substance moves all the spheres immediately. Hence it need not be everywhere.

So, then, it is evident that to be in a place appertains quite differently to a body, to an angel, and to God. For a body is in a place in a circumscribed fashion, since it is measured by the place. An angel, however, is not there in a circumscribed fashion, since he is not measured by the place, but definitively, because he is in a place in such a manner that he is not in another. But God is neither circumscriptively nor definitively there, because He is everywhere.

From this we can easily gather an answer to the objections: because the entire subject to which the angelic power is immediately applied, is reputed as one place, even though it be continuous.

THIRD ARTICLE [I, Q. 52, Art. 3]

Whether Several Angels Can Be at the Same Time in the Same Place?

Objection 1: It would seem that several angels can be at the same time in the same place. For several bodies cannot be at the same time in the same place, because they fill the place. But the angels do not fill a place, because only a body fills a place, so that it be not empty, as appears from the Philosopher (Phys. iv, text 52,58). Therefore several angels can be in the one place.

Obj. 2: Further, there is a greater difference between an angel and a body than there is between two angels. But an angel and a body are at the one time in the one place: because there is no place which is not filled with a sensible body, as we find proved in Phys. iv, text. 58. Much more, then, can two angels be in the same place.

Obj. 3: Further, the soul is in every part of the body, according to Augustine (De Trin. vi). But demons, although they do not obsess souls, do obsess bodies occasionally; and thus the soul and the demon are at the one time in the same place; and consequently for the same reason all other spiritual substances.

*On the contrary,* There are not two souls in the same body. Therefore for a like reason there are not two angels in the same place.

*I answer that,* There are not two angels in the same place. The reason of this is because it is impossible for two complete causes to be the causes immediately of one and the same thing. This is evident in every class of causes: for there is one proximate form of one thing, and there is one proximate mover, although there may be several remote movers. Nor can it be objected that several individuals may row a boat, since no one of them is a perfect mover, because no one man's strength is sufficient for moving the boat; while all together are as one mover, in so far as their united strengths all combine in producing the one movement. Hence, since the angel is said to be in one place by the fact that his power touches the place immediately by way of a perfect container, as was said (A. 1), there can be but one angel in one place.

Reply Obj. 1: Several angels are not hindered from being in the same place because of their filling the place; but for another reason, as has been said.

Reply Obj. 2: An angel and a body are not in a place in the same way; hence the conclusion does not follow.

Reply Obj. 3: Not even a demon and a soul are compared to a body according to the same relation of causality; since the soul is its form, while the demon is not. Hence the inference does not follow.

# QUESTION 53

OF THE LOCAL MOVEMENT OF THE ANGELS (In Three Articles)

We must next consider the local movement of the angels; under which heading there are three points of inquiry:

(1) Whether an angel can be moved locally.

(2) Whether in passing from place to place he passes through intervening space?

(3) Whether the angel's movement is in time or instantaneous?

FIRST ARTICLE [I, Q. 53, Art. 1]

Whether an Angel Can Be Moved Locally?

Objection 1: It seems that an angel cannot be moved locally. For, as the Philosopher proves (Phys. vi, text 32, 86) "nothing which is devoid of parts is moved"; because, while it is in the term *wherefrom,* it is not moved; nor while it is in the term *whereto,* for it is then already moved; consequently it remains that everything which is moved, while it is being moved, is partly in the term *wherefrom* and partly in the term *whereto.* But an angel is without parts. Therefore an angel cannot be moved locally.

Obj. 2: Further, movement is "the act of an imperfect being," as the Philosopher says (Phys. iii, text 14). But a beatified angel is not imperfect. Consequently a beatified angel is not moved locally.

Obj. 3: Further, movement is simply because of want. But the holy angels have no want. Therefore the holy angels are not moved locally.

*On the contrary,* It is the same thing for a beatified angel to be moved as for a beatified soul to be moved. But it must necessarily be said that a blessed soul is moved locally, because it is an article of faith that Christ's soul descended into Hell. Therefore a beatified angel is moved locally.

*I answer that,* A beatified angel can be moved locally. As, however, to be in a place belongs equivocally to a body and to an angel, so likewise does local movement. For a body is in a place in so far as it is contained under the place, and is commensurate with the place. Hence it is necessary for local movement of a body to be commensurate with the place, and according to its exigency. Hence it is that the continuity of movement is according to the continuity of magnitude; and according to priority and posteriority of local movement, as the Philosopher says (Phys. iv, text 99). But an angel is not in a place as commensurate and contained, but rather as containing it. Hence it is not necessary for the local movement of an angel to be commensurate with the place, nor for it to be according to the exigency of the place, so as to have continuity therefrom; but it is a non-continuous movement. For since the angel is in a place only by virtual contact, as was said above (Q. 52, A. 1), it follows necessarily that the movement of an angel in a place is nothing else than the various contacts of various places successively, and not at once; because an angel cannot be in several places at one time, as was said above (Q. 52, A. 2). Nor is it necessary for these contacts to be continuous. Nevertheless a certain kind of continuity can be found in such contacts. Because, as was said above (Q. 52, A. 1), there is nothing to hinder us from assigning a divisible place to an angel according to virtual contact; just as a divisible place is assigned to a body by contact of magnitude. Hence as a body successively, and not all at once, quits the place in which it was before, and thence arises continuity in its local movement; so likewise an angel can successively quit the divisible place in which he was before, and so his movement will be continuous. And he can all at once quit the whole place, and in the same instant apply himself to the whole of another place, and thus his movement will not be continuous.

Reply Obj. 1: This argument fails of its purpose for a twofold reason. First of all, because Aristotle's demonstration deals with what is indivisible according to quantity, to which responds a place necessarily indivisible. And this cannot be said of an angel.

Secondly, because Aristotle's demonstration deals with movement which is continuous. For if the movement were not continuous, it might be said that a thing is moved where it is in the term *wherefrom,* and while it is in the term *whereto* : because the very succession of "wheres," regarding the same thing, would be called movement: hence, in whichever of those "wheres" the thing might be, it could be said to be moved. But the continuity of movement prevents this; because nothing which is continuous is in its term, as is clear, because the line is not in the point. Therefore it is necessary for the thing moved to be not totally in either of the terms while it is being moved; but partly in the one, and partly in the other. Therefore, according as the angel's movement is not continuous, Aristotle's demonstration does not hold good. But according as the angel's movement is held to be continuous, it can be so granted, that, while an angel is in movement, he is partly in the term *wherefrom,* and partly in the term *whereto* (yet so that such partiality be not referred to the angel's substance, but to the place); because at the outset of his continuous movement the angel is in the whole divisible place from which he begins to be moved; but while he is actually in movement, he is in part of the first place which he quits, and in part of the second place which he occupies. This very fact that he can occupy the parts of two places appertains to the angel from this, that he can occupy a divisible place by applying his power; as a body does by application of magnitude. Hence it follows regarding a body which is movable according to place, that it is divisible according to magnitude; but regarding an angel, that his power can be applied to something which is divisible.

Reply Obj. 2: The movement of that which is in potentiality is the act of an imperfect agent. But the movement which is by application of energy is the act of one in act: because energy implies actuality.

Reply Obj. 3: The movement of that which is in potentiality is the act of an imperfect but the movement of what is in act is not for any need of its own, but for another's need. In this way, because of our need, the angel is moved locally, according to Heb. 1:14: "They are all [*Vulg.: 'Are they not all ... ?'] ministering spirits, sent to minister for them who receive the inheritance of salvation."

SECOND ARTICLE [I, Q. 53, Art. 2]

Whether an Angel Passes Through Intermediate Space?

Objection 1: It would seem that an angel does not pass through intermediate space. For everything that passes through a middle space first travels along a place of its own dimensions, before passing through a greater. But the place responding to an angel, who is indivisible, is confined to a point. Therefore if the angel passes through middle space, he must reckon infinite points in his movement: which is not possible.

Obj. 2: Further, an angel is of simpler substance

than the soul. But our soul by taking thought can pass from one extreme to another without going through the middle: for I can think of France and afterwards of Syria, without ever thinking of Italy, which stands between them. Therefore much more can an angel pass from one extreme to another without going through the middle.

*On the contrary,* If the angel be moved from one place to another, then, when he is in the term "whither," he is no longer in motion, but is changed. But a process of changing precedes every actual change: consequently he was being moved while existing in some place. But he was not moved so long as he was in the term "whence." Therefore, he was moved while he was in mid-space: and so it was necessary for him to pass through intervening space.

*I answer that,* As was observed above in the preceding article, the local motion of an angel can be continuous, and non-continuous. If it be continuous, the angel cannot pass from one extreme to another without passing through the mid-space; because, as is said by the Philosopher (Phys. v, text 22; vi, text 77), "The middle is that into which a thing which is continually moved comes, before arriving at the last into which it is moved"; because the order of first and last in continuous movement, is according to the order of the first and last in magnitude, as he says (Phys. iv, text 99).

But if an angel's movement be not continuous, it is possible for him to pass from one extreme to another without going through the middle: which is evident thus. Between the two extreme limits there are infinite intermediate places; whether the places be taken as divisible or as indivisible. This is clearly evident with regard to places which are indivisible; because between every two points that are infinite intermediate points, since no two points follow one another without a middle, as is proved in Phys. vi, text. 1. And the same must of necessity be said of divisible places: and this is shown from the continuous movement of a body. For a body is not moved from place to place except in time. But in the whole time which measures the movement of a body, there are not two "nows" in which the body moved is not in one place and in another; for if it were in one and the same place in two "nows," it would follow that it would be at rest there; since to be at rest is nothing else than to be in the same place now and previously. Therefore since there are infinite "nows" between the first and the last "now" of the time which measures the movement, there must be infinite places between the first from which the movement begins, and the last where the movement ceases. This again is made evident from sensible experience. Let there be a body of a palm's length, and let there be a plane measuring two palms, along which it travels; it is evident that the first place from which the movement starts is that of the one palm; and the place wherein the movement ends is that of the other palm. Now it is clear that when it begins to move, it gradually quits the first palm and enters the second. According, then, as the magnitude of the palm is divided, even so are the intermediate places multiplied; because every distinct point in the magnitude of the first palm is the beginning of a place, and a distinct point in the magnitude of the other palm is the limit of the same. Accordingly, since magnitude is infinitely divisible and the points in every magnitude are likewise infinite in potentiality, it follows that between every two places there are infinite intermediate places.

Now a movable body only exhausts the infinity of the intermediate places by the continuity of its movement; because, as the intermediate places are infinite in potentiality, so likewise must there be reckoned some infinitudes in movement which is continuous. Consequently, if the movement be not continuous, then all the parts of the movement will be actually numbered. If, therefore, any movable body be moved, but not by continuous movement, it follows, either that it does not pass through all the intermediate places, or else that it actually numbers infinite places: which is not possible. Accordingly, then, as the angel's movement is not continuous, he does not pass through all intermediate places.

Now, the actual passing from one extreme to the other, without going through the mid-space, is quite in keeping with an angel's nature; but not with that of a body, because a body is measured by and contained under a place; hence it is bound to follow the laws of place in its movement. But an angel's substance is not subject to place as contained thereby, but is above it as containing it: hence it is under his control to apply himself to a place just as he wills, either through or without the intervening place.

Reply Obj. 1: The place of an angel is not taken as equal to him according to magnitude, but according to contact of power: and so the angel's place can be divisible, and is not always a mere point. Yet even the intermediate divisible places are infinite, as was said above: but they are consumed by the continuity of the movement, as is evident from the foregoing.

Reply Obj. 2: While an angel is moved locally, his essence is applied to various places: but the soul's essence is not applied to the things thought of, but rather the things thought of are in it. So there is no comparison.

Reply Obj. 3: In continuous movement the actual change is not a part of the movement, but its conclusion; hence movement must precede change. Accordingly such movement is through the mid-space. But in movement which is not continuous, the change is a part, as a unit is a part of number: hence the succession of the various places, even without the mid-space, constitutes such movement.

THIRD ARTICLE [I, Q. 53, Art. 3]

Whether the Movement of an Angel Is Instantaneous?

Objection 1: It would seem that an angel's movement is instantaneous. For the greater the power of the mover, and the less the moved resist the mover, the more rapid is the movement. But the power of an angel moving himself exceeds beyond all proportion the power which moves a body. Now the proportion of velocities is reckoned according to the lessening of the time. But between one length of time and any other length of time there is proportion. If therefore a body is moved in time, an angel is moved in an instant.

Obj. 2: Further, the angel's movement is simpler than any bodily change. But some bodily change is effected in an instant, such as illumination; both because the subject is not illuminated successively, as it gets hot successively; and because a ray does not reach sooner what is near than what is remote. Much more therefore is the angel's movement instantaneous.

Obj. 3: Further, if an angel be moved from place to place in time, it is manifest that in the last instant of such time he is in the term *whereto* : but in the whole of the preceding time, he is either in the place immediately preceding, which is taken as the term *wherefrom* ; or else he is partly in the one, and partly in the other, it follows that he is divisible; which is impossible. Therefore during the whole of the preceding time he is in the term *wherefrom.* Therefore he rests there: since to be at rest is to be in the same place now and previously, as was said (A. 2). Therefore it follows that he is not moved except in the last instant of time.

*On the contrary,* In every change there is a before and after. Now the before and after of movement is reckoned by time. Consequently every movement, even of an angel, is in time, since there is a before and after in it.

*I answer that,* Some have maintained that the local movement of an angel is instantaneous. They said that when an angel is moved from place to place, during the whole of the preceding time he is in the term *wherefrom* ; but in the last instant of such time he is in the term *whereto.* Nor is there any need for a medium between the terms, just as there is no medium between time and the limit of time. But there is a mid-time between two "nows" of time: hence they say that a last "now" cannot be assigned in which it was in the term *wherefrom,* just as in illumination, and in the substantial generation of fire, there is no last instant to be assigned in which the air was dark, or in which the matter was under the privation of the form of fire: but a last time can be assigned, so that in the last instant of such time there is light in the air, or the form of fire in the matter. And so illumination and substantial generation are called instantaneous movements.

But this does not hold good in the present case; and it is shown thus. It is of the nature of rest that the subject in repose be not otherwise disposed now than it was before: and therefore in every "now" of time which measures rest, the subject reposing is in the same "where" in the first, in the middle, and in the last "now." On the other hand, it is of the very nature of movement for the subject moved to be otherwise now than it was before: and therefore in every "now" of time which measures movement, the movable subject is in various dispositions; hence in the last "now" it must have a different form from what it had before. So it is evident that to rest during the whole time in some (disposition), for instance, in whiteness, is to be in it in every instant of such time. Hence it is not possible for anything to rest in one term during the whole of the preceding time, and afterwards in the last instant of that time to be in the other term. But this is possible in movement: because to be moved in any whole time, is not to be in the same disposition in every instant of that time. Therefore all instantaneous changes of the kind are terms of a continuous movement: just as generation is the term of the alteration of matter, and illumination is the term of the local movement of the illuminating body. Now the local movement of an angel is not the term of any other continuous movement, but is of itself, depending upon no other movement. Consequently it is impossible to say that he is in any place during the whole time, and that in the last "now" he is in another place: but some "now" must be assigned in which he was last in the preceding place. But where there are many "nows" succeeding one another, there is necessarily time; since time is nothing else than the reckoning of before and after in movement. It remains, then, that the movement of an angel is in time. It is in continuous time if his movement be continuous, and in non-continuous time if his movement is non-continuous for, as was said (A. 1), his movement can be of either kind, since the continuity of time comes of the continuity of movement, as the Philosopher says (Phys. iv, text 99).

But that time, whether it be continuous or not, is not the same as the time which measures the movement of the heavens, and whereby all corporeal things are measured, which have their changeableness from the movement of the heavens; because the angel's movement does not depend upon the movement of the heavens.

Reply Obj. 1: If the time of the angel's movement be not continuous, but a kind of succession of 'nows,' it will have no proportion to the time which measures the movement of corporeal things, which is continuous; since it is not of the same nature. If, however, it be continuous, it is indeed proportionable, not, indeed, because of the proportion of the mover and the movable, but on account of the proportion of the magnitudes in which the movement exists. Besides, the swiftness of the angel's movement is not measured by the quantity of his power, but according to the determination of his will.

Reply Obj. 2: Illumination is the term of a movement; and is an alteration, not a local movement, as though the light were understood to be moved to what is near, before being moved to what is remote. But the angel's movement is local, and, besides, it is not the term of movement; hence there is no comparison.

Reply Obj. 3: This objection is based on continuous time. But the same time of an angel's movement can be non-continuous. So an angel can be in one place in one instant, and in another place in the next instant, without any time intervening. If the time of the angel's movement be continuous, he is changed through infinite places throughout the whole time which precedes the last 'now'; as was already shown (A. 2). Nevertheless he is partly in one of the continuous places, and partly in another, not because his substance is susceptible of parts, but because his power is applied to a part of the first place and to a part of the second, as was said above (A. 2).

## QUESTION 54

OF THE KNOWLEDGE OF THE ANGELS (In Five Articles)

After considering what belongs to the angel's substance, we now proceed to his knowledge. This investigation will be fourfold. In the first place inquiry must be made into his power of knowledge: secondly, into his medium of knowledge: thirdly, into the objects known: and fourthly, into the manner whereby he knows them.

Under the first heading there are five points of inquiry:

(1) Is the angel's understanding his substance?

(2) Is his being his understanding?

(3) Is his substance his power of intelligence?

(4) Is there in the angels an active and a passive intellect?

(5) Is there in them any other power of knowledge besides the intellect?

FIRST ARTICLE [I, Q. 54, Art. 1]

Whether an Angel's Act of Understanding Is His Substance?

Objection 1: It would seem that the angel's act of understanding is his substance. For the angel is both higher and simpler than the active intellect of a soul. But the substance of the active intellect is its own action; as is evident from Aristotle (De Anima iii) and from his Commentator [*Averroes, A.D. 1126-1198]. Therefore much more is the angel's substance his action—that is, his act of understanding.

Obj. 2: Further, the Philosopher says (Metaph. xii, text 39) that "the action of the intellect is life." But "since in living things to live is to be," as he says (De Anima ii, text 37), it seems that life is essence. Therefore the action of the intellect is the essence of an angel who understands.

Obj. 3: Further, if the extremes be one, then the middle does not differ from them; because extreme is farther from extreme than the middle is. But in an angel the intellect and the object understood are the same, at least in so far as he understands his own essence. Therefore the act of understanding, which is between the intellect and the thing understood, is one with the substance of the angel who understands.

*On the contrary,* The action of anything differs more from its substance than does its existence. But no creature's existence is its substance, for this belongs to God only, as is evident from what was said above (Q. 3, A. 4). Therefore neither the action of an angel, nor of any other creature, is its substance.

*I answer that,* It is impossible for the action of an angel, or of any creature, to be its own substance. For an action is properly the actuality of a power; just as existence is the actuality of a substance or of an essence. Now it is impossible for anything which is not a pure act, but which has some admixture of potentiality, to be its own actuality: because actuality is opposed to potentiality. But God alone is pure act. Hence only in God is His substance the same as His existence and His action.

Besides, if an angel's act of understanding were his substance, it would be necessary for it to be subsisting. Now a subsisting act of intelligence can be but one; just as an abstract thing that subsists. Consequently an angel's substance would neither be distinguished from God's substance, which is His very act of understanding subsisting in itself, nor from the substance of another angel.

Also, if the angel were his own act of understanding, there could then be no degrees of understanding more or less perfectly; for this comes about through the diverse participation of the act of understanding.

Reply Obj. 1: When the active intellect is said to be its own action, such predication is not essential, but concomitant, because, since its very nature consists in act, instantly, so far as lies in itself, action accompanies it: which cannot be said of the passive intellect, for this has no actions until after it has been reduced to act.

Reply Obj. 2: The relation between "life" and "to live" is not the same as that between "essence" and "to be"; but rather as that between "a race" and "to run," one of which signifies the act in the abstract, and the other in the concrete. Hence it does not follow, if "to live" is "to be," that "life" is "essence." Although life is sometimes put for the essence, as Augustine says (De Trin. x), "Memory and understanding and will are one essence, one life": yet it is not taken in this sense by the Philosopher, when he says that "the act of the intellect is life."

Reply Obj. 3: The action which is transient, passing to some extrinsic object, is really a medium between the agent and the subject receiving the action. The action which remains within the agent, is not really a medium between the agent and the object, but only according to the manner of expression; for it really follows the union of the object with the agent. For the act of understanding is brought about by the union of the object understood with the one who understands it, as an effect which differs from both.

SECOND ARTICLE [I, Q. 54, Art. 2]

Whether in the Angel to Understand Is to Exist?

Objection 1: It would seem that in the angel to understand is to exist. For in living things to live is to be, as the Philosopher says (De Anima ii, text. 37). But to "understand is in a sense to live" (De Anima ii, text. 37). Therefore in the angel to understand is to exist.

Obj. 2: Further, cause bears the same relation to cause, as effect to effect. But the form whereby the angel exists is the same as the form by which he understands at least himself. Therefore in the angel to understand is to exist.

*On the contrary,* The angel's act of understanding is his movement, as is clear from Dionysius (Div. Nom. iv). But to exist is not movement. Therefore in the angel to be is not to understand.

*I answer that,* The action of the angel, as also the action of any creature, is not his existence. For as it is said (Metaph. ix, text. 16), there is a twofold class of action; one which passes out to something beyond, and causes passion in it, as burning and cutting; and another which does not pass outwards, but which remains within the agent, as to feel, to understand, to will; by such actions nothing outside is changed, but the whole action takes place within the agent. It is quite clear regarding the first kind of action that it cannot be the agent's very existence: because the agent's existence is signified as within him, while such an action denotes something as issuing from the agent into the thing done. But the second action of its own nature has infinity, either simple or relative. As an example of simple infinity, we have the act "to understand," of which the object is "the true"; and the act "to will," of which the object is "the good"; each of which is convertible with being; and so, to understand and to will, of themselves, bear relation to all things, and each receives its species from its object. But the act of sensation is relatively infinite, for it bears relation to all sensible things; as sight does to all things visible. Now the being of every creature is restricted to one in genus and species; God's being alone is simply infinite, comprehending all things in itself, as Dionysius says (Div. Nom. v). Hence the Divine nature alone is its own act of understanding and its own act of will.

Reply Obj. 1: Life is sometimes taken for the existence of the living subject: sometimes also for a vital operation, that is, for one whereby something is shown to be living. In this way the Philosopher says that to understand is, in a sense, to live: for there he distinguishes the various grades of living things according to the various functions of life.

Reply Obj. 2: The essence of an angel is the reason of his entire existence, but not the reason of his whole act of understanding, since he cannot understand everything by his essence. Consequently in its own specific nature as such an essence, it is compared to the existence of the angel, whereas to his act of understanding it is compared as included in the idea of a more universal object, namely, truth and being. Thus it is evident, that, although the form is the same, yet it is not the principle of existence and of understanding according to the same formality. On this account it does not follow that in the angel "to be" is the same as 'to understand.'

THIRD ARTICLE [I, Q. 54, Art. 3]

Whether an Angel's Power of Intelligence Is His Essence?

Objection 1: It would seem that in an angel the power or faculty of understanding is not different from his essence. For, "mind" and "intellect" express the power of understanding. But in many passages of his writings, Dionysius styles angels "intellects" and "minds." Therefore the angel is his own power of intelligence.

Obj. 2: Further, if the angel's power of intelligence be anything besides his essence, then it must needs be an accident; for that which is besides the essence of anything, we call it accident. But "a simple form cannot be a subject," as Boethius states (De Trin. 1). Thus an angel would not be a simple form, which is contrary to what has been previously said (Q. 50, A. 2).

Obj. 3: Further, Augustine (Confess. xii) says, that God made the angelic nature "nigh unto Himself," while He made primary matter "nigh unto nothing"; from this it would seem that the angel is of a simpler nature than primary matter, as being closer to God. But primary matter is its own power. Therefore much more is an angel his own power of intelligence.

*On the contrary,* Dionysius says (Coel. Hier. xi) that "the angels are divided into substance, power, and operation." Therefore substance, power, and operation, are all distinct in them.

*I answer that,* Neither in an angel nor in any creature, is the power or operative faculty the same as its essence: which is made evident thus. Since every power is ordained to an act, then according to the diversity of acts must be the diversity of powers; and on this account it is said that each proper act responds to its proper power. But in every creature the essence differs from the existence, and is compared to it as potentiality is to act, as is evident from what has been already said (Q. 44, A. 1). Now the act to which the operative power is compared is operation. But in the angel to understand is not the same as to exist, nor is any operation in him, nor in any other created thing, the same as his existence.

Hence the angel's essence is not his power of intelligence: nor is the essence of any creature its power of operation.

Reply Obj. 1: An angel is called "intellect" and "mind," because all his knowledge is intellectual: whereas the knowledge of a soul is partly intellectual and partly sensitive.

Reply Obj. 2: A simple form which is pure act cannot be the subject of accident, because subject is compared to accident as potentiality is to act. God alone is such a form: and of such is Boethius speaking there. But a simple form which is not its own existence, but is compared to it as potentiality is to act, can be the subject of accident; and especially of such accident as follows the species: for such accident belongs to the form—whereas an accident which belongs to the individual, and which does not belong to the whole species, results from the matter, which is the principle of individuation. And such a simple form is an angel.

Reply Obj. 3: The power of matter is a potentiality in regard to substantial being itself, whereas the power of operation regards accidental being. Hence there is no comparison.

FOURTH ARTICLE [I, Q. 54, Art. 4]

Whether There Is an Active and a Passive Intellect in an Angel?

Objection 1: It would seem that there is both an active and a passive intellect in an angel. The Philosopher says (De Anima iii, text. 17) that, "in the soul, just as in every nature, there is something whereby it can become all things, and there is something whereby it can make all things." But an angel is a kind of nature. Therefore there is an active and a passive intellect in an angel.

Obj. 2: Further, the proper function of the passive intellect is to receive; whereas to enlighten is the proper function of the active intellect, as is made clear in *De Anima* iii, text. 2, 3, 18. But an angel receives enlightenment from a higher angel, and enlightens a lower one. Therefore there is in him an active and a passive intellect.

*On the contrary,* The distinction of active and passive intellect in us is in relation to the phantasms, which are compared to the passive intellect as colors to the sight; but to the active intellect as colors to the light, as is clear from De Anima iii, text. 18. But this is not so in the angel. Therefore there is no active and passive intellect in the angel.

*I answer that,* The necessity for admitting a passive intellect in us is derived from the fact that we understand sometimes only in potentiality, and not actually. Hence there must exist some power, which, previous to the act of understanding, is in potentiality to intelligible things, but which becomes actuated in their regard when it apprehends them, and still more when it reflects upon them. This is the power which is denominated the passive intellect. The necessity for admitting an active intellect is due to this—that the natures of the material things which we understand do not exist outside the soul, as immaterial and actually intelligible, but are only intelligible in potentiality so long as they are outside the soul. Consequently it is necessary that there should be some power capable of rendering such natures actually intelligible: and this power in us is called the active intellect.

But each of these necessities is absent from the angels. They are neither sometimes understanding only in potentiality, with regard to such things as they naturally apprehend; nor, again, are their intelligible objects intelligible in potentiality, but they are actually such; for they first and principally understand immaterial things, as will appear later (Q. 84, A. 7; Q. 85, A. 1). Therefore there cannot be an active and a passive intellect in them, except equivocally.

Reply Obj. 1: As the words themselves show, the Philosopher understands those two things to be in every nature in which there chances to be generation or making. Knowledge, however, is not generated in the angels, but is present naturally. Hence there is no need for admitting an active and a passive intellect in them.

Reply Obj. 2: It is the function of the active intellect to enlighten, not another intellect, but things which are intelligible in potentiality, in so far as by abstraction it makes them to be actually intelligible. It belongs to the passive intellect to be in potentiality with regard to things which are naturally capable of being known, and sometimes to apprehend them actually. Hence for one angel to enlighten another does not belong to the notion of an active intellect: neither does it belong to the passive intellect for the angel to be enlightened with regard to supernatural mysteries, to the knowledge of which he is sometimes in potentiality. But if anyone wishes to call these by the names of active and passive intellect, he will then be speaking equivocally; and it is not about names that we need trouble.

FIFTH ARTICLE [I, Q. 54, Art. 5]

Whether There Is Only Intellectual Knowledge in the Angels?

Objection 1: It would seem that the knowledge of the angels is not exclusively intellectual. For Augustine says (De Civ. Dei viii) that in the angels there is "life which understands and feels." Therefore there is a sensitive faculty in them as well.

Obj. 2: Further, Isidore says (De Summo Bono) that the angels have learnt many things by experience. But experience comes of many remembrances, as stated in *Metaph.* i, 1. Consequently they have likewise a power of memory.

Obj. 3: Further, Dionysius says (Div. Nom. iv) that there is a sort of "perverted phantasy" in the demons. But phantasy belongs to the imaginative faculty. Therefore the power of the imagination is in the demons; and for the same reason it is in the angels, since they are of the same nature.

*On the contrary,* Gregory says (Hom. 29 in Ev.), that "man senses in common with the brutes, and understands with the angels."

*I answer that,* In our soul there are certain powers whose operations are exercised by corporeal organs; such powers are acts of sundry parts of the body, as sight of the eye, and hearing of the ear. There are some other powers of the soul whose operations are not performed through bodily organs, as intellect and will: these are not acts of any parts of the body. Now the angels have no bodies naturally joined to them, as is manifest from what has been said already (Q. 51, A. 1). Hence of the soul's powers only intellect and will can belong to them.

The Commentator (Metaph. xii) says the same thing, namely, that the separated substances are divided into intellect and will. And it is in keeping with the order of the universe for the highest intellectual creature to be entirely intelligent; and not in part, as is our soul. For this reason the angels are called "intellects" and "minds," as was said above (A. 3, ad 1).

A twofold answer can be returned to the contrary objections. First, it may be replied that those authorities are speaking according to the opinion of such men as contended that angels and demons have bodies naturally united to them. Augustine often makes use of this opinion in his books, although he does not mean to assert it; hence he says (De Civ. Dei xxi) that "such an inquiry does not call for much labor." Secondly, it may be said that such authorities and the like are to be understood by way of similitude. Because, since sense has a sure apprehension of its proper sensible object, it is a common usage of speech, when we understand something for certain, to say that we "sense it." And hence it is that we use the word "sentence." Experience can be attributed to the angels according to the likeness of the things known, although not by likeness of the faculty knowing them. We have experience when we know single objects through the senses: the angels likewise know single objects, as we shall show (Q. 57, A. 2), yet not through the senses. But memory can be allowed in the angels, according as Augustine (De Trin. x) puts it in the mind; although it cannot belong to them in so far as it is a part of the sensitive soul. In like fashion 'a perverted phantasy' is attributed to demons, since they have a false practical estimate of what is the true good; while deception in us comes properly from the phantasy, whereby we sometimes hold fast to images of things as to the things themselves, as is manifest in sleepers and lunatics.

# QUESTION 55

OF THE MEDIUM OF THE ANGELIC KNOWLEDGE (In Three Articles)

Next in order, the question arises as to the medium of the angelic knowledge. Under this heading there are three points of inquiry:

(1) Do the angels know everything by their substance, or by some species?

(2) If by species, is it by connatural species, or is it by such as they have derived from things?

(3) Do the higher angels know by more universal species than the lower angels?

FIRST ARTICLE [I, Q. 55, Art. 1]

Whether the Angels Know All Things by Their Substance?

Objection 1: It would seem that the angels know all things by their substance. For Dionysius says (Div. Nom. vii) that "the angels, according to the proper nature of a mind, know the things which are happening upon earth." But the angel's nature is his essence. Therefore the angel knows things by his essence.

Obj. 2: Further, according to the Philosopher (Metaph. xii, text. 51; *De Anima* iii, text. 15), "in things which are without matter, the intellect is the same as the object understood." But the object understood is the same as the one who understands it, as regards that whereby it is understood. Therefore in things without matter, such as the angels, the medium whereby the object is understood is the very substance of the one understanding it.

Obj. 3: Further, everything which is contained in another is there according to the mode of the container. But an angel has an intellectual nature. Therefore whatever is in him is there in an intelligible mode. But all things are in him: because the lower orders of beings are essentially in the higher, while the higher are in the lower participatively: and therefore Dionysius says (Div. Nom. iv) that God "enfolds the whole in the whole," i.e. all in all. Therefore the angel knows all things in his substance.

*On the contrary,* Dionysius says (Div. Nom. iv) that "the angels are enlightened by the forms of things." Therefore they know by the forms of things, and not by their own substance.

*I answer that,* The medium through which the intellect understands, is compared to the intellect understanding it as its form, because it is by the form that the agent acts. Now in order that the faculty may be perfectly completed by the form, it is necessary for all things to which the faculty extends to be contained under the form. Hence it is that in things which are corruptible, the form does not perfectly complete the potentiality of the matter: because the potentiality of the matter extends to more things than are contained under this or that form. But the intellective power of the angel extends to understanding all things: because the object of the intellect is universal being or universal truth. The angel's essence, however, does not comprise all things in itself, since it is an essence restricted to a genus and species. This is proper to the Divine essence, which is infinite, simply and perfectly to comprise all things in Itself. Therefore God alone knows all things by His essence. But an angel cannot know all things by his essence; and his intellect must be perfected by some species in order to know things.

Reply Obj. 1: When it is said that the angel knows things according to his own nature, the words "according to" do not determine the medium of such knowledge, since the medium is the similitude of the thing known; but they denote the knowing power, which belongs to the angel of his own nature.

Reply Obj. 2: As the sense in act is the sensible in act, as stated in *De Anima* ii, text. 53, not so that the sensitive power is the sensible object's likeness contained in the sense, but because one thing is made from both as from act and potentiality: so likewise the intellect in act is said to be the thing understood in act, not that the substance of the intellect is itself the similitude by which it understands, but because that similitude is its form. Now, it is precisely the same thing to say "in things which are without matter, the intellect is the same thing as the object understood," as to say that "the intellect in act is the thing understood in act"; for a thing is actually understood, precisely because it is immaterial.

Reply Obj. 3: The things which are beneath the angel, and those which are above him, are in a measure in his substance, not indeed perfectly, nor according to their own proper formality—because the angel's essence, as being finite, is distinguished by its own formality from other things—but according to some common formality. Yet all things are perfectly and according to their own formality in God's essence, as in the first and universal operative power, from which proceeds whatever is proper or common to anything. Therefore God has a proper knowledge of all things by His own essence: and this the angel has not, but only a common knowledge.

SECOND ARTICLE [I, Q. 55, Art. 2]

Whether the Angels Understand by Species Drawn from Things?

Objection 1: It would seem that the angels understand by species drawn from things. For everything understood is apprehended by some likeness within him who understands it. But the likeness of the thing existing in another is there either by way of an exemplar, so that the likeness is the cause of the thing; or else by way of an image, so that it is caused by such thing. All knowledge, then, of the person understanding must either be the cause of the object understood, or else caused by it. Now the angel's knowledge is not the cause of existing things; that belongs to the Divine knowledge alone. Therefore it is necessary for the species, by which the angelic mind understands, to be derived from things.

Obj. 2: Further, the angelic light is stronger than the light of the active intellect of the soul. But the light of the active intellect abstracts intelligible species from phantasms. Therefore the light of the angelic mind can also abstract species from sensible things. So there is nothing to hinder us from saying that the angel understands through species drawn from things.

Obj. 3: Further, the species in the intellect are indifferent to what is present or distant, except in so far as they are taken from sensible objects. Therefore, if the angel does not understand by species drawn from things, his knowledge would be indifferent as to things present and distant; and so he would be moved locally to no purpose.

*On the contrary,* Dionysius says (Div. Nom. vii) that the "angels do not gather their Divine knowledge from things divisible or sensible."

*I answer that,* The species whereby the angels understand are not drawn from things, but are connatural to them. For we must observe that there is a similarity between the distinction and order of spiritual substances and the distinction and order of corporeal substances. The highest bodies have in their nature a potentiality which is fully perfected by the form; whereas in the lower bodies the potentiality of matter is not entirely perfected by the form, but receives from some agent, now one form, now another. In like fashion also the lower intellectual substances —that is to say, human souls—have a power of understanding which is not naturally complete, but is successively completed in them by their drawing intelligible species from things. But in the higher spiritual substances—that is, the angels—the power of understanding is naturally complete by intelligible species, in so far as they have such species connatural to them, so as to understand all things which they can know naturally.

The same is evident from the manner of existence of such substances. The lower spiritual substances—that is, souls—have a nature akin to a body, in so far as they are the forms of bodies: and consequently from their very mode of existence it behooves them to seek their intelligible perfection from bodies, and through bodies; otherwise they would be united with bodies to no purpose. On the other hand, the higher substances—that is, the angels—are utterly free from bodies, and subsist immaterially and in their own intelligible nature; consequently they attain their intelligible perfection through an intelligible outpouring, whereby they received from God the species of things known, together with their intellectual nature. Hence Augustine says (Gen. ad lit. ii, 8): "The other things which are lower than the angels are so created that they first receive existence in the knowledge of the rational creature, and then in their own nature."

Reply Obj. 1: There are images of creatures in the angel's mind, not, indeed derived from creatures, but from God, Who is the cause of creatures, and in Whom the likenesses of creatures first exist. Hence Augustine says (Gen. ad lit. ii, 8) that, "As the type, according to which the creature is fashioned, is in the Word of God before the creature which is fashioned, so the knowledge of the same type exists first in the intellectual creature, and is afterwards the very fashioning of the creature."

Reply Obj. 2: To go from one extreme to the other it is necessary to pass through the middle. Now the nature of a form in the imagination, which form is without matter but not without material conditions, stands midway between the nature of a form which is in matter, and the nature of a form which is in the intellect by abstraction from matter and from material conditions. Consequently, however powerful the angelic mind might be, it could not reduce material forms to an intelligible condition, except it were first to reduce them to the nature of imagined forms; which is impossible, since the angel has no imagination, as was said above (Q. 54, A. 5). Even granted that he could abstract intelligible species from material things, yet he would not do so; because he would not need them, for he has connatural intelligible species.

Reply Obj. 3: The angel's knowledge is quite indifferent as to what is near or distant. Nevertheless his local movement is not purposeless on that account: for he is not moved to a place for the purpose of acquiring knowledge, but for the purpose of operation.

THIRD ARTICLE [I, Q. 55, Art. 3]

Whether the Higher Angels Understand by More Universal Species Than the Lower Angels?

Objection 1: It would seem that the higher angels do not understand by more universal species than the lower angels. For the universal, seemingly, is what is abstracted from particulars. But angels do not understand by species abstracted from things. Therefore it cannot be said that the species of the angelic intellect are more or less universal.

Obj. 2: Further, whatever is known in detail is more perfectly known than what is known generically; because to know anything generically is, in a fashion, midway between potentiality and act. If, therefore, the higher angels know by more universal species than the lower, it follows that the higher have a more imperfect knowledge than the lower; which is not befitting.

Obj. 3: Further, the same cannot be the proper type of many. But if the higher angel knows various things by one universal form, which the lower angel knows by several special forms, it follows that the higher angel uses one universal form for knowing various things. Therefore he will not be able to have a proper knowledge of each; which seems unbecoming.

*On the contrary,* Dionysius says (Coel. Hier. xii) that the higher angels have a more universal knowledge than the lower. And in De Causis it is said that the higher angels have more universal forms.

*I answer that,* For this reason are some things of a more exalted nature, because they are nearer to and more like unto the first, which is God. Now in God the whole plenitude of intellectual knowledge is contained in one thing, that is to say, in the Divine essence, by which God knows all things. This plenitude of knowledge is found in created intellects in a lower manner, and less simply. Consequently it is necessary for the lower intelligences to know by many forms what God knows by one, and by so many forms the more according as the intellect is lower.

Thus the higher the angel is, by so much the fewer species will he be able to apprehend the whole mass of intelligible objects. Therefore his forms must be more universal; each one of them, as it were, extending to more things. An example of this can in some measure be observed in ourselves. For some people there are who cannot grasp an intelligible truth, unless it be explained to them in every part and detail; this comes of their weakness of intellect: while there are others of stronger intellect, who can grasp many things from few.

Reply Obj. 1: It is accidental to the universal to be abstracted from particulars, in so far as the intellect knowing it derives its knowledge from things. But if there be an intellect which does not derive its knowledge from things, the universal which it knows will not be abstracted from things, but in a measure will be pre-existing to them; either according to the order of causality, as the universal ideas of things are in the Word of God; or at least in the order of nature, as the universal ideas of things are in the angelic mind.

Reply Obj. 2: To know anything universally can be taken in two senses. In one way, on the part of the thing known, namely, that only the universal nature of the thing is known. To know a thing thus is something less perfect: for he would have but an imperfect knowledge of a man who only knew him to be an animal. In another way, on the part of the medium of such knowledge. In this way it is more perfect to know a thing in the universal; for the intellect, which by one universal medium can know each of the things which are properly contained in it, is more perfect than one which cannot.

Reply Obj. 3: The same cannot be the proper and adequate type of several things. But if it be eminent, then it can be taken as the proper type and likeness of many. Just as in man, there is a universal prudence with respect to all the acts of the virtues; which can be taken as the proper type and likeness of that prudence which in the lion leads to acts of magnanimity, and in the fox to acts of wariness; and so on of the rest. The Divine essence, on account of Its eminence, is in like fashion taken as the proper type of each thing contained therein: hence each one is likened to It according to its proper type. The same applies to the universal form which is in the mind of the angel, so that, on account of its excellence, many things can be known through it with a proper knowledge.

## QUESTION 56

OF THE ANGEL'S KNOWLEDGE OF IMMATERIAL THINGS (In Three Articles)

We now inquire into the knowledge of the angels with regard to the objects known by them. We shall treat of their knowledge, first, of immaterial things, secondly of things material. Under the first heading there are three points of inquiry:

(1) Does an angel know himself?

(2) Does one angel know another?

(3) Does the angel know God by his own natural principles?

FIRST ARTICLE [I, Q. 56, Art 1]

Whether an Angel Knows Himself?

Objection 1: It would seem that an angel does not know himself. For Dionysius says that "the angels do not know their own powers" (Coel. Hier. vi). But, when the substance is known, the power is known. Therefore an angel does not know his own essence.

Obj. 2: Further, an angel is a single substance, otherwise he would not act, since acts belong to single subsistences. But nothing single is intelligible. Therefore, since the angel possesses only knowledge which is intellectual, no angel can know himself.

Obj. 3: Further, the intellect is moved by the intelligible object: because, as stated in *De Anima* iii, 4 understanding is a kind of passion. But nothing is moved by or is passive to itself; as appears in corporeal things. Therefore the angel cannot understand himself.

*On the contrary,* Augustine says (Gen. ad lit. ii) that "the angel knew himself when he was established, that is, enlightened by truth."

*I answer that,* As is evident from what has been previously said (Q. 14, A. 2; Q. 54, A. 2), the object is on a different footing in an immanent, and in a transient, action. In a transient action the object or matter into which the action passes is something separate from the agent, as the thing heated is from what gave it heat, and the building from the builder; whereas in an immanent action, for the action to proceed, the object must be united with the agent; just as the sensible object must be in contact with sense, in order that sense may actually perceive. And the object which is united to a faculty bears the same relation to actions of this kind as does the form which is the principle of action in other agents: for, as heat is the formal principle of heating in the fire, so is the species of the thing seen the formal principle of sight to the eye.

It must, however, be borne in mind that this image of the object exists sometimes only potentially in the knowing faculty; and then there is only knowledge in potentiality; and in order that there may be actual knowledge, it is required that the faculty of knowledge be actuated by the species. But if it always actually possesses the species, it can thereby have actual knowledge without any preceding change or reception. From this it is evident that it is not of the nature of knower, as knowing, to be moved by the object, but as knowing in potentiality. Now, for the form to be the principle of the action, it makes no difference whether it be inherent in something else, or self-subsisting; because heat would give forth heat none the less if it were self-subsisting, than it does by inhering in something else. So therefore, if in the order of intelligible beings there be any subsisting intelligible form, it will understand itself. And since an angel is immaterial, he is a subsisting form; and, consequently, he is actually intelligible. Hence it follows that he understands himself by his form, which is his substance.

Reply Obj. 1: That is the text of the old translation, which is amended in the new one, and runs thus: "furthermore they," that is to say the angels, "knew their own powers": instead of which the old translation read—"and furthermore they do not know their own powers." Although even the letter of the old translation might be kept in this respect, that the angels do not know their own power perfectly; according as it proceeds from the order of the Divine Wisdom, Which to the angels is incomprehensible.

Reply Obj. 2: We have no knowledge of single corporeal things, not because of their particularity, but on account of the matter, which is their principle of individuation. Accordingly, if there be any single things subsisting without matter, as the angels are, there is nothing to prevent them from being actually intelligible.

Reply Obj. 3: It belongs to the intellect, in so far as it is in potentiality, to be moved and to be passive. Hence this does not happen in the angelic intellect, especially as regards the fact that he understands himself. Besides the action of the intellect is not of the same nature as the action found in corporeal things, which passes into some other matter.

SECOND ARTICLE [I, Q. 56, Art. 2]

Whether One Angel Knows Another?

Objection 1: It would seem that one angel does not know another. For the Philosopher says (De Anima iii, text. 4), that if the human intellect were to have in itself any one of the sensible things, then such a nature existing within it would prevent it from apprehending external things; as likewise, if the pupil of the eye were colored with some particular color, it could not see every color. But as the human intellect is disposed for understanding corporeal things, so is the angelic mind for understanding immaterial things. Therefore, since the angelic intellect has within itself some one determinate nature from the number of such natures, it would seem that it cannot understand other natures.

Obj. 2: Further, it is stated in *De Causis* that "every intelligence knows what is above it, in so far as it is caused by it; and what is beneath it, in so far as it is its cause." But one angel is not the cause of another. Therefore one angel does not know another.

Obj. 3: Further, one angel cannot be known to another angel by the essence of the one knowing; because all knowledge is effected by way of a likeness. But the essence of the angel knowing is not like the essence of the angel known, except generically; as is clear from what has been said before (Q. 50, A. 4; Q. 55, A. 1, ad 3). Hence, it follows that one angel would not have a particular knowledge of another, but only a general knowledge. In like manner it cannot be said that one angel knows another by the essence of the angel known; because that whereby the intellect understands is something within the intellect; whereas the Trinity alone can penetrate the mind. Again, it cannot be said that one angel knows the other by a species; because that species would not differ from the angel understood, since each is immaterial. Therefore in no way does it appear that one angel can understand another.

Obj. 4: Further, if one angel did understand another, this would be either by an innate species; and so it would follow that, if God were now to create another angel, such an angel could not be known by the existing angels; or else he would have to be known by a species drawn from things; and so it would follow that the higher angels could not know the lower, from whom they receive nothing. Therefore in no way does it seem that one angel knows another.

*On the contrary,* We read in De Causis that "every intelligence knows the things which are not corrupted."

*I answer that,* As Augustine says (Gen. ad lit. lit. ii), such things as pre-existed from eternity in the Word of God, came forth from Him in two ways: first, into the angelic mind; and secondly, so as to subsist in their own natures. They proceeded into the angelic mind in such a way, that God impressed upon the angelic mind the images of the things which He produced in their own natural being. Now in the Word of God from eternity there existed not only the forms of corporeal things, but likewise the forms of all spiritual creatures. So in every one of these spiritual creatures, the forms of all things, both corporeal and spiritual, were impressed by the Word of God; yet so that in every angel there was impressed the form of his own species according to both its natural and its intelligible condition, so that he should subsist in the nature of his species, and understand himself by it; while the forms of other spiritual and corporeal natures were impressed in him only according to their intelligible natures, so that by such impressed species he might know corporeal and spiritual creatures.

Reply Obj. 1: The spiritual natures of the angels are distinguished from one another in a certain order, as was already observed (Q. 50, A. 4, ad 1, 2). So the nature of an angel does not hinder him from knowing the other angelic natures, since both the higher and lower bear affinity to his nature, the only difference being according to their various degrees of perfection.

Reply Obj. 2: The nature of cause and effect does not lead one angel to know another, except on account of likeness, so far as cause and effect are alike. Therefore if likeness without causality be admitted in the angels, this will suffice for one to know another.

Reply Obj. 3: One angel knows another by the species of such angel existing in his intellect, which differs from the angel whose image it is, not according to material and immaterial nature, but according to natural and intentional existence. The angel is himself a subsisting form in his natural being; but his species in the intellect of another angel is not so, for there it possesses only an intelligible existence. As the form of color on the wall has a natural existence; but, in the deferent medium, it has only intentional existence.

Reply Obj. 4: God made every creature proportionate to the universe which He determined to make. Therefore had God resolved to make more angels or more natures of things, He would have impressed more intelligible species in the angelic minds; as a builder who, if he had intended to build a larger house, would have made larger foundations. Hence, for God to add a new creature to the universe, means that He would add a new intelligible species to an angel.

THIRD ARTICLE [I, Q. 56, Art. 3]

Whether an Angel Knows God by His Own Natural Principles?

Objection 1: It would seem that the angels cannot know God by their natural principles. For Dionysius says (Div. Nom. i) that God "by His incomprehensible might is placed above all heavenly minds." Afterwards he adds that, "since He is above all substances, He is remote from all knowledge."

Obj. 2: Further, God is infinitely above the intellect of an angel. But what is infinitely beyond cannot be reached. Therefore it appears that an angel cannot know God by his natural principles.

Obj. 3: Further, it is written (1 Cor. 13:12): "We see now through a glass in a dark manner; but then face to face." From this it appears that there is a twofold knowledge of God; the one, whereby He is seen in His essence, according to which He is said to be seen face to face; the other whereby He is seen in the mirror of creatures. As was already shown (Q. 12, A. 4), an angel cannot have the former knowledge by his natural principles. Nor does vision through a mirror belong to the angels, since they do not derive their knowledge of God from sensible things, as Dionysius observes (Div. Nom. vii). Therefore the angels cannot know God by their natural powers.

*On the contrary,* The angels are mightier in knowledge than men. Yet men can know God through their natural principles; according to Rom. 1:19: "what is known of God is manifest in them." Therefore much more so can the angels.

*I answer that,* The angels can have some knowledge of God by their own principles. In evidence whereof it must be borne in mind that a thing is known in three ways: first, by the presence of its essence in the knower, as light can be seen in the eye; and so we have said that an angel knows himself—secondly, by the presence of its similitude in the power which knows it, as a stone is seen by the eye from its image being in the eye—thirdly, when the image of the object known is not drawn directly from the object itself, but from something else in which it is made to appear, as when we behold a man in a mirror.

To the first-named class that knowledge of God is likened by which He is seen through His essence; and knowledge such as this cannot accrue to any creature from its natural principles, as was said above (Q. 12, A. 4). The third class comprises the knowledge whereby we know God while we are on earth, by His likeness reflected in creatures, according to Rom. 1:20: "The invisible things of God are clearly seen, being understood by the things that are made." Hence, too, we are said to see God in a mirror. But the knowledge, whereby according to his natural principles the angel knows God, stands midway between these two; and is likened to that knowledge whereby a thing is seen through the species abstracted from it. For since God's image is impressed on the very nature of the angel in his essence, the angel knows God in as much as he is the image of God. Yet he does not behold God's essence; because no created likeness is sufficient to represent the Divine essence. Such knowledge then approaches rather to the specular kind; because the angelic nature is itself a kind of mirror representing the Divine image.

Reply Obj. 1: Dionysius is speaking of the knowledge of comprehension, as his words expressly state. In this way God is not known by any created intellect.

Reply Obj. 2: Since an angel's intellect and essence are infinitely remote from God, it follows that he cannot comprehend Him; nor can he see God's essence through his own nature. Yet it does not follow on that account that he can have no knowledge of Him at all: because, as God is infinitely remote from the angel, so the knowledge which God has of Himself is infinitely above the knowledge which an angel has of Him.

Reply Obj. 3: The knowledge which an angel has of God is midway between these two kinds of knowledge; nevertheless it approaches more to one of them, as was said above.

## QUESTION 57

OF THE ANGEL'S KNOWLEDGE OF MATERIAL THINGS (In Five Articles)

We next investigate the material objects which are known by the angels. Under this heading there are five points of inquiry:

(1) Whether the angels know the natures of material things?

(2) Whether they know single things?

(3) Whether they know the future?

(4) Whether they know secret thoughts?

(5) Whether they know all mysteries of grace?

FIRST ARTICLE [I, Q. 57, Art. 1]

Whether the Angels Know Material Things?

Objection 1: It would seem that the angels do not know material things. For the object understood is the perfection of him who understands it. But material things cannot be the perfections of angels, since they are beneath them. Therefore the angels do not know material things.

Obj. 2: Further, intellectual vision is only of such things as exist within the soul by their essence, as is said in the gloss [*On 2 Cor. 12:2, taken from Augustine (Gen. ad lit. xii. 28)]. But the material things cannot enter by their essence into man's soul, nor into the angel's mind. Therefore they cannot be known by intellectual vision, but only by imaginary vision, whereby the images of bodies are apprehended, and by sensible vision, which regards bodies in themselves. Now there is neither imaginary nor sensible vision in the angels, but only intellectual. Therefore the angels cannot know material things.

Obj. 3: Further, material things are not actually intelligible, but are knowable by apprehension of sense and of imagination, which does not exist in angels. Therefore angels do not know material things.

*On the contrary,* Whatever the lower power can do, the higher can do likewise. But man's intellect, which in the order of nature is inferior to the angel's, can know material things. Therefore much more can the mind of an angel.

*I answer that,* The established order of things is for the higher beings to be more perfect than the lower; and for whatever is contained deficiently, partially, and in manifold manner in the lower beings, to be contained in the higher eminently, and in a certain degree of fulness and simplicity. Therefore, in God, as in the highest source of things, all things pre-exist supersubstantially in respect of His simple Being itself, as Dionysius says (Div. Nom. 1). But among other creatures the angels are nearest to God, and resemble Him most; hence they share more fully and more perfectly in the Divine goodness, as Dionysius says (Coel. Hier. iv). Consequently, all material things pre-exist in the angels more simply and less materially even than in themselves, yet in a more manifold manner and less perfectly than in God.

Now whatever exists in any subject, is contained in it after the manner of such subject. But the angels are intellectual beings of their own nature. Therefore, as God knows material things by His essence, so do the angels know them, forasmuch as they are in the angels by their intelligible species.

Reply Obj. 1: The thing understood is the perfection of the one who understands, by reason of the intelligible species which he has in his intellect. And thus the intelligible species which are in the intellect of an angel are perfections and acts in regard to that intellect.

Reply Obj. 2: Sense does not apprehend the essences of things, but only their outward accidents. In like manner neither does the imagination; for it apprehends only the images of bodies. The intellect alone apprehends the essences of things. Hence it is said (De Anima iii, text. 26) that the object of the intellect is "what a thing is," regarding which it does not err; as neither does sense regarding its proper sensible object. So therefore the essences of material things are in the intellect of man and angels, as the thing understood is in him who understands, and not according to their real natures. But some things are in an intellect or in the soul according to both natures; and in either case there is intellectual vision.

Reply Obj. 3: If an angel were to draw his knowledge of material things from the material things themselves, he would require to make them actually intelligible by a process of abstraction. But he does not derive his knowledge of them from the material things themselves; he has knowledge of material things by actually intelligible species of things, which species are connatural to him; just as our intellect has, by species which it makes intelligible by abstraction.

SECOND ARTICLE [I, Q. 57, Art. 2]

Whether an Angel Knows Singulars?

Objection 1: It would seem that angels do not know singulars. For the Philosopher says (Poster. i, text. 22): "The sense has for its object singulars, but the intellect, universals." Now, in the angels there is no power of understanding save the intellectual power, as is evident from what was said above (Q. 54, A. 5). Consequently they do not know singulars.

Obj. 2: Further, all knowledge comes about by some assimilation of the knower to the object known. But it is not possible for any assimilation to exist between an angel and a singular object, in so far as it is singular; because, as was observed above (Q. 50, A. 2), an angel is immaterial, while matter is the principle of singularity. Therefore the angel cannot know singulars.

Obj. 3: Further, if an angel does know singulars, it is either by singular or by universal species. It is not by singular species; because in this way he would require to have an infinite number of species. Nor is it by universal species; since the universal is not the sufficient principle for knowing the singular as such, because singular things are not known in the universal except potentially. Therefore the angel does not know singulars.

*On the contrary,* No one can guard what he does not know. But angels guard individual men, according to Ps. 90:11: "He hath given His angels charge over Thee." Consequently the angels know singulars.

*I answer that,* Some have denied to the angels all knowledge of singulars. In the first place this derogates from the Catholic faith, which asserts that these lower things are administered by angels, according to Heb. 1:14: "They are all ministering spirits." Now, if they had no knowledge of singulars, they could exercise no provision over what is going on in this world; since acts belong to individuals: and this is against the text of Eccles. 5:5: "Say not before the angel: There is no providence." Secondly, it is also contrary to the teachings of philosophy, according to which the angels are stated to be the movers of the heavenly spheres, and to move them according to their knowledge and will.

Consequently others have said that the angel possesses knowledge of singulars, but in their universal causes, to which all particular effects are reduced; as if the astronomer were to foretell a coming eclipse from the dispositions of the movements of the heavens. This opinion does not escape the aforesaid implications; because, to know a singular, merely in its universal causes, is not to know it as singular, that is, as it exists here and now. The astronomer, knowing from computation of the heavenly movements that an eclipse is about to happen, knows it in the universal; yet he does not know it as taking place now, except by the senses. But administration, providence and movement are of singulars, as they are here and now existing.

Therefore, it must be said differently, that, as man by his various powers of knowledge knows all classes of things, apprehending universals and immaterial things by his intellect, and things singular and corporeal by the senses, so an angel knows both by his one mental power. For the order of things runs in this way, that the higher a thing is, so much the more is its power united and far-reaching: thus in man himself it is manifest that the common sense which is higher than the proper sense, although it is but one faculty, knows everything apprehended by the five outward senses, and some other things which no outer sense knows; for example, the difference between white and sweet. The same is to be observed in other cases. Accordingly, since an angel is above man in the order of nature, it is unreasonable to say that a man knows by any one of his powers something which an angel by his one faculty of knowledge, namely, the intellect, does not know. Hence Aristotle pronounces it ridiculous to say that a discord, which is known to us, should be unknown to God (De Anima i, text. 80; *Metaph.* text. 15).

The manner in which an angel knows singular things can be considered from this, that, as things proceed from God in order that they may subsist in their own natures, so likewise they proceed in order that they may exist in the angelic mind. Now it is clear that there comes forth from God not only whatever belongs to their universal nature, but likewise all that goes to make up their principles of individuation; since He is the cause of the entire substance of the thing, as to both its matter and its form. And for as much as He causes, does He know; for His knowledge is the cause of a thing, as was shown above (Q. 14, A. 8). Therefore as by His essence, by which He causes all things, God is the likeness of all things, and knows all things, not only as to their universal natures, but also as to their singularity; so through the species imparted to them do the angels know things, not only as to their universal nature, but likewise in their individual conditions, in so far as they are the manifold representations of that one simple essence.

Reply Obj. 1: The Philosopher is speaking of our intellect, which apprehends only by a process of abstraction; and by such abstraction from material conditions the thing abstracted becomes a universal. Such a manner of understanding is not in keeping with the nature of the angels, as was said above (Q. 55, A. 2, A. 3 ad 1), and consequently there is no comparison.

Reply Obj. 2: It is not according to their nature that the angels are likened to material things, as one thing resembles another by agreement in genus, species, or accident; but as the higher bears resemblance to the lower, as the sun does to fire. Even in this way there is in God a resemblance of all things, as to both matter and form, in so far as there pre-exists in Him as in its cause whatever is to be found in things. For the same reason, the species in the angel's intellect, which are images drawn from the Divine essence, are the images of things not only as to their form, but also as to their matter.

Reply Obj. 3: Angels know singulars by universal forms, which nevertheless are the images of things both as to their universal, and as to their individuating principles. How many things can be known by the same species, has been already stated above (Q. 55, A. 3, ad 3).

THIRD ARTICLE [I, Q. 57, Art. 3]

Whether Angels Know the Future?

Objection 1: It would seem that the angels know future events. For angels are mightier in knowledge than men. But some men know many future events. Therefore much more do the angels.

Obj. 2: Further, the present and the future are differences of time. But the angel's intellect is above time; because, as is said in *De Causis*, "an intelligence keeps pace with eternity," that is, aeviternity. Therefore, to the angel's mind, past and future are not different, but he knows each indifferently.

Obj. 3: Further, the angel does not understand by species derived from things, but by innate universal species. But universal species refer equally to present, past, and future. Therefore it appears that the angels know indifferently things past, present, and future.

Obj. 4: Further, as a thing is spoken of as distant by reason of time, so is it by reason of place. But angels know things which are distant according to place. Therefore they likewise know things distant according to future time.

*On the contrary,* Whatever is the exclusive sign of the Divinity, does not belong to the angels. But to know future events is the exclusive sign of the Divinity, according to Isa. 41:23: "Show the things that are to come hereafter, and we shall know that ye are gods." Therefore the angels do not know future events.

*I answer that,* The future can be known in two ways. First, it can be known in its cause. And thus, future events which proceed necessarily from their causes, are known with sure knowledge; as that the sun will rise tomorrow. But events which proceed from their causes in the majority of cases, are not known for certain, but conjecturally; thus the doctor knows beforehand the health of the patient. This manner of knowing future events exists in the angels, and by so much the more than it does in us, as they understand the causes of things both more universally and more perfectly; thus doctors who penetrate more deeply into the causes of an ailment can pronounce a surer verdict on the future issue thereof. But events which proceed from their causes in the minority of cases are quite unknown; such as casual and chance events.

In another way future events are known in themselves. To know the future in this way belongs to God alone; and not merely to know those events which happen of necessity, or in the majority of cases, but even casual and chance events; for God sees all things in His eternity, which, being simple, is present to all time, and embraces all time. And therefore God's one glance is cast over all things which happen in all time as present before Him; and He beholds all things as they are in themselves, as was said before when dealing with God's knowledge (Q. 14, A. 13). But the mind of an angel, and every created intellect, fall far short of God's eternity; hence the future as it is in itself cannot be known by any created intellect.

Reply Obj. 1: Men cannot know future things except in their causes, or by God's revelation. The angels know the future in the same way, but much more distinctly.

Reply Obj. 2: Although the angel's intellect is above that time according to which corporeal movements are reckoned, yet there is a time in his mind according to the succession of intelligible concepts; of which Augustine says (Gen. ad lit. viii) that "God moves the spiritual creature according to time." And thus, since there is succession in the angel's intellect, not all things that happen through all time, are present to the angelic mind.

Reply Obj. 3: Although the species in the intellect of an angel, in so far as they are species, refer equally to things present, past, and future; nevertheless the present, past, and future; nevertheless the present, past, and future do not bear the same relations to the species. Present things have a nature according to which they resemble the species in the mind of an angel: and so they can be known thereby. Things which are yet to come have not yet a nature whereby they are likened to such species; consequently, they cannot be known by those species.

Reply Obj. 4: Things distant according to place are already existing in nature; and share in some species, whose image is in the angel; whereas this is not true of future things, as has been stated. Consequently there is no comparison.

FOURTH ARTICLE [I, Q. 57, Art. 4]

Whether Angels Know Secret Thoughts?

Objection 1: It would seem that the angels know secret thoughts. For Gregory (Moral. xviii), explaining Job 28:17: "Gold or crystal cannot equal it," says that "then," namely in the bliss of those rising from the dead, "one shall be as evident to another as he is to himself, and when once the mind of each is seen, his conscience will at the same time be penetrated." But those who rise shall be like the angels, as is stated (Matt. 22:30). Therefore an angel can see what is in another's conscience.

Obj. 2: Further, intelligible species bear the same relation to the intellect as shapes do to bodies. But when the body is seen its shape is seen. Therefore, when an intellectual substance is seen, the intelligible species within it is also seen. Consequently, when one angel beholds another, or even a soul, it seems that he can see the thoughts of both.

Obj. 3: Further, the ideas of our intellect resemble the angel more than do the images in our imagination; because the former are actually understood, while the latter are understood only potentially. But the images in our imagination can be known by an angel as corporeal things are known: because the imagination is a corporeal faculty. Therefore it seems that an angel can know the thoughts of the intellect.

*On the contrary,* What is proper to God does not belong to the angels. But it is proper to God to read the secrets of hearts, according to Jer. 17:9: "The heart is perverse above all things, and unsearchable; who can know it? I am the Lord, Who search the heart." Therefore angels do not know the secrets of hearts.

*I answer that,* A secret thought can be known in two ways: first, in its effect. In this way it can be known not only by an angel, but also by man; and with so much the greater subtlety according as the effect is the more hidden. For thought is sometimes discovered not merely by outward act, but also by change of countenance; and doctors can tell some passions of the soul by the mere pulse. Much more then can angels, or even demons, the more deeply they penetrate those occult bodily modifications. Hence Augustine says (De divin. daemon.) that demons "sometimes with the greatest faculty learn man's dispositions, not only when expressed by speech, but even when conceived in thought, when the soul expresses them by certain signs in the body"; although (Retract. ii, 30) he says "it cannot be asserted how this is done."

In another way thoughts can be known as they are in the mind, and affections as they are in the will: and thus God alone can know the thoughts of hearts and affections of wills. The reason of this is, because the rational creature is subject to God only, and He alone can work in it Who is its principal object and last end: this will be developed later (Q. 63, A. 1; Q. 105, A. 5). Consequently all that is in the will, and all things that depend only on the will, are known to God alone. Now it is evident that it depends entirely on the will for anyone actually to consider anything; because a man who has a habit of knowledge, or any intelligible species, uses them at will. Hence the Apostle says (1 Cor. 2:11): "For what man knoweth the things of a man, but the spirit of a man that is in him?"

Reply Obj. 1: In the present life one man's thought is not known by another owing to a twofold hindrance; namely, on account of the grossness of the body, and because the will shuts up its secrets. The first obstacle will be removed at the Resurrection, and does not exist at all in the angels; while the second will remain, and is in the angels now. Nevertheless the brightness of the body will show forth the quality of the soul; as to its amount of grace and of glory. In this way one will be able to see the mind of another.

Reply Obj. 2: Although one angel sees the intelligible species of another, by the fact that the species are proportioned to the rank of these substances according to greater or lesser universality, yet it does not follow that one knows how far another makes use of them by actual consideration.

Reply Obj. 3: The appetite of the brute does not control its act, but follows the impression of some other corporeal or spiritual cause. Since, therefore, the angels know corporeal things and their dispositions, they can thereby know what is passing in the appetite or in the imaginative apprehension of the brute beasts, and even of man, in so far as the sensitive appetite sometimes, through following some bodily impression, influences his conduct, as always happens in brutes. Yet the angels do not necessarily know the movement of the sensitive appetite and the imaginative apprehension of man in so far as these are moved by the will and reason; because, even the lower part of the soul has some share of reason, as obeying its ruler, as is said in *Ethics* iii, 12. But it does not follow that, if the angel knows what is passing through man's sensitive appetite or imagination, he knows what is in the thought or will: because the intellect or will is not subject to the sensitive appetite or the imagination, but can make various uses of them.

FIFTH ARTICLE [I, Q. 57, Art. 5]

Whether the Angels Know the Mysteries of Grace?

Objection 1: It would seem that the angels know mysteries of grace. For, the mystery of the Incarnation is the most excellent of all mysteries. But the angels knew of it from the beginning; for Augustine says (Gen. ad lit. v, 19): "This mystery was hidden in God through the ages, yet so that it was known to the princes and powers in heavenly places." And the Apostle says (1 Tim. 3:16): "That great mystery of godliness appeared unto angels*." [*Vulg.: 'Great is the mystery of godliness, which ... appeared unto angels.'] Therefore the angels know the mysteries of grace.

Obj. 2: Further, the reasons of all mysteries of grace are contained in the Divine wisdom. But the angels behold God's wisdom, which is His essence. Therefore they know the mysteries of grace.

Obj. 3: Further, the prophets are enlightened by the angels, as is clear from Dionysius (Coel. Hier. iv). But the prophets knew mysteries of grace; for it is said (Amos 3:7): "For the Lord God doth nothing without revealing His secret to His servants the prophets." Therefore angels know the mysteries of grace.

*On the contrary,* No one learns what he knows already. Yet even the highest angels seek out and learn mysteries of grace. For it is stated (Coel. Hier. vii) that "Sacred Scripture describes some heavenly essences as questioning Jesus, and learning from Him the knowledge of His Divine work for us; and Jesus as teaching them directly": as is evident in Isa. 63:1, where, on the angels asking, "Who is he who cometh up from Edom?" Jesus answered, "It is I, Who speak justice." Therefore the angels do not know mysteries of grace.

*I answer that,* There is a twofold knowledge in the angel. The first is his natural knowledge, according to which he knows things both by his essence, and by innate species. By such knowledge the angels cannot know mysteries of grace. For these mysteries depend upon the pure will of God: and if an angel cannot learn the thoughts of another angel, which depend upon the will of such angel, much less can he ascertain what depends entirely upon God's will. The Apostle reasons in this fashion (1 Cor. 2:11): "No one knoweth the things of a man [*Vulg.: 'What man knoweth the things of a man, but ... ?'], but the spirit of a man that is in him." So, "the things also that are of God no man knoweth but the Spirit of God."

There is another knowledge of the angels, which renders them happy; it is the knowledge whereby they see the Word, and things in the Word. By such vision they know mysteries of grace, but not all mysteries: nor do they all know them equally; but just as God wills them to learn by revelation; as the Apostle says (1 Cor. 2:10): "But to us God hath revealed them through His Spirit"; yet so that the higher angels beholding the Divine wisdom more clearly, learn more and deeper mysteries in the vision of God, which mysteries they communicate to the lower angels by enlightening them. Some of these mysteries they knew from the very beginning of their creation; others they are taught afterwards, as befits their ministrations.

Reply Obj. 1: One can speak in two ways of the mystery of the Incarnation. First of all, in general; and in this way it was revealed to all from the commencement of their beatitude. The reason of this is, that this is a kind of general principle to which all their duties are ordered. For "all are [*Vulg.: 'Are they not all.'] ministering spirits, sent to minister for them who shall receive the inheritance of salvation" (Heb. 1:14); and this is brought about by the mystery of the Incarnation. Hence it was necessary for all of them to be instructed in this mystery from the very beginning.

We can speak of the mystery of the Incarnation in another way, as to its special conditions. Thus not all the angels were instructed on all points from the beginning; even the higher angels learned these afterwards, as appears from the passage of Dionysius already quoted.

Reply Obj. 2: Although the angels in bliss behold the Divine wisdom, yet they do not comprehend it. So it is not necessary for them to know everything hidden in it.

Reply Obj. 3: Whatever the prophets knew by revelation of the mysteries of grace, was revealed in a more excellent way to the angels. And although God revealed in general to the prophets what He was one day to do regarding the salvation of the human race, still the apostles knew some particulars of the same, which the prophets did not know. Thus we read (Eph. 3:4, 5): "As you reading, may understand my knowledge in the mystery of Christ, which in other generations was not known to the sons of men, as it is now revealed to His holy apostles." Among the prophets also, the later ones knew what the former did not know; according to Ps. 118:100: "I have had understanding above ancients," and Gregory says: "The knowledge of Divine things increased as time went on" (Hom. xvi in Ezech.).

## QUESTION 58

OF THE MODE OF ANGELIC KNOWLEDGE (In Seven Articles)

After the foregoing we have now to treat of the mode of the angelic knowledge, concerning which there are seven points of inquiry:

(1) Whether the angel's intellect be sometimes in potentiality, and sometimes in act?

(2) Whether the angel can understand many things at the same time?

(3) Whether the angel's knowledge is discursive?

(4) Whether he understands by composing and dividing?

(5) Whether there can be error in the angel's intellect?

(6) Whether his knowledge can be styled as morning and evening?

(7) Whether the morning and evening knowledge are the same, or do they differ?

FIRST ARTICLE [I, Q. 58, Art. 1]

Whether the Angel's Intellect Is Sometimes in Potentiality, Sometimes in Act?

Objection 1: It would seem that the angel's intellect is sometimes in potentiality and sometimes in act. For movement is the act of what is in potentiality, as stated in *Phys.* iii, 6. But the angels' minds are moved by understanding, as Dionysius says (Div. Nom. iv). Therefore the angelic minds are sometimes in potentiality.

Obj. 2: Further, since desire is of a thing not possessed but possible to have, whoever desires to know anything is in potentiality thereto. But it is said (1 Pet. 1:12): "On Whom the angels desire to look." Therefore the angel's intellect is sometimes in potentiality.

Obj. 3: Further, in the book *De Causis* it is stated that "an intelligence understands according to the mode of its substance." But the angel's intelligence has some admixture of potentiality. Therefore it sometimes understands potentially.

*On the contrary,* Augustine says (Gen. ad lit. ii): "Since the angels were created, in the eternity of the Word, they enjoy holy and devout contemplation." Now a contemplating intellect is not in potentiality, but in act. Therefore the intellect of an angel is not in potentiality.

*I answer that,* As the Philosopher states (De Anima iii, text. 8; Phys. viii, 32), the intellect is in potentiality in two ways; first, "as before learning or discovering," that is, before it has the habit of knowledge; secondly, as "when it possesses the habit of knowledge, but does not actually consider." In the first way an angel's intellect is never in potentiality with regard to the things to which his natural knowledge extends. For, as the higher, namely, the heavenly, bodies have no potentiality to existence, which is not fully actuated, in the same way the heavenly intellects, the angels, have no intelligible potentiality which is not fully completed by connatural intelligible species. But with regard to things divinely revealed to them, there is nothing to hinder them from being in potentiality: because even the heavenly bodies are at times in potentiality to being enlightened by the sun.

In the second way an angel's intellect can be in potentiality with regard to things learnt by natural knowledge; for he is not always actually considering everything that he knows by natural knowledge. But as to the knowledge of the Word, and of the things he beholds in the Word, he is never in this way in potentiality; because he is always actually beholding the Word, and the things he sees in the Word. For the bliss of the angels consists in such vision; and beatitude does not consist in habit, but in act, as the Philosopher says (Ethic. i, 8).

Reply Obj. 1: Movement is taken there not as the act of something imperfect, that is, of something existing in potentiality, but as the act of something perfect, that is, of one actually existing. In this way understanding and feeling are termed movements, as stated in *De Anima* iii, text. 28.

Reply Obj. 2: Such desire on the part of the angels does not exclude the object desired, but weariness thereof. Or they are said to desire the vision of God with regard to fresh revelations, which they receive from God to fit them for the tasks which they have to perform.

Reply Obj. 3: In the angel's substance there is no potentiality divested of act. In the same way, the angel's intellect is never so in potentiality as to be without act.

SECOND ARTICLE [I, Q. 58, Art. 2]

Whether an Angel Can Understand Many Things at the Same Time?

Objection 1: It would seem that an angel cannot understand many things at the same time. For the Philosopher says (Topic. ii, 4) that "it may happen that we know many things, but understand only one."

Obj. 2: Further, nothing is understood unless the intellect be informed by an intelligible species; just at the body is formed by shape. But one body cannot be formed into many shapes. Therefore neither can one intellect simultaneously understand various intelligible things.

Obj. 3: Further, to understand is a kind of movement. But no movement terminates in various terms. Therefore many things cannot be understood altogether.

*On the contrary,* Augustine says (Gen. ad lit. iv, 32): "The spiritual faculty of the angelic mind comprehends most easily at the same time all things that it wills."

*I answer that,* As unity of term is requisite for unity of movement, so is unity of object required for unity of operation. Now it happens that several things may be taken as several or as one; like the parts of a continuous whole. For if each of the parts be considered severally they are many: consequently neither by sense nor by intellect are they grasped by one operation, nor all at once. In another way they are taken as forming one in the whole; and so they are grasped both by sense and intellect all at once and by one operation; as long as the entire continuous whole is considered, as is stated in *De Anima* iii, text. 23. In this way our intellect understands together both the subject and the predicate, as forming parts of one proposition; and also two things compared together, according as they agree in one point of comparison. From this it is evident that many things, in so far as they are distinct, cannot be understood at once; but in so far as they are comprised under one intelligible concept, they can be understood together. Now everything is actually intelligible according as its image is in the intellect. All things, then, which can be known by one intelligible species, are known as one intelligible object, and therefore are understood simultaneously. But things known by various intelligible species, are apprehended as different intelligible objects.

Consequently, by such knowledge as the angels have of things through the Word, they know all things under one intelligible species, which is the Divine essence. Therefore, as regards such knowledge, they know all things at once: just as in heaven "our thoughts will not be fleeting, going and returning from one thing to another, but we shall survey all our knowledge at the same time by one glance," as Augustine says (De Trin. xv, 16). But by that knowledge wherewith the angels know things by innate species, they can at one time know all things which can be comprised under one species; but not such as are under various species.

Reply Obj. 1: To understand many things as one, is, so to speak, to understand one thing.

Reply Obj. 2: The intellect is informed by the intelligible species which it has within it. So it can behold at the same time many intelligible objects under one species; as one body can by one shape be likened to many bodies.

To the third objection the answer is the same as the first.

THIRD ARTICLE [I, Q. 58, Art. 3]

Whether an Angel's Knowledge Is Discursive?

Objection 1: It would seem that the knowledge of an angel is discursive. For the discursive movement of the mind comes from one thing being known through another. But the angels know one thing through another; for they know creatures through the Word. Therefore the intellect of an angel knows by discursive method.

Obj. 2: Further, whatever a lower power can do, the higher can do. But the human intellect can syllogize, and know causes in effects; all of which is the discursive method. Therefore the intellect of the angel, which is higher in the order of nature, can with greater reason do this.

Obj. 3: Further, Isidore (De sum. bono i, 10) says that "demons learn more things by experience." But experimental knowledge is discursive: for, "one experience comes of many remembrances, and one universal from many experiences," as Aristotle observes (Poster. ii; *Metaph.* vii). Therefore an angel's knowledge is discursive.

*On the contrary,* Dionysius says (Div. Nom. vii) that the "angels do not acquire Divine knowledge from separate discourses, nor are they led to something particular from something common."

*I answer that,* As has often been stated (A. 1; Q. 55, A. 1), the angels hold that grade among spiritual substances which the heavenly bodies hold among corporeal substances: for Dionysius calls them "heavenly minds" (loc. cit.). Now, the difference between heavenly and earthly bodies is this, that earthly bodies obtain their last perfection by chance and movement: while the heavenly bodies have their last perfection at once from their very nature. So, likewise, the lower, namely, the human, intellects obtain their perfection in the knowledge of truth by a kind of movement and discursive intellectual operation; that is to say, as they advance from one known thing to another. But, if from the knowledge of a known principle they were straightway to perceive as known all its consequent conclusions, then there would be no discursive process at all. Such is the condition of the angels, because in the truths which they know naturally, they at once behold all things whatsoever that can be known in them.

Therefore they are called "intellectual beings": because even with ourselves the things which are instantly grasped by the mind are said to be understood [intelligi]; hence "intellect" is defined as the habit of first principles. But human souls which acquire knowledge of truth by the discursive method are called "rational"; and this comes of the feebleness of their intellectual light. For if they possessed the fulness of intellectual light, like the angels, then in the first aspect of principles they would at once comprehend their whole range, by perceiving whatever could be reasoned out from them.

Reply Obj. 1: Discursion expresses movement of a kind. Now all movement is from something before to something after. Hence discursive knowledge comes about according as from something previously known one attains to the knowledge of what is afterwards known, and which was previously unknown. But if in the thing perceived something else be seen at the same time, as an object and its image are seen simultaneously in a mirror, it is not discursive knowledge. And in this way the angels know things in the Word.

Reply Obj. 2: The angels can syllogize, in the sense of knowing a syllogism; and they see effects in causes, and causes in effects: yet they do not acquire knowledge of an unknown truth in this way, by syllogizing from causes to effect, or from effect to cause.

Reply Obj. 3: Experience is affirmed of angels and demons simply by way of similitude, forasmuch as they know sensible things which are present, yet without any discursion withal.

FOURTH ARTICLE [I, Q. 58, Art. 4]

Whether the Angels Understand by Composing and Dividing?

Objection 1: It would seem that the angels understand by composing and dividing. For, where there is multiplicity of things understood, there is composition of the same, as is said in *De Anima* iii, text. 21. But there is a multitude of things understood in the angelic mind; because angels apprehend different things by various species, and not all at one time. Therefore there is composition and division in the angel's mind.

Obj. 2: Further, negation is far more remote from affirmation than any two opposite natures are; because the first of distinctions is that of affirmation and negation. But the angel knows certain distant natures not by one, but by diverse species, as is evident from what was said (A. 2). Therefore he must know affirmation and negation by diverse species. And so it seems that he understands by composing and dividing.

Obj. 3: Further, speech is a sign of the intellect. But in speaking to men, angels use affirmative and negative expressions, which are signs of composition and of division in the intellect; as is manifest from many passages of Sacred Scripture. Therefore it seems that the angel understands by composing and dividing.

*On the contrary,* Dionysius says (Div. Nom. vii) that "the intellectual power of the angel shines forth with the clear simplicity of divine concepts." But a simple intelligence is without composition and division. Therefore the angel understands without composition or division.

*I answer that,* As in the intellect, when reasoning, the conclusion is compared with the principle, so in the intellect composing and dividing, the predicate is compared with the subject. For if our intellect were to see at once the truth of the conclusion in the principle, it would never understand by discursion and reasoning. In like manner, if the intellect in apprehending the quiddity of the subject were at once to have knowledge of all that can be attributed to, or removed from, the subject, it would never understand by composing and dividing, but only by understanding the essence. Thus it is evident that for the self-same reason our intellect understands by discursion, and by composing and dividing, namely, that in the first apprehension of anything newly apprehended it does not at once grasp all that is virtually contained in it. And this comes from the weakness of the intellectual light within us, as has been said (A. 3). Hence, since the intellectual light is perfect in the angel, for he is a pure and most clear mirror, as Dionysius says (Div. Nom. iv), it follows that as the angel does not understand by reasoning, so neither does he by composing and dividing.

Nevertheless, he understands the composition and the division of enunciations, just as he apprehends the reasoning of syllogisms: for he understands simply, such things as are composite, things movable immovably, and material things immaterially.

Reply Obj. 1: Not every multitude of things understood causes composition, but a multitude of such things understood that one of them is attributed to, or denied of, another. When an angel apprehends the nature of anything, he at the same time understands whatever can be either attributed to it, or denied of it. Hence, in apprehending a nature, he by one simple perception grasps all that we can learn by composing and dividing.

Reply Obj. 2: The various natures of things differ less as to their mode of existing than do affirmation and negation. Yet, as to the way in which they are known, affirmation and negation have something more in common; because directly the truth of an affirmation is known, the falsehood of the opposite negation is known also.

Reply Obj. 3: The fact that angels use affirmative and negative forms of speech, shows that they know both composition and division: yet not that they know by composing and dividing, but by knowing simply the nature of a thing.

FIFTH ARTICLE [I, Q. 58, Art. 5]

Whether There Can Be Falsehood in the Intellect of an Angel?

Objection 1: It would seem that there can be falsehood in the angel's intellect. For perversity appertains to falsehood. But, as Dionysius says (Div. Nom. iv), there is "a perverted fancy" in the demons. Therefore it seems that there can be falsehood in the intellect of the angels.

Obj. 2: Further, nescience is the cause of estimating falsely. But, as Dionysius says (Eccl. Hier. vi), there can be nescience in the angels. Therefore it seems there can be falsehood in them.

Obj. 3: Further, everything which falls short of the truth of wisdom, and which has a depraved reason, has falsehood or error in its intellect. But Dionysius (Div. Nom. vii) affirms this of the demons. Therefore it seems that there can be error in the minds of the angels.

*On the contrary,* The Philosopher says (De Anima iii, text. 41) that "the intelligence is always true." Augustine likewise says (QQ. 83, qu. 32) that "nothing but what is true can be the object of intelligence" Therefore there can be neither deception nor falsehood in the angel's knowledge.

*I answer that,* The truth of this question depends partly upon what has gone before. For it has been said (A. 4) that an angel understands not by composing and dividing, but by understanding what a thing is. Now the intellect is always true as regards what a thing is, just as the sense regarding its proper object, as is said in De Anima iii, text. 26. But by accident, deception and falsehood creep in, when we understand the essence of a thing by some kind of composition, and this happens either when we take the definition of one thing for another, or when the parts of a definition do not hang together, as if we were to accept as the definition of some creature, "a four-footed flying beast," for there is no such animal. And this comes about in things composite, the definition of which is drawn from diverse elements, one of which is as matter to the other. But there is no room for error in understanding simple quiddities, as is stated in *Metaph.* ix, text. 22; for either they are not grasped at all, and so we know nothing respecting them; or else they are known precisely as they exist.

So therefore, no falsehood, error, or deception can exist of itself in the mind of any angel; yet it does so happen accidentally; but very differently from the way it befalls us. For we sometimes get at the quiddity of a thing by a composing and dividing process, as when, by division and demonstration, we seek out the truth of a definition. Such is not the method of the angels; but through the (knowledge of the) essence of a thing they know everything that can be said regarding it. Now it is quite evident that the quiddity of a thing can be a source of knowledge with regard to everything belonging to such thing, or excluded from it; but not of what may be dependent on God's supernatural ordinance. Consequently, owing to their upright will, from their knowing the nature of every creature, the good angels form no judgments as to the nature of the qualities therein, save under the Divine ordinance; hence there can be no error or falsehood in them. But since the minds of demons are utterly perverted from the Divine wisdom, they at times form their opinions of things simply according to the natural conditions of the same. Nor are they ever deceived as to the natural properties of anything; but they can be misled with regard to supernatural matters; for example, on seeing a dead man, they may suppose that he will not rise again, or, on beholding Christ, they may judge Him not to be God.

From all this the answers to the objections of both sides of the question are evident. For the perversity of the demons comes of their not being subject to the Divine wisdom; while nescience is in the angels as regards things knowable, not naturally but supernaturally. It is, furthermore, evident that their understanding of what a thing is, is always true, save accidentally, according as it is, in an undue manner, referred to some composition or division.

SIXTH ARTICLE [I, Q. 58, A. 6]

Whether There Is a "Morning" and an "Evening" Knowledge in the Angels?

Objection 1: It would seem that there is neither an evening nor a morning knowledge in the angels; because evening and morning have an admixture of darkness. But there is no darkness in the knowledge of an angel; since there is no error nor falsehood. Therefore the angelic knowledge ought not to be termed morning and evening knowledge.

Obj. 2: Further, between evening and morning the night intervenes; while noonday falls between morning and evening. Consequently, if there be a morning and an evening knowledge in the angels, for the same reason it appears that there ought to be a noonday and a night knowledge.

Obj. 3: Further, knowledge is diversified according to the difference of the objects known: hence the Philosopher says (De Anima iii, text. 38), "The sciences are divided just as things are." But there is a threefold existence of things: to wit, in the Word; in their own natures; and in the angelic knowledge, as Augustine observes (Gen. ad lit. ii, 8). If, therefore, a morning and an evening knowledge be admitted in the angels, because of the existence of things in the Word, and in their own nature, then there ought to be admitted a third class of knowledge, on account of the existence of things in the angelic mind.

*On the contrary,* Augustine (Gen. ad lit. iv, 22, 31; De Civ. Dei xii, 7, 20) divides the knowledge of the angels into morning and evening knowledge.

*I answer that,* The expression "morning" and "evening" knowledge was devised by Augustine; who interprets the six days wherein God made all things, not as ordinary days measured by the solar circuit, since the sun was only made on the fourth day, but as one day, namely, the day of angelic knowledge as directed to six classes of things. As in the ordinary day, morning is the beginning, and evening the close of day, so, their knowledge of the primordial being of things is called morning knowledge; and this is according as things exist in the Word. But their knowledge of the very being of the thing created, as it stands in its own nature, is termed evening knowledge; because the being of things flows from the Word, as from a kind of primordial principle; and this flow is terminated in the being which they have in themselves.

Reply Obj. 1: Evening and morning knowledge in the angelic knowledge are not taken as compared to an admixture of darkness, but as compared to beginning and end. Or else it can be said, as Augustine puts it (Gen. ad lit. iv, 23), that there is nothing to prevent us from calling something light in comparison with one thing, and darkness with respect to another. In the same way the life of the faithful and the just is called light in comparison with the wicked, according to Eph. 5:8: "You were heretofore darkness; but now, light in the Lord": yet this very life of the faithful, when set in contrast to the life of glory, is termed darkness, according to 2 Pet. 1:19: "You have the firm prophetic word, whereunto you do well to attend, as to a light that shineth in a dark place." So the angel's knowledge by which he knows things in their own nature, is day in comparison with ignorance or error; yet it is dark in comparison with the vision of the Word.

Reply Obj. 2: The morning and evening knowledge belong to the day, that is, to the enlightened angels, who are quite apart from the darkness, that is, from the evil spirits. The good angels, while knowing the creature, do not adhere to it, for that would be to turn to darkness and to night; but they refer this back to the praise of God, in Whom, as in their principle, they know all things. Consequently after "evening" there is no night, but "morning"; so that morning is the end of the preceding day, and the beginning of the following, in so far as the angels refer to God's praise their knowledge of the preceding work. Noonday is comprised under the name of day, as the middle between the two extremes. Or else the noon can be referred to their knowledge of God Himself, Who has neither beginning nor end.

Reply Obj. 3: The angels themselves are also creatures. Accordingly the existence of things in the angelic knowledge is comprised under evening knowledge, as also the existence of things in their own nature.

SEVENTH ARTICLE [I, Q. 58, Art. 7]

Whether the Morning and Evening Knowledge Are One?

Objection 1: It would seem that the morning and the evening knowledge are one. For it is said (Gen. 1:5): "There was evening and morning, one day." But by the expression "day" the knowledge of the angels is to be understood, as Augustine says (Gen. ad lit. iv, 23). Therefore the morning and evening knowledge of the angels are one and the same.

Obj. 2: Further, it is impossible for one faculty to have two operations at the same time. But the angels are always using their morning knowledge; because they are always beholding God and things in God, according to Matt. 18:10. Therefore, if the evening knowledge were different from the morning, the angel could never exercise his evening knowledge.

Obj. 3: Further, the Apostle says (1 Cor. 13:10): "When that which is perfect is come, then that which is in part shall be done away." But, if the evening knowledge be different from the morning, it is compared to it as the less perfect to the perfect. Therefore the evening knowledge cannot exist together with the morning knowledge.

*On the contrary,* Augustine says (Gen. ad lit. iv, 24): "There is a vast difference between knowing anything as it is in the Word of God, and as it is in its own nature; so that the former belongs to the day, and the latter to the evening."

*I answer that,* As was observed (A. 6), the evening knowledge is that by which the angels know things in their proper nature. This cannot be understood as if they drew their knowledge from the proper nature of things, so that the preposition "in" denotes the form of a principle; because, as has been already stated (Q. 55, A. 2), the angels do not draw their knowledge from things. It follows, then, that when we say "in their proper nature" we refer to the aspect of the thing known in so far as it is an object of knowledge; that is to say, that the evening knowledge is in the angels in so far as they know the being of things which those things have in their own nature.

Now they know this through a twofold medium, namely, by innate ideas, or by the forms of things existing in the Word. For by beholding the Word, they know not merely the being of things as existing in the Word, but the being as possessed by the things themselves; as God by contemplating Himself sees that being which things have in their own nature. It, therefore, it be called evening knowledge, in so far as when the angels behold the Word, they know the being which things have in their proper nature, then the morning and the evening knowledge are essentially one and the same, and only differ as to the things known. If it be called evening knowledge, in so far as through innate ideas they know the being which things have in their own natures, then the morning and the evening knowledge differ. Thus Augustine seems to understand it when he assigns one as inferior to the other.

Reply Obj. 1: The six days, as Augustine understands them, are taken as the six classes of things known by the angels; so that the day's unit is taken according to the unit of the thing understood; which, nevertheless, can be apprehended by various ways of knowing it.

Reply Obj. 2: There can be two operations of the same faculty at the one time, one of which is referred to the other; as is evident when the will at the same time wills the end and the means to the end; and the intellect at the same instant perceives principles and conclusions through those principles, when it has already acquired knowledge. As Augustine says (Gen. ad lit. iv, 24), the evening knowledge is referred to the morning knowledge in the angels; hence there is nothing to hinder both from being at the same time in the angels.

Reply Obj. 3: On the coming of what is perfect, the opposite imperfect is done away: just as faith, which is of the things that are not seen, is made void when vision succeeds. But the imperfection of the evening knowledge is not opposed to the perfection of the morning knowledge. For that a thing be known in itself, is not opposite to its being known in its cause. Nor, again, is there any inconsistency in knowing a thing through two mediums, one of which is more perfect and the other less perfect; just as we can have a demonstrative and a probable medium for reaching the same conclusion. In like manner a thing can be known by the angel through the uncreated Word, and through an innate idea.

## QUESTION 59

THE WILL OF THE ANGELS (FOUR ARTICLES)

In the next place we must treat of things concerning the will of the angels. In the first place we shall treat of the will itself; secondly, of its movement, which is love. Under the first heading there are four points of inquiry:

(1) Whether there is will in the angels?

(2) Whether the will of the angel is his nature, or his intellect?

(3) Is there free-will in the angels?

(4) Is there an irascible and a concupiscible appetite in them?

FIRST ARTICLE [I, Q. 59, Art. 1]

Whether There Is Will in the Angels?

Objection 1: It would seem that there is no will in the angels. For as the Philosopher says (De Anima iii, text. 42), "The will is in the reason." But there is no reason in the angels, but something higher than reason. Therefore there is no will in the angels, but something higher than the will.

Obj. 2: Further, the will is comprised under the appetite, as is evident from the Philosopher (De Anima iii, text. 42). But the appetite argues something imperfect; because it is a desire of something not as yet possessed. Therefore, since there is no imperfection in the angels, especially in the blessed ones, it seems that there is no will in them.

Obj. 3: Further, the Philosopher says (De Anima ii, text. 54) that the will is a mover which is moved; for it is moved by the appetible object understood. Now the angels are immovable, since they are incorporeal. Therefore there is no will in the angels.

*On the contrary,* Augustine says (De Trin. x, 11,12) that the image of the Trinity is found in the soul according to memory, understanding, and will. But God's image is found not only in the soul of man, but also in the angelic mind, since it also is capable of knowing God. Therefore there is will in the angels.

*I answer that,* We must necessarily place a will in the angels. In evidence thereof, it must be borne in mind that, since all things flow from the Divine will, all things in their own way are inclined by appetite towards good, but in different ways. Some are inclined to good by their natural inclination, without knowledge, as plants and inanimate bodies. Such inclination towards good is called "a natural appetite." Others, again, are inclined towards good, but with some knowledge; not that they know the aspect of goodness, but that they apprehend some particular good; as in the sense, which knows the sweet, the white, and so on. The inclination which follows this apprehension is called "a sensitive appetite." Other things, again, have an inclination towards good, but with a knowledge whereby they perceive the aspect of goodness; this belongs to the intellect. This is most perfectly inclined towards what is good; not, indeed, as if it were merely guided by another towards some particular good only, like things devoid of knowledge, nor towards some particular good only, as things which have only sensitive knowledge, but as inclined towards good in general. Such inclination is termed "will." Accordingly, since the angels by their intellect know the universal aspect of goodness, it is manifest that there is a will in them.

Reply Obj. 1: Reason surpasses sense in a different way from that in which intellect surpasses reason. Reason surpasses sense according to the diversity of the objects known; for sense judges of particular objects, while reason judges of universals. Therefore there must be one appetite tending towards good in the abstract, which appetite belongs to reason; and another with a tendency towards particular good, which appetite belongs to sense. But intellect and reason differ as to their manner of knowing; because the intellect knows by simple intuition, while reason knows by a process of discursion from one thing to another. Nevertheless by such discursion reason comes to know what intellect learns without it, namely, the universal. Consequently the object presented to the appetitive faculty on the part of reason and on the part of intellect is the same. Therefore in the angels, who are purely intellectual, there is no appetite higher than the will.

Reply Obj. 2: Although the name of the appetitive part is derived from seeking things not yet possessed, yet the appetitive part reaches out not to these things only, but also to many other things; thus the name of a stone [lapis] is derived from injuring the foot [laesione pedis], though not this alone belongs to a stone. In the same way the irascible faculty is so denominated from anger [ira]; though at the same time there are several other passions in it, as hope, daring, and the rest.

Reply Obj. 3: The will is called a mover which is moved, according as to will and to understand are termed movements of a kind; and there is nothing to prevent movement of this kind from existing in the angels, since such movement is the act of a perfect agent, as stated in *De Anima* iii, text. 28.

SECOND ARTICLE [I, Q. 59, Art. 2]

Whether in the Angels the Will Differs from the Intellect?

Objection 1: It would seem that in the angel the will does not differ from the intellect and from the nature. For an angel is more simple than a natural body. But a natural body is inclined through its form towards its end, which is its good. Therefore much more so is the angel. Now the angel's form is either the nature in which he subsists, or else it is some species within his intellect. Therefore the angel inclines towards the good through his own nature, or through an intelligible species. But such inclination towards the good belongs to the will. Therefore the will of the angel does not differ from his nature or his intellect.

Obj. 2: Further, the object of the intellect is the true, while the object of the will is the good. Now the good and the true differ, not really but only logically [*Cf. Q. 16, A. 4]. Therefore will and intellect are not really different.

Obj. 3: Further, the distinction of common and proper does not differentiate the faculties; for the same power of sight perceives color and whiteness. But the good and the true seem to be mutually related as common to particular; for the true is a particular good, to wit, of the intellect. Therefore the will, whose object is the good, does not differ from the intellect, whose object is the true.

*On the contrary,* The will in the angels regards good things only, while their intellect regards both good and bad things, for they know both. Therefore the will of the angels is distinct from their intellect.

*I answer that,* In the angels the will is a special faculty or power, which is neither their nature nor their intellect. That it is not their nature is manifest from this, that the nature or essence of a thing is completely comprised within it: whatever, then, extends to anything beyond it, is not its essence. Hence we see in natural bodies that the inclination to being does not come from anything superadded to the essence, but from the matter which desires being before possessing it, and from the form which keeps it in such being when once it exists. But the inclination towards something extrinsic comes from something superadded to the essence; as tendency to a place comes from gravity or lightness, while the inclination to make something like itself comes from the active qualities.

Now the will has a natural tendency towards good. Consequently there alone are essence and will identified where all good is contained within the essence of him who wills; that is to say, in God, Who wills nothing beyond Himself except on account of His goodness. This cannot be said of any creature, because infinite goodness is quite foreign to the nature of any created thing. Accordingly, neither the will of the angel, nor that of any creature, can be the same thing as its essence.

In like manner neither can the will be the same thing as the intellect of angel or man. Because knowledge comes about in so far as the object known is within the knower; consequently the intellect extends itself to what is outside it, according as what, in its essence, is outside it is disposed to be somehow within it. On the other hand, the will goes out to what is beyond it, according as by a kind of inclination it tends, in a manner, to what is outside it. Now it belongs to one faculty to have within itself something which is outside it, and to another faculty to tend to what is outside it. Consequently intellect and will must necessarily be different powers in every creature. It is not so with God, for He has within Himself universal being, and the universal good. Therefore both intellect and will are His nature.

Reply Obj. 1: A natural body is moved to its own being by its substantial form: while it is inclined to something outside by something additional, as has been said.

Reply Obj. 2: Faculties are not differentiated by any material difference of their objects, but according to their formal distinction, which is taken from the nature of the object as such. Consequently the diversity derived from the notion of good and true suffices for the difference of intellect from will.

Reply Obj. 3: Because the good and the true are really convertible, it follows that the good is apprehended by the intellect as something true; while the true is desired by the will as something good. Nevertheless, the diversity of their aspects is sufficient for diversifying the faculties, as was said above (ad 2).

THIRD ARTICLE [I, Q. 59, Art. 3]

Whether There Is Free-Will in the Angels?

Objection 1: It would seem that there is no free-will in the angels. For the act of free-will is to choose. But there can be no choice with the angels, because choice is "the desire of something after taking counsel," while counsel is "a kind of inquiry," as stated in *Ethic.* iii, 3. But the angels' knowledge is not the result of inquiring, for this belongs to the discursiveness of reason. Therefore it appears that there is no free-will in the angels.

Obj. 2: Further, free-will implies indifference to alternatives. But in the angels on the part of their intellect there is no such indifference; because, as was observed already (Q. 58, A. 5), their intellect is not deceived as to things which are naturally intelligible to them. Therefore neither on the part of their appetitive faculty can there be free-will.

Obj. 3: Further, the natural endowments of the angels belong to them according to degrees of more or less; because in the higher angels the intellectual nature is more perfect than in the lower. But the free-will does not admit of degrees. Therefore there is no free-will in them.

*On the contrary,* Free-will is part of man's dignity. But the angels' dignity surpasses that of men. Therefore, since free-will is in men, with much more reason is it in the angels.

*I answer that,* Some things there are which act, not from any previous judgment, but, as it were, moved and made to act by others; just as the arrow is directed to the target by the archer. Others act from some kind of judgment; but not from free-will, such as irrational animals; for the sheep flies from the wolf by a kind of judgment whereby it esteems it to be hurtful to itself: such a judgment is not a free one, but implanted by nature. Only an agent endowed with an intellect can act with a judgment which is free, in so far as it apprehends the common note of goodness; from which it can judge this or the other thing to be good. Consequently, wherever there is intellect, there is free-will. It is therefore manifest that just as there is intellect, so is there free-will in the angels, and in a higher degree of perfection than in man.

Reply Obj. 1: The Philosopher is speaking of choice, as it is in man. As a man's estimate in speculative matters differs from an angel's in this, that the one needs not to inquire, while the other does so need; so is it in practical matters. Hence there is choice in the angels, yet not with the inquisitive deliberation of counsel, but by the sudden acceptance of truth.

Reply Obj. 2: As was observed already (A. 2), knowledge is effected by the presence of the known within the knower. Now it is a mark of imperfection in anything not to have within it what it should naturally have. Consequently an angel would not be perfect in his nature, if his intellect were not determined to every truth which he can know naturally. But the act of the appetitive faculty comes of this, that the affection is directed to something outside. Yet the perfection of a thing does not come from everything to which it is inclined, but only from something which is higher than it. Therefore it does not argue imperfection in an angel if his will be not determined with regard to things beneath him; but it would argue imperfection in him, were he to be indeterminate to what is above him.

Reply Obj. 3: Free-will exists in a nobler manner in the higher angels than it does in the lower, as also does the judgment of the intellect. Yet it is true that liberty, in so far as the removal of compulsion is considered, is not susceptible of greater and less degree; because privations and negations are not lessened nor increased directly of themselves; but only by their cause, or through the addition of some qualification.

FOURTH ARTICLE [I, Q. 59, Art. 4]

Whether There Is an Irascible and a Concupiscible Appetite in the Angels?

Objection 1: It would seem that there is an irascible and a concupiscible appetite in the angels. For Dionysius says (Div. Nom. iv) that in the demons there is "unreasonable fury and wild concupiscence." But demons are of the same nature as angels; for sin has not altered their nature. Therefore there is an irascible and a concupiscible appetite in the angels.

Obj. 2: Further, love and joy are in the concupiscible; while anger, hope, and fear are in the irascible appetite. But in the Sacred Scriptures these things are attributed both to the good and to the wicked angels. Therefore there is an irascible and a concupiscible appetite in the angels.

Obj. 3: Further, some virtues are said to reside in the irascible appetite and some in the concupiscible: thus charity and temperance appear to be in the concupiscible, while hope and fortitude are in the irascible. But these virtues are in the angels. Therefore there is both a concupiscible and an irascible appetite in the angels.

*On the contrary,* The Philosopher says (De Anima iii, text. 42) that the irascible and concupiscible are in the sensitive part, which does not exist in angels. Consequently there is no irascible or concupiscible appetite in the angels.

*I answer that,* The intellective appetite is not divided into irascible and concupiscible; only the sensitive appetite is so divided. The reason of this is because, since the faculties are distinguished from one another not according to the material but only by the formal distinction of objects, if to any faculty there respond an object according to some common idea, there will be no distinction of faculties according to the diversity of the particular things contained under that common idea. Just as if the proper object of the power of sight be color as such, then there are not several powers of sight distinguished according to the difference of black and white: whereas if the proper object of any faculty were white, as white, then the faculty of seeing white would be distinguished from the faculty of seeing black.

Now it is quite evident from what has been said (A. 1; Q. 16, A. 1), that the object of the intellective appetite, otherwise known as the will, is good according to the common aspect of goodness; nor can there be any appetite except of what is good. Hence, in the intellective part, the appetite is not divided according to the distinction of some particular good things, as the sensitive appetite is divided, which does not crave for what is good according to its common aspect, but for some particular good object. Accordingly, since there exists in the angels only an intellective appetite, their appetite is not distinguished into irascible and concupiscible, but remains undivided; and it is called the will.

Reply Obj. 1: Fury and concupiscence are metaphorically said to be in the demons, as anger is sometimes attributed to God;—on account of the resemblance in the effect.

Reply Obj. 2: Love and joy, in so far as they are passions, are in the concupiscible appetite, but in so far as they express a simple act of the will, they are in the intellective part: in this sense to love is to wish well to anyone; and to be glad is for the will to repose in some good possessed. Universally speaking, none of these things is said of the angels, as by way of passions; as Augustine says (De Civ. Dei ix).

Reply Obj. 3: Charity, as a virtue, is not in the concupiscible appetite, but in the will; because the object of the concupiscible appetite is the good as delectable to the senses. But the Divine goodness, which is the object of charity, is not of any such kind. For the same reason it must be said that hope does not exist in the irascible appetite; because the object of the irascible appetite is something arduous belonging to the sensible order, which the virtue of hope does not regard; since the object of hope is arduous and divine. Temperance, however, considered as a human virtue, deals with the desires of sensible pleasures, which belong to the concupiscible faculty. Similarly, fortitude regulates daring and fear, which reside in the irascible part. Consequently temperance, in so far as it is a human virtue, resides in the concupiscible part, and fortitude in the irascible. But they do not exist in the angels in this manner. For in them there are no passions of concupiscence, nor of fear and daring, to be regulated by temperance and fortitude. But temperance is predicated of them according as in moderation they display their will in conformity with the Divine will. Fortitude is likewise attributed to them, in so far as they firmly carry out the Divine will. All of this is done by their will, and not by the irascible or concupiscible appetite.

# QUESTION 60

OF THE LOVE OR DILECTION OF THE ANGELS (In Five Articles)

The next subject for our consideration is that act of the will which is love or dilection; because every act of the appetitive faculty comes of love.

Under this heading there are five points of inquiry:

(1) Whether there is natural love in the angels?

(2) Whether there is in them love of choice?

(3) Whether the angel loves himself with natural love or with love of choice?

(4) Whether one angel loves another with natural love as he loves himself?

(5) Whether the angel loves God more than self with natural love?

FIRST ARTICLE [I, Q. 60, Art. 1]

Whether There Is Natural Love or Dilection in an Angel?

Objection 1: It would seem that there is no natural love or dilection in the angels. For, natural love is contradistinguished from intellectual love, as stated by Dionysius (Div. Nom. iv). But an angel's love is intellectual. Therefore it is not natural.

Obj. 2: Further, those who love with natural love are more acted upon than active in themselves; for nothing has control over its own nature. Now the angels are not acted upon, but act of themselves; because they possess free-will, as was shown above (Q. 59, A. 3). Consequently there is no natural love in them.

Obj. 3: Further, every love is either ordinate or inordinate. Now ordinate love belongs to charity; while inordinate love belongs to wickedness. But neither of these belongs to nature; because charity is above nature, while wickedness is against nature. Therefore there is no natural love in the angels.

*On the contrary,* Love results from knowledge; for, nothing is loved except it be first known, as Augustine says (De Trin. x, 1,2). But there is natural knowledge in the angels. Therefore there is also natural love.

*I answer that,* We must necessarily place natural love in the angels. In evidence of this we must bear in mind that what comes first is always sustained in what comes after it. Now nature comes before intellect, because the nature of every subject is its essence. Consequently whatever belongs to nature must be preserved likewise in such subjects as have intellect. But it is common to every nature to have some inclination; and this is its natural appetite or love. This inclination is found to exist differently in different natures; but in each according to its mode. Consequently, in the intellectual nature there is to be found a natural inclination coming from the will; in the sensitive nature, according to the sensitive appetite; but in a nature devoid of knowledge, only according to the tendency of the nature to something. Therefore, since an angel is an intellectual nature, there must be a natural love in his will.

Reply Obj. 1: Intellectual love is contradistinguished from that natural love, which is merely natural, in so far as it belongs to a nature which has not likewise the perfection of either sense or intellect.

Reply Obj. 2: All things in the world are moved to act by something else except the First Agent, Who acts in such a manner that He is in no way moved to act by another; and in Whom nature and will are the same. So there is nothing unfitting in an angel being moved to act in so far as such natural inclination is implanted in him by the Author of his nature. Yet he is not so moved to act that he does not act himself, because he has free-will.

Reply Obj. 3: As natural knowledge is always true, so is natural love well regulated; because natural love is nothing else than the inclination implanted in nature by its Author. To say that a natural inclination is not well regulated, is to derogate from the Author of nature. Yet the rectitude of natural love is different from the rectitude of charity and virtue: because the one rectitude perfects the other; even so the truth of natural knowledge is of one kind, and the truth of infused or acquired knowledge is of another.

SECOND ARTICLE [I, Q. 60, Art. 2]

Whether There Is Love of Choice in the Angels?

Objection 1: It would seem that there is no love of choice in the angels. For love of choice appears to be rational love; since choice follows counsel, which lies in inquiry, as stated in *Ethic.* iii, 3. Now rational love is contrasted with intellectual, which is proper to angels, as is said (Div. Nom. iv). Therefore there is no love of choice in the angels.

Obj. 2: Further, the angels have only natural knowledge besides such as is infused: since they do not proceed from principles to acquire the knowledge of conclusions. Hence they are disposed to everything they can know, as our intellect is disposed towards first principles, which it can know naturally. Now love follows knowledge, as has been already stated (A. 1; Q. 16, A. 1). Consequently, besides their infused love, there is only natural love in the angels. Therefore there is no love of choice in them.

*On the contrary,* We neither merit nor demerit by our natural acts. But by their love the angels merit or demerit. Therefore there is love of choice in them.

*I answer that,* There exists in the angels a natural love, and a love of choice. Their natural love is the principle of their love of choice; because, what belongs to that which precedes, has always the nature of a principle. Wherefore, since nature is first in everything, what belongs to nature must be a principle in everything.

This is clearly evident in man, with respect to both his intellect and his will. For the intellect knows principles naturally; and from such knowledge in man comes the knowledge of conclusions, which are known by him not naturally, but by discovery, or by teaching. In like manner, the end acts in the will in the same way as the principle does in the intellect, as is laid down in *Phys.* ii, text. 89. Consequently the will tends naturally to its last end; for every man naturally wills happiness: and all other desires are caused by this natural desire; since whatever a man wills he wills on account of the end. Therefore the love of that good, which a man naturally wills as an end, is his natural love; but the love which comes of this, which is of something loved for the end's sake, is the love of choice.

There is however a difference on the part of the intellect and on the part of the will. Because, as was stated already (Q. 59, A. 2), the mind's knowledge is brought about by the inward presence of the known within the knower. It comes of the imperfection of man's intellectual nature that his mind does not simultaneously possess all things capable of being understood, but only a few things from which he is moved in a measure to grasp other things. The act of the appetitive faculty, *on the contrary,* follows the inclination of man towards things; some of which are good in themselves, and consequently are appetible in themselves; others being good only in relation to something else, and being appetible on account of something else. Consequently it does not argue imperfection in the person desiring, for him to seek one thing naturally as his end, and something else from choice as ordained to such end. Therefore, since the intellectual nature of the angels is perfect, only natural and not deductive knowledge is to be found in them, but there is to be found in them both natural love and love of choice.

In saying all this, we are passing over all that regards things which are above nature, since nature is not the sufficient principle thereof: but we shall speak of them later on (Q. 62).

Reply Obj. 1: Not all love of choice is rational love, according as rational is distinguished from intellectual love. For rational love is so called which follows deductive knowledge: but, as was said above (Q. 59, A. 3, ad 1), when treating of free-will, every choice does not follow a discursive act of the reason; but only human choice. Consequently the conclusion does not follow.

The reply to the second objection follows from what has been said.

THIRD ARTICLE [I, Q. 60, Art. 4]

Whether the Angel Loves Himself with Both Natural Love, and Love of Choice?

Objection 1: It would seem that the angel does not love himself both with natural love and a love of choice. For, as was said (A. 2), natural love regards the end itself; while love of choice regards the means to the end. But the same thing, with regard to the same, cannot be both the end and a means to the end. Therefore natural love and the love of choice cannot have the same object.

Obj. 2: Further, as Dionysius observes (Div. Nom. iv): "Love is a uniting and a binding power." But uniting and binding imply various things brought together. Therefore the angel cannot love himself.

Obj. 3: Further, love is a kind of movement. But every movement tends towards something else. Therefore it seems that an angel cannot love himself with either natural or elective love.

*On the contrary,* The Philosopher says (Ethic. ix, 8): "Love for others comes of love for oneself."

*I answer that,* Since the object of love is good, and good is to be found both in substance and in accident, as is clear from *Ethic.* i, 6, a thing may be loved in two ways; first of all as a subsisting good; and secondly as an accidental or inherent good. That is loved as a subsisting good, which is so loved that we wish well to it. But that which we wish unto another, is loved as an accidental or inherent good: thus knowledge is loved, not that any good may come to it but that it may be possessed. This kind of love has been called by the name "concupiscence" while the first is called "friendship."

Now it is manifest that in things devoid of knowledge, everything naturally seeks to procure what is good for itself; as fire seeks to mount upwards. Consequently both angel and man naturally seek their own good and perfection. This is to love self. Hence angel and man naturally love self, in so far as by natural appetite each desires what is good for self. On the other hand, each loves self with the love of choice, in so far as from choice he wishes for something which will benefit himself.

Reply Obj. 1: It is not under the same but under quite different aspects that an angel or a man loves self with natural and with elective love, as was observed above.

Reply Obj. 2: As to be one is better than to be united, so there is more oneness in love which is directed to self than in love which unites one to others. Dionysius used the terms "uniting" and "binding" in order to show the derivation of love from self to things outside self; as uniting is derived from unity.

Reply Obj. 3: As love is an action which remains within the agent, so also is it a movement which abides within the lover, but does not of necessity tend towards something else; yet it can be reflected back upon the lover so that he loves himself; just as knowledge is reflected back upon the knower, in such a way that he knows himself.

FOURTH ARTICLE [I, Q. 60, Art. 4]

Whether an Angel Loves Another with Natural Love As He Loves Himself?

Objection 1: It would seem that an angel does not love another with natural love as he loves himself. For love follows knowledge. But an angel does not know another as he knows himself: because he knows himself by his essence, while he knows another by his similitude, as was said above (Q. 56, AA. 1, 2). Therefore it seems that one angel does not love another with natural love as he loves himself.

Obj. 2: Further, the cause is more powerful than the effect; and the principle than what is derived from it. But love for another comes of love for self, as the Philosopher says (Ethic. ix, 8). Therefore one angel does not love another as himself, but loves himself more.

Obj. 3: Further, natural love is of something as an end, and is unremovable. But no angel is the end of another; and again, such love can be severed from him, as is the case with the demons, who have no love for the good angels. Therefore an angel does not love another with natural love as he loves himself.

*On the contrary,* That seems to be a natural property which is found in all, even in such as devoid of reason. But, "every beast loves its like," as is said, Ecclus. 13:19. Therefore an angel naturally loves another as he loves himself.

*I answer that,* As was observed (A. 3), both angel and man naturally love self. Now what is one with a thing, is that thing itself: consequently every thing loves what is one with itself. So, if this be one with it by natural union, it loves it with natural love; but if it be one with it by non-natural union, then it loves it with non-natural love. Thus a man loves his fellow townsman with a social love, while he loves a blood relation with natural affection, in so far as he is one with him in the principle of natural generation.

Now it is evident that what is generically or specifically one with another, is the one according to nature. And so everything loves another which is one with it in species, with a natural affection, in so far as it loves its own species. This is manifest even in things devoid of knowledge: for fire has a natural inclination to communicate its form to another thing, wherein consists this other thing's good; as it is naturally inclined to seek its own good, namely, to be borne upwards.

So then, it must be said that one angel loves another with natural affection, in so far as he is one with him in nature. But so far as an angel has something else in common with another angel, or differs from him in other respects, he does not love him with natural love.

Reply Obj. 1: The expression 'as himself' can in one way qualify the knowledge and the love on the part of the one known and loved: and thus one angel knows another as himself, because he knows the other to be even as he knows himself to be. In another way the expression can qualify the knowledge and the love on the part of the knower and lover. And thus one angel does not know another as himself, because he knows himself by his essence, and the other not by the other's essence. In like manner he does not love another as he loves himself, because he loves himself by his own will; but he does not love another by the other's will.

Reply Obj. 2: The expression "as" does not denote equality, but likeness. For since natural affection rests upon natural unity, the angel naturally loves less what is less one with him. Consequently he loves more what is numerically one with himself, than what is one only generically or specifically. But it is natural for him to have a like love for another as for himself, in this respect, that as he loves self in wishing well to self, so he loves another in wishing well to him.

Reply Obj. 3: Natural love is said to be of the end, not as of that end to which good is willed, but rather as of that good which one wills for oneself, and in consequence for another, as united to oneself. Nor can such natural love be stripped from the wicked angels, without their still retaining a natural affection towards the good angels, in so far as they share the same nature with them. But they hate them, in so far as they are unlike them according to righteousness and unrighteousness.

FIFTH ARTICLE [I, Q. 60, Art. 5]

Whether an angel by natural love loves God more than he loves himself?

Objection 1: It would seem that the angel does not love God by natural love more than he loves himself. For, as was stated (A. 4), natural love rests upon natural union. Now the Divine nature is far above the angelic nature. Therefore, according to natural love, the angel loves God less than self, or even than another angel.

Obj. 2: Further, "That on account of which a thing is such, is yet more so." But every one loves another with natural love for his own sake: because one thing loves another as good for itself. Therefore the angel does not love God more than self with natural love.

Obj. 3: Further, nature is self-centered in its operation; for we behold every agent acting naturally for its own preservation. But nature's operation would not be self-centered were it to tend towards anything else more than to nature itself. Therefore the angel does not love God more than himself from natural love.

Obj. 4: Further, it is proper to charity to love God more than self. But to love from charity is not natural to the angels; for "it is poured out upon their hearts by the Holy Spirit Who is given to them," as Augustine says (De Civ. Dei xii, 9). Therefore the angels do not love God more than themselves by natural love.

Obj. 5: Further, natural love lasts while nature endures. But the love of God more than self does not remain in the angel or man who sins; for Augustine says (De Civ. Dei xiv), "Two loves have made two cities; namely love of self unto the contempt of God has made the earthly city; while love of God unto the contempt of self has made the heavenly city." Therefore it is not natural to love God more than self.

*On the contrary,* All the moral precepts of the law come of the law of nature. But the precept of loving God more than self is a moral precept of the law. Therefore, it is of the law of nature. Consequently from natural love the angel loves God more than himself.

*I answer that,* There have been some who maintained that an angel loves God more than himself with natural love, both as to the love of concupiscence, through his seeking the Divine good for himself rather than his own good; and, in a fashion, as to the love of friendship, in so far as he naturally desires a greater good to God than to himself; because he naturally wishes God to be God, while as for himself, he wills to have his own nature. But absolutely speaking, out of the natural love he loves himself more than he does God, because he naturally loves himself before God, and with greater intensity.

The falsity of such an opinion stands in evidence, if one but consider whither natural movement tends in the natural order of things; because the natural tendency of things devoid of reason shows the nature of the natural inclination residing in the will of an intellectual nature. Now, in natural things, everything which, as such, naturally belongs to another, is principally, and more strongly inclined to that other to which it belongs, than towards itself. Such a natural tendency is evidenced from things which are moved according to nature: because "according as a thing is moved naturally, it has an inborn aptitude to be thus moved," as stated in Phys. ii, text. 78. For we observe that the part naturally exposes itself in order to safeguard the whole; as, for instance, the hand is without deliberation exposed to the blow for the whole body's safety. And since reason copies nature, we find the same inclination among the social virtues; for it behooves the virtuous citizen to expose himself to the danger of death for the public weal of the state; and if man were a natural part of the city, then such inclination would be natural to him.

Consequently, since God is the universal good, and under this good both man and angel and all creatures are comprised, because every creature in regard to its entire being naturally belongs to God, it follows that from natural love angel and man alike love God before themselves and with a greater love. Otherwise, if either of them loved self more than God, it would follow that natural love would be perverse, and that it would not be perfected but destroyed by charity.

Reply Obj. 1: Such reasoning holds good of things adequately divided whereof one is not the cause of the existence and goodness of the other; for in such natures each loves itself naturally more than it does the other, inasmuch as it is more one with itself than it is with the other. But where one is the whole cause of the existence and goodness of the other, that one is naturally more loved than self; because, as we said above, each part naturally loves the whole more than itself: and each individual naturally loves the good of the species more than its own individual good. Now God is not only the good of one species, but is absolutely the universal good; hence everything in its own way naturally loves God more than itself.

Reply Obj. 2: When it is said that God is loved by an angel "in so far" as He is good to the angel, if the expression "in so far" denotes an end, then it is false; for he does not naturally love God for his own good, but for God's sake. If it denotes the nature of love on the lover's part, then it is true; for it would not be in the nature of anyone to love God, except from this—that everything is dependent on that good which is God.

Reply Obj. 3: Nature's operation is self-centered not merely as to certain particular details, but much more as to what is common; for everything is inclined to preserve not merely its individuality, but likewise its species. And much more has everything a natural inclination towards what is the absolutely universal good.

Reply Obj. 4: God, in so far as He is the universal good, from Whom every natural good depends, is loved by everything with natural love. So far as He is the good which of its very nature beatifies all with supernatural beatitude, He is love with the love of charity.

Reply Obj. 5: Since God's substance and universal goodness are one and the same, all who behold God's essence are by the same movement of love moved towards the Divine essence as it is distinct from other things, and according as it is the universal good. And because He is naturally loved by all so far as He is the universal good, it is impossible that whoever sees Him in His essence should not love Him. But such as do not behold His essence, know Him by some particular effects, which are sometimes opposed to their will. So in this way they are said to hate God; yet nevertheless, so far as He is the universal good of all, every thing naturally loves God more than itself.

## QUESTION 61

OF THE PRODUCTION OF THE ANGELS IN THE ORDER OF NATURAL BEING (In Four Articles)

After dealing with the nature of the angels, their knowledge and will, it now remains for us to treat of their creation, or, speaking in a general way, of their origin. Such consideration is threefold. In the first place we must see how they were brought into natural existence; secondly, how they were made perfect in grace or glory; and thirdly, how some of them became wicked.

Under the first heading there are four points of inquiry:

(1) Whether the angel has a cause of his existence?

(2) Whether he has existed from eternity?

(3) Whether he was created before corporeal creatures?

(4) Whether the angels were created in the empyrean heaven?

FIRST ARTICLE [I, Q. 61, Art. 1]

Whether the Angels Have a Cause of Their Existence?

Objection 1: It would seem that the angels have no cause of their existence. For the first chapter of Genesis treats of things created by God. But there is no mention of angels. Therefore the angels were not created by God.

Obj. 2: Further, the Philosopher says (Metaph. viii, text. 16) that if any substance be a form without matter, "straightway it has being and unity of itself, and has no cause of its being and unity." But the angels are immaterial forms, as was shown above (Q. 50, A. 2). Therefore they have no cause of their being.

Obj. 3: Further, whatever is produced by any agent, from the very fact of its being produced, receives form from it. But since the angels are forms, they do not derive their form from any agent. Therefore the angels have no active cause.

*On the contrary,* It is said (Ps. 148:2): "Praise ye Him, all His angels"; and further on, verse 5: "For He spoke and they were made."

*I answer that,* It must be affirmed that angels and everything existing, except God, were made by God. God alone is His own existence; while in everything else the essence differs from the existence, as was shown above (Q. 3, A. 4). From this it is clear that God alone exists of His own essence: while all other things have their existence by participation. Now whatever exists by participation is caused by what exists essentially; as everything ignited is caused by fire. Consequently the angels, of necessity, were made by God.

Reply Obj. 1: Augustine says (De Civ. Dei xi, 50) that the angels were not passed over in that account of the first creation of things, but are designated by the name "heavens" or of "light." And they were either passed over, or else designated by the names of corporeal things, because Moses was addressing an uncultured people, as yet incapable of understanding an incorporeal nature; and if it had been divulged that there were creatures existing beyond corporeal nature, it would have proved to them an occasion of idolatry, to which they were inclined, and from which Moses especially meant to safeguard them.

Reply Obj. 2: Substances that are subsisting forms have no 'formal' cause of their existence and unity, nor such active cause as produces its effect by changing the matter from a state of potentiality to actuality; but they have a cause productive of their entire substance.

From this the solution of the third difficulty is manifest.

SECOND ARTICLE [I, Q. 61, Art. 2]

Whether the Angel Was Produced by God from Eternity?

Objection 1: It would seem that the angel was produced by God from eternity. For God is the cause of the angel by His being: for He does not act through something besides His essence. But His being is eternal. Therefore He produced the angels from eternity.

Obj. 2: Further, everything which exists at one period and not at another, is subject to time. But the angel is above time, as is laid down in the book *De Causis.* Therefore the angel is not at one time existing and at another non-existing, but exists always.

Obj. 3: Further, Augustine (De Trin. xiii) proves the soul's incorruptibility by the fact that the mind is capable of truth. But as truth is incorruptible, so is it eternal. Therefore the intellectual nature of the soul and of the angel is not only incorruptible, but likewise eternal.

*On the contrary,* It is said (Prov. 8:22), in the person of begotten Wisdom: "The Lord possessed me in the beginning of His ways, before He made anything from the beginning." But, as was shown above (A. 1), the angels were made by God. Therefore at one time the angels were not.

*I answer that,* God alone, Father, Son and Holy Ghost, is from eternity. Catholic Faith holds this without doubt; and everything to the contrary must be rejected as heretical. For God so produced creatures that He made them "from nothing"; that is, after they had not been.

Reply Obj. 1: God's being is His will. So the fact that God produced the angels and other creatures by His being does not exclude that He made them also by His will. But, as was shown above (Q. 19, A. 3; Q. 46, A. 1), God's will does not act by necessity in producing creatures. Therefore He produced such as He willed, and when He willed.

Reply Obj. 2: An angel is above that time which is the measure of the movement of the heavens; because he is above every movement of a corporeal nature. Nevertheless he is not above time which is the measure of the succession of his existence after his non-existence, and which is also the measure of the succession which is in his operations. Hence Augustine says (Gen. ad lit. viii, 20,21) that "God moves the spiritual creature according to time."

Reply Obj. 3: Angels and intelligent souls are incorruptible by the very fact of their having a nature whereby they are capable of truth. But they did not possess this nature from eternity; it was bestowed upon them when God Himself willed it. Consequently it does not follow that the angels existed from eternity.

THIRD ARTICLE [I, Q. 61, Art. 3]

Whether the Angels Were Created Before the Corporeal World?

Objection 1: It would seem that the angels were created before the corporeal world. For Jerome says (In Ep. ad Tit. i, 2): "Six thousand years of our time have not yet elapsed; yet how shall we measure the time, how shall we count the ages, in which the Angels, Thrones, Dominations, and the other orders served God?" Damascene also says (De Fide Orth. ii): "Some say that the angels were begotten before all creation; as Gregory the Theologian declares, He first of all devised the angelic and heavenly powers, and the devising was the making thereof."

Obj. 2: Further, the angelic nature stands midway between the Divine and the corporeal natures. But the Divine nature is from eternity; while corporeal nature is from time. Therefore the angelic nature was produced ere time was made, and after eternity.

Obj. 3: Further, the angelic nature is more remote from the corporeal nature than one corporeal nature is from another. But one corporeal nature was made before another; hence the six days of the production of things are set forth in the opening of Genesis. Much more, therefore, was the angelic nature made before every corporeal nature.

*On the contrary,* It is said (Gen. 1:1): "In the beginning God created heaven and earth." Now, this would not be true if anything had been created previously. Consequently the angels were not created before corporeal nature.

*I answer that,* There is a twofold opinion on this point to be found in the writings of the Fathers. The more probable one holds that the angels were created at the same time as corporeal creatures. For the angels are part of the universe: they do not constitute a universe of themselves; but both they and corporeal natures unite in constituting one universe. This stands in evidence from the relationship of creature to creature; because the mutual relationship of creatures makes up the good of the universe. But no part is perfect if separate from the whole. Consequently it is improbable that God, Whose "works are perfect," as it is said Deut. 32:4, should have created the angelic creature before other creatures. At the same time the contrary is not to be deemed erroneous; especially on account of the opinion of Gregory Nazianzen, "whose authority in Christian doctrine is of such weight that no one has ever raised objection to his teaching, as is also the case with the doctrine of Athanasius," as Jerome says.

Reply Obj. 1: Jerome is speaking according to the teaching of the Greek Fathers; all of whom hold the creation of the angels to have taken place previously to that of the corporeal world.

Reply Obj. 2: God is not a part of, but far above, the whole universe, possessing within Himself the entire perfection of the universe in a more eminent way. But an angel is a part of the universe. Hence the comparison does not hold.

Reply Obj. 3: All corporeal creatures are one in matter; while the angels do not agree with them in matter. Consequently the creation of the matter of the corporeal creature involves in a manner the creation of all things; but the creation of the angels does not involve creation of the universe.

If the contrary view be held, then in the text of Gen. 1, "In the beginning God created heaven and earth," the words, "In the beginning," must be interpreted, "In the Son," or "In the beginning of time": but not, "In the beginning, before which there was nothing," unless we say "Before which there was nothing of the nature of corporeal creatures."

FOURTH ARTICLE [I, Q. 61, Art. 4]

Whether the Angels Were Created in the Empyrean Heaven?

Objection 1: It would seem that the angels were not created in the empyrean heaven. For the angels are incorporeal substances. Now a substance which is incorporeal is not dependent upon a body for its existence; and as a consequence, neither is it for its creation. Therefore the angels were not created in any corporeal place.

Obj. 2: Further, Augustine remarks (Gen. ad lit. iii, 10), that the angels were created in the upper atmosphere: therefore not in the empyrean heaven.

Obj. 3: Further, the empyrean heaven is said to be the highest heaven. If therefore the angels were created in the empyrean heaven, it would not beseem them to mount up to a still higher heaven. And this is contrary to what is said in Isaias, speaking in the person of the sinning angel: "I will ascend into heaven" (Isa. 14:13).

*On the contrary,* Strabus, commenting on the text "In the beginning God created heaven and earth," says: "By heaven he does not mean the visible firmament, but the empyrean, that is, the fiery or intellectual firmament, which is not so styled from its heat, but from its splendor; and which was filled with angels directly it was made."

*I answer that,* As was observed (A. 3), the universe is made up of corporeal and spiritual creatures. Consequently spiritual creatures were so created as to bear some relationship to the corporeal creature, and to rule over every corporeal creature. Hence it was fitting for the angels to be created in the highest corporeal place, as presiding over all corporeal nature; whether it be styled the empyrean heaven, or whatever else it be called. So Isidore says that the highest heaven is the heaven of the angels, explaining the passage of Deut. 10:14: "Behold heaven is the Lord's thy God, and the heaven of heaven."

Reply Obj. 1: The angels were created in a corporeal place, not as if depending upon a body either as to their existence or as to their being made; because God could have created them before all corporeal creation, as many holy Doctors hold. They were made in a corporeal place in order to show their relationship to corporeal nature, and that they are by their power in touch with bodies.

Reply Obj. 2: By the uppermost atmosphere Augustine possibly means the highest part of heaven, to which the atmosphere has a kind of affinity owing to its subtlety and transparency. Or else he is not speaking of all the angels; but only of such as sinned, who, in the opinion of some, belonged to the inferior orders. But there is nothing to hinder us from saying that the higher angels, as having an exalted and universal power over all corporeal things, were created in the highest place of the corporeal creature; while the other angels, as having more restricted powers, were created among the inferior bodies.

Reply Obj. 3: Isaias is not speaking there of any corporeal heaven, but of the heaven of the Blessed Trinity; unto which the sinning angel wished to ascend, when he desired to be equal in some manner to God, as will appear later on (Q. 63, A. 3).

## QUESTION 62

OF THE PERFECTION OF THE ANGELS IN THE ORDER OF GRACE AND OF GLORY (In Nine Articles)

In due sequence we have to inquire how the angels were made in the order of grace and of glory; under which heading there are nine points of inquiry:

(1) Were the angels created in beatitude?

(2) Did they need grace in order to turn to God?

(3) Were they created in grace?

(4) Did they merit their beatitude?

(5) Did they at once enter into beatitude after merit?

(6) Did they receive grace and glory according to their natural capacities?

(7) After entering glory, did their natural love and knowledge remain?

(8) Could they have sinned afterwards?

(9) After entering into glory, could they advance farther?

FIRST ARTICLE [I, Q. 62, Art. 1]

Whether the Angels Were Created in Beatitude?

Objection 1: It would seem that the angels were created in beatitude. For it is stated (De Eccl. Dogm. xxix) that "the angels who continue in the beatitude wherein they were created, do not of their nature possess the excellence they have." Therefore the angels were created in beatitude.

Obj. 2: Further, the angelic nature is nobler than the corporeal creature. But the corporeal creature straightway from its creation was made perfect and complete; nor did its lack of form take precedence in time, but only in nature, as Augustine says (Gen. ad lit. i, 15). Therefore neither did God create the angelic nature imperfect and incomplete. But its formation and perfection are derived from its beatitude, whereby it enjoys God. Therefore it was created in beatitude.

Obj. 3: Further, according to Augustine (Gen. ad lit. iv, 34; v, 5), the things which we read of as being made in the works of the six days, were made together at one time; and so all the six days must have existed instantly from the beginning of creation. But, according to his exposition, in those six days, "the morning" was the angelic knowledge, according to which they knew the Word and things in the Word. Therefore straightway from their creation they knew the Word, and things in the Word. But the bliss of the angels comes of seeing the Word. Consequently the angels were in beatitude straightway from the very beginning of their creation.

*On the contrary,* To be established or confirmed in good is of the nature of beatitude. But the angels were not confirmed in good as soon as they were created; the fall of some of them shows this. Therefore the angels were not in beatitude from their creation.

*I answer that,* By the name of beatitude is understood the ultimate perfection of rational or of intellectual nature; and hence it is that it is naturally desired, since everything naturally desires its ultimate perfection. Now there is a twofold ultimate perfection of rational or of intellectual nature. The first is one which it can procure of its own natural power; and this is in a measure called beatitude or happiness. Hence Aristotle (Ethic. x) says that man's ultimate happiness consists in his most perfect contemplation, whereby in this life he can behold the best intelligible object; and that is God. Above this happiness there is still another, which we look forward to in the future, whereby "we shall see God as He is." This is beyond the nature of every created intellect, as was shown above (Q. 12, A. 4).

So, then, it remains to be said, that, as regards this first beatitude, which the angel could procure by his natural power, he was created already blessed. Because the angel does not acquire such beatitude by any progressive action, as man does, but, as was observed above (Q. 58, AA. 3, 4), is straightway in possession thereof, owing to his natural dignity. But the angels did not have from the beginning of their creation that ultimate beatitude which is beyond the power of nature; because such beatitude is no part of their nature, but its end; and consequently they ought not to have it immediately from the beginning.

Reply Obj. 1: Beatitude is there taken for that natural perfection which the angel had in the state of innocence.

Reply Obj. 2: The corporeal creature instantly in the beginning of its creation could not have the perfection to which it is brought by its operation; consequently, according to Augustine (Gen. ad. lit. v, 4, 23; viii, 3), the growing of plants from the earth did not take place at once among the first works, in which only the germinating power of the plants was bestowed upon the earth. In the same way, the angelic creature in the beginning of its existence had the perfection of its nature; but it did not have the perfection to which it had to come by its operation.

Reply Obj. 3: The angel has a twofold knowledge of the Word; the one which is natural, and the other according to glory. He has a natural knowledge whereby he knows the Word through a similitude thereof shining in his nature; and he has a knowledge of glory whereby he knows the Word through His essence. By both kinds of knowledge the angel knows things in the Word; imperfectly by his natural knowledge, and perfectly by his knowledge of glory. Therefore the first knowledge of things in the Word was present to the angel from the outset of his creation; while the second was not, but only when the angels became blessed by turning to the good. And this is properly termed their morning knowledge.

SECOND ARTICLE [I, Q. 62, Art. 2]

Whether an Angel Needs Grace in Order to Turn to God?

Objection 1: It would seem that the angel had no need of grace in order to turn to God. For, we have no need of grace for what we can accomplish naturally. But the angel naturally turns to God: because he loves God naturally, as is clear from what has been said (Q. 60, A. 5). Therefore an angel did not need grace in order to turn to God.

Obj. 2: Further, seemingly we need help only for difficult tasks. Now it was not a difficult task for the angel to turn to God; because there was no obstacle in him to such turning. Therefore the angel had no need of grace in order to turn to God.

Obj. 3: Further, to turn oneself to God is to dispose oneself for grace; hence it is said (Zech. 1:3): "Turn ye to Me, and I will turn to you." But we do not stand in need of grace in order to prepare ourselves for grace: for thus we should go on to infinity. Therefore the angel did not need grace to turn to God.

*On the contrary,* It was by turning to God that the angel reached to beatitude. If, then, he had needed no grace in order to turn to God, it would follow that he did not require grace in order to possess everlasting life. But this is contrary to the saying of the Apostle (Rom. 6:23): "The grace of God is life everlasting."

*I answer that,* The angels stood in need of grace in order to turn to God, as the object of beatitude. For, as was observed above (Q. 60, A. 2) the natural movement of the will is the principle of all things that we will. But the will's natural inclination is directed towards what is in keeping with its nature. Therefore, if there is anything which is above nature, the will cannot be inclined towards it, unless helped by some other supernatural principle. Thus it is clear that fire has a natural tendency to give forth heat, and to generate fire; whereas to generate flesh is beyond the natural power of fire; consequently, fire has no tendency thereto, except in so far as it is moved instrumentally by the nutritive soul.

Now it was shown above (Q. 12, AA. 4, 5), when we were treating of God's knowledge, that to see God in His essence, wherein the ultimate beatitude of the rational creature consists, is beyond the nature of every created intellect. Consequently no rational creature can have the movement of the will directed towards such beatitude, except it be moved thereto by a supernatural agent. This is what we call the help of grace. Therefore it must be said that an angel could not of his own will be turned to such beatitude, except by the help of grace.

Reply Obj. 1: The angel loves God naturally, so far as God is the author of his natural being. But here we are speaking of turning to God, so far as God bestows beatitude by the vision of His essence.

Reply Obj. 2: A thing is "difficult" which is beyond a power; and this happens in two ways. First of all, because it is beyond the natural capacity of the power. Thus, if it can be attained by some help, it is said to be "difficult"; but if it can in no way be attained, then it is "impossible"; thus it is impossible for a man to fly. In another way a thing may be beyond the power, not according to the natural order of such power, but owing to some intervening hindrance; as to mount upwards is not contrary to the natural order of the motive power of the soul; because the soul, considered in itself, can be moved in any direction; but is hindered from so doing by the weight of the body; consequently it is difficult for a man to mount upwards. To be turned to his ultimate beatitude is difficult for man, both because it is beyond his nature, and because he has a hindrance from the corruption of the body and infection of sin. But it is difficult for an angel, only because it is supernatural.

Reply Obj. 3: Every movement of the will towards God can be termed a conversion to God. And so there is a threefold turning to God. The first is by the perfect love of God; this belongs to the creature enjoying the possession of God; and for such conversion, consummate grace is required. The next turning to God is that which merits beatitude; and for this there is required habitual grace, which is the principle of merit. The third conversion is that whereby a man disposes himself so that he may have grace; for this no habitual grace is required; but the operation of God, Who draws the soul towards Himself, according to Lament. 5:21: "Convert us, O Lord, to Thee, and we shall be converted." Hence it is clear that there is no need to go on to infinity.

THIRD ARTICLE [I, Q. 62, Art. 3]

Whether the Angels Were Created in Grace?

Objection 1: It would seem that the angels were not created in grace. For Augustine says (Gen. ad lit. ii, 8) that the angelic nature was first made without form, and was called "heaven": but afterwards it received its form, and was then called "light." But such formation comes from grace. Therefore they were not created in grace.

Obj. 2: Further, grace turns the rational creature towards God. If, therefore, the angel had been created in grace, no angel would ever have turned away from God.

Obj. 3: Further, grace comes midway between nature and glory. But the angels were not beatified in their creation. Therefore it seems that they were not created in grace; but that they were first created in nature only, and then received grace, and that last of all they were beatified.

*On the contrary,* Augustine says (De Civ. Dei xii, 9), "Who wrought the good will of the angels? Who, save Him Who created them with His will, that is, with the pure love wherewith they cling to Him; at the same time building up their nature and bestowing grace on them?"

*I answer that,* Although there are conflicting opinions on this point, some holding that the angels were created only in a natural state, while others maintain that they were created in grace; yet it seems more probable, and more in keeping with the sayings of holy men, that they were created in sanctifying grace. For we see that all things which, in the process of time, being created by the work of Divine Providence, were produced by the operation of God, were created in the first fashioning of things according to seedlike forms, as Augustine says (Gen. ad lit. viii, 3), such as trees, animals, and the rest. Now it is evident that sanctifying grace bears the same relation to beatitude as the seedlike form in nature does to the natural effect; hence (1 John 3:9) grace is called the "seed" of God. As, then, in Augustine's opinion it is contended that the seedlike forms of all natural effects were implanted in the creature when corporeally created, so straightway from the beginning the angels were created in grace.

Reply Obj. 1: Such absence of form in the angels can be understood either by comparison with their formation in glory; and so the absence of formation preceded formation by priority of time. Or else it can be understood of the formation according to grace: and so it did not precede in the order of time, but in the order of nature; as Augustine holds with regard to the formation of corporeal things (Gen. ad lit. i, 15).

Reply Obj. 2: Every form inclines the subject after the mode of the subject's nature. Now it is the mode of an intellectual nature to be inclined freely towards the objects it desires. Consequently the movement of grace does not impose necessity; but he who has grace can fail to make use of it, and can sin.

Reply Obj. 3: Although in the order of nature grace comes midway between nature and glory, nevertheless, in the order of time, in created nature, glory is not simultaneous with nature; because glory is the end of the operation of nature helped by grace. But grace stands not as the end of operation, because it is not of works, but as the principle of right operation. Therefore it was fitting for grace to be given straightway with nature.

FOURTH ARTICLE [I, Q. 62, Art. 4]

Whether an Angel Merits His Beatitude?

Objection 1: It would seem that the angel did not merit his beatitude. For merit arises from the difficulty of the meritorious act. But the angel experienced no difficulty in acting rightly. Therefore righteous action was not meritorious for him.

Obj. 2: Further, we do not merit by merely natural operations. But it was quite natural for the angel to turn to God. Therefore he did not thereby merit beatitude.

Obj. 3: Further, if a beatified angel merited his beatitude, he did so either before he had it, or else afterwards. But it was not before; because, in the opinion of many, he had no grace before whereby to merit it. Nor did he merit it afterwards, because thus he would be meriting it now; which is clearly false, because in that case a lower angel could by meriting rise up to the rank of a higher, and the distinct degrees of grace would not be permanent; which is not admissible. Consequently the angel did not merit his beatitude.

*On the contrary,* It is stated (Apoc. 21:17) that the "measure of the angel" in that heavenly Jerusalem is "the measure of a man." Therefore the same is the case with the angel.

*I answer that,* Perfect beatitude is natural only to God, because existence and beatitude are one and the same thing in Him. Beatitude, however, is not of the nature of the creature, but is its end. Now everything attains its last end by its operation. Such operation leading to the end is either productive of the end, when such end is not beyond the power of the agent working for the end, as the healing art is productive of health; or else it is deserving of the end, when such end is beyond the capacity of the agent striving to attain it; wherefore it is looked for from another's bestowing. Now it is evident from what has gone before (AA. 1, 2; Q. 12, AA. 4, 5), ultimate beatitude exceeds both the angelic and the human nature. It remains, then, that both man and angel merited their beatitude.

And if the angel was created in grace, without which there is no merit, there would be no difficulty in saying that he merited beatitude: as also, if one were to say that he had grace in any way before he had glory.

But if he had no grace before entering upon beatitude, it would then have to be said that he had beatitude without merit, even as we have grace. This, however, is quite foreign to the idea of beatitude; which conveys the notion of an end, and is the reward of virtue, as even the Philosopher says (Ethic. i, 9). Or else it will have to be said, as some others have maintained, that the angels merit beatitude by their present ministrations, while in beatitude. This is quite contrary, again, to the notion of merit: since merit conveys the idea of a means to an end; while what is already in its end cannot, properly speaking, be moved towards such end; and so no one merits to produce what he already enjoys. Or else it will have to be said that one and the same act of turning to God, so far as it comes of free-will, is meritorious; and so far as it attains the end, is the fruition of beatitude. Even this view will not stand, because free-will is not the sufficient cause of merit; and, consequently, an act cannot be meritorious as coming from free-will, except in so far as it is informed by grace; but it cannot at the same time be informed by imperfect grace, which is the principle of meriting, and by perfect grace, which is the principle of enjoying. Hence it does not appear to be possible for anyone to enjoy beatitude, and at the same time to merit it.

Consequently it is better to say that the angel had grace ere he was admitted to beatitude, and that by such grace he merited beatitude.

Reply Obj. 1: The angel's difficulty of working righteously does not come from any contrariety or hindrance of natural powers; but from the fact that the good work is beyond his natural capacity.

Reply Obj. 2: An angel did not merit beatitude by natural movement towards God; but by the movement of charity, which comes of grace.

The answer to the Third Objection is evident from what we have said.

FIFTH ARTICLE [I, Q. 62, Art. 5]

Whether the Angel Obtained Beatitude Immediately After One Act of Merit?

Objection 1: It would seem that the angel did not possess beatitude instantly after one act of merit. For it is more difficult for a man to do well than for an angel. But man is not rewarded at once after one act of merit. Therefore neither was the angel.

Obj. 2: Further, an angel could act at once, and in an instant, from the very outset of his creation, for even natural bodies begin to be moved in the very instant of their creation; and if the movement of a body could be instantaneous, like operations of mind and will, it would have movement in the first instant of its generation. Consequently, if the angel merited beatitude by one act of his will, he merited it in the first instant of his creation; and so, if their beatitude was not retarded, then the angels were in beatitude in the first instant.

Obj. 3: Further, there must be many intervals between things which are far apart. But the beatific state of the angels is very far remote from their natural condition: while merit comes midway between. Therefore the angel would have to pass through many stages of merit in order to reach beatitude.

*On the contrary,* Man's soul and an angel are ordained alike for beatitude: consequently equality with angels is promised to the saints. Now the soul separated from the body, if it has merit deserving beatitude, enters at once into beatitude, unless there be some obstacle. Therefore so does an angel. Now an angel instantly, in his first act of charity, had the merit of beatitude. Therefore, since there was no obstacle within him, he passed at once into beatitude by only one meritorious act.

*I answer that,* The angel was beatified instantly after the first act of charity, whereby he merited beatitude. The reason whereof is because grace perfects nature according to the manner of the nature; as every perfection is received in the subject capable of perfection, according to its mode. Now it is proper to the angelic nature to receive its natural perfection not by passing from one stage to another; but to have it at once naturally, as was shown above (A. 1; Q. 58, AA. 3, 4). But as the angel is of his nature inclined to natural perfection, so is he by merit inclined to glory. Hence instantly after merit the angel secured beatitude. Now the merit of beatitude in angel and man alike can be from merely one act; because man merits beatitude by every act informed by charity. Hence it remains that an angel was beatified straightway after one act of charity.

Reply Obj. 1: Man was not intended to secure his ultimate perfection at once, like the angel. Hence a longer way was assigned to man than to the angel for securing beatitude.

Reply Obj. 2: The angel is above the time of corporeal things; hence the various instants regarding the angels are not to be taken except as reckoning the succession of their acts. Now their act which merited beatitude could not be in them simultaneously with the act of beatitude, which is fruition; since the one belongs to imperfect grace, and the other to consummate grace. Consequently, it remains for different instants to be conceived, in one of which the angel merited beatitude, and in another was beatified.

Reply Obj. 3: It is of the nature of an angel instantly to attain the perfection unto which he is ordained. Consequently, only one meritorious act is required; which act can so far be called an interval as through it the angel is brought to beatitude.

SIXTH ARTICLE [I, Q. 62, Art. 6]

Whether the Angels Receive Grace and Glory According to the Degree of Their Natural Gifts?

Objection 1: It would seem that the angels did not receive grace and glory according to the degree of their natural gifts. For grace is bestowed of God's absolute will. Therefore the degree of grace depends on God's will, and not on the degree of their natural gifts.

Obj. 2: Further, a moral act seems to be more closely allied with grace than nature is; because a moral act is preparatory to grace. But grace does not come "of works," as is said Rom. 11:6. Therefore much less does the degree of grace depend upon the degree of their natural gifts.

Obj. 3: Further, man and angel are alike ordained for beatitude or grace. But man does not receive more grace according to the degree of his natural gifts. Therefore neither does the angel.

*On the contrary,* Is the saying of the Master of the Sentences (Sent. ii, D, 3) that "those angels who were created with more subtle natures and of keener intelligence in wisdom, were likewise endowed with greater gifts of grace."

*I answer that,* It is reasonable to suppose that gifts of graces and perfection of beatitude were bestowed on the angels according to the degree of their natural gifts. The reason for this can be drawn from two sources. First of all, on the part of God, Who, in the order of His wisdom, established various degrees in the angelic nature. Now as the angelic nature was made by God for attaining grace and beatitude, so likewise the grades of the angelic nature seem to be ordained for the various degrees of grace and glory; just as when, for example, the builder chisels the stones for building a house, from the fact that he prepares some more artistically and more fittingly than others, it is clear that he is setting them apart for the more ornate part of the house. So it seems that God destined those angels for greater gifts of grace and fuller beatitude, whom He made of a higher nature.

Secondly, the same is evident on the part of the angel. The angel is not a compound of different natures, so that the inclination of the one thwarts or retards the tendency of the other; as happens in man, in whom the movement of his intellective part is either retarded or thwarted by the inclination of his sensitive part. But when there is nothing to retard or thwart it, nature is moved with its whole energy. So it is reasonable to suppose that the angels who had a higher nature, were turned to God more mightily and efficaciously. The same thing happens in men, since greater grace and glory are bestowed according to the greater earnestness of their turning to God. Hence it appears that the angels who had the greater natural powers, had the more grace and glory.

Reply Obj. 1: As grace comes of God's will alone, so likewise does the nature of the angel: and as God's will ordained nature for grace, so did it ordain the various degrees of nature to the various degrees of grace.

Reply Obj. 2: The acts of the rational creature are from the creature itself; whereas nature is immediately from God. Accordingly it seems rather that grace is bestowed according to degree of nature than according to works.

Reply Obj. 3: Diversity of natural gifts is in one way in the angels, who are themselves different specifically; and in quite another way in men, who differ only numerically. For specific difference is on account of the end; while numerical difference is because of the matter. Furthermore, there is something in man which can thwart or impede the movement of his intellective nature; but not in the angels. Consequently the argument is not the same for both.

SEVENTH ARTICLE [I, Q. 62, Art. 7]

Whether Natural Knowledge and Love Remain in the Beatified Angels?

Objection 1: It would seem that natural knowledge and love do not remain in the beatified angels. For it is said (1 Cor. 13:10): "When that which is perfect is come, then that which is in part shall be done away." But natural love and knowledge are imperfect in comparison with beatified knowledge and love. Therefore, in beatitude, natural knowledge and love cease.

Obj. 2: Further, where one suffices, another is superfluous. But the knowledge and love of glory suffice for the beatified angels. Therefore it would be superfluous for their natural knowledge and love to remain.

Obj. 3: Further, the same faculty has not two simultaneous acts, as the same line cannot, at the same end, be terminated in two points. But the beatified angels are always exercising their beatified knowledge and love; for, as is said *Ethic.* i, 8, happiness consists not in habit, but in act. Therefore there can never be natural knowledge and love in the angels.

*On the contrary,* So long as a nature endures, its operation remains. But beatitude does not destroy nature, since it is its perfection. Therefore it does not take away natural knowledge and love.

*I answer that,* Natural knowledge and love remain in the angels. For as principles of operations are mutually related, so are the operations themselves. Now it is manifest that nature is to beatitude as first to second; because beatitude is superadded to nature. But the first must ever be preserved in the second. Consequently nature must be preserved in beatitude: and in like manner the act of nature must be preserved in the act of beatitude.

Reply Obj. 1: The advent of a perfection removes the opposite imperfection. Now the imperfection of nature is not opposed to the perfection of beatitude, but underlies it; as the imperfection of the power underlies the perfection of the form, and the power is not taken away by the form, but the privation which is opposed to the form. In the same way, the imperfection of natural knowledge is not opposed to the perfection of the knowledge in glory; for nothing hinders us from knowing a thing through various mediums, as a thing may be known at the one time through a probable medium and through a demonstrative one. In like manner, an angel can know God by His essence, and this appertains to his knowledge of glory; and at the same time he can know God by his own essence, which belongs to his natural knowledge.

Reply Obj. 2: All things which make up beatitude are sufficient of themselves. But in order for them to exist, they presuppose the natural gifts; because no beatitude is self-subsisting, except the uncreated beatitude.

Reply Obj. 3: There cannot be two operations of the one faculty at the one time, except the one be ordained to the other. But natural knowledge and love are ordained to the knowledge and love of glory. Accordingly there is nothing to hinder natural knowledge and love from existing in the angel conjointly with those of glory.

EIGHTH ARTICLE [I, Q. 62, Art. 8]

Whether a Beatified Angel Can Sin?

Objection 1: It would seem that a beatified angel can sin. For, as as said above (A. 7), beatitude does not do away with nature. But it is of the very notion of created nature, that it can fail. Therefore a beatified angel can sin.

Obj. 2: Further, the rational powers are referred to opposites, as the Philosopher observes (Metaph. iv, text. 3). But the will of the angel in beatitude does not cease to be rational. Therefore it is inclined towards good and evil.

Obj. 3: Further, it belongs to the liberty of free-will for man to be able to choose good or evil. But the freedom of will is not lessened in the beatified angels. Therefore they can sin.

*On the contrary,* Augustine says (Gen. ad lit. xi) that "there is in the holy angels that nature which cannot sin." Therefore the holy angels cannot sin.

*I answer that,* The beatified angels cannot sin. The reason for this is, because their beatitude consists in seeing God through His essence. Now, God's essence is the very essence of goodness. Consequently the angel beholding God is disposed towards God in the same way as anyone else not seeing God is to the common form of goodness. Now it is impossible for any man either to will or to do anything except aiming at what is good; or for him to wish to turn away from good precisely as such. Therefore the beatified angel can neither will nor act, except as aiming towards God. Now whoever wills or acts in this manner cannot sin. Consequently the beatified angel cannot sin.

Reply Obj. 1: Created good, considered in itself, can fail. But from its perfect union with the uncreated good, such as is the union of beatitude, it is rendered unable to sin, for the reason already alleged.

Reply Obj. 2: The rational powers are referred to opposites in the things to which they are not inclined naturally; but as to the things whereunto they have a natural tendency, they are not referred to opposites. For the intellect cannot but assent to naturally known principles; in the same way, the will cannot help clinging to good, formally as good; because the will is naturally ordained to good as to its proper object. Consequently the will of the angels is referred to opposites, as to doing many things, or not doing them. But they have no tendency to opposites with regard to God Himself, Whom they see to be the very nature of goodness; but in all things their aim is towards God, which ever alternative they choose, that is not sinful.

Reply Obj. 3: Free-will in its choice of means to an end is disposed just as the intellect is to conclusions. Now it is evident that it belongs to the power of the intellect to be able to proceed to different conclusions, according to given principles; but for it to proceed to some conclusion by passing out of the order of the principles, comes of its own defect. Hence it belongs to the perfection of its liberty for the free-will to be able to choose between opposite things, keeping the order of the end in view; but it comes of the defect of liberty for it to choose anything by turning away from the order of the end; and this is to sin. Hence there is greater liberty of will in the angels, who cannot sin, than there is in ourselves, who can sin.

NINTH ARTICLE [I, Q. 62, Art. 3]

Whether the Beatified Angels Advance in Beatitude?

Objection 1: It would seem that the beatified angels can advance in beatitude. For charity is the principle of merit. But there is perfect charity in the angels. Therefore the beatified angels can merit. Now, as merit increases, the reward of beatitude increases. Therefore the beatified angels can progress in beatitude.

Obj. 2: Further, Augustine says (De Doctr. Christ. i) that "God makes use of us for our own gain, and for His own goodness. The same thing happens to the angels, whom He uses for spiritual ministrations"; since "they are all [*Vulg.: 'Are they not all ... ?'] ministering spirits, sent to minister for them who shall receive the inheritance of salvation" (Heb. 1:14). This would not be for their profit were they not to merit thereby, nor to advance to beatitude. It remains, then, that the beatified angels can merit, and can advance in beatitude.

Obj. 3: Further, it argues imperfection for anyone not occupying the foremost place not to be able to advance. But the angels are not in the highest degree of beatitude. Therefore if unable to ascend higher, it would appear that there is imperfection and defect in them; which is not admissible.

*On the contrary,* Merit and progress belong to this present condition of life. But angels are not wayfarers travelling towards beatitude, they are already in possession of beatitude. Consequently the beatified angels can neither merit nor advance in beatitude.

*I answer that,* In every movement the mover's intention is centered upon one determined end, to which he intends to lead the movable subject; because intention looks to the end, to which infinite progress is repugnant. Now it is evident, since the rational creature cannot of its own power attain to its beatitude, which consists in the vision of God, as is clear from what has gone before (Q. 12, A. 4), that it needs to be moved by God towards its beatitude. Therefore there must be some one determined thing to which every rational creature is directed as to its last end.

Now this one determinate object cannot, in the vision of God, consist precisely in that which is seen; for the Supreme Truth is seen by all the blessed in various degrees: but it is on the part of the mode of vision, that diverse terms are fixed beforehand by the intention of Him Who directs towards the end. For it is impossible that as the rational creature is led on to the vision of the Supreme Essence, it should be led on in the same way to the supreme mode of vision, which is comprehension, for this belongs to God only; as is evident from what was said above (Q. 12, A. 7; Q. 14, A. 3). But since infinite efficacy is required for comprehending God, while the creature's efficacy in beholding is only finite; and since every finite being is in infinite degrees removed from the infinite; it comes to pass that the rational creature understands God more or less clearly according to infinite degrees. And as beatitude consists in vision, so the degree of vision lies in a determinate mode of the vision.

Therefore every rational creature is so led by God to the end of its beatitude, that from God's predestination it is brought even to a determinate degree of beatitude. Consequently, when that degree is once secured, it cannot pass to a higher degree.

Reply Obj. 1: Merit belongs to a subject which is moving towards its end. Now the rational creature is moved towards its end, not merely passively, but also by working actively. If the end is within the power of the rational creature, then its action is said to procure the end; as man acquires knowledge by reflection: but if the end be beyond its power, and is looked for from another, then the action will be meritorious of such end. But what is already in the ultimate term is not said to be moved, but to have been moved. Consequently, to merit belongs to the imperfect charity of this life; whereas perfect charity does not merit but rather enjoys the reward. Even as in acquired habits, the operation preceding the habit is productive of the habit; but the operation from an acquired habit is both perfect and enjoyable. In the same way the act of perfect charity has no quality of merit, but belongs rather to the perfection of the reward.

Reply Obj. 2: A thing can be termed useful in two ways. First of all, as being on the way to an end; and so the merit of beatitude is useful. Secondly, as the part is useful for the whole; as the wall for a house. In this way the angelic ministerings are useful for the beatified angels, inasmuch as they are a part of their beatitude; for to pour out acquired perfection upon others is of the nature of what is perfect, considered as perfect.

Reply Obj. 3: Although a beatified angel is not absolutely in the highest degree of beatitude, yet, in his own regard he is in the highest degree, according to Divine predestination. Nevertheless the joy of the angels can be increased with regard to the salvation of such as are saved by their ministrations, according to Luke 15:10: "There is [Vulg.'shall be'] joy before the angels of God upon one sinner doing penance." Such joy belongs to their accidental reward, which can be increased unto judgment day. Hence some writers say that they can merit as to their accidental reward. But it is better to say that the Blessed can in no wise merit without being at the same time a wayfarer and a comprehensor; like Christ, Who alone was such. For the Blessed acquire such joy from the virtue of their beatitude, rather than merit it.

## QUESTION 63

THE MALICE OF THE ANGELS WITH REGARD TO SIN (In Nine Articles)

In the next place we must consider how angels became evil: first of all with regard to the evil of fault; and secondly, as to the evil of punishment. Under the first heading there are nine points for consideration:

(1) Can there be evil of fault in the angels?

(2) What kind of sins can be in them?

(3) What did the angel seek in sinning?

(4) Supposing that some became evil by a sin of their own choosing, are any of them naturally evil?

(5) Supposing that it is not so, could any one of them become evil in the first instant of his creation by an act of his own will?

(6) Supposing that he did not, was there any interval between his creation and fall?

(7) Was the highest of them who fell, absolutely the highest among the angels?

(8) Was the sin of the foremost angel the cause of the others sinning?

(9) Did as many sin as remained steadfast?

FIRST ARTICLE [I, Q. 63, Art. 1]

Whether the Evil of Fault Can Be in the Angels?

Objection 1: It would seem that there can be no evil of fault in the angels. For there can be no evil except in things which are in potentiality, as is said by the Philosopher (Metaph. ix, text. 19), because the subject of privation is a being in potentiality. But the angels have not being in potentiality, since they are subsisting forms. Therefore there can be no evil in them.

Obj. 2: Further, the angels are higher than the heavenly bodies. But philosophers say that there cannot be evil in the heavenly bodies. Therefore neither can there be in the angels.

Obj. 3: Further, what is natural to a thing is always in it. But it is natural for the angels to be moved by the movement of love towards God. Therefore such love cannot be withdrawn from them. But in loving God they do not sin. Consequently the angels cannot sin.

Obj. 4: Further, desire is only of what is good or apparently good. Now for the angels there can be no apparent good which is not a true good; because in them either there can be no error at all, or at least not before guilt. Therefore the angels can desire only what it truly good. But no one sins by desiring what is truly good. Consequently the angel does not sin by desire.

*On the contrary,* It is said (Job 4:18): "In His angels He found wickedness."

*I answer that,* An angel or any other rational creature considered in his own nature, can sin; and to whatever creature it belongs not to sin, such creature has it as a gift of grace, and not from the condition of nature. The reason of this is, because sinning is nothing else than a deviation from that rectitude which an act ought to have; whether we speak of sin in nature, art, or morals. That act alone, the rule of which is the very virtue of the agent, can never fall short of rectitude. Were the craftsman's hand the rule itself engraving, he could not engrave the wood otherwise than rightly; but if the rightness of engraving be judged by another rule, then the engraving may be right or faulty. Now the Divine will is the sole rule of God's act, because it is not referred to any higher end. But every created will has rectitude of act so far only as it is regulated according to the Divine will, to which the last end is to be referred: as every desire of a subordinate ought to be regulated by the will of his superior; for instance, the soldier's will, according to the will of his commanding officer. Thus only in the Divine will can there be no sin; whereas there can be sin in the will of every creature; considering the condition of its nature.

Reply Obj. 1: In the angels there is no potentiality to natural existence. Yet there is potentiality in their intellective part, as regards their being inclined to this or the other object. In this respect there can be evil in them.

Reply Obj. 2: The heavenly bodies have none but a natural operation. Therefore as there can be no evil of corruption in their nature; so neither can there be evil of disorder in their natural action. But besides their natural action there is the action of free-will in the angels, by reason of which evil may be in them.

Reply Obj. 3: It is natural for the angel to turn to God by the movement of love, according as God is the principle of his natural being. But for him to turn to God as the object of supernatural beatitude, comes of infused love, from which he could be turned away by sinning.

Reply Obj. 4: Mortal sin occurs in two ways in the act of free-will. First, when something evil is chosen; as man sins by choosing adultery, which is evil of itself. Such sin always comes of ignorance or error; otherwise what is evil would never be chosen as good. The adulterer errs in the particular, choosing this delight of an inordinate act as something good to be performed now, from the inclination of passion or of habit; even though he does not err in his universal judgment, but retains a right opinion in this respect. In this way there can be no sin in the angel; because there are no passions in the angels to fetter reason or intellect, as is manifest from what has been said above (Q. 59, A. 4); nor, again, could any habit inclining to sin precede their first sin. In another way sin comes of free-will by choosing something good in itself, but not according to proper measure or rule; so that the defect which induces sin is only on the part of the choice which is not properly regulated, but not on the part of the thing chosen; as if one were to pray, without heeding the order established by the Church. Such a sin does not presuppose ignorance, but merely absence of consideration of the things which ought to be considered. In this way the angel sinned, by seeking his own good, from his own free-will, insubordinately to the rule of the Divine will.

SECOND ARTICLE [I, Q. 63, Art. 2]

Whether Only the Sin of Pride and Envy Can Exist in an Angel?

Objection 1: It would seem that there can be other sins in the angels besides those of pride and envy. Because whosoever can delight in any kind of sin, can fall into the sin itself. But the demons delight even in the obscenities of carnal sins; as Augustine says (De Civ. Dei xiv, 3). Therefore there can also be carnal sins in the demons.

Obj. 2: Further, as pride and envy are spiritual sins, so are sloth, avarice, and anger. But spiritual sins are concerned with the spirit, just as carnal sins are with the flesh. Therefore not only can there be pride and envy in the angels; but likewise sloth and avarice.

Obj. 3: Further, according to Gregory (Moral. xxxi), many vices spring from pride; and in like manner from envy. But, if the cause is granted, the effect follows. If, therefore, there can be pride and envy in the angels, for the same reason there can likewise be other vices in them.

*On the contrary,* Augustine says (De Civ. Dei xiv, 3) that the devil "is not a fornicator nor a drunkard, nor anything of the like sort; yet he is proud and envious."

*I answer that,* Sin can exist in a subject in two ways: first of all by actual guilt, and secondly by affection. As to guilt, all sins are in the demons; since by leading men to sin they incur the guilt of all sins. But as to affection only those sins can be in the demons which can belong to a spiritual nature. Now a spiritual nature cannot be affected by such pleasures as appertain to bodies, but only by such as are in keeping with spiritual things; because nothing is affected except with regard to something which is in some way suited to its nature. But there can be no sin when anyone is incited to good of the spiritual order; unless in such affection the rule of the superior be not kept. Such is precisely the sin of pride—not to be subject to a superior when subjection is due. Consequently the first sin of the angel can be none other than pride.

Yet, as a consequence, it was possible for envy also to be in them, since for the appetite to tend to the desire of something involves on its part resistance to anything contrary. Now the envious man repines over the good possessed by another, inasmuch as he deems his neighbor's good to be a hindrance to his own. But another's good could not be deemed a hindrance to the good coveted by the wicked angel, except inasmuch as he coveted a singular excellence, which would cease to be singular because of the excellence of some other. So, after the sin of pride, there followed the evil of envy in the sinning angel, whereby he grieved over man's good, and also over the Divine excellence, according as against the devil's will God makes use of man for the Divine glory.

Reply Obj. 1: The demons do not delight in the obscenities of the sins of the flesh, as if they themselves were disposed to carnal pleasures: it is wholly through envy that they take pleasure in all sorts of human sins, so far as these are hindrances to a man's good.

Reply Obj. 2: Avarice, considered as a special kind of sin, is the immoderate greed of temporal possessions which serve the use of human life, and which can be estimated in value of money; to these demons are not at all inclined, any more than they are to carnal pleasures. Consequently avarice properly so called cannot be in them. But if every immoderate greed of possessing any created good be termed avarice, in this way avarice is contained under the pride which is in the demons. Anger implies passion, and so does concupiscence; consequently they can only exist metaphorically in the demons. Sloth is a kind of sadness, whereby a man becomes sluggish in spiritual exercises because they weary the body; which does not apply to the demons. So it is evident that pride and envy are the only spiritual sins which can be found in demons; yet so that envy is not to be taken for a passion, but for a will resisting the good of another.

Reply Obj. 3: Under envy and pride, as found in the demons, are comprised all other sins derived from them.

THIRD ARTICLE [I, Q. 63, Art. 3]

Whether the Devil Desired to Be As God?

Objection 1: It would seem that the devil did not desire to be as God. For what does not fall under apprehension, does not fall under desire; because the good which is apprehended moves the appetite, whether sensible, rational, or intellectual; and sin consists only in such desire. But for any creature to be God's equal does not fall under apprehension, because it implies a contradiction; for it the finite equals the infinite, then it would itself be infinite. Therefore an angel could not desire to be as God.

Obj. 2: Further, the natural end can always be desired without sin. But to be likened unto God is the end to which every creature naturally tends. If, therefore, the angel desired to be as God, not by equality, but by likeness, it would seem that he did not thereby sin.

Obj. 3: Further, the angel was created with greater fulness of wisdom than man. But no man, save a fool, ever makes choice of being the equal of an angel, still less of God; because choice regards only things which are possible, regarding which one takes deliberation. Therefore much less did the angel sin by desiring to be as God.

*On the contrary,* It is said, in the person of the devil (Isa. 14:13, 14), "I will ascend into heaven ... I will be like the Most High." And Augustine (De Qu. Vet. Test. cxiii) says that being "inflated with pride, he wished to be called God."

*I answer that,* Without doubt the angel sinned by seeking to be as God. But this can be understood in two ways: first, by equality; secondly, by likeness. He could not seek to be as God in the first way; because by natural knowledge he knew that this was impossible: and there was no habit preceding his first sinful act, nor any passion fettering his mind, so as to lead him to choose what was impossible by failing in some particular; as sometimes happens in ourselves. And even supposing it were possible, it would be against the natural desire; because there exists in everything the natural desire of preserving its own nature; which would not be preserved were it to be changed into another nature. Consequently, no creature of a lower order can ever covet the grade of a higher nature; just as an ass does not desire to be a horse: for were it to be so upraised, it would cease to be itself. But herein the imagination plays us false; for one is liable to think that, because a man seeks to occupy a higher grade as to accidentals, which can increase without the destruction of the subject, he can also seek a higher grade of nature, to which he could not attain without ceasing to exist. Now it is quite evident that God surpasses the angels, not merely in accidentals, but also in degree of nature; and one angel, another. Consequently it is impossible for one angel of lower degree to desire equality with a higher; and still more to covet equality with God.

To desire to be as God according to likeness can happen in two ways. In one way, as to that likeness whereby everything is made to be likened unto God. And so, if anyone desire in this way to be Godlike, he commits no sin; provided that he desires such likeness in proper order, that is to say, that he may obtain it of God. But he would sin were he to desire to be like unto God even in the right way, as of his own, and not of God's power. In another way one may desire to be like unto God in some respect which is not natural to one; as if one were to desire to create heaven and earth, which is proper to God; in which desire there would be sin. It was in this way that the devil desired to be as God. Not that he desired to resemble God by being subject to no one else absolutely; for so he would be desiring his own 'not-being'; since no creature can exist except by holding its existence under God. But he desired resemblance with God in this respect—by desiring, as his last end of beatitude, something which he could attain by the virtue of his own nature, turning his appetite away from supernatural beatitude, which is attained by God's grace. Or, if he desired as his last end that likeness of God which is bestowed by grace, he sought to have it by the power of his own nature; and not from Divine assistance according to God's ordering. This harmonizes with Anselm's opinion, who says [*De casu diaboli, iv.] that "he sought that to which he would have come had he stood fast." These two views in a manner coincide; because according to both, he sought to have final beatitude of his own power, whereas this is proper to God alone.

Since, then, what exists of itself is the cause of what exists of another, it follows from this furthermore that he sought to have dominion over others; wherein he also perversely wished to be like unto God.

From this we have the answer to all the objections.

FOURTH ARTICLE [I, Q. 63, Art. 4]

Whether Any Demons Are Naturally Wicked?

Objection 1: It would seem that some demons are naturally wicked. For Porphyry says, as quoted by Augustine (De Civ. Dei x, 11): "There is a class of demons of crafty nature, pretending that they are gods and the souls of the dead." But to be deceitful is to be evil. Therefore some demons are naturally wicked.

Obj. 2: Further, as the angels are created by God, so are men. But some men are naturally wicked, of whom it is said (Wis. 12:10): "Their malice is natural." Therefore some angels may be naturally wicked.

Obj. 3: Further, some irrational animals have wicked dispositions by nature: thus the fox is naturally sly, and the wolf naturally rapacious; yet they are God's creatures. Therefore, although the demons are God's creatures, they may be naturally wicked.

*On the contrary,* Dionysius says (Div. Nom. iv) that "the demons are not naturally wicked."

*I answer that,* Everything which exists, so far as it exists and has a particular nature, tends naturally towards some good; since it comes from a good principle; because the effect always reverts to its principle. Now a particular good may happen to have some evil connected with it; thus fire has this evil connected with it that it consumes other things: but with the universal good no evil can be connected. If, then, there be anything whose nature is inclined towards some particular good, it can tend naturally to some evil; not as evil, but accidentally, as connected with some good. But if anything of its nature be inclined to good in general, then of its own nature it cannot be inclined to evil. Now it is manifest that every intellectual nature is inclined towards good in general, which it can apprehend and which is the object of the will. Hence, since the demons are intellectual substances, they can in no wise have a natural inclination towards any evil whatsoever; consequently they cannot be naturally evil.

Reply Obj. 1: Augustine rebukes Porphyry for saying that the demons are naturally deceitful; himself maintaining that they are not naturally so, but of their own will. Now the reason why Porphyry held that they are naturally deceitful was that, as he contended, demons are animals with a sensitive nature. Now the sensitive nature is inclined towards some particular good, with which evil may be connected. In this way, then, it can have a natural inclination to evil; yet only accidentally, inasmuch as evil is connected with good.

Reply Obj. 2: The malice of some men can be called natural, either because of custom which is a second nature; or on account of the natural proclivity on the part of the sensitive nature to some inordinate passion, as some people are said to be naturally wrathful or lustful; but not on the part of the intellectual nature.

Reply Obj. 3: Brute beasts have a natural inclination in their sensitive nature towards certain particular goods, with which certain evils are connected; thus the fox in seeking its food has a natural inclination to do so with a certain skill coupled with deceit. Wherefore it is not evil in the fox to be sly, since it is natural to him; as it is not evil in the dog to be fierce, as Dionysius observes (De Div. Nom. iv).

FIFTH ARTICLE [I, Q. 63, Art. 5]

Whether the Devil Was Wicked by the Fault of His Own Will in the First Instant of His Creation?

Objection 1: It would seem that the devil was wicked by the fault of his own will in the first instant of his creation. For it is said of the devil (John 8:44): "He was a murderer from the beginning."

Obj. 2: Further, according to Augustine (Gen. ad lit. i, 15), the lack of form in the creature did not precede its formation in order of time, but merely in order of nature. Now according to him (Gen. ad lit. ii, 8), the "heaven," which is said to have been created in the beginning, signifies the angelic nature while as yet not fully formed: and when it is said that God said: "Be light made: and light was made," we are to understand the full formation of the angel by turning to the Word. Consequently, the nature of the angel was created, and light was made, in the one instant. But at the same moment that light was made, it was made distinct from "darkness," whereby the angels who sinned are denoted. Therefore in the first instant of their creation some of the angels were made blessed, and some sinned.

Obj. 3: Further, sin is opposed to merit. But some intellectual nature can merit in the first instant of its creation; as the soul of Christ, or also the good angels. Therefore the demons likewise could sin in the first instant of their creation.

Obj. 4: Further, the angelic nature is more powerful than the corporeal nature. But a corporeal thing begins to have its operation in the first instant of its creation; as fire begins to move upwards in the first instant it is produced. Therefore the angel could also have his operation in the first instant of his creation. Now this operation was either ordinate or inordinate. If ordinate, then, since he had grace, he thereby merited beatitude. But with the angels the reward follows immediately upon merit; as was said above (Q. 62, A. 5). Consequently they would have become blessed at once; and so would never have sinned, which is false. It remains, then, that they sinned by inordinate action in their first instant.

*On the contrary,* It is written (Gen. 1:31): "God saw all the things that He had made, and they were very good." But among them were also the demons. Therefore the demons were at some time good.

*I answer that,* Some have maintained that the demons were wicked straightway in the first instant of their creation; not by their nature, but by the sin of their own will; because, as soon as he was made, the devil refused righteousness. To this opinion, as Augustine says (De Civ. Dei xi, 13), if anyone subscribes, he does not agree with those Manichean heretics who say that the devil's nature is evil of itself. Since this opinion, however, is in contradiction with the authority of Scripture—for it is said of the devil under the figure of the prince of Babylon (Isa. 14:12): "How art thou fallen ... O Lucifer, who didst rise in the morning!" and it is said to the devil in the person of the King of Tyre (Ezech. 28:13): "Thou wast in the pleasures of the paradise of God,"—consequently, this opinion was reasonably rejected by the masters as erroneous.

Hence others have said that the angels, in the first instant of their creation, could have sinned, but did not. Yet this view also is repudiated by some, because, when two operations follow one upon the other, it seems impossible for each operation to terminate in the one instant. Now it is clear that the angel's sin was an act subsequent to his creation. But the term of the creative act is the angel's very being, while the term of the sinful act is the being wicked. It seems, then, an impossibility for the angel to have been wicked in the first instant of his existence.

This argument, however, does not satisfy. For it holds good only in such movements as are measured by time, and take place successively; thus, if local movement follows a change, then the change and the local movement cannot be terminated in the same instant. But if the changes are instantaneous, then all at once and in the same instant there can be a term to the first and the second change; thus in the same instant in which the moon is lit up by the sun, the atmosphere is lit up by the moon. Now, it is manifest that creation is instantaneous; so also is the movement of free-will in the angels; for, as has been already stated, they have no occasion for comparison or discursive reasoning (Q. 58, A. 3). Consequently, there is nothing to hinder the term of creation and of free-will from existing in the same instant.

We must therefore reply that, *on the contrary,* it was impossible for the angel to sin in the first instant by an inordinate act of free-will. For although a thing can begin to act in the first instant of its existence, nevertheless, that operation which begins with the existence comes of the agent from which it drew its nature; just as upward movement in fire comes of its productive cause. Therefore, if there be anything which derives its nature from a defective cause, which can be the cause of a defective action, it can in the first instant of its existence have a defective operation; just as the leg, which is defective from birth, through a defect in the principle of generation, begins at once to limp. But the agent which brought the angels into existence, namely, God, cannot be the cause of sin. Consequently it cannot be said that the devil was wicked in the first instant of his creation.

Reply Obj. 1: As Augustine says (De Civ. Dei xi, 15), when it is stated that "the devil sins from the beginning," "he is not to be thought of as sinning from the beginning wherein he was created, but from the beginning of sin": that is to say, because he never went back from his sin.

Reply Obj. 2: That distinction of light and darkness, whereby the sins of the demons are understood by the term darkness, must be taken as according to God's foreknowledge. Hence Augustine says (De Civ. Dei xi, 15), that "He alone could discern light and darkness, Who also could foreknow, before they fell, those who would fall."

Reply Obj. 3: All that is in merit is from God; and consequently an angel could merit in the first instant of his creation. The same reason does not hold good of sin; as has been said.

Reply Obj. 4: God did not distinguish between the angels before the turning away of some of them, and the turning of others to Himself, as Augustine says (De Civ. Dei xi, 15). Therefore, as all were created in grace, all merited in their first instant. But some of them at once placed an impediment to their beatitude, thereby destroying their preceding merit; and consequently they were deprived of the beatitude which they had merited.

SIXTH ARTICLE [I, Q. 63, Art. 6]

Whether There Was Any Interval Between the Creation and the Fall of the Angel?

Objection 1: It would seem that there was some interval between the angel's creation and his fall. For, it is said (Ezech. 28:15): "Thou didst walk perfect [*Vulg.: 'Thou hast walked in the midst of the stones of fire; thou wast perfect ...'] in thy ways from the day of thy creation until iniquity was found in thee." But since walking is continuous movement, it requires an interval. Therefore there was some interval between the devil's creation and his fall.

Obj. 2: Further, Origen says (Hom. i in Ezech.) that "the serpent of old did not from the first walk upon his breast and belly"; which refers to his sin. Therefore the devil did not sin at once after the first instant of his creation.

Obj. 3: Further, capability of sinning is common alike to man and angel. But there was some delay between man's formation and his sin. Therefore, for the like reason there was some interval between the devil's formation and his sin.

Obj. 4: Further, the instant wherein the devil sinned was distinct from the instant wherein he was created. But there is a middle time between every two instants. Therefore there was an interval between his creation and his fall.

*On the contrary,* It is said of the devil (John 8:44): "He stood not in the truth": and, as Augustine says (De Civ. Dei xi, 15), "we must understand this in the sense, that he was in the truth, but did not remain in it."

*I answer that,* There is a twofold opinion on this point. But the more probable one, which is also more in harmony with the teachings of the Saints, is that the devil sinned at once after the first instant of his creation. This must be maintained if it be held that he elicited an act of free-will in the first instant of his creation, and that he was created in grace; as we have said (Q. 62, A. 3). For since the angels attain beatitude by one meritorious act, as was said above (Q. 62, A. 5), if the devil, created in grace, merited in the first instant, he would at once have received beatitude after that first instant, if he had not placed an impediment by sinning.

If, however, it be contended that the angel was not created in grace, or that he could not elicit an act of free-will in the first instant, then there is nothing to prevent some interval being interposed between his creation and fall.

Reply Obj. 1: Sometimes in Holy Scripture spiritual instantaneous movements are represented by corporeal movements which are measured by time. In this way by "walking" we are to understand the movement of free-will tending towards good.

Reply Obj. 2: Origen says, "The serpent of old did not from the first walk upon his breast and belly," because of the first instant in which he was not wicked.

Reply Obj. 3: An angel has an inflexible free-will after once choosing; consequently, if after the first instant, in which he had a natural movement to good, he had not at once placed a barrier to beatitude, he would have been confirmed in good. It is not so with man; and therefore the argument does not hold good.

Reply Obj. 4: It is true to say that there is a middle time between every two instants, so far as time is continuous, as it is proved *Phys.* vi, text. 2. But in the angels, who are not subject to the heavenly movement, which is primarily measured by continuous time, time is taken to mean the succession of their mental acts, or of their affections. So the first instant in the angels is understood to respond to the operation of the angelic mind, whereby it introspects itself by its evening knowledge because on the first day evening is mentioned, but not morning. This operation was good in them all. From such operation some of them were converted to the praise of the Word by their morning knowledge while others, absorbed in themselves, became night, "swelling up with pride," as Augustine says (Gen. ad lit. iv, 24). Hence the first act was common to them all; but in their second they were separated. Consequently they were all of them good in the first instant; but in the second the good were set apart from the wicked.

SEVENTH ARTICLE [I, Q. 63, Art. 7]

Whether the Highest Angel Among Those Who Sinned Was the Highest of All?

Objection 1: It would seem that the highest among the angels who sinned was not the highest of all. For it is stated (Ezech. 28:14): "Thou wast a cherub stretched out, and protecting, and I set thee in the holy mountain of God." Now the order of the Cherubim is under the order of the Seraphim, as Dionysius says (Coel. Hier. vi, vii). Therefore, the highest angel among those who sinned was not the highest of all.

Obj. 2: Further, God made intellectual nature in order that it might attain to beatitude. If therefore the highest of the angels sinned, it follows that the Divine ordinance was frustrated in the noblest creature which is unfitting.

Obj. 3: Further, the more a subject is inclined towards anything, so much the less can it fall away from it. But the higher an angel is, so much the more is he inclined towards God. Therefore so much the less can he turn away from God by sinning. And so it seems that the angel who sinned was not the highest of all, but one of the lower angels.

*On the contrary,* Gregory (Hom. xxxiv in Ev.) says that the chief angel who sinned, "being set over all the hosts of angels, surpassed them in brightness, and was by comparison the most illustrious among them."

*I answer that,* Two things have to be considered in sin, namely, the proneness to sin, and the motive for sinning. If, then, in the angels we consider the proneness to sin, it seems that the higher angels were less likely to sin than the lower. On this account Damascene says (De Fide Orth. ii), that the highest of those who sinned was set over the terrestrial order. This opinion seems to agree with the view of the Platonists, which Augustine quotes (De Civ. Dei vii, 6, 7; x, 9, 10, 11). For they said that all the gods were good; whereas some of the demons were good, and some bad; naming as 'gods' the intellectual substances which are above the lunar sphere, and calling by the name of "demons" the intellectual substances which are beneath it, yet higher than men in the order of nature. Nor is this opinion to be rejected as contrary to faith; because the whole corporeal creation is governed by God through the angels, as Augustine says (De Trin. iii, 4,5). Consequently there is nothing to prevent us from saying that the lower angels were divinely set aside for presiding over the lower bodies, the higher over the higher bodies; and the highest to stand before God. And in this sense Damascene says (De Fide Orth. ii) that they who fell were of the lower grade of angels; yet in that order some of them remained good.

But if the motive for sinning be considered, we find that it existed in the higher angels more than in the lower. For, as has been said (A. 2), the demons' sin was pride; and the motive of pride is excellence, which was greater in the higher spirits. Hence Gregory says that he who sinned was the very highest of all. This seems to be the more probable view: because the angels' sin did not come of any proneness, but of free choice alone. Consequently that argument seems to have the more weight which is drawn from the motive in sinning. Yet this must not be prejudicial to the other view; because there might be some motive for sinning in him also who was the chief of the lower angels.

Reply Obj. 1: Cherubim is interpreted "fulness of knowledge," while "Seraphim" means "those who are on fire," or "who set on fire." Consequently Cherubim is derived from knowledge; which is compatible with mortal sin; but Seraphim is derived from the heat of charity, which is incompatible with mortal sin. Therefore the first angel who sinned is called, not a Seraph, but a Cherub.

Reply Obj. 2: The Divine intention is not frustrated either in those who sin, or in those who are saved; for God knows beforehand the end of both; and He procures glory from both, saving these of His goodness, and punishing those of His justice. But the intellectual creature, when it sins, falls away from its due end. Nor is this unfitting in any exalted creature; because the intellectual creature was so made by God, that it lies within its own will to act for its end.

Reply Obj. 3: However great was the inclination towards good in the highest angel, there was no necessity imposed upon him: consequently it was in his power not to follow it.

EIGHTH ARTICLE [I, Q. 63, Art. 8]

Whether the Sin of the Highest Angel Was the Cause of the Others Sinning?

Objection 1: It would seem that the sin of the highest angel was not the cause of the others sinning. For the cause precedes the effect. But, as Damascene observes (De Fide Orth. ii), they all sinned at one time. Therefore the sin of one was not the cause of the others' sinning.

Obj. 2: Further, an angel's first sin can only be pride, as was shown above (A. 2). But pride seeks excellence. Now it is more contrary to excellence for anyone to be subject to an inferior than to a superior; and so it does not appear that the angels sinned by desiring to be subject to a higher angel rather than to God. Yet the sin of one angel would have been the cause of the others sinning, if he had induced them to be his subjects. Therefore it does not appear that the sin of the highest angel was the cause of the others sinning.

Obj. 3: Further, it is a greater sin to wish to be subject to another against God, than to wish to be over another against God; because there is less motive for sinning. If, therefore, the sin of the foremost angel was the cause of the others sinning, in that he induced them to subject themselves to him, then the lower angels would have sinned more deeply than the highest one; which is contrary to a gloss on Ps. 103:26: "This dragon which Thou hast formed—He who was the more excellent than the rest in nature, became the greater in malice." Therefore the sin of the highest angel was not the cause of the others sinning.

*On the contrary,* It is said (Apoc. 12:4) that the dragon "drew" with him "the third part of the stars of heaven."

*I answer that,* The sin of the highest angel was the cause of the others sinning; not as compelling them, but as inducing them by a kind of exhortation. A token thereof appears in this, that all the demons are subjects of that highest one; as is evident from our Lord's words: "Go [Vulg. 'Depart from Me'], you cursed, into everlasting fire, which was prepared for the devil and his angels" (Matt. 25:41). For the order of Divine justice exacts that whosoever consents to another's evil suggestion, shall be subjected to him in his punishment; according to (2 Pet. 2:19): "By whom a man is overcome, of the same also he is the slave."

Reply Obj. 1: Although the demons all sinned in the one instant, yet the sin of one could be the cause of the rest sinning. For the angel needs no delay of time for choice, exhortation, or consent, as man, who requires deliberation in order to choose and consent, and vocal speech in order to exhort; both of which are the work of time. And it is evident that even man begins to speak in the very instant when he takes thought; and in the last instant of speech, another who catches his meaning can assent to what is said; as is especially evident with regard to primary concepts, "which everyone accepts directly they are heard" [*Boethius, De Hebdom.].

Taking away, then, the time for speech and deliberation which is required in us; in the same instant in which the highest angel expressed his affection by intelligible speech, it was possible for the others to consent thereto.

Reply Obj. 2: Other things being equal, the proud would rather be subject to a superior than to an inferior. Yet he chooses rather to be subject to an inferior than to a superior, if he can procure an advantage under an inferior which he cannot under a superior. Consequently it was not against the demons' pride for them to wish to serve an inferior by yielding to his rule; for they wanted to have him as their prince and leader, so that they might attain their ultimate beatitude of their own natural powers; especially because in the order of nature they were even then subject to the highest angel.

Reply Obj. 3: As was observed above (Q. 62, A. 6), an angel has nothing in him to retard his action, and with his whole might he is moved to whatsoever he is moved, be it good or bad. Consequently since the highest angel had greater natural energy than the lower angels, he fell into sin with intenser energy, and therefore he became the greater in malice.

NINTH ARTICLE [I, Q. 63, Art. 9]

Whether Those Who Sinned Were As Many As Those Who Remained Firm?

Objection 1: It would seem that more angels sinned than stood firm. For, as the Philosopher says (Ethic. ii, 6): "Evil is in many, but good is in few."

Obj. 2: Further, justice and sin are to be found in the same way in men and in angels. But there are more wicked men to be found than good; according to Eccles. 1:15: "The number of fools is infinite." Therefore for the same reason it is so with the angels.

Obj. 3: Further, the angels are distinguished according to persons and orders. Therefore if more angelic persons stood firm, it would appear that those who sinned were not from all the orders.

*On the contrary,* It is said (4 Kings 6:16): "There are more with us than with them": which is expounded of the good angels who are with us to aid us, and the wicked spirits who are our foes.

*I answer that,* More angels stood firm than sinned. Because sin is contrary to the natural inclination; while that which is against the natural order happens with less frequency; for nature procures its effects either always, or more often than not.

Reply Obj. 1: The Philosopher is speaking with regard to men, in whom evil comes to pass from seeking after sensible pleasures, which are known to most men, and from forsaking the good dictated by reason, which good is known to the few. In the angels there is only an intellectual nature; hence the argument does not hold.

And from this we have the answer to the second difficulty.

Reply Obj. 3: According to those who hold that the chief devil belonged to the lower order of the angels, who are set over earthly affairs, it is evident that some of every order did not fall, but only those of the lowest order. According to those who maintain that the chief devil was of the highest order, it is probable that some fell of every order; just as men are taken up into every order to supply for the angelic ruin. In this view the liberty of free-will is more established; which in every degree of creature can be turned to evil. In the Sacred Scripture, however, the names of some orders, as of Seraphim and Thrones, are not attributed to demons; since they are derived from the ardor of love and from God's indwelling, which are not consistent with mortal sin. Yet the names of Cherubim, Powers, and Principalities are attributed to them; because these names are derived from knowledge and from power, which can be common to both good and bad.

## QUESTION 64

THE PUNISHMENT OF THE DEMONS (In Four Articles)

It now remains as a sequel to deal with the punishment of the demons; under which heading there are four points of inquiry:

(1) Of their darkness of intellect;
(2) Of their obstinacy of will;
(3) Of their grief;
(4) Of their place of punishment.

FIRST ARTICLE [I, Q. 64, Art. 1]

Whether the Demons' Intellect Is Darkened by Privation of the Knowledge of All Truth?

Objection 1: It would seem that the demons' intellect is darkened by being deprived of the knowledge of all truth. For if they knew any truth at all, they would most of all know themselves; which is to know separated substances. But this is not in keeping with their unhappiness: for this seems to belong to great happiness, insomuch as that some writers have assigned as man's last happiness the knowledge of the separated substances. Therefore the demons are deprived of all knowledge of truth.

Obj. 2: Further, what is most manifest in its nature, seems to be specially manifest to the angels, whether good or bad. That the same is not manifest with regard to ourselves, comes from the weakness of our intellect which draws its knowledge from phantasms; as it comes from the weakness of its eye that the owl cannot behold the light of the sun. But the demons cannot know God, Who is most manifest of Himself, because He is the sovereign truth; and this is because they are not clean of heart, whereby alone can God be seen. Therefore neither can they know other things.

Obj. 3: Further, according to Augustine (Gen. ad lit. iv, 22), the proper knowledge of the angels is twofold; namely, morning and evening. But the demons have no morning knowledge, because they do not see things in the Word; nor have they the evening knowledge, because this evening knowledge refers the things known to the Creator's praise (hence, after "evening" comes "morning" [Gen. 1]). Therefore the demons can have no knowledge of things.

Obj. 4: Further, the angels at their creation knew the mystery of the kingdom of God, as Augustine says (Gen. ad lit. v, 19; De Civ. Dei xi). But the demons are deprived of such knowledge: "for if they had known it, they would never have crucified the Lord of glory," as is said 1 Cor. 2:8. Therefore, for the same reason, they are deprived of all other knowledge of truth.

Obj. 5: Further, whatever truth anyone knows is known either naturally, as we know first principles; or by deriving it from someone else, as we know by learning; or by long experience, as the things we learn by discovery. Now, the demons cannot know the truth by their own nature, because, as Augustine says (De Civ. Dei xi, 33), the good angels are separated from them as light is from darkness; and every manifestation is made through light, as is said Eph. 5:13. In like manner they cannot learn by revelation, nor by learning from the good angels: because "there is no fellowship of light with darkness [*Vulg.: 'What fellowship hath ... ?']" (2 Cor. 6:14). Nor can they learn by long experience: because experience comes of the senses. Consequently there is no knowledge of truth in them.

*On the contrary,* Dionysius says (Div. Nom. iv) that, "certain gifts were bestowed upon the demons which, we say, have not been changed at all, but remain entire and most brilliant." Now, the knowledge of truth stands among those natural gifts. Consequently there is some knowledge of truth in them.

*I answer that,* The knowledge of truth is twofold: one which comes of nature, and one which comes of grace. The knowledge which comes of grace is likewise twofold: the first is purely speculative, as when Divine secrets are imparted to an individual; the other is effective, and produces love for God; which knowledge properly belongs to the gift of wisdom.

Of these three kinds of knowledge the first was neither taken away nor lessened in the demons. For it follows from the very nature of the angel, who, according to his nature, is an intellect or mind: since on account of the simplicity of his substance, nothing can be withdrawn from his nature, so as to punish him by subtracting from his natural powers, as a man is punished by being deprived of a hand or a foot or of something else. Therefore Dionysius says (Div. Nom. iv) that the natural gifts remain entire in them. Consequently their natural knowledge was not diminished. The second kind of knowledge, however, which comes of grace, and consists in speculation, has not been utterly taken away from them, but lessened; because, of these Divine secrets only so much is revealed to them as is necessary; and that is done either by means of the angels, or "through some temporal workings of Divine power," as Augustine says (De Civ. Dei ix, 21); but not in the same degree as to the holy angels, to whom many more things are revealed, and more fully, in the Word Himself. But of the third knowledge, as likewise of charity, they are utterly deprived.

Reply Obj. 1: Happiness consists in self-application to something higher. The separated substances are above us in the order of nature; hence man can have happiness of a kind by knowing the separated substances, although his perfect happiness consists in knowing the first substance, namely, God. But it is quite natural for one separate substance to know another; as it is natural for us to know sensible natures. Hence, as man's happiness does not consist in knowing sensible natures; so neither does the angel's happiness consist in knowing separated substances.

Reply Obj. 2: What is most manifest in its nature is hidden from us by its surpassing the bounds of our intellect; and not merely because our intellect draws knowledge from phantasms. Now the Divine substance surpasses the proportion not only of the human intellect, but even of the angelic. Consequently, not even an angel can of his own nature know God's substance. Yet on account of the perfection of his intellect he can of his nature have a higher knowledge of God than man can have. Such knowledge of God remains also in the demons. Although they do not possess the purity which comes with grace, nevertheless they have purity of nature; and this suffices for the knowledge of God which belongs to them from their nature.

Reply Obj. 3: The creature is darkness in comparison with the excellence of the Divine light; and therefore the creature's knowledge in its own nature is called "evening" knowledge. For the evening is akin to darkness, yet it possesses some light: but when the light fails utterly, then it is night. So then the knowledge of things in their own nature, when referred to the praise of the Creator, as it is in the good angels, has something of the Divine light, and can be called evening knowledge; but if it be not referred to God, as is the case with the demons, it is not called evening, but "nocturnal" knowledge. Accordingly we read in Gen. 1:5 that the darkness, which God separated from the light, "He called night."

Reply Obj. 4: All the angels had some knowledge from the very beginning respecting the mystery of God's kingdom, which found its completion in Christ; and most of all from the moment when they were beatified by the vision of the Word, which vision the demons never had. Yet all the angels did not fully and equally apprehend it; hence the demons much less fully understood the mystery of the Incarnation, when Christ was in the world. For, as Augustine observes (De Civ. Dei ix, 21), "It was not manifested to them as it was to the holy angels, who enjoy a participated eternity of the Word; but it was made known by some temporal effects, so as to strike terror into them." For had they fully and certainly known that He was the Son of God and the effect of His passion, they would never have procured the crucifixion of the Lord of glory.

Reply Obj. 5: The demons know a truth in three ways: first of all by the subtlety of their nature; for although they are darkened by privation of the light of grace, yet they are enlightened by the light of their intellectual nature: secondly, by revelation from the holy angels; for while not agreeing with them in conformity of will, they do agree, nevertheless, by their likeness of intellectual nature, according to which they can accept what is manifested by others: thirdly, they know by long experience; not as deriving it from the senses; but when the similitude of their innate intelligible species is completed in individual things, they know some things as present, which they previously did not know would come to pass, as we said when dealing with the knowledge of the angels (Q. 57, A. 3, ad 3).

SECOND ARTICLE [I, Q. 64, Art. 2]

Whether the Will of the Demons Is Obstinate in Evil?

Objection 1: It would seem that the will of the demons is not obstinate in evil. For liberty of will belongs to the nature of an intellectual being, which nature remains in the demons, as we said above (A. 1). But liberty of will is directly and firstly ordained to good rather than to evil. Therefore the demons' will is not so obstinate in evil as not to be able to return to what is good.

Obj. 2: Further, since God's mercy is infinite, it is greater than the demons' malice, which is finite. But no one returns from the malice of sin to the goodness of justice save through God's mercy. Therefore the demons can likewise return from their state of malice to the state of justice.

Obj. 3: Further, if the demons have a will obstinate in evil, then their will would be especially obstinate in the sin whereby they fell. But that sin, namely, pride, is in them no longer; because the motive for the sin no longer endures, namely, excellence. Therefore the demon is not obstinate in malice.

Obj. 4: Further, Gregory says (Moral. iv) that man can be reinstated by another, since he fell through another. But, as was observed already (Q. 63, A. 8), the lower demons fell through the highest one. Therefore their fall can be repaired by another. Consequently they are not obstinate in malice.

Obj. 5: Further, whoever is obstinate in malice, never performs any good work. But the demon performs some good works: for he confesses the truth, saying to Christ: "I know Who Thou art, the holy one of God" (Mark 1:24). "The demons" also "believe and tremble" (James 2:19). And Dionysius observes (Div. Nom. iv), that "they desire what is good and best, which is, to be, to live, to understand." Therefore they are not obstinate in malice.

*On the contrary,* It is said (Ps. 73:23): "The pride of them that hate Thee, ascendeth continually"; and this is understood of the demons. Therefore they remain ever obstinate in their malice.

*I answer that,* It was Origen's opinion [*Peri Archon i. 6] that every will of the creature can by reason of free-will be inclined to good and evil; with the exception of the soul of Christ on account of the union of the Word. Such a statement deprives angels and saints of true beatitude, because everlasting stability is of the very nature of true beatitude; hence it is termed "life everlasting." It is also contrary to the authority of Sacred Scripture, which declares that demons and wicked men shall be sent "into everlasting punishment," and the good brought "into everlasting life." Consequently such an opinion must be considered erroneous; while according to Catholic Faith, it must be held firmly both that the will of the good angels is confirmed in good, and that the will of the demons is obstinate in evil.

We must seek for the cause of this obstinacy, not in the gravity of the sin, but in the condition of their nature or state. For as Damascene says (De Fide Orth. ii), "death is to men, what the fall is to the angels." Now it is clear that all the mortal sins of men, grave or less grave, are pardonable before death; whereas after death they are without remission and endure for ever.

To find the cause, then, of this obstinacy, it must be borne in mind that the appetitive power is in all things proportioned to the apprehensive, whereby it is moved, as the movable by its mover. For the sensitive appetite seeks a particular good; while the will seeks the universal good, as was said above (Q. 59, A. 1); as also the sense apprehends particular objects, while the intellect considers universals. Now the angel's apprehension differs from man's in this respect, that the angel by his intellect apprehends immovably, as we apprehend immovably first principles which are the object of the habit of "intelligence"; whereas man by his reason apprehends movably, passing from one consideration to another; and having the way open by which he may proceed to either of two opposites. Consequently man's will adheres to a thing movably, and with the power of forsaking it and of clinging to the opposite; whereas the angel's will adheres fixedly and immovably. Therefore, if his will be considered before its adhesion, it can freely adhere either to this or to its opposite (namely, in such things as he does not will naturally); but after he has once adhered, he clings immovably. So it is customary to say that man's free-will is flexible to the opposite both before and after choice; but the angel's free-will is flexible either opposite before the choice, but not after. Therefore the good angels who adhered to justice, were confirmed therein; whereas the wicked ones, sinning, are obstinate in sin. Later on we shall treat of the obstinacy of men who are damned (Suppl., Q. 98, AA. 1, 2).

Reply Obj. 1: The good and wicked angels have free-will, but according to the manner and condition of their state, as has been said.

Reply Obj. 2: God's mercy delivers from sin those who repent. But such as are not capable of repenting, cling immovably to sin, and are not delivered by the Divine mercy.

Reply Obj. 3: The devil's first sin still remains in him according to desire; although not as to his believing that he can obtain what he desired. Even so, if a man were to believe that he can commit murder, and wills to commit it, and afterwards the power is taken from him; nevertheless, the will to murder can stay with him, so that he would he had done it, or still would do it if he could.

Reply Obj. 4: The fact that man sinned from another's suggestion, is not the whole cause of man's sin being pardonable. Consequently the argument does not hold good.

Reply Obj. 5: A demon's act is twofold. One comes of deliberate will; and this is properly called his own act. Such an act on the demon's part is always wicked; because, although at times he does something good, yet he does not do it well; as when he tells the truth in order to deceive; and when he believes and confesses, yet not willingly, but compelled by the evidence of things. Another kind of act is natural to the demon; this can be good and bears witness to the goodness of nature. Yet he abuses even such good acts to evil purpose.

THIRD ARTICLE [I, Q. 64, Art. 3]

Whether There Is Sorrow in the Demons?

Objection 1: It would seem that there is no sorrow in the demons. For since sorrow and joy are opposites, they cannot be together in the same subject. But there is joy in the demons: for Augustine writing against the Maniches (De Gen. Contra Manich. ii, 17) says: "The devil has power over them who despise God's commandments, and he rejoices over this sinister power." Therefore there is no sorrow in the demons.

Obj. 2: Further, sorrow is the cause of fear, for those things cause fear while they are future, which cause sorrow when they are present. But there is no fear in the demons, according to Job 41:24, "Who was made to fear no one." Therefore there is no grief in the demons.

Obj. 3: Further, it is a good thing to be sorry for evil. But the demons can do no good action. Therefore they cannot be sorry, at least for the evil of sin; which applies to the worm of conscience.

*On the contrary,* The demon's sin is greater than man's sin. But man is punished with sorrow on account of the pleasure taken in sin, according to Apoc. 18:7, "As much as she hath glorified herself, and lived in delicacies, so much torment and sorrow give ye to her." Consequently much more is the devil punished with the grief of sorrow, because he especially glorified himself.

*I answer that,* Fear, sorrow, joy, and the like, so far as they are passions, cannot exist in the demons; for thus they are proper to the sensitive appetite, which is a power in a corporeal organ. According, however, as they denote simple acts of the will, they can be in the demons. And it must be said that there is sorrow in them; because sorrow, as denoting a simple act of the will, is nothing else than the resistance of the will to what is, or to what is not. Now it is evident that the demons would wish many things not to be, which are, and others to be, which are not: for, out of envy, they would wish others to be damned, who are saved. Consequently, sorrow must be said to exist in them: and especially because it is of the very notion of punishment for it to be repugnant to the will. Moreover, they are deprived of happiness, which they desire naturally; and their wicked will is curbed in many respects.

Reply Obj. 1: Joy and sorrow about the same thing are opposites, but not about different things. Hence there is nothing to hinder a man from being sorry for one thing, and joyful for another; especially so far as sorrow and joy imply simple acts of the will; because, not merely in different things, but even in one and the same thing, there can be something that we will, and something that we will not.

Reply Obj. 2: As there is sorrow in the demons over present evil, so also there is fear of future evil. Now when it is said, "He was made to fear no one," this is to be understood of the fear of God which restrains from sin. For it is written elsewhere that "the devils believe and tremble" (James 2:19).

Reply Obj. 3: To be sorry for the evil of sin on account of the sin bears witness to the goodness of the will, to which the evil of sin is opposed. But to be sorry for the evil of punishment, or for the evil of sin on account of the punishment, bears witness to the goodness of nature, to which the evil of punishment is opposed. Hence Augustine says (De Civ. Dei xix, 13), that "sorrow for good lost by punishment, is the witness to a good nature." Consequently, since the demon has a perverse and obstinate will, he is not sorry for the evil of sin.

FOURTH ARTICLE [I, Q. 64, Art. 4]

Whether Our Atmosphere Is the Demons' Place of Punishment?

Objection 1: It would seem that this atmosphere is not the demons' place of punishment. For a demon is a spiritual nature. But a spiritual nature is not affected by place. Therefore there is no place of punishment for demons.

Obj. 2: Further, man's sin is not graver than the demons'. But man's place of punishment is hell. Much more, therefore, is it the demons' place of punishment; and consequently not the darksome atmosphere.

Obj. 3: Further, the demons are punished with the pain of fire. But there is no fire in the darksome atmosphere. Therefore the darksome atmosphere is not the place of punishment for the demons.

*On the contrary,* Augustine says (Gen. ad lit. iii, 10), that "the darksome atmosphere is as a prison to the demons until the judgment day."

*I answer that,* The angels in their own nature stand midway between God and men. Now the order of Divine providence so disposes, that it procures the welfare of the inferior orders through the superior. But man's welfare is disposed by Divine providence in two ways: first of all, directly, when a man is brought unto good and withheld from evil; and this is fittingly done through the good angels. In another way, indirectly, as when anyone assailed is exercised by fighting against opposition. It was fitting for this procuring of man's welfare to be brought about through the wicked spirits, lest they should cease to be of service in the natural order. Consequently a twofold place of punishment is due to the demons: one, by reason of their sin, and this is hell; and another, in order that they may tempt men, and thus the darksome atmosphere is their due place of punishment.

Now the procuring of men's salvation is prolonged even to the judgment day: consequently, the ministry of the angels and wrestling with demons endure until then. Hence until then the good angels are sent to us here; and the demons are in this dark atmosphere for our trial: although some of them are even now in hell, to torment those whom they have led astray; just as some of the good angels are with the holy souls in heaven. But after the judgment day all the wicked, both men and angels, will be in hell, and the good in heaven.

Reply Obj. 1: A place is not penal to angel or soul as if affecting the nature by changing it, but as affecting the will by saddening it: because the angel or the soul apprehends that it is in a place not agreeable to its will.

Reply Obj. 2: One soul is not set over another in the order of nature, as the demons are over men in the order of nature; consequently there is no parallel.

Reply Obj. 3: Some have maintained that the pain of sense for demons and souls is postponed until the judgment day: and that the beatitude of the saints is likewise postponed until the judgment day. But this is erroneous, and contrary to the teaching of the Apostle (2 Cor. 5:1): "If our earthly house of this habitation be dissolved, we have a house in heaven." Others, again, while not admitting the same of souls, admit it as to demons. But it is better to say that the same judgment is passed upon wicked souls and wicked angels, even as on good souls and good angels.

Consequently, it must be said that, although a heavenly place belongs to the glory of the angels, yet their glory is not lessened by their coming to us, for they consider that place to be their own; in the same way as we say that the bishop's honor is not lessened while he is not actually sitting on his throne. In like manner it must be said, that although the demons are not actually bound within the fire of hell while they are in this dark atmosphere, nevertheless their punishment is none the less; because they know that such confinement is their due. Hence it is said in a gloss upon James 3:6: "They carry fire of hell with them wherever they go." Nor is this contrary to what is said (Luke 8:31), "They besought the Lord not to cast them into the abyss"; for they asked for this, deeming it to be a punishment for them to be cast out of a place where they could injure men. Hence it is stated, "They [Vulg. 'He'] besought Him that He would not expel them [Vulg. 'him'] out of the country" (Mark 5:10).

TREATISE ON THE WORK OF THE SIX DAYS (QQ. 65-74)

# QUESTION 65

THE WORK OF CREATION OF CORPOREAL CREATURES (In Four Articles)

From the consideration of spiritual creatures we proceed to that of corporeal creatures, in the production of which, as Holy Scripture makes mention, three works are found, namely, the work of creation, as given in the words, "In the beginning God created heaven and earth"; the work of distinction as given in the words, "He divided the light from the darkness, and the waters that are above the firmament from the waters that are under the firmament"; and the work of adornment, expressed thus, "Let there be lights in the firmament."

First, then, we must consider the work of creation; secondly, the work of distinction; and thirdly, the work of adornment. Under the first head there are four points of inquiry:

(1) Whether corporeal creatures are from God?

(2) Whether they were created on account of God's goodness?

(3) Whether they were created by God through the medium of the angels?

(4) Whether the forms of bodies are from the angels or immediately from God.

FIRST ARTICLE [I, Q. 65, Art. 1]

Whether Corporeal Creatures Are from God?

Objection 1: It would seem that corporeal creatures are not from God. For it is said (Eccles. 3:14): "I have learned that all the works which God hath made, continue for ever." But visible bodies do not continue for ever, for it is said (2 Cor. 4:18): "The things which are seen are temporal, but the things which are not seen are eternal." Therefore God did not make visible bodies.

Obj. 2: Further, it is said (Gen. 1:31): "God saw all things that He had made, and they were very good." But corporeal creatures are evil, since we find them harmful in many ways; as may be seen in serpents, in the sun's heat, and other things. Now a thing is called evil, in so far as it is harmful. Corporeal creatures, therefore, are not from God.

Obj. 3: Further, what is from God does not withdraw us from God, but leads us to Him. But corporeal creatures withdraw us from God. Hence the Apostle (2 Cor. 4:18): "While we look not at the things which are seen." Corporeal creatures, therefore, are not from God.

*On the contrary,* It is said (Ps. 145:6): "Who made heaven and earth, the sea, and all things that are in them."

*I answer that,* Certain heretics maintain that visible things are not created by the good God, but by an evil principle, and allege in proof of their error the words of the Apostle (2 Cor. 4:4), "The god of this world hath blinded the minds of unbelievers." But this position is altogether untenable. For, if things that differ agree in some point, there must be some cause for that agreement, since things diverse in nature cannot be united of themselves. Hence whenever in different things some one thing common to all is found, it must be that these different things receive that one thing from some one cause, as different bodies that are hot receive their heat from fire. But being is found to be common to all things, however otherwise different. There must, therefore, be one principle of being from which all things in whatever way existing have their being, whether they are invisible and spiritual, or visible and corporeal. But the devil is called the god of this world, not as having created it, but because worldlings serve him, of whom also the Apostle says, speaking in the same sense, "Whose god is their belly" (Phil. 3:19).

Reply Obj. 1: All the creatures of God in some respects continue for ever, at least as to matter, since what is created will never be annihilated, even though it be corruptible. And the nearer a creature approaches God, Who is immovable, the more it also is immovable. For corruptible creatures endure for ever as regards their matter, though they change as regards their substantial form. But incorruptible creatures endure with respect to their substance, though they are mutable in other respects, such as place, for instance, the heavenly bodies; or the affections, as spiritual creatures. But the Apostle's words, "The things which are seen are temporal," though true even as regards such things considered in themselves (in so far as every visible creature is subject to time, either as to being or as to movement), are intended to apply to visible things in so far as they are offered to man as rewards. For such rewards, as consist in these visible things, are temporal; while those that are invisible endure for ever. Hence he said before (2 Cor. 4:17): "It worketh for us ... an eternal weight of glory."

Reply Obj. 2: Corporeal creatures according to their nature are good, though this good is not universal, but partial and limited, the consequence of which is a certain opposition of contrary qualities, though each quality is good in itself. To those, however, who estimate things, not by the nature thereof, but by the good they themselves can derive therefrom, everything which is harmful to themselves seems simply evil. For they do not reflect that what is in some way injurious to one person, to another is beneficial, and that even to themselves the same thing may be evil in some respects, but good in others. And this could not be, if bodies were essentially evil and harmful.

Reply Obj. 3: Creatures of themselves do not withdraw us from God, but lead us to Him; for "the invisible things of God are clearly seen, being understood by the things that are made" (Rom. 1:20). If, then, they withdraw men from God, it is the fault of those who use them foolishly. Thus it is said (Wis. 14:11): "Creatures are turned into a snare to the feet of the unwise." And the very fact that they can thus withdraw us from God proves that they came from Him, for they cannot lead the foolish away from God except by the allurements of some good that they have from Him.

SECOND ARTICLE [I, Q. 65, Art. 2]

Whether Corporeal Things Were Made on Account of God's Goodness?

Objection 1: It would seem that corporeal creatures were not made on account of God's goodness. For it is said (Wis. 1:14) that God "created all things that they might be." Therefore all things were created for their own being's sake, and not on account of God's goodness.

Obj. 2: Further, good has the nature of an end; therefore the greater good in things is the end of the lesser good. But spiritual creatures are related to corporeal creatures, as the greater good to the lesser. Corporeal creatures, therefore, are created for the sake of spiritual creatures, and not on account of God's goodness.

Obj. 3: Further, justice does not give unequal things except to the unequal. Now God is just: therefore inequality not created by God must precede all inequality created by Him. But an inequality not created by God can only arise from free-will, and consequently all inequality results from the different movements of free-will. Now, corporeal creatures are unequal to spiritual creatures. Therefore the former were made on account of movements of free-will, and not on account of God's goodness.

*On the contrary,* It is said (Prov. 16:4): "The Lord hath made all things for Himself."

*I answer that,* Origen laid down [*Peri Archon

ii.] that corporeal creatures were not made according to God's original purpose, but in punishment of the sin of spiritual creatures. For he maintained that God in the beginning made spiritual creatures only, and all of equal nature; but that of these by the use of free-will some turned to God, and, according to the measure of their conversion, were given a higher or a lower rank, retaining their simplicity; while others turned from God, and became bound to different kinds of bodies according to the degree of their turning away. But this position is erroneous. In the first place, because it is contrary to Scripture, which, after narrating the production of each kind of corporeal creatures, subjoins, "God saw that it was good" (Gen. 1), as if to say that everything was brought into being for the reason that it was good for it to be. But according to Origen's opinion, the corporeal creature was made, not because it was good that it should be, but that the evil in another might be punished. Secondly, because it would follow that the arrangement, which now exists, of the corporeal world would arise from mere chance. For it the sun's body was made what it is, that it might serve for a punishment suitable to some sin of a spiritual creature, it would follow, if other spiritual creatures had sinned in the same way as the one to punish whom the sun had been created, that many suns would exist in the world; and so of other things. But such a consequence is altogether inadmissible. Hence we must set aside this theory as false, and consider that the entire universe is constituted by all creatures, as a whole consists of its parts.

Now if we wish to assign an end to any whole, and to the parts of that whole, we shall find, first, that each and every part exists for the sake of its proper act, as the eye for the act of seeing; secondly, that less honorable parts exist for the more honorable, as the senses for the intellect, the lungs for the heart; and, thirdly, that all parts are for the perfection of the whole, as the matter for the form, since the parts are, as it were, the matter of the whole. Furthermore, the whole man is on account of an extrinsic end, that end being the fruition of God. So, therefore, in the parts of the universe also every creature exists for its own proper act and perfection, and the less noble for the nobler, as those creatures that are less noble than man exist for the sake of man, whilst each and every creature exists for the perfection of the entire universe. Furthermore, the entire universe, with all its parts, is ordained towards God as its end, inasmuch as it imitates, as it were, and shows forth the Divine goodness, to the glory of God. Reasonable creatures, however, have in some special and higher manner God as their end, since they can attain to Him by their own operations, by knowing and loving Him. Thus it is plain that the Divine goodness is the end of all corporeal things.

Reply Obj. 1: In the very fact of any creature possessing being, it represents the Divine being and Its goodness. And, therefore, that God created all things, that they might have being, does not exclude that He created them for His own goodness.

Reply Obj. 2: The proximate end does not exclude the ultimate end. Therefore that corporeal creatures were, in a manner, made for the sake of the spiritual, does not prevent their being made on account of God's goodness.

Reply Obj. 3: Equality of justice has its place in retribution, since equal rewards or punishments are due to equal merit or demerit. But this does not apply to things as at first instituted. For just as an architect, without injustice, places stones of the same kind in different parts of a building, not on account of any antecedent difference in the stones, but with a view to securing that perfection of the entire building, which could not be obtained except by the different positions of the stones; even so, God from the beginning, to secure perfection in the universe, has set therein creatures of various and unequal natures, according to His wisdom, and without injustice, since no diversity of merit is presupposed.

THIRD ARTICLE [I, Q. 65, Art. 3]

Whether Corporeal Creatures Were Produced by God Through the Medium of the Angels?

Objection 1: It would seem that corporeal creatures were produced by God through the medium of the angels. For, as all things are governed by the Divine wisdom, so by it were all things made, according to Ps. 103:24: "Thou hast made all things in wisdom." But "it belongs to wisdom to ordain," as stated in the beginning of the *Metaphysics* (i, 2). Hence in the government of things the lower is ruled by the higher in a certain fitting order, as Augustine says (De Trin. iii, 4). Therefore in the production of things it was ordained that the corporeal should be produced by the spiritual, as the lower by the higher.

Obj. 2: Further, diversity of effects shows diversity of causes, since like always produces like. If then all creatures, both spiritual and corporeal, were produced immediately by God, there would be no diversity in creatures, for one would not be further removed from God than another. But this is clearly false; for the Philosopher says that some things are corruptible because they are far removed from God (De Gen. et Corrup. ii, text. 59).

Obj. 3: Further, infinite power is not required to produce a finite effect. But every corporeal thing is finite. Therefore, it could be, and was, produced by the finite power of spiritual creatures: for in suchlike beings there is no distinction between what is and what is possible: especially as no dignity befitting a nature is denied to that nature, unless it be in punishment of a fault.

*On the contrary,* It is said (Gen. 1:1): "In the beginning God created heaven and earth"; by which are understood corporeal creatures. These, therefore, were produced immediately by God.

*I answer that,* Some have maintained that creatures proceeded from God by degrees, in such a way that the first creature proceeded from Him immediately, and in its turn produced another, and so on until the production of corporeal creatures. But this position is untenable, since the first production of corporeal creatures is by creation, by which matter itself is produced: for in the act of coming into being the imperfect must be made before the perfect: and it is impossible that anything should be created, save by God alone.

In proof whereof it must be borne in mind that the higher the cause, the more numerous the objects to which its causation extends. Now the underlying principle in things is always more universal than that which informs and restricts it; thus, being is more universal than living, living than understanding, matter than form. The more widely, then, one thing underlies others, the more directly does that thing proceed from a higher cause. Thus the thing that underlies primarily all things, belongs properly to the causality of the supreme cause. Therefore no secondary cause can produce anything, unless there is presupposed in the thing produced something that is caused by a higher cause. But creation is the production of a thing in its entire substance, nothing being presupposed either uncreated or created. Hence it remains that nothing can create except God alone, Who is the first cause. Therefore, in order to show that all bodies were created immediately by God, Moses said: "In the beginning God created heaven and earth."

Reply Obj. 1: In the production of things an order exists, but not such that one creature is created by another, for that is impossible; but rather such that by the Divine wisdom diverse grades are constituted in creatures.

Reply Obj. 2: God Himself, though one, has knowledge of many and different things without detriment to the simplicity of His nature, as has been shown above (Q. 15, A. 2); so that by His wisdom He is the cause of diverse things as known by Him, even as an artificer, by apprehending diverse forms, produces diverse works of art.

Reply Obj. 3: The amount of the power of an agent is measured not only by the thing made, but also by the manner of making it; for one and the same thing is made in one way by a higher power, in another by a lower. But the production of finite things, where nothing is presupposed as existing, is the work of infinite power, and, as such, can belong to no creature.

FOURTH ARTICLE [I, Q. 65, Art. 4]

Whether the Forms of Bodies Are from the Angels?

Objection 1: It would seem that the forms of bodies come from the angels. For Boethius says (De Trin. i): "From forms that are without matter come the forms that are in matter." But forms that are without matter are spiritual substances, and forms that are in matter are the forms of bodies. Therefore, the forms of bodies are from spiritual substances.

Obj. 2: Further, all that is such by participation is reduced to that which is such by its essence. But spiritual substances are forms essentially, whereas corporeal creatures have forms by participation. Therefore the forms of corporeal things are derived from spiritual substances.

Obj. 3: Further, spiritual substances have more power of causation than the heavenly bodies. But the heavenly bodies give form to things here below, for which reason they are said to cause generation and corruption. Much more, therefore, are material forms derived from spiritual substances.

*On the contrary,* Augustine says (De Trin. iii, 8): "We must not suppose that this corporeal matter serves the angels at their nod, but rather that it obeys God thus." But corporeal matter may be said thus to serve that from which it receives its form. Corporeal forms, then, are not from the angels, but from God.

*I answer that,* It was the opinion of some that all corporeal forms are derived from spiritual substances, which we call the angels. And there are two ways in which this has been stated. For Plato held that the forms of corporeal matter are derived from, and formed by, forms immaterially subsisting, by a kind of participation. Thus he held that there exists an immaterial man, and an immaterial horse, and so forth, and that from such the individual sensible things that we see are constituted, in so far as in corporeal matter there abides the impression received from these separate forms, by a kind of assimilation, or as he calls it, "participation" (Phaedo xlix). And, according to the Platonists, the order of forms corresponds to the order of those separate substances; for example, that there is a single separate substance, which is horse and the cause of all horses, whilst above this is separate life, or *per se* life, as they term it, which is the cause of all life, and that above this again is that which they call being itself, which is the cause of all being. Avicenna, however, and certain others, have maintained that the forms of corporeal things do not subsist *per se* in matter, but in the intellect only. Thus they say that from forms existing in the intellect of spiritual creatures (called "intelligences" by them, but "angels" by us) proceed all the forms of corporeal matter, as the form of his handiwork proceeds from the forms in the mind of the craftsman. This theory seems to be the same as that of certain heretics of modern times, who say that God indeed created all things, but that the devil formed corporeal matter, and differentiated it into species.

But all these opinions seem to have a common origin; they all, in fact, sought for a cause of forms as though the form were of itself brought into being. Whereas, as Aristotle (Metaph. vii, text. 26, 27,

28), proves, what is, properly speaking, made, is the "composite." Now, such are the forms of corruptible things that at one time they exist and at another exist not, without being themselves generated or corrupted, but by reason of the generation or corruption of the "composite"; since even forms have not being, but composites have being through forms: for, according to a thing's mode of being, is the mode in which it is brought into being. Since, then, like is produced from like, we must not look for the cause of corporeal forms in any immaterial form, but in something that is composite, as this fire is generated by that fire. Corporeal forms, therefore, are caused, not as emanations from some immaterial form, but by matter being brought from potentiality into act by some composite agent. But since the composite agent, which is a body, is moved by a created spiritual substance, as Augustine says (De Trin. iii, 4, 5), it follows further that even corporeal forms are derived from spiritual substances, not emanating from them, but as the term of their movement. And, further still, the species of the angelic intellect, which are, as it were, the seminal types of corporeal forms, must be referred to God as the first cause. But in the first production of corporeal creatures no transmutation from potentiality to act can have taken place, and accordingly, the corporeal forms that bodies had when first produced came immediately form God, whose bidding alone matter obeys, as its own proper cause. To signify this, Moses prefaces each work with the words, "God said, Let this thing be," or "that," to denote the formation of all things by the Word of God, from Whom, according to Augustine [*Tract. i. in Joan. and Gen. ad lit. i. 4], is "all form and fitness and concord of parts."

Reply Obj. 1: By immaterial forms Boethius understands the types of things in the mind of God. Thus the Apostle says (Heb. 11:3): "By faith we understand that the world was framed by the Word of God; that from invisible things visible things might be made." But if by immaterial forms he understands the angels, we say that from them come material forms, not by emanation, but by motion.

Reply Obj. 2: Forms received into matter are to be referred, not to self-subsisting forms of the same type, as the Platonists held, but either to intelligible forms of the angelic intellect, from which they proceed by movement, or, still higher, to the types in the Divine intellect, by which the seeds of forms are implanted in created things, that they may be able to be brought by movement into act.

Reply Obj. 3: The heavenly bodies inform earthly ones by movement, not by emanation.

# QUESTION 66

ON THE ORDER OF CREATION TOWARDS DISTINCTION (In Four Articles)

We must next consider the work of distinction; first, the ordering of creation towards distinction; secondly, the distinction itself. Under the first head there are four points of inquiry:

(1) Whether formlessness of created matter preceded in time its formation?

(2) Whether the matter of all corporeal things is the same?

(3) Whether the empyrean heaven was created contemporaneously with formless matter?

(4) Whether time was created simultaneously with it?

FIRST ARTICLE [I, Q. 66, Art. 1]

Objection 1: It would seem that formlessness of matter preceded in time its formation. For it is said (Gen. 1:2): "The earth was void and empty," or "invisible and shapeless," according to another version [*Septuagint]; by which is understood the formlessness of matter, as Augustine says (Confess. xii, 12). Therefore matter was formless until it received its form.

Obj. 2: Further, nature in its working imitates the working of God, as a secondary cause imitates a first cause. But in the working of nature formlessness precedes form in time. It does so, therefore, in the Divine working.

Obj. 3: Further, matter is higher than accident, for matter is part of substance. But God can effect that accident exist without substance, as in the Sacrament of the Altar. He could, therefore, cause matter to exist without form.

*On the contrary,* An imperfect effect proves imperfection in the agent. But God is an agent absolutely perfect; wherefore it is said of Him (Deut. 32:4): "The works of God are perfect." Therefore the work of His creation was at no time formless. Further, the formation of corporeal creatures was effected by the work of distinction. But confusion is opposed to distinction, as formlessness to form. If, therefore, formlessness preceded in time the formation of matter, it follows that at the beginning confusion, called by the ancients chaos, existed in the corporeal creation.

*I answer that,* On this point holy men differ in opinion. Augustine for instance (Gen. ad lit. i, 15), believes that the formlessness of matter was not prior in time to its formation, but only in origin or the order of nature, whereas others, as Basil (Hom. ii In Hexaem.), Ambrose (In Hexaem. i), and Chrysostom (Hom. ii In Gen.), hold that formlessness of matter preceded in time its formation. And although these opinions seem mutually contradictory, in reality they differ but little; for Augustine takes the formlessness of matter in a different sense from the others. In his sense it means the absence of all form, and if we thus understand it we cannot say that the formlessness of matter was prior in time either to its formation or to its distinction. As to formation, the argument is clear. For if formless matter preceded in duration, it already existed; for this is implied by duration, since the end of creation is being in act: and act itself is a form. To say, then, that matter preceded, but without form, is to say that being existed actually, yet without act, which is a contradiction in terms. Nor can it be said that it possessed some common form, on which afterwards supervened the different forms that distinguish it. For this would be to hold the opinion of the ancient natural philosophers, who maintained that primary matter was some corporeal thing in act, as fire, air, water, or some intermediate substance. Hence, it followed that to be made means merely to be changed; for since that preceding form bestowed actual substantial being, and made some particular thing to be, it would result that the supervening form would not simply make an actual being, but 'this' actual being; which is the proper effect of an accidental form. Thus the consequent forms would be merely accidents, implying not generation, but alteration. Hence we must assert that primary matter was not created altogether formless, nor under any one common form, but under distinct forms. And so, if the formlessness of matter be taken as referring to the condition of primary matter, which in itself is formless, this formlessness did not precede in time its formation or distinction, but only in origin and nature, as Augustine says; in the same way as potentiality is prior to act, and the part to the whole. But the other holy writers understand by formlessness, not the exclusion of all form, but the absence of that beauty and comeliness which are now apparent in the corporeal creation. Accordingly they say that the formlessness of corporeal matter preceded its form in duration. And so, when this is considered, it appears that Augustine agrees with them in some respects, and in others disagrees, as will be shown later (Q. 69, A. 1; Q. 74, A. 2).

As far as may be gathered from the text of Genesis a threefold beauty was wanting to corporeal creatures, for which reason they are said to be without form. For the beauty of light was wanting to all that transparent body which we call the heavens, whence it is said that "darkness was upon the fact of the deep." And the earth lacked beauty in two ways: first, that beauty which it acquired when its watery veil was withdrawn, and so we read that "the earth was void," or "invisible," inasmuch as the waters covered and concealed it from view; secondly, that which it derives from being adorned by herbs and plants, for which reason it is called "empty," or, according to another reading [*Septuagint], "shapeless"—that is, unadorned. Thus after mention of two created natures, the heaven and the earth, the formlessness of the heaven is indicated by the words, "darkness was upon the face of the deep," since the air is included under heaven; and the formlessness of the earth, by the words, "the earth was void and empty."

Reply Obj. 1: The word earth is taken differently in this passage by Augustine, and by other writers. Augustine holds that by the words "earth" and "water," in this passage, primary matter itself is signified on account of its being impossible for Moses to make the idea of such matter intelligible to an ignorant people, except under the similitude of well-known objects. Hence he uses a variety of figures in speaking of it, calling it not water only, nor earth only, lest they should think it to be in very truth water or earth. At the same time it has so far a likeness to earth, in that it is susceptible of form, and to water in its adaptability to a variety of forms. In this respect, then, the earth is said to be "void and empty," or "invisible and shapeless," that matter is known by means of form. Hence, considered in itself, it is called "invisible" or "void," and its potentiality is completed by form; thus Plato says that matter is "place" [*Timaeus, quoted by Aristotle, Phys. iv, text. 15]. But other holy writers understand by earth the element of earth, and we have said (A. 1) how, in this sense, the earth was, according to them, without form.

Reply Obj. 2: Nature produces effect in act from being in potentiality; and consequently in the operations of nature potentiality must precede act in time, and formlessness precede form. But God produces being in act out of nothing, and can, therefore, produce a perfect thing in an instant, according to the greatness of His power.

Reply Obj. 3: Accident, inasmuch as it is a form, is a kind of act; whereas matter, as such, is essentially being in potentiality. Hence it is more repugnant that matter should be in act without form, than for accident to be without subject.

In reply to the first argument in the contrary sense, we say that if, according to some holy writers, formlessness was prior in time to the informing of matter, this arose, not from want of power on God's part, but from His wisdom, and from the design of preserving due order in the disposition of creatures by developing perfection from imperfection.

In reply to the second argument, we say that certain of the ancient natural philosophers maintained confusion devoid of all distinction; except Anaxagoras, who taught that the intellect alone was distinct and without admixture. But previous to the work of distinction Holy Scripture enumerates several kinds of differentiation, the first being that of the heaven from the earth, in which even a material distinction is expressed, as will be shown later (A. 3; Q. 68, A. 1). This is signified by the words, "In the beginning God created heaven and earth." The second distinction mentioned is that of the elements according to their forms, since both earth and water are named. That air and fire are not mentioned by name is due to the fact that the corporeal nature of these would not be so evident as that of earth and water, to the ignorant people to whom Moses spoke. Plato (Timaeus xxvi), nevertheless, understood air to be signified by the words, "Spirit of God," since spirit is another name for air, and considered that by the word heaven is meant fire, for he held heaven to be composed of fire, as Augustine relates (De Civ. Dei viii, 11). But Rabbi Moses (Perplex. ii), though otherwise agreeing with Plato, says that fire is signified by the word darkness, since, said he, fire does not shine in its own sphere. However, it seems more reasonable to hold to what we stated above; because by the words "Spirit of God" Scripture usually means the Holy Ghost, Who is said to "move over the waters," not, indeed, in bodily shape, but as the craftsman's will may be said to move over the material to which he intends to give a form. The third distinction is that of place; since the earth is said to be under the waters that rendered it invisible, whilst the air, the subject of darkness, is described as being above the waters, in the words: "Darkness was upon the face of the deep." The remaining distinctions will appear from what follows (Q. 71).

SECOND ARTICLE [I, Q. 66, Art. 2]

Whether the Formless Matter of All Corporeal Things Is the Same?

Objection 1: It would seem that the formless matter of all corporeal things is the same. For Augustine says (Confess. xii, 12): "I find two things Thou hast made, one formed, the other formless," and he says that the latter was the earth invisible and shapeless, whereby, he says, the matter of all corporeal things is designated. Therefore the matter of all corporeal things is the same.

Obj. 2: Further, the Philosopher says (Metaph. v, text. 10): "Things that are one in genus are one in matter." But all corporeal things are in the same genus of body. Therefore the matter of all bodies is the same.

Obj. 3: Further, different acts befit different potentialities, and the same act befits the same potentiality. But all bodies have the same form, corporeity. Therefore all bodies have the same matter.

Obj. 4: Further, matter, considered in itself, is only in potentiality. But distinction is due to form. Therefore matter considered in itself is the same in all corporeal things.

*On the contrary,* Things of which the matter is the same are mutually interchangeable and mutually active or passive, as is said (De Gener. i, text. 50). But heavenly and earthly bodies do not act upon each other mutually. Therefore their matter is not the same.

*I answer that,* On this question the opinions of philosophers have differed. Plato and all who preceded Aristotle held that all bodies are of the nature of the four elements. Hence because the four elements have one common matter, as their mutual generation and corruption prove, it followed that the matter of all bodies is the same. But the fact of the incorruptibility of some bodies was ascribed by Plato, not to the condition of matter, but to the will of the artificer, God, Whom he represents as saying to the heavenly bodies: "By your own nature you are subject to dissolution, but by My will you are indissoluble, for My will is more powerful than the link that binds you together." But this theory Aristotle (De Caelo i, text. 5) disproves by the natural movements of bodies. For since, he says, the heavenly bodies have a natural movement, different from that of the elements, it follows that they have a different nature from them. For movement in a circle, which is proper to the heavenly bodies, is not by contraries, whereas the movements of the elements are mutually opposite, one tending upwards, another downwards: so, therefore, the heavenly body is without contrariety, whereas the elemental bodies have contrariety in their nature. And as generation and corruption are from contraries, it follows that, whereas the elements are corruptible, the heavenly bodies are incorruptible. But in spite of this difference of natural corruption and incorruption, Avicebron taught unity of matter in all bodies, arguing from their unity of form. And, indeed, if corporeity were one form in itself, on which the other forms that distinguish bodies from each other supervene, this argument would necessarily be true; for this form of corporeity would inhere in matter immutably and so far all bodies would be incorruptible. But corruption would then be merely accidental through the disappearance of successive forms—that is to say, it would be corruption, not pure and simple, but partial, since a being in act would subsist under the transient form. Thus the ancient natural philosophers taught that the substratum of bodies was some actual being, such as air or fire. But supposing that no form exists in corruptible bodies which remains subsisting beneath generation and corruption, it follows necessarily that the matter of corruptible and incorruptible bodies is not the same. For matter, as it is in itself, is in potentiality to form.

Considered in itself, then, it is in potentiality in respect to all those forms to which it is common, and in receiving any one form it is in act only as regards that form. Hence it remains in potentiality to all other forms. And this is the case even where some forms are more perfect than others, and contain these others virtually in themselves. For potentiality in itself is indifferent with respect to perfection and imperfection, so that under an imperfect form it is in potentiality to a perfect form, and *vice versa.* Matter, therefore, whilst existing under the form of an incorruptible body, would be in potentiality to the form of a corruptible body; and as it does not actually possess the latter, it has both form and the privation of form; for want of a form in that which is in potentiality thereto is privation. But this condition implies corruptibility. It is therefore impossible that bodies by nature corruptible, and those by nature incorruptible, should possess the same matter.

Neither can we say, as Averroes [*De Substantia Orbis ii.] imagines, that a heavenly body itself is the matter of the heaven—being in potentiality with regard to place, though not to being, and that its form is a separate substance united to it as its motive force. For it is impossible to suppose any being in act, unless in its totality it be act and form, or be something which has act or form. Setting aside, then, in thought, the separate substance stated to be endowed with motive power, if the heavenly body is not something having form—that is, something composed of a form and the subject of that form—it follows that in its totality it is form and act. But every such thing is something actually understood, which the heavenly bodies are not, being sensible. It follows, then, that the matter of the heavenly bodies, considered in itself, is in potentiality to that form alone which it actually possesses. Nor does it concern the point at issue to inquire whether this is a soul or any other thing. Hence this form perfects this matter in such a way that there remains in it no potentiality with respect to being, but only to place, as Aristotle [*De Coelo i, text. 20] says. So, then, the matter of the heavenly bodies and of the elements is not the same, except by analogy, in so far as they agree in the character of potentiality.

Reply Obj. 1: Augustine follows in this the opinion of Plato, who does not admit a fifth essence. Or we may say that formless matter is one with the unity of order, as all bodies are one in the order of corporeal creatures.

Reply Obj. 2: If genus is taken in a physical sense, corruptible and incorruptible things are not in the same genus, on account of their different modes of potentiality, as is said in *Metaph.* x, text. 26. Logically considered, however, there is but one genus of all bodies, since they are all included in the one notion of corporeity.

Reply Obj. 3: The form of corporeity is not one and the same in all bodies, being no other than the various forms by which bodies are distinguished, as stated above.

Reply Obj. 4: As potentiality is directed towards act, potential beings are differentiated by their different acts, as sight is by color, hearing by sound. Therefore for this reason the matter of the celestial bodies is different from that of the elemental, because the matter of the celestial is not in potentiality to an elemental form.

THIRD ARTICLE [I, Q. 66, Art. 3]

Whether the Empyrean Heaven Was Created at the Same Time As Formless Matter?

Objection 1: It would seem that the empyrean heaven was not created at the same time as formless matter. For the empyrean, if it is anything at all, must be a sensible body. But all sensible bodies are movable, and the empyrean heaven is not movable. For if it were so, its movement would be ascertained by the movement of some visible body, which is not the case. The empyrean heaven, then, was not created contemporaneously with formless matter.

Obj. 2: Further, Augustine says (De Trin. iii, 4) that "the lower bodies are governed by the higher in a certain order." If, therefore, the empyrean heaven is the highest of bodies, it must necessarily exercise some influence on bodies below it. But this does not seem to be the case, especially as it is presumed to be without movement; for one body cannot move another unless itself also be moved. Therefore the empyrean heaven was not created together with formless matter.

Obj. 3: Further, if it is held that the empyrean heaven is the place of contemplation, and not ordained to natural effects; *on the contrary,* Augustine says (De Trin. iv, 20): "In so far as we mentally apprehend eternal things, so far are we not of this world"; from which it is clear that contemplation lifts the mind above the things of this world. Corporeal place, therefore, cannot be the seat of contemplation.

Obj. 4: Further, among the heavenly bodies exists a body, partly transparent and partly luminous, which we call the sidereal heaven. There exists also a heaven wholly transparent, called by some the aqueous or crystalline heaven. If, then, there exists a still higher heaven, it must be wholly luminous. But this cannot be, for then the air would be constantly illuminated, and there would be no night. Therefore the empyrean heaven was not created together with formless matter.

*On the contrary,* Strabus says that in the passage, "In the beginning God created heaven and earth," heaven denotes not the visible firmament, but the empyrean or fiery heaven.

*I answer that,* The empyrean heaven rests only on the authority of Strabus and Bede, and also of Basil; all of whom agree in one respect, namely, in holding it to be the place of the blessed. Strabus and Bede say that as soon as created it was filled with angels; and Basil [*Hom. ii. in Hexaem.] says: "Just as the lost are driven into the lowest darkness, so the reward for worthy deeds is laid up in the light beyond this world, where the just shall obtain the abode of rest." But they differ in the reasons on which they base their statement. Strabus and Bede teach that there is an empyrean heaven, because the firmament, which they take to mean the sidereal heaven, is said to have been made, not in the beginning, but on the second day: whereas the reason given by Basil is that otherwise God would seem to have made darkness His first work, as the Manicheans falsely assert, when they call the God of the Old Testament the God of darkness. These reasons, however, are not very cogent. For the question of the firmament, said to have been made on the second day, is solved in one way by Augustine, and in another by other holy writers. But the question of the darkness is explained according to Augustine [*Gen. ad lit. i; vii.], by supposing that formlessness, signified by darkness, preceded form not by duration, but by origin. According to others, however, since darkness is no creature, but a privation of light, it is a proof of Divine wisdom, that the things it created from nothing it produced first of all in an imperfect state, and afterwards brought them to perfection. But a better reason can be drawn from the state of glory itself. For in the reward to come a two-fold glory is looked for, spiritual and corporeal, not only in the human body to be glorified, but in the whole world which is to be made new. Now the spiritual glory began with the beginning of the world, in the blessedness of the angels, equality with whom is promised to the saints. It was fitting, then, that even from the beginning, there should be made some beginning of bodily glory in something corporeal, free at the very outset from the servitude of corruption and change, and wholly luminous, even as the whole bodily creation, after the Resurrection, is expected to be. So, then, that heaven is called the empyrean, i.e. fiery, not from its heat, but from its brightness. It is to be noticed, however, that Augustine (De Civ. Dei x, 9, 27) says that Porphyry sets the demons apart from the angels by supposing that the former inhabit the air, the latter the ether, or empyrean. But Porphyry, as a Platonist, held the heaven, known as sidereal, to be fiery, and therefore called it empyrean or ethereal, taking ethereal to denote the burning of flame, and not as Aristotle understands it, swiftness of movement (De Coel. i, text. 22). This much has been said to prevent anyone from supposing that Augustine maintained an empyrean heaven in the sense understood by modern writers.

Reply Obj. 1: Sensible corporeal things are movable in the present state of the world, for by the movement of corporeal creatures is secured by the multiplication of the elements. But when glory is finally consummated, the movement of bodies will cease. And such must have been from the beginning the condition of the empyrean.

Reply Obj. 2: It is sufficiently probable, as some assert, that the empyrean heaven, having the state of glory for its ordained end, does not influence inferior bodies of another order—those, namely, that are directed only to natural ends. Yet it seems still more probable that it does influence bodies that are moved, though itself motionless, just as angels of the highest rank, who assist [*Infra, Q. 112, A. 3], influence those of lower degree who act as messengers, though they themselves are not sent, as Dionysius teaches (Coel. Hier. xii). For this reason it may be said that the influence of the empyrean upon that which is called the first heaven, and is moved, produces therein not something that comes and goes as a result of movement, but something of a fixed and stable nature, as the power of conservation or causation, or something of the kind pertaining to dignity.

Reply Obj. 3: Corporeal place is assigned to contemplation, not as necessary, but as congruous, that the splendor without may correspond to that which is within. Hence Basil (Hom. ii in Hexaem.) says: "The ministering spirit could not live in darkness, but made his habitual dwelling in light and joy."

Reply Obj. 4: As Basil says (Hom. ii in Hexaem.): "It is certain that the heaven was created spherical in shape, of dense body, and sufficiently strong to separate what is outside it from what it encloses. On this account it darkens the region external to it, the light by which itself is lit up being shut out from that region." But since the body of the firmament, though solid, is transparent, for that it does not exclude light (as is clear from the fact that we can see the stars through the intervening heavens), we may also say that the empyrean has light, not condensed so as to emit rays, as the sun does, but of a more subtle nature. Or it may have the brightness of glory which differs from mere natural brightness.

FOURTH ARTICLE [I, Q. 66, Art. 4]

Whether Time Was Created Simultaneously with Formless Matter?

Objection 1: It would seem that time was not created simultaneously with formless matter. For Augustine says (Confess. xii, 12): "I find two things that Thou didst create before time was, the primary corporeal matter, and the angelic nature. "Therefore time was not created with formless matter.

Obj. 2: Further, time is divided by day and night. But in the beginning there was neither day nor night, for these began when "God divided the light from the darkness." Therefore in the beginning time was not.

Obj. 3: Further, time is the measure of the firmament's movement; and the firmament is said to have been made on the second day. Therefore in the beginning time was not.

Obj. 4: Further, movement precedes time, and therefore should be reckoned among the first things created, rather than time.

Obj. 5: Further, as time is the extrinsic measure of created things, so is place. Place, then, as truly as time, must be reckoned among the things first created.

*On the contrary,* Augustine says (Gen. ad lit. i, 3): "Both spiritual and corporeal creatures were created at the beginning of time."

*I answer that,* It is commonly said that the first things created were these four—the angelic nature, the empyrean heaven, formless corporeal matter, and time. It must be observed, however, that this is not the opinion of Augustine. For he (Confess. xii, 12) specifies only two things as first created—the angelic nature and corporeal matter—making no mention of the empyrean heaven. But these two, namely, the angelic nature and formless matter, precede the formation, by nature only, and not by duration; and therefore, as they precede formation, so do they precede movement and time. Time, therefore, cannot be included among them. But the enumeration above given is that of other holy writers, who hold that the formlessness of matter preceded by duration its form, and this view postulates the existence of time as the measure of duration: for otherwise there would be no such measure.

Reply Obj. 1: The teaching of Augustine rests on the opinion that the angelic nature and formless matter precede time by origin or nature.

Reply Obj. 2: As in the opinion of some holy writers matter was in some measure formless before it received its full form, so time was in a manner formless before it was fully formed and distinguished into day and night.

Reply Obj. 3: If the movement of the firmament did not begin immediately from the beginning, then the time that preceded was the measure, not of the firmament's movement, but of the first movement of whatsoever kind. For it is accidental to time to be the measure of the firmament's movement, in so far as this is the first movement. But if the first movement was another than this, time would have been its measure, for everything is measured by the first of its kind. And it must be granted that forthwith from the beginning, there was movement of some kind, at least in the succession of concepts and affections in the angelic mind: while movement without time cannot be conceived, since time is nothing else than "the measure of priority and succession in movement."

Reply Obj. 4: Among the first created things are to be reckoned those which have a general relationship to things. And, therefore, among these time must be included, as having the nature of a common measure; but not movement, which is related only to the movable subject.

Reply Obj. 5: Place is implied as existing in the empyrean heaven, this being the boundary of the universe. And since place has reference to things permanent, it was created at once in its totality. But time, as not being permanent, was created in its beginning: even as actually we cannot lay hold of any part of time save the "now."

## QUESTION 67

ON THE WORK OF DISTINCTION IN ITSELF (In Four Articles)

We must consider next the work of distinction in itself. First, the work of the first day; secondly, the work of the second day; thirdly the work of the third day.

Under the first head there are four points of inquiry:

(1) Whether the word light is used in its proper sense in speaking of spiritual things?

(2) Whether light, in corporeal things, is itself corporeal?

(3) Whether light is a quality?

(4) Whether light was fittingly made on the first day?

FIRST ARTICLE [I, Q. 67, Art. 1]

Whether the Word "Light" Is Used in Its Proper Sense in Speaking of Spiritual Things?

Objection 1: It would seem that "light" is used in its proper sense in spiritual things. For Augustine says (Gen. ad lit. iv, 28) that "in spiritual things light is better and surer: and that Christ is not called Light in the same sense as He is called the Stone; the former is to be taken literally, and the latter metaphorically."

Obj. 2: Further, Dionysius (Div. Nom. iv) includes Light among the intellectual names of God. But such names are used in their proper sense in spiritual things. Therefore light is used in its proper sense in spiritual matters.

Obj. 3: Further, the Apostle says (Eph. 5:13): "All that is made manifest is light." But to be made manifest belongs more properly to spiritual things than to corporeal. Therefore also does light.

*On the contrary,* Ambrose says (De Fide ii) that "Splendor" is among those things which are said of God metaphorically.

*I answer that,* Any word may be used in two ways—that is to say, either in its original application or in its more extended meaning. This is clearly shown in the word "sight," originally applied to the act of the sense, and then, as sight is the noblest and most trustworthy of the senses, extended in common speech to all knowledge obtained through the other senses. Thus we say, "Seeing how it tastes," or "smells," or "burns." Further, sight is applied to knowledge obtained through the intellect, as in those words: "Blessed are the clean of heart, for they shall see God" (Matt. 5:8). And thus it is with the word light. In its primary meaning it signifies that which makes manifest to the sense of sight; afterwards it was extended to that which makes manifest to cognition of any kind. If, then, the word is taken in its strict and primary meaning, it is to be understood metaphorically when applied to spiritual things, as Ambrose says (De Fide ii). But if taken in its common and extended use, as applied to manifestation of every kind, it may properly be applied to spiritual things.

The answer to the objections will sufficiently appear from what has been said.

SECOND ARTICLE [I, Q. 67, Art. 2]

Whether Light Is a Body?

Objection 1: It would seem that light is a body. For Augustine says (De Lib. Arb. iii, 5) that "light takes the first place among bodies."Therefore light is a body.

Obj. 2: Further, the Philosopher says (Topic. v, 2) that "light is a species of fire." But fire is a body, and therefore so is light.

Obj. 3: Further, the powers of movement, intersection, reflection, belong properly to bodies; and all these are attributes of light and its rays. Moreover, different rays of light, as Dionysius says (Div. Nom. ii) are united and separated, which seems impossible unless they are bodies. Therefore light is a body.

*On the contrary,* Two bodies cannot occupy the same place simultaneously. But this is the case with light and air. Therefore light is not a body.

*I answer that,* Light cannot be a body, for three evident reasons. First, on the part of place. For the place of any one body is different from that of any other, nor is it possible, naturally speaking, for any two bodies of whatever nature, to exist simultaneously in the same place; since contiguity requires distinction of place.

The second reason is from movement. For if light were a body, its diffusion would be the local movement of a body. Now no local movement of a body can be instantaneous, as everything that moves from one place to another must pass through the intervening space before reaching the end: whereas the diffusion of light is instantaneous. Nor can it be argued that the time required is too short to be perceived; for though this may be the case in short distances, it cannot be so in distances so great as that which separates the East from the West. Yet as soon as the sun is at the horizon, the whole hemisphere is illuminated from end to end. It must also be borne in mind on the part of movement that whereas all bodies have their natural determinate movement, that of light is indifferent as regards direction, working equally in a circle as in a straight line. Hence it appears that the diffusion of light is not the local movement of a body.

The third reason is from generation and corruption. For if light were a body, it would follow that whenever the air is darkened by the absence of the luminary, the body of light would be corrupted, and its matter would receive a new form. But unless we are to say that darkness is a body, this does not appear to be the case. Neither does it appear from what matter a body can be daily generated large enough to fill the intervening hemisphere. Also it would be absurd to say that a body of so great a bulk is corrupted by the mere absence of the luminary. And should anyone reply that it is not corrupted, but approaches and moves around with the sun, we may ask why it is that when a lighted candle is obscured by the intervening object the whole room is darkened? It is not that the light is condensed round the candle when this is done, since it burns no more brightly then than it burned before.

Since, therefore, these things are repugnant, not only to reason, but to common sense, we must conclude that light cannot be a body.

Reply Obj. 1: Augustine takes light to be a luminous body in act—in other words, to be fire, the noblest of the four elements.

Reply Obj. 2: Aristotle pronounces light to be fire existing in its own proper matter: just as fire in aerial matter is "flame," or in earthly matter is "burning coal." Nor must too much attention be paid to the instances adduced by Aristotle in his works on logic, as he merely mentions them as the more or less probable opinions of various writers.

Reply Obj. 3: All these properties are assigned to light metaphorically, and might in the same way be attributed to heat. For because movement from place to place is naturally first in the order of movement as is proved *Phys.* viii, text. 55, we use terms belonging to local movement in speaking of alteration and movement of all kinds. For even the word distance is derived from the idea of remoteness of place, to that of all contraries, as is said *Metaph.* x, text. 13.

THIRD ARTICLE [I, Q. 67, Art. 3]

Whether Light Is a Quality?

Objection 1: It would seem that light is not a quality. For every quality remains in its subject, though the active cause of the quality be removed, as heat remains in water removed from the fire. But light does not remain in the air when the source of light is withdrawn. Therefore light is not a quality.

Obj. 2: Further, every sensible quality has its opposite, as cold is opposed to heat, blackness to whiteness. But this is not the case with light since darkness is merely a privation of light. Light therefore is not a sensible quality.

Obj. 3: Further, a cause is more potent than its effect. But the light of the heavenly bodies is a cause of substantial forms of earthly bodies, and also gives to colors their immaterial being, by making them actually visible. Light, then, is not a sensible quality, but rather a substantial or spiritual form.

*On the contrary,* Damascene (De Fide Orth. i) says that light is a species of quality.

*I answer that,* Some writers have said that the light in the air has not a natural being such as the color on a wall has, but only an intentional being, as a similitude of color in the air. But this cannot be the case for two reasons. First, because light gives a name to the air, since by it the air becomes actually luminous. But color does not do this, for we do not speak of the air as colored. Secondly, because light produces natural effects, for by the rays of the sun bodies are warmed, and natural changes cannot be brought about by mere intentions. Others have said that light is the sun's substantial form, but this also seems impossible for two reasons. First, because substantial forms are not of themselves objects of the senses; for the object of the intellect is what a thing is, as is said *De Anima* iii, text. 26: whereas light is visible of itself. In the second place, because it is impossible that what is the substantial form of one thing should be the accidental form of another; since substantial forms of their very nature constitute species: wherefore the substantial form always and everywhere accompanies the species. But light is not the substantial form of air, for if it were, the air would be destroyed when light is withdrawn. Hence it cannot be the substantial form of the sun.

We must say, then, that as heat is an active quality consequent on the substantial form of fire, so light is an active quality consequent on the substantial form of the sun, or of another body that is of itself luminous, if there is any such body. A proof of this is that the rays of different stars produce different effects according to the diverse natures of bodies.

Reply Obj. 1: Since quality is consequent upon substantial form, the mode in which the subject receives a quality differs as the mode differs in which a subject receives a substantial form. For when matter receives its form perfectly, the qualities consequent upon the form are firm and enduring; as when, for instance, water is converted into fire. When, however, substantial form is received imperfectly, so as to be, as it were, in process of being received, rather than fully impressed, the consequent quality lasts for a time but is not permanent; as may be seen when water which has been heated returns in time to its natural state. But light is not produced by the transmutation of matter, as though matter were in receipt of a substantial form, and light were a certain inception of substantial form. For this reason light disappears on the disappearance of its active cause.

Reply Obj. 2: It is accidental to light not to have a contrary, forasmuch as it is the natural quality of the first corporeal cause of change, which is itself removed from contrariety.

Reply Obj. 3: As heat acts towards perfecting the form of fire, as an instrumental cause, by virtue of the substantial form, so does light act instrumentally, by virtue of the heavenly bodies, towards producing substantial forms; and towards rendering colors actually visible, inasmuch as it is a quality of the first sensible body.

FOURTH ARTICLE [I, Q. 67, Art. 4]

Whether the Production of Light Is Fittingly Assigned to the First Day?

Objection 1: It would seem that the production of light is not fittingly assigned to the first day. For light, as stated above (A. 3), is a quality. But qualities are accidents, and as such should have, not the first, but a subordinate place. The production of light, then, ought not to be assigned to the first day.

Obj. 2: Further, it is light that distinguishes night from day, and this is effected by the sun, which is recorded as having been made on the fourth day. Therefore the production of light could not have been on the first day.

Obj. 3: Further, night and day are brought about by the circular movement of a luminous body. But movement of this kind is an attribute of the firmament, and we read that the firmament was made on the second day. Therefore the production of light, dividing night from day, ought not to be assigned to the first day.

Obj. 4: Further, if it be said that spiritual light is here spoken of, it may be replied that the light made on the first day dispels the darkness. But in the beginning spiritual darkness was not, for even the demons were in the beginning good, as has been shown (Q. 63, A. 5). Therefore the production of light ought not to be assigned to the first day.

*On the contrary,* That without which there could not be day, must have been made on the first day. But there can be no day without light. Therefore light must have been made on the first day.

*I answer that,* There are two opinions as to the production of light. Augustine seems to say (De Civ. Dei xi, 9,33) that Moses could not have fittingly passed over the production of the spiritual creature, and therefore when we read, "In the beginning God created heaven and earth," a spiritual nature as yet formless is to be understood by the word "heaven," and formless matter of the corporeal creature by the word "earth." And spiritual nature was formed first, as being of higher dignity than corporeal. The forming, therefore, of this spiritual nature is signified by the production of light, that is to say, of spiritual light. For a spiritual nature receives its form by the enlightenment whereby it is led to adhere to the Word of God.

Other writers think that the production of spiritual creatures was purposely omitted by Moses, and give various reasons. Basil [*Hom. i in Hexaem.] says that Moses begins his narrative from the beginning of time which belongs to sensible things; but that the spiritual or angelic creation is passed over, as created beforehand.

Chrysostom [*Hom. ii in Genes.] gives as a reason for the omission that Moses was addressing an ignorant people, to whom material things alone appealed, and whom he was endeavoring to withdraw from the service of idols. It would have been to them a pretext for idolatry if he had spoken to them of natures spiritual in substance and nobler than all corporeal creatures; for they would have paid them Divine worship, since they were prone to worship as gods even the sun, moon, and stars, which was forbidden them (Deut. 4).

But mention is made of several kinds of formlessness, in regard to the corporeal creature. One is where we read that "the earth was void and empty," and another where it is said that "darkness was upon the face of the deep." Now it seems to be required, for two reasons, that the formlessness of darkness should be removed first of all by the production of light. In the first place because light is a quality of the first body, as was stated (A. 3), and thus by means of light it was fitting that the world should first receive its form. The second reason is because light is a common quality. For light is common to terrestrial and celestial bodies. But as in knowledge we proceed from general principles, so do we in work of every kind. For the living thing is generated before the animal, and the animal before the man, as is shown in *De Gener. Anim.* ii, 3. It was fitting, then, as an evidence of the Divine wisdom, that among the works of distinction the production of light should take first place, since light is a form of the primary body, and because it is more common quality.

Basil [*Hom. ii in Hexaem.], indeed, adds a third reason: that all other things are made manifest by light. And there is yet a fourth, already touched upon in the objections; that day cannot be unless light exists, which was made therefore on the first day.

Reply Obj. 1: According to the opinion of those who hold that the formlessness of matter preceded its form in duration, matter must be held to have been created at the beginning with substantial forms, afterwards receiving those that are accidental, among which light holds the first place.

Reply Obj. 2: In the opinion of some the light here spoken of was a kind of luminous nebula, and that on the making of the sun this returned to the matter of which it had been formed. But this cannot well be maintained, as in the beginning of Genesis Holy Scripture records the institution of that order of nature which henceforth is to endure. We cannot, then, say that what was made at that time afterwards ceased to exist.

Others, therefore, held that this luminous nebula continues in existence, but so closely attached to the sun as to be indistinguishable. But this is as much as to say that it is superfluous, whereas none of God's works have been made in vain. On this account it is held by some that the sun's body was made out of this nebula. This, too, is impossible to those at least who believe that the sun is different in its nature from the four elements, and naturally incorruptible. For in that case its matter cannot take on another form.

I answer, then, with Dionysius (Div. Nom. iv), that the light was the sun's light, formless as yet, being already the solar substance, and possessing illuminative power in a general way, to which was afterwards added the special and determinative power required to produce determinate effects. Thus, then, in the production of this light a triple distinction was made between light and darkness. First, as to the cause, forasmuch as in the substance of the sun we have the cause of light, and in the opaque nature of the earth the cause of darkness. Secondly, as to place, for in one hemisphere there was light, in the other darkness. Thirdly, as to time; because there was light for one and darkness for another in the same hemisphere; and this is signified by the words, "He called the light day, and the darkness night."

Reply Obj. 3: Basil says (Hom. ii in Hexaem.) that day and night were then caused by expansion and contraction of light, rather than by movement. But Augustine objects to this (Gen. ad lit. i), that there was no reason for this vicissitude of expansion and contraction since there were neither men nor animals on the earth at that time, for whose service this was required. Nor does the nature of a luminous body seem to admit of the withdrawal of light, so long as the body is actually present; though this might be effected by a miracle. As to this, however, Augustine remarks (Gen. ad lit. i) that in the first founding of the order of nature we must not look for miracles, but for what is in accordance with nature. We hold, then, that the movement of the heavens is twofold. Of these movements, one is common to the entire heaven, and is the cause of day and night. This, as it seems, had its beginning on the first day. The other varies in proportion as it affects various bodies, and by its variations is the cause of the succession of days, months, and years. Thus it is, that in the account of the first day the distinction between day and night alone is mentioned; this distinction being brought about by the common movement of the heavens. The further distinction into successive days, seasons, and years recorded as begun on the fourth day, in the words, "let them be for seasons, and for days, and years" is due to proper movements.

Reply Obj. 4: As Augustine teaches (Confess. xii; Gen. ad lit. 1, 15), formlessness did not precede forms in duration; and so we must understand the production of light to signify the formation of spiritual creatures, not, indeed, with the perfection of glory, in which they were not created, but with the perfection of grace, which they possessed from their creation as said above (Q. 62, A. 3). Thus the division of light from darkness will denote the distinction of the spiritual creature from other created things as yet without form. But if all created things received their form at the same time, the darkness must be held to mean the spiritual darkness of the wicked, not as existing from the beginning but such as God foresaw would exist.

# QUESTION 68

ON THE WORK OF THE SECOND DAY (In Four Articles)

We must next consider the work of the second day. Under this head there are four points of inquiry:

(1) Whether the firmament was made on the second day?

(2) Whether there are waters above the firmament?

(3) Whether the firmament divides waters from waters?

(4) Whether there is more than one heaven?

FIRST ARTICLE [I, Q. 68, Art. 1]

Whether the Firmament Was Made on the Second Day?

Objection 1: It would seem that the firmament was not made on the second day. For it is said (Gen. 1:8): "God called the firmament heaven." But the heaven existed before days, as is clear from the words, "In the beginning God created heaven and earth." Therefore the firmament was not made on the second day.

Obj. 2: Further, the work of the six days is ordered conformably to the order of Divine wisdom. Now it would ill become the Divine wisdom to make afterwards that which is naturally first. But though the firmament naturally precedes the earth and the waters, these are mentioned before the formation of light, which was on the first day. Therefore the firmament was not made on the second day.

Obj. 3: Further, all that was made in the six days was formed out of matter created before days began. But the firmament cannot have been formed out of pre-existing matter, for if so it would be liable to generation and corruption. Therefore the firmament was not made on the second day.

*On the contrary,* It is written (Gen. 1:6): "God said: let there be a firmament," and further on (verse 8); "And the evening and morning were the second day."

*I answer that,* In discussing questions of this kind two rules are to be observed, as Augustine teaches (Gen. ad lit. i, 18). The first is, to hold the truth of Scripture without wavering. The second is that since Holy Scripture can be explained in a multiplicity of senses, one should adhere to a particular explanation, only in such measure as to be ready to abandon it, if it be proved with certainty to be false; lest Holy Scripture be exposed to the ridicule of unbelievers, and obstacles be placed to their believing.

We say, therefore, that the words which speak of the firmament as made on the second day can be understood in two senses. They may be understood, first, of the starry firmament, on which point it is necessary to set forth the different opinions of philosophers. Some of these believed it to be composed of the elements; and this was the opinion of Empedocles, who, however, held further that the body of the firmament was not susceptible of dissolution, because its parts are, so to say, not in disunion, but in harmony. Others held the firmament to be of the nature of the four elements, not, indeed, compounded of them, but being as it were a simple element. Such was the opinion of Plato, who held that element to be fire. Others, again, have held that the heaven is not of the nature of the four elements, but is itself a fifth body, existing over and above these. This is the opinion of Aristotle (De Coel. i, text. 6,32).

According to the first opinion, it may, strictly speaking, be granted that the firmament was made, even as to substance, on the second day. For it is part of the work of creation to produce the substance of the elements, while it belongs to the work of distinction and adornment to give forms to the elements that pre-exist.

But the belief that the firmament was made, as to its substance, on the second day is incompatible with the opinion of Plato, according to whom the making of the firmament implies the production of the element of fire. This production, however, belongs to the work of creation, at least, according to those who hold that formlessness of matter preceded in time its formation, since the first form received by matter is the elemental.

Still less compatible with the belief that the substance of the firmament was produced on the second day is the opinion of Aristotle, seeing that the mention of days denotes succession of time, whereas the firmament, being naturally incorruptible, is of a matter not susceptible of change of form; wherefore it could not be made out of matter existing antecedently in time.

Hence to produce the substance of the firmament belongs to the work of creation. But its formation, in some degree, belongs to the second day, according to both opinions: for as Dionysius says (Div. Nom. iv), the light of the sun was without form during the first three days, and afterwards, on the fourth day, received its form.

If, however, we take these days to denote merely sequence in the natural order, as Augustine holds (Gen. ad lit. iv, 22,24), and not succession in time, there is then nothing to prevent our saying, whilst holding any one of the opinions given above, that the substantial formation of the firmament belongs to the second day.

Another possible explanation is to understand by the firmament that was made on the second day, not that in which the stars are set, but the part of the atmosphere where the clouds are collected, and which has received the name firmament from the firmness and density of the air. "For a body is called firm," that is dense and solid, "thereby differing from a mathematical body" as is remarked by Basil (Hom. iii in Hexaem.). If, then, this explanation is adopted none of these opinions will be found repugnant to reason. Augustine, in fact (Gen. ad lit. ii, 4), recommends it thus: "I consider this view of the question worthy of all commendation, as neither contrary to faith nor difficult to be proved and believed."

Reply Obj. 1: According to Chrysostom (Hom. iii in Genes.), Moses prefaces his record by speaking of the works of God collectively, in the words, "In the beginning God created heaven and earth," and then proceeds to explain them part by part; in somewhat the same way as one might say: "This house was constructed by that builder," and then add: "First, he laid the foundations, then built the walls, and thirdly, put on the roof." In accepting this explanation we are, therefore, not bound to hold that a different heaven is spoken of in the words: "In the beginning God created heaven and earth," and when we read that the firmament was made on the second day.

We may also say that the heaven recorded as created in the beginning is not the same as that made on the second day; and there are several senses in which this may be understood. Augustine says (Gen. ad lit. i, 9) that the heaven recorded as made on the first day is the formless spiritual nature, and that the heaven of the second day is the corporeal heaven. According to Bede (Hexaem. i) and Strabus, the heaven made on the first day is the empyrean, and the firmament made on the second day, the starry heaven. According to Damascene (De Fide Orth. ii) that of the first day was spherical in form and without stars, the same, in fact, that the philosophers speak of, calling it the ninth sphere, and the primary movable body that moves with diurnal movement: while by the firmament made on the second day he understands the starry heaven. According to another theory, touched upon by Augustine [*Gen. ad lit. ii, 1] the heaven made on the first day was the starry heaven, and the firmament made on the second day was that region of the air where the clouds are collected, which is also called heaven, but equivocally. And to show that the word is here used in an equivocal sense, it is expressly said that "God called the firmament heaven"; just as in a preceding verse it said that "God called the light day" (since the word "day" is also used to denote a space of twenty-four hours). Other instances of a similar use occur, as pointed out by Rabbi Moses.

The second and third objections are sufficiently answered by what has been already said.

SECOND ARTICLE [I, Q. 68, Art. 2]

Whether There Are Waters Above the Firmament?

Objection 1: It would seem that there are not waters above the firmament. For water is heavy by nature, and heavy things tend naturally downwards, not upwards. Therefore there are not waters above the firmament.

Obj. 2: Further, water is fluid by nature, and fluids cannot rest on a sphere, as experience shows. Therefore, since the firmament is a sphere, there cannot be water above it.

Obj. 3: Further, water is an element, and appointed to the generation of composite bodies, according to the relation in which imperfect things stand towards perfect. But bodies of composite nature have their place upon the earth, and not above the firmament, so that water would be useless there. But none of God's works are useless. Therefore there are not waters above the firmament.

*On the contrary,* It is written (Gen. 1:7): "(God) divided the waters that were under the firmament, from those that were above the firmament."

I answer with Augustine (Gen. ad lit. ii, 5) that, "These words of Scripture have more authority than the most exalted human intellect. Hence, whatever these waters are, and whatever their mode of existence, we cannot for a moment doubt that they are there." As to the nature of these waters, all are not agreed. Origen says (Hom. i in Gen.) that the waters that are above the firmament are "spiritual substances." Wherefore it is written (Ps. 148:4): "Let the waters that are above the heavens praise the name of the Lord," and (Dan. 3:60): "Ye waters that are above the heavens, bless the Lord."To this Basil answers (Hom. iii in Hexaem.) that these words do not mean that these waters are rational creatures, but that "the thoughtful contemplation of them by those who understand fulfils the glory of the Creator." Hence in the same context, fire, hail, and other like creatures, are invoked in the same way, though no one would attribute reason to these.

We must hold, then, these waters to be material, but their exact nature will be differently defined according as opinions on the firmament differ. For if by the firmament we understand the starry heaven, and as being of the nature of the four elements, for the same reason it may be believed that the waters above the heaven are of the same nature as the elemental waters. But if by the firmament we understand the starry heaven, not, however, as being of the nature of the four elements, then the waters above the firmament will not be of the same nature as the elemental waters, but just as, according to Strabus, one heaven is called empyrean, that is, fiery, solely on account of its splendor: so this other heaven will be called aqueous solely on account of its transparence; and this heaven is above the starry heaven. Again, if the firmament is held to be of other nature than the elements, it may still be said to divide the waters, if we understand by water not the element but formless matter. Augustine, in fact, says (Super Gen. cont. Manich. i, 5,7) that whatever divides bodies from bodies can be said to divide waters from waters.

If, however, we understand by the firmament that part of the air in which the clouds are collected, then the waters above the firmament must rather be the vapors resolved from the waters which are raised above a part of the atmosphere, and from which the rain falls. But to say, as some writers alluded to by Augustine (Gen. ad lit. ii, 4), that waters resolved into vapor may be lifted above the starry heaven, is a mere absurdity. The solid nature of the firmament, the intervening region of fire, wherein all vapor must be consumed, the tendency in light and rarefied bodies to drift to one spot beneath the vault of the moon, as well as the fact that vapors are perceived not to rise even to the tops of the higher mountains, all to go to show the impossibility of this. Nor is it less absurd to say, in support of this opinion, that bodies may be rarefied infinitely, since natural bodies cannot be infinitely rarefied or divided, but up to a certain point only.

Reply Obj. 1: Some have attempted to solve this difficulty by supposing that in spite of the natural gravity of water, it is kept in its place above the firmament by the Divine power. Augustine (Gen. ad lit. ii, 1), however will not admit this solution, but says "It is our business here to inquire how God has constituted the natures of His creatures, not how far it may have pleased Him to work on them by way of miracle." We leave this view, then, and answer that according to the last two opinions on the firmament and the waters the solution appears from what has been said. According to the first opinion, an order of the elements must be supposed different from that given by Aristotle, that is to say, that the waters surrounding the earth are of a dense consistency, and those around the firmament of a rarer consistency, in proportion to the respective density of the earth and of the heaven.

Or by the water, as stated, we may understand the matter of bodies to be signified.

Reply Obj. 2: The solution is clear from what has been said, according to the last two opinions. But according to the first opinion, Basil gives two replies (Hom. iii in Hexaem.). He answers first, that a body seen as concave beneath need not necessarily be rounded, or convex, above. Secondly, that the waters above the firmament are not fluid, but exist outside it in a solid state, as a mass of ice, and that this is the crystalline heaven of some writers.

Reply Obj. 3: According to the third opinion given, the waters above the firmament have been raised in the form of vapors, and serve to give rain to the earth. But according to the second opinion, they are above the heaven that is wholly transparent and starless. This, according to some, is the primary mobile, the cause of the daily revolution of the entire heaven, whereby the continuance of generation is secured. In the same way the starry heaven, by the zodiacal movement, is the cause whereby different bodies are generated or corrupted, through the rising and setting of the stars, and their various influences. But according to the first opinion these waters are set there to temper the heat of the celestial bodies, as Basil supposes (Hom. iii in Hexaem.). And Augustine says (Gen. ad lit. ii, 5) that some have considered this to be proved by the extreme cold of Saturn owing to its nearness to the waters that are above the firmament.

THIRD ARTICLE [I, Q. 68, Art. 3]

Whether the Firmament Divides Waters from Waters?

Objection 1: It would seem that the firmament does not divide waters from waters. For bodies that are of one and the same species have naturally one and the same place. But the Philosopher says (Topic. i, 6): "All water is the same species." Water therefore cannot be distinct from water by place.

Obj. 2: Further, should it be said that the waters above the firmament differ in species from those under the firmament, it may be argued, *on the contrary,* that things distinct in species need nothing else to distinguish them. If then, these waters differ in species, it is not the firmament that distinguishes them.

Obj. 3: Further, it would appear that what distinguishes waters from waters must be something which is in contact with them on either side, as a wall standing in the midst of a river. But it is evident that the waters below do not reach up to the firmament. Therefore the firmament does not divide the waters from the waters.

*On the contrary,* It is written (Gen. 1:6): "Let there be a firmament made amidst the waters; and let it divide the waters from the waters."

*I answer that,* The text of Genesis, considered superficially, might lead to the adoption of a theory similar to that held by certain philosophers of antiquity, who taught that water was a body infinite in dimension, and the primary element of all bodies. Thus in the words, "Darkness was upon the face of the deep," the word "deep" might be taken to mean the infinite mass of water, understood as the principle of all other bodies. These philosophers also taught that not all corporeal things are confined beneath the heaven perceived by our senses, but that a body of water, infinite in extent, exists above that heaven. On this view the firmament of heaven might be said to divide the waters without from those within—that is to say, from all bodies under the heaven, since they took water to be the principle of them all.

As, however, this theory can be shown to be false by solid reasons, it cannot be held to be the sense of Holy Scripture. It should rather be considered that Moses was speaking to ignorant people, and that out of condescension to their weakness he put before them only such things as are apparent to sense. Now even the most uneducated can perceive by their senses that earth and water are corporeal, whereas it is not evident to all that air also is corporeal, for there have even been philosophers who said that air is nothing, and called a space filled with air a vacuum.

Moses, then, while he expressly mentions water and earth, makes no express mention of air by name, to avoid setting before ignorant persons something beyond their knowledge. In order, however, to express the truth to those capable of understanding it, he implies in the words: "Darkness was upon the face of the deep," the existence of air as attendant, so to say, upon the water. For it may be understood from these words that over the face of the water a transparent body was extended, the subject of light and darkness, which, in fact, is the air.

Whether, then, we understand by the firmament the starry heaven, or the cloudy region of the air, it is true to say that it divides the waters from the waters, according as we take water to denote formless matter, or any kind of transparent body, as fittingly designated under the name of waters. For the starry heaven divides the lower transparent bodies from the higher, and the cloudy region divides that higher part of the air, where the rain and similar things are generated, from the lower part, which is connected with the water and included under that name.

Reply Obj. 1: If by the firmament is understood the starry heaven, the waters above are not of the same species as those beneath. But if by the firmament is understood the cloudy region of the air, both these waters are of the same species, and two places are assigned to them, though not for the same purpose, the higher being the place of their begetting, the lower, the place of their repose.

Reply Obj. 2: If the waters are held to differ in species, the firmament cannot be said to divide the waters, as the cause of their destruction, but only as the boundary of each.

Reply Obj. 3: On account of the air and other similar bodies being invisible, Moses includes all such bodies under the name of water, and thus it is evident that waters are found on each side of the firmament, whatever be the sense in which the word is used.

FOURTH ARTICLE [I, Q. 68, Art. 4]

Whether There Is Only One Heaven?

Objection 1: It would seem that there is only one heaven. For the heaven is contrasted with the earth, in the words, "In the beginning God created heaven and earth." But there is only one earth. Therefore there is only one heaven.

Obj. 2: Further, that which consists of the entire sum of its own matter, must be one; and such is the heaven, as the Philosopher proves (De Coel. i, text. 95). Therefore there is but one heaven.

Obj. 3: Further, whatever is predicated of many things univocally is predicated of them according to some common notion. But if there are more heavens than one, they are so called univocally, for if equivocally only, they could not properly be called many. If, then, they are many, there must be some common notion by reason of which each is called heaven, but this common notion cannot be assigned. Therefore there cannot be more than one heaven.

*On the contrary,* It is said (Ps. 148:4): "Praise Him, ye heavens of heavens."

*I answer that,* On this point there seems to be a diversity of opinion between Basil and Chrysostom. The latter says that there is only one heaven (Hom. iv in Gen.), and that the words 'heavens of heavens' are merely the translation of the Hebrew idiom according to which the word is always used in the plural, just as in Latin there are many nouns that are wanting in the singular. On the other hand, Basil (Hom. iii in Hexaem.), whom Damascene follows (De Fide Orth. ii), says that there are many heavens. The difference, however, is more nominal than real. For Chrysostom means by the one heaven the whole body that is above the earth and the water, for which reason the birds that fly in the air are called birds of heaven [*Ps. 8:9]. But since in this body there are many distinct parts, Basil said that there are more heavens than one.

In order, then, to understand the distinction of heavens, it must be borne in mind that Scripture speaks of heaven in a threefold sense. Sometimes it uses the word in its proper and natural meaning, when it denotes that body on high which is luminous actually or potentially, and incorruptible by nature. In this body there are three heavens; the first is the empyrean, which is wholly luminous; the second is the aqueous or crystalline, wholly transparent; and the third is called the starry heaven, in part transparent, and in part actually luminous, and divided into eight spheres. One of these is the sphere of the fixed stars; the other seven, which may be called the seven heavens, are the spheres of the planets.

In the second place, the name heaven is applied to a body that participates in any property of the heavenly body, as sublimity and luminosity, actual or potential. Thus Damascene (De Fide Orth. ii) holds as one heaven all the space between the waters and the moon's orb, calling it the aerial. According to him, then, there are three heavens, the aerial, the starry, and one higher than both these, of which the Apostle is understood to speak when he says of himself that he was "rapt to the third heaven."

But since this space contains two elements, namely, fire and air, and in each of these there is what is called a higher and a lower region Rabanus subdivides this space into four distinct heavens. The higher region of fire he calls the fiery heaven; the lower, the Olympian heaven from a lofty mountain of that name: the higher region of air he calls, from its brightness, the ethereal heaven; the lower, the aerial. When, therefore, these four heavens are added to the three enumerated above, there are seven corporeal heavens in all, in the opinion of Rabanus.

Thirdly, there are metaphorical uses of the word heaven, as when this name is applied to the Blessed Trinity, Who is the Light and the Most High Spirit. It is explained by some, as thus applied, in the words, "I will ascend into heaven"; whereby the evil spirit is represented as seeking to make himself equal with God. Sometimes also spiritual blessings, the recompense of the Saints, from being the highest of all good gifts, are signified by the word heaven, and, in fact, are so signified, according to Augustine (De Serm. Dom. in Monte), in the words, "Your reward is very great in heaven" (Matt. 5:12).

Again, three kinds of supernatural visions, bodily, imaginative, and intellectual, are called sometimes so many heavens, in reference to which Augustine (Gen. ad lit. xii) expounds Paul's rapture "to the third heaven."

Reply Obj. 1: The earth stands in relation to the heaven as the centre of a circle to its circumference. But as one center may have many circumferences, so, though there is but one earth, there may be many heavens.

Reply Obj. 2: The argument holds good as to the heaven, in so far as it denotes the entire sum of corporeal creation, for in that sense it is one.

Reply Obj. 3: All the heavens have in common sublimity and some degree of luminosity, as appears from what has been said.

# QUESTION 69

ON THE WORK OF THE THIRD DAY (In Two Articles)

We next consider the work of the third day. Under this head there are two points of inquiry:

(1) About the gathering together of the waters.

(2) About the production of plants.

FIRST ARTICLE [I, Q. 69, Art. 1]

Whether It Was Fitting That the Gathering Together of the Waters Should Take Place, As Recorded, on the Third Day?

Objection 1: It would seem that it was not fitting that the gathering together of the waters should take place on the third day. For what was made on the first and second days is expressly said to have been "made" in the words, "God said: Be light made," and "Let there be a firmament made."But the third day is contradistinguished from the first and the second days. Therefore the work of the third day should have been described as a making not as a gathering together.

Obj. 2: Further, the earth hitherto had been completely covered by the waters, wherefore it was described as "invisible" [* See Q. 66, A. 1, Obj. 1]. There was then no place on the earth to which the waters could be gathered together.

Obj. 3: Further, things which are not in continuous contact cannot occupy one place. But not all the waters are in continuous contact, and therefore all were not gathered together into one place.

Obj. 4: Further, a gathering together is a mode of local movement. But the waters flow naturally, and take their course towards the sea. In their case, therefore, a Divine precept of this kind was unnecessary.

Obj. 5: Further, the earth is given its name at its first creation by the words, "In the beginning God created heaven and earth." Therefore the imposition of its name on the third day seems to be recorded without necessity.

*On the contrary,* The authority of Scripture suffices.

*I answer that,* It is necessary to reply differently to this question according to the different interpretations given by Augustine and other holy writers. In all these works, according to Augustine (Gen. ad lit. i, 15; iv, 22, 34; De Gen. Contr. Manich. i, 5, 7), there is no order of duration, but only of origin and nature. He says that the formless spiritual and formless corporeal natures were created first of all, and that the latter are at first indicated by the words "earth" and "water." Not that this formlessness preceded formation, in time, but only in origin; nor yet that one formation preceded another in duration, but merely in the order of nature. Agreeably, then, to this order, the formation of the highest or spiritual nature is recorded in the first place, where it is said that light was made on the first day. For as the spiritual nature is higher than the corporeal, so the higher bodies are nobler than the lower. Hence the formation of the higher bodies is indicated in the second place, by the words, "Let there be made a firmament," by which is to be understood the impression of celestial forms on formless matter, that preceded with priority not of time, but of origin only. But in the third place the impression of elemental forms on formless matter is recorded, also with a priority of origin only. Therefore the words, "Let the waters be gathered together, and the dry land appear," mean that corporeal matter was impressed with the substantial form of water, so as to have such movement, and with the substantial form of earth, so as to have such an appearance.

According, however, to other holy writers [* See Q. 66, A. 1], an order of duration in the works is to be understood, by which is meant that the formlessness of matter precedes its formation, and one form another, in order of time. Nevertheless, they do not hold that the formlessness of matter implies the total absence of form, since heaven, earth, and water already existed, since these three are named as already clearly perceptible to the senses; rather they understand by formlessness the want of due distinction and of perfect beauty, and in respect of these three Scripture mentions three kinds of formlessness. Heaven, the highest of them, was without form so long as "darkness" filled it, because it was the source of light. The formlessness of water, which holds the middle place, is called the "deep," because, as Augustine says (Contr. Faust. xxii, 11), this word signifies the mass of waters without order. Thirdly, the formless state of the earth is touched upon when the earth is said to be "void" or "invisible," because it was covered by the waters. Thus, then, the formation of the highest body took place on the first day. And since time results from the movement of the heaven, and is the numerical measure of the movement of the highest body, from this formation, resulted the distinction of time, namely, that of night and day. On the second day the intermediate body, water, was formed, receiving from the firmament a sort of distinction and order (so that water be understood as including certain other things, as explained above (Q. 68, A. 3)). On the third day the earth, the lowest body, received its form by the withdrawal of the waters, and there resulted the distinction in the lowest body, namely, of land and sea. Hence Scripture, having clearly expressed the formless state of the earth, by saying that it was "invisible" or "void," expresses the manner in which it received its form by the equally suitable words, "Let the dry land appear."

Reply Obj. 1: According to Augustine [*Gen. ad lit. ii, 7, 8; iii, 20], Scripture does not say of the work of the third day, that it was made, as it says of those that precede, in order to show that higher and spiritual forms, such as the angels and the heavenly bodies, are perfect and stable in being, whereas inferior forms are imperfect and mutable. Hence the impression of such forms is signified by the gathering of the waters, and the appearing of the land. For "water," to use Augustine's words, "glides and flows away, the earth abides" (Gen. ad lit. ii, 11). Others, again, hold that the work of the third day was perfected on that day only as regards movement from place to place, and that for this reason Scripture had no reason to speak of it as made.

Reply Obj. 2: This argument is easily solved, according to Augustine's opinion (De Gen. Contr. Manich. i), because we need not suppose that the earth was first covered by the waters, and that these were afterwards gathered together, but that they were produced in this very gathering together. But according to the other writers there are three solutions, which Augustine gives (Gen. ad lit. i, 12). The first supposes that the waters are heaped up to a greater height at the place where they were gathered together, for it has been proved in regard to the Red Sea, that the sea is higher than the land, as Basil remarks (Hom. iv in Hexaem.). The second explains the water that covered the earth as being rarefied or nebulous, which was afterwards condensed when the waters were gathered together. The third suggests the existence of hollows in the earth, to receive the confluence of waters. Of the above the first seems the most probable.

Reply Obj. 3: All the waters have the sea as their goal, into which they flow by channels hidden or apparent, and this may be the reason why they are said to be gathered together into one place. Or, "one place" is to be understood not simply, but as contrasted with the place of the dry land, so that the sense would be, "Let the waters be gathered together in one place," that is, apart from the dry land. That the waters occupied more places than one seems to be implied by the words that follow, "The gathering together of the waters He called Seas."

Reply Obj. 4: The Divine command gives bodies their natural movement and by these natural movements they are said to "fulfill His word." Or we may say that it was according to the nature of water completely to cover the earth, just as the air completely surrounds both water and earth; but as a necessary means towards an end, namely, that plants and animals might be on the earth, it was necessary for the waters to be withdrawn from a portion of the earth. Some philosophers attribute this uncovering of the earth's surface to the action of the sun lifting up the vapors and thus drying the land. Scripture, however, attributes it to the Divine power, not only in the Book of Genesis, but also Job 38:10 where in the person of the Lord it is said, "I set My bounds around the sea," and Jer. 5:22, where it is written: "Will you not then fear Me, saith the Lord, who have set the sand a bound for the sea?"

Reply Obj. 5: According to Augustine (De Gen. Contr. Manich. i), primary matter is meant by the word earth, where first mentioned, but in the present passage it is to be taken for the element itself. Again it may be said with Basil (Hom. iv in Hexaem.), that the earth is mentioned in the first passage in respect of its nature, but here in respect of its principal property, namely, dryness. Wherefore it is written: "He called the dry land, Earth." It may also be said with Rabbi Moses, that the expression, "He called," denotes throughout an equivocal use of the name imposed. Thus we find it said at first that "He called the light Day": for the reason that later on a period of twenty-four hours is also called day, where it is said that "there was evening and morning, one day." In like manner it is said that "the firmament," that is, the air, "He called heaven": for that which was first created was also called "heaven." And here, again, it is said that "the dry land," that is, the part from which the waters had withdrawn, "He called, Earth," as distinct from the sea; although the name earth is equally applied to that which is covered with waters or not. So by the expression "He called" we are to understand throughout that the nature or property He bestowed corresponded to the name He gave.

SECOND ARTICLE [I, Q. 69, Art. 2]

Whether It Was Fitting That the Production of Plants Should Take Place on the Third Day?

Objection 1: It would seem that it was not fitting that the production of plants should take place on the third day. For plants have life, as animals have. But the production of animals belongs to the work, not of distinction, but of adornment. Therefore the production of plants, as also belonging to the work of adornment, ought not to be recorded as taking place on the third day, which is devoted to the work of distinction.

Obj. 2: Further, a work by which the earth is accursed should have been recorded apart from the work by which it receives its form. But the words of Gen. 3:17, "Cursed is the earth in thy work, thorns and thistles shall it bring forth to thee," show that by the production of certain plants the earth was accursed. Therefore the production of plants in general should not have been recorded on the third day, which is concerned with the work of formation.

Obj. 3: Further, as plants are firmly fixed to the earth, so are stones and metals, which are, nevertheless, not mentioned in the work of formation. Plants, therefore, ought not to have been made on the third day.

*On the contrary,* It is said (Gen. 1:12): "The earth brought forth the green herb," after which there follows, "The evening and the morning were the third day."

*I answer that,* On the third day, as said (A. 1), the formless state of the earth comes to an end. But this state is described as twofold. On the one hand, the earth was "invisible" or "void," being covered by the waters; on the other hand, it was "shapeless" or "empty," that is, without that comeliness which it owes to the plants that clothe it, as it were, with a garment. Thus, therefore, in either respect this formless state ends on the third day: first, when "the waters were gathered together into one place and the dry land appeared"; secondly, when "the earth brought forth the green herb." But concerning the production of plants, Augustine's opinion differs from that of others. For other commentators, in accordance with the surface meaning of the text, consider that the plants were produced in act in their various species on this third day; whereas Augustine (Gen. ad lit. v, 5; viii, 3) says that the earth is said to have then produced plants and trees in their causes, that is, it received then the power to produce them. He supports this view by the authority of Scripture, for it is said (Gen. 2:4, 5): "These are the generations of the heaven and the earth, when they were created, in the day that … God made the heaven and the earth, and every plant of the field before it sprung up in the earth, and every herb of the ground before it grew." Therefore, the production of plants in their causes, within the earth, took place before they sprang up from the earth's surface. And this is confirmed by reason, as follows. In these first days God created all things in their origin or causes, and from this work He subsequently rested. Yet afterwards, by governing His creatures, in the work of propagation, "He worketh until now." Now the production of plants from the earth is a work of propagation, and therefore they were not produced in act on the third day, but in their causes only. However, in accordance with other writers, it may be said that the first constitution of species belongs to the work of the six days, but the reproduction among them of like from like, to the government of the universe. And Scripture indicates this in the words, "before it sprung up in the earth," and "before it grew," that is, before like was produced from like; just as now happens in the natural course by the production of seed. Wherefore Scripture says pointedly (Gen. 1:11): "Let the earth bring forth the green herb, and such as may seed," as indicating the production of perfect species, from which the seed of others should arise. Nor does the question where the seminal power may reside, whether in root, stem, or fruit, affect the argument.

Reply Obj. 1: Life in plants is hidden, since they lack sense and local movement, by which the animate and the inanimate are chiefly discernible. And therefore, since they are firmly fixed in the earth, their production is treated as a part of the earth's formation.

Reply Obj. 2: Even before the earth was accursed, thorns and thistles had been produced, either virtually or actually. But they were not produced in punishment of man; as though the earth, which he tilled to gain his food, produced unfruitful and noxious plants. Hence it is said: "Shall it bring forth *to thee.*"

Reply Obj. 3: Moses put before the people such things only as were manifest to their senses, as we have said (Q. 67, A. 4; Q. 68, A. 3). But minerals are generated in hidden ways within the bowels of the earth. Moreover they seem hardly specifically distinct from earth, and would seem to be species thereof. For this reason, therefore, he makes no mention of them.

## QUESTION 70

OF THE WORK OF ADORNMENT, AS REGARDS THE FOURTH DAY (In Three Articles)

We must next consider the work of adornment, first as to each day by itself, secondly as to all seven days in general.

In the first place, then, we consider the work of the fourth day, secondly, that of the fifth day, thirdly, that of the sixth day, and fourthly, such matters as belong to the seventh day.

Under the first head there are three points of inquiry:

(1) As to the production of the lights;
(2) As to the end of their production;
(3) Whether they are living beings?

FIRST ARTICLE [I, Q. 70, Art. 1]

Whether the Lights Ought to Have Been Produced on the Fourth Day?

Objection 1: It would seem that the lights ought not to have been produced on the fourth day. For the heavenly luminaries are by nature incorruptible bodies: wherefore their matter cannot exist without their form. But as their matter was produced in the work of creation, before there was any day, so therefore were their forms. It follows, then, that the lights were not produced on the fourth day.

Obj. 2: Further, the luminaries are, as it were, vessels of light. But light was made on the first day. The luminaries, therefore, should have been made on the first day, not on the fourth.

Obj. 3: Further, the lights are fixed in the firmament, as plants are fixed in the earth. For, the Scripture says: "He set them in the firmament." But plants are described as produced when the earth, to which they are attached, received its form. The lights, therefore, should have been produced at the same time as the firmament, that is to say, on the second day.

Obj. 4: Further, plants are an effect of the sun, moon, and other heavenly bodies. Now, cause precedes effect in the order of nature. The lights, therefore, ought not to have been produced on the fourth day, but on the third day.

Obj. 5: Further, as astronomers say, there are many stars larger than the moon. Therefore the sun and the moon alone are not correctly described as the "two great lights."

*On the contrary,* Suffices the authority of Scripture.

*I answer that,* In recapitulating the Divine works, Scripture says (Gen. 2:1): "So the heavens and the earth were finished and all the furniture of them," thereby indicating that the work was threefold. In the first work, that of "creation," the heaven and the earth were produced, but as yet without form. In the second, or work of "distinction," the heaven and the earth were perfected, either by adding substantial form to formless matter, as Augustine holds (Gen. ad lit. ii, 11), or by giving them the order and beauty due to them, as other holy writers suppose. To these two works is added the work of adornment, which is distinct from perfect[ion]. For the perfection of the heaven and the earth regards, seemingly, those things that belong to them intrinsically, but the adornment, those that are extrinsic, just as the perfection of a man lies in his proper parts and forms, and his adornment, in clothing or such like. Now just as distinction of certain things is made most evident by their local movement, as separating one from another; so the work of adornment is set forth by the production of things having movement in the heavens, and upon the earth. But it has been stated above (Q. 69, A. 1), that three things are recorded as created, namely, the heaven, the water, and the earth; and these three received their form from the three days' work of distinction, so that heaven was formed on the first day; on the second day the waters were separated; and on the third day, the earth was divided into sea and dry land. So also is it in the work of adornment; on the first day of this work, which is the fourth of creation, are produced the lights, to adorn the heaven by their movements; on the second day, which is the fifth, birds and fishes are called into being, to make beautiful the intermediate element, for they move in air and water, which are here taken as one; while on the third day, which is the sixth, animals are brought forth, to move upon the earth and adorn it. It must also here be noted that Augustine's opinion (Gen. ad lit. v, 5) on the production of lights is not at variance with that of other holy writers, since he says that they were made actually, and not merely virtually, for the firmament has not the power of producing lights, as the earth has of producing plants. Wherefore Scripture does not say: "Let the firmament produce lights," though it says: "Let the earth bring forth the green herb."

Reply Obj. 1: In Augustine's opinion there is no difficulty here; for he does not hold a succession of time in these works, and so there was no need for the matter of the lights to exist under another form. Nor is there any difficulty in the opinion of those who hold the heavenly bodies to be of the nature of the four elements, for it may be said that they were formed out of matter already existing, as animals and plants were formed. For those, however, who hold the heavenly bodies to be of another nature from the elements, and naturally incorruptible, the answer must be that the lights were substantially created at the beginning, but that their substance, at first formless, is formed on this day, by receiving not its substantial form, but a determination of power. As to the fact that the lights are not mentioned as existing from the beginning, but only as made on the fourth day, Chrysostom (Hom. vi in Gen.) explains this by the need of guarding the people from the danger of idolatry: since the lights are proved not to be gods, by the fact that they were not from the beginning.

Reply Obj. 2: No difficulty exists if we follow Augustine in holding the light made on the first day to be spiritual, and that made on this day to be corporeal. If, however, the light made on the first day is understood to be itself corporeal, then it must be held to have been produced on that day merely as light in general; and that on the fourth day the lights received a definite power to produce determinate effects. Thus we observe that the rays of the sun have one effect, those of the moon another, and so forth. Hence, speaking of such a determination of power, Dionysius (Div. Nom. iv) says that the sun's light which previously was without form, was formed on the fourth day.

Reply Obj. 3: According to Ptolemy the heavenly luminaries are not fixed in the spheres, but have their own movement distinct from the movement of the spheres. Wherefore Chrysostom says (Hom. vi in Gen.) that He is said to have set them in the firmament, not because He fixed them there immovably, but because He bade them to be there, even as He placed man in Paradise, to be there. In the opinion of Aristotle, however, the stars are fixed in their orbits, and in reality have no other movement but that of the spheres; and yet our senses perceive the movement of the luminaries and not that of the spheres (De Coel. ii, text. 43). But Moses describes what is obvious to sense, out of condescension to popular ignorance, as we have already said (Q. 67, A. 4; Q. 68, A. 3). The objection, however, falls to the ground if we regard the firmament made on the second day as having a natural distinction from that in which the stars are placed, even though the distinction is not apparent to the senses, the testimony of which Moses follows, as stated above (De Coel. ii, text. 43). For although to the senses there appears but one firmament; if we admit a higher and a lower firmament, the lower will be that which was made on the second day, and on the fourth the stars were fixed in the higher firmament.

Reply Obj. 4: In the words of Basil (Hom. v in Hexaem.), plants were recorded as produced before the sun and moon, to prevent idolatry, since those who believe the heavenly bodies to be gods, hold that plants originate primarily from these bodies. Although as Chrysostom remarks (Hom. vi in Gen.), the sun, moon, and stars cooperate in the work of production by their movements, as the husbandman cooperates by his labor.

Reply Obj. 5: As Chrysostom says, the two lights are called great, not so much with regard to their dimensions as to their influence and power. For though the stars be of greater bulk than the moon, yet the influence of the moon is more perceptible to the senses in this lower world. Moreover, as far as the senses are concerned, its apparent size is greater.

SECOND ARTICLE [I, Q. 70, Art. 2]

Whether the Cause Assigned for the Production of the Lights Is Reasonable?

Objection 1: It would seem that the cause assigned for the production of the lights is not reasonable. For it is said (Jer. 10:2): "Be not afraid of the signs of heaven, which the heathens fear." Therefore the heavenly lights were not made to be signs.

Obj. 2: Further, sign is contradistinguished from cause. But the lights are the cause of what takes place upon the earth. Therefore they are not signs.

Obj. 3: Further, the distinction of seasons and days began from the first day. Therefore the lights were not made "for seasons, and days, and years," that is, in order to distinguish them.

Obj. 4: Further, nothing is made for the sake of that which is inferior to itself, "since the end is better than the means" (Topic. iii). But the lights are nobler than the earth. Therefore they were not made "to enlighten it."

Obj. 5: Further, the new moon cannot be said "to rule the night." But such it probably did when first made; for men begin to count from the new moon. The moon, therefore, was not made "to rule the night."

*On the contrary,* Suffices the authority of Scripture.

*I answer that,* As we have said above (Q. 65, A. 2), a corporeal creature can be considered as made either for the sake of its proper act, or for other creatures, or for the whole universe, or for the glory of God. Of these reasons only that which points out the usefulness of these things to man, is touched upon by Moses, in order to withdraw his people from idolatry. Hence it is written (Deut. 4:19): "Lest perhaps lifting up thy eyes to heaven, thou see the sun and the moon and all the stars of heaven, and being deceived by error thou adore and serve them, which the Lord thy God created for the service of all nations." Now, he explains this service at the beginning of Genesis as threefold. First, the lights are of service to man, in regard to sight, which directs him in his works, and is most useful for perceiving objects. In reference to this he says: "Let them shine in the firmament and give life to the earth." Secondly, as regards the changes of the seasons, which prevent weariness, preserve health, and provide for the necessities of food; all of which things could not be secured if it were always summer or winter. In reference to this he says: "Let them be for seasons, and for days, and years." Thirdly, as regards the convenience of business and work, in so far as the lights are set in the heavens to indicate fair or foul weather, as favorable to various occupations. And in this respect he says: "Let them be for signs."

Reply Obj. 1: The lights in the heaven are set for signs of changes effected in corporeal creatures, but not of those changes which depend upon the free-will.

Reply Obj. 2: We are sometimes brought to the knowledge of hidden effects through their sensible causes, and conversely. Hence nothing prevents a sensible cause from being a sign. But he says "signs," rather than "causes," to guard against idolatry.

Reply Obj. 3: The general division of time into day and night took place on the first day, as regards the diurnal movement, which is common to the whole heaven and may be understood to have begun on that first day. But the particular distinctions of days and seasons and years, according as one day is hotter than another, one season than another, and one year than another, are due to certain particular movements of the stars: which movements may have had their beginning on the fourth day.

Reply Obj. 4: Light was given to the earth for the service of man, who, by reason of his soul, is nobler than the heavenly bodies. Nor is it untrue to say that a higher creature may be made for the sake of a lower, considered not in itself, but as ordained to the good of the universe.

Reply Obj. 5: When the moon is at its perfection it rises in the evening and sets in the morning, and thus it rules the night, and it was probably made in its full perfection as were plants yielding seed, as also were animals and man himself. For although the perfect is developed from the imperfect by natural processes, yet the perfect must exist simply before the imperfect. Augustine, however (Gen. ad lit. ii), does not say this, for he says that it is not unfitting that God made things imperfect, which He afterwards perfected.

THIRD ARTICLE [I, Q. 70, Art. 3]

Whether the Lights of Heaven Are Living Beings?

Objection 1: It would seem that the lights of heaven are living beings. For the nobler a body is, the more nobly it should be adorned. But a body less noble than the heaven, is adorned with living beings, with fish, birds, and the beasts of the field. Therefore the lights of heaven, as pertaining to its adornment, should be living beings also.

Obj. 2: Further, the nobler a body is, the nobler must be its form. But the sun, moon, and stars are nobler bodies than plants or animals, and must therefore have nobler forms. Now the noblest of all forms is the soul, as being the first principle of life. Hence Augustine (De Vera Relig. xxix) says: "Every living substance stands higher in the order of nature than one that has not life." The lights of heaven, therefore, are living beings.

Obj. 3: Further, a cause is nobler than its effect. But the sun, moon, and stars are a cause of life, as is especially evidenced in the case of animals generated from putrefaction, which receive life from the power of the sun and stars. Much more, therefore, have the heavenly bodies a living soul.

Obj. 4: Further, the movement of the heaven and the heavenly bodies are natural (De Coel. i, text. 7, 8): and natural movement is from an intrinsic principle. Now the principle of movement in the heavenly bodies is a substance capable of apprehension, and is moved as the desirer is moved by the object desired (Metaph. xii, text. 36). Therefore, seemingly, the apprehending principle is intrinsic to the heavenly bodies: and consequently they are living beings.

Obj. 5: Further, the first of movables is the heaven. Now, of all things that are endowed with movement the first moves itself, as is proved in *Phys.* viii, text. 34, because, what is such of itself precedes that which is by another. But only beings that are living move themselves, as is shown in the same book (text. 27). Therefore the heavenly bodies are living beings.

*On the contrary,* Damascene says (De Fide Orth. ii), "Let no one esteem the heavens or the heavenly bodies to be living things, for they have neither life nor sense."

*I answer that,* Philosophers have differed on this question. Anaxagoras, for instance, as Augustine mentions (De Civ. Dei xviii, 41), "was condemned by the Athenians for teaching that the sun was a fiery mass of stone, and neither a god nor even a living being." On the other hand, the Platonists held that the heavenly bodies have life. Nor was there less diversity of opinion among the Doctors of the Church. It was the belief of Origen (Peri Archon i) and Jerome that these bodies were alive, and the latter seems to explain in that sense the words (Eccles. 1:6), "The spirit goeth forward, surveying all places round about." But Basil (Hom. iii, vi in Hexaem.) and Damascene (De Fide Orth. ii) maintain that the heavenly bodies are inanimate. Augustine leaves the matter in doubt, without committing himself to either theory, though he goes so far as to say that if the heavenly bodies are really living beings, their souls must be akin to the angelic nature (Gen. ad lit. ii, 18; Enchiridion lviii).

In examining the truth of this question, where such diversity of opinion exists, we shall do well to bear in mind that the union of soul and body exists for the sake of the soul and not of the body; for the form does not exist for the matter, but the matter for the form. Now the nature and power of the soul are apprehended through its operation, which is to a certain extent its end. Yet for some of these operations, as sensation and nutrition, our body is a necessary instrument. Hence it is clear that the sensitive and nutritive souls must be united to a body in order to exercise their functions. There are, however, operations of the soul, which are not exercised through the medium of the body, though the body ministers, as it were, to their production. The intellect, for example, makes use of the phantasms derived from the bodily senses, and thus far is dependent on the body, although capable of existing apart from it. It is not, however, possible that the functions of nutrition, growth, and generation, through which the nutritive soul operates, can be exercised by the heavenly bodies, for such operations are incompatible with a body naturally incorruptible. Equally impossible is it that the functions of the sensitive soul can appertain to the heavenly body, since all the senses depend on the sense of touch, which perceives elemental qualities, and all the organs of the senses require a certain proportion in the admixture of elements, whereas the nature of the heavenly bodies is not elemental. It follows, then, that of the operations of the soul the only ones left to be attributed to the heavenly bodies are those of understanding and moving; for appetite follows both sensitive and intellectual perception, and is in proportion thereto. But the operations of the intellect, which does not act through the body, do not need a body as their instrument, except to supply phantasms through the senses. Moreover, the operations of the sensitive soul, as we have seen, cannot be attributed to the heavenly bodies. Accordingly, the union of a soul to a heavenly body cannot be for the purpose of the operations of the intellect. It remains, then, only to consider whether the movement of the heavenly bodies demands a soul as the motive power, not that the soul, in order to move the heavenly body, need be united to the latter as its form; but by contact of power, as a mover is united to that which he moves. Wherefore Aristotle (Phys. viii, text. 42, 43), after showing that the first mover is made up of two parts, the moving and the moved, goes on to show the nature of the union between these two parts. This, he says, is effected by contact which is mutual if both are bodies; on the part of one only, if one is a body and the other not. The Platonists explain the union of soul and body in the same way, as a contact of a moving power with the object moved, and since Plato holds the heavenly bodies to be living beings, this means nothing else but that substances of spiritual nature are united to them, and act as their moving power. A proof that the heavenly bodies are moved by the direct influence and contact of some spiritual substance, and not, like bodies of specific gravity, by nature, lies in the fact that whereas nature moves to one fixed end which having attained, it rests; this does not appear in the movement of heavenly bodies. Hence it follows that they are moved by some intellectual substances. Augustine appears to be of the same opinion when he expresses his belief that all corporeal things are ruled by God through the spirit of life (De Trin. iii, 4).

From what has been said, then, it is clear that the heavenly bodies are not living beings in the same sense as plants and animals, and that if they are called so, it can only be equivocally. It will also be seen that the difference of opinion between those who affirm, and those who deny, that these bodies have life, is not a difference of things but of words.

Reply Obj. 1: Certain things belong to the adornment of the universe by reason of their proper movement; and in this way the heavenly luminaries agree with others that conduce to that adornment, for they are moved by a living substance.

Reply Obj. 2: One being may be nobler than another absolutely, but not in a particular respect. While, then, it is not conceded that the souls of heavenly bodies are nobler than the souls of animals absolutely it must be conceded that they are superior to them with regard to their respective forms, since their form perfects their matter entirely, which is not in potentiality to other forms; whereas a soul does not do this. Also as regards movement the power that moves the heavenly bodies is of a nobler kind.

Reply Obj. 3: Since the heavenly body is a mover moved, it is of the nature of an instrument, which acts in virtue of the agent: and therefore since this agent is a living substance the heavenly body can impart life in virtue of that agent.

Reply Obj. 4: The movements of the heavenly bodies are natural, not on account of their active principle, but on account of their passive principle; that is to say, from a certain natural aptitude for being moved by an intelligent power.

Reply Obj. 5: The heaven is said to move itself in as far as it is compounded of mover and moved; not by the union of the mover, as the form, with the moved, as the matter, but by contact with the motive power, as we have said. So far, then, the principle that moves it may be called intrinsic, and consequently its movement natural with respect to that active principle; just as we say that voluntary movement is natural to the animal as animal (Phys. viii, text. 27).

# QUESTION 71

ON THE WORK OF THE FIFTH DAY (In One Article)

We must next consider the work of the fifth day.

Objection 1: It would seem that this work is not fittingly described. For the waters produce that which the power of water suffices to produce. But the power of water does not suffice for the production of every kind of fishes and birds since we find that many of them are generated from seed. Therefore the words, "Let the waters bring forth the creeping creature having life, and the fowl that may fly over the earth," do not fittingly describe this work.

Obj. 2: Further, fishes and birds are not produced from water only, but earth seems to predominate over water in their composition, as is shown by the fact that their bodies tend naturally to the earth and rest upon it. It is not, then, fittingly said that fishes and birds are produced from water.

Obj. 3: Further, fishes move in the waters, and birds in the air. If, then, fishes are produced from the waters, birds ought to be produced from the air, and not from the waters.

Obj. 4: Further, not all fishes creep through the waters, for some, as seals, have feet and walk on land. Therefore the production of fishes is not sufficiently described by the words, "Let the waters bring forth the creeping creature having life."

Obj. 5: Further, land animals are more perfect than birds and fishes which appears from the fact that they have more distinct limbs, and generation of a higher order. For they bring forth living beings, whereas birds and fishes bring forth eggs. But the more perfect has precedence in the order of nature. Therefore fishes and birds ought not to have been produced on the fifth day, before land animals.

*On the contrary,* Suffices the authority of Scripture.

*I answer that,* As said above, (Q. 70, A. 1), the order of the work of adornment corresponds to the order of the work of distinction. Hence, as among the three days assigned to the work of distinction, the middle, or second, day is devoted to the work of distinction of water, which is the intermediate body, so in the three days of the work of adornment, the middle day, which is the fifth, is assigned to the adornment of the intermediate body, by the production of birds and fishes. As, then, Moses makes mention of the lights and the light on the fourth day, to show that the fourth day corresponds to the first day on which he had said that the light was made, so on this fifth day he mentions the waters and the firmament of heaven to show that the fifth day corresponds to the second. It must, however, be observed that Augustine differs from other writers in his opinion about the production of fishes and birds, as he differs about the production of plants. For while others say that fishes and birds were produced on the fifth day actually, he holds that the nature of the waters produced them on that day potentially.

Reply Obj. 1: It was laid down by Avicenna that animals of all kinds can be generated by various minglings of the elements, and naturally, without any kind of seed. This, however, seems repugnant to the fact that nature produces its effects by determinate means, and consequently, those things that are naturally generated from seed cannot be generated naturally in any other way. It ought, then, rather to be said that in the natural generation of all animals that are generated from seed, the active principle lies in the formative power of the seed, but that in the case of animals generated from putrefaction, the formative power of is the influence of the heavenly bodies. The material principle, however, in the generation of either kind of animals, is either some element, or something compounded of the elements. But at the first beginning of the world the active principle was the Word of God, which produced animals from material elements, either in act, as some holy writers say, or virtually, as Augustine teaches. Not as though the power possessed by water or earth of producing all animals resides in the earth and the water themselves, as Avicenna held, but in the power originally given to the elements of producing them from elemental matter by the power of seed or the influence of the stars.

Reply Obj. 2: The bodies of birds and fishes may be considered from two points of view. If considered in themselves, it will be evident that the earthly element must predominate, since the element that is least active, namely, the earth, must be the most abundant in quantity in order that the mingling may be duly tempered in the body of the animal. But if considered as by nature constituted to move with certain specific motions, thus they have some special affinity with the bodies in which they move; and hence the words in which their generation is described.

Reply Obj. 3: The air, as not being so apparent to the senses, is not enumerated by itself, but with other things: partly with the water, because the lower region of the air is thickened by watery exhalations; partly with the heaven as to the higher region. But birds move in the lower part of the air, and so are said to fly "beneath the firmament," even if the firmament be taken to mean the region of clouds. Hence the production of birds is ascribed to the water.

Reply Obj. 4: Nature passes from one extreme to another through the medium; and therefore there are creatures of intermediate type between the animals of the air and those of the water, having something in common with both; and they are reckoned as belonging to that class to which they are most allied, through the characters possessed in common with that class, rather than with the other. But in order to include among fishes all such intermediate forms as have special characters like to theirs, the words, "Let the waters bring forth the creeping creature having life," are followed by these: "God created great whales," etc.

Reply Obj. 5: The order in which the production of these animals is given has reference to the order of those bodies which they are set to adorn, rather than to the superiority of the animals themselves. Moreover, in generation also the more perfect is reached through the less perfect.

# QUESTION 72

ON THE WORK OF THE SIXTH DAY (In One Article)

We must now consider the work of the sixth day.

Objection 1: It would seem that this work is not fittingly described. For as birds and fishes have a living soul, so also have land animals. But these animals are not themselves living souls. Therefore the words, "Let the earth bring forth the living creature," should rather have been, "Let the earth bring forth the living four-footed creatures."

Obj. 2: Further, a genus ought not to be opposed to its species. But beasts and cattle are quadrupeds. Therefore quadrupeds ought not to be enumerated as a class with beasts and cattle.

Obj. 3: Further, as animals belong to a determinate genus and species, so also does man. But in the making of man nothing is said of his genus and species, and therefore nothing ought to have been said about them in the production of other animals, whereas it is said "according to its genus" and "in its species."

Obj. 4: Further, land animals are more like man, whom God is recorded to have blessed, than are birds and fishes. But as birds and fishes are said to be blessed, this should have been said, with much more reason, of the other animals as well.

Obj. 5: Further, certain animals are generated from putrefaction, which is a kind of corruption. But corruption is repugnant to the first founding of the world. Therefore such animals should not have been produced at that time.

Obj. 6: Further, certain animals are poisonous, and injurious to man. But there ought to have been nothing injurious to man before man sinned. Therefore such animals ought not to have been made by God at all, since He is the Author of good; or at least not until man had sinned.

*On the contrary,* Suffices the authority of Scripture.

*I answer that,* As on the fifth day the intermediate body, namely, the water, is adorned, and thus that day corresponds to the second day; so the sixth day, on which the lowest body, or the earth, is adorned by the production of land animals, corresponds to the third day. Hence the earth is mentioned in both places. And here again Augustine says (Gen. ad lit. v) that the production was potential, and other holy writers that it was actual.

Reply Obj. 1: The different grades of life which are found in different living creatures can be discovered from the various ways in which Scripture speaks of them, as Basil says (Hom. viii in Hexaem.). The life of plants, for instance, is very imperfect and difficult to discern, and hence, in speaking of their production, nothing is said of their life, but only their generation is mentioned, since only in generation is a vital act observed in them. For the powers of nutrition and growth are subordinate to the generative life, as will be shown later on (Q. 78, A. 2). But amongst animals, those that live on land are, generally speaking, more perfect than birds and fishes, not because the fish is devoid of memory, as Basil upholds (Hom. viii in Hexaem.) and Augustine rejects (Gen. ad lit. iii), but because their limbs are more distinct and their generation of a higher order, (yet some imperfect animals, such as bees and ants, are more intelligent in certain ways). Scripture, therefore, does not call fishes "living creatures," but "creeping creatures having life"; whereas it does call land animals "living creatures" on account of their more perfect life, and seems to imply that fishes are merely bodies having in them something of a soul, whilst land animals, from the higher perfection of their life, are, as it were, living souls with bodies subject to them. But the life of man, as being the most perfect grade, is not said to be produced, like the life of other animals, by earth or water, but immediately by God.

Reply Obj. 2: By "cattle," domestic animals are signified, which in any way are of service to man: but by "beasts," wild animals such as bears and lions are designated. By "creeping things" those animals are meant which either have no feet and cannot rise from the earth, as serpents, or those whose feet are too short to lift them far from the ground, as the lizard and tortoise. But since certain animals, as deer and goats, seem to fall under none of these classes, the word "quadrupeds" is added. Or perhaps the word "quadruped" is used first as being the genus, to which the others are added as species, for even some reptiles, such as lizards and tortoises, are four-footed.

Reply Obj. 3: In other animals, and in plants, mention is made of genus and species, to denote the generation of like from like. But it was unnecessary to do so in the case of man, as what had already been said of other creatures might be understood of him. Again, animals and plants may be said to be produced according to their kinds, to signify their remoteness from the Divine image and likeness, whereas man is said to be made "to the image and likeness of God."

Reply Obj. 4: The blessing of God gives power to multiply by generation, and, having been mentioned in the preceding account of the making of birds and fishes, could be understood of the beasts of the earth, without requiring to be repeated. The blessing, however, is repeated in the case of man, since in him generation of children has a special relation to the number of the elect [*Cf. Augustine, Gen. ad lit. iii, 12], and to prevent anyone from saying that there was any sin whatever in the act of begetting children. As to plants, since they experience neither desire of propagation, nor sensation in generating, they are deemed unworthy of a formal blessing.

Reply Obj. 5: Since the generation of one thing is the corruption of another, it was not incompatible with the first formation of things, that from the corruption of the less perfect the more perfect should be generated. Hence animals generated from the corruption of inanimate things, or of plants, may have been generated then. But those generated from corruption of animals could not have been produced then otherwise than potentially.

Reply Obj. 6: In the words of Augustine (Super. Gen. contr. Manich. i): "If an unskilled person enters the workshop of an artificer he sees in it many appliances of which he does not understand the use, and which, if he is a foolish fellow, he considers unnecessary. Moreover, should he carelessly fall into the fire, or wound himself with a sharp-edged tool, he is under the impression that many of the things there are hurtful; whereas the craftsman, knowing their use, laughs at his folly. And thus some people presume to find fault with many things in this world, through not seeing the reasons for their existence. For though not required for the furnishing of our house, these things are necessary for the perfection of the universe." And, since man before he sinned would have used the things of this world conformably to the order designed, poisonous animals would not have injured him.

# QUESTION 73

ON THE THINGS THAT BELONG TO THE SEVENTH DAY (In Three Articles)

We must next consider the things that belong to the seventh day. Under this head there are three points of inquiry:

(1) About the completion of the works;

(2) About the resting of God;

(3) About the blessing and sanctifying of this day.

FIRST ARTICLE [I, Q. 73, Art. 1]

Whether the Completion of the Divine Works Ought to Be Ascribed to the Seventh Day?

Objection 1: It would seem that the completion of the Divine works ought not to be ascribed to the seventh day. For all things that are done in this world belong to the Divine works. But the consummation of the world will be at the end of the world (Matt. 13:39, 40). Moreover, the time of Christ's Incarnation is a time of completion, wherefore it is called "the time of fulness [*Vulg.: 'the fulness of time']" (Gal. 4:4). And Christ Himself, at the moment of His death, cried out, "It is consummated" (John 19:30). Hence the completion of the Divine works does not belong to the seventh day.

Obj. 2: Further, the completion of a work is an act in itself. But we do not read that God acted at all on the seventh day, but rather that He rested from all His work. Therefore the completion of the works does not belong to the seventh day.

Obj. 3: Further, nothing is said to be complete to which many things are added, unless they are merely superfluous, for a thing is called perfect to which nothing is wanting that it ought to possess. But many things were made after the seventh day, as the production of many individual beings, and even of certain new species that are frequently appearing, especially in the case of animals generated from putrefaction. Also, God creates daily new souls. Again, the work of the Incarnation was a new work, of which it is said (Jer. 31:22): "The Lord hath created a new thing upon the earth." Miracles also are new works, of which it is said (Eccles. 36:6): "Renew thy signs, and work new miracles." Moreover, all things will be made new when the Saints are glorified, according to Apoc. 21:5: "And He that sat on the throne said: Behold I make all things new." Therefore the completion of the Divine works ought not to be attributed to the seventh day.

*On the contrary,* It is said (Gen. 2:2): "On the seventh day God ended His work which He had made."

*I answer that,* The perfection of a thing is twofold, the first perfection and the second perfection. The *first* perfection is that according to which a thing is substantially perfect, and this perfection is the form of the whole; which form results from the whole having its parts complete. But the *second* perfection is the end, which is either an operation, as the end of the harpist is to play the harp; or something that is attained by an operation, as the end of the builder is the house that he makes by building. But the first perfection is the cause of the second, because the form is the principle of operation. Now the final perfection, which is the end of the whole universe, is the perfect beatitude of the Saints at the consummation of the world; and the first perfection is the completeness of the universe at its first founding, and this is what is ascribed to the seventh day.

Reply Obj. 1: The first perfection is the cause of the second, as above said. Now for the attaining of beatitude two things are required, nature and grace. Therefore, as said above, the perfection of beatitude will be at the end of the world. But this consummation existed previously in its causes, as to nature, at the first founding of the world, as to grace, in the Incarnation of Christ. For, "Grace and truth came by Jesus Christ" (John 1:17). So, then, on the seventh day was the consummation of nature, in Christ's Incarnation the consummation of grace, and at the end of the world will be the consummation of glory.

Reply Obj. 2: God did act on the seventh day, not by creating new creatures, but by directing and moving His creatures to the work proper to them, and thus He made some beginning of the *second* perfection. So that, according to our version of the Scripture, the completion of the works is attributed to the seventh day, though according to another it is assigned to the sixth. Either version, however, may stand, since the completion of the universe as to the completeness of its parts belongs to the sixth day, but its completion as regards their operation, to the seventh. It may also be added that in continuous movement, so long as any movement further is possible, movement cannot be called completed till it comes to rest, for rest denotes consummation of movement. Now God might have made many other creatures besides those which He made in the six days, and hence, by the fact that He ceased making them on the seventh day, He is said on that day to have consummated His work.

Reply Obj. 3: Nothing entirely new was afterwards made by God, but all things subsequently made had in a sense been made before in the work of the six days. Some things, indeed, had a previous experience materially, as the rib from the side of Adam out of which God formed Eve; whilst others existed not only in matter but also in their causes, as those individual creatures that are now generated existed in the first of their kind. Species, also, that are new, if any such appear, existed beforehand in various active powers; so that animals, and perhaps even new species of animals, are produced by putrefaction by the power which the stars and elements received at the beginning. Again, animals of new kinds arise occasionally from the connection of individuals belonging to different species, as the mule is the offspring of an ass and a mare; but even these existed previously in their causes, in the works of the six days. Some also existed beforehand by way of similitude, as the souls now created. And the work of the Incarnation itself was thus foreshadowed, for as we read (Phil. 2:7), The Son of God "was made in the likeness of men." And again, the glory that is spiritual was anticipated in the angels by way of similitude; and that of the body in the heaven, especially the empyrean. Hence it is written (Eccles. 1:10), "Nothing under the sun is new, for it hath already gone before, in the ages that were before us."

SECOND ARTICLE [I, Q. 73, Art. 2]

Whether God Rested on the Seventh Day from All His Work?

Objection 1: It would seem that God did not rest on the seventh day from all His work. For it is said (John 5:17), "My Father worketh until now, and I work." God, then, did not rest on the seventh day from all His work.

Obj. 2: Further, rest is opposed to movement, or to labor, which movement causes. But, as God produced His work without movement and without labor, He cannot be said to have rested on the seventh day from His work.

Obj. 3: Further, should it be said that God rested on the seventh day by causing man to rest; against this it may be argued that rest is set down in contradistinction to His work; now the words "God created" or "made" this thing or the other cannot be explained to mean that He made man create or make these things. Therefore the resting of God cannot be explained as His making man to rest.

*On the contrary,* It is said (Gen. 2:2): "God rested on the seventh day from all the work which He had done."

*I answer that,* Rest is, properly speaking, opposed to movement, and consequently to the labor that arises from movement. But although movement, strictly speaking, is a quality of bodies, yet the word is applied also to spiritual things, and in a twofold sense. On the one hand, every operation may be called a movement, and thus the Divine goodness is said to move and go forth to its object, in communicating itself to that object, as Dionysius says (Div. Nom. ii). On the other hand, the desire that tends to an object outside itself, is said to move towards it. Hence rest is taken in two senses, in one sense meaning a cessation from work, in the other, the satisfying of desire. Now, in either sense God is said to have rested on the seventh day. First, because He ceased from creating new creatures on that day, for, as said above (A. 1, ad 3), He made nothing afterwards that had not existed previously, in some degree, in the first works; secondly, because He Himself had no need of the things that He had made, but was happy in the fruition of Himself. Hence, when all things were made He is not said to have rested "in" His works, as though needing them for His own happiness, but to have rested "from" them, as in fact resting in Himself, as He suffices for Himself and fulfils His own desire. And even though from all eternity He rested in Himself, yet the rest in Himself, which He took after He had finished His works, is that rest which belongs to the seventh day. And this, says Augustine, is the meaning of God's resting from His works on that day (Gen. ad lit. iv).

Reply Obj. 1: God indeed "worketh until now" by preserving and providing for the creatures He has made, but not by the making of new ones.

Reply Obj. 2: Rest is here not opposed to labor or to movement, but to the production of new creatures, and to the desire tending to an external object.

Reply Obj. 3: Even as God rests in Himself alone and is happy in the enjoyment of Himself, so our own sole happiness lies in the enjoyment of God. Thus, also, He makes us find rest in Himself, both from His works and our own. It is not, then, unreasonable to say that God rested in giving rest to us. Still, this explanation must not be set down as the only one, and the other is the first and principal explanation.

THIRD ARTICLE [I, Q. 73, Art. 3]

Whether Blessing and Sanctifying Are Due to the Seventh Day?

Objection 1: It would seem that blessing and sanctifying are not due to the seventh day. For it is usual to call a time blessed or holy for that some good thing has happened in it, or some evil been avoided. But whether God works or ceases from work nothing accrues to Him or is lost to Him. Therefore no special blessing or sanctifying are due to the seventh day.

Obj. 2: Further, the Latin "benedictio" [blessing] is derived from "bonitas" [goodness]. But it is the nature of good to spread and communicate itself, as Dionysius says (Div. Nom. iv). The days, therefore, in which God produced creatures deserved a blessing rather than the day on which He ceased producing them.

Obj. 3: Further, over each creature a blessing was pronounced, as upon each work it was said, "God saw that it was good." Therefore it was not necessary that after all had been produced, the seventh day should be blessed.

*On the contrary,* It is written (Gen. 2:3), "God blessed the seventh day and sanctified it, because in it He had rested from all His work."

*I answer that,* As said above (A. 2), God's rest on the seventh day is understood in two ways. First, in that He ceased from producing new works, though He still preserves and provides for the creatures He has made. Secondly, in that after all His works He rested in Himself. According to the first meaning, then, a blessing befits the seventh day, since, as we explained (Q. 72, ad 4), the blessing referred to the increase by multiplication; for which reason God said to the creatures which He blessed: "Increase and multiply." Now, this increase is effected through God's Providence over His creatures, securing the generation of like from like. And according to the second meaning, it is right that the seventh day should have been sanctified, since the special sanctification of every creature consists in resting in God. For this reason things dedicated to God are said to be sanctified.

Reply Obj. 1: The seventh day is said to be sanctified not because anything can accrue to God, or be taken from Him, but because something is added to creatures by their multiplying, and by their resting in God.

Reply Obj. 2: In the first six days creatures were produced in their first causes, but after being thus produced, they are multiplied and preserved, and this work also belongs to the Divine goodness. And the perfection of this goodness is made most clear by the knowledge that in it alone God finds His own rest, and we may find ours in its fruition.

Reply Obj. 3: The good mentioned in the works of each day belongs to the first institution of nature; but the blessing attached to the seventh day, to its propagation.

# QUESTION 74

ON ALL THE SEVEN DAYS IN COMMON (In Three Articles)

We next consider all the seven days in common: and there are three points of inquiry:

(1) As to the sufficiency of these days;

(2) Whether they are all one day, or more than one?

(3) As to certain modes of speaking which Scripture uses in narrating the works of the six days.

FIRST ARTICLE [I, Q. 74, Art. 1]

Whether these days are sufficiently enumerated?

Objection 1: It would seem that these days are not sufficiently enumerated. For the work of creation is no less distinct from the works of distinction and adornment than these two works are from one another. But separate days are assigned to distinction and to adornment, and therefore separate days should be assigned to creation.

Obj. 2: Further, air and fire are nobler elements than earth and water. But one day is assigned to the distinction of water, and another to the distinction of the land. Therefore, other days ought to be devoted to the distinction of fire and air.

Obj. 3: Further, fish differ from birds as much as birds differ from the beasts of the earth, whereas man differs more from other animals than all animals whatsoever differ from each other. But one day is devoted to the production of fishes, and another to that of the beast of the earth. Another day, then, ought to be assigned to the production of birds and another to that of man.

Obj. 4: Further, it would seem, on the other hand, that some of these days are superfluous. Light, for instance, stands to the luminaries in the relation of accident to subject. But the subject is produced at the same time as the accident proper to it. The light and the luminaries, therefore, ought not to have been produced on different days.

Obj. 5: Further, these days are devoted to the first instituting of the world. But as on the seventh day nothing was instituted, that day ought not to be enumerated with the others.

*I answer that,* The reason of the distinction of these days is made clear by what has been said above (Q. 70, A. 1), namely, that the parts of the world had first to be distinguished, and then each part adorned and filled, as it were, by the beings that inhabit it. Now the parts into which the corporeal creation is divided are three, according to some holy writers, these parts being the heaven, or highest part, the water, or middle part, and the earth, or the lowest part. Thus the Pythagoreans teach that perfection consists in three things, the beginning, the middle, and the end. The first part, then, is distinguished on the first day, and adorned on the fourth, the middle part distinguished on the middle day, and adorned on the fifth, and the third part distinguished on the third day, and adorned on the sixth. But Augustine, while agreeing with the above writers as to the last three days, differs as to the first three, for, according to him, spiritual creatures are formed on the first day, and corporeal on the two others, the higher bodies being formed on the first these two days, and the lower on the second. Thus, then, the perfection of the Divine works corresponds to the perfection of the number six, which is the sum of its aliquot parts, one, two, three; since one day is assigned to the forming of spiritual creatures, two to that of corporeal creatures, and three to the work of adornment.

Reply Obj. 1: According to Augustine, the work of creation belongs to the production of formless matter, and of the formless spiritual nature, both of which are outside of time, as he himself says (Confess. xii, 12). Thus, then, the creation of either is set down before there was any day. But it may also be said, following other holy writers, that the works of distinction and adornment imply certain changes in the creature which are measurable by time; whereas the work of creation lies only in the Divine act producing the substance of beings instantaneously. For this reason, therefore, every work of distinction and adornment is said to take place "in a day," but creation "in the beginning" which denotes something indivisible.

Reply Obj. 2: Fire and air, as not distinctly known by the unlettered, are not expressly named by Moses among the parts of the world, but reckoned with the intermediate part, or water, especially as regards the lowest part of the air; or with the heaven, to which the higher region of air approaches, as Augustine says (Gen. ad lit. ii, 13).

Reply Obj. 3: The production of animals is recorded with reference to their adorning the various parts of the world, and therefore the days of their production are separated or united according as the animals adorn the same parts of the world, or different parts.

Reply Obj. 4: The nature of light, as existing in a subject, was made on the first day; and the making of the luminaries on the fourth day does not mean that their substance was produced anew, but that they then received a form that they had not before, as said above (Q. 70, [A. 1] ad 2).

Reply Obj. 5: According to Augustine (Gen. ad lit. iv, 15), after all that has been recorded that is assigned to the six days, something distinct is attributed to the seventh—namely, that on it God rested in Himself from His works: and for this reason it was right that the seventh day should be mentioned after the six. It may also be said, with the other writers, that the world entered on the seventh day upon a new state, in that nothing new was to be added to it, and that therefore the seventh day is mentioned after the six, from its being devoted to cessation from work.

SECOND ARTICLE [I, Q. 74, Art. 2]

Whether All These Days Are One Day?

Objection 1: It would seem that all these days are one day. For it is written (Gen. 2:4, 5): "These are the generations of the heaven and the earth, when they were created, in the day that the Lord ... made the heaven and the earth, and every plant of the field, before it sprung up in the earth." Therefore the day in which God made "the heaven and the earth, and every plant of the field," is one and the same day. But He made the heaven and the earth on the first day, or rather before there was any day, but the plant of the field He made on the third day. Therefore the first and third days are but one day, and for a like reason all the rest.

Obj. 2: Further, it is said (Ecclus. 18:1): "He that liveth for ever, created all things together." But this would not be the case if the days of these works were more than one. Therefore they are not many but one only.

Obj. 3: Further, on the seventh day God ceased from all new works. If, then, the seventh day is distinct from the other days, it follows that He did not make that day; which is not admissible.

Obj. 4: Further, the entire work ascribed to one day God perfected in an instant, for with each work are the words (God) "said .... and it was ... done." If, then, He had kept back His next work to another day, it would follow that for the remainder of a day He would have ceased from working and left it vacant, which would be superfluous. The day, therefore, of the preceding work is one with the day of the work that follows.

*On the contrary,* It is written (Gen. 1), "The evening and the morning were the second day ... the third day," and so on. But where there is a second and third there are more than one. There was not, therefore, only one day.

*I answer that,* On this question Augustine differs from other expositors. His opinion is that all the days that are called seven, are one day represented in a sevenfold aspect (Gen. ad lit. iv, 22; De Civ. Dei xi, 9; Ad Orosium xxvi); while others consider there were seven distinct days, not one only. Now, these two opinions, taken as explaining the literal text of Genesis, are certainly widely different. For Augustine understands by the word "day," the knowledge in the mind of the angels, and hence, according to him, the first day denotes their knowledge of the first of the Divine works, the second day their knowledge of the second work, and similarly with the rest. Thus, then, each work is said to have been wrought in some one of these days, inasmuch as God wrought nothing in the universe without impressing the knowledge thereof on the angelic mind; which can know many things at the same time, especially in the Word, in Whom all angelic knowledge is perfected and terminated. So the distinction of days denotes the natural order of the things known, and not a succession in the knowledge acquired, or in the things produced. Moreover, angelic knowledge is appropriately called "day," since light, the cause of day, is to be found in spiritual things, as Augustine observes (Gen. ad lit. iv, 28). In the opinion of the others, however, the days signify a succession both in time, and in the things produced.

If, however, these two explanations are looked at as referring to the mode of production, they will be found not greatly to differ, if the diversity of opinion existing on two points, as already shown (Q. 67, A. 1; Q. 69, A. 1), between Augustine and other writers is taken into account. First, because Augustine takes the earth and the water as first created, to signify matter totally without form; but the making of the firmament, the gathering of the waters, and the appearing of dry land, to denote the impression of forms upon corporeal matter. But other holy writers take the earth and the water, as first created, to signify the elements of the universe themselves existing under the proper forms, and the works that follow to mean some sort of distinction in bodies previously existing, as also has been shown (Q. 67, AA. 1, 4; Q. 69, A. 1). Secondly, some writers hold that plants and animals were produced actually in the work of the six days; Augustine, that they were produced potentially. Now the opinion of Augustine, that the works of the six days were simultaneous, is consistent with either view of the mode of production. For the other writers agree with him that in the first production of things matter existed under the substantial form of the elements, and agree with him also that in the first instituting of the world animals and plants did not exist actually. There remains, however, a difference as to four points; since, according to the latter, there was a time, after the production of creatures, in which light did not exist, the firmament had not been formed, and the earth was still covered by the waters, nor had the heavenly bodies been formed, which is the fourth difference; which are not consistent with Augustine's explanation. In order, therefore, to be impartial, we must meet the arguments of either side.

Reply Obj. 1: On the day on which God created the heaven and the earth, He created also every plant of the field, not, indeed, actually, but "before it sprung up in the earth," that is, potentially. And this work Augustine ascribes to the third day, but other writers to the first instituting of the world.

Reply Obj. 2: God created all things together so far as regards their substance in some measure formless. But He did not create all things together, so far as regards that formation of things which lies in distinction and adornment. Hence the word "creation" is significant.

Reply Obj. 3: On the seventh day God ceased from making new things, but not from providing for their increase, and to this latter work it belongs that the first day is succeeded by other days.

Reply Obj. 4: All things were not distinguished

and adorned together, not from a want of power on God's part, as requiring time in which to work, but that due order might be observed in the instituting of the world. Hence it was fitting that different days should be assigned to the different states of the world, as each succeeding work added to the world a fresh state of perfection.

Reply Obj. 5: According to Augustine, the order of days refers to the natural order of the works attributed to the days.

THIRD ARTICLE [I, Q. 74, Art. 3]

Whether Scripture Uses Suitable Words to Express the Work of the Six Days?

Objection 1: It would seem the Scripture does not use suitable words to express the works of the six days. For as light, the firmament, and other similar works were made by the Word of God, so were the heaven and the earth. For "all things were made by Him" (John 1:3). Therefore in the creation of heaven and earth, as in the other works, mention should have been made of the Word of God.

Obj. 2: Further, the water was created by God, yet its creation is not mentioned. Therefore the creation of the world is not sufficiently described.

Obj. 3: Further, it is said (Gen. 1:31): "God saw all the things that He had made, and they were very good." It ought, then, to have been said of each work, "God saw that it was good." The omission, therefore, of these words in the work of creation and in that of the second day, is not fitting.

Obj. 4: Further, the Spirit of God is God Himself. But it does not befit God to move and to occupy place. Therefore the words, "The Spirit of God moved over the waters," are unbecoming.

Obj. 5: Further, what is already made is not made over again. Therefore to the words, "God said: Let the firmament be made ... and it was so," it is superfluous to add, "God made the firmament." And the like is to be said of other works.

Obj. 6: Further, evening and morning do not sufficiently divide the day, since the day has many parts. Therefore the words, "The evening and morning were the second day" or, "the third day," are not suitable.

Obj. 7: Further, "first," not "one," corresponds to "second" and "third." It should therefore have been said that, "The evening and the morning were the first day," rather than "one day."

Reply Obj. 1: According to Augustine (Gen. ad lit. i, 4), the person of the Son is mentioned both in the first creation of the world, and in its distinction and adornment, but differently in either place. For distinction and adornment belong to the work by which the world receives its form. But as the giving form to a work of art is by means of the form of the art in the mind of the artist, which may be called his intelligible word, so the giving form to every creature is by the word of God; and for this reason in the works of distinction and adornment the Word is mentioned. But in creation the Son is mentioned as the beginning, by the words, "In the beginning God created," since by creation is understood the production of formless matter. But according to those who hold that the elements were created from the first under their proper forms, another explanation must be given; and therefore Basil says (Hom. ii, iii in Hexaem.) that the words, "God said," signify a Divine command. Such a command, however, could not have been given before creatures had been produced that could obey it.

Reply Obj. 2: According to Augustine (De Civ. Dei ix, 33), by the heaven is understood the formless spiritual nature, and by the earth, the formless matter of all corporeal things, and thus no creature is omitted. But, according to Basil (Hom. i in Hexaem.), the heaven and the earth, as the two extremes, are alone mentioned, the intervening things being left to be understood, since all these move heavenwards, if light, or earthwards, if heavy. And others say that under the word, "earth," Scripture is accustomed to include all the four elements as (Ps. 148:7,8) after the words, "Praise the Lord from the earth," is added, "fire, hail, snow, and ice."

Reply Obj. 3: In the account of the creation there is found something to correspond to the words, "God saw that it was good," used in the work of distinction and adornment, and this appears from the consideration that the Holy Spirit is Love. Now, "there are two things," says Augustine (Gen. ad lit. i, 8) which came from God's love of His creatures, their existence and their permanence. That they might then exist, and exist permanently, "the Spirit of God," it is said, "moved over the waters"—that is to say, over that formless matter, signified by water, even as the love of the artist moves over the materials of his art, that out of them he may form his work. And the words, "God saw that it was good," signify that the things that He had made were to endure, since they express a certain satisfaction taken by God in His works, as of an artist in his art: not as though He knew the creature otherwise, or that the creature was pleasing to Him otherwise, than before He made it. Thus in either work, of creation and of formation, the Trinity of Persons is implied. In creation the Person of the Father is indicated by God the Creator, the Person of the Son by the beginning, in which He created, and the Person of the Holy Ghost by the Spirit that moved over the waters. But in the formation, the Person of the Father is indicated by God that speaks, and the Person of the Son by the Word in which He speaks, and the Person of the Holy Spirit by the satisfaction with which God saw that what was made was good. And if the words, "God saw that it was good," are not said of the work of the second day, this is because the work of distinguishing the waters was only begun on that day, but perfected on the third. Hence these words, that are said of the third day, refer also to the second. Or it may be that Scripture does not use these words of approval of the second day's work, because this is concerned with the distinction of things not evident to the senses of mankind. Or, again, because by the firmament is simply understood the cloudy region of the air, which is not one of the permanent parts of the universe, nor of the principal divisions of the world. The above three reasons are given by Rabbi Moses [*Perplex. ii.], and to these may be added a mystical one derived from numbers and assigned by some writers, according to whom the work of the second day is not marked with approval because the second number is an imperfect number, as receding from the perfection of unity.

Reply Obj. 4: Rabbi Moses (Perplex. ii) understands by the "Spirit of the Lord," the air or the wind, as Plato also did, and says that it is so called according to the custom of Scripture, in which these things are throughout attributed to God. But according to the holy writers, the Spirit of the Lord signifies the Holy Ghost, Who is said to "move over the water"—that is to say, over what Augustine holds to mean formless matter, lest it should be supposed that God loved of necessity the works He was to produce, as though He stood in need of them. For love of that kind is subject to, not superior to, the object of love. Moreover, it is fittingly implied that the Spirit moved over that which was incomplete and unfinished, since that movement is not one of place, but of pre-eminent power, as Augustine says (Gen. ad lit. i, 7). It is the opinion, however, of Basil (Hom. ii in Hexaem.) that the Spirit moved over the element of water, "fostering and quickening its nature and impressing vital power, as the hen broods over her chickens." For water has especially a life-giving power, since many animals are generated in water, and the seed of all animals is liquid. Also the life of the soul is given by the water of baptism, according to John 3:5: "Unless a man be born again of water and the Holy Ghost, he cannot enter into the kingdom of God."

Reply Obj. 5: According to Augustine (Gen. ad lit. i, 8), these three phrases denote the threefold being of creatures; first, their being in the Word, denoted by the command "Let ... be made"; secondly, their being in the angelic mind, signified by the words, "It was ... done"; thirdly, their being in their proper nature, by the words, "He made." And because the formation of the angels is recorded on the first day, it was not necessary there to add, "He made." It may also be said, following other writers, that the words, "He said," and "Let ... be made," denote God's command, and the words, "It was done," the fulfilment of that command. But as it was necessary, for the sake of those especially who have asserted that all visible things were made by the angels, to mention how things were made, it is added, in order to remove that error, that God Himself made them. Hence, in each work, after the words, "It was done," some act of God is expressed by some such words as, "He made," or, "He divided," or, "He called."

Reply Obj. 6: According to Augustine (Gen. ad lit. iv, 22, 30), by the "evening" and the "morning" are understood the evening and the morning knowledge of the angels, which has been explained (Q. 58, A. 6, 7). But, according to Basil (Hom. ii in Hexaem.), the entire period takes its name, as is customary, from its more important part, the day. An instance of this is found in the words of Jacob, "The days of my pilgrimage," where night is not mentioned at all. But the evening and the morning are mentioned as being the ends of the day, since day begins with morning and ends with evening, or because evening denotes the beginning of night, and morning the beginning of day. It seems fitting, also, that where the first distinction of creatures is described, divisions of time should be denoted only by what marks their beginning. And the reason for mentioning the evening first is that as the evening ends the day, which begins with the light, the termination of the light at evening precedes the termination of the darkness, which ends with the morning. But Chrysostom's explanation is that thereby it is intended to show that the natural day does not end with the evening, but with the morning (Hom. v in Gen.).

Reply Obj. 7: The words "one day" are used when day is first instituted, to denote that one day is made up of twenty-four hours. Hence, by mentioning "one," the measure of a natural day is fixed. Another reason may be to signify that a day is completed by the return of the sun to the point from which it commenced its course. And yet another, because at the completion of a week of seven days, the first day returns which is one with the eighth day. The three reasons assigned above are those given by Basil (Hom. ii in Hexaem.).

TREATISE ON MAN (QQ. 75-102)

# QUESTION 75

OF MAN WHO IS COMPOSED OF A SPIRITUAL AND A CORPOREAL SUBSTANCE: AND IN THE FIRST PLACE, CONCERNING WHAT BELONGS TO THE ESSENCE OF THE SOUL (In Seven Articles)

Having treated of the spiritual and of the corporeal creature, we now proceed to treat of man, who is composed of a spiritual and corporeal substance. We shall treat first of the nature of man, and secondly of his origin. Now the theologian considers the nature of man in relation to the soul; but not in relation to the body, except in so far as the body has relation to the soul. Hence the first object of our consideration will be the soul. And since Dionysius (Ang. Hier. xi) says that three things are to be found in spiritual substances—essence, power, and operation—we shall treat first of what belongs to the essence of the soul; secondly, of what belongs to its power; thirdly, of what belongs to its operation.

Concerning the first, two points have to be considered; the first is the nature of the soul considered in itself; the second is the union of the soul with the body. Under the first head there are seven points of inquiry.

(1) Whether the soul is a body?

(2) Whether the human soul is a subsistence?

(3) Whether the souls of brute animals are subsistent?

(4) Whether the soul is man, or is man composed of soul and body?

(5) Whether the soul is composed of matter and form?

(6) Whether the soul is incorruptible?

(7) Whether the soul is of the same species as an angel?

FIRST ARTICLE [I, Q. 75, Art. 1]

Whether the Soul Is a Body?

Objection 1: It would seem that the soul is a body. For the soul is the moving principle of the body. Nor does it move unless moved. First, because seemingly nothing can move unless it is itself moved, since nothing gives what it has not; for instance, what is not hot does not give heat. Secondly, because if there be anything that moves and is not moved, it must be the cause of eternal, unchanging movement, as we find proved Phys. viii, 6; and this does not appear to be the case in the movement of an animal, which is caused by the soul. Therefore the soul is a mover moved. But every mover moved is a body. Therefore the soul is a body.

Obj. 2: Further, all knowledge is caused by means of a likeness. But there can be no likeness of a body to an incorporeal thing. If, therefore, the soul were not a body, it could not have knowledge of corporeal things.

Obj. 3: Further, between the mover and the moved there must be contact. But contact is only between bodies. Since, therefore, the soul moves the body, it seems that the soul must be a body.

*On the contrary,* Augustine says (De Trin. vi, 6) that the soul "is simple in comparison with the body, inasmuch as it does not occupy space by its bulk."

*I answer that,* To seek the nature of the soul, we must premise that the soul is defined as the first principle of life of those things which live: for we call living things "animate," [*i.e. having a soul] and those things which have no life, "inanimate." Now life is shown principally by two actions, knowledge and movement. The philosophers of old, not being able to rise above their imagination, supposed that the principle of these actions was something corporeal: for they asserted that only bodies were real things; and that what is not corporeal is nothing: hence they maintained that the soul is something corporeal. This opinion can be proved to be false in many ways; but we shall make use of only one proof, based on universal and certain principles, which shows clearly that the soul is not a body.

It is manifest that not every principle of vital action is a soul, for then the eye would be a soul, as it is a principle of vision; and the same might be applied to the other instruments of the soul: but it is the *first* principle of life, which we call the soul. Now, though a body may be a principle of life, as the heart is a principle of life in an animal, yet nothing corporeal can be the first principle of life. For it is clear that to be a principle of life, or to be a living thing, does not belong to a body as such; since, if that were the case, every body would be a living thing, or a principle of life. Therefore a body is competent to be a living thing or even a principle of life, as "such" a body. Now that it is actually such a body, it owes to some principle which is called its act. Therefore the soul, which is the first principle of life, is not a body, but the act of a body; thus heat, which is the principle of calefaction, is not a body, but an act of a body.

Reply Obj. 1: As everything which is in motion must be moved by something else, a process which cannot be prolonged indefinitely, we must allow that not every mover is moved. For, since to be moved is to pass from potentiality to actuality, the mover gives what it has to the thing moved, inasmuch as it causes it to be in act. But, as is shown in *Phys.* viii, 6, there is a mover which is altogether immovable, and not moved either essentially, or accidentally; and such a mover can cause an invariable movement. There is, however, another kind of mover, which, though not moved essentially, is moved accidentally; and for this reason it does not cause an invariable movement; such a mover, is the soul. There is, again, another mover, which is moved essentially—namely, the body. And because the philosophers of old believed that nothing existed but bodies, they maintained that every mover is moved; and that the soul is moved directly, and is a body.

Reply Obj. 2: The likeness of a thing known is not of necessity actually in the nature of the knower; but given a thing which knows potentially, and afterwards knows actually, the likeness of the thing known must be in the nature of the knower, not actually, but only potentially; thus color is not actually in the pupil of the eye, but only potentially. Hence it is necessary, not that the likeness of corporeal things should be actually in the nature of the soul, but that there be a potentiality in the soul for such a likeness. But the ancient philosophers omitted to distinguish between actuality and potentiality; and so they held that the soul must be a body in order to have knowledge of a body; and that it must be composed of the principles of which all bodies are formed in order to know all bodies.

Reply Obj. 3: There are two kinds of contact; of "quantity," and of "power." By the former a body can be touched only by a body; by the latter a body can be touched by an incorporeal thing, which moves that body.

SECOND ARTICLE [I, Q. 75, Art. 2]

Whether the Human Soul Is Something Subsistent?

Objection 1: It would seem that the human soul is not something subsistent. For that which subsists is said to be "this particular thing." Now "this particular thing" is said not of the soul, but of that which is composed of soul and body. Therefore the soul is not something subsistent.

Obj. 2: Further, everything subsistent operates. But the soul does not operate; for, as the Philosopher says (De Anima i, 4), "to say that the soul feels or understands is like saying that the soul weaves or builds." Therefore the soul is not subsistent.

Obj. 3: Further, if the soul were subsistent, it would have some operation apart from the body. But it has no operation apart from the body, not even that of understanding: for the act of understanding does not take place without a phantasm, which cannot exist apart from the body. Therefore the human soul is not something subsistent.

*On the contrary,* Augustine says (De Trin. x, 7): "Who understands that the nature of the soul is that of a substance and not that of a body, will see that those who maintain the corporeal nature of the soul, are led astray through associating with the soul those things without which they are unable to think of any nature—i.e. imaginary pictures of corporeal things." Therefore the nature of the human intellect is not only incorporeal, but it is also a substance, that is, something subsistent.

*I answer that,* It must necessarily be allowed that the principle of intellectual operation which we call the soul, is a principle both incorporeal and subsistent. For it is clear that by means of the intellect man can have knowledge of all corporeal things. Now whatever knows certain things cannot have any of them in its own nature; because that which is in it naturally would impede the knowledge of anything else. Thus we observe that a sick man's tongue being vitiated by a feverish and bitter humor, is insensible to anything sweet, and everything seems bitter to it. Therefore, if the intellectual principle contained the nature of a body it would be unable to know all bodies. Now every body has its own determinate nature. Therefore it is impossible for the intellectual principle to be a body. It is likewise impossible for it to understand by means of a bodily organ; since the determinate nature of that organ would impede knowledge of all bodies; as when a certain determinate color is not only in the pupil of the eye, but also in a glass vase, the liquid in the vase seems to be of that same color.

Therefore the intellectual principle which we call the mind or the intellect has an operation *per se* apart from the body. Now only that which subsists can have an operation *per se*. For nothing can operate but what is actual: for which reason we do not say that heat imparts heat, but that what is hot gives heat. We must conclude, therefore, that the human soul, which is called the intellect or the mind, is something incorporeal and subsistent.

Reply Obj. 1: "This particular thing" can be taken in two senses. Firstly, for anything subsistent; secondly, for that which subsists, and is complete in a specific nature. The former sense excludes the inherence of an accident or of a material form; the latter excludes also the imperfection of the part, so that a hand can be called "this particular thing" in the first sense, but not in the second. Therefore, as the human soul is a part of human nature, it can indeed be called "this particular thing," in the first sense, as being something subsistent; but not in the second, for in this sense, what is composed of body and soul is said to be "this particular thing."

Reply Obj. 2: Aristotle wrote those words as expressing not his own opinion, but the opinion of those who said that to understand is to be moved, as is clear from the context. Or we may reply that to operate *per se* belongs to what exists per se. But for a thing to exist *per se*, it suffices sometimes that it be not inherent, as an accident or a material form; even though it be part of something. Nevertheless, that is rightly said to subsist *per se,* which is neither inherent in the above sense, nor part of anything else. In this sense, the eye or the hand cannot be said to subsist *per se* ; nor can it for that reason be said to operate *per se*. Hence the operation of the parts is through each part attributed to the whole. For we say that man sees with the eye, and feels with the hand, and not in the same sense as when we say that what is hot gives heat by its heat; for heat, strictly speaking, does not give heat. We may therefore say that the soul understands, as the eye sees; but it is more correct to say that man understands through the soul.

Reply Obj. 3: The body is necessary for the action of the intellect, not as its origin of action, but on the part of the object; for the phantasm is to the intellect what color is to the sight. Neither does such a dependence on the body prove the intellect to be non-subsistent; otherwise it would follow that an animal is non-subsistent, since it requires external objects of the senses in order to perform its act of perception.

THIRD ARTICLE [I, Q. 75, Art. 3]

Whether the Souls of Brute Animals Are Subsistent?

Objection 1: It would seem that the souls of brute animals are subsistent. For man is of the same genus as other animals; and, as we have just shown (A. 2), the soul of man is subsistent. Therefore the souls of other animals are subsistent.

Obj. 2: Further, the relation of the sensitive faculty to sensible objects is like the relation of the intellectual faculty to intelligible objects. But the intellect, apart from the body, apprehends intelligible objects. Therefore the sensitive faculty, apart from the body, perceives sensible objects. Therefore, since the souls of brute animals are sensitive, it follows that they are subsistent; just as the human intellectual soul is subsistent.

Obj. 3: Further, the soul of brute animals moves the body. But the body is not a mover, but is moved. Therefore the soul of brute animals has an operation apart from the body.

*On the contrary,* Is what is written in the book De Eccl. Dogm. xvi, xvii: "Man alone we believe to have a subsistent soul: whereas the souls of animals are not subsistent."

*I answer that,* The ancient philosophers made no distinction between sense and intellect, and referred both to a corporeal principle, as has been said (A. 1). Plato, however, drew a distinction between intellect and sense; yet he referred both to an incorporeal principle, maintaining that sensing, just as understanding, belongs to the soul as such. From this it follows that even the souls of brute animals are subsistent. But Aristotle held that of the operations of the soul, understanding alone is performed without a corporeal organ. On the other hand, sensation and the consequent operations of the sensitive soul are evidently accompanied with change in the body; thus in the act of vision, the pupil of the eye is affected by a reflection of color: and so with the other senses. Hence it is clear that the sensitive soul has no *per se* operation of its own, and that every operation of the sensitive soul belongs to the composite. Wherefore we conclude that as the souls of brute animals have no *per se* operations they are not subsistent. For the operation of anything follows the mode of its being.

Reply Obj. 1: Although man is of the same genus as other animals, he is of a different species. Specific difference is derived from the difference of form; nor does every difference of form necessarily imply a diversity of genus.

Reply Obj. 2: The relation of the sensitive faculty to the sensible object is in one way the same as that of the intellectual faculty to the intelligible object, in so far as each is in potentiality to its object. But in another way their relations differ, inasmuch as the impression of the object on the sense is accompanied with change in the body; so that excessive strength of the sensible corrupts sense; a thing that never occurs in the case of the intellect. For an intellect that understands the highest of intelligible objects is more able afterwards to understand those that are lower. If, however, in the process of intellectual operation the body is weary, this result is accidental, inasmuch as the intellect requires the operation of the sensitive powers in the production of the phantasms.

Reply Obj. 3: Motive power is of two kinds. One, the appetitive power, commands motion. The operation of this power in the sensitive soul is not apart from the body; for anger, joy, and passions of a like nature are accompanied by a change in the body. The other motive power is that which executes motion in adapting the members for obeying the appetite; and the act of this power does not consist in moving, but in being moved. Whence it is clear that to move is not an act of the sensitive soul without the body.

FOURTH ARTICLE [I, Q. 75, Art. 4]

Whether the Soul Is Man?

Objection 1: It would seem that the soul is man. For it is written (2 Cor. 4:16): "Though our outward man is corrupted, yet the inward man is renewed day by day." But that which is within man is the soul. Therefore the soul is the inward man.

Obj. 2: Further, the human soul is a substance. But it is not a universal substance. Therefore it is a particular substance. Therefore it is a "hypostasis" or a person; and it can only be a human person. Therefore the soul is man; for a human person is a man.

*On the contrary,* Augustine (De Civ. Dei xix, 3) commends Varro as holding "that man is not a mere soul, nor a mere body; but both soul and body."

*I answer that,* The assertion "the soul is man," can be taken in two senses. First, that man is a soul; though this particular man, Socrates, for instance, is not a soul, but composed of soul and body. I say this, forasmuch as some held that the form alone belongs to the species; while matter is part of the individual, and not the species. This cannot be true; for to the nature of the species belongs what the definition signifies; and in natural things the definition does not signify the form only, but the form and the matter. Hence in natural things the matter is part of the species; not, indeed, signate matter, which is the principle of individuality; but the common matter. For as it belongs to the notion of this particular man to be composed of this soul, of this flesh, and of these bones; so it belongs to the notion of man to be composed of soul, flesh, and bones; for whatever belongs in common to the substance of all the individuals contained under a given species, must belong to the substance of the species.

It may also be understood in this sense, that this soul is this man; and this could be held if it were supposed that the operation of the sensitive soul were proper to it, apart from the body; because in that case all the operations which are attributed to man would belong to the soul only; and whatever performs the operations proper to a thing, is that thing; wherefore that which performs the operations of a man is man. But it has been shown above (A. 3) that sensation is not the operation of the soul only. Since, then, sensation is an operation of man, but not proper to him, it is clear that man is not a soul only, but something composed of soul and body. Plato, through supposing that sensation was proper to the soul, could maintain man to be a soul making use of the body.

Reply Obj. 1: According to the Philosopher (Ethic. ix, 8), a thing seems to be chiefly what is princip[al] in it; thus what the governor of a state does, the state is said to do. In this way sometimes what is princip[al] in man is said to be man; sometimes, indeed, the intellectual part which, in accordance with truth, is called the "inward" man; and sometimes the sensitive part with the body is called man in the opinion of those whose observation does not go beyond the senses. And this is called the "outward" man.

Reply Obj. 2: Not every particular substance is a hypostasis or a person, but that which has the complete nature of its species. Hence a hand, or a foot, is not called a hypostasis, or a person; nor, likewise, is the soul alone so called, since it is a part of the human species.

FIFTH ARTICLE [I, Q. 75, Art. 5]

Whether the Soul Is Composed of Matter and Form?

Objection 1: It would seem that the soul is composed of matter and form. For potentiality is opposed to actuality. Now, whatsoever things are in actuality participate of the First Act, which is God; by participation of Whom, all things are good, are beings, and are living things, as is clear from the teaching of Dionysius (Div. Nom. v). Therefore whatsoever things are in potentiality participate of the first potentiality. But the first potentiality is primary matter. Therefore, since the human soul is, after a manner, in potentiality; which appears from the fact that sometimes a man is potentially understanding; it seems that the human soul must participate of primary matter, as part of itself.

Obj. 2: Further, wherever the properties of matter are found, there matter is. But the properties of matter are found in the soul—namely, to be a subject, and to be changed, for it is a subject to science, and virtue; and it changes from ignorance to knowledge and from vice to virtue. Therefore matter is in the soul.

Obj. 3: Further, things which have no matter, have no cause of their existence, as the Philosopher says *Metaph.* viii (Did. vii, 6). But the soul has a cause of its existence, since it is created by God. Therefore the soul has matter.

Obj. 4: Further, what has no matter, and is a form only, is a pure act, and is infinite. But this belongs to God alone. Therefore the soul has matter.

*On the contrary,* Augustine (Gen. ad lit. vii, 7,8,9) proves that the soul was made neither of corporeal matter, nor of spiritual matter.

*I answer that,* The soul has no matter. We may consider this question in two ways. First, from the notion of a soul in general; for it belongs to the notion of a soul to be the form of a body. Now, either it is a form by virtue of itself, in its entirety, or by virtue of some part of itself. If by virtue of itself in its entirety, then it is impossible that any part of it should be matter, if by matter we understand something purely potential: for a form, as such, is an act; and that which is purely potentiality cannot be part of an act, since potentiality is repugnant to actuality as being opposite thereto. If, however, it be a form by virtue of a part of itself, then we call that part the soul: and that matter, which it actualizes first, we call the "primary animate."

Secondly, we may proceed from the specific notion of the human soul inasmuch as it is intellectual. For it is clear that whatever is received into something is received according to the condition of the recipient. Now a thing is known in as far as its form is in the knower. But the intellectual soul knows a thing in its nature absolutely: for instance, it knows a stone absolutely as a stone; and therefore the form of a stone absolutely, as to its proper formal idea, is in the intellectual soul. Therefore the intellectual soul itself is an absolute form, and not something composed of matter and form. For if the intellectual soul were composed of matter and form, the forms of things would be received into it as individuals, and so it would only know the individual: just as it happens with the sensitive powers which receive forms in a corporeal organ; since matter is the principle by which forms are individualized. It follows, therefore, that the intellectual soul, and every intellectual substance which has knowledge of forms absolutely, is exempt from composition of matter and form.

Reply Obj. 1: The First Act is the universal principle of all acts; because It is infinite, virtually "precontaining all things," as Dionysius says (Div. Nom. v). Wherefore things participate of It not as a part of themselves, but by diffusion of Its processions. Now as potentiality is receptive of act, it must be proportionate to act. But the acts received which proceed from the First Infinite Act, and are participations thereof, are diverse, so that there cannot be one potentiality which receives all acts, as there is one act, from which all participated acts are derived; for then the receptive potentiality would equal the active potentiality of the First Act. Now the receptive potentiality in the intellectual soul is other than the receptive potentiality of first matter, as appears from the diversity of the things received by each. For primary matter receives individual forms; whereas the intelligence receives absolute forms. Hence the existence of such a potentiality in the intellectual soul does not prove that the soul is composed of matter and form.

Reply Obj. 2: To be a subject and to be changed belong to matter by reason of its being in potentiality. As, therefore, the potentiality of the intelligence is one thing and the potentiality of primary matter another, so in each is there a different reason of subjection and change. For the intelligence is subject to knowledge, and is changed from ignorance to knowledge, by reason of its being in potentiality with regard to the intelligible species.

Reply Obj. 3: The form causes matter to be, and so does the agent; wherefore the agent causes matter to be, so far as it actualizes it by transmuting it to the act of a form. A subsistent form, however, does not owe its existence to some formal principle, nor has it a cause transmuting it from potentiality to act. So after the words quoted above, the Philosopher concludes, that in things composed of matter and form "there is no other cause but that which moves from potentiality to act; while whatsoever things have no matter are simply beings at once." [*The Leonine edition has, "simpliciter sunt quod vere entia aliquid." The Parma edition of St. Thomas's Commentary on Aristotle has, "statim per se unum quiddam est ... et ens quiddam."]

Reply Obj. 4: Everything participated is compared to the participator as its act. But whatever created form be supposed to subsist "per se," must have existence by participation; for "even life," or anything of that sort, "is a participator of existence," as Dionysius says (Div. Nom. v). Now participated existence is limited by the capacity of the participator; so that God alone, Who is His own existence, is pure act and infinite. But in intellectual substances there is composition of actuality and potentiality, not, indeed, of matter and form, but of form and participated existence. Wherefore some say that they are composed of that "whereby they are" and that "which they are"; for existence itself is that by which a thing is.

SIXTH ARTICLE [I, Q. 75, Art. 6]

Whether the Human Soul Is Incorruptible?

Objection 1: It would seem that the human soul is corruptible. For those things that have a like beginning and process seemingly have a like end. But the beginning, by generation, of men is like that of animals, for they are made from the earth. And the process of life is alike in both; because "all things breathe alike, and man hath nothing more than the beast," as it is written (Eccles. 3:19). Therefore, as the same text concludes, "the death of man and beast is one, and the condition of both is equal." But the souls of brute animals are corruptible. Therefore, also, the human soul is corruptible.

Obj. 2: Further, whatever is out of nothing can return to nothingness; because the end should correspond to the beginning. But as it is written (Wis. 2:2), "We are born of nothing"; which is true, not only of the body, but also of the soul. Therefore, as is concluded in the same passage, "After this we shall be as if we had not been," even as to our soul.

Obj. 3: Further, nothing is without its own proper operation. But the operation proper to the soul, which is to understand through a phantasm, cannot be without the body. For the soul understands nothing without a phantasm; and there is no phantasm without the body as the Philosopher says (De Anima i, 1). Therefore the soul cannot survive the dissolution of the body.

*On the contrary,* Dionysius says (Div. Nom. iv) that human souls owe to Divine goodness that they are "intellectual," and that they have "an incorruptible substantial life."

*I answer that,* We must assert that the intellectual principle which we call the human soul is incorruptible. For a thing may be corrupted in two ways—*per se,* and accidentally. Now it is impossible for any substance to be generated or corrupted accidentally, that is, by the generation or corruption of something else. For generation and corruption belong to a thing, just as existence belongs to it, which is acquired by generation and lost by corruption. Therefore, whatever has existence *per se* cannot be generated or corrupted except "per se"; while things which do not subsist, such as accidents and material forms, acquire existence or lose it through the generation or corruption of composite things. Now it was shown above (AA. 2, 3) that the souls of brutes are not self-subsistent, whereas the human soul is; so that the souls of brutes are corrupted, when their bodies are corrupted; while the human soul could not be corrupted unless it were corrupted *per se.* This, indeed, is impossible, not only as regards the human soul, but also as regards anything subsistent that is a form alone. For it is clear that what belongs to a thing by virtue of itself is inseparable from it; but existence belongs to a form, which is an act, by virtue of itself. Wherefore matter acquires actual existence as it acquires the form; while it is corrupted so far as the form is separated from it. But it is impossible for a form to be separated from itself; and therefore it is impossible for a subsistent form to cease to exist.

Granted even that the soul is composed of matter and form, as some pretend, we should nevertheless have to maintain that it is incorruptible. For corruption is found only where there is contrariety; since generation and corruption are from contraries and into contraries. Wherefore the heavenly bodies, since they have no matter subject to contrariety, are incorruptible. Now there can be no contrariety in the intellectual soul; for it receives according to the manner of its existence, and those things which it receives are without contrariety; for the notions even of contraries are not themselves contrary, since contraries belong to the same knowledge. Therefore it is impossible for the intellectual soul to be corruptible. Moreover we may take a sign of this from the fact that everything naturally aspires to existence after its own manner. Now, in things that have knowledge, desire ensues upon knowledge. The senses indeed do not know existence, except under the conditions of "here" and "now," whereas the intellect apprehends existence absolutely, and for all time; so that everything that has an intellect naturally desires always to exist. But a natural desire cannot be in vain. Therefore every intellectual substance is incorruptible.

Reply Obj. 1: Solomon reasons thus in the person of the foolish, as expressed in the words of Wisdom 2. Therefore the saying that man and animals have a like beginning in generation is true of the body; for all animals alike are made of earth. But it is not true of the soul. For the souls of brutes are produced by some power of the body; whereas the human soul is produced by God. To signify this it is written as to other animals: "Let the earth bring forth the living soul" (Gen. 1:24): while of man it is written (Gen. 2:7) that "He breathed into his face the breath of life." And so in the last chapter of Ecclesiastes (12:7) it is concluded: "(Before) the dust return into its earth from whence it was; and the spirit return to God Who gave it." Again the process of life is alike as to the body, concerning which it is written (Eccles. 3:19): "All things breathe alike," and (Wis. 2:2), "The breath in our nostrils is smoke." But the process is not alike of the soul; for man is intelligent, whereas animals are not. Hence it is false to say: "Man has nothing more than beasts." Thus death comes to both alike as to the body, by not as to the soul.

Reply Obj. 2: As a thing can be created by reason, not of a passive potentiality, but only of the active potentiality of the Creator, Who can produce something out of nothing, so when we say that a thing can be reduced to nothing, we do not imply in the creature a potentiality to non-existence, but in the Creator the power of ceasing to sustain existence. But a thing is said to be corruptible because there is in it a potentiality to non-existence.

Reply Obj. 3: To understand through a phantasm is the proper operation of the soul by virtue of its union with the body. After separation from the body it will have another mode of understanding, similar to other substances separated from bodies, as will appear later on (Q. 89, A. 1).

SEVENTH ARTICLE [I, Q. 75, Art. 7]

Whether the Soul Is of the Same Species As an Angel?

Objection 1: It would seem that the soul is of the same species as an angel. For each thing is ordained to its proper end by the nature of its species, whence is derived its inclination for that end. But the end of the soul is the same as that of an angel—namely, eternal happiness. Therefore they are of the same species.

Obj. 2: Further, the ultimate specific difference is the noblest, because it completes the nature of the species. But there is nothing nobler either in an angel or in the soul than their intellectual nature. Therefore the soul and the angel agree in the ultimate specific difference: therefore they belong to the same species.

Obj. 3: Further, it seems that the soul does not differ from an angel except in its union with the body. But as the body is outside the essence of the soul, it seems that it does not belong to its species. Therefore the soul and angel are of the same species.

*On the contrary,* Things which have different natural operations are of different species. But the natural operations of the soul and of an angel are different; since, as Dionysius says (Div. Nom. vii), "Angelic minds have simple and blessed intelligence, not gathering their knowledge of Divine things from visible things." Subsequently he says the contrary to this of the soul. Therefore the soul and an angel are not of the same species.

*I answer that,* Origen (Peri Archon iii, 5) held that human souls and angels are all of the same species; and this because he supposed that in these substances the difference of degree was accidental, as resulting from their free-will: as we have seen above (Q. 47, A. 2). But this cannot be; for in incorporeal substances there cannot be diversity of number without diversity of species and inequality of nature; because, as they are not composed of matter and form, but are subsistent forms, it is clear that there is necessarily among them a diversity of species. For a separate form cannot be understood otherwise than as one of a single species; thus, supposing a separate whiteness to exist, it could only be one; forasmuch as one whiteness does not differ from another except as in this or that subject. But diversity of species is always accompanied with a diversity of nature; thus in species of colors one is more perfect than another; and the same applies to other species, because differences which divide a genus are contrary to one another. Contraries, however, are compared to one another as the perfect to the imperfect, since the "principle of contrariety is habit, and privation thereof," as is written, *Metaph.* x (Did. ix, 4). The same would follow if the aforesaid substances were composed of matter and form. For if the matter of one be distinct from the matter of another, it follows that either the form is the principle of the distinction of matter—that is to say, that the matter is distinct on account of its relation to divers forms; and even then there would result a difference of species and inequality of nature: or else the matter is the principle of the distinction of forms. But one matter cannot be distinct from another, except by a distinction of quantity, which has no place in these incorporeal substances, such as an angel and the soul. So that it is not possible for the angel and the soul to be of the same species. How it is that there can be many souls of one species will be explained later (Q. 76, A. 2, ad 1).

Reply Obj. 1: This argument proceeds from the proximate and natural end. Eternal happiness is the ultimate and supernatural end.

Reply Obj. 2: The ultimate specific difference is the noblest because it is the most determinate, in the same way as actuality is nobler than potentiality. Thus, however, the intellectual faculty is not the noblest, because it is indeterminate and common to many degrees of intellectuality; as the sensible faculty is common to many degrees in the sensible nature. Hence, as all sensible things are not of one species, so neither are all intellectual things of one species.

Reply Obj. 3: The body is not of the essence of the soul; but the soul by the nature of its essence can be united to the body, so that, properly speaking, not the soul alone, but the "composite," is the species. And the very fact that the soul in a certain way requires the body for its operation, proves that the soul is endowed with a grade of intellectuality inferior to that of an angel, who is not united to a body.

## QUESTION 76

OF THE UNION OF BODY AND SOUL (In Eight Articles)

We now consider the union of the soul with the body; and concerning this there are eight points of inquiry:

(1) Whether the intellectual principle is united to the body as its form?

(2) Whether the intellectual principle is multiplied numerically according to the number of bodies; or is there one intelligence for all men?

(3) Whether in the body the form of which is an intellectual principle, there is some other soul?

(4) Whether in the body there is any other substantial form?

(5) Of the qualities required in the body of which the intellectual principle is the form?

(6) Whether it be united to such a body by means of another body?

(7) Whether by means of an accident?

(8) Whether the soul is wholly in each part of the body?

FIRST ARTICLE [I, Q. 76, Art. 1]

Whether the Intellectual Principle Is United to the Body As Its Form?

Objection 1: It seems that the intellectual principle is not united to the body as its form. For the Philosopher says (De Anima iii, 4) that the intellect is "separate," and that it is not the act of any body. Therefore it is not united to the body as its form.

Obj. 2: Further, every form is determined according to the nature of the matter of which it is the form; otherwise no proportion would be required between matter and form. Therefore if the intellect were united to the body as its form, since every body has a determinate nature, it would follow that the intellect has a determinate nature; and thus, it would not be capable of knowing all things, as is clear from what has been said (Q. 75, A. 2); which is contrary to the nature of the intellect. Therefore the intellect is not united to the body as its form.

Obj. 3: Further, whatever receptive power is an act of a body, receives a form materially and individually; for what is received must be received according to the condition of the receiver. But the form of the thing understood is not received into the intellect materially and individually, but rather immaterially and universally: otherwise the intellect would not be capable of the knowledge of immaterial and universal objects, but only of individuals, like the senses. Therefore the intellect is not united to the body as its form.

Obj. 4: Further, power and action have the same subject; for the same subject is what can, and does, act. But the intellectual action is not the action of a body, as appears from above (Q. 75, A. 2). Therefore neither is the intellectual faculty a power of the body. But virtue or power cannot be more abstract or more simple than the essence from which the faculty or power is derived. Therefore neither is the substance of the intellect the form of a body.

Obj. 5: Further, whatever has *per se* existence is not united to the body as its form; because a form is that by which a thing exists: so that the very existence of a form does not belong to the form by itself. But the intellectual principle has *per se* existence and is subsistent, as was said above (Q. 75, A. 2). Therefore it is not united to the body as its form.

Obj. 6: Further, whatever exists in a thing by reason of its nature exists in it always. But to be united to matter belongs to the form by reason of its nature; because form is the act of matter, not by an accidental quality, but by its own essence; otherwise matter and form would not make a thing substantially one, but only accidentally one. Therefore a form cannot be without its own proper matter. But the intellectual principle, since it is incorruptible, as was shown above (Q. 75, A. 6), remains separate from the body, after the dissolution of the body. Therefore the intellectual principle is not united to the body as its form.

*On the contrary,* According to the Philosopher, Metaph. viii (Did. vii 2), difference is derived from the form. But the difference which constitutes man is "rational," which is applied to man on account of his intellectual principle. Therefore the intellectual principle is the form of man.

*I answer that,* We must assert that the intellect which is the principle of intellectual operation is the form of the human body. For that whereby primarily anything acts is a form of the thing to which the act is to be attributed: for instance, that whereby a body is primarily healed is health, and that whereby the soul knows primarily is knowledge; hence health is a form of the body, and knowledge is a form of the soul. The reason is because nothing acts except so far as it is in act; wherefore a thing acts by that whereby it is in act. Now it is clear that the first thing by which the body lives is the soul. And as life appears through various operations in different degrees of living things, that whereby we primarily perform each of all these vital actions is the soul. For the soul is the primary principle of our nourishment, sensation, and local movement; and likewise of our understanding. Therefore this principle by which we primarily understand, whether it be called the intellect or the intellectual soul, is the form of the body. This is the demonstration used by Aristotle (De Anima ii, 2).

But if anyone says that the intellectual soul is not the form of the body he must first explain how it is that this action of understanding is the action of this particular man; for each one is conscious that it is himself who understands. Now an action may be attributed to anyone in three ways, as is clear from the Philosopher (Phys. v, 1); for a thing is said to move or act, either by virtue of its whole self, for instance, as a physician heals; or by virtue of a part, as a man sees by his eye; or through an accidental quality, as when we say that something that is white builds, because it is accidental to the builder to be white. So when we say that Socrates or Plato understands, it is clear that this is not attributed to him accidentally; since it is ascribed to him as man, which is predicated of him essentially. We must therefore say either that Socrates understands by virtue of his whole self, as Plato maintained, holding that man is an intellectual soul; or that intelligence is a part of Socrates. The first cannot stand, as was shown above (Q. 75, A. 4), for this reason, that it is one and the same man who is conscious both that he understands, and that he senses. But one cannot sense without a body: therefore the body must be some part of man. It follows therefore that the intellect by which Socrates understands is a part of Socrates, so that in some way it is united to the body of Socrates.

The Commentator held that this union is through the intelligible species, as having a double subject, in the possible intellect, and in the phantasms which are in the corporeal organs. Thus through the intelligible species the possible intellect is linked to the body of this or that particular man. But this link or union does not sufficiently explain the fact, that the act of the intellect is the act of Socrates. This can be clearly seen from comparison with the sensitive faculty, from which Aristotle proceeds to consider things relating to the intellect. For the relation of phantasms to the intellect is like the relation of colors to the sense of sight, as he says *De Anima* iii, 5,7. Therefore, as the species of colors are in the sight, so are the species of phantasms in the possible intellect. Now it is clear that because the colors, the images of which are in the sight, are on a wall, the action of seeing is not attributed to the wall: for we do not say that the wall sees, but rather that it is seen. Therefore, from the fact that the species of phantasms are in the possible intellect, it does not follow that Socrates, in whom are the phantasms, understands, but that he or his phantasms are understood.

Some, however, tried to maintain that the intellect is united to the body as its motor; and hence that the intellect and body form one thing so that the act of the intellect could be attributed to the whole. This is, however, absurd for many reasons. First, because the intellect does not move the body except through the appetite, the movement of which presupposes the operation of the intellect. The reason therefore why Socrates understands is not because he is moved by his intellect, but rather, contrariwise, he is moved by his intellect because he understands. Secondly, because since Socrates is an individual in a nature of one essence composed of matter and form, if the intellect be not the form, it follows that it must be outside the essence, and then the intellect is the whole Socrates as a motor to the thing moved. Whereas the act of intellect remains in the agent, and does not pass into something else, as does the action of heating. Therefore the action of understanding cannot be attributed to Socrates for the reason that he is moved by his intellect. Thirdly, because the action of a motor is never attributed to the thing moved, except as to an instrument; as the action of a carpenter to a saw. Therefore if understanding is attributed to Socrates, as the action of what moves him, it follows that it is attributed to him as to an instrument. This is contrary to the teaching of the Philosopher, who holds that understanding is not possible through a corporeal instrument (De Anima iii, 4). Fourthly, because, although the action of a part be attributed to the whole, as the action of the eye is attributed to a man; yet it is never attributed to another part, except perhaps indirectly; for we do not say that the hand sees because the eye sees. Therefore if the intellect and Socrates are united in the above manner, the action of the intellect cannot be attributed to Socrates. If, however, Socrates be a whole composed of a union of the intellect with whatever else belongs to Socrates, and still the intellect be united to those other things only as a motor, it follows that Socrates is not one absolutely, and consequently neither a being absolutely, for a thing is a being according as it is one.

There remains, therefore, no other explanation than that given by Aristotle—namely, that this particular man understands, because the intellectual principle is his form. Thus from the very operation of the intellect it is made clear that the intellectual principle is united to the body as its form.

The same can be clearly shown from the nature of the human species. For the nature of each thing is shown by its operation. Now the proper operation of man as man is to understand; because he thereby surpasses all other animals. Whence Aristotle concludes (Ethic. x, 7) that the ultimate happiness of man must consist in this operation as properly belonging to him. Man must therefore derive his species from that which is the principle of this operation. But the species of anything is derived from its form. It follows therefore that the intellectual principle is the proper form of man.

But we must observe that the nobler a form is, the more it rises above corporeal matter, the less it is merged in matter, and the more it excels matter by its power and its operation; hence we find that the form of a mixed body has another operation not caused by its elemental qualities. And the higher we advance in the nobility of forms, the more we find that the power of the form excels the elementary matter; as the vegetative soul excels the form of the metal, and the sensitive soul excels the vegetative soul. Now the human soul is the highest and noblest of forms. Wherefore it excels corporeal matter in its power by the fact that it has an operation and a power in which corporeal matter has no share whatever. This power is called the intellect.

It is well to remark that if anyone holds that the soul is composed of matter and form, it would follow that in no way could the soul be the form of the body. For since the form is an act, and matter is only in potentiality, that which is composed of matter and form cannot be the form of another by virtue of itself as a whole. But if it is a form by virtue of some part of itself, then that part which is the form we call the soul, and that of which it is the form we call the "primary animate," as was said above (Q. 75, A. 5).

Reply Obj. 1: As the Philosopher says (Phys. ii, 2), the ultimate natural form to which the consideration of the natural philosopher is directed is indeed separate; yet it exists in matter. He proves this from the fact that "man and the sun generate man from matter." It is separate indeed according to its intellectual power, because the intellectual power does not belong to a corporeal organ, as the power of seeing is the act of the eye; for understanding is an act which cannot be performed by a corporeal organ, like the act of seeing. But it exists in matter so far as the soul itself, to which this power belongs, is the form of the body, and the term of human generation. And so the Philosopher says (De Anima iii) that the intellect is separate, because it is not the faculty of a corporeal organ.

From this it is clear how to answer the Second and Third objections: since, in order that man may be able to understand all things by means of his intellect, and that his intellect may understand immaterial things and universals, it is sufficient that the intellectual power be not the act of the body.

Reply Obj. 4: The human soul, by reason of its perfection, is not a form merged in matter, or entirely embraced by matter. Therefore there is nothing to prevent some power thereof not being the act of the body, although the soul is essentially the form of the body.

Reply Obj. 5: The soul communicates that existence in which it subsists to the corporeal matter, out of which and the intellectual soul there results unity of existence; so that the existence of the whole composite is also the existence of the soul. This is not the case with other non-subsistent forms. For this reason the human soul retains its own existence after the dissolution of the body; whereas it is not so with other forms.

Reply Obj. 6: To be united to the body belongs to the soul by reason of itself, as it belongs to a light body by reason of itself to be raised up. And as a light body remains light, when removed from its proper place, retaining meanwhile an aptitude and an inclination for its proper place; so the human soul retains its proper existence when separated from the body, having an aptitude and a natural inclination to be united to the body.

SECOND ARTICLE [I, Q. 76, Art. 2]

Whether the Intellectual Principle Is Multiplied According to the Number of Bodies?

Objection 1: It would seem that the intellectual principle is not multiplied according to the number of bodies, but that there is one intellect in all men. For an immaterial substance is not multiplied in number within one species. But the human soul is an immaterial substance; since it is not composed of matter and form as was shown above (Q. 75, A. 5). Therefore there are not many human souls in one species. But all men are of one species. Therefore there is but one intellect in all men.

Obj. 2: Further, when the cause is removed, the effect is also removed. Therefore, if human souls were multiplied according to the number of bodies, it follows that the bodies being removed, the number of souls would not remain; but from all the souls there would be but a single remainder. This is heretical; for it would do away with the distinction of rewards and punishments.

Obj. 3: Further, if my intellect is distinct from your intellect, my intellect is an individual, and so is yours; for individuals are things which differ in number but agree in one species. Now whatever is received into anything must be received according to the condition of the receiver. Therefore the species of things would be received individually into my intellect, and also into yours: which is contrary to the nature of the intellect which knows universals.

Obj. 4: Further, the thing understood is in the intellect which understands. If, therefore, my intellect is distinct from yours, what is understood by me must be distinct from what is understood by you; and consequently it will be reckoned as something individual, and be only potentially something understood; so that the common intention will have to be abstracted from both; since from things diverse something intelligible common to them may be abstracted. But this is contrary to the nature of the intellect; for then the intellect would seem not to be distinct from the imagination. It seems, therefore, to follow that there is one intellect in all men.

Obj. 5: Further, when the disciple receives knowledge from the master, it cannot be said that the master's knowledge begets knowledge in the disciple, because then also knowledge would be an active form, such as heat is, which is clearly false. It seems, therefore, that the same individual knowledge which is in the master is communicated to the disciple; which cannot be, unless there is one intellect in both. Seemingly, therefore, the intellect of the disciple and master is but one; and, consequently, the same applies to all men.

Obj. 6: Further, Augustine (De Quant. Animae xxxii) says: "If I were to say that there are many human souls, I should laugh at myself." But the soul seems to be one chiefly on account of the intellect. Therefore there is one intellect of all men.

*On the contrary,* The Philosopher says (Phys. ii, 3) that the relation of universal causes to universals is like the relation of particular causes to individuals. But it is impossible that a soul, one in species, should belong to animals of different species. Therefore it is impossible that one individual intellectual soul should belong to several individuals.

*I answer that,* It is absolutely impossible for one intellect to belong to all men. This is clear if, as Plato maintained, man is the intellect itself. For it would follow that Socrates and Plato are one man; and that they are not distinct from each other, except by something outside the essence of each. The distinction between Socrates and Plato would be no other than that of one man with a tunic and another with a cloak; which is quite absurd.

It is likewise clear that this is impossible if, according to the opinion of Aristotle (De Anima ii, 2), it is supposed that the intellect is a part or a power of the soul which is the form of man. For it is impossible for many distinct individuals to have one form, as it is impossible for them to have one existence, for the form is the principle of existence.

Again, this is clearly impossible, whatever one may hold as to the manner of the union of the intellect to this or that man. For it is manifest that, supposing there is one principal agent, and two instruments, we can say that there is one agent absolutely, but several actions; as when one man touches several things with his two hands, there will be one who touches, but two contacts. If, *on the contrary,* we suppose one instrument and several principal agents, we might say that there are several agents, but one act; for example, if there be many drawing a ship by means of a rope; there will be many drawing, but one pull. If, however, there is one principal agent, and one instrument, we say that there is one agent and one action, as when the smith strikes with one hammer, there is one striker and one stroke. Now it is clear that no matter how the intellect is united or coupled to this or that man, the intellect has the precedence of all the other things which appertain to man; for the sensitive powers obey the intellect, and are at its service. Therefore, if we suppose two men to have several intellects and one sense—for instance, if two men had one eye—there would be several seers, but one sight. But if there is one intellect, no matter how diverse may be all those things of which the intellect makes use as instruments, in no way is it possible to say that Socrates and Plato are otherwise than one understanding man. And if to this we add that to understand, which is the act of the intellect, is not affected by any organ other than the intellect itself; it will further follow that there is but one agent and one action: that is to say that all men are but one "understander," and have but one act of understanding, in regard, that is, of one intelligible object.

However, it would be possible to distinguish my intellectual action from yours by the distinction of the phantasms—that is to say, were there one phantasm of a stone in me, and another in you—if the phantasm itself, as it is one thing in me and another in you, were a form of the possible intellect; since the same agent according to divers forms produces divers actions; as, according to divers forms of things with regard to the same eye, there are divers visions. But the phantasm itself is not a form of the possible intellect; it is the intelligible species abstracted from the phantasm that is a form. Now in one intellect, from different phantasms of the same species, only one intelligible species is abstracted; as appears in one man, in whom there may be different phantasms of a stone; yet from all of them only one intelligible species of a stone is abstracted; by which the intellect of that one man, by one operation, understands the nature of a stone, notwithstanding the diversity of phantasms. Therefore, if there were one intellect for all men, the diversity of phantasms which are in this one and that one would not cause a diversity of intellectual operation in this man and that man. It follows, therefore, that it is altogether impossible and unreasonable to maintain that there exists one intellect for all men.

Reply Obj. 1: Although the intellectual soul, like an angel, has no matter from which it is produced, yet it is the form of a certain matter; in which it is unlike an angel. Therefore, according to the division of matter, there are many souls of one species; while it is quite impossible for many angels to be of one species.

Reply Obj. 2: Everything has unity in the same way that it has being; consequently we must judge of the multiplicity of a thing as we judge of its being. Now it is clear that the intellectual soul, by virtue of its very being, is united to the body as its form; yet, after the dissolution of the body, the intellectual soul retains its own being. In like manner the multiplicity of souls is in proportion to the multiplicity of the bodies; yet, after the dissolution of the bodies, the souls retain their multiplied being.

Reply Obj. 3: Individuality of the intelligent being, or of the species whereby it understands, does not exclude the understanding of universals; otherwise, since separate intellects are subsistent substances, and consequently individual, they could not understand universals. But the materiality of the knower, and of the species whereby it knows, impedes the knowledge of the universal. For as every action is according to the mode of the form by which the agent acts, as heating is according to the mode of the heat; so knowledge is according to the mode of the species by which the knower knows.

Now it is clear that common nature becomes distinct and multiplied by reason of the individuating principles which come from the matter. Therefore if the form, which is the means of knowledge, is material—that is, not abstracted from material conditions—its likeness to the nature of a species or genus will be according to the distinction and multiplication of that nature by means of individuating principles; so that knowledge of the nature of a thing in general will be impossible. But if the species be abstracted from the conditions of individual matter, there will be a likeness of the nature without those things which make it distinct and multiplied; thus there will be knowledge of the universal. Nor does it matter, as to this particular point, whether there be one intellect or many; because, even if there were but one, it would necessarily be an individual intellect, and the species whereby it understands, an individual species.

Reply Obj. 4: Whether the intellect be one or many, what is understood is one; for what is understood is in the intellect, not according to its own nature, but according to its likeness; for "the stone is not in the soul, but its likeness is," as is said, De Anima iii, 8. Yet it is the stone which is understood, not the likeness of the stone; except by a reflection of the intellect on itself: otherwise, the objects of sciences would not be things, but only intelligible species. Now it happens that different things, according to different forms, are likened to the same thing. And since knowledge is begotten according to the assimilation of the knower to the thing known, it follows that the same thing may happen to be known by several knowers; as is apparent in regard to the senses; for several see the same color, according to different likenesses. In the same way several intellects understand one object understood. But there is this difference, according to the opinion of Aristotle, between the sense and the intelligence—that a thing is perceived by the sense according to the disposition which it has outside the soul—that is, in its individuality; whereas the nature of the thing understood is indeed outside the soul, but the mode according to which it exists outside the soul is not the mode according to which it is understood. For the common nature is understood as apart from the individuating principles; whereas such is not its mode of existence outside the soul. But, according to the opinion of Plato, the thing understood exists outside the soul in the same condition as those under which it is understood; for he supposed that the natures of things exist separate from matter.

Reply Obj. 5: One knowledge exists in the disciple and another in the master. How it is caused will be shown later on (Q. 117, A. 1).

Reply Obj. 6: Augustine denies a plurality of souls, that would involve a plurality of species.

THIRD ARTICLE [I, Q. 76, Art. 3]

Whether Besides the Intellectual Soul There Are in Man Other Souls Essentially Different from One Another?

Objection 1: It would seem that besides the intellectual soul there are in man other souls essentially different from one another, such as the sensitive soul and the nutritive soul. For corruptible and incorruptible are not of the same substance. But the intellectual soul is incorruptible; whereas the other souls, as the sensitive and the nutritive, are corruptible, as was shown above (Q. 75, A. 6). Therefore in man the essence of the intellectual soul, the sensitive soul, and the nutritive soul, cannot be the same.

Obj. 2: Further, if it be said that the sensitive soul in man is incorruptible; *on the contrary,* "corruptible and incorruptible differ generically," says the Philosopher, *Metaph.* x (Did. ix, 10). But the sensitive soul in the horse, the lion, and other brute animals, is corruptible. If, therefore, in man it be incorruptible, the sensitive soul in man and brute animals will not be of the same genus. Now an animal is so called from its having a sensitive soul; and, therefore, "animal" will not be one genus common to man and other animals, which is absurd.

Obj. 3: Further, the Philosopher says, *Metaph.* viii (Did. vii, 2), that the genus is taken from the matter, and difference from the form. But "rational," which is the difference constituting man, is taken from the intellectual soul; while he is called "animal" by reason of his having a body animated by a sensitive soul. Therefore the intellectual soul may be compared to the body animated by a sensitive soul, as form to matter. Therefore in man the intellectual soul is not essentially the same as the sensitive soul, but presupposes it as a material subject.

*On the contrary,* It is said in the book De Ecclesiasticis Dogmatibus xv: "Nor do we say that there are two souls in one man, as James and other Syrians write; one, animal, by which the body is animated, and which is mingled with the blood; the other, spiritual, which obeys the reason; but we say that it is one and the same soul in man, that both gives life to the body by being united to it, and orders itself by its own reasoning."

*I answer that,* Plato held that there were several souls in one body, distinct even as to organs, to which souls he referred the different vital actions, saying that the nutritive power is in the liver, the concupiscible in the heart, and the power of knowledge in the brain. Which opinion is rejected by Aristotle (De Anima ii, 2), with regard to those parts of the soul which use corporeal organs; for this reason, that in those animals which continue to live when they have been divided in each part are observed the operations of the soul, as sense and appetite. Now this would not be the case if the various principles of the soul's operations were essentially different, and distributed in the various parts of the body. But with regard to the intellectual part, he seems to leave it in doubt whether it be "only logically" distinct from the other parts of the soul, "or also locally."

The opinion of Plato might be maintained if, as he held, the soul was supposed to be united to the body, not as its form, but as its motor. For it involves nothing unreasonable that the same movable thing be moved by several motors; and still less if it be moved according to its various parts. If we suppose, however, that the soul is united to the body as its form, it is quite impossible for several essentially different souls to be in one body. This can be made clear by three different reasons.

In the first place, an animal would not be absolutely one, in which there were several souls. For nothing is absolutely one except by one form, by which a thing has existence: because a thing has from the same source both existence and unity; and therefore things which are denominated by various forms are not absolutely one; as, for instance, "a white man." If, therefore, man were *living* by one form, the vegetative soul, and *animal* by another form, the sensitive soul, and *man* by another form, the intellectual soul, it would follow that man is not absolutely one. Thus Aristotle argues, *Metaph.* viii (Did. vii, 6), against Plato, that if the idea of an animal is distinct from the idea of a biped, then a biped animal is not absolutely one. For this reason, against those who hold that there are several souls in the body, he asks (De Anima i, 5), "what contains them?"—that is, what makes them one? It cannot be said that they are united by the one body; because rather does the soul contain the body and make it one, than the reverse.

Secondly, this is proved to be impossible by the manner in which one thing is predicated of another. Those things which are derived from various forms are predicated of one another, either accidentally, (if the forms are not ordered to one another, as when we say that something white is sweet), or essentially, in the second manner of essential predication, (if the forms are ordered one to another, the subject belonging to the definition of the predicate; as a surface is presupposed to color; so that if we say that a body with a surface is colored, we have the second manner of essential predication.) Therefore, if we have one form by which a thing is an animal, and another form by which it is a man, it follows either that one of these two things could not be predicated of the other, except accidentally, supposing these two forms not to be ordered to one another—or that one would be predicated of the other according to the second manner of essential predication, if one soul be presupposed to the other. But both of these consequences are clearly false: because "animal" is predicated of man essentially and not accidentally; and man is not part of the definition of an animal, but the other way about. Therefore of necessity by the same form a thing is animal and man; otherwise man would not really be the thing which is an animal, so that animal can be essentially predicated of man.

Thirdly, this is shown to be impossible by the fact that when one operation of the soul is intense it impedes another, which could never be the case unless the principle of action were essentially one.

We must therefore conclude that in man the sensitive soul, the intellectual soul, and the nutritive soul are numerically one soul. This can easily be explained, if we consider the differences of species and forms. For we observe that the species and forms of things differ from one another, as the perfect and imperfect; as in the order of things, the animate are more perfect than the inanimate, and animals more perfect than plants, and man than brute animals; and in each of these genera there are various degrees. For this reason Aristotle, *Metaph.* viii (Did. vii, 3), compares the species of things to numbers, which differ in species by the addition or subtraction of unity. And (De Anima ii, 3) he compares the various souls to the species of figures, one of which contains another; as a pentagon contains and exceeds a tetragon. Thus the intellectual soul contains virtually whatever belongs to the sensitive soul of brute animals, and to the nutritive souls of plants. Therefore, as a surface which is of a pentagonal shape, is not tetragonal by one shape, and pentagonal by another—since a tetragonal shape would be superfluous as contained in the pentagonal—so neither is Socrates a man by one soul, and animal by another; but by one and the same soul he is both animal and man.

Reply Obj. 1: The sensitive soul is incorruptible, not by reason of its being sensitive, but by reason of its being intellectual. When, therefore, a soul is sensitive only, it is corruptible; but when with sensibility it has also intellectuality, it is incorruptible. For although sensibility does not give incorruptibility, yet it cannot deprive intellectuality of its incorruptibility.

Reply Obj. 2: Not forms, but composites, are classified either generically or specifically. Now man is corruptible like other animals. And so the difference of corruptible and incorruptible which is on the part of the forms does not involve a generic difference between man and the other animals.

Reply Obj. 3: The embryo has first of all a soul which is merely sensitive, and when this is removed, it is supplanted by a more perfect soul, which is both sensitive and intellectual: as will be shown further on (Q. 118, A. 2, ad 2).

Reply Obj. 4: We must not consider the diversity of natural things as proceeding from the various logical notions or intentions, which flow from our manner of understanding, because reason can apprehend one and the same thing in various ways. Therefore since, as we have said, the intellectual soul contains virtually what belongs to the sensitive soul, and something more, reason can consider separately what belongs to the power of the sensitive soul, as something imperfect and material. And because it observes that this is something common to man and to other animals, it forms thence the notion of the genus; while that wherein the intellectual soul exceeds the sensitive soul, it takes as formal and perfecting; thence it gathers the "difference" of man.

FOURTH ARTICLE [I, Q. 76, Art. 4]

Whether in Man There Is Another Form Besides the Intellectual Soul?

Objection 1: It would seem that in man there is another form besides the intellectual soul. For the Philosopher says (De Anima ii, 1), that "the soul is the act of a physical body which has life potentially." Therefore the soul is to the body as a form of matter. But the body has a substantial form by which it is a body. Therefore some other substantial form in the body precedes the soul.

Obj. 2: Further, man moves himself as every animal does. Now everything that moves itself is divided into two parts, of which one moves, and the other is moved, as the Philosopher proves (Phys. viii, 5). But the part which moves is the soul. Therefore the other part must be such that it can be moved. But primary matter cannot be moved (Phys. v, 1), since it is a being only potentially; indeed everything that is moved is a body. Therefore in man and in every animal there must be another substantial form, by which the body is constituted.

Obj. 3: Further, the order of forms depends on their relation to primary matter; for "before" and "after" apply by comparison to some beginning. Therefore if there were not in man some other substantial form besides the rational soul, and if this were to inhere immediately to primary matter; it would follow that it ranks among the most imperfect forms which inhere to matter immediately.

Obj. 4: Further, the human body is a mixed body. Now mingling does not result from matter alone; for then we should have mere corruption. Therefore the forms of the elements must remain in a mixed body; and these are substantial forms. Therefore in the human body there are other substantial forms besides the intellectual soul.

*On the contrary,* Of one thing there is but one substantial being. But the substantial form gives substantial being. Therefore of one thing there is but one substantial form. But the soul is the substantial form of man. Therefore it is impossible for there to be in man another substantial form besides the intellectual soul.

*I answer that,* If we suppose that the intellectual soul is not united to the body as its form, but only as its motor, as the Platonists maintain, it would necessarily follow that in man there is another substantial form, by which the body is established in its being as movable by the soul. If, however, the intellectual soul be united to the body as its substantial form, as we have said above (A. 1), it is impossible for another substantial form besides the intellectual soul to be found in man.

In order to make this evident, we must consider that the substantial form differs from the accidental form in this, that the accidental form does not make a thing to be "simply," but to be "such," as heat does not make a thing to be simply, but only to be hot. Therefore by the coming of the accidental form a thing is not said to be made or generated simply, but to be made such, or to be in some particular condition; and in like manner, when an accidental form is removed, a thing is said to be corrupted, not simply, but relatively. Now the substantial form gives being simply; therefore by its coming a thing is said to be generated simply; and by its removal to be corrupted simply. For this reason, the old natural philosophers, who held that primary matter was some actual being—for instance, fire or air, or something of that sort—maintained that nothing is generated simply, or corrupted simply; and stated that "every becoming is nothing but an alteration," as we read, *Phys.* i, 4. Therefore, if besides the intellectual soul there pre-existed in matter another substantial form by which the subject of the soul were made an actual being, it would follow that the soul does not give being simply; and consequently that it is not the substantial form: and so at the advent of the soul there would not be simple generation; nor at its removal simple corruption, all of which is clearly false.

Whence we must conclude, that there is no other substantial form in man besides the intellectual soul; and that the soul, as it virtually contains the sensitive and nutritive souls, so does it virtually contain all inferior forms, and itself alone does whatever the imperfect forms do in other things. The same is to be said of the sensitive soul in brute animals, and of the nutritive soul in plants, and universally of all more perfect forms with regard to the imperfect.

Reply Obj. 1: Aristotle does not say that the soul is the act of a body only, but "the act of a physical organic body which has life potentially"; and that this potentiality "does not reject the soul." Whence it is clear that when the soul is called the act, the soul itself is included; as when we say that heat is the act of what is hot, and light of what is lucid; not as though lucid and light were two separate things, but because a thing is made lucid by the light. In like manner, the soul is said to be the "act of a body," etc., because by the soul it is a body, and is organic, and has life potentially. Yet the first act is said to be in potentiality to the second act, which is operation; for such a potentiality "does not reject"—that is, does not exclude—the soul.

Reply Obj. 2: The soul does not move the body by its essence, as the form of the body, but by the motive power, the act of which presupposes the body to be already actualized by the soul: so that the soul by its motive power is the part which moves; and the animate body is the part moved.

Reply Obj. 3: We observe in matter various degrees of perfection, as existence, living, sensing, and understanding. Now what is added is always more perfect. Therefore that form which gives matter only the first degree of perfection is the most imperfect; while that form which gives the first, second, and third degree, and so on, is the most perfect: and yet it inheres to matter immediately.

Reply Obj. 4: Avicenna held that the substantial forms of the elements remain entire in the mixed body; and that the mixture is made by the contrary qualities of the elements being reduced to an average. But this is impossible, because the various forms of the elements must necessarily be in various parts of matter; for the distinction of which we must suppose dimensions, without which matter cannot be divisible. Now matter subject to dimension is not to be found except in a body. But various bodies cannot be in the same place. Whence it follows that elements in the mixed body would be distinct as to situation. And then there would not be a real mixture which is in respect of the whole; but only a mixture apparent to sense, by the juxtaposition of particles.

Averroes maintained that the forms of elements, by reason of their imperfection, are a medium between accidental and substantial forms, and so can be "more" or "less"; and therefore in the mixture they are modified and reduced to an average, so that one form emerges from them. But this is even still more impossible. For the substantial being of each thing consists in something indivisible, and every addition and subtraction varies the species, as in numbers, as stated in *Metaph.* viii (Did. vii, 3); and consequently it is impossible for any substantial form to receive "more" or "less." Nor is it less impossible for anything to be a medium between substance and accident.

Therefore we must say, in accordance with the Philosopher (De Gener. i, 10), that the forms of the elements remain in the mixed body, not actually but virtually. For the proper qualities of the elements remain, though modified; and in them is the power of the elementary forms. This quality of the mixture is the proper disposition for the substantial form of the mixed body; for instance, the form of a stone, or of any sort of soul.

FIFTH ARTICLE [I, Q. 76, Art. 5]

Whether the Intellectual Soul Is Properly United to Such a Body?

Objection 1: It would seem that the intellectual soul is improperly united to such a body. For matter must be proportionate to the form. But the intellectual soul is incorruptible. Therefore it is not properly united to a corruptible body.

Obj. 2: Further, the intellectual soul is a perfectly immaterial form; a proof whereof is its operation in which corporeal matter does not share. But the more subtle is the body, the less has it of matter. Therefore the soul should be united to a most subtle body, to fire, for instance, and not to a mixed body, still less to a terrestrial body.

Obj. 3: Further, since the form is the principle of the species, one form cannot produce a variety of species. But the intellectual soul is one form. Therefore, it should not be united to a body which is composed of parts belonging to various species.

Obj. 4: Further, what is susceptible of a more perfect form should itself be more perfect. But the intellectual soul is the most perfect of souls. Therefore since the bodies of other animals are naturally provided with a covering, for instance, with hair instead of clothes, and hoofs instead of shoes; and are, moreover, naturally provided with arms, as claws, teeth, and horns; it seems that the intellectual soul should not have been united to a body which is imperfect as being deprived of the above means of protection.

*On the contrary,* The Philosopher says (De Anima ii, 1), that "the soul is the act of a physical organic body having life potentially."

*I answer that,* Since the form is not for the matter, but rather the matter for the form, we must gather from the form the reason why the matter is such as it is; and not conversely. Now the intellectual soul, as we have seen above (Q. 55, A. 2) in the order of nature, holds the lowest place among intellectual substances; inasmuch as it is not naturally gifted with the knowledge of truth, as the angels are; but has to gather knowledge from individual things by way of the senses, as Dionysius says (Div. Nom. vii). But nature never fails in necessary things: therefore the intellectual soul had to be endowed not only with the power of understanding, but also with the power of feeling. Now the action of the senses is not performed without a corporeal instrument. Therefore it behooved the intellectual soul to be united to a body fitted to be a convenient organ of sense.

Now all the other senses are based on the sense of touch. But the organ of touch requires to be a medium between contraries, such as hot and cold, wet and dry, and the like, of which the sense of touch has the perception; thus it is in potentiality with regard to contraries, and is able to perceive them. Therefore the more the organ of touch is reduced to an equable complexion, the more sensitive will be the touch. But the intellectual soul has the power of sense in all its completeness; because what belongs to the inferior nature pre-exists more perfectly in the superior, as Dionysius says (Div. Nom. v). Therefore the body to which the intellectual soul is united should be a mixed body, above others reduced to the most equable complexion. For this reason among animals, man has the best sense of touch. And among men, those who have the best sense of touch have the best intelligence. A sign of which is that we observe "those who are refined in body are well endowed in mind," as stated in *De Anima* ii, 9.

Reply Obj. 1: Perhaps someone might attempt

to answer this by saying that before sin the human body was incorruptible. This answer does not seem sufficient; because before sin the human body was immortal not by nature, but by a gift of Divine grace; otherwise its immortality would not be forfeited through sin, as neither was the immortality of the devil.

Therefore we answer otherwise by observing that in matter two conditions are to be found; one which is chosen in order that the matter be suitable to the form; the other which follows by force of the first disposition. The artisan, for instance, for the form of the saw chooses iron adapted for cutting through hard material; but that the teeth of the saw may become blunt and rusted, follows by force of the matter itself. So the intellectual soul requires a body of equable complexion, which, however, is corruptible by force of its matter. If, however, it be said that God could avoid this, we answer that in the formation of natural things we do not consider what God might do; but what is suitable to the nature of things, as Augustine says (Gen. ad lit. ii, 1). God, however, provided in this case by applying a remedy against death in the gift of grace.

Reply Obj. 2: A body is not necessary to the intellectual soul by reason of its intellectual operation considered as such; but on account of the sensitive power, which requires an organ of equable temperament. Therefore the intellectual soul had to be united to such a body, and not to a simple element, or to a mixed body, in which fire was in excess; because otherwise there could not be an equability of temperament. And this body of an equable temperament has a dignity of its own by reason of its being remote from contraries, thereby resembling in a way a heavenly body.

Reply Obj. 3: The parts of an animal, for instance, the eye, hand, flesh, and bones, and so forth, do not make the species; but the whole does, and therefore, properly speaking, we cannot say that these are of different species, but that they are of various dispositions. This is suitable to the intellectual soul, which, although it be one in its essence, yet on account of its perfection, is manifold in power: and therefore, for its various operations it requires various dispositions in the parts of the body to which it is united. For this reason we observe that there is a greater variety of parts in perfect than in imperfect animals; and in these a greater variety than in plants.

Reply Obj. 4: The intellectual soul as comprehending universals, has a power extending to the infinite; therefore it cannot be limited by nature to certain fixed natural notions, or even to certain fixed means whether of defence or of clothing, as is the case with other animals, the souls of which are endowed with knowledge and power in regard to fixed particular things. Instead of all these, man has by nature his reason and his hands, which are "the organs of organs" (De Anima iii), since by their means man can make for himself instruments of an infinite variety, and for any number of purposes.

SIXTH ARTICLE [I, Q. 76, Art. 6]

Whether the Intellectual Soul Is United to the Body Through the Medium of Accidental Dispositions?

Objection 1: It would seem that the intellectual soul is united to the body through the medium of accidental dispositions. For every form exists in its proper disposed matter. But dispositions to a form are accidents. Therefore we must presuppose accidents to be in matter before the substantial form; and therefore before the soul, since the soul is a substantial form.

Obj. 2: Further, various forms of one species require various parts of matter. But various parts of matter are unintelligible without division in measurable quantities. Therefore we must suppose dimensions in matter before the substantial forms, which are many belonging to one species.

Obj. 3: Further, what is spiritual is connected with what is corporeal by virtual contact. But the virtue of the soul is its power. Therefore it seems that the soul is united to the body by means of a power, which is an accident.

*On the contrary,* Accident is posterior to substance, both in the order of time and in the order of reason, as the Philosopher says, Metaph. vii (Did. vi, 1). Therefore it is unintelligible that any accidental form exist in matter before the soul, which is the substantial form.

*I answer that,* If the soul were united to the body, merely as a motor, there would be nothing to prevent the existence of certain dispositions mediating between the soul and the body; *on the contrary,* they would be necessary, for on the part of the soul would be required the power to move the body; and on the part of the body, a certain aptitude to be moved by the soul.

If, however, the intellectual soul is united to the body as the substantial form, as we have already said above (A. 1), it is impossible for any accidental disposition to come between the body and the soul, or between any substantial form whatever and its matter. The reason is because since matter is in potentiality to all manner of acts in a certain order, what is absolutely first among the acts must be understood as being first in matter. Now the first among all acts is existence. Therefore, it is impossible for matter to be apprehended as hot, or as having quantity, before it is actual. But matter has actual existence by the substantial form, which makes it to exist absolutely, as we have said above (A. 4). Wherefore it is impossible for any accidental dispositions to pre-exist in matter before the substantial form, and consequently before the soul.

Reply Obj. 1: As appears from what has been already said (A. 4), the more perfect form virtually contains whatever belongs to the inferior forms; therefore while remaining one and the same, it perfects matter according to the various degrees of perfection. For the same essential form makes man an actual being, a body, a living being, an animal, and a man. Now it is clear that to every genus follow its own proper accidents. Therefore as matter is apprehended as perfected in its existence, before it is understood as corporeal, and so on; so those accidents which belong to existence are understood to exist before corporeity; and thus dispositions are understood in matter before the form, not as regards all its effects, but as regards the subsequent effect.

Reply Obj. 2: Dimensions of quantity are accidents consequent to the corporeity which belongs to the whole matter. Wherefore matter, once understood as corporeal and measurable, can be understood as distinct in its various parts, and as receptive of different forms according to the further degrees of perfection. For although it is essentially the same form which gives matter the various degrees of perfection, as we have said (ad 1), yet it is considered as different when brought under the observation of reason.

Reply Obj. 3: A spiritual substance which is united to a body as its motor only, is united thereto by power or virtue. But the intellectual soul is united by its very being to the body as a form; and yet it guides and moves the body by its power and virtue.

SEVENTH ARTICLE [I, Q. 76, Art. 7]

Whether the Soul Is United to the Animal Body by Means of a Body?

Objection 1: It seems that the soul is united to the animal body by means of a body. For Augustine says (Gen. ad lit. vii, 19), that "the soul administers the body by light," that is, by fire, "and by air, which is most akin to a spirit." But fire and air are bodies. Therefore the soul is united to the human body by means of a body.

Obj. 2: Further, a link between two things seems to be that thing the removal of which involves the cessation of their union. But when breathing ceases, the soul is separated from the body. Therefore the breath, which is a subtle body, is the means of union between soul and body.

Obj. 3: Further, things which are very distant from one another, are not united except by something between them. But the intellectual soul is very distant from the body, both because it is incorporeal, and because it is incorruptible. Therefore it seems to be united to the body by means of an incorruptible body, and such would be some heavenly light, which would harmonize the elements, and unite them together.

*On the contrary,* The Philosopher says (De Anima ii, 1): "We need not ask if the soul and body are one, as neither do we ask if wax and its shape are one." But the shape is united to the wax without a body intervening. Therefore also the soul is thus united to the body.

*I answer that,* If the soul, according to the Platonists, were united to the body merely as a motor, it would be right to say that some other bodies must intervene between the soul and body of man, or any animal whatever; for a motor naturally moves what is distant from it by means of something nearer.

If, however, the soul is united to the body as its form, as we have said (A. 1), it is impossible for it to be united by means of another body. The reason of this is that a thing is one, according as it is a being. Now the form, through itself, makes a thing to be actual since it is itself essentially an act; nor does it give existence by means of something else. Wherefore the unity of a thing composed of matter and form, is by virtue of the form itself, which by reason of its very nature is united to matter as its act. Nor is there any other cause of union except the agent, which causes matter to be in act, as the Philosopher says, *Metaph.* viii (Did. vii, 6).

From this it is clear how false are the opinions of those who maintained the existence of some mediate bodies between the soul and body of man. Of these certain Platonists said that the intellectual soul has an incorruptible body naturally united to it, from which it is never separated, and by means of which it is united to the corruptible body of man. Others said that the soul is united to the body by means of a corporeal spirit. Others said it is united to the body by means of light, which, they say, is a body and of the nature of the fifth essence; so that the vegetative soul would be united to the body by means of the light of the sidereal heaven; the sensible soul, by means of the light of the crystal heaven; and the intellectual soul by means of the light of the empyrean heaven. Now all this is fictitious and ridiculous: for light is not a body; and the fifth essence does not enter materially into the composition of a mixed body (since it is unchangeable), but only virtually: and lastly, because the soul is immediately united to the body as the form to matter.

Reply Obj. 1: Augustine speaks there of the soul as it moves the body; whence he uses the word "administration." It is true that it moves the grosser parts of the body by the more subtle parts. And the first instrument of the motive power is a kind of spirit, as the Philosopher says in De causa motus animalium (De mot. animal. x).

Reply Obj. 2: The union of soul and body ceases at the cessation of breath, not because this is the means of union, but because of the removal of that disposition by which the body is disposed for such a union. Nevertheless the breath is a means of moving, as the first instrument of motion.

Reply Obj. 3: The soul is indeed very distant from the body, if we consider the condition of each separately: so that if each had a separate existence, many means of connection would have to intervene. But inasmuch as the soul is the form of the body, it has not an existence apart from the existence of the body, but by its own existence is united to the body immediately. This is the case with every form which, if considered as an act, is very distant from matter, which is a being only in potentiality.

EIGHTH ARTICLE [I, Q. 76, Art. 8]

Whether the Soul Is in Each Part of the Body?

Objection 1: It would seem that the whole soul is not in each part of the body; for the Philosopher says in *De causa motus animalium* (De mot. animal. x): "It is not necessary for the soul to be in each part of the body; it suffices that it be in some principle of the body causing the other parts to live, for each part has a natural movement of its own."

Obj. 2: Further, the soul is in the body of which it is the act. But it is the act of an organic body. Therefore it exists only in an organic body. But each part of the human body is not an organic body. Therefore the whole soul is not in each part.

Obj. 3: Further, the Philosopher says (De Anima ii, 1) that the relation of a part of the soul to a part of the body, such as the sight to the pupil of the eye, is the same as the relation of the soul to the whole body of an animal. If, therefore, the whole soul is in each part of the body, it follows that each part of the body is an animal.

Obj. 4: Further, all the powers of the soul are rooted in the essence of the soul. If, therefore, the whole soul be in each part of the body, it follows that all the powers of the soul are in each part of the body; thus the sight will be in the ear, and hearing in the eye, and this is absurd.

Obj. 5: Further, if the whole soul is in each part of the body, each part of the body is immediately dependent on the soul. Thus one part would not depend on another; nor would one part be nobler than another; which is clearly untrue. Therefore the soul is not in each part of the body.

*On the contrary,* Augustine says (De Trin. vi, 6), that "in each body the whole soul is in the whole body, and in each part is entire."

*I answer that,* As we have said, if the soul were united to the body merely as its motor, we might say that it is not in each part of the body, but only in one part through which it would move the others. But since the soul is united to the body as its form, it must necessarily be in the whole body, and in each part thereof. For it is not an accidental form, but the substantial form of the body. Now the substantial form perfects not only the whole, but each part of the whole. For since a whole consists of parts, a form of the whole which does not give existence to each of the parts of the body, is a form consisting in composition and order, such as the form of a house; and such a form is accidental. But the soul is a substantial form; and therefore it must be the form and the act, not only of the whole, but also of each part. Therefore, on the withdrawal of the soul, as we do not speak of an animal or a man unless equivocally, as we speak of a painted animal or a stone animal; so is it with the hand, the eye, the flesh and bones, as the Philosopher says (De Anima ii, 1). A proof of which is, that on the withdrawal of the soul, no part of the body retains its proper action; although that which retains its species, retains the action of the species. But act is in that which it actuates: wherefore the soul must be in the whole body, and in each part thereof.

That it is entire in each part thereof, may be concluded from this, that since a whole is that which is divided into parts, there are three kinds of totality, corresponding to three kinds of division. There is a whole which is divided into parts of quantity, as a whole line, or a whole body. There is also a whole which is divided into logical and essential parts: as a thing defined is divided into the parts of a definition, and a composite into matter and form. There is, further, a third kind of whole which is potential, divided into virtual parts. The first kind of totality does not apply to forms, except perhaps accidentally; and then only to those forms, which have an indifferent relationship to a quantitative whole and its parts; as whiteness, as far as its essence is concerned, is equally disposed to be in the whole surface and in each part of the surface; and, therefore, the surface being divided, the whiteness is accidentally divided. But a form which requires variety in the parts, such as a soul, and specially the soul of perfect animals, is not equally related to the whole and the parts: hence it is not divided accidentally when the whole is divided. So therefore quantitative totality cannot be attributed to the soul, either essentially or accidentally. But the second kind of totality, which depends on logical and essential perfection, properly and essentially belongs to forms: and likewise the virtual totality, because a form is the principle of operation.

Therefore if it be asked whether the whole whiteness is in the whole surface and in each part thereof, it is necessary to distinguish. If we mean quantitative totality which whiteness has accidentally, then the whole whiteness is not in each part of the surface. The same is to be said of totality of power: since the whiteness which is in the whole surface moves the sight more than the whiteness which is in a small part thereof. But if we mean totality of species and essence, then the whole whiteness is in each part of a surface.

Since, however, the soul has not quantitative totality, neither essentially, nor accidentally, as we have seen; it is enough to say that the whole soul is in each part of the body, by totality of perfection and of essence, but not by totality of power. For it is not in each part of the body, with regard to each of its powers; but with regard to sight, it is in the eye; and with regard to hearing, it is in the ear; and so forth. We must observe, however, that since the soul requires variety of parts, its relation to the whole is not the same as its relation to the parts; for to the whole it is compared primarily and essentially, as to its proper and proportionate perfectible; but to the parts, secondarily, inasmuch as they are ordained to the whole.

Reply Obj. 1: The Philosopher is speaking there of the motive power of the soul.

Reply Obj. 2: The soul is the act of an organic body, as of its primary and proportionate perfectible.

Reply Obj. 3: An animal is that which is composed of a soul and a whole body, which is the soul's primary and proportionate perfectible. Thus the soul is not in a part. Whence it does not follow that a part of an animal is an animal.

Reply Obj. 4: Some of the powers of the soul are in it according as it exceeds the entire capacity of the body, namely the intellect and the will; whence these powers are not said to be in any part of the body. Other powers are common to the soul and body; wherefore each of these powers need not be wherever the soul is, but only in that part of the body, which is adapted to the operation of such a power.

Reply Obj. 5: One part of the body is said to be nobler than another, on account of the various powers, of which the parts of the body are the organs. For that part which is the organ of a nobler power, is a nobler part of the body: as also is that part which serves the same power in a nobler manner.

## QUESTION 77

OF THOSE THINGS WHICH BELONG TO THE POWERS OF THE SOUL IN GENERAL (In Eight Articles)

We proceed to consider those things which belong to the powers of the soul; first, in general, secondly, in particular. Under the first head there are eight points of inquiry:

(1) Whether the essence of the soul is its power?

(2) Whether there is one power of the soul, or several?

(3) How the powers of the soul are distinguished from one another?

(4) Of the orders of the powers, one to another;

(5) Whether the powers of the soul are in it as in their subject?

(6) Whether the powers flow from the essence of the soul?

(7) Whether one power rises from another?

(8) Whether all the powers of the soul remain in the soul after death?

FIRST ARTICLE [I, Q. 77, Art. 1]

Whether the Essence of the Soul Is Its Power?

Objection 1: It would seem that the essence of the soul is its power. For Augustine says (De Trin. ix, 4), that "mind, knowledge, and love are in the soul substantially, or, which is the same thing, essentially": and (De Trin. x, 11), that "memory, understanding, and will are one life, one mind, one essence."

Obj. 2: Further, the soul is nobler than primary matter. But primary matter is its own potentiality. Much more therefore is the soul its own power.

Obj. 3: Further, the substantial form is simpler than the accidental form; a sign of which is that the substantial form is not intensified or relaxed, but is indivisible. But the accidental form is its own power. Much more therefore is that substantial form which is the soul.

Obj. 4: Further, we sense by the sensitive power and we understand by the intellectual power. But "that by which we first sense and understand" is the soul, according to the Philosopher (De Anima ii, 2). Therefore the soul is its own power.

Obj. 5: Further, whatever does not belong to the essence is an accident. Therefore if the power of the soul is something else besides the essence thereof, it is an accident, which is contrary to Augustine, who says that the foregoing (see Obj. 1) "are not in the soul as in a subject as color or shape, or any other quality, or quantity, are in a body; for whatever is so, does not exceed the subject in which it is: Whereas the mind can love and know other things" (De Trin. ix, 4).

Obj. 6: Further, "a simple form cannot be a subject." But the soul is a simple form; since it is not composed of matter and form, as we have said above (Q. 75, A. 5). Therefore the power of the soul cannot be in it as in a subject.

Obj. 7: Further, an accident is not the principle of a substantial difference. But sensitive and rational are substantial differences; and they are taken from sense and reason, which are powers of the soul. Therefore the powers of the soul are not accidents; and so it would seem that the power of the soul is its own essence.

*On the contrary,* Dionysius (Coel. Hier. xi) says that "heavenly spirits are divided into essence, power, and operation." Much more, then, in the soul is the essence distinct from the virtue or power.

*I answer that,* It is impossible to admit that the power of the soul is its essence, although some have maintained it. For the present purpose this may be proved in two ways. First, because, since power and act divide being and every kind of being, we must refer a power and its act to the same genus. Therefore, if the act be not in the genus of substance, the power directed to that act cannot be in the genus of substance. Now the operation of the soul is not in the genus of substance; for this belongs to God alone, whose operation is His own substance. Wherefore the Divine power which is the principle of His operation is the Divine Essence itself. This cannot be true either of the soul, or of any creature; as we have said above when speaking of the angels (Q. 54, A. 3). Secondly, this may be also shown to be impossible in the soul. For the soul by its very essence is an act. Therefore if the very essence of the soul were the immediate principle of operation, whatever has a soul would always have actual vital actions, as that which has a soul is always an actually living thing. For as a form the soul is not an act ordained to a further act, but the ultimate term of generation. Wherefore, for it to be in potentiality to another act, does not belong to it according to its essence, as a form, but according to its power. So the soul itself, as the subject of its power, is called the first act, with a further relation to the second act. Now we observe that what has a soul is not always actual with respect to its vital operations; whence also it is said in the definition of the soul, that it is "the act of a body having life potentially"; which potentiality, however, "does not exclude the soul." Therefore it follows that the essence of the soul is not its power. For nothing is in potentiality by reason of an act, as act.

Reply Obj. 1: Augustine is speaking of the mind as it knows and loves itself. Thus knowledge and love as referred to the soul as known and loved, are substantially or essentially in the soul, for the very substance or essence of the soul is known and loved. In the same way are we to understand what he says in the other passage, that those things are "one life, one mind, one essence." Or, as some say, this passage is true in the sense in which the potential whole is predicated of its parts, being midway between the universal whole, and the integral whole. For the universal whole is in each part according to its entire essence and power; as animal in a man and in a horse; and therefore it is properly predicated of each part. But the integral whole is not in each part, neither according to its whole essence, nor according to its whole power. Therefore in no way can it be predicated of each part; yet in a way it is predicated, though improperly, of all the parts together; as if we were to say that the wall, roof, and foundations are a house. But the potential whole is in each part according to its whole essence, not, however, according to its whole power. Therefore in a way it can be predicated of each part, but not so properly as the universal whole. In this sense, Augustine says that the memory, understanding, and the will are the one essence of the soul.

Reply Obj. 2: The act to which primary matter is in potentiality is the substantial form. Therefore the potentiality of matter is nothing else but its essence.

Reply Obj. 3: Action belongs to the composite, as does existence; for to act belongs to what exists. Now the composite has substantial existence through the substantial form; and it operates by the power which results from the substantial form. Hence an active accidental form is to the substantial form of the agent (for instance, heat compared to the form of fire) as the power of the soul is to the soul.

Reply Obj. 4: That the accidental form is a principle of action is due to the substantial form. Therefore the substantial form is the first principle of action; but not the proximate principle. In this sense the Philosopher says that "the soul is that whereby we understand and sense."

Reply Obj. 5: If we take accident as meaning what is divided against substance, then there can be no medium between substance and accident; because they are divided by affirmation and negation, that is, according to existence in a subject, and non-existence in a subject. In this sense, as the power of the soul is not its essence, it must be an accident; and it belongs to the second species of accident, that of quality. But if we take accident as one of the five universals, in this sense there is a medium between substance and accident. For the substance is all that belongs to the essence of a thing; whereas whatever is beyond the essence of a thing cannot be called accident in this sense; but only what is not caused by the essential principle of the species. For the 'proper' does not belong to the essence of a thing, but is caused by the essential principles of the species; wherefore it is a medium between the essence and accident thus understood. In this sense the powers of the soul may be said to be a medium between substance and accident, as being natural properties of the soul. When Augustine says that knowledge and love are not in the soul as accidents in a subject, this must be understood in the sense given above, inasmuch as they are compared to the soul, not as loving and knowing, but as loved and known. His argument proceeds in this sense; for if love were in the soul loved as in a subject, it would follow that an accident transcends its subject, since even other things are loved through the soul.

Reply Obj. 6: Although the soul is not composed of matter and form, yet it has an admixture of potentiality, as we have said above (Q. 75, A. 5, ad 4); and for this reason it can be the subject of an accident. The statement quoted is verified in God, Who is the Pure Act; in treating of which subject Boethius employs that phrase (De Trin. i).

Reply Obj. 7: Rational and sensitive, as differences, are not taken from the powers of sense and reason, but from the sensitive and rational soul itself. But because substantial forms, which in themselves are unknown to us, are known by their accidents; nothing prevents us from sometimes substituting accidents for substantial differences.

SECOND ARTICLE [I, Q. 77, Art. 2]

Whether There Are Several Powers of the Soul?

Objection 1: It would seem that there are not several powers of the soul. For the intellectual soul approaches nearest to the likeness of God. But in God there is one simple power: and therefore also in the intellectual soul.

Obj. 2: Further, the higher a power is, the more unified it is. But the intellectual soul excels all other forms in power. Therefore above all others it has one virtue or power.

Obj. 3: Further, to operate belongs to what is in act. But by the one essence of the soul, man has actual existence in the different degrees of perfection, as we have seen above (Q. 76, AA. 3, 4). Therefore by the one power of the soul he performs operations of various degrees.

*On the contrary,* The Philosopher places several powers in the soul (De Anima ii, 2,3).

*I answer that,* Of necessity we must place several powers in the soul. To make this evident, we observe that, as the Philosopher says (De Coelo ii, 12), the lowest order of things cannot acquire perfect goodness, but they acquire a certain imperfect goodness, by few movements; and those which belong to a higher order acquire perfect goodness by many movements; and those yet higher acquire perfect goodness by few movements; and the highest perfection is found in those things which acquire perfect goodness without any movement whatever. Thus he is least of all disposed of health, who can only acquire imperfect health by means of a few remedies; better disposed is he who can acquire perfect health by means of many remedies; and better still, he who can by few remedies; best of all is he who has perfect health without any remedies. We conclude, therefore, that things which are below man acquire a certain limited goodness; and so they have a few determinate operations and powers. But man can acquire universal and perfect goodness, because he can acquire beatitude. Yet he is in the last degree, according to his nature, of those to whom beatitude is possible; therefore the human soul requires many and various operations and powers. But to angels a smaller variety of powers is sufficient. In God there is no power or action beyond His own Essence.

There is yet another reason why the human soul abounds in a variety of powers—because it is on the confines of spiritual and corporeal creatures; and therefore the powers of both meet together in the soul.

Reply Obj. 1: The intellectual soul approaches to the Divine likeness, more than inferior creatures, in being able to acquire perfect goodness; although by many and various means; and in this it falls short of more perfect creatures.

Reply Obj. 2: A unified power is superior if it extends to equal things: but a multiform power is superior to it, if it is over many things.

Reply Obj. 3: One thing has one substantial existence, but may have several operations. So there is one essence of the soul, with several powers.

THIRD ARTICLE [I, Q. 77, Art. 3]

Whether the Powers Are Distinguished by Their Acts and Objects?

Objection 1: It would seem that the powers of the soul are not distinguished by acts and objects. For nothing is determined to its species by what is subsequent and extrinsic to it. But the act is subsequent to the power; and the object is extrinsic to it. Therefore the soul's powers are not specifically distinct by acts and objects.

Obj. 2: Further, contraries are what differ most from each other. Therefore if the powers are distinguished by their objects, it follows that the same power could not have contrary objects. This is clearly false in almost all the powers; for the power of vision extends to white and black, and the power to taste to sweet and bitter.

Obj. 3: Further, if the cause be removed, the effect is removed. Hence if the difference of powers came from the difference of objects, the same object would not come under different powers. This is clearly false; for the same thing is known by the cognitive power, and desired by the appetitive.

Obj. 4: Further, that which of itself is the cause of anything, is the cause thereof, wherever it is. But various objects which belong to various powers, belong also to some one power; as sound and color belong to sight and hearing, which are different powers, yet they come under the one power of common sense. Therefore the powers are not distinguished according to the difference of their objects.

*On the contrary,* Things that are subsequent are distinguished by what precedes. But the Philosopher says (De Anima ii, 4) that "acts and operations precede the powers according to reason; and these again are preceded by their opposites," that is their objects. Therefore the powers are distinguished according to their acts and objects.

*I answer that,* A power as such is directed to an act. Wherefore we seek to know the nature of a power from the act to which it is directed, and consequently the nature of a power is diversified, as the nature of the act is diversified. Now the nature of an act is diversified according to the various natures of the objects. For every act is either of an active power or of a passive power. Now, the object is to the act of a passive power, as the principle and moving cause: for color is the principle of vision, inasmuch as it moves the sight. On the other hand, to the act of an active power the object is a term and end; as the object of the power of growth is perfect quantity, which is the end of growth. Now, from these two things an act receives its species, namely, from its principle, or from its end or term; for the act of heating differs from the act of cooling, in this, that the former proceeds from something hot, which is the active principle, to heat; the latter from something cold, which is the active principle, to cold. Therefore the powers are of necessity distinguished by their acts and objects.

Nevertheless, we must observe that things which are accidental do not change the species. For since to be colored is accidental to an animal, its species is not changed by a difference of color, but by a difference in that which belongs to the nature of an animal, that is to say, by a difference in the sensitive soul, which is sometimes rational, and sometimes otherwise. Hence "rational" and "irrational" are differences dividing animal, constituting its various species. In like manner therefore, not any variety of objects diversifies the powers of the soul, but a difference in that to which the power of its very nature is directed. Thus the senses of their very nature are directed to the passive quality which of itself is divided into color, sound, and the like, and therefore there is one sensitive power with regard to color, namely, the sight, and another with regard to sound, namely, hearing. But it is accidental to a passive quality, for instance, to something colored, to be a musician or a grammarian, great or small, a man or a stone. Therefore by reason of such differences the powers of the soul are not distinct.

Reply Obj. 1: Act, though subsequent in existence to power, is, nevertheless, prior to it in intention and logically; as the end is with regard to the agent. And the object, although extrinsic, is, nevertheless, the principle or end of the action; and those conditions which are intrinsic to a thing, are proportionate to its principle and end.

Reply Obj. 2: If any power were to have one of two contraries as such for its object, the other contrary would belong to another power. But the power of the soul does not regard the nature of the contrary as such, but rather the common aspect of both contraries; as sight does not regard white as such, but as color. This is because of two contraries one, in a manner, includes the idea of the other, since they are to one another as perfect and imperfect.

Reply Obj. 3: Nothing prevents things which coincide in subject, from being considered under different aspects; therefore they can belong to various powers of the soul.

Reply Obj. 4: The higher power of itself regards a more universal formality of the object than the lower power; because the higher a power is, to a greater number of things does it extend. Therefore many things are combined in the one formality of the object, which the higher power considers of itself; while they differ in the formalities regarded by the lower powers of themselves. Thus it is that various objects belong to various lower powers; which objects, however, are subject to one higher power.

FOURTH ARTICLE [I, Q. 77, Art. 4]

Whether Among the Powers of the Soul There Is Order?

Objection 1: It would seem that there is no order among the powers of the soul. For in those things which come under one division, there is no before and after, but all are naturally simultaneous. But the powers of the soul are contradistinguished from one another. Therefore there is no order among them.

Obj. 2: Further, the powers of the soul are referred to their objects and to the soul itself. On the part of the soul, there is not order among them, because the soul is one. In like manner the objects are various and dissimilar, as color and sound. Therefore there is no order among the powers of the soul.

Obj. 3: Further, where there is order among powers, we find that the operation of one depends on the operation of another. But the action of one power of the soul does not depend on that of another; for sight can act independently of hearing, and conversely. Therefore there is no order among the powers of the soul.

*On the contrary,* The Philosopher (De Anima ii, 3) compares the parts or powers of the soul to figures. But figures have an order among themselves. Therefore the powers of the soul have order.

*I answer that,* Since the soul is one, and the powers are many; and since a number of things that proceed from one must proceed in a certain order; there must be some order among the powers of the soul. Accordingly we may observe a triple order among them, two of which correspond to the dependence of one power on another; while the third is taken from the order of the objects. Now the dependence of one power on another can be taken in two ways; according to the order of nature, forasmuch as perfect things are by their nature prior to imperfect things; and according to the order of generation and time; forasmuch as from being imperfect, a thing comes to be perfect. Thus, according to the first kind of order among the powers, the intellectual powers are prior to the sensitive powers; wherefore they direct them and command them. Likewise the sensitive powers are prior in this order to the powers of the nutritive soul.

In the second kind of order, it is the other way about. For the powers of the nutritive soul are prior by way of generation to the powers of the sensitive soul; for which, therefore, they prepare the body. The same is to be said of the sensitive powers with regard to the intellectual. But in the third kind of order, certain sensitive powers are ordered among themselves, namely, sight, hearing, and smelling. For the visible naturally comes first; since it is common to higher and lower bodies. But sound is audible in the air, which is naturally prior to the mingling of elements, of which smell is the result.

Reply Obj. 1: The species of a given genus are to one another as before and after, like numbers and figures, if considered in their nature; although they may be said to be simultaneous, according as they receive the predication of the common genus.

Reply Obj. 2: This order among the powers of the soul is both on the part of the soul (which, though it be one according to its essence, has a certain aptitude to various acts in a certain order) and on the part of the objects, and furthermore on the part of the acts, as we have said above.

Reply Obj. 3: This argument is verified as regards those powers among which order of the third kind exists. Those powers among which the two other kinds of order exist are such that the action of one depends on another.

FIFTH ARTICLE [I, Q. 77, Art. 5]

Whether All the Powers of the Soul Are in the Soul As Their Subject?

Objection 1: It would seem that all the powers of the soul are in the soul as their subject. For as the powers of the body are to the body; so are the powers of the soul to the soul. But the body is the subject of the corporeal powers. Therefore the soul is the subject of the powers of the soul.

Obj. 2: Further, the operations of the powers of the soul are attributed to the body by reason of the soul; because, as the Philosopher says (De Anima ii, 2), "The soul is that by which we sense and understand primarily." But the natural principles of the operations of the soul are the powers. Therefore the powers are primarily in the soul.

Obj. 3: Further, Augustine says (Gen. ad lit. xii, 7,24) that the soul senses certain things, not through the body, in fact, without the body, as fear and such like; and some things through the body. But if the sensitive powers were not in the soul alone as their subject, the soul could not sense anything without the body. Therefore the soul is the subject of the sensitive powers; and for a similar reason, of all the other powers.

*On the contrary,* The Philosopher says (De Somno et Vigilia i) that "sensation belongs neither to the soul, nor to the body, but to the composite." Therefore the sensitive power is in "the composite" as its subject. Therefore the soul alone is not the subject of all the powers.

*I answer that,* The subject of operative power is that which is able to operate, for every accident denominates its proper subject. Now the same is that which is able to operate, and that which does operate. Wherefore the "subject of power" is of necessity "the subject of operation," as again the Philosopher says in the beginning of *De Somno et Vigilia.* Now, it is clear from what we have said above (Q. 75, AA. 2, 3; Q. 76, A. 1, ad 1), that some operations of the soul are performed without a corporeal organ, as understanding and will. Hence the powers of these operations are in the soul as their subject. But some operations of the soul are performed by means of corporeal organs; as sight by the eye, and hearing by the ear. And so it is with all the other operations of the nutritive and sensitive parts. Therefore the powers which are the principles of these operations have their subject in the composite, and not in the soul alone.

Reply Obj. 1: All the powers are said to belong to the soul, not as their subject, but as their principle; because it is by the soul that the composite has the power to perform such operations.

Reply Obj. 2: All such powers are primarily in the soul, as compared to the composite; not as in their subject, but as in their principle.

Reply Obj. 3: Plato's opinion was that sensation is an operation proper to the soul, just as understanding is. Now in many things relating to Philosophy Augustine makes use of the opinions of Plato, not asserting them as true, but relating them. However, as far as the present question is concerned, when it is said that the soul senses some things with the body, and some without the body, this can be taken in two ways. Firstly, the words "with the body or without the body" may determine the act of sense in its mode of proceeding from the sentient. Thus the soul senses nothing without the body, because the action of sensation cannot proceed from the soul except by a corporeal organ. Secondly, they may be understood as determining the act of sense on the part of the object sensed. Thus the soul senses some things with the body, that is, things existing in the body, as when it feels a wound or something of that sort; while it senses some things without the body, that is, which do not exist in the body, but only in the apprehension of the soul, as when it feels sad or joyful on hearing something.

SIXTH ARTICLE [I, Q. 77, Art. 6]

Whether the Powers of the Soul Flow from Its Essence?

Objection 1: It would seem that the powers of the soul do not flow from its essence. For different things do not proceed from one simple thing. But the essence of the soul is one and simple. Since, therefore, the powers of the soul are many and various, they cannot proceed from its essence.

Obj. 2: Further, that from which a thing proceeds is its cause. But the essence of the soul cannot be said to be the cause of the powers; as is clear if one considers the different kinds of causes. Therefore the powers of the soul do not flow from its essence.

Obj. 3: Further, emanation involves some sort of movement. But nothing is moved by itself, as the Philosopher proves (Phys. vii, 1,2); except, perhaps, by reason of a part of itself, as an animal is said to be moved by itself, because one part thereof moves and another is moved. Neither is the soul moved, as the Philosopher proves (De Anima i, 4). Therefore the soul does not produce its powers within itself.

*On the contrary,* The powers of the soul are its natural properties. But the subject is the cause of its proper accidents; whence also it is included in the definition of accident, as is clear from Metaph. vii (Did. vi, 4). Therefore the powers of the soul proceed from its essence as their cause.

*I answer that,* The substantial and the accidental form partly agree and partly differ. They agree in this, that each is an act; and that by each of them something is after a manner actual. They differ, however, in two respects. First, because the substantial form makes a thing to exist absolutely, and its subject is something purely potential. But the accidental form does not make a thing to exist absolutely but to be such, or so great, or in some particular condition; for its subject is an actual being. Hence it is clear that actuality is observed in the substantial form prior to its being observed in the subject: and since that which is first in a genus is the cause in that genus, the substantial form causes existence in its subject. On the other hand, actuality is observed in the subject of the accidental form prior to its being observed in the accidental form; wherefore the actuality of the accidental form is caused by the actuality of the subject. So the subject, forasmuch as it is in potentiality, is receptive of the accidental form: but forasmuch as it is in act, it produces it. This I say of the proper and *per se* accident; for with regard to the extraneous accident, the subject is receptive only, the accident being caused by an extrinsic agent. Secondly, substantial and accidental forms differ, because, since that which is the less principal exists for the sake of that which is the more principal, matter therefore exists on account of the substantial form; while *on the contrary,* the accidental form exists on account of the completeness of the subject.

Now it is clear, from what has been said (A. 5), that either the subject of the soul's powers is the soul itself alone, which can be the subject of an accident, forasmuch as it has something of potentiality, as we have said above (A. 1, ad 6); or else this subject is the composite. Now the composite is actual by the soul. Whence it is clear that all the powers of the soul, whether their subject be the soul alone, or the composite, flow from the essence of the soul, as from their principle; because it has already been said that the accident is caused by the subject according as it is actual, and is received into it according as it is in potentiality.

Reply Obj. 1: From one simple thing many things may proceed naturally, in a certain order; or again if there be diversity of recipients. Thus, from the one essence of the soul many and various powers proceed; both because order exists among these powers; and also by reason of the diversity of the corporeal organs.

Reply Obj. 2: The subject is both the final cause, and in a way the active cause, of its proper accident. It is also as it were the material cause, inasmuch as it is receptive of the accident. From this we may gather that the essence of the soul is the cause of all its powers, as their end, and as their active principle; and of some as receptive thereof.

Reply Obj. 3: The emanation of proper accidents from their subject is not by way of transmutation, but by a certain natural resultance; thus one thing results naturally from another, as color from light.

SEVENTH ARTICLE [I, Q. 77, Art. 7]

Whether One Power of the Soul Arises from Another?

Objection 1: It would seem that one power of the soul does not arise from another. For if several things arise together, one of them does not arise from another. But all the powers of the soul are created at the same time with the soul. Therefore one of them does not arise from another.

Obj. 2: Further, the power of the soul arises from the soul as an accident from the subject. But one power of the soul cannot be the subject of another; because nothing is the accident of an accident. Therefore one power does not arise from another.

Obj. 3: Further, one opposite does not arise from the other opposite; but everything arises from that which is like it in species. Now the powers of the soul are oppositely divided, as various species. Therefore one of them does not proceed from another.

*On the contrary,* Powers are known by their actions. But the action of one power is caused by the action of another power, as the action of the imagination by the action of the senses. Therefore one power of the soul is caused by another.

*I answer that,* In those things which proceed from one according to a natural order, as the first is the cause of all, so that which is nearer to the first is, in a way, the cause of those which are more remote. Now it has been shown above (A. 4) that among the powers of the soul there are several kinds of order. Therefore one power of the soul proceeds from the essence of the soul by the medium of another. But since the essence of the soul is compared to the powers both as a principle active and final, and as a receptive principle, either separately by itself, or together with the body; and since the agent and the end are more perfect, while the receptive principle, as such, is less perfect; it follows that those powers of the soul which precede the others, in the order of perfection and nature, are the principles of the others, after the manner of the end and active principle. For we see that the senses are for the sake of the intelligence, and not the other way about. The senses, moreover, are a certain imperfect participation of the intelligence; wherefore, according to their natural origin, they proceed from the intelligence as the imperfect from the perfect. But considered as receptive principles, the more perfect powers are principles with regard to the others; thus the soul, according as it has the sensitive power, is considered as the subject, and as something material with regard to the intelligence. On this account, the more imperfect powers precede the others in the order of generation, for the animal is generated before the man.

Reply Obj. 1: As the power of the soul flows from the essence, not by a transmutation, but by a certain natural resultance, and is simultaneous with the soul, so is it the case with one power as regards another.

Reply Obj. 2: An accident cannot of itself be the subject of an accident; but one accident is received prior to another into substance, as quantity prior to quality. In this sense one accident is said to be the subject of another; as surface is of color, inasmuch as substance receives an accident through the means of another. The same thing may be said of the powers of the soul.

Reply Obj. 3: The powers of the soul are opposed to one another, as perfect and imperfect; as also are the species of numbers and figures. But this opposition does not prevent the origin of one from another, because imperfect things naturally proceed from perfect things.

EIGHTH ARTICLE [I, Q. 77, Art. 8]

Whether All the Powers Remain in the Soul When Separated from the Body?

Objection 1: It would seem that all the powers of the soul remain in the soul separated from the body. For we read in the book *De Spiritu et Anima* that "the soul withdraws from the body, taking with itself sense and imagination, reason and intelligence, concupiscibility and irascibility."

Obj. 2: Further, the powers of the soul are its natural properties. But properties are always in that to which they belong; and are never separated from it. Therefore the powers of the soul are in it even after death.

Obj. 3: Further, the powers even of the sensitive soul are not weakened when the body becomes weak; because, as the Philosopher says (De Anima i, 4), "If an old man were given the eye of a young man, he would see even as well as a young man." But weakness is the road to corruption. Therefore the powers of the soul are not corrupted when the body is corrupted, but remain in the separated soul.

Obj. 4: Further, memory is a power of the sensitive soul, as the Philosopher proves (De Memor. et Remin. 1). But memory remains in the separated soul; for it was said to the rich glutton whose soul was in hell: "Remember that thou didst receive good things during thy lifetime" (Luke 16:25). Therefore memory remains in the separated soul; and consequently the other powers of the sensitive part.

Obj. 5: Further, joy and sorrow are in the concupiscible part, which is a power of the sensitive soul. But it is clear that separate souls grieve or rejoice at the pains or rewards which they receive. Therefore the concupiscible power remains in the separate soul.

Obj. 6: Further, Augustine says (Gen. ad lit. xii, 32) that, as the soul, when the body lies senseless, yet not quite dead, sees some things by imaginary vision; so also when by death the soul is quite separate from the body. But the imagination is a power of the sensitive part. Therefore the power of the sensitive part remains in the separate soul; and consequently all the other powers.

*On the contrary,* It is said (De Eccl. Dogm. xix) that "of two substances only does man consist; the soul with its reason, and the body with its senses." Therefore the body being dead, the sensitive powers do not remain.

*I answer that,* As we have said already (AA. 5, 6, 7), all the powers of the soul belong to the soul alone as their principle. But some powers belong to the soul alone as their subject; as the intelligence and the will. These powers must remain in the soul, after the destruction of the body. But other powers are subjected in the composite; as all the powers of the sensitive and nutritive parts. Now accidents cannot remain after the destruction of the subject. Wherefore, the composite being destroyed, such powers do not remain actually; but they remain virtually in the soul, as in their principle or root.

So it is false that, as some say, these powers remain in the soul even after the corruption of the body. It is much more false that, as they say also, the acts of these powers remain in the separate soul; because these powers have no act apart from the corporeal organ.

Reply Obj. 1: That book has no authority, and so what is there written can be despised with the same facility as it was said; although we may say that the soul takes with itself these powers, not actually but virtually.

Reply Obj. 2: These powers, which we say do not actually remain in the separate soul, are not the properties of the soul alone, but of the composite.

Reply Obj. 3: These powers are said not to be weakened when the body becomes weak, because the soul remains unchangeable, and is the virtual principle of these powers.

Reply Obj. 4: The recollection spoken of there is to be taken in the same way as Augustine (De Trin. x, 11; xiv, 7) places memory in the mind; not as a part of the sensitive soul.

Reply Obj. 5: In the separate soul, sorrow and joy are not in the sensitive, but in the intellectual appetite, as in the angels.

Reply Obj. 6: Augustine in that passage is speaking as inquiring, not as asserting. Wherefore he retracted some things which he had said there (Retrac. ii, 24).

# QUESTION 78

OF THE SPECIFIC POWERS OF THE SOUL (In Four Articles)

We next treat of the powers of the soul specifically. The theologian, however, has only to inquire specifically concerning the intellectual and appetitive powers, in which the virtues reside. And since the knowledge of these powers depends to a certain extent on the other powers, our consideration of the powers of the soul taken specifically will be divided into three parts: first, we shall consider those powers which are a preamble to the intellect; secondly, the intellectual powers; thirdly, the appetitive powers.

Under the first head there are four points of inquiry:

(1) The powers of the soul considered generally;
(2) The various species of the vegetative part;
(3) The exterior senses;
(4) The interior senses.

FIRST ARTICLE [I, Q. 78, Art. 1]

Whether There Are to Be Distinguished Five Genera of Powers in the Soul?

Objection 1: It would seem that there are not to

be distinguished five genera of powers in the soul—namely, vegetative, sensitive, appetitive, locomotive, and intellectual. For the powers of the soul are called its parts. But only three parts of the soul are commonly assigned—namely, the vegetative soul, the sensitive soul, and the rational soul. Therefore there are only three genera of powers in the soul, and not five.

Obj. 2: Further, the powers of the soul are the principles of its vital operations. Now, in four ways is a thing said to live. For the Philosopher says (De Anima ii, 2): "In several ways a thing is said to live, and even if only one of these is present, the thing is said to live; as intellect and sense, local movement and rest, and lastly, movement of decrease and increase due to nourishment." Therefore there are only four genera of powers of the soul, as the appetitive is excluded.

Obj. 3: Further, a special kind of soul ought not to be assigned as regards what is common to all the powers. Now desire is common to each power of the soul. For sight desires an appropriate visible object; whence we read (Ecclus. 40:22): "The eye desireth favor and beauty, but more than these green sown fields." In the same way every other power desires its appropriate object. Therefore the appetitive power should not be made a special genus of the powers of the soul.

Obj. 4: Further, the moving principle in animals is sense, intellect or appetite, as the Philosopher says (De Anima iii, 10). Therefore the motive power should not be added to the above as a special genus of soul.

*On the contrary,* The Philosopher says (De Anima ii, 3), "The powers are the vegetative, the sensitive, the appetitive, the locomotion, and the intellectual."

*I answer that,* There are five genera of powers of the soul, as above numbered. Of these, three are called souls, and four are called modes of living. The reason of this diversity lies in the various souls being distinguished accordingly as the operation of the soul transcends the operation of the corporeal nature in various ways; for the whole corporeal nature is subject to the soul, and is related to it as its matter and instrument. There exists, therefore, an operation of the soul which so far exceeds the corporeal nature that it is not even performed by any corporeal organ; and such is the operation of the *rational soul.* Below this, there is another operation of the soul, which is indeed performed through a corporeal organ, but not through a corporeal quality, and this is the operation of the *sensitive soul;* for though hot and cold, wet and dry, and other such corporeal qualities are required for the work of the senses, yet they are not required in such a way that the operation of the senses takes place by virtue of such qualities; but only for the proper disposition of the organ. The lowest of the operations of the soul is that which is performed by a corporeal organ, and by virtue of a corporeal quality. Yet this transcends the operation of the corporeal nature; because the movements of bodies are caused by an extrinsic principle, while these operations are from an intrinsic principle; for this is common to all the operations of the soul; since every animate thing, in some way, moves itself. Such is the operation of the vegetative soul; for digestion, and what follows, is caused instrumentally by the action of heat, as the Philosopher says (De Anima ii, 4).

Now the powers of the soul are distinguished generically by their objects. For the higher a power is, the more universal is the object to which it extends, as we have said above (Q. 77, A. 3, ad 4). But the object of the soul's operation may be considered in a triple order. For in the soul there is a power the object of which is only the body that is united to that soul; the powers of this genus are called "vegetative" for the vegetative power acts only on the body to which the soul is united. There is another genus in the powers of the soul, which genus regards a more universal object—namely, every sensible body, not only the body to which the soul is united. And there is yet another genus in the powers of the soul, which genus regards a still more universal object—namely, not only the sensible body, but all being in universal. Wherefore it is evident that the latter two genera of the soul's powers have an operation in regard not merely to that which is united to them, but also to something extrinsic. Now, since whatever operates must in some way be united to the object about which it operates, it follows of necessity that this something extrinsic, which is the object of the soul's operation, must be related to the soul in a twofold manner. First, inasmuch as this something extrinsic has a natural aptitude to be united to the soul, and to be by its likeness in the soul. In this way there are two kinds of powers—namely, the "sensitive" in regard to the less common object—the sensible body; and the "intellectual," in regard to the most common object—universal being. Secondly, forasmuch as the soul itself has an inclination and tendency to the something extrinsic. And in this way there are again two kinds of powers in the soul: one—the "appetitive"—in respect of which the soul is referred to something extrinsic as to an end, which is first in the intention; the other—the "locomotive" power—in respect of which the soul is referred to something extrinsic as to the term of its operation and movement; for every animal is moved for the purpose of realizing its desires and intentions.

The modes of living are distinguished according to the degrees of living things. There are some living things in which there exists only vegetative power, as the plants. There are others in which with the vegetative there exists also the sensitive, but not the locomotive power; such as immovable animals, as shellfish. There are others which besides this have locomotive powers, as perfect animals, which require many things for their life, and consequently movement to seek necessaries of life from a distance. And there are some living things which with these have intellectual power—namely, men. But the appetitive power does not constitute a degree of living things; because wherever there is sense there is also appetite (De Anima ii, 3).

Thus the first two objections are hereby solved.

Reply Obj. 3: The "natural appetite" is that inclination which each thing has, of its own nature, for something; wherefore by its natural appetite each power desires something suitable to itself. But the "animal appetite" results from the form apprehended; this sort of appetite requires a special power of the soul—mere apprehension does not suffice. For a thing is desired as it exists in its own nature, whereas in the apprehensive power it exists not according to its own nature, but according to its likeness. Whence it is clear that sight desires naturally a visible object for the purpose of its act only—namely, for the purpose of seeing; but the animal by the appetitive power desires the thing seen, not merely for the purpose of seeing it, but also for other purposes. But if the soul did not require things perceived by the senses, except on account of the actions of the senses, that is, for the purpose of sensing them; there would be no need for a special genus of appetitive powers, since the natural appetite of the powers would suffice.

Reply Obj. 4: Although sense and appetite are principles of movement in perfect animals, yet sense and appetite, as such, are not sufficient to cause movement, unless another power be added to them; for immovable animals have sense and appetite, and yet they have not the power of motion. Now this motive power is not only in the appetite and sense as commanding the movement, but also in the parts of the body, to make them obey the appetite of the soul which moves them. Of this we have a sign in the fact that when the members are deprived of their natural disposition, they do not move in obedience to the appetite.

SECOND ARTICLE [I, Q. 78, Art. 2]

Whether the Parts of the Vegetative Soul Are Fittingly Described As the Nutritive, Augmentative, and Generative?

Objection 1: It would seem that the parts of the vegetative soul are not fittingly described—namely, the nutritive, augmentative, and generative. For these are called "natural" forces. But the powers of the soul are above the natural forces. Therefore we should not class the above forces as powers of the soul.

Obj. 2: Further, we should not assign a particular power of the soul to that which is common to living and non-living things. But generation is common to all things that can be generated and corrupted, whether living or not living. Therefore the generative force should not be classed as a power of the soul.

Obj. 3: Further, the soul is more powerful than the body. But the body by the same force gives species and quantity; much more, therefore, does the soul. Therefore the augmentative power of the soul is not distinct from the generative power.

Obj. 4: Further, everything is preserved in being by that whereby it exists. But the generative power is that whereby a living thing exists. Therefore by the same power the living thing is preserved. Now the nutritive force is directed to the preservation of the living thing (De Anima ii, 4), being "a power which is capable of preserving whatever receives it." Therefore we should not distinguish the nutritive power from the generative.

*On the contrary,* The Philosopher says (De Anima ii, 2,4) that the operations of this soul are "generation, the use of food," and (cf. De Anima iii, 9) "growth."

*I answer that,* The vegetative part has three powers. For the vegetative part, as we have said (A. 1), has for its object the body itself, living by the soul; for which body a triple operation of the soul is required. One is whereby it acquires existence, and to this is directed the *generative* power. Another is whereby the living body acquires its due quantity; to this is directed the *augmentative* power. Another is whereby the body of a living thing is preserved in its existence and in its due quantity; to this is directed the *nutritive* power.

We must, however, observe a difference among these powers. The nutritive and the augmentative have their effect where they exist, since the body itself united to the soul grows and is preserved by the augmentative and nutritive powers which exist in one and the same soul. But the generative power has its effect, not in one and the same body but in another; for a thing cannot generate itself. Therefore the generative power, in a way, approaches to the dignity of the sensitive soul, which has an operation extending to extrinsic things, although in a more excellent and more universal manner; for that which is highest in an inferior nature approaches to that which is lowest in the higher nature, as is made clear by Dionysius (Div. Nom. vii). Therefore, of these three powers, the generative has the greater finality, nobility, and perfection, as the Philosopher says (De Anima ii, 4), for it belongs to a thing which is already perfect to "produce another like unto itself." And the generative power is served by the augmentative and nutritive powers; and the augmentative power by the nutritive.

Reply Obj. 1: Such forces are called natural, both because they produce an effect like that of nature, which also gives existence, quantity and preservation (although the above forces accomplish these things in a more perfect way); and because those forces perform their actions instrumentally, through the active and passive qualities, which are the principles of natural actions.

Reply Obj. 2: Generation of inanimate things is

entirely from an extrinsic source; whereas the generation of living things is in a higher way, through something in the living thing itself, which is the semen containing the principle productive of the body. Therefore there must be in the living thing a power that prepares this semen; and this is the generative power.

Reply Obj. 3: Since the generation of living things is from a semen, it is necessary that in the beginning an animal of small size be generated. For this reason it must have a power in the soul, whereby it is brought to its appropriate size. But the inanimate body is generated from determinate matter by an extrinsic agent; therefore it receives at once its nature and its quantity, according to the condition of the matter.

Reply Obj. 4: As we have said above (A. 1), the operation of the vegetative principle is performed by means of heat, the property of which is to consume humidity. Therefore, in order to restore the humidity thus lost, the nutritive power is required, whereby the food is changed into the substance of the body. This is also necessary for the action of the augmentative and generative powers.

THIRD ARTICLE [I, Q. 78, Art. 3]

Whether the Five Exterior Senses Are Properly Distinguished?

Objection 1: It would seem inaccurate to distinguish five exterior senses. For sense can know accidents. But there are many kinds of accidents. Therefore, as powers are distinguished by their objects, it seems that the senses are multiplied according to the number of the kinds of accidents.

Obj. 2: Further, magnitude and shape, and other things which are called "common sensibles," are "not sensibles by accident," but are contradistinguished from them by the Philosopher (De Anima ii, 6). Now the diversity of objects, as such, diversifies the powers. Since, therefore, magnitude and shape are further from color than sound is, it seems that there is much more need for another sensitive power than can grasp magnitude or shape than for that which grasps color or sound.

Obj. 3: Further, one sense regards one contrariety; as sight regards white and black. But the sense of touch grasps several contraries; such as hot or cold, damp or dry, and suchlike. Therefore it is not a single sense but several. Therefore there are more than five senses.

Obj. 4: Further, a species is not divided against its genus. But taste is a kind of touch. Therefore it should not be classed as a distinct sense of touch.

*On the contrary,* The Philosopher says (De Anima iii, 1): "There is no other besides the five senses."

*I answer that,* The reason of the distinction and number of the senses has been assigned by some to the organs in which one or other of the elements preponderate, as water, air, or the like. By others it has been assigned to the medium, which is either in conjunction or extrinsic and is either water or air, or such like. Others have ascribed it to the various natures of the sensible qualities, according as such quality belongs to a simple body or results from complexity. But none of these explanations is apt. For the powers are not for the organs, but the organs for the powers; wherefore there are not various powers for the reason that there are various organs; *on the contrary,* for this has nature provided a variety of organs, that they might be adapted to various powers. In the same way nature provided various mediums for the various senses, according to the convenience of the acts of the powers. And to be cognizant of the natures of sensible qualities does not pertain to the senses, but to the intellect.

The reason of the number and distinction of the exterior senses must therefore be ascribed to that which belongs to the senses properly and *per se.* Now, sense is a passive power, and is naturally immuted by the exterior sensible. Wherefore the exterior cause of such immutation is what is per se perceived by the sense, and according to the diversity of that exterior cause are the sensitive powers diversified.

Now, immutation is of two kinds, one natural, the other spiritual. Natural immutation takes place by the form of the immuter being received according to its natural existence, into the thing immuted, as heat is received into the thing heated. Whereas spiritual immutation takes place by the form of the immuter being received, according to a spiritual mode of existence, into the thing immuted, as the form of color is received into the pupil which does not thereby become colored. Now, for the operation of the senses, a spiritual immutation is required, whereby an intention of the sensible form is effected in the sensile organ. Otherwise, if a natural immutation alone sufficed for the sense's action, all natural bodies would feel when they undergo alteration.

But in some senses we find spiritual immutation only, as in *sight:* while in others we find not only spiritual but also a natural immutation; either on the part of the object only, or likewise on the part of the organ. On the part of the object we find natural immutation, as to place, in sound which is the object of *hearing;* for sound is caused by percussion and commotion of air: and we find natural immutation by alteration, in odor which is the object of *smelling;* for in order to exhale an odor, a body must be in a measure affected by heat. On the part of an organ, natural immutation takes place in *touch* and taste; for the hand that touches something hot becomes hot, while the tongue is moistened by the humidity of the flavored morsel. But the organs of smelling and hearing are not affected in their respective operations by any natural immutation unless indirectly.

Now, the sight, which is without natural immutation either in its organ or in its object, is the most spiritual, the most perfect, and the most universal of all the senses. After this comes the hearing and then the smell, which require a natural immutation on the part of the object; while local motion is more perfect than, and naturally prior to, the motion of alteration, as the Philosopher proves (Phys. viii, 7). Touch and taste are the most material of all: of the distinction of which we shall speak later on (ad 3, 4). Hence it is that the three other senses are not exercised through a medium united to them, to obviate any natural immutation in their organ; as happens as regards these two senses.

Reply Obj. 1: Not every accident has in itself a power of immutation but only qualities of the third species, which are the principles of alteration: therefore only suchlike qualities are the objects of the senses; because "the senses are affected by the same things whereby inanimate bodies are affected," as stated in Phys. vii, 2.

Reply Obj. 2: Size, shape, and the like, which are called "common sensibles," are midway between "accidental sensibles" and "proper sensibles," which are the objects of the senses. For the proper sensibles first, and of their very nature, affect the senses; since they are qualities that cause alteration. But the common sensibles are all reducible to quantity. As to size and number, it is clear that they are species of quantity. Shape is a quality about quantity, since the notion of shape consists of fixing the bounds of magnitude. Movement and rest are sensed according as the subject is affected in one or more ways in the magnitude of the subject or of its local distance, as in the movement of growth or of locomotion, or again, according as it is affected in some sensible qualities, as in the movement of alteration; and thus to sense movement and rest is, in a way, to sense one thing and many. Now quantity is the proximate subject of the qualities that cause alteration, as surface is of color. Therefore the common sensibles do not move the senses first and of their own nature, but by reason of the sensible quality; as the surface by reason of color. Yet they are not accidental sensibles, for they produce a certain variety in the immutation of the senses. For sense is immuted differently by a large and by a small surface: since whiteness itself is said to be great or small, and therefore it is divided according to its proper subject.

Reply Obj. 3: As the Philosopher seems to say (De Anima ii, 11), the sense of touch is generically one, but is divided into several specific senses, and for this reason it extends to various contrarieties; which senses, however, are not separate from one another in their organ, but are spread throughout the whole body, so that their distinction is not evident. But taste, which perceives the sweet and the bitter, accompanies touch in the tongue, but not in the whole body; so it is easily distinguished from touch. We might also say that all those contrarieties agree, each in some proximate genus, and all in a common genus, which is the common and formal object of touch. Such common genus is, however, unnamed, just as the proximate genus of hot and cold is unnamed.

Reply Obj. 4: The sense of taste, according to a saying of the Philosopher (De Anima ii, 9), is a kind of touch existing in the tongue only. It is not distinct from touch in general, but only from the species of touch distributed in the body. But if touch is one sense only, on account of the common formality of its object: we must say that taste is distinguished from touch by reason of a different formality of immutation. For touch involves a natural, and not only a spiritual, immutation in its organ, by reason of the quality which is its proper object. But the organ of taste is not necessarily immuted by a natural immutation by reason of the quality which is its proper object, so that the tongue itself becomes sweet and bitter: but by reason of a quality which is a preamble to, and on which is based, the flavor, which quality is moisture, the object of touch.

FOURTH ARTICLE [I, Q. 78, Art. 4]

Whether the Interior Senses Are Suitably Distinguished?

Objection 1: It would seem that the interior senses are not suitably distinguished. For the common is not divided against the proper. Therefore the common sense should not be numbered among the interior sensitive powers, in addition to the proper exterior senses.

Obj. 2: Further, there is no need to assign an interior power of apprehension when the proper and exterior sense suffices. But the proper and exterior senses suffice for us to judge of sensible things; for each sense judges of its proper object. In like manner they seem to suffice for the perception of their own actions; for since the action of the sense is, in a way, between the power and its object, it seems that sight must be much more able to perceive its own vision, as being nearer to it, than the color; and in like manner with the other senses. Therefore for this there is no need to assign an interior power, called the common sense.

Obj. 3: Further, according to the Philosopher (De Memor. et Remin. i), the imagination and the memory are passions of the "first sensitive." But passion is not divided against its subject. Therefore memory and imagination should not be assigned as powers distinct from the senses.

Obj. 4: Further, the intellect depends on the senses less than any power of the sensitive part. But the intellect knows nothing but what it receives from the senses; whence we read (Poster. i, 8), that "those who lack one sense lack one kind of knowledge." Therefore much less should we assign to the sensitive part a power, which they call the "estimative" power, for the perception of intentions which the sense does not perceive.

Obj. 5: Further, the action of the cogitative power, which consists in comparing, adding and dividing, and the action of the reminiscence, which consists in the use of a kind of syllogism for the sake of inquiry, is not less distant from the actions of the estimative and memorative powers, than the action of the estimative is from the action of the imagination. Therefore either we must add the cognitive and reminiscitive to the estimative and memorative powers, or the estimative and memorative powers should not be made distinct from the imagination.

Obj. 6: Further, Augustine (Gen. ad lit. xii, 6, 7, 24) describes three kinds of vision; namely, corporeal, which is the action of the sense; spiritual, which is an action of the imagination or phantasy; and intellectual, which is an action of the intellect. Therefore there is no interior power between the sense and intellect, besides the imagination.

*On the contrary,* Avicenna (De Anima iv, 1) assigns five interior sensitive powers; namely, "common sense, phantasy, imagination, and the estimative and memorative powers."

*I answer that,* As nature does not fail in necessary things, there must needs be as many actions of the sensitive soul as may suffice for the life of a perfect animal. If any of these actions cannot be reduced to the same one principle, they must be assigned to diverse powers; since a power of the soul is nothing else than the proximate principle of the soul's operation.

Now we must observe that for the life of a perfect animal, the animal should apprehend a thing not only at the actual time of sensation, but also when it is absent. Otherwise, since animal motion and action follow apprehension, an animal would not be moved to seek something absent: the contrary of which we may observe specially in perfect animals, which are moved by progression, for they are moved towards something apprehended and absent. Therefore an animal through the sensitive soul must not only receive the species of sensible things, when it is actually affected by them, but it must also retain and preserve them. Now to receive and retain are, in corporeal things, reduced to diverse principles; for moist things are apt to receive, but retain with difficulty, while it is the reverse with dry things. Wherefore, since the sensitive power is the act of a corporeal organ, it follows that the power which receives the species of sensible things must be distinct from the power which preserves them.

Again we must observe that if an animal were moved by pleasing and disagreeable things only as affecting the sense, there would be no need to suppose that an animal has a power besides the apprehension of those forms which the senses perceive, and in which the animal takes pleasure, or from which it shrinks with horror. But the animal needs to seek or to avoid certain things, not only because they are pleasing or otherwise to the senses, but also on account of other advantages and uses, or disadvantages: just as the sheep runs away when it sees a wolf, not on account of its color or shape, but as a natural enemy: and again a bird gathers together straws, not because they are pleasant to the sense, but because they are useful for building its nest. Animals, therefore, need to perceive such intentions, which the exterior sense does not perceive. And some distinct principle is necessary for this; since the perception of sensible forms comes by an immutation caused by the sensible, which is not the case with the perception of those intentions.

Thus, therefore, for the reception of sensible forms, the "proper sense" and the *common sense* are appointed, and of their distinction we shall speak farther on (ad 1, 2). But for the retention and preservation of these forms, the "phantasy" or "imagination" is appointed; which are the same, for phantasy or imagination is as it were a storehouse of forms received through the senses. Furthermore, for the apprehension of intentions which are not received through the senses, the "estimative" power is appointed: and for the preservation thereof, the "memorative" power, which is a storehouse of such-like intentions. A sign of which we have in the fact that the principle of memory in animals is found in some such intention, for instance, that something is harmful or otherwise. And the very formality of the past, which memory observes, is to be reckoned among these intentions.

Now, we must observe that as to sensible forms there is no difference between man and other animals; for they are similarly immuted by the extrinsic sensible. But there is a difference as to the above intentions: for other animals perceive these intentions only by some natural instinct, while man perceives them by means of coalition of ideas. Therefore the power by which in other animals is called the natural estimative, in man is called the "cogitative," which by some sort of collation discovers these intentions. Wherefore it is also called the "particular reason," to which medical men assign a certain particular organ, namely, the middle part of the head: for it compares individual intentions, just as the intellectual reason compares universal intentions. As to the memorative power, man has not only memory, as other animals have in the sudden recollection of the past; but also "reminiscence" by syllogistically, as it were, seeking for a recollection of the past by the application of individual intentions. Avicenna, however, assigns between the estimative and the imaginative, a fifth power, which combines and divides imaginary forms: as when from the imaginary form of gold, and imaginary form of a mountain, we compose the one form of a golden mountain, which we have never seen. But this operation is not to be found in animals other than man, in whom the imaginative power suffices thereto. To man also does Averroes attribute this action in his book *De sensu et sensibilibus* (viii). So there is no need to assign more than four interior powers of the sensitive part—namely, the common sense, the imagination, and the estimative and memorative powers.

Reply Obj. 1: The interior sense is called "common" not by predication, as if it were a genus; but as the common root and principle of the exterior senses.

Reply Obj. 2: The proper sense judges of the proper sensible by discerning it from other things which come under the same sense; for instance, by discerning white from black or green. But neither sight nor taste can discern white from sweet: because what discerns between two things must know both. Wherefore the discerning judgment must be assigned to the common sense; to which, as to a common term, all apprehensions of the senses must be referred: and by which, again, all the intentions of the senses are perceived; as when someone sees that he sees. For this cannot be done by the proper sense, which only knows the form of the sensible by which it is immuted, in which immutation the action of sight is completed, and from immutation follows another in the common sense which perceives the act of vision.

Reply Obj. 3: As one power arises from the soul by means of another, as we have seen above (Q. 77, A. 7), so also the soul is the subject of one power through another. In this way the imagination and the memory are called passions of the "first sensitive."

Reply Obj. 4: Although the operation of the intellect has its origin in the senses: yet, in the thing apprehended through the senses, the intellect knows many things which the senses cannot perceive. In like manner does the estimative power, though in a less perfect manner.

Reply Obj. 5: The cogitative and memorative powers in man owe their excellence not to that which is proper to the sensitive part; but to a certain affinity and proximity to the universal reason, which, so to speak, overflows into them. Therefore they are not distinct powers, but the same, yet more perfect than in other animals.

Reply Obj. 6: Augustine calls that vision spiritual which is effected by the images of bodies in the absence of bodies. Whence it is clear that it is common to all interior apprehensions.

# QUESTION 79

OF THE INTELLECTUAL POWERS (In Thirteen Articles)

The next question concerns the intellectual powers, under which head there are thirteen points of inquiry:

(1) Whether the intellect is a power of the soul, or its essence?

(2) If it be a power, whether it is a passive power?

(3) If it is a passive power, whether there is an active intellect?

(4) Whether it is something in the soul?

(5) Whether the active intellect is one in all?

(6) Whether memory is in the intellect?

(7) Whether the memory be distinct from the intellect?

(8) Whether the reason is a distinct power from the intellect?

(9) Whether the superior and inferior reason are distinct powers?

(10) Whether the intelligence is distinct from the intellect?

(11) Whether the speculative and practical intellect are distinct powers?

(12) Whether "synderesis" is a power of the intellectual part?

(13) Whether the conscience is a power of the intellectual part?

FIRST ARTICLE [I, Q. 79, Art. 1]

Whether the Intellect Is a Power of the Soul?

Objection 1: It would seem that the intellect is not a power of the soul, but the essence of the soul. For the intellect seems to be the same as the mind. Now the mind is not a power of the soul, but the essence; for Augustine says (De Trin. ix, 2): "Mind and spirit are not relative things, but denominate the essence." Therefore the intellect is the essence of the soul.

Obj. 2: Further, different genera of the soul's powers are not united in some one power, but only in the essence of the soul. Now the appetitive and the intellectual are different genera of the soul's powers as the Philosopher says (De Anima ii, 3), but they are united in the mind, for Augustine (De Trin. x, 11) places the intelligence and will in the mind. Therefore the mind and intellect of man is of the very essence of the soul and not a power thereof.

Obj. 3: Further, according to Gregory, in a homily for the Ascension (xxix in Ev.), "man understands with the angels." But angels are called "minds" and "intellects." Therefore the mind and intellect of man are not a power of the soul, but the soul itself.

Obj. 4: Further, a substance is intellectual by the fact that it is immaterial. But the soul is immaterial through its essence. Therefore it seems that the soul must be intellectual through its essence.

*On the contrary,* The Philosopher assigns the intellectual faculty as a power of the soul (De Anima ii, 3).

*I answer that,* In accordance with what has been already shown (Q. 54, A. 3; Q. 77, A. 1) it is necessary to say that the intellect is a power of the soul, and not the very essence of the soul. For then alone the essence of that which operates is the immediate principle of operation, when operation itself is its being: for as power is to operation as its act, so is the essence to being. But in God alone His action of understanding is His very Being. Wherefore in

God alone is His intellect His essence: while in other intellectual creatures, the intellect is a power.

Reply Obj. 1: Sense is sometimes taken for the power, and sometimes for the sensitive soul; for the sensitive soul takes its name from its chief power, which is sense. And in like manner the intellectual soul is sometimes called intellect, as from its chief power; and thus we read (De Anima i, 4), that the "intellect is a substance." And in this sense also Augustine says that the mind is spirit and essence (De Trin. ix, 2; xiv, 16).

Reply Obj. 2: The appetitive and intellectual powers are different genera of powers in the soul, by reason of the different formalities of their objects. But the appetitive power agrees partly with the intellectual power and partly with the sensitive in its mode of operation either through a corporeal organ or without it: for appetite follows apprehension. And in this way Augustine puts the will in the mind; and the Philosopher, in the reason (De Anima iii, 9).

Reply Obj. 3: In the angels there is no other power besides the intellect, and the will, which follows the intellect. And for this reason an angel is called a "mind" or an "intellect"; because his whole power consists in this. But the soul has many other powers, such as the sensitive and nutritive powers, and therefore the comparison fails.

Reply Obj. 4: The immateriality of the created intelligent substance is not its intellect; and through its immateriality it has the power of intelligence. Wherefore it follows not that the intellect is the substance of the soul, but that it is its virtue and power.

SECOND ARTICLE [I, Q. 79, Art. 2]

Whether the Intellect Is a Passive Power?

Objection 1: It would seem that the intellect is not a passive power. For everything is passive by its matter, and acts by its form. But the intellectual power results from the immateriality of the intelligent substance. Therefore it seems that the intellect is not a passive power.

Obj. 2: Further, the intellectual power is incorruptible, as we have said above (Q. 79, A. 6). But "if the intellect is passive, it is corruptible" (De Anima iii, 5). Therefore the intellectual power is not passive.

Obj. 3: Further, the "agent is nobler than the patient," as Augustine (Gen. ad lit. xii, 16) and Aristotle (De Anima iii, 5) says. But all the powers of the vegetative part are active; yet they are the lowest among the powers of the soul. Much more, therefore, all the intellectual powers, which are the highest, are active.

*On the contrary,* The Philosopher says (De Anima iii, 4) that "to understand is in a way to be passive."

*I answer that,* To be passive may be taken in three ways. Firstly, in its most strict sense, when from a thing is taken something which belongs to it by virtue either of its nature, or of its proper inclination: as when water loses coolness by heating, and as when a man becomes ill or sad. Secondly, less strictly, a thing is said to be passive, when something, whether suitable or unsuitable, is taken away from it. And in this way not only he who is ill is said to be passive, but also he who is healed; not only he that is sad, but also he that is joyful; or whatever way he be altered or moved. Thirdly, in a wide sense a thing is said to be passive, from the very fact that what is in potentiality to something receives that to which it was in potentiality, without being deprived of anything. And accordingly, whatever passes from potentiality to act, may be said to be passive, even when it is perfected. And thus with us to understand is to be passive. This is clear from the following reason. For the intellect, as we have seen above (Q. 78, A. 1), has an operation extending to universal being. We may therefore see whether the intellect be in act or potentiality by observing first of all the nature of the relation of the intellect to universal being. For we find an intellect whose relation to universal being is that of the act of all being: and such is the Divine intellect, which is the Essence of God, in which originally and virtually, all being pre-exists as in its first cause. And therefore the Divine intellect is not in potentiality, but is pure act. But no created intellect can be an act in relation to the whole universal being; otherwise it would needs be an infinite being. Wherefore every created intellect is not the act of all things intelligible, by reason of its very existence; but is compared to these intelligible things as a potentiality to act.

Now, potentiality has a double relation to act. There is a potentiality which is always perfected by its act: as the matter of the heavenly bodies (Q. 58, A. 1). And there is another potentiality which is not always in act, but proceeds from potentiality to act; as we observe in things that are corrupted and generated. Wherefore the angelic intellect is always in act as regards those things which it can understand, by reason of its proximity to the first intellect, which is pure act, as we have said above. But the human intellect, which is the lowest in the order of intelligence and most remote from the perfection of the Divine intellect, is in potentiality with regard to things intelligible, and is at first "like a clean tablet on which nothing is written," as the Philosopher says (De Anima iii, 4). This is made clear from the fact, that at first we are only in potentiality to understand, and afterwards we are made to understand actually. And so it is evident that with us to understand is "in a way to be passive"; taking passion in the third sense. And consequently the intellect is a passive power.

Reply Obj. 1: This objection is verified of passion in the first and second senses, which belong to primary matter. But in the third sense passion is in anything which is reduced from potentiality to act.

Reply Obj. 2: "Passive intellect" is the name given by some to the sensitive appetite, in which are the passions of the soul; which appetite is also called "rational by participation," because it "obeys the reason" (Ethic. i, 13). Others give the name of passive intellect to the cogitative power, which is called the "particular reason." And in each case "passive" may be taken in the two first senses; forasmuch as this so-called intellect is the act of a corporeal organ. But the intellect which is in potentiality to things intelligible, and which for this reason Aristotle calls the "possible" intellect (De Anima iii, 4) is not passive except in the third sense: for it is not an act of a corporeal organ. Hence it is incorruptible.

Reply Obj. 3: The agent is nobler than the patient, if the action and the passion are referred to the same thing: but not always, if they refer to different things. Now the intellect is a passive power in regard to the whole universal being: while the vegetative power is active in regard to some particular thing, namely, the body as united to the soul. Wherefore nothing prevents such a passive force being nobler than such an active one.

THIRD ARTICLE [I, Q. 79, Art. 3]

Whether There Is an Active Intellect?

Objection 1: It would seem that there is no active intellect. For as the senses are to things sensible, so is our intellect to things intelligible. But because sense is in potentiality to things sensible, the sense is not said to be active, but only passive. Therefore, since our intellect is in potentiality to things intelligible, it seems that we cannot say that the intellect is active, but only that it is passive.

Obj. 2: Further, if we say that also in the senses there is something active, such as light: *on the contrary,* light is required for sight, inasmuch as it makes the medium to be actually luminous; for color of its own nature moves the luminous medium. But in the operation of the intellect there is no appointed medium that has to be brought into act. Therefore there is no necessity for an active intellect.

Obj. 3: Further, the likeness of the agent is received into the patient according to the nature of the patient. But the passive intellect is an immaterial power. Therefore its immaterial nature suffices for forms to be received into it immaterially. Now a form is intelligible in act from the very fact that it is immaterial. Therefore there is no need for an active intellect to make the species actually intelligible.

*On the contrary,* The Philosopher says (De Anima iii, 5), "As in every nature, so in the soul is there something by which it becomes all things, and something by which it makes all things." Therefore we must admit an active intellect.

*I answer that,* According to the opinion of Plato, there is no need for an active intellect in order to make things actually intelligible; but perhaps in order to provide intellectual light to the intellect, as will be explained farther on (A. 4). For Plato supposed that the forms of natural things subsisted apart from matter, and consequently that they are intelligible: since a thing is actually intelligible from the very fact that it is immaterial. And he called such forms "species or ideas"; from a participation of which, he said that even corporeal matter was formed, in order that individuals might be naturally established in their proper genera and species: and that our intellect was formed by such participation in order to have knowledge of the genera and species of things. But since Aristotle did not allow that forms of natural things exist apart from matter, and as forms existing in matter are not actually intelligible; it follows that the natures or forms of the sensible things which we understand are not actually intelligible. Now nothing is reduced from potentiality to act except by something in act; as the senses as made actual by what is actually sensible. We must therefore assign on the part of the intellect some power to make things actually intelligible, by abstraction of the species from material conditions. And such is the necessity for an active intellect.

Reply Obj. 1: Sensible things are found in act outside the soul; and hence there is no need for an active sense. Wherefore it is clear that in the nutritive part all the powers are active, whereas in the sensitive part all are passive: but in the intellectual part, there is something active and something passive.

Reply Obj. 2: There are two opinions as to the effect of light. For some say that light is required for sight, in order to make colors actually visible. And according to this the active intellect is required for understanding, in like manner and for the same reason as light is required for seeing. But in the opinion of others, light is required for sight; not for the colors to become actually visible; but in order that the medium may become actually luminous, as the Commentator says on *De Anima* ii. And according to this, Aristotle's comparison of the active intellect to light is verified in this, that as it is required for understanding, so is light required for seeing; but not for the same reason.

Reply Obj. 3: If the agent pre-exist, it may well happen that its likeness is received variously into various things, on account of their dispositions. But if the agent does not pre-exist, the disposition of the recipient has nothing to do with the matter. Now the intelligible in act is not something existing in nature; if we consider the nature of things sensible, which do not subsist apart from matter. And therefore in order to understand them, the immaterial nature of the passive intellect would not suffice but for the presence of the active intellect which makes things actually intelligible by way of abstraction.

FOURTH ARTICLE [I, Q. 79, Art. 4]

Whether the Active Intellect Is Something in the Soul?

Objection 1: It would seem that the active intellect is not something in the soul. For the effect of the active intellect is to give light for the purpose of understanding. But this is done by something higher than the soul: according to John 1:9, "He was the true light that enlighteneth every man coming into this world." Therefore the active intellect is not something in the soul.

Obj. 2: Further, the Philosopher (De Anima iii, 5) says of the active intellect, "that it does not sometimes understand and sometimes not understand." But our soul does not always understand: sometimes it understands, sometimes it does not understand. Therefore the active intellect is not something in our soul.

Obj. 3: Further, agent and patient suffice for action. If, therefore, the passive intellect, which is a passive power, is something belonging to the soul; and also the active intellect, which is an active power: it follows that a man would always be able to understand when he wished, which is clearly false. Therefore the active intellect is not something in our soul.

Obj. 4: Further, the Philosopher (De Anima iii, 5) says that the active intellect is a "substance in actual being." But nothing can be in potentiality and in act with regard to the same thing. If, therefore, the passive intellect, which is in potentiality to all things intelligible, is something in the soul, it seems impossible for the active intellect to be also something in our soul.

Obj. 5: Further, if the active intellect is something in the soul, it must be a power. For it is neither a passion nor a habit; since habits and passions are not in the nature of agents in regard to the passivity of the soul; but rather passion is the very action of the passive power; while habit is something which results from acts. But every power flows from the essence of the soul. It would therefore follow that the active intellect flows from the essence of the soul. And thus it would not be in the soul by way of participation from some higher intellect: which is unfitting. Therefore the active intellect is not something in our soul.

*On the contrary,* The Philosopher says (De Anima iii, 5), that "it is necessary for these differences," namely, the passive and active intellect, "to be in the soul."

*I answer that,* The active intellect, of which the Philosopher speaks, is something in the soul. In order to make this evident, we must observe that above the intellectual soul of man we must needs suppose a superior intellect, from which the soul acquires the power of understanding. For what is such by participation, and what is mobile, and what is imperfect always requires the pre-existence of something essentially such, immovable and perfect. Now the human soul is called intellectual by reason of a participation in intellectual power; a sign of which is that it is not wholly intellectual but only in part. Moreover it reaches to the understanding of truth by arguing, with a certain amount of reasoning and movement. Again it has an imperfect understanding; both because it does not understand everything, and because, in those things which it does understand, it passes from potentiality to act. Therefore there must needs be some higher intellect, by which the soul is helped to understand.

Wherefore some held that this intellect, substantially separate, is the active intellect, which by lighting up the phantasms as it were, makes them to be actually intelligible. But, even supposing the existence of such a separate active intellect, it would still be necessary to assign to the human soul some power participating in that superior intellect, by which power the human soul makes things actually intelligible. Just as in other perfect natural things, besides the universal active causes, each one is endowed with its proper powers derived from those universal causes: for the sun alone does not generate man; but in man is the power of begetting man: and in like manner with other perfect animals. Now among these lower things nothing is more perfect than the human soul. Wherefore we must say that in the soul is some power derived from a higher intellect, whereby it is able to light up the phantasms. And we know this by experience, since we perceive that we abstract universal forms from their particular conditions, which is to make them actually intelligible. Now no action belongs to anything except through some principle formally inherent therein; as we have said above of the passive intellect (Q. 76, A. 1). Therefore the power which is the principle of this action must be something in the soul. For this reason Aristotle (De Anima iii, 5) compared the active intellect to light, which is something received into the air: while Plato compared the separate intellect impressing the soul to the sun, as Themistius says in his commentary on *De Anima* iii. But the separate intellect, according to the teaching of our faith, is God Himself, Who is the soul's Creator, and only beatitude; as will be shown later on (Q. 90, A. 3; I-II, Q. 3, A. 7). Wherefore the human soul derives its intellectual light from Him, according to Ps. 4:7, "The light of Thy countenance, O Lord, is signed upon us."

Reply Obj. 1: That true light enlightens as a universal cause, from which the human soul derives a particular power, as we have explained.

Reply Obj. 2: The Philosopher says those words not of the active intellect, but of the intellect in act: of which he had already said: "Knowledge in act is the same as the thing." Or, if we refer those words to the active intellect, then they are said because it is not owing to the active intellect that sometimes we do, and sometimes we do not understand, but to the intellect which is in potentiality.

Reply Obj. 3: If the relation of the active intellect to the passive were that of the active object to a power, as, for instance, of the visible in act to the sight; it would follow that we could understand all things instantly, since the active intellect is that which makes all things (in act). But now the active intellect is not an object, rather is it that whereby the objects are made to be in act: for which, besides the presence of the active intellect, we require the presence of phantasms, the good disposition of the sensitive powers, and practice in this sort of operation; since through one thing understood, other things come to be understood, as from terms are made propositions, and from first principles, conclusions. From this point of view it matters not whether the active intellect is something belonging to the soul, or something separate from the soul.

Reply Obj. 4: The intellectual soul is indeed actually immaterial, but it is in potentiality to determinate species. *On the contrary,* phantasms are actual images of certain species, but are immaterial in potentiality. Wherefore nothing prevents one and the same soul, inasmuch as it is actually immaterial, having one power by which it makes things actually immaterial, by abstraction from the conditions of individual matter: which power is called the "active intellect"; and another power, receptive of such species, which is called the "passive intellect" by reason of its being in potentiality to such species.

Reply Obj. 5: Since the essence of the soul is immaterial, created by the supreme intellect, nothing prevents that power which it derives from the supreme intellect, and whereby it abstracts from matter, flowing from the essence of the soul, in the same way as its other powers.

FIFTH ARTICLE [I, Q. 79, Art. 5]

Whether the Active Intellect Is One in All?

Objection 1: It would seem that there is one active intellect in all. For what is separate from the body is not multiplied according to the number of bodies. But the active intellect is "separate," as the Philosopher says (De Anima iii, 5). Therefore it is not multiplied in the many human bodies, but is one for all men.

Obj. 2: Further, the active intellect is the cause of the universal, which is one in many. But that which is the cause of unity is still more itself one. Therefore the active intellect is the same in all.

Obj. 3: Further, all men agree in the first intellectual concepts. But to these they assent by the active intellect. Therefore all agree in one active intellect.

*On the contrary,* The Philosopher says (De Anima iii, 5) that the active intellect is as a light. But light is not the same in the various things enlightened. Therefore the same active intellect is not in various men.

*I answer that,* The truth about this question depends on what we have already said (A. 4). For if the active intellect were not something belonging to the soul, but were some separate substance, there would be one active intellect for all men. And this is what they mean who hold that there is one active intellect for all. But if the active intellect is something belonging to the soul, as one of its powers, we are bound to say that there are as many active intellects as there are souls, which are multiplied according to the number of men, as we have said above (Q. 76, A. 2). For it is impossible that one same power belong to various substances.

Reply Obj. 1: The Philosopher proves that the active intellect is separate, by the fact that the passive intellect is separate: because, as he says (De Anima iii, 5), "the agent is more noble than the patient." Now the passive intellect is said to be separate, because it is not the act of any corporeal organ. And in the same sense the active intellect is also called "separate"; but not as a separate substance.

Reply Obj. 2: The active intellect is the cause of the universal, by abstracting it from matter. But for this purpose it need not be the same intellect in all intelligent beings; but it must be one in its relationship to all those things from which it abstracts the universal, with respect to which things the universal is one. And this befits the active intellect inasmuch as it is immaterial.

Reply Obj. 3: All things which are of one species enjoy in common the action which accompanies the nature of the species, and consequently the power which is the principle of such action; but not so as that power be identical in all. Now to know the first intelligible principles is the action belonging to the human species. Wherefore all men enjoy in common the power which is the principle of this action: and this power is the active intellect. But there is no need for it to be identical in all. Yet it must be derived by all from one principle. And thus the possession by all men in common of the first principles proves the unity of the separate intellect, which Plato compares to the sun; but not the unity of the active intellect, which Aristotle compares to light.

SIXTH ARTICLE [I, Q. 79, Art. 6]

Whether Memory Is in the Intellectual Part of the Soul?

Objection 1: It would seem that memory is not in the intellectual part of the soul. For Augustine says (De Trin. xii, 2,3,8) that to the higher part of the soul belongs those things which are not "common to man and beast." But memory is common to man and beast, for he says (De Trin. xii, 2, 3, 8) that "beasts can sense corporeal things through the senses of the body, and commit them to memory." Therefore memory does not belong to the intellectual part of the soul.

Obj. 2: Further, memory is of the past. But the past is said of something with regard to a fixed time. Memory, therefore, knows a thing under a condition of a fixed time; which involves knowledge under the conditions of "here" and "now." But this is not the province of the intellect, but of the sense. Therefore memory is not in the intellectual part, but only in the sensitive.

Obj. 3: Further, in the memory are preserved the species of those things of which we are not actually thinking. But this cannot happen in the intellect, because the intellect is reduced to act by the fact that the intelligible species are received into it. Now the intellect in act implies understanding in act; and therefore the intellect actually understands all things of which it has the species. Therefore the memory is not in the intellectual part.

*On the contrary,* Augustine says (De Trin. x, 11) that "memory, understanding, and will are one mind."

*I answer that,* Since it is of the nature of the memory to preserve the species of those things which are not actually apprehended, we must first of all consider whether the intelligible species can thus be preserved in the intellect: because Avicenna held that this was impossible. For he admitted that this could happen in the sensitive part, as to some powers, inasmuch as they are acts of corporeal organs, in which certain species may be preserved apart from actual apprehension. But in the intellect, which has no corporeal organ, nothing but what is intelligible exists. Wherefore every thing of which the likeness exists in the intellect must be actually understood. Thus, therefore, according to him, as soon as we cease to understand something actually, the species of that thing ceases to be in our intellect, and if we wish to understand that thing anew, we must turn to the active intellect, which he held to be a separate substance, in order that the intelligible species may thence flow again into our passive intellect. And from the practice and habit of turning to the active intellect there is formed, according to him, a certain aptitude in the passive intellect for turning to the active intellect; which aptitude he calls the habit of knowledge. According, therefore, to this supposition, nothing is preserved in the intellectual part that is not actually understood: wherefore it would not be possible to admit memory in the intellectual part.

But this opinion is clearly opposed to the teaching of Aristotle. For he says (De Anima iii, 4) that, when the passive intellect "is identified with each thing as knowing it, it is said to be in act," and that "this happens when it can operate of itself. And, even then, it is in potentiality, but not in the same way as before learning and discovering." Now, the passive intellect is said to be each thing, inasmuch as it receives the intelligible species of each thing. To the fact, therefore, that it receives the species of intelligible things it owes its being able to operate when it wills, but not so that it be always operating: for even then is it in potentiality in a certain sense, though otherwise than before the act of understanding—namely, in the sense that whoever has habitual knowledge is in potentiality to actual consideration.

The foregoing opinion is also opposed to reason. For what is received into something is received according to the conditions of the recipient. But the intellect is of a more stable nature, and is more immovable than corporeal nature. If, therefore, corporeal matter holds the forms which it receives, not only while it actually does something through them, but also after ceasing to act through them, much more cogent reason is there for the intellect to receive the species unchangeably and lastingly, whether it receive them from things sensible, or derive them from some superior intellect. Thus, therefore, if we take memory only for the power of retaining species, we must say that it is in the intellectual part. But if in the notion of memory we include its object as something past, then the memory is not in the intellectual, but only in the sensitive part, which apprehends individual things. For past, as past, since it signifies being under a condition of fixed time, is something individual.

Reply Obj. 1: Memory, if considered as retentive of species, is not common to us and other animals. For species are not retained in the sensitive part of the soul only, but rather in the body and soul united: since the memorative power is the act of some organ. But the intellect in itself is retentive of species, without the association of any corporeal organ. Wherefore the Philosopher says (De Anima iii, 4) that "the soul is the seat of the species, not the whole soul, but the intellect."

Reply Obj. 2: The condition of past may be referred to two things—namely, to the object which is known, and to the act of knowledge. These two are found together in the sensitive part, which apprehends something from the fact of its being immuted by a present sensible: wherefore at the same time an animal remembers to have sensed before in the past, and to have sensed some past sensible thing. But as concerns the intellectual part, the past is accidental, and is not in itself a part of the object of the intellect. For the intellect understands man, as man: and to man, as man, it is accidental that he exist in the present, past, or future. But on the part of the act, the condition of past, even as such, may be understood to be in the intellect, as well as in the senses. Because our soul's act of understanding is an individual act, existing in this or that time, inasmuch as a man is said to understand now, or yesterday, or tomorrow. And this is not incompatible with the intellectual nature: for such an act of understanding, though something individual, is yet an immaterial act, as we have said above of the intellect (Q. 76, A. 1); and therefore, as the intellect understands itself, though it be itself an individual intellect, so also it understands its act of understanding, which is an individual act, in the past, present, or future. In this way, then, the notion of memory, in as far as it regards past events, is preserved in the intellect, forasmuch as it understands that it previously understood: but not in the sense that it understands the past as something "here" and "now."

Reply Obj. 3: The intelligible species is sometimes in the intellect only in potentiality, and then the intellect is said to be in potentiality. Sometimes the intelligible species is in the intellect as regards the ultimate completion of the act, and then it understands in act. And sometimes the intelligible species is in a middle state, between potentiality and act: and then we have habitual knowledge. In this way the intellect retains the species, even when it does not understand in act.

SEVENTH ARTICLE [I, Q. 79, Art. 7]

Whether the Intellectual Memory Is a Power Distinct from the Intellect?

Objection 1: It would seem that the intellectual memory is distinct from the intellect. For Augustine (De Trin. x, 11) assigns to the soul memory, understanding, and will. But it is clear that the memory is a distinct power from the will. Therefore it is also distinct from the intellect.

Obj. 2: Further, the reason of distinction among the powers in the sensitive part is the same as in the intellectual part. But memory in the sensitive part is distinct from sense, as we have said (Q. 78, A. 4). Therefore memory in the intellectual part is distinct from the intellect.

Obj. 3: Further, according to Augustine (De Trin. x, 11; xi, 7), memory, understanding, and will are equal to one another, and one flows from the other. But this could not be if memory and intellect were the same power. Therefore they are not the same power.

*On the contrary,* From its nature the memory is the treasury or storehouse of species. But the Philosopher (De Anima iii) attributes this to the intellect, as we have said (A. 6, ad 1). Therefore the memory is not another power from the intellect.

*I answer that,* As has been said above (Q. 77, A. 3), the powers of the soul are distinguished by the different formal aspects of their objects: since each power is defined in reference to that thing to which it is directed and which is its object. It has also been said above (Q. 59, A. 4) that if any power by its nature be directed to an object according to the common ratio of the object, that power will not be differentiated according to the individual differences of that object: just as the power of sight, which regards its object under the common ratio of color, is not differentiated by differences of black and white. Now, the intellect regards its object under the common ratio of being: since the passive intellect is that "in which all are in potentiality." Wherefore the passive intellect is not differentiated by any difference of being. Nevertheless there is a distinction between the power of the active intellect and of the passive intellect: because as regards the same object, the active power which makes the object to be in act must be distinct from the passive power, which is moved by the object existing in act. Thus the active power is compared to its object as a being in act is to a being in potentiality; whereas the passive power, *on the contrary,* is compared to its object as being in potentiality is to a being in act. Therefore there can be no other difference of powers in the intellect, but that of passive and active. Wherefore it is clear that memory is not a distinct power from the intellect: for it belongs to the nature of a passive power to retain as well as to receive.

Reply Obj. 1: Although it is said (3 Sent. D, 1) that memory, intellect, and will are three powers, this is not in accordance with the meaning of Augustine, who says expressly (De Trin. xiv) that "if we take memory, intelligence, and will as always present in the soul, whether we actually attend to them or not, they seem to pertain to the memory only. And by intelligence I mean that by which we understand when actually thinking; and by will I mean that love or affection which unites the child and its parent." Wherefore it is clear that Augustine does not take the above three for three powers; but by memory he understands the soul's habit of retention; by intelligence, the act of the intellect; and by will, the act of the will.

Reply Obj. 2: Past and present may differentiate the sensitive powers, but not the intellectual powers, for the reason give above.

Reply Obj. 3: Intelligence arises from memory, as act from habit; and in this way it is equal to it, but not as a power to a power.

EIGHTH ARTICLE [I, Q. 79, Art. 8]

Whether the Reason Is Distinct from the Intellect?

Objection 1: It would seem that the reason is a distinct power from the intellect. For it is stated in *De Spiritu et Anima* that "when we wish to rise from lower things to higher, first the sense comes to our aid, then imagination, then reason, then the intellect." Therefore the reason is distinct from the intellect, as imagination is from sense.

Obj. 2: Further, Boethius says (De Consol. iv, 6), that intellect is compared to reason, as eternity to time. But it does not belong to the same power to be in eternity and to be in time. Therefore reason and intellect are not the same power.

Obj. 3: Further, man has intellect in common with the angels, and sense in common with the brutes. But reason, which is proper to man, whence he is called a rational animal, is a power distinct from sense. Therefore is it equally true to say that it is distinct from the intellect, which properly belongs to the angel: whence they are called intellectual.

*On the contrary,* Augustine says (Gen. ad lit. iii, 20) that "that in which man excels irrational animals is reason, or mind, or intelligence or whatever appropriate name we like to give it." Therefore, reason, intellect and mind are one power.

*I answer that,* Reason and intellect in man cannot be distinct powers. We shall understand this clearly if we consider their respective actions. For to understand is simply to apprehend intelligible truth: and to reason is to advance from one thing understood to another, so as to know an intelligible truth. And therefore angels, who according to their nature, possess perfect knowledge of intelligible truth, have no need to advance from one thing to another; but apprehend the truth simply and without mental discussion, as Dionysius says (Div. Nom. vii). But man arrives at the knowledge of intelligible truth by advancing from one thing to another; and therefore he is called rational. Reasoning, therefore, is compared to understanding, as movement is to rest, or acquisition to possession; of which one belongs to the perfect, the other to the imperfect. And since movement always proceeds from something immovable, and ends in something at rest; hence it is that human reasoning, by way of inquiry and discovery, advances from certain things simply understood—namely, the first principles; and, again, by way of judgment returns by analysis to first principles, in the light of which it examines what it has found. Now it is clear that rest and movement are not to be referred to different powers, but to one and the same, even in natural things: since by the same nature a thing is moved towards a certain place, and rests in that place. Much more, therefore, by the same power do we understand and reason: and so it is clear that in man reason and intellect are the same power.

Reply Obj. 1: That enumeration is made according to the order of actions, not according to the distinction of powers. Moreover, that book is not of great authority.

Reply Obj. 2: The answer is clear from what we have said. For eternity is compared to time as immovable to movable. And thus Boethius compared the intellect to eternity, and reason to time.

Reply Obj. 3: Other animals are so much lower than man that they cannot attain to the knowledge of truth, which reason seeks. But man attains, although imperfectly, to the knowledge of intelligible truth, which angels know. Therefore in the angels the power of knowledge is not of a different genus from that which is in the human reason, but is compared to it as the perfect to the imperfect.

NINTH ARTICLE [I, Q. 79, Art. 9]

Whether the Higher and Lower Reason Are Distinct Powers?

Objection 1: It would seem that the higher and lower reason are distinct powers. For Augustine says (De Trin. xii, 4,7), that the image of the Trinity is in the higher part of the reason, and not in the lower. But the parts of the soul are its powers. Therefore the higher and lower reason are two powers.

Obj. 2: Further, nothing flows from itself. Now, the lower reason flows from the higher, and is ruled and directed by it. Therefore the higher reason is another power from the lower.

Obj. 3: Further, the Philosopher says (Ethic. vi, 1) that "the scientific part" of the soul, by which the soul knows necessary things, is another principle, and another part from the "opinionative" and "reasoning" part by which it knows contingent things. And he proves this from the principle that for those things which are "generically different, generically different parts of the soul are ordained." Now contingent and necessary are generically different, as corruptible and incorruptible. Since, therefore, necessary is the same as eternal, and temporal the same as contingent, it seems that what the Philosopher calls the "scientific" part must be the same as the higher reason, which, according to Augustine (De Trin. xii, 7) "is intent on the consideration and consultation of things eternal"; and that what the Philosopher calls the "reasoning" or "opinionative" part is the same as the lower reason, which, according to Augustine, "is intent on the disposal of temporal things." Therefore the higher reason is another power than the lower.

Obj. 4: Further, Damascene says (De Fide Orth. ii) that "opinion rises from the imagination: then the mind by judging of the truth or error of the opinion discovers the truth: whence *mens* (mind) is derived from *metiendo* (measuring). And therefore the intellect regards those things which are already subject to judgment and true decision." Therefore the opinionative power, which is the lower reason, is distinct from the mind and the intellect, by which we may understand the higher reason.

*On the contrary,* Augustine says (De Trin. xii, 4) that "the higher and lower reason are only distinct by their functions." Therefore they are not two powers.

*I answer that,* The higher and lower reason, as they are understood by Augustine, can in no way be two powers of the soul. For he says that "the higher reason is that which is intent on the contemplation and consultation of things eternal": forasmuch as in contemplation it sees them in themselves, and in consultation it takes its rules of action from them. But he calls the lower reason that which "is intent on the disposal of temporal things." Now these two—namely, eternal and temporal—are related to our knowledge in this way, that one of them is the means of knowing the other. For by way of discovery, we come through knowledge of temporal things to that of things eternal, according to the words of the Apostle (Rom. 1:20), "The invisible things of God are clearly seen, being understood by the things that are made": while by way of judgment, from eternal things already known, we judge of temporal things, and according to laws of things eternal we dispose of temporal things.

But it may happen that the medium and what is attained thereby belong to different habits: as the first indemonstrable principles belong to the habit of the intellect; whereas the conclusions which we draw from them belong to the habit of science. And so it happens that from the principles of geometry we draw a conclusion in another science—for example, perspective. But the power of the reason is such that both medium and term belong to it. For the act of the reason is, as it were, a movement from one thing to another. But the same movable thing passes through the medium and reaches the end. Wherefore the higher and lower reasons are one and the same power. But according to Augustine they are distinguished by the functions of their actions, and according to their various habits: for wisdom is attributed to the higher reason, science to the lower.

Reply Obj. 1: We speak of parts, in whatever way a thing is divided. And so far as reason is divided according to its various acts, the higher and lower reason are called parts; but not because they are different powers.

Reply Obj. 2: The lower reason is said to flow from the higher, or to be ruled by it, as far as the principles made use of by the lower reason are drawn from and directed by the principles of the higher reason.

Reply Obj. 3: The "scientific" part, of which the Philosopher speaks, is not the same as the higher reason: for necessary truths are found even among temporal things, of which natural science and mathematics treat. And the "opinionative" and "ratiocinative" part is more limited than the lower reason; for it regards only things contingent. Neither must we say, without any qualification, that a power, by which the intellect knows necessary things, is distinct from a power by which it knows contingent things: because it knows both under the same objective aspect—namely, under the aspect of being and truth. Wherefore it perfectly knows necessary things which have perfect being in truth; since it penetrates to their very essence, from which it demonstrates their proper accidents. On the other hand, it knows contingent things, but imperfectly; forasmuch as they have but imperfect being and truth. Now perfect and imperfect in the action do not vary the power, but they vary the actions as to the mode of acting, and consequently the principles of the actions and the habits themselves. And therefore the Philosopher postulates two lesser parts of the soul—namely, the "scientific" and the "ratiocinative," not because they are two powers, but because they are distinct according to a different aptitude for receiving various habits, concerning the variety of which he inquires. For contingent and necessary, though differing according to their proper genera, nevertheless agree in the common aspect of being, which the intellect considers, and to which they are variously compared as perfect and imperfect.

Reply Obj. 4: That distinction given by Damascene is according to the variety of acts, not according to the variety of powers. For "opinion" signifies an act of the intellect which leans to one side of a contradiction, whilst in fear of the other. While to "judge" or "measure" [mensurare] is an act of the intellect, applying certain principles to examine propositions. From this is taken the word "mens" [mind]. Lastly, to "understand" is to adhere to the formed judgment with approval.

TENTH ARTICLE [I, Q. 79, Art. 10]

Whether Intelligence Is a Power Distinct from Intellect?

Objection 1: It would seem that the intelligence is another power than the intellect. For we read in *De Spiritu et Anima* that "when we wish to rise from lower to higher things, first the sense comes to our aid, then imagination, then reason, then intellect, and afterwards intelligence." But imagination and sense are distinct powers. Therefore also intellect and intelligence are distinct.

Obj. 2: Further, Boethius says (De Consol. v, 4) that "sense considers man in one way, imagination in another, reason in another, intelligence in another." But intellect is the same power as reason. Therefore, seemingly, intelligence is a distinct power from intellect, as reason is a distinct power from imagination or sense.

Obj. 3: Further, "actions came before powers," as the Philosopher says (De Anima ii, 4). But intelligence is an act separate from others attributed to the intellect. For Damascene says (De Fide Orth. ii) that "the first movement is called intelligence; but that intelligence which is about a certain thing is called intention; that which remains and conforms the soul to that which is understood is called invention, and invention when it remains in the same man, examining and judging of itself, is called phronesis (that is, wisdom), and phronesis if dilated makes thought, that is, orderly internal speech; from which, they say, comes speech expressed by the tongue." Therefore it seems that intelligence is some special power.

*On the contrary,* The Philosopher says (De Anima iii, 6) that "intelligence is of indivisible things in which there is nothing false." But the knowledge of these things belongs to the intellect. Therefore intelligence is not another power than the intellect.

*I answer that,* This word "intelligence" properly signifies the intellect's very act, which is to understand. However, in some works translated from the Arabic, the separate substances which we call angels are called "intelligences," and perhaps for this reason, that such substances are always actually understanding. But in works translated from the Greek, they are called "intellects" or "minds." Thus intelligence is not distinct from intellect, as power is from power; but as act is from power. And such a division is recognized even by the philosophers. For sometimes they assign four intellects—namely, the "active" and "passive" intellects, the intellect "in habit," and the "actual" intellect. Of which four the active and passive intellects are different powers; just as in all things the active power is distinct from the passive. But three of these are distinct, as three states of the passive intellect, which is sometimes in potentiality only, and thus it is called passive; sometimes it is in the first act, which is knowledge, and thus it is called intellect in habit; and sometimes it is in the second act, which is to consider, and thus it is called intellect in act, or actual intellect.

Reply Obj. 1: If this authority is accepted, intelligence there means the act of the intellect. And thus it is divided against intellect as act against power.

Reply Obj. 2: Boethius takes intelligence as meaning that act of the intellect which transcends the act of the reason. Wherefore he also says that reason alone belongs to the human race, as intelligence alone belongs to God, for it belongs to God to understand all things without any investigation.

Reply Obj. 3: All those acts which Damascene enumerates belong to one power—namely, the intellectual power. For this power first of all only apprehends something; and this act is called "intelligence." Secondly, it directs what it apprehends to the knowledge of something else, or to some operation; and this is called "intention." And when it goes on in search of what it "intends," it is called "invention." When, by reference to something known for certain, it examines what it has found, it is said to know or to be wise, which belongs to "phronesis" or "wisdom"; for "it belongs to the wise man to judge," as the Philosopher says (Metaph. i, 2). And when once it has obtained something for certain, as being fully examined, it thinks about the means of making it known to others; and this is the ordering of "interior speech," from which proceeds "external speech." For every difference of acts does not make the powers vary, but only what cannot be reduced to the one same principle, as we have said above (Q. 78, A. 4).

ELEVENTH ARTICLE [I, Q. 79, Art. 11]

Whether the Speculative and Practical Intellects Are Distinct Powers?

Objection 1: It would seem that the speculative and practical intellects are distinct powers. For the apprehensive and motive are different kinds of powers, as is clear from *De Anima* ii, 3. But the speculative intellect is merely an apprehensive power; while the practical intellect is a motive power. Therefore they are distinct powers.

Obj. 2: Further, the different nature of the object differentiates the power. But the object of the speculative intellect is *truth*, and of the practical is good; which differ in nature. Therefore the speculative and practical intellect are distinct powers.

Obj. 3: Further, in the intellectual part, the practical intellect is compared to the speculative, as the estimative is to the imaginative power in the sensitive part. But the estimative differs from the imaginative, as power form power, as we have said above (Q. 78, A. 4). Therefore also the speculative intellect differs from the practical.

*On the contrary,* The speculative intellect by extension becomes practical (De Anima iii, 10). But one power is not changed into another. Therefore the speculative and practical intellects are not distinct powers.

*I answer that,* The speculative and practical intellects are not distinct powers. The reason of which is that, as we have said above (Q. 77, A. 3), what is accidental to the nature of the object of a power, does not differentiate that power; for it is accidental to a thing colored to be man, or to be great or small; hence all such things are apprehended by the same power of sight. Now, to a thing apprehended by the intellect, it is accidental whether it be directed to operation or not, and according to this the speculative and practical intellects differ. For it is the speculative intellect which directs what it apprehends, not to operation, but to the consideration of truth; while the practical intellect is that which directs what it apprehends to operation. And this is what the Philosopher says (De Anima iii, 10); that "the speculative differs from the practical in its end." Whence each is named from its end: the one speculative, the other practical—i.e. operative.

Reply Obj. 1: The practical intellect is a motive power, not as executing movement, but as directing towards it; and this belongs to it according to its mode of apprehension.

Reply Obj. 2: Truth and good include one another; for truth is something good, otherwise it would not be desirable; and good is something true, otherwise it would not be intelligible. Therefore as the object of the appetite may be something true, as having the aspect of good, for example, when some one desires to know the truth; so the object of the practical intellect is good directed to the operation, and under the aspect of truth. For the practical intellect knows truth, just as the speculative, but it directs the known truth to operation.

Reply Obj. 3: Many differences differentiate the sensitive powers, which do not differentiate the intellectual powers, as we have said above (A. 7, ad 2; Q. 77, A. 3, ad 4).

TWELFTH ARTICLE [I, Q. 79, Art. 12]

Whether Synderesis Is a Special Power of the Soul Distinct from the Others?

Objection 1: It would seem that "synderesis" is a special power, distinct from the others. For those things which fall under one division, seem to be of the same genus. But in the gloss of Jerome on Ezech. 1:6, "synderesis" is divided against the irascible, the concupiscible, and the rational, which are powers. Therefore "synderesis" is a power.

Obj. 2: Further, opposite things are of the same genus. But "synderesis" and sensuality seem to be opposed to one another because "synderesis" always incites to good; while sensuality always incites to evil: whence it is signified by the serpent, as is clear from Augustine (De Trin. xii, 12,13). It seems, therefore, that "synderesis" is a power just as sensuality is.

Obj. 3: Further, Augustine says (De Lib. Arb. ii, 10) that in the natural power of judgment there are certain "rules and seeds of virtue, both true and unchangeable." And this is what we call synderesis. Since, therefore, the unchangeable rules which guide our judgment belong to the reason as to its higher part, as Augustine says (De Trin. xii, 2), it seems that "synderesis" is the same as reason: and thus it is a power.

*On the contrary,* According to the Philosopher (Metaph. viii, 2), "rational powers regard opposite things." But "synderesis" does not regard opposites, but inclines to good only. Therefore "synderesis" is not a power. For if it were a power it would be a rational power, since it is not found in brute animals.

*I answer that,* "Synderesis" is not a power but a habit; though some held that it is a power higher than reason; while others [*Cf. Alexander of Hales, Sum. Theol. II, Q. 73] said that it is reason itself, not as reason, but as a nature. In order to make this clear we must observe that, as we have said above (A. 8), man's act of reasoning, since it is a kind of movement, proceeds from the understanding of certain things—namely, those which are naturally known without any investigation on the part of reason, as from an immovable principle—and ends also at the understanding, inasmuch as by means of those principles naturally known, we judge of those things which we have discovered by reasoning. Now it is clear that, as the speculative reason argues about speculative things, so that practical reason argues about practical things. Therefore we must have, bestowed on us by nature, not only speculative principles, but also practical principles. Now the first speculative principles bestowed on us by nature do not belong to a special power, but to a special habit, which is called "the understanding of principles," as the Philosopher explains (Ethic. vi, 6). Wherefore the first practical principles, bestowed on us by nature, do not belong to a special power, but to a special natural habit, which we call "synderesis." Whence "synderesis" is said to incite to good, and to murmur at evil, inasmuch as through first principles we proceed to discover, and judge of what we have discovered. It is therefore clear that "synderesis" is not a power, but a natural habit.

Reply Obj. 1: The division given by Jerome is taken from the variety of acts, and not from the variety of powers; and various acts can belong to one power.

Reply Obj. 2: In like manner, the opposition of sensuality to "syneresis" is an opposition of acts, and not of the different species of one genus.

Reply Obj. 3: Those unchangeable notions are the first practical principles, concerning which no one errs; and they are attributed to reason as to a power, and to "synderesis" as to a habit. Wherefore we judge naturally both by our reason and by "synderesis."

THIRTEENTH ARTICLE [I, Q. 79, Art. 13]

Whether Conscience Be a Power?

Objection 1: It would seem that conscience is a power; for Origen says [*Commentary on Rom. 2:15] that "conscience is a correcting and guiding spirit accompanying the soul, by which it is led away from evil and made to cling to good." But in the soul, spirit designates a power—either the mind itself, according to the text (Eph. 4:13), "Be ye renewed in the spirit of your mind"—or the imagination, whence imaginary vision is called spiritual, as Augustine says (Gen. ad lit. xii, 7,24). Therefore conscience is a power.

Obj. 2: Further, nothing is a subject of sin, except a power of the soul. But conscience is a subject of sin; for it is said of some that "their mind and conscience are defiled" (Titus 1:15). Therefore it seems that conscience is a power.

Obj. 3: Further, conscience must of necessity be either an act, a habit, or a power. But it is not an act; for thus it would not always exist in man. Nor is it a habit; for conscience is not one thing but many, since we are directed in our actions by many habits of knowledge. Therefore conscience is a power.

*On the contrary,* Conscience can be laid aside. But a power cannot be laid aside. Therefore conscience is not a power.

*I answer that,* Properly speaking, conscience is not a power, but an act. This is evident both from the very name and from those things which in the common way of speaking are attributed to conscience. For conscience, according to the very nature of the word, implies the relation of knowledge to something: for conscience may be resolved into "cum alio scientia," i.e. knowledge applied to an individual case. But the application of knowledge to something is done by some act. Wherefore from this explanation of the name it is clear that conscience is an act.

The same is manifest from those things which are attributed to conscience. For conscience is said to witness, to bind, or incite, and also to accuse, torment, or rebuke. And all these follow the application of knowledge or science to what we do: which application is made in three ways. One way in so far as we recognize that we have done or not done something; "Thy conscience knoweth that thou hast often spoken evil of others" (Eccles. 7:23), and according to this, conscience is said to witness. In another way, so far as through the conscience we judge that something should be done or not done; and in this sense, conscience is said to incite or to bind. In the third way, so far as by conscience we judge that something done is well done or ill done, and in this sense conscience is said to excuse, accuse, or torment. Now, it is clear that all these things follow the actual application of knowledge to what we do. Wherefore, properly speaking, conscience denominates an act. But since habit is a principle of act, sometimes the name conscience is given to the first natural habit—namely, "synderesis": thus Jerome calls "synderesis" conscience (Gloss. Ezech. 1:6); Basil [*Hom. in princ. Proverb.], the "natural power of judgment," and Damascene [*De Fide Orth. iv. 22] says that it is the "law of our intellect." For it is customary for causes and effects to be called after one another.

Reply Obj. 1: Conscience is called a spirit, so far as spirit is the same as mind; because conscience is a certain pronouncement of the mind.

Reply Obj. 2: The conscience is said to be defiled, not as a subject, but as the thing known is in knowledge; so far as someone knows he is defiled.

Reply Obj. 3: Although an act does not always remain in itself, yet it always remains in its cause, which is power and habit. Now all the habits by which conscience is formed, although many, nevertheless have their efficacy from one first habit, the habit of first principles, which is called "synderesis." And for this special reason, this habit is sometimes called conscience, as we have said above.

## QUESTION 80

OF THE APPETITIVE POWERS IN GENERAL (In Two Articles)

Next we consider the appetitive powers, concerning which there are four heads of consideration: first, the appetitive powers in general; second, sensuality; third, the will; fourth, the free-will. Under the first there are two points of inquiry:

(1) Whether the appetite should be considered a special power of the soul?

(2) Whether the appetite should be divided into intellectual and sensitive as distinct powers?

FIRST ARTICLE [I, Q. 80, Art. 1]

Whether the Appetite Is a Special Power of the Soul?

Objection 1: It would seem that the appetite is not a special power of the soul. For no power of the soul is to be assigned for those things which are common to animate and to inanimate things. But appetite is common to animate and inanimate things: since "all desire good," as the Philosopher says (Ethic. i, 1). Therefore the appetite is not a special power of the soul.

Obj. 2: Further, powers are differentiated by their objects. But what we desire is the same as what we know. Therefore the appetitive power is not distinct from the apprehensive power.

Obj. 3: Further, the common is not divided from the proper. But each power of the soul desires some particular desirable thing—namely its own suitable object. Therefore, with regard to this object which is the desirable in general, we should not assign some particular power distinct from the others, called the appetitive power.

*On the contrary,* The Philosopher distinguishes (De Anima ii, 3) the appetitive from the other powers. Damascene also (De Fide Orth. ii, 22) distinguishes the appetitive from the cognitive powers.

*I answer that,* It is necessary to assign an appetitive power to the soul. To make this evident, we must observe that some inclination follows every form: for example, fire, by its form, is inclined to rise, and to generate its like. Now, the form is found to have a more perfect existence in those things which participate knowledge than in those which lack knowledge. For in those which lack knowledge, the form is found to determine each thing only to its own being—that is, to its nature. Therefore this natural form is followed by a natural inclination, which is called the natural appetite. But in those things which have knowledge, each one is determined to its own natural being by its natural form, in such a manner that it is nevertheless receptive of the species of other things: for example, sense receives the species of all things sensible, and the intellect, of all things intelligible, so that the soul of man is, in a way, all things by sense and intellect: and thereby, those things that have knowledge, in a way, approach to a likeness to God, "in Whom all things pre-exist," as Dionysius says (Div. Nom. v).

Therefore, as forms exist in those things that have knowledge in a higher manner and above the manner of natural forms; so must there be in them an inclination surpassing the natural inclination, which is called the natural appetite. And this superior inclination belongs to the appetitive power of the soul, through which the animal is able to desire what it apprehends, and not only that to which it is inclined by its natural form. And so it is necessary to assign an appetitive power to the soul.

Reply Obj. 1: Appetite is found in things which have knowledge, above the common manner in which it is found in all things, as we have said above. Therefore it is necessary to assign to the soul a particular power.

Reply Obj. 2: What is apprehended and what is desired are the same in reality, but differ in aspect: for a thing is apprehended as something sensible or intelligible, whereas it is desired as suitable or good. Now, it is diversity of aspect in the objects, and not material diversity, which demands a diversity of powers.

Reply Obj. 3: Each power of the soul is a form or nature, and has a natural inclination to something. Wherefore each power desires by the natural appetite that object which is suitable to itself. Above which natural appetite is the animal appetite, which follows the apprehension, and by which something is desired not as suitable to this or that power, such as sight for seeing, or sound for hearing; but simply as suitable to the animal.

SECOND ARTICLE [I, Q. 80, Art. 2]

Whether the Sensitive and Intellectual Appetites Are Distinct Powers?

Objection 1: It would seem that the sensitive and intellectual appetites are not distinct powers. For powers are not differentiated by accidental differences, as we have seen above (Q. 77, A. 3). But it is accidental to the appetible object whether it be apprehended by the sense or by the intellect. Therefore the sensitive and intellectual appetites are not distinct powers.

Obj. 2: Further, intellectual knowledge is of universals; and so it is distinct from sensitive knowledge, which is of individual things. But there is no place for this distinction in the appetitive part: for since the appetite is a movement of the soul to individual things, seemingly every act of the appetite regards an individual thing. Therefore the intellectual appetite is not distinguished from the sensitive.

Obj. 3: Further, as under the apprehensive power, the appetitive is subordinate as a lower power, so also is the motive power. But the motive power which in man follows the intellect is not distinct from the motive power which in animals follows sense. Therefore, for a like reason, neither is there distinction in the appetitive part.

*On the contrary,* The Philosopher (De Anima iii, 9) distinguishes a double appetite, and says (De Anima iii, 11) that the higher appetite moves the lower.

*I answer that,* We must needs say that the intellectual appetite is a distinct power from the sensitive appetite. For the appetitive power is a passive power, which is naturally moved by the thing apprehended: wherefore the apprehended appetible is a mover which is not moved, while the appetite is a mover moved, as the Philosopher says in De Anima*iii, 10 and*Metaph. xii (Did. xi, 7). Now things passive and movable are differentiated according to the distinction of the corresponding active and motive principles; because the motive must be proportionate to the movable, and the active to the passive: indeed, the passive power itself has its very nature from its relation to its active principle. Therefore, since what is apprehended by the intellect and what is apprehended by sense are generically different; consequently, the intellectual appetite is distinct from the sensitive.

Reply Obj. 1: It is not accidental to the thing desired to be apprehended by the sense or the intellect; *on the contrary,* this belongs to it by its nature; for the appetible does not move the appetite except as it is apprehended. Wherefore differences in the thing apprehended are of themselves differences of the appetible. And so the appetitive powers are distinct according to the distinction of the things apprehended, as their proper objects.

Reply Obj. 2: The intellectual appetite, though it tends to individual things which exist outside the soul, yet tends to them as standing under the universal; as when it desires something because it is good. Wherefore the Philosopher says (Rhetoric. ii, 4) that hatred can regard a universal, as when "we hate every kind of thief." In the same way by the intellectual appetite we may desire the immaterial good, which is not apprehended by sense, such as knowledge, virtue, and suchlike.

## QUESTION 81

OF THE POWER OF SENSUALITY (In Three Articles)

Next we have to consider the power of sensuality, concerning which there are three points of inquiry:

(1) Whether sensuality is only an appetitive power?

(2) Whether it is divided into irascible and concupiscible as distinct powers?

(3) Whether the irascible and concupiscible powers obey reason?

FIRST ARTICLE [I, Q. 81, Art. 1]

Whether Sensuality Is Only Appetitive?

Objection 1: It would seem that sensuality is not only appetitive, but also cognitive. For Augustine says (De Trin. xii, 12) that "the sensual movement of the soul which is directed to the bodily senses is common to us and beasts." But the bodily senses belong to the apprehensive powers. Therefore sensuality is a cognitive power.

Obj. 2: Further, things which come under one division seem to be of one genus. But Augustine (De Trin. xii, 12) divides sensuality against the higher and lower reason, which belong to knowledge. Therefore sensuality also is apprehensive.

Obj. 3: Further, in man's temptations sensuality stands in the place of the "serpent." But in the temptation of our first parents, the serpent presented himself as one giving information and proposing sin, which belong to the cognitive power. Therefore sensuality is a cognitive power.

*On the contrary,* Sensuality is defined as "the appetite of things belonging to the body."

*I answer that,* The name sensuality seems to be taken from the sensual movement, of which Augustine speaks (De Trin. xii, 12, 13), just as the name of a power is taken from its act; for instance, sight from seeing. Now the sensual movement is an appetite following sensitive apprehension. For the act of the apprehensive power is not so properly called a movement as the act of the appetite: since the operation of the apprehensive power is completed in the very fact that the thing apprehended is in the one that apprehends: while the operation of the appetitive power is completed in the fact that he who desires is borne towards the thing desirable. Therefore the operation of the apprehensive power is likened to rest: whereas the operation of the appetitive power is rather likened to movement. Wherefore by sensual movement we understand the operation of the appetitive power: so that sensuality is the name of the sensitive appetite.

Reply Obj. 1: By saying that the sensual movement of the soul is directed to the bodily senses, Augustine does not give us to understand that the bodily senses are included in sensuality, but rather that the movement of sensuality is a certain inclination to the bodily senses, since we desire things which are apprehended through the bodily senses. And thus the bodily senses appertain to sensuality as a preamble.

Reply Obj. 2: Sensuality is divided against higher and lower reason, as having in common with them the act of movement: for the apprehensive power, to which belong the higher and lower reason, is a motive power; as is appetite, to which appertains sensuality.

Reply Obj. 3: The serpent not only showed and proposed sin, but also incited to the commission of sin. And in this, sensuality is signified by the serpent.

SECOND ARTICLE [I, Q. 81, Art. 2]

Whether the Sensitive Appetite Is Divided into the Irascible and Concupiscible As Distinct Powers?

Objection 1: It would seem that the sensitive appetite is not divided into the irascible and concupiscible as distinct powers. For the same power of the soul regards both sides of a contrariety, as sight regards both black and white, according to the Philosopher (De Anima ii, 11). But suitable and harmful are contraries. Since, then, the concupiscible power regards what is suitable, while the irascible is concerned with what is harmful, it seems that irascible and concupiscible are the same power in the soul.

Obj. 2: Further, the sensitive appetite regards only what is suitable according to the senses. But such is the object of the concupiscible power. Therefore there is no sensitive appetite differing from the concupiscible.

Obj. 3: Further, hatred is in the irascible part: for Jerome says on Matt. 13:33: "We ought to have the hatred of vice in the irascible power." But hatred is contrary to love, and is in the concupiscible part. Therefore the concupiscible and irascible are the same powers.

*On the contrary,* Gregory of Nyssa (Nemesius, De Natura Hominis) and Damascene (De Fide Orth. ii, 12) assign two parts to the sensitive appetite, the irascible and the concupiscible.

*I answer that,* The sensitive appetite is one generic power, and is called sensuality; but it is divided into two powers, which are species of the sensitive appetite—the irascible and the concupiscible. In order to make this clear, we must observe that in natural corruptible things there is needed an inclination not only to the acquisition of what is suitable and to the avoiding of what is harmful, but also to resistance against corruptive and contrary agencies which are a hindrance to the acquisition of what is suitable, and are productive of harm. For example, fire has a natural inclination, not only to rise from a lower position, which is unsuitable to it, towards a higher position which is suitable, but also to resist whatever destroys or hinders its action. Therefore, since the sensitive appetite is an inclination following sensitive apprehension, as natural appetite is an inclination following the natural form, there must needs be in the sensitive part two appetitive powers—one through which the soul is simply inclined to seek what is suitable, according to the senses, and to fly from what is hurtful, and this is called the concupiscible: and another, whereby an animal resists these attacks that hinder what is suitable, and inflict harm, and this is called the irascible. Whence we say that its object is something arduous, because its tendency is to overcome and rise above obstacles. Now these two are not to be reduced to one principle: for sometimes the soul busies itself with unpleasant things, against the inclination of the concupiscible appetite, in order that, following the impulse of the irascible appetite, it may fight against obstacles. Wherefore also the passions of the irascible appetite counteract the passions of the concupiscible appetite: since the concupiscence, on being aroused, diminishes anger; and anger being roused, diminishes concupiscence in many cases. This is clear also from the fact that the irascible is, as it were, the champion and defender of the concupiscible when it rises up against what hinders the acquisition of the suitable things which the concupiscible desires, or against what inflicts harm, from which the concupiscible flies. And for this reason all the passions of the irascible appetite rise from the passions of the concupiscible appetite and terminate in them; for instance, anger rises from sadness, and having wrought vengeance, terminates in joy. For this reason also the quarrels of animals are about things concupiscible—namely, food and sex, as the Philosopher says [*De Animal. Histor. viii.].

Reply Obj. 1: The concupiscible power regards both what is suitable and what is unsuitable. But the object of the irascible power is to resist the onslaught of the unsuitable.

Reply Obj. 2: As in the apprehensive powers of the sensitive part there is an estimative power, which perceives those things which do not impress the senses, as we have said above (Q. 78, A. 2); so also in the sensitive appetite there is a certain appetitive power which regards something as suitable, not because it pleases the senses, but because it is useful to the animal for self-defense: and this is the irascible power.

Reply Obj. 3: Hatred belongs simply to the concupiscible appetite: but by reason of the strife which arises from hatred, it may belong to the irascible appetite.

THIRD ARTICLE [I, Q. 81, Art. 3]

Whether the irascible and concupiscible appetites obey reason?

Objection 1: It would seem that the irascible and concupiscible appetites do not obey reason. For irascible and concupiscible are parts of sensuality. But sensuality does not obey reason, wherefore it is signified by the serpent, as Augustine says (De Trin. xii, 12,13). Therefore the irascible and concupiscible appetites do not obey reason.

Obj. 2: Further, what obeys a certain thing does not resist it. But the irascible and concupiscible appetites resist reason: according to the Apostle (Rom. 7:23): "I see another law in my members fighting against the law of my mind." Therefore the irascible and concupiscible appetites do not obey reason.

Obj. 3: Further, as the appetitive power is inferior to the rational part of the soul, so also is the sensitive power. But the sensitive part of the soul does not obey reason: for we neither hear nor see just when we wish. Therefore, in like manner, neither do the powers of the sensitive appetite, the irascible and concupiscible, obey reason.

*On the contrary,* Damascene says (De Fide Orth. ii, 12) that "the part of the soul which is obedient and amenable to reason is divided into concupiscence and anger."

*I answer that,* In two ways the irascible and concupiscible powers obey the higher part, in which are the intellect or reason, and the will; first, as to reason, secondly as to the will. They obey the reason in their own acts, because in other animals the sensitive appetite is naturally moved by the estimative power; for instance, a sheep, esteeming the wolf as an enemy, is afraid. In man the estimative power, as we have said above (Q. 78, A. 4), is replaced by the cogitative power, which is called by some "the particular reason," because it compares individual intentions. Wherefore in man the sensitive appetite is naturally moved by this particular reason. But this same particular reason is naturally guided and moved according to the universal reason: wherefore in syllogistic matters particular conclusions are drawn from universal propositions. Therefore it is clear that the universal reason directs the sensitive appetite, which is divided into concupiscible and irascible; and this appetite obeys it. But because to draw particular conclusions from universal principles is not the work of the intellect, as such, but of the reason: hence it is that the irascible and concupiscible are said to obey the reason rather than to obey the intellect. Anyone can experience this in himself: for by applying certain universal considerations, anger or fear or the like may be modified or excited.

To the will also is the sensitive appetite subject in execution, which is accomplished by the motive power. For in other animals movement follows at once the concupiscible and irascible appetites: for instance, the sheep, fearing the wolf, flees at once, because it has no superior counteracting appetite. *On the contrary,* man is not moved at once, according to the irascible and concupiscible appetites: but he awaits the command of the will, which is the superior appetite. For wherever there is order among a number of motive powers, the second only moves by virtue of the first: wherefore the lower appetite is not sufficient to cause movement, unless the higher appetite consents. And this is what the Philosopher says (De Anima iii, 11), that "the higher appetite moves the lower appetite, as the higher sphere moves the lower." In this way, therefore, the irascible and concupiscible are subject to reason.

Reply Obj. 1: Sensuality is signified by the serpent, in what is proper to it as a sensitive power. But the irascible and concupiscible powers denominate the sensitive appetite rather on the part of the act, to which they are led by the reason, as we have said.

Reply Obj. 2: As the Philosopher says (Polit. i, 2): "We observe in an animal a despotic and a politic principle: for the soul dominates the body by a despotic power; but the intellect dominates the appetite by a politic and royal power." For a power is called despotic whereby a man rules his slaves, who have not the right to resist in any way the orders of the one that commands them, since they have nothing of their own. But that power is called politic and royal by which a man rules over free subjects, who, though subject to the government of the ruler, have nevertheless something of their own, by reason of which they can resist the orders of him who commands. And so, the soul is said to rule the body by a despotic power, because the members of the body cannot in any way resist the sway of the soul, but at the soul's command both hand and foot, and whatever member is naturally moved by voluntary movement, are moved at once. But the intellect or reason is said to rule the irascible and concupiscible by a politic power: because the sensitive appetite has something of its own, by virtue whereof it can resist the commands of reason. For the sensitive appetite is naturally moved, not only by the estimative power in other animals, and in man by the cogitative power which the universal reason guides, but also by the imagination and sense. Whence it is that we experience that the irascible and concupiscible powers do resist reason, inasmuch as we sense or imagine something pleasant, which reason forbids, or unpleasant, which reason commands. And so from the fact that the irascible and concupiscible resist reason in something, we must not conclude that they do not obey.

Reply Obj. 3: The exterior senses require for action exterior sensible things, whereby they are affected, and the presence of which is not ruled by reason. But the interior powers, both appetitive and apprehensive, do not require exterior things. Therefore they are subject to the command of reason, which can not only incite or modify the affections of the appetitive power, but can also form the phantasms of the imagination.

## QUESTION 82

OF THE WILL (In Five Articles)

We next consider the will. Under this head there are five points of inquiry:

(1) Whether the will desires something of necessity?

(2) Whether it desires everything of necessity?

(3) Whether it is a higher power than the intellect?

(4) Whether the will moves the intellect?

(5) Whether the will is divided into irascible and concupiscible?

FIRST ARTICLE [I, Q. 82, Art. 1]

Whether the Will Desires Something of Necessity?

Objection 1: It would seem that the will desires nothing of necessity. For Augustine says (De Civ. Dei v, 10) that it anything is necessary, it is not voluntary. But whatever the will desires is voluntary. Therefore nothing that the will desires is desired of necessity.

Obj. 2: Further, the rational powers, according to the Philosopher (Metaph. viii, 2), extend to opposite things. But the will is a rational power, because, as he says (De Anima iii, 9), "the will is in the reason." Therefore the will extends to opposite things, and therefore it is determined to nothing of necessity.

Obj. 3: Further, by the will we are masters of our own actions. But we are not masters of that which is of necessity. Therefore the act of the will cannot be necessitated.

*On the contrary,* Augustine says (De Trin. xiii, 4) that "all desire happiness with one will." Now if this were not necessary, but contingent, there would at least be a few exceptions. Therefore the will desires something of necessity.

*I answer that,* The word "necessity" is employed in many ways. For that which must be is necessary. Now that a thing must be may belong to it by an intrinsic principle—either material, as when we say that everything composed of contraries is of necessity corruptible—or formal, as when we say that it is necessary for the three angles of a triangle to be equal to two right angles. And this is "natural" and "absolute necessity." In another way, that a thing must be, belongs to it by reason of something extrinsic, which is either the end or the agent. On the part of the end, as when without it the end is not to be attained or so well attained: for instance, food is said to be necessary for life, and a horse is necessary for a journey. This is called "necessity of end," and sometimes also "utility." On the part of the agent, a thing must be, when someone is forced by some agent, so that he is not able to do the contrary. This is called "necessity of coercion."

Now this necessity of coercion is altogether repugnant to the will. For we call that violent which is against the inclination of a thing. But the very movement of the will is an inclination to something. Therefore, as a thing is called natural because it is according to the inclination of nature, so a thing is called voluntary because it is according to the inclination of the will. Therefore, just as it is impossible for a thing to be at the same time violent and natural, so it is impossible for a thing to be absolutely coerced or violent, and voluntary.

But necessity of end is not repugnant to the will, when the end cannot be attained except in one way: thus from the will to cross the sea, arises in the will the necessity to wish for a ship.

In like manner neither is natural necessity repugnant to the will. Indeed, more than this, for as the intellect of necessity adheres to the first principles, the will must of necessity adhere to the last end, which is happiness: since the end is in practical matters what the principle is in speculative matters. For what befits a thing naturally and immovably must be the root and principle of all else appertaining thereto, since the nature of a thing is the first in everything, and every movement arises from something immovable.

Reply Obj. 1: The words of Augustine are to be understood of the necessity of coercion. But natural necessity "does not take away the liberty of the will," as he says himself (De Civ. Dei v, 10).

Reply Obj. 2: The will, so far as it desires a thing naturally, corresponds rather to the intellect as regards natural principles than to the reason, which extends to opposite things. Wherefore in this respect it is rather an intellectual than a rational power.

Reply Obj. 3: We are masters of our own actions by reason of our being able to choose this or that. But choice regards not the end, but "the means to the end," as the Philosopher says (Ethic. iii, 9). Wherefore the desire of the ultimate end does not regard those actions of which we are masters.

SECOND ARTICLE [I, Q. 82, Art. 2]

Whether the Will Desires of Necessity, Whatever It Desires?

Objection 1: It would seem that the will desires all things of necessity, whatever it desires. For Dionysius says (Div. Nom. iv) that "evil is outside the scope of the will." Therefore the will tends of necessity to the good which is proposed to it.

Obj. 2: Further, the object of the will is compared to the will as the mover to the thing movable. But the movement of the movable necessarily follows the mover. Therefore it seems that the will's object moves it of necessity.

Obj. 3: Further, as the thing apprehended by sense is the object of the sensitive appetite, so the thing apprehended by the intellect is the object of the intellectual appetite, which is called the will. But what is apprehended by the sense moves the sensitive appetite of necessity: for Augustine says (Gen. ad lit. ix, 14) that "animals are moved by things seen." Therefore it seems that whatever is apprehended by the intellect moves the will of necessity.

*On the contrary,* Augustine says (Retract. i, 9) that "it is the will by which we sin and live well," and so the will extends to opposite things. Therefore it does not desire of necessity all things whatsoever it desires.

*I answer that,* The will does not desire of necessity whatsoever it desires. In order to make this evident we must observe that as the intellect naturally and of necessity adheres to the first principles, so the will adheres to the last end, as we have said already (A. 1). Now there are some things intelligible which have not a necessary connection with the first principles; such as contingent propositions, the denial of which does not involve a denial of the first principles. And to such the intellect does not assent of necessity. But there are some propositions which have a necessary connection with the first principles: such as demonstrable conclusions, a denial of which involves a denial of the first principles. And to these the intellect assents of necessity, when once it is aware of the necessary connection of these conclusions with the principles; but it does not assent of necessity until through the demonstration it recognizes the necessity of such connection. It is the same with the will. For there are certain individual goods which have not a necessary connection with happiness, because without them a man can be happy: and to such the will does not adhere of necessity. But there are some things which have a necessary connection with happiness, by means of which things man adheres to God, in Whom alone true happiness consists. Nevertheless, until through the certitude of the Divine Vision the necessity of such connection be shown, the will does not adhere to God of necessity, nor to those things which are of God. But the will of the man who sees God in His essence of necessity adheres to God, just as now we desire of necessity to be happy. It is therefore clear that the will does not desire of necessity whatever it desires.

Reply Obj. 1: The will can tend to nothing except under the aspect of good. But because good is of many kinds, for this reason the will is not of necessity determined to one.

Reply Obj. 2: The mover, then, of necessity causes movement in the thing movable, when the power of the mover exceeds the thing movable, so that its entire capacity is subject to the mover. But as the capacity of the will regards the universal and perfect good, its capacity is not subjected to any individual good. And therefore it is not of necessity moved by it.

Reply Obj. 3: The sensitive power does not compare different things with each other, as reason does: but it simply apprehends some one thing. Therefore, according to that one thing, it moves the sensitive appetite in a determinate way. But the reason is a power that compares several things together: therefore from several things the intellectual appetite—that is, the will—may be moved; but not of necessity from one thing.

THIRD ARTICLE [I, Q. 82, Art. 3]

Whether the Will Is a Higher Power Than the Intellect?

Objection 1: It would seem that the will is a higher power than the intellect. For the object of the will is good and the end. But the end is the first and highest cause. Therefore the will is the first and highest power.

Obj. 2: Further, in the order of natural things we observe a progress from imperfect things to perfect. And this also appears in the powers of the soul: for sense precedes the intellect, which is more noble. Now the act of the will, in the natural order, follows the act of the intellect. Therefore the will is a more noble and perfect power than the intellect.

Obj. 3: Further, habits are proportioned to their powers, as perfections to what they make perfect. But the habit which perfects the will—namely, charity—is more noble than the habits which perfect the intellect: for it is written (1 Cor. 13:2): "If I should know all mysteries, and if I should have all faith, and have not charity, I am nothing." Therefore the will is a higher power than the intellect.

*On the contrary,* The Philosopher holds the intellect to be the higher power than the intellect.

*I answer that,* The superiority of one thing over another can be considered in two ways: "absolutely" and "relatively." Now a thing is considered to be such absolutely which is considered such in itself: but relatively as it is such with regard to something else. If therefore the intellect and will be considered with regard to themselves, then the intellect is the higher power. And this is clear if we compare their respective objects to one another. For the object of the intellect is more simple and more absolute than the object of the will; since the object of the intellect is the very idea of appetible good; and the appetible good, the idea of which is in the intellect, is the object of the will. Now the more simple and the more abstract a thing is, the nobler and higher it is in itself; and therefore the object of the intellect is higher than the object of the will. Therefore, since the proper nature of a power is in its order to its object, it follows that the intellect in itself and absolutely is higher and nobler than the will. But relatively and by comparison with something else, we find that the will is sometimes higher than the intellect, from the fact that the object of the will occurs in something higher than that in which occurs the object of the intellect. Thus, for instance, I might say that hearing is relatively nobler than sight, inasmuch as something in which there is sound is nobler than something in which there is color, though color is nobler and simpler than sound. For as we have said above (Q. 16, A. 1; Q. 27, A. 4), the action of the intellect consists in this—that the idea of the thing understood is in the one who understands; while the act of the will consists in this—that the will is inclined to the thing itself as existing in itself. And therefore the Philosopher says in *Metaph.* vi (Did. v, 2) that "good and evil," which are objects of the will, "are in things," but "truth and error," which are objects of the intellect, "are in the mind."

When, therefore, the thing in which there is good is nobler than the soul itself, in which is the idea understood; by comparison with such a thing, the will is higher than the intellect. But when the thing which is good is less noble than the soul, then even in comparison with that thing the intellect is higher than the will. Wherefore the love of God is better than the knowledge of God; but, *on the contrary*, the knowledge of corporeal things is better than the love thereof. Absolutely, however, the intellect is nobler than the will.

Reply Obj. 1: The aspect of causality is perceived by comparing one thing to another, and in such a comparison the idea of good is found to be nobler: but truth signifies something more absolute, and extends to the idea of good itself: wherefore even good is something true. But, again, truth is something good: forasmuch as the intellect is a thing, and truth its end. And among other ends this is the most excellent: as also is the intellect among the other powers.

Reply Obj. 2: What precedes in order of generation and time is less perfect: for in one and in the same thing potentiality precedes act, and imperfection precedes perfection. But what precedes absolutely and in the order of nature is more perfect: for thus act precedes potentiality. And in this way the intellect precedes the will, as the motive power precedes the thing movable, and as the active precedes the passive; for good which is understood moves the will.

Reply Obj. 3: This reason is verified of the will as compared with what is above the soul. For charity is the virtue by which we love God.

FOURTH ARTICLE [I, Q. 82, Art. 4]

Whether the Will Moves the Intellect?

Objection 1: It would seem that the will does not move the intellect. For what moves excels and precedes what is moved, because what moves is an agent, and "the agent is nobler than the patient," as Augustine says (Gen. ad lit. xii, 16), and the Philosopher (De Anima iii, 5). But the intellect excels and precedes the will, as we have said above (A. 3). Therefore the will does not move the intellect.

Obj. 2: Further, what moves is not moved by what is moved, except perhaps accidentally. But the intellect moves the will, because the good apprehended by the intellect moves without being moved; whereas the appetite moves and is moved. Therefore the intellect is not moved by the will.

Obj. 3: Further, we can will nothing but what we understand. If, therefore, in order to understand, the will moves by willing to understand, that act of the will must be preceded by another act of the intellect, and this act of the intellect by another act of the will, and so on indefinitely, which is impossible. Therefore the will does not move the intellect.

*On the contrary,* Damascene says (De Fide Orth. ii, 26): "It is in our power to learn an art or not, as we list." But a thing is in our power by the will, and we learn art by the intellect. Therefore the will moves the intellect.

*I answer that,* A thing is said to move in two ways: First, as an end; for instance, when we say that the end moves the agent. In this way the intellect moves the will, because the good understood is the object of the will, and moves it as an end. Secondly, a thing is said to move as an agent, as what alters moves what is altered, and what impels moves what is impelled. In this way the will moves the intellect and all the powers of the soul, as Anselm says (Eadmer, De Similitudinibus). The reason is, because wherever we have order among a number of active powers, that power which regards the universal end moves the powers which regard particular ends. And we may observe this both in nature and in things politic. For the heaven, which aims at the universal preservation of things subject to generation and corruption, moves all inferior bodies, each of which aims at the preservation of its own species or of the individual. The king also, who aims at the common good of the whole kingdom, by his rule moves all the governors of cities, each of whom rules over his own particular city. Now the object of the will is good and the end in general, and each power is directed to some suitable good proper to it, as sight is directed to the perception of color, and the intellect to the knowledge of truth. Therefore the will as agent moves all the powers of the soul to their respective acts, except the natural powers of the vegetative part, which are not subject to our will.

Reply Obj. 1: The intellect may be considered in two ways: as apprehensive of universal being and truth, and as a thing and a particular power having a determinate act. In like manner also the will may be considered in two ways: according to the common nature of its object—that is to say, as appetitive of universal good—and as a determinate power of the soul having a determinate act. If, therefore, the intellect and the will be compared with one another according to the universality of their respective objects, then, as we have said above (A. 3), the intellect is simply higher and nobler than the will. If, however, we take the intellect as regards the common nature of its object and the will as a determinate power, then again the intellect is higher and nobler than the will, because under the notion of being and truth is contained both the will itself, and its act, and its object. Wherefore the intellect understands the will, and its act, and its object, just as it understands other species of things, as stone or wood, which are contained in the common notion of being and truth. But if we consider the will as regards the common nature of its object, which is good, and the intellect as a thing and a special power; then the intellect itself, and its act, and its object, which is truth, each of which is some species of good, are contained under the common notion of good. And in this way the will is higher than the intellect, and can move it. From this we can easily understand why these powers include one another in their acts, because the intellect understands that the will wills, and the will wills the intellect to understand. In the same way good is contained in truth, inasmuch as it is an understood truth, and truth in good, inasmuch as it is a desired good.

Reply Obj. 2: The intellect moves the will in one sense, and the will moves the intellect in another, as we have said above.

Reply Obj. 3: There is no need to go on indefinitely, but we must stop at the intellect as preceding all the rest. For every movement of the will must be preceded by apprehension, whereas every apprehension is not preceded by an act of the will; but the principle of counselling and understanding is an intellectual principle higher than our intellect—namely, God—as also Aristotle says (Eth. Eudemic. vii, 14), and in this way he explains that there is no need to proceed indefinitely.

FIFTH ARTICLE [I, Q. 82, Art. 5]

Whether We Should Distinguish Irascible and Concupiscible Parts in the Superior Appetite?

Objection 1: It would seem that we ought to distinguish irascible and concupiscible parts in the superior appetite, which is the will. For the concupiscible power is so called from "concupiscere" (to desire), and the irascible part from "irasci" (to be angry). But there is a concupiscence which cannot belong to the sensitive appetite, but only to the intellectual, which is the will; as the concupiscence of wisdom, of which it is said (Wis. 6:21): "The concupiscence of wisdom bringeth to the eternal kingdom." There is also a certain anger which cannot belong to the sensitive appetite, but only to the intellectual; as when our anger is directed against vice. Wherefore Jerome commenting on Matt. 13:33 warns us "to have the hatred of vice in the irascible part." Therefore we should distinguish irascible and concupiscible parts of the intellectual soul as well as in the sensitive.

Obj. 2: Further, as is commonly said, charity is in the concupiscible, and hope in the irascible part. But they cannot be in the sensitive appetite, because their objects are not sensible, but intellectual. Therefore we must assign an irascible and concupiscible power to the intellectual part.

Obj. 3: Further, it is said (De Spiritu et Anima) that "the soul has these powers"—namely, the irascible, concupiscible, and rational—"before it is united to the body." But no power of the sensitive part belongs to the soul alone, but to the soul and body united, as we have said above (Q. 78, AA. 5, 8). Therefore the irascible and concupiscible powers are in the will, which is the intellectual appetite.

*On the contrary,* Gregory of Nyssa (Nemesius, De Nat. Hom.) says that the irrational part of the soul is divided into the desiderative and irascible, and Damascene says the same (De Fide Orth. ii, 12). And the Philosopher says (De Anima iii, 9) "that the will is in reason, while in the irrational part of the soul are concupiscence and anger," or "desire and animus."

*I answer that,* The irascible and concupiscible are not parts of the intellectual appetite, which is called the will. Because, as was said above (Q. 59, A. 4; Q. 79, A. 7), a power which is directed to an object according to some common notion is not differentiated by special differences which are contained under that common notion. For instance, because sight regards the visible thing under the common notion of something colored, the visual power is not multiplied according to the different kinds of color: but if there were a power regarding white as white, and not as something colored, it would be distinct from a power regarding black as black.

Now the sensitive appetite does not consider the common notion of good, because neither do the senses apprehend the universal. And therefore the parts of the sensitive appetite are differentiated by the different notions of particular good: for the concupiscible regards as proper to it the notion of good, as something pleasant to the senses and suitable to nature: whereas the irascible regards the notion of good as something that wards off and repels what is hurtful. But the will regards good according to the common notion of good, and therefore in the will, which is the intellectual appetite, there is no differentiation of appetitive powers, so that there be in the intellectual appetite an irascible power distinct from a concupiscible power: just as neither on the part of the intellect are the apprehensive powers multiplied, although they are on the part of the senses.

Reply Obj. 1: Love, concupiscence, and the like can be understood in two ways. Sometimes they are taken as passions—arising, that is, with a certain commotion of the soul. And thus they are commonly understood, and in this sense they are only in the sensitive appetite. They may, however, be taken in another way, as far as they are simple affections without passion or commotion of the soul, and thus they are acts of the will. And in this sense, too, they are attributed to the angels and to God. But if taken in this sense, they do not belong to different powers, but only to one power, which is called the will.

Reply Obj. 2: The will itself may be said to [be] irascible, as far as it wills to repel evil, not from any sudden movement of a passion, but from a judgment of the reason. And in the same way the will may be said to be concupiscible on account of its desire for good. And thus in the irascible and concupiscible are charity and hope—that is, in the will as ordered to such acts. And in this way, too, we may understand the words quoted (De Spiritu et Anima); that the irascible and concupiscible powers are in the soul before it is united to the body (as long as we understand priority of nature, and not of time), although there is no need to have faith in what that book says. Whence the answer to the third objection is clear.

## QUESTION 83

OF FREE-WILL (In Four Articles)

We now inquire concerning free-will. Under this head there are four points of inquiry:

(1) Whether man has free-will?

(2) What is free-will—a power, an act, or a habit?

(3) If it is a power, is it appetitive or cognitive?

(4) If it is appetitive, is it the same power as the will, or distinct?

FIRST ARTICLE [I, Q. 83, Art. 1]

Whether Man Has Free-Will?

Objection 1: It would seem that man has not free-will. For whoever has free-will does what he wills. But man does not what he wills; for it is written (Rom. 7:19): "For the good which I will I do not, but the evil which I will not, that I do." Therefore man has not free-will.

Obj. 2: Further, whoever has free-will has in his power to will or not to will, to do or not to do. But this is not in man's power: for it is written (Rom. 9:16): "It is not of him that willeth"—namely, to will—"nor of him that runneth"—namely, to run. Therefore man has not free-will.

Obj. 3: Further, what is "free is cause of itself," as the Philosopher says (Metaph. i, 2). Therefore what is moved by another is not free. But God moves the will, for it is written (Prov. 21:1): "The heart of the king is in the hand of the Lord; whithersoever He will He shall turn it" and (Phil. 2:13): "It is God Who worketh in you both to will and to accomplish." Therefore man has not free-will.

Obj. 4: Further, whoever has free-will is master of his own actions. But man is not master of his own actions: for it is written (Jer. 10:23): "The way of a man is not his: neither is it in a man to walk." Therefore man has not free-will.

Obj. 5: Further, the Philosopher says (Ethic. iii, 5): "According as each one is, such does the end seem to him." But it is not in our power to be of one quality or another; for this comes to us from nature. Therefore it is natural to us to follow some particular end, and therefore we are not free in so doing.

*On the contrary,* It is written (Ecclus. 15:14): "God made man from the beginning, and left him in the hand of his own counsel"; and the gloss adds: "That is of his free-will."

*I answer that,* Man has free-will: otherwise counsels, exhortations, commands, prohibitions, rewards, and punishments would be in vain. In order to make this evident, we must observe that some things act without judgment; as a stone moves downwards; and in like manner all things which lack knowledge. And some act from judgment, but not a free judgment; as brute animals. For the sheep, seeing the wolf, judges it a thing to be shunned, from a natural and not a free judgment, because it judges, not from reason, but from natural instinct. And the same thing is to be said of any judgment of brute animals. But man acts from judgment, because by his apprehensive power he judges that something should be avoided or sought. But because this judgment, in the case of some particular act, is not from a natural instinct, but from some act of comparison in the reason, therefore he acts from free judgment and retains the power of being inclined to various things. For reason in contingent matters may follow opposite courses, as we see in dialectic syllogisms and rhetorical arguments. Now particular operations are contingent, and therefore in such matters the judgment of reason may follow opposite courses, and is not determinate to one. And forasmuch as man is rational is it necessary that man have a free-will.

Reply Obj. 1: As we have said above (Q. 81, A. 3, ad 2), the sensitive appetite, though it obeys the reason, yet in a given case can resist by desiring what the reason forbids. This is therefore the good which man does not when he wishes—namely, "not to desire against reason," as Augustine says.

Reply Obj. 2: Those words of the Apostle are not to be taken as though man does not wish or does not run of his free-will, but because the free-will is not sufficient thereto unless it be moved and helped by God.

Reply Obj. 3: Free-will is the cause of its own movement, because by his free-will man moves himself to act. But it does not of necessity belong to liberty that what is free should be the first cause of itself, as neither for one thing to be cause of another need it be the first cause. God, therefore, is the first cause, Who moves causes both natural and voluntary. And just as by moving natural causes He does not prevent their acts being natural, so by moving voluntary causes He does not deprive their actions of being voluntary: but rather is He the cause of this very thing in them; for He operates in each thing according to its own nature.

Reply Obj. 4: "Man's way" is said "not to be his" in the execution of his choice, wherein he may be impeded, whether he will or not. The choice itself, however, is in us, but presupposes the help of God.

Reply Obj. 5: Quality in man is of two kinds: natural and adventitious. Now the natural quality may be in the intellectual part, or in the body and its powers. From the very fact, therefore, that man is such by virtue of a natural quality which is in the intellectual part, he naturally desires his last end, which is happiness. Which desire, indeed, is a natural desire, and is not subject to free-will, as is clear from what we have said above (Q. 82, AA. 1, 2). But on the part of the body and its powers man may be such by virtue of a natural quality, inasmuch as he is of such a temperament or disposition due to any impression whatever produced by corporeal causes, which cannot affect the intellectual part, since it is not the act of a corporeal organ. And such as a man is by virtue of a corporeal quality, such also does his end seem to him, because from such a disposition a man is inclined to choose or reject something. But these inclinations are subject to the judgment of reason, which the lower appetite obeys, as we have said (Q. 81, A. 3). Wherefore this is in no way prejudicial to free-will.

The adventitious qualities are habits and passions, by virtue of which a man is inclined to one thing rather than to another. And yet even these inclinations are subject to the judgment of reason. Such qualities, too, are subject to reason, as it is in our power either to acquire them, whether by causing them or disposing ourselves to them, or to reject them. And so there is nothing in this that is repugnant to free-will.

SECOND ARTICLE [I, Q. 83, Art. 2]

Whether Free-Will Is a Power?

Objection 1: It would seem that free-will is not a power. For free-will is nothing but a free judgment. But judgment denominates an act, not a power. Therefore free-will is not a power.

Obj. 2: Further, free-will is defined as "the faculty of the will and reason." But faculty denominates a facility of power, which is due to a habit. Therefore free-will is a habit. Moreover Bernard says (De Gratia et Lib. Arb. 1,2) that free-will is "the soul's habit of disposing of itself." Therefore it is not a power.

Obj. 3: Further, no natural power is forfeited through sin. But free-will is forfeited through sin; for Augustine says that "man, by abusing free-will, loses both it and himself." Therefore free-will is not a power.

*On the contrary,* Nothing but a power, seemingly, is the subject of a habit. But free-will is the subject of grace, by the help of which it chooses what is good. Therefore free-will is a power.

*I answer that,* Although free-will [*Liberum arbitrium—i.e. free judgment] in its strict sense denotes an act, in the common manner of speaking we call free-will, that which is the principle of the act by which man judges freely. Now in us the principle of an act is both power and habit; for we say that we know something both by knowledge and by the intellectual power. Therefore free-will must be either a power or a habit, or a power with a habit. That it is neither a habit nor a power together with a habit, can be clearly proved in two ways. First of all, because, if it is a habit, it must be a natural habit; for it is natural to man to have a free-will. But there is not natural habit in us with respect to those things which come under free-will: for we are naturally inclined to those things of which we have natural habits—for instance, to assent to first principles: while those things to which we are naturally inclined are not subject to free-will, as we have said of the desire of happiness (Q. 82, AA. 1, 2). Wherefore it is against the very notion of free-will that it should be a natural habit. And that it should be a non-natural habit is against its nature. Therefore in no sense is it a habit.

Secondly, this is clear because habits are defined as that "by reason of which we are well or ill disposed with regard to actions and passions" (Ethic. ii, 5); for by temperance we are well-disposed as regards concupiscences, and by intemperance ill-disposed: and by knowledge we are well-disposed to the act of the intellect when we know the truth, and by the contrary ill-disposed. But the free-will is indifferent to good and evil choice: wherefore it is impossible for free-will to be a habit. Therefore it is a power.

Reply Obj. 1: It is not unusual for a power to be named from its act. And so from this act, which is a free judgment, is named the power which is the principle of this act. Otherwise, if free-will denominated an act, it would not always remain in man.

Reply Obj. 2: Faculty sometimes denominates a power ready for operation, and in this sense faculty is used in the definition of free-will. But Bernard takes habit, not as divided against power, but as signifying a certain aptitude by which a man has some sort of relation to an act. And this may be both by a power and by a habit: for by a power man is, as it were, empowered to do the action, and by the habit he is apt to act well or ill.

Reply Obj. 3: Man is said to have lost free-will by falling into sin, not as to natural liberty, which is freedom from coercion, but as regards freedom from fault and unhappiness. Of this we shall treat later in the treatise on Morals in the second part of this work (I-II, Q. 85, seqq.; Q. 109).

THIRD ARTICLE [I, Q. 83, Art. 3]

Whether Free-will Is an Appetitive Power?

Objection 1: It would seem that free-will is not an appetitive, but a cognitive power. For Damascene (De Fide Orth. ii, 27) says that "free-will straightway accompanies the rational nature." But reason is a cognitive power. Therefore free-will is a cognitive power.

Obj. 2: Further, free-will is so called as though it were a free judgment. But to judge is an act of a cognitive power. Therefore free-will is a cognitive power.

Obj. 3: Further, the principal function of free-will is to choose. But choice seems to belong to knowledge, because it implies a certain comparison of one thing to another, which belongs to the cognitive power. Therefore free-will is a cognitive power.

*On the contrary,* The Philosopher says (Ethic. iii, 3) that choice is "the desire of those things which are in us." But desire is an act of the appetitive power: therefore choice is also. But free-will is that by which we choose. Therefore free-will is an appetitive power.

*I answer that,* The proper act of free-will is choice: for we say that we have a free-will because we can take one thing while refusing another; and this is to choose. Therefore we must consider the nature of free-will, by considering the nature of choice. Now two things concur in choice: one on the part of the cognitive power, the other on the part of the appetitive power. On the part of the cognitive power, counsel is required, by which we judge one thing to be preferred to another: and on the part of the appetitive power, it is required that the appetite should accept the judgment of counsel. Therefore Aristotle (Ethic. vi, 2) leaves it in doubt whether choice belongs principally to the appetitive or the cognitive power: since he says that choice is either "an appetitive intellect or an intellectual appetite." But (Ethic. iii, 3) he inclines to its being an intellectual appetite when he describes choice as "a desire proceeding from counsel." And the reason of this is because the proper object of choice is the means to the end: and this, as such, is in the nature of that good which is called useful: wherefore since good, as such, is the object of the appetite, it follows that choice is principally an act of the appetitive power. And thus free-will is an appetitive power.

Reply Obj. 1: The appetitive powers accompany the apprehensive, and in this sense Damascene says that free-will straightway accompanies the rational power.

Reply Obj. 2: Judgment, as it were, concludes and terminates counsel. Now counsel is terminated, first, by the judgment of reason; secondly, by the acceptation of the appetite: whence the Philosopher (Ethic. iii, 3) says that, "having formed a judgment by counsel, we desire in accordance with that counsel." And in this sense choice itself is a judgment from which free-will takes its name.

Reply Obj. 3: This comparison which is implied in the choice belongs to the preceding counsel, which is an act of reason. For though the appetite does not make comparisons, yet forasmuch as it is moved by the apprehensive power which does compare, it has some likeness of comparison by choosing one in preference to another.

FOURTH ARTICLE [I, Q. 83, Art. 4]

Whether Free-will Is a Power Distinct from the Will?

Objection 1: It would seem that free-will is a power distinct from the will. For Damascene says (De Fide Orth. ii, 22) that *thelesis* is one thing and *boulesis* another. But thelesis is the will, while *boulesis* seems to be the free-will, because boulesis, according to him, is will as concerning an object by way of comparison between two things. Therefore it seems that free-will is a distinct power from the will.

Obj. 2: Further, powers are known by their acts. But choice, which is the act of free-will, is distinct from the act of willing, because "the act of the will regards the end, whereas choice regards the means to the end" (Ethic. iii, 2). Therefore free-will is a distinct power from the will.

Obj. 3: Further, the will is the intellectual appetite. But in the intellect there are two powers—the active and the passive. Therefore, also on the part of the intellectual appetite, there must be another power besides the will. And this, seemingly, can only be free-will. Therefore free-will is a distinct power from the will.

*On the contrary,* Damascene says (De Fide Orth. iii, 14) free-will is nothing else than the will.

*I answer that,* The appetitive powers must be proportionate to the apprehensive powers, as we have said above (Q. 64, A. 2). Now, as on the part of the intellectual apprehension we have intellect and reason, so on the part of the intellectual appetite we have will, and free-will which is nothing else but the power of choice. And this is clear from their relations to their respective objects and acts. For the act of *understanding* implies the simple acceptation of something; whence we say that we understand first principles, which are known of themselves without any comparison. But to *reason,* properly speaking, is to come from one thing to the knowledge of another: wherefore, properly speaking, we reason about conclusions, which are known from the principles. In like manner on the part of the appetite to "will" implies the simple appetite for something: wherefore the will is said to regard the end, which is desired for itself. But to "choose" is to desire something for the sake of obtaining something else: wherefore, properly speaking, it regards the means to the end. Now, in matters of knowledge, the principles are related to the conclusion to which we assent on account of the principles: just as, in appetitive matters, the end is related to the means, which is desired on account of the end. Wherefore it is evident that as the intellect is to reason, so is the will to the power of choice, which is free-will. But it has been shown above (Q. 79, A. 8) that it belongs to the same power both to understand and to reason, even as it belongs to the same power to be at rest and to be in movement. Wherefore it belongs also to the same power to will and to choose: and on this account the will and the free-will are not two powers, but one.

Reply Obj. 1: *Boulesis* is distinct from thelesis on account of a distinction, not of powers, but of acts.

Reply Obj. 2: Choice and will—that is, the act of willing—are different acts: yet they belong to the same power, as also to understand and to reason, as we have said.

Reply Obj. 3: The intellect is compared to the will as moving the will. And therefore there is no need to distinguish in the will an active and a passive will.

# QUESTION 84

HOW THE SOUL WHILE UNITED TO THE BODY UNDERSTANDS CORPOREAL THINGS BENEATH IT (In Eight Articles)

We now have to consider the acts of the soul in regard to the intellectual and the appetitive powers: for the other powers of the soul do not come directly under the consideration of the theologian. Furthermore, the acts of the appetitive part of the soul come under the consideration of the science of morals; wherefore we shall treat of them in the second part of this work, to which the consideration of moral matters belongs. But of the acts of the intellectual part we shall treat now.

In treating of these acts we shall proceed in the following order: First, we shall inquire how the soul understands when united to the body; secondly, how it understands when separated therefrom.

The former of these inquiries will be threefold:

(1) How the soul understands bodies which are beneath it;

(2) How it understands itself and things contained in itself;

(3) How it understands immaterial substances, which are above it.

In treating of the knowledge of corporeal things there are three points to be considered:

(1) Through what does the soul know them?

(2) How and in what order does it know them?

(3) What does it know in them?

Under the first head there are eight points of inquiry:

(1) Whether the soul knows bodies through the intellect?

(2) Whether it understands them through its essence, or through any species?

(3) If through some species, whether the species of all things intelligible are naturally innate in the soul?

(4) Whether these species are derived by the soul from certain separate immaterial forms?

(5) Whether our soul sees in the eternal ideas all that it understands?

(6) Whether it acquires intellectual knowledge from the senses?

(7) Whether the intellect can, through the species of which it is possessed, actually understand, without turning to the phantasms?

(8) Whether the judgment of the intellect is hindered by an obstacle in the sensitive powers?

FIRST ARTICLE [I, Q. 84, Art. 1]

Whether the Soul Knows Bodies Through the Intellect?

Objection 1: It would seem that the soul does not know bodies through the intellect. For Augustine says (Soliloq. ii, 4) that "bodies cannot be understood by the intellect; nor indeed anything corporeal unless it can be perceived by the senses." He says also (Gen. ad lit. xii, 24) that intellectual vision is of those things that are in the soul by their essence. But such are not bodies. Therefore the soul cannot know bodies through the intellect.

Obj. 2: Further, as sense is to the intelligible, so is the intellect to the sensible. But the soul can by no means, through the senses, understand spiritual things, which are intelligible. Therefore by no means can it, through the intellect, know bodies, which are sensible.

Obj. 3: Further, the intellect is concerned with things that are necessary and unchangeable. But all bodies are mobile and changeable. Therefore the soul cannot know bodies through the intellect.

*On the contrary,* Science is in the intellect. If, therefore, the intellect does not know bodies, it follows that there is no science of bodies; and thus perishes natural science, which treats of mobile bodies.

*I answer that,* It should be said in order to elucidate this question, that the early philosophers, who inquired into the natures of things, thought there was nothing in the world save bodies. And because they observed that all bodies are mobile, and considered them to be ever in a state of flux, they were of opinion that we can have no certain knowledge of the true nature of things. For what is in a continual state of flux, cannot be grasped with any degree of certitude, for it passes away ere the mind can form a judgment thereon: according to the saying of Heraclitus, that "it is not possible twice to touch a drop of water in a passing torrent," as the Philosopher relates (Metaph. iv, Did. iii, 5).

After these came Plato, who, wishing to save the certitude of our knowledge of truth through the intellect, maintained that, besides these things corporeal, there is another genus of beings, separate from matter and movement, which beings he called species or "ideas," by participation of which each one of these singular and sensible things is said to be either a man, or a horse, or the like. Wherefore he said that sciences and definitions, and whatever appertains to the act of the intellect, are not referred to these sensible bodies, but to those beings immaterial and separate: so that according to this the soul does not understand these corporeal things, but the separate species thereof.

Now this may be shown to be false for two reasons. First, because, since those species are immaterial and immovable, knowledge of movement and matter would be excluded from science (which knowledge is proper to natural science), and likewise all demonstration through moving and material causes. Secondly, because it seems ridiculous, when we seek for knowledge of things which are to us manifest, to introduce other beings, which cannot be the substance of those others, since they differ from them essentially: so that granted that we have a knowledge of those separate substances, we cannot for that reason claim to form a judgment concerning these sensible things.

Now it seems that Plato strayed from the truth because, having observed that all knowledge takes place through some kind of similitude, he thought that the form of the thing known must of necessity be in the knower in the same manner as in the thing known. Then he observed that the form of the thing understood is in the intellect under conditions of universality, immateriality, and immobility: which is apparent from the very operation of the intellect, whose act of understanding has a universal extension, and is subject to a certain amount of necessity: for the mode of action corresponds to the mode of the agent's form. Wherefore he concluded that the things which we understand must have in themselves an existence under the same conditions of immateriality and immobility.

But there is no necessity for this. For even in sensible things it is to be observed that the form is otherwise in one sensible than in another: for instance, whiteness may be of great intensity in one, and of a less intensity in another: in one we find whiteness with sweetness, in another without sweetness. In the same way the sensible form is conditioned differently in the thing which is external to the soul, and in the senses which receive the forms of sensible things without receiving matter, such as the color of gold without receiving gold. So also the intellect, according to its own mode, receives under conditions of immateriality and immobility, the species of material and mobile bodies: for the received is in the receiver according to the mode of the receiver. We must conclude, therefore, that through the intellect the soul knows bodies by a knowledge which is immaterial, universal, and necessary.

Reply Obj. 1: These words of Augustine are to be understood as referring to the medium of intellectual knowledge, and not to its object. For the intellect knows bodies by understanding them, not indeed through bodies, nor through material and corporeal species; but through immaterial and intelligible species, which can be in the soul by their own essence.

Reply Obj. 2: As Augustine says (De Civ. Dei xxii, 29), it is not correct to say that as the sense knows only bodies so the intellect knows only spiritual things; for it follows that God and the angels would not know corporeal things. The reason of this diversity is that the lower power does not extend to those things that belong to the higher power; whereas the higher power operates in a more excellent manner those things which belong to the lower power.

Reply Obj. 3: Every movement presupposes something immovable: for when a change of quality occurs, the substance remains unmoved; and when there is a change of substantial form, matter remains unmoved. Moreover the various conditions of mutable things are themselves immovable; for instance, though Socrates be not always sitting, yet it is an immovable truth that whenever he does sit he remains in one place. For this reason there is nothing to hinder our having an immovable science of movable things.

SECOND ARTICLE [I, Q. 84, Art. 2]

Whether the Soul Understands Corporeal Things Through Its Essence?

Objection 1: It would seem that the soul understands corporeal things through its essence. For Augustine says (De Trin. x, 5) that the soul "collects and lays hold of the images of bodies which are formed in the soul and of the soul: for in forming them it gives them something of its own substance." But the soul understands bodies by images of bodies. Therefore the soul knows bodies through its essence, which it employs for the formation of such images, and from which it forms them.

Obj. 2: Further, the Philosopher says (De Anima iii, 8) that "the soul, after a fashion, is everything." Since, therefore, like is known by like, it seems that the soul knows corporeal things through itself.

Obj. 3: Further, the soul is superior to corporeal creatures. Now lower things are in higher things in a more eminent way than in themselves, as Dionysius says (Coel. Hier. xii). Therefore all corporeal creatures exist in a more excellent way in the soul than in themselves. Therefore the soul can know corporeal creatures through its essence.

*On the contrary,* Augustine says (De Trin. ix, 3) that "the mind gathers knowledge of corporeal things through the bodily senses." But the soul itself cannot be known through the bodily senses. Therefore it does not know corporeal things through itself.

*I answer that,* The ancient philosophers held that the soul knows bodies through its essence. For it was universally admitted that "like is known by like." But they thought that the form of the thing known is in the knower in the same mode as in the thing known. The Platonists however were of a contrary opinion. For Plato, having observed that the intellectual soul has an immaterial nature, and an immaterial mode of knowledge, held that the forms of things known subsist immaterially. While the earlier natural philosophers, observing that things known are corporeal and material, held that things known must exist materially even in the soul that knows them. And therefore, in order to ascribe to the soul a knowledge of all things, they held that it has the same nature in common with all. And because the nature of a result is determined by its principles, they ascribed to the soul the nature of a principle; so that those who thought fire to be the principle of all, held that the soul had the nature of fire; and in like manner as to air and water. Lastly, Empedocles, who held the existence of our four material elements and two principles of movement, said that the soul was composed of these. Consequently, since they held that things exist in the soul materially, they maintained that all the soul's knowledge is material, thus failing to discern intellect from sense.

But this opinion will not hold. First, because in the material principle of which they spoke, the various results do not exist save in potentiality. But a thing is not known according as it is in potentiality, but only according as it is in act, as is shown *Metaph.* ix (Did. viii, 9): wherefore neither is a power known except through its act. It is therefore insufficient to ascribe to the soul the nature of the principles in order to explain the fact that it knows all, unless we further admit in the soul natures and forms of each individual result, for instance, of bone, flesh, and the like; thus does Aristotle argue against Empedocles (De Anima i, 5). Secondly, because if it were necessary for the thing known to exist materially in the knower, there would be no reason why things which have a material existence outside the soul should be devoid of knowledge; why, for instance, if by fire the soul knows fire, that fire also which is outside the soul should not have knowledge of fire.

We must conclude, therefore, that material things known must needs exist in the knower, not materially, but immaterially. The reason of this is, because the act of knowledge extends to things outside the knower: for we know things even that are external to us. Now by matter the form of a thing is determined to some one thing. Wherefore it is clear that knowledge is in inverse ratio of materiality. And consequently things that are not receptive of forms save materially, have no power of knowledge whatever—such as plants, as the Philosopher says (De Anima ii, 12). But the more immaterially a thing receives the form of the thing known, the more perfect is its knowledge. Therefore the intellect which abstracts the species not only from matter, but also from the individuating conditions of matter, has more perfect knowledge than the senses, which receive the form of the thing known, without matter indeed, but subject to material conditions. Moreover, among the senses, sight has the most perfect knowledge, because it is the least material, as we have remarked above (Q. 78, A. 3): while among intellects the more perfect is the more immaterial.

It is therefore clear from the foregoing, that if there be an intellect which knows all things by its essence, then its essence must needs have all things in itself immaterially; thus the early philosophers held that the essence of the soul, that it may know all things, must be actually composed of the principles of all material things. Now this is proper to God, that His Essence comprise all things immaterially as effects pre-exist virtually in their cause. God alone, therefore, understands all things through His Essence: but neither the human soul nor the angels can do so.

Reply Obj. 1: Augustine in that passage is speaking of an imaginary vision, which takes place through the image of bodies. To the formation of such images the soul gives part of its substance, just as a subject is given in order to be informed by some form. In this way the soul makes such images from itself; not that the soul or some part of the soul be turned into this or that image; but just as we say that a body is made into something colored because of its being informed with color. That this is the sense, is clear from what follows. For he says that the soul "keeps something"—namely, not informed with such image—"which is able freely to judge of the species of these images": and that this is the "mind" or "intellect." And he says that the part which is informed with these images—namely, the imagination—is "common to us and beasts."

Reply Obj. 2: Aristotle did not hold that the soul is actually composed of all things, as did the earlier philosophers; he said that the soul is all things, "after a fashion," forasmuch as it is in potentiality to all—through the senses, to all things sensible—through the intellect, to all things intelligible.

Reply Obj. 3: Every creature has a finite and determinate essence. Wherefore although the essence of the higher creature has a certain likeness to the lower creature, forasmuch as they have something in common generically, yet it has not a complete likeness thereof, because it is determined to a certain species other than the species of the lower creature. But the Divine Essence is a perfect likeness of all, whatsoever may be found to exist in things created, being the universal principle of all.

THIRD ARTICLE [I, Q. 84, Art. 3]

Whether the Soul Understands All Things Through Innate Species?

Objection 1: It would seem that the soul understands all things through innate species. For Gregory says, in a homily for the Ascension (xxix in Ev.), that "man has understanding in common with the angels." But angels understand all things through innate species: wherefore in the book *De Causis* it is said that "every intelligence is full of forms." Therefore the soul also has innate species of things, by means of which it understands corporeal things.

Obj. 2: Further, the intellectual soul is more excellent than corporeal primary matter. But primary matter was created by God under the forms to which it has potentiality. Therefore much more is the intellectual soul created by God under intelligible species. And so the soul understands corporeal things through innate species.

Obj. 3: Further, no one can answer the truth except concerning what he knows. But even a person untaught and devoid of acquired knowledge, answers the truth to every question if put to him in orderly fashion, as we find related in the Meno (xv seqq.) of Plato, concerning a certain individual. Therefore we have some knowledge of things even before we acquire knowledge; which would not be the case unless we had innate species. Therefore the soul understands corporeal things through innate species.

*On the contrary,* The Philosopher, speaking of the intellect, says (De Anima iii, 4) that it is like "a tablet on which nothing is written."

*I answer that,* Since form is the principle of action, a thing must be related to the form which is the principle of an action, as it is to that action: for instance, if upward motion is from lightness, then that which only potentially moves upwards must needs be only potentially light, but that which actually moves upwards must needs be actually light. Now we observe that man sometimes is only a potential knower, both as to sense and as to intellect. And he is reduced from such potentiality to act—through the action of sensible objects on his senses, to the act of sensation—by instruction or discovery, to the act of understanding. Wherefore we must say that the cognitive soul is in potentiality both to the images which are the principles of sensing, and to those which are the principles of understanding. For this reason Aristotle (De Anima iii, 4) held that the intellect by which the soul understands has no innate species, but is at first in potentiality to all such species.

But since that which has a form actually, is sometimes unable to act according to that form on account of some hindrance, as a light thing may be hindered from moving upwards; for this reason did Plato hold that naturally man's intellect is filled with all intelligible species, but that, by being united to the body, it is hindered from the realization of its act. But this seems to be unreasonable. First, because, if the soul has a natural knowledge of all things, it seems impossible for the soul so far to forget the existence of such knowledge as not to know itself to be possessed thereof: for no man forgets what he knows naturally; that, for instance, the whole is larger than the part, and such like. And especially unreasonable does this seem if we suppose that it is natural to the soul to be united to the body, as we have established above ([Q. 76] , A. 1): for it is unreasonable that the natural operation of a thing be totally hindered by that which belongs to it naturally. Secondly, the falseness of this opinion is clearly proved from the fact that if a sense be wanting, the knowledge of what is apprehended through that sense is wanting also: for instance, a man who is born blind can have no knowledge of colors. This would not be the case if the soul had innate images of all intelligible things. We must therefore conclude that the soul does not know corporeal things through innate species.

Reply Obj. 1: Man indeed has intelligence in common with the angels, but not in the same degree of perfection: just as the lower grades of bodies, which merely exist, according to Gregory (Homily on Ascension, xxix In Ev.), have not the same degree of perfection as the higher bodies. For the matter of the lower bodies is not totally completed by its form, but is in potentiality to forms which it has not: whereas the matter of heavenly bodies is totally completed by its form, so that it is not in potentiality to any other form, as we have said above (Q. 66, A. 2). In the same way the angelic intellect is perfected by intelligible species, in accordance with its nature; whereas the human intellect is in potentiality to such species.

Reply Obj. 2: Primary matter has substantial being through its form, consequently it had need to be created under some form: else it would not be in act. But when once it exists under one form it is in potentiality to others. On the other hand, the intellect does not receive substantial being through the intelligible species; and therefore there is no comparison.

Reply Obj. 3: If questions be put in an orderly fashion they proceed from universal self-evident principles to what is particular. Now by such a process knowledge is produced in the mind of the learner. Wherefore when he answers the truth to a subsequent question, this is not because he had knowledge previously, but because he thus learns for the first time. For it matters not whether the teacher proceed from universal principles to conclusions by questioning or by asserting; for in either case the mind of the listener is assured of what follows by that which preceded.

FOURTH ARTICLE [I, Q. 84, Art. 4]

Whether the Intelligible Species Are Derived by the Soul from Certain Separate Forms?

Objection 1: It would seem that the intelligible species are derived by the soul from some separate forms. For whatever is such by participation is caused by what is such essentially; for instance, that which is on fire is reduced to fire as the cause thereof. But the intellectual soul forasmuch as it is actually understanding, participates the thing understood: for, in a way, the intellect in act is the thing understood in act. Therefore what in itself and in its essence is understood in act, is the cause that the intellectual soul actually understands. Now that which in its essence is actually understood is a form existing without matter. Therefore the intelligible species, by which the soul understands, are caused by some separate forms.

Obj. 2: Further, the intelligible is to the intellect, as the sensible is to the sense. But the sensible species which are in the senses, and by which we sense, are caused by the sensible object which exists actually outside the soul. Therefore the intelligible species, by which our intellect understands, are caused by some things actually intelligible, existing outside the soul. But these can be nothing else than forms separate from matter. Therefore the intelligible forms of our intellect are derived from some separate substances.

Obj. 3: Further, whatever is in potentiality is reduced to act by something actual. If, therefore, our intellect, previously in potentiality, afterwards actually understands, this must needs be caused by some intellect which is always in act. But this is a separate intellect. Therefore the intelligible species, by which we actually understand, are caused by some separate substances.

*On the contrary,* If this were true we should not need the senses in order to understand. And this is proved to be false especially from the fact that if a man be wanting in a sense, he cannot have any knowledge of the sensibles corresponding to that sense.

*I answer that,* Some have held that the intelligible species of our intellect are derived from certain separate forms or substances. And this in two ways. For Plato, as we have said (A. 1), held that the forms of sensible things subsist by themselves without matter; for instance, the form of a man which he called *per se* man, and the form or idea of a horse which is called *per se* horse, and so forth. He said therefore that these forms are participated both by our soul and by corporeal matter; by our soul, to the effect of knowledge thereof, and by corporeal matter to the effect of existence: so that, just as corporeal matter by participating the idea of a stone, becomes an individuating stone, so our intellect, by participating the idea of a stone, is made to understand a stone. Now participation of an idea takes place by some image of the idea in the participator, just as a model is participated by a copy. So just as he held that the sensible forms, which are in corporeal matter, are derived from the ideas as certain images thereof: so he held that the intelligible species of our intellect are images of the ideas, derived therefrom. And for this reason, as we have said above (A. 1), he referred sciences and definitions to those ideas.

But since it is contrary to the nature of sensible things that their forms should subsist without matter, as Aristotle proves in many ways (Metaph. vi), Avicenna (De Anima v) setting this opinion aside, held that the intelligible species of all sensible things, instead of subsisting in themselves without matter, pre-exist immaterially in the separate intellects: from the first of which, said he, such species are derived by a second, and so on to the last separate intellect which he called the "active intelligence," from which, according to him, intelligible species flow into our souls, and sensible species into corporeal matter. And so Avicenna agrees with Plato in this, that the intelligible species of our intellect are derived from certain separate forms; but these Plato held to subsist of themselves, while Avicenna placed them in the "active intelligence." They differ, too, in this respect, that Avicenna held that the intelligible species do not remain in our intellect after it has ceased actually to understand, and that it needs to turn (to the active intellect) in order to receive them anew. Consequently he does not hold that the soul has innate knowledge, as Plato, who held that the participated ideas remain immovably in the soul.

But in this opinion no sufficient reason can be assigned for the soul being united to the body. For it cannot be said that the intellectual soul is united to the body for the sake of the body: for neither is form for the sake of matter, nor is the mover for the sake of the moved, but rather the reverse. Especially does the body seem necessary to the intellectual soul, for the latter's proper operation which is to understand: since as to its being the soul does not depend on the body. But if the soul by its very nature had an inborn aptitude for receiving intelligible species through the influence of only certain separate principles, and were not to receive them from the senses, it would not need the body in order to understand: wherefore to no purpose would it be united to the body.

But if it be said that our soul needs the senses in order to understand, through being in some way awakened by them to the consideration of those things, the intelligible species of which it receives from the separate principles: even this seems an insufficient explanation. For this awakening does not seem necessary to the soul, except in as far as it is overcome by sluggishness, as the Platonists expressed it, and by forgetfulness, through its union with the body: and thus the senses would be of no use to the intellectual soul except for the purpose of removing the obstacle which the soul encounters through its union with the body. Consequently the reason of the union of the soul with the body still remains to be sought.

And if it be said with Avicenna, that the senses are necessary to the soul, because by them it is aroused to turn to the "active intelligence" from which it receives the species: neither is this a sufficient explanation. Because if it is natural for the soul to understand through species derived from the "active intelligence," it follows that at times the soul of an individual wanting in one of the senses can turn to the active intelligence, either from the inclination of its very nature, or through being roused by another sense, to the effect of receiving the intelligible species of which the corresponding sensible species are wanting. And thus a man born blind could have knowledge of colors; which is clearly untrue. We must therefore conclude that the intelligible species, by which our soul understands, are not derived from separate forms.

Reply Obj. 1: The intelligible species which are participated by our intellect are reduced, as to their first cause, to a first principle which is by its essence intelligible—namely, God. But they proceed from that principle by means of the sensible forms and material things, from which we gather knowledge, as Dionysius says (Div. Nom. vii).

Reply Obj. 2: Material things, as to the being which they have outside the soul, may be actually sensible, but not actually intelligible. Wherefore there is no comparison between sense and intellect.

Reply Obj. 3: Our passive intellect is reduced from potentiality to act by some being in act, that is, by the active intellect, which is a power of the soul, as we have said (Q. 79, A. 4); and not by a separate intelligence, as proximate cause, although perchance as remote cause.

FIFTH ARTICLE [I, Q. 84, Art. 5]

Whether the Intellectual Soul Knows Material Things in the Eternal Types?

Objection 1: It would seem that the intellectual soul does not know material things in the eternal types. For that in which anything is known must itself be known more and previously. But the intellectual soul of man, in the present state of life, does not know the eternal types: for it does not know God in Whom the eternal types exist, but is "united to God as to the unknown," as Dionysius says (Myst. Theolog. i). Therefore the soul does not know all in the eternal types.

Obj. 2: Further, it is written (Rom. 1:20) that "the invisible things of God are clearly seen ... by the things that are made." But among the invisible things of God are the eternal types. Therefore the eternal types are known through creatures and not the converse.

Obj. 3: Further, the eternal types are nothing else but ideas, for Augustine says (QQ. 83, qu. 46) that "ideas are permanent types existing in the Divine mind." If therefore we say that the intellectual soul knows all things in the eternal types, we come back to the opinion of Plato who said that all knowledge is derived from them.

*On the contrary,* Augustine says (Confess. xii, 25): "If we both see that what you say is true, and if we both see that what I say is true, where do we see this, I pray? Neither do I see it in you, nor do you see it in me: but we both see it in the unchangeable truth which is above our minds." Now the unchangeable truth is contained in the eternal types. Therefore the intellectual soul knows all true things in the eternal types.

*I answer that,* As Augustine says (De Doctr. Christ. ii, 11): "If those who are called philosophers said by chance anything that was true and consistent with our faith, we must claim it from them as from unjust possessors. For some of the doctrines of the heathens are spurious imitations or superstitious inventions, which we must be careful to avoid when we renounce the society of the heathens." Consequently whenever Augustine, who was imbued with the doctrines of the Platonists, found in their teaching anything consistent with faith, he adopted it: and those thing which he found contrary to faith he amended. Now Plato held, as we have said above (A. 4), that the forms of things subsist of themselves apart from matter; and these he called ideas, by participation of which he said that our intellect knows all things: so that just as corporeal matter by participating the idea of a stone becomes a stone, so our intellect, by participating the same idea, has knowledge of a stone. But since it seems contrary to faith that forms of things themselves, outside the things themselves and apart from matter, as the Platonists held, asserting that *per se* life or *per se* wisdom are creative substances, as Dionysius relates (Div. Nom. xi); therefore Augustine (QQ. 83, qu. 46), for the ideas defended by Plato, substituted the types of all creatures existing in the Divine mind, according to which types all things are made in themselves, and are known to the human soul.

When, therefore, the question is asked: Does the human soul know all things in the eternal types? we must reply that one thing is said to be known in another in two ways. First, as in an object itself known; as one may see in a mirror the images of things reflected therein. In this way the soul, in the present state of life, cannot see all things in the eternal types; but the blessed who see God, and all things in Him, thus know all things in the eternal types. Secondly, one thing is said to be known in another as in a principle of knowledge: thus we might say that we see in the sun what we see by the sun. And thus we must needs say that the human soul knows all things in the eternal types, since by participation of these types we know all things. For the intellectual light itself which is in us, is nothing else than a participated likeness of the uncreated light, in which are contained the eternal types. Whence it is written (Ps. 4:6, 7), "Many say: Who showeth us good things?" which question the Psalmist answers, "The light of Thy countenance, O Lord, is signed upon us," as though he were to say: By the seal of the Divine light in us, all things are made known to us.

But since besides the intellectual light which is in us, intelligible species, which are derived from things, are required in order for us to have knowledge of material things; therefore this same knowledge is not due merely to a participation of the eternal types, as the Platonists held, maintaining that the mere participation of ideas sufficed for knowledge. Wherefore Augustine says (De Trin. iv, 16): "Although the philosophers prove by convincing arguments that all things occur in time according to the eternal types, were they able to see in the eternal types, or to find out from them how many kinds of animals there are and the origin of each? Did they not seek for this information from the story of times and places?"

But that Augustine did not understand all things to be known in their "eternal types" or in the "unchangeable truth," as though the eternal types themselves were seen, is clear from what he says (QQ. 83, qu. 46)—viz. that "not each and every rational soul can be said to be worthy of that vision," namely, of the eternal types, "but only those that are holy and pure," such as the souls of the blessed.

From what has been said the objections are easily solved.

SIXTH ARTICLE [I, Q. 84, Art. 6]

Whether Intellectual Knowledge Is Derived from Sensible Things?

Objection 1: It would seem that intellectual knowledge is not derived from sensible things. For Augustine says (QQ. 83, qu. 9) that "we cannot expect to learn the fulness of truth from the senses of the body." This he proves in two ways. First, because "whatever the bodily senses reach, is continually being changed; and what is never the same cannot be perceived." Secondly, because, "whatever we perceive by the body, even when not present to the senses, may be present to the imagination, as when we are asleep or angry: yet we cannot discern by the senses, whether what we perceive be the sensible object or the deceptive image thereof. Now nothing can be perceived which cannot be distinguished from its counterfeit." And so he concludes that we cannot expect to learn the truth from the senses. But intellectual knowledge apprehends the truth. Therefore intellectual knowledge cannot be conveyed by the senses.

Obj. 2: Further, Augustine says (Gen. ad lit. xii, 16): "We must not think that the body can make any impression on the spirit, as though the spirit were to supply the place of matter in regard to the body's action; for that which acts is in every way more excellent than that which it acts on." Whence he concludes that "the body does not cause its image in the spirit, but the spirit causes it in itself." Therefore intellectual knowledge is not derived from sensible things.

Obj. 3: Further, an effect does not surpass the power of its cause. But intellectual knowledge extends beyond sensible things: for we understand some things which cannot be perceived by the senses. Therefore intellectual knowledge is not derived from sensible things.

*On the contrary,* The Philosopher says (Metaph. i, 1; Poster. ii, 15) that the principle of knowledge is in the senses.

*I answer that,* On this point the philosophers held three opinions. For Democritus held that "all knowledge is caused by images issuing from the bodies we think of and entering into our souls," as Augustine says in his letter to Dioscorus (cxviii, 4). And Aristotle says (De Somn. et Vigil.) that Democritus held that knowledge is caused by a "discharge of images." And the reason for this opinion was that both Democritus and the other early philosophers did not distinguish between intellect and sense, as Aristotle relates (De Anima iii, 3). Consequently, since the sense is affected by the sensible, they thought that all our knowledge is affected by this mere impression brought about by sensible things. Which impression Democritus held to be caused by a discharge of images.

Plato, on the other hand, held that the intellect is distinct from the senses: and that it is an immaterial power not making use of a corporeal organ for its action. And since the incorporeal cannot be affected by the corporeal, he held that intellectual knowledge is not brought about by sensible things affecting the intellect, but by separate intelligible forms being participated by the intellect, as we have said above (AA. 4 ,5). Moreover he held that sense is a power operating of itself. Consequently neither is sense, since it is a spiritual power, affected by the sensible: but the sensible organs are affected by the sensible, the result being that the soul is in a way roused to form within itself the species of the sensible. Augustine seems to touch on this opinion (Gen. ad lit. xii, 24) where he says that the "body feels not, but the soul through the body, which it makes use of as a kind of messenger, for reproducing within itself what is announced from without." Thus according to Plato, neither does intellectual knowledge proceed from sensible knowledge, nor sensible knowledge exclusively from sensible things; but these rouse the sensible soul to the sentient act, while the senses rouse the intellect to the act of understanding.

Aristotle chose a middle course. For with Plato he agreed that intellect and sense are different. But he held that the sense has not its proper operation without the cooperation of the body; so that to feel is not an act of the soul alone, but of the "composite." And he held the same in regard to all the operations of the sensitive part. Since, therefore, it is not unreasonable that the sensible objects which are outside the soul should produce some effect in the "composite," Aristotle agreed with Democritus in this, that the operations of the sensitive part are caused by the impression of the sensible on the sense: not by a discharge, as Democritus said, but by some kind of operation. For Democritus maintained that every operation is by way of a discharge of atoms, as we gather from De Gener. i, 8. But Aristotle held that the intellect has an operation which is independent of the body's cooperation. Now nothing corporeal can make an impression on the incorporeal. And therefore in order to cause the intellectual operation according to Aristotle, the impression caused by the sensible does not suffice, but something more noble is required, for "the agent is more noble than the patient," as he says (De Gener. i, 5). Not, indeed, in the sense that the intellectual operation is effected in us by the mere impression of some superior beings, as Plato held; but that the higher and more noble agent which he calls the active intellect, of which we have spoken above (Q. 79, AA. 3, 4) causes the phantasms received from the senses to be actually intelligible, by a process of abstraction.

According to this opinion, then, on the part of the phantasms, intellectual knowledge is caused by the senses. But since the phantasms cannot of themselves affect the passive intellect, and require to be made actually intelligible by the active intellect, it cannot be said that sensible knowledge is the total and perfect cause of intellectual knowledge, but rather that it is in a way the material cause.

Reply Obj. 1: Those words of Augustine mean that we must not expect the entire truth from the senses. For the light of the active intellect is needed, through which we achieve the unchangeable truth of changeable things, and discern things themselves from their likeness.

Reply Obj. 2: In this passage Augustine speaks not of intellectual but of imaginary knowledge. And since, according to the opinion of Plato, the imagination has an operation which belongs to the soul only, Augustine, in order to show that corporeal images are impressed on the imagination, not by bodies but by the soul, uses the same argument as Aristotle does in proving that the active intellect must be separate, namely, because "the agent is more noble than the patient." And without doubt, according to the above opinion, in the imagination there must needs be not only a passive but also an active power. But if we hold, according to the opinion of Aristotle, that the action of the imagination is an action of the "composite," there is no difficulty; because the sensible body is more noble than the organ of the animal, in so far as it is compared to it as a being in act to a being in potentiality; even as the object actually colored is compared to the pupil which is potentially colored. It may, however, be said, although the first impression of the imagination is through the agency of the sensible, since "fancy is movement produced in accordance with sensation" (De Anima iii, 3), that nevertheless there is in man an operation which by synthesis and analysis forms images of various things, even of things not perceived by the senses. And Augustine's words may be taken in this sense.

Reply Obj. 3: Sensitive knowledge is not the entire cause of intellectual knowledge. And therefore it is not strange that intellectual knowledge should extend further than sensitive knowledge.

SEVENTH ARTICLE [I, Q. 84, Art. 7]

Whether the Intellect Can Actually Understand Through the Intelligible Species of Which It Is Possessed, Without Turning to the Phantasms?

Objection 1: It would seem that the intellect can actually understand through the intelligible species of which it is possessed, without turning to the phantasms. For the intellect is made actual by the intelligible species by which it is informed. But if the intellect is in act, it understands. Therefore the intelligible species suffices for the intellect to understand actually, without turning to the phantasms.

Obj. 2: Further, the imagination is more dependent on the senses than the intellect on the imagination. But the imagination can actually imagine in the absence of the sensible. Therefore much more can the intellect understand without turning to the phantasms.

Obj. 3: There are no phantasms of incorporeal things: for the imagination does not transcend time and space. If, therefore, our intellect cannot understand anything actually without turning to the phantasms, it follows that it cannot understand anything incorporeal. Which is clearly false: for we understand truth, and God, and the angels.

*On the contrary,* The Philosopher says (De Anima iii, 7) that "the soul understands nothing without a phantasm."

*I answer that,* In the present state of life in which the soul is united to a passible body, it is impossible for our intellect to understand anything actually, except by turning to the phantasms. First of all because the intellect, being a power that does not make use of a corporeal organ, would in no way be hindered in its act through the lesion of a corporeal organ, if for its act there were not required the act of some power that does make use of a corporeal organ. Now sense, imagination and the other powers belonging to the sensitive part, make use of a corporeal organ. Wherefore it is clear that for the intellect to understand actually, not only when it acquires fresh knowledge, but also when it applies knowledge already acquired, there is need for the act of the imagination and of the other powers. For when the act of the imagination is hindered by a lesion of the corporeal organ, for instance in a case of frenzy; or when the act of the memory is hindered, as in the case of lethargy, we see that a man is hindered from actually understanding things of which he had a previous knowledge. Secondly, anyone can experience this of himself, that when he tries to understand something, he forms certain phantasms to serve him by way of examples, in which as it were he examines what he is desirous of understanding. For this reason it is that when we wish to help someone to understand something, we lay examples before him, from which he forms phantasms for the purpose of understanding.

Now the reason of this is that the power of knowledge is proportioned to the thing known. Wherefore the proper object of the angelic intellect, which is entirely separate from a body, is an intelligible substance separate from a body. Whereas the proper object of the human intellect, which is united to a body, is a quiddity or nature existing in corporeal matter; and through such natures of visible things it rises to a certain knowledge of things invisible. Now it belongs to such a nature to exist in an individual, and this cannot be apart from corporeal matter: for instance, it belongs to the nature of a stone to be in an individual stone, and to the nature of a horse to be in an individual horse, and so forth. Wherefore the nature of a stone or any material thing cannot be known completely and truly, except in as much as it is known as existing in the individual. Now we apprehend the individual through the senses and the imagination. And, therefore, for the intellect to understand actually its proper object, it must of necessity turn to the phantasms in order to perceive the universal nature existing in the individual. But if the proper object of our intellect were a separate form; or if, as the Platonists say, the natures of sensible things subsisted apart from the individual; there would be no need for the intellect to turn to the phantasms whenever it understands.

Reply Obj. 1: The species preserved in the passive intellect exist there habitually when it does not understand them actually, as we have said above (Q. 79, A. 6). Wherefore for us to understand actually, the fact that the species are preserved does not suffice; we need further to make use of them in a manner befitting the things of which they are the species, which things are natures existing in individuals.

Reply Obj. 2: Even the phantasm is the likeness of an individual thing; wherefore the imagination does not need any further likeness of the individual, whereas the intellect does.

Reply Obj. 3: Incorporeal things, of which there are no phantasms, are known to us by comparison with sensible bodies of which there are phantasms. Thus we understand truth by considering a thing of which we possess the truth; and God, as Dionysius says (Div. Nom. i), we know as cause, by way of excess and by way of remotion. Other incorporeal substances we know, in the present state of life, only by way of remotion or by some comparison to corporeal things. And, therefore, when we understand something about these things, we need to turn to phantasms of bodies, although there are no phantasms of the things themselves.

EIGHTH ARTICLE [I, Q. 84, Art. 8]

Whether the Judgment of the Intellect Is Hindered Through Suspension of the Sensitive Powers?

Objection 1: It would seem that the judgment of the intellect is not hindered by suspension of the sensitive powers. For the superior does not depend on the inferior. But the judgment of the intellect is higher than the senses. Therefore the judgment of the intellect is not hindered through suspension of the senses.

Obj. 2: Further, to syllogize is an act of the intellect. But during sleep the senses are suspended, as is said in *De Somn. et Vigil.* i and yet it sometimes happens to us to syllogize while asleep. Therefore the judgment of the intellect is not hindered through suspension of the senses.

*On the contrary,* What a man does while asleep, against the moral law, is not imputed to him as a sin; as Augustine says (Gen. ad lit. xii, 15). But this would not be the case if man, while asleep, had free use of his reason and intellect. Therefore the judgment of the intellect is hindered by suspension of the senses.

*I answer that,* As we have said above (A. 7), our intellect's proper and proportionate object is the nature of a sensible thing. Now a perfect judgment concerning anything cannot be formed, unless all that pertains to that thing's nature be known; especially if that be ignored which is the term and end of judgment. Now the Philosopher says (De Coel. iii), that "as the end of a practical science is action, so the end of natural science is that which is perceived principally through the senses"; for the smith does not seek knowledge of a knife except for the purpose of action, in order that he may produce a certain individual knife; and in like manner the natural philosopher does not seek to know the nature of a stone and of a horse, save for the purpose of knowing the essential properties of those things which he perceives with his senses. Now it is clear that a smith cannot judge perfectly of a knife unless he knows the action of the knife: and in like manner the natural philosopher cannot judge perfectly of natural things, unless he knows sensible things. But in the present state of life whatever we understand, we know by comparison to natural sensible things. Consequently it is not possible for our intellect to form a perfect judgment, while the senses are suspended, through which sensible things are known to us.

Reply Obj. 1: Although the intellect is superior to the senses, nevertheless in a manner it receives from the senses, and its first and principal objects are founded in sensible things. And therefore suspension of the senses necessarily involves a hindrance to the judgment of the intellect.

Reply Obj. 2: The senses are suspended in the sleeper through certain evaporations and the escape of certain exhalations, as we read in De Somn. et Vigil. iii. And, therefore, according to the amount of such evaporation, the senses are more or less suspended. For when the amount is considerable, not only are the senses suspended, but also the imagination, so that there are no phantasms; thus does it happen, especially when a man falls asleep after eating and drinking copiously. If, however, the evaporation be somewhat less, phantasms appear, but distorted and without sequence; thus it happens in a case of fever. And if the evaporation be still more attenuated, the phantasms will have a certain sequence: thus especially does it happen towards the end of sleep in sober men and those who are gifted with a strong imagination. If the evaporation be very slight, not only does the imagination retain its freedom, but also the common sense is partly freed; so that sometimes while asleep a man may judge that what he sees is a dream, discerning, as it were, between things, and their images. Nevertheless, the common sense remains partly suspended; and therefore, although it discriminates some images from the reality, yet is it always deceived in some particular. Therefore, while man is asleep, according as sense and imagination are free, so is the judgment of his intellect unfettered, though not entirely. Consequently, if a man syllogizes while asleep, when he wakes up he invariably recognizes a flaw in some respect.

## QUESTION 85

OF THE MODE AND ORDER OF UNDERSTANDING (In Eight Articles)

We come now to consider the mode and order of understanding. Under this head there are eight points of inquiry:

(1) Whether our intellect understands by abstracting the species from the phantasms?

(2) Whether the intelligible species abstracted from the phantasms are what our intellect understands, or that whereby it understands?

(3) Whether our intellect naturally first understands the more universal?

(4) Whether our intellect can know many things at the same time?

(5) Whether our intellect understands by the process of composition and division?

(6) Whether the intellect can err?

(7) Whether one intellect can understand better than another?

(8) Whether our intellect understands the indivisible before the divisible?

FIRST ARTICLE [I, Q. 85, Art. 1]

Whether Our Intellect Understands Corporeal and Material Things by Abstraction from Phantasms?

Objection 1: It would seem that our intellect does not understand corporeal and material things by abstraction from the phantasms. For the intellect is false if it understands an object otherwise than as it really is. Now the forms of material things do not exist as abstracted from the particular things represented by the phantasms. Therefore, if we understand material things by abstraction of the species from the phantasm, there will be error in the intellect.

Obj. 2: Further, material things are those natural things which include matter in their definition. But nothing can be understood apart from that which enters into its definition. Therefore material things cannot be understood apart from matter. Now matter is the principle of individualization. Therefore material things cannot be understood by abstraction of the universal from the particular, which is the process whereby the intelligible species is abstracted from the phantasm.

Obj. 3: Further, the Philosopher says (De Anima iii, 7) that the phantasm is to the intellectual soul what color is to the sight. But seeing is not caused by abstraction of species from color, but by color impressing itself on the sight. Therefore neither does the act of understanding take place by abstraction of something from the phantasm, but by the phantasm impressing itself on the intellect.

Obj. 4: Further, the Philosopher says (De Anima iii, 5) there are two things in the intellectual soul—the passive intellect and the active intellect. But it does not belong to the passive intellect to abstract the intelligible species from the phantasm, but to receive them when abstracted. Neither does it seem to be the function of the active intellect, which is related to the phantasm, as light is to color; since light does not abstract anything from color, but rather streams on to it. Therefore in no way do we understand by abstraction from phantasms.

Obj. 5: Further, the Philosopher (De Anima iii, 7) says that "the intellect understands the species in the phantasm"; and not, therefore, by abstraction.

*On the contrary,* The Philosopher says (De Anima iii, 4) that "things are intelligible in proportion as they are separate from matter." Therefore material things must needs be understood according as they are abstracted from matter and from material images, namely, phantasms.

*I answer that,* As stated above (Q. 84, A. 7), the object of knowledge is proportionate to the power of knowledge. Now there are three grades of the cognitive powers. For one cognitive power, namely, the sense, is the act of a corporeal organ. And therefore the object of every sensitive power is a form as existing in corporeal matter. And since such matter is the principle of individuality, therefore every power of the sensitive part can only have knowledge of the individual. There is another grade of cognitive power which is neither the act of a corporeal organ, nor in any way connected with corporeal matter; such is the angelic intellect, the object of whose cognitive power is therefore a form existing apart from matter: for though angels know material things, yet they do not know them save in something immaterial, namely, either in themselves or in God. But the human intellect holds a middle place: for it is not the act of an organ; yet it is a power of the soul which is the form of the body, as is clear from what we have said above (Q. 76, A. 1). And therefore it is proper to it to know a form existing individually in corporeal matter, but not as existing in this individual matter. But to know what is in individual matter, not as existing in such matter, is to abstract the form from individual matter which is represented by the phantasms. Therefore we must needs say that our intellect understands material things by abstracting from the phantasms; and through material things thus considered we acquire some knowledge of immaterial things, just as, *on the contrary,* angels know material things through the immaterial.

But Plato, considering only the immateriality of the human intellect, and not its being in a way united to the body, held that the objects of the intellect are separate ideas; and that we understand not by abstraction, but by participating things abstract, as stated above (Q. 84, A. 1).

Reply Obj. 1: Abstraction may occur in two ways: First, by way of composition and division; thus we may understand that one thing does not exist in some other, or that it is separate therefrom. Secondly, by way of simple and absolute consideration; thus we understand one thing without considering the other. Thus for the intellect to abstract one from another things which are not really abstract from one another, does, in the first mode of abstraction, imply falsehood. But, in the second mode of abstraction, for the intellect to abstract things which are not really abstract from one another, does not involve falsehood, as clearly appears in the case of the senses. For if we understood or said that color is not in a colored body, or that it is separate from it, there would be error in this opinion or assertion. But if we consider color and its properties, without reference to the apple which is colored; or if we express in word what we thus understand, there is no error in such an opinion or assertion, because an apple is not essential to color, and therefore color can be understood independently of the apple. Likewise, the things which belong to the species of a material thing, such as a stone, or a man, or a horse, can be thought of apart from the individualizing principles which do not belong to the notion of the species. This is what we mean by abstracting the universal from the particular, or the intelligible species from the phantasm; that is, by considering the nature of the species apart from its individual qualities represented by the phantasms. If, therefore, the intellect is said to be false when it understands a thing otherwise than as it is, that is so, if the word "otherwise" refers to the thing understood; for the intellect is false when it understands a thing otherwise than as it is; and so the intellect would be false if it abstracted the species of a stone from its matter in such a way as to regard the species as not existing in matter, as Plato held. But it is not so, if the word "otherwise" be taken as referring to the one who understands. For it is quite true that the mode of understanding, in one who understands, is not the same as the mode of a thing in existing: since the thing understood is immaterially in the one who understands, according to the mode of the intellect, and not materially, according to the mode of a material thing.

Reply Obj. 2: Some have thought that the species of a natural thing is a form only, and that matter is not part of the species. If that were so, matter would not enter into the definition of natural things. Therefore it must be said otherwise, that matter is twofold, common, and "signate" or individual; common, such as flesh and bone; and individual, as this flesh and these bones. The intellect therefore abstracts the species of a natural thing from the individual sensible matter, but not from the common sensible matter; for example, it abstracts the species of man from "this flesh and these bones," which do not belong to the species as such, but to the individual (Metaph. vii, Did. vi, 10), and need not be considered in the species: whereas the species of man cannot be abstracted by the intellect from "flesh and bones."

Mathematical species, however, can be abstracted by the intellect from sensible matter, not only from individual, but also from common matter; not from common intelligible matter, but only from individual matter. For sensible matter is corporeal matter as subject to sensible qualities, such as being cold or hot, hard or soft, and the like: while intelligible matter is substance as subject to quantity. Now it is manifest that quantity is in substance before other sensible qualities are. Hence quantities, such as number, dimension, and figures, which are the terminations of quantity, can be considered apart from sensible qualities; and this is to abstract them from sensible matter; but they cannot be considered without understanding the substance which is subject to the quantity; for that would be to abstract them from common intelligible matter. Yet they can be considered apart from this or that substance; for that is to abstract them from individual intelligible matter. But some things can be abstracted even from common intelligible matter, such as "being," "unity," "power," "act," and the like; all these can exist without matter, as is plain regarding immaterial things. Because Plato failed to consider the twofold kind of abstraction, as above explained (ad 1), he held that all those things which we have stated to be abstracted by the intellect, are abstract in reality.

Reply Obj. 3: Colors, as being in individual corporeal matter, have the same mode of existence as the power of sight: therefore they can impress their own image on the eye. But phantasms, since they are images of individuals, and exist in corporeal organs, have not the same mode of existence as the human intellect, and therefore have not the power of themselves to make an impression on the passive intellect. This is done by the power of the active intellect which by turning towards the phantasm produces in the passive intellect a certain likeness which represents, as to its specific conditions only, the thing reflected in the phantasm. It is thus that the intelligible species is said to be abstracted from the phantasm; not that the identical form which previously was in the phantasm is subsequently in the passive intellect, as a body transferred from one place to another.

Reply Obj. 4: Not only does the active intellect throw light on the phantasm: it does more; by its own power it abstracts the intelligible species from the phantasm. It throws light on the phantasm, because, just as the sensitive part acquires a greater power by its conjunction with the intellectual part, so by the power of the active intellect the phantasms are made more fit for the abstraction therefrom of intelligible intentions. Furthermore, the active intellect abstracts the intelligible species from the phantasm, forasmuch as by the power of the active intellect we are able to disregard the conditions of individuality, and to take into our consideration the specific nature, the image of which informs the passive intellect.

Reply Obj. 5: Our intellect both abstracts the intelligible species from the phantasms, inasmuch as it considers the natures of things in universal, and, nevertheless, understands these natures in the phantasms since it cannot understand even the things of which it abstracts the species, without turning to the phantasms, as we have said above (Q. 84, A. 7).

SECOND ARTICLE [I, Q. 85, Art. 2]

Whether the Intelligible Species Abstracted from the Phantasm Is Related to Our Intellect As That Which Is Understood?

Objection 1: It would seem that the intelligible species abstracted from the phantasm is related to our intellect as that which is understood. For the understood in act is in the one who understands: since the understood in act is the intellect itself in act. But nothing of what is understood is in the intellect actually understanding, save the abstracted intelligible species. Therefore this species is what is actually understood.

Obj. 2: Further, what is actually understood must be in something; else it would be nothing. But it is not in something outside the soul: for, since what is outside the soul is material, nothing therein can be actually understood. Therefore what is actually understood is in the intellect. Consequently it can be nothing else than the aforesaid intelligible species.

Obj. 3: Further, the Philosopher says (1 Peri Herm. i) that "words are signs of the passions in the soul." But words signify the things understood, for we express by word what we understand. Therefore these passions of the soul—viz. the intelligible species, are what is actually understood.

*On the contrary,* The intelligible species is to the intellect what the sensible image is to the sense. But the sensible image is not what is perceived, but rather that by which sense perceives. Therefore the intelligible species is not what is actually understood, but that by which the intellect understands.

*I answer that,* Some have asserted that our intellectual faculties know only the impression made on them; as, for example, that sense is cognizant only of the impression made on its own organ. According to this theory, the intellect understands only its own impression, namely, the intelligible species which it has received, so that this species is what is understood.

This is, however, manifestly false for two reasons. First, because the things we understand are the objects of science; therefore if what we understand is merely the intelligible species in the soul, it would follow that every science would not be concerned with objects outside the soul, but only with the intelligible species within the soul; thus, according to the teaching of the Platonists all science is about ideas, which they held to be actually understood [*Q. 84, A. 1]]. Secondly, it is untrue, because it would lead to the opinion of the ancients who maintained that "whatever seems, is true" [*Aristotle, *Metaph.* iii. 5, and that consequently contradictories are true simultaneously. For if the faculty knows its own impression only, it can judge of that only. Now a thing seems according to the impression made on the cognitive faculty. Consequently the cognitive faculty will always judge of its own impression as such; and so every judgment will be true: for instance, if taste perceived only its own impression, when anyone with a healthy taste perceives that honey is sweet, he would judge truly; and if anyone with a corrupt taste perceives that honey is bitter, this would be equally true; for each would judge according to the impression on his taste. Thus every opinion would be equally true; in fact, every sort of apprehension.

Therefore it must be said that the intelligible species is related to the intellect as that by which it understands: which is proved thus. There is a twofold action (Metaph. ix, Did. viii, 8), one which remains in the agent; for instance, to see and to understand; and another which passes into an external object; for instance, to heat and to cut; and each of these actions proceeds in virtue of some form. And as the form from which proceeds an act tending to something external is the likeness of the object of the action, as heat in the heater is a likeness of the thing heated; so the form from which proceeds an action remaining in the agent is the likeness of the object. Hence that by which the sight sees is the likeness of the visible thing; and the likeness of the thing understood, that is, the intelligible species, is the form by which the intellect understands. But since the intellect reflects upon itself, by such reflection it understands both its own act of intelligence, and the species by which it understands. Thus the intelligible species is that which is understood secondarily; but that which is primarily understood is the object, of which the species is the likeness. This also appears from the opinion of the ancient philosophers, who said that "like is known by like." For they said that the soul knows the earth outside itself, by the earth within itself; and so of the rest. If, therefore, we take the species of the earth instead of the earth, according to Aristotle (De Anima iii, 8), who says "that a stone is not in the soul, but only the likeness of the stone"; it follows that the soul knows external things by means of its intelligible species.

Reply Obj. 1: The thing understood is in the intellect by its own likeness; and it is in this sense that we say that the thing actually understood is the intellect in act, because the likeness of the thing understood is the form of the intellect, as the likeness of a sensible thing is the form of the sense in act. Hence it does not follow that the intelligible species abstracted is what is actually understood; but rather that it is the likeness thereof.

Reply Obj. 2: In these words "the thing actually understood" there is a double implication—the thing which is understood, and the fact that it is understood. In like manner the words "abstract universal" imply two things, the nature of a thing and its abstraction or universality. Therefore the nature itself to which it occurs to be understood, abstracted or considered as universal is only in individuals; but that it is understood, abstracted or considered as universal is in the intellect. We see something similar to this is in the senses. For the sight sees the color of the apple apart from its smell. If therefore it be asked where is the color which is seen apart from the smell, it is quite clear that the color which is seen is only in the apple: but that it be perceived apart from the smell, this is owing to the sight, forasmuch as the faculty of sight receives the likeness of color and not of smell. In like manner humanity understood is only in this or that man; but that humanity be apprehended without conditions of individuality, that is, that it be abstracted and consequently considered as universal, occurs to humanity inasmuch as it is brought under the consideration of the intellect, in which there is a likeness of the specific nature, but not of the principles of individuality.

Reply Obj. 3: There are two operations in the sensitive part. One, in regard of impression only, and thus the operation of the senses takes place by the senses being impressed by the sensible. The other is formation, inasmuch as the imagination forms for itself an image of an absent thing, or even of something never seen. Both of these operations are found in the intellect. For in the first place there is the passion of the passive intellect as informed by the intelligible species; and then the passive intellect thus informed forms a definition, or a division, or a composition, expressed by a word. Wherefore the concept conveyed by a word is its definition; and a proposition conveys the intellect's division or composition. Words do not therefore signify the intelligible species themselves; but that which the intellect forms for itself for the purpose of judging of external things.

THIRD ARTICLE [I, Q. 85, Art. 3]

Whether the More Universal Is First in Our Intellectual Cognition?

Objection 1: It would seem that the more universal is not first in our intellectual cognition. For what is first and more known in its own nature, is secondarily and less known in relation to ourselves. But universals come first as regards their nature, because "that is first which does not involve the existence of its correlative" (Categor. ix). Therefore the universals are secondarily known as regards our intellect.

Obj. 2: Further, the composition precedes the simple in relation to us. But universals are the more simple. Therefore they are known secondarily by us.

Obj. 3: Further, the Philosopher says (Phys. i, 1), that the object defined comes in our knowledge before the parts of its definition. But the more universal is part of the definition of the less universal, as "animal" is part of the definition of "man." Therefore the universals are secondarily known by us.

Obj. 4: Further, we know causes and principles by their effects. But universals are principles. Therefore universals are secondarily known by us.

*On the contrary,* "We must proceed from the universal to the singular and individual" (Phys. i, 1)

*I answer that,* In our knowledge there are two things to be considered. First, that intellectual knowledge in some degree arises from sensible knowledge: and, because sense has singular and individual things for its object, and intellect has the universal for its object, it follows that our knowledge of the former comes before our knowledge of the latter. Secondly, we must consider that our intellect proceeds from a state of potentiality to a state of actuality; and every power thus proceeding from potentiality to actuality comes first to an incomplete act, which is the medium between potentiality and actuality, before accomplishing the perfect act. The perfect act of the intellect is complete knowledge, when the object is distinctly and determinately known; whereas the incomplete act is imperfect knowledge, when the object is known indistinctly, and as it were confusedly. A thing thus imperfectly known, is known partly in act and partly in potentiality, and hence the Philosopher says (Phys. i, 1), that "what is manifest and certain is known to us at first confusedly; afterwards we know it by distinguishing its principles and elements." Now it is evident that to know an object that comprises many things, without proper knowledge of each thing contained in it, is to know that thing confusedly. In this way we can have knowledge not only of the universal whole, which contains parts potentially, but also of the integral whole; for each whole can be known confusedly, without its parts being known. But to know distinctly what is contained in the universal whole is to know the less common, as to "animal" indistinctly is to know it as "animal"; whereas to know "animal" distinctly is know it as "rational" or "irrational animal," that is, to know a man or a lion: therefore our intellect knows "animal" before it knows man; and the same reason holds in comparing any more universal idea with the less universal.

Moreover, as sense, like the intellect, proceeds from potentiality to act, the same order of knowledge appears in the senses. For by sense we judge of the more common before the less common, in reference both to place and time; in reference to place, when a thing is seen afar off it is seen to be a body before it is seen to be an animal; and to be an animal before it is seen to be a man, and to be a man before it seen to be Socrates or Plato; and the same is true as regards time, for a child can distinguish man from not man before he distinguishes this man from that, and therefore "children at first call men fathers, and later on distinguish each one from the others" (Phys. i, 1). The reason of this is clear: because he who knows a thing indistinctly is in a state of potentiality as regards its principle of distinction; as he who knows genus is in a state of potentiality as regards "difference." Thus it is evident that indistinct knowledge is midway between potentiality and act.

We must therefore conclude that knowledge of the singular and individual is prior, as regards us, to the knowledge of the universal; as sensible knowledge is prior to intellectual knowledge. But in both sense and intellect the knowledge of the more common precedes the knowledge of the less common.

Reply Obj. 1: The universal can be considered in two ways. First, the universal nature may be considered together with the intention of universality. And since the intention of universality—viz. the relation of one and the same to many—is due to intellectual abstraction, the universal thus considered is a secondary consideration. Hence it is said (De Anima i, 1) that the "universal animal is either nothing or something secondary." But according to Plato, who held that universals are subsistent, the universal considered thus would be prior to the particular, for the latter, according to him, are mere participations of the subsistent universals which he called ideas.

Secondly, the universal can be considered in the nature itself—for instance, animality or humanity as existing in the individual. And thus we must distinguish two orders of nature: one, by way of generation and time; and thus the imperfect and the potential come first. In this way the more common comes first in the order of nature; as appears clearly in the generation of man and animal; for "the animal is generated before man," as the Philosopher says (De Gener. Animal ii, 3). The other order is the order of perfection or of the intention of nature: for instance, act considered absolutely is naturally prior to potentiality, and the perfect to the imperfect: thus the less common comes naturally before the more common; as man comes before animal. For the intention of nature does not stop at the generation of animal but goes on to the generation of man.

Reply Obj. 2: The more common universal may be compared to the less common, as the whole, and as the part. As the whole, considering that in the more universal is potentially contained not only the less universal, but also other things, as in "animal" is contained not only "man" but also "horse." As part, considering that the less common contains in its idea not only the more common, but also more; as "man" contains not only "animal" but also "rational." Therefore "animal" in itself comes into our knowledge before "man"; but "man" comes before "animal" considered as part of the same idea.

Reply Obj. 3: A part can be known in two ways. First, absolutely considered in itself; and thus nothing prevents the parts being known before the whole, as stones are known before a house is known. Secondly as belonging to a certain whole; and thus we must needs know the whole before its parts. For we know a house vaguely before we know its different parts. So likewise principles of definition are known before the thing defined is known; otherwise the thing defined would not be known at all. But as parts of the definition they are known after. For we know man vaguely as man before we know how to distinguish all that belongs to human nature.

Reply Obj. 4: The universal, as understood with the intention of universality, is, indeed, in a way, a principle of knowledge, in so far as the intention of universality results from the mode of understanding by way of abstraction. But what is a principle of knowledge is not of necessity a principle of existence, as Plato thought: since at times we know a cause through its effect, and substance through accidents. Wherefore the universal thus considered, according to the opinion of Aristotle, is neither a principle of existence, nor a substance, as he makes clear (Metaph. vii, Did. vi, 13). But if we consider the generic or specific nature itself as existing in the singular, thus in a way it is in the nature of a formal principle in regard to the singulars: for the singular is the result of matter, while the idea of species is from the form. But the generic nature is compared to the specific nature rather after the fashion of a material principle, because the generic nature is taken from that which is material in a thing, while the idea of species is taken from that which is formal: thus the notion of animal is taken from the sensitive part, whereas the notion of man is taken from the intellectual part. Thus it is that the ultimate intention of nature is to the species and not to the individual, or the genus: because the form is the end of generation, while matter is for the sake of the form. Neither is it necessary that, as regards us, knowledge of any cause or principle should be secondary: since at times through sensible causes we become acquainted with unknown effects, and sometimes conversely.

FOURTH ARTICLE [I, Q. 85, Art. 4]

Whether We Can Understand Many Things at the Same Time?

Objection 1: It would seem that we can understand many things at the same time. For intellect is above time, whereas the succession of before and after belongs to time. Therefore the intellect does not understand different things in succession, but at the same time.

Obj. 2: Further, there is nothing to prevent different forms not opposed to each other from actually being in the same subject, as, for instance, color and smell are in the apple. But intelligible species are not opposed to each other. Therefore there is nothing to prevent the same intellect being in act as regards different intelligible species, and thus it can understand many things at the same time.

Obj. 3: Further, the intellect understands a whole at the same time, such as a man or a house. But a whole contains many parts. Therefore the intellect understands many things at the same time.

Obj. 4: Further, we cannot know the difference between two things unless we know both at the same time (De Anima iii, 2), and the same is to be said of any other comparison. But our intellect knows the difference and comparison between one thing and another. Therefore it knows many things at the same time.

*On the contrary,* It is said (Topic. ii, 10) that "understanding is of one thing only, knowledge is of many."

*I answer that,* The intellect can, indeed, understand many things as one, but not as many: that is to say by *one* but not by many intelligible species. For the mode of every action follows the form which is the principle of that action. Therefore whatever things the intellect can understand under one species, it can understand at the same time: hence it is that God sees all things at the same time, because He sees all in one, that is, in His Essence. But whatever things the intellect understands under different species, it does not understand at the same time. The reason of this is that it is impossible for one and the same subject to be perfected at the same time by many forms of one genus and diverse species, just as it is impossible for one and the same body at the same time to have different colors or different shapes. Now all intelligible species belong to one genus, because they are the perfections of one intellectual faculty: although the things which the species represent belong to different genera. Therefore it is impossible for one and the same intellect to be perfected at the same time by different intelligible species so as actually to understand different things.

Reply Obj. 1: The intellect is above that time, which is the measure of the movement of corporeal things. But the multitude itself of intelligible species causes a certain vicissitude of intelligible operations, according as one operation succeeds another. And this vicissitude is called time by Augustine, who says (Gen. ad lit. viii, 20, 22), that "God moves the spiritual creature through time."

Reply Obj. 2: Not only is it impossible for opposite forms to exist at the same time in the same subject, but neither can any forms belonging to the same genus, although they be not opposed to one another, as is clear from the examples of colors and shapes.

Reply Obj. 3: Parts can be understood in two ways. First, in a confused way, as existing in the whole, and thus they are known through the one form of the whole, and so are known together. In another way they are known distinctly: thus each is known by its species; and so they are not understood at the same time.

Reply Obj. 4: If the intellect sees the difference or comparison between one thing and another, it knows both in relation to their difference or comparison; just, as we have said above (ad 3), as it knows the parts in the whole.

FIFTH ARTICLE [I, Q. 85, Art. 5]

Whether Our Intellect Understands by Composition and Division?

Objection 1: It would seem that our intellect does not understand by composition and division. For composition and division are only of many; whereas the intellect cannot understand many things at the same time. Therefore it cannot understand by composition and division.

Obj. 2: Further, every composition and division implies past, present, or future time. But the intellect abstracts from time, as also from other individual conditions. Therefore the intellect does not understand by composition and division.

Obj. 3: Further, the intellect understands things by a process of assimilation to them. But composition and division are not in things, for nothing is in things but what is signified by the predicate and the subject, and which is one and the same, provided that the composition be true, for "man" is truly what "animal" is. Therefore the intellect does not act by composition and division.

*On the contrary,* Words signify the conceptions of the intellect, as the Philosopher says (Peri Herm. i). But in words we find composition and division, as appears in affirmative and negative propositions. Therefore the intellect acts by composition and division.

*I answer that,* The human intellect must of necessity understand by composition and division. For since the intellect passes from potentiality to act, it has a likeness to things which are generated, which do not attain to perfection all at once but acquire it by degrees: so likewise the human intellect does not acquire perfect knowledge by the first act of apprehension; but it first apprehends something about its object, such as its quiddity, and this is its first and proper object; and then it understands the properties, accidents, and the various relations of the essence. Thus it necessarily compares one thing with another by composition or division; and from one composition and division it proceeds to another, which is the process of reasoning.

But the angelic and the Divine intellect, like all incorruptible things, have their perfection at once from the beginning. Hence the angelic and the Divine intellect have the entire knowledge of a thing at once and perfectly; and hence also in knowing the quiddity of a thing they know at once whatever we can know by composition, division, and reasoning. Therefore the human intellect knows by composition, division and reasoning. But the Divine intellect and the angelic intellect know, indeed, composition, division, and reasoning, not by the process itself, but by understanding the simple essence.

Reply Obj. 1: Composition and division of the

intellect are made by differentiating and comparing. Hence the intellect knows many things by composition and division, as by knowing the difference and comparison of things.

Reply Obj. 2: Although the intellect abstracts from the phantasms, it does not understand actually without turning to the phantasms, as we have said (A. 1; Q. 84, A. 7). And forasmuch as it turns to the phantasms, composition and division of the intellect involve time.

Reply Obj. 3: The likeness of a thing is received into the intellect according to the mode of the intellect, not according to the mode of the thing. Wherefore something on the part of the thing corresponds to the composition and division of the intellect; but it does not exist in the same way in the intellect and in the thing. For the proper object of the human intellect is the quiddity of a material thing, which comes under the action of the senses and the imagination. Now in a material thing there is a twofold composition. First, there is the composition of form with matter; and to this corresponds that composition of the intellect whereby the universal whole is predicated of its part: for the genus is derived from common matter, while the difference that completes the species is derived from the form, and the particular from individual matter. The second comparison is of accident with subject: and to this real composition corresponds that composition of the intellect, whereby accident is predicated of subject, as when we say "the man is white." Nevertheless composition of the intellect differs from composition of things; for in the latter the things are diverse, whereas composition of the intellect is a sign of the identity of the components. For the above composition of the intellect does not imply that "man" and "whiteness" are identical, but the assertion, "the man is white," means that "the man is something having whiteness": and the subject, which is a man, is identified with a subject having whiteness. It is the same with the composition of form and matter: for animal signifies that which has a sensitive nature; rational, that which has an intellectual nature; man, that which has both; and Socrates that which has all these things together with individual matter; and according to this kind of identity our intellect predicates the composition of one thing with another.

SIXTH ARTICLE [I, Q. 85, Art. 6]

Whether the Intellect Can Be False?

Objection 1: It would seem that the intellect can be false; for the Philosopher says (Metaph. vi, Did. v, 4) that "truth and falsehood are in the mind." But the mind and intellect are the same, as is shown above (Q. 79, A. 1). Therefore falsehood may be in the mind.

Obj. 2: Further, opinion and reasoning belong to the intellect. But falsehood exists in both. Therefore falsehood can be in the intellect.

Obj. 3: Further, sin is in the intellectual faculty. But sin involves falsehood: for "those err that work evil" (Prov. 14:22). Therefore falsehood can be in the intellect.

*On the contrary,* Augustine says (QQ. 83, qu. 32), that "everyone who is deceived, does not rightly understand that wherein he is deceived." And the Philosopher says (De Anima iii, 10), that "the intellect is always true."

*I answer that,* The Philosopher (De Anima iii, 6) compares intellect with sense on this point. For sense is not deceived in its proper object, as sight in regard to color; [unless] accidentally through some hindrance occurring to the sensile organ—for example, the taste of a fever-stricken person judges a sweet thing to be bitter, through his tongue being vitiated by ill humors. Sense, however, may be deceived as regards common sensible objects, as size or figure; when, for example, it judges the sun to be only a foot in diameter, whereas in reality it exceeds the earth in size. Much more is sense deceived concerning accidental sensible objects, as when it judges that vinegar is honey by reason of the color being the same. The reason of this is evident; for every faculty, as such, is *per se* directed to its proper object; and things of this kind are always the same. Hence, as long as the faculty exists, its judgment concerning its own proper object does not fail. Now the proper object of the intellect is the "quiddity" of a material thing; and hence, properly speaking, the intellect is not at fault concerning this quiddity; whereas it may go astray as regards the surroundings of the thing in its essence or quiddity, in referring one thing to another, as regards composition or division, or also in the process of reasoning. Therefore, also in regard to those propositions, which are understood, the intellect cannot err, as in the case of first principles from which arises infallible truth in the certitude of scientific conclusions.

The intellect, however, may be accidentally deceived in the quiddity of composite things, not by the defect of its organ, for the intellect is a faculty that is independent of an organ; but on the part of the composition affecting the definition, when, for instance, the definition of a thing is false in relation to something else, as the definition of a circle applied to a triangle; or when a definition is false in itself as involving the composition of things incompatible; as, for instance, to describe anything as "a rational winged animal." Hence as regards simple objects not subject to composite definitions we cannot be deceived unless, indeed, we understand nothing whatever about them, as is said *Metaph.* ix, Did. viii, 10.

Reply Obj. 1: The Philosopher says that falsehood is in the intellect in regard to composition and division. The same answer applies to the Second Objection concerning opinion and reasoning, and to the Third Objection, concerning the error of the sinner, who errs in the practical judgment of the appetible object. But in the absolute consideration of the quiddity of a thing, and of those things which are known thereby, the intellect is never deceived. In this sense are to be understood the authorities quoted in proof of the opposite conclusion.

SEVENTH ARTICLE [I, Q. 85, Art. 7]

Whether One Person Can Understand One and the Same Thing Better Than Another Can?

Objection 1: It would seem that one person cannot understand one and the same thing better than another can. For Augustine says (QQ. 83, qu. 32), "Whoever understands a thing otherwise than as it is, does not understand it at all. Hence it is clear that there is a perfect understanding, than which none other is more perfect: and therefore there are not infinite degrees of understanding a thing: nor can one person understand a thing better than another can."

Obj. 2: Further, the intellect is true in its act of understanding. But truth, being a certain equality between thought and thing, is not subject to more or less; for a thing cannot be said to be more or less equal. Therefore a thing cannot be more or less understood.

Obj. 3: Further, the intellect is the most formal of all that is in man. But different forms cause different species. Therefore if one man understands better than another, it would seem that they do not belong to the same species.

*On the contrary,* Experience shows that some understand more profoundly than do others; as one who carries a conclusion to its first principles and ultimate causes understands it better than the one who reduces it only to its proximate causes.

*I answer that,* A thing being understood more by one than by another may be taken in two senses. First, so that the word "more" be taken as determining the act of understanding as regards the thing understood; and thus, one cannot understand the same thing more than another, because to understand it otherwise than as it is, either better or worse, would entail being deceived, and such a one would not understand it, as Augustine argues (QQ. 83, qu. 32). In another sense the word "more" can be taken as determining the act of understanding on the part of him who understands; and so one may understand the same thing better than someone else, through having a greater power of understanding: just as a man may see a thing better with his bodily sight, whose power is greater, and whose sight is more perfect. The same applies to the intellect in two ways. First, as regards the intellect itself, which is more perfect. For it is plain that the better the disposition of a body, the better the soul allotted to it; which clearly appears in things of different species: and the reason thereof is that act and form are received into matter according to matter's capacity: thus because some men have bodies of better disposition, their souls have a greater power of understanding, wherefore it is said (De Anima ii, 9), that "it is to be observed that those who have soft flesh are of apt mind." Secondly, this occurs in regard to the lower powers of which the intellect has need in its operation: for those in whom the imaginative, cogitative, and memorative powers are of better disposition, are better disposed to understand.

The reply to the First Objection is clear from the above; likewise the reply to the Second, for the truth of the intellect consists in the intellect understanding a thing as it is.

Reply Obj. 3: The difference of form which is due only to the different disposition of matter, causes not a specific but only a numerical difference: for different individuals have different forms, diversified according to the difference of matter.

EIGHTH ARTICLE [I, Q. 85, Art. 8]

Whether the Intellect Understands the Indivisible Before the Divisible?

Objection 1: It would seem that the intellect understands the indivisible before the divisible. For the Philosopher says (Phys. i, 1) that "we understand and know from the knowledge of principles and elements." But principles are indivisible, and elements are of divisible things. Therefore the indivisible is known to us before the divisible.

Obj. 2: Further, the definition of a thing contains what is known previously, for a definition "proceeds from the first and more known," as is said *Topic.* vi, 4. But the indivisible is part of the definition of the divisible; as a point comes into the definition of a line; for as Euclid says, "a line is length without breadth, the extremities of which are points"; also unity comes into the definition of number, for "number is multitude measured by one," as is said *Metaph.* x, Did. ix, 6. Therefore our intellect understands the indivisible before the divisible.

Obj. 3: Further, "Like is known by like." But the indivisible is more like to the intellect than is the divisible; because "the intellect is simple" (De Anima iii, 4). Therefore our intellect first knows the indivisible.

*On the contrary,* It is said (De Anima iii, 6) that "the indivisible is expressed as a privation." But privation is known secondarily. Therefore likewise is the indivisible.

*I answer that,* The object of our intellect in its present state is the quiddity of a material thing, which it abstracts from the phantasms, as above stated (Q. 84, A. 7). And since that which is known first and of itself by our cognitive power is its proper object, we must consider its relationship to that quiddity in order to discover in what order the indivisible is known. Now the indivisible is threefold, as is said *De Anima* iii, 6. First, the continuous is indivisible, since actually it is undivided, although potentially divisible: and this indivisible is known to us before its division, which is a division into parts: because confused knowledge is prior to distinct knowledge, as we have said above (A. 3).

Secondly, the indivisible is so called in relation to species, as man's reason is something indivisible. This way, also, the indivisible is understood before its division into logical parts, as we have said above (De Anima iii, 6); and again before the intellect disposes and divides by affirmation and negation. The reason of this is that both these kinds of indivisible are understood by the intellect of itself, as being its proper object. The third kind of indivisible is what is altogether indivisible, as a point and unity, which cannot be divided either actually or potentially. And this indivisible is known secondarily, through the privation of divisibility. Wherefore a point is defined by way of privation "as that which has no parts"; and in like manner the notion of "one" is that is "indivisible," as stated in *Metaph.* x, Did. ix, 1. And the reason of this is that this indivisible has a certain opposition to a corporeal being, the quiddity of which is the primary and proper object of the intellect.

But if our intellect understood by participation of certain separate indivisible (forms), as the Platonists maintained, it would follow that a like indivisible is understood primarily; for according to the Platonists what is first is first participated by things.

Reply Obj. 1: In the acquisition of knowledge, principles and elements are not always (known) first: for sometimes from sensible effects we arrive at the knowledge of principles and intelligible causes. But in perfect knowledge, the knowledge of effects always depends on the knowledge of principles and elements: for as the Philosopher says in the same passage: "Then do we consider that we know, when we can resolve principles into their causes."

Reply Obj. 2: A point is not included in the definition of a line in general: for it is manifest that in a line of indefinite length, and in a circular line, there is no point, save potentially. Euclid defines a finite straight line: and therefore he mentions a point in the definition, as the limit in the definition of that which is limited. Unity is the measure of number: wherefore it is included in the definition of a measured number. But it is not included in the definition of the divisible, but rather conversely.

Reply Obj. 3: The likeness through which we understand is the species of the known in the knower; therefore a thing is known first, not on account of its natural likeness to the cognitive power, but on account of the power's aptitude for the object: otherwise sight would perceive hearing rather than color.

# QUESTION 86

WHAT OUR INTELLECT KNOWS IN MATERIAL THINGS (In Four Articles)

We now have to consider what our intellect knows in material things. Under this head there are four points of inquiry:

(1) Whether it knows singulars?

(2) Whether it knows the infinite?

(3) Whether it knows contingent things?

(4) Whether it knows future things?

FIRST ARTICLE [I, Q. 86, Art. 4]

Whether Our Intellect Knows Singulars?

Objection 1: It would seem that our intellect knows singulars. For whoever knows composition, knows the terms of composition. But our intellect knows this composition; "Socrates is a man": for it belongs to the intellect to form a proposition. Therefore our intellect knows this singular, Socrates.

Obj. 2: Further, the practical intellect directs to action. But action has relation to singular things. Therefore the intellect knows the singular.

Obj. 3: Further, our intellect understands itself. But in itself it is a singular, otherwise it would have no action of its own; for actions belong to singulars. Therefore our intellect knows singulars.

Obj. 4: Further, a superior power can do whatever is done by an inferior power. But sense knows the singular. Much more, therefore, can the intellect know it.

*On the contrary,* The Philosopher says (Phys. i, 5), that "the universal is known by reason; and the singular is known by sense."

*I answer that,* Our intellect cannot know the singular in material things directly and primarily. The reason of this is that the principle of singularity in material things is individual matter, whereas our intellect, as have said above (Q. 85, A. 1), understands by abstracting the intelligible species from such matter. Now what is abstracted from individual matter is the universal. Hence our intellect knows directly the universal only. But indirectly, and as it were by a kind of reflection, it can know the singular, because, as we have said above (Q. 85, A. 7), even after abstracting the intelligible species, the intellect, in order to understand, needs to turn to the phantasms in which it understands the species, as is said *De Anima* iii, 7. Therefore it understands the universal directly through the intelligible species, and indirectly the singular represented by the phantasm. And thus it forms the proposition "Socrates is a man." Wherefore the reply to the first objection is clear.

Reply Obj. 2: The choice of a particular thing to be done is as the conclusion of a syllogism formed by the practical intellect, as is said *Ethic.* vii, 3. But a singular proposition cannot be directly concluded from a universal proposition, except through the medium of a singular proposition. Therefore the universal principle of the practical intellect does not move save through the medium of the particular apprehension of the sensitive part, as is said *De Anima* iii, 11.

Reply Obj. 3: Intelligibility is incompatible with the singular not as such, but as material, for nothing can be understood otherwise than immaterially. Therefore if there be an immaterial singular such as the intellect, there is no reason why it should not be intelligible.

Reply Obj. 4: The higher power can do what the lower power can, but in a more eminent way. Wherefore what the sense knows materially and concretely, which is to know the singular directly, the intellect knows immaterially and in the abstract, which is to know the universal.

SECOND ARTICLE [I, Q. 86, Art. 2]

Whether Our Intellect Can Know the Infinite?

Objection 1: It would seem that our intellect can know the infinite. For God excels all infinite things. But our intellect can know God, as we have said above (Q. 12, A. 1). Much more, therefore, can our intellect know all other infinite things.

Obj. 2: Further, our intellect can naturally know genera and species. But there is an infinity of species in some genera, as in number, proportion, and figure. Therefore our intellect can know the infinite.

Obj. 3: Further, if one body can coexist with another in the same place, there is nothing to prevent an infinite number of bodies being in one place. But one intelligible species can exist with another in the same intellect, for many things can be habitually known at the same time. Therefore our intellect can have an habitual knowledge of an infinite number of things.

Obj. 4: Further, as the intellect is not a corporeal faculty, as we have said (Q. 76, A. 1), it appears to be an infinite power. But an infinite power has a capacity for an infinite object. Therefore our intellect can know the infinite.

*On the contrary,* It is said (Phys. i, 4) that "the infinite, considered as such, is unknown."

*I answer that,* Since a faculty and its object are proportional to each other, the intellect must be related to the infinite, as is its object, which is the quiddity of a material thing. Now in material things the infinite does not exist actually, but only potentially, in the sense of one succeeding another, as is said Phys. iii, 6. Therefore infinity is potentially in our mind through its considering successively one thing after another: because never does our intellect understand so many things, that it cannot understand more.

On the other hand, our intellect cannot understand the infinite either actually or habitually. Not actually, for our intellect cannot know actually at the same time, except what it knows through one species. But the infinite is not represented by one species, for if it were it would be something whole and complete. Consequently it cannot be understood except by a successive consideration of one part after another, as is clear from its definition (Phys. iii, 6): for the infinite is that "from which, however much we may take, there always remains something to be taken." Thus the infinite could not be known actually, unless all its parts were counted: which is impossible.

For the same reason we cannot have habitual knowledge of the infinite: because in us habitual knowledge results from actual consideration: since by understanding we acquire knowledge, as is said *Ethic.* ii, 1. Wherefore it would not be possible for us to have a habit of an infinity of things distinctly known, unless we had already considered the entire infinity thereof, counting them according to the succession of our knowledge: which is impossible. And therefore neither actually nor habitually can our intellect know the infinite, but only potentially as explained above.

Reply Obj. 1: As we have said above (Q. 7, A. 1), God is called infinite, because He is a form unlimited by matter; whereas in material things, the term "infinite" is applied to that which is deprived of any formal term. And form being known in itself, whereas matter cannot be known without form, it follows that the material infinite is in itself unknowable. But the formal infinite, God, is of Himself known; but He is unknown to us by reason of our feeble intellect, which in its present state has a natural aptitude for material objects only. Therefore we cannot know God in our present life except through material effects. In the future life this defect of intellect will be removed by the state of glory, when we shall be able to see the Essence of God Himself, but without being able to comprehend Him.

Reply Obj. 2: The nature of our mind is to know species abstracted from phantasms; therefore it cannot know actually or habitually species of numbers or figures that are not in the imagination, except in a general way and in their universal principles; and this is to know them potentially and confusedly.

Reply Obj. 3: If two or more bodies were in the same place, there would be no need for them to occupy the place successively, in order for the things placed to be counted according to this succession of occupation. On the other hand, the intelligible species enter into our intellect successively; since many things cannot be actually understood at the same time: and therefore there must be a definite and not an infinite number of species in our intellect.

Reply Obj. 4: As our intellect is infinite in power, so does it know the infinite. For its power is indeed infinite inasmuch as it is not terminated by corporeal matter. Moreover it can know the universal, which is abstracted from individual matter, and which consequently is not limited to one individual, but, considered in itself, extends to an infinite number of individuals.

THIRD ARTICLE [I, Q. 86, Art. 3]

Whether Our Intellect Can Know Contingent Things?

Objection 1: It would seem that the intellect cannot know contingent things: because, as the Philosopher says (Ethic. vi, 6), the objects of understanding, wisdom and knowledge are not contingent, but necessary things.

Obj. 2: Further, as stated in Phys. iv, 12, "what sometimes is and sometimes is not, is measured by time." Now the intellect abstracts from time, and from other material conditions. Therefore, as it is proper to a contingent thing sometime to be and sometime not to be, it seems that contingent things are not known by the intellect.

*On the contrary,* All knowledge is in the intellect. But some sciences are of the contingent things, as the moral sciences, the objects of which are human actions subject to free-will; and again, the natural sciences in as far as they relate to things generated and corruptible. Therefore the intellect knows contingent things.

*I answer that,* Contingent things can be considered in two ways; either as contingent, or as containing some element of necessity, since every contingent thing has in it something necessary: for example, that Socrates runs, is in itself contingent; but the relation of running to motion is necessary, for it is necessary that Socrates move if he runs. Now contingency arises from matter, for contingency is a potentiality to be or not to be, and potentiality belongs to matter; whereas necessity results from form, because whatever is consequent on form is of necessity in the subject. But matter is the individualizing principle: whereas the universal comes from the abstraction of the form from the particular matter. Moreover it was laid down above (A. 1) that the intellect of itself and directly has the universal for its object; while the object of sense is the singular, which in a certain way is the indirect object of the intellect, as we have said above (A. 1). Therefore the contingent, considered as such, is known directly by sense and indirectly by the intellect; while the universal and necessary principles of contingent things are known only by the intellect. Hence if we consider the objects of science in their universal principles, then all science is of necessary things. But if we consider the things themselves, thus some sciences are of necessary things, some of contingent things.

From which the replies to the objections are clear.

FOURTH ARTICLE [I, Q. 86, Art. 4]

Whether Our Intellect Can Know the Future?

Objection 1: It would seem that our intellect knows the future. For our intellect knows by means of intelligible species abstracted from the "here" and "now," and related indifferently to all time. But it can know the present. Therefore it can know the future.

Obj. 2: Further, man, while his senses are in suspense, can know some future things, as in sleep, and in frenzy. But the intellect is freer and more vigorous when removed from sense. Therefore the intellect of its own nature can know the future.

Obj. 3: The intellectual knowledge of man is superior to any knowledge of brutes. But some animals know the future; thus crows by their frequent cawing foretell rain. Therefore much more can the intellect know the future.

*On the contrary,* It is written (Eccles. 8:6, 7), "There is a great affliction for man, because he is ignorant of things past; and things to come he cannot know by any messenger."

*I answer that,* We must apply the same distinction to future things, as we applied above (A. 3) to contingent things. For future things considered as subject to time are singular, and the human intellect knows them by reflection only, as stated above (A. 1). But the principles of future things may be universal; and thus they may enter the domain of the intellect and become the objects of science.

Speaking, however, of the knowledge of the future in a general way, we must observe that the future may be known in two ways: either in itself, or in its cause. The future cannot be known in itself save by God alone; to Whom even that is present which in the course of events is future, forasmuch as from eternity His glance embraces the whole course of time, as we have said above when treating of God's knowledge (Q. 14, A. 13). But forasmuch as it exists in its cause, the future can be known by us also. And if, indeed, the cause be such as to have a necessary connection with its future result, then the future is known with scientific certitude, just as the astronomer foresees the future eclipse. If, however, the cause be such as to produce a certain result more frequently than not, then can the future be known more or less conjecturally, according as its cause is more or less inclined to produce the effect.

Reply Obj. 1: This argument considers that knowledge which is drawn from universal causal principles; from these the future may be known, according to the order of the effects to the cause.

Reply Obj. 2: As Augustine says (Confess. xii [*Gen. ad lit. xii. 13]), the soul has a certain power of forecasting, so that by its very nature it can know the future; hence when withdrawn from corporeal sense, and, as it were, concentrated on itself, it shares in the knowledge of the future. Such an opinion would be reasonable if we were to admit that the soul receives knowledge by participating the ideas as the Platonists maintained, because in that case the soul by its nature would know the universal causes of all effects, and would only be impeded in its knowledge by the body, and hence when withdrawn from the corporeal senses it would know the future.

But since it is connatural to our intellect to know things, not thus, but by receiving its knowledge from the senses; it is not natural for the soul to know the future when withdrawn from the senses: rather does it know the future by the impression of superior spiritual and corporeal causes; of spiritual causes, when by Divine power the human intellect is enlightened through the ministry of angels, and the phantasms are directed to the knowledge of future events; or, by the influence of demons, when the imagination is moved regarding the future known to the demons, as explained above (Q. 57, A. 3). The soul is naturally more inclined to receive these impressions of spiritual causes when it is withdrawn from the senses, as it is then nearer to the spiritual world, and freer from external distractions. The same may also come from superior corporeal causes. For it is clear that superior bodies influence inferior bodies. Hence, in consequence of the sensitive faculties being acts of corporeal organs, the influence of the heavenly bodies causes the imagination to be affected, and so, as the heavenly bodies cause many future events, the imagination receives certain images of some such events. These images are perceived more at night and while we sleep than in the daytime and while we are awake, because, as stated in De Somn. et Vigil. ii [*De Divinat. per somn. ii], "impressions made by day are evanescent. The night air is calmer, when silence reigns, hence bodily impressions are made in sleep, when slight internal movements are felt more than in wakefulness, and such movements produce in the imagination images from which the future may be foreseen."

Reply Obj. 3: Brute animals have no power above the imagination wherewith to regulate it, as man has his reason, and therefore their imagination follows entirely the influence of the heavenly bodies. Thus from such animals' movements some future things, such as rain and the like, may be known rather than from human movements directed by reason. Hence the Philosopher says (De Somn. et Vig.), that "some who are most imprudent are most far-seeing; for their intelligence is not burdened with cares, but is as it were barren and bare of all anxiety moving at the caprice of whatever is brought to bear on it."

# QUESTION 87

HOW THE INTELLECTUAL SOUL KNOWS ITSELF AND ALL WITHIN ITSELF (In Four Articles)

We have now to consider how the intellectual soul knows itself and all within itself. Under this head there are four points of inquiry:

(1) Whether the soul knows itself by its own essence?

(2) Whether it knows its own habits?

(3) How does the intellect know its own act?

(4) How does it know the act of the will?

FIRST ARTICLE [I, Q. 87, Art. 1]

Whether the Intellectual Soul Knows Itself by Its Essence?

Objection 1: It would seem that the intellectual soul knows itself by its own essence. For Augustine says (De Trin. ix, 3), that "the mind knows itself, because it is incorporeal."

Obj. 2: Further, both angels and human souls belong to the genus of intellectual substance. But an angel understands itself by its own essence. Therefore likewise does the human soul.

Obj. 3: Further, "in things void of matter, the intellect and that which is understood are the same" (De Anima iii, 4). But the human mind is void of matter, not being the act of a body as stated above (Q. 76, A. 1). Therefore the intellect and its object are the same in the human mind; and therefore the human mind understands itself by its own essence.

*On the contrary,* It is said (De Anima iii, 4) that "the intellect understands itself in the same way as it understands other things." But it understands other things, not by their essence, but by their similitudes. Therefore it does not understand itself by its own essence.

*I answer that,* Everything is knowable so far as it is in act, and not, so far as it is in potentiality (Metaph. ix, Did. viii, 9): for a thing is a being, and is true, and therefore knowable, according as it is actual. This is quite clear as regards sensible things, for the eye does not see what is potentially, but what is actually colored. In like manner it is clear that the intellect, so far as it knows material things, does not know save what is in act: and hence it does not know primary matter except as proportionate to form, as is stated Phys. i, 7. Consequently immaterial substances are intelligible by their own essence according as each one is actual by its own essence.

Therefore it is that the Essence of God, the pure and perfect act, is simply and perfectly in itself intelligible; and hence God by His own Essence knows Himself, and all other things also. The angelic essence belongs, indeed, to the genus of intelligible things as *act,* but not as a *pure act,* nor as a complete act, and hence the angel's act of intelligence is not completed by his essence. For although an angel understands himself by his own essence, still he cannot understand all other things by his own essence; for he knows things other than himself by their likenesses. Now the human intellect is only a potentiality in the genus of intelligible beings, just as primary matter is a potentiality as regards sensible beings; and hence it is called "possible" [*Possibilis—elsewhere in this translation rendered "passive"—Ed.]. Therefore in its essence the human mind is potentially understanding. Hence it has in itself the power to understand, but not to be understood, except as it is made actual. For even the Platonists asserted that an order of intelligible beings existed above the order of intellects, forasmuch as the intellect understands only by participation of the intelligible; for they said that the participator is below what it participates.

If, therefore, the human intellect, as the Platonists held, became actual by participating separate intelligible forms, it would understand itself by such participation of incorporeal beings. But as in this life our intellect has material and sensible things for its proper natural object, as stated above (Q. 84, A. 7), it understands itself according as it is made actual by the species abstracted from sensible things, through the light of the active intellect, which not only actuates the intelligible things themselves, but also, by their instrumentality, actuates the passive intellect. Therefore the intellect knows itself not by its essence, but by its act. This happens in two ways: In the first place, singularly, as when Socrates or Plato perceives that he has an intellectual soul because he perceives that he understands. In the second place, universally, as when we consider the nature of the human mind from knowledge of the intellectual act. It is true, however, that the judgment and force of this knowledge, whereby we know the nature of the soul, comes to us according to the derivation of our intellectual light from the Divine Truth which contains the types of all things as above stated (Q. 84, A. 5). Hence Augustine says (De Trin. ix, 6): "We gaze on the inviolable truth whence we can as perfectly as possible define, not what each man's mind is, but what it ought to be in the light of the eternal types." There is, however, a difference between these two kinds of knowledge, and it consists in this, that the mere presence of the mind suffices for the first; the mind itself being the principle of action whereby it perceives itself, and hence it is said to know itself by its own presence. But as regards the second kind of knowledge, the mere presence of the mind does not suffice, and there is further required a careful and subtle inquiry. Hence many are ignorant of the soul's nature, and many have erred about it. So Augustine says (De Trin. x, 9), concerning such mental inquiry: "Let the mind strive not to see itself as if it were absent, but to discern itself as present"—i.e. to know how it differs from other things; which is to know its essence and nature.

Reply Obj. 1: The mind knows itself by means of itself, because at length it acquires knowledge of itself, though led thereto by its own act: because it is itself that it knows, since it loves itself, as he says in the same passage. For a thing can be called self-evident in two ways, either because we can know it by nothing else except itself, as first principles are called self-evident; or because it is not accidentally knowable, as color is visible of itself, whereas substance is visible by its accident.

Reply Obj. 2: The essence of an angel is an act in the genus of intelligible things, and therefore it is both intellect and the thing understood. Hence an angel apprehends his own essence through itself: not so the human mind, which is either altogether in potentiality to intelligible things—as is the passive intellect—or is the act of intelligible things abstracted from the phantasms—as is the active intellect.

Reply Obj. 3: This saying of the Philosopher is universally true in every kind of intellect. For as sense in act is the sensible in act, by reason of the sensible likeness which is the form of sense in act, so likewise the intellect in act is the object understood in act, by reason of the likeness of the thing understood, which is the form of the intellect in act. So the human intellect, which becomes actual by the species of the object understood, is itself understood by the same species as by its own form. Now to say that in "things without matter the intellect and what is understood are the same," is equal to saying that "as regards things actually understood the intellect and what is understood are the same." For a thing is actually understood in that it is immaterial. But a distinction must be drawn: since the essences of some things are immaterial—as the separate substances called angels, each of which is understood and understands, whereas there are other things whose essences are not wholly immaterial, but only the abstract likenesses thereof. Hence the Commentator says (De Anima iii) that the proposition quoted is true only of separate substances; because in a sense it is verified in their regard, and not in regard of other substances, as already stated (Reply Obj. 2).

SECOND ARTICLE [I, Q. 87, Art. 2]

Whether Our Intellect Knows the Habits of the Soul by Their Essence?

Objection 1: It would seem that our intellect knows the habits of the soul by their essence. For Augustine says (De Trin. xiii, 1): "Faith is not seen in the heart wherein it abides, as the soul of a man may be seen by another from the movement of the body; but we know most certainly that it is there, and conscience proclaims its existence"; and the same principle applies to the other habits of the soul. Therefore the habits of the soul are not known by their acts, but by themselves.

Obj. 2: Further, material things outside the soul are known by their likeness being present in the soul, and are said therefore to be known by their likenesses. But the soul's habits are present by their essence in the soul. Therefore the habits of the soul are known by their essence.

Obj. 3: Further, "whatever is the cause of a thing being such is still more so." But habits and intelligible species cause things to be known by the soul. Therefore they are still more known by the soul in themselves.

*On the contrary,* Habits like powers are the principles of acts. But as is said (De Anima ii, 4), "acts and operations are logically prior to powers." Therefore in the same way they are prior to habits; and thus habits, like the powers, are known by their acts.

*I answer that,* A habit is a kind of medium between mere power and mere act. Now, it has been said (A. 1) that nothing is known but as it is actual: therefore so far as a habit fails in being a perfect act, it falls short in being of itself knowable, and can be known only by its act; thus, for example, anyone knows he has a habit from the fact that he can produce the act proper to that habit; or he may inquire into the nature and idea of the habit by considering the act. The first kind of knowledge of the habit arises from its being present, for the very fact of its presence causes the act whereby it is known. The second kind of knowledge of the habit arises from a careful inquiry, as is explained above of the mind (A. 1).

Reply Obj. 1: Although faith is not known by external movement of the body, it is perceived by the subject wherein it resides, by the interior act of the heart. For no one knows that he has faith unless he knows that he believes.

Reply Obj. 2: Habits are present in our intellect, not as its object since, in the present state of life, our intellect's object is the nature of a material thing as stated above (Q. 84, A. 7), but as that by which it understands.

Reply Obj. 3: The axiom, "whatever is the cause of a thing being such, is still more so," is true of things that are of the same order, for instance, of the same kind of cause; for example, we may say that health is desirable on account of life, and therefore life is more desirable still. But if we take things of different orders the axiom is not true: for we may say that health is caused by medicine, but it does not follow that medicine is more desirable than health, for health belongs to the order of final causes, whereas medicine belongs to the order of efficient causes. So of two things belonging essentially to the order of the objects of knowledge, the one which is the cause of the other being known, is the more known, as principles are more known than conclusions. But habit as such does not belong to the order of objects of knowledge; nor are things known on account of the habit, as on account of an object known, but as on account of a disposition or form whereby the subject knows: and therefore the argument does not prove.

THIRD ARTICLE [I, Q. 87, Art. 3]

Whether Our Intellect Knows Its Own Act?

Objection 1: It would seem that our intellect does not know its own act. For what is known is the object of the knowing faculty. But the act differs from the object. Therefore the intellect does not know its own act.

Obj. 2: Further, whatever is known is known by some act. If, then, the intellect knows its own act, it knows it by some act, and again it knows that act by some other act; this is to proceed indefinitely, which seems impossible.

Obj. 3: Further, the intellect has the same relation to its act as sense has to its act. But the proper sense does not feel its own act, for this belongs to the common sense, as stated *De Anima* iii, 2. Therefore neither does the intellect understand its own act.

*On the contrary,* Augustine says (De Trin. x, 11), "I understand that I understand."

*I answer that,* As stated above (AA. 1, 2) a thing is intelligible according as it is in act. Now the ultimate perfection of the intellect consists in its own operation: for this is not an act tending to something else in which lies the perfection of the work accomplished, as building is the perfection of the thing built; but it remains in the agent as its perfection and act, as is said *Metaph.* ix, Did. viii, 8. Therefore the first thing understood of the intellect is its own act of understanding. This occurs in different ways with different intellects. For there is an intellect, namely, the Divine, which is Its own act of intelligence, so that in God the understanding of His intelligence, and the understanding of His Essence, are one and the same act, because His Essence is His act of understanding. But there is another intellect, the angelic, which is not its own act of understanding, as we have said above (Q. 79, A. 1), and yet the first object of that act is the angelic essence. Wherefore although there is a logical distinction between the act whereby he understands that he understands, and that whereby he understands his essence, yet he understands both by one and the same act; because to understand his own essence is the proper perfection of his essence, and by one and the same act is a thing, together with its perfection, understood. And there is yet another, namely, the human intellect, which neither is its own act of understanding, nor is its own essence the first object of its act of understanding, for this object is the nature of a material thing. And therefore that which is first known by the human intellect is an object of this kind, and that which is known secondarily is the act by which that object is known; and through the act the intellect itself is known, the perfection of which is this act of understanding. For this reason did the Philosopher assert that objects are known before acts, and acts before powers (De Anima ii, 4).

Reply Obj. 1: The object of the intellect is something universal, namely, *being* and the true, in which the act also of understanding is comprised. Wherefore the intellect can understand its own act. But not primarily, since the first object of our intellect, in this state of life, is not every being and everything true, but *being* and true, as considered in material things, as we have said above (Q. 84, A. 7), from which it acquires knowledge of all other things.

Reply Obj. 2: The intelligent act of the human intellect is not the act and perfection of the material nature understood, as if the nature of the material thing and intelligent act could be understood by one act; just as a thing and its perfection are understood by one act. Hence the act whereby the intellect understands a stone is distinct from the act whereby it understands that it understands a stone; and so on. Nor is there any difficulty in the intellect being thus potentially infinite, as explained above (Q. 86, A. 2).

Reply Obj. 3: The proper sense feels by reason of the immutation in the material organ caused by the external sensible. A material object, however, cannot immute itself; but one is immuted by another, and therefore the act of the proper sense is perceived by the common sense. The intellect, *on the contrary,* does not perform the act of understanding by the material immutation of an organ; and so there is no comparison.

FOURTH ARTICLE [I, Q. 87, Art. 4]

Whether the Intellect Understands the Act of the Will?

Objection 1: It would seem that the intellect does not understand the act of the will. For nothing is known by the intellect, unless it be in some way present in the intellect. But the act of the will is not in the intellect; since the will and the intellect are distinct. Therefore the act of the will is not known by the intellect.

Obj. 2: Further, the act is specified by the object. But the object of the will is not the same as the object of the intellect. Therefore the act of the will is specifically distinct from the object of the intellect, and therefore the act of the will is not known by the intellect.

Obj. 3: Augustine (Confess. x, 17) says of the soul's affections that "they are known neither by images as bodies are known; nor by their presence, like the arts; but by certain notions." Now it does not seem that there can be in the soul any other notions of things but either the essences of things known or the likenesses thereof. Therefore it seems impossible for the intellect to known such affections of the soul as the acts of the will.

*On the contrary,* Augustine says (De Trin. x, 11), "I understand that I will."

*I answer that,* As stated above (Q. 59, A. 1), the act of the will is nothing but an inclination consequent on the form understood; just as the natural appetite is an inclination consequent on the natural form. Now the inclination of a thing resides in it according to its mode of existence; and hence the natural inclination resides in a natural thing naturally, and the inclination called the sensible appetite is in the sensible thing sensibly; and likewise the intelligible inclination, which is the act of the will, is in the intelligent subject intelligibly as in its principle and proper subject. Hence the Philosopher expresses himself thus (De Anima iii, 9)—that "the will is in the reason." Now whatever is intelligibly in an intelligent subject, is understood by that subject. Therefore the act of the will is understood by the intellect, both inasmuch as one knows that one wills; and inasmuch as one knows the nature of this act, and consequently, the nature of its principle which is the habit or power.

Reply Obj. 1: This argument would hold good if the will and the intellect were in different subjects, as they are distinct powers; for then whatever was in the will would not be in the intellect. But as both are rooted in the same substance of the soul, and since one is in a certain way the principle of the other, consequently what is in the will is, in a certain way, also in the intellect.

Reply Obj. 2: The "good" and the "true" which are the objects of the will and of the intellect, differ logically, but one is contained in the other, as we have said above (Q. 82, A. 4, ad 1; Q. 16, A. 4, ad 1); for the true is good and the good is true. Therefore the objects of the will fall under the intellect, and those of the intellect can fall under the will.

Reply Obj. 3: The affections of the soul are in the intellect not by similitude only, like bodies; nor by being present in their subject, as the arts; but as the thing caused is in its principle, which contains some notion of the thing caused. And so Augustine says that the soul's affections are in the memory by certain notions.

## QUESTION 88

HOW THE HUMAN SOUL KNOWS WHAT IS ABOVE ITSELF (In Three Articles)

We must now consider how the human soul knows what is above itself, viz. immaterial substances. Under this head there are three points of inquiry:

(1) Whether the human soul in the present state of life can understand the immaterial substances called angels, in themselves?

(2) Whether it can arrive at the knowledge thereof by the knowledge of material things?

(3) Whether God is the first object of our knowledge?

FIRST ARTICLE [I, Q. 88, Art. 1]

Whether the Human Soul in the Present State of Life Can Understand Immaterial Substances in Themselves?

Objection 1: It would seem that the human soul in the present state of life can understand immaterial substances in themselves. For Augustine (De Trin. ix, 3) says: "As the mind itself acquires the knowledge of corporeal things by means of the corporeal senses, so it gains from itself the knowledge of incorporeal things." But these are the immaterial substances. Therefore the human mind understands immaterial substances.

Obj. 2: Further, like is known by like. But the human mind is more akin to immaterial than to material things; since its own nature is immaterial, as is clear from what we have said above (Q. 76, A. 1). Since then our mind understands material things, much more is it able to understand immaterial things.

Obj. 3: Further, the fact that objects which are in themselves most sensible are not most felt by us, comes from sense being corrupted by their very excellence. But the intellect is not subject to such a corrupting influence from its object, as is stated *De Anima* iii, 4. Therefore things which are in themselves in the highest degree of intelligibility, are likewise to us most intelligible. As material things, however, are intelligible only so far as we make them actually so by abstracting them from material conditions, it is clear that those substances are more intelligible in themselves whose nature is immaterial. Therefore they are much more known to us than are material things.

Obj. 4: Further, the Commentator says (Metaph. ii) that "nature would be frustrated in its end" were we unable to understand abstract substances, "because it would have made what in itself is naturally intelligible not to be understood at all." But in nature nothing is idle or purposeless. Therefore immaterial substances can be understood by us.

Obj. 5: Further, as sense is to the sensible, so is intellect to the intelligible. But our sight can see all things corporeal, whether superior and incorruptible; or lower and corruptible. Therefore our intellect can understand all intelligible substances, even the superior and immaterial.

*On the contrary,* It is written (Wis. 9:16): "The things that are in heaven, who shall search out?" But these substances are said to be in heaven, according to Matt. 18:10, "Their angels in heaven," etc. Therefore immaterial substances cannot be known by human investigation.

*I answer that,* In the opinion of Plato, immaterial substances are not only understood by us, but are the objects we understand first of all. For Plato taught that immaterial subsisting forms, which he called "Ideas," are the proper objects of our intellect, and thus first and *per se* understood by us; and, further, that material objects are known by the soul inasmuch as phantasy and sense are mixed up with the mind. Hence the purer the intellect is, so much the more clearly does it perceive the intelligible truth of immaterial things.

But in Aristotle's opinion, which experience corroborates, our intellect in its present state of life has a natural relationship to the natures of material things; and therefore it can only understand by turning to the phantasms, as we have said above (Q. 84, A. 7). Thus it clearly appears that immaterial substances which do not fall under sense and imagination, cannot first and *per se* be known by us, according to the mode of knowledge which experience proves us to have.

Nevertheless Averroes (Comment. De Anima iii) teaches that in this present life man can in the end arrive at the knowledge of separate substances by being coupled or united to some separate substance, which he calls the "active intellect," and which, being a separate substance itself, can naturally understand separate substances. Hence, when it is perfectly united to us so that by its means we are able to understand perfectly, we also shall be able to understand separate substances, as in the present life through the medium of the passive intellect united to us, we can understand material things. Now he said that the active intellect is united to us, thus. For since we understand by means of both the active intellect and intelligible objects, as, for instance, we understand conclusions by principles understood; it is clear that the active intellect must be compared to the objects understood, either as the principal agent is to the instrument, or as form to matter. For an action is ascribed to two principles in one of these two ways; to a principal agent and to an instrument, as cutting to the workman and the saw; to a form and its subject, as heating to heat and fire. In both these ways the active intellect can be compared to the intelligible object as perfection is to the perfectible, and as act is to potentiality. Now a subject is made perfect and receives its perfection at one and the same time, as the reception of what is actually visible synchronizes with the reception of light in the eye. Therefore the passive intellect receives the intelligible object and the active intellect together; and the more numerous the intelligible objects received, so much the nearer do we come to the point of perfect union between ourselves and the active intellect; so much so that when we understand all the intelligible objects, the active intellect becomes one with us, and by its instrumentality we can understand all things material and immaterial. In this he makes the ultimate happiness of man to consist. Nor, as regards the present inquiry, does it matter whether the passive intellect in that state of happiness understands separate substances by the instrumentality of the active intellect, as he himself maintains, or whether (as he says Alexander holds) the passive intellect can never understand separate substances (because according to him it is corruptible), but man understands separate substances by means of the active intellect.

This opinion, however, is untrue. First, because, supposing the active intellect to be a separate substance, we could not formally understand by its instrumentality, for the medium of an agent's formal action consists in its form and act, since every agent acts according to its actuality, as was said of the passive intellect (Q. 70, A. 1). Secondly, this opinion is untrue, because in the above explanation, the active intellect, supposing it to be a separate substance, would not be joined to us in its substance, but only in its light, as participated in things understood; and would not extend to the other acts of the active intellect so as to enable us to understand immaterial substances; just as when we see colors set off by the sun, we are not united to the substance of the sun so as to act like the sun, but its light only is united to us, that we may see the colors. Thirdly, this opinion is untrue, because granted that, as above explained, the active intellect were united to us in substance, still it is not said that it is wholly so united in regard to one intelligible object, or two; but rather in regard to all intelligible objects. But all such objects together do not equal the force of the active intellect, as it is a much greater thing to understand separate substances than to understand all material things. Hence it clearly follows that the knowledge of all material things would not make the active intellect to be so united to us as to enable us by its instrumentality to understand separate substances.

Fourthly, this opinion is untrue, because it is hardly possible for anyone in this world to understand all material things: and thus no one, or very few, could reach to perfect felicity; which is against what the Philosopher says (Ethic. i, 9), that happiness is a "kind of common good, communicable to all capable of virtue." Further, it is unreasonable that only the few of any species attain to the end of the species.

Fifthly, the Philosopher expressly says (Ethic. i, 10), that happiness is "an operation according to perfect virtue"; and after enumerating many virtues in the tenth book, he concludes (Ethic. i, 7) that ultimate happiness consisting in the knowledge of the highest things intelligible is attained through the virtue of wisdom, which in the sixth chapter he had named as the chief of speculative sciences. Hence Aristotle clearly places the ultimate felicity of man in the knowledge of separate substances, obtainable by speculative science; and not by being united to the active intellect as some imagined.

Sixthly, as was shown above (Q. 79, A. 4), the active intellect is not a separate substance; but a faculty of the soul, extending itself actively to the same objects to which the passive intellect extends receptively; because, as is stated (De Anima iii, 5), the passive intellect is "all things potentially," and the active intellect is "all things in act." Therefore both intellects, according to the present state of life, extend to material things only, which are made actually intelligible by the active intellect, and are received in the passive intellect. Hence in the present state of life we cannot understand separate immaterial substances in themselves, either by the passive or by the active intellect.

Reply Obj. 1: Augustine may be taken to mean that the knowledge of incorporeal things in the mind can be gained by the mind itself. This is so true that philosophers also say that the knowledge concerning the soul is a principle for the knowledge of separate substances. For by knowing itself, it attains to some knowledge of incorporeal substances, such as is within its compass; not that the knowledge of itself gives it a perfect and absolute knowledge of them.

Reply Obj. 2: The likeness of nature is not a sufficient cause of knowledge; otherwise what Empedocles said would be true—that the soul needs to have the nature of all in order to know all. But knowledge requires that the likeness of the thing known be in the knower, as a kind of form thereof. Now our passive intellect, in the present state of life, is such that it can be informed with similitudes abstracted from phantasms: and therefore it knows material things rather than immaterial substances.

Reply Obj. 3: There must needs be some proportion between the object and the faculty of knowledge; such as of the active to the passive, and of perfection to the perfectible. Hence that sensible objects of great power are not grasped by the senses, is due not merely to the fact that they corrupt the organ, but also to their being improportionate to the sensitive power. And thus it is that immaterial substances are improportionate to our intellect, in our present state of life, so that it cannot understand them.

Reply Obj. 4: This argument of the Commentator fails in several ways. First, because if separate substances are not understood by us, it does not follow that they are not understood by any intellect; for they are understood by themselves, and by one another.

Secondly, to be understood by us is not the end of separate substances: while only that is vain and purposeless, which fails to attain its end. It does not follow, therefore, that immaterial substances are purposeless, even if they are not understood by us at all.

Reply Obj. 5: Sense knows bodies, whether superior or inferior, in the same way, that is, by the sensible acting on the organ. But we do not understand material and immaterial substances in the same way. The former we understand by a process of abstraction, which is impossible in the case of the latter, for there are no phantasms of what is immaterial.

SECOND ARTICLE [I, Q. 88, Art. 2]

Whether Our Intellect Can Understand Immaterial Substances Through Its Knowledge of Material Things?

Objection 1: It would seem that our intellect can know immaterial substances through the knowledge of material things. For Dionysius says (Coel. Hier. i) that "the human mind cannot be raised up to immaterial contemplation of the heavenly hierarchies, unless it is led thereto by material guidance according to its own nature." Therefore we can be led by material things to know immaterial substances.

Obj. 2: Further, science resides in the intellect. But there are sciences and definitions of immaterial substances; for Damascene defines an angel (De Fide Orth. ii, 3); and we find angels treated of both in theology and philosophy. Therefore immaterial substances can be understood by us.

Obj. 3: Further, the human soul belongs to the genus of immaterial substances. But it can be understood by us through its act by which it understands material things. Therefore also other material substances can be understood by us, through their material effects.

Obj. 4: Further, the only cause which cannot be comprehended through its effects is that which is infinitely distant from them, and this belongs to God alone. Therefore other created immaterial substances can be understood by us through material things.

*On the contrary,* Dionysius says (Div. Nom. i) that "intelligible things cannot be understood through sensible things, nor composite things through simple, nor incorporeal through corporeal."

*I answer that,* Averroes says (De Anima iii) that a philosopher named Avempace [*Ibn-Badja, Arabian Philosopher; ob. 1183] taught that by the understanding of natural substances we can be led, according to true philosophical principles, to the knowledge of immaterial substances. For since the nature of our intellect is to abstract the quiddity of material things from matter, anything material residing in that abstracted quiddity can again be made subject to abstraction; and as the process of abstraction cannot go on forever, it must arrive at length at some immaterial quiddity, absolutely without matter; and this would be the understanding of immaterial substance.

Now this opinion would be true, were immaterial substances the forms and species of these material things; as the Platonists supposed. But supposing, *on the contrary,* that immaterial substances differ altogether from the quiddity of material things, it follows that however much our intellect abstract the quiddity of material things from matter, it could never arrive at anything akin to immaterial substance. Therefore we are not able perfectly to understand immaterial substances through material substances.

Reply Obj. 1: From material things we can rise to some kind of knowledge of immaterial things, but not to the perfect knowledge thereof; for there is no proper and adequate proportion between material and immaterial things, and the likenesses drawn from material things for the understanding of immaterial things are very dissimilar therefrom, as Dionysius says (Coel. Hier. ii).

Reply Obj. 2: Science treats of higher things principally by way of negation. Thus Aristotle (De Coel. i, 3) explains the heavenly bodies by denying to them inferior corporeal properties. Hence it follows that much less can immaterial substances be known by us in such a way as to make us know their quiddity; but we may have a scientific knowledge of them by way of negation and by their relation to material things.

Reply Obj. 3: The human soul understands itself through its own act of understanding, which is proper to it, showing perfectly its power and nature. But the power and nature of immaterial substances cannot be perfectly known through such act, nor through any other material thing, because there is no proportion between the latter and the power of the former.

Reply Obj. 4: Created immaterial substances are not in the same natural genus as material substances, for they do not agree in power or in matter; but they belong to the same logical genus, because even immaterial substances are in the predicament of substance, as their essence is distinct from their existence. But God has no connection with material things, as regards either natural genus or logical genus; because God is in no genus, as stated above (Q. 3, A. 5). Hence through the likeness derived from material things we can know something positive concerning the angels, according to some common notion, though not according to the specific nature; whereas we cannot acquire any such knowledge at all about God.

THIRD ARTICLE [I, Q. 88, Art. 3]

Whether God Is the First Object Known by the Human Mind?

Objection 1: It would seem that God is the first object known by the human mind. For that object in which all others are known, and by which we judge others, is the first thing known to us; as light is to the eye, and first principles to the intellect. But we know all things in the light of the first truth, and thereby judge of all things, as Augustine says (De Trin. xii, 2; De Vera Relig. xxxi); [*Confess. xii, 25]. Therefore God is the first object known to us.

Obj. 2: Further, whatever causes a thing to be such is more so. But God is the cause of all our knowledge; for He is "the true light which enlighteneth every man that cometh into this world" (John 1:9). Therefore God is our first and most known object.

Obj. 3: Further, what is first known in the image is the exemplar to which it is made. But in our mind is the image of God, as Augustine says (De Trin. xii, 4,7). Therefore God is the first object known to our mind.

*On the contrary,* "No man hath seen God at any time" (John 1:18).

*I answer that,* Since the human intellect in the present state of life cannot understand even immaterial created substances (A. 1), much less can it understand the essence of the uncreated substance. Hence it must be said simply that God is not the first object of our knowledge. Rather do we know God through creatures, according to the Apostle (Rom. 1:20), "the invisible things of God are clearly seen, being understood by the things that are made": while the first object of our knowledge in this life is the "quiddity of a material thing," which is the proper object of our intellect, as appears above in many passages (Q. 84, A. 7; Q. 85, A. 8; Q. 87, A. 2, ad 2)

Reply Obj. 1: We see and judge of all things in the light of the first truth, forasmuch as the light itself of our mind, whether natural or gratuitous, is nothing else than the impression of the first truth upon it, as stated above (Q. 12, A. 2). Hence, as the light itself of our intellect is not the object it understands, much less can it be said that God is the first object known by our intellect.

Reply Obj. 2: The axiom, "Whatever causes a thing to be such is more so," must be understood of things belonging to one and the same order, as explained above (Q. 81, A. 2, ad 3). Other things than God are known because of God; not as if He were the first known object, but because He is the first cause of our faculty of knowledge.

Reply Obj. 3: If there existed in our souls a perfect image of God, as the Son is the perfect image of the Father, our mind would know God at once. But the image in our mind is imperfect; hence the argument does not prove.

# QUESTION 89

OF THE KNOWLEDGE OF THE SEPARATED SOUL (In Eight Articles)

We must now consider the knowledge of the separated soul. Under this head there are eight points of inquiry:

(1) Whether the soul separated from the body can understand?

(2) Whether it understands separate substances?

(3) Whether it understands all natural things?

(4) Whether it understands individuals and singulars?

(5) Whether the habits of knowledge acquired in this life remain?

(6) Whether the soul can use the habit of knowledge here acquired?

(7) Whether local distance impedes the separated soul's knowledge?

(8) Whether souls separated from the body know what happens here?

FIRST ARTICLE [I, Q. 89, Art. 1]

Whether the Separated Soul Can Understand Anything?

Objection 1: It would seem that the soul separated from the body can understand nothing at all. For the Philosopher says (De Anima i, 4) that "the understanding is corrupted together with its interior principle." But by death all human interior principles are corrupted. Therefore also the intellect itself is corrupted.

Obj. 2: Further, the human soul is hindered from understanding when the senses are tied, and by a distracted imagination, as explained above (Q. 84, AA. 7,8). But death destroys the senses and imagination, as we have shown above (Q. 77, A. 8). Therefore after death the soul understands nothing.

Obj. 3: Further, if the separated soul can understand, this must be by means of some species. But it does not understand by means of innate species, because it has none such; being at first "like a tablet on which nothing is written": nor does it understand by species abstracted from things, for it does not then possess organs of sense and imagination which are necessary for the abstraction of species: nor does it understand by means of species, formerly abstracted and retained in the soul; for if that were so, a child's soul would have no means of understanding at all: nor does it understand by means of intelligible species divinely infused, for such knowledge would not be natural, such as we treat of now, but the effect of grace. Therefore the soul apart from the body understands nothing.

*On the contrary,* The Philosopher says (De Anima i, 1), "If the soul had no proper operation, it could not be separated from the body." But the soul is separated from the body; therefore it has a proper operation and above all, that which consists in intelligence. Therefore the soul can understand when it is apart from the body.

*I answer that,* The difficulty in solving this question arises from the fact that the soul united to the body can understand only by turning to the phantasms, as experience shows. Did this not proceed from the soul's very nature, but accidentally through its being bound up with the body, as the Platonists said, the difficulty would vanish; for in that case when the body was once removed, the soul would at once return to its own nature, and would understand intelligible things simply, without turning to the phantasms, as is exemplified in the case of other separate substances. In that case, however, the union of soul and body would not be for the soul's good, for evidently it would understand worse in the body than out of it; but for the good of the body, which would be unreasonable, since matter exists on account of the form, and not the form for the sake of matter. But if we admit that the nature of the soul requires it to understand by turning to the phantasms, it will seem, since death does not change its nature, that it can then naturally understand nothing; as the phantasms are wanting to which it may turn.

To solve this difficulty we must consider that as nothing acts except so far as it is actual, the mode of action in every agent follows from its mode of existence. Now the soul has one mode of being when in the body, and another when apart from it, its nature remaining always the same; but this does not mean that its union with the body is an accidental thing, for, *on the contrary,* such union belongs to its very nature, just as the nature of a light object is not changed, when it is in its proper place, which is natural to it, and outside its proper place, which is beside its nature. The soul, therefore, when united to the body, consistently with that mode of existence, has a mode of understanding, by turning to corporeal phantasms, which are in corporeal organs; but when it is separated from the body, it has a mode of understanding, by turning to simply intelligible objects, as is proper to other separate substances. Hence it is as natural for the soul to understand by turning to the phantasms as it is for it to be joined to the body; but to be separated from the body is not in accordance with its nature, and likewise to understand without turning to the phantasms is not natural to it; and hence it is united to the body in order that it may have an existence and an operation suitable to its nature. But here again a difficulty arises. For since nature is always ordered to what is best, and since it is better to understand by turning to simply intelligible objects than by turning to the phantasms; God should have ordered the soul's nature so that the nobler way of understanding would have been natural to it, and it would not have needed the body for that purpose.

In order to resolve this difficulty we must consider that while it is true that it is nobler in itself to understand by turning to something higher than to understand by turning to phantasms, nevertheless such a mode of understanding was not so perfect as regards what was possible to the soul. This will appear if we consider that every intellectual substance possesses intellective power by the influence of the Divine light, which is one and simple in its first principle, and the farther off intellectual creatures are from the first principle so much the more is the light divided and diversified, as is the case with lines radiating from the centre of a circle. Hence it is that God by His one Essence understands all things; while the superior intellectual substances understand by means of a number of species, which nevertheless are fewer and more universal and bestow a deeper comprehension of things, because of the efficaciousness of the intellectual power of such natures: whereas the inferior intellectual natures possess a greater number of species, which are less universal, and bestow a lower degree of comprehension, in proportion as they recede from the intellectual power of the higher natures. If, therefore, the inferior substances received species in the same degree of universality as the superior substances, since they are not so strong in understanding, the knowledge which they would derive through them would be imperfect, and of a general and confused nature. We can see this to a certain extent in man, for those who are of weaker intellect fail to acquire perfect knowledge through the universal conceptions of those who have a better understanding, unless things are explained to them singly and in detail. Now it is clear that in the natural order human souls hold the lowest place among intellectual substances. But the perfection of the universe required various grades of being. If, therefore, God had willed souls to understand in the same way as separate substances, it would follow that human knowledge, so far from being perfect, would be confused and general. Therefore to make it possible for human souls to possess perfect and proper knowledge, they were so made that their nature required them to be joined to bodies, and thus to receive the proper and adequate knowledge of sensible things from the sensible things themselves; thus we see in the case of uneducated men that they have to be taught by sensible examples.

It is clear then that it was for the soul's good that it was united to a body, and that it understands by turning to the phantasms. Nevertheless it is possible for it to exist apart from the body, and also to understand in another way.

Reply Obj. 1: The Philosopher's words carefully examined will show that he said this on the previous supposition that understanding is a movement of body and soul as united, just as sensation is, for he had not as yet explained the difference between intellect and sense. We may also say that he is referring to the way of understanding by turning to phantasms. This is also the meaning of the second objection.

Reply Obj. 3: The separated soul does not understand by way of innate species, nor by species abstracted then, nor only by species retained, and this the objection proves; but the soul in that state understands by means of participated species arising from the influence of the Divine light, shared by the soul as by other separate substances; though in a lesser degree. Hence as soon as it ceases to act by turning to corporeal (phantasms), the soul turns at once to the superior things; nor is this way of knowledge unnatural, for God is the author of the influx of both of the light of grace and of the light of nature.

SECOND ARTICLE [I, Q. 89, Art. 2]

Whether the Separated Soul Understands Separate Substances?

Objection 1: It would seem that the separated soul does not understand separate substances. For the soul is more perfect when joined to the body than when existing apart from it, being an essential part of human nature; and every part of a whole is more perfect when it exists in that whole. But the soul in the body does not understand separate substances as shown above (Q. 88, A. 1). Therefore much less is it able to do so when apart from the body.

Obj. 2: Further, whatever is known is known either by its presence or by its species. But separate substances cannot be known to the soul by their presence, for God alone can enter into the soul; nor by means of species abstracted by the soul from an angel, for an angel is more simple than a soul. Therefore the separated soul cannot at all understand separate substances.

Obj. 3: Further, some philosophers said that the ultimate happiness of man consists in the knowledge of separate substances. If, therefore, the separated soul can understand separate substances, its happiness would be secured by its separation alone; which cannot be reasonably be said.

*On the contrary,* Souls apart from the body know

other separated souls; as we see in the case of the rich man in hell, who saw Lazarus and Abraham (Luke 16:23). Therefore separated souls see the devils and the angels.

*I answer that,* Augustine says (De Trin. ix, 3), "our mind acquires the knowledge of incorporeal things by itself"—i.e. by knowing itself (Q. 88, A. 1, ad 1). Therefore from the knowledge which the separated soul has of itself, we can judge how it knows other separate things. Now it was said above (A. 1), that as long as it is united to the body the soul understands by turning to phantasms, and therefore it does not understand itself save through becoming actually intelligent by means of ideas abstracted from phantasms; for thus it understands itself through its own act, as shown above (Q. 87, A. 1). When, however, it is separated from the body, it understands no longer by turning to phantasms, but by turning to simply intelligible objects; hence in that state it understands itself through itself. Now, every separate substance "understands what is above itself and what is below itself, according to the mode of its substance" (De Causis viii): for a thing is understood according as it is in the one who understands; while one thing is in another according to the nature of that in which it is. And the mode of existence of a separated soul is inferior to that of an angel, but is the same as that of other separated souls. Therefore the soul apart from the body has perfect knowledge of other separated souls, but it has an imperfect and defective knowledge of the angels so far as its natural knowledge is concerned. But the knowledge of glory is otherwise.

Reply Obj. 1: The separated soul is, indeed, less perfect considering its nature in which it communicates with the nature of the body: but it has a greater freedom of intelligence, since the weight and care of the body is a clog upon the clearness of its intelligence in the present life.

Reply Obj. 2: The separated soul understands the angels by means of divinely impressed ideas; which, however, fail to give perfect knowledge of them, forasmuch as the nature of the soul is inferior to that of an angel.

Reply Obj. 3: Man's ultimate happiness consists not in the knowledge of any separate substances; but in the knowledge of God, Who is seen only by grace. The knowledge of other separate substances if perfectly understood gives great happiness—not final and ultimate happiness. But the separated soul does not understand them perfectly, as was shown above in this article.

THIRD ARTICLE [I, Q. 89, Art. 3]

Whether the Separated Soul Knows All Natural Things?

Objection 1: It would seem that the separated soul knows all natural things. For the types of all natural things exist in separate substances. Therefore, as separated souls know separate substances, they also know all natural things.

Obj. 2: Further, whoever understands the greater intelligible, will be able much more to understand the lesser intelligible. But the separated soul understands immaterial substances, which are in the highest degree of intelligibility. Therefore much more can it understand all natural things which are in a lower degree of intelligibility.

*On the contrary,* The devils have greater natural knowledge than the separated soul; yet they do not know all natural things, but have to learn many things by long experience, as Isidore says (De Summo Bono i). Therefore neither can the separated soul know all natural things.

*I answer that,* As stated above (A. 1), the separated soul, like the angels, understands by means of species, received from the influence of the Divine light. Nevertheless, as the soul by nature is inferior to an angel, to whom this kind of knowledge is natural, the soul apart from the body through such species does not receive perfect knowledge, but only a general and confused kind of knowledge. Separated souls, therefore, have the same relation through such species to imperfect and confused knowledge of natural things as the angels have to the perfect knowledge thereof. Now angels through such species know all natural things perfectly; because all that God has produced in the respective natures of natural things has been produced by Him in the angelic intelligence, as Augustine says (Gen. ad lit. ii, 8). Hence it follows that separated souls know all natural things not with a certain and proper knowledge, but in a general and confused manner.

Reply Obj. 1: Even an angel does not understand all natural things through his substance, but through certain species, as stated above (Q. 87, A. 1). So it does not follow that the soul knows all natural things because it knows separate substances after a fashion.

Reply Obj. 2: As the soul separated from the body does not perfectly understand separate substances, so neither does it know all natural things perfectly; but it knows them confusedly, as above explained in this article.

Reply Obj. 3: Isidore speaks of the knowledge of the future which neither angels, nor demons, nor separated souls, know except so far as future things pre-exist in their causes or are known by Divine revelation. But we are here treating of the knowledge of natural things.

Reply Obj. 4: Knowledge acquired here by study is proper and perfect; the knowledge of which we speak is confused. Hence it does not follow that to study in order to learn is useless.

FOURTH ARTICLE [I, Q. 89, Art. 4]

Whether the Separated Soul Knows Singulars?

Objection 1: It would seem that the separated soul does not know singulars. For no cognitive power besides the intellect remains in the separated soul, as is clear from what has been said above (Q. 77, A. 8). But the intellect cannot know singulars, as we have shown (Q. 86, A. 1). Therefore the separated soul cannot know singulars.

Obj. 2: Further, the knowledge of the singular is more determinate than knowledge of the universal. But the separated soul has no determinate knowledge of the species of natural things, therefore much less can it know singulars.

Obj. 3: Further, if it knew the singulars, yet not by sense, for the same reason it would know all singulars. But it does not know all singulars. Therefore it knows none.

*On the contrary,* The rich man in hell said: "I have five brethren" (Luke 16:28).

*I answer that,* Separated souls know some singulars, but not all, not even all present singulars. To understand this, we must consider that there is a twofold way of knowing things, one by means of abstraction from phantasms, and in this way singulars cannot be directly known by the intellect, but only indirectly, as stated above (Q. 86, A. 1). The other way of understanding is by the infusion of species by God, and in that way it is possible for the intellect to know singulars. For as God knows all things, universal and singular, by His Essence, as the cause of universal and individual principles (Q. 14, A. 2), so likewise separate substances can know singulars by species which are a kind of participated similitude of the Divine Essence. There is a difference, however, between angels and separated souls in the fact that through these species the angels have a perfect and proper knowledge of things; whereas separated souls have only a confused knowledge. Hence the angels, by reason of their perfect intellect, through these species, know not only the specific natures of things, but also the singulars contained in those species; whereas separated souls by these species know only those singulars to which they are determined by former knowledge in this life, or by some affection, or by natural aptitude, or by the disposition of the Divine order; because whatever is received into anything is conditioned according to the mode of the recipient.

Reply Obj. 1: The intellect does not know the singular by way of abstraction; neither does the separated soul know it thus; but as explained above.

Reply Obj. 2: The knowledge of the separated soul is confined to those species or individuals to which the soul has some kind of determinate relation, as we have said.

Reply Obj. 3: The separated soul has not the same relation to all singulars, but one relation to some, and another to others. Therefore there is not the same reason why it should know all singulars.

FIFTH ARTICLE [I, Q. 89, Art. 5]

Whether the Habit of Knowledge Here Acquired Remains in the Separated Soul?

Objection 1: It would seem that the habit of knowledge acquired in this life does not remain in the soul separated from the body: for the Apostle says: "Knowledge shall be destroyed" (1 Cor. 13:8).

Obj. 2: Further, some in this world who are less good enjoy knowledge denied to others who are better. If, therefore, the habit of knowledge remained in the soul after death, it would follow that some who are less good would, even in the future life, excel some who are better; which seems unreasonable.

Obj. 3: Further, separated souls will possess knowledge by influence of the Divine light. Supposing, therefore, that knowledge here acquired remained in the separated soul, it would follow that two forms of the same species would co-exist in the same subject which cannot be.

Obj. 4: Further, the Philosopher says (Praedic. vi, 4, 5), that "a habit is a quality hard to remove: yet sometimes knowledge is destroyed by sickness or the like." But in this life there is no change so thorough as death. Therefore it seems that the habit of knowledge is destroyed by death.

*On the contrary,* Jerome says (Ep. liii, ad Paulinum), "Let us learn on earth that kind of knowledge which will remain with us in heaven."

*I answer that,* Some say that the habit of knowledge resides not in the intellect itself, but in the sensitive powers, namely, the imaginative, cogitative, and memorative, and that the intelligible species are not kept in the passive intellect. If this were true, it would follow that when the body is destroyed by death, knowledge here acquired would also be entirely destroyed.

But, since knowledge resides in the intellect, which is "the abode of species," as the Philosopher says (De Anima iii, 4), the habit of knowledge here acquired must be partly in the aforesaid sensitive powers and partly in the intellect. This can be seen by considering the very actions from which knowledge arises. For "habits are like the actions whereby they are acquired" (Ethic. ii, 1). Now the actions of the intellect, by which knowledge is here acquired, are performed by the mind turning to the phantasms in the aforesaid sensitive powers. Hence through such acts the passive intellect acquires a certain facility in considering the species received: and the aforesaid sensitive powers acquire a certain aptitude in seconding the action of the intellect when it turns to them to consider the intelligible object. But as the intellectual act resides chiefly and formally in the intellect itself, whilst it resides materially and dispositively in the inferior powers, the same distinction is to be applied to habit.

Knowledge, therefore, acquired in the present life does not remain in the separated soul, as regards what belongs to the sensitive powers; but as regards what belongs to the intellect itself, it must remain; because, as the Philosopher says (De Long. et Brev. Vitae ii), a form may be corrupted in two ways; first, directly, when corrupted by its contrary, as heat, by cold; and secondly, indirectly, when its subject is corrupted. Now it is evident that human knowledge is not corrupted through corruption of the subject, for the intellect is an incorruptible faculty, as above stated (Q. 79, A. 2, ad 2). Neither can the intelligible species in the passive intellect be corrupted by their contrary; for there is no contrary to intelligible "intentions," above all as regards simple intelligence of "what a thing is." But contrariety may exist in the intellect as regards mental composition and division, or also reasoning; so far as what is false in statement or argument is contrary to truth. And thus knowledge may be corrupted by its contrary when a false argument seduces anyone from the knowledge of truth. For this reason the Philosopher in the above work mentions two ways in which knowledge is corrupted directly: namely, "forgetfulness" on the part of the memorative power, and "deception" on the part of a false argument. But these have no place in the separated soul. Therefore we must conclude that the habit of knowledge, so far as it is in the intellect, remains in the separated soul.

Reply Obj. 1: The Apostle is not speaking of knowledge as a habit, but as to the act of knowing; and hence he says, in proof of the assertion quoted, "Now, I know in part."

Reply Obj. 2: As a less good man may exceed a better man in bodily stature, so the same kind of man may have a habit of knowledge in the future life which a better man may not have. Such knowledge, however, cannot be compared with the other prerogatives enjoyed by the better man.

Reply Obj. 3: These two kinds of knowledge are not of the same species, so there is no impossibility.

Reply Obj. 4: This objection considers the corruption of knowledge on the part of the sensitive powers.

SIXTH ARTICLE [I, Q. 89, Art. 6]

Whether the Act of Knowledge Acquired Here Remains in the Separated Soul?

Objection 1: It would seem that the act of knowledge here acquired does not remain in the separated soul. For the Philosopher says (De Anima i, 4), that when the body is corrupted, "the soul neither remembers nor loves." But to consider what is previously known is an act of memory. Therefore the separated soul cannot retain an act of knowledge here acquired.

Obj. 2: Further, intelligible species cannot have greater power in the separated soul than they have in the soul united to the body. But in this life we cannot understand by intelligible species without turning to phantasms, as shown above (Q. 84, A. 7). Therefore the separated soul cannot do so, and thus it cannot understand at all by intelligible species acquired in this life.

Obj. 3: Further, the Philosopher says (Ethic. ii, 1), that "habits produce acts similar to those whereby they are acquired." But the habit of knowledge is acquired here by acts of the intellect turning to phantasms: therefore it cannot produce any other acts. These acts, however, are not adapted to the separated soul. Therefore the soul in the state of separation cannot produce any act of knowledge acquired in this life.

*On the contrary,* It was said to Dives in hell (Luke 16:25): "Remember thou didst receive good things in thy lifetime."

*I answer that,* Action offers two things for our consideration—its species and its mode. Its species comes from the object, whereto the faculty of knowledge is directed by the (intelligible) species, which is the object's similitude; whereas the mode is gathered from the power of the agent. Thus that a person see a stone is due to the species of the stone in his eye; but that he see it clearly, is due to the eye's visual power. Therefore as the intelligible species remain in the separated soul, as stated above (A. 5), and since the state of the separated soul is not the same as it is in this life, it follows that through the intelligible species acquired in this life the soul apart from the body can understand what it understood formerly, but in a different way; not by turning to phantasms, but by a mode suited to a soul existing apart from the body. Thus the act of knowledge here acquired remains in the separated soul, but in a different way.

Reply Obj. 1: The Philosopher speaks of remembrance, according as memory belongs to the sensitive part, but not as belonging in a way to the intellect, as explained above (Q. 79, A. 6).

Reply Obj. 2: The different mode of intelligence is produced by the different state of the intelligent soul; not by diversity of species.

Reply Obj. 3: The acts which produce a habit are like the acts caused by that habit, in species, but not in mode. For example, to do just things, but not justly, that is, pleasurably, causes the habit of political justice, whereby we act pleasurably. (Cf. Aristotle, Ethic. v, 8: Magn. Moral. i, 34).

SEVENTH ARTICLE [I, Q. 89, Art. 7]

Whether Local Distance Impedes the Knowledge in the Separated Soul?

Objection 1: It would seem that local distance impedes the separated soul's knowledge. For Augustine says (De Cura pro Mort. xiii), that "the souls of the dead are where they cannot know what is done here." But they know what is done among themselves. Therefore local distance impedes the knowledge in the separated soul.

Obj. 2: Further, Augustine says (De Divin. Daemon. iii), that "the demons' rapidity of movement enables them to tell things unknown to us." But agility of movement would be useless in that respect unless their knowledge was impeded by local distance; which, therefore, is a much greater hindrance to the knowledge of the separated soul, whose nature is inferior to the demon's.

Obj. 3: Further, as there is distance of place, so is there distance of time. But distance of time impedes knowledge in the separated soul, for the soul is ignorant of the future. Therefore it seems that distance of place also impedes its knowledge.

*On the contrary,* It is written (Luke 16:23), that Dives, "lifting up his eyes when he was in torment, saw Abraham afar off." Therefore local distance does not impede knowledge in the separated soul.

*I answer that,* Some have held that the separated soul knows the singular by abstraction from the sensible. If that were so, it might be that local distance would impede its knowledge; for either the sensible would need to act upon the soul, or the soul upon the sensible, and in either case a determinate distance would be necessary. This is, however, impossible because abstraction of the species from the sensible is done through the senses and other sensible faculties which do not remain actually in the soul apart from the body. But the soul when separated understands singulars by species derived from the Divine light, which is indifferent to what is near or distant. Hence knowledge in the separated soul is not hindered by local distance.

Reply Obj. 1: Augustine says that the souls of the departed cannot see what is done here, not because they are "there," as if impeded by local distance; but for some other cause, as we shall explain (A. 8).

Reply Obj. 2: Augustine speaks there in accordance with the opinion that demons have bodies naturally united to them, and so have sensitive powers, which require local distance. In the same book he expressly sets down this opinion, though apparently rather by way of narration than of assertion, as we may gather from *De Civ. Dei* xxi, 10.

Reply Obj. 3: The future, which is distant in time, does not actually exist, and therefore is not knowable in itself, because so far as a thing falls short of being, so far does it fall short of being knowable. But what is locally distant exists actually, and is knowable in itself. Hence we cannot argue from distance of time to distance of place.

EIGHTH ARTICLE [I, Q. 89, Art. 8]

Whether Separated Souls Know What Takes Place on Earth?

Objection 1: It would seem that separated souls know what takes place on earth; for otherwise they would have no care for it, as they have, according to what Dives said (Luke 16:27, 28), "I have five brethren ... he may testify unto them, lest they also come into the place of torments." Therefore separated souls know what passes on earth.

Obj. 2: Further, the dead often appear to the living, asleep or awake, and tell them of what takes place there; as Samuel appeared to Saul (1 Kings 28:11). But this could not be unless they knew what takes place here. Therefore they know what takes place on earth.

Obj. 3: Further, separated souls know what happens among themselves. If, therefore, they do not know what takes place among us, it must be by reason of local distance; which has been shown to be false (A. 7).

*On the contrary,* It is written (Job 14:21): "He will not understand whether his children come to honor or dishonor."

*I answer that,* By natural knowledge, of which we are treating now, the souls of the dead do not know what passes on earth. This follows from what has been laid down (A. 4), since the separated soul has knowledge of singulars, by being in a way determined to them, either by some vestige of previous knowledge or affection, or by the Divine order. Now the souls departed are in a state of separation from the living, both by Divine order and by their mode of existence, whilst they are joined to the world of incorporeal spiritual substances; and hence they are ignorant of what goes on among us. Whereof Gregory gives the reason thus: "The dead do not know how the living act, for the life of the spirit is far from the life of the flesh; and so, as corporeal things differ from incorporeal in genus, so they are distinct in knowledge" (Moral. xii). Augustine seems to say the same (De Cura pro Mort. xiii), when he asserts that, "the souls of the dead have no concern in the affairs of the living."

Gregory and Augustine, however, seem to be divided in opinion as regards the souls of the blessed in heaven, for Gregory continues the passage above quoted: "The case of the holy souls is different, for since they see the light of Almighty God, we cannot believe that external things are unknown to them." But Augustine (De Cura pro Mort. xiii) expressly says: "The dead, even the saints do not know what is done by the living or by their own children," as a gloss quotes on the text, "Abraham hath not known us" (Isa. 63:16). He confirms this opinion by saying that he was not visited, nor consoled in sorrow by his mother, as when she was alive; and he could not think it possible that she was less kind when in a happier state; and again by the fact that the Lord promised to king Josias that he should die, lest he should see his people's afflictions (4 Kings 22:20). Yet Augustine says this in doubt; and premises, "Let every one take, as he pleases, what I say." Gregory, on the other hand, is positive, since he says, "We cannot believe." His opinion, indeed, seems to be the more probable one—that the souls of the blessed who see God do know all that passes here. For they are equal to the angels, of whom Augustine says that they know what happens among those living on earth. But as the souls of the blessed are most perfectly united to Divine justice, they do not suffer from sorrow, nor do they interfere in mundane affairs, except in accordance with Divine justice.

Reply Obj. 1: The souls of the departed may care for the living, even if ignorant of their state; just as we care for the dead by pouring forth prayer on their behalf, though we are ignorant of their state. Moreover, the affairs of the living can be made known to them not immediately, but the souls who pass hence thither, or by angels and demons, or even by "the revelation of the Holy Ghost," as Augustine says in the same book.

Reply Obj. 2: That the dead appear to the living in any way whatever is either by the special dispensation of God; in order that the souls of the dead may interfere in affairs of the living—and this is to be accounted as miraculous. Or else such apparitions occur through the instrumentality of bad or good angels, without the knowledge of the departed; as may likewise happen when the living appear, without their own knowledge, to others living, as Augustine says in the same book. And so it may be said of Samuel that he appeared through Divine revelation; according to Ecclus. 46:23, "he slept, and told the king the end of his life." Or, again, this apparition was procured by the demons; unless, indeed, the authority of Ecclesiasticus be set aside through not being received by the Jews as canonical Scripture.

Reply Obj. 3: This kind of ignorance does not proceed from the obstacle of local distance, but from the cause mentioned above.

## QUESTION 90

OF THE FIRST PRODUCTION OF MAN'S SOUL (In Four Articles)

After the foregoing we must consider the first production of man, concerning which there are four subjects of treatment:

(1) the production of man himself;

(2) the end of this production;

(3) the state and condition of the first man;

(4) the place of his abode.

Concerning the production of man, there are three things to be considered:

(1) the production of man's soul;

(2) the production of man's body;

(3) the production of the woman.

Under the first head there are four points of inquiry:

(1) Whether man's soul was something made, or was of the Divine substance?

(2) Whether, if made, it was created?

(3) Whether it was made by angelic instrumentality?

(4) Whether it was made before the body?

FIRST ARTICLE [I, Q. 90, Art. 1]

Whether the Soul Was Made or Was of God's Substance?

Objection 1: It would seem that the soul was not made, but was God's substance. For it is written (Gen. 2:7): "God formed man of the slime of the earth, and breathed into his face the breath of life, and man was made a living soul." But he who breathes sends forth something of himself. Therefore the soul, whereby man lives, is of the Divine substance.

Obj. 2: Further, as above explained (Q. 75, A. 5), the soul is a simple form. But a form is an act. Therefore the soul is a pure act; which applies to God alone. Therefore the soul is of God's substance.

Obj. 3: Further, things that exist and do [not] differ are the same. But God and the mind exist, and in no way differ, for they could only be differentiated by certain differences, and thus would be composite. Therefore God and the human mind are the same.

*On the contrary,* Augustine (De Orig. Animae iii, 15) mentions certain opinions which he calls "exceedingly and evidently perverse, and contrary to the Catholic Faith," among which the first is the opinion that "God made the soul not out of nothing, but from Himself."

*I answer that,* To say that the soul is of the Divine substance involves a manifest improbability. For, as is clear from what has been said (Q. 77, A. 2; Q. 79, A. 2; Q. 84, A. 6), the human soul is sometimes in a state of potentiality to the act of intelligence —acquires its knowledge somehow from things—and thus has various powers; all of which are incompatible with the Divine Nature, Which is a pure act—receives nothing from any other—and admits of no variety in itself, as we have proved (Q. 3, AA. 1, 7; Q. 9, A. 1).

This error seems to have originated from two statements of the ancients. For those who first began to observe the nature of things, being unable to rise above their imagination, supposed that nothing but bodies existed. Therefore they said that God was a body, which they considered to be the principle of other bodies. And since they held that the soul was of the same nature as that body which they regarded as the first principle, as is stated *De Anima* i, 2, it followed that the soul was of the nature of God Himself. According to this supposition, also, the Manichaeans, thinking that God was corporeal light, held that the soul was part of that light bound up with the body.

Then a further step in advance was made, and some surmised the existence of something incorporeal, not apart from the body, but the form of a body; so that Varro said, "God is a soul governing the world by movement and reason," as Augustine relates (De Civ. Dei vii, 6 [*The words as quoted are to be found iv. 31.]). So some supposed man's soul to be part of that one soul, as man is a part of the whole world; for they were unable to go so far as to understand the different degrees of spiritual substance, except according to the distinction of bodies.

But, all these theories are impossible, as proved above (Q. 3, AA. 1, 8; and Q. 75, A. 1), wherefore it is evidently false that the soul is of the substance of God.

Reply Obj. 1: The term "breathe" is not to be taken in the material sense; but as regards the act of God, to breathe (spirare), is the same as to *make a spirit.* Moreover, in the material sense, man by breathing does not send forth anything of his own substance, but an extraneous thing.

Reply Obj. 2: Although the soul is a simple form in its essence, yet it is not its own existence, but is a being by participation, as above explained (Q. 75, A. 5, ad 4). Therefore it is not a pure act like God.

Reply Obj. 3: That which differs, properly speaking, differs in something; wherefore we seek for difference where we find also resemblance. For this reason things which differ must in some way be compound; since they differ in something, and in something resemble each other. In this sense, although all that differ are diverse, yet all things that are diverse do not differ. For simple things are diverse; yet do not differ from one another by differences which enter into their composition. For instance, a man and a horse differ by the difference of rational and irrational; but we cannot say that these again differ by some further difference.

SECOND ARTICLE [I, Q. 90, Art. 2]

Whether the Soul Was Produced by Creation?

Objection 1: It would seem that the soul was not produced by creation. For that which has in itself something material is produced from matter. But the soul is in part material, since it is not a pure act. Therefore the soul was made of matter; and hence it was not created.

Obj. 2: Further, every actuality of matter is educed from the potentiality of that matter; for since matter is in potentiality to act, any act pre-exists in matter potentially. But the soul is the act of corporeal matter, as is clear from its definition. Therefore the soul is educed from the potentiality of matter.

Obj. 3: Further, the soul is a form. Therefore, if the soul is created, all other forms also are created. Thus no forms would come into existence by generation; which is not true.

*On the contrary,* It is written (Gen. 1:27): "God created man to His own image." But man is like to God in his soul. Therefore the soul was created.

*I answer that,* The rational soul can be made only by creation; which, however, is not true of other forms. The reason is because, since to be made is the way to existence, a thing must be made in such a way as is suitable to its mode of existence. Now that properly exists which itself has existence; as it were, subsisting in its own existence. Wherefore only substances are properly and truly called beings; whereas an accident has not existence, but something is (modified) by it, and so far is it called a being; for instance, whiteness is called a being, because by it something is white. Hence it is said *Metaph.* vii, Did. vi, 1 that an accident should be described as "of something rather than as something." The same is to be said of all non-subsistent forms. Therefore, properly speaking, it does not belong to any non-existing form to be made; but such are said to be made through the composite substances being made. On the other hand, the rational soul is a subsistent form, as above explained (Q. 75, A. 2). Wherefore it is competent to be and to be made. And since it cannot be made of pre-existing matter—whether corporeal, which would render it a corporeal being—or spiritual, which would involve the transmutation of one spiritual substance into another, we must conclude that it cannot exist except by creation.

Reply Obj. 1: The soul's simple essence is as the material element, while its participated existence is its formal element; which participated existence necessarily co-exists with the soul's essence, because existence naturally follows the form. The same reason holds if the soul is supposed to be composed of some spiritual matter, as some maintain; because the said matter is not in potentiality to another form, as neither is the matter of a celestial body; otherwise the soul would be corruptible. Wherefore the soul cannot in any way be made of pre-existent matter.

Reply Obj. 2: The production of act from the potentiality of matter is nothing else but something becoming actually that previously was in potentiality. But since the rational soul does not depend in its existence on corporeal matter, and is subsistent, and exceeds the capacity of corporeal matter, as we have seen (Q. 75, A. 2), it is not educed from the potentiality of matter.

Reply Obj. 3: As we have said, there is no comparison between the rational soul and other forms.

THIRD ARTICLE [I, Q. 90, Art. 3]

Whether the Rational Soul Is Produced by God Immediately?

Objection 1: It would seem that the rational soul is not immediately made by God, but by the instrumentality of the angels. For spiritual things have more order than corporeal things. But inferior bodies are produced by means of the superior, as Dionysius says (Div. Nom. iv). Therefore also the inferior spirits, who are the rational souls, are produced by means of the superior spirits, the angels.

Obj. 2: Further, the end corresponds to the beginning of things; for God is the beginning and end of all. Therefore the issue of things from their beginning corresponds to the forwarding of them to their end. But "inferior things are forwarded by the higher," as Dionysius says (Eccl. Hier. v); therefore also the inferior are produced into existence by the higher, and souls by angels.

Obj. 3: Further, "perfect is that which can produce its like," as is stated *Metaph.* v. But spiritual substances are much more perfect than corporeal. Therefore, since bodies produce their like in their own species, much more are angels able to produce something specifically inferior to themselves; and such is the rational soul.

*On the contrary,* It is written (Gen. 2:7) that God Himself "breathed into the face of man the breath of life."

*I answer that,* Some have held that angels, acting by the power of God, produce rational souls. But this is quite impossible, and is against faith. For it has been proved that the rational soul cannot be produced except by creation. Now, God alone can create; for the first agent alone can act without presupposing the existence of anything; while the second cause always presupposes something derived from the first cause, as above explained (Q. 75, A. 3): and every agent, that presupposes something to its act, acts by making a change therein. Therefore everything else acts by producing a change, whereas God alone acts by creation. Since, therefore, the rational soul cannot be produced by a change in matter, it cannot be produced, save immediately by God.

Thus the replies to the objections are clear. For that bodies produce their like or something inferior to themselves, and that the higher things lead forward the inferior—all these things are effected through a certain transmutation.

FOURTH ARTICLE [I, Q. 90, Art. 4]

Whether the Human Soul Was Produced Before the Body?

Objection 1: It would seem that the human soul was made before the body. For the work of creation preceded the work of distinction and adornment, as shown above (Q. 66, A. 1; Q. 70, A. 1). But the soul was made by creation; whereas the body was made at the end of the work of adornment. Therefore the soul of man was made before the body.

Obj. 2: Further, the rational soul has more in common with the angels than with the brute animals. But angels were created before bodies, or at least, at the beginning with corporeal matter; whereas the body of man was formed on the sixth day, when also the animals were made. Therefore the soul of man was created before the body.

Obj. 3: Further, the end is proportionate to the beginning. But in the end the soul outlasts the body. Therefore in the beginning it was created before the body.

*On the contrary,* The proper act is produced in its proper potentiality. Therefore since the soul is the proper act of the body, the soul was produced in the body.

*I answer that,* Origen (Peri Archon i, 7,8) held that not only the soul of the first man, but also the souls of all men were created at the same time as the angels, before their bodies: because he thought that all spiritual substances, whether souls or angels, are equal in their natural condition, and differ only by merit; so that some of them—namely, the souls of men or of heavenly bodies—are united to bodies while others remain in their different orders entirely free from matter. Of this opinion we have already spoken (Q. 47, A. 2); and so we need say nothing about it here.

Augustine, however (Gen. ad lit. vii, 24), says that the soul of the first man was created at the same time as the angels, before the body, for another reason; because he supposes that the body of man, during the work of the six days, was produced, not actually, but only as to some "causal virtues"; which cannot be said of the soul, because neither was it made of any pre-existing corporeal or spiritual matter, nor could it be produced from any created virtue. Therefore it seems that the soul itself, during the work of the six days, when all things were made, was created, together with the angels; and that afterwards, by its own will, was joined to the service of the body. But he does not say this by way of assertion; as his words prove. For he says (Gen. ad lit. vii, 29): "We may believe, if neither Scripture nor reason forbid, that man was made on the sixth day, in the sense that his body was created as to its causal virtue in the elements of the world, but that the soul was already created."

Now this could be upheld by those who hold that the soul has of itself a complete species and nature, and that it is not united to the body as its form, but as its administrator. But if the soul is united to the body as its form, and is naturally a part of human nature, the above supposition is quite impossible. For it is clear that God made the first things in their perfect natural state, as their species required. Now the soul, as a part of human nature, has its natural perfection only as united to the body. Therefore it would have been unfitting for the soul to be created without the body.

Therefore, if we admit the opinion of Augustine about the work of the six days (Q. 74, A. 2), we may say that the human soul preceded in the work of the six days by a certain generic similitude, so far as it has intellectual nature in common with the angels; but was itself created at the same time as the body. According to the other saints, both the body and soul of the first man were produced in the work of the six days.

Reply Obj. 1: If the soul by its nature were a complete species, so that it might be created as to itself, this reason would prove that the soul was created by itself in the beginning. But as the soul is naturally the form of the body, it was necessarily created, not separately, but in the body.

Reply Obj. 2: The same observation applies to the second objection. For if the soul had a species of itself it would have something still more in common with the angels. But, as the form of the body, it belongs to the animal genus, as a formal principle.

Reply Obj. 3: That the soul remains after the body, is due to a defect of the body, namely, death. Which defect was not due when the soul was first created.

## QUESTION 91

THE PRODUCTION OF THE FIRST MAN'S BODY (FOUR ARTICLES)

We have now to consider the production of the first man's body. Under this head there are four points of inquiry:

(1) The matter from which it was produced;
(2) The author by whom it was produced;
(3) The disposition it received in its production;
(4) The mode and order of its production.

FIRST ARTICLE [I, Q. 91, Art. 1]

Whether the Body of the First Man Was Made of the Slime of the Earth?

Objection 1: It would seem that the body of the first man was not made of the slime of the earth. For it is an act of greater power to make something out of nothing than out of something; because "not being" is farther off from actual existence than "being in potentiality." But since man is the most honorable of God's lower creatures, it was fitting that in the production of man's body, the power of God should be most clearly shown. Therefore it should not have been made of the slime of the earth, but out of nothing.

Obj. 2: Further, the heavenly bodies are nobler than earthly bodies. But the human body has the greatest nobility; since it is perfected by the noblest form, which is the rational soul. Therefore it should not be made of an earthly body, but of a heavenly body.

Obj. 3: Further, fire and air are nobler than earth and water, as is clear from their subtlety. Therefore, since the human body is most noble, it should rather have been made of fire and air than of the slime of the earth.

Obj. 4: Further, the human body is composed of the four elements. Therefore it was not made of the slime of the earth, but of the four elements.

*On the contrary,* It is written (Gen. 2:7): "God made man of the slime of the earth."

*I answer that,* As God is perfect in His works, He bestowed perfection on all of them according to their capacity: "God's works are perfect" (Deut. 32:4). He Himself is simply perfect by the fact that "all things are pre-contained" in Him, not as component parts, but as "united in one simple whole," as Dionysius says (Div. Nom. v); in the same way as various effects pre-exist in their cause, according to its one virtue. This perfection is bestowed on the angels, inasmuch as all things which are produced by God in nature through various forms come under their knowledge. But on man this perfection is bestowed in an inferior way. For he does not possess a natural knowledge of all natural things, but is in a manner composed of all things, since he has in himself a rational soul of the genus of spiritual substances, and in likeness to the heavenly bodies he is removed from contraries by an equable temperament. As to the elements, he has them in their very substance, yet in such a way that the higher elements, fire and air, predominate in him by their power; for life is mostly found where there is heat, which is from fire; and where there is humor, which is of the air. But the inferior elements abound in man by their substance; otherwise the mingling of elements would not be evenly balanced, unless the inferior elements, which have the less power, predominated in quantity. Therefore the body of man is said to have been formed from the slime of the earth; because earth and water mingled are called slime, and for this reason man is called "a little world," because all creatures of the world are in a way to be found in him.

Reply Obj. 1: The power of the Divine Creator was manifested in man's body when its matter was produced by creation. But it was fitting that the human body should be made of the four elements, that man might have something in common with the inferior bodies, as being something between spiritual and corporeal substances.

Reply Obj. 2: Although the heavenly body is in itself nobler than the earthly body, yet for the acts of the rational soul the heavenly body is less adapted. For the rational soul receives the knowledge of truth in a certain way through the senses, the organs of which cannot be formed of a heavenly body which is impassible. Nor is it true that something of the fifth essence enters materially into the composition of the human body, as some say, who suppose that the soul is united to the body by means of light. For, first of all, what they say is false—that light is a body. Secondly, it is impossible for something to be taken from the fifth essence, or from a heavenly body, and to be mingled with the elements, since a heavenly body is impassible; wherefore it does not enter into the composition of mixed bodies, except as in the effects of its power.

Reply Obj. 3: If fire and air, whose action is of greater power, predominated also in quantity in the human body, they would entirely draw the rest into themselves, and there would be no equality in the mingling, such as is required in the composition of man, for the sense of touch, which is the foundation of the other senses. For the organ of any particular sense must not actually have the contraries of which that sense has the perception, but only potentially; either in such a way that it is entirely void of the whole genus of such contraries—thus, for instance, the pupil of the eye is without color, so as to be in potentiality as regards all colors; which is not possible in the organ of touch, since it is composed of the very elements, the qualities of which are perceived by that sense—or so that the organ is a medium between two contraries, as much needs be the case with regard to touch; for the medium is in potentiality to the extremes.

Reply Obj. 4: In the slime of the earth are earth, and water binding the earth together. Of the other elements, Scripture makes no mention, because they are less in quantity in the human body, as we have said; and because also in the account of the Creation no mention is made of fire and air, which are not perceived by senses of uncultured men such as those to whom the Scripture was immediately addressed.

SECOND ARTICLE [I, Q. 91, Art. 2]

Whether the Human Body Was Immediately Produced by God?

Objection 1: It would seem that the human body was not produced by God immediately. For Augustine says (De Trin. iii, 4), that "corporeal things are disposed by God through the angels." But the human body was made of corporeal matter, as stated above (A. 1). Therefore it was produced by the instrumentality of the angels, and not immediately by God.

Obj. 2: Further, whatever can be made by a created power, is not necessarily produced immediately by God. But the human body can be produced by the created power of a heavenly body; for even certain animals are produced from putrefaction by the active power of a heavenly body; and Albumazar says that man is not generated where heat and cold are extreme, but only in temperate regions. Therefore the human body was not necessarily produced immediately by God.

Obj. 3: Further, nothing is made of corporeal matter except by some material change. But all corporeal change is caused by a movement of a heavenly body, which is the first movement. Therefore, since the human body was produced from corporeal matter, it seems that a heavenly body had part in its production.

Obj. 4: Further, Augustine says (Gen. ad lit. vii, 24) that man's body was made during the work of the six days, according to the causal virtues which God inserted in corporeal creatures; and that afterwards it was actually produced. But what pre-exists in the corporeal creature by reason of causal virtues can be produced by some corporeal body. Therefore the human body was produced by some created power, and not immediately by God.

*On the contrary,* It is written (Ecclus. 17:1): "God created man out of the earth."

*I answer that,* The first formation of the human body could not be by the instrumentality of any created power, but was immediately from God. Some, indeed, supposed that the forms which are in corporeal matter are derived from some immaterial forms; but the Philosopher refutes this opinion (Metaph. vii), for the reason that forms cannot be made in themselves, but only in the composite, as we have explained (Q. 65, A. 4); and because the agent must be like its effect, it is not fitting that a pure form, not existing in matter, should produce a form which is in matter, and which form is only made by the fact that the composite is made. So a form which is in matter can only be the cause of another form that is in matter, according as composite is made by composite. Now God, though He is absolutely immaterial, can alone by His own power produce matter by creation: wherefore He alone can produce a form in matter, without the aid of any preceding material form. For this reason the angels cannot transform a body except by making use of something in the nature of a seed, as Augustine says (De Trin. iii, 19). Therefore as no pre-existing body has been formed whereby another body of the same species could be generated, the first human body was of necessity made immediately by God.

Reply Obj. 1: Although the angels are the ministers of God, as regards what He does in bodies, yet God does something in bodies beyond the angels' power, as, for instance, raising the dead, or giving sight to the blind: and by this power He formed the body of the first man from the slime of the earth. Nevertheless the angels could act as ministers in the formation of the body of the first man, in the same way as they will do at the last resurrection by collecting the dust.

Reply Obj. 2: Perfect animals, produced from seed, cannot be made by the sole power of a heavenly body, as Avicenna imagined; although the power of a heavenly body may assist by co-operation in the work of natural generation, as the Philosopher says (Phys. ii, 26), "man and the sun beget man from matter." For this reason, a place of moderate temperature is required for the production of man and other animals. But the power of heavenly bodies suffices for the production of some imperfect animals from properly disposed matter: for it is clear that more conditions are required to produce a perfect than an imperfect thing.

Reply Obj. 3: The movement of the heavens causes natural changes; but not changes that surpass the order of nature, and are caused by the Divine Power alone, as for the dead to be raised to life, or the blind to see: like to which also is the making of man from the slime of the earth.

Reply Obj. 4: An effect may be said to pre-exist in the causal virtues of creatures, in two ways. First, both in active and in passive potentiality, so that not only can it be produced out of pre-existing matter, but also that some pre-existing creature can produce it. Secondly, in passive potentiality only; that is, that out of pre-existing matter it can be produced by God. In this sense, according to Augustine, the human body pre-existed in the previous work in their causal virtues.

THIRD ARTICLE [I, Q. 91, Art. 3]

Whether the Body of Man Was Given an Apt Disposition?

Objection 1: It would seem that the body of man was not given an apt disposition. For since man is the noblest of animals, his body ought to be the best disposed in what is proper to an animal, that is, in sense and movement. But some animals have sharper senses and quicker movement than man; thus dogs have a keener smell, and birds a swifter flight. Therefore man's body was not aptly disposed.

Obj. 2: Further, perfect is what lacks nothing. But the human body lacks more than the body of other animals, for these are provided with covering and natural arms of defense, in which man is lacking. Therefore the human body is very imperfectly disposed.

Obj. 3: Further, man is more distant from plants than he is from the brutes. But plants are erect in stature, while brutes are prone in stature. Therefore man should not be of erect stature.

*On the contrary,* It is written (Eccles. 7:30): "God made man right."

*I answer that,* All natural things were produced by the Divine art, and so may be called God's works of art. Now every artist intends to give to his work the best disposition; not absolutely the best, but the best as regards the proposed end; and even if this entails some defect, the artist cares not: thus, for instance, when man makes himself a saw for the purpose of cutting, he makes it of iron, which is suitable for the object in view; and he does not prefer to make it of glass, though this be a more beautiful material, because this very beauty would be an obstacle to the end he has in view. Therefore God gave to each natural being the best disposition; not absolutely so, but in the view of its proper end. This is what the Philosopher says (Phys. ii, 7): "And because it is better so, not absolutely, but for each one's substance."

Now the proximate end of the human body is the rational soul and its operations; since matter is for the sake of the form, and instruments are for the action of the agent. I say, therefore, that God fashioned the human body in that disposition which was best, as most suited to such a form and to such operations. If defect exists in the disposition of the human body, it is well to observe that such defect arises as a necessary result of the matter, from the conditions required in the body, in order to make it suitably proportioned to the soul and its operations.

Reply Obj. 1: The sense of touch, which is the foundation of the other senses, is more perfect in man than in any other animal; and for this reason man must have the most equable temperament of all animals. Moreover man excels all other animals in the interior sensitive powers, as is clear from what we have said above (Q. 78, A. 4). But by a kind of necessity, man falls short of the other animals in some of the exterior senses; thus of all animals he has the least sense of smell. For man needs the largest brain as compared to the body; both for his greater freedom of action in the interior powers required for the intellectual operations, as we have seen above (Q. 84, A. 7); and in order that the low temperature of the brain may modify the heat of the heart, which has to be considerable in man for him to be able to stand erect. So that size of the brain, by reason of its humidity, is an impediment to the smell, which requires dryness. In the same way, we may suggest a reason why some animals have a keener sight, and a more acute hearing than man; namely, on account of a hindrance to his senses arising necessarily from the perfect equability of his temperament. The same reason suffices to explain why some animals are more rapid in movement than man, since this excellence of speed is inconsistent with the equability of the human temperament.

Reply Obj. 2: Horns and claws, which are the weapons of some animals, and toughness of hide and quantity of hair or feathers, which are the clothing of animals, are signs of an abundance of the earthly element; which does not agree with the equability and softness of the human temperament. Therefore such things do not suit the nature of man. Instead of these, he has reason and hands whereby he can make himself arms and clothes, and other necessaries of life, of infinite variety. Wherefore the hand is called by Aristotle (De Anima iii, 8), "the organ of organs." Moreover this was more becoming to the rational nature, which is capable of conceiving an infinite number of things, so as to make for itself an infinite number of instruments.

Reply Obj. 3: An upright stature was becoming to man for four reasons. First, because the senses are given to man, not only for the purpose of procuring the necessaries of life, which they are bestowed on other animals, but also for the purpose of knowledge. Hence, whereas the other animals take delight in the objects of the senses only as ordered to food and sex, man alone takes pleasure in the beauty of sensible objects for its own sake. Therefore, as the senses are situated chiefly in the face, other animals have the face turned to the ground, as it were for the purpose of seeking food and procuring a livelihood; whereas man has his face erect, in order that by the senses, and chiefly by sight, which is more subtle and penetrates further into the differences of things, he may freely survey the sensible objects around him, both heavenly and earthly, so as to gather intelligible truth from all things. Secondly, for the greater freedom of the acts of the interior powers; the brain, wherein these actions are, in a way, performed, not being low down, but lifted up above other parts of the body. Thirdly, because if man's stature were prone to the ground he would need to use his hands as fore-feet; and thus their utility for other purposes would cease. Fourthly, because if man's stature were prone to the ground, and he used his hands as fore-feet, he would be obliged to take hold of his food with his mouth. Thus he would have a protruding mouth, with thick and hard lips, and also a hard tongue, so as to keep it from being hurt by exterior things; as we see in other animals. Moreover, such an attitude would quite hinder speech, which is reason's proper operation.

Nevertheless, though of erect stature, man is far above plants. For man's superior part, his head, is turned towards the superior part of the world, and his inferior part is turned towards the inferior world; and therefore he is perfectly disposed as to the general situation of his body. Plants have the superior part turned towards the lower world, since their roots correspond to the mouth; and their inferior part towards the upper world. But brute animals have a middle disposition, for the superior part of the animal is that by which it takes food, and the inferior part that by which it rids itself of the surplus.

FOURTH ARTICLE [I, Q. 91, Art. 4]

Whether the Production of the Human Body Is Fittingly Described in Scripture?

Objection 1: It would seem that the production of the human body is not fittingly described in Scripture. For, as the human body was made by God, so also were the other works of the six days. But in the other works it is written, "God said; Let it be made, and it was made." Therefore the same should have been said of man.

Obj. 2: Further, the human body was made by God immediately, as explained above (A. 2). Therefore it was not fittingly said, "Let us make man."

Obj. 3: Further, the form of the human body is the soul itself which is the breath of life. Therefore, having said, "God made man of the slime of the earth," he should not have added: "And He breathed into him the breath of life."

Obj. 4: Further, the soul, which is the breath of life, is in the whole body, and chiefly in the heart. Therefore it was not fittingly said: "He breathed into his face the breath of life."

Obj. 5: Further, the male and female sex belong to the body, while the image of God belongs to the soul. But the soul, according to Augustine (Gen. ad lit. vii, 24), was made before the body. Therefore having said: "To His image He made them," he should not have added, "male and female He created them."

*On the contrary,* Is the authority of Scripture.

Reply Obj. 1: As Augustine observes (Gen. ad lit. vi, 12), man surpasses other things, not in the fact that God Himself made man, as though He did not make other things; since it is written (Ps. 101:26), "The work of Thy hands is the heaven," and elsewhere (Ps. 94:5), "His hands laid down the dry land"; but in this, that man is made to God's image. Yet in describing man's production, Scripture uses a special way of speaking, to show that other things were made for man's sake. For we are accustomed to do with more deliberation and care what we have chiefly in mind.

Reply Obj. 2: We must not imagine that when God said "Let us make man," He spoke to the angels, as some were perverse enough to think. But by these words is signified the plurality of the Divine Person, Whose image is more clearly expressed in man.

Reply Obj. 3: Some have thought that man's body was formed first in priority of time, and that afterwards the soul was infused into the formed body. But it is inconsistent with the perfection of the production of things, that God should have made either the body without the soul, or the soul without the body, since each is a part of human nature. This is especially unfitting as regards the body, for the body depends on the soul, and not the soul on the body.

To remove the difficulty some have said that the words, "God made man," must be understood of the production of the body with the soul; and that the subsequent words, "and He breathed into his face the breath of life," should be understood of the Holy Ghost; as the Lord breathed on His Apostles, saying, "Receive ye the Holy Ghost" (John 20:22). But this explanation, as Augustine says (De Civ. Dei xiii, 24), is excluded by the very words of Scripture. For we read farther on, "And man was made a living soul"; which words the Apostle (1 Cor. 15:45) refers not to spiritual life, but to animal life. Therefore, by breath of life we must understand the soul, so that the words, "He breathed into his face the breath of life," are a sort of exposition of what goes before; for the soul is the form of the body.

Reply Obj. 4: Since vital operations are more clearly seen in man's face, on account of the senses which are there expressed; therefore Scripture says that the breath of life was breathed into man's face.

Reply Obj. 5: According to Augustine (Gen. ad lit. iv, 34), the works of the six days were done all at one time; wherefore according to him man's soul, which he holds to have been made with the angels, was not made before the sixth day; but on the sixth day both the soul of the first man was made actually, and his body in its causal elements. But other doctors hold that on the sixth day both body and soul of man were actually made.

# QUESTION 92

THE PRODUCTION OF THE WOMAN (In Four Articles)

We must next consider the production of the woman. Under this head there are four points of inquiry:

(1) Whether the woman should have been made in that first production of things?

(2) Whether the woman should have been made from man?

(3) Whether of man's rib?

(4) Whether the woman was made immediately by God?

FIRST ARTICLE [I, Q. 92, Art. 1]

Whether the Woman Should Have Been Made in the First Production of Things?

Objection 1: It would seem that the woman should not have been made in the first production of things. For the Philosopher says (De Gener. ii, 3), that "the female is a misbegotten male." But nothing misbegotten or defective should have been in the first production of things. Therefore woman should not have been made at that first production.

Obj. 2: Further, subjection and limitation were a result of sin, for to the woman was it said after sin (Gen. 3:16): "Thou shalt be under the man's power"; and Gregory says that, "Where there is no sin, there is no inequality." But woman is naturally of less strength and dignity than man; "for the agent is always more honorable than the patient," as Augustine says (Gen. ad lit. xii, 16). Therefore woman should not have been made in the first production of things before sin.

Obj. 3: Further, occasions of sin should be cut off. But God foresaw that the woman would be an occasion of sin to man. Therefore He should not have made woman.

*On the contrary,* It is written (Gen. 2:18): "It is not good for man to be alone; let us make him a helper like to himself."

*I answer that,* It was necessary for woman to be made, as the Scripture says, as a *helper* to man; not, indeed, as a helpmate in other works, as some say, since man can be more efficiently helped by another man in other works; but as a helper in the work of generation. This can be made clear if we observe the mode of generation carried out in various living things. Some living things do not possess in themselves the power of generation, but are generated by some other specific agent, such as some plants and animals by the influence of the heavenly bodies, from some fitting matter and not from seed: others possess the active and passive generative power together; as we see in plants which are generated from seed; for the noblest vital function in plants is generation. Wherefore we observe that in these the active power of generation invariably accompanies the passive power. Among perfect animals the active power of generation belongs to the male sex, and the passive power to the female. And as among animals there is a vital operation nobler than generation, to which their life is principally directed; therefore the male sex is not found in continual union with the female in perfect animals, but only at the time of coition; so that we may consider that by this means the male and female are one, as in plants they are always united; although in some cases one of them preponderates, and in some the other. But man is yet further ordered to a still nobler vital action, and that is intellectual operation. Therefore there was greater reason for the distinction of these two forces in man; so that the female should be produced separately from the male; although they are carnally united for generation. Therefore directly after the formation of woman, it was said: "And they shall be two in one flesh" (Gen. 2:24).

Reply Obj. 1: As regards the individual nature, woman is defective and misbegotten, for the active force in the male seed tends to the production of a perfect likeness in the masculine sex; while the production of woman comes from defect in the active force or from some material indisposition, or even from some external influence; such as that of a south wind, which is moist, as the Philosopher observes (De Gener. Animal. iv, 2). On the other hand, as regards human nature in general, woman is not misbegotten, but is included in nature's intention as directed to the work of generation. Now the general intention of nature depends on God, Who is the universal Author of nature. Therefore, in producing nature, God formed not only the male but also the female.

Reply Obj. 2: Subjection is twofold. One is servile, by virtue of which a superior makes use of a subject for his own benefit; and this kind of subjection began after sin. There is another kind of subjection which is called economic or civil, whereby the superior makes use of his subjects for their own benefit and good; and this kind of subjection existed even before sin. For good order would have been wanting in the human family if some were not governed by others wiser than themselves. So by such a kind of subjection woman is naturally subject to man, because in man the discretion of reason predominates. Nor is inequality among men excluded by the state of innocence, as we shall prove (Q. 96, A. 3).

Reply Obj. 3: If God had deprived the world of all those things which proved an occasion of sin, the universe would have been imperfect. Nor was it fitting for the common good to be destroyed in order that individual evil might be avoided; especially as God is so powerful that He can direct any evil to a good end.

SECOND ARTICLE [I, Q. 92, Art. 2]

Whether Woman Should Have Been Made from Man?

Objection 1: It would seem that woman should not have been made from man. For sex belongs both to man and animals. But in the other animals the female was not made from the male. Therefore neither should it have been so with man.

Obj. 2: Further, things of the same species are of the same matter. But male and female are of the same species. Therefore, as man was made of the slime of the earth, so woman should have been made of the same, and not from man.

Obj. 3: Further, woman was made to be a helpmate to man in the work of generation. But close relationship makes a person unfit for that office; hence near relations are debarred from intermarriage, as is written (Lev. 18:6). Therefore woman should not have been made from man.

*On the contrary,* It is written (Ecclus. 17:5): "He created of him," that is, out of man, "a helpmate like to himself," that is, woman.

*I answer that,* When all things were first formed, it was more suitable for the woman to be made from man than (for the female to be from the male) in other animals. First, in order thus to give the first man a certain dignity consisting in this, that as God is the principle of the whole universe, so the first man, in likeness to God, was the principle of the whole human race. Wherefore Paul says that "God made the whole human race from one" (Acts 17:26). Secondly, that man might love woman all the more, and cleave to her more closely, knowing her to be fashioned from himself. Hence it is written (Gen. 2:23, 24): "She was taken out of man, wherefore a man shall leave father and mother, and shall cleave to his wife." This was most necessary as regards the human race, in which the male and female live together for life; which is not the case with other animals. Thirdly, because, as the Philosopher says (Ethic. viii, 12), the human male and female are united, not only for generation, as with other animals, but also for the purpose of domestic life, in which each has his or her particular duty, and in which the man is the head of the woman. Wherefore it was suitable for the woman to be made out of man, as out of her principle. Fourthly, there is a sacramental reason for this. For by this is signified that the Church takes her origin from Christ. Wherefore the Apostle says (Eph. 5:32): "This is a great sacrament; but I speak in Christ and in the Church."

Reply Obj. 1 is clear from the foregoing.

Reply Obj. 2: Matter is that from which something is made. Now created nature has a determinate principle; and since it is determined to one thing, it has also a determinate mode of proceeding. Wherefore from determinate matter it produces something in a determinate species. On the other hand, the Divine Power, being infinite, can produce things of the same species out of any matter, such as a man from the slime of the earth, and a woman from out of man.

Reply Obj. 3: A certain affinity arises from natural generation, and this is an impediment to matrimony. Woman, however, was not produced from man by natural generation, but by the Divine Power alone. Wherefore Eve is not called the daughter of Adam; and so this argument does not prove.

THIRD ARTICLE [I, Q. 92, Art. 3]

Whether the Woman Was Fittingly Made from the Rib of Man?

Objection 1: It would seem that the woman should not have been formed from the rib of man. For the rib was much smaller than the woman's body. Now from a smaller thing a larger thing can be made only—either by addition (and then the woman ought to have been described as made out of that which was added, rather than out of the rib itself)—or by rarefaction, because, as Augustine says (Gen. ad lit. x): "A body cannot increase in bulk except by rarefaction." But the woman's body is not more rarefied than man's—at least, not in the proportion of a rib to Eve's body. Therefore Eve was not formed from a rib of Adam.

Obj. 2: Further, in those things which were first created there was nothing superfluous. Therefore a rib of Adam belonged to the integrity of his body. So, if a rib was removed, his body remained imperfect; which is unreasonable to suppose.

Obj. 3: Further, a rib cannot be removed from man without pain. But there was no pain before sin. Therefore it was not right for a rib to be taken from the man, that Eve might be made from it.

*On the contrary,* It is written (Gen. 2:22): "God built the rib, which He took from Adam, into a woman."

*I answer that,* It was right for the woman to be made from a rib of man. First, to signify the social union of man and woman, for the woman should neither "use authority over man," and so she was not made from his head; nor was it right for her to be subject to man's contempt as his slave, and so she was not made from his feet. Secondly, for the sacramental signification; for from the side of Christ sleeping on the Cross the Sacraments flowed—namely, blood and water—on which the Church was established.

Reply Obj. 1: Some say that the woman's body was formed by a material increase, without anything being added; in the same way as our Lord multiplied the five loaves. But this is quite impossible. For such an increase of matter would either be by a change of the very substance of the matter itself, or by a change of its dimensions. Not by change of the substance of the matter, both because matter, considered in itself, is quite unchangeable, since it has a potential existence, and has nothing but the nature of a subject, and because quantity and size are extraneous to the essence of matter itself. Wherefore multiplication of matter is quite unintelligible, as long as the matter itself remains the same without anything added to it; unless it receives greater dimensions. This implies rarefaction, which is for the same matter to receive greater dimensions, as the Philosopher says (Phys. iv). To say, therefore, that the same matter is enlarged, without being rarefied, is to combine contradictories—viz. the definition with the absence of the thing defined.

Wherefore, as no rarefaction is apparent in such multiplication of matter, we must admit an addition of matter: either by creation, or which is more probable, by conversion. Hence Augustine says (Tract. xxiv in Joan.) that "Christ filled five thousand men with five loaves, in the same way as from a few seeds He produces the harvest of corn"—that is, by transformation of the nourishment. Nevertheless, we say that the crowds were fed with five loaves, or that woman was made from the rib, because an addition was made to the already existing matter of the loaves and of the rib.

Reply Obj. 2: The rib belonged to the integral perfection of Adam, not as an individual, but as the principle of the human race; just as the semen belongs to the perfection of the begetter, and is released by a natural and pleasurable operation. Much more, therefore, was it possible that by the Divine power the body of the woman should be produced from the man's rib.

From this it is clear how to answer the third objection.

FOURTH ARTICLE [I, Q. 92, Art. 4]

Whether the Woman Was Formed Immediately by God?

Objection 1: It would seem that the woman was not formed immediately by God. For no individual is produced immediately by God from another individual alike in species. But the woman was made from a man who is of the same species. Therefore she was not made immediately by God.

Obj. 2: Further, Augustine (De Trin. iii, 4) says that corporeal things are governed by God through the angels. But the woman's body was formed from corporeal matter. Therefore it was made through the ministry of the angels, and not immediately by God.

Obj. 3: Further, those things which pre-exist in creatures as to their causal virtues are produced by the power of some creature, and not immediately by God. But the woman's body was produced in its causal virtues among the first created works, as Augustine says (Gen. ad lit. ix, 15). Therefore it was not produced immediately by God.

*On the contrary,* Augustine says, in the same work: "God alone, to Whom all nature owes its existence, could form or build up the woman from the man's rib."

*I answer that,* As was said above (A. 2, ad 2), the natural generation of every species is from some determinate matter. Now the matter whence man is naturally begotten is the human semen of man or woman. Wherefore from any other matter an individual of the human species cannot naturally be generated. Now God alone, the Author of nature, can produce an effect into existence outside the ordinary course of nature. Therefore God alone could produce either a man from the slime of the earth, or a woman from the rib of man.

Reply Obj. 1: This argument is verified when an individual is begotten, by natural generation, from that which is like it in the same species.

Reply Obj. 2: As Augustine says (Gen. ad lit. ix, 15), we do not know whether the angels were employed by God in the formation of the woman; but it is certain that, as the body of man was not formed by the angels from the slime of the earth, so neither was the body of the woman formed by them from the man's rib.

Reply Obj. 3: As Augustine says (Gen. ad lit. ix, 18): "The first creation of things did not demand that woman should be made thus; it made it possible for her to be thus made." Therefore the body of the woman did indeed pre-exist in these causal virtues, in the things first created; not as regards active potentiality, but as regards a potentiality passive in relation to the active potentiality of the Creator.

## QUESTION 93

THE END OR TERM OF THE PRODUCTION OF MAN (In Nine Articles)

We now treat of the end or term of man's production, inasmuch as he is said to be made "to the image and likeness of God." There are under this head nine points of inquiry:

(1) Whether the image of God is in man?

(2) Whether the image of God is in irrational creatures?

(3) Whether the image of God is in the angels more than in man?

(4) Whether the image of God is in every man?

(5) Whether the image of God is in man by comparison with the Essence, or with all the Divine Persons, or with one of them?

(6) Whether the image of God is in man, as to his mind only?

(7) Whether the image of God is in man's power or in his habits and acts?

(8) Whether the image of God is in man by comparison with every object?

(9) Of the difference between "image" and "likeness."

FIRST ARTICLE [I, Q. 93, Art. 1]

Whether the Image of God Is in Man?

Objection 1: It would seem that the image of God is not in man. For it is written (Isa. 40:18): "To whom have you likened God? or what image will you make for Him?"

Obj. 2: Further, to be the image of God is the property of the First-Begotten, of Whom the Apostle says (Col. 1:15): "Who is the image of the invisible God, the First-Born of every creature." Therefore the image of God is not to be found in man.

Obj. 3: Further, Hilary says (De Synod [*Super i can]. Synod. Ancyr.) that "an image is of the same species as that which it represents"; and he also says that "an image is the undivided and united likeness of one thing adequately representing another." But there is no species common to both God and man; nor can there be a comparison of equality between God and man. Therefore there can be no image of God in man.

*On the contrary,* It is written (Gen. 1:26): "Let Us make man to Our own image and likeness."

*I answer that,* As Augustine says (QQ. 83, qu. 74): "Where an image exists, there forthwith is likeness; but where there is likeness, there is not necessarily an image." Hence it is clear that likeness is essential to an image; and that an image adds something to likeness—namely, that it is copied from something else. For an "image" is so called because it is produced as an imitation of something else; wherefore, for instance, an egg, however much like and equal to another egg, is not called an image of the other egg, because it is not copied from it.

But equality does not belong to the essence of an image; for as Augustine says (QQ. 83, qu. 74): "Where there is an image there is not necessarily equality," as we see in a person's image reflected in a glass. Yet this is of the essence of a perfect image; for in a perfect image nothing is wanting that is to be found in that of which it is a copy. Now it is manifest that in man there is some likeness to God, copied from God as from an exemplar; yet this likeness is not one of equality, for such an exemplar infinitely excels its copy. Therefore there is in man a likeness to God; not, indeed, a perfect likeness, but imperfect. And Scripture implies the same when it says that man was made "to" God's likeness; for the preposition "to" signifies a certain approach, as of something at a distance.

Reply Obj. 1: The Prophet speaks of bodily images made by man. Therefore he says pointedly: "What image will you make for Him?" But God made a spiritual image to Himself in man.

Reply Obj. 2: The First-Born of creatures is the perfect Image of God, reflecting perfectly that of which He is the Image, and so He is said to be the "Image," and never "to the image." But man is said to be both "image" by reason of the likeness; and "to the image" by reason of the imperfect likeness. And since the perfect likeness to God cannot be except in an identical nature, the Image of God exists in His first-born Son; as the image of the king is in his son, who is of the same nature as himself: whereas it exists in man as in an alien nature, as the image of the king is in a silver coin, as Augustine says explains in *De decem Chordis* (Serm. ix, al, xcvi, De Tempore).

Reply Obj. 3: As unity means absence of division, a species is said to be the same as far as it is one. Now a thing is said to be one not only numerically, specifically, or generically, but also according to a certain analogy or proportion. In this sense a creature is one with God, or like to Him; but when Hilary says "of a thing which adequately represents another," this is to be understood of a perfect image.

SECOND ARTICLE [I, Q. 93, Art. 2]

Whether the Image of God Is to Be Found in Irrational Creatures?

Objection 1: It would seem that the image of God is to be found in irrational creatures. For Dionysius says (Div. Nom. ii): "Effects are contingent images of their causes." But God is the cause not only of rational, but also of irrational creatures. Therefore the image of God is to be found in irrational creatures.

Obj. 2: Further, the more distinct a likeness is, the nearer it approaches to the nature of an image. But Dionysius says (Div. Nom. iv) that "the solar ray has a very great similitude to the Divine goodness." Therefore it is made to the image of God.

Obj. 3: Further, the more perfect anything is in goodness, the more it is like God. But the whole universe is more perfect in goodness than man; for though each individual thing is good, all things together are called "very good" (Gen. 1:31). Therefore the whole universe is to the image of God, and not only man.

Obj. 4: Further, Boethius (De Consol. iii) says of God: "Holding the world in His mind, and forming it into His image." Therefore the whole world is to the image of God, and not only the rational creature.

*On the contrary,* Augustine says (Gen. ad lit. vi, 12): "Man's excellence consists in the fact that God made him to His own image by giving him an intellectual soul, which raises him above the beasts of the field." Therefore things without intellect are not made to God's image.

*I answer that,* Not every likeness, not even what is copied from something else, is sufficient to make an image; for if the likeness be only generic, or existing by virtue of some common accident, this does not suffice for one thing to be the image of another. For instance, a worm, though from man it may originate, cannot be called man's image, merely because of the generic likeness. Nor, if anything is made white like something else, can we say that it is the image of that thing; for whiteness is an accident belonging to many species. But the nature of an image requires likeness in species; thus the image of the king exists in his son: or, at least, in some specific accident, and chiefly in the shape; thus, we speak of a man's image in copper. Whence Hilary says pointedly that "an image is of the same species."

Now it is manifest that specific likeness follows the ultimate difference. But some things are like to God first and most commonly because they exist; secondly, because they live; and thirdly because they know or understand; and these last, as Augustine says (QQ. 83, qu. 51) "approach so near to God in likeness, that among all creatures nothing comes nearer to Him." It is clear, therefore, that intellectual creatures alone, properly speaking, are made to God's image.

Reply Obj. 1: Everything imperfect is a participation of what is perfect. Therefore even what falls short of the nature of an image, so far as it possesses any sort of likeness to God, participates in some degree the nature of an image. So Dionysius says that effects are "contingent images of their causes"; that is, as much as they happen ( *contingit* ) to be so, but not absolutely.

Reply Obj. 2: Dionysius compares the solar ray to Divine goodness, as regards its causality; not as regards its natural dignity which is involved in the idea of an image.

Reply Obj. 3: The universe is more perfect in goodness than the intellectual creature as regards extension and diffusion; but intensively and collectively the likeness to the Divine goodness is found rather in the intellectual creature, which has a capacity for the highest good. Or else we may say that a part is not rightly divided against the whole, but only against another part. Wherefore, when we say that the intellectual nature alone is to the image of God, we do not mean that the universe in any part is not to God's image, but that the other parts are excluded.

Reply Obj. 4: Boethius here uses the word "image" to express the likeness which the product of an art bears to the artistic species in the mind of the artist. Thus every creature is an image of the exemplar type thereof in the Divine mind. We are not, however, using the word "image" in this sense; but as it implies a likeness in nature, that is, inasmuch as all things, as being, are like to the First Being; as living, like to the First Life; and as intelligent, like to the Supreme Wisdom.

THIRD ARTICLE [I, Q. 93, Art. 3]

Whether the Angels Are More to the Image of God Than Man Is?

Objection 1: It would seem that the angels are not more to the image of God than man is. For Augustine says in a sermon *de Imagine* xliii (de verbis Apost. xxvii) that God granted to no other creature besides man to be to His image. Therefore it is not true to say that the angels are more than man to the image of God.

Obj. 2: Further, according to Augustine (QQ. 83, qu. 51), "man is so much to God's image that God did not make any creature to be between Him and man: and therefore nothing is more akin to Him." But a creature is called God's image so far as it is akin to God. Therefore the angels are not more to the image of God than man.

Obj. 3: Further, a creature is said to be to God's image so far as it is of an intellectual nature. But the intellectual nature does not admit of intensity or remissness; for it is not an accidental thing, since it is a substance. Therefore the angels are not more to the image of God than man.

*On the contrary,* Gregory says (Hom. in Evang. xxxiv): "The angel is called a "seal of resemblance" (Ezech. 28:12) because in him the resemblance of the Divine image is wrought with greater expression.

*I answer that,* We may speak of God's image in two ways. First, we may consider in it that in which the image chiefly consists, that is, the intellectual nature. Thus the image of God is more perfect in the angels than in man, because their intellectual nature is more perfect, as is clear from what has been said (Q. 58, A. 3; Q. 79, A. 8). Secondly, we may consider the image of God in man as regards its accidental qualities, so far as to observe in man a certain imitation of God, consisting in the fact that man proceeds from man, as God from God; and also in the fact that the whole human soul is in the whole body, and again, in every part, as God is in regard to the whole world. In these and the like things the image of God is more perfect in man than it is in the angels. But these do not of themselves belong to the nature of the Divine image in man, unless we presuppose the first likeness, which is in the intellectual nature; otherwise even brute animals would be to God's image. Therefore, as in their intellectual nature, the angels are more to the image of God than man is, we must grant that, absolutely speaking, the angels are more to the image of God than man is, but that in some respects man is more like to God.

Reply Obj. 1: Augustine excludes the inferior creatures bereft of reason from the image of God; but not the angels.

Reply Obj. 2: As fire is said to be specifically the most subtle of bodies, while, nevertheless, one kind of fire is more subtle than another; so we say that nothing is more like to God than the human soul in its generic and intellectual nature, because as Augustine had said previously, "things which have knowledge, are so near to Him in likeness that of all creatures none are nearer." Wherefore this does not mean that the angels are not more to God's image.

Reply Obj. 3: When we say that substance does not admit of more or less, we do not mean that one species of substance is not more perfect than another; but that one and the same individual does not participate in its specific nature at one time more than at another; nor do we mean that a species of substance is shared among different individuals in a greater or lesser degree.

FOURTH ARTICLE [I, Q. 93, Art. 4]

Whether the Image of God Is Found in Every Man?

Objection 1: It would seem that the image of God is not found in every man. For the Apostle says that "man is the image of God, but woman is the image [Vulg. glory] of man" (1 Cor. 11:7). Therefore, as woman is an individual of the human species, it is clear that every individual is not an image of God.

Obj. 2: Further, the Apostle says (Rom. 8:29): "Whom God foreknew, He also predestined to be made conformable to the image of His Son." But all men are not predestined. Therefore all men have not the conformity of image.

Obj. 3: Further, likeness belongs to the nature of the image, as above explained (A. 1). But by sin man becomes unlike God. Therefore he loses the image of God.

*On the contrary,* It is written (Ps. 38:7): "Surely man passeth as an image."

*I answer that,* Since man is said to be the image of God by reason of his intellectual nature, he is the most perfectly like God according to that in which he can best imitate God in his intellectual nature. Now the intellectual nature imitates God chiefly in this, that God understands and loves Himself. Wherefore we see that the image of God is in man in three ways. First, inasmuch as man possesses a natural aptitude for understanding and loving God; and this aptitude consists in the very nature of the mind, which is common to all men. Secondly, inasmuch as man actually and habitually knows and loves God, though imperfectly; and this image consists in the conformity of grace. Thirdly, inasmuch as man knows and loves God perfectly; and this image consists in the likeness of glory. Wherefore on the words, "The light of Thy countenance, O Lord, is signed upon us" (Ps. 4:7), the gloss distinguishes a threefold image of "creation," of "re-creation," and of "likeness." The first is found in all men, the second only in the just, the third only in the blessed.

Reply Obj. 1: The image of God, in its principal signification, namely the intellectual nature, is found both in man and in woman. Hence after the words, "To the image of God He created him," it is added, "Male and female He created them" (Gen. 1:27). Moreover it is said "them" in the plural, as Augustine (Gen. ad lit. iii, 22) remarks, lest it should be thought that both sexes were united in one individual. But in a secondary sense the image of God is found in man, and not in woman: for man is the beginning and end of woman; as God is the beginning and end of every creature. So when the Apostle had said that "man is the image and glory of God, but woman is the glory of man," he adds his reason for saying this: "For man is not of woman, but woman of man; and man was not created for woman, but woman for man."

Reply Obj. 2 and 3: These reasons refer to the image consisting in the conformity of grace and glory.

FIFTH ARTICLE [I, Q. 93, Art. 5]

Whether the Image of God Is in Man According to the Trinity of Persons?

Objection 1: It would seem that the image of God does not exist in man as to the Trinity of Persons. For Augustine says (Fulgentius De Fide ad Petrum i): "One in essence is the Godhead of the Holy Trinity; and one is the image to which man was made." And Hilary (De Trin. v) says: "Man is made to the image of that which is common in the Trinity." Therefore the image of God in man is of the Divine Essence, and not of the Trinity of Persons.

Obj. 2: Further, it is said (De Eccl. Dogmat.) that the image of God in man is to be referred to eternity. Damascene also says (De Fide Orth. ii, 12) that the image of God in man belongs to him as "an intelligent being endowed with free-will and self-movement." Gregory of Nyssa (De Homin. Opificio xvi) also asserts that, when Scripture says that "man was made to the image of God, it means that human nature was made a participator of all good: for the Godhead is the fulness of goodness." Now all these things belong more to the unity of the Essence than to the distinction of the Persons. Therefore the image of God in man regards, not the Trinity of Persons, but the unity of the Essence.

Obj. 3: Further, an image leads to the knowledge of that of which it is the image. Therefore, if there is in man the image of God as to the Trinity of Persons; since man can know himself by his natural reason, it follows that by his natural knowledge man could know the Trinity of the Divine Persons; which is untrue, as was shown above (Q. 32, A. 1).

Obj. 4: Further, the name of Image is not applicable to any of the Three Persons, but only to the Son; for Augustine says (De Trin. vi, 2) that "the Son alone is the image of the Father." Therefore, if in man there were an image of God as regards the Person, this would not be an image of the Trinity, but only of the Son.

*On the contrary,* Hilary says (De Trin. iv): "The plurality of the Divine Persons is proved from the fact that man is said to have been made to the image of God."

*I answer that,* as we have seen (Q. 40, A. 2), the distinction of the Divine Persons is only according to origin, or, rather, relations of origin. Now the mode of origin is not the same in all things, but in each thing is adapted to the nature thereof; animated things being produced in one way, and inanimate in another; animals in one way, and plants in another. Wherefore it is manifest that the distinction of the Divine Persons is suitable to the Divine Nature; and therefore to be to the image of God by imitation of the Divine Nature does not exclude being to the same image by the representation of the Divine Persons: but rather one follows from the other. We must, therefore, say that in man there exists the image of God, both as regards the Divine Nature and as regards the Trinity of Persons; for also in God Himself there is one Nature in Three Persons.

Thus it is clear how to solve the first two objections.

Reply Obj. 3: This argument would avail if the image of God in man represented God in a perfect manner. But, as Augustine says (De Trin. xv, 6), there is a great difference between the trinity within ourselves and the Divine Trinity. Therefore, as he there says: "We see, rather than believe, the trinity which is in ourselves; whereas we believe rather than see that God is Trinity."

Reply Obj. 4: Some have said that in man there is an image of the Son only. Augustine rejects this opinion (De Trin. xii, 5,6). First, because as the Son is like to the Father by a likeness of essence, it would follow of necessity if man were made in likeness to the Son, that he is made to the likeness of the Father. Secondly, because if man were made only to the image of the Son, the Father would not have said, "Let Us make man to Our own image and likeness"; but "to Thy image." When, therefore, it is written, "He made him to the image of God," the sense is not that the Father made man to the image of the Son only, Who is God, as some explained it, but that the Divine Trinity made man to Its image, that is, of the whole Trinity. When it is said that God "made man to His image," this can be understood in two ways: first, so that this preposition "to" points to the term of the making, and then the sense is, "Let Us make man in such a way that Our image may be in him." Secondly, this preposition 'to' may point to the exemplar cause, as when we say, "This book is made (like) to that one." Thus the image of God is the very Essence of God, Which is incorrectly called an image forasmuch as image is put for the exemplar. Or, as some say, the Divine Essence is called an image because thereby one Person imitates another.

SIXTH ARTICLE [I, Q. 93, Art. 6]

Whether the Image of God Is in Man As Regards the Mind Only?

Objection 1: It would seem that the image of God is not only in man's mind. For the Apostle says (1 Cor. 11:7) that "the man is the image ... of God." But man is not only mind. Therefore the image of God is to be observed not only in his mind.

Obj. 2: Further, it is written (Gen. 1:27): "God created man to His own image; to the image of God He created him; male and female He created them." But the distinction of male and female is in the body. Therefore the image of God is also in the body, and not only in the mind.

Obj. 3: Further, an image seems to apply principally to the shape of a thing. But shape belongs to the body. Therefore the image of God is to be seen in man's body also, and not in his mind.

Obj. 4: Further, according to Augustine (Gen. ad lit. xii, 7,24) there is a threefold vision in us, "corporeal," "spiritual," or imaginary, and "intellectual." Therefore, if in the intellectual vision that belongs to the mind there exists in us a trinity by reason of which we are made to the image of God, for the like reason there must be another trinity in the others.

*On the contrary,* The Apostle says (Eph. 4:23,24): "Be renewed in the spirit of your mind, and put on the new man." Whence we are given to understand that our renewal which consists in putting on the new man, belongs to the mind. Now, he says (Col. 3:10): "Putting on the new" man; "him who is renewed unto knowledge" of God, "according to the image of Him that created him," where the renewal which consists in putting on the new man is ascribed to the image of God. Therefore to be to the image of God belongs to the mind only.

*I answer that,* While in all creatures there is some kind of likeness to God, in the rational creature alone we find a likeness of "image" as we have explained above (AA. 1,2); whereas in other creatures we find a likeness by way of a "trace." Now the intellect or mind is that whereby the rational creature excels other creatures; wherefore this image of God is not found even in the rational creature except in the mind; while in the other parts, which the rational creature may happen to possess, we find the likeness of a "trace," as in other creatures to which, in reference to such parts, the rational creature can be likened. We may easily understand the reason of this if we consider the way in which a "trace," and the way in which an "image," represents anything. An "image" represents something by likeness in species, as we have said; while a "trace" represents something by way of an effect, which represents the cause in such a way as not to attain to the likeness of species. For imprints which are left by the movements of animals are called "traces": so also ashes are a trace of fire, and desolation of the land a trace of a hostile army.

Therefore we may observe this difference between rational creatures and others, both as to the representation of the likeness of the Divine Nature in creatures, and as to the representation in them of the uncreated Trinity. For as to the likeness of the Divine Nature, rational creatures seem to attain, after a fashion, to the representation of the species, inasmuch as they imitate God, not only in being and life, but also in intelligence, as above explained (A. 2); whereas other creatures do not understand, although we observe in them a certain trace of the Intellect that created them, if we consider their disposition. Likewise as the uncreated Trinity is distinguished by the procession of the Word from the Speaker, and of Love from both of these, as we have seen (Q. 28, A. 3); so we may say that in rational creatures wherein we find a procession of the word in the intellect, and a procession of the love in the will, there exists an image of the uncreated Trinity, by a certain representation of the species. In other creatures, however, we do not find the principle of the word, and the word and love; but we do see in them a certain trace of the existence of these in the Cause that produced them. For in the fact that a creature has a modified and finite nature, proves that it proceeds from a principle; while its species points to the (mental) word of the maker, just as the shape of a house points to the idea of the architect; and order points to the maker's love by reason of which he directs the effect to a good end; as also the use of the house points to the will of the architect. So we find in man a likeness to God by way of an "image" in his mind; but in the other parts of his being by way of a "trace."

Reply Obj. 1: Man is called to the image of God; not that he is essentially an image; but that the image of God is impressed on his mind; as a coin is an image of the king, as having the image of the king. Wherefore there is no need to consider the image of God as existing in every part of man.

Reply Obj. 2: As Augustine says (De Trin. xii, 5), some have thought that the image of God was not in man individually, but severally. They held that "the man represents the Person of the Father; those born of man denote the person of the Son; and that the woman is a third person in likeness to the Holy Ghost, since she so proceeded from man as not to be his son or daughter." All of this is manifestly absurd; first, because it would follow that the Holy

Ghost is the principle of the Son, as the woman is the principle of the man's offspring; secondly, because one man would be only the image of one Person; thirdly, because in that case Scripture should not have mentioned the image of God in man until after the birth of the offspring. Therefore we must understand that when Scripture had said, "to the image of God He created him," it added, "male and female He created them," not to imply that the image of God came through the distinction of sex, but that the image of God belongs to both sexes, since it is in the mind, wherein there is no sexual distinction. Wherefore the Apostle (Col. 3:10), after saying, "According to the image of Him that created him," added, "Where there is neither male nor female" [*these words are in reality from Gal. 3:28] (Vulg. "neither Gentile nor Jew").

Reply Obj. 3: Although the image of God in man is not to be found in his bodily shape, yet because "the body of man alone among terrestrial animals is not inclined prone to the ground, but is adapted to look upward to heaven, for this reason we may rightly say that it is made to God's image and likeness, rather than the bodies of other animals," as Augustine remarks (QQ. 83, qu. 51). But this is not to be understood as though the image of God were in man's body; but in the sense that the very shape of the human body represents the image of God in the soul by way of a trace.

Reply Obj. 4: Both in the corporeal and in the imaginary vision we may find a trinity, as Augustine says (De Trin. xi, 2). For in corporeal vision there is first the species of the exterior body; secondly, the act of vision, which occurs by the impression on the sight of a certain likeness of the said species; thirdly, the intention of the will applying the sight to see, and to rest on what is seen.

Likewise, in the imaginary vision we find first the species kept in the memory; secondly, the vision itself, which is caused by the penetrative power of the soul, that is, the faculty of imagination, informed by the species; and thirdly, we find the intention of the will joining both together. But each of these trinities falls short of the Divine image. For the species of the external body is extrinsic to the essence of the soul; while the species in the memory, though not extrinsic to the soul, is adventitious to it; and thus in both cases the species falls short of representing the connaturality and co-eternity of the Divine Persons. The corporeal vision, too, does not proceed only from the species of the external body, but from this, and at the same time from the sense of the seer; in like manner imaginary vision is not from the species only which is preserved in the memory, but also from the imagination. For these reasons the procession of the Son from the Father alone is not suitably represented. Lastly the intention of the will joining the two together, does not proceed from them either in corporeal or spiritual vision. Wherefore the procession of the Holy Ghost from the Father and the Son is not thus properly represented.

SEVENTH ARTICLE [I, Q. 93, Art. 7]

Whether the Image of God Is to Be Found in the Acts of the Soul?

Objection 1: It would seem that the image of God is not found in the acts of the soul. For Augustine says (De Civ. Dei xi, 26), that "man was made to God's image, inasmuch as we exist and know that we exist, and love this existence and knowledge." But to exist does not signify an act. Therefore the image of God is not to be found in the soul's acts.

Obj. 2: Further, Augustine (De Trin. ix, 4) assigns God's image in the soul to these three things—mind, knowledge, and love. But mind does not signify an act, but rather the power or the essence of the intellectual soul. Therefore the image of God does not extend to the acts of the soul.

Obj. 3: Further, Augustine (De Trin. x, 11) assigns the image of the Trinity in the soul to "memory, understanding, and will." But these three are "natural powers of the soul," as the Master of the Sentences says (1 Sent. D iii). Therefore the image of God is in the powers, and does not extend to the acts of the soul.

Obj. 4: Further, the image of the Trinity always remains in the soul. But an act does not always remain. Therefore the image of God does not extend to the acts.

*On the contrary,* Augustine (De Trin. xi, 2 seqq.) assigns the trinity in the lower part of the soul, in relation to the actual vision, whether sensible or imaginative. Therefore, also, the trinity in the mind, by reason of which man is like to God's image, must be referred to actual vision.

*I answer that,* As above explained (A. 2), a certain representation of the species belongs to the nature of an image. Hence, if the image of the Divine Trinity is to be found in the soul, we must look for it where the soul approaches the nearest to a representation of the species of the Divine Persons. Now the Divine Persons are distinct from each other by reason of the procession of the Word from the Speaker, and the procession of Love connecting Both. But in our soul word "cannot exist without actual thought," as Augustine says (De Trin. xiv, 7). Therefore, first and chiefly, the image of the Trinity is to be found in the acts of the soul, that is, inasmuch as from the knowledge which we possess, by actual thought we form an internal word; and thence break forth into love. But, since the principles of acts are the habits and powers, and everything exists virtually in its principle, therefore, secondarily and consequently, the image of the Trinity may be considered as existing in the powers, and still more in the habits, forasmuch as the acts virtually exist therein.

Reply Obj. 1: Our being bears the image of God so far as it is proper to us, and excels that of the other animals, that is to say, in so far as we are endowed with a mind. Therefore, this trinity is the same as that which Augustine mentions (De Trin. ix, 4), and which consists in mind, knowledge, and love.

Reply Obj. 2: Augustine observed this trinity, first, as existing in the mind. But because the mind, though it knows itself entirely in a certain degree, yet also in a way does not know itself—namely, as being distinct from others (and thus also it searches itself, as Augustine subsequently proves—De Trin. x, 3,4); therefore, as though knowledge were not in equal proportion to mind, he takes three things in the soul which are proper to the mind, namely, memory, understanding, and will; which everyone is conscious of possessing; and assigns the image of the Trinity pre-eminently to these three, as though the first assignation were in part deficient.

Reply Obj. 3: As Augustine proves (De Trin. xiv, 7), we may be said to understand, will, and to love certain things, both when we actually consider them, and when we do not think of them. When they are not under our actual consideration, they are objects of our memory only, which, in his opinion, is nothing else than habitual retention of knowledge and love [*Cf. Q. 79, A. 7, ad 1]. "But since," as he says, "a word cannot be there without actual thought (for we think everything that we say, even if we speak with that interior word belonging to no nation's tongue), this image chiefly consists in these three things, memory, understanding, and will. And by understanding I mean here that whereby we understand with actual thought; and by will, love, or dilection I mean that which unites this child with its parent." From which it is clear that he places the image of the Divine Trinity more in actual understanding and will, than in these as existing in the habitual retention of the memory; although even thus the image of the Trinity exists in the soul in a certain degree, as he says in the same place. Thus it is clear that memory, understanding, and will are not three powers as stated in the Sentences.

Reply Obj. 4: Someone might answer by referring to Augustine's statement (De Trin. xiv, 6), that "the mind ever remembers itself, ever understands itself, ever loves itself"; which some take to mean that the soul ever actually understands, and loves itself. But he excludes this interpretation by adding that "it does not always think of itself as actually distinct from other things." Thus it is clear that the soul always understands and loves itself, not actually but habitually; though we might say that by perceiving its own act, it understands itself whenever it understands anything. But since it is not always actually understanding, as in the case of sleep, we must say that these acts, although not always actually existing, yet ever exist in their principles, the habits and powers. Wherefore, Augustine says (De Trin. xiv, 4): "If the rational soul is made to the image of God in the sense that it can make use of reason and intellect to understand and consider God, then the image of God was in the soul from the beginning of its existence."

EIGHTH ARTICLE [I, Q. 93, Art. 8]

Whether the Image of the Divine Trinity Is in the Soul Only by Comparison with God As Its Object?

Objection 1: It would seem that the image of the Divine Trinity is in the soul not only by comparison with God as its object. For the image of the Divine Trinity is to be found in the soul, as shown above (A. 7), according as the word in us proceeds from the speaker; and love from both. But this is to be found in us as regards any object. Therefore the image of the Divine Trinity is in our mind as regards any object.

Obj. 2: Further, Augustine says (De Trin. xii, 4) that "when we seek trinity in the soul, we seek it in the whole of the soul, without separating the process of reasoning in temporal matters from the consideration of things eternal." Therefore the image of the Trinity is to be found in the soul, even as regards temporal objects.

Obj. 3: Further, it is by grace that we can know and love God. If, therefore, the image of the Trinity is found in the soul by reason of the memory, understanding, and will or love of God, this image is not in man by nature but by grace, and thus is not common to all.

Obj. 4: Further, the saints in heaven are most perfectly conformed to the image of God by the beatific vision; wherefore it is written (2 Cor. 3:18): "We ... are transformed into the same image from glory to glory." But temporal things are known by the beatific vision. Therefore the image of God exists in us even according to temporal things.

*On the contrary,* Augustine says (De Trin. xiv, 12): "The image of God exists in the mind, not because it has a remembrance of itself, loves itself, and understands itself; but because it can also remember, understand, and love God by Whom it was made." Much less, therefore, is the image of God in the soul, in respect of other objects.

*I answer that,* As above explained (AA. 2, 7), image means a likeness which in some degree, however small, attains to a representation of the species. Wherefore we need to seek in the image of the Divine Trinity in the soul some kind of representation of species of the Divine Persons, so far as this is possible to a creature. Now the Divine Persons, as above stated (AA. 6, 7), are distinguished from each other according to the procession of the word from the speaker, and the procession of love from both. Moreover the Word of God is born of God by the knowledge of Himself; and Love proceeds from God according as He loves Himself. But it is clear that diversity of objects diversifies the species of word and love; for in the human mind the species of a stone is specifically different from that of a horse, which also the love regarding each of them is specifically different. Hence we refer the Divine image in man to the verbal concept born of the knowledge of God, and to the love derived therefrom. Thus the image of God is found in the soul according as the soul turns to God, or possesses a nature that enables it to turn to God. Now the mind may turn towards an object in two ways: directly and immediately, or indirectly and mediately; as, for instance, when anyone sees a man reflected in a looking-glass he may be said to be turned towards that man. So Augustine says (De Trin. xiv, 8), that "the mind remembers itself, understands itself, and loves itself. If we perceive this, we perceive a trinity, not, indeed, God, but, nevertheless, rightly called the image of God." But this is due to the fact, not that the mind reflects on itself absolutely, but that thereby it can furthermore turn to God, as appears from the authority quoted above (Arg. On the contrary).

Reply Obj. 1: For the notion of an image it is not enough that something proceed from another, but it is also necessary to observe what proceeds and whence it proceeds; namely, that what is Word of God proceeds from knowledge of God.

Reply Obj. 2: In all the soul we may see a kind of trinity, not, however, as though besides the action of temporal things and the contemplation of eternal things, "any third thing should be required to make up the trinity," as he adds in the same passage. But in that part of the reason which is concerned with temporal things, "although a trinity may be found; yet the image of God is not to be seen there," as he says farther on; forasmuch as this knowledge of temporal things is adventitious to the soul. Moreover even the habits whereby temporal things are known are not always present; but sometimes they are actually present, and sometimes present only in memory even after they begin to exist in the soul. Such is clearly the case with faith, which comes to us temporally for this present life; while in the future life faith will no longer exist, but only the remembrance of faith.

Reply Obj. 3: The meritorious knowledge and love of God can be in us only by grace. Yet there is a certain natural knowledge and love as seen above (Q. 12, A. 12; Q. 56, A. 3; Q. 60, A. 5). This, too, is natural that the mind, in order to understand God, can make use of reason, in which sense we have already said that the image of God abides ever in the soul; "whether this image of God be so obsolete," as it were clouded, "as almost to amount to nothing," as in those who have not the use of reason; "or obscured and disfigured," as in sinners; or "clear and beautiful," as in the just; as Augustine says (De Trin. xiv, 6).

Reply Obj. 4: By the vision of glory temporal things will be seen in God Himself; and such a vision of things temporal will belong to the image of God. This is what Augustine means (De Trin. xiv, 6), when he says that "in that nature to which the mind will blissfully adhere, whatever it sees it will see as unchangeable"; for in the Uncreated Word are the types of all creatures.

NINTH ARTICLE [I, Q. 93, Art. 9]

Whether "Likeness" Is Properly Distinguished from "Image"?

Objection 1: It would seem that "likeness" is not properly distinguished from "image." For genus is not properly distinguished from species. Now, "likeness" is to "image" as genus to species: because, "where there is image, forthwith there is likeness, but not conversely" as Augustine says (QQ. 83, qu. 74). Therefore "likeness" is not properly to be distinguished from "image."

Obj. 2: Further, the nature of the image consists not only in the representation of the Divine Persons, but also in the representation of the Divine Essence, to which representation belong immortality and indivisibility. So it is not true to say that the "likeness is in the essence because it is immortal and indivisible; whereas the image is in other things" (Sent. ii, D, xvi).

Obj. 3: Further, the image of God in man is threefold—the image of nature, of grace, and of glory, as above explained (A. 4). But innocence and righteousness belong to grace. Therefore it is incorrectly said (Sent. ii, D, xvi) "that the image is taken from the memory, the understanding and the will, while the likeness is from innocence and righteousness."

Obj. 4: Further, knowledge of truth belongs to the intellect, and love of virtue to the will; which two things are parts of the image. Therefore it is incorrect to say (Sent. ii, D, xvi) that "the image consists in the knowledge of truth, and the likeness in the love of virtue."

*On the contrary,* Augustine says (QQ. 83, qu. 51): "Some consider that these two were mentioned not without reason, namely "image" and "likeness," since, if they meant the same, one would have sufficed."

*I answer that,* Likeness is a kind of unity, for oneness in quality causes likeness, as the Philosopher says (Metaph. v, Did. iv, 15). Now, since "one" is a transcendental, it is both common to all, and adapted to each single thing, just as the good and the true. Wherefore, as the good can be compared to each individual thing both as its preamble, and as subsequent to it, as signifying some perfection in it, so also in the same way there exists a kind of comparison between "likeness" and "image." For the good is a preamble to man, inasmuch as man is an individual good; and, again, the good is subsequent to man, inasmuch as we may say of a certain man that he is good, by reason of his perfect virtue. In like manner, likeness may be considered in the light of a preamble to image, inasmuch as it is something more general than image, as we have said above (A. 1): and, again, it may be considered as subsequent to image, inasmuch as it signifies a certain perfection of image. For we say that an image is like or unlike what it represents, according as the representation is perfect or imperfect. Thus likeness may be distinguished from image in two ways: first as its preamble and existing in more things, and in this sense likeness regards things which are more common than the intellectual properties, wherein the image is properly to be seen. In this sense it is stated (QQ. 83, qu. 51) that "the spirit" (namely, the mind) without doubt was made to the image of God. "But the other parts of man," belonging to the soul's inferior faculties, or even to the body, "are in the opinion of some made to God's likeness." In this sense he says (De Quant. Animae ii) that the likeness of God is found in the soul's incorruptibility; for corruptible and incorruptible are differences of universal beings. But likeness may be considered in another way, as signifying the expression and perfection of the image. In this sense Damascene says (De Fide Orth. ii, 12) that the image implies "an intelligent being, endowed with free-will and self-movement, whereas likeness implies a likeness of power, as far as this may be possible in man." In the same sense "likeness" is said to belong to "the love of virtue": for there is no virtue without love of virtue.

Reply Obj. 1: "Likeness" is not distinct from "image" in the general notion of "likeness" (for thus it is included in "image"); but so far as any "likeness" falls short of "image," or again, as it perfects the idea of "image."

Reply Obj. 2: The soul's essence belongs to the "image," as representing the Divine Essence in those things which belong to the intellectual nature; but not in those conditions subsequent to general notions of being, such as simplicity and indissolubility.

Reply Obj. 3: Even certain virtues are natural to the soul, at least, in their seeds, by reason of which we may say that a natural "likeness" exists in the soul. Nor it is unfitting to us the term "image" from one point of view and from another the term "likeness."

Reply Obj. 4: Love of the word, which is knowledge loved, belongs to the nature of "image"; but love of virtue belongs to "likeness," as virtue itself belongs to likeness.

## QUESTION 94

OF THE STATE AND CONDITION OF THE FIRST MAN AS REGARDS HIS INTELLECT (In Four Articles)

We next consider the state or condition of the first man; first, as regards his soul; secondly, as regards his body. Concerning the first there are two things to be considered:

(1) The condition of man as to his intellect;

(2) the condition of man as to his will.

Under the first head there are four points of inquiry:

(1) Whether the first man saw the Essence of God?

(2) Whether he could see the separate substances, that is, the angels?

(3) Whether he possessed all knowledge?

(4) Whether he could err or be deceived?

FIRST ARTICLE [I, Q. 94, Art. 1]

Whether the First Man Saw God Through His Essence?

Objection 1: It would seem that the first man saw God through His Essence. For man's happiness consists in the vision of the Divine Essence. But the first man, "while established in paradise, led a life of happiness in the enjoyment of all things," as Damascene says (De Fide Orth. ii, 11). And Augustine says (De Civ. Dei xiv, 10): "If man was gifted with the same tastes as now, how happy must he have been in paradise, that place of ineffable happiness!" Therefore the first man in paradise saw God through His Essence.

Obj. 2: Further, Augustine says (De Civ. Dei xiv, loc. cit.) that "the first man lacked nothing which his good-will might obtain." But our good-will can obtain nothing better than the vision of the Divine Essence. Therefore man saw God through His Essence.

Obj. 3: Further, the vision of God in His Essence is whereby God is seen without a medium or enigma. But man in the state of innocence "saw God immediately," as the Master of the Sentences asserts (Sent. iv, D, i). He also saw without an enigma, for an enigma implies obscurity, as Augustine says (De Trin. xv, 9). Now, obscurity resulted from sin. Therefore man in the primitive state saw God through His Essence.

*On the contrary,* The Apostle says (1 Cor. 15:46): "That was not first which is spiritual, but that which is natural." But to see God through His Essence is most spiritual. Therefore the first man in the primitive state of his natural life did not see God through His Essence.

*I answer that,* The first man did not see God through His Essence if we consider the ordinary state of that life; unless, perhaps, it be said that he saw God in a vision, when "God cast a deep sleep upon Adam" (Gen. 2:21). The reason is because, since in the Divine Essence is beatitude itself, the intellect of a man who sees the Divine Essence has the same relation to God as a man has to beatitude. Now it is clear that man cannot willingly be turned away from beatitude, since naturally and necessarily he desires it, and shuns unhappiness. Wherefore no one who sees the Essence of God can willingly turn away from God, which means to sin. Hence all who see God through His Essence are so firmly established in the love of God, that for eternity they can never sin. Therefore, as Adam did sin, it is clear that he did not see God through His Essence.

Nevertheless he knew God with a more perfect knowledge than we do now. Thus in a sense his knowledge was midway between our knowledge in the present state, and the knowledge we shall have in heaven, when we see God through His Essence. To make this clear, we must consider that the vision of God through His Essence is contradistinguished from the vision of God through His creatures. Now the higher the creature is, and the more like it is to God, the more clearly is God seen in it; for instance, a man is seen more clearly through a mirror in which his image is the more clearly expressed. Thus God is seen in a much more perfect manner through His intelligible effects than through those which are only sensible or corporeal. But in his present state man is impeded as regards the full and clear consideration of intelligible creatures, because he is distracted by and occupied with sensible things. Now, it is written (Eccles. 7:30): "God made man right." And man was made right by God in this sense, that in him the lower powers were subjected to the higher, and the higher nature was made so as not to be impeded by the lower. Wherefore the first man was not impeded by exterior things from a clear and steady contemplation of the intelligible effects which he perceived by the radiation of the first truth, whether by a natural or by a gratuitous knowledge. Hence Augustine says (Gen. ad lit. xi, 33) that, "perhaps God used to speak to the first man as He speaks to the angels; by shedding on his mind a ray of the unchangeable truth, yet without bestowing on him the experience of which the angels are capable in the participation of the Divine Essence." Therefore, through these intelligible effects of God, man knew God then more clearly than we know Him now.

Reply Obj. 1: Man was happy in paradise, but not with that perfect happiness to which he was destined, which consists in the vision of the Divine Essence. He was, however, endowed with "a life of happiness in a certain measure," as Augustine says (Gen. ad lit. xi, 18), so far as he was gifted with natural integrity and perfection.

Reply Obj. 2: A good will is a well-ordered will; but the will of the first man would have been ill-ordered had he wished to have, while in the state of merit, what had been promised to him as a reward.

Reply Obj. 3: A medium (of knowledge) is twofold; one through which, and, at the same time, in which, something is seen, as, for example, a man is seen through a mirror, and is seen with the mirror: another kind of medium is that whereby we attain to the knowledge of something unknown; such as the medium in a demonstration. God was seen without this second kind of medium, but not without the first kind. For there was no need for the first man to attain to the knowledge of God by demonstration drawn from an effect, such as we need; since he knew God simultaneously in His effects, especially in the intelligible effects, according to His capacity. Again, we must remark that the obscurity which is implied in the word enigma may be of two kinds: first, so far as every creature is something obscure when compared with the immensity of the Divine light; and thus Adam saw God in an enigma, because he saw Him in a created effect: secondly, we may take obscurity as an effect of sin, so far as man is impeded in the consideration of intelligible things by being preoccupied with sensible things; in which sense Adam did not see God in an enigma.

SECOND ARTICLE [I, Q. 94, Art. 2]

Whether Adam in the State of Innocence Saw the Angels Through Their Essence?

Objection 1: It would seem that Adam, in the state of innocence, saw the angels through their essence. For Gregory says (Dialog. iv, 1): "In paradise man was accustomed to enjoy the words of God; and by purity of heart and loftiness of vision to have the company of the good angels."

Obj. 2: Further, the soul in the present state is impeded from the knowledge of separate substances by union with a corruptible body which "is a load upon the soul," as is written Wis. 9:15. Wherefore the separate soul can see separate substances, as above explained (Q. 89, A. 2). But the body of the first man was not a load upon his soul; for the latter was not corruptible. Therefore he was able to see separate substances.

Obj. 3: Further, one separate substance knows another separate substance, by knowing itself (De Causis xiii). But the soul of the first man knew itself. Therefore it knew separate substances.

*On the contrary,* The soul of Adam was of the same nature as ours. But our souls cannot now understand separate substances. Therefore neither could Adam's soul.

*I answer that,* The state of the human soul may be distinguished in two ways. First, from a diversity of mode in its natural existence; and in this point the state of the separate soul is distinguished from the state of the soul joined to the body. Secondly, the state of the soul is distinguished in relation to integrity and corruption, the state of natural existence remaining the same: and thus the state of innocence is distinct from the state of man after sin. For man's soul, in the state of innocence, was adapted to perfect and govern the body; wherefore the first man is said to have been made into a "living soul"; that is, a soul giving life to the body—namely animal life. But he was endowed with integrity as to this life, in that the body was entirely subject to the soul, hindering it in no way, as we have said above (A. 1). Now it is clear from what has been already said (Q. 84, A. 7; Q. 85, A. 1; Q. 89, A. 1) that since the soul is adapted to perfect and govern the body, as regards animal life, it is fitting that it should have that mode of understanding which is by turning to phantasms. Wherefore this mode of understanding was becoming to the soul of the first man also.

Now, in virtue of this mode of understanding, there are three degrees of movement in the soul, as Dionysius says (Div. Nom. iv). The first is by the soul "passing from exterior things to concentrate its powers on itself"; the second is by the soul ascending "so as to be associated with the united superior powers," namely the angels; the third is when the soul is "led on" yet further "to the supreme good," that is, to God.

In virtue of the first movement of the soul from exterior things to itself, the soul's knowledge is perfected. This is because the intellectual operation of the soul has a natural order to external things, as we have said above (Q. 87, A. 3): and so by the knowledge thereof, our intellectual operation can be known perfectly, as an act through its object. And through the intellectual operation itself, the human intellect can be known perfectly, as a power through its proper act. But in the second movement we do not find perfect knowledge. Because, since the angel does not understand by turning to phantasms, but by a far more excellent process, as we have said above (Q. 55, A. 2); the above-mentioned mode of knowledge, by which the soul knows itself, is not sufficient to lead it to the knowledge of an angel. Much less does the third movement lead to perfect knowledge: for even the angels themselves, by the fact that they know themselves, are not able to arrive at the knowledge of the Divine Substance, by reason of its surpassing excellence. Therefore the soul of the first man could not see the angels in their essence. Nevertheless he had a more excellent mode of knowledge regarding the angels than we possess, because his knowledge of intelligible things within him was more certain and fixed than our knowledge. And it was on account of this excellence of knowledge that Gregory says that "he enjoyed the company of the angelic spirits."

This makes clear the reply to the first objection.

Reply Obj. 2: That the soul of the first man fell short of the knowledge regarding separate substances, was not owing to the fact that the body was a load upon it; but to the fact that its connatural object fell short of the excellence of separate substances. We, in our present state, fall short on account of both these reasons.

Reply Obj. 3: The soul of the first man was not able to arrive at knowledge of separate substances by means of its self-knowledge, as we have shown above; for even each separate substance knows others in its own measure.

THIRD ARTICLE [I, Q. 94, Art. 3]

Whether the First Man Knew All Things?

Objection 1: It would seem that the first man did not know all things. For if he had such knowledge it would be either by acquired species, or by connatural species, or by infused species. Not, however, by acquired species; for this kind of knowledge is acquired by experience, as stated in *Metaph.* i, 1; and the first man had not then gained experience of all things. Nor through connatural species, because he was of the same nature as we are; and our soul, as Aristotle says (De Anima iii, 4), is "like a clean tablet on which nothing is written." And if his knowledge came by infused species, it would have been of a different kind from ours, which we acquire from things themselves.

Obj. 2: Further, individuals of the same species have the same way of arriving at perfection. Now other men have not, from the beginning, knowledge of all things, but they acquire it in the course of time according to their capacity. Therefore neither did Adam know all things when he was first created.

Obj. 3: Further, the present state of life is given to man in order that his soul may advance in knowledge and merit; indeed, the soul seems to be united to the body for that purpose. Now man would have advanced in merit in that state of life; therefore also in knowledge. Therefore he was not endowed with knowledge of all things.

*On the contrary,* Man named the animals (Gen. 2:20). But names should be adapted to the nature of things. Therefore Adam knew the animals' natures; and in like manner he was possessed of the knowledge of all other things.

*I answer that,* In the natural order, perfection comes before imperfection, as act precedes potentiality; for whatever is in potentiality is made actual only by something actual. And since God created things not only for their own existence, but also that they might be the principles of other things; so creatures were produced in their perfect state to be the principles as regards others. Now man can be the principle of another man, not only by generation of the body, but also by instruction and government. Hence, as the first man was produced in his perfect state, as regards his body, for the work of generation, so also was his soul established in a perfect state to instruct and govern others.

Now no one can instruct others unless he has knowledge, and so the first man was established by God in such a manner as to have knowledge of all those things for which man has a natural aptitude. And such are whatever are virtually contained in the first self-evident principles, that is, whatever truths man is naturally able to know. Moreover, in order to direct his own life and that of others, man needs to know not only those things which can be naturally known, but also things surpassing natural knowledge; because the life of man is directed to a supernatural end: just as it is necessary for us to know the truths of faith in order to direct our own lives. Wherefore the first man was endowed with such a knowledge of these supernatural truths as was necessary for the direction of human life in that state. But those things which cannot be known by merely human effort, and which are not necessary for the direction of human life, were not known by the first man; such as the thoughts of men, future contingent events, and some individual facts, as for instance the number of pebbles in a stream; and the like.

Reply Obj. 1: The first man had knowledge of all things by divinely infused species. Yet his knowledge was not different from ours; as the eyes which Christ gave to the man born blind were not different from those given by nature.

Reply Obj. 2: To Adam, as being the first man, was due a degree of perfection which was not due to other men, as is clear from what is above explained.

Reply Obj. 3: Adam would have advanced in natural knowledge, not in the number of things known, but in the manner of knowing; because what he knew speculatively he would subsequently have known by experience. But as regards supernatural knowledge, he would also have advanced as regards the number of things known, by further revelation; as the angels advance by further enlightenment. Moreover there is no comparison between advance in knowledge and advance in merit; since one man cannot be a principle of merit to another, although he can be to another a principle of knowledge.

FOURTH ARTICLE [I, Q. 94, Art. 4]

Whether Man in His First State Could Be Deceived?

Objection 1: It would seem that man in his primitive state could have been deceived. For the Apostle says (1 Tim. 2:14) that "the woman being seduced was in the transgression."

Obj. 2: Further, the Master says (Sent. ii, D, xxi) that, "the woman was not frightened at the serpent speaking, because she thought that he had received the faculty of speech from God." But this was untrue. Therefore before sin the woman was deceived.

Obj. 3: Further, it is natural that the farther off anything is from us, the smaller it seems to be. Now, the nature of the eyes is not changed by sin. Therefore this would have been the case in the state of innocence. Wherefore man would have been deceived in the size of what he saw, just as he is deceived now.

Obj. 4: Further, Augustine says (Gen. ad lit. xii, 2) that, in sleep the soul adheres to the images of things as if they were the things themselves. But in the state of innocence man would have eaten and consequently have slept and dreamed. Therefore he would have been deceived, adhering to images as to realities.

Obj. 5: Further, the first man would have been ignorant of other men's thoughts, and of future contingent events, as stated above (A. 3). So if anyone had told him what was false about these things, he would have been deceived.

*On the contrary,* Augustine says (De Lib. Arb. iii, 18): "To regard what is true as false, is not natural to man as created; but is a punishment of man condemned."

*I answer that,* in the opinion of some, deception may mean two things; namely, any slight surmise, in which one adheres to what is false, as though it were true, but without the assent of belief—or it may mean a firm belief. Thus before sin Adam could not be deceived in either of these ways as regards those things to which his knowledge extended; but as regards things to which his knowledge did not extend, he might have been deceived, if we take deception in the wide sense of the term for any surmise without assent of belief. This opinion was held with the idea that it is not derogatory to man to entertain a false opinion in such matters, and that provided he does not assent rashly, he is not to be blamed.

Such an opinion, however, is not fitting as regards the integrity of the primitive state of life; because, as Augustine says (De Civ. Dei xiv, 10), in that state of life "sin was avoided without struggle, and while it remained so, no evil could exist." Now it is clear that as truth is the good of the intellect, so falsehood is its evil, as the Philosopher says (Ethic. vi, 2). So that, as long as the state of innocence continued, it was impossible for the human intellect to assent to falsehood as if it were truth. For as some perfections, such as clarity, were lacking in the bodily members of the first man, though no evil could be therein; so there could be in his intellect the absence of some knowledge, but no false opinion.

This is clear also from the very rectitude of the primitive state, by virtue of which, while the soul remained subject to God, the lower faculties in man were subject to the higher, and were no impediment to their action. And from what has preceded (Q. 85, A. 6), it is clear that as regards its proper object the intellect is ever true; and hence it is never deceived of itself; but whatever deception occurs must be ascribed to some lower faculty, such as the imagination or the like. Hence we see that when the natural power of judgment is free we are not deceived by such images, but only when it is not free, as is the case in sleep. Therefore it is clear that the rectitude of the primitive state was incompatible with deception of the intellect.

Reply Obj. 1: Though the woman was deceived before she sinned in deed, still it was not till she had already sinned by interior pride. For Augustine says (Gen. ad lit. xi, 30) that "the woman could not have believed the words of the serpent, had she not already acquiesced in the love of her own power, and in a presumption of self-conceit."

Reply Obj. 2: The woman thought that the serpent had received this faculty, not as acting in accordance with nature, but by virtue of some supernatural operation. We need not, however, follow the Master of the Sentences in this point.

Reply Obj. 3: Were anything presented to the imagination or sense of the first man, not in accordance with the nature of things, he would not have been deceived, for his reason would have enabled him to judge the truth.

Reply Obj. 4: A man is not accountable for what occurs during sleep; as he has not then the use of his reason, wherein consists man's proper action.

Reply Obj. 5: If anyone had said something untrue as regards future contingencies, or as regards secret thoughts, man in the primitive state would not have believed it was so: but he might have believed that such a thing was possible; which would not have been to entertain a false opinion.

It might also be said that he would have been divinely guided from above, so as not to be deceived in a matter to which his knowledge did not extend.

If any object, as some do, that he was not guided, when tempted, though he was then most in need of guidance, we reply that man had already sinned in his heart, and that he failed to have recourse to the Divine aid.

## QUESTION 95

OF THINGS PERTAINING TO THE FIRST MAN'S WILL—NAMELY, GRACE AND RIGHTEOUSNESS (In Four Articles)

We next consider what belongs to the will of the first man; concerning which there are two points of treatment:

(1) the grace and righteousness of the first man;

(2) the use of righteousness as regards his dominion over other things.

Under the first head there are four points of inquiry:

(1) Whether the first man was created in grace?

(2) Whether in the state of innocence he had passions of the soul?

(3) Whether he had all virtues?

(4) Whether what he did would have been as meritorious as now?

FIRST ARTICLE [I, Q. 95, Art. 1]

Whether the First Man Was Created in Grace?

Objection 1: It would seem that the first man was not created in grace. For the Apostle, distinguishing between Adam and Christ, says (1 Cor. 15:45): "The first Adam was made into a living soul; the last Adam into a quickening spirit." But the spirit is quickened by grace. Therefore Christ alone was made in grace.

Obj. 2: Further, Augustine says (QQ. Vet. et Nov. Test., qu. 123) [*Work of an anonymous author, among the supposititious works of St. Augustine] that "Adam did not possess the Holy Ghost." But whoever possesses grace has the Holy Ghost. Therefore Adam was not created in grace.

Obj. 3: Further, Augustine says (De Correp. et Grat. x) that "God so ordered the life of the angels and men, as to show first what they could do by free-will, then what they could do by His grace, and by the discernment of righteousness." God thus first created men and angels in the state of natural free-will only; and afterwards bestowed grace on them.

Obj. 4: Further, the Master says (Sent. ii, D, xxiv): "When man was created he was given sufficient help to stand, but not sufficient to advance." But whoever has grace can advance by merit. Therefore the first man was not created in grace.

Obj. 5: Further, the reception of grace requires the consent of the recipient, since thereby a kind of spiritual marriage takes place between God and the soul. But consent presupposes existence. Therefore man did not receive grace in the first moment of his creation.

Obj. 6: Further, nature is more distant from grace than grace is from glory, which is but grace consummated. But in man grace precedes glory. Therefore much more did nature precede grace.

*On the contrary,* Man and angel are both ordained to grace. But the angels were created in grace, for Augustine says (De Civ. Dei xii, 9): "God at the same time fashioned their nature and endowed them with grace." Therefore man also was created in grace.

*I answer that,* Some say that man was not created in grace; but that it was bestowed on him subsequently before sin: and many authorities of the Saints declare that man possessed grace in the state of innocence.

But the very rectitude of the primitive state, wherewith man was endowed by God, seems to require that, as others say, he was created in grace, according to Eccles. 7:30, "God made man right." For this rectitude consisted in his reason being subject to God, the lower powers to reason, and the body to the soul: and the first subjection was the cause of both the second and the third; since while reason was subject to God, the lower powers remained subject to reason, as Augustine says [*Cf. De Civ. Dei xiii, 13; De Pecc. Merit. et Remiss. i, 16]. Now it is clear that such a subjection of the body to the soul and of the lower powers to reason, was not from nature; otherwise it would have remained after sin; since even in the demons the natural gifts remained after sin, as Dionysius declared (Div. Nom. iv). Hence it is clear that also the primitive subjection by virtue of which reason was subject to God, was not a merely natural gift, but a supernatural endowment of grace; for it is not possible that the effect should be of greater efficiency than the cause. Hence Augustine says (De Civ. Dei xiii, 13) that, "as soon as they disobeyed the Divine command, and forfeited Divine grace, they were ashamed of their nakedness, for they felt the impulse of disobedience in the flesh, as though it were a punishment corresponding to their own disobedience." Hence if the loss of grace dissolved the obedience of the flesh to the soul, we may gather that the inferior powers were subjected to the soul through grace existing therein.

Reply Obj. 1: The Apostle in these words means to show that there is a spiritual body, if there is an animal body, inasmuch as the spiritual life of the body began in Christ, who is "the firstborn of the dead," as the body's animal life began in Adam. From the Apostle's words, therefore, we cannot gather that Adam had no spiritual life in his soul; but that he had not spiritual life as regards the body.

Reply Obj. 2: As Augustine says in the same passage, it is not disputed that Adam, like other just souls, was in some degree gifted with the Holy Ghost; but "he did not possess the Holy Ghost, as the faithful possess Him now," who are admitted to eternal happiness directly after death.

Reply Obj. 3: This passage from Augustine does not assert that angels or men were created with natural free-will before they possessed grace; but that God shows first what their free-will could do before being confirmed in grace, and what they acquired afterwards by being so confirmed.

Reply Obj. 4: The Master here speaks according to the opinion of those who held that man was not created in grace, but only in a state of nature. We may also say that, though man was created in grace, yet it was not by virtue of the nature wherein he was created that he could advance by merit, but by virtue of the grace which was added.

Reply Obj. 5: As the motion of the will is not continuous there is nothing against the first man having consented to grace even in the first moment of his existence.

Reply Obj. 6: We merit glory by an act of grace; but we do not merit grace by an act of nature; hence the comparison fails.

SECOND ARTICLE [I, Q. 95, Art. 2]

Whether Passions Existed in the Soul of the First Man?

Objection 1: It would seem that the first man's soul had no passions. For by the passions of the soul "the flesh lusteth against the spirit" (Gal. 5:7). But this did not happen in the state of innocence. Therefore in the state of innocence there were no passions of the soul.

Obj. 2: Further, Adam's soul was nobler than his body. But his body was impassible. Therefore no passions were in his soul.

Obj. 3: Further, the passions of the soul are restrained by the moral virtues. But in Adam the moral virtues were perfect. Therefore the passions were entirely excluded from him.

*On the contrary,* Augustine says (De Civ. Dei xiv, 10) that "in our first parents there was undisturbed love of God," and other passions of the soul.

*I answer that,* The passions of the soul are in the sensual appetite, the object of which is good and evil. Wherefore some passions of the soul are directed to what is good, as love and joy; others to what is evil, as fear and sorrow. And since in the primitive state, evil was neither present nor imminent, nor was any good wanting which a good-will could desire to have then, as Augustine says (De Civ. Dei xiv, 10), therefore Adam had no passion with evil as its object; such as fear, sorrow, and the like; neither had he passions in respect of good not possessed, but to be possessed then, as burning concupiscence. But those passions which regard present good, as joy and love; or which regard future good to be had at the proper time, as desire and hope that casteth not down, existed in the state of innocence; otherwise, however, than as they exist in ourselves. For our sensual appetite, wherein the passions reside, is not entirely subject to reason; hence at times our passions forestall and hinder reason's judgment; at other times they follow reason's judgment, accordingly as the sensual appetite obeys reason to some extent. But in the state of innocence the inferior appetite was wholly subject to reason: so that in that state the passions of the soul existed only as consequent upon the judgment of reason.

Reply Obj. 1: The flesh lusts against the spirit by the rebellion of the passions against reason; which could not occur in the state of innocence.

Reply Obj. 2: The human body was impassible in the state of innocence as regards the passions which alter the disposition of nature, as will be explained later on (Q. 97, A. 2); likewise the soul was impassible as regards the passions which impede the free use of reason.

Reply Obj. 3: Perfection of moral virtue does not wholly take away the passions, but regulates them; for the temperate man desires as he ought to desire, and what he ought to desire, as stated in *Ethic.* iii, 11.

THIRD ARTICLE [I, Q. 95, Art. 3]

Whether Adam Had All the Virtues?

Objection 1: It would seem that Adam had not all the virtues. For some virtues are directed to curb passions: thus immoderate concupiscence is restrained by temperance, and immoderate fear by fortitude. But in the state of innocence no immoderation existed in the passions. Therefore neither did these virtues then exist.

Obj. 2: Further, some virtues are concerned with the passions which have evil as their object; as meekness with anger; fortitude with fear. But these passions did not exist in the state of innocence, as stated above (A. 2). Therefore neither did those virtues exist then.

Obj. 3: Further, penance is a virtue that regards sin committed. Mercy, too, is a virtue concerned with unhappiness. But in the state of innocence neither sin nor unhappiness existed. Therefore neither did those virtues exist.

Obj. 4: Further, perseverance is a virtue. But Adam possessed it not; as proved by his subsequent sin. Therefore he possessed not every virtue.

Obj. 5: Further, faith is a virtue. But it did not exist in the state of innocence; for it implies an obscurity of knowledge which seems to be incompatible with the perfection of the primitive state.

*On the contrary,* Augustine says, in a homily (Serm. contra Judaeos): "The prince of sin overcame Adam who was made from the slime of the earth to the image of God, adorned with modesty, restrained by temperance, refulgent with brightness."

*I answer that,* in the state of innocence man in a certain sense possessed all the virtues; and this can be proved from what precedes. For it was shown above (A. 1) that such was the rectitude of the primitive state, that reason was subject to God, and the lower powers to reason. Now the virtues are nothing but those perfections whereby reason is directed to God, and the inferior powers regulated according to the dictate of reason, as will be explained in the Treatise on the Virtues (I-II, Q. 63, A. 2). Wherefore the rectitude of the primitive state required that man should in a sense possess every virtue.

It must, however, be noted that some virtues of their very nature do not involve imperfection, such as charity and justice; and these virtues did exist in the primitive state absolutely, both in habit and in act. But other virtues are of such a nature as to imply imperfection either in their act, or on the part of the matter. If such imperfection be consistent with the perfection of the primitive state, such virtues necessarily existed in that state; as faith, which is of things not seen, and hope which is of things not yet possessed. For the perfection of that state did not extend to the vision of the Divine Essence, and the possession of God with the enjoyment of final beatitude. Hence faith and hope could exist in the primitive state, both as to habit and as to act. But any virtue which implies imperfection incompatible with the perfection of the primitive state, could exist in that state as a habit, but not as to the act; for instance, penance, which is sorrow for sin committed; and mercy, which is sorrow for others' unhappiness; because sorrow, guilt, and unhappiness are incompatible with the perfection of the primitive state. Wherefore such virtues existed as habits in the first man, but not as to their acts; for he was so disposed that he would repent, if there had been a sin to repent for; and had he seen unhappiness in his neighbor, he would have done his best to remedy it. This is in accordance with what the Philosopher says, "Shame, which regards what is ill done, may be found in a virtuous man, but only conditionally; as being so disposed that he would be ashamed if he did wrong" (Ethic. iv, 9).

Reply Obj. 1: It is accidental to temperance and fortitude to subdue superabundant passion, in so far as they are in a subject which happens to have superabundant passions, and yet those virtues are *per se* competent to moderate the passions.

Reply Obj. 2: Passions which have evil for their object were incompatible with the perfection of the primitive state, if that evil be in the one affected by the passion; such as fear and sorrow. But passions which relate to evil in another are not incompatible with the perfection of the primitive state; for in that state man could hate the demons' malice, as he could love God's goodness. Thus the virtues which relate to such passions could exist in the primitive state, in habit and in act. Virtues, however, relating to passions which regard evil in the same subject, if relating to such passions only, could not exist in the primitive state in act, but only in habit, as we have said above of penance and of mercy. But other virtues there are which have relation not to such passions only, but to others; such as temperance, which relates not only to sorrow, but also to joy; and fortitude, which relates not only to fear, but also to daring and hope. Thus the act of temperance could exist in the primitive state, so far as it moderates pleasure; and in like manner, fortitude, as moderating daring and hope, but not as moderating sorrow and fear.

Reply Obj. 3: appears from what has been said above.

Reply Obj. 4: Perseverance may be taken in two ways: in one sense as a particular virtue, signifying a habit whereby a man makes a choice of persevering in good; in that sense Adam possessed perseverance. In another sense it is taken as a circumstance of virtue; signifying a certain uninterrupted continuation of virtue; in which sense Adam did not possess perseverance.

Reply Obj. 5: appears from what has been said above.

FOURTH ARTICLE [I, Q. 95, Art. 4]

Whether the Actions of the First Man Were Less Meritorious Than Ours Are?

Objection 1: It would seem that the actions of the first man were less meritorious than ours are. For grace is given to us through the mercy of God, Who succors most those who are most in need. Now we are more in need of grace than was man in the state of innocence. Therefore grace is more copiously poured out upon us; and since grace is the source of merit, our actions are more meritorious.

Obj. 2: Further, struggle and difficulty are required for merit; for it is written (2 Tim. 2:5): "He ... is not crowned except he strive lawfully" and the Philosopher says (Ethic. ii, 3): "The object of virtue is the difficult and the good." But there is more strife and difficulty now. Therefore there is greater efficacy for merit.

Obj. 3: Further, the Master says (Sent. ii., D, xxiv) that "man would not have merited in resisting temptation; whereas he does merit now, when he resists." Therefore our actions are more meritorious than in the primitive state.

*On the contrary,* if such were the case, man would be better off after sinning.

*I answer that,* Merit as regards degree may be gauged in two ways. First, in its root, which is grace and charity. Merit thus measured corresponds in degree to the essential reward, which consists in the enjoyment of God; for the greater the charity whence our actions proceed, the more perfectly shall we enjoy God. Secondly, the degree of merit is measured by the degree of the action itself. This degree is of two kinds, absolute and proportional. The widow who put two mites into the treasury performed a deed of absolutely less degree than the others who put great sums therein. But in proportionate degree the widow gave more, as Our Lord said; because she gave more in proportion to her means. In each of these cases the degree of merit corresponds to the accidental reward, which consists in rejoicing for created good.

We conclude therefore that in the state of innocence man's works were more meritorious than after sin was committed, if we consider the degree of merit on the part of grace, which would have been more copious as meeting with no obstacle in hu man nature: and in like manner, if we consider the absolute degree of the work done; because, as man would have had greater virtue, he would have performed greater works. But if we consider the proportionate degree, a greater reason for merit exists after sin, on account of man's weakness; because a small deed is more beyond the capacity of one who works with difficulty than a great deed is beyond one who performs it easily.

Reply Obj. 1: After sin man requires grace for more things than before sin; but he does not need grace more; forasmuch as man even before sin required grace to obtain eternal life, which is the chief reason for the need of grace. But after sin man required grace also for the remission of sin, and for the support of his weakness.

Reply Obj. 2: Difficulty and struggle belong to the degree of merit according to the proportionate degree of the work done, as above explained. It is also a sign of the will's promptitude striving after what is difficult to itself: and the promptitude of the will is caused by the intensity of charity. Yet it may happen that a person performs an easy deed with as prompt a will as another performs an arduous deed; because he is ready to do even what may be difficult to him. But the actual difficulty, by its penal character, enables the deed to satisfy for sin.

Reply Obj. 3: The first man would not have gained merit in resisting temptation, according to the opinion of those who say that he did not possess grace; even as now there is no merit to those who have not grace. But in this point there is a difference, inasmuch as in the primitive state there was no interior impulse to evil, as in our present state. Hence man was more able then than now to resist temptation even without grace.

## QUESTION 96

OF THE MASTERSHIP BELONGING TO MAN IN THE STATE OF INNOCENCE (In Four Articles)

We next consider the mastership which belonged to man in the state of innocence. Under this head there are four points of inquiry:

(1) Whether man in the state of innocence was master over the animals?

(2) Whether he was master over all creatures?

(3) Whether in the state of innocence all men were equal?

(4) Whether in that state man would have been master over men?

FIRST ARTICLE [I, Q. 96, Art. 1]

Whether Adam in the State of Innocence Had Mastership Over the Animals?

Objection 1: It would seem that in the state of innocence Adam had no mastership over the animals. For Augustine says (Gen. ad lit. ix, 14), that the animals were brought to Adam, under the direction of the angels, to receive their names from him. But the angels need not have intervened thus, if man himself were master over the animals. Therefore in the state of innocence man had no mastership of the animals.

Obj. 2: Further, it is unfitting that elements hostile to one another should be brought under the mastership of one. But many animals are hostile to one another, as the sheep and the wolf. Therefore all animals were not brought under the mastership of man.

Obj. 3: Further, Jerome says [*The words quoted are not in St. Jerome's works. St. Thomas may have had in mind Bede, Hexaem., as quoted in the Glossa ordinaria on Gen. 1:26]: "God gave man mastership over the animals, although before sin he had no need of them: for God foresaw that after sin animals would become useful to man." Therefore, at least before sin, it was unfitting for man to make use of his mastership.

Obj. 4: Further, it is proper to a master to command. But a command is not given rightly save to a rational being. Therefore man had no mastership over the irrational animals.

*On the contrary,* It is written (Gen. 1:26): "Let him have dominion over the fishes of the sea, and the birds of the air, and the beasts of the earth" [Vulg."and the whole earth"].

*I answer that,* As above stated (Q. 95, A. 1) for his disobedience to God, man was punished by the disobedience of those creatures which should be subject to him. Therefore in the state of innocence, before man had disobeyed, nothing disobeyed him that was naturally subject to him. Now all animals are naturally subject to man. This can be proved in three ways. First, from the order observed by nature; for just as in the generation of things we perceive a certain order of procession of the perfect from the imperfect (thus matter is for the sake of form; and the imperfect form, for the sake of the perfect), so also is there order in the use of natural things; thus the imperfect are for the use of the perfect; as the plants make use of the earth for their nourishment, and animals make use of plants, and man makes use of both plants and animals. Therefore it is in keeping with the order of nature, that man should be master over animals. Hence the Philosopher says (Polit. i, 5) that the hunting of wild animals is just and natural, because man thereby exercises a natural right. Secondly, this is proved by the order of Divine Providence which always governs inferior things by the superior. Wherefore, as man, being made to the image of God, is above other animals, these are rightly subject to his government. Thirdly, this is proved from a property of man and of other animals. For we see in the latter a certain participated prudence of natural instinct, in regard to certain particular acts; whereas man possesses a universal prudence as regards all practical matters. Now whatever is participated is subject to what is essential and universal. Therefore the subjection of other animals to man is proved to be natural.

Reply Obj. 1: A higher power can do many things that an inferior power cannot do to those which are subject to them. Now an angel is naturally higher than man. Therefore certain things in regard to animals could be done by angels, which could not be done by man; for instance, the rapid gathering together of all the animals.

Reply Obj. 2: In the opinion of some, those animals which now are fierce and kill others, would, in that state, have been tame, not only in regard to man, but also in regard to other animals. But this is quite unreasonable. For the nature of animals was not changed by man's sin, as if those whose nature now it is to devour the flesh of others, would then have lived on herbs, as the lion and falcon. Nor does Bede's gloss on Gen. 1:30, say that trees and herbs were given as food to all animals and birds, but to some. Thus there would have been a natural antipathy between some animals. They would not, however, on this account have been excepted from the mastership of man: as neither at present are they for that reason excepted from the mastership of God, Whose Providence has ordained all this. Of this Providence man would have been the executor, as appears even now in regard to domestic animals, since fowls are given by men as food to the trained falcon.

Reply Obj. 3: In the state of innocence man would not have had any bodily need of animals—neither for clothing, since then they were naked and not ashamed, there being no inordinate motions of concupiscence—nor for food, since they fed on the trees of paradise—nor to carry him about, his body being strong enough for that purpose. But man needed animals in order to have experimental knowledge of their natures. This is signified by the fact that God led the animals to man, that he might give them names expressive of their respective natures.

Reply Obj. 4: All animals by their natural instinct have a certain participation of prudence and reason: which accounts for the fact that cranes follow their leader, and bees obey their queen. So all animals would have obeyed man of their own accord, as in the present state some domestic animals obey him.

SECOND ARTICLE [I, Q. 96, Art. 2]

Whether Man Had Mastership Over All Other Creatures?

Objection 1: It would seem that in the state of innocence man would not have had mastership over all other creatures. For an angel naturally has a greater power than man. But, as Augustine says (De Trin. iii, 8), "corporeal matter would not have obeyed even the holy angels." Much less therefore would it have obeyed man in the state of innocence.

Obj. 2: Further, the only powers of the soul existing in plants are nutritive, augmentative, and generative. Now these do not naturally obey reason; as we can see in the case of any one man. Therefore, since it is by his reason that man is competent to have mastership, it seems that in the state of innocence man had no dominion over plants.

Obj. 3: Further, whosoever is master of a thing, can change it. But man could not have changed the course of the heavenly bodies; for this belongs to God alone, as Dionysius says (Ep. ad Polycarp. vii). Therefore man had no dominion over them.

*On the contrary,* It is written (Gen. 1:26): "That he may have dominion over ... every creature."

*I answer that,* Man in a certain sense contains all things; and so according as he is master of what is within himself, in the same way he can have mastership over other things. Now we may consider four things in man: his *reason,* which makes him like to the angels; his *sensitive powers,* whereby he is like the animals; his natural forces,*which liken him to the plants; and*the body itself, wherein he is like to inanimate things. Now in man reason has the position of a master and not of a subject. Wherefore man had no mastership over the angels in the primitive state; so when we read "all creatures," we must understand the creatures which are not made to God's image. Over the sensitive powers, as the irascible and concupiscible, which obey reason in some degree, the soul has mastership by commanding. So in the state of innocence man had mastership over the animals by commanding them. But of the natural powers and the body itself man is master not by commanding, but by using them. Thus also in the state of innocence man's mastership over plants and inanimate things consisted not in commanding or in changing them, but in making use of them without hindrance.

The answers to the objections appear from the above.

THIRD ARTICLE [I, Q. 96, Art. 3]

Whether Men Were Equal in the State of Innocence?

Objection 1: It would seem that in the state of innocence all would have been equal. For Gregory says (Moral. xxi): "Where there is no sin, there is no inequality." But in the state of innocence there was no sin. Therefore all were equal.

Obj. 2: Further, likeness and equality are the basis of mutual love, according to Ecclus. 13:19, "Every beast loveth its like; so also every man him that is nearest to himself." Now in that state there was among men an abundance of love, which is the bond of peace. Therefore all were equal in the state of innocence.

Obj. 3: Further, the cause ceasing, the effect also ceases. But the cause of present inequality among men seems to arise, on the part of God, from the fact that He rewards some and punishes others; and on the part of nature, from the fact that some, through a defect of nature, are born weak and deficient, others strong and perfect, which would not have been the case in the primitive state. Therefore, etc.

*On the contrary,* It is written (Rom. 13:1): "The things which are of God, are well ordered" [Vulg."-Those that are, are ordained of God"]. But order chiefly consists in inequality; for Augustine says (De Civ. Dei xix, 13): "Order disposes things equal and unequal in their proper place." Therefore in the primitive state, which was most proper and orderly, inequality would have existed.

*I answer that,* We must needs admit that in the primitive state there would have been some inequality, at least as regards sex, because generation depends upon diversity of sex: and likewise as regards age; for some would have been born of others; nor would sexual union have been sterile.

Moreover, as regards the soul, there would have been inequality as to righteousness and knowledge. For man worked not of necessity, but of his own free-will, by virtue of which man can apply himself, more or less, to action, desire, or knowledge; hence some would have made a greater advance in virtue and knowledge than others.

There might also have been bodily disparity. For the human body was not entirely exempt from the laws of nature, so as not to receive from exterior sources more or less advantage and help: since indeed it was dependent on food wherewith to sustain life.

So we may say that, according to the climate, or the movement of the stars, some would have been born more robust in body than others, and also greater, and more beautiful, and all ways better disposed; so that, however, in those who were thus surpassed, there would have been no defect or fault either in soul or body.

Reply Obj. 1: By those words Gregory means to exclude such inequality as exists between virtue and vice; the result of which is that some are placed in subjection to others as a penalty.

Reply Obj. 2: Equality is the cause of equality in mutual love. Yet between those who are unequal there can be a greater love than between equals; although there be not an equal response: for a father naturally loves his son more than a brother loves his brother; although the son does not love his father as much as he is loved by him.

Reply Obj. 3: The cause of inequality could be on the part of God; not indeed that He would punish some and reward others, but that He would exalt some above others; so that the beauty of order would the more shine forth among men. Inequality might also arise on the part of nature as above described, without any defect of nature.

FOURTH ARTICLE [I, Q. 96, Art. 4]

Whether in the State of Innocence Man Would Have Been Master Over Man?

Objection 1: It would seem that in the state of innocence man would not have been master over man. For Augustine says (De Civ. Dei xix, 15): "God willed that man, who was endowed with reason and made to His image, should rule over none but irrational creatures; not over men, but over cattle."

Obj. 2: Further, what came into the world as a penalty for sin would not have existed in the state of innocence. But man was made subject to man as a penalty; for after sin it was said to the woman (Gen. 3:16): "Thou shalt be under thy husband's power." Therefore in the state of innocence man would not have been subject to man.

Obj. 3: Further, subjection is opposed to liberty. But liberty is one of the chief blessings, and would not have been lacking in the state of innocence, "where nothing was wanting that man's good-will could desire," as Augustine says (De Civ. Dei xiv, 10). Therefore man would not have been master over man in the state of innocence.

*On the contrary,* The condition of man in the state of innocence was not more exalted than the condition of the angels. But among the angels some rule over others; and so one order is called that of "Dominations." Therefore it was not beneath the dignity of the state of innocence that one man should be subject to another.

*I answer that,* Mastership has a twofold meaning. First, as opposed to slavery, in which sense a master means one to whom another is subject as a slave. In another sense mastership is referred in a general sense to any kind of subject; and in this sense even he who has the office of governing and directing free men, can be called a master. In the state of innocence man could have been a master of men, not in the former but in the latter sense. This distinction is founded on the reason that a slave differs from a free man in that the latter has the disposal of himself, as is stated in the beginning of the *Metaphysics,* whereas a slave is ordered to another. So that one man is master of another as his slave when he refers the one whose master he is, to his own—namely the master's use. And since every man's proper good is desirable to himself, and consequently it is a grievous matter to anyone to yield to another what ought to be one's own, therefore such dominion implies of necessity a pain inflicted on the subject; and consequently in the state of innocence such a mastership could not have existed between man and man.

But a man is the master of a free subject, by directing him either towards his proper welfare, or to the common good. Such a kind of mastership would have existed in the state of innocence between man and man, for two reasons. First, because man is naturally a social being, and so in the state of innocence he would have led a social life. Now a social life cannot exist among a number of people unless under the presidency of one to look after the common good; for many, as such, seek many things, whereas one attends only to one. Wherefore the Philosopher says, in the beginning of the *Politics,* that wherever many things are directed to one, we shall always find one at the head directing them. Secondly, if one man surpassed another in knowledge and virtue, this would not have been fitting unless these gifts conduced to the benefit of others, according to 1 Pet. 4:10, "As every man hath received grace, ministering the same one to another." Wherefore Augustine says (De Civ. Dei xix, 14): "Just men command not by the love of domineering, but by the service of counsel": and (De Civ. Dei xix, 15): "The natural order of things requires this; and thus did God make man."

From this appear the replies to the objections which are founded on the first-mentioned mode of mastership.

# QUESTION 97

OF THE PRESERVATION OF THE INDIVIDUAL IN THE PRIMITIVE STATE (In Four Articles)

We next consider what belongs to the bodily state of the first man: first, as regards the preservation of the individual; secondly, as regards the preservation of the species.

Under the first head there are four points of inquiry:

(1) Whether man in the state of innocence was immortal?

(2) Whether he was impassible?

(3) Whether he stood in need of food?

(4) Whether he would have obtained immortality by the tree of life?

FIRST ARTICLE [I, Q. 97, Art. 1]

Whether in the State of Innocence Man Would Have Been Immortal?

Objection 1: It would seem that in the state of innocence man was not immortal. For the term "mortal" belongs to the definition of man. But if you take away the definition, you take away the thing defined. Therefore as long as man was man he could not be immortal.

Obj. 2: Further, corruptible and incorruptible are generically distinct, as the Philosopher says (Metaph. x, Did. ix, 10). But there can be no passing from one genus to another. Therefore if the first man was incorruptible, man could not be corruptible in the present state.

Obj. 3: Further, if man were immortal in the state of innocence, this would have been due either to nature or to grace. Not to nature, for since nature does not change within the same species, he would also have been immortal now. Likewise neither would this be owing to grace; for the first man recovered grace by repentance, according to Wis. 10:2: "He brought him out of his sins." Hence he would have regained his immortality; which is clearly not the case. Therefore man was not immortal in the state of innocence.

Obj. 4: Further, immortality is promised to man as a reward, according to Apoc. 21:4: "Death shall be no more." But man was not created in the state of reward, but that he might deserve the reward. Therefore man was not immortal in the state of innocence.

*On the contrary,* It is written (Rom. 5:12): "By sin death came into the world." Therefore man was immortal before sin.

*I answer that,* A thing may be incorruptible in three ways. First, on the part of matter—that is to say, either because it possesses no matter, like an angel; or because it possesses matter that is in potentiality to one form only, like the heavenly bodies. Such things as these are incorruptible by their very nature. Secondly, a thing is incorruptible in its form, inasmuch as being by nature corruptible, yet it has an inherent disposition which preserves it wholly from corruption; and this is called incorruptibility of glory; because as Augustine says (Ep. ad Dioscor.): "God made man's soul of such a powerful nature, that from its fulness of beatitude, there redounds to the body a fulness of health, with the vigor of incorruption." Thirdly, a thing may be incorruptible on the part of its efficient cause; in this sense man was incorruptible and immortal in the state of innocence. For, as Augustine says (QQ. Vet. et Nov. Test. qu. 19 [*Work of an anonymous author], among the supposititious works of St. Augustine): "God made man immortal as long as he did not sin; so that he might achieve for himself life or death." For man's body was indissoluble not by reason of any intrinsic vigor of immortality, but by reason of a supernatural force given by God to the soul, whereby it was enabled to preserve the body from all corruption so long as it remained itself subject to God. This entirely agrees with reason; for since the rational soul surpasses the capacity of corporeal matter, as above explained (Q. 76, A. 1), it was most properly endowed at the beginning with the power of preserving the body in a manner surpassing the capacity of corporeal matter.

Reply Obj. 1 and 2: These objections are founded on natural incorruptibility and immortality.

Reply Obj. 3: This power of preserving the body was not natural to the soul, but was the gift of grace. And though man recovered grace as regards remission of guilt and the merit of glory; yet he did not recover immortality, the loss of which was an effect of sin; for this was reserved for Christ to accomplish, by Whom the defect of nature was to be restored into something better, as we shall explain further on (III, Q. 14, A. 4, ad 1).

Reply Obj. 4: The promised reward of the immortality of glory differs from the immortality which was bestowed on man in the state of innocence.

SECOND ARTICLE [I, Q. 97, Art. 2]

Whether in the State of Innocence Man Would Have Been Passible?

Objection 1: It would seem that in the state of innocence man was passible. For "sensation is a kind of passion." But in the state of innocence man would have been sensitive. Therefore he would have been passible.

Obj. 2: Further, sleep is a kind of passion. Now, man slept in the state of innocence, according to Gen. 2:21, "God cast a deep sleep upon Adam." Therefore he would have been passible.

Obj. 3: Further, the same passage goes on to say that "He took a rib out of Adam." Therefore he was passible even to the degree of the cutting out of part of his body.

Obj. 4: Further, man's body was soft. But a soft body is naturally passible as regards a hard body; therefore if a hard body had come in contact with the soft body of the first man, the latter would have suffered from the impact. Therefore the first man was passible.

*On the contrary,* Had man been passible, he would have been also corruptible, because, as the Philosopher says (Top. vi, 3): "Excessive suffering wastes the very substance."

*I answer that,* "Passion" may be taken in two senses. First, in its proper sense, and thus a thing is said to suffer when changed from its natural disposition. For passion is the effect of action; and in nature contraries are mutually active or passive, according as one thing changes another from its natural disposition. Secondly, "passion" can be taken in a general sense for any kind of change, even if belonging to the perfecting process of nature. Thus understanding and sensation are said to be passions. In this second sense, man was passible in the state of innocence, and was passive both in soul and body. In the first sense, man was impassible, both in soul and body, as he was likewise immortal; for he could curb his passion, as he could avoid death, so long as he refrained from sin.

Thus it is clear how to reply to the first two objections; since sensation and sleep do not remove from man his natural disposition, but are ordered to his natural welfare.

Reply Obj. 3: As already explained (Q. 92, A. 3, ad 2), the rib was in Adam as the principle of the human race, as the semen in man, who is a principle through generation. Hence as man does not suffer any natural deterioration by seminal issue; so neither did he through the separation of the rib.

Reply Obj. 4: Man's body in the state of innocence could be preserved from suffering injury from a hard body; partly by the use of his reason, whereby he could avoid what was harmful; and partly also by Divine Providence, so preserving him, that nothing of a harmful nature could come upon him unawares.

THIRD ARTICLE [I, Q. 97, Art. 3]

Whether in the State of Innocence Man Had Need of Food?

Objection 1: It would seem that in the state of innocence man did not require food. For food is necessary for man to restore what he has lost. But Adam's body suffered no loss, as being incorruptible. Therefore he had no need of food.

Obj. 2: Further, food is needed for nourishment. But nourishment involves passibility. Since, then, man's body was impassible; it does not appear how food could be needful to him.

Obj. 3: Further, we need food for the preservation of life. But Adam could preserve his life otherwise; for had he not sinned, he would not have died. Therefore he did not require food.

Obj. 4: Further, the consumption of food involves voiding of the surplus, which seems unsuitable to the state of innocence. Therefore it seems that man did not take food in the primitive state.

*On the contrary,* It is written (Gen. 2:16): "Of every tree in paradise ye shall [Vulg. 'thou shalt'] eat."

*I answer that,* In the state of innocence man had an animal life requiring food; but after the resurrection he will have a spiritual life needing no food. In order to make this clear, we must observe that the rational soul is both soul and spirit. It is called a soul by reason of what it possesses in common with other souls—that is, as giving life to the body; whence it is written (Gen. 2:7): "Man was made into a living soul"; that is, a soul giving life to the body. But the soul is called a spirit according to what properly belongs to itself, and not to other souls, as possessing an intellectual immaterial power.

Thus in the primitive state, the rational soul communicated to the body what belonged to itself as a soul; and so the body was called "animal" [*From 'anima,' a soul; Cf. 1 Cor. 15:44 seqq.], through having its life from the soul. Now the first principle of life in these inferior creatures as the Philosopher says (De Anima ii, 4) is the vegetative soul: the operations of which are the use of food, generation, and growth. Wherefore such operations befitted man in the state of innocence. But in the final state, after the resurrection, the soul will, to a certain extent, communicate to the body what properly belongs to itself as a spirit; immortality to everyone, impassibility, glory, and power to the good, whose bodies will be called "spiritual." So, after the resurrection, man will not require food; whereas he required it in the state of innocence.

Reply Obj. 1: As Augustine says (QQ. Vet. et Nov. Test. qu. 19 [*Works of an anonymous author], among the supposititious works of St. Augustine): "How could man have an immortal body, which was sustained by food? Since an immortal being needs neither food nor drink." For we have explained (A. 1) that the immortality of the primitive state was based on a supernatural force in the soul, and not on any intrinsic disposition of the body: so that by the action of heat, the body might lose part of its humid qualities; and to prevent the entire consumption of the humor, man was obliged to take food.

Reply Obj. 2: A certain passion and alteration attends nutriment, on the part of the food changed into the substance of the thing nourished. So we cannot thence conclude that man's body was passible, but that the food taken was passible; although this kind of passion conduced to the perfection of the nature.

Reply Obj. 3: If man had not taken food he would have sinned; as he also sinned by taking the forbidden fruit. For he was told at the same time, to abstain from the tree of knowledge of good and evil, and to eat of every other tree of Paradise.

Reply Obj. 4: Some say that in the state of innocence man would not have taken more than necessary food, so that there would have been nothing superfluous; which, however, is unreasonable to suppose, as implying that there would have been no faecal matter. Wherefore there was need for voiding the surplus, yet so disposed by God as to be decorous and suitable to the state.

FOURTH ARTICLE [I, Q. 97, Art. 4]

Whether in the State of Innocence Man Would Have Acquired Immortality by the Tree of Life?

Objection 1: It would seem that the tree of life could not be the cause of immortality. For nothing can act beyond its own species; as an effect does not exceed its cause. But the tree of life was corruptible, otherwise it could not be taken as food; since food is changed into the substance of the thing nourished. Therefore the tree of life could not give incorruptibility or immortality.

Obj. 2: Further, effects caused by the forces of plants and other natural agencies are natural. If therefore the tree of life caused immortality, this would have been natural immortality.

Obj. 3: Further, this would seem to be reduced to the ancient fable, that the gods, by eating a certain food, became immortal; which the Philosopher ridicules (Metaph. iii, Did. ii, 4).

*On the contrary,* It is written (Gen. 3:22): "Lest perhaps he put forth his hand, and take of the tree of life, and eat, and live for ever." Further, Augustine says (QQ. Vet. et Nov. Test. qu. 19 [*Work of an anonymous author], among the supposititious works of St. Augustine): "A taste of the tree of life warded off corruption of the body; and even after sin man would have remained immortal, had he been allowed to eat of the tree of life."

*I answer that,* The tree of life in a certain degree was the cause of immortality, but not absolutely. To understand this, we must observe that in the primitive state man possessed, for the preservation of life, two remedies, against two defects. One of these defects was the lost of humidity by the action of natural heat, which acts as the soul's instrument: as a remedy against such loss man was provided with food, taken from the other trees of paradise, as now we are provided with the food, which we take for the same purpose. The second defect, as the Philosopher says (De Gener. i, 5), arises from the fact that the humor which is caused from extraneous sources, being added to the humor already existing, lessens the specific active power: as water added to wine takes at first the taste of wine, then, as more water is added, the strength of the wine is diminished, till the wine becomes watery. In like manner, we may observe that at first the active force of the species is so strong that it is able to transform so much of the food as is required to replace the lost tissue, as well as what suffices for growth; later on, however, the assimilated food does not suffice for growth, but only replaces what is lost. Last of all, in old age, it does not suffice even for this purpose; whereupon the body declines, and finally dies from natural causes. Against this defect man was provided with a remedy in the tree of life; for its effect was to strengthen the force of the species against the weakness resulting from the admixture of extraneous nutriment. Wherefore Augustine says (De Civ. Dei xiv, 26): "Man had food to appease his hunger, drink to slake his thirst; and the tree of life to banish the breaking up of old age"; and (QQ. Vet. et Nov. Test. qu. 19 [*Work of an anonymous author], among the supposititious works of St. Augustine) "The tree of life, like a drug, warded off all bodily corruption."

Yet it did not absolutely cause immortality; for neither was the soul's intrinsic power of preserving the body due to the tree of life, nor was it of such efficiency as to give the body a disposition to immortality, whereby it might become indissoluble; which is clear from the fact that every bodily power is finite; so the power of the tree of life could not go so far as to give the body the prerogative of living for an infinite time, but only for a definite time. For it is manifest that the greater a force is, the more durable is its effect; therefore, since the power of the tree of life was finite, man's life was to be preserved for a definite time by partaking of it once; and when that time had elapsed, man was to be either transferred to a spiritual life, or had need to eat once more of the tree of life.

From this the replies to the objections clearly appear. For the first proves that the tree of life did not absolutely cause immortality; while the others show that it caused incorruption by warding off corruption, according to the explanation above given.

## QUESTION 98

OF THE PRESERVATION OF THE SPECIES (In Two Articles)

We next consider what belongs to the preservation of the species; and, first, of generation; secondly, of the state of the offspring. Under the first head there are two points of inquiry:

(1) Whether in the state of innocence there would have been generation?

(2) Whether generation would have been through coition?

FIRST ARTICLE [Q. 98, Art. 1]

Whether in the State of Innocence Generation Existed?

Objection 1: It would seem there would have been no generation in the state of innocence. For, as stated in *Phys.* v, 5, "corruption is contrary to generation." But contraries affect the same subject: also there would have been no corruption in the state of innocence. Therefore neither would there have been generation.

Obj. 2: Further, the object of generation is the preservation in the species of that which is corruptible in the individual. Wherefore there is no generation in those individual things which last for ever. But in the state of innocence man would have lived for ever. Therefore in the state of innocence there would have been no generation.

Obj. 3: Further, by generation man is multiplied. But the multiplication of masters requires the division of property, to avoid confusion of mastership. Therefore, since man was made master of the animals, it would have been necessary to make a division of rights when the human race increased by generation. This is against the natural law, according to which all things are in common, as Isidore says (Etym. v, 4). Therefore there would have been no generation in the state of innocence.

*On the contrary,* It is written (Gen. 1:28): "Increase and multiply, and fill the earth." But this increase could not come about save by generation, since the original number of mankind was two only. Therefore there would have been generation in the state of innocence.

*I answer that,* In the state of innocence there would have been generation of offspring for the multiplication of the human race; otherwise man's sin would have been very necessary, for such a great blessing to be its result. We must, therefore, observe that man, by his nature, is established, as it were, midway between corruptible and incorruptible creatures, his soul being naturally incorruptible, while his body is naturally corruptible. We must also observe that nature's purpose appears to be different as regards corruptible and incorruptible things. For that seems to be the direct purpose of nature, which is invariable and perpetual; while what is only for a time is seemingly not the chief purpose of nature, but as it were, subordinate to something else; otherwise, when it ceased to exist, nature's purpose would become void.

Therefore, since in things corruptible none is everlasting and permanent except the species, it follows that the chief purpose of nature is the good of the species; for the preservation of which natural generation is ordained. On the other hand, incorruptible substances survive, not only in the species, but also in the individual; wherefore even the individuals are included in the chief purpose of nature.

Hence it belongs to man to beget offspring, on the part of the naturally corruptible body. But on the part of the soul, which is incorruptible, it is fitting that the multitude of individuals should be the direct purpose of nature, or rather of the Author of nature, Who alone is the Creator of the human soul. Wherefore, to provide for the multiplication of the human race, He established the begetting of offspring even in the state of innocence.

Reply Obj. 1: In the state of innocence the human body was in itself corruptible, but it could be preserved from corruption by the soul. Therefore, since generation belongs to things corruptible, man was not to be deprived thereof.

Reply Obj. 2: Although generation in the state of innocence might not have been required for the preservation of the species, yet it would have been required for the multiplication of the individual.

Reply Obj. 3: In our present state a division of possessions is necessary on account of the multiplicity of masters, inasmuch as community of possession is a source of strife, as the Philosopher says (Politic. ii, 5). In the state of innocence, however, the will of men would have been so ordered that without any danger of strife they would have used in common, according to each one's need, those things of which they were masters—a state of things to be observed even now among many good men.

SECOND ARTICLE [I, Q. 98, Art. 2]

Whether in the State of Innocence There Would Have Been Generation by Coition?

Objection 1: It would seem that generation by coition would not have existed in the state of innocence. For, as Damascene says (De Fide Orth. ii, 11; iv, 25), the first man in the terrestrial Paradise was "like an angel." But in the future state of the resurrection, when men will be like the angels, "they shall neither marry nor be married," as is written Matt. 22:30. Therefore neither in paradise would there have been generation by coition.

Obj. 2: Further, our first parents were created at the age of perfect development. Therefore, if generation by coition had existed before sin, they would have had intercourse while still in paradise: which was not the case according to Scripture (Gen. 4:1).

Obj. 3: Further, in carnal intercourse, more than at any other time, man becomes like the beasts, on account of the vehement delight which he takes therein; whence contingency is praiseworthy, whereby man refrains from such pleasures. But man is compared to beasts by reason of sin, according to Ps. 48:13: "Man, when he was in honor, did not understand; he is compared to senseless beasts, and is become like to them." Therefore, before sin, there would have been no such intercourse of man and woman.

Obj. 4: Further, in the state of innocence there would have been no corruption. But virginal integrity is corrupted by intercourse. Therefore there would have been no such thing in the state of innocence.

*On the contrary,* God made man and woman before sin (Gen. 1, 2). But nothing is void in God's works. Therefore, even if man had not sinned, there would have been such intercourse, to which the distinction of sex is ordained. Moreover, we are told that woman was made to be a help to man (Gen. 2:18, 20). But she is not fitted to help man except in generation, because another man would have proved a more effective help in anything else. Therefore there would have been such generation also in the state of innocence.

*I answer that,* Some of the earlier doctors, considering the nature of concupiscence as regards generation in our present state, concluded that in the state of innocence generation would not have been effected in the same way. Thus Gregory of Nyssa says (De Hom. Opif. xvii) that in paradise the human race would have been multiplied by some other means, as the angels were multiplied without coition by the operation of the Divine Power. He adds that God made man male and female before sin, because He foreknew the mode of generation which would take place after sin, which He foresaw. But this is unreasonable. For what is natural to man was neither acquired nor forfeited by sin. Now it is clear that generation by coition is natural to man by reason of his animal life, which he possessed even before sin, as above explained (Q. 97, A. 3), just as it is natural to other perfect animals, as the corporeal members make it clear. So we cannot allow that these members would not have had a natural use, as other members had, before sin.

Thus, as regards generation by coition, there are, in the present state of life, two things to be considered. One, which comes from nature, is the union of man and woman; for in every act of generation there is an active and a passive principle. Wherefore, since wherever there is distinction of sex, the active principle is male and the passive is female; the order of nature demands that for the purpose of generation there should be concurrence of male and female. The second thing to be observed is a certain deformity of excessive concupiscence, which in the state of innocence would not have existed, when the lower powers were entirely subject to reason. Wherefore Augustine says (De Civ. Dei xiv, 26): "We must be far from supposing that offspring could not be begotten without concupiscence. All the bodily members would have been equally moved by the will, without ardent or wanton incentive, with calmness of soul and body."

Reply Obj. 1: In paradise man would have been like an angel in his spirituality of mind, yet with an animal life in his body. After the resurrection man will be like an angel, spiritualized in soul and body. Wherefore there is no parallel.

Reply Obj. 2: As Augustine says (Gen. ad lit. ix, 4), our first parents did not come together in paradise, because on account of sin they were ejected from paradise shortly after the creation of the woman; or because, having received the general Divine command relative to generation, they awaited the special command relative to time.

Reply Obj. 3: Beasts are without reason. In this way man becomes, as it were, like them in coition, because he cannot moderate concupiscence. In the state of innocence nothing of this kind would have happened that was not regulated by reason, not because delight of sense was less, as some say (rather indeed would sensible delight have been the greater in proportion to the greater purity of nature and the greater sensibility of the body), but because the force of concupiscence would not have so inordinately thrown itself into such pleasure, being curbed by reason, whose place it is not to lessen sensual pleasure, but to prevent the force of concupiscence from cleaving to it immoderately. By "immoderately" I mean going beyond the bounds of reason, as a sober person does not take less pleasure in food taken in moderation than the glutton, but his concupiscence lingers less in such pleasures. This is what Augustine means by the words quoted, which do not exclude intensity of pleasure from the state of innocence, but ardor of desire and restlessness of the mind. Therefore continence would not have been praiseworthy in the state of innocence, whereas it is praiseworthy in our present state, not because it removes fecundity, but because it excludes inordinate desire. In that state fecundity would have been without lust.

Reply Obj. 4: As Augustine says (De Civ. Dei xiv, 26): In that state "intercourse would have been without prejudice to virginal integrity; this would have remained intact, as it does in the menses. And just as in giving birth the mother was then relieved, not by groans of pain, but by the instigations of maturity; so in conceiving, the union was one, not of lustful desire, but of deliberate action."

## QUESTION 99

OF THE CONDITION OF THE OFFSPRING AS TO THE BODY (In Two Articles)

We must now consider the condition of the offspring—first, as regards the body; secondly, as regards virtue; thirdly, in knowledge. Under the first head there are two points of inquiry:

(1) Whether in the state of innocence children would have had full powers of the body immediately after birth?

(2) Whether all infants would have been of the male sex?

FIRST ARTICLE [I, Q. 99, Art. 1]

Whether in the State of Innocence Children Would Have Had Perfect Strength of Body As to the Use of Its Members Immediately After Birth?

Objection 1: It would seem that in the state of innocence children would have had perfect strength of the body, as to the use of its members, immediately after birth. For Augustine says (De Pecc. Merit. et Remiss. i, 38): "This weakness of the body befits their weakness of mind." But in the state of innocence there would have been no weakness of mind. Therefore neither would there have been weakness of body in infants.

Obj. 2: Further, some animals at birth have sufficient strength to use their members. But man is nobler than other animals. Therefore much more is it natural to man to have strength to use his members at birth; and thus it appears to be a punishment of sin that he has not that strength.

Obj. 3: Further, inability to secure a proffered pleasure causes affliction. But if children had not full strength in the use of their limbs, they would often have been unable to procure something pleasurable offered to them; and so they would have been afflicted, which was not possible before sin. Therefore, in the state of innocence, children would not have been deprived of the use of their limbs.

Obj. 4: Further, the weakness of old age seems to correspond to that of infancy. But in the state of innocence there would have been no weakness of old age. Therefore neither would there have been such weakness in infancy.

*On the contrary,* Everything generated is first imperfect. But in the state of innocence children would have been begotten by generation. Therefore from the first they would have been imperfect in bodily size and power.

*I answer that,* By faith alone do we hold truths which are above nature, and what we believe rests on authority. Wherefore, in making any assertion, we must be guided by the nature of things, except in those things which are above nature, and are made known to us by Divine authority. Now it is clear that it is as natural as it is befitting to the principles of human nature that children should not have sufficient strength for the use of their limbs immediately after birth. Because in proportion to other animals man has naturally a larger brain. Wherefore it is natural, on account of the considerable humidity of the brain in children, that the nerves which are instruments of movement, should not be apt for moving the limbs. On the other hand, no Catholic doubts it possible for a child to have, by Divine power, the use of its limbs immediately after birth.

Now we have it on the authority of Scripture that "God made man right" (Eccles. 7:30), which rightness, as Augustine says (De Civ. Dei xiv, 11), consists in the perfect subjection of the body to the soul. As, therefore, in the primitive state it was impossible to find in the human limbs anything repugnant to man's well-ordered will, so was it impossible for those limbs to fail in executing the will's commands. Now the human will is well ordered when it tends to acts which are befitting to man. But the same acts are not befitting to man at every season of life. We must, therefore, conclude that children would not have had sufficient strength for the use of their limbs for the purpose of performing every kind of act; but only for the acts befitting the state of infancy, such as suckling, and the like.

Reply Obj. 1: Augustine is speaking of the weakness which we observe in children even as regards those acts which befit the state of infancy; as is clear from his preceding remark that "even when close to the breast, and longing for it, they are more apt to cry than to suckle."

Reply Obj. 2: The fact that some animals have the use of their limbs immediately after birth, is due, not to their superiority, since more perfect animals are not so endowed; but to the dryness of the brain, and to the operations proper to such animals being imperfect, so that a small amount of strength suffices them.

Reply Obj. 3 is clear from what we have said above. We may add that they would have desired nothing except with an ordinate will; and only what was befitting to their state of life.

Reply Obj. 4: In the state of innocence man would have been born, yet not subject to corruption. Therefore in that state there could have been certain infantile defects which result from birth; but not senile defects leading to corruption.

SECOND ARTICLE [I, Q. 99, Art. 2]

Whether, in the Primitive State, Women Would Have Been Born?

Objection 1: It would seem that in the primitive state woman would not have been born. For the Philosopher says (De Gener. Animal. ii, 3) that woman is a "misbegotten male," as though she were a product outside the purpose of nature. But in that state nothing would have been unnatural in human generation. Therefore in that state women would not have been born.

Obj. 2: Further, every agent produces its like, unless prevented by insufficient power or ineptness of matter: thus a small fire cannot burn green wood. But in generation the active force is in the male. Since, therefore, in the state of innocence man's active force was not subject to defect, nor was there inept matter on the part of the woman, it seems that males would always have been born.

Obj. 3: Further, in the state of innocence generation is ordered to the multiplication of the human race. But the race would have been sufficiently multiplied by the first man and woman, from the fact that they would have lived for ever. Therefore, in the state of innocence, there was no need for women to be born.

*On the contrary,* Nature's process in generation would have been in harmony with the manner in which it was established by God. But God established male and female in human nature, as it is written (Gen. 1, 2). Therefore also in the state of innocence male and female would have been born.

*I answer that,* Nothing belonging to the completeness of human nature would have been lacking in the state of innocence. And as different grades belong to the perfection of the universe, so also diversity of sex belongs to the perfection of human nature. Therefore in the state of innocence, both sexes would have been begotten.

Reply Obj. 1: Woman is said to be a "misbegotten male," as being a product outside the purpose of nature considered in the individual case: but not against the purpose of universal nature, as above explained (Q. 92, A. 1, ad 2).

Reply Obj. 2: The generation of woman is not occasioned either by a defect of the active force or by inept matter, as the objection proposes; but sometimes by an extrinsic accidental cause; thus the Philosopher says (De Animal. Histor. vi, 19): "The northern wind favors the generation of males, and the southern wind that of females": sometimes also by some impression in the soul (of the parents), which may easily have some effect on the body (of the child). Especially was this the case in the state of innocence, when the body was more subject to the soul; so that by the mere will of the parent the sex of the offspring might be diversified.

Reply Obj. 3: The offspring would have been begotten to an animal life, as to the use of food and generation. Hence it was fitting that all should generate, and not only the first parents. From this it seems to follow that males and females would have been in equal number.

## QUESTION 100

OF THE CONDITION OF THE OFFSPRING AS REGARDS RIGHTEOUSNESS (In Two Articles)

We now have to consider the condition of the offspring as to righteousness. Under this head there are two points of inquiry:

(1) Whether men would have been born in a state of righteousness?

(2) Whether they would have been born confirmed in righteousness?

FIRST ARTICLE [I, Q. 100, Art. 1]

Whether Men Would Have Been Born in a State of Righteousness?

Objection 1: It would seem that in the state of innocence men would not have been born in a state of righteousness. For Hugh of St. Victor says (De Sacram. i): "Before sin the first man would have begotten children sinless; but not heirs to their father's righteousness."

Obj. 2: Further, righteousness is effected by grace, as the Apostle says (Rom. 5:16, 21). Now grace is not transfused from one to another, for thus it would be natural; but is infused by God alone. Therefore children would not have been born righteous.

Obj. 3: Further, righteousness is in the soul. But the soul is not transmitted from the parent. Therefore neither would righteousness have been transmitted from parents, to the children.

*On the contrary,* Anselm says (De Concep. Virg. x): "As long as man did not sin, he would have begotten children endowed with righteousness together with the rational soul."

*I answer that,* Man naturally begets a specific likeness to himself. Hence whatever accidental qualities result from the nature of the species, must be alike in parent and child, unless nature fails in its operation, which would not have occurred in the state of innocence. But individual accidents do not necessarily exist alike in parent and child. Now original righteousness, in which the first man was created, was an accident pertaining to the nature of the species, not as caused by the principles of the species, but as a gift conferred by God on the entire human nature. This is clear from the fact that opposites are of the same genus; and original sin, which is opposed to original righteousness, is called the sin of nature, wherefore it is transmitted from the parent to the offspring; and for this reason also, the children would have been assimilated to their parents as regards original righteousness.

Reply Obj. 1: These words of Hugh are to be understood as referring, not to the habit of righteousness, but to the execution of the act thereof.

Reply Obj. 2: Some say that children would have been born, not with the righteousness of grace, which is the principle of merit, but with original righteousness. But since the root of original righteousness, which conferred righteousness on the first man when he was made, consists in the supernatural subjection of the reason to God, which subjection results from sanctifying grace, as above explained (Q. 95, A. 1), we must conclude that if children were born in original righteousness, they would also have been born in grace; thus we have said above that the first man was created in grace (Q. 95, A. 1). This grace, however, would not have been natural, for it would not have been transfused by virtue of the semen; but would have been conferred on man immediately on his receiving a rational soul. In the same way the rational soul, which is not transmitted by the parent, is infused by God as soon as the human body is apt to receive it.

From this the reply to the third objection is clear.

SECOND ARTICLE [I, Q. 100, Art. 2]

Whether in the State of Innocence Children Would Have Been Born Confirmed in Righteousness?

Objection 1: It would seem that in the state of innocence children would have been born confirmed in righteousness. For Gregory says (Moral. iv) on the words of Job 3:13: "For now I should have been asleep, etc.": "If no sinful corruption had infected our first parent, he would not have begotten 'children of hell'; no children would have been born of him but such as were destined to be saved by the Redeemer." Therefore all would have been born confirmed in righteousness.

Obj. 2: Further, Anselm says (Cur Deus Homo i, 18): "If our first parents had lived so as not to yield to temptation, they would have been confirmed in grace, so that with their offspring they would have been unable to sin any more." Therefore the children would have been born confirmed in righteousness.

Obj. 3: Further, good is stronger than evil. But by the sin of the first man there resulted, in those born of him, the necessity of sin. Therefore, if the first man had persevered in righteousness, his descendants would have derived from him the necessity of preserving righteousness.

Obj. 4: Further, the angels who remained faithful to God, while the others sinned, were at once confirmed in grace, so as to be unable henceforth to sin. In like manner, therefore, man would have been confirmed in grace if he had persevered. But he would have begotten children like himself. Therefore they also would have been born confirmed in righteousness.

*On the contrary,* Augustine says (De Civ. Dei xiv, 10): "Happy would have been the whole human race if neither they—that is our first parents—had committed any evil to be transmitted to their descendants, nor any of their race had committed any sin for which they would have been condemned." From which words we gather that even if our first parents had not sinned, any of their descendants might have done evil; and therefore they would not have been born confirmed in righteousness.

*I answer that,* It does not seem possible that in the state of innocence children would have been born confirmed in righteousness. For it is clear that at their birth they would not have had greater perfection than their parents at the time of begetting. Now the parents, as long as they begot children, would not have been confirmed in righteousness. For the rational creature is confirmed in righteousness through the beatitude given by the clear vision of God; and when once it has seen God, it cannot but cleave to Him Who is the essence of goodness, wherefrom no one can turn away, since nothing is desired or loved but under the aspect of good. I say this according to the general law; for it may be otherwise in the case of special privilege, such as we believe was granted to the Virgin Mother of God. And as soon as Adam had attained to that happy state of seeing God in His Essence, he would have become spiritual in soul and body; and his animal life would have ceased, wherein alone there is generation. Hence it is clear that children would not have been born confirmed in righteousness.

Reply Obj. 1: If Adam had not sinned, he would not have begotten "children of hell" in the sense that they would contract from him sin which is the cause of hell: yet by sinning of their own free-will they could have become "children of hell." If, however, they did not become "children of hell" by falling into sin, this would not have been owing to their being confirmed in righteousness, but to Divine Providence preserving them free from sin.

Reply Obj. 2: Anselm does not say this by way of assertion, but only as an opinion, which is clear from his mode of expression as follows: "It seems that if they had lived, etc."

Reply Obj. 3: This argument is not conclusive, though Anselm seems to have been influenced by it, as appears from his words above quoted. For the necessity of sin incurred by the descendants would not have been such that they could not return to righteousness, which is the case only with the damned. Wherefore neither would the parents have transmitted to their descendants the necessity of not sinning, which is only in the blessed.

Reply Obj. 4: There is no comparison between man and the angels; for man's free-will is changeable, both before and after choice; whereas the angel's is not changeable, as we have said above in treating of the angels (Q. 64, A. 2).

# QUESTION 101

OF THE CONDITION OF THE OFFSPRING AS REGARDS KNOWLEDGE (In Two Articles)

We next consider the condition of the offspring as to knowledge. Under this head there are two points of inquiry:

(1) Whether in the state of innocence children would have been born with perfect knowledge?

(2) Whether they would have had perfect use of reason at the moment of birth?

FIRST ARTICLE [I, Q. 101, Art. 1]

Whether in the State of Innocence Children Would Have Been Born with Perfect Knowledge?

Objection 1: It would seem that in the state of innocence children would have been born with perfect knowledge. For Adam would have begotten children like himself. But Adam was gifted with perfect knowledge (Q. 94, A. 3). Therefore children would have been born of him with perfect knowledge.

Obj. 2: Further, ignorance is a result of sin, as Bede says (Cf. I-II, Q. 85, A. 3). But ignorance is privation of knowledge. Therefore before sin children would have had perfect knowledge as soon as they were born.

Obj. 3: Further, children would have been gifted with righteousness from birth. But knowledge is required for righteousness, since it directs our actions. Therefore they would also have been gifted with knowledge.

*On the contrary,* The human soul is naturally "like a blank tablet on which nothing is written," as the Philosopher says (De Anima iii, 4). But the nature of the soul is the same now as it would have been in the state of innocence. Therefore the souls of children would have been without knowledge at birth.

*I answer that,* As above stated (Q. 99, A. 1), as regards belief in matters which are above nature, we rely on authority alone; and so, when authority is wanting, we must be guided by the ordinary course of nature. Now it is natural for man to acquire knowledge through the senses, as above explained (Q. 55, A. 2; Q. 84, A. 6); and for this reason is the soul united to the body, that it needs it for its proper operation; and this would not be so if the soul were endowed at birth with knowledge not acquired through the sensitive powers. We must conclude then, that, in the state of innocence, children would not have been born with perfect knowledge; but in course of time they would have acquired knowledge without difficulty by discovery or learning.

Reply Obj. 1: The perfection of knowledge was an individual accident of our first parent, so far as he was established as the father and instructor of the whole human race. Therefore he begot children like himself, not in that respect, but only in those accidents which were natural or conferred gratuitously on the whole nature.

Reply Obj. 2: Ignorance is privation of knowledge due at some particular time; and this would not have been in children from their birth, for they would have possessed the knowledge due to them at that time. Hence, no ignorance would have been in them, but only nescience in regard to certain matters. Such nescience was even in the holy angels, according to Dionysius (Coel. Hier. vii).

Reply Obj. 3: Children would have had sufficient knowledge to direct them to deeds of righteousness, in which men are guided by universal principles of right; and this knowledge of theirs would have been much more complete than what we have now by nature, as likewise their knowledge of other universal principles.

SECOND ARTICLE [I, Q. 101, Art. 2]

Whether Children Would Have Had Perfect Use of Reason at Birth?

Objection 1: It would seem that children would have had perfect use of reason at birth. For that children have not perfect use of reason in our present state, is due to the soul being weighed down by the body; which was not the case in paradise, because, as it is written, "The corruptible body is a load upon the soul" (Wis. 9:15). Therefore, before sin and the corruption which resulted therefrom, children would have had the perfect use of reason at birth.

Obj. 2: Further, some animals at birth have the use of their natural powers, as the lamb at once flees from the wolf. Much more, therefore, would men in the state of innocence have had perfect use of reason at birth.

*On the contrary,* In all things produced by generation nature proceeds from the imperfect to the perfect. Therefore children would not have had the perfect use of reason from the very outset.

*I answer that,* As above stated (Q. 84, A. 7), the use of reason depends in a certain manner on the use of the sensitive powers; wherefore, while the senses are tired and the interior sensitive powers hampered, man has not the perfect use of reason, as we see in those who are asleep or delirious. Now the sensitive powers are situate in corporeal organs; and therefore, so long as the latter are hindered, the action of the former is of necessity hindered also; and likewise, consequently, the use of reason. Now children are hindered in the use of these powers on account of the humidity of the brain; wherefore they have perfect use neither of these powers nor of reason. Therefore, in the state of innocence, children would not have had the perfect use of reason, which they would have enjoyed later on in life. Yet they would have had a more perfect use than they have now, as to matters regarding that particular state, as explained above regarding the use of their limbs (Q. 99, A. 1).

Reply Obj. 1: The corruptible body is a load upon the soul, because it hinders the use of reason even in those matters which belong to man at all ages.

Reply Obj. 2: Even other animals have not at birth such a perfect use of their natural powers as they have later on. This is clear from the fact that birds teach their young to fly; and the like may be observed in other animals. Moreover a special impediment exists in man from the humidity of the brain, as we have said above (Q. 99, A. 1).

# QUESTION 102

OF MAN'S ABODE, WHICH IS PARADISE (In Four Articles)

We next consider man's abode, which is paradise. Under this head there are four points of inquiry:

(1) Whether paradise is a corporeal place?

(2) Whether it is a place apt for human habitation?

(3) For what purpose was man placed in paradise?

(4) Whether he should have been created in paradise?

FIRST ARTICLE [I, Q. 102, Art. 1]

Whether Paradise Is a Corporeal Place?

Objection 1: It would seem that paradise is not a corporeal place. For Bede [*Strabus, Gloss on Gen. 2:8] says that "paradise reaches to the lunar circle." But no earthly place answers that description, both because it is contrary to the nature of the earth to be raised up so high, and because beneath the moon is the region of fire, which would consume the earth. Therefore paradise is not a corporeal place.

Obj. 2: Further, Scripture mentions four rivers as rising in paradise (Gen. 2:10). But the rivers there mentioned have visible sources elsewhere, as is clear from the Philosopher (Meteor. i). Therefore paradise is not a corporeal place.

Obj. 3: Further, although men have explored the entire habitable world, yet none have made mention of the place of paradise. Therefore apparently it is not a corporeal place.

Obj. 4: Further, the tree of life is described as growing in paradise. But the tree of life is a spiritual thing, for it is written of Wisdom that "She is a tree of life to them that lay hold on her" (Prov. 3:18). Therefore paradise also is not a corporeal, but a spiritual place.

Obj. 5: Further, if paradise be a corporeal place, the trees also of paradise must be corporeal. But it seems they were not; for corporeal trees were produced on the third day, while the planting of the trees of paradise is recorded after the work of the six days. Therefore paradise was not a corporeal place.

*On the contrary,* Augustine says (Gen. ad lit. viii, 1): "Three general opinions prevail about paradise. Some understand a place merely corporeal; others a place entirely spiritual; while others, whose opinion, I confess, pleases me, hold that paradise was both corporeal and spiritual."

*I answer that,* As Augustine says (De Civ. Dei xiii, 21): "Nothing prevents us from holding, within proper limits, a spiritual paradise; so long as we believe in the truth of the events narrated as having there occurred." For whatever Scripture tells us about paradise is set down as matter of history; and wherever Scripture makes use of this method, we must hold to the historical truth of the narrative as a foundation of whatever spiritual explanation we may offer. And so paradise, as Isidore says (Etym. xiv, 3), "is a place situated in the east, its name being the Greek for garden." It was fitting that it should be in the east; for it is to be believed that it was situated in the most excellent part of the earth. Now the east is the right hand on the heavens, as the Philosopher explains (De Coel. ii, 2); and the right hand is nobler than the left: hence it was fitting that God should place the earthly paradise in the east.

Reply Obj. 1: Bede's assertion is untrue, if taken in its obvious sense. It may, however, be explained to mean that paradise reaches to the moon, not literally, but figuratively; because, as Isidore says (Etym. xiv, 3), the atmosphere there is "a continually even temperature"; and in this respect it is like the heavenly bodies, which are devoid of opposing elements. Mention, however, is made of the moon rather than of other bodies, because, of all the heavenly bodies, the moon is nearest to us, and is, moreover, the most akin to the earth; hence it is observed to be overshadowed by clouds so as to be almost obscured. Others say that paradise reached to the moon—that is, to the middle space of the air, where rain, and wind, and the like arise; because the moon is said to have influence on such changes. But in this sense it would not be a fit place for human dwelling, through being uneven in temperature, and not attuned to the human temperament, as is the lower atmosphere in the neighborhood of the earth.

Reply Obj. 2: Augustine says (Gen. ad lit. viii, 7): "It is probable that man has no idea where paradise was, and that the rivers, whose sources are said to be known, flowed for some distance underground, and then sprang up elsewhere. For who is not aware that such is the case with some other streams?"

Reply Obj. 3: The situation of paradise is shut off from the habitable world by mountains, or seas, or some torrid region, which cannot be crossed; and so people who have written about topography make no mention of it.

Reply Obj. 4: The tree of life is a material tree, and so called because its fruit was endowed with a life-preserving power as above stated (Q. 97, A. 4). Yet it had a spiritual signification; as the rock in the desert was of a material nature, and yet signified Christ. In like manner the tree of the knowledge of good and evil was a material tree, so called in view of future events; because, after eating of it, man was to learn, by experience of the consequent punishment, the difference between the good of obedience and the evil of rebellion. It may also be said to signify spiritually the free-will as some say.

Reply Obj. 5: According to Augustine (Gen. ad lit. v, 5, viii, 3), the plants were not actually produced on the third day, but in their seminal virtues; whereas, after the work of the six days, the plants, both of paradise and others, were actually produced. According to other holy writers, we ought to say that all the plants were actually produced on the third day, including the trees of paradise; and what is said of the trees of paradise being planted after the work of the six days is to be understood, they say, by way of recapitulation. Whence our text reads: "The Lord God had planted a paradise of pleasure from the beginning" (Gen. 2:8).

SECOND ARTICLE [I, Q. 102, Art. 2]

Whether Paradise Was a Place Adapted to Be the Abode of Man?

Objection 1: It would seem that paradise was not a place adapted to be the abode of man. For man and angels are similarly ordered to beatitude. But the angels from the very beginning of their existence were made to dwell in the abode of the blessed—that is, the empyrean heaven. Therefore the place of man's habitation should have been there also.

Obj. 2: Further, if some definite place were required for man's abode, this would be required on the part either of the soul or of the body. If on the part of the soul, the place would be in heaven, which is adapted to the nature of the soul; since the desire of heaven is implanted in all. On the part of the body, there was no need for any other place than the one provided for other animals. Therefore paradise was not at all adapted to be the abode of man.

Obj. 3: Further, a place which contains nothing is useless. But after sin, paradise was not occupied by man. Therefore if it were adapted as a dwelling-place for man, it seems that God made paradise to no purpose.

Obj. 4: Further, since man is of an even temperament, a fitting place for him should be of even temperature. But paradise was not of an even temperature; for it is said to have been on the equator—a situation of extreme heat, since twice in the year the sun passes vertically over the heads of its inhabitants. Therefore paradise was not a fit dwelling-place for man.

*On the contrary,* Damascene says (De Fide Orth. ii, 11): "Paradise was a divinely ordered region, and worthy of him who was made to God's image."

*I answer that,* As above stated (Q. 97, A. 1), Man was incorruptible and immortal, not because his body had a disposition to incorruptibility, but because in his soul there was a power preserving the body from corruption. Now the human body may be corrupted from within or from without. From within, the body is corrupted by the consumption of the humors, and by old age, as above explained (Q. 97, A. 4), and man was able to ward off such corruption by food. Among those things which corrupt the body from without, the chief seems to be an atmosphere of unequal temperature; and to such corruption a remedy is found in an atmosphere of equable nature. In paradise both conditions were found; because, as Damascene says (De Fide Orth. ii, 11): "Paradise was permeated with the all pervading brightness of a temperate, pure, and exquisite atmosphere, and decked with ever-flowering plants." Whence it is clear that paradise was most fit to be a dwelling-place for man, and in keeping with his original state of immortality.

Reply Obj. 1: The empyrean heaven is the highest of corporeal places, and is outside the region of change. By the first of these two conditions, it is a fitting abode for the angelic nature: for, as Augustine says (De Trin. ii), "God rules corporeal creatures through spiritual creatures." Hence it is fitting that the spiritual nature should be established above the entire corporeal nature, as presiding over it. By the second condition, it is a fitting abode for the state of beatitude, which is endowed with the highest degree of stability. Thus the abode of beatitude was suited to the very nature of the angel; therefore he was created there. But it is not suited to man's nature, since man is not set as a ruler over the entire corporeal creation: it is a fitting abode for man in regard only to his beatitude. Wherefore he was not placed from the beginning in the empyrean heaven, but was destined to be transferred thither in the state of his final beatitude.

Reply Obj. 2: It is ridiculous to assert that any particular place is natural to the soul or to any spiritual substances, though some particular place may have a certain fitness in regard to spiritual substances. For the earthly paradise was a place adapted to man, as regards both his body and his soul—that is, inasmuch as in his soul was the force which preserved the human body from corruption. This could not be said of the other animals. Therefore, as Damascene says (De Fide Orth. ii, 11): "No irrational animal inhabited paradise"; although, by a certain dispensation, the animals were brought thither by God to Adam; and the serpent was able to trespass therein by the complicity of the devil.

Reply Obj. 3: Paradise did not become useless through being unoccupied by man after sin, just as immortality was not conferred on man in vain, though he was to lose it. For thereby we learn God's kindness to man, and what man lost by sin. Moreover, some say that Enoch and Elias still dwell in that paradise.

Reply Obj. 4: Those who say that paradise was on the equinoctial line are of opinion that such a situation is most temperate, on account of the unvarying equality of day and night; that it is never too cold there, because the sun is never too far off; and never too hot, because, although the sun passes over the heads of the inhabitants, it does not remain long in that position. However, Aristotle distinctly says (Meteor. ii, 5) that such a region is uninhabitable on account of the heat. This seems to be more probable; because, even those regions where the sun does not pass vertically overhead, are extremely hot on account of the mere proximity of the sun. But whatever be the truth of the matter, we must hold that paradise was situated in a most temperate situation, whether on the equator or elsewhere.

THIRD ARTICLE [I, Q. 102, Art. 3]

Whether Man Was Placed in Paradise to Dress It and Keep It?

Objection 1: It would seem that man was not placed in paradise to dress and keep it. For what was brought on him as a punishment of sin would not have existed in paradise in the state of innocence. But the cultivation of the soil was a punishment of sin (Gen. 3:17). Therefore man was not placed in paradise to dress and keep it.

Obj. 2: Further, there is no need of a keeper when there is no fear of trespass with violence. But in paradise there was no fear of trespass with violence. Therefore there was no need for man to keep paradise.

Obj. 3: Further, if man was placed in paradise to dress and keep it, man would apparently have been made for the sake of paradise, and not contrariwise; which seems to be false. Therefore man was not place in paradise to dress and keep it.

*On the contrary,* It is written (Gen. 2: 15): "The Lord God took man and placed in the paradise of pleasure, to dress and keep it."

*I answer that,* As Augustine says (Gen. ad lit. viii, 10), these words in Genesis may be understood in two ways. First, in the sense that God placed man in paradise that He might Himself work in man and keep him, by sanctifying him (for if this work cease, man at once relapses into darkness, as the air grows dark when the light ceases to shine); and by keeping man from all corruption and evil. Secondly, that man might dress and keep paradise, which dressing would not have involved labor, as it did after sin; but would have been pleasant on account of man's practical knowledge of the powers of nature. Nor would man have kept paradise against a trespasser; but he would have striven to keep paradise for himself lest he should lose it by sin. All of which was for man's good; wherefore paradise was ordered to man's benefit, and not conversely.

Whence the Replies to the Objections are made clear.

FOURTH ARTICLE [I, Q. 102, Art. 4]

Whether Man Was Created in Paradise?

Objection 1: It would seem that man was created in paradise. For the angel was created in his dwelling-place—namely, the empyrean heaven. But before sin paradise was a fitting abode for man. Therefore it seems that man was created in paradise.

Obj. 2: Further, other animals remain in the place where they are produced, as the fish in the water, and walking animals on the earth from which they were made. Now man would have remained in paradise after he was created (Q. 97, A. 4). Therefore he was created in paradise.

Obj. 3: Further, woman was made in paradise. But man is greater than woman. Therefore much more should man have been made in paradise.

*On the contrary,* It is written (Gen. 2:15): "God took man and placed him in paradise."

*I answer that,* Paradise was a fitting abode for man as regards the incorruptibility of the primitive state. Now this incorruptibility was man's, not by nature, but by a supernatural gift of God. Therefore that this might be attributed to God, and not to human nature, God made man outside of paradise, and afterwards placed him there to live there during the whole of his animal life; and, having attained to the spiritual life, to be transferred thence to heaven.

Reply Obj. 1: The empyrean heaven was a fitting abode for the angels as regards their nature, and therefore they were created there.

In the same way I reply to the second objection, for those places befit those animals in their nature.

Reply Obj. 3: Woman was made in paradise, not by reason of her own dignity, but on account of the dignity of the principle from which her body was formed. For the same reason the children would have been born in paradise, where their parents were already.

TREATISE ON THE CONSERVATION AND GOVERNMENT OF CREATURES (QQ. 103-119)

# QUESTION 103

OF THE GOVERNMENT OF THINGS IN GENERAL (In Eight Articles)

Having considered the creation of things and their distinction, we now consider in the third place the government thereof, and (1) the government of things in general; (2) in particular, the effects of this government. Under the first head there are eight points of inquiry:

(1) Whether the world is governed by someone?

(2) What is the end of this government?

(3) Whether the world is governed by one?

(4) Of the effects of this government?

(5) Whether all things are subject to Divine government?

(6) Whether all things are immediately governed by God?

(7) Whether the Divine government is frustrated in anything?

(8) Whether anything is contrary to the Divine Providence?

FIRST ARTICLE [I, Q. 103, Art. 1]

Whether the World Is Governed by Anyone?

Objection 1: It would seem that the world is not governed by anyone. For it belongs to those things to be governed, which move or work for an end. But natural things which make up the greater part of the world do not move, or work for an end; for they have no knowledge of their end. Therefore the world is not governed.

Obj. 2: Further, those things are governed which are moved towards an object. But the world does not appear to be so directed, but has stability in itself. Therefore it is not governed.

Obj. 3: Further, what is necessarily determined by its own nature to one particular thing, does not require any external principle of government. But the principal parts of the world are by a certain necessity determined to something particular in their actions and movements. Therefore the world does not require to be governed.

*On the contrary,* It is written (Wis. 14:3): "But Thou, O Father, governest all things by Thy Providence." And Boethius says (De Consol. iii): "Thou Who governest this universe by mandate eternal."

*I answer that,* Certain ancient philosophers denied the government of the world, saying that all things happened by chance. But such an opinion can be refuted as impossible in two ways. First, by observation of things themselves: for we observe that in nature things happen always or nearly always for the best; which would not be the case unless some sort of providence directed nature towards good as an end; which is to govern. Wherefore the unfailing order we observe in things is a sign of their being governed; for instance, if we enter a well-ordered house we gather therefrom the intention of him that put it in order, as Tullius says (De Nat. Deorum ii), quoting Aristotle [*Cleanthes]. Secondly, this is clear from a consideration of Divine goodness, which, as we have said above (Q. 44, A. 4; Q. 65, A. 2), was the cause of the production of things in existence. For as "it belongs to the best to produce the best," it is not fitting that the supreme goodness of God should produce things without giving them their perfection. Now a thing's ultimate perfection consists in the attainment of its end. Therefore it belongs to the Divine goodness, as it brought things into existence, so to lead them to their end: and this is to govern.

Reply Obj. 1: A thing moves or operates for an end in two ways. First, in moving itself to the end, as man and other rational creatures; and such things have knowledge of their end, and of the means to the end. Secondly, a thing is said to move or operate for an end, as though moved or directed by another thereto, as an arrow directed to the target by the archer, who knows the end unknown to the arrow. Wherefore, as the movement of the arrow towards a definite end shows clearly that it is directed by someone with knowledge, so the unvarying course of natural things which are without knowledge, shows clearly that the world is governed by some reason.

Reply Obj. 2: In all created things there is a stable element, at least primary matter; and something belonging to movement, if under movement we include operation. And things need governing as to both: because even that which is stable, since it is created from nothing, would return to nothingness were it not sustained by a governing hand, as will be explained later (Q. 104, A. 1).

Reply Obj. 3: The natural necessity inherent in those beings which are determined to a particular thing, is a kind of impression from God, directing them to their end; as the necessity whereby an arrow is moved so as to fly towards a certain point is an impression from the archer, and not from the arrow. But there is a difference, inasmuch as that which creatures receive from God is their nature, while that which natural things receive from man in addition to their nature is somewhat violent. Wherefore, as the violent necessity in the movement of the arrow shows the action of the archer, so the natural necessity of things shows the government of Divine Providence.

SECOND ARTICLE [I, Q. 103, Art. 2]

Whether the End of the Government of the World Is Something Outside the World?

Objection 1: It would seem that the end of the government of the world is not something existing outside the world. For the end of the government of a thing is that whereto the thing governed is brought. But that whereto a thing is brought is some good in the thing itself; thus a sick man is brought back to health, which is something good in him. Therefore the end of government of things is some good not outside, but within the things themselves.

Obj. 2: Further, the Philosopher says (Ethic. i, 1): "Some ends are an operation; some are a work"—i.e. produced by an operation. But nothing can be produced by the whole universe outside itself; and operation exists in the agent. Therefore nothing extrinsic can be the end of the government of things.

Obj. 3: Further, the good of the multitude seems to consist in order, and peace which is the "tranquillity of order," as Augustine says (De Civ. Dei xix, 13). But the world is composed of a multitude of things. Therefore the end of the government of the world is the peaceful order in things themselves. Therefore the end of the government of the world is not an extrinsic good.

*On the contrary,* It is written (Prov. 16:4): "The Lord hath made all things for Himself." But God is outside the entire order of the universe. Therefore the end of all things is something extrinsic to them.

*I answer that,* As the end of a thing corresponds to its beginning, it is not possible to be ignorant of the end of things if we know their beginning. Therefore, since the beginning of all things is something outside the universe, namely, God, it is clear from what has been expounded above (Q. 44, AA. 1, 2), that we must conclude that the end of all things is some extrinsic good. This can be proved by reason. For it is clear that good has the nature of an end; wherefore, a particular end of anything consists in some particular good; while the universal end of all things is the Universal Good; Which is good of Itself by virtue of Its Essence, Which is the very essence of goodness; whereas a particular good is good by participation. Now it is manifest that in the whole created universe there is not a good which is not such by participation. Wherefore that good which is the end of the whole universe must be a good outside the universe.

Reply Obj. 1: We may acquire some good in many ways: first, as a form existing in us, such as health or knowledge; secondly, as something done by us, as a builder attains his end by building a house; thirdly, as something good possessed or acquired by us, as the buyer of a field attains his end when he enters into possession. Wherefore nothing prevents something outside the universe being the good to which it is directed.

Reply Obj. 2: The Philosopher is speaking of the ends of various arts; for the end of some arts consists in the operation itself, as the end of a harpist is to play the harp; whereas the end of other arts consists in something produced, as the end of a builder is not the act of building, but the house he builds. Now it may happen that something extrinsic is the end not only as made, but also as possessed or acquired or even as represented, as if we were to say that Hercules is the end of the statue made to represent him. Therefore we may say that some good outside the whole universe is the end of the government of the universe, as something possessed and represented; for each thing tends to a participation thereof, and to an assimilation thereto, as far as is possible.

Reply Obj. 3: A good existing in the universe, namely, the order of the universe, is an end thereof; this, however, is not its ultimate end, but is ordered to the extrinsic good as to the end: thus the order in an army is ordered to the general, as stated in *Metaph.* xii, Did. xi, 10.

THIRD ARTICLE [I, Q. 103, Art. 3]

Whether the World Is Governed by One?

Objection 1: It would seem that the world is not governed by one. For we judge the cause by the effect. Now, we see in the government of the universe that things are not moved and do not operate uniformly, but some contingently and some of necessity in variously different ways. Therefore the world is not governed by one.

Obj. 2: Further, things which are governed by one do not act against each other, except by the incapacity or unskillfulness of the ruler; which cannot apply to God. But created things agree not together, and act against each other; as is evident in the case of contraries. Therefore the world is not governed by one.

Obj. 3: Further, in nature we always find what is the better. But it "is better that two should be together than one" (Eccles. 4:9). Therefore the world is not governed by one, but by many.

*On the contrary,* We confess our belief in one God and one Lord, according to the words of the Apostle (1 Cor. 8:6): "To us there is but one God, the Father ... and one Lord": and both of these pertain to government. For to the Lord belongs dominion over subjects; and the name of God is taken from Providence as stated above (Q. 13, A. 8). Therefore the world is governed by one.

*I answer that,* We must of necessity say that the world is governed by one. For since the end of the government of the world is that which is essentially good, which is the greatest good; the government of the world must be the best kind of government. Now the best government is the government by one. The reason of this is that government is nothing but the directing of the things governed to the end; which consists in some good. But unity belongs to the idea of goodness, as Boethius proves (De Consol. iii, 11) from this, that, as all things desire good, so do they desire unity; without which they would cease to exist. For a thing so far exists as it is one. Whence we observe that things resist division, as far as they can; and the dissolution of a thing arises from defect therein. Therefore the intention of a ruler over a multitude is unity, or peace. Now the proper cause of unity is one. For it is clear that several cannot be the cause of unity or concord, except so far as they are united. Furthermore, what is one in itself is a more apt and a better cause of unity than several things united. Therefore a multitude is better governed by one than by several. From this it follows that the government of the world, being the best form of government, must be by one. This is expressed by the Philosopher (Metaph. xii, Did. xi, 10): "Things refuse to be ill governed; and multiplicity of authorities is a bad thing, therefore there should be one ruler."

Reply Obj. 1: Movement is "the act of a thing moved, caused by the mover." Wherefore dissimilarity of movements is caused by diversity of things moved, which diversity is essential to the perfection of the universe (Q. 47, AA. 1,2; Q. 48, A. 2), and not by a diversity of governors.

Reply Obj. 2: Although contraries do not agree with each other in their proximate ends, nevertheless they agree in the ultimate end, so far as they are included in the one order of the universe.

Reply Obj. 3: If we consider individual goods, then two are better than one. But if we consider the essential good, then no addition is possible.

FOURTH ARTICLE [I, Q. 103, Art. 4]

Whether the Effect of Government Is One or Many?

Objection 1: It would seem that there is but one effect of the government of the world and not many. For the effect of government is that which is caused in the things governed. This is one, namely, the good which consists in order; as may be seen in the example of an army. Therefore the government of the world has but one effect.

Obj. 2: Further, from one there naturally proceeds but one. But the world is governed by one as we have proved (A. 3). Therefore also the effect of this government is but one.

Obj. 3: Further, if the effect of government is not one by reason of the unity of the Governor, it must be many by reason of the many things governed. But these are too numerous to be counted. Therefore we cannot assign any definite number to the effects of government.

*On the contrary,* Dionysius says (Div. Nom. xii): "God contains all and fills all by His providence and perfect goodness." But government belongs to providence. Therefore there are certain definite effects of the Divine government.

*I answer that,* The effect of any action may be judged from its end; because it is by action that the attainment of the end is effected. Now the end of the government of the world is the essential good, to the participation and similarity of which all things tend. Consequently the effect of the government of the world may be taken in three ways. First, on the part of the end itself; and in this way there is but one effect, that is, assimilation to the supreme good. Secondly, the effect of the government of the world may be considered on the part of those things by means of which the creature is made like to God. Thus there are, in general, two effects of the government. For the creature is assimilated to God in two things; first, with regard to this, that God is good; and so the creature becomes like Him by being good; and secondly, with regard to this, that God is the cause of goodness in others; and so the creature becomes like God by moving others to be good. Wherefore there are two effects of government, the preservation of things in their goodness, and the moving of things to good. Thirdly, we may consider in the individual the effects of the government of the world; and in this way they are without number.

Reply Obj. 1: The order of the universe includes both the preservation of things created by God and their movement. As regards these two things we find order among them, inasmuch as one is better than another; and one is moved by another.

From what has been said above, we can gather the replies to the other two objections.

FIFTH ARTICLE [I, Q. 103, Art. 5]

Whether All Things Are Subject to the Divine Government?

Objection 1: It would seem that not all things are subject to the Divine government. For it is written (Eccles. 9:11): "I saw that under the sun the race is not to the swift, nor the battle to the strong, nor bread to the wise, nor riches to the learned, nor favor to the skillful, but time and chance in all." But things subject to the Divine government are not ruled by chance. Therefore those things which are under the sun are not subject to the Divine government.

Obj. 2: Further, the Apostle says (1 Cor. 9:9): "God hath no care for oxen." But he that governs has care for the things he governs. Therefore all things are not subject to the Divine government.

Obj. 3: Further, what can govern itself needs not to be governed by another. But the rational creature can govern itself; since it is master of its own act, and acts of itself; and is not made to act by another, which seems proper to things which are governed. Therefore all things are not subject to the Divine government.

*On the contrary,* Augustine says (De Civ. Dei v, 11): "Not only heaven and earth, not only man and angel, even the bowels of the lowest animal, even the wing of the bird, the flower of the plant, the leaf of the tree, hath God endowed with every fitting detail of their nature." Therefore all things are subject to His government.

*I answer that,* For the same reason is God the ruler of things as He is their cause, because the same gives existence as gives perfection; and this belongs to government. Now God is the cause not indeed only of some particular kind of being, but of the whole universal being, as proved above (Q. 44, AA. 1, 2). Wherefore, as there can be nothing which is not created by God, so there can be nothing which is not subject to His government. This can also be proved from the nature of the end of government. For a man's government extends over all those things which come under the end of his government. Now the end of the Divine government is the Divine goodness; as we have shown (A. 2). Wherefore, as there can be nothing that is not ordered to the Divine goodness as its end, as is clear from what we have said above (Q. 44, A. 4; Q. 65, A. 2), so it is impossible for anything to escape from the Divine government.

Foolish therefore was the opinion of those who said that the corruptible lower world, or individual things, or that even human affairs, were not subject to the Divine government. These are represented as saying, "God hath abandoned the earth" (Ezech. 9:9).

Reply Obj. 1: These things are said to be under the sun which are generated and corrupted according to the sun's movement. In all such things we find chance: not that everything is casual which occurs in such things; but that in each one there is an element of chance. And the very fact that an element of chance is found in those things proves that they are subject to government of some kind. For unless corruptible things were governed by a higher being, they would tend to nothing definite, especially those which possess no kind of knowledge. So nothing would happen unintentionally; which constitutes the nature of chance. Wherefore to show how things happen by chance and yet according to the ordering of a higher cause, he does not say absolutely that he observes chance in all things, but "time and chance," that is to say, that defects may be found in these things according to some order of time.

Reply Obj. 2: Government implies a certain change effected by the governor in the things governed. Now every movement is the act of a movable thing, caused by the moving principle, as is laid down *Phys.* iii, 3. And every act is proportionate to that of which it is an act. Consequently, various movable things must be moved variously, even as regards movement by one and the same mover. Thus by the one art of the Divine governor, various things are variously governed according to their variety. Some, according to their nature, act of themselves, having dominion over their actions; and these are governed by God, not only in this, that they are moved by God Himself, Who works in them interiorly; but also in this, that they are induced by Him to do good and to fly from evil, by precepts and prohibitions, rewards and punishments. But irrational creatures which do not act but are acted upon, are not thus governed by God. Hence, when the Apostle says that "God hath no care for oxen," he does not wholly withdraw them from the Divine government, but only as regards the way in which rational creatures are governed.

Reply Obj. 3: The rational creature governs itself by its intellect and will, both of which require to be governed and perfected by the Divine intellect and will. Therefore above the government whereby the rational creature governs itself as master of its own act, it requires to be governed by God.

SIXTH ARTICLE [I, Q. 103, Art. 6]

Whether all things are immediately governed by God?

Objection 1: It would seem that all things are governed by God immediately. For Gregory of Nyssa (Nemesius, De Nat. Hom.) reproves the opinion of Plato who divides providence into three parts. The first he ascribes to the supreme god, who watches over heavenly things and all universals; the second providence he attributes to the secondary deities, who go the round of the heavens to watch over generation and corruption; while he ascribes a third providence to certain spirits who are guardians on earth of human actions. Therefore it seems that all things are immediately governed by God.

Obj. 2: Further, it is better that a thing be done by one, if possible, than by many, as the Philosopher says (Phys. viii, 6). But God can by Himself govern all things without any intermediary cause. Therefore it seems that He governs all things immediately.

Obj. 3: Further, in God nothing is defective or imperfect. But it seems to be imperfect in a ruler to govern by means of others; thus an earthly king, by reason of his not being able to do everything himself, and because he cannot be everywhere at the same time, requires to govern by means of ministers. Therefore God governs all things immediately.

*On the contrary,* Augustine says (De Trin. iii, 4): "As the lower and grosser bodies are ruled in a certain orderly way by bodies of greater subtlety and power; so all bodies are ruled by the rational spirit of life; and the sinful and unfaithful spirit is ruled by the good and just spirit of life; and this spirit by God Himself."

*I answer that,* In government there are two things to be considered; the design of government, which is providence itself; and the execution of the design. As to the design of government, God governs all things immediately; whereas in its execution, He governs some things by means of others.

The reason of this is that as God is the very essence of goodness, so everything must be attributed to God in its highest degree of goodness. Now the highest degree of goodness in any practical order, design or knowledge (and such is the design of government) consists in knowing the individuals acted upon; as the best physician is not the one who can only give his attention to general principles, but who can consider the least details; and so on in other things. Therefore we must say that God has the design of the government of all things, even of the very least.

But since things which are governed should be brought to perfection by government, this government will be so much the better in the degree the things governed are brought to perfection. Now it is a greater perfection for a thing to be good in itself and also the cause of goodness in others, than only to be good in itself. Therefore God so governs things that He makes some of them to be causes of others in government; as a master, who not only imparts knowledge to his pupils, but gives also the faculty of teaching others.

Reply Obj. 1: Plato's opinion is to be rejected, because he held that God did not govern all things immediately, even in the design of government; this is clear from the fact that he divided providence, which is the design of government, into three parts.

Reply Obj. 2: If God governed alone, things would be deprived of the perfection of causality. Wherefore all that is effected by many would not be accomplished by one.

Reply Obj. 3: That an earthly king should have ministers to execute his laws is a sign not only of his being imperfect, but also of his dignity; because by the ordering of ministers the kingly power is brought into greater evidence.

SEVENTH ARTICLE [I, Q. 103, Art. 7]

Whether Anything Can Happen Outside the Order of the Divine Government?

Objection 1: It would seem possible that something may occur outside the order of the Divine government. For Boethius says (De Consol. iii) that "God disposes all for good." Therefore, if nothing happens outside the order of the Divine government, it would follow that no evil exists.

Obj. 2: Further, nothing that is in accordance with the pre-ordination of a ruler occurs by chance. Therefore, if nothing occurs outside the order of the Divine government, it follows that there is nothing fortuitous and casual.

Obj. 3: Further, the order of Divine Providence is certain and unchangeable; because it is in accordance with the eternal design. Therefore, if nothing happens outside the order of the Divine government, it follows that all things happen by necessity, and nothing is contingent; which is false. Therefore it is possible for something to occur outside the order of the Divine government.

*On the contrary,* It is written (Esther 13:9): "O Lord, Lord, almighty King, all things are in Thy power, and there is none that can resist Thy will."

*I answer that,* It is possible for an effect to result outside the order of some particular cause; but not outside the order of the universal cause. The reason of this is that no effect results outside the order of a particular cause, except through some other impeding cause; which other cause must itself be reduced to the first universal cause; as indigestion may occur outside the order of the nutritive power by some such impediment as the coarseness of the food, which again is to be ascribed to some other cause, and so on till we come to the first universal cause. Therefore as God is the first universal cause, not of one genus only, but of all being in general, it is impossible for anything to occur outside the order of the Divine government; but from the very fact that from one point of view something seems to evade the order of Divine providence considered in regard to one particular cause, it must necessarily come back to that order as regards some other cause.

Reply Obj. 1: There is nothing wholly evil in the world, for evil is ever founded on good, as shown above (Q. 48, A. 3). Therefore something is said to be evil through its escaping from the order of some particular good. If it wholly escaped from the order of the Divine government, it would wholly cease to exist.

Reply Obj. 2: Things are said to be fortuitous as regards some particular cause from the order of which they escape. But as to the order of Divine providence, "nothing in the world happens by chance," as Augustine declares (QQ. 83, qu. 24).

Reply Obj. 3: Certain effects are said to be contingent as compared to their proximate causes, which may fail in their effects; and not as though anything could happen entirely outside the order of Divine government. The very fact that something occurs outside the order of some proximate cause, is owing to some other cause, itself subject to the Divine government.

EIGHTH ARTICLE [I, Q. 103, Art. 8]

Whether anything can resist the order of the Divine government?

Objection 1: It would seem possible that some resistance can be made to the order of the Divine government. For it is written (Isa. 3:8): "Their tongue and their devices are against the Lord."

Obj. 2: Further, a king does not justly punish those who do not rebel against his commands. Therefore if no one rebelled against God's commands, no one would be justly punished by God.

Obj. 3: Further, everything is subject to the order of the Divine government. But some things oppose others. Therefore some things rebel against the order of the Divine government.

*On the contrary,* Boethius says (De Consol. iii): "There is nothing that can desire or is able to resist this sovereign good. It is this sovereign good therefore that ruleth all mightily and ordereth all sweetly," as is said (Wis. 8) of Divine wisdom.

*I answer that,* We may consider the order of Divine providence in two ways: in general, inasmuch as it proceeds from the governing cause of all; and in particular, inasmuch as it proceeds from some particular cause which executes the order of the Divine government.

Considered in the first way, nothing can resist the order of the Divine government. This can be proved in two ways: firstly from the fact that the order of the Divine government is wholly directed to good, and everything by its own operation and effort tends to good only, "for no one acts intending evil," as Dionysius says (Div. Nom. iv): secondly from the fact that, as we have said above (A. 1, ad 3; A. 5, ad 2), every inclination of anything, whether natural or voluntary, is nothing but a kind of impression from the first mover; as the inclination of the arrow towards a fixed point is nothing but an impulse received from the archer. Wherefore every agent, whether natural or free, attains to its divinely appointed end, as though of its own accord. For this reason God is said "to order all things sweetly."

Reply Obj. 1: Some are said to think or speak, or act against God: not that they entirely resist the order of the Divine government; for even the sinner intends the attainment of a certain good: but because they resist some particular good, which belongs to their nature or state. Therefore they are justly punished by God.

Reply Obj. 2 is clear from the above.

Reply Obj. 3: From the fact that one thing opposes another, it follows that some one thing can resist the order of a particular cause; but not that order which depends on the universal cause of all things.

## QUESTION 104

THE SPECIAL EFFECTS OF THE DIVINE GOVERNMENT (In Four Articles)

We next consider the effects of the Divine government in particular; concerning which four points of inquiry arise:

(1) Whether creatures need to be kept in existence by God?

(2) Whether they are immediately preserved by God?

(3) Whether God can reduce anything to nothingness?

(4) Whether anything is reduced to nothingness?

FIRST ARTICLE [I, Q. 104, Art. 1]

Whether Creatures Need to Be Kept in Being by God?

Objection 1: It would seem that creatures do not

need to be kept in being by God. For what cannot not-be, does not need to be kept in being; just as that which cannot depart, does not need to be kept from departing. But some creatures by their very nature cannot not-be. Therefore not all creatures need to be kept in being by God. The middle proposition is proved thus. That which is included in the nature of a thing is necessarily in that thing, and its contrary cannot be in it; thus a multiple of two must necessarily be even, and cannot possibly be an odd number. Now form brings being with itself, because everything is actually in being, so far as it has form. But some creatures are subsistent forms, as we have said of the angels (Q. 50, AA. 2, 5): and thus to be is in them of themselves. The same reasoning applies to those creatures whose matter is in potentiality to one form only, as above explained of heavenly bodies (Q. 66, A. 2). Therefore such creatures as these have in their nature to be necessarily, and cannot not-be; for there can be no potentiality to not-being, either in the form which has being of itself, or in matter existing under a form which it cannot lose, since it is not in potentiality to any other form.

Obj. 2: Further, God is more powerful than any created agent. But a created agent, even after ceasing to act, can cause its effect to be preserved in being; thus the house continues to stand after the builder has ceased to build; and water remains hot for some time after the fire has ceased to heat. Much more, therefore, can God cause His creature to be kept in being, after He has ceased to create it.

Obj. 3: Further, nothing violent can occur, except there be some active cause thereof. But tendency to not-being is unnatural and violent to any creature, since all creatures naturally desire to be. Therefore no creature can tend to not-being, except through some active cause of corruption. Now there are creatures of such a nature that nothing can cause them to corrupt; such are spiritual substances and heavenly bodies. Therefore such creatures cannot tend to not-being, even if God were to withdraw His action.

Obj. 4: Further, if God keeps creatures in being, this is done by some action. Now every action of an agent, if that action be efficacious, produces something in the effect. Therefore the preserving power of God must produce something in the creature. But this is not so; because this action does not give being to the creature, since being is not given to that which already is: nor does it add anything new to the creature; because either God would not keep the creature in being continually, or He would be continually adding something new to the creature; either of which is unreasonable. Therefore creatures are not kept in being by God.

*On the contrary,* It is written (Heb. 1:3): "Upholding all things by the word of His power."

*I answer that,* Both reason and faith bind us to say that creatures are kept in being by God. To make this clear, we must consider that a thing is preserved by another in two ways. First, indirectly, and accidentally; thus a person is said to preserve anything by removing the cause of its corruption, as a man may be said to preserve a child, whom he guards from falling into the fire. In this way God preserves some things, but not all, for there are some things of such a nature that nothing can corrupt them, so that it is not necessary to keep them from corruption. Secondly, a thing is said to preserve another *per se* and directly, namely, when what is preserved depends on the preserver in such a way that it cannot exist without it. In this manner all creatures need to be preserved by God. For the being of every creature depends on God, so that not for a moment could it subsist, but would fall into nothingness were it not kept in being by the operation of the Divine power, as Gregory says (Moral. xvi).

This is made clear as follows: Every effect depends on its cause, so far as it is its cause. But we must observe that an agent may be the cause of the *becoming* of its effect, but not directly of its *being.* This may be seen both in artificial and in natural beings: for the builder causes the house in its *becoming,* but he is not the direct cause of its *being.* For it is clear that the being of the house is a result of its form, which consists in the putting together and arrangement of the materials, and results from the natural qualities of certain things. Thus a cook dresses the food by applying the natural activity of fire; thus a builder constructs a house, by making use of cement, stones, and wood which are able to be put together in a certain order and to preserve it. Therefore the *being* of a house depends on the nature of these materials, just as its *becoming* depends on the action of the builder. The same principle applies to natural things. For if an agent is not the cause of a form as such, neither will it be directly the cause of *being* which results from that form; but it will be the cause of the effect, in its *becoming* only.

Now it is clear that of two things in the same species one cannot directly cause the other's form as such, since it would then be the cause of its own form, which is essentially the same as the form of the other; but it can be the cause of this form for as much as it is in matter—in other words, it may be the cause that "this matter" receives *this form.* And this is to be the cause of becoming, as when man begets man, and fire causes fire. Thus whenever a natural effect is such that it has an aptitude to receive from its active cause an impression specifically the same as in that active cause, then the *becoming* of the effect, but not its being, depends on the agent.

Sometimes, however, the effect has not this aptitude to receive the impression of its cause, in the same way as it exists in the agent: as may be seen clearly in all agents which do not produce an effect of the same species as themselves: thus the heavenly bodies cause the generation of inferior bodies which differ from them in species. Such an agent can be the cause of a form as such, and not merely as existing in this matter, consequently it is not merely the cause of *becoming* but also the cause of being.

Therefore as the becoming of a thing cannot continue when that action of the agent ceases which causes the *becoming* of the effect: so neither can the *being* of a thing continue after that action of the agent has ceased, which is the cause of the effect not only in *becoming* but also in being. This is why hot water retains heat after the cessation of the fire's action; while, *on the contrary,* the air does not continue to be lit up, even for a moment, when the sun ceases to act upon it, because water is a matter susceptive of the fire's heat in the same way as it exists in the fire. Wherefore if it were to be reduced to the perfect form of fire, it would retain that form always; whereas if it has the form of fire imperfectly and inchoately, the heat will remain for a time only, by reason of the imperfect participation of the principle of heat. On the other hand, air is not of such a nature as to receive light in the same way as it exists in the sun, which is the principle of light. Therefore, since it has not root in the air, the light ceases with the action of the sun.

Now every creature may be compared to God, as the air is to the sun which enlightens it. For as the sun possesses light by its nature, and as the air is enlightened by sharing the sun's nature; so God alone is Being in virtue of His own Essence, since His Essence is His existence; whereas every creature has being by participation, so that its essence is not its existence. Therefore, as Augustine says (Gen. ad lit. iv, 12): "If the ruling power of God were withdrawn from His creatures, their nature would at once cease, and all nature would collapse." In the same work (Gen. ad lit. viii, 12) he says: "As the air becomes light by the presence of the sun, so is man enlightened by the presence of God, and in His absence returns at once to darkness."

Reply Obj. 1: *Being* naturally results from the form of a creature, given the influence of the Divine action; just as light results from the diaphanous nature of the air, given the action of the sun. Wherefore the potentiality to not-being in spiritual creatures and heavenly bodies is rather something in God, Who can withdraw His influence, than in the form or matter of those creatures.

Reply Obj. 2: God cannot grant to a creature to be preserved in being after the cessation of the Divine influence: as neither can He make it not to have received its being from Himself. For the creature needs to be preserved by God in so far as the being of an effect depends on the cause of its being. So that there is no comparison with an agent that is not the cause of *being* but only of becoming.

Reply Obj. 3: This argument holds in regard to that preservation which consists in the removal of corruption: but all creatures do not need to be preserved thus, as stated above.

Reply Obj. 4: The preservation of things by God is a continuation of that action whereby He gives existence, which action is without either motion or time; so also the preservation of light in the air is by the continual influence of the sun.

SECOND ARTICLE [I, Q. 104, Art. 2]

Whether God Preserves Every Creature Immediately?

Objection 1: It would seem that God preserves every creature immediately. For God creates and preserves things by the same action, as above stated (A. 1, ad 4). But God created all things immediately. Therefore He preserves all things immediately.

Obj. 2: Further, a thing is nearer to itself than to another. But it cannot be given to a creature to preserve itself; much less therefore can it be given to a creature to preserve another. Therefore God preserves all things without any intermediate cause preserving them.

Obj. 3: Further, an effect is kept in being by the cause, not only of its *becoming,* but also of its being. But all created causes do not seem to cause their effects except in their *becoming,* for they cause only by moving, as above stated (Q. 45, A. 3). Therefore they do not cause so as to keep their effects in being.

*On the contrary,* A thing is kept in being by that which gives it being. But God gives being by means of certain intermediate causes. Therefore He also keeps things in being by means of certain causes.

*I answer that,* As stated above (A. 1), a thing keeps another in being in two ways; first, indirectly and accidentally, by removing or hindering the action of a corrupting cause; secondly, directly and *per se,* by the fact that that on it depends the other's being, as the being of the effect depends on the cause. And in both ways a created thing keeps another in being. For it is clear that even in corporeal things there are many causes which hinder the action of corrupting agents, and for that reason are called preservatives; just as salt preserves meat from putrefaction; and in like manner with many other things. It happens also that an effect depends on a creature as to its being. For when we have a series of causes depending on one another, it necessarily follows that, while the effect depends first and principally on the first cause, it also depends in a secondary way on all the middle causes. Therefore the first cause is the principal cause of the preservation of the effect which is to be referred to the middle causes in a secondary way; and all the more so, as the middle cause is higher and nearer to the first cause.

For this reason, even in things corporeal, the preservation and continuation of things is ascribed to the higher causes: thus the Philosopher says (Metaph. xii, Did. xi, 6), that the first, namely the diurnal movement is the cause of the continuation of things generated; whereas the second movement, which is from the zodiac, is the cause of diversity owing to generation and corruption. In like manner astrologers ascribe to Saturn, the highest of the planets, those things which are permanent and fixed. So we conclude that God keeps certain things in being, by means of certain causes.

Reply Obj. 1: God created all things immediately, but in the creation itself He established an order among things, so that some depend on others, by which they are preserved in being, though He remains the principal cause of their preservation.

Reply Obj. 2: Since an effect is preserved by its proper cause on which it depends; just as no effect can be its own cause, but can only produce another effect, so no effect can be endowed with the power of self-preservation, but only with the power of preserving another.

Reply Obj. 3: No created nature can be the cause of another, as regards the latter acquiring a new form, or disposition, except by virtue of some change; for the created nature acts always on something presupposed. But after causing the form or disposition in the effect, without any fresh change in the effect, the cause preserves that form or disposition; as in the air, when it is lit up anew, we must allow some change to have taken place, while the preservation of the light is without any further change in the air due to the presence of the source of light.

THIRD ARTICLE [I, Q. 104, Art. 3]

Whether God Can Annihilate Anything?

Objection 1: It would seem that God cannot annihilate anything. For Augustine says (QQ. 83, qu. 21) that "God is not the cause of anything tending to non-existence." But He would be such a cause if He were to annihilate anything. Therefore He cannot annihilate anything.

Obj. 2: Further, by His goodness God is the cause why things exist, since, as Augustine says (De Doctr. Christ. i, 32): "Because God is good, we exist." But God cannot cease to be good. Therefore He cannot cause things to cease to exist; which would be the case were He to annihilate anything.

Obj. 3: Further, if God were to annihilate anything it would be by His action. But this cannot be; because the term of every action is existence. Hence even the action of a corrupting cause has its term in something generated; for when one thing is generated another undergoes corruption. Therefore God cannot annihilate anything.

*On the contrary,* It is written (Jer. 10:24): "Correct me, O Lord, but yet with judgment; and not in Thy fury, lest Thou bring me to nothing."

*I answer that,* Some have held that God, in giving existence to creatures, acted from natural necessity. Were this true, God could not annihilate anything, since His nature cannot change. But, as we have said above (Q. 19, A. 4), such an opinion is entirely false, and absolutely contrary to the Catholic faith, which confesses that God created things of His own free-will, according to Ps. 134:6: "Whatsoever the Lord pleased, He hath done." Therefore that God gives existence to a creature depends on His will; nor does He preserve things in existence otherwise than by continually pouring out existence into them, as we have said. Therefore, just as before things existed, God was free not to give them existence, and not to make them; so after they are made, He is free not to continue their existence; and thus they would cease to exist; and this would be to annihilate them.

Reply Obj. 1: Non-existence has no direct cause; for nothing is a cause except inasmuch as it has existence, and a being essentially as such is a cause of something existing. Therefore God cannot cause a thing to tend to non-existence, whereas a creature has this tendency of itself, since it is produced from nothing. But indirectly God can be the cause of things being reduced to non-existence, by withdrawing His action therefrom.

Reply Obj. 2: God's goodness is the cause of things, not as though by natural necessity, because the Divine goodness does not depend on creatures; but by His free-will. Wherefore, as without prejudice to His goodness, He might not have produced things into existence, so, without prejudice to His goodness, He might not preserve things in existence.

Reply Obj. 3: If God were to annihilate anything, this would not imply an action on God's part; but a mere cessation of His action.

FOURTH ARTICLE [I, Q. 104, Art. 4]

Whether Anything Is Annihilated?

Objection 1: It would seem that something is annihilated. For the end corresponds to the beginning. But in the beginning there was nothing but God. Therefore all things must tend to this end, that there shall be nothing but God. Therefore creatures will be reduced to nothing.

Obj. 2: Further, every creature has a finite power. But no finite power extends to the infinite. Wherefore the Philosopher proves (Phys. viii, 10) that, "a finite power cannot move in infinite time." Therefore a creature cannot last for an infinite duration; and so at some time it will be reduced to nothing.

Obj. 3: Further, forms and accidents have no matter as part of themselves. But at some time they cease to exist. Therefore they are reduced to nothing.

*On the contrary,* It is written (Eccles. 3:14): "I have learned that all the works that God hath made continue for ever."

*I answer that,* Some of those things which God does in creatures occur in accordance with the natural course of things; others happen miraculously, and not in accordance with the natural order, as will be explained (Q. 105, A. 6). Now whatever God wills to do according to the natural order of things may be observed from their nature; but those things which occur miraculously, are ordered for the manifestation of grace, according to the Apostle, "To each one is given the manifestation of the Spirit, unto profit" (1 Cor. 12:7); and subsequently he mentions, among others, the working of miracles.

Now the nature of creatures shows that none of them is annihilated. For, either they are immaterial, and therefore have no potentiality to non-existence; or they are material, and then they continue to exist, at least in matter, which is incorruptible, since it is the subject of generation and corruption. Moreover, the annihilation of things does not pertain to the manifestation of grace; since rather the power and goodness of God are manifested by the preservation of things in existence. Wherefore we must conclude by denying absolutely that anything at all will be annihilated.

Reply Obj. 1: That things are brought into existence from a state of non-existence, clearly shows the power of Him Who made them; but that they should be reduced to nothing would hinder that manifestation, since the power of God is conspicuously shown in His preserving all things in existence, according to the Apostle: "Upholding all things by the word of His power" (Heb. 1:3).

Reply Obj. 2: A creature's potentiality to existence is merely receptive; the active power belongs to God Himself, from Whom existence is derived. Wherefore the infinite duration of things is a consequence of the infinity of the Divine power. To some things, however, is given a determinate power of duration for a certain time, so far as they may be hindered by some contrary agent from receiving the influx of existence which comes from Him Whom finite power cannot resist, for an infinite, but only for a fixed time. So things which have no contrary, although they have a finite power, continue to exist for ever.

Reply Obj. 3: Forms and accidents are not complete beings, since they do not subsist: but each one of them is something "of a being"; for it is called a being, because something is by it. Yet so far as their mode of existence is concerned, they are not entirely reduced to nothingness; not that any part of them survives, but that they remain in the potentiality of the matter, or of the subject.

# QUESTION 105

OF THE CHANGE OF CREATURES BY GOD (In Eight Articles)

We now consider the second effect of the Divine government, i.e. the change of creatures; and first, the change of creatures by God; secondly, the change of one creature by another.

Under the first head there are eight points of inquiry:

(1) Whether God can move immediately the matter to the form?

(2) Whether He can immediately move a body?

(3) Whether He can move the intellect?

(4) Whether He can move the will?

(5) Whether God works in every worker?

(6) Whether He can do anything outside the order imposed on things?

(7) Whether all that God does is miraculous?

(8) Of the diversity of miracles.

FIRST ARTICLE [I, Q. 105, Art. 1]

Whether God Can Move the Matter Immediately to the Form?

Objection 1: It would seem that God cannot move the matter immediately to receive the form. For as the Philosopher proves (Metaph. vii, Did. vi, 8), nothing can bring a form into any particular matter, except that form which is in matter; because, like begets like. But God is not a form in matter. Therefore He cannot cause a form in matter.

Obj. 2: Further, any agent inclined to several effects will produce none of them, unless it is determined to a particular one by some other cause; for, as the Philosopher says (De Anima iii, 11), a general assertion does not move the mind, except by means of some particular apprehension. But the Divine power is the universal cause of all things. Therefore it cannot produce any particular form, except by means of a particular agent.

Obj. 3: As universal being depends on the first universal cause, so determinate being depends on determinate particular causes; as we have seen above (Q. 104, A. 2). But the determinate being of a particular thing is from its own form. Therefore the forms of things are produced by God, only by means of particular causes.

*On the contrary,* It is written (Gen. 2:7): "God formed man of the slime of the earth."

*I answer that,* God can move matter immediately to form; because whatever is in passive potentiality can be reduced to act by the active power which extends over that potentiality. Therefore, since the Divine power extends over matter, as produced by God, it can be reduced to act by the Divine power: and this is what is meant by matter being moved to a form; for a form is nothing else but the act of matter.

Reply Obj. 1: An effect is assimilated to the active cause in two ways. First, according to the same species; as man is generated by man, and fire by fire. Secondly, by being virtually contained in the cause; as the form of the effect is virtually contained in its cause: thus animals produced by putrefaction, and plants, and minerals are like the sun and stars, by whose power they are produced. In this way the effect is like its active cause as regards all that over which the power of that cause extends. Now the power of God extends to both matter and form; as we have said above (Q. 14, A. 2; Q. 44, A. 2); wherefore if a composite thing be produced, it is likened to God by way of a virtual inclusion; or it is likened to the composite generator by a likeness of species. Therefore just as the composite generator can move matter to a form by generating a composite thing like itself; so also can God. But no other form not existing in matter can do this; because the power of no other separate substance extends over matter. Hence angels and demons operate on visible matter; not by imprinting forms in matter, but by making use of corporeal seeds.

Reply Obj. 2: This argument would hold if God were to act of natural necessity. But since He acts by His will and intellect, which knows the particular and not only the universal natures of all forms, it follows that He can determinately imprint this or that form on matter.

Reply Obj. 3: The fact that secondary causes are ordered to determinate effects is due to God; wherefore since God ordains other causes to certain effects He can also produce certain effects by Himself without any other cause.

SECOND ARTICLE [I, Q. 105, Art. 2]

Whether God Can Move a Body Immediately?

Objection 1: It would seem that God cannot move a body immediately. For as the mover and the moved must exist simultaneously, as the Philosopher says (Phys. vii, 2), it follows that there must be some contact between the mover and moved. But there can be no contact between God and a body; for Dionysius says (Div. Nom. 1): "There is no contact with God." Therefore God cannot move a body immediately.

Obj. 2: Further, God is the mover unmoved. But such also is the desirable object when apprehended. Therefore God moves as the object of desire and apprehension. But He cannot be apprehended except by the intellect, which is neither a body nor a corporeal power. Therefore God cannot move a body immediately.

Obj. 3: Further, the Philosopher proves (Phys. viii, 10) that an infinite power moves instantaneously. But it is impossible for a body to be moved in one instant; for since every movement is between opposites, it follows that two opposites would exist at once in the same subject, which is impossible. Therefore a body cannot be moved immediately by an infinite power. But God's power is infinite, as we have explained (Q. 25, A. 2). Therefore God cannot move a body immediately.

*On the contrary,* God produced the works of the six days immediately among which is included the movements of bodies, as is clear from Gen. 1:9 "Let the waters be gathered together into one place." Therefore God alone can move a body immediately.

*I answer that,* It is erroneous to say that God cannot Himself produce all the determinate effects which are produced by any created cause. Wherefore, since bodies are moved immediately by created causes, we cannot possibly doubt that God can move immediately any bodies whatever. This indeed follows from what is above stated (A. 1). For every movement of any body whatever, either results from a form, as the movements of things heavy and light result from the form which they have from their generating cause, for which reason the generator is called the mover; or else tends to a form, as heating tends to the form of heat. Now it belongs to the same cause, to imprint a form, to dispose to that form, and to give the movement which results from that form; for fire not only generates fire, but it also heats and moves things upwards. Therefore, as God can imprint form immediately in matter, it follows that He can move any body whatever in respect of any movement whatever.

Reply Obj. 1: There are two kinds of contact; corporeal contact, when two bodies touch each other; and virtual contact, as the cause of sadness is said to touch the one made sad. According to the first kind of contact, God, as being incorporeal, neither touches, nor is touched; but according to virtual contact He touches creatures by moving them; but He is not touched, because the natural power of no creature can reach up to Him. Thus did Dionysius understand the words, "There is no contact with God"; that is, so that God Himself be touched.

Reply Obj. 2: God moves as the object of desire and apprehension; but it does not follow that He always moves as being desired and apprehended by that which is moved; but as being desired and known by Himself; for He does all things for His own goodness.

Reply Obj. 3: The Philosopher (Phys. viii, 10) intends to prove that the power of the first mover is not a power of the first mover *of bulk,* by the following argument. The power of the first mover is infinite (which he proves from the fact that the first mover can move in infinite time). Now an infinite power, if it were a power *of bulk,* would move without time, which is impossible; therefore the infinite power of the first mover must be in something which is not measured by its bulk. Whence it is clear that for a body to be moved without time can only be the result of an infinite power. The reason is that every power of bulk moves in its entirety; since it moves by the necessity of its nature. But an infinite power surpasses out of all proportion any finite power. Now the greater the power of the mover, the greater is the velocity of the movement. Therefore, since a finite power moves in a determinate time, it follows that an infinite power does not move in any time; for between one time and any other time there is some proportion. On the other hand, a power which is not in bulk is the power of an intelligent being, which operates in its effects according to what is fitting to them; and therefore, since it cannot be fitting for a body to be moved without time, it does not follow that it moves without time.

THIRD ARTICLE [I, Q. 105, Art. 3]

Whether God Moves the Created Intellect Immediately?

Objection 1: It would seem that God does not immediately move the created intellect. For the action of the intellect is governed by its own subject; since it does not pass into external matter; as stated in *Metaph.* ix, Did. viii, 8. But the action of what is moved by another does not proceed from that wherein it is; but from the mover. Therefore the intellect is not moved by another; and so apparently God cannot move the created intellect.

Obj. 2: Further, anything which in itself is a sufficient principle of movement, is not moved by another. But the movement of the intellect is its act of understanding; in the sense in which we say that to understand or to feel is a kind of movement, as the Philosopher says (De Anima iii, 7). But the intellectual light which is natural to the soul, is a sufficient principle of understanding. Therefore it is not moved by another.

Obj. 3: Further, as the senses are moved by the sensible, so the intellect is moved by the intelligible. But God is not intelligible to us, and exceeds the capacity of our intellect. Therefore God cannot move our intellect.

*On the contrary,* The teacher moves the intellect of the one taught. But it is written (Ps. 93:10) that God "teaches man knowledge." Therefore God moves the human intellect.

*I answer that,* As in corporeal movement that is called the mover which gives the form that is the principle of movement, so that is said to move the intellect, which is the cause of the form that is the principle of the intellectual operation, called the movement of the intellect. Now there is a twofold principle of intellectual operation in the intelligent being; one which is the intellectual power itself, which principle exists in the one who understands in potentiality; while the other is the principle of actual understanding, namely, the likeness of the thing understood in the one who understands. So a thing is said to move the intellect, whether it gives to him who understands the power of understanding; or impresses on him the likeness of the thing understood.

Now God moves the created intellect in both ways. For He is the First immaterial Being; and as intellectuality is a result of immateriality, it follows that He is the First intelligent Being. Therefore since in each order the first is the cause of all that follows, we must conclude that from Him proceeds all intellectual power. In like manner, since He is the First Being, and all other beings pre-exist in Him as in their First Cause, it follows that they exist intelligibly in Him, after the mode of His own Nature. For as the intelligible types of everything exist first of all in God, and are derived from Him by other intellects in order that these may actually understand; so also are they derived by creatures that they may subsist. Therefore God so moves the created intellect, inasmuch as He gives it the intellectual power, whether natural, or superadded; and impresses on the created intellect the intelligible species, and maintains and preserves both power and species in existence.

Reply Obj. 1: The intellectual operation is performed by the intellect in which it exists, as by a secondary cause; but it proceeds from God as from its first cause. For by Him the power to understand is given to the one who understands.

Reply Obj. 2: The intellectual light together with the likeness of the thing understood is a sufficient principle of understanding; but it is a secondary principle, and depends upon the First Principle.

Reply Obj. 3: The intelligible object moves our human intellect, so far as, in a way, it impresses on it its own likeness, by means of which the intellect is able to understand it. But the likenesses which God impresses on the created intellect are not sufficient to enable the created intellect to understand Him through His Essence, as we have seen above (Q. 12, A. 2; Q. 56, A. 3). Hence He moves the created intellect, and yet He cannot be intelligible to it, as we have explained (Q. 12, A. 4).

FOURTH ARTICLE [I, Q. 105, Art. 4]

Whether God Can Move the Created Will?

Objection 1: It would seem that God cannot move the created will. For whatever is moved from without, is forced. But the will cannot be forced. Therefore it is not moved from without; and therefore cannot be moved by God.

Obj. 2: Further, God cannot make two contradictories to be true at the same time. But this would follow if He moved the will; for to be voluntarily moved means to be moved from within, and not by another. Therefore God cannot move the will.

Obj. 3: Further, movement is attributed to the mover rather than to the one moved; wherefore homicide is not ascribed to the stone, but to the thrower. Therefore, if God moves the will, it follows that voluntary actions are not imputed to man for reward or blame. But this is false. Therefore God does not move the will.

*On the contrary,* It is written (Phil. 2:13): "It is God who worketh in us [Vulgate—'you'] both to will and to accomplish."

*I answer that,* As the intellect is moved by the object and by the Giver of the power of intelligence, as stated above (A. 3), so is the will moved by its object, which is good, and by Him who creates the power of willing. Now the will can be moved by good as its object, but by God alone sufficiently and efficaciously. For nothing can move a movable thing sufficiently unless the active power of the mover surpasses or at least equals the potentiality of the thing movable. Now the potentiality of the will extends to the universal good; for its object is the universal good; just as the object of the intellect is the universal being. But every created good is some particular good; God alone is the universal good.

Whereas He alone fills the capacity of the will, and moves it sufficiently as its object. In like manner the power of willing is caused by God alone. For to will is nothing but to be inclined towards the object of the will, which is universal good. But to incline towards the universal good belongs to the First Mover, to Whom the ultimate end is proportionate; just as in human affairs to him that presides over the community belongs the directing of his subjects to the common weal. Wherefore in both ways it belongs to God to move the will; but especially in the second way by an interior inclination of the will.

Reply Obj. 1: A thing moved by another is forced if moved against its natural inclination; but if it is moved by another giving to it the proper natural inclination, it is not forced; as when a heavy body is made to move downwards by that which produced it, then it is not forced. In like manner God, while moving the will, does not force it, because He gives the will its own natural inclination.

Reply Obj. 2: To be moved voluntarily, is to be moved from within, that is, by an interior principle: yet this interior principle may be caused by an exterior principle; and so to be moved from within is not repugnant to being moved by another.

Reply Obj. 3: If the will were so moved by another as in no way to be moved from within itself, the act of the will would not be imputed for reward or blame. But since its being moved by another does not prevent its being moved from within itself, as we have stated (ad 2), it does not thereby forfeit the motive for merit or demerit.

FIFTH ARTICLE [I, Q. 105, Art. 5]

Whether God Works in Every Agent?

Objection 1: It would seem that God does not work in every agent. For we must not attribute any insufficiency to God. If therefore God works in every agent, He works sufficiently in each one. Hence it would be superfluous for the created agent to work at all.

Obj. 2: Further, the same work cannot proceed at the same time from two sources; as neither can one and the same movement belong to two movable things. Therefore if the creature's operation is from God operating in the creature, it cannot at the same time proceed from the creature; and so no creature works at all.

Obj. 3: Further, the maker is the cause of the operation of the thing made, as giving it the form whereby it operates. Therefore, if God is the cause of the operation of things made by Him, this would be inasmuch as He gives them the power of operating. But this is in the beginning, when He makes them. Thus it seems that God does not operate any further in the operating creature.

*On the contrary,* It is written (Isa. 26:12): "Lord, Thou hast wrought all our works in [Vulg.: 'for'] us."

*I answer that,* Some have understood God to work in every agent in such a way that no created power has any effect in things, but that God alone is the ultimate cause of everything wrought; for instance, that it is not fire that gives heat, but God in the fire, and so forth. But this is impossible. First, because the order of cause and effect would be taken away from created things: and this would imply lack of power in the Creator: for it is due to the power of the cause, that it bestows active power on its effect. Secondly, because the active powers which are seen to exist in things, would be bestowed on things to no purpose, if these wrought nothing through them. Indeed, all things created would seem, in a way, to be purposeless, if they lacked an operation proper to them; since the purpose of everything is its operation. For the less perfect is always for the sake of the more perfect: and consequently as the matter is for the sake of the form, so the form which is the first act, is for the sake of its operation, which is the second act; and thus operation is the end of the creature. We must therefore understand that God works in things in such a manner that things have their proper operation.

In order to make this clear, we must observe that as there are few kinds of causes; matter is not a principle of action, but is the subject that receives the effect of action. On the other hand, the end, the agent, and the form are principles of action, but in a certain order. For the first principle of action is the end which moves the agent; the second is the agent; the third is the form of that which the agent applies to action (although the agent also acts through its own form); as may be clearly seen in things made by art. For the craftsman is moved to action by the end, which is the thing wrought, for instance a chest or a bed; and applies to action the axe which cuts through its being sharp.

Thus then does God work in every worker, according to these three things. First as an end. For since every operation is for the sake of some good, real or apparent; and nothing is good either really or apparently, except in as far as it participates in a likeness to the Supreme Good, which is God; it follows that God Himself is the cause of every operation as its end. Again it is to be observed that where there are several agents in order, the second always acts in virtue of the first; for the first agent moves the second to act. And thus all agents act in virtue of God Himself: and therefore He is the cause of action in every agent. Thirdly, we must observe that God not only moves things to operate, as it were applying their forms and powers to operation, just as the workman applies the axe to cut, who nevertheless at times does not give the axe its form; but He also gives created agents their forms and preserves them in being. Therefore He is the cause of action not only by giving the form which is the principle of action, as the generator is said to be the cause of movement in things heavy and light; but also as preserving the forms and powers of things; just as the sun is said to be the cause of the manifestation of colors, inasmuch as it gives and preserves the light by which colors are made manifest. And since the form of a thing is within the thing, and all the more, as it approaches nearer to the First and Universal Cause; and because in all things God Himself is properly the cause of universal being which is innermost in all things; it follows that in all things God works intimately. For this reason in Holy Scripture the operations of nature are attributed to God as operating in nature, according to Job 10:11: "Thou hast clothed me with skin and flesh: Thou hast put me together with bones and sinews."

Reply Obj. 1: God works sufficiently in things as First Agent, but it does not follow from this that the operation of secondary agents is superfluous.

Reply Obj. 2: One action does not proceed from two agents of the same order. But nothing hinders the same action from proceeding from a primary and a secondary agent.

Reply Obj. 3: God not only gives things their form, but He also preserves them in existence, and applies them to act, and is moreover the end of every action, as above explained.

SIXTH ARTICLE [I, Q. 105, Art. 6]

Whether God Can Do Anything Outside the Established Order of Nature?

Objection 1: It would seem that God cannot do anything outside the established order of nature. For Augustine (Contra Faust. xxvi, 3) says: "God the Maker and Creator of each nature, does nothing against nature." But that which is outside the natural order seems to be against nature. Therefore God can do nothing outside the natural order.

Obj. 2: Further, as the order of justice is from God, so is the order of nature. But God cannot do anything outside the order of justice; for then He would do something unjust. Therefore He cannot do anything outside the order of nature.

Obj. 3: Further, God established the order of nature. Therefore it God does anything outside the order of nature, it would seem that He is changeable; which cannot be said.

*On the contrary,* Augustine says (Contra Faust. xxvi, 3): "God sometimes does things which are contrary to the ordinary course of nature."

*I answer that,* From each cause there results a certain order to its effects, since every cause is a principle; and so, according to the multiplicity of causes, there results a multiplicity of orders, subjected one to the other, as cause is subjected to cause. Wherefore a higher cause is not subjected to a cause of a lower order; but conversely. An example of this may be seen in human affairs. On the father of a family depends the order of the household; which order is contained in the order of the city; which order again depends on the ruler of the city; while this last order depends on that of the king, by whom the whole kingdom is ordered.

If therefore we consider the order of things depending on the first cause, God cannot do anything against this order; for, if He did so, He would act against His foreknowledge, or His will, or His goodness. But if we consider the order of things depending on any secondary cause, thus God can do something outside such order; for He is not subject to the order of secondary causes; but, *on the contrary,* this order is subject to Him, as proceeding from Him, not by a natural necessity, but by the choice of His own will; for He could have created another order of things. Wherefore God can do something outside this order created by Him, when He chooses, for instance by producing the effects of secondary causes without them, or by producing certain effects to which secondary causes do not extend. So Augustine says (Contra Faust. xxvi, 3): "God acts against the wonted course of nature, but by no means does He act against the supreme law; because He does not act against Himself."

Reply Obj. 1: In natural things something may happen outside this natural order, in two ways. It may happen by the action of an agent which did not give them their natural inclination; as, for example, when a man moves a heavy body upwards, which does not owe to him its natural inclination to move downwards; and that would be against nature. It may also happen by the action of the agent on whom the natural inclination depends; and this is not against nature, as is clear in the ebb and flow of the tide, which is not against nature; although it is against the natural movement of water in a downward direction; for it is owing to the influence of a heavenly body, on which the natural inclination of lower bodies depends. Therefore since the order of nature is given to things by God; if He does anything outside this order, it is not against nature. Wherefore Augustine says (Contra Faust. xxvi, 3): "That is natural to each thing which is caused by Him from Whom is all mode, number, and order in nature."

Reply Obj. 2: The order of justice arises by relation to the First Cause, Who is the rule of all justice; and therefore God can do nothing against such order.

Reply Obj. 3: God fixed a certain order in things in such a way that at the same time He reserved to Himself whatever he intended to do otherwise than by a particular cause. So when He acts outside this order, He does not change.

SEVENTH ARTICLE [I, Q. 105, Art. 7]

Whether Whatever God Does Outside the Natural Order Is Miraculous?

Objection 1: It would seem that not everything which God does outside the natural order of things, is miraculous. For the creation of the world, and of souls, and the justification of the unrighteous, are done by God outside the natural order; as not being accomplished by the action of any natural cause. Yet these things are not called miracles. Therefore not everything that God does outside the natural order is a miracle.

Obj. 2: Further, a miracle is "something difficult, which seldom occurs, surpassing the faculty of nature, and going so far beyond our hopes as to compel our astonishment" [*St. Augustine, De utilitate credendi xvi.]. But some things outside the order of nature are not arduous; for they occur in small things, such as the recovery and healing of the sick. Nor are they of rare occurrence, since they happen frequently; as when the sick were placed in the streets, to be healed by the shadow of Peter (Acts 5:15). Nor do they surpass the faculty of nature; as when people are cured of a fever. Nor are they beyond our hopes, since we all hope for the resurrection of the dead, which nevertheless will be outside the course of nature. Therefore not all things are outside the course of nature are miraculous.

Obj. 3: Further, the word miracle is derived from admiration. Now admiration concerns things manifest to the senses. But sometimes things happen outside the order of nature, which are not manifest to the senses; as when the Apostles were endowed with knowledge without studying or being taught. Therefore not everything that occurs outside the order of nature is miraculous.

*On the contrary,* Augustine says (Contra Faust. xxvi, 3): "Where God does anything against that order of nature which we know and are accustomed to observe, we call it a miracle."

*I answer that,* The word miracle is derived from admiration, which arises when an effect is manifest, whereas its cause is hidden; as when a man sees an eclipse without knowing its cause, as the Philosopher says in the beginning of his *Metaphysics.* Now the cause of a manifest effect may be known to one, but unknown to others. Wherefore a thing is wonderful to one man, and not at all to others: as an eclipse is to a rustic, but not to an astronomer. Now a miracle is so called as being full of wonder; as having a cause absolutely hidden from all: and this cause is God. Wherefore those things which God does outside those causes which we know, are called miracles.

Reply Obj. 1: Creation, and the justification of the unrighteous, though done by God alone, are not, properly speaking, miracles, because they are not of a nature to proceed from any other cause; so they do not occur outside the order of nature, since they do not belong to that order.

Reply Obj. 2: An arduous thing is called a miracle, not on account of the excellence of the thing wherein it is done, but because it surpasses the faculty of nature: likewise a thing is called unusual, not because it does not often happen, but because it is outside the usual natural course of things. Furthermore, a thing is said to be above the faculty of nature, not only by reason of the substance of the thing done, but also on account of the manner and order in which it is done. Again, a miracle is said to go beyond the hope "of nature," not above the hope "of grace," which hope comes from faith, whereby we believe in the future resurrection.

Reply Obj. 3: The knowledge of the Apostles, although not manifest in itself, yet was made manifest in its effect, from which it was shown to be wonderful.

EIGHTH ARTICLE [I, Q. 105, Art. 8]

Whether One Miracle Is Greater Than Another?

Objection 1: It would seem that one miracle is not greater than another. For Augustine says (Epist. ad Volusian. cxxxvii): "In miraculous deeds, the whole measure of the deed is the power of the doer." But by the same power of God all miracles are done. Therefore one miracle is not greater than another.

Obj. 2: Further, the power of God is infinite. But the infinite exceeds the finite beyond all proportion; and therefore no more reason exists to wonder at one effect thereof than at another. Therefore one miracle is not greater than another.

*On the contrary,* The Lord says, speaking of miraculous works (John 14:12): "The works that I do, he also shall do, and greater than these shall he do."

*I answer that,* Nothing is called a miracle by comparison with the Divine Power; because no action is of any account compared with the power of God, according to Isa. 40:15: "Behold the Gentiles are as a drop from a bucket, and are counted as the smallest grain of a balance." But a thing is called a miracle by comparison with the power of nature which it surpasses. So the more the power of nature is surpassed, the greater the miracle. Now the power of nature is surpassed in three ways: firstly, in the substance of the deed, for instance, if two bodies occupy the same place, or if the sun goes backwards; or if a human body is glorified: such things nature is absolutely unable to do; and these hold the highest rank among miracles. Secondly, a thing surpasses the power of nature, not in the deed, but in that wherein it is done; as the raising of the dead, and giving sight to the blind, and the like; for nature can give life, but not to the dead; and such hold the second rank in miracles. Thirdly, a thing surpasses nature's power in the measure and order in which it is done; as when a man is cured of a fever suddenly, without treatment or the usual process of nature; or as when the air is suddenly condensed into rain, by Divine power without a natural cause, as occurred at the prayers of Samuel and Elias; and these hold the lowest place in miracles. Moreover, each of these kinds has various degrees, according to the different ways in which the power of nature is surpassed.

From this is clear how to reply to the objections, arguing as they do from the Divine power.

## QUESTION 106

HOW ONE CREATURE MOVES ANOTHER (In Four Articles)

We next consider how one creature moves another. This consideration will be threefold:

(1) How the angels move, who are purely spiritual creatures;

(2) How bodies move;

(3) How man moves, who is composed of a spiritual and a corporeal nature.

Concerning the first point, there are three things to be considered:

(1) How an angel acts on an angel;

(2) How an angel acts on a corporeal nature;

(3) How an angel acts on man.

The first of these raises the question of the enlightenment and speech of the angels; and of their mutual coordination, both of the good and of the bad angels.

Concerning their enlightenment there are four points of inquiry:

(1) Whether one angel moves the intellect of another by enlightenment?

(2) Whether one angel moves the will of another?

(3) Whether an inferior angel can enlighten a superior angel?

(4) Whether a superior angel enlightens an inferior angel in all that he knows himself?

FIRST ARTICLE [I, Q. 106, Art. 1]

Whether One Angel Enlightens Another?

Objection 1: It would seem that one angel does not enlighten another. For the angels possess now the same beatitude which we hope to obtain. But one man will not then enlighten another, according to Jer. 31:34: "They shall teach no more every man his neighbor, and every man his brother." Therefore neither does an angel enlighten another now.

Obj. 2: Further, light in the angels is threefold; of nature, of grace, and of glory. But an angel is enlightened in the light of nature by the Creator; in the light of grace by the Justifier; in the light of glory by the Beatifier; all of which comes from God. Therefore one angel does not enlighten another.

Obj. 3: Further, light is a form in the mind. But the rational mind is "informed by God alone, without created intervention," as Augustine says (QQ. 83, qu. 51). Therefore one angel does not enlighten the mind of another.

*On the contrary,* Dionysius says (Coel. Hier. viii) that "the angels of the second hierarchy are cleansed, enlightened and perfected by the angels of the first hierarchy."

*I answer that,* One angel enlightens another. To make this clear, we must observe that intellectual light is nothing else than a manifestation of truth, according to Eph. 5:13: "All that is made manifest is light." Hence to enlighten means nothing else but to communicate to others the manifestation of the known truth; according to the Apostle (Eph. 3:8): "To me the least of all the saints is given this grace ... to enlighten all men, that they may see what is the dispensation of the mystery which hath been hidden from eternity in God." Therefore one angel is said to enlighten another by manifesting the truth which he knows himself. Hence Dionysius says (Coel. Hier. vii): "Theologians plainly show that the orders of the heavenly beings are taught Divine science by the higher minds."

Now since two things concur in the intellectual operation, as we have said (Q. 105, A. 3), namely, the intellectual power, and the likeness of the thing understood; in both of these one angel can notify the known truth to another. First, by strengthening his intellectual power; for just as the power of an imperfect body is strengthened by the neighborhood of a more perfect body—for instance, the less hot is made hotter by the presence of what is hotter; so the intellectual power of an inferior angel is strengthened by the superior angel turning to him: since in spiritual things, for one thing to turn to another, corresponds to neighborhood in corporeal things. Secondly, one angel manifests the truth to another as regards the likeness of the thing understood. For the superior angel receives the knowledge of truth by a kind of universal conception, to receive which the inferior angel's intellect is not sufficiently powerful, for it is natural to him to receive truth in a more particular manner. Therefore the superior angel distinguishes, in a way, the truth which he conceives universally, so that it can be grasped by the inferior angel; and thus he proposes it to his knowledge. Thus it is with us that the teacher, in order to adapt himself to others, divides into many points the knowledge which he possesses in the universal. This is thus expressed by Dionysius (Coel. Hier. xv): "Every intellectual substance with provident power divides and multiplies the uniform knowledge bestowed on it by one nearer to God, so as to lead its inferiors upwards by analogy."

Reply Obj. 1: All the angels, both inferior and superior, see the Essence of God immediately, and in this respect one does not teach another. It is of this truth that the prophet speaks; wherefore he adds: "They shall teach no more every man his brother, saying: 'Know the Lord': for all shall know Me, from the least of them even to the greatest." But all the types of the Divine works, which are known in God as in their cause, God knows in Himself, because He comprehends Himself; but of others who see God, each one knows the more types, the more perfectly he sees God. Hence a superior angel knows more about the types of the Divine works than an inferior angel, and concerning these the former enlightens the latter; and as to this Dionysius says (Div. Nom. iv) that the angels "are enlightened by the types of existing things."

Reply Obj. 2: An angel does not enlighten another by giving him the light of nature, grace, or glory; but by strengthening his natural light, and by manifesting to him the truth concerning the state of nature, of grace, and of glory, as explained above.

Reply Obj. 3: The rational mind is formed immediately by God, either as the image from the exemplar, forasmuch as it is made to the image of God alone; or as the subject by the ultimate perfecting form: for the created mind is always considered to be unformed, except it adhere to the first truth; while the other kinds of enlightenment that proceed from man or angel, are, as it were, dispositions to this ultimate form.

SECOND ARTICLE [I, Q. 106, Art. 2]

Whether one angel moves another angel's will?

Objection 1: It would seem that one angel can move another angel's will. Because, according to Dionysius quoted above (A. 1), as one angel enlightens another, so does he cleanse and perfect another. But cleansing and perfecting seem to belong to the will: for the former seems to point to the stain of sin which appertains to will; while to be perfected is to obtain an end, which is the object of the will. Therefore an angel can move another angel's will.

Obj. 2: Further, as Dionysius says (Coel. Hier. vii): "The names of the angels designate their properties." Now the Seraphim are so called because they "kindle" or "give heat": and this is by love which belongs to the will. Therefore one angel moves another angel's will.

Obj. 3: Further, the Philosopher says (De Anima iii, 11) that the higher appetite moves the lower. But as the intellect of the superior angel is higher, so also is his will. It seems, therefore, that the superior angel can change the will of another angel.

*On the contrary,* To him it belongs to change the will, to whom it belongs to bestow righteousness: for righteousness is the rightness of the will. But God alone bestows righteousness. Therefore one angel cannot change another angel's will.

*I answer that,* As was said above (Q. 105, A. 4), the will is changed in two ways; on the part of the object, and on the part of the power. On the part of the object, both the good itself which is the object of the will, moves the will, as the appetible moves the appetite; and he who points out the object, as, for instance, one who proves something to be good. But as we have said above (Q. 105, A. 4), other goods in a measure incline the will, yet nothing sufficiently moves the will save the universal good, and that is God. And this good He alone shows, that it may be seen by the blessed, Who, when Moses asked: "Show me Thy glory," answered: "I will show thee all good" (Ex. 33:18, 19). Therefore an angel does not move the will sufficiently, either as the object or as showing the object. But he inclines the will as something lovable, and as manifesting some created good ordered to God's goodness. And thus he can incline the will to the love of the creature or of God, by way of persuasion.

But on the part of the power the will cannot be moved at all save by God. For the operation of the will is a certain inclination of the willer to the thing willed. And He alone can change this inclination, Who bestowed on the creature the power to will: just as that agent alone can change the natural inclination, which can give the power to which follows that natural inclination. Now God alone gave to the creature the power to will, because He alone is the author of the intellectual nature. Therefore an angel cannot move another angel's will.

Reply Obj. 1: Cleansing and perfecting are to be understood according to the mode of enlightenment. And since God enlightens by changing the intellect and will, He cleanses by removing defects of intellect and will, and perfects unto the end of the intellect and will. But the enlightenment caused by an angel concerns the intellect, as explained above (A. 1); therefore an angel is to be understood as cleansing from the defect of nescience in the intellect; and as perfecting unto the consummate end of the intellect, and this is the knowledge of truth. Thus Dionysius says (Eccl. Hier. vi): that "in the heavenly hierarchy the chastening of the inferior essence is an enlightening of things unknown, that leads them to more perfect knowledge." For instance, we might say that corporeal sight is cleansed by the removal of darkness; enlightened by the diffusion of light; and perfected by being brought to the perception of the colored object.

Reply Obj. 2: One angel can induce another to love God by persuasion as explained above.

Reply Obj. 3: The Philosopher speaks of the lower sensitive appetite which can be moved by the superior intellectual appetite, because it belongs to the same nature of the soul, and because the inferior appetite is a power in a corporeal organ. But this does not apply to the angels.

THIRD ARTICLE [I, Q. 106, Art. 3]

Whether an Inferior Angel Can Enlighten a Superior Angel?

Objection 1: It would seem that an inferior angel can enlighten a superior angel. For the ecclesiastical hierarchy is derived from, and represents the heavenly hierarchy; and hence the heavenly Jerusalem is called "our mother" (Gal. 4:26). But in the Church even superiors are enlightened and taught by their inferiors, as the Apostle says (1 Cor. 14:31): "You may all prophesy one by one, that all may learn and all may be exhorted." Therefore, likewise in the heavenly hierarchy, the superiors can be enlightened by inferiors.

Obj. 2: Further, as the order of corporeal substances depends on the will of God, so also does the order of spiritual substances. But, as was said above (Q. 105, A. 6), God sometimes acts outside the order of corporeal substances. Therefore He also sometimes acts outside the order of spiritual substances, by enlightening inferior otherwise than through their superiors. Therefore in that way the inferiors enlightened by God can enlighten superiors.

Obj. 3: Further, one angel enlightens the other to whom he turns, as was above explained (A. 1). But since this turning to another is voluntary, the highest angel can turn to the lowest passing over the others. Therefore he can enlighten him immediately; and thus the latter can enlighten his superiors.

*On the contrary,* Dionysius says that "this is the Divine unalterable law, that inferior things are led to God by the superior" (Coel. Hier. iv; Eccl. Hier. v).

*I answer that,* The inferior angels never enlighten the superior, but are always enlightened by them. The reason is, because, as above explained (Q. 105, A. 6), one order is under another, as cause is under cause; and hence as cause is ordered to cause, so is order to order. Therefore there is no incongruity if sometimes anything is done outside the order of the inferior cause, to be ordered to the superior cause, as in human affairs the command of the president is passed over from obedience to the prince. So it happens that God works miraculously outside the order of corporeal nature, that men may be ordered to the knowledge of Him. But the passing over of the order that belongs to spiritual substances in no way belongs to the ordering of men to God; since the angelic operations are not made known to us; as are the operations of sensible bodies. Thus the order which belongs to spiritual substances is never passed over by God; so that the inferiors are always moved by the superior, and not conversely.

Reply Obj. 1: The ecclesiastical hierarchy imitates the heavenly in some degree, but not by a perfect likeness. For in the heavenly hierarchy the perfection of the order is in proportion to its nearness to God; so that those who are the nearer to God are the more sublime in grade, and more clear in knowledge; and on that account the superiors are never enlightened by the inferiors, whereas in the ecclesiastical hierarchy, sometimes those who are the nearer to God in sanctity, are in the lowest grade, and are not conspicuous for science; and some also are eminent in one kind of science, and fail in another; and on that account superiors may be taught by inferiors.

Reply Obj. 2: As above explained, there is no similarity between what God does outside the order of corporeal nature, and that of spiritual nature. Hence the argument does not hold.

Reply Obj. 3: An angel turns voluntarily to enlighten another angel, but the angel's will is ever regulated by the Divine law which made the order in the angels.

FOURTH ARTICLE [I, Q. 106, Art. 4]

Whether the Superior Angel Enlightens the Inferior As Regards All He Himself Knows?

Objection 1: It would seem that the superior angel does not enlighten the inferior concerning all he himself knows. For Dionysius says (Coel. Hier. xii) that the superior angels have a more universal knowledge; and the inferior a more particular and individual knowledge. But more is contained under a universal knowledge than under a particular knowledge. Therefore not all that the superior angels know, is known by the inferior, through these being enlightened by the former.

Obj. 2: Further, the Master of the Sentences (ii, D, 11) says that the superior angels had long known the Mystery of the Incarnation, whereas the inferior angels did not know it until it was accomplished. Thus we find that on some of the angels inquiring, as it were, in ignorance: "Who is this King of glory?" other angels, who knew, answered: "The Lord of Hosts, He is the King of glory," as Dionysius expounds (Coel. Hier. vii). But this would not apply if the superior angels enlightened the inferior concerning all they know themselves. Therefore they do not do so.

Obj. 3: Further, if the superior angels enlighten the inferior about all they know, nothing that the superior angels know would be unknown to the inferior angels. Therefore the superior angels could communicate nothing more to the inferior; which appears open to objection. Therefore the superior angels enlighten the inferior in all things.

*On the contrary,* Gregory [*Peter Lombard, Sent. ii, D, ix; Cf. Gregory, Hom. xxxiv, in Ev.] says: "In that heavenly country, though there are some excellent gifts, yet nothing is held individually." And Dionysius says: "Each heavenly essence communicates to the inferior the gift derived from the superior" (Coel. Hier. xv), as quoted above (A. 1).

*I answer that,* Every creature participates in the Divine goodness, so as to diffuse the good it possesses to others; for it is of the nature of good to communicate itself to others. Hence also corporeal agents give their likeness to others so far as they can. So the more an agent is established in the share of the Divine goodness, so much the more does it strive to transmit its perfections to others as far as possible. Hence the Blessed Peter admonishes those who by grace share in the Divine goodness; saying: "As every man hath received grace, ministering the same one to another; as good stewards of the manifold grace of God" (1 Pet. 4:10). Much more therefore do the holy angels, who enjoy the plenitude of participation of the Divine goodness, impart the same to those below them.

Nevertheless this gift is not received so excellently by the inferior as by the superior angels; and therefore the superior ever remain in a higher order, and have a more perfect knowledge; as the master understands the same thing better than the pupil who learns from him.

Reply Obj. 1: The knowledge of the superior angels is said to be more universal as regards the more eminent mode of knowledge.

Reply Obj. 2: The Master's words are not to be understood as if the inferior angels were entirely ignorant of the Mystery of the Incarnation but that they did not know it as fully as the superior angels; and that they progressed in the knowledge of it afterwards when the Mystery was accomplished.

Reply Obj. 3: Till the Judgment Day some new things are always being revealed by God to the highest angels, concerning the course of the world, and especially the salvation of the elect. Hence there is always something for the superior angels to make known to the inferior.

## QUESTION 107

THE SPEECH OF THE ANGELS (In Five Articles)

We next consider the speech of the angels. Here there are five points of inquiry:

(1) Whether one angel speaks to another?

(2) Whether the inferior speaks to the superior?

(3) Whether an angel speaks to God?

(4) Whether the angelic speech is subject to local distance?

(5) Whether all the speech of one angel to another is known to all?

FIRST ARTICLE [I, Q. 107, Art. 1]

Whether One Angel Speaks to Another?

Objection 1: It would seem that one angel does not speak to another. For Gregory says (Moral. xviii) that, in the state of the resurrection "each one's body will not hide his mind from his fellows." Much less, therefore, is one angel's mind hidden from another. But speech manifests to another what lies hidden in the mind. Therefore it is not necessary that one angel should speak to another.

Obj. 2: Further, speech is twofold; interior, whereby one speaks to oneself; and exterior, whereby one speaks to another. But exterior speech takes place by some sensible sign, as by voice, or gesture, or some bodily member, as the tongue, or the fingers, and this cannot apply to the angels. Therefore one angel does not speak to another.

Obj. 3: Further, the speaker incites the hearer to listen to what he says. But it does not appear that one angel incites another to listen; for this happens among us by some sensible sign. Therefore one angel does not speak to another.

*On the contrary,* The Apostle says (1 Cor. 13:1): "If I speak with the tongues of men and of angels."

*I answer that,* The angels speak in a certain way. But, as Gregory says (Moral. ii): "It is fitting that our mind, rising above the properties of bodily speech, should be lifted to the sublime and unknown methods of interior speech."

To understand how one angel speaks to another, we must consider that, as we explained above (Q. 82, A. 4), when treating of the actions and powers of the soul, the will moves the intellect to its operation. Now an intelligible object is present to the intellect in three ways; first, habitually, or in the memory, as Augustine says (De Trin. xiv, 6, 7); secondly, as actually considered or conceived; thirdly, as related to something else. And it is clear that the intelligible object passes from the first to the second stage by the command of the will, and hence in the definition of habit these words occur, "which anyone uses when he wills." So likewise the intelligible object passes from the second to the third stage by the will; for by the will the concept of the mind is ordered to something else, as, for instance, either to the performing of an action, or to being made known to another. Now when the mind turns itself to the actual consideration of any habitual knowledge, then a person speaks to himself; for the concept of the mind is called "the interior word." And by the fact that the concept of the angelic mind is ordered to be made known to another by the will of the angel himself, the concept of one angel is made known to another; and in this way one angel speaks to another; for to speak to another only means to make known the mental concept to another.

Reply Obj. 1: Our mental concept is hidden by a twofold obstacle. The first is in the will, which can retain the mental concept within, or can direct it externally. In this way God alone can see the mind of another, according to 1 Cor. 2:11: "What man knoweth the things of a man, but the spirit of a man that is in him?" The other obstacle whereby the mental concept is excluded from another one's knowledge, comes from the body; and so it happens that even when the will directs the concept of the mind to make itself known, it is not at once make known to another; but some sensible sign must be used. Gregory alludes to this fact when he says (Moral. ii): "To other eyes we seem to stand aloof as it were behind the wall of the body; and when we wish to make ourselves known, we go out as it were by the door of the tongue to show what we really are." But an angel is under no such obstacle, and so he can make his concept known to another at once.

Reply Obj. 2: External speech, made by the voice, is a necessity for us on account of the obstacle of the body. Hence it does not befit an angel; but only interior speech belongs to him, and this includes not only the interior speech by mental concept, but also its being ordered to another's knowledge by the will. So the tongue of an angel is called metaphorically the angel's power, whereby he manifests his mental concept.

Reply Obj. 3: There is no need to draw the attention of the good angels, inasmuch as they always see each other in the Word; for as one ever sees the other, so he ever sees what is ordered to himself. But because by their very nature they can speak to each other, and even now the bad angels speak to each other, we must say that the intellect is moved by the intelligible object just as sense is affected by the sensible object. Therefore, as sense is aroused by the sensible object, so the mind of an angel can be aroused to attention by some intelligible power.

SECOND ARTICLE [I, Q. 107, Art. 2]

Whether the Inferior Angel Speaks to the Superior?

Objection 1: It would seem that the inferior angel does not speak to the superior. For on the text (1 Cor. 13:1), "If I speak with the tongues of men and of angels," a gloss remarks that the speech of the angels is an enlightenment whereby the superior enlightens the inferior. But the inferior never enlightens the superior, as was above explained (Q. 106, A. 3). Therefore neither do the inferior speak to the superior.

Obj. 2: Further, as was said above (Q. 106, A. 1), to enlighten means merely to acquaint one man of what is known to another; and this is to speak. Therefore to speak and to enlighten are the same; so the same conclusion follows.

Obj. 3: Further, Gregory says (Moral. ii): "God speaks to the angels by the very fact that He shows to their hearts His hidden and invisible things." But this is to enlighten them. Therefore, whenever God speaks, He enlightens. In the same way every angelic speech is an enlightening. Therefore an inferior angel can in no way speak to a superior angel.

*On the contrary,* According to the exposition of Dionysius (Coel. Hier. vii), the inferior angels said to the superior: "Who is this King of Glory?"

*I answer that,* The inferior angels can speak to the superior. To make this clear, we must consider that every angelic enlightening is an angelic speech; but on the other hand, not every speech is an enlightening; because, as we have said (A. 1), for one angel to speak to another angel means nothing else, but that by his own will he directs his mental concept in such a way, that it becomes known to the other. Now what the mind conceives may be reduced to a twofold principle; to God Himself, Who is the primal truth; and to the will of the one who understands, whereby we actually consider anything. But because truth is the light of the intellect, and God Himself is the rule of all truth; the manifestation of what is conceived by the mind, as depending on the primary truth, is both speech and enlightenment; for example, when one man says to another: "Heaven was created by God"; or, "Man is an animal." The manifestation, however, of what depends on the will of the one who understands, cannot be called an enlightenment, but is only a speech; for instance, when one says to another: "I wish to learn this; I wish to do this or that." The reason is that the created will is not a light, nor a rule of truth; but participates of light. Hence to communicate what comes from the created will is not, as such, an enlightening. For to know what you may will, or what you may understand does not belong to the perfection of my intellect; but only to know the truth in reality.

Now it is clear that the angels are called superior or inferior by comparison with this principle, God; and therefore enlightenment, which depends on the principle which is God, is conveyed only by the superior angels to the inferior. But as regards the will as the principle, he who wills is first and supreme; and therefore the manifestation of what belongs to the will, is conveyed to others by the one who wills. In that manner both the superior angels speak to the inferior, and the inferior speak to the superior.

From this clearly appear the replies to the first and second objections.

Reply Obj. 3: Every speech of God to the angels is an enlightening; because since the will of God is the rule of truth, it belongs to the perfection and enlightenment of the created mind to know even what God wills. But the same does not apply to the will of the angels, as was explained above.

THIRD ARTICLE [I, Q. 107, Art. 3]

Whether an Angel Speaks to God?

Objection 1: It would seem that an angel does not speak to God. For speech makes known something to another. But an angel cannot make known anything to God, Who knows all things. Therefore an angel does not speak to God.

Obj. 2: Further, to speak is to order the mental concept in reference to another, as was shown above (A. 1). But an angel ever orders his mental concept to God. So if an angel speaks to God, he ever speaks to God; which in some ways appears to be unreasonable, since an angel sometimes speaks to another angel. Therefore it seems that an angel never speaks to God.

*On the contrary,* It is written (Zech. 1:12): "The angel of the Lord answered and said: O Lord of hosts, how long wilt Thou not have mercy on Jerusalem." Therefore an angel speaks to God.

*I answer that,* As was said above (AA. 1, 2), the angel speaks by ordering his mental concept to something else. Now one thing is ordered to another in a twofold manner. In one way for the purpose of giving one thing to another, as in natural things the agent is ordered to the patient, and in human speech the teacher is ordered to the learner; and in this sense an angel in no way speaks to God either of what concerns the truth, or of whatever depends on the created will; because God is the principle and source of all truth and of all will. In another way one thing is ordered to another to receive something, as in natural things the passive is ordered to the agent, and in human speech the disciple to the master; and in this way an angel speaks to God, either by consulting the Divine will of what ought to be done, or by admiring the Divine excellence which he can never comprehend; thus Gregory says (Moral. ii) that "the angels speak to God, when by contemplating what is above themselves they rise to emotions of admiration."

Reply Obj. 1: Speech is not always for the purpose of making something known to another; but is sometimes finally ordered to the purpose of manifesting something to the speaker himself; as when the disciples ask instruction from the master.

Reply Obj. 2: The angels are ever speaking to God in the sense of praising and admiring Him and His works; but they speak to Him by consulting Him about what ought to be done whenever they have to perform any new work, concerning which they desire enlightenment.

FOURTH ARTICLE [I, Q. 107, Art. 4]

Whether Local Distance Influences the Angelic Speech?

Objection 1: It would seem that local distance affects the angelic speech. For as Damascene says (De Fide Orth. i, 13): "An angel works where he is." But speech is an angelic operation. Therefore, as an angel is in a determinate place, it seems that an angel's speech is limited by the bounds of that place.

Obj. 2: Further, a speaker cries out on account of the distance of the hearer. But it is said of the Seraphim that "they cried one to another" (Isa. 6:3). Therefore in the angelic speech local distance has some effect.

*On the contrary,* It is said that the rich man in hell spoke to Abraham, notwithstanding the local distance (Luke 16:24). Much less therefore does local distance impede the speech of one angel to another.

*I answer that,* The angelic speech consists in an intellectual operation, as explained above (AA. 1, 2, 3). And the intellectual operation of an angel abstracts from the "here and now." For even our own intellectual operation takes place by abstraction from the "here and now," except accidentally on the part of the phantasms, which do not exist at all in an angel. But as regards whatever is abstracted from "here and now," neither difference of time nor local distance has any influence whatever. Hence in the angelic speech local distance is no impediment.

Reply Obj. 1: The angelic speech, as above explained (A. 1, ad 2), is interior; perceived, nevertheless, by another; and therefore it exists in the angel who speaks, and consequently where the angel is who speaks. But as local distance does not prevent one angel seeing another, so neither does it prevent an angel perceiving what is ordered to him on the part of another; and this is to perceive his speech.

Reply Obj. 2: The cry mentioned is not a bodily voice raised by reason of the local distance; but is taken to signify the magnitude of what is said, or the intensity of the affection, according to what Gregory says (Moral. ii): "The less one desires, the less one cries out."

FIFTH ARTICLE [I, Q. 107, Art. 5]

Whether All the Angels Know What One Speaks to Another?

Objection 1: It would seem that all the angels know what one speaks to another. For unequal local distance is the reason why all men do not know what one man says to another. But in the angelic speech local distance has no effect, as above explained (A. 4). Therefore all the angels know what one speaks to another.

Obj. 2: Further, all the angels have the intellectual power in common. So if the mental concept of one ordered to another is known by one, it is for the same reason known by all.

Obj. 3: Further, enlightenment is a kind of speech. But the enlightenment of one angel by another extends to all the angels, because, as Dionysius says (Coel. Hier. xv): "Each one of the heavenly beings communicates what he learns to the others." Therefore the speech of one angel to another extends to all.

*On the contrary,* One man can speak to another alone; much more can this be the case among the angels.

*I answer that,* As above explained (AA. 1, 2), the mental concept of one angel can be perceived by another when the angel who possesses the concept refers it by his will to another. Now a thing can be ordered through some cause to one thing and not to another; consequently the concept of one (angel) may be known by one and not by another; and therefore an angel can perceive the speech of one angel to another; whereas others do not, not through the obstacle of local distance, but on account of the will so ordering, as explained above.

From this appear the replies to the first and second objections.

Reply Obj. 3: Enlightenment is of those truths that emanate from the first rule of truth, which is the principle common to all the angels; and in that way all enlightenments are common to all. But speech may be of something ordered to the principle of the created will, which is proper to each angel; and in this way it is not necessary that these speeches should be common to all.

# QUESTION 108

OF THE ANGELIC DEGREES OF HIERARCHIES AND ORDERS (In Eight Articles)

We next consider the degrees of the angels in their hierarchies and orders; for it was said above (Q. 106, A. 3), that the superior angels enlighten the inferior angels; and not conversely.

Under this head there are eight points of inquiry:

(1) Whether all the angels belong to one hierarchy?

(2) Whether in one hierarchy there is only one order?

(3) Whether in one order there are many angels?

(4) Whether the distinction of hierarchies and orders is natural?

(5) Of the names and properties of each order.

(6) Of the comparison of the orders to one another.

(7) Whether the orders will outlast the Day of Judgment?

(8) Whether men are taken up into the angelic orders?

FIRST ARTICLE [I, Q. 108, Art. 1]

Whether All the Angels Are of One Hierarchy?

Objection 1: It would seem that all the angels belong to one hierarchy. For since the angels are supreme among creatures, it is evident that they are ordered for the best. But the best ordering of a multitude is for it to be governed by one authority, as the Philosopher shows (Metaph. xii, Did. xi, 10; Polit. iii, 4). Therefore as a hierarchy is nothing but a sacred principality, it seems that all the angels belong to one hierarchy.

Obj. 2: Further, Dionysius says (Coel. Hier. iii) that "hierarchy is order, knowledge, and action." But all the angels agree in one order towards God, Whom they know, and by Whom in their actions they are ruled. Therefore all the angels belong to one hierarchy.

Obj. 3: Further, the sacred principality called hierarchy is to be found among men and angels. But all men are of one hierarchy. Therefore likewise all the angels are of one hierarchy.

*On the contrary,* Dionysius (Coel. Hier. vi) distinguishes three hierarchies of angels.

*I answer that,* Hierarchy means a "sacred" principality, as above explained. Now principality includes two things: the prince himself and the multitude ordered under the prince. Therefore because there is one God, the Prince not only of all the angels but also of men and all creatures; so there is one hierarchy, not only of all the angels, but also of all rational creatures, who can be participators of sacred things; according to Augustine (De Civ. Dei xii, 1): "There are two cities, that is, two societies, one of the good angels and men, the other of the wicked." But if we consider the principality on the part of the multitude ordered under the prince, then principality is said to be "one" accordingly as the multitude can be subject in *one* way to the government of the prince. And those that cannot be governed in the same way by a prince belong to different principalities: thus, under one king there are different cities, which are governed by different laws and administrators. Now it is evident that men do not receive the Divine enlightenments in the same way as do the angels; for the angels receive them in their intelligible purity, whereas men receive them under sensible signs, as Dionysius says (Coel. Hier. i). Therefore there must needs be a distinction between the human and the angelic hierarchy. In the same manner we distinguish three angelic hierarchies. For it was shown above (Q. 55, A. 3), in treating of the angelic knowledge, that the superior angels have a more universal knowledge of the truth than the inferior angels. This universal knowledge has three grades among the angels. For the types of things, concerning which the angels are enlightened, can be considered in a threefold manner. First as preceding from God as the first universal principle, which mode of knowledge belongs to the first hierarchy, connected immediately with God, and, "as it were, placed in the vestibule of God," as Dionysius says (Coel. Hier. vii). Secondly, forasmuch as these types depend on the universal created causes which in some way are already multiplied; which mode belongs to the second hierarchy. Thirdly, forasmuch as these types are applied to particular things as depending on their causes; which mode belongs to the lowest hierarchy. All this will appear more clearly when we treat of each of the orders (A. 6). In this way are the hierarchies distinguished on the part of the multitude of subjects.

Hence it is clear that those err and speak against the opinion of Dionysius who place a hierarchy in the Divine Persons, and call it the "supercelestial" hierarchy. For in the Divine Persons there exists, indeed, a natural order, but there is no hierarchical order, for as Dionysius says (Coel. Hier. iii): "The hierarchical order is so directed that some be cleansed, enlightened, and perfected; and that others cleanse, enlighten, and perfect"; which far be it from us to apply to the Divine Persons.

Reply Obj. 1: This objection considers principality on the part of the ruler, inasmuch as a multitude is best ruled by one ruler, as the Philosopher asserts in those passages.

Reply Obj. 2: As regards knowing God Himself, Whom all see in one way—that is, in His essence—there is no hierarchical distinction among the angels; but there is such a distinction as regards the types of created things, as above explained.

Reply Obj. 3: All men are of one species, and have one connatural mode of understanding; which is not the case in the angels: and hence the same argument does not apply to both.

SECOND ARTICLE [I, Q. 108, Art. 2]

Whether There Are Several Orders in One Hierarchy?

Objection 1: It would seem that in the one hierarchy there are not several orders. For when a definition is multiplied, the thing defined is also multiplied. But hierarchy is order, as Dionysius says (Coel. Hier. iii). Therefore, if there are many orders, there is not one hierarchy only, but many.

Obj. 2: Further, different orders are different grades, and grades among spirits are constituted by different spiritual gifts. But among the angels all the spiritual gifts are common to all, for "nothing is possessed individually" (Sent. ii, D, ix). Therefore there are not different orders of angels.

Obj. 3: Further, in the ecclesiastical hierarchy the orders are distinguished according to the actions of "cleansing," "enlightening," and "perfecting." For the order of deacons is "cleansing," the order of priests, is "enlightening," and of bishops "perfecting," as Dionysius says (Eccl. Hier. v). But each of the angels cleanses, enlightens, and perfects. Therefore there is no distinction of orders among the angels.

*On the contrary,* The Apostle says (Eph. 1:20,21) that "God has set the Man Christ above all principality and power, and virtue, and dominion": which are the various orders of the angels, and some of them belong to one hierarchy, as will be explained (A. 6).

*I answer that,* As explained above, one hierarchy is one principality—that is, one multitude ordered in one way under the rule of a prince. Now such a multitude would not be ordered, but confused, if there were not in it different orders. So the nature of a hierarchy requires diversity of orders.

This diversity of order arises from the diversity of offices and actions, as appears in one city where there are different orders according to the different actions; for there is one order of those who judge, and another of those who fight, and another of those who labor in the fields, and so forth.

But although one city thus comprises several orders, all may be reduced to three, when we consider that every multitude has a beginning, a middle, and an end. So in every city, a threefold order of men is to be seen, some of whom are supreme, as the nobles; others are the last, as the common people, while others hold a place between these, as the middle-class [populus honorabilis]. In the same way we find in each angelic hierarchy the orders distinguished according to their actions and offices, and all this diversity is reduced to three—namely, to the summit, the middle, and the base; and so in every hierarchy Dionysius places three orders (Coel. Hier. vi).

Reply Obj. 1: Order is twofold. In one way it is taken as the order comprehending in itself different grades; and in that way a hierarchy is called an order. In another way one grade is called an order; and in that sense the several orders of one hierarchy are so called.

Reply Obj. 2: All things are possessed in common by the angelic society, some things, however, being held more excellently by some than by others. Each gift is more perfectly possessed by the one who can communicate it, than by the one who cannot communicate it; as the hot thing which can communicate heat is more perfect that what is unable to give heat. And the more perfectly anyone can communicate a gift, the higher grade he occupies, as he is in the more perfect grade of mastership who can teach a higher science. By this similitude we can reckon the diversity of grades or orders among the angels, according to their different offices and actions.

Reply Obj. 3: The inferior angel is superior to the highest man of our hierarchy, according to the words, "He that is the lesser in the kingdom of heaven, is greater than he"—namely, John the Baptist, than whom "there hath not risen a greater among them that are born of women" (Matt. 11:11). Hence the lesser angel of the heavenly hierarchy can not only cleanse, but also enlighten and perfect, and in a higher way than can the orders of our hierarchy. Thus the heavenly orders are not distinguished by reason of these, but by reason of other different acts.

THIRD ARTICLE [I, Q. 108, Art. 3]

Whether There Are Many Angels in One Order?

Objection 1: It seems that there are not many angels in one order. For it was shown above (Q. 50, A. 4), that all the angels are unequal. But equals belong to one order. Therefore there are not many angels in one order.

Obj. 2: Further, it is superfluous for a thing to be done by many, which can be done sufficiently by one. But that which belongs to one angelic office can be done sufficiently by one angel; so much more sufficiently than the one sun does what belongs to the office of the sun, as the angel is more perfect than a heavenly body. If, therefore, the orders are distinguished by their offices, as stated above (A. 2), several angels in one order would be superfluous.

Obj. 3: Further, it was said above (Obj. 1) that all the angels are unequal. Therefore, if several angels (for instance, three or four), are of one order, the lowest one of the superior order will be more akin to the highest of the inferior order than with the highest of his own order; and thus he does not seem to be more of one order with the latter than with the former. Therefore there are not many angels of one order.

*On the contrary,* It is written: "The Seraphim cried to one another" (Isa. 6:3). Therefore there are many angels in the one order of the Seraphim.

*I answer that,* Whoever knows anything perfectly, is able to distinguish its acts, powers, and nature, down to the minutest details, whereas he who knows a thing in an imperfect manner can only distinguish it in a general way, and only as regards a few points. Thus, one who knows natural things imperfectly, can distinguish their orders in a general way, placing the heavenly bodies in one order, inanimate inferior bodies in another, plants in another, and animals in another; whilst he who knows natural things perfectly, is able to distinguish different orders in the heavenly bodies themselves, and in each of the other orders.

Now our knowledge of the angels is imperfect, as Dionysius says (Coel. Hier. vi). Hence we can only distinguish the angelic offices and orders in a general way, so as to place many angels in one order. But if we knew the offices and distinctions of the angels perfectly, we should know perfectly that each angel has his own office and his own order among things, and much more so than any star, though this be hidden from us.

Reply Obj. 1: All the angels of one order are in some way equal in a common similitude, whereby they are placed in that order; but absolutely speaking they are not equal. Hence Dionysius says (Coel. Hier. x) that in one and the same order of angels there are those who are first, middle, and last.

Reply Obj. 2: That special distinction of orders and offices wherein each angel has his own office and order, is hidden from us.

Reply Obj. 3: As in a surface which is partly white and partly black, the two parts on the borders of white and black are more akin as regards their position than any other two white parts, but are less akin in quality; so two angels who are on the boundary of two orders are more akin in propinquity of nature than one of them is akin to the others of its own order, but less akin in their fitness for similar offices, which fitness, indeed, extends to a definite limit.

FOURTH ARTICLE [I, Q. 108, Art. 4]

Whether the Distinction of Hierarchies and Orders Comes from the Angelic Nature?

Objection 1: It would seem that the distinction of hierarchies and of orders is not from the nature of the angels. For hierarchy is "a sacred principality," and Dionysius places in its definition that it "approaches a resemblance to God, as far as may be" (Coel. Hier. iii). But sanctity and resemblance to God is in the angels by grace, and not by nature. Therefore the distinction of hierarchies and orders in the angels is by grace, and not by nature.

Obj. 2: Further, the Seraphim are called "burning" or "kindling," as Dionysius says (Coel. Hier. vii). This belongs to charity which comes not from nature but from grace; for "it is poured forth in our hearts by the Holy Ghost Who is given to us" (Rom. 5:5): "which is said not only of holy men, but also of the holy angels," as Augustine says (De Civ. Dei xii). Therefore the angelic orders are not from nature, but from grace.

Obj. 3: Further, the ecclesiastical hierarchy is copied from the heavenly. But the orders among men are not from nature, but by the gift of grace; for it is not a natural gift for one to be a bishop, and another a priest, and another a deacon. Therefore neither in the angels are the orders from nature, but from grace only.

*On the contrary,* The Master says (ii, D. 9) that "an angelic order is a multitude of heavenly spirits, who are likened to each other by some gift of grace, just as they agree also in the participation of natural gifts." Therefore the distinction of orders among the angels is not only by gifts of grace, but also by gifts of nature.

*I answer that,* The order of government, which is the order of a multitude under authority, is derived from its end. Now the end of the angels may be considered in two ways. First, according to the faculty of nature, so that they may know and love God by natural knowledge and love; and according to their relation to this end the orders of the angels are distinguished by natural gifts. Secondly, the end of the angelic multitude can be taken from what is above their natural powers, which consists in the vision of the Divine Essence, and in the unchangeable fruition of His goodness; to which end they can reach only by grace; and hence as regards this end, the orders in the angels are adequately distinguished by the gifts of grace, but dispositively by natural gifts, forasmuch as to the angels are given gratuitous gifts according to the capacity of their natural gifts; which is not the case with men, as above explained (Q. 62, A. 6). Hence among men the orders are distinguished according to the gratuitous gifts only, and not according to natural gifts.

From the above the replies to the objections are evident.

FIFTH ARTICLE [I, Q. 108, Art. 5]

Whether the Orders of the Angels Are Properly Named?

Objection 1: It would seem that the orders of the angels are not properly named. For all the heavenly spirits are called angels and heavenly virtues. But common names should not be appropriated to individuals. Therefore the orders of the angels and virtues are ineptly named.

Obj. 2: Further, it belongs to God alone to be Lord, according to the words, "Know ye that the Lord He is God" (Ps. 99:3). Therefore one order of the heavenly spirits is not properly called "Dominations."

Obj. 3: Further, the name "Domination" seems to imply government and likewise the names "Principalities" and "Powers." Therefore these three names do not seem to be properly applied to three orders.

Obj. 4: Further, archangels are as it were angel princes. Therefore this name ought not to be given to any other order than to the "Principalities."

Obj. 5: Further, the name "Seraphim" is derived from ardor, which pertains to charity; and the name "Cherubim" from knowledge. But charity and knowledge are gifts common to all the angels. Therefore they ought not to be names of any particular orders.

Obj. 6: Further, Thrones are seats. But from the fact that God knows and loves the rational creature He is said to sit within it. Therefore there ought not to be any order of "Thrones" besides the "Cherubim" and "Seraphim." Therefore it appears that the orders of angels are not properly styled.

On the contrary is the authority of Holy Scripture wherein they are so named. For the name "Seraphim" is found in Isa. 6:2; the name "Cherubim" in Ezech. 1 (Cf. 10:15,20); "Thrones" in Col. 1:16; "Dominations," "Virtues," "Powers," and "Principalities" are mentioned in Eph. 1:21; the name "Archangels" in the canonical epistle of St. Jude (9), and the name "Angels" is found in many places of Scripture.

*I answer that,* As Dionysius says (Coel. Hier. vii), in the names of the angelic orders it is necessary to observe that the proper name of each order expresses its property. Now to see what is the property of each order, we must consider that in coordinated things, something may be found in a threefold manner: by way of property, by way of excess, and by way of participation. A thing is said to be in another by way of property, if it is adequate and proportionate to its nature: by excess when an attribute is less than that to which it is attributed, but is possessed thereby in an eminent manner, as we have stated (Q. 13, A. 2) concerning all the names which are attributed to God: by participation, when an attribute is possessed by something not fully but partially; thus holy men are called gods by participation. Therefore, if anything is to be called by a name designating its property, it ought not to be named from what it participates imperfectly, nor from that which it possesses in excess, but from that which is adequate thereto; as, for instance, when we wish properly to name a man, we should call him a "rational substance," but not an "intellectual substance," which latter is the proper name of an angel; because simple intelligence belongs to an angel as a property, and to man by participation; nor do we call him a "sensible substance," which is the proper name of a brute; because sense is less than the property of a man, and belongs to man in a more excellent way than to other animals.

So we must consider that in the angelic orders all spiritual perfections are common to all the angels, and that they are all more excellently in the superior than in the inferior angels. Further, as in these perfections there are grades, the superior perfection belongs to the superior order as its property, whereas it belongs to the inferior by participation; and conversely the inferior perfection belongs to the inferior order as its property, and to the superior by way of excess; and thus the superior order is denominated from the superior perfection.

So in this way Dionysius (Coel. Hier. vii) explains the names of the orders accordingly as they befit the spiritual perfections they signify. Gregory, on the other hand, in expounding these names (Hom. xxxiv in Evang.) seems to regard more the exterior ministrations; for he says that "angels are so called as announcing the least things; and the archangels in the greatest; by the virtues miracles are wrought; by the powers hostile powers are repulsed; and the principalities preside over the good spirits themselves."

Reply Obj. 1: Angel means "messenger." So all the heavenly spirits, so far as they make known Divine things, are called "angels." But the superior angels enjoy a certain excellence, as regards this manifestation, from which the superior orders are denominated. The lowest order of angels possess no excellence above the common manifestation; and therefore it is denominated from manifestation only; and thus the common name remains as it were proper to the lowest order, as Dionysius says (Coel. Hier. v). Or we may say that the lowest order can be specially called the order of "angels," forasmuch as they announce things to us immediately.

"Virtue" can be taken in two ways. First, commonly, considered as the medium between the essence and the operation, and in that sense all the heavenly spirits are called heavenly virtues, as also "heavenly essences." Secondly, as meaning a certain excellence of strength; and thus it is the proper name of an angelic order. Hence Dionysius says (Coel. Hier. viii) that the "name 'virtues' signifies a certain virile and immovable strength"; first, in regard of those Divine operations which befit them; secondly, in regard to receiving Divine gifts. Thus it signifies that they undertake fearlessly the Divine behests appointed to them; and this seems to imply strength of mind.

Reply Obj. 2: As Dionysius says (Div. Nom. xii): "Dominion is attributed to God in a special manner, by way of excess: but the Divine word gives the more illustrious heavenly princes the name of Lord by participation, through whom the inferior angels receive the Divine gifts." Hence Dionysius also states (Coel. Hier. viii) that the name "Domination" means first "a certain liberty, free from servile condition and common subjection, such as that of plebeians, and from tyrannical oppression," endured sometimes even by the great. Secondly, it signifies "a certain rigid and inflexible supremacy which does not bend to any servile act, or to the act of those who are subject to or oppressed by tyrants." Thirdly, it signifies "the desire and participation of the true dominion which belongs to God." Likewise the name of each order signifies the participation of what belongs to God; as the name "Virtues" signifies the participation of the Divine virtue; and the same principle applies to the rest.

Reply Obj. 3: The names "Domination," "Power," and "Principality" belong to government in different ways. The place of a lord is only to prescribe what is to be done. So Gregory says (Hom. xxiv in Evang.), that "some companies of the angels, because others are subject to obedience to them, are called dominations." The name "Power" points out a kind of order, according to what the Apostle says, "He that resisteth the power, resisteth the ordination of God" (Rom. 13:2). And so Dionysius says (Coel. Hier. viii) that the name "Power" signifies a kind of ordination both as regards the reception of Divine things, and as regards the Divine actions performed by superiors towards inferiors by leading them to things above. Therefore, to the order of "Powers" it belongs to regulate what is to be done by those who are subject to them. To preside [principari] as Gregory says (Hom. xxiv in Ev.) is "to be first among others," as being first in carrying out what is ordered to be done. And so Dionysius says (Coel. Hier. ix) that the name of "Principalities" signifies "one who leads in a sacred order." For those who lead others, being first among them, are properly called "princes," according to the words, "Princes went before joined with singers" (Ps. 67:26).

Reply Obj. 4: The "Archangels," according to Dionysius (Coel. Hier. ix), are between the "Principalities" and the "Angels." A medium compared to one extreme seems like the other, as participating in the nature of both extremes; thus tepid seems cold compared to hot, and hot compared to cold. So the "Archangels" are called the "angel princes"; forasmuch as they are princes as regards the "Angels," and angels as regards the Principalities. But according to Gregory (Hom. xxiv in Ev.) they are called "Archangels," because they preside over the one order of the "Angels"; as it were, announcing greater things: and the "Principalities" are so called as presiding over all the heavenly "Virtues" who fulfil the Divine commands.

Reply Obj. 5: The name "Seraphim" does not come from charity only, but from the excess of charity, expressed by the word ardor or fire. Hence Dionysius (Coel. Hier. vii) expounds the name "Seraphim" according to the properties of fire, containing an excess of heat. Now in fire we may consider three things. First, the movement which is upwards and continuous. This signifies that they are borne inflexibly towards God. Secondly, the active force which is "heat," which is not found in fire simply, but exists with a certain sharpness, as being of most penetrating action, and reaching even to the smallest things, and as it were, with superabundant fervor; whereby is signified the action of these angels, exercised powerfully upon those who are subject to them, rousing them to a like fervor, and cleansing them wholly by their heat. Thirdly we consider in fire the quality of clarity, or brightness; which signifies that these angels have in themselves an inextinguishable light, and that they also perfectly enlighten others.

In the same way the name "Cherubim" comes from a certain excess of knowledge; hence it is interpreted "fulness of knowledge," which Dionysius (Coel. Hier. vii) expounds in regard to four things: the perfect vision of God; the full reception of the Divine Light; their contemplation in God of the beauty of the Divine order; and in regard to the fact that possessing this knowledge fully, they pour it forth copiously upon others.

Reply Obj. 6: The order of the "Thrones" excels the inferior orders as having an immediate knowledge of the types of the Divine works; whereas the "Cherubim" have the excellence of knowledge and the "Seraphim" the excellence of ardor. And although these two excellent attributes include the third, yet the gift belonging to the "Thrones" does not include the other two; and so the order of the "Thrones" is distinguished from the orders of the "Cherubim" and the "Seraphim." For it is a common rule in all things that the excellence of the inferior is contained in the superior, but not conversely. But Dionysius (Coel. Hier. vii) explains the name "Thrones" by its relation to material seats, in which we may consider four things. First, the site; because seats are raised above the earth, and to the angels who are called "Thrones" are raised up to the immediate knowledge of the types of things in God. Secondly, because in material seats is displayed strength, forasmuch as a person sits firmly on them. But here the reverse is the case; for the angels themselves are made firm by God. Thirdly, because the seat receives him who sits thereon, and he can be carried thereupon; and so the angels receive God in themselves, and in a certain way bear Him to the inferior creatures. Fourthly, because in its shape, a seat is open on one side to receive the sitter; and thus are the angels promptly open to receive God and to serve Him.

SIXTH ARTICLE [I, Q. 108, Art. 6]

Whether the Grades of the Orders Are Properly Assigned?

Objection 1: It would seem that the grades of the orders are not properly assigned. For the order of prelates is the highest. But the names of "Dominations," "Principalities," and "Powers" of themselves imply prelacy. Therefore these orders ought not to be supreme.

Obj. 2: Further, the nearer an order is to God, the higher it is. But the order of "Thrones" is the nearest to God; for nothing is nearer to the sitter than the seat. Therefore the order of the "Thrones" is the highest.

Obj. 3: Further, knowledge comes before love, and intellect is higher than will. Therefore the order of "Cherubim" seems to be higher than the "Seraphim."

Obj. 4: Further, Gregory (Hom. xxiv in Evang.) places the "Principalities" above the "Powers." These therefore are not placed immediately above the Archangels, as Dionysius says (Coel. Hier. ix).

*On the contrary,* Dionysius (Coel. Hier. vii), places in the highest hierarchy the "Seraphim" as the first, the "Cherubim" as the middle, the "Thrones" as the last; in the middle hierarchy he places the "Dominations," as the first, the "Virtues" in the middle, the "Powers" last; in the lowest hierarchy the "Principalities" first, then the "Archangels," and lastly the "Angels."

*I answer that,* The grades of the angelic orders are assigned by Gregory (Hom. xxiv in Ev.) and Dionysius (Coel. Hier. vii), who agree as regards all except the "Principalities" and "Virtues." For Dionysius places the "Virtues" beneath the "Dominations," and above the "Powers"; the "Principalities" beneath the "Powers" and above the "Archangels." Gregory, however, places the "Principalities" between the "Dominations" and the "Powers"; and the "Virtues" between the "Powers" and the "Archangels." Each of these placings may claim authority from the words of the Apostle, who (Eph. 1:20,21) enumerates the middle orders, beginning from the lowest saying that "God set Him," i.e. Christ, "on His right hand in the heavenly places above all Principality and Power, and Virtue, and Dominion." Here he places "Virtues" between "Powers" and "Dominations," according to the placing of Dionysius. Writing however to the Colossians (1:16), numbering the same orders from the highest, he says: "Whether Thrones, or Dominations, or Principalities, or Powers, all things were created by Him and in Him." Here he places the "Principalities" between "Dominations" and "Powers," as does also Gregory.

Let us then first examine the reason for the ordering of Dionysius, in which we see, that, as said above (A. 1), the highest hierarchy contemplates the ideas of things in God Himself; the second in the universal causes; and third in their application to particular effects. And because God is the end not only of the angelic ministrations, but also of the whole creation, it belongs to the first hierarchy to consider the end; to the middle one belongs the universal disposition of what is to be done; and to the last belongs the application of this disposition to the effect, which is the carrying out of the work; for it is clear that these three things exist in every kind of operation. So Dionysius, considering the properties of the orders as derived from their names, places in the first hierarchy those orders the names of which are taken from their relation to God, the "Seraphim," "Cherubim," and "Thrones"; and he places in the middle hierarchy those orders whose names denote a certain kind of common government or disposition—the "Dominations," "Virtues," and "Powers"; and he places in the third hierarchy the orders whose names denote the execution of the work, the "Principalities," "Angels," and "Archangels."

As regards the end, three things may be considered. For firstly we consider the end; then we acquire perfect knowledge of the end; thirdly, we fix our intention on the end; of which the second is an addition to the first, and the third an addition to both. And because God is the end of creatures, as the leader is the end of an army, as the Philosopher says (Metaph. xii, Did. xi, 10); so a somewhat similar order may be seen in human affairs. For there are some who enjoy the dignity of being able with familiarity to approach the king or leader; others in addition are privileged to know his secrets; and others above these ever abide with him, in a close union. According to this similitude, we can understand the disposition in the orders of the first hierarchy; for the "Thrones" are raised up so as to be the familiar recipients of God in themselves, in the sense of knowing immediately the types of things in Himself; and this is proper to the whole of the first hierarchy. The "Cherubim" know the Divine secrets supereminently; and the "Seraphim" excel in what is the supreme excellence of all, in being united to God Himself; and all this in such a manner that the whole of this hierarchy can be called the "Thrones"; as, from what is common to all the heavenly spirits together, they are all called "Angels."

As regards government, three things are comprised therein, the first of which is to appoint those things which are to be done, and this belongs to the "Dominations"; the second is to give the power of carrying out what is to be done, which belongs to the "Virtues"; the third is to order how what has been commanded or decided to be done can be carried out by others, which belongs to the "Powers."

The execution of the angelic ministrations consists in announcing Divine things. Now in the execution of any action there are beginners and leaders; as in singing, the precentors; and in war, generals and officers; this belongs to the "Principalities." There are others who simply execute what is to be done; and these are the "Angels." Others hold a middle place; and these are the "Archangels," as above explained.

This explanation of the orders is quite a reasonable one. For the highest in an inferior order always has affinity to the lowest in the higher order; as the lowest animals are near to the plants. Now the first order is that of the Divine Persons, which terminates in the Holy Ghost, Who is Love proceeding, with Whom the highest order of the first hierarchy has affinity, denominated as it is from the fire of love. The lowest order of the first hierarchy is that of the "Thrones," who in their own order are akin to the "Dominations"; for the "Thrones," according to Gregory (Hom. xxiv in Ev.), are so called "because through them God accomplishes His judgments," since they are enlightened by Him in a manner adapted to the immediate enlightening of the second hierarchy, to which belongs the disposition of the Divine ministrations. The order of the "Powers" is akin to the order of the "Principalities"; for as it belongs to the "Powers" to impose order on those subject to them, this ordering is plainly shown at once in the name of "Principalities," who, as presiding over the government of peoples and kingdoms (which occupies the first and principal place in the Divine ministrations), are the first in the execution thereof; "for the good of a nation is more divine than the good of one man" (Ethic. i, 2); and hence it is written, "The prince of the kingdom of the Persians resisted me" (Dan. 10:13).

The disposition of the orders which is mentioned by Gregory is also reasonable. For since the "Dominations" appoint and order what belongs to the Divine ministrations, the orders subject to them are arranged according to the disposition of those things in which the Divine ministrations are effected. Still, as Augustine says (De Trin. iii), "bodies are ruled in a certain order; the inferior by the superior; and all of them by the spiritual creature, and the bad spirit by the good spirit." So the first order after the "Dominations" is called that of "Principalities," who rule even over good spirits; then the "Powers," who coerce the evil spirits; even as evil-doers are coerced by earthly powers, as it is written (Rom. 13:3,4). After these come the "Virtues," which have power over corporeal nature in the working of miracles; after these are the "Angels" and the "Archangels," who announce to men either great things above reason, or small things within the purview of reason.

Reply Obj. 1: The angels' subjection to God is greater than their presiding over inferior things; and the latter is derived from the former. Thus the orders which derive their name from presiding are not the first and highest; but rather the orders deriving their name from their nearness and relation to God.

Reply Obj. 2: The nearness to God designated by the name of the "Thrones," belongs also to the "Cherubim" and "Seraphim," and in a more excellent way, as above explained.

Reply Obj. 3: As above explained (Q. 27, A. 3), knowledge takes place accordingly as the thing known is in the knower; but love as the lover is united to the object loved. Now higher things are in a nobler way in themselves than in lower things; whereas lower things are in higher things in a nobler way than they are in themselves. Therefore to know lower things is better than to love them; and to love the higher things, God above all, is better than to know them.

Reply Obj. 4: A careful comparison will show that little or no difference exists in reality between the dispositions of the orders according to Dionysius and Gregory. For Gregory expounds the name "Principalities" from their "presiding over good spirits," which also agrees with the "Virtues" accordingly as this name expressed a certain strength, giving efficacy to the inferior spirits in the execution of the Divine ministrations. Again, according to Gregory, the "Virtues" seem to be the same as "Principalities" of Dionysius. For to work miracles holds the first place in the Divine ministrations; since thereby the way is prepared for the announcements of the "Archangels" and the "Angels."

SEVENTH ARTICLE [I, Q. 108, Art. 7]

Whether the Orders Will Outlast the Day of Judgment?

Objection 1: It would seem that the orders of angels will not outlast the Day of Judgment. For the Apostle says (1 Cor. 15:24), that Christ will "bring to naught all principality and power, when He shall have delivered up the kingdom to God and the Father," and this will be in the final consummation. Therefore for the same reason all others will be abolished in that state.

Obj. 2: Further, to the office of the angelic orders it belongs to cleanse, enlighten, and perfect. But after the Day of Judgment one angel will not cleanse, enlighten, or perfect another, because they will not advance any more in knowledge. Therefore the angelic orders would remain for no purpose.

Obj. 3: Further, the Apostle says of the angels (Heb. 1:14), that "they are all ministering spirits, sent to minister to them who shall receive the inheritance of salvation"; whence it appears that the angelic offices are ordered for the purpose of leading men to salvation. But all the elect are in pursuit of salvation until the Day of Judgment. Therefore the angelic offices and orders will not outlast the Day of Judgment.

*On the contrary,* It is written (Judges 5:20): "Stars remaining in their order and courses," which is applied to the angels. Therefore the angels will ever remain in their orders.

*I answer that,* In the angelic orders we may consider two things; the distinction of grades, and the execution of their offices. The distinction of grades among the angels takes place according to the difference of grace and nature, as above explained (A. 4); and these differences will ever remain in the angels; for these differences of natures cannot be taken from them unless they themselves be corrupted. The difference of glory will also ever remain in them according to the difference of preceding merit. As to the execution of the angelic offices, it will to a certain degree remain after the Day of Judgment, and to a certain degree will cease. It will cease accordingly as their offices are directed towards leading others to their end; but it will remain, accordingly as it agrees with the attainment of the end. Thus also the various ranks of soldiers have different duties to perform in battle and in triumph.

Reply Obj. 1: The principalities and powers will come to an end in that final consummation as regards their office of leading others to their end; because when the end is attained, it is no longer necessary to tend towards the end. This is clear from the words of the Apostle, "When He shall have delivered up the kingdom of God and the Father," i.e. when He shall have led the faithful to the enjoyment of God Himself.

Reply Obj. 2: The actions of angels over the other angels are to be considered according to a likeness to our own intellectual actions. In ourselves we find many intellectual actions which are ordered according to the order of cause and effect; as when we gradually arrive at one conclusion by many middle terms. Now it is manifest that the knowledge of a conclusion depends on all the preceding middle terms not only in the new acquisition of knowledge, but also as regards the keeping of the knowledge acquired. A proof of this is that when anyone forgets any of the preceding middle terms he can have opinion or belief about the conclusion, but not knowledge; as he is ignorant of the order of the causes. So, since the inferior angels know the types of the Divine works by the light of the superior angels, their knowledge depends on the light of the superior angels not only as regards the acquisition of knowledge, but also as regards the preserving of the knowledge possessed. So, although after the Judgment the inferior angels will not progress in the knowledge of some things, still this will not prevent their being enlightened by the superior angels.

Reply Obj. 3: Although after the Day of Judgment men will not be led any more to salvation by the ministry of the angels, still those who are already saved will be enlightened through the angelic ministry.

EIGHTH ARTICLE [I, Q. 108, Art. 8]

Whether Men Are Taken Up into the Angelic Orders?

Objection 1: It would seem that men are not taken up into the orders of the angels. For the human hierarchy is stationed beneath the lowest heavenly hierarchy, as the lowest under the middle hierarchy and the middle beneath the first. But the angels of the lowest hierarchy are never transferred into the middle, or the first. Therefore neither are men transferred to the angelic orders.

Obj. 2: Further, certain offices belong to the orders of the angels, as to guard, to work miracles, to coerce the demons, and the like; which do not appear to belong to the souls of the saints. Therefore they are not transferred to the angelic orders.

Obj. 3: Further, as the good angels lead on to good, so do the demons to what is evil. But it is erroneous to say that the souls of bad men are changed into demons; for Chrysostom rejects this (Hom. xxviii in Matt.). Therefore it does not seem that the souls of the saints will be transferred to the orders of angels.

*On the contrary,* The Lord says of the saints that, "they will be as the angels of God" (Matt. 22:30). *I answer that,* As above explained (AA. 4,7), the orders of the angels are distinguished according to the conditions of nature and according to the gifts of grace. Considered only as regards the grade of nature, men can in no way be assumed into the angelic orders; for the natural distinction will always remain. In view of this distinction, some asserted that men can in no way be transferred to an equality with the angels; but this is erroneous, contradicting as it does the promise of Christ saying that the children of the resurrection will be equal to the angels in heaven (Luke 20:36). For whatever belongs to nature is the material part of an order; whilst that which perfects is from grace which depends on the liberality of God, and not on the order of nature. Therefore by the gift of grace men can merit glory in such a degree as to be equal to the angels, in each of the angelic grades; and this implies that men are taken up into the orders of the angels. Some, however, say that not all who are saved are assumed into the angelic orders, but only virgins or the perfect; and that the other will constitute their own order, as it were, corresponding to the whole society of the angels. But this is against what Augustine says (De Civ. Dei xii, 9), that "there will not be two societies of men and angels, but only one; because the beatitude of all is to cleave to God alone."

Reply Obj. 1: Grace is given to the angels in proportion to their natural gifts. This, however, does not apply to men, as above explained (A. 4; Q. 62, A. 6). So, as the inferior angels cannot be transferred to the natural grade of the superior, neither can they be transferred to the superior grade of grace; whereas men can ascend to the grade of grace, but not of nature.

Reply Obj. 2: The angels according to the order of nature are between us and God; and therefore according to the common law not only human affairs are administered by them, but also all corporeal matters. But holy men even after this life are of the same nature with ourselves; and hence according to the common law they do not administer human affairs, "nor do they interfere in the things of the living," as Augustine says (De cura pro mortuis xiii, xvi). Still, by a certain special dispensation it is sometimes granted to some of the saints to exercise these offices; by working miracles, by coercing the demons, or by doing something of that kind, as Augustine says (De cura pro mortuis xvi).

Reply Obj. 3: It is not erroneous to say that men are transferred to the penalty of demons; but some erroneously stated that the demons are nothing but souls of the dead; and it is this that Chrysostom rejects.

# QUESTION 109

THE ORDERING OF THE BAD ANGELS (In Four Articles)

We now consider the ordering of the bad angels; concerning which there are four points of inquiry:

(1) Whether there are orders among the demons?

(2) Whether among them there is precedence?

(3) Whether one enlightens another?

(4) Whether they are subject to the precedence of the good angels?

FIRST ARTICLE [I, Q. 109, Art. 1]

Whether There Are Orders Among the Demons?

Objection 1: It would seem that there are no orders among the demons. For order belongs to good, as also mode, and species, as Augustine says (De Nat. Boni iii); and *on the contrary,* disorder belongs to evil. But there is nothing disorderly in the good angels. Therefore in the bad angels there are no orders.

Obj. 2: Further, the angelic orders are contained under a hierarchy. But the demons are not in a hierarchy, which is defined as a holy principality; for they are void of all holiness. Therefore among the demons there are no orders.

Obj. 3: Further, the demons fell from every one of the angelic orders; as is commonly supposed. Therefore, if some demons are said to belong to an order, as falling from that order, it would seem necessary to give them the names of each of those orders. But we never find that they are called "Seraphim," or "Thrones," or "Dominations." Therefore on the same ground they are not to be placed in any other order.

*On the contrary,* The Apostle says (Eph. 6:12): "Our wrestling ... is against principalities and powers, against the rulers of the world of this darkness."

*I answer that,* As explained above (Q. 108, AA. 4, 7, 8), order in the angels is considered both according to the grade of nature; and according to that of grace. Now grace has a twofold state, the imperfect, which is that of merit; and the perfect, which is that of consummate glory.

If therefore we consider the angelic orders in the light of the perfection of glory, then the demons are not in the angelic orders, and never were. But if we consider them in relation to imperfect grace, in that view the demons were at the time in the orders of angels, but fell away from them, according to what was said above (Q. 62, A. 3), that all the angels were created in grace. But if we consider them in the light of nature, in that view they are still in those orders; because they have not lost their natural gifts; as Dionysius says (Div. Nom. iv).

Reply Obj. 1: Good can exist without evil; whereas evil cannot exist without good (Q. 49, A. 3); so there is order in the demons, as possessing a good nature.

Reply Obj. 2: If we consider the ordering of the demons on the part of God Who orders them, it is sacred; for He uses the demons for Himself; but on the part of the demons' will it is not a sacred thing, because they abuse their nature for evil.

Reply Obj. 3: The name "Seraphim" is given from the ardor of charity; and the name "Thrones" from the Divine indwelling; and the name "Dominations" imports a certain liberty; all of which are opposed to sin; and therefore these names are not given to the angels who sinned.

SECOND ARTICLE [I, Q. 109, Art. 2]

Whether among the demons there is precedence?

Objection 1: It would seem that there is no precedence among the demons. For every precedence is according to some order of justice. But the demons are wholly fallen from justice. Therefore there is no precedence among them.

Obj. 2: Further, there is no precedence where obedience and subjection do not exist. But these cannot be without concord; which is not to be found among the demons, according to the text, "Among the proud there are always contentions" (Prov. 13:10). Therefore there is no precedence among the demons.

Obj. 3: If there be precedence among them it is either according to nature, or according to their sin or punishment. But it is not according to their nature, for subjection and service do not come from nature but from subsequent sin; neither is it according to sin or punishment, because in that case the superior demons who have sinned the most grievously, would be subject to the inferior. Therefore there is no precedence among the demons.

*On the contrary,* On 1 Cor. 15:24 the gloss says: "While the world lasts, angels will preside over angels, men over men, and demons over demons."

*I answer that,* Since action follows the nature of a thing, where natures are subordinate, actions also must be subordinate to each other. Thus it is in corporeal things, for as the inferior bodies by natural order are below the heavenly bodies, their actions and movements are subject to the actions and movements of the heavenly bodies. Now it is plain from what we have said (A. 1), that the demons are by natural order subject to others; and hence their actions are subject to the action of those above them, and this is what we mean by precedence—that the action of the subject should be under the action of the prelate. So the very natural disposition of the demons requires that there should be authority among them. This agrees too with Divine wisdom, which leaves nothing inordinate, which "reacheth from end to end mightily, and ordereth all things sweetly" (Wis. 8:1).

Reply Obj. 1: The authority of the demons is not founded on their justice, but on the justice of God ordering all things.

Reply Obj. 2: The concord of the demons, whereby some obey others, does not arise from mutual friendships, but from their common wickedness whereby they hate men, and fight against God's justice. For it belongs to wicked men to be joined to and subject to those whom they see to be stronger, in order to carry out their own wickedness.

Reply Obj. 3: The demons are not equal in nature; and so among them there exists a natural precedence; which is not the case with men, who are naturally equal. That the inferior are subject to the superior, is not for the benefit of the superior, but rather to their detriment; because since to do evil belongs in a pre-eminent degree to unhappiness, it follows that to preside in evil is to be more unhappy.

THIRD ARTICLE [I, Q. 109, Art. 3]

Whether There Is Enlightenment in the Demons?

Objection 1: It would seem that enlightenment is in the demons. For enlightenment means the manifestation of the truth. But one demon can manifest truth to another, because the superior excel in natural knowledge. Therefore the superior demons can enlighten the inferior.

Obj. 2: Further, a body abounding in light can enlighten a body deficient in light, as the sun enlightens the moon. But the superior demons abound in the participation of natural light. Therefore it seems that the superior demons can enlighten the inferior.

*On the contrary,* Enlightenment is not without cleansing and perfecting, as stated above (Q. 106, A. 1). But to cleanse does not befit the demons, according to the words: "What can be made clean by the unclean?" (Ecclus. 34:4). Therefore neither can they enlighten.

*I answer that,* There can be no enlightenment properly speaking among the demons. For, as above explained (Q. 107, A. 2), enlightenment properly speaking is the manifestation of the truth in reference to God, Who enlightens every intellect. Another kind of manifestation of the truth is speech, as when one angel manifests his concept to another. Now the demon's perversity does not lead one to order another to God, but rather to lead away from the Divine order; and so one demon does not enlighten another; but one can make known his mental concept to another by way of speech.

Reply Obj. 1: Not every kind of manifestation of the truth is enlightenment, but only that which is above described.

Reply Obj. 2: According to what belongs to natural knowledge, there is no necessary manifestation of the truth either in the angels, or in the demons, because, as above explained (Q. 55, A. 2; Q. 58, A. 2; Q. 79, A. 2), they know from the first all that belongs to their natural knowledge. So the greater fulness of natural light in the superior demons does not prove that they can enlighten others.

FOURTH ARTICLE [I, Q. 109, Art. 4]

Whether the Good Angels Have Precedence Over the Bad Angels?

Objection 1: It would seem that the good angels have no precedence over the bad angels. For the angels' precedence is especially connected with enlightenment. But the bad angels, being darkness, are not enlightened by the good angels. Therefore the good angels do not rule over the bad.

Obj. 2: Further, superiors are responsible as regards negligence for the evil deeds of their subjects. But the demons do much evil. Therefore if they are subject to the good angels, it seems that negligence is to be charged to the good angels; which cannot be admitted.

Obj. 3: Further, the angels' precedence follows upon the order of nature, as above explained (A. 2). But if the demons fell from every order, as is commonly said, many of the demons are superior to many good angels in the natural order. Therefore the good angels have no precedence over all the bad angels.

*On the contrary,* Augustine says (De Trin. iii), that "the treacherous and sinful spirit of life is ruled by the rational, pious, and just spirit of life"; and Gregory says (Hom. xxxiv) that "the Powers are the angels to whose charge are subjected the hostile powers."

*I answer that,* The whole order of precedence is first and originally in God; and it is shared by creatures accordingly as they are the nearer to God. For those creatures, which are more perfect and nearer to God, have the power to act on others. Now the greatest perfection and that which brings them nearest to God belongs to the creatures who enjoy God, as the holy angels; of which perfection the demons are deprived; and therefore the good angels have precedence over the bad, and these are ruled by them.

Reply Obj. 1: Many things concerning Divine mysteries are made known by the holy angels to the bad angels, whenever the Divine justice requires the demons to do anything for the punishment of the evil; or for the trial of the good; as in human affairs the judge's assessors make known his sentence to the executioners. This revelation, if compared to the angelic revealers, can be called an enlightenment, forasmuch as they direct it to God; but it is not an enlightenment on the part of the demons, for these do not direct it to God; but to the fulfilment of their own wickedness.

Reply Obj. 2: The holy angels are the ministers of the Divine wisdom. Hence as the Divine wisdom permits some evil to be done by bad angels or men, for the sake of the good that follows; so also the good angels do not entirely restrain the bad from inflicting harm.

Reply Obj. 3: An angel who is inferior in the natural order presides over demons, although these may be naturally superior; because the power of Divine justice to which the good angels cleave, is stronger than the natural power of the angels. Hence likewise among men, "the spiritual man judgeth all things" (1 Cor. 2:15), and the Philosopher says (Ethic. iii, 4; x, 5) that "the virtuous man is the rule and measure of all human acts."

## QUESTION 110

HOW ANGELS ACT ON BODIES (In Four Articles)

We now consider how the angels preside over the corporeal creatures. Under this head there are four points of inquiry:

(1) Whether the corporeal creature is governed by the angels?

(2) Whether the corporeal creature obeys the mere will of the angels?

(3) Whether the angels by their own power can immediately move bodies locally?

(4) Whether the good or bad angels can work miracles?

FIRST ARTICLE [I, Q. 110, Art. 1]

Whether the Corporeal Creature Is Governed by the Angels?

Objection 1: It would seem that the corporeal creature is not governed by angels. For whatever possesses a determinate mode of action, needs not to be governed by any superior power; for we require to be governed lest we do what we ought not. But corporeal things have their actions determined by the nature divinely bestowed upon them. Therefore they do not need the government of angels.

Obj. 2: Further, the lowest things are ruled by the superior. But some corporeal things are inferior, and others are superior. Therefore they need not be governed by the angels.

Obj. 3: Further, the different orders of the angels are distinguished by different offices. But if corporeal creatures were ruled by the angels, there would be as many angelic offices as there are species of things. So also there would be as many orders of angels as there are species of things; which is against what is laid down above (Q. 108, A. 2). Therefore the corporeal creature is not governed by angels.

*On the contrary,* Augustine says (De Trin. iii, 4) that "all bodies are ruled by the rational spirit of life"; and Gregory says (Dial. iv, 6), that "in this visible world nothing takes place without the agency of the invisible creature."

*I answer that,* It is generally found both in human affairs and in natural things that every particular power is governed and ruled by the universal power; as, for example, the bailiff's power is governed by the power of the king. Among the angels also, as explained above (Q. 55, A. 3; Q. 108, A. 1), the superior angels who preside over the inferior possess a more universal knowledge. Now it is manifest that the power of any individual body is more particular than the power of any spiritual substance; for every corporeal form is a form individualized by matter, and determined to the "here and now"; whereas immaterial forms are absolute and intelligible. Therefore, as the inferior angels who have the less universal forms, are ruled by the superior; so are all corporeal things ruled by the angels. This is not only laid down by the holy doctors, but also by all philosophers who admit the existence of incorporeal substances.

Reply Obj. 1: Corporeal things have determinate actions; but they exercise such actions only according as they are moved; because it belongs to a body not to act unless moved. Hence a corporeal creature must be moved by a spiritual creature.

Reply Obj. 2: The reason alleged is according to the opinion of Aristotle who laid down (Metaph. xi, 8) that the heavenly bodies are moved by spiritual substances; the number of which he endeavored to assign according to the number of motions apparent in the heavenly bodies. But he did not say that there were any spiritual substances with immediate rule over the inferior bodies, except perhaps human souls; and this was because he did not consider that any operations were exercised in the inferior bodies except the natural ones for which the movement of the heavenly bodies sufficed. But because we assert that many things are done in the inferior bodies besides the natural corporeal actions, for which the movements of the heavenly bodies are not sufficient; therefore in our opinion we must assert that the angels possess an immediate presidency not only over the heavenly bodies, but also over the inferior bodies.

Reply Obj. 3: Philosophers have held different opinions about immaterial substances. For Plato laid down that immaterial substances were types and species of sensible bodies; and that some were more universal than others; and so he held that immaterial substances preside immediately over all sensible bodies, and different ones over different bodies. But Aristotle held that immaterial substances are not the species of sensible bodies, but something higher and more universal; and so he did not attribute to them any immediate presiding over single bodies, but only over the universal agents, the heavenly bodies. Avicenna followed a middle course. For he agreed with Plato in supposing some spiritual substance to preside immediately in the sphere of active and passive elements; because, as Plato also said, he held that the forms of these sensible things are derived from immaterial substances. But he differed from Plato because he supposed only one immaterial substance to preside over all inferior bodies, which he called the "active intelligence."

The holy doctors held with the Platonists that different spiritual substances were placed over corporeal things. For Augustine says (QQ. 83, qu. 79): "Every visible thing in this world has an angelic power placed over it"; and Damascene says (De Fide Orth. ii, 4): "The devil was one of the angelic powers who presided over the terrestrial order"; and Origen says on the text, "When the ass saw the angel" (Num. 22:23), that "the world has need of angels who preside over beasts, and over the birth of animals, and trees, and plants, and over the increase of all other things" (Hom. xiv in Num.). The reason of this, however, is not that an angel is more fitted by his nature to preside over animals than over plants; because each angel, even the least, has a higher and more universal power than any kind of corporeal things: the reason is to be sought in the order of Divine wisdom, Who places different rulers over different things. Nor does it follow that there are more than nine orders of angels, because, as above expounded (Q. 108, A. 2), the orders are distinguished by their general offices. Hence as according to Gregory all the angels whose proper office it is to preside over the demons are of the order of the "powers"; so to the order of the "virtues" do those angels seem to belong who preside over purely corporeal creatures; for by their ministration miracles are sometimes performed.

SECOND ARTICLE [I, Q. 110, Art. 2]

Whether Corporeal Matter Obeys the Mere Will of an Angel?

Objection 1: It would seem that corporeal matter obeys the mere will of an angel. For the power of an angel excels the power of the soul. But corporeal matter obeys a conception of the soul; for the body of man is changed by a conception of the soul as regards heat and cold, and sometimes even as regards health and sickness. Therefore much more is corporeal matter changed by a conception of an angel.

Obj. 2: Further, whatever can be done by an inferior power, can be done by a superior power. Now the power of an angel is superior to corporeal power. But a body by its power is able to transform corporeal matter; as appears when fire begets fire. Therefore much more efficaciously can an angel by his power transform corporeal matter.

Obj. 3: Further, all corporeal nature is under angelic administration, as appears above (A. 1), and thus it appears that bodies are as instruments to the angels, for an instrument is essentially a mover moved. Now in effects there is something that is due to the power of their principal agents, and which cannot be due to the power of the instrument; and this it is that takes the principal place in the effect. For example, digestion is due to the force of natural heat, which is the instrument of the nutritive soul: but that living flesh is thus generated is due to the power of the soul. Again the cutting of the wood is from the saw; but that it assumes the length the form of a bed is from the design of the [joiner's] art. Therefore the substantial form which takes the principal place in the corporeal effects, is due to the angelic power. Therefore matter obeys the angels in receiving its form.

*On the contrary,* Augustine says "It is not to be thought, that this visible matter obeys these rebel angels; for it obeys God alone."

*I answer that,* The Platonists [*Phaedo. xlix: Tim. (Did.) vol. ii, p. 218] asserted that the forms which are in matter are caused by immaterial forms, because they said that the material forms are participations of immaterial forms. Avicenna followed them in this opinion to some extent, for he said that all forms which are in matter proceed from the concept of the *intellect;* and that corporeal agents only dispose [matter] for the forms. They seem to have been deceived on this point, through supposing a form to be something made *per se,* so that it would be the effect of a formal principle. But, as the Philosopher proves (Metaph. vii, Did. vi, 8), what is made, properly speaking, is the *composite:* for this properly speaking, is, as it were, what subsists. Whereas the form is called a being, not as that which is, but as that by which something is; and consequently neither is a form, properly speaking, made; for that is made which is; since to be is nothing but the way to existence.

Now it is manifest that what is made is like to the maker, forasmuch as every agent makes its like. So whatever makes natural things, has a likeness to the composite; either because it is composite itself, as when fire begets fire, or because the whole "composite" as to both matter and form is within its power; and this belongs to God alone. Therefore every informing of matter is either immediately from God, or form some corporeal agent; but not immediately from an angel.

Reply Obj. 1: Our soul is united to the body as the form; and so it is not surprising for the body to be formally changed by the soul's concept; especially as the movement of the sensitive appetite, which is accompanied with a certain bodily change, is subject to the command of reason. An angel, however, has not the same connection with natural bodies; and hence the argument does not hold.

Reply Obj. 2: Whatever an inferior power can do, that a superior power can do, not in the same way, but in a more excellent way; for example, the intellect knows sensible things in a more excellent way than sense knows them. So an angel can change corporeal matter in a more excellent way than can corporeal agents, that is by moving the corporeal agents themselves, as being the superior cause.

Reply Obj. 3: There is nothing to prevent some natural effect taking place by angelic power, for which the power of corporeal agents would not suffice. This, however, is not to obey an angel's will (as neither does matter obey the mere will of a cook, when by regulating the fire according to the prescription of his art he produces a dish that the fire could not have produced by itself); since to reduce matter to the act of the substantial form does not exceed the power of a corporeal agent; for it is natural for like to make like.

THIRD ARTICLE [I, Q. 110, Art. 3]

Whether Bodies Obey the Angels As Regards Local Motion?

Objection 1: It would seem that bodies do not obey the angels in local motion. For the local motion of natural bodies follows on their forms. But the angels do not cause the forms of natural bodies, as stated above (A. 2). Therefore neither can they cause in them local motion.

Obj. 2: Further, the Philosopher (Phys. viii, 7) proves that local motion is the first of all movements. But the angels cannot cause other movements by a formal change of the matter. Therefore neither can they cause local motion.

Obj. 3: Further, the corporeal members obey the concept of the soul as regards local movement, as having in themselves some principle of life. In natural bodies, however, there is no vital principle. Therefore they do not obey the angels in local motion.

*On the contrary,* Augustine says (De Trin. iii, 8,9) that the angels use corporeal seed to produce certain effects. But they cannot do this without causing local movement. Therefore bodies obey them in local motion.

*I answer that,* As Dionysius says (Div. Nom. vii): "Divine wisdom has joined the ends of the first to the principles of the second." Hence it is clear that the inferior nature at its highest point is in conjunction with superior nature. Now corporeal nature is below the spiritual nature. But among all corporeal movements the most perfect is local motion, as the Philosopher proves (Phys. viii, 7). The reason of this is that what is moved locally is not as such in potentiality to anything intrinsic, but only to something extrinsic—that is, to place. Therefore the corporeal nature has a natural aptitude to be moved immediately by the spiritual nature as regards place. Hence also the philosophers asserted that the supreme bodies are moved locally by the spiritual substances; whence we see that the soul moves the body first and chiefly by a local motion.

Reply Obj. 1: There are in bodies other local movements besides those which result from the forms; for instance, the ebb and flow of the sea does not follow from the substantial form of the water, but from the influence of the moon; and much more can local movements result from the power of spiritual substances.

Reply Obj. 2: The angels, by causing local motion, as the first motion, can thereby cause other movements; that is, by employing corporeal agents to produce these effects, as a workman employs fire to soften iron.

Reply Obj. 3: The power of an angel is not so limited as is the power of the soul. Hence the motive power of the soul is limited to the body united to it, which is vivified by it, and by which it can move other things. But an angel's power is not limited to any body; hence it can move locally bodies not joined to it.

FOURTH ARTICLE [I, Q. 110, Art. 4]

Whether Angels Can Work Miracles?

Objection 1: It would seem that the angels can work miracles. For Gregory says (Hom. xxxiv in Evang.): "Those spirits are called virtues by whom signs and miracles are usually done."

Obj. 2: Further, Augustine says (QQ. 83, qu. 79) that "magicians work miracles by private contracts; good Christians by public justice, bad Christians by the signs of public justice." But magicians work miracles because they are "heard by the demons," as he says elsewhere in the same work [*Cf. Liber xxi, Sentent., sent. 4: among the supposititious works of St. Augustine]. Therefore the demons can work miracles. Therefore much more can the good angels.

Obj. 3: Further, Augustine says in the same work [*Cf. Liber xxi, Sentent., sent. 4: among the supposititious works of St. Augustine] that "it is not absurd to believe that all the things we see happen may be brought about by the lower powers that dwell in our atmosphere." But when an effect of natural causes is produced outside the order of the natural cause, we call it a miracle, as, for instance, when anyone is cured of a fever without the operation of nature. Therefore the angels and demons can work miracles.

Obj. 4: Further, superior power is not subject to the order of an inferior cause. But corporeal nature is inferior to an angel. Therefore an angel can work outside the order of corporeal agents; which is to work miracles.

*On the contrary,* It is written of God (Ps. 135:4): "Who alone doth great wonders."

*I answer that,* A miracle properly so called is when something is done outside the order of nature. But it is not enough for a miracle if something is done outside the order of any particular nature; for otherwise anyone would perform a miracle by throwing a stone upwards, as such a thing is outside the order of the stone's nature. So for a miracle is required that it be against the order of the whole created nature. But God alone can do this, because, whatever an angel or any other creature does by its own power, is according to the order of created nature; and thus it is not a miracle. Hence God alone can work miracles.

Reply Obj. 1: Some angels are said to work miracles; either because God works miracles at their request, in the same way as holy men are said to work miracles; or because they exercise a kind of ministry in the miracles which take place; as in collecting the dust in the general resurrection, or by doing something of that kind.

Reply Obj. 2: Properly speaking, as said above, miracles are those things which are done outside the order of the whole created nature. But as we do not know all the power of created nature, it follows that when anything is done outside the order of created nature by a power unknown to us, it is called a miracle as regards ourselves. So when the demons do anything of their own natural power, these things are called "miracles" not in an absolute sense, but in reference to ourselves. In this way the magicians work miracles through the demons; and these are said to be done by "private contracts," forasmuch as every power of the creature, in the universe, may be compared to the power of a private person in a city. Hence when a magician does anything by compact with the devil, this is done as it were by private contract. On the other hand, the Divine justice is in the whole universe as the public law is in the city. Therefore good Christians, so far as they work miracles by Divine justice, are said to work miracles by "public justice": but bad Christians by the "signs of public justice," as by invoking the name of Christ, or by making use of other sacred signs.

Reply Obj. 3: Spiritual powers are able to effect whatever happens in this visible world, by employing corporeal seeds by local movement.

Reply Obj. 4: Although the angels can do something which is outside the order of corporeal nature, yet they cannot do anything outside the whole created order, which is essential to a miracle, as above explained.

## QUESTION 111

THE ACTION OF THE ANGELS ON MAN (In Four Articles)

We now consider the action of the angels on man, and inquire:

(1) How far they can change them by their own natural power;

(2) How they are sent by God to the ministry of men;

(3) How they guard and protect men.

Under the first head there are four points of inquiry:

(1) Whether an angel can enlighten the human intellect?

(2) Whether he can change man's will?

(3) Whether he can change man's imagination?

(4) Whether he can change man's senses?

FIRST ARTICLE [I, Q. 111, Art. 1]

Whether an Angel Can Enlighten Man?

Objection 1: It would seem that an angel cannot enlighten man. For man is enlightened by faith; hence Dionysius (Eccl. Hier. iii) attributes enlightenment to baptism, as "the sacrament of faith." But faith is immediately from God, according to Eph. 2:8: "By grace you are saved through faith, and that not of yourselves, for it is the gift of God." Therefore man is not enlightened by an angel; but immediately by God.

Obj. 2: Further, on the words, "God hath manifested it to them" (Rom. 1:19), the gloss observes that "not only natural reason availed for the manifestation of Divine truths to men, but God also revealed them by His work," that is, by His creature. But both are immediately from God—that is, natural reason and the creature. Therefore God enlightens man immediately.

Obj. 3: Further, whoever is enlightened is conscious of being enlightened. But man is not conscious of being enlightened by angels. Therefore he is not enlightened by them.

*On the contrary,* Dionysius says (Coel. Hier. iv) that the revelation of Divine things reaches men through the ministry of the angels. But such revelation is an enlightenment as we have stated (Q. 106, A. 1; Q. 107, A. 2). Therefore men are enlightened by the angels.

*I answer that,* Since the order of Divine Providence disposes that lower things be subject to the actions of higher, as explained above (Q. 109, A. 2); as the inferior angels are enlightened by the superior, so men, who are inferior to the angels, are enlightened by them.

The modes of each of these kinds of enlightenment are in one way alike and in another way unlike. For, as was shown above (Q. 106, A. 1), the enlightenment which consists in making known Divine truth has two functions; namely, according as the inferior intellect is strengthened by the action of the superior intellect, and according as the intelligible species which are in the superior intellect are proposed to the inferior so as to be grasped thereby. This takes place in the angels when the superior angel divides his universal concept of the truth according to the capacity of the inferior angel, as explained above (Q. 106, A. 1).

The human intellect, however, cannot grasp the universal truth itself unveiled; because its nature requires it to understand by turning to the phantasms, as above explained (Q. 84, A. 7). So the angels propose the intelligible truth to men under the similitudes of sensible things, according to what Dionysius says (Coel. Hier. i), that, "It is impossible for the divine ray to shine on us, otherwise than shrouded by the variety of the sacred veils." On the other hand, the human intellect as the inferior, is strengthened by the action of the angelic intellect. And in these two ways man is enlightened by an angel.

Reply Obj. 1: Two dispositions concur in the virtue of faith; first, the habit of the intellect whereby it is disposed to obey the will tending to Divine truth. For the intellect assents to the truth of faith, not as convinced by the reason, but as commanded by the will; hence Augustine says, "No one believes except willingly." In this respect faith comes from God alone. Secondly, faith requires that what is to be believed be proposed to the believer; which is accomplished by man, according to Rom. 10:17, "Faith cometh by hearing"; principally, however, by the angels, by whom Divine things are revealed to men. Hence the angels have some part in the enlightenment of faith. Moreover, men are enlightened by the angels not only concerning what is to be believed; but also as regards what is to be done.

Reply Obj. 2: Natural reason, which is immediately from God, can be strengthened by an angel, as we have said above. Again, the more the human intellect is strengthened, so much higher an intelligible truth can be elicited from the species derived from creatures. Thus man is assisted by an angel so that he may obtain from creatures a more perfect knowledge of God.

Reply Obj. 3: Intellectual operation and enlightenment can be understood in two ways. First, on the part of the object understood; thus whoever understands or is enlightened, knows that he understands or is enlightened, because he knows that the object is made known to him. Secondly, on the part of the principle; and thus it does not follow that whoever understands a truth, knows what the intellect is, which is the principle of the intellectual operation. In like manner not everyone who is enlightened by an angel, knows that he is enlightened by him.

SECOND ARTICLE [I, Q. 111, Art. 3]

Whether the Angels Can Change the Will of Man?

Objection 1: It would seem that the angels can change the will of man. For, upon the text, "Who maketh His angels spirits and His ministers a flame of fire" (Heb. 1:7), the gloss notes that "they are fire, as being spiritually fervent, and as burning away our vices." This could not be, however, unless they changed the will. Therefore the angels can change the will.

Obj. 2: Further, Bede says (Super Matth. xv, 11), that, "the devil does not send wicked thoughts, but kindles them." Damascene, however, says that he also sends them; for he remarks that "every malicious act and unclean passion is contrived by the demons and put into men" (De Fide Orth. ii, 4); in like manner also the good angels introduce and kindle good thoughts. But this could only be if they changed the will. Therefore the will is changed by them.

Obj. 3: Further, the angel, as above explained, enlightens the human intellect by means of the phantasms. But as the imagination which serves the intellect can be changed by an angel, so can the sensitive appetite which serves the will, because it also is a faculty using a corporeal organ. Therefore as the angel enlightens the mind, so can he change the will.

*On the contrary,* To change the will belongs to God alone, according to Prov. 21:1: "The heart of the king is in the hand of the Lord, whithersoever He will He shall turn it."

*I answer that,* The will can be changed in two ways. First, from within; in which way, since the movement of the will is nothing but the inclination of the will to the thing willed, God alone can thus change the will, because He gives the power of such an inclination to the intellectual nature. For as the natural inclination is from God alone Who gives the nature, so the inclination of the will is from God alone, Who causes the will.

Secondly, the will is moved from without. As regards an angel, this can be only in one way—by the good apprehended by the intellect. Hence in as far as anyone may be the cause why anything be apprehended as an appetible good, so far does he move the will. In this way also God alone can move the will efficaciously; but an angel and man move the will by way of persuasion, as above explained (Q. 106, A. 2).

In addition to this mode the human will can be moved from without in another way; namely, by the passion residing in the sensitive appetite: thus by concupiscence or anger the will is inclined to will something. In this manner the angels, as being able to rouse these passions, can move the will, not however by necessity, for the will ever remains free to consent to, or to resist, the passion.

Reply Obj. 1: Those who act as God's ministers, either men or angels, are said to burn away vices, and to incite to virtue by way of persuasion.

Reply Obj. 2: The demon cannot put thoughts in our minds by causing them from within, since the act of the cogitative faculty is subject to the will; nevertheless the devil is called the kindler of thoughts, inasmuch as he incites to thought, by the desire of the things thought of, by way of persuasion, or by rousing the passions. Damascene calls this kindling "a putting in" because such a work is accomplished within. But good thoughts are attributed to a higher principle, namely, God, though they may be procured by the ministry of the angels.

Reply Obj. 3: The human intellect in its present state can understand only by turning to the phantasms; but the human will can will something following the judgment of reason rather than the passion of the sensitive appetite. Hence the comparison does not hold.

THIRD ARTICLE [I, Q. 111, Art. 3]

Whether an Angel Can Change Man's Imagination?

Objection 1: It would seem that an angel cannot change man's imagination. For the phantasy, as is said *De Anima* iii, is "a motion caused by the sense in act." But if this motion were caused by an angel, it would not be caused by the sense in act. Therefore it is contrary to the nature of the phantasy, which is the act of the imaginative faculty, to be changed by an angel.

Obj. 2: Further, since the forms in the imagination are spiritual, they are nobler than the forms existing in sensible matter. But an angel cannot impress forms upon sensible matter (Q. 110, A. 2). Therefore he cannot impress forms on the imagination, and so he cannot change it.

Obj. 3: Further, Augustine says (Gen. ad lit. xii, 12): "One spirit by intermingling with another can communicate his knowledge to the other spirit by these images, so that the latter either understands it himself, or accepts it as understood by the other." But it does not seem that an angel can be mingled with the human imagination, nor that the imagination can receive the knowledge of an angel. Therefore it seems that an angel cannot change the imagination.

Obj. 4: Further, in the imaginative vision man cleaves to the similitudes of the things as to the things themselves. But in this there is deception. So as a good angel cannot be the cause of deception, it seems that he cannot cause the imaginative vision, by changing the imagination.

*On the contrary,* Those things which are seen in dreams are seen by imaginative vision. But the angels reveal things in dreams, as appears from Matt. 1:20; 2:13, 19 in regard to the angel who appeared to Joseph in dreams. Therefore an angel can move the imagination.

*I answer that,* Both a good and a bad angel by their own natural power can move the human imagination. This may be explained as follows. For it was said above (Q. 110, A. 3), that corporeal nature obeys the angel as regards local movement, so that whatever can be caused by the local movement of bodies is subject to the natural power of the angels. Now it is manifest that imaginative apparitions are sometimes caused in us by the local movement of animal spirits and humors. Hence Aristotle says (De Somn. et Vigil.) [*De Insomniis iii], when assigning the cause of visions in dreams, that "when an animal sleeps, the blood descends in abundance to the sensitive principle, and movements descend with it," that is, the impressions left from the movements are preserved in the animal spirits, "and move the sensitive principle"; so that a certain appearance ensues, as if the sensitive principle were being then changed by the external objects themselves. Indeed, the commotion of the spirits and humors may be so great that such appearances may even occur to those who are awake, as is seen in mad people, and the like. So, as this happens by a natural disturbance of the humors, and sometimes also by the will of man who voluntarily imagines what he previously experienced, so also the same may be done by the power of a good or a bad angel, sometimes with alienation from the bodily senses, sometimes without such alienation.

Reply Obj. 1: The first principle of the imagination is from the sense in act. For we cannot imagine what we have never perceived by the senses, either wholly or partly; as a man born blind cannot imagine color. Sometimes, however, the imagination is informed in such a way that the act of the imaginative movement arises from the impressions preserved within.

Reply Obj. 2: An angel changes the imagination, not indeed by the impression of an imaginative form in no way previously received from the senses (for he cannot make a man born blind imagine color), but by local movement of the spirits and humors, as above explained.

Reply Obj. 3: The commingling of the angelic spirit with the human imagination is not a mingling of essences, but by reason of an effect which he produces in the imagination in the way above stated; so that he shows man what he [the angel] knows, but not in the way he knows.

Reply Obj. 4: An angel causing an imaginative vision, sometimes enlightens the intellect at the same time, so that it knows what these images signify; and then there is no deception. But sometimes by the angelic operation the similitudes of things only appear in the imagination; but neither then is deception caused by the angel, but by the defect in the intellect to whom such things appear. Thus neither was Christ a cause of deception when He spoke many things to the people in parables, which He did not explain to them.

FOURTH ARTICLE [I, Q. 111, Art. 4]

Whether an Angel Can Change the Human Senses?

Objection 1: It seems that an angel cannot change the human senses. For the sensitive operation is a vital operation. But such an operation does not come from an extrinsic principle. Therefore the sensitive operation cannot be caused by an angel.

Obj. 2: Further, the sensitive operation is nobler than the nutritive. But the angel cannot change the nutritive power, nor other natural forms. Therefore neither can he change the sensitive power.

Obj. 3: Further, the senses are naturally moved by the sensible objects. But an angel cannot change the order of nature (Q. 110, A. 4). Therefore an angel cannot change the senses; but these are changed always by the sensible object.

*On the contrary,* The angels who overturned Sodom, "struck the people of Sodom with blindness or *aorasia* , so that they could not find the door" (Gen. 19:11). [*It is worth noting that these are the only two passages in the Greek version where the word *aorasia* appears. It expresses, in fact, the effect produced on the people of Sodom—namely, dazzling (French version, "eblouissement"), which the Latin "caecitas" (blindness) does not necessarily imply.] The same is recorded of the Syrians whom Eliseus led into Samaria (4 Kings 6:18).

*I answer that,* The senses may be changed in a twofold manner; from without, as when affected by the sensible object: and from within, for we see that the senses are changed when the spirits and humors are disturbed; as for example, a sick man's tongue, charged with choleric humor, tastes everything as bitter, and the like with the other senses. Now an angel, by his natural power, can work a change in the senses both ways. For an angel can offer the senses a sensible object from without, formed by nature or by the angel himself, as when he assumes a body, as we have said above (Q. 51, A. 2). Likewise he can move the spirits and humors from within, as above remarked, whereby the senses are changed in various ways.

Reply Obj. 1: The principle of the sensitive operation cannot be without the interior principle which is the sensitive power; but this interior principle can be moved in many ways by the exterior principle, as above explained.

Reply Obj. 2: By the interior movement of the spirits and humors an angel can do something towards changing the act of the nutritive power, and also of the appetitive and sensitive power, and of any other power using a corporeal organ.

Reply Obj. 3: An angel can do nothing outside the entire order of creatures; but he can outside some particular order of nature, since he is not subject to that order; thus in some special way an angel can work a change in the senses outside the common mode of nature.

# QUESTION 112

THE MISSION OF THE ANGELS (In Four Articles)

We next consider the mission of the angels. Under this head arise four points of inquiry:

(1) Whether any angels are sent on works of ministry?

(2) Whether all are sent?

(3) Whether those who are sent, assist?

(4) From what orders they are sent.

FIRST ARTICLE [I, Q. 112, Art. 1]

Whether the Angels Are Sent on Works of Ministry?

Objection 1: It would seem that the angels are not sent on works of ministry. For every mission is to some determinate place. But intellectual actions do not determine a place, for intellect abstracts from the "here" and "now." Since therefore the angelic actions are intellectual, it appears that the angels are not sent to perform their own actions.

Obj. 2: Further, the empyrean heaven is the place that beseems the angelic dignity. Therefore if they are sent to us in ministry, it seems that something of their dignity would be lost; which is unseemly.

Obj. 3: Further, external occupation hinders the contemplation of wisdom; hence it is said: "He that is less in action, shall receive wisdom" (Ecclus. 38:25). So if some angels are sent on external ministrations, they would seemingly be hindered from contemplation. But the whole of their beatitude consists in the contemplation of God. So if they were sent, their beatitude would be lessened; which is unfitting.

Obj. 4: Further, to minister is the part of an inferior; hence it is written (Luke 22:27): "Which is the greater, he that sitteth at table, or he that serveth? is not he that sitteth at table?" But the angels are naturally greater than we are. Therefore they are not sent to administer to us.

*On the contrary,* It is written (Ex. 23:20): "Behold I will send My angels who shall go before thee."

*I answer that,* From what has been said above (Q. 108, A. 6), it may be shown that some angels are sent in ministry by God. For, as we have already stated (Q. 43, A. 1), in treating of the mission of the Divine Persons, he is said to be sent who in any way proceeds from another so as to begin to be where he was not, or to be in another way, where he already was. Thus the Son, or the Holy Ghost is said to be sent as proceeding from the Father by origin; and begins to be in a new way, by grace or by the nature assumed, where He was before by the presence of His Godhead; for it belongs to God to be present everywhere, because, since He is the universal agent, His power reaches to all being, and hence He exists in all things (Q. 8, A. 1). An angel's power, however, as a particular agent, does not reach to the whole universe, but reaches to one thing in such a way as not to reach another; and so he is "here" in such a manner as not to be "there." But it is clear from what was above stated (Q. 110, A. 1), that the corporeal creature is governed by the angels. Hence, whenever an angel has to perform any work concerning a corporeal creature, the angel applies himself anew to that body by his power; and in that way begins to be there afresh. Now all this takes place by Divine command. Hence it follows that an angel is sent by God.

Yet the action performed by the angel who is sent, proceeds from God as from its first principle, at Whose nod and by Whose authority the angels work; and is reduced to God as to its last end. Now this is what is meant by a minister: for a minister is an intelligent instrument; while an instrument is moved by another, and its action is ordered to another. Hence angels' actions are called "ministries"; and for this reason they are said to be sent in ministry.

Reply Obj. 1: An operation can be intellectual in two ways. In one way, as dwelling in the intellect itself, as contemplation; such an operation does not demand to occupy a place; indeed, as Augustine says (De Trin. iv, 20): "Even we ourselves as mentally tasting something eternal, are not in this world." In another sense an action is said to be intellectual because it is regulated and commanded by some intellect; in that sense the intellectual operations evidently have sometimes a determinate place.

Reply Obj. 2: The empyrean heaven belongs to the angelic dignity by way of congruity; forasmuch as it is congruous that the higher body should be attributed to that nature which occupies a rank above bodies. Yet an angel does not derive his dignity from the empyrean heaven; so when he is not actually in the empyrean heaven, nothing of his dignity is lost, as neither does a king lessen his dignity when not actually sitting on his regal throne, which suits his dignity.

Reply Obj. 3: In ourselves the purity of contemplation is obscured by exterior occupation; because we give ourselves to action through the sensitive faculties, the action of which when intense impedes the action of the intellectual powers. An angel, *on the contrary,* regulates his exterior actions by intellectual operation alone. Hence it follows that his external occupations in no respect impede his contemplation; because given two actions, one of which is the rule and the reason of the other, one does not hinder but helps the other. Wherefore Gregory says (Moral. ii) that "the angels do not go abroad in such a manner as to lose the delights of inward contemplation."

Reply Obj. 4: In their external actions the angels chiefly minister to God, and secondarily to us; not because we are superior to them, absolutely speaking, but because, since every man or angel by cleaving to God is made one spirit with God, he is thereby superior to every creature. Hence the Apostle says (Phil. 2:3): "Esteeming others better than themselves."

SECOND ARTICLE [I, Q. 112, Art. 2]

Whether All the Angels Are Sent in Ministry?

Objection 1: It would seem that all the angels are sent in ministry. For the Apostle says (Heb. 1:14): "All are ministering spirits, sent to minister" [Vulg. 'Are they not all ... ?'].

Obj. 2: Further, among the orders, the highest is that of the Seraphim, as stated above (Q. 108, A.

6). But a Seraph was sent to purify the lips of the prophet (Isa. 6:6, 7). Therefore much more are the inferior orders sent.

Obj. 3: Further, the Divine Persons infinitely excel all the angelic orders. But the Divine Persons are sent. Therefore much more are even the highest angels sent.

Obj. 4: Further, if the superior angels are not sent to the external ministries, this can only be because the superior angels execute the Divine ministries by means of the inferior angels. But as all the angels are unequal, as stated above (Q. 50, A. 4), each angel has an angel inferior to himself except the last one. Therefore only the last angel would be sent in ministry; which contradicts the words, "Thousands of thousands ministered to Him" (Dan. 7:10).

*On the contrary,* Gregory says (Hom. xxxiv in Evang.), quoting the statement of Dionysius (Coel. Hier. xiii), that "the higher ranks fulfil no exterior service."

*I answer that,* As appears from what has been said above (Q. 106, A. 3; Q. 110, A. 1), the order of Divine Providence has so disposed not only among the angels, but also in the whole universe, that inferior things are administered by the superior. But the Divine dispensation, however, this order is sometimes departed from as regards corporeal things, for the sake of a higher order, that is, according as it is suitable for the manifestation of grace. That the man born blind was enlightened, that Lazarus was raised from the dead, was accomplished immediately by God without the action of the heavenly bodies. Moreover both good and bad angels can work some effect in these bodies independently of the heavenly bodies, by the condensation of the clouds to rain, and by producing some such effects. Nor can anyone doubt that God can immediately reveal things to men without the help of the angels, and the superior angels without the inferior. From this standpoint some have said that according to the general law the superior angels are not sent, but only the inferior; yet that sometimes, by Divine dispensation, the superior angels also are sent.

It may also be said that the Apostle wishes to prove that Christ is greater than the angels who were chosen as the messengers of the law; in order that He might show the excellence of the new over the old law. Hence there is no need to apply this to any other angels besides those who were sent to give the law.

Reply Obj. 2: According to Dionysius (Coel. Hier. xiii), the angel who was sent to purify the prophet's lips was one of the inferior order; but was called a "Seraph," that is, "kindling " in an equivocal sense, because he came to "kindle" the lips of the prophet. It may also be said that the superior angels communicate their own proper gifts whereby they are denominated, through the ministry of the inferior angels. Thus one of the Seraphim is described as purifying by fire the prophet's lips, not as if he did so immediately, but because an inferior angel did so by his power; as the Pope is said to absolve a man when he gives absolution by means of someone else.

Reply Obj. 3: The Divine Persons are not sent in ministry, but are said to be sent in an equivocal sense, as appears from what has been said (Q. 43, A. 1).

Reply Obj. 4: A manifold grade exists in the Divine ministries. Hence there is nothing to prevent angels though unequal from being sent immediately in ministry, in such a manner however that the superior are sent to the higher ministries, and the lower to the inferior ministries.

THIRD ARTICLE [I, Q. 112, Art. 3]

Whether All the Angels Who Are Sent, Assist?

Objection 1: It would seem that the angels who are sent also assist. For Gregory says (Hom. xxxiv in Evang.): "So the angels are sent, and assist; for, though the angelic spirit is limited, yet the supreme Spirit, God, is not limited."

Obj. 2: Further, the angel was sent to minister to Tobias. Yet he said, "I am the angel Raphael, one of the seven who stand before the Lord" (Tob. 12:15). Therefore the angels who are sent, assist.

Obj. 3: Further, every holy angel is nearer to God than Satan is. Yet Satan assisted God, according to Job 1:6: "When the sons of God came to stand before the Lord, Satan also was present among them." Therefore much more do the angels, who are sent to minister, assist.

Obj. 4: Further, if the inferior angels do not assist, the reason is because they receive the Divine enlightenment, not immediately, but through the superior angels. But every angel receives the Divine enlightenment from a superior, except the one who is highest of all. Therefore only the highest angel would assist; which is contrary to the text of Dan. 7:10: "Ten thousand times a hundred thousand stood before Him." Therefore the angels who are sent also assist.

*On the contrary,* Gregory says, on Job 25:3: "Is there any numbering of His soldiers?" (Moral. xvii): "Those powers assist, who do not go forth as messengers to men." Therefore those who are sent in ministry do not assist.

*I answer that,* The angels are spoken of as "assisting" and "administering," after the likeness of those who attend upon a king; some of whom ever wait upon him, and hear his commands immediately; while others there are to whom the royal commands are conveyed by those who are in attendance—for instance, those who are placed at the head of the administration of various cities; these are said to administer, not to assist.

We must therefore observe that all the angels gaze upon the Divine Essence immediately; in regard to which all, even those who minister, are said to assist. Hence Gregory says (Moral. ii) that "those who are sent on the external ministry of our salvation can always assist and see the face of the Father." Yet not all the angels can perceive the secrets of the Divine mysteries in the clearness itself of the Divine Essence; but only the superior angels who announce them to the inferior: and in that respect only the superior angels belonging to the highest hierarchy are said to assist, whose special prerogative it is to be enlightened immediately by God.

From this may be deduced the reply to the first and second objections, which are based on the first mode of assisting.

Reply Obj. 3: Satan is not described as having assisted, but as present among the assistants; for, as Gregory says (Moral. ii), "though he has lost beatitude, still he has retained a nature like to the angels."

Reply Obj. 4: All the assistants see some things immediately in the glory of the Divine Essence; and so it may be said that it is the prerogative of the whole of the highest hierarchy to be immediately enlightened by God; while the higher ones among them see more than is seen by the inferior; some of whom enlighten others: as also among those who assist the king, one knows more of the king's secrets than another.

FOURTH ARTICLE [I, Q. 112, Art. 4]

Whether All the Angels of the Second Hierarchy Are Sent?

Objection 1: It would seem that all the angels of the second hierarchy are sent. For all the angels either assist, or minister, according to Dan. 7:10. But the angels of the second hierarchy do not assist; for they are enlightened by the angels of the first hierarchy, as Dionysius says (Coel. Hier. viii). Therefore all the angels of the second hierarchy are sent in ministry.

Obj. 2: Further, Gregory says (Moral. xvii) that "there are more who minister than who assist." This would not be the case if the angels of the second hierarchy were not sent in ministry. Therefore all the angels of the second hierarchy are sent to minister.

*On the contrary,* Dionysius says (Coel. Hier. viii) that the "Dominations are above all subjection." But to be sent implies subjection. Therefore the dominations are not sent to minister.

*I answer that,* As above stated (A. 1), to be sent to external ministry properly belongs to an angel according as he acts by Divine command in respect of any corporeal creature; which is part of the execution of the Divine ministry. Now the angelic properties are manifested by their names, as Dionysius says (Coel. Hier. vii); and therefore the angels of those orders are sent to external ministry whose names signify some kind of administration. But the name "dominations" does not signify any such administration, but only disposition and command in administering. On the other hand, the names of the inferior orders imply administration, for the "Angels" and "Archangels" are so called from "announcing"; the "Virtues" and "Powers" are so called in respect of some act; and it is right that the "Prince," according to what Gregory says (Hom. xxxiv in Evang.), "be first among the workers." Hence it belongs to these five orders to be sent to external ministry; not to the four superior orders.

Reply Obj. 1: The Dominations are reckoned among the ministering angels, not as exercising but as disposing and commanding what is to be done by others; thus an architect does not put his hands to the production of his art, but only disposes and orders what others are to do.

Reply Obj. 2: A twofold reason may be given in assigning the number of the assisting and ministering angels. For Gregory says that those who minister are more numerous than those who assist; because he takes the words (Dan. 7:10) "thousands of thousands ministered to Him," not in a multiple but in a partitive sense, to mean "thousands out of thousands"; thus the number of those who minister is indefinite, and signifies excess; while the number of assistants is finite as in the words added, "and ten thousand times a hundred thousand assisted Him." This explanation rests on the opinion of the Platonists, who said that the nearer things are to the one first principle, the smaller they are in number; as the nearer a number is to unity, the lesser it is than multitude. This opinion is verified as regards the number of orders, as six administer and three assist.

Dionysius, however, (Coel. Hier. xiv) declares that the multitude of angels surpasses all the multitude of material things; so that, as the superior bodies exceed the inferior in magnitude to an immeasurable degree, so the superior incorporeal natures surpass all corporeal natures in multitude; because whatever is better is more intended and more multiplied by God. Hence, as the assistants are superior to the ministers there will be more assistants than ministers. In this way, the words "thousands of thousands" are taken by way of multiplication, to signify "a thousand times a thousand." And because ten times a hundred is a thousand, if it were said "ten times a hundred thousand" it would mean that there are as many assistants as ministers: but since it is written "ten thousand times a hundred thousand," we are given to understand that the assistants are much more numerous than the ministers. Nor is this said to signify that this is the precise number of angels, but rather that it is much greater, in that it exceeds all material multitude. This is signified by the multiplication together of all the greatest numbers, namely ten, a hundred, and a thousand, as Dionysius remarks in the same passage.

## QUESTION 113

OF THE GUARDIANSHIP OF THE GOOD ANGELS (In Eight Articles)

We next consider the guardianship exercised by the good angels; and their warfare against the bad angels. Under the first head eight points of inquiry arise:

(1) Whether men are guarded by the angels?

(2) Whether to each man is assigned a single guardian angel?

(3) Whether the guardianship belongs only to the lowest order of angels?

(4) Whether it is fitting for each man to have an angel guardian?

(5) When does an angel's guardianship of a man begin?

(6) Whether the angel guardians always watch over men?

(7) Whether the angel grieves over the loss of the one guarded?

(8) Whether rivalry exists among the angels as regards their guardianship?

FIRST ARTICLE [I, Q. 113, Art. 1]

Whether Men Are Guarded by the Angels?

Objection 1: It would seem that men are not guarded by the angels. For guardians are deputed to some because they either know not how, or are not able, to guard themselves, as children and the sick. But man is able to guard himself by his free-will; and knows how by his natural knowledge of natural law. Therefore man is not guarded by an angel.

Obj. 2: Further, a strong guard makes a weaker one superfluous. But men are guarded by God, according to Ps. 120:4: "He shall neither slumber nor sleep, that keepeth Israel." Therefore man does not need to be guarded by an angel.

Obj. 3: Further, the loss of the guarded redounds to the negligence of the guardian; hence it was said to a certain one: "Keep this man; and if he shall slip away, thy life shall be for his life" (3 Kings 20:39). Now many perish daily through falling into sin; whom the angels could help by visible appearance, or by miracles, or in some such-like way. The angels would therefore be negligent if men are given to their guardianship. But that is clearly false. Therefore the angels are not the guardians of men.

*On the contrary,* It is written (Ps. 90:11): "He hath given His angels charge over thee, to keep thee in all thy ways."

*I answer that,* According to the plan of Divine Providence, we find that in all things the movable and variable are moved and regulated by the immovable and invariable; as all corporeal things by immovable spiritual substances, and the inferior bodies by the superior which are invariable in substance. We ourselves also are regulated as regards conclusions, about which we may have various opinions, by the principles which we hold in an invariable manner. It is moreover manifest that as regards things to be done human knowledge and affection can vary and fail from good in many ways; and so it was necessary that angels should be deputed for the guardianship of men, in order to regulate them and move them to good.

Reply Obj. 1: By free-will man can avoid evil to a certain degree, but not in any sufficient degree; forasmuch as he is weak in affection towards good on account of the manifold passions of the soul. Likewise universal natural knowledge of the law, which by nature belongs to man, to a certain degree directs man to good, but not in a sufficient degree; because in the application of the universal principles of law to particular actions man happens to be deficient in many ways. Hence it is written (Wis. 9:14): "The thoughts of mortal men are fearful, and our counsels uncertain." Thus man needs to be guarded by the angels.

Reply Obj. 2: Two things are required for a good action; first, that the affection be inclined to good, which is effected in us by the habit of mortal virtue. Secondly, that reason should discover the proper methods to make perfect the good of virtue; this the Philosopher (Ethic. vi) attributes to prudence. As regards the first, God guards man immediately by infusing into him grace and virtues; as regards the second, God guards man as his universal instructor, Whose precepts reach man by the medium of the angels, as above stated (Q. 111, A. 1).

Reply Obj. 3: As men depart from the natural instinct of good by reason of a sinful passion, so also do they depart from the instigation of the good angels, which takes place invisibly when they enlighten man that he may do what is right. Hence that men perish is not to be imputed to the negligence of the angels but to the malice of men. That they sometimes appear to men visibly outside the ordinary course of nature comes from a special grace of God, as likewise that miracles occur outside the order of nature.

SECOND ARTICLE [I, Q. 113, Art. 2]

Whether Each Man Is Guarded by an Angel?

Objection 1: It would seem that each man is not guarded by an angel. For an angel is stronger than a man. But one man suffices to guard many men. Therefore much more can one angel guard many men.

Obj. 2: Further, the lower things are brought to God through the medium of the higher, as Dionysius says (Coel. Hier. iv, xiii). But as all the angels are unequal (Q. 50, A. 4), there is only one angel between whom and men there is no medium. Therefore there is only one angel who immediately keeps men.

Obj. 3: Further, the greater angels are deputed to the greater offices. But it is not a greater office to keep one man more than another; since all men are naturally equal. Since therefore of all the angels one is greater than another, as Dionysius says (Coel. Hier. x), it seems that different men are not guarded by different angels.

*On the contrary,* On the text, "Their angels in heaven," etc. (Matt. 8:10), Jerome says: "Great is the dignity of souls, for each one to have an angel deputed to guard it from its birth."

*I answer that,* Each man has an angel guardian appointed to him. This rests upon the fact that the guardianship of angels belongs to the execution of Divine providence concerning men. But God's providence acts differently as regards men and as regards other corruptible creatures, for they are related differently to incorruptibility. For men are not only incorruptible in the common species, but also in the proper forms of each individual, which are the rational souls, which cannot be said of other incorruptible things. Now it is manifest that the providence of God is chiefly exercised towards what remains for ever; whereas as regards things which pass away, the providence of God acts so as to order their existence to the things which are perpetual. Thus the providence of God is related to each man as it is to every genus or species of things corruptible. But, according to Gregory (Hom. xxxiv in Evang.), the different orders are deputed to the different genera of things, for instance, the "Powers" to coerce the demons, the "Virtues" to work miracles in things corporeal; while it is probable that the different species are presided over by different angels of the same order. Hence it is also reasonable to suppose that different angels are appointed to the guardianship of different men.

Reply Obj. 1: A guardian may be assigned to a man for two reasons: first, inasmuch as a man is an individual, and thus to one man one guardian is due; and sometimes several are appointed to guard one. Secondly, inasmuch as a man is part of a community, and thus one man is appointed as guardian of a whole community; to whom it belongs to provide what concerns one man in his relation to the whole community, such as external works, which are sources of strength or weakness to others. But angel guardians are given to men also as regards invisible and occult things, concerning the salvation of each one in his own regard. Hence individual angels are appointed to guard individual men.

Reply Obj. 2: As above stated (Q. 112, A. 3, ad 4), all the angels of the first hierarchy are, as to some things, enlightened by God directly; but as to other things, only the superior are directly enlightened by God, and these reveal them to the inferior. And the same also applies to the inferior orders: for a lower angel is enlightened in some respects by one of the highest, and in other respects by the one immediately above him. Thus it is possible that some one angel enlightens a man immediately, and yet has other angels beneath him whom he enlightens.

Reply Obj. 3: Although men are equal in nature, still inequality exists among them, according as Divine Providence orders some to the greater, and others to the lesser things, according to Ecclus. 33:11, 12: "With much knowledge the Lord hath divided them, and diversified their ways: some of them hath He blessed and exalted, and some of them hath He cursed and brought low." Thus it is a greater office to guard one man than another.

THIRD ARTICLE [I, Q. 113, Art. 3]

Whether to Guard Men Belongs Only to the Lowest Order of Angels?

Objection 1: It would seem that the guardianship of men does not belong only to the lowest order of the angels. For Chrysostom says that the text (Matt. 18:10), "Their angels in heaven," etc. is to be understood not of any angels but of the highest. Therefore the superior angels guard men.

Obj. 2: Further, the Apostle says that angels "are sent to minister for them who shall receive the inheritance of salvation" (Heb. 1:14); and thus it seems that the mission of the angels is directed to the guardianship of men. But five orders are sent in external ministry (Q. 112, A. 4). Therefore all the angels of the five orders are deputed to the guardianship of men.

Obj. 3: Further, for the guardianship of men it seems especially necessary to coerce the demons, which belongs most of all to the Powers, according to Gregory (Hom. xxxiv in Evang.); and to work miracles, which belongs to the Virtues. Therefore these orders are also deputed to the work of guardianship, and not only the lowest order.

*On the contrary,* In the Psalm (90) the guardianship of men is attributed to the angels; who belong to the lowest order, according to Dionysius (Coel. Hier. v, ix).

*I answer that,* As above stated (A. 2), man is guarded in two ways; in one way by particular guardianship, according as to each man an angel is appointed to guard him; and such guardianship belongs to the lowest order of the angels, whose place it is, according to Gregory, to announce the "lesser things"; for it seems to be the least of the angelic offices to procure what concerns the salvation of only one man. The other kind of guardianship is universal, multiplied according to the different orders. For the more universal an agent is, the higher it is. Thus the guardianship of the human race belongs to the order of "Principalities," or perhaps to the "Archangels," whom we call the angel princes. Hence, Michael, whom we call an archangel, is also styled "one of the princes" (Dan. 10:13). Moreover all corporeal creatures are guarded by the "Virtues"; and likewise the demons by the "Powers," and the good spirits by the "Principalities," according to Gregory's opinion (Hom. xxxiv in Ev.).

Reply Obj. 1: Chrysostom can be taken to mean the highest in the lowest order of angels; for, as Dionysius says (Coel. Hier. x) in each order there are first, middle, and last. It is, however, probable that the greater angels are deputed to keep those chosen by God for the higher degree of glory.

Reply Obj. 2: Not all the angels who are sent have guardianship of individual men; but some orders have a universal guardianship, greater or less, as above explained.

Reply Obj. 3: Even inferior angels exercise the office of the superior, as they share in their gifts, and they are executors of the superiors' power; and in this way all the angels of the lowest order can coerce the demons, and work miracles.

FOURTH ARTICLE [I, Q. 113, Art. 4]

Whether Angels Are Appointed to the Guardianship of All Men?

Objection 1: It would seem that angels are not appointed to the guardianship of all men. For it is written of Christ (Phil. 2:7) that "He was made in the likeness of men, and in habit found as a man." If therefore angels are appointed to the guardianship of all men, Christ also would have had an angel guardian. But this is unseemly, for Christ is greater than all the angels. Therefore angels are not appointed to the guardianship of all men.

Obj. 2: Further, Adam was the first of all men. But it was not fitting that he should have an angel guardian, at least in the state of innocence: for then he was not beset by any dangers. Therefore angels are not appointed to the guardianship of all men.

Obj. 3: Further, angels are appointed to the guardianship of men, that they may take them by the hand and guide them to eternal life, encourage them to good works, and protect them against the assaults of the demons. But men who are foreknown to damnation, never attain to eternal life. Infidels, also, though at times they perform good works, do not perform them well, for they have not a right intention: for "faith directs the intention" as Augustine says (Enarr. ii in Ps. 31). Moreover, the coming of Antichrist will be "according to the working of Satan," as it is written (2 Thess. 2:9). Therefore angels are not deputed to the guardianship of all men.

*On the contrary,* is the authority of Jerome quoted above (A. 2), for he says that "each soul has an angel appointed to guard it."

*I answer that,* Man while in this state of life, is, as it were, on a road by which he should journey towards heaven. On this road man is threatened by many dangers both from within and from without, according to Ps. 159:4: "In this way wherein I walked, they have hidden a snare for me." And therefore as guardians are appointed for men who have to pass by an unsafe road, so an angel guardian is assigned to each man as long as he is a wayfarer. When, however, he arrives at the end of life he no longer has a guardian angel; but in the kingdom he will have an angel to reign with him, in hell a demon to punish him.

Reply Obj. 1: Christ as man was guided immediately by the Word of God: wherefore He needed not be guarded by an angel. Again as regards His soul, He was a comprehensor, although in regard to His passible body, He was a wayfarer. In this latter respect it was right that He should have not a guardian angel as superior to Him, but a ministering angel as inferior to Him. Whence it is written (Matt. 4:11) that "angels came and ministered to Him."

Reply Obj. 2: In the state of innocence man was not threatened by any peril from within: because within him all was well ordered, as we have said above (Q. 95, AA. 1, 3). But peril threatened from without on account of the snares of the demons; as was proved by the event. For this reason he needed a guardian angel.

Reply Obj. 3: Just as the foreknown, the infidels, and even Antichrist, are not deprived of the interior help of natural reason; so neither are they deprived of that exterior help granted by God to the whole human race—namely the guardianship of the angels. And although the help which they receive therefrom does not result in their deserving eternal life by good works, it does nevertheless conduce to their being protected from certain evils which would hurt both themselves and others. For even the demons are held off by the good angels, lest they hurt as much as they would. In like manner Antichrist will not do as much harm as he would wish.

FIFTH ARTICLE [I, Q. 113, Art. 5]

Whether an Angel Is Appointed to Guard a Man from His Birth?

Objection 1: It would seem that an angel is not appointed to guard a man from his birth. For angels are "sent to minister for them who shall receive the inheritance of salvation," as the Apostle says (Heb. 1:14). But men begin to receive the inheritance of salvation, when they are baptized. Therefore an angel is appointed to guard a man from the time of his baptism, not of his birth.

Obj. 2: Further, men are guarded by angels in as far as angels enlighten and instruct them. But children are not capable of instruction as soon as they are born, for they have not the use of reason. Therefore angels are not appointed to guard children as soon as they are born.

Obj. 3: Further, a child has a rational soul for some time before birth, just as well as after. But it does not appear that an angel is appointed to guard a child before its birth, for they are not then admitted to the sacraments of the Church. Therefore angels are not appointed to guard men from the moment of their birth.

*On the contrary,* Jerome says ( vide A. 4) that "each soul has an angel appointed to guard it from its birth."

*I answer that,* as Origen observes (Tract. v, super Matt.) there are two opinions on this matter. For some have held that the angel guardian is appointed at the time of baptism, others, that he is appointed at the time of birth. The latter opinion Jerome approves (loc. cit.), and with reason. For those benefits which are conferred by God on man as a Christian, begin with his baptism; such as receiving the Eucharist, and the like. But those which are conferred by God on man as a rational being, are bestowed on him at his birth, for then it is that he receives that nature. Among the latter benefits we must count the guardianship of angels, as we have said above (AA. 1, 4). Wherefore from the very moment of his birth man has an angel guardian appointed to him.

Reply Obj. 1: Angels are sent to minister, and that efficaciously indeed, for those who shall receive the inheritance of salvation, if we consider the ultimate effect of their guardianship, which is the realizing of that inheritance. But for all that, the angelic ministrations are not withdrawn for others although they are not so efficacious as to bring them to salvation: efficacious, nevertheless, they are, inasmuch as they ward off many evils.

Reply Obj. 2: Guardianship is ordained to enlightenment by instruction, as to its ultimate and principal effect. Nevertheless it has many other effects consistent with childhood; for instance to ward off the demons, and to prevent both bodily and spiritual harm.

Reply Obj. 3: As long as the child is in the mother's womb it is not entirely separate, but by reason of a certain intimate tie, is still part of her: just as the fruit while hanging on the tree is part of the tree. And therefore it can be said with some degree of probability, that the angel who guards the mother guards the child while in the womb. But at its birth, when it becomes separate from the mother, an angel guardian is appointed to it; as Jerome, above quoted, says.

SIXTH ARTICLE [I, Q. 113, Art. 6]

Whether the Angel Guardian Ever Forsakes a Man?

Objection 1: It would seem that the angel guardian sometimes forsakes the man whom he is appointed to guard. For it is said (Jer. 51:9) in the person of the angels: "We would have cured Babylon, but she is not healed: let us forsake her." And (Isa. 5:5) it is written: "I will take away the hedge"—that is, "the guardianship of the angels" [gloss]—"and it shall be wasted."

Obj. 2: Further, God's guardianship excels that of the angels. But God forsakes man at times, according to Ps. 21:2: "O God, my God, look upon me: why hast Thou forsaken me?" Much rather therefore does an angel guardian forsake man.

Obj. 3: Further, according to Damascene (De Fide Orth. ii, 3), "When the angels are here with us, they are not in heaven." But sometimes they are in heaven. Therefore sometimes they forsake us.

*On the contrary,* The demons are ever assailing us, according to 1 Pet. 5:8: "Your adversary the devil, as a roaring lion, goeth about, seeking whom he may devour." Much more therefore do the good angels ever guard us.

*I answer that,* As appears above (A. 2), the guardianship of the angels is an effect of Divine providence in regard to man. Now it is evident that neither man, nor anything at all, is entirely withdrawn from the providence of God: for in as far as a thing participates being, so far is it subject to the providence that extends over all being. God indeed is said to forsake man, according to the ordering of His providence, but only in so far as He allows man to suffer some defect of punishment or of fault. In like manner it must be said that the angel guardian never forsakes a man entirely, but sometimes he leaves him in some particular, for instance by not preventing him from being subject to some trouble, or even from falling into sin, according to the ordering of Divine judgments. In this sense Babylon and the House of Israel are said to have been forsaken by the angels, because their angel guardians did not prevent them from being subject to tribulation.

From this the answers are clear to the first and second objections.

Reply Obj. 3: Although an angel may forsake a man sometimes locally, he does not for that reason forsake him as to the effect of his guardianship: for even when he is in heaven he knows what is happening to man; nor does he need time for his local motion, for he can be with man in an instant.

SEVENTH ARTICLE [I, Q. 113, Art. 7]

Whether Angels Grieve for the Ills of Those Whom They Guard?

Objection 1: It would seem that angels grieve for the ills of those whom they guard. For it is written (Isa. 33:7): "The angels of peace shall weep bitterly." But weeping is a sign of grief and sorrow. Therefore angels grieve for the ills of those whom they guard.

Obj. 2: Further, according to Augustine (De Civ. Dei xiv, 15), "sorrow is for those things that happen against our will." But the loss of the man whom he has guarded is against the guardian angel's will. Therefore angels grieve for the loss of men.

Obj. 3: Further, as sorrow is contrary to joy, so penance is contrary to sin. But angels rejoice about one sinner doing penance, as we are told, Luke 15:7. Therefore they grieve for the just man who falls into sin.

Obj. 4: Further, on Numbers 18:12: "Whatsoever first-fruits they offer," etc. the gloss of Origen says: "The angels are brought to judgment as to whether men have fallen through their negligence or through their own fault." But it is reasonable for anyone to grieve for the ills which have brought him to judgment. Therefore angels grieve for men's sins.

*On the contrary,* Where there is grief and sorrow, there is not perfect happiness: wherefore it is written (Apoc. 21:4): "Death shall be no more, nor mourning, nor crying, nor sorrow." But the angels are perfectly happy. Therefore they have no cause for grief.

*I answer that,* Angels do not grieve, either for sins or for the pains inflicted on men. For grief and sorrow, according to Augustine (De Civ. Dei xiv, 15) are for those things which occur against our will. But nothing happens in the world contrary to the will of the angels and the other blessed, because their will cleaves entirely to the ordering of Divine justice; while nothing happens in the world save what is effected or permitted by Divine justice. Therefore simply speaking, nothing occurs in the world against the will of the blessed. For as the Philosopher says (Ethic. iii, 1) that is called simply voluntary, which a man wills in a particular case, and at a particular time, having considered all the circumstances; although universally speaking, such a thing would not be voluntary: thus the sailor does not will the casting of his cargo into the sea, considered universally and absolutely, but on account of the threatened danger of his life, he wills it. Wherefore this is voluntary rather than involuntary, as stated in the same passage. Therefore universally and absolutely speaking the angels do not will sin and the pains inflicted on its account: but they do will the fulfilment of the ordering of Divine justice in this matter, in respect of which some are subjected to pains and are allowed to fall into sin.

Reply Obj. 1: These words of Isaias may be understood of the angels, i.e. the messengers, of Ezechias, who wept on account of the words of Rabsaces, as related Isa. 37:2 seqq.: this would be the literal sense. According to the allegorical sense the "angels of peace" are the apostles and preachers who weep for men's sins. If according to the anagogical sense this passage be expounded of the blessed angels, then the expression is metaphorical, and signifies that universally speaking the angels will the salvation of mankind: for in this sense we attribute passions to God and the angels.

The reply to the second objection appears from what has been said.

Reply Obj. 3: Both in man's repentance and in man's sin there is one reason for the angel's joy, namely the fulfilment of the ordering of the Divine Providence.

Reply Obj. 4: The angels are brought into judgment for the sins of men, not as guilty, but as witnesses to convict man of weakness.

EIGHTH ARTICLE [I, Q. 113, Art. 8]

Whether There Can Be Strife or Discord Among the Angels?

Objection 1: It would seem that there can be [no] strife or discord among the angels. For it is written (Job 25:2): "Who maketh peace in His high places." But strife is opposed to peace. Therefore among the high angels there is no strife.

Obj. 2: Further, where there is perfect charity and just authority there can be no strife. But all this exists among the angels. Therefore there is no strife among the angels.

Obj. 3: Further, if we say that angels strive for those whom they guard, one angel must needs take one side, and another angel the opposite side. But if one side is in the right the other side is in the wrong. It will follow therefore, that a good angel is a compounder of wrong; which is unseemly. Therefore there is no strife among good angels.

*On the contrary,* It is written (Dan. 10:13): "The prince of the kingdom of the Persians resisted me one and twenty days." But this prince of the Persians was the angel deputed to the guardianship of the kingdom of the Persians. Therefore one good angel resists the others; and thus there is strife among them.

*I answer that,* The raising of this question is occasioned by this passage of Daniel. Jerome explains it by saying that the prince of the kingdom of the Persians is the angel who opposed the setting free of the people of Israel, for whom Daniel was praying, his prayers being offered to God by Gabriel. And this resistance of his may have been caused by some prince of the demons having led the Jewish captives in Persia into sin; which sin was an impediment to the efficacy of the prayer which Daniel put up for that same people.

But according to Gregory (Moral. xvii), the prince of the kingdom of Persia was a good angel appointed to the guardianship of that kingdom. To see therefore how one angel can be said to resist another, we must note that the Divine judgments in regard to various kingdoms and various men are executed by the angels. Now in their actions, the angels are ruled by the Divine decree. But it happens at times in various kingdoms or various men there are contrary merits or demerits, so that one of them is subject to or placed over another. As to what is the ordering of Divine wisdom on such matters, the angels cannot know it unless God reveal it to them: and so they need to consult Divine wisdom thereupon. Wherefore forasmuch as they consult the Divine will concerning various contrary and opposing merits, they are said to resist one another: not that their wills are in opposition, since they are all of one mind as to the fulfilment of the Divine decree; but that the things about which they seek knowledge are in opposition.

From this the answers to the objections are clear.

# QUESTION 114

OF THE ASSAULTS OF THE DEMONS (In Five Articles)

We now consider the assaults of the demons. Under this head there are five points of inquiry:

(1) Whether men are assailed by the demons?

(2) Whether to tempt is proper to the devil?

(3) Whether all the sins of men are to be set down to the assaults or temptations of the demons?

(4) Whether they can work real miracles for the purpose of leading men astray?

(5) Whether the demons who are overcome by men, are hindered from making further assaults?

FIRST ARTICLE [I, Q. 114, Art. 1]

Whether Men Are Assailed by the Demons?

Objection 1: It would seem that men are not assailed by the demons. For angels are sent by God to guard man. But demons are not sent by God: for the demons' intention is the loss of souls; whereas God's is the salvation of souls. Therefore demons are not deputed to assail man.

Obj. 2: Further, it is not a fair fight, for the weak to be set against the strong, and the ignorant against the astute. But men are weak and ignorant, whereas the demons are strong and astute. It is not therefore to be permitted by God, the author of all justice, that men should be assailed by demons.

Obj. 3: Further, the assaults of the flesh and the world are enough for man's exercise. But God permits His elect to be assailed that they may be exercised. Therefore there is no need for them to be assailed by the demons.

*On the contrary,* The Apostle says (Eph. 6:12): "Our wrestling is not against flesh and blood; but against Principalities and Powers, against the rulers of the world of this darkness, against the spirits of wickedness in the high places."

*I answer that,* Two things may be considered in the assault of the demons—the assault itself, and the ordering thereof. The assault itself is due to the malice of the demons, who through envy endeavor to hinder man's progress; and through pride usurp a semblance of Divine power, by deputing certain ministers to assail man, as the angels of God in their various offices minister to man's salvation. But the ordering of the assault is from God, Who knows how to make orderly use of evil by ordering it to good. On the other hand, in regard to the angels, both their guardianship and the ordering thereof are to be referred to God as their first author.

Reply Obj. 1: The wicked angels assail men in two ways. Firstly by instigating them to sin; and thus they are not sent by God to assail us, but are sometimes permitted to do so according to God's just judgments. But sometimes their assault is a punishment to man: and thus they are sent by God; as the lying spirit was sent to punish Achab, King of Israel, as is related in 3 Kings 22:20. For punishment is referred to God as its first author. Nevertheless the demons who are sent to punish, do so with an intention other than that for which they are sent; for they punish from hatred or envy; whereas they are sent by God on account of His justice.

Reply Obj. 2: In order that the conditions of the fight be not unequal, there is as regards man the promised recompense, to be gained principally through the grace of God, secondarily through the guardianship of the angels. Wherefore (4 Kings 6:16), Eliseus said to his servant: "Fear not, for there are more with us than with them."

Reply Obj. 3: The assault of the flesh and the world would suffice for the exercise of human weakness: but it does not suffice for the demon's malice, which makes use of both the above in assailing men. But by the Divine ordinance this tends to the glory of the elect.

SECOND ARTICLE [I, Q. 114, Art. 2]

Whether to Tempt Is Proper to the Devil?

Objection 1: It would seem that to tempt is not proper to the devil. For God is said to tempt, according to Gen. 22:1, "God tempted Abraham." Moreover man is tempted by the flesh and the world. Again, man is said to tempt God, and to tempt man. Therefore it is not proper to the devil to tempt.

Obj. 2: Further, to tempt is a sign of ignorance. But the demons know what happens among men. Therefore the demons do not tempt.

Obj. 3: Further, temptation is the road to sin. Now sin dwells in the will. Since therefore the demons cannot change man's will, as appears from what has been said above (Q. 111, A. 2), it seems that it is not in their province to tempt.

*On the contrary,* It is written (1 Thess. 3:5): "Lest perhaps he that tempteth should have tempted you": to which the gloss adds, "that is, the devil, whose office it is to tempt."

*I answer that,* To tempt is, properly speaking, to make trial of something. Now we make trial of something in order to know something about it: hence the immediate end of every tempter is knowledge. But sometimes another end, either good or bad, is sought to be acquired through that knowledge; a good end, when, for instance, one desires to know of someone, what sort of a man he is as to knowledge, or virtue, with a view to his promotion; a bad end, when that knowledge is sought with the purpose of deceiving or ruining him.

From this we can gather how various beings are said to tempt in various ways. For man is said to tempt, sometimes indeed merely for the sake of knowing something; and for this reason it is a sin to tempt God; for man, being uncertain as it were, presumes to make an experiment of God's power. Sometimes too he tempts in order to help, sometimes in order to hurt. The devil, however, always tempts in order to hurt by urging man into sin. In this sense it is said to be his proper office to tempt: for thought at times man tempts thus, he does this as minister of the devil. God is said to tempt that He may know, in the same sense as that is said to know which makes others to know. Hence it is written (Deut. 13:3): "The Lord your God trieth you, that it may appear whether you love him."

The flesh and the world are said to tempt as the instruments or matter of temptations; inasmuch as one can know what sort of man someone is, according as he follows or resists the desires of the flesh, and according as he despises worldly advantages and adversity: of which things the devil also makes use in tempting.

Thus the reply to the first objection is clear.

Reply Obj. 2: The demons know what happens outwardly among men; but the inward disposition of man God alone knows, Who is the "weigher of spirits" (Prov. 16:2). It is this disposition that makes man more prone to one vice than to another: hence the devil tempts, in order to explore this inward disposition of man, so that he may tempt him to that vice to which he is most prone.

Reply Obj. 3: Although a demon cannot change the will, yet, as stated above (Q. 111, A. 3), he can change the inferior powers of man, in a certain degree: by which powers, though the will cannot be forced, it can nevertheless be inclined.

THIRD ARTICLE [I, Q. 114, Art. 3]

Whether All Sins Are Due to the Temptation of the Devil?

Objection 1: It would seem that all sins are due to the temptation of the devil. For Dionysius says (Div. Nom. iv) that "the multitude of demons is the cause of all evils, both to themselves and to others." And Damascene says (De Fide Orth. ii, 4) that "all malice and all uncleanness have been devised by the devil."

Obj. 2: Further, of every sinner can be said what the Lord said of the Jews (John 8:44): "You are of your father the devil." But this was in as far as they sinned through the devil's instigation. Therefore every sin is due to the devil's instigation.

Obj. 3: Further, as angels are deputed to guard men, so demons are deputed to assail men. But every good thing we do is due to the suggestion of the good angels: because the Divine gifts are borne to us by the angels. Therefore all the evil we do, is due to the instigation of the devil.

*On the contrary,* It is written (De Eccl. Dogmat. xlix): "Not all our evil thoughts are stirred up by the devil, but sometimes they arise from the movement of our free-will."

*I answer that,* One thing can be the cause of another in two ways; directly and indirectly. Indirectly as when an agent is the cause of a disposition to a certain effect, it is said to be the occasional and indirect cause of that effect: for instance, we might say that he who dries the wood is the cause of the wood burning. In this way we must admit that the devil is the cause of all our sins; because he it was who instigated the first man to sin, from whose sin there resulted a proneness to sin in the whole human race: and in this sense we must take the words of Damascene and Dionysius.

But a thing is said to be the direct cause of something, when its action tends directly thereunto. And in this way the devil is not the cause of every sin: for all sins are not committed at the devil's instigation, but some are due to the free-will and the corruption of the flesh. For, as Origen says (Peri Archon iii), even if there were no devil, men would have the desire for food and love and such like pleasures; with regard to which many disorders may arise unless those desires are curbed by reason, especially if we presuppose the corruption of our natures. Now it is in the power of the free-will to curb this appetite and keep it in order. Consequently there is no need for all sins to be due to the instigation of the devil. But those sins which are due thereto man perpetrates "through being deceived by the same blandishments as were our first parents," as Isidore says (De Summo Bono ii).

Thus the answer to the first objection is clear.

Reply Obj. 2: When man commits sin without being thereto instigated by the devil, he nevertheless becomes a child of the devil thereby, in so far as he imitates him who was the first to sin.

Reply Obj. 3: Man can of his own accord fall into sin: but he cannot advance in merit without the Divine assistance, which is borne to man by the ministry of the angels. For this reason the angels take part in all our good works: whereas all our sins are not due to the demons' instigation. Nevertheless there is no kind of sin which is not sometimes due to the demons' suggestion.

FOURTH ARTICLE [I, Q. 114, Art. 4]

Whether Demons Can Lead Men Astray by Means of Real Miracles?

Objection 1: It would seem that the demons cannot lead men astray by means of real miracles. For the activity of the demons will show itself especially in the works of Antichrist. But as the Apostle says (2 Thess. 2:9), his "coming is according to the working of Satan, in all power, and signs, and lying wonders." Much more therefore at other times do the demons perform lying wonders.

Obj. 2: Further, true miracles are wrought by some corporeal change. But demons are unable to change the nature of a body; for Augustine says (De Civ. Dei xviii, 18): "I cannot believe that the human body can receive the limbs of a beast by means of a demon's art or power." Therefore the demons cannot work real miracles.

Obj. 3: Further, an argument is useless which may prove both ways. If therefore real miracles can be wrought by demons, to persuade one of what is false, they will be useless to confirm the teaching of the faith. This is unfitting; for it is written (Mk. 16:20): "The Lord working withal, and confirming the word with signs that followed."

*On the contrary,* Augustine says (Q. 83) [*Lib. xxi, Sent. sent 4, among the supposititious works of St. Augustine]: "Often by means of the magic art miracles are wrought like those which are wrought by the servants of God."

*I answer that,* As is clear from what has been said above (Q. 110, A. 4), if we take a miracle in the strict sense, the demons cannot work miracles, nor can any creature, but God alone: since in the strict sense a miracle is something done outside the order of the entire created nature, under which order every power of a creature is contained. But sometimes miracle may be taken in a wide sense, for whatever exceeds the human power and experience. And thus demons can work miracles, that is, things which rouse man's astonishment, by reason of their being beyond his power and outside his sphere of knowledge. For even a man by doing what is beyond the power and knowledge of another, leads him to marvel at what he has done, so that in a way he seems to that man to have worked a miracle.

It is to be noted, however, that although these works of demons which appear marvelous to us are not real miracles, they are sometimes nevertheless something real. Thus the magicians of Pharaoh by the demons' power produced real serpents and frogs. And "when fire came down from heaven and at one blow consumed Job's servants and sheep; when the storm struck down his house and with it his children—these were the work of Satan, not phantoms"; as Augustine says (De Civ. Dei xx, 19).

Reply Obj. 1: As Augustine says in the same place, the works of Antichrist may be called lying wonders, "either because he will deceive men's senses by means of phantoms, so that he will not really do what he will seem to do; or because, if he work real prodigies, they will lead those into falsehood who believe in him."

Reply Obj. 2: As we have said above (Q. 110, A. 2), corporeal matter does not obey either good or bad angels at their will, so that demons be able by their power to transmute matter from one form to another; but they can employ certain seeds that exist in the elements of the world, in order to produce these effects, as Augustine says (De Trin. iii, 8, 9). Therefore it must be admitted that all the transformation of corporeal things which can be produced by certain natural powers, to which we must assign the seeds above mentioned, can alike be produced by the operation of the demons, by the employment of these seeds; such as the transformation of certain things into serpents or frogs, which can be produced by putrefaction. *On the contrary,* those transformations which cannot be produced by the power of nature, cannot in reality be effected by the operation of the demons; for instance, that the human body be changed into the body of a beast, or that the body of a dead man return to life. And if at times something of this sort seems to be effected by the operation of demons, it is not real but a mere semblance of reality.

Now this may happen in two ways. Firstly, from within; in this way a demon can work on man's imagination and even on his corporeal senses, so that something seems otherwise that it is, as explained above (Q. 111, AA. 3,4). It is said indeed that this can be done sometimes by the power of certain bodies. Secondly, from without: for just as he can from the air form a body of any form and shape, and assume it so as to appear in it visibly: so, in the same way he can clothe any corporeal thing with any corporeal form, so as to appear therein. This is what Augustine says (De Civ. Dei xviii, 18): "Man's imagination, which whether thinking or dreaming, takes the forms of an innumerable number of things, appears to other men's senses, as it were embodied in the semblance of some animal." This not to be understood as though the imagination itself or the images formed therein were identified with that which appears embodied to the senses of another man: but that the demon, who forms an image in a man's imagination, can offer the same picture to another man's senses.

Reply Obj. 3: As Augustine says (QQ. 83, qu. 79): "When magicians do what holy men do, they do it for a different end and by a different right. The former do it for their own glory; the latter, for the glory of God: the former, by certain private compacts; the latter by the evident assistance and command of God, to Whom every creature is subject."

FIFTH ARTICLE [I, Q. 114, Art. 5]

Whether a Demon Who Is Overcome by Man, Is for This Reason Hindered from Making Further Assaults?

Objection 1: It would seem that a demon who is overcome by a man, is not for that reason hindered from any further assault. For Christ overcame the tempter most effectively. Yet afterwards the demon assailed Him by instigating the Jews to kill Him. Therefore it is not true that the devil when conquered ceases his assaults.

Obj. 2: Further, to inflict punishment on one who has been worsted in a fight, is to incite him to a sharper attack. But this is not befitting God's mercy. Therefore the conquered demons are not prevented from further assaults.

*On the contrary,* It is written (Matt. 4:11): "Then the devil left Him," i.e. Christ Who overcame.

*I answer that,* Some say that when once a demon has been overcome he can no more tempt any man at all, neither to the same nor to any other sin. And others say that he can tempt others, but not the same man. This seems more probable as long as we understand it to be so for a certain definite time: wherefore (Luke 4:13) it is written: "All temptation being ended, the devil departed from Him for a time." There are two reasons for this. One is on the part of God's clemency; for as Chrysostom says (Super Matt. Hom. v) [*In the Opus Imperfectum, among his supposititious works], "the devil does not tempt man for just as long as he likes, but for as long as God allows; for although He allows him to tempt for a short time, He orders him off on account of our weakness." The other reason is taken from the astuteness of the devil. As to this, Ambrose says on Luke 4:13: "The devil is afraid of persisting, because he shrinks from frequent defeat." That the devil does nevertheless sometimes return to the assault, is apparent from Matt. 12:44: "I will return into my house from whence I came out."

From what has been said, the objections can easily be solved.

## QUESTION 115

OF THE ACTION OF THE CORPOREAL CREATURE (In Six Articles)

We have now to consider the action of the corporeal creature; and fate, which is ascribed to certain bodies. Concerning corporeal actions there are six points of inquiry:

(1) Whether a body can be active?

(2) Whether there exist in bodies certain seminal virtues?

(3) Whether the heavenly bodies are the causes of what is done here by the inferior bodies?

(4) Whether they are the cause of human acts?

(5) Whether demons are subject to their influence?

(6) Whether the heavenly bodies impose necessity on those things which are subject to their influence?

FIRST ARTICLE [I, Q. 115, Art. 1]

Whether a Body Can Be Active?

Objection 1: It would seem that no bodies are active. For Augustine says (De Civ. Dei v, 9): "There are things that are acted upon, but do not act; such are bodies: there is one Who acts but is not acted upon; this is God: there are things that both act and are acted upon; these are the spiritual substances."

Obj. 2: Further, every agent except the first agent requires in its work a subject susceptible of its action. But there is not substance below the corporeal substance which can be susceptible of the latter's action; since it belongs to the lowest degree of beings. Therefore corporeal substance is not active.

Obj. 3: Further, every corporeal substance is limited by quantity. But quantity hinders substance from movement and action, because it surrounds it and penetrates it: just as a cloud hinders the air from receiving light. A proof of this is that the more a body increases in quantity, the heavier it is and the more difficult to move. Therefore no corporeal substance is active.

Obj. 4: Further, the power of action in every agent is according to its propinquity to the first active cause. But bodies, being most composite, are most remote from the first active cause, which is most simple. Therefore no bodies are active.

Obj. 5: Further, if a body is an agent, the term of its action is either a substantial, or an accidental form. But it is not a substantial form; for it is not possible to find in a body any principle of action, save an active quality, which is an accident; and an accident cannot be the cause of a substantial form, since the cause is always more excellent than the effect. Likewise, neither is it an accidental form, for "an accident does not extend beyond its subject," as Augustine says (De Trin. ix, 4). Therefore no bodies are active.

*On the contrary,* Dionysius says (Coel. Hier. xv) that among other qualities of corporeal fire, "it shows its greatness in its action and power on that of which it lays hold."

*I answer that,* It is apparent to the senses that some bodies are active. But concerning the action of bodies there have been three errors. For some denied all action to bodies. This is the opinion of Avicebron in his book on *The Fount of Life,* where, by the arguments mentioned above, he endeavors to prove that no bodies act, but that all the actions which seem to be the actions of bodies, are the actions of some spiritual power that penetrates all bodies: so that, according to him, it is not fire that heats, but a spiritual power which penetrates, by means of the fire. And this opinion seems to be derived from that of Plato. For Plato held that all forms existing in corporeal matter are participated thereby, and determined and limited thereto; and that separate forms are absolute and as it were universal; wherefore he said that these separate forms are the causes of forms that exist in matter. Therefore inasmuch as the form which is in corporeal matter is determined to this matter individualized by quantity, Avicebron held that the corporeal form is held back and imprisoned by quantity, as the principle of individuality, so as to be unable by action to extend to any other matter: and that the spiritual and immaterial form alone, which is not hedged in by quantity, can issue forth by acting on something else.

But this does not prove that the corporeal form is not an agent, but that it is not a universal agent. For in proportion as a thing is participated, so, of necessity, must that be participated which is proper thereto; thus in proportion to the participation of light is the participation of visibility. But to act, which is nothing else than to make something to be in act, is essentially proper to an act as such; wherefore every agent produces its like. So therefore to the fact of its being a form not determined by matter subject to quantity, a thing owes its being an agent indeterminate and universal: but to the fact that it is determined to this matter, it owes its being an agent limited and particular. Wherefore if the form of fire were separate, as the Platonists supposed, it would be, in a fashion, the cause of every ignition. But this form of fire which is in this corporeal matter, is the cause of this ignition which passes from this body to that. Hence such an action is effected by the contact of two bodies.

But this opinion of Avicebron goes further than that of Plato. For Plato held only substantial forms to be separate; while he referred accidents to the material principles which are "the great" and "the small," which he considered to be the first contraries, by others considered to the "the rare" and "the dense." Consequently both Plato and Avicenna, who follows him to a certain extent, held that corporeal agents act through their accidental forms, by disposing matter for the substantial form; but that the ultimate perfection attained by the introduction of the substantial form is due to an immaterial principle. And this is the second opinion concerning the action of bodies; of which we have spoken above when treating of the creation (Q. 45, A. 8).

The third opinion is that of Democritus, who held that action takes place through the issue of atoms from the corporeal agent, while passion consists in the reception of the atoms in the pores of the passive body. This opinion is disproved by Aristotle (De Gener. i, 8, 9). For it would follow that a body would not be passive as a whole, and the quantity of the active body would be diminished through its action; which things are manifestly untrue.

We must therefore say that a body acts forasmuch as it is in act, on a body forasmuch as it is in potentiality.

Reply Obj. 1: This passage of Augustine is to be understood of the whole corporeal nature considered as a whole, which thus has no nature inferior to it, on which it can act; as the spiritual nature acts on the corporeal, and the uncreated nature on the created. Nevertheless one body is inferior to another, forasmuch as it is in potentiality to that which the other has in act.

From this follows the solution of the second objection. But it must be observed, when Avicebron argues thus, "There is a mover who is not moved, to wit, the first maker of all; therefore, on the other hand, there exists something moved which is purely passive," that this is to be conceded. But this latter is primary matter, which is a pure potentiality, just as God is pure act. Now a body is composed of potentiality and act; and therefore it is both active and passive.

Reply Obj. 3: Quantity does not entirely hinder the corporeal form from action, as stated above; but from being a universal agent, forasmuch as a form is individualized through being in matter subject to quantity. The proof taken from the weight of bodies is not to the purpose. First, because addition of quantity does not cause weight; as is proved (De Coelo et Mundo iv, 2). Secondly, it is false that weight retards movement; *on the contrary,* the heavier a thing, the greater its movement, if we consider the movement proper thereto. Thirdly, because action is not effected by local movement, as Democritus held: but by something being reduced from potentiality to act.

Reply Obj. 4: A body is not that which is most distant from God; for it participates something of a likeness to the Divine Being, forasmuch as it has a form. That which is most distant from God is primary matter; which is in no way active, since it is a pure potentiality.

Reply Obj. 5: The term of a body's action is both an accidental form and a substantial form. For the active quality, such as heat, although itself an accident, acts nevertheless by virtue of the substantial form, as its instrument: wherefore its action can terminate in a substantial form; thus natural heat, as the instrument of the soul, has an action terminating in the generation of flesh. But by its own virtue it produces an accident. Nor is it against the nature of an accident to surpass its subject in acting, but it is to surpass it in being; unless indeed one were to imagine that an accident transfers its identical self from the agent to the patient; thus Democritus explained action by an issue of atoms.

SECOND ARTICLE [I, Q. 115, Art. 2]

Whether There Are Any Seminal Virtues in Corporeal Matter?

Objection 1: It would seem that there are no seminal virtues in corporeal matter. For virtue ( *ratio* ) implies something of a spiritual order. But in corporeal matter nothing exists spiritually, but only materially, that is, according to the mode of that in which it is. Therefore there are no seminal virtues in corporeal matter.

Obj. 2: Further, Augustine (De Trin. iii, 8, 9) says that demons produce certain results by employing with a hidden movement certain seeds, which they know to exist in matter. But bodies, not virtues, can be employed with local movement. Therefore it is unreasonable to say that there are seminal virtues in corporeal matter.

Obj. 3: Further, seeds are active principles. But there are no active principles in corporeal matter; since, as we have said above, matter is not competent to act (A. 1, ad 2, 4). Therefore there are no seminal virtues in corporeal matter.

Obj. 4: Further, there are said to be certain "causal virtues" (Augustine, De Gen. ad lit. v, 4) which seem to suffice for the production of things. But seminal virtues are not causal virtues: for miracles are outside the scope of seminal virtues, but not of causal virtues. Therefore it is unreasonable to say that there are seminal virtues in corporeal matter.

*On the contrary,* Augustine says (De Trin. iii, 8): "Of all the things which are generated in a corporeal and visible fashion, certain seeds lie hidden in the corporeal things of this world."

*I answer that,* It is customary to name things after what is more perfect, as the Philosopher says (De Anima ii, 4). Now in the whole corporeal nature, living bodies are the most perfect: wherefore the word "nature" has been transferred from living things to all natural things. For the word itself, "nature," as the Philosopher says (Metaph. v, Did. iv, 4), was first applied to signify the generation of living things, which is called "nativity": and because living things are generated from a principle united to them, as fruit from a tree, and the offspring from the mother, to whom it is united, consequently the word "nature" has been applied to every principle of movement existing in that which is moved. Now it is manifest that the active and passive principles of the generation of living things are the seeds from which living things are generated. Therefore Augustine fittingly gave the name of "seminal virtues" [seminales rationes] to all those active and passive virtues which are the principles of natural generation and movement.

These active and passive virtues may be considered in several orders. For in the first place, as Augustine says (Gen. ad lit. vi, 10), they are principally and originally in the Word of God, as *typal ideas.* Secondly, they are in the elements of the world, where they were produced altogether at the beginning, as in *universal causes.* Thirdly, they are in those things which, in the succession of time, are produced by universal causes, for instance in this plant, and in that animal, as in *particular causes.* Fourthly, they are in the *seeds* produced from animals and plants. And these again are compared to further particular effects, as the primordial universal causes to the first effects produced.

Reply Obj. 1: These active and passive virtues of natural things, though not called "virtues" (rationes) by reason of their being in corporeal matter, can nevertheless be so called in respect of their origin, forasmuch as they are the effect of the typal ideas [rationes ideales].

Reply Obj. 2: These active and passive virtues are in certain parts of corporeal things: and when they are employed with local movement for the production of certain results, we speak of the demons as employing seeds.

Reply Obj. 3: The seed of the male is the active principle in the generation of an animal. But that can be called seed also which the female contributes as the passive principle. And thus the word "seed" covers both active and passive principles.

Reply Obj. 4: From the words of Augustine when speaking of these seminal virtues, it is easy to gather that they are also causal virtues, just as seed is a kind of cause: for he says (De Trin. iii, 9) that, "as a mother is pregnant with the unborn offspring, so is the world itself pregnant with the causes of unborn things." Nevertheless, the "typal ideas" can be called "causal virtues," but not, strictly speaking, "seminal virtues," because seed is not a separate principle; and because miracles are not wrought outside the scope of causal virtues. Likewise neither are miracles wrought outside the scope of the passive virtues so implanted in the creature, that the latter can be used to any purpose that God commands. But miracles are said to be wrought outside the scope of the natural active virtues, and the passive potentialities which are ordered to such active virtues, and this is what is meant when we say that they are wrought outside the scope of seminal virtues.

THIRD ARTICLE [I, Q. 115, Art. 3]

Whether the Heavenly Bodies Are the Cause of What Is Produced in Bodies Here Below?

Objection 1: It would seem that the heavenly bodies are not the cause of what is produced in bodies here below. For Damascene says (De Fide Orth. ii, 7): "We say that they"—namely, the heavenly bodies—"are not the cause of generation or corruption: they are rather signs of storms and atmospheric changes."

Obj. 2: Further, for the production of anything, an agent and matter suffice. But in things here below there is passive matter; and there are contrary agents—heat and cold, and the like. Therefore for the production of things here below, there is no need to ascribe causality to the heavenly bodies.

Obj. 3: Further, the agent produces its like. Now it is to be observed that everything which is produced here below is produced through the action of heat and cold, moisture and dryness, and other such qualities, which do not exist in heavenly bodies. Therefore the heavenly bodies are not the cause of what is produced here below.

Obj. 4: Further, Augustine says (De Civ. Dei v, 6): "Nothing is more corporeal than sex." But sex is not caused by the heavenly bodies: a sign of this is that of twins born under the same constellation, one may be male, the other female. Therefore the heavenly bodies are not the cause of things produced in bodies here below.

*On the contrary,* Augustine says (De Trin. iii, 4): "Bodies of a grosser and inferior nature are ruled in a certain order by those of a more subtle and powerful nature." And Dionysius (Div. Nom. iv) says that "the light of the sun conduces to the generation of sensible bodies, moves them to life, gives them nourishment, growth, and perfection."

*I answer that,* Since every multitude proceeds from unity; and since what is immovable is always in the same way of being, whereas what is moved has many ways of being: it must be observed that throughout the whole of nature, all movement proceeds from the immovable. Therefore the more immovable certain things are, the more are they the cause of those things which are most movable. Now the heavenly bodies are of all bodies the most immovable, for they are not moved save locally. Therefore the movements of bodies here below, which are various and multiform, must be referred to the movement of the heavenly bodies, as to their cause.

Reply Obj. 1: These words of Damascene are to be understood as denying that the heavenly bodies are the first cause of generation and corruption here below; for this was affirmed by those who held that the heavenly bodies are gods.

Reply Obj. 2: The active principles of bodies here below are only the active qualities of the elements, such as hot and cold and the like. If therefore the substantial forms of inferior bodies were not diversified save according to accidents of that kind, the principles of which the early natural philosophers held to be the "rare" and the "dense"; there would be no need to suppose some principle above these inferior bodies, for they would be of themselves sufficient to act. But to anyone who considers the matter aright, it is clear that those accidents are merely material dispositions in regard to the substantial forms of natural bodies. Now matter is not of itself sufficient to act. And therefore it is necessary to suppose some active principle above these material dispositions.

This is why the Platonists maintained the existence of separate species, by participation of which the inferior bodies receive their substantial forms. But this does not seem enough. For the separate species, since they are supposed to be immovable, would always have the same mode of being: and consequently there would be no variety in the generation and corruption of inferior bodies: which is clearly false.

Therefore it is necessary, as the Philosopher says (De Gener. ii, 10), to suppose a movable principle, which by reason of its presence or absence causes variety in the generation and corruption of inferior bodies. Such are the heavenly bodies. Consequently whatever generates here below, moves to the production of the species, as the instrument of a heavenly body: thus the Philosopher says (Phys. ii, 2) that "man and the sun generate man."

Reply Obj. 3: The heavenly bodies have not a specific likeness to the bodies here below. Their likeness consists in this, that by reason of their universal power, whatever is generated in inferior bodies, is contained in them. In this way also we say that all things are like God.

Reply Obj. 4: The actions of heavenly bodies are variously received in inferior bodies, according to the various dispositions of matter. Now it happens at times that the matter in the human conception is not wholly disposed to the male sex; wherefore it is formed sometimes into a male, sometimes into a female. Augustine quotes this as an argument against divination by stars: because the effects of the stars are varied even in corporeal things, according to the various dispositions of matter.

FOURTH ARTICLE [I, Q. 115, Art. 4]

Whether the Heavenly Bodies Are the Cause of Human Actions?

Objection 1: It would seem that the heavenly bodies are the cause of human actions. For since the heavenly bodies are moved by spiritual substances, as stated above (Q. 110, A. 3), they act by virtue thereof as their instruments. But those spiritual substances are superior to our souls. Therefore it seems that they can cause impressions on our souls, and thereby cause human actions.

Obj. 2: Further, every multiform is reducible to a uniform principle. But human actions are various and multiform. Therefore it seems that they are reducible to the uniform movements of heavenly bodies, as to their principles.

Obj. 3: Further, astrologers often foretell the truth concerning the outcome of wars, and other human actions, of which the intellect and will are the principles. But they could not do this by means of the heavenly bodies, unless these were the cause of human actions. Therefore the heavenly bodies are the cause of human actions.

*On the contrary,* Damascene says (De Fide Orth. ii, 7) that "the heavenly bodies are by no means the cause of human actions."

*I answer that,* The heavenly bodies can directly and of themselves act on bodies, as stated above (A. 3). They can act directly indeed on those powers of the soul which are the acts of corporeal organs, but accidentally: because the acts of such powers must needs be hindered by obstacles in the organs; thus an eye when disturbed cannot see well. Wherefore if the intellect and will were powers affixed to corporeal organs, as some maintained, holding that intellect does not differ from sense; it would follow of necessity that the heavenly bodies are the cause of human choice and action. It would also follow that man is led by natural instinct to his actions, just as other animals, in which there are powers other than those which are affixed to corporeal organs: for whatever is done here below in virtue of the action of heavenly bodies, is done naturally. It would therefore follow that man has no free-will, and that he would have determinate actions, like other natural things. All of which is manifestly false, and contrary to human habit. It must be observed, however, that indirectly and accidentally, the impressions of heavenly bodies can reach the intellect and will, forasmuch, namely, as both intellect and will receive something from the inferior powers which are affixed to corporeal organs. But in this the intellect and will are differently situated. For the intellect, of necessity, receives from the inferior apprehensive powers: wherefore if the imaginative, cogitative, or memorative powers be disturbed, the action of the intellect is, of necessity, disturbed also. The will, *on the contrary,* does not, of necessity, follow the inclination of the inferior appetite; for although the passions in the irascible and concupiscible have a certain force in inclining the will; nevertheless the will retains the power of following the passions or repressing them. Therefore the impressions of the heavenly bodies, by virtue of which the inferior powers can be changed, has less influence on the will, which is the proximate cause of human actions, than on the intellect.

To maintain therefore that heavenly bodies are the cause of human actions is proper to those who hold that intellect does not differ from sense. Wherefore some of these said that "such is the will of men, as is the day which the father of men and of gods brings on" (Odyssey xviii 135). Since, therefore, it is manifest that intellect and will are not acts of corporeal organs, it is impossible that heavenly bodies be the cause of human actions.

Reply Obj. 1: The spiritual substances, that move the heavenly bodies, do indeed act on corporeal things by means of the heavenly bodies; but they act immediately on the human intellect by enlightening it. On the other hand, they cannot compel the will, as stated above (Q. 111, A. 2).

Reply Obj. 2: Just as the multiformity of corporeal movements is reducible to the uniformity of the heavenly movement as to its cause: so the multiformity of actions proceeding from the intellect and the will is reduced to a uniform principle which is the Divine intellect and will.

Reply Obj. 3: The majority of men follow their passions, which are movements of the sensitive appetite, in which movements of the heavenly bodies can cooperate: but few are wise enough to resist these passions. Consequently astrologers are able to foretell the truth in the majority of cases, especially in a general way. But not in particular cases; for nothing prevents man resisting his passions by his free-will. Wherefore the astrologers themselves are wont to say that "the wise man is stronger than the stars" [*Ptolemy, Centiloquium, prop. 5], forasmuch as, to wit, he conquers his passions.

FIFTH ARTICLE [I, Q. 115, Art. 5]

Whether Heavenly Bodies Can Act on the Demons?

Objection 1: It would seem that heavenly bodies can act on the demons. For the demons, according to certain phases of the moon, can harass men, who on that account are called lunatics, as appears from Matt. 4:24 and 17:14. But this would not be if they were not subject to the heavenly bodies. Therefore the demons are subject to them.

Obj. 2: Further, necromancers observe certain constellations in order to invoke the demons. But these would not be invoked through the heavenly bodies unless they were subject to them. Therefore they are subject to them.

Obj. 3: Further, heavenly bodies are more powerful than inferior bodies. But the demons are confined to certain inferior bodies, namely, "herbs, stones, animals, and to certain sounds and words, forms and figures," as Porphyry says, quoted by Augustine (De Civ. Dei x, 11). Much more therefore are the demons subject to the action of heavenly bodies.

*On the contrary,* The demons are superior in the order of nature, to the heavenly bodies. But the "agent is superior to the patient," as Augustine says (Gen. ad lit. xii, 16). Therefore the demons are not subject to the action of heavenly bodies.

*I answer that,* There have been three opinions about the demons. In the first place the Peripatetics denied the existence of demons; and held that what is ascribed to the demons, according to the necromantic art, is effected by the power of the heavenly bodies. This is what Augustine (De Civ. Dei x, 11) relates as having been held by Porphyry, namely, that "on earth men fabricate certain powers useful in producing certain effects of the stars." But this opinion is manifestly false. For we know by experience that many things are done by demons, for which the power of heavenly bodies would in no way suffice: for instance, that a man in a state of delirium should speak an unknown tongue, recite poetry and authors of whom he has no previous knowledge; that necromancers make statues to speak and move, and other like things.

For this reason the Platonists were led to hold that demons are "animals with an aerial body and a passive soul," as Apuleius says, quoted by Augustine (De Civ. Dei viii, 16). And this is the second of the opinions mentioned above: according to which it could be said that demons are subject to heavenly bodies in the same way as we have said man is subject thereto (A. 4). But this opinion is proved to be false from what we have said above (Q. 51, A. 1): for we hold that demons are spiritual substances not united to bodies. Hence it is clear that they are subject to the action of heavenly bodies neither essentially nor accidentally, neither directly nor indirectly.

Reply Obj. 1: That demons harass men, according to certain phases of the moon, happens in two ways. Firstly, they do so in order to "defame God's creature," namely, the moon; as Jerome (In Matt. iv, 24) and Chrysostom (Hom. lvii in Matt.) say. Secondly, because as they are unable to effect anything save by means of the natural forces, as stated above (Q. 114, A. 4, ad 2) they take into account the aptitude of bodies for the intended result. Now it is manifest that "the brain is the most moist of all the parts of the body," as Aristotle says [*De Part. Animal. ii, 7: De Sens. et Sensato ii: De Somn. et Vigil. iii]: wherefore it is the most subject to the action of the moon, the property of which is to move what is moist. And it is precisely in the brain that animal forces culminate: wherefore the demons, according to certain phases of the moon, disturb man's imagination, when they observe that the brain is thereto disposed.

Reply Obj. 2: Demons when summoned through certain constellations, come for two reasons. Firstly, in order to lead man into the error of believing that there is some Divine power in the stars. Secondly, because they consider that under certain constellations corporeal matter is better disposed for the result for which they are summoned.

Reply Obj. 3: As Augustine says (De Civ. Dei xxi, 6), the "demons are enticed through various kinds of stones, herbs, trees, animals, songs, rites, not as an animal is enticed by food, but as a spirit by signs"; that is to say, forasmuch as these things are offered to them in token of the honor due to God, of which they are covetous.

SIXTH ARTICLE [I, Q. 115, Art. 6]

Whether Heavenly Bodies Impose Necessity on Things Subject to Their Action?

Objection 1: It would seem that heavenly bodies impose necessity on things subject to their action. For given a sufficient cause, the effect follows of necessity. But heavenly bodies are a sufficient cause of their effects. Since, therefore, heavenly bodies, with their movements and dispositions, are necessary beings; it seems that their effects follow of necessity.

Obj. 2: Further, an agent's effect results of necessity in matter, when the power of the agent is such that it can subject the matter to itself entirely. But the entire matter of inferior bodies is subject to the power of heavenly bodies, since this is a higher power than theirs. Therefore the effect of the heavenly bodies is of necessity received in corporeal matter.

Obj. 3: Further, if the effect of the heavenly body does not follow of necessity, this is due to some hindering cause. But any corporeal cause, that might possibly hinder the effect of a heavenly body, must of necessity be reducible to some heavenly principle: since the heavenly bodies are the causes of all that takes place here below. Therefore, since also that heavenly principle is necessary, it follows that the effect of the heavenly body is necessarily hindered. Consequently it would follow that all that takes place here below happens of necessity.

*On the contrary,* The Philosopher says (De Somn. et Vigil. [*De Divin. per Somn. ii]): "It is not incongruous that many of the signs observed in bodies, of occurrences in the heavens, such as rain and wind, should not be fulfilled." Therefore not all the effects of heavenly bodies take place of necessity.

*I answer that,* This question is partly solved by what was said above (A. 4); and in part presents some difficulty. For it was shown that although the action of heavenly bodies produces certain inclinations in corporeal nature, the will nevertheless does not of necessity follow these inclinations. Therefore there is nothing to prevent the effect of heavenly bodies being hindered by the action of the will, not only in man himself, but also in other things to which human action extends.

But in natural things there is no such principle, endowed with freedom to follow or not to follow the impressions produced by heavenly agents. Wherefore it seems that in such things at least, everything happens of necessity; according to the reasoning of some of the ancients who supposing that everything that is, has a cause; and that, given the cause, the effect follows of necessity; concluded that all things happen of necessity. This opinion is refuted by Aristotle (Metaph. vi, Did. v, 3) as to this double supposition.

For in the first place it is not true that, given any cause whatever, the effect must follow of necessity. For some causes are so ordered to their effects, as to produce them, not of necessity, but in the majority of cases, and in the minority to fail in producing them. But that such causes do fail in the minority of cases is due to some hindering cause; consequently the above-mentioned difficulty seems not to be avoided, since the cause in question is hindered of necessity.

Therefore we must say, in the second place, that everything that is a being *per se,* has a cause; but what is accidentally, has not a cause, because it is not truly a being, since it is not truly one. For (that a thing is) "white" has a cause, likewise (that a man is) "musical" has not a cause, but (that a being is) "white-musical" has not a cause, because it is not truly a being, nor truly one. Now it is manifest that a cause which hinders the action of a cause so ordered to its effect as to produce it in the majority of cases, clashes sometimes with this cause by accident: and the clashing of these two causes, inasmuch as it is accidental, has no cause. Consequently what results from this clashing of causes is not to be reduced to a further pre-existing cause, from which it follows of necessity. For instance, that some terrestrial body take fire in the higher regions of the air and fall to the earth, is caused by some heavenly power: again, that there be on the surface of the earth some combustible matter, is reducible to some heavenly principle. But that the burning body should alight on this matter and set fire to it, is not caused by a heavenly body, but is accidental. Consequently not all the effects of heavenly bodies result of necessity.

Reply Obj. 1: The heavenly bodies are causes of effects that take place here below, through the means of particular inferior causes, which can fail in their effects in the minority of cases.

Reply Obj. 2: The power of a heavenly body is not infinite. Wherefore it requires a determinate disposition in matter, both as to local distance and as to other conditions, in order to produce its effect. Therefore as local distance hinders the effect of a heavenly body (for the sun has not the same effect in heat in Dacia as in Ethiopia); so the grossness of matter, its low or high temperature or other such disposition, can hinder the effect of a heavenly body.

Reply Obj. 3: Although the cause that hinders the effect of another cause can be reduced to a heavenly body as its cause; nevertheless the clashing of two causes, being accidental, is not reduced to the causality of a heavenly body, as stated above.

ON FATE (In Four Articles)

We come now to the consideration of fate. Under this head there are four points of inquiry:

(1) Is there such a thing as fate?

(2) Where is it?

(3) Is it unchangeable?

(4) Are all things subject to fate?

FIRST ARTICLE [I, Q. 116, Art. 1]

Whether There Be Such a Thing As Fate?

Objection 1: It would seem that fate is nothing. For Gregory says in a homily for the Epiphany (Hom. x in Evang.): "Far be it from the hearts of the faithful to think that fate is anything real."

Obj. 2: Further, what happens by fate is not unforeseen, for as Augustine says (De Civ. Dei v, 4), "fate is understood to be derived from the verb 'fari' which means to speak"; as though things were said to happen by fate, which are "fore-spoken" by one who decrees them to happen. Now what is foreseen is neither lucky nor chance-like. If therefore things happen by fate, there will be neither luck nor chance in the world.

*On the contrary,* What does not exist cannot be defined. But Boethius (De Consol. iv) defines fate thus: "Fate is a disposition inherent to changeable things, by which Providence connects each one with its proper order."

*I answer that,* In this world some things seem to happen by luck or chance. Now it happens sometimes that something is lucky or chance-like as compared to inferior causes, which, if compared to some higher cause, is directly intended. For instance, if two servants are sent by their master to the same place; the meeting of the two servants in regard to themselves is by chance; but as compared to the master, who had ordered it, it is directly intended.

So there were some who refused to refer to a higher cause such events which by luck or chance take place here below. These denied the existence of fate and Providence, as Augustine relates of Tully (De Civ. Dei v, 9). And this is contrary to what we have said above about Providence (Q. 22, A. 2).

On the other hand, some have considered that everything that takes place here below by luck or by chance, whether in natural things or in human affairs, is to be reduced to a superior cause, namely, the heavenly bodies. According to these fate is nothing else than "a disposition of the stars under which each one is begotten or born" [*Cf. St. Augustine , loc. cit., v, 1, 8, 9]. But this will not hold. First, as to human affairs: because we have proved above (Q. 115, A. 4) that human actions are not subject to the action of heavenly bodies, save accidentally and indirectly. Now the cause of fate, since it has the ordering of things that happen by fate, must of necessity be directly and of itself the cause of what takes place. Secondly, as to all things that happen accidentally: for it has been said (Q. 115, A. 6) that what is accidental, is properly speaking neither a being, nor a unity. But every action of nature terminates in some one thing. Wherefore it is impossible for that which is accidental to be the proper effect of an active natural principle. No natural cause can therefore have for its proper effect that a man intending to dig a grave finds a treasure. Now it is manifest that a acts after the manner of a natural principle: wherefore its effects in this world are natural. It is therefore impossible that any active power of a heavenly body be the cause of what happens by accident here below, whether by luck or by chance.

We must therefore say that what happens here by accident, both in natural things and in human affairs, is reduced to a preordaining cause, which is Divine Providence. For nothing hinders that which happens by accident being considered as one by an intellect: otherwise the intellect could not form this proposition: "The digger of a grave found a treasure." And just as an intellect can apprehend this so can it effect it; for instance, someone who knows a place where a treasure is hidden, might instigate a rustic, ignorant of this, to dig a grave there. Consequently, nothing hinders what happens here by accident, by luck or by chance, being reduced to some ordering cause which acts by the intellect, especially the Divine intellect. For God alone can change the will, as shown above (Q. 105, A. 4). Consequently the ordering of human actions, the principle of which is the will, must be ascribed to God alone.

So therefore inasmuch as all that happens here below is subject to Divine Providence, as being pre-ordained, and as it were "fore-spoken," we can admit the existence of fate: although the holy doctors avoided the use of this word, on account of those who twisted its application to a certain force in the position of the stars. Hence Augustine says (De Civ. Dei v, 1): "If anyone ascribes human affairs to fate, meaning thereby the will or power of God, let him keep to his opinion, but hold his tongue." For this reason Gregory denies the existence of fate: wherefore the first objection's solution is manifest.

Reply Obj. 2: Nothing hinders certain things happening by luck or by chance, if compared to their proximate causes: but not if compared to Divine Providence, whereby "nothing happens at random in the world," as Augustine says (QQ. 83, qu. 24).

SECOND ARTICLE [I, Q. 116, Art. 2]

Whether Fate Is in Created Things?

Objection 1: It would seem that fate is not in created things. For Augustine says (De Civ. Dei v, 1) that the "Divine will or power is called fate." But the Divine will or power is not in creatures, but in God. Therefore fate is not in creatures but in God.

Obj. 2: Further, fate is compared to things that happen by fate, as their cause; as the very use of the word proves. But the universal cause that of itself effects what takes place by accident here below, is God alone, as stated above (A. 1). Therefore fate is in God, and not in creatures.

Obj. 3: Further, if fate is in creatures, it is either a substance or an accident: and whichever it is it must be multiplied according to the number of creatures. Since, therefore, fate seems to be one thing only, it seems that fate is not in creatures, but in God.

*On the contrary,* Boethius says (De Consol. iv): "Fate is a disposition inherent to changeable things."

*I answer that,* As is clear from what has been stated above (Q. 22, A. 3; Q. 103, A. 6), Divine Providence produces effects through mediate causes. We can therefore consider the ordering of the effects in two ways. Firstly, as being in God Himself: and thus the ordering of the effects is called Providence. But if we consider this ordering as being in the mediate causes ordered by God to the production of certain effects, thus it has the nature of fate. This is what Boethius says (De Consol. iv): "Fate is worked out when Divine Providence is served by certain spirits; whether by the soul, or by all nature itself which obeys Him, whether by the heavenly movements of the stars, whether by the angelic power, or by the ingenuity of the demons, whether by some of these, or by all, the chain of fate is forged." Of each of these things we have spoken above (A. 1; Q. 104, A. 2; Q. 110, A. 1; Q. 113; Q. 114). It is therefore manifest that fate is in the created causes themselves, as ordered by God to the production of their effects.

Reply Obj. 1: The ordering itself of second causes, which Augustine (De Civ. Dei v, 8) calls the "series of causes," has not the nature of fate, except as dependent on God. Wherefore the Divine power or will can be called fate, as being the cause of fate. But essentially fate is the very disposition or "series," i.e. order, of second causes.

Reply Obj. 2: Fate has the nature of a cause, just as much as the second causes themselves, the ordering of which is called fate.

Reply Obj. 3: Fate is called a disposition, not that disposition which is a species of quality, but in the sense in which it signifies order, which is not a substance, but a relation. And if this order be considered in relation to its principle, it is one; and thus fate is one. But if it be considered in relation to its effects, or to the mediate causes, this fate is multiple. In this sense the poet wrote: "Thy fate draws thee."

THIRD ARTICLE [I, Q. 116, Art. 3]

Whether Fate Is Unchangeable?

Objection 1: It seems that fate is not unchangeable. For Boethius says (De Consol. iv): "As reasoning is to the intellect, as the begotten is to that which is, as time to eternity, as the circle to its centre; so is the fickle chain of fate to the unwavering simplicity of Providence."

Obj. 2: Further, the Philosopher says (Topic. ii, 7): "If we be moved, what is in us is moved." But fate is a "disposition inherent to changeable things," as Boethius says (De Consol. iv). Therefore fate is changeable.

Obj. 3: Further, if fate is unchangeable, what is subject to fate happens unchangeably and of necessity. But things ascribed to fate seem principally to be contingencies. Therefore there would be no contingencies in the world, but all things would happen of necessity.

*On the contrary,* Boethius says (De Consol. iv) that fate is an unchangeable disposition.

*I answer that,* The disposition of second causes which we call fate, can be considered in two ways: firstly, in regard to the second causes, which are thus disposed or ordered; secondly, in regard to the first principle, namely, God, by Whom they are ordered. Some, therefore, have held that the series itself o[f] dispositions of causes is in itself necessary, so that all things would happen of necessity; for this reason that each effect has a cause, and given a cause the effect must follow of necessity. But this is false, as proved above (Q. 115, A. 6).

Others, on the other hand, held that fate is changeable, even as dependent on Divine Providence. Wherefore the Egyptians said that fate could be changed by certain sacrifices, as Gregory of Nyssa says (Nemesius, De Homine). This too has been disproved above for the reason that it is repugnant to Divine Providence.

We must therefore say that fate, considered in regard to second causes, is changeable; but as subject to Divine Providence, it derives a certain unchangeableness, not of absolute but of conditional necessity. In this sense we say that this conditional is true and necessary: "If God foreknew that this would happen, it will happen." Wherefore Boethius, having said that the chain of fate is fickle, shortly afterwards adds—"which, since it is derived from an unchangeable Providence must also itself be unchangeable."

From this the answers to the objections are clear.

FOURTH ARTICLE [I, Q. 116, Art. 4]

Whether All Things Are Subject to Fate?

Objection 1: It seems that all things are subject to fate. For Boethius says (De Consol. iv): "The chain of fate moves the heaven and the stars, tempers the elements to one another, and models them by a reciprocal transformation. By fate all things that are born into the world and perish are renewed in a uniform progression of offspring and seed." Nothing therefore seems to be excluded from the domain of fate.

Obj. 2: Further, Augustine says (De Civ. Dei v, 1) that fate is something real, as referred to the Divine will and power. But the Divine will is cause of all things that happen, as Augustine says (De Trin. iii, 1 seqq.). Therefore all things are subject to fate.

Obj. 3: Further, Boethius says (De Consol. iv) that fate "is a disposition inherent to changeable things." But all creatures are changeable, and God alone is truly unchangeable, as stated above (Q. 9, A. 2). Therefore fate is in all things.

*On the contrary,* Boethius says (De Consol. iv) that "some things subject to Providence are above the ordering of fate."

*I answer that,* As stated above (A. 2), fate is the ordering of second causes to effects foreseen by God. Whatever, therefore, is subject to second causes, is subject also to fate. But whatever is done immediately by God, since it is not subject to second causes, neither is it subject to fate; such are creation, the glorification of spiritual substances, and the like. And this is what Boethius says (De Consol. iv): viz. that "those things which are nigh to God have a state of immobility, and exceed the changeable order of fate." Hence it is clear that "the further a thing is from the First Mind, the more it is involved in the chain of fate"; since so much the more it is bound up with second causes.

Reply Obj. 1: All the things mentioned in this passage are done by God by means of second causes; for this reason they are contained in the order of fate. But it is not the same with everything else, as stated above.

Reply Obj. 2: Fate is to be referred to the Divine will and power, as to its first principle. Consequently it does not follow that whatever is subject to the Divine will or power, is subject also to fate, as already stated.

Reply Obj. 3: Although all creatures are in some way changeable, yet some of them do not proceed from changeable created causes. And these, therefore, are not subject to fate, as stated above.

# QUESTION 117

OF THINGS PERTAINING TO THE ACTION OF MAN (In Four Articles)

We have next to consider those things which pertain to the action of man, who is composed of a created corporeal and spiritual nature. In the first place we shall consider that action (in general) and secondly in regard to the propagation of man from man. As to the first, there are four points of inquiry:

(1) Whether one man can teach another, as being the cause of his knowledge?

(2) Whether man can teach an angel?

(3) Whether by the power of his soul man can change corporeal matter?

(4) Whether the separate soul of man can move bodies by local movement?

FIRST ARTICLE [I, Q. 117, Art. 1]

Whether One Man Can Teach Another?

Objection 1: It would seem that one man cannot teach another. For the Lord says (Matt. 22:8): "Be not you called Rabbi": on which the gloss of Jerome says, "Lest you give to men the honor due to God." Therefore to be a master is properly an honor due to God. But it belongs to a master to teach. Therefore man cannot teach, and this is proper to God.

Obj. 2: Further, if one man teaches another this is only inasmuch as he acts through his own knowledge, so as to cause knowledge in the other. But a quality through which anyone acts so as to produce his like, is an active quality. Therefore it follows that knowledge is an active quality just as heat is.

Obj. 3: Further, for knowledge we require intellectual light, and the species of the thing understood. But a man cannot cause either of these in another man. Therefore a man cannot by teaching cause knowledge in another man.

Obj. 4: Further, the teacher does nothing in regard to a disciple save to propose to him certain signs, so as to signify something by words or gestures. But it is not possible to teach anyone so as to cause knowledge in him, by putting signs before him. For these are signs either of things that he knows, or of things he does not know. If of things that he knows, he to whom these signs are proposed is already in the possession of knowledge, and does not acquire it from the master. If they are signs of things that he does not know, he can learn nothing therefrom: for instance, if one were to speak Greek to a man who only knows Latin, he would learn nothing thereby. Therefore in no way can a man cause knowledge in another by teaching him.

*On the contrary,* The Apostle says (1 Tim. 2:7): "Whereunto I am appointed a preacher and an apostle ... a doctor of the Gentiles in faith and truth."

*I answer that,* On this question there have been various opinions. For Averroes, commenting on *De Anima* iii, maintains that all men have one passive intellect in common, as stated above (Q. 76, A. 2). From this it follows that the same intelligible species belong to all men. Consequently he held that one man does not cause another to have a knowledge distinct from that which he has himself; but that he communicates the identical knowledge which he has himself, by moving him to order rightly the phantasms in his soul, so that they be rightly disposed for intelligible apprehension. This opinion is true so far as knowledge is the same in disciple and master, if we consider the identity of the thing known: for the same objective truth is known by both of them. But so far as he maintains that all men have but one passive intellect, and the same intelligible species, differing only as to various phantasms, his opinion is false, as stated above (Q. 76, A. 2).

Besides this, there is the opinion of the Platonists, who held that our souls are possessed of knowledge from the very beginning, through the participation of separate forms, as stated above (Q. 84, AA. 3, 4); but that the soul is hindered, through its union with the body, from the free consideration of those things which it knows. According to this, the disciple does not acquire fresh knowledge from his master, but is roused by him to consider what he knows; so that to learn would be nothing else than to remember. In the same way they held that natural agents only dispose (matter) to receive forms, which matter acquires by a participation of separate substances. But against this we have proved above (Q. 79, A. 2; Q. 84, A. 3) that the passive intellect of the human soul is in pure potentiality to intelligible (species), as Aristotle says (De Anima iii, 4).

We must therefore decide the question differently, by saying that the teacher causes knowledge in the learner, by reducing him from potentiality to act, as the Philosopher says (Phys. viii, 4). In order to make this clear, we must observe that of effects proceeding from an exterior principle, some proceed from the exterior principle alone; as the form of a house is caused to be in matter by art alone: whereas other effects proceed sometimes from an exterior principle, sometimes from an interior principle: thus health is caused in a sick man, sometimes by an exterior principle, namely by the medical art, sometimes by an interior principle as when a man is healed by the force of nature. In these latter effects two things must be noticed. First, that art in its work imitates nature for just as nature heals a man by alteration, digestion, rejection of the matter that caused the sickness, so does art. Secondly, we must remark that the exterior principle, art, acts, not as principal agent, but as helping the principal agent, but as helping the principal agent, which is the interior principle, by strengthening it, and by furnishing it with instruments and assistance, of which the interior principle makes use in producing the effect. Thus the physician strengthens nature, and employs food and medicine, of which nature makes use for the intended end.

Now knowledge is acquired in man, both from an interior principle, as is clear in one who procures knowledge by his own research; and from an exterior principle, as is clear in one who learns (by instruction). For in every man there is a certain principle of knowledge, namely the light of the active intellect, through which certain universal principles of all the sciences are naturally understood as soon as proposed to the intellect. Now when anyone applies these universal principles to certain particular things, the memory or experience of which he acquires through the senses; then by his own research advancing from the known to the unknown, he obtains knowledge of what he knew not before. Wherefore anyone who teaches, leads the disciple from things known by the latter, to the knowledge of things previously unknown to him; according to what the Philosopher says (Poster. i, 1): "All teaching and all learning proceed from previous knowledge."

Now the master leads the disciple from things known to knowledge of the unknown, in a twofold manner. Firstly, by proposing to him certain helps or means of instruction, which his intellect can use for the acquisition of science: for instance, he may put before him certain less universal propositions, of which nevertheless the disciple is able to judge from previous knowledge: or he may propose to him some sensible examples, either by way of likeness or of opposition, or something of the sort, from which the intellect of the learner is led to the knowledge of truth previously unknown. Secondly, by strengthening the intellect of the learner; not, indeed, by some active power as of a higher nature, as explained above (Q. 106, A. 1; Q. 111, A. 1) of the angelic enlightenment, because all human intellects are of one grade in the natural order; but inasmuch as he proposes to the disciple the order of principles to conclusions, by reason of his not having sufficient collating power to be able to draw the conclusions from the principles. Hence the Philosopher says (Poster. i, 2) that "a demonstration is a syllogism that causes knowledge." In this way a demonstrator causes his hearer to know.

Reply Obj. 1: As stated above, the teacher only brings exterior help as the physician who heals: but just as the interior nature is the principal cause of the healing, so the interior light of the intellect is the principal cause of knowledge. But both of these are from God. Therefore as of God is it written: "Who healeth all thy diseases" (Ps. 102:3); so of Him is it written: "He that teacheth man knowledge" (Ps. 93:10), inasmuch as "the light of His countenance is signed upon us" (Ps. 4:7), through which light all things are shown to us.

Reply Obj. 2: As Averroes argues, the teacher does not cause knowledge in the disciple after the manner of a natural active cause. Wherefore knowledge need not be an active quality: but is the principle by which one is directed in teaching, just as art is the principle by which one is directed in working.

Reply Obj. 3: The master does not cause the intellectual light in the disciple, nor does he cause the intelligible species directly: but he moves the disciple by teaching, so that the latter, by the power of his intellect, forms intelligible concepts, the signs of which are proposed to him from without.

Reply Obj. 4: The signs proposed by the master to the disciple are of things known in a general and confused manner; but not known in detail and distinctly. Therefore when anyone acquires knowledge by himself, he cannot be called self-taught, or be said to have his own master because perfect knowledge did not precede in him, such as is required in a master.

SECOND ARTICLE [I, Q. 117, Art. 2]

Whether Man Can Teach the Angels?

Objection 1: It would seem that men teach angels. For the Apostle says (Eph. 3:10): "That the manifold wisdom of God may be made known to the principalities and powers in the heavenly places through the Church." But the Church is the union of all the faithful. Therefore some things are made known to angels through men.

Obj. 2: Further, the superior angels, who are enlightened immediately concerning Divine things by God, can instruct the inferior angels, as stated above (Q. 116, A. 1; Q. 112, A. 3). But some men are instructed immediately concerning Divine things by the Word of God; as appears principally of the apostles from Heb. 1:1, 2: "Last of all, in these days (God) hath spoken to us by His Son." Therefore some men have been able to teach the angels.

Obj. 3: Further, the inferior angels are instructed by the superior. But some men are higher than some angels; since some men are taken up to the highest angelic orders, as Gregory says in a homily (Hom. xxxiv in Evang.). Therefore some of the inferior angels can be instructed by men concerning Divine things.

*On the contrary,* Dionysius says (Div. Nom. iv) that every Divine enlightenment is borne to men by the ministry of the angels. Therefore angels are not instructed by men concerning Divine things.

*I answer that,* As stated above (Q. 107, A. 2), the inferior angels can indeed speak to the superior angels, by making their thoughts known to them; but concerning Divine things superior angels are never enlightened by inferior angels. Now it is manifest that in the same way as inferior angels are subject to the superior, the highest men are subject even to the lowest angels. This is clear from Our Lord's words (Matt. 11:11): "There hath not risen among them that are born of woman a greater than John the Baptist; yet he that is lesser in the kingdom of heaven is greater than he." Therefore angels are never enlightened by men concerning Divine things. But men can by means of speech make known to angels the thoughts of their hearts: because it belongs to God alone to know the heart's secrets.

Reply Obj. 1: Augustine (Gen. ad lit. v, 19) thus explains this passage of the Apostle, who in the preceding verses says: "To me, the least of all the saints, is given this grace ... to enlighten all men, that they may see what is the dispensation of the mystery which hath been hidden from eternity in God. Hidden, yet so that the multiform wisdom of God was made known to the principalities and powers in the heavenly places—that is, through the Church." As though he were to say: This mystery was hidden from men, but not from the Church in heaven, which is contained in the principalities and powers who knew it "from all ages, but not before all ages: because the Church was at first there, where after the resurrection this Church composed of men will be gathered together."

It can also be explained otherwise that "what is hidden, is known by the angels, not only in God, but also here where when it takes place and is made public," as Augustine says further on (Gen. ad lit. v, 19). Thus when the mysteries of Christ and the Church were fulfilled by the apostles, some things concerning these mysteries became apparent to the angels, which were hidden from them before. In this way we can understand what Jerome says (Comment. in Ep. ad Eph.)—that from the preaching of the apostles the angels learned certain mysteries; that is to say, through the preaching of the apostles, the mysteries were realized in the things themselves: thus by the preaching of Paul the Gentiles were converted, of which mystery the Apostle is speaking in the passage quoted.

Reply Obj. 2: The apostles were instructed immediately by the Word of God, not according to His Divinity, but according as He spoke in His human nature. Hence the argument does not prove.

Reply Obj. 3: Certain men in this state of life are greater than certain angels, not actually, but virtually; forasmuch as they have such great charity that they can merit a higher degree of beatitude than that possessed by certain angels. In the same way we might say that the seed of a great tree is virtually greater than a small tree, though actually it is much smaller.

THIRD ARTICLE [I, Q. 117, Art. 3]

Whether Man by the Power of His Soul Can Change Corporeal Matter?

Objection 1: It would seem that man by the power of his soul can change corporeal matter. For Gregory says (Dialog. ii, 30): "Saints work miracles sometimes by prayer, sometimes by their power: thus Peter, by prayer, raised the dead Tabitha to life, and by his reproof delivered to death the lying Ananias and Saphira." But in the working of miracles a change is wrought in corporeal matter. Therefore men, by the power of the soul, can change corporeal matter.

Obj. 2: Further, on these words (Gal. 3:1): "Who hath bewitched you, that you should not obey the truth?" the gloss says that "some have blazing eyes, who by a single look bewitch others, especially children." But this would not be unless the power of the soul could change corporeal matter. Therefore man can change corporeal matter by the power of his soul.

Obj. 3: Further, the human body is nobler than other inferior bodies. But by the apprehension of the human soul the human body is changed to heat and cold, as appears when a man is angry or afraid: indeed this change sometimes goes so far as to bring on sickness and death. Much more, then, can the human soul by its power change corporeal matter.

*On the contrary,* Augustine says (De Trin. iii, 8): "Corporeal matter obeys God alone at will."

*I answer that,* As stated above (Q. 110, A. 2), corporeal matter is not changed to (the reception of) a form save either by some agent composed of matter and form, or by God Himself, in whom both matter and form pre-exist virtually, as in the primordial cause of both. Wherefore of the angels also we have stated (Q. 110, A. 2) that they cannot change corporeal matter by their natural power, except by employing corporeal agents for the production of certain effects. Much less therefore can the soul, by its natural power, change corporeal matter, except by means of bodies.

Reply Obj. 1: The saints are said to work miracles by the power of grace, not of nature. This is clear from what Gregory says in the same place: "Those who are sons of God, in power, as John says—what wonder is there that they should work miracles by that power?"

Reply Obj. 2: Avicenna assigns the cause of bewitchment to the fact that corporeal matter has a natural tendency to obey spiritual substance rather than natural contrary agents. Therefore when the soul is of strong imagination, it can change corporeal matter. This he says is the cause of the "evil eye."

But it has been shown above (Q. 110, A. 2) that corporeal matter does not obey spiritual substances at will, but the Creator alone. Therefore it is better to say, that by a strong imagination the (corporeal) spirits of the body united to that soul are changed, which change in the spirits takes place especially in the eyes, to which the more subtle spirits can reach. And the eyes infect the air which is in contact with them to a certain distance: in the same way as a new and clear mirror contracts a tarnish from the look of a "menstruata," as Aristotle says (De Somn. et Vigil.; [*De Insomniis ii]).

Hence then when a soul is vehemently moved to wickedness, as occurs mostly in little old women, according to the above explanation, the countenance becomes venomous and hurtful, especially to children, who have a tender and most impressionable body. It is also possible that by God's permission, or from some hidden deed, the spiteful demons co-operate in this, as the witches may have some compact with them.

Reply Obj. 3: The soul is united to the body as its form; and the sensitive appetite, which obeys the reason in a certain way, as stated above (Q. 81, A. 3), it is the act of a corporeal organ. Therefore at the apprehension of the human soul, the sensitive appetite must needs be moved with an accompanying corporeal operation. But the apprehension of the human soul does not suffice to work a change in exterior bodies, except by means of a change in the body united to it, as stated above (ad 2).

FOURTH ARTICLE [I, Q. 117, Art. 4]

Whether the Separate Human Soul Can Move Bodies at Least Locally?

Objection 1: It seems that the separate human soul can move bodies at least locally. For a body naturally obeys a spiritual substance as to local motion, as stated above (Q. 110, A. 5). But the separate soul is a spiritual substance. Therefore it can move exterior bodies by its command.

Obj. 2: Further, in the Itinerary of Clement it is said in the narrative of Nicetas to Peter, that Simon Magus, by sorcery retained power over the soul of a child that he had slain, and that through this soul he worked magical wonders. But this could not have been without some corporeal change at least as to place. Therefore, the separate soul has the power to move bodies locally.

*On the contrary,* the Philosopher says (De Anima i, 3) that the soul cannot move any other body whatsoever but its own.

*I answer that,* The separate soul cannot by its natural power move a body. For it is manifest that, even while the soul is united to the body, it does not move the body except as endowed with life: so that if one of the members become lifeless, it does not obey the soul as to local motion. Now it is also manifest that no body is quickened by the separate soul. Therefore within the limits of its natural power the separate soul cannot command the obedience of a body; though, by the power of God, it can exceed those limits.

Reply Obj. 1: There are certain spiritual substances whose powers are not determinate to certain bodies; such are the angels who are naturally unfettered by a body; consequently various bodies may obey them as to movement. But if the motive power of a separate substance is naturally determinate to move a certain body, that substance will not be able to move a body of higher degree, but only one of lower degree: thus according to philosophers the mover of the lower heaven cannot move the higher heaven. Wherefore, since the soul is by its nature determinate to move the body of which it is the form, it cannot by its natural power move any other body.

Reply Obj. 2: As Augustine (De Civ. Dei x, 11) and Chrysostom (Hom. xxviii in Matt.) say, the demons often pretend to be the souls of the dead, in order to confirm the error of heathen superstition. It is therefore credible that Simon Magus was deceived by some demon who pretended to be the soul of the child whom the magician had slain.

## QUESTION 118

OF THE PRODUCTION OF MAN FROM MAN AS TO THE SOUL (In Three Articles)

We next consider the production of man from man: first, as to the soul; secondly, as to the body.

Under the first head there are three points of inquiry:

(1) Whether the sensitive soul is transmitted with the semen?

(2) Whether the intellectual soul is thus transmitted?

(3) Whether all souls were created at the same time?

FIRST ARTICLE [I, Q. 118, Art. 1]

Whether the Sensitive Soul Is Transmitted with the Semen?

Objection 1: It would seem that the sensitive soul is not transmitted with the semen, but created by God. For every perfect substance, not composed of matter and form, that begins to exist, acquires existence not by generation, but by creation: for nothing is generated save from matter. But the sensitive soul is a perfect substance, otherwise it could not move the body; and since it is the form of a body, it is not composed of matter and form. Therefore it begins to exist not by generation but by creation.

Obj. 2: Further, in living things the principle of generation is the generating power; which, since it is one of the powers of the vegetative soul, is of a lower order than the sensitive soul. Now nothing acts beyond its species. Therefore the sensitive soul cannot be caused by the animal's generating power.

Obj. 3: Further, the generator begets its like: so that the form of the generator must be actually in the cause of generation. But neither the sensitive soul itself nor any part thereof is actually in the semen, for no part of the sensitive soul is elsewhere than in some part of the body; while in the semen there is not even a particle of the body, because there is not a particle of the body which is not made from the semen and by the power thereof. Therefore the sensitive soul is not produced through the semen.

Obj. 4: Further, if there be in the semen any principle productive of the sensitive soul, this principle either remains after the animal is begotten, or it does not remain. Now it cannot remain. For either it would be identified with the sensitive soul of the begotten animal; which is impossible, for thus there would be identity between begetter and begotten, maker and made: or it would be distinct therefrom; and again this is impossible, for it has been proved above (Q. 76, A. 4) that in one animal there is but one formal principle, which is the soul. If on the other hand the aforesaid principle does not remain, this again seems to be impossible: for thus an agent would act to its own destruction, which cannot be. Therefore the sensitive soul cannot be generated from the semen.

*On the contrary,* The power in the semen is to the animal seminally generated, as the power in the elements of the world is to animals produced from these elements—for instance by putrefaction. But in the latter animals the soul is produced by the elemental power, according to Gen. 1:20: "Let the waters bring forth the creeping creatures having life." Therefore also the souls of animals seminally generated are produced by the seminal power.

*I answer that,* Some have held that the sensitive souls of animals are created by God (Q. 65, A. 4). This opinion would hold if the sensitive soul were subsistent, having being and operation of itself. For thus, as having being and operation of itself, to be made would needs be proper to it. And since a simple and subsistent thing cannot be made except by creation, it would follow that the sensitive soul would arrive at existence by creation.

But this principle is false—namely, that being and operation are proper to the sensitive soul, as has been made clear above (Q. 75, A. 3): for it would not cease to exist when the body perishes. Since, therefore, it is not a subsistent form, its relation to existence is that of the corporeal forms, to which existence does not belong as proper to them, but which are said to exist forasmuch as the subsistent composites exist through them.

Wherefore to be made is proper to composites. And since the generator is like the generated, it follows of necessity that both the sensitive soul, and all other like forms are naturally brought into existence by certain corporeal agents that reduce the matter from potentiality to act, through some corporeal power of which they are possessed.

Now the more powerful an agent, the greater scope its action has: for instance, the hotter a body, the greater the distance to which its heat carries. Therefore bodies not endowed with life, which are the lowest in the order of nature, generate their like, not through some medium, but by themselves; thus fire by itself generates fire. But living bodies, as being more powerful, act so as to generate their like, both without and with a medium. Without a medium—in the work of nutrition, in which flesh generates flesh: with a medium—in the act of generation, because the semen of the animal or plant derives a certain active force from the soul of the generator, just as the instrument derives a certain motive power from the principal agent. And as it matters not whether we say that something is moved by the instrument or by the principal agent, so neither does it matter whether we say that the soul of the generated is caused by the soul of the generator, or by some seminal power derived therefrom.

Reply Obj. 1: The sensitive soul is not a perfect self-subsistent substance. We have said enough (Q. 25, A. 3) on this point, nor need we repeat it here.

Reply Obj. 2: The generating power begets not only by its own virtue but by that of the whole soul, of which it is a power. Therefore the generating power of a plant generates a plant, and that of an animal begets an animal. For the more perfect the soul is, to so much a more perfect effect is its generating power ordained.

Reply Obj. 3: This active force which is in the semen, and which is derived from the soul of the generator, is, as it were, a certain movement of this soul itself: nor is it the soul or a part of the soul, save virtually; thus the form of a bed is not in the saw or the axe, but a certain movement towards that form. Consequently there is no need for this active force to have an actual organ; but it is based on the (vital) spirit in the semen which is frothy, as is attested by its whiteness. In which spirit, moreover, there is a certain heat derived from the power of the heavenly bodies, by virtue of which the inferior bodies also act towards the production of the species as stated above (Q. 115, A. 3, ad 2). And since in this (vital) spirit the power of the soul is concurrent with the power of a heavenly body, it has been said that "man and the sun generate man." Moreover, elemental heat is employed instrumentally by the soul's power, as also by the nutritive power, as stated (De Anima ii, 4).

Reply Obj. 4: In perfect animals, generated by coition, the active force is in the semen of the male, as the Philosopher says (De Gener. Animal. ii, 3); but the foetal matter is provided by the female. In this matter, the vegetative soul exists from the very beginning, not as to the second act, but as to the first act, as the sensitive soul is in one who sleeps. But as soon as it begins to attract nourishment, then it already operates in act. This matter therefore is transmuted by the power which is in the semen of the male, until it is actually informed by the sensitive soul; not as though the force itself which was in the semen becomes the sensitive soul; for thus, indeed, the generator and generated would be identical; moreover, this would be more like nourishment and growth than generation, as the Philosopher says. And after the sensitive soul, by the power of the active principle in the semen, has been produced in one of the principal parts of the thing generated, then it is that the sensitive soul of the offspring begins to work towards the perfection of its own body, by nourishment and growth. As to the active power which was in the semen, it ceases to exist, when the semen is dissolved and the (vital) spirit thereof vanishes. Nor is there anything unreasonable in this, because this force is not the principal but the instrumental agent; and the movement of an instrument ceases when once the effect has been produced.

SECOND ARTICLE [I, Q. 118, Art. 2]

Whether the Intellectual Soul Is Produced from the Semen?

Objection 1: It would seem that the intellectual soul is produced from the semen. For it is written (Gen. 46:26): "All the souls that came out of [Jacob's] thigh, sixty-six." But nothing is produced from the thigh of a man, except from the semen. Therefore the intellectual soul is produced from the semen.

Obj. 2: Further, as shown above (Q. 76, A. 3), the intellectual, sensitive, and nutritive souls are, in substance, one soul in man. But the sensitive soul in man is generated from the semen, as in other animals; wherefore the Philosopher says (De Gener. Animal. ii, 3) that the animal and the man are not made at the same time, but first of all the animal is made having a sensitive soul. Therefore also the intellectual soul is produced from the semen.

Obj. 3: Further, it is one and the same agent whose action is directed to the matter and to the form: else from the matter and the form there would not result something simply one. But the intellectual soul is the form of the human body, which is produced by the power of the semen. Therefore the intellectual soul also is produced by the power of the semen.

Obj. 4: Further, man begets his like in species. But the human species is constituted by the rational soul. Therefore the rational soul is from the begetter.

Obj. 5: Further, it cannot be said that God concurs in sin. But if the rational soul be created by God, sometimes God concurs in the sin of adultery, since sometimes offspring is begotten of illicit intercourse. Therefore the rational soul is not created by God.

*On the contrary,* It is written in De Eccl. Dogmat. xiv that "the rational soul is not engendered by coition."

*I answer that,* It is impossible for an active power existing in matter to extend its action to the production of an immaterial effect. Now it is manifest that the intellectual principle in man transcends matter; for it has an operation in which the body takes no part whatever. It is therefore impossible for the seminal power to produce the intellectual principle.

Again, the seminal power acts by virtue of the soul of the begetter according as the soul of the begetter is the act of the body, making use of the body in its operation. Now the body has nothing whatever to do in the operation of the intellect. Therefore the power of the intellectual principle, as intellectual, cannot reach the semen. Hence the Philosopher says (De Gener. Animal. ii, 3): "It follows that the intellect alone comes from without."

Again, since the intellectual soul has an operation independent of the body, it is subsistent, as proved above (Q. 75, A. 2): therefore to be and to be made are proper to it. Moreover, since it is an immaterial substance it cannot be caused through generation, but only through creation by God. Therefore to hold that the intellectual soul is caused by the begetter, is nothing else than to hold the soul to be non-subsistent and consequently to perish with the body. It is therefore heretical to say that the intellectual soul is transmitted with the semen.

Reply Obj. 1: In the passage quoted, the part is put instead of the whole, the soul for the whole man, by the figure of synecdoche.

Reply Obj. 2: Some say that the vital functions observed in the embryo are not from its soul, but from the soul of the mother; or from the formative power of the semen. Both of these explanations are false; for vital functions such as feeling, nourishment, and growth cannot be from an extrinsic principle. Consequently it must be said that the soul is in the embryo; the nutritive soul from the beginning, then the sensitive, lastly the intellectual soul.

Therefore some say that in addition to the vegetative soul which existed first, another, namely the sensitive, soul supervenes; and in addition to this, again another, namely the intellectual soul. Thus there would be in man three souls of which one would be in potentiality to another. This has been disproved above (Q. 76, A. 3).

Therefore others say that the same soul which was at first merely vegetative, afterwards through the action of the seminal power, becomes a sensitive soul; and finally this same soul becomes intellectual, not indeed through the active seminal power, but by the power of a higher agent, namely God enlightening (the soul) from without. For this reason the Philosopher says that the intellect comes from without. But this will not hold. First, because no substantial form is susceptible of more or less; but addition of greater perfection constitutes another species, just as the addition of unity constitutes another species of number. Now it is not possible for the same identical form to belong to different species. Secondly, because it would follow that the generation of an animal would be a continuous movement, proceeding gradually from the imperfect to the perfect, as happens in alteration. Thirdly, because it would follow that the generation of a man or an animal is not generation simply, because the subject thereof would be a being in act. For if the vegetative soul is from the beginning in the matter of offspring, and is subsequently gradually brought to perfection; this will imply addition of further perfection without corruption of the preceding perfection. And this is contrary to the nature of generation properly so called. Fourthly, because either that which is caused by the action of God is something subsistent: and thus it must needs be essentially distinct from the pre-existing form, which was non-subsistent; and we shall then come back to the opinion of those who held the existence of several souls in the body—or else it is not subsistent, but a perfection of the pre-existing soul: and from this it follows of necessity that the intellectual soul perishes with the body, which cannot be admitted.

There is again another explanation, according to those who held that all men have but one intellect in common: but this has been disproved above (Q. 76, A. 2).

We must therefore say that since the generation of one thing is the corruption of another, it follows of necessity that both in men and in other animals, when a more perfect form supervenes the previous form is corrupted: yet so that the supervening form contains the perfection of the previous form, and something in addition. It is in this way that through many generations and corruptions we arrive at the ultimate substantial form, both in man and other animals. This indeed is apparent to the senses in animals generated from putrefaction. We conclude therefore that the intellectual soul is created by God at the end of human generation, and this soul is at the same time sensitive and nutritive, the pre-existing forms being corrupted.

Reply Obj. 3: This argument holds in the case of diverse agents not ordered to one another. But where there are many agents ordered to one another, nothing hinders the power of the higher agent from reaching to the ultimate form; while the powers of the inferior agents extend only to some disposition of matter: thus in the generation of an animal, the seminal power disposes the matter, but the power of the soul gives the form. Now it is manifest from what has been said above (Q. 105, A. 5; Q. 110, A. 1) that the whole of corporeal nature acts as the instrument of a spiritual power, especially of God. Therefore nothing hinders the formation of the body from being due to a corporeal power, while the intellectual soul is from God alone.

Reply Obj. 4: Man begets his like, forasmuch as by his seminal power the matter is disposed for the reception of a certain species of form.

Reply Obj. 5: In the action of the adulterer, what is of nature is good; in this God concurs. But what there is of inordinate lust is evil; in this God does not concur.

THIRD ARTICLE [I, Q. 118, Art. 3]

Whether Human Souls Were Created Together at the Beginning of the World?

Objection 1: It would seem that human souls were created together at the beginning of the world. For it is written (Gen. 2:2): "God rested Him from all His work which He had done." This would not be true if He created new souls every day. Therefore all souls were created at the same time.

Obj. 2: Further, spiritual substances before all others belong to the perfection of the universe. If therefore souls were created with the bodies, every day innumerable spiritual substances would be added to the perfection of the universe: consequently at the beginning the universe would have been imperfect. This is contrary to Gen. 2:2, where it is said that "God ended" all "His work."

Obj. 3: Further, the end of a thing corresponds to its beginning. But the intellectual soul remains, when the body perishes. Therefore it began to exist before the body.

*On the contrary,* It is said (De Eccl. Dogmat. xiv, xviii) that "the soul is created together with the body."

*I answer that,* Some have maintained that it is accidental to the intellectual soul to be united to the body, asserting that the soul is of the same nature as those spiritual substances which are not united to a body. These, therefore, stated that the souls of men were created together with the angels at the beginning. But this statement is false. Firstly, in the very principle on which it is based. For if it were accidental to the soul to be united to the body, it would follow that man who results from this union is a being by accident; or that the soul is a man, which is false, as proved above (Q. 75, A. 4). Moreover, that the human soul is not of the same nature as the angels, is proved from the different mode of understanding, as shown above (Q. 55, A. 2; Q. 85, A. 1): for man understands through receiving from the senses, and turning to phantasms, as stated above (Q. 84, AA. 6, 7; Q. 85, A. 1). For this reason the soul needs to be united to the body, which is necessary to it for the operation of the sensitive part: whereas this cannot be said of an angel.

Secondly, this statement can be proved to be false in itself. For if it is natural to the soul to be united to the body, it is unnatural to it to be without a body, and as long as it is without a body it is deprived of its natural perfection. Now it was not fitting that God should begin His work with things imperfect and unnatural, for He did not make man without a hand or a foot, which are natural parts of a man. Much less, therefore, did He make the soul without a body.

But if someone say that it is not natural to the soul to be united to the body, he must give the reason why it is united to a body. And the reason must be either because the soul so willed, or for some other reason. If because the soul willed it—this seems incongruous. First, because it would be unreasonable of the soul to wish to be united to the body, if it did not need the body: for if it did need it, it would be natural for it to be united to it, since "nature does not fail in what is necessary." Secondly, because there would be no reason why, having been created from the beginning of the world, the soul should, after such a long time, come to wish to be united to the body. For a spiritual substance is above time, and superior to the heavenly revolutions. Thirdly, because it would seem that this body was united to this soul by chance: since for this union to take place two wills would have to concur—to wit, that of the incoming soul, and that of the begetter. If, however, this union be neither voluntary nor natural on the part of the soul, then it must be the result of some violent cause, and to the soul would have something of a penal and afflicting nature. This is in keeping with the opinion of Origen, who held that souls were embodied in punishment of sin. Since, therefore, all these opinions are unreasonable, we must simply confess that souls were not created before bodies, but are created at the same time as they are infused into them.

Reply Obj. 1: God is said to have rested on the seventh day, not from all work, since we read (John 5:17): "My Father worketh until now"; but from the creation of any new genera and species, which may not have already existed in the first works. For in this sense, the souls which are created now, existed already, as to the likeness of the species, in the first works, which included the creation of Adam's soul.

Reply Obj. 2: Something can be added every day to the perfection of the universe, as to the number of individuals, but not as to the number of species.

Reply Obj. 3: That the soul remains without the body is due to the corruption of the body, which was a result of sin. Consequently it was not fitting that God should make the soul without the body from the beginning: for as it is written (Wis. 1:13, 16): "God made not death ... but the wicked with works and words have called it to them."

## QUESTION 119

OF THE PROPAGATION OF MAN AS TO THE BODY (In Two Articles)

We now consider the propagation of man, as to the body. Concerning this there are two points of inquiry:

(1) Whether any part of the food is changed into true human nature?

(2) Whether the semen, which is the principle of human generation, is produced from the surplus food?

FIRST ARTICLE [I, Q. 119, Art. 1]

Whether Some Part of the Food Is Changed into True Human Nature?

Objection 1: It would seem that none of the food is changed into true human nature. For it is written (Matt. 15:17): "Whatsoever entereth into the mouth, goeth into the belly, and is cast out into the privy." But what is cast out is not changed into the reality of human nature. Therefore none of the food is changed into true human nature.

Obj. 2: Further, the Philosopher (De Gener. i, 5) distinguishes flesh belonging to the species from flesh belonging to "matter"; and says that the latter "comes and goes." Now what is formed from food comes and goes. Therefore what is produced from food is flesh belonging to matter, not to the species. But what belongs to true human nature belongs to the species. Therefore the food is not changed into true human nature.

Obj. 3: Further, the "radical humor" seems to belong to the reality of human nature; and if it be lost, it cannot be recovered, according to physicians. But it could be recovered if the food were changed into the humor. Therefore food is not changed into true human nature.

Obj. 4: Further, if the food were changed into true human nature, whatever is lost in man could be restored. But man's death is due only to the loss of something. Therefore man would be able by taking food to insure himself against death in perpetuity.

Obj. 5: Further, if the food is changed into true human nature, there is nothing in man which may not recede or be repaired: for what is generated in a man from his food can both recede and be repaired. If therefore a man lived long enough, it would follow that in the end nothing would be left in him of what belonged to him at the beginning. Consequently he would not be numerically the same man throughout his life; since for the thing to be numerically the same, identity of matter is necessary. But this is incongruous. Therefore the food is not changed into true human nature.

*On the contrary,* Augustine says (De Vera Relig. xi): "The bodily food when corrupted, that is, having lost its form, is changed into the texture of the members." But the texture of the members belongs to true human nature. Therefore the food is changed into the reality of human nature.

*I answer that,* According to the Philosopher (Metaph. ii), "The relation of a thing to truth is the same as its relation to being." Therefore that belongs to the true nature of any thing which enters into the constitution of that nature. But nature can be considered in two ways: firstly, in general according to the species; secondly, as in the individual. And whereas the form and the common matter belong to a thing's true nature considered in general; individual signate matter, and the form individualized by that matter belong to the true nature considered in this particular individual. Thus a soul and body belong to the true human nature in general, but to the true human nature of Peter and Martin belong this soul and this body.

Now there are certain things whose form cannot exist but in one individual matter: thus the form of the sun cannot exist save in the matter in which it actually is. And in this sense some have said that the human form cannot exist but in a certain individual matter, which, they said, was given that form at the very beginning in the first man. So that whatever may have been added to that which was derived by posterity from the first parent, does not belong to the truth of human nature, as not receiving in truth the form of human nature.

But, said they, that matter which, in the first man, was the subject of the human form, was multiplied in itself: and in this way the multitude of human bodies is derived from the body of the first man. According to these, the food is not changed into true human nature; we take food, they stated, in order to help nature to resist the action of natural heat, and prevent the consumption of the "radical humor"; just as lead or tin is mixed with silver to prevent its being consumed by fire.

But this is unreasonable in many ways. Firstly, because it comes to the same that a form can be produced in another matter, or that it can cease to be in its proper matter; wherefore all things that can be generated are corruptible, and conversely. Now it is manifest that the human form can cease to exist in this (particular) matter which is its subject: else the human body would not be corruptible. Consequently it can begin to exist in another matter, so that something else be changed into true human nature. Secondly, because in all beings whose entire matter is contained in one individual there is only one individual in the species: as is clearly the case with the sun, moon and such like. Thus there would only be one individual of the human species. Thirdly, because multiplication of matter cannot be understood otherwise than either in respect of quantity only, as in things which are rarefied, so that their matter increases in dimensions; or in respect of the substance itself of the matter. But as long as the substance alone of matter remains, it cannot be said to be multiplied; for multitude cannot consist in the addition of a thing to itself, since of necessity it can only result from division. Therefore some other substance must be added to matter, either by creation, or by something else being changed into it. Consequently no matter can be multiplied save either by rarefaction as when air is made from water; or by the change of some other things, as fire is multiplied by the addition of wood; or lastly by creation. Now it is manifest that the multiplication of matter in the human body does not occur by rarefaction: for thus the body of a man of perfect age would be more imperfect than the body of a child. Nor does it occur by creation of fresh matter: for, according to Gregory (Moral. xxxii): "All things were created together as to the substance of matter, but not as to the specific form." Consequently the multiplication of the human body can only be the result of the food being changed into the true human nature. Fourthly, because, since man does not differ from animals and plants in regard to the vegetative soul, it would follow that the bodies of animals and plants do not increase through a change of nourishment into the body so nourished, but through some kind of multiplication. Which multiplication cannot be natural: since the matter cannot naturally extend beyond a certain fixed quantity; nor again does anything increase naturally, save either by rarefaction or the change of something else into it. Consequently the whole process of generation and nourishment, which are called "natural forces," would be miraculous. Which is altogether inadmissible.

Wherefore others have said that the human form can indeed begin to exist in some other matter, if we consider the human nature in general: but not if we consider it as in this individual. For in the individual the form remains confined to a certain determinate matter, on which it is first imprinted at the generation of that individual, so that it never leaves that matter until the ultimate dissolution of the individual. And this matter, say they, principally belongs to the true human nature. But since this matter does not suffice for the requisite quantity, some other matter must be added, through the change of food into the substance of the individual partaking thereof, in such a quantity as suffices for the increase required. And this matter, they state, belongs secondarily to the true human nature: because it is not required for the primary existence of the individual, but for the quantity due to him. And if anything further is produced from the food, this does not belong to true human nature, properly speaking. However, this also is inadmissible. First, because this opinion judges of living bodies as of inanimate bodies; in which, although there be a power of generating their like in species, there is not the power of generating their like in the individual; which power in living bodies is the nutritive power. Nothing, therefore, would be added to living bodies by their nutritive power, if their food were not changed into their true nature. Secondly, because the active seminal power is a certain impression derived from the soul of the begetter, as stated above (Q. 118, A. 1). Hence it cannot have a greater power in acting, than the soul from which it is derived. If, therefore, by the seminal power a certain matter truly assumes the form of human nature, much more can the soul, by the nutritive power, imprint the true form of human nature on the food which is assimilated. Thirdly, because food is needed not only for growth, else at the term of growth, food would be needful no longer; but also to renew that which is lost by the action of natural heat. But there would be no renewal, unless what is formed from the food, took the place of what is lost. Wherefore just as that which was there previously belonged to true human nature, so also does that which is formed from the food.

Therefore, according to others, it must be said that the food is really changed into the true human nature by reason of its assuming the specific form of flesh, bones and such like parts. This is what the Philosopher says (De Anima ii, 4): "Food nourishes inasmuch as it is potentially flesh."

Reply Obj. 1: Our Lord does not say that the "whole" of what enters into the mouth, but "all"—because something from every kind of food is cast out into the privy. It may also be said that whatever is generated from food, can be dissolved by natural heat, and be cast aside through the pores, as Jerome expounds the passage.

Reply Obj. 2: By flesh belonging to the species, some have understood that which first receives the human species, which is derived from the begetter: this, they say, lasts as long as the individual does. By flesh belonging to the matter these understand what is generated from food: and this, they say, does not always remain, but as it comes so it goes. But this is contrary to the mind of Aristotle. For he says there, that "just as in things which have their species in matter"—for instance, wood or stone—"so in flesh, there is something belonging to the species, and something belonging to matter." Now it is clear that this distinction has no place in inanimate things, which are not generated seminally, or nourished. Again, since what is generated from food is united to, by mixing with, the body so nourished, just as water is mixed with wine, as the Philosopher says there by way of example: that which is added, and that to which it is added, cannot be different natures, since they are already made one by being mixed together. Therefore there is no reason for saying that one is destroyed by natural heat, while the other remains.

It must therefore be said that this distinction of the Philosopher is not of different kinds of flesh, but of the same flesh considered from different points of view. For if we consider the flesh according to the species, that is, according to that which is formed therein, thus it remains always: because the nature of flesh always remains together with its natural disposition. But if we consider flesh according to matter, then it does not remain, but is gradually destroyed and renewed: thus in the fire of a furnace, the form of fire remains, but the matter is gradually consumed, and other matter is substituted in its place.

Reply Obj. 3: The "radical humor" is said to comprise whatever the virtue of the species is founded on. If this be taken away it cannot be renewed; as when a man's hand or foot is amputated. But the "nutritive humor" is that which has not yet received perfectly the specific nature, but is on the way thereto; such is the blood, and the like. Wherefore if such be taken away, the virtue of the species remains in its root, which is not destroyed.

Reply Obj. 4: Every virtue of a passible body is weakened by continuous action, because such agents are also patient. Therefore the transforming virtue is strong at first so as to be able to transform not only enough for the renewal of what is lost, but also for growth. Later on it can only transform enough for the renewal of what is lost, and then growth ceases. At last it cannot even do this; and then begins decline. In fine, when this virtue fails altogether, the animal dies. Thus the virtue of wine that transforms the water added to it, is weakened by further additions of water, so as to become at length watery, as the Philosopher says by way of example (De Gener. i, 5).

Reply Obj. 5: As the Philosopher says (De Gener. i, 5), when a certain matter is directly transformed into fire, then fire is said to be generated anew: but when matter is transformed into a fire already existing, then fire is said to be fed. Wherefore if the entire matter together loses the form of fire, and another matter transformed into fire, there will be another distinct fire. But if, while one piece of wood is burning, other wood is laid on, and so on until the first piece is entirely consumed, the same identical fire will remain all the time: because that which is added passes into what pre-existed. It is the same with living bodies, in which by means of nourishment that is renewed which was consumed by natural heat.

SECOND ARTICLE [I, Q. 119, Art. 2]

Whether the Semen Is Produced from Surplus Food?

Objection 1: It would seem that the semen is not produced from the surplus food, but from the substance of the begetter. For Damascene says (De Fide Orth. i, 8) that "generation is a work of nature, producing, from the substance of the begetter, that which is begotten." But that which is generated is produced from the semen. Therefore the semen is produced from the substance of the begetter.

Obj. 2: Further, the son is like his father, in respect of that which he receives from him. But if the semen from which something is generated, is produced from the surplus food, a man would receive nothing from his grandfather and his ancestors in whom the food never existed. Therefore a man would not be more like to his grandfather or ancestors, than to any other men.

Obj. 3: Further, the food of the generator is sometimes the flesh of cows, pigs and suchlike. If therefore, the semen were produced from surplus food, the man begotten of such semen would be more akin to the cow and the pig, than to his father or other relations.

Obj. 4: Further, Augustine says (Gen. ad lit. x, 20) that we were in Adam "not only by seminal virtue, but also in the very substance of the body." But this would not be, if the semen were produced from surplus food. Therefore the semen is not produced therefrom.

*On the contrary,* The Philosopher proves in many ways (De Gener. Animal. i, 18) that "the semen is surplus food."

*I answer that,* This question depends in some way on what has been stated above (A. 1; Q. 118, A. 1). For if human nature has a virtue for the communication of its form to alien matter not only in another, but also in its own subject; it is clear that the food which at first is dissimilar, becomes at length similar through the form communicated to it. Now it belongs to the natural order that a thing should be reduced from potentiality to act gradually: hence in things generated we observe that at first each is imperfect and is afterwards perfected. But it is clear that the common is to the proper and determinate, as imperfect is to perfect: therefore we see that in the generation of an animal, the animal is generated first, then the man or the horse. So therefore food first of all receives a certain common virtue in regard to all the parts of the body, which virtue is subsequently determinate to this or that part.

Now it is not possible that the semen be a kind of solution from what is already transformed into the substance of the members. For this solution, if it does not retain the nature of the member it is taken from, it would no longer be of the nature of the begetter, and would be due to a process of corruption; and consequently it would not have the power of transforming something else into the likeness of that nature. But if it retained the nature of the member it is taken from, then, since it is limited to a certain part of the body, it would not have the power of moving towards (the production of) the whole nature, but only the nature of that part. Unless one were to say that the solution is taken from all the parts of the body, and that it retains the nature of each part. Thus the semen would be a small animal in act; and generation of animal from animal would be a mere division, as mud is generated from mud, and as animals which continue to live after being cut in two: which is inadmissible.

It remains to be said, therefore, that the semen is not something separated from what was before the actual whole; rather is it the whole, though potentially, having the power, derived from the soul of the begetter, to produce the whole body, as stated above (A. 1; Q. 108, A. 1). Now that which is in potentiality to the whole, is that which is generated from the food, before it is transformed into the substance of the members. Therefore the semen is taken from this. In this sense the nutritive power is said to serve the generative power: because what is transformed by the nutritive power is employed as semen by the generative power. A sign of this, according to the Philosopher, is that animals of great size, which require much food, have little semen in proportion to the size of their bodies, and generate seldom; in like manner fat men, and for the same reason.

Reply Obj. 1: Generation is from the substance of the begetter in animals and plants, inasmuch as the semen owes its virtue to the form of the begetter, and inasmuch as it is in potentiality to the substance.

Reply Obj. 2: The likeness of the begetter to the begotten is on account not of the matter, but of the form of the agent that generates its like. Wherefore in order for a man to be like his grandfather, there is no need that the corporeal seminal matter should have been in the grandfather; but that there be in the semen a virtue derived from the soul of the grandfather through the father. In like manner the third objection is answered. For kinship is not in relation to matter, but rather to the derivation of the forms.

Reply Obj. 4: These words of Augustine are not to be understood as though the immediate seminal virtue, or the corporeal substance from which this individual was formed were actually in Adam: but so that both were in Adam as in principle. For even the corporeal matter, which is supplied by the mother, and which he calls the corporeal substance, is originally derived from Adam: and likewise the active seminal power of the father, which is the immediate seminal virtue (in the production) of this man.

But Christ is said to have been in Adam according to the "corporeal substance," not according to the seminal virtue. Because the matter from which His Body was formed, and which was supplied by the Virgin Mother, was derived from Adam; whereas the active virtue was not derived from Adam, because His Body was not formed by the seminal virtue of a man, but by the operation of the Holy Ghost. For "such a birth was becoming to Him," [*Hymn for Vespers at Christmas; Breviary, O. P.], WHO IS ABOVE ALL GOD FOR EVER BLESSED. Amen.

---

**The End**

# SUMMA THEOLOGICA PART I-II ("Prima Secundae")

## DEDICATION

To the Blessed Virgin Mary Immaculate Seat of Wisdom

FIRST PART OF THE SECOND PART ["I-II," "Prima Secundae"]

TREATISE ON THE LAST END (QQ. 1-5)

## PROLOGUE

Since, as Damascene states (De Fide Orth. ii, 12), man is said to be made in God's image, in so far as the image implies "an intelligent being endowed with free-will and self-movement": now that we have treated of the exemplar, i.e. God, and of those things which came forth from the power of God in accordance with His will; it remains for us to treat of His image, i.e. man, inasmuch as he too is the principle of his actions, as having free-will and control of his actions.

## QUESTION 1

OF MAN'S LAST END (In Eight Articles)

In this matter we shall consider first the last end of human life; and secondly, those things by means of which man may advance towards this end, or stray from the path: for the end is the rule of whatever is ordained to the end. And since the last end of human life is stated to be happiness, we must consider (1) the last end in general; (2) happiness.

Under the first head there are eight points of inquiry:

(1) Whether it belongs to man to act for an end?

(2) Whether this is proper to the rational nature?

(3) Whether a man's actions are specified by their end?

(4) Whether there is any last end of human life?

(5) Whether one man can have several last ends?

(6) Whether man ordains all to the last end?

(7) Whether all men have the same last end?

(8) Whether all other creatures concur with man in that last end?

FIRST ARTICLE [I-II, Q. 1, Art. 1]

Whether It Belongs to Man to Act for an End?

Objection 1: It would seem that it does not belong to man to act for an end. For a cause is naturally first. But an end, in its very name, implies something that is last. Therefore an end is not a cause. But that for which a man acts, is the cause of his action; since this preposition "for" indicates a relation of causality. Therefore it does not belong to man to act for an end.

Obj. 2: Further, that which is itself the last end is not for an end. But in some cases the last end is an action, as the Philosopher states (Ethic. i, 1). Therefore man does not do everything for an end.

Obj. 3: Further, then does a man seem to act for an end, when he acts deliberately. But man does many things without deliberation, sometimes not even thinking of what he is doing; for instance when one moves one's foot or hand, or scratches one's beard, while intent on something else. Therefore man does not do everything for an end.

*On the contrary,* All things contained in a genus are derived from the principle of that genus. Now the end is the principle in human operations, as the Philosopher states (Phys. ii, 9). Therefore it belongs to man to do everything for an end.

*I answer that,* Of actions done by man those alone are properly called "human," which are proper to man as man. Now man differs from irrational animals in this, that he is master of his actions. Wherefore those actions alone are properly called human, of which man is master. Now man is master of his actions through his reason and will; whence, too, the free-will is defined as "the faculty and will of reason." Therefore those actions are properly called human which proceed from a deliberate will. And if any other actions are found in man, they can be called actions "of a man," but not properly "human" actions, since they are not proper to man as man. Now it is clear that whatever actions proceed from a power, are caused by that power in accordance with the nature of its object. But the object of the will is the end and the good. Therefore all human actions must be for an end.

Reply Obj. 1: Although the end be last in the order of execution, yet it is first in the order of the agent's intention. And it is this way that it is a cause.

Reply Obj. 2: If any human action be the last end, it must be voluntary, else it would not be human, as stated above. Now an action is voluntary in one of two ways: first, because it is commanded by the will, e.g. to walk, or to speak; secondly, because it is elicited by the will, for instance the very act of willing. Now it is impossible for the very act elicited by the will to be the last end. For the object of the will is the end, just as the object of sight is color: wherefore just as the first visible cannot be the act of seeing, because every act of seeing is directed to a visible object; so the first appetible, i.e. the end, cannot be the very act of willing. Consequently it follows that if a human action be the last end, it must be an action commanded by the will: so that there, some action of man, at least the act of willing, is for the end. Therefore whatever a man does, it is true to say that man acts for an end, even when he does that action in which the last end consists.

Reply Obj. 3: Such like actions are not properly human actions; since they do not proceed from deliberation of the reason, which is the proper principle of human actions. Therefore they have indeed an imaginary end, but not one that is fixed by reason.

SECOND ARTICLE [I-II, Q. 1, Art. 2]

Whether It Is Proper to the Rational Nature to Act for an End?

Objection 1: It would seem that it is proper to the rational nature to act for an end. For man, to whom it belongs to act for an end, never acts for an unknown end. On the other hand, there are many things that have no knowledge of an end; either because they are altogether without knowledge, as insensible creatures: or because they do not apprehend the idea of an end as such, as irrational animals. Therefore it seems proper to the rational nature to act for an end.

Obj. 2: Further, to act for an end is to order one's action to an end. But this is the work of reason. Therefore it does not belong to things that lack reason.

Obj. 3: Further, the good and the end is the object of the will. But "the will is in the reason" (De Anima iii, 9). Therefore to act for an end belongs to none but a rational nature.

*On the contrary,* The Philosopher proves (Phys. ii, 5) that "not only mind but also nature acts for an end."

*I answer that,* Every agent, of necessity, acts for an end. For if, in a number of causes ordained to one another, the first be removed, the others must, of necessity, be removed also. Now the first of all causes is the final cause. The reason of which is that matter does not receive form, save in so far as it is moved by an agent; for nothing reduces itself from potentiality to act. But an agent does not move except out of intention for an end. For if the agent were not determinate to some particular effect, it would not do one thing rather than another: consequently in order that it produce a determinate effect, it must, of necessity, be determined to some certain one, which has the nature of an end. And just as this determination is effected, in the rational nature, by the "rational appetite," which is called the will; so, in other things, it is caused by their natural inclination, which is called the "natural appetite."

Nevertheless it must be observed that a thing tends to an end, by its action or movement, in two ways: first, as a thing, moving itself to the end, as man; secondly, as a thing moved by another to the end, as an arrow tends to a determinate end through being moved by the archer who directs his action to the end. Therefore those things that are possessed of reason, move themselves to an end; because they have dominion over their actions through their free-will, which is the "faculty of will and reason." But those things that lack reason tend to an end, by natural inclination, as being moved by another and not by themselves; since they do not know the nature of an end as such, and consequently cannot ordain anything to an end, but can be ordained to an end only by another. For the entire irrational nature is in comparison to God as an instrument to the principal agent, as stated above (I, Q. 22, A. 2, ad 4; Q. 103, A. 1, ad 3). Consequently it is proper to the rational nature to tend to an end, as directing ( *agens* ) and leading itself to the end: whereas it is proper to the irrational nature to tend to an end, as directed or led by another, whether it apprehend the end, as do irrational animals, or do not apprehend it, as is the case of those things which are altogether void of knowledge.

Reply Obj. 1: When a man of himself acts for an end, he knows the end: but when he is directed or led by another, for instance, when he acts at another's command, or when he is moved under another's compulsion, it is not necessary that he should know the end. And it is thus with irrational creatures.

Reply Obj. 2: To ordain towards an end belongs to that which directs itself to an end: whereas to be ordained to an end belongs to that which is directed by another to an end. And this can belong to an irrational nature, but owing to some one possessed of reason. Reply Obj. 3: The object of the will is the end and the good in universal. Consequently there can be no will in those things that lack reason and intellect, since they cannot apprehend the universal; but they have a natural appetite or a sensitive appetite, determinate to some particular good. Now it is clear that particular causes are moved by a universal cause: thus the governor of a city, who intends the common good, moves, by his command, all the particular departments of the city. Consequently all things that lack reason are, of necessity, moved to their particular ends by some rational will which extends to the universal good, namely by the Divine will.

THIRD ARTICLE [I-II, Q. 1, Art. 3]

Whether Human Acts Are Specified by Their End?

Objection 1: It would seem that human acts are not specified by their end. For the end is an extrinsic cause. But everything is specified by an intrinsic principle. Therefore human acts are not specified by their end.

Obj. 2: Further, that which gives a thing its species should exist before it. But the end comes into existence afterwards. Therefore a human act does not derive its species from the end.

Obj. 3: Further, one thing cannot be in more than one species. But one and the same act may happen to be ordained to various ends. Therefore the end does not give the species to human acts.

*On the contrary,* Augustine says (De Mor. Eccl. et Manich. ii, 13): "According as their end is worthy of blame or praise so are our deeds worthy of blame or praise."

*I answer that,* Each thing receives its species in respect of an act and not in respect of potentiality; wherefore things composed of matter and form are established in their respective species by their own forms. And this is also to be observed in proper movements. For since movements are, in a way, divided into action and passion, each of these receives its species from an act; action indeed from the act which is the principle of acting, and passion from the act which is the terminus of the movement. Wherefore heating, as an action, is nothing else than a certain movement proceeding from heat, while heating as a passion is nothing else than a movement towards heat: and it is the definition that shows the specific nature. And either way, human acts, whether they be considered as actions, or as passions, receive their species from the end. For human acts can be considered in both ways, since man moves himself, and is moved by himself. Now it has been stated above (A. 1) that acts are called human, inasmuch as they proceed from a deliberate will. Now the object of the will is the good and the end. And hence it is clear that the principle of human acts, in so far as they are human, is the end. In like manner it is their terminus: for the human act terminates at that which the will intends as the end; thus in natural agents the form of the thing generated is conformed to the form of the generator. And since, as Ambrose says (Prolog. super Luc.) "morality is said properly of man," moral acts properly speaking receive their species from the end, for moral acts are the same as human acts.

Reply Obj. 1: The end is not altogether extrinsic to the act, because it is related to the act as principle or terminus; and thus it just this that is essential to an act, viz. to proceed from something, considered as action, and to proceed towards something, considered as passion.

Reply Obj. 2: The end, in so far as it pre-exists in the intention, pertains to the will, as stated above (A. 1, ad 1). And it is thus that it gives the species to the human or moral act.

Reply Obj. 3: One and the same act, in so far as it proceeds once from the agent, is ordained to but one proximate end, from which it has its species: but it can be ordained to several remote ends, of which one is the end of the other. It is possible, however, that an act which is one in respect of its natural species, be ordained to several ends of the will: thus this act "to kill a man," which is but one act in respect of its natural species, can be ordained, as to an end, to the safeguarding of justice, and to the satisfying of anger: the result being that there would be several acts in different species of morality: since in one way there will be an act of virtue, in another, an act of vice. For a movement does not receive its species from that which is its terminus accidentally, but only from that which is its *per se* terminus. Now moral ends are accidental to a natural thing, and conversely the relation to a natural end is accidental to morality. Consequently there is no reason why acts which are the same considered in their natural species, should not be diverse, considered in their moral species, and conversely.

FOURTH ARTICLE [I-II, Q. 1, Art. 4]

Whether There Is One Last End of Human Life?

Objection 1: It would seem that there is no last end of human life, but that we proceed to infinity. For good is essentially diffusive, as Dionysius states (Div. Nom. iv). Consequently if that which proceeds from good is itself good, the latter must needs diffuse some other good: so that the diffusion of good goes on indefinitely. But good has the nature of an end. Therefore there is an indefinite series of ends.

Obj. 2: Further, things pertaining to the reason can be multiplied to infinity: thus mathematical quantities have no limit. For the same reason the species of numbers are infinite, since, given any number, the reason can think of one yet greater. But desire of the end is consequent on the apprehension of the reason. Therefore it seems that there is also an infinite series of ends.

Obj. 3: Further, the good and the end is the object of the will. But the will can react on itself an infinite number of times: for I can will something, and will to will it, and so on indefinitely. Therefore there is an infinite series of ends of the human will, and there is no last end of the human will.

*On the contrary,* The Philosopher says (Metaph. ii, 2) that "to suppose a thing to be indefinite is to deny that it is good." But the good is that which has the nature of an end. Therefore it is contrary to the nature of an end to proceed indefinitely. Therefore it is necessary to fix one last end.

*I answer that,* Absolutely speaking, it is not possible to proceed indefinitely in the matter of ends, from any point of view. For in whatsoever things there is an essential order of one to another, if the first be removed, those that are ordained to the first, must of necessity be removed also. Wherefore the Philosopher proves (Phys. viii, 5) that we cannot proceed to infinitude in causes of movement, because then there would be no first mover, without which neither can the others move, since they move only through being moved by the first mover. Now there is to be observed a twofold order in ends—the order of intention and the order of execution: and in either of these orders there must be something first. For that which is first in the order of intention, is the principle, as it were, moving the appetite; consequently, if you remove this principle, there will be nothing to move the appetite. On the other hand, the principle in execution is that wherein operation has its beginning; and if this principle be taken away, no one will begin to work. Now the principle in the intention is the last end; while the principle in execution is the first of the things which are ordained to the end. Consequently, on neither side is it possible to go to infinity since if there were no last end, nothing would be desired, nor would any action have its term, nor would the intention of the agent be at rest; while if there is no first thing among those that are ordained to the end, none would begin to work at anything, and counsel would have no term, but would continue indefinitely.

On the other hand, nothing hinders infinity from being in things that are ordained to one another not essentially but accidentally; for accidental causes are indeterminate. And in this way it happens that there is an accidental infinity of ends, and of things ordained to the end.

Reply Obj. 1: The very nature of good is that something flows from it, but not that it flows from something else. Since, therefore, good has the nature of end, and the first good is the last end, this argument does not prove that there is no last end; but that from the end, already supposed, we may proceed downwards indefinitely towards those things that are ordained to the end. And this would be true if we considered but the power of the First Good, which is infinite. But, since the First Good diffuses itself according to the intellect, to which it is proper to flow forth into its effects according to a certain fixed form; it follows that there is a certain measure to the flow of good things from the First Good from Which all other goods share the power of diffusion. Consequently the diffusion of goods does not proceed indefinitely but, as it is written (Wis. 11:21), God disposes all things "in number, weight and measure."

Reply Obj. 2: In things which are of themselves, reason begins from principles that are known naturally, and advances to some term. Wherefore the Philosopher proves (Poster. i, 3) that there is no infinite process in demonstrations, because there we find a process of things having an essential, not an accidental, connection with one another. But in those things which are accidentally connected, nothing hinders the reason from proceeding indefinitely. Now it is accidental to a stated quantity or number, as such, that quantity or unity be added to it. Wherefore in such like things nothing hinders the reason from an indefinite process.

Reply Obj. 3: This multiplication of acts of the will reacting on itself, is accidental to the order of ends. This is clear from the fact that in regard to one and the same end, the will reacts on itself indifferently once or several times.

FIFTH ARTICLE [I-II, Q. 1, Art. 5]

Whether One Man Can Have Several Last Ends?

Objection 1: It would seem possible for one man's will to be directed at the same time to several things, as last ends. For Augustine says (De Civ. Dei xix, 1) that some held man's last end to consist in four things, viz. "in pleasure, repose, the gifts of nature, and virtue." But these are clearly more than one thing. Therefore one man can place the last end of his will in many things.

Obj. 2: Further, things not in opposition to one another do not exclude one another. Now there are many things which are not in opposition to one another. Therefore the supposition that one thing is the last end of the will does not exclude others.

Obj. 3: Further, by the fact that it places its last end in one thing, the will does not lose its freedom. But before it placed its last end in that thing, e.g. pleasure, it could place it in something else, e.g. riches. Therefore even after having placed his last end in pleasure, a man can at the same time place his last end in riches. Therefore it is possible for one man's will to be directed at the same time to several things, as last ends.

*On the contrary,* That in which a man rests as in his last end, is master of his affections, since he takes therefrom his entire rule of life. Hence of gluttons it is written (Phil. 3:19): "Whose god is their belly": viz. because they place their last end in the pleasures of the belly. Now according to Matt. 6:24, "No man can serve two masters," such, namely, as are not ordained to one another. Therefore it is impossible for one man to have several last ends not ordained to one another.

*I answer that,* It is impossible for one man's will to be directed at the same time to diverse things, as last ends. Three reasons may be assigned for this. First, because, since everything desires its own perfection, a man desires for his ultimate end, that which he desires as his perfect and crowning good. Hence Augustine (De Civ. Dei xix, 1): "In speaking of the end of good we mean now, not that it passes away so as to be no more, but that it is perfected so as to be complete." It is therefore necessary for the last end so to fill man's appetite, that nothing is left besides it for man to desire. Which is not possible, if something else be required for his perfection. Consequently it is not possible for the appetite so to tend to two things, as though each were its perfect good.

The second reason is because, just as in the process of reasoning, the principle is that which is naturally known, so in the process of the rational appetite, i.e. the will, the principle needs to be that which is naturally desired. Now this must needs be one: since nature tends to one thing only. But the principle in the process of the rational appetite is the last end. Therefore that to which the will tends, as to its last end, is one.

The third reason is because, since voluntary actions receive their species from the end, as stated above (A. 3), they must needs receive their genus from the last end, which is common to them all: just as natural things are placed in a genus according to a common form. Since, then, all things that can be desired by the will, belong, as such, to one genus, the last end must needs be one. And all the more because in every genus there is one first principle; and the last end has the nature of a first principle, as stated above. Now as the last end of man, simply as man, is to the whole human race, so is the last end of any individual man to that individual. Therefore, just as of all men there is naturally one last end, so the will of an individual man must be fixed on one last end.

Reply Obj. 1: All these several objects were considered as one perfect good resulting therefrom, by those who placed in them the last end.

Reply Obj. 2: Although it is possible to find several things which are not in opposition to one another, yet it is contrary to a thing's perfect good, that anything besides be required for that thing's perfection.

Reply Obj. 3: The power of the will does not extend to making opposites exist at the same time. Which would be the case were it to tend to several diverse objects as last ends, as has been shown above (ad 2).

SIXTH ARTICLE [I-II, Q. 1, Art. 6]

Whether Man Wills All, Whatsoever He Wills, for the Last End?

Objection 1: It would seem that man does not will all, whatsoever he wills, for the last end. For things ordained to the last end are said to be serious matter, as being useful. But jests are foreign to serious matter. Therefore what man does in jest, he ordains not to the last end.

Obj. 2: Further, the Philosopher says at the beginning of his Metaphysics (i. 2) that speculative science is sought for its own sake. Now it cannot be said that each speculative science is the last end. Therefore man does not desire all, whatsoever he desires, for the last end.

Obj. 3: Further, whosoever ordains something to an end, thinks of that end. But man does not always think of the last end in all that he desires or does. Therefore man neither desires nor does all for the last end.

*On the contrary,* Augustine says (De Civ. Dei xix, 1): "That is the end of our good, for the sake of which we love other things, whereas we love it for its own sake."

*I answer that,* Man must, of necessity, desire all, whatsoever he desires, for the last end. This is evident for two reasons. First, because whatever man desires, he desires it under the aspect of good. And if he desire it, not as his perfect good, which is the last end, he must, of necessity, desire it as tending to the perfect good, because the beginning of anything is always ordained to its completion; as is clearly the case in effects both of nature and of art. Wherefore every beginning of perfection is ordained to complete perfection which is achieved through the last end. Secondly, because the last end stands in the same relation in moving the appetite, as the first mover in other movements. Now it is clear that secondary moving causes do not move save inasmuch as they are moved by the first mover. Therefore secondary objects of the appetite do not move the appetite, except as ordained to the first object of the appetite, which is the last end.

Reply Obj. 1: Actions done jestingly are not directed to any external end; but merely to the good of the jester, in so far as they afford him pleasure or relaxation. But man's consummate good is his last end.

Reply Obj. 2: The same applies to speculative science; which is desired as the scientist's good, included in complete and perfect good, which is the ultimate end.

Reply Obj. 3: One need not always be thinking of the last end, whenever one desires or does something: but the virtue of the first intention, which was in respect of the last end, remains in every desire directed to any object whatever, even though one's thoughts be not actually directed to the last end. Thus while walking along the road one needs not to be thinking of the end at every step.

SEVENTH ARTICLE [I-II, Q. 1, Art. 7]

Whether All Men Have the Same Last End?

Objection 1: It would seem that all men have not the same last end. For before all else the unchangeable good seems to be the last end of man. But some turn away from the unchangeable good, by sinning. Therefore all men have not the same last end.

Obj. 2: Further, man's entire life is ruled according to his last end. If, therefore, all men had the same last end, they would not have various pursuits in life. Which is evidently false.

Obj. 3: Further, the end is the term of action. But actions are of individuals. Now although men agree in their specific nature, yet they differ in things pertaining to individuals. Therefore all men have not the same last end.

*On the contrary,* Augustine says (De Trin. xiii, 3) that all men agree in desiring the last end, which is happiness.

*I answer that,* We can speak of the last end in two ways: first, considering only the aspect of last end; secondly, considering the thing in which the aspect of last end is realized. So, then, as to the aspect of last end, all agree in desiring the last end: since all desire the fulfilment of their perfection, and it is precisely this fulfilment in which the last end consists, as stated above (A. 5). But as to the thing in which this aspect is realized, all men are not agreed as to their last end: since some desire riches as their consummate good; some, pleasure; others, something else. Thus to every taste the sweet is pleasant but to some, the sweetness of wine is most pleasant, to others, the sweetness of honey, or of something similar. Yet that sweet is absolutely the best of all pleasant things, in which he who has the best taste takes most pleasure. In like manner that good is most complete which the man with well disposed affections desires for his last end.

Reply Obj. 1: Those who sin turn from that in which their last end really consists: but they do not turn away from the intention of the last end, which intention they mistakenly seek in other things.

Reply Obj. 2: Various pursuits in life are found among men by reason of the various things in which men seek to find their last end.

Reply Obj. 3: Although actions are of individuals, yet their first principle of action is nature, which tends to one thing, as stated above (A. 5).

EIGHTH ARTICLE [I-II, Q. 1, Art. 8]

Whether Other Creatures Concur in That Last End?

Objection 1: It would seem that all other creatures concur in man's last end. For the end corresponds to the beginning. But man's beginning—i.e. God—is also the beginning of all else. Therefore all other things concur in man's last end.

Obj. 2: Further, Dionysius says (Div. Nom. iv) that "God turns all things to Himself as to their last end." But He is also man's last end; because He alone is to be enjoyed by man, as Augustine says (De Doctr. Christ. i, 5, 22). Therefore other things, too, concur in man's last end.

Obj. 3: Further, man's last end is the object of the will. But the object of the will is the universal good, which is the end of all. Therefore other things, too, concur in man's last end.

*On the contrary,* man's last end is happiness; which all men desire, as Augustine says (De Trin. xiii, 3, 4). But "happiness is not possible for animals bereft of reason," as Augustine says (QQ. 83, qu. 5). Therefore other things do not concur in man's last end.

*I answer that,* As the Philosopher says (Phys. ii, 2), the end is twofold—the end "for which" and the end "by which"; viz. the thing itself in which is found the aspect of good, and the use or acquisition of that thing. Thus we say that the end of the movement of a weighty body is either a lower place as "thing," or to be in a lower place, as "use"; and the end of the miser is money as "thing," or possession of money as "use."

If, therefore, we speak of man's last end as of the thing which is the end, thus all other things concur in man's last end, since God is the last end of man and of all other things. If, however, we speak of man's last end, as of the acquisition of the end, then irrational creatures do not concur with man in this end. For man and other rational creatures attain to their last end by knowing and loving God: this is not possible to other creatures, which acquire their last end, in so far as they share in the Divine likeness, inasmuch as they are, or live, or even know.

Hence it is evident how the objections are solved: since happiness means the acquisition of the last end.

## QUESTION 2

OF THOSE THINGS IN WHICH MAN'S HAPPINESS CONSISTS (In Eight Articles)

We have now to consider happiness: and (1) in what it consists; (2) what it is; (3) how we can obtain it.

Concerning the first there are eight points of inquiry:

(1) Whether happiness consists in wealth?
(2) Whether in honor?
(3) Whether in fame or glory?
(4) Whether in power?
(5) Whether in any good of the body?
(6) Whether in pleasure?
(7) Whether in any good of the soul?
(8) Whether in any created good?

FIRST ARTICLE [I-II, Q. 2, Art. 1]

Whether Man's Happiness Consists in Wealth?

Objection 1: It would seem that man's happiness consists in wealth. For since happiness is man's last end, it must consist in that which has the greatest hold on man's affections. Now this is wealth: for it is written (Eccles. 10:19): "All things obey money." Therefore man's happiness consists in wealth.

Obj. 2: Further, according to Boethius (De Consol. iii), happiness is "a state of life made perfect by the aggregate of all good things." Now money seems to be the means of possessing all things: for, as the Philosopher says (Ethic. v, 5), money was invented, that it might be a sort of guarantee for the acquisition of whatever man desires. Therefore happiness consists in wealth.

Obj. 3: Further, since the desire for the sovereign good never fails, it seems to be infinite. But this is the case with riches more than anything else; since "a covetous man shall not be satisfied with riches" (Eccles. 5:9). Therefore happiness consists in wealth.

*On the contrary,* Man's good consists in retaining happiness rather than in spreading it. But as Boethius says (De Consol. ii), "wealth shines in giving rather than in hoarding: for the miser is hateful, whereas the generous man is applauded." Therefore man's happiness does not consist in wealth.

*I answer that,* It is impossible for man's happiness to consist in wealth. For wealth is twofold, as the Philosopher says (Polit. i, 3), viz. natural and artificial. Natural wealth is that which serves man as a remedy for his natural wants: such as food, drink, clothing, cars, dwellings, and such like, while artificial wealth is that which is not a direct help to nature, as money, but is invented by the art of man, for the convenience of exchange, and as a measure of things salable.

Now it is evident that man's happiness cannot consist in natural wealth. For wealth of this kind is sought for the sake of something else, viz. as a support of human nature: consequently it cannot be man's last end, rather is it ordained to man as to its end. Wherefore in the order of nature, all such things are below man, and made for him, according to Ps. 8:8: "Thou hast subjected all things under his feet."

And as to artificial wealth, it is not sought save for the sake of natural wealth; since man would not seek it except because, by its means, he procures for himself the necessaries of life. Consequently much less can it be considered in the light of the last end. Therefore it is impossible for happiness, which is the last end of man, to consist in wealth.

Reply Obj. 1: All material things obey money, so far as the multitude of fools is concerned, who know no other than material goods, which can be obtained for money. But we should take our estimation of human goods not from the foolish but from the wise: just as it is for a person whose sense of taste is in good order, to judge whether a thing is palatable.

Reply Obj. 2: All things salable can be had for money: not so spiritual things, which cannot be sold. Hence it is written (Prov. 17:16): "What doth it avail a fool to have riches, seeing he cannot buy wisdom."

Reply Obj. 3: The desire for natural riches is not infinite: because they suffice for nature in a certain measure. But the desire for artificial wealth is infinite, for it is the servant of disordered concupiscence, which is not curbed, as the Philosopher makes clear (Polit. i, 3). Yet this desire for wealth is infinite otherwise than the desire for the sovereign good. For the more perfectly the sovereign good is possessed, the more it is loved, and other things despised: because the more we possess it, the more we know it. Hence it is written (Ecclus. 24:29): "They that eat me shall yet hunger." Whereas in the desire for wealth and for whatsoever temporal goods, the contrary is the case: for when we already possess them, we despise them, and seek others: which is the sense of Our Lord's words (John 4:13): "Whosoever drinketh of this water," by which temporal goods are signified, "shall thirst again." The reason of this is that we realize more their insufficiency when we possess them: and this very fact shows that they are imperfect, and the sovereign good does not consist therein.

SECOND ARTICLE [I-II, Q. 2, Art. 2]

Whether Man's Happiness Consists in Honors?

Objection 1: It would seem that man's happiness consists in honors. For happiness or bliss is "the reward of virtue," as the Philosopher says (Ethic. i, 9). But honor more than anything else seems to be that by which virtue is rewarded, as the Philosopher says (Ethic. iv, 3). Therefore happiness consists especially in honor.

Obj. 2: Further, that which belongs to God and to persons of great excellence seems especially to be happiness, which is the perfect good. But that is honor, as the Philosopher says (Ethic. iv, 3). Moreover, the Apostle says (1 Tim. 1:17): "To ... the only God be honor and glory." Therefore happiness consists in honor.

Obj. 3: Further, that which man desires above all is happiness. But nothing seems more desirable to man than honor: since man suffers loss in all other things, lest he should suffer loss of honor. Therefore happiness consists in honor.

*On the contrary,* Happiness is in the happy. But honor is not in the honored, but rather in him who honors, and who offers deference to the person honored, as the Philosopher says (Ethic. i, 5). Therefore happiness does not consist in honor.

*I answer that,* It is impossible for happiness to consist in honor. For honor is given to a man on account of some excellence in him; and consequently it is a sign and attestation of the excellence that is in the person honored. Now a man's excellence is in proportion, especially to his happiness, which is man's perfect good; and to its parts, i.e. those goods by which he has a certain share of happiness. And therefore honor can result from happiness, but happiness cannot principally consist therein.

Reply Obj. 1: As the Philosopher says (Ethic. i, 5), honor is not that reward of virtue, for which the virtuous work: but they receive honor from men by way of reward, "as from those who have nothing greater to offer." But virtue's true reward is happiness itself, for which the virtuous work: whereas if they worked for honor, it would no longer be a virtue, but ambition.

Reply Obj. 2: Honor is due to God and to persons of great excellence as a sign of attestation of excellence already existing: not that honor makes them excellent.

Reply Obj. 3: That man desires honor above all else, arises from his natural desire for happiness, from which honor results, as stated above. Wherefore man seeks to be honored especially by the wise, on whose judgment he believes himself to be excellent or happy.

THIRD ARTICLE [I-II, Q. 2, Art. 3]

Whether Man's Happiness Consists in Fame or Glory?

Objection 1: It would seem that man's happiness consists in glory. For happiness seems to consist in that which is paid to the saints for the trials they have undergone in the world. But this is glory: for the Apostle says (Rom. 8:18): "The sufferings of this time are not worthy to be compared with the glory to come, that shall be revealed in us." Therefore happiness consists in glory.

Obj. 2: Further, good is diffusive of itself, as stated by Dionysius (Div. Nom. iv). But man's good is spread abroad in the knowledge of others by glory more than by anything else: since, according to Ambrose [*Augustine, Contra Maxim. Arian. ii. 13], glory consists "in being well known and praised." Therefore man's happiness consists in glory.

Obj. 3: Further, happiness is the most enduring good. Now this seems to be fame or glory; because by this men attain to eternity after a fashion. Hence Boethius says (De Consol. ii): "You seem to beget unto yourselves eternity, when you think of your fame in future time." Therefore man's happiness consists in fame or glory.

*On the contrary,* Happiness is man's true good. But it happens that fame or glory is false: for as Boethius says (De Consol. iii), "many owe their renown to the lying reports spread among the people. Can anything be more shameful? For those who receive false fame, must needs blush at their own praise." Therefore man's happiness does not consist in fame or glory.

*I answer that,* Man's happiness cannot consist in human fame or glory. For glory consists "in being well known and praised," as Ambrose [*Augustine, Contra Maxim. Arian. ii, 13] says. Now the thing known is related to human knowledge otherwise than to God's knowledge: for human knowledge is caused by the things known, whereas God's knowledge is the cause of the things known. Wherefore the perfection of human good, which is called happiness, cannot be caused by human knowledge: but rather human knowledge of another's happiness proceeds from, and, in a fashion, is caused by, human happiness itself, inchoate or perfect. Consequently man's happiness cannot consist in fame or glory. On the other hand, man's good depends on God's knowledge as its cause. And therefore man's beatitude depends, as on its cause, on the glory which man has with God; according to Ps. 90:15, 16: "I will deliver him, and I will glorify him; I will fill him with length of days, and I will show him my salvation."

Furthermore, we must observe that human knowledge often fails, especially in contingent singulars, such as are human acts. For this reason human glory is frequently deceptive. But since God cannot be deceived, His glory is always true; hence it is written (2 Cor. 10:18): "He ... is approved ... whom God commendeth."

Reply Obj. 1: The Apostle speaks, then, not of the glory which is with men, but of the glory which is from God, with His Angels. Hence it is written (Mk. 8:38): "The Son of Man shall confess him in the glory of His Father, before His angels" [*St. Thomas joins Mk. 8:38 with Luke 12:8 owing to a possible variant in his text, or to the fact that he was quoting from memory].

Reply Obj. 2: A man's good which, through fame or glory, is in the knowledge of many, if this knowledge be true, must needs be derived from good existing in the man himself: and hence it presupposes perfect or inchoate happiness. But if the knowledge be false, it does not harmonize with the thing: and thus good does not exist in him who is looked upon as famous. Hence it follows that fame can nowise make man happy.

Reply Obj. 3: Fame has no stability; in fact, it is easily ruined by false report. And if sometimes it endures, this is by accident. But happiness endures of itself, and for ever.

FOURTH ARTICLE [I-II, Q. 2, Art. 4]

Whether Man's Happiness Consists in Power?

Objection 1: It would seem that happiness consists in power. For all things desire to become like to God, as to their last end and first beginning. But men who are in power, seem, on account of the similarity of power, to be most like to God: hence also in Scripture they are called "gods" (Ex. 22:28), "Thou shalt not speak ill of the gods." Therefore happiness consists in power.

Obj. 2: Further, happiness is the perfect good. But the highest perfection for man is to be able to rule others; which belongs to those who are in power. Therefore happiness consists in power.

Obj. 3: Further, since happiness is supremely desirable, it is contrary to that which is before all to be shunned. But, more than aught else, men shun servitude, which is contrary to power. Therefore happiness consists in power.

*On the contrary,* Happiness is the perfect good. But power is most imperfect. For as Boethius says (De Consol. iii), "the power of man cannot relieve the gnawings of care, nor can it avoid the thorny path of anxiety": and further on: "Think you a man is powerful who is surrounded by attendants, whom he inspires with fear indeed, but whom he fears still more?"

*I answer that,* It is impossible for happiness to consist in power; and this for two reasons. First because power has the nature of principle, as is stated in *Metaph.* v, 12, whereas happiness has the nature of last end. Secondly, because power has relation to good and evil: whereas happiness is man's proper and perfect good. Wherefore some happiness might consist in the good use of power, which is by virtue, rather than in power itself.

Now four general reasons may be given to prove that happiness consists in none of the foregoing external goods. First, because, since happiness is man's supreme good, it is incompatible with any evil. Now all the foregoing can be found both in good and in evil men. Secondly, because, since it is the nature of happiness to "satisfy of itself," as stated in *Ethic.* i, 7, having gained happiness, man cannot lack any needful good. But after acquiring any one of the foregoing, man may still lack many goods that are necessary to him; for instance, wisdom, bodily health, and such like. Thirdly, because, since happiness is the perfect good, no evil can accrue to anyone therefrom. This cannot be said of the foregoing: for it is written (Eccles. 5:12) that "riches" are sometimes "kept to the hurt of the owner"; and the same may be said of the other three. Fourthly, because man is ordained to happiness through principles that are in him; since he is ordained thereto naturally. Now the four goods mentioned above are due rather to external causes, and in most cases to fortune; for which reason they are called goods of fortune. Therefore it is evident that happiness nowise consists in the foregoing.

Reply Obj. 1: God's power is His goodness:

hence He cannot use His power otherwise than well. But it is not so with men. Consequently it is not enough for man's happiness, that he become like God in power, unless he become like Him in goodness also.

Reply Obj. 2: Just as it is a very good thing for a man to make good use of power in ruling many, so is it a very bad thing if he makes a bad use of it. And so it is that power is towards good and evil.

Reply Obj. 3: Servitude is a hindrance to the good use of power: therefore is it that men naturally shun it; not because man's supreme good consists in power.

FIFTH ARTICLE [I-II, Q. 2, Art. 5]

Whether Man's Happiness Consists in Any Bodily Good?

Objection 1: It would seem that man's happiness consists in bodily goods. For it is written (Ecclus. 30:16): "There is no riches above the riches of the health of the body." But happiness consists in that which is best. Therefore it consists in the health of the body.

Obj. 2: Further, Dionysius says (Div. Nom. v), that "to be" is better than "to live," and "to live" is better than all that follows. But for man's being and living, the health of the body is necessary. Since, therefore, happiness is man's supreme good, it seems that health of the body belongs more than anything else to happiness.

Obj. 3: Further, the more universal a thing is, the higher the principle from which it depends; because the higher a cause is, the greater the scope of its power. Now just as the causality of the efficient cause consists in its flowing into something, so the causality of the end consists in its drawing the appetite. Therefore, just as the First Cause is that which flows into all things, so the last end is that which attracts the desire of all. But being itself is that which is most desired by all. Therefore man's happiness consists most of all in things pertaining to his being, such as the health of the body.

*On the contrary,* Man surpasses all other animals in regard to happiness. But in bodily goods he is surpassed by many animals; for instance, by the elephant in longevity, by the lion in strength, by the stag in fleetness. Therefore man's happiness does not consist in goods of the body.

*I answer that,* It is impossible for man's happiness to consist in the goods of the body; and this for two reasons. First, because, if a thing be ordained to another as to its end, its last end cannot consist in the preservation of its being. Hence a captain does not intend as a last end, the preservation of the ship entrusted to him, since a ship is ordained to something else as its end, viz. to navigation. Now just as the ship is entrusted to the captain that he may steer its course, so man is given over to his will and reason; according to Ecclus. 15:14: "God made man from the beginning and left him in the hand of his own counsel." Now it is evident that man is ordained to something as his end: since man is not the supreme good. Therefore the last end of man's reason and will cannot be the preservation of man's being.

Secondly, because, granted that the end of man's will and reason be the preservation of man's being, it could not be said that the end of man is some good of the body. For man's being consists in soul and body; and though the being of the body depends on the soul, yet the being of the human soul depends not on the body, as shown above (I, Q. 75, A. 2); and the very body is for the soul, as matter for its form, and the instruments for the man that puts them into motion, that by their means he may do his work. Wherefore all goods of the body are ordained to the goods of the soul, as to their end. Consequently happiness, which is man's last end, cannot consist in goods of the body.

Reply Obj. 1: Just as the body is ordained to the soul, as its end, so are external goods ordained to the body itself. And therefore it is with reason that the good of the body is preferred to external goods, which are signified by "riches," just as the good of the soul is preferred to all bodily goods.

Reply Obj. 2: Being taken simply, as including all perfection of being, surpasses life and all that follows it; for thus being itself includes all these. And in this sense Dionysius speaks. But if we consider being itself as participated in this or that thing, which does not possess the whole perfection of being, but has imperfect being, such as the being of any creature; then it is evident that being itself together with an additional perfection is more excellent. Hence in the same passage Dionysius says that things that live are better than things that exist, and intelligent better than living things.

Reply Obj. 3: Since the end corresponds to the beginning; this argument proves that the last end is the first beginning of being, in Whom every perfection of being is: Whose likeness, according to their proportion, some desire as to being only, some as to living being, some as to being which is living, intelligent and happy. And this belongs to few.

SIXTH ARTICLE [I-II, Q. 2, Art. 5]

Whether Man's Happiness Consists in Pleasure?

Objection 1: It would seem that man's happiness consists in pleasure. For since happiness is the last end, it is not desired for something else, but other things for it. But this answers to pleasure more than to anything else: "for it is absurd to ask anyone what is his motive in wishing to be pleased" (Ethic. x, 2). Therefore happiness consists principally in pleasure and delight.

Obj. 2: Further, "the first cause goes more deeply into the effect than the second cause" (De Causis i). Now the causality of the end consists in its attracting the appetite. Therefore, seemingly that which moves most the appetite, answers to the notion of the last end. Now this is pleasure: and a sign of this is that delight so far absorbs man's will and reason, that it causes him to despise other goods. Therefore it seems that man's last end, which is happiness, consists principally in pleasure.

Obj. 3: Further, since desire is for good, it seems that what all desire is best. But all desire delight; both wise and foolish, and even irrational creatures. Therefore delight is the best of all. Therefore happiness, which is the supreme good, consists in pleasure.

*On the contrary,* Boethius says (De Consol. iii): "Any one that chooses to look back on his past excesses, will perceive that pleasures had a sad ending: and if they can render a man happy, there is no reason why we should not say that the very beasts are happy too."

*I answer that,* Because bodily delights are more generally known, "the name of pleasure has been appropriated to them" (Ethic. vii, 13), although other delights excel them: and yet happiness does not consist in them. Because in every thing, that which pertains to its essence is distinct from its proper accident: thus in man it is one thing that he is a mortal rational animal, and another that he is a risible animal. We must therefore consider that every delight is a proper accident resulting from happiness, or from some part of happiness; since the reason that a man is delighted is that he has some fitting good, either in reality, or in hope, or at least in memory. Now a fitting good, if indeed it be the perfect good, is precisely man's happiness: and if it is imperfect, it is a share of happiness, either proximate, or remote, or at least apparent. Therefore it is evident that neither is delight, which results from the perfect good, the very essence of happiness, but something resulting therefrom as its proper accident.

But bodily pleasure cannot result from the perfect good even in that way. For it results from a good apprehended by sense, which is a power of the soul, which power makes use of the body. Now good pertaining to the body, and apprehended by sense, cannot be man's perfect good. For since the rational soul excels the capacity of corporeal matter, that part of the soul which is independent of a corporeal organ, has a certain infinity in regard to the body and those parts of the soul which are tied down to the body: just as immaterial things are in a way infinite as compared to material things, since a form is, after a fashion, contracted and bounded by matter, so that a form which is independent of matter is, in a way, infinite. Therefore sense, which is a power of the body, knows the singular, which is determinate through matter: whereas the intellect, which is a power independent of matter, knows the universal, which is abstracted from matter, and contains an infinite number of singulars. Consequently it is evident that good which is fitting to the body, and which causes bodily delight through being apprehended by sense, is not man's perfect good, but is quite a trifle as compared with the good of the soul. Hence it is written (Wis. 7:9) that "all gold in comparison of her, is as a little sand." And therefore bodily pleasure is neither happiness itself, nor a proper accident of happiness.

Reply Obj. 1: It comes to the same whether we desire good, or desire delight, which is nothing else than the appetite's rest in good: thus it is owing to the same natural force that a weighty body is borne downwards and that it rests there. Consequently just as good is desired for itself, so delight is desired for itself and not for anything else, if the preposition "for" denote the final cause. But if it denote the formal or rather the motive cause, thus delight is desirable for something else, i.e. for the good, which is the object of that delight, and consequently is its principle, and gives it its form: for the reason that delight is desired is that it is rest in the thing desired.

Reply Obj. 2: The vehemence of desire for sensible delight arises from the fact that operations of the senses, through being the principles of our knowledge, are more perceptible. And so it is that sensible pleasures are desired by the majority.

Reply Obj. 3: All desire delight in the same way as they desire good: and yet they desire delight by reason of the good and not conversely, as stated above (ad 1). Consequently it does not follow that delight is the supreme and essential good, but that every delight results from some good, and that some delight results from that which is the essential and supreme good.

SEVENTH ARTICLE [I-II, Q. 2, Art. 7]

Whether Some Good of the Soul Constitutes Man's Happiness?

Objection 1: It would seem that some good of the soul constitutes man's happiness. For happiness is man's good. Now this is threefold: external goods, goods of the body, and goods of the soul. But happiness does not consist in external goods, nor in goods of the body, as shown above (AA. 4, 5). Therefore it consists in goods of the soul.

Obj. 2: Further, we love that for which we desire good, more than the good that we desire for it: thus we love a friend for whom we desire money, more than we love money. But whatever good a man desires, he desires it for himself. Therefore he loves himself more than all other goods. Now happiness is what is loved above all: which is evident from the fact that for its sake all else is loved and desired. Therefore happiness consists in some good of man himself: not, however, in goods of the body; therefore, in goods of the soul.

Obj. 3: Further, perfection is something belonging to that which is perfected. But happiness is a perfection of man. Therefore happiness is something belonging to man. But it is not something belonging to the body, as shown above (A. 5). Therefore it is something belonging to the soul; and thus it consists in goods of the soul.

*On the contrary,* As Augustine says (De Doctr.

Christ. i, 22), "that which constitutes the life of happiness is to be loved for its own sake." But man is not to be loved for his own sake, but whatever is in man is to be loved for God's sake. Therefore happiness consists in no good of the soul.

*I answer that,* As stated above (Q. 1, A. 8), the end is twofold: namely, the thing itself, which we desire to attain, and the use, namely, the attainment or possession of that thing. If, then, we speak of man's last end, it is impossible for man's last end to be the soul itself or something belonging to it. Because the soul, considered in itself, is as something existing in potentiality: for it becomes knowing actually, from being potentially knowing; and actually virtuous, from being potentially virtuous. Now since potentiality is for the sake of act as for its fulfilment, that which in itself is in potentiality cannot be the last end. Therefore the soul itself cannot be its own last end.

In like manner neither can anything belonging to it, whether power, habit, or act. For that good which is the last end, is the perfect good fulfilling the desire. Now man's appetite, otherwise the will, is for the universal good. And any good inherent to the soul is a participated good, and consequently a portioned good. Therefore none of them can be man's last end.

But if we speak of man's last end, as to the attainment or possession thereof, or as to any use whatever of the thing itself desired as an end, thus does something of man, in respect of his soul, belong to his last end: since man attains happiness through his soul. Therefore the thing itself which is desired as end, is that which constitutes happiness, and makes man happy; but the attainment of this thing is called happiness. Consequently we must say that happiness is something belonging to the soul; but that which constitutes happiness is something outside the soul.

Reply Obj. 1: Inasmuch as this division includes all goods that man can desire, thus the good of the soul is not only power, habit, or act, but also the object of these, which is something outside. And in this way nothing hinders us from saying that what constitutes happiness is a good of the soul.

Reply Obj. 2: As far as the proposed objection is concerned, happiness is loved above all, as the good desired; whereas a friend is loved as that for which good is desired; and thus, too, man loves himself. Consequently it is not the same kind of love in both cases. As to whether man loves anything more than himself with the love of friendship there will be occasion to inquire when we treat of Charity.

Reply Obj. 3: Happiness, itself, since it is a perfection of the soul, is an inherent good of the soul; but that which constitutes happiness, viz. which makes man happy, is something outside his soul, as stated above.

EIGHTH ARTICLE [I-II, Q. 2, Art. 8]

Whether Any Created Good Constitutes Man's Happiness?

Objection 1: It would seem that some created good constitutes man's happiness. For Dionysius says (Div. Nom. vii) that Divine wisdom "unites the ends of first things to the beginnings of second things," from which we may gather that the summit of a lower nature touches the base of the higher nature. But man's highest good is happiness. Since then the angel is above man in the order of nature, as stated in the First Part (Q. 111, A. 1), it seems that man's happiness consists in man somehow reaching the angel.

Obj. 2: Further, the last end of each thing is that which, in relation to it, is perfect: hence the part is for the whole, as for its end. But the universe of creatures which is called the macrocosm, is compared to man who is called the microcosm (Phys. viii, 2), as perfect to imperfect. Therefore man's happiness consists in the whole universe of creatures.

Obj. 3: Further, man is made happy by that which lulls his natural desire. But man's natural desire does not reach out to a good surpassing his capacity. Since then man's capacity does not include that good which surpasses the limits of all creation, it seems that man can be made happy by some created good. Consequently some created good constitutes man's happiness.

*On the contrary,* Augustine says (De Civ. Dei xix, 26): "As the soul is the life of the body, so God is man's life of happiness: of Whom it is written: 'Happy is that people whose God is the Lord' (Ps. 143:15)."

*I answer that,* It is impossible for any created good to constitute man's happiness. For happiness is the perfect good, which lulls the appetite altogether; else it would not be the last end, if something yet remained to be desired. Now the object of the will, i.e. of man's appetite, is the universal good; just as the object of the intellect is the universal true. Hence it is evident that naught can lull man's will, save the universal good. This is to be found, not in any creature, but in God alone; because every creature has goodness by participation. Wherefore God alone can satisfy the will of man, according to the words of Ps. 102:5: "Who satisfieth thy desire with good things." Therefore God alone constitutes man's happiness.

Reply Obj. 1: The summit of man does indeed touch the base of the angelic nature, by a kind of likeness; but man does not rest there as in his last end, but reaches out to the universal fount itself of good, which is the common object of happiness of all the blessed, as being the infinite and perfect good.

Reply Obj. 2: If a whole be not the last end, but ordained to a further end, then the last end of a part thereof is not the whole itself, but something else. Now the universe of creatures, to which man is compared as part to whole, is not the last end, but is ordained to God, as to its last end. Therefore the last end of man is not the good of the universe, but God himself.

Reply Obj. 3: Created good is not less than that good of which man is capable, as of something intrinsic and inherent to him: but it is less than the good of which he is capable, as of an object, and which is infinite. And the participated good which is in an angel, and in the whole universe, is a finite and restricted good.

# QUESTION 3

WHAT IS HAPPINESS (In Eight Articles)

We have now to consider (1) what happiness is, and (2) what things are required for it.

Concerning the first there are eight points of inquiry:

(1) Whether happiness is something uncreated?

(2) If it be something created, whether it is an operation?

(3) Whether it is an operation of the sensitive, or only of the intellectual part?

(4) If it be an operation of the intellectual part, whether it is an operation of the intellect, or of the will?

(5) If it be an operation of the intellect, whether it is an operation of the speculative or of the practical intellect?

(6) If it be an operation of the speculative intellect, whether it consists in the consideration of speculative sciences?

(7) Whether it consists in the consideration of separate substances viz. angels?

(8) Whether it consists in the sole contemplation of God seen in His Essence?

FIRST ARTICLE [I-II, Q. 3, Art. 1]

Whether Happiness Is Something Uncreated?

Objection 1: It would seem that happiness is something uncreated. For Boethius says (De Consol. iii): "We must needs confess that God is happiness itself."

Obj. 2: Further, happiness is the supreme good. But it belongs to God to be the supreme good. Since, then, there are not several supreme goods, it seems that happiness is the same as God.

Obj. 3: Further, happiness is the last end, to which man's will tends naturally. But man's will should tend to nothing else as an end, but to God, Who alone is to be enjoyed, as Augustine says (De Doctr. Christ. i, 5, 22). Therefore happiness is the same as God.

*On the contrary,* Nothing made is uncreated. But man's happiness is something made; because according to Augustine (De Doctr. Christ. i, 3): "Those things are to be enjoyed which make us happy." Therefore happiness is not something uncreated.

*I answer that,* As stated above (Q. 1, A. 8; Q. 2, A. 7), our end is twofold. First, there is the thing itself which we desire to attain: thus for the miser, the end is money. Secondly there is the attainment or possession, the use or enjoyment of the thing desired; thus we may say that the end of the miser is the possession of money; and the end of the intemperate man is to enjoy something pleasurable. In the first sense, then, man's last end is the uncreated good, namely, God, Who alone by His infinite goodness can perfectly satisfy man's will. But in the second way, man's last end is something created, existing in him, and this is nothing else than the attainment or enjoyment of the last end. Now the last end is called happiness. If, therefore, we consider man's happiness in its cause or object, then it is something uncreated; but if we consider it as to the very essence of happiness, then it is something created.

Reply Obj. 1: God is happiness by His Essence: for He is happy not by acquisition or participation of something else, but by His Essence. On the other hand, men are happy, as Boethius says (De Consol. iii), by participation; just as they are called "gods," by participation. And this participation of happiness, in respect of which man is said to be happy, is something created.

Reply Obj. 2: Happiness is called man's supreme good, because it is the attainment or enjoyment of the supreme good.

Reply Obj. 3: Happiness is said to be the last end, in the same way as the attainment of the end is called the end.

SECOND ARTICLE [I-II, Q. 3, Art. 2]

Whether Happiness Is an Operation?

Objection 1: It would seem that happiness is not an operation. For the Apostle says (Rom. 6:22): "You have your fruit unto sanctification, and the end, life everlasting." But life is not an operation, but the very being of living things. Therefore the last end, which is happiness, is not an operation.

Obj. 2: Further, Boethius says (De Consol. iii) that happiness is "a state made perfect by the aggregate of all good things." But state does not indicate operation. Therefore happiness is not an operation.

Obj. 3: Further, happiness signifies something existing in the happy one: since it is man's final perfection. But the meaning of operation does not imply anything existing in the operator, but rather something proceeding therefrom. Therefore happiness is not an operation.

Obj. 4: Further, happiness remains in the happy one. Now operation does not remain, but passes. Therefore happiness is not an operation.

Obj. 5: Further, to one man there is one happiness. But operations are many. Therefore happiness is not an operation.

Obj. 6: Further, happiness is in the happy one uninterruptedly. But human operation is often interrupted; for instance, by sleep, or some other occupation, or by cessation. Therefore happiness is not an operation.

*On the contrary,* The Philosopher says (Ethic. i, 13) that "happiness is an operation according to perfect virtue."

*I answer that,* In so far as man's happiness is something created, existing in him, we must needs say that it is an operation. For happiness is man's supreme perfection. Now each thing is perfect in so far as it is actual; since potentiality without act is imperfect. Consequently happiness must consist in man's last act. But it is evident that operation is the last act of the operator, wherefore the Philosopher calls it "second act" (De Anima ii, 1): because that which has a form can be potentially operating, just as he who knows is potentially considering. And hence it is that in other things, too, each one is said to be "for its operation" (De Coel ii, 3). Therefore man's happiness must of necessity consist in an operation.

Reply Obj. 1: Life is taken in two senses. First for the very being of the living. And thus happiness is not life: since it has been shown (Q. 2, A. 5) that the being of a man, no matter in what it may consist, is not that man's happiness; for of God alone is it true that His Being is His Happiness. Secondly, life means the operation of the living, by which operation the principle of life is made actual: thus we speak of active and contemplative life, or of a life of pleasure. And in this sense eternal life is said to be the last end, as is clear from John 17:3: "This is eternal life, that they may know Thee, the only true God."

Reply Obj. 2: Boethius, in defining happiness, considered happiness in general: for considered thus it is the perfect common good; and he signified this by saying that happiness is "a state made perfect by the aggregate of all good things," thus implying that the state of a happy man consists in possessing the perfect good. But Aristotle expressed the very essence of happiness, showing by what man is established in this state, and that it is by some kind of operation. And so it is that he proves happiness to be "the perfect good" (Ethic. i, 7).

Reply Obj. 3: As stated in *Metaph.* ix, 7 action is twofold. One proceeds from the agent into outward matter, such as "to burn" and "to cut." And such an operation cannot be happiness: for such an operation is an action and a perfection, not of the agent, but rather of the patient, as is stated in the same passage. The other is an action that remains in the agent, such as to feel, to understand, and to will: and such an action is a perfection and an act of the agent. And such an operation can be happiness.

Reply Obj. 4: Since happiness signifies some final perfection; according as various things capable of happiness can attain to various degrees of perfection, so must there be various meanings applied to happiness. For in God there is happiness essentially; since His very Being is His operation, whereby He enjoys no other than Himself. In the happy angels, the final perfection is in respect of some operation, by which they are united to the Uncreated Good: and this operation of theirs is one only and everlasting. But in men, according to their present state of life, the final perfection is in respect of an operation whereby man is united to God: but this operation neither can be continual, nor, consequently, is it one only, because operation is multiplied by being discontinued. And for this reason in the present state of life, perfect happiness cannot be attained by man. Wherefore the Philosopher, in placing man's happiness in this life (Ethic. i, 10), says that it is imperfect, and after a long discussion, concludes: "We call men happy, but only as men." But God has promised us perfect happiness, when we shall be "as the angels ... in heaven" (Matt. 22:30).

Consequently in regard to this perfect happiness, the objection fails: because in that state of happiness, man's mind will be united to God by one, continual, everlasting operation. But in the present life, in as far as we fall short of the unity and continuity of that operation so do we fall short of perfect happiness. Nevertheless it is a participation of happiness: and so much the greater, as the operation can be more continuous and more one. Consequently the active life, which is busy with many things, has less of happiness than the contemplative life, which is busied with one thing, i.e. the contemplation of truth. And if at any time man is not actually engaged in this operation, yet since he can always easily turn to it, and since he ordains the very cessation, by sleeping or occupying himself otherwise, to the aforesaid occupation, the latter seems, as it were, continuous. From these remarks the replies to Objections 5 and 6 are evident.

THIRD ARTICLE [I-II, Q. 3, Art. 3]

Whether Happiness Is an Operation of the Sensitive Part, or of the Intellective Part Only?

Objection 1: It would seem that happiness consists in an operation of the senses also. For there is no more excellent operation in man than that of the senses, except the intellective operation. But in us the intellective operation depends on the sensitive: since "we cannot understand without a phantasm" (De Anima iii, 7). Therefore happiness consists in an operation of the senses also.

Obj. 2: Further, Boethius says (De Consol. iii) that happiness is "a state made perfect by the aggregate of all good things." But some goods are sensible, which we attain by the operation of the senses. Therefore it seems that the operation of the senses is needed for happiness.

Obj. 3: Further, happiness is the perfect good, as we find proved in *Ethic.* i, 7: which would not be true, were not man perfected thereby in all his parts. But some parts of the soul are perfected by sensitive operations. Therefore sensitive operation is required for happiness.

*On the contrary,* Irrational animals have the sensitive operation in common with us: but they have not happiness in common with us. Therefore happiness does not consist in a sensitive operation.

*I answer that,* A thing may belong to happiness in three ways: (1) essentially, (2) antecedently, (3) consequently. Now the operation of sense cannot belong to happiness essentially. For man's happiness consists essentially in his being united to the Uncreated Good, Which is his last end, as shown above (A. 1): to Which man cannot be united by an operation of his senses. Again, in like manner, because, as shown above (Q. 2, A. 5), man's happiness does not consist in goods of the body, which goods alone, however, we attain through the operation of the senses.

Nevertheless the operations of the senses can belong to happiness, both antecedently and consequently: antecedently, in respect of imperfect happiness, such as can be had in this life, since the operation of the intellect demands a previous operation of the sense; consequently, in that perfect happiness which we await in heaven; because at the resurrection, "from the very happiness of the soul," as Augustine says (Ep. ad Dioscor.) "the body and the bodily senses will receive a certain overflow, so as to be perfected in their operations"; a point which will be explained further on when we treat of the resurrection (Suppl. QQ. 82-85). But then the operation whereby man's mind is united to God will not depend on the senses.

Reply Obj. 1: This objection proves that the operation of the senses is required antecedently for imperfect happiness, such as can be had in this life.

Reply Obj. 2: Perfect happiness, such as the angels have, includes the aggregate of all good things, by being united to the universal source of all good; not that it requires each individual good. But in this imperfect happiness, we need the aggregate of those goods that suffice for the most perfect operation of this life.

Reply Obj. 3: In perfect happiness the entire man is perfected, in the lower part of his nature, by an overflow from the higher. But in the imperfect happiness of this life, it is otherwise; we advance from the perfection of the lower part to the perfection of the higher part.

FOURTH ARTICLE [I-II, Q. 3, Art. 4]

Whether, If Happiness Is in the Intellective Part, It Is an Operation of the Intellect or of the Will?

Objection 1: It would seem that happiness consists in an act of the will. For Augustine says (De Civ. Dei xix, 10, 11), that man's happiness consists in peace; wherefore it is written (Ps. 147:3): "Who hath placed peace in thy end [Douay: 'borders']". But peace pertains to the will. Therefore man's happiness is in the will.

Obj. 2: Further, happiness is the supreme good. But good is the object of the will. Therefore happiness consists in an operation of the will.

Obj. 3: Further, the last end corresponds to the first mover: thus the last end of the whole army is victory, which is the end of the general, who moves all the men. But the first mover in regard to operations is the will: because it moves the other powers, as we shall state further on (Q. 9, AA. 1, 3). Therefore happiness regards the will.

Obj. 4: Further, if happiness be an operation, it must needs be man's most excellent operation. But the love of God, which is an act of the will, is a more excellent operation than knowledge, which is an operation of the intellect, as the Apostle declares (1 Cor. 13). Therefore it seems that happiness consists in an act of the will.

Obj. 5: Further, Augustine says (De Trin. xiii, 5) that "happy is he who has whatever he desires, and desires nothing amiss." And a little further on (6) he adds: "He is most happy who desires well, whatever he desires: for good things make a man happy, and such a man already possesses some good—i.e. a good will." Therefore happiness consists in an act of the will.

*On the contrary,* Our Lord said (John 17:3): "This is eternal life: that they may know Thee, the only true God." Now eternal life is the last end, as stated above (A. 2, ad 1). Therefore man's happiness consists in the knowledge of God, which is an act of the intellect.

*I answer that,* As stated above (Q. 2, A. 6) two things are needed for happiness: one, which is the essence of happiness: the other, that is, as it were, its proper accident, i.e. the delight connected with it. I say, then, that as to the very essence of happiness, it is impossible for it to consist in an act of the will. For it is evident from what has been said (AA. 1, 2; Q. 2, A. 7) that happiness is the attainment of the last end. But the attainment of the end does not consist in the very act of the will. For the will is directed to the end, both absent, when it desires it; and present, when it is delighted by resting therein. Now it is evident that the desire itself of the end is not the attainment of the end, but is a movement towards the end: while delight comes to the will from the end being present; and not conversely, is a thing made present, by the fact that the will delights in it. Therefore, that the end be present to him who desires it, must be due to something else than an act of the will.

This is evidently the case in regard to sensible ends. For if the acquisition of money were through an act of the will, the covetous man would have it from the very moment that he wished for it. But at the moment it is far from him; and he attains it, by grasping it in his hand, or in some like manner; and then he delights in the money got. And so it is with an intelligible end. For at first we desire to attain an intelligible end; we attain it, through its being made present to us by an act of the intellect; and then the delighted will rests in the end when attained.

So, therefore, the essence of happiness consists in an act of the intellect: but the delight that results from happiness pertains to the will. In this sense Augustine says (Confess. x, 23) that happiness is "joy in truth," because, to wit, joy itself is the consummation of happiness.

Reply Obj. 1: Peace pertains to man's last end, not as though it were the very essence of happiness; but because it is antecedent and consequent thereto: antecedent, in so far as all those things are removed which disturb and hinder man in attaining the last end: consequent inasmuch as when man has attained his last end, he remains at peace, his desire being at rest.

Reply Obj. 2: The will's first object is not its act: just as neither is the first object of the sight, vision, but a visible thing. Wherefore, from the very fact that happiness belongs to the will, as the will's first object, it follows that it does not belong to it as its act.

Reply Obj. 3: The intellect apprehends the end before the will does: yet motion towards the end begins in the will. And therefore to the will belongs that which last of all follows the attainment of the end, viz. delight or enjoyment.

Reply Obj. 4: Love ranks above knowledge in moving, but knowledge precedes love in attaining: for "naught is loved save what is known," as Augustine says (De Trin. x, 1). Consequently we first attain an intelligible end by an act of the intellect; just as we first attain a sensible end by an act of sense.

Reply Obj. 5: He who has whatever he desires, is happy, because he has what he desires: and this indeed is by something other than the act of his will. But to desire nothing amiss is needed for happiness, as a necessary disposition thereto. And a good will is reckoned among the good things which make a man happy, forasmuch as it is an inclination of the will: just as a movement is reduced to the genus of its terminus, for instance, "alteration" to the genus "quality."

FIFTH ARTICLE [I-II, Q. 3, Art. 5]

Whether Happiness Is an Operation of the Speculative, or of the Practical Intellect?

Objection 1: It would seem that happiness is an operation of the practical intellect. For the end of every creature consists in becoming like God. But man is like God, by his practical intellect, which is the cause of things understood, rather than by his speculative intellect, which derives its knowledge from things. Therefore man's happiness consists in an operation of the practical intellect rather than of the speculative.

Obj. 2: Further, happiness is man's perfect good. But the practical intellect is ordained to the good rather than the speculative intellect, which is ordained to the true. Hence we are said to be good, in reference to the perfection of the practical intellect, but not in reference to the perfection of the speculative intellect, according to which we are said to be knowing or understanding. Therefore man's happiness consists in an act of the practical intellect rather than of the speculative.

Obj. 3: Further, happiness is a good of man himself. But the speculative intellect is more concerned with things outside man; whereas the practical intellect is concerned with things belonging to man himself, viz. his operations and passions. Therefore man's happiness consists in an operation of the practical intellect rather than of the speculative.

*On the contrary,* Augustine says (De Trin. i, 8) that "contemplation is promised us, as being the goal of all our actions, and the everlasting perfection of our joys."

*I answer that,* Happiness consists in an operation of the speculative rather than of the practical intellect. This is evident for three reasons. First because if man's happiness is an operation, it must needs be man's highest operation. Now man's highest operation is that of his highest power in respect of its highest object: and his highest power is the intellect, whose highest object is the Divine Good, which is the object, not of the practical but of the speculative intellect. Consequently happiness consists principally in such an operation, viz. in the contemplation of Divine things. And since that "seems to be each man's self, which is best in him," according to *Ethic.* ix, 8, and x, 7, therefore such an operation is most proper to man and most delightful to him.

Secondly, it is evident from the fact that contemplation is sought principally for its own sake. But the act of the practical intellect is not sought for its own sake but for the sake of action: and these very actions are ordained to some end. Consequently it is evident that the last end cannot consist in the active life, which pertains to the practical intellect.

Thirdly, it is again evident, from the fact that in the contemplative life man has something in common with things above him, viz. with God and the angels, to whom he is made like by happiness. But in things pertaining to the active life, other animals also have something in common with man, although imperfectly.

Therefore the last and perfect happiness, which we await in the life to come, consists entirely in contemplation. But imperfect happiness, such as can be had here, consists first and principally, in an operation of the practical intellect directing human actions and passions, as stated in *Ethic.* x, 7, 8.

Reply Obj. 1: The asserted likeness of the practical intellect to God is one of proportion; that is to say, by reason of its standing in relation to what it knows, as God does to what He knows. But the likeness of the speculative intellect to God is one of union and "information"; which is a much greater likeness. And yet it may be answered that, in regard to the principal thing known, which is His Essence, God has not practical but merely speculative knowledge.

Reply Obj. 2: The practical intellect is ordained to good which is outside of it: but the speculative intellect has good within it, viz. the contemplation of truth. And if this good be perfect, the whole man is perfected and made good thereby: such a good the practical intellect has not; but it directs man thereto.

Reply Obj. 3: This argument would hold, if man himself were his own last end; for then the consideration and direction of his actions and passions would be his happiness. But since man's last end is something outside of him, to wit, God, to Whom we reach out by an operation of the speculative intellect; therefore, man's happiness consists in an operation of the speculative intellect rather than of the practical intellect.

SIXTH ARTICLE [I-II, Q. 3, Art. 6]

Whether Happiness Consists in the Consideration of Speculative Sciences?

Objection 1: It would seem that man's happiness consists in the consideration of speculative sciences. For the Philosopher says (Ethic. i, 13) that "happiness is an operation according to perfect virtue." And in distinguishing the virtues, he gives no more than three speculative virtues—"knowledge," "wisdom" and "understanding," which all belong to the consideration of speculative sciences. Therefore man's final happiness consists in the consideration of speculative sciences.

Obj. 2: Further, that which all desire for its own sake, seems to be man's final happiness. Now such is the consideration of speculative sciences; because, as stated in *Metaph.* i, 1, "all men naturally desire to know"; and, a little farther on (2), it is stated that speculative sciences are sought for their own sakes. Therefore happiness consists in the consideration of speculative sciences.

Obj. 3: Further, happiness is man's final perfection. Now everything is perfected, according as it is reduced from potentiality to act. But the human intellect is reduced to act by the consideration of speculative sciences. Therefore it seems that in the consideration of these sciences, man's final happiness consists.

*On the contrary,* It is written (Jer. 9:23): "Let not the wise man glory in his wisdom": and this is said in reference to speculative sciences. Therefore man's final happiness does not consist in the consideration of these.

*I answer that,* As stated above (A. 2, ad 4), man's happiness is twofold, one perfect, the other imperfect. And by perfect happiness we are to understand that which attains to the true notion of happiness; and by imperfect happiness that which does not attain thereto, but partakes of some particular likeness of happiness. Thus perfect prudence is in man, with whom is the idea of things to be done; while imperfect prudence is in certain irrational animals, who are possessed of certain particular instincts in respect of works similar to works of prudence.

Accordingly perfect happiness cannot consist essentially in the consideration of speculative sciences. To prove this, we must observe that the consideration of a speculative science does not extend beyond the scope of the principles of that science: since the entire science is virtually contained in its principles. Now the first principles of speculative sciences are received through the senses, as the Philosopher clearly states at the beginning of the *Metaphysics* (i, 1), and at the end of the Posterior Analytics (ii, 15). Wherefore the entire consideration of speculative sciences cannot extend farther than knowledge of sensibles can lead. Now man's final happiness, which is his final perfection cannot consist in the knowledge of sensibles. For a thing is not perfected by something lower, except in so far as the lower partakes of something higher. Now it is evident that the form of a stone or of any sensible, is lower than man. Consequently the intellect is not perfected by the form of a stone, as such, but inasmuch as it partakes of a certain likeness to that which is above the human intellect, viz. the intelligible light, or something of the kind. Now whatever is by something else is reduced to that which is of itself. Therefore man's final perfection must needs be through knowledge of something above the human intellect. But it has been shown (I, Q. 88, A. 2), that man cannot acquire through sensibles, the knowledge of separate substances, which are above the human intellect. Consequently it follows that man's happiness cannot consist in the consideration of speculative sciences. However, just as in sensible forms there is a participation of the higher substances, so the consideration of speculative sciences is a certain participation of true and perfect happiness.

Reply Obj. 1: In his book on Ethics the Philosopher treats of imperfect happiness, such as can be had in this life, as stated above (A. 2, ad 4).

Reply Obj. 2: Not only is perfect happiness naturally desired, but also any likeness or participation thereof.

Reply Obj. 3: Our intellect is reduced to act, in a fashion, by the consideration of speculative sciences, but not to its final and perfect act.

SEVENTH ARTICLE [I-II, Q. 3, Art. 7]

Whether Happiness Consists in the Knowledge of Separate Substances, Namely, Angels?

Objection 1: It would seem that man's happiness consists in the knowledge of separate substances, namely, angels. For Gregory says in a homily (xxvi in Evang.): "It avails nothing to take part in the feasts of men, if we fail to take part in the feasts of angels"; by which he means final happiness. But we can take part in the feasts of the angels by contemplating them. Therefore it seems that man's final happiness consists in contemplating the angels.

Obj. 2: Further, the final perfection of each thing is for it to be united to its principle: wherefore a circle is said to be a perfect figure, because its beginning and end coincide. But the beginning of human knowledge is from the angels, by whom men are enlightened, as Dionysius says (Coel. Hier. iv). Therefore the perfection of the human intellect consists in contemplating the angels.

Obj. 3: Further, each nature is perfect, when united to a higher nature; just as the final perfection of a body is to be united to the spiritual nature. But above the human intellect, in the natural order, are the angels. Therefore the final perfection of the human intellect is to be united to the angels by contemplation.

*On the contrary,* It is written (Jer. 9:24): "Let him that glorieth, glory in this, that he understandeth and knoweth Me." Therefore man's final glory or happiness consists only in the knowledge of God.

*I answer that,* As stated above (A. 6), man's perfect happiness consists not in that which perfects the intellect by some participation, but in that which is so by its essence. Now it is evident that whatever is the perfection of a power is so in so far as the proper formal object of that power belongs to it. Now the proper object of the intellect is the true. Therefore the contemplation of whatever has participated truth, does not perfect the intellect with its final perfection. Since, therefore, the order of things is the same in being and in truth (Metaph. ii, 1); whatever are beings by participation, are true by participation. Now angels have being by participation: because in God alone is His Being His Essence, as shown in the First Part (Q. 44, A. 1). It follows that contemplation of Him makes man perfectly happy. However, there is no reason why we should not admit a certain imperfect happiness in the contemplation of the angels; and higher indeed than in the consideration of speculative science.

Reply Obj. 1: We shall take part in the feasts of the angels, by contemplating not only the angels, but, together with them, also God Himself.

Reply Obj. 2: According to those that hold human souls to be created by the angels, it seems fitting enough, that man's happiness should consist in the contemplation of the angels, in the union, as it were, of man with his beginning. But this is erroneous, as stated in the First Part (Q. 90, A. 3). Wherefore the final perfection of the human intellect is by union with God, Who is the first principle both of the creation of the soul and of its enlightenment. Whereas the angel enlightens as a minister, as stated in the First Part (Q. 111, A. 2, ad 2). Consequently, by his ministration he helps man to attain to happiness; but he is not the object of man's happiness.

Reply Obj. 3: The lower nature may reach the higher in two ways. First, according to a degree of the participating power: and thus man's final perfection will consist in his attaining to a contemplation such as that of the angels. Secondly, as the object is attained by the power: and thus the final perfection of each power is to attain that in which is found the fulness of its formal object.

EIGHTH ARTICLE [I-II, Q. 3, Art. 8]

Whether Man's Happiness Consists in the Vision of the Divine Essence?

Objection 1: It would seem that man's happiness does not consist in the vision of the Divine Essence. For Dionysius says (Myst. Theol. i) that by that which is highest in his intellect, man is united to God as to something altogether unknown. But that which is seen in its essence is not altogether unknown. Therefore the final perfection of the intellect, namely, happiness, does not consist in God being seen in His Essence.

Obj. 2: Further, the higher the perfection belongs to the higher nature. But to see His own Essence is the perfection proper to the Divine intellect. Therefore the final perfection of the human intellect does not reach to this, but consists in something less.

*On the contrary,* It is written (1 John 3:2): "When He shall appear, we shall be like to Him; and [Vulg.: 'because'] we shall see Him as He is."

*I answer that,* Final and perfect happiness can consist in nothing else than the vision of the Divine Essence. To make this clear, two points must be observed. First, that man is not perfectly happy, so long as something remains for him to desire and seek: secondly, that the perfection of any power is determined by the nature of its object. Now the object of the intellect is "what a thing is," i.e. the essence of a thing, according to *De Anima* iii, 6. Wherefore the intellect attains perfection, in so far as it knows the essence of a thing. If therefore an intellect knows the essence of some effect, whereby it is not possible to know the essence of the cause, i.e. to know of the cause "what it is"; that intellect cannot be said to reach that cause simply, although it may be able to gather from the effect the knowledge that the cause is. Consequently, when man knows an effect, and knows that it has a cause, there naturally remains in the man the desire to know about the cause, "what it is." And this desire is one of wonder, and causes inquiry, as is stated in the beginning of the *Metaphysics* (i, 2). For instance, if a man, knowing the eclipse of the sun, consider that it must be due to some cause, and know not what that cause is, he wonders about it, and from wondering proceeds to inquire. Nor does this inquiry cease until he arrive at a knowledge of the essence of the cause.

If therefore the human intellect, knowing the essence of some created effect, knows no more of God than "that He is"; the perfection of that intellect does not yet reach simply the First Cause, but there remains in it the natural desire to seek the cause. Wherefore it is not yet perfectly happy. Consequently, for perfect happiness the intellect needs to reach the very Essence of the First Cause. And thus it will have its perfection through union with God as with that object, in which alone man's happiness consists, as stated above (AA. 1, 7; Q. 2, A. 8).

Reply Obj. 1: Dionysius speaks of the knowledge of wayfarers journeying towards happiness.

Reply Obj. 2: As stated above (Q. 1, A. 8), the end has a twofold acceptation. First, as to the thing itself which is desired: and in this way, the same thing is the end of the higher and of the lower nature, and indeed of all things, as stated above (Q. 1, A. 8). Secondly, as to the attainment of this thing; and thus the end of the higher nature is different from that of the lower, according to their respective habitudes to that thing. So then in the happiness of God, Who, in understanding his Essence, comprehends It, is higher than that of a man or angel who sees It indeed, but comprehends It not.

# QUESTION 4

OF THOSE THINGS THAT ARE REQUIRED FOR HAPPINESS (In Eight Articles)

We have now to consider those things that are required for happiness: and concerning this there are eight points of inquiry:

(1) Whether delight is required for happiness?

(2) Which is of greater account in happiness, delight or vision?

(3) Whether comprehension is required?

(4) Whether rectitude of the will is required?

(5) Whether the body is necessary for man's happiness?

(6) Whether any perfection of the body is necessary?

(7) Whether any external goods are necessary?

(8) Whether the fellowship of friends is necessary?

FIRST ARTICLE [I-II, Q. 4, Art. 1]

Whether Delight Is Required for Happiness?

Objection 1: It would seem that delight is not required for happiness. For Augustine says (De Trin. i, 8) that "vision is the entire reward of faith." But the prize or reward of virtue is happiness, as the Philosopher clearly states (Ethic. i, 9). Therefore nothing besides vision is required for happiness.

Obj. 2: Further, happiness is "the most self-sufficient of all goods," as the Philosopher declares (Ethic. i, 7). But that which needs something else is not self-sufficient. Since then the essence of happiness consists in seeing God, as stated above (Q. 3, A. 8); it seems that delight is not necessary for happiness.

Obj. 3: Further, the "operation of bliss or happiness should be unhindered" (Ethic. vii, 13). But delight hinders the operation of the intellect: since it destroys the estimate of prudence (Ethic. vi, 5). Therefore delight is not necessary for happiness.

*On the contrary,* Augustine says (Confess. x, 23) that happiness is "joy in truth."

*I answer that,* One thing may be necessary for another in four ways. First, as a preamble and preparation to it: thus instruction is necessary for science. Secondly, as perfecting it: thus the soul is necessary for the life of the body. Thirdly, as helping it from without: thus friends are necessary for some undertaking. Fourthly, as something attendant on it: thus we might say that heat is necessary for fire. And in this way delight is necessary for happiness. For it is caused by the appetite being at rest in the good attained. Wherefore, since happiness is nothing else but the attainment of the Sovereign Good, it cannot be without concomitant delight.

Reply Obj. 1: From the very fact that a reward is given to anyone, the will of him who deserves it is at rest, and in this consists delight. Consequently, delight is included in the very notion of reward.

Reply Obj. 2: The very sight of God causes delight. Consequently, he who sees God cannot need delight.

Reply Obj. 3: Delight that is attendant upon the operation of the intellect does not hinder it, rather does it perfect it, as stated in *Ethic.* x, 4: since what we do with delight, we do with greater care and perseverance. On the other hand, delight which is extraneous to the operation is a hindrance thereto: sometimes by distracting the attention because, as already observed, we are more attentive to those things that delight us; and when we are very attentive to one thing, we must needs be less attentive to another: sometimes on account of opposition; thus a sensual delight that is contrary to reason, hinders the estimate of prudence more than it hinders the estimate of the speculative intellect.

SECOND ARTICLE [I-II, Q. 4, Art. 2]

Whether in Happiness Vision Ranks Before Delight?

Objection 1: It would seem that in happiness, delight ranks before vision. For "delight is the perfection of operation" (Ethic. x, 4). But perfection ranks before the thing perfected. Therefore delight ranks before the operation of the intellect, i.e. vision.

Obj. 2: Further, that by reason of which a thing is desirable, is yet more desirable. But operations are desired on account of the delight they afford: hence, too, nature has adjusted delight to those operations which are necessary for the preservation of the individual and of the species, lest animals should disregard such operations. Therefore, in happiness, delight ranks before the operation of the intellect, which is vision.

Obj. 3: Further, vision corresponds to faith; while delight or enjoyment corresponds to charity. But charity ranks before faith, as the Apostle says (1 Cor. 13:13). Therefore delight or enjoyment ranks before vision.

*On the contrary,* The cause is greater than its effect. But vision is the cause of delight. Therefore vision ranks before delight.

*I answer that,* The Philosopher discusses this

question (Ethic. x, 4), and leaves it unsolved. But if one consider the matter carefully, the operation of the intellect which is vision, must needs rank before delight. For delight consists in a certain repose of the will. Now that the will finds rest in anything, can only be on account of the goodness of that thing in which it reposes. If therefore the will reposes in an operation, the will's repose is caused by the goodness of the operation. Nor does the will seek good for the sake of repose; for thus the very act of the will would be the end, which has been disproved above (Q. 1, A. 1, ad 2;Q. 3, A. 4): but it seeks to be at rest in the operation, because that operation is its good. Consequently it is evident that the operation in which the will reposes ranks before the resting of the will therein.

Reply Obj. 1: As the Philosopher says (Ethic. x, 4) "delight perfects operation as vigor perfects youth," because it is a result of youth. Consequently delight is a perfection attendant upon vision; but not a perfection whereby vision is made perfect in its own species.

Reply Obj. 2: The apprehension of the senses does not attain to the universal good, but to some particular good which is delightful. And consequently, according to the sensitive appetite which is in animals, operations are sought for the sake of delight. But the intellect apprehends the universal good, the attainment of which results in delight: wherefore its purpose is directed to good rather than to delight. Hence it is that the Divine intellect, which is the Author of nature, adjusted delights to operations on account of the operations. And we should form our estimate of things not simply according to the order of the sensitive appetite, but rather according to the order of the intellectual appetite.

Reply Obj. 3: Charity does not seek the beloved good for the sake of delight: it is for charity a consequence that it delights in the good gained which it loves. Thus delight does not answer to charity as its end, but vision does, whereby the end is first made present to charity.

THIRD ARTICLE [I-II, Q. 4, Art. 3]

Whether Comprehension Is Necessary for Happiness?

Objection 1: It would seem that comprehension is not necessary for happiness. For Augustine says (Ad Paulinam de Videndo Deum; [*Cf. Serm. xxxciii De Verb. Dom.]): "To reach God with the mind is happiness, to comprehend Him is impossible." Therefore happiness is without comprehension.

Obj. 2: Further, happiness is the perfection of man as to his intellective part, wherein there are no other powers than the intellect and will, as stated in the First Part (QQ. 79 and following). But the intellect is sufficiently perfected by seeing God, and the will by enjoying Him. Therefore there is no need for comprehension as a third.

Obj. 3: Further, happiness consists in an operation. But operations are determined by their objects: and there are two universal objects, the true and the good: of which the true corresponds to vision, and good to delight. Therefore there is no need for comprehension as a third.

*On the contrary,* The Apostle says (1 Cor. 9:24): "So run that you may comprehend [Douay: 'obtain']." But happiness is the goal of the spiritual race: hence he says (2 Tim. 4:7, 8): "I have fought a good fight, I have finished my course, I have kept the faith; as to the rest there is laid up for me a crown of justice." Therefore comprehension is necessary for Happiness.

*I answer that,* Since Happiness consists in gaining the last end, those things that are required for Happiness must be gathered from the way in which man is ordered to an end. Now man is ordered to an intelligible end partly through his intellect, and partly through his will: through his intellect, in so far as a certain imperfect knowledge of the end pre-exists in the intellect: through the will, first by love which is the will's first movement towards anything; secondly, by a real relation of the lover to the thing beloved, which relation may be threefold. For sometimes the thing beloved is present to the lover: and then it is no longer sought for. Sometimes it is not present, and it is impossible to attain it: and then, too, it is not sought for. But sometimes it is possible to attain it, yet it is raised above the capability of the attainer, so that he cannot have it forthwith; and this is the relation of one that hopes, to that which he hopes for, and this relation alone causes a search for the end. To these three, there are a corresponding three in Happiness itself. For perfect knowledge of the end corresponds to imperfect knowledge; presence of the end corresponds to the relation of hope; but delight in the end now present results from love, as already stated (A. 2, ad 3). And therefore these three must concur with Happiness; to wit, vision, which is perfect knowledge of the intelligible end; comprehension, which implies presence of the end; and delight or enjoyment, which implies repose of the lover in the object beloved.

Reply Obj. 1: Comprehension is twofold. First, inclusion of the comprehended in the comprehensor; and thus whatever is comprehended by the finite, is itself finite. Wherefore God cannot be thus comprehended by a created intellect. Secondly, comprehension means nothing but the holding of something already present and possessed: thus one who runs after another is said to comprehend [*In English we should say 'catch.'] him when he lays hold on him. And in this sense comprehension is necessary for Happiness.

Reply Obj. 2: Just as hope and love pertain to the will, because it is the same one that loves a thing, and that tends towards it while not possessed, so, too, comprehension and delight belong to the will, since it is the same that possesses a thing and reposes therein.

Reply Obj. 3: Comprehension is not a distinct operation from vision; but a certain relation to the end already gained. Wherefore even vision itself, or the thing seen, inasmuch as it is present, is the object of comprehension.

FOURTH ARTICLE [I-II, Q. 4, Art. 4]

Whether Rectitude of the Will Is Necessary for Happiness?

Objection 1: It would seem that rectitude of the will is not necessary for Happiness. For Happiness consists essentially in an operation of the intellect, as stated above (Q. 3, A. 4). But rectitude of the will, by reason of which men are said to be clean of heart, is not necessary for the perfect operation of the intellect: for Augustine says (Retract. i, 4) "I do not approve of what I said in a prayer: O God, Who didst will none but the clean of heart to know the truth. For it can be answered that many who are not clean of heart, know many truths." Therefore rectitude of the will is not necessary for Happiness.

Obj. 2: Further, what precedes does not depend on what follows. But the operation of the intellect precedes the operation of the will. Therefore Happiness, which is the perfect operation of the intellect, does not depend on rectitude of the will.

Obj. 3: Further, that which is ordained to another as its end, is not necessary, when the end is already gained; as a ship, for instance, after arrival in port. But rectitude of will, which is by reason of virtue, is ordained to Happiness as to its end. Therefore, Happiness once obtained, rectitude of the will is no longer necessary.

*On the contrary,* It is written (Matt. 5:8): "Blessed are the clean of heart; for they shall see God": and (Heb. 12:14): "Follow peace with all men, and holiness; without which no man shall see God."

*I answer that,* Rectitude of will is necessary for Happiness both antecedently and concomitantly. Antecedently, because rectitude of the will consists in being duly ordered to the last end. Now the end in comparison to what is ordained to the end is as form compared to matter. Wherefore, just as matter cannot receive a form, unless it be duly disposed thereto, so nothing gains an end, except it be duly ordained thereto. And therefore none can obtain Happiness, without rectitude of the will. Concomitantly, because as stated above (Q. 3, A. 8), final Happiness consists in the vision of the Divine Essence, Which is the very essence of goodness. So that the will of him who sees the Essence of God, of necessity, loves, whatever he loves, in subordination to God; just as the will of him who sees not God's Essence, of necessity, loves whatever he loves, under the common notion of good which he knows. And this is precisely what makes the will right. Wherefore it is evident that Happiness cannot be without a right will.

[Reply Obj. 1: Augustine is speaking of knowledge of truth that is not the essence of goodness itself.]

Reply Obj. 2: Every act of the will is preceded by an act of the intellect: but a certain act of the will precedes a certain act of the intellect. For the will tends to the final act of the intellect which is happiness. And consequently right inclination of the will is required antecedently for happiness, just as the arrow must take a right course in order to strike the target.

Reply Obj. 3: Not everything that is ordained to the end, ceases with the getting of the end: but only that which involves imperfection, such as movement. Hence the instruments of movement are no longer necessary when the end has been gained: but the due order to the end is necessary.

FIFTH ARTICLE [I-II, Q. 4, Art. 5]

Whether the Body Is Necessary for Man's Happiness?

Objection 1: It would seem that the body is necessary for Happiness. For the perfection of virtue and grace presupposes the perfection of nature. But Happiness is the perfection of virtue and grace. Now the soul, without the body, has not the perfection of nature; since it is naturally a part of human nature, and every part is imperfect while separated from its whole. Therefore the soul cannot be happy without the body.

Obj. 2: Further, Happiness is a perfect operation, as stated above (Q. 3, AA. 2, 5). But perfect operation follows perfect being: since nothing operates except in so far as it is an actual being. Since, therefore, the soul has not perfect being, while it is separated from the body, just as neither has a part, while separate from its whole; it seems that the soul cannot be happy without the body.

Obj. 3: Further, Happiness is the perfection of man. But the soul, without the body, is not man. Therefore Happiness cannot be in the soul separated from the body.

Obj. 4: Further, according to the Philosopher (Ethic. vii, 13) "the operation of bliss," in which operation happiness consists, is "not hindered." But the operation of the separate soul is hindered; because, as Augustine says (Gen. ad lit. xii, 35), the soul "has a natural desire to rule the body, the result of which is that it is held back, so to speak, from tending with all its might to the heavenward journey," i.e. to the vision of the Divine Essence. Therefore the soul cannot be happy without the body.

Obj. 5: Further, Happiness is the sufficient good and lulls desire. But this cannot be said of the separated soul; for it yet desires to be united to the body, as Augustine says (Gen. ad lit. xii, 35). Therefore the soul is not happy while separated from the body.

Obj. 6: Further, in Happiness man is equal to the angels. But the soul without the body is not equal to the angels, as Augustine says (Gen. ad lit. xii, 35). Therefore it is not happy.

*On the contrary,* It is written (Apoc. 14:13): "Happy [Douay: 'blessed'] are the dead who die in the Lord."

*I answer that,* Happiness is twofold; the one is imperfect and is had in this life; the other is perfect, consisting in the vision of God. Now it is evident that the body is necessary for the happiness of this life. For the happiness of this life consists in an operation of the intellect, either speculative or practical. And the operation of the intellect in this life cannot be without a phantasm, which is only in a bodily organ, as was shown in the First Part (Q. 84, AA. 6, 7). Consequently that happiness which can be had in this life, depends, in a way, on the body. But as to perfect Happiness, which consists in the vision of God, some have maintained that it is not possible to the soul separated from the body; and have said that the souls of saints, when separated from their bodies, do not attain to that Happiness until the Day of Judgment, when they will receive their bodies back again. And this is shown to be false, both by authority and by reason. By authority, since the Apostle says (2 Cor. 5:6): "While we are in the body, we are absent from the Lord"; and he points out the reason of this absence, saying: "For we walk by faith and not by sight." Now from this it is clear that so long as we walk by faith and not by sight, bereft of the vision of the Divine Essence, we are not present to the Lord. But the souls of the saints, separated from their bodies, are in God's presence; wherefore the text continues: "But we are confident and have a good will to be absent ... from the body, and to be present with the Lord." Whence it is evident that the souls of the saints, separated from their bodies, "walk by sight," seeing the Essence of God, wherein is true Happiness.

Again this is made clear by reason. For the intellect needs not the body, for its operation, save on account of the phantasms, wherein it looks on the intelligible truth, as stated in the First Part (Q. 84, A. 7). Now it is evident that the Divine Essence cannot be seen by means of phantasms, as stated in the First Part (Q. 12, A. 3). Wherefore, since man's perfect Happiness consists in the vision of the Divine Essence, it does not depend on the body. Consequently, without the body the soul can be happy.

We must, however, notice that something may belong to a thing's perfection in two ways. First, as constituting the essence thereof; thus the soul is necessary for man's perfection. Secondly, as necessary for its well-being: thus, beauty of body and keenness of perfection belong to man's perfection. Wherefore though the body does not belong in the first way to the perfection of human Happiness, yet it does in the second way. For since operation depends on a thing's nature, the more perfect is the soul in its nature, the more perfectly it has its proper operation, wherein its happiness consists. Hence, Augustine, after inquiring (Gen. ad lit. xii, 35) "whether that perfect Happiness can be ascribed to the souls of the dead separated from their bodies," answers "that they cannot see the Unchangeable Substance, as the blessed angels see It; either for some other more hidden reason, or because they have a natural desire to rule the body."

Reply Obj. 1: Happiness is the perfection of the soul on the part of the intellect, in respect of which the soul transcends the organs of the body; but not according as the soul is the natural form of the body. Wherefore the soul retains that natural perfection in respect of which happiness is due to it, though it does not retain that natural perfection in respect of which it is the form of the body.

Reply Obj. 2: The relation of the soul to being is not the same as that of other parts: for the being of the whole is not that of any individual part: wherefore, either the part ceases altogether to be, when the whole is destroyed, just as the parts of an animal, when the animal is destroyed; or, if they remain, they have another actual being, just as a part of a line has another being from that of the whole line. But the human soul retains the being of the composite after the destruction of the body: and this because the being of the form is the same as that of its matter, and this is the being of the composite. Now the soul subsists in its own being, as stated in the First Part (Q. 75, A. 2). It follows, therefore, that after being separated from the body it has perfect being and that consequently it can have a perfect operation; although it has not the perfect specific nature.

Reply Obj. 3: Happiness belongs to man in respect of his intellect: and, therefore, since the intellect remains, it can have Happiness. Thus the teeth of an Ethiopian, in respect of which he is said to be white, can retain their whiteness, even after extraction.

Reply Obj. 4: One thing is hindered by another in two ways. First, by way of opposition; thus cold hinders the action of heat: and such a hindrance to operation is repugnant to Happiness. Secondly, by way of some kind of defect, because, to wit, that which is hindered has not all that is necessary to make it perfect in every way: and such a hindrance to operation is not incompatible with Happiness, but prevents it from being perfect in every way. And thus it is that separation from the body is said to hold the soul back from tending with all its might to the vision of the Divine Essence. For the soul desires to enjoy God in such a way that the enjoyment also may overflow into the body, as far as possible. And therefore, as long as it enjoys God, without the fellowship of the body, its appetite is at rest in that which it has, in such a way, that it would still wish the body to attain to its share.

Reply Obj. 5: The desire of the separated soul is entirely at rest, as regards the thing desired; since, to wit, it has that which suffices its appetite. But it is not wholly at rest, as regards the desirer, since it does not possess that good in every way that it would wish to possess it. Consequently, after the body has been resumed, Happiness increases not in intensity, but in extent.

Reply Obj. 6: The statement made (Gen. ad lit. xii, 35) to the effect that "the souls of the departed see not God as the angels do," is not to be understood as referring to inequality of quantity; because even now some souls of the Blessed are raised to the higher orders of the angels, thus seeing God more clearly than the lower angels. But it refers to inequality of proportion: because the angels, even the lowest, have every perfection of Happiness that they ever will have, whereas the separated souls of the saints have not.

SIXTH ARTICLE [I-II, Q. 4, Art. 6]

Whether Perfection of the Body Is Necessary for Happiness?

Objection 1: It would seem that perfection of the body is not necessary for man's perfect Happiness. For perfection of the body is a bodily good. But it has been shown above (Q. 2) that Happiness does not consist in bodily goods. Therefore no perfect disposition of the body is necessary for man's Happiness.

Obj. 2: Further, man's Happiness consists in the vision of the Divine Essence, as shown above (Q. 3, A. 8). But the body has no part in this operation, as shown above (A. 5). Therefore no disposition of the body is necessary for Happiness.

Obj. 3: Further, the more the intellect is abstracted from the body, the more perfectly it understands. But Happiness consists in the most perfect operation of the intellect. Therefore the soul should be abstracted from the body in every way. Therefore, in no way is a disposition of the body necessary for Happiness.

*On the contrary,* Happiness is the reward of virtue; wherefore it is written (John 13:17): "You shall be blessed, if you do them." But the reward promised to the saints is not only that they shall see and enjoy God, but also that their bodies shall be well-disposed; for it is written (Isa. 66:14): "You shall see and your heart shall rejoice, and your bones shall flourish like a herb." Therefore good disposition of the body is necessary for Happiness.

*I answer that,* If we speak of that happiness which man can acquire in this life, it is evident that a well-disposed body is of necessity required for it. For this happiness consists, according to the Philosopher (Ethic. i, 13) in "an operation according to perfect virtue"; and it is clear that man can be hindered, by indisposition of the body, from every operation of virtue.

But speaking of perfect Happiness, some have maintained that no disposition of body is necessary for Happiness; indeed, that it is necessary for the soul to be entirely separated from the body. Hence Augustine (De Civ. Dei xxii, 26) quotes the words of Porphyry who said that "for the soul to be happy, it must be severed from everything corporeal." But this is unreasonable. For since it is natural to the soul to be united to the body; it is not possible for the perfection of the soul to exclude its natural perfection.

Consequently, we must say that perfect disposition of the body is necessary, both antecedently and consequently, for that Happiness which is in all ways perfect. Antecedently, because, as Augustine says (Gen. ad lit. xii, 35), "if the body be such, that the governance thereof is difficult and burdensome, like unto flesh which is corruptible and weighs upon the soul, the mind is turned away from that vision of the highest heaven." Whence he concludes that, "when this body will no longer be 'natural,' but 'spiritual,' then will it be equalled to the angels, and that will be its glory, which erstwhile was its burden." Consequently, because from the Happiness of the soul there will be an overflow on to the body, so that this too will obtain its perfection. Hence Augustine says (Ep. ad Dioscor.) that "God gave the soul such a powerful nature that from its exceeding fulness of happiness the vigor of incorruption overflows into the lower nature."

Reply Obj. 1: Happiness does not consist in bodily good as its object: but bodily good can add a certain charm and perfection to Happiness.

Reply Obj. 2: Although the body has no part in that operation of the intellect whereby the Essence of God is seen, yet it might prove a hindrance thereto. Consequently, perfection of the body is necessary, lest it hinder the mind from being lifted up.

Reply Obj. 3: The perfect operation of the intellect requires indeed that the intellect be abstracted from this corruptible body which weighs upon the soul; but not from the spiritual body, which will be wholly subject to the spirit. On this point we shall treat in the Third Part of this work (Suppl., Q. 82, seqq.).

SEVENTH ARTICLE [I-II, Q. 4, Art. 7]

Whether Any External Goods Are Necessary for Happiness?

Objection 1: It would seem that external goods also are necessary for Happiness. For that which is promised the saints for reward, belongs to Happiness. But external goods are promised the saints; for instance, food and drink, wealth and a kingdom: for it is said (Luke 22:30): "That you may eat and drink at My table in My kingdom": and (Matt. 6:20): "Lay up to yourselves treasures in heaven": and (Matt. 25:34): "Come, ye blessed of My Father, possess you the kingdom." Therefore external goods are necessary for Happiness.

Obj. 2: Further, according to Boethius (De Consol. iii): happiness is "a state made perfect by the aggregate of all good things." But some of man's goods are external, although they be of least account, as Augustine says (De Lib. Arb. ii, 19). Therefore they too are necessary for Happiness.

Obj. 3: Further, Our Lord said (Matt. 5:12): "Your reward is very great in heaven." But to be in heaven implies being in a place. Therefore at least external place is necessary for Happiness.

*On the contrary,* It is written (Ps. 72:25): "For what have I in heaven? and besides Thee what do I desire upon earth?" As though to say: "I desire nothing but this, "—"It is good for me to adhere to my God." Therefore nothing further external is necessary for Happiness.

*I answer that,* For imperfect happiness, such as can be had in this life, external goods are necessary, not as belonging to the essence of happiness, but by serving as instruments to happiness, which consists in an operation of virtue, as stated in *Ethic.* i, 13. For man needs in this life, the necessaries of the body, both for the operation of contemplative virtue, and for the operation of active virtue, for which latter he needs also many other things by means of which to perform its operations.

On the other hand, such goods as these are nowise necessary for perfect Happiness, which consists in seeing God. The reason of this is that all suchlike external goods are requisite either for the support of the animal body; or for certain operations which belong to human life, which we perform by means of the animal body: whereas that perfect Happiness which consists in seeing God, will be either in the soul separated from the body, or in the soul united to the body then no longer animal but spiritual. Consequently these external goods are nowise necessary for that Happiness, since they are ordained to the animal life. And since, in this life, the felicity of contemplation, as being more Godlike, approaches nearer than that of action to the likeness of that perfect Happiness, therefore it stands in less need of these goods of the body as stated in *Ethic.* x, 8.

Reply Obj. 1: All those material promises contained in Holy Scripture, are to be understood metaphorically, inasmuch as Scripture is wont to express spiritual things under the form of things corporeal, in order "that from things we know, we may rise to the desire of things unknown," as Gregory says (Hom. xi in Evang.). Thus food and drink signify the delight of Happiness; wealth, the sufficiency of God for man; the kingdom, the lifting up of man to union of God.

Reply Obj. 2: These goods that serve for the animal life, are incompatible with that spiritual life wherein perfect Happiness consists. Nevertheless in that Happiness there will be the aggregate of all good things, because whatever good there be in these things, we shall possess it all in the Supreme Fount of goodness.

Reply Obj. 3: According to Augustine (De Serm. Dom. in Monte i, 5), it is not material heaven that is described as the reward of the saints, but a heaven raised on the height of spiritual goods. Nevertheless a bodily place, viz. the empyrean heaven, will be appointed to the Blessed, not as a need of Happiness, but by reason of a certain fitness and adornment.

EIGHTH ARTICLE [I-II, Q. 4, Art. 8]

Whether the Fellowship of Friends Is Necessary for Happiness?

Objection 1: It would seem that friends are necessary for Happiness. For future Happiness is frequently designated by Scripture under the name of "glory." But glory consists in man's good being brought to the notice of many. Therefore the fellowship of friends is necessary for Happiness.

Obj. 2: Further, Boethius [*Seneca, Ep. 6] says that "there is no delight in possessing any good whatever, without someone to share it with us." But delight is necessary for Happiness. Therefore fellowship of friends is also necessary.

Obj. 3: Further, charity is perfected in Happiness. But charity includes the love of God and of our neighbor. Therefore it seems that fellowship of friends is necessary for Happiness.

*On the contrary,* It is written (Wis. 7:11): "All good things came to me together with her," i.e. with divine wisdom, which consists in contemplating God. Consequently nothing else is necessary for Happiness.

*I answer that,* If we speak of the happiness of this life, the happy man needs friends, as the Philosopher says (Ethic. ix, 9), not, indeed, to make use of them, since he suffices himself; nor to delight in them, since he possesses perfect delight in the operation of virtue; but for the purpose of a good operation, viz. that he may do good to them; that he may delight in seeing them do good; and again that he may be helped by them in his good work. For in order that man may do well, whether in the works of the active life, or in those of the contemplative life, he needs the fellowship of friends.

But if we speak of perfect Happiness which will be in our heavenly Fatherland, the fellowship of friends is not essential to Happiness; since man has the entire fulness of his perfection in God. But the fellowship of friends conduces to the well-being of Happiness. Hence Augustine says (Gen. ad lit. viii, 25) that "the spiritual creatures receive no other interior aid to happiness than the eternity, truth, and charity of the Creator. But if they can be said to be helped from without, perhaps it is only by this that they see one another and rejoice in God, at their fellowship."

Reply Obj. 1: That glory which is essential to Happiness, is that which man has, not with man but with God.

Reply Obj. 2: This saying is to be understood of the possession of good that does not fully satisfy. This does not apply to the question under consideration; because man possesses in God a sufficiency of every good.

Reply Obj. 3: Perfection of charity is essential to Happiness, as to the love of God, but not as to the love of our neighbor. Wherefore if there were but one soul enjoying God, it would be happy, though having no neighbor to love. But supposing one neighbor to be there, love of him results from perfect love of God. Consequently, friendship is, as it were, concomitant with perfect Happiness.

# QUESTION 5

OF THE ATTAINMENT OF HAPPINESS (In Eight Articles)

We must now consider the attainment of Happiness. Under this heading there are eight points of inquiry:

(1) Whether man can attain Happiness?

(2) Whether one man can be happier than another?

(3) Whether any man can be happy in this life?

(4) Whether Happiness once had can be lost?

(5) Whether man can attain Happiness by means of his natural powers?

(6) Whether man attains Happiness through the action of some higher creature?

(7) Whether any actions of man are necessary in order that man may obtain Happiness of God?

(8) Whether every man desires Happiness?

FIRST ARTICLE [I-II, Q. 5, Art. 1]

Whether Man Can Attain Happiness?

Objection 1: It would seem that man cannot attain happiness. For just as the rational is above the sensible nature, so the intellectual is above the rational, as Dionysius declares (Div. Nom. iv, vi, vii) in several passages. But irrational animals that have the sensitive nature only, cannot attain the end of the rational nature. Therefore neither can man, who is of rational nature, attain the end of the intellectual nature, which is Happiness.

Obj. 2: Further, True Happiness consists in seeing God, Who is pure Truth. But from his very nature, man considers truth in material things: wherefore "he understands the intelligible species in the phantasm" (De Anima iii, 7). Therefore he cannot attain Happiness.

Obj. 3: Further, Happiness consists in attaining the Sovereign Good. But we cannot arrive at the top without surmounting the middle. Since, therefore, the angelic nature through which man cannot mount is midway between God and human nature; it seems that he cannot attain Happiness.

*On the contrary,* It is written (Ps. 93:12): "Blessed is the man whom Thou shalt instruct, O Lord."

*I answer that,* Happiness is the attainment of the Perfect Good. Whoever, therefore, is capable of the Perfect Good can attain Happiness. Now, that man is capable of the Perfect Good, is proved both because his intellect can apprehend the universal and perfect good, and because his will can desire it. And therefore man can attain Happiness. This can be proved again from the fact that man is capable of seeing God, as stated in the First Part (Q. 12, A. 1): in which vision, as we stated above (Q. 3, A. 8) man's perfect Happiness consists.

Reply Obj. 1: The rational exceeds the sensitive nature, otherwise than the intellectual surpasses the rational. For the rational exceeds the sensitive nature in respect of the object of its knowledge: since the senses have no knowledge whatever of the universal, whereas the reason has knowledge thereof. But the intellectual surpasses the rational nature, as to the mode of knowing the same intelligible truth: for the intellectual nature grasps forthwith the truth which the rational nature reaches by the inquiry of reason, as was made clear in the First Part (Q. 58, A. 3; Q. 79, A. 8). Therefore reason arrives by a kind of movement at that which the intellect grasps. Consequently the rational nature can attain Happiness, which is the perfection of the intellectual nature: but otherwise than the angels. Because the angels attained it forthwith after the beginning of their creation: whereas man attains if after a time. But the sensitive nature can nowise attain this end.

Reply Obj. 2: To man in the present state of life the natural way of knowing intelligible truth is by means of phantasms. But after this state of life, he has another natural way, as was stated in the First Part (Q. 84, A. 7; Q. 89, A. 1).

Reply Obj. 3: Man cannot surmount the angels in the degree of nature so as to be above them naturally. But he can surmount them by an operation of the intellect, by understanding that there is above the angels something that makes men happy; and when he has attained it, he will be perfectly happy.

SECOND ARTICLE [I-II, Q. 5, Art. 2]

Whether One Man Can Be Happier Than Another?

Objection 1: It would seem that one man cannot be happier than another. For Happiness is "the reward of virtue," as the Philosopher says (Ethic. i, 9). But equal reward is given for all the works of virtue; because it is written (Matt. 20:10) that all who labor in the vineyard "received every man a penny"; for, as Gregory says (Hom. xix in Evang.), "each was equally rewarded with eternal life." Therefore one man cannot be happier than another.

Obj. 2: Further, Happiness is the supreme good. But nothing can surpass the supreme. Therefore one man's Happiness cannot be surpassed by another's.

Obj. 3: Further, since Happiness is "the perfect and sufficient good" (Ethic. i, 7) it brings rest to man's desire. But his desire is not at rest, if he yet lacks some good that can be got. And if he lack nothing that he can get, there can be no still greater good. Therefore either man is not happy; or, if he be happy, no other Happiness can be greater.

*On the contrary,* It is written (John 14:2): "In My Father's house there are many mansions"; which, according to Augustine (Tract. lxvii in Joan.) signify "the diverse dignities of merits in the one eternal life." But the dignity of eternal life which is given according to merit, is Happiness itself. Therefore there are diverse degrees of Happiness, and Happiness is not equally in all.

*I answer that,* As stated above (Q. 1, A. 8; Q. 2, A. 7), Happiness implies two things, to wit, the last end itself, i.e. the Sovereign Good; and the attainment or enjoyment of that same Good. As to that Good itself, Which is the object and cause of Happiness, one Happiness cannot be greater than another, since there is but one Sovereign Good, namely, God, by enjoying Whom, men are made happy. But as to the attainment or enjoyment of this Good, one man can be happier than another; because the more a man enjoys this Good the happier he is. Now, that one man enjoys God more than another, happens through his being better disposed or ordered to the enjoyment of Him. And in this sense one man can be happier than another.

Reply Obj. 1: The one penny signifies that Happiness is one in its object. But the many mansions signify the manifold Happiness in the divers degrees of enjoyment.

Reply Obj. 2: Happiness is said to be the supreme good, inasmuch as it is the perfect possession or enjoyment of the Supreme Good.

Reply Obj. 3: None of the Blessed lacks any desirable good; since they have the Infinite Good Itself, Which is "the good of all good," as Augustine says (Enarr. in Ps. 134). But one is said to be happier than another, by reason of diverse participation of the same good. And the addition of other goods does not increase Happiness, since Augustine says (Confess. v, 4): "He who knows Thee, and others besides, is not the happier for knowing them, but is happy for knowing Thee alone."

THIRD ARTICLE [I-II, Q. 5, Art. 3]

Whether One Can Be Happy in This Life?

Objection 1: It would seem that Happiness can be had in this life. For it is written (Ps. 118:1): "Blessed are the undefiled in the way, who walk in the law of the Lord." But this happens in this life. Therefore one can be happy in this life.

Obj. 2: Further, imperfect participation in the Sovereign Good does not destroy the nature of Happiness, otherwise one would not be happier than another. But men can participate in the Sovereign Good in this life, by knowing and loving God, albeit imperfectly. Therefore man can be happy in this life.

Obj. 3: Further, what is said by many cannot be altogether false: since what is in many, comes, apparently, from nature; and nature does not fail altogether. Now many say that Happiness can be had in this life, as appears from Ps. 143:15: "They have called the people happy that hath these things," to wit, the good things in this life. Therefore one can be happy in this life.

*On the contrary,* It is written (Job 14:1): "Man born of a woman, living for a short time, is filled with many miseries." But Happiness excludes misery. Therefore man cannot be happy in this life.

*I answer that,* A certain participation of Happiness can be had in this life: but perfect and true Happiness cannot be had in this life. This may be seen from a twofold consideration.

First, from the general notion of happiness. For since happiness is a "perfect and sufficient good," it excludes every evil, and fulfils every desire. But in this life every evil cannot be excluded. For this present life is subject to many unavoidable evils; to ignorance on the part of the intellect; to inordinate affection on the part of the appetite, and to many penalties on the part of the body; as Augustine sets forth in De Civ. Dei xix, 4. Likewise neither can the desire for good be satiated in this life. For man naturally desires the good, which he has, to be abiding. Now the goods of the present life pass away; since life itself passes away, which we naturally desire to have, and would wish to hold abidingly, for man naturally shrinks from death. Wherefore it is impossible to have true Happiness in this life.

Secondly, from a consideration of the specific nature of Happiness, viz. the vision of the Divine Essence, which man cannot obtain in this life, as was shown in the First Part (Q. 12, A. 11). Hence it is evident that none can attain true and perfect Happiness in this life.

Reply Obj. 1: Some are said to be happy in this life, either on account of the hope of obtaining Happiness in the life to come, according to Rom. 8:24: "We are saved by hope"; or on account of a certain participation of Happiness, by reason of a kind of enjoyment of the Sovereign Good.

Reply Obj. 2: The imperfection of participated Happiness is due to one of two causes. First, on the part of the object of Happiness, which is not seen in Its Essence: and this imperfection destroys the nature of true Happiness. Secondly, the imperfection may be on the part of the participator, who indeed attains the object of Happiness, in itself, namely, God: imperfectly, however, in comparison with the way in which God enjoys Himself. This imperfection does not destroy the true nature of Happiness; because, since Happiness is an operation, as stated above (Q. 3, A. 2), the true nature of Happiness is taken from the object, which specifies the act, and not from the subject.

Reply Obj. 3: Men esteem that there is some kind of happiness to be had in this life, on account of a certain likeness to true Happiness. And thus they do not fail altogether in their estimate.

FOURTH ARTICLE [I-II, Q. 5, Art. 4]

Whether Happiness Once Had Can Be Lost?

Objection 1: It would seem that Happiness can be lost. For Happiness is a perfection. But every perfection is in the thing perfected according to the mode of the latter. Since then man is, by his nature, changeable, it seems that Happiness is participated by man in a changeable manner. And consequently it seems that man can lose Happiness.

Obj. 2: Further, Happiness consists in an act of the intellect; and the intellect is subject to the will. But the will can be directed to opposites. Therefore it seems that it can desist from the operation whereby man is made happy: and thus man will cease to be happy.

Obj. 3: Further, the end corresponds to the beginning. But man's Happiness has a beginning, since man was not always happy. Therefore it seems that it has an end.

*On the contrary,* It is written (Matt. 25:46) of the righteous that "they shall go ... into life everlasting," which, as above stated (A. 2), is the Happiness of the saints. Now what is eternal ceases not. Therefore Happiness cannot be lost.

*I answer that,* If we speak of imperfect happiness, such as can be had in this life, in this sense it can be lost. This is clear of contemplative happiness, which is lost either by forgetfulness, for instance, when knowledge is lost through sickness; or again by certain occupations, whereby a man is altogether withdrawn from contemplation.

This is also clear of active happiness: since man's will can be changed so as to fall to vice from the virtue, in whose act that happiness principally consists. If, however, the virtue remain unimpaired, outward changes can indeed disturb such like happiness, in so far as they hinder many acts of virtue; but they cannot take it away altogether because there still remains an act of virtue, whereby man bears these trials in a praiseworthy manner. And since the happiness of this life can be lost, a circumstance that appears to be contrary to the nature of happiness, therefore did the Philosopher state (Ethic. i, 10) that some are happy in this life, not simply, but "as men," whose nature is subject to change.

But if we speak of that perfect Happiness which we await after this life, it must be observed that Origen (Peri Archon. ii, 3), following the error of certain Platonists, held that man can become unhappy after the final Happiness.

This, however, is evidently false, for two reasons. First, from the general notion of happiness. For since happiness is the "perfect and sufficient good," it must needs set man's desire at rest and exclude every evil. Now man naturally desires to hold to the good that he has, and to have the surety of his holding: else he must of necessity be troubled with the fear of losing it, or with the sorrow of knowing that he will lose it. Therefore it is necessary for true Happiness that man have the assured opinion of never losing the good that he possesses. If this opinion be true, it follows that he never will lose happiness: but if it be false, it is in itself an evil that he should have a false opinion: because the false is the evil of the intellect, just as the true is its good, as stated in *Ethic.* vi, 2. Consequently he will no longer be truly happy, if evil be in him.

Secondly, it is again evident if we consider the specific nature of Happiness. For it has been shown above (Q. 3, A. 8) that man's perfect Happiness consists in the vision of the Divine Essence. Now it is impossible for anyone seeing the Divine Essence, to wish not to see It. Because every good that one possesses and yet wishes to be without, is either insufficient, something more sufficing being desired in its stead; or else has some inconvenience attached to it, by reason of which it becomes wearisome. But the vision of the Divine Essence fills the soul with all good things, since it unites it to the source of all goodness; hence it is written (Ps. 16:15): "I shall be satisfied when Thy glory shall appear"; and (Wis. 7:11): "All good things came to me together with her," i.e. with the contemplation of wisdom. In like manner neither has it any inconvenience attached to it; because it is written of the contemplation of wisdom (Wis. 8:16): "Her conversation hath no bitterness, nor her company any tediousness." It is thus evident that the happy man cannot forsake Happiness of his own accord. Moreover, neither can he lose Happiness, through God taking it away from him. Because, since the withdrawal of Happiness is a punishment, it cannot be enforced by God, the just Judge, except for some fault; and he that sees God cannot fall into a fault, since rectitude of the will, of necessity, results from that vision as was shown above (Q. 4, A. 4). Nor again can it be withdrawn by any other agent. Because the mind that is united to God is raised above all other things: and consequently no other agent can sever the mind from that union. Therefore it seems unreasonable that as time goes on, man should pass from happiness to misery, and vice versa; because such like vicissitudes of time can only be for such things as are subject to time and movement.

Reply Obj. 1: Happiness is consummate perfection, which excludes every defect from the happy. And therefore whoever has happiness has it altogether unchangeably: this is done by the Divine power, which raises man to the participation of eternity which transcends all change.

Reply Obj. 2: The will can be directed to opposites, in things which are ordained to the end; but it is ordained, of natural necessity, to the last end. This is evident from the fact that man is unable not to wish to be happy.

Reply Obj. 3: Happiness has a beginning owing to the condition of the participator: but it has no end by reason of the condition of the good, the participation of which makes man happy. Hence the beginning of happiness is from one cause, its endlessness is from another.

FIFTH ARTICLE [I-II, Q. 5, Art. 5]

Whether Man Can Attain Happiness by His Natural Powers?

Objection 1: It would seem that man can attain Happiness by his natural powers. For nature does not fail in necessary things. But nothing is so necessary to man as that by which he attains the last end. Therefore this is not lacking to human nature. Therefore man can attain Happiness by his natural powers.

Obj. 2: Further, since man is more noble than

irrational creatures, it seems that he must be better equipped than they. But irrational creatures can attain their end by their natural powers. Much more therefore can man attain Happiness by his natural powers.

Obj. 3: Further, Happiness is a "perfect operation," according to the Philosopher (Ethic. vii, 13). Now the beginning of a thing belongs to the same principle as the perfecting thereof. Since, therefore, the imperfect operation, which is as the beginning in human operations, is subject to man's natural power, whereby he is master of his own actions; it seems that he can attain to perfect operation, i.e. Happiness, by his natural powers.

*On the contrary,* Man is naturally the principle of his action, by his intellect and will. But final Happiness prepared for the saints, surpasses the intellect and will of man; for the Apostle says (1 Cor. 2:9) "Eye hath not seen, nor ear heard, neither hath it entered into the heart of man, what things God hath prepared for them that love Him." Therefore man cannot attain Happiness by his natural powers.

*I answer that,* Imperfect happiness that can be had in this life, can be acquired by man by his natural powers, in the same way as virtue, in whose operation it consists: on this point we shall speak further on (Q. 63). But man's perfect Happiness, as stated above (Q. 3, A. 8), consists in the vision of the Divine Essence. Now the vision of God's Essence surpasses the nature not only of man, but also of every creature, as was shown in the First Part (Q. 12, A. 4). For the natural knowledge of every creature is in keeping with the mode of his substance: thus it is said of the intelligence (De Causis; Prop. viii) that "it knows things that are above it, and things that are below it, according to the mode of its substance." But every knowledge that is according to the mode of created substance, falls short of the vision of the Divine Essence, which infinitely surpasses all created substance. Consequently neither man, nor any creature, can attain final Happiness by his natural powers.

Reply Obj. 1: Just as nature does not fail man in necessaries, although it has not provided him with weapons and clothing, as it provided other animals, because it gave him reason and hands, with which he is able to get these things for himself; so neither did it fail man in things necessary, although it gave him not the wherewithal to attain Happiness: since this it could not do. But it did give him free-will, with which he can turn to God, that He may make him happy. "For what we do by means of our friends, is done, in a sense, by ourselves" (Ethic. iii, 3).

Reply Obj. 2: The nature that can attain perfect good, although it needs help from without in order to attain it, is of more noble condition than a nature which cannot attain perfect good, but attains some imperfect good, although it need no help from without in order to attain it, as the Philosopher says (De Coel. ii, 12). Thus he is better disposed to health who can attain perfect health, albeit by means of medicine, than he who can attain but imperfect health, without the help of medicine. And therefore the rational creature, which can attain the perfect good of happiness, but needs the Divine assistance for the purpose, is more perfect than the irrational creature, which is not capable of attaining this good, but attains some imperfect good by its natural powers.

Reply Obj. 3: When imperfect and perfect are of the same species, they can be caused by the same power. But this does not follow of necessity, if they be of different species: for not everything, that can cause the disposition of matter, can produce the final perfection. Now the imperfect operation, which is subject to man's natural power, is not of the same species as that perfect operation which is man's happiness: since operation takes its species from its object. Consequently the argument does not prove.

SIXTH ARTICLE [I-II, Q. 5, Art. 6]

Whether Man Attains Happiness Through the Action of Some Higher Creature?

Objection 1: It would seem that man can be made happy through the action of some higher creature, viz. an angel. For since we observe a twofold order in things—one, of the parts of the universe to one another, the other, of the whole universe to a good which is outside the universe; the former order is ordained to the second as to its end (Metaph. xii, 10). Thus the mutual order of the parts of an army is dependent on the order of the parts of an army is dependent on the order of the whole army to the general. But the mutual order of the parts of the universe consists in the higher creatures acting on the lower, as stated in the First Part (Q. 109, A. 2): while happiness consists in the order of man to a good which is outside the universe, i.e. God. Therefore man is made happy, through a higher creature, viz. an angel, acting on him.

Obj. 2: Further, that which is such in potentiality, can be reduced to act, by that which is such actually: thus what is potentially hot, is made actually hot, by something that is actually hot. But man is potentially happy. Therefore he can be made actually happy by an angel who is actually happy.

Obj. 3: Further, Happiness consists in an operation of the intellect as stated above (Q. 3, A. 4). But an angel can enlighten man's intellect as shown in the First Part (Q. 111, A. 1). Therefore an angel can make a man happy.

*On the contrary,* It is written (Ps. 83:12): "The Lord will give grace and glory."

*I answer that,* Since every creature is subject to the laws of nature, from the very fact that its power and action are limited: that which surpasses created nature, cannot be done by the power of any creature. Consequently if anything need to be done that is above nature, it is done by God immediately; such as raising the dead to life, restoring sight to the blind, and such like. Now it has been shown above (A. 5) that Happiness is a good surpassing created nature. Therefore it is impossible that it be bestowed through the action of any creature: but by God alone is man made happy, if we speak of perfect Happiness. If, however, we speak of imperfect happiness, the same is to be said of it as of the virtue, in whose act it consists.

Reply Obj. 1: It often happens in the case of active powers ordained to one another, that it belongs to the highest power to reach the last end, while the lower powers contribute to the attainment of that last end, by causing a disposition thereto: thus to the art of sailing, which commands the art of shipbuilding, it belongs to use a ship for the end for which it was made. Thus, too, in the order of the universe, man is indeed helped by the angels in the attainment of his last end, in respect of certain preliminary dispositions thereto: whereas he attains the last end itself through the First Agent, which is God.

Reply Obj. 2: When a form exists perfectly and naturally in something, it can be the principle of action on something else: for instance a hot thing heats through heat. But if a form exist in something imperfectly, and not naturally, it cannot be the principle whereby it is communicated to something else: thus the *intention* of color which is in the pupil, cannot make a thing white; nor indeed can everything enlightened or heated give heat or light to something else; for if they could, enlightening and heating would go on to infinity. But the light of glory, whereby God is seen, is in God perfectly and naturally; whereas in any creature, it is imperfectly and by likeness or participation. Consequently no creature can communicate its Happiness to another.

Reply Obj. 3: A happy angel enlightens the intellect of a man or of a lower angel, as to certain notions of the Divine works: but not as to the vision of the Divine Essence, as was stated in the First Part (Q. 106, A. 1): since in order to see this, all are immediately enlightened by God.

SEVENTH ARTICLE [I-II, Q. 5, Art. 7]

Whether Any Good Works Are Necessary That Man May Receive Happiness from God?

Objection 1: It would seem that no works of man are necessary that he may obtain Happiness from God. For since God is an agent of infinite power, He requires before acting, neither matter, nor disposition of matter, but can forthwith produce the whole effect. But man's works, since they are not required for Happiness, as the efficient cause thereof, as stated above (A. 6), can be required only as dispositions thereto. Therefore God who does not require dispositions before acting, bestows Happiness without any previous works.

Obj. 2: Further, just as God is the immediate cause of Happiness, so is He the immediate cause of nature. But when God first established nature, He produced creatures without any previous disposition or action on the part of the creature, but made each one perfect forthwith in its species. Therefore it seems that He bestows Happiness on man without any previous works.

Obj. 3: Further, the Apostle says (Rom. 4:6) that Happiness is of the man "to whom God reputeth justice without works." Therefore no works of man are necessary for attaining Happiness.

*On the contrary,* It is written (John 13:17): "If you know these things, you shall be blessed if you do them." Therefore Happiness is obtained through works.

*I answer that,* Rectitude of the will, as stated above (Q. 4, A. 4), is necessary for Happiness; since it is nothing else than the right order of the will to the last end; and it is therefore necessary for obtaining the end, just as the right disposition of matter, in order to receive the form. But this does not prove that any work of man need precede his Happiness: for God could make a will having a right tendency to the end, and at the same time attaining the end; just as sometimes He disposes matter and at the same time introduces the form. But the order of Divine wisdom demands that it should not be thus; for as is stated in *De Coelo* ii, 12, "of those things that have a natural capacity for the perfect good, one has it without movement, some by one movement, some by several." Now to possess the perfect good without movement, belongs to that which has it naturally: and to have Happiness naturally belongs to God alone. Therefore it belongs to God alone not to be moved towards Happiness by any previous operation. Now since Happiness surpasses every created nature, no pure creature can becomingly gain Happiness, without the movement of operation, whereby it tends thereto. But the angel, who is above man in the natural order, obtained it, according to the order of Divine wisdom, by one movement of a meritorious work, as was explained in the First Part (Q. 62, A. 5); whereas man obtains it by many movements of works which are called merits. Wherefore also according to the Philosopher (Ethic. i, 9), happiness is the reward of works of virtue.

Reply Obj. 1: Works are necessary to man in order to gain Happiness; not on account of the insufficiency of the Divine power which bestows Happiness, but that the order in things be observed.

Reply Obj. 2: God produced the first creatures so that they are perfect forthwith, without any previous disposition or operation of the creature; because He instituted the first individuals of the various species, that through them nature might be propagated to their progeny. In like manner, because Happiness was to be bestowed on others through Christ, who is God and Man, "Who," according to Heb. 2:10, "had brought many children into glory"; therefore, from the very beginning of

His conception, His soul was happy, without any previous meritorious operation. But this is peculiar to Him: for Christ's merit avails baptized children for the gaining of Happiness, though they have no merits of their own; because by Baptism they are made members of Christ.

Reply Obj. 3: The Apostle is speaking of the Happiness of Hope, which is bestowed on us by sanctifying grace, which is not given on account of previous works. For grace is not a term of movement, as Happiness is; rather is it the principle of the movement that tends towards Happiness.

EIGHTH ARTICLE [I-II, Q. 5, Art. 8]

Whether Every Man Desires Happiness?

Objection 1: It would seem that not all desire Happiness. For no man can desire what he knows not; since the apprehended good is the object of the appetite (De Anima iii, 10). But many know not what Happiness is. This is evident from the fact that, as Augustine says (De Trin. xiii, 4), "some thought that Happiness consists in pleasures of the body; some, in a virtue of the soul; some in other things." Therefore not all desire Happiness.

Obj. 2: Further, the essence of Happiness is the vision of the Divine Essence, as stated above (Q. 3, A. 8). But some consider it impossible for man to see the Divine Essence; wherefore they desire it not. Therefore all men do not desire Happiness.

Obj. 3: Further, Augustine says (De Trin. xiii, 5) that "happy is he who has all he desires, and desires nothing amiss." But all do not desire this; for some desire certain things amiss, and yet they wish to desire such things. Therefore all do not desire Happiness.

*On the contrary,* Augustine says (De Trin. xiii, 3): "If that actor had said: 'You all wish to be happy; you do not wish to be unhappy,' he would have said that which none would have failed to acknowledge in his will." Therefore everyone desires to be happy.

*I answer that,* Happiness can be considered in two ways. First according to the general notion of happiness: and thus, of necessity, every man desires happiness. For the general notion of happiness consists in the perfect good, as stated above (AA. 3, 4). But since good is the object of the will, the perfect good of a man is that which entirely satisfies his will. Consequently to desire happiness is nothing else than to desire that one's will be satisfied. And this everyone desires. Secondly we may speak of Happiness according to its specific notion, as to that in which it consists. And thus all do not know Happiness; because they know not in what thing the general notion of happiness is found. And consequently, in this respect, not all desire it. Wherefore the reply to the first Objection is clear.

Reply Obj. 2: Since the will follows the apprehension of the intellect or reason; just as it happens that where there is no real distinction, there may be a distinction according to the consideration of reason; so does it happen that one and the same thing is desired in one way, and not desired in another. So that happiness may be considered as the final and perfect good, which is the general notion of happiness: and thus the will naturally and of necessity tends thereto, as stated above. Again it can be considered under other special aspects, either on the part of the operation itself, or on the part of the operating power, or on the part of the object; and thus the will does not tend thereto of necessity.

Reply Obj. 3: This definition of Happiness given by some—"Happy is the man that has all he desires," or, "whose every wish is fulfilled," is a good and adequate definition, if it be understood in a certain way; but an inadequate definition if understood in another. For if we understand it simply of all that man desires by his natural appetite, thus it is true that he who has all that he desires, is happy: since nothing satisfies man's natural desire, except the perfect good which is Happiness. But if we understand it of those things that man desires according to the apprehension of the reason, thus it does not belong to Happiness, to have certain things that man desires; rather does it belong to unhappiness, in so far as the possession of such things hinders man from having all that he desires naturally; thus it is that reason sometimes accepts as true things that are a hindrance to the knowledge of truth. And it was through taking this into consideration that Augustine added so as to include perfect Happiness—that he "desires nothing amiss": although the first part suffices if rightly understood, to wit, that "happy is he who has all he desires."

TREATISE ON HUMAN ACTS: ACTS PECULIAR TO MAN (QQ. 6-21)

# QUESTION 6

OF THE VOLUNTARY AND THE INVOLUNTARY (In Eight Articles)

Since therefore Happiness is to be gained by means of certain acts, we must in due sequence consider human acts, in order to know by what acts we may obtain Happiness, and by what acts we are prevented from obtaining it. But because operations and acts are concerned with things singular, consequently all practical knowledge is incomplete unless it take account of things in detail. The study of Morals, therefore, since it treats of human acts, should consider first the general principles; and secondly matters of detail.

In treating of the general principles, the points that offer themselves for our consideration are (1) human acts themselves; (2) their principles. Now of human acts some are proper to man; others are common to man and animals. And since Happiness is man's proper good, those acts which are proper to man have a closer connection with Happiness than have those which are common to man and the other animals. First, then, we must consider those acts which are proper to man; secondly, those acts which are common to man and the other animals, and are called Passions. The first of these points offers a twofold consideration: (1) What makes a human act? (2) What distinguishes human acts?

And since those acts are properly called human which are voluntary, because the will is the rational appetite, which is proper to man; we must consider acts in so far as they are voluntary.

First, then, we must consider the voluntary and involuntary in general; secondly, those acts which are voluntary, as being elicited by the will, and as issuing from the will immediately; thirdly, those acts which are voluntary, as being commanded by the will, which issue from the will through the medium of the other powers.

And because voluntary acts have certain circumstances, according to which we form our judgment concerning them, we must first consider the voluntary and the involuntary, and afterwards, the circumstances of those acts which are found to be voluntary or involuntary. Under the first head there are eight points of inquiry:

(1) Whether there is anything voluntary in human acts?

(2) Whether in irrational animals?

(3) Whether there can be voluntariness without any action?

(4) Whether violence can be done to the will?

(5) Whether violence causes involuntariness?

(6) Whether fear causes involuntariness?

(7) Whether concupiscence causes involuntariness?

(8) Whether ignorance causes involuntariness?

FIRST ARTICLE [I-II, Q. 6, Art. 1]

Whether There Is Anything Voluntary in Human Acts?

Objection 1: It would seem that there is nothing voluntary in human acts. For that is voluntary "which has its principle within itself," as Gregory of Nyssa [*Nemesius, De Natura Hom. xxxii.], Damascene (De Fide Orth. ii, 24), and Aristotle (Ethic. iii, 1) declare. But the principle of human acts is not in man himself, but outside him: since man's appetite is moved to act, by the appetible object which is outside him, and is as a "mover unmoved" (De Anima iii, 10). Therefore there is nothing voluntary in human acts.

Obj. 2: Further, the Philosopher (Phys. viii, 2) proves that in animals no new movement arises that is not preceded by a motion from without. But all human acts are new, since none is eternal. Consequently, the principle of all human acts is from without: and therefore there is nothing voluntary in them.

Obj. 3: Further, he that acts voluntarily, can act of himself. But this is not true of man; for it is written (John 15:5): "Without Me you can do nothing." Therefore there is nothing voluntary in human acts.

*On the contrary,* Damascene says (De Fide Orth. ii) that "the voluntary is an act consisting in a rational operation." Now such are human acts. Therefore there is something voluntary in human acts.

*I answer that,* There must needs be something voluntary in human acts. In order to make this clear, we must take note that the principle of some acts or movements is within the agent, or that which is moved; whereas the principle of some movements or acts is outside. For when a stone is moved upwards, the principle of this movement is outside the stone: whereas when it is moved downwards, the principle of this movement is in the stone. Now of those things that are moved by an intrinsic principle, some move themselves, some not. For since every agent or thing moved, acts or is moved for an end, as stated above (Q. 1, A. 2); those are perfectly moved by an intrinsic principle, whose intrinsic principle is one not only of movement but of movement for an end. Now in order for a thing to be done for an end, some knowledge of the end is necessary. Therefore, whatever so acts or is moved by an intrinsic principle, that it has some knowledge of the end, has within itself the principle of its act, so that it not only acts, but acts for an end. On the other hand, if a thing has no knowledge of the end, even though it have an intrinsic principle of action or movement, nevertheless the principle of acting or being moved for an end is not in that thing, but in something else, by which the principle of its action towards an end is not in that thing, but in something else, by which the principle of its action towards an end is imprinted on it. Wherefore such like things are not said to move themselves, but to be moved by others. But those things which have a knowledge of the end are said to move themselves because there is in them a principle by which they not only act but also act for an end. And consequently, since both are from an intrinsic principle, to wit, that they act and that they act for an end, the movements of such things are said to be voluntary: for the word "voluntary" implies that their movements and acts are from their own inclination. Hence it is that, according to the definitions of Aristotle, Gregory of Nyssa, and Damascene [*See Objection 1], the voluntary is defined not only as having "a principle within" the agent, but also as implying "knowledge." Therefore, since man especially knows the end of his work, and moves himself, in his acts especially is the voluntary to be found.

Reply Obj. 1: Not every principle is a first principle. Therefore, although it is essential to the voluntary act that its principle be within the agent, nevertheless it is not contrary to the nature of the voluntary act that this intrinsic principle be caused or moved by an extrinsic principle: because it is not essential to the voluntary act that its intrinsic principle be a first principle. Yet again it must be observed that a principle of movement may happen to be first in a genus, but not first simply: thus in the genus of things subject to alteration, the first principle of alteration is a heavenly body, which nevertheless is not the first mover simply, but is moved locally by a higher mover. And so the intrinsic principle of the voluntary act, i.e. the cognitive and appetitive power, is the first principle in the genus of appetitive movement, although it is moved by an extrinsic principle according to other species of movement.

Reply Obj. 2: New movements in animals are indeed preceded by a motion from without; and this in two respects. First, in so far as by means of an extrinsic motion an animal's senses are confronted with something sensible, which, on being apprehended, moves the appetite. Thus a lion, on seeing a stag in movement and coming towards him, begins to be moved towards the stag. Secondly, in so far as some extrinsic motion produces a physical change in an animal's body, as in the case of cold or heat; and through the body being affected by the motion of an outward body, the sensitive appetite which is the power of a bodily organ, is also moved indirectly; thus it happens that through some alteration in the body the appetite is roused to the desire of something. But this is not contrary to the nature of voluntariness, as stated above (ad 1), for such movements caused by an extrinsic principle are of another genus of movement.

Reply Obj. 3: God moves man to act, not only by proposing the appetible to the senses, or by effecting a change in his body, but also by moving the will itself; because every movement either of the will or of nature, proceeds from God as the First Mover. And just as it is not incompatible with nature that the natural movement be from God as the First Mover, inasmuch as nature is an instrument of God moving it: so it is not contrary to the essence of a voluntary act, that it proceed from God, inasmuch as the will is moved by God. Nevertheless both natural and voluntary movements have this in common, that it is essential that they should proceed from a principle within the agent.

SECOND ARTICLE [I-II, Q. 6, Art. 2]

Whether There Is Anything Voluntary in Irrational Animals?

Objection 1: It would seem that there is nothing voluntary in irrational animals. For a thing is called "voluntary" from *voluntas* (will). Now since the will is in the reason (De Anima iii, 9), it cannot be in irrational animals. Therefore neither is there anything voluntary in them.

Obj. 2: Further, according as human acts are voluntary, man is said to be master of his actions. But irrational animals are not masters of their actions; for "they act not; rather are they acted upon," as Damascene says (De Fide Orth. ii, 27). Therefore there is no such thing as a voluntary act in irrational animals.

Obj. 3: Further, Damascene says (De Fide Orth. 24) that "voluntary acts lead to praise and blame." But neither praise nor blame is due to the acts of irrational minds. Therefore such acts are not voluntary.

*On the contrary,* The Philosopher says (Ethic. iii, 2) that "both children and irrational animals participate in the voluntary." The same is said by Damascene (De Fide Orth. 24) and Gregory of Nyssa [*Nemesius, De Nat. Hom. xxxii.].

*I answer that,* As stated above (A. 1), it is essential to the voluntary act that its principle be within the agent, together with some knowledge of the end. Now knowledge of the end is twofold; perfect and imperfect. Perfect knowledge of the end consists in not only apprehending the thing which is the end, but also in knowing it under the aspect of end, and the relationship of the means to that end. And such knowledge belongs to none but the rational nature. But imperfect knowledge of the end consists in mere apprehension of the end, without knowing it under the aspect of end, or the relationship of an act to the end. Such knowledge of the end is exercised by irrational animals, through their senses and their natural estimative power.

Consequently perfect knowledge of the end leads to the perfect voluntary; inasmuch as, having apprehended the end, a man can, from deliberating about the end and the means thereto, be moved, or not, to gain that end. But imperfect knowledge of the end leads to the imperfect voluntary; inasmuch as the agent apprehends the end, but does not deliberate, and is moved to the end at once. Wherefore the voluntary in its perfection belongs to none but the rational nature: whereas the imperfect voluntary is within the competency of even irrational animals.

Reply Obj. 1: The will is the name of the rational appetite; and consequently it cannot be in things devoid of reason. But the word "voluntary" is derived from "voluntas" (will), and can be extended to those things in which there is some participation of will, by way of likeness thereto. It is thus that voluntary action is attributed to irrational animals, in so far as they are moved to an end, through some kind of knowledge.

Reply Obj. 2: The fact that man is master of his actions, is due to his being able to deliberate about them: for since the deliberating reason is indifferently disposed to opposite things, the will can be inclined to either. But it is not thus that voluntariness is in irrational animals, as stated above.

Reply Obj. 3: Praise and blame are the result of the voluntary act, wherein is the perfect voluntary; such as is not to be found in irrational animals.

THIRD ARTICLE [I-II, Q. 6, Art. 3]

Whether There Can Be Voluntariness Without Any Act?

Objection 1: It would seem that voluntariness cannot be without any act. For that is voluntary which proceeds from the will. But nothing can proceed from the will, except through some act, at least an act of the will. Therefore there cannot be voluntariness without act.

Obj. 2: Further, just as one is said to wish by an act of the will, so when the act of the will ceases, one is said not to wish. But not to wish implies involuntariness, which is contrary to voluntariness. Therefore there can be nothing voluntary when the act of the will ceases.

Obj. 3: Further, knowledge is essential to the voluntary, as stated above (AA. 1, 2). But knowledge involves an act. Therefore voluntariness cannot be without some act.

*On the contrary,* The word "voluntary" is applied to that of which we are masters. Now we are masters in respect of to act and not to act, to will and not to will. Therefore just as to act and to will are voluntary, so also are not to act and not to will.

*I answer that,* Voluntary is what proceeds from the will. Now one thing proceeds from another in two ways. First, directly; in which sense something proceeds from another inasmuch as this other acts; for instance, heating from heat. Secondly, indirectly; in which sense something proceeds from another through this other not acting; thus the sinking of a ship is set down to the helmsman, from his having ceased to steer. But we must take note that the cause of what follows from want of action is not always the agent as not acting; but only then when the agent can and ought to act. For if the helmsman were unable to steer the ship or if the ship's helm be not entrusted to him, the sinking of the ship would not be set down to him, although it might be due to his absence from the helm.

Since, then, the will by willing and acting, is able, and sometimes ought, to hinder not-willing and not-acting; this not-willing and not-acting is imputed to, as though proceeding from, the will. And thus it is that we can have the voluntary without an act; sometimes without outward act, but with an interior act; for instance, when one wills not to act; and sometimes without even an interior act, as when one does not will to act.

Reply Obj. 1: We apply the word "voluntary" not only to that which proceeds from the will directly, as from its action; but also to that which proceeds from it indirectly as from its inaction.

Reply Obj. 2: "Not to wish" is said in two senses. First, as though it were one word, and the infinitive of "I-do-not-wish." Consequently just as when I say "I do not wish to read," the sense is, "I wish not to read"; so "not to wish to read" is the same as "to wish not to read," and in this sense "not to wish" implies involuntariness. Secondly it is taken as a sentence: and then no act of the will is affirmed. And in this sense "not to wish" does not imply involuntariness.

Reply Obj. 3: Voluntariness requires an act of knowledge in the same way as it requires an act of will; namely, in order that it be in one's power to consider, to wish and to act. And then, just as not to wish, and not to act, when it is time to wish and to act, is voluntary, so is it voluntary not to consider.

FOURTH ARTICLE [I-II, Q. 6, Art. 4]

Whether Violence Can Be Done to the Will?

Objection 1: It would seem that violence can be done to the will. For everything can be compelled by that which is more powerful. But there is something, namely, God, that is more powerful than the human will. Therefore it can be compelled, at least by Him.

Obj. 2: Further, every passive subject is compelled by its active principle, when it is changed by it. But the will is a passive force: for it is a "mover moved" (De Anima iii, 10). Therefore, since it is sometimes moved by its active principle, it seems that sometimes it is compelled.

Obj. 3: Further, violent movement is that which is contrary to nature. But the movement of the will is sometimes contrary to nature; as is clear of the will's movement to sin, which is contrary to nature, as Damascene says (De Fide Orth. iv, 20). Therefore the movement of the will can be compelled.

*On the contrary,* Augustine says (De Civ. Dei v, 10) that what is done by the will is not done of necessity. Now, whatever is done under compulsion is done of necessity: consequently what is done by the will, cannot be compelled. Therefore the will cannot be compelled to act.

*I answer that,* The act of the will is twofold: one is its immediate act, as it were, elicited by it, namely, "to wish"; the other is an act of the will commanded by it, and put into execution by means of some other power, such as "to walk" and "to speak," which are commanded by the will to be executed by means of the motive power.

As regards the commanded acts of the will, then, the will can suffer violence, in so far as violence can prevent the exterior members from executing the will's command. But as to the will's own proper act, violence cannot be done to the will.

The reason of this is that the act of the will is nothing else than an inclination proceeding from the interior principle of knowledge: just as the natural appetite is an inclination proceeding from an interior principle without knowledge. Now what is compelled or violent is from an exterior principle. Consequently it is contrary to the nature of the will's own act, that it should be subject to compulsion and violence: just as it is also contrary to the nature of a natural inclination or movement. For a stone may have an upward movement from violence, but that this violent movement be from its natural inclination is impossible. In like manner a man may be dragged by force: but it is contrary to the very notion of violence, that he be dragged of his own will.

Reply Obj. 1: God Who is more powerful than the human will, can move the will of man, according to Prov. 21:1: "The heart of the king is in the hand of the Lord; whithersoever He will He shall turn it." But if this were by compulsion, it would no longer be by an act of the will, nor would the will itself be moved, but something else against the will.

Reply Obj. 2: It is not always a violent movement, when a passive subject is moved by its active principle; but only when this is done against the interior inclination of the passive subject. Otherwise every alteration and generation of simple bodies would be unnatural and violent: whereas they are natural by reason of the natural interior aptitude of the matter or subject to such a disposition. In like manner when the will is moved, according to its own inclination, by the appetible object, this movement is not violent but voluntary.

Reply Obj. 3: That to which the will tends by sinning, although in reality it is evil and contrary to the rational nature, nevertheless is apprehended as something good and suitable to nature, in so far as it is suitable to man by reason of some pleasurable sensation or some vicious habit.

FIFTH ARTICLE [I-II, Q. 6, Art. 5]

Whether Violence Causes Involuntariness?

Objection 1: It would seem that violence does not cause involuntariness. For we speak of voluntariness and involuntariness in respect of the will. But violence cannot be done to the will, as shown above (A. 4). Therefore violence cannot cause involuntariness.

Obj. 2: Further, that which is done involuntarily is done with grief, as Damascene (De Fide Orth. ii, 24) and the Philosopher (Ethic. iii, 5) say. But sometimes a man suffers compulsion without being grieved thereby. Therefore violence does not cause involuntariness.

Obj. 3: Further, what is from the will cannot be involuntary. But some violent actions proceed from the will: for instance, when a man with a heavy body goes upwards; or when a man contorts his limbs in a way contrary to their natural flexibility. Therefore violence does not cause involuntariness.

*On the contrary,* The Philosopher (Ethic. iii, 1) and Damascene (De Fide Orth. ii, 24) say that "things done under compulsion are involuntary."

*I answer that,* Violence is directly opposed to the voluntary, as likewise to the natural. For the voluntary and the natural have this in common, that both are from an intrinsic principle; whereas violence is from an extrinsic principle. And for this reason, just as in things devoid of knowledge, violence effects something against nature: so in things endowed with knowledge, it effects something against the will. Now that which is against nature is said to be "unnatural"; and in like manner that which is against the will is said to be "involuntary." Therefore violence causes involuntariness.

Reply Obj. 1: The involuntary is opposed to the voluntary. Now it has been said (A. 4) that not only the act, which proceeds immediately from the will, is called voluntary, but also the act commanded by the will. Consequently, as to the act which proceeds immediately from the will, violence cannot be done to the will, as stated above (A. 4): wherefore violence cannot make that act involuntary. But as to the commanded act, the will can suffer violence: and consequently in this respect violence causes involuntariness.

Reply Obj. 2: As that is said to be natural, which is according to the inclination of nature; so that is said to be voluntary, which is according to the inclination of the will. Now a thing is said to be natural in two ways. First, because it is from nature as from an active principle: thus it is natural for fire to produce heat. Secondly, according to a passive principle; because, to wit, there is in nature an inclination to receive an action from an extrinsic principle: thus the movement of the heavens is said to be natural, by reason of the natural aptitude in a heavenly body to receive such movement; although the cause of that movement is a voluntary agent. In like manner an act is said to be voluntary in two ways. First, in regard to action, for instance, when one wishes to be passive to another. Hence when action is brought to bear on something, by an extrinsic agent, as long as the will to suffer that action remains in the passive subject, there is not violence simply: for although the patient does nothing by way of action, he does something by being willing to suffer. Consequently this cannot be called involuntary.

Reply Obj. 3: As the Philosopher says (Phys. viii, 4) the movement of an animal, whereby at times an animal is moved against the natural inclination of the body, although it is not natural to the body, is nevertheless somewhat natural to the animal, to which it is natural to be moved according to its appetite. Accordingly this is violent, not simply but in a certain respect. The same remark applies in the case of one who contorts his limbs in a way that is contrary to their natural disposition. For this is violent in a certain respect, i.e. as to that particular limb; but not simply, i.e. as to the man himself.

SIXTH ARTICLE [I-II, Q. 6, Art. 6]

Whether Fear Causes Involuntariness Simply?

Objection 1: It would seem that fear causes involuntariness simply. For just as violence regards that which is contrary to the will at the time, so fear regards a future evil which is repugnant to the will. But violence causes involuntariness simply. Therefore fear too causes involuntariness simply.

Obj. 2: Further, that which is such of itself, remains such, whatever be added to it: thus what is hot of itself, as long as it remains, is still hot, whatever be added to it. But that which is done through fear, is involuntary in itself. Therefore, even with the addition of fear, it is involuntary.

Obj. 3: Further, that which is such, subject to a condition, is such in a certain respect; whereas what is such, without any condition, is such simply: thus what is necessary, subject to a condition, is necessary in some respect: but what is necessary absolutely, is necessary simply. But that which is done through fear, is absolutely involuntary; and is not voluntary, save under a condition, namely, in order that the evil feared may be avoided. Therefore that which is done through fear, is involuntary simply.

*On the contrary,* Gregory of Nyssa [*Nemesius, De Nat. Hom. xxx.] and the Philosopher (Ethic. iii, 1) say that such things as are done through fear are "voluntary rather than involuntary."

*I answer that,* As the Philosopher says (Ethic. iii) and likewise Gregory of Nyssa in his book on Man (Nemesius, De Nat. Hom. xxx), such things are done through fear "are of a mixed character," being partly voluntary and partly involuntary. For that which is done through fear, considered in itself, is not voluntary; but it becomes voluntary in this particular case, in order, namely, to avoid the evil feared.

But if the matter be considered aright, such things are voluntary rather than involuntary; for they are voluntary simply, but involuntary in a certain respect. For a thing is said to be simply, according as it is in act; but according as it is only in apprehension, it is not simply, but in a certain respect. Now that which is done through fear, is in act in so far as it is done. For, since acts are concerned with singulars; and the singular, as such, is here and now; that which is done is in act, in so far as it is here and now and under other individuating circumstances. And that which is done through fear is voluntary, inasmuch as it is here and now, that is to say, in so far as, under the circumstances, it hinders a greater evil which was feared; thus the throwing of the cargo into the sea becomes voluntary during the storm, through fear of the danger: wherefore it is clear that it is voluntary simply. And hence it is that what is done out of fear is essentially voluntary, because its principle is within. But if we consider what is done through fear, as outside this particular case, and inasmuch as it is repugnant to the will, this is merely a consideration of the mind. And consequently what is done through fear is involuntary, considered in that respect, that is to say, outside the actual circumstances of the case.

Reply Obj. 1: Things done through fear and compulsion differ not only according to present and future time, but also in this, that the will does not consent, but is moved entirely counter to that which is done through compulsion: whereas what is done through fear, becomes voluntary, because the will is moved towards it, albeit not for its own sake, but on account of something else, that is, in order to avoid an evil which is feared. For the conditions of a voluntary act are satisfied, if it be done on account of something else voluntary: since the voluntary is not only what we wish, for its own sake, as an end, but also what we wish for the sake of something else, as an end. It is clear therefore that in what is done from compulsion, the will does nothing inwardly; whereas in what is done through fear, the will does something. Accordingly, as Gregory of Nyssa [*Nemesius, De Nat. Hom. xxx.] says, in order to exclude things done through fear, a violent action is defined as not only one, "the princip[le] whereof is from without," but with the addition, "in which he that suffers violence concurs not at all"; because the will of him that is in fear, does concur somewhat in that which he does through fear.

Reply Obj. 2: Things that are such absolutely, remain such, whatever be added to them; for instance, a cold thing, or a white thing: but things that are such relatively, vary according as they are compared with different things. For what is big in comparison with one thing, is small in comparison with another. Now a thing is said to be voluntary, not only for its own sake, as it were absolutely; but also for the sake of something else, as it were relatively. Accordingly, nothing prevents a thing which was not voluntary in comparison with one thing, from becoming voluntary when compared with another.

Reply Obj. 3: That which is done through fear, is voluntary without any condition, that is to say, according as it is actually done: but it is involuntary, under a certain condition, that is to say, if such a fear were not threatening. Consequently, this argument proves rather the opposite.

SEVENTH ARTICLE [I-II, Q. 6, Art. 7]

Whether Concupiscence Causes Involuntariness?

Objection 1: It would seem that concupiscence causes involuntariness. For just as fear is a passion, so is concupiscence. But fear causes involuntariness to a certain extent. Therefore concupiscence does so too.

Obj. 2: Further, just as the timid man through fear acts counter to that which he proposed, so does the incontinent, through concupiscence. But fear causes involuntariness to a certain extent. Therefore concupiscence does so also.

Obj. 3: Further, knowledge is necessary for voluntariness. But concupiscence impairs knowledge; for the Philosopher says (Ethic. vi, 5) that "delight," or the lust of pleasure, "destroys the judgment of prudence." Therefore concupiscence causes involuntariness.

*On the contrary,* Damascene says (De Fide Orth. ii, 24): "The involuntary act deserves mercy or indulgence, and is done with regret." But neither of these can be said of that which is done out of concupiscence. Therefore concupiscence does not cause involuntariness.

*I answer that,* Concupiscence does not cause involuntariness, but on the contrary makes something to be voluntary. For a thing is said to be voluntary, from the fact that the will is moved to it. Now concupiscence inclines the will to desire the object of concupiscence. Therefore the effect of concupiscence is to make something to be voluntary rather than involuntary.

Reply Obj. 1: Fear regards evil, but concupiscence regards good. Now evil of itself is counter to the will, whereas good harmonizes with the will. Therefore fear has a greater tendency than concupiscence to cause involuntariness.

Reply Obj. 2: He who acts from fear retains the repugnance of the will to that which he does, considered in itself. But he that acts from concupiscence, e.g. an incontinent man, does not retain his former will whereby he repudiated the object of his concupiscence; for his will is changed so that he desires that which previously he repudiated. Accordingly, that which is done out of fear is involuntary, to a certain extent, but that which is done from concupiscence is nowise involuntary. For the man who yields to concupiscence acts counter to that which he purposed at first, but not counter to that which he desires now; whereas the timid man acts counter to that which in itself he desires now.

Reply Obj. 3: If concupiscence were to destroy knowledge altogether, as happens with those whom concupiscence has rendered mad, it would follow that concupiscence would take away voluntariness. And yet properly speaking it would not result in the act being involuntary, because in things bereft of reason, there is neither voluntary nor involuntary. But sometimes in those actions which are done from concupiscence, knowledge is not completely destroyed, because the power of knowing is not taken away entirely, but only the actual consideration in some particular possible act. Nevertheless, this itself is voluntary, according as by voluntary we mean that which is in the power of the will, for example "not to act" or "not to will," and in like manner "not to consider"; for the will can resist the passion, as we shall state later on (Q. 10, A. 3; Q. 77, A.)

EIGHTH ARTICLE [I-II, Q. 6, Art. 8]

Whether Ignorance Causes Involuntariness?

Objection 1: It would seem that ignorance does not cause involuntariness. For "the involuntary act deserves pardon," as Damascene says (De Fide Orth. ii, 24). But sometimes that which is done through ignorance does not deserve pardon, according to 1 Cor. 14:38: "If any man know not, he shall not be known." Therefore ignorance does not cause involuntariness.

Obj. 2: Further, every sin implies ignorance; according to Prov. 14:22: "They err, that work evil." If, therefore, ignorance causes involuntariness, it would follow that every sin is involuntary: which is opposed to the saying of Augustine, that "every sin is voluntary" (De Vera Relig. xiv).

Obj. 3: Further, "involuntariness is not without sadness," as Damascene says (De Fide Orth. ii, 24). But some things are done out of ignorance, but without sadness: for instance, a man may kill a foe, whom he wishes to kill, thinking at the time that he is killing a stag. Therefore ignorance does not cause involuntariness.

*On the contrary,* Damascene (De Fide Orth. ii, 24) and the Philosopher (Ethic. iii, 1) say that "what is done through ignorance is involuntary."

*I answer that,* If ignorance causes involuntariness, it is in so far as it deprives one of knowledge, which is a necessary condition of voluntariness, as was declared above (A. 1). But it is not every ignorance that deprives one of this knowledge. Accordingly, we must take note that ignorance has a threefold relationship to the act of the will: in one way, "concomitantly"; in another, "consequently"; in a third way, "antecedently." "Concomitantly," when there is ignorance of what is done; but, so that even if it were known, it would be done. For then, ignorance does not induce one to wish this to be done, but it just happens that a thing is at the same time done, and not known: thus in the example given (Obj. 3) a man did indeed wish to kill his foe, but killed him in ignorance, thinking to kill a stag. And ignorance of this kind, as the Philosopher states (Ethic. iii, 1), does not cause involuntariness, since it is not the cause of anything that is repugnant to the will: but it causes "non-voluntariness," since that which is unknown cannot be actually willed. Ignorance is "consequent" to the act of the will, in so far as ignorance itself is voluntary: and this happens in two ways, in accordance with the two aforesaid modes of voluntary (A. 3). First, because the act of the will is brought to bear on the ignorance: as when a man wishes not to know, that he may have an excuse for sin, or that he may not be withheld from sin; according to Job 21:14: "We desire not the knowledge of Thy ways." And this is called "affected ignorance." Secondly, ignorance is said to be voluntary, when it regards that which one can and ought to know: for in this sense "not to act" and "not to will" are said to be voluntary, as stated above (A. 3). And ignorance of this kind happens, either when one does not actually consider what one can and ought to consider; this is called "ignorance of evil choice," and arises from some passion or habit: or when one does not take the trouble to acquire the knowledge which one ought to have; in which sense, ignorance of the general principles of law, which one to know, is voluntary, as being due to negligence. Accordingly, if in either of these ways, ignorance is voluntary, it cannot cause involuntariness simply. Nevertheless it causes involuntariness in a certain respect, inasmuch as it precedes the movement of the will towards the act, which movement would not be, if there were knowledge. Ignorance is "antecedent" to the act of the will, when it is not voluntary, and yet is the cause of man's willing what he would not will otherwise. Thus a man may be ignorant of some circumstance of his act, which he was not bound to know, the result being that he does that which he would not do, if he knew of that circumstance; for instance, a man, after taking proper precaution, may not know that someone is coming along the road, so that he shoots an arrow and slays a passer-by. Such ignorance causes involuntariness simply.

From this may be gathered the solution of the objections. For the first objection deals with ignorance of what a man is bound to know. The second, with ignorance of choice, which is voluntary to a certain extent, as stated above. The third, with that ignorance which is concomitant with the act of the will.

## QUESTION 7

OF THE CIRCUMSTANCES OF HUMAN ACTS (In Four Articles)

We must now consider the circumstances of human acts: under which head there are four points of inquiry:

(1) What is a circumstance?

(2) Whether a theologian should take note of the circumstances of human acts?

(3) How many circumstances are there?

(4) Which are the most important of them?

FIRST ARTICLE [I-II, Q. 7, Art. 1]

Whether a Circumstance Is an Accident of a Human Act?

Objection 1: It would seem that a circumstance is not an accident of a human act. For Tully says (De Invent. Rhetor. i) that a circumstance is that from "which an orator adds authority and strength to his argument." But oratorical arguments are derived principally from things pertaining to the essence of a thing, such as the definition, the genus, the species, and the like, from which also Tully declares that an orator should draw his arguments. Therefore a circumstance is not an accident of a human act.

Obj. 2: Further, "to be in" is proper to an accident. But that which surrounds ( *circumstat* ) is rather out than in. Therefore the circumstances are not accidents of human acts.

Obj. 3: Further, an accident has no accident. But human acts themselves are accidents. Therefore the circumstances are not accidents of acts.

*On the contrary,* The particular conditions of any singular thing are called its individuating accidents. But the Philosopher (Ethic. iii, 1) calls the circumstances particular things [* ta kath' ekasta ], i.e. the particular conditions of each act. Therefore the circumstances are individual accidents of human acts.

*I answer that,* Since, according to the Philosopher (Peri Herm. i), "words are the signs of what we understand," it must needs be that in naming things we follow the process of intellectual knowledge. Now our intellectual knowledge proceeds from the better known to the less known. Accordingly with us, names of more obvious things are transferred so as to signify things less obvious: and hence it is that, as stated in *Metaph.* x, 4, "the notion of distance has been transferred from things that are apart locally, to all kinds of opposition": and in like manner words that signify local movement are employed to designate all other movements, because bodies which are circumscribed by place, are best known to us. And hence it is that the word "circumstance" has passed from located things to human acts.

Now in things located, that is said to surround something, which is outside it, but touches it, or is placed near it. Accordingly, whatever conditions are outside the substance of an act, and yet in some way touch the human act, are called circumstances. Now what is outside a thing's substance, while it belongs to that thing, is called its accident. Wherefore the circumstances of human acts should be called their accidents.

Reply Obj. 1: The orator gives strength to his argument, in the first place, from the substance of the act; and secondly, from the circumstances of the act. Thus a man becomes indictable, first, through being guilty of murder; secondly, through having done it fraudulently, or from motives of greed or at a holy time or place, and so forth. And so in the passage quoted, it is said pointedly that the orator "adds strength to his argument," as though this were something secondary.

Reply Obj. 2: A thing is said to be an accident of something in two ways. First, from being in that thing: thus, whiteness is said to be an accident of Socrates. Secondly, because it is together with that thing in the same subject: thus, whiteness is an accident of the art of music, inasmuch as they meet in the same subject, so as to touch one another, as it were. And in this sense circumstances are said to be the accidents of human acts.

Reply Obj. 3: As stated above (ad 2), an accident is said to be the accident of an accident, from the fact that they meet in the same subject. But this happens in two ways. First, in so far as two accidents are both related to the same subject, without any relation to one another; as whiteness and the art of music in Socrates. Secondly, when such accidents are related to one another; as when the subject receives one accident by means of the other; for instance, a body receives color by means of its surface. And thus also is one accident said to be in another; for we speak of color as being in the surface.

Accordingly, circumstances are related to acts in both these ways. For some circumstances that have a relation to acts, belong to the agent otherwise than through the act; as place and condition of person; whereas others belong to the agent by reason of the act, as the manner in which the act is done.

SECOND ARTICLE [I-II, Q. 7, Art. 2]

Whether Theologians Should Take Note of the Circumstances of Human Acts?

Objection 1: It would seem that theologians

should not take note of the circumstances of human acts. Because theologians do not consider human acts otherwise than according to their quality of good or evil. But it seems that circumstances cannot give quality to human acts; for a thing is never qualified, formally speaking, by that which is outside it; but by that which is in it. Therefore theologians should not take note of the circumstances of acts.

Obj. 2: Further, circumstances are the accidents of acts. But one thing may be subject to an infinity of accidents; hence the Philosopher says (Metaph. vi, 2) that "no art or science considers accidental being, except only the art of sophistry." Therefore the theologian has not to consider circumstances.

Obj. 3: Further, the consideration of circumstances belongs to the orator. But oratory is not a part of theology. Therefore it is not a theologian's business to consider circumstances.

*On the contrary,* Ignorance of circumstances causes an act to be involuntary, according to Damascene (De Fide Orth. ii, 24) and Gregory of Nyssa [*Nemesius, De Nat. Hom. xxxi.]. But involuntariness excuses from sin, the consideration of which belongs to the theologian. Therefore circumstances also should be considered by the theologian.

*I answer that,* Circumstances come under the consideration of the theologian, for a threefold reason. First, because the theologian considers human acts, inasmuch as man is thereby directed to Happiness. Now, everything that is directed to an end should be proportionate to that end. But acts are made proportionate to an end by means of a certain commensurateness, which results from the due circumstances. Hence the theologian has to consider the circumstances. Secondly, because the theologian considers human acts according as they are found to be good or evil, better or worse: and this diversity depends on circumstances, as we shall see further on (Q. 18, AA. 10, 11; Q. 73, A. 7). Thirdly, because the theologian considers human acts under the aspect of merit and demerit, which is proper to human acts; and for this it is requisite that they be voluntary. Now a human act is deemed to be voluntary or involuntary, according to knowledge or ignorance of circumstances, as stated above (Q. 6, A. 8). Therefore the theologian has to consider circumstances.

Reply Obj. 1: Good directed to the end is said to be useful; and this implies some kind of relation: wherefore the Philosopher says (Ethic. i, 6) that "the good in the genus 'relation' is the useful." Now, in the genus "relation" a thing is denominated not only according to that which is inherent in the thing, but also according to that which is extrinsic to it: as may be seen in the expressions "right" and "left," "equal" and "unequal," and such like. Accordingly, since the goodness of acts consists in their utility to the end, nothing hinders their being called good or bad according to their proportion to extrinsic things that are adjacent to them.

Reply Obj. 2: Accidents which are altogether accidental are neglected by every art, by reason of their uncertainty and infinity. But such like accidents are not what we call circumstances; because circumstances although, as stated above (A. 1), they are extrinsic to the act, nevertheless are in a kind of contact with it, by being related to it. Proper accidents, however, come under the consideration of art.

Reply Obj. 3: The consideration of circumstances belongs to the moralist, the politician, and the orator. To the moralist, in so far as with respect to circumstances we find or lose the mean of virtue in human acts and passions. To the politician and to the orator, in so far as circumstances make acts to be worthy of praise or blame, of excuse or indictment. In different ways, however: because where the orator persuades, the politician judges. To the theologian this consideration belongs, in all the aforesaid ways: since to him all the other arts are subservient: for he has to consider virtuous and vicious acts, just as the moralist does; and with the orator and politician he considers acts according as they are deserving of reward or punishment.

THIRD ARTICLE [I-II, Q. 7, Art. 3]

Whether the Circumstances Are Properly Set Forth in the Third Book of Ethics?

Objection 1: It would seem that the circumstances are not properly set forth in *Ethic.* iii, 1. For a circumstance of an act is described as something outside the act. Now time and place answer to this description. Therefore there are only two circumstances, to wit, "when" and "where."

Obj. 2: Further, we judge from the circumstances whether a thing is well or ill done. But this belongs to the mode of an act. Therefore all the circumstances are included under one, which is the "mode of acting."

Obj. 3: Further, circumstances are not part of the substance of an act. But the causes of an act seem to belong to its substance. Therefore no circumstance should be taken from the cause of the act itself. Accordingly, neither "who," nor "why," nor "about what," are circumstances: since "who" refers to the efficient cause, "why" to the final cause, and "about what" to the material cause.

On the contrary is the authority of the Philosopher in *Ethic.* iii, 1.

*I answer that,* Tully, in his Rhetoric (De Invent. Rhetor. i), gives seven circumstances, which are contained in this verse:

"Quis, quid, ubi, quibus auxiliis, cur, quomodo, quando—

"Who, what, where, by what aids, why, how, and when."

For in acts we must take note of "who" did it, "by what aids" or "instruments" he did it, "what" he did, "where" he did it, "why" he did it, "how" and "when" he did it. But Aristotle in *Ethic.* iii, 1 adds yet another, to wit, "about what," which Tully includes in the circumstance "what."

The reason of this enumeration may be set down as follows. For a circumstance is described as something outside the substance of the act, and yet in a way touching it. Now this happens in three ways: first, inasmuch as it touches the act itself; secondly, inasmuch as it touches the cause of the act; thirdly, inasmuch as it touches the effect. It touches the act itself, either by way of measure, as "time" and "place"; or by qualifying the act as the "mode of acting." It touches the effect when we consider "what" is done. It touches the cause of the act, as to the final cause, by the circumstance "why"; as to the material cause, or object, in the circumstance "about what"; as to the principal efficient cause, in the circumstance "who"; and as to the instrumental efficient cause, in the circumstance "by what aids."

Reply Obj. 1: Time and place surround ( *circumstant* ) the act by way of measure; but the others surround the act by touching it in any other way, while they are extrinsic to the substance of the act.

Reply Obj. 2: This mode "well" or "ill" is not a circumstance, but results from all the circumstances. But the mode which refers to a quality of the act is a special circumstance; for instance, that a man walk fast or slowly; that he strike hard or gently, and so forth.

Reply Obj. 3: A condition of the cause, on which the substance of the act depends, is not a circumstance; it must be an additional condition. Thus, in regard to the object, it is not a circumstance of theft that the object is another's property, for this belongs to the substance of the act; but that it be great or small. And the same applies to the other circumstances which are considered in reference to the other causes. For the end that specifies the act is not a circumstance, but some additional end. Thus, that a valiant man act *valiantly for the sake of* the good of the virtue o[f] fortitude, is not a circumstance; but if he act valiantly for the sake of the delivery of the state, or of Christendom, or some such purpose. The same is to be said with regard to the circumstance "what"; for that a man by pouring water on someone should happen to wash him, is not a circumstance of the washing; but that in doing so he give him a chill, or scald him; heal him or harm him, these are circumstances.

FOURTH ARTICLE [I-II, Q. 7, Art. 4]

Whether the Most Important Circumstances Are "Why" and "In What the Act Consists"?

Objection 1: It would seem that these are not the most important circumstances, namely, "why" and those "in which the act is, [* hen ois e praxis *]" as stated in*Ethic. iii, 1. For those in which the act is seem to be place and time: and these do not seem to be the most important of the circumstances, since, of them all, they are the most extrinsic to the act. Therefore those things in which the act is are not the most important circumstances.

Obj. 2: Further, the end of a thing is extrinsic to it. Therefore it is not the most important circumstance.

Obj. 3: Further, that which holds the foremost place in regard to each thing, is its cause and its form. But the cause of an act is the person that does it; while the form of an act is the manner in which it is done. Therefore these two circumstances seem to be of the greatest importance.

*On the contrary,* Gregory of Nyssa [*Nemesius, De Nat. Hom. xxxi.] says that "the most important circumstances" are "why it is done" and "what is done."

*I answer that,* As stated above (Q. 1, A. 1), acts are properly called human, inasmuch as they are voluntary. Now, the motive and object of the will is the end. Therefore that circumstance is the most important of all which touches the act on the part of the end, viz. the circumstance "why": and the second in importance, is that which touches the very substance of the act, viz. the circumstance "what he did." As to the other circumstances, they are more or less important, according as they more or less approach to these.

Reply Obj. 1: By those things "in which the act is" the Philosopher does not mean time and place, but those circumstances that are affixed to the act itself. Wherefore Gregory of Nyssa [*Nemesius, De Nat. Hom. xxxi], as though he were explaining the dictum of the Philosopher, instead of the latter's term—"in which the act is"—said, "what is done."

Reply Obj. 2: Although the end is not part of the substance of the act, yet it is the most important cause of the act, inasmuch as it moves the agent to act. Wherefore the moral act is specified chiefly by the end.

Reply Obj. 3: The person that does the act is the cause of that act, inasmuch as he is moved thereto by the end; and it is chiefly in this respect that he is directed to the act; while other conditions of the person have not such an important relation to the act. As to the mode, it is not the substantial form of the act, for in an act the substantial form depends on the object and term or end; but it is, as it were, a certain accidental quality of the act.

## QUESTION 8

OF THE WILL, IN REGARD TO WHAT IT WILLS (In Three Articles)

We must now consider the different acts of the will; and in the first place, those acts which belong to the will itself immediately, as being elicited by the will; secondly, those acts which are commanded by the will.

Now the will is moved to the end, and to the means to the end; we must therefore consider: (1) those acts of the will whereby it is moved to the end; and (2) those whereby it is moved to the means. And since it seems that there are three acts of the will in reference to the end; viz. "volition," "enjoyment," and "intention"; we must consider: (1) volition; (2) enjoyment; (3) intention. Concerning the first, three things must be considered:

(1) Of what things is the will?

(2) By what is the will moved?

(3) How is it moved?

Under the first head there are three points of inquiry:

(1) Whether the will is of good only?

(2) Whether it is of the end only, or also of the means?

(3) If in any way it be of the means, whether it be moved to the end and to the means, by the same movement?

FIRST ARTICLE [I-II, Q. 8, Art. 1]

Whether the Will Is of Good Only?

Objection 1: It would seem that the will is not of good only. For the same power regards opposites; for instance, sight regards white and black. But good and evil are opposites. Therefore the will is not only of good, but also of evil.

Obj. 2: Further, rational powers can be directed to opposite purposes, according to the Philosopher (Metaph. ix, 2). But the will is a rational power, since it is "in the reason," as is stated in *De Anima* iii, 9. Therefore the will can be directed to opposites; and consequently its volition is not confined to good, but extends to evil.

Obj. 3: Further, good and being are convertible. But volition is directed not only to beings, but also to non-beings. For sometimes we wish "not to walk," or "not to speak"; and again at times we wish for future things, which are not actual beings. Therefore the will is not of good only.

*On the contrary,* Dionysius says (Div. Nom. iv) that "evil is outside the scope of the will," and that "all things desire good."

*I answer that,* The will is a rational appetite. Now every appetite is only of something good. The reason of this is that the appetite is nothing else than an inclination of a person desirous of a thing towards that thing. Now every inclination is to something like and suitable to the thing inclined. Since, therefore, everything, inasmuch as it is being and substance, is a good, it must needs be that every inclination is to something good. And hence it is that the Philosopher says (Ethic. i, 1) that "the good is that which all desire."

But it must be noted that, since every inclination results from a form, the natural appetite results from a form existing in the nature of things: while the sensitive appetite, as also the intellective or rational appetite, which we call the will, follows from an apprehended form. Therefore, just as the natural appetite tends to good existing in a thing; so the animal or voluntary appetite tends to a good which is apprehended. Consequently, in order that the will tend to anything, it is requisite, not that this be good in very truth, but that it be apprehended as good. Wherefore the Philosopher says (Phys. ii, 3) that "the end is a good, or an apparent good."

Reply Obj. 1: The same power regards opposites, but it is not referred to them in the same way. Accordingly, the will is referred both to good and evil: but to good by desiring it: to evil, by shunning it. Wherefore the actual desire of good is called "volition" [*In Latin, 'voluntas'. To avoid confusion with "voluntas" (the will) St. Thomas adds a word of explanation, which in the translation may appear superfluous.], meaning thereby the act of the will; for it is in this sense that we are now speaking of the will. On the other hand, the shunning of evil is better described as "nolition": wherefore, just as volition is of good, so nolition is of evil.

Reply Obj. 2: A rational power is not to be directed to all opposite purposes, but to those which are contained under its proper object; for no power seeks other than its proper object. Now, the object of the will is good. Wherefore the will can be directed to such opposite purposes as are contained under good, such as to be moved or to be at rest, to speak or to be silent, and such like: for the will can be directed to either under the aspect of good.

Reply Obj. 3: That which is not a being in nature, is considered as a being in the reason, wherefore negations and privations are said to be "beings of reason." In this way, too, future things, in so far as they are apprehended, are beings. Accordingly, in so far as such like are beings, they are apprehended under the aspect of good; and it is thus that the will is directed to them. Wherefore the Philosopher says (Ethic. v, 1) that "to lack evil is considered as a good."

SECOND ARTICLE [I-II, Q. 8, Art. 2]

Whether Volition Is of the End Only, or Also of the Means?

Objection 1: It would seem that volition is not of the means, but of the end only. For the Philosopher says (Ethic. iii, 2) that "volition is of the end, while choice is of the means."

Obj. 2: Further, "For objects differing in genus there are corresponding different powers of the soul" (Ethic. vi, 1). Now, the end and the means are in different genera of good: because the end, which is a good either of rectitude or of pleasure, is in the genus "quality," or "action," or "passion"; whereas the good which is useful, and is directed to and end, is in the genus "relation" (Ethic. i, 6). Therefore, if volition is of the end, it is not of the means.

Obj. 3: Further, habits are proportionate to powers, since they are perfections thereof. But in those habits which are called practical arts, the end belongs to one, and the means to another art; thus the use of a ship, which is its end, belongs to the (art of the) helmsman; whereas the building of the ship, which is directed to the end, belongs to the art of the shipwright. Therefore, since volition is of the end, it is not of the means.

*On the contrary,* In natural things, it is by the same power that a thing passes through the middle space, and arrives at the terminus. But the means are a kind of middle space, through which one arrives at the end or terminus. Therefore, if volition is of the end, it is also of the means.

*I answer that,* The word "voluntas" sometimes designates the power of the will, sometimes its act [*See note to A. 1, Reply Obj. 1]. Accordingly, if we speak of the will as a power, thus it extends both to the end and to the means. For every power extends to those things in which may be considered the aspect of the object of that power in any way whatever: thus the sight extends to all things whatsoever that are in any way colored. Now the aspect of good, which is the object of the power of the will, may be found not only in the end, but also in the means.

If, however, we speak of the will in regard to its act, then, properly speaking, volition is of the end only. Because every act denominated from a power, designates the simple act of that power: thus "to understand" designates the simple act of the understanding. Now the simple act of a power is referred to that which is in itself the object of that power. But that which is good and willed in itself is the end. Wherefore volition, properly speaking, is of the end itself. On the other hand, the means are good and willed, not in themselves, but as referred to the end. Wherefore the will is directed to them, only in so far as it is directed to the end: so that what it wills in them, is the end. Thus, to understand, is properly directed to things that are known in themselves, i.e. first principles: but we do not speak of understanding with regard to things known through first principles, except in so far as we see the principles in those things. For in morals the end is what principles are in speculative science (Ethic. viii, 8).

Reply Obj. 1: The Philosopher is speaking of the will in reference to the simple act of the will; not in reference to the power of the will.

Reply Obj. 2: There are different powers for objects that differ in genus and are on an equality; for instance, sound and color are different genera of sensibles, to which are referred hearing and sight. But the useful and the righteous are not on an equality, but are as that which is of itself, and that which is in relation to another. Now such like objects are always referred to the same power; for instance, the power of sight perceives both color and light by which color is seen.

Reply Obj. 3: Not everything that diversifies habits, diversifies the powers: since habits are certain determinations of powers to certain special acts. Moreover, every practical art considers both the end and the means. For the art of the helmsman does indeed consider the end, as that which it effects; and the means, as that which it commands. On the other hand, the ship-building art considers the means as that which it effects; but it considers that which is the end, as that to which it refers what it effects. And again, in every practical art there is an end proper to it and means that belong properly to that art.

THIRD ARTICLE [I-II, Q. 8, Art. 3]

Whether the Will Is Moved by the Same Act to the End and to the Means?

Objection 1: It would seem that the will is moved by the same act, to the end and to the means. Because according to the Philosopher (Topic. iii, 2) "where one thing is on account of another there is only one." But the will does not will the means save on account of the end. Therefore it is moved to both by the same act.

Obj. 2: Further, the end is the reason for willing the means, just as light is the reason of seeing colors. But light and colors are seen by the same act. Therefore it is the same movement of the will, whereby it wills the end and the means.

Obj. 3: Further, it is one and the same natural movement which tends through the middle space to the terminus. But the means are in comparison to the end, as the middle space is to the terminus. Therefore it is the same movement of the will whereby it is directed to the end and to the means.

*On the contrary,* Acts are diversified according to their objects. But the end is a different species of good from the means, which are a useful good. Therefore the will is not moved to both by the same act.

*I answer that,* Since the end is willed in itself, whereas the means, as such, are only willed for the end, it is evident that the will can be moved to the end, without being moved to the means; whereas it cannot be moved to the means, as such, unless it is moved to the end. Accordingly the will is moved to the end in two ways: first, to the end absolutely and in itself; secondly, as the reason for willing the means. Hence it is evident that the will is moved by one and the same movement, to the end, as the reason for willing the means; and to the means themselves. But it is another act whereby the will is moved to the end absolutely. And sometimes this act precedes the other in time; for example when a man first wills to have health, and afterwards deliberating by what means to be healed, wills to send for the doctor to heal him. The same happens in regard to the intellect: for at first a man understands the principles in themselves; but afterwards he understands them in the conclusions, inasmuch as he assents to the conclusions on account of the principles.

Reply Obj. 1: This argument holds in respect of the will being moved to the end as the reason for willing the means.

Reply Obj. 2: Whenever color is seen, by the same act the light is seen; but the light can be seen without the color being seen. In like manner whenever a man wills the means, by the same act he wills the end; but not the conversely.

Reply Obj. 3: In the execution of a work, the means are as the middle space, and the end, as the terminus. Wherefore just as natural movement sometimes stops in the middle and does not reach the terminus; so sometimes one is busy with the means, without gaining the end. But in willing it is the reverse: the will through (willing) the end comes to will the means; just as the intellect arrives at the conclusions through the principles which are called "means." Hence it is that sometimes the intellect understands a mean, and does not proceed thence to the conclusion. And in like manner the will sometimes wills the end, and yet does not proceed to will the means.

The solution to the argument in the contrary sense is clear from what has been said above (A. 2, ad 2). For the useful and the righteous are not species of good in an equal degree, but are as that which is for its own sake and that which is for the sake of something else: wherefore the act of the will can be directed to one and not to the other; but not conversely.

# QUESTION 9

OF THAT WHICH MOVES THE WILL (In Six Articles)

We must now consider what moves the will: and under this head there are six points of inquiry:

(1) Whether the will is moved by the intellect?

(2) Whether it is moved by the sensitive appetite?

(3) Whether the will moves itself?

(4) Whether it is moved by an extrinsic principle?

(5) Whether it is moved by a heavenly body?

(6) Whether the will is moved by God alone as by an extrinsic principle?

FIRST ARTICLE [I-II, Q. 9, Art. 1]

Whether the Will Is Moved by the Intellect?

Objection 1: It would seem that the will is not moved by the intellect. For Augustine says on Ps. 118:20: "My soul hath coveted to long for Thy justifications: The intellect flies ahead, the desire follows sluggishly or not at all: we know what is good, but deeds delight us not." But it would not be so, if the will were moved by the intellect: because movement of the movable results from motion of the mover. Therefore the intellect does not move the will.

Obj. 2: Further, the intellect in presenting the appetible object to the will, stands in relation to the will, as the imagination in representing the appetible object to the sensitive appetite. But the imagination, in presenting the appetible object, does not remove the sensitive appetite: indeed sometimes our imagination affects us no more than what is set before us in a picture, and moves us not at all (De Anima ii, 3). Therefore neither does the intellect move the will.

Obj. 3: Further, the same is not mover and moved in respect of the same thing. But the will moves the intellect; for we exercise the intellect when we will. Therefore the intellect does not move the will.

*On the contrary,* The Philosopher says (De Anima iii, 10) that "the appetible object is a mover not moved, whereas the will is a mover moved."

*I answer that,* A thing requires to be moved by something in so far as it is in potentiality to several things; for that which is in potentiality needs to be reduced to act by something actual; and to do this is to move. Now a power of the soul is seen to be in potentiality to different things in two ways: first, with regard to acting and not acting; secondly, with regard to this or that action. Thus the sight sometimes sees actually, and sometimes sees not: and sometimes it sees white, and sometimes black. It needs therefore a mover in two respects, viz. as to the exercise or use of the act, and as to the determination of the act. The first of these is on the part of the subject, which is sometimes acting, sometimes not acting: while the other is on the part of the object, by reason of which the act is specified.

The motion of the subject itself is due to some agent. And since every agent acts for an end, as was shown above (Q. 1, A. 2), the principle of this motion lies in the end. And hence it is that the art which is concerned with the end, by its command moves the art which is concerned with the means; just as the "art of sailing commands the art of shipbuilding" (Phys. ii, 2). Now good in general, which has the nature of an end, is the object of the will. Consequently, in this respect, the will moves the other powers of the soul to their acts, for we make use of the other powers when we will. For the end and perfection of every other power, is included under the object of the will as some particular good: and always the art or power to which the universal end belongs, moves to their acts the arts or powers to which belong the particular ends included in the universal end. Thus the leader of an army, who intends the common good—i.e. the order of the whole army—by his command moves one of the captains, who intends the order of one company.

On the other hand, the object moves, by determining the act, after the manner of a formal principle, whereby in natural things actions are specified, as heating by heat. Now the first formal principle is universal "being" and "truth," which is the object of the intellect. And therefore by this kind of motion the intellect moves the will, as presenting its object to it.

Reply Obj. 1: The passage quoted proves, not that the intellect does not move, but that it does not move of necessity.

Reply Obj. 2: Just as the imagination of a form without estimation of fitness or harmfulness, does not move the sensitive appetite; so neither does the apprehension of the true without the aspect of goodness and desirability. Hence it is not the speculative intellect that moves, but the practical intellect (De Anima iii, 9).

Reply Obj. 3: The will moves the intellect as to the exercise of its act; since even the true itself which is the perfection of the intellect, is included in the universal good, as a particular good. But as to the determination of the act, which the act derives from the object, the intellect moves the will; since the good itself is apprehended under a special aspect as contained in the universal true. It is therefore evident that the same is not mover and moved in the same respect.

SECOND ARTICLE [I-II, Q. 9, Art. 2]

Whether the Will Is Moved by the Sensitive Appetite?

Objection 1: It would seem that the will cannot be moved by the sensitive appetite. For "to move and to act is more excellent than to be passive," as Augustine says (Gen. ad lit. xii, 16). But the sensitive appetite is less excellent than the will which is the intellectual appetite; just as sense is less excellent than intellect. Therefore the sensitive appetite does not move the will.

Obj. 2: Further, no particular power can produce a universal effect. But the sensitive appetite is a particular power, because it follows the particular apprehension of sense. Therefore it cannot cause the movement of the will, which movement is universal, as following the universal apprehension of the intellect.

Obj. 3: Further, as is proved in *Phys.* viii, 5, the mover is not moved by that which it moves, in such a way that there be reciprocal motion. But the will moves the sensitive appetite, inasmuch as the sensitive appetite obeys the reason. Therefore the sensitive appetite does not move the will.

*On the contrary,* It is written (James 1:14): "Every man is tempted by his own concupiscence, being drawn away and allured." But man would not be drawn away by his concupiscence, unless his will were moved by the sensitive appetite, wherein concupiscence resides. Therefore the sensitive appetite moves the will.

*I answer that,* As stated above (A. 1), that which is apprehended as good and fitting, moves the will by way of object. Now, that a thing appear to be good and fitting, happens from two causes: namely, from the condition, either of the thing proposed, or of the one to whom it is proposed. For fitness is spoken of by way of relation; hence it depends on both extremes. And hence it is that taste, according as it is variously disposed, takes to a thing in various ways, as being fitting or unfitting. Wherefore as the Philosopher says (Ethic. iii, 5): "According as a man is, such does the end seem to him."

Now it is evident that according to a passion of the sensitive appetite man is changed to a certain disposition. Wherefore according as man is affected by a passion, something seems to him fitting, which does not seem so when he is not so affected: thus that seems good to a man when angered, which does not seem good when he is calm. And in this way, the sensitive appetite moves the will, on the part of the object.

Reply Obj. 1: Nothing hinders that which is better simply and in itself, from being less excellent in a certain respect. Accordingly the will is simply more excellent than the sensitive appetite: but in respect of the man in whom a passion is predominant, in so far as he is subject to that passion, the sensitive appetite is more excellent.

Reply Obj. 2: Men's acts and choices are in reference to singulars. Wherefore from the very fact that the sensitive appetite is a particular power, it has great influence in disposing man so that something seems to him such or otherwise, in particular cases.

Reply Obj. 3: As the Philosopher says (Polit. i, 2), the reason, in which resides the will, moves, by its command, the irascible and concupiscible powers, not, indeed, "by a despotic sovereignty," as a slave is moved by his master, but by a "royal and politic sovereignty," as free men are ruled by their governor, and can nevertheless act counter to his commands. Hence both irascible and concupiscible can move counter to the will: and accordingly nothing hinders the will from being moved by them at times.

THIRD ARTICLE [I-II, Q. 9, Art. 3]

Whether the Will Moves Itself?

Objection 1: It would seem that the will does not move itself. For every mover, as such, is in act: whereas what is moved, is in potentiality; since "movement is the act of that which is in potentiality, as such" [*Aristotle, *Phys.* iii, 1]. Now the same is not in potentiality and in act, in respect of the same. Therefore nothing moves itself. Neither, therefore, can the will move itself.

Obj. 2: Further, the movable is moved on the mover being present. But the will is always present to itself. If, therefore, it moved itself, it would always be moving itself, which is clearly false.

Obj. 3: Further, the will is moved by the intellect, as stated above (A. 1). If, therefore, the will move itself, it would follow that the same thing is at once moved immediately by two movers; which seems unreasonable. Therefore the will does not move itself.

*On the contrary,* The will is mistress of its own act, and to it belongs to will and not to will. But this would not be so, had it not the power to move itself to will. Therefore it moves itself.

*I answer that,* As stated above (A. 1), it belongs to the will to move the other powers, by reason of the end which is the will's object. Now, as stated above (Q. 8, A. 2), the end is in things appetible, what the principle is in things intelligible. But it is evident that the intellect, through its knowledge of the principle, reduces itself from potentiality to act, as to its knowledge of the conclusions; and thus it moves itself. And, in like manner, the will, through its volition of the end, moves itself to will the means.

Reply Obj. 1: It is not in respect of the same that the will moves itself and is moved: wherefore neither is it in act and in potentiality in respect of the same. But forasmuch as it actually wills the end, it reduces itself from potentiality to act, in respect of the means, so as, in a word, to will them actually.

Reply Obj. 2: The power of the will is always actually present to itself; but the act of the will, whereby it wills an end, is not always in the will. But it is by this act that it moves itself. Accordingly it does not follow that it is always moving itself.

Reply Obj. 3: The will is moved by the intellect, otherwise than by itself. By the intellect it is moved on the part of the object: whereas it is moved by itself, as to the exercise of its act, in respect of the end.

FOURTH ARTICLE [I-II, Q. 9, Art. 4]

Whether the Will Is Moved by an Exterior Principle?

Objection 1: It would seem that the will is not moved by anything exterior. For the movement of the will is voluntary. But it is essential to the voluntary act that it be from an intrinsic principle, just as it is essential to the natural act. Therefore the movement of the will is not from anything exterior.

Obj. 2: Further, the will cannot suffer violence, as was shown above (Q. 6, A. 4). But the violent act is one "the principle of which is outside the agent" [*Aristotle, *Ethic.* iii, 1]. Therefore the will cannot be moved by anything exterior.

Obj. 3: Further, that which is sufficiently moved by one mover, needs not to be moved by another. But the will moves itself sufficiently. Therefore it is not moved by anything exterior.

*On the contrary,* The will is moved by the object, as stated above (A. 1). But the object of the will can be something exterior, offered to the sense. Therefore the will can be moved by something exterior.

*I answer that,* As far as the will is moved by the object, it is evident that it can be moved by something exterior. But in so far as it is moved in the exercise of its act, we must again hold it to be moved by some exterior principle.

For everything that is at one time an agent actually, and at another time an agent in potentiality, needs to be moved by a mover. Now it is evident that the will begins to will something, whereas previously it did not will it. Therefore it must, of necessity, be moved by something to will it. And, indeed, it moves itself, as stated above (A. 3), in so far as through willing the end it reduces itself to the act of willing the means. Now it cannot do this without the aid of counsel: for when a man wills to be healed, he begins to reflect how this can be attained, and through this reflection he comes to the conclusion that he can be healed by a physician: and this he wills. But since he did not always actually will to have health, he must, of necessity, have begun, through something moving him, to will to be healed. And if the will moved itself to will this, it must, of necessity, have done this with the aid of counsel following some previous volition. But this process could not go on to infinity. Wherefore we must, of necessity, suppose that the will advanced to its first movement in virtue of the instigation of some exterior mover, as Aristotle concludes in a chapter of the Eudemian Ethics (vii, 14).

Reply Obj. 1: It is essential to the voluntary act that its principle be within the agent: but it is not necessary that this inward principle be the first principle unmoved by another. Wherefore though the voluntary act has an inward proximate principle, nevertheless its first principle is from without. Thus, too, the first principle of the natural movement is from without, that, to wit, which moves nature.

Reply Obj. 2: For an act to be violent it is not enough that its principle be extrinsic, but we must add "without the concurrence of him that suffers violence." This does not happen when the will is moved by an exterior principle: for it is the will that wills, though moved by another. But this movement would be violent, if it were counter to the movement of the will: which in the present case is impossible; since then the will would will and not will the same thing.

Reply Obj. 3: The will moves itself sufficiently in one respect, and in its own order, that is to say as proximate agent; but it cannot move itself in every respect, as we have shown. Wherefore it needs to be moved by another as first mover.

FIFTH ARTICLE [I-II, Q. 9, Art. 5]

Whether the Will Is Moved by a Heavenly Body?

Objection 1: It would seem that the human will is moved by a heavenly body. For all various and multiform movements are reduced, as to their cause, to a uniform movement which is that of the heavens, as is proved in *Phys.* viii, 9. But human movements are various and multiform, since they begin to be, whereas previously they were not. Therefore they are reduced, as to their cause, to the movement of the heavens, which is uniform according to its nature.

Obj. 2: Further, according to Augustine (De Trin. iii, 4) "the lower bodies are moved by the higher." But the movements of the human body, which are caused by the will, could not be reduced to the movement of the heavens, as to their cause, unless the will too were moved by the heavens. Therefore the heavens move the human will.

Obj. 3: Further, by observing the heavenly bodies astrologers foretell the truth about future human acts, which are caused by the will. But this would not be so, if the heavenly bodies could not move man's will. Therefore the human will is moved by a heavenly body.

*On the contrary,* Damascene says (De Fide Orth. ii, 7) that "the heavenly bodies are not the causes of our acts." But they would be, if the will, which is the principle of human acts, were moved by the heavenly bodies. Therefore the will is not moved by the heavenly bodies.

*I answer that,* It is evident that the will can be moved by the heavenly bodies in the same way as it is moved by its object; that is to say, in so far as exterior bodies, which move the will, through being offered to the senses, and also the organs themselves of the sensitive powers, are subject to the movements of the heavenly bodies.

But some have maintained that heavenly bodies have an influence on the human will, in the same way as some exterior agent moves the will, as to the exercise of its act. But this is impossible. For the "will," as stated in *De Anima* iii, 9, "is in the reason." Now the reason is a power of the soul, not bound to a bodily organ: wherefore it follows that the will is a power absolutely incorporeal and immaterial. But it is evident that no body can act on what is incorporeal, but rather the reverse: because things incorporeal and immaterial have a power more formal and more universal than any corporeal things whatever. Therefore it is impossible for a heavenly body to act directly on the intellect or will. For this reason Aristotle (De Anima iii, 3) ascribed to those who held that intellect differs not from sense, the theory that "such is the will of men, as is the day which the father of men and of gods bring on" [*Odyssey xviii. 135] (referring to Jupiter, by whom they understand the entire heavens). For all the sensitive powers, since they are acts of bodily organs, can be moved accidentally, by the heavenly bodies, i.e. through those bodies being moved, whose acts they are.

But since it has been stated (A. 2) that the intellectual appetite is moved, in a fashion, by the sensitive appetite, the movements of the heavenly bodies have an indirect bearing on the will; in so far as the will happens to be moved by the passions of the sensitive appetite.

Reply Obj. 1: The multiform movements of the human will are reduced to some uniform cause, which, however, is above the intellect and will. This can be said, not of any body, but of some superior immaterial substance. Therefore there is no need for the movement of the will to be referred to the movement of the heavens, as to its cause.

Reply Obj. 2: The movements of the human body are reduced, as to their cause, to the movement of a heavenly body, in so far as the disposition suitable to a particular movement, is somewhat due to the influence of heavenly bodies; also, in so far as the sensitive appetite is stirred by the influence of heavenly bodies; and again, in so far as exterior bodies are moved in accordance with the movement of heavenly bodies, at whose presence, the will begins to will or not to will something; for instance, when the body is chilled, we begin to wish to make the fire. But this movement of the will is on the part of the object offered from without: not on the part of an inward instigation.

Reply Obj. 3: As stated above (Cf. I, Q. 84, AA. 6, 7), the sensitive appetite is the act of a bodily organ. Wherefore there is no reason why man should not be prone to anger or concupiscence, or some like passion, by reason of the influence of heavenly bodies, just as by reason of his natural complexion. But the majority of men are led by the passions, which the wise alone resist. Consequently, in the majority of cases predictions about human acts, gathered from the observation of heavenly bodies, are fulfilled. Nevertheless, as Ptolemy says (Centiloquium v), "the wise man governs the stars"; which is a though to say that by resisting his passions, he opposes his will, which is free and nowise subject to the movement of the heavens, to such like effects of the heavenly bodies.

Or, as Augustine says (Gen. ad lit. ii, 15): "We must confess that when the truth is foretold by astrologers, this is due to some most hidden inspiration, to which the human mind is subject without knowing it. And since this is done in order to deceive man, it must be the work of the lying spirits."

SIXTH ARTICLE [I-II, Q. 9, Art. 6]

Whether the Will Is Moved by God Alone, As Exterior Principle?

Objection 1: It would seem that the will is not moved by God alone as exterior principle. For it is natural that the inferior be moved by its superior: thus the lower bodies are moved by the heavenly bodies. But there is something which is higher than the will of man and below God, namely, the angel. Therefore man's will can be moved by an angel also, as exterior principle.

Obj. 2: Further, the act of the will follows the act of the intellect. But man's intellect is reduced to act, not by God alone, but also by the angel who enlightens it, as Dionysius says (Coel. Hier. iv). For the same reason, therefore, the will also is moved by an angel.

Obj. 3: Further, God is not the cause of other than good things, according to Gen. 1:31: "God saw all the things that He had made, and they were very good." If, therefore man's will were moved by God alone, it would never be moved to evil: and yet it is the will whereby "we sin and whereby we do right," as Augustine says (Retract. i, 9).

*On the contrary,* It is written (Phil. 2:13): "It is God Who worketh in us" [Vulg.'you'] "both to will and to accomplish."

*I answer that,* The movement of the will is from within, as also is the movement of nature. Now although it is possible for something to move a natural thing, without being the cause of the thing moved, yet that alone, which is in some way the cause of a thing's nature, can cause a natural movement in that thing. For a stone is moved upwards by a man, who is not the cause of the stone's nature, but this movement is not natural to the stone; but the natural movement of the stone is caused by no other than the cause of its nature. Wherefore it is said in *Phys.* vii, 4, that the generator moves locally heavy and light things. Accordingly man endowed with a will is sometimes moved by something that is not his cause; but that his voluntary movement be from an exterior principle that is not the cause of his will, is impossible.

Now the cause of the will can be none other than God. And this is evident for two reasons. First, because the will is a power of the rational soul, which is caused by God alone, by creation, as was stated in the First Part (Q. 90, A. 2). Secondly, it is evident from the fact that the will is ordained to the universal good. Wherefore nothing else can be the cause of the will, except God Himself, Who is the universal good: while every other good is good by participation, and is some particular good, and a particular cause does not give a universal inclination. Hence neither can primary matter, which is potentiality to all forms, be created by some particular agent.

Reply Obj. 1: An angel is not above man in such a way as to be the cause of his will, as the heavenly bodies are the causes of natural forms, from which result the natural movements of natural bodies.

Reply Obj. 2: Man's intellect is moved by an angel, on the part of the object, which by the power of the angelic light is proposed to man's knowledge. And in this way the will also can be moved by a creature from without, as stated above (A. 4).

Reply Obj. 3: God moves man's will, as the Universal Mover, to the universal object of the will, which is good. And without this universal motion, man cannot will anything. But man determines himself by his reason to will this or that, which is true or apparent good. Nevertheless, sometimes God moves some specially to the willing of something determinate, which is good; as in the case of those whom He moves by grace, as we shall state later on (Q. 109, A. 2).

# QUESTION 10

OF THE MANNER IN WHICH THE WILL IS MOVED (In Four Articles)

We must now consider the manner in which the will is moved. Under this head there are four points of inquiry:

(1) Whether the will is moved to anything naturally?

(2) Whether it is moved of necessity by its object?

(3) Whether it is moved of necessity by the lower appetite?

(4) Whether it is moved of necessity by the exterior mover which is God?

FIRST ARTICLE [I-II, Q. 10, Art. 1]

Whether the Will Is Moved to Anything Naturally?

Objection 1: It would seem that the will is not moved to anything naturally. For the natural agent is condivided with the voluntary agent, as stated at the beginning of *Phys.* ii, 1. Therefore the will is not moved to anything naturally.

Obj. 2: Further, that which is natural is in a thing always: as "being hot" is in fire. But no movement is always in the will. Therefore no movement is natural to the will.

Obj. 3: Further, nature is determinate to one thing: whereas the will is referred to opposites. Therefore the will wills nothing naturally.

*On the contrary,* The movement of the will follows the movement of the intellect. But the intellect understands some things naturally. Therefore the will, too, wills some things naturally.

*I answer that,* As Boethius says (De Duabus Nat.) and the Philosopher also (Metaph. v, 4) the word "nature" is used in a manifold sense. For sometimes it stands for the intrinsic principle in movable things. In this sense nature is either matter or the material form, as stated in *Phys.* ii, 1. In another sense nature stands for any substance, or even for any being. And in this sense, that is said to be natural to a thing which befits it in respect of its substance. And this is that which of itself is in a thing. Now all things that do not of themselves belong to the thing in which they are, are reduced to something which belongs of itself to that thing, as to their principle. Wherefore, taking nature in this sense, it is necessary that the principle of whatever belongs to a thing, be a natural principle. This is evident in regard to the intellect: for the principles of intellectual knowledge are naturally known. In like manner the principle of voluntary movements must be something naturally willed.

Now this is good in general, to which the will tends naturally, as does each power to its object; and again it is the last end, which stands in the same relation to things appetible, as the first principles of demonstrations to things intelligible: and, speaking generally, it is all those things which belong to the willer according to his nature. For it is not only things pertaining to the will that the will desires, but also that which pertains to each power, and to the entire man. Wherefore man wills naturally not only the object of the will, but also other things that are appropriate to the other powers; such as the knowledge of truth, which befits the intellect; and to be and to live and other like things which regard the natural well-being; all of which are included in the object of the will, as so many particular goods.

Reply Obj. 1: The will is distinguished from nature as one kind of cause from another; for some things happen naturally and some are done voluntarily. There is, however, another manner of causing that is proper to the will, which is mistress of its act, besides the manner proper to nature, which is determinate to one thing. But since the will is founded on some nature, it is necessary that the movement proper to nature be shared by the will, to some extent: just as what belongs to a previous cause is shared by a subsequent cause. Because in every thing, being itself, which is from nature, precedes volition, which is from the will. And hence it is that the will wills something naturally.

Reply Obj. 2: In the case of natural things, that which is natural, as a result of the form only, is always in them actually, as heat is in fire. But that which is natural as a result of matter, is not always in them actually, but sometimes only in potentiality: because form is act, whereas matter is potentiality. Now movement is "the act of that which is in potentiality" (Aristotle, *Phys.* iii, 1). Wherefore that which belongs to, or results from, movement, in regard to natural things, is not always in them. Thus fire does not always move upwards, but only when it is outside its own place. [*The Aristotelian theory was that fire's proper place is the fiery heaven, i.e. the Empyrean.] And in like manner it is not necessary that the will (which is reduced from potentiality to act, when it wills something), should always be in the act of volition; but only when it is in a certain determinate disposition. But God's will, which is pure act, is always in the act of volition.

Reply Obj. 3: To every nature there is one thing corresponding, proportionate, however, to that nature. For to nature considered as a genus, there corresponds something one generically; and to nature as species there corresponds something one specifically; and to the individualized nature there corresponds some one individual. Since, therefore, the will is an immaterial power like the intellect, some one general thing corresponds to it, naturally which is the good; just as to the intellect there corresponds some one general thing, which is the true, or being, or "what a thing is." And under good in general are included many particular goods, to none of which is the will determined.

SECOND ARTICLE [I-II, Q. 10, Art. 2]

Whether the Will Is Moved, of Necessity, by Its Object?

Objection 1: It seems that the will is moved, of necessity, by its object. For the object of the will is compared to the will as mover to movable, as stated in *De Anima* iii, 10. But a mover, if it be sufficient, moves the movable of necessity. Therefore the will can be moved of necessity by its object.

Obj. 2: Further, just as the will is an immaterial power, so is the intellect: and both powers are ordained to a universal object, as stated above (A. 1, ad 3). But the intellect is moved, of necessity, by its object: therefore the will also, by its object.

Obj. 3: Further, whatever one wills, is either the end, or something ordained to an end. But, seemingly, one wills an end necessarily: because it is like the principle in speculative matters, to which principle one assents of necessity. Now the end is the reason for willing the means; and so it seems that we will the means also necessarily. Therefore the will is moved of necessity by its object.

*On the contrary,* The rational powers, according to the Philosopher (Metaph. ix, 2) are directed to opposites. But the will is a rational power, since it is in the reason, as stated in De Anima iii, 9. Therefore the will is directed to opposites. Therefore it is not moved, of necessity, to either of the opposites.

*I answer that,* The will is moved in two ways: first, as to the exercise of its act; secondly, as to the specification of its act, derived from the object. As to the first way, no object moves the will necessarily, for no matter what the object be, it is in man's power not to think of it, and consequently not to will it actually. But as to the second manner of motion, the will is moved by one object necessarily, by another not. For in the movement of a power by its object, we must consider under what aspect the object moves the power. For the visible moves the sight, under the aspect of color actually visible. Wherefore if color be offered to the sight, it moves the sight necessarily: unless one turns one's eyes away; which belongs to the exercise of the act. But if the sight were confronted with something not in all respects colored actually, but only so in some respects, and in other respects not, the sight would not of necessity see such an object: for it might look at that part of the object which is not actually colored, and thus it would not see it. Now just as the actually colored is the object of sight, so is good the object of the will. Wherefore if the will be offered an object which is good universally and from every point of view, the will tends to it of necessity, if it wills anything at all; since it cannot will the opposite. If, on the other hand, the will is offered an object that is not good from every point of view, it will not tend to it of necessity. And since lack of any good whatever, is a non-good, consequently, that good alone which is perfect and lacking in nothing, is such a good that the will cannot not-will it: and this is Happiness. Whereas any other particular goods, in so far as they are lacking in some good, can be regarded as non-goods: and from this point of view, they can be set aside or approved by the will, which can tend to one and the same thing from various points of view.

Reply Obj. 1: The sufficient mover of a power is none but that object that in every respect presents the aspect of the mover of that power. If, on the other hand, it is lacking in any respect, it will not move of necessity, as stated above.

Reply Obj. 2: The intellect is moved, of necessity, by an object which is such as to be always and necessarily true: but not by that which may be either true or false—viz. by that which is contingent: as we have said of the good.

Reply Obj. 3: The last end moves the will necessarily, because it is the perfect good. In like manner whatever is ordained to that end, and without which the end cannot be attained, such as "to be" and "to live," and the like. But other things without which the end can be gained, are not necessarily willed by one who wills the end: just as he who assents to the principle, does not necessarily assent to the conclusions, without which the principles can still be true.

THIRD ARTICLE [I-II, Q. 10, Art. 3]

Whether the Will Is Moved, of Necessity, by the Lower Appetite?

Objection 1: It would seem that the will is moved of necessity by a passion of the lower appetite. For the Apostle says (Rom. 7:19): "The good which I will I do not; but the evil which I will not, that I do": and this is said by reason of concupiscence, which is a passion. Therefore the will is moved of necessity by a passion.

Obj. 2: Further, as stated in *Ethic.* iii, 5, "according as a man is, such does the end seem to him." But it is not in man's power to cast aside a passion at once. Therefore it is not in man's power not to will that to which the passion inclines him.

Obj. 3: Further, a universal cause is not applied to a particular effect, except by means of a particular cause: wherefore the universal reason does not move save by means of a particular estimation, as stated in *De Anima* iii, 11. But as the universal reason is to the particular estimation, so is the will to the sensitive appetite. Therefore the will is not moved to will something particular, except through the sensitive appetite. Therefore, if the sensitive appetite happen to be disposed to something, by reason of a passion, the will cannot be moved in a contrary sense.

*On the contrary,* It is written (Gen. 4:7): "Thy lust [Vulg. 'The lust thereof'] shall be under thee, and thou shalt have dominion over it." Therefore man's will is not moved of necessity by the lower appetite.

*I answer that,* As stated above (Q. 9, A. 2), the passion of the sensitive appetite moves the will, in so far as the will is moved by its object: inasmuch as, to wit, man through being disposed in such and such a way by a passion, judges something to be fitting and good, which he would not judge thus were it not for the passion. Now this influence of a passion on man occurs in two ways. First, so that his reason is wholly bound, so that he has not the use of reason: as happens in those who through a violent access of anger or concupiscence become furious or insane, just as they may from some other bodily disorder; since such like passions do not take place without some change in the body. And of such the same is to be said as of irrational animals, which follow, of necessity, the impulse of their passions: for in them there is neither movement of reason, nor, consequently, of will.

Sometimes, however, the reason is not entirely engrossed by the passion, so that the judgment of reason retains, to a certain extent, its freedom: and thus the movement of the will remains in a certain degree. Accordingly in so far as the reason remains free, and not subject to the passion, the will's movement, which also remains, does not tend of necessity to that whereto the passion inclines it. Consequently, either there is no movement of the will in that man, and the passion alone holds its sway: or if there be a movement of the will, it does not necessarily follow the passion.

Reply Obj. 1: Although the will cannot prevent the movement of concupiscence from arising, of which the Apostle says: "The evil which I will not, that I do—i.e. I desire"; yet it is in the power of the will not to will to desire or not to consent to concupiscence. And thus it does not necessarily follow the movement of concupiscence.

Reply Obj. 2: Since there is in man a twofold nature, intellectual and sensitive; sometimes man is such and such uniformly in respect of his whole soul: either because the sensitive part is wholly subject to his reason, as in the virtuous; or because reason is entirely engrossed by passion, as in a madman. But sometimes, although reason is clouded by passion, yet something of this reason remains free. And in respect of this, man can either repel the passion entirely, or at least hold himself in check so as not to be led away by the passion. For when thus disposed, since man is variously disposed according to the various parts of the soul, a thing appears to him otherwise according to his reason, than it does according to a passion.

Reply Obj. 3: The will is moved not only by the universal good apprehended by the reason, but also by good apprehended by sense. Wherefore he can be moved to some particular good independently of a passion of the sensitive appetite. For we will and do many things without passion, and through choice alone; as is most evident in those cases wherein reason resists passion.

FOURTH ARTICLE [I-II, Q. 10, Art. 4]

Whether the Will Is Moved of Necessity by the Exterior Mover Which Is God?

Objection 1: It would seem that the will is moved of necessity by God. For every agent that cannot be resisted moves of necessity. But God cannot be resisted, because His power is infinite; wherefore it is written (Rom. 9:19): "Who resisteth His will?" Therefore God moves the will of necessity.

Obj. 2: Further, the will is moved of necessity to whatever it wills naturally, as stated above (A. 2, ad 3). But "whatever God does in a thing is natural to it," as Augustine says (Contra Faust. xxvi, 3). Therefore the will wills of necessity everything to which God moves it.

Obj. 3: Further, a thing is possible, if nothing impossible follows from its being supposed. But something impossible follows from the supposition that the will does not will that to which God moves it: because in that case God's operation would be ineffectual. Therefore it is not possible for the will not to will that to which God moves it. Therefore it wills it of necessity.

*On the contrary,* It is written (Ecclus. 15:14): "God made man from the beginning, and left him in the hand of his own counsel." Therefore He does not of necessity move man's will.

*I answer that,* As Dionysius says (Div. Nom. iv) "it belongs to Divine providence, not to destroy but to preserve the nature of things." Wherefore it moves all things in accordance with their conditions; so that from necessary causes through the Divine motion, effects follow of necessity; but from contingent causes, effects follow contingently. Since, therefore, the will is an active principle, not determinate to one thing, but having an indifferent relation to many things, God so moves it, that He does not determine it of necessity to one thing, but its movement remains contingent and not necessary, except in those things to which it is moved naturally.

Reply Obj. 1: The Divine will extends not only to the doing of something by the thing which He moves, but also to its being done in a way which is fitting to the nature of that thing. And therefore it would be more repugnant to the Divine motion, for the will to be moved of necessity, which is not fitting to its nature; than for it to be moved freely, which is becoming to its nature.

Reply Obj. 2: That is natural to a thing, which God so works in it that it may be natural to it: for thus is something becoming to a thing, according as God wishes it to be becoming. Now He does not wish that whatever He works in things should be natural to them, for instance, that the dead should rise again. But this He does wish to be natural to each thing—that it be subject to the Divine power.

Reply Obj. 3: If God moves the will to anything, it is incompatible with this supposition, that the will be not moved thereto. But it is not impossible simply. Consequently it does not follow that the will is moved by God necessarily.

## QUESTION 11

OF ENJOYMENT [*Or, Fruition], WHICH IS AN ACT OF THE WILL (In Four Articles)

We must now consider enjoyment: concerning which there are four points of inquiry:

(1) Whether to enjoy is an act of the appetitive power?

(2) Whether it belongs to the rational creature alone, or also to irrational animals?

(3) Whether enjoyment is only of the last end?

(4) Whether it is only of the end possessed?

FIRST ARTICLE [I-II, Q. 11, Art. 1]

Whether to Enjoy Is an Act of the Appetitive Power?

Objection 1: It would seem that to enjoy belongs not only to the appetitive power. For to enjoy seems nothing else than to receive the fruit. But it is the intellect, in whose act Happiness consists, as shown above (Q. 3, A. 4), that receives the fruit of human life, which is Happiness. Therefore to enjoy is not an act of the appetitive power, but of the intellect.

Obj. 2: Further, each power has its proper end, which is its perfection: thus the end of sight is to know the visible; of the hearing, to perceive sounds; and so forth. But the end of a thing is its fruit. Therefore to enjoy belongs to each power, and not only to the appetite.

Obj. 3: Further, enjoyment implies a certain delight. But sensible delight belongs to sense, which delights in its object: and for the same reason, intellectual delight belongs to the intellect. Therefore enjoyment belongs to the apprehensive, and not to the appetitive power.

*On the contrary,* Augustine says (De Doctr. Christ. i, 4; and De Trin. x, 10, 11): "To enjoy is to adhere lovingly to something for its own sake." But love belongs to the appetitive power. Therefore also to enjoy is an act of the appetitive power.

*I answer that,* Fruitio (enjoyment) and fructus (fruit) seem to refer to the same, one being derived from the other; which from which, matters not for our purpose; though it seems probable that the one which is more clearly known, was first named. Now those things are most manifest to us which appeal most to the senses: wherefore it seems that the word "fruition" is derived from sensible fruits. But sensible fruit is that which we expect the tree to produce in the last place, and in which a certain sweetness is to be perceived. Hence fruition seems to have relation to love, or to the delight which one has in realizing the longed-for term, which is the end. Now the end and the good is the object of the appetitive power. Wherefore it is evident that fruition is the act of the appetitive power.

Reply Obj. 1: Nothing hinders one and the same thing from belonging, under different aspects, to different powers. Accordingly the vision of God, as vision, is an act of the intellect, but as a good and an end, is the object of the will. And as such is the fruition thereof: so that the intellect attains this end, as the executive power, but the will as the motive power, moving (the powers) towards the end and enjoying the end attained.

Reply Obj. 2: The perfection and end of every other power is contained in the object of the appetitive power, as the proper is contained in the common, as stated above (Q. 9, A. 1). Hence the perfection and end of each power, in so far as it is a good, belongs to the appetitive power. Wherefore the appetitive power moves the other powers to their ends; and itself realizes the end, when each of them reaches the end.

Reply Obj. 3: In delight there are two things: perception of what is becoming; and this belongs to the apprehensive power; and complacency in that which is offered as becoming: and this belongs to the appetitive power, in which power delight is formally completed.

SECOND ARTICLE [I-II, Q. 11, Art. 2]

Whether to Enjoy Belongs to the Rational Creature Alone, or Also to Irrational Animals?

Objection 1: It would seem that to enjoy belongs to men alone. For Augustine says (De Doctr. Christ. i, 22) that "it is given to us men to enjoy and to use." Therefore other animals cannot enjoy.

Obj. 2: Further, to enjoy relates to the last end. But irrational animals cannot obtain the last end. Therefore it is not for them to enjoy.

Obj. 3: Further, just as the sensitive appetite is beneath the intellectual appetite, so is the natural appetite beneath the sensitive. If, therefore, to enjoy belongs to the sensitive appetite, it seems that for the same reason it can belong to the natural appetite. But this is evidently false, since the latter cannot delight in anything. Therefore the sensitive appetite cannot enjoy: and accordingly enjoyment is not possible for irrational animals.

*On the contrary,* Augustine says (QQ. 83, qu. 30): "It is not so absurd to suppose that even beasts enjoy their food and any bodily pleasure."

*I answer that,* As was stated above (A. 1) to enjoy is not the act of the power that achieves the end as executor, but of the power that commands the achievement; for it has been said to belong to the appetitive power. Now things void of reason have indeed a power of achieving an end by way of execution, as that by which a heavy body has a downward tendency, whereas a light body has an upward tendency. Yet the power of command in respect of the end is not in them, but in some higher nature, which moves all nature by its command, just as in things endowed with knowledge, the appetite moves the other powers to their acts. Wherefore it is clear that things void of knowledge, although they attain an end, have no enjoyment of the end: this is only for those that are endowed with knowledge.

Now knowledge of the end is twofold: perfect and imperfect. Perfect knowledge of the end, is that whereby not only is that known which is the end and the good, but also the universal formality of the end and the good; and such knowledge belongs to the rational nature alone. On the other hand, imperfect knowledge is that by which the end and the good are known in the particular. Such knowledge is in irrational animals: whose appetitive powers do not command with freedom, but are moved according to a natural instinct to whatever they apprehend. Consequently, enjoyment belongs to the rational nature, in a perfect degree; to irrational animals, imperfectly; to other creatures, not at all.

Reply Obj. 1: Augustine is speaking there of perfect enjoyment.

Reply Obj. 2: Enjoyment need not be of the last end simply; but of that which each one chooses for his last end.

Reply Obj. 3: The sensitive appetite follows some knowledge; not so the natural appetite, especially in things void of knowledge.

Reply Obj. 4: Augustine is speaking there of imperfect enjoyment. This is clear from his way of speaking: for he says that "it is not so absurd to suppose that even beasts enjoy," that is, as it would be, if one were to say that they "use."

THIRD ARTICLE [I-II, Q. 11, Art. 3]

Whether Enjoyment Is Only of the Last End?

Objection 1: It would seem that enjoyment is not only of the last end. For the Apostle says (Philem. 20): "Yea, brother, may I enjoy thee in the Lord." But it is evident that Paul had not placed his last end in a man. Therefore to enjoy is not only of the last end.

Obj. 2: Further, what we enjoy is the fruit. But the Apostle says (Gal. 5:22): "The fruit of the Spirit is charity, joy, peace," and other like things, which are not in the nature of the last end. Therefore enjoyment is not only of the last end.

Obj. 3: Further, the acts of the will reflect on one another; for I will to will, and I love to love. But to enjoy is an act of the will: since "it is the will with which we enjoy," as Augustine says (De Trin. x, 10). Therefore a man enjoys his enjoyment. But the last end of man is not enjoyment, but the uncreated good alone, which is God. Therefore enjoyment is not only of the last end.

*On the contrary,* Augustine says (De Trin. x, 11): "A man does not enjoy that which he desires for the sake of something else." But the last end alone is that which man does not desire for the sake of something else. Therefore enjoyment is of the last end alone.

*I answer that,* As stated above (A. 1) the notion of fruit implies two things: first that it should come last; second, that it should calm the appetite with a certain sweetness and delight. Now a thing is last either simply or relatively; simply, if it be referred to nothing else; relatively, if it is the last in a particular series. Therefore that which is last simply, and in which one delights as in the last end, is properly called fruit; and this it is that one is properly said to enjoy. But that which is delightful not in itself, but is desired, only as referred to something else, e.g. a bitter potion for the sake of health, can nowise be called fruit. And that which has something delightful about it, to which a number of preceding things are referred, may indeed be called fruit in a certain manner; but we cannot be said to enjoy it properly or as though it answered perfectly to the notion of fruit. Hence Augustine says (De Trin. x, 10) that "we enjoy what we know, when the delighted will is at rest therein." But its rest is not absolute save in the possession of the last end: for as long as something is looked for, the movement of the will remains in suspense, although it has reached something. Thus in local movement, although any point between the two terms is a beginning and an end, yet it is not considered as an actual end, except when the movement stops there.

Reply Obj. 1: As Augustine says (De Doctr. Christ. i, 33), "if he had said, 'May I enjoy thee,' without adding 'in the Lord,' he would seem to have set the end of his love in him. But since he added that he set his end in the Lord, he implied his desire to enjoy Him": as if we were to say that he expressed his enjoyment of his brother not as a term but as a means.

Reply Obj. 2: Fruit bears one relation to the tree that bore it, and another to man that enjoys it. To the tree indeed that bore it, it is compared as effect to cause; to the one enjoying it, as the final object of his longing and the consummation of his delight. Accordingly these fruits mentioned by the Apostle are so called because they are certain effects of the Holy Ghost in us, wherefore they are called "fruits of the spirit": but not as though we are to enjoy them as our last end. Or we may say with Ambrose that they are called fruits because "we should desire them for their own sake": not indeed as though they were not ordained to the last end; but because they are such that we ought to find pleasure in them.

Reply Obj. 3: As stated above (Q. 1, A. 8; Q. 2, A. 7), we speak of an end in a twofold sense: first, as being the thing itself; secondly, as the attainment thereof. These are not, of course, two ends, but one end, considered in itself, and in its relation to something else. Accordingly God is the last end, as that which is ultimately sought for: while the enjoyment is as the attainment of this last end. And so, just as God is not one end, and the enjoyment of God, another: so it is the same enjoyment whereby we enjoy God, and whereby we enjoy our enjoyment of God. And the same applies to created happiness which consists in enjoyment.

FOURTH ARTICLE [I-II, Q. 11, Art. 4]

Whether Enjoyment Is Only of the End Possessed?

Objection 1: It would seem that enjoyment is only of the end possessed. For Augustine says (De Trin. x, 1) that "to enjoy is to use joyfully, with the joy, not of hope, but of possession." But so long as a thing is not had, there is joy, not of possession, but of hope. Therefore enjoyment is only of the end possessed.

Obj. 2: Further, as stated above (A. 3), enjoyment is not properly otherwise than of the last end: because this alone gives rest to the appetite. But the appetite has no rest save in the possession of the end. Therefore enjoyment, properly speaking, is only of the end possessed.

Obj. 3: Further, to enjoy is to lay hold of the fruit. But one does not lay hold of the fruit until one is in possession of the end. Therefore enjoyment is only of the end possessed.

*On the contrary,* "to enjoy is to adhere lovingly to something for its own sake," as Augustine says (De Doctr. Christ. i, 4). But this is possible, even in regard to a thing which is not in our possession. Therefore it is possible to enjoy the end even though it be not possessed.

*I answer that,* To enjoy implies a certain relation of the will to the last end, according as the will has something by way of last end. Now an end is possessed in two ways; perfectly and imperfectly. Perfectly, when it is possessed not only in intention but also in reality; imperfectly, when it is possessed in intention only. Perfect enjoyment, therefore, is of the end already possessed: but imperfect enjoyment is also of the end possessed not really, but only in intention.

Reply Obj. 1: Augustine speaks there of perfect enjoyment.

Reply Obj. 2: The will is hindered in two ways from being at rest. First on the part of the object; by reason of its not being the last end, but ordained to something else: secondly on the part of the one who desires the end, by reason of his not being yet in possession of it. Now it is the object that specifies an act: but on the agent depends the manner of acting, so that the act be perfect or imperfect, as compared with the actual circumstances of the agent. Therefore enjoyment of anything but the last end is not enjoyment properly speaking, as falling short of the nature of enjoyment. But enjoyment of the last end, not yet possessed, is enjoyment properly speaking, but imperfect, on account of the imperfect way in which it is possessed.

Reply Obj. 3: One is said to lay hold of or to have an end, not only in reality, but also in intention, as stated above.

## QUESTION 12

OF INTENTION (In Five Articles)

We must now consider Intention: concerning which there are five points of inquiry:

(1) Whether intention is an act of intellect or of the will?

(2) Whether it is only of the last end?

(3) Whether one can intend two things at the same time?

(4) Whether intention of the end is the same act as volition of the means?

(5) Whether intention is within the competency of irrational animals?

FIRST ARTICLE [I-II, Q. 12, Art. 1]

Whether Intention Is an Act of the Intellect or of the Will?

Objection 1: It would seem that intention is an act of the intellect, and not of the will. For it is written (Matt. 6:22): "If thy eye be single, thy whole body shall be lightsome": where, according to Augustine (De Serm. Dom. in Monte ii, 13) the eye signifies intention. But since the eye is the organ of sight, it signifies the apprehensive power. Therefore intention is not an act of the appetitive but of the apprehensive power.

Obj. 2: Further, Augustine says (De Serm. Dom. in Monte ii, 13) that Our Lord spoke of intention as a light, when He said (Matt. 6:23): "If the light that is in thee be darkness," etc. But light pertains to knowledge. Therefore intention does too.

Obj. 3: Further, intention implies a kind of ordaining to an end. But to ordain is an act of reason. Therefore intention belongs not to the will but to the reason.

Obj. 4: Further, an act of the will is either of the end or of the means. But the act of the will in respect of the end is called volition, or enjoyment; with regard to the means, it is choice, from which intention is distinct. Therefore it is not an act of the will.

*On the contrary,* Augustine says (De Trin. xi, 4, 8, 9) that "the intention of the will unites the sight to the object seen; and the images retained in the memory, to the penetrating gaze of the soul's inner thought." Therefore intention is an act of the will.

*I answer that,* Intention, as the very word denotes, signifies, "to tend to something." Now both the action of the mover and the movement of thing moved, tend to something. But that the movement of the thing moved tends to anything, is due to the action of the mover. Consequently intention belongs first and principally to that which moves to the end: hence we say that an architect or anyone who is in authority, by his command moves others to that which he intends. Now the will moves all the other powers of the soul to the end, as shown above (Q. 9, A. 1). Wherefore it is evident that intention, properly speaking, is an act of the will.

Reply Obj. 1: The eye designates intention figuratively, not because intention has reference to knowledge, but because it presupposes knowledge, which proposes to the will the end to which the latter moves; thus we foresee with the eye whither we should tend with our bodies.

Reply Obj. 2: Intention is called a light because it is manifest to him who intends. Wherefore works are called darkness because a man knows what he intends, but knows not what the result may be, as Augustine expounds (De Serm. Dom. in Monte ii, 13).

Reply Obj. 3: The will does not ordain, but tends to something according to the order of reason. Consequently this word "intention" indicates an act of the will, presupposing the act whereby the reason orders something to the end.

Reply Obj. 4: Intention is an act of the will in regard to the end. Now the will stands in a threefold relation to the end. First, absolutely; and thus we have "volition," whereby we will absolutely to have health, and so forth. Secondly, it considers the end, as its place of rest; and thus "enjoyment" regards the end. Thirdly, it considers the end as the term towards which something is ordained; and thus "intention" regards the end. For when we speak of intending to have health, we mean not only that we have it, but that we will have it by means of something else.

SECOND ARTICLE [I-II, Q. 12, Art. 2]

Whether Intention Is Only of the Last End?

Objection 1: It would seem that intention is only of the last end. For it is said in the book of Prosper's Sentences (Sent. 100): "The intention of the heart is a cry to God." But God is the last end of the human heart. Therefore intention is always regards the last end.

Obj. 2: Further, intention regards the end as the terminus, as stated above (A. 1, ad 4). But a terminus is something last. Therefore intention always regards the last end.

Obj. 3: Further, just as intention regards the end, so does enjoyment. But enjoyment is always of the last end. Therefore intention is too.

*On the contrary,* There is but one last end of human wills, viz. Happiness, as stated above (Q. 1, A. 7). If, therefore, intentions were only of the last end, men would not have different intentions: which is evidently false.

*I answer that,* As stated above (A. 1, ad 4), intention regards the end as a terminus of the movement of the will. Now a terminus of movement may be taken in two ways. First, the very last terminus, when the movement comes to a stop; this is the terminus of the whole movement. Secondly, some point midway, which is the beginning of one part of the movement, and the end or terminus of the other. Thus in the movement from A to C through B, C is the last terminus, while B is a terminus, but not the last. And intention can be both. Consequently though intention is always of the end, it need not be always of the last end.

Reply Obj. 1: The intention of the heart is called a cry to God, not that God is always the object of intention, but because He sees our intention. Or because, when we pray, we direct our intention to God, which intention has the force of a cry.

Reply Obj. 2: A terminus is something last, not always in respect of the whole, but sometimes in respect of a part.

Reply Obj. 3: Enjoyment implies rest in the end; and this belongs to the last end alone. But intention implies movement towards an end, not rest. Wherefore the comparison proves nothing.

THIRD ARTICLE [I-II, Q. 12, Art. 3]

Whether One Can Intend Two Things at the Same Time?

Objection 1: It would seem that one cannot intend several things at the same time. For Augustine says (De Serm. Dom. in Monte ii, 14, 16, 17) that man's intention cannot be directed at the same time to God and to bodily benefits. Therefore, for the same reason, neither to any other two things.

Obj. 2: Further, intention designates a movement of the will towards a terminus. Now there cannot be several termini in the same direction of one movement. Therefore the will cannot intend several things at the same time.

Obj. 3: Further, intention presupposes an act of reason or of the intellect. But "it is not possible to understand several things at the same time," according to the Philosopher (Topic. ii, 10). Therefore neither is it possible to intend several things at the same time.

*On the contrary,* Art imitates nature. Now nature intends two purposes by means of one instrument: thus "the tongue is for the purpose of taste and speech" (De Anima ii, 8). Therefore, for the same reason, art or reason can at the same time direct one thing to two ends: so that one can intend several ends at the same time.

*I answer that,* The expression "two things" may be taken in two ways: they may be ordained to one another or not so ordained. And if they be ordained to one another, it is evident, from what has been said, that a man can intend several things at the same time. For intention is not only of the last end, as stated above (A. 2), but also of an intermediary end. Now a man intends at the same time, both the proximate and the last end; as the mixing of a medicine and the giving of health.

But if we take two things that are not ordained to one another, thus also a man can intend several things at the same time. This is evident from the fact that a man prefers one thing to another because it is the better of the two. Now one of the reasons for which one thing is better than another is that it is available for more purposes: wherefore one thing can be chosen in preference to another, because of the greater number of purposes for which it is available: so that evidently a man can intend several things at the same time.

Reply Obj. 1: Augustine means to say that man cannot at the same time direct his attention to God and to bodily benefits, as to two last ends: since, as stated above (Q. 1, A. 5), one man cannot have several last ends.

Reply Obj. 2: There can be several termini ordained to one another, of the same movement and in the same direction; but not unless they be ordained to one another. At the same time it must be observed that what is not one in reality may be taken as one by the reason. Now intention is a movement of the will to something already ordained by the reason, as stated above (A. 1, ad 3). Wherefore where we have many things in reality, we may take them as one term of intention, in so far as the reason takes them as one: either because two things concur in the integrity of one whole, as a proper measure of heat and cold conduce to health; or because two things are included in one which may be intended. For instance, the acquiring of wine and clothing is included in wealth, as in something common to both; wherefore nothing hinders the man who intends to acquire wealth, from intending both the others.

Reply Obj. 3: As stated in the First Part (Q. 12, A. 10; Q. 58, A. 2; Q. 85, A. 4), it is possible to understand several things at the same time, in so far as, in some way, they are one.

FOURTH ARTICLE [I-II, Q. 12, Art. 4]

Whether Intention of the End Is the Same Act As the Volition of the Means?

Objection 1: It would seem that the intention of the end and the volition of the means are not one and the same movement. For Augustine says (De Trin. xi, 6) that "the will to see the window, has for its end the seeing of the window; and is another act from the will to see, through the window, the passersby." But that I should will to see the passersby, through the window, belongs to intention; whereas that I will to see the window, belongs to the volition of the means. Therefore intention of the end and the willing of the means are distinct movements of the will.

Obj. 2: Further, acts are distinct according to their objects. But the end and the means are distinct objects. Therefore the intention of the end and the willing of the means are distinct movements of the will.

Obj. 3: Further, the willing of the means is called choice. But choice and intention are not the same. Therefore intention of the end and the willing of the means are not the same movement of the will.

*On the contrary,* The means in relation to the end, are as the mid-space to the terminus. Now it is all the same movement that passes through the mid-space to the terminus, in natural things. Therefore in things pertaining to the will, the intention of the end is the same movement as the willing of the means.

*I answer that,* The movement of the will to the end and to the means can be considered in two ways. First, according as the will is moved to each of the aforesaid absolutely and in itself. And thus there are really two movements of the will to them. Secondly, it may be considered accordingly as the will is moved to the means for the sake of the end: and thus the movement of the will to the end and its movement to the means are one and the same thing. For when I say: "I wish to take medicine for the sake of health," I signify no more than one movement of my will. And this is because the end is the reason for willing the means. Now the object, and that by reason of which it is an object, come under the same act; thus it is the same act of sight that perceives color and light, as stated above (Q. 8, A. 3, ad 2). And the same applies to the intellect; for if it consider principle and conclusion absolutely, it considers each by a distinct act; but when it assents to the conclusion on account of the principles, there is but one act of the intellect.

Reply Obj. 1: Augustine is speaking of seeing the window and of seeing, through the window, the passersby, according as the will is moved to either absolutely.

Reply Obj. 2: The end, considered as a thing, and the means to that end, are distinct objects of the will. But in so far as the end is the formal object in willing the means, they are one and the same object.

Reply Obj. 3: A movement which is one as to the subject, may differ, according to our way of looking at it, as to its beginning and end, as in the case of ascent and descent (Phys. iii, 3). Accordingly, in so far as the movement of the will is to the means, as ordained to the end, it is called "choice": but the movement of the will to the end as acquired by the means, is called "intention." A sign of this is that we can have intention of the end without having determined the means which are the object of choice.

FIFTH ARTICLE [I-II, Q. 12, Art. 5]

Whether Intention Is Within the Competency of Irrational Animals?

Objection 1: It would seem that irrational animals intend the end. For in things void of reason nature stands further apart from the rational nature, than does the sensitive nature in irrational animals. But nature intends the end even in things void of reason, as is proved in *Phys.* ii, 8. Much more, therefore, do irrational animals intend the end.

Obj. 2: Further, just as intention is of the end, so is enjoyment. But enjoyment is in irrational animals, as stated above (Q. 11, A. 2). Therefore intention is too.

Obj. 3: Further, to intend an end belongs to one who acts for an end; since to intend is nothing else than to tend to something. But irrational animals act for an end; for an animal is moved either to seek food, or to do something of the kind. Therefore irrational animals intend an end.

*On the contrary,* Intention of an end implies ordaining something to an end: which belongs to reason. Since therefore irrational animals are void of reason, it seems that they do not intend an end.

*I answer that,* As stated above (A. 1), to intend is to tend to something; and this belongs to the mover and to the moved. According, therefore, as that which is moved to an end by another is said to intend the end, thus nature is said to intend an end, as being moved to its end by God, as the arrow is moved by the archer. And in this way, irrational animals intend an end, inasmuch as they are moved to something by natural instinct. The other way of intending an end belongs to the mover; according as he ordains the movement of something, either his own or another's, to an end. This belongs to reason alone. Wherefore irrational animals do not intend an end in this way, which is to intend properly and principally, as stated above (A. 1).

Reply Obj. 1: This argument takes intention in the sense of being moved to an end.

Reply Obj. 2: Enjoyment does not imply the ordaining of one thing to another, as intention does, but absolute repose in the end.

Reply Obj. 3: Irrational animals are moved to an end, not as though they thought that they can gain the end by this movement; this belongs to one that intends; but through desiring the end by natural instinct, they are moved to an end, moved, as it were, by another, like other things that are moved naturally.

# QUESTION 13

OF CHOICE, WHICH IS AN ACT OF THE WILL WITH REGARD TO THE MEANS (In Six Articles)

We must now consider the acts of the will with regard to the means. There are three of them: to choose, to consent, and to use. And choice is preceded by counsel. First of all, then, we must consider choice: secondly, counsel; thirdly, consent; fourthly, use.

Concerning choice there are six points of inquiry:

(1) Of what power is it the act; of the will or of the reason?

(2) Whether choice is to be found in irrational animals?

(3) Whether choice is only the means, or sometimes also of the end?

(4) Whether choice is only of things that we do ourselves?

(5) Whether choice is only of possible things?

(6) Whether man chooses of necessity or freely?

FIRST ARTICLE [I-II, Q. 13, Art. 1]

Whether Choice Is an Act of Will or of Reason?

Objection 1: It would seem that choice is an act, not of will but of reason. For choice implies comparison, whereby one is given preference to another. But to compare is an act of reason. Therefore choice is an act of reason.

Obj. 2: Further, it is for the same faculty to form a syllogism, and to draw the conclusion. But, in practical matters, it is the reason that forms syllogisms. Since therefore choice is a kind of conclusion in practical matters, as stated in *Ethic.* vii, 3, it seems that it is an act of reason.

Obj. 3: Further, ignorance does not belong to the will but to the cognitive power. Now there is an "ignorance of choice," as is stated in *Ethic.* iii, 1. Therefore it seems that choice does not belong to the will but to the reason.

*On the contrary,* The Philosopher says (Ethic. iii, 3) that choice is "the desire of things in our power." But desire is an act of will. Therefore choice is too.

*I answer that,* The word choice implies something belonging to the reason or intellect, and something belonging to the will: for the Philosopher says (Ethic. vi, 2) that choice is either "intellect influenced by appetite or appetite influenced by intellect." Now whenever two things concur to make one, one of them is formal in regard to the other. Hence Gregory of Nyssa [*Nemesius, De Nat. Hom. xxxiii.] says that choice "is neither desire only, nor counsel only, but a combination of the two. For just as we say that an animal is composed of soul and body, and that it is neither a mere body, nor a mere soul, but both; so is it with choice."

Now we must observe, as regards the acts of the soul, that an act belonging essentially to some power or habit, receives a form or species from a higher power or habit, according as an inferior is ordained by a superior: for if a man were to perform an act of fortitude for the love of God, that act is materially an act of fortitude, but formally, an act of charity. Now it is evident that, in a sense, reason precedes the will and ordains its act: in so far as the will tends to its object, according to the order of reason, since the apprehensive power presents the object to the appetite. Accordingly, that act whereby the will tends to something proposed to it as being good, through being ordained to the end by the reason, is materially an act of the will, but formally an act of the reason. Now in such like matters the substance of the act is as the matter in comparison to the order imposed by the higher power. Wherefore choice is substantially not an act of the reason but of the will: for choice is accomplished in a certain movement of the soul towards the good which is chosen. Consequently it is evidently an act of the appetitive power.

Reply Obj. 1: Choice implies a previous comparison; not that it consists in the comparison itself.

Reply Obj. 2: It is quite true that it is for the reason to draw the conclusion of a practical syllogism; and it is called "a decision" or "judgment," to be followed by "choice." And for this reason the conclusion seems to belong to the act of choice, as to that which results from it.

Reply Obj. 3: In speaking "of ignorance of choice," we do not mean that choice is a sort of knowledge, but that there is ignorance of what ought to be chosen.

SECOND ARTICLE [I-II, Q. 13, Art. 2]

Whether Choice Is to Be Found in Irrational Animals?

Objection 1: It would seem that irrational animals are able to choose. For choice "is the desire of certain things on account of an end," as stated in *Ethic.* iii, 2, 3. But irrational animals desire something on account of an end: since they act for an end, and from desire. Therefore choice is in irrational animals.

Obj. 2: Further, the very word *electio* (choice) seems to signify the taking of something in preference to others. But irrational animals take something in preference to others: thus we can easily see for ourselves that a sheep will eat one grass and refuse another. Therefore choice is in irrational animals.

Obj. 3: Further, according to *Ethic.* vi, 12, "it is from prudence that a man makes a good choice of means." But prudence is found in irrational animals: hence it is said in the beginning of *Metaph.* i, 1 that "those animals which, like bees, cannot hear sounds, are prudent by instinct." We see this plainly, in wonderful cases of sagacity manifested in the works of various animals, such as bees, spiders, and dogs. For a hound in following a stag, on coming to a crossroad, tries by scent whether the stag has passed by the first or the second road: and if he find that the stag has not passed there, being thus assured, takes to the third road without trying the scent; as though he were reasoning by way of exclusion, arguing that the stag must have passed by this way, since he did not pass by the others, and there is no other road. Therefore it seems that irrational animals are able to choose.

*On the contrary,* Gregory of Nyssa [*Nemesius, De Nat. Hom. xxxiii.] says that "children and irrational animals act willingly but not from choice." Therefore choice is not in irrational animals.

*I answer that,* Since choice is the taking of one thing in preference to another it must of necessity be in respect of several things that can be chosen. Consequently in those things which are altogether determinate to one there is no place for choice. Now the difference between the sensitive appetite and the will is that, as stated above (Q. 1, A. 2, ad 3), the sensitive appetite is determinate to one particular thing, according to the order of nature; whereas the will, although determinate to one thing in general, viz. the good, according to the order of nature, is nevertheless indeterminate in respect of particular goods. Consequently choice belongs properly to the will, and not to the sensitive appetite which is all that irrational animals have. Wherefore irrational animals are not competent to choose.

Reply Obj. 1: Not every desire of one thing on account of an end is called choice: there must be a certain discrimination of one thing from another. And this cannot be except when the appetite can be moved to several things.

Reply Obj. 2: An irrational animal takes one thing in preference to another, because its appetite is naturally determinate to that thing. Wherefore as soon as an animal, whether by its sense or by its imagination, is offered something to which its appetite is naturally inclined, it is moved to that alone, without making any choice. Just as fire is moved upwards and not downwards, without its making any choice.

Reply Obj. 3: As stated in *Phys.* iii, 3 "movement is the act of the movable, caused by a mover." Wherefore the power of the mover appears in the movement of that which it moves. Accordingly, in all things moved by reason, the order of reason which moves them is evident, although the things themselves are without reason: for an arrow through the motion of the archer goes straight towards the target, as though it were endowed with reason to direct its course. The same may be seen in the movements of clocks and all engines put together by the art of man. Now as artificial things are in comparison to human art, so are all natural things in comparison to the Divine art. And accordingly order is to be seen in things moved by nature, just as in things moved by reason, as is stated in *Phys.* ii. And thus it is that in the works of irrational animals we notice certain marks of sagacity, in so far as they have a natural inclination to set about their actions in a most orderly manner through being ordained by the Supreme art. For which reason, too, certain animals are called prudent or sagacious; and not because they reason or exercise any choice about things. This is clear from the fact that all that share in one nature, invariably act in the same way.

THIRD ARTICLE [I-II, Q. 13, Art. 3]

Whether Choice Is Only of the Means, or Sometimes Also of the End?

Objection 1: It would seem that choice is not only of the means. For the Philosopher says (Ethic. vi, 12) that "virtue makes us choose aright; but it is not the part of virtue, but of some other power to direct aright those things which are to be done for its sake." But that for the sake of which something is done is the end. Therefore choice is of the end.

Obj. 2: Further, choice implies preference of one thing to another. But just as there can be preference of means, so can there be preference of ends. Therefore choice can be of ends, just as it can be of means.

*On the contrary,* The Philosopher says (Ethic. iii, 2) that "volition is of the end, but choice of the means."

*I answer that,* As already stated (A. 1, ad 2), choice results from the decision or judgment which is, as it were, the conclusion of a practical syllogism. Hence that which is the conclusion of a practical syllogism, is the matter of choice. Now in practical things the end stands in the position of a principle, not of a conclusion, as the Philosopher says (Phys. ii, 9). Wherefore the end, as such, is not a matter of choice.

But just as in speculative knowledge nothing hinders the principle of one demonstration or of one science, from being the conclusion of another demonstration or science; while the first indemonstrable principle cannot be the conclusion of any demonstration or science; so too that which is the end in one operation, may be ordained to something as an end. And in this way it is a matter of choice. Thus in the work of a physician health is the end: wherefore it is not a matter of choice for a physician, but a matter of principle. Now the health of the body is ordained to the good of the soul, consequently with one who has charge of the soul's health, health or sickness may be a matter of choice; for the Apostle says (2 Cor. 12:10): "For when I am weak, then am I powerful." But the last end is nowise a matter of choice.

Reply Obj. 1: The proper ends of virtues are ordained to Happiness as to their last end. And thus it is that they can be a matter of choice.

Reply Obj. 2: As stated above (Q. 1, A. 5), there is but one last end. Accordingly wherever there are several ends, they can be the subject of choice, in so far as they are ordained to a further end.

FOURTH ARTICLE [I-II, Q. 13, Art. 4]

Whether Choice Is of Those Things Only That Are Done by Us?

Objection 1: It would seem that choice is not only in respect of human acts. For choice regards the means. Now, not only acts, but also the organs, are means (Phys. ii, 3). Therefore choice is not only concerned with human acts.

Obj. 2: Further, action is distinct from contemplation. But choice has a place even in contemplation; in so far as one opinion is preferred to another. Therefore choice is not concerned with human acts alone.

Obj. 3: Further, men are chosen for certain posts, whether secular or ecclesiastical, by those who exercise no action in their regard. Therefore choice is not concerned with human acts alone.

*On the contrary,* The Philosopher says (Ethic. iii, 2) that "no man chooses save what he can do himself."

*I answer that,* Just as intention regards the end, so does choice regard the means. Now the end is either an action or a thing. And when the end is a thing, some human action must intervene; either in so far as man produces the thing which is the end, as the physician produces health (wherefore the production of health is said to be the end of the physician); or in so far as man, in some fashion, uses or enjoys the thing which is the end; thus for the miser, money or the possession of money is the end. The same is to be said of the means. For the means must needs be either an action; or a thing, with some action intervening whereby man either makes the thing which is the means, or puts it to some use. And thus it is that choice is always in regard to human acts.

Reply Obj. 1: The organs are ordained to the end, inasmuch as man makes use of them for the sake of the end.

Reply Obj. 2: In contemplation itself there is the act of the intellect assenting to this or that opinion. It is exterior action that is put in contradistinction to contemplation.

Reply Obj. 3: When a man chooses someone for a bishopric or some high position in the state, he chooses to name that man to that post. Else, if he had no right to act in the appointment of the bishop or official, he would have no right to choose. Likewise, whenever we speak of one thing being chosen in preference to another, it is in conjunction with some action of the chooser.

FIFTH ARTICLE [I-II, Q. 13, Art. 5]

Whether Choice Is Only of Possible Things?

Objection 1: It would seem that choice is not only of possible things. For choice is an act of the will, as stated above (A. 1). Now there is "a willing of impossibilities" (Ethic. iii, 2). Therefore there is also a choice of impossibilities.

Obj. 2: Further, choice is of things done by us, as stated above (A. 4). Therefore it matters not, as far as the act of choosing is concerned, whether one choose that which is impossible in itself, or that which is impossible to the chooser. Now it often happens that we are unable to accomplish what we choose: so that this proves to be impossible to us. Therefore choice is of the impossible.

Obj. 3: Further, to try to do a thing is to choose to do it. But the Blessed Benedict says (Regula lxviii) that if the superior command what is impossible, it should be attempted. Therefore choice can be of the impossible.

*On the contrary,* The Philosopher says (Ethic. iii, 2) that "there is no choice of impossibilities."

*I answer that,* As stated above (A. 4), our choice is always concerned with our actions. Now whatever is done by us, is possible to us. Therefore we must needs say that choice is only of possible things.

Moreover, the reason for choosing a thing is that it conduces to an end. But what is impossible cannot conduce to an end. A sign of this is that when men in taking counsel together come to something that is impossible to them, they depart, as being unable to proceed with the business.

Again, this is evident if we examine the previous process of the reason. For the means, which are the object of choice, are to the end, as the conclusion is to the principle. Now it is clear that an impossible conclusion does not follow from a possible principle. Wherefore an end cannot be possible, unless the means be possible. Now no one is moved to the impossible. Consequently no one would tend to the end, save for the fact that the means appear to be possible. Therefore the impossible is not the object of choice.

Reply Obj. 1: The will stands between the intellect and the external action: for the intellect proposes to the will its object, and the will causes the external action. Hence the principle of the movement in the will is to be found in the intellect, which apprehends something under the universal notion of good: but the term or perfection of the will's act is to be observed in its relation to the action whereby a man tends to the attainment of a thing; for the movement of the will is from the soul to the thing. Consequently the perfect act of the will is in respect of something that is good for one to do. Now this cannot be something impossible. Wherefore the complete act of the will is only in respect of what is possible and good for him that wills. But the incomplete act of the will is in respect of the impossible; and by some is called "velleity," because, to wit, one would will ( *vellet* ) such a thing, were it possible. But choice is an act of the will, fixed on something to be done by the chooser. And therefore it is by no means of anything but what is possible.

Reply Obj. 2: Since the object of the will is the apprehended good, we must judge of the object of the will according as it is apprehended. And so, just as sometimes the will tends to something which is apprehended as good, and yet is not really good; so is choice sometimes made of something apprehended as possible to the chooser, and yet impossible to him.

Reply Obj. 3: The reason for this is that the subject should not rely on his own judgment to decide whether a certain thing is possible; but in each case should stand by his superior's judgment.

SIXTH ARTICLE [I-II, Q. 13, Art. 6]

Whether Man Chooses of Necessity or Freely?

Objection 1: It would seem that man chooses of necessity. For the end stands in relation to the object of choice, as the principle of that which follows from the principles, as declared in *Ethic.* vii, 8. But conclusions follow of necessity from their principles. Therefore man is moved of necessity from (willing) the end of the choice (of the means).

Obj. 2: Further, as stated above (A. 1, ad 2), choice follows the reason's judgment of what is to be done. But reason judges of necessity about some things: on account of the necessity of the premises. Therefore it seems that choice also follows of necessity.

Obj. 3: Further, if two things are absolutely equal, man is not moved to one more than to the other; thus if a hungry man, as Plato says (Cf. De Coelo ii, 13), be confronted on either side with two portions of food equally appetizing and at an equal distance, he is not moved towards one more than to the other; and he finds the reason of this in the immobility of the earth in the middle of the world. Now, if that which is equally (eligible) with something else cannot be chosen, much less can that be chosen which appears as less (eligible). Therefore if two or more things are available, of which one appears to be more (eligible), it is impossible to choose any of the others. Therefore that which appears to hold the first place is chosen of necessity. But every act of choosing is in regard to something that seems in some way better. Therefore every choice is made necessarily.

*On the contrary,* Choice is an act of a rational power; which according to the Philosopher (Metaph. ix, 2) stands in relation to opposites.

*I answer that,* Man does not choose of necessity. And this is because that which is possible not to be, is not of necessity. Now the reason why it is possible not to choose, or to choose, may be gathered from a twofold power in man. For man can will and not will, act and not act; again, he can will this or that, and do this or that. The reason of this is seated in the very power of the reason. For the will can tend to whatever the reason can apprehend as good. Now the reason can apprehend as good, not only this, viz. "to will" or "to act," but also this, viz. "not to will" or "not to act." Again, in all particular goods, the reason can consider an aspect of some good, and the lack of some good, which has the aspect of evil: and in this respect, it can apprehend any single one of such goods as to be chosen or to be avoided. The perfect good alone, which is Happiness, cannot be apprehended by the reason as an evil, or as lacking in any way. Consequently man wills Happiness of necessity, nor can he will not to be happy, or to be unhappy. Now since choice is not of the end, but of the means, as stated above (A. 3); it is not of the perfect good, which is Happiness, but of other particular goods. Therefore man chooses not of necessity, but freely.

Reply Obj. 1: The conclusion does not always of necessity follow from the principles, but only when the principles cannot be true if the conclusion is not true. In like manner, the end does not always necessitate in man the choosing of the means, because the means are not always such that the end cannot be gained without them; or, if they be such, they are not always considered in that light.

Reply Obj. 2: The reason's decision or judgment of what is to be done is about things that are contingent and possible to us. In such matters the conclusions do not follow of necessity from principles that are absolutely necessary, but from such as are so conditionally; as, for instance, "If he runs, he is in motion."

Reply Obj. 3: If two things be proposed as equal under one aspect, nothing hinders us from considering in one of them some particular point of superiority, so that the will has a bent towards that one rather than towards the other.

## QUESTION 14

OF COUNSEL, WHICH PRECEDES CHOICE (In Six Articles)

We must now consider counsel; concerning which there are six points of inquiry:

(1) Whether counsel is an inquiry?

(2) Whether counsel is of the end or of the means?

(3) Whether counsel is only of things that we do?

(4) Whether counsel is of all things that we do?

(5) Whether the process of counsel is one of analysis?

(6) Whether the process of counsel is indefinite?

FIRST ARTICLE [I-II, Q. 14, Art. 1]

Whether Counsel Is an Inquiry?

Objection 1: It would seem that counsel is not an inquiry. For Damascene says (De Fide Orth. ii, 22) that counsel is "an act of the appetite." But inquiry is not an act of the appetite. Therefore counsel is not an inquiry.

Obj. 2: Further, inquiry is a discursive act of the intellect: for which reason it is not found in God, Whose knowledge is not discursive, as we have shown in the First Part (Q. 14, A. 7). But counsel is ascribed to God: for it is written (Eph. 1:11) that "He worketh all things according to the counsel of His will." Therefore counsel is not inquiry.

Obj. 3: Further, inquiry is of doubtful matters. But counsel is given in matters that are certainly good; thus the Apostle says (1 Cor. 7:25): "Now concerning virgins I have no commandment of the Lord: but I give counsel." Therefore counsel is not an inquiry.

*On the contrary,* Gregory of Nyssa [*Nemesius, De Nat. Hom. xxxiv.] says: "Every counsel is an inquiry; but not every inquiry is a counsel."

*I answer that,* Choice, as stated above (Q. 13, A. 1, ad 2; A. 3), follows the judgment of the reason about what is to be done. Now there is much uncertainty in things that have to be done; because actions are concerned with contingent singulars, which by reason of their vicissitude, are uncertain. Now in things doubtful and uncertain the reason does not pronounce judgment, without previous inquiry: wherefore the reason must of necessity institute an inquiry before deciding on the objects of choice; and this inquiry is called counsel. Hence the Philosopher says (Ethic. iii, 2) that choice is the "desire of what has been already counselled."

Reply Obj. 1: When the acts of two powers are ordained to one another, in each of them there is something belonging to the other power: consequently each act can be denominated from either power. Now it is evident that the act of the reason giving direction as to the means, and the act of the will tending to these means according to the reason's direction, are ordained to one another. Consequently there is to be found something of the reason, viz. order, in that act of the will, which is choice: and in counsel, which is an act of reason, something of the will—both as matter (since counsel is of what man wills to do)—and as motive (because it is from willing the end, that man is moved to take counsel in regard to the means). And therefore, just as the Philosopher says (Ethic. vi, 2) that choice "is intellect influenced by appetite," thus pointing out that both concur in the act of choosing; so Damascene says (De Fide Orth. ii, 22) that counsel is "appetite based on inquiry," so as to show that counsel belongs, in a way, both to the will, on whose behalf and by whose impulsion the inquiry is made, and to the reason that executes the inquiry.

Reply Obj. 2: The things that we say of God must be understood without any of the defects which are to be found in us: thus in us science is of conclusions derived by reasoning from causes to effects: but science when said of God means sure knowledge of all effects in the First Cause, without any reasoning process. In like manner we ascribe counsel to God, as to the certainty of His knowledge or judgment, which certainty in us arises from the inquiry of counsel. But such inquiry has no place in God; wherefore in this respect it is not ascribed to God: in which sense Damascene says (De Fide Orth. ii, 22): "God takes not counsel: those only take counsel who lack knowledge."

Reply Obj. 3: It may happen that things which are most certainly good in the opinion of wise and spiritual men are not certainly good in the opinion of many, or at least of carnal-minded men. Consequently in such things counsel may be given.

SECOND ARTICLE [I-II, Q. 14, Art. 2]

Whether Counsel Is of the End, or Only of the Means?

Objection 1: It would seem that counsel is not only of the means but also of the end. For whatever is doubtful, can be the subject of inquiry. Now in things to be done by man there happens sometimes a doubt as to the end and not only as to the means. Since therefore inquiry as to what is to be done is counsel, it seems that counsel can be of the end.

Obj. 2: Further, the matter of counsel is human actions. But some human actions are ends, as stated in *Ethic.* i, 1. Therefore counsel can be of the end.

*On the contrary,* Gregory of Nyssa [*Nemesius, De Nat. Hom. xxxiv.] says that "counsel is not of the end, but of the means."

*I answer that,* The end is the principle in practical matters: because the reason of the means is to be found in the end. Now the principle cannot be called in question, but must be presupposed in every inquiry. Since therefore counsel is an inquiry, it is not of the end, but only of the means. Nevertheless it may happen that what is the end in regard to some things, is ordained to something else; just as also what is the principle of one demonstration, is the conclusion of another: and consequently that which is looked upon as the end in one inquiry, may be looked upon as the means in another; and thus it will become an object of counsel.

Reply Obj. 1: That which is looked upon as an end, is already fixed: consequently as long as there is any doubt about it, it is not looked upon as an end. Wherefore if counsel is taken about it, it will be counsel not about the end, but about the means.

Reply Obj. 2: Counsel is about operations, in so far as they are ordained to some end. Consequently if any human act be an end, it will not, as such, be the matter of counsel.

THIRD ARTICLE [I-II, Q. 14, Art. 3]

Whether Counsel Is Only of Things That We Do?

Objection 1: It would seem that counsel is not only of things that we do. For counsel implies some kind of conference. But it is possible for many to confer about things that are not subject to movement, and are not the result of our actions, such as the nature of various things. Therefore counsel is not only of things that we do.

Obj. 2: Further, men sometimes seek counsel about things that are laid down by law; hence we speak of counsel at law. And yet those who seek counsel thus, have nothing to do in making the laws. Therefore counsel is not only of things that we do.

Obj. 3: Further, some are said to take consultation about future events; which, however, are not in our power. Therefore counsel is not only of things that we do.

Obj. 4: Further, if counsel were only of things that we do, no one would take counsel about what another does. But this is clearly untrue. Therefore counsel is not only of things that we do.

*On the contrary,* Gregory of Nyssa [*Nemesius, De Nat. Hom. xxxiv.] says: "We take counsel of things that are within our competency and that we are able to do."

*I answer that,* Counsel properly implies a conference held between several; the very word ( *consilium* ) denotes this, for it means a sitting together ( *considium* ), from the fact that many sit together in order to confer with one another. Now we must take note that in contingent particular cases, in order that anything be known for certain, it is necessary to take several conditions or circumstances into consideration, which it is not easy for one to consider, but are considered by several with greater certainty, since what one takes note of, escapes the notice of another; whereas in necessary and universal things, our view is brought to bear on matters much more absolute and simple, so that one man by himself may be sufficient to consider these things. Wherefore the inquiry of counsel is concerned, properly speaking, with contingent singulars. Now the knowledge of the truth in such matters does not rank so high as to be desirable of itself, as is the knowledge of things universal and necessary; but it is desired as being useful towards action, because actions bear on things singular and contingent. Consequently, properly speaking, counsel is about things done by us.

Reply Obj. 1: Counsel implies conference, not of any kind, but about what is to be done, for the reason given above.

Reply Obj. 2: Although that which is laid down by the law is not due to the action of him who seeks counsel, nevertheless it directs him in his action: since the mandate of the law is one reason for doing something.

Reply Obj. 3: Counsel is not only about what is done, but also about whatever has relation to what is done. And for this reason we speak of consulting about future events, in so far as man is induced to do or omit something, through the knowledge of future events.

Reply Obj. 4: We seek counsel about the actions

of others, in so far as they are, in some way, one with us; either by union of affection—thus a man is solicitous about what concerns his friend, as though it concerned himself; or after the manner of an instrument, for the principal agent and the instrument are, in a way, one cause, since one acts through the other; thus the master takes counsel about what he would do through his servant.

FOURTH ARTICLE [I-II, Q. 14, Art. 4]

Whether Counsel Is About All Things That We Do?

Objection 1: It would seem that counsel is about all things that we have to do. For choice is the "desire of what is counselled" as stated above (A. 1). But choice is about all things that we do. Therefore counsel is too.

Obj. 2: Further, counsel implies the reason's inquiry. But, whenever we do not act through the impulse of passion, we act in virtue of the reason's inquiry. Therefore there is counsel about everything that we do.

Obj. 3: Further, the Philosopher says (Ethic. iii, 3) that "if it appears that something can be done by more means than one, we take counsel by inquiring whereby it may be done most easily and best; but if it can be accomplished by one means, how it can be done by this." But whatever is done, is done by one means or by several. Therefore counsel takes place in all things that we do.

*On the contrary,* Gregory of Nyssa [*Nemesius, De Nat. Hom. xxxiv.] says that "counsel has no place in things that are done according to science or art."

*I answer that,* Counsel is a kind of inquiry, as stated above (A. 1). But we are wont to inquire about things that admit of doubt; hence the process of inquiry, which is called an argument, "is a reason that attests something that admitted of doubt" [*Cicero, *Topic.* ad Trebat.]. Now, that something in relation to human acts admits of no doubt, arises from a twofold source. First, because certain determinate ends are gained by certain determinate means: as happens in the arts which are governed by certain fixed rules of action; thus a writer does not take counsel how to form his letters, for this is determined by art. Secondly, from the fact that it little matters whether it is done this or that way; this occurs in minute matters, which help or hinder but little with regard to the end aimed at; and reason looks upon small things as mere nothings. Consequently there are two things of which we do not take counsel, although they conduce to the end, as the Philosopher says (Ethic. iii, 3): namely, minute things, and those which have a fixed way of being done, as in works produced by art, with the exception of those arts that admit of conjecture such as medicine, commerce, and the like, as Gregory of Nyssa says [*Nemesius, De Nat. Hom. xxiv.].

Reply Obj. 1: Choice presupposes counsel by reason of its judgment or decision. Consequently when the judgment or decision is evident without inquiry, there is no need for the inquiry of counsel.

Reply Obj. 2: In matters that are evident, the reason makes no inquiry, but judges at once. Consequently there is no need of counsel in all that is done by reason.

Reply Obj. 3: When a thing can be accomplished by one means, but in different ways, doubt may arise, just as when it can be accomplished by several means: hence the need of counsel. But when not only the means, but also the way of using the means, is fixed, then there is no need of counsel.

FIFTH ARTICLE [I-II, Q. 14, Art. 5]

Whether the Process of Counsel Is One of Analysis?

Objection 1: It would seem that the process of counsel is not one of analysis. For counsel is about things that we do. But the process of our actions is not one of analysis, but rather one of synthesis, viz. from the simple to the composite. Therefore counsel does not always proceed by way of analysis.

Obj. 2: Further, counsel is an inquiry of the reason. But reason proceeds from things that precede to things that follow, according to the more appropriate order. Since then, the past precedes the present, and the present precedes the future, it seems that in taking counsel one should proceed from the past and present to the future: which is not an analytical process. Therefore the process of counsel is not one of analysis.

Obj. 3: Further, counsel is only of such things as are possible to us, according to *Ethic.* iii, 3. But the question as to whether a certain thing is possible to us, depends on what we are able or unable to do, in order to gain such and such an end. Therefore the inquiry of counsel should begin from things present.

*On the contrary,* The Philosopher says (Ethic. iii, 3) that "he who takes counsel seems to inquire and analyze."

*I answer that,* In every inquiry one must begin from some principle. And if this principle precedes both in knowledge and in being, the process is not analytic, but synthetic: because to proceed from cause to effect is to proceed synthetically, since causes are more simple than effects. But if that which precedes in knowledge is later in the order of being, the process is one of analysis, as when our judgment deals with effects, which by analysis we trace to their simple causes. Now the principle in the inquiry of counsel is the end, which precedes indeed in intention, but comes afterwards into execution. Hence the inquiry of counsel must needs be one of analysis, beginning that is to say, from that which is intended in the future, and continuing until it arrives at that which is to be done at once.

Reply Obj. 1: Counsel is indeed about action. But actions take their reason from the end; and consequently the order of reasoning about actions is contrary to the order of actions.

Reply Obj. 2: Reason begins with that which is first according to reason; but not always with that which is first in point of time.

Reply Obj. 3: We should not want to know whether something to be done for an end be possible, if it were not suitable for gaining that end. Hence we must first inquire whether it be conducive to the end, before considering whether it be possible.

SIXTH ARTICLE [I-II, Q. 14, Art. 6]

Whether the Process of Counsel Is Indefinite?

Objection 1: It would seem that the process of counsel is indefinite. For counsel is an inquiry about the particular things with which action is concerned. But singulars are infinite. Therefore the process of counsel is indefinite.

Obj. 2: Further, the inquiry of counsel has to consider not only what is to be done, but how to avoid obstacles. But every human action can be hindered, and an obstacle can be removed by some human reason. Therefore the inquiry about removing obstacles can go on indefinitely.

Obj. 3: Further, the inquiry of demonstrative science does not go on indefinitely, because one can come to principles that are self-evident, which are absolutely certain. But such like certainty is not to be had in contingent singulars, which are variable and uncertain. Therefore the inquiry of counsel goes on indefinitely.

*On the contrary,* "No one is moved to that which he cannot possibly reach" (De Coelo i, 7). But it is impossible to pass through the infinite. If therefore the inquiry of counsel is infinite, no one would begin to take counsel. Which is clearly untrue.

*I answer that,* The inquiry of counsel is actually finite on both sides, on that of its principle and on that of its term. For a twofold principle is available in the inquiry of counsel. One is proper to it, and belongs to the very genus of things pertaining to operation: this is the end which is not the matter of counsel, but is taken for granted as its principle, as stated above (A. 2). The other principle is taken from another genus, so to speak; thus in demonstrative sciences one science postulates certain things from another, without inquiring into them. Now these principles which are taken for granted in the inquiry of counsel are any facts received through the senses—for instance, that this is bread or iron: and also any general statements known either through speculative or through practical science; for instance, that adultery is forbidden by God, or that man cannot live without suitable nourishment. Of such things counsel makes no inquiry. But the term of inquiry is that which we are able to do at once. For just as the end is considered in the light of a principle, so the means are considered in the light of a conclusion. Wherefore that which presents itself as to be done first, holds the position of an ultimate conclusion whereat the inquiry comes to an end. Nothing however prevents counsel from being infinite potentially, for as much as an infinite number of things may present themselves to be inquired into by means of counsel.

Reply Obj. 1: Singulars are infinite; not actually, but only potentially.

Reply Obj. 2: Although human action can be hindered, the hindrance is not always at hand. Consequently it is not always necessary to take counsel about removing the obstacle.

Reply Obj. 3: In contingent singulars, something may be taken for certain, not simply, indeed, but for the time being, and as far as it concerns the work to be done. Thus that Socrates is sitting is not a necessary statement; but that he is sitting, as long as he continues to sit, is necessary; and this can be taken for a certain fact.

## QUESTION 15

OF CONSENT, WHICH IS AN ACT OF THE WILL IN REGARD TO THE MEANS (In Four Articles)

We must now consider consent; concerning which there are four points of inquiry:

(1) Whether consent is an act of the appetitive or of the apprehensive power?

(2) Whether it is to be found in irrational animals?

(3) Whether it is directed to the end or to the means?

(4) Whether consent to an act belongs to the higher part of the soul only?

FIRST ARTICLE [I-II, Q. 15, Art. 1]

Whether Consent Is an Act of the Appetitive or of the Apprehensive Power?

Objection 1: It would seem that consent belongs only to the apprehensive part of the soul. For Augustine (De Trin. xii, 12) ascribes consent to the higher reason. But the reason is an apprehensive power. Therefore consent belongs to an apprehensive power.

Obj. 2: Further, consent is "co-sense." But sense is an apprehensive power. Therefore consent is the act of an apprehensive power.

Obj. 3: Further, just as assent is an application of the intellect to something, so is consent. But assent belongs to the intellect, which is an apprehensive power. Therefore consent also belongs to an apprehensive power.

*On the contrary,* Damascene says (De Fide Orth. ii, 22) that "if a man judge without affection for that of which he judges, there is no sentence," i.e. consent. But affection belongs to the appetitive power. Therefore consent does also.

*I answer that,* Consent implies application of sense to something. Now it is proper to sense to take cognizance of things present; for the imagination apprehends the similitude of corporeal things, even in the absence of the things of which they bear the likeness; while the intellect apprehends universal ideas, which it can apprehend indifferently, whether the singulars be present or absent. And since the act of an appetitive power is a kind of inclination to the thing itself, the application of the appetitive power to the thing, in so far as it cleaves to it, gets by a kind of similitude, the name of sense, since, as it were, it acquires direct knowledge of the thing to which it cleaves, in so far as it takes complacency in it. Hence it is written (Wis. 1:1): "Think of ( *Sentite* ) the Lord in goodness." And on these grounds consent is an act of the appetitive power.

Reply Obj. 1: As stated in *De Anima* iii, 9, "the will is in the reason." Hence, when Augustine ascribes consent to the reason, he takes reason as including the will.

Reply Obj. 2: Sense, properly speaking, belongs to the apprehensive faculty; but by way of similitude, in so far as it implies seeking acquaintance, it belongs to the appetitive power, as stated above.

Reply Obj. 3: *Assentire* (to assent) is, to speak, ad aliud sentire (to feel towards something); and thus it implies a certain distance from that to which assent is given. But *consentire* (to consent) is "to feel with," and this implies a certain union to the object of consent. Hence the will, to which it belongs to tend to the thing itself, is more properly said to consent: whereas the intellect, whose act does not consist in a movement towards the thing, but rather the reverse, as we have stated in the First Part (Q. 16, A. 1; Q. 27, A. 4; Q. 59, A. 2), is more properly said to assent: although one word is wont to be used for the other [*In Latin rather than in English.]. We may also say that the intellect assents, in so far as it is moved by the will.

SECOND ARTICLE [I-II, Q. 15, Art. 2]

Whether Consent Is to Be Found in Irrational Animals?

Objection 1: It would seem that consent is to be found in irrational animals. For consent implies a determination of the appetite to one thing. But the appetite of irrational animals is determinate to one thing. Therefore consent is to be found in irrational animals.

Obj. 2: Further, if you remove what is first, you remove what follows. But consent precedes the accomplished act. If therefore there were no consent in irrational animals, there would be no act accomplished; which is clearly false.

Obj. 3: Further, men are sometimes said to consent to do something, through some passion; desire, for instance, or anger. But irrational animals act through passion. Therefore they consent.

*On the contrary,* Damascene says (De Fide Orth. ii, 22) that "after judging, man approves and embraces the judgment of his counselling, and this is called the sentence," i.e. consent. But counsel is not in irrational animals. Therefore neither is consent.

*I answer that,* Consent, properly speaking, is not in irrational animals. The reason of this is that consent implies an application of the appetitive movement to something as to be done. Now to apply the appetitive movement to the doing of something, belongs to the subject in whose power it is to move the appetite: thus to touch a stone is an action suitable to a stick, but to apply the stick so that it touch the stone, belongs to one who has the power of moving the stick. But irrational animals have not the command of the appetitive movement; for this is in them through natural instinct. Hence in the irrational animal, there is indeed the movement of the appetite, but it does not apply that movement to some particular thing. And hence it is that the irrational animal is not properly said to consent: this is proper to the rational nature, which has the command of the appetitive movement, and is able to apply or not to apply it to this or that thing.

Reply Obj. 1: In irrational animals the determination of the appetite to a particular thing is merely passive: whereas consent implies a determination of the appetite, which is active rather than merely passive.

Reply Obj. 2: If the first be removed, then what follows is removed, provided that, properly speaking, it follow from that only. But if something can follow from several things, it is not removed by the fact that one of them is removed; thus if hardening is the effect of heat and of cold (since bricks are hardened by the fire, and frozen water is hardened by the cold), then by removing heat it does not follow that there is no hardening. Now the accomplishment of an act follows not only from consent, but also from the impulse of the appetite, such as is found in irrational animals.

Reply Obj. 3: The man who acts through passion is able not to follow the passion: whereas irrational animals have not that power. Hence the comparison fails.

THIRD ARTICLE [I-II, Q. 15, Art. 3]

Whether Consent Is Directed to the End or to the Means?

Objection 1: It would seem that consent is directed to the end. Because that on account of which a thing is such is still more such. But it is on account of the end that we consent to the means. Therefore, still more do we consent to the end.

Obj. 2: Further, the act of the intemperate man is his end, just as the act of the virtuous man is his end. But the intemperate man consents to his own act. Therefore consent can be directed to the end.

Obj. 3: Further, desire of the means is choice, as stated above (Q. 13, A. 1). If therefore consent were only directed to the means it would nowise differ from choice. And this is proved to be false by the authority of Damascene who says (De Fide Orth. ii, 22) that "after the approval" which he calls "the sentence," "comes the choice." Therefore consent is not only directed to the means.

*On the contrary,* Damascene says (De Fide Orth. ii, 22) that the "sentence," i.e. the consent, takes place "when a man approves and embraces the judgment of his counsel." But counsel is only about the means. Therefore the same applies to consent.

*I answer that,* Consent is the application of the appetitive movement to something that is already in the power of him who causes the application. Now the order of action is this: First there is the apprehension of the end; then the desire of the end; then the counsel about the means; then the desire of the means. Now the appetite tends to the last end naturally: wherefore the application of the appetitive movement to the apprehended end has not the nature of consent, but of simple volition. But as to those things which come under consideration after the last end, in so far as they are directed to the end, they come under counsel: and so counsel can be applied to them, in so far as the appetitive movement is applied to the judgment resulting from counsel. But the appetitive movement to the end is not applied to counsel: rather is counsel applied to it, because counsel presupposes the desire of the end. On the other hand, the desire of the means presupposes the decision of counsel. And therefore the application of the appetitive movement to counsel's decision is consent, properly speaking. Consequently, since counsel is only about the means, consent, properly speaking, is of nothing else but the means.

Reply Obj. 1: Just as the knowledge of conclusions through the principles is science, whereas the knowledge of the principles is not science, but something higher, namely, understanding; so do we consent to the means on account of the end, in respect of which our act is not consent but something greater, namely, volition.

Reply Obj. 2: Delight in his act, rather than the act itself, is the end of the intemperate man, and for sake of this delight he consents to that act.

Reply Obj. 3: Choice includes something that consent has not, namely, a certain relation to something to which something else is preferred: and therefore after consent there still remains a choice. For it may happen that by aid of counsel several means have been found conducive to the end, and through each of these meeting with approval, consent has been given to each: but after approving of many, we have given our preference to one by choosing it. But if only one meets with approval, then consent and choice do not differ in reality, but only in our way of looking at them; so that we call it consent, according as we approve of doing that thing; but choice according as we prefer it to those that do not meet with our approval.

FOURTH ARTICLE [I-II, Q. 15, Art. 4]

Whether Consent to the Act Belongs Only to the Higher Part of the Soul?

Objection 1: It would seem that consent to the act does not always belong to the higher reason. For "delight follows action, and perfects it, just as beauty perfects youth" [* oion tois akmaiois he hora —as youthful vigor perfects a man in his prime] (Ethic. x, 4). But consent to delight belongs to the lower reason, as Augustine says (De Trin. xii, 12). Therefore consent to the act does not belong only to the higher reason.

Obj. 2: Further, an act to which we consent is said to be voluntary. But it belongs to many powers to produce voluntary acts. Therefore the higher reason is not alone in consenting to the act.

Obj. 3: Further, "the higher reason is that which is intent on the contemplation and consultation of things eternal," as Augustine says (De Trin. xii, 7). But man often consents to an act not for eternal, but for temporal reasons, or even on account of some passion of the soul. Therefore consent to an act does not belong to the higher reason alone.

*On the contrary,* Augustine says (De Trin. xii, 12): "It is impossible for man to make up his mind to commit a sin, unless that mental faculty which has the sovereign power of urging his members to, or restraining them from, act, yield to the evil deed and become its slave."

*I answer that,* The final decision belongs to him who holds the highest place, and to whom it belongs to judge of the others; for as long as judgment about some matter remains to be pronounced, the final decision has not been given. Now it is evident that it belongs to the higher reason to judge of all: since it is by the reason that we judge of sensible things; and of things pertaining to human principles we judge according to Divine principles, which is the function of the higher reason. Wherefore as long as a man is uncertain whether he resists or not, according to Divine principles, no judgment of the reason can be considered in the light of a final decision. Now the final decision of what is to be done is consent to the act. Therefore consent to the act belongs to the higher reason; but in that sense in which the reason includes the will, as stated above (A. 1, ad 1).

Reply Obj. 1: Consent to delight in the work done belongs to the higher reason, as also does consent to the work; but consent to delight in thought belongs to the lower reason, just as to the lower reason it belongs to think. Nevertheless the higher reason exercises judgment on the fact of thinking or not thinking, considered as an action; and in like manner on the delight that results. But in so far as the act of thinking is considered as ordained to a further act, it belongs to the lower reason. For that which is ordained to something else, belongs to a lower art or power than does the end to which it is ordained: hence the art which is concerned with the end is called the master or principal art.

Reply Obj. 2: Since actions are called voluntary from the fact that we consent to them, it does not follow that consent is an act of each power, but of the will which is in the reason, as stated above (A. 1, ad 1), and from which the voluntary act is named.

Reply Obj. 3: The higher reason is said to consent not only because it always moves to act, according to the eternal reasons; but also because it fails to dissent according to those same reasons.

## QUESTION 16

OF USE, WHICH IS AN ACT OF THE WILL IN REGARD TO THE MEANS (In Four Articles)

We must now consider use; concerning which there are four points of inquiry:

(1) Whether use is an act of the will?

(2) Whether it is to be found in irrational animals?

(3) Whether it regards the means only, or the end also?

(4) Of the relation of use to choice.

FIRST ARTICLE [I-II, Q. 16, Art. 1]

Whether Use Is an Act of the Will?

Objection 1: It would seem that use is not an act of the will. For Augustine says (De Doctr. Christ. i, 4) that "to use is to refer that which is the object of use to the obtaining of something else." But "to refer" something to another is an act of the reason to which it belongs to compare and to direct. Therefore use is an act of the reason and not of the will.

Obj. 2: Further, Damascene says (De Fide Orth. ii, 22) that man "goes forward to the operation, and this is called impulse; then he makes use (of the powers) and this is called use." But operation belongs to the executive power; and the act of the will does not follow the act of the executive power, on the contrary execution comes last. Therefore use is not an act of the will.

Obj. 3: Further, Augustine says (QQ. 83, qu. 30): "All things that were made were made for man's use, because reason with which man is endowed uses all things by its judgment of them." But judgment of things created by God belongs to the speculative reason; which seems to be altogether distinct from the will, which is the principle of human acts. Therefore use is not an act of the will.

*On the contrary,* Augustine says (De Trin. x, 11): "To use is to apply to something to purpose of the will."

*I answer that,* The use of a thing implies the application of that thing to an operation: hence the operation to which we apply a thing is called its use; thus the use of a horse is to ride, and the use of a stick is to strike. Now we apply to an operation not only the interior principles of action, viz. the powers of the soul or the members of the body; as the intellect, to understand; and the eye, to see; but also external things, as a stick, to strike. But it is evident that we do not apply external things to an operation save through the interior principles which are either the powers of the soul, or the habits of those powers, or the organs which are parts of the body. Now it has been shown above (Q. 9, A. 1) that it is the will which moves the soul's powers to their acts, and this is to apply them to operation. Hence it is evident that first and principally use belongs to the will as first mover; to the reason, as directing; and to the other powers as executing the operation, which powers are compared to the will which applies them to act, as the instruments are compared to the principal agent. Now action is properly ascribed, not to the instrument, but to the principal agent, as building is ascribed to the builder, not to his tools. Hence it is evident that use is, properly speaking, an act of the will.

Reply Obj. 1: Reason does indeed refer one thing to another; but the will tends to that which is referred by the reason to something else. And in this sense to use is to refer one thing to another.

Reply Obj. 2: Damascene is speaking of use in so far as it belongs to the executive powers.

Reply Obj. 3: Even the speculative reason is applied by the will to the act of understanding or judging. Consequently the speculative reason is said to use, in so far as it is moved by the will, in the same way as the other powers.

SECOND ARTICLE [I-II, Q. 16, Art. 2]

Whether Use Is to Be Found in Irrational Animals?

Objection 1: It would seem that use is to be found in irrational animals. For it is better to enjoy than to use, because, as Augustine says (De Trin. x, 10): "We use things by referring them to something else which we are to enjoy." But enjoyment is to be found in irrational animals, as stated above (Q. 11, A. 2). Much more, therefore, is it possible for them to use.

Obj. 2: Further, to apply the members to action is to use them. But irrational animals apply their members to action; for instance, their feet, to walk; their horns, to strike. Therefore it is possible for irrational animals to use.

*On the contrary,* Augustine says (QQ. 83, qu. 30): "None but a rational animal can make use of a thing."

*I answer that,* as stated above (A. 1), to use is to apply an active principle to action: thus to consent is to apply the appetitive movement to the desire of something, as stated above (Q. 15, AA. 1, 2, 3). Now he alone who has the disposal of a thing, can apply it to something else; and this belongs to him alone who knows how to refer it to something else, which is an act of the reason. And therefore none but a rational animal consents and uses.

Reply Obj. 1: To enjoy implies the absolute movement of the appetite to the appetible: whereas to use implies a movement of the appetite to something as directed to something else. If therefore we compare use and enjoyment in respect of their objects, enjoyment is better than use; because that which is appetible absolutely is better than that which is appetible only as directed to something else. But if we compare them in respect of the apprehensive power that precedes them, greater excellence is required on the part of use: because to direct one thing to another is an act of reason; whereas to apprehend something absolutely is within the competency even of sense.

Reply Obj. 2: Animals by means of their members do something from natural instinct; not through knowing the relation of their members to these operations. Wherefore, properly speaking, they do not apply their members to action, nor do they use them.

THIRD ARTICLE [I-II, Q. 16, Art. 3]

Whether Use Regards Also the Last End?

Objection 1: It would seem that use can regard also the last end. For Augustine says (De Trin. x, 11): "Whoever enjoys, uses." But man enjoys the last end. Therefore he uses the last end.

Obj. 2: Further, "to use is to apply something to the purpose of the will" (De Trin. x, 11). But the last end, more than anything else, is the object of the will's application. Therefore it can be the object of use.

Obj. 3: Further, Hilary says (De Trin. ii) that "Eternity is in the Father, Likeness in the Image," i.e. in the Son, "Use in the Gift," i.e. in the Holy Ghost. But the Holy Ghost, since He is God, is the last end. Therefore the last end can be the object of use.

*On the contrary,* Augustine says (QQ. 83, qu. 30): "No one rightly uses God, but one enjoys Him." But God alone is the last end. Therefore we cannot use the last end.

*I answer that,* Use, as stated above (A. 1), implies the application of one thing to another. Now that which is applied to another is regarded in the light of means to an end; and consequently use always regards the means. For this reason things that are adapted to a certain end are said to be "useful"; in fact their very usefulness is sometimes called use.

It must, however, be observed that the last end may be taken in two ways: first, simply; secondly, in respect of an individual. For since the end, as stated above (Q. 1, A. 8; Q. 2, A. 7), signifies sometimes the thing itself, and sometimes the attainment or possession of that thing (thus the miser's end is either money or the possession of it); it is evident that, simply speaking, the last end is the thing itself; for the possession of money is good only inasmuch as there is some good in money. But in regard to the individual, the obtaining of money is the last end; for the miser would not seek for money, save that he might have it. Therefore, simply and properly speaking, a man enjoys money, because he places his last end therein; but in so far as he seeks to possess it, he is said to use it.

Reply Obj. 1: Augustine is speaking of use in general, in so far as it implies the relation of an end to the enjoyment which a man seeks in that end.

Reply Obj. 2: The end is applied to the purpose of the will, that the will may find rest in it. Consequently this rest in the end, which is the enjoyment thereof, is in this sense called use of the end. But the means are applied to the will's purpose, not only in being used as means, but as ordained to something else in which the will finds rest.

Reply Obj. 3: The words of Hilary refer to use as applicable to rest in the last end; just as, speaking in a general sense, one may be said to use the end for the purpose of attaining it, as stated above. Hence Augustine says (De Trin. vi, 10) that "this love, delight, felicity, or happiness, is called use by him."

FOURTH ARTICLE [I-II, Q. 16, Art. 4]

Whether Use Precedes Choice?

Objection 1: It would seem that use precedes choice. For nothing follows after choice, except execution. But use, since it belongs to the will, precedes execution. Therefore it precedes choice also.

Obj. 2: Further, the absolute precedes the relative. Therefore the less relative precedes the more relative. But choice implies two relations: one, of the thing chosen, in relation to the end; the other, of the thing chosen, in respect of that to which it is preferred; whereas use implies relation to the end only. Therefore use precedes choice.

Obj. 3: Further, the will uses the other powers in so far as it removes them. But the will moves itself, too, as stated above (Q. 9, A. 3). Therefore it uses itself, by applying itself to act. But it does this when it consents. Therefore there is use in consent. But consent precedes choice as stated above (Q. 15, A. 3, ad 3). Therefore use does also.

*On the contrary,* Damascene says (De Fide Orth. ii, 22) that "the will after choosing has an impulse to the operation, and afterwards it uses (the powers)." Therefore use follows choice.

*I answer that,* The will has a twofold relation to the thing willed. One, according as the thing willed is, in a way, in the willing subject, by a kind of proportion or order to the thing willed. Wherefore those things that are naturally proportionate to a certain end, are said to desire that end naturally. Yet to have an end thus is to have it imperfectly. Now every imperfect thing tends to perfection. And therefore both the natural and the voluntary appetite tend to have the end in reality; and this is to have it perfectly. This is the second relation of the will to the thing willed.

Now the thing willed is not only the end, but also the means. And the last act that belongs to the first relation of the will to the means, is choice; for there the will becomes fully proportionate, by willing the means fully. Use, on the other hand, belongs to the second relation of the will, in respect of which it tends to the realization of the thing willed. Wherefore it is evident that use follows choice; provided that by use we mean the will's use of the executive power in moving it. But since the will, in a way, moves the reason also, and uses it, we may take the use of the means, as consisting in the consideration of the reason, whereby it refers the means to the end. In this sense use precedes choice.

Reply Obj. 1: The motion of the will to the execution of the work, precedes execution, but follows choice. And so, since use belongs to that very motion of the will, it stands between choice and execution.

Reply Obj. 2: What is essentially relative is after the absolute; but the thing to which relation is referred need not come after. Indeed, the more a cause precedes, the more numerous the effects to which it has relation.

Reply Obj. 3: Choice precedes use, if they be referred to the same object. But nothing hinders the use of one thing preceding the choice of another. And since the acts of the will react on one another, in each act of the will we can find both consent and choice and use; so that we may say that the will consents to choose, and consents to consent, and uses itself in consenting and choosing. And such acts as are ordained to that which precedes, precede also.

# QUESTION 17

OF THE ACTS COMMANDED BY THE WILL (In Nine Articles)

We must now consider the acts commanded by the will; under which head there are nine points of inquiry:

(1) Whether command is an act of the will or of the reason?

(2) Whether command belongs to irrational animals?

(3) Of the order between command and use;

(4) Whether command and the commanded act are one act or distinct?

(5) Whether the act of the will is commanded?

(6) Whether the act of the reason is commanded?

(7) Whether the act of the sensitive appetite is commanded?

(8) Whether the act of the vegetal soul is commanded?

(9) Whether the acts of the external members are commanded?

FIRST ARTICLE [I-II, Q. 17, Art. 1]

Whether Command Is an Act of the Reason or of the Will?

Objection 1: It would seem that command is not an act of the reason but of the will. For command is a kind of motion; because Avicenna says that there are four ways of moving, "by perfecting, by disposing, by commanding, and by counselling." But it belongs to the will to move all the other powers of the soul, as stated above (Q. 9, A. 1). Therefore command is an act of the will.

Obj. 2: Further, just as to be commanded belongs to that which is subject, so, seemingly, to command belongs to that which is most free. But the root of liberty is especially in the will. Therefore to command belongs to the will.

Obj. 3: Further, command is followed at once by act. But the act of the reason is not followed at once by act: for he who judges that a thing should be done, does not do it at once. Therefore command is not an act of the reason, but of the will.

*On the contrary,* Gregory of Nyssa [*Nemesius, De Nat. Hom. xvi.] and the Philosopher (Ethic. i, 13) say that "the appetite obeys reason." Therefore command is an act of the reason.

*I answer that,* Command is an act of the reason presupposing, however, an act of the will. In proof of this, we must take note that, since the acts of the reason and of the will can be brought to bear on one another, in so far as the reason reasons about willing, and the will wills to reason, the result is that the act of the reason precedes the act of the will, and conversely. And since the power of the preceding act continues in the act that follows, it happens sometimes that there is an act of the will in so far as it retains in itself something of an act of the reason, as we have stated in reference to use and choice; and conversely, that there is an act of the reason in so far as it retains in itself something of an act of the will.

Now, command is essentially indeed an act of the reason: for the commander orders the one commanded to do something, by way of intimation or declaration; and to order thus by intimating or declaring is an act of the reason. Now the reason can intimate or declare something in two ways. First, absolutely: and this intimation is expressed by a verb in the indicative mood, as when one person says to another: "This is what you should do." Sometimes, however, the reason intimates something to a man by moving him thereto; and this intimation is expressed by a verb in the imperative mood; as when it is said to someone: "Do this." Now the first mover, among the powers of the soul, to the doing of an act is the will, as stated above (Q. 9, A. 1). Since therefore the second mover does not move, save in virtue of the first mover, it follows that the very fact that the reason moves by commanding, is due to the power of the will. Consequently it follows that command is an act of the reason, presupposing an act of the will, in virtue of which the reason, by its command, moves (the power) to the execution of the act.

Reply Obj. 1: To command is to move, not anyhow, but by intimating and declaring to another; and this is an act of the reason.

Reply Obj. 2: The root of liberty is the will as the subject thereof; but it is the reason as its cause. For the will can tend freely towards various objects, precisely because the reason can have various perceptions of good. Hence philosophers define the free-will as being "a free judgment arising from reason," implying that reason is the root of liberty.

Reply Obj. 3: This argument proves that command is an act of reason not absolutely, but with a kind of motion as stated above.

SECOND ARTICLE [I-II, Q. 17, Art. 2]

Whether Command Belongs to Irrational Animals?

Objection 1: It would seem that command belongs to irrational animals. Because, according to Avicenna, "the power that commands movement is the appetite; and the power that executes movement is in the muscles and nerves." But both powers are in irrational animals. Therefore command is to be found in irrational animals.

Obj. 2: Further, the condition of a slave is that of one who receives commands. But the body is compared to the soul as a slave to his master, as the Philosopher says (Polit. i, 2). Therefore the body is commanded by the soul, even in irrational animals, since they are composed of soul and body.

Obj. 3: Further, by commanding, man has an impulse towards an action. But impulse to action is to be found in irrational animals, as Damascene says (De Fide Orth. ii, 22). Therefore command is to be found in irrational animals.

*On the contrary,* Command is an act of reason, as stated above (A. 1). But in irrational animals there is no reason. Neither, therefore, is there command.

*I answer that,* To command is nothing else than to direct someone to do something, by a certain motion of intimation. Now to direct is the proper act of reason. Wherefore it is impossible that irrational animals should command in any way, since they are devoid of reason.

Reply Obj. 1: The appetitive power is said to command movement, in so far as it moves the commanding reason. But this is only in man. In irrational animals the appetitive power is not, properly speaking, a commanding faculty, unless command be taken loosely for motion.

Reply Obj. 2: The body of the irrational animal is competent to obey; but its soul is not competent to command, because it is not competent to direct. Consequently there is no ratio there of commander and commanded; but only of mover and moved.

Reply Obj. 3: Impulse to action is in irrational animals otherwise than in man. For the impulse of man to action arises from the directing reason; wherefore his impulse is one of command. On the other hand, the impulse of the irrational animal arises from natural instinct; because as soon as they apprehend the fitting or the unfitting, their appetite is moved naturally to pursue or to avoid. Wherefore they are directed by another to act; and they themselves do not direct themselves to act. Consequently in them is impulse but not command.

THIRD ARTICLE [I-II, Q. 17, Art. 3]

Whether Use Precedes Command?

Objection 1: It would seem that use precedes command. For command is an act of the reason presupposing an act of the will, as stated above (A. 1). But, as we have already shown (Q. 16, A. 1), use is an act of the will. Therefore use precedes command.

Obj. 2: Further, command is one of those things that are ordained to the end. But use is of those things that are ordained to the end. Therefore it seems that use precedes command.

Obj. 3: Further, every act of a power moved by the will is called use; because the will uses the other powers, as stated above (Q. 16, A. 1). But command is an act of the reason as moved by the will, as stated above (A. 1). Therefore command is a kind of use. Now the common precedes the proper. Therefore use precedes command.

*On the contrary,* Damascene says (De Fide Orth. ii, 22) that impulse to action precedes use. But impulse to operation is given by command. Therefore command precedes use.

*I answer that,* use of that which is directed to the end, in so far as it is in the reason referring this to the end, precedes choice, as stated above (Q. 16, A. 4). Wherefore still more does it precede command. On the other hand, use of that which is directed to the end, in so far as it is subject to the executive power, follows command; because use in the user is united to the act of the thing used; for one does not use a stick before doing something with the stick. But command is not simultaneous with the act of the thing to which the command is given: for it naturally precedes its fulfilment, sometimes, indeed, by priority of time. Consequently it is evident that command precedes use.

Reply Obj. 1: Not every act of the will precedes this act of the reason which is command; but an act of the will precedes, viz. choice; and an act of the will follows, viz. use. Because after counsel's decision, which is reason's judgment, the will chooses; and after choice, the reason commands that power which has to do what was chosen; and then, last of all, someone's will begins to use, by executing the command of reason; sometimes it is another's will, when one commands another; sometimes the will of the one that commands, when he commands himself to do something.

Reply Obj. 2: Just as act ranks before power, so does the object rank before the act. Now the object of use is that which is directed to the end. Consequently, from the fact that command [itself is directed to the end, it may be concluded that command] precedes, rather than that it follows use.

Reply Obj. 3: Just as the act of the will in using the reason for the purpose of command, precedes the command; so also we may say that this act whereby the will uses the reason, is preceded by a command of reason; since the acts of these powers react on one another.

FOURTH ARTICLE [I-II, Q. 17, Art. 4]

Whether Command and the Commanded Act Are One Act, or Distinct?

Objection 1: It would seem that the commanded act is not one with the command itself. For the acts of different powers are themselves distinct. But the commanded act belongs to one power, and the command to another; since one is the power that commands, and the other is the power that receives the command. Therefore the commanded act is not one with the command.

Obj. 2: Further, whatever things can be separate from one another, are distinct: for nothing is severed from itself. But sometimes the commanded act is separate from the command: for sometimes the command is given, and the commanded act follows not. Therefore command is a distinct act from the act commanded.

Obj. 3: Further, whatever things are related to one another as precedent and consequent, are distinct. But command naturally precedes the commanded act. Therefore they are distinct.

*On the contrary,* The Philosopher says (Topic. iii, 2) that "where one thing is by reason of another, there is but one." But there is no commanded act unless by reason of the command. Therefore they are one.

*I answer that,* Nothing prevents certain things being distinct in one respect, and one in another respect. Indeed, every multitude is one in some respect, as Dionysius says (Div. Nom. xiii). But a difference is to be observed in this, that some are simply many, and one in a particular aspect: while with others it is the reverse. Now "one" is predicated in the same way as "being." And substance is being simply, whereas accident or being "of reason" is a being only in a certain respect. Wherefore those things that are one in substance are one simply, though many in a certain respect. Thus, in the genus substance, the whole composed of its integral or essential parts, is one simply: because the whole is being and substance simply, and the parts are being and substances in the whole. But those things which are distinct in substance, and one according to an accident, are distinct simply, and one in a certain respect: thus many men are one people, and many stones are one heap; which is unity of composition or order. In like manner also many individuals that are one in genus or species are many simply, and one in a certain respect: since to be one in genus or species is to be one according to the consideration of the reason.

Now just as in the genus of natural things, a whole is composed of matter and form (e.g. man, who is one natural being, though he has many parts, is composed of soul and body); so, in human acts, the act of a lower power is in the position of matter in regard to the act of a higher power, in so far as the lower power acts in virtue of the higher power moving it: for thus also the act of the first mover is as the form in regard to the act of its instrument. Hence it is evident that command and the commanded act are one human act, just as a whole is one, yet in its parts, many.

Reply Obj. 1: If the distinct powers are not ordained to one another, their acts are diverse simply. But when one power is the mover of the other, then their acts are, in a way, one: since "the act of the mover and the act of the thing moved are one act" (Phys. iii, 3).

Reply Obj. 2: The fact that command and the commanded act can be separated from one another shows that they are different parts. Because the parts of a man can be separated from one another, and yet they form one whole.

Reply Obj. 3: In those things that are many in parts, but one as a whole, nothing hinders one part from preceding another. Thus the soul, in a way, precedes the body; and the heart, the other members.

FIFTH ARTICLE [I-II, Q. 17, Art. 5]

Whether the Act of the Will Is Commanded?

Objection 1: It would seem that the act of the will is not commanded. For Augustine says (Confess. viii, 9): "The mind commands the mind to will, and yet it does not." But to will is the act of the will. Therefore the act of the will is not commanded.

Obj. 2: Further, to receive a command belongs to one who can understand the command. But the will cannot understand the command; for the will differs from the intellect, to which it belongs to understand. Therefore the act of the will is not commanded.

Obj. 3: Further, if one act of the will is commanded, for the same reason all are commanded. But if all the acts of the will are commanded, we must needs proceed to infinity; because the act of the will precedes the act of reason commanding, as stated above (A. 1); for if that act of the will be also commanded, this command will be preceded by another act of the reason, and so on to infinity. But to proceed to infinity is not possible. Therefore the act of the will is not commanded.

*On the contrary,* Whatever is in our power, is subject to our command. But the acts of the will, most of all, are in our power; since all our acts are said to be in our power, in so far as they are voluntary. Therefore the acts of the will are commanded by us.

*I answer that,* As stated above (A. 1), command is nothing else than the act of the reason directing, with a certain motion, something to act. Now it is evident that the reason can direct the act of the will: for just as it can judge it to be good to will something, so it can direct by commanding man to will. From this it is evident that an act of the will can be commanded.

Reply Obj. 1: As Augustine says (Confess. viii, 9) when the mind commands itself perfectly to will, then already it wills: but that sometimes it commands and wills not, is due to the fact that it commands imperfectly. Now imperfect command arises from the fact that the reason is moved by opposite motives to command or not to command: wherefore it fluctuates between the two, and fails to command perfectly.

Reply Obj. 2: Just as each of the members of the body works not for itself alone but for the whole body; thus it is for the whole body that the eye sees; so is it with the powers of the soul. For the intellect understands, not for itself alone, but for all the powers; and the will wills not only for itself, but for all the powers too. Wherefore man, in so far as he is endowed with intellect and will, commands the act of the will for himself.

Reply Obj. 3: Since command is an act of reason, that act is commanded which is subject to reason. Now the first act of the will is not due to the direction of the reason but to the instigation of nature, or of a higher cause, as stated above (Q. 9, A. 4). Therefore there is no need to proceed to infinity.

SIXTH ARTICLE [I-II, Q. 17, Art. 6]

Whether the Act of the Reason Is Commanded?

Objection 1: It would seem that the act of the reason cannot be commanded. For it seems impossible for a thing to command itself. But it is the reason that commands, as stated above (A. 1). Therefore the act of the reason is not commanded.

Obj. 2: Further, that which is essential is different from that which is by participation. But the power whose act is commanded by reason, is rational by participation, as stated in *Ethic.* i, 13. Therefore the act of that power, which is essentially rational, is not commanded.

Obj. 3: Further, that act is commanded, which is in our power. But to know and judge the truth, which is the act of reason, is not always in our power. Therefore the act of the reason cannot be commanded.

*On the contrary,* That which we do of our free-will, can be done by our command. But the acts of the reason are accomplished through the free-will: for Damascene says (De Fide Orth. ii, 22) that "by his free-will man inquires, considers, judges, approves." Therefore the acts of the reason can be commanded.

*I answer that,* Since the reason reacts on itself, just as it directs the acts of other powers, so can it direct its own act. Consequently its act can be commanded.

But we must take note that the act of the reason may be considered in two ways. First, as to the exercise of the act. And considered thus, the act of the reason can always be commanded: as when one is told to be attentive, and to use one's reason. Secondly, as to the object; in respect of which two acts of the reason have to be noticed. One is the act whereby it apprehends the truth about something. This act is not in our power: because it happens in virtue of a natural or supernatural light. Consequently in this respect, the act of the reason is not in our power, and cannot be commanded. The other act of the reason is that whereby it assents to what it apprehends. If, therefore, that which the reason apprehends is such that it naturally assents thereto, e.g. the first principles, it is not in our power to assent or dissent to the like: assent follows naturally, and consequently, properly speaking, is not subject to our command. But some things which are apprehended do not convince the intellect to such an extent as not to leave it free to assent or dissent, or at least suspend its assent or dissent, on account of some cause or other; and in such things assent or dissent is in our power, and is subject to our command.

Reply Obj. 1: Reason commands itself, just as the will moves itself, as stated above (Q. 9, A. 3), that is to say, in so far as each power reacts on its own acts, and from one thing tends to another.

Reply Obj. 2: On account of the diversity of objects subject to the act of the reason, nothing prevents the reason from participating in itself: thus the knowledge of principles is participated in the knowledge of the conclusions.

The reply to the third object is evident from what has been said.

SEVENTH ARTICLE [I-II, Q. 17, Art. 7]

Whether the Act of the Sensitive Appetite Is Commanded?

Objection 1: It would seem that the act of the sensitive appetite is not commanded. For the Apostle says (Rom. 7:15): "For I do not that good which I will": and a gloss explains this by saying that man lusts, although he wills not to lust. But to lust is an act of the sensitive appetite. Therefore the act of the sensitive appetite is not subject to our command.

Obj. 2: Further, corporeal matter obeys God alone, to the effect of formal transmutation, as was shown in the First Part (Q. 65, A. 4; Q. 91, A. 2; Q. 110, A. 2). But the act of the sensitive appetite is accompanied by a formal transmutation of the body, consisting in heat or cold. Therefore the act of the sensitive appetite is not subject to man's command.

Obj. 3: Further, the proper motive principle of the sensitive appetite is something apprehended by sense or imagination. But it is not always in our power to apprehend something by sense or imagination. Therefore the act of the sensitive appetite is not subject to our command.

*On the contrary,* Gregory of Nyssa [*Nemesius, De Nat. Hom. xvi.] says: "That which obeys reason is twofold, the concupiscible and the irascible," which belong to the sensitive appetite. Therefore the act of the sensitive appetite is subject to the command of reason.

*I answer that,* An act is subject to our command, in so far as it is in our power, as stated above (A. 5). Consequently in order to understand in what manner the act of the sensitive appetite is subject to the command of reason, we must consider in what manner it is in our power. Now it must be observed that the sensitive appetite differs from the intellective appetite, which is called the will, in the fact that the sensitive appetite is a power of a corporeal organ, whereas the will is not. Again, every act of a power that uses a corporeal organ, depends not only on a power of the soul, but also on the disposition of that corporeal organ: thus the act of vision depends on the power of sight, and on the condition of the eye, which condition is a help or a hindrance to that act. Consequently the act of the sensitive appetite depends not only on the appetitive power, but also on the disposition of the body.

Now whatever part the power of the soul takes in the act, follows apprehension. And the apprehension of the imagination, being a particular apprehension, is regulated by the apprehension of reason, which is universal; just as a particular active power is regulated by a universal active power. Consequently in this respect the act of the sensitive appetite is subject to the command of reason. On the other hand, condition or disposition of the body is not subject to the command of reason: and consequently in this respect, the movement of the sensitive appetite is hindered from being wholly subject to the command of reason.

Moreover it happens sometimes that the movement of the sensitive appetite is aroused suddenly in consequence of an apprehension of the imagination of sense. And then such movement occurs without the command of reason: although reason could have prevented it, had it foreseen. Hence the Philosopher says (Polit. i, 2) that the reason governs the irascible and concupiscible not by a "despotic supremacy," which is that of a master over his slave; but by a "politic and royal supremacy," whereby the free are governed, who are not wholly subject to command.

Reply Obj. 1: That man lusts, although he wills not to lust, is due to a disposition of the body, whereby the sensitive appetite is hindered from perfect compliance with the command of reason. Hence the Apostle adds (Rom. 7:15): "I see another law in my members, fighting against the law of my mind." This may also happen through a sudden movement of concupiscence, as stated above.

Reply Obj. 2: The condition of the body stands in a twofold relation to the act of the sensitive appetite. First, as preceding it: thus a man may be disposed in one way or another, in respect of his body, to this or that passion. Secondly, as consequent to it: thus a man becomes heated through anger. Now the condition that precedes, is not subject to the command of reason: since it is due either to nature, or to some previous movement, which cannot cease at once. But the condition that is consequent, follows the command of reason: since it results from the local movement of the heart, which has various movements according to the various acts of the sensitive appetite.

Reply Obj. 3: Since the external sensible is necessary for the apprehension of the senses, it is not in our power to apprehend anything by the senses, unless the sensible be present; which presence of the sensible is not always in our power. For it is then that man can use his senses if he will so to do; unless there be some obstacle on the part of the organ. On the other hand, the apprehension of the imagination is subject to the ordering of reason, in proportion to the strength or weakness of the imaginative power. For that man is unable to imagine the things that reason considers, is either because they cannot be imagined, such as incorporeal things; or because of the weakness of the imaginative power, due to some organic indisposition.

EIGHTH ARTICLE [I-II, Q. 17, Art. 8]

Whether the Act of the Vegetal Soul Is Commanded?

Objection 1: It would seem that the acts of the vegetal soul are subject to the command of reason. For the sensitive powers are of higher rank than the vegetal powers. But the powers of the sensitive soul are subject to the command of reason. Much more, therefore, are the powers of the vegetal soul.

Obj. 2: Further, man is called a "little world" [*Aristotle, *Phys.* viii. 2], because the soul is in the body, as God is in the world. But God is in the world in such a way, that everything in the world obeys His command. Therefore all that is in man, even the powers of the vegetal soul, obey the command of reason.

Obj. 3: Further, praise and blame are awarded only to such acts as are subject to the command of reason. But in the acts of the nutritive and generative power, there is room for praise and blame, virtue and vice: as in the case of gluttony and lust, and their contrary virtues. Therefore the acts of these powers are subject to the command of reason.

*On the contrary,* Gregory of Nyssa [*Nemesius, De Nat. Hom. xxii.] says that "the nutritive and generative power is one over which the reason has no control."

*I answer that,* Some acts proceed from the natural appetite, others from the animal, or from the intellectual appetite: for every agent desires an end in some way. Now the natural appetite does not follow from some apprehension, as [d]o the animal and the intellectual appetite. But the reason commands by way of apprehensive power. Wherefore those acts that proceed from the intellective or the animal appetite, can be commanded by reason: but not those acts that proceed from the natural appetite. And such are the acts of the vegetal soul; wherefore Gregory of Nyssa (Nemesius, De Nat. Hom. xxii) says "that generation and nutrition belong to what are called natural powers." Consequently the acts of the vegetal soul are not subject to the command of reason.

Reply Obj. 1: The more immaterial an act is, the more noble it is, and the more is it subject to the command of reason. Hence the very fact that the acts of the vegetal soul do not obey reason, shows that they rank lowest.

Reply Obj. 2: The comparison holds in a certain respect: because, to wit, as God moves the world, so the soul moves the body. But it does not hold in every respect: for the soul did not create the body out of nothing, as God created the world; for which reason the world is wholly subject to His command.

Reply Obj. 3: Virtue and vice, praise and blame do not affect the acts themselves of the nutritive and generative power, i.e. digestion, and formation of the human body; but they affect the acts of the sensitive part, that are ordained to the acts of generation and nutrition; for example the desire for pleasure in the act of taking food or in the act of generation, and the right or wrong use thereof.

NINTH ARTICLE [I-II, Q. 17, Art. 9]

Whether the Acts of the External Members Are Commanded?

Objection 1: It would seem that the members of the body do not obey reason as to their acts. For it is evident that the members of the body are more distant from the reason, than the powers of the vegetal soul. But the powers of the vegetal soul do not obey reason, as stated above (A. 8). Therefore much less do the members of the body obey.

Obj. 2: Further, the heart is the principle of animal movement. But the movement of the heart is not subject to the command of reason: for Gregory of Nyssa [*Nemesius, De Nat. Hom. xxii.] says that "the pulse is not controlled by reason." Therefore the movement of the bodily members is not subject to the command of reason.

Obj. 3: Further, Augustine says (De Civ. Dei xiv, 16) that "the movement of the genital members is sometimes inopportune and not desired; sometimes when sought it fails, and whereas the heart is warm with desire, the body remains cold." Therefore the movements of the members are not obedient to reason.

*On the contrary,* Augustine says (Confess. viii, 9): "The mind commands a movement of the hand, and so ready is the hand to obey, that scarcely can one discern obedience from command."

*I answer that,* The members of the body are organs of the soul's powers. Consequently according as the powers of the soul stand in respect of obedience to reason, so do the members of the body stand in respect thereof. Since then the sensitive powers are subject to the command of reason, whereas the natural powers are not; therefore all movements of members, that are moved by the sensitive powers, are subject to the command of reason; whereas those movements of members, that arise from the natural powers, are not subject to the command of reason.

Reply Obj. 1: The members do not move themselves, but are moved through the powers of the soul; of which powers, some are in closer contact with the reason than are the powers of the vegetal soul.

Reply Obj. 2: In things pertaining to intellect and will, that which is according to nature stands first, whence all other things are derived: thus from the knowledge of principles that are naturally known, is derived knowledge of the conclusions; and from volition of the end naturally desired, is derived the choice of the means. So also in bodily movements the principle is according to nature. Now the principle of bodily movements begins with the movement of the heart. Consequently the movement of the heart is according to nature, and not according to the will: for like a proper accident, it results from life, which follows from the union of soul and body. Thus the movement of heavy and light things results from their substantial form: for which reason they are said to be moved by their generator, as the Philosopher states (Phys. viii, 4). Wherefore this movement is called "vital." For which reason Gregory of Nyssa (Nemesius, De Nat. Hom. xxii) says that, just as the movement of generation and nutrition does not obey reason, so neither does the pulse which is a vital movement. By the pulse he means the movement of the heart which is indicated by the pulse veins.

Reply Obj. 3: As Augustine says (De Civ. Dei xiv, 17, 20) it is in punishment of sin that the movement of these members does not obey reason: in this sense, that the soul is punished for its rebellion against God, by the insubmission of that member whereby original sin is transmitted to posterity.

But because, as we shall state later on, the effect of the sin of our first parent was that his nature was left to itself, through the withdrawal of the supernatural gift which God had bestowed on man, we must consider the natural cause of this particular member's insubmission to reason. This is stated by Aristotle (De Causis Mot. Animal.) who says that "the movements of the heart and of the organs of generation are involuntary," and that the reason of this is as follows. These members are stirred at the occasion of some apprehension; in so far as the intellect and imagination represent such things as arouse the passions of the soul, of which passions these movements are a consequence. But they are not moved at the command of the reason or intellect, because these movements are conditioned by a certain natural change of heat and cold, which change is not subject to the command of reason. This is the case with these two organs in particular, because each is as it were a separate animal being, in so far as it is a principle of life; and the principle is virtually the whole. For the heart is the principle of the senses; and from the organ of generation proceeds the seminal virtue, which is virtually the entire animal. Consequently they have their proper movements naturally: because principles must needs be natural, as stated above (Reply Obj. 2).

## QUESTION 18

OF THE GOOD AND EVIL OF HUMAN ACTS, IN GENERAL (In Eleven Articles)

We must now consider the good and evil of human acts. First, how a human act is good or evil; secondly, what results from the good or evil of a human act, as merit or demerit, sin and guilt.

Under the first head there will be a threefold consideration: the first will be of the good and evil of human acts, in general; the second, of the good and evil of internal acts; the third, of the good and evil of external acts.

Concerning the first there are eleven points of inquiry:

(1) Whether every human action is good, or are there evil actions?

(2) Whether the good or evil of a human action is derived from its object?

(3) Whether it is derived from a circumstance?

(4) Whether it is derived from the end?

(5) Whether a human action is good or evil in its species?

(6) Whether an action has the species of good or evil from its end?

(7) Whether the species derived from the end is contained under the species derived from the object, as under its genus, or conversely?

(8) Whether any action is indifferent in its species?

(9) Whether an individual action can be indifferent?

(10) Whether a circumstance places a moral action in the species of good or evil?

(11) Whether every circumstance that makes an action better or worse, places the moral action in the species of good or evil?

FIRST ARTICLE [I-II, Q. 18, Art. 1]

Whether Every Human Action Is Good, or Are There Evil Actions?

Objection 1: It would seem that every human action is good, and that none is evil. For Dionysius says (Div. Nom. iv) that evil acts not, save in virtue of the good. But no evil is done in virtue of the good. Therefore no action is evil.

Obj. 2: Further, nothing acts except in so far as it is in act. Now a thing is evil, not according as it is in act, but according as its potentiality is void of act; whereas in so far as its potentiality is perfected by act, it is good, as stated in *Metaph.* ix, 9. Therefore nothing acts in so far as it is evil, but only according as it is good. Therefore every action is good, and none is evil.

Obj. 3: Further, evil cannot be a cause, save accidentally, as Dionysius declares (Div. Nom. iv). But every action has some effect which is proper to it. Therefore no action is evil, but every action is good.

*On the contrary,* Our Lord said (John 3:20): "Every one that doth evil, hateth the light." Therefore some actions of man are evil.

*I answer that,* We must speak of good and evil in actions as of good and evil in things: because such as everything is, such is the act that it produces. Now in things, each one has so much good as it has being: since good and being are convertible, as was stated in the First Part (Q. 5, AA. 1, 3). But God alone has the whole plenitude of His Being in a certain unity: whereas every other thing has its proper fulness of being in a certain multiplicity. Wherefore it happens with some things, that they have being in some respect, and yet they are lacking in the fulness of being due to them. Thus the fulness of human being requires a compound of soul and body, having all the powers and instruments of knowledge and movement: wherefore if any man be lacking in any of these, he is lacking in something due to the fulness of his being. So that as much as he has of being, so much has he of goodness: while so far as he is lacking in goodness, and is said to be evil: thus a blind man is possessed of goodness inasmuch as he lives; and of evil, inasmuch as he lacks sight. That, however, which has nothing of being or goodness, could not be said to be either evil or good. But since this same fulness of being is of the very essence of good, if a thing be lacking in its due fulness of being, it is not said to be good simply, but in a certain respect, inasmuch as it is a being; although it can be called a being simply, and a non-being in a certain respect, as was stated in the First Part (Q. 5, A. 1, ad 1). We must therefore say that every action has goodness, in so far as it has being; whereas it is lacking in goodness, in so far as it is lacking in something that is due to its fulness of being; and thus it is said to be evil: for instance if it lacks the quantity determined by reason, or its due place, or something of the kind.

Reply Obj. 1: Evil acts in virtue of deficient goodness. For if there were nothing of good there, there would be neither being nor possibility of action. On the other hand if good were not deficient, there would be no evil. Consequently the action done is a deficient good, which is good in a certain respect, but simply evil.

Reply Obj. 2: Nothing hinders a thing from being in act in a certain respect, so that it can act; and in a certain respect deficient in act, so as to cause a deficient act. Thus a blind man has in act the power of walking, whereby he is able to walk; but inasmuch as he is deprived of sight he suffers a defect in walking by stumbling when he walks.

Reply Obj. 3: An evil action can have a proper effect, according to the goodness and being that it has. Thus adultery is the cause of human generation, inasmuch as it implies union of male and female, but not inasmuch as it lacks the order of reason.

SECOND ARTICLE [I-II, Q. 18, Art. 2]

Whether the Good or Evil of a Man's Action Is Derived from Its Object?

Objection 1: It would seem that the good or evil of an action is not derived from its object. For the object of any action is a thing. But "evil is not in things, but in the sinner's use of them," as Augustine says (De Doctr. Christ. iii, 12). Therefore the good or evil of a human action is not derived from their object.

Obj. 2: Further, the object is compared to the action as its matter. But the goodness of a thing is not from its matter, but rather from the form, which is an act. Therefore good and evil in actions is not derived from their object.

Obj. 3: Further, the object of an active power is compared to the action as effect to cause. But the goodness of a cause does not depend on its effect; rather is it the reverse. Therefore good or evil in actions is not derived from their object.

*On the contrary,* It is written (Osee 9:10): "They became abominable as those things which they loved." Now man becomes abominable to God on account of the malice of his action. Therefore the malice of his action is according to the evil objects that man loves. And the same applies to the goodness of his action.

*I answer that,* as stated above (A. 1) the good or evil of an action, as of other things, depends on its fulness of being or its lack of that fulness. Now the first thing that belongs to the fulness of being seems to be that which gives a thing its species. And just as a natural thing has its species from its form, so an action has its species from its object, as movement from its term. And therefore just as the primary goodness of a natural thing is derived from its form, which gives it its species, so the primary goodness of a moral action is derived from its suitable object: hence some call such an action "good in its genus"; for instance, "to make use of what is one's own." And just as, in natural things, the primary evil is when a generated thing does not realize its specific form (for instance, if instead of a man, something else be generated); so the primary evil in moral actions is that which is from the object, for instance, "to take what belongs to another." And this action is said to be "evil in its genus," genus here standing for species, just as we apply the term "mankind" to the whole human species.

Reply Obj. 1: Although external things are good in themselves, nevertheless they have not always a due proportion to this or that action. And so, inasmuch as they are considered as objects of such actions, they have not the quality of goodness.

Reply Obj. 2: The object is not the matter "of which" (a thing is made), but the matter "about which" (something is done); and stands in relation to the act as its form, as it were, through giving it its species.

Reply Obj. 3: The object of the human action is not always the object of an active power. For the appetitive power is, in a way, passive; in so far as it is moved by the appetible object; and yet it is a principle of human actions. Nor again have the objects of the active powers always the nature of an effect, but only when they are already transformed: thus food when transformed is the effect of the nutritive power; whereas food before being transformed stands in relation to the nutritive power as the matter about which it exercises its operation. Now since the object is in some way the effect of the active power, it follows that it is the term of its action, and consequently that it gives it its form and species, since movement derives its species from its term. Moreover, although the goodness of an action is not caused by the goodness of its effect, yet an action is said to be good from the fact that it can produce a good effect. Consequently the very proportion of an action to its effect is the measure of its goodness.

THIRD ARTICLE [I-II, Q. 18, Art. 3]

Whether Man's Action Is Good or Evil from a Circumstance?

Objection 1: It would seem that an action is not good or evil from a circumstance. For circumstances stand around ( *circumstant* ) an action, as being outside it, as stated above (Q. 7, A. 1). But "good and evil are in things themselves," as is stated in Metaph. vi, 4. Therefore an action does not derive goodness or malice from a circumstance.

Obj. 2: Further, the goodness or malice of an action is considered principally in the doctrine of morals. But since circumstances are accidents of actions, it seems that they are outside the scope of art: because "no art takes notice of what is accidental" (Metaph. vi, 2). Therefore the goodness or malice of an action is not taken from a circumstance.

Obj. 3: Further, that which belongs to a thing, in respect of its substance, is not ascribed to it in respect of an accident. But good and evil belong to an action in respect of its substance; because an action can be good or evil in its genus as stated above (A. 2). Therefore an action is not good or bad from a circumstance.

*On the contrary,* the Philosopher says (Ethic. ii, 3) that a virtuous man acts as he should, and when he should, and so on in respect of the other circumstances. Therefore, on the other hand, the vicious man, in the matter of each vice, acts when he should not, or where he should not, and so on with the other circumstances. Therefore human actions are good or evil according to circumstances.

*I answer that,* In natural things, it is to be noted that the whole fulness of perfection due to a thing, is not from the mere substantial form, that gives it its species; since a thing derives much from supervening accidents, as man does from shape, color, and the like; and if any one of these accidents be out of due proportion, evil is the result. So it is with action. For the plenitude of its goodness does not consist wholly in its species, but also in certain additions which accrue to it by reason of certain accidents: and such are its due circumstances. Wherefore if something be wanting that is requisite as a due circumstance the action will be evil.

Reply Obj. 1: Circumstances are outside an action, inasmuch as they are not part of its essence; but they are in an action as accidents thereof. Thus, too, accidents in natural substances are outside the essence.

Reply Obj. 2: Every accident is not accidentally in its subject; for some are proper accidents; and of these every art takes notice. And thus it is that the circumstances of actions are considered in the doctrine of morals.

Reply Obj. 3: Since good and being are convertible; according as being is predicated of substance and of accident, so is good predicated of a thing both in respect of its essential being, and in respect of its accidental being; and this, both in natural things and in moral actions.

FOURTH ARTICLE [I-II, Q. 18, Art. 4]

Whether a Human Action Is Good or Evil from Its End?

Objection 1: It would seem that the good and evil in human actions are not from the end. For Dionysius says (Div. Nom. iv) that "nothing acts with a view to evil." If therefore an action were good or evil from its end, no action would be evil. Which is clearly false.

Obj. 2: Further, the goodness of an action is something in the action. But the end is an extrinsic cause. Therefore an action is not said to be good or bad according to its end.

Obj. 3: Further, a good action may happen to be ordained to an evil end, as when a man gives an alms from vainglory; and conversely, an evil action may happen to be ordained to a good end, as a theft committed in order to give something to the poor. Therefore an action is not good or evil from its end.

*On the contrary,* Boethius says (De Differ. Topic. ii) that "if the end is good, the thing is good, and if the end be evil, the thing also is evil."

*I answer that,* The disposition of things as to goodness is the same as their disposition as to being. Now in some things the being does not depend on another, and in these it suffices to consider their being absolutely. But there are things the being of which depends on something else, and hence in their regard we must consider their being in its relation to the cause on which it depends. Now just as the being of a thing depends on the agent, and the form, so the goodness of a thing depends on its end. Hence in the Divine Persons, Whose goodness does not depend on another, the measure of goodness is not taken from the end. Whereas human actions, and other things, the goodness of which depends on something else, have a measure of goodness from the end on which they depend, besides that goodness which is in them absolutely.

Accordingly a fourfold goodness may be considered in a human action. First, that which, as an action, it derives from its genus; because as much as it has of action and being so much has it of goodness, as stated above (A. 1). Secondly, it has goodness according to its species; which is derived from its suitable object. Thirdly, it has goodness from its circumstances, in respect, as it were, of its accidents. Fourthly, it has goodness from its end, to which it is compared as to the cause of its goodness.

Reply Obj. 1: The good in view of which one acts is not always a true good; but sometimes it is a true good, sometimes an apparent good. And in the latter event, an evil action results from the end in view.

Reply Obj. 2: Although the end is an extrinsic cause, nevertheless due proportion to the end, and relation to the end, are inherent to the action.

Reply Obj. 3: Nothing hinders an action that is good in one of the ways mentioned above, from lacking goodness in another way. And thus it may happen that an action which is good in its species or in its circumstances is ordained to an evil end, or vice versa. However, an action is not good simply, unless it is good in all those ways: since "evil results from any single defect, but good from the complete cause," as Dionysius says (Div. Nom. iv).

FIFTH ARTICLE [I-II, Q. 18, Art. 5]

Whether a Human Action Is Good or Evil in Its Species?

Objection 1: It would seem that good and evil in moral actions do not make a difference of species. For the existence of good and evil in actions is in conformity with their existence in things, as stated above (A. 1). But good and evil do not make a specific difference in things; for a good man is specifically the same as a bad man. Therefore neither do they make a specific difference in actions.

Obj. 2: Further, since evil is a privation, it is a non-being. But non-being cannot be a difference, according to the Philosopher (Metaph. iii, 3). Since therefore the difference constitutes the species, it seems that an action is not constituted in a species through being evil. Consequently good and evil do not diversify the species of human actions.

Obj. 3: Further, acts that differ in species produce different effects. But the same specific effect results from a good and from an evil action: thus a man is born of adulterous or of lawful wedlock. Therefore good and evil actions do not differ in species.

Obj. 4: Further, actions are sometimes said to be good or bad from a circumstance, as stated above (A. 3). But since a circumstance is an accident, it does not give an action its species. Therefore human actions do not differ in species on account of their goodness or malice.

*On the contrary,* According to the Philosopher (Ethic ii. 1) "like habits produce like actions." But a good and a bad habit differ in species, as liberality and prodigality. Therefore also good and bad actions differ in species.

*I answer that,* Every action derives its species from its object, as stated above (A. 2). Hence it follows that a difference of object causes a difference of species in actions. Now, it must be observed that a difference of objects causes a difference of species in actions, according as the latter are referred to one active principle, which does not cause a difference in actions, according as they are referred to another active principle. Because nothing accidental constitutes a species, but only that which is essential; and a difference of object may be essential in reference to one active principle, and accidental in reference to another. Thus to know color and to know sound, differ essentially in reference to sense, but not in reference to the intellect.

Now in human actions, good and evil are predicated in reference to the reason; because as Dionysius says (Div. Nom. iv), "the good of man is to be in accordance with reason," and evil is "to be against reason." For that is good for a thing which suits it in regard to its form; and evil, that which is against the order of its form. It is therefore evident that the difference of good and evil considered in reference to the object is an essential difference in relation to reason; that is to say, according as the object is suitable or unsuitable to reason. Now certain actions are called human or moral, inasmuch as they proceed from the reason. Consequently it is evident that good and evil diversify the species in human actions; since essential differences cause a difference of species.

Reply Obj. 1: Even in natural things, good and evil, inasmuch as something is according to nature, and something against nature, diversify the natural species; for a dead body and a living body are not of the same species. In like manner, good, inasmuch as it is in accord with reason, and evil, inasmuch as it is against reason, inasmuch as it is against reason, diversify the moral species.

Reply Obj. 2: Evil implies privation, not absolute, but affecting some potentiality. For an action is said to be evil in its species, not because it has no object at all; but because it has an object in disaccord with reason, for instance, to appropriate another's property. Wherefore in so far as the object is something positive, it can constitute the species of an evil act.

Reply Obj. 3: The conjugal act and adultery, as compared to reason, differ specifically and have effects specifically different; because the other deserves praise and reward, the other, blame and punishment. But as compared to the generative power, they do not differ in species; and thus they have one specific effect.

Reply Obj. 4: A circumstance is sometimes taken as the essential difference of the object, as compared to reason; and then it can specify a moral act. And it must needs be so whenever a circumstance transforms an action from good to evil; for a circumstance would not make an action evil, except through being repugnant to reason.

SIXTH ARTICLE [I-II, Q. 18, Art. 6]

Whether an Action Has the Species of Good or Evil from Its End?

Objection 1: It would seem that the good and evil which are from the end do not diversify the species of actions. For actions derive their species from the object. But the end is altogether apart from the object. Therefore the good and evil which are from the end do not diversify the species of an action.

Obj. 2: Further, that which is accidental does not constitute the species, as stated above (A. 5). But it is accidental to an action to be ordained to some particular end; for instance, to give alms from vainglory. Therefore actions are not diversified as to species, according to the good and evil which are from the end.

Obj. 3: Further, acts that differ in species, can be ordained to the same end: thus to the end of vainglory, actions of various virtues and vices can be ordained. Therefore the good and evil which are taken from the end, do not diversify the species of action.

*On the contrary,* It has been shown above (Q. 1, A. 3) that human actions derive their species from the end. Therefore good and evil in respect of the end diversify the species of actions.

*I answer that,* Certain actions are called human, inasmuch as they are voluntary, as stated above (Q. 1, A. 1). Now, in a voluntary action, there is a twofold action, viz. the interior action of the will, and the external action: and each of these actions has its object. The end is properly the object of the interior act of the will: while the object of the external action, is that on which the action is brought to bear. Therefore just as the external action takes its species from the object on which it bears; so the interior act of the will takes its species from the end, as from its own proper object.

Now that which is on the part of the will is formal in regard to that which is on the part of the external action: because the will uses the limbs to act as instruments; nor have external actions any measure of morality, save in so far as they are voluntary. Consequently the species of a human act is considered formally with regard to the end, but materially with regard to the object of the external action. Hence the Philosopher says (Ethic. v, 2) that "he who steals that he may commit adultery, is strictly speaking, more adulterer than thief."

Reply Obj. 1: The end also has the character of an object, as stated above.

Reply Obj. 2: Although it is accidental to the external action to be ordained to some particular end, it is not accidental to the interior act of the will, which act is compared to the external act, as form to matter.

Reply Obj. 3: When many actions, differing in species, are ordained to the same end, there is indeed a diversity of species on the part of the external actions; but unity of species on the part of the internal action.

SEVENTH ARTICLE [I-II, Q. 18, Art. 7]

Whether the Species Derived from the End Is Contained Under the Species Derived from the Object, As Under Its Genus, or Conversely?

Objection 1: It would seem that the species of goodness derived from the end is contained under the species of goodness derived from the object, as a species is contained under its genus; for instance, when a man commits a theft in order to give alms. For an action takes its species from its object, as stated above (AA. 2, 6). But it is impossible for a thing to be contained under another species, if this species be not contained under the proper species of that thing; because the same thing cannot be contained in different species that are not subordinate to one another. Therefore the species which is taken from the end, is contained under the species which is taken from the object.

Obj. 2: Further, the last difference always constitutes the most specific species. But the difference derived from the end seems to come after the difference derived from the object: because the end is something last. Therefore the species derived from the end, is contained under the species derived from the object, as its most specific species.

Obj. 3: Further, the more formal a difference is, the more specific it is: because difference is compared to genus, as form to matter. But the species derived from the end, is more formal than that which is derived from the object, as stated above (A. 6). Therefore the species derived from the end is contained under the species derived from the object, as the most specific species is contained under the subaltern genus.

*On the contrary,* Each genus has its determinate differences. But an action of one same species on the part of its object, can be ordained to an infinite number of ends: for instance, theft can be ordained to an infinite number of good and bad ends. Therefore the species derived from the end is not contained under the species derived from the object, as under its genus.

*I answer that,* The object of the external act can stand in a twofold relation to the end of the will: first, as being of itself ordained thereto; thus to fight well is of itself ordained to victory; secondly, as being ordained thereto accidentally; thus to take what belongs to another is ordained accidentally to the giving of alms. Now the differences that divide a genus, and constitute the species of that genus, must, as the Philosopher says (Metaph. vii, 12), divide that genus essentially: and if they divide it accidentally, the division is incorrect: as, if one were to say: "Animals are divided into rational and irrational; and the irrational into animals with wings, and animals without wings"; for "winged" and "wingless" are not essential determinations of the irrational being. But the following division would be correct: "Some animals have feet, some have no feet: and of those that have feet, some have two feet, some four, some many": because the latter division is an essential determination of the former. Accordingly when the object is not of itself ordained to the end, the specific difference derived from the object is not an essential determination of the species derived from the end, nor is the reverse the case. Wherefore one of these species is not under the other; but then the moral action is contained under two species that are disparate, as it were. Consequently we say that he that commits theft for the sake of adultery, is guilty of a twofold malice in one action. On the other hand, if the object be of itself ordained to the end, one of these differences is an essential determination of the other. Wherefore one of these species will be contained under the other.

It remains to be considered which of the two is contained under the other. In order to make this clear, we must first of all observe that the more particular the form is from which a difference is taken, the more specific is the difference. Secondly, that the more universal an agent is, the more universal a form does it cause. Thirdly, that the more remote an end is, the more universal the agent to which it corresponds; thus victory, which is the last end of the army, is the end intended by the commander in chief; while the right ordering of this or that regiment is the end intended by one of the lower officers. From all this it follows that the specific difference derived from the end, is more general; and that the difference derived from an object which of itself is ordained to that end, is a specific difference in relation to the former. For the will, the proper object of which is the end, is the universal mover in respect of all the powers of the soul, the proper objects of which are the objects of their particular acts.

Reply Obj. 1: One and the same thing, considered in its substance, cannot be in two species, one of which is not subordinate to the other. But in respect of those things which are superadded to the substance, one thing can be contained under different species. Thus one and the same fruit, as to its color, is contained under one species, i.e. a white thing: and, as to its perfume, under the species of sweet-smelling things. In like manner an action which, as to its substance, is in one natural species, considered in respect to the moral conditions that are added to it, can belong to two species, as stated above (Q. 1, A. 3, ad 3).

Reply Obj. 2: The end is last in execution; but first in the intention of the reason, in regard to which moral actions receive their species.

Reply Obj. 3: Difference is compared to genus as form to matter, inasmuch as it actualizes the genus. On the other hand, the genus is considered as more formal than the species, inasmuch as it is something more absolute and less contracted. Wherefore also the parts of a definition are reduced to the genus of formal cause, as is stated in *Phys.* ii, 3. And in this sense the genus is the formal cause of the species; and so much the more formal, as it is more universal.

EIGHTH ARTICLE [I-II, Q. 18, Art. 8]

Whether Any Action Is Indifferent in Its Species?

Objection 1: It would seem that no action is indifferent in its species. For evil is the privation of good, according to Augustine (Enchiridion xi). But privation and habit are immediate contraries, according to the Philosopher (Categor. viii). Therefore there is not such thing as an action that is indifferent in its species, as though it were between good and evil.

Obj. 2: Further, human actions derive their species from their end or object, as stated above (A. 6; Q. 1, A. 3). But every end and every object is either good or bad. Therefore every human action is good or evil according to its species. None, therefore, is indifferent in its species.

Obj. 3: Further, as stated above (A. 1), an action is said to be good, when it has its due complement of goodness; and evil, when it lacks that complement. But every action must needs either have the entire plenitude of its goodness, or lack it in some respect. Therefore every action must needs be either good or bad in its species, and none is indifferent.

*On the contrary,* Augustine says (De Serm. Dom. in Monte ii, 18) that "there are certain deeds of a middle kind, which can be done with a good or evil mind, of which it is rash to form a judgment." Therefore some actions are indifferent according to their species.

*I answer that,* As stated above (AA. 2, 5), every action takes its species from its object; while human action, which is called moral, takes its species from the object, in relation to the principle of human actions, which is the reason. Wherefore if the object of an action includes something in accord with the order of reason, it will be a good action according to its species; for instance, to give alms to a person in want. On the other hand, if it includes something repugnant to the order of reason, it will be an evil act according to its species; for instance, to steal, which is to appropriate what belongs to another. But it may happen that the object of an action does not include something pertaining to the order of reason; for instance, to pick up a straw from the ground, to walk in the fields, and the like: and such actions are indifferent according to their species.

Reply Obj. 1: Privation is twofold. One is privation "as a result" ( *privatum esse* ), and this leaves nothing, but takes all away: thus blindness takes away sight altogether; darkness, light; and death, life. Between this privation and the contrary habit, there can be no medium in respect of the proper subject. The other is privation "in process" ( *privari* ): thus sickness is privation of health; not that it takes health away altogether, but that it is a kind of road to the entire loss of health, occasioned by death. And since this sort of privation leaves something, it is not always the immediate contrary of the opposite habit. In this way evil is a privation of good, as Simplicius says in his commentary on the Categories: because it does not take away all good, but leaves some. Consequently there can be something between good and evil.

Reply Obj. 2: Every object or end has some goodness or malice, at least natural to it: but this does not imply moral goodness or malice, which is considered in relation to the reason, as stated above. And it is of this that we are here treating.

Reply Obj. 3: Not everything belonging to an action belongs also to its species. Wherefore although an action's specific nature may not contain all that belongs to the full complement of its goodness, it is not therefore an action specifically bad; nor is it specifically good. Thus a man in regard to his species is neither virtuous nor wicked.

NINTH ARTICLE [I-II, Q. 18, Art. 9]

Whether an Individual Action Can Be Indifferent?

Objection 1: It would seem that an individual action can be indifferent. For there is no species that does not, or cannot, contain an individual. But an action can be indifferent in its species, as stated above (A. 8). Therefore an individual action can be indifferent.

Obj. 2: Further, individual actions cause like habits, as stated in *Ethic.* ii, 1. But a habit can be indifferent: for the Philosopher says (Ethic. iv, 1) that those who are of an even temper and prodigal disposition are not evil; and yet it is evident that they are not good, since they depart from virtue; and thus they are indifferent in respect of a habit. Therefore some individual actions are indifferent.

Obj. 3: Further, moral good belongs to virtue, while moral evil belongs to vice. But it happens sometimes that a man fails to ordain a specifically indifferent action to a vicious or virtuous end. Therefore an individual action may happen to be indifferent.

*On the contrary,* Gregory says in a homily (vi in Evang.): "An idle word is one that lacks either the usefulness of rectitude or the motive of just necessity or pious utility." But an idle word is an evil, because "men ... shall render an account of it in the day of judgment" (Matt. 12:36): while if it does not lack the motive of just necessity or pious utility, it is good. Therefore every word is either good or bad. For the same reason every other action is either good or bad. Therefore no individual action is indifferent.

*I answer that,* It sometimes happens that an action is indifferent in its species, but considered in the individual it is good or evil. And the reason of this is because a moral action, as stated above (A. 3), derives its goodness not only from its object, whence it takes its species; but also from the circumstances, which are its accidents, as it were; just as something belongs to a man by reason of his individual accidents, which does not belong to him by reason of his species. And every individual action must needs have some circumstance that makes it good or bad, at least in respect of the intention of the end. For since it belongs to the reason to direct; if an action that proceeds from deliberate reason be not directed to the due end, it is, by that fact alone, repugnant to reason, and has the character of evil. But if it be directed to a due end, it is in accord with reason; wherefore it has the character of good. Now it must needs be either directed or not directed to a due end. Consequently every human action that proceeds from deliberate reason, if it be considered in the individual, must be good or bad.

If, however, it does not proceed from deliberate reason, but from some act of the imagination, as when a man strokes his beard, or moves his hand or foot; such an action, properly speaking, is not moral or human; since this depends on the reason. Hence it will be indifferent, as standing apart from the genus of moral actions.

Reply Obj. 1: For an action to be indifferent in its species can be understood in several ways. First in such a way that its species demands that it remain indifferent; and the objection proceeds along this line. But no action can be specifically indifferent thus: since no object of human action is such that it cannot be directed to good or evil, either through its end or through a circumstance. Secondly, specific indifference of an action may be due to the fact that as far as its species is concerned, it is neither good nor bad. Wherefore it can be made good or bad by something else. Thus man, as far as his species is concerned, is neither white nor black; nor is it a condition of his species that he should not be black or white; but blackness or whiteness is superadded to man by other principles than those of his species.

Reply Obj. 2: The Philosopher states that a man is evil, properly speaking, if he be hurtful to others. And accordingly, he says that the prodigal is not evil, because he hurts none save himself. And the same applies to all others who are not hurtful to other men. But we say here that evil, in general, is all that is repugnant to right reason. And in this sense every individual action is either good or bad, as stated above.

Reply Obj. 3: Whenever an end is intended by deliberate reason, it belongs either to the good of some virtue, or to the evil of some vice. Thus, if a man's action is directed to the support or repose of his body, it is also directed to the good of virtue, provided he direct his body itself to the good of virtue. The same clearly applies to other actions.

TENTH ARTICLE [I-II, Q. 18, Art. 10]

Whether a Circumstance Places a Moral Action in the Species of Good or Evil?

Objection 1: It would seem that a circumstance cannot place a moral action in the species of good or evil. For the species of an action is taken from its object. But circumstances differ from the object. Therefore circumstances do not give an action its species.

Obj. 2: Further, circumstances are as accidents in relation to the moral action, as stated above (Q. 7, A. 1). But an accident does not constitute the species. Therefore a circumstance does not constitute a species of good or evil.

Obj. 3: Further, one thing is not in several species. But one action has several circumstances. Therefore a circumstance does not place a moral action in a species of good or evil.

*On the contrary,* Place is a circumstance. But place makes a moral action to be in a certain species of evil; for theft of a thing from a holy place is a sacrilege. Therefore a circumstance makes a moral action to be specifically good or bad.

*I answer that,* Just as the species of natural things are constituted by their natural forms, so the species of moral actions are constituted by forms as conceived by the reason, as is evident from what was said above (A. 5). But since nature is determinate to one thing, nor can a process of nature go on to infinity, there must needs be some ultimate form, giving a specific difference, after which no further specific difference is possible. Hence it is that in natural things, that which is accidental to a thing, cannot be taken as a difference constituting the species. But the process of reason is not fixed to one particular term, for at any point it can still proceed further. And consequently that which, in one action, is taken as a circumstance added to the object that specifies the action, can again be taken by the directing reason, as the principal condition of the object that determines the action's species. Thus to appropriate another's property is specified by reason of the property being "another's," and in this respect it is placed in the species of theft; and if we consider that action also in its bearing on place or time, then this will be an additional circumstance. But since the reason can direct as to place, time, and the like, it may happen that the condition as to place, in relation to the object, is considered as being in disaccord with reason: for instance, reason forbids damage to be done to a holy place. Consequently to steal from a holy place has an additional repugnance to the order of reason. And thus place, which was first of all considered as a circumstance, is considered here as the principal condition of the object, and as itself repugnant to reason. And in this way, whenever a circumstance has a special relation to reason, either for or against, it must needs specify the moral action whether good or bad.

Reply Obj. 1: A circumstance, in so far as it specifies an action, is considered as a condition of the object, as stated above, and as being, as it were, a specific difference thereof.

Reply Obj. 2: A circumstance, so long as it is but a circumstance, does not specify an action, since thus it is a mere accident: but when it becomes a principal condition of the object, then it does specify the action.

Reply Obj. 3: It is not every circumstance that places the moral action in the species of good or evil; since not every circumstance implies accord or disaccord with reason. Consequently, although one action may have many circumstances, it does not follow that it is in many species. Nevertheless there is no reason why one action should not be in several, even disparate, moral species, as said above (A. 7, ad 1; Q. 1, A. 3, ad 3).

ELEVENTH ARTICLE [I-II, Q. 18, Art. 11]

Whether Every Circumstance That Makes an Action Better or Worse, Places a Moral Action in a Species of Good or Evil?

Objection 1: It would seem that every circumstance relating to good or evil, specifies an action. For good and evil are specific differences of moral actions. Therefore that which causes a difference in the goodness or malice of a moral action, causes a specific difference, which is the same as to make it differ in species. Now that which makes an action better or worse, makes it differ in goodness and malice. Therefore it causes it to differ in species. Therefore every circumstance that makes an action better or worse, constitutes a species.

Obj. 2: Further, an additional circumstance either has in itself the character of goodness or malice, or it has not. If not, it cannot make the action better or worse; because what is not good, cannot make a greater good; and what is not evil, cannot make a greater evil. But if it has in itself the character of good or evil, for this very reason it has a certain species of good or evil. Therefore every circumstance that makes an action better or worse, constitutes a new species of good or evil.

Obj. 3: Further, according to Dionysius (Div. Nom. iv), "evil is caused by each single defect." Now every circumstance that increases malice, has a special defect. Therefore every such circumstance adds a new species of sin. And for the same reason, every circumstance that increases goodness, seems to add a new species of goodness: just as every unity added to a number makes a new species of number; since the good consists in "number, weight, and measure" (I, Q. 5, A. 5).

*On the contrary,* More and less do not change a species. But more and less is a circumstance of additional goodness or malice. Therefore not every circumstance that makes a moral action better or worse, places it in a species of good or evil.

*I answer that,* As stated above (A. 10), a circumstance gives the species of good or evil to a moral action, in so far as it regards a special order of reason. Now it happens sometimes that a circumstance does not regard a special order of reason in respect of good or evil, except on the supposition of another previous circumstance, from which the moral action takes its species of good or evil. Thus to take something in a large or small quantity, does not regard the order of reason in respect of good or evil, except a certain other condition be presupposed, from which the action takes its malice or goodness; for instance, if what is taken belongs to another, which makes the action to be discordant with reason. Wherefore to take what belongs to another in a large or small quantity, does not change the species of the sin. Nevertheless it can aggravate or diminish the sin. The same applies to other evil or good actions. Consequently not every circumstance that makes a moral action better or worse, changes its species.

Reply Obj. 1: In things which can be more or less intense, the difference of more or less does not change the species: thus by differing in whiteness through being more or less white a thing is not changed in regard to its species of color. In like manner that which makes an action to be more or less good or evil, does not make the action differ in species.

Reply Obj. 2: A circumstance that aggravates a sin, or adds to the goodness of an action, sometimes has no goodness or malice in itself, but in regard to some other condition of the action, as stated above. Consequently it does not add a new species, but adds to the goodness or malice derived from this other condition of the action.

Reply Obj. 3: A circumstance does not always involve a distinct defect of its own; sometimes it causes a defect in reference to something else. In like manner a circumstance does not always add further perfection, except in reference to something else. And, for as much as it does, although it may add to the goodness or malice, it does not always change the species of good or evil.

## QUESTION 19

OF THE GOODNESS AND MALICE OF THE INTERIOR ACT OF THE WILL (In Ten Articles)

We must now consider the goodness of the interior act of the will; under which head there are ten points of inquiry:

(1) Whether the goodness of the will depends on the object?

(2) Whether it depends on the object alone?

(3) Whether it depends on reason?

(4) Whether it depends on the eternal law?

(5) Whether erring reason binds?

(6) Whether the will is evil if it follows the erring reason against the law of God?

(7) Whether the goodness of the will in regard to the means, depends on the intention of the end?

(8) Whether the degree of goodness or malice in the will depends on the degree of good or evil in the intention?

(9) Whether the goodness of the will depends on its conformity to the Divine Will?

(10) Whether it is necessary for the human will, in order to be good, to be conformed to the Divine Will, as regards the thing willed?

FIRST ARTICLE [I-II, Q. 19, Art. 1]

Whether the Goodness of the Will Depends on the Object?

Objection 1: It would seem that the goodness of the will does not depend on the object. For the will cannot be directed otherwise than to what is good: since "evil is outside the scope of the will," as Dionysius says (Div. Nom. iv). If therefore the goodness of the will depended on the object, it would follow that every act of the will is good, and none bad.

Obj. 2: Further, good is first of all in the end: wherefore the goodness of the end, as such, does not depend on any other. But, according to the Philosopher (Ethic. vi, 5), "goodness of action is the end, but goodness of making is never the end": because the latter is always ordained to the thing made, as to its end. Therefore the goodness of the act of the will does not depend on any object.

Obj. 3: Further, such as a thing is, such does it make a thing to be. But the object of the will is good, by reason of the goodness of nature. Therefore it cannot give moral goodness to the will. Therefore the moral goodness of the will does not depend on the object.

*On the contrary,* the Philosopher says (Ethic. v, 1) that justice is that habit "from which men wish for just things": and accordingly, virtue is a habit from which men wish for good things. But a good will is one which is in accordance with virtue. Therefore the goodness of the will is from the fact that a man wills that which is good.

*I answer that,* Good and evil are essential differences of the act of the will. Because good and evil of themselves regard the will; just as truth and falsehood regard reason; the act of which is divided essentially by the difference of truth and falsehood, for as much as an opinion is said to be true or false. Consequently good and evil will are acts differing in species. Now the specific difference in acts is according to objects, as stated above (Q. 18, A. 5). Therefore good and evil in the acts of the will is derived properly from the objects.

Reply Obj. 1: The will is not always directed to what is truly good, but sometimes to the apparent good; which has indeed some measure of good, but not of a good that is simply suitable to be desired. Hence it is that the act of the will is not always good, but sometimes evil.

Reply Obj. 2: Although an action can, in a certain way, be man's last end; nevertheless such action is not an act of the will, as stated above (Q. 1, A. 1, ad 2).

Reply Obj. 3: Good is presented to the will as its object by the reason: and in so far as it is in accord with reason, it enters the moral order, and causes moral goodness in the act of the will: because the reason is the principle of human and moral acts, as stated above (Q. 18, A. 5).

SECOND ARTICLE [I-II, Q. 19, Art. 2]

Whether the goodness of the will depends on the object alone?

Objection 1: It would seem that the goodness of the will does not depend on the object alone. For the end has a closer relationship to the will than to any other power. But the acts of the other powers derive goodness not only from the object but also from the end, as we have shown above (Q. 18, A. 4). Therefore the act also of the will derives goodness not only from the object but also from the end.

Obj. 2: Further, the goodness of an action is derived not only from the object but also from the circumstances, as stated above (Q. 18, A. 3). But according to the diversity of circumstances there may be diversity of goodness and malice in the act of the will: for instance, if a man will, when he ought, where he ought, as much as he ought, and how he ought, or if he will as he ought not. Therefore the goodness of the will depends not only on the object, but also on the circumstances.

Obj. 3: Further, ignorance of circumstances excuses malice of the will, as stated above (Q. 6, A. 8). But it would not be so, unless the goodness or malice of the will depended on the circumstances. Therefore the goodness and malice of the will depend on the circumstances, and not only on the object.

*On the contrary,* An action does not take its species from the circumstances as such, as stated above (Q. 18, A. 10, ad 2). But good and evil are specific differences of the act of the will, as stated above (A. 1). Therefore the goodness and malice of the will depend, not on the circumstances, but on the object alone.

*I answer that,* In every genus, the more a thing is first, the more simple it is, and the fewer the principles of which it consists: thus primary bodies are simple. Hence it is to be observed that the first things in every genus, are, in some way, simple and consist of one principle. Now the principle of the goodness and malice of human actions is taken from the act of the will. Consequently the goodness and malice of the act of the will depend on some one thing; while the goodness and malice of other acts may depend on several things.

Now that one thing which is the principle in each genus, is not something accidental to that genus, but something essential thereto: because whatever is accidental is reduced to something essential, as to its principle. Therefore the goodness of the will's act depends on that one thing alone, which of itself causes goodness in the act; and that one thing is the object, and not the circumstances, which are accidents, as it were, of the act.

Reply Obj. 1: The end is the object of the will, but not of the other powers. Hence, in regard to the act of the will, the goodness derived from the object, does not differ from that which is derived from the end, as they differ in the acts of the other powers; except perhaps accidentally, in so far as one end depends on another, and one act of the will on another.

Reply Obj. 2: Given that the act of the will is fixed on some good, no circumstances can make that act bad. Consequently when it is said that a man wills a good when he ought not, or where he ought not, this can be understood in two ways. First, so that this circumstance is referred to the thing willed. And thus the act of the will is not fixed on something good: since to will to do something when it ought not to be done, is not to will something good. Secondly, so that the circumstance is referred to the act of willing. And thus, it is impossible to will something good when one ought not to, because one ought always to will what is good: except, perhaps, accidentally, in so far as a man by willing some particular good, is prevented from willing at the same time another good which he ought to will at that time. And then evil results, not from his willing that particular good, but from his not willing the other. The same applies to the other circumstances.

Reply Obj. 3: Ignorance of circumstances excuses malice of the will, in so far as the circumstance affects the thing willed: that is to say, in so far as a man ignores the circumstances of the act which he wills.

THIRD ARTICLE [I-II, Q. 19, Art. 3]

Whether the Goodness of the Will Depends on Reason?

Objection 1: It would seem that the goodness of the will does not depend on reason. For what comes first does not depend on what follows. But the good belongs to the will before it belongs to reason, as is clear from what has been said above (Q. 9, A. 1). Therefore the goodness of the will does not depend on reason.

Obj. 2: Further, the Philosopher says (Ethic. vi, 2) that the goodness of the practical intellect is "a truth that is in conformity with right desire." But right desire is a good will. Therefore the goodness of the practical reason depends on the goodness of the will, rather than conversely.

Obj. 3: Further, the mover does not depend on that which is moved, but vice versa. But the will moves the reason and the other powers, as stated above (Q. 9, A. 1). Therefore the goodness of the will does not depend on reason.

*On the contrary,* Hilary says (De Trin. x): "It is an unruly will that persists in its desires in opposition to reason." But the goodness of the will consists in not being unruly. Therefore the goodness of the will depends on its being subject to reason.

*I answer that,* As stated above (AA. 1, 2), the goodness of the will depends properly on the object. Now the will's object is proposed to it by reason. Because the good understood is the proportionate object of the will; while sensitive or imaginary good is proportionate not to the will but to the sensitive appetite: since the will can tend to the universal good, which reason apprehends; whereas the sensitive appetite tends only to the particular good, apprehended by the sensitive power. Therefore the goodness of the will depends on reason, in the same way as it depends on the object.

Reply Obj. 1: The good considered as such, i.e. as appetible, pertains to the will before pertaining to the reason. But considered as true it pertains to the reason, before, under the aspect of goodness, pertaining to the will: because the will cannot desire a good that is not previously apprehended by reason.

Reply Obj. 2: The Philosopher speaks here of the practical intellect, in so far as it counsels and reasons about the means: for in this respect it is perfected by prudence. Now in regard to the means, the rectitude of the reason depends on its conformity with the desire of a due end: nevertheless the very desire of the due end presupposes on the part of reason a right apprehension of the end.

Reply Obj. 3: The will moves the reason in one way: the reason moves the will in another, viz. on the part of the object, as stated above (Q. 9, A. 1).

FOURTH ARTICLE [I-II, Q. 19, Art. 4]

Whether the Goodness of the Will Depends on the Eternal Law?

Objection 1: It would seem that the goodness of the human will does not depend on the eternal law. Because to one thing there is one rule and one measure. But the rule of the human will, on which its goodness depends, is right reason. Therefore the goodness of the will does not depend on the eternal law.

Obj. 2: Further, "a measure is homogeneous with the thing measured" (Metaph. x, 1). But the eternal law is not homogeneous with the human will. Therefore the eternal law cannot be the measure on which the goodness of the human will depends.

Obj. 3: Further, a measure should be most certain. But the eternal law is unknown to us. Therefore it cannot be the measure on which the goodness of our will depends.

*On the contrary,* Augustine says (Contra Faust. xxii, 27) that "sin is a deed, word or desire against the eternal law." But malice of the will is the root of sin. Therefore, since malice is contrary to goodness, the goodness of the will depends on the eternal law.

*I answer that,* Wherever a number of causes are subordinate to one another, the effect depends more on the first than on the second cause: since the second cause acts only in virtue of the first. Now it is from the eternal law, which is the Divine Reason, that human reason is the rule of the human will, from which the human derives its goodness. Hence it is written (Ps. 4:6, 7): "Many say: Who showeth us good things? The light of Thy countenance, O Lord, is signed upon us": as though to say: "The light of our reason is able to show us good things, and guide our will, in so far as it is the light (i.e. derived from) Thy countenance." It is therefore evident that the goodness of the human will depends on the eternal law much more than on human reason: and when human reason fails we must have recourse to the Eternal Reason.

Reply Obj. 1: To one thing there are not several proximate measures; but there can be several measures if one is subordinate to the other.

Reply Obj. 2: A proximate measure is homogeneous with the thing measured; a remote measure is not.

Reply Obj. 3: Although the eternal law is unknown to us according as it is in the Divine Mind: nevertheless, it becomes known to us somewhat, either by natural reason which is derived therefrom as its proper image; or by some sort of additional revelation.

FIFTH ARTICLE [I-II, Q. 19, Art. 5]

Whether the Will Is Evil When It Is at Variance with Erring Reason?

Objection 1: It would seem that the will is not evil when it is at variance with erring reason. Because the reason is the rule of the human will, in so far as it is derived from the eternal law, as stated above (A. 4). But erring reason is not derived from the eternal law. Therefore erring reason is not the rule of the human will. Therefore the will is not evil, if it be at variance with erring reason.

Obj. 2: Further, according to Augustine, the command of a lower authority does not bind if it be contrary to the command of a higher authority: for instance, if a provincial governor command something that is forbidden by the emperor. But erring reason sometimes proposes what is against the command of a higher power, namely, God Whose power is supreme. Therefore the decision of an erring reason does not bind. Consequently the will is not evil if it be at variance with erring reason.

Obj. 3: Further, every evil will is reducible to some species of malice. But the will that is at variance with erring reason is not reducible to some species of malice. For instance, if a man's reason err in telling him to commit fornication, his will in not willing to do so, cannot be reduced to any species of malice. Therefore the will is not evil when it is at variance with erring reason.

*On the contrary,* As stated in the First Part (Q. 79, A. 13), conscience is nothing else than the application of knowledge to some action. Now knowledge is in the reason. Therefore when the will is at variance with erring reason, it is against conscience. But every such will is evil; for it is written (Rom. 14:23): "All that is not of faith"—i.e. all that is against conscience—"is sin." Therefore the will is evil when it is at variance with erring reason.

*I answer that,* Since conscience is a kind of dictate of the reason, for it is an application of knowledge to action, as was stated in the First Part (Q. 19, A. 13), to inquire whether the will is evil when it is at variance with erring reason, is the same as to inquire "whether an erring conscience binds." On this matter, some distinguished three kinds of actions: for some are good generically; some are indifferent; some are evil generically. And they say that if reason or conscience tell us to do something which is good generically, there is no error: and in like manner if it tell us not to do something which is evil generically; since it is the same reason that prescribes what is good and forbids what is evil. On the other hand if a man's reason or conscience tells him that he is bound by precept to do what is evil in itself; or that what is good in itself, is forbidden, then his reason or conscience errs. In like manner if a man's reason or conscience tell him, that what is indifferent in itself, for instance to raise a straw from the ground, is forbidden or commanded, his reason or conscience errs. They say, therefore, that reason or conscience when erring in matters of indifference, either by commanding or by forbidding them, binds: so that the will which is at variance with that erring reason is evil and sinful. But they say that when reason or conscience errs in commanding what is evil in itself, or in forbidding what is good in itself and necessary for salvation, it does not bind; wherefore in such cases the will which is at variance with erring reason or conscience is not evil.

But this is unreasonable. For in matters of indifference, the will that is at variance with erring reason or conscience, is evil in some way on account of the object, on which the goodness or malice of the will depends; not indeed on account of the object according as it is in its own nature; but according as it is accidentally apprehended by reason as something evil to do or to avoid. And since the object of the will is that which is proposed by the reason, as stated above (A. 3), from the very fact that a thing is proposed by the reason as being evil, the will by tending thereto becomes evil. And this is the case not only in indifferent matters, but also in those that are good or evil in themselves. For not only indifferent matters can receive the character of goodness or malice accidentally; but also that which is good, can receive the character of evil, or that which is evil, can receive the character of goodness, on account of the reason apprehending it as such. For instance, to refrain from fornication is good: yet the will does not tend to this good except in so far as it is proposed by the reason. If, therefore, the erring reason propose it as an evil, the will tends to it as to something evil. Consequently the will is evil, because it wills evil, not indeed that which is evil in itself, but that which is evil accidentally, through being apprehended as such by the reason. In like manner, to believe in Christ is good in itself, and necessary for salvation: but the will does not tend thereto, except inasmuch as it is proposed by the reason. Consequently if it be proposed by the reason as something evil, the will tends to it as to something evil: not as if it were evil in itself, but because it is evil accidentally, through the apprehension of the reason. Hence the Philosopher says (Ethic. vii, 9) that "properly speaking the incontinent man is one who does not follow right reason; but accidentally, he is also one who does not follow false reason." We must therefore conclude that, absolutely speaking, every will at variance with reason, whether right or erring, is always evil.

Reply Obj. 1: Although the judgment of an erring reason is not derived from God, yet the erring reason puts forward its judgment as being true, and consequently as being derived from God, from Whom is all truth.

Reply Obj. 2: The saying of Augustine holds good when it is known that the inferior authority prescribes something contrary to the command of the higher authority. But if a man were to believe the command of the proconsul to be the command of the emperor, in scorning the command of the proconsul he would scorn the command of the emperor. In like manner if a man were to know that human reason was dictating something contrary to God's commandment, he would not be bound to abide by reason: but then reason would not be entirely erroneous. But when erring reason proposes something as being commanded by God, then to scorn the dictate of reason is to scorn the commandment of God.

Reply Obj. 3: Whenever reason apprehends something as evil, it apprehends it under some species of evil; for instance, as being something contrary to a divine precept, or as giving scandal, or for some such like reason. And then that evil is reduced to that species of malice.

SIXTH ARTICLE [I-II, Q. 19, Art. 6]

Whether the Will Is Good When It Abides by Erring Reason?

Objection 1: It would seem that the will is good when it abides by erring reason. For just as the will, when at variance with the reason, tends to that which reason judges to be evil; so, when in accord with reason, it tends to what reason judges to be good. But the will is evil when it is at variance with reason, even when erring. Therefore even when it abides by erring reason, the will is good.

Obj. 2: Further, the will is always good, when it abides by the commandment of God and the eternal law. But the eternal law and God's commandment are proposed to us by the apprehension of the reason, even when it errs. Therefore the will is good, even when it abides by erring reason.

Obj. 3: Further, the will is evil when it is at variance with erring reason. If, therefore, the will is evil also when it abides by erring reason, it seems that the will is always evil when in conjunction with erring reason: so that in such a case a man would be in a dilemma, and, of necessity, would sin: which is unreasonable. Therefore the will is good when it abides by erring reason.

*On the contrary,* The will of those who slew the apostles was evil. And yet it was in accord with the erring reason, according to John 16:2: "The hour cometh, that whosoever killeth you, will think that he doth a service to God." Therefore the will can be evil, when it abides by erring reason.

*I answer that,* Whereas the previous question is the same as inquiring "whether an erring conscience binds"; so this question is the same as inquiring "whether an erring conscience excuses." Now this question depends on what has been said above about ignorance. For it was said (Q. 6, A. 8) that ignorance sometimes causes an act to be involuntary, and sometimes not. And since moral good and evil consist in action in so far as it is voluntary, as was stated above (A. 2); it is evident that when ignorance causes an act to be involuntary, it takes away the character of moral good and evil; but not, when it does not cause the act to be involuntary. Again, it has been stated above (Q. 6, A. 8) that when ignorance is in any way willed, either directly or indirectly, it does not cause the act to be involuntary. And I call that ignorance "directly" voluntary, to which the act of the will tends: and that, "indirectly" voluntary, which is due to negligence, by reason of a man not wishing to know what he ought to know, as stated above (Q. 6, A. 8).

If then reason or conscience err with an error that is voluntary, either directly, or through negligence, so that one errs about what one ought to know; then such an error of reason or conscience does not excuse the will, that abides by that erring reason or conscience, from being evil. But if the error arise from ignorance of some circumstance, and without any negligence, so that it cause the act to be involuntary, then that error of reason or conscience excuses the will, that abides by that erring reason, from being evil. For instance, if erring reason tell a man that he should go to another man's wife, the will that abides by that erring reason is evil; since this error arises from ignorance of the Divine Law, which he is bound to know. But if a man's reason, errs in mistaking another for his wife, and if he wish to give her her right when she asks for it, his will is excused from being evil: because this error arises from ignorance of a circumstance, which ignorance excuses, and causes the act to be involuntary.

Reply Obj. 1: As Dionysius says (Div. Nom. iv), "good results from the entire cause, evil from each particular defect." Consequently in order that the thing to which the will tends be called evil, it suffices, either that it be evil in itself, or that it be apprehended as evil. But in order for it to be good, it must be good in both ways.

Reply Obj. 2: The eternal law cannot err, but human reason can. Consequently the will that abides by human reason, is not always right, nor is it always in accord with the eternal law.

Reply Obj. 3: Just as in syllogistic arguments, granted one absurdity, others must needs follow; so in moral matters, given one absurdity, others must follow too. Thus suppose a man to seek vainglory, he will sin, whether he does his duty for vainglory or whether he omit to do it. Nor is he in a dilemma about the matter: because he can put aside his evil intention. In like manner, suppose a man's reason or conscience to err through inexcusable ignorance, then evil must needs result in the will. Nor is this man in a dilemma: because he can lay aside his error, since his ignorance is vincible and voluntary.

SEVENTH ARTICLE [I-II, Q. 19, Art. 7]

Whether the Goodness of the Will, As Regards the Means, Depends on the Intention of the End?

Objection 1: It would seem that the goodness of the will does not depend on the intention of the end. For it has been stated above (A. 2) that the goodness of the will depends on the object alone. But as regards the means, the object of the will is one thing, and the end intended is another. Therefore in such matters the goodness of the will does not depend on the intention of the end.

Obj. 2: Further, to wish to keep God's commandment, belongs to a good will. But this can be referred to an evil end, for instance, to vainglory or covetousness, by willing to obey God for the sake of temporal gain. Therefore the goodness of the will does not depend on the intention of the end.

Obj. 3: Further, just as good and evil diversify the will, so do they diversify the end. But malice of the will does not depend on the malice of the end intended; since a man who wills to steal in order to give alms, has an evil will, although he intends a good end. Therefore neither does the goodness of the will depend on the goodness of the end intended.

*On the contrary,* Augustine says (Confess. ix, 3) that God rewards the intention. But God rewards a thing because it is good. Therefore the goodness of the will depends on the intention of the end.

*I answer that,* The intention may stand in a twofold relation to the act of the will; first, as preceding it, secondly as following [*Leonine edn.: 'accompanying'] it. The intention precedes the act of the will causally, when we will something because we intend a certain end. And then the order to the end is considered as the reason of the goodness of the thing willed: for instance, when a man wills to fast for God's sake; because the act of fasting is specifically good from the very fact that it is done for God's sake. Wherefore, since the goodness of the will depends on the goodness of the thing willed, as stated above (AA. 1, 2), it must, of necessity, depend on the intention of the end.

On the other hand, intention follows the act of the will, when it is added to a preceding act of the will; for instance, a man may will to do something, and may afterwards refer it to God. And then the goodness of the previous act of the will does not depend on the subsequent intention, except in so far as that act is repeated with the subsequent intention.

Reply Obj. 1: When the intention is the cause of the act of willing, the order to the end is considered as the reason of the goodness of the object, as stated above.

Reply Obj. 2: The act of the will cannot be said to be good, if an evil intention is the cause of willing. For when a man wills to give an alms for the sake of vainglory, he wills that which is good in itself, under a species of evil; and therefore, as willed by him, it is evil. Wherefore his will is evil. If, however, the intention is subsequent to the act of the will, then the latter may be good: and the intention does not spoil that act of the will which preceded, but that which is repeated.

Reply Obj. 3: As we have already stated (A. 6, ad 1), "evil results from each particular defect, but good from the whole and entire cause." Hence, whether the will tend to what is evil in itself, even under the species of good; or to the good under the species of evil, it will be evil in either case. But in order for the will to be good, it must tend to the good under the species of good; in other words, it must will the good for the sake of the good.

EIGHTH ARTICLE [I-II, Q. 19, Art. 8]

Whether the Degree of Goodness or Malice in the Will Depends on the Degree of Good or Evil in the Intention?

Objection 1: It would seem that the degree of goodness in the will depends on the degree of good in the intention. Because on Matt. 12:35, "A good man out of the good treasure of his heart bringeth forth that which is good," a gloss says: "A man does as much good as he intends." But the intention gives goodness not only to the external action, but also to the act of the will, as stated above (A. 7). Therefore the goodness of a man's will is according to the goodness of his intention.

Obj. 2: Further, if you add to the cause, you add to the effect. But the goodness of the intention is the cause of the good will. Therefore a man's will is good, according as his intention is good.

Obj. 3: Further, in evil actions, a man sins in proportion to his intention: for if a man were to throw a stone with a murderous intention, he would be guilty of murder. Therefore, for the same reason, in good actions, the will is good in proportion to the good intended.

*On the contrary,* The intention can be good, while the will is evil. Therefore, for the same reason, the intention can be better, and the will less good.

*I answer that,* In regard to both the act, and the intention of the end, we may consider a twofold quantity: one, on the part of the object, by reason of a man willing or doing a good that is greater; the other, taken from the intensity of the act, according as a man wills or acts intensely; and this is more on the part of the agent.

If then we speak of these respective quantities from the point of view of the object, it is evident that the quantity in the act does not depend on the quantity in the intention. With regard to the external act this may happen in two ways. First, through the object that is ordained to the intended end not being proportionate to that end; for instance, if a man were to give ten pounds, he could not realize his intention, if he intended to buy a thing worth a hundred pounds. Secondly, on account of the obstacles that may supervene in regard to the exterior action, which obstacles we are unable to remove: for instance, a man intends to go to Rome, and encounters obstacles, which prevent him from going. On the other hand, with regard to the interior act of the will, this happens in only one way: because the interior acts of the will are in our power, whereas the external actions are not. But the will can will an object that is not proportionate to the intended end: and thus the will that tends to that object considered absolutely, is not so good as the intention. Yet because the intention also belongs, in a way, to the act of the will, inasmuch, to wit, as it is the reason thereof; it comes to pass that the quantity of goodness in the intention redounds upon the act of the will; that is to say, in so far as the will wills some great good for an end, although that by which it wills to gain so great a good, is not proportionate to that good.

But if we consider the quantity in the intention and in the act, according to their respective intensity, then the intensity of the intention redounds upon the interior act and the exterior act of the will: since the intention stands in relation to them as a kind of form, as is clear from what has been said above (Q. 12, A. 4; Q. 18, A. 6). And yet considered materially, while the intention is intense, the interior or exterior act may be not so intense, materially speaking: for instance, when a man does not will with as much intensity to take medicine as he wills to regain health. Nevertheless the very fact of intending health intensely, redounds, as a formal principle, upon the intense volition of medicine.

We must observe, however, that the intensity of the interior or exterior act, may be referred to the intention as its object: as when a man intends to will intensely, or to do something intensely. And yet it does not follow that he wills or acts intensely; because the quantity of goodness in the interior or exterior act does not depend on the quantity of the good intended, as is shown above. And hence it is that a man does not merit as much as he intends to merit: because the quantity of merit is measured by the intensity of the act, as we shall show later on (Q. 20, A. 4; Q. 114, A. 4).

Reply Obj. 1: This gloss speaks of good as in the estimation of God, Who considers principally the intention of the end. Wherefore another gloss says on the same passage that "the treasure of the heart is the intention, according to which God judges our works." For the goodness of the intention, as stated above, redounds, so to speak, upon the goodness of the will, which makes even the external act to be meritorious in God's sight.

Reply Obj. 2: The goodness of the intention is not the whole cause of a good will. Hence the argument does not prove.

Reply Obj. 3: The mere malice of the intention suffices to make the will evil: and therefore too, the will is as evil as the intention is evil. But the same reasoning does not apply to goodness, as stated above (ad 2).

NINTH ARTICLE [I-II, Q. 19, Art. 9]

Whether the Goodness of the Will Depends on Its Conformity to the Divine Will?

Objection 1: It would seem that the goodness of the human will does not depend on its conformity to the Divine will. Because it is impossible for man's will to be conformed to the Divine will; as appears from the word of Isa. 55:9: "As the heavens are exalted above the earth, so are My ways exalted above your ways, and My thoughts above your thoughts." If therefore goodness of the will depended on its conformity to the Divine will, it would follow that it is impossible for man's will to be good. Which is inadmissible.

Obj. 2: Further, just as our wills arise from the Divine will, so does our knowledge flow from the Divine knowledge. But our knowledge does not require to be conformed to God's knowledge; since God knows many things that we know not. Therefore there is no need for our will to be conformed to the Divine will.

Obj. 3: Further, the will is a principle of action. But our action cannot be conformed to God's. Therefore neither can our will be conformed to His.

*On the contrary,* It is written (Matt. 26:39): "Not as I will, but as Thou wilt": which words He said, because "He wishes man to be upright and to tend to God," as Augustine expounds in the Enchiridion [*Enarr. in Ps. 32, serm. i.]. But the rectitude of the will is its goodness. Therefore the goodness of the will depends on its conformity to the Divine will.

*I answer that,* As stated above (A. 7), the goodness of the will depends on the intention of the end. Now the last end of the human will is the Sovereign Good, namely, God, as stated above (Q. 1, A. 8; Q. 3, A. 1). Therefore the goodness of the human will requires it to be ordained to the Sovereign Good, that is, to God.

Now this Good is primarily and essentially compared to the Divine will, as its proper object. Again, that which is first in any genus is the measure and rule of all that belongs to that genus. Moreover, everything attains to rectitude and goodness, in so far as it is in accord with its proper measure. Therefore, in order that man's will be good it needs to be conformed to the Divine will.

Reply Obj. 1: The human will cannot be conformed to the will of God so as to equal it, but only so as to imitate it. In like manner human knowledge is conformed to the Divine knowledge, in so far as it knows truth: and human action is conformed to the Divine, in so far as it is becoming to the agent: and this by way of imitation, not by way of equality.

From the above may be gathered the replies to the Second and Third Objections.

TENTH ARTICLE [I-II, Q. 19, Art. 10]

Whether It Is Necessary for the Human Will, in Order to Be Good, to Be Conformed to the Divine Will, As Regards the Thing Willed?

Objection 1: It would seem that the human will need not always be conformed to the Divine will, as regards the thing willed. For we cannot will what we know not: since the apprehended good is the object of the will. But in many things we know not what God wills. Therefore the human will cannot be conformed to the Divine will as to the thing willed.

Obj. 2: Further, God wills to damn the man whom He foresees about to die in mortal sin. If therefore man were bound to conform his will to the Divine will, in the point of the thing willed, it would follow that a man is bound to will his own damnation. Which is inadmissible.

Obj. 3: Further, no one is bound to will what is against filial piety. But if man were to will what God wills, this would sometimes be contrary to filial piety: for instance, when God wills the death of a father: if his son were to will it also, it would be against filial piety. Therefore man is not bound to conform his will to the Divine will, as to the thing willed.

*On the contrary,* (1) On Ps. 32:1, "Praise becometh the upright," a gloss says: "That man has an upright heart, who wills what God wills." But everyone is bound to have an upright heart. Therefore everyone is bound to will what God wills.

(2) Moreover, the will takes its form from the object, as does every act. If therefore man is bound to conform his will to the Divine will, it follows that he is bound to conform it, as to the thing willed.

(3) Moreover, opposition of wills arises from men willing different things. But whoever has a will in opposition to the Divine will, has an evil will. Therefore whoever does not conform his will to the Divine will, as to the thing willed, has an evil will.

*I answer that,* As is evident from what has been said above (AA. 3, 5), the will tends to its object, according as it is proposed by the reason. Now a thing may be considered in various ways by the reason, so as to appear good from one point of view, and not good from another point of view. And therefore if a man's will wills a thing to be, according as it appears to be good, his will is good: and the will of another man, who wills that thing not to be, according as it appears evil, is also good. Thus a judge has a good will, in willing a thief to be put to death, because this is just: while the will of another—e.g. the thief's wife or son, who wishes him not to be put to death, inasmuch as killing is a natural evil, is also good.

Now since the will follows the apprehension of the reason or intellect; the more universal the aspect of the apprehended good, the more universal the good to which the will tends. This is evident in the example given above: because the judge has care of the common good, which is justice, and therefore he wishes the thief's death, which has the aspect of good in relation to the common estate; whereas the thief's wife has to consider the private good of the family, and from this point of view she wishes her husband, the thief, not to be put to death. Now the good of the whole universe is that which is apprehended by God, Who is the Maker and Governor of all things: hence whatever He wills, He wills it under the aspect of the common good; this is His own Goodness, which is the good of the whole universe. On the other hand, the apprehension of a creature, according to its nature, is of some particular good, proportionate to that nature. Now a thing may happen to be good under a particular aspect, and yet not good under a universal aspect, or vice versa, as stated above. And therefore it comes to pass that a certain will is good from willing something considered under a particular aspect, which thing God wills not, under a universal aspect, and vice versa. And hence too it is, that various wills of various men can be good in respect of opposite things, for as much as, under various aspects, they wish a particular thing to be or not to be.

But a man's will is not right in willing a particular good, unless he refer it to the common good as an end: since even the natural appetite of each part is ordained to the common good of the whole. Now it is the end that supplies the formal reason, as it were, of willing whatever is directed to the end. Consequently, in order that a man will some particular good with a right will, he must will that particular good materially, and the Divine and universal good, formally. Therefore the human will is bound to be conformed to the Divine will, as to that which is willed formally, for it is bound to will the Divine and universal good; but not as to that which is willed materially, for the reason given above.

At the same time in both these respects, the human will is conformed to the Divine, in a certain degree. Because inasmuch as it is conformed to the Divine will in the common aspect of the thing willed, it is conformed thereto in the point of the last end. While, inasmuch as it is not conformed to the Divine will in the thing willed materially, it is conformed to that will considered as efficient cause; since the proper inclination consequent to nature, or to the particular apprehension of some particular thing, comes to a thing from God as its efficient cause. Hence it is customary to say that a man's will, in this respect, is conformed to the Divine will, because it wills what God wishes him to will.

There is yet another kind of conformity in respect of the formal cause, consisting in man's willing something from charity, as God wills it. And this conformity is also reduced to the formal conformity, that is in respect of the last end, which is the proper object of charity.

Reply Obj. 1: We can know in a general way what God wills. For we know that whatever God wills, He wills it under the aspect of good. Consequently whoever wills a thing under any aspect of good, has a will conformed to the Divine will, as to the reason of the thing willed. But we know not what God wills in particular: and in this respect we are not bound to conform our will to the Divine will.

But in the state of glory, every one will see in each thing that he wills, the relation of that thing to what God wills in that particular matter. Consequently he will conform his will to God in all things not only formally, but also materially.

Reply Obj. 2: God does not will the damnation of a man, considered precisely as damnation, nor a man's death, considered precisely as death, because, "He wills all men to be saved" (1 Tim. 2:4); but He wills such things under the aspect of justice. Wherefore in regard to such things it suffices for man to will the upholding of God's justice and of the natural order.

Wherefore the reply to the Third Objection is evident.

To the first argument advanced in a contrary sense, it should be said that a man who conforms his will to God's, in the aspect of reason of the thing willed, wills what God wills, more than the man, who conforms his will to God's, in the point of the very thing willed; because the will tends more to the end, than to that which is on account of the end.

To the second, it must be replied that the species and form of an act are taken from the object considered formally, rather than from the object considered materially.

To the third, it must be said that there is no opposition of wills when several people desire different things, but not under the same aspect: but there is opposition of wills, when under one and the same aspect, one man wills a thing which another wills not. But there is no question of this here.

# QUESTION 20

OF GOODNESS AND MALICE IN EXTERNAL HUMAN ACTIONS (In Six Articles)

We must next consider goodness and malice as to external actions: under which head there are six points of inquiry:

(1) Whether goodness and malice is first in the act of the will, or in the external action?

(2) Whether the whole goodness or malice of the external action depends on the goodness of the will?

(3) Whether the goodness and malice of the interior act are the same as those of the external action?

(4) Whether the external action adds any goodness or malice to that of the interior act?

(5) Whether the consequences of an external action increase its goodness or malice?

(6) Whether one and the same external action can be both good and evil?

FIRST ARTICLE [I-II, Q. 20, Art. 1]

Whether Goodness or Malice Is First in the Action of the Will, or in the External Action?

Objection 1: It would seem that good and evil are in the external action prior to being in the act of the will. For the will derives goodness from its object, as stated above (Q. 19, AA. 1, 2). But the external action is the object of the interior act of the will: for a man is said to will to commit a theft, or to will to give an alms. Therefore good and evil are in the external action, prior to being in the act of the will.

Obj. 2: Further, the aspect of good belongs first to the end: since what is directed to the end receives the aspect of good from its relation to the end. Now whereas the act of the will cannot be an end, as stated above (Q. 1, A. 1, ad 2), the act of another power can be an end. Therefore good is in the act of some other power prior to being in the act of the will.

Obj. 3: Further, the act of the will stands in a formal relation to the external action, as stated above (Q. 18, A. 6). But that which is formal is subsequent; since form is something added to matter. Therefore good and evil are in the external action, prior to being in the act of the will.

*On the contrary,* Augustine says (Retract. i, 9) that "it is by the will that we sin, and that we behave aright." Therefore moral good and evil are first in the will.

*I answer that,* External actions may be said to be good or bad in two ways. First, in regard to their genus, and the circumstances connected with them: thus the giving of alms, if the required conditions be observed, is said to be good. Secondly, a thing is said to be good or evil, from its relation to the end: thus the giving of alms for vainglory is said to be evil. Now, since the end is the will's proper object, it is evident that this aspect of good or evil, which the external action derives from its relation to the end, is to be found first of all in the act of the will, whence it passes to the external action. On the other hand, the goodness or malice which the external action has of itself, on account of its being about due matter and its being attended by due circumstances, is not derived from the will, but rather from the reason. Consequently, if we consider the goodness of the external action, in so far as it comes from reason's ordination and apprehension, it is prior to the goodness of the act of the will: but if we consider it in so far as it is in the execution of the action done, it is subsequent to the goodness of the will, which is its principle.

Reply Obj. 1: The exterior action is the object of the will, inasmuch as it is proposed to the will by the reason, as good apprehended and ordained by the reason: and thus it is prior to the good in the act of the will. But inasmuch as it is found in the execution of the action, it is an effect of the will, and is subsequent to the will.

Reply Obj. 2: The end precedes in the order of intention, but follows in the order of execution.

Reply Obj. 3: A form as received into matter, is subsequent to matter in the order of generation, although it precedes it in the order of nature: but inasmuch as it is in the active cause, it precedes in every way. Now the will is compared to the exterior action, as its efficient cause. Wherefore the goodness of the act of the will, as existing in the active cause, is the form of the exterior action.

SECOND ARTICLE [I-II, Q. 20, Art. 2]

Whether the Whole Goodness and Malice of the External Action Depends on the Goodness of the Will?

Objection 1: It would seem that the whole goodness and malice of the external action depend on the goodness of the will. For it is written (Matt. 7:18): "A good tree cannot bring forth evil fruit, neither can an evil tree bring forth good fruit." But, according to the gloss, the tree signifies the will, and fruit signifies works. Therefore, it is impossible for the interior act of the will to be good, and the external action evil, or vice versa.

Obj. 2: Further, Augustine says (Retract. i, 9) that there is no sin without the will. If therefore there is no sin in the will, there will be none in the external action. And so the whole goodness or malice of the external action depends on the will.

Obj. 3: Further, the good and evil of which we are speaking now are differences of the moral act. Now differences make an essential division in a genus, according to the Philosopher (Metaph. vii, 12). Since therefore an act is moral from being voluntary, it seems that goodness and malice in an act are derived from the will alone.

*On the contrary,* Augustine says (Contra Mendac. vii), that "there are some actions which neither a good end nor a good will can make good."

*I answer that,* As stated above (A. 1), we may consider a twofold goodness or malice in the external action: one in respect of due matter and circumstances; the other in respect of the order to the end. And that which is in respect of the order to the end, depends entirely on the will: while that which is in respect of due matter or circumstances, depends on the reason: and on this goodness depends the goodness of the will, in so far as the will tends towards it.

Now it must be observed, as was noted above (Q. 19, A. 6, ad 1), that for a thing to be evil, one single defect suffices, whereas, for it to be good simply, it is not enough for it to be good in one point only, it must be good in every respect. If therefore the will be good, both from its proper object and from its end, if follows that the external action is good. But if the will be good from its intention of the end, this is not enough to make the external action good: and if the will be evil either by reason of its intention of the end, or by reason of the act willed, it follows that the external action is evil.

Reply Obj. 1: If the good tree be taken to signify the good will, it must be in so far as the will derives goodness from the act willed and from the end intended.

Reply Obj. 2: A man sins by his will, not only when he wills an evil end; but also when he wills an evil act.

Reply Obj. 3: Voluntariness applies not only to the interior act of the will, but also to external actions, inasmuch as they proceed from the will and the reason. Consequently the difference of good and evil is applicable to both the interior and external act.

THIRD ARTICLE [I-II, Q. 20, Art. 3]

Whether the Goodness and Malice of the External Action Are the Same As Those of the Interior Act?

Objection 1: It would seem that the goodness and malice of the interior act of the will are not the same as those of the external action. For the principle of the interior act is the interior apprehensive or appetitive power of the soul; whereas the principle of the external action is the power that accomplishes the movement. Now where the principles of action are different, the actions themselves are different. Moreover, it is the action which is the subject of goodness or malice: and the same accident cannot be in different subjects. Therefore the goodness of the interior act cannot be the same as that of the external action.

Obj. 2: Further, "A virtue makes that, which has it, good, and renders its action good also" (Ethic. ii, 6). But the intellective virtue in the commanding power is distinct from the moral virtue in the power commanded, as is declared in *Ethic.* i, 13. Therefore the goodness of the interior act, which belongs to the commanding power, is distinct from the goodness of the external action, which belongs to the power commanded.

Obj. 3: Further, the same thing cannot be cause and effect; since nothing is its own cause. But the goodness of the interior act is the cause of the goodness of the external action, or vice versa, as stated above (AA. 1, 2). Therefore it is not the same goodness in each.

*On the contrary,* It was shown above (Q. 18, A. 6) that the act of the will is the form, as it were, of the external action. Now that which results from the material and formal element is one thing. Therefore there is but one goodness of the internal and external act.

*I answer that,* As stated above (Q. 17, A. 4), the interior act of the will, and the external action, considered morally, are one act. Now it happens sometimes that one and the same individual act has several aspects of goodness or malice, and sometimes that it has but one. Hence we must say that sometimes the goodness or malice of the interior act is the same as that of the external action, and sometimes not. For as we have already said (AA. 1, 2), these two goodnesses or malices, of the internal and external acts, are ordained to one another. Now it may happen, in things that are subordinate to something else, that a thing is good merely from being subordinate; thus a bitter draught is good merely because it procures health. Wherefore there are not two goodnesses, one the goodness of health, and the other the goodness of the draught; but one and the same. On the other hand it happens sometimes that that which is subordinate to something else, has some aspect of goodness in itself, besides the fact of its being subordinate to some other good: thus a palatable medicine can be considered in the light of a pleasurable good, besides being conducive to health.

We must therefore say that when the external action derives goodness or malice from its relation to the end only, then there is but one and the same goodness of the act of the will which of itself regards the end, and of the external action, which regards the end through the medium of the act of the will. But when the external action has goodness or malice of itself, i.e. in regard to its matter and circumstances, then the goodness of the external action is distinct from the goodness of the will in regarding the end; yet so that the goodness of the end passes into the external action, and the goodness of the matter and circumstances passes into the act of the will, as stated above (AA. 1, 2).

Reply Obj. 1: This argument proves that the internal and external actions are different in the physical order: yet distinct as they are in that respect, they combine to form one thing in the moral order, as stated above (Q. 17, A. 4).

Reply Obj. 2: As stated in *Ethic.* vi, 12, a moral virtue is ordained to the act of that virtue, which act is the end, as it were, of that virtue; whereas prudence, which is in the reason, is ordained to things directed to the end. For this reason various virtues are necessary. But right reason in regard to the very end of a virtue has no other goodness than the goodness of that virtue, in so far as the goodness of the reason is participated in each virtue.

Reply Obj. 3: When a thing is derived by one thing from another, as from a univocal efficient cause, then it is not the same in both: thus when a hot thing heats, the heat of the heater is distinct from the heat of the thing heated, although it be the same specifically. But when a thing is derived from one thing from another, according to analogy or proportion, then it is one and the same in both: thus the healthiness which is in medicine or urine is derived from the healthiness of the animal's body; nor is health as applied to urine and medicine, distinct from health as applied to the body of an animal, of which health medicine is the cause, and urine the sign. It is in this way that the goodness of the external action is derived from the goodness of the will, and vice versa; viz. according to the order of one to the other.

FOURTH ARTICLE [I-II, Q. 20, Art. 4]

Whether the External Action Adds Any Goodness or Malice to That of the Interior Act?

Objection 1: It would seem that the external action does not add any goodness or malice to that of the interior action. For Chrysostom says (Hom. xix in Matt.): "It is the will that is rewarded for doing good, or punished for doing evil." Now works are the witnesses of the will. Therefore God seeks for works not on His own account, in order to know how to judge; but for the sake of others, that all may understand how just He is. But good or evil is to be estimated according to God's judgment rather than according to the judgment of man. Therefore the external action adds no goodness or malice to that of the interior act.

Obj. 2: Further, the goodness and malice of the interior and external acts are one and the same, as stated above (A. 3). But increase is the addition of one thing to another. Therefore the external action does not add to the goodness or malice of the interior act.

Obj. 3: Further, the entire goodness of created things does not add to the Divine Goodness, because it is entirely derived therefrom. But sometimes the entire goodness of the external action is derived from the goodness of the interior act, and sometimes conversely, as stated above (AA. 1, 2). Therefore neither of them adds to the goodness or malice of the other.

*On the contrary,* Every agent intends to attain good and avoid evil. If therefore by the external action no further goodness or malice be added, it is to no purpose that he who has a good or an evil will, does a good deed or refrains from an evil deed. Which is unreasonable.

*I answer that,* If we speak of the goodness which the external action derives from the will tending to the end, then the external action adds nothing to this goodness, unless it happens that the will in itself is made better in good things, or worse in evil things. This, seemingly, may happen in three ways. First in point of number; if, for instance, a man wishes to do something with a good or an evil end in view, and does not do it then, but afterwards wills and does it, the act of his will is doubled and a double good, or a double evil is the result. Secondly, in point of extension: when, for instance, a man wishes to do something for a good or an evil end, and is hindered by some obstacle, whereas another man perseveres in the movement of the will until he accomplish it in deed; it is evident that the will of the latter is more lasting in good or evil, and in this respect, is better or worse. Thirdly, in point of intensity: for there are certain external actions, which, in so far as they are pleasurable, or painful, are such as naturally to make the will more intense or more remiss; and it is evident that the more intensely the will tends to good or evil, the better or worse it is.

On the other hand, if we speak of the goodness which the external action derives from its matter and due circumstances, thus it stands in relation to the will as its term and end. And in this way it adds to the goodness or malice of the will; because every inclination or movement is perfected by attaining its end or reaching its term. Wherefore the will is not perfect, unless it be such that, given the opportunity, it realizes the operation. But if this prove impossible, as long as the will is perfect, so as to realize the operation if it could; the lack of perfection derived from the external action, is simply involuntary. Now just as the involuntary deserves neither punishment nor reward in the accomplishment of good or evil deeds, so neither does it lessen reward or punishment, if a man through simple involuntariness fail to do good or evil.

Reply Obj. 1: Chrysostom is speaking of the case where a man's will is complete, and does not refrain from the deed save through the impossibility of achievement.

Reply Obj. 2: This argument applies to that goodness which the external action derives from the will as tending to the end. But the goodness which the external action takes from its matter and circumstances, is distinct from that which it derives from the end; but it is not distinct from that which it has from the very act willed, to which it stands in the relation of measure and cause, as stated above (AA. 1, 2).

From this the reply to the Third Objection is evident.

FIFTH ARTICLE [I-II, Q. 20, Art. 5]

Whether the Consequences of the External Action Increase Its Goodness or Malice?

Objection 1: It would seem that the consequences of the external action increase its goodness or malice. For the effect pre-exists virtually in its cause. But the consequences result from the action as an effect from its cause. Therefore they pre-exist virtually in actions. Now a thing is judged to be good or bad according to its virtue, since a virtue "makes that which has it to be good" (Ethic. ii, 6). Therefore the consequences increase the goodness or malice of an action.

Obj. 2: Further, the good actions of his hearers are consequences resulting from the words of a preacher. But such goods as these redound to the merit of the preacher, as is evident from Phil. 4:1: "My dearly beloved brethren, my joy and my crown." Therefore the consequences of an action increase its goodness or malice.

Obj. 3: Further, punishment is not increased, unless the fault increases: wherefore it is written (Deut. 25:2): "According to the measure of the sin shall the measure also of the stripes be." But the punishment is increased on account of the consequences; for it is written (Ex. 21:29): "But if the ox was wont to push with his horn yesterday and the day before, and they warned his master, and he did not shut him up, and he shall kill a man or a woman, then the ox shall be stoned, and his owner also shall be put to death." But he would not have been put to death, if the ox, although he had not been shut up, had not killed a man. Therefore the consequences increase the goodness or malice of an action.

Obj. 4: Further, if a man do something which may cause death, by striking, or by sentencing, and if death does not ensue, he does not contract irregularity: but he would if death were to ensue. Therefore the consequence of an action increase its goodness or malice.

*On the contrary,* The consequences do not make an action that was evil, to be good; nor one that was good, to be evil. For instance, if a man give an alms to a poor man who makes bad use of the alms by committing a sin, this does not undo the good done by the giver; and, in like manner, if a man bear patiently a wrong done to him, the wrongdoer is not thereby excused. Therefore the consequences of an action doe not increase its goodness or malice.

*I answer that,* The consequences of an action are either foreseen or not. If they are foreseen, it is evident that they increase the goodness or malice. For when a man foresees that many evils may follow from his action, and yet does not therefore desist therefrom, this shows his will to be all the more inordinate.

But if the consequences are not foreseen, we must make a distinction. Because if they follow from the nature of the action and in the majority of cases, in this respect, the consequences increase the goodness or malice of that action: for it is evident that an action is specifically better, if better results can follow from it; and specifically worse, if it is of a nature to produce worse results. On the other hand, if the consequences follow by accident and seldom, then they do not increase the goodness or malice of the action: because we do not judge of a thing according to that which belongs to it by accident, but only according to that which belongs to it of itself.

Reply Obj. 1: The virtue of a cause is measured by the effect that flows from the nature of the cause, not by that which results by accident.

Reply Obj. 2: The good actions done by the hearers, result from the preacher's words, as an effect that flows from their very nature. Hence they redound to the merit of the preacher: especially when such is his intention.

Reply Obj. 3: The consequences for which that man is ordered to be punished, both follow from the nature of the cause, and are supposed to be foreseen. For this reason they are reckoned as punishable.

Reply Obj. 4: This argument would prove if irregularity were the result of the fault. But it is not the result of the fault, but of the fact, and of the obstacle to the reception of a sacrament.

SIXTH ARTICLE [I-II, Q. 20, Art. 6]

Whether One and the Same External Action Can Be Both Good and Evil?

Objection 1: It would seem that one and the same external action can be both good and evil. For "movement, if continuous, is one and the same" (Phys. v, 4). But one continuous movement can be both good and bad: for instance, a man may go to church continuously, intending at first vainglory, and afterwards the service of God. Therefore one and the same action can be both good and bad.

Obj. 2: Further, according to the Philosopher (Phys. iii, 3), action and passion are one act. But the passion may be good, as Christ's was; and the action evil, as that of the Jews. Therefore one and the same act can be both good and evil.

Obj. 3: Further, since a servant is an instrument, as it were, of his master, the servant's action is his master's, just as the action of a tool is the workman's action. But it may happen that the servant's action result from his master's good will, and is therefore good: and from the evil will of the servant, and is therefore evil. Therefore the same action can be both good and evil.

*On the contrary,* The same thing cannot be the subject of contraries. But good and evil are contraries. Therefore the same action cannot be both good and evil.

*On the contrary,* The same thing cannot be the subject of contraries. But good and evil are contraries. Therefore the same action cannot be both good and evil.

*I answer that,* Nothing hinders a thing from being one, in so far as it is in one genus, and manifold, in so far as it is referred to another genus. Thus a continuous surface is one, considered as in the genus of quantity; and yet it is manifold, considered as to the genus of color, if it be partly white, and partly black. And accordingly, nothing hinders an action from being one, considered in the natural order; whereas it is not one, considered in the moral order; and vice versa, as we have stated above (A. 3, ad 1; Q. 18, A. 7, ad 1). For continuous walking is one action, considered in the natural order: but it may resolve itself into many actions, considered in the moral order, if a change take place in the walker's will, for the will is the principle of moral actions. If therefore we consider one action in the moral order, it is impossible for it to be morally both good and evil. Whereas if it be one as to natural and not moral unity, it can be both good and evil.

Reply Obj. 1: This continual movement which proceeds from various intentions, although it is one in the natural order, is not one in the point of moral unity.

Reply Obj. 2: Action and passion belong to the moral order, in so far as they are voluntary. And therefore in so far as they are voluntary in respect of wills that differ, they are two distinct things, and good can be in one of them while evil is in the other.

Reply Obj. 3: The action of the servant, in so far as it proceeds from the will of the servant, is not the master's action: but only in so far as it proceeds from the master's command. Wherefore the evil will of the servant does not make the action evil in this respect.

# QUESTION 21

OF THE CONSEQUENCES OF HUMAN ACTIONS BY REASON OF THEIR GOODNESS AND MALICE (In Four Articles)

We have now to consider the consequences of human actions by reason of their goodness and malice: and under this head there are four points of inquiry:

(1) Whether a human action is right or sinful by reason of its being good or evil?

(2) Whether it thereby deserves praise or blame?

(3) Whether accordingly, it is meritorious or demeritorious?

(4) Whether it is accordingly meritorious or demeritorious before God?

FIRST ARTICLE [I-II, Q. 21, Art. 1]

Whether a Human Action Is Right or Sinful, in So Far As It Is Good or Evil?

Objection 1: It seems that a human action is not right or sinful, in so far as it is good or evil. For "monsters are the sins of nature" (Phys. ii, 8). But monsters are not actions, but things engendered outside the order of nature. Now things that are produced according to art and reason imitate those that are produced according to nature (Phys. ii, 8). Therefore an action is not sinful by reason of its being inordinate and evil.

Obj. 2: Further, sin, as stated in *Phys.* ii, 8 occurs in nature and art, when the end intended by nature or art is not attained. But the goodness or malice of a human action depends, before all, on the intention of the end, and on its achievement. Therefore it seems that the malice of an action does not make it sinful.

Obj. 3: Further, if the malice of an action makes it sinful, it follows that wherever there is evil, there is sin. But this is false: since punishment is not a sin, although it is an evil. Therefore an action is not sinful by reason of its being evil.

*On the contrary,* As shown above (Q. 19, A. 4),

the goodness of a human action depends principally on the Eternal Law: and consequently its malice consists in its being in disaccord with the Eternal Law. But this is the very nature of sin; for Augustine says (Contra Faust. xxii, 27) that "sin is a word, deed, or desire, in opposition to the Eternal Law." Therefore a human action is sinful by reason of its being evil.

*I answer that,* Evil is more comprehensive than sin, as also is good than right. For every privation of good, in whatever subject, is an evil: whereas sin consists properly in an action done for a certain end, and lacking due order to that end. Now the due order to an end is measured by some rule. In things that act according to nature, this rule is the natural force that inclines them to that end. When therefore an action proceeds from a natural force, in accord with the natural inclination to an end, then the action is said to be right: since the mean does not exceed its limits, viz. the action does not swerve from the order of its active principle to the end. But when an action strays from this rectitude, it comes under the notion of sin.

Now in those things that are done by the will, the proximate rule is the human reason, while the supreme rule is the Eternal Law. When, therefore, a human action tends to the end, according to the order of reason and of the Eternal Law, then that action is right: but when it turns aside from that rectitude, then it is said to be a sin. Now it is evident from what has been said (Q. 19, AA. 3, 4) that every voluntary action that turns aside from the order of reason and of the Eternal Law, is evil, and that every good action is in accord with reason and the Eternal Law. Hence it follows that a human action is right or sinful by reason of its being good or evil.

Reply Obj. 1: Monsters are called sins, inasmuch as they result from a sin in nature's action.

Reply Obj. 2: The end is twofold; the last end, and the proximate end. In the sin of nature, the action does indeed fail in respect of the last end, which is the perfection of the thing generated; but it does not fail in respect of any proximate end whatever; since when nature works it forms something. In like manner, the sin of the will always fails as regards the last end intended, because no voluntary evil action can be ordained to happiness, which is the last end: and yet it does not fail in respect of some proximate end: intended and achieved by the will. Wherefore also, since the very intention of this end is ordained to the last end, this same intention may be right or sinful.

Reply Obj. 3: Each thing is ordained to its end by its action: and therefore sin, which consists in straying from the order to the end, consists properly in an action. On the other hand, punishment regards the person of the sinner, as was stated in the First Part (Q. 48, A. 5, ad 4; A. 6, ad 3).

SECOND ARTICLE [I-II, Q. 21, Art. 2]

Whether a Human Action Deserves Praise or Blame, by Reason of Its Being Good or Evil?

Objection 1: It would seem that a human action does not deserve praise or blame by reason of its being good or evil. For "sin happens even in things done by nature" (Phys. ii, 8). And yet natural things are not deserving of praise or blame (Ethic. iii, 5). Therefore a human action does not deserve blame, by reason of its being evil or sinful; and, consequently, neither does it deserve praise, by reason of its being good.

Obj. 2: Further, just as sin occurs in moral actions, so does it happen in the productions of art: because as stated in *Phys.* ii, 8 "it is a sin in a grammarian to write badly, and in a doctor to give the wrong medicine." But the artist is not blamed for making something bad: because the artist's work is such, that he can produce a good or a bad thing, just as he lists. Therefore it seems that neither is there any reason for blaming a moral action, in the fact that it is evil.

Obj. 3: Further, Dionysius says (Div. Nom. iv) that evil is "weak and incapable." But weakness or inability either takes away or diminishes guilt. Therefore a human action does not incur guilt from being evil.

*On the contrary,* The Philosopher says (De Virt. et Vit. i) that "virtuous deeds deserve praise, while deeds that are opposed to virtue deserve censure and blame." But good actions are virtuous; because "virtue makes that which has it, good, and makes its action good" (Ethic. ii, 6): wherefore actions opposed to virtue are evil. Therefore a human action deserves praise or blame, through being good or evil.

*I answer that,* Just as evil is more comprehensive than sin, so is sin more comprehensive than blame. For an action is said to deserve praise or blame, from its being imputed to the agent: since to praise or to blame means nothing else than to impute to someone the malice or goodness of his action. Now an action is imputed to an agent, when it is in his power, so that he has dominion over it: because it is through his will that man has dominion over his actions, as was made clear above (Q. 1, AA. 1, 2). Hence it follows that good or evil, in voluntary actions alone, renders them worthy of praise or blame: and in such like actions, evil, sin and guilt are one and the same thing.

Reply Obj. 1: Natural actions are not in the power of the natural agent: since the action of nature is determinate. And, therefore, although there be sin in natural actions, there is no blame.

Reply Obj. 2: Reason stands in different relations to the productions of art, and to moral actions. In matters of art, reason is directed to a particular end, which is something devised by reason: whereas in moral matters, it is directed to the general end of all human life. Now a particular end is subordinate to the general end. Since therefore sin is a departure from the order to the end, as stated above (A. 1), sin may occur in two ways, in a production of art. First, by a departure from the particular end intended by the artist: and this sin will be proper to the art; for instance, if an artist produce a bad thing, while intending to produce something good; or produce something good, while intending to produce something bad. Secondly, by a departure from the general end of human life: and then he will be said to sin, if he intend to produce a bad work, and does so in effect, so that another is taken in thereby. But this sin is not proper to the artist as such, but as man. Consequently for the former sin the artist is blamed as an artist; while for the latter he is blamed as a man. On the other hand, in moral matters, where we take into consideration the order of reason to the general end of human life, sin and evil are always due to a departure from the order of reason to the general end of human life. Wherefore man is blamed for such a sin, both as man and as a moral being. Hence the Philosopher says (Ethic. vi, 5) that "in art, he who sins voluntarily is preferable; but in prudence, as in the moral virtues," which prudence directs, "he is the reverse."

Reply Obj. 3: Weakness that occurs in voluntary evils, is subject to man's power: wherefore it neither takes away nor diminishes guilt.

THIRD ARTICLE [I-II, Q. 21, Art. 3]

Whether a Human Action Is Meritorious or Demeritorious in So Far As It Is Good or Evil?

Objection 1: It would seem that a human action is not meritorious or demeritorious on account of its goodness or malice. For we speak of merit or demerit in relation to retribution, which has no place save in matters relating to another person. But good or evil actions are not all related to another person, for some are related to the person of the agent. Therefore not every good or evil human action is meritorious or demeritorious.

Obj. 2: Further, no one deserves punishment or reward for doing as he chooses with that of which he is master: thus if a man destroys what belongs to him, he is not punished, as if he had destroyed what belongs to another. But man is master of his own actions. Therefore a man does not merit punishment or reward, through putting his action to a good or evil purpose.

Obj. 3: Further, if a man acquire some good for himself, he does not on that account deserve to be benefited by another man: and the same applies to evil. Now a good action is itself a kind of good and perfection of the agent: while an inordinate action is his evil. Therefore a man does not merit or demerit, from the fact that he does a good or an evil deed.

*On the contrary,* It is written (Isa. 3:10, 11): "Say to the just man that it is well; for he shall eat the fruit of his doings. Woe to the wicked unto evil; for the reward of his hands shall be given him."

*I answer that,* We speak of merit and demerit, in relation to retribution, rendered according to justice. Now, retribution according to justice is rendered to a man, by reason of his having done something to another's advantage or hurt. It must, moreover, be observed that every individual member of a society is, in a fashion, a part and member of the whole society. Wherefore, any good or evil, done to the member of a society, redounds on the whole society: thus, who hurts the hand, hurts the man. When, therefore, anyone does good or evil to another individual, there is a twofold measure of merit or demerit in his action: first, in respect of the retribution owed to him by the individual to whom he has done good or harm; secondly, in respect of the retribution owed to him by the whole of society. Now when a man ordains his action directly for the good or evil of the whole society, retribution is owed to him, before and above all, by the whole society; secondarily, by all the parts of society. Whereas when a man does that which conduces to his own benefit or disadvantage, then again is retribution owed to him, in so far as this too affects the community, forasmuch as he is a part of society: although retribution is not due to him, in so far as it conduces to the good or harm of an individual, who is identical with the agent: unless, perchance, he owe retribution to himself, by a sort of resemblance, in so far as man is said to be just to himself.

It is therefore evident that a good or evil action deserves praise or blame, in so far as it is in the power of the will: that it is right or sinful, according as it is ordained to the end; and that its merit or demerit depends on the recompense for justice or injustice towards another.

Reply Obj. 1: A man's good or evil actions, although not ordained to the good or evil of another individual, are nevertheless ordained to the good or evil of another, i.e. the community.

Reply Obj. 2: Man is master of his actions; and yet, in so far as he belongs to another, i.e. the community, of which he forms part, he merits or demerits, inasmuch as he disposes his actions well or ill: just as if he were to dispense well or ill other belongings of his, in respect of which he is bound to serve the community.

Reply Obj. 3: This very good or evil, which a man does to himself by his action, redounds to the community, as stated above.

FOURTH ARTICLE [I-II, Q. 21, Art. 4]

Whether a Human Action Is Meritorious or Demeritorious Before God, According As It Is Good or Evil?

Objection 1: It would seem that man's actions, good or evil, are not meritorious or demeritorious in the sight of God. Because, as stated above (A. 3), merit and demerit imply relation to retribution for good or harm done to another. But a man's action, good or evil, does no good or harm to God; for it is written (Job 35:6, 7): "If thou sin, what shalt thou hurt Him? ... And if thou do justly, what shalt thou give Him?" Therefore a human action, good or evil, is not meritorious or demeritorious in the sight of God.

Obj. 2: Further, an instrument acquires no merit or demerit in the sight of him that uses it; because the entire action of the instrument belongs to the user. Now when man acts he is the instrument of the Divine power which is the principal cause of his action; hence it is written (Isa. 10:15): "Shall the axe boast itself against him that cutteth with it? Or shall the saw exalt itself against him by whom it is drawn?" where man while acting is evidently compared to an instrument. Therefore man merits or demerits nothing in God's sight, by good or evil deeds.

Obj. 3: Further, a human action acquires merit or demerit through being ordained to someone else. But not all human actions are ordained to God. Therefore not every good or evil action acquires merit or demerit in God's sight.

*On the contrary,* It is written (Eccles. 12:14): "All things that are done, God will bring into judgment ... whether it be good or evil." Now judgment implies retribution, in respect of which we speak of merit and demerit. Therefore every human action, both good and evil, acquires merit or demerit in God's sight.

*I answer that,* A human action, as stated above (A. 3), acquires merit or demerit, through being ordained to someone else, either by reason of himself, or by reason of the community: and in each way, our actions, good and evil, acquire merit or demerit, in the sight of God. On the part of God Himself, inasmuch as He is man's last end; and it is our duty to refer all our actions to the last end, as stated above (Q. 19, A. 10). Consequently, whoever does an evil deed, not referable to God, does not give God the honor due to Him as our last end. On the part of the whole community of the universe, because in every community, he who governs the community, cares, first of all, for the common good; wherefore it is his business to award retribution for such things as are done well or ill in the community. Now God is the governor and ruler of the whole universe, as stated in the First Part (Q. 103, A. 5): and especially of rational creatures. Consequently it is evident that human actions acquire merit or demerit in reference to Him: else it would follow that human actions are no business of God's.

Reply Obj. 1: God in Himself neither gains nor loses anything by the action of man: but man, for his part, takes something from God, or offers something to Him, when he observes or does not observe the order instituted by God.

Reply Obj. 2: Man is so moved, as an instrument, by God, that, at the same time, he moves himself by his free-will, as was explained above (Q. 9, A. 6, ad 3). Consequently, by his action, he acquires merit or demerit in God's sight.

Reply Obj. 3: Man is not ordained to the body politic, according to all that he is and has; and so it does not follow that every action of his acquires merit or demerit in relation to the body politic. But all that man is, and can, and has, must be referred to God: and therefore every action of man, whether good or bad, acquires merit or demerit in the sight of God, as far as the action itself is concerned.

TREATISE ON THE PASSIONS (QQ. 22-48)

## QUESTION 22

OF THE SUBJECT OF THE SOUL'S PASSIONS (In Three Articles)

We must now consider the passions of the soul: first, in general; secondly, in particular. Taking them in general, there are four things to be considered: (1) Their subject: (2) The difference between them: (3) Their mutual relationship: (4) Their malice and goodness.

Under the first head there are three points of inquiry:

(1) Whether there is any passion in the soul?

(2) Whether passion is in the appetitive rather than in the apprehensive part?

(3) Whether passion is in the sensitive appetite rather than in the intellectual appetite, which is called the will?

FIRST ARTICLE [I-II, Q. 22, Art. 1]

Whether Any Passion Is in the Soul?

Objection 1: It would seem that there is no passion in the soul. Because passivity belongs to matter. But the soul is not composed of matter and form, as stated in the First Part (Q. 75, A. 5). Therefore there is no passion in the soul.

Obj. 2: Further, passion is movement, as is stated in *Phys.* iii, 3. But the soul is not moved, as is proved in De Anima i, 3. Therefore passion is not in the soul.

Obj. 3: Further, passion is the road to corruption; since "every passion, when increased, alters the substance," as is stated in *Topic.* vi, 6. But the soul is incorruptible. Therefore no passion is in the soul.

*On the contrary,* The Apostle says (Rom. 7:5): "When we were in the flesh, the passions of sins which were by the law, did the work in our members." Now sins are, properly speaking, in the soul. Therefore passions also, which are described as being "of sins," are in the soul.

*I answer that,* The word "passive" is used in three ways. First, in a general way, according as whatever receives something is passive, although nothing is taken from it: thus we may say that the air is passive when it is lit up. But this is to be perfected rather than to be passive. Secondly, the word "passive" is employed in its proper sense, when something is received, while something else is taken away: and this happens in two ways. For sometimes that which is lost is unsuitable to the thing: thus when an animal's body is healed, and loses sickness. At other times the contrary occurs: thus to ail is to be passive; because the ailment is received and health is lost. And here we have passion in its most proper acceptation. For a thing is said to be passive from its being drawn to the agent: and when a thing recedes from what is suitable to it, then especially does it appear to be drawn to something else. Moreover in *De Generat.* i, 3 it is stated that when a more excellent thing is generated from a less excellent, we have generation simply, and corruption in a particular respect: whereas the reverse is the case, when from a more excellent thing, a less excellent is generated. In these three ways it happens that passions are in the soul. For in the sense of mere reception, we speak of "feeling and understanding as being a kind of passion" (De Anima i, 5). But passion, accompanied by the loss of something, is only in respect of a bodily transmutation; wherefore passion properly so called cannot be in the soul, save accidentally, in so far, to wit, as the *composite* is passive. But here again we find a difference; because when this transmutation is for the worse, it has more of the nature of a passion, than when it is for the better: hence sorrow is more properly a passion than joy.

Reply Obj. 1: It belongs to matter to be passive in such a way as to lose something and to be transmuted: hence this happens only in those things that are composed of matter and form. But passivity, as implying mere reception, need not be in matter, but can be in anything that is in potentiality. Now, though the soul is not composed of matter and form, yet it has something of potentiality, in respect of which it is competent to receive or to be passive, according as the act of understanding is a kind of passion, as stated in *De Anima* iii, 4.

Reply Obj. 2: Although it does not belong to the soul in itself to be passive and to be moved, yet it belongs accidentally as stated in *De Anima* i, 3.

Reply Obj. 3: This argument is true of passion accompanied by transmutation to something worse. And passion, in this sense, is not found in the soul, except accidentally: but the composite, which is corruptible, admits of it by reason of its own nature.

SECOND ARTICLE [I-II, Q. 22, Art. 2]

Whether Passion Is in the Appetitive Rather Than in the Apprehensive Part?

Objection 1: It would seem that passion is in the apprehensive part of the soul rather than in the appetitive. Because that which is first in any genus, seems to rank first among all things that are in that genus, and to be their cause, as is stated in *Metaph.* ii, 1. Now passion is found to be in the apprehensive, before being in the appetitive part: for the appetitive part is not affected unless there be a previous passion in the apprehensive part. Therefore passion is in the apprehensive part more than in the appetitive.

Obj. 2: Further, what is more active is less passive; for action is contrary to passion. Now the appetitive part is more active than the apprehensive part. Therefore it seems that passion is more in the apprehensive part.

Obj. 3: Further, just as the sensitive appetite is the power of a corporeal organ, so is the power of sensitive apprehension. But passion in the soul occurs, properly speaking, in respect of a bodily transmutation. Therefore passion is not more in the sensitive appetitive than in the sensitive apprehensive part.

*On the contrary,* Augustine says (De Civ. Dei ix, 4) that "the movement of the soul, which the Greeks called *pathe* , are styled by some of our writers, Cicero [*"Those things which the Greeks call *pathe* , we prefer to call disturbances rather than diseases" (Tusc. iv. 5)] for instance, disturbances; by some, affections or emotions; while others rendering the Greek more accurately, call them passions." From this it is evident that the passions of the soul are the same as affections. But affections manifestly belong to the appetitive, and not to the apprehensive part. Therefore the passions are in the appetitive rather than in the apprehensive part.

*I answer that,* As we have already stated (A. 1) the word "passion" implies that the patient is drawn to that which belongs to the agent. Now the soul is drawn to a thing by the appetitive power rather than by the apprehensive power: because the soul has, through its appetitive power, an order to things as they are in themselves: hence the Philosopher says (Metaph. vi, 4) that "good and evil," i.e. the objects of the appetitive power, "are in things themselves." On the other hand the apprehensive power is not drawn to a thing, as it is in itself; but knows it by reason of an "intention" of the thing, which "intention" it has in itself, or receives in its own way. Hence we find it stated (Metaph. vi, 4) that "the true and the false," which pertain to knowledge, "are not in things, but in the mind." Consequently it is evident that the nature of passion is consistent with the appetitive, rather than with the apprehensive part.

Reply Obj. 1: In things relating to perfection the case is the opposite, in comparison to things that pertain to defect. Because in things relating to perfection, intensity is in proportion to the approach to one first principle; to which the nearer a thing approaches, the more intense it is. Thus the intensity of a thing possessed of light depends on its approach to something endowed with light in a supreme degree, to which the nearer a thing approaches the more light it possesses. But in things that relate to defect, intensity depends, not on approach to something supreme, but [o]n receding from that which is perfect; because therein consists the very notion of privation and defect. Wherefore the less a thing recedes from that which stands first, the less intense it is: and the result is that at first we always find some small defect, which afterwards increases as it goes on. Now passion pertains to defect, because it belongs to a thing according as it is in potentiality. Wherefore in those things that approach to the Supreme Perfection, i.e. to God, there is but little potentiality and passion: while in other things, consequently, there is more. Hence also, in the supreme, i.e. the apprehensive, power of the soul, passion is found less than in the other powers.

Reply Obj. 2: The appetitive power is said to be more active, because it is, more than the apprehensive power, the principle of the exterior action: and this for the same reason that it is more passive, namely, its being related to things as existing in themselves: since it is through the external action that we come into contact with things.

Reply Obj. 3: As stated in the First Part (Q. 78, A. 3) the organs of the soul can be changed in two ways. First, by a spiritual change, in respect of which the organ receives an "intention" of the object. And this is essential to the act of the sensitive apprehension: thus is the eye changed by the object visible, not by being colored, but by receiving an intention of color. But the organs are receptive of another and natural change, which affects their natural disposition; for instance, when they become hot or cold, or undergo some similar change. And whereas this kind of change is accidental to the act of the sensitive apprehension; for instance, if the eye be wearied through gazing intently at something or be overcome by the intensity of the object: on the other hand, it is essential to the act of the sensitive appetite; wherefore the material element in the definitions of the movements of the appetitive part, is the natural change of the organ; for instance, "anger is" said to be "a kindling of the blood about the heart." Hence it is evident that the notion of passion is more consistent with the act of the sensitive appetite, than with that of the sensitive apprehension, although both are actions of a corporeal organ.

THIRD ARTICLE [I-II, Q. 22, Art. 3]

Whether Passion Is in the Sensitive Appetite Rather Than in the Intellectual Appetite, Which Is Called the Will?

Objection 1: It would seem that passion is not more in the sensitive than in the intellectual appetite. For Dionysius declares (Div. Nom. ii) Hierotheus "to be taught by a kind of yet more Godlike instruction; not only by learning Divine things, but also by suffering ( *patiens* ) them." But the sensitive appetite cannot "suffer" Divine things, since its object is the sensible good. Therefore passion is in the intellectual appetite, just as it is also in the sensitive appetite.

Obj. 2: Further, the more powerful the active force, the more intense the passion. But the object of the intellectual appetite, which is the universal good, is a more powerful active force than the object of the sensitive appetite, which is a particular good. Therefore passion is more consistent with the intellectual than with the sensitive appetite.

Obj. 3: Further, joy and love are said to be passions. But these are to be found in the intellectual and not only in the sensitive appetite: else they would not be ascribed by the Scriptures to God and the angels. Therefore the passions are not more in the sensitive than in the intellectual appetite.

*On the contrary,* Damascene says (De Fide Orth. ii, 22), while describing the animal passions: "Passion is a movement of the sensitive appetite when we imagine good or evil: in other words, passion is a movement of the irrational soul, when we think of good or evil."

*I answer that,* As stated above (A. 1) passion is properly to be found where there is corporeal transmutation. This corporeal transmutation is found in the act of the sensitive appetite, and is not only spiritual, as in the sensitive apprehension, but also natural. Now there is no need for corporeal transmutation in the act of the intellectual appetite: because this appetite is not exercised by means of a corporeal organ. It is therefore evident that passion is more properly in the act of the sensitive appetite, than in that of the intellectual appetite; and this is again evident from the definitions of Damascene quoted above.

Reply Obj. 1: By "suffering" Divine things is meant being well affected towards them, and united to them by love: and this takes place without any alteration in the body.

Reply Obj. 2: Intensity of passion depends not only on the power of the agent, but also on the passibility of the patient: because things that are disposed to passion, suffer much even from petty agents. Therefore although the object of the intellectual appetite has greater activity than the object of the sensitive appetite, yet the sensitive appetite is more passive.

Reply Obj. 3: When love and joy and the like are ascribed to God or the angels, or to man in respect of his intellectual appetite, they signify simple acts of the will having like effects, but without passion. Hence Augustine says (De Civ. Dei ix, 5): "The holy angels feel no anger while they punish ... no fellow-feeling with misery while they relieve the unhappy: and yet ordinary human speech is wont to ascribe to them also these passions by name, because, although they have none of our weakness, their acts bear a certain resemblance to ours."

## QUESTION 23

HOW THE PASSIONS DIFFER FROM ONE ANOTHER (In Four Articles)

We must now consider how the passions differ from one another: and under this head there are four points of inquiry:

(1) Whether the passions of the concupiscible part are different from those of the irascible part?

(2) Whether the contrariety of passions in the irascible part is based on the contrariety of good and evil?

(3) Whether there is any passion that has no contrary?

(4) Whether, in the same power, there are any passions, differing in species, but not contrary to one another?

FIRST ARTICLE [I-II, Q. 23, Art. 1]

Whether the Passions of the Concupiscible Part Are Different from Those of the Irascible Part?

Objection 1: It would seem that the same passions are in the irascible and concupiscible parts. For the Philosopher says (Ethic. ii, 5) that the passions of the soul are those emotions "which are followed by joy or sorrow." But joy and sorrow are in the concupiscible part. Therefore all the passions are in the concupiscible part, and not some in the irascible, others in the concupiscible part.

Obj. 2: Further, on the words of Matt. 13:33, "The kingdom of heaven is like to leaven," etc., Jerome's gloss says: "We should have prudence in the reason; hatred of vice in the irascible faculty; desire of virtue, in the concupiscible part." But hatred is in the concupiscible faculty, as also is love, of which it is the contrary, as is stated in *Topic.* ii, 7. Therefore the same passion is in the concupiscible and irascible faculties.

Obj. 3: Further, passions and actions differ specifically according to their objects. But the objects of the irascible and concupiscible passions are the same, viz. good and evil. Therefore the same passions are in the irascible and concupiscible faculties.

*On the contrary,* The acts of the different powers differ in species; for instance, to see, and to hear. But the irascible and the concupiscible are two powers into which the sensitive appetite is divided, as stated in the First Part (Q. 81, A. 2). Therefore, since the passions are movements of the sensitive appetite, as stated above (Q. 22, A. 3), the passions of the irascible faculty are specifically distinct from those of the concupiscible part.

*I answer that,* The passions of the irascible part differ in species from those of the concupiscible faculty. For since different powers have different objects, as stated in the First Part (Q. 77, A. 3), the passions of different powers must of necessity be referred to different objects. Much more, therefore, do the passions of different faculties differ in species; since a greater difference in the object is required to diversify the species of the powers, than to diversify the species of passions or actions. For just as in the physical order, diversity of genus arises from diversity in the potentiality of matter, while diversity of species arises from diversity of form in the same matter; so in the acts of the soul, those that belong to different powers, differ not only in species but also in genus, while acts and passions regarding different specific objects, included under the one common object of a single power, differ as the species of that genus.

In order, therefore, to discern which passions are in the irascible, and which in the concupiscible, we must take the object of each of these powers. For we have stated in the First Part (Q. 81, A. 2), that the object of the concupiscible power is sensible good or evil, simply apprehended as such, which causes pleasure or pain. But, since the soul must, of necessity, experience difficulty or struggle at times, in acquiring some such good, or in avoiding some such evil, in so far as such good or evil is more than our animal nature can easily acquire or avoid; therefore this very good or evil, inasmuch as it is of an arduous or difficult nature, is the object of the irascible faculty. Therefore whatever passions regard good or evil absolutely, belong to the concupiscible power; for instance, joy, sorrow, love, hatred, and such like: whereas those passions which regard good or bad as arduous, through being difficult to obtain or avoid, belong to the irascible faculty; such are daring, fear, hope and the like.

Reply Obj. 1: As stated in the First Part (Q. 81, A. 2), the irascible faculty is bestowed on animals, in order to remove the obstacles that hinder the concupiscible power from tending towards its object, either by making some good difficult to obtain, or by making some evil hard to avoid. The result is that all the irascible passions terminate in the concupiscible passions: and thus it is that even the passions which are in the irascible faculty are followed by joy and sadness which are in the concupiscible faculty.

Reply Obj. 2: Jerome ascribes hatred of vice to the irascible faculty, not by reason of hatred, which is properly a concupiscible passion; but on account of the struggle, which belongs to the irascible power.

Reply Obj. 3: Good, inasmuch as it is delightful, moves the concupiscible power. But if it prove difficult to obtain, from this very fact it has a certain contrariety to the concupiscible power: and hence the need of another power tending to that good. The same applies to evil. And this power is the irascible faculty. Consequently the concupiscible passions are specifically different from the irascible passions.

SECOND ARTICLE [I-II, Q. 23, Art. 2]

Whether the Contrariety of the Irascible Passions Is Based on the Contrariety of Good and Evil?

Objection 1: It would seem that the contrariety of the irascible passions is based on no other contrariety than that of good and evil. For the irascible passions are ordained to the concupiscible passions, as stated above (A. 1, ad 1). But the contrariety of the concupiscible passions is no other than that of good and evil; take, for instance, love and hatred, joy and sorrow. Therefore the same applies to the irascible passions.

Obj. 2: Further, passions differ according to their objects; just as movements differ according to their termini. But there is no other contrariety of movements, except that of the termini, as is stated in *Phys.* v, 3. Therefore there is no other contrariety of passions, save that of the objects. Now the object of the appetite is good or evil. Therefore in no appetitive power can there be contrariety of passions other than that of good and evil.

Obj. 3: Further, "every passion of the soul is by way of approach and withdrawal," as Avicenna declares in his sixth book of *Physics.* Now approach results from the apprehension of good; withdrawal, from the apprehension of evil: since just as "good is what all desire" (Ethic. i, 1), so evil is what all shun. Therefore, in the passions of the soul, there can be no other contrariety than that of good and evil.

*On the contrary,* Fear and daring are contrary to one another, as stated in Ethic. iii, 7. But fear and daring do not differ in respect of good and evil: because each regards some kind of evil. Therefore not every contrariety of the irascible passions is that of good and evil.

*I answer that,* Passion is a kind of movement, as stated in Phys. iii, 3. Therefore contrariety of passions is based on contrariety of movements or changes. Now there is a twofold contrariety in changes and movements, as stated in *Phys.* v, 5. One is according to approach and withdrawal in respect of the same term: and this contrariety belongs properly to changes, i.e. to generation, which is a change *to being,* and to corruption, which is a change from being. The other contrariety is according to opposition of termini, and belongs properly to movements: thus whitening, which is movement from black to white, is contrary to blackening, which is movement from white to black.

Accordingly there is a twofold contrariety in the passions of the soul: one, according to contrariety of objects, i.e. of good and evil; the other, according to approach and withdrawal in respect of the same term. In the concupiscible passions the former contrariety alone is to be found; viz. that which is based on the objects: whereas in the irascible passions, we find both forms of contrariety. The reason of this is that the object of the concupiscible faculty, as stated above (A. 1), is sensible good or evil considered absolutely. Now good, as such, cannot be a term wherefrom, but only a term whereto, since nothing shuns good as such; *on the contrary,* all things desire it. In like manner, nothing desires evil, as such; but all things shun it: wherefore evil cannot have the aspect of a term whereto, but only of a term wherefrom. Accordingly every concupiscible passion in respect of good, tends to it, as love, desire and joy; while every concupiscible passion in respect of evil, tends from it, as hatred, avoidance or dislike, and sorrow. Wherefore, in the concupiscible passions, there can be no contrariety of approach and withdrawal in respect of the same object.

On the other hand, the object of the irascible faculty is sensible good or evil, considered not absolutely, but under the aspect of difficulty or arduousness. Now the good which is difficult or arduous, considered as good, is of such a nature as to produce in us a tendency to it, which tendency pertains to the passion of *hope;* whereas, considered as arduous or difficult, it makes us turn from it; and this pertains to the passion of *despair.* In like manner the arduous evil, considered as an evil, has the aspect of something to be shunned; and this belongs to the passion of *fear:* but it also contains a reason for tending to it, as attempting something arduous, whereby to escape being subject to evil; and this tendency is called *daring.* Consequently, in the irascible passions we find contrariety in respect of good and evil (as between hope and fear): and also contrariety according to approach and withdrawal in respect of the same term (as between daring and fear).

From what has been said the replies to the objections are evident.

THIRD ARTICLE [I-II, Q. 23, Art. 3]

Whether Any Passion of the Soul Has No Contrary?

Objection 1: It would seem that every passion of the soul has a contrary. For every passion of the soul is either in the irascible or in the concupiscible faculty, as stated above (A. 1). But both kinds of passion have their respective modes of contrariety. Therefore every passion of the soul has its contrary.

Obj. 2: Further, every passion of the soul has either good or evil for its object; for these are the common objects of the appetitive part. But a passion having good for its object, is contrary to a passion having evil for its object. Therefore every passion has a contrary.

Obj. 3: Further, every passion of the soul is in respect of approach or withdrawal, as stated above (A. 2). But every approach has a corresponding contrary withdrawal, and vice versa. Therefore every passion of the soul has a contrary.

*On the contrary,* Anger is a passion of the soul. But no passion is set down as being contrary to anger, as stated in Ethic. iv, 5. Therefore not every passion has a contrary.

*I answer that,* The passion of anger is peculiar in this, that it cannot have a contrary, either according to approach and withdrawal, or according to the contrariety of good and evil. For anger is caused by a difficult evil already present: and when such an evil is present, the appetite must needs either succumb, so that it does not go beyond the limits of *sadness,* which is a concupiscible passion; or else it has a movement of attack on the hurtful evil, which movement is that of *anger.* But it cannot have a movement of withdrawal: because the evil is supposed to be already present or past. Thus no passion is contrary to anger according to contrariety of approach and withdrawal.

In like manner neither can there be according to contrariety of good and evil. Because the opposite of present evil is good obtained, which can be no longer have the aspect of arduousness or difficulty. Nor, when once good is obtained, does there remain any other movement, except the appetite's repose in the good obtained; which repose belongs to joy, which is a passion of the concupiscible faculty.

Accordingly no movement of the soul can be contrary to the movement of anger, and nothing else than cessation from its movement is contrary thereto; thus the Philosopher says (Rhet. ii, 3) that "calm is contrary to anger," by opposition not of contrariety but of negation or privation.

From what has been said the replies to the objections are evident.

FOURTH ARTICLE [I-II, Q. 23, Art. 4]

Whether in the Same Power, There Are Any Passions, Specifically Different, but Not Contrary to One Another?

Objection 1: It would seem that there cannot be, in the same power, specifically different passions that are not contrary to one another. For the passions of the soul differ according to their objects. Now the objects of the soul's passions are good and evil; and on this distinction is based the contrariety of the passions. Therefore no passions of the same power, that are not contrary to one another, differ specifically.

Obj. 2: Further, difference of species implies a difference of form. But every difference of form is in respect of some contrariety, as stated in *Metaph.* x, 8. Therefore passions of the same power, that are not contrary to one another, do not differ specifically.

Obj. 3: Further, since every passion of the soul consists in approach or withdrawal in respect of good or evil, it seems that every difference in the passions of the soul must needs arise from the difference of good and evil; or from the difference of approach and withdrawal; or from degrees in approach or withdrawal. Now the first two differences cause contrariety in the passions of the soul, as stated above (A. 2): whereas the third difference does not diversify the species; else the species of the soul's passions would be infinite. Therefore it is not possible for passions of the same power to differ in species, without being contrary to one another.

*On the contrary,* Love and joy differ in species, and are in the concupiscible power; and yet they are not contrary to one another; rather, in fact, one causes the other. Therefore in the same power there are passions that differ in species without being contrary to one another.

*I answer that,* Passions differ in accordance with their active causes, which, in the case of the passions of the soul, are their objects. Now, the difference in active causes may be considered in two ways: first, from the point of view of their species or nature, as fire differs from water; secondly, from the point of view of the difference in their active power. In the passions of the soul we can treat the difference of their active or motive causes in respect of their motive power, as if they were natural agents. For every mover, in a fashion, either draws the patient to itself, or repels it from itself. Now in drawing it to itself, it does three things in the patient. Because, in the first place, it gives the patient an inclination or aptitude to tend to the mover: thus a light body, which is above, bestows lightness on the body generated, so that it has an inclination or aptitude to be above. Secondly, if the generated body be outside its proper place, the mover gives it movement towards that place. Thirdly, it makes it to rest, when it shall have come to its proper place: since to the same cause are due, both rest in a place, and the movement to that place. The same applies to the cause of repulsion.

Now, in the movements of the appetitive faculty, good has, as it were, a force of attraction, while evil has a force of repulsion. In the first place, therefore, good causes, in the appetitive power, a certain inclination, aptitude or connaturalness in respect of good: and this belongs to the passion of *love:* the corresponding contrary of which is *hatred* in respect of evil. Secondly, if the good be not yet possessed, it causes in the appetite a movement towards the attainment of the good beloved: and this belongs to the passion of *desire* or concupiscence: and contrary to it, in respect of evil, is the passion of *aversion* or dislike. Thirdly, when the good is obtained, it causes the appetite to rest, as it were, in the good obtained: and this belongs to the passion of *delight* or joy; the contrary of which, in respect of evil, is *sorrow* or sadness.

On the other hand, in the irascible passions, the aptitude, or inclination to seek good, or to shun evil, is presupposed as arising from the concupiscible faculty, which regards good or evil absolutely. And in respect of good not yet obtained, we have *hope* and despair. In respect of evil not yet present we have *fear* and daring. But in respect of good obtained there is no irascible passion: because it is no longer considered in the light of something arduous, as stated above (A. 3). But evil already present gives rise to the passion of *anger.*

Accordingly it is clear that in the concupiscible faculty there are three couples of passions; viz. love and hatred, desire and aversion, joy and sadness. In like manner there are three groups in the irascible faculty; viz. hope and despair, fear and daring, and anger which has no contrary passion.

Consequently there are altogether eleven passions differing specifically; six in the concupiscible faculty, and five in the irascible; and under these all the passions of the soul are contained.

From this the replies to the objections are evident.

## QUESTION 24

OF GOOD AND EVIL IN THE PASSIONS OF THE SOUL (In Four Articles)

We must now consider good and evil in the passions of the soul: and under this head there are four points of inquiry:

(1) Whether moral good and evil can be found in the passions of the soul?

(2) Whether every passion of the soul is morally evil?

(3) Whether every passion increases or decreases the goodness or malice of an act?

(4) Whether any passion is good or evil specifically?

FIRST ARTICLE [I-II, Q. 24, Art. 1]

Whether Moral Good and Evil Can Be Found in the Passions of the Soul?

Objection 1: It would seem that no passion of the soul is morally good or evil. For moral good and evil are proper to man: since "morals are properly predicated of man," as Ambrose says (Super Luc. Prolog.). But passions are not proper to man, for he has them in common with other animals. Therefore no passion of the soul is morally good or evil.

Obj. 2: Further, the good or evil of man consists in "being in accord, or in disaccord with reason," as Dionysius says (Div. Nom. iv). Now the passions of the soul are not in the reason, but in the sensitive appetite, as stated above (Q. 22, A. 3). Therefore they have no connection with human, i.e. moral, good or evil.

Obj. 3: Further, the Philosopher says (Ethic. ii, 5) that "we are neither praised nor blamed for our passions." But we are praised and blamed for moral good and evil. Therefore the passions are not morally good or evil.

*On the contrary,* Augustine says (De Civ. Dei xiv, 7) while speaking of the passions of the soul: "They are evil if our love is evil; good if our love is good."

*I answer that,* We may consider the passions of the soul in two ways: first, in themselves; secondly, as being subject to the command of the reason and will. If then the passions be considered in themselves, to wit, as movements of the irrational appetite, thus there is no moral good or evil in them, since this depends on the reason, as stated above (Q. 18, A. 5). If, however, they be considered as subject to the command of the reason and will, then moral good and evil are in them. Because the sensitive appetite is nearer than the outward members to the reason and will; and yet the movements and actions of the outward members are morally good or evil, inasmuch as they are voluntary. Much more, therefore, may the passions, in so far as they are voluntary, be called morally good or evil. And they are said to be voluntary, either from being commanded by the will, or from not being checked by the will.

Reply Obj. 1: These passions, considered in themselves, are common to man and other animals: but, as commanded by the reason, they are proper to man.

Reply Obj. 2: Even the lower appetitive powers are called rational, in so far as "they partake of reason in some sort" (Ethic. i, 13).

Reply Obj. 3: The Philosopher says that we are neither praised nor blamed for our passions considered absolutely; but he does not exclude their becoming worthy of praise or blame, in so far as they are subordinate to reason. Hence he continues: "For the man who fears or is angry, is not praised ... or blamed, but the man who is angry in a certain way, i.e. according to, or against reason."

SECOND ARTICLE [I-II, Q. 24, Art. 2]

Whether Every Passion of the Soul Is Evil Morally?

Objection 1: It would seem that all the passions of the soul are morally evil. For Augustine says (De Civ. Dei ix, 4) that "some call the soul's passions diseases or disturbances of the soul" [*Cf. Q. 22, A. 2, footnote]. But every disease or disturbance of the soul is morally evil. Therefore every passion of the soul is evil morally.

Obj. 2: Further, Damascene says (De Fide Orth. ii, 22) that "movement in accord with nature is an action, but movement contrary to nature is passion." But in movements of the soul, what is against nature is sinful and morally evil: hence he says elsewhere (De Fide Orth. ii, 4) that "the devil turned from that which is in accord with nature to that which is against nature." Therefore these passions are morally evil.

Obj. 3: Further, whatever leads to sin, has an aspect of evil. But these passions lead to sin: wherefore they are called "the passions of sins" (Rom. 7:5). Therefore it seems that they are morally evil.

*On the contrary,* Augustine says (De Civ. Dei xiv, 9) that "all these emotions are right in those whose love is rightly placed ... For they fear to sin, they desire to persevere; they grieve for sin, they rejoice in good works."

*I answer that,* On this question the opinion of the Stoics differed from that of the Peripatetics: for the Stoics held that all passions are evil, while the Peripatetics maintained that moderate passions are good. This difference, although it appears great in words, is nevertheless, in reality, none at all, or but little, if we consider the intent of either school. For the Stoics did not discern between sense and intellect; and consequently neither between the intellectual and sensitive appetite. Hence they did not discriminate the passions of the soul from the movements of the will, in so far as the passions of the soul are in the sensitive appetite, while the simple movements of the will are in the intellectual appetite: but every rational movement of the appetitive part they call will, while they called passion, a movement that exceeds the limits of reason. Wherefore Cicero, following their opinion (De Tusc. Quaest. iii, 4) calls all passions "diseases of the soul": whence he argues that "those who are diseased are unsound; and those who are unsound are wanting in sense." Hence we speak of those who are wanting in sense of being "unsound."

On the other hand, the Peripatetics give the name of "passions" to all the movements of the sensitive appetite. Wherefore they esteem them good, when they are controlled by reason; and evil when they are not controlled by reason. Hence it is evident that Cicero was wrong in disapproving (De Tusc. Quaest. iii, 4) of the Peripatetic theory of a mean in the passions, when he says that "every evil, though moderate, should be shunned; for, just as a body, though it be moderately ailing, is not sound; so, this mean in the diseases or passions of the soul, is not sound." For passions are not called "diseases" or "disturbances" of the soul, save when they are not controlled by reason.

Hence the reply to the First Objection is evident.

Reply Obj. 2: In every passion there is an increase or decrease in the natural movement of the heart, according as the heart is moved more or less intensely by contraction and dilatation; and hence it derives the character of passion. But there is no need for passion to deviate always from the order of natural reason.

Reply Obj. 3: The passions of the soul, in so far as they are contrary to the order of reason, incline us to sin: but in so far as they are controlled by reason, they pertain to virtue.

THIRD ARTICLE [I-II, Q. 24, Art. 3]

Whether Passion Increases or Decreases the Goodness or Malice of an Act?

Objection 1: It would seem that every passion decreases the goodness of a moral action. For anything that hinders the judgment of reason, on which depends the goodness of a moral act, consequently decreases the goodness of the moral act. But every passion hinders the judgment of reason: for Sallust says (Catilin.): "All those that take counsel about matters of doubt, should be free from hatred, anger, friendship and pity." Therefore passion decreases the goodness of a moral act.

Obj. 2: Further, the more a man's action is like to God, the better it is: hence the Apostle says (Eph. 5:1): "Be ye followers of God, as most dear children." But "God and the holy angels feel no anger when they punish ... no fellow-feeling with misery when they relieve the unhappy," as Augustine says (De Civ. Dei ix, 5). Therefore it is better to do such like deeds without than with a passion of the soul.

Obj. 3: Further, just as moral evil depends on its relation to reason, so also does moral good. But moral evil is lessened by passion: for he sins less, who sins from passion, than he who sins deliberately. Therefore he does a better deed, who does well without passion, than he who does with passion.

*On the contrary,* Augustine says (De Civ. Dei ix, 5) that "the passion of pity is obedient to reason, when pity is bestowed without violating right, as when the poor are relieved, or the penitent forgiven." But nothing that is obedient to reason lessens the moral good. Therefore a passion of the soul does not lessen moral good.

*I answer that,* As the Stoics held that every passion of the soul is evil, they consequently held that every passion of the soul lessens the goodness of an act; since the admixture of evil either destroys good altogether, or makes it to be less good. And this is true indeed, if by passions we understand none but the inordinate movements of the sensitive appetite, considered as disturbances or ailments. But if we give the name of passions to all the movements of the sensitive appetite, then it belongs to the perfection of man's good that his passions be moderated by reason. For since man's good is founded on reason as its root, that good will be all the more perfect, according as it extends to more things pertaining to man. Wherefore no one questions the fact that it belongs to the perfection of moral good, that the actions of the outward members be controlled by the law of reason. Hence, since the sensitive appetite can obey reason, as stated above (Q. 17, A. 7), it belongs to the perfection of moral or human good, that the passions themselves also should be controlled by reason.

Accordingly just as it is better that man should both will good and do it in his external act; so also does it belong to the perfection of moral good, that man should be moved unto good, not only in respect of his will, but also in respect of his sensitive appetite; according to Ps. 83:3: "My heart and my flesh have rejoiced in the living God": where by "heart" we are to understand the intellectual appetite, and by "flesh" the sensitive appetite.

Reply Obj. 1: The passions of the soul may stand in a twofold relation to the judgment of reason. First, antecedently: and thus, since they obscure the judgment of reason, on which the goodness of the moral act depends, they diminish the goodness of the act; for it is more praiseworthy to do a work of charity from the judgment of reason than from the mere passion of pity. In the second place, consequently: and this in two ways. First, by way of redundance: because, to wit, when the higher part of the soul is intensely moved to anything, the lower part also follows that movement: and thus the passion that results in consequence, in the sensitive appetite, is a sign of the intensity of the will, and so indicates greater moral goodness. Secondly, by way of choice; when, to wit, a man, by the judgment of his reason, chooses to be affected by a passion in order to work more promptly with the co-operation of the sensitive appetite. And thus a passion of the soul increases the goodness of an action.

Reply Obj. 2: In God and the angels there is no sensitive appetite, nor again bodily members: and so in them good does not depend on the right ordering of passions or of bodily actions, as it does in us.

Reply Obj. 3: A passion that tends to evil, and precedes the judgment of reason, diminishes sin; but if it be consequent in either of the ways mentioned above (Reply Obj. 1), it aggravates the sin, or else it is a sign of its being more grievous.

FOURTH ARTICLE [I-II, Q. 24, Art. 4]

Whether Any Passion Is Good or Evil in Its Species?

Objection 1: It would seem that no passion of the soul is good or evil morally according to its species. Because moral good and evil depend on reason. But the passions are in the sensitive appetite; so that accordance with reason is accidental to them. Since, therefore, nothing accidental belongs to a thing's species, it seems that no passion is good or evil according to its species.

Obj. 2: Further, acts and passions take their species from their object. If, therefore, any passion were good or evil, according to its species, it would follow that those passions the object of which is good, are specifically good, such as love, desire and joy: and that those passions, the object of which is evil, are specifically evil, as hatred, fear and sadness. But this is clearly false. Therefore no passion is good or evil according to its species.

Obj. 3: Further, there is no species of passion that is not to be found in other animals. But moral good is in man alone. Therefore no passion of the soul is good or evil according to its species.

*On the contrary,* Augustine says (De Civ. Dei ix, 5) that "pity is a kind of virtue." Moreover, the Philosopher says (Ethic. ii, 7) that modesty is a praiseworthy passion. Therefore some passions are good or evil according to their species.

*I answer that,* We ought, seemingly, to apply to passions what has been said in regard to acts (Q. 18, AA. 5, 6; Q. 20, A. 1)—viz. that the species of a passion, as the species of an act, can be considered from two points of view. First, according to its natural genus; and thus moral good and evil have no connection with the species of an act or passion. Secondly, according to its moral genus, inasmuch as it is voluntary and controlled by reason. In this way moral good and evil can belong to the species of a passion, in so far as the object to which a passion tends, is, of itself, in harmony or in discord with reason: as is clear in the case of *shame* which is base fear; and of *envy* which is sorrow for another's good: for thus passions belong to the same species as the external act.

Reply Obj. 1: This argument considers the passions in their natural species, in so far as the sensitive appetite is considered in itself. But in so far as the sensitive appetite obeys reason, good and evil of reason are no longer accidentally in the passions of the appetite, but essentially.

Reply Obj. 2: Passions having a tendency to good, are themselves good, if they tend to that which is truly good, and in like manner, if they turn away from that which is truly evil. On the other hand, those passions which consist in aversion from good, and a tendency to evil, are themselves evil.

Reply Obj. 3: In irrational animals the sensitive appetite does not obey reason. Nevertheless, in so far as they are led by a kind of estimative power, which is subject to a higher, i.e. the Divine reason, there is a certain likeness of moral good in them, in regard to the soul's passions.

## QUESTION 25

OF THE ORDER OF THE PASSIONS TO ONE ANOTHER (In Four Articles)

We must now consider the order of the passions to one another: and under this head there are four points of inquiry:

(1) The relation of the irascible passions to the concupiscible passions;

(2) The relation of the concupiscible passions to one another;

(3) The relation of the irascible passions to one another;

(4) The four principal passions.

FIRST ARTICLE [I-II, Q. 25, Art. 1]

Whether the Irascible Passions Precede the Concupiscible Passions, or Vice Versa?

Objection 1: It would seem that the irascible passions precede the concupiscible passions. For the order of the passions is that of their objects. But the object of the irascible faculty is the difficult good, which seems to be the highest good. Therefore the irascible passions seem to precede the concupiscible passions.

Obj. 2: Further, the mover precedes that which is moved. But the irascible faculty is compared to the concupiscible, as mover to that which is moved: since it is given to animals, for the purpose of removing the obstacles that hinder the concupiscible faculty from enjoying its object, as stated above (Q. 23, A. 1, ad 1; I, Q. 81, A. 2). Now "that which removes an obstacle, is a kind of mover" (Phys. viii, 4). Therefore the irascible passions precede the concupiscible passions.

Obj. 3: Further, joy and sadness are concupiscible passions. But joy and sadness succeed to the irascible passions: for the Philosopher says (Ethic. iv, 5) that "retaliation causes anger to cease, because it produces pleasure instead of the previous pain." Therefore the concupiscible passions follow the irascible passions.

*On the contrary,* The concupiscible passions regard the absolute good, while the irascible passions regard a restricted, viz. the difficult, good. Since, therefore, the absolute good precedes the restricted good, it seems that the concupiscible passions precede the irascible.

*I answer that,* In the concupiscible passions there is more diversity than in the passions of the irascible faculty. For in the former we find something relating to movement—e.g. desire; and something belonging to repose, e.g. joy and sadness. But in the irascible passions there is nothing pertaining to repose, and only that which belongs to movement. The reason of this is that when we find rest in a thing, we no longer look upon it as something difficult or arduous; whereas such is the object of the irascible faculty.

Now since rest is the end of movement, it is first in the order of intention, but last in the order of execution. If, therefore, we compare the passions of the irascible faculty with those concupiscible passions that denote rest in good, it is evident that in the order of execution, the irascible passions take precedence of such like passions of the concupiscible faculty: thus hope precedes joy, and hence causes it, according to the Apostle (Rom. 12:12): "Rejoicing in hope." But the concupiscible passion which denotes rest in evil, viz. sadness, comes between two irascible passions: because it follows fear; since we become sad when we are confronted by the evil that we feared: while it precedes the movement of anger; since the movement of self-vindication, that results from sadness, is the movement of anger. And because it is looked upon as a good thing to pay back the evil done to us; when the angry man has achieved this he rejoices. Thus it is evident that every passion of the irascible faculty terminates in a concupiscible passion denoting rest, viz. either in joy or in sadness.

But if we compare the irascible passions to those concupiscible passions that denote movement, then it is clear that the latter take precedence: because the passions of the irascible faculty add something to those of the concupiscible faculty; just as the object of the irascible adds the aspect of arduousness or difficulty to the object of the concupiscible faculty. Thus hope adds to desire a certain effort, and a certain raising of the spirits to the realization of the arduous good. In like manner fear adds to aversion or detestation a certain lowness of spirits, on account of difficulty in shunning the evil.

Accordingly the passions of the irascible faculty stand between those concupiscible passions that denote movement towards good or evil, and those concupiscible passions that denote rest in good or evil. And it is therefore evident that the irascible passions both arise from and terminate in the passions of the concupiscible faculty.

Reply Obj. 1: This argument would prove, if the formal object of the concupiscible faculty were something contrary to the arduous, just as the formal object of the irascible faculty is that which is arduous. But because the object of the concupiscible faculty is good absolutely, it naturally precedes the object of the irascible, as the common precedes the proper.

Reply Obj. 2: The remover of an obstacle is not a direct but an accidental mover: and here we are speaking of passions as directly related to one another. Moreover, the irascible passion removes the obstacle that hinders the concupiscible from resting in its object. Wherefore it only follows that the irascible passions precede those concupiscible passions that connote rest. The third objection leads to the same conclusion.

SECOND ARTICLE [I-II, Q. 25, Art. 2]

Whether Love Is the First of the Concupiscible Passions?

Objection 1: It would seem that love is not the first of the concupiscible passions. For the concupiscible faculty is so called from concupiscence, which is the same passion as desire. But "things are named from their chief characteristic" (De Anima ii, 4). Therefore desire takes precedence of love.

Obj. 2: Further, love implies a certain union; since it is a "uniting and binding force," as Dionysius says (Div. Nom. iv). But concupiscence or desire is a movement towards union with the thing coveted or desired. Therefore desire precedes love.

Obj. 3: Further, the cause precedes its effect. But pleasure is sometimes the cause of love: since some love on account of pleasure (Ethic. viii, 3, 4). Therefore pleasure precedes love; and consequently love is not the first of the concupiscible passions.

*On the contrary,* Augustine says (De Civ. Dei xiv, 7, 9) that all the passions are caused by love: since "love yearning for the beloved object, is desire; and, having and enjoying it, is joy." Therefore love is the first of the concupiscible passions.

*I answer that,* Good and evil are the object of the concupiscible faculty. Now good naturally precedes evil; since evil is privation of good. Wherefore all the passions, the object of which is good, are naturally before those, the object of which is evil—that is to say, each precedes its contrary passion: because the quest of a good is the reason for shunning the opposite evil.

Now good has the aspect of an end, and the end is indeed first in the order of intention, but last in the order of execution. Consequently the order of the concupiscible passions can be considered either in the order of intention or in the order of execution. In the order of execution, the first place belongs to that which takes place first in the thing that tends to the end. Now it is evident that whatever tends to an end, has, in the first place, an aptitude or proportion to that end, for nothing tends to a disproportionate end; secondly, it is moved to that end; thirdly, it rests in the end, after having attained it. And this very aptitude or proportion of the appetite to good is love, which is complacency in good; while movement towards good is desire or concupiscence; and rest in good is joy or pleasure. Accordingly in this order, love precedes desire, and desire precedes pleasure. But in the order of intention, it is the reverse: because the pleasure intended causes desire and love. For pleasure is the enjoyment of the good, which enjoyment is, in a way, the end, just as the good itself is, as stated above (Q. 11, A. 3, ad 3).

Reply Obj. 1: We name a thing as we understand it, for "words are signs of thoughts," as the Philosopher states (Peri Herm. i, 1). Now in most cases we know a cause by its effect. But the effect of love, when the beloved object is possessed, is pleasure: when it is not possessed, it is desire or concupiscence: and, as Augustine says (De Trin. x, 12), "we are more sensible to love, when we lack that which we love." Consequently of all the concupiscible passions, concupiscence is felt most; and for this reason the power is named after it.

Reply Obj. 2: The union of lover and beloved is twofold. There is real union, consisting in the conjunction of one with the other. This union belongs to joy or pleasure, which follows desire. There is also an affective union, consisting in an aptitude or proportion, in so far as one thing, from the very fact of its having an aptitude for and an inclination to another, partakes of it: and love betokens such a union. This union precedes the movement of desire.

Reply Obj. 3: Pleasure causes love, in so far as it precedes love in the order of intention.

THIRD ARTICLE [I-II, Q. 25, Art. 3]

Whether Hope Is the First of the Irascible Passions?

Objection 1: It would seem that hope is not the first of the irascible passions. Because the irascible faculty is denominated from anger. Since, therefore, "things are names from their chief characteristic" (cf. A. 2, Obj. 1), it seems that anger precedes and surpasses hope.

Obj. 2: Further, the object of the irascible faculty is something arduous. Now it seems more arduous to strive to overcome a contrary evil that threatens soon to overtake us, which pertains to daring; or an evil actually present, which pertains to anger; than to strive simply to obtain some good. Again, it seems more arduous to strive to overcome a present evil, than a future evil. Therefore anger seems to be a stronger passion than daring, and daring, than hope. And consequently it seems that hope does not precede them.

Obj. 3: Further, when a thing is moved towards an end, the movement of withdrawal precedes the movement of approach. But fear and despair imply withdrawal from something; while daring and hope imply approach towards something. Therefore fear and despair precede hope and daring.

*On the contrary,* The nearer a thing is to the first, the more it precedes others. But hope is nearer to love, which is the first of the passions. Therefore hope is the first of the passions in the irascible faculty.

*I answer that,* As stated above (A. 1) all irascible passions imply movement towards something. Now this movement of the irascible faculty towards something may be due to two causes: one is the mere aptitude or proportion to the end; and this pertains to love or hatred; [the other is the presence of good or evil itself,] and this belongs to sadness or joy. As a matter of fact, the presence of good produces no passion in the irascible, as stated above (Q. 23, AA. 3, 4); but the presence of evil gives rise to the passion of anger.

Since then in the order of generation or execution, proportion or aptitude to the end precedes the achievement of the end; it follows that, of all the irascible passions, anger is the last in the order of generation. And among the other passions of the irascible faculty, which imply a movement arising from love of good or hatred of evil, those whose object is good, viz. hope and despair, must naturally precede those whose object is evil, viz. daring and fear: yet so that hope precedes despair; since hope is a movement towards good as such, which is essentially attractive, so that hope tends to good directly; whereas despair is a movement away from good, a movement which is consistent with good, not as such, but in respect of something else, wherefore its tendency from good is accidental, as it were. In like manner fear, through being a movement from evil, precedes daring. And that hope and despair naturally precede fear and daring is evident from this—that as the desire of good is the reason for avoiding evil, so hope and despair are the reason for fear and daring: because daring arises from the hope of victory, and fear arises from the despair of overcoming. Lastly, anger arises from daring: for no one is angry while seeking vengeance, unless he dare to avenge himself, as Avicenna observes in the sixth book of his *Physics.* Accordingly, it is evident that hope is the first of all the irascible passions.

And if we wish to know the order of all the passions in the way of generation, love and hatred are first; desire and aversion, second; hope and despair, third; fear and daring, fourth; anger, fifth; sixth and last, joy and sadness, which follow from all the passions, as stated in *Ethic.* ii, 5: yet so that love precedes hatred; desire precedes aversion; hope precedes despair; fear precedes daring; and joy precedes sadness, as may be gathered from what has been stated above.

Reply Obj. 1: Because anger arises from the other passions, as an effect from the causes that precede it, it is from anger, as being more manifest than the other passions, that the power takes its name.

Reply Obj. 2: It is not the arduousness but the good that is the reason for approach or desire. Consequently hope, which regards good more directly, takes precedence: although at times daring or even anger regards something more arduous.

Reply Obj. 3: The movement of the appetite is essentially and directly towards the good as towards its proper object; its movement from evil results from this. For the movement of the appetitive part is in proportion, not to natural movement, but to the intention of nature, which intends the end before intending the removal of a contrary, which removal is desired only for the sake of obtaining the end.

FOURTH ARTICLE [I-II, Q. 25, Art. 4]

Whether These Are the Four Principal Passions: Joy, Sadness, Hope and Fear?

Objection 1: It would seem that joy, sadness, hope and fear are not the four principal passions. For Augustine (De Civ. Dei xiv, 3, 7 sqq.) omits hope and puts desire in its place.

Obj. 2: Further, there is a twofold order in the passions of the soul: the order of intention, and the order of execution or generation. The principal passions should therefore be taken, either in the order of intention; and thus joy and sadness, which are the final passions, will be the principal passions; or in the order of execution or generation, and thus love will be the principal passion. Therefore joy and sadness, hope and fear should in no way be called the four principal passions.

Obj. 3: Further, just as daring is caused by hope, so fear is caused by despair. Either, therefore, hope and despair should be reckoned as principal passions, since they cause others: or hope and daring, from being akin to one another.

*On the contrary,* Boethius (De Consol. i) in enumerating the four principal passions, says:

"Banish joys: banish fears: Away with hope: away with tears."

*I answer that,* These four are commonly called the principal passions. Two of them, viz. joy and sadness, are said to be principal because in them all the other passions have their completion and end; wherefore they arise from all the other passions, as is stated in *Ethic.* ii, 5. Fear and hope are principal passions, not because they complete the others simply, but because they complete them as regards the movement of the appetite towards something: for in respect of good, movement begins in love, goes forward to desire, and ends in hope; while in respect of evil, it begins in hatred, goes on to aversion, and ends in fear. Hence it is customary to distinguish these four passions in relation to the present and the future: for movement regards the future, while rest is in something present: so that joy relates to present good, sadness relates to present evil; hope regards future good, and fear, future evil.

As to the other passions that regard good or evil, present or future, they all culminate in these four. For this reason some have said that these four are the principal passions, because they are general passions; and this is true, provided that by hope and fear we understand the appetite's common tendency to desire or shun something.

Reply Obj. 1: Augustine puts desire or covetousness in place of hope, in so far as they seem to regard the same object, viz. some future good.

Reply Obj. 2: These are called principal passions, in the order of intention and completion. And though fear and hope are not the last passions simply, yet they are the last of those passions that tend towards something as future. Nor can the argument be pressed any further except in the case of anger: yet neither can anger be reckoned a principal passion, because it is an effect of daring, which cannot be a principal passion, as we shall state further on (Reply Obj. 3).

Reply Obj. 3: Despair implies movement away from good; and this is, as it were, accidental: and daring implies movement towards evil; and this too is accidental. Consequently these cannot be principal passions; because that which is accidental cannot be said to be principal. And so neither can anger be called a principal passion, because it arises from daring.

## QUESTION 26

OF THE PASSIONS OF THE SOUL IN PARTICULAR: AND FIRST, OF LOVE (In Four Articles)

We have now to consider the soul's passions in particular, and (1) the passions of the concupiscible faculty; (2) the passions of the irascible faculty.

The first of these considerations will be threefold: since we shall consider (1) Love and hatred; (2) Desire and aversion; (3) Pleasure and sadness.

Concerning love, three points must be considered: (1) Love itself; (2) The cause of love; (3) The effects of love. Under the first head there are four points of inquiry:

(1) Whether love is in the concupiscible power?

(2) Whether love is a passion?

(3) Whether love is the same as dilection?

(4) Whether love is properly divided into love of friendship, and love of concupiscence?

FIRST ARTICLE [I-II, Q. 26, Art. 1]

Whether Love Is in the Concupiscible Power?

Objection 1: It would seem that love is not in the concupiscible power. For it is written (Wis. 8:2): "Her," namely wisdom, "have I loved, and have sought her out from my youth." But the concupiscible power, being a part of the sensitive appetite, cannot tend to wisdom, which is not apprehended by the senses. Therefore love is not in the concupiscible power.

Obj. 2: Further, love seems to be identified with every passion: for Augustine says (De Civ. Dei xiv, 7): "Love, yearning for the object beloved, is desire; having and enjoying it, is joy; fleeing what is contrary to it, is fear; and feeling what is contrary to it, is sadness." But not every passion is in the concupiscible power; indeed, fear, which is mentioned in this passage, is in the irascible power. Therefore we must not say absolutely that love is in the concupiscible power.

Obj. 3: Further, Dionysius (Div. Nom. iv) mentions a "natural love." But natural love seems to pertain rather to the natural powers, which belong to the vegetal soul. Therefore love is not simply in the concupiscible power.

*On the contrary,* The Philosopher says (Topic. ii, 7) that "love is in the concupiscible power."

*I answer that,* Love is something pertaining to the appetite; since good is the object of both. Wherefore love differs according to the difference of appetites. For there is an appetite which arises from an apprehension existing, not in the subject of the appetite, but in some other: and this is called the *natural appetite.* Because natural things seek what is suitable to them according to their nature, by reason of an apprehension which is not in them, but in the Author of their nature, as stated in the First Part (Q. 6, A. 1, ad 2; Q. 103, A. 1, ad 1, 3). And there is another appetite arising from an apprehension in the subject of the appetite, but from necessity and not from free-will. Such is, in irrational animals, the *sensitive appetite,* which, however, in man, has a certain share of liberty, in so far as it obeys reason. Again, there is another appetite following freely from an apprehension in the subject of the appetite. And this is the rational or intellectual appetite, which is called the *will.*

Now in each of these appetites, the name "love" is given to the principle of movement towards the end loved. In the natural appetite the principle of this movement is the appetitive subject's connaturalness with the thing to which it tends, and may be called "natural love": thus the connaturalness of a heavy body for the centre, is by reason of its weight and may be called "natural love." In like manner the aptitude of the sensitive appetite or of the will to some good, that is to say, its very complacency in good is called "sensitive love," or "intellectual" or "rational love." So that sensitive love is in the sensitive appetite, just as intellectual love is in the intellectual appetite. And it belongs to the concupiscible power, because it regards good absolutely, and not under the aspect of difficulty, which is the object of the irascible faculty.

Reply Obj. 1: The words quoted refer to intellectual or rational love.

Reply Obj. 2: Love is spoken of as being fear, joy, desire and sadness, not essentially but causally.

Reply Obj. 3: Natural love is not only in the powers of the vegetal soul, but in all the soul's powers, and also in all the parts of the body, and universally in all things: because, as Dionysius says (Div. Nom. iv), "Beauty and goodness are beloved by all things"; since each single thing has a connaturalness with that which is naturally suitable to it.

SECOND ARTICLE [I-II, Q. 26, Art. 2]

Whether Love Is a Passion?

Objection 1: It would seem that love is not a passion. For no power is a passion. But every love is a power, as Dionysius says (Div. Nom. iv). Therefore love is not a passion.

Obj. 2: Further, love is a kind of union or bond, as Augustine says (De Trin. viii, 10). But a union or bond is not a passion, but rather a relation. Therefore love is not a passion.

Obj. 3: Further, Damascene says (De Fide Orth. ii, 22) that passion is a movement. But love does not imply the movement of the appetite; for this is desire, of which movement love is the principle. Therefore love is not a passion.

*On the contrary,* The Philosopher says (Ethic. viii, 5) that "love is a passion."

*I answer that,* Passion is the effect of the agent on the patient. Now a natural agent produces a twofold effect on the patient: for in the first place it gives it the form; and secondly it gives it the movement that results from the form. Thus the generator gives the generated body both weight and the movement resulting from weight: so that weight, from being the principle of movement to the place, which is connatural to that body by reason of its weight, can, in a way, be called "natural love." In the same way the appetible object gives the appetite, first, a certain adaptation to itself, which consists in complacency in that object; and from this follows movement towards the appetible object. For "the appetitive movement is circular," as stated in *De Anima* iii, 10; because the appetible object moves the appetite, introducing itself, as it were, into its intention; while the appetite moves towards the realization of the appetible object, so that the movement ends where it began. Accordingly, the first change wrought in the appetite by the appetible object is called "love," and is nothing else than complacency in that object; and from this complacency results a movement towards that same object, and this movement is "desire"; and lastly, there is rest which is "joy." Since, therefore, love consists in a change wrought in the appetite by the appetible object, it is evident that love is a passion: properly so called, according as it is in the concupiscible faculty; in a wider and extended sense, according as it is in the will.

Reply Obj. 1: Since power denotes a principle of movement or action, Dionysius calls love a power, in so far as it is a principle of movement in the appetite.

Reply Obj. 2: Union belongs to love in so far as by reason of the complacency of the appetite, the lover stands in relation to that which he loves, as though it were himself or part of himself. Hence it is clear that love is not the very relation of union, but that union is a result of love. Hence, too, Dionysius says that "love is a unitive force" (Div. Nom. iv), and the Philosopher says (Polit. ii, 1) that union is the work of love.

Reply Obj. 3: Although love does not denote the movement of the appetite in tending towards the appetible object, yet it denotes that movement whereby the appetite is changed by the appetible object, so as to have complacency therein.

THIRD ARTICLE [I-II, Q. 26, Art. 3]

Whether Love Is the Same As Dilection?

Objection 1: It would seem that love is the same as dilection. For Dionysius says (Div. Nom. iv) that love is to dilection, "as four is to twice two, and as a rectilinear figure is to one composed of straight lines." But these have the same meaning. Therefore love and dilection denote the same thing.

Obj. 2: Further, the movements of the appetite differ by reason of their objects. But the objects of dilection and love are the same. Therefore these are the same.

Obj. 3: Further, if dilection and love differ, it seems that it is chiefly in the fact that "dilection refers to good things, love to evil things, as some have maintained," according to Augustine (De Civ. Dei xiv, 7). But they do not differ thus; because as Augustine says (De Civ. Dei xiv, 7) the holy Scripture uses both words in reference to either good or bad things. Therefore love and dilection do not differ: thus indeed Augustine concludes (De Civ. Dei xiv, 7) that "it is not one thing to speak of love, and another to speak of dilection."

*On the contrary,* Dionysius says (Div. Nom. iv) that "some holy men have held that love means something more Godlike than dilection does."

*I answer that,* We find four words referring in a way, to the same thing: viz. love, dilection, charity and friendship. They differ, however, in this, that "friendship," according to the Philosopher (Ethic. viii, 5), "is like a habit," whereas "love" and "dilection" are expressed by way of act or passion; and "charity" can be taken either way.

Moreover these three express act in different ways. For love has a wider signification than the others, since every dilection or charity is love, but not vice versa. Because dilection implies, in addition to love, a choice ( *electionem* ) made beforehand, as the very word denotes: and therefore dilection is not in the concupiscible power, but only in the will, and only in the rational nature. Charity denotes, in addition to love, a certain perfection of love, in so far as that which is loved is held to be of great price, as the word itself implies [*Referring to the Latin "carus" (dear)].

Reply Obj. 1: Dionysius is speaking of love and dilection, in so far as they are in the intellectual appetite; for thus love is the same as dilection.

Reply Obj. 2: The object of love is more general than the object of dilection: because love extends to more than dilection does, as stated above.

Reply Obj. 3: Love and dilection differ, not in respect of good and evil, but as stated. Yet in the intellectual faculty love is the same as dilection. And it is in this sense that Augustine speaks of love in the passage quoted: hence a little further on he adds that "a right will is well-directed love, and a wrong will is ill-directed love." However, the fact that love, which is concupiscible passion, inclines many to evil, is the reason why some assigned the difference spoken of.

Reply Obj. 4: The reason why some held that, even when applied to the will itself, the word "love" signifies something more Godlike than "dilection," was because love denotes a passion, especially in so far as it is in the sensitive appetite; whereas dilection presupposes the judgment of reason. But it is possible for man to tend to God by love, being as it were passively drawn by Him, more than he can possibly be drawn thereto by his reason, which pertains to the nature of dilection, as stated above. And consequently love is more Godlike than dilection.

FOURTH ARTICLE [I-II, Q. 26, Art. 4]

Whether Love Is Properly Divided into Love of Friendship and Love of Concupiscence?

Objection 1: It would seem that love is not properly divided into love of friendship and love of concupiscence. For "love is a passion, while friendship is a habit," according to the Philosopher (Ethic. viii, 5). But habit cannot be the member of a division of passions. Therefore love is not properly divided into love of concupiscence and love of friendship.

Obj. 2: Further, a thing cannot be divided by another member of the same division; for man is not a member of the same division as "animal." But concupiscence is a member of the same division as love, as a passion distinct from love. Therefore concupiscence is not a division of love.

Obj. 3: Further, according to the Philosopher (Ethic. viii, 3) friendship is threefold, that which is founded on *usefulness,* that which is founded on pleasure, and that which is founded on goodness. But useful and pleasant friendship are not without concupiscence. Therefore concupiscence should not be contrasted with friendship.

*On the contrary,* We are said to love certain things, because we desire them: thus "a man is said to love wine, on account of its sweetness which he desires"; as stated in Topic. ii, 3. But we have no friendship for wine and suchlike things, as stated in Ethic. viii, 2. Therefore love of concupiscence is distinct from love of friendship.

*I answer that,* As the Philosopher says (Rhet. ii, 4), "to love is to wish good to someone." Hence the movement of love has a twofold tendency: towards the good which a man wishes to someone (to himself or to another) and towards that to which he wishes some good. Accordingly, man has love of concupiscence towards the good that he wishes to another, and love of friendship towards him to whom he wishes good.

Now the members of this division are related as primary and secondary: since that which is loved with the love of friendship is loved simply and for itself; whereas that which is loved with the love of concupiscence, is loved, not simply and for itself, but for something else. For just as that which has existence, is a being simply, while that which exists in another is a relative being; so, because good is convertible with being, the good, which itself has goodness, is good simply; but that which is another's good, is a relative good. Consequently the love with which a thing is loved, that it may have some good, is love simply; while the love, with which a thing is loved, that it may be another's good, is relative love.

Reply Obj. 1: Love is not divided into friendship and concupiscence, but into love of friendship, and love of concupiscence. For a friend is, properly speaking, one to whom we wish good: while we are said to desire, what we wish for ourselves.

Hence the Reply to the Second Objection.

Reply Obj. 3: When friendship is based on usefulness or pleasure, a man does indeed wish his friend some good: and in this respect the character of friendship is preserved. But since he refers this good further to his own pleasure or use, the result is that friendship of the useful or pleasant, in so far as it is connected with love of concupiscence, loses the character to true friendship.

# QUESTION 27

OF THE CAUSE OF LOVE (In Four Articles)

We must now consider the cause of love: and under this head there are four points of inquiry:

(1) Whether good is the only cause of love?

(2) Whether knowledge is a cause of love?

(3) Whether likeness is a cause of love?

(4) Whether any other passion of the soul is a cause of love?

FIRST ARTICLE [I-II, Q. 27, Art. 1]

Whether Good Is the Only Cause of Love?

Objection 1: It would seem that good is not the only cause of love. For good does not cause love, except because it is loved. But it happens that evil also is loved, according to Ps. 10:6: "He that loveth iniquity, hateth his own soul": else, every love would be good. Therefore good is not the only cause of love.

Obj. 2: Further, the Philosopher says (Rhet. ii, 4) that "we love those who acknowledge their evils." Therefore it seems that evil is the cause of love.

Obj. 3: Further, Dionysius says (Div. Nom. iv) that not "the good" only but also "the beautiful is beloved by all."

*On the contrary,* Augustine says (De Trin. viii, 3): "Assuredly the good alone is beloved." Therefore good alone is the cause of love.

*I answer that,* As stated above (Q. 26, A. 1), Love belongs to the appetitive power which is a passive faculty. Wherefore its object stands in relation to it as the cause of its movement or act. Therefore the cause of love must needs be love's object. Now the proper object of love is the good; because, as stated above (Q. 26, AA. 1, 2), love implies a certain connaturalness or complacency of the lover for the thing beloved, and to everything, that thing is a good, which is akin and proportionate to it. It follows, therefore, that good is the proper cause of love.

Reply Obj. 1: Evil is never loved except under the aspect of good, that is to say, in so far as it is good in some respect, and is considered as being good simply. And thus a certain love is evil, in so far as it tends to that which is not simply a true good. It is in this way that man "loves iniquity," inasmuch as, by means of iniquity, some good is gained; pleasure, for instance, or money, or such like.

Reply Obj. 2: Those who acknowledge their evils, are beloved, not for their evils, but because they acknowledge them, for it is a good thing to acknowledge one's faults, in so far as it excludes insincerity or hypocrisy.

Reply Obj. 3: The beautiful is the same as the good, and they differ in aspect only. For since good is what all seek, the notion of good is that which calms the desire; while the notion of the beautiful is that which calms the desire, by being seen or known. Consequently those senses chiefly regard the beautiful, which are the most cognitive, viz. sight and hearing, as ministering to reason; for we speak of beautiful sights and beautiful sounds. But in reference to the other objects of the other senses, we do not use the expression "beautiful," for we do not speak of beautiful tastes, and beautiful odors. Thus it is evident that beauty adds to goodness a relation to the cognitive faculty: so that "good" means that which simply pleases the appetite; while the "beautiful" is something pleasant to apprehend.

SECOND ARTICLE [I-II, Q. 27, Art. 2]

Whether Knowledge Is a Cause of Love?

Objection 1: It would seem that knowledge is not a cause of love. For it is due to love that a thing is sought. But some things are sought without being known, for instance, the sciences; for since "to have them is the same as to know them," as Augustine says (QQ. 83, qu. 35), if we knew them we should have them, and should not seek them. Therefore knowledge is not the cause of love.

Obj. 2: Further, to love what we know not seems like loving something more than we know it. But some things are loved more than they are known: thus in this life God can be loved in Himself, but cannot be known in Himself. Therefore knowledge is not the cause of love.

Obj. 3: Further, if knowledge were the cause of love, there would be no love, where there is no knowledge. But in all things there is love, as Dionysius says (Div. Nom. iv); whereas there is not knowledge in all things. Therefore knowledge is not the cause of love.

*On the contrary,* Augustine proves (De Trin. x, 1, 2) that "none can love what he does not know."

*I answer that,* As stated above (A. 1), good is the cause of love, as being its object. But good is not the object of the appetite, except as apprehended. And therefore love demands some apprehension of the good that is loved. For this reason the Philosopher (Ethic. ix, 5, 12) says that bodily sight is the beginning of sensitive love: and in like manner the contemplation of spiritual beauty or goodness is the beginning of spiritual love. Accordingly knowledge is the cause of love for the same reason as good is, which can be loved only if known.

Reply Obj. 1: He who seeks science, is not entirely without knowledge thereof: but knows something about it already in some respect, either in a general way, or in some one of its effects, or from having heard it commended, as Augustine says (De Trin. x, 1, 2). But to have it is not to know it thus, but to know it perfectly.

Reply Obj. 2: Something is required for the perfection of knowledge, that is not requisite for the perfection of love. For knowledge belongs to the reason, whose function it is to distinguish things which in reality are united, and to unite together, after a fashion, things that are distinct, by comparing one with another. Consequently the perfection of knowledge requires that man should know distinctly all that is in a thing, such as its parts, powers, and properties. On the other hand, love is in the appetitive power, which regards a thing as it is in itself: wherefore it suffices, for the perfection of love, that a thing be loved according as it is known in itself. Hence it is, therefore, that a thing is loved more than it is known; since it can be loved perfectly, even without being perfectly known. This is most evident in regard to the sciences, which some love through having a certain general knowledge of them: for instance, they know that rhetoric is a science that enables man to persuade others; and this is what they love in rhetoric. The same applies to the love of God.

Reply Obj. 3: Even natural love, which is in all things, is caused by a kind of knowledge, not indeed existing in natural things themselves, but in Him Who created their nature, as stated above (Q. 26, A. 1; cf. I, Q. 6, A. 1, ad 2).

THIRD ARTICLE [I-II, Q. 27, Art. 3]

Whether Likeness Is a Cause of Love?

Objection 1: It would seem that likeness is not a cause of love. For the same thing is not the cause of contraries. But likeness is the cause of hatred; for it is written (Prov. 13:10) that "among the proud there are always contentions"; and the Philosopher says (Ethic. viii, 1) that "potters quarrel with one another." Therefore likeness is not a cause of love.

Obj. 2: Further, Augustine says (Confess. iv, 14) that "a man loves in another that which he would not be himself: thus he loves an actor, but would not himself be an actor." But it would not be so, if likeness were the proper cause of love; for in that case a man would love in another, that which he possesses himself, or would like to possess. Therefore likeness is not a cause of love.

Obj. 3: Further, everyone loves that which he needs, even if he have it not: thus a sick man loves health, and a poor man loves riches. But in so far as he needs them and lacks them, he is unlike them. Therefore not only likeness but also unlikeness is a cause of love.

Obj. 4: Further, the Philosopher says (Rhet. ii, 4) that "we love those who bestow money and health on us; and also those who retain their friendship for the dead." But all are not such. Therefore likeness is not a cause of love.

*On the contrary,* It is written (Ecclus. 13:19): "Every beast loveth its like."

*I answer that,* Likeness, properly speaking, is a cause of love. But it must be observed that likeness between things is twofold. One kind of likeness arises from each thing having the same quality actually: for example, two things possessing the quality of whiteness are said to be alike. Another kind of likeness arises from one thing having potentially and by way of inclination, a quality which the other has actually: thus we may say that a heavy body existing outside its proper place is like another heavy body that exists in its proper place: or again, according as potentiality bears a resemblance to its act; since act is contained, in a manner, in the potentiality itself.

Accordingly the first kind of likeness causes love of friendship or well-being. For the very fact that two men are alike, having, as it were, one form, makes them to be, in a manner, one in that form: thus two men are one thing in the species of humanity, and two white men are one thing in whiteness. Hence the affections of one tend to the other, as being one with him; and he wishes good to him as to himself. But the second kind of likeness causes love of concupiscence, or friendship founded on usefulness or pleasure: because whatever is in potentiality, as such, has the desire for its act; and it takes pleasure in its realization, if it be a sentient and cognitive being.

Now it has been stated above (Q. 26, A. 4), that in the love of concupiscence, the lover, properly speaking, loves himself, in willing the good that he desires. But a man loves himself more than another: because he is one with himself substantially, whereas with another he is one only in the likeness of some form. Consequently, if this other's likeness to him arising from the participation of a form, hinders him from gaining the good that he loves, he becomes hateful to him, not for being like him, but for hindering him from gaining his own good. This is why "potters quarrel among themselves," because they hinder one another's gain: and why "there are contentions among the proud," because they hinder one another in attaining the position they covet.

Hence the Reply to the First Objection is evident.

Reply Obj. 2: Even when a man loves in another what he loves not in himself, there is a certain likeness of proportion: because as the latter is to that which is loved in him, so is the former to that which he loves in himself: for instance, if a good singer love a good writer, we can see a likeness of proportion, inasmuch as each one has that which is becoming to him in respect of his art.

Reply Obj. 3: He that loves what he needs, bears a likeness to what he loves, as potentiality bears a likeness to its act, as stated above.

Reply Obj. 4: According to the same likeness of potentiality to its act, the illiberal man loves the man who is liberal, in so far as he expects from him something which he desires. The same applies to the man who is constant in his friendship as compared to one who is inconstant. For in either case friendship seems to be based on usefulness. We might also say that although not all men have these virtues in the complete habit, yet they have them according to certain seminal principles in the reason, in force of which principles the man who is not virtuous loves the virtuous man, as being in conformity with his own natural reason.

FOURTH ARTICLE [I-II, Q. 27, Art. 4]

Whether Any Other Passion of the Soul Is a Cause of Love?

Objection 1: It would seem that some other passion can be the cause of love. For the Philosopher (Ethic. viii, 3) says that some are loved for the sake of the pleasure they give. But pleasure is a passion. Therefore another passion is a cause of love.

Obj. 2: Further, desire is a passion. But we love some because we desire to receive something from them: as happens in every friendship based on usefulness. Therefore another passion is a cause of love.

Obj. 3: Further, Augustine says (De Trin. x, 1): "When we have no hope of getting a thing, we love it but half-heartedly or not at all, even if we see how beautiful it is." Therefore hope too is a cause of love.

*On the contrary,* All the other emotions of the soul are caused by love, as Augustine says (De Civ. Dei xiv, 7, 9).

*I answer that,* There is no other passion of the soul that does not presuppose love of some kind. The reason is that every other passion of the soul implies either movement towards something, or rest in something. Now every movement towards something, or rest in something, arises from some kinship or aptness to that thing; and in this does love consist. Therefore it is not possible for any other passion of the soul to be universally the cause of every love. But it may happen that some other passion is the cause of some particular love: just as one good is the cause of another.

Reply Obj. 1: When a man loves a thing for the pleasure it affords, his love is indeed caused by pleasure; but that very pleasure is caused, in its turn, by another preceding love; for none takes pleasure save in that which is loved in some way.

Reply Obj. 2: Desire for a thing always presupposes love for that thing. But desire of one thing can be the cause of another thing's being loved; thus he that desires money, for this reason loves him from whom he receives it.

Reply Obj. 3: Hope causes or increases love; both by reason of pleasure, because it causes pleasure; and by reason of desire, because hope strengthens desire, since we do not desire so intensely that which we have no hope of receiving. Nevertheless hope itself is of a good that is loved.

## QUESTION 28

OF THE EFFECTS OF LOVE (In Six Articles)

We now have to consider the effects of love: under which head there are six points of inquiry:

(1) Whether union is an effect of love?

(2) Whether mutual indwelling is an effect of love?

(3) Whether ecstasy is an effect of love?

(4) Whether zeal is an effect of love?

(5) Whether love is a passion that is hurtful to the lover?

(6) Whether love is cause of all that the lover does?

FIRST ARTICLE [I-II, Q. 28, Art. 1]

Whether Union Is an Effect of Love?

Objection 1: It would seem that union is not an effect of love. For absence is incompatible with union. But love is compatible with absence; for the Apostle says (Gal. 4:18): "Be zealous for that which is good in a good thing always" (speaking of himself, according to a gloss), "and not only when I am present with you." Therefore union is not an effect of love.

Obj. 2: Further, every union is either according to essence, thus form is united to matter, accident to subject, and a part to the whole, or to another part in order to make up the whole: or according to likeness, in genus, species, or accident. But love does not cause union of essence; else love could not be between things essentially distinct. On the other hand, love does not cause union of likeness, but rather is caused by it, as stated above (Q. 27, A. 3). Therefore union is not an effect of love.

Obj. 3: Further, the sense in act is the sensible in act, and the intellect in act is the thing actually understood. But the lover in act is not the beloved in act. Therefore union is the effect of knowledge rather than of love.

*On the contrary,* Dionysius says (Div. Nom. iv) that every love is a "unitive love."

*I answer that,* The union of lover and beloved is twofold. The first is real union; for instance, when the beloved is present with the lover. The second is union of affection: and this union must be considered in relation to the preceding apprehension; since movement of the appetite follows apprehension. Now love being twofold, viz. love of concupiscence and love of friendship; each of these arises from a kind of apprehension of the oneness of the thing loved with the lover. For when we love a thing, by desiring it, we apprehend it as belonging to our well-being. In like manner when a man loves another with the love of friendship, he wills good to him, just as he wills good to himself: wherefore he apprehends him as his other self, in so far, to wit, as he wills good to him as to himself. Hence a friend is called a man's "other self" (Ethic. ix, 4), and Augustine says (Confess. iv, 6), "Well did one say to his friend: Thou half of my soul."

The first of these unions is caused *effectively* by love; because love moves man to desire and seek the presence of the beloved, as of something suitable and belonging to him. The second union is caused *formally* by love; because love itself is this union or bond. In this sense Augustine says (De Trin. viii, 10) that "love is a vital principle uniting, or seeking to unite two together, the lover, to wit, and the beloved." For in describing it as "uniting" he refers to the union of affection, without which there is no love: and in saying that "it seeks to unite," he refers to real union.

Reply Obj. 1: This argument is true of real union. That is necessary to pleasure as being its cause; desire implies the real absence of the beloved: but love remains whether the beloved be absent or present.

Reply Obj. 2: Union has a threefold relation to love. There is union which causes love; and this is substantial union, as regards the love with which one loves oneself; while as regards the love wherewith one loves other things, it is the union of likeness, as stated above (Q. 27, A. 3). There is also a union which is essentially love itself. This union is according to a bond of affection, and is likened to substantial union, inasmuch as the lover stands to the object of his love, as to himself, if it be love of friendship; as to something belonging to himself, if it be love of concupiscence. Again there is a union, which is the effect of love. This is real union, which the lover seeks with the object of his love. Moreover this union is in keeping with the demands of love: for as the Philosopher relates (Polit. ii, 1), "Aristophanes stated that lovers would wish to be united both into one," but since "this would result in either one or both being destroyed," they seek a suitable and becoming union—to live together, speak together, and be united together in other like things.

Reply Obj. 3: Knowledge is perfected by the thing known being united, through its likeness, to the knower. But the effect of love is that the thing itself which is loved, is, in a way, united to the lover, as stated above. Consequently the union caused by love is closer than that which is caused by knowledge.

SECOND ARTICLE [I-II, Q. 28, Art. 2]

Whether Mutual Indwelling Is an Effect of Love?

Objection 1: It would seem that love does not cause mutual indwelling, so that the lover be in the beloved and vice versa. For that which is in another is contained in it. But the same cannot be container and contents. Therefore love cannot cause mutual indwelling, so that the lover be in the beloved and vice versa.

Obj. 2: Further, nothing can penetrate within a whole, except by means of a division of the whole. But it is the function of the reason, not of the appetite where love resides, to divide things that are really united. Therefore mutual indwelling is not an effect of love.

Obj. 3: Further, if love involves the lover being in the beloved and vice versa, it follows that the beloved is united to the lover, in the same way as the lover is united to the beloved. But the union itself is love, as stated above (A. 1). Therefore it follows that the lover is always loved by the object of his love; which is evidently false. Therefore mutual indwelling is not an effect of love.

*On the contrary,* It is written (1 John 4:16): "He that abideth in charity abideth in God, and God in him." Now charity is the love of God. Therefore, for the same reason, every love makes the beloved to be in the lover, and vice versa.

*I answer that,* This effect of mutual indwelling may be understood as referring both to the apprehensive and to the appetitive power. Because, as to the apprehensive power, the beloved is said to be in the lover, inasmuch as the beloved abides in the apprehension of the lover, according to Phil. 1:7, "For that I have you in my heart": while the lover is said to be in the beloved, according to apprehension, inasmuch as the lover is not satisfied with a superficial apprehension of the beloved, but strives to gain an intimate knowledge of everything pertaining to the beloved, so as to penetrate into his very soul. Thus it is written concerning the Holy Ghost, Who is God's Love, that He "searcheth all things, yea the deep things of God" (1 Cor. 2:10).

As the appetitive power, the object loved is said to be in the lover, inasmuch as it is in his affections, by a kind of complacency: causing him either to take pleasure in it, or in its good, when present; or, in the absence of the object loved, by his longing, to tend towards it with the love of concupiscence, or towards the good that he wills to the beloved, with the love of friendship: not indeed from any extrinsic cause (as when we desire one thing on account of another, or wish good to another on account of something else), but because the complacency in the beloved is rooted in the lover's heart. For this reason we speak of love as being "intimate"; and "of the bowels of charity." On the other hand, the lover is in the beloved, by the love of concupiscence and by the love of friendship, but not in the same way. For the love of concupiscence is not satisfied with any external or superficial possession or enjoyment of the beloved; but seeks to possess the beloved perfectly, by penetrating into his heart, as it were. Whereas, in the love of friendship, the lover is in the beloved, inasmuch as he reckons what is good or evil to his friend, as being so to himself; and his friend's will as his own, so that it seems as though he felt the good or suffered the evil in the person of his friend. Hence it is proper to friends "to desire the same things, and to grieve and rejoice at the same," as the Philosopher says (Ethic. ix, 3 and Rhet. ii, 4). Consequently in so far as he reckons what affects his friend as affecting himself, the lover seems to be in the beloved, as though he were become one with him: but in so far as, on the other hand, he wills and acts for his friend's sake as for his own sake, looking on his friend as identified with himself, thus the beloved is in the lover.

In yet a third way, mutual indwelling in the love of friendship can be understood in regard to reciprocal love: inasmuch as friends return love for love, and both desire and do good things for one another.

Reply Obj. 1: The beloved is contained in the lover, by being impressed on his heart and thus becoming the object of his complacency. On the other hand, the lover is contained in the beloved, inasmuch as the lover penetrates, so to speak, into the beloved. For nothing hinders a thing from being both container and contents in different ways: just as a genus is contained in its species, and vice versa.

Reply Obj. 2: The apprehension of the reason precedes the movement of love. Consequently, just as the reason divides, so does the movement of love penetrate into the beloved, as was explained above.

Reply Obj. 3: This argument is true of the third kind of mutual indwelling, which is not to be found in every kind of love.

THIRD ARTICLE [I-II, Q. 28, Art. 3]

Whether Ecstasy Is an Effect of Love?

Objection 1: It would seem that ecstasy is not an effect of love. For ecstasy seems to imply loss of reason. But love does not always result in loss of reason: for lovers are masters of themselves at times. Therefore love does not cause ecstasy.

Obj. 2: Further, the lover desires the beloved to be united to him. Therefore he draws the beloved to himself, rather than betakes himself into the beloved, going forth out from himself as it were.

Obj. 3: Further, love unites the beloved to the lover, as stated above (A. 1). If, therefore, the lover goes out from himself, in order to betake himself into the beloved, it follows that the lover always loves the beloved more than himself: which is evidently false. Therefore ecstasy is not an effect of love.

*On the contrary,* Dionysius says (Div. Nom. iv) that "the Divine love produces ecstasy," and that "God Himself suffered ecstasy through love." Since therefore according to the same author (Div. Nom. iv), every love is a participated likeness of the Divine Love, it seems that every love causes ecstasy.

*I answer that,* To suffer ecstasy means to be placed outside oneself. This happens as to the apprehensive power and as to the appetitive power. As to the apprehensive power, a man is said to be placed outside himself, when he is placed outside the knowledge proper to him. This may be due to his being raised to a higher knowledge; thus, a man is said to suffer ecstasy, inasmuch as he is placed outside the connatural apprehension of his sense and reason, when he is raised up so as to comprehend things that surpass sense and reason: or it may be due to his being cast down into a state of debasement; thus a man may be said to suffer ecstasy, when he is overcome by violent passion or madness. As to the appetitive power, a man is said to suffer ecstasy, when that power is borne towards something else, so that it goes forth out from itself, as it were.

The first of these ecstasies is caused by love dispositively in so far, namely, as love makes the lover dwell on the beloved, as stated above (A. 2), and to dwell intently on one thing draws the mind from other things. The second ecstasy is caused by love directly; by love of friendship, simply; by love of concupiscence not simply but in a restricted sense. Because in love of concupiscence, the lover is carried out of himself, in a certain sense; in so far, namely, as not being satisfied with enjoying the good that he has, he seeks to enjoy something outside himself. But since he seeks to have this extrinsic good for himself, he does not go out from himself simply, and this movement remains finally within him. On the other hand, in the love of friendship, a man's affection goes out from itself simply; because he wishes and does good to his friend, by caring and providing for him, for his sake.

Reply Obj. 1: This argument is true of the first kind of ecstasy.

Reply Obj. 2: This argument applies to love of concupiscence, which, as stated above, does not cause ecstasy simply.

Reply Obj. 3: He who loves, goes out from himself, in so far as he wills the good of his friend and works for it. Yet he does not will the good of his friend more than his own good: and so it does not follow that he loves another more than himself.

FOURTH ARTICLE [I-II, Q. 28, Art. 4]

Whether Zeal Is an Effect of Love?

Objection 1: It would seem that zeal is not an effect of love. For zeal is a beginning of contention; wherefore it is written (1 Cor. 3:3): "Whereas there is among you zeal [Douay: 'envying'] and contention," etc. But contention is incompatible with love. Therefore zeal is not an effect of love.

Obj. 2: Further, the object of love is the good, which communicates itself to others. But zeal is opposed to communication; since it seems an effect of zeal, that a man refuses to share the object of his love with another: thus husbands are said to be jealous of ( *zelare* ) their wives, because they will not share them with others. Therefore zeal is not an effect of love.

Obj. 3: Further, there is no zeal without hatred, as neither is there without love: for it is written (Ps. 72:3): "I had a zeal on occasion of the wicked." Therefore it should not be set down as an effect of love any more than of hatred.

*On the contrary,* Dionysius says (Div. Nom. iv): "God is said to be a zealot, on account of his great love for all things."

*I answer that,* Zeal, whatever way we take it, arises from the intensity of love. For it is evident that the more intensely a power tends to anything, the more vigorously it withstands opposition or resistance. Since therefore love is "a movement towards the object loved," as Augustine says (QQ. 83, qu. 35), an intense love seeks to remove everything that opposes it.

But this happens in different ways according to love of concupiscence, and love of friendship. For in love of concupiscence he who desires something intensely, is moved against all that hinders his gaining or quietly enjoying the object of his love. It is thus that husbands are said to be jealous of their wives, lest association with others prove a hindrance to their exclusive individual rights. In like manner those who seek to excel, are moved against those who seem to excel, as though these were a hindrance to their excelling. And this is the zeal of envy, of which it is written (Ps. 36:1): "Be not emulous of evil doers, nor envy ( *zelaveris* ) them that work iniquity."

On the other hand, love of friendship seeks the friend's good: wherefore, when it is intense, it causes a man to be moved against everything that opposes the friend's good. In this respect, a man is said to be zealous on behalf of his friend, when he makes a point of repelling whatever may be said or done against the friend's good. In this way, too, a man is said to be zealous on God's behalf, when he endeavors, to the best of his means, to repel whatever is contrary to the honor or will of God; according to 3 Kings 19:14: "With zeal I have been zealous for the Lord of hosts." Again on the words of John 2:17: "The zeal of Thy house hath eaten me up," a gloss says that "a man is eaten up with a good zeal, who strives to remedy whatever evil he perceives; and if he cannot, bears with it and laments it."

Reply Obj. 1: The Apostle is speaking in this passage of the zeal of envy; which is indeed the cause of contention, not against the object of love, but for it, and against that which is opposed to it.

Reply Obj. 2: Good is loved inasmuch as it can be communicated to the lover. Consequently whatever hinders the perfection of this communication, becomes hateful. Thus zeal arises from love of good. But through defect of goodness, it happens that certain small goods cannot, in their entirety, be possessed by many at the same time: and from the love of such things arises the zeal of envy. But it does not arise, properly speaking, in the case of those things which, in their entirety, can be possessed by many: for no one envies another the knowledge of truth, which can be known entirely by many; except perhaps one may envy another his superiority in the knowledge of it.

Reply Obj. 3: The very fact that a man hates whatever is opposed to the object of his love, is the effect of love. Hence zeal is set down as an effect of love rather than of hatred.

FIFTH ARTICLE [I-II, Q. 28, Art. 5]

Whether Love Is a Passion That Wounds the Lover?

Objection 1: It would seem that love wounds the lover. For languor denotes a hurt in the one that languishes. But love causes languor: for it is written (Cant 2:5): "Stay me up with flowers, compass me about with apples; because I languish with love." Therefore love is a wounding passion.

Obj. 2: Further, melting is a kind of dissolution. But love melts that in which it is: for it is written (Cant 5:6): "My soul melted when my beloved spoke." Therefore love is a dissolvent: therefore it is a corruptive and a wounding passion.

Obj. 3: Further, fervor denotes a certain excess of heat; which excess has a corruptive effect. But love causes fervor: for Dionysius (Coel. Hier. vii) in reckoning the properties belonging to the Seraphim's love, includes "hot" and "piercing" and "most fervent." Moreover it is said of love (Cant 8:6) that "its lamps are fire and flames." Therefore love is a wounding and corruptive passion.

*On the contrary,* Dionysius says (Div. Nom. iv) that "everything loves itself with a love that holds it together," i.e. that preserves it. Therefore love is not a wounding passion, but rather one that preserves and perfects.

*I answer that,* As stated above (Q. 26, AA. 1, 2; Q. 27, A. 1), love denotes a certain adapting of the appetitive power to some good. Now nothing is hurt by being adapted to that which is suitable to it; rather, if possible, it is perfected and bettered. But if a thing be adapted to that which is not suitable to it, it is hurt and made worse thereby. Consequently love of a suitable good perfects and betters the lover; but love of a good which is unsuitable to the lover, wounds and worsens him. Wherefore man is perfected and bettered chiefly by the love of God: but is wounded and worsened by the love of sin, according to Osee 9:10: "They became abominable, as those things which they loved."

And let this be understood as applying to love in respect of its formal element, i.e. in regard to the appetite. But in respect of the material element in the passion of love, i.e. a certain bodily change, it happens that love is hurtful, by reason of this change being excessive: just as it happens in the senses, and in every act of a power of the soul that is exercised through the change of some bodily organ.

In reply to the objections, it is to be observed

that four proximate effects may be ascribed to love: viz. melting, enjoyment, languor, and fervor. Of these the first is "melting," which is opposed to freezing. For things that are frozen, are closely bound together, so as to be hard to pierce. But it belongs to love that the appetite is fitted to receive the good which is loved, inasmuch as the object loved is in the lover, as stated above (A. 2). Consequently the freezing or hardening of the heart is a disposition incompatible with love: while melting denotes a softening of the heart, whereby the heart shows itself to be ready for the entrance of the beloved. If, then, the beloved is present and possessed, pleasure or enjoyment ensues. But if the beloved be absent, two passions arise; viz. sadness at its absence, which is denoted by "languor" (hence Cicero in *De Tusc. Quaest.* iii, 11 applies the term "ailment" chiefly to sadness); and an intense desire to possess the beloved, which is signified by "fervor." And these are the effects of love considered formally, according to the relation of the appetitive power to its object. But in the passion of love, other effects ensue, proportionate to the above, in respect of a change in the organ.

SIXTH ARTICLE [I-II, Q. 28, Art. 6]

Whether Love Is Cause of All That the Lover Does?

Objection 1: It would seem that the lover does not do everything from love. For love is a passion, as stated above (Q. 26, A. 2). But man does not do everything from passion: but some things he does from choice, and some things from ignorance, as stated in *Ethic.* v, 8. Therefore not everything that a man does, is done from love.

Obj. 2: Further, the appetite is a principle of movement and action in all animals, as stated in *De Anima* iii, 10. If, therefore, whatever a man does is done from love, the other passions of the appetitive faculty are superfluous.

Obj. 3: Further, nothing is produced at one and the same time by contrary causes. But some things are done from hatred. Therefore all things are not done from love.

*On the contrary,* Dionysius says (Div. Nom. iv) that "all things, whatever they do, they do for the love of good."

*I answer that,* Every agent acts for an end, as stated above (Q. 1, A. 2). Now the end is the good desired and loved by each one. Wherefore it is evident that every agent, whatever it be, does every action from love of some kind.

Reply Obj. 1: This objection takes love as a passion existing in the sensitive appetite. But here we are speaking of love in a general sense, inasmuch as it includes intellectual, rational, animal, and natural love: for it is in this sense that Dionysius speaks of love in chapter iv of *De Divinis Nominibus.*

Reply Obj. 2: As stated above (A. 5; Q. 27, A. 4) desire, sadness and pleasure, and consequently all the other passions of the soul, result from love. Wherefore every act that proceeds from any passion, proceeds also from love as from a first cause: and so the other passions, which are proximate causes, are not superfluous.

Reply Obj. 3: Hatred also is a result of love, as we shall state further on (Q. 29, A. 2).

# QUESTION 29

OF HATRED (In Six Articles)

We must now consider hatred: concerning which there are six points of inquiry:

(1) Whether evil is the cause and the object of hatred?

(2) Whether love is the cause of hatred?

(3) Whether hatred is stronger than love?

(4) Whether a man can hate himself?

(5) Whether a man can hate the truth?

(6) Whether a thing can be the object of universal hatred?

FIRST ARTICLE [I-II, Q. 29, Art. 1]

Whether Evil Is the Cause and Object of Hatred?

Objection 1: It would seem that evil is not the object and cause of hatred. For everything that exists, as such, is good. If therefore evil be the object of hatred, it follows that nothing but the lack of something can be the object of hatred: which is clearly untrue.

Obj. 2: Further, hatred of evil is praiseworthy; hence (2 Macc. 3:1) some are praised for that "the laws were very well kept, because of the godliness of Onias the high-priest, and the hatred of their souls [Douay: 'his soul'] had no evil." If, therefore, nothing but evil be the object of hatred, it would follow that all hatred is commendable: and this is clearly false.

Obj. 3: Further, the same thing is not at the same time both good and evil. But the same thing is lovable and hateful to different subjects. Therefore hatred is not only of evil, but also of good.

*On the contrary,* Hatred is the opposite of love. But the object of love is good, as stated above (Q. 26, A. 1; Q. 27, A. 1). Therefore the object of hatred is evil.

*I answer that,* Since the natural appetite is the result of apprehension (though this apprehension is not in the same subject as the natural appetite), it seems that what applies to the inclination of the natural appetite, applies also to the animal appetite, which does result from an apprehension in the same subject, as stated above (Q. 26, A. 1). Now, with regard to the natural appetite, it is evident, that just as each thing is naturally attuned and adapted to that which is suitable to it, wherein consists natural love; so has it a natural dissonance from that which opposes and destroys it; and this is natural hatred. So, therefore, in the animal appetite, or in the intellectual appetite, love is a certain harmony of the appetite with that which is apprehended as suitable; while hatred is dissonance of the appetite from that which is apprehended as repugnant and hurtful. Now, just as whatever is suitable, as such, bears the aspect of good; so whatever is repugnant, as such, bears the aspect of evil. And therefore, just as good is the object of love, so evil is the object of hatred.

Reply Obj. 1: Being, as such, has not the aspect of repugnance but only of fittingness; because being is common to all things. But being, inasmuch as it is this determinate being, has an aspect of repugnance to some determinate being. And in this way, one being is hateful to another, and is evil; though not in itself, but by comparison with something else.

Reply Obj. 2: Just as a thing may be apprehended as good, when it is not truly good; so a thing may be apprehended as evil, whereas it is not truly evil. Hence it happens sometimes that neither hatred of evil nor love of good is good.

Reply Obj. 3: To different things the same thing may be lovable or hateful: in respect of the natural appetite, owing to one and the same thing being naturally suitable to one thing, and naturally unsuitable to another: thus heat is becoming to fire and unbecoming to water: and in respect of the animal appetite, owing to one and the same thing being apprehended by one as good, by another as bad.

SECOND ARTICLE [I-II, Q. 29, Art. 2]

Whether Love Is a Cause of Hatred?

Objection 1: It would seem that love is not a cause of hatred. For "the opposite members of a division are naturally simultaneous" (Praedic. x). But love and hatred are opposite members of a division, since they are contrary to one another. Therefore they are naturally simultaneous. Therefore love is not the cause of hatred.

Obj. 2: Further, of two contraries, one is not the cause of the other. But love and hatred are contraries. Therefore love is not the cause of hatred.

Obj. 3: Further, that which follows is not the cause of that which precedes. But hatred precedes love, seemingly: since hatred implies a turning away from evil, whereas love implies a turning towards good. Therefore love is not the cause of hatred.

*On the contrary,* Augustine says (De Civ. Dei xiv, 7, 9) that all emotions are caused by love. Therefore hatred also, since it is an emotion of the soul, is caused by love.

*I answer that,* As stated above (A. 1), love consists in a certain agreement of the lover with the object loved, while hatred consists in a certain disagreement or dissonance. Now we should consider in each thing, what agrees with it, before that which disagrees: since a thing disagrees with another, through destroying or hindering that which agrees with it. Consequently love must needs precede hatred; and nothing is hated, save through being contrary to a suitable thing which is loved. And hence it is that every hatred is caused by love.

Reply Obj. 1: The opposite members of a division are sometimes naturally simultaneous, both really and logically; e.g. two species of animal, or two species of color. Sometimes they are simultaneous logically, while, in reality, one precedes, and causes the other; e.g. the species of numbers, figures and movements. Sometimes they are not simultaneous either really or logically; e.g. substance and accident; for substance is in reality the cause of accident; and being is predicated of substance before it is predicated of accident, by a priority of reason, because it is not predicated of accident except inasmuch as the latter is in substance. Now love and hatred are naturally simultaneous, logically but not really. Wherefore nothing hinders love from being the cause of hatred.

Reply Obj. 2: Love and hatred are contraries if considered in respect of the same thing. But if taken in respect of contraries, they are not themselves contrary, but consequent to one another: for it amounts to the same that one love a certain thing, or that one hate its contrary. Thus love of one thing is the cause of one's hating its contrary.

Reply Obj. 3: In the order of execution, the turning away from one term precedes the turning towards the other. But the reverse is the case in the order of intention: since approach to one term is the reason for turning away from the other. Now the appetitive movement belongs rather to the order of intention than to that of execution. Wherefore love precedes hatred: because each is an appetitive movement.

THIRD ARTICLE [I-II, Q. 29, Art. 3]

Whether Hatred Is Stronger Than Love?

Objection 1: It would seem that hatred is stronger than love. For Augustine says (QQ. 83, qu. 36): "There is no one who does not flee from pain, more than he desires pleasure." But flight from pain pertains to hatred; while desire for pleasure belongs to love. Therefore hatred is stronger than love.

Obj. 2: Further, the weaker is overcome by the stronger. But love is overcome by hatred: when, that is to say, love is turned into hatred. Therefore hatred is stronger than love.

Obj. 3: Further, the emotions of the soul are shown by their effects. But man insists more on repelling what is hateful, than on seeking what is pleasant: thus also irrational animals refrain from pleasure for fear of the whip, as Augustine instances (QQ. 83, qu. 36). Therefore hatred is stronger than love.

*On the contrary,* Good is stronger than evil; because "evil does nothing except in virtue of good," as Dionysius says (Div. Nom. iv). But hatred and love differ according to the difference of good and evil. Therefore love is stronger than hatred.

*I answer that,* It is impossible for an effect to be stronger than its cause. Now every hatred arises from some love as its cause, as above stated (A. 2).

Therefore it is impossible for hatred to be stronger than love absolutely.

But furthermore, love must needs be, absolutely speaking, stronger than hatred. Because a thing is moved to the end more strongly than to the means. Now turning away from evil is directed as a means to the gaining of good. Wherefore, absolutely speaking, the soul's movement in respect of good is stronger than its movement in respect of evil.

Nevertheless hatred sometimes seems to be stronger than love, for two reasons. First, because hatred is more keenly felt than love. For, since the sensitive perception is accompanied by a certain impression; when once the impression has been received it is not felt so keenly as in the moment of receiving it. Hence the heat of a hectic fever, though greater, is nevertheless not felt so much as the heat of tertian fever; because the heat of the hectic fever is habitual and like a second nature. For this reason, love is felt more keenly in the absence of the object loved; thus Augustine says (De Trin. x, 12) that "love is felt more keenly when we lack what we love." And for the same reason, the unbecomingness of that which is hated is felt more keenly than the becomingness of that which is loved. Secondly, because comparison is made between a hatred and a love which are not mutually corresponding. Because, according to different degrees of good there are different degrees of love to which correspond different degrees of hatred. Wherefore a hatred that corresponds to a greater love, moves us more than a lesser love.

Hence it is clear how to reply to the First Objection. For the love of pleasure is less than the love of self-preservation, to which corresponds flight from pain. Wherefore we flee from pain more than we love pleasure.

Reply Obj. 2: Hatred would never overcome love, were it not for the greater love to which that hatred corresponds. Thus man loves himself, more than he loves his friend: and because he loves himself, his friend is hateful to him, if he oppose him.

Reply Obj. 3: The reason why we act with greater insistence in repelling what is hateful, is because we feel hatred more keenly.

FOURTH ARTICLE [I-II, Q. 29, Art. 4]

Whether a Man Can Hate Himself?

Objection 1: It would seem that a man can hate himself. For it is written (Ps. 10:6): "He that loveth iniquity, hateth his own soul." But many love iniquity. Therefore many hate themselves.

Obj. 2: Further, him we hate, to whom we wish and work evil. But sometimes a man wishes and works evil to himself, e.g. a man who kills himself. Therefore some men hate themselves.

Obj. 3: Further, Boethius says (De Consol. ii) that "avarice makes a man hateful"; whence we may conclude that everyone hates a miser. But some men are misers. Therefore they hate themselves.

*On the contrary,* The Apostle says (Eph. 5:29) that "no man ever hated his own flesh."

*I answer that,* Properly speaking, it is impossible for a man to hate himself. For everything naturally desires good, nor can anyone desire anything for himself, save under the aspect of good: for "evil is outside the scope of the will," as Dionysius says (Div. Nom. iv). Now to love a man is to will good to him, as stated above (Q. 26, A. 4). Consequently, a man must, of necessity, love himself; and it is impossible for a man to hate himself, properly speaking.

But accidentally it happens that a man hates himself: and this in two ways. First, on the part of the good which a man wills to himself. For it happens sometimes that what is desired as good in some particular respect, is simply evil; and in this way, a man accidentally wills evil to himself; and thus hates himself. Secondly, in regard to himself, to whom he wills good. For each thing is that which is predominant in it; wherefore the state is said to do what the king does, as if the king were the whole state. Now it is clear that man is principally the mind of man. And it happens that some men account themselves as being principally that which they are in their material and sensitive nature. Wherefore they love themselves according to what they take themselves to be, while they hate that which they really are, by desiring what is contrary to reason. And in both these ways, "he that loveth iniquity hateth" not only "his own soul," but also himself.

Wherefore the reply to the First Objection is evident.

Reply Obj. 2: No man wills and works evil to himself, except he apprehend it under the aspect of good. For even they who kill themselves, apprehend death itself as a good, considered as putting an end to some unhappiness or pain.

Reply Obj. 3: The miser hates something accidental to himself, but not for that reason does he hate himself: thus a sick man hates his sickness for the very reason that he loves himself. Or we may say that avarice makes man hateful to others, but not to himself. In fact, it is caused by inordinate self-love, in respect of which, man desires temporal goods for himself more than he should.

FIFTH ARTICLE [I-II, Q. 29, Art. 5]

Whether a Man Can Hate the Truth?

Objection 1: It would seem that a man cannot hate the truth. For good, true, and being are convertible. But a man cannot hate good. Neither, therefore, can he hate the truth.

Obj. 2: Further, "All men have a natural desire for knowledge," as stated in the beginning of the *Metaphysics* (i, 1). But knowledge is only of truth. Therefore truth is naturally desired and loved. But that which is in a thing naturally, is always in it. Therefore no man can hate the truth.

Obj. 3: Further, the Philosopher says (Rhet. ii, 4) that "men love those who are straightforward." But there can be no other motive for this save truth. Therefore man loves the truth naturally. Therefore he cannot hate it.

*On the contrary,* The Apostle says (Gal. 4:16): "Am I become your enemy because I tell you the truth?" [*St. Thomas quotes the passage, probably from memory, as though it were an assertion: "I am become," etc.]

*I answer that,* Good, true and being are the same in reality, but differ as considered by reason. For good is considered in the light of something desirable, while being and true are not so considered: because good is "what all things seek." Wherefore good, as such, cannot be the object of hatred, neither in general nor in particular. Being and truth in general cannot be the object of hatred: because disagreement is the cause of hatred, and agreement is the cause of love; while being and truth are common to all things. But nothing hinders some particular being or some particular truth being an object of hatred, in so far as it is considered as hurtful and repugnant; since hurtfulness and repugnance are not incompatible with the notion of being and truth, as they are with the notion of good.

Now it may happen in three ways that some particular truth is repugnant or hurtful to the good we love. First, according as truth is in things as in its cause and origin. And thus man sometimes hates a particular truth, when he wishes that what is true were not true. Secondly, according as truth is in man's knowledge, which hinders him from gaining the object loved: such is the case of those who wish not to know the truth of faith, that they may sin freely; in whose person it is said (Job 21:14): "We desire not the knowledge of Thy ways." Thirdly, a particular truth is hated, as being repugnant, inasmuch as it is in the intellect of another man: as, for instance, when a man wishes to remain hidden in his sin, he hates that anyone should know the truth about his sin. In this respect, Augustine says (Confess. x, 23) that men "love truth when it enlightens, they hate it when it reproves." This suffices for the Reply to the First Objection.

Reply Obj. 2: The knowledge of truth is lovable in itself: hence Augustine says that men love it when it enlightens. But accidentally, the knowledge of truth may become hateful, in so far as it hinders one from accomplishing one's desire.

Reply Obj. 3: The reason why we love those who are straightforward is that they make known the truth, and the knowledge of the truth, considered in itself, is a desirable thing.

SIXTH ARTICLE [I-II, Q. 29, Art. 6]

Whether Anything Can Be an Object of Universal Hatred?

Objection 1: It would seem that a thing cannot be an object of universal hatred. Because hatred is a passion of the sensitive appetite, which is moved by an apprehension in the senses. But the senses cannot apprehend the universal. Therefore a thing cannot be an object of universal hatred.

Obj. 2: Further, hatred is caused by disagreement; and where there is disagreement, there is nothing in common. But the notion of universality implies something in common. Therefore nothing can be the object of universal hatred.

Obj. 3: Further, the object of hatred is evil. But "evil is in things, and not in the mind" (Metaph. vi, 4). Since therefore the universal is in the mind only, which abstracts the universal from the particular, it would seem that hatred cannot have a universal object.

*On the contrary,* The Philosopher says (Rhet. ii, 4) that "anger is directed to something singular, whereas hatred is also directed to a thing in general; for everybody hates the thief and the backbiter."

*I answer that,* There are two ways of speaking of the universal: first, as considered under the aspect of universality; secondly, as considered in the nature to which it is ascribed: for it is one thing to consider the universal man, and another to consider a man as man. If, therefore, we take the universal, in the first way, no sensitive power, whether of apprehension or of appetite, can attain the universal: because the universal is obtained by abstraction from individual matter, on which every sensitive power is based.

Nevertheless the sensitive powers, both of apprehension and of appetite, can tend to something universally. Thus we say that the object of sight is color considered generically; not that the sight is cognizant of universal color, but because the fact that color is cognizant by the sight, is attributed to color, not as being this particular color, but simply because it is color. Accordingly hatred in the sensitive faculty can regard something universally: because this thing, by reason of its common nature, and not merely as an individual, is hostile to the animal—for instance, a wolf in regard to a sheep. Hence a sheep hates the wolf universally. On the other hand, anger is always caused by something in particular: because it is caused by some action of the one that hurts us; and actions proceed from individuals. For this reason the Philosopher says (Rhet. ii, 4) that "anger is always directed to something singular, whereas hatred can be directed to a thing in general."

But according as hatred is in the intellectual part, since it arises from the universal apprehension of the intellect, it can regard the universal in both ways.

Reply Obj. 1: The senses do not apprehend the universal, as such: but they apprehend something to which the character of universality is given by abstraction.

Reply Obj. 2: That which is common to all cannot be a reason of hatred. But nothing hinders a thing from being common to many, and at variance with others, so as to be hateful to them.

Reply Obj. 3: This argument considers the universal under the aspect of universality: and thus it does not come under the sensitive apprehension or appetite.

## QUESTION 30

OF CONCUPISCENCE (In Four Articles)

We have now to consider concupiscence: under which head there are four points of inquiry:

(1) Whether concupiscence is in the sensitive appetite only?

(2) Whether concupiscence is a specific passion?

(3) Whether some concupiscences are natural, and some not natural?

(4) Whether concupiscence is infinite?

FIRST ARTICLE [I-II, Q. 30, Art. 1]

Whether Concupiscence Is in the Sensitive Appetite Only?

Objection 1: It would seem that concupiscence is not only in the sensitive appetite. For there is a concupiscence of wisdom, according to Wis. 6:21: "The concupiscence [Douay: 'desire'] of wisdom bringeth to the everlasting kingdom." But the sensitive appetite can have no tendency to wisdom. Therefore concupiscence is not only in the sensitive appetite.

Obj. 2: Further, the desire for the commandments of God is not in the sensitive appetite: in fact the Apostle says (Rom. 7:18): "There dwelleth not in me, that is to say, in my flesh, that which is good." But desire for God's commandments is an act of concupiscence, according to Ps. 118:20: "My soul hath coveted ( *concupivit* ) to long for thy justifications." Therefore concupiscence is not only in the sensitive appetite.

Obj. 3: Further, to each power, its proper good is a matter of concupiscence. Therefore concupiscence is in each power of the soul, and not only in the sensitive appetite.

*On the contrary,* Damascene says (De Fide Orth. ii, 12) that "the irrational part which is subject and amenable to reason, is divided into the faculties of concupiscence and anger. This is the irrational part of the soul, passive and appetitive." Therefore concupiscence is in the sensitive appetite.

*I answer that,* As the Philosopher says (Rhet. i, 11), "concupiscence is a craving for that which is pleasant." Now pleasure is twofold, as we shall state later on (Q. 31, AA. 3, 4): one is in the intelligible good, which is the good of reason; the other is in good perceptible to the senses. The former pleasure seems to belong to soul alone: whereas the latter belongs to both soul and body: because the sense is a power seated in a bodily organ: wherefore sensible good is the good of the whole composite. Now concupiscence seems to be the craving for this latter pleasure, since it belongs to the united soul and body, as is implied by the Latin word "concupiscentia." Therefore, properly speaking, concupiscence is in the sensitive appetite, and in the concupiscible faculty, which takes its name from it.

Reply Obj. 1: The craving for wisdom, or other spiritual goods, is sometimes called concupiscence; either by reason of a certain likeness; or on account of the craving in the higher part of the soul being so vehement that it overflows into the lower appetite, so that the latter also, in its own way, tends to the spiritual good, following the lead of the higher appetite, the result being that the body itself renders its service in spiritual matters, according to Ps. 83:3: "My heart and my flesh have rejoiced in the living God."

Reply Obj. 2: Properly speaking, desire may be not only in the lower, but also in the higher appetite. For it does not imply fellowship in craving, as concupiscence does; but simply movement towards the thing desired.

Reply Obj. 3: It belongs to each power of the soul to seek its proper good by the natural appetite, which does not arise from apprehension. But the craving for good, by the animal appetite, which arises from apprehension, belongs to the appetitive power alone. And to crave a thing under the aspect of something delightful to the senses, wherein concupiscence properly consists, belongs to the concupiscible power.

SECOND ARTICLE [I-II, Q. 30, Art. 2]

Whether Concupiscence Is a Specific Passion?

Objection 1: It would seem that concupiscence is not a specific passion of the concupiscible power. For passions are distinguished by their objects. But the object of the concupiscible power is something delightful to the senses; and this is also the object of concupiscence, as the Philosopher declares (Rhet. i, 11). Therefore concupiscence is not a specific passion of the concupiscible faculty.

Obj. 2: Further, Augustine says (QQ. 83, qu. 33) that "covetousness is the love of transitory things": so that it is not distinct from love. But all specific passions are distinct from one another. Therefore concupiscence is not a specific passion in the concupiscible faculty.

Obj. 3: Further, to each passion of the concupiscible faculty there is a specific contrary passion in that faculty, as stated above (Q. 23, A. 4). But no specific passion of the concupiscible faculty is contrary to concupiscence. For Damascene says (De Fide Orth. ii, 12) that "good when desired gives rise to concupiscence; when present, it gives joy: in like manner, the evil we apprehend makes us fear, the evil that is present makes us sad": from which we gather that as sadness is contrary to joy, so is fear contrary to concupiscence. But fear is not in the concupiscible, but in the irascible part. Therefore concupiscence is not a specific passion of the concupiscible faculty.

*On the contrary,* Concupiscence is caused by love, and tends to pleasure, both of which are passions of the concupiscible faculty. Hence it is distinguished from the other concupiscible passions, as a specific passion.

*I answer that,* As stated above (A. 1; Q. 23, A. 1), the good which gives pleasure to the senses is the common object of the concupiscible faculty. Hence the various concupiscible passions are distinguished according to the differences of that good. Now the diversity of this object can arise from the very nature of the object, or from a diversity in its active power. The diversity, derived from the nature of the active object, causes a material difference of passions: while the difference in regard to its active power causes a formal diversity of passions, in respect of which the passions differ specifically.

Now the nature of the motive power of the end or of the good, differs according as it is really present, or absent: because, according as it is present, it causes the faculty to find rest in it; whereas, according as it is absent, it causes the faculty to be moved towards it. Wherefore the object of sensible pleasure causes love, inasmuch as, so to speak, it attunes and conforms the appetite to itself; it causes concupiscence, inasmuch as, when absent, it draws the faculty to itself; and it causes pleasure, inasmuch as, when present, it makes the faculty to find rest in itself. Accordingly, concupiscence is a passion differing *in species* from both love and pleasure. But concupiscences of this or that pleasurable object differ *in number.*

Reply Obj. 1: Pleasurable good is the object of concupiscence, not absolutely, but considered as absent: just as the sensible, considered as past, is the object of memory. For these particular conditions diversify the species of passions, and even of the powers of the sensitive part, which regards particular things.

Reply Obj. 2: In the passage quoted we have causal, not essential predication: for covetousness is not essentially love, but an effect of love. We may also say that Augustine is taking covetousness in a wide sense, for any movement of the appetite in respect of good to come: so that it includes both love and hope.

Reply Obj. 3: The passion which is directly contrary to concupiscence has no name, and stands in relation to evil, as concupiscence in regard to good. But since, like fear, it regards the absent evil; sometimes it goes by the name of fear, just as hope is sometimes called covetousness. For a small good or evil is reckoned as though it were nothing: and consequently every movement of the appetite in future good or evil is called hope or fear, which regard good and evil as arduous.

THIRD ARTICLE [I-II, Q. 30, Art. 3]

Whether Some Concupiscences Are Natural, and Some Not Natural?

Objection 1: It would seem that concupiscences are not divided into those which are natural and those which are not. For concupiscence belongs to the animal appetite, as stated above (A. 1, ad 3). But the natural appetite is contrasted with the animal appetite. Therefore no concupiscence is natural.

Obj. 2: Further, material differences makes no difference of species, but only numerical difference; a difference which is outside the purview of science. But if some concupiscences are natural, and some not, they differ only in respect of their objects; which amounts to a material difference, which is one of number only. Therefore concupiscences should not be divided into those that are natural and those that are not.

Obj. 3: Further, reason is contrasted with nature, as stated in *Phys.* ii, 5. If therefore in man there is a concupiscence which is not natural, it must needs be rational. But this is impossible: because, since concupiscence is a passion, it belongs to the sensitive appetite, and not to the will, which is the rational appetite. Therefore there are no concupiscences which are not natural.

*On the contrary,* The Philosopher (Ethic. iii, 11 and Rhetor. i, 11) distinguishes natural concupiscences from those that are not natural.

*I answer that,* As stated above (A. 1), concupiscence is the craving for pleasurable good. Now a thing is pleasurable in two ways. First, because it is suitable to the nature of the animal; for example, food, drink, and the like: and concupiscence of such pleasurable things is said to be natural. Secondly, a thing is pleasurable because it is apprehended as suitable to the animal: as when one apprehends something as good and suitable, and consequently takes pleasure in it: and concupiscence of such pleasurable things is said to be not natural, and is more wont to be called "cupidity."

Accordingly concupiscences of the first kind, or natural concupiscences, are common to men and other animals: because to both is there something suitable and pleasurable according to nature: and in these all men agree; wherefore the Philosopher (Ethic. iii, 11) calls them "common" and "necessary." But concupiscences of the second kind are proper to men, to whom it is proper to devise something as good and suitable, beyond that which nature requires. Hence the Philosopher says (Rhet. i, 11) that the former concupiscences are "irrational," but the latter, "rational." And because different men reason differently, therefore the latter are also called (Ethic. iii, 11) "peculiar and acquired," i.e. in addition to those that are natural.

Reply Obj. 1: The same thing that is the object of the natural appetite, may be the object of the animal appetite, once it is apprehended. And in this way there may be an animal concupiscence of food, drink, and the like, which are objects of the natural appetite.

Reply Obj. 2: The difference between those concupiscences that are natural and those that are not, is not merely a material difference; it is also, in a way, formal, in so far as it arises from a difference in the active object. Now the object of the appetite is the apprehended good. Hence diversity of the active object follows from diversity of apprehension: according as a thing is apprehended as suitable, either by absolute apprehension, whence arise natural concupiscences, which the Philosopher calls "irrational" (Rhet. i, 11); or by apprehension together with deliberation, whence arise those concupiscences that are not natural, and which for this very reason the Philosopher calls "rational" (Rhet. i, 11).

Reply Obj. 3: Man has not only universal reason, pertaining to the intellectual faculty; but also particular reason pertaining to the sensitive faculty, as stated in the First Part (Q. 78, A. 4; Q. 81, A. 3): so that even rational concupiscence may pertain to the sensitive appetite. Moreover the sensitive appetite can be moved by the universal reason also, through the medium of the particular imagination.

FOURTH ARTICLE [I-II, Q. 30, Art. 4]

Whether Concupiscence Is Infinite?

Objection 1: It would seem that concupiscence is not infinite. For the object of concupiscence is good, which has the aspect of an end. But where there is infinity there is no end (Metaph. ii, 2). Therefore concupiscence cannot be infinite.

Obj. 2: Further, concupiscence is of the fitting good, since it proceeds from love. But the infinite is without proportion, and therefore unfitting. Therefore concupiscence cannot be infinite.

Obj. 3: Further, there is no passing through infinite things: and thus there is no reaching an ultimate term in them. But the subject of concupiscence is not delighted until he attain the ultimate term. Therefore, if concupiscence were infinite, no delight would ever ensue.

*On the contrary,* The Philosopher says (Polit. i, 3) that "since concupiscence is infinite, men desire an infinite number of things."

*I answer that,* As stated above (A. 3), concupiscence is twofold; one is natural, the other is not natural. Natural concupiscence cannot be actually infinite: because it is of that which nature requires; and nature ever tends to something finite and fixed. Hence man never desires infinite meat, or infinite drink. But just as in nature there is potential successive infinity, so can this kind of concupiscence be infinite successively; so that, for instance, after getting food, a man may desire food yet again; and so of anything else that nature requires: because these bodily goods, when obtained, do not last for ever, but fail. Hence Our Lord said to the woman of Samaria (John 4:13): "Whosoever drinketh of this water, shall thirst again."

But non-natural concupiscence is altogether infinite. Because, as stated above (A. 3), it follows from the reason, and it belongs to the reason to proceed to infinity. Hence he that desires riches, may desire to be rich, not up to a certain limit, but to be simply as rich as possible.

Another reason may be assigned, according to the Philosopher (Polit. i, 3), why a certain concupiscence is finite, and another infinite. Because concupiscence of the end is always infinite: since the end is desired for its own sake, e.g. health: and thus greater health is more desired, and so on to infinity; just as, if a white thing of itself dilates the sight, that which is more white dilates yet more. On the other hand, concupiscence of the means is not infinite, because the concupiscence of the means is in suitable proportion to the end. Consequently those who place their end in riches have an infinite concupiscence of riches; whereas those who desire riches, on account of the necessities of life, desire a finite measure of riches, sufficient for the necessities of life, as the Philosopher says (Polit. i, 3). The same applies to the concupiscence of any other things.

Reply Obj. 1: Every object of concupiscence is taken as something finite: either because it is finite in reality, as being once actually desired; or because it is finite as apprehended. For it cannot be apprehended as infinite, since the infinite is that "from which, however much we may take, there always remains something to be taken" (Phys. iii, 6).

Reply Obj. 2: The reason is possessed of infinite power, in a certain sense, in so far as it can consider a thing infinitely, as appears in the addition of numbers and lines. Consequently, the infinite, taken in a certain way, is proportionate to reason. In fact the universal which the reason apprehends, is infinite in a sense, inasmuch as it contains potentially an infinite number of singulars.

Reply Obj. 3: In order that a man be delighted, there is no need for him to realize all that he desires: for he delights in the realization of each object of his concupiscence.

# QUESTION 31

OF DELIGHT [*Or, Pleasure] CONSIDERED IN ITSELF (In Eight Articles)

We must now consider delight and sadness. Concerning delight four things must be considered: (1) Delight in itself; (2) The causes of delight; (3) Its effects; (4) Its goodness and malice.

Under the first head there are eight points of inquiry:

(1) Whether delight is a passion?

(2) Whether delight is subject to time?

(3) Whether it differs from joy?

(4) Whether it is in the intellectual appetite?

(5) Of the delights of the higher appetite compared with the delight of the lower;

(6) Of sensible delights compared with one another;

(7) Whether any delight is non-natural?

(8) Whether one delight can be contrary to another?

FIRST ARTICLE [I-II, Q. 31, Art. 1]

Whether Delight Is a Passion?

Objection 1: It would seem that delight is not a passion. For Damascene (De Fide Orth. ii, 22) distinguishes operation from passion, and says that "operation is a movement in accord with nature, while passion is a movement contrary to nature." But delight is an operation, according to the Philosopher (Ethic. vii, 12; x, 5). Therefore delight is not a passion.

Obj. 2: Further, "To be passive is to be moved," as stated in *Phys.* iii, 3. But delight does not consist in being moved, but in having been moved; for it arises from good already gained. Therefore delight is not a passion.

Obj. 3: Further, delight is a kind of a perfection of the one who is delighted; since it "perfects operation," as stated in *Ethic.* x, 4, 5. But to be perfected does not consist in being passive or in being altered, as stated in Phys. vii, 3 and De Anima ii, 5. Therefore delight is not a passion.

*On the contrary,* Augustine (De Civ. Dei ix, 2; xiv, 5 seqq) reckons delight, joy, or gladness among the other passions of the soul.

*I answer that,* The movements of the sensitive appetite, are properly called passions, as stated above (Q. 22, A. 3). Now every emotion arising from a sensitive apprehension, is a movement of the sensitive appetite: and this must needs be said of delight, since, according to the Philosopher (Rhet. i, 11) "delight is a certain movement of the soul and a sensible establishing thereof all at once, in keeping with the nature of the thing."

In order to understand this, we must observe that just as in natural things some happen to attain to their natural perfections, so does this happen in animals. And though movement towards perfection does not occur all at once, yet the attainment of natural perfection does occur all at once. Now there is this difference between animals and other natural things, that when these latter are established in the state becoming their nature, they do not perceive it, whereas animals do. And from this perception there arises a certain movement of the soul in the sensitive appetite; which movement is called delight. Accordingly by saying that delight is "a movement of the soul," we designate its genus. By saying that it is "an establishing in keeping with the thing's nature," i.e. with that which exists in the thing, we assign the cause of delight, viz. the presence of a becoming good. By saying that this establishing is "all at once," we mean that this establishing is to be understood not as in the process of establishment, but as in the fact of complete establishment, in the term of the movement, as it were: for delight is not a "becoming" as Plato [*Phileb. 32, 33] maintained, but a "complete fact," as stated in *Ethic.* vii, 12. Lastly, by saying that this establishing is "sensible," we exclude the perfections of insensible things wherein there is no delight. It is therefore evident that, since delight is a movement of the animal appetite arising from an apprehension of sense, it is a passion of the soul.

Reply Obj. 1: Connatural operation, which is unhindered, is a second perfection, as stated in *De Anima* ii, 1: and therefore when a thing is established in its proper connatural and unhindered operation, delight follows, which consists in a state of completion, as observed above. Accordingly when we say that delight is an operation, we designate, not its essence, but its cause.

Reply Obj. 2: A twofold movement is to be observed in an animal: one, according to the intention of the end, and this belongs to the appetite; the other, according to the execution, and this belongs to the external operation. And so, although in him who has already gained the good in which he delights, the movement of execution ceases, by which he tends to the end; yet the movement of the appetitive faculty does not cease, since, just as before it desired that which it had not, so afterwards does it delight in that which is possesses. For though delight is a certain repose of the appetite, if we consider the presence of the pleasurable good that satisfies the appetite, nevertheless there remains the impression made on the appetite by its object, by reason of which delight is a kind of movement.

Reply Obj. 3: Although the name of passion is more appropriate to those passions which have a corruptive and evil tendency, such as bodily ailments, as also sadness and fear in the soul; yet some passions have a tendency to something good, as stated above (Q. 23, AA. 1, 4): and in this sense delight is called a passion.

SECOND ARTICLE [I-II, Q. 31, Art. 2]

Whether Delight Is in Time?

Objection 1: It would seem that delight is in time. For "delight is a kind of movement," as the Philosopher says (Rhet. i, 11). But all movement is in time. Therefore delight is in time.

Obj. 2: Further, a thing is said to last long and to be morose in respect of time. But some pleasures are called morose. Therefore pleasure is in time.

Obj. 3: Further, the passions of the soul are of one same genus. But some passions of the soul are in time. Therefore delight is too.

*On the contrary,* The Philosopher says (Ethic. x, 4) that "no one takes pleasure according to time."

*I answer that,* A thing may be in time in two ways: first, by itself; secondly, by reason of something else, and accidentally as it were. For since time is the measure of successive things, those things are of themselves said to be in time, to which succession or something pertaining to succession is essential: such are movement, repose, speech and such like. On the other hand, those things are said to be in time, by reason of something else and not of themselves, to which succession is not essential, but which are subject to something successive. Thus the fact of being a man is not essentially something successive; since it is not a movement, but the term of a movement or change, viz. of this being begotten: yet, because human being is subject to changeable causes, in this respect, to be a man is in time.

Accordingly, we must say that delight, of itself indeed, is not in time: for it regards good already gained, which is, as it were, the term of the movement. But if this good gained be subject to change, the delight therein will be in time accidentally: whereas if it be altogether unchangeable, the delight therein will not be in time, either by reason of itself or accidentally.

Reply Obj. 1: As stated in *De Anima* iii, 7, movement is twofold. One is "the act of something imperfect, i.e. of something existing in potentiality, as such": this movement is successive and is in time. Another movement is "the act of something perfect, i.e. of something existing in act," e.g. to understand, to feel, and to will and such like, also to have delight. This movement is not successive, nor is it of itself in time.

Reply Obj. 2: Delight is said to be long lasting or morose, according as it is accidentally in time.

Reply Obj. 3: Other passions have not for their object a good obtained, as delight has. Wherefore there is more of the movement of the imperfect in them than in delight. And consequently it belongs more to delight not to be in time.

THIRD ARTICLE [I-II, Q. 31, Art. 3]

Whether Delight Differs from Joy?

Objection 1: It would seem that delight is altogether the same as joy. Because the passions of the soul differ according to their objects. But delight and joy have the same object, namely, a good obtained. Therefore joy is altogether the same as delight.

Obj. 2: Further, one movement does not end in two terms. But one and the same movement, that of desire, ends in joy and delight. Therefore delight and joy are altogether the same.

Obj. 3: Further, if joy differs from delight, it seems that there is equal reason for distinguishing gladness, exultation, and cheerfulness from delight, so that they would all be various passions of the soul. But this seems to be untrue. Therefore joy does not differ from delight.

*On the contrary,* We do not speak of joy in irrational animals; whereas we do speak of delight in them. Therefore joy is not the same as delight.

*I answer that,* Joy, as Avicenna states (De Anima iv), is a kind of delight. For we must observe that, just as some concupiscences are natural, and some not natural, but consequent to reason, as stated above (Q. 30, A. 3), so also some delights are natural, and some are not natural but rational. Or, as Damascene (De Fide Orth. ii, 13) and Gregory of Nyssa [*Nemesius, De Nat. Hom. xviii.] put it, "some delights are of the body, some are of the soul"; which amounts to the same. For we take delight both in those things which we desire naturally, when we get them, and in those things which we desire as a result of reason. But we do not speak of joy except when delight follows reason; and so we do not ascribe joy to irrational animals, but only delight.

Now whatever we desire naturally, can also be the object of reasoned desire and delight, but not vice versa. Consequently whatever can be the object of delight, can also be the object of joy in rational beings. And yet everything is not always the object of joy; since sometimes one feels a certain delight in the body, without rejoicing thereat according to reason. And accordingly delight extends to more things than does joy.

Reply Obj. 1: Since the object of the appetite of the soul is an apprehended good, diversity of apprehension pertains, in a way, to diversity of the object. And so delights of the soul, which are also called joys, are distinct from bodily delights, which are not called otherwise than delights: as we have observed above in regard to concupiscences (Q. 30, A. 3, ad 2).

Reply Obj. 2: A like difference is to be observed in concupiscences also: so that delight corresponds to concupiscence, while joy corresponds to desire, which seems to pertain more to concupiscence of the soul. Hence there is a difference of repose corresponding to the difference of movement.

Reply Obj. 3: These other names pertaining to delight are derived from the effects of delight; for *laetitia* (gladness) is derived from the "dilation" of the heart, as if one were to say "latitia"; "exultation" is derived from the exterior signs of inward delight, which appear outwardly in so far as the inward joy breaks forth from its bounds; and "cheerfulness" is so called from certain special signs and effects of gladness. Yet all these names seem to belong to joy; for we do not employ them save in speaking of rational beings.

FOURTH ARTICLE [I-II, Q. 31, Art. 4]

Whether Delight Is in the Intellectual Appetite?

Objection 1: It would seem that delight is not in the intellectual appetite. Because the Philosopher says (Rhet. i, 11) that "delight is a sensible movement." But sensible movement is not in an intellectual power. Therefore delight is not in the intellectual appetite.

Obj. 2: Further, delight is a passion. But every passion is in the sensitive appetite. Therefore delight is only in the sensitive appetite.

Obj. 3: Further, delight is common to us and to the irrational animals. Therefore it is not elsewhere than in that power which we have in common with irrational animals.

*On the contrary,* It is written (Ps. 36:4): "Delight in the Lord." But the sensitive appetite cannot reach to God; only the intellectual appetite can. Therefore delight can be in the intellectual appetite.

*I answer that,* As stated above (A. 3), a certain delight arises from the apprehension of the reason. Now on the reason apprehending something, not only the sensitive appetite is moved, as regards its application to some particular thing, but also the intellectual appetite, which is called the will. And accordingly in the intellectual appetite or will there is that delight which is called joy, but not bodily delight.

However, there is this difference of delight in either power, that delight of the sensitive appetite is accompanied by a bodily transmutation, whereas delight of the intellectual appetite is nothing but the mere movement of the will. Hence Augustine says (De Civ. Dei xiv, 6) that "desire and joy are nothing else but a volition of consent to the things we wish."

Reply Obj. 1: In this definition of the Philosopher, he uses the word "sensible" in its wide acceptation for any kind of perception. For he says (Ethic. x, 4) that "delight is attendant upon every sense, as it is also upon every act of the intellect and contemplation." Or we may say that he is defining delight of the sensitive appetite.

Reply Obj. 2: Delight has the character of passion, properly speaking, when accompanied by bodily transmutation. It is not thus in the intellectual appetite, but according to simple movement: for thus it is also in God and the angels. Hence the Philosopher says (Ethic. vii, 14) that "God rejoices by one simple act": and Dionysius says at the end of *De Coel. Hier.*, that "the angels are not susceptible to our passible delight, but rejoice together with God with the gladness of incorruption."

Reply Obj. 3: In us there is delight, not only in common with dumb animals, but also in common with angels. Wherefore Dionysius says (De Coel. Hier.) that "holy men often take part in the angelic delights." Accordingly we have delight, not only in the sensitive appetite, which we have in common with dumb animals, but also in the intellectual appetite, which we have in common with the angels.

FIFTH ARTICLE [I-II, Q. 31, Art. 5]

Whether Bodily and Sensible Pleasures Are Greater Than Spiritual and Intellectual Pleasures?

Objection 1: It would seem that bodily and sensible pleasures are greater than spiritual and intelligible pleasures. For all men seek some pleasure, according to the Philosopher (Ethic. x, 2, 4). But more seek sensible pleasures, than intelligible spiritual pleasures. Therefore bodily pleasures are greater.

Obj. 2: Further, the greatness of a cause is known by its effect. But bodily pleasures have greater effects; since "they alter the state of the body, and in some they cause madness" (Ethic. vii, 3). Therefore bodily pleasures are greater.

Obj. 3: Further, bodily pleasures need to be tempered and checked, by reason of their vehemence: whereas there is no need to check spiritual pleasures. Therefore bodily pleasures are greater.

*On the contrary,* It is written (Ps. 118:103): "How sweet are Thy words to my palate; more than honey to my mouth!" And the Philosopher says (Ethic. x, 7) that "the greatest pleasure is derived from the operation of wisdom."

*I answer that,* As stated above (A. 1), pleasure arises from union with a suitable object perceived or known. Now, in the operations of the soul, especially of the sensitive and intellectual soul, it must be noted that, since they do not pass into outward matter, they are acts or perfections of the agent, e.g. to understand, to feel, to will and the like: because actions which pass into outward matter, are actions and perfections rather of the matter transformed; for "movement is the act produced by the mover in the thing moved" (Phys. iii, 3). Accordingly the aforesaid actions of the sensitive and intellectual soul, are themselves a certain good of the agent, and are known by sense and intellect. Wherefore from them also does pleasure arise, and not only from their objects.

If therefore we compare intellectual pleasures with sensible pleasures, according as we delight in the very actions, for instance in sensitive and in intellectual knowledge; without doubt intellectual pleasures are much greater than sensible pleasures. For man takes much more delight in knowing something, by understanding it, than in knowing something by perceiving it with his sense. Because intellectual knowledge is more perfect; and because it is better known, since the intellect reflects on its own act more than sense does. Moreover intellectual knowledge is more beloved: for there is no one who would not forfeit his bodily sight rather than his intellectual vision, as beasts or fools are deprived thereof, as Augustine says in De Civ. Dei (De Trin. xiv, 14).

If, however, intellectual spiritual pleasures be compared with sensible bodily pleasures, then, in themselves and absolutely speaking, spiritual pleasures are greater. And this appears from the consideration of the three things needed for pleasure, viz. the good which is brought into conjunction, that to which it is conjoined, and the conjunction itself. For spiritual good is both greater and more beloved than bodily good: a sign whereof is that men abstain from even the greatest bodily pleasures, rather than suffer loss of honor which is an intellectual good. Likewise the intellectual faculty is much more noble and more knowing than the sensitive faculty. Also the conjunction is more intimate, more perfect and more firm. More intimate, because the senses stop at the outward accidents of a thing, whereas the intellect penetrates to the essence; for the object of the intellect is "what a thing is." More perfect, because the conjunction of the sensible to the sense implies movement, which is an imperfect act: wherefore sensible pleasures are not perceived all at once, but some part of them is passing away, while some other part is looked forward to as yet to be realized, as is manifest in pleasures of the table and in sexual pleasures: whereas intelligible things are without movement: hence pleasures of this kind are realized all at once. More firm; because the objects of bodily pleasure are corruptible, and soon pass away; whereas spiritual goods are incorruptible.

On the other hand, in relation to us, bodily pleasures are more vehement, for three reasons. First, because sensible things are more known to us, than intelligible things. Secondly, because sensible pleasures, through being passions of the sensitive appetite, are accompanied by some alteration in the body: whereas this does not occur in spiritual pleasures, save by reason of a certain reaction of the superior appetite on the lower. Thirdly, because bodily pleasures are sought as remedies for bodily defects or troubles, whence various griefs arise. Wherefore bodily pleasures, by reason of their succeeding griefs of this kind, are felt the more, and consequently are welcomed more than spiritual pleasures, which have no contrary griefs, as we shall state farther on (Q. 35, A. 5).

Reply Obj. 1: The reason why more seek bodily pleasures is because sensible goods are known better and more generally: and, again, because men need pleasures as remedies for many kinds of sorrow and sadness: and since the majority cannot attain spiritual pleasures, which are proper to the virtuous, hence it is that they turn aside to seek those of the body.

Reply Obj. 2: Bodily transmutation arises more from bodily pleasures, inasmuch as they are passions of the sensitive appetite.

Reply Obj. 3: Bodily pleasures are realized in the sensitive faculty which is governed by reason: wherefore they need to be tempered and checked by reason. But spiritual pleasures are in the mind, which is itself the rule: wherefore they are in themselves both sober and moderate.

SIXTH ARTICLE [I-II, Q. 31, Art. 6]

Whether the Pleasures of Touch Are Greater Than the Pleasures Afforded by the Other Senses?

Objection 1: It would seem that the pleasures of touch are not greater than the pleasures afforded by the other senses. Because the greatest pleasure seems to be that without which all joy is at an end. But such is the pleasure afforded by the sight, according to the words of Tob. 5:12: "What manner of joy shall be to me, who sit in darkness, and see not the light of heaven?" Therefore the pleasure afforded by the sight is the greatest of sensible pleasures.

Obj. 2: Further, "every one finds treasure in what he loves," as the Philosopher says (Rhet. i, 11). But "of all the senses the sight is loved most" [*Metaph. i, 1]. Therefore the greatest pleasure seems to be afforded by sight.

Obj. 3: Further, the beginning of friendship which is for the sake of the pleasant is principally sight. But pleasure is the cause of such friendship. Therefore the greatest pleasure seems to be afforded by sight.

*On the contrary,* The Philosopher says (Ethic. iii, 10), that the greatest pleasures are those which are afforded by the touch.

*I answer that,* As stated above (Q. 25, A. 2, ad 1; Q. 27, A. 4, ad 1), everything gives pleasure according as it is loved. Now, as stated in *Metaph.* i, 1, the senses are loved for two reasons: for the purpose of knowledge, and on account of their usefulness. Wherefore the senses afford pleasure in both these ways. But because it is proper to man to apprehend knowledge itself as something good, it follows that the former pleasures of the senses, i.e. those which arise from knowledge, are proper to man: whereas pleasures of the senses, as loved for their usefulness, are common to all animals.

If therefore we speak of that sensible pleasure which is by reason of knowledge, it is evident that the sight affords greater pleasure than any other sense. On the other hand, if we speak of that sensible pleasure which is by reason of usefulness, then the greatest pleasure is afforded by the touch. For the usefulness of sensible things is gauged by their relation to the preservation of the animal's nature. Now the sensible objects of touch bear the closest relation to this usefulness: for the touch takes cognizance of those things which are vital to an animal, namely, of things hot and cold and the like. Wherefore in this respect, the pleasures of touch are greater as being more closely related to the end. For this reason, too, other animals which do not experience sensible pleasure save by reason of usefulness, derive no pleasure from the other senses except as subordinated to the sensible objects of the touch: "for dogs do not take delight in the smell of hares, but in eating them; ... nor does the lion feel pleasure in the lowing of an ox, but in devouring it" (Ethic. iii, 10).

Since then the pleasure afforded by touch is the greatest in respect of usefulness, and the pleasure afforded by sight the greatest in respect of knowledge; if anyone wish to compare these two, he will find that the pleasure of touch is, absolutely speaking, greater than the pleasure of sight, so far as the latter remains within the limits of sensible pleasure. Because it is evident that in everything, that which is natural is most powerful: and it is to these pleasures of the touch that the natural concupiscences, such as those of food, sexual union, and the like, are ordained. If, however, we consider the pleasures of sight, inasmuch sight is the handmaid of the mind, then the pleasures of sight are greater, forasmuch as intellectual pleasures are greater than sensible.

Reply Obj. 1: Joy, as stated above (A. 3), denotes pleasure of the soul; and this belongs principally to the sight. But natural pleasure belongs principally to the touch.

Reply Obj. 2: The sight is loved most, "on account of knowledge, because it helps us to distinguish many things," as is stated in the same passage (Metaph. i, 1).

Reply Obj. 3: Pleasure causes carnal love in one way; the sight, in another. For pleasure, especially that which is afforded by the touch, is the final cause of the friendship which is for the sake of the pleasant: whereas the sight is a cause like that from which a movement has its beginning, inasmuch as the beholder on seeing the lovable object receives an impression of its image, which entices him to love it and to seek its delight.

SEVENTH ARTICLE [I-II, Q. 31, Art. 7]

Whether Any Pleasure Is Not Natural?

Objection 1: It would seem that no pleasure is not natural. For pleasure is to the emotions of the soul what repose is to bodies. But the appetite of a natural body does not repose save in a connatural place. Neither, therefore, can the repose of the animal appetite, which is pleasure, be elsewhere than in something connatural. Therefore no pleasure is non-natural.

Obj. 2: Further, what is against nature is violent. But "whatever is violent causes grief" (Metaph. v, 5). Therefore nothing which is unnatural can give pleasure.

Obj. 3: Further, the fact of being established in one's own nature, if perceived, gives rise to pleasure, as is evident from the Philosopher's definition quoted above (A. 1). But it is natural to every thing to be established in its nature; because natural movement tends to a natural end. Therefore every pleasure is natural.

*On the contrary,* The Philosopher says (Ethic. vii, 5, 6) that some things are pleasant "not from nature but from disease."

*I answer that,* We speak of that as being natural, which is in accord with nature, as stated in *Phys.* ii, 1. Now, in man, nature can be taken in two ways. First, inasmuch as intellect and reason is the principal part of man's nature, since in respect thereof he has his own specific nature. And in this sense, those pleasures may be called natural to man, which are derived from things pertaining to man in respect of his reason: for instance, it is natural to man to take pleasure in contemplating the truth and in doing works of virtue. Secondly, nature in man may be taken as contrasted with reason, and as denoting that which is common to man and other animals, especially that part of man which does not obey reason. And in this sense, that which pertains to the preservation of the body, either as regards the individual, as food, drink, sleep, and the like, or as regards the species, as sexual intercourse, are said to afford man natural pleasure. Under each kind of pleasures, we find some that are *not natural* speaking absolutely, and yet connatural in some respect. For it happens in an individual that some one of the natural principles of the species is corrupted, so that something which is contrary to the specific nature, becomes accidentally natural to this individual: thus it is natural to this hot water to give heat. Consequently it happens that something which is not natural to man, either in regard to reason, or in regard to the preservation of the body, becomes connatural to this individual man, on account of there being some corruption of nature in him. And this corruption may be either on the part of the body—from some ailment; thus to a man suffering from fever, sweet things seem bitter, and vice versa—or from an evil temperament; thus some take pleasure in eating earth and coals and the like; or on the part of the soul; thus from custom some take pleasure in cannibalism or in the unnatural intercourse of man and beast, or other such things, which are not in accord with human nature.

This suffices for the answers to the objections.

EIGHTH ARTICLE [I-II, Q. 31, Art. 8]

Whether One Pleasure Can Be Contrary to Another?

Objection 1: It would seem that one pleasure cannot be contrary to another. Because the passions of the soul derive their species and contrariety from their objects. Now the object of pleasure is the good. Since therefore good is not contrary to good, but "good is contrary to evil, and evil to good," as stated in Praedic. viii; it seems that one pleasure is not contrary to another.

Obj. 2: Further, to one thing there is one contrary, as is proved in *Metaph.* x, 4. But sadness is contrary to pleasure. Therefore pleasure is not contrary to pleasure.

Obj. 3: Further, if one pleasure is contrary to another, this is only on account of the contrariety of the things which give pleasure. But this difference is material: whereas contrariety is a difference of form, as stated in *Metaph.* x, 4. Therefore there is no contrariety between one pleasure and another.

*On the contrary,* Things of the same genus that impede one another are contraries, as the Philosopher states (Phys. viii, 8). But some pleasures impede one another, as stated in Ethic. x, 5. Therefore some pleasures are contrary to one another.

*I answer that,* Pleasure, in the emotions of the soul, is likened to repose in natural bodies, as stated above (Q. 23, A. 4). Now one repose is said to be contrary to another when they are in contrary termini; thus, "repose in a high place is contrary to repose in a low place" (Phys. v, 6). Wherefore it happens in the emotions of the soul that one pleasure is contrary to another.

Reply Obj. 1: This saying of the Philosopher is to be understood of good and evil as applied to virtues and vices: because one vice may be contrary to another vice, whereas no virtue can be contrary to another virtue. But in other things nothing prevents one good from being contrary to another, such as hot and cold, of which the former is good in relation to fire, the latter, in relation to water. And in this way one pleasure can be contrary to another. That this is impossible with regard to the good of virtue, is due to the fact that virtue's good depends on fittingness in relation to some one thing—i.e. the reason.

Reply Obj. 2: Pleasure, in the emotions of the soul, is likened to natural repose in bodies: because its object is something suitable and connatural, so to speak. But sadness is like a violent repose; because its object is disagreeable to the animal appetite, just as the place of violent repose is disagreeable to the natural appetite. Now natural repose is contrary both to violent repose of the same body, and to the natural repose of another, as stated in *Phys*. v, 6. Wherefore pleasure is contrary to both to another pleasure and to sadness.

Reply Obj. 3: The things in which we take pleasure, since they are the objects of pleasure, cause not only a material, but also a formal difference, if the formality of pleasurableness be different. Because difference in the formal object causes a specific difference in acts and passions, as stated above (Q. 23, AA. 1, 4; Q. 30, A. 2).

# QUESTION 32

OF THE CAUSE OF PLEASURE (In Eight Articles)

We must now consider the causes of pleasure: and under this head there are eight points of inquiry:

(1) Whether operation is the proper cause of pleasure?

(2) Whether movement is a cause of pleasure?

(3) Whether hope and memory cause pleasure?

(4) Whether sadness causes pleasure?

(5) Whether the actions of others are a cause of pleasure to us?

(6) Whether doing good to another is a cause of pleasure?

(7) Whether likeness is a cause of pleasure?

(8) Whether wonder is a cause of pleasure?

FIRST ARTICLE [I-II, Q. 32, Art. 1]

Whether Operation Is the Proper Cause of Pleasure?

Objection 1: It would seem that operation is not the proper and first cause of pleasure. For, as the Philosopher says (Rhet. i, 11), "pleasure consists in a perception of the senses," since knowledge is requisite for pleasure, as stated above (Q. 31, A. 1). But the objects of operations are knowable before the operations themselves. Therefore operation is not the proper cause of pleasure.

Obj. 2: Further, pleasure consists especially in an end gained: since it is this that is chiefly desired. But the end is not always an operation, but is sometimes the effect of the operation. Therefore operation is not the proper and direct cause of pleasure.

Obj. 3: Further, leisure and rest consist in cessation from work: and they are objects of pleasure (Rhet. i, 11). Therefore operation is not the proper cause of pleasure.

*On the contrary,* The Philosopher says (Ethic. vii, 12, 13; x, 4) that "pleasure is a connatural and uninterrupted operation."

*I answer that,* As stated above (Q. 31, A. 1), two things are requisite for pleasure: namely, the attainment of the suitable good, and knowledge of this attainment. Now each of these consists in a kind of operation: because actual knowledge is an operation; and the attainment of the suitable good is by means of an operation. Moreover, the proper operation itself is a suitable good. Wherefore every pleasure must needs be the result of some operation.

Reply Obj. 1: The objects of operations are not pleasurable save inasmuch as they are united to us; either by knowledge alone, as when we take pleasure in thinking of or looking at certain things; or in some other way in addition to knowledge; as when a man takes pleasure in knowing that he has something good—riches, honor, or the like; which would not be pleasurable unless they were apprehended as possessed. For as the Philosopher observes (Polit. ii, 2) "we take great pleasure in looking upon a thing as our own, by reason of the natural love we have for ourselves." Now to have such like things is nothing else but to use them or to be able to use them: and this is through some operation. Wherefore it is evident that every pleasure is traced to some operation as its cause.

Reply Obj. 2: Even when it is not an operation, but the effect of an operation, that is the end, this effect is pleasant in so far as possessed or effected: and this implies use or operation.

Reply Obj. 3: Operations are pleasant, in so far as they are proportionate and connatural to the agent. Now, since human power is finite, operation is proportionate thereto according to a certain measure. Wherefore if it exceed that measure, it will be no longer proportionate or pleasant, but, *on the contrary,* painful and irksome. And in this sense, leisure and play and other things pertaining to repose, are pleasant, inasmuch as they banish sadness which results from labor.

SECOND ARTICLE [I-II, Q. 32, Art. 2]

Whether Movement Is a Cause of Pleasure?

Objection 1: It would seem that movement is not a cause of pleasure. Because, as stated above (Q. 31, A. 1), the good which is obtained and is actually possessed, is the cause of pleasure: wherefore the Philosopher says (Ethic. vii, 12) that pleasure is not compared with generation, but with the operation of a thing already in existence. Now that which is being moved towards something has it not as yet; but, so to speak, is being generated in its regard, forasmuch as generation or corruption are united to every movement, as stated in *Phys.* viii, 3. Therefore movement is not a cause of pleasure.

Obj. 2: Further, movement is the chief cause of toil and fatigue in our works. But operations through being toilsome and fatiguing are not pleasant but disagreeable. Therefore movement is not a cause of pleasure.

Obj. 3: Further, movement implies a certain innovation, which is the opposite of custom. But things "which we are accustomed to, are pleasant," as the Philosopher says (Rhet. i, 11). Therefore movement is not a cause of pleasure.

*On the contrary,* Augustine says (Confess. viii, 3): "What means this, O Lord my God, whereas Thou art everlasting joy to Thyself, and some things around Thee evermore rejoice in Thee? What means this, that this portion of things ebbs and flows alternately displeased and reconciled?" From these words we gather that man rejoices and takes pleasure in some kind of alterations: and therefore movement seems to cause pleasure.

*I answer that,* Three things are requisite for pleasure; two, i.e. the one that is pleased and the pleasurable object conjoined to him; and a third, which is knowledge of this conjunction: and in respect of these three, movement is pleasant, as the Philosopher says (Ethic. vii, 14 and Rhetor. i, 11). For as far as we who feel pleasure are concerned, change is pleasant to us because our nature is changeable: for which reason that which is suitable to us at one time is not suitable at another; thus to warm himself at a fire is suitable to man in winter but not in summer. Again, on the part of the pleasing good which is united to us, change is pleasant. Because the continued action of an agent increases its effect: thus the longer a person remains near the fire, the more he is warmed and dried. Now the natural mode of being consists in a certain measure; and therefore when the continued presence of a pleasant object exceeds the measure of one's natural mode of being, the removal of that object becomes pleasant. On the part of the knowledge itself (change becomes pleasant), because man desires to know something whole and perfect: when therefore a thing cannot be apprehended all at once as a whole, change in such a thing is pleasant, so that one part may pass and another succeed, and thus the whole be perceived. Hence Augustine says (Confess. iv, 11): "Thou wouldst not have the syllables stay, but fly away, that others may come, and thou hear the whole. And so whenever any one thing is made up of many, all of which do not exist together, all would please collectively more than they do severally, if all could be perceived collectively."

If therefore there be any thing, whose nature is unchangeable; the natural mode of whose being cannot be exceeded by the continuation of any pleasing object; and which can behold the whole object of its delight at once—to such a one change will afford no delight. And the more any pleasures approach to this, the more are they capable of being continual.

Reply Obj. 1: Although the subject of movement has not yet perfectly that to which it is moved, nevertheless it is beginning to have something thereof: and in this respect movement itself has something of pleasure. But it falls short of the perfection of pleasure; because the more perfect pleasures regard things that are unchangeable. Moreover movement becomes the cause of pleasure, in so far as thereby something which previously was unsuitable, becomes suitable or ceases to be, as stated above.

Reply Obj. 2: Movement causes toil and fatigue, when it exceeds our natural aptitude. It is not thus that it causes pleasure, but by removing the obstacles to our natural aptitude.

Reply Obj. 3: What is customary becomes pleasant, in so far as it becomes natural: because custom is like a second nature. But the movement which gives pleasure is not that which departs from custom, but rather that which prevents the corruption of the natural mode of being, that might result from continued operation. And thus from the same cause of connaturalness, both custom and movement become pleasant.

THIRD ARTICLE [I-II, Q. 32, Art. 3]

Whether Hope and Memory Cause Pleasure?

Objection 1: It would seem that memory and hope do not cause pleasure. Because pleasure is caused by present good, as Damascene says (De Fide Orth. ii, 12). But hope and memory regard what is absent: since memory is of the past, and hope of the future. Therefore memory and hope do not cause pleasure.

Obj. 2: Further, the same thing is not the cause of contraries. But hope causes affliction, according to Prov. 13:12: "Hope that is deferred afflicteth the soul." Therefore hope does not cause pleasure.

Obj. 3: Further, just as hope agrees with pleasure in regarding good, so also do desire and love. Therefore hope should not be assigned as a cause of pleasure, any more than desire or love.

*On the contrary,* It is written (Rom. 12:12): "Rejoicing in hope"; and (Ps. 76:4): "I remembered God, and was delighted."

*I answer that,* Pleasure is caused by the presence of suitable good, in so far as it is felt, or perceived in any way. Now a thing is present to us in two ways. First, in knowledge—i.e. according as the thing known is in the knower by its likeness; secondly, in reality—i.e. according as one thing is in real conjunction of any kind with another, either actually or potentially. And since real conjunction is greater than conjunction by likeness, which is the conjunction of knowledge; and again, since actual is greater than potential conjunction: therefore the greatest pleasure is that which arises from sensation which requires the presence of the sensible object. The second place belongs to the pleasure of hope, wherein there is pleasurable conjunction, not only in respect of apprehension, but also in respect of the faculty or power of obtaining the pleasurable object. The third place belongs to the pleasure of memory, which has only the conjunction of apprehension.

Reply Obj. 1: Hope and memory are indeed of things which, absolutely speaking, are absent: and yet those are, after a fashion, present, i.e. either according to apprehension only; or according to apprehension and possibility, at least supposed, of attainment.

Reply Obj. 2: Nothing prevents the same thing, in different ways, being the cause of contraries. And so hope, inasmuch as it implies a present appraising of a future good, causes pleasure; whereas, inasmuch as it implies absence of that good, it causes affliction.

Reply Obj. 3: Love and concupiscence also cause pleasure. For everything that is loved becomes pleasing to the lover, since love is a kind of union or connaturalness of lover and beloved. In like manner every object of desire is pleasing to the one that desires, since desire is chiefly a craving for pleasure. However hope, as implying a certainty of the real presence of the pleasing good, that is not implied either by love or by concupiscence, is reckoned in preference to them as causing pleasure; and also in preference to memory, which is of that which has already passed away.

FOURTH ARTICLE [I-II, Q. 32, Art. 4]

Whether sadness causes pleasure?

Objection 1: It would seem that sadness does not cause pleasure. For nothing causes its own contrary. But sadness is contrary to pleasure. Therefore it does not cause it.

Obj. 2: Further, contraries have contrary effects. But pleasures, when called to mind, cause pleasure. Therefore sad things, when remembered, cause sorrow and not pleasure.

Obj. 3: Further, as sadness is to pleasure, so is hatred to love. But hatred does not cause love, but rather the other way about, as stated above (Q. 29, A. 2). Therefore sadness does not cause pleasure.

*On the contrary,* It is written (Ps. 41:4): "My tears have been my bread day and night": where bread denotes the refreshment of pleasure. Therefore tears, which arise from sadness, can give pleasure.

*I answer that,* Sadness may be considered in two ways: as existing actually, and as existing in the memory: and in both ways sadness can cause pleasure. Because sadness, as actually existing, causes pleasure, inasmuch as it brings to mind that which is loved, the absence of which causes sadness; and yet the mere thought of it gives pleasure. The recollection of sadness becomes a cause of pleasure, on account of the deliverance which ensued: because absence of evil is looked upon as something good; wherefore so far as a man thinks that he has been delivered from that which caused him sorrow and pain, so much reason has he to rejoice. Hence Augustine says in *De Civ. Dei* xxii, 31 [*Gregory, Moral. iv.] that "oftentimes in joy we call to mind sad things ... and in the season of health we recall past pains without feeling pain ... and in proportion are the more filled with joy and gladness": and again (Confess. viii, 3) he says that "the more peril there was in the battle, so much the more joy will there be in the triumph."

Reply Obj. 1: Sometimes accidentally a thing is the cause of its contrary: thus "that which is cold sometimes causes heat," as stated in *Phys.* viii, 1. In like manner sadness is the accidental cause of pleasure, in so far as it gives rise to the apprehension of something pleasant.

Reply Obj. 2: Sad things, called to mind, cause pleasure, not in so far as they are sad and contrary to pleasant things; but in so far as man is delivered from them. In like manner the recollection of pleasant things, by reason of these being lost, may cause sadness.

Reply Obj. 3: Hatred also can be the accidental cause of love: i.e. so far as some love one another, inasmuch as they agree in hating one and the same thing.

FIFTH ARTICLE [I-II, Q. 32, Art. 5]

Whether the Actions of Others Are a Cause of Pleasure to Us?

Objection 1: It would seem that the actions of others are not a cause of pleasure to us. Because the cause of pleasure is our own good when conjoined to us. But the actions of others are not conjoined to us. Therefore they are not a cause of pleasure to us.

Obj. 2: Further, the action is the agent's own good. If, therefore, the actions of others are a cause of pleasure to us, for the same reason all goods belonging to others will be pleasing to us: which is evidently untrue.

Obj. 3: Further, action is pleasant through proceeding from an innate habit; hence it is stated in *Ethic.* ii, 3 that "we must reckon the pleasure which follows after action, as being the sign of a habit existing in us." But the actions of others do not proceed from habits existing in us, but, sometimes, from habits existing in the agents. Therefore the actions of others are not pleasing to us, but to the agents themselves.

*On the contrary,* It is written in the second canonical epistle of John (verse 4): "I was exceeding glad that I found thy children walking in truth."

*I answer that,* As stated above (A. 1; Q. 31, A. 1), two things are requisite for pleasure, namely, the attainment of one's proper good, and the knowledge of having obtained it. Wherefore the action of another may cause pleasure to us in three ways. First, from the fact that we obtain some good through the action of another. And in this way, the actions of those who do some good to us, are pleasing to us: since it is pleasant to be benefited by another. Secondly, from the fact that another's action makes us to know or appreciate our own good: and for this reason men take pleasure in being praised or honored by others, because, to wit, they thus become aware of some good existing in themselves. And since this appreciation receives greater weight from the testimony of good and wise men, hence men take greater pleasure in being praised and honored by them. And because a flatterer appears to praise, therefore flattery is pleasing to some. And as love is for something good, while admiration is for something great, so it is pleasant to be loved and admired by others, inasmuch as a man thus becomes aware of his own goodness or greatness, through their giving pleasure to others. Thirdly, from the fact that another's actions, if they be good, are reckoned as one's own good, by reason of the power of love, which makes a man to regard his friend as one with himself. And on account of hatred, which makes one to reckon another's good as being in opposition to oneself, the evil action of an enemy becomes an object of pleasure: whence it is written (1 Cor. 13:6) that charity "rejoiceth not in iniquity, but rejoiceth with the truth."

Reply Obj. 1: Another's action may be conjoined to me, either by its effect, as in the first way, or by knowledge, as in the second way; or by affection, as in the third way.

Reply Obj. 2: This argument avails for the third mode, but not for the first two.

Reply Obj. 3: Although the actions of another do not proceed from habits that are in me, yet they either produce in me something that gives pleasure; or they make me appreciate or know a habit of mind; or they proceed from the habit of one who is united to me by love.

SIXTH ARTICLE [I-II, Q. 32, Art. 6]

Whether Doing Good to Another Is a Cause of Pleasure?

Objection 1: It would seem that doing good to another is not a cause of pleasure. Because pleasure is caused by one's obtaining one's proper good, as stated above (AA. 1, 5; Q. 31, A. 1). But doing good pertains not to the obtaining but to the spending of one's proper good. Therefore it seems to be the cause of sadness rather than of pleasure.

Obj. 2: Further, the Philosopher says (Ethic. iv, 1) that "illiberality is more connatural to man than prodigality." Now it is a mark of prodigality to do good to others; while it is a mark of illiberality to desist from doing good. Since therefore everyone takes pleasure in a connatural operation, as stated in *Ethic.* vii, 14 and x, 4, it seems that doing good to others is not a cause of pleasure.

Obj. 3: Further, contrary effects proceed from contrary causes. But man takes a natural pleasure in certain kinds of ill-doing, such as overcoming, contradicting or scolding others, or, if he be angry, in punishing them, as the Philosopher says (Rhet. i, 11). Therefore doing good to others is a cause of sadness rather than pleasure.

*On the contrary,* The Philosopher says (Polit. ii, 2) that "it is most pleasant to give presents or assistance to friends and strangers."

*I answer that,* Doing good to another may give pleasure in three ways. First, in consideration of the effect, which is the good conferred on another. In this respect, inasmuch as through being united to others by love, we look upon their good as being our own, we take pleasure in the good we do to others, especially to our friends, as in our own good. Secondly, in consideration of the end; as when a man, from doing good to another, hopes to get some good for himself, either from God or from man: for hope is a cause of pleasure. Thirdly, in consideration of the principle: and thus, doing good to another, can give pleasure in respect of a threefold principle. One is the faculty of doing good: and in this regard, doing good to another becomes pleasant, in so far as it arouses in man an imagination of abundant good existing in him, whereof he is able to give others a share. Wherefore men take pleasure in their children, and in their own works, as being things on which they bestow a share of their own good. Another principle is man's habitual inclination to do good, by reason of which doing good becomes connatural to him: for which reason the liberal man takes pleasure in giving to others. The third principle is the motive: for instance when a man is moved by one whom he loves, to do good to someone: for whatever we do or suffer for a friend is pleasant, because love is the principal cause of pleasure.

Reply Obj. 1: Spending gives pleasure as showing forth one's good. But in so far as it empties us of our own good it may be a cause of sadness; for instance when it is excessive.

Reply Obj. 2: Prodigality is an excessive spending, which is unnatural: wherefore prodigality is said to be contrary to nature.

Reply Obj. 3: To overcome, to contradict, and to punish, give pleasure, not as tending to another's ill, but as pertaining to one's own good, which man loves more than he hates another's ill. For it is naturally pleasant to overcome, inasmuch as it makes a man to appreciate his own superiority. Wherefore all those games in which there is a striving for the mastery, and a possibility of winning it, afford the greatest pleasure: and speaking generally all contests, in so far as they admit hope of victory. To contradict and to scold can give pleasure in two ways. First, as making man imagine himself to be wise and excellent; since it belongs to wise men and elders to reprove and to scold. Secondly, in so far as by scolding and reproving, one does good to another: for this gives one pleasure, as stated above. It is pleasant to an angry man to punish, in so far as he thinks himself to be removing an apparent slight, which seems to be due to a previous hurt: for when a man is hurt by another, he seems to be slighted thereby; and therefore he wishes to be quit of this slight by paying back the hurt. And thus it is clear that doing good to another may be of itself pleasant: whereas doing evil to another is not pleasant, except in so far as it seems to affect one's own good.

SEVENTH ARTICLE [I-II, Q. 32, Art. 7]

Whether Likeness Is a Cause of Pleasure?

Objection 1: It would seem that likeness is not a cause of pleasure. Because ruling and presiding seem to imply a certain unlikeness. But "it is natural to take pleasure in ruling and presiding," as stated in *Rhetor.* i, 11. Therefore unlikeness, rather than likeness, is a cause of pleasure.

Obj. 2: Further, nothing is more unlike pleasure than sorrow. But those who are burdened by sorrow are most inclined to seek pleasures, as the Philosopher says (Ethic. vii, 14). Therefore unlikeness, rather than likeness, is a cause of pleasure.

Obj. 3: Further, those who are satiated with certain delights, derive not pleasure but disgust from them; as when one is satiated with food. Therefore likeness is not a cause of pleasure.

*On the contrary,* Likeness is a cause of love, as above stated (Q. 27, A. 3): and love is the cause of pleasure. Therefore likeness is a cause of pleasure.

*I answer that,* Likeness is a kind of unity; hence that which is like us, as being one with us, causes pleasure; just at it causes love, as stated above (Q. 27, A. 3). And if that which is like us does not hurt our own good, but increase it, it is pleasurable simply; for instance one man in respect of another, one youth in relation to another. But if it be hurtful to our own good, thus accidentally it causes disgust or sadness, not as being like and one with us, but as hurtful to that which is yet more one with us.

Now it happens in two ways that something like is hurtful to our own good. First, by destroying the measure of our own good, by a kind of excess; because good, especially bodily good, as health, is conditioned by a certain measure: wherefore superfluous good or any bodily pleasure, causes disgust. Secondly, by being directly contrary to one's own good: thus a potter dislikes other potters, not because they are potters, but because they deprive him of his own excellence or profits, which he seeks as his own good.

Reply Obj. 1: Since ruler and subject are in communion with one another, there is a certain likeness between them: but this likeness is conditioned by a certain superiority, since ruling and presiding pertain to the excellence of a man's own good: because they belong to men who are wise and better than others; the result being that they give man an idea of his own excellence. Another reason is that by ruling and presiding, a man does good to others, which is pleasant.

Reply Obj. 2: That which gives pleasure to the sorrowful man, though it be unlike sorrow, bears some likeness to the man that is sorrowful: because sorrows are contrary to his own good. Wherefore the sorrowful man seeks pleasure as making for his own good, in so far as it is a remedy for its contrary. And this is why bodily pleasures, which are contrary to certain sorrows, are more sought than intellectual pleasures, which have no contrary sorrow, as we shall state later on (Q. 35, A. 5). And this explains why all animals naturally desire pleasure: because animals ever work through sense and movement. For this reason also young people are most inclined to seek pleasures; on account of the many changes to which they are subject, while yet growing. Moreover this is why the melancholic has a strong desire for pleasures, in order to drive away sorrow: because his "body is corroded by a base humor," as stated in *Ethic.* vii, 14.

Reply Obj. 3: Bodily goods are conditioned by a certain fixed measure: wherefore surfeit of such things destroys the proper good, and consequently gives rise to disgust and sorrow, through being contrary to the proper good of man.

EIGHTH ARTICLE [I-II, Q. 32, Art. 8]

Whether Wonder Is a Cause of Pleasure?

Objection 1: It would seem that wonder is not a cause of pleasure. Because wonder is the act of one who is ignorant of the nature of something, as Damascene says. But knowledge, rather than ignorance, is a cause of pleasure. Therefore wonder is not a cause of pleasure.

Obj. 2: Further, wonder is the beginning of wisdom, being as it were, the road to the search of truth, as stated in the beginning of *Metaph.* i, 2. But "it is more pleasant to think of what we know, than to seek what we know not," as the Philosopher says (Ethic. x, 7): since in the latter case we encounter difficulties and hindrances, in the former not; while pleasure arises from an operation which is unhindered, as stated in *Ethic.* vii, 12, 13. Therefore wonder hinders rather than causes pleasure.

Obj. 3: Further, everyone takes pleasure in what he is accustomed to: wherefore the actions of habits acquired by custom, are pleasant. But "we wonder at what is unwonted," as Augustine says (Tract. xxiv in Joan.). Therefore wonder is contrary to the cause of pleasure.

*On the contrary,* The Philosopher says (Rhet. i, 11) that wonder is the cause of pleasure.

*I answer that,* It is pleasant to get what one desires, as stated above (Q. 23, A. 4): and therefore the greater the desire for the thing loved, the greater the pleasure when it is attained: indeed the very increase of desire brings with it an increase of pleasure, according as it gives rise to the hope of obtaining that which is loved, since it was stated above (A. 3, ad 3) that desire resulting from hope is a cause of pleasure. Now wonder is a kind of desire for knowledge; a desire which comes to man when he sees an effect of which the cause either is unknown to him, or surpasses his knowledge or faculty of understanding. Consequently wonder is a cause of pleasure, in so far as it includes a hope of getting the knowledge which one desires to have. For this reason whatever is wonderful is pleasing, for instance things that are scarce. Also, representations of things, even of those which are not pleasant in themselves, give rise to pleasure; for the soul rejoices in comparing one thing with another, because comparison of one thing with another is the proper and connatural act of the reason, as the Philosopher says (Poet. iv). This again is why "it is more delightful to be delivered from great danger, because it is something wonderful," as stated in *Rhetor.* i, 11.

Reply Obj. 1: Wonder gives pleasure, not because it implies ignorance, but in so far as it includes the desire of learning the cause, and in so far as the wonderer learns something new, i.e. that the cause is other than he had thought it to be. [*According to another reading:—that he is other than he thought himself to be.]

Reply Obj. 2: Pleasure includes two things; rest in the good, and perception of this rest. As to the former therefore, since it is more perfect to contemplate the known truth, than to seek for the unknown, the contemplation of what we know, is in itself more pleasing than the research of what we do not know. Nevertheless, as to the second, it happens that research is sometimes more pleasing accidentally, in so far as it proceeds from a greater desire: for greater desire is awakened when we are conscious of our ignorance. This is why man takes the greatest pleasure in finding or learning things for the first time.

Reply Obj. 3: It is pleasant to do what we are wont to do, inasmuch as this is connatural to us, as it were. And yet things that are of rare occurrence can be pleasant, either as regards knowledge, from the fact that we desire to know something about them, in so far as they are wonderful; or as regards action, from the fact that "the mind is more inclined by desire to act intensely in things that are new," as stated in *Ethic.* x, 4, since more perfect operation causes more perfect pleasure.

# QUESTION 33

OF THE EFFECTS OF PLEASURE (In Four Articles)

We must now consider the effects of pleasure; and under this head there are four points of inquiry:

(1) Whether expansion is an effect of pleasure?

(2) Whether pleasure causes thirst or desire for itself?

(3) Whether pleasure hinders the use of reason?

(4) Whether pleasure perfects operation?

FIRST ARTICLE [I-II, Q. 33, Art. 1]

Whether Expansion Is an Effect of Pleasure?

Objection 1: It would seem that expansion is not an effect of pleasure. For expansion seems to pertain more to love, according to the Apostle (2 Cor. 6:11): "Our heart is enlarged." Wherefore it is written (Ps. 118:96) concerning the precept of charity: "Thy commandment is exceeding broad." But pleasure is a distinct passion from love. Therefore expansion is not an effect of pleasure.

Obj. 2: Further, when a thing expands it is enabled to receive more. But receiving pertains to desire, which is for something not yet possessed. Therefore expansion seems to belong to desire rather than to pleasure.

Obj. 3: Further, contraction is contrary to expansion. But contraction seems to belong to pleasure, for the hand closes on that which we wish to grasp firmly: and such is the affection of appetite in regard to that which pleases it. Therefore expansion does not pertain to pleasure.

*On the contrary,* In order to express joy, it is written (Isa. 60:5): "Thou shall see and abound, thy heart shall wonder and be enlarged." Moreover pleasure is called by the name of "laetitia" as being derived from "dilatatio" (expansion), as stated above (Q. 31, A. 3, ad 3).

*I answer that,* Breadth ( latitudo )is a dimension of bodily magnitude: hence it is not applied to the emotions of the soul, save metaphorically. Now expansion denotes a kind of movement towards breadth; and it belongs to pleasure in respect of the two things requisite for pleasure. One of these is on the part of the apprehensive power, which is cognizant of the conjunction with some suitable good. As a result of this apprehension, man perceives that he has attained a certain perfection, which is a magnitude of the spiritual order: and in this respect man's mind is said to be magnified or expanded by pleasure. The other requisite for pleasure is on the part of the appetitive power, which acquiesces in the pleasurable object, and rests therein, offering, as it were, to enfold it within itself. And thus man's affection is expanded by pleasure, as though it surrendered itself to hold within itself the object of its pleasure.

Reply Obj. 1: In metaphorical expressions nothing hinders one and the same thing from being attributed to different things according to different likenesses. And in this way expansion pertains to love by reason of a certain spreading out, in so far as the affection of the lover spreads out to others, so as to care, not only for his own interests, but also for what concerns others. On the other hand expansion pertains to pleasure, in so far as a thing becomes more ample in itself so as to become more capacious.

Reply Obj. 2: Desire includes a certain expansion arising from the imagination of the thing desired; but this expansion increases at the presence of the pleasurable object: because the mind surrenders itself more to that object when it is already taking pleasure in it, than when it desires it before possessing it; since pleasure is the end of desire.

Reply Obj. 3: He that takes pleasure in a thing holds it fast, by clinging to it with all his might: but he opens his heart to it that he may enjoy it perfectly.

SECOND ARTICLE [I-II, Q. 33, Art. 2]

Whether Pleasure Causes Thirst or Desire for Itself?

Objection 1: It would seem that pleasure does not cause desire for itself. Because all movement ceases when repose is reached. But pleasure is, as it were, a certain repose of the movement of desire, as stated above (Q. 23, A. 4; Q. 25, A. 2). Therefore the movement of desire ceases when pleasure is reached. Therefore pleasure does not cause desire.

Obj. 2: Further, a thing does not cause its contrary. But pleasure is, in a way, contrary to desire, on the part of the object: since desire regards a good which is not yet possessed, whereas pleasure regards the good that is possessed. Therefore pleasure does not cause desire for itself.

Obj. 3: Further, distaste is incompatible with desire. But pleasure often causes distaste. Therefore it does not cause desire.

*On the contrary,* Our Lord said (John 4:13): "Whosoever drinketh of this water, shall thirst again": where, according to Augustine (Tract. xv in Joan.), water denotes pleasures of the body.

*I answer that,* Pleasure can be considered in two ways; first, as existing in reality; secondly, as existing in the memory. Again thirst, or desire, can be taken in two ways; first, properly, as denoting a craving for something not possessed; secondly, in general, as excluding distaste.

Considered as existing in reality, pleasure does not of itself cause thirst or desire for itself, but only accidentally; provided we take thirst or desire as denoting a craving for some thing not possessed: because pleasure is an emotion of the appetite in respect of something actually present. But it may happen that what is actually present is not perfectly possessed: and this may be on the part of the thing possessed, or on the part of the possessor. On the part of the thing possessed, this happens through the thing possessed not being a simultaneous whole; wherefore one obtains possession of it successively, and while taking pleasure in what one has, one desires to possess the remainder: thus if a man is pleased with the first part of a verse, he desires to hear the second part, as Augustine says (Confess. iv, 11). In this way nearly all bodily pleasures cause thirst for themselves, until they are fully realized, because pleasures of this kind arise from some movement: as is evident in pleasures of the table. On the part of the possessor, this happens when a man possesses a thing which is perfect in itself, yet does not possess it perfectly, but obtains possession of it little by little. Thus in this life, a faint perception of Divine knowledge affords us delight, and delight sets up a thirst or desire for perfect knowledge; in which sense we may understand the words of Ecclus. 24:29: "They that drink me shall yet thirst."

On the other hand, if by thirst or desire we understand the mere intensity of the emotion, that excludes distaste, thus more than all others spiritual pleasures cause thirst or desire for themselves. Because bodily pleasures become distasteful by reason of their causing an excess in the natural mode of being, when they are increased or even when they are protracted; as is evident in the case of pleasures of the table. This is why, when a man arrives at the point of perfection in bodily pleasures, he wearies of them, and sometimes desires another kind. Spiritual pleasures, *on the contrary,* do not exceed the natural mode of being, but perfect nature. Hence when their point of perfection is reached, then do they afford the greatest delight: except, perchance, accidentally, in so far as the work of contemplation is accompanied by some operation of the bodily powers, which tire from protracted activity. And in this sense also we may understand those words of Ecclus. 24:29: "They that drink me shall yet thirst": for, even of the angels, who know God perfectly, and delight in Him, it is written (1 Pet. 1:12) that they "desire to look at Him."

Lastly, if we consider pleasure, not as existing in reality, but as existing in the memory, thus it has of itself a natural tendency to cause thirst and desire for itself: when, to wit, man returns to that disposition, in which he was when he experienced the pleasure that is past. But if he be changed from that disposition, the memory of that pleasure does not give him pleasure, but distaste: for instance, the memory of food in respect of a man who has eaten to repletion.

Reply Obj. 1: When pleasure is perfect, then it includes complete rest; and the movement of desire, tending to what was not possessed, ceases. But when it is imperfect, then the desire, tending to what was not possessed, does not cease altogether.

Reply Obj. 2: That which is possessed imperfectly, is possessed in one respect, and in another respect is not possessed. Consequently it may be the object of desire and pleasure at the same time.

Reply Obj. 3: Pleasures cause distaste in one way, desire in another, as stated above.

THIRD ARTICLE [I-II, Q. 33, Art. 3]

Whether Pleasure Hinders the Use of Reason?

Objection 1: It would seem that pleasure does not hinder the use of reason. Because repose facilitates very much the due use of reason: wherefore the Philosopher says (Phys. vii, 3) that "while we sit and rest, the soul is inclined to knowledge and prudence"; and it is written (Wis. 8:16): "When I go into my house, I shall repose myself with her," i.e. wisdom. But pleasure is a kind of repose. Therefore it helps rather than hinders the use of reason.

Obj. 2: Further, things which are not in the same subject though they be contraries, do not hinder one another. But pleasure is in the appetitive faculty, while the use of reason is in the apprehensive power. Therefore pleasure does not hinder the use of reason.

Obj. 3: Further, that which is hindered by another, seems to be moved, as it were, thereby. But the use of an apprehensive power moves pleasure rather than is moved by it: because it is the cause of pleasure. Therefore pleasure does not hinder the use of reason.

*On the contrary,* The Philosopher says (Ethic. vi, 5), that "pleasure destroys the estimate of prudence."

*I answer that,* As is stated in Ethic. x, 5, "appropriate pleasures increase activity ... whereas pleasures arising from other sources are impediments to activity." Accordingly there is a certain pleasure that is taken in the very act of reason, as when one takes pleasure in contemplating or in reasoning: and such pleasure does not hinder the act of reason, but helps it; because we are more attentive in doing that which gives us pleasure, and attention fosters activity.

On the other hand bodily pleasures hinder the use of reason in three ways. First, by distracting the reason. Because, as we have just observed, we attend much to that which pleases us. Now when the attention is firmly fixed on one thing, it is either weakened in respect of other things, or it is entirely withdrawn from them; and thus if the bodily pleasure be great, either it entirely hinders the use of reason, by concentrating the mind's attention on itself; or else it hinders it considerably. Secondly, by being contrary to reason. Because some pleasures, especially those that are in excess, are contrary to the order of reason: and in this sense the Philosopher says that "bodily pleasures destroy the estimate of prudence, but not the speculative estimate," to which they are not opposed, "for instance that the three angles of a triangle are together equal to two right angles." In the first sense, however, they hinder both estimates. Thirdly, by fettering the reason: in so far as bodily pleasure is followed by a certain alteration in the body, greater even than in the other passions, in proportion as the appetite is more vehemently affected towards a present than towards an absent thing. Now such bodily disturbances hinder the use of reason; as may be seen in the case of drunkards, in whom the use of reason is fettered or hindered.

Reply Obj. 1: Bodily pleasure implies indeed repose of the appetite in the object of pleasure; which repose is sometimes contrary to reason; but on the part of the body it always implies alteration. And in respect of both points, it hinders the use of reason.

Reply Obj. 2: The powers of the appetite and of apprehension are indeed distinct parts, but belonging to the one soul. Consequently when the soul is very intent on the action of one part, it is hindered from attending to a contrary act of the other part.

Reply Obj. 3: The use of reason requires the due use of the imagination and of the other sensitive powers, which are exercised through a bodily organ. Consequently alteration in the body hinders the use of reason, because it hinders the act of the imagination and of the other sensitive powers.

FOURTH ARTICLE [I-II, Q. 33, Art. 4]

Whether Pleasure Perfects Operation?

Objection 1: It would seem that pleasure does not perfect operation. For every human operation depends on the use of reason. But pleasure hinders the use of reason, as stated above (A. 3). Therefore pleasure does not perfect, but weakens human operation.

Obj. 2: Further, nothing perfects itself or its cause. But pleasure is an operation (Ethic. vii, 12; x, 4), i.e. either in its essence or in its cause. Therefore pleasure does not perfect operation.

Obj. 3: Further, if pleasure perfects operation, it does so either as end, or as form, or as agent. But not as end; because operation is not sought for the sake of pleasure, but rather the reverse, as stated above (Q. 4, A. 2): nor as agent, because rather is it the operation that causes pleasure: nor again as form, because, according to the Philosopher (Ethic. x, 4), "pleasure does not perfect operation, as a habit does." Therefore pleasure does not perfect operation.

*On the contrary,* The Philosopher says (Ethic. x, 4) that "pleasure perfects operation."

*I answer that,* Pleasure perfects operation in two ways. First, as an end: not indeed according as an end is that on "account of which a thing is"; but according as every good which is added to a thing and completes it, can be called its end. And in this sense the Philosopher says (Ethic. x, 4) that "pleasure perfects operation ... as some end added to it": that is to say, inasmuch as to this good, which is operation, there is added another good, which is pleasure, denoting the repose of the appetite in a good that is presupposed. Secondly, as agent; not indeed directly, for the Philosopher says (Ethic. x, 4) that "pleasure perfects operation, not as a physician makes a man healthy, but as health does": but it does so indirectly; inasmuch as the agent, through taking pleasure in his action, is more eagerly intent on it, and carries it out with greater care. And in this sense it is said in *Ethic.* x, 5 that "pleasures increase their appropriate activities, and hinder those that are not appropriate."

Reply Obj. 1: It is not every pleasure that hinders the act of reason, but only bodily pleasure; for this arises, not from the act of reason, but from the act of the concupiscible faculty, which act is intensified by pleasure. *On the contrary,* pleasure that arises from the act of reason, strengthens the use of reason.

Reply Obj. 2: As stated in *Phys.* ii, 3 two things may be causes of one another, if one be the efficient, the other the final cause. And in this way, operation is the efficient cause of pleasure, while pleasure perfects operation by way of final cause, as stated above.

The Reply to the Third Objection is evident for what has been said.

## QUESTION 34

OF THE GOODNESS AND MALICE OF PLEASURES (In Four Articles)

We must now consider the goodness and malice of pleasures: under which head there are four points of inquiry:

(1) Whether every pleasure is evil?

(2) If not, whether every pleasure is good?

(3) Whether any pleasure is the greatest good?

(4) Whether pleasure is the measure or rule by which to judge of moral good and evil?

FIRST ARTICLE [I-II, Q. 34, Art. 1]

Whether Every Pleasure Is Evil?

Objection 1: It would seem that every pleasure is evil. For that which destroys prudence and hinders the use of reason, seems to be evil in itself: since man's good is to be "in accord with reason," as Dionysius says (Div. Nom. iv). But pleasure destroys prudence and hinders the use of reason; and so much the more, as the pleasure is greater: wherefore "in sexual pleasures," which are the greatest of all, "it is impossible to understand anything," as stated in *Ethic.* vii, 11. Moreover, Jerome says in his commentary on Matthew [*Origen, Hom. vi in Num.] that "at the time of conjugal intercourse, the presence of the Holy Ghost is not vouchsafed, even if it be a prophet that fulfils the conjugal duty." Therefore pleasure is evil in itself; and consequently every pleasure is evil.

Obj. 2: Further, that which the virtuous man shuns, and the man lacking in virtue seeks, seems to be evil in itself, and should be avoided; because, as stated in *Ethic.* x, 5 "the virtuous man is a kind of measure and rule of human actions"; and the Apostle says (1 Cor. 2:15): "The spiritual man judgeth all things." But children and dumb animals, in whom there is no virtue, seek pleasure: whereas the man who is master of himself does not. Therefore pleasures are evil in themselves and should be avoided.

Obj. 3: Further, "virtue and art are concerned about the difficult and the good" (Ethic. ii, 3). But no art is ordained to pleasure. Therefore pleasure is not something good.

*On the contrary,* It is written (Ps. 36:4): "Delight in the Lord." Since, therefore, Divine authority leads to no evil, it seems that not every pleasure is evil.

*I answer that,* As stated in Ethic. x, 2, 3, some have maintained that all pleasure is evil. The reason seems to have been that they took account only of sensible and bodily pleasures which are more manifest; since, also in other respects, the ancient philosophers did not discriminate between the intelligible and the sensible, nor between intellect and sense (De Anima iii, 3). And they held that all bodily pleasures should be reckoned as bad, and thus that man, being prone to immoderate pleasures, arrives at the mean of virtue by abstaining from pleasure. But they were wrong in holding this opinion. Because, since none can live without some sensible and bodily pleasure, if they who teach that all pleasures are evil, are found in the act of taking pleasure; men will be more inclined to pleasure by following the example of their works instead of listening to the doctrine of their words: since, in human actions and passions, wherein experience is of great weight, example moves more than words.

We must therefore say that some pleasures are good, and that some are evil. For pleasure is a repose of the appetitive power in some loved good, and resulting from some operation; wherefore we assign a twofold reason for this assertion. The first is in respect of the good in which a man reposes with pleasure. For good and evil in the moral order depend on agreement or disagreement with reason, as stated above (Q. 18, A. 5): just as in the order of nature, a thing is said to be natural, if it agrees with nature, and unnatural, if it disagrees. Accordingly, just as in the natural order there is a certain natural repose, whereby a thing rests in that which agrees with its nature, for instance, when a heavy body rests down below; and again an unnatural repose, whereby a thing rests in that which disagrees with its nature, as when a heavy body rests up aloft: so, in the moral order, there is a good pleasure, whereby the higher or lower appetite rests in that which is in accord with reason; and an evil pleasure, whereby the appetite rests in that which is discordant from reason and the law of God.

The second reason can be found by considering the actions, some of which are good, some evil. Now pleasures which are conjoined to actions are more akin to those actions, than desires, which precede them in point of time. Wherefore, since the desires of good actions are good, and of evil actions, evil; much more are the pleasures of good actions good, and those of evil actions evil.

Reply Obj. 1: As stated above (Q. 33, A. 3), it is not the pleasures which result from an act of reason, that hinder the reason or destroy prudence, but extraneous pleasures, such as the pleasures of the body. These indeed hinder the use of reason, as stated above (Q. 33, A. 3), either by contrariety of the appetite that rests in something repugnant to reason, which makes the pleasure morally bad; or by fettering the reason: thus in conjugal intercourse, though the pleasure be in accord with reason, yet it hinders the use of reason, on account of the accompanying bodily change. But in this case the pleasure is not morally evil; as neither is sleep, whereby the reason is fettered, morally evil, if it be taken according to reason: for reason itself demands that the use of reason be interrupted at times. We must add, however, that although this fettering of the reason through the pleasure of conjugal intercourse has no moral malice, since it is neither a mortal nor a venial sin; yet it proceeds from a kind of moral malice, namely, from the sin of our first parent; because, as stated in the First Part (Q. 98, A. 2) the case was different in the state of innocence.

Reply Obj. 2: The temperate man does not shun all pleasures, but those that are immoderate, and contrary to reason. The fact that children and dumb animals seek pleasures, does not prove that all pleasures are evil: because they have from God their natural appetite, which is moved to that which is naturally suitable to them.

Reply Obj. 3: Art is not concerned with all kinds of good, but with the making of external things, as we shall state further on (Q. 57, A. 3). But actions and passions, which are within us, are more the concern of prudence and virtue than of art. Nevertheless there is an art of making pleasure, namely, "the art of cookery and the art of making arguments," as stated in *Ethic.* vii, 12.

SECOND ARTICLE [I-II, Q. 34, Art. 2]

Whether Every Pleasure Is Good?

Objection 1: It would seem that every pleasure is good. Because as stated in the First Part (Q. 5, A. 6) there are three kinds of good: the virtuous, the useful, and the pleasant. But everything virtuous is good; and in like manner everything useful is good. Therefore also every pleasure is good.

Obj. 2: Further, that which is not sought for the sake of something else, is good in itself, as stated in *Ethic.* i, 6, 7. But pleasure is not sought for the sake of something else; for it seems absurd to ask anyone why he seeks to be pleased. Therefore pleasure is good in itself. Now that which is predicated of a thing considered in itself, is predicated thereof universally. Therefore every pleasure is good.

Obj. 3: Further, that which is desired by all, seems to be good of itself: because good is "what all things seek," as stated in *Ethic.* i, 1. But everyone seeks some kind of pleasure, even children and dumb animals. Therefore pleasure is good in itself: and consequently all pleasure is good.

*On the contrary,* It is written (Prov. 2:14): "Who are glad when they have done evil, and rejoice in most wicked things."

*I answer that,* While some of the Stoics maintained that all pleasures are evil, the Epicureans held that pleasure is good in itself, and that consequently all pleasures are good. They seem to have thus erred through not discriminating between that which is good simply, and that which is good in respect of a particular individual. That which is good simply, is good in itself. Now that which is not good in itself, may be good in respect of some individual in two ways. In one way, because it is suitable to him by reason of a disposition in which he is now, which disposition, however, is not natural: thus it is sometimes good for a leper to eat things that are poisonous, which are not suitable simply to the human temperament. In another way, through something unsuitable being esteemed suitable. And since pleasure is the repose of the appetite in some good, if the appetite reposes in that which is good simply, the pleasure will be pleasure simply, and good simply. But if a man's appetite repose in that which is good, not simply, but in respect of that particular man, then his pleasure will not be pleasure simply, but a pleasure to him; neither will it be good simply, but in a certain respect, or an apparent good.

Reply Obj. 1: The virtuous and the useful depend on accordance with reason, and consequently nothing is virtuous or useful, without being good. But the pleasant depends on agreement with the appetite, which tends sometimes to that which is discordant from reason. Consequently not every object of pleasure is good in the moral order which depends on the order of reason.

Reply Obj. 2: The reason why pleasure is not sought for the sake of something else is because it is repose in the end. Now the end may be either good or evil; although nothing can be an end except in so far as it is good in respect of such and such a man: and so too with regard to pleasure.

Reply Obj. 3: All things seek pleasure in the same way as they seek good: since pleasure is the repose of the appetite in good. But, just as it happens that not every good which is desired, is of itself and verily good; so not every pleasure is of itself and verily good.

THIRD ARTICLE [I-II, Q. 34, Art. 3]

Whether Any Pleasure Is the Greatest Good?

Objection 1: It would seem that no pleasure is the greatest good. Because nothing generated is the greatest good: since generation cannot be the last end. But pleasure is a consequence of generation: for the fact that a thing takes pleasure is due to its being established in its own nature, as stated above (Q. 31, A. 1). Therefore no pleasure is the greatest good.

Obj. 2: Further, that which is the greatest good cannot be made better by addition. But pleasure is made better by addition; since pleasure together with virtue is better than pleasure without virtue. Therefore pleasure is not the greatest good.

Obj. 3: Further, that which is the greatest good is universally good, as being good of itself: since that which is such of itself is prior to and greater than that which is such accidentally. But pleasure is not universally good, as stated above (A. 2). Therefore pleasure is not the greatest good.

*On the contrary,* Happiness is the greatest good: since it is the end of man's life. But Happiness is not without pleasure: for it is written (Ps. 15:11): "Thou shalt fill me with joy with Thy countenance; at Thy right hand are delights even to the end."

*I answer that,* Plato held neither with the Stoics, who asserted that all pleasures are evil, nor with the Epicureans, who maintained that all pleasures are good; but he said that some are good, and some evil; yet, so that no pleasure be the sovereign or greatest good. But, judging from his arguments, he fails in two points. First, because, from observing that sensible and bodily pleasure consists in a certain movement and "becoming," as is evident in satiety from eating and the like; he concluded that all pleasure arises from some "becoming" and movement: and from this, since "becoming" and movement are the acts of something imperfect, it would follow that pleasure is not of the nature of ultimate perfection. But this is seen to be evidently false as regards intellectual pleasures: because one takes pleasure, not only in the "becoming" of knowledge, for instance, when one learns or wonders, as stated above (Q. 32, A. 8, ad 2); but also in the act of contemplation, by making use of knowledge already acquired.

Secondly, because by greatest good he understood that which is the supreme good simply, i.e. the good as existing apart from, and unparticipated by, all else, in which sense God is the Supreme Good; whereas we are speaking of the greatest good in human things. Now the greatest good of everything is its last end. And the end, as stated above (Q. 1, A. 8; Q. 2, A. 7) is twofold; namely, the thing itself, and the use of that thing; thus the miser's end is either money or the possession of money. Accordingly, man's last end may be said to be either God Who is the Supreme Good simply; or the enjoyment of God, which implies a certain pleasure in the last end. And in this sense a certain pleasure of man may be said to be the greatest among human goods.

Reply Obj. 1: Not every pleasure arises from a "becoming"; for some pleasures result from perfect operations, as stated above. Accordingly nothing prevents some pleasure being the greatest good, although every pleasure is not such.

Reply Obj. 2: This argument is true of the greatest good simply, by participation of which all things are good; wherefore no addition can make it better: whereas in regard to other goods, it is universally true that any good becomes better by the addition of another good. Moreover it might be said that pleasure is not something extraneous to the operation of virtue, but that it accompanies it, as stated in *Ethic.* i, 8.

Reply Obj. 3: That pleasure is the greatest good is due not to the mere fact that it is pleasure, but to the fact that it is perfect repose in the perfect good. Hence it does not follow that every pleasure is supremely good, or even good at all. Thus a certain science is supremely good, but not every science is.

FOURTH ARTICLE [I-II, Q. 34, Art. 4]

Whether Pleasure Is the Measure or Rule by Which to Judge of Moral Good or Evil?

Objection 1: It would seem that pleasure is not the measure or rule of moral good and evil. Because "that which is first in a genus is the measure of all the rest" (Metaph. x, 1). But pleasure is not the first thing in the moral genus, for it is preceded by love and desire. Therefore it is not the rule of goodness and malice in moral matters.

Obj. 2: Further, a measure or rule should be uniform; hence that movement which is the most uniform, is the measure and rule of all movements (Metaph. x, 1). But pleasures are various and multiform: since some of them are good, and some evil. Therefore pleasure is not the measure and rule of morals.

Obj. 3: Further, judgment of the effect from its cause is more certain than judgment of cause from effect. Now goodness or malice of operation is the cause of goodness or malice of pleasure: because "those pleasures are good which result from good operations, and those are evil which arise from evil operations," as stated in *Ethic.* x, 5. Therefore pleasures are not the rule and measure of moral goodness and malice.

*On the contrary,* Augustine, commenting on Ps. 7:10 "The searcher of hearts and reins is God," says: "The end of care and thought is the pleasure which each one aims at achieving." And the Philosopher says (Ethic. vii, 11) that "pleasure is the architect," i.e. the principal, "end [*St. Thomas took *finis* as being the nominative, whereas it is the genitive—*tou telous*; and the Greek reads "He" (i.e. the political philosopher), "is the architect of the end."], in regard to which, we say absolutely that this is evil, and that, good."

*I answer that,* Moral goodness or malice depends chiefly on the will, as stated above (Q. 20, A. 1); and it is chiefly from the end that we discern whether the will is good or evil. Now the end is taken to be that in which the will reposes: and the repose of the will and of every appetite in the good is pleasure. And therefore man is reckoned to be good or bad chiefly according to the pleasure of the human will; since that man is good and virtuous, who takes pleasure in the works of virtue; and that man evil, who takes pleasure in evil works.

On the other hand, pleasures of the sensitive appetite are not the rule of moral goodness and malice; since food is universally pleasurable to the sensitive appetite both of good and of evil men. But the will of the good man takes pleasure in them in accordance with reason, to which the will of the evil man gives no heed.

Reply Obj. 1: Love and desire precede pleasure in the order of generation. But pleasure precedes them in the order of the end, which serves a principle in actions; and it is by the principle, which is the rule and measure of such matters, that we form our judgment.

Reply Obj. 2: All pleasures are uniform in the point of their being the repose of the appetite in something good: and in this respect pleasure can be a rule or measure. Because that man is good, whose will rests in the true good: and that man evil, whose will rests in evil.

Reply Obj. 3: Since pleasure perfects operation as its end, as stated above (Q. 33, A. 4); an operation cannot be perfectly good, unless there be also pleasure in good: because the goodness of a thing depends on its end. And thus, in a way, the goodness of the pleasure is the cause of goodness in the operation.

## QUESTION 35

OF PAIN OR SORROW, IN ITSELF (In Eight Articles)

We have now to consider pain and sorrow: concerning which we must consider: (1) Sorrow or pain in itself; (2) Its cause; (3) Its effects; (4) Its remedies; (5) Its goodness or malice.

Under the first head there are eight points of inquiry:

(1) Whether pain is a passion of the soul?

(2) Whether sorrow is the same as pain?

(3) Whether sorrow or pain is contrary [to] pleasure?

(4) Whether all sorrow is contrary to all pleasure?

(5) Whether there is a sorrow contrary to the pleasure of contemplation?

(6) Whether sorrow is to be shunned more than pleasure is to be sought?

(7) Whether exterior pain is greater than interior?

(8) Of the species of sorrow.

FIRST ARTICLE [I-II, Q. 35, Art. 1]

Whether Pain Is a Passion of the Soul?

Objection 1: It would seem that pain is not a passion of the soul. Because no passion of the soul is in the body. But pain can be in the body, since Augustine says (De Vera Relig. xii), that "bodily pain is a sudden corruption of the well-being of that thing which the soul, by making evil use of it, made subject to corruption." Therefore pain is not a passion of the soul.

Obj. 2: Further, every passion of the soul belongs to the appetitive faculty. But pain does not belong to the appetitive, but rather to the apprehensive part: for Augustine says (De Nat. Boni xx) that "bodily pain is caused by the sense resisting a more powerful body." Therefore pain is not a passion of the soul.

Obj. 3: Further, every passion of the soul belongs to the animal appetite. But pain does not belong to the animal appetite, but rather to the natural appetite; for Augustine says (Gen. ad lit. viii, 14): "Had not some good remained in nature, we should feel no pain in being punished by the loss of good." Therefore pain is not a passion of the soul.

*On the contrary,* Augustine (De Civ. Dei xiv, 8) reckons pain among the passions of the soul; quoting Virgil (Aeneid, vi, 733):

"hence wild desires and grovelling fears And human laughter, human tears." [Translation: Conington.]

*I answer that,* Just as two things are requisite for pleasure; namely, conjunction with good and perception of this conjunction; so also two things are requisite for pain: namely, conjunction with some evil (which is in so far evil as it deprives one of some good), and perception of this conjunction. Now whatever is conjoined, if it have not the aspect of good or evil in regard to the being to which it is conjoined, cannot cause pleasure or pain. Whence it is evident that something under the aspect of good or evil is the object of the pleasure or pain. But good and evil, as such, are objects of the appetite. Consequently it is clear that pleasure and pain belong to the appetite.

Now every appetitive movement or inclination consequent to apprehension, belongs to the intellective or sensitive appetite: since the inclination of the natural appetite is not consequent to an apprehension of the subject of that appetite, but to the apprehension of another, as stated in the First Part (Q. 103, AA. 1, 3). Since then pleasure and pain presuppose some sense or apprehension in the same subject, it is evident that pain, like pleasure, is in the intellective or sensitive appetite.

Again every movement of the sensitive appetite is called a passion, as stated above (Q. 22, AA. 1, 3): and especially those which tend to some defect. Consequently pain, according as it is in the sensitive appetite, is most properly called a passion of the soul: just as bodily ailments are properly called passions of the body. Hence Augustine (De Civ. Dei xiv, 7, 8 [*Quoting Cicero]) reckons pain especially as being a kind of ailment.

Reply Obj. 1: We speak of the body, because the cause of pain is in the body: as when we suffer something hurtful to the body. But the movement of pain is always in the soul; since "the body cannot feel pain unless the soul feel it," as Augustine says (Super Psalm. 87:4).

Reply Obj. 2: We speak of pain of the senses, not as though it were an act of the sensitive power; but because the senses are required for bodily pain, in the same way as for bodily pleasure.

Reply Obj. 3: Pain at the loss of good proves the goodness of the nature, not because pain is an act of the natural appetite, but because nature desires something as good, the removal of which being perceived, there results the passion of pain in the sensitive appetite.

SECOND ARTICLE [I-II, Q. 35, Art. 2]

Whether Sorrow Is the Same As Pain?

Objection 1: It would seem that sorrow is not pain. For Augustine says (De Civ. Dei xiv, 7) that "pain is used to express bodily suffering." But sorrow is used more in reference to the soul. Therefore sorrow is not pain.

Obj. 2: Further, pain is only in respect of present evil. But sorrow can refer to both past and future evil: thus repentance is sorrow for the past, and anxiety for the future. Therefore sorrow is quite different from pain.

Obj. 3: Further, pain seems not to follow save from the sense of touch. But sorrow can arise from all the senses. Therefore sorrow is not pain, and extends to more objects.

*On the contrary,* The Apostle says (Rom. 9:2): "I have great sorrow [Douay: 'sadness'] and continual pain [Douay: 'sorrow'] in my heart," thus denoting the same thing by sorrow and pain.

*I answer that,* Pleasure and pain can arise from a twofold apprehension, namely, from the apprehension of an exterior sense; and from the interior apprehension of the intellect or of the imagination. Now the interior apprehension extends to more objects than the exterior apprehension: because whatever things come under the exterior apprehension, come under the interior, but not conversely. Consequently that pleasure alone which is caused by an interior apprehension is called joy, as stated above (Q. 31, A. 3): and in like manner that pain alone which is caused by an interior apprehension, is called sorrow. And just as that pleasure which is caused by an exterior apprehension, is called pleasure but not joy; so too that pain which is caused by an exterior apprehension, is called pain indeed but not sorrow. Accordingly sorrow is a species of pain, as joy is a species of pleasure.

Reply Obj. 1: Augustine is speaking there of the use of the word: because "pain" is more generally used in reference to bodily pains, which are better known, than in reference to spiritual pains.

Reply Obj. 2: External sense perceives only what is present; but the interior cognitive power can perceive the present, past and future. Consequently sorrow can regard present, past and future: whereas bodily pain, which follows apprehension of the external sense, can only regard something present.

Reply Obj. 3: The sensibles of touch are painful, not only in so far as they are disproportionate to the apprehensive power, but also in so far as they are contrary to nature: whereas the objects of the other senses can indeed be disproportionate to the apprehensive power, but they are not contrary to nature, save as they are subordinate to the sensibles of touch. Consequently man alone, who is a perfectly cognizant animal, takes pleasure in the objects of the other senses for their own sake; whereas other animals take no pleasure in them save as referable to the sensibles of touch, as stated in *Ethic.* iii, 10. Accordingly, in referring to the objects of the other senses, we do not speak of pain in so far as it is contrary to natural pleasure: but rather of sorrow, which is contrary to joy. So then if pain be taken as denoting bodily pain, which is its more usual meaning, then it is contrasted with sorrow, according to the distinction of interior and exterior apprehension; although, on the part of the objects, pleasure extends further than does bodily pain. But if pain be taken in a wide sense, then it is the genus of sorrow, as stated above.

THIRD ARTICLE [I-II, Q. 35, Art. 3]

Whether Sorrow or Pain Is Contrary to Pleasure?

Objection 1: It would seem that sorrow is not contrary to pleasure. For one of two contraries is not the cause of the other. But sorrow can be the cause of pleasure; for it is written (Matt. 5:5): "Blessed are they that mourn, for they shall be comforted." Therefore they are not contrary to one another.

Obj. 2: Further, one contrary does not denominate the other. But to some, pain or sorrow gives pleasure: thus Augustine says (Confess. iii, 2) that in stage-plays sorrow itself gives pleasure: and (Confess. iv, 5) that "weeping is a bitter thing, and yet it sometimes pleases us." Therefore pain is not contrary to pleasure.

Obj. 3: Further, one contrary is not the matter of the other; because contraries cannot co-exist together. But sorrow can be the matter of pleasure; for Augustine says (De Poenit. xiii): "The penitent should ever sorrow, and rejoice in his sorrow." The Philosopher too says (Ethic. ix, 4) that, on the other hand, "the evil man feels pain at having been pleased." Therefore pleasure and pain are not contrary to one another.

*On the contrary,* Augustine says (De Civ. Dei xiv, 6) that "joy is the volition of consent to the things we wish: and that sorrow is the volition of dissent from the things we do not wish." But consent and dissent are contraries. Therefore pleasure and sorrow are contrary to one another.

*I answer that,* As the Philosopher says (Metaph. x, 4), contrariety is a difference in respect of a form. Now the form or species of a passion or movement is taken from the object or term. Consequently, since the objects of pleasure and sorrow or pain, viz. present good and present evil, are contrary to one another, it follows that pain and pleasure are contrary to one another.

Reply Obj. 1: Nothing hinders one contrary causing the other accidentally: and thus sorrow can be the cause of pleasure. In one way, in so far as from sorrow at the absence of something, or at the presence of its contrary, one seeks the more eagerly for something pleasant: thus a thirsty man seeks more eagerly the pleasure of a drink, as a remedy for the pain he suffers. In another way, in so far as, from a strong desire for a certain pleasure, one does not shrink from undergoing pain, so as to obtain that pleasure. In each of these ways, the sorrows of the present life lead us to the comfort of the future life. Because by the mere fact that man mourns for his sins, or for the delay of glory, he merits the consolation of eternity. In like manner a man merits it when he shrinks not from hardships and straits in order to obtain it.

Reply Obj. 2: Pain itself can be pleasurable accidentally in so far as it is accompanied by wonder, as in stage-plays; or in so far as it recalls a beloved object to one's memory, and makes one feel one's love for the thing, whose absence gives us pain. Consequently, since love is pleasant, both pain and whatever else results from love, forasmuch as they remind us of our love, are pleasant. And, for this reason, we derive pleasure even from pains depicted on the stage: in so far as, in witnessing them, we perceive ourselves to conceive a certain love for those who are there represented.

Reply Obj. 3: The will and the reason reflect on their own acts, inasmuch as the acts themselves of the will and reason are considered under the aspect of good or evil. In this way sorrow can be the matter of pleasure, or vice versa, not essentially but accidentally: that is, in so far as either of them is considered under the aspect of good or evil.

FOURTH ARTICLE [I-II, Q. 35, Art. 4]

Whether All Sorrow Is Contrary to All Pleasure?

Objection 1: It would seem that all sorrow is contrary to all pleasure. Because, just as whiteness and blackness are contrary species of color, so pleasure and sorrow are contrary species of the soul's passions. But whiteness and blackness are universally contrary to one another. Therefore pleasure and sorrow are so too.

Obj. 2: Further, remedies are made of things contrary (to the evil). But every pleasure is a remedy for all manner of sorrow, as the Philosopher declares (Ethic. vii, 14). Therefore every pleasure is contrary to every sorrow.

Obj. 3: Further, contraries are hindrances to one another. But every sorrow hinders any kind of pleasure: as is evident from *Ethic.* x, 5. Therefore every sorrow is contrary to every pleasure.

*On the contrary,* The same thing is not the cause of contraries. But joy for one thing, and sorrow for the opposite thing, proceed from the same habit: thus from charity it happens that we "rejoice with them that rejoice," and "weep with them that weep" (Rom. 12:15). Therefore not every sorrow is contrary to every pleasure.

*I answer that,* As the Philosopher says (Metaph. x, 4), contrariety is a difference in respect of a form. Now a form may be generic or specific. Consequently things may be contraries in respect of a generic form, as virtue and vice; or in respect of a specific form, as justice and injustice.

Now we must observe that some things are specified by absolute forms, e.g. substances and qualities; whereas other things are specified in relation to something extrinsic, e.g. passions and movements, which derive their species from their terms or objects. Accordingly in those things that are specified by absolute forms, it happens that species contained under contrary genera are not contrary as to their specific nature: but it does not happen for them to have any affinity or fittingness to one another. For intemperance and justice, which are in the contrary genera of virtue and vice, are not contrary to one another in respect of their specific nature; and yet they have no affinity or fittingness to one another. On the other hand, in those things that are specified in relation to something extrinsic, it happens that species belonging to contrary genera, are not only not contrary to one another, but also that they have a certain mutual affinity or fittingness. The reason of this is that where there is one same relation to two contraries, there is contrariety; e.g. to approach to a white thing, and to approach to a black thing, are contraries; whereas contrary relations to contrary things, implies a certain likeness, e.g. to recede from something white, and to approach to something black. This is most evident in the case of contradiction, which is the principle of opposition: because opposition consists in affirming and denying the same thing, e.g. "white" and "non-white"; while there is fittingness and likeness in the affirmation of one contrary and the denial of the other, as, if I were to say "black" and "not white."

Now sorrow and pleasure, being passions, are specified by their objects. According to their respective genera, they are contrary to one another: since one is a kind of *pursuit,* the other a kind of *avoidance,* which "are to the appetite, what affirmation and denial are to the intellect" (Ethic. vi, 2). Consequently sorrow and pleasure in respect of the same object, are specifically contrary to one another: whereas sorrow and pleasure in respect of objects that are not contrary but disparate, are not specifically contrary to one another, but are also disparate; for instance, sorrow at the death of a friend, and pleasure in contemplation. If, however, those diverse objects be contrary to one another, then pleasure and sorrow are not only specifically contrary, but they also have a certain mutual fittingness and affinity: for instance to rejoice in good and to sorrow for evil.

Reply Obj. 1: Whiteness and blackness do not take their species from their relationship to something extrinsic, as pleasure and sorrow do: wherefore the comparison does not hold.

Reply Obj. 2: Genus is taken from matter, as is stated in *Metaph.* viii, 2; and in accidents the subject takes the place of matter. Now it has been said above that pleasure and sorrow are generically contrary to one another. Consequently in every sorrow the subject has a disposition contrary to the disposition of the subject of pleasure: because in every pleasure the appetite is viewed as accepting what it possesses, and in every sorrow, as avoiding it. And therefore on the part of the subject every pleasure is a remedy for any kind of sorrow, and every sorrow is a hindrance of all manner of pleasure: but chiefly when pleasure is opposed to sorrow specifically.

Wherefore the Reply to the Third Objection is evident. Or we may say that, although not every sorrow is specifically contrary to every pleasure, yet they are contrary to one another in regard to their effects: since one has the effect of strengthening the animal nature, while the other results in a kind of discomfort.

FIFTH ARTICLE [I-II, Q. 35, Art. 5]

Whether There Is Any Sorrow Contrary to the Pleasure of Contemplation?

Objection 1: It would seem that there is a sorrow that is contrary to the pleasure of contemplation. For the Apostle says (2 Cor. 7:10): "The sorrow that is according to God, worketh penance steadfast unto salvation." Now to look at God belongs to the higher reason, whose act is to give itself to contemplation, according to Augustine (De Trin. xii, 3, 4). Therefore there is a sorrow contrary to the pleasure of contemplation.

Obj. 2: Further, contrary things have contrary effects. If therefore the contemplation of one contrary gives pleasure, the other contrary will give sorrow: and so there will be a sorrow contrary to the pleasure of contemplation.

Obj. 3: Further, as the object of pleasure is good, so the object of sorrow is evil. But contemplation can be an evil: since the Philosopher says (Metaph. xii, 9) that "it is unfitting to think of certain things." Therefore sorrow can be contrary to the pleasure of contemplation.

Obj. 4: Further, any work, so far as it is unhindered, can be a cause of pleasure, as stated in *Ethic.* vii, 12, 13; x, 4. But the work of contemplation can be hindered in many ways, either so as to destroy it altogether, or as to make it difficult. Therefore in contemplation there can be a sorrow contrary to the pleasure.

Obj. 5: Further, affliction of the flesh is a cause of sorrow. But, as it is written (Eccles. 12:12) "much study is an affliction of the flesh." Therefore contemplation admits of sorrow contrary to its pleasure.

*On the contrary,* It is written (Wis. 8:16): "Her," i.e. wisdom's, "conversation hath no bitterness nor her company any tediousness; but joy and gladness." Now the conversation and company of wisdom are found in contemplation. Therefore there is no sorrow contrary to the pleasure of contemplation.

*I answer that,* The pleasure of contemplation can be understood in two ways. In one way, so that contemplation is the cause, but not the object of pleasure: and then pleasure is taken not in contemplating but in the thing contemplated. Now it is possible to contemplate something harmful and sorrowful, just as to contemplate something suitable and pleasant. Consequently if the pleasure of contemplation be taken in this way, nothing hinders some sorrow being contrary to the pleasure of contemplation.

In another way, the pleasure of contemplation is understood, so that contemplation is its object and cause; as when one takes pleasure in the very act of contemplating. And thus, according to Gregory of Nyssa [*Nemesius, De Nat. Hom. xviii.], "no sorrow is contrary to that pleasure which is about contemplation": and the Philosopher says the same (Topic. i, 13; Ethic. x, 3). This, however, is to be understood as being the case properly speaking. The reason is because sorrow is of itself contrary to pleasure in a contrary object: thus pleasure in heat is contrary to sorrow caused by cold. But there is no contrary to the object of contemplation: because contraries, as apprehended by the mind, are not contrary, but one is the means of knowing the other. Wherefore, properly speaking, there cannot be a sorrow contrary to the pleasure of contemplation. Nor has it any sorrow annexed to it, as bodily pleasures have, which are like remedies against certain annoyances; thus a man takes pleasure in drinking through being troubled with thirst, but when the thirst is quite driven out, the pleasure of drinking ceases also. Because the pleasure of contemplation is not caused by one's being quit of an annoyance, but by the fact that contemplation is pleasant in itself: for pleasure is not a "becoming" but a perfect operation, as stated above (Q. 31, A. 1).

Accidentally, however, sorrow is mingled with the pleasure of contemplation; and this in two ways: first, on the part of an organ, secondly, through some impediment in the apprehension. On the part of an organ, sorrow or pain is mingled with apprehension, directly, as regards the apprehensive powers of the sensitive part, which have a bodily organ; either from the sensible object disagreeing with the normal condition of the organ, as the taste of something bitter, and the smell of something foul; or from the sensible object, though agreeable, being so continuous in its action on the sense, that it exceeds the normal condition of the organ, as stated above (Q. 33, A. 2), the result being that an apprehension which at first was pleasant becomes tedious. But these two things cannot occur directly in the contemplation of the mind; because the mind has no corporeal organ: wherefore it was said in the authority quoted above that intellectual contemplation has neither "bitterness," nor "tediousness." Since, however, the human mind, in contemplation, makes use of the sensitive powers of apprehension, to whose acts weariness is incidental; therefore some affliction or pain is indirectly mingled with contemplation.

Nevertheless, in neither of these ways, is the pain thus accidentally mingled with contemplation, contrary to the pleasure thereof. Because pain caused by a hindrance to contemplation, is not contrary to the pleasure of contemplation, but rather is in affinity and in harmony with it, as is evident from what has been said above (A. 4): while pain or sorrow caused by bodily weariness, does not belong to the same genus, wherefore it is altogether disparate. Accordingly it is evident that no sorrow is contrary to pleasure taken in the very act of contemplation; nor is any sorrow connected with it save accidentally.

Reply Obj. 1: The "sorrow which is according to God," is not caused by the very act of intellectual contemplation, but by something which the mind contemplates: viz. by sin, which the mind considers as contrary to the love of God.

Reply Obj. 2: Things which are contrary according to nature are not contrary according as they exist in the mind: for things that are contrary in reality are not contrary in the order of thought; indeed rather is one contrary the reason for knowing the other. Hence one and the same science considers contraries.

Reply Obj. 3: Contemplation, in itself, is never evil, since it is nothing else than the consideration of truth, which is the good of the intellect: it can, however, be evil accidentally, i.e. in so far as the contemplation of a less noble object hinders the contemplation of a more noble object; or on the part of the object contemplated, to which the appetite is inordinately attached.

Reply Obj. 4: Sorrow caused by a hindrance to contemplation, is not contrary to the pleasure of contemplation, but is in harmony with it, as stated above.

Reply Obj. 5: Affliction of the flesh affects contemplation accidentally and indirectly, as stated above.

SIXTH ARTICLE [I-II, Q. 35, Art. 6]

Whether Sorrow Is to Be Shunned More Than Pleasure Is to Be Sought?

Objection 1: It would seem that sorrow is to be shunned more than pleasure is to be sought. For Augustine says (QQ. 83, qu. 63): "There is nobody that does not shun sorrow more than he seeks pleasure." Now that which all agree in doing, seems to be natural. Therefore it is natural and right for sorrow to be shunned more than pleasure is sought.

Obj. 2: Further, the action of a contrary conduces to rapidity and intensity of movement: for "hot water freezes quicker and harder," as the Philosopher says (Meteor. i, 12). But the shunning of sorrow is due to the contrariety of the cause of sorrow; whereas the desire for pleasure does not arise from any contrariety, but rather from the suitableness of the pleasant object. Therefore sorrow is shunned more eagerly than pleasure is sought.

Obj. 3: Further, the stronger the passion which a man resists according to reason, the more worthy is he of praise, and the more virtuous: since "virtue is concerned with the difficult and the good" (Ethic. ii, 3). But the brave man who resists the movement of shunning sorrow, is more virtuous than the temperate man, who resists the movement of desire for pleasure: since the Philosopher says (Rhet. ii, 4) that "the brave and the just are chiefly praised." Therefore the movement of shunning sorrow is more eager than the movement of seeking pleasure.

*On the contrary,* Good is stronger than evil, as Dionysius declares (Div. Nom. iv). But pleasure is desirable for the sake of the good which is its object; whereas the shunning of sorrow is on account of evil. Therefore the desire for pleasure is more eager than the shunning of sorrow.

*I answer that,* The desire for pleasure is of itself more eager than the shunning of sorrow. The reason of this is that the cause of pleasure is a suitable good; while the cause of pain or sorrow is an unsuitable evil. Now it happens that a certain good is suitable without any repugnance at all: but it is not possible for any evil to be so unsuitable as not to be suitable in some way. Wherefore pleasure can be entire and perfect: whereas sorrow is always partial. Therefore desire for pleasure is naturally greater than the shunning of sorrow. Another reason is because the good, which is the object of pleasure, is sought for its own sake: whereas the evil, which is the object of sorrow, is to be shunned as being a privation of good: and that which is by reason of itself is stronger than that which is by reason of something else. Moreover we find a confirmation of this in natural movements. For every natural movement is more intense in the end, when a thing approaches the term that is suitable to its nature, than at the beginning, when it leaves the term that is unsuitable to its nature: as though nature were more eager in tending to what is suitable to it, than in shunning what is unsuitable. Therefore the inclination of the appetitive power is, of itself, more eager in tending to pleasure than in shunning sorrow.

But it happens accidentally that a man shuns sorrow more eagerly than he seeks pleasure: and this for three reasons. First, on the part of the apprehension. Because, as Augustine says (De Trin. x, 12), "love is felt more keenly, when we lack that which we love." Now from the lack of what we love, sorrow results, which is caused either by the loss of some loved good, or by the presence of some contrary evil. But pleasure suffers no lack of the good loved, for it rests in possession of it. Since then love is the cause of pleasure and sorrow, the latter is the more shunned, according as love is the more keenly felt on account of that which is contrary to it. Secondly, on the part of the cause of sorrow or pain, which cause is repugnant to a good that is more loved than the good in which we take pleasure. For we love the natural well-being of the body more than the pleasure of eating: and consequently we would leave the pleasure of eating and the like, from fear of the pain occasioned by blows or other such causes, which are contrary to the well-being of the body. Thirdly, on the part of the effect: namely, in so far as sorrow hinders not only one pleasure, but all.

Reply Obj. 1: The saying of Augustine that "sorrow is shunned more than pleasure is sought" is true accidentally but not simply. And this is clear from what he says after: "Since we see that the most savage animals are deterred from the greatest pleasures by fear of pain," which pain is contrary to life which is loved above all.

Reply Obj. 2: It is not the same with movement from within and movement from without. For movement from within tends to what is suitable more than it recedes from that which is unsuitable; as we remarked above in regard to natural movement. But movement from without is intensified by the very opposition: because each thing strives in its own way to resist anything contrary to it, as aiming at its own preservation. Hence violent movement is intense at first, and slackens towards the end. Now the movement of the appetitive faculty is from within: since it tends from the soul to the object. Consequently pleasure is, of itself, more to be sought than sorrow is to be shunned. But the movement of the sensitive faculty is from without, as it were from the object of the soul. Consequently the more contrary a thing is the more it is felt. And then too, accidentally, in so far as the senses are requisite for pleasure and pain, pain is shunned more than pleasure is sought.

Reply Obj. 3: A brave man is not praised because, in accordance with reason, he is not overcome by any kind of sorrow or pain whatever, but because he is not overcome by that which is concerned with the dangers of death. And this kind of sorrow is more shunned, than pleasures of the table or of sexual intercourse are sought, which latter pleasures are the object of temperance: thus life is loved more than food and sexual pleasure. But the temperate man is praised for refraining from pleasures of touch, more than for not shunning the pains which are contrary to them, as is stated in *Ethic.* iii, 11.

SEVENTH ARTICLE [I-II, Q. 35, Art. 7]

Whether Outward Pain Is Greater Than Interior Sorrow?

Objection 1: It would seem that outward pain is greater than interior sorrow of the heart. Because outward pain arises from a cause repugnant to the well-being of the body in which is life: whereas interior sorrow is caused by some evil in the imagination. Since, therefore, life is loved more than an imagined good, it seems that, according to what has been said above (A. 6), outward pain is greater than interior sorrow.

Obj. 2: Further, the reality moves more than its likeness does. But outward pain arises from the real conjunction of some contrary; whereas inward sorrow arises from the apprehended likeness of a contrary. Therefore outward pain is greater than inward sorrow.

Obj. 3: Further, a cause is known by its effect. But outward pain has more striking effects: since man dies sooner of outward pain than of interior sorrow. Therefore outward pain is greater and is shunned more than interior sorrow.

*On the contrary,* it is written (Ecclus. 25:17): "The sadness of the heart is every wound [Douay: 'plague'], and the wickedness of a woman is all evil." Therefore, just as the wickedness of a woman surpasses all other wickedness, as the text implies; so sadness of the heart surpasses every outward wound.

*I answer that,* Interior and exterior pain agree in one point and differ in two. They agree in this, that each is a movement of the appetitive power, as stated above (A. 1). But they differ in respect of those two things which are requisite for pain and pleasure; namely, in respect of the cause, which is a conjoined good or evil; and in respect of the apprehension. For the cause of outward pain is a conjoined evil repugnant to the body; while the cause of inward pain is a conjoined evil repugnant to the appetite. Again, outward pain arises from an apprehension of sense, chiefly of touch; while inward pain arises from an interior apprehension, of the imagination or of the reason.

If then we compare the cause of inward pain to the cause of outward pain, the former belongs, of itself, to the appetite to which both these pains belong: while the latter belongs to the appetite directly. Because inward pain arises from something being repugnant to the appetite itself, while outward pain arises from something being repugnant to the appetite, through being repugnant to the body. Now, that which is of itself is always prior to that which is by reason of another. Wherefore, from this point of view, inward pain surpasses outward pain. In like manner also on the part of apprehension: because the apprehension of reason and imagination is of a higher order than the apprehension of the sense of touch. Consequently inward pain is, simply and of itself, more keen than outward pain: a sign whereof is that one willingly undergoes outward pain in order to avoid inward pain: and in so far as outward pain is not repugnant to the interior appetite, it becomes in a manner pleasant and agreeable by way of inward joy. Sometimes, however, outward pain is accompanied by inward pain, and then the pain is increased. Because inward pain is not only greater than outward pain, it is also more universal: since whatever is repugnant to the body, can be repugnant to the interior appetite; and whatever is apprehended by sense may be apprehended by imagination and reason, but not conversely. Hence in the passage quoted above it is said expressively: "Sadness of the heart is every wound," because even the pains of outward wounds are comprised in the interior sorrows of the heart.

Reply Obj. 1: Inward pain can also arise from things that are destructive of life. And then the comparison of inward to outward pain must not be taken in reference to the various evils that cause pain; but in regard to the various ways in which this cause of pain is compared to the appetite.

Reply Obj. 2: Inward pain is not caused by the apprehended likeness of a thing: for a man is not inwardly pained by the apprehended likeness itself, but by the thing which the likeness represents. And this thing is all the more perfectly apprehended by means of its likeness, as this likeness is more immaterial and abstract. Consequently inward pain is, of itself, greater, as being caused by a greater evil, forasmuch as evil is better known by an inward apprehension.

Reply Obj. 3: Bodily changes are more liable to be caused by outward pain, both from the fact that outward pain is caused by a corruptive conjoined corporally, which is a necessary condition of the sense of touch; and from the fact that the outward sense is more material than the inward sense, just as the sensitive appetite is more material than the intellective. For this reason, as stated above (Q. 22, A. 3; Q. 31, A. 5), the body undergoes a greater change from the movement of the sensitive appetite: and, in like manner, from outward than from inward pain.

EIGHTH ARTICLE [I-II, Q. 35, Art. 8]

Whether There Are Only Four Species of Sorrow?

Objection 1: It would seem that Damascene's (De Fide Orth. ii, 14) division of sorrow into four species is incorrect; viz. into "torpor, distress," which Gregory of Nyssa [*Nemesius, De Nat. Hom. xix.] calls "anxiety,"—"pity," and "envy." For sorrow is contrary to pleasure. But there are not several species of pleasure. Therefore it is incorrect to assign different species of sorrow.

Obj. 2: Further, *Repentance* is a species of sorrow; and so are indignation and jealousy, as the Philosopher states (Rhet. ii, 9, 11). But these are not included in the above species. Therefore this division is insufficient.

Obj. 3: Further, the members of a division should be things that are opposed to one another. But these species are not opposed to one another. For according to Gregory [*Nemesius, De Nat. Hom. xix.] "torpor is sorrow depriving of speech; anxiety is the sorrow that weighs down; envy is sorrow for another's good; pity is sorrow for another's wrongs." But it is possible for one to sorrow for another's wrongs, and for another's good, and at the same time to be weighed down inwardly, and outwardly to be speechless. Therefore this division is incorrect.

*On the contrary,* stands the twofold authority of Gregory of Nyssa [*Nemesius] and of Damascene.

*I answer that,* It belongs to the notion of a species that it is something added to the genus. But a thing can be added to a genus in two ways. First, as something belonging of itself to the genus, and virtually contained therein: thus "rational" is added to "animal." Such an addition makes true species of a genus: as the Philosopher says (Metaph. vii, 12; viii, 2, 3). But, secondly, a thing may be added to a genus, that is, as it were, foreign to the notion conveyed by that genus: thus "white" or something of the kind may be added to "animal." Such an addition does not make true species of the genus, according to the usual sense in which we speak of genera and species. But sometimes a thing is said to be a species of a certain genus, through having something foreign to that genus indeed, but to which the notion of that genus is applicable: thus a live coal or a flame is said to be a species of fire, because in each of them the nature of fire is applied to a foreign matter. In like manner we speak of astronomy and perspective as being species of mathematics, inasmuch as the principles of mathematics are applied to natural matter.

In accordance with this manner of speaking, the species of sorrow are reckoned by an application of the notion of sorrow to something foreign to it. This foreign matter may be taken on the part of the cause or the object, or of the effect. For the proper object of sorrow is *one's own evil.* Hence sorrow may be concerned for an object foreign to it either through one's being sorry for an evil that is not one's own; and thus we have *pity* which is sorrow for another's evil, considered, however, as one's own: or through one's being sorry for something that is neither evil nor one's own, but another's good, considered, however, as one's own evil: and thus we have *envy.* The proper effect of sorrow consists in a certain *flight of the appetite.* Wherefore the foreign element in the effect of sorrow, may be taken so as to affect the first part only, by excluding flight: and thus we have *anxiety* which weighs on the mind, so as to make escape seem impossible: hence it is also called *perplexity.* If, however, the mind be weighed down so much, that even the limbs become motionless, which belongs to *torpor,* then we have the foreign element affecting both, since there is neither flight, nor is the effect in the appetite. And the reason why torpor especially is said to deprive one of speech is because of all the external movements the voice is the best expression of the inward thought and desire, not only in men, but also in other animals, as is stated in *Polit.* i, 1.

Reply Obj. 1: Pleasure is caused by good, which has only one meaning: and so pleasure is not divided into several species as sorrow is; for the latter is caused by evil, which "happens in many ways," as Dionysius says (Div. Nom. iv).

Reply Obj. 2: Repentance is for one's own evil, which is the proper object of sorrow: wherefore it does not belong to these species. Jealousy and indignation are included in envy, as we shall explain later (II-II, Q. 36, A. 2).

Reply Obj. 3: This division is not according to opposite species; but according to the diversity of foreign matter to which the notion of sorrow is applied, as stated above.

## QUESTION 36

OF THE CAUSES OF SORROW OR PAIN (In Four Articles)

We must now consider the causes of sorrow: under which head there are four points of inquiry:

(1) Whether sorrow is caused by the loss of a good or rather by the presence of an evil?

(2) Whether desire is a cause of sorrow?

(3) Whether the craving for unity is a cause of sorrow?

(4) Whether an irresistible power is a cause of sorrow?

FIRST ARTICLE [I-II, Q. 36, Art. 1]

Whether Sorrow Is Caused by the Loss of Good or by the Presence of Evil?

Objection 1: It would seem that sorrow is caused by the loss of a good rather than by the presence of an evil. For Augustine says (De viii QQ. Dulcit. qu. 1) that sorrow is caused by the loss of temporal goods. Therefore, in like manner, every sorrow is caused by the loss of some good.

Obj. 2: Further, it was said above (Q. 35, A. 4) that the sorrow which is contrary to a pleasure, has the same object as that pleasure. But the object of pleasure is good, as stated above (Q. 23, A. 4; Q. 31, A. 1; Q. 35, A. 3). Therefore sorrow is caused chiefly by the loss of good.

Obj. 3: Further, according to Augustine (De Civ. Dei xiv, 7, 9), love is the cause of sorrow, as of the other emotions of the soul. But the object of love is good. Therefore pain or sorrow is felt for the loss of good rather than for an evil that is present.

*On the contrary,* Damascene says (De Fide Orth. ii, 12) that "the dreaded evil gives rise to fear, the present evil is the cause of sorrow."

*I answer that,* If privations, as considered by the mind, were what they are in reality, this question would seem to be of no importance. For, as stated in the First Part (Q. 14, A. 10; Q. 48, A. 3), evil is the privation of good: and privation is in reality nothing else than the lack of the contrary habit; so that, in this respect, to sorrow for the loss of good, would be the same as to sorrow for the presence of evil. But sorrow is a movement of the appetite in consequence of an apprehension: and even a privation, as apprehended, has the aspect of a being, wherefore it is called "a being of reason." And in this way evil, being a privation, is regarded as a "contrary." Accordingly, so far as the movement of the appetite is concerned, it makes a difference which of the two it regards chiefly, the present evil or the good which is lost.

Again, since the movement of the animal appetite holds the same place in the actions of the soul, as natural movement in natural things; the truth of the matter is to be found by considering natural movements. For if, in natural movements, we observe those of approach and withdrawal, approach is of itself directed to something suitable to nature; while withdrawal is of itself directed to something contrary to nature; thus a heavy body, of itself, withdraws from a higher place, and approaches naturally to a lower place. But if we consider the cause of both these movements, viz. gravity, then gravity itself inclines towards the lower place more than it withdraws from the higher place, since withdrawal from the latter is the reason for its downward tendency.

Accordingly, since, in the movements of the appetite, sorrow is a kind of flight or withdrawal, while pleasure is a kind of pursuit or approach; just as pleasure regards first the good possessed, as its proper object, so sorrow regards the evil that is present. On the other hand love, which is the cause of pleasure and sorrow, regards good rather than evil: and therefore, forasmuch as the object is the cause of a passion, the present evil is more properly the cause of sorrow or pain, than the good which is lost.

Reply Obj. 1: The loss itself of good is apprehended as an evil, just as the loss of evil is apprehended as a good: and in this sense Augustine says that pain results from the loss of temporal goods.

Reply Obj. 2: Pleasure and its contrary pain have the same object, but under contrary aspects: because if the presence of a particular thing be the object of pleasure, the absence of that same thing is the object of sorrow. Now one contrary includes the privation of the other, as stated in *Metaph.* x, 4: and consequently sorrow in respect of one contrary is, in a way, directed to the same thing under a contrary aspect.

Reply Obj. 3: When many movements arise from one cause, it does not follow that they all regard chiefly that which the cause regards chiefly, but only the first of them. And each of the others regards chiefly that which is suitable to it according to its own nature.

SECOND ARTICLE [I-II, Q. 36, Art. 2]

Whether Desire Is a Cause of Sorrow?

Objection 1: It would seem that desire is not a cause of pain or sorrow. Because sorrow of itself regards evil, as stated above (A. 1): whereas desire is a movement of the appetite towards good. Now movement towards one contrary is not a cause of movement towards the other contrary. Therefore desire is not a cause of pain.

Obj. 2: Further, pain, according to Damascene (De Fide Orth. ii, 12), is caused by something present; whereas the object of desire is something future. Therefore desire is not a cause of pain.

Obj. 3: Further, that which is pleasant in itself is not a cause of pain. But desire is pleasant in itself, as the Philosopher says (Rhet. i, 11). Therefore desire is not a cause of pain or sorrow.

*On the contrary,* Augustine says (Enchiridion xxiv): "When ignorance of things necessary to be done, and desire of things hurtful, found their way in: error and pain stole an entrance in their company." But ignorance is the cause of error. Therefore desire is a cause of sorrow.

*I answer that,* Sorrow is a movement of the animal appetite. Now, as stated above (A. 1), the appetitive movement is likened to the natural appetite; a likeness, that may be assigned to a twofold cause; one, on the part of the end, the other, on the part of the principle of movement. Thus, on the part of the end, the cause of a heavy body's downward movement is the lower place; while the principle of that movement is a natural inclination resulting from gravity.

Now the cause of the appetitive movement, on the part of the end, is the object of that movement. And thus, it has been said above (A. 1) that the cause of pain or sorrow is a present evil. On the other hand, the cause, by way of principle, of that movement, is the inward inclination of the appetite; which inclination regards, first of all, the good, and in consequence, the rejection of a contrary evil. Hence the first principle of this appetitive movement is love, which is the first inclination of the appetite towards the possession of good: while the second principle is hatred, which is the first inclination of the appetite towards the avoidance of evil. But since concupiscence or desire is the first effect of love, which gives rise to the greatest pleasure, as stated above (Q. 32, A. 6); hence it is that Augustine often speaks of desire or concupiscence in the sense of love, as was also stated (Q. 30, A. 2, ad 2): and in this sense he says that desire is the universal cause of sorrow. Sometimes, however, desire taken in its proper sense, is the cause of sorrow. Because whatever hinders a movement from reaching its end is contrary to that movement. Now that which is contrary to the movement of the appetite, is a cause of sorrow. Consequently, desire becomes a cause of sorrow, in so far as we sorrow for the delay of a desired good, or for its entire removal. But it cannot be a universal cause of sorrow: since we sorrow more for the loss of present good, in which we have already taken pleasure, than for the withdrawal of future good which we desire to have.

Reply Obj. 1: The inclination of the appetite to the possession of good causes the inclination of the appetite to fly from evil, as stated above. And hence it is that the appetitive movements that regard good, are reckoned as causing the appetitive movements that regard evil.

Reply Obj. 2: That which is desired, though really future, is, nevertheless, in a way, present, inasmuch as it is hoped for. Or we may say that although the desired good itself is future, yet the hindrance is reckoned as present, and so gives rise to sorrow.

Reply Obj. 3: Desire gives pleasure, so long as there is hope of obtaining that which is desired. But, when hope is removed through the presence of an obstacle, desire causes sorrow.

THIRD ARTICLE [I-II, Q. 36, Art. 3]

Whether the Craving for Unity Is a Cause of Sorrow?

Objection 1: It would seem that the craving for unity is not a cause of sorrow. For the Philosopher says (Ethic. x, 3) that "this opinion," which held repletion to be the cause of pleasure, and division [*Aristotle wrote *endeian* , 'want'; St. Thomas, in the Latin version, read 'incisionem'; should he have read 'indigentiam'?], the cause of sorrow, "seems to have originated in pains and pleasures connected with food." But not every pleasure or sorrow is of this kind. Therefore the craving for unity is not the universal cause of sorrow; since repletion pertains to unity, and division is the cause of multitude.

Obj. 2: Further, every separation is opposed to unity. If therefore sorrow were caused by a craving for unity, no separation would be pleasant: and this is clearly untrue as regards the separation of whatever is superfluous.

Obj. 3: Further, for the same reason we desire the conjunction of good and the removal of evil. But as conjunction regards unity, since it is a kind of union; so separation is contrary to unity. Therefore the craving for unity should not be reckoned, rather than the craving for separation, as causing sorrow.

*On the contrary,* Augustine says (De Lib. Arb. iii, 23), that "from the pain that dumb animals feel, it is quite evident how their souls desire unity, in ruling and quickening their bodies. For what else is pain but a feeling of impatience of division or corruption?"

*I answer that,* Forasmuch as the desire or craving for good is reckoned as a cause of sorrow, so must a craving for unity, and love, be accounted as causing sorrow. Because the good of each thing consists in a certain unity, inasmuch as each thing has, united in itself, the elements of which its perfection consists: wherefore the Platonists held that *one* is a principle, just as good is. Hence everything naturally desires unity, just as it desires goodness: and therefore, just as love or desire for good is a cause of sorrow, so also is the love or craving for unity.

Reply Obj. 1: Not every kind of union causes perfect goodness, but only that on which the perfect being of a thing depends. Hence neither does the desire of any kind of unity cause pain or sorrow, as some have maintained: whose opinion is refuted by the Philosopher from the fact that repletion is not always pleasant; for instance, when a man has eaten to repletion, he takes no further pleasure in eating; because repletion or union of this kind, is repugnant rather than conducive to perfect being. Consequently sorrow is caused by the craving, not for any kind of unity, but for that unity in which the perfection of nature consists.

Reply Obj. 2: Separation can be pleasant, either because it removes something contrary to a thing's perfection, or because it has some union connected with it, such as union of the sense to its object.

Reply Obj. 3: Separation from things hurtful and corruptive is desired, in so far as they destroy the unity which is due. Wherefore the desire for such like separation is not the first cause of sorrow, whereas the craving for unity is.

FOURTH ARTICLE [I-II, Q. 36, Art. 4]

Whether an Irresistible Power Is a Cause of Sorrow?

Objection 1: It would seem that a greater power should not be reckoned a cause of sorrow. For that which is in the power of the agent is not present but future. But sorrow is for present evil. Therefore a greater power is not a cause of sorrow.

Obj. 2: Further, hurt inflicted is the cause of sorrow. But hurt can be inflicted even by a lesser power. Therefore a greater power should not be reckoned as a cause of sorrow.

Obj. 3: Further, the interior inclinations of the soul are the causes of the movements of appetite. But a greater power is something external. Therefore it should not be reckoned as a cause of sorrow.

*On the contrary,* Augustine says (De Nat. Boni xx): "Sorrow in the soul is caused by the will resisting a stronger power: while pain in the body is caused by sense resisting a stronger body."

*I answer that,* As stated above (A. 1), a present evil, is cause of sorrow or pain, by way of object. Therefore that which is the cause of the evil being present, should be reckoned as causing pain or sorrow. Now it is evident that it is contrary to the inclination of the appetite to be united with a present evil: and whatever is contrary to a thing's inclination does not happen to it save by the action of something stronger. Wherefore Augustine reckons a greater power as being the cause of sorrow.

But it must be noted that if the stronger power goes so far as to transform the contrary inclination into its own inclination there will be no longer repugnance or violence: thus if a stronger agent, by its action on a heavy body, deprives it of its downward tendency, its consequent upward tendency is not violent but natural to it.

Accordingly if some greater power prevail so far as to take away from the will or the sensitive appetite, their respective inclinations, pain or sorrow will not result therefrom; such is the result only when the contrary inclination of the appetite remains. And hence Augustine says (De Nat. Boni xx) that sorrow is caused by the will "resisting a stronger power": for were it not to resist, but to yield by consenting, the result would be not sorrow but pleasure.

Reply Obj. 1: A greater power causes sorrow, as acting not potentially but actually, i.e. by causing the actual presence of the corruptive evil.

Reply Obj. 2: Nothing hinders a power which is not simply greater, from being greater in some respect: and accordingly it is able to inflict some harm. But if it be nowise stronger, it can do no harm at all: wherefore it cannot bring about that which causes sorrow.

Reply Obj. 3: External agents can be the causes of appetitive movements, in so far as they cause the presence of the object: and it is thus that a greater power is reckoned to be the cause of sorrow.

# QUESTION 37

OF THE EFFECTS OF PAIN OR SORROW (In Four Articles)

We must now consider the effects of pain or of sorrow: under which head there are four points of inquiry:

(1) Whether pain deprives one of the power to learn?

(2) Whether the effect of sorrow or pain is to burden the soul?

(3) Whether sorrow or pain weakens all activity?

(4) Whether sorrow is more harmful to the body than all the other passions of the soul?

FIRST ARTICLE [I-II, Q. 37, Art. 1]

Whether Pain Deprives One of the Power to Learn?

Objection 1: It would seem that pain does not deprive one of the power to learn. For it is written (Isa. 26:9): "When Thou shalt do Thy judgments on the earth, the inhabitants of the world shall learn justice": and further on (verse 16): "In the tribulation of murmuring Thy instruction was with them." But the judgments of God and tribulation cause sorrow in men's hearts. Therefore pain or sorrow, far from destroying, increases the power of learning.

Obj. 2: Further, it is written (Isa. 28:9): "Whom shall He teach knowledge? And whom shall He make to understand the hearing? Them that are weaned from the milk, that are drawn away from the breasts," i.e. from pleasures. But pain and sorrow are most destructive of pleasure; since sorrow hinders all pleasure, as stated in *Ethic.* vii, 14: and (Ecclus. 11:29) it is stated that "the affliction of an hour maketh one forget great delights." Therefore pain, instead of taking away, increases the faculty of learning.

Obj. 3: Further, inward sorrow surpasses outward pain, as stated above (Q. 35, A. 7). But man can learn while sorrowful. Much more, therefore, can he learn while in bodily pain.

*On the contrary,* Augustine says (Soliloq. i, 12): "Although during those days I was tormented with a violent tooth-ache, I was not able to turn over in my mind other things than those I had already learnt; and as to learning anything, I was quite unequal to it, because it required undivided attention."

*I answer that,* Since all the powers of the soul are rooted in the one essence of the soul, it must needs happen, when the intention of the soul is strongly drawn towards the action of one power, that it is withdrawn from the action of another power: because the soul, being one, can only have one intention. The result is that if one thing draws upon itself the entire intention of the soul, or a great portion thereof, anything else requiring considerable attention is incompatible therewith.

Now it is evident that sensible pain above all draws the soul's attention to itself; because it is natural for each thing to tend wholly to repel whatever is contrary to it, as may be observed even in natural things. It is likewise evident that in order to learn anything new, we require study and effort with a strong intention, as is clearly stated in Prov. 2:4, 5: "If thou shalt seek wisdom as money, and shall dig for her as for a treasure, then shalt thou understand learning" [Vulg: 'the fear of the Lord']. Consequently if the pain be acute, man is prevented at the time from learning anything: indeed it can be so acute, that, as long as it lasts, a man is unable to give his attention even to that which he knew already. However a difference is to be observed according to the difference of love that a man has for learning or for considering: because the greater his love, the more will he retain the intention of his mind so as to prevent it from turning entirely to the pain.

Reply Obj. 1: Moderate sorrow, that does not cause the mind to wander, can conduce to the acquisition of learning especially in regard to those things by which a man hopes to be freed from sorrow. And thus, "in the tribulation of murmuring," men are more apt to be taught by God.

Reply Obj. 2: Both pleasure and pain, in so far as they draw upon themselves the soul's intention, hinder the reason from the act of consideration, wherefore it is stated in *Ethic.* vii, 11 that "in the moment of sexual pleasure, a man cannot understand anything." Nevertheless pain attracts the soul's intention more than pleasure does: thus we observe in natural things that the action of a natural body is more intense in regard to its contrary; for instance, hot water is more accessible to the action of cold, and in consequence freezes harder. If therefore pain or sorrow be moderate, it can conduce accidentally to the facility of learning, in so far as it takes away an excess of pleasure. But, of itself, it is a hindrance; and if it be intense, it prevents it altogether.

Reply Obj. 3: External pain arises from hurt done to the body, so that it involves bodily transmutation more than inward sorrow does: and yet the latter is greater in regard to the formal element of pain, which belongs to the soul. Consequently bodily pain is a greater hindrance to contemplation which requires complete repose, than inward sorrow is. Nevertheless if inward sorrow be very intense, it attracts the intention, so that man is unable to learn anything for the first time: wherefore on account of sorrow Gregory interrupted his commentary on Ezechiel (Hom. xxii in Ezechiel).

SECOND ARTICLE [I-II, Q. 37, Art. 2]

Whether the Effect of Sorrow or Pain Is to Burden the Soul?

Objection 1: It would seem that it is not an effect of sorrow to burden the soul. For the Apostle says (2 Cor. 7:11): "Behold this self-same thing, that you were made sorrowful according to God, how great carefulness it worketh in you: yea, defence, yea indignation," etc. Now carefulness and indignation imply that the soul is uplifted, which is contrary to being depressed. Therefore depression is not an effect of sorrow.

Obj. 2: Further, sorrow is contrary to pleasure. But the effect of pleasure is expansion: the opposite of which is not depression but contraction. Therefore depression should not be reckoned as an effect of sorrow.

Obj. 3: Further, sorrow consumes those who are inflicted therewith, as may be gathered from the words of the Apostle (2 Cor. 2:7): "Lest perhaps such an one be swallowed up with overmuch sorrow." But that which is depressed is not consumed; nay, it is weighed down by something heavy, whereas that which is consumed enters within the consumer. Therefore depression should not be reckoned an effect of sorrow.

*On the contrary,* Gregory of Nyssa [*Nemesius, De Nat. Hom. xix.] and Damascene (De Fide Orth. ii, 14) speak of "depressing sorrow."

*I answer that,* The effects of the soul's passions are sometimes named metaphorically, from a likeness to sensible bodies: for the reason that the movements of the animal appetite are like the inclinations of the natural appetite. And in this way fervor is ascribed to love, expansion to pleasure, and depression to sorrow. For a man is said to be depressed, through being hindered in his own movement by some weight. Now it is evident from what has been said above (Q. 23, A. 4; Q. 25, A. 4; Q. 36, A. 1) that sorrow is caused by a present evil: and this evil, from the very fact that it is repugnant to the movement of the will, depresses the soul, inasmuch as it hinders it from enjoying that which it wishes to enjoy. And if the evil which is the cause of sorrow be not so strong as to deprive one of the hope of avoiding it, although the soul be depressed in so far as, for the present, it fails to grasp that which it craves for; yet it retains the movement whereby to repulse that evil. If, on the other hand, the strength of the evil be such as to exclude the hope of evasion, then even the interior movement of the afflicted soul is absolutely hindered, so that it cannot turn aside either this way or that. Sometimes even the external movement of the body is paralyzed, so that a man becomes completely stupefied.

Reply Obj. 1: That uplifting of the soul ensues from the sorrow which is according to God, because it brings with it the hope of the forgiveness of sin.

Reply Obj. 2: As far as the movement of the appetite is concerned, contraction and depression amount to the same: because the soul, through being depressed so as to be unable to attend freely to outward things, withdraws to itself, closing itself up as it were.

Reply Obj. 3: Sorrow is said to consume man, when the force of the afflicting evil is such as to shut out all hope of evasion: and thus also it both depresses and consumes at the same time. For certain things, taken metaphorically, imply one another, which taken literally, appear to exclude one another.

THIRD ARTICLE [I-II, Q. 37, Art. 3]

Whether Sorrow or Pain Weakens All Activity?

Objection 1: It would seem that sorrow does not weaken all activity. Because carefulness is caused by sorrow, as is clear from the passage of the Apostle quoted above (A. 2, Obj. 1). But carefulness conduces to good work: wherefore the Apostle says (2 Tim. 2:15): "Carefully study to present thyself ... a workman that needeth not to be ashamed." Therefore sorrow is not a hindrance to work, but helps one to work well.

Obj. 2: Further, sorrow causes desire in many cases, as stated in *Ethic.* vii, 14. But desire causes intensity of action. Therefore sorrow does too.

Obj. 3: Further, as some actions are proper to the joyful, so are others proper to the sorrowful; for instance, to mourn. Now a thing is improved by that which is suitable to it. Therefore certain actions are not hindered but improved by reason of sorrow.

*On the contrary,* The Philosopher says (Ethic. x, 4) that "pleasure perfects action," whereas on the other hand, "sorrow hinders it" (Ethic. x, 5).

*I answer that,* As stated above (A. 2), sorrow at times does not depress or consume the soul, so as to shut out all movement, internal or external; but certain movements are sometimes caused by sorrow itself. Accordingly action stands in a twofold relation to sorrow. First, as being the object of sorrow: and thus sorrow hinders any action: for we never do that which we do with sorrow, so well as that which we do with pleasure, or without sorrow. The reason for this is that the will is the cause of human actions: and consequently when we do something that gives pain, the action must of necessity be weakened in consequence. Secondly, action stands in relation to sorrow, as to its principle and cause: and such action must needs be improved by sorrow: thus the more one sorrows on account of a certain thing, the more one strives to shake off sorrow, provided there is a hope of shaking it off: otherwise no movement or action would result from that sorrow.

From what has been said the replies to the objections are evident.

FOURTH ARTICLE [I-II, Q. 37, Art. 4]

Whether Sorrow Is More Harmful to the Body Than the Other Passions of the Soul?

Objection 1: It would seem that sorrow is not most harmful to the body. For sorrow has a spiritual existence in the soul. But those things which have only a spiritual existence do not cause a transmutation in the body: as is evident with regard to the images of colors, which images are in the air and do not give color to bodies. Therefore sorrow is not harmful to the body.

Obj. 2: Further if it be harmful to the body, this can only be due to its having a bodily transmutation in conjunction with it. But bodily transmutation takes place in all the passions of the soul, as stated above (Q. 22, AA. 1, 3). Therefore sorrow is not more harmful to the body than the other passions of the soul.

Obj. 3: Further, the Philosopher says (Ethic. vii, 3) that "anger and desire drive some to madness": which seems to be a very great harm, since reason is the most excellent thing in man. Moreover, despair seems to be more harmful than sorrow; for it is the cause of sorrow. Therefore sorrow is not more harmful to the body than the other passions of the soul.

*On the contrary,* It is written (Prov. 17:22): "A joyful mind maketh age flourishing: a sorrowful spirit drieth up the bones": and (Prov. 25:20): "As a moth doth by a garment, and a worm by the wood: so the sadness of a man consumeth the heart": and (Ecclus. 38:19): "Of sadness cometh death."

*I answer that,* Of all the soul's passions, sorrow is most harmful to the body. The reason of this is because sorrow is repugnant to man's life in respect of the species of its movement, and not merely in respect of its measure or quantity, as is the case with the other passions of the soul. For man's life consists in a certain movement, which flows from the heart to the other parts of the body: and this movement is befitting to human nature according to a certain fixed measure. Consequently if this movement goes beyond the right measure, it will be repugnant to man's life in respect of the measure of quantity; but not in respect of its specific character: whereas if this movement be hindered in its progress, it will be repugnant to life in respect of its species.

Now it must be noted that, in all the passions of the soul, the bodily transmutation which is their material element, is in conformity with and in proportion to the appetitive movement, which is the formal element: just as in everything matter is proportionate to form. Consequently those passions that imply a movement of the appetite in pursuit of something, are not repugnant to the vital movement as regards its species, but they may be repugnant thereto as regards its measure: such are love, joy, desire and the like; wherefore these passions conduce to the well-being of the body; though, if they be excessive, they may be harmful to it. On the other hand, those passions which denote in the appetite a movement of flight or contraction, are repugnant to the vital movement, not only as regards its measure, but also as regards its species; wherefore they are simply harmful: such are fear and despair, and above all sorrow which depresses the soul by reason of a present evil, which makes a stronger impression than future evil.

Reply Obj. 1: Since the soul naturally moves the body, the spiritual movement of the soul is naturally the cause of bodily transmutation. Nor is there any parallel with spiritual images, because they are not naturally ordained to move such other bodies as are not naturally moved by the soul.

Reply Obj. 2: Other passions imply a bodily transmutation which is specifically in conformity with the vital movement: whereas sorrow implies a transmutation that is repugnant thereto, as stated above.

Reply Obj. 3: A lesser cause suffices to hinder the use of reason, than to destroy life: since we observe that many ailments deprive one of the use of reason, before depriving one of life. Nevertheless fear and anger cause very great harm to the body, by reason of the sorrow which they imply, and which arises from the absence of the thing desired. Moreover sorrow too sometimes deprives man of the use of reason: as may be seen in those who through sorrow become a prey to melancholy or madness.

# QUESTION 38

OF THE REMEDIES OF SORROW OR PAIN (In Four Articles)

We must now consider the remedies of pain or sorrow: under which head there are five points of inquiry:

(1) Whether pain or sorrow is assuaged by every pleasure?

(2) Whether it is assuaged by weeping?

(3) Whether it is assuaged by the sympathy of friends?

(4) Whether it is assuaged by contemplating the truth?

(5) Whether it is assuaged by sleep and baths?

FIRST ARTICLE [I-II, Q. 38, Art. 1]

Whether Pain or Sorrow Is Assuaged by Every Pleasure?

Objection 1: It would seem that not every pleasure assuages every pain or sorrow. For pleasure does not assuage sorrow, save in so far as it is contrary to it: for "remedies work by contraries" (Ethic. ii, 3). But not every pleasure is contrary to every sorrow; as stated above (Q. 35, A. 4). Therefore not every pleasure assuages every sorrow.

Obj. 2: Further, that which causes sorrow does not assuage it. But some pleasures cause sorrow; since, as stated in *Ethic.* ix, 4, "the wicked man feels pain at having been pleased." Therefore not every pleasure assuages sorrow.

Obj. 3: Further, Augustine says (Confess. iv, 7) that he fled from his country, where he had been wont to associate with his friend, now dead: "for so should his eyes look for him less, where they were not wont to see him." Hence we may gather that those things which united us to our dead or absent friends, become burdensome to us when we mourn their death or absence. But nothing united us more than the pleasures we enjoyed in common. Therefore these very pleasures become burdensome to us when we mourn. Therefore not every pleasure assuages every sorrow.

*On the contrary,* The Philosopher says (Ethic. vii, 14) that "sorrow is driven forth by pleasure, both by a contrary pleasure and by any other, provided it be intense."

*I answer that,* As is evident from what has been said above (Q. 23, A. 4), pleasure is a kind of repose of the appetite in a suitable good; while sorrow arises from something unsuited to the appetite. Consequently in movements of the appetite pleasure is to sorrow, what, in bodies, repose is to weariness, which is due to a non-natural transmutation; for sorrow itself implies a certain weariness or ailing of the appetitive faculty. Therefore just as all repose of the body brings relief to any kind of weariness, ensuing from any non-natural cause; so every pleasure brings relief by assuaging any kind of sorrow, due to any cause whatever.

Reply Obj. 1: Although not every pleasure is specifically contrary to every sorrow, yet it is generically, as stated above (Q. 35, A. 4). And consequently, on the part of the disposition of the subject, any sorrow can be assuaged by any pleasure.

Reply Obj. 2: The pleasures of wicked men are not a cause of sorrow while they are enjoyed, but afterwards: that is to say, in so far as wicked men repent of those things in which they took pleasure. This sorrow is healed by contrary pleasures.

Reply Obj. 3: When there are two causes inclining to contrary movements, each hinders the other; yet the one which is stronger and more persistent, prevails in the end. Now when a man is made sorrowful by those things in which he took pleasure in common with a deceased or absent friend, there are two causes producing contrary movements. For the thought of the friend's death or absence, inclines him to sorrow: whereas the present good inclines him to pleasure. Consequently each is modified by the other. And yet, since the perception of the present moves more strongly than the memory of the past, and since love of self is more persistent than love of another; hence it is that, in the end, the pleasure drives out the sorrow. Wherefore a little further on (Confess. iv, 8) Augustine says that his "sorrow gave way to his former pleasures."

SECOND ARTICLE [I-II, Q. 38, Art. 2]

Whether Pain or Sorrow Is Assuaged by Tears?

Objection 1: It would seem that tears do not assuage sorrow. Because no effect diminishes its cause. But tears or groans are an effect of sorrow. Therefore they do not diminish sorrow.

Obj. 2: Further, just as tears or groans are an effect of sorrow, so laughter is an effect of joy. But laughter does not lessen joy. Therefore tears do not lessen sorrow.

Obj. 3: Further, when we weep, the evil that saddens us is present to the imagination. But the image of that which saddens us increases sorrow, just as the image of a pleasant thing adds to joy. Therefore it seems that tears do not assuage sorrow.

*On the contrary,* Augustine says (Confess. iv, 7) that when he mourned the death of his friend, "in groans and in tears alone did he find some little refreshment."

*I answer that,* Tears and groans naturally assuage sorrow: and this for two reasons. First, because a hurtful thing hurts yet more if we keep it shut up, because the soul is more intent on it: whereas if it be allowed to escape, the soul's intention is dispersed as it were on outward things, so that the inward sorrow is lessened. This is why men, burdened with sorrow, make outward show of their sorrow, by tears or groans or even by words, their sorrow is assuaged. Secondly, because an action, that befits a man according to his actual disposition, is always pleasant to him. Now tears and groans are actions befitting a man who is in sorrow or pain; and consequently they become pleasant to him. Since then, as stated above (A. 1), every pleasure assuages sorrow or pain somewhat, it follows that sorrow is assuaged by weeping and groans.

Reply Obj. 1: This relation of the cause to effect is opposed to the relation existing between the cause of sorrow and the sorrowing man. For every effect is suited to its cause, and consequently is pleasant to it; but the cause of sorrow is disagreeable to him that sorrows. Hence the effect of sorrow is not related to him that sorrows in the same way as the cause of sorrow is. For this reason sorrow is assuaged by its effect, on account of the aforesaid contrariety.

Reply Obj. 2: The relation of effect to cause is like the relation of the object of pleasure to him that takes pleasure in it: because in each case the one agrees with the other. Now every like thing increases its like. Therefore joy is increased by laughter and the other effects of joy: except they be excessive, in which case, accidentally, they lessen it.

Reply Obj. 3: The image of that which saddens us, considered in itself, has a natural tendency to increase sorrow: yet from the very fact that a man imagines himself to be doing that which is fitting according to his actual state, he feels a certain amount of pleasure. For the same reason if laughter escapes a man when he is so disposed that he thinks he ought to weep, he is sorry for it, as having done something unbecoming to him, as Cicero says (De Tusc. Quaest. iii, 27).

THIRD ARTICLE [I-II, Q. 38, Art. 3]

Whether Pain or Sorrow Are Assuaged by the Sympathy of Friends?

Objection 1: It would seem that the sorrow of sympathizing friends does not assuage our own sorrow. For contraries have contrary effects. Now as Augustine says (Confess. viii, 4), "when many rejoice together, each one has more exuberant joy, for they are kindled and inflamed one by the other." Therefore, in like manner, when many are sorrowful, it seems that their sorrow is greater.

Obj. 2: Further, friendship demands mutual love, as Augustine declares (Confess. iv, 9). But a sympathizing friend is pained at the sorrow of his friend with whom he sympathizes. Consequently the pain of a sympathizing friend becomes, to the friend in sorrow, a further cause of sorrow: so that, his pain being doubled his sorrow seems to increase.

Obj. 3: Further, sorrow arises from every evil affecting a friend, as though it affected oneself: since "a friend is one's other self" (Ethic. ix, 4, 9). But sorrow is an evil. Therefore the sorrow of the sympathizing friend increases the sorrow of the friend with whom he sympathizes.

*On the contrary,* The Philosopher says (Ethic. ix, 11) that those who are in pain are consoled when their friends sympathize with them.

*I answer that,* When one is in pain, it is natural that the sympathy of a friend should afford consolation: whereof the Philosopher indicates a twofold reason (Ethic. ix, 11). The first is because, since sorrow has a depressing effect, it is like a weight whereof we strive to unburden ourselves: so that when a man sees others saddened by his own sorrow, it seems as though others were bearing the burden with him, striving, as it were, to lessen its weight; wherefore the load of sorrow becomes lighter for him: something like what occurs in the carrying of bodily burdens. The second and better reason is because when a man's friends condole with him, he sees that he is loved by them, and this affords him pleasure, as stated above (Q. 32, A. 5). Consequently, since every pleasure assuages sorrow, as stated above (A. 1), it follows that sorrow is mitigated by a sympathizing friend.

Reply Obj. 1: In either case there is a proof of friendship, viz. when a man rejoices with the joyful, and when he sorrows with the sorrowful. Consequently each becomes an object of pleasure by reason of its cause.

Reply Obj. 2: The friend's sorrow itself would be a cause of sorrow: but consideration of its cause, viz. his love, gives rise rather to pleasure.

And this suffices for the reply to the Third Objection.

FOURTH ARTICLE [I-II, Q. 38, Art. 4]

Whether Pain and Sorrow Are Assuaged by the Contemplation of Truth?

Objection 1: It would seem that the contemplation of truth does not assuage sorrow. For it is written (Eccles. 1:18): "He that addeth knowledge addeth also sorrow" [Vulg.: 'labor']. But knowledge pertains to the contemplation of truth. Therefore the contemplation of truth does not assuage sorrow.

Obj. 2: Further, the contemplation of truth belongs to the speculative intellect. But "the speculative intellect is not a principle of movement"; as stated in *De Anima* iii, 11. Therefore, since joy and sorrow are movements of the soul, it seems that the contemplation of truth does not help to assuage sorrow.

Obj. 3: Further, the remedy for an ailment should be applied to the part which ails. But contemplation of truth is in the intellect. Therefore it does not assuage bodily pain, which is in the senses.

*On the contrary,* Augustine says (Soliloq. i, 12): "It seemed to me that if the light of that truth were to dawn on our minds, either I should not feel that pain, or at least that pain would seem nothing to me."

*I answer that,* As stated above (Q. 3, A. 5), the greatest of all pleasures consists in the contemplation of truth. Now every pleasure assuages pain as stated above (A. 1): hence the contemplation of truth assuages pain or sorrow, and the more so, the more perfectly one is a lover of wisdom. And therefore in the midst of tribulations men rejoice in the contemplation of Divine things and of future Happiness, according to James 1:2: "My brethren, count it all joy, when you shall fall into divers temptations": and, what is more, even in the midst of bodily tortures this joy is found; as the "martyr Tiburtius, when he was walking barefoot on the burning coals, said: Methinks, I walk on roses, in the name of Jesus Christ." [*Cf. Dominican Breviary, August 11th, commemoration of St. Tiburtius.]

Reply Obj. 1: "He that addeth knowledge, addeth sorrow," either on account of the difficulty and disappointment in the search for truth; or because knowledge makes man acquainted with many things that are contrary to his will. Accordingly, on the part of the things known, knowledge causes sorrow: but on the part of the contemplation of truth, it causes pleasure.

Reply Obj. 2: The speculative intellect does not move the mind on the part of the thing contemplated: but on the part of contemplation itself, which is man's good and naturally pleasant to him.

Reply Obj. 3: In the powers of the soul there is an overflow from the higher to the lower powers: and accordingly, the pleasure of contemplation, which is in the higher part, overflows so as to mitigate even that pain which is in the senses.

FIFTH ARTICLE [I-II, Q. 38, Art. 5]

Whether Pain and Sorrow Are Assuaged by Sleep and Baths?

Objection 1: It would seem that sleep and baths do not assuage sorrow. For sorrow is in the soul: whereas sleep and baths regard the body. Therefore they do not conduce to the assuaging of sorrow.

Obj. 2: Further, the same effect does not seem to ensue from contrary causes. But these, being bodily things, are incompatible with the contemplation of truth which is a cause of the assuaging of sorrow, as stated above (A. 4). Therefore sorrow is not mitigated by the like.

Obj. 3: Further, sorrow and pain, in so far as they affect the body, denote a certain transmutation of the heart. But such remedies as these seem to pertain to the outward senses and limbs, rather than to the interior disposition of the heart. Therefore they do not assuage sorrow.

*On the contrary,* Augustine says (Confess. ix, 12): "I had heard that the bath had its name [* *Balneum,* from the Greek balaneion ] ... from the fact of its driving sadness from the mind." And further on, he says: "I slept, and woke up again, and found my grief not a little assuaged": and quotes the words from the hymn of Ambrose [*Cf. Sarum Breviary: First Sunday after the octave of the Epiphany, Hymn for first Vespers], in which it is said that "Sleep restores the tired limbs to labor, refreshes the weary mind, and banishes sorrow."

*I answer that,* As stated above (Q. 37, A. 4), sorrow, by reason of its specific nature, is repugnant to the vital movement of the body; and consequently whatever restores the bodily nature to its due state of vital movement, is opposed to sorrow and assuages it. Moreover such remedies, from the very fact that they bring nature back to its normal state, are causes of pleasure; for this is precisely in what pleasure consists, as stated above (Q. 31, A. 1). Therefore, since every pleasure assuages sorrow, sorrow is assuaged by such like bodily remedies.

Reply Obj. 1: The normal disposition of the body, so far as it is felt, is itself a cause of pleasure, and consequently assuages sorrow.

Reply Obj. 2: As stated above (Q. 31, A. 8), one pleasure hinders another; and yet every pleasure assuages sorrow. Consequently it is not unreasonable that sorrow should be assuaged by causes which hinder one another.

Reply Obj. 3: Every good disposition of the body reacts somewhat on the heart, which is the beginning and end of bodily movements, as stated in *De Causa Mot. Animal.* xi.

## QUESTION 39

OF THE GOODNESS AND MALICE OF SORROW OR PAIN (In Four Articles)

We must now consider the goodness and malice of pain or sorrow: under which head there are four points of inquiry:

(1) Whether all sorrow is evil?
(2) Whether sorrow can be a virtuous good?
(3) Whether it can be a useful good?
(4) Whether bodily pain is the greatest evil?

FIRST ARTICLE [I-II, Q. 39, Art. 1]

Whether All Sorrow Is Evil?

Objection 1: It would seem that all sorrow is evil. For Gregory of Nyssa [*Nemesius, De Nat. Hom. xix.] says: "All sorrow is evil, from its very nature." Now what is naturally evil, is evil always and everywhere. Therefore, all sorrow is evil.

Obj. 2: Further, that which all, even the virtuous, avoid, is evil. But all avoid sorrow, even the virtuous, since as stated in *Ethic.* vii, 11, "though the prudent man does not aim at pleasure, yet he aims at avoiding sorrow." Therefore sorrow is evil.

Obj. 3: Further, just as bodily evil is the object and cause of bodily pain, so spiritual evil is the object and cause of sorrow in the soul. But every bodily pain is a bodily evil. Therefore every spiritual sorrow is an evil of the soul.

*On the contrary,* Sorrow for evil is contrary to pleasure in evil. But pleasure in evil is evil: wherefore in condemnation of certain men, it is written (Prov. 2:14), that "they were glad when they had done evil." Therefore sorrow for evil is good.

*I answer that,* A thing may be good or evil in two ways: first considered simply and in itself; and thus all sorrow is an evil, because the mere fact of a man's appetite being uneasy about a present evil, is itself an evil, because it hinders the response of the appetite in good. Secondly, a thing is said to be good or evil, on the supposition of something else: thus shame is said to be good, on the supposition of a shameful deed done, as stated in *Ethic.* iv, 9. Accordingly, supposing the presence of something saddening or painful, it is a sign of goodness if a man is in sorrow or pain on account of this present evil. For if he were not to be in sorrow or pain, this could only be either because he feels it not, or because he does not reckon it as something unbecoming, both of which are manifest evils. Consequently it is a condition of goodness, that, supposing an evil to be present, sorrow or pain should ensue. Wherefore Augustine says (Gen. ad lit. viii, 14): "It is also a good thing that he sorrows for the good he has lost: for had not some good remained in his nature, he could not be punished by the loss of good." Because, however, in the science of Morals, we consider things individually—for actions are concerned about individuals—that which is good on some supposition, should be considered as good: just as that which is voluntary on some supposition, is judged to be voluntary, as stated in *Ethic.* iii, 1, and likewise above (Q. 6, A. 6).

Reply Obj. 1: Gregory of Nyssa [*Nemesius] is speaking of sorrow on the part of the evil that causes it, but not on the part of the subject that feels and rejects the evil. And from this point of view, all shun sorrow, inasmuch as they shun evil: but they do not shun the perception and rejection of evil. The same also applies to bodily pain: because the perception and rejection of bodily evil is the proof of the goodness of nature.

This suffices for the Replies to the Second and Third Objections.

SECOND ARTICLE [I-II, Q. 39, Art. 2]

Whether Sorrow Can Be a Virtuous Good?

Objection 1: It would seem that sorrow is not a virtuous good. For that which leads to hell is not a virtuous good. But, as Augustine says (Gen. ad lit. xii, 33), "Jacob seems to have feared lest he should be troubled overmuch by sorrow, and so, instead of entering into the rest of the blessed, be consigned to the hell of sinners." Therefore sorrow is not a virtuous good.

Obj. 2: Further, the virtuous good is praiseworthy and meritorious. But sorrow lessens praise or merit: for the Apostle says (2 Cor. 9:7): "Everyone, as he hath determined in his heart, not with sadness, or of necessity." Therefore sorrow is not a virtuous good.

Obj. 3: Further, as Augustine says (De Civ. Dei xiv, 15), "sorrow is concerned about those things which happen against our will." But not to will those things which are actually taking place, is to have a will opposed to the decree of God, to Whose providence whatever is done is subject. Since, then, conformity of the human to the Divine will is a condition of the rectitude of the will, as stated above (Q. 19, A. 9), it seems that sorrow is incompatible with rectitude of the will, and that consequently it is not virtuous.

*On the contrary,* Whatever merits the reward of eternal life is virtuous. But such is sorrow; as is evident from Matt. 5:5: "Blessed are they that mourn, for they shall be comforted." Therefore sorrow is a virtuous good.

*I answer that,* In so far as sorrow is good, it can be a virtuous good. For it has been said above (A. 1) that sorrow is a good inasmuch as it denotes perception and rejection of evil. These two things, as regards bodily pain, are a proof of the goodness of nature, to which it is due that the senses perceive, and that nature shuns, the harmful thing that causes pain. As regards interior sorrow, perception of the evil is sometimes due to a right judgment of reason; while the rejection of the evil is the act of the will, well disposed and detesting that evil. Now every virtuous good results from these two things, the rectitude of the reason and the will. Wherefore it is evident that sorrow may be a virtuous good.

Reply Obj. 1: All the passions of the soul should be regulated according to the rule of reason, which is the root of the virtuous good; but excessive sorrow, of which Augustine is speaking, oversteps this rule, and therefore it fails to be a virtuous good.

Reply Obj. 2: Just as sorrow for an evil arises from a right will and reason, which detest the evil, so sorrow for a good is due to a perverse reason and will, which detest the good. Consequently such sorrow is an obstacle to the praise and merit of the virtuous good; for instance, when a man gives an alms sorrowfully.

Reply Obj. 3: Some things do actually happen, not because God wills, but because He permits them to happen—such as sins. Consequently a will that is opposed to sin, whether in oneself or in another, is not discordant from the Divine will. Penal evils happen actually, even by God's will. But it is not necessary for the rectitude of his will, that man should will them in themselves: but only that he should not revolt against the order of Divine justice, as stated above (Q. 19, A. 10).

THIRD ARTICLE [I-II, Q. 39, Art. 3]

Whether Sorrow Can Be a Useful Good?

Objection 1: It would seem that sorrow cannot be a useful good. For it is written (Ecclus. 30:25): "Sadness hath killed many, and there is no profit in it."

Obj. 2: Further, choice is of that which is useful to an end. But sorrow is not an object of choice; in fact, "a thing without sorrow is to be chosen rather than the same thing with sorrow" (Topic. iii, 2). Therefore sorrow is not a useful good.

Obj. 3: Further, "Everything is for the sake of its own operation," as stated in *De Coelo* ii, 3. But "sorrow hinders operation," as stated in Ethic. x, 5. Therefore sorrow is not a useful good.

*On the contrary,* The wise man seeks only that which is useful. But according to Eccles. 7:5, "the heart of the wise is where there is mourning, and the heart of fools where there is mirth." Therefore sorrow is useful.

*I answer that,* A twofold movement of the appetite ensues from a present evil. One is that whereby the appetite is opposed to the present evil; and, in this respect, sorrow is of no use; because that which is present, cannot be not present. The other movement arises in the appetite to the effect of avoiding or expelling the saddening evil: and, in this respect, sorrow is of use, if it be for something which ought to be avoided. Because there are two reasons for which it may be right to avoid a thing. First, because it should be avoided in itself, on account of its being contrary to good; for instance, sin. Wherefore sorrow for sin is useful as inducing a man to avoid sin: hence the Apostle says (2 Cor. 7:9): "I am glad: not because you were made sorrowful, but because you were made sorrowful unto penance." Secondly, a thing is to be avoided, not as though it were evil in itself, but because it is an occasion of evil; either through one's being attached to it, and loving it too much, or through one's being thrown headlong thereby into an evil, as is evident in the case of temporal goods. And, in this respect, sorrow for temporal goods may be useful; according to Eccles. 7:3: "It is better to go to the house of mourning, than to the house of feasting: for in that we are put in mind of the end of all."

Moreover, sorrow for that which ought to be avoided is always useful, since it adds another motive for avoiding it. Because the very evil is in itself a thing to be avoided: while everyone avoids sorrow for its own sake, just as everyone seeks the good, and pleasure in the good. Therefore just as pleasure in the good makes one seek the good more earnestly, so sorrow for evil makes one avoid evil more eagerly.

Reply Obj. 1: This passage is to be taken as referring to excessive sorrow, which consumes the soul: for such sorrow paralyzes the soul, and hinders it from shunning evil, as stated above (Q. 37, A. 2).

Reply Obj. 2: Just as any object of choice becomes less eligible by reason of sorrow, so that which ought to be shunned is still more to be shunned by reason of sorrow: and, in this respect, sorrow is useful.

Reply Obj. 3: Sorrow caused by an action hinders that action: but sorrow for the cessation of an action, makes one do it more earnestly.

FOURTH ARTICLE [I-II, Q. 39, Art. 4]

Whether Bodily Pain Is the Greatest Evil?

Objection 1: It would seem that pain is the greatest evil. Because "the worst is contrary to the best" (Ethic. viii, 10). But a certain pleasure is the greatest good, viz. the pleasure of bliss. Therefore a certain pain is the greatest evil.

Obj. 2: Further, happiness is man's greatest good, because it is his last end. But man's Happiness consists in his "having whatever he will, and in willing naught amiss," as stated above (Q. 3, A. 4, Obj. 5; Q. 5, A. 8, Obj. 3). Therefore man's greatest good consists in the fulfilment of his will. Now pain consists in something happening contrary to the will, as Augustine declares (De Civ. Dei xiv, 6, 15). Therefore pain is man's greatest evil.

Obj. 3: Further, Augustine argues thus (Soliloq. i, 12): "We are composed of two parts, i.e. of a soul and a body, whereof the body is the inferior. Now the sovereign good is the greatest good of the better part: while the supreme evil is the greatest evil of the inferior part. But wisdom is the greatest good of the soul; while the worst thing in the body is pain. Therefore man's greatest good is to be wise: while his greatest evil is to suffer pain."

*On the contrary,* Guilt is a greater evil than punishment, as was stated in the First Part (Q. 48, A. 6). But sorrow or pain belongs to the punishment of sin, just as the enjoyment of changeable things is an evil of guilt. For Augustine says (De Vera Relig. xii): "What is pain of the soul, except for the soul to be deprived of that which it was wont to enjoy, or had hoped to enjoy? And this is all that is called evil, i.e. sin, and the punishment of sin." Therefore sorrow or pain is not man's greatest evil.

*I answer that,* It is impossible for any sorrow or pain to be man's greatest evil. For all sorrow or pain is either for something that is truly evil, or for something that is apparently evil, but good in reality. Now pain or sorrow for that which is truly evil cannot be the greatest evil: for there is something worse, namely, either not to reckon as evil that which is really evil, or not to reject it. Again, sorrow or pain, for that which is apparently evil, but really good, cannot be the greatest evil, for it would be worse to be altogether separated from that which is truly good. Hence it is impossible for any sorrow or pain to be man's greatest evil.

Reply Obj. 1: Pleasure and sorrow have two good points in common: namely, a true judgment concerning good and evil; and the right order of the will in approving of good and rejecting evil. Thus it is clear that in pain or sorrow there is a good, by the removal of which they become worse: and yet there is not an evil in every pleasure, by the removal of which the pleasure is better. Consequently, a pleasure can be man's highest good, in the way above stated (Q. 34, A. 3): whereas sorrow cannot be man's greatest evil.

Reply Obj. 2: The very fact of the will being opposed to evil is a good. And for this reason, sorrow or pain cannot be the greatest evil; because it has an admixture of good.

Reply Obj. 3: That which harms the better thing is worse than that which harms the worse. Now a thing is called evil "because it harms," as Augustine says (Enchiridion xii). Therefore that which is an evil to the soul is a greater evil than that which is an evil to the body. Therefore this argument does not prove: nor does Augustine give it as his own, but as taken from another [*Cornelius Celsus].

# QUESTION 40

OF THE IRASCIBLE PASSIONS, AND FIRST, OF HOPE AND DESPAIR (In Eight Articles)

We must now consider the irascible passions: (1) Hope and despair; (2) Fear and daring; (3) Anger. Under first head there are eight points of inquiry:

(1) Whether hope is the same as desire or cupidity?

(2) Whether hope is in the apprehensive, or in the appetitive faculty?

(3) Whether hope is in dumb animals?

(4) Whether despair is contrary to hope?

(5) Whether experience is a cause of hope?

(6) Whether hope abounds in young men and drunkards?

(7) Concerning the order of hope to love;

(8) Whether love conduces to action?

FIRST ARTICLE [I-II, Q. 40, Art. 1]

Whether Hope Is the Same As Desire or Cupidity?

Objection 1: It would seem that hope is the same as desire or cupidity. Because hope is reckoned as one of the four principal passions. But Augustine in setting down the four principal passions puts cupidity in the place of hope (De Civ. Dei xiv, 3, 7). Therefore hope is the same as cupidity or desire.

Obj. 2: Further, passions differ according to their objects. But the object of hope is the same as the object of cupidity or desire, viz. the future good. Therefore hope is the same as cupidity or desire.

Obj. 3: If it be said that hope, in addition to desire, denotes the possibility of obtaining the future good; *on the contrary,* whatever is accidental to the object does not make a different species of passion. But possibility of acquisition is accidental to a future good, which is the object of cupidity or desire, and of hope. Therefore hope does not differ specifically from desire or cupidity.

*On the contrary,* To different powers belong different species of passions. But hope is in the irascible power; whereas desire or cupidity is in the concupiscible. Therefore hope differs specifically from desire or cupidity.

*I answer that,* The species of a passion is taken from the object. Now, in the object of hope, we may note four conditions. First, that it is something good; since, properly speaking, hope regards only the good; in this respect, hope differs from fear, which regards evil. Secondly, that it is future; for hope does not regard that which is present and already possessed: in this respect, hope differs from joy which regards a present good. Thirdly, that it must be something arduous and difficult to obtain, for we do not speak of any one hoping for trifles, which are in one's power to have at any time: in this respect, hope differs from desire or cupidity, which regards the future good absolutely: wherefore it belongs to the concupiscible, while hope belongs to the irascible faculty. Fourthly, that this difficult thing is something possible to obtain: for one does not hope for that which one cannot get at all: and, in this respect, hope differs from despair. It is therefore evident that hope differs from desire, as the irascible passions differ from the concupiscible. For this reason, moreover, hope presupposes desire: just as all irascible passions presuppose the passions of the concupiscible faculty, as stated above (Q. 25, A. 1).

Reply Obj. 1: Augustine mentions desire instead of hope, because each regards future good; and because the good which is not arduous is reckoned as nothing: thus implying that desire seems to tend chiefly to the arduous good, to which hope tends likewise.

Reply Obj. 2: The object of hope is the future good considered, not absolutely, but as arduous and difficult of attainment, as stated above.

Reply Obj. 3: The object of hope adds not only possibility to the object of desire, but also difficulty: and this makes hope belong to another power, viz. the irascible, which regards something difficult, as stated in the First Part (Q. 81, A. 2). Moreover, possibility and impossibility are not altogether accidental to the object of the appetitive power: because the appetite is a principle of movement; and nothing is moved to anything except under the aspect of being possible; for no one is moved to that which he reckons impossible to get. Consequently hope differs from despair according to the difference of possible and impossible.

SECOND ARTICLE [I-II, Q. 40, Art. 2]

Whether Hope Is in the Apprehensive or in the Appetitive Power?

Objection 1: It would seem that hope belongs to the cognitive power. Because hope, seemingly, is a kind of awaiting; for the Apostle says (Rom. 8:25): "If we hope for that which we see not; we wait for it with patience." But awaiting seems to belong to the cognitive power, which we exercise by *looking out.* Therefore hope belongs to the cognitive power.

Obj. 2: Further, apparently hope is the same as confidence; hence when a man hopes he is said to be confident, as though to hope and to be confident were the same thing. But confidence, like faith, seems to belong to the cognitive power. Therefore hope does too.

Obj. 3: Further, certainty is a property of the cognitive power. But certainty is ascribed to hope. Therefore hope belongs to the cognitive power.

*On the contrary,* Hope regards good, as stated above (A. 1). Now good, as such, is not the object of the cognitive, but of the appetitive power. Therefore hope belongs, not to the cognitive, but to the appetitive power.

*I answer that,* Since hope denotes a certain stretching out of the appetite towards good, it evidently belongs to the appetitive power; since movement towards things belongs properly to the appetite: whereas the action of the cognitive power is accomplished not by the movement of the knower towards things, but rather according as the things known are in the knower. But since the cognitive power moves the appetite, by presenting its object to it; there arise in the appetite various movements according to various aspects of the apprehended object. For the apprehension of good gives rise to one kind of movement in the appetite, while the apprehension of evil gives rise to another: in like manner various movements arise from the apprehension of something present and of something future; of something considered absolutely, and of something considered as arduous; of something possible, and of something impossible. And accordingly hope is a movement of the appetitive power ensuing from the apprehension of a future good, difficult but possible to obtain; namely, a stretching forth of the appetite to such a good.

Reply Obj. 1: Since hope regards a possible good, there arises in man a twofold movement of hope; for a thing may be possible to him in two ways, viz. by his own power, or by another's. Accordingly when a man hopes to obtain something by his own power, he is not said to wait for it, but simply to hope for it. But, properly speaking, he is said to await that which he hopes to get by another's help, as though to await ( *exspectare* ) implied keeping one's eyes on another ( ex alio spectare ), in so far as the apprehensive power, by going ahead, not only keeps its eye on the good which man intends to get, but also on the thing by whose power he hopes to get it; according to Ecclus. 51:10, "I looked for the succor of men." Wherefore the movement of hope is sometimes called expectation, on account of the preceding inspection of the cognitive power.

Reply Obj. 2: When a man desires a thing and reckons that he can get it, he believes that he can get it, he believes that he will get it; and from this belief which precedes in the cognitive power, the ensuing movement in the appetite is called confidence. Because the movement of the appetite takes its name from the knowledge that precedes it, as an effect from a cause which is better known; for the apprehensive power knows its own act better than that of the appetite.

Reply Obj. 3: Certainty is ascribed to the movement, not only of the sensitive, but also of the natural appetite; thus we say that a stone is certain to tend downwards. This is owing to the inerrancy which the movement of the sensitive or even natural appetite derives from the certainty of the knowledge that precedes it.

THIRD ARTICLE [I-II, Q. 40, Art. 3]

Whether Hope Is in Dumb Animals?

Objection 1: It would seem that there is no hope in dumb animals. Because hope is for some future good, as Damascene says (De Fide Orth. ii, 12). But knowledge of the future is not in the competency of dumb animals, whose knowledge is confined to the senses and does not extend to the future. Therefore there is no hope in dumb animals.

Obj. 2: Further, the object of hope is a future good, possible of attainment. But possible and impossible are differences of the true and the false, which are only in the mind, as the Philosopher states (Metaph. vi, 4). Therefore there is no hope in dumb animals, since they have no mind.

Obj. 3: Further, Augustine says (Gen. ad lit. ix, 14) that "animals are moved by the things that they see." But hope is of things unseen: "for what a man seeth, why doth he hope for?" (Rom. 8:24). Therefore there is no hope in dumb animals.

*On the contrary,* Hope is an irascible passion. But the irascible faculty is in dumb animals. Therefore hope is also.

*I answer that,* The internal passions of animals can be gathered from their outward movements: from which it is clear that hope is in dumb animals. For if a dog see a hare, or a hawk see a bird, too far off, it makes no movement towards it, as having no hope to catch it: whereas, if it be near, it makes a movement towards it, as being in hopes of catching it. Because as stated above (Q. 1, A. 2; Q. 26, A. 1; Q. 35, A. 1), the sensitive appetite of dumb animals, and likewise the natural appetite of insensible things, result from the apprehension of an intellect, just as the appetite of the intellectual nature, which is called the will. But there is a difference, in that the will is moved by an apprehension of the intellect in the same subject; whereas the movement of the natural appetite results from the apprehension of the separate Intellect, Who is the Author of nature; as does also the sensitive appetite of dumb animals, who act from a certain natural instinct. Consequently, in the actions of irrational animals and of other natural things, we observe a procedure which is similar to that which we observe in the actions of art: and in this way hope and despair are in dumb animals.

Reply Obj. 1: Although dumb animals do not know the future, yet an animal is moved by its natural instinct to something future, as though it foresaw the future. Because this instinct is planted in them by the Divine Intellect that foresees the future.

Reply Obj. 2: The object of hope is not the possible as differentiating the true, for thus the possible ensues from the relation of a predicate to a subject. The object of hope is the possible as compared to a power. For such is the division of the possible given in *Metaph*. v, 12, i.e. into the two kinds we have just mentioned.

Reply Obj. 3: Although the thing which is future does not come under the object of sight; nevertheless through seeing something present, an animal's appetite is moved to seek or avoid something future.

FOURTH ARTICLE [I-II, Q. 40, Art. 4]

Whether Despair Is Contrary to Hope?

Objection 1: It would seem that despair is not contrary to hope. Because "to one thing there is one contrary" (Metaph. x, 5). But fear is contrary to hope. Therefore despair is not contrary to hope.

Obj. 2: Further, contraries seem to bear on the same thing. But hope and despair do not bear on the same thing: since hope regards the good, whereas despair arises from some evil that is in the way of obtaining good. Therefore hope is not contrary to despair.

Obj. 3: Further, movement is contrary to movement: while repose is in opposition to movement as a privation thereof. But despair seems to imply immobility rather than movement. Therefore it is not contrary to hope, which implies movement of stretching out towards the hoped-for good.

*On the contrary,* The very name of despair ( desperatio ) implies that it is contrary to hope ( spes ).

*I answer that,* As stated above (Q. 23, A. 2), there is a twofold contrariety of movements. One is in respect of approach to contrary terms: and this contrariety alone is to be found in the concupiscible passions, for instance between love and hatred. The other is according to approach and withdrawal with regard to the same term; and is to be found in the irascible passions, as stated above (Q. 23, A. 2). Now the object of hope, which is the arduous good, has the character of a principle of attraction, if it be considered in the light of something attainable; and thus hope tends thereto, for it denotes a kind of approach. But in so far as it is considered as unobtainable, it has the character of a principle of repulsion, because, as stated in *Ethic.* iii, 3, "when men come to an impossibility they disperse." And this is how despair stands in regard to this object, wherefore it implies a movement of withdrawal: and consequently it is contrary to hope, as withdrawal is to approach.

Reply Obj. 1: Fear is contrary to hope, because their objects, i.e. good and evil, are contrary: for this contrariety is found in the irascible passions, according as they ensue from the passions of the concupiscible. But despair is contrary to hope, only by contrariety of approach and withdrawal.

Reply Obj. 2: Despair does not regard evil as such; sometimes however it regards evil accidentally, as making the difficult good impossible to obtain. But it can arise from the mere excess of good.

Reply Obj. 3: Despair implies not only privation of hope, but also a recoil from the thing desired, by reason of its being esteemed impossible to get. Hence despair, like hope, presupposes desire; because we neither hope for nor despair of that which we do not desire to have. For this reason, too, each of them regards the good, which is the object of desire.

FIFTH ARTICLE [I-II, Q. 40, Art. 5]

Whether Experience Is a Cause of Hope?

Objection 1: It would seem that experience is not a cause of hope. Because experience belongs to the cognitive power; wherefore the Philosopher says (Ethic. ii, 1) that "intellectual virtue needs experience and time." But hope is not in the cognitive power, but in the appetite, as stated above (A. 2). Therefore experience is not a cause of hope.

Obj. 2: Further, the Philosopher says (Rhet. ii, 13) that "the old are slow to hope, on account of their experience"; whence it seems to follow that experience causes want of hope. But the same cause is not productive of opposites. Therefore experience is not a cause of hope.

Obj. 3: Further, the Philosopher says (De Coel. ii, 5) that "to have something to say about everything, without leaving anything out, is sometimes a proof of folly." But to attempt everything seems to point to great hopes; while folly arises from inexperience. Therefore inexperience, rather than experience, seems to be a cause of hope.

*On the contrary,* The Philosopher says (Ethic. iii, 8) "some are hopeful, through having been victorious often and over many opponents": which seems to pertain to experience. Therefore experience is a cause of hope.

*I answer that,* As stated above (A. 1), the object of hope is a future good, difficult but possible to obtain. Consequently a thing may be a cause of hope, either because it makes something possible to a man: or because it makes him think something possible. In the first way hope is caused by everything that increases a man's power; e.g. riches, strength, and, among others, experience: since by experience man acquires the faculty of doing something easily, and the result of this is hope. Wherefore Vegetius says (De Re Milit. i): "No one fears to do that which he is sure of having learned well."

In the second way, hope is caused by everything that makes man think that he can obtain something: and thus both teaching and persuasion may be a cause of hope. And then again experience is a cause of hope, in so far as it makes him reckon something possible, which before his experience he looked upon as impossible. However, in this way, experience can cause a lack of hope: because just as it makes a man think possible what he had previously thought impossible; so, conversely, experience makes a man consider as impossible that which hitherto he had thought possible. Accordingly experience causes hope in two ways, despair in one way: and for this reason we may say rather that it causes hope.

Reply Obj. 1: Experience in matters pertaining to action not only produces knowledge; it also causes a certain habit, by reason of custom, which renders the action easier. Moreover, the intellectual virtue itself adds to the power of acting with ease: because it shows something to be possible; and thus is a cause of hope.

Reply Obj. 2: The old are wanting in hope because of their experience, in so far as experience makes them think something impossible. Hence he adds (Rhet. ii, 13) that "many evils have befallen them."

Reply Obj. 3: Folly and inexperience can be a cause of hope accidentally as it were, by removing the knowledge which would help one to judge truly a thing to be impossible. Wherefore inexperience is a cause of hope, for the same reason as experience causes lack of hope.

SIXTH ARTICLE [I-II, Q. 40, Art. 6]

Whether Hope Abounds in Young Men and Drunkards?

Objection 1: It would seem that youth and drunkenness are not causes of hope. Because hope implies certainty and steadiness; so much so that it is compared to an anchor (Heb. 6:19). But young men and drunkards are wanting in steadiness; since their minds are easily changed. Therefore youth and drunkenness are not causes of hope.

Obj. 2: Further, as stated above (A. 5), the cause of hope is chiefly whatever increases one's power. But youth and drunkenness are united to weakness. Therefore they are not causes of hope.

Obj. 3: Further, experience is a cause of hope, as stated above (A. 5). But youth lacks experience. Therefore it is not a cause of hope.

*On the contrary,* The Philosopher says (Ethic. iii, 8) that "drunken men are hopeful": and (Rhet. ii, 12) that "the young are full of hope."

*I answer that,* Youth is a cause of hope for three reasons, as the Philosopher states in *Rhet.* ii, 12: and these three reasons may be gathered from the three conditions of the good which is the object of hope—namely, that it is future, arduous and possible, as stated above (A. 1). For youth has much of the future before it, and little of the past: and therefore since memory is of the past, and hope of the future, it has little to remember and lives very much in hope. Again, youths, on account of the heat of their nature, are full of spirit; so that their heart expands: and it is owing to the heart being expanded that one tends to that which is arduous; wherefore youths are spirited and hopeful. Likewise they who have not suffered defeat, nor had experience of obstacles to their efforts, are prone to count a thing possible to them. Wherefore youths, through inexperience of obstacles and of their own shortcomings, easily count a thing possible; and consequently are of good hope. Two of these causes are also in those who are in drink—viz. heat and high spirits, on account of wine, and heedlessness of dangers and shortcomings. For the same reason all foolish and thoughtless persons attempt everything and are full of hope.

Reply Obj. 1: Although youths and men in drink lack steadiness in reality, yet they are steady in their own estimation, for they think that they will steadily obtain that which they hope for.

In like manner, in reply to the Second Objection, we must observe that young people and men in drink are indeed unsteady in reality: but, in their own estimation, they are capable, for they know not their shortcomings.

Reply Obj. 3: Not only experience, but also lack of experience, is, in some way, a cause of hope, as explained above (A. 5, ad 3).

SEVENTH ARTICLE [I-II, Q. 40, Art. 7]

Whether Hope Is a Cause of Love?

Objection 1: It would seem that hope is not a cause of love. Because, according to Augustine (De Civ. Dei xiv, 7, 9), love is the first of the soul's emotions. But hope is an emotion of the soul. Therefore love precedes hope, and consequently hope does not cause love.

Obj. 2: Further, desire precedes hope. But desire is caused by love, as stated above (Q. 25, A. 2). Therefore hope, too, follows love, and consequently is not its cause.

Obj. 3: Further, hope causes pleasure, as stated above (Q. 32, A. 3). But pleasure is only of the good that is loved. Therefore love precedes hope.

*On the contrary,* The gloss commenting on Matt. 1:2, "Abraham begot Isaac, and Isaac begot Jacob," says, i.e. "faith begets hope, and hope begets charity." But charity is love. Therefore love is caused by hope.

*I answer that,* Hope can regard two things. For it regards as its object, the good which one hopes for. But since the good we hope for is something difficult but possible to obtain; and since it happens sometimes that what is difficult becomes possible to us, not through ourselves but through others; hence it is that hope regards also that by which something becomes possible to us.

In so far, then, as hope regards the good we hope to get, it is caused by love: since we do not hope save for that which we desire and love. But in so far as hope regards one through whom something becomes possible to us, love is caused by hope, and not vice versa. Because by the very fact that we hope that good will accrue to us through someone, we are moved towards him as to our own good; and thus we begin to love him. Whereas from the fact that we love someone we do not hope in him, except accidentally, that is, in so far as we think that he returns our love. Wherefore the fact of being loved by another makes us hope in him; but our love for him is caused by the hope we have in him.

Wherefore the Replies to the Objections are evident.

EIGHTH ARTICLE [I-II, Q. 40, Art. 8]

Whether Hope Is a Help or a Hindrance to Action?

Objection 1: It would seem that hope is not a help but a hindrance to action. Because hope implies security. But security begets negligence which hinders action. Therefore hope is a hindrance to action.

Obj. 2: Further, sorrow hinders action, as stated above (Q. 37, A. 3). But hope sometimes causes sorrow: for it is written (Prov. 13:12): "Hope that is deferred afflicteth the soul." Therefore hope hinders action.

Obj. 3: Further, despair is contrary to hope, as stated above (A. 4). But despair, especially in matters of war, conduces to action; for it is written (2 Kings 2:26), that "it is dangerous to drive people to despair." Therefore hope has a contrary effect, namely, by hindering action.

*On the contrary,* It is written (1 Cor. 9:10) that "he that plougheth should plough in hope ... to receive fruit": and the same applies to all other actions.

*I answer that,* Hope of its very nature is a help to action by making it more intense: and this for two reasons. First, by reason of its object, which is a good, difficult but possible. For the thought of its being difficult arouses our attention; while the thought that it is possible is no drag on our effort. Hence it follows that by reason of hope man is intent on his action. Secondly, on account of its effect. Because hope, as stated above (Q. 32, A. 3), causes pleasure; which is a help to action, as stated above (Q. 33, A. 4). Therefore hope is conducive to action.

Reply Obj. 1: Hope regards a good to be obtained; security regards an evil to be avoided. Wherefore security seems to be contrary to fear rather than to belong to hope. Yet security does not beget negligence, save in so far as it lessens the idea of difficulty: whereby it also lessens the character of hope: for the things in which a man fears no hindrance, are no longer looked upon as difficult.

Reply Obj. 2: Hope of itself causes pleasure; it is by accident that it causes sorrow, as stated above (Q. 32, A. 3, ad 2).

Reply Obj. 3: Despair threatens danger in war, on account of a certain hope that attaches to it. For they who despair of flight, strive less to fly, but hope to avenge their death: and therefore in this hope they fight the more bravely, and consequently prove dangerous to the foe.

## QUESTION 41

OF FEAR, IN ITSELF (In Four Articles)

We must now consider, in the first place, fear; and, secondly, daring. With regard to fear, four things must be considered: (1) Fear, in itself; (2) Its object; (3) Its cause; (4) Its effect. Under the first head there are four points of inquiry:

(1) Whether fear is a passion of the soul?

(2) Whether fear is a special passion?

(3) Whether there is a natural fear?

(4) Of the species of fear.

FIRST ARTICLE [I-II, Q. 41, Art. 1]

Whether Fear Is a Passion of the Soul?

Objection 1: It would seem that fear is not a passion of the soul. For Damascene says (De Fide Orth. iii, 23) that "fear is a power, by way of *systole* "—i.e. of contraction—"desirous of vindicating nature." But no virtue is a passion, as is proved in Ethic. ii, 5. Therefore fear is not a passion.

Obj. 2: Further, every passion is an effect due to the presence of an agent. But fear is not of something present, but of something future, as Damascene declares (De Fide Orth. ii, 12). Therefore fear is not a passion.

Obj. 3: Further, every passion of the soul is a movement of the sensitive appetite, in consequence of an apprehension of the senses. But sense apprehends, not the future but the present. Since, then, fear is of future evil, it seems that it is not a passion of the soul.

*On the contrary,* Augustine (De Civ. Dei xiv, 5, seqq.) reckons fear among the other passions of the soul.

*I answer that,* Among the other passions of the soul, after sorrow, fear chiefly has the character of passion. For as we have stated above (Q. 22), the notion of passion implies first of all a movement of a passive power—i.e. of a power whose object is compared to it as its active principle: since passion is the effect of an agent. In this way, both *to feel* and to understand are passions. Secondly, more properly speaking, passion is a movement of the appetitive power; and more properly still, it is a movement of an appetitive power that has a bodily organ, such movement being accompanied by a bodily transmutation. And, again, most properly those movements are called passions, which imply some deterioration. Now it is evident that fear, since it regards evil, belongs to the appetitive power, which of itself regards good and evil. Moreover, it belongs to the sensitive appetite: for it is accompanied by a certain transmutation—i.e. contraction—as Damascene says (Cf. Obj. 1). Again, it implies relation to evil as overcoming, so to speak, some particular good. Wherefore it has most properly the character of passion; less, however, than sorrow, which regards the present evil: because fear regards future evil, which is not so strong a motive as present evil.

Reply Obj. 1: Virtue denotes a principle of action: wherefore, in so far as the interior movements of the appetitive faculty are principles of external action, they are called virtues. But the Philosopher denies that passion is a virtue by way of habit.

Reply Obj. 2: Just as the passion of a natural body is due to the bodily presence of an agent, so is the passion of the soul due to the agent being present to the soul, although neither corporally nor really present: that is to say, in so far as the evil which is really future, is present in the apprehension of the soul.

Reply Obj. 3: The senses do not apprehend the future: but from apprehending the present, an animal is moved by natural instinct to hope for a future good, or to fear a future evil.

SECOND ARTICLE [I-II, Q. 41, Art. 2]

Whether Fear Is a Special Passion?

Objection 1: It would seem that fear is not a special passion. For Augustine says (QQ. 83, qu. 33) that "the man who is not distraught by fear, is neither harassed by desire, nor wounded by sickness"—i.e. sorrow—"nor tossed about in transports of empty joys." Wherefore it seems that, if fear be set aside, all the other passions are removed. Therefore fear is not a special but a general passion.

Obj. 2: Further, the Philosopher says (Ethic. vi, 2) that "pursuit and avoidance in the appetite are what affirmation and denial are in the intellect." But denial is nothing special in the intellect, as neither is affirmation, but something common to many. Therefore neither is avoidance anything special in the appetite. But fear is nothing but a kind of avoidance of evil. Therefore it is not a special passion.

Obj. 3: Further, if fear were a special passion, it would be chiefly in the irascible part. But fear is also in the concupiscible: since the Philosopher says (Rhet. ii, 5) that "fear is a kind of sorrow"; and Damascene says (De Fide Orth. iii, 23) that fear is "a power of desire": and both sorrow and desire are in the concupiscible faculty, as stated above (Q. 23, A. 4). Therefore fear is not a special passion, since it belongs to different powers.

*On the contrary,* Fear is condivided with the other passions of the soul, as is clear from Damascene (De Fide Orth. ii, 12, 15).

*I answer that,* The passions of the soul derive their species from their objects: hence that is a special passion, which has a special object. Now fear has a special object, as hope has. For just as the object of hope is a future good, difficult but possible to obtain; so the object of fear is a future evil, difficult and irresistible. Consequently fear is a special passion of the soul.

Reply Obj. 1: All the passions of the soul arise from one source, viz. love, wherein they are connected with one another. By reason of this connection, when fear is put aside, the other passions of the soul are dispersed; not, however, as though it were a general passion.

Reply Obj. 2: Not every avoidance in the appetite is fear, but avoidance of a special object, as stated. Wherefore, though avoidance be something common, yet fear is a special passion.

Reply Obj. 3: Fear is nowise in the concupiscible: for it regards evil, not absolutely, but as difficult or arduous, so as to be almost unavoidable. But since the irascible passions arise from the passions of the concupiscible faculty, and terminate therein, as stated above (Q. 25, A. 1); hence it is that what belongs to the concupiscible is ascribed to fear. For fear is called sorrow, in so far as the object of fear causes sorrow when present: wherefore the Philosopher says (Rhet. ii, 5) that fear arises "from the representation of a future evil which is either corruptive or painful." In like manner desire is ascribed by Damascene to fear, because just as hope arises from the desire of good, so fear arises from avoidance of evil; while avoidance of evil arises from the desire of good, as is evident from what has been said above (Q. 25, A. 2; Q. 29, A. 2; Q. 36, A. 2).

THIRD ARTICLE [I-II, Q. 41, Art. 3]

Whether There Is a Natural Fear?

Objection 1: It would seem that there is a natural fear. For Damascene says (De Fide Orth. iii, 23) that "there is a natural fear, through the soul refusing to be severed from the body."

Obj. 2: Further, fear arises from love, as stated above (A. 2, ad 1). But there is a natural love, as Dionysius says (Div. Nom. iv). Therefore there is also a natural fear.

Obj. 3: Further, fear is opposed to hope, as stated above (Q. 40, A. 4, ad 1). But there is a hope of nature, as is evident from Rom. 4:18, where it is said of Abraham that "against hope" of nature, "he believed in hope" of grace. Therefore there is also a fear of nature.

*On the contrary,* That which is natural is common to things animate and inanimate. But fear is not in things inanimate. Therefore there is no natural fear.

*I answer that,* A movement is said to be natural, because nature inclines thereto. Now this happens in two ways. First, so that it is entirely accomplished by nature, without any operation of the apprehensive faculty: thus to have an upward movement is natural to fire, and to grow is the natural movement of animals and plants. Secondly, a movement is said to be natural, if nature inclines thereto, though it be accomplished by the apprehensive faculty alone: since, as stated above (Q. 10, A. 1), the movements of the cognitive and appetitive faculties are reducible to nature as to their first principle. In this way, even the acts of the apprehensive power, such as understanding, feeling, and remembering, as well as the movements of the animal appetite, are sometimes said to be natural.

And in this sense we may say that there is a natural fear; and it is distinguished from non-natural fear, by reason of the diversity of its object. For, as the Philosopher says (Rhet. ii, 5), there is a fear of "corruptive evil," which nature shrinks from on account of its natural desire to exist; and such fear is said to be natural. Again, there is a fear of "painful evil," which is repugnant not to nature, but to the desire of the appetite; and such fear is not natural. In this sense we have stated above (Q. 26, A. 1; Q. 30, A. 3; Q. 31, A. 7) that love, desire, and pleasure are divisible into natural and non-natural.

But in the first sense of the word "natural," we must observe that certain passions of the soul are sometimes said to be natural, as love, desire, and hope; whereas the others cannot be called natural. The reason of this is because love and hatred, desire and avoidance, imply a certain inclination to pursue what is good or to avoid what is evil; which inclination is to be found in the natural appetite also. Consequently there is a natural love; while we may also speak of desire and hope as being even in natural things devoid of knowledge. On the other hand the other passions of the soul denote certain movements, whereto the natural inclination is nowise sufficient. This is due either to the fact that perception or knowledge is essential to these passions (thus we have said, Q. 31, AA. 1, 3; Q. 35, A. 1, that apprehension is a necessary condition of pleasure and sorrow), wherefore things devoid of knowledge cannot be said to take pleasure or to be sorrowful: or else it is because such like movements are contrary to the very nature of natural inclination: for instance, despair flies from good on account of some difficulty; and fear shrinks from repelling a contrary evil; both of which are contrary to the inclination of nature. Wherefore such like passions are in no way ascribed to inanimate beings.

Thus the Replies to the Objections are evident.

FOURTH ARTICLE [I-II, Q. 41, Art. 4]

Whether the Species of Fear Are Suitably Assigned?

Objection 1: It would seem that six species of fear are unsuitably assigned by Damascene (De Fide Orth. ii, 15); namely, "laziness, shamefacedness, shame, amazement, stupor, and anxiety." Because, as the Philosopher says (Rhet. ii, 5), "fear regards a saddening evil." Therefore the species of fear should correspond to the species of sorrow. Now there are four species of sorrow, as stated above (Q. 35, A. 8). Therefore there should only be four species of fear corresponding to them.

Obj. 2: Further, that which consists in an action of our own is in our power. But fear regards an evil that surpasses our power, as stated above (A. 2). Therefore laziness, shamefacedness, and shame, which regard our own actions, should not be reckoned as species of fear.

Obj. 3: Further, fear is of the future, as stated above (AA. 1, 2). But "shame regards a disgraceful deed already done," as Gregory of Nyssa [*Nemesius, De Nat. Hom. xx.] says. Therefore shame is not a species of fear.

Obj. 4: Further, fear is only of evil. But amazement and stupor regard great and unwonted things, whether good or evil. Therefore amazement and stupor are not species of fear.

Obj. 5: Further, Philosophers have been led by amazement to seek the truth, as stated in the beginning of *Metaph.* But fear leads to flight rather than to search. Therefore amazement is not a species of fear.

On the contrary suffices the authority of Damascene and Gregory of Nyssa [*Nemesius] (Cf. Obj. 1, 3).

*I answer that,* As stated above (A. 2), fear regards a future evil which surpasses the power of him that fears, so that it is irresistible. Now man's evil, like his good, may be considered either in his action or in external things. In his action he has a twofold evil to fear. First, there is the toil that burdens his nature: and hence arises *laziness,* as when a man shrinks from work for fear of too much toil. Secondly, there is the disgrace which damages him in the opinion of others. And thus, if disgrace is feared in a deed that is yet to be done, there is *shamefacedness* ; if, however, it be a deed already done, there is *shame.*

On the other hand, the evil that consists in external things may surpass man's faculty of resistance in three ways. First by reason of its magnitude; when, that is to say, a man considers some great evil the outcome of which he is unable to gauge: and then there is *amazement.* Secondly, by reason of its being unwonted; because, to wit, some unwonted evil arises before us, and on that account is great in our estimation: and then there is *stupor,* which is caused by the representation of something unwonted. Thirdly, by reason of its being unforeseen: thus future misfortunes are feared, and fear of this kind is called *anxiety.*

Reply Obj. 1: Those species of sorrow given above are not derived from the diversity of objects, but from the diversity of effects, and for certain special reasons. Consequently there is no need for those species of sorrow to correspond with these species of fear, which are derived from the proper division of the object of fear itself.

Reply Obj. 2: A deed considered as being actually done, is in the power of the doer. But it is possible to take into consideration something connected with the deed, and surpassing the faculty of the doer, for which reason he shrinks from the deed. It is in this sense that laziness, shamefacedness, and shame are reckoned as species of fear.

Reply Obj. 3: The past deed may be the occasion of fear of future reproach or disgrace: and in this sense shame is a species of fear.

Reply Obj. 4: Not every amazement and stupor are species of fear, but that amazement which is caused by a great evil, and that stupor which arises from an unwonted evil. Or else we may say that, just as laziness shrinks from the toil of external work, so amazement and stupor shrink from the difficulty of considering a great and unwonted thing, whether good or evil: so that amazement and stupor stand in relation to the act of the intellect, as laziness does to external work.

Reply Obj. 5: He who is amazed shrinks at present from forming a judgment of that which amazes him, fearing to fall short of the truth, but inquires afterwards: whereas he who is overcome by stupor fears both to judge at present, and to inquire afterwards. Wherefore amazement is a beginning of philosophical research: whereas stupor is a hindrance thereto.

## QUESTION 42

OF THE OBJECT OF FEAR (In Six Articles)

We must now consider the object of fear: under which head there are six points of inquiry:

(1) Whether good or evil is the object of fear?

(2) Whether evil of nature is the object of fear?

(3) Whether the evil of sin is an object of fear?

(4) Whether fear itself can be feared?

(5) Whether sudden things are especially feared?

(6) Whether those things are more feared against which there is no remedy?

FIRST ARTICLE [I-II, Q. 42, Art. 1]

Whether the Object of Fear Is Good or Evil?

Objection 1: It would seem that good is the object of fear. For Augustine says (QQ. 83, qu. 83) that "we fear nothing save to lose what we love and possess, or not to obtain that which we hope for." But that which we love is good. Therefore fear regards good as its proper object.

Obj. 2: Further, the Philosopher says (Rhet. ii, 5) that "power and to be above another is a thing to be feared." But this is a good thing. Therefore good is the object of fear.

Obj. 3: Further, there can be no evil in God. But we are commanded to fear God, according to Ps. 33:10: "Fear the Lord, all ye saints." Therefore even the good is an object of fear.

*On the contrary,* Damascene says (De Fide Orth. ii, 12) that fear is of future evil.

*I answer that,* Fear is a movement of the appetitive power. Now it belongs to the appetitive power to pursue and to avoid, as stated in *Ethic.* vi, 2: and pursuit is of good, while avoidance is of evil. Consequently whatever movement of the appetitive power implies pursuit, has some good for its object: and whatever movement implies avoidance, has an evil for its object. Wherefore, since fear implies an avoidance, in the first place and of its very nature it regards evil as its proper object.

It can, however, regard good also, in so far as referable to evil. This can be in two ways. In one way, inasmuch as an evil causes privation of good. Now a thing is evil from the very fact that it is a privation of some good. Wherefore, since evil is shunned because it is evil, it follows that it is shunned because it deprives one of the good that one pursues through love thereof. And in this sense Augustine says that there is no cause for fear, save loss of the good we love.

In another way, good stands related to evil as its cause: in so far as some good can by its power bring harm to the good we love: and so, just as hope, as stated above (Q. 40, A. 7), regards two things, namely, the good to which it tends, and the thing through which there is a hope of obtaining the desired good; so also does fear regard two things, namely, the evil from which it shrinks, and that good which, by its power, can inflict that evil. In this way God is feared by man, inasmuch as He can inflict punishment, spiritual or corporal. In this way, too, we fear the power of man; especially when it has been thwarted, or when it is unjust, because then it is more likely to do us a harm.

In like manner one fears *to be over another,* i.e. to lean on another, so that it is in his power to do us a harm: thus a man fears another, who knows him to be guilty of a crime, lest he reveal it to others.

This suffices for the Replies to the Objections.

SECOND ARTICLE [I-II, Q. 42, Art. 2]

Whether Evil of Nature Is an Object of Fear?

Objection 1: It would seem that evil of nature is not an object of fear. For the Philosopher says (Rhet. ii, 5) that "fear makes us take counsel." But we do not take counsel about things which happen naturally, as stated in *Ethic.* iii, 3. Therefore evil of nature is not an object of fear.

Obj. 2: Further, natural defects such as death and the like are always threatening man. If therefore such like evils were an object of fear, man would needs be always in fear.

Obj. 3: Further, nature does not move to contraries. But evil of nature is an effect of nature. Therefore if a man shrinks from such like evils through fear thereof, this is not an effect of nature. Therefore natural fear is not of the evil of nature; and yet it seems that it should be.

*On the contrary,* The Philosopher says (Ethic. iii, 6) that "the most terrible of all things is death," which is an evil of nature.

*I answer that,* As the Philosopher says (Rhet. ii, 5), fear is caused by the "imagination of a future evil which is either corruptive or painful." Now just as a painful evil is that which is contrary to the will, so a corruptive evil is that which is contrary to nature: and this is the evil of nature. Consequently evil of nature can be the object of fear.

But it must be observed that evil of nature sometimes arises from a natural cause; and then it is called evil of nature, not merely from being a privation of the good of nature, but also from being an effect of nature; such are natural death and other like defects. But sometimes evil of nature arises from a non-natural cause; such as violent death inflicted by an assailant. In either case evil of nature is feared to a certain extent, and to a certain extent not. For since fear arises "from the imagination of future evil," as the Philosopher says (Rhet. ii, 5), whatever removes the imagination of the future evil, removes fear also. Now it may happen in two ways that an evil may not appear as about to be. First, through being remote and far off: for, on account of the distance, such a thing is considered as though it were not to be. Hence we either do not fear it, or fear it but little; for, as the Philosopher says (Rhet. ii, 5), "we do not fear things that are very far off; since all know that they shall die, but as death is not near, they heed it not." Secondly, a future evil is considered as though it were not to be, on account of its being inevitable, wherefore we look upon it as already present. Hence the Philosopher says (Rhet. ii, 5) that "those who are already on the scaffold, are not afraid," seeing that they are on the very point of a death from which there is no escape; "but in order that a man be afraid, there must be some hope of escape for him."

Consequently evil of nature is not feared if it be not apprehended as future: but if evil of nature, that is corruptive, be apprehended as near at hand, and yet with some hope of escape, then it will be feared.

Reply Obj. 1: The evil of nature sometimes is not an effect of nature, as stated above. But in so far as it is an effect of nature, although it may be impossible to avoid it entirely, yet it may be possible to delay it. And with this hope one may take counsel about avoiding it.

Reply Obj. 2: Although evil of nature ever threatens, yet it does not always threaten from near at hand: and consequently it is not always feared.

Reply Obj. 3: Death and other defects of nature are the effects of the common nature; and yet the individual nature rebels against them as far as it can. Accordingly, from the inclination of the individual nature arise pain and sorrow for such like evils, when present; fear when threatening in the future.

THIRD ARTICLE [I-II, Q. 42, Art. 3]

Whether the Evil of Sin Is an Object of Fear?

Objection 1: It would seem that the evil of sin can be an object of fear. For Augustine says on the canonical Epistle of John (Tract. ix), that "by chaste fear man fears to be severed from God." Now nothing but sin severs us from God; according to Isa. 59:2: "Your iniquities have divided between you and your God." Therefore the evil of sin can be an object of fear.

Obj. 2: Further, Cicero says (Quaest. Tusc. iv, 4, 6) that "we fear when they are yet to come, those things which give us pain when they are present." But it is possible for one to be pained or sorrowful on account of the evil of sin. Therefore one can also fear the evil of sin.

Obj. 3: Further, hope is contrary to fear. But the good of virtue can be the object of hope, as the Philosopher declares (Ethic. ix, 4): and the Apostle says (Gal. 5:10): "I have confidence in you in the Lord, that you will not be of another mind." Therefore fear can regard evil of sin.

Obj. 4: Further, shame is a kind of fear, as stated above (Q. 41, A. 4). But shame regards a disgraceful deed, which is an evil of sin. Therefore fear does so likewise.

*On the contrary,* The Philosopher says (Rhet. ii, 5) that "not all evils are feared, for instance that someone be unjust or slow."

*I answer that,* As stated above (Q. 40, A. 1; Q. 41, A. 2), as the object of hope is a future good difficult but possible to obtain, so the object of fear is a future evil, arduous and not to be easily avoided. From this we may gather that whatever is entirely subject to our power and will, is not an object of fear; and that nothing gives rise to fear save what is due to an external cause. Now human will is the proper cause of the evil of sin: and consequently evil of sin, properly speaking, is not an object of fear.

But since the human will may be inclined to sin by an extrinsic cause; if this cause have a strong power of inclination, in that respect a man may fear the evil of sin, in so far as it arises from that extrinsic cause: as when he fears to dwell in the company of wicked men, lest he be led by them to sin. But, properly speaking, a man thus disposed, fears the being led astray rather than the sin considered in its proper nature, i.e. as a voluntary act; for considered in this light it is not an object of fear to him.

Reply Obj. 1: Separation from God is a punishment resulting from sin: and every punishment is, in some way, due to an extrinsic cause.

Reply Obj. 2: Sorrow and fear agree in one point, since each regards evil: they differ, however, in two points. First, because sorrow is about present evil, whereas fear is future evil. Secondly, because sorrow, being in the concupiscible faculty, regards evil absolutely; wherefore it can be about any evil, great or small; whereas fear, being in the irascible part, regards evil with the addition of a certain arduousness or difficulty; which difficulty ceases in so far as a thing is subject to the will. Consequently not all things that give us pain when they are present, make us fear when they are yet to come, but only some things, namely, those that are difficult.

Reply Obj. 3: Hope is of good that is obtainable. Now one may obtain a good either of oneself, or through another: and so, hope may be of an act of virtue, which lies within our own power. On the other hand, fear is of an evil that does not lie in our own power: and consequently the evil which is feared is always from an extrinsic cause; while the good that is hoped for may be both from an intrinsic and from an extrinsic cause.

Reply Obj. 4: As stated above (Q. 41, A. 4, ad 2, 3), shame is not fear of the very act of sin, but of the disgrace or ignominy which arises therefrom, and which is due to an extrinsic cause.

FOURTH ARTICLE [I-II, Q. 42, Art. 4]

Whether Fear Itself Can Be Feared?

Objection 1: It would seem that fear cannot be feared. For whatever is feared, is prevented from being lost, through fear thereof: thus a man who fears to lose his health, keeps it, through fearing its loss. If therefore a man be afraid of fear, he will keep himself from fear by being afraid: which seems absurd.

Obj. 2: Further, fear is a kind of flight. But nothing flies from itself. Therefore fear cannot be the object of fear.

Obj. 3: Further, fear is about the future. But fear is present to him that fears. Therefore it cannot be the object of his fear.

*On the contrary,* A man can love his own love, and can grieve at his own sorrow. Therefore, in like manner, he can fear his own fear.

*I answer that,* As stated above (A. 3), nothing can be an object of fear, save what is due to an extrinsic cause; but not that which ensues from our own will. Now fear partly arises from an extrinsic cause, and is partly subject to the will. It is due to an extrinsic cause, in so far as it is a passion resulting from the imagination of an imminent evil. In this sense it is possible for fear to be the object of fear, i.e. a man may fear lest he should be threatened by the necessity of fearing, through being assailed by some great evil. It is subject to the will, in so far as the lower appetite obeys reason; wherefore man is able to drive fear away. In this sense fear cannot be the object of fear, as Augustine says (QQ. 83, qu. 33). Lest, however, anyone make use of his arguments, in order to prove that fear cannot be at all be the object of fear, we must add a solution to the same.

Reply Obj. 1: Not every fear is identically the same; there are various fears according to the various objects of fear. Nothing, then, prevents a man from keeping himself from fearing one thing, by fearing another, so that the fear which he has preserves him from the fear which he has not.

Reply Obj. 2: Since fear of an imminent evil is not identical with the fear of the fear of imminent evil; it does not follow that a thing flies from itself, or that it is the same flight in both cases.

Reply Obj. 3: On account of the various kinds of fear already alluded to (ad 2) a man's present fear may have a future fear for its object.

FIFTH ARTICLE [I-II, Q. 42, Art. 5]

Whether Sudden Things Are Especially Feared?

Objection 1: It would seem that unwonted and sudden things are not especially feared. Because, as hope is about good things, so fear is about evil things. But experience conduces to the increase of hope in good things. Therefore it also adds to fear in evil things.

Obj. 2: Further, the Philosopher says (Rhet. ii, 5) that "those are feared most, not who are quick-tempered, but who are gentle and cunning." Now it is clear that those who are quick-tempered are more subject to sudden emotions. Therefore sudden things are less to be feared.

Obj. 3: Further, we think less about things that happen suddenly. But the more we think about a thing, the more we fear it; hence the Philosopher says (Ethic. iii, 8) that "some appear to be courageous through ignorance, but as soon as they discover that the case is different from what they expected, they run away." Therefore sudden things are feared less.

*On the contrary,* Augustine says (Confess. ii, 6): "Fear is startled at things unwonted and sudden, which endanger things beloved, and takes forethought for their safety."

*I answer that,* As stated above (A. 3; Q. 41, A. 2), the object of fear is an imminent evil, which can be repelled, but with difficulty. Now this is due to one of two causes: to the greatness of the evil, or to the weakness of him that fears; while unwontedness and suddenness conduce to both of these causes. First, it helps an imminent evil to seem greater. Because all material things, whether good or evil, the more we consider them, the smaller they seem. Consequently, just as sorrow for a present evil is mitigated in course of time, as Cicero states (De Quaest. Tusc. iii, 30); so, too, fear of a future evil is diminished by thinking about it beforehand. Secondly, unwontedness and suddenness increase the weakness of him that fears, in so far as they deprive him of the remedies with which he might otherwise provide himself to forestall the coming evil, were it not for the evil taking him by surprise.

Reply Obj. 1: The object of hope is a good that is possible to obtain. Consequently whatever increases a man's power, is of a nature to increase hope, and, for the same reason, to diminish fear, since fear is about an evil which cannot be easily repelled. Since, therefore, experience increases a man's power of action, therefore, as it increases hope, so does it diminish fear.

Reply Obj. 2: Those who are quick-tempered do not hide their anger; wherefore the harm they do others is not so sudden, as not to be foreseen. On the other hand, those who are gentle or cunning hide their anger; wherefore the harm which may be impending from them, cannot be foreseen, but takes one by surprise. For this reason the Philosopher says that such men are feared more than others.

Reply Obj. 3: Bodily good or evil, considered in itself, seems greater at first. The reason for this is that a thing is more obvious when seen in juxtaposition with its contrary. Hence, when a man passes unexpectedly from penury to wealth, he thinks more of his wealth on account of his previous poverty: while, on the other hand, the rich man who suddenly becomes poor, finds poverty all the more disagreeable. For this reason sudden evil is feared more, because it seems more to be evil. However, it may happen through some accident that the greatness of some evil is hidden; for instance if the foe hides himself in ambush: and then it is true that evil inspires greater fear through being much thought about.

SIXTH ARTICLE [I-II, Q. 42, Art. 6]

Whether Those Things Are More Feared, for Which There Is No Remedy?

Objection 1: It would seem that those things are not more to be feared, for which there is no remedy. Because it is a condition of fear, that there be some hope of safety, as stated above (A. 2). But an evil that cannot be remedied leaves no hope of escape. Therefore such things are not feared at all.

Obj. 2: Further, there is no remedy for the evil of death: since, in the natural course of things, there is no return from death to life. And yet death is not the most feared of all things, as the Philosopher says (Rhet. ii, 5). Therefore those things are not feared most, for which there is no remedy.

Obj. 3: Further, the Philosopher says (Ethic. i, 6) that "a thing which lasts long is no better than that which lasts but one day: nor is that which lasts for ever any better than that which is not everlasting": and the same applies to evil. But things that cannot be remedied seem to differ from other things, merely in the point of their lasting long or for ever. Consequently they are not therefore any worse or more to be feared.

*On the contrary,* the Philosopher says (Rhet. ii, 5) that "those things are most to be feared which when done wrong cannot be put right … or for which there is no help, or which are not easy."

*I answer that,* The object of fear is evil: consequently whatever tends to increase evil, conduces to the increase of fear. Now evil is increased not only in its species of evil, but also in respect of circumstances, as stated above (Q. 18, A. 3). And of all the circumstances, longlastingness, or even everlastingness, seems to have the greatest bearing on the increase of evil. Because things that exist in time are measured, in a way, according to the duration of time: wherefore if it be an evil to suffer something for a certain length of time, we should reckon the evil doubled, if it be suffered for twice that length of time. And accordingly, to suffer the same thing for an infinite length of time, i.e. for ever, implies, so to speak, an infinite increase. Now those evils which, after they have come, cannot be remedied at all, or at least not easily, are considered as lasting for ever or for a long time: for which reason they inspire the greatest fear.

Reply Obj. 1: Remedy for an evil is twofold. One, by which a future evil is warded off from coming. If such a remedy be removed, there is an end to hope and consequently to fear; wherefore we do not speak now of remedies of that kind. The other remedy is one by which an already present evil is removed: and of such a remedy we speak now.

Reply Obj. 2: Although death be an evil without remedy, yet, since it threatens not from near, it is not feared, as stated above (A. 2).

Reply Obj. 3: The Philosopher is speaking there of things that are good in themselves, i.e., good specifically. And such like good is no better for lasting long or for ever: its goodness depends on its very nature.

## QUESTION 43

OF THE CAUSE OF FEAR (In Two Articles)

We must now consider the cause of fear: under which head there are two points of inquiry:

(1) Whether love is the cause of fear?

(2) Whether defect is the cause of fear?

FIRST ARTICLE [I-II, Q. 43, Art. 1]

Whether Love Is the Cause of Fear?

Objection 1: It would seem that love is not the cause of fear. For that which leads to a thing is its cause. But "fear leads to the love of charity" as Augustine says on the canonical epistle of John (Tract. ix). Therefore fear is the cause of love, and not conversely.

Obj. 2: Further, the Philosopher says (Rhet. ii, 5) that "those are feared most from whom we dread the advent of some evil." But the dread of evil being caused by someone, makes us hate rather than love him. Therefore fear is caused by hate rather than by love.

Obj. 3: Further, it has been stated above (Q. 42, A. 3) that those things which occur by our own doing are not fearful. But that which we do from love, is done from our inmost heart. Therefore fear is not caused by love.

*On the contrary,* Augustine says (QQ. 83, qu. 33): "There can be no doubt that there is no cause for fear save the loss of what we love, when we possess it, or the failure to obtain what we hope for." Therefore all fear is caused by our loving something: and consequently love is the cause of fear.

*I answer that,* The objects of the soul's passions stand in relation thereto as the forms to things natural or artificial: because the passions of the soul take their species from their objects, as the aforesaid things do from their forms. Therefore, just as whatever is a cause of the form, is a cause of the thing constituted by that form, so whatever is a cause, in any way whatever, of the object, is a cause of the passion. Now a thing may be a cause of the object, either by way of efficient cause, or by way of material disposition. Thus the object of pleasure is good apprehended as suitable and conjoined: and its efficient cause is that which causes the conjunction, or the suitableness, or goodness, or apprehension of that good thing; while its cause by way of material disposition, is a habit or any sort of disposition by reason of which this conjoined good becomes suitable or is apprehended as such.

Accordingly, as to the matter in question, the object of fear is something reckoned as an evil to come, near at hand and difficult to avoid. Therefore that which can inflict such an evil, is the efficient cause of the object of fear, and, consequently, of fear itself. While that which renders a man so disposed that thing is such an evil to him, is a cause of fear and of its object, by way of material disposition. And thus it is that love causes fear: since it is through his loving a certain good, that whatever deprives a man of that good is an evil to him, and that consequently he fears it as an evil.

Reply Obj. 1: As stated above (Q. 42, A. 1), fear, of itself and in the first place, regards the evil from which it recoils as being contrary to some loved good: and thus fear, of itself, is born of love. But, in the second place, it regards the cause from which that evil ensues: so that sometimes, accidentally, fear gives rise to love; in so far as, for instance, through fear of God's punishments, man keeps His commandments, and thus begins to hope, while hope leads to love, as stated above (Q. 40, A. 7).

Reply Obj. 2: He, from whom evil is expected, is indeed hated at first; but afterwards, when once we begin to hope for good from him, we begin to love him. But the good, the contrary evil of which is feared, was loved from the beginning.

Reply Obj. 3: This argument is true of that which is the efficient cause of the evil to be feared: whereas love causes fear by way of material disposition, as stated above.

SECOND ARTICLE [I-II, Q. 43, Art. 2]

Whether Defect Is the Cause of Fear?

Objection 1: It would seem that defect is not a cause of fear. Because those who are in power are very much feared. But defect is contrary to power. Therefore defect is not a cause of fear.

Obj. 2: Further, the defect of those who are already being executed is extreme. But such like do not fear as stated in *Rhet.* ii, 5. Therefore defect is not a cause of fear.

Obj. 3: Further, contests arise from strength not from defect. But "those who contend fear those who contend with them" (Rhet. ii, 5). Therefore defect is not a cause of fear.

*On the contrary,* Contraries ensue from contrary causes. But "wealth, strength, a multitude of friends, and power drive fear away" (Rhet. ii, 5). Therefore fear is caused by lack of these.

*I answer that,* As stated above (A. 1), fear may be set down to a twofold cause: one is by way of a material disposition, on the part of him that fears; the other is by way of efficient cause, on the part of the person feared. As to the first then, some defect is, of itself, the cause of fear: for it is owing to some lack of power that one is unable easily to repulse a threatening evil. And yet, in order to cause fear, this defect must be according to a measure. For the defect which causes fear of a future evil, is less than the defect caused by evil present, which is the object of sorrow. And still greater would be the defect, if perception of the evil, or love of the good whose contrary is feared, were entirely absent.

But as to the second, power and strength are, of themselves, the cause of fear: because it is owing to the fact that the cause apprehended as harmful is powerful, that its effect cannot be repulsed. It may happen, however, in this respect, that some defect causes fear accidentally, in so far as owing to some defect someone wishes to hurt another; for instance, by reason of injustice, either because that other has already done him a harm, or because he fears to be harmed by him.

Reply Obj. 1: This argument is true of the cause of fear, on the part of the efficient cause.

Reply Obj. 2: Those who are already being executed, are actually suffering from a present evil; wherefore their defect exceeds the measure of fear.

Reply Obj. 3: Those who contend with one another are afraid, not on account of the power which enables them to contend: but on account of the lack of power, owing to which they are not confident of victory.

## QUESTION 44

OF THE EFFECTS OF FEAR (In Four Articles)

We must now consider the effects of fear: under which head there are four points of inquiry:

(1) Whether fear causes contraction?

(2) Whether it makes men suitable for counsel?

(3) Whether it makes one tremble?

(4) Whether it hinders action?

FIRST ARTICLE [I-II, Q. 44, Art. 1]

Whether Fear Causes Contraction?

Objection 1: It would seem that fear does not cause contraction. For when contraction takes place, the heat and vital spirits are withdrawn inwardly. But accumulation of heat and vital spirits in the interior parts of the body, dilates the heart unto endeavors of daring, as may be seen in those who are angered: while the contrary happens in those who are afraid. Therefore fear does not cause contraction.

Obj. 2: Further, when, as a result of contraction, the vital spirits and heat are accumulated in the interior parts, man cries out, as may be seen in those who are in pain. But those who fear utter nothing: on the contrary they lose their speech. Therefore fear does not cause contraction.

Obj. 3: Further, shame is a kind of fear, as stated above (Q. 41, A. 4). But "those who are ashamed blush," as Cicero (De Quaest. Tusc. iv, 8), and the Philosopher (Ethic. iv, 9) observe. But blushing is an indication, not of contraction, but of the reverse. Therefore contraction is not an effect of fear.

*On the contrary,* Damascene says (De Fide Orth. ii, 23) that "fear is a power according to systole ," i.e. contraction.

*I answer that,* As stated above (Q. 28, A. 5), in the passions of the soul, the formal element is the movement of the appetitive power, while the bodily transmutation is the material element. Both of these are mutually proportionate; and consequently the bodily transmutation assumes a resemblance to and the very nature of the appetitive movement. Now, as to the appetitive movement of the soul, fear implies a certain contraction: the reason of which is that fear arises from the imagination of some threatening evil which is difficult to repel, as stated above (Q. 41, A. 2). But that a thing be difficult to repel is due to lack of power, as stated above (Q. 43, A. 2): and the weaker a power is, the fewer the things to which it extends. Wherefore from the very imagination that causes fear there ensues a certain contraction in the appetite. Thus we observe in one who is dying that nature withdraws inwardly, on account of the lack of power: and again we see the inhabitants of a city, when seized with fear, leave the outskirts, and, as far as possible, make for the inner quarters. It is in resemblance to this contraction, which pertains to the appetite of the soul, that in fear a similar contraction of heat and vital spirits towards the inner parts takes place in regard to the body.

Reply Obj. 1: As the Philosopher says (De Problem. xxvii, 3), although in those who fear, the vital spirits recede from outer to the inner parts of the body, yet the movement of vital spirits is not the same in those who are angry and those who are afraid. For in those who are angry, by reason of the heat and subtlety of the vital spirits, which result from the craving for vengeance, the inward movement has an upward direction: wherefore the vital spirits and heat concentrate around the heart: the result being that an angry man is quick and brave in attacking. But in those who are afraid, on account of the condensation caused by cold, the vital spirits have a downward movement; the said cold being due to the imagined lack of power. Consequently the heat and vital spirits abandon the heart instead of concentrating around it: the result being that a man who is afraid is not quick to attack, but is more inclined to run away.

Reply Obj. 2: To everyone that is in pain, whether man or animal, it is natural to use all possible means of repelling the harmful thing that causes pain but its presence: thus we observe that animals, when in pain, attack with their jaws or with their horns. Now the greatest help for all purposes, in animals, is heat and vital spirits: wherefore when they are in pain, their nature stores up the heat and vital spirits within them, in order to make use thereof in repelling the harmful object. Hence the Philosopher says (De Problem. xxvii, 9) when the vital spirits and heat are concentrated together within, they require to find a vent in the voice: for which reason those who are in pain can scarcely refrain from crying aloud. On the other hand, in those who are afraid, the internal heat and vital spirits move from the heart downwards, as stated above (ad 1): wherefore fear hinders speech which ensues from the emission of the vital spirits in an upward direction through the mouth: the result being that fear makes its subject speechless. For this reason, too, fear "makes its subject tremble," as the Philosopher says (De Problem. xxvii, 1, 6, 7).

Reply Obj. 3: Mortal perils are contrary not only to the appetite of the soul, but also to nature. Consequently in such like fear, there is contraction not only in the appetite, but also in the corporeal nature: for when an animal is moved by the imagination of death, it experiences a contraction of heat towards the inner parts of the body, as though it were threatened by a natural death. Hence it is that "those who are in fear of death turn pale" (Ethic. iv, 9). But the evil that shame fears, is contrary, not to nature, but only to the appetite of the soul. Consequently there results a contraction in this appetite, but not in the corporeal nature; in fact, the soul, as though contracted in itself, is free to set the vital spirits and heat in movement, so that they spread to the outward parts of the body: the result being that those who are ashamed blush.

SECOND ARTICLE [I-II, Q. 44, Art. 2]

Whether Fear Makes One Suitable for Counsel?

Objection 1: It would seem that fear does not make one suitable for counsel. For the same thing cannot be conducive to counsel, and a hindrance thereto. But fear hinders counsel: because every passion disturbs repose, which is requisite for the good use of reason. Therefore fear does not make a man suitable for counsel.

Obj. 2: Further, counsel is an act of reason, in thinking and deliberating about the future. But a certain fear "drives away all thought, and dislocates the mind," as Cicero observes (De Quaest. Tusc. iv, 8). Therefore fear does not conduce to counsel, but hinders it.

Obj. 3: Further, just as we have recourse to counsel in order to avoid evil, so do we, in order to attain good things. But whereas fear is of evil to be avoided, so is hope of good things to be obtained. Therefore fear is not more conducive to counsel, than hope is.

*On the contrary,* The Philosopher says (Rhet. ii, 5) that "fear makes men of counsel."

*I answer that,* A man of counsel may be taken in two ways. First, from his being willing or anxious to take counsel. And thus fear makes men of counsel. Because, as the Philosopher says (Ethic. iii, 3), "we take counsel on great matters, because therein we distrust ourselves." Now things which make us afraid, are not simply evil, but have a certain magnitude, both because they seem difficult to repel, and because they are apprehended as near to us, as stated above (Q. 42, A. 2). Wherefore men seek for counsel especially when they are afraid.

Secondly, a man of counsel means one who is apt for giving good counsel: and in this sense, neither fear nor any passion makes men of counsel. Because when a man is affected by a passion, things seem to him greater or smaller than they really are: thus to a lover, what he loves seems better; to him that fears, what he fears seems more dreadful. Consequently owing to the want of right judgment, every passion, considered in itself, hinders the faculty of giving good counsel.

This suffices for the Reply to the First Objection.

Reply Obj. 2: The stronger a passion is, the greater the hindrance is it to the man who is swayed by it. Consequently, when fear is intense, man does indeed wish to take counsel, but his thoughts are so disturbed, that he can find no counsel. If, however, the fear be slight, so as to make a man wish to take counsel, without gravely disturbing the reason; it may even make it easier for him to take good counsel, by reason of his ensuing carefulness.

Reply Obj. 3: Hope also makes man a good counsellor: because, as the Philosopher says (Rhet. ii, 5), "no man takes counsel in matters he despairs of," nor about impossible things, as he says in *Ethic.* iii, 3. But fear incites to counsel more than hope does. Because hope is of good things, as being possible of attainment; whereas fear is of evil things, as being difficult to repel, so that fear regards the aspect of difficulty more than hope does. And it is in matters of difficulty, especially when we distrust ourselves, that we take counsel, as stated above.

THIRD ARTICLE [I-II, Q. 44, Art. 3]

Whether Fear Makes One Tremble?

Objection 1: It would seem that trembling is not an effect of fear. Because trembling is occasioned by cold; thus we observe that a cold person trembles. Now fear does not seem to make one cold, but rather to cause a parching heat: a sign whereof is that those who fear are thirsty, especially if their fear be very great, as in the case of those who are being led to execution. Therefore fear does not cause trembling.

Obj. 2: Further, faecal evacuation is occasioned by heat; hence laxative medicines are generally warm. But these evacuations are often caused by fear. Therefore fear apparently causes heat; and consequently does not cause trembling.

Obj. 3: Further, in fear, the heat is withdrawn from the outer to the inner parts of the body. If, therefore, man trembles in his outward parts, through the heat being withdrawn thus; it seems that fear should cause this trembling in all the external members. But such is not the case. Therefore trembling of the body is not caused by fear.

*On the contrary,* Cicero says (De Quaest. Tusc. iv, 8) that "fear is followed by trembling, pallor and chattering of the teeth."

*I answer that,* As stated above (A. 1), in fear there takes place a certain contraction from the outward to the inner parts of the body, the result being that the outer parts become cold; and for this reason trembling is occasioned in these parts, being caused by a lack of power in controlling the members: which lack of power is due to the want of heat, which is the instrument whereby the soul moves those members, as stated in *De Anima* ii, 4.

Reply Obj. 1: When the heat withdraws from the outer to the inner parts, the inward heat increases, especially in the inferior or nutritive parts. Consequently the humid element being spent, thirst ensues; sometimes indeed the result is a loosening of the bowels, and urinary or even seminal evacuation. Or else such like evacuations are due to contraction of the abdomen and testicles, as the Philosopher says (De Problem. xxii, 11).

This suffices for the Reply to the Second Objection.

Reply Obj. 3: In fear, heat abandons the heart, with a downward movement: hence in those who are afraid the heart especially trembles, as also those members which are connected with the breast where the heart resides. Hence those who fear tremble especially in their speech, on account of the tracheal artery being near the heart. The lower lip, too, and the lower jaw tremble, through their connection with the heart; which explains the chattering of the teeth. For the same reason the arms and hands tremble. Or else because the aforesaid members are more mobile. For which reason the knees tremble in those who are afraid, according to Isa. 35:3: "Strengthen ye the feeble hands, and confirm the trembling [Vulg.: 'weak'] knees."

FOURTH ARTICLE [I-II, Q. 44, Art. 4]

Whether Fear Hinders Action?

Objection 1: It would seem that fear hinders action. For action is hindered chiefly by a disturbance in the reason, which directs action. But fear disturbs reason, as stated above (A. 2). Therefore fear hinders action.

Obj. 2: Further, those who fear while doing anything, are more apt to fail: thus a man who walks on a plank placed aloft, easily falls through fear; whereas, if he were to walk on the same plank down below, he would not fall, through not being afraid. Therefore fear hinders action.

Obj. 3: Further, laziness or sloth is a kind of fear. But laziness hinders action. Therefore fear does too.

*On the contrary,* The Apostle says (Phil. 2:12): "With fear and trembling work out your salvation": and he would not say this if fear were a hindrance to a good work. Therefore fear does not hinder a good action.

*I answer that,* Man's exterior actions are caused by the soul as first mover, but by the bodily members as instruments. Now action may be hindered both by defect of the instrument, and by defect of the principal mover. On the part of the bodily instruments, fear, considered in itself, is always apt to hinder exterior action, on account of the outward members being deprived, through fear, of their heat. But on the part of the soul, if the fear be moderate, without much disturbance of the reason, it conduces to working well, in so far as it causes a certain solicitude, and makes a man take counsel and work with greater attention. If, however, fear increases so much as to disturb the reason, it hinders action even on the part of the soul. But of such a fear the Apostle does not speak.

This suffices for the Reply to the First Objection.

Reply Obj. 2: He that falls from a plank placed aloft, suffers a disturbance of his imagination, through fear of the fall that is pictured to his imagination.

Reply Obj. 3: Everyone in fear shuns that which he fears: and therefore, since laziness is a fear of work itself as being toilsome, it hinders work by withdrawing the will from it. But fear of other things conduces to action, in so far as it inclines the will to do that whereby a man escapes from what he fears.

## QUESTION 45

OF DARING (In Four Articles)

We must now consider daring: under which head there are four points of inquiry:

(1) Whether daring is contrary to fear?

(2) How is daring related to hope?

(3) Of the cause of daring;

(4) Of its effect.

FIRST ARTICLE [I-II, Q. 45, Art. 1]

Whether Daring Is Contrary to Fear?

Objection 1: It would seem that daring is not contrary to fear. For Augustine says (QQ. 83, qu. 31) that "daring is a vice." Now vice is contrary to virtue. Since, therefore, fear is not a virtue but a passion, it seems that daring is not contrary to fear.

Obj. 2: Further, to one thing there is one contrary. But hope is contrary to fear. Therefore daring is not contrary to fear.

Obj. 3: Further, every passion excludes its opposite. But fear excludes safety; for Augustine says (Confess. ii, 6) that "fear takes forethought for safety." Therefore safety is contrary to fear. Therefore daring is not contrary to fear.

*On the contrary,* The Philosopher says (Rhet. ii, 5) that "daring is contrary to fear."

*I answer that,* It is of the essence of contraries to be "farthest removed from one another," as stated in *Metaph.* x, 4. Now that which is farthest removed from fear, is daring: since fear turns away from the future hurt, on account of its victory over him that fears it; whereas daring turns on threatened danger because of its own victory over that same danger. Consequently it is evident that daring is contrary to fear.

Reply Obj. 1: Anger, daring and all the names of the passions can be taken in two ways. First, as denoting absolutely movements of the sensitive appetite in respect of some object, good or bad: and thus they are names of passions. Secondly, as denoting besides this movement, a straying from the order of reason: and thus they are names of vices. It is in this sense that Augustine speaks of daring: but we are speaking of it in the first sense.

Reply Obj. 2: To one thing, in the same respect, there are not several contraries; but in different respects nothing prevents one thing having several contraries. Accordingly it has been said above (Q. 23, A. 2; Q. 40, A. 4) that the irascible passions admit of a twofold contrariety: one, according to the opposition of good and evil, and thus fear is contrary to hope: the other, according to the opposition of approach and withdrawal, and thus daring is contrary to fear, and despair contrary to hope.

Reply Obj. 3: Safety does not denote something contrary to fear, but merely the exclusion of fear: for he is said to be safe, who fears not. Wherefore safety is opposed to fear, as a privation: while daring is opposed thereto as a contrary. And as contrariety implies privation, so daring implies safety.

SECOND ARTICLE [I-II, Q. 45, Art. 2]

Whether Daring Ensues from Hope?

Objection 1: It would seem that daring does not ensue from hope. Because daring regards evil and fearful things, as stated in *Ethic.* iii, 7. But hope regards good things, as stated above (Q. 40, A. 1). Therefore they have different objects and are not in the same order. Therefore daring does not ensue from hope.

Obj. 2: Further, just as daring is contrary to fear, so is despair contrary to hope. But fear does not ensue from despair: in fact, despair excludes fear, as the Philosopher says (Rhet. ii, 5). Therefore daring does not result from hope.

Obj. 3: Further, daring is intent on something good, viz. victory. But it belongs to hope to tend to that which is good and difficult. Therefore daring is the same as hope; and consequently does not result from it.

*On the contrary,* The Philosopher says (Ethic. iii, 8) that "those are hopeful are full of daring." Therefore it seems that daring ensues from hope.

*I answer that,* As we have often stated (Q. 22, A. 2; Q. 35, A. 1; Q. 41, A. 1), all these passions belong to the appetitive power. Now every movement of the appetitive power is reducible to one either of pursuit or of avoidance. Again, pursuit or avoidance is of something either by reason of itself or by reason of something else. By reason of itself, good is the object of pursuit, and evil, the object of avoidance: but by reason of something else, evil can be the object of pursuit, through some good attaching to it; and good can be the object of avoidance, through some evil attaching to it. Now that which is by reason of something else, follows that which is by reason of itself. Consequently pursuit of evil follows pursuit of good; and avoidance of good follows avoidance of evil. Now these four things belong to four passions, since pursuit of good belongs to hope, avoidance of evil to fear, the pursuit of the fearful evil belongs to daring, and the avoidance of good to despair. It follows, therefore, that daring results from hope; since it is in the hope of overcoming the threatening object of fear, that one attacks it boldly. But despair results from fear: since the reason why a man despairs is because he fears the difficulty attaching to the good he should hope for.

Reply Obj. 1: This argument would hold, if good and evil were not co-ordinate objects. But because evil has a certain relation to good, since it comes after good, as privation comes after habit; consequently daring which pursues evil, comes after hope which pursues good.

Reply Obj. 2: Although good, absolutely speaking, is prior to evil, yet avoidance of evil precedes avoidance of good; just as the pursuit of good precedes the pursuit of evil. Consequently just as hope precedes daring, so fear precedes despair. And just as fear does not always lead to despair, but only when it is intense; so hope does not always lead to daring, save only when it is strong.

Reply Obj. 3: Although the object of daring is an evil to which, in the estimation of the daring man, the good of victory is conjoined; yet daring regards the evil, and hope regards the conjoined good. In like manner despair regards directly the good which it turns away from, while fear regards the conjoined evil. Hence, properly speaking, daring is not a part of hope, but its effect: just as despair is an effect, not a part, of fear. For this reason, too, daring cannot be a principal passion.

THIRD ARTICLE [I-II, Q. 45, Art. 3]

Whether Some Defect Is a Cause of Daring?

Objection 1: It would seem that some defect is a cause of daring. For the Philosopher says (De Problem. xxvii, 4) that "lovers of wine are strong and daring." But from wine ensues the effect of drunkenness. Therefore daring is caused by a defect.

Obj. 2: Further, the Philosopher says (Rhet. ii, 5) that "those who have no experience of danger are bold." But want of experience is a defect. Therefore daring is caused by a defect.

Obj. 3: Further, those who have suffered wrongs are wont to be daring; "like the beasts when beaten," as stated in *Ethic.* iii, 5. But the suffering of wrongs pertains to defect. Therefore daring is caused by a defect.

*On the contrary,* The Philosopher says (Rhet. ii, 5) that the cause of daring "is the presence in the imagination of the hope that the means of safety are nigh, and that the things to be feared are either non-existent or far off." But anything pertaining to defect implies either the removal of the means of safety, or the proximity of something to be feared. Therefore nothing pertaining to defect is a cause of daring.

*I answer that,* As stated above (AA. 1, 2) daring results from hope and is contrary to fear: wherefore whatever is naturally apt to cause hope or banish fear, is a cause of daring. Since, however, fear and hope, and also daring, being passions, consist in a movement of the appetite, and in a certain bodily transmutation; a thing may be considered as the cause of daring in two ways, whether by raising hope, or by banishing fear; in one way, in the part of the appetitive movement; in another way, on the part of the bodily transmutation.

On the part of the appetitive movement which follows apprehension, hope that leads to daring is roused by those things that make us reckon victory as possible. Such things regard either our own power, as bodily strength, experience of dangers, abundance of wealth, and the like; or they regard the powers of others, such as having a great number of friends or any other means of help, especially if a man trust in the Divine assistance: wherefore "those are more daring, with whom it is well in regard to godlike things," as the Philosopher says (Rhet. ii, 5). Fear is banished, in this way, by the removal of threatening causes of fear; for instance, by the fact that a man has no enemies, through having harmed nobody, so that he is not aware of any imminent danger; since those especially appear to be threatened by danger, who have harmed others.

On the part of the bodily transmutation, daring is caused through the incitement of hope and the banishment of fear, by those things which raise the temperature about the heart. Wherefore the Philosopher says (De Part. Animal. iii, 4) that "those whose heart is small in size, are more daring; while animals whose heart is large are timid; because the natural heat is unable to give the same degree of temperature to a large as to a small heart; just as a fire does not heat a large house as well as it does a small house." He says also (De Problem. xxvii, 4), that "those whose lungs contain much blood, are more daring, through the heat in the heart that results therefrom." He says also in the same passage that "lovers of wine are more daring, on account of the heat of the wine": hence it has been said above (Q. 40, A. 6) that drunkenness conduces to hope, since the heat in the heart banishes fear and raises hope, by reason of the dilatation and enlargement of the heart.

Reply Obj. 1: Drunkenness causes daring, not through being a defect, but through dilating the heart: and again through making a man think greatly of himself.

Reply Obj. 2: Those who have no experience of dangers are more daring, not on account of a defect, but accidentally, i.e. in so far as through being inexperienced they do not know their own failings, nor the dangers that threaten. Hence it is that the removal of the cause of fear gives rise to daring.

Reply Obj. 3: As the Philosopher says (Rhet. ii, 5)

"those who have been wronged are courageous, because they think that God comes to the assistance of those who suffer unjustly."

Hence it is evident that no defect causes daring except accidentally, i.e. in so far as some excellence attaches thereto, real or imaginary, either in oneself or in another.

FOURTH ARTICLE [I-II, Q. 45, Art. 4]

Whether the Brave Are More Eager at First Than in the Midst of Danger?

Objection 1: It would seem that the daring are not more eager at first than in the midst of danger. Because trembling is caused by fear, which is contrary to daring, as stated above (A. 1; Q. 44, A. 3). But the daring sometimes tremble at first, as the Philosopher says (De Problem. xxvii, 3). Therefore they are not more eager at first than in the midst of danger.

Obj. 2: Further, passion is intensified by an increase in its object: thus since a good is lovable, what is better is yet more lovable. But the object of daring is something difficult. Therefore the greater the difficulty, the greater the daring. But danger is more arduous and difficult when present. It is then therefore that daring is greatest.

Obj. 3: Further, anger is provoked by the infliction of wounds. But anger causes daring; for the Philosopher says (Rhet. ii, 5) that "anger makes man bold." Therefore when man is in the midst of danger and when he is being beaten, then is he most daring.

*On the contrary,* It is said in Ethic. iii, 7 that "the daring are precipitate and full of eagerness before the danger, yet in the midst of dangers they stand aloof."

*I answer that,* Daring, being a movement of the sensitive appetite, follows an apprehension of the sensitive faculty. But the sensitive faculty cannot make comparisons, nor can it inquire into circumstances; its judgment is instantaneous. Now it happens sometimes that it is impossible for a man to take note in an instant of all the difficulties of a certain situation: hence there arises the movement of daring to face the danger; so that when he comes to experience the danger, he feels the difficulty to be greater than he expected, and so gives way.

On the other hand, reason discusses all the difficulties of a situation. Consequently men of fortitude who face danger according to the judgment of reason, at first seem slack, because they face the danger not from passion but with due deliberation. Yet when they are in the midst of danger, they experience nothing unforeseen, but sometimes the difficulty turns out to be less than they anticipated; wherefore they are more persevering. Moreover, it may be because they face the danger on account of the good of virtue which is the abiding object of their will, however great the danger may prove: whereas men of daring face the danger on account of a mere thought giving rise to hope and banishing fear, as stated above (A. 3).

Reply Obj. 1: Trembling does occur in men of daring, on account of the heat being withdrawn from the outer to the inner parts of the body, as occurs also in those who are afraid. But in men of daring the heat withdraws to the heart; whereas in those who are afraid, it withdraws to the inferior parts.

Reply Obj. 2: The object of love is good simply, wherefore if it be increased, love is increased simply. But the object of daring is a compound of good and evil; and the movement of daring towards evil presupposes the movement of hope towards good. If, therefore, so much difficulty be added to the danger that it overcomes hope, the movement of daring does not ensue, but fails. But if the movement of daring does ensue, the greater the danger, the greater is the daring considered to be.

Reply Obj. 3: Hurt does not give rise to anger unless there be some kind of hope, as we shall see later on (Q. 46, A. 1). Consequently if the danger be so great as to banish all hope of victory, anger does not ensue. It is true, however, that if anger does ensue, there will be greater daring.

# QUESTION 46

OF ANGER, IN ITSELF (In Eight Articles)

We must now consider anger: and (1) anger in itself; (2) the cause of anger and its remedy; (3) the effect of anger.

Under the first head there are eight points of inquiry:

(1) Whether anger is a special passion?

(2) Whether the object of anger is good or evil?

(3) Whether anger is in the concupiscible faculty?

(4) Whether anger is accompanied by an act of reason?

(5) Whether anger is more natural than desire?

(6) Whether anger is more grievous than hatred?

(7) Whether anger is only towards those with whom we have a relation of justice?

(8) Of the species of anger.

FIRST ARTICLE [I-II, Q. 46, Art. 1]

Whether Anger Is a Special Passion?

Objection 1: It would seem that anger is not a special passion. For the irascible power takes its name from anger ( *ira* ). But there are several passions in this power, not only one. Therefore anger is not one special passion.

Obj. 2: Further, to every special passion there is a contrary passion; as is evident by going through them one by one. But no passion is contrary to anger, as stated above (Q. 23, A. 3). Therefore anger is not a special passion.

Obj. 3: Further, one special passion does not include another. But anger includes several passions: since it accompanies sorrow, pleasure, and hope, as the Philosopher states (Rhet. ii, 2). Therefore anger is not a special passion.

*On the contrary,* Damascene (De Fide Orth. ii, 16) calls anger a special passion: and so does Cicero (De Quaest. Tusc. iv, 7).

*I answer that,* A thing is said to be general in two ways. First, by predication; thus "animal" is general in respect of all animals. Secondly, by causality; thus the sun is the general cause of all things generated here below, according to Dionysius (Div. Nom. iv). Because just as a genus contains potentially many differences, according to a likeness of matter; so an efficient cause contains many effects according to its active power. Now it happens that an effect is produced by the concurrence of various causes; and since every cause remains somewhat in its effect, we may say that, in yet a third way, an effect which is due to the concurrence of several causes, has a certain generality, inasmuch as several causes are, in a fashion, actually existing therein.

Accordingly in the first way, anger is not a general passion but is condivided with the other passions, as stated above (Q. 23, A. 4). In like manner, neither is it in the second way: since it is not a cause of the other passions. But in this way, love may be called a general passion, as Augustine declares (De Civ. Dei xiv, 7, 9), because love is the primary root of all the other passions, as stated above (Q. 27, A. 4). But, in a third way, anger may be called a general passion, inasmuch as it is caused by a concurrence of several passions. Because the movement of anger does not arise save on account of some pain inflicted, and unless there be desire and hope of revenge: for, as the Philosopher says (Rhet. ii, 2), "the angry man hopes to punish; since he craves for revenge as being possible." Consequently if the person, who inflicted the injury, excel very much, anger does not ensue, but only sorrow, as Avicenna states (De Anima iv, 6).

Reply Obj. 1: The irascible power takes its name from "ira" (anger), not because every movement of that power is one of anger; but because all its movements terminate in anger; and because, of all these movements, anger is the most patent.

Reply Obj. 2: From the very fact that anger is caused by contrary passions, i.e. by hope, which is of good, and by sorrow, which is of evil, it includes in itself contrariety: and consequently it has no contrary outside itself. Thus also in mixed colors there is no contrariety, except that of the simple colors from which they are made.

Reply Obj. 3: Anger includes several passions, not indeed as a genus includes several species; but rather according to the inclusion of cause and effect.

SECOND ARTICLE [I-II, Q. 46, Art. 2]

Whether the Object of Anger Is Good or Evil?

Objection 1: It would seem that the object of anger is evil. For Gregory of Nyssa says [*Nemesius, De Nat. Hom. xxi.] that anger is "the sword-bearer of desire," inasmuch, to wit, as it assails whatever obstacle stands in the way of desire. But an obstacle has the character of evil. Therefore anger regards evil as its object.

Obj. 2: Further, anger and hatred agree in their effect, since each seeks to inflict harm on another. But hatred regards evil as its object, as stated above (Q. 29, A. 1). Therefore anger does also.

Obj. 3: Further, anger arises from sorrow; wherefore the Philosopher says (Ethic. viii, 6) that "anger acts with sorrow." But evil is the object of sorrow. Therefore it is also the object of anger.

*On the contrary,* Augustine says (Confess. ii, 6) that "anger craves for revenge." But the desire for revenge is a desire for something good: since revenge belongs to justice. Therefore the object of anger is good.

Moreover, anger is always accompanied by hope, wherefore it causes pleasure, as the Philosopher says (Rhet. ii, 2). But the object of hope and of pleasure is good. Therefore good is also the object of anger.

*I answer that,* The movement of the appetitive power follows an act of the apprehensive power. Now the apprehensive power apprehends a thing in two ways. First, by way of an incomplex object, as when we understand what a man is; secondly, by way of a complex object, as when we understand that whiteness is in a man. Consequently in each of these ways the appetitive power can tend to both good and evil: by way of a simple and incomplex object, when the appetite simply follows and adheres to good, or recoils from evil: and such movements are desire, hope, pleasure, sorrow, and so forth: by way of a complex object, as when the appetite is concerned with some good or evil being in, or being done to, another, either seeking this or recoiling from it. This is evident in the case of love and hatred: for we love someone, in so far as we wish some good to be in him; and we hate someone, in so far as we wish some evil to be in him. It is the same with anger; for when a man is angry, he wishes to be avenged on someone. Hence the movement of anger has a twofold tendency: viz. to vengeance itself, which it desires and hopes for as being a good, wherefore it takes pleasure in it; and to the person on whom it seeks vengeance, as to something contrary and hurtful, which bears the character of evil.

We must, however, observe a twofold difference in this respect, between anger on the one side, and hatred and love on the other. The first difference is that anger always regards two objects: whereas love and hatred sometimes regard but one object, as when a man is said to love wine or something of the kind, or to hate it. The second difference is, that both the objects of love are good: since the lover wishes good to someone, as to something agreeable to himself: while both the objects of hatred bear the character of evil: for the man who hates, wishes evil to someone, as to something disagreeable to him. Whereas anger regards one object under the aspect of evil, viz. the noxious person, on whom it seeks to be avenged. Consequently it is a passion somewhat made up of contrary passions.

This suffices for the Replies to the Objections.

THIRD ARTICLE [I-II, Q. 46, Art. 3]

Whether Anger Is in the Concupiscible Faculty?

Objection 1: It would seem that anger is in the concupiscible faculty. For Cicero says (De Quaest. Tusc. iv, 9) that anger is a kind of "desire." But desire is in the concupiscible faculty. Therefore anger is too.

Obj. 2: Further, Augustine says in his Rule, that "anger grows into hatred": and Cicero says (De Quaest. Tusc. iv, 9) that "hatred is inveterate anger." But hatred, like love, is a concupiscible passion. Therefore anger is in the concupiscible faculty.

Obj. 3: Further, Damascene (De Fide Orth. ii, 16) and Gregory of Nyssa [*Nemesius, De Nat. Hom. xxi.] say that "anger is made up of sorrow and desire." Both of these are in the concupiscible faculty. Therefore anger is a concupiscible passion.

*On the contrary,* The concupiscible is distinct from the irascible faculty. If, therefore, anger were in the concupiscible power, the irascible would not take its name from it.

*I answer that,* As stated above (Q. 23, A. 1), the passions of the irascible part differ from the passions of the concupiscible faculty, in that the objects of the concupiscible passions are good and evil absolutely considered, whereas the objects of the irascible passions are good and evil in a certain elevation or arduousness. Now it has been stated (A. 2) that anger regards two objects: viz. the vengeance that it seeks; and the person on whom it seeks vengeance; and in respect of both, anger requires a certain arduousness: for the movement of anger does not arise, unless there be some magnitude about both these objects; since "we make no ado about things that are naught or very minute," as the Philosopher observes (Rhet. ii, 2). It is therefore evident that anger is not in the concupiscible, but in the irascible faculty.

Reply Obj. 1: Cicero gives the name of desire to any kind of craving for a future good, without discriminating between that which is arduous and that which is not. Accordingly he reckons anger as a kind of desire, inasmuch as it is a desire of vengeance. In this sense, however, desire is common to the irascible and concupiscible faculties.

Reply Obj. 2: Anger is said to grow into hatred, not as though the same passion which at first was anger, afterwards becomes hatred by becoming inveterate; but by a process of causality. For anger when it lasts a long time engenders hatred.

Reply Obj. 3: Anger is said to be composed of sorrow and desire, not as though they were its parts, but because they are its causes: and it has been said above (Q. 25, A. 2) that the concupiscible passions are the causes of the irascible passions.

FOURTH ARTICLE [I-II, Q. 46, Art. 4]

Whether Anger Requires an Act of Reason?

Objection 1: It would seem that anger does not require an act of reason. For, since anger is a passion, it is in the sensitive appetite. But the sensitive appetite follows an apprehension, not of reason, but of the sensitive faculty. Therefore anger does not require an act of reason.

Obj. 2: Further, dumb animals are devoid of reason: and yet they are seen to be angry. Therefore anger does not require an act of reason.

Obj. 3: Further, drunkenness fetters the reason; whereas it is conducive to anger. Therefore anger does not require an act of reason.

*On the contrary,* The Philosopher says (Ethic. vii, 6) that "anger listens to reason somewhat."

*I answer that,* As stated above (A. 2), anger is a desire for vengeance. Now vengeance implies a comparison between the punishment to be inflicted and the hurt done; wherefore the Philosopher says (Ethic. vii, 6) that "anger, as if it had drawn the inference that it ought to quarrel with such a person, is therefore immediately exasperated." Now to compare and to draw an inference is an act of reason. Therefore anger, in a fashion, requires an act of reason.

Reply Obj. 1: The movement of the appetitive power may follow an act of reason in two ways. In the first way, it follows the reason in so far as the reason commands: and thus the will follows reason, wherefore it is called the rational appetite. In another way, it follows reason in so far as the reason denounces, and thus anger follows reason. For the Philosopher says (De Problem. xxviii, 3) that "anger follows reason, not in obedience to reason's command, but as a result of reason's denouncing the injury." Because the sensitive appetite is subject to the reason, not immediately but through the will.

Reply Obj. 2: Dumb animals have a natural instinct imparted to them by the Divine Reason, in virtue of which they are gifted with movements, both internal and external, like unto rational movements, as stated above (Q. 40, A. 3).

Reply Obj. 3: As stated in *Ethic.* vii, 6, "anger listens somewhat to reason" in so far as reason denounces the injury inflicted, "but listens not perfectly," because it does not observe the rule of reason as to the measure of vengeance. Anger, therefore, requires an act of reason; and yet proves a hindrance to reason. Wherefore the Philosopher says (De Problem. iii, 2, 27) that whose who are very drunk, so as to be incapable of the use of reason, do not get angry: but those who are slightly drunk, do get angry, through being still able, though hampered, to form a judgment of reason.

FIFTH ARTICLE [I-II, Q. 46, Art. 5]

Whether Anger Is More Natural Than Desire?

Objection 1: It would seem that anger is not more natural than desire. Because it is proper to man to be by nature a gentle animal. But "gentleness is contrary to anger," as the Philosopher states (Rhet. ii, 3). Therefore anger is no more natural than desire, in fact it seems to be altogether unnatural to man.

Obj. 2: Further, reason is contrasted with nature: since those things that act according to reason, are not said to act according to nature. Now "anger requires an act of reason, but desire does not," as stated in *Ethic.* vii, 6. Therefore desire is more natural than anger.

Obj. 3: Further, anger is a craving for vengeance: while desire is a craving for those things especially which are pleasant to the touch, viz. for pleasures of the table and for sexual pleasures. But these things are more natural to man than vengeance. Therefore desire is more natural than anger.

*On the contrary,* The Philosopher says (Ethic. vii, 6) that "anger is more natural than desire."

*I answer that,* By "natural" we mean that which is caused by nature, as stated in *Phys.* ii, 1. Consequently the question as to whether a particular passion is more or less natural cannot be decided without reference to the cause of that passion. Now the cause of a passion, as stated above (Q. 36, A. 2), may be considered in two ways: first, on the part of the object; secondly, on the part of the subject. If then we consider the cause of anger and of desire, on the part of the object, thus desire, especially of pleasures of the table, and of sexual pleasures, is more natural than anger; in so far as these pleasures are more natural to man than vengeance.

If, however, we consider the cause of anger on the part of the subject, thus anger, in a manner, is more natural; and, in a manner, desire is more natural. Because the nature of an individual man may be considered either as to the generic, or as to the specific nature, or again as to the particular temperament of the individual. If then we consider the generic nature, i.e. the nature of this man considered as an animal; thus desire is more natural than anger; because it is from this very generic nature that man is inclined to desire those things which tend to preserve in him the life both of the species and of the individual. If, however, we consider the specific nature, i.e. the nature of this man as a rational being; then anger is more natural to man than desire, in so far as anger follows reason more than desire does. Wherefore the Philosopher says (Ethic. iv, 5) that "revenge" which pertains to anger "is more natural to man than meekness": for it is natural to everything to rise up against things contrary and hurtful. And if we consider the nature of the individual, in respect of his particular temperament, thus anger is more natural than desire; for the reason that anger is prone to ensue from the natural tendency to anger, more than desire, or any other passion, is to ensue from a natural tendency to desire, which tendencies result from a man's individual temperament. Because disposition to anger is due to a bilious temperament; and of all the humors, the bile moves quickest; for it is like fire. Consequently he that is temperamentally disposed to anger is sooner incensed with anger, than he that is temperamentally disposed to desire, is inflamed with desire: and for this reason the Philosopher says (Ethic. vii, 6) that a disposition to anger is more liable to be transmitted from parent to child, than a disposition to desire.

Reply Obj. 1: We may consider in man both the natural temperament on the part of the body, and the reason. On the part of the bodily temperament, a man, considered specifically, does not naturally excel others either in anger or in any other passion, on account of the moderation of his temperament. But other animals, for as much as their temperament recedes from this moderation and approaches to an extreme disposition, are naturally disposed to some excess of passion, such as the lion in daring, the hound in anger, the hare in fear, and so forth. On the part of reason, however, it is natural to man, both to be angry and to be gentle: in so far as reason somewhat causes anger, by denouncing the injury which causes anger; and somewhat appeases anger, in so far as the angry man "does not listen perfectly to the command of reason," as stated above (A. 4, ad 3).

Reply Obj. 2: Reason itself belongs to the nature of man: wherefore from the very fact that anger requires an act of reason, it follows that it is, in a manner, natural to man.

Reply Obj. 3: This argument regards anger and desire on the part of the object.

SIXTH ARTICLE [I-II, Q. 46, Art. 6]

Whether Anger Is More Grievous Than Hatred?

Objection 1: It would seem that anger is more grievous than hatred. For it is written (Prov. 27:4) that "anger hath no mercy, nor fury when it breaketh forth." But hatred sometimes has mercy. Therefore anger is more grievous than hatred.

Obj. 2: Further, it is worse to suffer evil and to grieve for it, than merely to suffer it. But when a man hates, he is contented if the object of his hatred suffer evil: whereas the angry man is not satisfied unless the object of his anger know it and be aggrieved thereby, as the Philosopher says (Rhet. ii, 4). Therefore, anger is more grievous than hatred.

Obj. 3: Further, a thing seems to be so much the more firm according as more things concur to set it up: thus a habit is all the more settled through being caused by several acts. But anger is caused by the concurrence of several passions, as stated above (A. 1): whereas hatred is not. Therefore anger is more settled and more grievous than hatred.

*On the contrary,* Augustine, in his Rule, compares hatred to "a beam," but anger to "a mote."

*I answer that,* The species and nature of a passion are taken from its object. Now the object of anger is the same in substance as the object of hatred; since, just as the hater wishes evil to him whom he hates, so does the angry man wish evil to him with whom he is angry. But there is a difference of aspect: for the hater wishes evil to his enemy, as evil, whereas the angry man wishes evil to him with whom he is angry, not as evil but in so far as it has an aspect of good, that is, in so far as he reckons it as just, since it is a means of vengeance. Wherefore also it has been said above (A. 2) that hatred implies application of evil to evil, whereas anger denotes application of good to evil. Now it is evident that to seek evil under the aspect of justice, is a lesser evil, than simply to seek evil to someone. Because to wish evil to someone under the aspect of justice, may be according to the virtue of justice, if it be in conformity with the order of reason; and anger fails only in this, that it does not obey the precept of reason in taking vengeance. Consequently it is evident that hatred is far worse and graver than anger.

Reply Obj. 1: In anger and hatred two points may be considered: namely, the thing desired, and the intensity of the desire. As to the thing desired, anger has more mercy than hatred has. For since hatred desires another's evil for evil's sake, it is satisfied with no particular measure of evil: because those things that are desired for their own sake, are desired without measure, as the Philosopher states (Polit. i, 3), instancing a miser with regard to riches. Hence it is written (Ecclus. 12:16): "An enemy ... if he find an opportunity, will not be satisfied with blood." Anger, on the other hand, seeks evil only under the aspect of a just means of vengeance. Consequently when the evil inflicted goes beyond the measure of justice according to the estimate of the angry man, then he has mercy. Wherefore the Philosopher says (Rhet. ii, 4) that "the angry man is appeased if many evils befall, whereas the hater is never appeased."

As to the intensity of the desire, anger excludes mercy more than hatred does; because the movement of anger is more impetuous, through the heating of the bile. Hence the passage quoted continues: "Who can bear the violence of one provoked?"

Reply Obj. 2: As stated above, an angry man wishes evil to someone, in so far as this evil is a means of just vengeance. Now vengeance is wrought by the infliction of a punishment: and the nature of punishment consists in being contrary to the will, painful, and inflicted for some fault. Consequently an angry man desires this, that the person whom he is hurting, may feel it and be in pain, and know that this has befallen him on account of the harm he has done the other. The hater, on the other hand, cares not for all this, since he desires another's evil as such. It is not true, however, that an evil is worse through giving pain: because "injustice and imprudence, although evil," yet, being voluntary, "do not grieve those in whom they are," as the Philosopher observes (Rhet. ii, 4).

Reply Obj. 3: That which proceeds from several causes, is more settled when these causes are of one kind: but it may be that one cause prevails over many others. Now hatred ensues from a more lasting cause than anger does. Because anger arises from an emotion of the soul due to the wrong inflicted; whereas hatred ensues from a disposition in a man, by reason of which he considers that which he hates to be contrary and hurtful to him. Consequently, as passion is more transitory than disposition or habit, so anger is less lasting than hatred; although hatred itself is a passion ensuing from this disposition. Hence the Philosopher says (Rhet. ii, 4) that "hatred is more incurable than anger."

SEVENTH ARTICLE [I-II, Q. 46, Art. 7]

Whether Anger Is Only Towards Those to Whom One Has an Obligation of Justice?

Objection 1: It would seem that anger is not only towards those to whom one has an obligation of justice. For there is no justice between man and irrational beings. And yet sometimes one is angry with irrational beings; thus, out of anger, a writer throws away his pen, or a rider strikes his horse. Therefore anger is not only towards those to whom one has an obligation of justice.

Obj. 2: Further, "there is no justice towards oneself ... nor is there justice towards one's own" (Ethic. v, 6). But sometimes a man is angry with himself; for instance, a penitent, on account of his sin; hence it is written (Ps. 4:5): "Be ye angry and sin not." Therefore anger is not only towards those with whom one has a relation of justice.

Obj. 3: Further, justice and injustice can be of one man towards an entire class, or a whole community: for instance, when the state injures an individual. But anger is not towards a class but only towards an individual, as the Philosopher states (Rhet. ii, 4). Therefore properly speaking, anger is not towards those with whom one is in relation of justice or injustice.

The contrary, however, may be gathered from the Philosopher (Rhet. ii, 2, 3).

*I answer that,* As stated above (A. 6), anger desires evil as being a means of just vengeance. Consequently, anger is towards those to whom we are just or unjust: since vengeance is an act of justice, and wrong-doing is an act of injustice. Therefore both on the part of the cause, viz. the harm done by another, and on the part of the vengeance sought by the angry man, it is evident that anger concerns those to whom one is just or unjust.

Reply Obj. 1: As stated above (A. 4, ad 2), anger, though it follows an act of reason, can nevertheless be in dumb animals that are devoid of reason, in so far as through their natural instinct they are moved by their imagination to something like rational action. Since then in man there is both reason and imagination, the movement of anger can be aroused in man in two ways. First, when only his imagination denounces the injury: and, in this way, man is aroused to a movement of anger even against irrational and inanimate beings, which movement is like that which occurs in animals against anything that injures them. Secondly, by the reason denouncing the injury: and thus, according to the Philosopher (Rhet. ii, 3), "it is impossible to be angry with insensible things, or with the dead": both because they feel no pain, which is, above all, what the angry man seeks in those with whom he is angry: and because there is no question of vengeance on them, since they can do us no harm.

Reply Obj. 2: As the Philosopher says (Ethic. v, 11), "metaphorically speaking there is a certain justice and injustice between a man and himself," in so far as the reason rules the irascible and concupiscible parts of the soul. And in this sense a man is said to be avenged on himself, and consequently, to be angry with himself. But properly, and in accordance with the nature of things, a man is never angry with himself.

Reply Obj. 3: The Philosopher (Rhet. ii, 4) assigns as one difference between hatred and anger, that "hatred may be felt towards a class, as we hate the entire class of thieves; whereas anger is directed only towards an individual." The reason is that hatred arises from our considering a quality as disagreeing with our disposition; and this may refer to a thing in general or in particular. Anger, on the other hand, ensues from someone having injured us by his action. Now all actions are the deeds of individuals: and consequently anger is always pointed at an individual. When the whole state hurts us, the whole state is reckoned as one individual [*Cf. Q. 29, A. 6].

EIGHTH ARTICLE [I-II, Q. 46, Art. 8]

Whether the Species of Anger Are Suitably Assigned?

Objection 1: It would seem that Damascene (De Fide Orth. ii, 16) unsuitably assigns three species of anger—"wrath," "ill-will" and "rancor." For no genus derives its specific differences from accidents. But these three are diversified in respect of an accident: because "the beginning of the movement of anger is called wrath ( *cholos* ), if anger continue it is called ill-will ( menis ); while rancor ( *kotos* ) is anger waiting for an opportunity of vengeance." Therefore these are not different species of anger.

Obj. 2: Further, Cicero says (De Quaest. Tusc. iv, 9) that " *excandescentia* (irascibility) is what the Greeks call thymosis , and is a kind of anger that arises and subsides intermittently"; while according to Damascene thymosis , is the same as kotos (rancor). Therefore kotos does not bide its time for taking vengeance, but in course of time spends itself.

Obj. 3: Further, Gregory (Moral. xxi, 4) gives three degrees of anger, namely, "anger without utterance, anger with utterance, and anger with perfection of speech," corresponding to the three degrees mentioned by Our Lord (Matt. 5:22): "Whosoever is angry with his brother" (thus implying "anger without utterance"), and then, "whosoever shall say to his brother, 'Raca'" (implying anger with utterance yet without full expression), and lastly, "whosoever shall say 'Thou fool'" (where we have "perfection of speech"). Therefore Damascene's division is imperfect, since it takes no account of utterance.

*On the contrary,* stands the authority of Damascene (De Fide Orth. ii, 16) and Gregory of Nyssa [*Nemesius, De Nat. Hom. xxi.].

*I answer that,* The species of anger given by Damascene and Gregory of Nyssa are taken from those things which give increase to anger. This happens in three ways. First from facility of the movement itself, and he calls this kind of anger *cholos* (bile) because it quickly aroused. Secondly, on the part of the grief that causes anger, and which dwells some time in the memory; this belongs to *menis* (ill-will) which is derived from menein (to dwell). Thirdly, on the part of that which the angry man seeks, viz. vengeance; and this pertains to *kotos* (rancor) which never rests until it is avenged [*Eph. 4:31: "Let all bitterness and anger and indignation ... be put away from you."]. Hence the Philosopher (Ethic. iv, 5) calls some angry persons *akrocholoi* (choleric), because they are easily angered; some he calls *pikroi* (bitter), because they retain their anger for a long time; and some he calls *chalepoi* (ill-tempered), because they never rest until they have retaliated [*Cf. II-II, Q. 158, A. 5].

Reply Obj. 1: All those things which give anger some kind of perfection are not altogether accidental to anger; and consequently nothing prevents them from causing a certain specific difference thereof.

Reply Obj. 2: Irascibility, which Cicero mentions, seems to pertain to the first species of anger, which consists in a certain quickness of temper, rather than to rancor ( *furor* ). And there is no reason why the Greek thymosis , which is denoted by the Latin furor, should not signify both quickness to anger, and firmness of purpose in being avenged.

Reply Obj. 3: These degrees are distinguished according to various effects of anger; and not according to degrees of perfection in the very movement of anger.

## QUESTION 47

OF THE CAUSE THAT PROVOKES ANGER, AND OF THE REMEDIES OF ANGER (In Four Articles) [*There is no further mention of these remedies in the text, except in A. 4].

We must now consider the cause that provokes anger, and its remedies. Under this head there are four points of inquiry:

(1) Whether the motive of anger is always something done against the one who is angry?

(2) Whether slight or contempt is the sole motive of anger?

(3) Of the cause of anger on the part of the angry person;

(4) Of the cause of anger on the part of the person with whom one is angry.

FIRST ARTICLE [I-II, Q. 47, Art. 1]

Whether the Motive of Anger Is Always Something Done Against the One Who Is Angry?

Objection 1: It would seem that the motive of anger is not always something done against the one who is angry. Because man, by sinning, can do nothing against God; since it is written (Job 35:6): "If thy iniquities be multiplied, what shalt thou do against Him?" And yet God is spoken of as being angry with man on account of sin, according to Ps. 105:40: "The Lord was exceedingly angry with His people." Therefore it is not always on account of something done against him, that a man is angry.

Obj. 2: Further, anger is a desire for vengeance. But one may desire vengeance for things done against others. Therefore we are not always angry on account of something done against us.

Obj. 3: Further, as the Philosopher says (Rhet. ii, 2) man is angry especially with those "who despise what he takes a great interest in; thus men who study philosophy are angry with those who despise philosophy," and so forth. But contempt of philosophy does not harm the philosopher. Therefore it is not always a harm done to us that makes us angry.

Obj. 4: Further, he that holds his tongue when another insults him, provokes him to greater anger, as Chrysostom observes (Hom. xxii, in Ep. ad Rom.). But by holding his tongue he does the other no harm. Therefore a man is not always provoked to anger by something done against him.

*On the contrary,* The Philosopher says (Rhet. ii, 4) that "anger is always due to something done to oneself: whereas hatred may arise without anything being done to us, for we hate a man simply because we think him such."

*I answer that,* As stated above (Q. 46, A. 6), anger is the desire to hurt another for the purpose of just vengeance. Now unless some injury has been done, there is no question of vengeance: nor does any injury provoke one to vengeance, but only that which is done to the person who seeks vengeance: for just as everything naturally seeks its own good, so does it naturally repel its own evil. But injury done by anyone does not affect a man unless in some way it be something done against him. Consequently the motive of a man's anger is always something done against him.

Reply Obj. 1: We speak of anger in God, not as of a passion of the soul but as of judgment of justice, inasmuch as He wills to take vengeance on sin. Because the sinner, by sinning, cannot do God any actual harm: but so far as he himself is concerned, he acts against God in two ways. First, in so far as he despises God in His commandments. Secondly, in so far as he harms himself or another; which injury redounds to God, inasmuch as the person injured is an object of God's providence and protection.

Reply Obj. 2: If we are angry with those who harm others, and seek to be avenged on them, it is because those who are injured belong in some way to us: either by some kinship or friendship, or at least because of the nature we have in common.

Reply Obj. 3: When we take a very great interest in a thing, we look upon it as our own good; so that if anyone despise it, it seems as though we ourselves were despised and injured.

Reply Obj. 4: Silence provokes the insulter to anger when he thinks it is due to contempt, as though his anger were slighted: and a slight is an action.

SECOND ARTICLE [I-II, Q. 47, Art. 2]

Whether the Sole Motive of Anger Is Slight or Contempt?

Objection 1: It would seem that slight or contempt is not the sole motive of anger. For Damascene says (De Fide Orth. ii, 16) that we are angry "when we suffer, or think that we are suffering, an injury." But one may suffer an injury without being despised or slighted. Therefore a slight is not the only motive of anger.

Obj. 2: Further, desire for honor and grief for a slight belong to the same subject. But dumb animals do not desire honor. Therefore they are not grieved by being slighted. And yet "they are roused to anger, when wounded," as the Philosopher says (Ethic. iii, 8). Therefore a slight is not the sole motive of anger.

Obj. 3: Further, the Philosopher (Rhet. ii, 2) gives many other causes of anger, for instance, "being forgotten by others; that others should rejoice in our misfortunes; that they should make known our evils; being hindered from doing as we like." Therefore being slighted is not the only motive for being angry.

*On the contrary,* The Philosopher says (Rhet. ii, 2) that anger is "a desire, with sorrow, for vengeance, on account of a seeming slight done unbecomingly."

*I answer that,* All the causes of anger are reduced to slight. For slight is of three kinds, as stated in Rhet. ii, 2, viz. "contempt," "despiteful treatment," i.e. hindering one from doing one's will, and "insolence": and all motives of anger are reduced to these three. Two reasons may be assigned for this. First, because anger seeks another's hurt as being a means of just vengeance: wherefore it seeks vengeance in so far as it seems just. Now just vengeance is taken only for that which is done unjustly; hence that which provokes anger is always something considered in the light of an injustice. Wherefore the Philosopher says (Rhet. ii, 3) that "men are not angry,—if they think they have wronged some one and are suffering justly on that account; because there is no anger at what is just." Now injury is done to another in three ways: namely, through ignorance, through passion, and through choice. Then, most of all, a man does an injustice, when he does an injury from choice, on purpose, or from deliberate malice, as stated in *Ethic.* v, 8. Wherefore we are most of all angry with those who, in our opinion, have hurt us on purpose. For if we think that some one has done us an injury through ignorance or through passion, either we are not angry with them at all, or very much less: since to do anything through ignorance or through passion takes away from the notion of injury, and to a certain extent calls for mercy and forgiveness. Those, on the other hand, who do an injury on purpose, seem to sin from contempt; wherefore we are angry with them most of all. Hence the Philosopher says (Rhet. ii, 3) that "we are either not angry at all, or not very angry with those who have acted through anger, because they do not seem to have acted slightingly."

The second reason is because a slight is opposed to a man's excellence: because "men think little of things that are not worth much ado" (Rhet. ii, 2). Now we seek for some kind of excellence from all our goods. Consequently whatever injury is inflicted on us, in so far as it is derogatory to our excellence, seems to savor of a slight.

Reply Obj. 1: Any other cause, besides contempt, through which a man suffers an injury, takes away from the notion of injury: contempt or slight alone adds to the motive of anger, and consequently is of itself the cause of anger.

Reply Obj. 2: Although a dumb animal does not seek honor as such, yet it naturally seeks a certain superiority, and is angry with anything derogatory thereto.

Reply Obj. 3: Each of those causes amounts to some kind of slight. Thus forgetfulness is a clear sign of slight esteem, for the more we think of a thing the more is it fixed in our memory. Again if a man does not hesitate by his remarks to give pain to another, this seems to show that he thinks little of him: and those too who show signs of hilarity when another is in misfortune, seem to care little about his good or evil. Again he that hinders another from carrying out his will, without deriving thereby any profit to himself, seems not to care much for his friendship. Consequently all those things, in so far as they are signs of contempt, provoke anger.

THIRD ARTICLE [I-II, Q. 47, Art. 3]

Whether a Man's Excellence Is the Cause of His Being Angry?

Objection 1: It would seem that a man's excellence is not the cause of his being more easily angry. For the Philosopher says (Rhet. ii, 2) that "some are angry especially when they are grieved, for instance, the sick, the poor, and those who are disappointed." But these things seem to pertain to defect. Therefore defect rather than excellence makes one prone to anger.

Obj. 2: Further, the Philosopher says (Rhet. ii, 2) that "some are very much inclined to be angry when they are despised for some failing or weakness of the existence of which there are grounds for suspicion; but if they think they excel in those points, they do not trouble." But a suspicion of this kind is due to some defect. Therefore defect rather than excellence is a cause of a man being angry.

Obj. 3: Further, whatever savors of excellence makes a man agreeable and hopeful. But the Philosopher says (Rhet. ii, 3) that "men are not angry when they play, make jokes, or take part in a feast, nor when they are prosperous or successful, nor in moderate pleasures and well-founded hope." Therefore excellence is not a cause of anger.

*On the contrary,* The Philosopher says (Rhet. ii, 9) that excellence makes men prone to anger.

*I answer that,* The cause of anger, in the man who is angry, may be taken in two ways. First in respect of the motive of anger: and thus excellence is the cause of a man being easily angered. Because the motive of anger is an unjust slight, as stated above (A. 2). Now it is evident that the more excellent a man is, the more unjust is a slight offered him in the matter in which he excels. Consequently those who excel in any matter, are most of all angry, if they be slighted in that matter; for instance, a wealthy man in his riches, or an orator in his eloquence, and so forth.

Secondly, the cause of anger, in the man who is angry, may be considered on the part of the disposition produced in him by the motive aforesaid. Now it is evident that nothing moves a man to anger except a hurt that grieves him: while whatever savors of defect is above all a cause of grief; since men who suffer from some defect are more easily hurt. And this is why men who are weak, or subject to some other defect, are more easily angered, since they are more easily grieved.

This suffices for the Reply to the First Objection.

Reply Obj. 2: If a man be despised in a matter in which he evidently excels greatly, he does not consider himself the loser thereby, and therefore is not grieved: and in this respect he is less angered. But in another respect, in so far as he is more undeservedly despised, he has more reason for being angry: unless perhaps he thinks that he is envied or insulted not through contempt but through ignorance, or some other like cause.

Reply Obj. 3: All these things hinder anger in so far as they hinder sorrow. But in another respect they are naturally apt to provoke anger, because they make it more unseemly to insult anyone.

FOURTH ARTICLE [I-II, Q. 47, Art. 4]

Whether a Person's Defect Is a Reason for Being More Easily Angry with Him?

Objection 1: It would seem that a person's defect is not a reason for being more easily angry with him. For the Philosopher says (Rhet. ii, 3) that "we are not angry with those who confess and repent and humble themselves; *on the contrary,* we are gentle with them. Wherefore dogs bite not those who sit down." But these things savor of littleness and defect. Therefore littleness of a person is a reason for being less angry with him.

Obj. 2: Further, there is no greater defect than death. But anger ceases at the sight of death. Therefore defect of a person does not provoke anger against him.

Obj. 3: Further, no one thinks little of a man through his being friendly towards him. But we are more angry with friends, if they offend us or refuse to help us; hence it is written (Ps. 54:13): "If my enemy had reviled me I would verily have borne with it." Therefore a person's defect is not a reason for being more easily angry with him.

*On the contrary,* The Philosopher says (Rhet. ii, 2) that "the rich man is angry with the poor man, if the latter despise him; and in like manner the prince is angry with his subject."

*I answer that,* As stated above (AA. 2, 3) unmerited contempt more than anything else is a provocative of anger. Consequently deficiency or littleness in the person with whom we are angry, tends to increase our anger, in so far as it adds to the unmeritedness of being despised. For just as the higher a man's position is, the more undeservedly he is despised; so the lower it is, the less reason he has for despising. Thus a nobleman is angry if he be insulted by a peasant; a wise man, if by a fool; a master, if by a servant.

If, however, the littleness or deficiency lessens the unmerited contempt, then it does not increase but lessens anger. In this way those who repent of their ill-deeds, and confess that they have done wrong, who humble themselves and ask pardon, mitigate anger, according to Prov. 15:1: "A mild answer breaketh wrath": because, to wit, they seem not to despise, but rather to think much of those before whom they humble themselves.

This suffices for the Reply to the First Objection.

Reply Obj. 2: There are two reasons why anger ceases at the sight of death. One is because the dead are incapable of sorrow and sensation; and this is chiefly what the angry seek in those with whom they are angered. Another reason is because the dead seem to have attained to the limit of evils. Hence anger ceases in regard to all who are grievously hurt, in so far as this hurt surpasses the measure of just retaliation.

Reply Obj. 3: To be despised by one's friends seems also a greater indignity. Consequently if they despise us by hurting or by failing to help, we are angry with them for the same reason for which we are angry with those who are beneath us.

## QUESTION 48

OF THE EFFECTS OF ANGER (In Four Articles)

We must now consider the effects of anger: under which head there are four points of inquiry:

(1) Whether anger causes pleasure?

(2) Whether above all it causes heat in the heart?

(3) Whether above all it hinders the use of reason?

(4) Whether it causes taciturnity?

FIRST ARTICLE [I-II, Q. 48, Art. 1]

Whether Anger Causes Pleasure?

Objection 1: It would seem that anger does not cause pleasure. Because sorrow excludes pleasure. But anger is never without sorrow, since, as stated in *Ethic.* vii, 6, "everyone that acts from anger, acts with pain." Therefore anger does not cause pleasure.

Obj. 2: Further, the Philosopher says (Ethic. iv, 5) that "vengeance makes anger to cease, because it substitutes pleasure for pain": whence we may gather that the angry man derives pleasure from vengeance, and that vengeance quells his anger. Therefore on the advent of pleasure, anger departs: and consequently anger is not an effect united with pleasure.

Obj. 3: Further, no effect hinders its cause, since it is conformed to its cause. But pleasure hinders anger as stated in *Rhet.* ii, 3. Therefore pleasure is not an effect of anger.

*On the contrary,* The Philosopher (Ethic. iv, 5) quotes the saying that anger is "Sweet to the soul as honey to the taste" (Iliad, xviii, 109, trl. Pope).

*I answer that,* As the Philosopher says (Ethic. vii, 14), pleasures, chiefly sensible and bodily pleasures, are remedies against sorrow: and therefore the greater the sorrow or anxiety, the more sensible are we to the pleasure which heals it, as is evident in the case of thirst which increases the pleasure of drink. Now it is clear from what has been said (Q. 47, AA. 1, 3), that the movement of anger arises from a wrong done that causes sorrow, for which sorrow vengeance is sought as a remedy. Consequently as soon as vengeance is present, pleasure ensues, and so much the greater according as the sorrow was greater. Therefore if vengeance be really present, perfect pleasure ensues, entirely excluding sorrow, so that the movement of anger ceases. But before vengeance is really present, it becomes present to the angry man in two ways: in one way, by hope; because none is angry except he hopes for vengeance, as stated above (Q. 46, A. 1); in another way, by thinking of it continually, for to everyone that desires a thing it is pleasant to dwell on the thought of what he desires; wherefore the imaginings of dreams are pleasant. Accordingly an angry man takes pleasure in thinking much about vengeance. This pleasure, however, is not perfect, so as to banish sorrow and consequently anger.

Reply Obj. 1: The angry man does not grieve and rejoice at the same thing; he grieves for the wrong done, while he takes pleasure in the thought and hope of vengeance. Consequently sorrow is to anger as its beginning; while pleasure is the effect or terminus of anger.

Reply Obj. 2: This argument holds in regard to pleasure caused by the real presence of vengeance, which banishes anger altogether.

Reply Obj. 3: Pleasure that precedes hinders sorrow from ensuing, and consequently is a hindrance to anger. But pleasure felt in taking vengeance follows from anger.

SECOND ARTICLE [I-II, Q. 48, Art. 2]

Whether Anger Above All Causes Fervor in the Heart?

Objection 1: It would seem that heat is not above all the effect of anger. For fervor, as stated above (Q. 28, A. 5; Q. 37, A. 2), belongs to love. But love, as above stated, is the beginning and cause of all the passions. Since then the cause is more powerful than its effect, it seems that anger is not the chief cause of fervor.

Obj. 2: Further, those things which, of themselves, arouse fervor, increase as time goes on; thus love grows stronger the longer it lasts. But in course of time anger grows weaker; for the Philosopher says (Rhet. ii, 3) that "time puts an end to anger." Therefore fervor is not the proper effect of anger.

Obj. 3: Further, fervor added to fervor produces greater fervor. But "the addition of a greater anger banishes already existing anger," as the Philosopher says (Rhet. ii, 3). Therefore anger does not cause fervor.

*On the contrary,* Damascene says (De Fide Orth. ii, 16) that "anger is fervor of the blood around the heart, resulting from an exhalation of the bile."

*I answer that,* As stated above (Q. 44, A. 1), the bodily transmutation that occurs in the passions of the soul is proportionate to the movement of the appetite. Now it is evident that every appetite, even the natural appetite, tends with greater force to repel that which is contrary to it, if it be present: hence we see that hot water freezes harder, as though the cold acted with greater force on the hot object. Since then the appetitive movement of anger is caused by some injury inflicted, as by a contrary that is present; it follows that the appetite tends with great force to repel the injury by the desire of vengeance; and hence ensues great vehemence and impetuosity in the movement of anger. And because the movement of anger is not one of recoil, which corresponds to the action of cold, but one of prosecution, which corresponds to the action of heat, the result is that the movement of anger produces fervor of the blood and vital spirits around the heart, which is the instrument of the soul's passions. And hence it is that, on account of the heart being so disturbed by anger, those chiefly who are angry betray signs thereof in their outer members. For, as Gregory says (Moral. v, 30) "the heart that is inflamed with the stings of its own anger beats quick, the body trembles, the tongue stammers, the countenance takes fire, the eyes grow fierce, they that are well known are not recognized. With the mouth indeed he shapes a sound, but the understanding knows not what it says."

Reply Obj. 1: "Love itself is not felt so keenly as in the absence of the beloved," as Augustine observes (De Trin. x, 12). Consequently when a man suffers from a hurt done to the excellence that he loves, he feels his love thereof the more: the result being that his heart is moved with greater heat to remove the hindrance to the object of his love; so that anger increases the fervor of love and makes it to be felt more.

Nevertheless, the fervor arising from heat differs according as it is to be referred to love or to anger. Because the fervor of love has a certain sweetness and gentleness; for it tends to the good that one loves: whence it is likened to the warmth of the air and of the blood. For this reason sanguine temperaments are more inclined to love; and hence the saying that "love springs from the liver," because of the blood being formed there. On the other hand, the fervor of anger has a certain bitterness with a tendency to destroy, for it seeks to be avenged on the contrary evil: whence it is likened to the heat of fire and of the bile, and for this reason Damascene says (De Fide Orth. ii, 16) that it "results from an exhalation of the bile whence it takes its name *chole*."

Reply Obj. 2: Time, of necessity, weakens all those things, the causes of which are impaired by time. Now it is evident that memory is weakened by time; for things which happened long ago easily slip from our memory. But anger is caused by the memory of a wrong done. Consequently the cause of anger is impaired little by little as time goes on, until at length it vanishes altogether. Moreover a wrong seems greater when it is first felt; and our estimate thereof is gradually lessened the further the sense of present wrong recedes into the past. The same applies to love, so long as the cause of love is in the memory alone; wherefore the Philosopher says (Ethic. viii, 5) that "if a friend's absence lasts long, it seems to make men forget their friendship." But in the presence of a friend, the cause of friendship is continually being multiplied by time: wherefore the friendship increases: and the same would apply to anger, were its cause continually multiplied.

Nevertheless the very fact that anger soon spends itself proves the strength of its fervor: for as a great fire is soon spent having burnt up all the fuel; so too anger, by reason of its vehemence, soon dies away.

Reply Obj. 3: Every power that is divided in itself is weakened. Consequently if a man being already angry with one, becomes angry with another, by this very fact his anger with the former is weakened. Especially is this so if his anger in the second case be greater: because the wrong done which aroused his former anger, will, in comparison with the second wrong, which is reckoned greater, seem to be of little or no account.

THIRD ARTICLE [I-II, Q. 48, Art. 3]

Whether Anger Above All Hinders the Use of Reason?

Objection 1: It would seem that anger does not hinder the use of reason. Because that which presupposes an act of reason, does not seem to hinder the use of reason. But "anger listens to reason," as stated in *Ethic.* vii, 6. Therefore anger does not hinder reason.

Obj. 2: Further, the more the reason is hindered, the less does a man show his thoughts. But the Philosopher says (Ethic. vii, 6) that "an angry man is not cunning but is open." Therefore anger does not seem to hinder the use of reason, as desire does; for desire is cunning, as he also states (Ethic. vii, 6.).

Obj. 3: Further, the judgment of reason becomes more evident by juxtaposition of the contrary: because contraries stand out more clearly when placed beside one another. But this also increases anger: for the Philosopher says (Rhet. ii, 2) that "men are more angry if they receive unwonted treatment; for instance, honorable men, if they be dishonored": and so forth. Therefore the same cause increases anger, and facilitates the judgment of reason. Therefore anger does not hinder the judgment of reason.

*On the contrary,* Gregory says (Moral. v, 30) that anger "withdraws the light of understanding, while by agitating it troubles the mind."

*I answer that,* Although the mind or reason makes no use of a bodily organ in its proper act, yet, since it needs certain sensitive powers for the execution of its act, the acts of which powers are hindered when the body is disturbed, it follows of necessity that any disturbance in the body hinders even the judgment of reason; as is clear in the case of drunkenness or sleep. Now it has been stated (A. 2) that anger, above all, causes a bodily disturbance in the region of the heart, so much as to effect even the outward members. Consequently, of all the passions, anger is the most manifest obstacle to the judgment of reason, according to Ps. 30:10: "My eye is troubled with wrath."

Reply Obj. 1: The beginning of anger is in the reason, as regards the appetitive movement, which is the formal element of anger. But the passion of anger forestalls the perfect judgment of reason, as though it listened but imperfectly to reason, on account of the commotion of the heat urging to instant action, which commotion is the material element of anger. In this respect it hinders the judgment of reason.

Reply Obj. 2: An angry man is said to be open, not because it is clear to him what he ought to do, but because he acts openly, without thought of hiding himself. This is due partly to the reason being hindered, so as not to discern what should be hidden and what done openly, nor to devise the means of hiding; and partly to the dilatation of the heart which pertains to magnanimity which is an effect of anger: wherefore the Philosopher says of the magnanimous man (Ethic. iv, 3) that "he is open in his hatreds and his friendships ... and speaks and acts openly." Desire, on the other hand, is said to lie low and to be cunning, because, in many cases, the pleasurable things that are desired, savor of shame and voluptuousness, wherein man wishes not to be seen. But in those things that savor of manliness and excellence, such as matters of vengeance, man seeks to be in the open.

Reply Obj. 3: As stated above (ad 1), the movement of anger begins in the reason, wherefore the juxtaposition of one contrary with another facilitates the judgment of reason, on the same grounds as it increases anger. For when a man who is possessed of honor or wealth, suffers a loss therein, the loss seems all the greater, both on account of the contrast, and because it was unforeseen. Consequently it causes greater grief: just as a great good, through being received unexpectedly, causes greater delight. And in proportion to the increase of the grief that precedes, anger is increased also.

FOURTH ARTICLE [I-II, Q. 48, Art. 4]

Whether Anger Above All Causes Taciturnity?

Objection 1: It would seem that anger does not cause taciturnity. Because taciturnity is opposed to speech. But increase in anger conduces to speech; as is evident from the degrees of anger laid down by Our Lord (Matt. 5:22): where He says: "Whosoever is angry with his brother"; and " ... whosoever shall say to his brother, 'Raca'"; and " ... whosoever shall say to his brother, 'Thou fool.'" Therefore anger does not cause taciturnity.

Obj. 2: Further, through failing to obey reason, man sometimes breaks out into unbecoming words: hence it is written (Prov. 25:28): "As a city that lieth open and is not compassed with walls, so is a man that cannot refrain his own spirit in speaking." But anger, above all, hinders the judgment of reason, as stated above (A. 3). Consequently above all it makes one break out into unbecoming words. Therefore it does not cause taciturnity.

Obj. 3: Further, it is written (Matt. 12:34): "Out of the abundance of the heart the mouth speaketh." But anger, above all, causes a disturbance in the heart, as stated above (A. 2). Therefore above all it conduces to speech. Therefore it does not cause taciturnity.

*On the contrary,* Gregory says (Moral. v, 30) that "when anger does not vent itself outwardly by the lips, inwardly it burns the more fiercely."

*I answer that,* As stated above (A. 3; Q. 46, A. 4), anger both follows an act of reason, and hinders the reason: and in both respects it may cause taciturnity. On the part of the reason, when the judgment of reason prevails so far, that although it does not curb the appetite in its inordinate desire for vengeance, yet it curbs the tongue from unbridled speech. Wherefore Gregory says (Moral. v, 30): "Sometimes when the mind is disturbed, anger, as if in judgment, commands silence." On the part of the impediment to reason because, as stated above (A. 2), the disturbance of anger reaches to the outward members, and chiefly to those members which reflect more distinctly the emotions of the heart, such as the eyes, face and tongue; wherefore, as observed above (A. 2), "the tongue stammers, the countenance takes fire, the eyes grow fierce." Consequently anger may cause such a disturbance, that the tongue is altogether deprived of speech; and taciturnity is the result.

Reply Obj. 1: Anger sometimes goes so far as to hinder the reason from curbing the tongue: but sometimes it goes yet farther, so as to paralyze the tongue and other outward members.

And this suffices for the Reply to the Second Objection.

Reply Obj. 3: The disturbance of the heart may sometimes superabound to the extend that the movements of the outward members are hindered by the inordinate movement of the heart. Thence ensue taciturnity and immobility of the outward members; and sometimes even death. If, however, the disturbance be not so great, then "out of the abundance of the heart" thus disturbed, the mouth proceeds to speak.

TREATISE ON HABITS (QQ. 49-54)

## QUESTION 49

OF HABITS IN GENERAL, AS TO THEIR SUBSTANCE (In Four Articles)

After treating of human acts and passions, we now pass on to the consideration of the principles of human acts, and firstly of intrinsic principles, secondly of extrinsic principles. The intrinsic principle is power and habit; but as we have treated of powers in the First Part (Q. 77, seqq.), it remains for us to consider them in general: in the second place we shall consider virtues and vices and other like habits, which are the principles of human acts.

Concerning habits in general there are four points to consider: First, the substance of habits; second, their subject; third, the cause of their generation, increase, and corruption; fourth, how they are distinguished from one another.

Under the first head, there are four points of inquiry:

(1) Whether habit is a quality?

(2) Whether it is a distinct species of quality?

(3) Whether habit implies an order to an act?

(4) Of the necessity of habit.

FIRST ARTICLE [I-II, Q. 49, Art. 1]

Whether Habit Is a Quality?

Objection 1: It would seem that habit is not a quality. For Augustine says (QQ. lxxxiii, qu. 73): "this word 'habit' is derived from the verb 'to have.'" But "to have" belongs not only to quality, but also to the other categories: for we speak of ourselves as "having" quantity and money and other like things. Therefore habit is not a quality.

Obj. 2: Further, habit is reckoned as one of the predicaments; as may be clearly seen in the *Book on the Predicaments* (Categor. vi). But one predicament is not contained under another. Therefore habit is not a quality.

Obj. 3: Further, "every habit is a disposition," as is stated in the *Book of the Predicaments* (Categor. vi). Now disposition is "the order of that which has parts," as stated in Metaph. v, text. 24. But this belongs to the predicament Position. Therefore habit is not a quality.

*On the contrary,* The Philosopher says in the Book of Predicaments (Categor. vi) that "habit is a quality which is difficult to change."

*I answer that,* This word habitus (habit) is derived from habere (to have). Now habit is taken from this word in two ways; in one way, inasmuch as man, or any other thing, is said to "have" something; in another way, inasmuch as a particular thing has a relation ( se habet ) either in regard to itself, or in regard to something else.

Concerning the first, we must observe that "to have," as said in regard to anything that is "had," is common to the various predicaments. And so the Philosopher puts "to have" among the "post-predicaments," so called because they result from the various predicaments; as, for instance, opposition, priority, posterity, and such like. Now among things which are had, there seems to be this distinction, that there are some in which there is no medium between the "haver" and that which is had: as, for instance, there is no medium between the subject and quality or quantity. Then there are some in which there is a medium, but only a relation: as, for instance, a man is said to have a companion or a friend. And, further, there are some in which there is a medium, not indeed an action or passion, but something after the manner of action or passion: thus, for instance, something adorns or covers, and something else is adorned or covered: wherefore the Philosopher says (Metaph. v, text. 25) that "a habit is said to be, as it were, an action or a passion of the haver and that which is had"; as is the case in those things which we have about ourselves. And therefore these constitute a special genus of things, which are comprised under the predicament of "habit": of which the Philosopher says (Metaph. v, text. 25) that "there is a habit between clothing and the man who is clothed."

But if "to have" be taken according as a thing has a relation in regard to itself or to something else; in that case habit is a quality; since this mode of having is in respect of some quality: and of this the Philosopher says (Metaph. v, text. 25) that "habit is a disposition whereby that which is disposed is disposed well or ill, and this, either in regard to itself or in regard to another: thus health is a habit." And in this sense we speak of habit now. Wherefore we must say that habit is a quality.

Reply Obj. 1: This argument takes "to have" in the general sense: for thus it is common to many predicaments, as we have said.

Reply Obj. 2: This argument takes habit in the sense in which we understand it to be a medium between the haver, and that which is had: and in this sense it is a predicament, as we have said.

Reply Obj. 3: Disposition does always, indeed, imply an order of that which has parts: but this happens in three ways, as the Philosopher goes on at once to says (Metaph. v, text. 25): namely, "either as to place, or as to power, or as to species." "In saying this," as Simplicius observes in his *Commentary on the Predicaments,* "he includes all dispositions: bodily dispositions, when he says 'as to place,'" and this belongs to the predicament "Position," which is the order of parts in a place: "when he says 'as to power,' he includes all those dispositions which are in course of formation and not yet arrived at perfect usefulness," such as inchoate science and virtue: "and when he says, 'as to species,' he includes perfect dispositions, which are called habits," such as perfected science and virtue.

SECOND ARTICLE [I-II, Q. 49, Art. 2]

Whether Habit Is a Distinct Species of Quality?

Objection 1: It would seem that habit is not a distinct species of quality. Because, as we have said (A. 1), habit, in so far as it is a quality, is "a disposition whereby that which is disposed is disposed well or ill." But this happens in regard to any quality: for a thing happens to be well or ill disposed in regard also to shape, and in like manner, in regard to heat and cold, and in regard to all such things. Therefore habit is not a distinct species of quality.

Obj. 2: Further, the Philosopher says in the *Book of the Predicaments* (Categor. vi), that heat and cold are dispositions or habits, just as sickness and health. Therefore habit or disposition is not distinct from the other species of quality.

Obj. 3: Further, "difficult to change" is not a difference belonging to the predicament of quality, but rather to movement or passion. Now, no genus should be contracted to a species by a difference of another genus; but "differences should be proper to a genus," as the Philosopher says in *Metaph.* vii, text. 42. Therefore, since habit is "a quality difficult to change," it seems not to be a distinct species of quality.

*On the contrary,* The Philosopher says in the Book of the Predicaments (Categor. vi) that "one species of quality is habit and disposition."

*I answer that,* The Philosopher in the Book of Predicaments (Categor. vi) reckons disposition and habit as the first species of quality. Now Simplicius, in his *Commentary on the Predicaments,* explains the difference of these species as follows. He says "that some qualities are natural, and are in their subject in virtue of its nature, and are always there: but some are adventitious, being caused from without, and these can be lost. Now the latter," i.e. those which are adventitious, "are habits and dispositions, differing in the point of being easily or difficultly lost. As to natural qualities, some regard a thing in the point of its being in a state of potentiality; and thus we have the second species of quality: while others regard a thing which is in act; and this either deeply rooted therein or only on its surface. If deeply rooted, we have the third species of quality: if on the surface, we have the fourth species of quality, as shape, and form which is the shape of an animated being." But this distinction of the species of quality seems unsuitable. For there are many shapes, and passion-like qualities, which are not natural but adventitious: and there are also many dispositions which are not adventitious but natural, as health, beauty, and the like. Moreover, it does not suit the order of the species, since that which is the more natural is always first.

Therefore we must explain otherwise the distinction of dispositions and habits from other qualities. For quality, properly speaking, implies a certain mode of substance. Now mode, as Augustine says (Gen. ad lit. iv, 3), "is that which a measure determines": wherefore it implies a certain determination according to a certain measure. Therefore, just as that in accordance with which the material potentiality ( *potentia materiae* ) is determined to its substantial being, is called quality, which is a difference affecting the substance, so that, in accordance with the potentiality of the subject is determined to its accidental being, is called an accidental quality, which is also a kind of difference, as is clear from the Philosopher (Metaph. v, text. 19).

Now the mode o[r] determination of the subject to accidental being may be taken in regard to the very nature of the subject, or in regard to action, and passion resulting from its natural principles, which are matter and form; or again in regard to quantity. If we take the mode or determination of the subject in regard to quantity, we shall then have the fourth species of quality. And because quantity, considered in itself, is devoid of movement, and does not imply the notion of good or evil, so it does not concern the fourth species of quality whether a thing be well or ill disposed, nor quickly or slowly transitory.

But the mode o[r] determination of the subject, in regard to action or passion, is considered in the second and third species of quality. And therefore in both, we take into account whether a thing be done with ease or difficulty; whether it be transitory or lasting. But in them, we do not consider anything pertaining to the notion of good or evil: because movements and passions have not the aspect of an end, whereas good and evil are said in respect of an end.

On the other hand, the mode or determination of the subject, in regard to the nature of the thing, belongs to the first species of quality, which is habit and disposition: for the Philosopher says (Phys. vii, text. 17), when speaking of habits of the soul and of the body, that they are "dispositions of the perfect to the best; and by perfect I mean that which is disposed in accordance with its nature." And since the form itself and the nature of a thing is the end and the cause why a thing is made (Phys. ii, text. 25), therefore in the first species we consider both evil and good, and also changeableness, whether easy or difficult; inasmuch as a certain nature is the end of generation and movement. And so the Philosopher (Metaph. v, text. 25) defines habit, a "disposition whereby someone is disposed, well or ill"; and in *Ethic.* ii, 4, he says that by "habits we are directed well or ill in reference to the passions." For when the mode is suitable to the thing's nature, it has the aspect of good: and when it is unsuitable, it has the aspect of evil. And since nature is the first object of consideration in anything, for this reason habit is reckoned as the first species of quality.

Reply Obj. 1: Disposition implies a certain order, as stated above (A. 1, ad 3). Wherefore a man is not said to be disposed by some quality except in relation to something else. And if we add "well or ill," which belongs to the essential notion of habit, we must consider the quality's relation to the nature, which is the end. So in regard to shape, or heat, or cold, a man is not said to be well or ill disposed, except by reason of a relation to the nature of a thing, with regard to its suitability or unsuitability. Consequently even shapes and passion-like qualities, in so far as they are considered to be suitable or unsuitable to the nature of a thing, belong to habits or dispositions: for shape and color, according to their suitability to the nature of thing, concern beauty; while heat and cold, according to their suitability to the nature of a thing, concern health. And in this way heat and cold are put, by the Philosopher, in the first species of quality.

Wherefore it is clear how to answer the second objection: though some give another solution, as Simplicius says in his *Commentary on the Predicaments.*

Reply Obj. 3: This difference, "difficult to change," does not distinguish habit from the other species of quality, but from disposition. Now disposition may be taken in two ways; in one way, as the genus of habit, for disposition is included in the definition of habit (Metaph. v, text. 25): in another way, according as it is divided against habit. Again, disposition, properly so called, can be divided against habit in two ways: first, as perfect and imperfect within the same species; and thus we call it a disposition, retaining the name of the genus, when it is had imperfectly, so as to be easily lost: whereas we call it a habit, when it is had perfectly, so as not to be lost easily. And thus a disposition becomes a habit, just as a boy becomes a man. Secondly, they may be distinguished as diverse species of the one subaltern genus: so that we call dispositions, those qualities of the first species, which by reason of their very nature are easily lost, because they have changeable causes; e.g. sickness and health: whereas we call habits those qualities which, by reason of their very nature, are not easily changed, in that they have unchangeable causes, e.g. sciences and virtues. And in this sense, disposition does not become habit. The latter explanation seems more in keeping with the intention of Aristotle: for in order to confirm this distinction he adduces the common mode of speaking, according to which, when a quality is, by reason of its nature, easily changeable, and, through some accident, becomes difficultly changeable, then it is called a habit: while the contrary happens in regard to qualities, by reason of their nature, difficultly changeable: for supposing a man to have a science imperfectly, so as to be liable to lose it easily, we say that he is disposed to that science, rather than that he has the science. From this it is clear that the word "habit" implies a certain lastingness: while the word "disposition" does not.

Nor does it matter that thus to be easy and difficult to change are specific differences (of a quality), although they belong to passion and movement, and not the genus of quality. For these differences, though apparently accidental to quality, nevertheless designate differences which are proper and essential to quality. In the same way, in the genus of substance we often take accidental instead of substantial differences, in so far as by the former, essential principles are designated.

THIRD ARTICLE [I-II, Q. 49, Art. 3]

Whether Habit Implies Order to an Act?

Objection 1: It would seem that habit does not imply order to an act. For everything acts according as it is in act. But the Philosopher says (De Anima iii, text 8), that "when one is become knowing by habit, one is still in a state of potentiality, but otherwise than before learning." Therefore habit does not imply the relation of a principle to an act.

Obj. 2: Further, that which is put in the definition of a thing, belongs to it essentially. But to be a principle of action, is put in the definition of power, as we read in *Metaph.* v, text. 17. Therefore to be the principle of an act belongs to power essentially. Now that which is essential is first in every genus. If therefore, habit also is a principle of act, it follows that it is posterior to power. And so habit and disposition will not be the first species of quality.

Obj. 3: Further, health is sometimes a habit, and so are leanness and beauty. But these do not indicate relation to an act. Therefore it is not essential to habit to be a principle of act.

*On the contrary,* Augustine says (De Bono Conjug. xxi) that "habit is that whereby something is done when necessary." And the Commentator says (De Anima iii) that "habit is that whereby we act when we will."

*I answer that,* To have relation to an act may belong to habit, both in regard to the nature of habit, and in regard to the subject in which the habit is. In regard to the nature of habit, it belongs to every habit to have relation to an act. For it is essential to habit to imply some relation to a thing's nature, in so far as it is suitable or unsuitable thereto. But a thing's nature, which is the end of generation, is further ordained to another end, which is either an operation, or the product of an operation, to which one attains by means of operation. Wherefore habit implies relation not only to the very nature of a thing, but also, consequently, to operation, inasmuch as this is the end of nature, or conducive to the end. Whence also it is stated (Metaph. v, text. 25) in the definition of habit, that it is a disposition whereby that which is disposed, is well or ill disposed either in regard to itself, that is to its nature, or in regard to something else, that is to the end.

But there are some habits, which even on the part of the subject in which they are, imply primarily and principally relation to an act. For, as we have said, habit primarily and of itself implies a relation to the thing's nature. If therefore the nature of a thing, in which the habit is, consists in this very relation to an act, it follows that the habit principally implies relation to an act. Now it is clear that the nature and the notion of power is that it should be a principle of act. Wherefore every habit is subjected in a power, implies principally relation to an act.

Reply Obj. 1: Habit is an act, in so far as it is a quality: and in this respect it can be a principle of operation. It is, however, in a state of potentiality in respect to operation. Wherefore habit is called first act, and operation, second act; as it is explained in *De Anima* ii, text. 5.

Reply Obj. 2: It is not the essence of habit to be related to power, but to be related to nature. And as nature precedes action, to which power is related, therefore habit is put before power as a species of quality.

Reply Obj. 3: Health is said to be a habit, or a habitual disposition, in relation to nature, as stated above. But in so far as nature is a principle of act, it consequently implies a relation to act. Wherefore the Philosopher says (De Hist. Animal. x, 1), that man, or one of his members, is called healthy, "when he can perform the operation of a healthy man." And the same applies to other habits.

FOURTH ARTICLE [I-II, Q. 49, Art. 4]

Whether Habits Are Necessary?

Objection 1: It would seem that habits are not necessary. For by habits we are well or ill disposed in respect of something, as stated above. But a thing is well or ill disposed by its form: for in respect of its form a thing is good, even as it is a being. Therefore there is no necessity for habits.

Obj. 2: Further, habit implies relation to an act. But power implies sufficiently a principle of act: for even the natural powers, without any habits, are principles of acts. Therefore there was no necessity for habits.

Obj. 3: Further, as power is related to good and evil, so also is habit: and as power does not always act, so neither does habit. Given, therefore, the powers, habits become superfluous.

*On the contrary,* Habits are perfections (Phys. vii, text. 17). But perfection is of the greatest necessity to a thing: since it is in the nature of an end. Therefore it is necessary that there should be habits.

*I answer that,* As we have said above (AA. 2, 3), habit implies a disposition in relation to a thing's nature, and to its operation or end, by reason of which disposition a thing is well or ill disposed thereto. Now for a thing to need to be disposed to something else, three conditions are necessary. The first condition is that which is disposed should be distinct from that to which it is disposed; and so, that it should be related to it as potentiality is to act. Whence, if there is a being whose nature is not composed of potentiality and act, and whose substance is its own operation, which itself is for itself, there we can find no room for habit and disposition, as is clearly the case in God.

The second condition is, that that which is in a state of potentiality in regard to something else, be capable of determination in several ways and to various things. Whence if something be in a state of potentiality in regard to something else, but in regard to that only, there we find no room for disposition and habit: for such a subject from its own nature has the due relation to such an act. Wherefore if a heavenly body be composed of matter and form, since that matter is not in a state of potentiality to another form, as we said in the First Part (Q. 56, A. 2) there is no need for disposition or habit in respect of the form, or even in respect of operation, since the nature of the heavenly body is not in a state of potentiality to more than one fixed movement.

The third condition is that in disposing the subject to one of those things to which it is in potentiality, several things should occur, capable of being adjusted in various ways: so as to dispose the subject well or ill to its form or to its operation. Wherefore the simple qualities of the elements which suit the natures of the elements in one single fixed way, are not called dispositions or habits, but "simple qualities": but we call dispositions or habits, such things as health, beauty, and so forth, which imply the adjustment of several things which may vary in their relative adjustability. For this reason the Philosopher says (Metaph. v, text. 24, 25) that "habit is a disposition": and disposition is "the order of that which has parts either as to place, or as to potentiality, or as to species," as we have said above (A. 1, ad 3). Wherefore, since there are many things for whose natures and operations several things must concur which may vary in their relative adjustability, it follows that habit is necessary.

Reply Obj. 1: By the form the nature of a thing is perfected: yet the subject needs to be disposed in regard to the form by some disposition. But the form itself is further ordained to operation, which is either the end, or the means to the end. And if the form is limited to one fixed operation, no further disposition, besides the form itself, is needed for the operation. But if the form be such that it can operate in diverse ways, as the soul; it needs to be disposed to its operations by means of habits.

Reply Obj. 2: Power sometimes has a relation to many things: and then it needs to be determined by something else. But if a power has not a relation to many things, it does not need a habit to determine it, as we have said. For this reason the natural forces do not perform their operations by means of habits: because they are of themselves determined to one mode of operation.

Reply Obj. 3: The same habit has not a relation to good and evil, as will be made clear further on (Q. 54, A. 3): whereas the same power has a relation to good and evil. And, therefore, habits are necessary that the powers be determined to good.

## QUESTION 50

OF THE SUBJECT OF HABITS (In Six Articles)

We consider next the subject of habits: and under this head there are six points of inquiry:

(1) Whether there is a habit in the body?

(2) Whether the soul is a subject of habit, in respect of its essence or in respect of its power?

(3) Whether in the powers of the sensitive part there can be a habit?

(4) Whether there is a habit in the intellect?

(5) Whether there is a habit in the will?

(6) Whether there is a habit in separate substances?

FIRST ARTICLE [I-II, Q. 50, Art. 1]

Whether There Is a Habit in the Body?

Objection 1: It would seem that there is not a habit in the body. For, as the Commentator says (De Anima iii), "a habit is that whereby we act when we will." But bodily actions are not subject to the will, since they are natural. Therefore there can be no habit in the body.

Obj. 2: Further, all bodily dispositions are easy to change. But habit is a quality, difficult to change. Therefore no bodily disposition can be a habit.

Obj. 3: Further, all bodily dispositions are subject to change. But change can only be in the third species of quality, which is divided against habit. Therefore there is no habit in the body.

*On the contrary,* The Philosopher says in the Book of Predicaments (De Categor. vi) that health of the body and incurable disease are called habits.

*I answer that,* As we have said above (Q. 49, AA. 2 seqq.), habit is a disposition of a subject which is in a state of potentiality either to form or to operation. Therefore in so far as habit implies disposition to operation, no habit is principally in the body as its subject. For every operation of the body proceeds either from a natural quality of the body or from the soul moving the body. Consequently, as to those operations which proceed from its nature, the body is not disposed by a habit: because the natural forces are determined to one mode of operation; and we have already said (Q. 49, A. 4) that it is when the subject is in potentiality to many things that a habitual disposition is required. As to the operations which proceed from the soul through the body, they belong principally to the soul, and secondarily to the body. Now habits are in proportion to their operations: whence "by like acts like habits are formed" (Ethic. ii, 1, 2). And therefore the dispositions to such operations are principally in the soul. But they can be secondarily in the body: to wit, in so far as the body is disposed and enabled with promptitude to help in the operations of the soul.

If, however, we speak of the disposition of the subject to form, thus a habitual disposition can be in the body, which is related to the soul as a subject is to its form. And in this way health and beauty and such like are called habitual dispositions. Yet they have not the nature of habit perfectly: because their causes, of their very nature, are easily changeable.

On the other hand, as Simplicius reports in his Commentary on the Predicaments, Alexander denied absolutely that habits or dispositions of the first species are in the body: and held that the first species of quality belonged to the soul alone. And he held that Aristotle mentions health and sickness in the Book on the Predicaments not as though they belonged to the first species of quality, but by way of example: so that he would mean that just as health and sickness may be easy or difficult to change, so also are all the qualities of the first species, which are called habits and dispositions. But this is clearly contrary to the intention of Aristotle: both because he speaks in the same way of health and sickness as examples, as of virtue and science; and because in *Phys.* vii, text. 17, he expressly mentions beauty and health among habits.

Reply Obj. 1: This objection runs in the sense of habit as a disposition to operation, and of those actions of the body which are from nature: but not in the sense of those actions which proceed from the soul, and the principle of which is the will.

Reply Obj. 2: Bodily dispositions are not simply difficult to change on account of the changeableness of their bodily causes. But they may be difficult to change by comparison to such a subject, because, to wit, as long as such a subject endures, they cannot be removed; or because they are difficult to change, by comparison to other dispositions. But qualities of the soul are simply difficult to change, on account of the unchangeableness of the subject.

And therefore he does not say that health which is difficult to change is a habit simply: but that it is "as a habit," as we read in the Greek [* *isos hexin* (Categor. viii)]. On the other hand, the qualities of the soul are called habits simply.

Reply Obj. 3: Bodily dispositions which are in the first species of quality, as some maintained, differ from qualities of the third species, in this, that the qualities of the third species consist in some "becoming" and movement, as it were, wherefore they are called passions or passible qualities. But when they have attained to perfection (specific perfection, so to speak), they have then passed into the first species of quality. But Simplicius in his *Commentary* disapproves of this; for in this way heating would be in the third species, and heat in the first species of quality; whereas Aristotle puts heat in the third.

Wherefore Porphyrius, as Simplicius reports (Commentary), says that passion or passion-like quality, disposition and habit, differ in bodies by way of intensity and remissness. For when a thing receives heat in this only that it is being heated, and not so as to be able to give heat, then we have passion, if it is transitory; or passion-like quality if it is permanent. But when it has been brought to the point that it is able to heat something else, then it is a disposition; and if it goes so far as to be firmly fixed and to become difficult to change, then it will be a habit: so that disposition would be a certain intensity of passion or passion-like quality, and habit an intensity or disposition. But Simplicius disapproves of this, for such intensity and remissness do not imply diversity on the part of the form itself, but on the part of the diverse participation thereof by the subject; so that there would be no diversity among the species of quality. And therefore we must say otherwise that, as was explained above (Q. 49, A. 2, ad 1), the adjustment of the passion-like qualities themselves, according to their suitability to nature, implies the notion of disposition: and so, when a change takes place in these same passion-like qualities, which are heat and cold, moisture and dryness, there results a change as to sickness and health. But change does not occur in regard to like habits and dispositions, primarily and of themselves.

SECOND ARTICLE [I-II, Q. 50, art. 2]

Whether the Soul Is the Subject of Habit in Respect of Its Essence or in Respect of Its Power?

Objection 1: It would seem that habit is in the soul in respect of its essence rather than in respect of its powers. For we speak of dispositions and habits in relation to nature, as stated above (Q. 49, A. 2). But nature regards the essence of the soul rather than the powers; because it is in respect of its essence that the soul is the nature of such a body and the form thereof. Therefore habits are in the soul in respect of its essence and not in respect of its powers.

Obj. 2: Further, accident is not the subject of accident. Now habit is an accident. But the powers of the soul are in the genus of accident, as we have said in the First Part (Q. 77, A. 1, ad 5). Therefore habit is not in the soul in respect of its powers.

Obj. 3: Further, the subject is prior to that which is in the subject. But since habit belongs to the first species of quality, it is prior to power, which belongs to the second species. Therefore habit is not in a power of the soul as its subject.

*On the contrary,* The Philosopher (Ethic. i, 13) puts various habits in the various powers of the soul.

*I answer that,* As we have said above (Q. 49, AA. 2, 3), habit implies a certain disposition in relation to nature or to operation. If therefore we take habit as having a relation to nature, it cannot be in the soul—that is, if we speak of human nature: for the soul itself is the form completing the human nature; so that, regarded in this way, habit or disposition is rather to be found in the body by reason of its relation to the soul, than in the soul by reason of its relation to the body. But if we speak of a higher nature, of which man may become a partaker, according to 2 Pet. 1, "that we may be partakers of the Divine Nature": thus nothing hinders some habit, namely, grace, from being in the soul in respect of its essence, as we shall state later on (Q. 110, A. 4).

On the other hand, if we take habit in its relation to operation, it is chiefly thus that habits are found in the soul: in so far as the soul is not determined to one operation, but is indifferent to many, which is a condition for a habit, as we have said above (Q. 49, A. 4). And since the soul is the principle of operation through its powers, therefore, regarded in this sense, habits are in the soul in respect of its powers.

Reply Obj. 1: The essence of the soul belongs to human nature, not as a subject requiring to be disposed to something further, but as a form and nature to which someone is disposed.

Reply Obj. 2: Accident is not of itself the subject of accident. But since among accidents themselves there is a certain order, the subject, according as it is under one accident, is conceived as the subject of a further accident. In this way we say that one accident is the subject of another; as superficies is the subject of color, in which sense power is the subject of habit.

Reply Obj. 3: Habit takes precedence of power, according as it implies a disposition to nature: whereas power always implies a relation to operation, which is posterior, since nature is the principle of operation. But the habit whose subject is a power, does not imply relation to nature, but to operation. Wherefore it is posterior to power. Or, we may say that habit takes precedence of power, as the complete takes precedence of the incomplete, and as act takes precedence of potentiality. For act is naturally prior to potentiality, though potentiality is prior in order of generation and time, as stated in *Metaph.* vii, text. 17; ix, text. 13.

THIRD ARTICLE [I-II, Q. 50, Art. 3]

Whether There Can Be Any Habits in the Powers of the Sensitive Part?

Objection 1: It would seem that there cannot be any habits in the powers of the sensitive part. For as the nutritive power is an irrational part, so is the sensitive power. But there can be no habits in the powers of the nutritive part. Therefore we ought not to put any habit in the powers of the sensitive part.

Obj. 2: Further, the sensitive parts are common to us and the brutes. But there are not any habits in brutes: for in them there is no will, which is put in the definition of habit, as we have said above (Q. 49, A. 3). Therefore there are no habits in the sensitive powers.

Obj. 3: Further, the habits of the soul are sciences and virtues: and just as science is related to the apprehensive power, so it virtue related to the appetitive power. But in the sensitive powers there are no sciences: since science is of universals, which the sensitive powers cannot apprehend. Therefore, neither can there be habits of virtue in the sensitive part.

*On the contrary,* The Philosopher says (Ethic. iii, 10) that "some virtues," namely, temperance and fortitude, "belong to the irrational part."

*I answer that,* The sensitive powers can be considered in two ways: first, according as they act from natural instinct: secondly, according as they act at the command of reason. According as they act from natural instinct, they are ordained to one thing, even as nature is; but according as they act at the command of reason, they can be ordained to various things. And thus there can be habits in them, by which they are well or ill disposed in regard to something.

Reply Obj. 1: The powers of the nutritive part have not an inborn aptitude to obey the command of reason, and therefore there are no habits in them. But the sensitive powers have an inborn aptitude to obey the command of reason; and therefore habits can be in them: for in so far as they obey reason, in a certain sense they are said to be rational, as stated in *Ethic.* i, 13.

Reply Obj. 2: The sensitive powers of dumb animals do not act at the command of reason; but if they are left to themselves, such animals act from natural instinct: and so in them there are no habits ordained to operations. There are in them, however, certain dispositions in relation to nature, as health and beauty. But whereas by man's reason brutes are disposed by a sort of custom to do things in this or that way, so in this sense, to a certain extent, we can admit the existence of habits in dumb animals: wherefore Augustine says (QQ. lxxxiii, qu. 36): "We find the most untamed beasts, deterred by fear of pain, from that wherein they took the keenest pleasure; and when this has become a custom in them, we say that they are tame and gentle." But the habit is incomplete, as to the use of the will, for they have not that power of using or of refraining, which seems to belong to the notion of habit: and therefore, properly speaking, there can be no habits in them.

Reply Obj. 3: The sensitive appetite has an inborn aptitude to be moved by the rational appetite, as stated in *De Anima* iii, text. 57: but the rational powers of apprehension have an inborn aptitude to receive from the sensitive powers. And therefore it is more suitable that habits should be in the powers of sensitive appetite than in the powers of sensitive apprehension, since in the powers of sensitive appetite habits do not exist except according as they act at the command of the reason. And yet even in the interior powers of sensitive apprehension, we may admit of certain habits whereby man has a facility of memory, thought or imagination: wherefore also the Philosopher says (De Memor. et Remin. ii) that "custom conduces much to a good memory": the reason of which is that these powers also are moved to act at the command of the reason.

On the other hand the exterior apprehensive powers, as sight, hearing and the like, are not susceptible of habits, but are ordained to their fixed acts, according to the disposition of their nature, just as the members of the body, for there are no habits in them, but rather in the powers which command their movements.

FOURTH ARTICLE [I-II, Q. 50, Art. 4]

Whether There Is Any Habit in the Intellect?

Objection 1: It would seem that there are no habits in the intellect. For habits are in conformity with operations, as stated above (A. 1). But the operations of man are common to soul and body, as stated in *De Anima* i, text. 64. Therefore also are habits. But the intellect is not an act of the body (De Anima iii, text. 6). Therefore the intellect is not the subject of a habit.

Obj. 2: Further, whatever is in a thing, is there according to the mode of that in which it is. But that which is form without matter, is act only: whereas what is composed of form and matter, has potentiality and act at the same time. Therefore nothing at the same time potential and actual can be in that which is form only, but only in that which is composed of matter and form. Now the intellect is form without matter. Therefore habit, which has potentiality at the same time as act, being a sort of medium between the two, cannot be in the intellect; but only in the *conjunction,* which is composed of soul and body.

Obj. 3: Further, habit is a disposition whereby we are well or ill disposed in regard to something, as is said (Metaph. v, text. 25). But that anyone should be well or ill disposed to an act of the intellect is due to some disposition of the body: wherefore also it is stated (De Anima ii, text. 94) that "we observe men with soft flesh to be quick witted." Therefore the habits of knowledge are not in the intellect, which is separate, but in some power which is the act of some part of the body.

*On the contrary,* The Philosopher (Ethic. vi, 2, 3, 10) puts science, wisdom and understanding, which is the habit of first principles, in the intellective part of the soul.

*I answer that,* concerning intellective habits there have been various opinions. Some, supposing that there was only one *possible* [*See First Part, Q. 79, A. 2, ad 2] intellect for all men, were bound to hold that habits of knowledge are not in the intellect itself, but in the interior sensitive powers. For it is manifest that men differ in habits; and so it was impossible to put the habits of knowledge directly in that, which, being only one, would be common to all men. Wherefore if there were but one single "possible" intellect of all men, the habits of science, in which men differ from one another, could not be in the "possible" intellect as their subject, but would be in the interior sensitive powers, which differ in various men.

Now, in the first place, this supposition is contrary to the mind of Aristotle. For it is manifest that the sensitive powers are rational, not by their essence, but only by participation (Ethic. i, 13). Now the Philosopher puts the intellectual virtues, which are wisdom, science and understanding, in that which is rational by its essence. Wherefore they are not in the sensitive powers, but in the intellect itself. Moreover he says expressly (De Anima iii, text. 8, 18) that when the "possible" intellect "is thus identified with each thing," that is, when it is reduced to act in respect of singulars by the intelligible species, "then it is said to be in act, as the knower is said to be in act; and this happens when the intellect can act of itself," i.e. by considering: "and even then it is in potentiality in a sense; but not in the same way as before learning and discovering." Therefore the "possible" intellect itself is the subject of the habit of science, by which the intellect, even though it be not actually considering, is able to consider. In the second place, this supposition is contrary to the truth. For as to whom belongs the operation, belongs also the power to operate, belongs also the habit. But to understand and to consider is the proper act of the intellect. Therefore also the habit whereby one considers is properly in the intellect itself.

Reply Obj. 1: Some said, as Simplicius reports in his *Commentary on the Predicaments,* that, since every operation of man is to a certain extent an operation of the *conjunctum,* as the Philosopher says (De Anima i, text. 64); therefore no habit is in the soul only, but in the *conjunctum.* And from this it follows that no habit is in the intellect, for the intellect is separate, as ran the argument, given above. But the argument is not cogent. For habit is not a disposition of the object to the power, but rather a disposition of the power to the object: wherefore the habit needs to be in that power which is principle of the act, and not in that which is compared to the power as its object.

Now the act of understanding is not said to be common to soul and body, except in respect of the phantasm, as is stated in *De Anima* , text. 66. But it is clear that the phantasm is compared as object to the passive intellect (De Anima iii, text. 3, 39). Whence it follows that the intellective habit is chiefly on the part of the intellect itself; and not on the part of the phantasm, which is common to soul and body. And therefore we must say that the "possible" intellect is the subject of habit, which is in potentiality to many: and this belongs, above all, to the "possible" intellect. Wherefore the "possible" intellect is the subject of intellectual habits.

Reply Obj. 2: As potentiality to sensible being belongs to corporeal matter, so potentiality to intellectual being belongs to the "possible" intellect. Wherefore nothing forbids habit to be in the "possible" intellect, for it is midway between pure potentiality and perfect act.

Reply Obj. 3: Because the apprehensive powers inwardly prepare their proper objects for the *possible intellect,* therefore it is by the good disposition of these powers, to which the good disposition of the body cooperates, that man is rendered apt to understand. And so in a secondary way the intellective habit can be in these powers. But principally it is in the "possible" intellect.

FIFTH ARTICLE [I-II, Q. 50, Art. 5]

Whether Any Habit Is in the Will?

Objection 1: It would seem that there is not a habit in the will. For the habit which is in the intellect is the intelligible species, by means of which the intellect actually understands. But the will does not act by means of species. Therefore the will is not the subject of habit.

Obj. 2: Further, no habit is allotted to the active intellect, as there is to the "possible" intellect, because the former is an active power. But the will is above all an active power, because it moves all the powers to their acts, as stated above (Q. 9, A. 1). Therefore there is no habit in the will.

Obj. 3: Further, in the natural powers there is no habit, because, by reason of their nature, they are determinate to one thing. But the will, by reason of its nature, is ordained to tend to the good which reason directs. Therefore there is no habit in the will.

*On the contrary,* Justice is a habit. But justice is in the will; for it is "a habit whereby men will and do that which is just" (Ethic. v, 1). Therefore the will is the subject of a habit.

*I answer that,* Every power which may be variously directed to act, needs a habit whereby it is well disposed to its act. Now since the will is a rational power, it may be variously directed to act. And therefore in the will we must admit the presence of a habit whereby it is well disposed to its act. Moreover, from the very nature of habit, it is clear that it is principally related to the will; inasmuch as habit "is that which one uses when one wills," as stated above (A. 1).

Reply Obj. 1: Even as in the intellect there is a species which is the likeness of the object; so in the will, and in every appetitive power there must be something by which the power is inclined to its object; for the act of the appetitive power is nothing but a certain inclination, as we have said above (Q. 6, A. 4; Q. 22, A. 2). And therefore in respect of those things to which it is inclined sufficiently by the nature of the power itself, the power needs no quality to incline it. But since it is necessary, for the end of human life, that the appetitive power be inclined to something fixed, to which it is not inclined by the nature of the power, which has a relation to many and various things, therefore it is necessary that, in the will and in the other appetitive powers, there be certain qualities to incline them, and these are called habits.

Reply Obj. 2: The active intellect is active only, and in no way passive. But the will, and every appetitive power, is both mover and moved (De Anima iii, text. 54). And therefore the comparison between them does not hold; for to be susceptible of habit belongs to that which is somehow in potentiality.

Reply Obj. 3: The will from the very nature of the power is inclined to the good of the reason. But because this good is varied in many ways, the will needs to be inclined, by means of a habit, to some fixed good of the reason, in order that action may follow more promptly.

SIXTH ARTICLE [I-II, Q. 50, Art. 6]

Whether There Are Habits in the Angels?

Objection 1: It would seem that there are no habits in the angels. For Maximus, commentator of Dionysius (Coel. Hier. vii), says: "It is not proper to suppose that there are intellectual (i.e. spiritual) powers in the divine intelligences (i.e. in the angels) after the manner of accidents, as in us: as though one were in the other as in a subject: for accident of any kind is foreign to them." But every habit is an accident. Therefore there are no habits in the angels.

Obj. 2: Further, as Dionysius says (Coel. Hier. iv): "The holy dispositions of the heavenly essences participate, above all other things, in God's goodness." But that which is of itself ( *per se* ) is prior to and more powerful than that which is by another ( per aliud ). Therefore the angelic essences are perfected of themselves unto conformity with God, and therefore not by means of habits. And this seems to have been the reasoning of Maximus, who in the same passage adds: "For if this were the case, surely their essence would not remain in itself, nor could it have been as far as possible deified of itself."

Obj. 3: Further, habit is a disposition (Metaph. v, text. 25). But disposition, as is said in the same book, is "the order of that which has parts." Since, therefore, angels are simple substances, it seems that there are no dispositions and habits in them.

*On the contrary,* Dionysius says (Coel. Hier. vii) that the angels of the first hierarchy are called: "Fire-bearers and Thrones and Outpouring of Wisdom, by which is indicated the godlike nature of their habits."

*I answer that,* Some have thought that there are no habits in the angels, and that whatever is said of them, is said essentially. Whence Maximus, after the words which we have quoted, says: "Their dispositions, and the powers which are in them, are essential, through the absence of matter in them." And Simplicius says the same in his *Commentary on the Predicaments:* "Wisdom which is in the soul is its habit: but that which is in the intellect, is its substance. For everything divine is sufficient of itself, and exists in itself."

Now this opinion contains some truth, and some error. For it is manifest from what we have said (Q. 49, A. 4) that only a being in potentiality is the subject of habit. So the above-mentioned commentators considered that angels are immaterial substances, and that there is no material potentiality in them, and on that account, excluded from them habit and any kind of accident. Yet since though there is no material potentiality in angels, there is still some potentiality in them (for to be pure act belongs to God alone), therefore, as far as potentiality is found to be in them, so far may habits be found in them. But because the potentiality of matter and the potentiality of intellectual substance are not of the same kind. Whence, Simplicius says in his *Commentary on the Predicaments* that: "The habits of the intellectual substance are not like the habits here below, but rather are they like simple and immaterial images which it contains in itself."

However, the angelic intellect and the human intellect differ with regard to this habit. For the human intellect, being the lowest in the intellectual order, is in potentiality as regards all intelligible things, just as primal matter is in respect of all sensible forms; and therefore for the understanding of all things, it needs some habit. But the angelic intellect is not as a pure potentiality in the order of intelligible things, but as an act; not indeed as pure act (for this belongs to God alone), but with an admixture of some potentiality: and the higher it is, the less potentiality it has. And therefore, as we said in the First Part (Q. 55, A. 1), so far as it is in potentiality, so far is it in need of habitual perfection by means of intelligible species in regard to its proper operation: but so far as it is in act, through its own essence it can understand some things, at least itself, and other things according to the mode of its substance, as stated in *De Causis:* and the more perfect it is, the more perfectly will it understand.

But since no angel attains to the perfection of God, but all are infinitely distant therefrom; for this reason, in order to attain to God Himself, through intellect and will, the angels need some habits, being as it were in potentiality in regard to that Pure Act. Wherefore Dionysius says (Coel. Hier. vii) that their habits are "godlike," that is to say, that by them they are made like to God.

But those habits that are dispositions to the natural being are not in angels, since they are immaterial.

Reply Obj. 1: This saying of Maximus must be understood of material habits and accidents.

Reply Obj. 2: As to that which belongs to angels by their essence, they do not need a habit. But as they are not so far beings of themselves, as not to partake of Divine wisdom and goodness, therefore, so far as they need to partake of something from without, so far do they need to have habits.

Reply Obj. 3: In angels there are no essential parts: but there are potential parts, in so far as their intellect is perfected by several species, and in so far as their will has a relation to several things.

# QUESTION 51

OF THE CAUSE OF HABITS, AS TO THEIR FORMATION (In Four Articles)

We must next consider the cause of habits: and firstly, as to their formation; secondly, as to their increase; thirdly, as to their diminution and corruption. Under the first head there are four points of inquiry:

(1) Whether any habit is from nature?

(2) Whether any habit is caused by acts?

(3) Whether any habit can be caused by one act?

(4) Whether any habits are infused in man by God?

FIRST ARTICLE [I-II, Q. 51, Art. 1]

Whether Any Habit Is from Nature?

Objection 1: It would seem that no habit is from nature. For the use of those things which are from nature does not depend on the will. But habit "is that which we use when we will," as the Commentator says on *De Anima* iii. Therefore habit is not from nature.

Obj. 2: Further, nature does not employ two where one is sufficient. But the powers of the soul are from nature. If therefore the habits of the powers were from nature, habit and power would be one.

Obj. 3: Further, nature does not fail in necessaries. But habits are necessary in order to act well, as we have stated above (Q. 49, A. 4). If therefore any habits were from nature, it seems that nature would not fail to cause all necessary habits: but this is clearly false. Therefore habits are not from nature.

*On the contrary,* In Ethic. vi, 6, among other habits, place is given to understanding of first principles, which habit is from nature: wherefore also first principles are said to be known naturally.

*I answer that,* One thing can be natural to another in two ways. First in respect of the specific nature, as the faculty of laughing is natural to man, and it is natural to fire to have an upward tendency. Secondly, in respect of the individual nature, as it is natural to Socrates or Plato to be prone to sickness or inclined to health, in accordance with their respective temperaments. Again, in respect of both natures, something may be called natural in two ways: first, because it entirely is from the nature; secondly, because it is partly from nature, and partly from an extrinsic principle. For instance, when a man is healed by himself, his health is entirely from nature; but when a man is healed by means of medicine, health is partly from nature, partly from an extrinsic principle.

Thus, then, if we speak of habit as a disposition of the subject in relation to form or nature, it may be natural in either of the foregoing ways. For there is a certain natural disposition demanded by the human species, so that no man can be without it. And this disposition is natural in respect of the specific nature. But since such a disposition has a certain latitude, it happens that different grades of this disposition are becoming to different men in respect of the individual nature. And this disposition may be either entirely from nature, or partly from nature, and partly from an extrinsic principle, as we have said of those who are healed by means of art.

But the habit which is a disposition to operation, and whose subject is a power of the soul, as stated above (Q. 50, A. 2), may be natural whether in respect of the specific nature or in respect of the individual nature: in respect of the specific nature, on the part of the soul itself, which, since it is the form of the body, is the specific principle; but in respect of the individual nature, on the part of the body, which is the material principle. Yet in neither way does it happen that there are natural habits in man, so that they be entirely from nature. In the angels, indeed, this does happen, since they have intelligible species naturally impressed on them, which cannot be said of the human soul, as we have said in the First Part (Q. 55, A. 2; Q. 84, A. 3).

There are, therefore, in man certain natural habits, owing their existence, partly to nature, and partly to some extrinsic principle: in one way, indeed, in the apprehensive powers; in another way, in the appetitive powers. For in the apprehensive powers there may be a natural habit by way of a beginning, both in respect of the specific nature, and in respect of the individual nature. This happens with regard to the specific nature, on the part of the soul itself: thus the understanding of first principles is called a natural habit. For it is owing to the very nature of the intellectual soul that man, having once grasped what is a whole and what is a part, should at once perceive that every whole is larger than its part: and in like manner with regard to other such principles. Yet what is a whole, and what is a part—this he cannot know except through the intelligible species which he has received from phantasms: and for this reason, the Philosopher at the end of the *Posterior Analytics* shows that knowledge of principles comes to us from the senses.

But in respect of the individual nature, a habit of knowledge is natural as to its beginning, in so far as one man, from the disposition of his organs of sense, is more apt than another to understand well, since we need the sensitive powers for the operation of the intellect.

In the appetitive powers, however, no habit is natural in its beginning, on the part of the soul itself, as to the substance of the habit; but only as to certain principles thereof, as, for instance, the principles of common law are called the "nurseries of virtue." The reason of this is because the inclination to its proper objects, which seems to be the beginning of a habit, does not belong to the habit, but rather to the very nature of the powers.

But on the part of the body, in respect of the individual nature, there are some appetitive habits by way of natural beginnings. For some are disposed from their own bodily temperament to chastity or meekness or such like.

Reply Obj. 1: This objection takes nature as divided against reason and will; whereas reason itself and will belong to the nature of man.

Reply Obj. 2: Something may be added even naturally to the nature of a power, while it cannot belong to the power itself. For instance, with regard to the angels, it cannot belong to the intellective power itself capable of knowing all things: for thus it would have to be the act of all things, which belongs to God alone. Because that by which something is known, must needs be the actual likeness of the thing known: whence it would follow, if the power of the angel knew all things by itself, that it was the likeness and act of all things. Wherefore there must needs be added to the angels' intellective power, some intelligible species, which are likenesses of things understood: for it is by participation of the Divine wisdom and not by their own essence, that their intellect can be actually those things which they understand. And so it is clear that not everything belonging to a natural habit can belong to the power.

Reply Obj. 3: Nature is not equally inclined to cause all the various kinds of habits: since some can be caused by nature, and some not, as we have said above. And so it does not follow that because some habits are natural, therefore all are natural.

SECOND ARTICLE [I-II, Q. 51, Art. 2]

Whether Any Habit Is Caused by Acts?

Objection 1: It would seem that no habit is caused by acts. For habit is a quality, as we have said above (Q. 49, A. 1). Now every quality is caused in a subject, according to the latter's receptivity. Since then the agent, inasmuch as it acts, does not receive but rather gives: it seems impossible for a habit to be caused in an agent by its own acts.

Obj. 2: Further, the thing wherein a quality is caused is moved to that quality, as may be clearly seen in that which is heated or cooled: whereas that which produces the act that causes the quality, moves, as may be seen in that which heats or cools. If therefore habits were caused in anything by its own act, it would follow that the same would be mover and moved, active and passive: which is impossible, as stated in Physics iii, 8.

Obj. 3: Further, the effect cannot be more noble than its cause. But habit is more noble than the act which precedes the habit; as is clear from the fact that the latter produces more noble acts. Therefore habit cannot be caused by an act which precedes the habit.

*On the contrary,* The Philosopher (Ethic. ii, 1, 2) teaches that habits of virtue and vice are caused by acts.

*I answer that,* In the agent there is sometimes only the active principle of its act: for instance in fire there is only the active principle of heating. And in such an agent a habit cannot be caused by its own act: for which reason natural things cannot become accustomed or unaccustomed, as is stated in *Ethic.* ii, 1. But a certain agent is to be found, in which there is both the active and the passive principle of its act, as we see in human acts. For the acts of the appetitive power proceed from that same power according as it is moved by the apprehensive power presenting the object: and further, the intellective power, according as it reasons about conclusions, has, as it were, an active principle in a self-evident proposition. Wherefore by such acts habits can be caused in their agents; not indeed with regard to the first active principle, but with regard to that principle of the act, which principle is a mover moved. For everything that is passive and moved by another, is disposed by the action of the agent; wherefore if the acts be multiplied a certain quality is formed in the power which is passive and moved, which quality is called a habit: just as the habits of moral virtue are caused in the appetitive powers, according as they are moved by the reason, and as the habits of science are caused in the intellect, according as it is moved by first propositions.

Reply Obj. 1: The agent, as agent, does not receive anything. But in so far as it moves through being moved by another, it receives something from that which moves it: and thus is a habit caused.

Reply Obj. 2: The same thing, and in the same respect, cannot be mover and moved; but nothing prevents a thing from being moved by itself as to different respects, as is proved in Physics viii, text. 28, 29.

Reply Obj. 3: The act which precedes the habit, in so far as it comes from an active principle, proceeds from a more excellent principle than is the habit caused thereby: just as the reason is a more excellent principle than the habit of moral virtue produced in the appetitive power by repeated acts, and as the understanding of first principles is a more excellent principle than the science of conclusions.

THIRD ARTICLE [I-II, Q. 51, Art. 3]

Whether a Habit Can Be Caused by One Act?

Objection 1: It would seem that a habit can be caused by one act. For demonstration is an act of reason. But science, which is the habit of one conclusion, is caused by one demonstration. Therefore habit can be caused by one act.

Obj. 2: Further, as acts happen to increase by multiplication so do they happen to increase by intensity. But a habit is caused by multiplication of acts. Therefore also if an act be very intense, it can be the generating cause of a habit.

Obj. 3: Further, health and sickness are habits. But it happens that a man is healed or becomes ill, by one act. Therefore one act can cause a habit.

*On the contrary,* The Philosopher (Ethic. i, 7): "As neither does one swallow nor one day make spring: so neither does one day nor a short time make a man blessed and happy." But "happiness is an operation in respect of a habit of perfect virtue" (Ethic. i, 7, 10, 13). Therefore a habit of virtue, and for the same reason, other habits, is not caused by one act.

*I answer that,* As we have said already (A. 2), habit is caused by act, because a passive power is moved by an active principle. But in order that some quality be caused in that which is passive the active principle must entirely overcome the passive. Whence we see that because fire cannot at once overcome the combustible, it does not enkindle at once; but it gradually expels contrary dispositions, so that by overcoming it entirely, it may impress its likeness on it. Now it is clear that the active principle which is reason, cannot entirely overcome the appetitive power in one act: because the appetitive power is inclined variously, and to many things; while the reason judges in a single act, what should be willed in regard to various aspects and circumstances. Wherefore the appetitive power is not thereby entirely overcome, so as to be inclined like nature to the same thing, in the majority of cases; which inclination belongs to the habit of virtue. Therefore a habit of virtue cannot be caused by one act, but only by many.

But in the apprehensive powers, we must observe that there are two passive principles: one is the *possible* (See First Part, Q. 79, A. 2, ad 2) intellect itself; the other is the intellect which Aristotle (De Anima iii, text. 20) calls "passive," and is the "particular reason," that is the cogitative power, with memory and imagination. With regard then to the former passive principle, it is possible for a certain active principle to entirely overcome, by one act, the power of its passive principle: thus one self-evident proposition convinces the intellect, so that it gives a firm assent to the conclusion, but a probable proposition cannot do this. Wherefore a habit of opinion needs to be caused by many acts of the reason, even on the part of the "possible" intellect: whereas a habit of science can be caused by a single act of the reason, so far as the *possible* intellect is concerned. But with regard to the lower apprehensive powers, the same acts need to be repeated many times for anything to be firmly impressed on the memory. And so the Philosopher says (De Memor. et Remin. 1) that "meditation strengthens memory." Bodily habits, however, can be caused by one act, if the active principle is of great power: sometimes, for instance, a strong dose of medicine restores health at once.

Hence the solutions to the objections are clear.

FOURTH ARTICLE [I-II, Q. 51, Art. 4]

Whether Any Habits Are Infused in Man by God?

Objection 1: It would seem that no habit is infused in man by God. For God treats all equally. If therefore He infuses habits into some, He would infuse them into all: which is clearly untrue.

Obj. 2: Further, God works in all things according to the mode which is suitable to their nature: for "it belongs to Divine providence to preserve nature," as Dionysius says (Div. Nom. iv). But habits are naturally caused in man by acts, as we have said above (A. 2). Therefore God does not cause habits to be in man except by acts.

Obj. 3: Further, if any habit be infused into man by God, man can by that habit perform many acts. But "from those acts a like habit is caused" (Ethic. ii, 1, 2). Consequently there will be two habits of the same species in the same man, one acquired, the other infused. Now this seems impossible: for the two forms of the same species cannot be in the same subject. Therefore a habit is not infused into man by God.

*On the contrary,* it is written (Ecclus. 15:5): "God filled him with the spirit of wisdom and understanding." Now wisdom and understanding are habits. Therefore some habits are infused into man by God.

*I answer that,* Some habits are infused by God into man, for two reasons.

The first reason is because there are some habits by which man is disposed to an end which exceeds the proportion of human nature, namely, the ultimate and perfect happiness of man, as stated above (Q. 5, A. 5). And since habits need to be in proportion with that to which man is disposed by them, therefore is it necessary that those habits, which dispose to this end, exceed the proportion of human nature. Wherefore such habits can never be in man except by Divine infusion, as is the case with all gratuitous virtues.

The other reason is, because God can produce the effects of second causes, without these second causes, as we have said in the First Part (Q. 105, A. 6). Just as, therefore, sometimes, in order to show His power, He causes health, without its natural cause, but which nature could have caused, so also, at times, for the manifestation of His power, He infuses into man even those habits which can be caused by a natural power. Thus He gave to the apostles the science of the Scriptures and of all tongues, which men can acquire by study or by custom, but not so perfectly.

Reply Obj. 1: God, in respect of His Nature, is the same to all, but in respect of the order of His Wisdom, for some fixed motive, gives certain things to some, which He does not give to others.

Reply Obj. 2: That God works in all according to their mode, does not hinder God from doing what nature cannot do: but it follows from this that He does nothing contrary to that which is suitable to nature.

Reply Obj. 3: Acts produced by an infused habit, do not cause a habit, but strengthen the already existing habit; just as the remedies of medicine given to a man who is naturally health, do not cause a kind of health, but give new strength to the health he had before.

## QUESTION 52

OF THE INCREASE OF HABITS (In Three Articles)

We have now to consider the increase of habits; under which head there are three points of inquiry:

(1) Whether habits increase?

(2) Whether they increase by addition?

(3) Whether each act increases the habit?

FIRST ARTICLE [I-II, Q. 52, Art. 1]

Whether Habits Increase?

Objection 1: It would seem that habits cannot increase. For increase concerns quantity (Phys. v, text. 18). But habits are not in the genus [of] quantity, but in that of quality. Therefore there can be no increase of habits.

Obj. 2: Further, habit is a perfection (Phys. vii, text. 17, 18). But since perfection conveys a notion of end and term, it seems that it cannot be more or less. Therefore a habit cannot increase.

Obj. 3: Further, those things which can be more or less are subject to alteration: for that which from being less hot becomes more hot, is said to be altered. But in habits there is no alteration, as is proved in *Phys.* vii, text. 15, 17. Therefore habits cannot increase.

*On the contrary,* Faith is a habit, and yet it increases: wherefore the disciples said to our Lord (Luke 17:5): "Lord, increase our faith." Therefore habits increase.

*I answer that,* Increase, like other things pertaining to quantity, is transferred from bodily quantities to intelligible spiritual things, on account of the natural connection of the intellect with corporeal things, which come under the imagination. Now in corporeal quantities, a thing is said to be great, according as it reaches the perfection of quantity due to it; wherefore a certain quantity is reputed great in man, which is not reputed great in an elephant. And so also in forms, we say a thing is great because it is perfect. And since good has the nature of perfection, therefore "in things which are great, but not in quantity, to be greater is the same as to be better," as Augustine says (De Trin. vi, 8).

Now the perfection of a form may be considered in two ways: first, in respect of the form itself: secondly, in respect of the participation of the form by its subject. In so far as we consider the perfections of a form in respect of the form itself, thus the form is said to be "little" or "great": for instance great or little health or science. But in so far as we consider the perfection of a form in respect of the participation thereof by the subject, it is said to be "more" or "less": for instance more or less white or healthy. Now this distinction is not to be understood as implying that the form has a being outside its matter or subject, but that it is one thing to consider the form according to its specific nature, and another to consider it in respect of its participation by a subject.

In this way, then, there were four opinions among philosophers concerning intensity and remission of habits and forms, as Simplicius relates in his *Commentary on the Predicaments.* For Plotinus and the other Platonists held that qualities and habits themselves were susceptible of more or less, for the reason that they were material and so had a certain want of definiteness, on account of the infinity of matter. Others, *on the contrary,* held that qualities and habits of themselves were not susceptible of more or less; but that the things affected by them ( *qualia* ) are said to be more or less, in respect of the participation of the subject: that, for instance, justice is not more or less, but the just thing. Aristotle alludes to this opinion in the *Predicaments* (Categor. vi). The third opinion was that of the Stoics, and lies between the two preceding opinions. For they held that some habits are of themselves susceptible of more and less, for instance, the arts; and that some are not, as the virtues. The fourth opinion was held by some who said that qualities and immaterial forms are not susceptible of more or less, but that material forms are.

In order that the truth in this matter be made clear, we must observe that [that], in respect of which a thing receives its species, must be something fixed and stationary, and as it were indivisible: for whatever attains to that thing, is contained under the species, and whatever recedes from it more or less, belongs to another species, more or less perfect. Wherefore, the Philosopher says (Metaph. viii, text. 10) that species of things are like numbers, in which addition or subtraction changes the species.

If, therefore, a form, or anything at all, receives its specific nature in respect of itself, or in respect of something belonging to it, it is necessary that, considered in itself, it be something of a definite nature, which can be neither more nor less. Such are heat, whiteness or other like qualities which are not denominated from a relation to something else: and much more so, substance, which is *per se* being. But those things which receive their species from something to which they are related, can be diversified, in respect of themselves, according to more or less: and nonetheless they remain in the same species, on account of the oneness of that to which they are related, and from which they receive their species. For example, movement is in itself more intense or more remiss: and yet it remains in the same species, on account of the oneness of the term by which it is specified. We may observe the same thing in health; for a body attains to the nature of health, according as it has a disposition suitable to an animal's nature, to which various dispositions may be suitable; which disposition is therefore variable as regards more or less, and withal the nature of health remains. Whence the Philosopher says (Ethic. x, 2, 3): "Health itself may be more or less: for the measure is not the same in all, nor is it always the same in one individual; but down to a certain point it may decrease and still remain health."

Now these various dispositions and measures of health are by way of excess and defect: wherefore if the name of health were given to the most perfect measure, then we should not speak of health as greater or less. Thus therefore it is clear how a quality or form may increase or decrease of itself, and how it cannot.

But if we consider a quality or form in respect of its participation by the subject, thus again we find that some qualities and forms are susceptible of more or less, and some not. Now Simplicius assigns the cause of this diversity to the fact that substance in itself cannot be susceptible of more or less, because it is *per se* being. And therefore every form which is participated substantially by its subject, cannot vary in intensity and remission: wherefore in the genus of substance nothing is said to be more or less. And because quantity is nigh to substance, and because shape follows on quantity, therefore is it that neither in these can there be such a thing as more or less. Whence the Philosopher says (Phys. vii, text. 15) that when a thing receives form and shape, it is not said to be altered, but to be made. But other qualities which are further removed from quantity, and are connected with passions and actions, are susceptible of more or less, in respect of their participation by the subject.

Now it is possible to explain yet further the reason of this diversity. For, as we have said, that from which a thing receives its species must remain indivisibly fixed and constant in something indivisible. Wherefore in two ways it may happen that a form cannot be participated more or less. First because the participator has its species in respect of that form. And for this reason no substantial form is participated more or less. Wherefore the Philosopher says (Metaph. viii, text. 10) that, "as a number cannot be more or less, so neither can that which is in the species of substance," that is, in respect of its participation of the specific form: "but in so far as substance may be with matter," i.e. in respect of material dispositions, "more or less are found in substance."

Secondly this may happen from the fact that the form is essentially indivisible: wherefore if anything participate that form, it must needs participate it in respect of its indivisibility. For this reason we do not speak of the species of number as varying in respect of more or less; because each species thereof is constituted by an indivisible unity. The same is to be said of the species of continuous quantity, which are denominated from numbers, as two-cubits-long, three-cubits-long, and of relations of quantity, as double and treble, and of figures of quantity, as triangle and tetragon.

This same explanation is given by Aristotle in the *Predicaments* (Categor. vi), where in explaining why figures are not susceptible of more or less, he says: "Things which are given the nature of a triangle or a circle, are accordingly triangles and circles": to wit, because indivisibility is essential to the motion of such, wherefore whatever participates their nature must participate it in its indivisibility.

It is clear, therefore, since we speak of habits and dispositions in respect of a relation to something (Phys. vii, text. 17), that in two ways intensity and remission may be observed in habits and dispositions. First, in respect of the habit itself: thus, for instance, we speak of greater or less health; greater or less science, which extends to more or fewer things. Secondly, in respect of participation by the subject: in so far as equal science or health is participated more in one than in another, according to a diverse aptitude arising either from nature, or from custom. For habit and disposition do not give species to the subject: nor again do they essentially imply indivisibility.

We shall say further on (Q. 66, A. 1) how it is with the virtues.

Reply Obj. 1: As the word "great" is taken from corporeal quantities and applied to the intelligible perfections of forms; so also is the word "growth," the term of which is something great.

Reply Obj. 2: Habit is indeed a perfection, but not a perfection which is the term of its subject; for instance, a term giving the subject its specific being. Nor again does the nature of a habit include the notion of term, as do the species of numbers. Wherefore there is nothing to hinder it from being susceptible of more or less.

Reply Obj. 3: Alteration is primarily indeed in the qualities of the third species; but secondarily it may be in the qualities of the first species: for, supposing an alteration as to hot and cold, there follows in an animal an alteration as to health and sickness. In like manner, if an alteration take place in the passions of the sensitive appetite, or the sensitive powers of apprehension, an alteration follows as to science and virtue (Phys. viii, text. 20).

SECOND ARTICLE [I-II, Q. 52, Art. 2]

Whether Habit Increases by Addition?

Objection 1: It would seem that the increase of habits is by way of addition. For the word "increase," as we have said, is transferred to forms, from corporeal quantities. But in corporeal quantities there is no increase without addition: wherefore (De Gener. i, text. 31) it is said that "increase is an addition to a magnitude already existing." Therefore in habits also there is no increase without addition.

Obj. 2: Further, habit is not increased except by means of some agent. But every agent does something in the passive subject: for instance, that which heats, causes heat in that which is heated. Therefore there is no increase without addition.

Obj. 3: Further, as that which is not white, is in potentiality to be white: so that which is less white, is in potentiality to be more white. But that which is not white, is not made white except by the addition of whiteness. Therefore that which is less white, is not made more white, except by an added whiteness.

*On the contrary,* The Philosopher says (Phys. iv, text. 84): "That which is hot is made hotter, without making, in the matter, something hot, that was not hot, when the thing was less hot." Therefore, in like manner, neither is any addition made in other forms when they increase.

*I answer that,* The solution of this question depends on what we have said above (A. 1). For we said that increase and decrease in forms which are capable of intensity and remissness, happen in one way not on the part of the very form considered in itself, through the diverse participation thereof by the subject. Wherefore such increase of habits and other forms, is not caused by an addition of form to form; but by the subject participating more or less perfectly, one and the same form. And just as, by an agent which is in act, something is made actually hot, beginning, as it were, to participate a form, not as though the form itself were made, as is proved in *Metaph.* vii, text. 32, so, by an intense action of the agent, something is made more hot, as it were participating the form more perfectly, not as though something were added to the form.

For if this increase in forms were understood to be by way of addition, this could only be either in the form itself or in the subject. If it be understood of the form itself, it has already been stated (A. 1) that such an addition or subtraction would change the species; even as the species of color is changed when a thing from being pale becomes white. If, on the other hand, this addition be understood as applying to the subject, this could only be either because one part of the subject receives a form which it had not previously (thus we may say cold increases in a man who, after being cold in one part of his body, is cold in several parts), or because some other subject is added sharing in the same form (as when a hot thing is added to another, or one white thing to another). But in either of these two ways we have not a more white or a more hot thing, but a greater white or hot thing.

Since, however, as stated above (A. 1), certain accidents are of themselves susceptible of more or less, in some of these we may find increase by addition. For movement increases by an addition either to the time it lasts, or to the course it follows: and yet the species remains the same on account of the oneness of the term. Yet movement increases the intensity as to participation in its subject: i.e. in so far as the same movement can be executed more or less speedily or readily. In like manner, science can increase in itself by addition; thus when anyone learns several conclusions of geometry, the same specific habit of science increases in that man. Yet a man's science increases, as to the subject's participation thereof, in intensity, in so far as one man is quicker and readier than another in considering the same conclusions.

As to bodily habits, it does not seem very probable that they receive increase by way of addition. For an animal is not said to be simply healthy or beautiful, unless it be such in all its parts. And if it be brought to a more perfect measure, this is the result of a change in the simple qualities, which are not susceptible of increase save in intensity on the part of the subject partaking of them.

How this question affects virtues we shall state further on (Q. 66, A. 1).

Reply Obj. 1: Even in bodily bulk increase is twofold. First, by addition of one subject to another; such is the increase of living things. Secondly, by mere intensity, without any addition at all; such is the case with things subject to rarefaction, as is stated in *Phys.* iv, text. 63.

Reply Obj. 2: The cause that increases a habit, always effects something in the subject, but not a new form. But it causes the subject to partake more perfectly of a pre-existing form, or it makes the form to extend further.

Reply Obj. 3: What is not already white, is potentially white, as not yet possessing the form of whiteness: hence the agent causes a new form in the subject. But that which is less hot or white, is not in potentiality to those forms, since it has them already actually: but it is in potentiality to a perfect mode of participation; and this it receives through the agent's action.

THIRD ARTICLE [I-II, Q. 52, Art. 3]

Whether Every Act Increases Its Habit?

Objection 1: It would seem that every act increases its habit. For when the cause is increased the effect is increased. Now acts are causes of habits, as stated above (Q. 51, A. 2). Therefore a habit increases when its acts are multiplied.

Obj. 2: Further, of like things a like judgment should be formed. But all the acts proceeding from one and the same habit are alike (Ethic. ii, 1, 2). Therefore if some acts increase a habit, every act should increase it.

Obj. 3: Further, like is increased by like. But any act is like the habit whence it proceeds. Therefore every act increases the habit.

*On the contrary,* Opposite effects do not result from the same cause. But according to Ethic. ii, 2, some acts lessen the habit whence they proceed, for instance if they be done carelessly. Therefore it is not every act that increases a habit.

*I answer that,* "Like acts cause like habits" (Ethic. ii, 1, 2). Now things are like or unlike not only in respect of their qualities being the same or various, but also in respect of the same or a different mode of participation. For it is not only black that is unlike white, but also less white is unlike more white, since there is movement from less white to more white, even as from one opposite to another, as stated in *Phys.* v, text. 52.

But since use of habits depends on the will, as was shown above (Q. 50, A. 5); just as one who has a habit may fail to use it or may act contrary to it; so may he happen to use the habit by performing an act that is not in proportion to the intensity of the habit. Accordingly, if the intensity of the act correspond in proportion to the intensity of the habit, or even surpass it, every such act either increases the habit or disposes to an increase thereof, if we may speak of the increase of habits as we do of the increase of an animal. For not every morsel of food actually increases the animal's size as neither does every drop of water hollow out the stone: but the multiplication of food results at last in an increase of the body. So, too, repeated acts cause a habit to grow. If, however, the act falls short of the intensity of the habit, such an act does not dispose to an increase of that habit, but rather to a lessening thereof.

From this it is clear how to solve the objections.

## QUESTION 53

HOW HABITS ARE CORRUPTED OR DIMINISHED (In Three Articles)

We must now consider how habits are lost or weakened; and under this head there are three points of inquiry:

(1) Whether a habit can be corrupted?

(2) Whether it can be diminished?

(3) How are habits corrupted or diminished?

FIRST ARTICLE [I-II, Q. 53, Art. 1]

Whether a Habit Can Be Corrupted?

Objection 1: It would seem that a habit cannot be corrupted. For habit is within its subject like a second nature; wherefore it is pleasant to act from habit. Now so long as a thing is, its nature is not corrupted. Therefore neither can a habit be corrupted so long as its subject remains.

Obj. 2: Further, whenever a form is corrupted, this is due either to corruption of its subject, or to its contrary: thus sickness ceases through corruption of the animal, or through the advent of health. Now science, which is a habit, cannot be lost through corruption of its subject: since "the intellect," which is its subject, "is a substance that is incorruptible" (De Anima i, text. 65). In like manner, neither can it be lost through the action of its contrary: since intelligible species are not contrary to one another (Metaph. vii, text. 52). Therefore the habit of science can nowise be lost.

Obj. 3: Further, all corruption results from some movement. But the habit of science, which is in the soul, cannot be corrupted by a direct movement of the soul itself, since the soul is not moved directly. It is, however, moved indirectly through the movement of the body: and yet no bodily change seems capable of corrupting the intelligible species residing in the intellect: since the intellect independently of the body is the proper abode of the species; for which reason it is held that habits are not lost either through old age or through death. Therefore science cannot be corrupted. For the same reason neither can habits of virtue be corrupted, since they also are in the rational soul, and, as the Philosopher declares (Ethic. i, 10), "virtue is more lasting than learning."

*On the contrary,* The Philosopher says (De Long. et Brev. Vitae ii) that "forgetfulness and deception are the corruption of science." Moreover, by sinning a man loses a habit of virtue: and again, virtues are engendered and corrupted by contrary acts (Ethic. ii, 2).

*I answer that,* A form is said to be corrupted directly by its contrary; indirectly, through its subject being corrupted. When therefore a habit has a corruptible subject, and a cause that has a contrary, it can be corrupted both ways. This is clearly the case with bodily habits—for instance, health and sickness. But those habits that have an incorruptible subject, cannot be corrupted indirectly. There are, however, some habits which, while residing chiefly in an incorruptible subject, reside nevertheless secondarily in a corruptible subject; such is the habit of science which is chiefly indeed in the "possible" intellect, but secondarily in the sensitive powers of apprehension, as stated above (Q. 50, A. 3, ad 3). Consequently the habit of science cannot be corrupted indirectly, on the part of the "possible" intellect, but only on the part of the lower sensitive powers.

We must therefore inquire whether habits of this kind can be corrupted directly. If then there be a habit having a contrary, either on the part of itself or on the part of its cause, it can be corrupted directly: but if it has no contrary, it cannot be corrupted directly. Now it is evident that an intelligible species residing in the "possible" intellect, has no contrary; nor can the active intellect, which is the cause of that species, have a contrary. Wherefore if in the "possible" intellect there be a habit caused immediately by the active intellect, such a habit is incorruptible both directly and indirectly. Such are the habits of the first principles, both speculative and practical, which cannot be corrupted by any forgetfulness or deception whatever: even as the Philosopher says about prudence (Ethic. vi, 5) that "it cannot be lost by being forgotten." There is, however, in the "possible" intellect a habit caused by the reason, to wit, the habit of conclusions, which is called science, to the cause of which something may be contrary in two ways. First, on the part of those very propositions which are the starting point of the reason: for the assertion "Good is not good" is contrary to the assertion "Good is good" (Peri Herm. ii). Secondly, on the part of the process of reasoning; forasmuch as a sophistical syllogism is contrary to a dialectic or demonstrative syllogism. Wherefore it is clear that a false reason can corrupt the habit of a true opinion or even of science. Hence the Philosopher, as stated above, says that "deception is the corruption of science." As to virtues, some of them are intellectual, residing in reason itself, as stated in *Ethic.* vi, 1: and to these applies what we have said of science and opinion. Some, however, viz. the moral virtues, are in the appetitive part of the soul; and the same may be said of the contrary vices. Now the habits of the appetitive part are caused therein because it is natural to it to be moved by the reason. Therefore a habit either of virtue or of vice, may be corrupted by a judgment of reason, whenever its motion is contrary to such vice or virtue, whether through ignorance, passion or deliberate choice.

Reply Obj. 1: As stated in *Ethic.* vii, 10, a habit is like a second nature, and yet it falls short of it. And so it is that while the nature of a thing cannot in any way be taken away from a thing, a habit is removed, though with difficulty.

Reply Obj. 2: Although there is no contrary to intelligible species, yet there can be a contrary to assertions and to the process of reason, as stated above.

Reply Obj. 3: Science is not taken away by movement of the body, if we consider the root itself of the habit, but only as it may prove an obstacle to the act of science; in so far as the intellect, in its act, has need of the sensitive powers, which are impeded by corporal transmutation. But the intellectual movement of the reason can corrupt the habit of science, even as regards the very root of the habit. In like manner a habit of virtue can be corrupted. Nevertheless when it is said that "virtue is more lasting than learning," this must be understood in respect, not of the subject or cause, but of the act: because the use of virtue continues through the whole of life, whereas the use of learning does not.

SECOND ARTICLE [I-II, Q. 53, Art. 2]

Whether a Habit Can Diminish?

Objection 1: It would seem that a habit cannot diminish. Because a habit is a simple quality and form. Now a simple thing is possessed either wholly or not at all. Therefore although a habit can be lost it cannot diminish.

Obj. 2: Further, if a thing is befitting an accident, this is by reason either of the accident or of its subject. Now a habit does not become more or less intense by reason of itself; else it would follow that a species might be predicated of its individuals more or less. And if it can become less intense as to its participation by its subject, it would follow that something is accidental to a habit, proper thereto and not common to the habit and its subject. Now whenever a form has something proper to it besides its subject, that form can be separate, as stated in *De Anima* i, text. 13. Hence it follows that a habit is a separable form; which is impossible.

Obj. 3: Further, the very notion and nature of a habit as of any accident, is inherence in a subject: wherefore any accident is defined with reference to its subject. Therefore if a habit does not become more or less intense in itself, neither can it in its inherence in its subject: and consequently it will be nowise less intense.

*On the contrary,* It is natural for contraries to be applicable to the same thing. Now increase and decrease are contraries. Since therefore a habit can increase, it seems that it can also diminish.

*I answer that,* Habits diminish, just as they increase, in two ways, as we have already explained (Q. 52, A. 1). And since they increase through the same cause as that which engenders them, so too they diminish by the same cause as that which corrupts them: since the diminishing of a habit is the road which leads to its corruption, even as, on the other hand, the engendering of a habit is a foundation of its increase.

Reply Obj. 1: A habit, considered in itself, is a simple form. It is not thus that it is subject to decrease; but according to the different ways in which its subject participates in it. This is due to the fact that the subject's potentiality is indeterminate, through its being able to participate a form in various ways, or to extend to a greater or a smaller number of things.

Reply Obj. 2: This argument would hold, if the essence itself of a habit were nowise subject to decrease. This we do not say; but that a certain decrease in the essence of a habit has its origin, not in the habit, but in its subject.

Reply Obj. 3: No matter how we take an accident,

its very notion implies dependence on a subject, but in different ways. For if we take an accident in the abstract, it implies relation to a subject, which relation begins in the accident and terminates in the subject: for "whiteness is that whereby a thing is white." Accordingly in defining an accident in the abstract, we do not put the subject as though it were the first part of the definition, viz. the genus; but we give it the second place, which is that of the difference; thus we say that *simitas* is "a curvature of the nose." But if we take accidents in the concrete, the relation begins in the subject and terminates in the concrete, the relation begins in the subject and terminates at the accident: for "a white thing" is "something that has whiteness." Accordingly in defining this kind of accident, we place the subject as the genus, which is the first part of a definition; for we say that a *simum* is a "snub-nose." Accordingly whatever is befitting an accident on the part of the subject, but is not of the very essence of the accident, is ascribed to that accident, not in the abstract, but in the concrete. Such are increase and decrease in certain accidents: wherefore to be more or less white is not ascribed to whiteness but to a white thing. The same applies to habits and other qualities; save that certain habits increase or diminish by a kind of addition, as we have already clearly explained (Q. 52, A. 2).

THIRD ARTICLE [I-II, Q. 53, Art. 3]

Whether a Habit Is Corrupted or Diminished Through Mere Cessation from Act?

Objection 1: It would seem that a habit is not corrupted or diminished through mere cessation from act. For habits are more lasting than passion-like qualities, as we have explained above (Q. 49, A. 2, ad 3; Q. 50, A. 1). But passion-like qualities are neither corrupted nor diminished by cessation from act: for whiteness is not lessened through not affecting the sight, nor heat through ceasing to make something hot. Therefore neither are habits diminished or corrupted through cessation from act.

Obj. 2: Further, corruption and diminution are changes. Now nothing is changed without a moving cause. Since therefore cessation from act does not imply a moving cause, it does not appear how a habit can be diminished or corrupted through cessation from act.

Obj. 3: Further, the habits of science and virtue are in the intellectual soul which is above time. Now those things that are above time are neither destroyed nor diminished by length of time. Neither, therefore, are such habits destroyed or diminished through length of time, if one fails for long to exercise them.

*On the contrary,* The Philosopher says (De Long. et Brev. Vitae ii) that not only "deception," but also "forgetfulness, is the corruption of science." Moreover he says (Ethic. viii, 5) that "want of intercourse has dissolved many a friendship." In like manner other habits of virtue are diminished or destroyed through cessation from act.

*I answer that,* As stated in Phys. vii, text. 27, a thing is a cause of movement in two ways. First, directly; and such a thing causes movement by reason of its proper form; thus fire causes heat. Secondly, indirectly; for instance, that which removes an obstacle. It is in this latter way that the destruction or diminution of a habit results through cessation from act, in so far, to wit, as we cease from exercising an act which overcame the causes that destroyed or weakened that habit. For it has been stated (A. 1) that habits are destroyed or diminished directly through some contrary agency. Consequently all habits that are gradually undermined by contrary agencies which need to be counteracted by acts proceeding from those habits, are diminished or even destroyed altogether by long cessation from act, as is clearly seen in the case both of science and of virtue. For it is evident that a habit of moral virtue makes a man ready to choose the mean in deeds and passions. And when a man fails to make use of his virtuous habit in order to moderate his own passions or deeds, the necessary result is that many passions and deeds fail to observe the mode of virtue, by reason of the inclination of the sensitive appetite and of other external agencies. Wherefore virtue is destroyed or lessened through cessation from act. The same applies to the intellectual habits, which render man ready to judge aright of those things that are pictured by his imagination. Hence when man ceases to make use of his intellectual habits, strange fancies, sometimes in opposition to them, arise in his imagination; so that unless those fancies be, as it were, cut off or kept back by frequent use of his intellectual habits, man becomes less fit to judge aright, and sometimes is even wholly disposed to the contrary, and thus the intellectual habit is diminished or even wholly destroyed by cessation from act.

Reply Obj. 1: Even heat would be destroyed through ceasing to give heat, if, for this same reason, cold which is destructive of heat were to increase.

Reply Obj. 2: Cessation from act is a moving cause, conducive of corruption or diminution, by removing the obstacles thereto, as explained above.

Reply Obj. 3: The intellectual part of the soul, considered in itself, is above time, but the sensitive part is subject to time, and therefore in course of time it undergoes change as to the passions of the sensitive part, and also as to the powers of apprehension. Hence the Philosopher says (Phys. iv. text. 117) that time makes us forget.

# QUESTION 54

OF THE DISTINCTION OF HABITS (In Four Articles)

We have now to consider the distinction of habits; and under this head there are four points of inquiry:

(1) Whether many habits can be in one power?

(2) Whether habits are distinguished by their objects?

(3) Whether habits are divided into good and bad?

(4) Whether one habit may be made up of many habits?

FIRST ARTICLE [I-II, Q. 54, Art. 1]

Whether Many Habits Can Be in One Power?

Objection 1: It would seem that there cannot be many habits in one power. For when several things are distinguished in respect of the same thing, if one of them be multiplied, the others are too. Now habits and powers are distinguished in respect of the same thing, viz. their acts and objects. Therefore they are multiplied in like manner. Therefore there cannot be many habits in one power.

Obj. 2: Further, a power is a simple force. Now in one simple subject there cannot be diversity of accidents; for the subject is the cause of its accidents; and it does not appear how diverse effects can proceed from one simple cause. Therefore there cannot be many habits in one power.

Obj. 3: Further, just as the body is informed by its shape, so is a power informed by a habit. But one body cannot be informed at the same time by various shapes. Therefore neither can a power be informed at the same time by many habits. Therefore several habits cannot be at the same time in one power.

*On the contrary,* The intellect is one power; wherein, nevertheless, are the habits of various sciences.

*I answer that,* As stated above (Q. 49, A. 4), habits are dispositions of a thing that is in potentiality to something, either to nature, or to operation, which is the end of nature. As to those habits which are dispositions to nature, it is clear that several can be in one same subject: since in one subject we may take parts in various ways, according to the various dispositions of which parts there are various habits. Thus, if we take the humors as being parts of the human body, according to their disposition in respect of human nature, we have the habit or disposition of health: while, if we take like parts, such as nerves, bones, and flesh, the disposition of these in respect of nature is strength or weakness; whereas, if we take the limbs, i.e. the hands, feet, and so on, the disposition of these in proportion to nature, is beauty: and thus there are several habits or dispositions in the same subject.

If, however, we speak of those habits that are dispositions to operation, and belong properly to the powers; thus, again, there may be several habits in one power. The reason for this is that the subject of a habit is a passive power, as stated above (Q. 51, A. 2): for it is only an active power that cannot be the subject of a habit, as was clearly shown above (Q. 51, A. 2). Now a passive power is compared to the determinate act of any species, as matter to form: because, just as matter is determinate to one form by one agent, so, too, is a passive power determined by the nature of one active object to an act specifically one. Wherefore, just as several objects can move one passive power, so can one passive power be the subject of several acts or perfections specifically diverse. Now habits are qualities or forms adhering to a power, and inclining that power to acts of a determinate species. Consequently several habits, even as several specifically different acts, can belong to one power.

Reply Obj. 1: Even as in natural things, diversity of species is according to the form, and diversity of genus, according to matter, as stated in *Metaph.* v, text. 33 (since things that differ in matter belong to different genera): so, too, generic diversity of objects entails a difference of powers (wherefore the Philosopher says in *Ethic.* vi, 1, that "those objects that differ generically belong to different departments of the soul"); while specific difference of objects entails a specific difference of acts, and consequently of habits also. Now things that differ in genus differ in species, but not vice versa. Wherefore the acts and habits of different powers differ in species: but it does not follow that different habits are in different powers, for several can be in one power. And even as several genera may be included in one genus, and several species be contained in one species; so does it happen that there are several species of habits and powers.

Reply Obj. 2: Although a power is simple as to its essence, it is multiple virtually, inasmuch as it extends to many specifically different acts. Consequently there is nothing to prevent many superficially different habits from being in one power.

Reply Obj. 3: A body is informed by its shape as by its own terminal boundaries: whereas a habit is not the terminal boundary of a power, but the disposition of a power to an act as to its ultimate term. Consequently one same power cannot have several acts at the same time, except in so far as perchance one act is comprised in another; just as neither can a body have several shapes, save in so far as one shape enters into another, as a three-sided in a four-sided figure. For the intellect cannot understand several things at the same time *actually;* and yet it can know several things at the same time *habitually.*

SECOND ARTICLE [I-II, Q. 54, Art. 2]

Whether Habits Are Distinguished by Their Objects?

Objection 1: It would seem that habits are not distinguished by their objects. For contraries differ in species. Now the same habit of science regards contraries: thus medicine regards the healthy and the unhealthy. Therefore habits are not distinguished by objects specifically distinct.

Obj. 2: Further, different sciences are different habits. But the same scientific truth belongs to different sciences: thus both the physicist and the astronomer prove the earth to be round, as stated in *Phys.* ii, text. 17. Therefore habits are not distinguished by their objects.

Obj. 3: Further, wherever the act is the same, the object is the same. But the same act can belong to different habits of virtue, if it be directed to different ends; thus to give money to anyone, if it be done for God's sake, is an act of charity; while, if it be done in order to pay a debt, it is an act of justice. Therefore the same object can also belong to different habits. Therefore diversity of habits does not follow diversity of objects.

*On the contrary,* Acts differ in species according to the diversity of their objects, as stated above (Q. 18, A. 5). But habits are dispositions to acts. Therefore habits also are distinguished according to the diversity of objects.

*I answer that,* A habit is both a form and a habit. Hence the specific distinction of habits may be taken in the ordinary way in which forms differ specifically; or according to that mode of distinction which is proper to habits. Accordingly forms are distinguished from one another in reference to the diversity of their active principles, since every agent produces its like in species. Habits, however, imply order to something: and all things that imply order to something, are distinguished according to the distinction of the things to which they are ordained. Now a habit is a disposition implying a twofold order: viz. to nature and to an operation consequent to nature.

Accordingly habits are specifically distinct in respect of three things. First, in respect of the active principles of such dispositions; secondly, in respect of nature; thirdly, in respect of specifically different objects, as will appear from what follows.

Reply Obj. 1: In distinguishing powers, or also habits, we must consider the object not in its material but in its formal aspect, which may differ in species or even in genus. And though the distinction between specific contraries is a real distinction yet they are both known under one aspect, since one is known through the other. And consequently in so far as they concur in the one aspect of cognoscibility, they belong to one cognitive habit.

Reply Obj. 2: The physicist proves the earth to be round by one means, the astronomer by another: for the latter proves this by means of mathematics, e.g. by the shapes of eclipses, or something of the sort; while the former proves it by means of physics, e.g. by the movement of heavy bodies towards the center, and so forth. Now the whole force of a demonstration, which is "a syllogism producing science," as stated in Poster. i, text. 5, depends on the mean. And consequently various means are as so many active principles, in respect of which the habits of science are distinguished.

Reply Obj. 3: As the Philosopher says (Phys. ii, text. 89; Ethic. vii, 8), the end is, in practical matters, what the principle is in speculative matters. Consequently diversity of ends demands a diversity of virtues, even as diversity of active principles does. Moreover the ends are objects of the internal acts, with which, above all, the virtues are concerned, as is evident from what has been said (Q. 18, A. 6; Q. 19, A. 2, ad 1; Q. 34, A. 4).

THIRD ARTICLE [I-II, Q. 54, Art. 3]

Whether Habits Are Divided into Good and Bad?

Objection 1: It would seem that habits are not divided into good and bad. For good and bad are contraries. Now the same habit regards contraries, as was stated above (A. 2, Obj. 1). Therefore habits are not divided into good and bad.

Obj. 2: Further, good is convertible with being; so that, since it is common to all, it cannot be accounted a specific difference, as the Philosopher declares (Topic. iv). Again, evil, since it is a privation and a non-being, cannot differentiate any being. Therefore habits cannot be specifically divided into good and evil.

Obj. 3: Further, there can be different evil habits about one same object; for instance, intemperance and insensibility about matters of concupiscence: and in like manner there can be several good habits; for instance, human virtue and heroic or godlike virtue, as the Philosopher clearly states (Ethic. vii, 1). Therefore, habits are not divided into good and bad.

*On the contrary,* A good habit is contrary to a bad habit, as virtue to vice. Now contraries are divided specifically into good and bad habits.

*I answer that,* As stated above (A. 2), habits are specifically distinct not only in respect of their objects and active principles, but also in their relation to nature. Now, this happens in two ways. First, by reason of their suitableness or unsuitableness to nature. In this way a good habit is specifically distinct from a bad habit: since a good habit is one which disposes to an act suitable to the agent's nature, while an evil habit is one which disposes to an act unsuitable to nature. Thus, acts of virtue are suitable to human nature, since they are according to reason, whereas acts of vice are discordant from human nature, since they are against reason. Hence it is clear that habits are distinguished specifically by the difference of good and bad.

Secondly, habits are distinguished in relation to nature, from the fact that one habit disposes to an act that is suitable to a lower nature, while another habit disposes to an act befitting a higher nature. And thus human virtue, which disposes to an act befitting human nature, is distinct from godlike or heroic virtue, which disposes to an act befitting some higher nature.

Reply Obj. 1: The same habit may be about contraries in so far as contraries agree in one common aspect. Never, however, does it happen that contrary habits are in one species: since contrariety of habits follows contrariety of aspect. Accordingly habits are divided into good and bad, namely, inasmuch as one habit is good, and another bad; but not by reason of one habit being [about] something good, and another about something bad.

Reply Obj. 2: It is not the good which is common to every being, that is a difference constituting the species of a habit; but some determinate good by reason of suitability to some determinate, viz. the human, nature. In like manner the evil that constitutes a difference of habits is not a pure privation, but something determinate repugnant to a determinate nature.

Reply Obj. 3: Several good habits about one same specific thing are distinct in reference to their suitability to various natures, as stated above. But several bad habits in respect of one action are distinct in reference to their diverse repugnance to that which is in keeping with nature: thus, various vices about one same matter are contrary to one virtue.

FOURTH ARTICLE [I-II, Q. 54, Art. 4]

Whether One Habit Is Made Up of Many Habits?

Objection 1: It would seem that one habit is made up of many habits. For whatever is engendered, not at once, but little by little, seems to be made up of several parts. But a habit is engendered, not at once, but little by little out of several acts, as stated above (Q. 51, A. 3). Therefore one habit is made up of several.

Obj. 2: Further, a whole is made up of its parts. Now many parts are assigned to one habit: thus Tully assigns many parts of fortitude, temperance, and other virtues. Therefore one habit is made up of many.

Obj. 3: Further, one conclusion suffices both for an act and for a habit of scientific knowledge. But many conclusions belong to but one science, to geometry, for instance, or to arithmetic. Therefore one habit is made up of many.

*On the contrary,* A habit, since it is a quality, is a simple form. But nothing simple is made up of many. Therefore one habit is not made up of many.

*I answer that,* A habit directed to operation, such as we are chiefly concerned with at present, is a perfection of a power. Now every perfection should be in proportion with that which it perfects. Hence, just as a power, while it is one, extends to many things, in so far as they have something in common, i.e. some general objective aspect, so also a habit extends to many things, in so far as they are related to one, for instance, to some specific objective aspect, or to one nature, or to one principle, as was clearly stated above (AA. 2, 3).

If then we consider a habit as to the extent of its object, we shall find a certain multiplicity therein. But since this multiplicity is directed to one thing, on which the habit is chiefly intent, hence it is that a habit is a simple quality, not composed to several habits, even though it extend to many things. For a habit does not extend to many things save in relation to one, whence it derives its unity.

Reply Obj. 1: That a habit is engendered little by little, is due, not to one part being engendered after another, but to the fact that the subject does not acquire all at once a firm and difficultly changeable disposition; and also to the fact that it begins by being imperfectly in the subject, and is gradually perfected. The same applies to other qualities.

Reply Obj. 2: The parts which are assigned to each cardinal virtue, are not integral parts that combine to form a whole; but subjective or potential parts, as we shall explain further on (Q. 57, A. 6, ad 4; II-II, Q. 48).

Reply Obj. 3: In any science, he who acquires, by demonstration, scientific knowledge of one conclusion, has the habit indeed, yet imperfectly. And when he obtains, by demonstration, the scientific knowledge of another conclusion, no additional habit is engendered in him: but the habit which was in him previously is perfected, forasmuch as it has increased in extent; because the conclusions and demonstrations of one science are coordinate, and one flows from another.

TREATISE ON HABITS IN PARTICULAR (QQ. 55-89): GOOD HABITS, i.e., VIRTUES (QQ. 55-70)

# QUESTION 55

OF THE VIRTUES, AS TO THEIR ESSENCE (In Four Articles)

We come now to the consideration of habits specifically. And since habits, as we have said (Q. 54, A. 3), are divided into good and bad, we must speak in the first place of good habits, which are virtues, and of other matters connected with them, namely the Gifts, Beatitudes and Fruits; in the second place, of bad habits, namely of vices and sins. Now five things must be considered about virtues: (1) the essence of virtue; (2) its subject; (3) the division of virtue; (4) the cause of virtue; (5) certain properties of virtue.

Under the first head, there are four points of inquiry:

(1) Whether human virtue is a habit?

(2) Whether it is an operative habit?

(3) Whether it is a good habit?

(4) Of the definition of virtue.

FIRST ARTICLE [I-II, Q. 55, Art. 1]

Whether Human Virtue Is a Habit?

Objection 1: It would seem that human virtue is not a habit: For virtue is "the limit of power" (De Coelo i, text. 116). But the limit of anything is reducible to the genus of that of which it is the limit; as a point is reducible to the genus of line. Therefore virtue is reducible to the genus of power, and not to the genus of habit.

Obj. 2: Further, Augustine says (De Lib. Arb. ii) [*Retract. ix; cf. De Lib. Arb. ii, 19] that "virtue is good use of free-will." But use of free-will is an act. Therefore virtue is not a habit, but an act.

Obj. 3: Further, we do not merit by our habits, but by our actions: otherwise a man would merit continually, even while asleep. But we do merit by our virtues. Therefore virtues are not habits, but acts.

Obj. 4: Further, Augustine says (De Moribus Eccl. xv) that "virtue is the order of love," and (QQ. lxxxiii, qu. 30) that "the ordering which is called virtue consists in enjoying what we ought to enjoy, and using what we ought to use." Now order, or ordering, denominates either an action or a relation. Therefore virtue is not a habit, but an action or a relation.

Obj. 5: Further, just as there are human virtues, so are there natural virtues. But natural virtues are not habits, but powers. Neither therefore are human virtues habits.

*On the contrary,* The Philosopher says (Categor. vi) that science and virtue are habits.

*I answer that,* Virtue denotes a certain perfection of a power. Now a thing's perfection is considered chiefly in regard to its end. But the end of power is act. Wherefore power is said to be perfect, according as it is determinate to its act.

Now there are some powers which of themselves are determinate to their acts; for instance, the active natural powers. And therefore these natural powers are in themselves called virtues. But the rational powers, which are proper to man, are not determinate to one particular action, but are inclined indifferently to many: and they are determinate to acts by means of habits, as is clear from what we have said above (Q. 49, A. 4). Therefore human virtues are habits.

Reply Obj. 1: Sometimes we give the name of a virtue to that to which the virtue is directed, namely, either to its object, or to its act: for instance, we give the name Faith, to that which we believe, or to the act of believing, as also to the habit by which we believe. When therefore we say that "virtue is the limit of power," virtue is taken for the object of virtue. For the furthest point to which a power can reach, is said to be its virtue; for instance, if a man can carry a hundredweight and not more, his virtue [*In English we should say 'strength,' which is the original signification of the Latin 'virtus': thus we speak of an engine being so many horse-power, to indicate its 'strength'] is put at a hundredweight, and not at sixty. But the objection takes virtue as being essentially the limit of power.

Reply Obj. 2: Good use of free-will is said to be a virtue, in the same sense as above (ad 1); that is to say, because it is that to which virtue is directed as to its proper act. For the act of virtue is nothing else than the good use of free-will.

Reply Obj. 3: We are said to merit by something in two ways. First, as by merit itself, just as we are said to run by running; and thus we merit by acts. Secondly, we are said to merit by something as by the principle whereby we merit, as we are said to run by the motive power; and thus are we said to merit by virtues and habits.

Reply Obj. 4: When we say that virtue is the order or ordering of love, we refer to the end to which virtue is ordered: because in us love is set in order by virtue.

Reply Obj. 5: Natural powers are of themselves determinate to one act: not so the rational powers. And so there is no comparison, as we have said.

SECOND ARTICLE [I-II, Q. 55, Art. 2]

Whether Human Virtue Is an Operative Habit?

Objection 1: It would seem that it is not essential to human virtue to be an operative habit. For Tully says (Tuscul. iv) that as health and beauty belong to the body, so virtue belongs to the soul. But health and beauty are not operative habits. Therefore neither is virtue.

Obj. 2: Further, in natural things we find virtue not only in reference to act, but also in reference to being: as is clear from the Philosopher (De Coelo i), since some have a virtue to be always, while some have a virtue to be not always, but at some definite time. Now as natural virtue is in natural things, so is human virtue in rational beings. Therefore also human virtue is referred not only to act, but also to being.

Obj. 3: Further, the Philosopher says (Phys. vii, text. 17) that virtue "is the disposition of a perfect thing to that which is best." Now the best thing to which man needs to be disposed by virtue is God Himself, as Augustine proves (De Moribus Eccl. 3, 6, 14) to Whom the soul is disposed by being made like to Him. Therefore it seems that virtue is a quality of the soul in reference to God, likening it, as it were, to Him; and not in reference to operation. It is not, therefore, an operative habit.

*On the contrary,* The Philosopher (Ethic. ii, 6) says that "virtue of a thing is that which makes its work good."

*I answer that,* Virtue, from the very nature of the word, implies some perfection of power, as we have said above (A. 1). Wherefore, since power [*The one Latin word *potentia* is rendered 'potentiality' in the first case, and 'power' in the second] is of two kinds, namely, power in reference to being, and power in reference to act; the perfection of each of these is called virtue. But power in reference to being is on the part of matter, which is potential being, whereas power in reference to act, is on the part of the form, which is the principle of action, since everything acts in so far as it is in act.

Now man is so constituted that the body holds the place of matter, the soul that of form. The body, indeed, man has in common with other animals; and the same is to be said of the forces which are common to the soul and body: and only those forces which are proper to the soul, namely, the rational forces, belong to man alone. And therefore, human virtue, of which we are speaking now, cannot belong to the body, but belongs only to that which is proper to the soul. Wherefore human virtue does not imply reference to being, but rather to act. Consequently it is essential to human virtue to be an operative habit.

Reply Obj. 1: Mode of action follows on the disposition of the agent: for such as a thing is, such is its act. And therefore, since virtue is the principle of some kind of operation, there must needs pre-exist in the operator in respect of virtue some corresponding disposition. Now virtue causes an ordered operation. Therefore virtue itself is an ordered disposition of the soul, in so far as, to wit, the powers of the soul are in some way ordered to one another, and to that which is outside. Hence virtue, inasmuch as it is a suitable disposition of the soul, is like health and beauty, which are suitable dispositions of the body. But this does not hinder virtue from being a principle of operation.

Reply Obj. 2: Virtue which is referred to being is not proper to man; but only that virtue which is referred to works of reason, which are proper to man.

Reply Obj. 3: As God's substance is His act, the highest likeness of man to God is in respect of some operation. Wherefore, as we have said above (Q. 3, A. 2), happiness or bliss by which man is made most perfectly conformed to God, and which is the end of human life, consists in an operation.

THIRD ARTICLE [I-II, Q. 55, Art. 3]

Whether Human Virtue Is a Good Habit?

Objection 1: It would seem that it is not essential to virtue that it should be a good habit. For sin is always taken in a bad sense. But there is a virtue even of sin; according to 1 Cor. 15:56: "The virtue [Douay: 'strength'] of sin is the Law." Therefore virtue is not always a good habit.

Obj. 2: Further, Virtue corresponds to power. But power is not only referred to good, but also to evil: according to Isa. 5: "Woe to you that are mighty to drink wine, and stout men at drunkenness." Therefore virtue also is referred to good and evil.

Obj. 3: Further, according to the Apostle (2 Cor. 12:9): "Virtue [Douay: 'power'] is made perfect in infirmity." But infirmity is an evil. Therefore virtue is referred not only to good, but also to evil.

*On the contrary,* Augustine says (De Moribus Eccl. vi): "No one can doubt that virtue makes the soul exceeding good": and the Philosopher says (Ethic. ii, 6): "Virtue is that which makes its possessor good, and his work good likewise."

*I answer that,* As we have said above (A. 1), virtue implies a perfection of power: wherefore the virtue of a thing is fixed by the limit of its power (De Coelo i). Now the limit of any power must needs be good: for all evil implies defect; wherefore Dionysius says (Div. Hom. ii) that every evil is a weakness. And for this reason the virtue of a thing must be regarded in reference to good. Therefore human virtue which is an operative habit, is a good habit, productive of good works.

Reply Obj. 1: Just as bad things are said metaphorically to be perfect, so are they said to be good: for we speak of a perfect thief or robber; and of a good thief or robber, as the Philosopher explains (Metaph. v, text. 21). In this way therefore virtue is applied to evil things: so that the "virtue" of sin is said to be law, in so far as occasionally sin is aggravated through the law, so as to attain to the limit of its possibility.

Reply Obj. 2: The evil of drunkenness and excessive drink, consists in a falling away from the order of reason. Now it happens that, together with this falling away from reason, some lower power is perfect in reference to that which belongs to its own kind, even in direct opposition to reason, or with some falling away therefrom. But the perfection of that power, since it is compatible with a falling away from reason, cannot be called a human virtue.

Reply Obj. 3: Reason is shown to be so much the more perfect, according as it is able to overcome or endure more easily the weakness of the body and of the lower powers. And therefore human virtue, which is attributed to reason, is said to be "made perfect in infirmity," not of the reason indeed, but of the body and of the lower powers.

FOURTH ARTICLE [I-II, Q. 55, Art. 4]

Whether Virtue Is Suitably Defined?

Objection 1: It would seem that the definition, usually given, of virtue, is not suitable, to wit: "Virtue is a good quality of the mind, by which we live righteously, of which no one can make bad use, which God works in us, without us." For virtue is man's goodness, since virtue it is that makes its subject good. But goodness does not seem to be good, as neither is whiteness white. It is therefore unsuitable to describe virtue as a "good quality."

Obj. 2: Further, no difference is more common than its genus; since it is that which divides the genus. But good is more common than quality, since it is convertible with being. Therefore "good" should not be put in the definition of virtue, as a difference of quality.

Obj. 3: Further, as Augustine says (De Trin. xii, 3): "When we come across anything that is not common to us and the beasts of the field, it is something appertaining to the mind." But there are virtues even of the irrational parts; as the Philosopher says (Ethic. iii, 10). Every virtue, therefore, is not a good quality "of the mind."

Obj. 4: Further, righteousness seems to belong to justice; whence the righteous are called just. But justice is a species of virtue. It is therefore unsuitable to put "righteous" in the definition of virtue, when we say that virtue is that "by which we live righteously."

Obj. 5: Further, whoever is proud of a thing, makes bad use of it. But many are proud of virtue, for Augustine says in his Rule, that "pride lies in wait for good works in order to slay them." It is untrue, therefore, "that no one can make bad use of virtue."

Obj. 6: Further, man is justified by virtue. But Augustine commenting on John 15:11: "He shall do greater things than these," says [*Tract. xxvii in Joan.: Serm. xv de Verb. Ap. 11]: "He who created thee without thee, will not justify thee without thee." It is therefore unsuitable to say that "God works virtue in us, without us."

*On the contrary,* We have the authority of Augustine from whose words this definition is gathered, and principally in De Libero Arbitrio ii, 19.

*I answer that,* This definition comprises perfectly the whole essential notion of virtue. For the perfect essential notion of anything is gathered from all its causes. Now the above definition comprises all the causes of virtue. For the formal cause of virtue, as of everything, is gathered from its genus and difference, when it is defined as "a good quality": for "quality" is the genus of virtue, and the difference, "good." But the definition would be more suitable if for "quality" we substitute "habit," which is the proximate genus.

Now virtue has no matter "out of which" it is formed, as neither has any other accident; but it has matter "about which" it is concerned, and matter "in which" it exists, namely, the subject. The matter about which virtue is concerned is its object, and this could not be included in the above definition, because the object fixes the virtue to a certain species, and here we are giving the definition of virtue in general. And so for material cause we have the subject, which is mentioned when we say that virtue is a good quality "of the mind."

The end of virtue, since it is an operative habit, is operation. But it must be observed that some operative habits are always referred to evil, as vicious habits: others are sometimes referred to good, sometimes to evil; for instance, opinion is referred both to the true and to the untrue: whereas virtue is a habit which is always referred to good: and so the distinction of virtue from those habits which are always referred to evil, is expressed in the words "by which we live righteously": and its distinction from those habits which are sometimes directed unto good, sometimes unto evil, in the words, "of which no one makes bad use."

Lastly, God is the efficient cause of infused virtue, to which this definition applies; and this is expressed in the words "which God works in us without us." If we omit this phrase, the remainder of the definition will apply to all virtues in general, whether acquired or infused.

Reply Obj. 1: That which is first seized by the intellect is being: wherefore everything that we apprehend we consider as being, and consequently as one, and as good, which are convertible with being. Wherefore we say that essence is being and is one and is good; and that oneness is being and one and good: and in like manner goodness. But this is not the case with specific forms, as whiteness and health; for everything that we apprehend, is not apprehended with the notion of white and healthy. We must, however, observe that, as accidents and non-subsistent forms are called beings, not as if they themselves had being, but because things are by them; so also are they called good or one, not by some distinct goodness or oneness, but because by them something is good or one. So also is virtue called good, because by it something is good.

Reply Obj. 2: Good, which is put in the definition of virtue, is not good in general which is convertible with being, and which extends further than quality, but the good as fixed by reason, with regard to which Dionysius says (Div. Nom. iv) "that the good of the soul is to be in accord with reason."

Reply Obj. 3: Virtue cannot be in the irrational part of the soul, except in so far as this participates in the reason (Ethic. i, 13). And therefore reason, or the mind, is the proper subject of virtue.

Reply Obj. 4: Justice has a righteousness of its own by which it puts those outward things right which come into human use, and are the proper matter of justice, as we shall show further on (Q. 60, A. 2; II-II, Q. 58, A. 8). But the righteousness which denotes order to a due end and to the Divine law, which is the rule of the human will, as stated above (Q. 19, A. 4), is common to all virtues.

Reply Obj. 5: One can make bad use of a virtue objectively, for instance by having evil thoughts about a virtue, e.g. by hating it, or by being proud of it: but one cannot make bad use of virtue as principle of action, so that an act of virtue be evil.

Reply Obj. 6: Infused virtue is caused in us by God without any action on our part, but not without our consent. This is the sense of the words, "which God works in us without us." As to those things which are done by us, God causes them in us, yet not without action on our part, for He works in every will and in every nature.

# QUESTION 56

OF THE SUBJECT OF VIRTUE (In Six Articles)

We now have to consider the subject of virtue, about which there are six points of inquiry:

(1) Whether the subject of virtue is a power of the soul?

(2) Whether one virtue can be in several powers?

(3) Whether the intellect can be the subject of virtue?

(4) Whether the irascible and concupiscible faculties can be the subject of virtue?

(5) Whether the sensitive powers of apprehension can be the subject of virtue?

(6) Whether the will can be the subject of virtue?

FIRST ARTICLE [I-II, Q. 56, Art. 1]

Whether the Subject of Virtue Is a Power of the Soul?

Objection 1: It would seem that the subject of virtue is not a power of the soul. For Augustine says (De Lib. Arb. ii, 19) that "virtue is that by which we live righteously." But we live by the essence of the soul, and not by a power of the soul. Therefore virtue is not a power, but in the essence of the soul.

Obj. 2: Further, the Philosopher says (Ethic. ii, 6) that "virtue is that which makes its possessor good, and his work good likewise." But as work is set up by power, so he that has a virtue is set up by the essence of the soul. Therefore virtue does not belong to the power, any more than to the essence of the soul.

Obj. 3: Further, power is in the second species of quality. But virtue is a quality, as we have said above (Q. 55, A. 4): and quality is not the subject of quality. Therefore a power of the soul is not the subject of virtue.

*On the contrary,* "Virtue is the limit of power" (De Coelo ii). But the limit is in that of which it is the limit. Therefore virtue is in a power of the soul.

*I answer that,* It can be proved in three ways that virtue belongs to a power of the soul. First, from the notion of the very essence of virtue, which implies perfection of a power; for perfection is in that which it perfects. Secondly, from the fact that virtue is an operative habit, as we have said above (Q. 55, A. 2): for all operation proceeds from the soul through a power. Thirdly, from the fact that virtue disposes to that which is best: for the best is the end, which is either a thing's operation, or something acquired by an operation proceeding from the thing's power. Therefore a power of the soul is the subject of virtue.

Reply Obj. 1: "To live" may be taken in two ways. Sometimes it is taken for the very existence of the living thing: in this way it belongs to the essence of the soul, which is the principle of existence in the living thing. But sometimes "to live" is taken for the operation of the living thing: in this sense, by virtue we live righteously, inasmuch as by virtue we perform righteous actions.

Reply Obj. 2: Good is either the end, or something referred to the end. And therefore, since the good of the worker consists in the work, this fact also, that virtue makes the worker good, is referred to the work, and consequently, to the power.

Reply Obj. 3: One accident is said to be the subject of another, not as though one accident could uphold another; but because one accident inheres to substance by means of another, as color to the body by means of the surface; so that surface is said to be the subject of color. In this way a power of the soul is said to be the subject of virtue.

SECOND ARTICLE [I-II, Q. 56, Art. 2]

Whether One Virtue Can Be in Several Powers?

Objection 1: It would seem that one virtue can be in several powers. For habits are known by their acts. But one act proceeds in various way from several powers: thus walking proceeds from the reason as directing, from the will as moving, and from the motive power as executing. Therefore also one habit can be in several powers.

Obj. 2: Further, the Philosopher says (Ethic. ii, 4) that three things are required for virtue, namely: "to know, to will, and to work steadfastly." But "to know" belongs to the intellect, and "to will" belongs to the will. Therefore virtue can be in several powers.

Obj. 3: Further, prudence is in the reason since it is "the right reason of things to be done" (Ethic. vi, 5). And it is also in the will: for it cannot exist together with a perverse will (Ethic. vi, 12). Therefore one virtue can be in two powers.

*On the contrary,* The subject of virtue is a power of the soul. But the same accident cannot be in several subjects. Therefore one virtue cannot be in several powers of the soul.

*I answer that,* It happens in two ways that one thing is subjected in two. First, so that it is in both on an equal footing. In this way it is impossible for one virtue to be in two powers: since diversity of powers follows the generic conditions of the objects, while diversity of habits follows the specific conditions thereof: and so wherever there is diversity of powers, there is diversity of habits; but not vice versa. In another way one thing can be subjected in two or more, not on an equal footing, but in a certain order. And thus one virtue can belong to several powers, so that it is in one chiefly, while it extends to others by a kind of diffusion, or by way of a disposition, in so far as one power is moved by another, and one power receives from another.

Reply Obj. 1: One act cannot belong to several powers equally, and in the same degree; but only from different points of view, and in various degrees.

Reply Obj. 2: "To know" is a condition required for moral virtue, inasmuch as moral virtue works according to right reason. But moral virtue is essentially in the appetite.

Reply Obj. 3: Prudence is really subjected in reason: but it presupposes as its principle the rectitude of the will, as we shall see further on (A. 3; Q. 57, A. 4).

THIRD ARTICLE [I-II, Q. 56, Art. 3]

Whether the Intellect Can Be the Subject of Virtue?

Objection 1: It would seem that the intellect is not the subject of virtue. For Augustine says (De Moribus Eccl. xv) that all virtue is love. But the subject of love is not the intellect, but the appetitive power alone. Therefore no virtue is in the intellect.

Obj. 2: Further, virtue is referred to good, as is clear from what has been said above (Q. 55, A. 3).

Now good is not the object of the intellect, but of the appetitive power. Therefore the subject of virtue is not the intellect, but the appetitive power.

Obj. 3: Further, virtue is that "which makes its possessor good," as the Philosopher says (Ethic. ii, 6). But the habit which perfects the intellect does not make its possessor good: since a man is not said to be a good man on account of his science or his art. Therefore the intellect is not the subject of virtue.

*On the contrary,* The mind is chiefly called the intellect. But the subject of virtue is the mind, as is clear from the definition, above given, of virtue (Q. 55, A. 4). Therefore the intellect is the subject of virtue.

*I answer that,* As we have said above (Q. 55, A. 3), a virtue is a habit by which we work well. Now a habit may be directed to a good act in two ways. First, in so far as by the habit a man acquires an aptness to a good act; for instance, by the habit of grammar man has the aptness to speak correctly. But grammar does not make a man always speak correctly: for a grammarian may be guilty of a barbarism or make a solecism: and the case is the same with other sciences and arts. Secondly, a habit may confer not only aptness to act, but also the right use of that aptness: for instance, justice not only gives man the prompt will to do just actions, but also makes him act justly.

And since good, and, in like manner, being, is said of a thing simply, in respect, not of what it is potentially, but of what it is actually: therefore from having habits of the latter sort, man is said simply to do good, and to be good; for instance, because he is just, or temperate; and in like manner as regards other such virtues. And since virtue is that "which makes its possessor good, and his work good likewise," these latter habits are called virtuous simply: because they make the work to be actually good, and the subject good simply. But the first kind of habits are not called virtues simply: because they do not make the work good except in regard to a certain aptness, nor do they make their possessor good simply. For through being gifted in science or art, a man is said to be good, not simply, but relatively; for instance, a good grammarian or a good smith. And for this reason science and art are often divided against virtue; while at other times they are called virtues (Ethic. vi, 2).

Hence the subject of a habit which is called a virtue in a relative sense, can be the intellect, and not only the practical intellect, but also the speculative, without any reference to the will: for thus the Philosopher (Ethic. vi, 3) holds that science, wisdom and understanding, and also art, are intellectual virtues. But the subject of a habit which is called a virtue simply, can only be the will, or some power in so far as it is moved by the will. And the reason of this is, that the will moves to their acts all those other powers that are in some way rational, as we have said above (Q. 9, A. 1; Q. 17, AA. 1, 5; I, Q. 82, A. 4): and therefore if man do well actually, this is because he has a good will. Therefore the virtue which makes a man to do well actually, and not merely to have the aptness to do well, must be either in the will itself; or in some power as moved by the will.

Now it happens that the intellect is moved by the will, just as are the other powers: for a man considers something actually, because he wills to do so. And therefore the intellect, in so far as it is subordinate to the will, can be the subject of virtue absolutely so called. And in this way the speculative intellect, or the reason, is the subject of Faith: for the intellect is moved by the command of the will to assent to what is of faith: for "no man believeth, unless he will" [*Augustine: Tract. xxvi in Joan.]. But the practical intellect is the subject of prudence. For since prudence is the right reason of things to be done, it is a condition thereof that man be rightly disposed in regard to the principles of this reason of things to be done, that is in regard to their ends, to which man is rightly disposed by the rectitude of the will, just as to the principles of speculative truth he is rightly disposed by the natural light of the active intellect. And therefore as the subject of science, which is the right reason of speculative truths, is the speculative intellect in its relation to the active intellect, so the subject of prudence is the practical intellect in its relation to the right will.

Reply Obj. 1: The saying of Augustine is to be understood of virtue simply so called: not that every virtue is love simply: but that it depends in some way on love, in so far as it depends on the will, whose first movement consists in love, as we have said above (Q. 25, AA. 1, 2, 3; Q. 27, A. 4; I, Q. 20, A. 1).

Reply Obj. 2: The good of each thing is its end: and therefore, as truth is the end of the intellect, so to know truth is the good act of the intellect. Whence the habit, which perfects the intellect in regard to the knowledge of truth, whether speculative or practical, is a virtue.

Reply Obj. 3: This objection considers virtue simply so called.

FOURTH ARTICLE [I-II, Q. 56, Art. 4]

Whether the Irascible and Concupiscible Powers Are the Subject of Virtue?

Objection 1: It would seem that the irascible and concupiscible powers cannot be the subject of virtue. For these powers are common to us and dumb animals. But we are now speaking of virtue as proper to man, since for this reason it is called human virtue. It is therefore impossible for human virtue to be in the irascible and concupiscible powers which are parts of the sensitive appetite, as we have said in the First Part (Q. 81, A. 2).

Obj. 2: Further, the sensitive appetite is a power which makes use of a corporeal organ. But the good of virtue cannot be in man's body: for the Apostle says (Rom. 7): "I know that good does not dwell in my flesh." Therefore the sensitive appetite cannot be the subject of virtue.

Obj. 3: Further, Augustine proves (De Moribus Eccl. v) that virtue is not in the body but in the soul, for the reason that the body is ruled by the soul: wherefore it is entirely due to his soul that a man make good use of his body: "For instance, if my coachman, through obedience to my orders, guides well the horses which he is driving; this is all due to me." But just as the soul rules the body, so also does the reason rule the sensitive appetite. Therefore that the irascible and concupiscible powers are rightly ruled, is entirely due to the rational powers. Now "virtue is that by which we live rightly," as we have said above (Q. 55, A. 4). Therefore virtue is not in the irascible and concupiscible powers, but only in the rational powers.

Obj. 4: Further, "the principal act of moral virtue is choice" (Ethic. viii, 13). Now choice is not an act of the irascible and concupiscible powers, but of the rational power, as we have said above (Q. 13, A. 2). Therefore moral virtue is not in the irascible and concupiscible powers, but in the reason.

*On the contrary,* Fortitude is assigned to the irascible power, and temperance to the concupiscible power. Whence the Philosopher (Ethic. iii, 10) says that "these virtues belong to the irrational part of the soul."

*I answer that,* The irascible and concupiscible powers can be considered in two ways. First, in themselves, in so far as they are parts of the sensitive appetite: and in this way they are not competent to be the subject of virtue. Secondly, they can be considered as participating in the reason, from the fact that they have a natural aptitude to obey reason. And thus the irascible or concupiscible power can be the subject of human virtue: for, in so far as it participates in the reason, it is the principle of a human act. And to these powers we must needs assign virtues.

For it is clear that there are some virtues in the irascible and concupiscible powers. Because an act, which proceeds from one power according as it is moved by another power, cannot be perfect, unless both powers be well disposed to the act: for instance, the act of a craftsman cannot be successful unless both the craftsman and his instrument be well disposed to act. Therefore in the matter of the operations of the irascible and concupiscible powers, according as they are moved by reason, there must needs be some habit perfecting in respect of acting well, not only the reason, but also the irascible and concupiscible powers. And since the good disposition of the power which moves through being moved, depends on its conformity with the power that moves it: therefore the virtue which is in the irascible and concupiscible powers is nothing else but a certain habitual conformity of these powers to reason.

Reply Obj. 1: The irascible and concupiscible powers considered in themselves, as parts of the sensitive appetite, are common to us and dumb animals. But in so far as they are rational by participation, and are obedient to the reason, they are proper to man. And in this way they can be the subject of human virtue.

Reply Obj. 2: Just as human flesh has not of itself the good of virtue, but is made the instrument of a virtuous act, inasmuch as being moved by reason, we "yield our members to serve justice"; so also, the irascible and concupiscible powers, of themselves indeed, have not the good of virtue, but rather the infection of the *fomes:* whereas, inasmuch as they are in conformity with reason, the good of reason is begotten in them.

Reply Obj. 3: The body is ruled by the soul, and the irascible and concupiscible powers by the reason, but in different ways. For the body obeys the soul blindly without any contradiction, in those things in which it has a natural aptitude to be moved by the soul: whence the Philosopher says (Polit. i, 3) that the "soul rules the body with a despotic command" as the master rules his slave: wherefore the entire movement of the body is referred to the soul. For this reason virtue is not in the body, but in the soul. But the irascible and concupiscible powers do not obey the reason blindly; *on the contrary,* they have their own proper movements, by which, at times, they go against reason, whence the Philosopher says (Polit. i, 3) that the "reason rules the irascible and concupiscible powers by a political command" such as that by which free men are ruled, who have in some respects a will of their own. And for this reason also must there be some virtues in the irascible and concupiscible powers, by which these powers are well disposed to act.

Reply Obj. 4: In choice there are two things, namely, the intention of the end, and this belongs to the moral virtue; and the preferential choice of that which is unto the end, and this belongs to prudence (Ethic. vi, 2, 5). But that the irascible and concupiscible powers have a right intention of the end in regard to the passions of the soul, is due to the good disposition of these powers. And therefore those moral virtues which are concerned with the passions are in the irascible and concupiscible powers, but prudence is in the reason.

FIFTH ARTICLE [I-II, Q. 56, Art. 5]

Whether the Sensitive Powers of Apprehension Are the Subject of Virtue?

Objection 1: It would seem that it is possible for virtue to be in the interior sensitive powers of apprehension. For the sensitive appetite can be the subject of virtue, in so far as it obeys reason. But the interior sensitive powers of apprehension obey reason: for the powers of imagination, of cogitation, and of memory [*Cf. I, Q. 78, A. 4] act at the command of reason. Therefore in these powers there can be virtue.

Obj. 2: Further, as the rational appetite, which is the will, can be hindered or helped in its act, by the sensitive appetite, so also can the intellect or reason be hindered or helped by the powers mentioned above. As, therefore, there can be virtue in the interior powers of appetite, so also can there be virtue in the interior powers of apprehension.

Obj. 3: Further, prudence is a virtue, of which Cicero (De Invent. Rhetor. ii) says that memory is a part. Therefore also in the power of memory there can be a virtue: and in like manner, in the other interior sensitive powers of apprehension.

*On the contrary,* All virtues are either intellectual or moral (Ethic. ii, 1). Now all the moral virtues are in the appetite; while the intellectual virtues are in the intellect or reason, as is clear from Ethic. vi, 1. Therefore there is no virtue in the interior sensitive powers of apprehension.

*I answer that,* In the interior sensitive powers of apprehension there are some habits. And this is made clear principally from what the Philosopher says (De Memoria ii), that "in remembering one thing after another, we become used to it; and use is a second nature." Now a habit of use is nothing else than a habit acquired by use, which is like unto nature. Wherefore Tully says of virtue in his *Rhetoric* that "it is a habit like a second nature in accord with reason." Yet, in man, that which he acquires by use, in his memory and other sensitive powers of apprehension, is not a habit properly so called, but something annexed to the habits of the intellective faculty, as we have said above (Q. 50, A. 4, ad 3).

Nevertheless even if there be habits in such powers, they cannot be virtues. For virtue is a perfect habit, by which it never happens that anything but good is done: and so virtue must needs be in that power which consummates the good act. But the knowledge of truth is not consummated in the sensitive powers of apprehension: for such powers prepare the way to the intellective knowledge. And therefore in these powers there are none of the virtues, by which we know truth: these are rather in the intellect or reason.

Reply Obj. 1: The sensitive appetite is related to the will, which is the rational appetite, through being moved by it. And therefore the act of the appetitive power is consummated in the sensitive appetite: and for this reason the sensitive appetite is the subject of virtue. Whereas the sensitive powers of apprehension are related to the intellect rather through moving it; for the reason that the phantasms are related to the intellective soul, as colors to sight (De Anima iii, text. 18). And therefore the act of knowledge is terminated in the intellect; and for this reason the cognoscitive virtues are in the intellect itself, or the reason.

And thus is made clear the Reply to the Second Objection.

Reply Obj. 3: Memory is not a part of prudence, as species is of a genus, as though memory were a virtue properly so called: but one of the conditions required for prudence is a good memory; so that, in a fashion, it is after the manner of an integral part.

SIXTH ARTICLE [I-II, Q. 56, Art. 6]

Whether the Will Can Be the Subject of Virtue?

Objection 1: It would seem that the will is not the subject of virtue. Because no habit is required for that which belongs to a power by reason of its very nature. But since the will is in the reason, it is of the very essence of the will, according to the Philosopher (De Anima iii, text. 42), to tend to that which is good, according to reason. And to this good every virtue is ordered, since everything naturally desires its own proper good; for virtue, as Tully says in his Rhetoric, is a "habit like a second nature in accord with reason." Therefore the will is not the subject of virtue.

Obj. 2: Further, every virtue is either intellectual or moral (Ethic. i, 13; ii, 1). But intellectual virtue is subjected in the intellect and reason, and not in the will: while moral virtue is subjected in the irascible and concupiscible powers which are rational by participation. Therefore no virtue is subjected in the will.

Obj. 3: Further, all human acts, to which virtues are ordained, are voluntary. If therefore there be a virtue in the will in respect of some human acts, in like manner there will be a virtue in the will in respect of all human acts. Either, therefore, there will be no virtue in any other power, or there will be two virtues ordained to the same act, which seems unreasonable. Therefore the will cannot be the subject of virtue.

*On the contrary,* Greater perfection is required in the mover than in the moved. But the will moves the irascible and concupiscible powers. Much more therefore should there be virtue in the will than in the irascible and concupiscible powers.

*I answer that,* Since the habit perfects the power in reference to act, then does the power need a habit perfecting it unto doing well, which habit is a virtue, when the power's own proper nature does not suffice for the purpose.

Now the proper nature of a power is seen in its relation to its object. Since, therefore, as we have said above (Q. 19, A. 3), the object of the will is the good of reason proportionate to the will, in respect of this the will does not need a virtue perfecting it. But if man's will is confronted with a good that exceeds its capacity, whether as regards the whole human species, such as Divine good, which transcends the limits of human nature, or as regards the individual, such as the good of one's neighbor, then does the will need virtue. And therefore such virtues as those which direct man's affections to God or to his neighbor are subjected in the will, as charity, justice, and such like.

Reply Obj. 1: This objection is true of those virtues which are ordained to the willer's own good; such as temperance and fortitude, which are concerned with the human passions, and the like, as is clear from what we have said (Q. 35, A. 6).

Reply Obj. 2: Not only the irascible and concupiscible powers are rational by participation but "the appetitive power altogether," i.e. in its entirety (Ethic. i, 13). Now the will is included in the appetitive power. And therefore whatever virtue is in the will must be a moral virtue, unless it be theological, as we shall see later on (Q. 62, A. 3).

Reply Obj. 3: Some virtues are directed to the good of moderated passion, which is the proper good of this or that man: and in these cases there is no need for virtue in the will, for the nature of the power suffices for the purpose, as we have said. This need exists only in the case of virtues which are directed to some extrinsic good.

## QUESTION 57

OF THE INTELLECTUAL VIRTUES (In Six Articles)

We now have to consider the various kinds of virtue: and (1) the intellectual virtues; (2) the moral virtues; (3) the theological virtues. Concerning the first there are six points of inquiry:

(1) Whether habits of the speculative intellect are virtues?

(2) Whether they are three, namely, wisdom, science and understanding?

(3) Whether the intellectual habit, which is art, is a virtue?

(4) Whether prudence is a virtue distinct from art?

(5) Whether prudence is a virtue necessary to man?

(6) Whether "eubulia," "synesis" and "gnome" are virtues annexed to prudence?

FIRST ARTICLE [I-II, Q. 57, Art. 1]

Whether the Habits of the Speculative Intellect Are Virtues?

Objection 1: It would seem that the habits of the speculative intellect are not virtues. For virtue is an operative habit, as we have said above (Q. 55, A. 2). But speculative habits are not operative: for speculative matter is distinct from practical, i.e. operative matter. Therefore the habits of the speculative intellect are not virtues.

Obj. 2: Further, virtue is about those things by which man is made happy or blessed: for "happiness is the reward of virtue" (Ethic. i, 9). Now intellectual habits do not consider human acts or other human goods, by which man acquires happiness, but rather things pertaining to nature or to God. Therefore such like habits cannot be called virtues.

Obj. 3: Further, science is a speculative habit. But science and virtue are distinct from one another as genera which are not subalternate, as the Philosopher proves in *Topic.* iv. Therefore speculative habits are not virtues.

*On the contrary,* The speculative habits alone consider necessary things which cannot be otherwise than they are. Now the Philosopher (Ethic. vi, 1) places certain intellectual virtues in that part of the soul which considers necessary things that cannot be otherwise than they are. Therefore the habits of the speculative intellect are virtues.

*I answer that,* Since every virtue is ordained to some good, as stated above (Q. 55, A. 3), a habit, as we have already observed (Q. 56, A. 3), may be called a virtue for two reasons: first, because it confers aptness in doing good; secondly, because besides aptness, it confers the right use of it. The latter condition, as above stated (Q. 55, A. 3), belongs to those habits alone which affect the appetitive part of the soul: since it is the soul's appetitive power that puts all the powers and habits to their respective uses.

Since, then, the habits of the speculative intellect do not perfect the appetitive part, nor affect it in any way, but only the intellective part; they may indeed be called virtues in so far as they confer aptness for a good work, viz. the consideration of truth (since this is the good work of the intellect): yet they are not called virtues in the second way, as though they conferred the right use of a power or habit. For if a man possess a habit of speculative science, it does not follow that he is inclined to make use of it, but he is made able to consider the truth in those matters of which he has scientific knowledge: that he make use of the knowledge which he has, is due to the motion of his will. Consequently a virtue which perfects the will, as charity or justice, confers the right use of these speculative habits. And in this way too there can be merit in the acts of these habits, if they be done out of charity: thus Gregory says (Moral. vi) that the "contemplative life has greater merit than the active life."

Reply Obj. 1: Work is of two kinds, exterior and interior. Accordingly the practical or active faculty which is contrasted with the speculative faculty, is concerned with exterior work, to which the speculative habit is not ordained. Yet it is ordained to the interior act of the intellect which is to consider the truth. And in this way it is an operative habit.

Reply Obj. 2: Virtue is about certain things in two ways. In the first place a virtue is about its object. And thus these speculative virtues are not about those things whereby man is made happy; except perhaps, in so far as the word "whereby" indicates the efficient cause or object of complete happiness, i.e. God, Who is the supreme object of contemplation. Secondly, a virtue is said to be about its acts: and in this sense the intellectual virtues are about those things whereby a man is made happy; both because the acts of these virtues can be meritorious, as stated above, and because they are a kind of beginning of perfect bliss, which consists in the contemplation of truth, as we have already stated (Q. 3, A. 7).

Reply Obj. 3: Science is contrasted with virtue taken in the second sense, wherein it belongs to the appetitive faculty.

SECOND ARTICLE [I-II, Q. 57, Art. 2]

Whether There Are Only Three Habits of the Speculative Intellect, Viz. Wisdom, Science and Understanding?

Objection 1: It would seem unfitting to distinguish three virtues of the speculative intellect, viz. wisdom, science and understanding. Because a species is a kind of science, as stated in *Ethic.* vi, 7. Therefore wisdom should not be condivided with science among the intellectual virtues.

Obj. 2: Further, in differentiating powers, habits and acts in respect of their objects, we consider chiefly the formal aspect of these objects, as we have already explained (I, Q. 77, A. 3). Therefore diversity of habits is taken, not from their material objects, but from the formal aspect of those objects. Now the principle of a demonstration is the formal aspect under which the conclusion is known. Therefore the understanding of principles should not be set down as a habit or virtue distinct from the knowledge of conclusions.

Obj. 3: Further, an intellectual virtue is one which resides in the essentially rational faculty. Now even the speculative reason employs the dialectic syllogism for the sake of argument, just as it employs the demonstrative syllogism. Therefore as science, which is the result of a demonstrative syllogism, is set down as an intellectual virtue, so also should opinion be.

*On the contrary,* The Philosopher (Ethic. vi, 1) reckons these three alone as being intellectual virtues, viz. wisdom, science and understanding.

*I answer that,* As already stated (A. 1), the virtues of the speculative intellect are those which perfect the speculative intellect for the consideration of truth: for this is its good work. Now a truth is subject to a twofold consideration—as known in itself, and as known through another. What is known in itself, is as a *principle,* and is at once understood by the intellect: wherefore the habit that perfects the intellect for the consideration of such truth is called *understanding,* which is the habit of principles.

On the other hand, a truth which is known through another, is understood by the intellect, not at once, but by means of the reason's inquiry, and is as a *term.* This may happen in two ways: first, so that it is the last in some particular genus; secondly, so that it is the ultimate term of all human knowledge. And, since "things that are knowable last from our standpoint, are knowable first and chiefly in their nature" (Phys. i, text. 2, 3); hence that which is last with respect to all human knowledge, is that which is knowable first and chiefly in its nature. And about these is *wisdom,* which considers the highest causes, as stated in Metaph. i, 1, 2. Wherefore it rightly judges all things and sets them in order, because there can be no perfect and universal judgment that is not based on the first causes. But in regard to that which is last in this or that genus of knowable matter, it is *science* which perfects the intellect. Wherefore according to the different kinds of knowable matter, there are different habits of scientific knowledge; whereas there is but one wisdom.

Reply Obj. 1: Wisdom is a kind of science, in so far as it has that which is common to all the sciences; viz. to demonstrate conclusions from principles. But since it has something proper to itself above the other sciences, inasmuch as it judges of them all, not only as to their conclusions, but also as to their first principles, therefore it is a more perfect virtue than science.

Reply Obj. 2: When the formal aspect of the object is referred to a power or habit by one same act, there is no distinction of habit or power in respect of the formal aspect and of the material object: thus it belongs to the same power of sight to see both color, and light, which is the formal aspect under which color is seen, and is seen at the same time as the color. On the other hand, the principles of a demonstration can be considered apart, without the conclusion being considered at all. Again they can be considered together with the conclusions, since the conclusions can be deduced from them. Accordingly, to consider the principles in this second way, belongs to science, which considers the conclusions also: while to consider the principles in themselves belongs to understanding.

Consequently, if we consider the point aright, these three virtues are distinct, not as being on a par with one another, but in a certain order. The same is to be observed in potential wholes, wherein one part is more perfect than another; for instance, the rational soul is more perfect than the sensitive soul; and the sensitive, than the vegetal. For it is thus that science depends on understanding as on a virtue of higher degree: and both of these depend on wisdom, as obtaining the highest place, and containing beneath itself both understanding and science, by judging both of the conclusions of science, and of the principles on which they are based.

Reply Obj. 3: As stated above (Q. 55, AA. 3, 4), a virtuous habit has a fixed relation to good, and is nowise referable to evil. Now the good of the intellect is truth, and falsehood is its evil. Wherefore those habits alone are called intellectual virtues, whereby we tell the truth and never tell a falsehood. But opinion and suspicion can be about both truth and falsehood: and so, as stated in *Ethic.* vi, 3, they are not intellectual virtues.

THIRD ARTICLE [I-II, Q. 57, Art. 3]

Whether the Intellectual Habit, Art, Is a Virtue?

Objection 1: It would seem that art is not an intellectual virtue. For Augustine says (De Lib. Arb. ii, 18, 19) that "no one makes bad use of virtue." But one may make bad use of art: for a craftsman can work badly according to the knowledge of his art. Therefore art is not a virtue.

Obj. 2: Further, there is no virtue of a virtue. But "there is a virtue of art," according to the Philosopher (Ethic. vi, 5). Therefore art is not a virtue.

Obj. 3: Further, the liberal arts excel the mechanical arts. But just as the mechanical arts are practical, so the liberal arts are speculative. Therefore, if art were an intellectual virtue, it would have to be reckoned among the speculative virtues.

*On the contrary,* The Philosopher (Ethic. vi, 3, 4) says that art is a virtue; and yet he does not reckon it among the speculative virtues, which, according to him, reside in the scientific part of the soul.

*I answer that,* Art is nothing else but "the right reason about certain works to be made." And yet the good of these things depends, not on man's appetitive faculty being affected in this or that way, but on the goodness of the work done. For a craftsman, as such, is commendable, not for the will with which he does a work, but for the quality of the work. Art, therefore, properly speaking, is an operative habit. And yet it has something in common with the speculative habits: since the quality of the object considered by the latter is a matter of concern to them also, but not how the human appetite may be affected towards that object. For as long as the geometrician demonstrates the truth, it matters not how his appetitive faculty may be affected, whether he be joyful or angry: even as neither does this matter in a craftsman, as we have observed. And so art has the nature of a virtue in the same way as the speculative habits, in so far, to wit, as neither art nor speculative habit makes a good work as regards the use of the habit, which is the property of a virtue that perfects the appetite, but only as regards the aptness to work well.

Reply Obj. 1: When anyone endowed with an art produces bad workmanship, this is not the work of that art, in fact it is contrary to the art: even as when a man lies, while knowing the truth, his words are not in accord with his knowledge, but contrary thereto. Wherefore, just as science has always a relation to good, as stated above (A. 2, ad 3), so it is with art: and it is for this reason that it is called a virtue. And yet it falls short of being a perfect virtue, because it does not make its possessor to use it well; for which purpose something further is requisite: although there cannot be a good use without the art.

Reply Obj. 2: In order that man may make good use of the art he has, he needs a good will, which is perfected by moral virtue; and for this reason the Philosopher says that there is a virtue of art; namely, a moral virtue, in so far as the good use of art requires a moral virtue. For it is evident that a craftsman is inclined by justice, which rectifies his will, to do his work faithfully.

Reply Obj. 3: Even in speculative matters there is something by way of work: e.g. the making of a syllogism or of a fitting speech, or the work of counting or measuring. Hence whatever habits are ordained to such like works of the speculative reason, are, by a kind of comparison, called arts indeed, but "liberal" arts, in order to distinguish them from those arts that are ordained to works done by the body, which arts are, in a fashion, servile, inasmuch as the body is in servile subjection to the soul, and man, as regards his soul, is free ( *liber* ). On the other hand, those sciences which are not ordained to any such like work, are called sciences simply, and not arts. Nor, if the liberal arts be more excellent, does it follow that the notion of art is more applicable to them.

FOURTH ARTICLE [I-II, Q. 57, Art. 4]

Whether Prudence Is a Distinct Virtue from Art?

Objection 1: It would seem that prudence is not a distinct virtue from art. For art is the right reason about certain works. But diversity of works does not make a habit cease to be an art; since there are various arts about works widely different. Since therefore prudence is also right reason about works, it seems that it too should be reckoned a virtue.

Obj. 2: Further, prudence has more in common with art than the speculative habits have; for they are both "about contingent matters that may be otherwise than they are" (Ethic. vi, 4, 5). Now some speculative habits are called arts. Much more, therefore, should prudence be called an art.

Obj. 3: Further, it belongs to prudence, "to be of good counsel" (Ethic. vi, 5). But counselling takes place in certain arts also, as stated in *Ethic.* iii, 3, e.g. in the arts of warfare, of seamanship, and of medicine. Therefore prudence is not distinct from art.

*On the contrary,* The Philosopher distinguishes prudence from art (Ethic. vi, 5).

*I answer that,* Where the nature of virtue differs, there is a different kind of virtue. Now it has been stated above (A. 1; Q. 56, A. 3) that some habits have the nature of virtue, through merely conferring aptness for a good work: while some habits are virtues, not only through conferring aptness for a good work, but also through conferring the use. But art confers the mere aptness for good work; since it does not regard the appetite; whereas prudence confers not only aptness for a good work, but also the use: for it regards the appetite, since it presupposes the rectitude thereof.

The reason for this difference is that art is the "right reason of things to be made"; whereas prudence is the "right reason of things to be done." Now "making" and "doing" differ, as stated in *Metaph.* ix, text. 16, in that "making" is an action passing into outward matter, e.g. "to build," "to saw," and so forth; whereas "doing" is an action abiding in the agent, e.g. "to see," "to will," and the like. Accordingly prudence stands in the same relation to such like human actions, consisting in the use of powers and habits, as art does to outward making: since each is the perfect reason about the things with which it is concerned. But perfection and rectitude of reason in speculative matters, depend on the principles from which reason argues; just as we have said above (A. 2, ad 2) that science depends on and presupposes understanding, which is the habit of principles. Now in human acts the end is what the principles are in speculative matters, as stated in *Ethic.* vii, 8. Consequently, it is requisite for prudence, which is right reason about things to be done, that man be well disposed with regard to the ends: and this depends on the rectitude of his appetite. Wherefore, for prudence there is need of a moral virtue, which rectifies the appetite. On the other hand the good of things made by art is not the good of man's appetite, but the good of those things themselves: wherefore art does not presuppose rectitude of the appetite. The consequence is that more praise is given to a craftsman who is at fault willingly, than to one who is unwillingly; whereas it is more contrary to prudence to sin willingly than unwillingly, since rectitude of the will is essential to prudence, but not to art. Accordingly it is evident that prudence is a virtue distinct from art.

Reply Obj. 1: The various kinds of things made by art are all external to man: hence they do not cause a different kind of virtue. But prudence is right reason about human acts themselves: hence it is a distinct kind of virtue, as stated above.

Reply Obj. 2: Prudence has more in common with art than a speculative habit has, if we consider their subject and matter: for they are both in the thinking part of the soul, and about things that may be otherwise than they are. But if we consider them as virtues, then art has more in common with the speculative habits, as is clear from what has been said.

Reply Obj. 3: Prudence is of good counsel about matters regarding man's entire life, and the end of human life. But in some arts there is counsel about matters concerning the ends proper to those arts. Hence some men, in so far as they are good counselors in matters of warfare, or seamanship, are said to be prudent officers or pilots, but not simply prudent: only those are simply prudent who give good counsel about all the concerns of life.

FIFTH ARTICLE [I-II, Q. 57, Art. 5]

Whether Prudence Is a Virtue Necessary to Man?

Objection 1: It would seem that prudence is not a virtue necessary to lead a good life. For as art is to things that are made, of which it is the right reason, so is prudence to things that are done, in respect of which we judge of a man's life: for prudence is the right reason about these things, as stated in *Ethic.* vi, 5. Now art is not necessary in things that are made, save in order that they be made, but not after they have been made. Neither, therefore is prudence necessary to man in order to lead a good life, after he has become virtuous; but perhaps only in order that he may become virtuous.

Obj. 2: Further, "It is by prudence that we are of good counsel," as stated in *Ethic.* vi, 5. But man can act not only from his own, but also from another's good counsel. Therefore man does not need prudence in order to lead a good life, but it is enough that he follow the counsels of prudent men.

Obj. 3: Further, an intellectual virtue is one by which one always tells the truth, and never a falsehood. But this does not seem to be the case with prudence: for it is not human never to err in taking counsel about what is to be done; since human actions are about things that may be otherwise than they are. Hence it is written (Wis. 9:14): "The thoughts of mortal men are fearful, and our counsels uncertain." Therefore it seems that prudence should not be reckoned an intellectual virtue.

*On the contrary,* It is reckoned with other virtues necessary for human life, when it is written (Wis. 8:7) of Divine Wisdom: "She teacheth temperance and prudence and justice and fortitude, which are such things as men can have nothing more profitable in life."

*I answer that,* Prudence is a virtue most necessary for human life. For a good life consists in good deeds. Now in order to do good deeds, it matters not only what a man does, but also how he does it; to wit, that he do it from right choice and not merely from impulse or passion. And, since choice is about things in reference to the end, rectitude of choice requires two things: namely, the due end, and something suitably ordained to that due end. Now man is suitably directed to his due end by a virtue which perfects the soul in the appetitive part, the object of which is the good and the end. And to that which is suitably ordained to the due end man needs to be rightly disposed by a habit in his reason, because counsel and choice, which are about things ordained to the end, are acts of the reason. Consequently an intellectual virtue is needed in the reason, to perfect the reason, and make it suitably affected towards things ordained to the end; and this virtue is prudence. Consequently prudence is a virtue necessary to lead a good life.

Reply Obj. 1: The good of an art is to be found, not in the craftsman, but in the product of the art, since art is right reason about things to be made: for since the making of a thing passes into external matter, it is a perfection not of the maker, but of the thing made, even as movement is the act of the thing moved: and art is concerned with the making of things. On the other hand, the good of prudence is in the active principle, whose activity is its perfection: for prudence is right reason about things to be done, as stated above (A. 4). Consequently art does not require of the craftsman that his act be a good act, but that his work be good. Rather would it be necessary for the thing made to act well (e.g. that a knife should carve well, or that a saw should cut well), if it were proper to such things to act, rather than to be acted on, because they have not dominion over their actions. Wherefore the craftsman needs art, not that he may live well, but that he may produce a good work of art, and have it in good keeping: whereas prudence is necessary to man, that he may lead a good life, and not merely that he may be a good man.

Reply Obj. 2: When a man does a good deed, not of his own counsel, but moved by that of another, his deed is not yet quite perfect, as regards his reason in directing him and his appetite in moving him. Wherefore, if he do a good deed, he does not do well simply; and yet this is required in order that he may lead a good life.

Reply Obj. 3: As stated in *Ethic.* vi, 2, truth is not the same for the practical as for the speculative intellect. Because the truth of the speculative intellect depends on conformity between the intellect and the thing. And since the intellect cannot be infallibly in conformity with things in contingent matters, but only in necessary matters, therefore no speculative habit about contingent things is an intellectual virtue, but only such as is about necessary things. On the other hand, the truth of the practical intellect depends on conformity with right appetite. This conformity has no place in necessary matters, which are not affected by the human will; but only in contingent matters which can be effected by us, whether they be matters of interior action, or the products of external work. Hence it is only about contingent matters that an intellectual virtue is assigned to the practical intellect, viz. art, as regards things to be made, and prudence, as regards things to be done.

SIXTH ARTICLE [I-II, Q. 57, Art. 6]

Whether "Eubulia," "Synesis," and "Gnome" Are Virtues Annexed to Prudence?

Objection 1: It would seem that " *eubulia, synesis* , and gnome " are unfittingly assigned as virtues annexed to prudence. For eubulia is "a habit whereby we take good counsel" (Ethic. vi, 9). Now it "belongs to prudence to take good counsel," as stated (Ethic. vi, 9). Therefore eubulia is not a virtue annexed to prudence, but rather is prudence itself.

Obj. 2: Further, it belongs to the higher to judge the lower. The highest virtue would therefore seem to be the one whose act is judgment. Now *synesis* enables us to judge well. Therefore *synesis* is not a virtue annexed to prudence, but rather is a principal virtue.

Obj. 3: Further, just as there are various matters to pass judgment on, so are there different points on which one has to take counsel. But there is one virtue referring to all matters of counsel. Therefore, in order to judge well of what has to be done, there is no need, besides *synesis,* of the virtue of gnome .

Obj. 4: Further, Cicero (De Invent. Rhet. iii) mentions three other parts of prudence; viz. "memory of the past, understanding of the present, and foresight of the future." Moreover, Macrobius (Super Somn. Scip. 1) mentions yet others: viz. "caution, docility," and the like. Therefore it seems that the above are not the only virtues annexed to prudence.

*On the contrary,* stands the authority of the Philosopher (Ethic. vi, 9, 10, 11), who assigns these three virtues as being annexed to prudence.

*I answer that,* Wherever several powers are subordinate to one another, that power is the highest which is ordained to the highest act. Now there are three acts of reason in respect of anything done by man: the first of these is counsel; the second, judgment; the third, command. The first two correspond to those acts of the speculative intellect, which are inquiry and judgment, for counsel is a kind of inquiry: but the third is proper to the practical intellect, in so far as this is ordained to operation; for reason does not have to command in things that man cannot do. Now it is evident that in things done by man, the chief act is that of command, to which all the rest are subordinate. Consequently, that virtue which perfects the command, viz. prudence, as obtaining the highest place, has other secondary virtues annexed to it, viz. *eustochia* , which perfects counsel; and *synesis* and gnome , which are parts of prudence in relation to judgment, and of whose distinction we shall speak further on (ad 3).

Reply Obj. 1: Prudence makes us be of good counsel, not as though its immediate act consisted in being of good counsel, but because it perfects the latter act by means of a subordinate virtue, viz. *euboulia* .

Reply Obj. 2: Judgment about what is to be done is directed to something further: for it may happen in some matter of action that a man's judgment is sound, while his execution is wrong. The matter does not attain to its final complement until the reason has commanded aright in the point of what has to be done.

Reply Obj. 3: Judgment of anything should be based on that thing's proper principles. But inquiry does not reach to the proper principles: because, if we were in possession of these, we should need no more to inquire, the truth would be already discovered. Hence only one virtue is directed to being of good counsel, wheres there are two virtues for good judgment: because difference is based not on common but on proper principles. Consequently, even in speculative matters, there is one science of dialectics, which inquires about all matters; whereas demonstrative sciences, which pronounce judgment, differ according to their different objects. *Synesis* and gnome differ in respect of the different rules on which judgment is based: for *synesis* judges of actions according to the common law; while *gnome* bases its judgment on the natural law, in those cases where the common law fails to apply, as we shall explain further on (II-II, Q. 51, A. 4).

Reply Obj. 4: Memory, understanding and foresight, as also caution and docility and the like, are not virtues distinct from prudence: but are, as it were, integral parts thereof, in so far as they are all requisite for perfect prudence. There are, moreover, subjective parts or species of prudence, e.g. domestic and political economy, and the like. But the three first names are, in a fashion, potential parts of prudence; because they are subordinate thereto, as secondary virtues to a principal virtue: and we shall speak of them later (II-II, Q. 48, seqq.).

## QUESTION 58

OF THE DIFFERENCE BETWEEN MORAL AND INTELLECTUAL VIRTUES (In Five Articles)

We must now consider moral virtues. We shall speak (1) of the difference between them and intellectual virtues; (2) of their distinction, one from another, in respect of their proper matter; (3) of the difference between the chief or cardinal virtues and the others.

Under the first head there are five points of inquiry:

(1) Whether every virtue is a moral virtue?

(2) Whether moral virtue differs from intellectual virtue?

(3) Whether virtue is adequately divided into moral and intellectual virtue?

(4) Whether there can be moral without intellectual virtue?

(5) Whether, on the other hand, there can be intellectual without moral virtue?

FIRST ARTICLE [I-II, Q. 58, Art. 1]

Whether Every Virtue Is a Moral Virtue?

Objection 1: It would seem that every virtue is a moral virtue. Because moral virtue is so called from the Latin *mos,* i.e. custom. Now, we can accustom ourselves to the acts of all the virtues. Therefore every virtue is a moral virtue.

Obj. 2: Further, the Philosopher says (Ethic. ii, 6) that moral virtue is "a habit of choosing the rational mean." But every virtue is a habit of choosing: since the acts of any virtue can be done from choice. And, moreover, every virtue consists in following the rational mean in some way, as we shall explain further on (Q. 64, AA. 1, 2, 3). Therefore every virtue is a moral virtue.

Obj. 3: Further, Cicero says (De Invent. Rhet. ii) that "virtue is a habit like a second nature, in accord with reason." But since every human virtue is directed to man's good, it must be in accord with reason: since man's good "consists in that which agrees with his reason," as Dionysius states (Div. Nom. iv). Therefore every virtue is a moral virtue.

*On the contrary,* The Philosopher [says] (Ethic. i, 13): "When we speak of a man's morals, we do not say that he is wise or intelligent, but that he is gentle or sober." Accordingly, then, wisdom and understanding are not moral virtues: and yet they are virtues, as stated above (Q. 57, A. 2). Therefore not every virtue is a moral virtue.

*I answer that,* In order to answer this question clearly, we must consider the meaning of the Latin word *mos;* for thus we shall be able to discover what a *moral* virtue is. Now mos has a twofold meaning. For sometimes it means custom, in which sense we read (Acts 15:1): "Except you be circumcised after the manner ( *morem* ) of Moses, you cannot be saved." Sometimes it means a natural or quasi-natural inclination to do some particular action, in which sense the word is applied to dumb animals. Thus we read (2 Macc. 1:2) that "rushing violently upon the enemy, like lions [*Leonum more, i.e. as lions are in the habit of doing], they slew them": and the word is used in the same sense in Ps. 67:7, where we read: "Who maketh men of one manner ( *moris* ) to dwell in a house." For both these significations there is but one word in Latin; but in the Greek there is a distinct word for each, for the word *ethos* is written sometimes with a long, and sometimes a short *e.*

Now *moral* virtue is so called from mos in the sense of a natural or quasi-natural inclination to do some particular action. And the other meaning of *mos,* i.e. custom, is akin to this: because custom becomes a second nature, and produces an inclination similar to a natural one. But it is evident that inclination to an action belongs properly to the appetitive power, whose function it is to move all the powers to their acts, as explained above (Q. 9, A. 1). Therefore not every virtue is a moral virtue, but only those that are in the appetitive faculty.

Reply Obj. 1: This argument takes *mos* in the sense of custom.

Reply Obj. 2: Every act of virtue can be done from choice: but no virtue makes us choose aright, save that which is in the appetitive part of the soul: for it has been stated above that choice is an act of the appetitive faculty (Q. 13, A. 1). Wherefore a habit of choosing, i.e. a habit which is the principle whereby we choose, is that habit alone which perfects the appetitive faculty: although the acts of other habits also may be a matter of choice.

Reply Obj. 3: "Nature is the principle of movement" (Phys. ii, text. 3). Now to move the faculties to act is the proper function of the appetitive power. Consequently to become as a second nature by consenting to the reason, is proper to those virtues which are in the appetitive faculty.

SECOND ARTICLE [I-II, Q. 58, Art. 2]

Whether Moral Virtue Differs from Intellectual Virtue?

Objection 1: It would seem that moral virtue does not differ from intellectual virtue. For Augustine says (De Civ. Dei iv, 21) "that virtue is the art of right conduct." But art is an intellectual virtue. Therefore moral and intellectual virtue do not differ.

Obj. 2: Further, some authors put science in the definition of virtues: thus some define perseverance as a "science or habit regarding those things to which we should hold or not hold"; and holiness as "a science which makes man to be faithful and to do his duty to God." Now science is an intellectual virtue. Therefore moral virtue should not be distinguished from intellectual virtue.

Obj. 3: Further, Augustine says (Soliloq. i, 6) that "virtue is the rectitude and perfection of reason." But this belongs to the intellectual virtues, as stated in *Ethic.* vi, 13. Therefore moral virtue does not differ from intellectual.

Obj. 4: Further, a thing does not differ from that which is included in its definition. But intellectual virtue is included in the definition of moral virtue: for the Philosopher says (Ethic. ii, 6) that "moral virtue is a habit of choosing the mean appointed by reason as a prudent man would appoint it." Now this right reason that fixes the mean of moral virtue, belongs to an intellectual virtue, as stated in *Ethic.* vi, 13. Therefore moral virtue does not differ from intellectual.

*On the contrary,* It is stated in Ethic. i, 13 that "there are two kinds of virtue: some we call intellectual; some moral."

*I answer that,* Reason is the first principle of all human acts; and whatever other principles of human acts may be found, they obey reason somewhat, but in various ways. For some obey reason blindly and without any contradiction whatever: such are the limbs of the body, provided they be in a healthy condition, for as soon as reason commands, the hand or the foot proceeds to action. Hence the Philosopher says (Polit. i, 3) that "the soul rules the body like a despot," i.e. as a master rules his slave, who has no right to rebel. Accordingly some held that all the active principles in man are subordinate to reason in this way. If this were true, for man to act well it would suffice that his reason be perfect. Consequently, since virtue is a habit perfecting man in view of his doing good actions, it would follow that it is only in the reason, so that there would be none but intellectual virtues. This was the opinion of Socrates, who said "every virtue is a kind of prudence," as stated in *Ethic.* vi, 13. Hence he maintained that as long as man is in possession of knowledge, he cannot sin; and that every one who sins, does so through ignorance.

Now this is based on a false supposition. Because the appetitive faculty obeys the reason, not blindly, but with a certain power of opposition; wherefore the Philosopher says (Polit. i, 3) that "reason commands the appetitive faculty by a politic power," whereby a man rules over subjects that are free, having a certain right of opposition. Hence Augustine says on Ps. 118 (Serm. 8) that "sometimes we understand (what is right) while desire is slow, or follows not at all," in so far as the habits or passions of the appetitive faculty cause the use of reason to be impeded in some particular action. And in this way, there is some truth in the saying of Socrates that so long as a man is in possession of knowledge he does not sin: provided, however, that this knowledge is made to include the use of reason in this individual act of choice.

Accordingly for a man to do a good deed, it is requisite not only that his reason be well disposed by means of a habit of intellectual virtue; but also that his appetite be well disposed by means of a habit of moral virtue. And so moral differs from intellectual virtue, even as the appetite differs from the reason. Hence just as the appetite is the principle of human acts, in so far as it partakes of reason, so are moral habits to be considered virtues in so far as they are in conformity with reason.

Reply Obj. 1: Augustine usually applies the term "art" to any form of right reason; in which sense art includes prudence which is the right reason about things to be done, even as art is the right reason about things to be made. Accordingly, when he says that "virtue is the art of right conduct," this applies to prudence essentially; but to other virtues, by participation, for as much as they are directed by prudence.

Reply Obj. 2: All such definitions, by whomsoever given, were based on the Socratic theory, and should be explained according to what we have said about art (ad 1).

The same applies to the Third Objection.

Reply Obj. 4: Right reason which is in accord with prudence is included in the definition of moral virtue, not as part of its essence, but as something belonging by way of participation to all the moral virtues, in so far as they are all under the direction of prudence.

THIRD ARTICLE [I-II, Q. 58, Art. 3]

Whether Virtue Is Adequately Divided into Moral and Intellectual?

Objection 1: It would seem that virtue is not adequately divided into moral and intellectual. For prudence seems to be a mean between moral and intellectual virtue, since it is reckoned among the intellectual virtues (Ethic. vi, 3, 5); and again is placed by all among the four cardinal virtues, which are moral virtues, as we shall show further on (Q. 61, A. 1). Therefore virtue is not adequately divided into intellectual and moral, as though there were no mean between them.

Obj. 2: Further, continency, perseverance, and patience are not reckoned to be intellectual virtues. Yet neither are they moral virtues; since they do not reduce the passions to a mean, and are consistent with an abundance of passion. Therefore virtue is not adequately divided into intellectual and moral.

Obj. 3: Further, faith, hope, and charity are virtues. Yet they are not intellectual virtues: for there are only five of these, viz. science, wisdom, understanding, prudence, and art, as stated above (Q. 57, AA. 2, 3, 5). Neither are they moral virtues; since they are not about the passions, which are the chief concern of moral virtue. Therefore virtue is not adequately divided into intellectual and moral.

*On the contrary,* The Philosopher says (Ethic. ii, 1) that "virtue is twofold, intellectual and moral."

*I answer that,* Human virtue is a habit perfecting man in view of his doing good deeds. Now, in man there are but two principles of human actions, viz. the intellect or reason and the appetite: for these are the two principles of movement in man as stated in De Anima iii, text. 48. Consequently every human virtue must needs be a perfection of one of these principles. Accordingly if it perfects man's speculative or practical intellect in order that his deed may be good, it will be an intellectual virtue: whereas if it perfects his appetite, it will be a moral virtue. It follows therefore that every human virtue is either intellectual or moral.

Reply Obj. 1: Prudence is essentially an intellectual virtue. But considered on the part of its matter, it has something in common with the moral virtues: for it is right reason about things to be done, as stated above (Q. 57, A. 4). It is in this sense that it is reckoned with the moral virtues.

Reply Obj. 2: Continency and perseverance are not perfections of the sensitive appetite. This is clear from the fact that passions abound in the continent and persevering man, which would not be the case if his sensitive appetite were perfected by a habit making it conformable to reason. Continency and perseverance are, however, perfections of the rational faculty, and withstand the passions lest reason be led astray. But they fall short of being virtues: since intellectual virtue, which makes reason to hold itself well in respect of moral matters, presupposes a right appetite of the end, so that it may hold itself aright in respect of principles, i.e. the ends, on which it builds its argument: and this is wanting in the continent and persevering man. Nor again can an action proceeding from two principles be perfect, unless each principle be perfected by the habit corresponding to that operation: thus, however perfect be the principal agent employing an instrument, it will produce an imperfect effect, if the instrument be not well disposed also. Hence if the sensitive faculty, which is moved by the rational faculty, is not perfect; however perfect the rational faculty may be, the resulting action will be imperfect: and consequently the principle of that action will not be a virtue. And for this reason, continency, desisting from pleasures, and perseverance in the midst of pains, are not virtues, but something less than a virtue, as the Philosopher maintains (Ethic. vii, 1, 9).

Reply Obj. 3: Faith, hope, and charity are superhuman virtues: for they are virtues of man as sharing in the grace of God.

FOURTH ARTICLE [I-II, Q. 58, Art. 4]

Whether There Can Be Moral Without Intellectual Virtue?

Objection 1: It would seem that moral can be without intellectual virtue. Because moral virtue, as Cicero says (De Invent. Rhet. ii) is "a habit like a second nature in accord with reason." Now though nature may be in accord with some sovereign reason that moves it, there is no need for that reason to be united to nature in the same subject, as is evident of natural things devoid of knowledge. Therefore in a man there may be a moral virtue like a second nature, inclining him to consent to his reason, without his reason being perfected by an intellectual virtue.

Obj. 2: Further, by means of intellectual virtue man obtains perfect use of reason. But it happens at times that men are virtuous and acceptable to God, without being vigorous in the use of reason. Therefore it seems that moral virtue can be without intellectual.

Obj. 3: Further moral virtue makes us inclined to do good works. But some, without depending on the judgment of reason, have a natural inclination to do good works. Therefore moral virtues can be without intellectual virtues.

*On the contrary,* Gregory says (Moral. xxii) that "the other virtues, unless we do prudently what we desire to do, cannot be real virtues." But prudence is an intellectual virtue, as stated above (Q. 57, A. 5). Therefore moral virtues cannot be without intellectual virtues.

*I answer that,* Moral virtue can be without some of the intellectual virtues, viz. wisdom, science, and art; but not without understanding and prudence. Moral virtue cannot be without prudence, because it is a habit of choosing, i.e. making us choose well. Now in order that a choice be good, two things are required. First, that the intention be directed to a due end; and this is done by moral virtue, which inclines the appetitive faculty to the good that is in accord with reason, which is a due end. Secondly, that man take rightly those things which have reference to the end: and this he cannot do unless his reason counsel, judge and command aright, which is the function of prudence and the virtues annexed to it, as stated above (Q. 57, AA. 5, 6). Wherefore there can be no moral virtue without prudence: and consequently neither can there be without understanding. For it is by the virtue of understanding that we know self-evident principles both in speculative and in practical matters. Consequently just as right reason in speculative matters, in so far as it proceeds from naturally known principles, presupposes the understanding of those principles, so also does prudence, which is the right reason about things to be done.

Reply Obj. 1: The inclination of nature in things devoid of reason is without choice: wherefore such an inclination does not of necessity require reason. But the inclination of moral virtue is with choice: and consequently in order that it may be perfect it requires that reason be perfected by intellectual virtue.

Reply Obj. 2: A man may be virtuous without having full use of reason as to everything, provided he have it with regard to those things which have to be done virtuously. In this way all virtuous men have full use of reason. Hence those who seem to be simple, through lack of worldly cunning, may possibly be prudent, according to Matt. 10:16: "Be ye therefore prudent (Douay: 'wise') as serpents, and simple as doves."

Reply Obj. 3: The natural inclination to a good of virtue is a kind of beginning of virtue, but is not perfect virtue. For the stronger this inclination is, the more perilous may it prove to be, unless it be accompanied by right reason, which rectifies the choice of fitting means towards the due end. Thus if a running horse be blind, the faster it runs the more heavily will it fall, and the more grievously will it be hurt. And consequently, although moral virtue be not right reason, as Socrates held, yet not only is it "according to right reason," in so far as it inclines man to that which is, according to right reason, as the Platonists maintained [*Cf. Plato, Meno xli.]; but also it needs to be "joined with right reason," as Aristotle declares (Ethic. vi, 13).

FIFTH ARTICLE [I-II, Q. 58, Art. 5]

Whether There Can Be Intellectual Without Moral Virtue?

Objection 1: It would seem that there can be intellectual without moral virtue. Because perfection of what precedes does not depend on the perfection of what follows. Now reason precedes and moves the sensitive appetite. Therefore intellectual virtue, which is a perfection of the reason, does not depend on moral virtue, which is a perfection of the appetitive faculty; and can be without it.

Obj. 2: Further, morals are the matter of prudence, even as things makeable are the matter of art. Now art can be without its proper matter, as a smith without iron. Therefore prudence can be without the moral virtues, although of all the intellectual virtues, it seems most akin to the moral virtues.

Obj. 3: Further, prudence is "a virtue whereby we are of good counsel" (Ethic. vi, 9). Now many are of good counsel without having the moral virtues. Therefore prudence can be without a moral virtue.

*On the contrary,* To wish to do evil is directly opposed to moral virtue; and yet it is not opposed to anything that can be without moral virtue. Now it is contrary to prudence "to sin willingly" (Ethic. vi, 5). Therefore prudence cannot be without moral virtue.

*I answer that,* Other intellectual virtues can, but prudence cannot, be without moral virtue. The reason for this is that prudence is the right reason about things to be done (and this, not merely in general, but also in particular); about which things actions are. Now right reason demands principles from which reason proceeds to argue. And when reason argues about particular cases, it needs not only universal but also particular principles. As to universal principles of action, man is rightly disposed by the natural understanding of principles, whereby he understands that he should do no evil; or again by some practical science. But this is not enough in order that man may reason aright about particular cases. For it happens sometimes that the aforesaid universal principle, known by means of understanding or science, is destroyed in a particular case by a passion: thus to one who is swayed by concupiscence, when he is overcome thereby, the object of his desire seems good, although it is opposed to the universal judgment of his reason. Consequently, as by the habit of natural understanding or of science, man is made to be rightly disposed in regard to the universal principles of action; so, in order that he be rightly disposed with regard to the particular principles of action, viz. the ends, he needs to be perfected by certain habits, whereby it becomes connatural, as it were, to man to judge aright to the end. This is done by moral virtue: for the virtuous man judges aright of the end of virtue, because "such a man is, such does the end seem to him" (Ethic. iii, 5). Consequently the right reason about things to be done, viz. prudence, requires man to have moral virtue.

Reply Obj. 1: Reason, as apprehending the end, precedes the appetite for the end: but appetite for the end precedes the reason, as arguing about the choice of the means, which is the concern of prudence. Even so, in speculative matters the understanding of principles is the foundation on which the syllogism of the reason is based.

Reply Obj. 2: It does not depend on the disposition of our appetite whether we judge well or ill of the principles of art, as it does, when we judge of the end which is the principle in moral matters: in the former case our judgment depends on reason alone. Hence art does not require a virtue perfecting the appetite, as prudence does.

Reply Obj. 3: Prudence not only helps us to be of good counsel, but also to judge and command well. This is not possible unless the impediment of the passions, destroying the judgment and command of prudence, be removed; and this is done by moral virtue.

## QUESTION 59

OF MORAL VIRTUE IN RELATION TO THE PASSIONS (In Five Articles)

We must now consider the difference of one moral virtue from another. And since those moral virtues which are about the passions, differ accordingly to the difference of passions, we must consider (1) the relation of virtue to passion; (2) the different kinds of moral virtue in relation to the passions. Under the first head there are five points of inquiry:

(1) Whether moral virtue is a passion?

(2) Whether there can be moral virtue with passion?

(3) Whether sorrow is compatible with moral virtue?

(4) Whether every moral virtue is about a passion?

(5) Whether there can be moral virtue without passion?

FIRST ARTICLE [I-II, Q. 59, Art. 1]

Whether Moral Virtue Is a Passion?

Objection 1: It would seem that moral virtue is a passion. Because the mean is of the same genus as the extremes. But moral virtue is a mean between two passions. Therefore moral virtue is a passion.

Obj. 2: Further, virtue and vice, being contrary to one another, are in the same genus. But some passions are reckoned to be vices, such as envy and anger. Therefore some passions are virtues.

Obj. 3: Further, pity is a passion, since it is sorrow for another's ills, as stated above (Q. 35, A. 8). Now "Cicero the renowned orator did not hesitate to call pity a virtue," as Augustine states in *De Civ. Dei* ix, 5. Therefore a passion may be a moral virtue.

*On the contrary,* It is stated in Ethic. ii, 5 that "passions are neither virtues nor vices."

*I answer that,* Moral virtue cannot be a passion. This is clear for three reasons. First, because a passion is a movement of the sensitive appetite, as stated above (Q. 22, A. 3): whereas moral virtue is not a movement, but rather a principle of the movement of the appetite, being a kind of habit. Secondly, because passions are not in themselves good or evil. For man's good or evil is something in reference to reason: wherefore the passions, considered in themselves, are referable both to good and evil, for as much as they may accord or disaccord with reason. Now nothing of this sort can be a virtue: since virtue is referable to good alone, as stated above (Q. 55, A. 3). Thirdly, because, granted that some passions are, in some way, referable to good only, or to evil only; even then the movement of passion, as passion, begins in the appetite, and ends in the reason, since the appetite tends to conformity with reason. On the other hand, the movement of virtue is the reverse, for it begins in the reason and ends in the appetite, inasmuch as the latter is moved by reason. Hence the definition of moral virtue (Ethic. ii, 6) states that it is "a habit of choosing the mean appointed by reason as a prudent man would appoint it."

Reply Obj. 1: Virtue is a mean between passions, not by reason of its essence, but on account of its effect; because, to wit, it establishes the mean between passions.

Reply Obj. 2: If by vice we understand a habit of doing evil deeds, it is evident that no passion is a vice. But if vice is taken to mean sin which is a vicious act, nothing hinders a passion from being a vice, or, on the other hand, from concurring in an act of virtue; in so far as a passion is either opposed to reason or in accordance with reason.

Reply Obj. 3: Pity is said to be a virtue, i.e. an act of virtue, in so far as "that movement of the soul is obedient to reason"; viz. "when pity is bestowed without violating right, as when the poor are relieved, or the penitent forgiven," as Augustine says (De Civ. Dei ix, 5). But if by pity we understand a habit perfecting man so that he bestows pity reasonably, nothing hinders pity, in this sense, from being a virtue. The same applies to similar passions.

SECOND ARTICLE [I-II, Q. 59, Art. 2]

Whether There Can Be Moral Virtue with Passion?

Objection 1: It would seem that moral virtue cannot be with passion. For the Philosopher says (Topic. iv) that "a gentle man is one who is not passionate; but a patient man is one who is passionate but does not give way." The same applies to all the moral virtues. Therefore all moral virtues are without passion.

Obj. 2: Further, virtue is a right affection of the soul, as health is to the body, as stated *Phys.* vii, text. 17: wherefore "virtue is a kind of health of the soul," as Cicero says (Quaest. Tusc. iv). But the soul's passions are "the soul's diseases," as he says in the same book. Now health is incompatible with disease. Therefore neither is passion compatible with virtue.

Obj. 3: Further, moral virtue requires perfect use of reason even in particular matters. But the passions are an obstacle to this: for the Philosopher says (Ethic. vi, 5) that "pleasures destroy the judgment of prudence": and Sallust says (Catilin.) that "when they," i.e. the soul's passions, "interfere, it is not easy for the mind to grasp the truth." Therefore passion is incompatible with moral virtue.

*On the contrary,* Augustine says (De Civ. Dei xiv, 6): "If the will is perverse, these movements," viz. the passions, "are perverse also: but if it is upright, they are not only blameless, but even praiseworthy." But nothing praiseworthy is incompatible with moral virtue. Therefore moral virtue does not exclude the passions, but is consistent with them.

*I answer that,* The Stoics and Peripatetics disagreed on this point, as Augustine relates (De Civ. Dei ix, 4). For the Stoics held that the soul's passions cannot be in a wise or virtuous man: whereas the Peripatetics, who were founded by Aristotle, as Augustine says (De Civ. Dei ix, 4), maintained that the passions are compatible with moral virtue, if they be reduced to the mean.

This difference, as Augustine observes (De Civ. Dei ix, 4), was one of words rather than of opinions. Because the Stoics, through not discriminating between the intellective appetite, i.e. the will, and the sensitive appetite, which is divided into irascible and concupiscible, did not, as the Peripatetics did, distinguish the passions from the other affections of the human soul, in the point of their being movements of the sensitive appetite, whereas the other emotions of the soul, which are not passions, are movements of the intellective appetite or will; but only in the point of the passions being, as they maintained, any emotions in disaccord with reason. These emotions could not be in a wise or virtuous man if they arose deliberately: while it would be possible for them to be in a wise man, if they arose suddenly: because, in the words of Aulus Gellius [*Noct. Attic. xix, 1], quoted by Augustine (De Civ. Dei ix, 4), "it is not in our power to call up the visions of the soul, known as its fancies; and when they arise from awesome things, they must needs disturb the mind of a wise man, so that he is slightly startled by fear, or depressed with sorrow," in so far as "these passions forestall the use of reason without his approving of such things or consenting thereto."

Accordingly, if the passions be taken for inordinate emotions, they cannot be in a virtuous man, so that he consent to them deliberately; as the Stoics maintained. But if the passions be taken for any movements of the sensitive appetite, they can be in a virtuous man, in so far as they are subordinate to reason. Hence Aristotle says (Ethic. ii, 3) that "some describe virtue as being a kind of freedom from passion and disturbance; this is incorrect, because the assertion should be qualified": they should have said virtue is freedom from those passions "that are not as they should be as to manner and time."

Reply Obj. 1: The Philosopher quotes this, as well as many other examples in his books on Logic, in order to illustrate, not his own mind, but that of others. It was the opinion of the Stoics that the passions of the soul were incompatible with virtue: and the Philosopher rejects this opinion (Ethic. ii, 3), when he says that virtue is not freedom from passion. It may be said, however, that when he says "a gentle man is not passionate," we are to understand this of inordinate passion.

Reply Obj. 2: This and all similar arguments which Tully brings forward in *De Tusc. Quaest.* iv take the passions in the execution of reason's command.

Reply Obj. 3: When a passion forestalls the judgment of reason, so as to prevail on the mind to give its consent, it hinders counsel and the judgment of reason. But when it follows that judgment, as through being commanded by reason, it helps towards the execution of reason's command.

THIRD ARTICLE [I-II, Q. 59, Art. 3]

Whether Sorrow Is Compatible with Moral Virtue?

Objection 1: It would seem that sorrow is incompatible with virtue. Because the virtues are effects of wisdom, according to Wis. 8:7: "She," i.e. Divine wisdom, "teacheth temperance, and prudence, and justice, and fortitude." Now the "conversation" of wisdom "hath no bitterness," as we read further on (verse 16). Therefore sorrow is incompatible with virtue also.

Obj. 2: Further, sorrow is a hindrance to work, as the Philosopher states (Ethic. vii, 13; x, 5). But a hindrance to good works is incompatible with virtue. Therefore sorrow is incompatible with virtue.

Obj. 3: Further, Tully calls sorrow a disease of the mind (De Tusc. Quaest. iv). But disease of the mind is incompatible with virtue, which is a good condition of the mind. Therefore sorrow is opposed to virtue and is incompatible with it.

*On the contrary,* Christ was perfect in virtue. But there was sorrow in Him, for He said (Matt. 26:38): "My soul is sorrowful even unto death." Therefore sorrow is compatible with virtue.

*I answer that,* As Augustine says (De Civ. Dei xiv, 8), the Stoics held that in the mind of the wise man there are three eupatheiai , i.e. "three good passions," in place of the three disturbances: viz. instead of covetousness, "desire"; instead of mirth, "joy"; instead of fear, "caution." But they denied that anything corresponding to sorrow could be in the mind of a wise man, for two reasons.

First, because sorrow is for an evil that is already present. Now they held that no evil can happen to a wise man: for they thought that, just as man's only good is virtue, and bodily goods are no good to man; so man's only evil is vice, which cannot be in a virtuous man. But this is unreasonable. For, since man is composed of soul and body, whatever conduces to preserve the life of the body, is some good to man; yet not his supreme good, because he can abuse it. Consequently the evil which is contrary to this good can be in a wise man, and can cause him moderate sorrow. Again, although a virtuous man can be without grave sin, yet no man is to be found to live without committing slight sins, according to 1 John 1:8: "If we say that we have no sin, we deceive ourselves." A third reason is because a virtuous man, though not actually in a state of sin, may have been so in the past. And he is to be commended if he sorrow for that sin, according to 2 Cor. 7:10: "The sorrow that is according to God worketh penance steadfast unto salvation." Fourthly, because he may praiseworthily sorrow for another's sin. Therefore sorrow is compatible with moral virtue in the same way as the other passions are when moderated by reason.

Their second reason for holding this opinion was that sorrow is about evil present, whereas fear is for evil to come: even as pleasure is about a present good, while desire is for a future good. Now the enjoyment of a good possessed, or the desire to have good that one possesses not, may be consistent with virtue: but depression of the mind resulting from sorrow for a present evil, is altogether contrary to reason: wherefore it is incompatible with virtue. But this is unreasonable. For there is an evil which can be present to the virtuous man, as we have just stated; which evil is rejected by reason. Wherefore the sensitive appetite follows reason's rejection by sorrowing for that evil; yet moderately, according as reason dictates. Now it pertains to virtue that the sensitive appetite be conformed to reason, as stated above (A. 1, ad 2). Wherefore moderated sorrow for an object which ought to make us sorrowful, is a mark of virtue; as also the Philosopher says (Ethic. ii, 6, 7). Moreover, this proves useful for avoiding evil: since, just as good is more readily sought for the sake of pleasure, so is evil more undauntedly shunned on account of sorrow.

Accordingly we must allow that sorrow for things pertaining to virtue is incompatible with virtue: since virtue rejoices in its own. On the other hand, virtue sorrows moderately for all that thwarts virtue, no matter how.

Reply Obj. 1: The passage quoted proves that the wise man is not made sorrowful by wisdom. Yet he sorrows for anything that hinders wisdom. Consequently there is no room for sorrow in the blessed, in whom there can be no hindrance to wisdom.

Reply Obj. 2: Sorrow hinders the work that makes us sorrowful: but it helps us to do more readily whatever banishes sorrow.

Reply Obj. 3: Immoderate sorrow is a disease of the mind: but moderate sorrow is the mark of a well-conditioned mind, according to the present state of life.

FOURTH ARTICLE [I-II, Q. 59, Art. 4]

Whether All the Moral Virtues Are About the Passions?

Objection 1: It would seem that all the moral virtues are about the passions. For the Philosopher says (Ethic. ii, 3) that "moral virtue is about objects of pleasure and sorrow." But pleasure and sorrow are passions, as stated above (Q. 23, A. 4; Q. 31, A. 1; Q. 35, AA. 1, 2). Therefore all the moral virtues are about the passions.

Obj. 2: Further, the subject of the moral virtues is a faculty which is rational by participation, as the Philosopher states (Ethic. i, 13). But the passions are in this part of the soul, as stated above (Q. 22, A. 3). Therefore every moral virtue is about the passions.

Obj. 3: Further, some passion is to be found in every moral virtue: and so either all are about the passions, or none are. But some are about the passions, as fortitude and temperance, as stated in *Ethic.* iii, 6, 10. Therefore all the moral virtues are about the passions.

*On the contrary,* Justice, which is a moral virtue, is not about the passions; as stated in Ethic. v, 1, seqq.

*I answer that,* Moral virtue perfects the appetitive part of the soul by directing it to good as defined by reason. Now good as defined by reason is that which is moderated or directed by reason. Consequently there are moral virtues about all matters that are subject to reason's direction and moderation. Now reason directs, not only the passions of the sensitive appetite, but also the operations of the intellective appetite, i.e. the will, which is not the subject of a passion, as stated above (Q. 22, A. 3). Therefore not all the moral virtues are about passions, but some are about passions, some about operations.

Reply Obj. 1: The moral virtues are not all about pleasures and sorrows, as being their proper matter; but as being something resulting from their proper acts. For every virtuous man rejoices in acts of virtue, and sorrows for the contrary. Hence the Philosopher, after the words quoted, adds, "if virtues are about actions and passions; now every action and passion is followed by pleasure or sorrow, so that in this way virtue is about pleasures and sorrows," viz. as about something that results from virtue.

Reply Obj. 2: Not only the sensitive appetite which is the subject of the passions, is rational by participation, but also the will, where there are no passions, as stated above.

Reply Obj. 3: Some virtues have passions as their proper matter, but some virtues not. Hence the comparison does not hold for all cases.

FIFTH ARTICLE [I-II, Q. 59, Art. 5]

Whether There Can Be Moral Virtue Without Passion?

Objection 1: It would seem that moral virtue can be without passion. For the more perfect moral virtue is, the more does it overcome the passions. Therefore at its highest point of perfection it is altogether without passion.

Obj. 2: Further, then is a thing perfect, when it is removed from its contrary and from whatever inclines to its contrary. Now the passions incline us to sin which is contrary to virtue: hence (Rom. 7:5) they are called "passions of sins." Therefore perfect virtue is altogether without passion.

Obj. 3: Further, it is by virtue that we are conformed to God, as Augustine declares (De Moribus Eccl. vi, xi, xiii). But God does all things without passion at all. Therefore the most perfect virtue is without any passion.

*On the contrary,* "No man is just who rejoices not in his deeds," as stated in Ethic. i, 8. But joy is a passion. Therefore justice cannot be without passion; and still less can the other virtues be.

*I answer that,* If we take the passions as being inordinate emotions, as the Stoics did, it is evident that in this sense perfect virtue is without the passions. But if by passions we understand any movement of the sensitive appetite, it is plain that moral virtues, which are about the passions as about their proper matter, cannot be without passions. The reason for this is that otherwise it would follow that moral virtue makes the sensitive appetite altogether idle: whereas it is not the function of virtue to deprive the powers subordinate to reason of their proper activities, but to make them execute the commands of reason, by exercising their proper acts. Wherefore just as virtue directs the bodily limbs to their due external acts, so does it direct the sensitive appetite to its proper regulated movements.

Those moral virtues, however, which are not about the passions, but about operations, can be without passions. Such a virtue is justice: because it applies the will to its proper act, which is not a passion. Nevertheless, joy results from the act of justice; at least in the will, in which case it is not a passion. And if this joy be increased through the perfection of justice, it will overflow into the sensitive appetite; in so far as the lower powers follow the movement of the higher, as stated above (Q. 17, A. 7; Q. 24, A. 3). Wherefore by reason of this kind of overflow, the more perfect a virtue is, the more does it cause passion.

Reply Obj. 1: Virtue overcomes inordinate passion; it produces ordinate passion.

Reply Obj. 2: It is inordinate, not ordinate, passion that leads to sin.

Reply Obj. 3: The good of anything depends on the condition of its nature. Now there is no sensitive appetite in God and the angels, as there is in man. Consequently good operation in God and the angels is altogether without passion, as it is without a body: whereas the good operation of man is with passion, even as it is produced with the body's help.

## QUESTION 60

HOW THE MORAL VIRTUES DIFFER FROM ONE ANOTHER (FIVE ARTICLES)

We must now consider how the moral virtues differ from one another: under which head there are five points of inquiry:

(1) Whether there is only one moral virtue?

(2) Whether those moral virtues which are about operations, are distinct from those which are about passions?

(3) Whether there is but one moral virtue about operations?

(4) Whether there are different moral virtues about different passions?

(5) Whether the moral virtues differ in point of the various objects of the passions?

FIRST ARTICLE [I-II, Q. 60, Art. 1]

Whether There Is Only One Moral Virtue?

Objection 1: It would seem that there is only one moral virtue. Because just as the direction of moral actions belongs to reason which is the subject of the intellectual virtues; so does their inclination belong to the appetite which is the subject of moral virtues. But there is only one intellectual virtue to direct all moral acts, viz. prudence. Therefore there is also but one moral virtue to give all moral acts their respective inclinations.

Obj. 2: Further, habits differ, not in respect of their material objects, but according to the formal aspect of their objects. Now the formal aspect of the good to which moral virtue is directed, is one thing, viz. the mean defined by reason. Therefore, seemingly, there is but one moral virtue.

Obj. 3: Further, things pertaining to morals are specified by their end, as stated above (Q. 1, A. 3). Now there is but one common end of all moral virtues, viz. happiness, while the proper and proximate ends are infinite in number. But the moral virtues themselves are not infinite in number. Therefore it seems that there is but one.

*On the contrary,* One habit cannot be in several powers, as stated above (Q. 56, A. 2). But the subject of the moral virtues is the appetitive part of the soul, which is divided into several powers, as stated in the First Part (Q. 80, A. 2; Q. 81, A. 2). Therefore there cannot be only one moral virtue.

*I answer that,* As stated above (Q. 58, AA. 1, 2, 3), the moral virtues are habits of the appetitive faculty. Now habits differ specifically according to the specific differences of their objects, as stated above (Q. 54, A. 2). Again, the species of the object of appetite, as of any thing, depends on its specific form which it receives from the agent. But we must observe that the matter of the passive subject bears a twofold relation to the agent. For sometimes it receives the form of the agent, in the same kind specifically as the agent has that form, as happens with all univocal agents, so that if the agent be one specifically, the matter must of necessity receive a form specifically one: thus the univocal effect of fire is of necessity something in the species of fire. Sometimes, however, the matter receives the form from the agent, but not in the same kind specifically as the agent, as is the case with non-univocal causes of generation: thus an animal is generated by the sun. In this case the forms received into matter are not of one species, but vary according to the adaptability of the matter to receive the influx of the agent: for instance, we see that owing to the one action of the sun, animals of various species are produced by putrefaction according to the various adaptability of matter.

Now it is evident that in moral matters the reason holds the place of commander and mover, while the appetitive power is commanded and moved. But the appetite does not receive the direction of reason univocally so to say; because it is rational, not essentially, but by participation (Ethic. i, 13). Consequently objects made appetible by the direction of reason belong to various species, according to their various relations to reason: so that it follows that moral virtues are of various species and are not one only.

Reply Obj. 1: The object of the reason is truth. Now in all moral matters, which are contingent matters of action, there is but one kind of truth. Consequently, there is but one virtue to direct all such matters, viz. prudence. On the other hand, the object of the appetitive power is the appetible good, which varies in kind according to its various relations to reason, the directing power.

Reply Obj. 2: This formal element is one generically, on account of the unity of the agent: but it varies in species, on account of the various relations of the receiving matter, as explained above.

Reply Obj. 3: Moral matters do not receive their species from the last end, but from their proximate ends: and these, although they be infinite in number, are not infinite in species.

SECOND ARTICLE [I-II, Q. 60, Art. 2]

Whether Moral Virtues About Operations Are Different from Those That Are About Passions?

Objection 1: It would seem that moral virtues are not divided into those which are about operations and those which are about passions. For the Philosopher says (Ethic. ii, 3) that moral virtue is "an operative habit whereby we do what is best in matters of pleasure or sorrow." Now pleasure and sorrow are passions, as stated above (Q. 31, A. 1; Q. 35, A. 1). Therefore the same virtue which is about passions is also about operations, since it is an operative habit.

Obj. 2: Further, the passions are principles of external action. If therefore some virtues regulate the passions, they must, as a consequence, regulate operations also. Therefore the same moral virtues are about both passions and operations.

Obj. 3: Further, the sensitive appetite is moved well or ill towards every external operation. Now movements of the sensitive appetite are passions. Therefore the same virtues that are about operations are also about passions.

*On the contrary,* The Philosopher reckons justice to be about operations; and temperance, fortitude and gentleness, about passions (Ethic. ii, 3, 7; v, 1, seqq.).

*I answer that,* Operation and passion stand in a twofold relation to virtue. First, as its effects; and in this way every moral virtue has some good operations as its product; and a certain pleasure or sorrow which are passions, as stated above (Q. 59, A. 4, ad 1).

Secondly, operation may be compared to moral virtue as the matter about which virtue is concerned: and in this sense those moral virtues which are about operations must needs differ from those which are about passions. The reason for this is that good and evil, in certain operations, are taken from the very nature of those operations, no matter how man may be affected towards them: viz. in so far as good and evil in them depend on their being commensurate with someone else. In operations of this kind there needs to be some power to regulate the operations in themselves: such are buying and selling, and all such operations in which there is an element of something due or undue to another. For this reason justice and its parts are properly about operations as their proper matter. On the other hand, in some operations, good and evil depend only on commensuration with the agent. Consequently good and evil in these operations depend on the way in which man is affected to them. And for this reason in such like operations virtue must needs be chiefly about internal emotions which are called the passions of the soul, as is evidently the case with temperance, fortitude and the like.

It happens, however, in operations which are directed to another, that the good of virtue is overlooked by reason of some inordinate passion of the soul. In such cases justice is destroyed in so far as the due measure of the external act is destroyed: while some other virtue is destroyed in so far as the internal passions exceed their due measure. Thus when through anger, one man strikes another, justice is destroyed in the undue blow; while gentleness is destroyed by the immoderate anger. The same may be clearly applied to other virtues.

This suffices for the Replies to the Objections. For the first considers operations as the effect of virtue, while the other two consider operation and passion as concurring in the same effect. But in some cases virtue is chiefly about operations, in others, about passions, for the reason given above.

THIRD ARTICLE [I-II, Q. 60, Art. 3]

Whether There Is Only One Moral Virtue About Operations?

Objection 1: It would seem that there is but one moral virtue about operations. Because the rectitude of all external operations seems to belong to justice. Now justice is but one virtue. Therefore there is but one virtue about operations.

Obj. 2: Further, those operations seem to differ most, which are directed on the one side to the good of the individual, and on the other to the good of the many. But this diversity does not cause diversity among the moral virtues: for the Philosopher says (Ethic. v, 1) that legal justice, which directs human acts to the common good, does not differ, save logically, from the virtue which directs a man's actions to one man only. Therefore diversity of operations does not cause a diversity of moral virtues.

Obj. 3: Further, if there are various moral virtues about various operations, diversity of moral virtues would needs follow diversity of operations. But this is clearly untrue: for it is the function of justice to establish rectitude in various kinds of commutations, and again in distributions, as is set down in *Ethic.* v, 2. Therefore there are not different virtues about different operations.

*On the contrary,* Religion is a moral virtue distinct from piety, both of which are about operations.

*I answer that,* All the moral virtues that are about operations agree in one general notion of justice, which is in respect of something due to another: but they differ in respect of various special notions. The reason for this is that in external operations, the order of reason is established, as we have stated (A. 2), not according as how man is affected towards such operations, but according to the becomingness of the thing itself; from which becomingness we derive the notion of something due which is the formal aspect of justice: for, seemingly, it pertains to justice that a man give another his due. Wherefore all such virtues as are about operations, bear, in some way, the character of justice. But the thing due is not of the same kind in all these virtues: for something is due to an equal in one way, to a superior, in another way, to an inferior, in yet another; and the nature of a debt differs according as it arises from a contract, a promise, or a favor already conferred. And corresponding to these various kinds of debt there are various virtues: e.g. *Religion* whereby we pay our debt to God; *Piety,* whereby we pay our debt to our parents or to our country; *Gratitude,* whereby we pay our debt to our benefactors, and so forth.

Reply Obj. 1: Justice properly so called is one special virtue, whose object is the perfect due, which can be paid in the equivalent. But the name of justice is extended also to all cases in which something due is rendered: in this sense it is not as a special virtue.

Reply Obj. 2: That justice which seeks the common good is another virtue from that which is directed to the private good of an individual: wherefore common right differs from private right; and Tully (De Inv. ii) reckons as a special virtue, piety which directs man to the good of his country. But that justice which directs man to the common good is a general virtue through its act of command: since it directs all the acts of the virtues to its own end, viz. the common good. And the virtues, in so far as they are commanded by that justice, receive the name of justice: so that virtue does not differ, save logically, from legal justice; just as there is only a logical difference between a virtue that is active of itself, and a virtue that is active through the command of another virtue.

Reply Obj. 3: There is the same kind of due in all the operations belonging to special justice. Consequently, there is the same virtue of justice, especially in regard to commutations. For it may be that distributive justice is of another species from commutative justice; but about this we shall inquire later on (II-II, Q. 61, A. 1).

FOURTH ARTICLE [I-II, Q. 60, Art. 4]

Whether There Are Different Moral Virtues About Different Passions?

Objection 1: It would seem that there are not different moral virtues about different passions. For there is but one habit about things that concur in their source and end: as is evident especially in the case of sciences. But the passions all concur in one source, viz. love; and they all terminate in the same end, viz. joy or sorrow, as we stated above (Q. 25, AA. 1, 2, 4; Q. 27, A. 4). Therefore there is but one moral virtue about all the passions.

Obj. 2: Further, if there were different moral virtues about different passions, it would follow that there are as many moral virtues as passions. But this clearly is not the case: since there is one moral virtue about contrary passions; namely, fortitude, about fear and daring; temperance, about pleasure and sorrow. Therefore there is no need for different moral virtues about different passions.

Obj. 3: Further, love, desire, and pleasure are passions of different species, as stated above (Q. 23, A. 4). Now there is but one virtue about all these three, viz. temperance. Therefore there are not different moral virtues about different passions.

*On the contrary,* Fortitude is about fear and daring; temperance about desire; meekness about anger; as stated in Ethic. iii, 6, 10; iv, 5.

*I answer that,* It cannot be said that there is only one moral virtue about all the passions: since some passions are not in the same power as other passions; for some belong to the irascible, others to the concupiscible faculty, as stated above (Q. 23, A. 1).

On the other hand, neither does every diversity of passions necessarily suffice for a diversity of moral virtues. First, because some passions are in contrary opposition to one another, such as joy and sorrow, fear and daring, and so on. About such passions as are thus in opposition to one another there must needs be one same virtue. Because, since moral virtue consists in a kind of mean, the mean in contrary passions stands in the same ratio to both, even as in the natural order there is but one mean between contraries, e.g. between black and white. Secondly, because there are different passions contradicting reason in the same manner, e.g. by impelling to that which is contrary to reason, or by withdrawing from that which is in accord with reason. Wherefore the different passions of the concupiscible faculty do not require different moral virtues, because their movements follow one another in a certain order, as being directed to the one same thing, viz. the attainment of some good or the avoidance of some evil: thus from love proceeds desire, and from desire we arrive at pleasure; and it is the same with the opposite passions, for hatred leads to avoidance or dislike, and this leads to sorrow. On the other hand, the irascible passions are not all of one order, but are directed to different things: for daring and fear are about some great danger; hope and despair are about some difficult good; while anger seeks to overcome something contrary which has wrought harm. Consequently there are different virtues about such like passions: e.g. temperance, about the concupiscible passions; fortitude, about fear and daring; magnanimity, about hope and despair; meekness, about anger.

Reply Obj. 1: All the passions concur in one common principle and end; but not in one proper principle or end: and so this does not suffice for the unity of moral virtue.

Reply Obj. 2: Just as in the natural order the same principle causes movement from one extreme and movement towards the other; and as in the intellectual order contraries have one common ratio; so too between contrary passions there is but one moral virtue, which, like a second nature, consents to reason's dictates.

Reply Obj. 3: Those three passions are directed to the same object in a certain order, as stated above: and so they belong to the same virtue.

FIFTH ARTICLE [I-II, Q. 60, Art. 5]

Whether the Moral Virtues Differ in Point of the Various Objects of the Passions?

Objection 1: It would seem that the moral virtues do not differ according to the objects of the passions. For just as there are objects of passions, so are there objects of operations. Now those moral virtues that are about operations, do not differ according to the objects of those operations: for the buying and selling either of a house or of a horse belong to the one same virtue of justice. Therefore neither do those moral virtues that are about passions differ according to the objects of those passions.

Obj. 2: Further, the passions are acts or movements of the sensitive appetite. Now it needs a greater difference to differentiate habits than acts. Hence diverse objects which do not diversify the species of passions, do not diversify the species of moral virtue: so that there is but one moral virtue about all objects of pleasure, and the same applies to the other passions.

Obj. 3: Further, more or less do not change a species. Now various objects of pleasure differ only by reason of being more or less pleasurable. Therefore all objects of pleasure belong to one species of virtue: and for the same reason so do all fearful objects, and the same applies to others. Therefore moral virtue is not diversified according to the objects of the passions.

Obj. 4: Further, virtue hinders evil, even as it produces good. But there are various virtues about the desires for good things: thus temperance is about desires for the pleasure of touch, and *eutrapelia* about pleasures in games. Therefore there should be different virtues about fears of evils.

*On the contrary,* Chastity is about sexual pleasures, abstinence about pleasures of the table, and eutrapelia about pleasures in games.

*I answer that,* The perfection of a virtue depends on the reason; whereas the perfection of a passion depends on the sensitive appetite. Consequently virtues must needs be differentiated according to their relation to reason, but the passions according to their relation to the appetite. Hence the objects of the passions, according as they are variously related to the sensitive appetite, cause the different species of passions: while, according as they are related to reason, they cause the different species of virtues. Now the movement of reason is not the same as that of the sensitive appetite. Wherefore nothing hinders a difference of objects from causing diversity of passions, without causing diversity of virtues, as when one virtue is about several passions, as stated above (A. 4); and again, a difference of objects from causing different virtues, without causing a difference of passions, since several virtues are directed about one passion, e.g. pleasure.

And because diverse passions belonging to diverse powers, always belong to diverse virtues, as stated above (A. 4); therefore a difference of objects that corresponds to a difference of powers always causes a specific difference of virtues—for instance the difference between that which is good absolutely speaking, and that which is good and difficult to obtain. Moreover since the reason rules man's lower powers in a certain order, and even extends to outward things; hence, one single object of the passions, according as it is apprehended by sense, imagination, or reason, and again, according as it belongs to the soul, body, or external things, has various relations to reason, and consequently is of a nature to cause a difference of virtues. Consequently man's good which is the object of love, desire and pleasure, may be taken as referred either to a bodily sense, or to the inner apprehension of the mind: and this same good may be directed to man's good in himself, either in his body or in his soul, or to man's good in relation to other men. And every such difference, being differently related to reason, differentiates virtues.

Accordingly, if we take a good, and it be something discerned by the sense of touch, and something pertaining to the upkeep of human life either in the individual or in the species, such as the pleasures of the table or of sexual intercourse, it will belong to the virtue of *temperance.* As regards the pleasures of the other senses, they are not intense, and so do not present much difficulty to the reason: hence there is no virtue corresponding to them; for virtue, "like art, is about difficult things" (Ethic. ii, 3).

On the other hand, good discerned not by the senses, but by an inner power, and belonging to man in himself, is like money and honor; the former, by its very nature, being employable for the good of the body, while the latter is based on the apprehension of the mind. These goods again may be considered either absolutely, in which way they concern the concupiscible faculty, or as being difficult to obtain, in which way they belong to the irascible part: which distinction, however, has no place in pleasurable objects of touch; since such are of base condition, and are becoming to man in so far as he has something in common with irrational animals. Accordingly in reference to money considered as a good absolutely, as an object of desire, pleasure, or love, there is *liberality* : but if we consider this good as difficult to get, and as being the object of our hope, there is *magnificence* [* megaloprepeia ]. With regard to that good which we call honor, taken absolutely, as the object of love, we have a virtue called *philotimia,* i.e. love of honor : while if we consider it as hard to attain, and as an object of hope, then we have *magnanimity.* Wherefore liberality and philotimia seem to be in the concupiscible part, while magnificence and magnanimity are in the irascible.

As regards man's good in relation to other men, it does not seem hard to obtain, but is considered absolutely, as the object of the concupiscible passions. This good may be pleasurable to a man in his behavior towards another either in some serious matter, in actions, to wit, that are directed by reason to a due end, or in playful actions, viz. that are done for mere pleasure, and which do not stand in the same relation to reason as the former. Now one man behaves towards another in serious matters, in two ways. First, as being pleasant in his regard, by becoming speech and deeds: and this belongs to a virtue which Aristotle (Ethic. ii, 7) calls "friendship" [* *philia* ], and may be rendered "affability." Secondly, one man behaves towards another by being frank with him, in words and deeds: this belongs to another virtue which (Ethic. iv, 7) he calls "truthfulness" [* *aletheia* ]. For frankness is more akin to the reason than pleasure, and serious matters than play. Hence there is another virtue about the pleasures of games, which the Philosopher calls *eutrapelia* (Ethic. iv, 8).

It is therefore evident that, according to Aristotle, there are ten moral virtues about the passions, viz. fortitude, temperance, liberality, magnificence, magnanimity, *philotimia,* gentleness, friendship, truthfulness, and eutrapelia, all of which differ in respect of their diverse matter, passions, or objects: so that if we add justice, which is about operations, there will be eleven in all.

Reply Obj. 1: All objects of the same specific operation have the same relation to reason: not so all the objects of the same specific passion; because operations do not thwart reason as the passions do.

Reply Obj. 2: Passions are not differentiated by the same rule as virtues are, as stated above.

Reply Obj. 3: More and less do not cause a difference of species, unless they bear different relations to reason.

Reply Obj. 4: Good is a more potent mover than evil: because evil does not cause movement save in virtue of good, as Dionysius states (Div. Nom. iv). Hence an evil does not prove an obstacle to reason, so as to require virtues unless that evil be great; there being, seemingly, one such evil corresponding to each kind of passion. Hence there is but one virtue, meekness, for every form of anger; and, again, but one virtue, fortitude, for all forms of daring. On the other hand, good involves difficulty, which requires virtue, even if it be not a great good in that particular kind of passion. Consequently there are various moral virtues about desires, as stated above.

# QUESTION 61

OF THE CARDINAL VIRTUES (In Five Articles)

We must now consider the cardinal virtues: under which head there are five points of inquiry:

(1) Whether the moral virtues should be called cardinal or principal virtues?

(2) Of their number;

(3) Which are they?

(4) Whether they differ from one another?

(5) Whether they are fittingly divided into social, perfecting, perfect, and exemplar virtues?

FIRST ARTICLE [I-II, Q. 61, Art. 1]

Whether the Moral Virtues Should Be Called Cardinal or Principal Virtues?

Objection 1: It would seem that moral virtues should not be called cardinal or principal virtues. For "the opposite members of a division are by nature simultaneous" (Categor. x), so that one is not principal rather than another. Now all the virtues are opposite members of the division of the genus "virtue." Therefore none of them should be called principal.

Obj. 2: Further, the end is principal as compared to the means. But the theological virtues are about the end; while the moral virtues are about the means. Therefore the theological virtues, rather than the moral virtues, should be called principal or cardinal.

Obj. 3: Further, that which is essentially so is principal in comparison with that which is so by participation. But the intellectual virtues belong to that which is essentially rational: whereas the moral virtues belong to that which is rational by participation, as stated above (Q. 58, A. 3). Therefore the intellectual virtues are principal, rather than the moral virtues.

*On the contrary,* Ambrose in explaining the words, "Blessed are the poor in spirit" (Luke 6:20) says: "We know that there are four cardinal virtues, viz. temperance, justice, prudence, and fortitude." But these are moral virtues. Therefore the moral virtues are cardinal virtues.

*I answer that,* When we speak of virtue simply, we are understood to speak of human virtue. Now human virtue, as stated above (Q. 56, A. 3), is one that answers to the perfect idea of virtue, which requires rectitude of the appetite: for such like virtue not only confers the faculty of doing well, but also causes the good deed done. On the other hand, the name virtue is applied to one that answers imperfectly to the idea of virtue, and does not require rectitude of the appetite: because it merely confers the faculty of doing well without causing the good deed to be done. Now it is evident that the perfect is principal as compared to the imperfect: and so those virtues which imply rectitude of the appetite are called principal virtues. Such are the moral virtues, and prudence alone, of the intellectual virtues, for it is also something of a moral virtue, as was clearly shown above (Q. 57, A. 4). Consequently, those virtues which are called principal or cardinal are fittingly placed among the moral virtues.

Reply Obj. 1: When a univocal genus is divided into its species, the members of the division are on a par in the point of the generic idea; although considered in their nature as things, one species may surpass another in rank and perfection, as man in respect of other animals. But when we divide an analogous term, which is applied to several things, but to one before it is applied to another, nothing hinders one from ranking before another, even in the point of the generic idea; as the notion of being is applied to substance principally in relation to accident. Such is the division of virtue into various kinds of virtue: since the good defined by reason is not found in the same way in all things.

Reply Obj. 2: The theological virtues are above man, as stated above (Q. 58, A. 3, ad 3). Hence they should properly be called not human, but "super-human" or godlike virtues.

Reply Obj. 3: Although the intellectual virtues, except in prudence, rank before the moral virtues, in the point of their subject, they do not rank before them as virtues; for a virtue, as such, regards good, which is the object of the appetite.

SECOND ARTICLE [I-II, Q. 61, Art. 5]

Whether There Are Four Cardinal Virtues?

Objection 1: It would seem that there are not four cardinal virtues. For prudence is the directing principle of the other moral virtues, as is clear from what has been said above (Q. 58, A. 4). But that which directs other things ranks before them. Therefore prudence alone is a principal virtue.

Obj. 2: Further, the principal virtues are, in a way, moral virtues. Now we are directed to moral works both by the practical reason, and by a right appetite, as stated in *Ethic.* vi, 2. Therefore there are only two cardinal virtues.

Obj. 3: Further, even among the other virtues one ranks higher than another. But in order that a virtue be principal, it needs not to rank above all the others, but above some. Therefore it seems that there are many more principal virtues.

*On the contrary,* Gregory says (Moral. ii): "The entire structure of good works is built on four virtues."

*I answer that,* Things may be numbered either in respect of their formal principles, or according to the subjects in which they are: and either way we find that there are four cardinal virtues.

For the formal principle of the virtue of which we speak now is good as defined by reason; which good is considered in two ways. First, as existing in the very act of reason: and thus we have one principal virtue, called "Prudence." Secondly, according as the reason puts its order into something else; either into operations, and then we have "Justice"; or into passions, and then we need two virtues. For the need of putting the order of reason into the passions is due to their thwarting reason: and this occurs in two ways. First, by the passions inciting to something against reason, and then the passions need a curb, which we call "Temperance." Secondly, by the passions withdrawing us from following the dictate of reason, e.g. through fear of danger or toil: and then man needs to be strengthened for that which reason dictates, lest he turn back; and to this end there is "Fortitude."

In like manner, we find the same number if we consider the subjects of virtue. For there are four subjects of the virtue we speak of now: viz. the power which is rational in its essence, and this is perfected by "Prudence"; and that which is rational by participation, and is threefold, the will, subject of "Justice," the concupiscible faculty, subject of "Temperance," and the irascible faculty, subject of "Fortitude."

Reply Obj. 1: Prudence is the principal of all the virtues simply. The others are principal, each in its own genus.

Reply Obj. 2: That part of the soul which is rational by participation is threefold, as stated above.

Reply Obj. 3: All the other virtues among which one ranks before another, are reducible to the above four, both as to the subject and as to the formal principle.

THIRD ARTICLE [I-II, Q. 61, Art. 3]

Whether Any Other Virtues Should Be Called Principal Rather Than These?

Objection 1: It would seem that other virtues should be called principal rather than these. For, seemingly, the greatest is the principal in any genus. Now "magnanimity has a great influence on all the virtues" (Ethic. iv, 3). Therefore magnanimity should more than any be called a principal virtue.

Obj. 2: Further, that which strengthens the other virtues should above all be called a principal virtue. But such is humility: for Gregory says (Hom. iv in Ev.) that "he who gathers the other virtues without humility is as one who carries straw against the wind." Therefore humility seems above all to be a principal virtue.

Obj. 3: Further, that which is most perfect seems to be principal. But this applies to patience, according to James 1:4: "Patience hath a perfect work." Therefore patience should be reckoned a principal virtue.

*On the contrary,* Cicero reduces all other virtues to these four (De Invent. Rhet. ii).

*I answer that,* As stated above (A. 2), these four are reckoned as cardinal virtues, in respect of the four formal principles of virtue as we understand it now. These principles are found chiefly in certain acts and passions. Thus the good which exists in the act of reason, is found chiefly in reason's command, but not in its counsel or its judgment, as stated above (Q. 57, A. 6). Again, good as defined by reason and put into our operations as something right and due, is found chiefly in commutations and distributions in respect of another person, and on a basis of equality. The good of curbing the passions is found chiefly in those passions which are most difficult to curb, viz. in the pleasures of touch. The good of being firm in holding to the good defined by reason, against the impulse of passion, is found chiefly in perils of death, which are most difficult to withstand.

Accordingly the above four virtues may be considered in two ways. First, in respect of their common formal principles. In this way they are called principal, being general, as it were, in comparison with all the virtues: so that, for instance, any virtue that causes good in reason's act of consideration, may be called prudence; every virtue that causes the good of right and due in operation, be called justice; every virtue that curbs and represses the passions, be called temperance; and every virtue that strengthens the mind against any passions whatever, be called fortitude. Many, both holy doctors, as also philosophers, speak about these virtues in this sense: and in this way the other virtues are contained under them. Wherefore all the objections fail.

Secondly, they may be considered in point of their being denominated, each one from that which is foremost in its respective matter, and thus they are specific virtues, condivided with the others. Yet they are called principal in comparison with the other virtues, on account of the importance of their matter: so that prudence is the virtue which commands; justice, the virtue which is about due actions between equals; temperance, the virtue which suppresses desires for the pleasures of touch; and fortitude, the virtue which strengthens against dangers of death. Thus again do the objections fail: because the other virtues may be principal in some other way, but these are called principal by reason of their matter, as stated above.

FOURTH ARTICLE [I-II, Q. 61, Art. 4]

Whether the Four Cardinal Virtues Differ from One Another?

Objection 1: It would seem that the above four virtues are not diverse and distinct from one another. For Gregory says (Moral. xxii, 1): "There is no true prudence, unless it be just, temperate and brave; no perfect temperance, that is not brave, just and prudent; no sound fortitude, that is not prudent, temperate and just; no real justice, without prudence, fortitude and temperance." But this would not be so, if the above virtues were distinct from one another: since the different species of one genus do not qualify one another. Therefore the aforesaid virtues are not distinct from one another.

Obj. 2: Further, among things distinct from one another the function of one is not attributed to another. But the function of temperance is attributed to fortitude: for Ambrose says (De Offic. xxxvi): "Rightly do we call it fortitude, when a man conquers himself, and is not weakened and bent by any enticement." And of temperance he says (De Offic. xliii, xlv) that it "safeguards the manner and order in all things that we decide to do and say." Therefore it seems that these virtues are not distinct from one another.

Obj. 3: Further, the Philosopher says (Ethic. ii, 4) that the necessary conditions of virtue are first of all "that a man should have knowledge; secondly, that he should exercise choice for a particular end; thirdly, that he should possess the habit and act with firmness and steadfastness." But the first of these seems to belong to prudence which is rectitude of reason in things to be done; the second, i.e. choice, belongs to temperance, whereby a man, holding his passions on the curb, acts, not from passion but from choice; the third, that a man should act for the sake of a due end, implies a certain rectitude, which seemingly belongs to justice; while the last, viz. firmness and steadfastness, belongs to fortitude. Therefore each of these virtues is general in comparison to other virtues. Therefore they are not distinct from one another.

*On the contrary,* Augustine says (De Moribus Eccl. xi) that "there are four virtues, corresponding to the various emotions of love," and he applies this to the four virtues mentioned above. Therefore the same four virtues are distinct from one another.

*I answer that,* As stated above (A. 3), these four virtues are understood differently by various writers. For some take them as signifying certain general conditions of the human mind, to be found in all the virtues: so that, to wit, prudence is merely a certain rectitude of discretion in any actions or matters whatever; justice, a certain rectitude of the mind, whereby a man does what he ought in any matters; temperance, a disposition of the mind, moderating any passions or operations, so as to keep them within bounds; and fortitude, a disposition whereby the soul is strengthened for that which is in accord with reason, against any assaults of the passions, or the toil involved by any operations. To distinguish these four virtues in this way does not imply that justice, temperance and fortitude are distinct virtuous habits: because it is fitting that every moral virtue, from the fact that it is a *habit,* should be accompanied by a certain firmness so as not to be moved by its contrary: and this, we have said, belongs to fortitude. Moreover, inasmuch as it is a *virtue,* it is directed to good which involves the notion of right and due; and this, we have said, belongs to justice. Again, owing to the fact that it is a *moral virtue* partaking of reason, it observes the mode of reason in all things, and does not exceed its bounds, which has been stated to belong to temperance. It is only in the point of having discretion, which we ascribed to prudence, that there seems to be a distinction from the other three, inasmuch as discretion belongs essentially to reason; whereas the other three imply a certain share of reason by way of a kind of application (of reason) to passions or operations. According to the above explanation, then, prudence would be distinct from the other three virtues: but these would not be distinct from one another; for it is evident that one and the same virtue is both habit, and virtue, and moral virtue.

Others, however, with better reason, take these four virtues, according as they have their special determinate matter; each of its own matter, in which special commendation is given to that general condition from which the virtue's name is taken as stated above (A. 3). In this way it is clear that the aforesaid virtues are distinct habits, differentiated in respect of their diverse objects.

Reply Obj. 1: Gregory is speaking of these four virtues in the first sense given above. It may also be said that these four virtues qualify one another by a kind of overflow. For the qualities of prudence overflow on to the other virtues in so far as they are directed by prudence. And each of the others overflows on to the rest, for the reason that whoever can do what is harder, can do what is less difficult. Wherefore whoever can curb his desires for the pleasures of touch, so that they keep within bounds, which is a very hard thing to do, for this very reason is more able to check his daring in dangers of death, so as not to go too far, which is much easier; and in this sense fortitude is said to be temperate. Again, temperance is said to be brave, by reason of fortitude overflowing into temperance: in so far, to wit, as he whose mind is strengthened by fortitude against dangers of death, which is a matter of very great difficulty, is more able to remain firm against the onslaught of pleasures; for as Cicero says (De Offic. i), "it would be inconsistent for a man to be unbroken by fear, and yet vanquished by cupidity; or that he should be conquered by lust, after showing himself to be unconquered by toil."

From this the Reply to the Second Objection is clear. For temperance observes the mean in all things, and fortitude keeps the mind unbent by the enticements of pleasures, either in so far as these virtues are taken to denote certain general conditions of virtue, or in the sense that they overflow on to one another, as explained above.

Reply Obj. 3: These four general conditions of virtue set down by the Philosopher, are not proper to the aforesaid virtues. They may, however, be appropriated to them, in the way above stated.

FIFTH ARTICLE [I-II, Q. 61, Art. 5]

Whether the Cardinal Virtues Are Fittingly Divided into Social Virtues, Perfecting, Perfect, and Exemplar Virtues?

Objection 1: It would seem that these four virtues are unfittingly divided into exemplar virtues, perfecting virtues, perfect virtues, and social virtues. For as Macrobius says (Super Somn. Scip. 1), the "exemplar virtues are such as exist in the mind of God." Now the Philosopher says (Ethic. x, 8) that "it is absurd to ascribe justice, fortitude, temperance, and prudence to God." Therefore these virtues cannot be exemplar.

Obj. 2: Further, the *perfect* virtues are those which are without any passion: for Macrobius says (Super Somn. Scip. 1) that "in a soul that is cleansed, temperance has not to check worldly desires, for it has forgotten all about them: fortitude knows nothing about the passions; it does not have to conquer them." Now it was stated above (Q. 59, A. 5) that the aforesaid virtues cannot be without passions. Therefore there is no such thing as *perfect* virtue.

Obj. 3: Further, he says (Macrobius: Super Somn. Scip. 1) that the "perfecting" virtues are those of the man "who flies from human affairs and devotes himself exclusively to the things of God." But it seems wrong to do this, for Cicero says (De Offic. i): "I reckon that it is not only unworthy of praise, but wicked for a man to say that he despises what most men admire, viz. power and office." Therefore there are no "perfecting" virtues.

Obj. 4: Further, he says (Macrobius: Super Somn. Scip. 1) that the "social" virtues are those "whereby good men work for the good of their country and for the safety of the city." But it is only legal justice that is directed to the common weal, as the Philosopher states (Ethic. v, 1). Therefore other virtues should not be called "social."

*On the contrary,* Macrobius says (Super Somn. Scip. 1): "Plotinus, together with Plato foremost among teachers of philosophy, says: 'The four kinds of virtue are fourfold: In the first place there are social* virtues; secondly, there are perfecting virtues [*Virtutes purgatoriae: literally meaning, cleansing virtues]; thirdly, there are perfect [*Virtutes purgati animi: literally, virtues of the clean soul] virtues; and fourthly, there are exemplar virtues.'" [*Cf. Chrysostom's fifteenth homily on St. Matthew, where he says: "The gentle, the modest, the merciful, the just man does not shut up his good deeds within himself ... He that is clean of heart and peaceful, and suffers persecution for the sake of the truth, lives for the common weal."]

*I answer that,* As Augustine says (De Moribus Eccl. vi), "the soul needs to follow something in order to give birth to virtue: this something is God: if we follow Him we shall live aright." Consequently the exemplar of human virtue must needs pre-exist in God, just as in Him pre-exist the types of all things. Accordingly virtue may be considered as existing originally in God, and thus we speak of "exemplar" virtues: so that in God the Divine Mind itself may be called prudence; while temperance is the turning of God's gaze on Himself, even as in us it is that which conforms the appetite to reason. God's fortitude is His unchangeableness; His justice is the observance of the Eternal Law in His works, as Plotinus states (Cf. Macrobius, Super Somn. Scip. 1).

Again, since man by his nature is a social [*See above note on Chrysostom] animal, these virtues, in so far as they are in him according to the condition of his nature, are called "social" virtues; since it is by reason of them that man behaves himself well in the conduct of human affairs. It is in this sense that we have been speaking of these virtues until now.

But since it behooves a man to do his utmost to strive onward even to Divine things, as even the Philosopher declares in *Ethic.* x, 7, and as Scripture often admonishes us—for instance: "Be ye ... perfect, as your heavenly Father is perfect" (Matt. 5:48), we must needs place some virtues between the social or human virtues, and the exemplar virtues which are Divine. Now these virtues differ by reason of a difference of movement and term: so that some are virtues of men who are on their way and tending towards the Divine similitude; and these are called "perfecting" virtues. Thus prudence, by contemplating the things of God, counts as nothing all things of the world, and directs all the thoughts of the soul to God alone: temperance, so far as nature allows, neglects the needs of the body; fortitude prevents the soul from being afraid of neglecting the body and rising to heavenly things; and justice consists in the soul giving a whole-hearted consent to follow the way thus proposed. Besides these there are the virtues of those who have already attained to the Divine similitude: these are called the "perfect virtues." Thus prudence sees nought else but the things of God; temperance knows no earthly desires; fortitude has no knowledge of passion; and justice, by imitating the Divine Mind, is united thereto by an everlasting covenant. Such as the virtues attributed to the Blessed, or, in this life, to some who are at the summit of perfection.

Reply Obj. 1: The Philosopher is speaking of these virtues according as they relate to human affairs; for instance, justice, about buying and selling; fortitude, about fear; temperance, about desires; for in this sense it is absurd to attribute them to God.

Reply Obj. 2: Human virtues, that is to say, virtues of men living together in this world, are about the passions. But the virtues of those who have attained to perfect bliss are without passions. Hence Plotinus says (Cf. Macrobius, Super Somn. Scip. 1) that "the social virtues check the passions," i.e. they bring them to the relative mean; "the second kind," viz. the perfecting virtues, "uproot them"; "the third kind," viz. the perfect virtues, "forget them; while it is impious to mention them in connection with virtues of the fourth kind," viz. the exemplar virtues. It may also be said that here he is speaking of passions as denoting inordinate emotions.

Reply Obj. 3: To neglect human affairs when necessity forbids is wicked; otherwise it is virtuous. Hence Cicero says a little earlier: "Perhaps one should make allowances for those who by reason of their exceptional talents have devoted themselves to learning; as also to those who have retired from public life on account of failing health, or for some other yet weightier motive; when such men yielded to others the power and renown of authority." This agrees with what Augustine says (De Civ. Dei xix, 19): "The love of truth demands a hallowed leisure; charity necessitates good works. If no one lays this burden on us we may devote ourselves to the study and contemplation of truth; but if the burden is laid on us it is to be taken up under the pressure of charity."

Reply Obj. 4: Legal justice alone regards the common weal directly: but by commanding the other virtues it draws them all into the service of the common weal, as the Philosopher declares (Ethic. v, 1). For we must take note that it concerns the human virtues, as we understand them here, to do well not only towards the community, but also towards the parts of the community, viz. towards the household, or even towards one individual.

## QUESTION 62

OF THE THEOLOGICAL VIRTUES (In Four Articles)

We must now consider the Theological Virtues: under which head there are four points of inquiry:

(1) Whether there are any theological virtues?

(2) Whether the theological virtues are distinct from the intellectual and moral virtues?

(3) How many, and which are they?

(4) Of their order.

FIRST ARTICLE [I-II, Q. 62, Art. 1]

Whether There Are Any Theological Virtues?

Objection 1: It would seem that there are not any theological virtues. For according to *Phys.* vii, text. 17, "virtue is the disposition of a perfect thing to that which is best: and by perfect, I mean that which is disposed according to nature." But that which is Divine is above man's nature. Therefore the theological virtues are not virtues of a man.

Obj. 2: Further, theological virtues are quasi-Divine virtues. But the Divine virtues are exemplars, as stated above (Q. 61, A. 5), which are not in us but in God. Therefore the theological virtues are not virtues of man.

Obj. 3: Further, the theological virtues are so called because they direct us to God, Who is the first beginning and last end of all things. But by the very nature of his reason and will, man is directed to his first beginning and last end. Therefore there is no need for any habits of theological virtue, to direct the reason and will to God.

*On the contrary,* The precepts of the Law are about acts of virtue. Now the Divine Law contains precepts about the acts of faith, hope, and charity: for it is written (Ecclus. 2:8, seqq.): "Ye that fear the

Lord believe Him," and again, "hope in Him," and again, "love Him." Therefore faith, hope, and charity are virtues directing us to God. Therefore they are theological virtues.

*I answer that,* Man is perfected by virtue, for those actions whereby he is directed to happiness, as was explained above (Q. 5, A. 7). Now man's happiness is twofold, as was also stated above (Q. 5, A. 5). One is proportionate to human nature, a happiness, to wit, which man can obtain by means of his natural principles. The other is a happiness surpassing man's nature, and which man can obtain by the power of God alone, by a kind of participation of the Godhead, about which it is written (2 Pet. 1:4) that by Christ we are made "partakers of the Divine nature." And because such happiness surpasses the capacity of human nature, man's natural principles which enable him to act well according to his capacity, do not suffice to direct man to this same happiness. Hence it is necessary for man to receive from God some additional principles, whereby he may be directed to supernatural happiness, even as he is directed to his connatural end, by means of his natural principles, albeit not without Divine assistance. Such like principles are called "theological virtues": first, because their object is God, inasmuch as they direct us aright to God: secondly, because they are infused in us by God alone: thirdly, because these virtues are not made known to us, save by Divine revelation, contained in Holy Writ.

Reply Obj. 1: A certain nature may be ascribed to a certain thing in two ways. First, essentially: and thus these theological virtues surpass the nature of man. Secondly, by participation, as kindled wood partakes of the nature of fire: and thus, after a fashion, man becomes a partaker of the Divine Nature, as stated above: so that these virtues are proportionate to man in respect of the Nature of which he is made a partaker.

Reply Obj. 2: These virtues are called Divine, not as though God were virtuous by reason of them, but because of them God makes us virtuous, and directs us to Himself. Hence they are not exemplar but exemplate virtues.

Reply Obj. 3: The reason and will are naturally directed to God, inasmuch as He is the beginning and end of nature, but in proportion to nature. But the reason and will, according to their nature, are not sufficiently directed to Him in so far as He is the object of supernatural happiness.

SECOND ARTICLE [I-II, Q. 62, Art. 2]

Whether the Theological Virtues Are Distinct from the Intellectual and Moral Virtues?

Objection 1: It would seem that the theological virtues are not distinct from the moral and intellectual virtues. For the theological virtues, if they be in a human soul, must needs perfect it, either as to the intellective, or as to the appetitive part. Now the virtues which perfect the intellective part are called intellectual; and the virtues which perfect the appetitive part, are called moral. Therefore, the theological virtues are not distinct from the moral and intellectual virtues.

Obj. 2: Further, the theological virtues are those which direct us to God. Now, among the intellectual virtues there is one which directs us to God: this is wisdom, which is about Divine things, since it considers the highest cause. Therefore the theological virtues are not distinct from the intellectual virtues.

Obj. 3: Further, Augustine (De Moribus Eccl. xv) shows how the four cardinal virtues are the "order of love." Now love is charity, which is a theological virtue. Therefore the moral virtues are not distinct from the theological.

*On the contrary,* That which is above man's nature is distinct from that which is according to his nature. But the theological virtues are above man's nature; while the intellectual and moral virtues are in proportion to his nature, as clearly shown above (Q. 58, A. 3). Therefore they are distinct from one another.

*I answer that,* As stated above (Q. 54, A. 2, ad 1), habits are specifically distinct from one another in respect of the formal difference of their objects. Now the object of the theological virtues is God Himself, Who is the last end of all, as surpassing the knowledge of our reason. On the other hand, the object of the intellectual and moral virtues is something comprehensible to human reason. Wherefore the theological virtues are specifically distinct from the moral and intellectual virtues.

Reply Obj. 1: The intellectual and moral virtues perfect man's intellect and appetite according to the capacity of human nature; the theological virtues, supernaturally.

Reply Obj. 2: The wisdom which the Philosopher (Ethic. vi, 3, 7) reckons as an intellectual virtue, considers Divine things so far as they are open to the research of human reason. Theological virtue, on the other hand, is about those same things so far as they surpass human reason.

Reply Obj. 3: Though charity is love, yet love is not always charity. When, then, it is stated that every virtue is the order of love, this can be understood either of love in the general sense, or of the love of charity. If it be understood of love, commonly so called, then each virtue is stated to be the order of love, in so far as each cardinal virtue requires ordinate emotions; and love is the root and cause of every emotion, as stated above (Q. 27, A. 4; Q. 28, A. 6, ad 2; Q. 41, A. 2, ad 1). If, however, it be understood of the love of charity, it does not mean that every other virtue is charity essentially: but that all other virtues depend on charity in some way, as we shall show further on (Q. 65, AA. 2, 5; II-II, Q. 23, A. 7).

THIRD ARTICLE [I-II, Q. 62, Art. 3]

Whether Faith, Hope, and Charity Are Fittingly Reckoned As Theological Virtues?

Objection 1: It would seem that faith, hope, and charity are not fittingly reckoned as three theological virtues. For the theological virtues are in relation to Divine happiness, what the natural inclination is in relation to the connatural end. Now among the virtues directed to the connatural end there is but one natural virtue, viz. the understanding of principles. Therefore there should be but one theological virtue.

Obj. 2: Further, the theological virtues are more perfect than the intellectual and moral virtues. Now faith is not reckoned among the intellectual virtues, but is something less than a virtue, since it is imperfect knowledge. Likewise hope is not reckoned among the moral virtues, but is something less than a virtue, since it is a passion. Much less therefore should they be reckoned as theological virtues.

Obj. 3: Further, the theological virtues direct man's soul to God. Now man's soul cannot be directed to God, save through the intellective part, wherein are the intellect and will. Therefore there should be only two theological virtues, one perfecting the intellect, the other, the will.

*On the contrary,* The Apostle says (1 Cor. 13:13): "Now there remain faith, hope, charity, these three."

*I answer that,* As stated above (A. 1), the theological virtues direct man to supernatural happiness in the same way as by the natural inclination man is directed to his connatural end. Now the latter happens in respect of two things. First, in respect of the reason or intellect, in so far as it contains the first universal principles which are known to us by the natural light of the intellect, and which are reason's starting-point, both in speculative and in practical matters. Secondly, through the rectitude of the will which tends naturally to good as defined by reason.

But these two fall short of the order of supernatural happiness, according to 1 Cor. 2:9: "The eye hath not seen, nor ear heard, neither hath it entered into the heart of man, what things God hath prepared for them that love Him." Consequently in respect of both the above things man needed to receive in addition something supernatural to direct him to a supernatural end. First, as regards the intellect, man receives certain supernatural principles, which are held by means of a Divine light: these are the articles of faith, about which is faith. Secondly, the will is directed to this end, both as to that end as something attainable—and this pertains to hope—and as to a certain spiritual union, whereby the will is, so to speak, transformed into that end—and this belongs to charity. For the appetite of a thing is moved and tends towards its connatural end naturally; and this movement is due to a certain conformity of the thing with its end.

Reply Obj. 1: The intellect requires intelligible species whereby to understand: consequently there is need of a natural habit in addition to the power. But the very nature of the will suffices for it to be directed naturally to the end, both as to the intention of the end and as to its conformity with the end. But the nature of the power is insufficient in either of these respects, for the will to be directed to things that are above its nature. Consequently there was need for an additional supernatural habit in both respects.

Reply Obj. 2: Faith and hope imply a certain imperfection: since faith is of things unseen, and hope, of things not possessed. Hence faith and hope, in things that are subject to human power, fall short of the notion of virtue. But faith and hope in things which are above the capacity of human nature surpass all virtue that is in proportion to man, according to 1 Cor. 1:25: "The weakness of God is stronger than men."

Reply Obj. 3: Two things pertain to the appetite, viz. movement to the end, and conformity with the end by means of love. Hence there must needs be two theological virtues in the human appetite, namely, hope and charity.

FOURTH ARTICLE [I-II, Q. 62, Art. 4]

Whether Faith Precedes Hope, and Hope Charity?

Objection 1: It would seem that the order of the theological virtues is not that faith precedes hope, and hope charity. For the root precedes that which grows from it. Now charity is the root of all the virtues, according to Eph. 3:17: "Being rooted and founded in charity." Therefore charity precedes the others.

Obj. 2: Further, Augustine says (De Doctr. Christ. i): "A man cannot love what he does not believe to exist. But if he believes and loves, by doing good works he ends in hoping." Therefore it seems that faith precedes charity, and charity hope.

Obj. 3: Further, love is the principle of all our emotions, as stated above (A. 2, ad 3). Now hope is a kind of emotion, since it is a passion, as stated above (Q. 25, A. 2). Therefore charity, which is love, precedes hope.

*On the contrary,* The Apostle enumerates them thus (1 Cor. 13:13): "Now there remain faith, hope, charity."

*I answer that,* Order is twofold: order of generation, and order of perfection. By order of generation, in respect of which matter precedes form, and the imperfect precedes the perfect, in one same subject faith precedes hope, and hope charity, as to their acts: because habits are all infused together. For the movement of the appetite cannot tend to anything, either by hoping or loving, unless that thing be apprehended by the sense or by the intellect. Now it is by faith that the intellect apprehends the object of hope and love. Hence in the order of generation, faith precedes hope and charity. In like manner a man loves a thing because he apprehends it as his good. Now from the very fact that a man hopes to be able to obtain some good through someone, he looks on the man in whom he hopes as a good of his own. Hence for the very reason that a man hopes in someone, he proceeds to love him: so that in the order of generation, hope precedes charity as regards their respective acts.

But in the order of perfection, charity precedes faith and hope: because both faith and hope are quickened by charity, and receive from charity their full complement as virtues. For thus charity is the mother and the root of all the virtues, inasmuch as it is the form of them all, as we shall state further on (II-II, Q. 23, A. 8).

This suffices for the Reply to the First Objection.

Reply Obj. 2: Augustine is speaking of that hope whereby a man hopes to obtain bliss through the merits which he has already: this belongs to hope quickened by and following charity. But it is possible for a man before having charity, to hope through merits not already possessed, but which he hopes to possess.

Reply Obj. 3: As stated above (Q. 40, A. 7), in treating of the passions, hope regards two things. One as its principal object, viz. the good hoped for. With regard to this, love always precedes hope: for good is never hoped for unless it be desired and loved. Hope also regards the person from whom a man hopes to be able to obtain some good. With regard to this, hope precedes love at first; though afterwards hope is increased by love. Because from the fact that a man thinks that he can obtain a good through someone, he begins to love him: and from the fact that he loves him, he then hopes all the more in him.

# QUESTION 63

OF THE CAUSE OF VIRTUES (In Four Articles)

We must now consider the cause of virtues; and under this head there are four points of inquiry:

(1) Whether virtue is in us by nature?

(2) Whether any virtue is caused in us by habituation?

(3) Whether any moral virtues are in us by infusion?

(4) Whether virtue acquired by habituation, is of the same species as infused virtue?

FIRST ARTICLE [I-II, Q. 63, Art. 1]

Whether Virtue Is in Us by Nature?

Objection 1: It would seem that virtue is in us by nature. For Damascene says (De Fide Orth. iii, 14): "Virtues are natural to us and are equally in all of us." And Antony says in his sermon to the monks: "If the will contradicts nature it is perverse, if it follow nature it is virtuous." Moreover, a gloss on Matt. 4:23, "Jesus went about," etc., says: "He taught them natural virtues, i.e. chastity, justice, humility, which man possesses naturally."

Obj. 2: Further, the virtuous good consists in accord with reason, as was clearly shown above (Q. 55, A. 4, ad 2). But that which accords with reason is natural to man; since reason is part of man's nature. Therefore virtue is in man by nature.

Obj. 3: Further, that which is in us from birth is said to be natural to us. Now virtues are in some from birth: for it is written (Job 31:18): "From my infancy mercy grew up with me; and it came out with me from my mother's womb." Therefore virtue is in man by nature.

*On the contrary,* Whatever is in man by nature is common to all men, and is not taken away by sin, since even in the demons natural gifts remain, as Dionysius states (Div. Nom. iv). But virtue is not in all men; and is cast out by sin. Therefore it is not in man by nature.

*I answer that,* With regard to corporeal forms, it has been maintained by some that they are wholly from within, by those, for instance, who upheld the theory of "latent forms" [*Anaxagoras; Cf. I, Q. 45, A. 8; Q. 65, A. 4]. Others held that forms are entirely from without, those, for instance, who thought that corporeal forms originated from some separate cause. Others, however, esteemed that they are partly from within, in so far as they pre-exist potentially in matter; and partly from without, in so far as they are brought into act by the agent.

In like manner with regard to sciences and virtues, some held that they are wholly from within, so that all virtues and sciences would pre-exist in the soul naturally, but that the hindrances to science and virtue, which are due to the soul being weighed down by the body, are removed by study and practice, even as iron is made bright by being polished. This was the opinion of the Platonists. Others said that they are wholly from without, being due to the inflow of the active intellect, as Avicenna maintained. Others said that sciences and virtues are within us by nature, so far as we are adapted to them, but not in their perfection: this is the teaching of the Philosopher (Ethic. ii, 1), and is nearer the truth.

To make this clear, it must be observed that there are two ways in which something is said to be natural to a man; one is according to his specific nature, the other according to his individual nature. And, since each thing derives its species from its form, and its individuation from matter, and, again, since man's form is his rational soul, while his matter is his body, whatever belongs to him in respect of his rational soul, is natural to him in respect of his specific nature; while whatever belongs to him in respect of the particular temperament of his body, is natural to him in respect of his individual nature. For whatever is natural to man in respect of his body, considered as part of his species, is to be referred, in a way, to the soul, in so far as this particular body is adapted to this particular soul.

In both these ways virtue is natural to man inchoatively. This is so in respect of the specific nature, in so far as in man's reason are to be found instilled by nature certain naturally known principles of both knowledge and action, which are the nurseries of intellectual and moral virtues, and in so far as there is in the will a natural appetite for good in accordance with reason. Again, this is so in respect of the individual nature, in so far as by reason of a disposition in the body, some are disposed either well or ill to certain virtues: because, to wit, certain sensitive powers are acts of certain parts of the body, according to the disposition of which these powers are helped or hindered in the exercise of their acts, and, in consequence, the rational powers also, which the aforesaid sensitive powers assist. In this way one man has a natural aptitude for science, another for fortitude, another for temperance: and in these ways, both intellectual and moral virtues are in us by way of a natural aptitude, inchoatively, but not perfectly, since nature is determined to one, while the perfection of these virtues does not depend on one particular mode of action, but on various modes, in respect of the various matters, which constitute the sphere of virtue's action, and according to various circumstances.

It is therefore evident that all virtues are in us by nature, according to aptitude and inchoation, but not according to perfection, except the theological virtues, which are entirely from without.

This suffices for the Replies to the Objections. For the first two argue about the nurseries of virtue which are in us by nature, inasmuch as we are rational beings. The third objection must be taken in the sense that, owing to the natural disposition which the body has from birth, one has an aptitude for pity, another for living temperately, another for some other virtue.

SECOND ARTICLE [I-II, Q. 63, Art. 2]

Whether Any Virtue Is Caused in Us by Habituation?

Objection 1: It would seem that virtues can not be caused in us by habituation. Because a gloss of Augustine [*Cf. Lib. Sentent. Prosperi cvi.] commenting on Rom. 14:23, "All that is not of faith is sin," says: "The whole life of an unbeliever is a sin: and there is no good without the Sovereign Good. Where knowledge of the truth is lacking, virtue is a mockery even in the best behaved people." Now faith cannot be acquired by means of works, but is caused in us by God, according to Eph. 2:8: "By grace you are saved through faith." Therefore no acquired virtue can be in us by habituation.

Obj. 2: Further, sin and virtue are contraries, so that they are incompatible. Now man cannot avoid sin except by the grace of God, according to Wis. 8:21: "I knew that I could not otherwise be continent, except God gave it." Therefore neither can any virtues be caused in us by habituation, but only by the gift of God.

Obj. 3: Further, actions which lead toward virtue, lack the perfection of virtue. But an effect cannot be more perfect than its cause. Therefore a virtue cannot be caused by actions that precede it.

*On the contrary,* Dionysius says (Div. Nom. iv) that good is more efficacious than evil. But vicious habits are caused by evil acts. Much more, therefore, can virtuous habits be caused by good acts.

*I answer that,* We have spoken above (Q. 51, AA. 2, 3) in a general way about the production of habits from acts; and speaking now in a special way of this matter in relation to virtue, we must take note that, as stated above (Q. 55, AA. 3, 4), man's virtue perfects him in relation to good. Now since the notion of good consists in "mode, species, and order," as Augustine states (De Nat. Boni. iii) or in "number, weight, and measure," as expressed in Wis. 11:21, man's good must needs be appraised with respect to some rule. Now this rule is twofold, as stated above (Q. 19, AA. 3, 4), viz. human reason and Divine Law. And since Divine Law is the higher rule, it extends to more things, so that whatever is ruled by human reason, is ruled by the Divine Law too; but the converse does not hold.

It follows that human virtue directed to the good which is defined according to the rule of human reason can be caused by human acts: inasmuch as such acts proceed from reason, by whose power and rule the aforesaid good is established. On the other hand, virtue which directs man to good as defined by the Divine Law, and not by human reason, cannot be caused by human acts, the principle of which is reason, but is produced in us by the Divine operation alone. Hence Augustine in giving the definition of the latter virtue inserts the words, "which God works in us without us" (Super Ps. 118, Serm. xxvi). It is also of these virtues that the First Objection holds good.

Reply Obj. 2: Mortal sin is incompatible with divinely infused virtue, especially if this be considered in its perfect state. But actual sin, even mortal, is compatible with humanly acquired virtue; because the use of a habit in us is subject to our will, as stated above (Q. 49, A. 3): and one sinful act does not destroy a habit of acquired virtue, since it is not an act but a habit, that is directly contrary to a habit. Wherefore, though man cannot avoid mortal sin without grace, so as never to sin mortally, yet he is not hindered from acquiring a habit of virtue, whereby he may abstain from evil in the majority of cases, and chiefly in matters most opposed to reason. There are also certain mortal sins which man can nowise avoid without grace, those, namely, which are directly opposed to the theological virtues, which are in us through the gift of grace. This, however, will be more fully explained later (Q. 109, A. 4).

Reply Obj. 3: As stated above (A. 1; Q. 51, A. 1), certain seeds or principles of acquired virtue pre-exist in us by nature. These principles are more excellent than the virtues acquired through them: thus the understanding of speculative principles is more excellent than the science of conclusions, and the natural rectitude of the reason is more excellent than the rectification of the appetite which results through the appetite partaking of reason, which rectification belongs to moral virtue. Accordingly human acts, in so far as they proceed from higher principles, can cause acquired human virtues.

THIRD ARTICLE [I-II, Q. 63, Art. 3]

Whether Any Moral Virtues Are in Us by Infusion?

Objection 1: It would seem that no virtues besides the theological virtues are infused in us by God. Because God does not do by Himself, save perhaps sometimes miraculously, those things that can be done by second causes; for, as Dionysius says (Coel. Hier. iv), "it is God's rule to bring about extremes through the mean." Now intellectual and moral virtues can be caused in us by our acts, as stated above (A. 2). Therefore it is not reasonable that they should be caused in us by infusion.

Obj. 2: Further, much less superfluity is found in God's works than in the works of nature. Now the theological virtues suffice to direct us to supernatural good. Therefore there are no other supernatural virtues needing to be caused in us by God.

Obj. 3: Further, nature does not employ two means where one suffices: much less does God. But God sowed the seeds of virtue in our souls, according to a gloss on Heb. 1 [*Cf. Jerome on Gal. 1: 15, 16]. Therefore it is unfitting for Him to cause in us other virtues by means of infusion.

*On the contrary,* It is written (Wis. 8:7): "She teacheth temperance and prudence and justice and fortitude."

*I answer that,* Effects must needs be proportionate to their causes and principles. Now all virtues, intellectual and moral, that are acquired by our actions, arise from certain natural principles pre-existing in us, as above stated (A. 1; Q. 51, A. 1): instead of which natural principles, God bestows on us the theological virtues, whereby we are directed to a supernatural end, as stated (Q. 62, A. 1). Wherefore we need to receive from God other habits corresponding, in due proportion, to the theological virtues, which habits are to the theological virtues, what the moral and intellectual virtues are to the natural principles of virtue.

Reply Obj. 1: Some moral and intellectual virtues can indeed be caused in us by our actions: but such are not proportionate to the theological virtues. Therefore it was necessary for us to receive, from God immediately, others that are proportionate to these virtues.

Reply Obj. 2: The theological virtues direct us sufficiently to our supernatural end, inchoatively: i.e. to God Himself immediately. But the soul needs further to be perfected by infused virtues in regard to other things, yet in relation to God.

Reply Obj. 3: The power of those naturally instilled principles does not extend beyond the capacity of nature. Consequently man needs in addition to be perfected by other principles in relation to his supernatural end.

FOURTH ARTICLE [I-II, Q. 63, Art. 4]

Whether Virtue by Habituation Belongs to the Same Species As Infused Virtue?

Objection 1: It would seem that infused virtue does not differ in species from acquired virtue. Because acquired and infused virtues, according to what has been said (A. 3), do not differ seemingly, save in relation to the last end. Now human habits and acts are specified, not by their last, but by their proximate end. Therefore the infused moral or intellectual virtue does not differ from the acquired virtue.

Obj. 2: Further, habits are known by their acts. But the act of infused and acquired temperance is the same, viz. to moderate desires of touch. Therefore they do not differ in species.

Obj. 3: Further, acquired and infused virtue differ as that which is wrought by God immediately, from that which is wrought by a creature. But the man whom God made, is of the same species as a man begotten naturally; and the eye which He gave to the man born blind, as one produced by the power of generation. Therefore it seems that acquired and infused virtue belong to the same species.

*On the contrary,* Any change introduced into the difference expressed in a definition involves a difference of species. But the definition of infused virtue contains the words, "which God works in us without us," as stated above (Q. 55, A. 4). Therefore acquired virtue, to which these words cannot apply, is not of the same species as infused virtue.

*I answer that,* There is a twofold specific difference among habits. The first, as stated above (Q. 54, A. 2; Q. 56, A. 2; Q. 60, A. 1), is taken from the specific and formal aspects of their objects. Now the object of every virtue is a good considered as in that virtue's proper matter: thus the object of temperance is a good in respect of the pleasures connected with the concupiscence of touch. The formal aspect of this object is from reason which fixes the mean in these concupiscences: while the material element is something on the part of the concupiscences. Now it is evident that the mean that is appointed in such like concupiscences according to the rule of human reason, is seen under a different aspect from the mean which is fixed according to Divine rule. For instance, in the consumption of food, the mean fixed by human reason, is that food should not harm the health of the body, nor hinder the use of reason: whereas, according to the Divine rule, it behooves man to "chastise his body, and bring it into subjection" (1 Cor. 9:27), by abstinence in food, drink and the like. It is therefore evident that infused and acquired temperance differ in species; and the same applies to the other virtues.

The other specific difference among habits is taken from the things to which they are directed: for a man's health and a horse's are not of the same species, on account of the difference between the natures to which their respective healths are directed. In the same sense, the Philosopher says (Polit. iii, 3) that citizens have diverse virtues according as they are well directed to diverse forms of government. In the same way, too, those infused moral virtues, whereby men behave well in respect of their being "fellow-citizens with the saints, and of the household [Douay: 'domestics'] of God" (Eph. 2:19), differ from the acquired virtues, whereby man behaves well in respect of human affairs.

Reply Obj. 1: Infused and acquired virtue differ not only in relation to the ultimate end, but also in relation to their proper objects, as stated.

Reply Obj. 2: Both acquired and infused temperance moderate desires for pleasures of touch, but for different reasons, as stated: wherefore their respective acts are not identical.

Reply Obj. 3: God gave the man born blind an eye for the same act as the act for which other eyes are formed naturally: consequently it was of the same species. It would be the same if God wished to give a man miraculously virtues, such as those that are acquired by acts. But the case is not so in the question before us, as stated.

## QUESTION 64

OF THE MEAN OF VIRTUE (In Four Articles)

We must now consider the properties of virtues: and (1) the mean of virtue, (2) the connection between virtues, (3) equality of virtues, (4) the duration of virtues. Under the first head there are four points of inquiry:

(1) Whether moral virtue observes the mean?

(2) Whether the mean of moral virtue is the real mean or the rational mean?

(3) Whether the intellectual virtues observe the mean?

(4) Whether the theological virtues do?

FIRST ARTICLE [I-II, Q. 64, Art. 1]

Whether Moral Virtues Observe the Mean?

Objection 1: It would seem that moral virtue does not observe the mean. For the nature of a mean is incompatible with that which is extreme. Now the nature of virtue is to be something extreme; for it is stated in *De Coelo* i that "virtue is the limit of power." Therefore moral virtue does not observe the mean.

Obj. 2: Further, the maximum is not a mean. Now some moral virtues tend to a maximum: for instance, magnanimity to very great honors, and magnificence to very large expenditure, as stated in *Ethic.* iv, 2, 3. Therefore not every moral virtue observes the mean.

Obj. 3: Further, if it is essential to a moral virtue to observe the mean, it follows that a moral virtue is not perfected, but the contrary corrupted, through tending to something extreme. Now some moral virtues are perfected by tending to something extreme; thus virginity, which abstains from all sexual pleasure, observes the extreme, and is the most perfect chastity: and to give all to the poor is the most perfect mercy or liberality. Therefore it seems that it is not essential to moral virtue that it should observe the mean.

*On the contrary,* The Philosopher says (Ethic. ii, 6) that "moral virtue is a habit of choosing the mean."

*I answer that,* As already explained (Q. 55, A. 3), the nature of virtue is that it should direct man to good. Now moral virtue is properly a perfection of the appetitive part of the soul in regard to some determinate matter: and the measure or rule of the appetitive movement in respect of appetible objects is the reason. But the good of that which is measured or ruled consists in its conformity with its rule: thus the good things made by art is that they follow the rule of art. Consequently, in things of this sort, evil consists in discordance from their rule or measure. Now this may happen either by their exceeding the measure or by their falling short of it; as is clearly the case in all things ruled or measured. Hence it is evident that the good of moral virtue consists in conformity with the rule of reason. Now it is clear that between excess and deficiency the mean is equality or conformity. Therefore it is evident that moral virtue observes the mean.

Reply Obj. 1: Moral virtue derives goodness from the rule of reason, while its matter consists in passions or operations. If therefore we compare moral virtue to reason, then, if we look at that which it has of reason, it holds the position of one extreme, viz. conformity; while excess and defect take the position of the other extreme, viz. deformity. But if we consider moral virtue in respect of its matter, then it holds the position of mean, in so far as it makes the passion conform to the rule of reason. Hence the Philosopher says (Ethic. ii, 6) that "virtue, as to its essence, is a mean state," in so far as the rule of virtue is imposed on its proper matter: "but it is an extreme in reference to the 'best' and the 'excellent,'" viz. as to its conformity with reason.

Reply Obj. 2: In actions and passions the mean and the extremes depend on various circumstances: hence nothing hinders something from being extreme in a particular virtue as to one circumstance, while the same thing is a mean in respect of other circumstances, through being in conformity with reason. This is the case with magnanimity and magnificence. For if we look at the absolute quantity of the respective objects of these virtues, we shall call it an extreme and a maximum: but if we consider the quantity in relation to other circumstances, then it has the character of a mean: since these virtues tend to this maximum in accordance with the rule of reason, i.e. *where* it is right, when it is right, and for an end that is right. There will be excess, if one tends to this maximum *when* it is not right, or *where* it is not right, or for an undue end; and there will be deficiency if one fails to tend thereto *where* one ought, and *when* one ought. This agrees with the saying of the Philosopher (Ethic. iv, 3) that the "magnanimous man observes the extreme in quantity, but the mean in the right mode of his action."

Reply Obj. 3: The same is to be said of virginity and poverty as of magnanimity. For virginity abstains from all sexual matters, and poverty from all wealth, for a right end, and in a right manner, i.e. according to God's word, and for the sake of eternal life. But if this be done in an undue manner, i.e. out of unlawful superstition, or again for vainglory, it will be in excess. And if it be not done when it ought to be done, or as it ought to be done, it is a vice by deficiency: for instance, in those who break their vows of virginity or poverty.

SECOND ARTICLE [I-II, Q. 64, Art. 2]

Whether the Mean of Moral Virtue Is the Real Mean, or the Rational Mean?

Objection 1: It would seem that the mean of moral virtue is not the rational mean, but the real mean. For the good of moral virtue consists in its observing the mean. Now, good, as stated in *Metaph.* ii, text. 8, is in things themselves. Therefore the mean of moral virtue is a real mean.

Obj. 2: Further, the reason is a power of apprehension. But moral virtue does not observe a mean between apprehensions, but rather a mean between operations or passions. Therefore the mean of moral virtue is not the rational, but the real mean.

Obj. 3: Further, a mean that is observed according to arithmetical or geometrical proportion is a real mean. Now such is the mean of justice, as stated in *Ethic.* v, 3. Therefore the mean of moral virtue is not the rational, but the real mean.

*On the contrary,* The Philosopher says (Ethic. ii, 6) that "moral virtue observes the mean fixed, in our regard, by reason."

*I answer that,* The rational mean can be understood in two ways. First, according as the mean is observed in the act itself of reason, as though the very act of reason were made to observe the mean: in this sense, since moral virtue perfects not the act of reason, but the act of the appetitive power, the mean of moral virtue is not the rational mean. Secondly, the mean of reason may be considered as that which the reason puts into some particular matter. In this sense every mean of moral virtue is a rational mean, since, as above stated (A. 1), moral virtue is said to observe the mean, through conformity with right reason.

But it happens sometimes that the rational mean is also the real mean: in which case the mean of moral virtue is the real mean, for instance, in justice. On the other hand, sometimes the rational mean is not the real mean, but is considered in relation to us: and such is the mean in all the other moral virtues. The reason for this is that justice is about operations, which deal with external things, wherein the right has to be established simply and absolutely, as stated above (Q. 60, A. 2): wherefore the rational mean in justice is the same as the real mean, in so far, to wit as justice gives to each one his due, neither more nor less. But the other moral virtues deal with interior passions wherein the right cannot be established in the same way, since men are variously situated in relation to their passions; hence the rectitude of reason has to be established in the passions, with due regard to us, who are moved in respect of the passions.

This suffices for the Replies to the Objections. For the first two arguments take the rational mean as being in the very act of reason, while the third argues from the mean of justice.

THIRD ARTICLE [I-II, Q. 64, Art. 3]

Whether the Intellectual Virtues Observe the Mean?

Objection 1: It would seem that the intellectual virtues do not observe the mean. Because moral virtue observes the mean by conforming to the rule of reason. But the intellectual virtues are in reason itself, so that they seem to have no higher rule. Therefore the intellectual virtues do not observe the mean.

Obj. 2: Further, the mean of moral virtue is fixed by an intellectual virtue: for it is stated in *Ethic.* ii, 6, that "virtue observes the mean appointed by reason, as a prudent man would appoint it." If therefore intellectual virtue also observe the mean, this mean will have to be appointed for them by another virtue, so that there would be an indefinite series of virtues.

Obj. 3: Further, a mean is, properly speaking, between contraries, as the Philosopher explains (Metaph. x, text. 22, 23). But there seems to be no contrariety in the intellect; since contraries themselves, as they are in the intellect, are not in opposition to one another, but are understood together, as white and black, healthy and sick. Therefore there is no mean in the intellectual virtues.

*On the contrary,* Art is an intellectual virtue; and yet there is a mean in art (Ethic. ii, 6). Therefore also intellectual virtue observes the mean.

*I answer that,* The good of anything consists in its observing the mean, by conforming with a rule or measure in respect of which it may happen to be excessive or deficient, as stated above (A. 1). Now intellectual virtue, like moral virtue, is directed to the good, as stated above (Q. 56, A. 3). Hence the good of an intellectual virtue consists in observing the mean, in so far as it is subject to a measure. Now the good of intellectual virtue is the true; in the case of contemplative virtue, it is the true taken absolutely (Ethic. vi, 2); in the case of practical virtue, it is the true in conformity with a right appetite.

Now truth apprehended by our intellect, if we consider it absolutely, is measured by things; since things are the measure of our intellect, as stated in *Metaph.* x, text. 5; because there is truth in what we think or say, according as the thing is so or not. Accordingly the good of speculative intellectual virtue consists in a certain mean, by way of conformity with things themselves, in so far as the intellect expresses them as being what they are, or as not being what they are not: and it is in this that the nature of truth consists. There will be excess if something false is affirmed, as though something were, which in reality it is not: and there will be deficiency if something is falsely denied, and declared not to be, whereas in reality it is.

The truth of practical intellectual virtue, if we consider it in relation to things, is by way of that which is measured; so that both in practical and in speculative intellectual virtues, the mean consists in conformity with things. But if we consider it in relation to the appetite, it has the character of a rule and measure. Consequently the rectitude of reason is the mean of moral virtue, and also the mean of prudence—of prudence as ruling and measuring, of moral virtue, as ruled and measured by that mean. In like manner the difference between excess and deficiency is to be applied in both cases.

Reply Obj. 1: Intellectual virtues also have their measure, as stated, and they observe the mean according as they conform to that measure.

Reply Obj. 2: There is no need for an indefinite series of virtues: because the measure and rule of intellectual virtue is not another kind of virtue, but things themselves.

Reply Obj. 3: The things themselves that are contrary have no contrariety in the mind, because one is the reason for knowing the other: nevertheless there is in the intellect contrariety of affirmation and negation, which are contraries, as stated at the end of *Peri Hermen[e]ias.* For though "to be" and "not to be" are not in contrary, but in contradictory opposition to one another, so long as we consider their signification in things themselves, for on the one hand we have "being" and on the other we have simply "non-being"; yet if we refer them to the act of the mind, there is something positive in both cases. Hence "to be" and "not to be" are contradictory: but the opinion stating that "good is good" is contrary to the opinion stating that "good is not good": and between two such contraries intellectual virtue observes the mean.

FOURTH ARTICLE [I-II, Q. 64, Art. 4]

Whether the Theological Virtues Observe the Mean?

Objection 1: It would seem that theological virtue observes the mean. For the good of other virtues consists in their observing the mean. Now the theological virtues surpass the others in goodness. Therefore much more does theological virtue observe the mean.

Obj. 2: Further, the mean of moral virtue depends on the appetite being ruled by reason; while the mean of intellectual virtue consists in the intellect being measured by things. Now theological virtue perfects both intellect and appetite, as stated above (Q. 62, A. 3). Therefore theological virtue also observes the mean.

Obj. 3: Further, hope, which is a theological virtue, is a mean between despair and presumption. Likewise faith holds a middle course between contrary heresies, as Boethius states (De Duab. Natur. vii): thus, by confessing one Person and two natures in Christ, we observe the mean between the heresy of Nestorius, who maintained the existence of two persons and two natures, and the heresy of Eutyches, who held to one person and one nature. Therefore theological virtue observes the mean.

*On the contrary,* Wherever virtue observes the mean it is possible to sin by excess as well as by deficiency. But there is no sinning by excess against God, Who is the object of theological virtue: for it is written (Ecclus. 43:33): "Blessing the Lord, exalt Him as much as you can: for He is above all praise." Therefore theological virtue does not observe the mean.

*I answer that,* As stated above (A. 1), the mean of virtue depends on conformity with virtue's rule or measure, in so far as one may exceed or fall short of that rule. Now the measure of theological virtue may be twofold. One is taken from the very nature of virtue, and thus the measure and rule of theological virtue is God Himself: because our faith is ruled according to Divine truth; charity, according to His goodness; hope, according to the immensity of His omnipotence and loving kindness. This measure surpasses all human power: so that never can we love God as much as He ought to be loved, nor believe and hope in Him as much as we should. Much less therefore can there be excess in such things. Accordingly the good of such virtues does not consist in a mean, but increases the more we approach to the summit.

The other rule or measure of theological virtue is by comparison with us: for although we cannot be borne towards God as much as we ought, yet we should approach to Him by believing, hoping and loving, according to the measure of our condition. Consequently it is possible to find a mean and extremes in theological virtue, accidentally and in reference to us.

Reply Obj. 1: The good of intellectual and moral virtues consists in a mean of reason by conformity with a measure that may be exceeded: whereas this is not so in the case of theological virtue, considered in itself, as stated above.

Reply Obj. 2: Moral and intellectual virtues perfect our intellect and appetite in relation to a created measure and rule; whereas the theological virtues perfect them in relation to an uncreated rule and measure. Wherefore the comparison fails.

Reply Obj. 3: Hope observes the mean between presumption and despair, in relation to us, in so far, to wit, as a man is said to be presumptuous, through hoping to receive from God a good in excess of his condition; or to despair through failing to hope for that which according to his condition he might hope for. But there can be no excess of hope in comparison with God, Whose goodness is infinite. In like manner faith holds a middle course between contrary heresies, not by comparison with its object, which is God, in Whom we cannot believe too much; but in so far as human opinion itself takes a middle position between contrary opinions, as was explained above.

# QUESTION 65

OF THE CONNECTION OF VIRTUES (In Five Articles)

We must now consider the connection of virtues: under which head there are five points of inquiry:

(1) Whether the moral virtues are connected with one another?

(2) Whether the moral virtues can be without charity?

(3) Whether charity can be without them?

(4) Whether faith and hope can be without charity?

(5) Whether charity can be without them?

FIRST ARTICLE [I-II, Q. 65, Art. 1]

Whether the Moral Virtues Are Connected with One Another?

Objection 1: It would seem that the moral virtues are not connected with one another. Because moral virtues are sometimes caused by the exercise of acts, as is proved in *Ethic.* ii, 1, 2. But man can exercise himself in the acts of one virtue, without exercising himself in the acts of some other virtue. Therefore it is possible to have one moral virtue without another.

Obj. 2: Further, magnificence and magnanimity are moral virtues. Now a man may have other moral virtues without having magnificence or magnanimity: for the Philosopher says (Ethic. iv, 2, 3) that "a poor man cannot be magnificent," and yet he may have other virtues; and (Ethic. iv) that "he who is worthy of small things, and so accounts his worth, is modest, but not magnanimous." Therefore the moral virtues are not connected with one another.

Obj. 3: Further, as the moral virtues perfect the appetitive part of the soul, so do the intellectual virtues perfect the intellective part. But the intellectual virtues are not mutually connected: since we may have one science, without having another. Neither, therefore, are the moral virtues connected with one another.

Obj. 4: Further, if the moral virtues are mutually connected, this can only be because they are united together in prudence. But this does not suffice to connect the moral virtues together. For, seemingly, one may be prudent about things to be done in relation to one virtue, without being prudent in those that concern another virtue: even as one may have the art of making certain things, without the art of making certain others. Now prudence is right reason about things to be done. Therefore the moral virtues are not necessarily connected with one another.

*On the contrary,* Ambrose says on Luke 6:20: "The virtues are connected and linked together, so that whoever has one, is seen to have several": and Augustine says (De Trin. vi, 4) that "the virtues that reside in the human mind are quite inseparable from one another": and Gregory says (Moral. xxii, 1) that "one virtue without the other is either of no account whatever, or very imperfect": and Cicero says (Quaest. Tusc. ii): "If you confess to not having one particular virtue, it must needs be that you have none at all."

*I answer that,* Moral virtue may be considered either as perfect or as imperfect. An imperfect moral virtue, temperance for instance, or fortitude, is nothing but an inclination in us to do some kind of good deed, whether such inclination be in us by nature or by habituation. If we take the moral virtues in this way, they are not connected: since we find men who, by natural temperament or by being accustomed, are prompt in doing deeds of liberality, but are not prompt in doing deeds of chastity.

But the perfect moral virtue is a habit that inclines us to do a good deed well; and if we take moral virtues in this way, we must say that they are connected, as nearly as all are agreed in saying. For this two reasons are given, corresponding to the different ways of assigning the distinction of the cardinal virtues. For, as we stated above (Q. 61, AA. 3, 4), some distinguish them according to certain general properties of the virtues: for instance, by saying that discretion belongs to prudence, rectitude to justice, moderation to temperance, and strength of mind to fortitude, in whatever matter we consider these properties to be. In this way the reason for the connection is evident: for strength of mind is not commended as virtuous, if it be without moderation or rectitude or discretion: and so forth. This, too, is the reason assigned for the connection by Gregory, who says (Moral. xxii, 1) that "a virtue cannot be perfect" as a virtue, "if isolated from the others: for there can be no true prudence without temperance, justice and fortitude": and he continues to speak in like manner of the other virtues (cf. Q. 61, A. 4, Obj. 1). Augustine also gives the same reason (De Trin. vi, 4).

Others, however, differentiate these virtues in respect of their matters, and it is in this way that Aristotle assigns the reason for their connection (Ethic. vi, 13). Because, as stated above (Q. 58, A. 4), no moral virtue can be without prudence; since it is proper to moral virtue to make a right choice, for it is an elective habit. Now right choice requires not only the inclination to a due end, which inclination is the direct outcome of moral virtue, but also correct choice of things conducive to the end, which choice is made by prudence, that counsels, judges, and commands in those things that are directed to the end. In like manner one cannot have prudence unless one has the moral virtues: since prudence is "right reason about things to be done," and the starting point of reason is the end of the thing to be done, to which end man is rightly disposed by moral virtue. Hence, just as we cannot have speculative science unless we have the understanding of the principles, so neither can we have prudence without the moral virtues: and from this it follows clearly that the moral virtues are connected with one another.

Reply Obj. 1: Some moral virtues perfect man as regards his general state, in other words, with regard to those things which have to be done in every kind of human life. Hence man needs to exercise himself at the same time in the matters of all moral virtues. And if he exercise himself, by good deeds, in all such matters, he will acquire the habits of all the moral virtues. But if he exercise himself by good deeds in regard to one matter, but not in regard to another, for instance, by behaving well in matters of anger, but not in matters of concupiscence; he will indeed acquire a certain habit of restraining his anger; but this habit will lack the nature of virtue, through the absence of prudence, which is wanting in matters of concupiscence. In the same way, natural inclinations fail to have the complete character of virtue, if prudence be lacking.

But there are some moral virtues which perfect man with regard to some eminent state, such as magnificence and magnanimity; and since it does not happen to all in common to be exercised in the matter of such virtues, it is possible for a man to have the other moral virtues, without actually having the habits of these virtues—provided we speak of acquired virtue. Nevertheless, when once a man has acquired those other virtues he possesses these in proximate potentiality. Because when, by practice, a man has acquired liberality in small gifts and expenditure, if he were to come in for a large sum of money, he would acquire the habit of magnificence with but little practice: even as a geometrician, by dint of little study, acquires scientific knowledge about some conclusion which had never been presented to his mind before. Now we speak of having a thing when we are on the point of having it, according to the saying of the Philosopher (Phys. ii, text. 56): "That which is scarcely lacking is not lacking at all."

This suffices for the Reply to the Second Objection.

Reply Obj. 3: The intellectual virtues are about divers matters having no relation to one another, as is clearly the case with the various sciences and arts. Hence we do not observe in them the connection that is to be found among the moral virtues, which are about passions and operations, that are clearly related to one another. For all the passions have their rise in certain initial passions, viz. love and hatred, and terminate in certain others, viz. pleasure and sorrow. In like manner all the operations that are the matter of moral virtue are related to one another, and to the passions. Hence the whole matter of moral virtues falls under the one rule of prudence.

Nevertheless, all intelligible things are related to first principles. And in this way, all the intellectual virtues depend on the understanding of principles; even as prudence depends on the moral virtues, as stated. On the other hand, the universal principles which are the object of the virtue of understanding of principles, do not depend on the conclusions, which are the objects of the other intellectual virtues, as do the moral virtues depend on prudence, because the appetite, in a fashion, moves the reason, and the reason the appetite, as stated above (Q. 9, A. 1; Q. 58, A. 5, ad 1).

Reply Obj. 4: Those things to which the moral virtues incline, are as the principles of prudence: whereas the products of art are not the principles, but the matter of art. Now it is evident that, though reason may be right in one part of the matter, and not in another, yet in no way can it be called right reason, if it be deficient in any principle whatever. Thus, if a man be wrong about the principle, "A whole is greater than its part," he cannot acquire the science of geometry, because he must necessarily wander from the truth in his conclusion. Moreover, things *done* are related to one another, but not things *made,* as stated above (ad 3). Consequently the lack of prudence in one department of things to be done, would result in a deficiency affecting other things to be done: whereas this does not occur in things to be made.

SECOND ARTICLE [I-II, Q. 65, Art. 2]

Whether Moral Virtues Can Be Without Charity?

Objection 1: It would seem that moral virtues can be without charity. For it is stated in the *Liber Sentent. Prosperi* vii, that "every virtue save charity may be common to the good and bad." But "charity can be in none except the good," as stated in the same book. Therefore the other virtues can be had without charity.

Obj. 2: Further, moral virtues can be acquired by means of human acts, as stated in *Ethic.* ii, 1, 2, whereas charity cannot be had otherwise than by infusion, according to Rom. 5:5: "The charity of God is poured forth in our hearts by the Holy Ghost Who is given to us." Therefore it is possible to have the other virtues without charity.

Obj. 3: Further, the moral virtues are connected together, through depending on prudence. But charity does not depend on prudence; indeed, it surpasses prudence, according to Eph. 3:19: "The charity of Christ, which surpasseth all knowledge." Therefore the moral virtues are not connected with charity, and can be without it.

*On the contrary,* It is written (1 John 3:14): "He that loveth not, abideth in death." Now the spiritual life is perfected by the virtues, since it is "by them" that "we lead a good life," as Augustine states (De Lib. Arb. ii, 17, 19). Therefore they cannot be without the love of charity.

*I answer that,* As stated above (Q. 63, A. 2), it is possible by means of human works to acquire moral virtues, in so far as they produce good works that are directed to an end not surpassing the natural power of man: and when they are acquired thus, they can be without charity, even as they were in many of the Gentiles. But in so far as they produce good works in proportion to a supernatural last end, thus they have the character of virtue, truly and perfectly; and cannot be acquired by human acts, but are infused by God. Such like moral virtues cannot be without charity. For it has been stated above (A. 1; Q. 58, AA. 4, 5) that the other moral virtues cannot be without prudence; and that prudence cannot be without the moral virtues, because these latter make man well disposed to certain ends, which are the starting-point of the procedure of prudence. Now for prudence to proceed aright, it is much more necessary that man be well disposed towards his ultimate end, which is the effect of charity, than that he be well disposed in respect of other ends, which is the effect of moral virtue: just as in speculative matters right reason has greatest need of the first indemonstrable principle, that "contradictories cannot both be true at the same time." It is therefore evident that neither can infused prudence be without charity; nor, consequently, the other moral virtues, since they cannot be without prudence.

It is therefore clear from what has been said that only the infused virtues are perfect, and deserve to be called virtues simply: since they direct man well to the ultimate end. But the other virtues, those, namely, that are acquired, are virtues in a restricted sense, but not simply: for they direct man well in respect of the last end in some particular genus of action, but not in respect of the last end simply. Hence a gloss of Augustine [*Cf. Lib. Sentent. Prosperi cvi.] on the words, "All that is not of faith is sin" (Rom. 14:23), says: "He that fails to acknowledge the truth, has no true virtue, even if his conduct be good."

Reply Obj. 1: Virtue, in the words quoted, denotes imperfect virtue. Else if we take moral virtue in its perfect state, "it makes its possessor good," and consequently cannot be in the wicked.

Reply Obj. 2: This argument holds good of virtue in the sense of acquired virtue.

Reply Obj. 3: Though charity surpasses science and prudence, yet prudence depends on charity, as stated: and consequently so do all the infused moral virtues.

THIRD ARTICLE [I-II, Q. 65, Art. 3]

Whether Charity Can Be Without Moral Virtue?

Objection 1: It would seem possible to have charity without the moral virtues. For when one thing suffices for a certain purpose, it is superfluous to employ others. Now charity alone suffices for the fulfilment of all the works of virtue, as is clear from 1 Cor. 13:4, seqq.: "Charity is patient, is kind," etc. Therefore it seems that if one has charity, other virtues are superfluous.

Obj. 2: Further, he that has a habit of virtue easily performs the works of that virtue, and those works are pleasing to him for their own sake: hence "pleasure taken in a work is a sign of habit" (Ethic. ii, 3). Now many have charity, being free from mortal sin, and yet they find it difficult to do works of virtue; nor are these works pleasing to them for their own sake, but only for the sake of charity. Therefore many have charity without the other virtues.

Obj. 3: Further, charity is to be found in every saint: and yet there are some saints who are without certain virtues. For Bede says (on Luke 17:10) that the saints are more humbled on account of their not having certain virtues, than rejoiced at the virtues they have. Therefore, if a man has charity, it does not follow of necessity that he has all the moral virtues.

*On the contrary,* The whole Law is fulfilled through charity, for it is written (Rom. 13:8): "He that loveth his neighbor, hath fulfilled the Law." Now it is not possible to fulfil the whole Law, without having all the moral virtues: since the law contains precepts about all acts of virtue, as stated in *Ethic.* v, 1, 2. Therefore he that has charity, has all the moral virtues. Moreover, Augustine says in a letter (Epis. clxvii) [*Cf. Serm. xxxix and xlvi de Temp.] that charity contains all the cardinal virtues.

*I answer that,* All the moral virtues are infused together with charity. The reason for this is that God operates no less perfectly in works of grace than in works of nature. Now, in the works of nature, we find that whenever a thing contains a principle of certain works, it has also whatever is necessary for their execution: thus animals are provided with organs whereby to perform the actions that their souls empower them to do. Now it is evident that charity, inasmuch as it directs man to his last end, is the principle of all the good works that are referable to his last end. Wherefore all the moral virtues must needs be infused together with charity, since it is through them that man performs each different kind of good work.

It is therefore clear that the infused moral virtues are connected, not only through prudence, but also on account of charity: and, again, that whoever loses charity through mortal sin, forfeits all the infused moral virtues.

Reply Obj. 1: In order that the act of a lower power be perfect, not only must there be perfection in the higher, but also in the lower power: for if the principal agent were well disposed, perfect action would not follow, if the instrument also were not well disposed. Consequently, in order that man work well in things referred to the end, he needs not only a virtue disposing him well to the end, but also those virtues which dispose him well to whatever is referred to the end: for the virtue which regards the end is the chief and moving principle in respect of those things that are referred to the end. Therefore it is necessary to have the moral virtues together with charity.

Reply Obj. 2: It happens sometimes that a man who has a habit, finds it difficult to act in accordance with the habit, and consequently feels no pleasure and complacency in the act, on account of some impediment supervening from without: thus a man who has a habit of science, finds it difficult to understand, through being sleepy or unwell. In like manner sometimes the habits of moral virtue experience difficulty in their works, by reason of certain ordinary dispositions remaining from previous acts. This difficulty does not occur in respect of acquired moral virtue: because the repeated acts by which they are acquired, remove also the contrary dispositions.

Reply Obj. 3: Certain saints are said not to have certain virtues, in so far as they experience difficulty in the acts of those virtues, for the reason stated; although they have the habits of all the virtues.

FOURTH ARTICLE [I-II, Q. 65, Art. 4]

Whether Faith and Hope Can Be Without Charity?

Objection 1: It would seem that faith and hope are never without charity. Because, since they are theological virtues, they seem to be more excellent than even the infused moral virtues. But the infused moral virtues cannot be without charity. Neither therefore can faith and hope be without charity.

Obj. 2: Further, "no man believes unwillingly" as Augustine says (Tract. xxvi in Joan.). But charity is in the will as a perfection thereof, as stated above (Q. 62, A. 3). Therefore faith cannot be without charity.

Obj. 3: Further, Augustine says (Enchiridion viii) that "there can be no hope without love." But love is charity: for it is of this love that he speaks. Therefore hope cannot be without charity.

*On the contrary,* A gloss on Matt. 1:2 says that "faith begets hope, and hope, charity." Now the begetter precedes the begotten, and can be without it. Therefore faith can be without hope; and hope, without charity.

*I answer that,* Faith and hope, like the moral virtues, can be considered in two ways; first in an inchoate state; secondly, as complete virtues. For since virtue is directed to the doing of good works, perfect virtue is that which gives the faculty of doing a perfectly good work, and this consists in not only doing what is good, but also in doing it well. Else, if what is done is good, but not well done, it will not be perfectly good; wherefore neither will the habit that is the principle of such an act, have the perfect character of virtue. For instance, if a man do what is just, what he does is good: but it will not be the work of a perfect virtue unless he do it well, i.e. by choosing rightly, which is the result of prudence; for which reason justice cannot be a perfect virtue without prudence.

Accordingly faith and hope can exist indeed in a fashion without charity: but they have not the perfect character of virtue without charity. For, since the act of faith is to believe in God; and since to believe is to assent to someone of one's own free will: to will not as one ought, will not be a perfect act of faith. To will as one ought is the outcome of charity which perfects the will: since every right movement of the will proceeds from a right love, as Augustine says (De Civ. Dei xiv, 9). Hence faith may be without charity, but not as a perfect virtue: just as temperance and fortitude can be without prudence. The same applies to hope. Because the act of hope consists in looking to God for future bliss. This act is perfect, if it is based on the merits which we have; and this cannot be without charity. But to expect future bliss through merits which one has not yet, but which one proposes to acquire at some future time, will be an imperfect act; and this is possible without charity. Consequently, faith and hope can be without charity; yet, without charity, they are not virtues properly so-called; because the nature of virtue requires that by it, we should not only do what is good, but also that we should do it well (Ethic. ii, 6).

Reply Obj. 1: Moral virtue depends on prudence: and not even infused prudence has the character of prudence without charity; for this involves the absence of due order to the first principle, viz. the ultimate end. On the other hand faith and hope, as such, do not depend either on prudence or charity; so that they can be without charity, although they are not virtues without charity, as stated.

Reply Obj. 2: This argument is true of faith considered as a perfect virtue.

Reply Obj. 3: Augustine is speaking here of that hope whereby we look to gain future bliss through merits which we have already; and this is not without charity.

FIFTH ARTICLE [I-II, Q. 65, Art. 5]

Whether Charity Can Be Without Faith and Hope?

Objection 1: It would seem that charity can be without faith and hope. For charity is the love of God. But it is possible for us to love God naturally, without already having faith, or hope in future bliss. Therefore charity can be without faith and hope.

Obj. 2: Further, charity is the root of all the virtues, according to Eph. 3:17: "Rooted and founded in charity." Now the root is sometimes without branches. Therefore charity can sometimes be without faith and hope, and the other virtues.

Obj. 3: Further, there was perfect charity in Christ. And yet He had neither faith nor hope: because He was a perfect comprehensor, as we shall explain further on (III, Q. 7, AA. 3, 4). Therefore charity can be without faith and hope.

*On the contrary,* The Apostle says (Heb. 11:6): "Without faith it is impossible to please God"; and this evidently belongs most to charity, according to Prov. 8:17: "I love them that love me." Again, it is by hope that we are brought to charity, as stated above (Q. 62, A. 4). Therefore it is not possible to have charity without faith and hope.

*I answer that,* Charity signifies not only the love of God, but also a certain friendship with Him; which implies, besides love, a certain mutual return of love, together with mutual communion, as stated in *Ethic.* viii, 2. That this belongs to charity is evident from 1 John 4:16: "He that abideth in charity, abideth in God, and God in him," and from 1 Cor. 1:9, where it is written: "God is faithful, by Whom you are called unto the fellowship of His Son." Now this fellowship of man with God, which consists in a certain familiar colloquy with Him, is begun here, in this life, by grace, but will be perfected in the future life, by glory; each of which things we hold by faith and hope. Wherefore just as friendship with a person would be impossible, if one disbelieved in, or despaired of, the possibility of their fellowship or familiar colloquy; so too, friendship with God, which is charity, is impossible without faith, so as to believe in this fellowship and colloquy with God, and to hope to attain to this fellowship. Therefore charity is quite impossible without faith and hope.

Reply Obj. 1: Charity is not any kind of love of God, but that love of God, by which He is loved as the object of bliss, to which object we are directed by faith and hope.

Reply Obj. 2: Charity is the root of faith and hope, in so far as it gives them the perfection of virtue. But faith and hope as such are the precursors of charity, as stated above (Q. 62, A. 4), and so charity is impossible without them.

Reply Obj. 3: In Christ there was neither faith nor hope, on account of their implying an imperfection. But instead of faith, He had manifest vision, and instead of hope, full comprehension [*See above, Q. 4, A. 3]: so that in Him was perfect charity.

# QUESTION 66

OF EQUALITY AMONG THE VIRTUES (In Six Articles)

We must now consider equality among the virtues: under which head there are six points of inquiry:

(1) Whether one virtue can be greater or less than another?

(2) Whether all the virtues existing together in one subject are equal?

(3) Of moral virtue in comparison with intellectual virtue;

(4) Of the moral virtues as compared with one another;

(5) Of the intellectual virtues in comparison with one another;

(6) Of the theological virtues in comparison with one another.

FIRST ARTICLE [I-II, Q. 66, Art. 1]

Whether One Virtue Can Be Greater or Less Than Another?

Objection 1: It would seem that one virtue cannot be greater or less than another. For it is written (Apoc. 21:16) that the sides of the city of Jerusalem are equal; and a gloss says that the sides denote the virtues. Therefore all virtues are equal; and consequently one cannot be greater than another.

Obj. 2: Further, a thing that, by its nature, consists in a maximum, cannot be more or less. Now the nature of virtue consists in a maximum, for virtue is "the limit of power," as the Philosopher states (De Coelo i, text. 116); and Augustine says (De Lib. Arb. ii, 19) that "virtues are very great boons, and no one can use them to evil purpose." Therefore it seems that one virtue cannot be greater or less than another.

Obj. 3: Further, the quantity of an effect is measured by the power of the agent. But perfect, viz. infused virtues, are from God Whose power is uniform and infinite. Therefore it seems that one virtue cannot be greater than another.

*On the contrary,* Wherever there can be increase and greater abundance, there can be inequality. Now virtues admit of greater abundance and increase: for it is written (Matt. 5:20): "Unless your justice abound more than that of the Scribes and Pharisees, you shall not enter into the kingdom of heaven": and (Prov. 15:5): "In abundant justice there is the greatest strength ( *virtus* )." Therefore it seems that a virtue can be greater or less than another.

*I answer that,* When it is asked whether one virtue can be greater than another, the question can be taken in two senses. First, as applying to virtues of different species. In this sense it is clear that one virtue is greater than another; since a cause is always more excellent than its effect; and among effects, those nearest to the cause are the most excellent. Now it is clear from what has been said (Q. 18, A. 5; Q. 61, A. 2) that the cause and root of human good is the reason. Hence prudence which perfects the reason, surpasses in goodness the other moral virtues which perfect the appetitive power, in so far as it partakes of reason. And among these, one is better than another, according as it approaches nearer to the reason. Consequently justice, which is in the will, excels the remaining moral virtues; and fortitude, which is in the irascible part, stands before temperance, which is in the concupiscible, which has a smaller share of reason, as stated in *Ethic.* vii, 6.

The question can be taken in another way, as referring to virtues of the same species. In this way, according to what was said above (Q. 52, A. 1), when we were treating of the intensity of habits, virtue may be said to be greater or less in two ways: first, in itself; secondly with regard to the subject that partakes of it. If we consider it in itself, we shall call it great or little, according to the things to which it extends. Now whosoever has a virtue, e.g. temperance, has it in respect of whatever temperance extends to. But this does not apply to science and art: for every grammarian does not know everything relating to grammar. And in this sense the Stoics said rightly, as Simplicius states in his Commentary on the Predicaments, that virtue cannot be more or less, as science and art can; because the nature of virtue consists in a maximum.

If, however, we consider virtue on the part of the subject, it may then be greater or less, either in relation to different times, or in different men. Because one man is better disposed than another to attain to the mean of virtue which is defined by right reason; and this, on account of either greater habituation, or a better natural disposition, or a more discerning judgment of reason, or again a greater gift of grace, which is given to each one "according to the measure of the giving of Christ," as stated in Eph. 4:9. And here the Stoics erred, for they held that no man should be deemed virtuous, unless he were, in the highest degree, disposed to virtue. Because the nature of virtue does not require that man should reach the mean of right reason as though it were an indivisible point, as the Stoics thought; but it is enough that he should approach the mean, as stated in *Ethic.* ii, 6. Moreover, one same indivisible mark is reached more nearly and more readily by one than by another: as may be seen when several archers aim at a fixed target.

Reply Obj. 1: This equality is not one of absolute quantity, but of proportion: because all virtues grow in a man proportionately, as we shall see further on (A. 2).

Reply Obj. 2: This "limit" which belongs to virtue, can have the character of something *more* or less good, in the ways explained above: since, as stated, it is not an indivisible limit.

Reply Obj. 3: God does not work by necessity of nature, but according to the order of His wisdom, whereby He bestows on men various measures of virtue, according to Eph. 4:7: "To every one of you [Vulg.: 'us'] is given grace according to the measure of the giving of Christ."

SECOND ARTICLE [I-II, Q. 66, Art. 2]

Whether All the Virtues That Are Together in One Man, Are Equal?

Objection 1: It would seem that the virtues in one same man are not all equally intense. For the Apostle says (1 Cor. 7:7): "Everyone hath his proper gift from God; one after this manner, and another after that." Now one gift would not be more proper than another to a man, if God infused all the virtues equally into each man. Therefore it seems that the virtues are not all equal in one and the same man.

Obj. 2: Further, if all the virtues were equally intense in one and the same man, it would follow that whoever surpasses another in one virtue, would surpass him in all the others. But this is clearly not the case: since various saints are specially praised for different virtues; e.g. Abraham for faith (Rom. 4), Moses for his meekness (Num. 7:3), Job for his patience (Tob. 2:12). This is why of each Confessor the Church sings: "There was not found his like in keeping the law of the most High," [*See *Lesson* in the Mass Statuit (Dominican Missal)], since each one was remarkable for some virtue or other. Therefore the virtues are not all equal in one and the same man.

Obj. 3: Further, the more intense a habit is, the greater one's pleasure and readiness in making use of it. Now experience shows that a man is more pleased and ready to make use of one virtue than of another. Therefore the virtues are not all equal in one and the same man.

*On the contrary,* Augustine says (De Trin. vi, 4) that "those who are equal in fortitude are equal in prudence and temperance," and so on. Now it would not be so, unless all the virtues in one man were equal. Therefore all virtues are equal in one man.

*I answer that,* As explained above (A. 1), the comparative greatness of virtues can be understood in two ways. First, as referring to their specific nature: and in this way there is no doubt that in a man one virtue is greater than another, for example, charity, than faith and hope. Secondly, it may be taken as referring to the degree of participation by the subject, according as a virtue becomes intense or remiss in its subject. In this sense all the virtues in one man are equal with an equality of proportion, in so far as their growth in man is equal: thus the fingers are unequal in size, but equal in proportion, since they grow in proportion to one another.

Now the nature of this equality is to be explained in the same way as the connection of virtues; for equality among virtues is their connection as to greatness. Now it has been stated above (Q. 65, A. 1) that a twofold connection of virtues may be assigned. The first is according to the opinion of those who understood these four virtues to be four general properties of virtues, each of which is found together with the other in any matter. In this way virtues cannot be said to be equal in any matter unless they have all these properties equal.

Augustine alludes to this kind of equality (De Trin. vi, 4) when he says: "If you say these men are equal in fortitude, but that one is more prudent than the other; it follows that the fortitude of the latter is less prudent. Consequently they are not really equal in fortitude, since the former's fortitude is more prudent. You will find that this applies to the other virtues if you run over them all in the same way."

The other kind of connection among virtues followed the opinion of those who hold these virtues to have their own proper respective matters (Q. 65, AA. 1, 2). In this way the connection among moral virtues results from prudence, and, as to the infused virtues, from charity, and not from the inclination, which is on the part of the subject, as stated above (Q. 65, A. 1). Accordingly the nature of the equality among virtues can also be considered on the part of prudence, in regard to that which is formal in all the moral virtues: for in one and the same man, so long as his reason has the same degree of perfection, the mean will be proportionately defined according to right reason in each matter of virtue.

But in regard to that which is material in the moral virtues, viz. the inclination to the virtuous act, one may be readier to perform the act of one virtue, than the act of another virtue, and this either from nature, or from habituation, or again by the grace of God.

Reply Obj. 1: This saying of the Apostle may be taken to refer to the gifts of gratuitous grace, which are not common to all, nor are all of them equal in the one same subject. We might also say that it refers to the measure of sanctifying grace, by reason of which one man has all the virtues in greater abundance than another man, on account of his greater abundance of prudence, or also of charity, in which all the infused virtues are connected.

Reply Obj. 2: One saint is praised chiefly for one virtue, another saint for another virtue, on account of his more admirable readiness for the act of one virtue than for the act of another virtue.

This suffices for the Reply to the Third Objection.

THIRD ARTICLE [I-II, Q. 66, Art. 3]

Whether the Moral Virtues Are Better Than the Intellectual Virtues?

Objection 1: It would seem that the moral virtues are better than the intellectual. Because that which is more necessary, and more lasting, is better. Now the moral virtues are "more lasting even than the sciences" (Ethic. i) which are intellectual virtues: and, moreover, they are more necessary for human life. Therefore they are preferable to the intellectual virtues.

Obj. 2: Further, virtue is defined as "that which makes its possessor good." Now man is said to be good in respect of moral virtue, and art in respect of intellectual virtue, except perhaps in respect of prudence alone. Therefore moral is better than intellectual virtue.

Obj. 3: Further, the end is more excellent than the means. But according to *Ethic.* vi, 12, "moral virtue gives right intention of the end; whereas prudence gives right choice of the means." Therefore moral virtue is more excellent than prudence, which is the intellectual virtue that regards moral matters.

*On the contrary,* Moral virtue is in that part of the soul which is rational by participation; while intellectual virtue is in the essentially rational part, as stated in Ethic. i, 13. Now rational by essence is more excellent than rational by participation. Therefore intellectual virtue is better than moral virtue.

*I answer that,* A thing may be said to be greater or less in two ways: first, simply; secondly, relatively. For nothing hinders something from being better simply, e.g. "learning than riches," and yet not better relatively, i.e. "for one who is in want" [*Aristotle, *Topic.* iii.]. Now to consider a thing simply is to consider it in its proper specific nature. Accordingly, a virtue takes its species from its object, as explained above (Q. 54, A. 2; Q. 60, A. 1). Hence, speaking simply, that virtue is more excellent, which has the more excellent object. Now it is evident that the object of the reason is more excellent than the object of the appetite: since the reason apprehends things in the universal, while the appetite tends to things themselves, whose being is restricted to the particular. Consequently, speaking simply, the intellectual virtues, which perfect the reason, are more excellent than the moral virtues, which perfect the appetite.

But if we consider virtue in its relation to act, then moral virtue, which perfects the appetite, whose function it is to move the other powers to act, as stated above (Q. 9, A. 1), is more excellent. And since virtue is so called from its being a principle of action, for it is the perfection of a power, it follows again that the nature of virtue agrees more with moral than with intellectual virtue, though the intellectual virtues are more excellent habits, simply speaking.

Reply Obj. 1: The moral virtues are more lasting than the intellectual virtues, because they are practised in matters pertaining to the life of the community. Yet it is evident that the objects of the sciences, which are necessary and invariable, are more lasting than the objects of moral virtue, which are certain particular matters of action. That the moral virtues are more necessary for human life, proves that they are more excellent, not simply, but relatively. Indeed, the speculative intellectual virtues, from the very fact that they are not referred to something else, as a useful thing is referred to an end, are more excellent. The reason for this is that in them we have a kind of beginning of that happiness which consists in the knowledge of truth, as stated above (Q. 3, A. 6).

Reply Obj. 2: The reason why man is said to be good simply, in respect of moral virtue, but not in respect of intellectual virtue, is because the appetite moves the other powers to their acts, as stated above (Q. 56, A. 3). Wherefore this argument, too, proves merely that moral virtue is better relatively.

Reply Obj. 3: Prudence directs the moral virtues not only in the choice of the means, but also in appointing the end. Now the end of each moral virtue is to attain the mean in the matter proper to that virtue; which mean is appointed according to the right ruling of prudence, as stated in *Ethic.* ii, 6; vi, 13.

FOURTH ARTICLE [I-II, Q. 66, Art. 4]

Whether Justice Is the Chief of the Moral Virtues?

Objection 1: It would seem that justice is not the chief of the moral virtues. For it is better to give of one's own than to pay what is due. Now the former belongs to liberality, the latter to justice. Therefore liberality is apparently a greater virtue than justice.

Obj. 2: Further, the chief quality of a thing is, seemingly, that in which it is most perfect. Now, according to Jam. 1:4, "Patience hath a perfect work." Therefore it would seem that patience is greater than justice.

Obj. 3: Further, "Magnanimity has a great influence on every virtue," as stated in *Ethic.* iv, 3. Therefore it magnifies even justice. Therefore it is greater than justice.

*On the contrary,* The Philosopher says (Ethic. v, 1) that "justice is the most excellent of the virtues."

*I answer that,* A virtue considered in its species may be greater or less, either simply or relatively. A virtue is said to be greater simply, whereby a greater rational good shines forth, as stated above (A. 1). In this way justice is the most excellent of all the moral virtues, as being most akin to reason. This is made evident by considering its subject and its object: its subject, because this is the will, and the will is the rational appetite, as stated above (Q. 8, A. 1; Q. 26, A. 1): its object or matter, because it is about operations, whereby man is set in order not only in himself, but also in regard to another. Hence "justice is the most excellent of virtues" (Ethic. v, 1). Among the other moral virtues, which are about the passions, the more excellent the matter in which the appetitive movement is subjected to reason, so much the more does the rational good shine forth in each. Now in things touching man, the chief of all is life, on which all other things depend. Consequently fortitude which subjects the appetitive movement to reason in matters of life and death, holds the first place among those moral virtues that are about the passions, but is subordinate to justice. Hence the Philosopher says (Rhet. 1) that "those virtues must needs be greatest which receive the most praise: since virtue is a power of doing good. Hence the brave man and the just man are honored more than others; because the former," i.e. fortitude, "is useful in war, and the latter," i.e. justice, "both in war and in peace." After fortitude comes temperance, which subjects the appetite to reason in matters directly relating to life, in the one individual, or in the one species, viz. in matters of food and of sex. And so these three virtues, together with prudence, are called principal virtues, in excellence also.

A virtue is said to be greater relatively, by reason of its helping or adorning a principal virtue: even as substance is more excellent simply than accident: and yet relatively some particular accident is more excellent than substance in so far as it perfects substance in some accidental mode of being.

Reply Obj. 1: The act of liberality needs to be founded on an act of justice, for "a man is not liberal in giving, unless he gives of his own" (Polit. ii, 3). Hence there could be no liberality apart from justice, which discerns between "meum" and "tuum": whereas justice can be without liberality. Hence justice is simply greater than liberality, as being more universal, and as being its foundation: while liberality is greater relatively since it is an ornament and an addition to justice.

Reply Obj. 2: Patience is said to have "a perfect work," by enduring evils, wherein it excludes not only unjust revenge, which is also excluded by justice; not only hatred, which is also suppressed by charity; nor only anger, which is calmed by gentleness; but also inordinate sorrow, which is the root of all the above. Wherefore it is more perfect and excellent through plucking up the root in this matter. It is not, however, more perfect than all the other virtues simply. Because fortitude not only endures trouble without being disturbed, but also fights against it if necessary. Hence whoever is brave is patient; but the converse does not hold, for patience is a part of fortitude.

Reply Obj. 3: There can be no magnanimity without the other virtues, as stated in *Ethic.* iv, 3. Hence it is compared to them as their ornament, so that relatively it is greater than all the others, but not simply.

FIFTH ARTICLE [I-II, Q. 66, Art. 5]

Whether Wisdom Is the Greatest of the Intellectual Virtues?

Objection 1: It would seem that wisdom is not the greatest of the intellectual virtues. Because the commander is greater than the one commanded. Now prudence seems to command wisdom, for it is stated in *Ethic.* i, 2 that political science, which belongs to prudence (Ethic. vi, 8), "orders that sciences should be cultivated in states, and to which of these each individual should devote himself, and to what extent." Since, then, wisdom is one of the sciences, it seems that prudence is greater than wisdom.

Obj. 2: Further, it belongs to the nature of virtue to direct man to happiness: because virtue is "the disposition of a perfect thing to that which is best," as stated in *Phys.* vii, text. 17. Now prudence is "right reason about things to be done," whereby man is brought to happiness: whereas wisdom takes no notice of human acts, whereby man attains happiness. Therefore prudence is a greater virtue than wisdom.

Obj. 3: Further, the more perfect knowledge is, the greater it seems to be. Now we can have more perfect knowledge of human affairs, which are the subject of science, than of Divine things, which are the object of wisdom, which is the distinction given by Augustine (De Trin. xii, 14): because Divine things are incomprehensible, according to Job 26:26: "Behold God is great, exceeding our knowledge." Therefore science is a greater virtue than wisdom.

Obj. 4: Further, knowledge of principles is more excellent than knowledge of conclusions. But wisdom draws conclusions from indemonstrable principles which are the object of the virtue of understanding, even as other sciences do. Therefore understanding is a greater virtue than wisdom.

*On the contrary,* The Philosopher says (Ethic. vi, 7) that wisdom is "the head" among "the intellectual virtues."

*I answer that,* As stated above (A. 3), the greatness of a virtue, as to its species, is taken from its object. Now the object of wisdom surpasses the objects of all the intellectual virtues: because wisdom considers the Supreme Cause, which is God, as stated at the beginning of the *Metaphysics.* And since it is by the cause that we judge of an effect, and by the higher cause that we judge of the lower effects; hence it is that wisdom exercises judgment over all the other intellectual virtues, directs them all, and is the architect of them all.

Reply Obj. 1: Since prudence is about human affairs, and wisdom about the Supreme Cause, it is impossible for prudence to be a greater virtue than wisdom, "unless," as stated in *Ethic.* vi, 7, "man were the greatest thing in the world." Wherefore we must say, as stated in the same book (Ethic. vi), that prudence does not command wisdom, but vice versa: because "the spiritual man judgeth all things; and he himself is judged by no man" (1 Cor. 2:15). For prudence has no business with supreme matters which are the object of wisdom: but its command covers things directed to wisdom, viz. how men are to obtain wisdom. Wherefore prudence, or political science, is, in this way, the servant of wisdom; for it leads to wisdom, preparing the way for her, as the doorkeeper for the king.

Reply Obj. 2: Prudence considers the means of acquiring happiness, but wisdom considers the very object of happiness, viz. the Supreme Intelligible. And if indeed the consideration of wisdom were perfect in respect of its object, there would be perfect happiness in the act of wisdom: but as, in this life, the act of wisdom is imperfect in respect of its principal object, which is God, it follows that the act of wisdom is a beginning or participation of future happiness, so that wisdom is nearer than prudence to happiness.

Reply Obj. 3: As the Philosopher says (De Anima i, text. 1), "one knowledge is preferable to another, either because it is about a higher object, or because it is more certain." Hence if the objects be equally good and sublime, that virtue will be greater which possesses more certain knowledge. But a virtue which is less certain about a higher and better object, is preferable to that which is more certain about an object of inferior degree. Wherefore the Philosopher says (De Coelo ii, text. 60) that "it is a great thing to be able to know something about celestial beings, though it be based on weak and probable reasoning"; and again (De Part. Animal. i, 5) that "it is better to know a little about sublime things, than much about mean things." Accordingly wisdom, to which knowledge about God pertains, is beyond the reach of man, especially in this life, so as to be his possession: for this "belongs to God alone" (Metaph. i, 2): and yet this little knowledge about God which we can have through wisdom is preferable to all other knowledge.

Reply Obj. 4: The truth and knowledge of indemonstrable principles depends on the meaning of the terms: for as soon as we know what is a whole, and what is a part, we know at once that every whole is greater than its part. Now to know the meaning of being and non-being, of whole and part, and of other things consequent to being, which are the terms whereof indemonstrable principles are constituted, is the function of wisdom: since universal being is the proper effect of the Supreme Cause, which is God. And so wisdom makes use of indemonstrable principles which are the object of understanding, not only by drawing conclusions from them, as other sciences do, but also by passing its judgment on them, and by vindicating them against those who deny them. Hence it follows that wisdom is a greater virtue than understanding.

SIXTH ARTICLE [I-II, Q. 66, Art. 6]

Whether Charity Is the Greatest of the Theological Virtues?

Objection 1: It would seem that charity is not the greatest of the theological virtues. Because, since faith is in the intellect, while hope and charity are in the appetitive power, it seems that faith is compared to hope and charity, as intellectual to moral virtue. Now intellectual virtue is greater than moral virtue, as was made evident above (Q. 62, A. 3). Therefore faith is greater than hope and charity.

Obj. 2: Further, when two things are added together, the result is greater than either one. Now hope results from something added to charity; for it presupposes love, as Augustine says (Enchiridion viii), and it adds a certain movement of stretching forward to the beloved. Therefore hope is greater than charity.

Obj. 3: Further, a cause is more noble than its effect. Now faith and hope are the cause of charity: for a gloss on Matt. 1:3 says that "faith begets hope, and hope charity." Therefore faith and hope are greater than charity.

*On the contrary,* The Apostle says (1 Cor. 13:13): "Now there remain faith, hope, charity, these three; but the greatest of these is charity."

*I answer that,* As stated above (A. 3), the greatness of a virtue, as to its species, is taken from its object. Now, since the three theological virtues look at God as their proper object, it cannot be said that any one of them is greater than another by reason of its having a greater object, but only from the fact that it approaches nearer than another to that object; and in this way charity is greater than the others. Because the others, in their very nature, imply a certain distance from the object: since faith is of what is not seen, and hope is of what is not possessed. But the love of charity is of that which is already possessed: since the beloved is, in a manner, in the lover, and, again, the lover is drawn by desire to union with the beloved; hence it is written (1 John 4:16): "He that abideth in charity, abideth in God, and God in him."

Reply Obj. 1: Faith and hope are not related to charity in the same way as prudence to moral virtue; and for two reasons. First, because the theological virtues have an object surpassing the human soul: whereas prudence and the moral virtues are about things beneath man. Now in things that are above man, to love them is more excellent than to know them. Because knowledge is perfected by the known being in the knower: whereas love is perfected by the lover being drawn to the beloved. Now that which is above man is more excellent in itself than in man: since a thing is contained according to the mode of the container. But it is the other way about in things beneath man. Secondly, because prudence moderates the appetitive movements pertaining to the moral virtues, whereas faith does not moderate the appetitive movement tending to God, which movement belongs to the theological virtues: it only shows the object. And this appetitive movement towards its object surpasses human knowledge, according to Eph. 3:19: "The charity of Christ which surpasseth all knowledge."

Reply Obj. 2: Hope presupposes love of that which a man hopes to obtain; and such love is love of concupiscence, whereby he who desires good, loves himself rather than something else. On the other hand, charity implies love of friendship, to which we are led by hope, as stated above (Q. 62, A. 4).

Reply Obj. 3: An efficient cause is more noble than its effect: but not a disposing cause. For otherwise the heat of fire would be more noble than the soul, to which the heat disposes the matter. It is in this way that faith begets hope, and hope charity: in the sense, to wit, that one is a disposition to the other.

# QUESTION 67

OF THE DURATION OF VIRTUES AFTER THIS LIFE (In Six Articles)

We must now consider the duration of virtues after this life, under which head there are six points of inquiry:

(1) Whether the moral virtues remain after this life?

(2) Whether the intellectual virtues remain?

(3) Whether faith remains?

(4) Whether hope remains?

(5) Whether anything remains of faith or hope?

(6) Whether charity remains?

FIRST ARTICLE [I-II, Q. 67, Art. 1]

Whether the Moral Virtues Remain After This Life?

Objection 1: It would seem that the moral virtues do not remain after this life. For in the future state of glory men will be like angels, according to Matt. 22:30. But it is absurd to put moral virtues in the angels [*"Whatever relates to moral action is petty, and unworthy of the gods" (Ethic. x, 8)], as stated in *Ethic.* x, 8. Therefore neither in man will there be moral virtues after this life.

Obj. 2: Further, moral virtues perfect man in the active life. But the active life does not remain after this life: for Gregory says (Moral. iv, 18): "The works of the active life pass away from the body." Therefore moral virtues do not remain after this life.

Obj. 3: Further, temperance and fortitude, which are moral virtues, are in the irrational parts of the soul, as the Philosopher states (Ethic. iii, 10). Now the irrational parts of the soul are corrupted, when the body is corrupted: since they are acts of bodily organs. Therefore it seems that the moral virtues do not remain after this life.

*On the contrary,* It is written (Wis. 1:15) that "justice is perpetual and immortal."

*I answer that,* As Augustine says (De Trin. xiv, 9), Cicero held that the cardinal virtues do not remain after this life; and that, as Augustine says (De Trin. xiv, 9), "in the other life men are made happy by the mere knowledge of that nature, than which nothing is better or more lovable, that Nature, to wit, which created all others." Afterwards he concludes that these four virtues remain in the future life, but after a different manner.

In order to make this evident, we must note that in these virtues there is a formal element, and a quasi-material element. The material element in these virtues is a certain inclination of the appetitive part to the passions and operations according to a certain mode: and since this mode is fixed by reason, the formal element is precisely this order of reason.

Accordingly we must say that these moral virtues do not remain in the future life, as regards their material element. For in the future life there will be no concupiscences and pleasures in matters of food and sex; nor fear and daring about dangers of death; nor distributions and commutations of things employed in this present life. But, as regards the formal element, they will remain most perfect, after this life, in the Blessed, in as much as each one's reason will have most perfect rectitude in regard to things concerning him in respect of that state of life: and his appetitive power will be moved entirely according to the order of reason, in things pertaining to that same state. Hence Augustine says (De Trin. xiv, 9) that "prudence will be there without any danger of error; fortitude, without the anxiety of bearing with evil; temperance, without the rebellion of the desires: so that prudence will neither prefer nor equal any good to God; fortitude will adhere to Him most steadfastly; and temperance will delight in Him Who knows no imperfection." As to justice, it is yet more evident what will be its act in that life, viz. "to be subject to God": because even in this life subjection to a superior is part of justice.

Reply Obj. 1: The Philosopher is speaking there of these moral virtues, as to their material element; thus he speaks of justice, as regards "commutations and distributions"; of fortitude, as to "matters of terror and danger"; of temperance, in respect of "lewd desires."

The same applies to the Second Objection. For those things that concern the active life, belong to the material element of the virtues.

Reply Obj. 3: There is a twofold state after this life; one before the resurrection, during which the soul will be separate from the body; the other, after the resurrection, when the souls will be reunited to their bodies. In this state of resurrection, the irrational powers will be in the bodily organs, just as they now are. Hence it will be possible for fortitude to be in the irascible, and temperance in the concupiscible part, in so far as each power will be perfectly disposed to obey the reason. But in the state preceding the resurrection, the irrational parts will not be in the soul actually, but only radically in its essence, as stated in the First Part (Q. 77, A. 8). Wherefore neither will these virtues be actually, but only in their root, i.e. in the reason and will, wherein are certain nurseries of these virtues, as stated above (Q. 63, A. 1). Justice, however, will remain because it is in the will. Hence of justice it is specially said that it is "perpetual and immortal"; both by reason of its subject, since the will is incorruptible; and because its act will not change, as stated.

SECOND ARTICLE [I-II, Q. 67, Art. 2]

Whether the Intellectual Virtues Remain After This Life?

Objection 1: It would seem that the intellectual virtues do not remain after this life. For the Apostle says (1 Cor. 13:8, 9) that "knowledge shall be destroyed," and he states the reason to be because "we know in part." Now just as the knowledge of science is in part, i.e. imperfect; so also is the knowledge of the other intellectual virtues, as long as this life lasts. Therefore all the intellectual virtues will cease after this life.

Obj. 2: Further, the Philosopher says (Categor. vi) that since science is a habit, it is a quality difficult to remove: for it is not easily lost, except by reason of some great change or sickness. But no bodily change is so great as that of death. Therefore science and the other intellectual virtues do not remain after death.

Obj. 3: Further, the intellectual virtues perfect the intellect so that it may perform its proper act well. Now there seems to be no act of the intellect after this life, since "the soul understands nothing without a phantasm" (De Anima iii, text. 30); and, after this life, the phantasms do not remain, since their only subject is an organ of the body. Therefore the intellectual virtues do not remain after this life.

*On the contrary,* The knowledge of what is universal and necessary is more constant than that of particular and contingent things. Now the knowledge of contingent particulars remains in man after this life; for instance, the knowledge of what one has done or suffered, according to Luke 16:25: "Son, remember that thou didst receive good things in thy life-time, and likewise Lazarus evil things." Much more, therefore, does the knowledge of universal and necessary things remain, which belong to science and the other intellectual virtues.

*I answer that,* As stated in the First Part (Q. 79, A. 6) some have held that the intelligible species do not remain in the passive intellect except when it actually understands; and that so long as actual consideration ceases, the species are not preserved save in the sensitive powers which are acts of bodily organs, viz. in the powers of imagination and memory. Now these powers cease when the body is corrupted: and consequently, according to this opinion, neither science nor any other intellectual virtue will remain after this life when once the body is corrupted.

But this opinion is contrary to the mind of Aristotle, who states (De Anima iii, text. 8) that "the possible intellect is in act when it is identified with each thing as knowing it; and yet, even then, it is in potentiality to consider it actually." It is also contrary to reason, because intelligible species are contained by the "possible" intellect immovably, according to the mode of their container. Hence the "possible" intellect is called "the abode of the species" (De Anima iii) because it preserves the intelligible species.

And yet the phantasms, by turning to which man understands in this life, by applying the intelligible species to them as stated in the First Part (Q. 84, A. 7; Q. 85, A. 1, ad 5), cease as soon as the body is corrupted. Hence, so far as the phantasms are concerned, which are the quasi-material element in the intellectual virtues, these latter cease when the body is destroyed: but as regards the intelligible species, which are in the "possible" intellect, the intellectual virtues remain. Now the species are the quasi-formal element of the intellectual virtues. Therefore these remain after this life, as regards their formal element, just as we have stated concerning the moral virtues (A. 1).

Reply Obj. 1: The saying of the Apostle is to be understood as referring to the material element in science, and to the mode of understanding; because, to it, neither do the phantasms remain, when the body is destroyed; nor will science be applied by turning to the phantasms.

Reply Obj. 2: Sickness destroys the habit of science as to its material element, viz. the phantasms, but not as to the intelligible species, which are in the "possible" intellect.

Reply Obj. 3: As stated in the First Part (Q. 89, A. 1), the separated soul has a mode of understanding, other than by turning to the phantasms. Consequently science remains, yet not as to the same mode of operation; as we have stated concerning the moral virtues (A. 1).

THIRD ARTICLE [I-II, Q. 67, Art. 3]

Whether Faith Remains After This Life?

Objection 1: It would seem that faith remains after this life. Because faith is more excellent than science. Now science remains after this life, as stated above (A. 2). Therefore faith remains also.

Obj. 2: Further, it is written (1 Cor. 3:11): "Other foundation no man can lay, but that which is laid; which is Christ Jesus," i.e. faith in Jesus Christ. Now if the foundation is removed, that which is built upon it remains no more. Therefore, if faith remains not after this life, no other virtue remains.

Obj. 3: Further, the knowledge of faith and the knowledge of glory differ as perfect from imperfect. Now imperfect knowledge is compatible with perfect knowledge: thus in an angel there can be "evening" and "morning" knowledge [*Cf. I, Q. 58, A. 6]; and a man can have science through a demonstrative syllogism, together with opinion through a probable syllogism, about one same conclusion. Therefore after this life faith also is compatible with the knowledge of glory.

*On the contrary,* The Apostle says (2 Cor. 5:6, 7): "While we are in the body, we are absent from the Lord: for we walk by faith and not by sight." But those who are in glory are not absent from the Lord, but present to Him. Therefore after this life faith does not remain in the life of glory.

*I answer that,* Opposition is of itself the proper cause of one thing being excluded from another, in so far, to wit, as wherever two things are opposite to one another, we find opposition of affirmation and negation. Now in some things we find opposition in respect of contrary forms; thus in colors we find white and black. In others we find opposition in respect of perfection and imperfection: wherefore in alterations, more and less are considered to be contraries, as when a thing from being less hot is made more hot (Phys. v, text. 19). And since perfect and imperfect are opposite to one another, it is impossible for perfection and imperfection to affect the same thing at the same time.

Now we must take note that sometimes imperfection belongs to a thing's very nature, and belongs to its species: even as lack of reason belongs to the very specific nature of a horse and an ox. And since a thing, so long as it remains the same identically, cannot pass from one species to another, it follows that if such an imperfection be removed, the species of that thing is changed: even as it would no longer be an ox or a horse, were it to be rational. Sometimes, however, the imperfection does not belong to the specific nature, but is accidental to the individual by reason of something else; even as sometimes lack of reason is accidental to a man, because he is asleep, or because he is drunk, or for some like reason; and it is evident, that if such an imperfection be removed, the thing remains substantially.

Now it is clear that imperfect knowledge belongs to the very nature of faith: for it is included in its definition; faith being defined as "the substance of things to be hoped for, the evidence of things that appear not" (Heb. 11:1). Wherefore Augustine says (Tract. xl in Joan.): "What is faith? Believing without seeing." But it is an imperfect knowledge that is of things unapparent or unseen. Consequently imperfect knowledge belongs to the very nature of faith: therefore it is clear that the knowledge of faith cannot be perfect and remain identically the same.

But we must also consider whether it is compatible with perfect knowledge: for there is nothing to prevent some kind of imperfect knowledge from being sometimes with perfect knowledge. Accordingly we must observe that knowledge can be imperfect in three ways: first, on the part of the knowable object; secondly, on the part of the medium; thirdly, on the part of the subject. The difference of perfect and imperfect knowledge on the part of the knowable object is seen in the "morning" and "evening" knowledge of the angels: for the "morning" knowledge is about things according to the being which they have in the Word, while the "evening" knowledge is about things according as they have being in their own natures, which being is imperfect in comparison with the First Being. On the part of the medium, perfect and imperfect knowledge are exemplified in the knowledge of a conclusion through a demonstrative medium, and through a probable medium. On the part of the subject the difference of perfect and imperfect knowledge applies to opinion, faith, and science. For it is essential to opinion that we assent to one of two opposite assertions with fear of the other, so that our adhesion is not firm: to science it is essential to have firm adhesion with intellectual vision, for science possesses certitude which results from the understanding of principles: while faith holds a middle place, for it surpasses opinion in so far as its adhesion is firm, but falls short of science in so far as it lacks vision.

Now it is evident that a thing cannot be perfect and imperfect in the same respect; yet the things which differ as perfect and imperfect can be together in the same respect in one and the same other thing. Accordingly, knowledge which is perfect on the part of the object is quite incompatible with imperfect knowledge about the same object; but they are compatible with one another in respect of the same medium or the same subject: for nothing hinders a man from having at one and the same time, through one and the same medium, perfect and imperfect knowledge about two things, one perfect, the other imperfect, e.g. about health and sickness, good and evil. In like manner knowledge that is perfect on the part of the medium is incompatible with imperfect knowledge through one and the same medium: but nothing hinders them being about the same subject or in the same subject: for one man can know the same conclusions through a probable and through a demonstrative medium. Again, knowledge that is perfect on the part of the subject is incompatible with imperfect knowledge in the same subject. Now faith, of its very nature, contains an imperfection on the part of the subject, viz. that the believer sees not what he believes: whereas bliss, of its very nature, implies perfection on the part of the subject, viz. that the Blessed see that which makes them happy, as stated above (Q. 3, A. 8). Hence it is manifest that faith and bliss are incompatible in one and the same subject.

Reply Obj. 1: Faith is more excellent than science, on the part of the object, because its object is the First Truth. Yet science has a more perfect mode of knowing its object, which is not incompatible with vision which is the perfection of happiness, as the mode of faith is incompatible.

Reply Obj. 2: Faith is the foundation in as much as it is knowledge: consequently when this knowledge is perfected, the foundation will be perfected also.

The Reply to the Third Objection is clear from what has been said.

FOURTH ARTICLE [I-II, Q. 67, Art. 4]

Whether Hope Remains After Death, in the State of Glory?

Objection 1: It would seem that hope remains after death, in the state of glory. Because hope perfects the human appetite in a more excellent manner than the moral virtues. But the moral virtues remain after this life, as Augustine clearly states (De Trin. xiv, 9). Much more then does hope remain.

Obj. 2: Further, fear is opposed to hope. But fear remains after this life: in the Blessed, filial fear, which abides for ever—in the lost, the fear of punishment. Therefore, in a like manner, hope can remain.

Obj. 3: Further, just as hope is of future good, so is desire. Now in the Blessed there is desire for future good; both for the glory of the body, which the souls of the Blessed desire, as Augustine declares (Gen. ad lit. xii, 35); and for the glory of the soul, according to Ecclus. 24:29: "They that eat me, shall yet hunger, and they that drink me, shall yet thirst," and 1 Pet. 1:12: "On Whom the angels desire to look." Therefore it seems that there can be hope in the Blessed after this life is past.

*On the contrary,* The Apostle says (Rom. 8:24): "What a man seeth, why doth he hope for?" But the Blessed see that which is the object of hope, viz. God. Therefore they do not hope.

*I answer that,* As stated above (A. 3), that which, in its very nature, implies imperfection of its subject, is incompatible with the opposite perfection in that subject. Thus it is evident that movement of its very nature implies imperfection of its subject, since it is "the act of that which is in potentiality as such" (Phys. iii): so that as soon as this potentiality is brought into act, the movement ceases; for a thing does not continue to become white, when once it is made white. Now hope denotes a movement towards that which is not possessed, as is clear from what we have said above about the passion of hope (Q. 40, AA. 1, 2). Therefore when we possess that which we hope for, viz. the enjoyment of God, it will no longer be possible to have hope.

Reply Obj. 1: Hope surpasses the moral virtues as to its object, which is God. But the acts of the moral virtues are not incompatible with the perfection of happiness, as the act of hope is; except perhaps, as regards their matter, in respect of which they do not remain. For moral virtue perfects the appetite, not only in respect of what is not yet possessed, but also as regards something which is in our actual possession.

Reply Obj. 2: Fear is twofold, servile and filial, as we shall state further on (II-II, Q. 19, A. 2). Servile fear regards punishment, and will be impossible in the life of glory, since there will no longer be possibility of being punished. Filial fear has two acts: one is an act of reverence to God, and with regard to this act, it remains: the other is an act of fear lest we be separated from God, and as regards this act, it does not remain. Because separation from God is in the nature of an evil: and no evil will be feared there, according to Prov. 1:33: "He ... shall enjoy abundance without fear of evils." Now fear is opposed to hope by opposition of good and evil, as stated above (Q. 23, A. 2; Q. 40, A. 1), and therefore the fear which will remain in glory is not opposed to hope. In the lost there can be fear of punishment, rather than hope of glory in the Blessed. Because in the lost there will be a succession of punishments, so that the notion of something future remains there, which is the object of fear: but the glory of the saints has no succession, by reason of its being a kind of participation of eternity, wherein there is neither past nor future, but only the present. And yet, properly speaking, neither in the lost is there fear. For, as stated above (Q. 42, A. 2), fear is never without some hope of escape: and the lost have no such hope. Consequently neither will there be fear in them; except speaking in a general way, in so far as any expectation of future evil is called fear.

Reply Obj. 3: As to the glory of the soul, there can be no desire in the Blessed, in so far as desire looks for something future, for the reason already given (ad 2). Yet hunger and thirst are said to be in them because they never weary, and for the same reason desire is said to be in the angels. With regard to the glory of the body, there can be desire in the souls of the saints, but not hope, properly speaking; neither as a theological virtue, for thus its object is God, and not a created good; nor in its general signification. Because the object of hope is something difficult, as stated above (Q. 40, A. 1): while a good whose unerring cause we already possess, is not compared to us as something difficult. Hence he that has money is not, properly speaking, said to hope for what he can buy at once. In like manner those who have the glory of the soul are not, properly speaking, said to hope for the glory of the body, but only to desire it.

FIFTH ARTICLE [I-II, Q. 67, Art. 5]

Whether Anything of Faith or Hope Remains in Glory?

Objection 1: It would seem that something of faith and hope remains in glory. For when that which is proper to a thing is removed, there remains what is common; thus it is stated in *De Causis* that "if you take away rational, there remains living, and when you remove living, there remains being." Now in faith there is something that it has in common with beatitude, viz. knowledge: and there is something proper to it, viz. darkness, for faith is knowledge in a dark manner. Therefore, the darkness of faith removed, the knowledge of faith still remains.

Obj. 2: Further, faith is a spiritual light of the soul, according to Eph. 1:17, 18: "The eyes of your heart enlightened ... in the knowledge of God"; yet this light is imperfect in comparison with the light of glory, of which it is written (Ps. 35:10): "In Thy light we shall see light." Now an imperfect light remains when a perfect light supervenes: for a candle is not extinguished when the sun's rays appear. Therefore it seems that the light of faith itself remains with the light of glory.

Obj. 3: Further, the substance of a habit does not cease through the withdrawal of its matter: for a man may retain the habit of liberality, though he have lost his money: yet he cannot exercise the act. Now the object of faith is the First Truth as unseen. Therefore when this ceases through being seen, the habit of faith can still remain.

*On the contrary,* Faith is a simple habit. Now a simple thing is either withdrawn entirely, or remains entirely. Since therefore faith does not remain entirely, but is taken away as stated above (A. 3), it seems that it is withdrawn entirely.

*I answer that,* Some have held that hope is taken away entirely: but that faith is taken away in part, viz. as to its obscurity, and remains in part, viz. as to the substance of its knowledge. And if this be understood to mean that it remains the same, not identically but generically, it is absolutely true; since faith is of the same genus, viz. knowledge, as the beatific vision. On the other hand, hope is not of the same genus as heavenly bliss: because it is compared to the enjoyment of bliss, as movement is to rest in the term of movement.

But if it be understood to mean that in heaven the knowledge of faith remains identically the same, this is absolutely impossible. Because when you remove a specific difference, the substance of the genus does not remain identically the same: thus if you remove the difference constituting whiteness, the substance of color does not remain identically the same, as though the identical color were at one time whiteness, and, at another, blackness. The reason is that genus is not related to difference as matter to form, so that the substance of the genus remains identically the same, when the difference is removed, as the substance of matter remains identically the same, when the form is changed: for genus and difference are not the parts of a species, else they would not be predicated of the species. But even as the species denotes the whole, i.e. the compound of matter and form in material things, so does the difference, and likewise the genus; the genus denotes the whole by signifying that which is material; the difference, by signifying that which is formal; the species, by signifying both. Thus, in man, the sensitive nature is as matter to the intellectual nature, and animal is predicated of that which has a sensitive nature, rational of that which has an intellectual nature, and man of that which has both. So that the one same whole is denoted by these three, but not under the same aspect.

It is therefore evident that, since the signification of the difference is confined to the genus if the difference be removed, the substance of the genus cannot remain the same: for the same animal nature does not remain, if another kind of soul constitute the animal. Hence it is impossible for the identical knowledge, which was previously obscure, to become clear vision. It is therefore evident that, in heaven, nothing remains of faith, either identically or specifically the same, but only generically.

Reply Obj. 1: If "rational" be withdrawn, the remaining "living" thing is the same, not identically, but generically, as stated.

Reply Obj. 2: The imperfection of candlelight is not opposed to the perfection of sunlight, since they do not regard the same subject: whereas the imperfection of faith and the perfection of glory are opposed to one another and regard the same subject. Consequently they are incompatible with one another, just as light and darkness in the air.

Reply Obj. 3: He that loses his money does not therefore lose the possibility of having money, and therefore it is reasonable for the habit of liberality to remain. But in the state of glory not only is the object of faith, which is the unseen, removed actually, but even its possibility, by reason of the unchangeableness of heavenly bliss: and so such a habit would remain to no purpose.

SIXTH ARTICLE [I-II, Q. 67, Art. 6]

Whether Charity Remains After This Life, in Glory?

Objection 1: It would seem that charity does not remain after this life, in glory. Because according to 1 Cor. 13:10, "when that which is perfect is come, that which is in part," i.e. that which is imperfect, "shall be done away." Now the charity of the wayfarer is imperfect. Therefore it will be done away when the perfection of glory is attained.

Obj. 2: Further, habits and acts are differentiated by their objects. But the object of love is good apprehended. Since therefore the apprehension of the present life differs from the apprehension of the life to come, it seems that charity is not the same in both cases.

Obj. 3: Further, things of the same kind can advance from imperfection to perfection by continuous increase. But the charity of the wayfarer can never attain to equality with the charity of heaven, however much it be increased. Therefore it seems that the charity of the wayfarer does not remain in heaven.

*On the contrary,* The Apostle says (1 Cor. 13:8): "Charity never falleth away."

*I answer that,* As stated above (A. 3), when the imperfection of a thing does not belong to its specific nature, there is nothing to hinder the identical thing passing from imperfection to perfection, even as man is perfected by growth, and whiteness by intensity. Now charity is love, the nature of which does not include imperfection, since it may relate to an object either possessed or not possessed, either seen or not seen. Therefore charity is not done away by the perfection of glory, but remains identically the same.

Reply Obj. 1: The imperfection of charity is accidental to it; because imperfection is not included in the nature of love. Now although that which is accidental to a thing be withdrawn, the substance remains. Hence the imperfection of charity being done away, charity itself is not done away.

Reply Obj. 2: The object of charity is not knowledge itself; if it were, the charity of the wayfarer would not be the same as the charity of heaven: its object is the thing known, which remains the same, viz. God Himself.

Reply Obj. 3: The reason why charity of the wayfarer cannot attain to the perfection of the charity of heaven, is a difference on the part of the cause: for vision is a cause of love, as stated in *Ethic.* ix, 5: and the more perfectly we know God, the more perfectly we love Him.

## QUESTION 68

OF THE GIFTS (In Eight Articles)

We now come to consider the Gifts; under which head there are eight points of inquiry:

(1) Whether the Gifts differ from the virtues?
(2) Of the necessity of the Gifts?
(3) Whether the Gifts are habits?
(4) Which, and how many are they?
(5) Whether the Gifts are connected?
(6) Whether they remain in heaven?
(7) Of their comparison with one another;
(8) Of their comparison with the virtues.

FIRST ARTICLE [I-II, Q. 68, Art. 1]

Whether the Gifts Differ from the Virtues?

Objection 1: It would seem that the gifts do not differ from the virtues. For Gregory commenting on Job 1:2, "There were born to him seven sons," says (Moral. i, 12): "Seven sons were born to us, when through the conception of heavenly thought, the seven virtues of the Holy Ghost take birth in us": and he quotes the words of Isa. 11:2, 3: "And the Spirit ... of understanding ... shall rest upon him," etc. where the seven gifts of the Holy Ghost are enumerated. Therefore the seven gifts of the Holy Ghost are virtues.

Obj. 2: Further, Augustine commenting on Matt. 12:45, "Then he goeth and taketh with him seven other spirits," etc., says (De Quaest. Evang. i, qu. 8): "The seven vices are opposed to the seven virtues of the Holy Ghost," i.e. to the seven gifts. Now the seven vices are opposed to the seven virtues, commonly so called. Therefore the gifts do not differ from the virtues commonly so called.

Obj. 3: Further, things whose definitions are the same, are themselves the same. But the definition of virtue applies to the gifts; for each gift is "a good quality of the mind, whereby we lead a good life," etc. [*Cf. Q. 55, A. 4]. Likewise the definition of a gift can apply to the infused virtues: for a gift is "an unreturnable giving," according to the Philosopher (Topic. iv, 4). Therefore the virtues and gifts do not differ from one another.

Obj. 4: Several of the things mentioned among the gifts, are virtues: for, as stated above (Q. 57, A. 2), wisdom, understanding, and knowledge are intellectual virtues, counsel pertains to prudence, piety to a kind of justice, and fortitude is a moral virtue. Therefore it seems that the gifts do not differ from the virtues.

*On the contrary,* Gregory (Moral. i, 12) distinguishes seven gifts, which he states to be denoted by the seven sons of Job, from the three theological virtues, which, he says, are signified by Job's three daughters. He also distinguishes (Moral. ii, 26) the same seven gifts from the four cardinal virtues, which he says were signified by the four corners of the house.

*I answer that,* If we speak of gift and virtue with regard to the notion conveyed by the words themselves, there is no opposition between them. Because the word "virtue" conveys the notion that it perfects man in relation to well-doing, while the word "gift" refers to the cause from which it proceeds. Now there is no reason why that which proceeds from one as a gift should not perfect another in well-doing: especially as we have already stated (Q. 63, A. 3) that some virtues are infused into us by God. Wherefore in this respect we cannot differentiate gifts from virtues. Consequently some have held that the gifts are not to be distinguished from the virtues. But there remains no less a difficulty for them to solve; for they must explain why some virtues are called gifts and some not; and why among the gifts there are some, fear, for instance, that are not reckoned virtues.

Hence it is that others have said that the gifts should be held as being distinct from the virtues; yet they have not assigned a suitable reason for this distinction, a reason, to wit, which would apply either to all the virtues, and to none of the gifts, or vice versa. For, seeing that of the seven gifts, four belong to the reason, viz. wisdom, knowledge, understanding and counsel, and three to the appetite, viz. fortitude, piety and fear; they held that the gifts perfect the free-will according as it is a faculty of the reason, while the virtues perfect it as a faculty of the will: since they observed only two virtues in the reason or intellect, viz. faith and prudence, the others being in the appetitive power or the affections. If this distinction were true, all the virtues would have to be in the appetite, and all the gifts in the reason.

Others observing that Gregory says (Moral. ii, 26) that "the gift of the Holy Ghost, by coming into the soul endows it with prudence, temperance, justice, and fortitude, and at the same time strengthens it against every kind of temptation by His sevenfold gift," said that the virtues are given us that we may do good works, and the gifts, that we may resist temptation. But neither is this distinction sufficient. Because the virtues also resist those temptations which lead to the sins that are contrary to the virtues; for everything naturally resists its contrary: which is especially clear with regard to charity, of which it is written (Cant. 8:7): "Many waters cannot quench charity."

Others again, seeing that these gifts are set down in Holy Writ as having been in Christ, according to Isa. 11:2, 3, said that the virtues are given simply that we may do good works, but the gifts, in order to conform us to Christ, chiefly with regard to His Passion, for it was then that these gifts shone with the greatest splendor. Yet neither does this appear to be a satisfactory distinction. Because Our Lord Himself wished us to be conformed to Him, chiefly in humility and meekness, according to Matt. 11:29: "Learn of Me, because I am meek and humble of heart," and in charity, according to John 15:12: "Love one another, as I have loved you." Moreover, these virtues were especially resplendent in Christ's Passion.

Accordingly, in order to differentiate the gifts from the virtues, we must be guided by the way in which Scripture expresses itself, for we find there that the term employed is "spirit" rather than "gift." For thus it is written (Isa. 11:2, 3): "The spirit ... of wisdom and of understanding ... shall rest upon him," etc.: from which words we are clearly given to understand that these seven are there set down as being in us by Divine inspiration. Now inspiration denotes motion from without. For it must be noted that in man there is a twofold principle of movement, one within him, viz. the reason; the other extrinsic to him, viz. God, as stated above (Q. 9, AA. 4, 6): moreover the Philosopher says this in the chapter On Good Fortune (Ethic. Eudem. vii, 8).

Now it is evident that whatever is moved must be proportionate to its mover: and the perfection of the mobile as such, consists in a disposition whereby it is disposed to be well moved by its mover. Hence the more exalted the mover, the more perfect must be the disposition whereby the mobile is made proportionate to its mover: thus we see that a disciple needs a more perfect disposition in order to receive a higher teaching from his master. Now it is manifest that human virtues perfect man according as it is natural for him to be moved by his reason in his interior and exterior actions. Consequently man needs yet higher perfections, whereby to be disposed to be moved by God. These perfections are called gifts, not only because they are infused by God, but also because by them man is disposed to become amenable to the Divine inspiration, according to Isa. 50:5: "The Lord ... hath opened my ear, and I do not resist; I have not gone back." Even the Philosopher says in the chapter On Good Fortune (Ethic. Eudem., vii, 8) that for those who are moved by Divine instinct, there is no need to take counsel according to human reason, but only to follow their inner promptings, since they are moved by a principle higher than human reason. This then is what some say, viz. that the gifts perfect man for acts which are higher than acts of virtue.

Reply Obj. 1: Sometimes these gifts are called virtues, in the broad sense of the word. Nevertheless, they have something over and above the virtues understood in this broad way, in so far as they are Divine virtues, perfecting man as moved by God. Hence the Philosopher (Ethic. vii, 1) above virtue commonly so called, places a kind of "heroic" or "divine virtue [* *arete heroike kai theia* ]," in respect of which some men are called "divine."

Reply Obj. 2: The vices are opposed to the virtues, in so far as they are opposed to the good as appointed by reason; but they are opposed to the gifts, in as much as they are opposed to the Divine instinct. For the same thing is opposed both to God and to reason, whose light flows from God.

Reply Obj. 3: This definition applies to virtue taken in its general sense. Consequently, if we wish to restrict it to virtue as distinguished from the gifts, we must explain the words, "whereby we lead a good life" as referring to the rectitude of life which is measured by the rule of reason. Likewise the gifts, as distinct from infused virtue, may be defined as something given by God in relation to His motion; something, to wit, that makes man to follow well the promptings of God.

Reply Obj. 4: Wisdom is called an intellectual virtue, so far as it proceeds from the judgment of reason: but it is called a gift, according as its work proceeds from the Divine prompting. The same applies to the other virtues.

SECOND ARTICLE [I-II, Q. 68, Art. 2]

Whether the Gifts Are Necessary to Man for Salvation?

Objection 1: It would seem that the gifts are not necessary to man for salvation. Because the gifts are ordained to a perfection surpassing the ordinary perfection of virtue. Now it is not necessary for man's salvation that he should attain to a perfection surpassing the ordinary standard of virtue; because such perfection falls, not under the precept, but under a counsel. Therefore the gifts are not necessary to man for salvation.

Obj. 2: Further, it is enough, for man's salvation, that he behave well in matters concerning God and matters concerning man. Now man's behavior to God is sufficiently directed by the theological virtues; and his behavior towards men, by the moral virtues. Therefore gifts are not necessary to man for salvation.

Obj. 3: Further, Gregory says (Moral. ii, 26) that "the Holy Ghost gives wisdom against folly, understanding against dullness, counsel against rashness, fortitude against fears, knowledge against ignorance, piety against hardness of our heart, and fear against pride." But a sufficient remedy for all these things is to be found in the virtues. Therefore the gifts are not necessary to man for salvation.

*On the contrary,* Of all the gifts, wisdom seems to be the highest, and fear the lowest. Now each of these is necessary for salvation: since of wisdom it is written (Wis. 7:28): "God loveth none but him that dwelleth with wisdom"; and of fear (Ecclus. 1:28): "He that is without fear cannot be justified." Therefore the other gifts that are placed between these are also necessary for salvation.

*I answer that,* As stated above (A. 1), the gifts are perfections of man, whereby he is disposed so as to be amenable to the promptings of God. Wherefore in those matters where the prompting of reason is not sufficient, and there is need for the prompting of the Holy Ghost, there is, in consequence, need for a gift.

Now man's reason is perfected by God in two ways: first, with its natural perfection, to wit, the natural light of reason; secondly, with a supernatural perfection, to wit, the theological virtues, as stated above (Q. 62, A. 1). And, though this latter perfection is greater than the former, yet the former is possessed by man in a more perfect manner than the latter: because man has the former in his full possession, whereas he possesses the latter imperfectly, since we love and know God imperfectly. Now it is evident that anything that has a nature or a form or a virtue perfectly, can of itself work according to them: not, however, excluding the operation of God, Who works inwardly in every nature and in every will. On the other hand, that which has a nature, or form, or virtue imperfectly, cannot of itself work, unless it be moved by another. Thus the sun which possesses light perfectly, can shine by itself; whereas the moon which has the nature of light imperfectly, sheds only a borrowed light. Again, a physician, who knows the medical art perfectly, can work by himself; but his pupil, who is not yet fully instructed, cannot work by himself, but needs to receive instructions from him.

Accordingly, in matters subject to human reason, and directed to man's connatural end, man can work through the judgment of his reason. If, however, even in these things man receive help in the shape of special promptings from God, this will be out of God's superabundant goodness: hence, according to the philosophers, not every one that had the acquired moral virtues, had also the heroic or divine virtues. But in matters directed to the supernatural end, to which man's reason moves him, according as it is, in a manner, and imperfectly, informed by the theological virtues, the motion of reason does not suffice, unless it receive in addition the prompting or motion of the Holy Ghost, according to Rom. 8:14, 17: "Whosoever are led by the Spirit of God, they are sons of God ... and if sons, heirs also": and Ps. 142:10: "Thy good Spirit shall lead me into the right land," because, to wit, none can receive the inheritance of that land of the Blessed, except he be moved and led thither by the Holy Ghost. Therefore, in order to accomplish this end, it is necessary for man to have the gift of the Holy Ghost.

Reply Obj. 1: The gifts surpass the ordinary perfection of the virtues, not as regards the kind of works (as the counsels surpass the commandments), but as regards the manner of working, in respect of man being moved by a higher principle.

Reply Obj. 2: By the theological and moral virtues, man is not so perfected in respect of his last end, as not to stand in continual need of being moved by the yet higher promptings of the Holy Ghost, for the reason already given.

Reply Obj. 3: Whether we consider human reason as perfected in its natural perfection, or as perfected by the theological virtues, it does not know all things, nor all possible things. Consequently it is unable to avoid folly and other like things mentioned in the objection. God, however, to Whose knowledge and power all things are subject, by His motion safeguards us from all folly, ignorance, dullness of mind and hardness of heart, and the rest. Consequently the gifts of the Holy Ghost, which make us amenable to His promptings, are said to be given as remedies to these defects.

THIRD ARTICLE [I-II, Q. 68, Art. 3]

Whether the Gifts of the Holy Ghost Are Habits?

Objection 1: It would seem that the gifts of the Holy Ghost are not habits. Because a habit is a quality abiding in man, being defined as "a quality difficult to remove," as stated in the *Predicaments* (Categor. vi). Now it is proper to Christ that the gifts of the Holy Ghost rest in Him, as stated in Isa. 11:2, 3: "He upon Whom thou shalt see the Spirit descending and remaining upon Him, He it is that baptizeth"; on which words Gregory comments as follows (Moral. ii, 27): "The Holy Ghost comes upon all the faithful; but, in a singular way, He dwells always in the Mediator." Therefore the gifts of the Holy Ghost are not habits.

Obj. 2: Further, the gifts of the Holy Ghost perfect man according as he is moved by the Spirit of God, as stated above (AA. 1, 2). But in so far as man is moved by the Spirit of God, he is somewhat like an instrument in His regard. Now to be perfected by a habit is befitting, not an instrument, but a principal agent. Therefore the gifts of the Holy Ghost are not habits.

Obj. 3: Further, as the gifts of the Holy Ghost are due to Divine inspiration, so is the gift of prophecy. Now prophecy is not a habit: for "the spirit of prophecy does not always reside in the prophets," as Gregory states (Hom. i in Ezechiel). Neither, therefore, are the gifts of the Holy Ghost.

*On the contrary,* Our Lord in speaking of the Holy Ghost said to His disciples (John 14:17): "He shall abide with you, and shall be in you." Now the Holy Ghost is not in a man without His gifts. Therefore His gifts abide in man. Therefore they are not merely acts or passions but abiding habits.

*I answer that,* As stated above (A. 1), the gifts are perfections of man, whereby he becomes amenable to the promptings of the Holy Ghost. Now it is evident from what has been already said (Q. 56, A. 4; Q. 58, A. 2), that the moral virtues perfect the appetitive power according as it partakes somewhat of the reason, in so far, to wit, as it has a natural aptitude to be moved by the command of reason. Accordingly the gifts of the Holy Ghost, as compared with the Holy Ghost Himself, are related to man, even as the moral virtues, in comparison with the reason, are related to the appetitive power. Now the moral virtues are habits, whereby the powers of appetite are disposed to obey reason promptly. Therefore the gifts of the Holy Ghost are habits whereby man is perfected to obey readily the Holy Ghost.

Reply Obj. 1: Gregory solves this objection (Moral. ii, 27) by saying that "by those gifts without which one cannot obtain life, the Holy Ghost ever abides in all the elect, but not by His other gifts." Now the seven gifts are necessary for salvation, as stated above (A. 2). Therefore, with regard to them, the Holy Ghost ever abides in holy men.

Reply Obj. 2: This argument holds, in the case of an instrument which has no faculty of action, but only of being acted upon. But man is not an instrument of that kind; for he is so acted upon, by the Holy Ghost, that he also acts himself, in so far as he has a free-will. Therefore he needs a habit.

Reply Obj. 3: Prophecy is one of those gifts which are for the manifestation of the Spirit, not for the necessity of salvation: hence the comparison fails.

FOURTH ARTICLE [I-II, Q. 68, Art. 4]

Whether the Seven Gifts of the Holy Ghost Are Suitably Enumerated?

Objection 1: It would seem that seven gifts of the Holy Ghost are unsuitably enumerated. For in that enumeration four are set down corresponding to the intellectual virtues, viz. wisdom, understanding, knowledge, and counsel, which corresponds to prudence; whereas nothing is set down corresponding to art, which is the fifth intellectual virtue. Moreover, something is included corresponding to justice, viz. piety, and something corresponding to fortitude, viz. the gift of fortitude; while there is nothing to correspond to temperance. Therefore the gifts are enumerated insufficiently.

Obj. 2: Further, piety is a part of justice. But no part of fortitude is assigned to correspond thereto, but fortitude itself. Therefore justice itself, and not piety, ought to have been set down.

Obj. 3: Further, the theological virtues, more than any, direct us to God. Since, then, the gifts perfect man according as he is moved by God, it seems that some gifts, corresponding to the theological virtues, should have been included.

Obj. 4: Further, even as God is an object of fear, so is He of love, of hope, and of joy. Now love, hope, and joy are passions condivided with fear. Therefore, as fear is set down as a gift, so ought the other three.

Obj. 5: Further, wisdom is added in order to direct understanding; counsel, to direct fortitude; knowledge, to direct piety. Therefore, some gift should have been added for the purpose of directing fear. Therefore the seven gifts of the Holy Ghost are unsuitably enumerated.

*On the contrary,* stands the authority of Holy Writ (Isa. 11:2, 3).

*I answer that,* As stated above (A. 3), the gifts are habits perfecting man so that he is ready to follow the promptings of the Holy Ghost, even as the moral virtues perfect the appetitive powers so that they obey the reason. Now just as it is natural for the appetitive powers to be moved by the command of reason, so it is natural for all the forces in man to be moved by the instinct of God, as by a superior power. Therefore whatever powers in man can be the principles of human actions, can also be the subjects of gifts, even as they are virtues; and such powers are the reason and appetite.

Now the reason is speculative and practical: and in both we find the apprehension of truth (which pertains to the discovery of truth), and judgment concerning the truth. Accordingly, for the apprehension of truth, the speculative reason is perfected by *understanding;* the practical reason, by *counsel.* In order to judge aright, the speculative reason is perfected by *wisdom* ; the practical reason by *knowledge.* The appetitive power, in matters touching a man's relations to another, is perfected by *piety;* in matters touching himself, it is perfected by *fortitude* against the fear of dangers; and against inordinate lust for pleasures, by *fear,* according to Prov. 15:27: "By the fear of the Lord every one declineth from evil," and Ps. 118:120: "Pierce Thou my flesh with Thy fear: for I am afraid of Thy judgments." Hence it is clear that these gifts extend to all those things to which the virtues, both intellectual and moral, extend.

Reply Obj. 1: The gifts of the Holy Ghost perfect man in matters concerning a good life: whereas art is not directed to such matters, but to external things that can be made, since art is the right reason, not about things to be done, but about things to be made (Ethic. vi, 4). However, we may say that, as regards the infusion of the gifts, the art is on the part of the Holy Ghost, Who is the principal mover, and not on the part of men, who are His organs when He moves them. The gift of fear corresponds, in a manner, to temperance: for just as it belongs to temperance, properly speaking, to restrain man from evil pleasures for the sake of the good appointed by reason, so does it belong to the gift of fear, to withdraw man from evil pleasures through fear of God.

Reply Obj. 2: Justice is so called from the rectitude of the reason, and so it is more suitably called a virtue than a gift. But the name of piety denotes the reverence which we give to our father and to our country. And since God is the Father of all, the worship of God is also called piety, as Augustine states (De Civ. Dei x, 1). Therefore the gift whereby a man, through reverence for God, works good to all, is fittingly called piety.

Reply Obj. 3: The mind of man is not moved by the Holy Ghost, unless in some way it be united to Him: even as the instrument is not moved by the craftsman, unless there by contact or some other kind of union between them. Now the primal union of man with God is by faith, hope and charity: and, consequently, these virtues are presupposed to the gifts, as being their roots. Therefore all the gifts correspond to these three virtues, as being derived therefrom.

Reply Obj. 4: Love, hope and joy have good for their object. Now God is the Sovereign Good: wherefore the names of these passions are transferred to the theological virtues which unite man to God. On the other hand, the object of fear is evil, which can nowise apply to God: hence fear does not denote union with God, but withdrawal from certain things through reverence for God. Hence it does not give its name to a theological virtue, but to a gift, which withdraws us from evil, for higher motives than moral virtue does.

Reply Obj. 5: Wisdom directs both the intellect and the affections of man. Hence two gifts are set down as corresponding to wisdom as their directing principle; on the part of the intellect, the gift of understanding; on the part of the affections, the gift of fear. Because the principal reason for fearing God is taken from a consideration of the Divine excellence, which wisdom considers.

FIFTH ARTICLE [I-II, Q. 68, Art. 5]

Whether the Gifts of the Holy Ghost Are Connected?

Objection 1: It would seem that the gifts are not connected, for the Apostle says (1 Cor. 12:8): "To one ... by the Spirit, is given the word of wisdom, and to another, the word of knowledge, according to the same Spirit." Now wisdom and knowledge are reckoned among the gifts of the Holy Ghost. Therefore the gifts of the Holy Ghost are given to divers men, and are not connected together in the same man.

Obj. 2: Further, Augustine says (De Trin. xiv, 1) that "many of the faithful have not knowledge, though they have faith." But some of the gifts, at least the gift of fear, accompany faith. Therefore it seems that the gifts are not necessarily connected together in one and the same man.

Obj. 3: Further, Gregory says (Moral. i) that wisdom "is of small account if it lack understanding, and understanding is wholly useless if it be not based upon wisdom ... Counsel is worthless, when the strength of fortitude is lacking thereto ... and fortitude is very weak if it be not supported by counsel ... Knowledge is nought if it hath not the use of piety ... and piety is very useless if it lack the discernment of knowledge ... and assuredly, unless it has these virtues with it, fear itself rises up to the doing of no good action": from which it seems that it is possible to have one gift without another. Therefore the gifts of the Holy Ghost are not connected.

*On the contrary,* Gregory prefaces the passage above quoted, with the following remark: "It is worthy of note in this feast of Job's sons, that by turns they fed one another." Now the sons of Job, of whom he is speaking, denote the gifts of the Holy Ghost. Therefore the gifts of the Holy Ghost are connected together by strengthening one another.

*I answer that,* The true answer to this question is easily gathered from what has been already set down. For it has been stated (A. 3) that as the powers of the appetite are disposed by the moral virtues as regards the governance of reason, so all the powers of the soul are disposed by the gifts as regards the motion of the Holy Ghost. Now the Holy Ghost dwells in us by charity, according to Rom. 5:5: "The charity of God is poured forth in our hearts by the Holy Ghost, Who is given to us," even as our reason is perfected by prudence. Wherefore, just as the moral virtues are united together in prudence, so the gifts of the Holy Ghost are connected together in charity: so that whoever has charity has all the gifts of the Holy Ghost, none of which can one possess without charity.

Reply Obj. 1: Wisdom and knowledge can be considered in one way as gratuitous graces, in so far, to wit, as man so far abounds in the knowledge of things Divine and human, that he is able both to instruct the believer and confound the unbeliever. It is in this sense that the Apostle speaks, in this passage, about wisdom and knowledge: hence he mentions pointedly the "word" of wisdom and the "word" of knowledge. They may be taken in another way for the gifts of the Holy Ghost: and thus wisdom and knowledge are nothing else but perfections of the human mind, rendering it amenable to the promptings of the Holy Ghost in the knowledge of things Divine and human. Consequently it is clear that these gifts are in all who are possessed of charity.

Reply Obj. 2: Augustine is speaking there of knowledge, while expounding the passage of the Apostle quoted above (Obj. 1): hence he is referring to knowledge, in the sense already explained, as a gratuitous grace. This is clear from the context which follows: "For it is one thing to know only what a man must believe in order to gain the blissful life, which is no other than eternal life; and another, to know how to impart this to godly souls, and to defend it against the ungodly, which latter the Apostle seems to have styled by the proper name of knowledge."

Reply Obj. 3: Just as the connection of the cardinal virtues is proved in one way from the fact that one is, in a manner, perfected by another, as stated above (Q. 65, A. 1); so Gregory wishes to prove the connection of the gifts, in the same way, from the fact that one cannot be perfect without the other. Hence he had already observed that "each particular virtue is to the last degree destitute, unless one virtue lend its support to another." We are therefore not to understand that one gift can be without another; but that if understanding were without wisdom, it would not be a gift; even as temperance, without justice, would not be a virtue.

SIXTH ARTICLE [I-II, Q. 68, Art. 6]

Whether the Gifts of the Holy Ghost Remain in Heaven?

Objection 1: It would seem that the gifts of the Holy Ghost do not remain in heaven. For Gregory says (Moral. ii, 26) that by means of His sevenfold gift the "Holy Ghost instructs the mind against all temptations." Now there will be no temptations in heaven, according to Isa. 11:9: "They shall not hurt, nor shall they kill in all My holy mountain." Therefore there will be no gifts of the Holy Ghost in heaven.

Obj. 2: Further, the gifts of the Holy Ghost are habits, as stated above (A. 3). But habits are of no use, where their acts are impossible. Now the acts of some gifts are not possible in heaven; for Gregory says (Moral. i, 15) that "understanding ... penetrates the truths heard ... counsel ... stays us from acting rashly ... fortitude ... has no fear of adversity ... piety satisfies the inmost heart with deeds of mercy," all of which are incompatible with the heavenly state. Therefore these gifts will not remain in the state of glory.

Obj. 3: Further, some of the gifts perfect man in the contemplative life, e.g. wisdom and understanding: and some in the active life, e.g. piety and fortitude. Now the active life ends with this as Gregory states (Moral. vi). Therefore not all the gifts of the Holy Ghost will be in the state of glory.

*On the contrary,* Ambrose says (De Spiritu Sancto i, 20): "The city of God, the heavenly Jerusalem is not washed with the waters of an earthly river: it is the Holy Ghost, of Whose outpouring we but taste, Who, proceeding from the Fount of life, seems to flow more abundantly in those celestial spirits, a seething torrent of sevenfold heavenly virtue."

*I answer that,* We may speak of the gifts in two ways: first, as to their essence; and thus they will be most perfectly in heaven, as may be gathered from the passage of Ambrose, just quoted. The reason for this is that the gifts of the Holy Ghost render the human mind amenable to the motion of the Holy Ghost: which will be especially realized in heaven, where God will be "all in all" (1 Cor. 15:28), and man entirely subject unto Him. Secondly, they may be considered as regards the matter about which their operations are: and thus, in the present life they have an operation about a matter, in respect of which they will have no operation in the state of glory. Considered in this way, they will not remain in the state of glory; just as we have stated to be the case with regard to the cardinal virtues (Q. 67, A. 1).

Reply Obj. 1: Gregory is speaking there of the gifts according as they are compatible with the present state: for it is thus that they afford us protection against evil temptations. But in the state of glory, where all evil will have ceased, we shall be perfected in good by the gifts of the Holy Ghost.

Reply Obj. 2: Gregory, in almost every gift, includes something that passes away with the present state, and something that remains in the future state. For he says that "wisdom strengthens the mind with the hope and certainty of eternal things"; of which two, hope passes, and certainty remains. Of understanding, he says "that it penetrates the truths heard, refreshing the heart and enlightening its darkness," of which, hearing passes away, since "they shall teach no more every man ... his brother" (Jer. 31:3, 4); but the enlightening of the mind remains. Of counsel he says that it "prevents us from being impetuous," which is necessary in the present life; and also that "it makes the mind full of reason," which is necessary even in the future state. Of fortitude he says that it "fears not adversity," which is necessary in the present life; and further, that it "sets before us the viands of confidence," which remains also in the future life. With regard to knowledge he mentions only one thing, viz. that "she overcomes the void of ignorance," which refers to the present state. When, however, he adds "in the womb of the mind," this may refer figuratively to the fulness of knowledge, which belongs to the future state. Of piety he says that "it satisfies the inmost heart with deeds of mercy." These words taken literally refer only to the present state: yet the inward regard for our neighbor, signified by "the inmost heart," belongs also to the future state, when piety will achieve, not works of mercy, but fellowship of joy. Of fear he says that "it oppresses the mind, lest it pride itself in present things," which refers to the present state, and that "it strengthens it with the meat of hope for the future," which also belongs to the present state, as regards hope, but may also refer to the future state, as regards being "strengthened" for things we hope are here, and obtain there.

Reply Obj. 3: This argument considers the gifts as to their matter. For the matter of the gifts will not be the works of the active life; but all the gifts will have their respective acts about things pertaining to the contemplative life, which is the life of heavenly bliss.

SEVENTH ARTICLE [I-II, Q. 68, Art. 7]

Whether the Gifts Are Set Down by Isaias in Their Order of Dignity?

Objection 1: It would seem that the gifts are not set down by Isaias in their order of dignity. For the principal gift is, seemingly, that which, more than the others, God requires of man. Now God requires of man fear, more than the other gifts: for it is written (Deut. 10:12): "And now, Israel, what doth the Lord thy God require of thee, but that thou fear the Lord thy God?" and (Malachi 1:6): "If ... I be a master, where is My fear?" Therefore it seems that fear, which is mentioned last, is not the lowest but the greatest of the gifts.

Obj. 2: Further, piety seems to be a kind of common good; since the Apostle says (1 Tim. 4:8): "Piety [Douay: 'Godliness'] is profitable to all things." Now a common good is preferable to particular goods. Therefore piety, which is given the last place but one, seems to be the most excellent gift.

Obj. 3: Further, knowledge perfects man's judgment, while counsel pertains to inquiry. But judgment is more excellent than inquiry. Therefore knowledge is a more excellent gift than counsel; and yet it is set down as being below it.

Obj. 4: Further, fortitude pertains to the appetitive power, while science belongs to reason. But reason is a more excellent power than the appetite. Therefore knowledge is a more excellent gift than fortitude; and yet the latter is given the precedence. Therefore the gifts are not set down in their order of dignity.

*On the contrary,* Augustine says [*De Serm. Dom. in Monte i, 4]: "It seems to me that the sevenfold operation of the Holy Ghost, of which Isaias speaks, agrees in degrees and expression with these" (of which we read in Matt. 5:3): "but there is a difference of order, for there" (viz. in Isaias) "the enumeration begins with the more excellent gifts, here, with the lower gifts."

*I answer that,* The excellence of the gifts can be measured in two ways: first, simply, viz. by comparison to their proper acts as proceeding from their principles; secondly, relatively, viz. by comparison to their matter. If we consider the excellence of the gifts simply, they follow the same rule as the virtues, as to their comparison one with another; because the gifts perfect man for all the acts of the soul's powers, even as the virtues do, as stated above (A. 4). Hence, as the intellectual virtues have the precedence of the moral virtues, and among the intellectual virtues, the contemplative are preferable to the active, viz. wisdom, understanding and science to prudence and art (yet so that wisdom stands before understanding, and understanding before science, and prudence and synesis before eubulia): so also among the gifts, wisdom, understanding, knowledge, and counsel are more excellent than piety, fortitude, and fear; and among the latter, piety excels fortitude, and fortitude fear, even as justice surpasses fortitude, and fortitude temperance. But in regard to their matter, fortitude and counsel precede knowledge and piety: because fortitude and counsel are concerned with difficult matters, whereas piety and knowledge regard ordinary matters. Consequently the excellence of the gifts corresponds with the order in which they are enumerated; but so far as wisdom and understanding are given the preference to the others, their excellence is considered simply, while, so far, as counsel and fortitude are preferred to knowledge and piety, it is considered with regard to their matter.

Reply Obj. 1: Fear is chiefly required as being the foundation, so to speak, of the perfection of the other gifts, for "the fear of the Lord is the beginning of wisdom" (Ps. 110:10; Ecclus. 1:16), and not as though it were more excellent than the others. Because, in the order of generation, man departs from evil on account of fear (Prov. 16:16), before doing good works, and which result from the other gifts.

Reply Obj. 2: In the words quoted from the Apostle, piety is not compared with all God's gifts, but only with "bodily exercise," of which he had said it "is profitable to little."

Reply Obj. 3: Although knowledge stands before counsel by reason of its judgment, yet counsel is more excellent by reason of its matter: for counsel is only concerned with matters of difficulty (Ethic. iii, 3), whereas the judgment of knowledge embraces all matters.

Reply Obj. 4: The directive gifts which pertain to the reason are more excellent than the executive gifts, if we consider them in relation to their acts as proceeding from their powers, because reason transcends the appetite as a rule transcends the thing ruled. But on the part of the matter, counsel is united to fortitude as the directive power to the executive, and so is knowledge united to piety: because counsel and fortitude are concerned with matters of difficulty, while knowledge and piety are concerned with ordinary matters. Hence counsel together with fortitude, by reason of their matter, are given the preference to knowledge and piety.

EIGHTH ARTICLE [I-II, Q. 68, Art. 8]

Whether the Virtues Are More Excellent Than the Gifts?

Objection 1: It would seem that the virtues are more excellent than the gifts. For Augustine says (De Trin. xv, 18) while speaking of charity: "No gift of God is more excellent than this. It is this alone which divides the children of the eternal kingdom from the children of eternal damnation. Other gifts are bestowed by the Holy Ghost, but, without charity, they avail nothing." But charity is a virtue. Therefore a virtue is more excellent than the gifts of the Holy Ghost.

Obj. 2: Further, that which is first naturally, seems to be more excellent. Now the virtues precede the gifts of the Holy Ghost; for Gregory says (Moral. ii, 26) that "the gift of the Holy Ghost in the mind it works on, forms first of all justice, prudence, fortitude, temperance ... and doth afterwards give it a temper in the seven virtues" (viz. the gifts), so "as against folly to bestow wisdom; against dullness, understanding; against rashness, counsel; against fear, fortitude; against ignorance, knowledge; against hardness of heart, piety; against piety, fear." Therefore the virtues are more excellent than the gifts.

Obj. 3: Further, Augustine says (De Lib. Arb. ii, 19) that "the virtues cannot be used to evil purpose." But it is possible to make evil use of the gifts, for Gregory says (Moral. i, 18): "We offer up the sacrifice of prayer ... lest wisdom may uplift; or understanding, while it runs nimbly, deviate from the right path; or counsel, while it multiplies itself, grow into confusion; that fortitude, while it gives confidence, may not make us rash; lest knowledge, while it knows and yet loves not, may swell the mind; lest piety, while it swerves from the right line, may become distorted; and lest fear, while it is unduly alarmed, may plunge us into the pit of despair." Therefore the virtues are more excellent than the gifts of the Holy Ghost.

*On the contrary,* The gifts are bestowed to assist the virtues and to remedy certain defects, as is shown in the passage quoted (Obj. 2), so that, seemingly, they accomplish what the virtues cannot. Therefore the gifts are more excellent than the virtues.

*I answer that,* As was shown above (Q. 58, A. 3; Q. 62, A. 1), there are three kinds of virtues: for some are theological, some intellectual, and some moral. The theological virtues are those whereby man's mind is united to God; the intellectual virtues are those whereby reason itself is perfected; and the moral virtues are those which perfect the powers of appetite in obedience to the reason. On the other hand the gifts of the Holy Ghost dispose all the powers of the soul to be amenable to the Divine motion.

Accordingly the gifts seem to be compared to the theological virtues, by which man is united to the Holy Ghost his Mover, in the same way as the moral virtues are compared to the intellectual virtues, which perfect the reason, the moving principle of the moral virtues. Wherefore as the intellectual virtues are more excellent than the moral virtues and control them, so the theological virtues are more excellent than the gifts of the Holy Ghost and regulate them. Hence Gregory says (Moral. i, 12) that "the seven sons," i.e. the seven gifts, "never attain the perfection of the number ten, unless all they do be done in faith, hope, and charity."

But if we compare the gifts to the other virtues, intellectual and moral, then the gifts have the precedence of the virtues. Because the gifts perfect the soul's powers in relation to the Holy Ghost their Mover; whereas the virtues perfect, either the reason itself, or the other powers in relation to reason: and it is evident that the more exalted the mover, the more excellent the disposition whereby the thing moved requires to be disposed. Therefore the gifts are more perfect than the virtues.

Reply Obj. 1: Charity is a theological virtue; and such we grant to be more perfect than the gifts.

Reply Obj. 2: There are two ways in which one thing precedes another. One is in order of perfection and dignity, as love of God precedes love of our neighbor: and in this way the gifts precede the intellectual and moral virtues, but follow the theological virtues. The other is the order of generation or disposition: thus love of one's neighbor precedes love of God, as regards the act: and in this way moral and intellectual virtues precede the gifts, since man, through being well subordinate to his own reason, is disposed to be rightly subordinate to God.

Reply Obj. 3: Wisdom and understanding and the like are gifts of the Holy Ghost, according as they are quickened by charity, which "dealeth not perversely" (1 Cor. 13:4). Consequently wisdom and understanding and the like cannot be used to evil purpose, in so far as they are gifts of the Holy Ghost. But, lest they depart from the perfection of charity, they assist one another. This is what Gregory means to say.

## QUESTION 69

OF THE BEATITUDES (In Four Articles)

We must now consider the beatitudes: under which head there are four points of inquiry:

(1) Whether the beatitudes differ from the gifts and virtues?

(2) Of the rewards of the beatitudes: whether they refer to this life?

(3) Of the number of the beatitudes;

(4) Of the fittingness of the rewards ascribed to the beatitudes.

FIRST ARTICLE [I-II, Q. 69, Art. 1]

Whether the Beatitudes Differ from the Virtues and Gifts?

Objection 1: It would seem that the beatitudes do not differ from the virtues and gifts. For Augustine (De Serm. Dom. in Monte i, 4) assigns the beatitudes recited by Matthew (v 3, seqq.) to the gifts of the Holy Ghost; and Ambrose in his commentary on Luke 6:20, seqq., ascribes the beatitudes mentioned there, to the four cardinal virtues. Therefore the beatitudes do not differ from the virtues and gifts.

Obj. 2: Further, there are but two rules of the human will: the reason and the eternal law, as stated above (Q. 19, A. 3; Q. 21, A. 1). Now the virtues perfect man in relation to reason; while the gifts perfect him in relation to the eternal law of the Holy Ghost, as is clear from what has been said (Q. 68, AA. 1, 3, seqq.). Therefore there cannot be anything else pertaining to the rectitude of the human will, besides the virtues and gifts. Therefore the beatitudes do not differ from them.

Obj. 3: Further, among the beatitudes are included meekness, justice, and mercy, which are said to be virtues. Therefore the beatitudes do not differ from the virtues and gifts.

*On the contrary,* Certain things are included among the beatitudes, that are neither virtues nor gifts, e.g. poverty, mourning, and peace. Therefore the beatitudes differ from the virtues and gifts.

*I answer that,* As stated above (Q. 2, A. 7; Q. 3, A. 1), happiness is the last end of human life. Now one is said to possess the end already, when one hopes to possess it; wherefore the Philosopher says (Ethic. i, 9) that "children are said to be happy because they are full of hope"; and the Apostle says (Rom. 8:24): "We are saved by hope." Again, we hope to obtain an end, because we are suitably moved towards that end, and approach thereto; and this implies some action. And a man is moved towards, and approaches the happy end by works of virtue, and above all by the works of the gifts, if we speak of eternal happiness, for which our reason is not sufficient, since we need to be moved by the Holy Ghost, and to be perfected with His gifts that we may obey and follow him. Consequently the beatitudes differ from the virtues and gifts, not as habit from habit, but as act from habit.

Reply Obj. 1: Augustine and Ambrose assign the beatitudes to the gifts and virtues, as acts are ascribed to habits. But the gifts are more excellent than the cardinal virtues, as stated above (Q. 68, A. 8). Wherefore Ambrose, in explaining the beatitudes propounded to the throng, assigns them to the cardinal virtues, whereas Augustine, who is explaining the beatitudes delivered to the disciples on the mountain, and so to those who were more perfect, ascribes them to the gifts of the Holy Ghost.

Reply Obj. 2: This argument proves that no other habits, besides the virtues and gifts, rectify human conduct.

Reply Obj. 3: Meekness is to be taken as denoting the act of meekness: and the same applies to justice and mercy. And though these might seem to be virtues, they are nevertheless ascribed to gifts, because the gifts perfect man in all matters wherein the virtues perfect him, as stated above (Q. 68, A. 2).

SECOND ARTICLE [I-II, Q. 69, Art. 2]

Whether the Rewards Assigned to the Beatitudes Refer to This Life?

Objection 1: It would seem that the rewards assigned to the beatitudes do not refer to this life. Because some are said to be happy because they hope for a reward, as stated above (A. 1). Now the object of hope is future happiness. Therefore these rewards refer to the life to come.

Obj. 2: Further, certain punishments are set down in opposition to the beatitudes, Luke 6:25, where we read: "Woe to you that are filled; for you shall hunger. Woe to you that now laugh, for you shall mourn and weep." Now these punishments do not refer to this life, because frequently men are not punished in this life, according to Job 21:13: "They spend their days in wealth." Therefore neither do the rewards of the beatitudes refer to this life.

Obj. 3: Further, the kingdom of heaven which is set down as the reward of poverty is the happiness of heaven, as Augustine says (De Civ. Dei xix) [*Cf. De Serm. Dom. in Monte i, 1]. Again, abundant fullness is not to be had save in the life to come, according to Ps. 16:15: "I shall be filled [Douay: 'satisfied'] when Thy glory shall appear." Again, it is only in the future life that we shall see God, and that our Divine sonship will be made manifest, according to 1 John 3:2: "We are now the sons of God; and it hath not yet appeared what we shall be. We know that, when He shall appear, we shall be like to Him, because we shall see Him as He is." Therefore these rewards refer to the future life.

*On the contrary,* Augustine says (De Serm. Dom. in Monte i, 4): "These promises can be fulfilled in this life, as we believe them to have been fulfilled in the apostles. For no words can express that complete change into the likeness even of an angel, which is promised to us after this life."

*I answer that,* Expounders of Holy Writ are not agreed in speaking of these rewards. For some, with Ambrose (Super Luc. v), hold that all these rewards refer to the life to come; while Augustine (De Serm. Dom. in Monte i, 4) holds them to refer to the present life; and Chrysostom in his homilies (In Matth. xv) says that some refer to the future, and some to the present life.

In order to make the matter clear we must take note that hope of future happiness may be in us for two reasons. First, by reason of our having a preparation for, or a disposition to future happiness; and this is by way of merit; secondly, by a kind of imperfect inchoation of future happiness in holy men, even in this life. For it is one thing to hope that the tree will bear fruit, when the leaves begin to appear, and another, when we see the first signs of the fruit.

Accordingly, those things which are set down as merits in the beatitudes, are a kind of preparation for, or disposition to happiness, either perfect or inchoate: while those that are assigned as rewards, may be either perfect happiness, so as to refer to the future life, or some beginning of happiness, such as is found in those who have attained perfection, in which case they refer to the present life. Because when a man begins to make progress in the acts of the virtues and gifts, it is to be hoped that he will arrive at perfection, both as a wayfarer, and as a citizen of the heavenly kingdom.

Reply Obj. 1: Hope regards future happiness as the last end: yet it may also regard the assistance of grace as that which leads to that end, according to Ps. 27:7: "In Him hath my heart hoped, and I have been helped."

Reply Obj. 2: Although sometimes the wicked do not undergo temporal punishment in this life, yet they suffer spiritual punishment. Hence Augustine says (Confess. i): "Thou hast decreed, and it is so, Lord—that the disordered mind should be its own punishment." The Philosopher, too, says of the wicked (Ethic. ix, 4) that "their soul is divided against itself ... one part pulls this way, another that"; and afterwards he concludes, saying: "If wickedness makes a man so miserable, he should strain every nerve to avoid vice." In like manner, although, on the other hand, the good sometimes do not receive material rewards in this life, yet they never lack spiritual rewards, even in this life, according to Matt. 19:29, and Mk. 10:30: "Ye shall receive a hundred times as much" even "in this time."

Reply Obj. 3: All these rewards will be fully consummated in the life to come: but meanwhile they are, in a manner, begun, even in this life. Because the "kingdom of heaven," as Augustine says (loc. cit.), can denote the beginning of perfect wisdom, in so far as "the spirit" begins to reign in men. The "possession" of the land denotes the well-ordered affections of the soul that rests, by its desire, on the solid foundation of the eternal inheritance, signified by "the land." They are "comforted" in this life, by receiving the Holy Ghost, Who is called the "Paraclete," i.e. the Comforter. They "have their fill," even in this life, of that food of which Our Lord said (John 4:34): "My meat is to do the will of Him that sent Me." Again, in this life, men "obtain" God's "Mercy." Again, the eye being cleansed by the gift of understanding, we can, so to speak, "see God." Likewise, in this life, those who are the "peacemakers" of their own movements, approach to likeness to God, and are called "the children of God." Nevertheless these things will be more perfectly fulfilled in heaven.

THIRD ARTICLE [I-II, Q. 69, Art. 3]

Whether the Beatitudes Are Suitably Enumerated?

Objection 1: It would seem that the beatitudes are unsuitably enumerated. For the beatitudes are assigned to the gifts, as stated above (A. 1, ad 1). Now some of the gifts, viz. wisdom and understanding, belong to the contemplative life: yet no beatitude is assigned to the act of contemplation, for all are assigned to matters connected with the active life. Therefore the beatitudes are insufficiently enumerated.

Obj. 2: Further, not only do the executive gifts belong to the active life, but also some of the directive gifts, e.g. knowledge and counsel: yet none of the beatitudes seems to be directly connected with the acts of knowledge or counsel. Therefore the beatitudes are insufficiently indicated.

Obj. 3: Further, among the executive gifts connected with the active life, fear is said to be connected with poverty, while piety seems to correspond to the beatitude of mercy: yet nothing is included directly connected with justice. Therefore the beatitudes are insufficiently enumerated.

Obj. 4: Further, many other beatitudes are mentioned in Holy Writ. Thus, it is written (Job 5:17): "Blessed is the man whom God correcteth"; and (Ps. i, 1): "Blessed is the man who hath not walked in the counsel of the ungodly"; and (Prov. 3:13): "Blessed is the man that findeth wisdom." Therefore the beatitudes are insufficiently enumerated.

Obj. 5: On the other hand, it seems that too many are mentioned. For there are seven gifts of the Holy Ghost: whereas eight beatitudes are indicated.

Obj. 6: Further, only four beatitudes are indicated in the sixth chapter of Luke. Therefore the seven or eight mentioned in Matthew 5 are too many.

*I answer that,* These beatitudes are most suitably enumerated. To make this evident it must be observed that beatitude has been held to consist in one of three things: for some have ascribed it to a sensual life, some, to an active life, and some, to a contemplative life [*See Q. 3]. Now these three kinds of happiness stand in different relations to future beatitude, by hoping for which we are said to be happy. Because sensual happiness, being false and contrary to reason, is an obstacle to future beatitude; while happiness of the active life is a disposition of future beatitude; and contemplative happiness, if perfect, is the very essence of future beatitude, and, if imperfect, is a beginning thereof.

And so Our Lord, in the first place, indicated certain beatitudes as removing the obstacle of sensual happiness. For a life of pleasure consists of two things. First, in the affluence of external goods, whether riches or honors; from which man is withdrawn—by a virtue so that he uses them in moderation—and by a gift, in a more excellent way, so that he despises them altogether. Hence the first beatitude is: "Blessed are the poor in spirit," which may refer either to the contempt of riches, or to the contempt of honors, which results from humility. Secondly, the sensual life consists in following the bent of one's passions, whether irascible or concupiscible. From following the irascible passions man is withdrawn—by a virtue, so that they are kept within the bounds appointed by the ruling of reason—and by a gift, in a more excellent manner, so that man, according to God's will, is altogether undisturbed by them: hence the second beatitude is: "Blessed are the meek." From following the concupiscible passions, man is withdrawn—by a virtue, so that man uses these passions in moderation—and by a gift, so that, if necessary, he casts them aside altogether; nay more, so that, if need be, he makes a deliberate choice of sorrow [*Cf. Q. 35, A. 3]; hence the third beatitude is: "Blessed are they that mourn."

Active life consists chiefly in man's relations with his neighbor, either by way of duty or by way of spontaneous gratuity. To the former we are disposed—by a virtue, so that we do not refuse to do our duty to our neighbor, which pertains to justice—and by a gift, so that we do the same much more heartily, by accomplishing works of justice with an ardent desire, even as a hungry and thirsty man eats and drinks with eager appetite. Hence the fourth beatitude is: "Blessed are they that hunger and thirst after justice." With regard to spontaneous favors we are perfected—by a virtue, so that we give where reason dictates we should give, e.g. to our friends or others united to us; which pertains to the virtue of liberality—and by a gift, so that, through reverence for God, we consider only the needs of those on whom we bestow our gratuitous bounty: hence it is written (Luke 14:12, 13): "When thou makest a dinner or supper, call not thy friends, nor thy brethren," etc ... "but ... call the poor, the maimed," etc.; which, properly, is to have mercy: hence the fifth beatitude is: "Blessed are the merciful."

Those things which concern the contemplative life, are either final beatitude itself, or some beginning thereof: wherefore they are included in the beatitudes, not as merits, but as rewards. Yet the effects of the active life, which dispose man for the contemplative life, are included in the beatitudes. Now the effect of the active life, as regards those virtues and gifts whereby man is perfected in himself, is the cleansing of man's heart, so that it is not defiled by the passions: hence the sixth beatitude is: "Blessed are the clean of heart." But as regards the virtues and gifts whereby man is perfected in relation to his neighbor, the effect of the active life is peace, according to Isa. 32:17: "The work of justice shall be peace": hence the seventh beatitude is "Blessed are the peacemakers."

Reply Obj. 1: The acts of the gifts which belong to the active life are indicated in the merits: but the acts of the gifts pertaining to the contemplative life are indicated in the rewards, for the reason given above. Because to "see God" corresponds to the gift of understanding; and to be like God by being adoptive "children of God," corresponds to the gift of wisdom.

Reply Obj. 2: In things pertaining to the active life, knowledge is not sought for its own sake, but for the sake of operation, as even the Philosopher states (Ethic. ii, 2). And therefore, since beatitude implies something ultimate, the beatitudes do not include the acts of those gifts which direct man in the active life, such acts, to wit, as are elicited by those gifts, as, e.g. to counsel is the act of counsel, and to judge, the act of knowledge: but, on the other hand, they include those operative acts of which the gifts have the direction, as, e.g. mourning in respect of knowledge, and mercy in respect of counsel.

Reply Obj. 3: In applying the beatitudes to the gifts we may consider two things. One is likeness of matter. In this way all the first five beatitudes may be assigned to knowledge and counsel as to their directing principles: whereas they must be distributed among the executive gifts: so that, to wit, hunger and thirst for justice, and mercy too, correspond to piety, which perfects man in his relations to others; meekness to fortitude, for Ambrose says on Luke 6:22: "It is the business of fortitude to conquer anger, and to curb indignation," fortitude being about the irascible passions: poverty and mourning to the gift of fear, whereby man withdraws from the lusts and pleasures of the world.

Secondly, we may consider the motives of the beatitudes: and, in this way, some of them will have to be assigned differently. Because the principal motive for meekness is reverence for God, which belongs to piety. The chief motive for mourning is knowledge, whereby man knows his failings and those of worldly things, according to Eccles. 1:18: "He that addeth knowledge, addeth also sorrow [Vulg: labor]." The principal motive for hungering after the works of justice is fortitude of the soul: and the chief motive for being merciful is God's counsel, according to Dan. 4:24: "Let my counsel be acceptable to the king [Vulg: to thee, O king]: and redeem thou thy sins with alms, and thy iniquities with works of mercy to the poor." It is thus that Augustine assigns them (De Serm. Dom. in Monte i, 4).

Reply Obj. 4: All the beatitudes mentioned in Holy Writ must be reduced to these, either as to the merits or as to the rewards: because they must all belong either to the active or to the contemplative life. Accordingly, when we read, "Blessed is the man whom the Lord correcteth," we must refer this to the beatitude of mourning: when we read, "Blessed is the man that hath not walked in the counsel of the ungodly," we must refer it to cleanness of heart: and when we read, "Blessed is the man that findeth wisdom," this must be referred to the reward of the seventh beatitude. The same applies to all others that can be adduced.

Reply Obj. 5: The eighth beatitude is a confirmation and declaration of all those that precede. Because from the very fact that a man is confirmed in poverty of spirit, meekness, and the rest, it follows that no persecution will induce him to renounce them. Hence the eighth beatitude corresponds, in a way, to all the preceding seven.

Reply Obj. 6: Luke relates Our Lord's sermon as addressed to the multitude (Luke 6:17). Hence he sets down the beatitudes according to the capacity of the multitude, who know no other happiness than pleasure, temporal and earthly: wherefore by these four beatitudes Our Lord excludes four things which seem to belong to such happiness. The first of these is abundance of external goods, which he sets aside by saying: "Blessed are ye poor." The second is that man be well off as to his body, in food and drink, and so forth; this he excludes by saying in the second place: "Blessed are ye that hunger." The third is that it should be well with man as to joyfulness of heart, and this he puts aside by saying: "Blessed are ye that weep now." The fourth is the outward favor of man; and this he excludes, saying, fourthly: "Blessed shall you be, when men shall hate you." And as Ambrose says on Luke 6:20, "poverty corresponds to temperance, which is unmoved by delights; hunger, to justice, since who hungers is compassionate and, through compassion gives; mourning, to prudence, which deplores perishable things; endurance of men's hatred belongs to fortitude."

FOURTH ARTICLE [I-II, Q. 69, Art. 4]

Whether the Rewards of the Beatitudes Are Suitably Enumerated?

Objection 1: It would seem that the rewards of the beatitudes are unsuitably enumerated. Because the kingdom of heaven, which is eternal life, contains all good things. Therefore, once given the kingdom of heaven, no other rewards should be mentioned.

Obj. 2: Further, the kingdom of heaven is assigned as the reward, both of the first and of the eighth beatitude. Therefore, on the same ground it should have been assigned to all.

Obj. 3: Further, the beatitudes are arranged in the ascending order, as Augustine remarks (De Serm. Dom. in Monte i, 4): whereas the rewards seem to be placed in the descending order, since to "possess the land" is less than to possess "the kingdom of heaven." Therefore these rewards are unsuitably enumerated.

*On the contrary,* stands the authority of Our Lord Who propounded these rewards.

*I answer that,* These rewards are most suitably assigned, considering the nature of the beatitudes in relation to the three kinds of happiness indicated above (A. 3). For the first three beatitudes concerned the withdrawal of man from those things in which sensual happiness consists: which happiness man desires by seeking the object of his natural desire, not where he should seek it, viz. in God, but in temporal and perishable things. Wherefore the rewards of the first three beatitudes correspond to these things which some men seek to find in earthly happiness. For men seek in external things, viz. riches and honors, a certain excellence and abundance, both of which are implied in the kingdom of heaven, whereby man attains to excellence and abundance of good things in God. Hence Our Lord promised the kingdom of heaven to the poor in spirit. Again, cruel and pitiless men seek by wrangling and fighting to destroy their enemies so as to gain security for themselves. Hence Our Lord promised the meek a secure and peaceful possession of the land of the living, whereby the solid reality of eternal goods is denoted. Again, men seek consolation for the toils of the present life, in the lusts and pleasures of the world. Hence Our Lord promises comfort to those that mourn.

Two other beatitudes belong to the works of active happiness, which are the works of virtues directing man in his relations to his neighbor: from which operations some men withdraw through inordinate love of their own good. Hence Our Lord assigns to these beatitudes rewards in correspondence with the motives for which men recede from them. For there are some who recede from acts of justice, and instead of rendering what is due, lay hands on what is not theirs, that they may abound in temporal goods. Wherefore Our Lord promised those who hunger after justice, that they shall have their fill. Some, again, recede from works of mercy, lest they be busied with other people's misery. Hence Our Lord promised the merciful that they should obtain mercy, and be delivered from all misery.

The last two beatitudes belong to contemplative happiness or beatitude: hence the rewards are assigned in correspondence with the dispositions included in the merit. For cleanness of the eye disposes one to see clearly: hence the clean of heart are promised that they shall see God. Again, to make peace either in oneself or among others, shows a man to be a follower of God, Who is the God of unity and peace. Hence, as a reward, he is promised the glory of the Divine sonship, consisting in perfect union with God through consummate wisdom.

Reply Obj. 1: As Chrysostom says (Hom. xv in Matth.), all these rewards are one in reality, viz. eternal happiness, which the human intellect cannot grasp. Hence it was necessary to describe it by means of various boons known to us, while observing due proportion to the merits to which those rewards are assigned.

Reply Obj. 2: Just as the eighth beatitude is a confirmation of all the beatitudes, so it deserves all the rewards of the beatitudes. Hence it returns to the first, that we may understand all the other rewards to be attributed to it in consequence. Or else, according to Ambrose (Super Luc. v), the kingdom of heaven is promised to the poor in spirit, as regards the glory of the soul; but to those who suffer persecution in their bodies, it is promised as regards the glory of the body.

Reply Obj. 3: The rewards are also arranged in ascending order. For it is more to possess the land of the heavenly kingdom than simply to have it: since we have many things without possessing them firmly and peacefully. Again, it is more to be comforted in the kingdom than to have and possess it, for there are many things the possession of which is accompanied by sorrow. Again, it is more to have one's fill than simply to be comforted, because fulness implies abundance of comfort. And mercy surpasses satiety, for thereby man receives more than he merited or was able to desire. And yet more is it to see God, even as he is a greater man who not only dines at court, but also sees the king's countenance. Lastly, the highest place in the royal palace belongs to the king's son.

## QUESTION 70

OF THE FRUITS OF THE HOLY GHOST (In Four Articles)

We must now consider the Fruits of the Holy Ghost: under which head there are four points of inquiry:

(1) Whether the fruits of the Holy Ghost are acts?

(2) Whether they differ from the beatitudes?

(3) Of their number?

(4) Of their opposition to the works of the flesh.

FIRST ARTICLE [I-II, Q. 70, Art. 1]

Whether the Fruits of the Holy Ghost Which the Apostle Enumerates (Gal. 5) Are Acts?

Objection 1: It would seem that the fruits of the Holy Ghost, enumerated by the Apostle (Gal. 5:22, 23), are not acts. For that which bears fruit, should not itself be called a fruit, else we should go on indefinitely. But our actions bear fruit: for it is written (Wis. 3:15): "The fruit of good labor is glorious," and (John 4:36): "He that reapeth receiveth wages, and gathereth fruit unto life everlasting." Therefore our actions are not to be called fruits.

Obj. 2: Further, as Augustine says (De Trin. x, 10), "we enjoy [*'Fruimur,' from which verb we have the Latin 'fructus' and the English 'fruit'] the things we know, when the will rests by rejoicing in them." But our will should not rest in our actions for their own sake. Therefore our actions should not be called fruits.

Obj. 3: Further, among the fruits of the Holy Ghost, the Apostle numbers certain virtues, viz. charity, meekness, faith, and chastity. Now virtues are not actions but habits, as stated above (Q. 55, A. 1). Therefore the fruits are not actions.

*On the contrary,* It is written (Matt. 12:33): "By the fruit the tree is known"; that is to say, man is known by his works, as holy men explain the passage. Therefore human actions are called fruits.

*I answer that,* The word "fruit" has been transferred from the material to the spiritual world. Now fruit, among material things, is the product of a plant when it comes to perfection, and has a certain sweetness. This fruit has a twofold relation: to the tree that produces it, and to the man who gathers the fruit from the tree. Accordingly, in spiritual matters, we may take the word "fruit" in two ways: first, so that the fruit of man, who is likened to the tree, is that which he produces; secondly, so that man's fruit is what he gathers.

Yet not all that man gathers is fruit, but only that which is last and gives pleasure. For a man has both a field and a tree, and yet these are not called fruits; but that only which is last, to wit, that which man intends to derive from the field and from the tree. In this sense man's fruit is his last end which is intended for his enjoyment.

If, however, by man's fruit we understand a product of man, then human actions are called fruits: because operation is the second act of the operator, and gives pleasure if it is suitable to him. If then man's operation proceeds from man in virtue of his reason, it is said to be the fruit of his reason: but if it proceeds from him in respect of a higher power, which is the power of the Holy Ghost, then man's operation is said to be the fruit of the Holy Ghost, as of a Divine seed, for it is written (1 John 3:9): "Whosoever is born of God, committeth no sin, for His seed abideth in him."

Reply Obj. 1: Since fruit is something last and final, nothing hinders one fruit bearing another fruit, even as one end is subordinate to another. And so our works, in so far as they are produced by the Holy Ghost working in us, are fruits: but, in so far as they are referred to the end which is eternal life, they should rather be called flowers: hence it is written (Ecclus. 24:23): "My flowers are the fruits of honor and riches."

Reply Obj. 2: When the will is said to delight in a thing for its own sake, this may be understood in two ways. First, so that the expression "for the sake of" be taken to designate the final cause; and in this way, man delights in nothing for its own sake, except the last end. Secondly, so that it expresses the formal cause; and in this way, a man may delight in anything that is delightful by reason of its form. Thus it is clear that a sick man delights in health, for its own sake, as in an end; in a nice medicine, not as in an end, but as in something tasty; and in a nasty medicine, nowise for its own sake, but only for the sake of something else. Accordingly we must say that man must delight in God for His own sake, as being his last end, and in virtuous deeds, not as being his end, but for the sake of their inherent goodness which is delightful to the virtuous. Hence Ambrose says (De Parad. xiii) that virtuous deeds are called fruits because "they refresh those that have them, with a holy and genuine delight."

Reply Obj. 3: Sometimes the names of the virtues are applied to their actions: thus Augustine writes (Tract. xl in Joan.): "Faith is to believe what thou seest not"; and (De Doctr. Christ. iii, 10): "Charity is the movement of the soul in loving God and our neighbor." It is thus that the names of the virtues are used in reckoning the fruits.

SECOND ARTICLE [I-II, Q. 70, Art. 2]

Whether the Fruits Differ from the Beatitudes?

Objection 1: It would seem that the fruits do not differ from the beatitudes. For the beatitudes are assigned to the gifts, as stated above (Q. 69, A. 1, ad 1). But the gifts perfect man in so far as he is moved by the Holy Ghost. Therefore the beatitudes themselves are fruits of the Holy Ghost.

Obj. 2: Further, as the fruit of eternal life is to future beatitude which is that of actual possession, so are the fruits of the present life to the beatitudes of the present life, which are based on hope. Now the fruit of eternal life is identified with future beatitude. Therefore the fruits of the present life are the beatitudes.

Obj. 3: Further, fruit is essentially something ultimate and delightful. Now this is the very nature of beatitude, as stated above (Q. 3, A. 1; Q. 4, A. 1). Therefore fruit and beatitude have the same nature, and consequently should not be distinguished from one another.

*On the contrary,* Things divided into different species, differ from one another. But fruits and beatitudes are divided into different parts, as is clear from the way in which they are enumerated. Therefore the fruits differ from the beatitudes.

*I answer that,* More is required for a beatitude than for a fruit. Because it is sufficient for a fruit to be something ultimate and delightful; whereas for a beatitude, it must be something perfect and excellent. Hence all the beatitudes may be called fruits, but not vice versa. For the fruits are any virtuous deeds in which one delights: whereas the beatitudes are none but perfect works, and which, by reason of their perfection, are assigned to the gifts rather than to the virtues, as already stated (Q. 69, A. 1, ad 1).

Reply Obj. 1: This argument proves the beatitudes to be fruits, but not that all the fruits are beatitudes.

Reply Obj. 2: The fruit of eternal life is ultimate and perfect simply: hence it nowise differs from future beatitude. On the other hand the fruits of the present life are not simply ultimate and perfect; wherefore not all the fruits are beatitudes.

Reply Obj. 3: More is required for a beatitude than for a fruit, as stated.

THIRD ARTICLE [I-II, Q. 70, Art. 3]

Whether the Fruits Are Suitably Enumerated by the Apostle?

Objection 1: It would seem that the fruits are unsuitably enumerated by the Apostle (Gal. 5:22, 23). Because, elsewhere, he says that there is only one fruit of the present life; according to Rom. 6:22: "You have your fruit unto sanctification." Moreover it is written (Isa. 27:9): "This is all the fruit ... that the sin ... be taken away." Therefore we should not reckon twelve fruits.

Obj. 2: Further, fruit is the product of spiritual seed, as stated (A. 1). But Our Lord mentions (Matt. 13:23) a threefold fruit as growing from a spiritual seed in a good ground, viz. "hundredfold, sixtyfold," and "thirtyfold." Therefore one should not reckon twelve fruits.

Obj. 3: Further, the very nature of fruit is to be something ultimate and delightful. But this does not apply to all the fruits mentioned by the Apostle: for patience and long-suffering seem to imply a painful object, while faith is not something ultimate, but rather something primary and fundamental. Therefore too many fruits are enumerated.

Obj. 4: On the other hand, It seems that they are enumerated insufficiently and incompletely. For it has been stated (A. 2) that all the beatitudes may be called fruits; yet not all are mentioned here. Nor is there anything corresponding to the acts of wisdom, and of many other virtues. Therefore it seems that the fruits are insufficiently enumerated.

*I answer that,* The number of the twelve fruits enumerated by the Apostle is suitable, and that there may be a reference to them in the twelve fruits of which it is written (Apoc. 22:2): "On both sides of the river was the tree bearing twelve fruits." Since, however, a fruit is something that proceeds from a source as from a seed or root, the difference between these fruits must be gathered from the various ways in which the Holy Ghost proceeds in us: which process consists in this, that the mind of man is set in order, first of all, in regard to itself; secondly, in regard to things that are near it; thirdly, in regard to things that are below it.

Accordingly man's mind is well disposed in regard to itself when it has a good disposition towards good things and towards evil things. Now the first disposition of the human mind towards the good is effected by love, which is the first of our emotions and the root of them all, as stated above (Q. 27, A. 4). Wherefore among the fruits of the Holy Ghost, we reckon "charity," wherein the Holy Ghost is given in a special manner, as in His own likeness, since He Himself is love. Hence it is written (Rom. 5:5): "The charity of God is poured forth in our hearts by the Holy Ghost, Who is given to us." The necessary result of the love of charity is joy: because every lover rejoices at being united to the beloved. Now charity has always actual presence in God Whom it loves, according to 1 John 4:16: "He that abideth in charity, abideth in God, and God in Him": wherefore the sequel of charity is "joy." Now the perfection of joy is peace in two respects. First, as regards freedom from outward disturbance; for it is impossible to rejoice perfectly in the beloved good, if one is disturbed in the enjoyment thereof; and again, if a man's heart is perfectly set at peace in one object, he cannot be disquieted by any other, since he accounts all others as nothing; hence it is written (Ps. 118:165): "Much peace have they that love Thy Law, and to them there is no stumbling-block," because, to wit, external things do not disturb them in their enjoyment of God. Secondly, as regards the calm of the restless desire: for he does not perfectly rejoice, who is not satisfied with the object of his joy. Now peace implies these two things, namely, that we be not disturbed by external things, and that our desires rest altogether in one object. Wherefore after charity and joy, "peace" is given the third place. In evil things the mind has a good disposition, in respect of two things. First, by not being disturbed whenever evil threatens: which pertains to "patience"; secondly, by not being disturbed, whenever good things are delayed; which belongs to "long suffering," since "to lack good is a kind of evil" (Ethic. v, 3).

Man's mind is well disposed as regards what is near him, viz. his neighbor, first, as to the will to do good; and to this belongs *goodness.* Secondly, as to the execution of well-doing; and to this belongs *benignity,* for the benign are those in whom the salutary flame ( *bonus ignis* ) of love has enkindled the desire to be kind to their neighbor. Thirdly, as to his suffering with equanimity the evils his neighbor inflicts on him. To this belongs *meekness,* which curbs anger. Fourthly, in the point of our refraining from doing harm to our neighbor not only through anger, but also through fraud or deceit. To this pertains *faith,* if we take it as denoting fidelity. But if we take it for the faith whereby we believe in God, then man is directed thereby to that which is above him, so that he subject his intellect and, consequently, all that is his, to God.

Man is well disposed in respect of that which is below him, as regards external action, by *modesty,* whereby we observe the mode in all our words and deeds: as regards internal desires, by *continency* and chastity: whether these two differ because chastity withdraws man from unlawful desires, continency also from lawful desires: or because the continent man is subject to concupiscence, but is not led away; whereas the chaste man is neither subject to, nor led away from them.

Reply Obj. 1: Sanctification is effected by all the virtues, by which also sins are taken away. Consequently fruit is mentioned there in the singular, on account of its being generically one, though divided into many species which are spoken of as so many fruits.

Reply Obj. 2: The hundredfold, sixtyfold, and thirtyfold fruits do not differ as various species of virtuous acts, but as various degrees of perfection, even in the same virtue. Thus continency of the married state is said to be signified by the thirtyfold fruit; the continency of widowhood, by the sixtyfold; and virginal continency, by the hundredfold fruit. There are, moreover, other ways in which holy men distinguish three evangelical fruits according to the three degrees of virtue: and they speak of three degrees, because the perfection of anything is considered with respect to its beginning, its middle, and its end.

Reply Obj. 3: The fact of not being disturbed by painful things is something to delight in. And as to faith, if we consider it as the foundation, it has the aspect of being ultimate and delightful, in as much as it contains certainty: hence a gloss expounds thus: "Faith, which is certainly about the unseen."

Reply Obj. 4: As Augustine says on Gal. 5:22, 23, "the Apostle had no intention of teaching us how many (either works of the flesh, or fruits of the Spirit) there are; but to show how the former should be avoided, and the latter sought after." Hence either more or fewer fruits might have been mentioned. Nevertheless, all the acts of the gifts and virtues can be reduced to these by a certain kind of fittingness, in so far as all the virtues and gifts must needs direct the mind in one of the above-mentioned ways. Wherefore the acts of wisdom and of any gifts directing to good, are reduced to charity, joy and peace. The reason why he mentions these rather than others, is that these imply either enjoyment of good things, or relief from evils, which things seem to belong to the notion of fruit.

FOURTH ARTICLE [I-II, Q. 70, Art. 4]

Whether the Fruits of the Holy Ghost Are Contrary to the Works of the Flesh?

Objection 1: It would seem that the fruits of the Holy Ghost are not contrary to the works of the flesh, which the Apostle enumerates (Gal. 5:19, seqq.). Because contraries are in the same genus. But the works of the flesh are not called fruits. Therefore the fruits of the Spirit are not contrary to them.

Obj. 2: Further, one thing has a contrary. Now the Apostle mentions more works of the flesh than fruits of the Spirit. Therefore the fruits of the Spirit and the works of the flesh are not contrary to one another.

Obj. 3: Further, among the fruits of the Spirit, the first place is given to charity, joy, and peace: to which, fornication, uncleanness, and immodesty, which are the first of the works of the flesh, are not opposed. Therefore the fruits of the Spirit are not contrary to the works of the flesh.

*On the contrary,* The Apostle says (Gal. 5:17) that "the flesh lusteth against the spirit, and the spirit against the flesh."

*I answer that,* The works of the flesh and the fruits of the Spirit may be taken in two ways. First, in general: and in this way the fruits of the Holy Ghost considered in general are contrary to the works of the flesh. Because the Holy Ghost moves the human mind to that which is in accord with reason, or rather to that which surpasses reason: whereas the fleshly, viz. the sensitive, appetite draws man to sensible goods which are beneath him. Wherefore, since upward and downward are contrary movements in the physical order, so in human actions the works of the flesh are contrary to the fruits of the Spirit.

Secondly, both fruits and fleshly works as enumerated may be considered singly, each according to its specific nature. And in this they are not of necessity contrary each to each: because, as stated above (A. 3, ad 4), the Apostle did not intend to enumerate all the works, whether spiritual or carnal. However, by a kind of adaptation, Augustine, commenting on Gal. 5:22, 23, contrasts the fruits with the carnal works, each to each. Thus "to fornication, which is the love of satisfying lust outside lawful wedlock, we may contrast charity, whereby the soul is wedded to God: wherein also is true chastity. By uncleanness we must understand whatever disturbances arise from fornication: and to these the joy of tranquillity is opposed. Idolatry, by reason of which war was waged against the Gospel of God, is opposed to peace. Against witchcrafts, enmities, contentions, emulations, wraths and quarrels, there is longsuffering, which helps us to bear the evils inflicted on us by those among whom we dwell; while kindness helps us to cure those evils; and goodness, to forgive them. In contrast to heresy there is faith; to envy, mildness; to drunkenness and revellings, contingency."

Reply Obj. 1: That which proceeds from a tree against the tree's nature, is not called its fruit, but rather its corruption. And since works of virtue are connatural to reason, while works of vice are contrary to nature, therefore it is that works of virtue are called fruits, but not so works of vice.

Reply Obj. 2: "Good happens in one way, evil in all manner of ways," as Dionysius says (Div. Nom. iv): so that to one virtue many vices are contrary. Consequently we must not be surprised if the works of the flesh are more numerous than the fruits of the spirit.

The Reply to the Third Objection is clear from what has been said.

EVIL HABITS, i.e. VICES AND SINS (QQ. 71-89)

# QUESTION 71

OF VICE AND SIN CONSIDERED IN THEMSELVES (In Six Articles)

We have in the next place to consider vice and sin: about which six points have to be considered: (1) Vice and sin considered in themselves; (2) their distinction; (3) their comparison with one another; (4) the subject of sin; (5) the cause of sin; (6) the effect of sin.

Under the first head there are six points of inquiry:

(1) Whether vice is contrary to virtue?

(2) Whether vice is contrary to nature?

(3) Which is worse, a vice or a vicious act?

(4) Whether a vicious act is compatible with virtue?

(5) Whether every sin includes action?

(6) Of the definition of sin proposed by Augustine (Contra Faust. xxii): "Sin is a word, deed, or desire against the eternal law."

FIRST ARTICLE [I-II, Q. 71, Art. 1]

Whether Vice Is Contrary to Virtue?

Objection 1: It would seem that vice is not contrary to virtue. For one thing has one contrary, as proved in *Metaph.* x, text. 17. Now sin and malice are contrary to virtue. Therefore vice is not contrary to it: since vice applies also to undue disposition of bodily members or of any things whatever.

Obj. 2: Further, virtue denotes a certain perfection of power. But vice does not denote anything relative to power. Therefore vice is not contrary to virtue.

Obj. 3: Further, Cicero (De Quaest. Tusc. iv) says that "virtue is the soul's health." Now sickness or disease, rather than vice, is opposed to health. Therefore vice is not contrary to virtue.

*On the contrary,* Augustine says (De Perfect. Justit. ii) that "vice is a quality in respect of which the soul is evil." But "virtue is a quality which makes its subject good," as was shown above (Q. 55, AA. 3, 4). Therefore vice is contrary to virtue.

*I answer that,* Two things may be considered in virtue—the essence of virtue, and that to which virtue is ordained. In the essence of virtue we may consider something directly, and we may consider something consequently. Virtue implies *directly* a disposition whereby the subject is well disposed according to the mode of its nature: wherefore the Philosopher says (Phys. vii, text. 17) that "virtue is a disposition of a perfect thing to that which is best; and by perfect I mean that which is disposed according to its nature." That which virtue implies *consequently* is that it is a kind of goodness: because the goodness of a thing consists in its being well disposed according to the mode of its nature. That to which virtue is directed is a good act, as was shown above (Q. 56, A. 3).

Accordingly three things are found to be contrary to virtue. One of these is *sin*, which is opposed to virtue in respect of that to which virtue is ordained: since, properly speaking, sin denotes an inordinate act; even as an act of virtue is an ordinate and due act: in respect of that which virtue implies consequently, viz. that it is a kind of goodness, the contrary of virtue is *malice* : while in respect of that which belongs to the essence of virtue directly, its contrary is *vice* : because the vice of a thing seems to consist in its not being disposed in a way befitting its nature: hence Augustine says (De Lib. Arb. iii): "Whatever is lacking for a thing's natural perfection may be called a vice."

Reply Obj. 1: These three things are contrary to virtue, but not in the same respect: for sin is opposed to virtue, according as the latter is productive of a good work; malice, according as virtue is a kind of goodness; while vice is opposed to virtue properly as such.

Reply Obj. 2: Virtue implies not only perfection of power, the principle of action; but also the due disposition of its subject. The reason for this is because a thing operates according as it is in act: so that a thing needs to be well disposed if it has to produce a good work. It is in this respect that vice is contrary to virtue.

Reply Obj. 3: As Cicero says (De Quaest. Tusc. iv), "disease and sickness are vicious qualities," for in speaking of the body he calls it disease "when the whole body is infected," for instance, with fever or the like; he calls it sickness "when the disease is attended with weakness"; and vice "when the parts of the body are not well compacted together." And although at times there may be disease in the body without sickness, for instance, when a man has a hidden complaint without being hindered outwardly from his wonted occupations; "yet, in the soul," as he says, "these two things are indistinguishable, except in thought." For whenever a man is ill-disposed inwardly, through some inordinate affection, he is rendered thereby unfit for fulfilling his duties: since "a tree is known by its fruit," i.e. man by his works, according to Matt. 12:33. But "vice of the soul," as Cicero says (De Quaest. Tusc. iv), "is a habit or affection of the soul discordant and inconsistent with itself through life": and this is to be found even without disease and sickness, e.g. when a man sins from weakness or passion. Consequently vice is of wider extent than sickness or disease; even as virtue extends to more things than health; for health itself is reckoned a kind of virtue (Phys. vii, text. 17). Consequently vice is reckoned as contrary to virtue, more fittingly than sickness or disease.

SECOND ARTICLE [I-II, Q. 71, Art. 2]

Whether Vice Is Contrary to Nature?

Objection 1: It would seem that vice is not contrary to nature. Because vice is contrary to virtue, as stated above (A. 1). Now virtue is in us, not by nature but by infusion or habituation, as stated above (Q. 63, AA. 1, 2, 3). Therefore vice is not contrary to nature.

Obj. 2: Further, it is impossible to become habituated to that which is contrary to nature: thus "a stone never becomes habituated to upward movement" (Ethic. ii, 1). But some men become habituated to vice. Therefore vice is not contrary to nature.

Obj. 3: Further, anything contrary to a nature, is not found in the greater number of individuals possessed of that nature. Now vice is found in the greater number of men; for it is written (Matt. 7:13): "Broad is the way that leadeth to destruction, and many there are who go in thereat." Therefore vice is not contrary to nature.

Obj. 4: Further, sin is compared to vice, as act to habit, as stated above (A. 1). Now sin is defined as "a word, deed, or desire, contrary to the Law of God," as Augustine shows (Contra Faust. xxii, 27). But the Law of God is above nature. Therefore we should say that vice is contrary to the Law, rather than to nature.

*On the contrary,* Augustine says (De Lib. Arb. iii, 13): "Every vice, simply because it is a vice, is contrary to nature."

*I answer that,* As stated above (A. 1), vice is contrary to virtue. Now the virtue of a thing consists in its being well disposed in a manner befitting its nature, as stated above (A. 1). Hence the vice of any thing consists in its being disposed in a manner not befitting its nature, and for this reason is that thing "vituperated," which word is derived from "vice" according to Augustine (De Lib. Arb. iii, 14).

But it must be observed that the nature of a thing is chiefly the form from which that thing derives its species. Now man derives his species from his rational soul: and consequently whatever is contrary to the order of reason is, properly speaking, contrary to the nature of man, as man; while whatever is in accord with reason, is in accord with the nature of man, as man. Now "man's good is to be in accord with reason, and his evil is to be against reason," as Dionysius states (Div. Nom. iv). Therefore human virtue, which makes a man good, and his work good, is in accord with man's nature, for as much as it accords with his reason: while vice is contrary to man's nature, in so far as it is contrary to the order of reason.

Reply Obj. 1: Although the virtues are not caused by nature as regards their perfection of being, yet they incline us to that which accords with reason, i.e. with the order of reason. For Cicero says (De Inv. Rhet. ii) that "virtue is a habit in accord with reason, like a second nature": and it is in this sense that virtue is said to be in accord with nature, and on the other hand that vice is contrary to nature.

Reply Obj. 2: The Philosopher is speaking there of a thing being against nature, in so far as "being against nature" is contrary to "being from nature": and not in so far as "being against nature" is contrary to "being in accord with nature," in which latter sense virtues are said to be in accord with nature, in as much as they incline us to that which is suitable to nature.

Reply Obj. 3: There is a twofold nature in man, rational nature, and the sensitive nature. And since it is through the operation of his senses that man accomplishes acts of reason, hence there are more who follow the inclinations of the sensitive nature, than who follow the order of reason: because more reach the beginning of a business than achieve its completion. Now the presence of vices and sins in man is owing to the fact that he follows the inclination of his sensitive nature against the order of his reason.

Reply Obj. 4: Whatever is irregular in a work of art, is unnatural to the art which produced that work. Now the eternal law is compared to the order of human reason, as art to a work of art. Therefore it amounts to the same that vice and sin are against the order of human reason, and that they are contrary to the eternal law. Hence Augustine says (De Lib. Arb. iii, 6) that "every nature, as such, is from God; and is a vicious nature, in so far as it fails from the Divine art whereby it was made."

THIRD ARTICLE [I-II, Q. 71, Art. 3]

Whether Vice Is Worse Than a Vicious Act?

Objection 1: It would seem that vice, i.e. a bad habit, is worse than a sin, i.e. a bad act. For, as the more lasting a good is, the better it is, so the longer an evil lasts, the worse it is. Now a vicious habit is more lasting than vicious acts, that pass forthwith. Therefore a vicious habit is worse than a vicious act.

Obj. 2: Further, several evils are more to be shunned than one. But a bad habit is virtually the cause of many bad acts. Therefore a vicious habit is worse than a vicious act.

Obj. 3: Further, a cause is more potent than its effect. But a habit produces its actions both as to their goodness and as to their badness. Therefore a habit is more potent than its act, both in goodness and in badness.

*On the contrary,* A man is justly punished for a vicious act; but not for a vicious habit, so long as no act ensues. Therefore a vicious action is worse than a vicious habit.

*I answer that,* A habit stands midway between power and act. Now it is evident that both in good and in evil, act precedes power, as stated in *Metaph.* ix, 19. For it is better to do well than to be able to do well, and in like manner, it is more blameworthy to do evil, than to be able to do evil: whence it also follows that both in goodness and in badness, habit stands midway between power and act, so that, to wit, even as a good or evil habit stands above the corresponding power in goodness or in badness, so does it stand below the corresponding act. This is also made clear from the fact that a habit is not called good or bad, save in so far as it induces to a good or bad act: wherefore a habit is called good or bad by reason of the goodness or badness of its act: so that an act surpasses its habit in goodness or badness, since "the cause of a thing being such, is yet more so."

Reply Obj. 1: Nothing hinders one thing from standing above another simply, and below it in some respect. Now a thing is deemed above another simply if it surpasses it in a point which is proper to both; while it is deemed above it in a certain respect, if it surpasses it in something which is accidental to both. Now it has been shown from the very nature of act and habit, that act surpasses habit both in goodness and in badness. Whereas the fact that habit is more lasting than act, is accidental to them, and is due to the fact that they are both found in a nature such that it cannot always be in action, and whose action consists in a transient movement. Consequently act simply excels in goodness and badness, but habit excels in a certain respect.

Reply Obj. 2: A habit is several acts, not simply, but in a certain respect, i.e. virtually. Wherefore this does not prove that habit precedes act simply, both in goodness and in badness.

Reply Obj. 3: Habit causes act by way of efficient causality: but act causes habit, by way of final causality, in respect of which we consider the nature of good and evil. Consequently act surpasses habit both in goodness and in badness.

FOURTH ARTICLE [I-II, Q. 71, Art. 4]

Whether Sin Is Compatible with Virtue?

Objection 1: It would seem that a vicious act, i.e. sin, is incompatible with virtue. For contraries cannot be together in the same subject. Now sin is, in some way, contrary to virtue, as stated above (A. 1). Therefore sin is incompatible with virtue.

Obj. 2: Further, sin is worse than vice, i.e. evil act than evil habit. But vice cannot be in the same subject with virtue: neither, therefore, can sin.

Obj. 3: Further, sin occurs in natural things, even as in voluntary matters (Phys. ii, text. 82). Now sin never happens in natural things, except through some corruption of the natural power; thus monsters are due to corruption of some elemental force in the seed, as stated in *Phys.* ii. Therefore no sin occurs in voluntary matters, except through the corruption of some virtue in the soul: so that sin and virtue cannot be together in the same subject.

*On the contrary,* The Philosopher says (Ethic. ii, 2, 3) that "virtue is engendered and corrupted by contrary causes." Now one virtuous act does not cause a virtue, as stated above (Q. 51, A. 3): and, consequently, one sinful act does not corrupt virtue. Therefore they can be together in the same subject.

*I answer that,* Sin is compared to virtue, as evil act to good habit. Now the position of a habit in the soul is not the same as that of a form in a natural thing. For the form of a natural thing produces, of necessity, an operation befitting itself; wherefore a natural form is incompatible with the act of a contrary form: thus heat is incompatible with the act of cooling, and lightness with downward movement (except perhaps violence be used by some extrinsic mover): whereas the habit that resides in the soul, does not, of necessity, produce its operation, but is used by man when he wills. Consequently man, while possessing a habit, may either fail to use the habit, or produce a contrary act; and so a man having a virtue may produce an act of sin. And this sinful act, so long as there is but one, cannot corrupt virtue, if we compare the act to the virtue itself as a habit: since, just as habit is not engendered by one act, so neither is it destroyed by one act as stated above (Q. 63, A. 2, ad 2). But if we compare the sinful act to the cause of the virtues, then it is possible for some virtues to be destroyed by one sinful act. For every mortal sin is contrary to charity, which is the root of all the infused virtues, as virtues; and consequently, charity being banished by one act of mortal sin, it follows that all the infused virtues are expelled *as virtues.* And I say [this] on account of faith and hope, whose habits remain unquickened after mortal sin, so that they are no longer virtues. On the other hand, since venial sin is neither contrary to charity, nor banishes it, as a consequence, neither does it expel the other virtues. As to the acquired virtues, they are not destroyed by one act of any kind of sin.

Accordingly, mortal sin is incompatible with the infused virtues, but is consistent with acquired virtue: while venial sin is compatible with virtues, whether infused or acquired.

Reply Obj. 1: Sin is contrary to virtue, not by reason of itself, but by reason of its act. Hence sin is incompatible with the act, but not with the habit, of virtue.

Reply Obj. 2: Vice is directly contrary to virtue, even as sin to virtuous act: and so vice excludes virtue, just as sin excludes acts of virtue.

Reply Obj. 3: The natural powers act of necessity, and hence so long as the power is unimpaired, no sin can be found in the act. On the other hand, the virtues of the soul do not produce their acts of necessity; hence the comparison fails.

FIFTH ARTICLE [I-II, Q. 71, Art. 5]

Whether Every Sin Includes an Action?

Objection 1: It would seem that every sin includes an action. For as merit is compared with virtue, even so is sin compared with vice. Now there can be no merit without an action. Neither, therefore, can there be sin without action.

Obj. 2: Further, Augustine says (De Lib. Arb. iii, 18) [*Cf. De Vera Relig. xiv.]: So "true is it that every sin is voluntary, that, unless it be voluntary, it is no sin at all." Now nothing can be voluntary, save through an act of the will. Therefore every sin implies an act.

Obj. 3: Further, if sin could be without act, it would follow that a man sins as soon as he ceases doing what he ought. Now he who never does something that he ought to do, ceases continually doing what he ought. Therefore it would follow that he sins continually; and this is untrue. Therefore there is no sin without an act.

*On the contrary,* It is written (James 4:17): "To him ... who knoweth to do good, and doth it not, to him it is a sin." Now "not to do" does not imply an act. Therefore sin can be without act.

*I answer that,* The reason for urging this question has reference to the sin of omission, about which there have been various opinions. For some say that in every sin of omission there is some act, either interior or exterior—interior, as when a man wills not to go to church, when he is bound to go—exterior, as when a man, at the very hour that he is bound to go to church (or even before), occupies himself in such a way that he is hindered from going. This seems, in a way, to amount to the same as the first, for whoever wills one thing that is incompatible with this other, wills, consequently, to go without this other: unless, perchance, it does not occur to him, that what he wishes to do, will hinder him from that which he is bound to do, in which case he might be deemed guilty of negligence. On the other hand, others say, that a sin of omission does not necessarily suppose an act: for the mere fact of not doing what one is bound to do is a sin.

Now each of these opinions has some truth in it. For if in the sin of omission we look merely at that in which the essence of the sin consists, the sin of omission will be sometimes with an interior act, as when a man wills *not to go to church:* while sometimes it will be without any act at all, whether interior or exterior, as when a man, at the time that he is bound to go to church, does not think of going or not going to church.

If, however, in the sin of omission, we consider also the causes, or occasions of the omission, then the sin of omission must of necessity include some act. For there is no sin of omission, unless we omit what we can do or not do: and that we turn aside so as not to do what we can do or not do, must needs be due to some cause or occasion, either united with the omission or preceding it. Now if this cause be not in man's power, the omission will not be sinful, as when anyone omits going to church on account of sickness: but if the cause or occasion be subject to the will, the omission is sinful; and such cause, in so far as it is voluntary, must needs always include some act, at least the interior act of the will: which act sometimes bears directly on the omission, as when a man wills *not to go to church,* because it is too much trouble; and in this case this act, of its very nature, belongs to the omission, because the volition of any sin whatever, pertains, of itself, to that sin, since voluntariness is essential to sin. Sometimes, however, the act of the will bears directly on something else which hinders man from doing what he ought, whether this something else be united with the omission, as when a man wills to play at the time he ought to go to church—or, precede the omission, as when a man wills to sit up late at night, the result being that he does not go to church in the morning. In this case the act, interior or exterior, is accidental to the omission, since the omission follows outside the intention, and that which is outside the intention is said to be accidental (Phys. ii, text. 49, 50). Wherefore it is evident that then the sin of omission has indeed an act united with, or preceding the omission, but that this act is accidental to the sin of omission.

Now in judging about things, we must be guided by that which is proper to them, and not by that which is accidental: and consequently it is truer to say that a sin can be without any act; else the circumstantial acts and occasions would be essential to other actual sins.

Reply Obj. 1: More things are required for good than for evil, since "good results from a whole and entire cause, whereas evil results from each single defect," as Dionysius states (Div. Nom. iv): so that sin may arise from a man doing what he ought not, or by his not doing what he ought; while there can be no merit, unless a man do willingly what he ought to do: wherefore there can be no merit without act, whereas there can be sin without act.

Reply Obj. 2: The term "voluntary" is applied not only to that on which the act of the will is brought to bear, but also to that which we have the power to do or not to do, as stated in *Ethic.* iii, 5. Hence even not to will may be called voluntary, in so far as man has it in his power to will, and not to will.

Reply Obj. 3: The sin of omission is contrary to an affirmative precept which binds always, but not for always. Hence, by omitting to act, a man sins only for the time at which the affirmative precept binds him to act.

SIXTH ARTICLE [I-II, Q. 71, Art. 6]

Whether Sin Is Fittingly Defined As a Word, Deed, or Desire Contrary to the Eternal Law?

Objection 1: It would seem that sin is unfittingly defined by saying: "Sin is a word, deed, or desire, contrary to the eternal law." Because "word," "deed," and "desire" imply an act; whereas not every sin implies an act, as stated above (A. 5). Therefore this definition does not include every sin.

Obj. 2: Further, Augustine says (De Duab. Anim. xii): "Sin is the will to retain or obtain what justice forbids." Now will is comprised under desire, in so far as desire denotes any act of the appetite. Therefore it was enough to say: "Sin is a desire contrary to the eternal law," nor was there need to add "word" or "deed."

Obj. 3: Further, sin apparently consists properly in aversion from the end: because good and evil are measured chiefly with regard to the end as explained above (Q. 1, A. 3; Q. 18, AA. 4, 6; Q. 20, AA. 2, 3): wherefore Augustine (De Lib. Arb. i) defines sin in reference to the end, by saying that "sin is nothing else than to neglect eternal things, and seek after temporal things": and again he says (Qq. lxxxii, qu. 30) that "all human wickedness consists in using what we should enjoy, and in enjoying what we should use." Now the definition in question contains no mention of aversion from our due end: therefore it is an insufficient definition of sin.

Obj. 4: Further, a thing is said to be forbidden, because it is contrary to the law. Now not all sins are evil through being forbidden, but some are forbidden because they are evil. Therefore sin in general should not be defined as being against the law of God.

Obj. 5: Further, a sin denotes a bad human act, as was explained above (A. 1). Now man's evil is to be against reason, as Dionysius states (Div. Nom. iv). Therefore it would have been better to say that sin is against reason than to say that it is contrary to the eternal law.

*On the contrary,* the authority of Augustine suffices (Contra Faust. xxii, 27).

*I answer that,* As was shown above (A. 1), sin is nothing else than a bad human act. Now that an act is a human act is due to its being voluntary, as stated above (Q. 1, A. 1), whether it be voluntary, as being elicited by the will, e.g. to will or to choose, or as being commanded by the will, e.g. the exterior actions of speech or operation. Again, a human act is evil through lacking conformity with its due measure: and conformity of measure in a thing depends on a rule, from which if that thing depart, it is incommensurate. Now there are two rules of the human will: one is proximate and homogeneous, viz. the human reason; the other is the first rule, viz. the eternal law, which is God's reason, so to speak. Accordingly Augustine (Contra Faust. xxii, 27) includes two things in the definition of sin; one, pertaining to the substance of a human act, and which is the matter, so to speak, of sin, when he says "word, deed, or desire"; the other, pertaining to the nature of evil, and which is the form, as it were, of sin, when he says, "contrary to the eternal law."

Reply Obj. 1: Affirmation and negation are reduced to one same genus: e.g. in Divine things, begotten and unbegotten are reduced to the genus "relation," as Augustine states (De Trin. v, 6, 7): and so "word" and "deed" denote equally what is said and what is not said, what is done and what is not done.

Reply Obj. 2: The first cause of sin is in the will, which commands all voluntary acts, in which alone is sin to be found: and hence it is that Augustine sometimes defines sin in reference to the will alone. But since external acts also pertain to the substance of sin, through being evil of themselves, as stated, it was necessary in defining sin to include something referring to external action.

Reply Obj. 3: The eternal law first and foremost directs man to his end, and in consequence, makes man to be well disposed in regard to things which are directed to the end: hence when he says, "contrary to the eternal law," he includes aversion from the end and all other forms of inordinateness.

Reply Obj. 4: When it is said that not every sin is evil through being forbidden, this must be understood of prohibition by positive law. If, however, the prohibition be referred to the natural law, which is contained primarily in the eternal law, but secondarily in the natural code of the human reason, then every sin is evil through being prohibited: since it is contrary to natural law, precisely because it is inordinate.

Reply Obj. 5: The theologian considers sin chiefly as an offense against God; and the moral philosopher, as something contrary to reason. Hence Augustine defines sin with reference to its being "contrary to the eternal law," more fittingly than with reference to its being contrary to reason; the more so, as the eternal law directs us in many things that surpass human reason, e.g. in matters of faith.

## QUESTION 72

OF THE DISTINCTION OF SINS (In Nine Articles)

We must now consider the distinction of sins or vices: under which head there are nine points of inquiry:

(1) Whether sins are distinguished specifically by their objects?

(2) Of the distinction between spiritual and carnal sins;

(3) Whether sins differ in reference to their causes?

(4) Whether they differ with respect to those who are sinned against?

(5) Whether sins differ in relation to the debt of punishment?

(6) Whether they differ in regard to omission and commission?

(7) Whether they differ according to their various stages?

(8) Whether they differ in respect of excess and deficiency?

(9) Whether they differ according to their various circumstances?

FIRST ARTICLE [I-II, Q. 72, Art. 1]

Whether Sins Differ in Species According to Their Objects?

Objection 1: It would seem that sins do not differ in species, according to their objects. For acts are said to be good or evil, in relation, chiefly, to their end, as shown above (Q. 1, A. 3; Q. 18, AA. 4, 6). Since then sin is nothing else than a bad human act, as stated above (Q. 71, A. 1), it seems that sins should differ specifically according to their ends rather than according to their objects.

Obj. 2: Further, evil, being a privation, differs specifically according to the different species of opposites. Now sin is an evil in the genus of human acts. Therefore sins differ specifically according to their opposites rather than according to their objects.

Obj. 3: Further, if sins differed specifically according to their objects, it would be impossible to find the same specific sin with diverse objects: and yet such sins are to be found. For pride is about things spiritual and material as Gregory says (Moral. xxxiv, 18); and avarice is about different kinds of things. Therefore sins do not differ in species according to their objects.

*On the contrary,* "Sin is a word, deed, or desire against God's law." Now words, deeds, and desires differ in species according to their various objects: since acts differ by their objects, as stated above (Q. 18, A. 2). Therefore sins, also differ in species according to their objects.

*I answer that,* As stated above (Q. 71, A. 6), two things concur in the nature of sin, viz. the voluntary act, and its inordinateness, which consists in departing from God's law. Of these two, one is referred essentially to the sinner, who intends such and such an act in such and such matter; while the other, viz. the inordinateness of the act, is referred accidentally to the intention of the sinner, for "no one acts intending evil," as Dionysius declares (Div. Nom. iv). Now it is evident that a thing derives its species from that which is essential and not from that which is accidental: because what is accidental is outside the specific nature. Consequently sins differ specifically on the part of the voluntary acts rather than of the inordinateness inherent to sin. Now voluntary acts differ in species according to their objects, as was proved above (Q. 18, A. 2). Therefore it follows that sins are properly distinguished in species by their objects.

Reply Obj. 1: The aspect of good is found chiefly in the end: and therefore the end stands in the relation of object to the act of the will which is at the root of every sin. Consequently it amounts to the same whether sins differ by their objects or by their ends.

Reply Obj. 2: Sin is not a pure privation but an act deprived of its due order: hence sins differ specifically according to the objects of their acts rather than according to their opposites, although, even if they were distinguished in reference to their opposite virtues, it would come to the same: since virtues differ specifically according to their objects, as stated above (Q. 60, A. 5).

Reply Obj. 3: In various things, differing in species or genus, nothing hinders our finding one formal aspect of the object, from which aspect sin receives its species. It is thus that pride seeks excellence in reference to various things; and avarice seeks abundance of things adapted to human use.

SECOND ARTICLE [I-II, Q. 72, Art. 2]

Whether Spiritual Sins Are Fittingly Distinguished from Carnal Sins?

Objection 1: It would seem that spiritual sins are unfittingly distinguished from carnal sins. For the Apostle says (Gal. 5:19): "The works of the flesh are manifest, which are fornication, uncleanness, immodesty, luxury, idolatry, witchcrafts," etc. from which it seems that all kinds of sins are works of the flesh. Now carnal sins are called works of the flesh. Therefore carnal sins should not be distinguished from spiritual sins.

Obj. 2: Further, whosoever sins, walks according to the flesh, as stated in Rom. 8:13: "If you live according to the flesh, you shall die. But if by the spirit you mortify the deeds of the flesh, you shall live." Now to live or walk according to the flesh seems to pertain to the nature of carnal sin. Therefore carnal sins should not be distinguished from spiritual sins.

Obj. 3: Further, the higher part of the soul, which is the mind or reason, is called the spirit, according to Eph. 4:23: "Be renewed in the spirit of your mind," where spirit stands for reason, according to a gloss. Now every sin, which is committed in accordance with the flesh, flows from the reason by its consent; since consent in a sinful act belongs to the higher reason, as we shall state further on (Q. 74, A. 7). Therefore the same sins are both carnal and spiritual, and consequently they should not be distinguished from one another.

Obj. 4: Further, if some sins are carnal specifically, this, seemingly, should apply chiefly to those sins whereby man sins against his own body. But, according to the Apostle (1 Cor. 6:18), "every sin that a man doth, is without the body: but he that committeth fornication, sinneth against his own body." Therefore fornication would be the only carnal sin, whereas the Apostle (Eph. 5:3) reckons covetousness with the carnal sins.

*On the contrary,* Gregory (Moral. xxxi, 17) says that "of the seven capital sins five are spiritual, and two carnal."

*I answer that,* As stated above (A. 1), sins take their species from their objects. Now every sin consists in the desire for some mutable good, for which man has an inordinate desire, and the possession of which gives him inordinate pleasure. Now, as explained above (Q. 31, A. 3), pleasure is twofold. One belongs to the soul, and is consummated in the mere apprehension of a thing possessed in accordance with desire; this can also be called spiritual pleasure, e.g. when one takes pleasure in human praise or the like. The other pleasure is bodily or natural, and is realized in bodily touch, and this can also be called carnal pleasure.

Accordingly, those sins which consist in spiritual pleasure, are called spiritual sins; while those which consist in carnal pleasure, are called carnal sins, e.g. gluttony, which consists in the pleasures of the table; and lust, which consists in sexual pleasures. Hence the Apostle says (2 Cor. 7:1): "Let us cleanse ourselves from all defilement of the flesh and of the spirit."

Reply Obj. 1: As a gloss says on the same passage, these vices are called works of the flesh, not as though they consisted in carnal pleasure; but flesh here denotes man, who is said to live according to the flesh, when he lives according to himself, as Augustine says (De Civ. Dei xiv, 2, 3). The reason of this is because every failing in the human reason is due in some way to the carnal sense.

This suffices for the Reply to the Second Objection.

Reply Obj. 3: Even in the carnal sins there is a spiritual act, viz. the act of reason: but the end of these sins, from which they are named, is carnal pleasure.

Reply Obj. 4: As the gloss says, "in the sin of fornication the soul is the body's slave in a special sense, because at the moment of sinning it can think of nothing else": whereas the pleasure of gluttony, although carnal, does not so utterly absorb the reason. It may also be said that in this sin, an injury is done to the body also, for it is defiled inordinately: wherefore by this sin alone is man said specifically to sin against his body. While covetousness, which is reckoned among the carnal sins, stands here for adultery, which is the unjust appropriation of another's wife. Again, it may be said that the thing in which the covetous man takes pleasure is something bodily, and in this respect covetousness is numbered with the carnal sins: but the pleasure itself does not belong to the body, but to the spirit, wherefore Gregory says (Moral. xxxi, 17) that it is a spiritual sin.

THIRD ARTICLE [I-II, Q. 72, Art. 3]

Whether Sins Differ Specifically in Reference to Their Causes?

Objection 1: It would seem that sins differ specifically in reference to their causes. For a thing takes its species from that whence it derives its being. Now sins derive their being from their causes. Therefore they take their species from them also. Therefore they differ specifically in reference to their causes.

Obj. 2: Further, of all the causes the material cause seems to have least reference to the species. Now the object in a sin is like its material cause. Since, therefore, sins differ specifically according to their objects, it seems that much more do they differ in reference to their other causes.

Obj. 3: Further, Augustine, commenting on Ps. 79:17, "Things set on fire and dug down," says that "every sin is due either to fear inducing false humility, or to love enkindling us to undue ardor." For it is written (1 John 2:16) that "all that is in the world, is the concupiscence of the flesh, or [Vulg.: 'and'] the concupiscence of the eyes, or [Vulg.: 'and'] the pride of life." Now a thing is said to be in the world on account of sin, in as much as the world denotes lovers of the world, as Augustine observes (Tract. ii in Joan.). Gregory, too (Moral. xxxi, 17), distinguishes all sins according to the seven capital vices. Now all these divisions refer to the causes of sins. Therefore, seemingly, sins differ specifically according to the diversity of their causes.

*On the contrary,* If this were the case all sins would belong to one species, since they are due to one cause. For it is written (Ecclus. 10:15) that "pride is the beginning of all sin," and (1 Tim. 6:10) that "the desire of money is the root of all evils." Now it is evident that there are various species of sins. Therefore sins do not differ specifically according to their different causes.

*I answer that,* Since there are four kinds of causes, they are attributed to various things in various ways. Because the *formal* and the *material* cause regard properly the substance of a thing; and consequently substances differ in respect of their matter and form, both in species and in genus. The *agent* and the end regard directly movement and operation: wherefore movements and operations differ specifically in respect of these causes; in different ways, however, because the natural active principles are always determined to the same acts; so that the different species of natural acts are taken not only from the objects, which are the ends or terms of those acts, but also from their active principles: thus heating and cooling are specifically distinct with reference to hot and cold. On the other hand, the active principles in voluntary acts, such as the acts of sins, are not determined, of necessity, to one act, and consequently from one active or motive principle, diverse species of sins can proceed: thus from fear engendering false humility man may proceed to theft, or murder, or to neglect the flock committed to his care; and these same things may proceed from love enkindling to undue ardor. Hence it is evident that sins do not differ specifically according to their various active or motive causes, but only in respect of diversity in the final cause, which is the end and object of the will. For it has been shown above (Q. 1, A. 3; Q. 18, AA. 4, 6) that human acts take their species from the end.

Reply Obj. 1: The active principles in voluntary acts, not being determined to one act, do not suffice for the production of human acts, unless the will be determined to one by the intention of the end, as the Philosopher proves (Metaph. ix, text. 15, 16), and consequently sin derives both its being and its species from the end.

Reply Obj. 2: Objects, in relation to external acts, have the character of matter "about which"; but, in relation to the interior act of the will, they have the character of end; and it is owing to this that they give the act its species. Nevertheless, even considered as the matter "about which," they have the character of term, from which movement takes its species (Phys. v, text. 4; *Ethic.* x, 4); yet even terms of movement specify movements, in so far as term has the character of end.

Reply Obj. 3: These distinctions of sins are given, not as distinct species of sins, but to show their various causes.

FOURTH ARTICLE [I-II, Q. 72, Art. 4]

Whether Sin Is Fittingly Divided into Sin Against God, Against Oneself, and Against One's Neighbor?

Objection 1: It would seem that sin is unfittingly divided into sin against God, against one's neighbor, and against oneself. For that which is common to all sins should not be reckoned as a part in the division of sin. But it is common to all sins to be against God: for it is stated in the definition of sin that it is "against God's law," as stated above (Q. 66, A. 6). Therefore sin against God should not be reckoned a part of the division of sin.

Obj. 2: Further, every division should consist of things in opposition to one another. But these three kinds of sin are not opposed to one another: for whoever sins against his neighbor, sins against himself and against God. Therefore sin is not fittingly divided into these three.

Obj. 3: Further, specification is not taken from things external. But God and our neighbor are external to us. Therefore sins are not distinguished specifically with regard to them: and consequently sin is unfittingly divided according to these three.

*On the contrary,* Isidore (De Summo Bono), in giving the division of sins, says that "man is said to sin against himself, against God, and against his neighbor."

*I answer that,* As stated above (Q. 71, AA. 1, 6), sin is an inordinate act. Now there should be a threefold order in man: one in relation to the rule of reason, in so far as all our actions and passions should be commensurate with the rule of reason: another order is in relation to the rule of the Divine Law, whereby man should be directed in all things: and if man were by nature a solitary animal, this twofold order would suffice. But since man is naturally a civic and social animal, as is proved in *Polit.* i, 2, hence a third order is necessary, whereby man is directed in relation to other men among whom he has to dwell. Of these orders the second contains the first and surpasses it. For whatever things are comprised under the order of reason, are comprised under the order of God Himself. Yet some things are comprised under the order of God, which surpass the human reason, such as matters of faith, and things due to God alone. Hence he that sins in such matters, for instance, by heresy, sacrilege, or blasphemy, is said to sin against God. In like manner, the first order includes the third and surpasses it, because in all things wherein we are directed in reference to our neighbor, we need to be directed according to the order of reason. Yet in some things we are directed according to reason, in relation to ourselves only, and not in reference to our neighbor; and when man sins in these matters, he is said to sin against himself, as is seen in the glutton, the lustful, and the prodigal. But when man sins in matters concerning his neighbor, he is said to sin against his neighbor, as appears in the thief and murderer. Now the things whereby man is directed to God, his neighbor, and himself are diverse. Wherefore this distinction of sins is in respect of their objects, according to which the species of sins are diversified: and consequently this distinction of sins is properly one of different species of sins: because the virtues also, to which sins are opposed, differ specifically in respect of these three. For it is evident from what has been said (Q. 62, AA. 1, 2, 3) that by the theological virtues man is directed to God; by temperance and fortitude, to himself; and by justice to his neighbor.

Reply Obj. 1: To sin against God is common to all sins, in so far as the order to God includes every human order; but in so far as order to God surpasses the other two orders, sin against God is a special kind of sin.

Reply Obj. 2: When several things, of which one includes another, are distinct from one another, this distinction is understood to refer, not to the part contained in another, but to that in which one goes beyond another. This may be seen in the division of numbers and figures: for a triangle is distinguished from a four-sided figure not in respect of its being contained thereby, but in respect of that in which it is surpassed thereby: and the same applies to the numbers three and four.

Reply Obj. 3: Although God and our neighbor are external to the sinner himself, they are not external to the act of sin, but are related to it as to its object.

FIFTH ARTICLE [I-II, Q. 72, Art. 5]

Whether the Division of Sins According to Their Debt of Punishment Diversifies Their Species?

Objection 1: It would seem that the division of sins according to their debt of punishment diversifies their species; for instance, when sin is divided into "mortal" and "venial." For things which are infinitely apart, cannot belong to the same species, nor even to the same genus. But venial and mortal sin are infinitely apart, since temporal punishment is due to venial sin, and eternal punishment to mortal sin; and the measure of the punishment corresponds to the gravity of the fault, according to Deut. 25:2: "According to the measure of the sin shall the measure be also of the stripes be." Therefore venial and mortal sins are not of the same genus, nor can they be said to belong to the same species.

Obj. 2: Further, some sins are mortal in virtue of their species [* *Ex genere,* genus in this case denoting the species], as murder and adultery; and some are venial in virtue of their species, as in an idle word, and excessive laughter. Therefore venial and mortal sins differ specifically.

Obj. 3: Further, just as a virtuous act stands in relation to its reward, so does sin stand in relation to punishment. But the reward is the end of the virtuous act. Therefore punishment is the end of sin. Now sins differ specifically in relation to their ends, as stated above (A. 1, ad 1). Therefore they are also specifically distinct according to the debt of punishment.

*On the contrary,* Those things that constitute a species are prior to the species, e.g. specific differences. But punishment follows sin as the effect thereof. Therefore sins do not differ specifically according to the debt of punishment.

*I answer that,* In things that differ specifically we find a twofold difference: the first causes the diversity of species, and is not to be found save in different species, e.g. "rational" and "irrational," "animate," and "inanimate": the other difference is consequent to specific diversity; and though, in some cases, it may [follow from the diversity of species], yet, in others, it may be found within the same species; thus "white" and "black" are consequent to the specific diversity of crow and swan, and yet this difference is found within the one species of man.

We must therefore say that the difference between venial and mortal sin, or any other difference is respect of the debt of punishment, cannot be a difference constituting specific diversity. For what is accidental never constitutes a species; and what is outside the agent's intention is accidental (Phys. ii, text. 50). Now it is evident that punishment is outside the intention of the sinner, wherefore it is accidentally referred to sin on the part of the sinner. Nevertheless it is referred to sin by an extrinsic principle, viz. the justice of the judge, who imposes various punishments according to the various manners of sin. Therefore the difference derived from the debt of punishment, may be consequent to the specific diversity of sins, but cannot constitute it.

Now the difference between venial and mortal sin is consequent to the diversity of that inordinateness which constitutes the notion of sin. For inordinateness is twofold, one that destroys the principle of order, and another which, without destroying the principle of order, implies inordinateness in the things which follow the principle: thus, in an animal's body, the frame may be so out of order that the vital principle is destroyed; this is the inordinateness of death; while, on the other hand, saving the vital principle, there may be disorder in the bodily humors; and then there is sickness. Now the principle of the entire moral order is the last end, which stands in the same relation to matters of action, as the indemonstrable principle does to matters of speculation (Ethic. vii, 8). Therefore when the soul is so disordered by sin as to turn away from its last end, viz. God, to Whom it is united by charity, there is mortal sin; but when it is disordered without turning away from God, there is venial sin. For even as in the body, the disorder of death which results from the destruction of the principle of life, is irreparable according to nature, while the disorder of sickness can be repaired by reason of the vital principle being preserved, so it is in matters concerning the soul. Because, in speculative matters, it is impossible to convince one who errs in the principles, whereas one who errs, but retains the principles, can be brought back to the truth by means of the principles. Likewise in practical matters, he who, by sinning, turns away from his last end, if we consider the nature of his sin, falls irreparably, and therefore is said to sin mortally and to deserve eternal punishment: whereas when a man sins without turning away from God, by the very nature of his sin, his disorder can be repaired, because the principle of the order is not destroyed; wherefore he is said to sin venially, because, to wit, he does not sin so as to deserve to be punished eternally.

Reply Obj. 1: Mortal and venial sins are infinitely apart as regards what they *turn away from*, not as regards what they turn to, viz. the object which specifies them. Hence nothing hinders the same species from including mortal and venial sins; for instance, in the species "adultery" the first movement is a venial sin; while an idle word, which is, generally speaking, venial, may even be a mortal sin.

Reply Obj. 2: From the fact that one sin is mortal by reason of its species, and another venial by reason of its species, it follows that this difference is consequent to the specific difference of sins, not that it is the cause thereof. And this difference may be found even in things of the same species, as stated above.

Reply Obj. 3: The reward is intended by him that merits or acts virtu[ous]ly; whereas the punishment is not intended by the sinner, but, *on the contrary*, is against his will. Hence the comparison fails.

SIXTH ARTICLE [I-II, Q. 72, Art. 6]

Whether Sins of Commission and Omission Differ Specifically?

Objection 1: It would seem that sins of commission and omission differ specifically. For "offense" and "sin" are condivided with one another (Eph. 2:1), where it is written: "When you were dead in your offenses and sins," which words a gloss explains, saying: "'Offenses,' by omitting to do what was commanded, and 'sins,' by doing what was forbidden." Whence it is evident that "offenses" here denotes sins of omission; while "sin" denotes sins of commission. Therefore they differ specifically, since they are contrasted with one another as different species.

Obj. 2: Further, it is essential to sin to be against God's law, for this is part of its definition, as is clear from what has been said (Q. 71, A. 6). Now in God's law, the affirmative precepts, against which is the sin of omission, are different from the negative precepts, against which is the sin of omission. Therefore sins of omission and commission differ specifically.

Obj. 3: Further, omission and commission differ as affirmation and negation. Now affirmation and negation cannot be in the same species, since negation has no species; for "there is neither species nor difference of non-being," as the Philosopher states (Phys. iv, text. 67). Therefore omission and commission cannot belong to the same species.

*On the contrary,* Omission and commission are found in the same species of sin. For the covetous man both takes what belongs to others, which is a sin of commission; and gives not of his own to whom he should give, which is a sin of omission. Therefore omission and commission do not differ specifically.

*I answer that,* There is a twofold difference in sins; a material difference and a formal difference: the material difference is to be observed in the natural species of the sinful act; while the formal difference is gathered from their relation to one proper end, which is also their proper object. Hence we find certain acts differing from one another in the material specific difference, which are nevertheless formally in the same species of sin, because they are directed to the one same end: thus strangling, stoning, and stabbing come under the one species of murder, although the actions themselves differ specifically according to the natural species. Accordingly, if we refer to the material species in sins of omission and commission, they differ specifically, using species in a broad sense, in so far as negation and privation may have a species. But if we refer to the formal species of sins of omission and commission, they do not differ specifically, because they are directed to the same end, and proceed from the same motive. For the covetous man, in order to hoard money, both robs, and omits to give what he ought, and in like manner, the glutton, to satiate his appetite, both eats too much and omits the prescribed fasts. The same applies to other sins: for in things, negation is always founded on affirmation, which, in a manner, is its cause. Hence in the physical order it comes under the same head, that fire gives forth heat, and that it does not give forth cold.

Reply Obj. 1: This division in respect of commission and omission, is not according to different formal species, but only according to material species, as stated.

Reply Obj. 2: In God's law, the necessity for various affirmative and negative precepts, was that men might be gradually led to virtue, first by abstaining from evil, being induced to this by the negative precepts, and afterwards by doing good, to which we are induced by the affirmative precepts. Wherefore the affirmative and negative precepts do not belong to different virtues, but to different degrees of virtue; and consequently they are not, of necessity, opposed to sins of different species. Moreover sin is not specified by that from which it turns away, because in this respect it is a negation or privation, but by that to which it turns, in so far as sin is an act. Consequently sins do not differ specifically according to the various precepts of the Law.

Reply Obj. 3: This objection considers the material diversity of sins. It must be observed, however, that although, properly speaking, negation is not in a species, yet it is allotted to a species by reduction to the affirmation on which it is based.

SEVENTH ARTICLE [I-II, Q. 72, Art. 7]

Whether Sins Are Fittingly Divided into Sins of Thought, Word, and Deed?

Objection 1: It would seem that sins are unfittingly divided into sins of thought, word, and deed. For Augustine (De Trin. xii, 12) describes three stages of sin, of which the first is "when the carnal sense offers a bait," which is the sin of thought; the second stage is reached "when one is satisfied with the mere pleasure of thought"; and the third stage, "when consent is given to the deed." Now these three belong to the sin of thought. Therefore it is unfitting to reckon sin of thought as one kind of sin.

Obj. 2: Further, Gregory (Moral. iv, 25) reckons four degrees of sin; the first of which is "a fault hidden in the heart"; the second, "when it is done openly"; the third, "when it is formed into a habit"; and the fourth, "when man goes so far as to presume on God's mercy or to give himself up to despair": where no distinction is made between sins of deed and sins of word, and two other degrees of sin are added. Therefore the first division was unfitting.

Obj. 3: Further, there can be no sin of word or deed unless there precede sin of thought. Therefore these sins do not differ specifically. Therefore they should not be condivided with one another.

*On the contrary,* Jerome in commenting on Ezech. 43:23, says: "The human race is subject to three kinds of sin, for when we sin, it is either by thought, or word, or deed."

*I answer that,* Things differ specifically in two ways: first, when each has the complete species; thus a horse and an ox differ specifically: secondly, when the diversity of species is derived from diversity of degree in generation or movement: thus the building is the complete generation of a house, while the laying of the foundations, and the setting up of the walls are incomplete species, as the Philosopher declares (Ethic. x, 4); and the same can apply to the generation of animals. Accordingly sins are divided into these three, viz. sins of thought, word, and deed, not as into various complete species: for the consummation of sin is in the deed, wherefore sins of deed have the complete species; but the first beginning of sin is its foundation, as it were, in the sin of thought; the second degree is the sin of word, in so far as man is ready to break out into a declaration of his thought; while the third degree consists in the consummation of the deed. Consequently these three differ in respect of the various degrees of sin. Nevertheless it is evident that these three belong to the one complete species of sin, since they proceed from the same motive. For the angry man, through desire of vengeance, is at first disturbed in thought, then he breaks out into words of abuse, and lastly he goes on to wrongful deeds; and the same applies to lust and to any other sin.

Reply Obj. 1: All sins of thought have the common note of secrecy, in respect of which they form one degree, which is, however, divided into three stages, viz. of cogitation, pleasure, and consent.

Reply Obj. 2: Sins of words and deed are both done openly, and for this reason Gregory (Moral. iv, 25) reckons them under one head: whereas Jerome (in commenting on Ezech. 43:23) distinguishes between them, because in sins of word there is nothing but manifestation which is intended principally; while in sins of deed, it is the consummation of the inward thought which is principally intended, and the outward manifestation is by way of sequel. Habit and despair are stages following the complete species of sin, even as boyhood and youth follow the complete generation of a man.

Reply Obj. 3: Sin of thought and sin of word are not distinct from the sin of deed when they are united together with it, but when each is found by itself: even as one part of a movement is not distinct from the whole movement, when the movement is continuous, but only when there is a break in the movement.

EIGHTH ARTICLE [I-II, Q. 72, Art. 8]

Whether Excess and Deficiency Diversify the Species of Sins?

Objection 1: It would seem that excess and deficiency do not diversify the species of sins. For excess and deficiency differ in respect of more and less. Now "more" and "less" do not diversify a species. Therefore excess and deficiency do not diversify the species of sins.

Obj. 2: Further, just as sin, in matters of action, is due to straying from the rectitude of reason, so falsehood, in speculative matters, is due to straying from the truth of the reality. Now the species of falsehood is not diversified by saying more or less than the reality. Therefore neither is the species of sin diversified by straying more or less from the rectitude of reason.

Obj. 3: Further, "one species cannot be made out of two," as Porphyry declares [*Isagog.; cf. Arist.

*Metaph.* i]. Now excess and deficiency are united in one sin; for some are at once illiberal and wasteful—illiberality being a sin of deficiency, and prodigality, by excess. Therefore excess and deficiency do not diversify the species of sins.

*On the contrary,* Contraries differ specifically, for "contrariety is a difference of form," as stated in Metaph. x, text. 13, 14. Now vices that differ according to excess and deficiency are contrary to one another, as illiberality to wastefulness. Therefore they differ specifically.

*I answer that,* While there are two things in sin, viz. the act itself and its inordinateness, in so far as sin is a departure from the order of reason and the Divine law, the species of sin is gathered, not from its inordinateness, which is outside the sinner's intention, as stated above (A. 1), but one the contrary, from the act itself as terminating in the object to which the sinner's intention is directed. Consequently wherever we find a different motive inclining the intention to sin, there will be a different species of sin. Now it is evident that the motive for sinning, in sins by excess, is not the same as the motive for sinning, in sins of deficiency; in fact, they are contrary to one another, just as the motive in the sin of intemperance is love for bodily pleasures, while the motive in the sin of insensibility is hatred of the same. Therefore these sins not only differ specifically, but are contrary to one another.

Reply Obj. 1: Although *more* and less do not cause diversity of species, yet they are sometimes consequent to specific difference, in so far as they are the result of diversity of form; thus we may say that fire is lighter than air. Hence the Philosopher says (Ethic. viii, 1) that "those who held that there are no different species of friendship, by reason of its admitting of degree, were led by insufficient proof." In this way to exceed reason or to fall short thereof belongs to sins specifically different, in so far as they result from different motives.

Reply Obj. 2: It is not the sinner's intention to depart from reason; and so sins of excess and deficiency do not become of one kind through departing from the one rectitude of reason. On the other hand, sometimes he who utters a falsehood, intends to hide the truth, wherefore in this respect, it matters not whether he tells more or less. If, however, departure from the truth be not outside the intention, it is evident that then one is moved by different causes to tell more or less; and in this respect there are different kinds of falsehood, as is evident of the *boaster,* who exceeds in telling untruths for the sake of fame, and the *cheat,* who tells less than the truth, in order to escape from paying his debts. This also explains how some false opinions are contrary to one another.

Reply Obj. 3: One may be prodigal and illiberal with regard to different objects: for instance one may be illiberal [*Cf. II-II, Q. 119, A. 1, ad 1] in taking what one ought not: and nothing hinders contraries from being in the same subject, in different respects.

NINTH ARTICLE [I-II, Q. 72, Art. 9]

Whether Sins Differ Specifically in Respect of Different Circumstances?

Objection 1: It would seem that vices and sins differ in respect of different circumstances. For, as Dionysius says (Div. Nom. iv), "evil results from each single defect." Now individual defects are corruptions of individual circumstances. Therefore from the corruption of each circumstance there results a corresponding species of sin.

Obj. 2: Further, sins are human acts. But human acts sometimes take their species from circumstances, as stated above (Q. 18, A. 10). Therefore sins differ specifically according as different circumstances are corrupted.

Obj. 3: Further, diverse species are assigned to gluttony, according to the words contained in the following verse:

"Hastily, sumptuously, too much, greedily, daintily."

Now these pertain to various circumstances, for "hastily" means sooner than is right; "too much," more than is right, and so on with the others. Therefore the species of sin is diversified according to the various circumstances.

*On the contrary,* The Philosopher says (Ethic. iii, 7; iv, 1) that "every vice sins by doing more than one ought, and when one ought not"; and in like manner as to the other circumstances. Therefore the species of sins are not diversified in this respect.

*I answer that,* As stated above (A. 8), wherever there is a special motive for sinning, there is a different species of sin, because the motive for sinning is the end and object of sin. Now it happens sometimes that although different circumstances are corrupted, there is but one motive: thus the illiberal man, for the same motive, takes when he ought not, where he ought not, and more than he ought, and so on with the circumstances, since he does this through an inordinate desire of hoarding money: and in such cases the corruption of different circumstances does not diversify the species of sins, but belongs to one and the same species.

Sometimes, however, the corruption of different circumstances arises from different motives: for instance that a man eat hastily, may be due to the fact that he cannot brook the delay in taking food, on account of a rapid exhaustion of the digestive humors; and that he desire too much food, may be due to a naturally strong digestion; that he desire choice meats, is due to his desire for pleasure in taking food. Hence in such matters, the corruption of different circumstances entails different species of sins.

Reply Obj. 1: Evil, as such, is a privation, and so it has different species in respect of the thing which the subject is deprived, even as other privations. But sin does not take its species from the privation or aversion, as stated above (A. 1), but from turning to the object of the act.

Reply Obj. 2: A circumstance never transfers an act from one species to another, save when there is another motive.

Reply Obj. 3: In the various species of gluttony there are various motives, as stated.

# QUESTION 73

OF THE COMPARISON OF ONE SIN WITH ANOTHER (In Ten Articles)

We must now consider the comparison of one sin with another: under which head there are ten points of inquiry:

(1) Whether all sins and vices are connected with one another?

(2) Whether all are equal?

(3) Whether the gravity of sin depends on its object?

(4) Whether it depends on the excellence of the virtue to which it is opposed?

(5) Whether carnal sins are more grievous than spiritual sins?

(6) Whether the gravity of sins depends on their causes?

(7) Whether it depends on their circumstances?

(8) Whether it depends on how much harm ensues?

(9) Whether on the position of the person sinned against?

(10) Whether sin is aggravated by reason of the excellence of the person sinning?

FIRST ARTICLE [I-II, Q. 73, Art. 1]

Whether All Sins Are Connected with One Another?

Objection 1: It would seem that all sins are connected. For it is written (James 2:10): "Whosoever shall keep the whole Law, but offend in one point, is become guilty of all." Now to be guilty of transgressing all the precepts of Law, is the same as to commit all sins, because, as Ambrose says (De Parad. viii), "sin is a transgression of the Divine law, and disobedience of the heavenly commandments." Therefore whoever commits one sin is guilty of all.

Obj. 2: Further, each sin banishes its opposite virtue. Now whoever lacks one virtue lacks them all, as was shown above (Q. 65, A. 1). Therefore whoever commits one sin, is deprived of all the virtues. Therefore whoever commits one sin, is guilty of all sins.

Obj. 3: Further, all virtues are connected, because they have a principle in common, as stated above (Q. 65, AA. 1, 2). Now as the virtues have a common principle, so have sins, because, as the love of God, which builds the city of God, is the beginning and root of all the virtues, so self-love, which builds the city of Babylon, is the root of all sins, as Augustine declares (De Civ. Dei xiv, 28). Therefore all vices and sins are also connected so that whoever has one, has them all.

*On the contrary,* Some vices are contrary to one another, as the Philosopher states (Ethic. ii, 8). But contraries cannot be together in the same subject. Therefore it is impossible for all sins and vices to be connected with one another.

*I answer that,* The intention of the man who acts according to virtue in pursuance of his reason, is different from the intention of the sinner in straying from the path of reason. For the intention of every man acting according to virtue is to follow the rule of reason, wherefore the intention of all the virtues is directed to the same end, so that all the virtues are connected together in the right reason of things to be done, viz. prudence, as stated above (Q. 65, A. 1). But the intention of the sinner is not directed to the point of straying from the path of reason; rather is it directed to tend to some appetible good whence it derives its species. Now these goods, to which the sinner's intention is directed when departing from reason, are of various kinds, having no mutual connection; in fact they are sometimes contrary to one another. Since, therefore, vices and sins take their species from that to which they turn, it is evident that, in respect of that which completes a sin's species, sins are not connected with one another. For sin does not consist in passing from the many to the one, as is the case with virtues, which are connected, but rather in forsaking the one for the many.

Reply Obj. 1: James is speaking of sin, not as regards the thing to which it turns and which causes the distinction of sins, as stated above (Q. 72, A. 1), but as regards that from which sin turns away, in as much as man, by sinning, departs from a commandment of the law. Now all the commandments of the law are from one and the same, as he also says in the same passage, so that the same God is despised in every sin; and in this sense he says that whoever "offends in one point, is become guilty of all," for as much as, by committing one sin, he incurs the debt of punishment through his contempt of God, which is the origin of all sins.

Reply Obj. 2: As stated above (Q. 71, A. 4), the opposite virtue is not banished by every act of sin; because venial sin does not destroy virtue; while mortal sin destroys infused virtue, by turning man away from God. Yet one act, even of mortal sin, does not destroy the habit of acquired virtue; though if such acts be repeated so as to engender a contrary habit, the habit of acquired virtue is destroyed, the destruction of which entails the loss of prudence, since when man acts against any virtue whatever, he acts against prudence, without which no moral virtue is possible, as stated above (Q. 58, A. 4; Q. 65, A. 1). Consequently all the moral virtues are destroyed as to the perfect and formal being of virtue, which they have in so far as they partake of prudence, yet there remain the inclinations to virtuous acts, which inclinations, however, are not virtues. Nevertheless it does not follow that for this reason man contracts all vices of sins—first, because several vices are opposed to one virtue, so that a virtue can be destroyed by one of them, without the others being present; secondly, because sin is directly opposed to virtue, as regards the virtue's inclination to act, as stated above (Q. 71, A. 1). Wherefore, as long as any virtuous inclinations remain, it cannot be said that man has the opposite vices or sins.

Reply Obj. 3: The love of God is unitive, in as much as it draws man's affections from the many to the one; so that the virtues, which flow from the love of God, are connected together. But self-love disunites man's affections among different things, in so far as man loves himself, by desiring for himself temporal goods, which are various and of many kinds: hence vices and sins, which arise from self-love, are not connected together.

SECOND ARTICLE [I-II, Q. 73, Art. 2]

Whether All Sins Are Equal?

Objection 1: It would seem that all sins are equal. Because sin is to do what is unlawful. Now to do what is unlawful is reproved in one and the same way in all things. Therefore sin is reproved in one and the same way. Therefore one sin is not graver than another.

Obj. 2: Further, every sin is a transgression of the rule of reason, which is to human acts what a linear rule is in corporeal things. Therefore to sin is the same as to pass over a line. But passing over a line occurs equally and in the same way, even if one go a long way from it or stay near it, since privations do not admit of more or less. Therefore all sins are equal.

Obj. 3: Further, sins are opposed to virtues. But all virtues are equal, as Cicero states (Paradox. iii). Therefore all sins are equal.

*On the contrary,* Our Lord said to Pilate (John 19:11): "He that hath delivered me to thee, hath the greater sin," and yet it is evident that Pilate was guilty of some sin. Therefore one sin is greater than another.

*I answer that,* The opinion of the Stoics, which Cicero adopts in the book on *Paradoxes* (Paradox. iii), was that all sins are equal: from which opinion arose the error of certain heretics, who not only hold all sins to be equal, but also maintain that all the pains of hell are equal. So far as can be gathered from the words of Cicero the Stoics arrived at their conclusion through looking at sin on the side of the privation only, in so far, to wit, as it is a departure from reason; wherefore considering simply that no privation admits of more or less, they held that all sins are equal. Yet, if we consider the matter carefully, we shall see that there are two kinds of privation. For there is a simple and pure privation, which consists, so to speak, in *being* corrupted; thus death is privation of life, and darkness is privation of light. Such like privations do not admit of more or less, because nothing remains of the opposite habit; hence a man is not less dead on the first day after his death, or on the third or fourth days, than after a year, when his corpse is already dissolved; and, in like manner, a house is no darker if the light be covered with several shades, than if it were covered by a single shade shutting out all the light. There is, however, another privation which is not simple, but retains something of the opposite habit; it consists in *becoming* corrupted rather than in being corrupted, like sickness which is a privation of the due commensuration of the humors, yet so that something remains of that commensuration, else the animal would cease to live: and the same applies to deformity and the like. Such privations admit of more or less on the part of what remains or the contrary habit. For it matters much in sickness or deformity, whether one departs more or less from the due commensuration of humors or members. The same applies to vices and sins: because in them the privation of the due commensuration of reason is such as not to destroy the order of reason altogether; else evil, if total, destroys itself, as stated in *Ethic.* iv, 5. For the substance of the act, or the affection of the agent could not remain, unless something remained of the order of reason. Therefore it matters much to the gravity of a sin whether one departs more or less from the rectitude of reason: and accordingly we must say that sins are not all equal.

Reply Obj. 1: To commit sin is unlawful on account of some inordinateness therein: wherefore those which contain a greater inordinateness are more unlawful, and consequently graver sins.

Reply Obj. 2: This argument looks upon sin as though it were a pure privation.

Reply Obj. 3: Virtues are proportionately equal in one and the same subject: yet one virtue surpasses another in excellence according to its species; and again, one man is more virtuous than another, in the same species of virtue, as stated above (Q. 66, AA. 1, 2). Moreover, even if virtues were equal, it would not follow that vices are equal, since virtues are connected, and vices or sins are not.

THIRD ARTICLE [I-II, Q. 73, Art. 3]

Whether the Gravity of Sins Varies According to Their Objects?

Objection 1: It would seem that the gravity of sins does not vary according to their objects. Because the gravity of a sin pertains to its mode or quality: whereas the object is the matter of the sin. Therefore the gravity of sins does not vary according to their various objects.

Obj. 2: Further, the gravity of a sin is the intensity of its malice. Now sin does not derive its malice from its proper object to which it turns, and which is some appetible good, but rather from that which it turns away from. Therefore the gravity of sins does not vary according to their various objects.

Obj. 3: Further, sins that have different objects are of different kinds. But things of different kinds cannot be compared with one another, as is proved in *Phys.* vii, text. 30, seqq. Therefore one sin is not graver than another by reason of the difference of objects.

*On the contrary,* Sins take their species from their objects, as was shown above (Q. 72, A. 1). But some sins are graver than others in respect of their species, as murder is graver than theft. Therefore the gravity of sins varies according to their objects.

*I answer that,* As is clear from what has been said (Q. 71, A. 5), the gravity of sins varies in the same way as one sickness is graver than another: for just as the good of health consists in a certain commensuration of the humors, in keeping with an animal's nature, so the good of virtue consists in a certain commensuration of the human act in accord with the rule of reason. Now it is evident that the higher the principle the disorder of which causes the disorder in the humors, the graver is the sickness: thus a sickness which comes on the human body from the heart, which is the principle of life, or from some neighboring part, is more dangerous. Wherefore a sin must needs be so much the graver, as the disorder occurs in a principle which is higher in the order of reason. Now in matters of action the reason directs all things in view of the end: wherefore the higher the end which attaches to sins in human acts, the graver the sin. Now the object of an act is its end, as stated above (Q. 72, A. 3, ad 2); and consequently the difference of gravity in sins depends on their objects. Thus it is clear that external things are directed to man as their end, while man is further directed to God as his end. Wherefore a sin which is about the very substance of man, e.g. murder, is graver than a sin which is about external things, e.g. theft; and graver still is a sin committed directly against God, e.g. unbelief, blasphemy, and the like: and in each of these grades of sin, one sin will be graver than another according as it is about a higher or lower principle. And forasmuch as sins take their species from their objects, the difference of gravity which is derived from the objects is first and foremost, as resulting from the species.

Reply Obj. 1: Although the object is the matter about which an act is concerned, yet it has the character of an end, in so far as the intention of the agent is fixed on it, as stated above (Q. 72, A. 3, ad 2). Now the form of a moral act depends on the end, as was shown above (Q. 72, A. 6; Q. 18, A. 6).

Reply Obj. 2: From the very fact that man turns unduly to some mutable good, it follows that he turns away from the immutable Good, which aversion completes the nature of evil. Hence the various degrees of malice in sins must needs follow the diversity of those things to which man turns.

Reply Obj. 3: All the objects of human acts are related to one another, wherefore all human acts are somewhat of one kind, in so far as they are directed to the last end. Therefore nothing prevents all sins from being compared with one another.

FOURTH ARTICLE [I-II, Q. 73, Art. 4]

Whether the Gravity of Sins Depends on the Excellence of the Virtues to Which They Are Opposed?

Objection 1: It would seem that the gravity of sins does not vary according to the excellence of the virtues to which they are opposed, so that, to wit, the graver sin is opposed to the greater virtue. For, according to Prov. 15:5, "In abundant justice there is the greatest strength." Now, as Our Lord says (Matt. 5:20, seqq.) abundant justice restrains anger, which is a less grievous sin than murder, which less abundant justice restrains. Therefore the least grievous sin is opposed to the greatest virtue.

Obj. 2: Further, it is stated in *Ethic.* ii, 3 that "virtue is about the difficult and the good": whence it seems to follow that the greater virtue is about what is more difficult. But it is a less grievous sin to fail in what is more difficult, than in what is less difficult. Therefore the less grievous sin is opposed to the greater virtue.

Obj. 3: Further, charity is a greater virtue than faith or hope (1 Cor. 13:13). Now hatred which is opposed to charity is a less grievous sin than unbelief or despair which are opposed to faith and hope. Therefore the less grievous sin is opposed to the greater virtue.

*On the contrary,* The Philosopher says (Ethic. 8:10) that the "worst is opposed to the best." Now in morals the best is the greatest virtue; and the worst is the most grievous sin. Therefore the most grievous sin is opposed to the greatest virtue.

*I answer that,* A sin is opposed to a virtue in two ways: first, principally and directly; that sin, to wit, which is about the same object: because contraries are about the same thing. In this way, the more grievous sin must needs be opposed to the greater virtue: because, just as the degrees of gravity in a sin depend on the object, so also does the greatness of a virtue, since both sin and virtue take their species from the object, as shown above (Q. 60, A. 5; Q. 72, A. 1). Wherefore the greatest sin must needs be directly opposed to the greatest virtue, as being furthest removed from it in the same genus. Secondly, the opposition of virtue to sin may be considered in respect of a certain extension of the virtue in checking sin. For the greater a virtue is, the further it removes man from the contrary sin, so that it withdraws man not only from that sin, but also from whatever leads to it. And thus it is evident that the greater a virtue is, the more it withdraws man also from less grievous sins: even as the more perfect health is, the more does it ward off even minor ailments. And in this way the less grievous sin is opposed to the greater virtue, on the part of the latter's effect.

Reply Obj. 1: This argument considers the opposition which consists in restraining from sin; for thus abundant justice checks even minor sins.

Reply Obj. 2: The greater virtue that is about a more difficult good is opposed directly to the sin which is about a more difficult evil. For in each case there is a certain superiority, in that the will is shown to be more intent on good or evil, through not being overcome by the difficulty.

Reply Obj. 3: Charity is not any kind of love, but the love of God: hence not any kind of hatred is opposed to it directly, but the hatred of God, which is the most grievous of all sins.

FIFTH ARTICLE [I-II, Q. 73, Art. 5]

Whether Carnal Sins Are of Less Guilt Than Spiritual Sins?

Objection 1: It would seem that carnal sins are not of less guilt than spiritual sins. Because adultery is a more grievous sin than theft: for it is written (Prov. 6:30, 32): "The fault is not so great when a man has stolen ... but he that is an adulterer, for the folly of his heart shall destroy his own soul." Now theft belongs to covetousness, which is a spiritual sin; while adultery pertains to lust, which is a carnal sin. Therefore carnal sins are of greater guilt than spiritual sins.

Obj. 2: Further, Augustine says in his commentary on Leviticus [*The quotation is from De Civ. Dei ii, 4 and iv, 31.] that "the devil rejoices chiefly in lust and idolatry." But he rejoices more in the greater sin. Therefore, since lust is a carnal sin, it seems that the carnal sins are of most guilt.

Obj. 3: Further, the Philosopher proves (Ethic. vii, 6) that "it is more shameful to be incontinent in lust than in anger." But anger is a spiritual sin, according to Gregory (Moral. xxxi, 17); while lust pertains to carnal sins. Therefore carnal sin is more grievous than spiritual sin.

*On the contrary,* Gregory says (Moral. xxxiii, 11) that carnal sins are of less guilt, but of more shame than spiritual sins.

*I answer that,* Spiritual sins are of greater guilt than carnal sins: yet this does not mean that each spiritual sin is of greater guilt than each carnal sin; but that, considering the sole difference between spiritual and carnal, spiritual sins are more grievous than carnal sins, other things being equal. Three reasons may be assigned for this. The first is on the part of the subject: because spiritual sins belong to the spirit, to which it is proper to turn to God, and to turn away from Him; whereas carnal sins are consummated in the carnal pleasure of the appetite, to which it chiefly belongs to turn to goods of the body; so that carnal sin, as such, denotes more a *turning to* something, and for that reason, implies a closer cleaving; whereas spiritual sin denotes more a *turning from* something, whence the notion of guilt arises; and for this reason it involves greater guilt. A second reason may be taken on the part of the person against whom sin is committed: because carnal sin, as such, is against the sinner's own body, which he ought to love less, in the order of charity, than God and his neighbor, against whom he commits spiritual sins, and consequently spiritual sins, as such, are of greater guilt. A third reason may be taken from the motive, since the stronger the impulse to sin, the less grievous the sin, as we shall state further on (A. 6). Now carnal sins have a stronger impulse, viz. our innate concupiscence of the flesh. Therefore spiritual sins, as such, are of greater guilt.

Reply Obj. 1: Adultery belongs not only to the sin of lust, but also to the sin of injustice, and in this respect may be brought under the head of covetousness, as a gloss observes on Eph. 5:5. "No fornicator, or unclean, or covetous person," etc.; so that adultery is so much more grievous than theft, as a man loves his wife more than his chattels.

Reply Obj. 2: The devil is said to rejoice chiefly in the sin of lust, because it is of the greatest adhesion, and man can with difficulty be withdrawn from it. "For the desire of pleasure is insatiable," as the Philosopher states (Ethic. iii, 12).

Reply Obj. 3: As the Philosopher himself says (Ethic. vii, 6), the reason why it is more shameful to be incontinent in lust than in anger, is that lust partakes less of reason; and in the same sense he says (Ethic. iii, 10) that "sins of intemperance are most worthy of reproach, because they are about those pleasures which are common to us and irrational animals": hence, by these sins man is, so to speak, brutalized; for which same reason Gregory says (Moral. xxxi, 17) that they are more shameful.

SIXTH ARTICLE [I-II, Q. 73, Art. 6]

Whether the Gravity of a Sin Depends on Its Cause?

Objection 1: It would seem that the gravity of a sin does not depend on its cause. Because the greater a sin's cause, the more forcibly it moves to sin, and so the more difficult is it to resist. But sin is lessened by the fact that it is difficult to resist; for it denotes weakness in the sinner, if he cannot easily resist sin; and a sin that is due to weakness is deemed less grievous. Therefore sin does not derive its gravity from its cause.

Obj. 2: Further, concupiscence is a general cause of sin; wherefore a gloss on Rom. 7:7, "For I had not known concupiscence," says: "The law is good, since by forbidding concupiscence, it forbids all evils." Now the greater the concupiscence by which man is overcome, the less grievous his sin. Therefore the gravity of a sin is diminished by the greatness of its cause.

Obj. 3: Further, as rectitude of the reason is the cause of a virtuous act, so defect in the reason seems to be the cause of sin. Now the greater the defect in the reason, the less grievous the sin: so much so that he who lacks the use of reason, is altogether excused from sin, and he who sins through ignorance, sins less grievously. Therefore the gravity of a sin is not increased by the greatness of its cause.

*On the contrary,* If the cause be increased, the effect is increased. Therefore the greater the cause of sin, the more grievous the sin.

*I answer that,* In the genus of sin, as in every other genus, two causes may be observed. The first is the direct and proper cause of sin, and is the will to sin: for it is compared to the sinful act, as a tree to its fruit, as a gloss observes on Matt. 7:18, "A good tree cannot bring forth evil fruit": and the greater this cause is, the more grievous will the sin be, since the greater the will to sin, the more grievously does man sin.

The other causes of sin are extrinsic and remote, as it were, being those whereby the will is inclined to sin. Among these causes we must make a distinction; for some of them induce the will to sin in accord with the very nature of the will: such is the end, which is the proper object of the will; and by a such like cause sin is made more grievous, because a man sins more grievously if his will is induced to sin by the intention of a more evil end. Other causes incline the will to sin, against the nature and order of the will, whose natural inclination is to be moved freely of itself in accord with the judgment of reason. Wherefore those causes which weaken the judgment of reason (e.g. ignorance), or which weaken the free movement of the will, (e.g. weakness, violence, fear, or the like), diminish the gravity of sin, even as they diminish its voluntariness; and so much so, that if the act be altogether involuntary, it is no longer sinful.

Reply Obj. 1: This argument considers the extrinsic moving cause, which diminishes voluntariness. The increase of such a cause diminishes the sin, as stated.

Reply Obj. 2: If concupiscence be understood to include the movement of the will, then, where there is greater concupiscence, there is a greater sin. But if by concupiscence we understand a passion, which is a movement of the concupiscible power, then a greater concupiscence, forestalling the judgment of reason and the movement of the will, diminishes the sin, because the man who sins, being stimulated by a greater concupiscence, falls through a more grievous temptation, wherefore he is less to be blamed. On the other hand, if concupiscence be taken in this sense follows the judgment of reason, and the movement of the will, then the greater concupiscence, the graver the sin: because sometimes the movement of concupiscence is redoubled by the will tending unrestrainedly to its object.

Reply Obj. 3: This argument considers the cause which renders the act involuntary, and such a cause diminishes the gravity of sin, as stated.

SEVENTH ARTICLE [I-II, Q. 73, Art. 7]

Whether a Circumstance Aggravates a Sin?

Objection 1: It would seem that a circumstance does not aggravate a sin. Because sin takes its gravity from its species. Now a circumstance does not specify a sin, for it is an accident thereof. Therefore the gravity of a sin is not taken from a circumstance.

Obj. 2: Further, a circumstance is either evil or not: if it is evil, it causes, of itself, a species of evil; and if it is not evil, it cannot make a thing worse. Therefore a circumstance nowise aggravates a sin.

Obj. 3: Further, the malice of a sin is derived from its turning away (from God). But circumstances affect sin on the part of the object to which it turns. Therefore they do not add to the sin's malice.

*On the contrary,* Ignorance of a circumstance diminishes sin: for he who sins through ignorance of a circumstance, deserves to be forgiven (Ethic. iii, 1). Now this would not be the case unless a circumstance aggravated a sin. Therefore a circumstance makes a sin more grievous.

*I answer that,* As the Philosopher says in speaking of habits of virtue (Ethic. ii, 1, 2), "it is natural for a thing to be increased by that which causes it." Now it is evident that a sin is caused by a defect in some circumstance: because the fact that a man departs from the order of reason is due to his not observing the due circumstances in his action. Wherefore it is evident that it is natural for a sin to be aggravated by reason of its circumstances. This happens in three ways. First, in so far as a circumstance draws a sin from one kind to another: thus fornication is the intercourse of a man with one who is not his wife: but if to this be added the circumstance that the latter is the wife of another, the sin is drawn to another kind of sin, viz. injustice, in so far as he usurps another's property; and in this respect adultery is a more grievous sin than fornication. Secondly, a circumstance aggravates a sin, not by drawing it into another genus, but only by multiplying the ratio of sin: thus if a wasteful man gives both when he ought not, and to whom he ought not to give, he commits the same kind of sin in more ways than if he were to merely to give to whom he ought not, and for that very reason his sin is more grievous; even as that sickness is the graver which affects more parts of the body. Hence Cicero says (Paradox. iii) that "in taking his father's life a man commits many sins; for he outrages one who begot him, who fed him, who educated him, to whom he owes his lands, his house, his position in the republic." Thirdly, a circumstance aggravates a sin by adding to the deformity which the sin derives from another circumstance: thus, taking another's property constitutes the sin of theft; but if to this be added the circumstance that much is taken of another's property, the sin will be more grievous; although in itself, to take more or less has not the character of a good or of an evil act.

Reply Obj. 1: Some circumstances do specify a moral act, as stated above (Q. 18, A. 10). Nevertheless a circumstance which does not give the species, may aggravate a sin; because, even as the goodness of a thing is weighed, not only in reference to its species, but also in reference to an accident, so the malice of an act is measured, not only according to the species of that act, but also according to a circumstance.

Reply Obj. 2: A circumstance may aggravate a sin either way. For if it is evil, it does not follow that it constitutes the sin's species; because it may multiply the ratio of evil within the same species, as stated above. And if it be not evil, it may aggravate a sin in relation to the malice of another circumstance.

Reply Obj. 3: Reason should direct the action not only as regards the object, but also as regards every circumstance. Therefore one may turn aside from the rule of reason through corruption of any single circumstance; for instance, by doing something when one ought not or where one ought not; and to depart thus from the rule of reason suffices to make the act evil. This turning aside from the rule of reason results from man's turning away from God, to Whom man ought to be united by right reason.

EIGHTH ARTICLE [I-II, Q. 73, Art. 8]

Whether Sin Is Aggravated by Reason of Its Causing More Harm?

Objection 1: It would seem that a sin is not aggravated by reason of its causing more harm. Because the harm done is an issue consequent to the sinful act. But the issue of an act does not add to its goodness or malice, as stated above (Q. 20, A. 5). Therefore a sin is not aggravated on account of its causing more harm.

Obj. 2: Further, harm is inflicted by sins against our neighbor. Because no one wishes to harm himself: and no one can harm God, according to Job 35:6, 8: "If thy iniquities be multiplied, what shalt thou do against Him? ... Thy wickedness may hurt a man that is like thee." If, therefore, sins were aggravated through causing more harm, it would follow that sins against our neighbor are more grievous than sins against God or oneself.

Obj. 3: Further, greater harm is inflicted on a man by depriving him of the life of grace, than by taking away his natural life; because the life of grace is better than the life of nature, so far that man ought to despise his natural life lest he lose the life of grace. Now, speaking absolutely, a man who leads a woman to commit fornication deprives her of the life of grace by leading her into mortal sin. If therefore a sin were more grievous on account of its causing a greater harm, it would follow that fornication, absolutely speaking, is a more grievous sin than murder, which is evidently untrue. Therefore a sin is not more grievous on account of its causing a greater harm.

*On the contrary,* Augustine says (De Lib. Arb. iii, 14): "Since vice is contrary to nature, a vice is the more grievous according as it diminishes the integrity of nature." Now the diminution of the integrity of nature is a harm. Therefore a sin is graver according as it does more harm.

*I answer that,* Harm may bear a threefold relation to sin. Because sometimes the harm resulting from a sin is foreseen and intended, as when a man does something with a mind to harm another, e.g. a murderer or a thief. In this case the quantity of harm aggravates the sin directly, because then the harm is the direct object of the sin. Sometimes the harm is foreseen, but not intended; for instance, when a man takes a short cut through a field, the result being that he knowingly injures the growing crops, although his intention is not to do this harm, but to commit fornication. In this case again the quantity of the harm done aggravates the sin; indirectly, however, in so far, to wit, as it is owing to his will being strongly inclined to sin, that a man does not forbear from doing, to himself or to another, a harm which he would not wish simply. Sometimes, however, the harm is neither foreseen nor intended: and then if this harm is connected with the sin accidentally, it does not aggravate the sin directly; but, on account of his neglecting to consider the harm that might ensue, a man is deemed punishable for the evil results of his action if it be unlawful. If, on the other hand, the harm follow directly from the sinful act, although it be neither foreseen nor intended, it aggravates the sin directly, because whatever is directly consequent to a sin, belongs, in a manner, to the very species of that sin: for instance, if a man is a notorious fornicator, the result is that many are scandalized; and although such was not his intention, nor was it perhaps foreseen by him, yet it aggravates his sin directly.

But this does not seem to apply to penal harm, which the sinner himself incurs. Such like harm, if accidentally connected with the sinful act, and if neither foreseen nor intended, does not aggravate a sin, nor does it correspond with the gravity of the sin: for instance, if a man in running to slay, slips and hurts his foot. If, on the other hand, this harm is directly consequent to the sinful act, although perhaps it be neither foreseen nor intended, then greater harm does not make greater sin, but, *on the contrary,* a graver sin calls for the infliction of a greater harm. Thus, an unbeliever who has heard nothing about the pains of hell, would suffer greater pain in hell for a sin of murder than for a sin of theft: but his sin is not aggravated on account of his neither intending nor foreseeing this, as it would be in the case of a believer, who, seemingly, sins more grievously in the very fact that he despises a greater punishment, that he may satisfy his desire to sin; but the gravity of this harm is caused by the sole gravity of sin.

Reply Obj. 1: As we have already stated (Q. 20, A. 5), in treating of the goodness and malice of external actions, the result of an action if foreseen and intended adds to the goodness and malice of an act.

Reply Obj. 2: Although the harm done aggravates a sin, it does not follow that this alone renders a sin more grievous: in fact, it is inordinateness which of itself aggravates a sin. Wherefore the harm itself that ensues aggravates a sin, in so far only as it renders the act more inordinate. Hence it does not follow, supposing harm to be inflicted chiefly by sins against our neighbor, that such sins are the most grievous, since a much greater inordinateness is to be found in sins which man commits against God, and in some which he commits against himself. Moreover we might say that although no man can do God any harm in His substance, yet he can endeavor to do so in things concerning Him, e.g. by destroying faith, by outraging holy things, which are most grievous sins. Again, a man sometimes knowingly and freely inflicts harm on himself, as in the case of suicide, though this be referred finally to some apparent good, for example, delivery from some anxiety.

Reply Obj. 3: This argument does not prove, for two reasons: first, because the murderer intends directly to do harm to his neighbors; whereas the fornicator who solicits the woman intends not harm but pleasure; secondly, because murder is the direct and sufficient cause of bodily death; whereas no man can of himself be the sufficient cause of another's spiritual death, because no man dies spiritually except by sinning of his own will.

NINTH ARTICLE [I-II, Q. 73, Art. 9]

Whether a Sin Is Aggravated by Reason of the Condition of the Person Against Whom It Is Committed?

Objection 1: It would seem that sin is not aggravated by reason of the condition of the person against whom it is committed. For if this were the case a sin would be aggravated chiefly by being committed against a just and holy man. But this does not aggravate a sin: because a virtuous man who bears a wrong with equanimity is less harmed by the wrong done him, than others, who, through being scandalized, are also hurt inwardly. Therefore the condition of the person against whom a sin is committed does not aggravate the sin.

Obj. 2: Further, if the condition of the person aggravated the sin, this would be still more the case if the person be near of kin, because, as Cicero says (Paradox. iii): "The man who kills his slave sins once: he that takes his father's life sins many times." But the kinship of a person sinned against does not apparently aggravate a sin, because every man is most akin to himself; and yet it is less grievous to harm oneself than another, e.g. to kill one's own, than another's horse, as the Philosopher declares (Ethic. v, 11). Therefore kinship of the person sinned against does not aggravate the sin.

Obj. 3: Further, the condition of the person who sins aggravates a sin chiefly on account of his position or knowledge, according to Wis. 6:7: "The mighty shall be mightily tormented," and Luke 12:47: "The servant who knew the will of his lord ... and did it not ... shall be beaten with many stripes." Therefore, in like manner, on the part of the person sinned against, the sin is made more grievous by reason of his position and knowledge. But, apparently, it is not a more grievous sin to inflict an injury on a rich and powerful person than on a poor man, since "there is no respect of persons with God" (Col. 3:25), according to Whose judgment the gravity of a sin is measured. Therefore the condition of the person sinned against does not aggravate the sin.

*On the contrary,* Holy Writ censures especially those sins that are committed against the servants of God. Thus it is written (3 Kings 19:14): "They have destroyed Thy altars, they have slain Thy prophets with the sword." Moreover much blame is attached to the sin committed by a man against those who are akin to him, according to Micah 7:6: "the son dishonoreth the father, and the daughter riseth up against her mother." Furthermore sins committed against persons of rank are expressly condemned: thus it is written (Job 34:18): "Who saith to the king: 'Thou art an apostate'; who calleth rulers ungodly." Therefore the condition of the person sinned against aggravates the sin.

*I answer that,* The person sinned against is, in a manner, the object of the sin. Now it has been stated above (A. 3) that the primary gravity of a sin is derived from its object; so that a sin is deemed to be so much the more grave, as its object is a more principal end. But the principal ends of human acts are God, man himself, and his neighbor: for whatever we do, it is on account of one of these that we do it; although one of them is subordinate to the other. Therefore the greater or lesser gravity of a sin, in respect of the person sinned against, may be considered on the part of these three.

First, on the part of God, to Whom man is the more closely united, as he is more virtuous or more sacred to God: so that an injury inflicted on such a person redounds on to God according to Zech. 2:8: "He that toucheth you, toucheth the apple of My eye." Wherefore a sin is the more grievous, according as it is committed against a person more closely united to God by reason of personal sanctity, or official station. On the part of man himself, it is evident that he sins all the more grievously, according as the person against whom he sins, is more united to him, either through natural affinity or kindness received or any other bond; because he seems to sin against himself rather than the other, and, for this very reason, sins all the more grievously, according to Ecclus. 14:5: "He that is evil to himself, to whom will he be good?" On the part of his neighbor, a man sins the more grievously, according as his sin affects more persons: so that a sin committed against a public personage, e.g. a sovereign prince who stands in the place of the whole people, is more grievous than a sin committed against a private person; hence it is expressly prohibited (Ex. 22:28): "The prince of thy people thou shalt not curse." In like manner it would seem that an injury done to a person of prominence, is all the more grave, on account of the scandal and the disturbance it would cause among many people.

Reply Obj. 1: He who inflicts an injury on a virtuous person, so far as he is concerned, disturbs him internally and externally; but that the latter is not disturbed internally is due to his goodness, which does not extenuate the sin of the injurer.

Reply Obj. 2: The injury which a man inflicts on himself in those things which are subject to the dominion of his will, for instance his possessions, is less sinful than if it were inflicted on another, because he does it of his own will; but in those things that are not subject to the dominion of his will, such as natural and spiritual goods, it is a graver sin to inflict an injury on oneself: for it is more grievous for a man to kill himself than another. Since, however, things belonging to our neighbor are not subject to the dominion of our will, the argument fails to prove, in respect of injuries done to such like things, that it is less grievous to sin in their regard, unless indeed our neighbor be willing, or give his approval.

Reply Obj. 3: There is no respect for persons if God punishes more severely those who sin against a person of higher rank; for this is done because such an injury redounds to the harm of many.

TENTH ARTICLE [I-II, Q. 73, Art. 10]

Whether the Excellence of the Person Sinning Aggravates the Sin?

Objection 1: It would seem that the excellence of the person sinning does not aggravate the sin. For man becomes great chiefly by cleaving to God, according to Ecclus. 25:13: "How great is he that findeth wisdom and knowledge! but there is none above him that feareth the Lord." Now the more a man cleaves to God, the less is a sin imputed to him: for it is written (2 Paral. 30: 18, 19): "The Lord Who is good will show mercy to all them, who with their whole heart seek the Lord the God of their fathers; and will not impute it to them that they are not sanctified." Therefore a sin is not aggravated by the excellence of the person sinning.

Obj. 2: Further, "there is no respect of persons with God" (Rom. 2:11). Therefore He does not punish one man more than another, for one and the same sin. Therefore a sin is not aggravated by the excellence of the person sinning.

Obj. 3: Further, no one should reap disadvantage from good. But he would, if his action were the more blameworthy on account of his goodness. Therefore a sin is not aggravated by reason of the excellence of the person sinning.

*On the contrary,* Isidore says (De Summo Bono ii, 18): "A sin is deemed so much the more grievous as the sinner is held to be a more excellent person."

*I answer that,* Sin is twofold. There is a sin which takes us unawares on account of the weakness of human nature: and such like sins are less imputable to one who is more virtuous, because he is less negligent in checking those sins, which nevertheless human weakness does not allow us to escape altogether. But there are other sins which proceed from deliberation: and these sins are all the more imputed to man according as he is more excellent. Four reasons may be assigned for this. First, because a more excellent person, e.g. one who excels in knowledge and virtue, can more easily resist sin; hence Our Lord said (Luke 12:47) that the "servant who knew the will of his lord ... and did it not ... shall be beaten with many stripes." Secondly, on account of ingratitude, because every good in which a man excels, is a gift of God, to Whom man is ungrateful when he sins: and in this respect any excellence, even in temporal goods, aggravates a sin, according to Wis. 6:7: "The mighty shall be mightily tormented." Thirdly, on account of the sinful act being specially inconsistent with the excellence of the person sinning: for instance, if a prince were to violate justice, whereas he is set up as the guardian of justice, or if a priest were to be a fornicator, whereas he has taken the vow of chastity. Fourthly, on account of the example or scandal; because, as Gregory says (Pastor. i, 2): "Sin becomes much more scandalous, when the sinner is honored for his position": and the sins of the great are much more notorious and men are wont to bear them with more indignation.

Reply Obj. 1: The passage quoted alludes to those things which are done negligently when we are taken unawares through human weakness.

Reply Obj. 2: God does not respect persons in punishing the great more severely, because their excellence conduces to the gravity of their sin, as stated.

Reply Obj. 3: The man who excels in anything reaps disadvantage, not from the good which he has, but from his abuse thereof.

# QUESTION 74

OF THE SUBJECT OF SIN (In Ten Articles)

We must now consider the subject of vice or sin: under which head there are ten points of inquiry:

(1) Whether the will can be the subject of sin?

(2) Whether the will alone is the subject of sin?

(3) Whether the sensuality can be the subject of sin?

(4) Whether it can be the subject of mortal sin?

(5) Whether the reason can be the subject of sin?

(6) Whether morose delectation or non-morose delectation be subjected in the higher reason?

(7) Whether the sin of consent in the act of sin is subjected in the higher reason?

(8) Whether the lower reason can be the subject of mortal sin?

(9) Whether the higher reason can be the subject of venial sin?

(10) Whether there can be in the higher reason a venial sin directed to its proper object?

FIRST ARTICLE [I-II, Q. 74, Art. 1]

Whether the Will Is a Subject of Sin?

Objection 1: It would seem that the will cannot be a subject of sin. For Dionysius says (Div. Nom. iv) that "evil is outside the will and the intention." But sin has the character of evil. Therefore sin cannot be in the will.

Obj. 2: Further, the will is directed either to the good or to what seems good. Now from the fact that will wishes the good, it does not sin: and that it wishes what seems good but is not truly good, points to a defect in the apprehensive power rather than in the will. Therefore sin is nowise in the will.

Obj. 3: Further, the same thing cannot be both subject and efficient cause of sin: because "the efficient and the material cause do not coincide" (Phys. 2, text. 70). Now the will is the efficient cause of sin: because the first cause of sinning is the will, as Augustine states (De Duabus Anim. x, 10, 11). Therefore it is not the subject of sin.

*On the contrary,* Augustine says (Retract. i, 9) that "it is by the will that we sin, and live righteously."

*I answer that,* Sin is an act, as stated above (Q. 71, AA. 1, 6). Now some acts pass into external matter, e.g. *to cut* and to burn : and such acts have for their matter and subject, the thing into which the action passes: thus the Philosopher states (Phys. iii, text. 18) that "movement is the act of the thing moved, caused by a mover." On the other hand, there are acts which do not pass into external matter, but remain in the agent, e.g. *to desire* and to know : and such are all moral acts, whether virtuous or sinful. Consequently the proper subject of sin must needs be the power which is the principle of the act. Now since it is proper to moral acts that they are voluntary, as stated above (Q. 1, A. 1; Q. 18, A. 6), it follows that the will, which is the principle of voluntary acts, both of good acts, and of evil acts or sins, is the principle of sins. Therefore it follows that sin is in the will as its subject.

Reply Obj. 1: Evil is said to be outside the will, because the will does not tend to it under the aspect of evil. But since some evil is an apparent good, the will sometimes desires an evil, and in this sense is in the will.

Reply Obj. 2: If the defect in the apprehensive power were nowise subject to the will, there would be no sin, either in the will, or in the apprehensive power, as in the case of those whose ignorance is invincible. It remains therefore that when there is in the apprehensive power a defect that is subject to the will, this defect also is deemed a sin.

Reply Obj. 3: This argument applies to those efficient causes whose actions pass into external matter, and which do not move themselves, but move other things; the contrary of which is to be observed in the will; hence the argument does not prove.

SECOND ARTICLE [I-II, Q. 74, Art. 2]

Whether the Will Alone Is the Subject of Sin?

Objection 1: It would seem that the will alone is the subject of sin. For Augustine says (De Duabus Anim. x, 10) that "no one sins except by the will." Now the subject of sin is the power by which we sin. Therefore the will alone is the subject of sin.

Obj. 2: Further, sin is an evil contrary to reason. Now good and evil pertaining to reason are the object of the will alone. Therefore the will alone is the subject of sin.

Obj. 3: Further, every sin is a voluntary act, because, as Augustine states (De Lib. Arb. iii, 18) [*Cf. De Vera Relig. xiv.], "so true is it that every sin is voluntary, that unless it be voluntary, it is no sin at all." Now the acts of the other powers are not voluntary, except in so far as those powers are moved by the will; nor does this suffice for them to be the subject of sin, because then even the external members of the body, which are moved by the will, would be a subject of sin; which is clearly untrue. Therefore the will alone is the subject of sin.

*On the contrary,* Sin is contrary to virtue: and contraries are about one same thing. But the other powers of the soul, besides the will, are the subject of virtues, as stated above (Q. 56). Therefore the will is not the only subject of sin.

*I answer that,* As was shown above (A. 1), whatever is the a principle of a voluntary act is a subject of sin. Now voluntary acts are not only those which are elicited by the will, but also those which are commanded by the will, as we stated above (Q. 6, A. 4) in treating of voluntariness. Therefore not only the will can be a subject of sin, but also all those powers which can be moved to their acts, or restrained from their acts, by the will; and these same powers are the subjects of good and evil moral habits, because act and habit belong to the same subject.

Reply Obj. 1: We do not sin except by the will as first mover; but we sin by the other powers as moved by the will.

Reply Obj. 2: Good and evil pertain to the will as its proper objects; but the other powers have certain determinate goods and evils, by reason of which they can be the subject of virtue, vice, and sin, in so far as they partake of will and reason.

Reply Obj. 3: The members of the body are not principles but merely organs of action: wherefore they are compared to the soul which moves them, as a slave who is moved but moves no other. On the other hand, the internal appetitive powers are compared to reason as free agents, because they both act and are acted upon, as is made clear in *Polit.* i, 3. Moreover, the acts of the external members are actions that pass into external matter, as may be seen in the blow that is inflicted in the sin of murder. Consequently there is no comparison.

THIRD ARTICLE [I-II, Q. 74, Art. 3]

Whether There Can Be Sin in the Sensuality?

Objection 1: It would seem that there cannot be sin in the sensuality. For sin is proper to man who is praised or blamed for his actions. Now sensuality is common to us and irrational animals. Therefore sin cannot be in the sensuality.

Obj. 2: Further, "no man sins in what he cannot avoid," as Augustine states (De Lib. Arb. iii, 18). But man cannot prevent the movement of the sensuality from being inordinate, since "the sensuality ever remains corrupt, so long as we abide in this mortal life; wherefore it is signified by the serpent," as Augustine declares (De Trin. xii, 12, 13). Therefore the inordinate movement of the sensuality is not a sin.

Obj. 3: Further, that which man himself does not do is not imputed to him as a sin. Now "that alone do we seem to do ourselves, which we do with the deliberation of reason," as the Philosopher says (Ethic. ix, 8). Therefore the movement of the sensuality, which is without the deliberation of reason, is not imputed to a man as a sin.

*On the contrary,* It is written (Rom. 7:19): "The good which I will I do not; but the evil which I will not, that I do": which words Augustine explains (Contra Julian. iii, 26; De Verb. Apost. xii, 2, 3), as referring to the evil of concupiscence, which is clearly a movement of the sensuality. Therefore there can be sin in the sensuality.

*I answer that,* As stated above (AA. 2, 3), sin may be found in any power whose act can be voluntary and inordinate, wherein consists the nature of sin. Now it is evident that the act of the sensuality, or sensitive appetite, is naturally inclined to be moved by the will. Wherefore it follows that sin can be in the sensuality.

Reply Obj. 1: Although some of the powers of the sensitive part are common to us and irrational animals, nevertheless, in us, they have a certain excellence through being united to the reason; thus we surpass other animals in the sensitive part for as much as we have the powers of cogitation and reminiscence, as stated in the First Part (Q. 78, A. 4). In the same way our sensitive appetite surpasses that of other animals by reason of a certain excellence consisting in its natural aptitude to obey the reason; and in this respect it can be the principle of a voluntary action, and, consequently, the subject of sin.

Reply Obj. 2: The continual corruption of the sensuality is to be understood as referring to the *fomes,* which is never completely destroyed in this life, since, though the stain of original sin passes, its effect remains. However, this corruption of the *fomes* does not hinder man from using his rational will to check individual inordinate movements, if he be presentient of them, for instance by turning his thoughts to other things. Yet while he is turning his thoughts to something else, an inordinate movement may arise about this also: thus when a man, in order to avoid the movements of concupiscence, turns his thoughts away from carnal pleasures, to the considerations of science, sometimes an unpremeditated movement of vainglory will arise. Consequently, a man cannot avoid all such movements, on account of the aforesaid corruption: but it is enough, for the conditions of a voluntary sin, that he be able to avoid each single one.

Reply Obj. 3: Man does not do perfectly himself what he does without the deliberation of reason, since the principal part of man does nothing therein: wherefore such is not perfectly a human act; and consequently it cannot be a perfect act of virtue or of sin, but is something imperfect of that kind. Therefore such movement of the sensuality as forestalls the reason, is a venial sin, which is something imperfect in the genus of sin.

FOURTH ARTICLE [I-II, Q. 74, Art. 4]

Whether Mortal Sin Can Be in the Sensuality?

Objection 1: It would seem that mortal sin can be in the sensuality. Because an act is discerned by its object. Now it is possible to commit a mortal sin about the objects of the sensuality, e.g. about carnal pleasures. Therefore the act of the sensuality can be a mortal sin, so that mortal sin can be found in the sensuality.

Obj. 2: Further, mortal sin is opposed to virtue. But virtue can be in the sensuality; for temperance and fortitude are virtues of the irrational parts, as the Philosopher states (Ethic. iii, 10). Therefore, since it is natural to contraries to be about the same subject, sensuality can be the subject of mortal sin.

Obj. 3: Further, venial sin is a disposition to mortal sin. Now disposition and habit are in the same subject. Since therefore venial sin may be in the sensuality, as stated above (A. 3, ad 3), mortal sin can be there also.

*On the contrary,* Augustine says (Retract. i, 23): "The inordinate movement of concupiscence, which is the sin of the sensuality, can even be in those who are in a state of grace," in whom, however, mortal sin is not to be found. Therefore the inordinate movement of the sensuality is not a mortal sin.

*I answer that,* Just as a disorder which destroys the principle of the body's life causes the body's death, so too a disorder which destroys the principle of spiritual life, viz. the last end, causes spiritual death, which is mortal sin, as stated above (Q. 72, A. 5). Now it belongs to the reason alone, and not to the sensuality, to order anything to the end: and disorder in respect of the end can only belong to the power whose function it is to order others to the end. Wherefore mortal sin cannot be in the sensuality, but only in the reason.

Reply Obj. 1: The act of the sensuality can concur towards a mortal sin: yet the fact of its being a mortal sin is due, not to its being an act of the sensuality, but to its being an act of reason, to whom the ordering to the end belongs. Consequently mortal sin is imputed, not to the sensuality, but to reason.

Reply Obj. 2: An act of virtue is perfected not only in that it is an act of the sensuality, but still more in the fact of its being an act of reason and will, whose function it is to choose: for the act of moral virtue is not without the exercise of choice: wherefore the act of moral virtue, which perfects the appetitive power, is always accompanied by an act of prudence, which perfects the rational power; and the same applies to mortal sin, as stated (ad 1).

Reply Obj. 3: A disposition may be related in three ways to that to which it disposes: for sometimes it is the same thing and is in the same subject; thus inchoate science is a disposition to perfect science: sometimes it is in the same subject, but is not the same thing; thus heat is a disposition to the form of fire: sometimes it is neither the same thing, nor in the same subject, as in those things which are subordinate to one another in such a way that we can arrive at one through the other, e.g. goodness of the imagination is a disposition to science which is in the intellect. In this way the venial sin that is in the sensuality, may be a disposition to mortal sin, which is in the reason.

FIFTH ARTICLE [I-II, Q. 74, Art. 5]

Whether Sin Can Be in the Reason?

Objection 1: It would seem that sin cannot be in the reason. For the sin of any power is a defect thereof. But the fault of the reason is not a sin, *on the contrary,* it excuses sin: for a man is excused from sin on account of ignorance. Therefore sin cannot be in the reason.

Obj. 2: Further, the primary object of sin is the will, as stated above (A. 1). Now reason precedes the will, since it directs it. Therefore sin cannot be in the reason.

Obj. 3: Further, there can be no sin except about things which are under our control. Now perfection and defect of reason are not among those things which are under our control: since by nature some are mentally deficient, and some shrewd-minded. Therefore no sin is in the reason.

*On the contrary,* Augustine says (De Trin. xii, 12) that sin is in the lower and in the higher reason.

*I answer that,* The sin of any power is an act of that power, as we have clearly shown (AA. 1, 2, 3). Now reason has a twofold act: one is its proper act in respect of its proper object, and this is the act of knowing the truth; the other is the act of reason as directing the other powers. Now in both of these ways there may be sin in the reason. First, in so far as it errs in the knowledge of truth, which error is imputed to the reason as a sin, when it is in ignorance or error about what it is able and ought to know: secondly, when it either commands the inordinate movements of the lower powers, or deliberately fails to check them.

Reply Obj. 1: This argument considers the defect in the proper act of the reason in respect of its proper object, and with regard to the case when it is a defect of knowledge about something which one is unable to know: for then this defect of reason is not a sin, and excuses from sin, as is evident with regard to the actions of madmen. If, however, the defect of reason be about something which a man is able and ought to know, he is not altogether excused from sin, and the defect is imputed to him as a sin. The defect which belongs only to the act of directing the other powers, is always imputed to reason as a sin, because it can always obviate this defect by means of its proper act.

Reply Obj. 2: As stated above (Q. 17, A. 1), when we were treating of the acts of the will and reason, the will moves and precedes the reason, in one way, and the reason moves and precedes the will in another: so that both the movement of the will can be called rational, and the act of the reason, voluntary. Accordingly sin is found in the reason, either through being a voluntary defect of the reason, or through the reason being the principle of the will's act.

The Reply to the Third Objection is evident from what has been said (ad 1).

SIXTH ARTICLE [I-II, Q. 74, Art. 6]

Whether the Sin of Morose Delectation Is in the Reason?

Objection 1: It would seem that the sin of morose delectation is not in the reason. For delectation denotes a movement of the appetitive power, as stated above (Q. 31, A. 1). But the appetitive power is distinct from the reason, which is an apprehensive power. Therefore morose delectation is not in the reason.

Obj. 2: Further, the object shows to which power an act belongs, since it is through the act that the power is directed to its object. Now a morose delectation is sometimes about sensible goods, and not about the goods of the reason. Therefore the sin of morose delectation is not in the reason.

Obj. 3: Further, a thing is said to be morose [*From the Latin *mora* —delay] through taking a length of time. But length of time is no reason why an act should belong to a particular power. Therefore morose delectation does not belong to the reason.

*On the contrary,* Augustine says (De Trin. xii, 12) that "if the consent to a sensual delectation goes no further than the mere thought of the pleasure, I deem this to be like as though the woman alone had partaken of the forbidden fruit." Now "the woman" denotes the lower reason, as he himself explains (De Trin. xii, 12). Therefore the sin of morose delectation is in the reason.

*I answer that,* As stated (A. 5), sin may be in the reason, not only in respect of reason's proper act, but sometimes in respect of its directing human actions. Now it is evident that reason directs not only external acts, but also internal passions. Consequently when the reason fails in directing the internal passions, sin is said to be in the reason, as also when it fails in directing external actions. Now it fails, in two ways, in directing internal passions: first, when it commands unlawful passions; for instance, when a man deliberately provokes himself to a movement of anger, or of lust: secondly, when it fails to check the unlawful movement of a passion; for instance, when a man, having deliberately considered that a rising movement of passion is inordinate, continues, notwithstanding, to dwell ( *immoratur* ) upon it, and fails to drive it away. And in this sense the sin of morose delectation is said to be in the reason.

Reply Obj. 1: Delectation is indeed in the appetitive power as its proximate principle; but it is in the reason as its first mover, in accordance with what has been stated above (A. 1), viz. that actions which do not pass into external matter are subjected in their principles.

Reply Obj. 2: Reason has its proper elicited act about its proper object; but it exercises the direction of all the objects of those lower powers that can be directed by the reason: and accordingly delectation about sensible objects comes also under the direction of reason.

Reply Obj. 3: Delectation is said to be morose not from a delay of time, but because the reason in deliberating dwells ( *immoratur* ) thereon, and fails to drive it away, "deliberately holding and turning over what should have been cast aside as soon as it touched the mind," as Augustine says (De Trin. xii, 12).

SEVENTH ARTICLE [I-II, Q. 74, Art. 7]

Whether the Sin of Consent to the Act Is in the Higher Reason?

Objection 1: It would seem that the sin of consent to the act is not in the higher reason. For consent is an act of the appetitive power, as stated above (Q. 15, A. 1): whereas the reason is an apprehensive power. Therefore the sin of consent to the act is not in the higher reason.

Obj. 2: Further, "the higher reason is intent on contemplating and consulting the eternal law," as Augustine states (De Trin. xii, 7). [* *Rationes aeternae,* cf. I, Q. 15, AA. 2, 3, where as in similar passages *ratio* has been rendered by the English type, because St. Thomas was speaking of the Divine *idea* as the archetype of the creature. Hence the type or idea is a rule of conduct, and is identified with the eternal law, (cf. A. 8, Obj. 1; A. 9)]. But sometimes consent is given to an act, without consulting the eternal law: since man does not always think about Divine things, whenever he consents to an act. Therefore the sin of consent to the act is not always in the higher reason.

Obj. 3: Further, just as man can regulate his external actions according to the eternal law, so can he regulate his internal pleasures or other passions. But "consent to a pleasure without deciding to fulfil it by deed, belongs to the lower reason," as Augustine states (De Trin. xii, 2). Therefore the consent to a sinful act should also be sometimes ascribed to the lower reason.

Obj. 4: Further, just as the higher reason excels the lower, so does the reason excel the imagination. Now sometimes man proceeds to act through the apprehension of the power of imagination, without any deliberation of his reason, as when, without premeditation, he moves his hand, or foot. Therefore sometimes also the lower reason may consent to a sinful act, independently of the higher reason.

*On the contrary,* Augustine says (De Trin. xii, 12): "If the consent to the evil use of things that can be perceived by the bodily senses, so far approves of any sin, as to point, if possible, to its consummation by deed, we are to understand that the woman has offered the forbidden fruit to her husband."

*I answer that,* Consent implies a judgment about the thing to which consent is given. For just as the speculative reason judges and delivers its sentence about intelligible matters, so the practical reason judges and pronounces sentence on matters of action. Now we must observe that in every case brought up for judgment, the final sentence belongs to the supreme court, even as we see that in speculative matters the final sentence touching any proposition is delivered by referring it to the first principles; since, so long as there remains a yet higher principle, the question can yet be submitted to it: wherefore the judgment is still in suspense, the final sentence not being as yet pronounced. But it is evident that human acts can be regulated by the rule of human reason, which rule is derived from the created things that man knows naturally; and further still, from the rule of the Divine law, as stated above (Q. 19, A. 4). Consequently, since the rule of the Divine law is the higher rule, it follows that the ultimate sentence, whereby the judgment is finally pronounced, belongs to the higher reason which is intent on the eternal types. Now when judgment has to be pronounced on several points, the final judgment deals with that which comes last; and, in human acts, the action itself comes last, and the delectation which is the inducement to the action is a preamble thereto. Therefore the consent to an action belongs properly to the higher reason, while the preliminary judgment which is about the delectation belongs to the lower reason, which delivers judgment in a lower court: although the higher reason can also judge of the delectation, since whatever is subject to the judgment of the lower court, is subject also to the judgment of the higher court, but not conversely.

Reply Obj. 1: Consent is an act of the appetitive power, not absolutely, but in consequence of an act of reason deliberating and judging, as stated above (Q. 15, A. 3). Because the fact that the consent is finally given to a thing is due to the fact that the will tends to that upon which the reason has already passed its judgment. Hence consent may be ascribed both to the will and to the reason.

Reply Obj. 2: The higher reason is said to consent, from the very fact that it fails to direct the human act according to the Divine law, whether or not it advert to the eternal law. For if it thinks of God's law, it holds it in actual contempt: and if not, it neglects it by a kind of omission. Therefore the consent to a sinful act always proceeds from the higher reason: because, as Augustine says (De Trin. xii, 12), "the mind cannot effectively decide on the commission of a sin, unless by its consent, whereby it wields its sovereign power of moving the members to action, or of restraining them from action, it become the servant or slave of the evil deed."

Reply Obj. 3: The higher reason, by considering the eternal law, can direct or restrain the internal delectation, even as it can direct or restrain the external action: nevertheless, before the judgment of the higher reason is pronounced the lower reason, while deliberating the matter in reference to temporal principles, sometimes approves of this delectation: and then the consent to the delectation belongs to the lower reason. If, however, after considering the eternal law, man persists in giving the same consent, such consent will then belong to the higher reason.

Reply Obj. 4: The apprehension of the power of imagination is sudden and indeliberate: wherefore it can cause an act before the higher or lower reason has time to deliberate. But the judgment of the lower reason is deliberate, and so requires time, during which the higher reason can also deliberate; consequently, if by its deliberation it does not check the sinful act, this will deservedly be imputed to it.

EIGHTH ARTICLE [I-II, Q. 74, Art. 8]

Whether Consent to Delectation Is a Mortal Sin?

Objection 1: It would seem that consent to delectation is not a mortal sin, for consent to delectation belongs to the lower reason, which does not consider the eternal types, i.e. the eternal law, and consequently does not turn away from them. Now every mortal sin consists in turning away from the Divine law, as is evident from Augustine's definition of mortal sin, which was quoted above (Q. 71, A. 6). Therefore consent to delectation is not a mortal sin.

Obj. 2: Further, consent to a thing is not evil, unless the thing to which consent is given be evil. Now "the cause of anything being such is yet more so," or at any rate not less. Consequently the thing to which a man consents cannot be a lesser evil than his consent. But delectation without deed is not a mortal sin, but only a venial sin. Therefore neither is the consent to the delectation a mortal sin.

Obj. 3: Further, delectations differ in goodness and malice, according to the difference of the deeds, as the Philosopher states (Ethic. x, 3, 5). Now the inward thought is one thing, and the outward deed, e.g. fornication, is another. Therefore the delectation consequent to the act of inward thought, differs in goodness and malice from the pleasure of fornication, as much as the inward thought differs from the outward deed; and consequently there is a like difference of consent on either hand. But the inward thought is not a mortal sin, nor is the consent to that thought: and therefore neither is the consent to the delectation.

Obj. 4: Further, the external act of fornication or adultery is a mortal sin, not by reason of the delectation, since this is found also in the marriage act, but by reason of an inordinateness in the act itself. Now he that consents to the delectation does not, for this reason, consent to the inordinateness of the act. Therefore he seems not to sin mortally.

Obj. 5: Further, the sin of murder is more grievous than simple fornication. Now it is not a mortal sin to consent to the delectation resulting from the thought of murder. Much less therefore is it a mortal sin to consent to the delectation resulting from the thought of fornication.

Obj. 6: Further, the Lord's prayer is recited every day for the remission of venial sins, as Augustine asserts (Enchiridion lxxviii). Now Augustine teaches that consent to delectation may be driven away by means of the Lord's Prayer: for he says (De Trin. xii, 12) that "this sin is much less grievous than if it be decided to fulfil it by deed: wherefore we ought to ask pardon for such thoughts also, and we should strike our breasts and say: 'Forgive us our trespasses.'" Therefore consent to delectation is a venial sin.

*On the contrary,* Augustine adds after a few words: "Man will be altogether lost unless, through the grace of the Mediator, he be forgiven those things which are deemed mere sins of thought, since without the will to do them, he desires nevertheless to enjoy them." But no man is lost except through mortal sin. Therefore consent to delectation is a mortal sin.

*I answer that,* There have been various opinions on this point, for some have held that consent to delectation is not a mortal sin, but only a venial sin, while others have held it to be a mortal sin, and this opinion is more common and more probable. For we must take note that since every delectation results from some action, as stated in *Ethic.* x, 4, and again, that since every delectation may be compared to two things, viz. to the operation from which it results, and to the object in which a person takes delight. Now it happens that an action, just as a thing, is an object of delectation, because the action itself can be considered as a good and an end, in which the person who delights in it, rests. Sometimes the action itself, which results in delectation, is the object of delectation, in so far as the appetitive power, to which it belongs to take delight in anything, is brought to bear on the action itself as a good: for instance, when a man thinks and delights in his thought, in so far as his thought pleases him; while at other times the delight consequent to an action, e.g. a thought, has for its object another action, as being the object of his thought; and then his thought proceeds from the inclination of the appetite, not indeed to the thought, but to the action thought of. Accordingly a man who is thinking of fornication, may delight in either of two things: first, in the thought itself, secondly, in the fornication thought of. Now the delectation in the thought itself results from the inclination of the appetite to the thought; and the thought itself is not in itself a mortal sin; sometimes indeed it is only a venial sin, as when a man thinks of such a thing for no purpose; and sometimes it is no sin at all, as when a man has a purpose in thinking of it; for instance, he may wish to preach or dispute about it. Consequently such affection or delectation in respect of the thought of fornication is not a mortal sin in virtue of its genus, but is sometimes a venial sin and sometimes no sin at all: wherefore neither is it a mortal sin to consent to such a thought. In this sense the first opinion is true.

But that a man in thinking of fornication takes pleasure in the act thought of, is due to his desire being inclined to this act. Wherefore the fact that a man consents to such a delectation, amounts to nothing less than a consent to the inclination of his appetite to fornication: for no man takes pleasure except in that which is in conformity with his appetite. Now it is a mortal sin, if a man deliberately chooses that his appetite be conformed to what is in itself a mortal sin. Wherefore such a consent to delectation in a mortal sin, is itself a mortal sin, as the second opinion maintains.

Reply Obj. 1: Consent to delectation may be not only in the lower reason, but also in the higher reason, as stated above (A. 7). Nevertheless the lower reason may turn away from the eternal types, for, though it is not intent on them, as regulating according to them, which is proper to the higher reason, yet, it is intent on them, as being regulated according to them: and by turning from them in this sense, it may sin mortally; since even the acts of the lower powers and of the external members may be mortal sins, in so far as the direction of the higher reason fails in directing them according to the eternal types.

Reply Obj. 2: Consent to a sin that is venial in its genus, is itself a venial sin, and accordingly one may conclude that the consent to take pleasure in a useless thought about fornication, is a venial sin. But delectation in the act itself of fornication is, in its genus, a mortal sin: and that it be a venial sin before the consent is given, is accidental, viz. on account of the incompleteness of the act: which incompleteness ceases when the deliberate consent has been given, so that therefore it has its complete nature and is a mortal sin.

Reply Obj. 3: This argument considers the delectation which has the thought for its object.

Reply Obj. 4: The delectation which has an external act for its object, cannot be without complacency in the external act as such, even though there be no decision to fulfil it, on account of the prohibition of some higher authority: wherefore the act is inordinate, and consequently the delectation will be inordinate also.

Reply Obj. 5: The consent to delectation, resulting from complacency in an act of murder thought of, is a mortal sin also: but not the consent to delectation resulting from complacency in the thought of murder.

Reply Obj. 6: The Lord's Prayer is to be said in order that we may be preserved not only from venial sin, but also from mortal sin.

NINTH ARTICLE [I-II, Q. 74, Art. 9]

Whether There Can Be Venial Sin in the Higher Reason As Directing the Lower Powers?

Objection 1: It would seem that there cannot be venial sin in the higher reason as directing the lower powers, i.e. as consenting to a sinful act. For Augustine says (De Trin. xii, 7) that the "higher reason is intent on considering and consulting the eternal law." But mortal sin consists in turning away from the eternal law. Therefore it seems that there can be no other than mortal sin in the higher reason.

Obj. 2: Further, the higher reason is the principle of the spiritual life, as the heart is of the body's life. But the diseases of the heart are deadly. Therefore the sins of the higher reason are mortal.

Obj. 3: Further, a venial sin becomes a mortal sin if it be done out of contempt. But it would seem impossible to commit even a venial sin, deliberately, without contempt. Since then the consent of the higher reason is always accompanied by deliberate consideration of the eternal law, it seems that it cannot be without mortal sin, on account of the contempt of the Divine law.

*On the contrary,* Consent to a sinful act belongs to the higher reason, as stated above (A. 7). But consent to an act of venial sin is itself a venial sin. Therefore a venial sin can be in the higher reason.

*I answer that,* As Augustine says (De Trin. xii, 7), the higher reason "is intent on contemplating or consulting the eternal law"; it contemplates it by considering its truth; it consults it by judging and directing other things according to it: and to this pertains the fact that by deliberating through the eternal types, it consents to an act or dissents from it. Now it may happen that the inordinateness of the act to which it consents, is not contrary to the eternal law, in the same way as mortal sin is, because it does not imply aversion from the last end, but is beside that law, as an act of venial sin is. Therefore when the higher reason consents to the act of a venial sin, it does not turn away from the eternal law: wherefore it sins, not mortally, but venially.

This suffices for the Reply to the First Objection.

Reply Obj. 2: Disease of the heart is twofold: one which is in the very substance of the heart, and affects its natural consistency, and such a disease is always mortal: the other is a disease of the heart consisting in some disorder either of the movement or of the parts surrounding the heart, and such a disease is not always mortal. In like manner there is mortal sin in the higher reason whenever the order itself of the higher reason to its proper object which is the eternal law, is destroyed; but when the disorder leaves this untouched, the sin is not mortal but venial.

Reply Obj. 3: Deliberate consent to a sin does not always amount to contempt of the Divine law, but only when the sin is contrary to the Divine law.

TENTH ARTICLE [I-II, Q. 74, Art. 10]

Whether Venial Sin Can Be in the Higher Reason As Such?

Objection 1: It would seem that venial sin cannot be in the higher reason as such, i.e. as considering the eternal law. For the act of a power is not found to fail except that power be inordinately disposed with regard to its object. Now the object of the higher reason is the eternal law, in respect of which there can be no disorder without mortal sin. Therefore there can be no venial sin in the higher reason as such.

Obj. 2: Further, since the reason is a deliberative power, there can be no act of reason without deliberation. Now every inordinate movement in things concerning God, if it be deliberate, is a mortal sin. Therefore venial sin is never in the higher reason as such.

Obj. 3: Further, it happens sometimes that a sin which takes us unawares, is a venial sin. Now a deliberate sin is a mortal sin, through the reason, in deliberating, having recourse to some higher good, by acting against which, man sins more grievously; just as when the reason in deliberating about an inordinate pleasurable act, considers that it is contrary to the law of God, it sins more grievously in consenting, than if it only considered that it is contrary to moral virtue. But the higher reason cannot have recourse to any higher tribunal than its own object. Therefore if a movement that takes us unawares is not a mortal sin, neither will the subsequent deliberation make it a mortal sin; which is clearly false. Therefore there can be no venial sin in the higher reason as such.

*On the contrary,* A sudden movement of unbelief is a venial sin. But it belongs to the higher reason as such. Therefore there can be a venial sin in the higher reason as such.

*I answer that,* The higher reason regards its own object otherwise than the objects of the lower powers that are directed by the higher reason. For it does not regard the objects of the lower powers, except in so far as it consults the eternal law about them, and so it does not regard them save by way of deliberation. Now deliberate consent to what is a mortal sin in its genus, is itself a mortal sin; and consequently the higher reason always sins mortally, if the acts of the lower powers to which it consents are mortal sins.

With regard to its own object it has a twofold act, viz. simple *intuition,* and deliberation, in respect of which it again consults the eternal law about its own object. But in respect of simple intuition, it can have an inordinate movement about Divine things, as when a man suffers a sudden movement of unbelief. And although unbelief, in its genus, is a mortal sin, yet a sudden movement of unbelief is a venial sin, because there is no mortal sin unless it be contrary to the law of God. Now it is possible for one of the articles of faith to present itself to the reason suddenly under some other aspect, before the eternal law, i.e. the law of God, is consulted, or can be consulted, on the matter; as, for instance, when a man suddenly apprehends the resurrection of the dead as impossible naturally, and rejects it, as soon as he had thus apprehended it, before he has had time to deliberate and consider that this is proposed to our belief in accordance with the Divine law. If, however, the movement of unbelief remains after this deliberation, it is a mortal sin. Therefore, in sudden movements, the higher reason may sin venially in respect of its proper object, even if it be a mortal sin in its genus; or it may sin mortally in giving a deliberate consent; but in things pertaining to the lower powers, it always sins mortally, in things which are mortal sins in their genus, but not in those which are venial sins in their genus.

Reply Obj. 1: A sin which is against the eternal law, though it be mortal in its genus, may nevertheless be venial, on account of the incompleteness of a sudden action, as stated.

Reply Obj. 2: In matters of action, the simple intuition of the principles from which deliberation proceeds, belongs to the reason, as well as the act of deliberation: even as in speculative matters it belongs to the reason both to syllogize and to form propositions: consequently the reason also can have a sudden movement.

Reply Obj. 3: One and the same thing may be the subject of different considerations, of which one is higher than the other; thus the existence of God may be considered, either as possible to be known by the human reason, or as delivered to us by Divine revelation, which is a higher consideration. And therefore, although the object of the higher reason is, in its nature, something sublime, yet it is reducible to some yet higher consideration: and in this way, that which in the sudden movement was not a mortal sin, becomes a mortal sin in virtue of the deliberation which brought it into the light of a higher consideration, as was explained above.

## QUESTION 75

OF THE CAUSES OF SIN, IN GENERAL (In Four Articles)

We must now consider the causes of sin: (1) in

general; (2) in particular. Under the first head there are four points of inquiry:

(1) Whether sin has a cause?

(2) Whether it has an internal cause?

(3) Whether it has an external cause?

(4) Whether one sin is the cause of another?

FIRST ARTICLE [I-II, Q. 75, Art. 1]

Whether Sin Has a Cause?

Objection 1: It would seem that sin has no cause. For sin has the nature of evil, as stated above (Q. 71, A. 6). But evil has no cause, as Dionysius says (Div. Nom. iv). Therefore sin has no cause.

Obj. 2: Further, a cause is that from which something follows of necessity. Now that which is of necessity, seems to be no sin, for every sin is voluntary. Therefore sin has no cause.

Obj. 3: Further, if sin has a cause, this cause is either good or evil. It is not a good, because good produces nothing but good, for "a good tree cannot bring forth evil fruit" (Matt. 7:18). Likewise neither can evil be the cause of sin, because the evil of punishment is a sequel to sin, and the evil of guilt is the same as sin. Therefore sin has no cause.

*On the contrary,* Whatever is done has a cause, for, according to Job 5:6, "nothing upon earth is done without a cause." But sin is something done; since it a "word, deed, or desire contrary to the law of God." Therefore sin has a cause.

*I answer that,* A sin is an inordinate act. Accordingly, so far as it is an act, it can have a direct cause, even as any other act; but, so far as it is inordinate, it has a cause, in the same way as a negation or privation can have a cause. Now two causes may be assigned to a negation: in the first place, absence of the cause of affirmation; i.e. the negation of the cause itself, is the cause of the negation in itself; since the result of removing the cause is the removal of the effect: thus the absence of the sun is the cause of darkness. In the second place, the cause of an affirmation, of which a negation is a sequel, is the accidental cause of the resulting negation: thus fire by causing heat in virtue of its principal tendency, consequently causes a privation of cold. The first of these suffices to cause a simple negation. But, since the inordinateness of sin and of every evil is not a simple negation, but the privation of that which something ought naturally to have, such an inordinateness must needs have an accidental efficient cause. For that which naturally is and ought to be in a thing, is never lacking except on account of some impeding cause. And accordingly we are wont to say that evil, which consists in a certain privation, has a deficient cause, or an accidental efficient cause. Now every accidental cause is reducible to the direct cause. Since then sin, on the part of its inordinateness, has an accidental efficient cause, and on the part of the act, a direct efficient cause, it follows that the inordinateness of sin is a result of the cause of the act. Accordingly then, the will lacking the direction of the rule of reason and of the Divine law, and intent on some mutable good, causes the act of sin directly, and the inordinateness of the act, indirectly, and beside the intention: for the lack of order in the act results from the lack of direction in the will.

Reply Obj. 1: Sin signifies not only the privation of good, which privation is its inordinateness, but also the act which is the subject of that privation, which has the nature of evil: and how this evil has a cause, has been explained.

Reply Obj. 2: If this definition is to be verified in all cases, it must be understood as applying to a cause which is sufficient and not impeded. For it happens that a thing is the sufficient cause of something else, and that the effect does not follow of necessity, on account of some supervening impediment: else it would follow that all things happen of necessity, as is proved in *Metaph.* vi, text. 5. Accordingly, though sin has a cause, it does not follow that this is a necessary cause, since its effect can be impeded.

Reply Obj. 3: As stated above, the will in failing to apply the rule of reason or of the Divine law, is the cause of sin. Now the fact of not applying the rule of reason or of the Divine law, has not in itself the nature of evil, whether of punishment or of guilt, before it is applied to the act. Wherefore accordingly, evil is not the cause of the first sin, but some good lacking some other good.

SECOND ARTICLE [I-II, Q. 75, Art. 2]

Whether Sin Has an Internal Cause?

Objection 1: It would seem that sin has no internal cause. For that which is within a thing is always in it. If therefore sin had an internal cause, man would always be sinning, since given the cause, the effect follows.

Obj. 2: Further, a thing is not its own cause. But the internal movements of a man are sins. Therefore they are not the cause of sin.

Obj. 3: Further, whatever is within man is either natural or voluntary. Now that which is natural cannot be the cause of sin, for sin is contrary to nature, as Damascene states (De Fide Orth. ii, 3; iv, 21); while that which is voluntary, if it be inordinate, is already a sin. Therefore nothing intrinsic can be the cause of the first sin.

*On the contrary,* Augustine says (De Duabus Anim. x, 10, 11; Retract. i, 9) that "the will is the cause of sin."

*I answer that,* As stated above (A. 1), the direct cause of sin must be considered on the part of the act. Now we may distinguish a twofold internal cause of human acts, one remote, the other proximate. The proximate internal cause of the human act is the reason and will, in respect of which man has a free-will; while the remote cause is the apprehension of the sensitive part, and also the sensitive appetite. For just as it is due to the judgment of reason, that the will is moved to something in accord with reason, so it is due to an apprehension of the senses that the sensitive appetite is inclined to something; which inclination sometimes influences the will and reason, as we shall explain further on (Q. 77, A. 1). Accordingly a double interior cause of sin may be assigned; one proximate, on the part of the reason and will; and the other remote, on the part of the imagination or sensitive appetite.

But since we have said above (A. 1, ad 3) that the cause of sin is some apparent good as motive, yet lacking the due motive, viz. the rule of reason or the Divine law, this motive which is an apparent good, appertains to the apprehension of the senses and to the appetite; while the lack of the due rule appertains to the reason, whose nature it is to consider this rule; and the completeness of the voluntary sinful act appertains to the will, so that the act of the will, given the conditions we have just mentioned, is already a sin.

Reply Obj. 1: That which is within a thing as its natural power, is always in it: but that which is within it, as the internal act of the appetitive or apprehensive power, is not always in it. Now the power of the will is the potential cause of sin, but is made actual by the preceding movements, both of the sensitive part, in the first place, and afterwards, of the reason. For it is because a thing is proposed as appetible to the senses, and because the appetite is inclined, that the reason sometimes fails to consider the due rule, so that the will produces the act of sin. Since therefore the movements that precede it are not always actual, neither is man always actually sinning.

Reply Obj. 2: It is not true that all the internal acts belong to the substance of sin, for this consists principally in the act of the will; but some precede and some follow the sin itself.

Reply Obj. 3: That which causes sin, as a power produces its act, is natural; and again, the movement of the sensitive part, from which sin follows, is natural sometimes, as, for instance, when anyone sins through appetite for food. Yet sin results in being unnatural from the very fact that the natural rule fails, which man, in accord with his nature, ought to observe.

THIRD ARTICLE [I-II, Q. 75, Art. 3]

Whether Sin Has an External Cause?

Objection 1: It would seem that sin has no external cause. For sin is a voluntary act. Now voluntary acts belong to principles that are within us, so that they have no external cause. Therefore sin has no external cause.

Obj. 2: Further, as nature is an internal principle, so is the will. Now in natural things sin can be due to no other than an internal cause; for instance, the birth of a monster is due to the corruption of some internal principle. Therefore in the moral order, sin can arise from no other than an internal cause. Therefore it has no external cause.

Obj. 3: Further, if the cause is multiplied, the effect is multiplied. Now the more numerous and weighty the external inducements to sin are, the less is a man's inordinate act imputed to him as a sin. Therefore nothing external is a cause of sin.

*On the contrary,* It is written (Num. 21:16): "Are not these they, that deceived the children of Israel by the counsel of Balaam, and made you transgress against the Lord by the sin of Phogor?" Therefore something external can be a cause of sin.

*I answer that,* As stated above (A. 2), the internal cause of sin is both the will, as completing the sinful act, and the reason, as lacking the due rule, and the appetite, as inclining to sin. Accordingly something external might be a cause of sin in three ways, either by moving the will itself immediately, or by moving the reason, or by moving the sensitive appetite. Now, as stated above (Q. 9, A. 6; Q. 10, A. 4), none can move the will inwardly save God alone, who cannot be a cause of sin, as we shall prove further on (Q. 79, A. 1). Hence it follows that nothing external can be a cause of sin, except by moving the reason, as a man or devil by enticing to sin; or by moving the sensitive appetite, as certain external sensibles move it. Yet neither does external enticement move the reason, of necessity, in matters of action, nor do things proposed externally, of necessity move the sensitive appetite, except perhaps it be disposed thereto in a certain way; and even the sensitive appetite does not, of necessity, move the reason and will. Therefore something external can be a cause moving to sin, but not so as to be a sufficient cause thereof: and the will alone is the sufficient completive cause of sin being accomplished.

Reply Obj. 1: From the very fact that the external motive causes of sin do not lead to sin sufficiently and necessarily, it follows that it remains in our power to sin or not to sin.

Reply Obj. 2: The fact that sin has an internal cause does not prevent its having an external cause; for nothing external is a cause of sin, except through the medium of the internal cause, as stated.

Reply Obj. 3: If the external causes inclining to sin be multiplied, the sinful acts are multiplied, because they incline to the sinful act in both greater numbers and greater frequency. Nevertheless the character of guilt is lessened, since this depends on the act being voluntary and in our power.

FOURTH ARTICLE [I-II, Q. 75, Art. 4]

Whether One Sin Is a Cause of Another?

Objection 1: It would seem that one sin cannot be the cause of another. For there are four kinds of cause, none of which will fit in with one sin causing another. Because the end has the character of good; which is inconsistent with sin, which has the character of evil. In like manner neither can a sin be an efficient cause, since "evil is not an efficient cause, but is weak and powerless," as Dionysius declares (Div. Nom. iv). The material and formal cause seems to have no place except in natural bodies, which are composed of matter and form. Therefore sin cannot have either a material or a formal cause.

Obj. 2: Further, "to produce its like belongs to a perfect thing," as stated in *Meteor.* iv, 2 [*Cf. De Anima ii.]. But sin is essentially something imperfect. Therefore one sin cannot be a cause of another.

Obj. 3: Further, if one sin is the cause of a second sin, in the same way, yet another sin will be the cause of the first, and thus we go on indefinitely, which is absurd. Therefore one sin is not the cause of another.

*On the contrary,* Gregory says on Ezechiel (Hom. xi): "A sin that is not quickly blotted out by repentance, is both a sin and a cause of sin."

*I answer that,* Forasmuch as a sin has a cause on the part of the act of sin, it is possible for one sin to be the cause of another, in the same way as one human act is the cause of another. Hence it happens that one sin may be the cause of another in respect of the four kinds of causes. First, after the manner of an efficient or moving cause, both directly and indirectly. Indirectly, as that which removes an impediment is called an indirect cause of movement: for when man, by one sinful act, loses grace, or charity, or shame, or anything else that withdraws him from sin, he thereby falls into another sin, so that the first sin is the accidental cause of the second. Directly, as when, by one sinful act, man is disposed to commit more readily another like act: because acts cause dispositions and habits inclining to like acts. Secondly, after the manner of a material cause, one sin is the cause of another, by preparing its matter: thus covetousness prepares the matter for strife, which is often about the wealth a man has amassed together. Thirdly, after the manner of a final cause, one sin causes another, in so far as a man commits one sin for the sake of another which is his end; as when a man is guilty of simony for the end of ambition, or fornication for the purpose of theft. And since the end gives the form to moral matters, as stated above (Q. 1, A. 3; Q. 18, AA. 4, 6), it follows that one sin is also the formal cause of another: because in the act of fornication committed for the purpose of theft, the former is material while the latter is formal.

Reply Obj. 1: Sin, in so far as it is inordinate, has the character of evil; but, in so far as it is an act, it has some good, at least apparent, for its end: so that, as an act, but not as being inordinate, it can be the cause, both final and efficient, of another sin. A sin has matter, not *of which* but about which it is: and it has its form from its end. Consequently one sin can be the cause of another, in respect of the four kinds of cause, as stated above.

Reply Obj. 2: Sin is something imperfect on account of its moral imperfection on the part of its inordinateness. Nevertheless, as an act it can have natural perfection: and thus it can be the cause of another sin.

Reply Obj. 3: Not every cause of one sin is another sin; so there is no need to go on indefinitely: for one may come to one sin which is not caused by another sin.

## QUESTION 76

OF THE CAUSES OF SIN, IN PARTICULAR (In Four Articles)

We must now consider the causes of sin, in particular, and (1) The internal causes of sin; (2) its external causes; and (3) sins which are the causes of other sins. In view of what has been said above (A. 2), the first consideration will be threefold: so that in the first place we shall treat of ignorance, which is the cause of sin on the part of reason; secondly, of weakness or passion, which is the cause of sin on the part of the sensitive appetite; thirdly, of malice, which is the cause of sin on the part of the will.

Under the first head, there are four points of inquiry:

(1) Whether ignorance is a cause of sin?
(2) Whether ignorance is a sin?
(3) Whether it excuses from sin altogether?
(4) Whether it diminishes sin?

FIRST ARTICLE [I-II, Q. 76, Art. 1]

Whether Ignorance Can Be a Cause of Sin?

Objection 1: It would seem that ignorance cannot be a cause of sin: because a non-being is not the cause of anything. Now ignorance is a non-being, since it is a privation of knowledge. Therefore ignorance is not a cause of sin.

Obj. 2: Further, causes of sin should be reckoned in respect of sin being a *turning to* something, as was stated above (Q. 75, A. 1). Now ignorance seems to savor of turning away from something. Therefore it should not be reckoned a cause of sin.

Obj. 3: Further, every sin is seated in the will. Now the will does not turn to that which is not known, because its object is the good apprehended. Therefore ignorance cannot be a cause of sin.

*On the contrary,* Augustine says (De Nat. et Grat. lxvii) "that some sin through ignorance."

*I answer that,* According to the Philosopher (Phys. viii, 27) a moving cause is twofold, direct and indirect. A direct cause is one that moves by its own power, as the generator is the moving cause of heavy and light things. An indirect cause, is either one that removes an impediment, or the removal itself of an impediment: and it is in this way that ignorance can be the cause of a sinful act; because it is a privation of knowledge perfecting the reason that forbids the act of sin, in so far as it directs human acts.

Now we must observe that the reason directs human acts in accordance with a twofold knowledge, universal and particular: because in conferring about what is to be done, it employs a syllogism, the conclusion of which is an act of judgment, or of choice, or an operation. Now actions are about singulars: wherefore the conclusion of a practical syllogism is a singular proposition. But a singular proposition does not follow from a universal proposition, except through the medium of a particular proposition: thus a man is restrained from an act of parricide, by the knowledge that it is wrong to kill one's father, and that this man is his father. Hence ignorance about either of these two propositions, viz. of the universal principle which is a rule of reason, or of the particular circumstance, could cause an act of parricide. Hence it is clear that not every kind of ignorance is the cause of a sin, but that alone which removes the knowledge which would prevent the sinful act. Consequently if a man's will be so disposed that he would not be restrained from the act of parricide, even though he recognized his father, his ignorance about his father is not the cause of his committing the sin, but is concomitant with the sin: wherefore such a man sins, not "through ignorance" but "in ignorance," as the Philosopher states (Ethic. iii, 1).

Reply Obj. 1: Non-being cannot be the direct cause of anything: but it can be an accidental cause, as being the removal of an impediment.

Reply Obj. 2: As knowledge, which is removed by ignorance, regards sin as turning towards something, so too, ignorance of this respect of a sin is the cause of that sin, as removing its impediment.

Reply Obj. 3: The will cannot turn to that which is absolutely unknown: but if something be known in one respect, and unknown in another, the will can will it. It is thus that ignorance is the cause of sin: for instance, when a man knows that what he is killing is a man, but not that it is his own father; or when one knows that a certain act is pleasurable, but not that it is a sin.

SECOND ARTICLE [I-II, Q. 76, Art. 2]

Whether Ignorance Is a Sin?

Objection 1: It would seem that ignorance is not a sin. For sin is "a word, deed or desire contrary to God's law," as stated above (Q. 71, A. 5). Now ignorance does not denote an act, either internal or external. Therefore ignorance is not a sin.

Obj. 2: Further, sin is more directly opposed to grace than to knowledge. Now privation of grace is not a sin, but a punishment resulting from sin. Therefore ignorance which is privation of knowledge is not a sin.

Obj. 3: Further, if ignorance is a sin, this can only be in so far as it is voluntary. But if ignorance is a sin, through being voluntary, it seems that the sin will consist in the act itself of the will, rather than in the ignorance. Therefore the ignorance will not be a sin, but rather a result of sin.

Obj. 4: Further, every sin is taken away by repentance, nor does any sin, except only original sin, pass as to guilt, yet remain in act. Now ignorance is not removed by repentance, but remains in act, all its guilt being removed by repentance. Therefore ignorance is not a sin, unless perchance it be original sin.

Obj. 5: Further, if ignorance be a sin, then a man will be sinning, as long as he remains in ignorance. But ignorance is continual in the one who is ignorant. Therefore a person in ignorance would be continually sinning, which is clearly false, else ignorance would be a most grievous sin. Therefore ignorance is not a sin.

*On the contrary,* Nothing but sin deserves punishment. But ignorance deserves punishment, according to 1 Cor. 14:38: "If any man know not, he shall not be known." Therefore ignorance is a sin.

*I answer that,* Ignorance differs from nescience, in that nescience denotes mere absence of knowledge; wherefore whoever lacks knowledge about anything, can be said to be nescient about it: in which sense Dionysius puts nescience in the angels (Coel. Hier. vii). On the other hand, ignorance denotes privation of knowledge, i.e. lack of knowledge of those things that one has a natural aptitude to know. Some of these we are under an obligation to know, those, to wit, without the knowledge of which we are unable to accomplish a due act rightly. Wherefore all are bound in common to know the articles of faith, and the universal principles of right, and each individual is bound to know matters regarding his duty or state. Meanwhile there are other things which a man may have a natural aptitude to know, yet he is not bound to know them, such as the geometrical theorems, and contingent particulars, except in some individual case. Now it is evident that whoever neglects to have or do what he ought to have or do, commits a sin of omission. Wherefore through negligence, ignorance of what one is bound to know, is a sin; whereas it is not imputed as a sin to man, if he fails to know what he is unable to know. Consequently ignorance of such like things is called "invincible," because it cannot be overcome by study. For this reason such like ignorance, not being voluntary, since it is not in our power to be rid of it, is not a sin: wherefore it is evident that no invincible ignorance is a sin. On the other hand, vincible ignorance is a sin, if it be about matters one is bound to know; but not, if it be about things one is not bound to know.

Reply Obj. 1: As stated above (Q. 71, A. 6, ad 1), when we say that sin is a "word, deed or desire," we include the opposite negations, by reason of which omissions have the character of sin; so that negligence, in as much as ignorance is a sin, is comprised in the above definition of sin; in so far as one omits to say what one ought, or to do what one ought, or to desire what one ought, in order to acquire the knowledge which we ought to have.

Reply Obj. 2: Although privation of grace is not a sin in itself, yet by reason of negligence in preparing oneself for grace, it may have the character of sin, even as ignorance; nevertheless even here there is a difference, since man can acquire knowledge by his acts, whereas grace is not acquired by acts, but by God's favor.

Reply Obj. 3: Just as in a sin of transgression, the sin consists not only in the act of the will, but also in the act willed, which is commanded by the will; so in a sin of omission not only the act of the will is a sin, but also the omission, in so far as it is in some way voluntary; and accordingly, the neglect to know, or even lack of consideration is a sin.

Reply Obj. 4: Although when the guilt has passed away through repentance, the ignorance remains, according as it is a privation of knowledge, nevertheless the negligence does not remain, by reason of which the ignorance is said to be a sin.

Reply Obj. 5: Just as in other sins of omission, man sins actually only at the time at which the affirmative precept is binding, so is it with the sin of ignorance. For the ignorant man sins actually indeed, not continually, but only at the time for acquiring the knowledge that he ought to have.

THIRD ARTICLE [I-II, Q. 76, Art. 3]

Whether Ignorance Excuses from Sin Altogether?

Objection 1: It would seem that ignorance excuses from sin altogether. For as Augustine says (Retract. i, 9), every sin is voluntary. Now ignorance causes involuntariness, as stated above (Q. 6, A. 8). Therefore ignorance excuses from sin altogether.

Obj. 2: Further, that which is done beside the intention, is done accidentally. Now the intention cannot be about what is unknown. Therefore what a man does through ignorance is accidental in human acts. But what is accidental does not give the species. Therefore nothing that is done through ignorance in human acts, should be deemed sinful or virtuous.

Obj. 3: Further, man is the subject of virtue and sin, inasmuch as he is partaker of reason. Now ignorance excludes knowledge which perfects the reason. Therefore ignorance excuses from sin altogether.

*On the contrary,* Augustine says (De Lib. Arb. iii, 18) that "some things done through ignorance are rightly reproved." Now those things alone are rightly reproved which are sins. Therefore some things done through ignorance are sins. Therefore ignorance does not altogether excuse from sin.

*I answer that,* Ignorance, by its very nature, renders the act which it causes involuntary. Now it has already been stated (AA. 1, 2) that ignorance is said to cause the act which the contrary knowledge would have prevented; so that this act, if knowledge were to hand, would be contrary to the will, which is the meaning of the word involuntary. If, however, the knowledge, which is removed by ignorance, would not have prevented the act, on account of the inclination of the will thereto, the lack of this knowledge does not make that man unwilling, but not willing, as stated in *Ethic.* iii, 1: and such like ignorance which is not the cause of the sinful act, as already stated, since it does not make the act to be involuntary, does not excuse from sin. The same applies to any ignorance that does not cause, but follows or accompanies the sinful act.

On the other hand, ignorance which is the cause of the act, since it makes it to be involuntary, of its very nature excuses from sin, because voluntariness is essential to sin. But it may fail to excuse altogether from sin, and this for two reasons. First, on the part of the thing itself which is not known. For ignorance excuses from sin, in so far as something is not known to be a sin. Now it may happen that a person ignores some circumstance of a sin, the knowledge of which circumstance would prevent him from sinning, whether it belong to the substance of the sin, or not; and nevertheless his knowledge is sufficient for him to be aware that the act is sinful; for instance, if a man strike someone, knowing that it is a man (which suffices for it to be sinful) and yet be ignorant of the fact that it is his father, (which is a circumstance constituting another species of sin); or, suppose that he is unaware that this man will defend himself and strike him back, and that if he had known this, he would not have struck him (which does not affect the sinfulness of the act). Wherefore, though this man sins through ignorance, yet he is not altogether excused, because, not withstanding, he has knowledge of the sin. Secondly, this may happen on the part of the ignorance itself, because, to wit, this ignorance is voluntary, either directly, as when a man wishes of set purpose to be ignorant of certain things that he may sin the more freely; or indirectly, as when a man, through stress of work or other occupations, neglects to acquire the knowledge which would restrain him from sin. For such like negligence renders the ignorance itself voluntary and sinful, provided it be about matters one is bound and able to know. Consequently this ignorance does not altogether excuse from sin. If, however, the ignorance be such as to be entirely involuntary, either through being invincible, or through being of matters one is not bound to know, then such like ignorance excuses from sin altogether.

Reply Obj. 1: Not every ignorance causes involuntariness, as stated above (Q. 6, A. 8). Hence not every ignorance excuses from sin altogether.

Reply Obj. 2: So far as voluntariness remains in the ignorant person, the intention of sin remains in him: so that, in this respect, his sin is not accidental.

Reply Obj. 3: If the ignorance be such as to exclude the use of reason entirely, it excuses from sin altogether, as is the case with madmen and imbeciles: but such is not always the ignorance that causes the sin; and so it does not always excuse from sin altogether.

FOURTH ARTICLE [I-II, Q. 76, Art. 4]

Whether Ignorance Diminishes a Sin?

Objection 1: It would seem that ignorance does not diminish a sin. For that which is common to all sins does not diminish sin. Now ignorance is common to all sins, for the Philosopher says (Ethic. iii, 1) that "every evil man is ignorant." Therefore ignorance does not diminish sin.

Obj. 2: Further, one sin added to another makes a greater sin. But ignorance is itself a sin, as stated above (A. 2). Therefore it does not diminish a sin.

Obj. 3: Further, the same thing does not both aggravate and diminish sin. Now ignorance aggravates sin; for Ambrose commenting on Rom. 2:4, "Knowest thou not that the benignity of God leadeth thee to penance?" says: "Thy sin is most grievous if thou knowest not." Therefore ignorance does not diminish sin.

Obj. 4: Further, if any kind of ignorance diminishes a sin, this would seem to be chiefly the case as regards the ignorance which removes the use of reason altogether. Now this kind of ignorance does not diminish sin, but increases it: for the Philosopher says (Ethic. iii, 5) that the "punishment is doubled for a drunken man." Therefore ignorance does not diminish sin.

*On the contrary,* Whatever is a reason for sin to be forgiven, diminishes sin. Now such is ignorance, as is clear from 1 Tim. 1:13: "I obtained ... mercy ... because I did it ignorantly." Therefore ignorance diminishes or alleviates sin.

*I answer that,* Since every sin is voluntary, ignorance can diminish sin, in so far as it diminishes its voluntariness; and if it does not render it less voluntary, it nowise alleviates the sin. Now it is evident that the ignorance which excuses from sin altogether (through making it altogether involuntary) does not diminish a sin, but does away with it altogether. On the other hand, ignorance which is not the cause of the sin being committed, but is concomitant with it, neither diminishes nor increases the sin.

Therefore sin cannot be alleviated by any ignorance, but only by such as is a cause of the sin being committed, and yet does not excuse from the sin altogether. Now it happens sometimes that such like ignorance is directly and essentially voluntary, as when a man is purposely ignorant that he may sin more freely, and ignorance of this kind seems rather to make the act more voluntary and more sinful, since it is through the will's intention to sin that he is willing to bear the hurt of ignorance, for the sake of freedom in sinning. Sometimes, however, the ignorance which is the cause of a sin being committed, is not directly voluntary, but indirectly or accidentally, as when a man is unwilling to work hard at his studies, the result being that he is ignorant, or as when a man willfully drinks too much wine, the result being that he becomes drunk and indiscreet, and this ignorance diminishes voluntariness and consequently alleviates the sin. For when a thing is not known to be a sin, the will cannot be said to consent to the sin directly, but only accidentally; wherefore, in that case there is less contempt, and therefore less sin.

Reply Obj. 1: The ignorance whereby "every evil man is ignorant," is not the cause of sin being committed, but something resulting from that cause, viz. of the passion or habit inclining to sin.

Reply Obj. 2: One sin added to another makes more sins, but it does not always make a sin greater, since, perchance, the two sins do not coincide, but are separate. It may happen, if the first diminishes the second, that the two together have not the same gravity as one of them alone would have; thus murder is a more grievous sin if committed by a man when sober, than if committed by a man when drunk, although in the latter case there are two sins: because drunkenness diminishes the sinfulness of the resulting sin more than its own gravity implies.

Reply Obj. 3: The words of Ambrose may be understood as referring to simply affected ignorance; or they may have reference to a species of the sin of ingratitude, the highest degree of which is that man even ignores the benefits he has received; or again, they may be an allusion to the ignorance of unbelief, which undermines the foundation of the spiritual edifice.

Reply Obj. 4: The drunken man deserves a "double punishment" for the two sins which he commits, viz. drunkenness, and the sin which results from his drunkenness: and yet drunkenness, on account of the ignorance connected therewith, diminishes the resulting sin, and more, perhaps, than the gravity of the drunkenness implies, as stated above (ad 2). It might also be said that the words quoted refer to an ordinance of the legislator named Pittacus, who ordered drunkards to be more severely punished if they assaulted anyone; having an eye, not to the indulgence which the drunkard might claim, but to expediency, since more harm is done by the drunk than by the sober, as the Philosopher observes (Polit. ii).

# QUESTION 77

OF THE CAUSE OF SIN, ON THE PART OF THE SENSITIVE APPETITE (In Eight Articles)

We must now consider the cause of sin, on the part of the sensitive appetite, as to whether a passion of the soul may be a cause of sin: and under this head there are eight points of inquiry:

(1) Whether a passion of the sensitive appetite can move or incline the will?

(2) Whether it can overcome the reason against the latter's knowledge?

(3) Whether a sin resulting from a passion is a sin of weakness?

(4) Whether the passion of self-love is the cause of every sin?

(5) Of three causes mentioned in 1 John 2:16: "Concupiscence of the eyes, Concupiscence of the flesh," and "Pride of life."

(6) Whether the passion which causes a sin diminishes it?

(7) Whether passion excuses from sin altogether?

(8) Whether a sin committed through passion can be mortal?

FIRST ARTICLE [I-II, Q. 77, Art. 1]

Whether the Will Is Moved by a Passion of the Sensitive Appetite?

Objection 1: It would seem that the will is not moved by a passion of the sensitive appetite. For no passive power is moved except by its object. Now the will is a power both passive and active, inasmuch as it is mover and moved, as the Philosopher says of the appetitive power in general (De Anima iii, text. 54). Since therefore the object of the will is not a passion of the sensitive appetite, but good defined by the reason, it seems that a passion of the sensitive appetite does not move the will.

Obj. 2: Further, the higher mover is not moved by the lower; thus the soul is not moved by the body. Now the will, which is the rational appetite, is compared to the sensitive appetite, as a higher mover to a lower: for the Philosopher says (De Anima iii, text. 57) that "the rational appetite moves the sensitive appetite, even as, in the heavenly bodies, one sphere moves another." Therefore the will cannot be moved by a passion of the sensitive appetite.

Obj. 3: Further, nothing immaterial can be moved by that which is material. Now the will is an immaterial power, because it does not use a corporeal organ, since it is in the reason, as stated in De Anima iii, text. 42: whereas the sensitive appetite is a material force, since it is seated in an organ of the body. Therefore a passion of the sensitive appetite cannot move the intellective appetite.

*On the contrary,* It is written (Dan. 13:56): "Lust hath perverted thy heart."

*I answer that,* A passion of the sensitive appetite cannot draw or move the will directly; but it can do so indirectly, and this in two ways. First, by a kind of distraction: because, since all the soul's powers are rooted in the one essence of the soul, it follows of necessity that, when one power is intent in its act, another power becomes remiss, or is even altogether impeded, in its act, both because all energy is weakened through being divided, so that, *on the contrary,* through being centered on one thing, it is less able to be directed to several; and because, in the operations of the soul, a certain attention is requisite, and if this be closely fixed on one thing, less attention is given to another. In this way, by a kind of distraction, when the movement of the sensitive appetite is enforced in respect of any passion whatever, the proper movement of the rational appetite or will must, of necessity, become remiss or altogether impeded.

Secondly, this may happen on the part of the will's object, which is good apprehended by reason. Because the judgment and apprehension of reason is impeded on account of a vehement and inordinate apprehension of the imagination and judgment of the estimative power, as appears in those who are out of their mind. Now it is evident that the apprehension of the imagination and the judgment of the estimative power follow the passion of the sensitive appetite, even as the verdict of the taste follows the disposition of the tongue: for which reason we observe that those who are in some kind of passion, do not easily turn their imagination away from the object of their emotion, the result being that the judgment of the reason often follows the passion of the sensitive appetite, and consequently the will's movement follows it also, since it has a natural inclination always to follow the judgment of the reason.

Reply Obj. 1: Although the passion of the sensitive appetite is not the direct object of the will, yet it occasions a certain change in the judgment about the object of the will, as stated.

Reply Obj. 2: The higher mover is not directly moved by the lower; but, in a manner, it can be moved by it indirectly, as stated.

The Third Objection is solved in like manner.

SECOND ARTICLE [I-II, Q. 77, Art. 2]

Whether the Reason Can Be Overcome by a Passion, Against Its Knowledge?

Objection 1: It would seem that the reason cannot be overcome by a passion, against its knowledge. For the stronger is not overcome by the weaker. Now knowledge, on account of its certitude, is the strongest thing in us. Therefore it cannot be overcome by a passion, which is weak and soon passes away.

Obj. 2: Further, the will is not directed save to the good or the apparent good. Now when a passion draws the will to that which is really good, it does not influence the reason against its knowledge; and when it draws it to that which is good apparently, but not really, it draws it to that which appears good to the reason. But what appears to the reason is in the knowledge of the reason. Therefore a passion never influences the reason against its knowledge.

Obj. 3: Further, if it be said that it draws the reason from its knowledge of something in general, to form a contrary judgment about a particular matter—*on the contrary,* if a universal and a particular proposition be opposed, they are opposed by contradiction, e.g. "Every man," and "Not every man." Now if two opinions contradict one another, they are contrary to one another, as stated in *Peri Herm.* ii. If therefore anyone, while knowing something in general, were to pronounce an opposite judgment in a particular case, he would have two contrary opinions at the same time, which is impossible.

Obj. 4: Further, whoever knows the universal, knows also the particular which he knows to be contained in the universal: thus who knows that every mule is sterile, knows that this particular animal is sterile, provided he knows it to be a mule, as is clear from *Poster.* i, text. 2. Now he who knows something in general, e.g. that "no fornication is lawful," knows this general proposition to contain, for example, the particular proposition, "This is an act of fornication." Therefore it seems that his knowledge extends to the particular.

Obj. 5: Further, according to the Philosopher (Peri Herm. i), "words express the thoughts of the mind." Now it often happens that man, while in a state of passion, confesses that what he has chosen is an evil, even in that particular case. Therefore he has knowledge, even in particular.

Therefore it seems that the passions cannot draw the reason against its universal knowledge; because it is impossible for it to have universal knowledge together with an opposite particular judgment.

*On the contrary,* The Apostle says (Rom. 7:23): "I see another law in my members, fighting against the law of my mind, and captivating me in the law of sin." Now the law that is in the members is concupiscence, of which he had been speaking previously. Since then concupiscence is a passion, it seems that a passion draws the reason counter to its knowledge.

*I answer that,* As the Philosopher states (Ethic. vii, 2), the opinion of Socrates was that knowledge can never be overcome by passion; wherefore he held every virtue to be a kind of knowledge, and every sin a kind of ignorance. In this he was somewhat right, because, since the object of the will is a good or an apparent good, it is never moved to an evil, unless that which is not good appear good in some respect to the reason; so that the will would never tend to evil, unless there were ignorance or error in the reason. Hence it is written (Prov. 14:22): "They err that work evil."

Experience, however, shows that many act contrary to the knowledge that they have, and this is confirmed by Divine authority, according to the words of Luke 12:47: "The servant who knew that the will of his lord ... and did not ... shall be beaten with many stripes," and of James 4:17: "To him ... who knoweth to do good, and doth it not, to him it is a sin." Consequently he was not altogether right, and it is necessary, with the Philosopher (Ethic. vii, 3) to make a distinction. Because, since man is directed to right action by a twofold knowledge, viz. universal and particular, a defect in either of them suffices to hinder the rectitude of the will and of the deed, as stated above (Q. 76, A. 1). It may happen, then, that a man has some knowledge in general, e.g. that no fornication is lawful, and yet he does not know in particular that this act, which is fornication, must not be done; and this suffices for the will not to follow the universal knowledge of the reason. Again, it must be observed that nothing prevents a thing which is known habitually from not being considered actually: so that it is possible for a man to have correct knowledge not only in general but also in particular, and yet not to consider his knowledge actually: and in such a case it does not seem difficult for a man to act counter to what he does not actually consider. Now, that a man sometimes fails to consider in particular what he knows habitually, may happen through mere lack of attention: for instance, a man who knows geometry, may not attend to the consideration of geometrical conclusions, which he is ready to consider at any moment. Sometimes man fails to consider actually what he knows habitually, on account of some hindrance supervening, e.g. some external occupation, or some bodily infirmity; and, in this way, a man who is in a state of passion, fails to consider in particular what he knows in general, in so far as the passions hinder him from considering it. Now it hinders him in three ways. First, by way of distraction, as explained above (A. 1). Secondly, by way of opposition, because a passion often inclines to something contrary to what man knows in general. Thirdly, by way of bodily transmutation, the result of which is that the reason is somehow fettered so as not to exercise its act freely; even as sleep or drunkenness, on account of some change wrought on the body, fetters the use of reason. That this takes place in the passions is evident from the fact that sometimes, when the passions are very intense, man loses the use of reason altogether: for many have gone out of their minds through excess of love or anger. It is in this way that passion draws the reason to judge in particular, against the knowledge which it has in general.

Reply Obj. 1: Universal knowledge, which is most certain, does not hold the foremost place in action, but rather particular knowledge, since actions are about singulars: wherefore it is not astonishing that, in matters of action, passion acts counter to universal knowledge, if the consideration of particular knowledge be lacking.

Reply Obj. 2: The fact that something appears good in particular to the reason, whereas it is not good, is due to a passion: and yet this particular judgment is contrary to the universal knowledge of the reason.

Reply Obj. 3: It is impossible for anyone to have an actual knowledge or true opinion about a universal affirmative proposition, and at the same time a false opinion about a particular negative proposition, or vice versa: but it may well happen that a man has true habitual knowledge about a universal affirmative proposition, and actually a false opinion about a particular negative: because an act is directly opposed, not to a habit, but to an act.

Reply Obj. 4: He that has knowledge in a universal, is hindered, on account of a passion, from reasoning about that universal, so as to draw the conclusion: but he reasons about another universal proposition suggested by the inclination of the passion, and draws his conclusion accordingly. Hence the Philosopher says (Ethic. vii, 3) that the syllogism of an incontinent man has four propositions, two particular and two universal, of which one is of the son, e.g. No fornication is lawful, and the other, of passion, e.g. Pleasure is to be pursued. Hence passion fetters the reason, and hinders it from arguing and concluding under the first proposition; so that while the passion lasts, the reason argues and concludes under the second.

Reply Obj. 5: Even as a drunken man sometimes gives utterance to words of deep signification, of which, however, he is incompetent to judge, his drunkenness hindering him; so that a man who is in a state of passion, may indeed say in words that he ought not to do so and so, yet his inner thought is that he must do it, as stated in *Ethic.* vii, 3.

THIRD ARTICLE [I-II, Q. 77, Art. 3]

Whether a Sin Committed Through Passion, Should Be Called a Sin of Weakness?

Objection 1: It would seem that a sin committed through passion should not be called a sin of weakness. For a passion is a vehement movement of the sensitive appetite, as stated above (A. 1). Now vehemence of movements is evidence of strength rather than of weakness. Therefore a sin committed through passion, should not be called a sin of weakness.

Obj. 2: Further, weakness in man regards that which is most fragile in him. Now this is the flesh; whence it is written (Ps. 77:39): "He remembered that they are flesh." Therefore sins of weakness should be those which result from bodily defects, rather than those which are due to a passion.

Obj. 3: Further, man does not seem to be weak in respect of things which are subject to his will. Now it is subject to man's will, whether he do or do not the things to which his passions incline him, according to Gen. 4:7: "Thy appetite shall be under thee [*Vulg.: 'The lust thereof shall be under thee.'], and thou shalt have dominion over it." Therefore sin committed through passion is not a sin of weakness.

*On the contrary,* Cicero (De Quaest. Tusc. iv) calls the passions diseases of the soul. Now weakness is another name for disease. Therefore a sin that arises from passion should be called a sin of weakness.

*I answer that,* The cause of sin is on the part of the soul, in which, chiefly, sin resides. Now weakness may be applied to the soul by way of likeness to weakness of the body. Accordingly, man's body is said to be weak, when it is disabled or hindered in the execution of its proper action, through some disorder of the body's parts, so that the humors and members of the human body cease to be subject to its governing and motive power. Hence a member is said to be weak, when it cannot do the work of a healthy member, the eye, for instance, when it cannot see clearly, as the Philosopher states (De Hist. Animal. x, 1). Therefore weakness of the soul is when the soul is hindered from fulfilling its proper action on account of a disorder in its parts. Now as the parts of the body are said to be out of order, when they fail to comply with the order of nature, so too the parts of the soul are said to be inordinate, when they are not subject to the order of reason, for the reason is the ruling power of the soul's parts. Accordingly, when the concupiscible or irascible power is affected by any passion contrary to the order of reason, the result being that an impediment arises in the aforesaid manner to the due action of man, it is said to be a sin of weakness. Hence the Philosopher (Ethic. vii, 8) compares the incontinent man to an epileptic, whose limbs move in a manner contrary to his intention.

Reply Obj. 1: Just as in the body the stronger the movement against the order of nature, the greater the weakness, so likewise, the stronger the movement of passion against the order of reason, the greater the weakness of the soul.

Reply Obj. 2: Sin consists chiefly in an act of the will, which is not hindered by weakness of the body: for he that is weak in body may have a will ready for action, and yet be hindered by a passion, as stated above (A. 1). Hence when we speak of sins of weakness, we refer to weakness of soul rather than of body. And yet even weakness of soul is called weakness of the flesh, in so far as it is owing to a condition of the flesh that the passions of the soul arise in us through the sensitive appetite being a power using a corporeal organ.

Reply Obj. 3: It is in the will's power to give or refuse its consent to what passion inclines us to do, and it is in this sense that our appetite is said to be under us; and yet this consent or dissent of the will is hindered in the way already explained (A. 1).

FOURTH ARTICLE [I-II, Q. 77, Art. 4]

Whether Self-love Is the Source of Every Sin?

Objection 1: It would seem that self-love is not the source of every sin. For that which is good and right in itself is not the proper cause of sin. Now love of self is a good and right thing in itself: wherefore man is commanded to love his neighbor as himself (Lev. 19:18). Therefore self-love cannot be the proper cause of sin.

Obj. 2: Further, the Apostle says (Rom. 7:8): "Sin taking occasion by the commandment wrought in me all manner of concupiscence"; on which words a gloss says that "the law is good, since by forbidding concupiscence, it forbids all evils," the reason for which is that concupiscence is the cause of every sin. Now concupiscence is a distinct passion from love, as stated above (Q. 3, A. 2; Q. 23, A. 4). Therefore self-love is not the cause of every sin.

Obj. 3: Further, Augustine in commenting on Ps. 79:17, "Things set on fire and dug down," says that "every sin is due either to love arousing us to undue ardor or to fear inducing false humility." Therefore self-love is not the only cause of sin.

Obj. 4: Further, as man sins at times through inordinate love of self, so does he sometimes through inordinate love of his neighbor. Therefore self-love is not the cause of every sin.

*On the contrary,* Augustine says (De Civ. Dei xiv, 28) that "self-love, amounting to contempt of God, builds up the city of Babylon." Now every sin makes man a citizen of Babylon. Therefore self-love is the cause of every sin.

*I answer that,* As stated above (Q. 75, A. 1), the proper and direct cause of sin is to be considered on the part of the adherence to a mutable good; in which respect every sinful act proceeds from inordinate desire for some temporal good. Now the fact that anyone desires a temporal good inordinately, is due to the fact that he loves himself inordinately; for to wish anyone some good is to love him. Therefore it is evident that inordinate love of self is the cause of every sin.

Reply Obj. 1: Well ordered self-love, whereby man desires a fitting good for himself, is right and natural; but it is inordinate self-love, leading to contempt of God, that Augustine (De Civ. Dei xiv, 28) reckons to be the cause of sin.

Reply Obj. 2: Concupiscence, whereby a man desires good for himself, is reduced to self-love as to its cause, as stated.

Reply Obj. 3: Man is said to love both the good he desires for himself, and himself to whom he desires it. Love, in so far as it is directed to the object of desire (e.g. a man is said to love wine or money) admits, as its cause, fear which pertains to avoidance of evil: for every sin arises either from inordinate desire for some good, or from inordinate avoidance of some evil. But each of these is reduced to self-love, since it is through loving himself that man either desires good things, or avoids evil things.

Reply Obj. 4: A friend is like another self (Ethic. ix): wherefore the sin which is committed through love for a friend, seems to be committed through self-love.

FIFTH ARTICLE [I-II, Q. 77, Art. 5]

Whether Concupiscence of the Flesh, Concupiscence of the Eyes, and Pride of Life Are Fittingly Described As Causes of Sin?

Objection 1: It would seem that "concupiscence of the flesh, concupiscence of the eyes, and pride of life" are unfittingly described as causes of sin. Because, according to the Apostle (1 Tim. 6:10), "covetousness [*Douay: 'The desire of money'] is the root of all evils." Now pride of life is not included in covetousness. Therefore it should not be reckoned among the causes of sin.

Obj. 2: Further, concupiscence of the flesh is aroused chiefly by what is seen by the eyes, according to Dan. 13:56: "Beauty hath deceived thee." Therefore concupiscence of the eyes should not be condivided with concupiscence of the flesh.

Obj. 3: Further, concupiscence is desire for pleasure, as stated above (Q. 30, A. 2). Now objects of pleasure are perceived not only by the sight, but also by the other senses. Therefore "concupiscence of the hearing" and of the other senses should also have been mentioned.

Obj. 4: Further, just as man is induced to sin, through inordinate desire of good things, so is he also, through inordinate avoidance of evil things, as stated above (A. 4, ad 3). But nothing is mentioned here pertaining to avoidance of evil. Therefore the causes of sin are insufficiently described.

*On the contrary,* It is written (1 John 2:16): "All that is in the world is concupiscence of the flesh, or [Vulg.: 'and'] pride of life." Now a thing is said to be "in the world" by reason of sin: wherefore it is written (1 John 5:19): "The whole world is seated in wickedness." Therefore these three are causes of sin.

*I answer that,* As stated above (A. 4), inordinate self-love is the cause of every sin. Now self-love includes inordinate desire of good: for a man desires good for the one he loves. Hence it is evident that inordinate desire of good is the cause of every sin. Now good is, in two ways, the object of the sensitive appetite, wherein are the passions which are the cause of sin: first, absolutely, according as it is the object of the concupiscible part; secondly, under the aspect of difficulty, according as it is the object of the irascible part, as stated above (Q. 23, A. 1). Again, concupiscence is twofold, as stated above (Q. 30, A. 3). One is natural, and is directed to those things which sustain the nature of the body, whether as regards the preservation of the individual, such as food, drink, and the like, or as regards the preservation of the species, such as sexual matters: and the inordinate appetite of such things is called "concupiscence of the flesh." The other is spiritual concupiscence, and is directed to those things which do not afford sustentation or pleasure in respect of the fleshly senses, but are delectable in respect of the apprehension or imagination, or some similar mode of perception; such are money, apparel, and the like; and this spiritual concupiscence is called "concupiscence of the eyes," whether this be taken as referring to the sight itself, of which the eyes are the organ, so as to denote curiosity according to Augustine's exposition (Confess. x); or to the concupiscence of things which are proposed outwardly to the eyes, so as to denote covetousness, according to the explanation of others.

The inordinate appetite of the arduous good pertains to the "pride of life"; for pride is the inordinate appetite of excellence, as we shall state further on (Q. 84, A. 2; II-II, Q. 162, A. 1).

It is therefore evident that all passions that are a cause of sin can be reduced to these three: since all the passions of the concupiscible part can be reduced to the first two, and all the irascible passions to the third, which is not divided into two because all the irascible passions conform to spiritual concupiscence.

Reply Obj. 1: "Pride of life" is included in covetousness according as the latter denotes any kind of appetite for any kind of good. How covetousness, as a special vice, which goes by the name of "avarice," is the root of all sins, shall be explained further on (Q. 84, A. 1).

Reply Obj. 2: "Concupiscence of the eyes" does not mean here the concupiscence for all things which can be seen by the eyes, but only for such things as afford, not carnal pleasure in respect of touch, but in respect of the eyes, i.e. of any apprehensive power.

Reply Obj. 3: The sense of sight is the most excellent of all the senses, and covers a larger ground, as stated in *Metaph.* i: and so its name is transferred to all the other senses, and even to the inner apprehensions, as Augustine states (De Verb. Dom., serm. xxxiii).

Reply Obj. 4: Avoidance of evil is caused by the appetite for good, as stated above (Q. 25, A. 2; Q. 39, A. 2); and so those passions alone are mentioned which incline to good, as being the causes of those which cause inordinately the avoidance of evil.

SIXTH ARTICLE [I-II, Q. 77, Art. 6]

Whether Sin Is Alleviated on Account of a Passion?

Objection 1: It would seem that sin is not alleviated on account of passion. For increase of cause adds to the effect: thus if a hot thing causes something to melt, a hotter will do so yet more. Now passion is a cause of sin, as stated (A. 5). Therefore the more intense the passion, the greater the sin. Therefore passion does not diminish sin, but increases it.

Obj. 2: Further, a good passion stands in the same relation to merit, as an evil passion does to sin. Now a good passion increases merit: for a man seems to merit the more, according as he is moved by a greater pity to help a poor man. Therefore an evil passion also increases rather than diminishes a sin.

Obj. 3: Further, a man seems to sin the more grievously, according as he sins with a more intense will. But the passion that impels the will makes it tend with greater intensity to the sinful act. Therefore passion aggravates a sin.

*On the contrary,* The passion of concupiscence is called a temptation of the flesh. But the greater the temptation that overcomes a man, the less grievous his sin, as Augustine states (De Civ. Dei iv, 12).

*I answer that,* Sin consists essentially in an act of the free will, which is a faculty of the will and reason; while passion is a movement of the sensitive appetite. Now the sensitive appetite can be related to the free-will, antecedently and consequently: antecedently, according as a passion of the sensitive appetite draws or inclines the reason or will, as stated above (AA. 1, 2; Q. 10, A. 3); and consequently, in so far as the movements of the higher powers redound on to the lower, since it is not possible for the will to be moved to anything intensely, without a passion being aroused in the sensitive appetite.

Accordingly if we take passion as preceding the sinful act, it must needs diminish the sin: because the act is a sin in so far as it is voluntary, and under our control. Now a thing is said to be under our control, through the reason and will: and therefore the more the reason and will do anything of their own accord, and not through the impulse of a passion, the more is it voluntary and under our control. In this respect passion diminishes sin, in so far as it diminishes its voluntariness.

On the other hand, a consequent passion does not diminish a sin, but increases it; or rather it is a sign of its gravity, in so far, to wit, as it shows the intensity of the will towards the sinful act; and so it is true that the greater the pleasure or the concupiscence with which anyone sins, the greater the sin.

Reply Obj. 1: Passion is the cause of sin on the part of that to which the sinner turns. But the gravity of a sin is measured on the part of that from which he turns, which results accidentally from his turning to something else—accidentally, i.e. beside his intention. Now an effect is increased by the increase, not of its accidental cause, but of its direct cause.

Reply Obj. 2: A good passion consequent to the judgment of reason increases merit; but if it precede, so that a man is moved to do well, rather by his passion than by the judgment of his reason, such a passion diminishes the goodness and praiseworthiness of his action.

Reply Obj. 3: Although the movement of the will incited by the passion is more intense, yet it is not so much the will's own movement, as if it were moved to sin by the reason alone.

SEVENTH ARTICLE [I-II, Q. 77, Art. 7]

Whether Passion Excuses from Sin Altogether?

Objection 1: It would seem that passion excuses from sin altogether. For whatever causes an act to be involuntary, excuses from sin altogether. But concupiscence of the flesh, which is a passion, makes an act to be involuntary, according to Gal. 5:17: "The flesh lusteth against the spirit ... so that you do not the things that you would." Therefore passion excuses from sin altogether.

Obj. 2: Further, passion causes a certain ignorance of a particular matter, as stated above (A. 2; Q. 76, A. 3). But ignorance of a particular matter excuses from sin altogether, as stated above (Q. 6, A. 8). Therefore passion excuses from sin altogether.

Obj. 3: Further, disease of the soul is graver than disease of the body. But bodily disease excuses from sin altogether, as in the case of mad people. Much more, therefore, does passion, which is a disease of the soul.

*On the contrary,* The Apostle (Rom. 7:5) speaks of the passions as "passions of sins," for no other reason than that they cause sin: which would not be the case if they excused from sin altogether. Therefore passion does not excuse from sin altogether.

*I answer that,* An act which, in its genus, is evil, cannot be excused from sin altogether, unless it be rendered altogether involuntary. Consequently, if the passion be such that it renders the subsequent act wholly involuntary, it entirely excuses from sin; otherwise, it does not excuse entirely. In this matter two points apparently should be observed: first, that a thing may be voluntary either *in itself,* as when the will tends towards it directly; or *in its cause,* when the will tends towards that cause and not towards the effect; as is the case with one who wilfully gets drunk, for in that case he is considered to do voluntarily whatever he does through being drunk. Secondly, we must observe that a thing is said to be voluntary "directly" or "indirectly"; directly, if the will tends towards it; indirectly, if the will could have prevented it, but did not.

Accordingly therefore we must make a distinction: because a passion is sometimes so strong as to take away the use of reason altogether, as in the case of those who are mad through love or anger; and then if such a passion were voluntary from the beginning, the act is reckoned a sin, because it is voluntary in its cause, as we have stated with regard to drunkenness. If, however, the cause be not voluntary but natural, for instance, if anyone through sickness or some such cause fall into such a passion as deprives him of the use of reason, his act is rendered wholly involuntary, and he is entirely excused from sin. Sometimes, however, the passion is not such as to take away the use of reason altogether; and then reason can drive the passion away, by turning to other thoughts, or it can prevent it from having its full effect; since the members are not put to work, except by the consent of reason, as stated above (Q. 17, A. 9): wherefore such a passion does not excuse from sin altogether.

Reply Obj. 1: The words, "So that you do not the things that you would" are not to be referred to outward deeds, but to the inner movement of concupiscence; for a man would wish never to desire evil, in which sense we are to understand the words of Rom. 7:19: "The evil which I will not, that I do." Or again they may be referred to the will as preceding the passion, as is the case with the incontinent, who act counter to their resolution on account of their concupiscence.

Reply Obj. 2: The particular ignorance which excuses altogether, is ignorance of a circumstance, which a man is unable to know even after taking due precautions. But passion causes ignorance of law in a particular case, by preventing universal knowledge from being applied to a particular act, which passion the reason is able to drive away, as stated.

Reply Obj. 3: Bodily disease is involuntary: there would be a comparison, however, if it were voluntary, as we have stated about drunkenness, which is a kind of bodily disease.

EIGHTH ARTICLE [I-II, Q. 77, Art. 8]

Whether a Sin Committed Through Passion Can Be Mortal?

Objection 1: It would seem that sin committed through passion cannot be mortal. Because venial sin is condivided with mortal sin. Now sin committed from weakness is venial, since it has in itself a motive for pardon ( *venia* ). Since therefore sin committed through passion is a sin of weakness, it seems that it cannot be mortal.

Obj. 2: Further, the cause is more powerful than its effect. But passion cannot be a mortal sin, for there is no mortal sin in the sensuality, as stated above (Q. 74, A. 4). Therefore a sin committed through passion cannot be mortal.

Obj. 3: Further, passion is a hindrance to reason, as explained above (AA. 1, 2). Now it belongs to the reason to turn to God, or to turn away from Him, which is the essence of a mortal sin. Therefore a sin committed through passion cannot be mortal.

*On the contrary,* The Apostle says (Rom. 7:5) that "the passions of the sins ... work [Vulg.: 'did work'] in our members to bring forth fruit unto death." Now it is proper to mortal sin to bring forth fruit unto death. Therefore sin committed through passion may be mortal.

*I answer that,* Mortal sin, as stated above (Q. 72, A. 5), consists in turning away from our last end which is God, which aversion pertains to the deliberating reason, whose function it is also to direct towards the end. Therefore that which is contrary to the last end can happen not to be a mortal sin, only when the deliberating reason is unable to come to the rescue, which is the case in sudden movements. Now when anyone proceeds from passion to a sinful act, or to a deliberate consent, this does not happen suddenly: and so the deliberating reason can come to the rescue here, since it can drive the passion away, or at least prevent it from having its effect, as stated above: wherefore if it does not come to the rescue, there is a mortal sin; and it is thus, as we see, that many murders and adulteries are committed through passion.

Reply Obj. 1: A sin may be venial in three ways. First, through its cause, i.e. through having cause to be forgiven, which cause lessens the sin; thus a sin that is committed through weakness or ignorance is said to be venial. Secondly, through its issue; thus every sin, through repentance, becomes venial, i.e. receives pardon ( *veniam* ). Thirdly, by its genus, e.g. an idle word. This is the only kind of venial sin that is opposed to mortal sin: whereas the objection regards the first kind.

Reply Obj. 2: Passion causes sin as regards the adherence to something. But that this be a mortal sin regards the aversion, which follows accidentally from the adherence, as stated above (A. 6, ad 1): hence the argument does not prove.

Reply Obj. 3: Passion does not always hinder the act of reason altogether: consequently the reason remains in possession of its free-will, so as to turn away from God, or turn to Him. If, however, the use of reason be taken away altogether, the sin is no longer either mortal or venial.

# QUESTION 78

OF THAT CAUSE OF SIN WHICH IS MALICE (In Four Articles)

We must now consider the cause of sin on the part of the will, viz. malice: and under this head there are four points of inquiry:

(1) Whether it is possible for anyone to sin through certain malice, i.e. purposely?

(2) Whether everyone that sins through habit, sins through certain malice?

(3) Whether every one that sins through certain malice, sins through habit?

(4) Whether it is more grievous to sin through certain malice, than through passion?

FIRST ARTICLE [I-II, Q. 78, Art. 1]

Whether Anyone Sins Through Certain Malice?

Objection 1: It would seem that no one sins purposely, or through certain malice. Because ignorance is opposed to purpose or certain malice. Now "every evil man is ignorant," according to the Philosopher (Ethic. iii, 1); and it is written (Prov. 14:22): "They err that work evil." Therefore no one sins through certain malice.

Obj. 2: Further, Dionysius says (Div. Nom. iv) that "no one works intending evil." Now to sin through malice seems to denote the intention of doing evil [*Alluding to the derivation of *malitia* (malice) from malum (evil)] in sinning, because an act is not denominated from that which is unintentional and accidental. Therefore no one sins through malice.

Obj. 3: Further, malice itself is a sin. If therefore malice is a cause of sin, it follows that sin goes on causing sin indefinitely, which is absurd. Therefore no one sins through malice.

*On the contrary,* It is written (Job 34:27): "[Who] as it were on purpose have revolted from God [Vulg.: 'Him'], and would not understand all His ways." Now to revolt from God is to sin. Therefore some sin purposely or through certain malice.

*I answer that,* Man like any other being has naturally an appetite for the good; and so if his appetite incline away to evil, this is due to corruption or disorder in some one of the principles of man: for it is thus that sin occurs in the actions of natural things. Now the principles of human acts are the intellect, and the appetite, both rational (i.e. the will) and sensitive. Therefore even as sin occurs in human acts, sometimes through a defect of the intellect, as when anyone sins through ignorance, and sometimes through a defect in the sensitive appetite, as when anyone sins through passion, so too does it occur through a defect consisting in a disorder of the will. Now the will is out of order when it loves more the lesser good. Again, the consequence of loving a thing less is that one chooses to suffer some hurt in its regard, in order to obtain a good that one loves more: as when a man, even knowingly, suffers the loss of a limb, that he may save his life which he loves more. Accordingly when an inordinate will loves some temporal good, e.g. riches or pleasure, more than the order of reason or Divine law, or Divine charity, or some such thing, it follows that it is willing to suffer the loss of some spiritual good, so that it may obtain possession of some temporal good. Now evil is merely the privation of some good; and so a man wishes knowingly a spiritual evil, which is evil simply, whereby he is deprived of a spiritual good, in order to possess a temporal good: wherefore he is said to sin through certain malice or on purpose, because he chooses evil knowingly.

Reply Obj. 1: Ignorance sometimes excludes the simple knowledge that a particular action is evil, and then man is said to sin through ignorance: sometimes it excludes the knowledge that a particular action is evil at this particular moment, as when he sins through passion: and sometimes it excludes the knowledge that a particular evil is not to be suffered for the sake of possessing a particular good, but not the simple knowledge that it is an evil: it is thus that a man is ignorant, when he sins through certain malice.

Reply Obj. 2: Evil cannot be intended by anyone for its own sake; but it can be intended for the sake of avoiding another evil, or obtaining another good, as stated above: and in this case anyone would choose to obtain a good intended for its own sake, without suffering loss of the other good; even as a lustful man would wish to enjoy a pleasure without offending God; but with the two set before him to choose from, he prefers sinning and thereby incurring God's anger, to being deprived of the pleasure.

Reply Obj. 3: The malice through which anyone sins, may be taken to denote habitual malice, in the sense in which the Philosopher (Ethic. v, 1) calls an evil habit by the name of malice, just as a good habit is called virtue: and in this way anyone is said to sin through malice when he sins through the inclination of a habit. It may also denote actual malice, whether by malice we mean the choice itself of evil (and thus anyone is said to sin through malice, in so far as he sins through making a choice of evil), or whether by malice we mean some previous fault that gives rise to a subsequent fault, as when anyone impugns the grace of his brother through envy. Nor does this imply that a thing is its own cause: for the interior act is the cause of the exterior act, and one sin is the cause of another; not indefinitely, however, since we can trace it back to some previous sin, which is not caused by any previous sin, as was explained above (Q. 75, A. 4, ad 3).

SECOND ARTICLE [I-II, Q. 78, Art. 2]

Whether Everyone That Sins Through Habit, Sins Through Certain Malice?

Objection 1: It would seem that not every one who sins through habit, sins through certain malice. Because sin committed through certain malice, seems to be most grievous. Now it happens sometimes that a man commits a slight sin through habit, as when he utters an idle word. Therefore sin committed from habit is not always committed through certain malice.

Obj. 2: Further, "Acts proceeding from habits are like the acts by which those habits were formed" (Ethic. ii, 1, 2). But the acts which precede a vicious habit are not committed through certain malice. Therefore the sins that arise from habit are not committed through certain malice.

Obj. 3: Further, when a man commits a sin through certain malice, he is glad after having done it, according to Prov. 2:14: "Who are glad when they have done evil, and rejoice in most wicked things": and this, because it is pleasant to obtain what we desire, and to do those actions which are connatural to us by reason of habit. But those who sin through habit, are sorrowful after committing a sin: because "bad men," i.e. those who have a vicious habit, "are full of remorse" (Ethic. ix, 4). Therefore sins that arise from habit are not committed through certain malice.

*On the contrary,* A sin committed through certain malice is one that is done through choice of evil. Now we make choice of those things to which we are inclined by habit, as stated in Ethic. vi, 2 with regard to virtuous habits. Therefore a sin that arises from habit is committed through certain malice.

*I answer that,* There is a difference between a sin committed by one who has the habit, and a sin committed by habit: for it is not necessary to use a habit, since it is subject to the will of the person who has that habit. Hence habit is defined as being "something we use when we will," as stated above (Q. 50, A. 1). And thus, even as it may happen that one who has a vicious habit may break forth into a virtuous act, because a bad habit does not corrupt reason altogether, something of which remains unimpaired, the result being that a sinner does some works which are generically good; so too it may happen sometimes that one who has a vicious habit, acts, not from that habit, but through the uprising of a passion, or again through ignorance. But whenever he uses the vicious habit he must needs sin through certain malice: because to anyone that has a habit, whatever is befitting to him in respect of that habit, has the aspect of something lovable, since it thereby becomes, in a way, connatural to him, according as custom and habit are a second nature. Now the very thing which befits a man in respect of a vicious habit, is something that excludes a spiritual good: the result being that a man chooses a spiritual evil, that he may obtain possession of what befits him in respect of that habit: and this is to sin through certain malice. Wherefore it is evident that whoever sins through habit, sins through certain malice.

Reply Obj. 1: Venial sin does not exclude spiritual good, consisting in the grace of God or charity. Wherefore it is an evil, not simply, but in a relative sense: and for that reason the habit thereof is not a simple but a relative evil.

Reply Obj. 2: Acts proceeding from habits are of like species as the acts from which those habits were formed: but they differ from them as perfect from imperfect. Such is the difference between sin committed through certain malice and sin committed through passion.

Reply Obj. 3: He that sins through habit is always glad for what he does through habit, as long as he uses the habit. But since he is able not to use the habit, and to think of something else, by means of his reason, which is not altogether corrupted, it may happen that while not using the habit he is sorry for what he has done through the habit. And so it often happens that such a man is sorry for his sin not because sin in itself is displeasing to him, but on account of his reaping some disadvantage from the sin.

THIRD ARTICLE [I-II, Q. 78, Art. 3]

Whether One Who Sins Through Certain Malice, Sins Through Habit?

Objection 1: It would seem that whoever sins through certain malice, sins through habit. For the Philosopher says (Ethic. v, 9) that "an unjust action is not done as an unjust man does it," i.e. through choice, "unless it be done through habit." Now to sin through certain malice is to sin through making a choice of evil, as stated above (A. 1). Therefore no one sins through certain malice, unless he has the habit of sin.

Obj. 2: Further, Origen says (Peri Archon iii) that "a man is not suddenly ruined and lost, but must needs fall away little by little." But the greatest fall seems to be that of the man who sins through certain malice. Therefore a man comes to sin through certain malice, not from the outset, but from inveterate custom, which may engender a habit.

Obj. 3: Further, whenever a man sins through certain malice, his will must needs be inclined of itself to the evil he chooses. But by the nature of that power man is inclined, not to evil but to good. Therefore if he chooses evil, this must be due to something supervening, which is passion or habit. Now when a man sins through passion, he sins not through certain malice, but through weakness, as stated (Q. 77, A. 3). Therefore whenever anyone sins through certain malice, he sins through habit.

*On the contrary,* The good habit stands in the same relation to the choice of something good, as the bad habit to the choice of something evil. But it happens sometimes that a man, without having the habit of a virtue, chooses that which is good according to that virtue. Therefore sometimes also a man, without having the habit of a vice, may choose evil, which is to sin through certain malice.

*I answer that,* The will is related differently to good and to evil. Because from the very nature of the power, it is inclined to the rational good, as its proper object; wherefore every sin is said to be contrary to nature. Hence, if a will be inclined, by its choice, to some evil, this must be occasioned by something else. Sometimes, in fact, this is occasioned through some defect in the reason, as when anyone sins through ignorance; and sometimes this arises through the impulse of the sensitive appetite, as when anyone sins through passion. Yet neither of these amounts to a sin through certain malice; for then alone does anyone sin through certain malice, when his will is moved to evil of its own accord. This may happen in two ways. First, through his having a corrupt disposition inclining him to evil, so that, in respect of that disposition, some evil is, as it were, suitable and similar to him; and to this thing, by reason of its suitableness, the will tends, as to something good, because everything tends, of its own accord, to that which is suitable to it. Moreover this corrupt disposition is either a habit acquired by custom, or a sickly condition on the part of the body, as in the case of a man who is naturally inclined to certain sins, by reason of some natural corruption in himself. Secondly, the will, of its own accord, may tend to an evil, through the removal of some obstacle: for instance, if a man be prevented from sinning, not through sin being in itself displeasing to him, but through hope of eternal life, or fear of hell, if hope give place to despair, or fear to presumption, he will end in sinning through certain malice, being freed from the bridle, as it were.

It is evident, therefore, that sin committed through certain malice, always presupposes some inordinateness in man, which, however, is not always a habit: so that it does not follow of necessity, if a man sins through certain malice, that he sins through habit.

Reply Obj. 1: To do an action as an unjust man does, may be not only to do unjust things through certain malice, but also to do them with pleasure, and without any notable resistance on the part of reason, and this occurs only in one who has a habit.

Reply Obj. 2: It is true that a man does not fall suddenly into sin from certain malice, and that something is presupposed; but this something is not always a habit, as stated above.

Reply Obj. 3: That which inclines the will to evil, is not always a habit or a passion, but at times is something else. Moreover, there is no comparison between choosing good and choosing evil: because evil is never without some good of nature, whereas good can be perfect without the evil of fault.

FOURTH ARTICLE [I-II, Q. 78, Art. 4]

Whether It Is More Grievous to Sin Through Certain Malice Than Through Passion?

Objection 1: It would seem that it is not more grievous to sin through certain malice than through passion. Because ignorance excuses from sin either altogether or in part. Now ignorance is greater in one who sins through certain malice, than in one who sins through passion; since he that sins through certain malice suffers from the worst form of ignorance, which according to the Philosopher (Ethic. vii, 8) is ignorance of principle, for he has a false estimation of the end, which is the principle in matters of action. Therefore there is more excuse for one who sins through certain malice, than for one who sins through passion.

Obj. 2: Further, the more a man is impelled to sin, the less grievous his sin, as is clear with regard to a man who is thrown headlong into sin by a more impetuous passion. Now he that sins through certain malice, is impelled by habit, the impulse of which is stronger than that of passion. Therefore to sin through habit is less grievous than to sin through passion.

Obj. 3: Further, to sin through certain malice is to sin through choosing evil. Now he that sins through passion, also chooses evil. Therefore he does not sin less than the man who sins through certain malice.

*On the contrary,* A sin that is committed on purpose, for this very reason deserves heavier punishment, according to Job 34:26: "He hath struck them as being wicked, in open sight, who, as it were, on purpose, have revolted from Him." Now punishment is not increased except for a graver fault. Therefore a sin is aggravated through being done on purpose, i.e. through certain malice.

*I answer that,* A sin committed through malice is more grievous than a sin committed through passion, for three reasons. First, because, as sin consists chiefly in an act of the will, it follows that, other things being equal, a sin is all the more grievous, according as the movement of the sin belongs more to the will. Now when a sin is committed through malice, the movement of sin belongs more to the will, which is then moved to evil of its own accord, than when a sin is committed through passion, when the will is impelled to sin by something extrinsic, as it were. Wherefore a sin is aggravated by the very fact that it is committed through certain malice, and so much the more, as the malice is greater; whereas it is diminished by being committed through passion, and so much the more, as the passion is stronger. Secondly, because the passion which incites the will to sin, soon passes away, so that man repents of his sin, and soon returns to his good intentions; whereas the habit, through which a man sins, is a permanent quality, so that he who sins through malice, abides longer in his sin. For this reason the Philosopher (Ethic. vii, 8) compares the intemperate man, who sins through malice, to a sick man who suffers from a chronic disease, while he compares the incontinent man, who sins through passion, to one who suffers intermittently. Thirdly, because he who sins through certain malice is ill-disposed in respect of the end itself, which is the principle in matters of action; and so the defect is more dangerous than in the case of the man who sins through passion, whose purpose tends to a good end, although this purpose is interrupted on account of the passion, for the time being. Now the worst of all defects is defect of principle. Therefore it is evident that a sin committed through malice is more grievous than one committed through passion.

Reply Obj. 1: Ignorance of choice, to which the objection refers, neither excuses nor diminishes a sin, as stated above (Q. 76, A. 4). Therefore neither does a greater ignorance of the kind make a sin to be less grave.

Reply Obj. 2: The impulse due to passion, is, as it were, due to a defect which is outside the will: whereas, by a habit, the will is inclined from within. Hence the comparison fails.

Reply Obj. 3: It is one thing to sin while choosing, and another to sin through choosing. For he that sins through passion, sins while choosing, but not through choosing, because his choosing is not for him the first principle of his sin; for he is induced through the passion, to choose what he would not choose, were it not for the passion. On the other hand, he that sins through certain malice, chooses evil of his own accord, in the way already explained (AA. 2, 3), so that his choosing, of which he has full control, is the principle of his sin: and for this reason he is said to sin "through" choosing.

## QUESTION 79

OF THE EXTERNAL CAUSES OF SIN (In Four Articles)

We must now consider the external causes of sin, and (1) on the part of God; (2) on the part of the devil; (3) on the part of man.

Under the first head there are four points of inquiry:

(1) Whether God is a cause of sin?

(2) Whether the act of sin is from God?

(3) Whether God is the cause of spiritual blindness and hardness of heart?

(4) Whether these things are directed to the salvation of those who are blinded or hardened?

FIRST ARTICLE [I-II, Q. 79, Art. 1]

Whether God Is a Cause of Sin?

Objection 1: It would seem that God is a cause of sin. For the Apostle says of certain ones (Rom. 1:28): "God delivered them up to a reprobate sense, to do those things which are not right [Douay: 'convenient']," and a gloss comments on this by saying that "God works in men's hearts, by inclining their wills to whatever He wills, whether to good or to evil." Now sin consists in doing what is not right, and in having a will inclined to evil. Therefore God is to man a cause of sin.

Obj. 2: Further, it is written (Wis. 14:11): "The creatures of God are turned to an abomination; and a temptation to the souls of men." But a temptation usually denotes a provocation to sin. Since therefore creatures were made by God alone, as was established in the First Part (Q. 44, A. 1), it seems that God is a cause of sin, by provoking man to sin.

Obj. 3: Further, the cause of the cause is the cause of the effect. Now God is the cause of the free-will, which itself is the cause of sin. Therefore God is the cause of sin.

Obj. 4: Further, every evil is opposed to good. But it is not contrary to God's goodness that He should cause the evil of punishment; since of this evil it is written (Isa. 45:7) that God creates evil, and (Amos 3:6): "Shall there be evil in the city which God [Vulg.: 'the Lord'] hath not done?" Therefore it is not incompatible with God's goodness that He should cause the evil of fault.

*On the contrary,* It is written (Wis. 11:25): "Thou ... hatest none of the things which Thou hast made." Now God hates sin, according to Wis. 14:9: "To God the wicked and his wickedness are hateful." Therefore God is not a cause of sin.

*I answer that,* Man is, in two ways, a cause either of his own or of another's sin. First, directly, namely by inclining his or another's will to sin; secondly, indirectly, namely by not preventing someone from sinning. Hence (Ezech. 3:18) it is said to the watchman: "If thou say not to the wicked: 'Thou shalt surely die' [*Vulg.: "If, when I say to the wicked, 'Thou shalt surely die,' thou declare it not to him."] ... I will require his blood at thy hand." Now God cannot be directly the cause of sin, either in Himself or in another, since every sin is a departure from the order which is to God as the end: whereas God inclines and turns all things to Himself as to their last end, as Dionysius states (Div. Nom. i): so that it is impossible that He should be either to Himself or to another the cause of departing from the order which is to Himself. Therefore He cannot be directly the cause of sin. In like manner neither can He cause sin indirectly. For it happens that God does not give some the assistance, whereby they may avoid sin, which assistance were He to give, they would not sin. But He does all this according to the order of His wisdom and justice, since He Himself is Wisdom and Justice: so that if someone sin it is not imputable to Him as though He were the cause of that sin; even as a pilot is not said to cause the wrecking of the ship, through not steering the ship, unless he cease to steer while able and bound to steer. It is therefore evident that God is nowise a cause of sin.

Reply Obj. 1: As to the words of the Apostle, the solution is clear from the text. For if God delivered some up to a reprobate sense, it follows that they already had a reprobate sense, so as to do what was not right. Accordingly He is said to deliver them up to a reprobate sense, in so far as He does not hinder them from following that reprobate sense, even as we are said to expose a person to danger if we do not protect him. The saying of Augustine (De Grat. et Lib. Arb. xxi, whence the gloss quoted is taken) to the effect that "God inclines men's wills to good and evil," is to be understood as meaning that He inclines the will directly to good; and to evil, in so far as He does not hinder it, as stated above. And yet even this is due as being deserved through a previous sin.

Reply Obj. 2: When it is said the "creatures of God are turned 'to' an abomination, and a temptation to the souls of men," the preposition "to" does not denote causality but sequel [*This is made clear by the Douay Version: the Latin "factae sunt in abominationem" admits of the translation "were made to be an abomination," which might imply causality.]; for God did not make the creatures that they might be an evil to man; this was the result of man's folly, wherefore the text goes on to say, "and a snare to the feet of the unwise," who, to wit, in their folly, use creatures for a purpose other than that for which they were made.

Reply Obj. 3: The effect which proceeds from the middle cause, according as it is subordinate to the first cause, is reduced to that first cause; but if it proceed from the middle cause, according as it goes outside the order of the first cause, it is not reduced to that first cause: thus if a servant do anything contrary to his master's orders, it is not ascribed to the master as though he were the cause thereof. In like manner sin, which the free-will commits against the commandment of God, is not attributed to God as being its cause.

Reply Obj. 4: Punishment is opposed to the good of the person punished, who is thereby deprived of some good or other: but fault is opposed to the good of subordination to God; and so it is directly opposed to the Divine goodness; consequently there is no comparison between fault and punishment.

SECOND ARTICLE [I-II, Q. 79, Art. 2]

Whether the Act of Sin Is from God?

Objection 1: It would seem that the act of sin is not from God. For Augustine says (De Perfect. Justit. ii) that "the act of sin is not a thing." Now whatever is from God is a thing. Therefore the act of sin is not from God.

Obj. 2: Further, man is not said to be the cause of sin, except because he is the cause of the sinful act: for "no one works, intending evil," as Dionysius states (Div. Nom. iv). Now God is not a cause of sin, as stated above (A. 1). Therefore God is not the cause of the act of sin.

Obj. 3: Further, some actions are evil and sinful in their species, as was shown above (Q. 18, AA. 2, 8). Now whatever is the cause of a thing, causes whatever belongs to it in respect of its species. If therefore God caused the act of sin, He would be the cause of sin, which is false, as was proved above (A. 1). Therefore God is not the cause of the act of sin.

*On the contrary,* The act of sin is a movement of the free-will. Now "the will of God is the cause of every movement," as Augustine declares (De Trin. iii, 4, 9). Therefore God's will is the cause of the act of sin.

*I answer that,* The act of sin is both a being and an act; and in both respects it is from God. Because every being, whatever the mode of its being, must be derived from the First Being, as Dionysius declares (Div. Nom. v). Again every action is caused by something existing in act, since nothing produces an action save in so far as it is in act; and every being in act is reduced to the First Act, viz. God, as to its cause, Who is act by His Essence. Therefore God is the cause of every action, in so far as it is an action. But sin denotes a being and an action with a defect: and this defect is from the created cause, viz. the free-will, as falling away from the order of the First Agent, viz. God. Consequently this defect is not reduced to God as its cause, but to the free-will: even as the defect of limping is reduced to a crooked leg as its cause, but not to the motive power, which nevertheless causes whatever there is of movement in the limping. Accordingly God is the cause of the act of sin: and yet He is not the cause of sin, because He does not cause the act to have a defect.

Reply Obj. 1: In this passage Augustine calls by the name of "thing," that which is a thing simply, viz. substance; for in this sense the act of sin is not a thing.

Reply Obj. 2: Not only the act, but also the defect, is reduced to man as its cause, which defect consists in man not being subject to Whom he ought to be, although he does not intend this principally. Wherefore man is the cause of the sin: while God is the cause of the act, in such a way, that nowise is He the cause of the defect accompanying the act, so that He is not the cause of the sin.

Reply Obj. 3: As stated above (Q. 72, A. 1), acts and habits do not take their species from the privation itself, wherein consists the nature of evil, but from some object, to which that privation is united: and so this defect which consists in not being from God, belongs to the species of the act consequently, and not as a specific difference.

THIRD ARTICLE [I-II, Q. 79, Art. 3]

Whether God Is the Cause of Spiritual Blindness and Hardness of Heart?

Objection 1: It would seem that God is not the cause of spiritual blindness and hardness of heart. For Augustine says (Qq. lxxxiii, qu. 3) that God is not the cause of that which makes man worse. Now man is made worse by spiritual blindness and hardness of heart. Therefore God is not the cause of spiritual blindness and hardness of heart.

Obj. 2: Further, Fulgentius says (De Dupl. Praedest. i, 19): "God does not punish what He causes." Now God punishes the hardened heart, according to Ecclus. 3:27: "A hard heart shall fear evil at the last." Therefore God is not the cause of hardness of heart.

Obj. 3: Further, the same effect is not put down to contrary causes. But the cause of spiritual blindness is said to be the malice of man, according to Wis. 2:21: "For their own malice blinded them," and again, according to 2 Cor. 4:4: "The god of this world hath blinded the minds of unbelievers": which causes seem to be opposed to God. Therefore God is not the cause of spiritual blindness and hardness of heart.

*On the contrary,* It is written (Isa. 6:10): "Blind the heart of this people, and make their ears heavy," and Rom. 9:18: "He hath mercy on whom He will, and whom He will He hardeneth."

*I answer that,* Spiritual blindness and hardness of heart imply two things. One is the movement of the human mind in cleaving to evil, and turning away from the Divine light; and as regards this, God is not the cause of spiritual blindness and hardness of heart, just as He is not the cause of sin. The other thing is the withdrawal of grace, the result of which is that the mind is not enlightened by God to see aright, and man's heart is not softened to live aright; and as regards this God is the cause of spiritual blindness and hardness of heart.

Now we must consider that God is the universal cause of the enlightening of souls, according to John 1:9: "That was the true light which enlighteneth every man that cometh into this world," even as the sun is the universal cause of the enlightening of bodies, though not in the same way; for the sun enlightens by necessity of nature, whereas God works freely, through the order of His wisdom. Now although the sun, so far as it is concerned, enlightens all bodies, yet if it be encountered by an obstacle in a body, it leaves it in darkness, as happens to a house whose window-shutters are closed, although the sun is in no way the cause of the house being darkened, since it does not act of its own accord in failing to light up the interior of the house; and the cause of this is the person who closed the shutters. On the other hand, God, of His own accord, withholds His grace from those in whom He finds an obstacle: so that the cause of grace being withheld is not only the man who raises an obstacle to grace; but God, Who, of His own accord, withholds His grace. In this way, God is the cause of spiritual blindness, deafness of ear, and hardness of heart.

These differ from one another in respect of the effects of grace, which both perfects the intellect by the gift of wisdom, and softens the affections by the fire of charity. And since two of the senses excel in rendering service to the intellect, viz. sight and hearing, of which the former assists "discovery," and the latter, "teaching," hence it is that spiritual "blindness" corresponds to sight, "heaviness of the ears" to hearing, and "hardness of heart" to the affections.

Reply Obj. 1: Blindness and hardheartedness, as regards the withholding of grace, are punishments, and therefore, in this respect, they make man no worse. It is because he is already worsened by sin that he incurs them, even as other punishments.

Reply Obj. 2: This argument considers hardheartedness in so far as it is a sin.

Reply Obj. 3: Malice is the demeritorious cause of blindness, just as sin is the cause of punishment: and in this way too, the devil is said to blind, in so far as he induces man to sin.

FOURTH ARTICLE [I-II, Q. 79, Art. 4]

Whether Blindness and Hardness of Heart Are Directed to the Salvation of Those Who Are Blinded and Hardened?

Objection 1: It would seem that blindness and hardness of heart are always directed to the salvation of those who are blinded and hardened. For Augustine says (Enchiridion xi) that "as God is supremely good, He would nowise allow evil to be done, unless He could draw some good from every evil." Much more, therefore, does He direct to some good, the evil of which He Himself is the cause. Now God is the cause of blindness and hardness of heart, as stated above (A. 3). Therefore they are directed to the salvation of those who are blinded and hardened.

Obj. 2: Further, it is written (Wis. 1:13) that "God hath no pleasure in the destruction of the ungodly [*Vulg.: 'God made not death, neither hath He pleasure in the destruction of the living.']." Now He would seem to take pleasure in their destruction, if He did not turn their blindness to their profit: just as a physician would seem to take pleasure in torturing the invalid, if he did not intend to heal the invalid when he prescribes a bitter medicine for him. Therefore God turns blindness to the profit of those who are blinded.

Obj. 3: Further, "God is not a respecter of persons" (Acts 10:34). Now He directs the blinding of some, to their salvation, as in the case of some of the Jews, who were blinded so as not to believe in Christ, and, through not believing, to slay Him, and afterwards were seized with compunction, and converted, as related by Augustine (De Quaest. Evang. iii). Therefore God turns all blindness to the spiritual welfare of those who are blinded.

Obj. 4: On the other hand, according to Rom. 3:8, evil should not be done, that good may ensue. Now blindness is an evil. Therefore God does not blind some for the sake of their welfare.

*I answer that,* Blindness is a kind of preamble to sin. Now sin has a twofold relation—to one thing directly, viz. to the sinner's damnation—to another, by reason of God's mercy or providence, viz. that the sinner may be healed, in so far as God permits some to fall into sin, that by acknowledging their sin, they may be humbled and converted, as Augustine states (De Nat. et Grat. xxii). Therefore blindness, of its very nature, is directed to the damnation of those who are blinded; for which reason it is accounted an effect of reprobation. But, through God's mercy, temporary blindness is directed medicinally to the spiritual welfare of those who are blinded. This mercy, however, is not vouchsafed to all those who are blinded, but only to the predestinated, to whom "all things work together unto good" (Rom. 8:28). Therefore as regards some, blindness is directed to their healing; but as regards others, to their damnation; as Augustine says (De Quaest. Evang. iii).

Reply Obj. 1: Every evil that God does, or permits to be done, is directed to some good; yet not always to the good of those in whom the evil is, but sometimes to the good of others, or of the whole universe: thus He directs the sin of tyrants to the good of the martyrs, and the punishment of the lost to the glory of His justice.

Reply Obj. 2: God does not take pleasure in the loss of man, as regards the loss itself, but by reason of His justice, or of the good that ensues from the loss.

Reply Obj. 3: That God directs the blindness of some to their spiritual welfare, is due to His mercy; but that the blindness of others is directed to their loss is due to His justice: and that He vouchsafes His mercy to some, and not to all, does not make God a respecter of persons, as explained in the First Part (Q. 23, A. 5, ad 3).

Reply Obj. 4: Evil of fault must not be done, that good may ensue; but evil of punishment must be inflicted for the sake of good.

# QUESTION 80

OF THE CAUSE OF SIN, AS REGARDS THE DEVIL (In Four Articles)

We must now consider the cause of sin, as regards the devil; and under this head there are four points of inquiry:

(1) Whether the devil is directly the cause of sin?

(2) Whether the devil induces us to sin, by persuading us inwardly?

(3) Whether he can make us sin of necessity?

(4) Whether all sins are due to the devil's suggestion?

FIRST ARTICLE [I-II, Q. 80, Art. 1]

Whether the Devil Is Directly the Cause of Man's Sinning?

Objection 1: It would seem that the devil is directly the cause of man's sinning. For sin consists directly in an act of the appetite. Now Augustine says (De Trin. iv, 12) that "the devil inspires his friends with evil desires"; and Bede, commenting on Acts 5:3, says that the devil "draws the mind to evil desires"; and Isidore says (De Summo Bono ii, 41; iii, 5) that the devil "fills men's hearts with secret lusts." Therefore the devil is directly the cause of sin.

Obj. 2: Further, Jerome says (Contra Jovin. ii, 2) that "as God is the perfecter of good, so is the devil the perfecter of evil." But God is directly the cause of our good. Therefore the devil is directly the cause of our sins.

Obj. 3: Further, the Philosopher says in a chapter of the *Eudeme[a]n Ethics* (vii, 18): "There must needs be some extrinsic principle of human counsel." Now human counsel is not only about good things but also about evil things. Therefore, as God moves man to take good counsel, and so is the cause of good, so the devil moves him to take evil counsel, and consequently is directly the cause of sin.

*On the contrary,* Augustine proves (De Lib. Arb. i, 11) that "nothing else than his own will makes man's mind the slave of his desire." Now man does not become a slave to his desires, except through sin. Therefore the cause of sin cannot be the devil, but man's own will alone.

*I answer that,* Sin is an action: so that a thing can be directly the cause of sin, in the same way as anyone is directly the cause of an action; and this can only happen by moving that action's proper principle to act. Now the proper principle of a sinful action is the will, since every sin is voluntary. Consequently nothing can be directly the cause of sin, except that which can move the will to act.

Now the will, as stated above (Q. 9, AA. 3, 4, 6), can be moved by two things: first by its object, inasmuch as the apprehended appetible is said to move the appetite: secondly by that agent which moves the will inwardly to will, and this is no other than the will itself, or God, as was shown above (Q. 9, AA. 3, 4, 6). Now God cannot be the cause of sin, as stated above (Q. 79, A. 1). Therefore it follows that in this respect, a man's will alone is directly the cause of his sin.

As regards the object, a thing may be understood as moving the will in three ways. First, the object itself which is proposed to the will: thus we say that food arouses man's desire to eat. Secondly, he that proposes or offers this object. Thirdly, he that persuades the will that the object proposed has an aspect of good, because he also, in a fashion, offers the will its proper object, which is a real or apparent good of reason. Accordingly, in the first way the sensible things, which approach from without, move a man's will to sin. In the second and third ways, either the devil or a man may incite to sin, either by offering an object of appetite to the senses, or by persuading the reason. But in none of these three ways can anything be the direct cause of sin, because the will is not, of necessity, moved by any object except the last end, as stated above (Q. 10, AA. 1, 2). Consequently neither the thing offered from without, nor he that proposes it, nor he that persuades, is the sufficient cause of sin. Therefore it follows that the devil is a cause of sin, neither directly nor sufficiently, but only by persuasion, or by proposing the object of appetite.

Reply Obj. 1: All these, and other like authorities, if we meet with them, are to be understood as denoting that the devil induces man to affection for a sin, either by suggesting to him, or by offering him objects of appetite.

Reply Obj. 2: This comparison is true in so far as the devil is somewhat the cause of our sins, even as God is in a certain way the cause of our good actions, but does not extend to the mode of causation: for God causes good things in us by moving the will inwardly, whereas the devil cannot move us in this way.

Reply Obj. 3: God is the universal principle of all inward movements of man; but that the human will be determined to an evil counsel, is directly due to the human will, and to the devil as persuading or offering the object of appetite.

SECOND ARTICLE [I-II, Q. 80, Art. 2]

Whether the Devil Can Induce Man to Sin, by Internal Instigations?

Objection 1: It would seem that the devil cannot induce man to sin, by internal instigations. Because the internal movements of the soul are vital functions. Now no vital functions can be exercised except by an intrinsic principle, not even those of the vegetal soul, which are the lowest of vital functions. Therefore the devil cannot instigate man to evil through his internal movements.

Obj. 2: Further, all the internal movements arise from the external senses according to the order of nature. Now it belongs to God alone to do anything beside the order of nature, as was stated in the First Part (Q. 110, A. 4). Therefore the devil cannot effect anything in man's internal movements, except in respect of things which are perceived by the external senses.

Obj. 3: Further, the internal acts of the soul are to understand and to imagine. Now the devil can do nothing in connection with either of these, because, as stated in the First Part (Q. 111, AA. 2, 3, ad 2), the devil cannot impress species on the human intellect, nor does it seem possible for him to produce imaginary species, since imaginary forms, being more spiritual, are more excellent than those which are in sensible matter, which, nevertheless, the devil is unable to produce, as is clear from what we have said in the First Part (Q. 110, A. 2; Q. 111, AA. 2, 3, ad 2). Therefore the devil cannot through man's internal movements induce him to sin.

*On the contrary,* In that case, the devil would never tempt man, unless he appeared visibly; which is evidently false.

*I answer that,* The interior part of the soul is intellective and sensitive; and the intellective part contains the intellect and the will. As regards the will, we have already stated (A. 1; I, Q. 111, A. 1) what is the devil's relation thereto. Now the intellect, of its very nature, is moved by that which enlightens it in the knowledge of truth, which the devil has no intention of doing in man's regard; rather does he darken man's reason so that it may consent to sin, which darkness is due to the imagination and sensitive appetite. Consequently the operation of the devil seems to be confined to the imagination and sensitive appetite, by moving either of which he can induce man to sin. For his operation may result in presenting certain forms to the imagination; and he is able to incite the sensitive appetite to some passion or other.

The reason of this is, that as stated in the First Part (Q. 110, A. 3), the corporeal nature has a natural aptitude to be moved locally by the spiritual nature: so that the devil can produce all those effects which can result from the local movement of bodies here below, except he be restrained by the Divine power. Now the representation of forms to the imagination is due, sometimes, to local movement: for the Philosopher says (De Somno et Vigil.) [*De Insomn. iii, iv.] that "when an animal sleeps, the blood descends in abundance to the sensitive principle, and the movements descend with it, viz. the impressions left by the action of sensible objects, which impressions are preserved by means of sensible species, and continue to move the apprehensive principle, so that they appear just as though the sensitive principles were being affected by them at the time." Hence such a local movement of the vital spirits or humors can be procured by the demons, whether man sleep or wake: and so it happens that man's imagination is brought into play.

In like manner, the sensitive appetite is incited to certain passions according to certain fixed movements of the heart and the vital spirits: wherefore the devil can cooperate in this also. And through certain passions being aroused in the sensitive appetite, the result is that man more easily perceives the movement or sensible image which is brought in the manner explained, before the apprehensive principle, since, as the Philosopher observes (De Somno et Virgil.: De Insomn. iii, iv), "lovers are moved, by even a slight likeness, to an apprehension of the beloved." It also happens, through the rousing of a passion, that what is put before the imagination, is judged, as being something to be pursued, because, to him who is held by a passion, whatever the passion inclines him to, seems good. In this way the devil induces man inwardly to sin.

Reply Obj. 1: Although vital functions are always from an intrinsic principle, yet an extrinsic agent can cooperate with them, even as external heat cooperates with the functions of the vegetal soul, that food may be more easily digested.

Reply Obj. 2: This apparition of imaginary forms is not altogether outside the order of nature, nor is it due to a command alone, but according to local movement, as explained above.

Consequently the Reply to the Third Objection is clear, because these forms are received originally from the senses.

THIRD ARTICLE [I-II, Q, 80, Art. 3]

Whether the Devil Can Induce Man to Sin of Necessity?

Objection 1: It would seem that the devil can induce man to sin of necessity. Because the greater can compel the lesser. Now it is said of the devil (Job 41:24) that "there is no power on earth that can compare with him." Therefore he can compel man to sin, while he dwells on the earth.

Obj. 2: Further, man's reason cannot be moved except in respect of things that are offered outwardly to the senses, or are represented to the imagination: because "all our knowledge arises from the senses, and we cannot understand without a phantasm" (De Anima iii, text. 30. 39). Now the devil can move man's imagination, as stated above (A. 2); and also the external senses, for Augustine says (Qq. lxxxiii, qu. 12) that "this evil," of which, to wit, the devil is the cause, "extends gradually through all the approaches to the senses, it adapts itself to shapes, blends with colors, mingles with sounds, seasons every flavor." Therefore it can incline man's reason to sin of necessity.

Obj. 3: Further, Augustine says (De Civ. Dei xix, 4) that "there is some sin when the flesh lusteth against the spirit." Now the devil can cause concupiscence of the flesh, even as other passions, in the way explained above (A. 2). Therefore he can induce man to sin of necessity.

*On the contrary,* It is written (1 Pet. 5:8): "Your adversary the devil, as a roaring lion, goeth about seeking whom he may devour." Now it would be useless to admonish thus, if it were true that man were under the necessity of succumbing to the devil. Therefore he cannot induce man to sin of necessity.

Further, it is likewise written (Jam. 4:7): "Be subject ... to God, but resist the devil, and he will fly from you," which would be said neither rightly nor truly, if the devil were able to compel us, in any way whatever, to sin; for then neither would it be possible to resist him, nor would he fly from those who do. Therefore he does not compel to sin.

*I answer that,* The devil, by his own power, unless he be restrained by God, can compel anyone to do an act which, in its genus, is a sin; but he cannot bring about the necessity of sinning. This is evident from the fact that man does not resist that which moves him to sin, except by his reason; the use of which the devil is able to impede altogether, by moving the imagination and the sensitive appetite; as is the case with one who is possessed. But then, the reason being thus fettered, whatever man may do, it is not imputed to him as a sin. If, however, the reason is not altogether fettered, then, in so far as it is free, it can resist sin, as stated above (Q. 77, A. 7). It is consequently evident that the devil can nowise compel man to sin.

Reply Obj. 1: Not every power that is greater than man, can move man's will; God alone can do this, as stated above (Q. 9, A. 6).

Reply Obj. 2: That which is apprehended by the senses or the imagination does not move the will, of necessity, so long as man has the use of reason; nor does such an apprehension always fetter the reason.

Reply Obj. 3: The lusting of the flesh against the spirit, when the reason actually resists it, is not a sin, but is matter for the exercise of virtue. That reason does not resist, is not in the devil's power; wherefore he cannot bring about the necessity of sinning.

FOURTH ARTICLE [I-II, Q. 80, Art. 4]

Whether All the Sins of Men Are Due to the Devil's Suggestion?

Objection 1: It would seem that all the sins of men are due to the devil's suggestion. For Dionysius says (Div. Nom. iv) that the "crowd of demons are the cause of all evils, both to themselves and to others."

Obj. 2: Further, whoever sins mortally, becomes the slave of the devil, according to John 8:34: "Whosoever committeth sin is the slave [Douay: 'servant'] of sin." Now "by whom a man is overcome, of the same also he is the slave" (2 Pet. 2:19). Therefore whoever commits a sin, has been overcome by the devil.

Obj. 3: Further, Gregory says (Moral. iv, 10) the sin of the devil is irreparable, because he sinned at no other's suggestion. Therefore, if any men were to sin of their own free-will and without suggestion from any other, their sin would be irremediable: which is clearly false. Therefore all the sins of men are due to the devil's suggestion.

*On the contrary,* It is written (De Eccl. Dogm. lxxxii): "Not all our evil thoughts are incited by the devil; sometimes they are due to a movement of the free-will."

*I answer that,* the devil is the occasional and indirect cause of all our sins, in so far as he induced the first man to sin, by reason of whose sin human nature is so infected, that we are all prone to sin: even as the burning of wood might be imputed to the man who dried the wood so as to make it easily inflammable. He is not, however, the direct cause of all the sins of men, as though each were the result of his suggestion. Origen proves this (Peri Archon iii, 2) from the fact that even if the devil were no more, men would still have the desire for food, sexual pleasures and the like; which desire might be inordinate, unless it were subordinate to reason, a matter that is subject to the free-will.

Reply Obj. 1: The crowd of demons are the cause of all our evils, as regards their original cause, as stated.

Reply Obj. 2: A man becomes another's slave not only by being overcome by him, but also by subjecting himself to him spontaneously: it is thus that one who sins of his own accord, becomes the slave of the devil.

Reply Obj. 3: The devil's sin was irremediable, not only because he sinned without another's suggestion; but also because he was not already prone to sin, on account of any previous sin; which can be said of no sin of man.

# QUESTION 81

OF THE CAUSE OF SIN, ON THE PART OF MAN (In Five Articles)

We must now consider the cause of sin, on the part of man. Now, while man, like the devil, is the cause of another's sin, by outward suggestion, he has a certain special manner of causing sin, by way of origin. Wherefore we must speak about original sin, the consideration of which will be three-fold: (1) Of its transmission; (2) of its essence; (3) of its subject.

Under the first head there are five points of inquiry:

(1) Whether man's first sin is transmitted, by way of origin to his descendants?

(2) Whether all the other sins of our first parent, or of any other parents, are transmitted to their descendants, by way of origin?

(3) Whether original sin is contracted by all those who are begotten of Adam by way of seminal generation?

(4) Whether it would be contracted by anyone formed miraculously from some part of the human body?

(5) Whether original sin would have been contracted if the woman, and not the man, had sinned?

FIRST ARTICLE [I-II, Q. 81, Art. 1]

Whether the First Sin of Our First Parent Is Contracted by His Descendants, by Way of Origin?

Objection 1: It would seem that the first sin of our first parent is not contracted by others, by way of origin. For it is written (Ezech. 18:20): "The son shall not bear the iniquity of the father." But he would bear the iniquity if he contracted it from him. Therefore no one contracts any sin from one of his parents by way of origin.

Obj. 2: Further, an accident is not transmitted by way of origin, unless its subject be also transmitted, since accidents do not pass from one subject to another. Now the rational soul which is the subject of sin, is not transmitted by way of origin, as was shown in the First Part (Q. 118, A. 2). Therefore neither can any sin be transmitted by way of origin.

Obj. 3: Further, whatever is transmitted by way of human origin, is caused by the semen. But the semen cannot cause sin, because it lacks the rational part of the soul, which alone can be a cause of sin. Therefore no sin can be contracted by way of origin.

Obj. 4: Further, that which is more perfect in nature, is more powerful in action. Now perfect flesh cannot infect the soul united to it, else the soul could not be cleansed of original sin, so long as it is united to the body. Much less, therefore, can the semen infect the soul.

Obj. 5: Further, the Philosopher says (Ethic. iii, 5): "No one finds fault with those who are ugly by nature, but only those who are so through want of exercise and through carelessness." Now those are said to be "naturally ugly," who are so from their origin. Therefore nothing which comes by way of origin is blameworthy or sinful.

*On the contrary,* The Apostle says (Rom. 5:12): "By one man sin entered into this world, and by sin death." Nor can this be understood as denoting imitation or suggestion, since it is written (Wis. 2:24): "By the envy of the devil, death came into this world." It follows therefore that through origin from the first man sin entered into the world.

*I answer that,* According to the Catholic Faith we are bound to hold that the first sin of the first man is transmitted to his descendants, by way of origin. For this reason children are taken to be baptized soon after their birth, to show that they have to be washed from some uncleanness. The contrary is part of the Pelagian heresy, as is clear from Augustine in many of his books [*For instance, Retract. i, 9; De Pecc. Merit. et Remiss. ix; Contra Julian. iii, 1; De Dono Persev. xi, xii.]

In endeavoring to explain how the sin of our first parent could be transmitted by way of origin to his descendants, various writers have gone about it in various ways. For some, considering that the subject of sin is the rational soul, maintained that the rational soul is transmitted with the semen, so that thus an infected soul would seem to produce other infected souls. Others, rejecting this as erroneous, endeavored to show how the guilt of the parent's soul can be transmitted to the children, even though the soul be not transmitted, from the fact that defects of the body are transmitted from parent to child—thus a leper may beget a leper, or a gouty man may be the father of a gouty son, on account of some seminal corruption, although this corruption is not leprosy or gout. Now since the body is proportionate to the soul, and since the soul's defects redound into the body, and vice versa, in like manner, say they, a culpable defect of the soul is passed on to the child, through the transmission of the semen, albeit the semen itself is not the subject of the guilt.

But all these explanations are insufficient. Because, granted that some bodily defects are transmitted by way of origin from parent to child, and granted that even some defects of the soul are transmitted in consequence, on account of a defect in the bodily habit, as in the case of idiots begetting idiots; nevertheless the fact of having a defect by the way of origin seems to exclude the notion of guilt, which is essentially something voluntary. Wherefore granted that the rational soul were transmitted, from the very fact that the stain on the child's soul is not in its will, it would cease to be a guilty stain binding its subject to punishment; for, as the Philosopher says (Ethic. iii, 5), "no one reproaches a man born blind; one rather takes pity on him."

Therefore we must explain the matter otherwise by saying that all men born of Adam may be considered as one man, inasmuch as they have one common nature, which they receive from their first parents; even as in civil matters, all who are members of one community are reputed as one body, and the whole community as one man. Indeed Porphyry says (Praedic., De Specie) that "by sharing the same species, many men are one man." Accordingly the multitude of men born of Adam, are as so many members of one body. Now the action of one member of the body, of the hand for instance, is voluntary not by the will of that hand, but by the will of the soul, the first mover of the members. Wherefore a murder which the hand commits would not be imputed as a sin to the hand, considered by itself as apart from the body, but is imputed to it as something belonging to man and moved by man's first moving principle. In this way, then, the disorder which is in this man born of Adam, is voluntary, not by his will, but by the will of his first parent, who, by the movement of generation, moves all who originate from him, even as the soul's will moves all the members to their actions. Hence the sin which is thus transmitted by the first parent to his descendants is called "original," just as the sin which flows from the soul into the bodily members is called "actual." And just as the actual sin that is committed by a member of the body, is not the sin of that member, except inasmuch as that member is a part of the man, for which reason it is called a "human sin"; so original sin is not the sin of this person, except inasmuch as this person receives his nature from his first parent, for which reason it is called the "sin of nature," according to Eph. 2:3: "We ... were by nature children of wrath."

Reply Obj. 1: The son is said not to bear the iniquity of his father, because he is not punished for his father's sin, unless he share in his guilt. It is thus in the case before us: because guilt is transmitted by the way of origin from father to son, even as actual sin is transmitted through being imitated.

Reply Obj. 2: Although the soul is not transmitted, because the power in the semen is not able to cause the rational soul, nevertheless the motion of the semen is a disposition to the transmission of the rational soul: so that the semen by its own power transmits the human nature from parent to child, and with that nature, the stain which infects it: for he that is born is associated with his first parent in his guilt, through the fact that he inherits his nature from him by a kind of movement which is that of generation.

Reply Obj. 3: Although the guilt is not actually in the semen, yet human nature is there virtually accompanied by that guilt.

Reply Obj. 4: The semen is the principle of generation, which is an act proper to nature, by helping it to propagate itself. Hence the soul is more infected by the semen, than by the flesh which is already perfect, and already affixed to a certain person.

Reply Obj. 5: A man is not blamed for that which he has from his origin, if we consider the man born, in himself. But it we consider him as referred to a principle, then he may be reproached for it: thus a man may from his birth be under a family disgrace, on account of a crime committed by one of his forbears.

SECOND ARTICLE [I-II, Q. 81, Art. 2]

Whether Also Other Sins of the First Parent or of Nearer Ancestors Are Transmitted to Their Descendants?

Objection 1: It would seem that also other sins, whether of the first parent or of nearer ancestors, are transmitted to their descendants. For punishment is never due unless for fault. Now some are punished by the judgment of God for the sin of their immediate parents, according to Ex. 20:5: "I am ... God ... jealous, visiting the iniquity of the fathers upon the children, unto the third and fourth generation." Furthermore, according to human law, the children of those who are guilty of high treason are disinherited. Therefore the guilt of nearer ancestors is also transmitted to their descendants.

Obj. 2: Further, a man can better transmit to another, that which he has of himself, than that which he has received from another: thus fire heats better than hot water does. Now a man transmits to his children, by the way, of origin, the sin which he has from Adam. Much more therefore should he transmit the sin which he has contracted of himself.

Obj. 3: Further, the reason why we contract original sin from our first parent is because we were in him as in the principle of our nature, which he corrupted. But we were likewise in our nearer ancestors, as in principles of our nature, which however it be corrupt, can be corrupted yet more by sin, according to Apoc. 22:11: "He that is filthy, let him be filthier still." Therefore children contract, by the way of origin, the sins of their nearer ancestors, even as they contract the sin of their first parent.

*On the contrary,* Good is more self-diffusive than evil. But the merits of the nearer ancestors are not transmitted to their descendants. Much less therefore are their sins.

*I answer that,* Augustine puts this question in the Enchiridion xlvi, xlvii, and leaves it unsolved. Yet if we look into the matter carefully we shall see that it is impossible for the sins of the nearer ancestors, or even any other but the first sin of our first parent to be transmitted by way of origin. The reason is that a man begets his like in species but not in individual. Consequently those things that pertain directly to the individual, such as personal actions and matters affecting them, are not transmitted by parents to their children: for a grammarian does not transmit to his son the knowledge of grammar that he has acquired by his own studies. On the other hand, those things that concern the nature of the species, are transmitted by parents to their children, unless there be a defect of nature: thus a man with eyes begets a son having eyes, unless nature fails. And if nature be strong, even certain accidents of the individual pertaining to natural disposition, are transmitted to the children, e.g. fleetness of body, acuteness of intellect, and so forth; but nowise those that are purely personal, as stated above.

Now just as something may belong to the person as such, and also something through the gift of grace, so may something belong to the nature as such, viz. whatever is caused by the principles of nature, and something too through the gift of grace. In this way original justice, as stated in the First Part (Q. 100, A. 1), was a gift of grace, conferred by God on all human nature in our first parent. This gift the first man lost by his first sin. Wherefore as that original justice together with the nature was to have been transmitted to his posterity, so also was its disorder. Other actual sins, however, whether of the first parent or of others, do not corrupt the nature as nature, but only as the nature of that person, i.e. in respect of the proneness to sin: and consequently other sins are not transmitted.

Reply Obj. 1: According to Augustine in his letter to Avitus [*Ep. ad Auxilium ccl.], children are never inflicted with spiritual punishment on account of their parents, unless they share in their guilt, either in their origin, or by imitation, because every soul is God's immediate property, as stated in Ezech. 18:4. Sometimes, however, by Divine or human judgment, children receive bodily punishment on their parents' account, inasmuch as the child, as to its body, is part of its father.

Reply Obj. 2: A man can more easily transmit that which he has of himself, provided it be transmissible. But the actual sins of our nearer ancestors are not transmissible, because they are purely personal, as stated above.

Reply Obj. 3: The first sin infects nature with a human corruption pertaining to nature; whereas other sins infect it with a corruption pertaining only to the person.

THIRD ARTICLE [I-II, Q. 81, Art. 3]

Whether the Sin of the First Parent Is Transmitted, by the Way of Origin, to All Men?

Objection 1: It would seem that the sin of the first parent is not transmitted, by the way of origin, to all men. Because death is a punishment consequent upon original sin. But not all those, who are born of the seed of Adam, will die: since those who will be still living at the coming of our Lord, will never die, as, seemingly, may be gathered from 1 Thess. 4:14: "We who are alive ... unto the coming of the Lord, shall not prevent them who have slept." Therefore they do not contract original sin.

Obj. 2: Further, no one gives another what he has not himself. Now a man who has been baptized has not original sin. Therefore he does not transmit it to his children.

Obj. 3: Further, the gift of Christ is greater than the sin of Adam, as the Apostle declares (Rom. 5:15, seqq). But the gift of Christ is not transmitted to all men: neither, therefore, is the sin of Adam.

*On the contrary,* The Apostle says (Rom. 5:12): "Death passed upon all men in whom all have sinned."

*I answer that,* According to the Catholic Faith we must firmly believe that, Christ alone excepted, all men descended from Adam contract original sin from him; else all would not need redemption [*Cf. Translator's note inserted before III, Q. 27] which is through Christ; and this is erroneous. The reason for this may be gathered from what has been stated (A. 1), viz. that original sin, in virtue of the sin of our first parent, is transmitted to his posterity, just as, from the soul's will, actual sin is transmitted to the members of the body, through their being moved by the will. Now it is evident that actual sin can be transmitted to all such members as have an inborn aptitude to be moved by the will. Therefore original sin is transmitted to all those who are moved by Adam by the movement of generation.

Reply Obj. 1: It is held with greater probability and more commonly that all those that are alive at the coming of our Lord, will die, and rise again shortly, as we shall state more fully in the Third Part (Suppl., Q. 78, A. 1, Obj. 1). If, however, it be true, as others hold, that they will never die, (an opinion which Jerome mentions among others in a letter to Minerius, on the Resurrection of the Body—Ep. cxix), then we must say in reply to the objection, that although they are not to die, the debt of death is none the less in them, and that the punishment of death will be remitted by God, since He can also forgive the punishment due for actual sins.

Reply Obj. 1: Original sin is taken away by Baptism as to the guilt, in so far as the soul recovers grace as regards the mind. Nevertheless original sin remains in its effect as regards the *fomes,* which is the disorder of the lower parts of the soul and of the body itself, in respect of which, and not of the mind, man exercises his power of generation. Consequently those who are baptized transmit original sin: since they do not beget as being renewed in Baptism, but as still retaining something of the oldness of the first sin.

Reply Obj. 3: Just as Adam's sin is transmitted to all who are born of Adam corporally, so is the grace of Christ transmitted to all that are begotten of Him spiritually, by faith and Baptism: and this, not only unto the removal of sin of their first parent, but also unto the removal of actual sins, and the obtaining of glory.

FOURTH ARTICLE [I-II, Q. 81, Art. 4]

Whether Original Sin Would Be Contracted by a Person Formed Miraculously from Human Flesh?

Objection 1: It would seem that original sin would be contracted by a person formed miraculously from human flesh. For a gloss on Gen. 4:1 says that "Adam's entire posterity was corrupted in his loins, because they were not severed from him in the place of life, before he sinned, but in the place of exile after he had sinned." But if a man were to be formed in the aforesaid manner, his flesh would be severed in the place of exile. Therefore it would contract original sin.

Obj. 2: Further, original sin is caused in us by the soul being infected through the flesh. But man's flesh is entirely corrupted. Therefore a man's soul would contract the infection of original sin, from whatever part of the flesh it was formed.

Obj. 3: Further, original sin comes upon all from our first parent, in so far as we were all in him when he sinned. But those who might be formed out of human flesh, would have been in Adam. Therefore they would contract original sin.

*On the contrary,* They would not have been in Adam according to seminal virtue, which alone is the cause of the transmission of original sin, as Augustine states (Gen. ad lit. x, 18, seqq.).

*I answer that,* As stated above (AA. 1, 3), original sin is transmitted from the first parent to his posterity, inasmuch as they are moved by him through generation, even as the members are moved by the soul to actual sin. Now there is no movement to generation except by the active power of generation: so that those alone contract original sin, who are descended from Adam through the active power of generation originally derived from Adam, i.e. who are descended from him through seminal power; for the seminal power is nothing else than the active power of generation. But if anyone were to be formed by God out of human flesh, it is evident that the active power would not be derived from Adam. Consequently he would not contract original sin: even as a hand would have no part in a human sin, if it were moved, not by the man's will, but by some external power.

Reply Obj. 1: Adam was not in the place of exile until after his sin. Consequently it is not on account of the place of exile, but on account of the sin, that original sin is transmitted to those to whom his active generation extends.

Reply Obj. 2: The flesh does not corrupt the soul, except in so far as it is the active principle in generation, as we have stated.

Reply Obj. 3: If a man were to be formed from human flesh, he would have been in Adam, "by way of bodily substance" [*The expression is St. Augustine's (Gen. ad lit. x). Cf. Summa Theologica, III, Q. 31, A. 6, Reply to First Objection.], but not according to seminal virtue, as stated above. Therefore he would not contract original sin.

FIFTH ARTICLE [I-II, Q. 81, Art. 5]

Whether If Eve, and Not Adam, Had Sinned, Their Children Would Have Contracted Original Sin?

Objection 1: It would seem that if Eve, and not Adam, had sinned, their children would have contracted original sin. Because we contract original sin from our parents, in so far as we were once in them, according to the word of the Apostle (Rom. 5:12): "In whom all have sinned." Now a man pre-exists in his mother as well as in his father. Therefore a man would have contracted original sin from his mother's sin as well as from his father's.

Obj. 2: Further, if Eve, and not Adam, had sinned, their children would have been born liable to suffering and death, since it is "the mother" that "provides the matter in generation" as the Philosopher states (De Gener. Animal. ii, 1, 4), when death and liability to suffering are the necessary results of matter. Now liability to suffering and the necessity of dying are punishments of original sin. Therefore if Eve, and not Adam, had sinned, their children would contract original sin.

Obj. 3: Further, Damascene says (De Fide Orth. iii, 3) that "the Holy Ghost came upon the Virgin," (of whom Christ was to be born without original sin) "purifying her." But this purification would not have been necessary, if the infection of original sin were not contracted from the mother. Therefore the infection of original sin is contracted from the mother: so that if Eve had sinned, her children would have contracted original sin, even if Adam had not sinned.

*On the contrary,* The Apostle says (Rom. 5:12): "By one man sin entered into this world." Now if the woman would have transmitted original sin to her children, he should have said that it entered by two, since both of them sinned, or rather that it entered by a woman, since she sinned first. Therefore original sin is transmitted to the children, not by the mother, but by the father.

*I answer that,* The solution of this question is made clear by what has been said. For it has been stated (A. 1) that original sin is transmitted by the first parent in so far as he is the mover in the begetting of his children: wherefore it has been said (A. 4) that if anyone were begotten materially only, of human flesh, they would not contract original sin. Now it is evident that in the opinion of philosophers, the active principle of generation is from the father, while the mother provides the matter. Therefore original sin is contracted, not from the mother, but from the father: so that, accordingly, if Eve, and not Adam, had sinned, their children would not contract original sin: whereas, if Adam, and not Eve, had sinned, they would contract it.

Reply Obj. 1: The child pre-exists in its father as in its active principle, and in its mother, as in its material and passive principle. Consequently the comparison fails.

Reply Obj. 2: Some hold that if Eve, and not Adam, had sinned, their children would be immune from the sin, but would have been subject to the necessity of dying and to other forms of suffering that are a necessary result of the matter which is provided by the mother, not as punishments, but as actual defects. This, however, seems unreasonable. Because, as stated in the First Part (Q. 97, AA. 1, 2, ad 4), immortality and impassibility, in the original state, were a result, not of the condition of matter, but of original justice, whereby the body was subjected to the soul, so long as the soul remained subject to God. Now privation of original justice is original sin. If, therefore, supposing Adam had not sinned, original sin would not have been transmitted to posterity on account of Eve's sin; it is evident that the children would not have been deprived of original justice: and consequently they would not have been liable to suffer and subject to the necessity of dying.

Reply Obj. 3: This prevenient purification in the Blessed Virgin was not needed to hinder the transmission of original sin, but because it behooved the Mother of God "to shine with the greatest purity" [*Cf. Anselm, De Concep. Virg. xviii.]. For nothing is worthy to receive God unless it be pure, according to Ps. 92:5: "Holiness becometh Thy House, O Lord."

# QUESTION 82

We must now consider original sin as to its essence, and under this head there are four points of inquiry:

(1) Whether original sin is a habit?

(2) Whether there is but one original sin in each man?

(3) Whether original sin is concupiscence?

(4) Whether original sin is equally in all?

FIRST ARTICLE [I-II, Q. 82, Art. 1]

Whether Original Sin Is a Habit?

Objection 1: It would seem that original sin is not a habit. For original sin is the absence of original justice, as Anselm states (De Concep. Virg. ii, iii, xxvi), so that original sin is a privation. But privation is opposed to habit. Therefore original sin is not a habit.

Obj. 2: Further, actual sin has the nature of fault more than original sin, in so far as it is more voluntary. Now the habit of actual sin has not the nature of a fault, else it would follow that a man while asleep, would be guilty of sin. Therefore no original habit has the nature of a fault.

Obj. 3: Further, in wickedness act always precedes habit, because evil habits are not infused, but acquired. Now original sin is not preceded by an act. Therefore original sin is not a habit.

*On the contrary,* Augustine says in his book on the Baptism of infants (De Pecc. Merit. et Remiss. i, 39) that on account of original sin little children have the aptitude of concupiscence though they have not the act. Now aptitude denotes some kind of habit. Therefore original sin is a habit.

*I answer that,* As stated above (Q. 49, A. 4; Q. 50, A. 1), habit is twofold. The first is a habit whereby power is inclined to an act: thus science and virtue are called habits. In this way original sin is not a habit. The second kind of habit is the disposition of a complex nature, whereby that nature is well or ill disposed to something, chiefly when such a disposition has become like a second nature, as in the case of sickness or health. In this sense original sin is a habit. For it is an inordinate disposition, arising from the destruction of the harmony which was essential to original justice, even as bodily sickness is an inordinate disposition of the body, by reason of the destruction of that equilibrium which is essential to health. Hence it is that original sin is called the "languor of nature" [*Cf. Augustine, In Ps. 118, serm. iii].

Reply Obj. 1: As bodily sickness is partly a privation, in so far as it denotes the destruction of the equilibrium of health, and partly something positive, viz. the very humors that are inordinately disposed, so too original sin denotes the privation of original justice, and besides this, the inordinate disposition of the parts of the soul. Consequently it is not a pure privation, but a corrupt habit.

Reply Obj. 2: Actual sin is an inordinateness of an act: whereas original sin, being the sin of nature, is an inordinate disposition of nature, and has the character of fault through being transmitted from our first parent, as stated above (Q. 81, A. 1). Now this inordinate disposition of nature is a kind of habit, whereas the inordinate disposition of an act is not: and for this reason original sin can be a habit, whereas actual sin cannot.

Reply Obj. 3: This objection considers the habit which inclines a power to an act: but original sin is not this kind of habit. Nevertheless a certain inclination to an inordinate act does follow from original sin, not directly, but indirectly, viz. by the removal of the obstacle, i.e. original justice, which hindered inordinate movements: just as an inclination to inordinate bodily movements results indirectly from bodily sickness. Nor is it necessary to say that original sin is a habit "infused," or a habit "acquired" (except by the act of our first parent, but not by our own act): but it is a habit "inborn" due to our corrupt origin.

SECOND ARTICLE [I-II, Q. 82, Art. 2]

Whether There Are Several Original Sins in One Man?

Objection 1: It would seem that there are many

original sins in one man. For it is written (Ps. 1:7): "Behold I was conceived in iniquities, and in sins did my mother conceive me." But the sin in which a man is conceived is original sin. Therefore there are several original sins in man.

Obj. 2: Further, one and the same habit does not incline its subject to contraries: since the inclination of habit is like that of nature which tends to one thing. Now original sin, even in one man, inclines to various and contrary sins. Therefore original sin is not one habit; but several.

Obj. 3: Further, original sin infects every part of the soul. Now the different parts of the soul are different subjects of sin, as shown above (Q. 74). Since then one sin cannot be in different subjects, it seems that original sin is not one but several.

*On the contrary,* It is written (John 1:29): "Behold the Lamb of God, behold Him Who taketh away the sin of the world": and the reason for the employment of the singular is that the "sin of the world" is original sin, as a gloss expounds this passage.

*I answer that,* In one man there is one original sin. Two reasons may be assigned for this. The first is on the part of the cause of original sin. For it has been stated (Q. 81, A. 2), that the first sin alone of our first parent was transmitted to his posterity. Wherefore in one man original sin is one in number; and in all men, it is one in proportion, i.e. in relation to its first principle. The second reason may be taken from the very essence of original sin. Because in every inordinate disposition, unity of species depends on the cause, while the unity of number is derived from the subject. For example, take bodily sickness: various species of sickness proceed from different causes, e.g. from excessive heat or cold, or from a lesion in the lung or liver; while one specific sickness in one man will be one in number. Now the cause of this corrupt disposition that is called original sin, is one only, viz. the privation of original justice, removing the subjection of man's mind to God. Consequently original sin is specifically one, and, in one man, can be only one in number; while, in different men, it is one in species and in proportion, but is numerically many.

Reply Obj. 1: The employment of the plural—"in sins"—may be explained by the custom of the Divine Scriptures in the frequent use of the plural for the singular, e.g. "They are dead that sought the life of the child"; or by the fact that all actual sins virtually pre-exist in original sin, as in a principle so that it is virtually many; or by the fact of there being many deformities in the sin of our first parent, viz. pride, disobedience, gluttony, and so forth; or by several parts of the soul being infected by original sin.

Reply Obj. 2: Of itself and directly, i.e. by its own form, one habit cannot incline its subject to contraries. But there is no reason why it should not do so, indirectly and accidentally, i.e. by the removal of an obstacle: thus, when the harmony of a mixed body is destroyed, the elements have contrary local tendencies. In like manner, when the harmony of original justice is destroyed, the various powers of the soul have various opposite tendencies.

Reply Obj. 3: Original sin infects the different parts of the soul, in so far as they are the parts of one whole; even as original justice held all the soul's parts together in one. Consequently there is but one original sin: just as there is but one fever in one man, although the various parts of the body are affected.

THIRD ARTICLE [I-II, Q. 82, Art. 3]

Whether Original Sin Is Concupiscence?

Objection 1: It would seem that original sin is not concupiscence. For every sin is contrary to nature, according to Damascene (De Fide Orth. ii, 4, 30). But concupiscence is in accordance with nature, since it is the proper act of the concupiscible faculty which is a natural power. Therefore concupiscence is not original sin.

Obj. 2: Further, through original sin "the passions of sins" are in us, according to the Apostle (Rom. 7:5). Now there are several other passions besides concupiscence, as stated above (Q. 23, A. 4). Therefore original sin is not concupiscence any more than another passion.

Obj. 3: Further, by original sin, all the parts of the soul are disordered, as stated above (A. 2, Obj. 3). But the intellect is the highest of the soul's parts, as the Philosopher states (Ethic. x, 7). Therefore original sin is ignorance rather than concupiscence.

*On the contrary,* Augustine says (Retract. i, 15): "Concupiscence is the guilt of original sin."

*I answer that,* Everything takes its species from its form: and it has been stated (A. 2) that the species of original sin is taken from its cause. Consequently the formal element of original sin must be considered in respect of the cause of original sin. But contraries have contrary causes. Therefore the cause of original sin must be considered with respect to the cause of original justice, which is opposed to it. Now the whole order of original justice consists in man's will being subject to God: which subjection, first and chiefly, was in the will, whose function it is to move all the other parts to the end, as stated above (Q. 9, A. 1), so that the will being turned away from God, all the other powers of the soul become inordinate. Accordingly the privation of original justice, whereby the will was made subject to God, is the formal element in original sin; while every other disorder of the soul's powers, is a kind of material element in respect of original sin. Now the inordinateness of the other powers of the soul consists chiefly in their turning inordinately to mutable good; which inordinateness may be called by the general name of concupiscence. Hence original sin is concupiscence, materially, but privation of original justice, formally.

Reply Obj. 1: Since, in man, the concupiscible power is naturally governed by reason, the act of concupiscence is so far natural to man, as it is in accord with the order of reason; while, in so far as it trespasses beyond the bounds of reason, it is, for a man, contrary to reason. Such is the concupiscence of original sin.

Reply Obj. 2: As stated above (Q. 25, A. 1), all the irascible passions are reducible to concupiscible passions, as holding the princip[al] place: and of these, concupiscence is the most impetuous in moving, and is felt most, as stated above (Q. 25, A. 2, ad 1). Therefore original sin is ascribed to concupiscence, as being the chief passion, and as including all the others, in a fashion.

Reply Obj. 3: As, in good things, the intellect and reason stand first, so conversely in evil things, the lower part of the soul is found to take precedence, for it clouds and draws the reason, as stated above (Q. 77, AA. 1, 2;Q. 80, A. 2). Hence original sin is called concupiscence rather than ignorance, although ignorance is comprised among the material defects of original sin.

FOURTH ARTICLE [I-II, Q. 82, Art. 4]

Whether Original Sin Is Equally in All?

Objection 1: It would seem that original sin is not equally in all. Because original sin is inordinate concupiscence, as stated above (A. 3). Now all are not equally prone to acts of concupiscence. Therefore original sin is not equally in all.

Obj. 2: Further, original sin is an inordinate disposition of the soul, just as sickness is an inordinate disposition of the body. But sickness is subject to degrees. Therefore original sin is subject to degrees.

Obj. 3: Further, Augustine says (De Nup. et Concep. i, 23) that "lust transmits original sin to the child." But the act of generation may be more lustful in one than in another. Therefore original sin may be greater in one than in another.

*On the contrary,* Original sin is the sin of nature, as stated above (Q. 81, A. 1). But nature is equally in all. Therefore original sin is too.

*I answer that,* There are two things in original sin: one is the privation of original justice; the other is the relation of this privation to the sin of our first parent, from whom it is transmitted to man through his corrupt origin. As to the first, original sin has no degrees, since the gift of original justice is taken away entirely; and privations that remove something entirely, such as death and darkness, cannot be more or less, as stated above (Q. 73, A. 2). In like manner, neither is this possible, as to the second: since all are related equally to the first principle of our corrupt origin, from which principle original sin takes the nature of guilt; for relations cannot be more or less. Consequently it is evident that original sin cannot be more in one than in another.

Reply Obj. 1: Through the bond of original justice being broken, which held together all the powers of the soul in a certain order, each power of the soul tends to its own proper movement, and the more impetuously, as it is stronger. Now it happens that some of the soul's powers are stronger in one man than in another, on account of the different bodily temperaments. Consequently if one man is more prone than another to acts of concupiscence, this is not due to original sin, because the bond of original justice is equally broken in all, and the lower parts of the soul are, in all, left to themselves equally; but it is due to the various dispositions of the powers, as stated.

Reply Obj. 2: Sickness of the body, even sickness of the same species, has not an equal cause in all; for instance if a fever be caused by corruption of the bile, the corruption may be greater or less, and nearer to, or further from a vital principle. But the cause of original sin is equal to all, so that there is no comparison.

Reply Obj. 3: It is not the actual lust that transmits original sin: for, supposing God were to grant to a man to feel no inordinate lust in the act of generation, he would still transmit original sin; we must understand this to be habitual lust, whereby the sensitive appetite is not kept subject to reason by the bonds of original justice. This lust is equally in all.

## QUESTION 83

OF THE SUBJECT OF ORIGINAL SIN (In Four Articles)

We must now consider the subject of original sin, under which head there are four points of inquiry:

(1) Whether the subject of original sin is the flesh rather than the soul?

(2) If it be the soul, whether this be through its essence, or through its powers?

(3) Whether the will prior to the other powers is the subject of original sin?

(4) Whether certain powers of the soul are specially infected, viz. the generative power, the concupiscible part, and the sense of touch?

FIRST ARTICLE [I-II, Q. 83, Art. 1]

Whether Original Sin Is More in the Flesh Than in the Soul?

Objection 1: It would seem that original sin is more in the flesh than in the soul. Because the rebellion of the flesh against the mind arises from the corruption of original sin. Now the root of this rebellion is seated in the flesh: for the Apostle says (Rom. 7:23): "I see another law in my members fighting against the law of my mind." Therefore original sin is seated chiefly in the flesh.

Obj. 2: Further, a thing is more in its cause than in its effect: thus heat is in the heating fire more than in the hot water. Now the soul is infected with the corruption of original sin by the carnal semen. Therefore original sin is in the flesh rather than in the soul.

Obj. 3: Further, we contract original sin from our first parent, in so far as we were in him by reason of seminal virtue. Now our souls were not in him thus, but only our flesh. Therefore original sin is not in the soul, but in the flesh.

Obj. 4: Further, the rational soul created by God is infused into the body. If therefore the soul were infected with original sin, it would follow that it is corrupted in its creation or infusion: and thus God would be the cause of sin, since He is the author of the soul's creation and fusion.

Obj. 5: Further, no wise man pours a precious liquid into a vessel, knowing that the vessel will corrupt the liquid. But the rational soul is more precious than any liquid. If therefore the soul, by being united with the body, could be corrupted with the infection of original sin, God, Who is wisdom itself, would never infuse the soul into such a body. And yet He does; wherefore it is not corrupted by the flesh. Therefore original sin is not in the soul but in the flesh.

*On the contrary,* The same is the subject of a virtue and of the vice or sin contrary to that virtue. But the flesh cannot be the subject of virtue: for the Apostle says (Rom. 7:18): "I know that there dwelleth not in me, that is to say, in my flesh, that which is good." Therefore the flesh cannot be the subject of original sin, but only the soul.

*I answer that,* One thing can be in another in two ways. First, as in its cause, either principal, or instrumental; secondly, as in its subject. Accordingly the original sin of all men was in Adam indeed, as in its principal cause, according to the words of the Apostle (Rom. 5:12): "In whom all have sinned": whereas it is in the bodily semen, as in its instrumental cause, since it is by the active power of the semen that original sin together with human nature is transmitted to the child. But original sin can nowise be in the flesh as its subject, but only in the soul.

The reason for this is that, as stated above (Q. 81, A. 1), original sin is transmitted from the will of our first parent to this posterity by a certain movement of generation, in the same way as actual sin is transmitted from any man's will to his other parts. Now in this transmission it is to be observed, that whatever accrues from the motion of the will consenting to sin, to any part of man that can in any way share in that guilt, either as its subject or as its instrument, has the character of sin. Thus from the will consenting to gluttony, concupiscence of food accrues to the concupiscible faculty, and partaking of food accrues to the hand and the mouth, which, in so far as they are moved by the will to sin, are the instruments of sin. But that further action is evoked in the nutritive power and the internal members, which have no natural aptitude for being moved by the will, does not bear the character of guilt.

Accordingly, since the soul can be the subject of guilt, while the flesh, of itself, cannot be the subject of guilt; whatever accrues to the soul from the corruption of the first sin, has the character of guilt, while whatever accrues to the flesh, has the character, not of guilt but of punishment: so that, therefore, the soul is the subject of original sin, and not the flesh.

Reply Obj. 1: As Augustine says (Retract. i, 27) [*Cf. QQ. lxxxiii, qu. 66], the Apostle is speaking, in that passage, of man already redeemed, who is delivered from guilt, but is still liable to punishment, by reason of which sin is stated to dwell "in the flesh." Consequently it follows that the flesh is the subject, not of guilt, but of punishment.

Reply Obj. 2: Original sin is caused by the semen as instrumental cause. Now there is no need for anything to be more in the instrumental cause than in the effect; but only in the principal cause: and, in this way, original sin was in Adam more fully, since in him it had the nature of actual sin.

Reply Obj. 3: The soul of any individual man was in Adam, in respect of his seminal power, not indeed as in its effective principle, but as in a dispositive principle: because the bodily semen, which is transmitted from Adam, does not of its own power produce the rational soul, but disposes the matter for it.

Reply Obj. 4: The corruption of original sin is nowise caused by God, but by the sin alone of our first parent through carnal generation. And so, since creation implies a relation in the soul to God alone, it cannot be said that the soul is tainted through being created. On the other hand, infusion implies relation both to God infusing and to the flesh into which the soul is infused. And so, with regard to God infusing, it cannot be said that the soul is stained through being infused; but only with regard to the body into which it is infused.

Reply Obj. 5: The common good takes precedence of private good. Wherefore God, according to His wisdom, does not overlook the general order of things (which is that such a soul be infused into such a body), lest this soul contract a singular corruption: all the more that the nature of the soul demands that it should not exist prior to its infusion into the body, as stated in the First Part (Q. 90, A. 4; Q. 118, A. 3). And it is better for the soul to be thus, according to its nature, than not to be at all, especially since it can avoid damnation, by means of grace.

SECOND ARTICLE [I-II, Q. 83, Art. 2]

Whether Original Sin Is in the Essence of the Soul Rather Than in the Powers?

Objection 1: It would seem that original sin is not in the essence of the soul rather than in the powers. For the soul is naturally apt to be the subject of sin, in respect of those parts which can be moved by the will. Now the soul is moved by the will, not as to its essence but only as to the powers. Therefore original sin is in the soul, not according to its essence, but only according to the powers.

Obj. 2: Further, original sin is opposed to original justice. Now original justice was in a power of the soul, because power is the subject of virtue. Therefore original sin also is in a power of the soul, rather than in its essence.

Obj. 3: Further, just as original sin is derived from the soul as from the flesh, so is it derived by the powers from the essence. But original sin is more in the soul than in the flesh. Therefore it is more in the powers than in the essence of the soul.

Obj. 4: Further, original sin is said to be concupiscence, as stated (Q. 82, A. 3). But concupiscence is in the powers of the soul. Therefore original sin is also.

*On the contrary,* Original sin is called the sin of nature, as stated above (Q. 81, A. 1). Now the soul is the form and nature of the body, in respect of its essence and not in respect of its powers, as stated in the First Part (Q. 76, A. 6). Therefore the soul is the subject of original sin chiefly in respect of its essence.

*I answer that,* The subject of a sin is chiefly that part of the soul to which the motive cause of that sin primarily pertains: thus if the motive cause of a sin is sensual pleasure, which regards the concupiscible power through being its proper object, it follows that the concupiscible power is the proper subject of that sin. Now it is evident that original sin is caused through our origin. Consequently that part of the soul which is first reached by man's origin, is the primary subject of original sin. Now the origin reaches the soul as the term of generation, according as it is the form of the body: and this belongs to the soul in respect of its essence, as was proved in the First Part (Q. 76, A. 6). Therefore the soul, in respect of its essence, is the primary subject of original sin.

Reply Obj. 1: As the motion of the will of an individual reaches to the soul's powers and not to its essence, so the motion of the will of the first generator, through the channel of generation, reaches first of all to the essence of the soul, as stated.

Reply Obj. 2: Even original justice pertained radically to the essence of the soul, because it was God's gift to human nature, to which the essence of the soul is related before the powers. For the powers seem to regard the person, in as much as they are the principles of personal acts. Hence they are the proper subjects of actual sins, which are the sins of the person.

Reply Obj. 3: The body is related to the soul as matter to form, which though it comes second in order of generation, nevertheless comes first in the order of perfection and nature. But the essence of the soul is related to the powers, as a subject to its proper accidents, which follow their subject both in the order of generation and in that of perfection. Consequently the comparison fails.

Reply Obj. 4: Concupiscence, in relation to original sin, holds the position of matter and effect, as stated above (Q. 82, A. 3).

THIRD ARTICLE [I-II, Q. 83, Art. 3]

Whether Original Sin Infects the Will Before the Other Powers?

Objection 1: It would seem that original sin does not infect the will before the other powers. For every sin belongs chiefly to that power by whose act it was caused. Now original sin is caused by an act of the generative power. Therefore it seems to belong to the generative power more than to the others.

Obj. 2: Further, original sin is transmitted through the carnal semen. But the other powers of the soul are more akin to the flesh than the will is, as is evident with regard to all the sensitive powers, which use a bodily organ. Therefore original sin is in them more than in the will.

Obj. 3: Further, the intellect precedes the will, for the object of the will is only the good understood. If therefore original sin infects all the powers of the soul, it seems that it must first of all infect the intellect, as preceding the others.

*On the contrary,* Original justice has a prior relation to the will, because it is "rectitude of the will," as Anselm states (De Concep. Virg. iii). Therefore original sin, which is opposed to it, also has a prior relation to the will.

*I answer that,* Two things must be considered in the infection of original sin. First, its inherence to its subject; and in this respect it regards first the essence of the soul, as stated above (A. 2). In the second place we must consider its inclination to act; and in this way it regards the powers of the soul. It must therefore regard first of all that power in which is seated the first inclination to commit a sin, and this is the will, as stated above (Q. 74, AA. 1, 2). Therefore original sin regards first of all the will.

Reply Obj. 1: Original sin, in man, is not caused by the generative power of the child, but by the act of the parental generative power. Consequently, it does not follow that the child's generative power is the subject of original sin.

Reply Obj. 2: Original sin spreads in two ways; from the flesh to the soul, and from the essence of the soul to the powers. The former follows the order of generation, the latter follows the order of perfection. Therefore, although the other, viz. the sensitive powers, are more akin to the flesh, yet, since the will, being the higher power, is more akin to the essence of the soul, the infection of original sin reaches it first.

Reply Obj. 3: The intellect precedes the will, in one way, by proposing its object to it. In another way, the will precedes the intellect, in the order of motion to act, which motion pertains to sin.

FOURTH ARTICLE [I-II, Q. 83, Art. 4]

Whether the Aforesaid Powers Are More Infected Than the Others?

Objection 1: It would seem that the aforesaid powers are not more infected than the others. For the infection of original sin seems to pertain more to that part of the soul which can be first the subject of sin. Now this is the rational part, and chiefly the will. Therefore that power is most infected by original sin.

Obj. 2: Further, no power of the soul is infected by guilt, except in so far as it can obey reason. Now the generative power cannot obey reason, as stated in *Ethic.* i, 13. Therefore the generative power is not the most infected by original sin.

Obj. 3: Further, of all the senses the sight is the most spiritual and the nearest to reason, in so far "as it shows us how a number of things differ" (Metaph. i). But the infection of guilt is first of all in the reason. Therefore the sight is more infected than touch.

*On the contrary,* Augustine says (De Civ. Dei xiv, 16, seqq., 24) that the infection of original sin is most apparent in the movements of the members of generation, which are not subject to reason. Now those members serve the generative power in the mingling of sexes, wherein there is the delectation of touch, which is the most powerful incentive to concupiscence. Therefore the infection of original sin regards these three chiefly, viz. the generative power, the concupiscible faculty and the sense of touch.

*I answer that,* Those corruptions especially are said to be infectious, which are of such a nature as to be transmitted from one subject to another: hence contagious diseases, such as leprosy and murrain and the like, are said to be infectious. Now the corruption of original sin is transmitted by the act of generation, as stated above (Q. 81, A. 1). Therefore the powers which concur in this act, are chiefly said to be infected. Now this act serves the generative power, in as much as it is directed to generation; and it includes delectation of the touch, which is the most powerful object of the concupiscible faculty. Consequently, while all the parts of the soul are said to be corrupted by original sin, these three are said specially to be corrupted and infected.

Reply Obj. 1: Original sin, in so far as it inclines to actual sins, belongs chiefly to the will, as stated above (A. 3). But in so far as it is transmitted to the offspring, it belongs to the aforesaid powers proximately, and to the will, remotely.

Reply Obj. 2: The infection of actual sin belongs only to the powers which are moved by the will of the sinner. But the infection of original sin is not derived from the will of the contractor, but through his natural origin, which is effected by the generative power. Hence it is this power that is infected by original sin.

Reply Obj. 3: Sight is not related to the act of generation except in respect of remote disposition, in so far as the concupiscible species is seen through the sight. But the delectation is completed in the touch. Wherefore the aforesaid infection is ascribed to the touch rather than to the sight.

## QUESTION 84

OF THE CAUSE OF SIN, IN RESPECT OF ONE SIN BEING THE CAUSE OF ANOTHER (In Four Articles)

We must now consider the cause of sin, in so far as one sin can be the cause of another. Under this head there are four points of inquiry:

(1) Whether covetousness is the root of all sins?

(2) Whether pride is the beginning of every sin?

(3) Whether other special sins should be called capital vices, besides pride and covetousness?

(4) How many capital vices there are, and which are they?

FIRST ARTICLE [I-II, Q. 84, Art. 1]

Whether Covetousness Is the Root of All Sins?

Objection 1: It would seem that covetousness is not the root of all sins. For covetousness, which is immoderate desire for riches, is opposed to the virtue of liberality. But liberality is not the root of all virtues. Therefore covetousness is not the root of all sins.

Obj. 2: Further, the desire for the means proceeds from desire for the end. Now riches, the desire for which is called covetousness, are not desired except as being useful for some end, as stated in *Ethic.* i, 5. Therefore covetousness is not the root of all sins, but proceeds from some deeper root.

Obj. 3: Further, it often happens that avarice, which is another name for covetousness, arises from other sins; as when a man desires money through ambition, or in order to sate his gluttony. Therefore it is not the root of all sins.

*On the contrary,* The Apostle says (1 Tim. 6:10): "The desire of money is the root of all evil."

*I answer that,* According to some, covetousness may be understood in different ways. First, as denoting inordinate desire for riches: and thus it is a special sin. Secondly, as denoting inordinate desire for any temporal good: and thus it is a genus comprising all sins, because every sin includes an inordinate turning to a mutable good, as stated above (Q. 72, A. 2). Thirdly, as denoting an inclination of a corrupt nature to desire corruptible goods inordinately: and they say that in this sense covetousness is the root of all sins, comparing it to the root of a tree, which draws its sustenance from earth, just as every sin grows out of the love of temporal things.

Now, though all this is true, it does not seem to explain the mind of the Apostle when he states that covetousness is the root of all sins. For in that passage he clearly speaks against those who, because they "will become rich, fall into temptation, and into the snare of the devil ... for covetousness is the root of all evils." Hence it is evident that he is speaking of covetousness as denoting the inordinate desire for riches. Accordingly, we must say that covetousness, as denoting a special sin, is called the root of all sins, in likeness to the root of a tree, in furnishing sustenance to the whole tree. For we see that by riches man acquires the means of committing any sin whatever, and of sating his desire for any sin whatever, since money helps man to obtain all manner of temporal goods, according to Eccles. 10:19: "All things obey money": so that in this desire for riches is the root of all sins.

Reply Obj. 1: Virtue and sin do not arise from the same source. For sin arises from the desire of mutable good; and consequently the desire of that good which helps one to obtain all temporal goods, is called the root of all sins. But virtue arises from the desire for the immutable God; and consequently charity, which is the love of God, is called the root of the virtues, according to Eph. 3:17: "Rooted and founded in charity."

Reply Obj. 2: The desire of money is said to be the root of sins, not as though riches were sought for their own sake, as being the last end; but because they are much sought after as useful for any temporal end. And since a universal good is more desirable than a particular good, they move the appetite more than any individual goods, which along with many others can be procured by means of money.

Reply Obj. 3: Just as in natural things we do not ask what always happens, but what happens most frequently, for the reason that the nature of corruptible things can be hindered, so as not always to act in the same way; so also in moral matters, we consider what happens in the majority of cases, not what happens invariably, for the reason that the will does not act of necessity. So when we say that covetousness is the root of all evils, we do not assert that no other evil can be its root, but that other evils more frequently arise therefrom, for the reason given.

SECOND ARTICLE [I-II, Q. 84, Art. 2]

Whether Pride Is the Beginning of Every Sin?

Objection 1: It would seem that pride is not the beginning of every sin. For the root is a beginning of a tree, so that the beginning of a sin seems to be the same as the root of sin. Now covetousness is the root of every sin, as stated above (A. 1). Therefore it is also the beginning of every sin, and not pride.

Obj. 2: Further, it is written (Ecclus. 10:14): "The beginning of the pride of man is apostasy [Douay: 'to fall off'] from God." But apostasy from God is a sin. Therefore another sin is the beginning of pride, so that the latter is not the beginning of every sin.

Obj. 3: Further, the beginning of every sin would seem to be that which causes all sins. Now this is inordinate self-love, which, according to Augustine (De Civ. Dei xiv), "builds up the city of Babylon." Therefore self-love and not pride, is the beginning of every sin.

*On the contrary,* It is written (Ecclus. 10:15): "Pride is the beginning of all sin."

*I answer that,* Some say pride is to be taken in three ways. First, as denoting inordinate desire to excel; and thus it is a special sin. Secondly, as denoting actual contempt of God, to the effect of not being subject to His commandment; and thus, they say, it is a generic sin. Thirdly, as denoting an inclination to this contempt, owing to the corruption of nature; and in this sense they say that it is the beginning of every sin, and that it differs from covetousness, because covetousness regards sin as turning towards the mutable good by which sin is, as it were, nourished and fostered, for which reason covetousness is called the "root"; whereas pride regards sin as turning away from God, to Whose commandment man refuses to be subject, for which reason it is called the "beginning," because the beginning of evil consists in turning away from God.

Now though all this is true, nevertheless it does not explain the mind of the wise man who said (Ecclus. 10:15): "Pride is the beginning of all sin." For it is evident that he is speaking of pride as denoting inordinate desire to excel, as is clear from what follows (verse 17): "God hath overturned the thrones of proud princes"; indeed this is the point of nearly the whole chapter. We must therefore say that pride, even as denoting a special sin, is the beginning of every sin. For we must take note that, in voluntary actions, such as sins, there is a twofold order, of intention, and of execution. In the former order, the principle is the end, as we have stated many times before (Q. 1, A. 1, ad 1; Q. 18, A. 7, ad 2; Q. 15, A. 1, ad 2; Q. 25, A. 2). Now man's end in acquiring all temporal goods is that, through their means, he may have some perfection and excellence. Therefore, from this point of view, pride, which is the desire to excel, is said to be the "beginning" of every sin. On the other hand, in the order of execution, the first place belongs to that which by furnishing the opportunity of fulfilling all desires of sin, has the character of a root, and such are riches; so that, from this point of view, covetousness is said to be the "root" of all evils, as stated above (A. 1).

This suffices for the Reply to the First Objection.

Reply Obj. 2: Apostasy from God is stated to be the beginning of pride, in so far as it denotes a turning away from God, because from the fact that man wishes not to be subject to God, it follows that he desires inordinately his own excellence in temporal things. Wherefore, in the passage quoted, apostasy from God does not denote the special sin, but rather that general condition of every sin, consisting in its turning away from God. It may also be said that apostasy from God is said to be the beginning of pride, because it is the first species of pride. For it is characteristic of pride to be unwilling to be subject to any superior, and especially to God; the result being that a man is unduly lifted up, in respect of the other species of pride.

Reply Obj. 3: In desiring to excel, man loves himself, for to love oneself is the same as to desire some good for oneself. Consequently it amounts to the same whether we reckon pride or self-love as the beginning of every evil.

THIRD ARTICLE [I-II, Q. 84, Art. 3]

Whether Any Other Special Sins, Besides Pride and Avarice, Should Be Called Capital?

Objection 1: It would seem that no other special sins, besides pride and avarice, should be called capital. Because "the head seems to be to an animal, what the root is to a plant," as stated in *De Anima* ii, text. 38: for the roots are like a mouth. If therefore covetousness is called the "root of all evils," it seems that it alone, and no other sin, should be called a capital vice.

Obj. 2: Further, the head bears a certain relation of order to the other members, in so far as sensation and movement follow from the head. But sin implies privation of order. Therefore sin has not the character of head: so that no sins should be called capital.

Obj. 3: Further, capital crimes are those which receive capital punishment. But every kind of sin comprises some that are punished thus. Therefore the capital sins are not certain specific sins.

*On the contrary,* Gregory (Moral. xxxi, 17) enumerates certain special vices under the name of capital.

*I answer that,* The word capital is derived from caput (a head). Now the head, properly speaking, is that part of an animal's body, which is the principle and director of the whole animal. Hence, metaphorically speaking, every principle is called a head, and even men who direct and govern others are called heads. Accordingly a capital vice is so called, in the first place, from "head" taken in the proper sense, and thus the name "capital" is given to a sin for which capital punishment is inflicted. It is not in this sense that we are now speaking of capital sins, but in another sense, in which the term "capital" is derived from head, taken metaphorically for a principle or director of others. In this way a capital vice is one from which other vices arise, chiefly by being their final cause, which origin is formal, as stated above (Q. 72, A. 6). Wherefore a capital vice is not only the principle of others, but is also their director and, in a way, their leader: because the art or habit, to which the end belongs, is always the principle and the commander in matters concerning the means. Hence Gregory (Moral. xxxi, 17) compares these capital vices to the "leaders of an army."

Reply Obj. 1: The term "capital" is taken from *caput* and applied to something connected with, or partaking of the head, as having some property thereof, but not as being the head taken literally. And therefore the capital vices are not only those which have the character of primary origin, as covetousness which is called the "root," and pride which is called the beginning, but also those which have the character of proximate origin in respect of several sins.

Reply Obj. 2: Sin lacks order in so far as it turns away from God, for in this respect it is an evil, and evil, according to Augustine (De Natura Boni iv), is "the privation of mode, species and order." But in so far as sin implies a turning to something, it regards some good: wherefore, in this respect, there can be order in sin.

Reply Obj. 3: This objection considers capital sin as so called from the punishment it deserves, in which sense we are not taking it here.

FOURTH ARTICLE [I-II, Q. 84, Art. 4]

Whether the Seven Capital Vices Are Suitably Reckoned?

Objection 1: It would seem that we ought not to reckon seven capital vices, viz. vainglory, envy, anger, sloth, covetousness, gluttony, lust. For sins are opposed to virtues. But there are four principal virtues, as stated above (Q. 61, A. 2). Therefore there are only four principal or capital vices.

Obj. 2: Further, the passions of the soul are causes of sin, as stated above (Q. 77). But there are four principal passions of the soul; two of which, viz. hope and fear, are not mentioned among the above sins, whereas certain vices are mentioned to which pleasure and sadness belong, since pleasure belongs to gluttony and lust, and sadness to sloth and envy. Therefore the principal sins are unfittingly enumerated.

Obj. 3: Further, anger is not a principal passion. Therefore it should not be placed among the principal vices.

Obj. 4: Further, just as covetousness or avarice is the root of sin, so is pride the beginning of sin, as stated above (A. 2). But avarice is reckoned to be one of the capital vices. Therefore pride also should be placed among the capital vices.

Obj. 5: Further, some sins are committed which cannot be caused through any of these: as, for instance, when one sins through ignorance, or when one commits a sin with a good intention, e.g. steals in order to give an alms. Therefore the capital vices are insufficiently enumerated.

*On the contrary,* stands the authority of Gregory who enumerates them in this way (Moral. xxxi, 17).

*I answer that,* As stated above (A. 3), the capital vices are those which give rise to others, especially by way of final cause. Now this kind of origin may take place in two ways. First, on account of the condition of the sinner, who is disposed so as to have a strong inclination for one particular end, the result being that he frequently goes forward to other sins. But this kind of origin does not come under the consideration of art, because man's particular dispositions are infinite in number. Secondly, on account of a natural relationship of the ends to one another: and it is in this way that most frequently one vice arises from another, so that this kind of origin can come under the consideration of art.

Accordingly therefore, those vices are called capital, whose ends have certain fundamental reasons for moving the appetite; and it is in respect of these fundamental reasons that the capital vices are differentiated. Now a thing moves the appetite in two ways. First, directly and of its very nature: thus good moves the appetite to seek it, while evil, for the same reason, moves the appetite to avoid it. Secondly, indirectly and on account of something else, as it were: thus one seeks an evil on account of some attendant good, or avoids a good on account of some attendant evil.

Again, man's good is threefold. For, in the first place, there is a certain good of the soul, which derives its aspect of appetibility, merely through being apprehended, viz. the excellence of honor and praise, and this good is sought inordinately by *vainglory.* Secondly, there is the good of the body, and this regards either the preservation of the individual, e.g. meat and drink, which good is pursued inordinately by *gluttony,* or the preservation of the species, e.g. sexual intercourse, which good is sought inordinately by *lust.* Thirdly, there is external good, viz. riches, to which *covetousness* is referred. These same four vices avoid inordinately the contrary evils.

Or again, good moves the appetite chiefly through possessing some property of happiness, which all men seek naturally. Now in the first place happiness implies perfection, since happiness is a perfect good, to which belongs excellence or renown, which is desired by *pride* or vainglory. Secondly, it implies satiety, which *covetousness* seeks in riches that give promise thereof. Thirdly, it implies pleasure, without which happiness is impossible, as stated in *Ethic.* i, 7; x, 6, 7, 8 and this gluttony and lust pursue.

On the other hand, avoidance of good on account of an attendant evil occurs in two ways. For this happens either in respect of one's own good, and thus we have *sloth,* which is sadness about one's spiritual good, on account of the attendant bodily labor: or else it happens in respect of another's good, and this, if it be without recrimination, belongs to *envy,* which is sadness about another's good as being a hindrance to one's own excellence, while if it be with recrimination with a view to vengeance, it is *anger.* Again, these same vices seek the contrary evils.

Reply Obj. 1: Virtue and vice do not originate in the same way: since virtue is caused by the subordination of the appetite to reason, or to the immutable good, which is God, whereas vice arises from the appetite for mutable good. Wherefore there is no need for the principal vices to be contrary to the principal virtues.

Reply Obj. 2: Fear and hope are irascible passions. Now all the passions of the irascible part arise from passions of the concupiscible part; and these are all, in a way, directed to pleasure or sorrow. Hence pleasure and sorrow have a prominent place among the capital sins, as being the most important of the passions, as stated above (Q. 25, A. 4).

Reply Obj. 3: Although anger is not a principal passion, yet it has a distinct place among the capital vices, because it implies a special kind of movement in the appetite, in so far as recrimination against another's good has the aspect of a virtuous good, i.e. of the right to vengeance.

Reply Obj. 4: Pride is said to be the beginning of every sin, in the order of the end, as stated above (A. 2): and it is in the same order that we are to consider the capital sin as being principal. Wherefore pride, like a universal vice, is not counted along with the others, but is reckoned as the "queen of them all," as Gregory states (Moral. xxxi, 27). But covetousness is said to be the root from another point of view, as stated above (AA. 1, 2).

Reply Obj. 5: These vices are called capital because others, most frequently, arise from them: so that nothing prevents some sins from arising out of other causes. Nevertheless we might say that all the sins which are due to ignorance, can be reduced to sloth, to which pertains the negligence of a man who declines to acquire spiritual goods on account of the attendant labor; for the ignorance that can cause sin, is due to negligence, as stated above (Q. 76, A. 2). That a man commit a sin with a good intention, seems to point to ignorance, in so far as he knows not that evil should not be done that good may come of it.

## QUESTION 85

OF THE EFFECTS OF SIN, AND, FIRST, OF THE CORRUPTION OF THE GOOD OF NATURE (In Six Articles)

We must now consider the effects of sin; and (1) the corruption of the good of nature; (2) the stain on the soul; (3) the debt of punishment.

Under the first head there are six points of inquiry:

(1) Whether the good of nature is diminished by sin?

(2) Whether it can be taken away altogether?

(3) Of the four wounds, mentioned by Bede, with which human nature is stricken in consequence of sin.

(4) Whether privation of mode, species and order is an effect of sin?

(5) Whether death and other bodily defects are the result of sin?

(6) Whether they are, in any way, natural to man?

FIRST ARTICLE [I-II, Q. 85, Art. 1]

Whether Sin Diminishes the Good of Nature?

Objection 1: It would seem that sin does not diminish the good of nature. For man's sin is no worse than the devil's. But natural good remains unimpaired in devils after sin, as Dionysius states (Div. Nom. iv). Therefore neither does sin diminish the good of human nature.

Obj. 2: Further, when that which follows is changed, that which precedes remains unchanged, since substance remains the same when its accidents are changed. But nature exists before the voluntary action. Therefore, when sin has caused a disorder in a voluntary act, nature is not changed on that account, so that the good of nature be diminished.

Obj. 3: Further, sin is an action, while diminution is a passion. Now no agent is passive by the very reason of its acting, although it is possible for it to act on one thing, and to be passive as regards another. Therefore he who sins, does not, by his sin, diminish the good of his nature.

Obj. 4: Further, no accident acts on its subject: because that which is patient is a potential being, while that which is subjected to an accident, is already an actual being as regards that accident. But sin is in the good of nature as an accident in a subject. Therefore sin does not diminish the good of nature, since to diminish is to act.

*On the contrary,* "A certain man going down from Jerusalem to Jericho (Luke 10:30), i.e. to the corruption of sin, was stripped of his gifts, and wounded in his nature," as Bede [*The quotation is from the Glossa Ordinaria of Strabo] expounds the passage. Therefore sin diminishes the good of nature.

*I answer that,* The good of human nature is threefold. First, there are the principles of which nature is constituted, and the properties that flow from them, such as the powers of the soul, and so forth. Secondly, since man has from nature an inclination to virtue, as stated above (Q. 60, A. 1; Q. 63, A. 1), this inclination to virtue is a good of nature. Thirdly, the gift of original justice, conferred on the whole of human nature in the person of the first man, may be called a good of nature.

Accordingly, the first-mentioned good of nature is neither destroyed nor diminished by sin. The third good of nature was entirely destroyed through the sin of our first parent. But the second good of nature, viz. the natural inclination to virtue, is diminished by sin. Because human acts produce an inclination to like acts, as stated above (Q. 50, A. 1). Now from the very fact that thing becomes inclined to one of two contraries, its inclination to the other contrary must needs be diminished. Wherefore as sin is opposed to virtue, from the very fact that a man sins, there results a diminution of that good of nature, which is the inclination to virtue.

Reply Obj. 1: Dionysius is speaking of the first-mentioned good of nature, which consists in "being, living and understanding," as anyone may see who reads the context.

Reply Obj. 2: Although nature precedes the voluntary action, it has an inclination to a certain voluntary action. Wherefore nature is not changed in itself, through a change in the voluntary action: it is the inclination that is changed in so far as it is directed to its term.

Reply Obj. 3: A voluntary action proceeds from various powers, active and passive. The result is that through voluntary actions something is caused or taken away in the man who acts, as we have stated when treating of the production of habits (Q. 51, A. 2).

Reply Obj. 4: An accident does not act effectively on its subject, but it acts on it formally, in the same sense as when we say that whiteness makes a thing white. In this way there is nothing to hinder sin from diminishing the good of nature; but only in so far as sin is itself a diminution of the good of nature, through being an inordinateness of action. But as regards the inordinateness of the agent, we must say that such like inordinateness is caused by the fact that in the acts of the soul, there is an active, and a passive element: thus the sensible object moves the sensitive appetite, and the sensitive appetite inclines the reason and will, as stated above (Q. 77, AA. 1, 2). The result of this is the inordinateness, not as though an accident acted on its own subject, but in so far as the object acts on the power, and one power acts on another and puts it out of order.

SECOND ARTICLE [I-II, Q. 85, Art. 2]

Whether the Entire Good of Human Nature Can Be Destroyed by Sin?

Objection 1: It would seem that the entire good of human nature can be destroyed by sin. For the good of human nature is finite, since human nature itself is finite. Now any finite thing is entirely taken away, if the subtraction be continuous. Since therefore the good of nature can be continually diminished by sin, it seems that in the end it can be entirely taken away.

Obj. 2: Further, in a thing of one nature, the whole and the parts are uniform, as is evidently the case with air, water, flesh and all bodies with similar parts. But the good of nature is wholly uniform. Since therefore a part thereof can be taken away by sin, it seems that the whole can also be taken away by sin.

Obj. 3: Further, the good of nature, that is weakened by sin, is aptitude for virtue. Now this aptitude is destroyed entirely in some on account of sin: thus the lost cannot be restored to virtue any more than the blind can to sight. Therefore sin can take away the good of nature entirely.

*On the contrary,* Augustine says (Enchiridion xiv) that "evil does not exist except in some good." But the evil of sin cannot be in the good of virtue or of grace, because they are contrary to it. Therefore it must be in the good of nature, and consequently it does not destroy it entirely.

*I answer that,* As stated above (A. 1), the good of nature, that is diminished by sin, is the natural inclination to virtue, which is befitting to man from the very fact that he is a rational being; for it is due to this that he performs actions in accord with reason, which is to act virtuously. Now sin cannot entirely take away from man the fact that he is a rational being, for then he would no longer be capable of sin. Wherefore it is not possible for this good of nature to be destroyed entirely.

Since, however, this same good of nature may be continually diminished by sin, some, in order to illustrate this, have made use of the example of a finite thing being diminished indefinitely, without being entirely destroyed. For the Philosopher says (Phys. i, text. 37) that if from a finite magnitude a continual subtraction be made in the same quantity, it will at last be entirely destroyed, for instance if from any finite length I continue to subtract the length of a span. If, however, the subtraction be made each time in the same proportion, and not in the same quantity, it may go on indefinitely, as, for instance, if a quantity be halved, and one half be diminished by half, it will be possible to go on thus indefinitely, provided that what is subtracted in each case be less than what was subtracted before. But this does not apply to the question at issue, since a subsequent sin does not diminish the good of nature less than a previous sin, but perhaps more, if it be a more grievous sin.

We must, therefore, explain the matter otherwise by saying that the aforesaid inclination is to be considered as a middle term between two others: for it is based on the rational nature as on its root, and tends to the good of virtue, as to its term and end. Consequently its diminution may be understood in two ways: first, on the part of its root, secondly, on the part of its term. In the first way, it is not diminished by sin, because sin does not diminish nature, as stated above (A. 1). But it is diminished in the second way, in so far as an obstacle is placed against its attaining its term. Now if it were diminished in the first way, it would needs be entirely destroyed at last by the rational nature being entirely destroyed. Since, however, it is diminished on the part of the obstacle which is placed against its attaining its term, it is evident that it can be diminished indefinitely, because obstacles can be placed indefinitely, inasmuch as man can go on indefinitely adding sin to sin: and yet it cannot be destroyed entirely, because the root of this inclination always remains. An example of this may be seen in a transparent body, which has an inclination to receive light, from the very fact that it is transparent; yet this inclination or aptitude is diminished on the part of supervening clouds, although it always remains rooted in the nature of the body.

Reply Obj. 1: This objection avails when diminution is made by subtraction. But here the diminution is made by raising obstacles, and this neither diminishes nor destroys the root of the inclination, as stated above.

Reply Obj. 2: The natural inclination is indeed wholly uniform: nevertheless it stands in relation both to its principle and to its term, in respect of which diversity of relation, it is diminished on the one hand, and not on the other.

Reply Obj. 3: Even in the lost the natural inclination to virtue remains, else they would have no remorse of conscience. That it is not reduced to act is owing to their being deprived of grace by Divine justice. Thus even in a blind man the aptitude to see remains in the very root of his nature, inasmuch as he is an animal naturally endowed with sight: yet this aptitude is not reduced to act, for the lack of a cause capable of reducing it, by forming the organ requisite for sight.

THIRD ARTICLE [I-II, Q. 85, Art. 3]

Whether Weakness, Ignorance, Malice and Concupiscence Are Suitably Reckoned As the Wounds of Nature Consequent Upon Sin?

Objection 1: It would seem that weakness, ignorance, malice and concupiscence are not suitably reckoned as the wounds of nature consequent upon sin. For one same thing is not both effect and cause of the same thing. But these are reckoned to be causes of sin, as appears from what has been said above (Q. 76, A. 1; Q. 77, AA. 3, 5; Q. 78, A. 1). Therefore they should not be reckoned as effects of sin.

Obj. 2: Further, malice is the name of a sin. Therefore it should have no place among the effects of sin.

Obj. 3: Further, concupiscence is something natural, since it is an act of the concupiscible power. But that which is natural should not be reckoned a wound of nature. Therefore concupiscence should not be reckoned a wound of nature.

Obj. 4: Further, it has been stated (Q. 77, A. 3) that to sin from weakness is the same as to sin from passion. But concupiscence is a passion. Therefore it should not be condivided with weakness.

Obj. 5: Further, Augustine (De Nat. et Grat. lxvii, 67) reckons "two things to be punishments inflicted on the soul of the sinner, viz. ignorance and difficulty," from which arise "error and vexation," which four do not coincide with the four in question. Therefore it seems that one or the other reckoning is incomplete.

*On the contrary,* The authority of Bede suffices [*Reference not known].

*I answer that,* As a result of original justice, the reason had perfect hold over the lower parts of the soul, while reason itself was perfected by God, and was subject to Him. Now this same original justice was forfeited through the sin of our first parent, as already stated (Q. 81, A. 2); so that all the powers of the soul are left, as it were, destitute of their proper order, whereby they are naturally directed to virtue; which destitution is called a wounding of nature.

Again, there are four of the soul's powers that can be subject of virtue, as stated above (Q. 61, A. 2), viz. the reason, where prudence resides, the will, where justice is, the irascible, the subject of fortitude, and the concupiscible, the subject of temperance. Therefore in so far as the reason is deprived of its order to the true, there is the wound of ignorance; in so far as the will is deprived of its order of good, there is the wound of malice; in so far as the irascible is deprived of its order to the arduous, there is the wound of weakness; and in so far as the concupiscible is deprived of its order to the delectable, moderated by reason, there is the wound of concupiscence.

Accordingly these are the four wounds inflicted on the whole of human nature as a result of our first parent's sin. But since the inclination to the good of virtue is diminished in each individual on account of actual sin, as was explained above (AA. 1, 2), these four wounds are also the result of other sins, in so far as, through sin, the reason is obscured, especially in practical matters, the will hardened to evil, good actions become more difficult and concupiscence more impetuous.

Reply Obj. 1: There is no reason why the effect of one sin should not be the cause of another: because the soul, through sinning once, is more easily inclined to sin again.

Reply Obj. 2: Malice is not to be taken here as a sin, but as a certain proneness of the will to evil, according to the words of Gen. 8:21: "Man's senses are prone to evil from his youth" [*Vulgate: 'The imagination and thought of man's heart are prone to evil from his youth.'].

Reply Obj. 3: As stated above (Q. 82, A. 3, ad 1), concupiscence is natural to man, in so far as it is subject to reason: whereas, in so far as it is goes beyond the bounds of reason, it is unnatural to man.

Reply Obj. 4: Speaking in a general way, every passion can be called a weakness, in so far as it weakens the soul's strength and clogs the reason. Bede, however, took weakness in the strict sense, as contrary to fortitude which pertains to the irascible.

Reply Obj. 5: The "difficulty" which is mentioned in this book of Augustine, includes the three wounds affecting the appetitive powers, viz. "malice," "weakness" and "concupiscence," for it is owing to these three that a man finds it difficult to tend to the good. "Error" and "vexation" are consequent wounds, since a man is vexed through being weakened in respect of the objects of his concupiscence.

FOURTH ARTICLE [I-II, Q. 85, Art. 4]

Whether Privation of Mode, Species and Order Is the Effect of Sin?

Objection 1: It would seem that privation of mode, species and order is not the effect of sin. For Augustine says (De Natura Boni iii) that "where these three abound, the good is great; where they are less, there is less good; where they are not, there is no good at all." But sin does not destroy the good of nature. Therefore it does not destroy mode, species and order.

Obj. 2: Further, nothing is its own cause. But sin itself is the "privation of mode, species and order," as Augustine states (De Natura Boni iv). Therefore privation of mode, species and order is not the effect of sin.

Obj. 3: Further, different effects result from different sins. Now since mode, species and order are diverse, their corresponding privations must be diverse also, and, consequently, must be the result of different sins. Therefore privation of mode, species and order is not the effect of each sin.

*On the contrary,* Sin is to the soul what weakness is to the body, according to Ps. 6:3, "Have mercy on me, O Lord, for I am weak." Now weakness deprives the body of mode, species and order.

*I answer that,* As stated in the First Part, Q. 5, A. 5, mode, species and order are consequent upon every created good, as such, and also upon every being. Because every being and every good as such depends on its form from which it derives its species. Again, any kind of form, whether substantial or accidental, of anything whatever, is according to some measure, wherefore it is stated in *Metaph.* viii, that "the forms of things are like numbers," so that a form has a certain *mode* corresponding to its measure. Lastly owing to its form, each thing has a relation of *order* to something else.

Accordingly there are different grades of mode, species and order, corresponding to the different degrees of good. For there is a good belonging to the very substance of nature, which good has its mode, species and order, and is neither destroyed nor diminished by sin. There is again the good of the natural inclination, which also has its mode, species and order; and this is diminished by sin, as stated above (AA. 1, 2), but is not entirely destroyed. Again, there is the good of virtue and grace: this too has its mode, species and order, and is entirely taken away by sin. Lastly, there is a good consisting in the ordinate act itself, which also has its mode, species and order, the privation of which is essentially sin. Hence it is clear both how sin is privation of mode, species and order, and how it destroys or diminishes mode, species and order.

This suffices for the Replies to the first two Objections.

Reply Obj. 3: Mode, species and order follow one from the other, as explained above: and so they are destroyed or diminished together.

FIFTH ARTICLE [I-II, Q. 85, Art. 5]

Whether Death and Other Bodily Defects Are the Result of Sin?

Objection 1: It would seem that death and other bodily defects are not the result of sin. Because equal causes have equal effects. Now these defects are not equal in all, but abound in some more than in others, whereas original sin, from which especially these defects seem to result, is equal in all, as stated above (Q. 82, A. 4). Therefore death and suchlike defects are not the result of sin.

Obj. 2: Further, if the cause is removed, the effect is removed. But these defects are not removed, when all sin is removed by Baptism or Penance. Therefore they are not the effect of sin.

Obj. 3: Further, actual sin has more of the character of guilt than original sin has. But actual sin does not change the nature of the body by subjecting it to some defect. Much less, therefore, does original sin. Therefore death and other bodily defects are not the result of sin.

*On the contrary,* The Apostle says (Rom. 5:12), "By one man sin entered into this world, and by sin death."

*I answer that,* One thing causes another in two ways: first, by reason of itself; secondly, accidentally. By reason of itself, one thing is the cause of another, if it produces its effect by reason of the power of its nature or form, the result being that the effect is directly intended by the cause. Consequently, as death and such like defects are beside the intention of the sinner, it is evident that sin is not, of itself, the cause of these defects. Accidentally, one thing is the cause of another if it causes it by removing an obstacle: thus it is stated in *Phys.* viii, text. 32, that "by displacing a pillar a man moves accidentally the stone resting thereon." In this way the sin of our first parent is the cause of death and all such like defects in human nature, in so far as by the sin of our first parent original justice was taken away, whereby not only were the lower powers of the soul held together under the control of reason, without any disorder whatever, but also the whole body was held together in subjection to the soul, without any defect, as stated in the First Part (Q. 97, A. 1). Wherefore, original justice being forfeited through the sin of our first parent; just as human nature was stricken in the soul by the disorder among the powers, as stated above (A. 3; Q. 82, A. 3), so also it became subject to corruption, by reason of disorder in the body.

Now the withdrawal of original justice has the character of punishment, even as the withdrawal of grace has. Consequently, death and all consequent bodily defects are punishments of original sin. And although the defects are not intended by the sinner, nevertheless they are ordered according to the justice of God Who inflicts them as punishments.

Reply Obj. 1: Causes that produce their effects of themselves, if equal, produce equal effects: for if such causes be increased or diminished, the effect is increased or diminished. But equal causes of an obstacle being removed, do not point to equal effects. For supposing a man employs equal force in displacing two columns, it does not follow that the movements of the stones resting on them will be equal; but that one will move with greater velocity, which has the greater weight according to the property of its nature, to which it is left when the obstacle to its falling is removed. Accordingly, when original justice is removed, the nature of the human body is left to itself, so that according to diverse natural temperaments, some men's bodies are subject to more defects, some to fewer, although original sin is equal in all.

Reply Obj. 2: Both original and actual sin are removed by the same cause that removes these defects, according to the Apostle (Rom. 8:11): "He ... shall quicken ... your mortal bodies, because of His Spirit that dwelleth in you": but each is done according to the order of Divine wisdom, at a fitting time. Because it is right that we should first of all be conformed to Christ's sufferings, before attaining to the immortality and impassibility of glory, which was begun in Him, and by Him acquired for us. Hence it behooves that our bodies should remain, for a time, subject to suffering, in order that we may merit the impassibility of glory, in conformity with Christ.

Reply Obj. 3: Two things may be considered in actual sin, the substance of the act, and the aspect of fault. As regards the substance of the act, actual sin can cause a bodily defect: thus some sicken and die through eating too much. But as regards the fault, it deprives us of grace which is given to us that we may regulate the acts of the soul, but not that we may ward off defects of the body, as original justice did. Wherefore actual sin does not cause those defects, as original sin does.

SIXTH ARTICLE [I-II, Q. 85, Art. 6]

Whether Death and Other Defects Are Natural to Man?

Objection 1: It would seem that death and such like defects are natural to man. For "the corruptible and the incorruptible differ generically" (Metaph. x, text. 26). But man is of the same genus as other animals which are naturally corruptible. Therefore man is naturally corruptible.

Obj. 2: Further, whatever is composed of contraries is naturally corruptible, as having within itself the cause of corruption. But such is the human body. Therefore it is naturally corruptible.

Obj. 3: Further, a hot thing naturally consumes moisture. Now human life is preserved by hot and moist elements. Since therefore the vital functions are fulfilled by the action of natural heat, as stated in *De Anima* ii, text. 50, it seems that death and such like defects are natural to man.

*On the contrary,* (1) God made in man whatever is natural to him. Now "God made not death" (Wis. 1:13). Therefore death is not natural to man.

(2) Further, that which is natural cannot be called either a punishment or an evil: since what is natural to a thing is suitable to it. But death and such like defects are the punishment of original sin, as stated above (A. 5). Therefore they are not natural to man.

(3) Further, matter is proportionate to form, and everything to its end. Now man's end is everlasting happiness, as stated above (Q. 2, A. 7; Q. 5, AA. 3, 4): and the form of the human body is the rational soul, as was proved in the First Part (Q. 75, A. 6). Therefore the human body is naturally incorruptible.

*I answer that,* We may speak of any corruptible thing in two ways; first, in respect of its universal nature, secondly, as regards its particular nature. A thing's particular nature is its own power of action and self-preservation. And in respect of this nature, every corruption and defect is contrary to nature, as stated in *De Coelo* ii, text. 37, since this power tends to the being and preservation of the thing to which it belongs.

On the other hand, the universal nature is an active force in some universal principle of nature, for instance in some heavenly body; or again belonging to some superior substance, in which sense God is said by some to be "the Nature Who makes nature." This force intends the good and the preservation of the universe, for which alternate generation and corruption in things are requisite: and in this respect corruption and defect in things are natural, not indeed as regards the inclination of the form which is the principle of being and perfection, but as regards the inclination of matter which is allotted proportionately to its particular form according to the discretion of the universal agent. And although every form intends perpetual being as far as it can, yet no form of a corruptible being can achieve its own perpetuity, except the rational soul; for the reason that the latter is not entirely subject to matter, as other forms are; indeed it has an immaterial operation of its own, as stated in the First Part (Q. 75, A. 2). Consequently as regards his form, incorruption is more natural to man than to other corruptible things. But since that very form has a matter composed of contraries, from the inclination of that matter there results corruptibility in the whole. In this respect man is naturally corruptible as regards the nature of his matter left to itself, but not as regards the nature of his form.

The first three objections argue on the side of the matter; while the other three argue on the side of the form. Wherefore in order to solve them, we must observe that the form of man which is the rational soul, in respect of its incorruptibility is adapted to its end, which is everlasting happiness: whereas the human body, which is corruptible, considered in respect of its nature, is, in a way, adapted to its form, and, in another way, it is not. For we may note a twofold condition in any matter, one which the agent chooses, and another which is not chosen by the agent, and is a natural condition of matter. Thus, a smith in order to make a knife, chooses a matter both hard and flexible, which can be sharpened so as to be useful for cutting, and in respect of this condition iron is a matter adapted for a knife: but that iron be breakable and inclined to rust, results from the natural disposition of iron, nor does the workman choose this in the iron, indeed he would do without it if he could: wherefore this disposition of matter is not adapted to the workman's intention, nor to the purpose of his art. In like manner the human body is the matter chosen by nature in respect of its being of a mixed temperament, in order that it may be most suitable as an organ of touch and of the other sensitive and motive powers. Whereas the fact that it is corruptible is due to a condition of matter, and is not chosen by nature: indeed nature would choose an incorruptible matter if it could. But God, to Whom every nature is subject, in forming man supplied the defect of nature, and by the gift of original justice, gave the body a certain incorruptibility, as was stated in the First Part (Q. 97, A. 1). It is in this sense that it is said that "God made not death," and that death is the punishment of sin.

This suffices for the Replies to the Objections.

# QUESTION 86

OF THE STAIN OF SIN (In Two Articles)

We must now consider the stain of sin; under which head there are two points of inquiry:

(1) Whether an effect of sin is a stain on the soul?

(2) Whether it remains in the soul after the act of sin?

FIRST ARTICLE [I-II, Q. 86, Art. 1]

Whether Sin Causes a Stain on the Soul?

Objection 1: It would seem that sin causes no stain on the soul. For a higher nature cannot be defiled by contact with a lower nature: hence the sun's ray is not defiled by contact with tainted bodies, as Augustine says (Contra Quinque Haereses v). Now the human soul is of a much higher nature than mutable things, to which it turns by sinning. Therefore it does not contract a stain from them by sinning.

Obj. 2: Further, sin is chiefly in the will, as stated above (Q. 74, AA. 1, 2). Now the will is in the reason, as stated in *DeAnima* iii, text. 42. But the reason or intellect is not stained by considering anything whatever; rather indeed is it perfected thereby. Therefore neither is the will stained by sin.

Obj. 3: Further, if sin causes a stain, this stain is either something positive, or a pure privation. If it be something positive, it can only be either a disposition or a habit: for it seems that nothing else can be caused by an act. But it is neither disposition nor habit: for it happens that a stain remains even after the removal of a disposition or habit; for instance, in a man who after committing a mortal sin of prodigality, is so changed as to fall into a sin of the opposite vice. Therefore the stain does not denote anything positive in the soul. Again, neither is it a pure privation. Because all sins agree on the part of aversion and privation of grace: and so it would follow that there is but one stain caused by all sins. Therefore the stain is not the effect of sin.

*On the contrary,* It was said to Solomon (Ecclus. 47:22): "Thou hast stained thy glory": and it is written (Eph. 5:27): "That He might present it to Himself a glorious church not having spot or wrinkle": and in each case it is question of the stain of sin. Therefore a stain is the effect of sin.

*I answer that,* A stain is properly ascribed to corporeal things, when a comely body loses its comeliness through contact with another body, e.g. a garment, gold or silver, or the like. Accordingly a stain is ascribed to spiritual things in like manner. Now man's soul has a twofold comeliness; one from the refulgence of the natural light of reason, whereby he is directed in his actions; the other, from the refulgence of the Divine light, viz. of wisdom and grace, whereby man is also perfected for the purpose of doing good and fitting actions. Now, when the soul cleaves to things by love, there is a kind of contact in the soul: and when man sins, he cleaves to certain things, against the light of reason and of the Divine law, as shown above (Q. 71, A. 6). Wherefore the loss of comeliness occasioned by this contact, is metaphorically called a stain on the soul.

Reply Obj. 1: The soul is not defiled by inferior things, by their own power, as though they acted on the soul: *on the contrary,* the soul, by its own action, defiles itself, through cleaving to them inordinately, against the light of reason and of the Divine law.

Reply Obj. 2: The action of the intellect is accomplished by the intelligible thing being in the intellect, according to the mode of the intellect, so that the intellect is not defiled, but perfected, by them. On the other hand, the act of the will consists in a movement towards things themselves, so that love attaches the soul to the thing loved. Thus it is that the soul is stained, when it cleaves inordinately, according to Osee 9:10: "They ... became abominable as those things were which they loved."

Reply Obj. 3: The stain is neither something positive in the soul, nor does it denote a pure privation: it denotes a privation of the soul's brightness in relation to its cause, which is sin; wherefore diverse sins occasion diverse stains. It is like a shadow, which is the privation of light through the interposition of a body, and which varies according to the diversity of the interposed bodies.

SECOND ARTICLE [I-II, Q. 86, Art. 2]

Whether the Stain Remains in the Soul After the Act of Sin?

Objection 1: It would seem that the stain does not remain in the soul after the act of sin. For after an action, nothing remains in the soul except habit or disposition. But the stain is not a habit or disposition, as stated above (A. 1, Obj. 3). Therefore the stain does not remain in the soul after the act of sin.

Obj. 2: Further, the stain is to the sin what the shadow is to the body, as stated above (A. 1, ad 3). But the shadow does not remain when the body has passed by. Therefore the stain does not remain in the soul when the act of sin is past.

Obj. 3: Further, every effect depends on its cause. Now the cause of the stain is the act of sin. Therefore when the act of sin is no longer there, neither is the stain in the soul.

*On the contrary,* It is written (Jos. 22:17): "Is it a small thing to you that you sinned with Beelphegor, and the stain of that crime remaineth in you [Vulg.: 'us'] to this day?"

*I answer that,* The stain of sin remains in the soul even when the act of sin is past. The reason for this is that the stain, as stated above (A. 1), denotes a blemish in the brightness of the soul, on account of its withdrawing from the light of reason or of the Divine law. And therefore so long as man remains out of this light, the stain of sin remains in him: but as soon as, moved by grace, he returns to the Divine light and to the light of reason, the stain is removed. For although the act of sin ceases, whereby man withdrew from the light of reason and of the Divine law, man does not at once return to the state in which he was before, and it is necessary that his will should have a movement contrary to the previous movement. Thus if one man be parted from another on account of some kind of movement, he is not reunited to him as soon as the movement ceases, but he needs to draw nigh to him and to return by a contrary movement.

Reply Obj. 1: Nothing positive remains in the soul after the act of sin, except the disposition or habit; but there does remain something privative, viz. the privation of union with the Divine light.

Reply Obj. 2: After the interposed body has passed by, the transparent body remains in the same position and relation as regards the illuminating body, and so the shadow passes at once. But when the sin is past, the soul does not remain in the same relation to God: and so there is no comparison.

Reply Obj. 3: The act of sin parts man from God, which parting causes the defect of brightness, just as local movement causes local parting. Wherefore, just as when movement ceases, local distance is not removed, so neither, when the act of sin ceases, is the stain removed.

# QUESTION 87

OF THE DEBT OF PUNISHMENT (In Eight Articles)

We must now consider the debt of punishment. We shall consider (1) the debt itself; (2) mortal and venial sin, which differ in respect of the punishment due to them.

Under the first head there are eight points of inquiry:

(1) Whether the debt of punishment is an effect of sin?

(2) Whether one sin can be the punishment of another?

(3) Whether any sin incurs a debt of eternal punishment?

(4) Whether sin incurs a debt of punishment that is infinite in quantity?

(5) Whether every sin incurs a debt of eternal and infinite punishment?

(6) Whether the debt of punishment can remain after sin?

(7) Whether every punishment is inflicted for a sin?

(8) Whether one person can incur punishment for another's sin?

FIRST ARTICLE [I-II, Q. 87, Art. 1]

Whether the Debt of Punishment Is an Effect of Sin?

Objection 1: It would seem that the debt of punishment is not an effect of sin. For that which is accidentally related to a thing, does not seem to be its proper effect. Now the debt of punishment is accidentally related to sin, for it is beside the intention of the sinner. Therefore the debt of punishment is not an effect of sin.

Obj. 2: Further, evil is not the cause of good. But punishment is good, since it is just, and is from God. Therefore it is not an effect of sin, which is evil.

Obj. 3: Further, Augustine says (Confess. i) that "every inordinate affection is its own punishment." But punishment does not incur a further debt of punishment, because then it would go on indefinitely. Therefore sin does not incur the debt of punishment.

*On the contrary,* It is written (Rom. 2:9): "Tribulation and anguish upon every soul of man that worketh evil." But to work evil is to sin. Therefore sin incurs a punishment which is signified by the words "tribulation and anguish."

*I answer that,* It has passed from natural things to human affairs that whenever one thing rises up against another, it suffers some detriment therefrom. For we observe in natural things that when one contrary supervenes, the other acts with greater energy, for which reason "hot water freezes more rapidly," as stated in *Meteor.* i, 12. Wherefore we find that the natural inclination of man is to repress those who rise up against him. Now it is evident that all things contained in an order, are, in a manner, one, in relation to the principle of that order. Consequently, whatever rises up against an order, is put down by that order or by the principle thereof. And because sin is an inordinate act, it is evident that whoever sins, commits an offense against an order: wherefore he is put down, in consequence, by that same order, which repression is punishment.

Accordingly, man can be punished with a threefold punishment corresponding to the three orders to which the human will is subject. In the first place a man's nature is subjected to the order of his own reason; secondly, it is subjected to the order of another man who governs him either in spiritual or in temporal matters, as a member either of the state or of the household; thirdly, it is subjected to the universal order of the Divine government. Now each of these orders is disturbed by sin, for the sinner acts against his reason, and against human and Divine law. Wherefore he incurs a threefold punishment; one, inflicted by himself, viz. remorse of conscience; another, inflicted by man; and a third, inflicted by God.

Reply Obj. 1: Punishment follows sin, inasmuch as this is an evil by reason of its being inordinate. Wherefore just as evil is accidental to the sinner's act, being beside his intention, so also is the debt of punishment.

Reply Obj. 2: Further, a just punishment may be inflicted either by God or by man: wherefore the punishment itself is the effect of sin, not directly but dispositively. Sin, however, makes man deserving of punishment, and that is an evil: for Dionysius says (Div. Nom. iv) that "punishment is not an evil, but to deserve punishment is." Consequently the debt of punishment is considered to be directly the effect of sin.

Reply Obj. 3: This punishment of the *inordinate affection* is due to sin as overturning the order of reason. Nevertheless sin incurs a further punishment, through disturbing the order of the Divine or human law.

SECOND ARTICLE [I-II, Q. 87, Art. 2]

Whether Sin Can Be the Punishment of Sin?

Objection 1: It would seem that sin cannot be the punishment of sin. For the purpose of punishment is to bring man back to the good of virtue, as the Philosopher declares (Ethic. x, 9). Now sin does not bring man back to the good of virtue, but leads him in the opposite direction. Therefore sin is not the punishment of sin.

Obj. 2: Further, just punishments are from God, as Augustine says (Qq. lxxxiii, qu. 82). But sin is not from God, and is an injustice. Therefore sin cannot be the punishment of sin.

Obj. 3: Further, the nature of punishment is to be something against the will. But sin is something from the will, as shown above (Q. 74, AA. 1, 2). Therefore sin cannot be the punishment of sin.

*On the contrary,* Gregory speaks (Hom. xi in Ezech.) that some sins are punishments of others.

*I answer that,* We may speak of sin in two ways: first, in its essence, as such; secondly, as to that which is accidental thereto. Sin as such can nowise be the punishment of another. Because sin considered in its essence is something proceeding from the will, for it is from this that it derives the character of guilt. Whereas punishment is essentially something against the will, as stated in the First Part (Q. 48, A. 5). Consequently it is evident that sin regarded in its essence can nowise be the punishment of sin.

On the other hand, sin can be the punishment of sin accidentally in three ways. First, when one sin is the cause of another, by removing an impediment thereto. For passions, temptations of the devil, and the like are causes of sin, but are impeded by the help of Divine grace which is withdrawn on account of sin. Wherefore since the withdrawal of grace is a punishment, and is from God, as stated above (Q. 79, A. 3), the result is that the sin which ensues from this is also a punishment accidentally. It is in this sense that the Apostle speaks (Rom. 1:24) when he says: "Wherefore God gave them up to the desires of their heart," i.e. to their passions; because, to wit, when men are deprived of the help of Divine grace, they are overcome by their passions. In this way sin is always said to be the punishment of a preceding sin. Secondly, by reason of the substance of the act, which is such as to cause pain, whether it be an interior act, as is clearly the case with anger or envy, or an exterior act, as is the case with one who endures considerable trouble and loss in order to achieve a sinful act, according to Wis. 5:7: "We wearied ourselves in the way of iniquity." Thirdly, on the part of the effect, so that one sin is said to be a punishment by reason of its effect. In the last two ways, a sin is a punishment not only in respect of a preceding sin, but also with regard to itself.

Reply Obj. 1: Even when God punishes men by permitting them to fall into sin, this is directed to the good of virtue. Sometimes indeed it is for the good of those who are punished, when, to wit, men arise from sin, more humble and more cautious. But it is always for the amendment of others, who seeing some men fall from sin to sin, are the more fearful of sinning. With regard to the other two ways, it is evident that the punishment is intended for the sinner's amendment, since the very fact that man endures toil and loss in sinning, is of a nature to withdraw man from sin.

Reply Obj. 2: This objection considers sin essentially as such: and the same answer applies to the Third Objection.

THIRD ARTICLE [I-II, Q. 87, Art. 3]

Whether Any Sin Incurs a Debt of Eternal Punishment?

Objection 1: It would seem that no sin incurs a debt of eternal punishment. For a just punishment is equal to the fault, since justice is equality: wherefore it is written (Isa. 27:8): "In measure against measure, when it shall be cast off, thou shalt judge it." Now sin is temporal. Therefore it does not incur a debt of eternal punishment.

Obj. 2: Further, "punishments are a kind of medicine" (Ethic. ii, 3). But no medicine should be infinite, because it is directed to an end, and "what is directed to an end, is not infinite," as the Philosopher states (Polit. i, 6). Therefore no punishment should be infinite.

Obj. 3: Further, no one does a thing always unless he delights in it for its own sake. But "God hath not pleasure in the destruction of men" [Vulg.: 'of the living']. Therefore He will not inflict eternal punishment on man.

Obj. 4: Further, nothing accidental is infinite. But punishment is accidental, for it is not natural to the one who is punished. Therefore it cannot be of infinite duration.

*On the contrary,* It is written (Matt. 25:46): "These shall go into everlasting punishment"; and (Mk. 3:29): "He that shall blaspheme against the Holy Ghost, shall never have forgiveness, but shall be guilty of an everlasting sin."

*I answer that,* As stated above (A. 1), sin incurs a debt of punishment through disturbing an order. But the effect remains so long as the cause remains. Wherefore so long as the disturbance of the order remains the debt of punishment must needs remain also. Now disturbance of an order is sometimes reparable, sometimes irreparable: because a defect which destroys the principle is irreparable, whereas if the principle be saved, defects can be repaired by virtue of that principle. For instance, if the principle of sight be destroyed, sight cannot be restored except by Divine power; whereas, if the principle of sight be preserved, while there arise certain impediments to the use of sight, these can be remedied by nature or by art. Now in every order there is a principle whereby one takes part in that order. Consequently if a sin destroys the principle of the order whereby man's will is subject to God, the disorder will be such as to be considered in itself, irreparable, although it is possible to repair it by the power of God. Now the principle of this order is the last end, to which man adheres by charity. Therefore whatever sins turn man away from God, so as to destroy charity, considered in themselves, incur a debt of eternal punishment.

Reply Obj. 1: Punishment is proportionate to sin in point of severity, both in Divine and in human judgments. In no judgment, however, as Augustine says (De Civ. Dei xxi, 11) is it requisite for punishment to equal fault in point of duration. For the fact that adultery or murder is committed in a moment does not call for a momentary punishment: in fact they are punished sometimes by imprisonment or banishment for life—sometimes even by death; wherein account is not taken of the time occupied in killing, but rather of the expediency of removing the murderer from the fellowship of the living, so that this punishment, in its own way, represents the eternity of punishment inflicted by God. Now according to Gregory (Dial. iv, 44) it is just that he who has sinned against God in his own eternity should be punished in God's eternity. A man is said to have sinned in his own eternity, not only as regards continual sinning throughout his whole life, but also because, from the very fact that he fixes his end in sin, he has the will to sin, everlastingly. Wherefore Gregory says (Dial. iv, 44) that the "wicked would wish to live without end, that they might abide in their sins for ever."

Reply Obj. 2: Even the punishment that is inflicted according to human laws, is not always intended as a medicine for the one who is punished, but sometimes only for others: thus when a thief is hanged, this is not for his own amendment, but for the sake of others, that at least they may be deterred from crime through fear of the punishment, according to Prov. 19:25: "The wicked man being scourged, the fool shall be wiser." Accordingly the eternal punishments inflicted by God on the reprobate, are medicinal punishments for those who refrain from sin through the thought of those punishments, according to Ps. 59:6: "Thou hast given a warning to them that fear Thee, that they may flee from before the bow, that Thy beloved may be delivered."

Reply Obj. 3: God does not delight in punishments for their own sake; but He does delight in the order of His justice, which requires them.

Reply Obj. 4: Although punishment is related indirectly to nature, nevertheless it is essentially related to the disturbance of the order, and to God's justice. Wherefore, so long as the disturbance lasts, the punishment endures.

FOURTH ARTICLE [I-II, Q. 87, Art. 4]

Whether Sin Incurs a Debt of Punishment Infinite in Quantity?

Objection 1: It would seem that sin incurs a debt of punishment infinite in quantity. For it is written (Jer. 10:24): "Correct me, O Lord, but yet with judgment: and not in Thy fury, lest Thou bring me to nothing." Now God's anger or fury signifies metaphorically the vengeance of Divine justice: and to be brought to nothing is an infinite punishment, even as to make a thing out of nothing denotes infinite power. Therefore according to God's vengeance, sin is awarded a punishment infinite in quantity.

Obj. 2: Further, quantity of punishment corresponds to quantity of fault, according to Deut. 25:2: "According to the measure of the sin shall the measure also of the stripes be." Now a sin which is committed against God, is infinite: because the gravity of a sin increases according to the greatness of the person sinned against (thus it is a more grievous sin to strike the sovereign than a private individual), and God's greatness is infinite. Therefore an infinite punishment is due for a sin committed against God.

Obj. 3: Further, a thing may be infinite in two ways, in duration, and in quantity. Now the punishment is infinite in duration. Therefore it is infinite in quantity also.

*On the contrary,* If this were the case, the punishments of all mortal sins would be equal; because one infinite is not greater than another.

*I answer that,* Punishment is proportionate to sin. Now sin comprises two things. First, there is the turning away from the immutable good, which is infinite, wherefore, in this respect, sin is infinite. Secondly, there is the inordinate turning to mutable good. In this respect sin is finite, both because the mutable good itself is finite, and because the movement of turning towards it is finite, since the acts of a creature cannot be infinite. Accordingly, in so far as sin consists in turning away from something, its corresponding punishment is the *pain of loss,* which also is infinite, because it is the loss of the infinite good, i.e. God. But in so far as sin turns inordinately to something, its corresponding punishment is the *pain of sense,* which is also finite.

Reply Obj. 1: It would be inconsistent with Divine justice for the sinner to be brought to nothing absolutely, because this would be incompatible with the perpetuity of punishment that Divine justice requires, as stated above (A. 3). The expression "to be brought to nothing" is applied to one who is deprived of spiritual goods, according to 1 Cor. 13:2: "If I ... have not charity, I am nothing."

Reply Obj. 2: This argument considers sin as turning away from something, for it is thus that man sins against God.

Reply Obj. 3: Duration of punishment corresponds to duration of fault, not indeed as regards the act, but on the part of the stain, for as long as this remains, the debt of punishment remains. But punishment corresponds to fault in the point of severity. And a fault which is irreparable, is such that, of itself, it lasts for ever; wherefore it incurs an everlasting punishment. But it is not infinite as regards the thing it turns to; wherefore, in this respect, it does not incur punishment of infinite quantity.

FIFTH ARTICLE [I-II, Q. 87, Art. 5]

Whether Every Sin Incurs a Debt of Eternal Punishment?

Objection 1: It would seem that every sin incurs a debt of eternal punishment. Because punishment, as stated above (A. 4), is proportionate to the fault. Now eternal punishment differs infinitely from temporal punishment: whereas no sin, apparently, differs infinitely from another, since every sin is a human act, which cannot be infinite. Since therefore some sins incur a debt of everlasting punishment, as stated above (A. 4), it seems that no sin incurs a debt of mere temporal punishment.

Obj. 2: Further, original sin is the least of all sins, wherefore Augustine says (Enchiridion xciii) that "the lightest punishment is incurred by those who are punished for original sin alone." But original sin incurs everlasting punishment, since children who have died in original sin through not being baptized, will never see the kingdom of God, as shown by our Lord's words (John 3:3): "Unless a man be born again, he cannot see the kingdom of God." Much more, therefore, will the punishments of all other sins be everlasting.

Obj. 3: Further, a sin does not deserve greater punishment through being united to another sin; for Divine justice has allotted its punishment to each sin. Now a venial sin deserves eternal punishment if it be united to a mortal sin in a lost soul, because in hell there is no remission of sins. Therefore venial sin by itself deserves eternal punishment. Therefore temporal punishment is not due for any sin.

*On the contrary,* Gregory says (Dial. iv, 39), that certain slighter sins are remitted after this life. Therefore all sins are not punished eternally.

*I answer that,* As stated above (A. 3), a sin incurs a debt of eternal punishment, in so far as it causes an irreparable disorder in the order of Divine justice, through being contrary to the very principle of that order, viz. the last end. Now it is evident that in some sins there is disorder indeed, but such as not to involve contrariety in respect of the last end, but only in respect of things referable to the end, in so far as one is too much or too little intent on them without prejudicing the order to the last end: as, for instance, when a man is too fond of some temporal thing, yet would not offend God for its sake, by breaking one of His commandments. Consequently such sins do not incur everlasting, but only temporal punishment.

Reply Obj. 1: Sins do not differ infinitely from one another in respect of their turning towards mutable good, which constitutes the substance of the sinful act; but they do differ infinitely in respect of their turning away from something. Because some sins consist in turning away from the last end, and some in a disorder affecting things referable to the end: and the last end differs infinitely from the things that are referred to it.

Reply Obj. 2: Original sin incurs everlasting punishment, not on account of its gravity, but by reason of the condition of the subject, viz. a human being deprived of grace, without which there is no remission of sin.

The same answer applies to the Third Objection about venial sin. Because eternity of punishment does not correspond to the quantity of the sin, but to its irremissibility, as stated above (A. 3).

SIXTH ARTICLE [I-II, Q. 87, Art. 6]

Whether the Debt of Punishment Remains After Sin?

Objection 1: It would seem that there remains no debt of punishment after sin. For if the cause be removed the effect is removed. But sin is the cause of the debt of punishment. Therefore, when the sin is removed, the debt of punishment ceases also.

Obj. 2: Further, sin is removed by man returning to virtue. Now a virtuous man deserves, not punishment, but reward. Therefore, when sin is removed, the debt of punishment no longer remains.

Obj. 3: Further, "Punishments are a kind of medicine" (Ethic. ii, 3). But a man is not given medicine after being cured of his disease. Therefore, when sin is removed the debt of punishment does not remain.

*On the contrary,* It is written (2 Kings xii. 13, 14): "David said to Nathan: I have sinned against the Lord. And Nathan said to David: The Lord also hath taken away thy sin; thou shalt not die. Nevertheless because thou hast given occasion to the enemies of the Lord to blaspheme ... the child that is born to thee shall die." Therefore a man is punished by God even after his sin is forgiven: and so the debt of punishment remains, when the sin has been removed.

*I answer that,* Two things may be considered in sin: the guilty act, and the consequent stain. Now it is evident that in all actual sins, when the act of sin has ceased, the guilt remains; because the act of sin makes man deserving of punishment, in so far as he transgresses the order of Divine justice, to which he cannot return except he pay some sort of penal compensation, which restores him to the equality of justice; so that, according to the order of Divine justice, he who has been too indulgent to his will, by transgressing God's commandments, suffers, either willingly or unwillingly, something contrary to what he would wish. This restoration of the equality of justice by penal compensation is also to be observed in injuries done to one's fellow men. Consequently it is evident that when the sinful or injurious act has ceased there still remains the debt of punishment.

But if we speak of the removal of sin as to the stain, it is evident that the stain of sin cannot be removed from the soul, without the soul being united to God, since it was through being separated from Him that it suffered the loss of its brightness, in which the stain consists, as stated above (Q. 86, A. 1). Now man is united to God by his will. Wherefore the stain of sin cannot be removed from man, unless his will accept the order of Divine justice, that is to say, unless either of his own accord he take upon himself the punishment of his past sin, or bear patiently the punishment which God inflicts on him; and in both ways punishment avails for satisfaction. Now when punishment is satisfactory, it loses somewhat of the nature of punishment: for the nature of punishment is to be against the will; and although satisfactory punishment, absolutely speaking, is against the will, nevertheless in this particular case and for this particular purpose, it is voluntary. Consequently it is voluntary simply, but involuntary in a certain respect, as we have explained when speaking of the voluntary and the involuntary (Q. 6, A. 6). We must, therefore, say that, when the stain of sin has been removed, there may remain a debt of punishment, not indeed of punishment simply, but of satisfactory punishment.

Reply Obj. 1: Just as after the act of sin has ceased, the stain remains, as stated above (Q. 86, A. 2), so the debt of punishment also can remain. But when the stain has been removed, the debt of punishment does not remain in the same way, as stated.

Reply Obj. 2: The virtuous man does not deserve

punishment simply, but he may deserve it as satisfactory: because his very virtue demands that he should do satisfaction for his offenses against God or man.

Reply Obj. 3: When the stain is removed, the wound of sin is healed as regards the will. But punishment is still requisite in order that the other powers of the soul be healed, since they were so disordered by the sin committed, so that, to wit, the disorder may be remedied by the contrary of that which caused it. Moreover punishment is requisite in order to restore the equality of justice, and to remove the scandal given to others, so that those who were scandalized at the sin many be edified by the punishment, as may be seen in the example of David quoted above.

SEVENTH ARTICLE [I-II, Q. 87, Art. 7]

Whether Every Punishment Is Inflicted for a Sin?

Objection 1: It would seem that not every punishment is inflicted for a sin. For it is written (John 9:3, 2) about the man born blind: "Neither hath this man sinned, nor his parents ... that he should be born blind." In like manner we see that many children, those also who have been baptized, suffer grievous punishments, fevers, for instance, diabolical possession, and so forth, and yet there is no sin in them after they have been baptized. Moreover before they are baptized, there is no more sin in them than in the other children who do not suffer such things. Therefore not every punishment is inflicted for a sin.

Obj. 2: Further, that sinners should thrive and that the innocent should be punished seem to come under the same head. Now each of these is frequently observed in human affairs, for it is written about the wicked (Ps. 72:5): "They are not in the labor of men: neither shall they be scourged like other men"; and (Job 21:7): "[Why then do] the wicked live, are [they] advanced, and strengthened with riches" (?)[*The words in brackets show the readings of the Vulgate]; and (Hab. 1:13): "Why lookest Thou upon the contemptuous [Vulg.: 'them that do unjust things'], and holdest Thy peace, when the wicked man oppresseth [Vulg.: 'devoureth'], the man that is more just than himself?" Therefore not every punishment is inflicted for a sin.

Obj. 3: Further, it is written of Christ (1 Pet. 2:22) that "He did no sin, nor was guile found in His mouth." And yet it is said (1 Pet. 2:21) that "He suffered for us." Therefore punishment is not always inflicted by God for sin.

*On the contrary,* It is written (Job 4:7, seqq.): "Who ever perished innocent? Or when were the just destroyed? *On the contrary,* I have seen those who work iniquity ... perishing by the blast of God"; and Augustine writes (Retract. i) that "all punishment is just, and is inflicted for a sin."

*I answer that,* As already stated (A. 6), punishment can be considered in two ways—simply, and as being satisfactory. A satisfactory punishment is, in a way, voluntary. And since those who differ as to the debt of punishment, may be one in will by the union of love, it happens that one who has not sinned, bears willingly the punishment for another: thus even in human affairs we see men take the debts of another upon themselves. If, however, we speak of punishment simply, in respect of its being something penal, it has always a relation to a sin in the one punished. Sometimes this is a relation to actual sin, as when a man is punished by God or man for a sin committed by him. Sometimes it is a relation to original sin: and this, either principally or consequently—principally, the punishment of original sin is that human nature is left to itself, and deprived of original justice: and consequently, all the penalties which result from this defect in human nature.

Nevertheless we must observe that sometimes a thing seems penal, and yet is not so simply. Because punishment is a species of evil, as stated in the First Part (Q. 48, A. 5). Now evil is privation of good. And since man's good is manifold, viz. good of the soul, good of the body, and external goods, it happens sometimes that man suffers the loss of a lesser good, that he may profit in a greater good, as when he suffers loss of money for the sake of bodily health, or loss of both of these, for the sake of his soul's health and the glory of God. In such cases the loss is an evil to man, not simply but relatively; wherefore it does not answer to the name of punishment simply, but of medicinal punishment, because a medical man prescribes bitter potions to his patients, that he may restore them to health. And since such like are not punishments properly speaking, they are not referred to sin as their cause, except in a restricted sense: because the very fact that human nature needs a treatment of penal medicines, is due to the corruption of nature which is itself the punishment of original sin. For there was no need, in the state of innocence, for penal exercises in order to make progress in virtue; so that whatever is penal in the exercise of virtue, is reduced to original sin as its cause.

Reply Obj. 1: Such like defects of those who are born with them, or which children suffer from, are the effects and the punishments of original sin, as stated above (Q. 85, A. 5); and they remain even after baptism, for the cause stated above (Q. 85, A. 5, ad 2): and that they are not equally in all, is due to the diversity of nature, which is left to itself, as stated above (Q. 85, A. 5, ad 1). Nevertheless, they are directed by Divine providence, to the salvation of men, either of those who suffer, or of others who are admonished by their means—and also to the glory of God.

Reply Obj. 2: Temporal and bodily goods are indeed goods of man, but they are of small account: whereas spiritual goods are man's chief goods. Consequently it belongs to Divine justice to give spiritual goods to the virtuous, and to award them as much temporal goods or evils, as suffices for virtue: for, as Dionysius says (Div. Nom. viii), "Divine justice does not enfeeble the fortitude of the virtuous man, by material gifts." The very fact that others receive temporal goods, is detrimental to their spiritual good; wherefore the psalm quoted concludes (verse 6): "Therefore pride hath held them fast."

Reply Obj. 3: Christ bore a satisfactory punishment, not for His, but for our sins.

EIGHTH ARTICLE [I-II, Q. 87, Art. 8]

Whether Anyone Is Punished for Another's Sin?

Objection 1: It would seem that one may be punished for another's sin. For it is written (Ex. 20:5): "I am ... God ... jealous, visiting the iniquity of the fathers upon the children, unto the third and fourth generation of them that hate Me"; and (Matt. 23:35): "That upon you may come all the just blood that hath been shed upon the earth."

Obj. 2: Further, human justice springs from Divine justice. Now, according to human justice, children are sometimes punished for their parents, as in the case of high treason. Therefore also according to Divine justice, one is punished for another's sin.

Obj. 3: Further, if it be replied that the son is punished, not for the father's sin, but for his own, inasmuch as he imitates his father's wickedness; this would not be said of the children rather than of outsiders, who are punished in like manner as those whose crimes they imitate. It seems, therefore, that children are punished, not for their own sins, but for those of their parents.

*On the contrary,* It is written (Ezech. 18:20): "The son shall not bear the iniquity of the father."

*I answer that,* If we speak of that satisfactory punishment, which one takes upon oneself voluntarily, one may bear another's punishment, in so far as they are, in some way, one, as stated above (A. 7). If, however, we speak of punishment inflicted on account of sin, inasmuch as it is penal, then each one is punished for his own sin only, because the sinful act is something personal. But if we speak of a punishment that is medicinal, in this way it does happen that one is punished for another's sin. For it has been stated (A. 7) that ills sustained in bodily goods or even in the body itself, are medicinal punishments intended for the health of the soul. Wherefore there is no reason why one should not have such like punishments inflicted on one for another's sin, either by God or by man; e.g. on children for their parents, or on servants for their masters, inasmuch as they are their property so to speak; in such a way, however, that, if the children or the servants take part in the sin, this penal ill has the character of punishment in regard to both the one punished and the one he is punished for. But if they do not take part in the sin, it has the character of punishment in regard to the one for whom the punishment is borne, while, in regard to the one who is punished, it is merely medicinal (except accidentally, if he consent to the other's sin), since it is intended for the good of his soul, if he bears it patiently.

With regard to spiritual punishments, these are not merely medicinal, because the good of the soul is not directed to a yet higher good. Consequently no one suffers loss in the goods of the soul without some fault of his own. Wherefore Augustine says (Ep. ad Avit.) [*Ep. ad Auxilium, ccl.], such like punishments are not inflicted on one for another's sin, because, as regards the soul, the son is not the father's property. Hence the Lord assigns the reason for this by saying (Ezech. 18:4): "All souls are Mine."

Reply Obj. 1: Both the passages quoted should, seemingly, be referred to temporal or bodily punishments, in so far as children are the property of their parents, and posterity, of their forefathers. Else, if they be referred to spiritual punishments, they must be understood in reference to the imitation of sin, wherefore in Exodus these words are added, "Of them that hate Me," and in the chapter quoted from Matthew (verse 32) we read: "Fill ye up then the measure of your fathers." The sins of the fathers are said to be punished in their children, because the latter are the more prone to sin through being brought up amid their parents' crimes, both by becoming accustomed to them, and by imitating their parents' example, conforming to their authority as it were. Moreover they deserve heavier punishment if, seeing the punishment of their parents, they fail to mend their ways. The text adds, "to the third and fourth generation," because men are wont to live long enough to see the third and fourth generation, so that both the children can witness their parents' sins so as to imitate them, and the parents can see their children's punishments so as to grieve for them.

Reply Obj. 2: The punishments which human justice inflicts on one for another's sin are bodily and temporal. They are also remedies or medicines against future sins, in order that either they who are punished, or others may be restrained from similar faults.

Reply Obj. 3: Those who are near of kin are said to be punished, rather than outsiders, for the sins of others, both because the punishment of kindred redounds somewhat upon those who sinned, as stated above, in so far as the child is the father's property, and because the examples and the punishments that occur in one's own household are more moving. Consequently when a man is brought up amid the sins of his parents, he is more eager to imitate them, and if he is not deterred by their punishments, he would seem to be the more obstinate, and, therefore, to deserve more severe punishment.

# QUESTION 88

OF VENIAL AND MORTAL SIN (In Six Articles)

In the next place, since venial and mortal sins differ in respect of the debt of punishment, we must consider them. First, we shall consider venial sin as compared with mortal sin; secondly, we shall consider venial sin in itself.

Under the first head there are six points of inquiry:

(1) Whether venial sin is fittingly condivided with mortal sin?

(2) Whether they differ generically?

(3) Whether venial sin is a disposition to mortal sin?

(4) Whether a venial sin can become mortal?

(5) Whether a venial sin can become mortal by reason of an aggravating circumstance?

(6) Whether a mortal sin can become venial?

FIRST ARTICLE [I-II, Q. 88, Art. 1]

Whether Venial Sin Is Fittingly Condivided with Mortal Sin?

Objection 1: It would seem that venial sin is unfittingly condivided with mortal sin. For Augustine says (Contra Faust. xxii, 27): "Sin is a word, deed or desire contrary to the eternal law." But the fact of being against the eternal law makes a sin to be mortal. Consequently every sin is mortal. Therefore venial sin is not condivided with mortal sin.

Obj. 2: Further, the Apostle says (1 Cor. 10:31): "Whether you eat or drink, or whatever else you do; do all to the glory of God." Now whoever sins breaks this commandment, because sin is not done for God's glory. Consequently, since to break a commandment is to commit a mortal sin, it seems that whoever sins, sins mortally.

Obj. 3: Further, whoever cleaves to a thing by love, cleaves either as enjoying it, or as using it, as Augustine states (De Doctr. Christ. i, 3, 4). But no person, in sinning, cleaves to a mutable good as using it: because he does not refer it to that good which gives us happiness, which, properly speaking, is to use, according to Augustine (De Doctr. Christ. i, 3, 4). Therefore whoever sins enjoys a mutable good. Now "to enjoy what we should use is human perverseness," as Augustine again says (Qq. lxxxiii, qu. 30). Therefore, since "perverseness" [*The Latin 'pervertere' means to overthrow, to destroy, hence 'perversion' of God's law is a mortal sin.] denotes a mortal sin, it seems that whoever sins, sins mortally.

Obj. 4: Further, whoever approaches one term, from that very fact turns away from the opposite. Now whoever sins, approaches a mutable good, and, consequently turns away from the immutable good, so that he sins mortally. Therefore venial sin is unfittingly condivided with mortal sin.

*On the contrary,* Augustine says (Tract. xli in Joan.), that "a crime is one that merits damnation, and a venial sin, one that does not." But a crime denotes a mortal sin. Therefore venial sin is fittingly condivided with mortal sin.

*I answer that,* Certain terms do not appear to be mutually opposed, if taken in their proper sense, whereas they are opposed if taken metaphorically: thus "to smile" is not opposed to "being dry"; but if we speak of the smiling meadows when they are decked with flowers and fresh with green hues this is opposed to drought. In like manner if mortal be taken literally as referring to the death of the body, it does not imply opposition to venial, nor belong to the same genus. But if mortal be taken metaphorically, as applied to sin, it is opposed to that which is venial.

For sin, being a sickness of the soul, as stated above (Q. 71, A. 1, ad 3; Q. 72, A. 5; Q. 74, A. 9, ad 2), is said to be mortal by comparison with a disease, which is said to be mortal, through causing an irreparable defect consisting in the corruption of a principle, as stated above (Q. 72, A. 5). Now the principle of the spiritual life, which is a life in accord with virtue, is the order to the last end, as stated above (Q. 72, A. 5; Q. 87, A. 3): and if this order be corrupted, it cannot be repaired by any intrinsic principle, but by the power of God alone, as stated above (Q. 87, A. 3), because disorders in things referred to the end, are repaired through the end, even as an error about conclusions can be repaired through the truth of the principles. Hence the defect of order to the last end cannot be repaired through something else as a higher principle, as neither can an error about principles. Wherefore such sins are called mortal, as being irreparable. On the other hand, sins which imply a disorder in things referred to the end, the order to the end itself being preserved, are reparable. These sins are called venial: because a sin receives its acquittal ( *veniam* ) when the debt of punishment is taken away, and this ceases when the sin ceases, as explained above (Q. 87, A. 6).

Accordingly, mortal and venial are mutually opposed as reparable and irreparable: and I say this with reference to the intrinsic principle, but not to the Divine power, which can repair all diseases, whether of the body or of the soul. Therefore venial sin is fittingly condivided with mortal sin.

Reply Obj. 1: The division of sin into venial and mortal is not a division of a genus into its species which have an equal share of the generic nature: but it is the division of an analogous term into its parts, of which it is predicated, of the one first, and of the other afterwards. Consequently the perfect notion of sin, which Augustine gives, applies to mortal sin. On the other hand, venial sin is called a sin, in reference to an imperfect notion of sin, and in relation to mortal sin: even as an accident is called a being, in relation to substance, in reference to the imperfect notion of being. For it is not *against* the law, since he who sins venially neither does what the law forbids, nor omits what the law prescribes to be done; but he acts *beside* the law, through not observing the mode of reason, which the law intends.

Reply Obj. 2: This precept of the Apostle is affirmative, and so it does not bind for all times. Consequently everyone who does not actually refer all his actions to the glory of God, does not therefore act against this precept. In order, therefore, to avoid mortal sin each time that one fails actually to refer an action to God's glory, it is enough to refer oneself and all that one has to God habitually. Now venial sin excludes only actual reference of the human act to God's glory, and not habitual reference: because it does not exclude charity, which refers man to God habitually. Therefore it does not follow that he who sins venially, sins mortally.

Reply Obj. 3: He that sins venially, cleaves to temporal good, not as enjoying it, because he does not fix his end in it, but as using it, by referring it to God, not actually but habitually.

Reply Obj. 4: Mutable good is not considered to be a term in contraposition to the immutable good, unless one's end is fixed therein: because what is referred to the end has not the character of finality.

SECOND ARTICLE [I-II, Q. 88, Art. 2]

Whether Mortal and Venial Sin Differ Generically?

Objection 1: It would seem that venial and mortal sin do not differ generically, so that some sins be generically mortal, and some generically venial. Because human acts are considered to be generically good or evil according to their matter or object, as stated above (Q. 18, A. 2). Now either mortal or venial sin may be committed in regard to any object or matter: since man can love any mutable good, either less than God, which may be a venial sin, or more than God, which is a mortal sin. Therefore venial and mortal sin do not differ generically.

Obj. 2: Further, as stated above (A. 1; Q. 72, A. 5; Q. 87, A. 3), a sin is called mortal when it is irreparable, venial when it can be repaired. Now irreparability belongs to sin committed out of malice, which, according to some, is irremissible: whereas reparability belongs to sins committed through weakness or ignorance, which are remissible. Therefore mortal and venial sin differ as sin committed through malice differs from sin committed through weakness or ignorance. But, in this respect, sins differ not in genus but in cause, as stated above (Q. 77, A. 8, ad 1). Therefore venial and mortal sin do not differ generically.

Obj. 3: Further, it was stated above (Q. 74, A. 3, ad 3; A. 10) that sudden movements both of the sensuality and of the reason are venial sins. But sudden movements occur in every kind of sin. Therefore no sins are generically venial.

*On the contrary,* Augustine, in a sermon on Purgatory (De Sanctis, serm. xli), enumerates certain generic venial sins, and certain generic mortal sins.

*I answer that,* Venial sin is so called from venia (pardon). Consequently a sin may be called venial, first of all, because it has been pardoned: thus Ambrose says that "penance makes every sin venial": and this is called venial "from the result." Secondly, a sin is called venial because it does not contain anything either partially or totally, to prevent its being pardoned: partially, as when a sin contains something diminishing its guilt, e.g. a sin committed through weakness or ignorance: and this is called venial "from the cause": totally, through not destroying the order to the last end, wherefore it deserves temporal, but not everlasting punishment. It is of this venial sin that we wish to speak now.

For as regards the first two, it is evident that they have no determinate genus: whereas venial sin, taken in the third sense, can have a determinate genus, so that one sin may be venial generically, and another generically mortal, according as the genus or species of an act is determined by its object. For, when the will is directed to a thing that is in itself contrary to charity, whereby man is directed to his last end, the sin is mortal by reason of its object. Consequently it is a mortal sin generically, whether it be contrary to the love of God, e.g. blasphemy, perjury, and the like, or against the love of one's neighbor, e.g. murder, adultery, and such like: wherefore such sins are mortal by reason of their genus. Sometimes, however, the sinner's will is directed to a thing containing a certain inordinateness, but which is not contrary to the love of God and one's neighbor, e.g. an idle word, excessive laughter, and so forth: and such sins are venial by reason of their genus.

Nevertheless, since moral acts derive their character of goodness and malice, not only from their objects, but also from some disposition of the agent, as stated above (Q. 18, AA. 4, 6), it happens sometimes that a sin which is venial generically by reason of its object, becomes mortal on the part of the agent, either because he fixes his last end therein, or because he directs it to something that is a mortal sin in its own genus; for example, if a man direct an idle word to the commission of adultery. In like manner it may happen, on the part of the agent, that a sin generically mortal because venial, by reason of the act being imperfect, i.e. not deliberated by reason, which is the proper principle of an evil act, as we have said above in reference to sudden movements of unbelief.

Reply Obj. 1: The very fact that anyone chooses something that is contrary to divine charity, proves that he prefers it to the love of God, and consequently, that he loves it more than he loves God. Hence it belongs to the genus of some sins, which are of themselves contrary to charity, that something is loved more than God; so that they are mortal by reason of their genus.

Reply Obj. 2: This argument considers those sins which are venial from their cause.

Reply Obj. 3: This argument considers those sins which are venial by reason of the imperfection of the act.

THIRD ARTICLE [I-II, Q. 88, Art. 3]

Whether Venial Sin Is a Disposition to Mortal Sin?

Objection 1: It would seem that venial sin is not a disposition to mortal sin. For one contrary does not dispose to another. But venial and mortal sin are condivided as contrary to one another, as stated above (A. 1). Therefore venial sin is not a disposition to mortal sin.

Obj. 2: Further, an act disposes to something of like species, wherefore it is stated in *Ethic.* ii, 1, 2, that "from like acts like dispositions and habits are engendered." But mortal and venial sin differ in genus or species, as stated above (A. 2). Therefore venial sin does not dispose to mortal sin.

Obj. 3: Further, if a sin is called venial because it disposes to mortal sin, it follows that whatever disposes to mortal sin is a venial sin. Now every good work disposes to mortal sin; wherefore Augustine says in his Rule (Ep. ccxi) that "pride lies in wait for good works that it may destroy them." Therefore even good works would be venial sins, which is absurd.

*On the contrary,* It is written (Ecclus. 19:1): "He that contemneth small things shall fall by little and little." Now he that sins venially seems to contemn small things. Therefore by little and little he is disposed to fall away together into mortal sin.

*I answer that,* A disposition is a kind of cause; wherefore as there is a twofold manner of cause, so is there a twofold manner of disposition. For there is a cause which moves directly to the production of the effect, as a hot thing heats: and there is a cause which moves indirectly, by removing an obstacle, as he who displaces a pillar is said to displace the stone that rests on it. Accordingly an act of sin disposes to something in two ways. First, directly, and thus it disposes to an act of like species. In this way, a sin generically venial does not, primarily and of its nature, dispose to a sin generically mortal, for they differ in species. Nevertheless, in this same way, a venial sin can dispose, by way of consequence, to a sin which is mortal on the part of the agent: because the disposition or habit may be so far strengthened by acts of venial sin, that the lust of sinning increases, and the sinner fixes his end in that venial sin: since the end for one who has a habit, as such, is to work according to that habit; and the consequence will be that, by sinning often venially, he becomes disposed to a mortal sin. Secondly, a human act disposes to something by removing an obstacle thereto. In this way a sin generically venial can dispose to a sin generically mortal. Because he that commits a sin generically venial, turns aside from some particular order; and through accustoming his will not to be subject to the due order in lesser matters, is disposed not to subject his will even to the order of the last end, by choosing something that is a mortal sin in its genus.

Reply Obj. 1: Venial and mortal sin are not condivided in contrariety to one another, as though they were species of one genus, as stated above (A. 1, ad 1), but as an accident is condivided with substance. Wherefore an accident can be a disposition to a substantial form, so can a venial sin dispose to mortal.

Reply Obj. 2: Venial sin is not like mortal sin in species; but it is in genus, inasmuch as they both imply a defect of due order, albeit in different ways, as stated (AA. 1, 2).

Reply Obj. 3: A good work is not, of itself, a disposition to mortal sin; but it can be the matter or occasion of mortal sin accidentally; whereas a venial sin, of its very nature, disposes to mortal sin, as stated.

FOURTH ARTICLE [I-II, Q. 88, Art. 4]

Whether a Venial Sin Can Become Mortal?

Objection 1: It would seem that a venial sin can become a mortal sin. For Augustine in explaining the words of John 3:36: "He that believeth not the Son, shall not see life," says (Tract. xii in Joan.): "The slightest," i.e. venial, "sins kill if we make little of them." Now a sin is called mortal through causing the spiritual death of the soul. Therefore a venial sin can become mortal.

Obj. 2: Further, a movement in the sensuality before the consent of reason, is a venial sin, but after consent, is a mortal sin, as stated above (Q. 74, A. 8, ad 2). Therefore a venial sin can become mortal.

Obj. 3: Further, venial and mortal sin differ as curable and incurable disease, as stated above (A. 1). But a curable disease may become incurable. Therefore a venial sin may become mortal.

Obj. 4: Further, a disposition may become a habit. Now venial sin is a disposition to mortal, as stated (A. 3). Therefore a venial sin can become mortal.

*I answer that,* The fact of a venial sin becoming a mortal sin may be understood in three ways. First, so that the same identical act be at first a venial, and then a mortal sin. This is impossible: because a sin, like any moral act, consists chiefly in an act of the will: so that an act is not one morally, if the will be changed, although the act be continuous physically. If, however, the will be not changed, it is not possible for a venial sin to become mortal.

Secondly, this may be taken to mean that a sin generically venial, becomes mortal. This is possible, in so far as one may fix one's end in that venial sin, or direct it to some mortal sin as end, as stated above (A. 2).

Thirdly, this may be understood in the sense of many venial sins constituting one mortal sin. If this be taken as meaning that many venial sins added together make one mortal sin, it is false, because all the venial sins in the world cannot incur a debt of punishment equal to that of one mortal sin. This is evident as regards the duration of the punishment, since mortal sin incurs a debt of eternal punishment, while venial sin incurs a debt of temporal punishment, as stated above (Q. 87, AA. 3, 5). It is also evident as regards the pain of loss, because mortal sins deserve to be punished by the privation of seeing God, to which no other punishment is comparable, as Chrysostom states (Hom. xxiv in Matth.). It is also evident as regards the pain of sense, as to the remorse of conscience; although as to the pain of fire, the punishments may perhaps not be improportionate to one another.

If, however, this be taken as meaning that many venial sins make one mortal sin dispositively, it is true, as was shown above (A. 3) with regard to the two different manners of disposition, whereby venial sin disposes to mortal sin.

Reply Obj. 1: Augustine is referring to the fact of many venial sins making one mortal sin dispositively.

Reply Obj. 2: The same movement of the sensuality which preceded the consent of reason can never become a mortal sin; but the movement of the reason in consenting is a mortal sin.

Reply Obj. 3: Disease of the body is not an act, but an abiding disposition; wherefore, while remaining the same disease, it may undergo change. On the other hand, venial sin is a transient act, which cannot be taken up again: so that in this respect the comparison fails.

Reply Obj. 4: A disposition that becomes a habit, is like an imperfect thing in the same species; thus imperfect science, by being perfected, becomes a habit. On the other hand, venial sin is a disposition to something differing generically, even as an accident which disposes to a substantial form, into which it is never changed.

FIFTH ARTICLE [I-II, Q. 88, Art. 5]

Whether a Circumstance Can Make a Venial Sin to Be Mortal?

Objection 1: It would seem that a circumstance can make a venial sin mortal. For Augustine says in a sermon on Purgatory (De Sanctis, serm. xli) that "if anger continue for a long time, or if drunkenness be frequent, they become mortal sins." But anger and drunkenness are not mortal but venial sins generically, else they would always be mortal sins. Therefore a circumstance makes a venial sin to be mortal.

Obj. 2: Further, the Master says (Sentent. ii, D, 24) that delectation, if morose [*See Q. 74, A. 6], is a mortal sin, but that if it be not morose, it is a venial sin. Now moroseness is a circumstance. Therefore a circumstance makes a venial sin to be mortal.

Obj. 3: Further, evil and good differ more than venial and mortal sin, both of which are generically evil. But a circumstance makes a good act to be evil, as when a man gives an alms for vainglory. Much more, therefore, can it make a venial sin to be mortal.

*On the contrary,* Since a circumstance is an accident, its quantity cannot exceed that of the act itself, derived from the act's genus, because the subject always excels its accident. If, therefore, an act be venial by reason of its genus, it cannot become mortal by reason of an accident: since, in a way, mortal sin infinitely surpasses the quantity of venial sin, as is evident from what has been said (Q. 72, A. 5, ad 1; Q. 87, A. 5, ad 1).

*I answer that,* As stated above (Q. 7, A. 1; Q. 18, A. 5, ad 4; AA. 10, 11), when we were treating of circumstances, a circumstance, as such, is an accident of the moral act: and yet a circumstance may happen to be taken as the specific difference of a moral act, and then it loses its nature of circumstance, and constitutes the species of the moral act. This happens in sins when a circumstance adds the deformity of another genus; thus when a man has knowledge of another woman than his wife, the deformity of his act is opposed to chastity; but if this other be another man's wife, there is an additional deformity opposed to justice which forbids one to take what belongs to another; and accordingly this circumstance constitutes a new species of sin known as adultery.

It is, however, impossible for a circumstance to make a venial sin become mortal, unless it adds the deformity of another species. For it has been stated above (A. 1) that the deformity of a venial sin consists in a disorder affecting things that are referred to the end, whereas the deformity of a mortal sin consists in a disorder about the last end. Consequently it is evident that a circumstance cannot make a venial sin to be mortal, so long as it remains a circumstance, but only when it transfers the sin to another species, and becomes, as it were, the specific difference of the moral act.

Reply Obj. 1: Length of time is not a circumstance that draws a sin to another species, nor is frequency or custom, except perhaps by something accidental supervening. For an action does not acquire a new species through being repeated or prolonged, unless by chance something supervene in the repeated or prolonged act to change its species, e.g. disobedience, contempt, or the like.

We must therefore reply to the objection by saying that since anger is a movement of the soul tending to the hurt of one's neighbor, if the angry movement tend to a hurt which is a mortal sin generically, such as murder or robbery, that anger will be a mortal sin generically: and if it be a venial sin, this will be due to the imperfection of the act, in so far as it is a sudden movement of the sensuality: whereas, if it last a long time, it returns to its generic nature, through the consent of reason. If, on the other hand, the hurt to which the angry movement tends, is a sin generically venial, for instance, if a man be angry with someone, so as to wish to say some trifling word in jest that would hurt him a little, the anger will not be mortal sin, however long it last, unless perhaps accidentally; for instance, if it were to give rise to great scandal or something of the kind.

With regard to drunkenness we reply that it is a mortal sin by reason of its genus; for, that a man, without necessity, and through the mere lust of wine, make himself unable to use his reason, whereby he is directed to God and avoids committing many sins, is expressly contrary to virtue. That it be a venial sin, is due some sort of ignorance or weakness, as when a man is ignorant of the strength of the wine, or of his own unfitness, so that he has no thought of getting drunk, for in that case the drunkenness is not imputed to him as a sin, but only the excessive drink. If, however, he gets drunk frequently, this ignorance no longer avails as an excuse, for his will seems to choose to give way to drunkenness rather than to refrain from excess of wine: wherefore the sin returns to its specific nature.

Reply Obj. 2: Morose delectation is not a mortal sin except in those matters which are mortal sins generically. In such matters, if the delectation be not morose, there is a venial sin through imperfection of the act, as we have said with regard to anger (ad 1): because anger is said to be lasting, and delectation to be morose, on account of the approval of the deliberating reason.

Reply Obj. 3: A circumstance does not make a good act to be evil, unless it constitute the species of a sin, as we have stated above (Q. 18, A. 5, ad 4).

SIXTH ARTICLE [I-II, Q. 88, Art. 6]

Whether a Mortal Sin Can Become Venial?

Objection 1: It would seem that a mortal sin can become venial. Because venial sin is equally distant from mortal, as mortal sin is from venial. But a venial sin can become mortal, as stated above (A. 5). Therefore also a mortal sin can become venial.

Obj. 2: Further, venial and mortal sin are said to differ in this, that he who sins mortally loves a creature more than God, while he who sins venially loves the creature less than God. Now it may happen that a person in committing a sin generically mortal, loves a creature less than God; for instance, if anyone being ignorant that simple fornication is a mortal sin, and contrary to the love of God, commits the sin of fornication, yet so as to be ready, for the love of God, to refrain from that sin if he knew that by committing it he was acting counter to the love of God. Therefore his will be a venial sin; and accordingly a mortal sin can become venial.

Obj. 3: Further, as stated above (A. 5, Obj. 3), good is more distant from evil, than venial from mortal sin. But an act which is evil in itself, can become good; thus to kill a man may be an act of justice, as when a judge condemns a thief to death. Much more therefore can a mortal sin become venial.

*On the contrary,* An eternal thing can never become temporal. But mortal sin deserves eternal punishment, whereas venial sin deserves temporal punishment. Therefore a mortal sin can never become venial.

*I answer that,* Venial and mortal differ as perfect and imperfect in the genus of sin, as stated above (A. 1, ad 1). Now the imperfect can become perfect, by some sort of addition: and, consequently, a venial sin can become mortal, by the addition of some deformity pertaining to the genus of mortal sin, as when a man utters an idle word for the purpose of fornication. On the other hand, the perfect cannot become imperfect, by addition; and so a mortal sin cannot become venial, by the addition of a deformity pertaining to the genus of venial sin, for the sin is not diminished if a man commit fornication in order to utter an idle word; rather is it aggravated by the additional deformity.

Nevertheless a sin which is generically mortal, can become venial by reason of the imperfection of the act, because then it does not completely fulfil the conditions of a moral act, since it is not a deliberate, but a sudden act, as is evident from what we have said above (A. 2). This happens by a kind of subtraction, namely, of deliberate reason. And since a moral act takes its species from deliberate reason, the result is that by such a subtraction the species of the act is destroyed.

Reply Obj. 1: Venial differs from mortal as imperfect from perfect, even as a boy differs from a man. But the boy becomes a man and not vice versa. Hence the argument does not prove.

Reply Obj. 2: If the ignorance be such as to excuse sin altogether, as the ignorance of a madman or an imbecile, then he that commits fornication in a state of such ignorance, commits no sin either mortal or venial. But if the ignorance be not invincible, then the ignorance itself is a sin, and contains within itself the lack of the love of God, in so far as a man neglects to learn those things whereby he can safeguard himself in the love of God.

Reply Obj. 3: As Augustine says (Contra Mendacium vii), "those things which are evil in themselves, cannot be well done for any good end." Now murder is the slaying of the innocent, and this can nowise be well done. But, as Augustine states (De Lib. Arb. i, 4, 5), the judge who sentences a thief to death, or the soldier who slays the enemy of the common weal, are not murderers.

## QUESTION 89

OF VENIAL SIN IN ITSELF (In Six Articles)

We must now consider venial sin in itself, and under this head there are six points of inquiry:

(1) Whether venial sin causes a stain in the soul?

(2) Of the different kinds of venial sin, as denoted by "wood," "hay," "stubble" (1 Cor. 3:12);

(3) Whether man could sin venially in the state of innocence?

(4) Whether a good or a wicked angel can sin venially?

(5) Whether the movements of unbelievers are venial sins?

(6) Whether venial sin can be in a man with original sin alone?

FIRST ARTICLE [I-II, Q. 89, Art. 1]

Whether Venial Sin Causes a Stain on the Soul?

Objection 1: It would seem that venial sin causes a stain in the soul. For Augustine says (De Poenit.) [*Hom. 50, inter. L., 2], that if venial sins be multiplied, they destroy the beauty of our souls so as to deprive us of the embraces of our heavenly spouse. But the stain of sin is nothing else but the loss of the soul's beauty. Therefore venial sins cause a stain in the soul.

Obj. 2: Further, mortal sin causes a stain in the soul, on account of the inordinateness of the act and of the sinner's affections. But, in venial sin, there is an inordinateness of the act and of the affections. Therefore venial sin causes a stain in the soul.

Obj. 3: Further, the stain on the soul is caused by contact with a temporal thing, through love thereof as stated above (Q. 86, A. 1). But, in venial sin, the soul is in contact with a temporal thing through inordinate love. therefore, venial sin brings a stain on the soul.

*On the contrary,* it is written, (Eph. 5:27): "That He might present it to Himself a glorious church, not having spot or wrinkle," on which the gloss says: "i.e., some grievous sin." Therefore it seems proper to mortal sin to cause a stain on the soul.

I answer that as stated above (Q. 86, A. 1), a stain denotes a loss of comeliness due to contact with something, as may be seen in corporeal matters, from which the term has been transferred to the soul, by way of similitude. Now, just as in the body there is a twofold comeliness, one resulting from the inward disposition of the members and colors, the other resulting from outward refulgence supervening, so too, in the soul, there is a twofold comeliness, one habitual and, so to speak, intrinsic, the other actual like an outward flash of light. Now venial sin is a hindrance to actual comeliness, but not to habitual comeliness, because it neither destroys nor diminishes the habit of charity and of the other virtues, as we shall show further on (II-II, Q. 24, A. 10; Q. 133, A. 1, ad 2), but only hinders their acts. On the other hand a stain denotes something permanent in the thing stained, wherefore it seems in the nature of a loss of habitual rather than of actual comeliness. Therefore, properly speaking, venial sin does not cause a stain in the soul. If, however, we find it stated anywhere that it does induce a stain, this is in a restricted sense, in so far as it hinders the comeliness that results from acts of virtue.

Reply Obj. 1: Augustine is speaking of the case in which many venial sins lead to mortal sin dispositively: because otherwise they would not sever the soul from its heavenly spouse.

Reply Obj. 2: In mortal sin the inordinateness of the act destroys the habit of virtue, but not in venial sin.

Reply Obj. 3: In mortal sin the soul comes into contact with a temporal thing as its end, so that the shedding of the light of grace, which accrues to those who, by charity, cleave to God as their last end, is entirely cut off. *On the contrary,* in venial sin, man does not cleave to a creature as his last end: hence there is no comparison.

SECOND ARTICLE [I-II, Q. 89, Art. 2]

Whether Venial Sins Are Suitably Designated As "Wood, Hay, and Stubble"?

Objection 1: It would seem that venial sins are unsuitably designated as "wood, hay, and stubble." Because wood, hay, and stubble are said (1 Cor. 3:12) to be built on a spiritual foundation. Now venial sins are something outside a spiritual foundation, even as false opinions are outside the pale of science. Therefore, venial sins are not suitably designated as wood, hay, and stubble.

Obj. 2: Further, he who builds wood, hay, and stubble, "shall be saved yet so as by fire" (1 Cor. 3:15). But sometimes the man who commits a venial sin, will not be saved, even by fire, e.g. when a man dies in mortal sin to which venial sins are attached. Therefore, venial sins are unsuitably designated by wood, hay, and stubble.

Obj. 3: Further, according to the Apostle (1 Cor. 3:12) those who build "gold, silver, precious stones," i.e. love of God and our neighbor, and good works, are others from those who build wood, hay, and stubble. But those even who love God and their neighbor, and do good works, commit venial sins: for it is written (1 John 1:8): "If we say that we have no sin, we deceive ourselves." Therefore venial sins are not suitably designated by these three.

Obj. 4: Further, there are many more than three differences and degrees of venial sins. Therefore they are unsuitably comprised under these three.

*On the contrary,* The Apostle says (1 Cor. 3:15) that the man who builds up wood, hay and stubble, "shall be saved yet so as by fire," so that he will suffer punishment, but not everlasting. Now the debt of temporal punishment belongs properly to venial sin, as stated above (Q. 87, A. 5). Therefore these three signify venial sins.

*I answer that,* Some have understood the "foundation" to be dead faith, upon which some build good works, signified by gold, silver, and precious stones, while others build mortal sins, which according to them are designated by wood, hay and stubble. But Augustine disapproves of this explanation (De Fide et Oper. xv), because, as the Apostle says (Gal. 5:21), he who does the works of the flesh, "shall not obtain the kingdom of God," which signifies to be saved; whereas the Apostle says that he who builds wood, hay, and stubble "shall be saved yet so as by fire." Consequently wood, hay, stubble cannot be understood to denote mortal sins.

Others say that wood, hay, stubble designate good works, which are indeed built upon the spiritual edifice, but are mixed with venial sins: as, when a man is charged with the care of a family, which is a good thing, excessive love of his wife or of his children or of his possessions insinuates itself into his life, under God however, so that, to wit, for the sake of these things he would be unwilling to do anything in opposition to God. But neither does this seem to be reasonable. For it is evident that all good works are referred to the love of God, and one's neighbor, wherefore they are designated by "gold," "silver," and "precious stones," and consequently not by "wood," "hay," and "stubble."

We must therefore say that the very venial sins that insinuate themselves into those who have a care for earthly things, are designated by wood, hay, and stubble. For just as these are stored in a house, without belonging to the substance of the house, and can be burnt, while the house is saved, so also venial sins are multiplied in a man, while the spiritual edifice remains, and for them, man suffers fire, either of temporal trials in this life, or of purgatory after this life, and yet he is saved for ever.

Reply Obj. 1: Venial sins are not said to be built upon the spiritual foundation, as though they were laid directly upon it, but because they are laid beside it; in the same sense as it is written (Ps. 136:1): "Upon the waters of Babylon," i.e. "beside the waters": because venial sins do not destroy the edifice.

Reply Obj. 2: It is not said that everyone who builds wood, hay and stubble, shall be saved as by fire, but only those who build "upon" the "foundation." And this foundation is not dead faith, as some have esteemed, but faith quickened by charity, according to Eph. 3:17: "Rooted and founded in charity." Accordingly, he that dies in mortal sin with venial sins, has indeed wood, hay, and stubble, but not built upon the spiritual edifice; and consequently he will not be saved so as by fire.

Reply Obj. 3: Although those who are withdrawn from the care of temporal things, sin venially sometimes, yet they commit but slight venial sins, and in most cases they are cleansed by the fervor of charity: wherefore they do not build up venial sins, because these do not remain long in them. But the venial sins of those who are busy about earthly things remain longer, because they are unable to have such frequent recourse to the fervor of charity in order to remove them.

Reply Obj. 4: As the Philosopher says (De Coelo i, text. 2), "all things are comprised under three, the beginning, the middle, the end." Accordingly all degrees of venial sins are reduced to three, viz. to "wood," which remains longer in the fire; "stubble," which is burnt up at once; and "hay," which is between these two: because venial sins are removed by fire, quickly or slowly, according as man is more or less attached to them.

THIRD ARTICLE [I-II, Q. 89, Art. 3]

Whether Man Could Commit a Venial Sin in the State of Innocence?

Objection 1: It would seem that man could commit a venial sin in the state of innocence. Because on 1 Tim. 2:14, "Adam was not seduced," a gloss says: "Having had no experience of God's severity, it was possible for him to be so mistaken as to think that what he had done was a venial sin." But he would not have thought this unless he could have committed a venial sin. Therefore he could commit a venial sin without sinning mortally.

Obj. 2: Further Augustine says (Gen. ad lit. xi, 5): "We must not suppose that the tempter would have overcome man, unless first of all there had arisen in man's soul a movement of vainglory which should have been checked." Now the vainglory which preceded man's defeat, which was accomplished through his falling into mortal sin, could be nothing more than a venial sin. In like manner, Augustine says (Gen. ad lit. xi, 5) that "man was allured by a certain desire of making the experiment, when he saw that the woman did not die when she had taken the forbidden fruit." Again there seems to have been a certain movement of unbelief in Eve, since she doubted what the Lord had said, as appears from her saying (Gen. 3:3): "Lest perhaps we die." Now these apparently were venial sins. Therefore man could commit a venial sin before he committed a mortal sin.

Obj. 3: Further, mortal sin is more opposed to the integrity of the original state, than venial sin is. Now man could sin mortally notwithstanding the integrity of the original state. Therefore he could also sin venially.

*On the contrary,* Every sin deserves some punishment. But nothing penal was possible in the state of innocence, as Augustine declares (De Civ. Dei xiv, 10). Therefore he could not commit a sin that would not deprive him of that state of integrity. But venial sin does not change man's state. Therefore he could not sin venially.

*I answer that,* It is generally admitted that man could not commit a venial sin in the state of innocence. This, however, is not to be understood as though on account of the perfection of his state, the sin which is venial for us would have been mortal for him, if he had committed it. Because the dignity of a person is circumstance that aggravates a sin, but it does not transfer it to another species, unless there be an additional deformity by reason of disobedience, or vow or the like, which does not apply to the question in point. Consequently what is venial in itself could not be changed into mortal by reason of the excellence of the original state. We must therefore understand this to mean that he could not sin venially, because it was impossible for him to commit a sin which was venial in itself, before losing the integrity of the original state by sinning mortally.

The reason for this is because venial sin occurs in us, either through the imperfection of the act, as in the case of sudden movements, in a genus of mortal sin or through some inordinateness in respect of things referred to the end, the due order of the end being safeguarded. Now each of these happens on account of some defect of order, by reason of the lower powers not being checked by the higher. Because the sudden rising of a movement of the sensuality in us is due to the sensuality not being perfectly subject to reason: and the sudden rising of a movement of reason itself is due, in us, to the fact that the execution of the act of reason is not subject to the act of deliberation which proceeds from a higher good, as stated above (Q. 74, A. 10); and that the human mind be out of order as regards things directed to the end, the due order of the end being safeguarded, is due to the fact that the things referred to the end are not infallibly directed under the end, which holds the highest place, being the beginning, as it were, in matters concerning the appetite, as stated above (Q. 10, AA. 1, 2, ad 3; Q. 72, A. 5). Now, in the state of innocence, as stated in the First Part (Q. 95, A. 1), there was an unerring stability of order, so that the lower powers were always subjected to the higher, so long as man remained subject to God, as Augustine says (De Civ. Dei xiv, 13). Hence there can be no inordinateness in man, unless first of all the highest part of man were not subject to God, which constitutes a mortal sin. From this it is evident that, in the state of innocence, man could not commit a venial sin, before committing a mortal sin.

Reply Obj. 1: In the passage quoted, venial is not taken in the same sense as we take it now; but by venial sin we mean that which is easily forgiven.

Reply Obj. 2: This vainglory which preceded man's downfall, was his first mortal sin, for it is stated to have preceded his downfall into the outward act of sin. This vainglory was followed, in the man, by the desire to make and experiment, and in the woman, by doubt, for she gave way to vainglory, merely through hearing the serpent mention the precept, as though she refused to be held in check by the precept.

Reply Obj. 3: Mortal sin is opposed to the integrity of the original state in the fact of its destroying that state: this a venial sin cannot do. And because the integrity of the primitive state is incompatible with any inordinateness whatever, the result is that the first man could not sin venially, before committing a mortal sin.

FOURTH ARTICLE [I-II, Q. 89, Art. 4]

Whether a Good or a Wicked Angel Can Sin Venially?

Objection 1: It seems that a good or wicked angel can sin venially. Because man agrees with the angels in the higher part of his soul which is called the mind, according to Gregory, who says (Hom. xxix in Evang.) that "man understands in common with the angels." But man can commit a venial sin in the higher part of his soul. Therefore an angel can commit a venial sin also.

Obj. 2: Further, He that can do more can do less. But an angel could love a created good more than God, and he did, by sinning mortally. Therefore he could also love a creature less than God inordinately, by sinning venially.

Obj. 3: Further, wicked angels seem to do things which are venial sins generically, by provoking men to laughter, and other like frivolities. Now the circumstance of the person does not make a mortal sin to be venial as stated above (A. 3), unless there is a special prohibition, which is not the case in point. Therefore an angel can sin venially.

*On the contrary,* The perfection of an angel is greater than that of man in the primitive state. But man could not sin venially in the primitive state, and much less, therefore, can an angel.

*I answer that,* An angel's intellect, as stated above in the First Part (Q. 58, A. 3; Q. 79, A. 8), is not discursive, i.e. it does not proceed from principles to conclusions, so as to understand both separately, as we do. Consequently, whenever the angelic intellect considers a conclusion, it must, of necessity, consider it in its principles. Now in matters of appetite, as we have often stated (Q. 8, A. 2; Q. 10, A. 1; Q. 72, A. 5), ends are like principles, while the means are like conclusions. Wherefore, an angel's mind is not directed to the means, except as they stand under the order to the end. Consequently, from their very nature, they can have no inordinateness in respect of the means, unless at the same time they have an inordinateness in respect of the end, and this is a mortal sin. Now good angels are not moved to the means, except in subordination to the due end which is God: wherefore all their acts are acts of charity, so that no venial sin can be in them. On the other hand, wicked angels are moved to nothing except in subordination to the end which is their sin of pride. Therefore they sin mortally in everything that they do of their own will. This does not apply to the appetite for the natural good, which appetite we have stated to be in them (I, Q. 63, A. 4; Q. 64, A. 2, ad 5).

Reply Obj. 1: Man does indeed agree with the angels in the mind or intellect, but he differs in his mode of understanding, as stated above.

Reply Obj. 2: An angel could not love a creature less than God, without, at the same time, either referring it to God, as the last end, or to some inordinate end, for the reason given above.

Reply Obj. 3: The demons incite man to all such things which seem venial, that he may become used to them, so as to lead him on to mortal sin. Consequently in all such things they sin mortally, on account of the end they have in view.

FIFTH ARTICLE [I-II, Q. 89, Art. 5]

Whether the First Movements of the Sensuality in Unbelievers Are Mortal Sin?

Objection 1: It would seem that the first movements of the sensuality in unbelievers are mortal sins. For the Apostle says (Rom. 8:1) that "there is ... no condemnation to them that are in Christ Jesus, who walk not according to the flesh": and he is speaking there of the concupiscence of the sensuality, as appears from the context (Rom. 7). Therefore the reason why concupiscence is not a matter of condemnation to those who walk not according to the flesh, i.e. by consenting to concupiscence, is because they are in Christ Jesus. But unbelievers are not in Christ Jesus. Therefore in unbelievers this is a matter of condemnation. Therefore the first movements of unbelievers are mortal sins.

Obj. 2: Further Anselm says (De Gratia et Lib. Arb. vii): "Those who are not in Christ, when they feel the sting of the flesh, follow the road of damnation, even if they walk not according to the flesh." But damnation is not due save to mortal sin. Therefore, since man feels the sting of the flesh in the first movements of the concupiscence, it seems that the first movements of concupiscence in unbelievers are mortal sins.

Obj. 3: Further, Anselm says (De Gratia et Lib. Arb. vii): "Man was so made that he was not liable to feel concupiscence." Now this liability seems to be remitted to man by the grace of Baptism, which the unbeliever has not. Therefore every act of concupiscence in an unbeliever, even without his consent, is a mortal sin, because he acts against his duty.

*On the contrary,* It is stated in Acts 10:34 that "God is not a respecter of persons." Therefore he does not impute to one unto condemnation, what He does not impute to another. But he does not impute first movements to believers, unto condemnation. Neither therefore does He impute them to unbelievers.

*I answer that,* It is unreasonable to say that the first movements of unbelievers are mortal sins, when they do not consent to them. This is evident for two reasons. First, because the sensuality itself could not be the subject of mortal sin, as stated above (Q. 79, A. 4). Now the sensuality has the same nature in unbelievers as in believers. Therefore it is not possible for the mere movements of the sensuality in unbelievers, to be mortal sins.

Secondly, from the state of the sinner. Because excellence of the person never diminishes sin, but, *on the contrary,* increases it, as stated above (Q. 73, A. 10). Therefore a sin is not less grievous in a believer than in an unbeliever, but much more so. For the sins of an unbeliever are more deserving of forgiveness, on account of their ignorance, according to 1 Tim. 1:13: "I obtained the mercy of God, because I did it ignorantly in my unbelief": whereas the sins of believers are more grievous on account of the sacraments of grace, according to Heb. 10:29: "How much more, do you think, he deserveth worse punishments ... who hath esteemed the blood of the testament unclean, by which he was sanctified?"

Reply Obj. 1: The Apostle is speaking of the condemnation due to original sin, which condemnation is remitted by the grace of Jesus Christ, although the *fomes* of concupiscence remain. Wherefore the fact that believers are subject to concupiscence is not in them a sign of the condemnation due to original sin, as it is in unbelievers.

In this way also is to be understood the saying of Anselm, wherefore the Reply to the Second Objection is evident.

Reply Obj. 3: This freedom from liability to concupiscence was a result of original justice. Wherefore that which is opposed to such liability pertains, not to actual but to original sin.

SIXTH ARTICLE [I-II, Q. 89, Art. 6]

Whether Venial Sin Can Be in Anyone with Original Sin Alone?

Objection 1: It would seem that venial sin can be in a man with original sin alone. For disposition precedes habit. Now venial sin is a disposition to mortal sin, as stated above (Q. 88, A. 3). Therefore in an unbeliever, in whom original sin is not remitted, venial sin exists before mortal sin: and so sometimes unbelievers have venial together with original sin, and without mortal sins.

Obj. 2: Further, venial sin has less in common, and less connection with mortal sin, than one mortal sin has with another. But an unbeliever in the state of original sin, can commit one mortal sin without committing another. Therefore he can also commit a venial sin without committing a mortal sin.

Obj. 3: Further, it is possible to fix the time at which a child is first able to commit an actual sin: and when the child comes to that time, it can stay a short time at least, without committing a mortal sin, because this happens in the worst criminals. Now it is possible for the child to sin venially during that space of time, however short it may be. Therefore venial sin can be in anyone with original sin alone and without mortal sin.

*On the contrary,* Man is punished for original sin in the children's limbo, where there is no pain of sense as we shall state further on (II-II, Q. 69, A. 6): whereas men are punished in hell for no other than mortal sin. Therefore there will be no place where a man can be punished for venial sin with no other than original sin.

*I answer that,* It is impossible for venial sin to be in anyone with original sin alone, and without mortal sin. The reason for this is because before a man comes to the age of discretion, the lack of years hinders the use of reason and excuses him from mortal sin, wherefore, much more does it excuse him from venial sin, if he does anything which is such generically. But when he begins to have the use of reason, he is not entirely excused from the guilt of venial or mortal sin. Now the first thing that occurs to a man to think about then, is to deliberate about himself. And if he then direct himself to the due end, he will, by means of grace, receive the remission of original sin: whereas if he does not then direct himself to the due end, as far as he is capable of discretion at that particular age, he will sin mortally, through not doing that which is in his power to do. Accordingly thenceforward there cannot be venial sin in him without mortal, until afterwards all sin shall have been remitted to him through grace.

Reply Obj. 1: Venial sin always precedes mortal sin not as a necessary, but as a contingent disposition, just as work sometimes disposes to fever, but not as heat disposes to the form of fire.

Reply Obj. 2: Venial sin is prevented from being with original sin alone, not on account of its want of connection or likeness, but on account of the lack of use of reason, as stated above.

Reply Obj. 3: The child that is beginning to have the use of reason can refrain from other mortal sins for a time, but it is not free from the aforesaid sin of omission, unless it turns to God as soon as possible. For the first thing that occurs to a man who has discretion, is to think of himself, and to direct other things to himself as to their end, since the end is the first thing in the intention. Therefore this is the time when man is bound by God's affirmative precept, which the Lord expressed by saying (Zech. 1:3): "Turn ye to Me ... and I will turn to you."

TREATISE ON LAW (QQ. 90-108)

## QUESTION 90

OF THE ESSENCE OF LAW (In Four Articles)

We have now to consider the extrinsic principles of acts. Now the extrinsic principle inclining to evil is the devil, of whose temptations we have spoken in the First Part (Q. 114). But the extrinsic principle moving to good is God, Who both instructs us by means of His Law, and assists us by His Grace: wherefore in the first place we must speak of law; in the second place, of grace.

Concerning law, we must consider: (1) Law itself in general; (2) its parts. Concerning law in general three points offer themselves for our consideration: (1) Its essence; (2) The different kinds of law; (3) The effects of law.

Under the first head there are four points of inquiry:

(1) Whether law is something pertaining to reason?

(2) Concerning the end of law;

(3) Its cause;

(4) The promulgation of law.

FIRST ARTICLE [I-II, Q. 90, Art. 1]

Whether Law Is Something Pertaining to Reason?

Objection 1: It would seem that law is not something pertaining to reason. For the Apostle says (Rom. 7:23): "I see another law in my members," etc. But nothing pertaining to reason is in the members; since the reason does not make use of a bodily organ. Therefore law is not something pertaining to reason.

Obj. 2: Further, in the reason there is nothing else but power, habit, and act. But law is not the power itself of reason. In like manner, neither is it a habit of reason: because the habits of reason are the intellectual virtues of which we have spoken above (Q. 57). Nor again is it an act of reason: because then law would cease, when the act of reason ceases, for instance, while we are asleep. Therefore law is nothing pertaining to reason.

Obj. 3: Further, the law moves those who are subject to it to act aright. But it belongs properly to the will to move to act, as is evident from what has been said above (Q. 9, A. 1). Therefore law pertains, not to the reason, but to the will; according to the words of the Jurist (Lib. i, ff., De Const. Prin. leg. i): "Whatsoever pleaseth the sovereign, has force of law."

*On the contrary,* It belongs to the law to command and to forbid. But it belongs to reason to command, as stated above (Q. 17, A. 1). Therefore law is something pertaining to reason.

*I answer that,* Law is a rule and measure of acts, whereby man is induced to act or is restrained from acting: for *lex* (law) is derived from *ligare* (to bind), because it binds one to act. Now the rule and measure of human acts is the reason, which is the first principle of human acts, as is evident from what has been stated above (Q. 1, A. 1, ad 3); since it belongs to the reason to direct to the end, which is the first principle in all matters of action, according to the Philosopher (Phys. ii). Now that which is the principle in any genus, is the rule and measure of that genus: for instance, unity in the genus of numbers, and the first movement in the genus of movements. Consequently it follows that law is something pertaining to reason.

Reply Obj. 1: Since law is a kind of rule and measure, it may be in something in two ways. First, as in that which measures and rules: and since this is proper to reason, it follows that, in this way, law is in the reason alone. Secondly, as in that which is measured and ruled. In this way, law is in all those things that are inclined to something by reason of some law: so that any inclination arising from a law, may be called a law, not essentially but by participation as it were. And thus the inclination of the members to concupiscence is called "the law of the members."

Reply Obj. 2: Just as, in external action, we may consider the work and the work done, for instance the work of building and the house built; so in the acts of reason, we may consider the act itself of reason, i.e. to understand and to reason, and something produced by this act. With regard to the speculative reason, this is first of all the definition; secondly, the proposition; thirdly, the syllogism or argument. And since also the practical reason makes use of a syllogism in respect of the work to be done, as stated above (Q. 13, A. 3; Q. 76, A. 1) and since as the Philosopher teaches (Ethic. vii, 3); hence we find in the practical reason something that holds the same position in regard to operations, as, in the speculative intellect, the proposition holds in regard to conclusions. Such like universal propositions of the practical intellect that are directed to actions have the nature of law. And these propositions are sometimes under our actual consideration, while sometimes they are retained in the reason by means of a habit.

Reply Obj. 3: Reason has its power of moving from the will, as stated above (Q. 17, A. 1): for it is due to the fact that one wills the end, that the reason issues its commands as regards things ordained to the end. But in order that the volition of what is commanded may have the nature of law, it needs to be in accord with some rule of reason. And in this sense is to be understood the saying that the will of the sovereign has the force of law; otherwise the sovereign's will would savor of lawlessness rather than of law.

SECOND ARTICLE [I-II, Q. 90, Art. 2]

Whether the Law Is Always Something Directed to the Common Good?

Objection 1: It would seem that the law is not always directed to the common good as to its end. For it belongs to law to command and to forbid. But commands are directed to certain individual goods. Therefore the end of the law is not always the common good.

Obj. 2: Further, the law directs man in his actions. But human actions are concerned with particular matters. Therefore the law is directed to some particular good.

Obj. 3: Further, Isidore says (Etym. v, 3): "If the law is based on reason, whatever is based on reason will be a law." But reason is the foundation not only of what is ordained to the common good, but also of that which is directed to private good. Therefore the law is not only directed to the good of all, but also to the private good of an individual.

*On the contrary,* Isidore says (Etym. v, 21) that "laws are enacted for no private profit, but for the common benefit of the citizens."

*I answer that,* As stated above (A. 1), the law belongs to that which is a principle of human acts, because it is their rule and measure. Now as reason is a principle of human acts, so in reason itself there is something which is the principle in respect of all the rest: wherefore to this principle chiefly and mainly law must needs be referred. Now the first principle in practical matters, which are the object of the practical reason, is the last end: and the last end of human life is bliss or happiness, as stated above (Q. 2, A. 7; Q. 3, A. 1). Consequently the law must needs regard principally the relationship to happiness. Moreover, since every part is ordained to the whole, as imperfect to perfect; and since one man is a part of the perfect community, the law must needs regard properly the relationship to universal happiness. Wherefore the Philosopher, in the above definition of legal matters mentions both happiness and the body politic: for he says (Ethic. v, 1) that we call those legal matters "just, which are adapted to produce and preserve happiness and its parts for the body politic": since the state is a perfect community, as he says in *Polit.* i, 1.

Now in every genus, that which belongs to it chiefly is the principle of the others, and the others belong to that genus in subordination to that thing: thus fire, which is chief among hot things, is the cause of heat in mixed bodies, and these are said to be hot in so far as they have a share of fire. Consequently, since the law is chiefly ordained to the common good, any other precept in regard to some individual work, must needs be devoid of the nature of a law, save in so far as it regards the common good. Therefore every law is ordained to the common good.

Reply Obj. 1: A command denotes an application of a law to matters regulated by the law. Now the order to the common good, at which the law aims, is applicable to particular ends. And in this way commands are given even concerning particular matters.

Reply Obj. 2: Actions are indeed concerned with particular matters: but those particular matters are referable to the common good, not as to a common genus or species, but as to a common final cause, according as the common good is said to be the common end.

Reply Obj. 3: Just as nothing stands firm with regard to the speculative reason except that which is traced back to the first indemonstrable principles, so nothing stands firm with regard to the practical reason, unless it be directed to the last end which is the common good: and whatever stands to reason in this sense, has the nature of a law.

THIRD ARTICLE [I-II, Q. 90, Art. 3]

Whether the Reason of Any Man Is Competent to Make Laws?

Objection 1: It would seem that the reason of any man is competent to make laws. For the Apostle says (Rom. 2:14) that "when the Gentiles, who have not the law, do by nature those things that are of the law ... they are a law to themselves." Now he says this of all in general. Therefore anyone can make a law for himself.

Obj. 2: Further, as the Philosopher says (Ethic. ii, 1), "the intention of the lawgiver is to lead men to virtue." But every man can lead another to virtue. Therefore the reason of any man is competent to make laws.

Obj. 3: Further, just as the sovereign of a state governs the state, so every father of a family governs his household. But the sovereign of a state can make laws for the state. Therefore every father of a family can make laws for his household.

*On the contrary,* Isidore says (Etym. v, 10): "A law is an ordinance of the people, whereby something is sanctioned by the Elders together with the Commonalty."

*I answer that,* A law, properly speaking, regards first and foremost the order to the common good. Now to order anything to the common good, belongs either to the whole people, or to someone who is the viceregent of the whole people. And therefore the making of a law belongs either to the whole people or to a public personage who has care of the whole people: since in all other matters the directing of anything to the end concerns him to whom the end belongs.

Reply Obj. 1: As stated above (A. 1, ad 1), a law is in a person not only as in one that rules, but also by participation as in one that is ruled. In the latter way each one is a law to himself, in so far as he shares the direction that he receives from one who rules him. Hence the same text goes on: "Who show the work of the law written in their hearts."

Reply Obj. 2: A private person cannot lead another to virtue efficaciously: for he can only advise, and if his advice be not taken, it has no coercive power, such as the law should have, in order to prove an efficacious inducement to virtue, as the Philosopher says (Ethic. x, 9). But this coercive power is vested in the whole people or in some public personage, to whom it belongs to inflict penalties, as we shall state further on (Q. 92, A. 2, ad 3; II-II, Q. 64, A. 3). Wherefore the framing of laws belongs to him alone.

Reply Obj. 3: As one man is a part of the household, so a household is a part of the state: and the state is a perfect community, according to *Polit.* i, 1. And therefore, as the good of one man is not the last end, but is ordained to the common good; so too the good of one household is ordained to the good of a single state, which is a perfect community. Consequently he that governs a family, can indeed make certain commands or ordinances, but not such as to have properly the force of law.

FOURTH ARTICLE [I-II, Q. 90, Art. 4]

Whether Promulgation Is Essential to a Law?

Objection 1: It would seem that promulgation is not essential to a law. For the natural law above all has the character of law. But the natural law needs no promulgation. Therefore it is not essential to a law that it be promulgated.

Obj. 2: Further, it belongs properly to a law to bind one to do or not to do something. But the obligation of fulfilling a law touches not only those in whose presence it is promulgated, but also others. Therefore promulgation is not essential to a law.

Obj. 3: Further, the binding force of a law extends even to the future, since "laws are binding in matters of the future," as the jurists say (Cod. 1, tit. De lege et constit. leg. vii). But promulgation concerns those who are present. Therefore it is not essential to a law.

*On the contrary,* It is laid down in the Decretals, dist. 4, that "laws are established when they are promulgated."

*I answer that,* As stated above (A. 1), a law is imposed on others by way of a rule and measure. Now a rule or measure is imposed by being applied to those who are to be ruled and measured by it. Wherefore, in order that a law obtain the binding force which is proper to a law, it must needs be applied to the men who have to be ruled by it. Such application is made by its being notified to them by promulgation. Wherefore promulgation is necessary for the law to obtain its force.

Thus from the four preceding articles, the definition of law may be gathered; and it is nothing else than an ordinance of reason for the common good, made by him who has care of the community, and promulgated.

Reply Obj. 1: The natural law is promulgated by the very fact that God instilled it into man's mind so as to be known by him naturally.

Reply Obj. 2: Those who are not present when a law is promulgated, are bound to observe the law, in so far as it is notified or can be notified to them by others, after it has been promulgated.

Reply Obj. 3: The promulgation that takes place now, extends to future time by reason of the durability of written characters, by which means it is continually promulgated. Hence Isidore says (Etym. v, 3; ii, 10) that " *lex* (law) is derived from legere (to read) because it is written."

# QUESTION 91

OF THE VARIOUS KINDS OF LAW (In Six Articles)

We must now consider the various kinds of law: under which head there are six points of inquiry:

(1) Whether there is an eternal law?

(2) Whether there is a natural law?

(3) Whether there is a human law?

(4) Whether there is a Divine law?

(5) Whether there is one Divine law, or several?

(6) Whether there is a law of sin?

FIRST ARTICLE [I-II, Q. 91, Art. 1]

Whether There Is an Eternal Law?

Objection 1: It would seem that there is no eternal law. Because every law is imposed on someone. But there was not someone from eternity on whom a law could be imposed: since God alone was from eternity. Therefore no law is eternal.

Obj. 2: Further, promulgation is essential to law. But promulgation could not be from eternity: because there was no one to whom it could be promulgated from eternity. Therefore no law can be eternal.

Obj. 3: Further, a law implies order to an end. But nothing ordained to an end is eternal: for the last end alone is eternal. Therefore no law is eternal.

*On the contrary,* Augustine says (De Lib. Arb. i, 6): "That Law which is the Supreme Reason cannot be understood to be otherwise than unchangeable and eternal."

*I answer that,* As stated above (Q. 90, A. 1, ad 2; AA. 3, 4), a law is nothing else but a dictate of practical reason emanating from the ruler who governs a perfect community. Now it is evident, granted that the world is ruled by Divine Providence, as was stated in the First Part (Q. 22, AA. 1, 2), that the whole community of the universe is governed by Divine Reason. Wherefore the very Idea of the government of things in God the Ruler of the universe, has the nature of a law. And since the Divine Reason's conception of things is not subject to time but is eternal, according to Prov. 8:23, therefore it is that this kind of law must be called eternal.

Reply Obj. 1: Those things that are not in themselves, exist with God, inasmuch as they are foreknown and preordained by Him, according to Rom. 4:17: "Who calls those things that are not, as those that are." Accordingly the eternal concept of the Divine law bears the character of an eternal law, in so far as it is ordained by God to the government of things foreknown by Him.

Reply Obj. 2: Promulgation is made by word of mouth or in writing; and in both ways the eternal law is promulgated: because both the Divine Word and the writing of the Book of Life are eternal. But the promulgation cannot be from eternity on the part of the creature that hears or reads.

Reply Obj. 3: The law implies order to the end actively, in so far as it directs certain things to the end; but not passively—that is to say, the law itself is not ordained to the end—except accidentally, in a governor whose end is extrinsic to him, and to which end his law must needs be ordained. But the end of the Divine government is God Himself, and His law is not distinct from Himself. Wherefore the eternal law is not ordained to another end.

SECOND ARTICLE [I-II, Q. 91, Art. 2]

Whether There Is in Us a Natural Law?

Objection 1: It would seem that there is no natural law in us. Because man is governed sufficiently by the eternal law: for Augustine says (De Lib. Arb. i) that "the eternal law is that by which it is right that all things should be most orderly." But nature does not abound in superfluities as neither does she fail in necessaries. Therefore no law is natural to man.

Obj. 2: Further, by the law man is directed, in his acts, to the end, as stated above (Q. 90, A. 2). But the directing of human acts to their end is not a function of nature, as is the case in irrational creatures, which act for an end solely by their natural appetite; whereas man acts for an end by his reason and will. Therefore no law is natural to man.

Obj. 3: Further, the more a man is free, the less is he under the law. But man is freer than all the animals, on account of his free-will, with which he is endowed above all other animals. Since therefore other animals are not subject to a natural law, neither is man subject to a natural law.

*On the contrary,* A gloss on Rom. 2:14: "When the Gentiles, who have not the law, do by nature those things that are of the law," comments as follows: "Although they have no written law, yet they have the natural law, whereby each one knows, and is conscious of, what is good and what is evil."

*I answer that,* As stated above (Q. 90, A. 1, ad 1), law, being a rule and measure, can be in a person in two ways: in one way, as in him that rules and measures; in another way, as in that which is ruled and measured, since a thing is ruled and measured, in so far as it partakes of the rule or measure. Wherefore, since all things subject to Divine providence are ruled and measured by the eternal law, as was stated above (A. 1); it is evident that all things partake somewhat of the eternal law, in so far as, namely, from its being imprinted on them, they derive their respective inclinations to their proper acts and ends. Now among all others, the rational creature is subject to Divine providence in the most excellent way, in so far as it partakes of a share of providence, by being provident both for itself and for others. Wherefore it has a share of the Eternal Reason, whereby it has a natural inclination to its proper act and end: and this participation of the eternal law in the rational creature is called the natural law. Hence the Psalmist after saying (Ps. 4:6): "Offer up the sacrifice of justice," as though someone asked what the works of justice are, adds: "Many say, Who showeth us good things?" in answer to which question he says: "The light of Thy countenance, O Lord, is signed upon us": thus implying that the light of natural reason, whereby we discern what is good and what is evil, which is the function of the natural law, is nothing else than an imprint on us of the Divine light. It is therefore evident that the natural law is nothing else than the rational creature's participation of the eternal law.

Reply Obj. 1: This argument would hold, if the natural law were something different from the eternal law: whereas it is nothing but a participation thereof, as stated above.

Reply Obj. 2: Every act of reason and will in us is based on that which is according to nature, as stated above (Q. 10, A. 1): for every act of reasoning is based on principles that are known naturally, and every act of appetite in respect of the means is derived from the natural appetite in respect of the last end. Accordingly the first direction of our acts to their end must needs be in virtue of the natural law.

Reply Obj. 3: Even irrational animals partake in their own way of the Eternal Reason, just as the rational creature does. But because the rational creature partakes thereof in an intellectual and rational manner, therefore the participation of the eternal law in the rational creature is properly called a law, since a law is something pertaining to reason, as stated above (Q. 90, A. 1). Irrational creatures, however, do not partake thereof in a rational manner, wherefore there is no participation of the eternal law in them, except by way of similitude.

THIRD ARTICLE [I-II, Q. 91, Art. 3]

Whether There Is a Human Law?

Objection 1: It would seem that there is not a human law. For the natural law is a participation of the eternal law, as stated above (A. 2). Now through the eternal law "all things are most orderly," as Augustine states (De Lib. Arb. i, 6). Therefore the natural law suffices for the ordering of all human affairs. Consequently there is no need for a human law.

Obj. 2: Further, a law bears the character of a measure, as stated above (Q. 90, A. 1). But human reason is not a measure of things, but vice versa, as stated in *Metaph.* x, text. 5. Therefore no law can emanate from human reason.

Obj. 3: Further, a measure should be most certain, as stated in *Metaph.* x, text. 3. But the dictates of human reason in matters of conduct are uncertain, according to Wis. 9:14: "The thoughts of mortal men are fearful, and our counsels uncertain." Therefore no law can emanate from human reason.

*On the contrary,* Augustine (De Lib. Arb. i, 6) distinguishes two kinds of law, the one eternal, the other temporal, which he calls human.

*I answer that,* As stated above (Q. 90, A. 1, ad 2), a law is a dictate of the practical reason. Now it is to be observed that the same procedure takes place in the practical and in the speculative reason: for each proceeds from principles to conclusions, as stated above (ibid.). Accordingly we conclude that just as, in the speculative reason, from naturally known indemonstrable principles, we draw the conclusions of the various sciences, the knowledge of which is not imparted to us by nature, but acquired by the efforts of reason, so too it is from the precepts of the natural law, as from general and indemonstrable principles, that the human reason needs to proceed to the more particular determination of certain matters. These particular determinations, devised by human reason, are called human laws, provided the other essential conditions of law be observed, as stated above (Q. 90, AA. 2, 3, 4). Wherefore Tully says in his *Rhetoric* (De Invent. Rhet. ii) that "justice has its source in nature; thence certain things came into custom by reason of their utility; afterwards these things which emanated from nature and were approved by custom, were sanctioned by fear and reverence for the law."

Reply Obj. 1: The human reason cannot have a full participation of the dictate of the Divine Reason, but according to its own mode, and imperfectly. Consequently, as on the part of the speculative reason, by a natural participation of Divine Wisdom, there is in us the knowledge of certain general principles, but not proper knowledge of each single truth, such as that contained in the Divine Wisdom; so too, on the part of the practical reason, man has a natural participation of the eternal law, according to certain general principles, but not as regards the particular determinations of individual cases, which are, however, contained in the eternal law. Hence the need for human reason to proceed further to sanction them by law.

Reply Obj. 2: Human reason is not, of itself, the rule of things: but the principles impressed on it by nature, are general rules and measures of all things relating to human conduct, whereof the natural reason is the rule and measure, although it is not the measure of things that are from nature.

Reply Obj. 3: The practical reason is concerned with practical matters, which are singular and contingent: but not with necessary things, with which the speculative reason is concerned. Wherefore human laws cannot have that inerrancy that belongs to the demonstrated conclusions of sciences. Nor is it necessary for every measure to be altogether unerring and certain, but according as it is possible in its own particular genus.

FOURTH ARTICLE [I-II, Q. 91, Art. 4]

Whether There Was Any Need for a Divine Law?

Objection 1: It would seem that there was no need for a Divine law. Because, as stated above (A. 2), the natural law is a participation in us of the eternal law. But the eternal law is a Divine law, as stated above (A. 1). Therefore there was no need for a Divine law in addition to the natural law, and human laws derived therefrom.

Obj. 2: Further, it is written (Ecclus. 15:14) that "God left man in the hand of his own counsel." Now counsel is an act of reason, as stated above (Q. 14, A. 1). Therefore man was left to the direction of his reason. But a dictate of human reason is a human law as stated above (A. 3). Therefore there is no need for man to be governed also by a Divine law.

Obj. 3: Further, human nature is more self-sufficing than irrational creatures. But irrational creatures have no Divine law besides the natural inclination impressed on them. Much less, therefore, should the rational creature have a Divine law in addition to the natural law.

*On the contrary,* David prayed God to set His law before him, saying (Ps. 118:33): "Set before me for a law the way of Thy justifications, O Lord."

*I answer that,* Besides the natural and the human law it was necessary for the directing of human conduct to have a Divine law. And this for four reasons. First, because it is by law that man is directed how to perform his proper acts in view of his last end. And indeed if man were ordained to no other end than that which is proportionate to his natural faculty, there would be no need for man to have any further direction of the part of his reason, besides the natural law and human law which is derived from it. But since man is ordained to an end of eternal happiness which is improportionate to man's natural faculty, as stated above (Q. 5, A. 5), therefore it was necessary that, besides the natural and the human law, man should be directed to his end by a law given by God.

Secondly, because, on account of the uncertainty of human judgment, especially on contingent and particular matters, different people form different judgments on human acts; whence also different and contrary laws result. In order, therefore, that man may know without any doubt what he ought to do and what he ought to avoid, it was necessary for man to be directed in his proper acts by a law given by God, for it is certain that such a law cannot err.

Thirdly, because man can make laws in those matters of which he is competent to judge. But man is not competent to judge of interior movements, that are hidden, but only of exterior acts which appear: and yet for the perfection of virtue it is necessary for man to conduct himself aright in both kinds of acts. Consequently human law could not sufficiently curb and direct interior acts; and it was necessary for this purpose that a Divine law should supervene.

Fourthly, because, as Augustine says (De Lib. Arb. i, 5, 6), human law cannot punish or forbid all evil deeds: since while aiming at doing away with all evils, it would do away with many good things, and would hinder the advance of the common good, which is necessary for human intercourse. In order, therefore, that no evil might remain unforbidden and unpunished, it was necessary for the Divine law to supervene, whereby all sins are forbidden.

And these four causes are touched upon in Ps. 118:8, where it is said: "The law of the Lord is unspotted," i.e. allowing no foulness of sin; "converting souls," because it directs not only exterior, but also interior acts; "the testimony of the Lord is faithful," because of the certainty of what is true and right; "giving wisdom to little ones," by directing man to an end supernatural and Divine.

Reply Obj. 1: By the natural law the eternal law is participated proportionately to the capacity of human nature. But to his supernatural end man needs to be directed in a yet higher way. Hence the additional law given by God, whereby man shares more perfectly in the eternal law.

Reply Obj. 2: Counsel is a kind of inquiry: hence it must proceed from some principles. Nor is it enough for it to proceed from principles imparted by nature, which are the precepts of the natural law, for the reasons given above: but there is need for certain additional principles, namely, the precepts of the Divine law.

Reply Obj. 3: Irrational creatures are not ordained to an end higher than that which is proportionate to their natural powers: consequently the comparison fails.

FIFTH ARTICLE [I-II, Q. 91, Art. 5]

Whether There Is but One Divine Law?

Objection 1: It would seem that there is but one Divine law. Because, where there is one king in one kingdom there is but one law. Now the whole of mankind is compared to God as to one king, according to Ps. 46:8: "God is the King of all the earth." Therefore there is but one Divine law.

Obj. 2: Further, every law is directed to the end which the lawgiver intends for those for whom he makes the law. But God intends one and the same thing for all men; since according to 1 Tim. 2:4: "He will have all men to be saved, and to come to the knowledge of the truth." Therefore there is but one Divine law.

Obj. 3: Further, the Divine law seems to be more akin to the eternal law, which is one, than the natural law, according as the revelation of grace is of a higher order than natural knowledge. Therefore much more is the Divine law but one.

*On the contrary,* The Apostle says (Heb. 7:12): "The priesthood being translated, it is necessary that a translation also be made of the law." But the priesthood is twofold, as stated in the same passage, viz. the levitical priesthood, and the priesthood of Christ. Therefore the Divine law is twofold, namely the Old Law and the New Law.

*I answer that,* As stated in the First Part (Q. 30, A. 3), distinction is the cause of number. Now things may be distinguished in two ways. First, as those things that are altogether specifically different, e.g. a horse and an ox. Secondly, as perfect and imperfect in the same species, e.g. a boy and a man: and in this way the Divine law is divided into Old and New. Hence the Apostle (Gal. 3:24, 25) compares the state of man under the Old Law to that of a child "under a pedagogue"; but the state under the New Law, to that of a full grown man, who is "no longer under a pedagogue."

Now the perfection and imperfection of these two laws is to be taken in connection with the three conditions pertaining to law, as stated above. For, in the first place, it belongs to law to be directed to the common good as to its end, as stated above (Q. 90, A. 2). This good may be twofold. It may be a sensible and earthly good; and to this, man was directly ordained by the Old Law: wherefore, at the very outset of the law, the people were invited to the earthly kingdom of the Chananaeans (Ex. 3:8, 17). Again it may be an intelligible and heavenly good: and to this, man is ordained by the New Law. Wherefore, at the very beginning of His preaching, Christ invited men to the kingdom of heaven, saying (Matt. 4:17): "Do penance, for the kingdom of heaven is at hand." Hence Augustine says (Contra Faust. iv) that "promises of temporal goods are contained in the Old Testament, for which reason it is called old; but the promise of eternal life belongs to the New Testament."

Secondly, it belongs to the law to direct human acts according to the order of righteousness (A. 4): wherein also the New Law surpasses the Old Law, since it directs our internal acts, according to Matt. 5:20: "Unless your justice abound more than that of the Scribes and Pharisees, you shall not enter into the kingdom of heaven." Hence the saying that "the Old Law restrains the hand, but the New Law controls the mind" ( Sentent. iii, D, xl).

Thirdly, it belongs to the law to induce men to observe its commandments. This the Old Law did by the fear of punishment: but the New Law, by love, which is poured into our hearts by the grace of Christ, bestowed in the New Law, but foreshadowed in the Old. Hence Augustine says (Contra Adimant. Manich. discip. xvii) that "there is little difference [*The 'little difference' refers to the Latin words 'timor' and 'amor'—'fear' and 'love.'] between the Law and the Gospel—fear and love."

Reply Obj. 1: As the father of a family issues different commands to the children and to the adults, so also the one King, God, in His one kingdom, gave one law to men, while they were yet imperfect, and another more perfect law, when, by the preceding law, they had been led to a greater capacity for Divine things.

Reply Obj. 2: The salvation of man could not be achieved otherwise than through Christ, according to Acts 4:12: "There is no other name ... given to men, whereby we must be saved." Consequently the law that brings all to salvation could not be given until after the coming of Christ. But before His coming it was necessary to give to the people, of whom Christ was to be born, a law containing certain rudiments of righteousness unto salvation, in order to prepare them to receive Him.

Reply Obj. 3: The natural law directs man by way of certain general precepts, common to both the perfect and the imperfect: wherefore it is one and the same for all. But the Divine law directs man also in certain particular matters, to which the perfect and imperfect do not stand in the same relation. Hence the necessity for the Divine law to be twofold, as already explained.

SIXTH ARTICLE [I-II, Q. 91, Art. 6]

Whether There Is a Law in the Fomes of Sin?

Objection 1: It would seem that there is no law of the *fomes* of sin. For Isidore says (Etym. v) that the "law is based on reason." But the *fomes* of sin is not based on reason, but deviates from it. Therefore the *fomes* has not the nature of a law.

Obj. 2: Further, every law is binding, so that those who do not obey it are called transgressors. But man is not called a transgressor, from not following the instigations of the *fomes;* but rather from his following them. Therefore the fomes has not the nature of a law.

Obj. 3: Further, the law is ordained to the common good, as stated above (Q. 90, A. 2). But the *fomes* inclines us, not to the common, but to our own private good. Therefore the *fomes* has not the nature of sin.

*On the contrary,* The Apostle says (Rom. 7:23): "I see another law in my members, fighting against the law of my mind."

*I answer that,* As stated above (A. 2; Q. 90, A. 1, ad 1), the law, as to its essence, resides in him that rules and measures; but, by way of participation, in that which is ruled and measured; so that every inclination or ordination which may be found in things subject to the law, is called a law by participation, as stated above (A. 2; Q. 90, A. 1, ad 1). Now those who are subject to a law may receive a twofold inclination from the lawgiver. First, in so far as he directly inclines his subjects to something; sometimes indeed different subjects to different acts; in this way we may say that there is a military law and a mercantile law. Secondly, indirectly; thus by the very fact that a lawgiver deprives a subject of some dignity, the latter passes into another order, so as to be under another law, as it were: thus if a soldier be turned out of the army, he becomes a subject of rural or of mercantile legislation.

Accordingly under the Divine Lawgiver various creatures have various natural inclinations, so that what is, as it were, a law for one, is against the law for another: thus I might say that fierceness is, in a way, the law of a dog, but against the law of a sheep or another meek animal. And so the law of man, which, by the Divine ordinance, is allotted to him, according to his proper natural condition, is that he should act in accordance with reason: and this law was so effective in the primitive state, that nothing either beside or against reason could take man unawares. But when man turned his back on God, he fell under the influence of his sensual impulses: in fact this happens to each one individually, the more he deviates from the path of reason, so that, after a fashion, he is likened to the beasts that are led by the impulse of sensuality, according to Ps. 48:21: "Man, when he was in honor, did not understand: he hath been compared to senseless beasts, and made like to them."

So, then, this very inclination of sensuality which is called the *fomes,* in other animals has simply the nature of a law (yet only in so far as a law may be said to be in such things), by reason of a direct inclination. But in man, it has not the nature of law in this way, rather is it a deviation from the law of reason. But since, by the just sentence of God, man is destitute of original justice, and his reason bereft of its vigor, this impulse of sensuality, whereby he is led, in so far as it is a penalty following from the Divine law depriving man of his proper dignity, has the nature of a law.

Reply Obj. 1: This argument considers the *fomes* in itself, as an incentive to evil. It is not thus that it has the nature of a law, as stated above, but according as it results from the justice of the Divine law: it is as though we were to say that the law allows a nobleman to be condemned to hard labor for some misdeed.

Reply Obj. 2: This argument considers law in the light of a rule or measure: for it is in this sense that those who deviate from the law become transgressors. But the *fomes* is not a law in this respect, but by a kind of participation, as stated above.

Reply Obj. 3: This argument considers the *fomes* as to its proper inclination, and not as to its origin. And yet if the inclination of sensuality be considered as it is in other animals, thus it is ordained to the common good, namely, to the preservation of nature in the species or in the individual. And this is in man also, in so far as sensuality is subject to reason. But it is called *fomes* in so far as it strays from the order of reason.

# QUESTION 92

OF THE EFFECTS OF LAW (In Two articles)

We must now consider the effects of law; under which head there are two points of inquiry:

(1) Whether an effect of law is to make men good?

(2) Whether the effects of law are to command, to forbid, to permit, and to punish, as the Jurist states?

FIRST ARTICLE [I-II, Q. 92, Art. 1]

Whether an Effect of Law Is to Make Men Good?

Objection 1: It seems that it is not an effect of law to make men good. For men are good through virtue, since virtue, as stated in *Ethic.* ii, 6 is "that which makes its subject good." But virtue is in man from God alone, because He it is Who "works it in us without us," as we stated above (Q. 55, A. 4) in giving the definition of virtue. Therefore the law does not make men good.

Obj. 2: Further, Law does not profit a man unless he obeys it. But the very fact that a man obeys a law is due to his being good. Therefore in man goodness is presupposed to the law. Therefore the law does not make men good.

Obj. 3: Further, Law is ordained to the common good, as stated above (Q. 90, A. 2). But some behave well in things regarding the community, who behave ill in things regarding themselves. Therefore it is not the business of the law to make men good.

Obj. 4: Further, some laws are tyrannical, as the Philosopher says (Polit. iii, 6). But a tyrant does not intend the good of his subjects, but considers only his own profit. Therefore law does not make men good.

*On the contrary,* The Philosopher says (Ethic. ii, 1) that the "intention of every lawgiver is to make good citizens."

*I answer that,* as stated above (Q. 90, A. 1, ad 2; AA. 3, 4), a law is nothing else than a dictate of reason in the ruler by whom his subjects are governed. Now the virtue of any subordinate thing consists in its being well subordinated to that by which it is regulated: thus we see that the virtue of the irascible and concupiscible faculties consists in their being obedient to reason; and accordingly "the virtue of every subject consists in his being well subjected to his ruler," as the Philosopher says (Polit. i). But every law aims at being obeyed by those who are subject to it. Consequently it is evident that the proper effect of law is to lead its subjects to their proper virtue: and since virtue is "that which makes its subject good," it follows that the proper effect of law is to make those to whom it is given, good, either simply or in some particular respect. For if the intention of the lawgiver is fixed on true good, which is the common good regulated according to Divine justice, it follows that the effect of the law is to make men good simply. If, however, the intention of the lawgiver is fixed on that which is not simply good, but useful or pleasurable to himself, or in opposition to Divine justice; then the law does not make men good simply, but in respect to that particular government. In this way good is found even in things that are bad of themselves: thus a man is called a good robber, because he works in a way that is adapted to his end.

Reply Obj. 1: Virtue is twofold, as explained above (Q. 63, A. 2), viz. acquired and infused. Now the fact of being accustomed to an action contributes to both, but in different ways; for it causes the acquired virtue; while it disposes to infused virtue, and preserves and fosters it when it already exists. And since law is given for the purpose of directing human acts; as far as human acts conduce to virtue, so far does law make men good. Wherefore the Philosopher says in the second book of the Politics (Ethic. ii) that "lawgivers make men good by habituating them to good works."

Reply Obj. 2: It is not always through perfect goodness of virtue that one obeys the law, but sometimes it is through fear of punishment, and sometimes from the mere dictates of reason, which is a beginning of virtue, as stated above (Q. 63, A. 1).

Reply Obj. 3: The goodness of any part is considered in comparison with the whole; hence Augustine says (Confess. iii) that "unseemly is the part that harmonizes not with the whole." Since then every man is a part of the state, it is impossible that a man be good, unless he be well proportionate to the common good: nor can the whole be well consistent unless its parts be proportionate to it. Consequently the common good of the state cannot flourish, unless the citizens be virtuous, at least those whose business it is to govern. But it is enough for the good of the community, that the other citizens be so far virtuous that they obey the commands of their rulers. Hence the Philosopher says (Polit. ii, 2) that "the virtue of a sovereign is the same as that of a good man, but the virtue of any common citizen is not the same as that of a good man."

Reply Obj. 4: A tyrannical law, through not being according to reason, is not a law, absolutely speaking, but rather a perversion of law; and yet in so far as it is something in the nature of a law, it aims at the citizens' being good. For all it has in the nature of a law consists in its being an ordinance made by a superior to his subjects, and aims at being obeyed by them, which is to make them good, not simply, but with respect to that particular government.

SECOND ARTICLE [I-II, Q. 92, Art. 2]

Whether the Acts of Law Are Suitably Assigned?

Objection 1: It would seem that the acts of law are not suitably assigned as consisting in "command, prohibition, permission, and punishment." For "every law is a general precept," as the Jurist states. But command and precept are the same. Therefore the other three are superfluous.

Obj. 2: Further, the effect of a law is to induce its subjects to be good, as stated above (A. 1). But counsel aims at a higher good than a command does. Therefore it belongs to law to counsel rather than to command.

Obj. 3: Further, just as punishment stirs a man to good deeds, so does reward. Therefore if to punish is reckoned an effect of law, so also is to reward.

Obj. 4: Further, the intention of a lawgiver is to make men good, as stated above (A. 1). But he that obeys the law, merely through fear of being punished, is not good: because "although a good deed may be done through servile fear, i.e. fear of punishment, it is not done well," as Augustine says (Contra duas Epist. Pelag. ii). Therefore punishment is not a proper effect of law.

*On the contrary,* Isidore says (Etym. v, 19): "Every law either permits something, as: 'A brave man may demand his reward'": or forbids something, as: "No man may ask a consecrated virgin in marriage": or punishes, as: "Let him that commits a murder be put to death."

*I answer that,* Just as an assertion is a dictate of reason asserting something, so is a law a dictate of reason, commanding something. Now it is proper to reason to lead from one thing to another. Wherefore just as, in demonstrative sciences, the reason leads us from certain principles to assent to the conclusion, so it induces us by some means to assent to the precept of the law.

Now the precepts of law are concerned with human acts, in which the law directs, as stated above (Q. 90, AA. 1, 2; Q. 91, A. 4). Again there are three kinds of human acts: for, as stated above (Q. 18, A. 8), some acts are good generically, viz. acts of virtue; and in respect of these the act of the law is a precept or command, for "the law commands all acts of virtue" (Ethic. v, 1). Some acts are evil generically, viz. acts of vice, and in respect of these the law forbids. Some acts are generically indifferent, and in respect of these the law permits; and all acts that are either not distinctly good or not distinctly bad may be called indifferent. And it is the fear of punishment that law makes use of in order to ensure obedience: in which respect punishment is an effect of law.

Reply Obj. 1: Just as to cease from evil is a kind of good, so a prohibition is a kind of precept: and accordingly, taking precept in a wide sense, every law is a kind of precept.

Reply Obj. 2: To advise is not a proper act of law, but may be within the competency even of a private person, who cannot make a law. Wherefore too the Apostle, after giving a certain counsel (1 Cor. 7:12) says: "I speak, not the Lord." Consequently it is not reckoned as an effect of law.

Reply Obj. 3: To reward may also pertain to anyone: but to punish pertains to none but the framer of the law, by whose authority the pain is inflicted. Wherefore to reward is not reckoned an effect of law, but only to punish.

Reply Obj. 4: From becoming accustomed to avoid evil and fulfill what is good, through fear of punishment, one is sometimes led on to do so likewise, with delight and of one's own accord. Accordingly, law, even by punishing, leads men on to being good.

# QUESTION 93

OF THE ETERNAL LAW (In Six Articles)

We must now consider each law by itself; and (1) The eternal law; (2) The natural law; (3) The human law; (4) The old law; (5) The new law, which is the law of the Gospel. Of the sixth law which is the law of the *fomes,* suffice what we have said when treating of original sin.

Concerning the first there are six points of inquiry:

(1) What is the eternal law?

(2) Whether it is known to all?

(3) Whether every law is derived from it?

(4) Whether necessary things are subject to the eternal law?

(5) Whether natural contingencies are subject to the eternal law?

(6) Whether all human things are subject to it?

FIRST ARTICLE [I-II, Q. 93, Art. 1]

Whether the Eternal Law Is a Sovereign Type [*Ratio] Existing in God?

Objection 1: It would seem that the eternal law is not a sovereign type existing in God. For there is only one eternal law. But there are many types of things in the Divine mind; for Augustine says (Qq. lxxxiii, qu. 46) that God "made each thing according to its type." Therefore the eternal law does not seem to be a type existing in the Divine mind.

Obj. 2: Further, it is essential to a law that it be promulgated by word, as stated above (Q. 90, A. 4). But Word is a Personal name in God, as stated in the First Part (Q. 34, A. 1): whereas type refers to the Essence. Therefore the eternal law is not the same as a Divine type.

Obj. 3: Further, Augustine says (De Vera Relig. xxx): "We see a law above our minds, which is called truth." But the law which is above our minds is the eternal law. Therefore truth is the eternal law. But the idea of truth is not the same as the idea of a type. Therefore the eternal law is not the same as the sovereign type.

*On the contrary,* Augustine says (De Lib. Arb. i, 6) that "the eternal law is the sovereign type, to which we must always conform."

*I answer that,* Just as in every artificer there pre-exists a type of the things that are made by his art, so too in every governor there must pre-exist the type of the order of those things that are to be done by those who are subject to his government. And just as the type of the things yet to be made by an art is called the art or exemplar of the products of that art, so too the type in him who governs the acts of his subjects, bears the character of a law, provided the other conditions be present which we have mentioned above (Q. 90). Now God, by His wisdom, is the Creator of all things in relation to which He stands as the artificer to the products of his art, as stated in the First Part (Q. 14, A. 8). Moreover He governs all the acts and movements that are to be found in each single creature, as was also stated in the First Part (Q. 103, A. 5). Wherefore as the type of the Divine Wisdom, inasmuch as by It all things are created, has the character of art, exemplar or idea; so the type of Divine Wisdom, as moving all things to their due end, bears the character of law. Accordingly the eternal law is nothing else than the type of Divine Wisdom, as directing all actions and movements.

Reply Obj. 1: Augustine is speaking in that passage of the ideal types which regard the proper nature of each single thing; and consequently in them there is a certain distinction and plurality, according to their different relations to things, as stated in the First Part (Q. 15, A. 2). But law is said to direct human acts by ordaining them to the common good, as stated above (Q. 90, A. 2). And things, which are in themselves different, may be considered as one, according as they are ordained to one common thing. Wherefore the eternal law is one since it is the type of this order.

Reply Obj. 2: With regard to any sort of word, two points may be considered: viz. the word itself, and that which is expressed by the word. For the spoken word is something uttered by the mouth of man, and expresses that which is signified by the human word. The same applies to the human mental word, which is nothing else than something conceived by the mind, by which man expresses his thoughts mentally. So then in God the Word conceived by the intellect of the Father is the name of a Person: but all things that are in the Father's knowledge, whether they refer to the Essence or to the Persons, or to the works of God, are expressed by this Word, as Augustine declares (De Trin. xv, 14). And among other things expressed by this Word, the eternal law itself is expressed thereby. Nor does it follow that the eternal law is a Personal name in God: yet it is appropriated to the Son, on account of the kinship between type and word.

Reply Obj. 3: The types of the Divine intellect do not stand in the same relation to things, as the types of the human intellect. For the human intellect is measured by things, so that a human concept is not true by reason of itself, but by reason of its being consonant with things, since "an opinion is true or false according as it answers to the reality." But the Divine intellect is the measure of things: since each thing has so far truth in it, as it represents the Divine intellect, as was stated in the First Part (Q. 16, A. 1). Consequently the Divine intellect is true in itself; and its type is truth itself.

SECOND ARTICLE [I-II, Q. 93, Art. 2]

Whether the Eternal Law Is Known to All?

Objection 1: It would seem that the eternal law is not known to all. Because, as the Apostle says (1 Cor. 2:11), "the things that are of God no man knoweth, but the Spirit of God." But the eternal law is a type existing in the Divine mind. Therefore it is unknown to all save God alone.

Obj. 2: Further, as Augustine says (De Lib. Arb. i, 6) "the eternal law is that by which it is right that all things should be most orderly." But all do not know how all things are most orderly. Therefore all do not know the eternal law.

Obj. 3: Further, Augustine says (De Vera Relig. xxxi) that "the eternal law is not subject to the judgment of man." But according to *Ethic.* i, "any man can judge well of what he knows." Therefore the eternal law is not known to us.

*On the contrary,* Augustine says (De Lib. Arb. i, 6) that "knowledge of the eternal law is imprinted on us."

*I answer that,* A thing may be known in two ways: first, in itself; secondly, in its effect, wherein some likeness of that thing is found: thus someone not seeing the sun in its substance, may know it by its rays. So then no one can know the eternal law, as it is in itself, except the blessed who see God in His Essence. But every rational creature knows it in its reflection, greater or less. For every knowledge of truth is a kind of reflection and participation of the eternal law, which is the unchangeable truth, as Augustine says (De Vera Relig. xxxi). Now all men know the truth to a certain extent, at least as to the common principles of the natural law: and as to the others, they partake of the knowledge of truth, some more, some less; and in this respect are more or less cognizant of the eternal law.

Reply Obj. 1: We cannot know the things that are of God, as they are in themselves; but they are made known to us in their effects, according to Rom. 1:20: "The invisible things of God ... are clearly seen, being understood by the things that are made."

Reply Obj. 2: Although each one knows the eternal law according to his own capacity, in the way explained above, yet none can comprehend it: for it cannot be made perfectly known by its effects. Therefore it does not follow that anyone who knows the eternal law in the way aforesaid, knows also the whole order of things, whereby they are most orderly.

Reply Obj. 3: To judge a thing may be understood in two ways. First, as when a cognitive power judges of its proper object, according to Job 12:11: "Doth not the ear discern words, and the palate of him that eateth, the taste?" It is to this kind of judgment that the Philosopher alludes when he says that "anyone can judge well of what he knows," by judging, namely, whether what is put forward is true. In another way we speak of a superior judging of a subordinate by a kind of practical judgment, as to whether he should be such and such or not. And thus none can judge of the eternal law.

THIRD ARTICLE [I-II, Q. 93, Art. 3]

Whether Every Law Is Derived from the Eternal Law?

Objection 1: It would seem that not every law is derived from the eternal law. For there is a law of the *fomes,* as stated above (Q. 91, A. 6), which is not derived from that Divine law which is the eternal law, since thereunto pertains the "prudence of the flesh," of which the Apostle says (Rom. 8:7), that "it cannot be subject to the law of God." Therefore not every law is derived from the eternal law.

Obj. 2: Further, nothing unjust can be derived from the eternal law, because, as stated above (A. 2, Obj. 2), "the eternal law is that, according to which it is right that all things should be most orderly." But some laws are unjust, according to Isa. 10:1: "Woe to them that make wicked laws." Therefore not every law is derived from the eternal law.

Obj. 3: Further, Augustine says (De Lib. Arb. i, 5) that "the law which is framed for ruling the people, rightly permits many things which are punished by Divine providence." But the type of Divine providence is the eternal law, as stated above (A. 1). Therefore not even every good law is derived from the eternal law.

*On the contrary,* Divine Wisdom says (Prov. 8:15): "By Me kings reign, and lawgivers decree just things." But the type of Divine Wisdom is the eternal law, as stated above (A. 1). Therefore all laws proceed from the eternal law.

*I answer that,* As stated above (Q. 90, AA. 1, 2), the law denotes a kind of plan directing acts towards an end. Now wherever there are movers ordained to one another, the power of the second mover must needs be derived from the power of the first mover; since the second mover does not move except in so far as it is moved by the first. Wherefore we observe the same in all those who govern, so that the plan of government is derived by secondary governors from the governor in chief; thus the plan of what is to be done in a state flows from the king's command to his inferior administrators: and again in things of art the plan of whatever is to be done by art flows from the chief craftsman to the under-craftsmen, who work with their hands. Since then the eternal law is the plan of government in the Chief Governor, all the plans of government in the inferior governors must be derived from the eternal law. But these plans of inferior governors are all other laws besides the eternal law. Therefore all laws, in so far as they partake of right reason, are derived from the eternal law. Hence Augustine says (De Lib. Arb. i, 6) that "in temporal law there is nothing just and lawful, but what man has drawn from the eternal law."

Reply Obj. 1: The *fomes* has the nature of law in man, in so far as it is a punishment resulting from Divine justice; and in this respect it is evident that it is derived from the eternal law. But in so far as it denotes a proneness to sin, it is contrary to the Divine law, and has not the nature of law, as stated above (Q. 91, A. 6).

Reply Obj. 2: Human law has the nature of law in so far as it partakes of right reason; and it is clear that, in this respect, it is derived from the eternal law. But in so far as it deviates from reason, it is called an unjust law, and has the nature, not of law but of violence. Nevertheless even an unjust law, in so far as it retains some appearance of law, though being framed by one who is in power, is derived from the eternal law; since all power is from the Lord God, according to Rom. 13:1.

Reply Obj. 3: Human law is said to permit certain things, not as approving them, but as being unable to direct them. And many things are directed by the Divine law, which human law is unable to direct, because more things are subject to a higher than to a lower cause. Hence the very fact that human law does not meddle with matters it cannot direct, comes under the ordination of the eternal law. It would be different, were human law to sanction what the eternal law condemns. Consequently it does not follow that human law is not derived from the eternal law, but that it is not on a perfect equality with it.

FOURTH ARTICLE [I-II, Q. 93, Art. 4]

Whether Necessary and Eternal Things Are Subject to the Eternal Law?

Objection 1: It would seem that necessary and eternal things are subject to the eternal law. For whatever is reasonable is subject to reason. But the Divine will is reasonable, for it is just. Therefore it is subject to (the Divine) reason. But the eternal law is the Divine reason. Therefore God's will is subject to the eternal law. But God's will is eternal. Therefore eternal and necessary things are subject to the eternal law.

Obj. 2: Further, whatever is subject to the King,

is subject to the King's law. Now the Son, according to 1 Cor. 15:28, 24, "shall be subject ... to God and the Father ... when He shall have delivered up the Kingdom to Him." Therefore the Son, Who is eternal, is subject to the eternal law.

Obj. 3: Further, the eternal law is Divine providence as a type. But many necessary things are subject to Divine providence: for instance, the stability of incorporeal substances and of the heavenly bodies. Therefore even necessary things are subject to the eternal law.

*On the contrary,* Things that are necessary cannot be otherwise, and consequently need no restraining. But laws are imposed on men, in order to restrain them from evil, as explained above (Q. 92, A. 2). Therefore necessary things are not subject to the eternal law.

*I answer that,* As stated above (A. 1), the eternal law is the type of the Divine government. Consequently whatever is subject to the Divine government, is subject to the eternal law: while if anything is not subject to the Divine government, neither is it subject to the eternal law. The application of this distinction may be gathered by looking around us. For those things are subject to human government, which can be done by man; but what pertains to the nature of man is not subject to human government; for instance, that he should have a soul, hands, or feet. Accordingly all that is in things created by God, whether it be contingent or necessary, is subject to the eternal law: while things pertaining to the Divine Nature or Essence are not subject to the eternal law, but are the eternal law itself.

Reply Obj. 1: We may speak of God's will in two ways. First, as to the will itself: and thus, since God's will is His very Essence, it is subject neither to the Divine government, nor to the eternal law, but is the same thing as the eternal law. Secondly, we may speak of God's will, as to the things themselves that God wills about creatures; which things are subject to the eternal law, in so far as they are planned by Divine Wisdom. In reference to these things God's will is said to be reasonable ( *rationalis* ): though regarded in itself it should rather be called their type ( *ratio* ).

Reply Obj. 2: God the Son was not made by God, but was naturally born of God. Consequently He is not subject to Divine providence or to the eternal law: but rather is Himself the eternal law by a kind of appropriation, as Augustine explains (De Vera Relig. xxxi). But He is said to be subject to the Father by reason of His human nature, in respect of which also the Father is said to be greater than He.

The third objection we grant, because it deals with those necessary things that are created.

Reply Obj. 4: As the Philosopher says (Metaph. v, text. 6), some necessary things have a cause of their necessity: and thus they derive from something else the fact that they cannot be otherwise. And this is in itself a most effective restraint; for whatever is restrained, is said to be restrained in so far as it cannot do otherwise than it is allowed to.

FIFTH ARTICLE [I-II, Q. 93, Art. 5]

Whether Natural Contingents Are Subject to the Eternal Law?

Objection 1: It would seem that natural contingents are not subject to the eternal law. Because promulgation is essential to law, as stated above (Q. 90, A. 4). But a law cannot be promulgated except to rational creatures, to whom it is possible to make an announcement. Therefore none but rational creatures are subject to the eternal law; and consequently natural contingents are not.

Obj. 2: Further, "Whatever obeys reason partakes somewhat of reason," as stated in *Ethic.* i. But the eternal law is the supreme type, as stated above (A. 1). Since then natural contingents do not partake of reason in any way, but are altogether void of reason, it seems that they are not subject to the eternal law.

Obj. 3: Further, the eternal law is most efficient. But in natural contingents defects occur. Therefore they are not subject to the eternal law.

*On the contrary,* It is written (Prov. 8:29): "When He compassed the sea with its bounds, and set a law to the waters, that they should not pass their limits."

*I answer that,* We must speak otherwise of the law of man, than of the eternal law which is the law of God. For the law of man extends only to rational creatures subject to man. The reason of this is because law directs the actions of those that are subject to the government of someone: wherefore, properly speaking, none imposes a law on his own actions. Now whatever is done regarding the use of irrational things subject to man, is done by the act of man himself moving those things, for these irrational creatures do not move themselves, but are moved by others, as stated above (Q. 1, A. 2). Consequently man cannot impose laws on irrational beings, however much they may be subject to him. But he can impose laws on rational beings subject to him, in so far as by his command or pronouncement of any kind, he imprints on their minds a rule which is a principle of action.

Now just as man, by such pronouncement, impresses a kind of inward principle of action on the man that is subject to him, so God imprints on the whole of nature the principles of its proper actions. And so, in this way, God is said to command the whole of nature, according to Ps. 148:6: "He hath made a decree, and it shall not pass away." And thus all actions and movements of the whole of nature are subject to the eternal law. Consequently irrational creatures are subject to the eternal law, through being moved by Divine providence; but not, as rational creatures are, through understanding the Divine commandment.

Reply Obj. 1: The impression of an inward active principle is to natural things, what the promulgation of law is to men: because law, by being promulgated, imprints on man a directive principle of human actions, as stated above.

Reply Obj. 2: Irrational creatures neither partake of nor are obedient to human reason: whereas they do partake of the Divine Reason by obeying it; because the power of Divine Reason extends over more things than human reason does. And as the members of the human body are moved at the command of reason, and yet do not partake of reason, since they have no apprehension subordinate to reason; so too irrational creatures are moved by God, without, on that account, being rational.

Reply Obj. 3: Although the defects which occur in natural things are outside the order of particular causes, they are not outside the order of universal causes, especially of the First Cause, i.e. God, from Whose providence nothing can escape, as stated in the First Part (Q. 22, A. 2). And since the eternal law is the type of Divine providence, as stated above (A. 1), hence the defects of natural things are subject to the eternal law.

SIXTH ARTICLE [I-II, Q. 93, Art. 6]

Whether All Human Affairs Are Subject to the Eternal Law?

Objection 1: It would seem that not all human affairs are subject to the eternal law. For the Apostle says (Gal. 5:18): "If you are led by the spirit you are not under the law." But the righteous who are the sons of God by adoption, are led by the spirit of God, according to Rom. 8:14: "Whosoever are led by the spirit of God, they are the sons of God." Therefore not all men are under the eternal law.

Obj. 2: Further, the Apostle says (Rom. 8:7): "The prudence [Vulg.: 'wisdom'] of the flesh is an enemy to God: for it is not subject to the law of God." But many are those in whom the prudence of the flesh dominates. Therefore all men are not subject to the eternal law which is the law of God.

Obj. 3: Further, Augustine says (De Lib. Arb. i, 6) that "the eternal law is that by which the wicked deserve misery, the good, a life of blessedness." But those who are already blessed, and those who are already lost, are not in the state of merit. Therefore they are not under the eternal law.

*On the contrary,* Augustine says (De Civ. Dei xix, 12): "Nothing evades the laws of the most high Creator and Governor, for by Him the peace of the universe is administered."

*I answer that,* There are two ways in which a thing is subject to the eternal law, as explained above (A. 5): first, by partaking of the eternal law by way of knowledge; secondly, by way of action and passion, i.e. by partaking of the eternal law by way of an inward motive principle: and in this second way, irrational creatures are subject to the eternal law, as stated above (A. 5). But since the rational nature, together with that which it has in common with all creatures, has something proper to itself inasmuch as it is rational, consequently it is subject to the eternal law in both ways; because while each rational creature has some knowledge of the eternal law, as stated above (A. 2), it also has a natural inclination to that which is in harmony with the eternal law; for "we are naturally adapted to the recipients of virtue" (Ethic. ii, 1).

Both ways, however, are imperfect, and to a certain extent destroyed, in the wicked; because in them the natural inclination to virtue is corrupted by vicious habits, and, moreover, the natural knowledge of good is darkened by passions and habits of sin. But in the good both ways are found more perfect: because in them, besides the natural knowledge of good, there is the added knowledge of faith and wisdom; and again, besides the natural inclination to good, there is the added motive of grace and virtue.

Accordingly, the good are perfectly subject to the eternal law, as always acting according to it: whereas the wicked are subject to the eternal law, imperfectly as to their actions, indeed, since both their knowledge of good, and their inclination thereto, are imperfect; but this imperfection on the part of action is supplied on the part of passion, in so far as they suffer what the eternal law decrees concerning them, according as they fail to act in harmony with that law. Hence Augustine says (De Lib. Arb. i, 15): "I esteem that the righteous act according to the eternal law; and (De Catech. Rud. xviii): Out of the just misery of the souls which deserted Him, God knew how to furnish the inferior parts of His creation with most suitable laws."

Reply Obj. 1: This saying of the Apostle may be understood in two ways. First, so that a man is said to be under the law, through being pinned down thereby, against his will, as by a load. Hence, on the same passage a gloss says that "he is under the law, who refrains from evil deeds, through fear of punishment threatened by the law, and not from love of virtue." In this way the spiritual man is not under the law, because he fulfils the law willingly, through charity which is poured into his heart by the Holy Ghost. Secondly, it can be understood as meaning that the works of a man, who is led by the Holy Ghost, are the works of the Holy Ghost rather than his own. Therefore, since the Holy Ghost is not under the law, as neither is the Son, as stated above (A. 4, ad 2); it follows that such works, in so far as they are of the Holy Ghost, are not under the law. The Apostle witnesses to this when he says (2 Cor. 3:17): "Where the Spirit of the Lord is, there is liberty."

Reply Obj. 2: The prudence of the flesh cannot be subject to the law of God as regards action; since it inclines to actions contrary to the Divine law: yet it is subject to the law of God, as regards passion; since it deserves to suffer punishment according to the law of Divine justice. Nevertheless in no man does the prudence of the flesh dominate so far as to destroy the whole good of his nature: and consequently there remains in man the inclination to act in accordance with the eternal law. For we have seen above (Q. 85, A. 2) that sin does not destroy entirely the good of nature.

Reply Obj. 3: A thing is maintained in the end and moved towards the end by one and the same cause: thus gravity which makes a heavy body rest in the lower place is also the cause of its being moved thither. We therefore reply that as it is according to the eternal law that some deserve happiness, others unhappiness, so is it by the eternal law that some are maintained in a happy state, others in an unhappy state. Accordingly both the blessed and the damned are under the eternal law.

# QUESTION 94

OF THE NATURAL LAW (In Six Articles)

We must now consider the natural law; concerning which there are six points of inquiry:

(1) What is the natural law?

(2) What are the precepts of the natural law?

(3) Whether all acts of virtue are prescribed by the natural law?

(4) Whether the natural law is the same in all?

(5) Whether it is changeable?

(6) Whether it can be abolished from the heart of man?

FIRST ARTICLE [I-II, Q. 94, Art. 1]

Whether the Natural Law Is a Habit?

Objection 1: It would seem that the natural law is a habit. Because, as the Philosopher says (Ethic. ii, 5), "there are three things in the soul: power, habit, and passion." But the natural law is not one of the soul's powers: nor is it one of the passions; as we may see by going through them one by one. Therefore the natural law is a habit.

Obj. 2: Further, Basil [*Damascene, De Fide Orth. iv, 22] says that the conscience or *synderesis* "is the law of our mind"; which can only apply to the natural law. But the "synderesis" is a habit, as was shown in the First Part (Q. 79, A. 12). Therefore the natural law is a habit.

Obj. 3: Further, the natural law abides in man always, as will be shown further on (A. 6). But man's reason, which the law regards, does not always think about the natural law. Therefore the natural law is not an act, but a habit.

*On the contrary,* Augustine says (De Bono Conjug. xxi) that "a habit is that whereby something is done when necessary." But such is not the natural law: since it is in infants and in the damned who cannot act by it. Therefore the natural law is not a habit.

*I answer that,* A thing may be called a habit in two ways. First, properly and essentially: and thus the natural law is not a habit. For it has been stated above (Q. 90, A. 1, ad 2) that the natural law is something appointed by reason, just as a proposition is a work of reason. Now that which a man does is not the same as that whereby he does it: for he makes a becoming speech by the habit of grammar. Since then a habit is that by which we act, a law cannot be a habit properly and essentially.

Secondly, the term habit may be applied to that which we hold by a habit: thus faith may mean that which we hold by faith. And accordingly, since the precepts of the natural law are sometimes considered by reason actually, while sometimes they are in the reason only habitually, in this way the natural law may be called a habit. Thus, in speculative matters, the indemonstrable principles are not the habit itself whereby we hold those principles, but are the principles the habit of which we possess.

Reply Obj. 1: The Philosopher proposes there to discover the genus of virtue; and since it is evident that virtue is a principle of action, he mentions only those things which are principles of human acts, viz. powers, habits and passions. But there are other things in the soul besides these three: there are acts; thus *to will* is in the one that wills; again, things known are in the knower; moreover its own natural properties are in the soul, such as immortality and the like.

Reply Obj. 2: *Synderesis* is said to be the law of our mind, because it is a habit containing the precepts of the natural law, which are the first principles of human actions.

Reply Obj. 3: This argument proves that the natural law is held habitually; and this is granted.

To the argument advanced in the contrary sense we reply that sometimes a man is unable to make use of that which is in him habitually, on account of some impediment: thus, on account of sleep, a man is unable to use the habit of science. In like manner, through the deficiency of his age, a child cannot use the habit of understanding of principles, or the natural law, which is in him habitually.

SECOND ARTICLE [I-II, Q. 94, Art. 2]

Whether the Natural Law Contains Several Precepts, or Only One?

Objection 1: It would seem that the natural law contains, not several precepts, but one only. For law is a kind of precept, as stated above (Q. 92, A. 2). If therefore there were many precepts of the natural law, it would follow that there are also many natural laws.

Obj. 2: Further, the natural law is consequent to human nature. But human nature, as a whole, is one; though, as to its parts, it is manifold. Therefore, either there is but one precept of the law of nature, on account of the unity of nature as a whole; or there are many, by reason of the number of parts of human nature. The result would be that even things relating to the inclination of the concupiscible faculty belong to the natural law.

Obj. 3: Further, law is something pertaining to reason, as stated above (Q. 90, A. 1). Now reason is but one in man. Therefore there is only one precept of the natural law.

*On the contrary,* The precepts of the natural law in man stand in relation to practical matters, as the first principles to matters of demonstration. But there are several first indemonstrable principles. Therefore there are also several precepts of the natural law.

*I answer that,* As stated above (Q. 91, A. 3), the precepts of the natural law are to the practical reason, what the first principles of demonstrations are to the speculative reason; because both are self-evident principles. Now a thing is said to be self-evident in two ways: first, in itself; secondly, in relation to us. Any proposition is said to be self-evident in itself, if its predicate is contained in the notion of the subject: although, to one who knows not the definition of the subject, it happens that such a proposition is not self-evident. For instance, this proposition, "Man is a rational being," is, in its very nature, self-evident, since who says "man," says "a rational being": and yet to one who knows not what a man is, this proposition is not self-evident. Hence it is that, as Boethius says (De Hebdom.), certain axioms or propositions are universally self-evident to all; and such are those propositions whose terms are known to all, as, "Every whole is greater than its part," and, "Things equal to one and the same are equal to one another." But some propositions are self-evident only to the wise, who understand the meaning of the terms of such propositions: thus to one who understands that an angel is not a body, it is self-evident that an angel is not circumscriptively in a place: but this is not evident to the unlearned, for they cannot grasp it.

Now a certain order is to be found in those things that are apprehended universally. For that which, before aught else, falls under apprehension, is *being* , the notion of which is included in all things whatsoever a man apprehends. Wherefore the first indemonstrable principle is that "the same thing cannot be affirmed and denied at the same time," which is based on the notion of *being* and *not-being*: and on this principle all others are based, as is stated in *Metaph.* iv, text. 9. Now as being is the first thing that falls under the apprehension simply, so *good* is the first thing that falls under the apprehension of the practical reason, which is directed to action: since every agent acts for an end under the aspect of good. Consequently the first principle of practical reason is one founded on the notion of good, viz. that "good is that which all things seek after." Hence this is the first precept of law, that "good is to be done and pursued, and evil is to be avoided." All other precepts of the natural law are based upon this: so that whatever the practical reason naturally apprehends as man's good (or evil) belongs to the precepts of the natural law as something to be done or avoided.

Since, however, good has the nature of an end, and evil, the nature of a contrary, hence it is that all those things to which man has a natural inclination, are naturally apprehended by reason as being good, and consequently as objects of pursuit, and their contraries as evil, and objects of avoidance. Wherefore according to the order of natural inclinations, is the order of the precepts of the natural law. Because in man there is first of all an inclination to good in accordance with the nature which he has in common with all substances: inasmuch as every substance seeks the preservation of its own being, according to its nature: and by reason of this inclination, whatever is a means of preserving human life, and of warding off its obstacles, belongs to the natural law. Secondly, there is in man an inclination to things that pertain to him more specially, according to that nature which he has in common with other animals: and in virtue of this inclination, those things are said to belong to the natural law, "which nature has taught to all animals" [*Pandect. Just. I, tit. i], such as sexual intercourse, education of offspring and so forth. Thirdly, there is in man an inclination to good, according to the nature of his reason, which nature is proper to him: thus man has a natural inclination to know the truth about God, and to live in society: and in this respect, whatever pertains to this inclination belongs to the natural law; for instance, to shun ignorance, to avoid offending those among whom one has to live, and other such things regarding the above inclination.

Reply Obj. 1: All these precepts of the law of nature have the character of one natural law, inasmuch as they flow from one first precept.

Reply Obj. 2: All the inclinations of any parts whatsoever of human nature, e.g. of the concupiscible and irascible parts, in so far as they are ruled by reason, belong to the natural law, and are reduced to one first precept, as stated above: so that the precepts of the natural law are many in themselves, but are based on one common foundation.

Reply Obj. 3: Although reason is one in itself, yet it directs all things regarding man; so that whatever can be ruled by reason, is contained under the law of reason.

THIRD ARTICLE [I-II, Q. 94, Art. 3]

Whether All Acts of Virtue Are Prescribed by the Natural Law?

Objection 1: It would seem that not all acts of virtue are prescribed by the natural law. Because, as stated above (Q. 90, A. 2) it is essential to a law that it be ordained to the common good. But some acts of virtue are ordained to the private good of the individual, as is evident especially in regards to acts of temperance. Therefore not all acts of virtue are the subject of natural law.

Obj. 2: Further, every sin is opposed to some virtuous act. If therefore all acts of virtue are prescribed by the natural law, it seems to follow that all sins are against nature: whereas this applies to certain special sins.

Obj. 3: Further, those things which are according to nature are common to all. But acts of virtue are not common to all: since a thing is virtuous in one, and vicious in another. Therefore not all acts of virtue are prescribed by the natural law.

*On the contrary,* Damascene says (De Fide Orth. iii, 4) that "virtues are natural." Therefore virtuous acts also are a subject of the natural law.

*I answer that,* We may speak of virtuous acts in two ways: first, under the aspect of virtuous; secondly, as such and such acts considered in their proper species. If then we speak of acts of virtue, considered as virtuous, thus all virtuous acts belong to the natural law. For it has been stated (A. 2) that to the natural law belongs everything to which a man is inclined according to his nature. Now each thing is inclined naturally to an operation that is suitable to it according to its form: thus fire is inclined to give heat. Wherefore, since the rational soul is the proper form of man, there is in every man a natural inclination to act according to reason: and this is to act according to virtue. Consequently, considered thus, all acts of virtue are prescribed by the natural law: since each one's reason naturally dictates to him to act virtuously. But if we speak of virtuous acts, considered in themselves, i.e. in their proper species, thus not all virtuous acts are prescribed by the natural law: for many things are done virtuously, to which nature does not incline at first; but which, through the inquiry of reason, have been found by men to be conducive to well-living.

Reply Obj. 1: Temperance is about the natural concupiscences of food, drink and sexual matters, which are indeed ordained to the natural common good, just as other matters of law are ordained to the moral common good.

Reply Obj. 2: By human nature we may mean either that which is proper to man—and in this sense all sins, as being against reason, are also against nature, as Damascene states (De Fide Orth. ii, 30): or we may mean that nature which is common to man and other animals; and in this sense, certain special sins are said to be against nature; thus contrary to sexual intercourse, which is natural to all animals, is unisexual lust, which has received the special name of the unnatural crime.

Reply Obj. 3: This argument considers acts in themselves. For it is owing to the various conditions of men, that certain acts are virtuous for some, as being proportionate and becoming to them, while they are vicious for others, as being out of proportion to them.

FOURTH ARTICLE [I-II, Q. 94, Art. 4]

Whether the Natural Law Is the Same in All Men?

Objection 1: It would seem that the natural law is not the same in all. For it is stated in the Decretals (Dist. i) that "the natural law is that which is contained in the Law and the Gospel." But this is not common to all men; because, as it is written (Rom. 10:16), "all do not obey the gospel." Therefore the natural law is not the same in all men.

Obj. 2: Further, "Things which are according to the law are said to be just," as stated in *Ethic.* v. But it is stated in the same book that nothing is so universally just as not to be subject to change in regard to some men. Therefore even the natural law is not the same in all men.

Obj. 3: Further, as stated above (AA. 2, 3), to the natural law belongs everything to which a man is inclined according to his nature. Now different men are naturally inclined to different things; some to the desire of pleasures, others to the desire of honors, and other men to other things. Therefore there is not one natural law for all.

*On the contrary,* Isidore says (Etym. v, 4): "The natural law is common to all nations."

*I answer that,* As stated above (AA. 2, 3), to the natural law belong those things to which a man is inclined naturally: and among these it is proper to man to be inclined to act according to reason. Now the process of reason is from the common to the proper, as stated in *Phys.* i. The speculative reason, however, is differently situated in this matter, from the practical reason. For, since the speculative reason is busied chiefly with necessary things, which cannot be otherwise than they are, its proper conclusions, like the universal principles, contain the truth without fail. The practical reason, on the other hand, is busied with contingent matters, about which human actions are concerned: and consequently, although there is necessity in the general principles, the more we descend to matters of detail, the more frequently we encounter defects. Accordingly then in speculative matters truth is the same in all men, both as to principles and as to conclusions: although the truth is not known to all as regards the conclusions, but only as regards the principles which are called common notions. But in matters of action, truth or practical rectitude is not the same for all, as to matters of detail, but only as to the general principles: and where there is the same rectitude in matters of detail, it is not equally known to all.

It is therefore evident that, as regards the general principles whether of speculative or of practical reason, truth or rectitude is the same for all, and is equally known by all. As to the proper conclusions of the speculative reason, the truth is the same for all, but is not equally known to all: thus it is true for all that the three angles of a triangle are together equal to two right angles, although it is not known to all. But as to the proper conclusions of the practical reason, neither is the truth or rectitude the same for all, nor, where it is the same, is it equally known by all. Thus it is right and true for all to act according to reason: and from this principle it follows as a proper conclusion, that goods entrusted to another should be restored to their owner. Now this is true for the majority of cases: but it may happen in a particular case that it would be injurious, and therefore unreasonable, to restore goods held in trust; for instance, if they are claimed for the purpose of fighting against one's country. And this principle will be found to fail the more, according as we descend further into detail, e.g. if one were to say that goods held in trust should be restored with such and such a guarantee, or in such and such a way; because the greater the number of conditions added, the greater the number of ways in which the principle may fail, so that it be not right to restore or not to restore.

Consequently we must say that the natural law, as to general principles, is the same for all, both as to rectitude and as to knowledge. But as to certain matters of detail, which are conclusions, as it were, of those general principles, it is the same for all in the majority of cases, both as to rectitude and as to knowledge; and yet in some few cases it may fail, both as to rectitude, by reason of certain obstacles (just as natures subject to generation and corruption fail in some few cases on account of some obstacle), and as to knowledge, since in some the reason is perverted by passion, or evil habit, or an evil disposition of nature; thus formerly, theft, although it is expressly contrary to the natural law, was not considered wrong among the Germans, as Julius Caesar relates (De Bello Gall. vi).

Reply Obj. 1: The meaning of the sentence quoted is not that whatever is contained in the Law and the Gospel belongs to the natural law, since they contain many things that are above nature; but that whatever belongs to the natural law is fully contained in them. Wherefore Gratian, after saying that "the natural law is what is contained in the Law and the Gospel," adds at once, by way of example, "by which everyone is commanded to do to others as he would be done by."

Reply Obj. 2: The saying of the Philosopher is to be understood of things that are naturally just, not as general principles, but as conclusions drawn from them, having rectitude in the majority of cases, but failing in a few.

Reply Obj. 3: As, in man, reason rules and commands the other powers, so all the natural inclinations belonging to the other powers must needs be directed according to reason. Wherefore it is universally right for all men, that all their inclinations should be directed according to reason.

FIFTH ARTICLE [I-II, Q. 94, Art. 5]

Whether the Natural Law Can Be Changed?

Objection 1: It would seem that the natural law can be changed. Because on Ecclus. 17:9, "He gave them instructions, and the law of life," the gloss says: "He wished the law of the letter to be written, in order to correct the law of nature." But that which is corrected is changed. Therefore the natural law can be changed.

Obj. 2: Further, the slaying of the innocent, adultery, and theft are against the natural law. But we find these things changed by God: as when God commanded Abraham to slay his innocent son (Gen. 22:2); and when he ordered the Jews to borrow and purloin the vessels of the Egyptians (Ex. 12:35); and when He commanded Osee to take to himself "a wife of fornications" (Osee 1:2). Therefore the natural law can be changed.

Obj. 3: Further, Isidore says (Etym. 5:4) that "the possession of all things in common, and universal freedom, are matters of natural law." But these things are seen to be changed by human laws. Therefore it seems that the natural law is subject to change.

*On the contrary,* It is said in the Decretals (Dist. v): "The natural law dates from the creation of the rational creature. It does not vary according to time, but remains unchangeable."

*I answer that,* A change in the natural law may be understood in two ways. First, by way of addition. In this sense nothing hinders the natural law from being changed: since many things for the benefit of human life have been added over and above the natural law, both by the Divine law and by human laws.

Secondly, a change in the natural law may be understood by way of subtraction, so that what previously was according to the natural law, ceases to be so. In this sense, the natural law is altogether unchangeable in its first principles: but in its secondary principles, which, as we have said (A. 4), are certain detailed proximate conclusions drawn from the first principles, the natural law is not changed so that what it prescribes be not right in most cases. But it may be changed in some particular cases of rare occurrence, through some special causes hindering the observance of such precepts, as stated above (A. 4).

Reply Obj. 1: The written law is said to be given for the correction of the natural law, either because it supplies what was wanting to the natural law; or because the natural law was perverted in the hearts of some men, as to certain matters, so that they esteemed those things good which are naturally evil; which perversion stood in need of correction.

Reply Obj. 2: All men alike, both guilty and innocent, die the death of nature: which death of nature is inflicted by the power of God on account of original sin, according to 1 Kings 2:6: "The Lord killeth and maketh alive." Consequently, by the command of God, death can be inflicted on any man, guilty or innocent, without any injustice whatever. In like manner adultery is intercourse with another's wife; who is allotted to him by the law emanating from God. Consequently intercourse with any woman, by the command of God, is neither adultery nor fornication. The same applies to theft, which is the taking of another's property. For whatever is taken by the command of God, to Whom all things belong, is not taken against the will of its owner, whereas it is in this that theft consists. Nor is it only in human things, that whatever is commanded by God is right; but also in natural things, whatever is done by God, is, in some way, natural, as stated in the First Part, Q. 105, A. 6, ad 1.

Reply Obj. 3: A thing is said to belong to the natural law in two ways. First, because nature inclines thereto: e.g. that one should not do harm to another. Secondly, because nature did not bring in the contrary: thus we might say that for man to be naked is of the natural law, because nature did not give him clothes, but art invented them. In this sense, "the possession of all things in common and universal freedom" are said to be of the natural law, because, to wit, the distinction of possessions and slavery were not brought in by nature, but devised by human reason for the benefit of human life. Accordingly the law of nature was not changed in this respect, except by addition.

SIXTH ARTICLE [I-II, Q. 94, Art. 6]

Whether the Law of Nature Can Be Abolished from the Heart of Man?

Objection 1: It would seem that the natural law can be abolished from the heart of man. Because on Rom. 2:14, "When the Gentiles who have not the law," etc. a gloss says that "the law of righteousness, which sin had blotted out, is graven on the heart of man when he is restored by grace." But the law of righteousness is the law of nature. Therefore the law of nature can be blotted out.

Obj. 2: Further, the law of grace is more efficacious than the law of nature. But the law of grace is blotted out by sin. Much more therefore can the law of nature be blotted out.

Obj. 3: Further, that which is established by law is made just. But many things are enacted by men, which are contrary to the law of nature. Therefore the law of nature can be abolished from the heart of man.

*On the contrary,* Augustine says (Confess. ii): "Thy law is written in the hearts of men, which iniquity itself effaces not." But the law which is written in men's hearts is the natural law. Therefore the natural law cannot be blotted out.

*I answer that,* As stated above (AA. 4, 5), there belong to the natural law, first, certain most general precepts, that are known to all; and secondly, certain secondary and more detailed precepts, which are, as it were, conclusions following closely from first principles. As to those general principles, the natural law, in the abstract, can nowise be blotted out from men's hearts. But it is blotted out in the case of a particular action, in so far as reason is hindered from applying the general principle to a particular point of practice, on account of concupiscence or some other passion, as stated above (Q. 77, A. 2). But as to the other, i.e. the secondary precepts, the natural law can be blotted out from the human heart, either by evil persuasions, just as in speculative matters errors occur in respect of necessary conclusions; or by vicious customs and corrupt habits, as among some men, theft, and even unnatural vices, as the Apostle states (Rom. i), were not esteemed sinful.

Reply Obj. 1: Sin blots out the law of nature in particular cases, not universally, except perchance in regard to the secondary precepts of the natural law, in the way stated above.

Reply Obj. 2: Although grace is more efficacious than nature, yet nature is more essential to man, and therefore more enduring.

Reply Obj. 3: This argument is true of the secondary precepts of the natural law, against which some legislators have framed certain enactments which are unjust.

# QUESTION 95

OF HUMAN LAW (In Four Articles)

We must now consider human law; and (1) this law considered in itself; (2) its power; (3) its mutability. Under the first head there are four points of inquiry:

(1) Its utility.
(2) Its origin.
(3) Its quality.
(4) Its division.

FIRST ARTICLE [I-II, Q. 95, Art. 1]

Whether It Was Useful for Laws to Be Framed by Men?

Objection 1: It would seem that it was not useful for laws to be framed by men. Because the purpose of every law is that man be made good thereby, as stated above (Q. 92, A. 1). But men are more to be induced to be good willingly by means of admonitions, than against their will, by means of laws. Therefore there was no need to frame laws.

Obj. 2: Further, As the Philosopher says (Ethic. v, 4), "men have recourse to a judge as to animate justice." But animate justice is better than inanimate justice, which contained in laws. Therefore it would have been better for the execution of justice to be entrusted to the decision of judges, than to frame laws in addition.

Obj. 3: Further, every law is framed for the direction of human actions, as is evident from what has been stated above (Q. 90, AA. 1, 2). But since human actions are about singulars, which are infinite in number, matter pertaining to the direction of human actions cannot be taken into sufficient consideration except by a wise man, who looks into each one of them. Therefore it would have been better for human acts to be directed by the judgment of wise men, than by the framing of laws. Therefore there was no need of human laws.

*On the contrary,* Isidore says (Etym. v, 20): "Laws were made that in fear thereof human audacity might be held in check, that innocence might be safeguarded in the midst of wickedness, and that the dread of punishment might prevent the wicked from doing harm." But these things are most necessary to mankind. Therefore it was necessary that human laws should be made.

*I answer that,* As stated above (Q. 63, A. 1; Q. 94, A. 3), man has a natural aptitude for virtue; but the perfection of virtue must be acquired by man by means of some kind of training. Thus we observe that man is helped by industry in his necessities, for instance, in food and clothing. Certain beginnings of these he has from nature, viz. his reason and his hands; but he has not the full complement, as other animals have, to whom nature has given sufficiency of clothing and food. Now it is difficult to see how man could suffice for himself in the matter of this training: since the perfection of virtue consists chiefly in withdrawing man from undue pleasures, to which above all man is inclined, and especially the young, who are more capable of being trained. Consequently a man needs to receive this training from another, whereby to arrive at the perfection of virtue. And as to those young people who are inclined to acts of virtue, by their good natural disposition, or by custom, or rather by the gift of God, paternal training suffices, which is by admonitions. But since some are found to be depraved, and prone to vice, and not easily amenable to words, it was necessary for such to be restrained from evil by force and fear, in order that, at least, they might desist from evil-doing, and leave others in peace, and that they themselves, by being habituated in this way, might be brought to do willingly what hitherto they did from fear, and thus become virtuous. Now this kind of training, which compels through fear of punishment, is the discipline of laws. Therefore in order that man might have peace and virtue, it was necessary for laws to be framed: for, as the Philosopher says (Polit. i, 2), "as man is the most noble of animals if he be perfect in virtue, so is he the lowest of all, if he be severed from law and righteousness"; because man can use his reason to devise means of satisfying his lusts and evil passions, which other animals are unable to do.

Reply Obj. 1: Men who are well disposed are led willingly to virtue by being admonished better than by coercion: but men who are evilly disposed are not led to virtue unless they are compelled.

Reply Obj. 2: As the Philosopher says (Rhet. i, 1), "it is better that all things be regulated by law, than left to be decided by judges": and this for three reasons. First, because it is easier to find a few wise men competent to frame right laws, than to find the many who would be necessary to judge aright of each single case. Secondly, because those who make laws consider long beforehand what laws to make; whereas judgment on each single case has to be pronounced as soon as it arises: and it is easier for man to see what is right, by taking many instances into consideration, than by considering one solitary fact. Thirdly, because lawgivers judge in the abstract and of future events; whereas those who sit in judgment judge of things present, towards which they are affected by love, hatred, or some kind of cupidity; wherefore their judgment is perverted.

Since then the animated justice of the judge is not found in every man, and since it can be deflected, therefore it was necessary, whenever possible, for the law to determine how to judge, and for very few matters to be left to the decision of men.

Reply Obj. 3: Certain individual facts which cannot be covered by the law "have necessarily to be committed to judges," as the Philosopher says in the same passage: for instance, "concerning something that has happened or not happened," and the like.

SECOND ARTICLE [I-II, Q. 95, Art. 2]

Whether Every Human Law Is Derived from the Natural Law?

Objection 1: It would seem that not every human law is derived from the natural law. For the Philosopher says (Ethic. v, 7) that "the legal just is that which originally was a matter of indifference." But those things which arise from the natural law are not matters of indifference. Therefore the enactments of human laws are not derived from the natural law.

Obj. 2: Further, positive law is contrasted with natural law, as stated by Isidore (Etym. v, 4) and the Philosopher (Ethic. v, 7). But those things which flow as conclusions from the general principles of the natural law belong to the natural law, as stated above (Q. 94, A. 4). Therefore that which is established by human law does not belong to the natural law.

Obj. 3: Further, the law of nature is the same for all; since the Philosopher says (Ethic. v, 7) that "the natural just is that which is equally valid everywhere." If therefore human laws were derived from the natural law, it would follow that they too are the same for all: which is clearly false.

Obj. 4: Further, it is possible to give a reason for things which are derived from the natural law. But "it is not possible to give the reason for all the legal enactments of the lawgivers," as the jurist says [*Pandect. Justin. lib. i, ff, tit. iii, v; De Leg. et Senat.]. Therefore not all human laws are derived from the natural law.

*On the contrary,* Tully says (Rhet. ii): "Things which emanated from nature and were approved by custom, were sanctioned by fear and reverence for the laws."

*I answer that,* As Augustine says (De Lib. Arb. i, 5) "that which is not just seems to be no law at all": wherefore the force of a law depends on the extent of its justice. Now in human affairs a thing is said to be just, from being right, according to the rule of reason. But the first rule of reason is the law of nature, as is clear from what has been stated above (Q. 91, A. 2, ad 2). Consequently every human law has just so much of the nature of law, as it is derived from the law of nature. But if in any point it deflects from the law of nature, it is no longer a law but a perversion of law.

But it must be noted that something may be derived from the natural law in two ways: first, as a conclusion from premises, secondly, by way of determination of certain generalities. The first way is like to that by which, in sciences, demonstrated conclusions are drawn from the principles: while the second mode is likened to that whereby, in the arts, general forms are particularized as to details: thus the craftsman needs to determine the general form of a house to some particular shape. Some things are therefore derived from the general principles of the natural law, by way of conclusions; e.g. that "one must not kill" may be derived as a conclusion from the principle that "one should do harm to no man": while some are derived therefrom by way of determination; e.g. the law of nature has it that the evil-doer should be punished; but that he be punished in this or that way, is a determination of the law of nature.

Accordingly both modes of derivation are found in the human law. But those things which are derived in the first way, are contained in human law not as emanating therefrom exclusively, but have some force from the natural law also. But those things which are derived in the second way, have no other force than that of human law.

Reply Obj. 1: The Philosopher is speaking of those enactments which are by way of determination or specification of the precepts of the natural law.

Reply Obj. 2: This argument avails for those things that are derived from the natural law, by way of conclusions.

Reply Obj. 3: The general principles of the natural law cannot be applied to all men in the same way on account of the great variety of human affairs: and hence arises the diversity of positive laws among various people.

Reply Obj. 4: These words of the Jurist are to be understood as referring to decisions of rulers in determining particular points of the natural law: on which determinations the judgment of expert and prudent men is based as on its principles; in so far, to wit, as they see at once what is the best thing to decide.

Hence the Philosopher says (Ethic. vi, 11) that in such matters, "we ought to pay as much attention to the undemonstrated sayings and opinions of persons who surpass us in experience, age and prudence, as to their demonstrations."

THIRD ARTICLE [I-II, Q. 95, Art. 3]

Whether Isidore's Description of the Quality of Positive Law Is Appropriate?

Objection 1: It would seem that Isidore's description of the quality of positive law is not appropriate, when he says (Etym. v, 21): "Law shall be virtuous, just, possible to nature, according to the custom of the country, suitable to place and time, necessary, useful; clearly expressed, lest by its obscurity it lead to misunderstanding; framed for no private benefit, but for the common good." Because he had previously expressed the quality of law in three conditions, saying that "law is anything founded on reason, provided that it foster religion, be helpful to discipline, and further the common weal." Therefore it was needless to add any further conditions to these.

Obj. 2: Further, Justice is included in honesty, as Tully says (De Offic. vii). Therefore after saying "honest" it was superfluous to add "just."

Obj. 3: Further, written law is condivided with custom, according to Isidore (Etym. ii, 10). Therefore it should not be stated in the definition of law that it is "according to the custom of the country."

Obj. 4: Further, a thing may be necessary in two ways. It may be necessary simply, because it cannot be otherwise: and that which is necessary in this way, is not subject to human judgment, wherefore human law is not concerned with necessity of this kind. Again a thing may be necessary for an end: and this necessity is the same as usefulness. Therefore it is superfluous to say both "necessary" and "useful."

*On the contrary,* stands the authority of Isidore.

*I answer that,* Whenever a thing is for an end, its form must be determined proportionately to that end; as the form of a saw is such as to be suitable for cutting (Phys. ii, text. 88). Again, everything that is ruled and measured must have a form proportionate to its rule and measure. Now both these conditions are verified of human law: since it is both something ordained to an end; and is a rule or measure ruled or measured by a higher measure. And this higher measure is twofold, viz. the Divine law and the natural law, as explained above (A. 2; Q. 93, A. 3). Now the end of human law is to be useful to man, as the Jurist states [*Pandect. Justin. lib. xxv, ff., tit. iii; De Leg. et Senat.]. Wherefore Isidore in determining the nature of law, lays down, at first, three conditions; viz. that it "foster religion," inasmuch as it is proportionate to the Divine law; that it be "helpful to discipline," inasmuch as it is proportionate to the nature law; and that it "further the common weal," inasmuch as it is proportionate to the utility of mankind.

All the other conditions mentioned by him are reduced to these three. For it is called virtuous because it fosters religion. And when he goes on to say that it should be "just, possible to nature, according to the customs of the country, adapted to place and time," he implies that it should be helpful to discipline. For human discipline depends first on the order of reason, to which he refers by saying "just": secondly, it depends on the ability of the agent; because discipline should be adapted to each one according to his ability, taking also into account the ability of nature (for the same burdens should not be laid on children as adults); and should be according to human customs; since man cannot live alone in society, paying no heed to others: thirdly, it depends on certain circumstances, in respect of which he says, "adapted to place and time." The remaining words, "necessary, useful," etc. mean that law should further the common weal: so that "necessity" refers to the removal of evils; "usefulness" to the attainment of good; "clearness of expression," to the need of preventing any harm ensuing from the law itself. And since, as stated above (Q. 90, A. 2), law is ordained to the common good, this is expressed in the last part of the description.

This suffices for the Replies to the Objections.

FOURTH ARTICLE [I-II, Q. 95, Art. 4]

Whether Isidore's Division of Human Laws Is Appropriate?

Objection 1: It would seem that Isidore wrongly divided human statutes or human law (Etym. v, 4, seqq.). For under this law he includes the "law of nations," so called, because, as he says, "nearly all nations use it." But as he says, "natural law is that which is common to all nations." Therefore the law of nations is not contained under positive human law, but rather under natural law.

Obj. 2: Further, those laws which have the same force, seem to differ not formally but only materially. But "statutes, decrees of the commonalty, senatorial decrees," and the like which he mentions (Etym. v, 9), all have the same force. Therefore they do not differ, except materially. But art takes no notice of such a distinction: since it may go on to infinity. Therefore this division of human laws is not appropriate.

Obj. 3: Further, just as, in the state, there are princes, priests and soldiers, so are there other human offices. Therefore it seems that, as this division includes *military law,* and public law, referring to priests and magistrates; so also it should include other laws pertaining to other offices of the state.

Obj. 4: Further, those things that are accidental should be passed over. But it is accidental to law that it be framed by this or that man. Therefore it is unreasonable to divide laws according to the names of lawgivers, so that one be called the "Cornelian" law, another the "Falcidian" law, etc.

*On the contrary,* The authority of Isidore (Obj. 1) suffices.

*I answer that,* A thing can of itself be divided in respect of something contained in the notion of that thing. Thus a soul either rational or irrational is contained in the notion of animal: and therefore animal is divided properly and of itself in respect of its being rational or irrational; but not in the point of its being white or black, which are entirely beside the notion of animal. Now, in the notion of human law, many things are contained, in respect of any of which human law can be divided properly and of itself. For in the first place it belongs to the notion of human law, to be derived from the law of nature, as explained above (A. 2). In this respect positive law is divided into the *law of nations* and civil law, according to the two ways in which something may be derived from the law of nature, as stated above (A. 2). Because, to the law of nations belong those things which are derived from the law of nature, as conclusions from premises, e.g. just buyings and sellings, and the like, without which men cannot live together, which is a point of the law of nature, since man is by nature a social animal, as is proved in *Polit.* i, 2. But those things which are derived from the law of nature by way of particular determination, belong to the civil law, according as each state decides on what is best for itself.

Secondly, it belongs to the notion of human law, to be ordained to the common good of the state. In this respect human law may be divided according to the different kinds of men who work in a special way for the common good: e.g. priests, by praying to God for the people; princes, by governing the people; soldiers, by fighting for the safety of the people. Wherefore certain special kinds of law are adapted to these men.

Thirdly, it belongs to the notion of human law, to be framed by that one who governs the community of the state, as shown above (Q. 90, A. 3). In this respect, there are various human laws according to the various forms of government. Of these, according to the Philosopher (Polit. iii, 10) one is *monarchy,* i.e. when the state is governed by one; and then we have *Royal Ordinances.* Another form is *aristocracy,* i.e. government by the best men or men of highest rank; and then we have the *Authoritative legal opinions* ( Responsa Prudentum *) and-* Decrees of the Senate ( Senatus consulta ). Another form is *oligarchy,* i.e. government by a few rich and powerful men; and then we have *Praetorian,* also called Honorary, law. Another form of government is that of the people, which is called *democracy,* and there we have Decrees of the commonalty ( *Plebiscita* ). There is also tyrannical government, which is altogether corrupt, which, therefore, has no corresponding law. Finally, there is a form of government made up of all these, and which is the best: and in this respect we have law sanctioned by the *Lords and Commons,* as stated by Isidore (Etym. v, 4, seqq.).

Fourthly, it belongs to the notion of human law to direct human actions. In this respect, according to the various matters of which the law treats, there are various kinds of laws, which are sometimes named after their authors: thus we have the *Lex Julia* about adultery, the *Lex Cornelia* concerning assassins, and so on, differentiated in this way, not on account of the authors, but on account of the matters to which they refer.

Reply Obj. 1: The law of nations is indeed, in

some way, natural to man, in so far as he is a reasonable being, because it is derived from the natural law by way of a conclusion that is not very remote from its premises. Wherefore men easily agreed thereto. Nevertheless it is distinct from the natural law, especially it is distinct from the natural law which is common to all animals.

The Replies to the other Objections are evident from what has been said.

# QUESTION 96

OF THE POWER OF HUMAN LAW (In Six Articles)

We must now consider the power of human law. Under this head there are six points of inquiry:

(1) Whether human law should be framed for the community?

(2) Whether human law should repress all vices?

(3) Whether human law is competent to direct all acts of virtue?

(4) Whether it binds man in conscience?

(5) Whether all men are subject to human law?

(6) Whether those who are under the law may act beside the letter of the law?

FIRST ARTICLE [I-II, Q. 96, Art. 1]

Whether Human Law Should Be Framed for the Community Rather Than for the Individual?

Objection 1: It would seem that human law should be framed not for the community, but rather for the individual. For the Philosopher says (Ethic. v, 7) that "the legal just ... includes all particular acts of legislation ... and all those matters which are the subject of decrees," which are also individual matters, since decrees are framed about individual actions. Therefore law is framed not only for the community, but also for the individual.

Obj. 2: Further, law is the director of human acts, as stated above (Q. 90, AA. 1, 2). But human acts are about individual matters. Therefore human laws should be framed, not for the community, but rather for the individual.

Obj. 3: Further, law is a rule and measure of human acts, as stated above (Q. 90, AA. 1, 2). But a measure should be most certain, as stated in *Metaph.* x. Since therefore in human acts no general proposition can be so certain as not to fail in some individual cases, it seems that laws should be framed not in general but for individual cases.

*On the contrary,* The Jurist says (Pandect. Justin. lib. i, tit. iii, art. ii; De legibus, etc.) that "laws should be made to suit the majority of instances; and they are not framed according to what may possibly happen in an individual case."

*I answer that,* Whatever is for an end should be proportionate to that end. Now the end of law is the common good; because, as Isidore says (Etym. v, 21) that "law should be framed, not for any private benefit, but for the common good of all the citizens." Hence human laws should be proportionate to the common good. Now the common good comprises many things. Wherefore law should take account of many things, as to persons, as to matters, and as to times. Because the community of the state is composed of many persons; and its good is procured by many actions; nor is it established to endure for only a short time, but to last for all time by the citizens succeeding one another, as Augustine says (De Civ. Dei ii, 21; xxii, 6).

Reply Obj. 1: The Philosopher (Ethic. v, 7) divides the legal just, i.e. positive law, into three parts. For some things are laid down simply in a general way: and these are the general laws. Of these he says that "the legal is that which originally was a matter of indifference, but which, when enacted, is so no longer": as the fixing of the ransom of a captive. Some things affect the community in one respect, and individuals in another. These are called "privileges," i.e. "private laws," as it were, because they regard private persons, although their power extends to many matters; and in regard to these, he adds, "and further, all particular acts of legislation." Other matters are legal, not through being laws, but through being applications of general laws to particular cases: such are decrees which have the force of law; and in regard to these, he adds "all matters subject to decrees."

Reply Obj. 2: A principle of direction should be applicable to many; wherefore (Metaph. x, text. 4) the Philosopher says that all things belonging to one genus, are measured by one, which is the principle in that genus. For if there were as many rules or measures as there are things measured or ruled, they would cease to be of use, since their use consists in being applicable to many things. Hence law would be of no use, if it did not extend further than to one single act. Because the decrees of prudent men are made for the purpose of directing individual actions; whereas law is a general precept, as stated above (Q. 92, A. 2, Obj. 2).

Reply Obj. 3: "We must not seek the same degree of certainty in all things" (Ethic. i, 3). Consequently in contingent matters, such as natural and human things, it is enough for a thing to be certain, as being true in the greater number of instances, though at times and less frequently it fail.

SECOND ARTICLE [I-II, Q. 96, Art. 2]

Whether It Belongs to the Human Law to Repress All Vices?

Objection 1: It would seem that it belongs to human law to repress all vices. For Isidore says (Etym. v, 20) that "laws were made in order that, in fear thereof, man's audacity might be held in check." But it would not be held in check sufficiently, unless all evils were repressed by law. Therefore human laws should repress all evils.

Obj. 2: Further, the intention of the lawgiver is to make the citizens virtuous. But a man cannot be virtuous unless he forbear from all kinds of vice. Therefore it belongs to human law to repress all vices.

Obj. 3: Further, human law is derived from the natural law, as stated above (Q. 95, A. 2). But all vices are contrary to the law of nature. Therefore human law should repress all vices.

*On the contrary,* We read in De Lib. Arb. i, 5: "It seems to me that the law which is written for the governing of the people rightly permits these things, and that Divine providence punishes them." But Divine providence punishes nothing but vices. Therefore human law rightly allows some vices, by not repressing them.

*I answer that,* As stated above (Q. 90, AA. 1, 2), law is framed as a rule or measure of human acts. Now a measure should be homogeneous with that which it measures, as stated in *Metaph.* x, text. 3, 4, since different things are measured by different measures. Wherefore laws imposed on men should also be in keeping with their condition, for, as Isidore says (Etym. v, 21), law should be "possible both according to nature, and according to the customs of the country." Now possibility or faculty of action is due to an interior habit or disposition: since the same thing is not possible to one who has not a virtuous habit, as is possible to one who has. Thus the same is not possible to a child as to a full-grown man: for which reason the law for children is not the same as for adults, since many things are permitted to children, which in an adult are punished by law or at any rate are open to blame. In like manner many things are permissible to men not perfect in virtue, which would be intolerable in a virtuous man.

Now human law is framed for a number of human beings, the majority of whom are not perfect in virtue. Wherefore human laws do not forbid all vices, from which the virtuous abstain, but only the more grievous vices, from which it is possible for the majority to abstain; and chiefly those that are to the hurt of others, without the prohibition of which human society could not be maintained: thus human law prohibits murder, theft and such like.

Reply Obj. 1: Audacity seems to refer to the assailing of others. Consequently it belongs to those sins chiefly whereby one's neighbor is injured: and these sins are forbidden by human law, as stated.

Reply Obj. 2: The purpose of human law is to lead men to virtue, not suddenly, but gradually. Wherefore it does not lay upon the multitude of imperfect men the burdens of those who are already virtuous, viz. that they should abstain from all evil. Otherwise these imperfect ones, being unable to bear such precepts, would break out into yet greater evils: thus it is written (Ps. 30:33): "He that violently bloweth his nose, bringeth out blood"; and (Matt. 9:17) that if "new wine," i.e. precepts of a perfect life, "is put into old bottles," i.e. into imperfect men, "the bottles break, and the wine runneth out," i.e. the precepts are despised, and those men, from contempt, break into evils worse still.

Reply Obj. 3: The natural law is a participation in us of the eternal law: while human law falls short of the eternal law. Now Augustine says (De Lib. Arb. i, 5): "The law which is framed for the government of states, allows and leaves unpunished many things that are punished by Divine providence. Nor, if this law does not attempt to do everything, is this a reason why it should be blamed for what it does." Wherefore, too, human law does not prohibit everything that is forbidden by the natural law.

THIRD ARTICLE [I-II, Q. 96, Art. 3]

Whether Human Law Prescribes Acts of All the Virtues?

Objection 1: It would seem that human law does not prescribe acts of all the virtues. For vicious acts are contrary to acts of virtue. But human law does not prohibit all vices, as stated above (A. 2). Therefore neither does it prescribe all acts of virtue.

Obj. 2: Further, a virtuous act proceeds from a virtue. But virtue is the end of law; so that whatever is from a virtue, cannot come under a precept of law. Therefore human law does not prescribe all acts of virtue.

Obj. 3: Further, law is ordained to the common good, as stated above (Q. 90, A. 2). But some acts of virtue are ordained, not to the common good, but to private good. Therefore the law does not prescribe all acts of virtue.

*On the contrary,* The Philosopher says (Ethic. v, 1) that the law "prescribes the performance of the acts of a brave man ... and the acts of the temperate man ... and the acts of the meek man: and in like manner as regards the other virtues and vices, prescribing the former, forbidding the latter."

*I answer that,* The species of virtues are distinguished by their objects, as explained above (Q. 54, A. 2; Q. 60, A. 1; Q. 62, A. 2). Now all the objects of virtues can be referred either to the private good of an individual, or to the common good of the multitude: thus matters of fortitude may be achieved either for the safety of the state, or for upholding the rights of a friend, and in like manner with the other virtues. But law, as stated above (Q. 90, A. 2) is ordained to the common good. Wherefore there is no virtue whose acts cannot be prescribed by the law. Nevertheless human law does not prescribe concerning all the acts of every virtue: but only in regard to those that are ordainable to the common good—either immediately, as when certain things are done directly for the common good—or mediately, as when a lawgiver prescribes certain things pertaining to good order, whereby the citizens are directed in the upholding of the common good of justice and peace.

Reply Obj. 1: Human law does not forbid all vicious acts, by the obligation of a precept, as neither does it prescribe all acts of virtue. But it forbids certain acts of each vice, just as it prescribes some acts of each virtue.

Reply Obj. 2: An act is said to be an act of virtue in two ways. First, from the fact that a man does something virtuous; thus the act of justice is to do what is right, and an act of fortitude is to do brave things: and in this way law prescribes certain acts of virtue. Secondly an act of virtue is when a man does a virtuous thing in a way in which a virtuous man does it. Such an act always proceeds from virtue: and it does not come under a precept of law, but is the end at which every lawgiver aims.

Reply Obj. 3: There is no virtue whose act is not ordainable to the common good, as stated above, either mediately or immediately.

FOURTH ARTICLE [I-II, Q. 96, Art. 4]

Whether Human Law Binds a Man in Conscience?

Objection 1: It would seem that human law does not bind man in conscience. For an inferior power has no jurisdiction in a court of higher power. But the power of man, which frames human law, is beneath the Divine power. Therefore human law cannot impose its precept in a Divine court, such as is the court of conscience.

Obj. 2: Further, the judgment of conscience depends chiefly on the commandments of God. But sometimes God's commandments are made void by human laws, according to Matt. 15:6: "You have made void the commandment of God for your tradition." Therefore human law does not bind a man in conscience.

Obj. 3: Further, human laws often bring loss of character and injury on man, according to Isa. 10:1 et seqq.: "Woe to them that make wicked laws, and when they write, write injustice; to oppress the poor in judgment, and do violence to the cause of the humble of My people." But it is lawful for anyone to avoid oppression and violence. Therefore human laws do not bind man in conscience.

*On the contrary,* It is written (1 Pet. 2:19): "This is thankworthy, if for conscience ... a man endure sorrows, suffering wrongfully."

*I answer that,* Laws framed by man are either just or unjust. If they be just, they have the power of binding in conscience, from the eternal law whence they are derived, according to Prov. 8:15: "By Me kings reign, and lawgivers decree just things." Now laws are said to be just, both from the end, when, to wit, they are ordained to the common good—and from their author, that is to say, when the law that is made does not exceed the power of the lawgiver—and from their form, when, to wit, burdens are laid on the subjects, according to an equality of proportion and with a view to the common good. For, since one man is a part of the community, each man in all that he is and has, belongs to the community; just as a part, in all that it is, belongs to the whole; wherefore nature inflicts a loss on the part, in order to save the whole: so that on this account, such laws as these, which impose proportionate burdens, are just and binding in conscience, and are legal laws.

On the other hand laws may be unjust in two ways: first, by being contrary to human good, through being opposed to the things mentioned above—either in respect of the end, as when an authority imposes on his subjects burdensome laws, conducive, not to the common good, but rather to his own cupidity or vainglory—or in respect of the author, as when a man makes a law that goes beyond the power committed to him—or in respect of the form, as when burdens are imposed unequally on the community, although with a view to the common good. The like are acts of violence rather than laws; because, as Augustine says (De Lib. Arb. i, 5), "a law that is not just, seems to be no law at all." Wherefore such laws do not bind in conscience, except perhaps in order to avoid scandal or disturbance, for which cause a man should even yield his right, according to Matt. 5:40, 41: "If a man ... take away thy coat, let go thy cloak also unto him; and whosoever will force thee one mile, go with him other two."

Secondly, laws may be unjust through being opposed to the Divine good: such are the laws of tyrants inducing to idolatry, or to anything else contrary to the Divine law: and laws of this kind must nowise be observed, because, as stated in Acts 5:29, "we ought to obey God rather than man."

Reply Obj. 1: As the Apostle says (Rom. 13:1, 2), all human power is from God ... "therefore he that resisteth the power," in matters that are within its scope, "resisteth the ordinance of God"; so that he becomes guilty according to his conscience.

Reply Obj. 2: This argument is true of laws that are contrary to the commandments of God, which is beyond the scope of (human) power. Wherefore in such matters human law should not be obeyed.

Reply Obj. 3: This argument is true of a law that inflicts unjust hurt on its subjects. The power that man holds from God does not extend to this: wherefore neither in such matters is man bound to obey the law, provided he avoid giving scandal or inflicting a more grievous hurt.

FIFTH ARTICLE [I-II, Q. 96, Art. 5]

Whether All Are Subject to the Law?

Objection 1: It would seem that not all are subject to the law. For those alone are subject to a law for whom a law is made. But the Apostle says (1 Tim. 1:9): "The law is not made for the just man." Therefore the just are not subject to the law.

Obj. 2: Further, Pope Urban says [*Decretals. caus. xix, qu. 2]: "He that is guided by a private law need not for any reason be bound by the public law." Now all spiritual men are led by the private law of the Holy Ghost, for they are the sons of God, of whom it is said (Rom. 8:14): "Whosoever are led by the Spirit of God, they are the sons of God." Therefore not all men are subject to human law.

Obj. 3: Further, the jurist says [*Pandect. Justin. i, ff., tit. 3, De Leg. et Senat.] that "the sovereign is exempt from the laws." But he that is exempt from the law is not bound thereby. Therefore not all are subject to the law.

*On the contrary,* The Apostle says (Rom. 13:1): "Let every soul be subject to the higher powers." But subjection to a power seems to imply subjection to the laws framed by that power. Therefore all men should be subject to human law.

*I answer that,* As stated above (Q. 90, AA. 1, 2; A. 3, ad 2), the notion of law contains two things: first, that it is a rule of human acts; secondly, that it has coercive power. Wherefore a man may be subject to law in two ways. First, as the regulated is subject to the regulator: and, in this way, whoever is subject to a power, is subject to the law framed by that power. But it may happen in two ways that one is not subject to a power. In one way, by being altogether free from its authority: hence the subjects of one city or kingdom are not bound by the laws of the sovereign of another city or kingdom, since they are not subject to his authority. In another way, by being under a yet higher law; thus the subject of a proconsul should be ruled by his command, but not in those matters in which the subject receives his orders from the emperor: for in these matters, he is not bound by the mandate of the lower authority, since he is directed by that of a higher. In this way, one who is simply subject to a law, may not be subject thereto in certain matters, in respect of which he is ruled by a higher law.

Secondly, a man is said to be subject to a law as the coerced is subject to the coercer. In this way the virtuous and righteous are not subject to the law, but only the wicked. Because coercion and violence are contrary to the will: but the will of the good is in harmony with the law, whereas the will of the wicked is discordant from it. Wherefore in this sense the good are not subject to the law, but only the wicked.

Reply Obj. 1: This argument is true of subjection by way of coercion: for, in this way, "the law is not made for the just men": because "they are a law to themselves," since they "show the work of the law written in their hearts," as the Apostle says (Rom. 2:14, 15). Consequently the law does not enforce itself upon them as it does on the wicked.

Reply Obj. 2: The law of the Holy Ghost is above all law framed by man: and therefore spiritual men, in so far as they are led by the law of the Holy Ghost, are not subject to the law in those matters that are inconsistent with the guidance of the Holy Ghost. Nevertheless the very fact that spiritual men are subject to law, is due to the leading of the Holy Ghost, according to 1 Pet. 2:13: "Be ye subject ... to every human creature for God's sake."

Reply Obj. 3: The sovereign is said to be "exempt from the law," as to its coercive power; since, properly speaking, no man is coerced by himself, and law has no coercive power save from the authority of the sovereign. Thus then is the sovereign said to be exempt from the law, because none is competent to pass sentence on him, if he acts against the law. Wherefore on Ps. 50:6: "To Thee only have I sinned," a gloss says that "there is no man who can judge the deeds of a king." But as to the directive force of law, the sovereign is subject to the law by his own will, according to the statement (Extra, De Constit. cap. Cum omnes) that "whatever law a man makes for another, he should keep himself. And a wise authority [*Dionysius Cato, Dist. de Moribus] says: 'Obey the law that thou makest thyself.'" Moreover the Lord reproaches those who "say and do not"; and who "bind heavy burdens and lay them on men's shoulders, but with a finger of their own they will not move them" (Matt. 23:3, 4). Hence, in the judgment of God, the sovereign is not exempt from the law, as to its directive force; but he should fulfil it to his own free-will and not of constraint. Again the sovereign is above the law, in so far as, when it is expedient, he can change the law, and dispense in it according to time and place.

SIXTH ARTICLE [I-II, Q. 96, Art. 6]

Whether He Who Is Under a Law May Act Beside the Letter of the Law?

Objection 1: It seems that he who is subject to a law may not act beside the letter of the law. For Augustine says (De Vera Relig. 31): "Although men judge about temporal laws when they make them, yet when once they are made they must pass judgment not on them, but according to them." But if anyone disregard the letter of the law, saying that he observes the intention of the lawgiver, he seems to pass judgment on the law. Therefore it is not right for one who is under the law to disregard the letter of the law, in order to observe the intention of the lawgiver.

Obj. 2: Further, he alone is competent to interpret the law who can make the law. But those who are subject to the law cannot make the law. Therefore they have no right to interpret the intention of the lawgiver, but should always act according to the letter of the law.

Obj. 3: Further, every wise man knows how to explain his intention by words. But those who framed the laws should be reckoned wise: for Wisdom says (Prov. 8:15): "By Me kings reign, and lawgivers decree just things." Therefore we should not judge of the intention of the lawgiver otherwise than by the words of the law.

*On the contrary,* Hilary says (De Trin. iv): "The meaning of what is said is according to the motive for saying it: because things are not subject to speech, but speech to things." Therefore we should take account of the motive of the lawgiver, rather than of his very words.

*I answer that,* As stated above (A. 4), every law is directed to the common weal of men, and derives the force and nature of law accordingly. Hence the jurist says [*Pandect. Justin. lib. i, ff., tit. 3, De Leg. et Senat.]: "By no reason of law, or favor of equity, is it allowable for us to interpret harshly, and render burdensome, those useful measures which have been enacted for the welfare of man." Now it happens often that the observance of some point of law conduces to the common weal in the majority of instances, and yet, in some cases, is very hurtful. Since then the lawgiver cannot have in view every single case, he shapes the law according to what happens most frequently, by directing his attention to the common good. Wherefore if a case arise wherein the observance of that law would be hurtful to the general welfare, it should not be observed. For instance, suppose that in a besieged city it be an established law that the gates of the city are to be kept closed, this is good for public welfare as a general rule: but, it were to happen that the enemy are in pursuit of certain citizens, who are defenders of the city, it would be a great loss to the city, if the gates were not opened to them: and so in that case the gates ought to be opened, contrary to the letter of the law, in order to maintain the common weal, which the lawgiver had in view.

Nevertheless it must be noted, that if the observance of the law according to the letter does not involve any sudden risk needing instant remedy, it is not competent for everyone to expound what is useful and what is not useful to the state: those alone can do this who are in authority, and who, on account of such like cases, have the power to dispense from the laws. If, however, the peril be so sudden as not to allow of the delay involved by referring the matter to authority, the mere necessity brings with it a dispensation, since necessity knows no law.

Reply Obj. 1: He who in a case of necessity acts beside the letter of the law, does not judge the law; but of a particular case in which he sees that the letter of the law is not to be observed.

Reply Obj. 2: He who follows the intention of the lawgiver, does not interpret the law simply; but in a case in which it is evident, by reason of the manifest harm, that the lawgiver intended otherwise. For if it be a matter of doubt, he must either act according to the letter of the law, or consult those in power.

Reply Obj. 3: No man is so wise as to be able to take account of every single case; wherefore he is not able sufficiently to express in words all those things that are suitable for the end he has in view. And even if a lawgiver were able to take all the cases into consideration, he ought not to mention them all, in order to avoid confusion: but should frame the law according to that which is of most common occurrence.

## QUESTION 97

OF CHANGE IN LAWS (In Four Articles)

We must now consider change in laws: under which head there are four points of inquiry:

(1) Whether human law is changeable?

(2) Whether it should be always changed, whenever anything better occurs?

(3) Whether it is abolished by custom, and whether custom obtains the force of law?

(4) Whether the application of human law should be changed by dispensation of those in authority?

FIRST ARTICLE [I-II, Q. 97, Art. 1]

Whether Human Law Should Be Changed in Any Way?

Objection 1: It would seem that human law should not be changed in any way at all. Because human law is derived from the natural law, as stated above (Q. 95, A. 2). But the natural law endures unchangeably. Therefore human law should also remain without any change.

Obj. 2: Further, as the Philosopher says (Ethic. v, 5), a measure should be absolutely stable. But human law is the measure of human acts, as stated above (Q. 90, AA. 1, 2). Therefore it should remain without change.

Obj. 3: Further, it is of the essence of law to be just and right, as stated above (Q. 95, A. 2). But that which is right once is right always. Therefore that which is law once, should be always law.

*On the contrary,* Augustine says (De Lib. Arb. i, 6): "A temporal law, however just, may be justly changed in course of time."

*I answer that,* As stated above (Q. 91, A. 3), human law is a dictate of reason, whereby human acts are directed. Thus there may be two causes for the just change of human law: one on the part of reason; the other on the part of man whose acts are regulated by law. The cause on the part of reason is that it seems natural to human reason to advance gradually from the imperfect to the perfect. Hence, in speculative sciences, we see that the teaching of the early philosophers was imperfect, and that it was afterwards perfected by those who succeeded them. So also in practical matters: for those who first endeavored to discover something useful for the human community, not being able by themselves to take everything into consideration, set up certain institutions which were deficient in many ways; and these were changed by subsequent lawgivers who made institutions that might prove less frequently deficient in respect of the common weal.

On the part of man, whose acts are regulated by law, the law can be rightly changed on account of the changed condition of man, to whom different things are expedient according to the difference of his condition. An example is proposed by Augustine (De Lib. Arb. i, 6): "If the people have a sense of moderation and responsibility, and are most careful guardians of the common weal, it is right to enact a law allowing such a people to choose their own magistrates for the government of the commonwealth. But if, as time goes on, the same people become so corrupt as to sell their votes, and entrust the government to scoundrels and criminals; then the right of appointing their public officials is rightly forfeit to such a people, and the choice devolves to a few good men."

Reply Obj. 1: The natural law is a participation of the eternal law, as stated above (Q. 91, A. 2), and therefore endures without change, owing to the unchangeableness and perfection of the Divine Reason, the Author of nature. But the reason of man is changeable and imperfect: wherefore his law is subject to change. Moreover the natural law contains certain universal precepts, which are everlasting: whereas human law contains certain particular precepts, according to various emergencies.

Reply Obj. 2: A measure should be as enduring as possible. But nothing can be absolutely unchangeable in things that are subject to change. And therefore human law cannot be altogether unchangeable.

Reply Obj. 3: In corporal things, right is predicated absolutely: and therefore, as far as itself is concerned, always remains right. But right is predicated of law with reference to the common weal, to which one and the same thing is not always adapted, as stated above: wherefore rectitude of this kind is subject to change.

SECOND ARTICLE [I-II, Q. 97, Art. 2]

Whether Human Law Should Always Be Changed, Whenever Something Better Occurs?

Objection 1: It would seem that human law should be changed, whenever something better occurs. Because human laws are devised by human reason, like other arts. But in the other arts, the tenets of former times give place to others, if something better occurs. Therefore the same should apply to human laws.

Obj. 2: Further, by taking note of the past we can provide for the future. Now unless human laws had been changed when it was found possible to improve them, considerable inconvenience would have ensued; because the laws of old were crude in many points. Therefore it seems that laws should be changed, whenever anything better occurs to be enacted.

Obj. 3: Further, human laws are enacted about single acts of man. But we cannot acquire perfect knowledge in singular matters, except by experience, which "requires time," as stated in *Ethic.* ii. Therefore it seems that as time goes on it is possible for something better to occur for legislation.

*On the contrary,* It is stated in the Decretals (Dist. xii, 5): "It is absurd, and a detestable shame, that we should suffer those traditions to be changed which we have received from the fathers of old."

*I answer that,* As stated above (A. 1), human law is rightly changed, in so far as such change is conducive to the common weal. But, to a certain extent, the mere change of law is of itself prejudicial to the common good: because custom avails much for the observance of laws, seeing that what is done contrary to general custom, even in slight matters, is looked upon as grave. Consequently, when a law is changed, the binding power of the law is diminished, in so far as custom is abolished. Wherefore human law should never be changed, unless, in some way or other, the common weal be compensated according to the extent of the harm done in this respect. Such compensation may arise either from some very great and every evident benefit conferred by the new enactment; or from the extreme urgency of the case, due to the fact that either the existing law is clearly unjust, or its observance extremely harmful. Wherefore the Jurist says [*Pandect. Justin. lib. i, ff., tit. 4, De Constit. Princip.] that "in establishing new laws, there should be evidence of the benefit to be derived, before departing from a law which has long been considered just."

Reply Obj. 1: Rules of art derive their force from reason alone: and therefore whenever something better occurs, the rule followed hitherto should be changed. But "laws derive very great force from custom," as the Philosopher states (Polit. ii, 5): consequently they should not be quickly changed.

Reply Obj. 2: This argument proves that laws ought to be changed: not in view of any improvement, but for the sake of a great benefit or in a case of great urgency, as stated above. This answer applies also to the Third Objection.

THIRD ARTICLE [I-II, Q. 97, Art. 3]

Whether Custom Can Obtain Force of Law?

Objection 1: It would seem that custom cannot obtain force of law, nor abolish a law. Because human law is derived from the natural law and from the Divine law, as stated above (Q. 93, A. 3; Q. 95, A. 2). But human custom cannot change either the law of nature or the Divine law. Therefore neither can it change human law.

Obj. 2: Further, many evils cannot make one good. But he who first acted against the law, did evil. Therefore by multiplying such acts, nothing good is the result. Now a law is something good; since it is a rule of human acts. Therefore law is not abolished by custom, so that the mere custom should obtain force of law.

Obj. 3: Further, the framing of laws belongs to those public men whose business it is to govern the community; wherefore private individuals cannot make laws. But custom grows by the acts of private individuals. Therefore custom cannot obtain force of law, so as to abolish the law.

*On the contrary,* Augustine says (Ep. ad Casulan. xxxvi): "The customs of God's people and the institutions of our ancestors are to be considered as laws. And those who throw contempt on the customs of the Church ought to be punished as those who disobey the law of God."

*I answer that,* All law proceeds from the reason and will of the lawgiver; the Divine and natural laws from the reasonable will of God; the human law from the will of man, regulated by reason. Now just as human reason and will, in practical matters, may be made manifest by speech, so may they be made known by deeds: since seemingly a man chooses as good that which he carries into execution. But it is evident that by human speech, law can be both changed and expounded, in so far as it manifests the interior movement and thought of human reason. Wherefore by actions also, especially if they be repeated, so as to make a custom, law can be changed and expounded; and also something can be established which obtains force of law, in so far as by repeated external actions, the inward movement of the will, and concepts of reason are most effectually declared; for when a thing is done again and again, it seems to proceed from a deliberate judgment of reason. Accordingly, custom has the force of a law, abolishes law, and is the interpreter of law.

Reply Obj. 1: The natural and Divine laws proceed from the Divine will, as stated above. Wherefore they cannot be changed by a custom proceeding from the will of man, but only by Divine authority. Hence it is that no custom can prevail over the Divine or natural laws: for Isidore says (Synon. ii, 16): "Let custom yield to authority: evil customs should be eradicated by law and reason."

Reply Obj. 2: As stated above (Q. 96, A. 6), human laws fail in some cases: wherefore it is possible sometimes to act beside the law; namely, in a case where the law fails; yet the act will not be evil. And when such cases are multiplied, by reason of some change in man, then custom shows that the law is no longer useful: just as it might be declared by the verbal promulgation of a law to the contrary. If, however, the same reason remains, for which the law was useful hitherto, then it is not the custom that prevails against the law, but the law that overcomes the custom: unless perhaps the sole reason for the law seeming useless, be that it is not "possible according to the custom of the country" [*Q. 95, A. 3], which has been stated to be one of the conditions of law. For it is not easy to set aside the custom of a whole people.

Reply Obj. 3: The people among whom a custom is introduced may be of two conditions. For if they are free, and able to make their own laws, the consent of the whole people expressed by a custom counts far more in favor of a particular observance, that does the authority of the sovereign, who has not the power to frame laws, except as representing the people. Wherefore although each individual cannot make laws, yet the whole people can. If however the people have not the free power to make their own laws, or to abolish a law made by a higher authority; nevertheless with such a people a prevailing custom obtains force of law, in so far as it is tolerated by those to whom it belongs to make laws for that people: because by the very fact that they tolerate it they seem to approve of that which is introduced by custom.

FOURTH ARTICLE [I-II, Q. 97, Art. 4]

Whether the Rulers of the People Can Dispense from Human Laws?

Objection 1: It would seem that the rulers of the people cannot dispense from human laws. For the law is established for the "common weal," as Isidore says (Etym. v, 21). But the common good should not be set aside for the private convenience of an individual: because, as the Philosopher says (Ethic. i, 2), "the good of the nation is more godlike than the good of one man." Therefore it seems that a man should not be dispensed from acting in compliance with the general law.

Obj. 2: Further, those who are placed over others are commanded as follows (Deut. 1:17): "You shall hear the little as well as the great; neither shall you respect any man's person, because it is the judgment of God." But to allow one man to do that which is equally forbidden to all, seems to be respect of persons. Therefore the rulers of a community cannot grant such dispensations, since this is against a precept of the Divine law.

Obj. 3: Further, human law, in order to be just, should accord with the natural and Divine laws: else it would not "foster religion," nor be "helpful to discipline," which is requisite to the nature of law, as laid down by Isidore (Etym. v, 3). But no man can dispense from the Divine and natural laws. Neither, therefore, can he dispense from the human law.

*On the contrary,* The Apostle says (1 Cor. 9:17): "A dispensation is committed to me."

*I answer that,* Dispensation, properly speaking, denotes a measuring out to individuals of some common goods: thus the head of a household is called a dispenser, because to each member of the household he distributes work and necessaries of life in due weight and measure. Accordingly in every community a man is said to dispense, from the very fact that he directs how some general precept is to be fulfilled by each individual. Now it happens at times that a precept, which is conducive to the common weal as a general rule, is not good for a particular individual, or in some particular case, either because it would hinder some greater good, or because it would be the occasion of some evil, as explained above (Q. 96, A. 6). But it would be dangerous to leave this to the discretion of each individual, except perhaps by reason of an evident and sudden emergency, as stated above (Q. 96, A. 6). Consequently he who is placed over a community is empowered to dispense in a human law that rests upon his authority, so that, when the law fails in its application to persons or circumstances, he may allow the precept of the law not to be observed. If however he grant this permission without any such reason, and of his mere will, he will be an unfaithful or an imprudent dispenser: unfaithful, if he has not the common good in view; imprudent, if he ignores the reasons for granting dispensations. Hence Our Lord says (Luke 12:42): "Who, thinkest thou, is the faithful and wise dispenser [Douay: steward], whom his lord setteth over his family?"

Reply Obj. 1: When a person is dispensed from observing the general law, this should not be done to the prejudice of, but with the intention of benefiting, the common good.

Reply Obj. 2: It is not respect of persons if unequal measures are served out to those who are themselves unequal. Wherefore when the condition of any person requires that he should reasonably receive special treatment, it is not respect of persons if he be the object of special favor.

Reply Obj. 3: Natural law, so far as it contains general precepts, which never fail, does not allow of dispensations. In other precepts, however, which are as conclusions of the general precepts, man sometimes grants a dispensation: for instance, that a loan should not be paid back to the betrayer of his country, or something similar. But to the Divine law each man stands as a private person to the public law to which he is subject. Wherefore just as none can dispense from public human law, except the man from whom the law derives its authority, or his delegate; so, in the precepts of the Divine law, which are from God, none can dispense but God, or the man to whom He may give special power for that purpose.

## QUESTION 98

OF THE OLD LAW (In Six Articles)

In due sequence we must now consider the Old Law; and (1) The Law itself; (2) Its precepts. Under the first head there are six points of inquiry:

(1) Whether the Old Law was good?

(2) Whether it was from God?

(3) Whether it came from Him through the angels?

(4) Whether it was given to all?

(5) Whether it was binding on all?

(6) Whether it was given at a suitable time?

FIRST ARTICLE [I-II, Q. 98, Art. 1]

Whether the Old Law Was Good?

Objection 1: It would seem that the Old Law was not good. For it is written (Ezech. 20:25): "I gave them statutes that were not good, and judgments in which they shall not live." But a law is not said to be good except on account of the goodness of the precepts that it contains. Therefore the Old Law was not good.

Obj. 2: Further, it belongs to the goodness of a law that it conduce to the common welfare, as Isidore says (Etym. v, 3). But the Old Law was not salutary; rather was it deadly and hurtful. For the Apostle says (Rom. 7:8, seqq.): "Without the law sin was dead. And I lived some time without the law. But when the commandment came sin revived; and I died." Again he says (Rom. 5:20): "Law entered in that sin might abound." Therefore the Old Law was not good.

Obj. 3: Further, it belongs to the goodness of the law that it should be possible to obey it, both according to nature, and according to human custom. But such the Old Law was not: since Peter said (Acts 15:10): "Why tempt you (God) to put a yoke on the necks of the disciples, which neither our fathers nor we have been able to bear?" Therefore it seems that the Old Law was not good.

*On the contrary,* The Apostle says (Rom. 7:12): "Wherefore the law indeed is holy, and the commandment holy, and just, and good."

*I answer that,* Without any doubt, the Old Law was good. For just as a doctrine is shown to be good by the fact that it accords with right reason, so is a law proved to be good if it accords with reason. Now the Old Law was in accordance with reason. Because it repressed concupiscence which is in conflict with reason, as evidenced by the commandment, "Thou shalt not covet thy neighbor's goods" (Ex. 20:17). Moreover the same law forbade all kinds of sin; and these too are contrary to reason. Consequently it is evident that it was a good law. The Apostle argues in the same way (Rom. 7): "I am delighted," says he (verse 22), "with the law of God, according to the inward man": and again (verse 16): "I consent to the law, that is good."

But it must be noted that the good has various degrees, as Dionysius states (Div. Nom. iv): for there is a perfect good, and an imperfect good. In things ordained to an end, there is perfect goodness when a thing is such that it is sufficient in itself to conduce to the end: while there is imperfect goodness when a thing is of some assistance in attaining the end, but is not sufficient for the realization thereof. Thus a medicine is perfectly good, if it gives health to a man; but it is imperfect, if it helps to cure him, without being able to bring him back to health. Again it must be observed that the end of human law is different from the end of Divine law. For the end of human law is the temporal tranquillity of the state, which end law effects by directing external actions, as regards those evils which might disturb the peaceful condition of the state. On the other hand, the end of the Divine law is to bring man to that end which is everlasting happiness; which end is hindered by any sin, not only of external, but also of internal action. Consequently that which suffices for the perfection of human law, viz. the prohibition and punishment of sin, does not suffice for the perfection of the Divine law: but it is requisite that it should make man altogether fit to partake of everlasting happiness. Now this cannot be done save by the grace of the Holy Ghost, whereby "charity" which fulfilleth the law ... "is spread abroad in our hearts" (Rom. 5:5): since "the grace of God is life everlasting" (Rom. 6:23). But the Old Law could not confer this grace, for this was reserved to Christ; because, as it is written (John

1:17), the law was given "by Moses, grace and truth came by Jesus Christ." Consequently the Old Law was good indeed, but imperfect, according to Heb. 7:19: "The law brought nothing to perfection."

Reply Obj. 1: The Lord refers there to the ceremonial precepts; which are said not to be good, because they did not confer grace unto the remission of sins, although by fulfilling these precepts man confessed himself a sinner. Hence it is said pointedly, "and judgments in which they shall not live"; i.e. whereby they are unable to obtain life; and so the text goes on: "And I polluted them," i.e. showed them to be polluted, "in their own gifts, when they offered all that opened the womb, for their offenses."

Reply Obj. 2: The law is said to have been deadly, as being not the cause, but the occasion of death, on account of its imperfection: in so far as it did not confer grace enabling man to fulfil what is prescribed, and to avoid what it forbade. Hence this occasion was not given to men, but taken by them. Wherefore the Apostle says (Rom. 5:11): "Sin, taking occasion by the commandment, seduced me, and by it killed me." In the same sense when it is said that "the law entered in that sin might abound," the conjunction "that" must be taken as consecutive and not final: in so far as men, taking occasion from the law, sinned all the more, both because a sin became more grievous after law had forbidden it, and because concupiscence increased, since we desire a thing the more from its being forbidden.

Reply Obj. 3: The yoke of the law could not be borne without the help of grace, which the law did not confer: for it is written (Rom. 9:16): "It is not him that willeth, nor of him that runneth," viz. that he wills and runs in the commandments of God, "but of God that showeth mercy." Wherefore it is written (Ps. 118:32): "I have run the way of Thy commandments, when Thou didst enlarge my heart," i.e. by giving me grace and charity.

SECOND ARTICLE [I-II, Q. 98, Art. 2]

Whether the Old Law Was from God?

Objection 1: It would seem that the Old Law was not from God. For it is written (Deut. 32:4): "The works of God are perfect." But the Law was imperfect, as stated above (A. 1). Therefore the Old Law was not from God.

Obj. 2: Further, it is written (Eccles. 3:14): "I have learned that all the works which God hath made continue for ever." But the Old Law does not continue for ever: since the Apostle says (Heb. 7:18): "There is indeed a setting aside of the former commandment, because of the weakness and unprofitableness thereof." Therefore the Old Law was not from God.

Obj. 3: Further, a wise lawgiver should remove, not only evil, but also the occasions of evil. But the Old Law was an occasion of sin, as stated above (A. 1, ad 2). Therefore the giving of such a law does not pertain to God, to Whom "none is like among the lawgivers" (Job 36:22).

Obj. 4: Further, it is written (1 Tim. 2:4) that God "will have all men to be saved." But the Old Law did not suffice to save man, as stated above (A. 1). Therefore the giving of such a law did not appertain to God. Therefore the Old Law was not from God.

*On the contrary,* Our Lord said (Matt. 15:6) while speaking to the Jews, to whom the Law was given: "You have made void the commandment of God for your tradition." And shortly before (verse 4) He had said: "Honor thy father and mother," which is contained expressly in the Old Law (Ex. 20:12; Deut. 5:16). Therefore the Old Law was from God.

*I answer that,* The Old Law was given by the good God, Who is the Father of Our Lord Jesus Christ. For the Old Law ordained men to Christ in two ways. First by bearing witness to Christ; wherefore He Himself says (Luke 24:44): "All things must needs be fulfilled, which are written in the law ... and in the prophets, and in the psalms, concerning Me": and (John 5:46): "If you did believe Moses, you would perhaps believe Me also; for he wrote of Me." Secondly, as a kind of disposition, since by withdrawing men from idolatrous worship, it enclosed ( *concludebat* ) them in the worship of one God, by Whom the human race was to be saved through Christ. Wherefore the Apostle says (Gal. 3:23): "Before the faith came, we were kept under the law shut up ( *conclusi* ), unto that faith which was to be revealed." Now it is evident that the same thing it is, which gives a disposition to the end, and which brings to the end; and when I say "the same," I mean that it does so either by itself or through its subjects. For the devil would not make a law whereby men would be led to Christ, Who was to cast him out, according to Matt. 12:26: "If Satan cast out Satan, his kingdom is divided" [Vulg.: 'he is divided against himself']. Therefore the Old Law was given by the same God, from Whom came salvation to man, through the grace of Christ.

Reply Obj. 1: Nothing prevents a thing being not perfect simply, and yet perfect in respect of time: thus a boy is said to be perfect, not simply, but with regard to the condition of time. So, too, precepts that are given to children are perfect in comparison with the condition of those to whom they are given, although they are not perfect simply. Hence the Apostle says (Gal. 3:24): "The law was our pedagogue in Christ."

Reply Obj. 2: Those works of God endure for ever which God so made that they would endure for ever; and these are His perfect works. But the Old Law was set aside when there came the perfection of grace; not as though it were evil, but as being weak and useless for this time; because, as the Apostle goes on to say, "the law brought nothing to perfection": hence he says (Gal. 3:25): "After the faith is come, we are no longer under a pedagogue."

Reply Obj. 3: As stated above (Q. 79, A. 4), God sometimes permits certain ones to fall into sin, that they may thereby be humbled. So also did He wish to give such a law as men by their own forces could not fulfill, so that, while presuming on their own powers, they might find themselves to be sinners, and being humbled might have recourse to the help of grace.

Reply Obj. 4: Although the Old Law did not suffice to save man, yet another help from God besides the Law was available for man, viz. faith in the Mediator, by which the fathers of old were justified even as we were. Accordingly God did not fail man by giving him insufficient aids to salvation.

THIRD ARTICLE [I-II, Q. 98, Art. 3]

Whether the Old Law Was Given Through the Angels?

Objection 1: It seems that the Old Law was not given through the angels, but immediately by God. For an angel means a "messenger"; so that the word "angel" denotes ministry, not lordship, according to Ps. 102:20, 21: "Bless the Lord, all ye His Angels ... you ministers of His." But the Old Law is related to have been given by the Lord: for it is written (Ex. 20:1): "And the Lord spoke ... these words," and further on: "I am the Lord Thy God." Moreover the same expression is often repeated in Exodus, and the later books of the Law. Therefore the Law was given by God immediately.

Obj. 2: Further, according to John 1:17, "the Law was given by Moses." But Moses received it from God immediately: for it is written (Ex. 33:11): "The Lord spoke to Moses face to face, as a man is wont to speak to his friend." Therefore the Old Law was given by God immediately.

Obj. 3: Further, it belongs to the sovereign alone to make a law, as stated above (Q. 90, A. 3). But God alone is Sovereign as regards the salvation of souls: while the angels are the "ministering spirits," as stated in Heb. 1:14. Therefore it was not meet for the Law to be given through the angels, since it is ordained to the salvation of souls.

*On the contrary,* The Apostle said (Gal. 3:19) that the Law was "given [Vulg.: 'ordained'] by angels in the hand of a Mediator." And Stephen said (Acts 7:53): "(Who) have received the Law by the disposition of angels."

*I answer that,* The Law was given by God through the angels. And besides the general reason given by Dionysius (Coel. Hier. iv), viz. that "the gifts of God should be brought to men by means of the angels," there is a special reason why the Old Law should have been given through them. For it has been stated (AA. 1, 2) that the Old Law was imperfect, and yet disposed man to that perfect salvation of the human race, which was to come through Christ. Now it is to be observed that wherever there is an order of powers or arts, he that holds the highest place, himself exercises the principal and perfect acts; while those things which dispose to the ultimate perfection are effected by him through his subordinates: thus the ship-builder himself rivets the planks together, but prepares the material by means of the workmen who assist him under his direction. Consequently it was fitting that the perfect law of the New Testament should be given by the incarnate God immediately; but that the Old Law should be given to men by the ministers of God, i.e. by the angels. It is thus that the Apostle at the beginning of his epistle to the Hebrews (1:2) proves the excellence of the New Law over the Old; because in the New Testament "God ... hath spoken to us by His Son," whereas in the Old Testament "the word was spoken by angels" (Heb. 2:2).

Reply Obj. 1: As Gregory says at the beginning of his Morals (Praef. chap. i), "the angel who is described to have appeared to Moses, is sometimes mentioned as an angel, sometimes as the Lord: an angel, in truth, in respect of that which was subservient to the external delivery; and the Lord, because He was the Director within, Who supported the effectual power of speaking." Hence also it is that the angel spoke as personating the Lord.

Reply Obj. 2: As Augustine says (Gen. ad lit. xii, 27), it is stated in Exodus that "the Lord spoke to Moses face to face"; and shortly afterwards we read, "'Show me Thy glory.' Therefore He perceived what he saw and he desired what he saw not." Hence he did not see the very Essence of God; and consequently he was not taught by Him immediately. Accordingly when Scripture states that "He spoke to him face to face," this is to be understood as expressing the opinion of the people, who thought that Moses was speaking with God mouth to mouth, when God spoke and appeared to him, by means of a subordinate creature, i.e. an angel and a cloud. Again we may say that this vision "face to face" means some kind of sublime and familiar contemplation, inferior to the vision of the Divine Essence.

Reply Obj. 3: It is for the sovereign alone to make a law by his own authority; but sometimes after making a law, he promulgates it through others. Thus God made the Law by His own authority, but He promulgated it through the angels.

FOURTH ARTICLE [I-II, Q, 98, Art. 4]

Whether the Old Law Should Have Been Given to the Jews Alone?

Objection 1: It would seem that the Old Law should not have been given to the Jews alone. For the Old Law disposed men for the salvation which was to come through Christ, as stated above (AA. 2, 3). But that salvation was to come not to the Jews alone but to all nations, according to Isa. 49:6: "It is a small thing that thou shouldst be my servant to raise up the tribes of Jacob, and to convert the dregs of Israel. Behold I have given thee to be the light of the Gentiles, that thou mayest be My salvation, even to the farthest part of the earth." Therefore the Old Law should have been given to all nations, and not to one people only.

Obj. 2: Further, according to Acts 10:34, 35,

"God is not a respecter of persons: but in every nation, he that feareth Him, and worketh justice, is acceptable to Him." Therefore the way of salvation should not have been opened to one people more than to another.

Obj. 3: Further, the law was given through the angels, as stated above (A. 3). But God always vouchsafed the ministrations of the angels not to the Jews alone, but to all nations: for it is written (Ecclus. 17:14): "Over every nation He set a ruler." Also on all nations He bestows temporal goods, which are of less account with God than spiritual goods. Therefore He should have given the Law also to all peoples.

*On the contrary,* It is written (Rom. 3:1, 2): "What advantage then hath the Jew? ... Much every way. First indeed, because the words of God were committed to them": and (Ps. 147:9): "He hath not done in like manner to every nation: and His judgments He hath not made manifest unto them."

*I answer that,* It might be assigned as a reason for the Law being given to the Jews rather than to other peoples, that the Jewish people alone remained faithful to the worship of one God, while the others turned away to idolatry; wherefore the latter were unworthy to receive the Law, lest a holy thing should be given to dogs.

But this reason does not seem fitting: because that people turned to idolatry, even after the Law had been made, which was more grievous, as is clear from Ex. 32 and from Amos 5:25, 26: "Did you offer victims and sacrifices to Me in the desert for forty years, O house of Israel? But you carried a tabernacle for your Moloch, and the image of your idols, the star of your god, which you made to yourselves." Moreover it is stated expressly (Deut. 9:6): "Know therefore that the Lord thy God giveth thee not this excellent land in possession for thy justices, for thou art a very stiff-necked people": but the real reason is given in the preceding verse: "That the Lord might accomplish His word, which He promised by oath to thy fathers Abraham, Isaac, and Jacob."

What this promise was is shown by the Apostle, who says (Gal. 3:16) that "to Abraham were the promises made and to his seed. He saith not, 'And to his seeds,' as of many: but as of one, 'And to thy seed,' which is Christ." And so God vouchsafed both the Law and other special boons to that people, on account of the promised made to their fathers that Christ should be born of them. For it was fitting that the people, of whom Christ was to be born, should be signalized by a special sanctification, according to the words of Lev. 19:2: "Be ye holy, because I ... am holy." Nor again was it on account of the merit of Abraham himself that this promise was made to him, viz. that Christ should be born of his seed: but of gratuitous election and vocation. Hence it is written (Isa. 41:2): "Who hath raised up the just one form the east, hath called him to follow him?"

It is therefore evident that it was merely from gratuitous election that the patriarchs received the promise, and that the people sprung from them received the law; according to Deut. 4:36, 37: "Ye did [Vulg.: 'Thou didst'] hear His words out of the midst of the fire, because He loved thy fathers, and chose their seed after them." And if again it asked why He chose this people, and not another, that Christ might be born thereof; a fitting answer is given by Augustine (Tract. super Joan. xxvi): "Why He draweth one and draweth not another, seek not thou to judge, if thou wish not to err."

Reply Obj. 1: Although the salvation, which was to come through Christ, was prepared for all nations, yet it was necessary that Christ should be born of one people, which, for this reason, was privileged above other peoples; according to Rom. 9:4: "To whom," namely the Jews, "belongeth the adoption as of children (of God) ... and the testament, and the giving of the Law ... whose are the fathers, and of whom is Christ according to the flesh."

Reply Obj. 2: Respect of persons takes place in those things which are given according to due; but it has no place in those things which are bestowed gratuitously. Because he who, out of generosity, gives of his own to one and not to another, is not a respecter of persons: but if he were a dispenser of goods held in common, and were not to distribute them according to personal merits, he would be a respecter of persons. Now God bestows the benefits of salvation on the human race gratuitously: wherefore He is not a respecter of persons, if He gives them to some rather than to others. Hence Augustine says (De Praedest. Sanct. viii): "All whom God teaches, he teaches out of pity; but whom He teaches not, out of justice He teaches not": for this is due to the condemnation of the human race for the sin of the first parent.

Reply Obj. 3: The benefits of grace are forfeited by man on account of sin: but not the benefits of nature. Among the latter are the ministries of the angels, which the very order of various natures demands, viz. that the lowest beings be governed through the intermediate beings: and also bodily aids, which God vouchsafes not only to men, but also to beasts, according to Ps. 35:7: "Men and beasts Thou wilt preserve, O Lord."

FIFTH ARTICLE [I-II, Q. 98, Art. 5]

Whether All Men Were Bound to Observe the Old Law?

Objection 1: It would seem that all men were bound to observe the Old Law. Because whoever is subject to the king, must needs be subject to his law. But the Old Law was given by God, Who is "King of all the earth" (Ps. 46:8). Therefore all the inhabitants of the earth were bound to observe the Law.

Obj. 2: Further, the Jews could not be saved without observing the Old Law: for it is written (Deut. 27:26): "Cursed be he that abideth not in the words of this law, and fulfilleth them not in work." If therefore other men could be saved without the observance of the Old Law, the Jews would be in a worse plight than other men.

Obj. 3: Further, the Gentiles were admitted to the Jewish ritual and to the observances of the Law: for it is written (Ex. 12:48): "If any stranger be willing to dwell among you, and to keep the Phase of the Lord, all his males shall first be circumcised, and then shall he celebrate it according to the manner; and he shall be as he that is born in the land." But it would have been useless to admit strangers to the legal observances according to Divine ordinance, if they could have been saved without the observance of the Law. Therefore none could be saved without observing the Law.

*On the contrary,* Dionysius says (Coel. Hier. ix) that many of the Gentiles were brought back to God by the angels. But it is clear that the Gentiles did not observe the Law. Therefore some could be saved without observing the Law.

*I answer that,* The Old Law showed forth the precepts of the natural law, and added certain precepts of its own. Accordingly, as to those precepts of the natural law contained in the Old Law, all were bound to observe the Old Law; not because they belonged to the Old Law, but because they belonged to the natural law. But as to those precepts which were added by the Old Law, they were not binding on any save the Jewish people alone.

The reason of this is because the Old Law, as stated above (A. 4), was given to the Jewish people, that it might receive a prerogative of holiness, in reverence for Christ Who was to be born of that people. Now whatever laws are enacted for the special sanctification of certain ones, are binding on them alone: thus clerics who are set aside for the service of God are bound to certain obligations to which the laity are not bound; likewise religious are bound by their profession to certain works of perfection, to which people living in the world are not bound. In like manner this people was bound to certain special observances, to which other peoples were not bound. Wherefore it is written (Deut. 18:13): "Thou shalt be perfect and without spot before the Lord thy God": and for this reason they used a kind of form of profession, as appears from Deut. 26:3: "I profess this day before the Lord thy God," etc.

Reply Obj. 1: Whoever are subject to a king, are bound to observe his law which he makes for all in general. But if he orders certain things to be observed by the servants of his household, others are not bound thereto.

Reply Obj. 2: The more a man is united to God, the better his state becomes: wherefore the more the Jewish people were bound to the worship of God, the greater their excellence over other peoples. Hence it is written (Deut. 4:8): "What other nation is there so renowned that hath ceremonies and just judgments, and all the law?" In like manner, from this point of view, the state of clerics is better than that of the laity, and the state of religious than that of folk living in the world.

Reply Obj. 3: The Gentiles obtained salvation more perfectly and more securely under the observances of the Law than under the mere natural law: and for this reason they were admitted to them. So too the laity are now admitted to the ranks of the clergy, and secular persons to those of the religious, although they can be saved without this.

SIXTH ARTICLE [I-II, Q. 98, Art. 6]

Whether the Old Law Was Suitably Given at the Time of Moses?

Objection 1: It would seem that the Old Law was not suitably given at the time of Moses. Because the Old Law disposed man for the salvation which was to come through Christ, as stated above (AA. 2, 3). But man needed this salutary remedy immediately after he had sinned. Therefore the Law should have been given immediately after sin.

Obj. 2: Further, the Old Law was given for the sanctification of those from whom Christ was to be born. Now the promise concerning the "seed, which is Christ" (Gal. 3:16) was first made to Abraham, as related in Gen. 12:7. Therefore the Law should have been given at once at the time of Abraham.

Obj. 3: Further, as Christ was born of those alone who descended from Noe through Abraham, to whom the promise was made; so was He born of no other of the descendants of Abraham but David, to whom the promise was renewed, according to 2 Kings 23:1: "The man to whom it was appointed concerning the Christ of the God of Jacob ... said." Therefore the Old Law should have been given after David, just as it was given after Abraham.

*On the contrary,* The Apostle says (Gal. 3:19) that the Law "was set because of transgressions, until the seed should come, to whom He made the promise, being ordained by angels in the hand of a Mediator": ordained, i.e. "given in orderly fashion," as the gloss explains. Therefore it was fitting that the Old Law should be given in this order of time.

*I answer that,* It was most fitting for the Law to be given at the time of Moses. The reason for this may be taken from two things in respect of which every law is imposed on two kinds of men. Because it is imposed on some men who are hard-hearted and proud, whom the law restrains and tames: and it is imposed on good men, who, through being instructed by the law, are helped to fulfil what they desire to do. Hence it was fitting that the Law should be given at such a time as would be appropriate for the overcoming of man's pride. For man was proud of two things, viz. of knowledge and of power. He was proud of his knowledge, as though his natural reason could suffice him for salvation: and accordingly, in order that his pride might be overcome in this matter, man was left to the guidance of his reason without the help of a written law: and man was able to learn from experience that his reason was deficient, since about the time of Abraham man had fallen headlong into idolatry and the most shameful vices. Wherefore, after those times, it was necessary for a written law to be given as a remedy for human ignorance: because "by the Law is the knowledge of sin" (Rom. 3:20). But, after man had been instructed by the Law, his pride was convinced of his weakness, through his being unable to fulfil what he knew. Hence, as the Apostle concludes (Rom. 8:3, 4), "what the Law could not do in that it was weak through the flesh, God sent [Vulg.: 'sending'] His own Son ... that the justification of the Law might be fulfilled in us."

With regard to good men, the Law was given to them as a help; which was most needed by the people, at the time when the natural law began to be obscured on account of the exuberance of sin: for it was fitting that this help should be bestowed on men in an orderly manner, so that they might be led from imperfection to perfection; wherefore it was becoming that the Old Law should be given between the law of nature and the law of grace.

Reply Obj. 1: It was not fitting for the Old Law to be given at once after the sin of the first man: both because man was so confident in his own reason, that he did not acknowledge his need of the Old Law; because as yet the dictate of the natural law was not darkened by habitual sinning.

Reply Obj. 2: A law should not be given save to the people, since it is a general precept, as stated above (Q. 90, AA. 2, 3); wherefore at the time of Abraham God gave men certain familiar, and, as it were, household precepts: but when Abraham's descendants had multiplied, so as to form a people, and when they had been freed from slavery, it was fitting that they should be given a law; for "slaves are not that part of the people or state to which it is fitting for the law to be directed," as the Philosopher says (Polit. iii, 2, 4, 5).

Reply Obj. 3: Since the Law had to be given to the people, not only those, of whom Christ was born, received the Law, but the whole people, who were marked with the seal of circumcision, which was the sign of the promise made to Abraham, and in which he believed, according to Rom. 4:11: hence even before David, the Law had to be given to that people as soon as they were collected together.

## QUESTION 99

OF THE PRECEPTS OF THE OLD LAW (In Six Articles)

We must now consider the precepts of the Old Law; and (1) how they are distinguished from one another; (2) each kind of precept. Under the first head there are six points of inquiry:

(1) Whether the Old Law contains several precepts or only one?

(2) Whether the Old Law contains any moral precepts?

(3) Whether it contains ceremonial precepts in addition to the moral precepts?

(4) Whether besides these it contains judicial precepts?

(5) Whether it contains any others besides these?

(6) How the Old Law induced men to keep its precepts.

FIRST ARTICLE [I-II, Q. 99, Art. 1]

Whether the Old Law Contains Only One Precept?

Objection 1: It would seem that the Old Law contains but one precept. Because a law is nothing else than a precept, as stated above (Q. 90, AA. 2, 3). Now there is but one Old Law. Therefore it contains but one precept.

Obj. 2: Further, the Apostle says (Rom. 13:9): "If there be any other commandment, it is comprised in this word: Thou shalt love thy neighbor as thyself." But this is only one commandment. Therefore the Old Law contained but one commandment.

Obj. 3: Further, it is written (Matt. 7:12): "All things ... whatsoever you would that men should do to you, do you also to them. For this is the Law and the prophets." But the whole of the Old Law is comprised in the Law and the prophets. Therefore the whole of the Old Law contains but one commandment.

*On the contrary,* The Apostle says (Eph. 2:15): "Making void the Law of commandments contained in decrees": where he is referring to the Old Law, as the gloss comments, on the passage. Therefore the Old Law comprises many commandments.

*I answer that,* Since a precept of law is binding, it is about something which must be done: and, that a thing must be done, arises from the necessity of some end. Hence it is evident that a precept implies, in its very idea, relation to an end, in so far as a thing is commanded as being necessary or expedient to an end. Now many things may happen to be necessary or expedient to an end; and, accordingly, precepts may be given about various things as being ordained to one end. Consequently we must say that all the precepts of the Old Law are one in respect of their relation to one end: and yet they are many in respect of the diversity of those things that are ordained to that end.

Reply Obj. 1: The Old Law is said to be one as being ordained to one end: yet it comprises various precepts, according to the diversity of the things which it directs to the end. Thus also the art of building is one according to the unity of its end, because it aims at the building of a house: and yet it contains various rules, according to the variety of acts ordained thereto.

Reply Obj. 2: As the Apostle says (1 Tim. 1:5), "the end of the commandment is charity"; since every law aims at establishing friendship, either between man and man, or between man and God. Wherefore the whole Law is comprised in this one commandment, "Thou shalt love thy neighbor as thyself," as expressing the end of all commandments: because love of one's neighbor includes love of God, when we love our neighbor for God's sake. Hence the Apostle put this commandment in place of the two which are about the love of God and of one's neighbor, and of which Our Lord said (Matt. 22:40): "On these two commandments dependeth the whole Law and the prophets."

Reply Obj. 3: As stated in *Ethic.* ix, 8, "friendship towards another arises from friendship towards oneself," in so far as man looks on another as on himself. Hence when it is said, "All things whatsoever you would that men should do to you, do you also to them," this is an explanation of the rule of neighborly love contained implicitly in the words, "Thou shalt love thy neighbor as thyself": so that it is an explanation of this commandment.

SECOND ARTICLE [I-II, Q. 99, Art. 2]

Whether the Old Law Contains Moral Precepts?

Objection 1: It would seem that the Old Law contains no moral precepts. For the Old Law is distinct from the law of nature, as stated above (Q. 91, AA. 4, 5; Q. 98, A. 5). But the moral precepts belong to the law of nature. Therefore they do not belong to the Old Law.

Obj. 2: Further, the Divine Law should have come to man's assistance where human reason fails him: as is evident in regard to things that are of faith, which are above reason. But man's reason seems to suffice for the moral precepts. Therefore the moral precepts do not belong to the Old Law, which is a Divine law.

Obj. 3: Further, the Old Law is said to be "the letter that killeth" (2 Cor. 3:6). But the moral precepts do not kill, but quicken, according to Ps. 118:93: "Thy justifications I will never forget, for by them Thou hast given me life." Therefore the moral precepts do not belong to the Old Law.

*On the contrary,* It is written (Ecclus. 17:9): "Moreover, He gave them discipline [Douay: 'instructions'] and the law of life for an inheritance." Now discipline belongs to morals; for this gloss on Heb. 12:11: "Now all chastisement ( disciplina )," etc., says: "Discipline is an exercise in morals by means of difficulties." Therefore the Law which was given by God comprised moral precepts.

*I answer that,* The Old Law contained some moral precepts; as is evident from Ex. 20:13, 15: "Thou shalt not kill," "Thou shalt not steal." This was reasonable: because, just as the principal intention of human law is to create friendship between man and man; so the chief intention of the Divine law is to establish man in friendship with God. Now since likeness is the reason of love, according to Ecclus. 13:19: "Every beast loveth its like"; there cannot possibly be any friendship of man to God, Who is supremely good, unless man become good: wherefore it is written (Lev. 19:2; 11:45): "You shall be holy, for I am holy." But the goodness of man is virtue, which "makes its possessor good" (Ethic. ii, 6). Therefore it was necessary for the Old Law to include precepts about acts of virtue: and these are the moral precepts of the Law.

Reply Obj. 1: The Old Law is distinct from the natural law, not as being altogether different from it, but as something added thereto. For just as grace presupposes nature, so must the Divine law presuppose the natural law.

Reply Obj. 2: It was fitting that the Divine law should come to man's assistance not only in those things for which reason is insufficient, but also in those things in which human reason may happen to be impeded. Now human reason could not go astray in the abstract, as to the universal principles of the natural law; but through being habituated to sin, it became obscured in the point of things to be done in detail. But with regard to the other moral precepts, which are like conclusions drawn from the universal principles of the natural law, the reason of many men went astray, to the extend of judging to be lawful, things that are evil in themselves. Hence there was need for the authority of the Divine law to rescue man from both these defects. Thus among the articles of faith not only are those things set forth to which reason cannot reach, such as the Trinity of the Godhead; but also those to which right reason can attain, such as the Unity of the Godhead; in order to remove the manifold errors to which reason is liable.

Reply Obj. 3: As Augustine proves (De Spiritu et Litera xiv), even the letter of the law is said to be the occasion of death, as to the moral precepts; in so far as, to wit, it prescribes what is good, without furnishing the aid of grace for its fulfilment.

THIRD ARTICLE [I-II, Q. 99, Art. 3]

Whether the Old Law Comprises Ceremonial, Besides Moral, Precepts?

Objection 1: It would seem that the Old Law does not comprise ceremonial, besides moral, precepts. For every law that is given to man is for the purpose of directing human actions. Now human actions are called moral, as stated above (Q. 1, A. 3). Therefore it seems that the Old Law given to men should not comprise other than moral precepts.

Obj. 2: Further, those precepts that are styled ceremonial seem to refer to the Divine worship. But Divine worship is the act of a virtue, viz. religion, which, as Tully says (De Invent. ii) "offers worship and ceremony to the Godhead." Since, then, the moral precepts are about acts of virtue, as stated above (A. 2), it seems that the ceremonial precepts should not be distinct from the moral.

Obj. 3: Further, the ceremonial precepts seem to be those which signify something figuratively. But, as Augustine observes (De Doctr. Christ. ii, 3, 4), "of all signs employed by men words hold the first place." Therefore there is no need for the Law to contain ceremonial precepts about certain figurative actions.

*On the contrary,* It is written (Deut. 4:13, 14): "Ten words ... He wrote in two tables of stone; and He commanded me at that time that I should teach you the ceremonies and judgments which you shall do." But the ten commandments of the Law are moral precepts. Therefore besides the moral precepts there are others which are ceremonial.

*I answer that,* As stated above (A. 2), the Divine law is instituted chiefly in order to direct men to God; while human law is instituted chiefly in order to direct men in relation to one another. Hence human laws have not concerned themselves with the institution of anything relating to Divine worship except as affecting the common good of mankind: and for this reason they have devised many institutions relating to Divine matters, according as it seemed expedient for the formation of human morals; as may be seen in the rites of the Gentiles. On the other hand the Divine law directed men to one another according to the demands of that order whereby man is directed to God, which order was the chief aim of that law. Now man is directed to God not only by the interior acts of the mind, which are faith, hope, and love, but also by certain external works, whereby man makes profession of his subjection to God: and it is these works that are said to belong to the Divine worship. This worship is called "ceremony,"—the *munia,* i.e. gifts, of Ceres (who was the goddess of fruits), as some say: because, at first, offerings were made to God from the fruits: or because, as Valerius Maximus states [*Fact. et Dict. Memor. i, 1], the word "ceremony" was introduced among the Latins, to signify the Divine worship, being derived from a town near Rome called "Caere": since, when Rome was taken by the Gauls, the sacred chattels of the Romans were taken thither and most carefully preserved. Accordingly those precepts of the Law which refer to the Divine worship are specially called ceremonial.

Reply Obj. 1: Human acts extend also to the Divine worship: and therefore the Old Law given to man contains precepts about these matters also.

Reply Obj. 2: As stated above (Q. 91, A. 3), the precepts of the natural law are general, and require to be determined: and they are determined both by human law and by Divine law. And just as these very determinations which are made by human law are said to be, not of natural, but of positive law; so the determinations of the precepts of the natural law, effected by the Divine law, are distinct from the moral precepts which belong to the natural law. Wherefore to worship God, since it is an act of virtue, belongs to a moral precept; but the determination of this precept, namely that He is to be worshipped by such and such sacrifices, and such and such offerings, belongs to the ceremonial precepts. Consequently the ceremonial precepts are distinct from the moral precepts.

Reply Obj. 3: As Dionysius says (Coel. Hier. i), the things of God cannot be manifested to men except by means of sensible similitudes. Now these similitudes move the soul more when they are not only expressed in words, but also offered to the senses. Wherefore the things of God are set forth in the Scriptures not only by similitudes expressed in words, as in the case of metaphorical expressions; but also by similitudes of things set before the eyes, which pertains to the ceremonial precepts.

FOURTH ARTICLE [I-II, Q. 99, Art. 4]

Whether, Besides the Moral and Ceremonial Precepts, There Are Also Judicial Precepts?

Objection 1: It would seem that there are no judicial precepts in addition to the moral and ceremonial precepts in the Old Law. For Augustine says (Contra Faust. vi, 2) that in the Old Law there are "precepts concerning the life we have to lead, and precepts regarding the life that is foreshadowed." Now the precepts of the life we have to lead are moral precepts; and the precepts of the life that is foreshadowed are ceremonial. Therefore besides these two kinds of precepts we should not put any judicial precepts in the Law.

Obj. 2: Further, a gloss on Ps. 118:102, "I have not declined from Thy judgments," says, i.e. "from the rule of life Thou hast set for me." But a rule of life belongs to the moral precepts. Therefore the judicial precepts should not be considered as distinct from the moral precepts.

Obj. 3: Further, judgment seems to be an act of justice, according to Ps. 93:15: "Until justice be turned into judgment." But acts of justice, like the acts of other virtues, belong to the moral precepts. Therefore the moral precepts include the judicial precepts, and consequently should not be held as distinct from them.

*On the contrary,* It is written (Deut. 6:1): "These are the precepts and ceremonies, and judgments": where "precepts" stands for "moral precepts" antonomastically. Therefore there are judicial precepts besides moral and ceremonial precepts.

*I answer that,* As stated above (AA. 2, 3), it belongs to the Divine law to direct men to one another and to God. Now each of these belongs in the abstract to the dictates of the natural law, to which dictates the moral precepts are to be referred: yet each of them has to be determined by Divine or human law, because naturally known principles are universal, both in speculative and in practical matters. Accordingly just as the determination of the universal principle about Divine worship is effected by the ceremonial precepts, so the determination of the general precepts of that justice which is to be observed among men is effected by the judicial precepts.

We must therefore distinguish three kinds of precept in the Old Law; viz. *moral* precepts, which are dictated by the natural law; *ceremonial* precepts, which are determinations of the Divine worship; and *judicial* precepts, which are determinations of the justice to be maintained among men. Wherefore the Apostle (Rom. 7:12) after saying that the "Law is holy," adds that "the commandment is just, and holy, and good": "just," in respect of the judicial precepts; "holy," with regard to the ceremonial precepts (since the word "sanctus"—"holy"—is applied to that which is consecrated to God); and "good," i.e. conducive to virtue, as to the moral precepts.

Reply Obj. 1: Both the moral and the judicial precepts aim at the ordering of human life: and consequently they are both comprised under one of the heads mentioned by Augustine, viz. under the precepts of the life we have to lead.

Reply Obj. 2: Judgment denotes execution of justice, by an application of the reason to individual cases in a determinate way. Hence the judicial precepts have something in common with the moral precepts, in that they are derived from reason; and something in common with the ceremonial precepts, in that they are determinations of general precepts. This explains why sometimes "judgments" comprise both judicial and moral precepts, as in Deut. 5:1: "Hear, O Israel, the ceremonies and judgments"; and sometimes judicial and ceremonial precepts, as in Lev. 18:4: "You shall do My judgments, and shall observe My precepts," where "precepts" denotes moral precepts, while "judgments" refers to judicial and ceremonial precepts.

Reply Obj. 3: The act of justice, in general, belongs to the moral precepts; but its determination to some special kind of act belongs to the judicial precepts.

FIFTH ARTICLE [I-II, Q. 99, Art. 5]

Whether the Old Law Contains Any Others Besides the Moral, Judicial, and Ceremonial Precepts?

Objection 1: It would seem that the Old Law contains others besides the moral, judicial, and ceremonial precepts. Because the judicial precepts belong to the act of justice, which is between man and man; while the ceremonial precepts belong to the act of religion, whereby God is worshipped. Now besides these there are many other virtues, viz. temperance, fortitude, liberality, and several others, as stated above (Q. 60, A. 5). Therefore besides the aforesaid precepts, the Old Law should comprise others.

Obj. 2: Further, it is written (Deut. 11:1): "Love the Lord thy God, and observe His precepts and ceremonies, His judgments and commandments." Now precepts concern moral matters, as stated above (A. 4). Therefore besides the moral, judicial and ceremonial precepts, the Law contains others which are called "commandments." [*The "commandments" (mandata) spoken of here and in the body of this article are not to be confused with the Commandments (praecepta) in the ordinary acceptance of the word.]

Obj. 3: Further, it is written (Deut. 6:17): "Keep the precepts of the Lord thy God, and the testimonies and ceremonies which I have [Vulg.: 'He hath'] commanded thee." Therefore in addition to the above, the Law comprises "testimonies."

Obj. 4: Further, it is written (Ps. 118:93): "Thy justifications (i.e. "Thy Law," according to a gloss) I will never forget." Therefore in the Old Law there are not only moral, ceremonial and judicial precepts, but also others, called "justifications."

*On the contrary,* It is written (Deut. 6:1): "These are the precepts and ceremonies and judgments which the Lord your God commanded ... you." And these words are placed at the beginning of the Law. Therefore all the precepts of the Law are included under them.

*I answer that,* Some things are included in the Law by way of precept; other things, as being ordained to the fulfilment of the precepts. Now the precepts refer to things which have to be done: and to their fulfilment man is induced by two considerations, viz. the authority of the lawgiver, and the benefit derived from the fulfilment, which benefit consists in the attainment of some good, useful, pleasurable or virtuous, or in the avoidance of some contrary evil. Hence it was necessary that in the Old Law certain things should be set forth to indicate the authority of God the lawgiver: e.g. Deut. 6:4: "Hear, O Israel, the Lord our God is one Lord"; and Gen. 1:1: "In the beginning God created heaven and earth": and these are called "testimonies." Again it was necessary that in the Law certain rewards should be appointed for those who observe the Law, and punishments for those who transgress; as it may be seen in Deut. 28: "If thou wilt hear the voice of the Lord thy God ... He will make thee higher than all the nations," etc.: and these are called "justifications," according as God punishes or rewards certain ones justly.

The things that have to be done do not come under the precept except in so far as they have the character of a duty. Now a duty is twofold: one according to the rule of reason; the other according to the rule of a law which prescribes that duty: thus the Philosopher distinguishes a twofold just—moral and legal (Ethic. v, 7).

Moral duty is twofold: because reason dictates that something must be done, either as being so necessary that without it the order of virtue would be destroyed; or as being useful for the better maintaining of the order of virtue. And in this sense some of the moral precepts are expressed by way of absolute command or prohibition, as "Thou shalt not kill," "Thou shalt not steal": and these are properly called "precepts." Other things are prescribed or forbidden, not as an absolute duty, but as something better to be done. These may be called "commandments"; because they are expressed by way of inducement and persuasion: an example whereof is seen in Ex. 22:26: "If thou take of thy neighbor a garment in pledge, thou shalt give it him again before sunset"; and in other like cases. Wherefore Jerome (Praefat. in Comment. super Marc.) says that "justice is in the precepts, charity in the commandments." Duty as fixed by the Law, belongs to the judicial precepts, as regards human affairs; to the ceremonial precepts, as regards Divine matters.

Nevertheless those ordinances also which refer to punishments and rewards may be called "testimonies," in so far as they testify to the Divine justice. Again all the precepts of the Law may be styled "justifications," as being executions of legal justice. Furthermore the commandments may be distinguished from the precepts, so that those things be called "precepts" which God Himself prescribed; and those things "commandments" which He enjoined ( *mandavit* ) through others, as the very word seems to denote.

From this it is clear that all the precepts of the Law are either moral, ceremonial, or judicial; and that other ordinances have not the character of a precept, but are directed to the observance of the precepts, as stated above.

Reply Obj. 1: Justice alone, of all the virtues, implies the notion of duty. Consequently moral matters are determinable by law in so far as they belong to justice: of which virtue religion is a part, as Tully says (De Invent. ii). Wherefore the legal just cannot be anything foreign to the ceremonial and judicial precepts.

The Replies to the other Objections are clear from what has been said.

SIXTH ARTICLE [I-II, Q. 99, Art. 6]

Whether the Old Law Should Have Induced Men to the Observance of Its Precepts, by Means of Temporal Promises and Threats?

Objection 1: It would seem that the Old Law should not have induced men to the observance of its precepts, by means of temporal promises and threats. For the purpose of the Divine law is to subject man to God by fear and love: hence it is written (Deut. 10:12): "And now, Israel, what doth the Lord thy God require of thee, but that thou fear the Lord thy God, and walk in His ways, and love Him?" But the desire for temporal goods leads man away from God: for Augustine says (Qq. lxxxiii, qu. 36), that "covetousness is the bane of charity." Therefore temporal promises and threats seem to be contrary to the intention of a lawgiver: and this makes a law worthy of rejection, as the Philosopher declares (Polit. ii, 6).

Obj. 2: Further, the Divine law is more excellent than human law. Now, in sciences, we notice that the loftier the science, the higher the means of persuasion that it employs. Therefore, since human law employs temporal threats and promises, as means of persuading man, the Divine law should have used, not these, but more lofty means.

Obj. 3: Further, the reward of righteousness and the punishment of guilt cannot be that which befalls equally the good and the wicked. But as stated in Eccles. 9:2, "all" temporal "things equally happen to the just and to the wicked, to the good and the evil, to the clean and to the unclean, to him that offereth victims, and to him that despiseth sacrifices." Therefore temporal goods or evils are not suitably set forth as punishments or rewards of the commandments of the Divine law.

*On the contrary,* It is written (Isa. 1:19, 20): "If you be willing, and will hearken to Me, you shall eat the good things of the land. But if you will not, and will provoke Me to wrath: the sword shall devour you."

*I answer that,* As in speculative sciences men are persuaded to assent to the conclusions by means of syllogistic arguments, so too in every law, men are persuaded to observe its precepts by means of punishments and rewards. Now it is to be observed that, in speculative sciences, the means of persuasion are adapted to the conditions of the pupil: wherefore the process of argument in sciences should be ordered becomingly, so that the instruction is based on principles more generally known. And thus also he who would persuade a man to the observance of any precepts, needs to move him at first by things for which he has an affection; just as children are induced to do something, by means of little childish gifts. Now it has been said above (Q. 98, AA. 1, 2, 3) that the Old Law disposed men to (the coming of) Christ, as the imperfect in comparison disposes to the perfect, wherefore it was given to a people as yet imperfect in comparison to the perfection which was to result from Christ's coming: and for this reason, that people is compared to a child that is still under a pedagogue (Gal. 3:24). But the perfection of man consists in his despising temporal things and cleaving to things spiritual, as is clear from the words of the Apostle (Phil. 3:13, 15): "Forgetting the things that are behind, I stretch [Vulg.: 'and stretching'] forth myself to those that are before ... Let us therefore, as many as are perfect, be thus minded." Those who are yet imperfect desire temporal goods, albeit in subordination to God: whereas the perverse place their end in temporalities. It was therefore fitting that the Old Law should conduct men to God by means of temporal goods for which the imperfect have an affection.

Reply Obj. 1: Covetousness whereby man places his end in temporalities, is the bane of charity. But the attainment of temporal goods which man desires in subordination to God is a road leading the imperfect to the love of God, according to Ps. 48:19: "He will praise Thee, when Thou shalt do well to him."

Reply Obj. 2: Human law persuades men by means of temporal rewards or punishments to be inflicted by men: whereas the Divine law persuades men by means of rewards or punishments to be received from God. In this respect it employs higher means.

Reply Obj. 3: As any one can see, who reads carefully the story of the Old Testament, the common weal of the people prospered under the Law as long as they obeyed it; and as soon as they departed from the precepts of the Law they were overtaken by many calamities. But certain individuals, although they observed the justice of the Law, met with misfortunes—either because they had already become spiritual (so that misfortune might withdraw them all the more from attachment to temporal things, and that their virtue might be tried)—or because, while outwardly fulfilling the works of the Law, their heart was altogether fixed on temporal goods, and far removed from God, according to Isa. 29:13 (Matt. 15:8): "This people honoreth Me with their lips; but their hearts is far from Me."

# QUESTION 100

OF THE MORAL PRECEPTS OF THE OLD LAW (In Twelve Articles)

We must now consider each kind of precept of the Old Law: and (1) the moral precepts, (2) the ceremonial precepts, (3) the judicial precepts. Under the first head there are twelve points of inquiry:

(1) Whether all the moral precepts of the Old Law belong to the law of nature?

(2) Whether the moral precepts of the Old Law are about the acts of all the virtues?

(3) Whether all the moral precepts of the Old Law are reducible to the ten precepts of the decalogue?

(4) How the precepts of the decalogue are distinguished from one another?

(5) Their number;

(6) Their order;

(7) The manner in which they were given;

(8) Whether they are dispensable?

(9) Whether the mode of observing a virtue comes under the precept of the Law?

(10) Whether the mode of charity comes under the precept?

(11) The distinction of other moral precepts;

(12) Whether the moral precepts of the Old Law justified man?

FIRST ARTICLE [I-II, Q. 100, Art. 1]

Whether All the Moral Precepts of the Old Law Belong to the Law of Nature?

Objection 1: It would seem that not all the moral precepts belong to the law of nature. For it is written (Ecclus. 17:9): "Moreover He gave them instructions, and the law of life for an inheritance." But instruction is in contradistinction to the law of nature; since the law of nature is not learnt, but instilled by natural instinct. Therefore not all the moral precepts belong to the natural law.

Obj. 2: Further, the Divine law is more perfect than human law. But human law adds certain things concerning good morals, to those that belong to the law of nature: as is evidenced by the fact that the natural law is the same in all men, while these moral institutions are various for various people. Much more reason therefore was there why the Divine law should add to the law of nature, ordinances pertaining to good morals.

Obj. 3: Further, just as natural reason leads to good morals in certain matters, so does faith: hence it is written (Gal. 5:6) that faith "worketh by charity." But faith is not included in the law of nature; since that which is of faith is above nature. Therefore not all the moral precepts of the Divine law belong to the law of nature.

*On the contrary,* The Apostle says (Rom. 2:14) that "the Gentiles, who have not the Law, do by nature those things that are of the Law": which must be understood of things pertaining to good morals. Therefore all the moral precepts of the Law belong to the law of nature.

*I answer that,* The moral precepts, distinct from the ceremonial and judicial precepts, are about things pertaining of their very nature to good morals. Now since human morals depend on their relation to reason, which is the proper principle of human acts, those morals are called good which accord with reason, and those are called bad which are discordant from reason. And as every judgment of speculative reason proceeds from the natural knowledge of first principles, so every judgment of practical reason proceeds from principles known naturally, as stated above (Q. 94, AA. 2, 4): from which principles one may proceed in various ways to judge of various matters. For some matters connected with human actions are so evident, that after very little consideration one is able at once to approve or disapprove of them by means of these general first principles: while some matters cannot be the subject of judgment without much consideration of the various circumstances, which all are not competent to do carefully, but only those who are wise: just as it is not possible for all to consider the particular conclusions of sciences, but only for those who are versed in philosophy: and lastly there are some matters of which man cannot judge unless he be helped by Divine instruction; such as the articles of faith.

It is therefore evident that since the moral precepts are about matters which concern good morals; and since good morals are those which are in accord with reason; and since also every judgment of human reason must needs by derived in some way from natural reason; it follows, of necessity, that all the moral precepts belong to the law of nature; but not all in the same way. For there are certain things which the natural reason of every man, of its own accord and at once, judges to be done or not to be done: e.g. "Honor thy father and thy mother," and "Thou shalt not kill," "Thou shalt not steal": and these belong to the law of nature absolutely. And there are certain things which, after a more careful consideration, wise men deem obligatory. Such belong to the law of nature, yet so that they need to be inculcated, the wiser teaching the less wise: e.g. "Rise up before the hoary head, and honor the person of the aged man," and the like. And there are some things, to judge of which, human reason needs Divine instruction, whereby we are taught about the things of God: e.g. "Thou shalt not make to thyself a graven thing, nor the likeness of anything"; "Thou shalt not take the name of the Lord thy God in vain."

This suffices for the Replies to the Objections.

SECOND ARTICLE [I-II, Q. 100, Art. 2]

Whether the Moral Precepts of the Law Are About All the Acts of Virtue?

Objection 1: It would seem that the moral precepts of the Law are not about all the acts of virtue. For observance of the precepts of the Old Law is called justification, according to Ps. 118:8: "I will keep Thy justifications." But justification is the execution of justice. Therefore the moral precepts are only about acts of justice.

Obj. 2: Further, that which comes under a precept has the character of a duty. But the character of duty belongs to justice alone and to none of the other virtues, for the proper act of justice consists in rendering to each one his due. Therefore the precepts of the moral law are not about the acts of the other virtues, but only about the acts of justice.

Obj. 3: Further, every law is made for the common good, as Isidore says (Etym. v, 21). But of all the virtues justice alone regards the common good, as the Philosopher says (Ethic. v, 1). Therefore the moral precepts are only about the acts of justice.

*On the contrary,* Ambrose says (De Paradiso viii) that "a sin is a transgression of the Divine law, and a disobedience to the commandments of heaven." But there are sins contrary to all the acts of virtue. Therefore it belongs to Divine law to direct all the acts of virtue.

*I answer that,* Since the precepts of the Law are ordained to the common good, as stated above (Q. 90, A. 2), the precepts of the Law must needs be diversified according to the various kinds of community: hence the Philosopher (Polit. iv, 1) teaches that the laws which are made in a state which is ruled by a king must be different from the laws of a state which is ruled by the people, or by a few powerful men in the state. Now human law is ordained for one kind of community, and the Divine law for another kind. Because human law is ordained for the civil community, implying mutual duties of man and his fellows: and men are ordained to one another by outward acts, whereby men live in communion with one another. This life in common of man with man pertains to justice, whose proper function consists in directing the human community. Wherefore human law makes precepts only about acts of justice; and if it commands acts of other virtues, this is only in so far as they assume the nature of justice, as the Philosopher explains (Ethic. v, 1).

But the community for which the Divine law is ordained, is that of men in relation to God, either in this life or in the life to come. And therefore the Divine law proposes precepts about all those matters whereby men are well ordered in their relations to God. Now man is united to God by his reason or mind, in which is God's image. Wherefore the Divine law proposes precepts about all those matters whereby human reason is well ordered. But this is effected by the acts of all the virtues: since the intellectual virtues set in good order the acts of the reason in themselves: while the moral virtues set in good order the acts of the reason in reference to the interior passions and exterior actions. It is therefore evident that the Divine law fittingly proposes precepts about the acts of all the virtues: yet so that certain matters, without which the order of virtue, which is the order of reason, cannot even exist, come under an obligation of precept; while other matters, which pertain to the well-being of perfect virtue, come under an admonition of counsel.

Reply Obj. 1: The fulfilment of the commandments of the Law, even of those which are about the acts of the other virtues, has the character of justification, inasmuch as it is just that man should obey God: or again, inasmuch as it is just that all that belongs to man should be subject to reason.

Reply Obj. 2: Justice properly so called regards the duty of one man to another: but all the other virtues regard the duty of the lower powers to reason. It is in relation to this latter duty that the Philosopher speaks (Ethic. v, 11) of a kind of metaphorical justice.

The Reply to the Third Objection is clear from what has been said about the different kinds of community.

THIRD ARTICLE [I-II, Q. 100, Art. 3]

Whether All the Moral Precepts of the Old Law Are Reducible to the Ten Precepts of the Decalogue?

Objection 1: It would seem that not all the moral precepts of the Old Law are reducible to the ten precepts of the decalogue. For the first and principal precepts of the Law are, "Thou shalt love the Lord thy God," and "Thou shalt love thy neighbor," as stated in Matt. 22:37, 39. But these two are not contained in the precepts of the decalogue. Therefore not all the moral precepts are contained in the precepts of the decalogue.

Obj. 2: Further, the moral precepts are not reducible to the ceremonial precepts, but rather vice versa. But among the precepts of the decalogue, one is ceremonial, viz. "Remember that thou keep holy the Sabbath-day." Therefore the moral precepts are not reducible to all the precepts of the decalogue.

Obj. 3: Further, the moral precepts are about all the acts of virtue. But among the precepts of the decalogue are only such as regard acts of justice; as may be seen by going through them all. Therefore the precepts of the decalogue do not include all the moral precepts.

*On the contrary,* The gloss on Matt. 5:11: "Blessed are ye when they shall revile you," etc. says that "Moses, after propounding the ten precepts, set them out in detail." Therefore all the precepts of the Law are so many parts of the precepts of the decalogue.

*I answer that,* The precepts of the decalogue differ from the other precepts of the Law, in the fact that God Himself is said to have given the precepts of the decalogue; whereas He gave the other precepts to the people through Moses. Wherefore the decalogue includes those precepts the knowledge of which man has immediately from God. Such are those which with but slight reflection can be gathered at once from the first general principles: and those also which become known to man immediately through divinely infused faith. Consequently two kinds of precepts are not reckoned among the precepts of the decalogue: viz. first general principles, for they need no further promulgation after being once imprinted on the natural reason to which they are self-evident; as, for instance, that one should do evil to no man, and other similar principles: and again those which the careful reflection of wise men shows to be in accord with reason; since the people receive these principles from God, through being taught by wise men. Nevertheless both kinds of precepts are contained in the precepts of the decalogue; yet in different ways. For the first general principles are contained in them, as principles in their proximate conclusions; while those which are known through wise men are contained, conversely, as conclusions in their principles.

Reply Obj. 1: Those two principles are the first general principles of the natural law, and are self-evident to human reason, either through nature or through faith. Wherefore all the precepts of the decalogue are referred to these, as conclusions to general principles.

Reply Obj. 2: The precept of the Sabbath observance is moral in one respect, in so far as it commands man to give some time to the things of God, according to Ps. 45:11: "Be still and see that I am God." In this respect it is placed among the precepts of the decalogue: but not as to the fixing of the time, in which respect it is a ceremonial precept.

Reply Obj. 3: The notion of duty is not so patent in the other virtues as it is in justice. Hence the precepts about the acts of the other virtues are not so well known to the people as are the precepts about acts of justice. Wherefore the acts of justice especially come under the precepts of the decalogue, which are the primary elements of the Law.

FOURTH ARTICLE [I-II, Q. 100, Art. 4]

Whether the Precepts of the Decalogue Are Suitably Distinguished from One Another?

Objection 1: It would seem that the precepts of the decalogue are unsuitably distinguished from one another. For worship is a virtue distinct from faith. Now the precepts are about acts of virtue. But that which is said at the beginning of the decalogue, "Thou shalt not have strange gods before Me," belongs to faith: and that which is added, "Thou shalt not make ... any graven thing," etc. belongs to worship. Therefore these are not one precept, as Augustine asserts (Qq. in Exod. qu. lxxi), but two.

Obj. 2: Further, the affirmative precepts in the Law are distinct from the negative precepts; e.g. "Honor thy father and thy mother," and, "Thou shalt not kill." But this, "I am the Lord thy God," is affirmative: and that which follows, "Thou shalt not have strange gods before Me," is negative. Therefore these are two precepts, and do not, as Augustine says (Qq. in Exod. qu. lxxi), make one.

Obj. 3: Further, the Apostle says (Rom. 7:7): "I had not known concupiscence, if the Law did not say: 'Thou shalt not covet.'" Hence it seems that this precept, "Thou shalt not covet," is one precept; and, therefore, should not be divided into two.

*On the contrary,* stands the authority of Augustine who, in commenting on Exodus (Qq. in Exod. qu. lxxi) distinguishes three precepts as referring to God, and seven as referring to our neighbor.

*I answer that,* The precepts of the decalogue are differently divided by different authorities. For Hesychius commenting on Lev. 26:26, "Ten women shall bake your bread in one oven," says that the precept of the Sabbath-day observance is not one of the ten precepts, because its observance, in the letter, is not binding for all time. But he distinguishes four precepts pertaining to God, the first being, "I am the Lord thy God"; the second, "Thou shalt not have strange gods before Me," (thus also Jerome distinguishes these two precepts, in his commentary on Osee 10:10, "On thy" [Vulg.: "their"] "two iniquities"); the third precept according to him is, "Thou shalt not make to thyself any graven thing"; and the fourth, "Thou shalt not take the name of the Lord thy God in vain." He states that there are six precepts pertaining to our neighbor; the first, "Honor thy father and thy mother"; the second, "Thou shalt not kill"; the third, "Thou shalt not commit adultery"; the fourth, "Thou shalt not steal"; the fifth, "Thou shalt not bear false witness"; the sixth, "Thou shalt not covet."

But, in the first place, it seems unbecoming for the precept of the Sabbath-day observance to be put among the precepts of the decalogue, if it nowise belonged to the decalogue. Secondly, because, since it is written (Matt. 6:24), "No man can serve two masters," the two statements, "I am the Lord thy God," and, "Thou shalt not have strange gods before Me" seem to be of the same nature and to form one precept. Hence Origen (Hom. viii in Exod.) who also distinguishes four precepts as referring to God, unites these two under one precept; and reckons in the second place, "Thou shalt not make ... any graven thing"; as third, "Thou shalt not take the name of the Lord thy God in vain"; and as fourth, "Remember that thou keep holy the Sabbath-day." The other six he reckons in the same way as Hesychius.

Since, however, the making of graven things or the likeness of anything is not forbidden except as to the point of their being worshipped as gods—for God commanded an image of the Seraphim [Vulg.: Cherubim] to be made and placed in the tabernacle, as related in Ex. 25:18—Augustine more fittingly unites these two, "Thou shalt not have strange gods before Me," and, "Thou shalt not make ... any graven thing," into one precept. Likewise to covet another's wife, for the purpose of carnal knowledge, belongs to the concupiscence of the flesh; whereas, to covet other things, which are desired for the purpose of possession, belongs to the concupiscence of the eyes; wherefore Augustine reckons as distinct precepts, that which forbids the coveting of another's goods, and that which prohibits the coveting of another's wife. Thus he distinguishes three precepts as referring to God, and seven as referring to our neighbor. And this is better.

Reply Obj. 1: Worship is merely a declaration of faith: wherefore the precepts about worship should not be reckoned as distinct from those about faith. Nevertheless precepts should be given about worship rather than about faith, because the precept about faith is presupposed to the precepts of the decalogue, as is also the precept of charity. For just as the first general principles of the natural law are self-evident to a subject having natural reason, and need no promulgation; so also to believe in God is a first and self-evident principle to a subject possessed of faith: "for he that cometh to God, must believe that He is" (Heb. 11:6). Hence it needs no other promulgation that the infusion of faith.

Reply Obj. 2: The affirmative precepts are distinct from the negative, when one is not comprised in the other: thus that man should honor his parents does not include that he should not kill another man; nor does the latter include the former. But when an affirmative precept is included in a negative, or vice versa, we do not find that two distinct precepts are given: thus there is not one precept saying that "Thou shalt not steal," and another binding one to keep another's property intact, or to give it back to its owner. In the same way there are not different precepts about believing in God, and about not believing in strange gods.

Reply Obj. 3: All covetousness has one common ratio: and therefore the Apostle speaks of the commandment about covetousness as though it were one. But because there are various special kinds of covetousness, therefore Augustine distinguishes different prohibitions against coveting: for covetousness differs specifically in respect of the diversity of actions or things coveted, as the Philosopher says (Ethic. x, 5).

FIFTH ARTICLE [I-II, Q. 100, Art. 5]

Whether the Precepts of the Decalogue Are Suitably Set Forth?

Objection 1: It would seem that the precepts of the decalogue are unsuitably set forth. Because sin, as stated by Ambrose (De Paradiso viii), is "a transgression of the Divine law and a disobedience to the commandments of heaven." But sins are distinguished according as man sins against God, or his neighbor, or himself. Since, then, the decalogue does not include any precepts directing man in his relations to himself, but only such as direct him in his relations to God and himself, it seems that the precepts of the decalogue are insufficiently enumerated.

Obj. 2: Further, just as the Sabbath-day observance pertained to the worship of God, so also did the observance of other solemnities, and the offering of sacrifices. But the decalogue contains a precept about the Sabbath-day observance. Therefore it should contain others also, pertaining to the other solemnities, and to the sacrificial rite.

Obj. 3: Further, as sins against God include the sin of perjury, so also do they include blasphemy, or other ways of lying against the teaching of God. But there is a precept forbidding perjury, "Thou shalt not take the name of the Lord thy God in vain." Therefore there should be also a precept of the decalogue forbidding blasphemy and false doctrine.

Obj. 4: Further, just as man has a natural affection for his parents, so has he also for his children. Moreover the commandment of charity extends to all our neighbors. Now the precepts of the decalogue are ordained unto charity, according to 1 Tim. 1:5: "The end of the commandment is charity." Therefore as there is a precept referring to parents, so should there have been some precepts referring to children and other neighbors.

Obj. 5: Further, in every kind of sin, it is possible to sin in thought or in deed. But in some kinds of sin, namely in theft and adultery, the prohibition of sins of deed, when it is said, "Thou shalt not commit adultery, Thou shalt not steal," is distinct from the prohibition of the sin of thought, when it is said, "Thou shalt not covet thy neighbor's goods," and, "Thou shalt not covet thy neighbor's wife." Therefore the same should have been done in regard to the sins of homicide and false witness.

Obj. 6: Further, just as sin happens through disorder of the concupiscible faculty, so does it arise through disorder of the irascible part. But some precepts forbid inordinate concupiscence, when it is said, "Thou shalt not covet." Therefore the decalogue should have included some precepts forbidding the disorders of the irascible faculty. Therefore it seems that the ten precepts of the decalogue are unfittingly enumerated.

*On the contrary,* It is written (Deut. 4:13): "He shewed you His covenant, which He commanded you to do, and the ten words that He wrote in two tablets of stone."

*I answer that,* As stated above (A. 2), just as the precepts of human law direct man in his relations to the human community, so the precepts of the Divine law direct man in his relations to a community or commonwealth of men under God. Now in order that any man may dwell aright in a community, two things are required: the first is that he behave well to the head of the community; the other is that he behave well to those who are his fellows and partners in the community. It is therefore necessary that the Divine law should contain in the first place precepts ordering man in his relations to God; and in the second place, other precepts ordering man in his relations to other men who are his neighbors and live with him under God.

Now man owes three things to the head of the community: first, fidelity; secondly, reverence; thirdly, service. Fidelity to his master consists in his not giving sovereign honor to another: and this is the sense of the first commandment, in the words "Thou shalt not have strange gods." Reverence to his master requires that he should do nothing injurious to him: and this is conveyed by the second commandment, "Thou shalt not take the name of the Lord thy God in vain." Service is due to the master in return for the benefits which his subjects receive from him: and to this belongs the third commandment of the sanctification of the Sabbath in memory of the creation of all things.

To his neighbors a man behaves himself well both in particular and in general. In particular, as to those to whom he is indebted, by paying his debts: and in this sense is to be taken the commandment about honoring one's parents. In general, as to all men, by doing harm to none, either by deed, or by word, or by thought. By deed, harm is done to one's neighbor—sometimes in his person, i.e. as to his personal existence; and this is forbidden by the words, "Thou shalt not kill": sometimes in a person united to him, as to the propagation of offspring; and this is prohibited by the words, "Thou shalt not commit adultery": sometimes in his possessions, which are directed to both the aforesaid; and with this regard to this it is said, "Thou shalt not steal." Harm done by word is forbidden when it is said, "Thou shalt not bear false witness against thy neighbor": harm done by thought is forbidden in the words, "Thou shalt not covet."

The three precepts that direct man in his behavior towards God may also be differentiated in this same way. For the first refers to deeds; wherefore it is said, "Thou shalt not make ... a graven thing": the second, to words; wherefore it is said, "Thou shalt not take the name of the Lord thy God in vain": the third, to thoughts; because the sanctification of the Sabbath, as the subject of a moral precept, requires repose of the heart in God. Or, according to Augustine (In Ps. 32: Conc. 1), by the first commandment we reverence the unity of the First Principle; by the second, the Divine truth; by the third, His goodness whereby we are sanctified, and wherein we rest as in our last end.

Reply Obj. 1: This objection may be answered in two ways. First, because the precepts of the decalogue can be reduced to the precepts of charity. Now there was need for man to receive a precept about loving God and his neighbor, because in this respect the natural law had become obscured on account of sin: but not about the duty of loving oneself, because in this respect the natural law retained its vigor: or again, because love of oneself is contained in the love of God and of one's neighbor: since true self-love consists in directing oneself to God. And for this reason the decalogue includes those precepts only which refer to our neighbor and to God.

Secondly, it may be answered that the precepts of the decalogue are those which the people received from God immediately; wherefore it is written (Deut. 10:4): "He wrote in the tables, according as He had written before, the ten words, which the Lord spoke to you." Hence the precepts of the decalogue need to be such as the people can understand at once. Now a precept implies the notion of duty. But it is easy for a man, especially for a believer, to understand that, of necessity, he owes certain duties to God and to his neighbor. But that, in matters which regard himself and not another, man has, of necessity, certain duties to himself, is not so evident: for, at the first glance, it seems that everyone is free in matters that concern himself. And therefore the precepts which prohibit disorders of a man with regard to himself, reach the people through the instruction of men who are versed in such matters; and, consequently, they are not contained in the decalogue.

Reply Obj. 2: All the solemnities of the Old Law were instituted in celebration of some Divine favor, either in memory of past favors, or in sign of some favor to come: in like manner all the sacrifices were offered up with the same purpose. Now of all the Divine favors to be commemorated the chief was that of the Creation, which was called to mind by the sanctification of the Sabbath; wherefore the reason for this precept is given in Ex. 20:11: "In six days the Lord made heaven and earth," etc. And of all future blessings, the chief and final was the repose of the mind in God, either, in the present life, by grace, or, in the future life, by glory; which repose was also foreshadowed in the Sabbath-day observance: wherefore it is written (Isa. 58:13): "If thou turn away thy foot from the Sabbath, from doing thy own will in My holy day, and call the Sabbath delightful, and the holy of the Lord glorious." Because these favors first and chiefly are borne in mind by men, especially by the faithful. But other solemnities were celebrated on account of certain particular favors temporal and transitory, such as the celebration of the Passover in memory of the past favor of the delivery from Egypt, and as a sign of the future Passion of Christ, which though temporal and transitory, brought us to the repose of the spiritual Sabbath. Consequently, the Sabbath alone, and none of the other solemnities and sacrifices, is mentioned in the precepts of the decalogue.

Reply Obj. 3: As the Apostle says (Heb. 6:16), "men swear by one greater than themselves; and an oath for confirmation is the end of all their controversy." Hence, since oaths are common to all, inordinate swearing is the matter of a special prohibition by a precept of the decalogue. According to one interpretation, however, the words, "Thou shalt not take the name of the Lord thy God in vain," are a prohibition of false doctrine, for one gloss expounds them thus: "Thou shalt not say that Christ is a creature."

Reply Obj. 4: That a man should not do harm to anyone is an immediate dictate of his natural reason: and therefore the precepts that forbid the doing of harm are binding on all men. But it is not an immediate dictate of natural reason that a man should do one thing in return for another, unless he happen to be indebted to someone. Now a son's debt to his father is so evident that one cannot get away from it by denying it: since the father is the principle of generation and being, and also of upbringing and teaching. Wherefore the decalogue does not prescribe deeds of kindness or service to be done to anyone except to one's parents. On the other hand parents do not seem to be indebted to their children for any favors received, but rather the reverse is the case. Again, a child is a part of his father; and "parents love their children as being a part of themselves," as the Philosopher states (Ethic. viii, 12). Hence, just as the decalogue contains no ordinance as to man's behavior towards himself, so, for the same reason, it includes no precept about loving one's children.

Reply Obj. 5: The pleasure of adultery and the usefulness of wealth, in so far as they have the character of pleasurable or useful good, are of themselves, objects of appetite: and for this reason they needed to be forbidden not only in the deed but also in the desire. But murder and falsehood are, of themselves, objects of repulsion (since it is natural for man to love his neighbor and the truth): and are desired only for the sake of something else. Consequently with regard to sins of murder and false witness, it was necessary to proscribe, not sins of thought, but only sins of deed.

Reply Obj. 6: As stated above (Q. 25, A. 1), all the passions of the irascible faculty arise from the passions of the concupiscible part. Hence, as the precepts of the decalogue are, as it were, the first elements of the Law, there was no need for mention of the irascible passions, but only of the concupiscible passions.

SIXTH ARTICLE [I-II, Q. 100, Art. 6]

Whether the Ten Precepts of the Decalogue Are Set in Proper Order?

Objection 1: It would seem that the ten precepts of the decalogue are not set in proper order. Because love of one's neighbor is seemingly previous to love of God, since our neighbor is better known to us than God is; according to 1 John 4:20: "He that loveth not his brother, whom he seeth, how can he love God, Whom he seeth not?" But the first three precepts belong to the love of God, while the other seven pertain to the love of our neighbor. Therefore the precepts of the decalogue are not set in proper order.

Obj. 2: Further, the acts of virtue are prescribed by the affirmative precepts, and acts of vice are forbidden by the negative precepts. But according to Boethius in his commentary on the *Categories* [*Lib. iv, cap. De Oppos.], vices should be uprooted before virtues are sown. Therefore among the precepts concerning our neighbor, the negative precepts should have preceded the affirmative.

Obj. 3: Further, the precepts of the Law are about men's actions. But actions of thought precede actions of word or outward deed. Therefore the precepts about not coveting, which regard our thoughts, are unsuitably placed last in order.

*On the contrary,* The Apostle says (Rom. 13:1): "The things that are of God, are well ordered" [Vulg.: 'Those that are, are ordained of God']. But the precepts of the decalogue were given immediately by God, as stated above (A. 3). Therefore they are arranged in becoming order.

*I answer that,* As stated above (AA. 3, 5, ad 1), the precepts of the decalogue are such as the mind of man is ready to grasp at once. Now it is evident that a thing is so much the more easily grasped by the reason, as its contrary is more grievous and repugnant to reason. Moreover, it is clear, since the order of reason begins with the end, that, for a man to be inordinately disposed towards his end, is supremely contrary to reason. Now the end of human life and society is God. Consequently it was necessary for the precepts of the decalogue, first of all, to direct man to God; since the contrary to this is most grievous. Thus also, in an army, which is ordained to the commander as to its end, it is requisite first that the soldier should be subject to the commander, and the opposite of this is most grievous; and secondly it is requisite that he should be in coordination with the other soldiers.

Now among those things whereby we are ordained to God, the first is that man should be subjected to Him faithfully, by having nothing in common with His enemies. The second is that he should show Him reverence: the third that he should offer Him service. Thus, in an army, it is a greater sin for a soldier to act treacherously and make a compact with the foe, than to be insolent to his commander: and this last is more grievous than if he be found wanting in some point of service to him.

As to the precepts that direct man in his behavior towards his neighbor, it is evident that it is more repugnant to reason, and a more grievous sin, if man does not observe the due order as to those persons to whom he is most indebted. Consequently, among those precepts that direct man in his relations to his neighbor, the first place is given to that one which regards his parents. Among the other precepts we again find the order to be according to the gravity of sin. For it is more grave and more repugnant to reason, to sin by deed than by word; and by word than by thought. And among sins of deed, murder which destroys life in one already living is more grievous than adultery, which imperils the life of the unborn child; and adultery is more grave than theft, which regards external goods.

Reply Obj. 1: Although our neighbor is better known than God by the way of the senses, nevertheless the love of God is the reason for the love of our neighbor, as shall be declared later on (II-II, Q. 25, A. 1; Q. 26, A. 2). Hence the precepts ordaining man to God demanded precedence of the others.

Reply Obj. 2: Just as God is the universal principle of being in respect of all things, so is a father a principle of being in respect of his son. Therefore the precept regarding parents was fittingly placed after the precepts regarding God. This argument holds in respect of affirmative and negative precepts about the same kind of deed: although even then it is not altogether cogent. For although in the order of execution, vices should be uprooted before virtues are sown, according to Ps. 33:15: "Turn away from evil, and do good," and Isa. 1:16, 17: "Cease to do perversely; learn to do well"; yet, in the order of knowledge, virtue precedes vice, because "the crooked line is known by the straight" (De Anima i): and "by the law is the knowledge of sin" (Rom. 3:20). Wherefore the affirmative precept demanded the first place. However, this is not the reason for the order, but that which is given above. Because in the precepts regarding God, which belongs to the first table, an affirmative precept is placed last, since its transgression implies a less grievous sin.

Reply Obj. 3: Although sin of thought stands first in the order of execution, yet its prohibition holds a later position in the order of reason.

SEVENTH ARTICLE [I-II, Q. 100, Art. 7]

Whether the Precepts of the Decalogue Are Suitably Formulated?

Objection 1: It would seem that the precepts of the decalogue are unsuitably formulated. Because the affirmative precepts direct man to acts of virtue, while the negative precepts withdraw him from acts of vice. But in every matter there are virtues and vices opposed to one another. Therefore in whatever matter there is an ordinance of a precept of the decalogue, there should have been an affirmative and a negative precept. Therefore it was unfitting that affirmative precepts should be framed in some matters, and negative precepts in others.

Obj. 2: Further, Isidore says (Etym. ii, 10) that every law is based on reason. But all the precepts of the decalogue belong to the Divine law. Therefore the reason should have been pointed out in each precept, and not only in the first and third.

Obj. 3: Further, by observing the precepts man deserves to be rewarded by God. But the Divine promises concern the rewards of the precepts. Therefore the promise should have been included in each precept, and not only in the second and fourth.

Obj. 4: Further, the Old Law is called "the law of fear," in so far as it induced men to observe the precepts, by means of the threat of punishments. But all the precepts of the decalogue belong to the Old Law. Therefore a threat of punishment should have been included in each, and not only in the first and second.

Obj. 5: Further, all the commandments of God should be retained in the memory: for it is written (Prov. 3:3): "Write them in the tables of thy heart." Therefore it was not fitting that mention of the memory should be made in the third commandment only. Consequently it seems that the precepts of the decalogue are unsuitably formulated.

*On the contrary,* It is written (Wis. 11:21) that "God made all things, in measure, number and weight." Much more therefore did He observe a suitable manner in formulating His Law.

*I answer that,* The highest wisdom is contained in the precepts of the Divine law: wherefore it is written (Deut. 4:6): "This is your wisdom and understanding in the sight of nations." Now it belongs to wisdom to arrange all things in due manner and order. Therefore it must be evident that the precepts of the Law are suitably set forth.

Reply Obj. 1: Affirmation of one thing always leads to the denial of its opposite: but the denial of one opposite does not always lead to the affirmation of the other. For it follows that if a thing is white, it is not black: but it does not follow that if it is not black, it is white: because negation extends further than affirmation. And hence too, that one ought not to do harm to another, which pertains to the negative precepts, extends to more persons, as a primary dictate of reason, than that one ought to do someone a service or kindness. Nevertheless it is a primary dictate of reason that man is a debtor in the point of rendering a service or kindness to those from whom he has received kindness, if he has not yet repaid the debt. Now there are two whose favors no man can sufficiently repay, viz. God and man's father, as stated in *Ethic.* viii, 14. Therefore it is that there are only two affirmative precepts; one about the honor due to parents, the other about the celebration of the Sabbath in memory of the Divine favor.

Reply Obj. 2: The reasons for the purely moral precepts are manifest; hence there was no need to add the reason. But some of the precepts include ceremonial matter, or a determination of a general moral precept; thus the first precept includes the determination, "Thou shalt not make a graven thing"; and in the third precept the Sabbath-day is fixed. Consequently there was need to state the reason in each case.

Reply Obj. 3: Generally speaking, men direct their actions to some point of utility. Consequently in those precepts in which it seemed that there would be no useful result, or that some utility might be hindered, it was necessary to add a promise of reward. And since parents are already on the way to depart from us, no benefit is expected from them: wherefore a promise of reward is added to the precept about honoring one's parents. The same applies to the precept forbidding idolatry: since thereby it seemed that men were hindered from receiving the apparent benefit which they think they can get by entering into a compact with the demons.

Reply Obj. 4: Punishments are necessary against those who are prone to evil, as stated in *Ethic.* x, 9. Wherefore a threat of punishment is only affixed to those precepts of the law which forbade evils to which men were prone. Now men were prone to idolatry by reason of the general custom of the nations. Likewise men are prone to perjury on account of the frequent use of oaths. Hence it is that a threat is affixed to the first two precepts.

Reply Obj. 5: The commandment about the Sabbath was made in memory of a past blessing. Wherefore special mention of the memory is made therein. Or again, the commandment about the Sabbath has a determination affixed to it that does not belong to the natural law, wherefore this precept needed a special admonition.

EIGHTH ARTICLE [I-II, Q. 100, Art. 8]

Whether the Precepts of the Decalogue Are Dispensable?

Objection 1: It would seem that the precepts of the decalogue are dispensable. For the precepts of the decalogue belong to the natural law. But the natural law fails in some cases and is changeable, like human nature, as the Philosopher says (Ethic. v, 7). Now the failure of law to apply in certain particular cases is a reason for dispensation, as stated above (Q. 96, A. 6; Q. 97, A. 4). Therefore a dispensation can be granted in the precepts of the decalogue.

Obj. 2: Further, man stands in the same relation to human law as God does to Divine law. But man can dispense with the precepts of a law made by man. Therefore, since the precepts of the decalogue are ordained by God, it seems that God can dispense with them. Now our superiors are God's viceregents on earth; for the Apostle says (2 Cor. 2:10): "For what I have pardoned, if I have pardoned anything, for your sakes have I done it in the person of Christ." Therefore superiors can dispense with the precepts of the decalogue.

Obj. 3: Further, among the precepts of the decalogue is one forbidding murder. But it seems that a dispensation is given by men in this precept: for instance, when according to the prescription of human law, such as evil-doers or enemies are lawfully slain. Therefore the precepts of the decalogue are dispensable.

Obj. 4: Further, the observance of the Sabbath is ordained by a precept of the decalogue. But a dispensation was granted in this precept; for it is written (1 Macc. 2:4): "And they determined in that day, saying: Whosoever shall come up to fight against us on the Sabbath-day, we will fight against him." Therefore the precepts of the decalogue are dispensable.

*On the contrary,* are the words of Isa. 24:5, where some are reproved for that "they have changed the ordinance, they have broken the everlasting covenant"; which, seemingly, apply principally to the precepts of the decalogue. Therefore the precepts of the decalogue cannot be changed by dispensation.

*I answer that,* As stated above (Q. 96, A. 6; Q. 97, A. 4), precepts admit of dispensation, when there occurs a particular case in which, if the letter of the law be observed, the intention of the lawgiver is frustrated. Now the intention of every lawgiver is directed first and chiefly to the common good; secondly, to the order of justice and virtue, whereby the common good is preserved and attained. If therefore there be any precepts which contain the very preservation of the common good, or the very order of justice and virtue, such precepts contain the intention of the lawgiver, and therefore are indispensable. For instance, if in some community a law were enacted, such as this—that no man should work for the destruction of the commonwealth, or betray the state to its enemies, or that no man should do anything unjust or evil, such precepts would not admit of dispensation. But if other precepts were enacted, subordinate to the above, and determining certain special modes of procedure, these latter precepts would admit of dispensation, in so far as the omission of these precepts in certain cases would not be prejudicial to the former precepts which contain the intention of the lawgiver. For instance if, for the safeguarding of the commonwealth, it were enacted in some city that from each ward some men should keep watch as sentries in case of siege, some might be dispensed from this on account of some greater utility.

Now the precepts of the decalogue contain the very intention of the lawgiver, who is God. For the precepts of the first table, which direct us to God, contain the very order to the common and final good, which is God; while the precepts of the second table contain the order of justice to be observed among men, that nothing undue be done to anyone, and that each one be given his due; for it is in this sense that we are to take the precepts of the decalogue. Consequently the precepts of the decalogue admit of no dispensation whatever.

Reply Obj. 1: The Philosopher is not speaking of the natural law which contains the very order of justice: for it is a never-failing principle that "justice should be preserved." But he is speaking in reference to certain fixed modes of observing justice, which fail to apply in certain cases.

Reply Obj. 2: As the Apostle says (2 Tim. 2:13), "God continueth faithful, He cannot deny Himself." But He would deny Himself if He were to do away with the very order of His own justice, since He is justice itself. Wherefore God cannot dispense a man so that it be lawful for him not to direct himself to God, or not to be subject to His justice, even in those matters in which men are directed to one another.

Reply Obj. 3: The slaying of a man is forbidden in the decalogue, in so far as it bears the character of something undue: for in this sense the precept contains the very essence of justice. Human law cannot make it lawful for a man to be slain unduly. But it is not undue for evil-doers or foes of the common weal to be slain: hence this is not contrary to the precept of the decalogue; and such a killing is no murder as forbidden by that precept, as Augustine observes (De Lib. Arb. i, 4). In like manner when a man's property is taken from him, if it be due that he should lose it, this is not theft or robbery as forbidden by the decalogue.

Consequently when the children of Israel, by God's command, took away the spoils of the Egyptians, this was not theft; since it was due to them by the sentence of God. Likewise when Abraham consented to slay his son, he did not consent to murder, because his son was due to be slain by the command of God, Who is Lord of life and death: for He it is Who inflicts the punishment of death on all men, both godly and ungodly, on account of the sin of our first parent, and if a man be the executor of that sentence by Divine authority, he will be no murderer any more than God would be. Again Osee, by taking unto himself a wife of fornications, or an adulterous woman, was not guilty either of adultery or of fornication: because he took unto himself one who was his by command of God, Who is the Author of the institution of marriage.

Accordingly, therefore, the precepts of the decalogue, as to the essence of justice which they contain, are unchangeable: but as to any determination by application to individual actions—for instance, that this or that be murder, theft or adultery, or not—in this point they admit of change; sometimes by Divine authority alone, namely, in such matters as are exclusively of Divine institution, as marriage and the like; sometimes also by human authority, namely in such matters as are subject to human jurisdiction: for in this respect men stand in the place of God: and yet not in all respects.

Reply Obj. 4: This determination was an interpretation rather than a dispensation. For a man is not taken to break the Sabbath, if he does something necessary for human welfare; as Our Lord proves (Matt. 12:3, seqq.).

NINTH ARTICLE [I-II, Q. 100, Art. 9]

Whether the Mode of Virtue Falls Under the Precept of the Law?

Objection 1: It would seem that the mode of virtue falls under the precept of the law. For the mode of virtue is that deeds of justice should be done justly, that deeds of fortitude should be done bravely, and in like manner as to the other virtues. But it is commanded (Deut. 26:20) that "thou shalt follow justly after that which is just." Therefore the mode of virtue falls under the precept.

Obj. 2: Further, that which belongs to the intention of the lawgiver comes chiefly under the precept. But the intention of the lawgiver is directed chiefly to make men virtuous, as stated in *Ethic.* ii: and it belongs to a virtuous man to act virtuously. Therefore the mode of virtue falls under the precept.

Obj. 3: Further, the mode of virtue seems to consist properly in working willingly and with pleasure. But this falls under a precept of the Divine law, for it is written (Ps. 99:2): "Serve ye the Lord with gladness"; and (2 Cor. 9:7): "Not with sadness or necessity: for God loveth a cheerful giver"; whereupon the gloss says: "Whatever ye do, do gladly; and then you will do it well; whereas if you do it sorrowfully, it is done in thee, not by thee." Therefore the mode of virtue falls under the precept of the law.

*On the contrary,* No man can act as a virtuous man acts unless he has the habit of virtue, as the Philosopher explains (Ethic. ii, 4; v, 8). Now whoever transgresses a precept of the law, deserves to be punished. Hence it would follow that a man who has not the habit of virtue, would deserve to be punished, whatever he does. But this is contrary to the intention of the law, which aims at leading man to virtue, by habituating him to good works. Therefore the mode of virtue does not fall under the precept.

*I answer that,* As stated above (Q. 90, A. 3, ad 2), a precept of law has compulsory power. Hence that on which the compulsion of the law is brought to bear, falls directly under the precept of the law. Now the law compels through fear of punishment, as stated in *Ethic.* x, 9, because that properly falls under the precept of the law, for which the penalty of the law is inflicted. But Divine law and human law are differently situated as to the appointment of penalties; since the penalty of the law is inflicted only for those things which come under the judgment of the lawgiver; for the law punishes in accordance with the verdict given. Now man, the framer of human law, is competent to judge only of outward acts; because "man seeth those things that appear," according to 1 Kings 16:7: while God alone, the framer of the Divine law, is competent to judge of the inward movements of wills, according to Ps. 7:10: "The searcher of hearts and reins is God."

Accordingly, therefore, we must say that the mode of virtue is in some sort regarded both by human and by Divine law; in some respect it is regarded by the Divine, but not by the human law; and in another way, it is regarded neither by the human nor by the Divine law. Now the mode of virtue consists in three things, as the Philosopher states in *Ethic.* ii. The first is that man should act "knowingly": and this is subject to the judgment of both Divine and human law; because what a man does in ignorance, he does accidentally. Hence according to both human and Divine law, certain things are judged in respect of ignorance to be punishable or pardonable.

The second point is that a man should act "deliberately," i.e. "from choice, choosing that particular action for its own sake"; wherein a twofold internal movement is implied, of volition and of intention, about which we have spoken above (QQ. 8, 12): and concerning these two, Divine law alone, and not human law, is competent to judge. For human law does not punish the man who wishes to slay, and slays not: whereas the Divine law does, according to Matt. 5:22: "Whosoever is angry with his brother, shall be in danger of the judgment."

The third point is that he should "act from a firm and immovable principle": which firmness belongs properly to a habit, and implies that the action proceeds from a rooted habit. In this respect, the mode of virtue does not fall under the precept either of Divine or of human law, since neither by man nor by God is he punished as breaking the law, who gives due honor to his parents and yet has not the habit of filial piety.

Reply Obj. 1: The mode of doing acts of justice, which falls under the precept, is that they be done in accordance with right; but not that they be done from the habit of justice.

Reply Obj. 2: The intention of the lawgiver is twofold. His aim, in the first place, is to lead men to something by the precepts of the law: and this is virtue. Secondly, his intention is brought to bear on the matter itself of the precept: and this is something leading or disposing to virtue, viz. an act of virtue. For the end of the precept and the matter of the precept are not the same: just as neither in other things is the end the same as that which conduces to the end.

Reply Obj. 3: That works of virtue should be done without sadness, falls under the precept of the Divine law; for whoever works with sadness works unwillingly. But to work with pleasure, i.e. joyfully or cheerfully, in one respect falls under the precept, viz. in so far as pleasure ensues from the love of God and one's neighbor (which love falls under the precept), and love causes pleasure: and in another respect does not fall under the precept, in so far as pleasure ensues from a habit; for "pleasure taken in a work proves the existence of a habit," as stated in *Ethic.* ii, 3. For an act may give pleasure either on account of its end, or through its proceeding from a becoming habit.

TENTH ARTICLE [I-II, Q. 100, Art. 10]

Whether the Mode of Charity Falls Under the Precept of the Divine Law?

Objection 1: It would seem that the mode of charity falls under the precept of the Divine law. For it is written (Matt. 19:17): "If thou wilt enter into life, keep the commandments": whence it seems to follow that the observance of the commandments suffices for entrance into life. But good works do not suffice for entrance into life, except they be done from charity: for it is written (1 Cor. 13:3): "If I should distribute all my goods to feed the poor, and if I should deliver my body to be burned, and have not charity, it profiteth me nothing." Therefore the mode of charity is included in the commandment.

Obj. 2: Further, the mode of charity consists properly speaking in doing all things for God. But this falls under the precept; for the Apostle says (1 Cor. 10:31): "Do all to the glory of God." Therefore the mode of charity falls under the precept.

Obj. 3: Further, if the mode of charity does not fall under the precept, it follows that one can fulfil the precepts of the law without having charity. Now what can be done without charity can be done without grace, which is always united to charity. Therefore one can fulfil the precepts of the law without grace. But this is the error of Pelagius, as Augustine declares (De Haeres. lxxxviii). Therefore the mode of charity is included in the commandment.

*On the contrary,* Whoever breaks a commandment sins mortally. If therefore the mode of charity falls under the precept, it follows that whoever acts otherwise than from charity sins mortally. But whoever has not charity, acts otherwise than from charity. Therefore it follows that whoever has not charity, sins mortally in whatever he does, however good this may be in itself: which is absurd.

*I answer that,* Opinions have been contrary on this question. For some have said absolutely that the mode of charity comes under the precept; and yet that it is possible for one not having charity to fulfil this precept: because he can dispose himself to receive charity from God. Nor (say they) does it follow that a man not having charity sins mortally whenever he does something good of its kind: because it is an affirmative precept that binds one to act from charity, and is binding not for all time, but only for such time as one is in a state of charity. On the other hand, some have said that the mode of charity is altogether outside the precept.

Both these opinions are true up to a certain point. Because the act of charity can be considered in two ways. First, as an act by itself: and thus it falls under the precept of the law which specially prescribes it, viz. "Thou shalt love the Lord thy God," and "Thou shalt love thy neighbor." In this sense, the first opinion is true. Because it is not impossible to observe this precept which regards the act of charity; since man can dispose himself to possess charity, and when he possesses it, he can use it. Secondly, the act of charity can be considered as being the mode of the acts of the other virtues, i.e. inasmuch as the acts of the other virtues are ordained to charity, which is "the end of the commandment," as stated in 1 Tim. i, 5: for it has been said above (Q. 12, A. 4) that the intention of the end is a formal mode of the act ordained to that end. In this sense the second opinion is true in saying that the mode of charity does not fall under the precept, that is to say that this commandment, "Honor thy father," does not mean that a man must honor his father from charity, but merely that he must honor him. Wherefore he that honors his father, yet has not charity, does not break this precept: although he does break the precept concerning the act of charity, for which reason he deserves to be punished.

Reply Obj. 1: Our Lord did not say, "If thou wilt enter into life, keep one commandment"; but "keep" all "the commandments": among which is included the commandment concerning the love of God and our neighbor.

Reply Obj. 2: The precept of charity contains the injunction that God should be loved from our whole heart, which means that all things would be referred to God. Consequently man cannot fulfil the precept of charity, unless he also refer all things to God. Wherefore he that honors his father and mother, is bound to honor them from charity, not in virtue of the precept, "Honor thy father and mother," but in virtue of the precept, "Thou shalt love the Lord thy God with thy whole heart." And since these are two affirmative precepts, not binding for all times, they can be binding, each one at a different time: so that it may happen that a man fulfils the precept of honoring his father and mother, without at the same time breaking the precept concerning the omission of the mode of charity.

Reply Obj. 3: Man cannot fulfil all the precepts of the law, unless he fulfil the precept of charity, which is impossible without charity. Consequently it is not possible, as Pelagius maintained, for man to fulfil the law without grace.

ELEVENTH ARTICLE [I-II, Q. 100, Art. 11]

Whether It Is Right to Distinguish Other Moral Precepts of the Law Besides the Decalogue?

Objection 1: It would seem that it is wrong to distinguish other moral precepts of the law besides the decalogue. Because, as Our Lord declared (Matt. 22:40), "on these two commandments" of charity "dependeth the whole law and the prophets." But these two commandments are explained by the ten commandments of the decalogue. Therefore there is no need for other moral precepts.

Obj. 2: Further, the moral precepts are distinct from the judicial and ceremonial precepts, as stated above (Q. 99, AA. 3, 4). But the determinations of the general moral precepts belong to the judicial and ceremonial precepts: and the general moral precepts are contained in the decalogue, or are even presupposed to the decalogue, as stated above (A. 3). Therefore it was unsuitable to lay down other moral precepts besides the decalogue.

Obj. 3: Further, the moral precepts are about the acts of all the virtues, as stated above (A. 2). Therefore, as the Law contains, besides the decalogue, moral precepts pertaining to religion, liberality, mercy, and chastity; so there should have been added some precepts pertaining to the other virtues, for instance, fortitude, sobriety, and so forth. And yet such is not the case. It is therefore unbecoming to distinguish other moral precepts in the Law besides those of the decalogue.

*On the contrary,* It is written (Ps. 18:8): "The law of the Lord is unspotted, converting souls." But man is preserved from the stain of sin, and his soul is converted to God by other moral precepts besides those of the decalogue. Therefore it was right for the Law to include other moral precepts.

*I answer that,* As is evident from what has been stated (Q. 99, AA. 3, 4), the judicial and ceremonial precepts derive their force from their institution alone: since before they were instituted, it seemed of no consequence whether things were done in this or that way. But the moral precepts derive their efficacy from the very dictate of natural reason, even if they were never included in the Law. Now of these there are three grades: for some are most certain, and so evident as to need no promulgation; such as the commandments of the love of God and our neighbor, and others like these, as stated above (A. 3), which are, as it were, the ends of the commandments; wherefore no man can have an erroneous judgment about them. Some precepts are more detailed, the reason of which even an uneducated man can easily grasp; and yet they need to be promulgated, because human judgment, in a few instances, happens to be led astray concerning them: these are the precepts of the decalogue. Again, there are some precepts the reason of which is not so evident to everyone, but only the wise; these are moral precepts added to the decalogue, and given to the people by God through Moses and Aaron.

But since the things that are evident are the principles whereby we know those that are not evident, these other moral precepts added to the decalogue are reducible to the precepts of the decalogue, as so many corollaries. Thus the first commandment of the decalogue forbids the worship of strange gods: and to this are added other precepts forbidding things relating to worship of idols: thus it is written (Deut. 18:10, 11): "Neither let there be found among you anyone that shall expiate his son or daughter, making them to pass through the fire: ... neither let there by any wizard nor charmer, nor anyone that consulteth pythonic spirits, or fortune-tellers, or that seeketh the truth from the dead." The second commandment forbids perjury. To this is added the prohibition of blasphemy (Lev. 24:15, seqq) and the prohibition of false doctrine (Deut. 13). To the third commandment are added all the ceremonial precepts. To the fourth commandment prescribing the honor due to parents, is added the precept about honoring the aged, according to Lev. 19:32: "Rise up before the hoary head, and honor the person of the aged man"; and likewise all the precepts prescribing the reverence to be observed towards our betters, or kindliness towards our equals or inferiors. To the fifth commandment, which forbids murder, is added the prohibition of hatred and of any kind of violence inflicted on our neighbor, according to Lev. 19:16: "Thou shalt not stand against the blood of thy neighbor": likewise the prohibition against hating one's brother (Lev. 19:17): "Thou shalt not hate thy brother in thy heart." To the sixth commandment which forbids adultery, is added the prohibition about whoredom, according to Deut. 23:17: "There shall be no whore among the daughters of Israel, nor whoremonger among the sons of Israel"; and the prohibition against unnatural sins, according to Lev. 28:22, 23: "Thou shalt not lie with mankind ... thou shalt not copulate with any beast." To the seventh commandment which prohibits theft, is added the precept forbidding usury, according to Deut. 23:19: "Thou shalt not lend to thy brother money to usury"; and the prohibition against fraud, according to Deut. 25:13: "Thou shalt not have divers weights in thy bag"; and universally all prohibitions relating to peculations and larceny. To the eighth commandment, forbidding false testimony, is added the prohibition against false judgment, according to Ex. 23:2: "Neither shalt thou yield in judgment, to the opinion of the most part, to stray from the truth"; and the prohibition against lying (Ex. 23:7): "Thou shalt fly lying," and the prohibition against detraction, according to Lev. 19:16: "Thou shalt not be a detractor, nor a whisperer among the people." To the other two commandments no further precepts are added, because thereby are forbidden all kinds of evil desires.

Reply Obj. 1: The precepts of the decalogue are ordained to the love of God and our neighbor as pertaining evidently to our duty towards them; but the other precepts are so ordained as pertaining thereto less evidently.

Reply Obj. 2: It is in virtue of their institution that the ceremonial and judicial precepts are determinations of the precepts of the decalogue, not by reason of a natural instinct, as in the case of the superadded moral precepts.

Reply Obj. 3: The precepts of a law are ordained for the common good, as stated above (Q. 90, A. 2). And since those virtues which direct our conduct towards others pertain directly to the common good, as also does the virtue of chastity, in so far as the generative act conduces to the common good of the species; hence precepts bearing directly on these virtues are given, both in the decalogue and in addition thereto. As to the act of fortitude there are the order to be given by the commanders in the war, which is undertaken for the common good: as is clear from Deut. 20:3, where the priest is commanded (to speak thus): "Be not afraid, do not give back." In like manner the prohibition of acts of gluttony is left to paternal admonition, since it is contrary to the good of the household; hence it is said (Deut. 21:20) in the person of parents: "He slighteth hearing our admonitions, he giveth himself to revelling, and to debauchery and banquetings."

TWELFTH ARTICLE [I-II, Q. 100, Art. 12]

Whether the Moral Precepts of the Old Law Justified Man?

Objection 1: It would seem that the moral precepts of the Old Law justified man. Because the Apostle says (Rom. 2:13): "For not the hearers of the Law are justified before God, but the doers of the Law shall be justified." But the doers of the Law are those who fulfil the precepts of the Law. Therefore the fulfilling of the precepts of the Law was a cause of justification.

Obj. 2: Further, it is written (Lev. 18:5): "Keep My laws and My judgments, which if a man do, he shall live in them." But the spiritual life of man is through justice. Therefore the fulfilling of the precepts of the Law was a cause of justification.

Obj. 3: Further, the Divine law is more efficacious than human law. But human law justifies man; since there is a kind of justice consisting in fulfilling the precepts of law. Therefore the precepts of the Law justified man.

*On the contrary,* The Apostle says (2 Cor. 3:6): "The letter killeth": which, according to Augustine (De Spir. et Lit. xiv), refers even to the moral precepts. Therefore the moral precepts did not cause justice.

*I answer that,* Just as "healthy" is said properly and first of that which is possessed of health, and secondarily of that which is a sign or a safeguard of health; so justification means first and properly the causing of justice; while secondarily and improperly, as it were, it may denote a sign of justice or a disposition thereto. If justice be taken in the last two ways, it is evident that it was conferred by the precepts of the Law; in so far, to wit, as they disposed men to the justifying grace of Christ, which they also signified, because as Augustine says (Contra Faust. xxii, 24), "even the life of that people foretold and foreshadowed Christ."

But if we speak of justification properly so called, then we must notice that it can be considered as in the habit or as in the act: so that accordingly justification may be taken in two ways. First, according as man is made just, by becoming possessed of the habit of justice: secondly, according as he does works of justice, so that in this sense justification is nothing else than the execution of justice. Now justice, like the other virtues, may denote either the acquired or the infused virtue, as is clear from what has been stated (Q. 63, A. 4). The acquired virtue is caused by works; but the infused virtue is caused by God Himself through His grace. The latter is true justice, of which we are speaking now, and in this respect of which a man is said to be just before God, according to Rom. 4:2: "If Abraham were justified by works, he hath whereof to glory, but not before God." Hence this justice could not be caused by moral precepts, which are about human actions: wherefore the moral precepts could not justify man by causing justice.

If, on the other hand, by justification we understand the execution of justice, thus all the precepts of the Law justified man, but in various ways. Because the ceremonial precepts taken as a whole contained something just in itself, in so far as they aimed at offering worship to God; whereas taken individually they contained that which is just, not in itself, but by being a determination of the Divine law. Hence it is said of these precepts that they did not justify man save through the devotion and obedience of those who complied with them. On the other hand the moral and judicial precepts, either in general or also in particular, contained that which is just in itself: but the moral precepts contained that which is just in itself according to that "general justice" which is "every virtue" according to *Ethic.* v, 1: whereas the judicial precepts belonged to "special justice," which is about contracts connected with the human mode of life, between one man and another.

Reply Obj. 1: The Apostle takes justification for the execution of justice.

Reply Obj. 2: The man who fulfilled the precepts of the Law is said to live in them, because he did not incur the penalty of death, which the Law inflicted on its transgressors: in this sense the Apostle quotes this passage (Gal. 3:12).

Reply Obj. 3: The precepts of human law justify man by acquired justice: it is not about this that we are inquiring now, but only about that justice which is before God.

# QUESTION 101

OF THE CEREMONIAL PRECEPTS IN THEMSELVES (In Four Articles)

We must now consider the ceremonial precepts: and first we must consider them in themselves; secondly, their cause; thirdly, their duration. Under the first head there are four points of inquiry:

(1) The nature of the ceremonial precepts;

(2) Whether they are figurative?

(3) Whether there should have been many of them?

(4) Of their various kinds.

FIRST ARTICLE [I-II, Q. 101, Art. 1]

Whether the Nature of the Ceremonial Precepts Consists in Their Pertaining to the Worship of God?

Objection 1: It would seem that the nature of the ceremonial precepts does not consist in their pertaining to the worship of God. Because, in the Old Law, the Jews were given certain precepts about abstinence from food (Lev. 11); and about refraining from certain kinds of clothes, e.g. (Lev. 19:19): "Thou shalt not wear a garment that is woven of two sorts"; and again (Num. 15:38): "To make to themselves fringes in the corners of their garments." But these are not moral precepts; since they do not remain in the New Law. Nor are they judicial precepts; since they do not pertain to the pronouncing of judgment between man and man. Therefore they are ceremonial precepts. Yet they seem in no way to pertain to the worship of God. Therefore the nature of the ceremonial precepts does not consist in their pertaining to Divine worship.

Obj. 2: Further, some state that the ceremonial precepts are those which pertain to solemnities; as though they were so called from the *cerei* (candles) which are lit up on those occasions. But many other things besides solemnities pertain to the worship of God. Therefore it does not seem that the ceremonial precepts are so called from their pertaining to the Divine worship.

Obj. 3: Further, some say that the ceremonial precepts are patterns, i.e. rules, of salvation: because the Greek *chaire* is the same as the Latin "salve." But all the precepts of the Law are rules of salvation, and not only those that pertain to the worship of God. Therefore not only those precepts which pertain to Divine worship are called ceremonial.

Obj. 4: Further, Rabbi Moses says (Doct. Perplex. iii) that the ceremonial precepts are those for which there is no evident reason. But there is evident reason for many things pertaining to the worship of God; such as the observance of the Sabbath, the feasts of the Passover and of the Tabernacles, and many other things, the reason for which is set down in the Law. Therefore the ceremonial precepts are not those which pertain to the worship of God.

*On the contrary,* It is written (Ex. 18:19, 20): "Be thou to the people in those things that pertain to God ... and ... shew the people the ceremonies and the manner of worshipping."

*I answer that,* As stated above (Q. 99, A. 4), the ceremonial precepts are determinations of the moral precepts whereby man is directed to God, just as the judicial precepts are determinations of the moral precepts whereby he is directed to his neighbor. Now man is directed to God by the worship due to Him. Wherefore those precepts are properly called ceremonial, which pertain to the Divine worship.

The reason for their being so called was given above (Q. 99, A. 3), when we established the distinction between the ceremonial and the other precepts.

Reply Obj. 1: The Divine worship includes not only sacrifices and the like, which seem to be directed to God immediately, but also those things whereby His worshippers are duly prepared to worship Him: thus too in other matters, whatever is preparatory to the end comes under the science whose object is the end. Accordingly those precepts of the Law which regard the clothing and food of God's worshippers, and other such matters, pertain to a certain preparation of the ministers, with the view of fitting them for the Divine worship: just as those who administer to a king make use of certain special observances. Consequently such are contained under the ceremonial precepts.

Reply Obj. 2: The alleged explanation of the name does not seem very probable: especially as the Law does not contain many instances of the lighting of candles in solemnities; since, even the lamps of the Candlestick were furnished with "oil of olives," as stated in Lev. 24:2. Nevertheless we may say that all things pertaining to the Divine worship were more carefully observed on solemn festivals: so that all ceremonial precepts may be included under the observance of solemnities.

Reply Obj. 3: Neither does this explanation of the name appear to be very much to the point, since the word "ceremony" is not Greek but Latin. We may say, however, that, since man's salvation is from God, those precepts above all seem to be rules of salvation, which direct man to God: and accordingly those which refer to Divine worship are called ceremonial precepts.

Reply Obj. 4: This explanation of the ceremonial precepts has a certain amount of probability: not that they are called ceremonial precisely because there is no evident reason for them; this is a kind of consequence. For, since the precepts referring to the Divine worship must needs be figurative, as we shall state further on (A. 2), the consequence is that the reason for them is not so very evident.

SECOND ARTICLE [I-II, Q. 101, Art. 2]

Whether the Ceremonial Precepts Are Figurative?

Objection 1: It would seem that the ceremonial precepts are not figurative. For it is the duty of every teacher to express himself in such a way as to be easily understood, as Augustine states (De Doctr. Christ. iv, 4, 10) and this seems very necessary in the framing of a law: because precepts of law are proposed to the populace; for which reason a law should be manifest, as Isidore declares (Etym. v, 21). If therefore the precepts of the Law were given as figures of something, it seems unbecoming that Moses should have delivered these precepts without explaining what they signified.

Obj. 2: Further, whatever is done for the worship of God, should be entirely free from unfittingness. But the performance of actions in representation of others, seems to savor of the theatre or of the drama: because formerly the actions performed in theatres were done to represent the actions of others. Therefore it seems that such things should not be done for the worship of God. But the ceremonial precepts are ordained to the Divine worship, as stated above (A. 1). Therefore they should not be figurative.

Obj. 3: Further, Augustine says (Enchiridion iii, iv) that "God is worshipped chiefly by faith, hope, and charity." But the precepts of faith, hope, and charity are not figurative. Therefore the ceremonial precepts should not be figurative.

Obj. 4: Further, Our Lord said (John 4:24): "God is a spirit, and they that adore Him, must adore Him in spirit and in truth." But a figure is not the very truth: in fact one is condivided with the other. Therefore the ceremonial precepts, which refer to the Divine worship, should not be figurative.

*On the contrary,* The Apostle says (Col. 2:16, 17): "Let no man ... judge you in meat or in drink, or in respect of a festival day, or of the new moon, or of the sabbaths, which are a shadow of things to come."

*I answer that,* As stated above (A. 1; Q. 99, AA. 3, 4), the ceremonial precepts are those which refer to the worship of God. Now the Divine worship is twofold: internal, and external. For since man is composed of soul and body, each of these should be applied to the worship of God; the soul by an interior worship; the body by an outward worship: hence it is written (Ps. 83:3): "My heart and my flesh have rejoiced in the living God." And as the body is ordained to God through the soul, so the outward worship is ordained to the internal worship. Now interior worship consists in the soul being united to God by the intellect and affections. Wherefore according to the various ways in which the intellect and affections of the man who worships God are rightly united to God, his external actions are applied in various ways to the Divine worship.

For in the state of future bliss, the human intellect will gaze on the Divine Truth in Itself. Wherefore the external worship will not consist in anything figurative, but solely in the praise of God, proceeding from the inward knowledge and affection, according to Isa. 51:3: "Joy and gladness shall be found therein, thanksgiving and the voice of praise."

But in the present state of life, we are unable to gaze on the Divine Truth in Itself, and we need the ray of Divine light to shine upon us under the form of certain sensible figures, as Dionysius states (Coel. Hier. i); in various ways, however, according to the various states of human knowledge. For under the Old Law, neither was the Divine Truth manifest in Itself, nor was the way leading to that manifestation as yet opened out, as the Apostle declares (Heb. 9:8). Hence the external worship of the Old Law needed to be figurative not only of the future truth to be manifested in our heavenly country, but also of Christ, Who is the way leading to that heavenly manifestation. But under the New Law this way is already revealed: and therefore it needs no longer to be foreshadowed as something future, but to be brought to our minds as something past or present: and the truth of the glory to come, which is not yet revealed, alone needs to be foreshadowed. This is what the Apostle says (Heb. 11:1): "The Law has [Vulg.: 'having'] a shadow of the good things to come, not the very image of the things": for a shadow is less than an image; so that the image belongs to the New Law, but the shadow to the Old.

Reply Obj. 1: The things of God are not to be revealed to man except in proportion to his capacity: else he would be in danger of downfall, were he to despise what he cannot grasp. Hence it was more beneficial that the Divine mysteries should be revealed to uncultured people under a veil of figures, that thus they might know them at least implicitly by using those figures to the honor of God.

Reply Obj. 2: Just as human reason fails to grasp poetical expressions on account of their being lacking in truth, so does it fail to grasp Divine things perfectly, on account of the sublimity of the truth they contain: and therefore in both cases there is need of signs by means of sensible figures.

Reply Obj. 3: Augustine is speaking there of internal worship; to which, however, external worship should be ordained, as stated above.

The same answer applies to the Fourth Objection: because men were taught by Him to practice more perfectly the spiritual worship of God.

THIRD ARTICLE [I-II, Q. 101, Art. 3]

Whether There Should Have Been Many Ceremonial Precepts?

Objection 1: It would seem that there should not have been many ceremonial precepts. For those things which conduce to an end should be proportionate to that end. But the ceremonial precepts, as stated above (AA. 1, 2), are ordained to the worship of God, and to the foreshadowing of Christ. Now "there is but one God, of Whom are all things ... and one Lord Jesus Christ, by Whom are all things" (1 Cor. 8:6). Therefore there should not have been many ceremonial precepts.

Obj. 2: Further, the great number of the ceremonial precepts was an occasion of transgression, according to the words of Peter (Acts 15:10): "Why tempt you God, to put a yoke upon the necks of the disciples, which neither our fathers nor we have been able to bear?" Now the transgression of the Divine precepts is an obstacle to man's salvation. Since, therefore, every law should conduce to man's salvation, as Isidore says (Etym. v, 3), it seems that the ceremonial precepts should not have been given in great number.

Obj. 3: Further, the ceremonial precepts referred to the outward and bodily worship of God, as stated above (A. 2). But the Law should have lessened this bodily worship: since it directed men to Christ, Who taught them to worship God "in spirit and in truth," as stated in John 4:23. Therefore there should not have been many ceremonial precepts.

*On the contrary,* (Osee 8:12): "I shall write to them [Vulg.: 'him'] My manifold laws"; and (Job 11:6): "That He might show thee the secrets of His wisdom, and that His Law is manifold."

*I answer that,* As stated above (Q. 96, A. 1), every law is given to a people. Now a people contains two kinds of men: some, prone to evil, who have to be coerced by the precepts of the law, as stated above (Q. 95, A. 1); some, inclined to good, either from nature or from custom, or rather from grace; and the like have to be taught and improved by means of the precepts of the law. Accordingly, with regard to both kinds of men it was expedient that the Old Law should contain many ceremonial precepts. For in that people there were many prone to idolatry; wherefore it was necessary to recall them by means of ceremonial precepts from the worship of idols to the worship of God. And since men served idols in many ways, it was necessary on the other hand to devise many means of repressing every single one: and again, to lay many obligations on such like men, in order that being burdened, as it were, by their duties to the Divine worship, they might have no time for the service of idols. As to those who were inclined to good, it was again necessary that there should be many ceremonial precepts; both because thus their mind turned to God in many ways, and more continually; and because the mystery of Christ, which was foreshadowed by these ceremonial precepts, brought many boons to the world, and afforded men many considerations, which needed to be signified by various ceremonies.

Reply Obj. 1: When that which conduces to an end is sufficient to conduce thereto, then one such thing suffices for one end: thus one remedy, if it be efficacious, suffices sometimes to restore men to health, and then the remedy needs not to be repeated. But when that which conduces to an end is weak and imperfect, it needs to be multiplied: thus many remedies are given to a sick man, when one is not enough to heal him. Now the ceremonies of the Old Law were weak and imperfect, both for representing the mystery of Christ, on account of its surpassing excellence; and for subjugating men's minds to God. Hence the Apostle says (Heb. 7:18, 19): "There is a setting aside of the former commandment because of the weakness and unprofitableness thereof, for the law brought nothing to perfection." Consequently these ceremonies needed to be in great number.

Reply Obj. 2: A wise lawgiver should suffer lesser transgressions, that the greater may be avoided. And therefore, in order to avoid the sin of idolatry, and the pride which would arise in the hearts of the Jews, were they to fulfil all the precepts of the Law, the fact that they would in consequence find many occasions of disobedience did not prevent God from giving them many ceremonial precepts.

Reply Obj. 3: The Old Law lessened bodily worship in many ways. Thus it forbade sacrifices to be offered in every place and by any person. Many such like things did it enact for the lessening of bodily worship; as Rabbi Moses, the Egyptian testifies (Doct. Perplex. iii). Nevertheless it behooved not to attenuate the bodily worship of God so much as to allow men to fall away into the worship of idols.

FOURTH ARTICLE [I-II, Q. 101, Art. 4]

Whether the Ceremonies of the Old Law Are Suitably Divided into Sacrifices, Sacred Things, Sacraments, and Observances?

Objection 1: It would seem that the ceremonies of the Old Law are unsuitably divided into "sacrifices, sacred things, sacraments, and observances." For the ceremonies of the Old Law foreshadowed Christ. But this was done only by the sacrifices, which foreshadowed the sacrifice in which Christ "delivered Himself an oblation and a sacrifice to God" (Eph. 5:2). Therefore none but the sacrifices were ceremonies.

Obj. 2: Further, the Old Law was ordained to the New. But in the New Law the sacrifice is the Sacrament of the Altar. Therefore in the Old Law there should be no distinction between "sacrifices" and "sacraments."

Obj. 3: Further, a "sacred thing" is something dedicated to God: in which sense the tabernacle and its vessels were said to be consecrated. But all the ceremonial precepts were ordained to the worship of God, as stated above (A. 1). Therefore all ceremonies were sacred things. Therefore "sacred things" should not be taken as a part of the ceremonies.

Obj. 4: Further, "observances" are so called from having to be observed. But all the precepts of the Law had to be observed: for it is written (Deut. 8:11): "Observe [Douay: 'Take heed'] and beware lest at any time thou forget the Lord thy God, and neglect His commandments and judgments and ceremonies." Therefore the "observances" should not be considered as a part of the ceremonies.

Obj. 5: Further, the solemn festivals are reckoned as part of the ceremonial: since they were a shadow of things to come (Col. 2:16, 17): and the same may be said of the oblations and gifts, as appears from the words of the Apostle (Heb. 9:9): and yet these do not seem to be inclined in any of those mentioned above. Therefore the above division of ceremonies is unsuitable.

*On the contrary,* In the Old Law each of the above is called a ceremony. For the sacrifices are called ceremonies (Num. 15:24): "They shall offer a calf ... and the sacrifices and libations thereof, as the ceremonies require." Of the sacrament of Order it is written (Lev. 7:35): "This is the anointing of Aaron and his sons in the ceremonies." Of sacred things also it is written (Ex. 38:21): "These are the instruments of the tabernacle of the testimony ... in the ceremonies of the Levites." And again of the observances it is written (3 Kings 9:6): "If you ... shall turn away from following Me, and will not observe [Douay: 'keep'] My ... ceremonies which I have set before you."

*I answer that,* As stated above (AA. 1, 2), the ceremonial precepts are ordained to the Divine worship. Now in this worship we may consider the worship itself, the worshippers, and the instruments of worship. The worship consists specially in *sacrifices,* which are offered up in honor of God. The instruments of worship refer to the *sacred things,* such as the tabernacle, the vessels and so forth. With regard to the worshippers two points may be considered. The first point is their preparation for Divine worship, which is effected by a sort of consecration either of the people or of the ministers; and to this the *sacraments* refer. The second point is their particular mode of life, whereby they are distinguished from those who do not worship God: and to this pertain the *observances,* for instance, in matters of food, clothing, and so forth.

Reply Obj. 1: It was necessary for the sacrifices to be offered both in some certain place and by some certain men: and all this pertained to the worship of God. Wherefore just as their sacrifices signified Christ the victim, so too their sacraments and sacred things foreshadowed the sacraments and sacred things of the New Law; while their observances foreshadowed the mode of life of the people under the New Law: all of which things pertain to Christ.

Reply Obj. 2: The sacrifice of the New Law, viz. the Eucharist, contains Christ Himself, the Author of our Sanctification: for He sanctified "the people by His own blood" (Heb. 13:12). Hence this Sacrifice is also a sacrament. But the sacrifices of the Old Law did not contain Christ, but foreshadowed Him; hence they are not called sacraments. In order to signify this there were certain sacraments apart from the sacrifices of the Old Law, which sacraments were figures of the sanctification to come. Nevertheless to certain consecrations certain sacrifices were united.

Reply Obj. 3: The sacrifices and sacraments were of course sacred things. But certain things were sacred, through being dedicated to the Divine worship, and yet were not sacrifices or sacraments: wherefore they retained the common designation of sacred things.

Reply Obj. 4: Those things which pertained to the mode of life of the people who worshipped God, retained the common designation of observances, in so far as they fell short of the above. For they were not called sacred things, because they had no immediate connection with the worship of God, such as the tabernacle and its vessels had. But by a sort of consequence they were matters of ceremony, in so far as they affected the fitness of the people who worshipped God.

Reply Obj. 5: Just as the sacrifices were offered in a fixed place, so were they offered at fixed times: for which reason the solemn festivals seem to be reckoned among the sacred things. The oblations and gifts are counted together with the sacrifices; hence the Apostle says (Heb. 5:1): "Every high-priest taken from among men, is ordained for men in things that appertain to God, that he may offer up gifts and sacrifices."

## QUESTION 102

OF THE CAUSES OF THE CEREMONIAL PRECEPTS (In Six Articles)

We must now consider the causes of the ceremonial precepts: under which head there are six points of inquiry:

(1) Whether there was any cause for the ceremonial precepts?

(2) Whether the cause of the ceremonial precepts was literal or figurative?

(3) The causes of the sacrifices;

(4) The causes of the sacrifices;

(5) The causes of the sacred things;

(6) The causes of the observances.

FIRST ARTICLE [I-II, Q. 102, Art. 1]

Whether There Was Any Cause for the Ceremonial Precepts?

Objection 1: It would seem that there was no cause for the ceremonial precepts. Because on Eph. 2:15, "Making void the law of the commandments," the gloss says, (i.e.) "making void the Old Law as to the carnal observances, by substituting decrees, i.e. evangelical precepts, which are based on reason." But if the observances of the Old Law were based on reason, it would have been useless to void them by the reasonable decrees of the New Law. Therefore there was no reason for the ceremonial observances of the Old Law.

Obj. 2: Further, the Old Law succeeded the law of nature. But in the law of nature there was a precept for which there was no reason save that man's obedience might be tested; as Augustine says (Gen. ad lit. viii, 6, 13), concerning the prohibition about the tree of life. Therefore in the Old Law there should have been some precepts for the purpose of testing man's obedience, having no reason in themselves.

Obj. 3: Further, man's works are called moral according as they proceed from reason. If therefore there is any reason for the ceremonial precepts, they would not differ from the moral precepts. It seems therefore that there was no cause for the ceremonial precepts: for the reason of a precept is taken from some cause.

*On the contrary,* It is written (Ps. 18:9): "The commandment of the Lord is lightsome, enlightening the eyes." But the ceremonial precepts are commandments of God. Therefore they are lightsome: and yet they would not be so, if they had no reasonable cause. Therefore the ceremonial precepts have a reasonable cause.

*I answer that,* Since, according to the Philosopher (Metaph. i, 2), it is the function of a "wise man to do everything in order," those things which proceed from the Divine wisdom must needs be well ordered, as the Apostle states (Rom. 13:1). Now there are two conditions required for things to be well ordered. First, that they be ordained to their due end, which is the principle of the whole order in matters of action: since those things that happen by chance outside the intention of the end, or which are not done seriously but for fun, are said to be inordinate. Secondly, that which is done in view of the end should be proportionate to the end. From this it follows that the reason for whatever conduces to the end is taken from the end: thus the reason for the disposition of a saw is taken from cutting, which is its end, as stated in *Phys.* ii, 9. Now it is evident that the ceremonial precepts, like all the other precepts of the Law, were institutions of Divine wisdom: hence it is written (Deut. 4:6): "This is your wisdom and understanding in the sight of nations." Consequently we must needs say that the ceremonial precepts were ordained to a certain end, wherefrom their reasonable causes can be gathered.

Reply Obj. 1: It may be said there was no reason for the observances of the Old Law, in the sense that there was no reason in the very nature of the thing done: for instance that a garment should not be made of wool and linen. But there could be a reason for them in relation to something else: namely, in so far as something was signified or excluded thereby. On the other hand, the decrees of the New Law, which refer chiefly to faith and the love of God, are reasonable from the very nature of the act.

Reply Obj. 2: The reason for the prohibition concerning the tree of knowledge of good and evil was not that this tree was naturally evil: and yet this prohibition was reasonable in its relation to something else, in as much as it signified something. And so also the ceremonial precepts of the Old Law were reasonable on account of their relation to something else.

Reply Obj. 3: The moral precepts in their very nature have reasonable causes: as for instance, "Thou shalt not kill," "Thou shalt not steal." But the ceremonial precepts have a reasonable cause in their relation to something else, as stated above.

SECOND ARTICLE [I-II, Q. 102, Art. 2]

Whether the Ceremonial Precepts Have a Literal Cause or Merely a Figurative Cause?

Objection 1: It would seem that the ceremonial precepts have not a literal, but merely a figurative cause. For among the ceremonial precepts, the chief was circumcision and the sacrifice of the paschal lamb. But neither of these had any but a figurative cause: because each was given as a sign. For it is written (Gen. 17:11): "You shall circumcise the flesh of your foreskin, that it may be a sign of the covenant between Me and you": and of the celebration of the Passover it is written (Ex. 13:9): "It shall be as a sign in thy hand, and as a memorial before thy eyes." Therefore much more did the other ceremonial precepts have none but a figurative reason.

Obj. 2: Further, an effect is proportionate to its cause. But all the ceremonial precepts are figurative, as stated above (Q. 101, A. 2). Therefore they have no other than a figurative cause.

Obj. 3: Further, if it be a matter of indifference whether a certain thing, considered in itself, be done in a particular way or not, it seems that it has not a literal cause. Now there are certain points in the ceremonial precepts, which appear to be a matter of indifference, as to whether they be done in one way or in another: for instance, the number of animals to be offered, and other such particular circumstances. Therefore there is no literal cause for the precepts of the Old Law.

*On the contrary,* Just as the ceremonial precepts foreshadowed Christ, so did the stories of the Old Testament: for it is written (1 Cor. 10:11) that "all (these things) happened to them in figure." Now in the stories of the Old Testament, besides the mystical or figurative, there is the literal sense. Therefore the ceremonial precepts had also literal, besides their figurative causes.

*I answer that,* As stated above (A. 1), the reason for whatever conduces to an end must be taken from that end. Now the end of the ceremonial precepts was twofold: for they were ordained to the Divine worship, for that particular time, and to the foreshadowing of Christ; just as the words of the prophets regarded the time being in such a way as to be utterances figurative of the time to come, as Jerome says on Osee 1:3. Accordingly the reasons for the ceremonial precepts of the Old Law can be taken in two ways. First, in respect of the Divine worship which was to be observed for that particular time: and these reasons are literal: whether they refer to the shunning of idolatry; or recall certain Divine benefits; or remind men of the Divine excellence; or point out the disposition of mind which was then required in those who worshipped God. Secondly, their reasons can be gathered from the point of view of their being ordained to foreshadow Christ: and thus their reasons are figurative and mystical: whether they be taken from Christ Himself and the Church, which pertains to the allegorical sense; or to the morals of the Christian people, which pertains to the moral sense; or to the state of future glory, in as much as we are brought thereto by Christ, which refers to the anagogical sense.

Reply Obj. 1: Just as the use of metaphorical expressions in Scripture belongs to the literal sense, because the words are employed in order to convey that particular meaning; so also the meaning of those legal ceremonies which commemorated certain Divine benefits, on account of which they were instituted, and of others similar which belonged to that time, does not go beyond the order of literal causes. Consequently when we assert that the cause of the celebration of the Passover was its signification of the delivery from Egypt, or that circumcision was a sign of God's covenant with Abraham, we assign the literal cause.

Reply Obj. 2: This argument would avail if the ceremonial precepts had been given merely as figures of things to come, and not for the purpose of worshipping God then and there.

Reply Obj. 3: As we have stated when speaking of human laws (Q. 96, AA. 1, 6), there is a reason for them in the abstract, but not in regard to particular conditions, which depend on the judgment of those who frame them; so also many particular determinations in the ceremonies of the Old Law have no literal cause, but only a figurative cause; whereas in the abstract they have a literal cause.

THIRD ARTICLE [I-II, Q. 102, Art. 3]

Whether a Suitable Cause Can Be Assigned for the Ceremonies Which Pertained to Sacrifices?

Objection 1: It would seem that no suitable cause can be assigned for the ceremonies pertaining to sacrifices. For those things which were offered in sacrifice, are those which are necessary for sustaining human life: such as certain animals and certain loaves. But God needs no such sustenance; according to Ps. 49:13: "Shall I eat the flesh of bullocks? Or shall I drink the blood of goats?" Therefore such sacrifices were unfittingly offered to God.

Obj. 2: Further, only three kinds of quadrupeds were offered in sacrifice to God, viz. oxen, sheep and goats; of birds, generally the turtledove and the dove; but specially, in the cleansing of a leper, an offering was made of sparrows. Now many other animals are more noble than these. Since therefore whatever is best should be offered to God, it seems that not only of these three should sacrifices have been offered to Him.

Obj. 3: Further, just as man has received from God the dominion over birds and beasts, so also has he received dominion over fishes. Consequently it was unfitting for fishes to be excluded from the divine sacrifices.

Obj. 4: Further, turtledoves and doves indifferently are commanded to be offered up. Since then the young of the dove are commanded to be offered, so also should the young of the turtledove.

Obj. 5: Further, God is the Author of life, not only of men, but also of animals, as is clear from Gen. 1:20, seqq. Now death is opposed to life. Therefore it was fitting that living animals rather than slain animals should be offered to God, especially as the Apostle admonishes us (Rom. 12:1), to present our bodies "a living sacrifice, holy, pleasing unto God."

Obj. 6: Further, if none but slain animals were offered in sacrifice to God, it seems that it mattered not how they were slain. Therefore it was unfitting that the manner of immolation should be determined, especially as regards birds (Lev. 1:15, seqq.).

Obj. 7: Further, every defect in an animal is a step towards corruption and death. If therefore slain animals were offered to God, it was unreasonable to forbid the offering of an imperfect animal, e.g. a lame, or a blind, or otherwise defective animal.

Obj. 8: Further, those who offer victims to God should partake thereof, according to the words of the Apostle (1 Cor. 10:18): "Are not they that eat of the sacrifices partakers of the altar?" It was therefore unbecoming for the offerers to be denied certain parts of the victims, namely, the blood, the fat, the breastbone and the right shoulder.

Objection 9: Further, just as holocausts were offered up in honor of God, so also were the peace-offerings and sin-offerings. But no female animals was offered up to God as a holocaust, although holocausts were offered of both quadrupeds and birds. Therefore it was inconsistent that female animals should be offered up in peace-offerings and sin-offerings, and that nevertheless birds should not be offered up in peace-offerings.

Objection 10: Further, all the peace-offerings seem to be of one kind. Therefore it was unfitting to make a distinction among them, so that it was forbidden to eat the flesh of certain peace-offerings on the following day, while it was allowed to eat the flesh of other peace-offerings, as laid down in Lev. 7:15, seqq.

Objection 11: Further, all sins agree in turning us from God. Therefore, in order to reconcile us to God, one kind of sacrifice should have been offered up for all sins.

Objection 12: Further, all animals that were offered up in sacrifice, were offered up in one way, viz. slain. Therefore it does not seem to be suitable that products of the soil should be offered up in various ways; for sometimes an offering was made of ears of corn, sometimes of flour, sometimes of bread, this being baked sometimes in an oven, sometimes in a pan, sometimes on a gridiron.

Objection 13: Further, whatever things are serviceable to us should be recognized as coming from God. It was therefore unbecoming that besides animals, nothing but bread, wine, oil, incense, and salt should be offered to God.

Objection 14: Further, bodily sacrifices denote the inward sacrifice of the heart, whereby man offers his soul to God. But in the inward sacrifice, the sweetness, which is denoted by honey, surpasses the pungency which salt represents; for it is written (Ecclus. 24:27): "My spirit is sweet above honey." Therefore it was unbecoming that the use of honey, and of leaven which makes bread savory, should be forbidden in a sacrifice; while the use was prescribed, of salt which is pungent, and of incense which has a bitter taste. Consequently it seems that things pertaining to the ceremonies of the sacrifices have no reasonable cause.

*On the contrary,* It is written (Lev. 1:13): "The priest shall offer it all and burn it all upon the altar, for a holocaust, and most sweet savor to the Lord." Now according to Wis. 7:28, "God loveth none but him that dwelleth with wisdom": whence it seems to follow that whatever is acceptable to God is wisely done. Therefore these ceremonies of the sacrifices were wisely done, as having reasonable causes.

*I answer that,* As stated above (A. 2), the ceremonies of the Old Law had a twofold cause, viz. a literal cause, according as they were intended for Divine worship; and a figurative or mystical cause, according as they were intended to foreshadow Christ: and on either hand the ceremonies pertaining to the sacrifices can be assigned to a fitting cause.

For, according as the ceremonies of the sacrifices were intended for the divine worship, the causes of the sacrifices can be taken in two ways. First, in so far as the sacrifice represented the directing of the mind to God, to which the offerer of the sacrifice was stimulated. Now in order to direct his mind to God aright, man must recognize that whatever he has is from God as from its first principle, and direct it to God as its last end. This was denoted in the offerings and sacrifices, by the fact that man offered some of his own belongings in honor of God, as though in recognition of his having received them from God, according to the saying of David (1 Paral. xxix, 14): "All things are Thine: and we have given Thee what we received of Thy hand." Wherefore in offering up sacrifices man made protestation that God is the first principle of the creation of all things, and their last end, to which all things must be directed. And since, for the human mind to be directed to God aright, it must recognize no first author of things other than God, nor place its end in any other; for this reason it was forbidden in the Law to offer sacrifice to any other but God, according to Ex. 22:20: "He that sacrificeth to gods, shall be put to death, save only to the Lord." Wherefore another reasonable cause may be assigned to the ceremonies of the sacrifices, from the fact that thereby men were withdrawn from offering sacrifices to idols. Hence too it is that the precepts about the sacrifices were not given to the Jewish people until after they had fallen into idolatry, by worshipping the molten calf: as though those sacrifices were instituted, that the people, being ready to offer sacrifices, might offer those sacrifices to God rather than to idols. Thus it is written (Jer. 7:22): "I spake not to your fathers and I commanded them not, in the day that I brought them out of the land of Egypt, concerning the matter of burnt-offerings and sacrifices."

Now of all the gifts which God vouchsafed to mankind after they had fallen away by sin, the chief is that He gave His Son; wherefore it is written (John 3:16): "God so loved the world, as to give His only-begotten Son; that whosoever believeth in Him, may not perish, but may have life everlasting." Consequently the chief sacrifice is that whereby Christ Himself "delivered Himself ... to God for an odor of sweetness" (Eph. 5:2). And for this reason all the other sacrifices of the Old Law were offered up in order to foreshadow this one individual and paramount sacrifice—the imperfect forecasting the perfect. Hence the Apostle says (Heb. 10:11) that the priest of the Old Law "often" offered "the same sacrifices, which can never take away sins: but" Christ offered "one sacrifice for sins, for ever." And since the reason of the figure is taken from that which the figure represents, therefore the reasons of the figurative sacrifices of the Old Law should be taken from the true sacrifice of Christ.

Reply Obj. 1: God did not wish these sacrifices to be offered to Him on account of the things themselves that were offered, as though He stood in need of them: wherefore it is written (Isa. 1:11): "I desire not holocausts of rams, and fat of fatlings, and blood of calves and lambs and buckgoats." But, as stated above, He wished them to be offered to Him, in order to prevent idolatry; in order to signify the right ordering of man's mind to God; and in order to represent the mystery of the Redemption of man by Christ.

Reply Obj. 2: In all the respects mentioned above (ad 1), there was a suitable reason for these animals, rather than others, being offered in sacrifice to God. First, in order to prevent idolatry. Because idolaters offered all other animals to their gods, or made use of them in their sorceries: while the Egyptians (among whom the people had been dwelling) considered it abominable to slay these animals, wherefore they used not to offer them in sacrifice to their gods. Hence it is written (Ex. 8:26): "We shall sacrifice the abominations of the Egyptians to the Lord our God." For they worshipped the sheep; they reverenced the ram (because demons appeared under the form thereof); while they employed oxen for agriculture, which was reckoned by them as something sacred.

Secondly, this was suitable for the aforesaid right ordering of man's mind to God: and in two ways. First, because it is chiefly by means of these animals that human life is sustained: and moreover they are most clean, and partake of a most clean food: whereas other animals are either wild, and not deputed to ordinary use among men: or, if they be tame, they have unclean food, as pigs and geese: and nothing but what is clean should be offered to God. These birds especially were offered in sacrifice because there were plenty of them in the land of promise. Secondly, because the sacrificing of these animals represented purity of heart. Because as the gloss says on Lev. 1, "We offer a calf, when we overcome the pride of the flesh; a lamb, when we restrain our unreasonable motions; a goat, when we conquer wantonness; a turtledove, when we keep chaste; unleavened bread, when we feast on the unleavened bread of sincerity." And it is evident that the dove denotes charity and simplicity of heart.

Thirdly, it was fitting that these animals should be offered, that they might foreshadow Christ. Because, as the gloss observes, "Christ is offered in the calf, to denote the strength of the cross; in the lamb, to signify His innocence; in the ram, to foreshadow His headship; and in the goat, to signify the likeness of 'sinful flesh' [*An allusion to Col. 2:11 (Textus Receptus)]. The turtledove and dove denoted the union of the two natures"; or else the turtledove signified chastity; while the dove was a figure of charity. "The wheat-flour foreshadowed the sprinkling of believers with the water of Baptism."

Reply Obj. 3: Fish through living in water are further removed from man than other animals, which, like man, live in the air. Again, fish die as soon as they are taken out of water; hence they could not be offered in the temple like other animals.

Reply Obj. 4: Among turtledoves the older ones are better than the young; while with doves the case is the reverse. Wherefore, as Rabbi Moses observes (Doct. Perplex. iii), turtledoves and young doves are commanded to be offered, because nothing should be offered to God but what is best.

Reply Obj. 5: The animals which were offered in sacrifice were slain, because it is by being killed that they become useful to man, forasmuch as God gave them to man for food. Wherefore also they were burnt with fire: because it is by being cooked that they are made fit for human consumption. Moreover the slaying of the animals signified the destruction of sins: and also that man deserved death on account of his sins; as though those animals were slain in man's stead, in order to betoken the expiation of sins. Again the slaying of these animals signified the slaying of Christ.

Reply Obj. 6: The Law fixed the special manner of slaying the sacrificial animals in order to exclude other ways of killing, whereby idolaters sacrificed animals to idols. Or again, as Rabbi Moses says (Doct. Perplex. iii), "the Law chose that manner of slaying which was least painful to the slain animal." This excluded cruelty on the part of the offerers, and any mangling of the animals slain.

Reply Obj. 7: It is because unclean animals are wont to be held in contempt among men, that it was forbidden to offer them in sacrifice to God: and for this reason too they were forbidden (Deut. 23:18) to offer "the hire of a strumpet or the price of a dog in the house of ... God." For the same reason they did not offer animals before the seventh day, because such were abortive as it were, the flesh being not yet firm on account of its exceeding softness.

Reply Obj. 8: There were three kinds of sacrifices. There was one in which the victim was entirely consumed by fire: this was called "a holocaust, i.e. all burnt." For this kind of sacrifice was offered to God specially to show reverence to His majesty, and love of His goodness: and typified the state of perfection as regards the fulfilment of the counsels. Wherefore the whole was burnt up: so that as the whole animal by being dissolved into vapor soared aloft, so it might denote that the whole man, and whatever belongs to him, are subject to the authority of God, and should be offered to Him.

Another sacrifice was the "sin-offering," which was offered to God on account of man's need for the forgiveness of sin: and this typifies the state of penitents in satisfying for sins. It was divided into two parts: for one part was burnt; while the other was granted to the use of the priests to signify that remission of sins is granted by God through the ministry of His priests. When, however, this sacrifice was offered for the sins of the whole people, or specially for the sin of the priest, the whole victim was burnt up. For it was not fitting that the priests should have the use of that which was offered for their own sins, to signify that nothing sinful should remain in them. Moreover, this would not be satisfaction for sin: for if the offering were granted to the use of those for whose sins it was offered, it would seem to be the same as if it had not been offered.

The third kind of sacrifice was called the "peace-offering," which was offered to God, either in thanksgiving, or for the welfare and prosperity of the offerers, in acknowledgment of benefits already received or yet to be received: and this typifies the state of those who are proficient in the observance of the commandments. These sacrifices were divided into three parts: for one part was burnt in honor of God; another part was allotted to the use of the priests; and the third part to the use of the offerers; in order to signify that man's salvation is from God, by the direction of God's ministers, and through the cooperation of those who are saved.

But it was the universal rule that the blood and fat were not allotted to the use either of the priests or of the offerers: the blood being poured out at the foot of the altar, in honor of God, while the fat was burnt upon the altar (Lev. 9:9, 10). The reason for this was, first, in order to prevent idolatry: because idolaters used to drink the blood and eat the fat of the victims, according to Deut. 32:38: "Of whose victims they eat the fat, and drank the wine of their drink-offerings." Secondly, in order to form them to a right way of living. For they were forbidden the use of the blood that they might abhor the shedding of human blood; wherefore it is written (Gen. 9:4, 5): "Flesh with blood you shall not eat: for I will require the blood of your lives": and they were forbidden to eat the fat, in order to withdraw them from lasciviousness; hence it is written (Ezech. 34:3): "You have killed that which was fat." Thirdly, on account of the reverence due to God: because blood is most necessary for life, for which reason "life" is said to be "in the blood" (Lev. 17:11, 14): while fat is a sign of abundant nourishment. Wherefore, in order to show that to God we owe both life and a sufficiency of all good things, the blood was poured out, and the fat burnt up in His honor. Fourthly, in order to foreshadow the shedding of Christ's blood, and the abundance of His charity, whereby He offered Himself to God for us.

In the peace-offerings, the breast-bone and the right shoulder were allotted to the use of the priest, in order to prevent a certain kind of divination which is known as "spatulamantia," so called because it was customary in divining to use the shoulder-blade ( *spatula* ), and the breast-bone of the animals offered in sacrifice; wherefore these things were taken away from the offerers. This is also denoted the priest's need of wisdom in the heart, to instruct the people—this was signified by the breast-bone, which covers the heart; and his need of fortitude, in order to bear with human frailty—and this was signified by the right shoulder.

Reply Obj. 9: Because the holocaust was the most perfect kind of sacrifice, therefore none but a male was offered for a holocaust: because the female is an imperfect animal. The offering of turtledoves and doves was on account of the poverty of the offerers, who were unable to offer bigger animals. And since peace-victims were offered freely, and no one was bound to offer them against his will, hence these birds were offered not among the peace-victims, but among the holocausts and victims for sin, which man was obliged to offer at times. Moreover these birds, on account of their lofty flight, were befitting the perfection of the holocausts: and were suitable for sin-offerings because their song is doleful.

Reply Obj. 10: The holocaust was the chief of all the sacrifices: because all was burnt in honor of God, and nothing of it was eaten. The second place in holiness, belongs to the sacrifice for sins, which was eaten in the court only, and on the very day of the sacrifice (Lev. 7:6, 15). The third place must be given to the peace-offerings of thanksgiving, which were eaten on the same day, but anywhere in Jerusalem. Fourth in order were the "ex-voto" peace-offerings, the flesh of which could be eaten even on the morrow. The reason for this order is that man is bound to God, chiefly on account of His majesty; secondly, on account of the sins he has committed; thirdly, because of the benefits he has already received from Him; fourthly, by reason of the benefits he hopes to receive from Him.

Reply Obj. 11: Sins are more grievous by reason of the state of the sinner, as stated above (Q. 73, A.

10): wherefore different victims are commanded to be offered for the sin of a priest, or of a prince, or of some other private individual. "But," as Rabbi Moses says (Doct. Perplex. iii), "we must take note that the more grievous the sin, the lower the species of animals offered for it. Wherefore the goat, which is a very base animal, was offered for idolatry; while a calf was offered for a priest's ignorance, and a ram for the negligence of a prince."

Reply Obj. 12: In the matter of sacrifices the Law had in view the poverty of the offerers; so that those who could not have a four-footed animal at their disposal, might at least offer a bird; and that he who could not have a bird might at least offer bread; and that if a man had not even bread he might offer flour or ears of corn.

The figurative cause is that the bread signifies Christ Who is the "living bread" (John 6:41, 51). He was indeed an ear of corn, as it were, during the state of the law of nature, in the faith of the patriarchs; He was like flour in the doctrine of the Law of the prophets; and He was like perfect bread after He had taken human nature; baked in the fire, i.e. formed by the Holy Ghost in the oven of the virginal womb; baked again in a pan by the toils which He suffered in the world; and consumed by fire on the cross as on a gridiron.

Reply Obj. 13: The products of the soil are useful to man, either as food, and of these bread was offered; or as drink, and of these wine was offered; or as seasoning, and of these oil and salt were offered; or as healing, and of these they offered incense, which both smells sweetly and binds easily together.

Now the bread foreshadowed the flesh of Christ; and the wine, His blood, whereby we were redeemed; oil betokens the grace of Christ; salt, His knowledge; incense, His prayer.

Reply Obj. 14: Honey was not offered in the sacrifices to God, both because it was wont to be offered in the sacrifices to idols; and in order to denote the absence of all carnal sweetness and pleasure from those who intend to sacrifice to God. Leaven was not offered, to denote the exclusion of corruption. Perhaps too, it was wont to be offered in the sacrifices to idols.

Salt, however, was offered, because it wards off the corruption of putrefaction: for sacrifices offered to God should be incorrupt. Moreover, salt signifies the discretion of wisdom, or again, mortification of the flesh.

Incense was offered to denote devotion of the heart, which is necessary in the offerer; and again, to signify the odor of a good name: for incense is composed of matter, both rich and fragrant. And since the sacrifice "of jealousy" did not proceed from devotion, but rather from suspicion, therefore incense was not offered therein (Num. 5:15).

FOURTH ARTICLE [I-II, Q. 102, Art. 4]

Whether Sufficient Reason Can Be Assigned for the Ceremonies Pertaining to Holy Things?

Objection 1: It would seem that no sufficient reason can be assigned for the ceremonies of the Old Law that pertain to holy things. For Paul said (Acts 17:24): "God Who made the world and all things therein; He being Lord of heaven and earth, dwelleth not in temples made by hands." It was therefore unfitting that in the Old Law a tabernacle or temple should be set up for the worship of God.

Obj. 2: Further, the state of the Old Law was not changed except by Christ. But the tabernacle denoted the state of the Old Law. Therefore it should not have been changed by the building of a temple.

Obj. 3: Further, the Divine Law, more than any other indeed, should lead man to the worship of God. But an increase of divine worship requires multiplication of altars and temples; as is evident in regard to the New Law. Therefore it seems that also under the Old Law there should have been not only one tabernacle or temple, but many.

Obj. 4: Further, the tabernacle or temple was ordained to the worship of God. But in God we should worship above all His unity and simplicity. Therefore it seems unbecoming for the tabernacle or temple to be divided by means of veils.

Obj. 5: Further, the power of the First Mover, i.e. God, appears first of all in the east, for it is in that quarter that the first movement begins. But the tabernacle was set up for the worship of God. Therefore it should have been built so as to point to the east rather than the west.

Obj. 6: Further, the Lord commanded (Ex. 20:4) that they should "not make ... a graven thing, nor the likeness of anything." It was therefore unfitting for graven images of the cherubim to be set up in the tabernacle or temple. In like manner, the ark, the propitiatory, the candlestick, the table, the two altars, seem to have been placed there without reasonable cause.

Obj. 7: Further, the Lord commanded (Ex. 20:24): "You shall make an altar of earth unto Me": and again (Ex. 20:26): "Thou shalt not go up by steps unto My altar." It was therefore unfitting that subsequently they should be commanded to make an altar of wood laid over with gold or brass; and of such a height that it was impossible to go up to it except by steps. For it is written (Ex. 27:1, 2): "Thou shalt make also an altar of setim wood, which shall be five cubits long, and as many broad ... and three cubits high ... and thou shalt cover it with brass": and (Ex. 30:1, 3): "Thou shalt make ... an altar to burn incense, of setim wood ... and thou shalt overlay it with the purest gold."

Obj. 8: Further, in God's works nothing should be superfluous; for not even in the works of nature is anything superfluous to be found. But one cover suffices for one tabernacle or house. Therefore it was unbecoming to furnish the tabernacle with many coverings, viz. curtains, curtains of goats' hair, rams' skins dyed red, and violet-colored skins (Ex. 26).

Objection 9: Further, exterior consecration signifies interior holiness, the subject of which is the soul. It was therefore unsuitable for the tabernacle and its vessels to be consecrated, since they were inanimate things.

Objection 10: Further, it is written (Ps. 33:2): "I will bless the Lord at all times, His praise shall always be in my mouth." But the solemn festivals were instituted for the praise of God. Therefore it was not fitting that certain days should be fixed for keeping solemn festivals; so that it seems that there was no suitable cause for the ceremonies relating to holy things.

*On the contrary,* The Apostle says (Heb. 8:4) that those who "offer gifts according to the law ... serve unto the example and shadow of heavenly things. As it was answered to Moses, when he was to finish the tabernacle: See, says He, that thou make all things according to the pattern which was shown thee on the mount." But that is most reasonable, which presents a likeness to heavenly things. Therefore the ceremonies relating to holy things had a reasonable cause.

*I answer that,* The chief purpose of the whole external worship is that man may give worship to God. Now man's tendency is to reverence less those things which are common, and indistinct from other things; whereas he admires and reveres those things which are distinct from others in some point of excellence. Hence too it is customary among men for kings and princes, who ought to be reverenced by their subjects, to be clothed in more precious garments, and to possess vaster and more beautiful abodes. And for this reason it behooved special times, a special abode, special vessels, and special ministers to be appointed for the divine worship, so that thereby the soul of man might be brought to greater reverence for God.

In like manner the state of the Old Law, as observed above (A. 2; Q. 100, A. 12; Q. 101, A. 2), was instituted that it might foreshadow the mystery of Christ. Now that which foreshadows something should be determinate, so that it may present some likeness thereto. Consequently, certain special points had to be observed in matters pertaining to the worship of God.

Reply Obj. 1: The divine worship regards two things: namely, God Who is worshipped; and men, who worship Him. Accordingly God, Who is worshipped, is confined to no bodily place: wherefore there was no need, on His part, for a tabernacle or temple to be set up. But men, who worship Him, are corporeal beings: and for their sake there was need for a special tabernacle or temple to be set up for the worship of God, for two reasons. First, that through coming together with the thought that the place was set aside for the worship of God, they might approach thither with greater reverence. Secondly, that certain things relating to the excellence of Christ's Divine or human nature might be signified by the arrangement of various details in such temple or tabernacle.

To this Solomon refers (3 Kings 8:27) when he says: "If heaven and the heavens of heavens cannot contain Thee, how much less this house which I have built" for Thee? And further on (3 Kings 8:29, 20) he adds: "That Thy eyes may be open upon this house ... of which Thou hast said: My name shall be there; ... that Thou mayest hearken to the supplication of Thy servant and of Thy people Israel." From this it is evident that the house of the sanctuary was set up, not in order to contain God, as abiding therein locally, but that God might be made known there by means of things done and said there; and that those who prayed there might, through reverence for the place, pray more devoutly, so as to be heard more readily.

Reply Obj. 2: Before the coming of Christ, the state of the Old Law was not changed as regards the fulfilment of the Law, which was effected in Christ alone: but it was changed as regards the condition of the people that were under the Law. Because, at first, the people were in the desert, having no fixed abode: afterwards they were engaged in various wars with the neighboring nations; and lastly, at the time of David and Solomon, the state of that people was one of great peace. And then for the first time the temple was built in the place which Abraham, instructed by God, had chosen for the purpose of sacrifice. For it is written (Gen. 22:2) that the Lord commanded Abraham to "offer" his son "for a holocaust upon one of the mountains which I will show thee": and it is related further on (Gen. 22:14) that "he calleth the name of that place, The Lord seeth," as though, according to the Divine prevision, that place were chosen for the worship of God. Hence it is written (Deut. 12:5, 6): "You shall come to the place which the Lord your God shall choose ... and you shall offer ... your holocausts and victims."

Now it was not meet for that place to be pointed out by the building of the temple before the aforesaid time; for three reasons assigned by Rabbi Moses. First, lest the Gentiles might seize hold of that place. Secondly, lest the Gentiles might destroy it. The third reason is lest each tribe might wish that place to fall to their lot, and strifes and quarrels be the result. Hence the temple was not built until they had a king who would be able to quell such quarrels. Until that time a portable tabernacle was employed for divine worship, no place being as yet fixed for the worship of God. This is the literal reason for the distinction between the tabernacle and the temple.

The figurative reason may be assigned to the fact that they signify a twofold state. For the tabernacle, which was changeable, signifies the state of the present changeable life: whereas the temple, which was fixed and stable, signifies the state of future life which is altogether unchangeable. For this reason it is said that in the building of the temple no sound was heard of hammer or saw, to signify that all movements of disturbance will be far removed from the future state. Or else the tabernacle signifies the state of the Old Law; while the temple built by Solomon betokens the state of the New Law. Hence the Jews alone worked at the building of the tabernacle; whereas the temple was built with the cooperation of the Gentiles, viz. the Tyrians and Sidonians.

Reply Obj. 3: The reason for the unity of the temple or tabernacle may be either literal or figurative. The literal reason was the exclusion of idolatry. For the Gentiles put up various temples to various gods: and so, to strengthen in the minds of men their belief in the unity of the Godhead, God wished sacrifices to be offered to Him in one place only. Another reason was in order to show that bodily worship is not acceptable of itself: and so they restrained from offering sacrifices anywhere and everywhere. But the worship of the New Law, in the sacrifice whereof spiritual grace is contained, is of itself acceptable to God; and consequently the multiplication of altars and temples is permitted in the New Law.

As to those matters that regarded the spiritual worship of God, consisting in the teaching of the Law and the Prophets, there were, even under the Old Law, various places, called synagogues, appointed for the people to gather together for the praise of God; just as now there are places called churches in which the Christian people gather together for the divine worship. Thus our church takes the place of both temple and synagogue: since the very sacrifice of the Church is spiritual; wherefore with us the place of sacrifice is not distinct from the place of teaching. The figurative reason may be that hereby is signified the unity of the Church, whether militant or triumphant.

Reply Obj. 4: Just as the unity of the temple or tabernacle betokened the unity of God, or the unity of the Church, so also the division of the tabernacle or temple signified the distinction of those things that are subject to God, and from which we arise to the worship of God. Now the tabernacle was divided into two parts: one was called the "Holy of Holies," and was placed to the west; the other was called the "Holy Place" [*Or 'Sanctuary'. The Douay version uses both expressions], which was situated to the east. Moreover there was a court facing the tabernacle. Accordingly there are two reasons for this distinction. One is in respect of the tabernacle being ordained to the worship of God. Because the different parts of the world are thus betokened by the division of the tabernacle. For that part which was called the Holy of Holies signified the higher world, which is that of spiritual substances: while that part which is called the Holy Place signified the corporeal world. Hence the Holy Place was separated from the Holy of Holies by a veil, which was of four different colors (denoting the four elements), viz. of linen, signifying earth, because linen, i.e. flax, grows out of the earth; purple, signifying water, because the purple tint was made from certain shells found in the sea; violet, signifying air, because it has the color of the air; and scarlet twice dyed, signifying fire: and this because matter composed of the four elements is a veil between us and incorporeal substances. Hence the high-priest alone, and that once a year, entered into the inner tabernacle, i.e. the Holy of Holies: whereby we are taught that man's final perfection consists in his entering into that (higher) world: whereas into the outward tabernacle, i.e. the Holy Place, the priests entered every day: whereas the people were only admitted to the court; because the people were able to perceived material things, the inner nature of which only wise men by dint of study are able to discover.

But with regard to the figurative reason, the outward tabernacle, which was called the Holy Place, betokened the state of the Old Law, as the Apostle says (Heb. 9:6, seqq.): because into that tabernacle "the priests always entered accomplishing the offices of sacrifices." But the inner tabernacle, which was called the Holy of Holies, signified either the glory of heaven or the spiritual state of the New Law to come. To the latter state Christ brought us; and this was signified by the high-priest entering alone, once a year, into the Holy of Holies. The veil betokened the concealing of the spiritual sacrifices under the sacrifices of old. This veil was adorned with four colors: viz. that of linen, to designate purity of the flesh; purple, to denote the sufferings which the saints underwent for God; scarlet twice dyed, signifying the twofold love of God and our neighbor; and violet, in token of heavenly contemplation. With regard to the state of the Old Law the people and the priests were situated differently from one another. For the people saw the mere corporeal sacrifices which were offered in the court: whereas the priests were intent on the inner meaning of the sacrifices, because their faith in the mysteries of Christ was more explicit. Hence they entered into the outer tabernacle. This outer tabernacle was divided from the court by a veil; because some matters relating to the mystery of Christ were hidden from the people, while they were known to the priests: though they were not fully revealed to them, as they were subsequently in the New Testament (cf. Eph. 3:5).

Reply Obj. 5: Worship towards the west was introduced in the Law to the exclusion of idolatry: because all the Gentiles, in reverence to the sun, worshipped towards the east; hence it is written (Ezech. 8:16) that certain men "had their backs towards the temple of the Lord, and their faces to the east, and they adored towards the rising of the sun." Accordingly, in order to prevent this, the tabernacle had the Holy of Holies to westward, that they might adore toward the west. A figurative reason may also be found in the fact that the whole state of the first tabernacle was ordained to foreshadow the death of Christ, which is signified by the west, according to Ps. 67:5: "Who ascendeth unto the west; the Lord is His name."

Reply Obj. 6: Both literal and figurative reasons may be assigned for the things contained in the tabernacle. The literal reason is in connection with the divine worship. And because, as already observed (ad 4), the inner tabernacle, called the Holy of Holies, signified the higher world of spiritual substances, hence that tabernacle contained three things, viz. "the ark of the testament in which was a golden pot that had manna, and the rod of Aaron that had blossomed, and the tables" (Heb. 9:4) on which were written the ten commandments of the Law. Now the ark stood between two "cherubim" that looked one towards the other: and over the ark was a table, called the "propitiatory," raised above the wings of the cherubim, as though it were held up by them; and appearing, to the imagination, to be the very seat of God. For this reason it was called the "propitiatory," as though the people received propitiation thence at the prayers of the high-priest. And so it was held up, so to speak, by the cherubim, in obedience, as it were, to God: while the ark of the testament was like the foot-stool to Him that sat on the propitiatory. These three things denote three things in that higher world: namely, God Who is above all, and incomprehensible to any creature. Hence no likeness of Him was set up; to denote His invisibility. But there was something to represent his seat; since, to wit, the creature, which is beneath God, as the seat under the sitter, is comprehensible. Again in that higher world there are spiritual substances called angels. These are signified by the two cherubim, looking one towards the other, to show that they are at peace with one another, according to Job 25:2: "Who maketh peace in ... high places." For this reason, too, there was more than one cherub, to betoken the multitude of heavenly spirits, and to prevent their receiving worship from those who had been commanded to worship but one God. Moreover there are, enclosed as it were in that spiritual world, the intelligible types of whatsoever takes place in this world, just as in every cause are enclosed the types of its effects, and in the craftsman the types of the works of his craft. This was betokened by the ark, which represented, by means of the three things it contained, the three things of greatest import in human affairs. These are wisdom, signified by the tables of the testament; the power of governing, betokened by the rod of Aaron; and life, betokened by the manna which was the means of sustenance. Or else these three things signified the three Divine attributes, viz. wisdom, in the tables; power, in the rod; goodness, in the manna—both by reason of its sweetness, and because it was through the goodness of God that it was granted to man, wherefore it was preserved as a memorial of the Divine mercy. Again, these three things were represented in Isaias' vision. For he "saw the Lord sitting upon a throne high and elevated"; and the seraphim standing by; and that the house was filled with the glory of the Lord; wherefrom the seraphim cried out: "All the earth is full of His glory" (Isa. 6:1, 3). And so the images of the seraphim were set up, not to be worshipped, for this was forbidden by the first commandment; but as a sign of their function, as stated above.

The outer tabernacle, which denotes this present world, also contained three things, viz. the "altar of incense," which was directly opposite the ark; the "table of proposition," with the twelve loaves of proposition on it, which stood on the northern side; and the "candlestick," which was placed towards the south. These three things seem to correspond to the three which were enclosed in the ark; and they represented the same things as the latter, but more clearly: because, in order that wise men, denoted by the priests entering the temple, might grasp the meaning of these types, it was necessary to express them more manifestly than they are in the Divine or angelic mind. Accordingly the candlestick betokened, as a sensible sign thereof, the wisdom which was expressed on the tables (of the Law) in intelligible words. The altar of incense signified the office of the priest, whose duty it was to bring the people to God: and this was signified also by the rod: because on that altar the sweet-smelling incense was burnt, signifying the holiness of the people acceptable to God: for it is written (Apoc. 8:3) that the smoke of the sweet-smelling spices signifies the "justifications of the saints" (cf. Apoc. 19:8). Moreover it was fitting that the dignity of the priesthood should be denoted, in the ark, by the rod, and, in the outer tabernacle, by the altar of incense: because the priest is the mediator between God and the people, governing the people by Divine power, denoted by the rod; and offering to God the fruit of His government, i.e. the holiness of the people, on the altar of incense, so to speak. The table signified the sustenance of life, just as the manna did: but the former, a more general and a coarser kind of nourishment; the latter, a sweeter and more delicate. Again, the candlestick was fittingly placed on the southern side, while the table was placed to the north: because the south is the right-hand side of the world, while the north is the left-hand side, as stated in De Coelo et Mundo ii; and wisdom, like other spiritual goods, belongs to the right hand, while temporal nourishment belongs on the left, according to Prov. 3:16: "In her left hand (are) riches and glory." And the priestly power is midway between temporal goods and spiritual wisdom; because thereby both spiritual wisdom and temporal goods are dispensed.

Another literal signification may be assigned.

For the ark contained the tables of the Law, in order to prevent forgetfulness of the Law, wherefore it is written (Ex. 24:12): "I will give thee two tables of stone, and the Law, and the commandments which I have written: that thou mayest teach them" to the children of Israel. The rod of Aaron was placed there to restrain the people from insubordination to the priesthood of Aaron; wherefore it is written (Num. 17:10): "Carry back the rod of Aaron into the tabernacle of the testimony, that it may be kept there for a token of the rebellious children of Israel." The manna was kept in the ark to remind them of the benefit conferred by God on the children of Israel in the desert; wherefore it is written (Ex. 16:32): "Fill a gomor of it, and let it be kept unto generations to come hereafter, that they may know the bread wherewith I fed you in the wilderness." The candlestick was set up to enhance the beauty of the temple, for the magnificence of a house depends on its being well lighted. Now the candlestick had seven branches, as Josephus observes (Antiquit. iii, 7, 8), to signify the seven planets, wherewith the whole world is illuminated. Hence the candlestick was placed towards the south; because for us the course of the planets is from that quarter. The altar of incense was instituted that there might always be in the tabernacle a sweet-smelling smoke; both through respect for the tabernacle, and as a remedy for the stenches arising from the shedding of blood and the slaying of animals. For men despise evil-smelling things as being vile, whereas sweet-smelling things are much appreciated. The table was placed there to signify that the priests who served the temple should take their food in the temple: wherefore, as stated in Matt. 12:4, it was lawful for none but the priests to eat the twelve loaves which were put on the table in memory of the twelve tribes. And the table was not placed in the middle directly in front of the propitiatory, in order to exclude an idolatrous rite: for the Gentiles, on the feasts of the moon, set up a table in front of the idol of the moon, wherefore it is written (Jer. 7:18): "The women knead the dough, to make cakes to the queen of heaven."

In the court outside the tabernacle was the altar of holocausts, on which sacrifices of those things which the people possessed were offered to God: and consequently the people who offered these sacrifices to God by the hands of the priest could be present in the court. But the priests alone, whose function it was to offer the people to God, could approach the inner altar, whereon the very devotion and holiness of the people was offered to God. And this altar was put up outside the tabernacle and in the court, to the exclusion of idolatrous worship: for the Gentiles placed altars inside the temples to offer up sacrifices thereon to idols.

The figurative reason for all these things may be taken from the relation of the tabernacle to Christ, who was foreshadowed therein. Now it must be observed that to show the imperfection of the figures of the Law, various figures were instituted in the temple to betoken Christ. For He was foreshadowed by the "propitiatory," since He is "a propitiation for our sins" (1 John 2:2). This propitiatory was fittingly carried by cherubim, since of Him it is written (Heb. 1:6): "Let all the angels of God adore Him." He is also signified by the ark: because just as the ark was made of setim-wood, so was Christ's body composed of most pure members. More over it was gilded: for Christ was full of wisdom and charity, which are betokened by gold. And in the ark was a golden pot, i.e. His holy soul, having manna, i.e. "all the fulness of the Godhead" (Col. 2:9). Also there was a rod in the ark, i.e. His priestly power: for "He was made a ... priest for ever" (Heb. 6:20). And therein were the tables of the Testament, to denote that Christ Himself is a lawgiver. Again, Christ was signified by the candlestick, for He said Himself (John 8:12): "I am the Light of the world"; while the seven lamps denoted the seven gifts of the Holy Ghost. He is also betokened in the table, because He is our spiritual food, according to John 6:41, 51: "I am the living bread": and the twelve loaves signified the twelve apostles, or their teaching. Or again, the candlestick and table may signify the Church's teaching, and faith, which also enlightens and refreshes. Again, Christ is signified by the two altars of holocausts and incense. Because all works of virtue must be offered to us to God through Him; both those whereby we afflict the body, which are offered, as it were, on the altar of holocausts; and those which, with greater perfection of mind, are offered to God in Christ, by the spiritual desires of the perfect, on the altar of incense, as it were, according to Heb. 13:15: "By Him therefore let us offer the sacrifice of praise always to God."

Reply Obj. 7: The Lord commanded an altar to be made for the offering of sacrifices and gifts, in honor of God, and for the upkeep of the ministers who served the tabernacle. Now concerning the construction of the altar the Lord issued a twofold precept. One was at the beginning of the Law (Ex. 20:24, seqq.) when the Lord commanded them to make "an altar of earth," or at least "not of hewn stones"; and again, not to make the altar high, so as to make it necessary to "go up" to it "by steps." This was in detestation of idolatrous worship: for the Gentiles made their altars ornate and high, thinking that there was something holy and divine in such things. For this reason, too, the Lord commanded (Deut. 16:21): "Thou shalt plant no grove, nor any tree near the altar of the Lord thy God": since idolaters were wont to offer sacrifices beneath trees, on account of the pleasantness and shade afforded by them. There was also a figurative reason for these precepts. Because we must confess that in Christ, Who is our altar, there is the true nature of flesh, as regards His humanity—and this is to make an altar of earth; and again, in regard to His Godhead, we must confess His equality with the Father—and this is "not to go up" to the altar by steps. Moreover we should not couple the doctrine of Christ to that of the Gentiles, which provokes men to lewdness.

But when once the tabernacle had been constructed to the honor of God, there was no longer reason to fear these occasions of idolatry. Wherefore the Lord commanded the altar of holocausts to be made of brass, and to be conspicuous to all the people; and the altar of incense, which was visible to none but the priests. Nor was brass so precious as to give the people an occasion for idolatry.

Since, however, the reason for the precept, "Thou shalt not go up by steps unto My altar" (Ex. 20:26) is stated to have been "lest thy nakedness be discovered," it should be observed that this too was instituted with the purpose of preventing idolatry, for in the feasts of Priapus the Gentiles uncovered their nakedness before the people. But later on the priests were prescribed the use of loin-cloths for the sake of decency: so that without any danger the altar could be placed so high that the priests when offering sacrifices would go up by steps of wood, not fixed but movable.

Reply Obj. 8: The body of the tabernacle consisted of boards placed on end, and covered on the inside with curtains of four different colors, viz. twisted linen, violet, purple, and scarlet twice dyed. These curtains, however, covered the sides only of the tabernacle; and the roof of the tabernacle was covered with violet-colored skins; and over this there was another covering of rams' skins dyed red; and over this there was a third curtain made of goats' hair, which covered not only the roof of the tabernacle, but also reached to the ground and covered the boards of the tabernacle on the outside. The literal reason of these coverings taken altogether was the adornment and protection of the tabernacle, that it might be an object of respect. Taken singly, according to some, the curtains denoted the starry heaven, which is adorned with various stars; the curtain (of goats' skin) signified the waters which are above the firmament; the skins dyed red denoted the empyrean heaven, where the angels are; the violet skins, the heaven of the Blessed Trinity.

The figurative meaning of these things is that the boards of which the tabernacle was constructed signify the faithful of Christ, who compose the Church. The boards were covered on the inner side by curtains of four colors: because the faithful are inwardly adorned with the four virtues: for "the twisted linen," as the gloss observes, "signifies the flesh refulgent with purity; violet signifies the mind desirous of heavenly things; purple denotes the flesh subject to passions; the twice dyed scarlet betokens the mind in the midst of the passions enlightened by the love of God and our neighbor." The coverings of the building designate prelates and doctors, who ought to be conspicuous for their heavenly manner of life, signified by the violet colored skins: and who should also be ready to suffer martyrdom, denoted by the skins dyed red; and austere of life and patient in adversity, betokened by the curtains of goats' hair, which were exposed to wind and rain, as the gloss observes.

Reply Obj. 9: The literal reason for the sanctification of the tabernacle and vessels was that they might be treated with greater reverence, being deputed, as it were, to the divine worship by this consecration. The figurative reason is that this sanctification signified the sanctification of the living tabernacle, i.e. the faithful of whom the Church of Christ is composed.

Reply Obj. 10: Under the Old Law there were seven temporal solemnities, and one continual solemnity, as may be gathered from Num. 28, 29. There was a continual feast, since the lamb was sacrificed every day, morning and evening: and this continual feast of an abiding sacrifice signified the perpetuity of Divine bliss. Of the temporal feasts the first was that which was repeated every week. This was the solemnity of the "Sabbath," celebrated in memory of the work of the creation of the universe. Another solemnity, viz. the "New Moon," was repeated every month, and was observed in memory of the work of the Divine government. For the things of this lower world owe their variety chiefly to the movement of the moon; wherefore this feast was kept at the new moon: and not at the full moon, to avoid the worship of idolaters who used to offer sacrifices to the moon at that particular time. And these two blessings are bestowed in common on the whole human race; and hence they were repeated more frequently.

The other five feasts were celebrated once a year: and they commemorated the benefits which had been conferred especially on that people. For there was the feast of the "Passover" in the first month to commemorate the blessing of being delivered out of Egypt. The feast of "Pentecost" was celebrated fifty days later, to recall the blessing of the giving of the Law. The other three feasts were kept in the seventh month, nearly the whole of which was solemnized by them, just as the seventh day. For on the first of the seventh month was the feast of "Trumpets," in memory of the delivery of Isaac, when Abraham found the ram caught by its horns, which they represented by the horns which they blew. The feast of Trumpets was a kind of invitation whereby they prepared themselves to keep the following feast which was kept on the tenth day. This was the feast of "Expiation," in memory of the blessing whereby, at the prayer of Moses, God forgave the people's sin of worshipping the calf. After this was the feast of "Scenopegia" or of "Tents," which was kept for seven days, to commemorate the blessing of being protected and led by God through the desert, where they lived in tents. Hence during this feast they had to take "the fruits of the fairest tree," i.e. the citron, "and the trees of dense foliage" [*Douay and A. V. and R. V. read: 'Boughs of thick trees'], i.e. the myrtle, which is fragrant, "and the branches of palm-trees, and willows of the brook," which retain their greenness a long time; and these are to be found in the Land of promise; to signify that God had brought them through the arid land of the wilderness to a land of delights. On the eighth day another feast was observed, of "Assembly and Congregation," on which the people collected the expenses necessary for the divine worship: and it signified the uniting of the people and the peace granted to them in the Land of promise.

The figurative reason for these feasts was that the continual sacrifice of the lamb foreshadowed the perpetuity of Christ, Who is the "Lamb of God," according to Heb. 13:8: "Jesus Christ yesterday and today, and the same for ever." The Sabbath signified the spiritual rest bestowed by Christ, as stated in Heb. 4. The Neomenia, which is the beginning of the new moon, signified the enlightening of the primitive Church by Christ's preaching and miracles. The feast of Pentecost signified the Descent of the Holy Ghost on the apostles. The feast of Trumpets signified the preaching of the apostles. The feast of Expiation signified the cleansing of the Christian people from sins: and the feast of Tabernacles signified their pilgrimage in this world, wherein they walk by advancing in virtue. The feast of Assembly or Congregation foreshadowed the assembly of the faithful in the kingdom of heaven: wherefore this feast is described as "most holy" (Lev. 23:36). These three feasts followed immediately on one another, because those who expiate their vices should advance in virtue, until they come to see God, as stated in Ps. 83:8.

FIFTH ARTICLE [I-II, Q. 102, Art. 5]

Whether There Can Be Any Suitable Cause for the Sacraments of the Old Law?

Objection 1: It would seem that there can be no suitable cause for the sacraments of the Old Law. Because those things that are done for the purpose of divine worship should not be like the observances of idolaters: since it is written (Deut. 12:31): "Thou shalt not do in like manner to the Lord thy God: for they have done to their gods all the abominations which the Lord abhorreth." Now worshippers of idols used to knive themselves to the shedding of blood: for it is related (3 Kings 18:28) that they "cut themselves after their manner with knives and lancets, till they were all covered with blood." For this reason the Lord commanded (Deut. 14:1): "You shall not cut yourselves nor make any baldness for the dead." Therefore it was unfitting for circumcision to be prescribed by the Law (Lev. 12:3).

Obj. 2: Further, those things which are done for the worship of God should be marked with decorum and gravity; according to Ps. 34:18: "I will praise Thee in a grave [Douay: 'strong'] people." But it seems to savor of levity for a man to eat with haste. Therefore it was unfittingly commanded (Ex. 12:11) that they should eat the Paschal lamb "in haste." Other things too relative to the eating of the lamb were prescribed, which seem altogether unreasonable.

Obj. 3: Further, the sacraments of the Old Law were figures of the sacraments of the New Law. Now the Paschal lamb signified the sacrament of the Eucharist, according to 1 Cor. 5:7: "Christ our Pasch is sacrificed." Therefore there should also have been some sacraments of the Old Law to foreshadow the other sacraments of the New Law, such as Confirmation, Extreme Unction, and Matrimony, and so forth.

Obj. 4: Further, purification can scarcely be done except by removing something impure. But as far as God is concerned, no bodily thing is reputed impure, because all bodies are God's creatures; and "every creature of God is good, and nothing to be rejected that is received with thanksgiving" (1 Tim. 4:4). It was therefore unfitting for them to be purified after contact with a corpse, or any similar corporeal infection.

Obj. 5: Further, it is written (Ecclus. 34:4): "What can be made clean by the unclean?" But the ashes of the red heifer [*Cf. Heb. 9:13] which was burnt, were unclean, since they made a man unclean: for it is stated (Num. 19:7, seqq.) that the priest who immolated her was rendered unclean "until the evening"; likewise he that burnt her; and he that gathered up her ashes. Therefore it was unfittingly prescribed there that the unclean should be purified by being sprinkled with those cinders.

Obj. 6: Further, sins are not something corporeal that can be carried from one place to another: nor can man be cleansed from sin by means of something unclean. It was therefore unfitting for the purpose of expiating the sins of the people that the priest should confess the sins of the children of Israel on one of the buck-goats, that it might carry them away into the wilderness: while they were rendered unclean by the other, which they used for the purpose of purification, by burning it together with the calf outside the camp; so that they had to wash their clothes and their bodies with water (Lev. 16).

Obj. 7: Further, what is already cleansed should not be cleansed again. It was therefore unfitting to apply a second purification to a man cleansed from leprosy, or to a house; as laid down in Lev. 14.

Obj. 8: Further, spiritual uncleanness cannot be cleansed by material water or by shaving the hair. Therefore it seems unreasonable that the Lord ordered (Ex. 30:18, seqq.) the making of a brazen laver with its foot, that the priests might wash their hands and feet before entering the temple; and that He commanded (Num. 8:7) the Levites to be sprinkled with the water of purification, and to shave all the hairs of their flesh.

Objection 9: Further, that which is greater cannot be cleansed by that which is less. Therefore it was unfitting that, in the Law, the higher and lower priests, as stated in Lev. 8 [*Cf. Ex. 29], and the Levites, according to Num. 8, should be consecrated with any bodily anointing, bodily sacrifices, and bodily oblations.

Objection 10: Further, as stated in 1 Kings 16:7, "Man seeth those things that appear, but the Lord beholdeth the heart." But those things that appear outwardly in man are the dispositions of his body and his clothes. Therefore it was unfitting for certain special garments to be appointed to the higher and lower priests, as related in Ex. 28 [*Cf. Lev. 8:7, seqq.]. It seems, moreover, unreasonable that anyone should be debarred from the priesthood on account of defects in the body, as stated in Lev. 21:17, seqq.: "Whosoever of thy seed throughout their families, hath a blemish, he shall not offer bread to his God ... if he be blind, if he be lame," etc. It seems, therefore, that the sacraments of the Old Law were unreasonable.

*On the contrary,* It is written (Lev. 20:8): "I am the Lord that sanctify you." But nothing unreasonable is done by God, for it is written (Ps. 103:24): "Thou hast made all things in wisdom." Therefore there was nothing without a reasonable cause in the sacraments of the Old Law, which were ordained to the sanctification of man.

*I answer that,* As stated above (Q. 101, A. 4), the sacraments are, properly speaking, things applied to the worshippers of God for their consecration so as, in some way, to depute them to the worship of God. Now the worship of God belonged in a general way to the whole people; but in a special way, it belonged to the priests and Levites, who were the ministers of divine worship. Consequently, in these sacraments of the Old Law, certain things concerned the whole people in general; while others belonged to the ministers.

In regard to both, three things were necessary. The first was to be established in the state of worshipping God: and this institution was brought about—for all in general, by circumcision, without which no one was admitted to any of the legal observances—and for the priests, by their consecration. The second thing required was the use of those things that pertain to divine worship. And thus, as to the people, there was the partaking of the paschal banquet, to which no uncircumcised man was admitted, as is clear from Ex. 12:43, seqq.: and, as to the priests, the offering of the victims, and the eating of the loaves of proposition and of other things that were allotted to the use of the priests. The third thing required was the removal of all impediments to divine worship, viz. of uncleannesses. And then, as to the people, certain purifications were instituted for the removal of certain external uncleannesses; and also expiations from sins; while, as to the priests and Levites, the washing of hands and feet and the shaving of the hair were instituted.

And all these things had reasonable causes, both literal, in so far as they were ordained to the worship of God for the time being, and figurative, in so far as they were ordained to foreshadow Christ: as we shall see by taking them one by one.

Reply Obj. 1: The chief literal reason for circumcision was in order that man might profess his belief in one God. And because Abraham was the first to sever himself from the infidels, by going out from his house and kindred, for this reason he was the first to receive circumcision. This reason is set forth by the Apostle (Rom. 4:9, seqq.) thus: "He received the sign of circumcision, a seal of the justice of the faith which he had, being uncircumcised"; because, to wit, we are told that "unto Abraham faith was reputed to justice," for the reason that "against hope he believed in hope," i.e. against the hope that is of nature he believed in the hope that is of grace, "that he might be made the father of many nations," when he was an old man, and his wife an old and barren woman. And in order that this declaration, and imitation of Abraham's faith, might be fixed firmly in the hearts of the Jews, they received in their flesh such a sign as they could not forget, wherefore it is written (Gen. 17:13): "My covenant shall be in your flesh for a perpetual covenant." This was done on the eighth day, because until then a child is very tender, and so might be seriously injured; and is considered as something not yet consolidated: wherefore neither are animals offered before the eighth day. And it was not delayed after that time, lest some might refuse the sign of circumcision on account of the pain: and also lest the parents, whose love for their children increases as they become used to their presence and as they grow older, should withdraw their children from circumcision. A second reason may have been the weakening of concupiscence in that member. A third motive may have been to revile the worship of Venus and Priapus, which gave honor to that part of the body. The Lord's prohibition extended only to the cutting of oneself in honor of idols: and such was not the circumcision of which we have been speaking.

The figurative reason for circumcision was that it foreshadowed the removal of corruption, which was to be brought about by Christ, and will be perfectly fulfilled in the eighth age, which is the age of those who rise from the dead. And since all corruption of guilt and punishment comes to us through our carnal origin, from the sin of our first parent, therefore circumcision was applied to the generative member. Hence the Apostle says (Col. 2:11): "You are circumcised" in Christ "with circumcision not made by hand in despoiling of the body of the flesh, but in the circumcision of" Our Lord Jesus "Christ."

Reply Obj. 2: The literal reason of the paschal banquet was to commemorate the blessing of being led by God out of Egypt. Hence by celebrating this banquet they declared that they belonged to that people which God had taken to Himself out of Egypt. For when they were delivered from Egypt, they were commanded to sprinkle the lamb's blood on the transoms of their house doors, as though declaring that they were averse to the rites of the Egyptians who worshipped the ram. Wherefore they were delivered by the sprinkling or rubbing of the blood of the lamb on the door-posts, from the danger of extermination which threatened the Egyptians.

Now two things are to be observed in their departure from Egypt: namely, their haste in going, for the Egyptians pressed them to go forth speedily, as related in Ex. 12:33; and there was danger that anyone who did not hasten to go with the crowd might be slain by the Egyptians. Their haste was shown in two ways. First by what they ate. For they were commanded to eat unleavened bread, as a sign "that it could not be leavened, the Egyptians pressing them to depart"; and to eat roast meat, for this took less time to prepare; and that they should not break a bone thereof, because in their haste there was no time to break bones. Secondly, as to the manner of eating. For it is written: "You shall gird your reins, and you shall have shoes on your feet, holding staves in your hands, and you shall eat in haste": which clearly designates men at the point of starting on a journey. To this also is to be referred the command: "In one house shall it be eaten, neither shall you carry forth of the flesh thereof out of the house": because, to wit, on account of their haste, they could not send any gifts of it.

The stress they suffered while in Egypt was denoted by the wild lettuces. The figurative reason is evident, because the sacrifice of the paschal lamb signified the sacrifice of Christ according to 1 Cor. 5:7: "Christ our pasch is sacrificed." The blood of the lamb, which ensured deliverance from the destroyer, by being sprinkled on the ransoms, signified faith in Christ's Passion, in the hearts and on the lips of the faithful, by which same Passion we are delivered from sin and death, according to 1 Pet. 1:18: "You were … redeemed … with the precious blood … of a lamb unspotted." The partaking of its flesh signified the eating of Christ's body in the Sacrament; and the flesh was roasted at the fire to signify Christ's Passion or charity. And it was eaten with unleavened bread to signify the blameless life of the faithful who partake of Christ's body, according to 1 Cor. 5:8: "Let us feast … with the unleavened bread of sincerity and truth." The wild lettuces were added to denote repentance for sins, which is required of those who receive the body of Christ. Their loins were girt in sign of chastity: and the shoes of their feet are the examples of our dead ancestors. The staves they were to hold in their hands denoted pastoral authority: and it was commanded that the paschal lamb should be eaten in one house, i.e. in a catholic church, and not in the conventicles of heretics.

Reply Obj. 3: Some of the sacraments of the New Law had corresponding figurative sacraments in the Old Law. For Baptism, which is the sacrament of Faith, corresponds to circumcision. Hence it is written (Col. 2:11, 12): "You are circumcised … in the circumcision of" Our Lord Jesus "Christ: buried with Him in Baptism." In the New Law the sacrament of the Eucharist corresponds to the banquet of the paschal lamb. The sacrament of Penance in the New Law corresponds to all the purifications of the Old Law. The sacrament of Orders corresponds to the consecration of the pontiff and of the priests. To the sacrament of Confirmation, which is the sacrament of the fulness of grace, there would be no corresponding sacrament of the Old Law, because the time of fulness had not yet come, since "the Law brought no man [Vulg.: 'nothing'] to perfection" (Heb. 7:19). The same applies to the sacrament of Extreme Unction, which is an immediate preparation for entrance into glory, to which the way was not yet opened out in the Old Law, since the price had not yet been paid. Matrimony did indeed exist under the Old Law, as a function of nature, but not as the sacrament of the union of Christ with the Church, for that union was not as yet brought about. Hence under the Old Law it was allowable to give a bill of divorce, which is contrary to the nature of the sacrament.

Reply Obj. 4: As already stated, the purifications of the Old Law were ordained for the removal of impediments to the divine worship: which worship is twofold; viz. spiritual, consisting in devotion of the mind to God; and corporal, consisting in sacrifices, oblations, and so forth. Now men are hindered in the spiritual worship by sins, whereby men were said to be polluted, for instance, by idolatry, murder, adultery, or incest. From such pollutions men were purified by certain sacrifices, offered either for the whole community in general, or also for the sins of individuals; not that those carnal sacrifices had of themselves the power of expiating sin; but that they signified that expiation of sins which was to be effected by Christ, and of which those of old became partakers by protesting their faith in the Redeemer, while taking part in the figurative sacrifices.

The impediments to external worship consisted in certain bodily uncleannesses; which were considered in the first place as existing in man, and consequently in other animals also, and in man's clothes, dwelling-place, and vessels. In man himself uncleanness was considered as arising partly from himself and partly from contact with unclean things. Anything proceeding from man was reputed unclean that was already subject to corruption, or exposed thereto: and consequently since death is a kind of corruption, the human corpse was considered unclean. In like manner, since leprosy arises from corruption of the humors, which break out externally and infect other persons, therefore were lepers also considered unclean; and, again, women suffering from a flow of blood, whether from weakness, or from nature (either at the monthly course or at the time of conception); and, for the same reason, men were reputed unclean if they suffered from a flow of seed, whether due to weakness, to nocturnal pollution, or to sexual intercourse. Because every humor issuing from man in the aforesaid ways involves some unclean infection. Again, man contracted uncleanness by touching any unclean thing whatever.

Now there was both a literal and a figurative reason for these uncleannesses. The literal reason was taken from the reverence due to those things that belong to the divine worship: both because men are not wont, when unclean, to touch precious things: and in order that by rarely approaching sacred things they might have greater respect for them. For since man could seldom avoid all the aforesaid uncleannesses, the result was that men could seldom approach to touch things belonging to the worship of God, so that when they did approach, they did so with greater reverence and humility. Moreover, in some of these the literal reason was that men should not be kept away from worshipping God through fear of coming in contact with lepers and others similarly afflicted with loathsome and contagious diseases. In others, again, the reason was to avoid idolatrous worship: because in their sacrificial rites the Gentiles sometimes employed human blood and seed. All these bodily uncleannesses were purified either by the mere sprinkling of water, or, in the case of those which were more grievous, by some sacrifice of expiation for the sin which was the occasion of the uncleanness in question.

The figurative reason for these uncleannesses was that they were figures of various sins. For the uncleanness of any corpse signifies the uncleanness of sin, which is the death of the soul. The uncleanness of leprosy betokened the uncleanness of heretical doctrine: both because heretical doctrine is contagious just as leprosy is, and because no doctrine is so false as not to have some truth mingled with error, just as on the surface of a leprous body one may distinguish the healthy parts from those that are infected. The uncleanness of a woman suffering from a flow of blood denotes the uncleanness of idolatry, on account of the blood which is offered up. The uncleanness of the man who has suffered seminal loss signifies the uncleanness of empty words, for "the seed is the word of God." The uncleanness of sexual intercourse and of the woman in child-birth signifies the uncleanness of original sin. The uncleanness of the woman in her periods signifies the uncleanness of a mind that is sensualized by pleasure. Speaking generally, the uncleanness contracted by touching an unclean thing denotes the uncleanness arising from consent in another's sin, according to 2 Cor. 6:17: "Go out from among them, and be ye separate … and touch not the unclean thing."

Moreover, this uncleanness arising from the touch was contracted even by inanimate objects; for whatever was touched in any way by an unclean man, became itself unclean. Wherein the Law attenuated the superstition of the Gentiles, who held that uncleanness was contracted not only by touch, but also by speech or looks, as Rabbi Moses states (Doct. Perplex. iii) of a woman in her periods. The mystical sense of this was that "to God the wicked and his wickedness are hateful alike" (Wis. 14:9).

There was also an uncleanness of inanimate things considered in themselves, such as the uncleanness of leprosy in a house or in clothes. For just as leprosy occurs in men through a corrupt humor causing putrefaction and corruption in the flesh; so, too, through some corruption and excess of humidity or dryness, there arises sometimes a kind of corruption in the stones with which a house is built, or in clothes. Hence the Law called this corruption by the name of leprosy, whereby a house or a garment was deemed to be unclean: both because all corruption savored of uncleanness, as stated above, and because the Gentiles worshipped their household gods as a preservative against this corruption. Hence the Law prescribed such houses, where this kind of corruption was of a lasting nature, to be destroyed; and such garments to be burnt, in order to avoid all occasion of idolatry. There was also an uncleanness of vessels, of which it is written (Num. 19:15): "The vessel that hath no cover, and binding over it, shall be unclean." The cause of this uncleanness was that anything unclean might easily drop into such vessels, so as to render them unclean. Moreover, this command aimed at the prevention of idolatry. For idolaters believed that if mice, lizards, or the like, which they used to sacrifice to the idols, fell into the vessels or into the water, these became more pleasing to the gods. Even now some women let down uncovered vessels in honor of the nocturnal deities which they call "Janae."

The figurative reason of these uncleannesses is that the leprosy of a house signified the uncleanness of the assembly of heretics; the leprosy of a linen garment signified an evil life arising from bitterness of mind; the leprosy of a woolen garment denoted the wickedness of flatterers; leprosy in the warp signified the vices of the soul; leprosy on the woof denoted sins of the flesh, for as the warp is in the woof, so is the soul in the body. The vessel that has neither cover nor binding, betokens a man who lacks the veil of taciturnity, and who is unrestrained by any severity of discipline.

Reply Obj. 5: As stated above (ad 4), there was a twofold uncleanness in the Law; one by way of corruption in the mind or in the body; and this was the graver uncleanness; the other was by mere contact with an unclean thing, and this was less grave, and was more easily expiated. Because the former uncleanness was expiated by sacrifices for sins, since all corruption is due to sin, and signifies sin: whereas the latter uncleanness was expiated by the mere sprinkling of a certain water, of which water we read in Num. 19. For there God commanded them to take a red cow in memory of the sin they had committed in worshipping a calf. And a cow is mentioned rather than a calf, because it was thus that the Lord was wont to designate the synagogue, according to Osee 4:16: "Israel hath gone astray like a wanton heifer": and this was, perhaps, because they worshipped heifers after the custom of Egypt, according to Osee 10:5: "(They) have worshipped the kine of Bethaven." And in detestation of the sin of idolatry it was sacrificed outside the camp; in fact, whenever sacrifice was offered up in expiation of the multitude of sins, it was all burnt outside the camp. Moreover, in order to show that this sacrifice cleansed the people from all their sins, "the priest" dipped "his finger in her blood," and sprinkled "it over against the door of the tabernacle seven times"; for the number seven signified universality. Further, the very sprinkling of blood pertained to the detestation of idolatry, in which the blood that was offered up was not poured out, but was collected together, and men gathered round it to eat in honor of the idols. Likewise it was burnt by fire, either because God appeared to Moses in a fire, and the Law was given from the midst of fire; or to denote that idolatry, together with all that was connected therewith, was to be extirpated altogether; just as the cow was burnt "with her skin and her flesh, her blood and dung being delivered to the flames." To this burning were added "cedar-wood, and hyssop, and scarlet twice dyed," to signify that just as cedar-wood is not liable to putrefaction, and scarlet twice dyed does not easily lose its color, and hyssop retains its odor after it has been dried; so also was this sacrifice for the preservation of the whole people, and for their good behavior and devotion. Hence it is said of the ashes of the cow: "That they may be reserved for the multitude of the children of Israel." Or, according to Josephus (Antiq. iii, 8, 9, 10), the four elements are indicated here: for "cedar-wood" was added to the fire, to signify the earth, on account of its earthiness; "hyssop," to signify the air, on account of its smell; "scarlet twice dyed," to signify water, for the same reason as purple, on account of the dyes which are taken out of the water: thus denoting the fact that this sacrifice was offered to the Creator of the four elements. And since this sacrifice was offered for the sin of idolatry, both "he that burned her," and "he that gathered up the ashes," and "he that sprinkled the water" in which the ashes were placed, were deemed unclean in detestation of that sin, in order to show that whatever was in any way connected with idolatry should be cast aside as being unclean. From this uncleanness they were purified by the mere washing of their clothes; nor did they need to be sprinkled with the water on account of this kind of uncleanness, because otherwise the process would have been unending, since he that sprinkled the water became unclean, so that if he were to sprinkle himself he would remain unclean; and if another were to sprinkle him, that one would have become unclean, and in like manner, whoever might sprinkle him, and so on indefinitely.

The figurative reason of this sacrifice was that the red cow signified Christ in respect of his assumed weakness, denoted by the female sex; while the color of the cow designated the blood of His Passion. And the "red cow was of full age," because all Christ's works are perfect, "in which there" was "no blemish"; "and which" had "not carried the yoke," because Christ was innocent, nor did He carry the yoke of sin. It was commanded to be taken to Moses, because they blamed Him for transgressing the law of Moses by breaking the Sabbath. And it was commanded to be delivered "to Eleazar the priest," because Christ was delivered into the hands of the priests to be slain. It was immolated "without the camp," because Christ "suffered outside the gate" (Heb. 13:12). And the priest dipped "his finger in her blood," because the mystery of Christ's Passion should be considered and imitated.

It was sprinkled "over against ... the tabernacle," which denotes the synagogue, to signify either the condemnation of the unbelieving Jews, or the purification of believers; and this "seven times," in token either of the seven gifts of the Holy Ghost, or of the seven days wherein all time is comprised. Again, all things that pertain to the Incarnation of Christ should be burnt with fire, i.e. they should be understood spiritually; for the "skin" and "flesh" signified Christ's outward works; the "blood" denoted the subtle inward force which quickened His external deeds; the "dung" betokened His weariness, His thirst, and all such like things pertaining to His weakness. Three things were added, viz. "cedar-wood," which denotes the height of hope or contemplation; "hyssop," in token of humility or faith; "scarlet twice dyed," which denotes twofold charity; for it is by these three that we should cling to Christ suffering. The ashes of this burning were gathered by "a man that is clean," because the relics of the Passion came into the possession of the Gentiles, who were not guilty of Christ's death. The ashes were put into water for the purpose of expiation, because Baptism receives from Christ's Passion the power of washing away sins. The priest who immolated and burned the cow, and he who burned, and he who gathered together the ashes, were unclean, as also he that sprinkled the water: either because the Jews became unclean through putting Christ to death, whereby our sins are expiated; and this, until the evening, i.e. until the end of the world, when the remnants of Israel will be converted; or else because they who handle sacred things with a view to the cleansing of others contract certain uncleannesses, as Gregory says (Pastor. ii, 5); and this until the evening, i.e. until the end of this life.

Reply Obj. 6: As stated above (ad 5), an uncleanness which was caused by corruption either of mind or of body was expiated by sin-offerings. Now special sacrifices were wont to be offered for the sins of individuals: but since some were neglectful about expiating such sins and uncleannesses; or, through ignorance, failed to offer this expiation; it was laid down that once a year, on the tenth day of the seventh month, a sacrifice of expiation should be offered for the whole people. And because, as the Apostle says (Heb. 7:28), "the Law maketh men priests, who have infirmity," it behooved the priest first of all to offer a calf for his own sins, in memory of Aaron's sin in fashioning the molten calf; and besides, to offer a ram for a holocaust, which signified that the priestly sovereignty denoted by the ram, who is the head of the flock, was to be ordained to the glory of God. Then he offered two he-goats for the people: one of which was offered in expiation of the sins of the multitude. For the he-goat is an evil-smelling animal; and from its skin clothes are made having a pungent odor; to signify the stench, uncleanness and the sting of sin. After this he-goat had been immolated, its blood was taken, together with the blood of the calf, into the Holy of Holies, and the entire sanctuary was sprinkled with it; to signify that the tabernacle was cleansed from the uncleanness of the children of Israel. But the corpses of the he-goat and calf which had been offered up for sin had to be burnt, to denote the destruction of sins. They were not, however, burnt on the altar: since none but holocausts were burnt thereon; but it was prescribed that they should be burnt without the camp, in detestation of sin: for this was done whenever sacrifice was offered for a grievous sin, or for the multitude of sins. The other goat was let loose into the wilderness: not indeed to offer it to the demons, whom the Gentiles worshipped in desert places, because it was unlawful to offer aught to them; but in order to point out the effect of the sacrifice which had been offered up. Hence the priest put his hand on its head, while confessing the sins of the children of Israel: as though that goat were to carry them away into the wilderness, where it would be devoured by wild beasts, because it bore the punishment of the people's sins. And it was said to bear the sins of the people, either because the forgiveness of the people's sins was signified by its being let loose, or because on its head written lists of sins were fastened.

The figurative reason of these things was that Christ was foreshadowed both by the calf, on account of His power; and by the ram, because He is the Head of the faithful; and by the he-goat, on account of "the likeness of sinful flesh" (Rom. 8:3). Moreover, Christ was sacrificed for the sins of both priests and people: since both those of high and those of low degree are cleansed from sin by His Passion. The blood of the calf and of the goat was brought into the Holies by the priest, because the entrance to the kingdom of heaven was opened to us by the blood of Christ's Passion. Their bodies were burnt without the camp, because "Christ suffered without the gate," as the Apostle declares (Heb. 13:12). The scape-goat may denote either Christ's Godhead Which went away into solitude when the Man Christ suffered, not by going to another place, but by restraining His power: or it may signify the base concupiscence which we ought to cast away from ourselves, while we offer up to Our Lord acts of virtue.

With regard to the uncleanness contracted by those who burnt these sacrifices, the reason is the same as that which we assigned (ad 5) to the sacrifice of the red heifer.

Reply Obj. 7: The legal rite did not cleanse the leper of his deformity, but declared him to be cleansed. This is shown by the words of Lev. 14:3, seqq., where it was said that the priest, "when he shall find that the leprosy is cleansed," shall command "him that is to be purified": consequently, the leper was already healed: but he was said to be purified in so far as the verdict of the priest restored him to the society of men and to the worship of God. It happened sometimes, however, that bodily leprosy was miraculously cured by the legal rite, when the priest erred in his judgment.

Now this purification of a leper was twofold: for, in the first place, he was declared to be clean; and, secondly, he was restored, as clean, to the society of men and to the worship of God, to wit, after seven days. At the first purification the leper who sought to be cleansed offered for himself "two living sparrows ... cedar-wood, and scarlet, and hyssop," in such wise that a sparrow and the hyssop should be tied to the cedar-wood with a scarlet thread, so that the cedar-wood was like the handle of an aspersory: while the hyssop and sparrow were that part of the aspersory which was dipped into the blood of the other sparrow which was "immolated ... over living waters." These things he offered as an antidote to the four defects of leprosy: for cedar-wood, which is not subject to putrefaction, was offered against the putrefaction; hyssop, which is a sweet-smelling herb, was offered up against the stench; a living sparrow was offered up against numbness; and scarlet, which has a vivid color, was offered up against the repulsive color of leprosy. The living sparrow was let loose to fly away into the plain, because the leper was restored to his former liberty.

On the eighth day he was admitted to divine worship, and was restored to the society of men; but only after having shaved all the hair of his body, and washed his clothes, because leprosy rots the hair, infects the clothes, and gives them an evil smell. Afterwards a sacrifice was offered for his sin, since leprosy was frequently a result of sin: and some of the blood of the sacrifice was put on the tip of the ear of the man that was to be cleansed, "and on the thumb of his right hand, and the great toe of his right foot"; because it is in these parts that leprosy is first diagnosed and felt. In this rite, moreover, three liquids were employed: viz. blood, against the corruption of the blood; oil, to denote the healing of the disease; and living waters, to wash away the filth.

The figurative reason was that the Divine and human natures in Christ were denoted by the two sparrows, one of which, in likeness of His human nature, was offered up in an earthen vessel over living waters, because the waters of Baptism are sanctified by Christ's Passion. The other sparrow, in token of His impassible Godhead, remained living, because the Godhead cannot die: hence it flew away, for the Godhead could not be encompassed by the Passion. Now this living sparrow, together with the cedar-wood and scarlet or cochineal, and hyssop, i.e. faith, hope and charity, as stated above (ad 5), was put into the water for the purpose of sprinkling, because we are baptized in the faith of the God-Man. By the waters of Baptism or of his tears man washes his clothes, i.e. his works, and all his hair, i.e. his thoughts. The tip of the right ear of the man to be cleansed is moistened with some the blood and oil, in order to strengthen his hearing against harmful words; and the thumb and toe of his right hand and foot are moistened that his deeds may be holy. Other matters pertaining to this purification, or to that also of any other uncleannesses, call for no special remark, beyond what applies to other sacrifices, whether for sins or for trespasses.

Reply Obj. 8 and 9: Just as the people were initiated by circumcision to the divine worship, so were the ministers by some special purification or consecration: wherefore they are commanded to be separated from other men, as being specially deputed, rather than others, to the ministry of the divine worship. And all that was done touching them in their consecration or institution, was with a view to show that they were in possession of a prerogative of purity, power and dignity. Hence three things were done in the institution of ministers: for first, they were purified; secondly, they were adorned [*'Ornabantur.' Some editions have 'ordinabantur'—'were ordained': the former reading is a reference to Lev. 8:7-9] and consecrated; thirdly, they were employed in the ministry. All in general used to be purified by washing in water, and by certain sacrifices; but the Levites in particular shaved all the hair of their bodies, as stated in Lev. 8 (cf. Num. 8).

With regard to the high-priests and priests the consecration was performed as follows. First, when they had been washed, they were clothed with certain special garments in designation of their dignity. In particular, the high-priest was anointed on the head with the oil of unction: to denote that the power of consecration was poured forth by him on to others, just as oil flows from the head on to the lower parts of the body; according to Ps. 132:2: "Like the precious ointment on the head that ran down upon the beard, the beard of Aaron." But the Levites received no other consecration besides being offered to the Lord by the children of Israel through the hands of the high-priest, who prayed for them. The lesser priests were consecrated on the hands only, which were to be employed in the sacrifices. The tip of their right ear and the thumb of their right hand, and the great toe of their right foot were tinged with the blood of the sacrificial animal, to denote that they should be obedient to God's law in offering the sacrifices (this is denoted by touching their right ear); and that they should be careful and ready in performing the sacrifices (this is signified by the moistening of the right foot and hand). They themselves and their garments were sprinkled with the blood of the animal that had been sacrificed, in memory of the blood of the lamb by which they had been delivered in Egypt. At their consecration the following sacrifices were offered: a calf, for sin, in memory of Aaron's sin in fashioning the molten calf; a ram, for a holocaust, in memory of the sacrifice of Abraham, whose obedience it behooved the high-priest to imitate; again, a ram of consecration, which was a peace-offering, in memory of the delivery from Egypt through the blood of the lamb; and a basket of bread, in memory of the manna vouchsafed to the people.

In reference to their being destined to the ministry, the fat of the ram, one roll of bread, and the right shoulder were placed on their hands, to show that they received the power of offering these things to the Lord: while the Levites were initiated to the ministry by being brought into the tabernacle of the covenant, as being destined to the ministry touching the vessels of the sanctuary.

The figurative reason of these things was that those who are to be consecrated to the spiritual ministry of Christ, should be first of all purified by the waters of Baptism, and by the waters of tears, in their faith in Christ's Passion, which is a sacrifice both of expiation and of purification. They have also to shave all the hair of their body, i.e. all evil thoughts. They should, moreover, be decked with virtues, and be consecrated with the oil of the Holy Ghost, and with the sprinkling of Christ's blood. And thus they should be intent on the fulfilment of their spiritual ministry.

Reply Obj. 10: As already stated (A. 4), the purpose of the Law was to induce men to have reverence for the divine worship: and this in two ways; first, by excluding from the worship of God whatever might be an object of contempt; secondly, by introducing into the divine worship all that seemed to savor of reverence. And, indeed, if this was observed in regard to the tabernacle and its vessels, and in the animals to be sacrificed, much more was it to be observed in the very ministers. Wherefore, in order to obviate contempt for the ministers, it was prescribed that they should have no bodily stain or defect: since men so deformed are wont to be despised by others. For the same reason it was also commanded that the choice of those who were to be destined to the service of God was not to be made in a broadcast manner from any family, but according to their descent from one particular stock, thus giving them distinction and nobility.

In order that they might be revered, special ornate vestments were appointed for their use, and a special form of consecration. This indeed is the general reason of ornate garments. But the high-priest in particular had eight vestments. First, he had a linen tunic. Secondly, he had a purple tunic; round the bottom of which were placed "little bells" and "pomegranates of violet, and purple, and scarlet twice dyed." Thirdly, he had the ephod, which covered his shoulders and his breast down to the girdle; and it was made of gold, and violet and purple, and scarlet twice dyed and twisted linen: and on his shoulders he bore two onyx stones, on which were graven the names of the children of Israel. Fourthly, he had the rational, made of the same material; it was square in shape, and was worn on the breast, and was fastened to the ephod. On this rational there were twelve precious stones set in four rows, on which also were graven the names of the children of Israel, in token that the priest bore the burden of the whole people, since he bore their names on his shoulders; and that it was his duty ever to think of their welfare, since he wore them on his breast, bearing them in his heart, so to speak. And the Lord commanded the "Doctrine and Truth" to be put in the rational: for certain matters regarding moral and dogmatic truth were written on it. The Jews indeed pretend that on the rational was placed a stone which changed color according to the various things which were about to happen to the children of Israel: and this they call the "Truth and Doctrine." Fifthly, he wore a belt or girdle made of the four colors mentioned above. Sixthly, there was the tiara or mitre which was made of linen. Seventhly, there was the golden plate which hung over his forehead; on it was inscribed the Lord's name. Eighthly, there were "the linen breeches to cover the flesh of their nakedness," when they went up to the sanctuary or altar. Of these eight vestments the lesser priests had four, viz. the linen tunic and breeches, the belt and the tiara.

According to some, the literal reason for these vestments was that they denoted the disposition of the terrestrial globe; as though the high-priest confessed himself to be the minister of the Creator of the world, wherefore it is written (Wis. 18:24): "In the robe" of Aaron "was the whole world" described. For the linen breeches signified the earth out of which the flax grows. The surrounding belt signified the ocean which surrounds the earth. The violet tunic denoted the air by its color: its little bells betoken the thunder; the pomegranates, the lightning. The ephod, by its many colors, signified the starry heaven; the two onyx stones denoted the two hemispheres, or the sun and moon. The twelve precious stones on the breast are the twelve signs of the zodiac: and they are said to have been placed on the rational because in heaven are the types ( *rationes* ) of earthly things, according to Job 38:33: "Dost thou know the order of heaven, and canst thou set down the reason ( *rationem* ) thereof on the earth?" The turban or tiara signified the empyrean: the golden plate was a token of God, the governor of the universe.

The figurative reason is evident. Because bodily stains or defects wherefrom the priests had to be immune, signify the various vices and sins from which they should be free. Thus it is forbidden that he should be blind, i.e. he ought not to be ignorant: he must not be lame, i.e. vacillating and uncertain of purpose: that he must have "a little, or a great, or a crooked nose," i.e. that he should not, from lack of discretion, exceed in one direction or in another, or even exercise some base occupation: for the nose signifies discretion, because it discerns odors. It is forbidden that he should have "a broken foot" or "hand," i.e. he should not lose the power of doing good works or of advancing in virtue. He is rejected, too, if he have a swelling either in front or behind [Vulg.: 'if he be crook-backed']: by which is signified too much love of earthly things: if he be blear-eyed, i.e. if his mind is darkened by carnal affections: for running of the eyes is caused by a flow of matter. He is also rejected if he had "a pearl in his eye," i.e. if he presumes in his own estimation that he is clothed in the white robe of righteousness. Again, he is rejected "if he have a continued scab," i.e. lustfulness of the flesh: also, if he have "a dry scurf," which covers the body without giving pain, and is a blemish on the comeliness of the members; which denotes avarice. Lastly, he is rejected "if he have a rupture" or hernia; through baseness rending his heart, though it appear not in his deeds.

The vestments denote the virtues of God's ministers. Now there are four things that are necessary to all His ministers, viz. chastity denoted by the breeches; a pure life, signified by the linen tunic; the moderation of discretion, betokened by the girdle; and rectitude of purpose, denoted by the mitre covering the head. But the high-priests needed four other things in addition to these. First, a continual recollection of God in their thoughts; and this was signified by the golden plate worn over the forehead, with the name of God engraved thereon. Secondly, they had to bear with the shortcomings of the people: this was denoted by the ephod which they bore on their shoulders. Thirdly, they had to carry the people in their mind and heart by the solicitude of charity, in token of which they wore the rational. Fourthly, they had to lead a godly life by performing works of perfection; and this was signified by the violet tunic. Hence little golden bells were fixed to the bottom of the violet tunic, which bells signified the teaching of divine things united in the high-priest to his godly mode of life. In addition to these were the pomegranates, signifying unity of faith and concord in good morals: because his doctrine should hold together in such a way that it should not rend asunder the unity of faith and peace.

SIXTH ARTICLE [I-II, Q. 102, Art. 6]

Whether There Was Any Reasonable Cause for the Ceremonial Observances?

Objection 1: It would seem that there was no reasonable cause for the ceremonial observances. Because, as the Apostle says (1 Tim. 4:4), "every creature of God is good, and nothing to be rejected that is received with thanksgiving." It was therefore unfitting that they should be forbidden to eat certain foods, as being unclean according to Lev. 11 [*Cf. Deut. 14].

Obj. 2: Further, just as animals are given to man for food, so also are herbs: wherefore it is written (Gen. 9:3): "As the green herbs have I delivered all" flesh "to you." But the Law did not distinguish any herbs from the rest as being unclean, although some are most harmful, for instance, those that are poisonous. Therefore it seems that neither should any animals have been prohibited as being unclean.

Obj. 3: Further, if the matter from which a thing is generated be unclean, it seems that likewise the thing generated therefrom is unclean. But flesh is generated from blood. Since therefore all flesh was not prohibited as unclean, it seems that in like manner neither should blood have been forbidden as unclean; nor the fat which is engendered from blood.

Obj. 4: Further, Our Lord said (Matt. 10:28; cf. Luke 12:4), that those should not be feared "that kill the body," since after death they "have no more that they can do": which would not be true if after death harm might come to man through anything done with his body. Much less therefore does it matter to an animal already dead how its flesh be cooked. Consequently there seems to be no reason in what is said, Ex. 23:19: "Thou shalt not boil a kid in the milk of its dam."

Obj. 5: Further, all that is first brought forth of man and beast, as being most perfect, is commanded to be offered to the Lord (Ex. 13). Therefore it is an unfitting command that is set forth in Lev. 19:23: "when you shall be come into the land, and shall have planted in it fruit trees, you shall take away the uncircumcision [*'Praeputia,' which Douay version renders 'first fruits'] of them," i.e. the first crops, and they "shall be unclean to you, neither shall you eat of them."

Obj. 6: Further, clothing is something extraneous to man's body. Therefore certain kinds of garments should not have been forbidden to the Jews: for instance (Lev. 19:19): "Thou shalt not wear a garment that is woven of two sorts": and (Deut. 22:5): "A woman shall not be clothed with man's apparel, neither shall a man use woman's apparel": and further on (Deut. 22:11): "Thou shalt not wear a garment that is woven of woolen and linen together."

Obj. 7: Further, to be mindful of God's commandments concerns not the body but the heart. Therefore it is unsuitably prescribed (Deut. 6:8, seqq.) that they should "bind" the commandments of God "as a sign" on their hands; and that they should "write them in the entry"; and (Num. 15:38, seqq.) that they should "make to themselves fringes in the corners of their garments, putting in them ribands of blue ... they may remember ... the commandments of the Lord."

Obj. 8: Further, the Apostle says (1 Cor. 9:9) that God does not "take care for oxen," and, therefore, neither of other irrational animals. Therefore without reason is it commanded (Deut. 22:6): "If thou find, as thou walkest by the way, a bird's nest in a tree ... thou shalt not take the dam with her young"; and (Deut. 25:4): "Thou shalt not muzzle the ox that treadeth out thy corn"; and (Lev. 19:19): "Thou shalt not make thy cattle to gender with beasts of any other kind."

Objection 9: Further, no distinction was made between clean and unclean plants. Much less therefore should any distinction have been made about the cultivation of plants. Therefore it was unfittingly prescribed (Lev. 19:19): "Thou shalt not sow thy field with different seeds"; and (Deut. 22:9, seqq.): "Thou shalt sow thy vineyard with divers seeds"; and: "Thou shalt not plough with an ox and an ass together."

Objection 10: Further, it is apparent that inanimate things are most of all subject to the power of man. Therefore it was unfitting to debar man from taking silver and gold of which idols were made, or anything they found in the houses of idols, as expressed in the commandment of the Law (Deut. 7:25, seqq.). It also seems an absurd commandment set forth in Deut. 23:13, that they should "dig round about and ... cover with earth that which they were eased of."

Objection 11: Further, piety is required especially in priests. But it seems to be an act of piety to assist at the burial of one's friends: wherefore Tobias is commended for so doing (Tob. 1:20, seqq.). In like manner it is sometimes an act of piety to marry a loose woman, because she is thereby delivered from sin and infamy. Therefore it seems inconsistent for these things to be forbidden to priests (Lev. 21).

*On the contrary,* It is written (Deut. 18:14): "But thou art otherwise instructed by the Lord thy God": from which words we may gather that these observances were instituted by God to be a special prerogative of that people. Therefore they are not without reason or cause.

*I answer that,* The Jewish people, as stated above (A. 5), were specially chosen for the worship of God, and among them the priests themselves were specially set apart for that purpose. And just as other things that are applied to the divine worship, need to be marked in some particular way so that they be worthy of the worship of God; so too in that people's, and especially the priests', mode of life, there needed to be certain special things befitting the divine worship, whether spiritual or corporal. Now the worship prescribed by the Law foreshadowed the mystery of Christ: so that whatever they did was a figure of things pertaining to Christ, according to 1 Cor. 10:11: "All these things happened to them in figures." Consequently the reasons for these observances may be taken in two ways, first according to their fittingness to the worship of God; secondly, according as they foreshadow something touching the Christian mode of life.

Reply Obj. 1: As stated above (A. 5, ad 4, 5), the Law distinguished a twofold pollution or uncleanness; one, that of sin, whereby the soul was defiled; and another consisting in some kind of corruption, whereby the body was in some way infected. Speaking then of the first-mentioned uncleanness, no kind of food is unclean, or can defile a man, by reason of its nature; wherefore we read (Matt. 15:11): "Not that which goeth into the mouth defileth a man; but what cometh out of the mouth, this defileth a man": which words are explained (Matt. 15:17) as referring to sins. Yet certain foods can defile the soul accidentally; in so far as man partakes of them against obedience or a vow, or from excessive concupiscence; or through their being an incentive to lust, for which reason some refrain from wine and flesh-meat.

If, however, we speak of bodily uncleanness, consisting in some kind of corruption, the flesh of certain animals is unclean, either because like the pig they feed on unclean things; or because their life is among unclean surroundings: thus certain animals, like moles and mice and such like, live underground, whence they contract a certain unpleasant smell; or because their flesh, through being too moist or too dry, engenders corrupt humors in the human body. Hence they were forbidden to eat the flesh of flat-footed animals, i.e. animals having an uncloven hoof, on account of their earthiness; and in like manner they were forbidden to eat the flesh of animals that have many clefts in their feet, because such are very fierce and their flesh is very dry, such as the flesh of lions and the like. For the same reason they were forbidden to eat certain birds of prey the flesh of which is very dry, and certain water-fowl on account of their exceeding humidity. In like manner certain fish lacking fins and scales were prohibited on account of their excessive moisture; such as eels and the like. They were, however, allowed to eat ruminants and animals with a divided hoof, because in such animals the humors are well absorbed, and their nature well balanced: for neither are they too moist, as is indicated by the hoof; nor are they too earthy, which is shown by their having not a flat but a cloven hoof. Of fishes they were allowed to partake of the drier kinds, of which the fins and scales are an indication, because thereby the moist nature of the fish is tempered. Of birds they were allowed to eat the tamer kinds, such as hens, partridges, and the like. Another reason was detestation of idolatry: because the Gentiles, and especially the Egyptians, among whom they had grown up, offered up these forbidden animals to their idols, or employed them for the purpose of sorcery: whereas they did not eat those animals which the Jews were allowed to eat, but worshipped them as gods, or abstained, for some other motive, from eating them, as stated above (A. 3, ad 2). The third reason was to prevent excessive care about food: wherefore they were allowed to eat those animals which could be procured easily and promptly.

With regard to blood and fat, they were forbidden to partake of those of any animals whatever without exception. Blood was forbidden, both in order to avoid cruelty, that they might abhor the shedding of human blood, as stated above (A. 3, ad 8); and in order to shun idolatrous rites whereby it was customary for men to collect the blood and to gather together around it for a banquet in honor of the idols, to whom they held the blood to be most acceptable. Hence the Lord commanded the blood to be poured out and to be covered with earth (Lev. 17:13). For the same reason they were forbidden to eat animals that had been suffocated or strangled: because the blood of these animals would not be separated from the body: or because this form of death is very painful to the victim; and the Lord wished to withdraw them from cruelty even in regard to irrational animals, so as to be less inclined to be cruel to other men, through being used to be kind to beasts. They were forbidden to eat the fat: both because idolaters ate it in honor of their gods; and because it used to be burnt in honor of God; and, again, because blood and fat are not nutritious, which is the cause assigned by Rabbi Moses (Doct. Perplex. iii). The reason why they were forbidden to eat the sinews is given in Gen. 32:32, where it is stated that "the children of Israel ... eat not the sinew ... because he touched the sinew of" Jacob's "thigh and it shrank."

The figurative reason for these things is that all these animals signified certain sins, in token of which those animals were prohibited. Hence Augustine says (Contra Faustum iv, 7): "If the swine and lamb be called in question, both are clean by nature, because all God's creatures are good: yet the lamb is clean, and the pig is unclean in a certain signification. Thus if you speak of a foolish, and of a wise man, each of these expressions is clean considered in the nature of the sound, letters and syllables of which it is composed: but in signification, the one is clean, the other unclean." The animal that chews the cud and has a divided hoof, is clean in signification. Because division of the hoof is a figure of the two Testaments: or of the Father and Son: or of the two natures in Christ: of the distinction of good and evil. While chewing the cud signifies meditation on the Scriptures and a sound understanding thereof; and whoever lacks either of these is spiritually unclean. In like manner those fish that have scales and fins are clean in signification. Because fins signify the heavenly or contemplative life; while scales signify a life of trials, each of which is required for spiritual cleanness. Of birds certain kinds were forbidden. In the eagle which flies at a great height, pride is forbidden: in the griffon which is hostile to horses and men, cruelty of powerful men is prohibited. The osprey, which feeds on very small birds, signifies those who oppress the poor. The kite, which is full of cunning, denotes those who are fraudulent in their dealings. The vulture, which follows an army, expecting to feed on the carcases of the slain, signifies those who like others to die or to fight among themselves that they may gain thereby. Birds of the raven kind signify those who are blackened by their lusts; or those who lack kindly feelings, for the raven did not return when once it had been let loose from the ark. The ostrich which, though a bird, cannot fly, and is always on the ground, signifies those who fight for God's cause, and at the same time are taken up with worldly business. The owl, which sees clearly at night, but cannot see in the daytime, denotes those who are clever in temporal affairs, but dull in spiritual matters. The gull, which both flies in the air and swims in the water, signifies those who are partial both to Circumcision and to Baptism: or else it denotes those who would fly by contemplation, yet dwell in the waters of sensual delights. The hawk, which helps men to seize the prey, is a figure of those who assist the strong to prey on the poor. The screech-owl, which seeks its food by night but hides by day, signifies the lustful man who seeks to lie hidden in his deeds of darkness. The cormorant, so constituted that it can stay a long time under water, denotes the glutton who plunges into the waters of pleasure. The ibis is an African bird with a long beak, and feeds on snakes; and perhaps it is the same as the stork: it signifies the envious man, who refreshes himself with the ills of others, as with snakes. The swan is bright in color, and by the aid of its long neck extracts its food from deep places on land or water: it may denote those who seek earthly profit though an external brightness of virtue. The bittern is a bird of the East: it has a long beak, and its jaws are furnished with follicules, wherein it stores its food at first, after a time proceeding to digest it: it is a figure of the miser, who is excessively careful in hoarding up the necessaries of life. The coot [*Douay: *porphyrion.* St. Thomas' description tallies with the coot or moorhen: though of course he is mistaken about the feet differing from one another.] has this peculiarity apart from other birds, that it has a webbed foot for swimming, and a cloven foot for walking: for it swims like a duck in the water, and walks like a partridge on land: it drinks only when it bites, since it dips all its food in water: it is a figure of a man who will not take advice, and does nothing but what is soaked in the water of his own will. The heron [*Vulg.: *herodionem* ], commonly called a falcon, signifies those whose "feet are swift to shed blood" (Ps. 13:3). The plover [*Here, again, the Douay translators transcribed from the Vulgate: *charadrion;* charadrius is the generic name for all plovers.], which is a garrulous bird, signifies the gossip. The hoopoe, which builds its nest on dung, feeds on foetid ordure, and whose song is like a groan, denotes worldly grief which works death in those who are unclean. The bat, which flies near the ground, signifies those who being gifted with worldly knowledge, seek none but earthly things. Of fowls and quadrupeds those alone were permitted which have the hind-legs longer than the forelegs, so that they can leap: whereas those were forbidden which cling rather to the earth: because those who abuse the doctrine of the four Evangelists, so that they are not lifted up thereby, are reputed unclean. By the prohibition of blood, fat and nerves, we are to understand the forbidding of cruelty, lust, and bravery in committing sin.

Reply Obj. 2: Men were wont to eat plants and other products of the soil even before the deluge: but the eating of flesh seems to have been introduced after the deluge; for it is written (Gen. 9:3): "Even as the green herbs have I delivered ... all" flesh "to you." The reason for this was that the eating of the products of the soil savors rather of a simple life; whereas the eating of flesh savors of delicate and over-careful living. For the soil gives birth to the herb of its own accord; and such like products of the earth may be had in great quantities with very little effort: whereas no small trouble is necessary either to rear or to catch an animal. Consequently God being wishful to bring His people back to a more simple way of living, forbade them to eat many kinds of animals, but not those things that are produced by the soil. Another reason may be that animals were offered to idols, while the products of the soil were not.

The Reply to the Third Objection is clear from what has been said (ad 1).

Reply Obj. 4: Although the kid that is slain has no perception of the manner in which its flesh is cooked, yet it would seem to savor of heartlessness if the dam's milk, which was intended for the nourishment of her offspring, were served up on the same dish. It might also be said that the Gentiles in celebrating the feasts of their idols prepared the flesh of kids in this manner, for the purpose of sacrifice or banquet: hence (Ex. 23) after the solemnities to be celebrated under the Law had been foretold, it is added: "Thou shalt not boil a kid in the milk of its dam." The figurative reason for this prohibition is this: the kid, signifying Christ, on account of "the likeness of sinful flesh" (Rom. 8:3), was not to be seethed, i.e. slain, by the Jews, "in the milk of its dam," i.e. during His infancy. Or else it signifies that the kid, i.e. the sinner, should not be boiled in the milk of its dam, i.e. should not be cajoled by flattery.

Reply Obj. 5: The Gentiles offered their gods the first-fruits, which they held to bring them good luck: or they burnt them for the purpose of secrecy. Consequently (the Israelites) were commanded to look upon the fruits of the first three years as unclean: for in that country nearly all the trees bear fruit in three years' time; those trees, to wit, that are cultivated either from seed, or from a graft, or from a cutting: but it seldom happens that the fruit-stones or seeds encased in a pod are sown: since it would take a longer time for these to bear fruit: and the Law considered what happened most frequently. The fruits, however, of the fourth year, as being the firstlings of clean fruits, were offered to God: and from the fifth year onward they were eaten.

The figurative reason was that this foreshadowed the fact that after the three states of the Law (the first lasting from Abraham to David, the second, until they were carried away to Babylon, the third until the time of Christ), the Fruit of the Law, i.e. Christ, was to be offered to God. Or again, that we must mistrust our first efforts, on account of their imperfection.

Reply Obj. 6: It is said of a man in Ecclus. 19:27, that "the attire of the body ... " shows "what he is." Hence the Lord wished His people to be distinguished from other nations, not only by the sign of the circumcision, which was in the flesh, but also by a certain difference of attire. Wherefore they were forbidden to wear garments woven of woolen and linen together, and for a woman to be clothed with man's apparel, or vice versa, for two reasons. First, to avoid idolatrous worship. Because the Gentiles, in their religious rites, used garments of this sort, made of various materials. Moreover in the worship of Mars, women put on men's armor; while, conversely, in the worship of Venus men donned women's attire. The second reason was to preserve them from lust: because the employment of various materials in the making of garments signified inordinate union of sexes, while the use of male attire by a woman, or vice versa, has an incentive to evil desires, and offers an occasion of lust. The figurative reason is that the prohibition of wearing a garment woven of woolen and linen signified that it was forbidden to unite the simplicity of innocence, denoted by wool, with the duplicity of malice, betokened by linen. It also signifies that woman is forbidden to presume to teach, or perform other duties of men: or that man should not adopt the effeminate manners of a woman.

Reply Obj. 7: As Jerome says on Matt. 23:6, "the Lord commanded them to make violet-colored fringes in the four corners of their garments, so that the Israelites might be distinguished from other nations." Hence, in this way, they professed to be Jews: and consequently the very sight of this sign reminded them of their law.

When we read: "Thou shalt bind them on thy hand, and they shall be ever before thy eyes [Vulg.: 'they shall be and shall move between thy eyes'], the Pharisees gave a false interpretation to these words, and wrote the decalogue of Moses on a parchment, and tied it on their foreheads like a wreath, so that it moved in front of their eyes": whereas the intention of the Lord in giving this commandment was that they should be bound in their hands, i.e. in their works; and that they should be before their eyes, i.e. in their thoughts. The violet-colored fillets which were inserted in their cloaks signify the godly intention which should accompany our every deed. It may, however, be said that, because they were a carnal-minded and stiff-necked people, it was necessary for them to be stirred by these sensible things to the observance of the Law.

Reply Obj. 8: Affection in man is twofold: it may be an affection of reason, or it may be an affection of passion. If a man's affection be one of reason, it matters not how man behaves to animals, because God has subjected all things to man's power, according to Ps. 8:8: "Thou hast subjected all things under his feet": and it is in this sense that the Apostle says that "God has no care for oxen"; because God does not ask of man what he does with oxen or other animals.

But if man's affection be one of passion, then it is moved also in regard to other animals: for since the passion of pity is caused by the afflictions of others; and since it happens that even irrational animals are sensible to pain, it is possible for the affection of pity to arise in a man with regard to the sufferings of animals. Now it is evident that if a man practice a pitiful affection for animals, he is all the more disposed to take pity on his fellow-men: wherefore it is written (Prov. 11:10): "The just regardeth the lives of his beasts: but the bowels of the wicked are cruel." Consequently the Lord, in order to inculcate pity to the Jewish people, who were prone to cruelty, wished them to practice pity even with regard to dumb animals, and forbade them to do certain things savoring of cruelty to animals. Hence He prohibited them to "boil a kid in the milk of its dam"; and to "muzzle the ox that treadeth out the corn"; and to slay "the dam with her young." It may, nevertheless, be also said that these prohibitions were made in hatred of idolatry. For the Egyptians held it to be wicked to allow the ox to eat of the grain while threshing the corn. Moreover certain sorcerers were wont to ensnare the mother bird with her young during incubation, and to employ them for the purpose of securing fruitfulness and good luck in bringing up children: also because it was held to be a good omen to find the mother sitting on her young.

As to the mingling of animals of divers species, the literal reason may have been threefold. The first was to show detestation for the idolatry of the Egyptians, who employed various mixtures in worshipping the planets, which produce various effects, and on various kinds of things according to their various conjunctions. The second reason was in condemnation of unnatural sins. The third reason was the entire removal of all occasions of concupiscence. Because animals of different species do not easily breed, unless this be brought about by man; and movements of lust are aroused by seeing such things. Wherefore in the Jewish traditions we find it prescribed as stated by Rabbi Moses that men shall turn away their eyes from such sights.

The figurative reason for these things is that the necessities of life should not be withdrawn from the ox that treadeth the corn, i.e. from the preacher bearing the sheaves of doctrine, as the Apostle states (1 Cor. 9:4, seqq.). Again, we should not take the dam with her young: because in certain things we have to keep the spiritual senses, i.e. the offspring, and set aside the observance of the letter, i.e. the mother, for instance, in all the ceremonies of the Law. It is also forbidden that a beast of burden, i.e. any of the common people, should be allowed to engender, i.e. to have any connection, with animals of another kind, i.e. with Gentiles or Jews.

Reply Obj. 9: All these minglings were forbidden in agriculture; literally, in detestation of idolatry. For the Egyptians in worshipping the stars employed various combinations of seeds, animals and garments, in order to represent the various connections of the stars. Or else all these minglings were forbidden in detestation of the unnatural vice.

They have, however, a figurative reason. For the prohibition: "Thou shalt not sow thy field with different seeds," is to be understood, in the spiritual sense, of the prohibition to sow strange doctrine in the Church, which is a spiritual vineyard. Likewise "the field," i.e. the Church, must not be sown "with different seeds," i.e. with Catholic and heretical doctrines. Neither is it allowed to plough "with an ox and an ass together"; thus a fool should not accompany a wise man in preaching, for one would hinder the other.

Reply Obj. 10: [*The Reply to the Tenth Objection is lacking in the codices. The solution given here is found in some editions, and was supplied by Nicolai.] Silver and gold were reasonably forbidden (Deut. 7) not as though they were not subject to the power of man, but because, like the idols themselves, all materials out of which idols were made, were anathematized as hateful in God's sight. This is clear from the same chapter, where we read further on (Deut. 7:26): "Neither shalt thou bring anything of the idol into thy house, lest thou become an anathema like it." Another reason was lest, by taking silver and gold, they should be led by avarice into idolatry to which the Jews were inclined. The other precept (Deut. 23) about covering up excretions, was just and becoming, both for the sake of bodily cleanliness; and in order to keep the air wholesome; and by reason of the respect due to the tabernacle of the covenant which stood in the midst of the camp, wherein the Lord was said to dwell; as is clearly set forth in the same passage, where after expressing the command, the reason thereof is at once added, to wit: "For the Lord thy God walketh in the midst of thy camp, to deliver thee, and to give up thy enemies to thee, and let thy camp be holy (i.e. clean), and let no uncleanness appear therein." The figurative reason for this precept, according to Gregory (Moral. xxxi), is that sins which are the fetid excretions of the mind should be covered over by repentance, that we may become acceptable to God, according to Ps. 31:1: "Blessed are they whose iniquities are forgiven, and whose sins are covered." Or else according to a gloss, that we should recognize the unhappy condition of human nature, and humbly cover and purify the stains of a puffed-up and proud spirit in the deep furrow of self-examination.

Reply Obj. 11: Sorcerers and idolatrous priests made use, in their rites, of the bones and flesh of dead men. Wherefore, in order to extirpate the customs of idolatrous worship, the Lord commanded that the priests of inferior degree, who at fixed times served in the temple, should not "incur an uncleanness at the death" of anyone except of those who were closely related to them, viz. their father or mother, and others thus near of kin to them. But the high-priest had always to be ready for the service of the sanctuary; wherefore he was absolutely forbidden to approach the dead, however nearly related to him. They were also forbidden to marry a "harlot" or "one that has been put away," or any other than a virgin: both on account of the reverence due to the priesthood, the honor of which would seem to be tarnished by such a marriage: and for the sake of the children who would be disgraced by the mother's shame: which was most of all to be avoided when the priestly dignity was passed on from father to son. Again, they were commanded to shave neither head nor beard, and not to make incisions in their flesh, in order to exclude the rites of idolatry. For the priests of the Gentiles shaved both head and beard, wherefore it is written (Bar 6:30): "Priests sit in their temples having their garments rent, and their heads and beards shaven." Moreover, in worshipping their idols "they cut themselves with knives and lancets" (3 Kings 18:28). For this reason the priests of the Old Law were commanded to do the contrary.

The spiritual reason for these things is that priests should be entirely free from dead works, i.e. sins. And they should not shave their heads, i.e. set wisdom aside; nor should they shave their beards, i.e. set aside the perfection of wisdom; nor rend their garments or cut their flesh, i.e. they should not incur the sin of schism.

## QUESTION 103

OF THE DURATION OF THE CEREMONIAL PRECEPTS (In Four Articles)

We must now consider the duration of the ceremonial precepts: under which head there are four points of inquiry:

(1) Whether the ceremonial precepts were in existence before the Law?

(2) Whether at the time of the Law the ceremonies of the Old Law had any power of justification?

(3) Whether they ceased at the coming of Christ?

(4) Whether it is a mortal sin to observe them after the coming of Christ?

FIRST ARTICLE [I-II, Q. 103, Art. 1]

Whether the Ceremonies of the Law Were in Existence Before the Law?

Objection 1: It would seem that the ceremonies of the Law were in existence before the Law. For sacrifices and holocausts were ceremonies of the Old Law, as stated above (Q. 101, A. 4). But sacrifices and holocausts preceded the Law: for it is written (Gen. 4:3, 4) that "Cain offered, of the fruits of the earth, gifts to the Lord," and that "Abel offered of the firstlings of his flock, and of their fat." Noe also "offered holocausts" to the Lord (Gen. 18:20), and Abraham did in like manner (Gen. 22:13). Therefore the ceremonies of the Old Law preceded the Law.

Obj. 2: Further, the erecting and consecrating of the altar were part of the ceremonies relating to holy things. But these preceded the Law. For we read (Gen. 13:18) that "Abraham ... built ... an altar the Lord"; and (Gen. 28:18) that "Jacob ... took the stone ... and set it up for a title, pouring oil upon the top of it." Therefore the legal ceremonies preceded the Law.

Obj. 3: Further, the first of the legal sacraments seems to have been circumcision. But circumcision preceded the Law, as appears from Gen. 17. In like manner the priesthood preceded the Law; for it is written (Gen. 14:18) that "Melchisedech ... was the priest of the most high God." Therefore the sacramental ceremonies preceded the Law.

Obj. 4: Further, the distinction of clean from unclean animals belongs to the ceremonies of observances, as stated above (Q. 100, 2, A. 6, ad 1). But this distinction preceded the Law; for it is written (Gen. 7:2, 3): "Of all clean beasts take seven and seven ... but of the beasts that are unclean, two and two." Therefore the legal ceremonies preceded the Law.

*On the contrary,* It is written (Deut. 6:1): "These are the precepts and ceremonies ... which the Lord your God commanded that I should teach you." But they would not have needed to be taught about these things, if the aforesaid ceremonies had been already in existence. Therefore the legal ceremonies did not precede the Law.

*I answer that,* As is clear from what has been said (Q. 101, A. 2; Q. 102, A. 2), the legal ceremonies were ordained for a double purpose; the worship of God, and the foreshadowing of Christ. Now whoever worships God must needs worship Him by means of certain fixed things pertaining to external worship. But the fixing of the divine worship belongs to the ceremonies; just as the determining of our relations with our neighbor is a matter determined by the judicial precepts, as stated above (Q. 99, A. 4). Consequently, as among men in general there were certain judicial precepts, not indeed established by Divine authority, but ordained by human reason; so also there were some ceremonies fixed, not by the authority of any law, but according to the will and devotion of those that worship God. Since, however, even before the Law some of the leading men were gifted with the spirit of prophecy, it is to be believed that a heavenly instinct, like a private law, prompted them to worship God in a certain definite way, which would be both in keeping with the interior worship, and a suitable token of Christ's mysteries, which were foreshadowed also by other things that they did, according to 1 Cor. 10:11: "All ... things happened to them in figure." Therefore there were some ceremonies before the Law, but they were not legal ceremonies, because they were not as yet established by legislation.

Reply Obj. 1: The patriarchs offered up these oblations, sacrifices and holocausts previously to the Law, out of a certain devotion of their own will, according as it seemed proper to them to offer up in honor of God those things which they had received from Him, and thus to testify that they worshipped God Who is the beginning and end of all.

Reply Obj. 2: They also established certain sacred things, because they thought that the honor due to God demanded that certain places should be set apart from others for the purpose of divine worship.

Reply Obj. 3: The sacrament of circumcision was established by command of God before the Law. Hence it cannot be called a sacrament of the Law as though it were an institution of the Law, but only as an observance included in the Law. Hence Our Lord said (John 7:20) that circumcision was "not of Moses, but of his fathers." Again, among those who worshipped God, the priesthood was in existence before the Law by human appointment, for the Law allotted the priestly dignity to the firstborn.

Reply Obj. 4: The distinction of clean from unclean animals was in vogue before the Law, not with regard to eating them, since it is written (Gen. 9:3): "Everything that moveth and liveth shall be meat for you": but only as to the offering of sacrifices because they used only certain animals for that purpose. If, however, they did make any distinction in regard to eating; it was not that it was considered illegal to eat such animals, since this was not forbidden by any law, but from dislike or custom: thus even now we see that certain foods are looked upon with disgust in some countries, while people partake of them in others.

SECOND ARTICLE [I-II, Q. 103, Art. 2]

Whether, at the Time of the Law, the Ceremonies of the Old Law Had Any Power of Justification?

Objection 1: It would seem that the ceremonies of the Old Law had the power of justification at the time of the Law. Because expiation from sin and consecration pertains to justification. But it is written (Ex. 39:21) that the priests and their apparel were consecrated by the sprinkling of blood and the anointing of oil; and (Lev. 16:16) that, by sprinkling the blood of the calf, the priest expiated "the sanctuary from the uncleanness of the children of Israel, and from their transgressions and ... their sins." Therefore the ceremonies of the Old Law had the power of justification.

Obj. 2: Further, that by which man pleases God pertains to justification, according to Ps. 10:8: "The Lord is just and hath loved justice." But some pleased God by means of ceremonies, according to Lev. 10:19: "How could I ... please the Lord in the ceremonies, having a sorrowful heart?" Therefore the ceremonies of the Old Law had the power of justification.

Obj. 3: Further, things relating to the divine worship regard the soul rather than the body, according to Ps. 18:8: "The Law of the Lord is unspotted, converting souls." But the leper was cleansed by means of the ceremonies of the Old Law, as stated in Lev. 14. Much more therefore could the ceremonies of the Old Law cleanse the soul by justifying it.

*On the contrary,* The Apostle says (Gal. 2) [*The first words of the quotation are from 3:21: St. Thomas probably quoting from memory, substituted them for 2:21, which runs thus: 'If justice be by the Law, then Christ died in vain.']: "If there had been a law given which could justify [Vulg.: 'give life'], Christ died in vain," i.e. without cause. But this is inadmissible. Therefore the ceremonies of the Old Law did not confer justice.

*I answer that,* As stated above (Q. 102, A. 5, ad 4), a twofold uncleanness was distinguished in the Old Law. One was spiritual and is the uncleanness of sin. The other was corporal, which rendered a man unfit for divine worship; thus a leper, or anyone that touched carrion, was said to be unclean: and thus uncleanness was nothing but a kind of irregularity. From this uncleanness, then, the ceremonies of the Old Law had the power to cleanse: because they were ordered by the Law to be employed as remedies for the removal of the aforesaid uncleannesses which were contracted in consequence of the prescription of the Law. Hence the Apostle says (Heb. 9:13) that "the blood of goats and of oxen, and the ashes of a heifer, being sprinkled, sanctify such as are defiled, to the cleansing of the flesh." And just as this uncleanness which was washed away by such like ceremonies, affected the flesh rather than the soul, so also the ceremonies themselves are called by the Apostle shortly before (Heb. 9:10) justices of the flesh: "justices of the flesh," says he, "being laid on them until the time of correction."

On the other hand, they had no power of cleansing from uncleanness of the soul, i.e. from the uncleanness of sin. The reason of this was that at no time could there be expiation from sin, except through Christ, "Who taketh away the sins [Vulg.: 'sin'] of the world" (John 1:29). And since the mystery of Christ's Incarnation and Passion had not yet really taken place, those ceremonies of the Old Law could not really contain in themselves a power flowing from Christ already incarnate and crucified, such as the sacraments of the New Law contain. Consequently they could not cleanse from sin: thus the Apostle says (Heb. 10:4) that "it is impossible that with the blood of oxen and goats sin should be taken away"; and for this reason he calls them (Gal. 4:9) "weak and needy elements": weak indeed, because they cannot take away sin; but this weakness results from their being needy, i.e. from the fact that they do not contain grace within themselves.

However, it was possible at the time of the Law, for the minds of the faithful, to be united by faith to Christ incarnate and crucified; so that they were justified by faith in Christ: of which faith the observance of these ceremonies was a sort of profession, inasmuch as they foreshadowed Christ. Hence in the Old Law certain sacrifices were offered up for sins, not as though the sacrifices themselves washed sins away, but because they were professions of faith which cleansed from sin. In fact, the Law itself implies this in the terms employed: for it is written (Lev. 4:26; 5:16) that in offering the sacrifice for sin "the priest shall pray for him ... and it shall be forgiven him," as though the sin were forgiven, not in virtue of the sacrifices, but through the faith and devotion of those who offered them. It must be observed, however, that the very fact that the ceremonies of the Old Law washed away uncleanness of the body, was a figure of that expiation from sins which was effected by Christ.

It is therefore evident that under the state of the Old Law the ceremonies had no power of justification.

Reply Obj. 1: That sanctification of priests and their sons, and of their apparel or of anything else belonging to them, by sprinkling them with blood, had no other effect but to appoint them to the divine worship, and to remove impediments from them, "to the cleansing of the flesh," as the Apostle states (Heb. 9:13) in token of that sanctification whereby "Jesus" sanctified "the people by His own blood" (Heb. 13:12). Moreover, the expiation must be understood as referring to the removal of these bodily uncleannesses, not to the forgiveness of sin. Hence even the sanctuary which could not be the subject of sin is stated to be expiated.

Reply Obj. 2: The priests pleased God in the ceremonies by their obedience and devotion, and by their faith in the reality foreshadowed; not by reason of the things considered in themselves.

Reply Obj. 3: Those ceremonies which were prescribed in the cleansing of a leper, were not ordained for the purpose of taking away the defilement of leprosy. This is clear from the fact that these ceremonies were not applied to a man until he was already healed: hence it is written (Lev. 14:3, 4) that the priest, "going out of the camp, when he shall find that the leprosy is cleansed, shall command him that is to be purified to offer," etc.; whence it is evident that the priest was appointed the judge of leprosy, not before, but after cleansing. But these ceremonies were employed for the purpose of taking away the uncleanness of irregularity. They do say, however, that if a priest were to err in his judgment, the leper would be cleansed miraculously by the power of God, but not in virtue of the sacrifice. Thus also it was by miracle that the thigh of the adulterous woman rotted, when she had drunk the water "on which" the priest had "heaped curses," as stated in Num. 5:19-27.

THIRD ARTICLE [I-II, Q. 103, Art. 3]

Whether the Ceremonies of the Old Law Ceased at the Coming of Christ?

Objection 1: It would seem that the ceremonies of the Old Law did not cease at the coming of Christ. For it is written (Bar. 4:1): "This is the book of the commandments of God, and the law that is for ever." But the legal ceremonies were part of the Law. Therefore the legal ceremonies were to last for ever.

Obj. 2: Further, the offering made by a leper after being cleansed was a ceremony of the Law. But the Gospel commands the leper, who has been cleansed, to make this offering (Matt. 8:4). Therefore the ceremonies of the Old Law did not cease at Christ's coming.

Obj. 3: Further, as long as the cause remains, the effect remains. But the ceremonies of the Old Law had certain reasonable causes, inasmuch as they were ordained to the worship of God, besides the fact that they were intended to be figures of Christ. Therefore the ceremonies of the Old Law should not have ceased.

Obj. 4: Further, circumcision was instituted as a sign of Abraham's faith: the observance of the sabbath, to recall the blessing of creation: and other solemnities, in memory of other Divine favors, as stated above (Q. 102, A. 4, ad 10; A. 5, ad 1). But Abraham's faith is ever to be imitated even by us: and the blessing of creation and other Divine favors should never be forgotten. Therefore at least circumcision and the other legal solemnities should not have ceased.

*On the contrary,* The Apostle says (Col. 2:16, 17): "Let no man ... judge you in meat or in drink, or in respect of a festival day, or of the new moon, or of the sabbaths, which are a shadow of things to come": and (Heb. 8:13): "In saying a new (testament), he hath made the former old: and that which decayeth and groweth old, is near its end."

*I answer that,* All the ceremonial precepts of the Old Law were ordained to the worship of God as stated above (Q. 101, AA. 1, 2). Now external worship should be in proportion to the internal worship, which consists in faith, hope and charity. Consequently exterior worship had to be subject to variations according to the variations in the internal worship, in which a threefold state may be distinguished. One state was in respect of faith and hope, both in heavenly goods, and in the means of obtaining them—in both of these considered as things to come. Such was the state of faith and hope in the Old Law. Another state of interior worship is that in which we have faith and hope in heavenly goods as things to come; but in the means of obtaining heavenly goods, as in things present or past. Such is the state of the New Law. The third state is that in which both are possessed as present; wherein nothing is believed in as lacking, nothing hoped for as being yet to come. Such is the state of the Blessed.

In this state of the Blessed, then, nothing in regard to worship of God will be figurative; there will be naught but "thanksgiving and voice of praise" (Isa. 51:3). Hence it is written concerning the city of the Blessed (Apoc. 21:22): "I saw no temple therein: for the Lord God Almighty is the temple thereof, and the Lamb." Proportionately, therefore, the ceremonies of the first-mentioned state which foreshadowed the second and third states, had need to cease at the advent of the second state; and other ceremonies had to be introduced which would be in keeping with the state of divine worship for that particular time, wherein heavenly goods are a thing of the future, but the Divine favors whereby we obtain the heavenly boons are a thing of the present.

Reply Obj. 1: The Old Law is said to be "for ever" simply and absolutely, as regards its moral precepts; but as regards the ceremonial precepts it lasts for even in respect of the reality which those ceremonies foreshadowed.

Reply Obj. 2: The mystery of the redemption of the human race was fulfilled in Christ's Passion: hence Our Lord said then: "It is consummated" (John 19:30). Consequently the prescriptions of the Law must have ceased then altogether through their reality being fulfilled. As a sign of this, we read that at the Passion of Christ "the veil of the temple was rent" (Matt. 27:51). Hence, before Christ's Passion, while Christ was preaching and working miracles, the Law and the Gospel were concurrent, since the mystery of Christ had already begun, but was not as yet consummated. And for this reason Our Lord, before His Passion, commanded the leper to observe the legal ceremonies.

Reply Obj. 3: The literal reasons already given (Q. 102) for the ceremonies refer to the divine worship, which was founded on faith in that which was to come. Hence, at the advent of Him Who was to come, both that worship ceased, and all the reasons referring thereto.

Reply Obj. 4: The faith of Abraham was commended in that he believed in God's promise concerning his seed to come, in which all nations were to blessed. Wherefore, as long as this seed was yet to come, it was necessary to make profession of Abraham's faith by means of circumcision. But now that it is consummated, the same thing needs to be declared by means of another sign, viz. Baptism, which, in this respect, took the place of circumcision, according to the saying of the Apostle (Col. 2:11, 12): "You are circumcised with circumcision not made by hand, in despoiling of the body of the flesh, but in the circumcision of Christ, buried with Him in Baptism."

As to the sabbath, which was a sign recalling the first creation, its place is taken by the "Lord's Day," which recalls the beginning of the new creature in the Resurrection of Christ. In like manner other solemnities of the Old Law are supplanted by new solemnities: because the blessings vouchsafed to that people, foreshadowed the favors granted us by Christ. Hence the feast of the Passover gave place to the feast of Christ's Passion and Resurrection: the feast of Pentecost when the Old Law was given, to the feast of Pentecost on which was given the Law of the living spirit: the feast of the New Moon, to Lady Day, when appeared the first rays of the sun, i.e. Christ, by the fulness of grace: the feast of Trumpets, to the feasts of the Apostles: the feast of Expiation, to the feasts of Martyrs and Confessors: the feast of Tabernacles, to the feast of the Church Dedication: the feast of the Assembly and Collection, to feast of the Angels, or else to the feast of All Hallows.

FOURTH ARTICLE [I-II, Q. 103, Art. 4]

Whether Since Christ's Passion the Legal Ceremonies Can Be Observed Without Committing Mortal Sin?

Objection 1: It would seem that since Christ's Passion the legal ceremonies can be observed without committing mortal sin. For we must not believe that the apostles committed mortal sin after receiving the Holy Ghost: since by His fulness they were "endued with power from on high" (Luke 24:49). But the apostles observed the legal ceremonies after the coming of the Holy Ghost: for it is stated (Acts 16:3) that Paul circumcised Timothy: and (Acts 21:26) that Paul, at the advice of James, "took the men, and ... being purified with them, entered into the temple, giving notice of the accomplishment of the days of purification, until an oblation should be offered for every one of them." Therefore the legal ceremonies can be observed since the Passion of Christ without mortal sin.

Obj. 2: Further, one of the legal ceremonies consisted in shunning the fellowship of Gentiles. But the first Pastor of the Church complied with this observance; for it is stated (Gal. 2:12) that, "when" certain men "had come" to Antioch, Peter "withdrew and separated himself" from the Gentiles. Therefore the legal ceremonies can be observed since Christ's Passion without committing mortal sin.

Obj. 3: Further, the commands of the apostles did not lead men into sin. But it was commanded by apostolic decree that the Gentiles should observe certain ceremonies of the Law: for it is written (Acts 15:28, 29): "It hath seemed good to the Holy Ghost and to us, to lay no further burden upon you than these necessary things: that you abstain from things sacrificed to idols, and from blood, and from things strangled, and from fornication." Therefore the legal ceremonies can be observed since Christ's Passion without committing mortal sin.

*On the contrary,* The Apostle says (Gal. 5:2): "If you be circumcised, Christ shall profit you nothing." But nothing save mortal sin hinders us from receiving Christ's fruit. Therefore since Christ's Passion it is a mortal sin to be circumcised, or to observe the other legal ceremonies.

*I answer that,* All ceremonies are professions of faith, in which the interior worship of God consists. Now man can make profession of his inward faith, by deeds as well as by words: and in either profession, if he make a false declaration, he sins mortally. Now, though our faith in Christ is the same as that of the fathers of old; yet, since they came before Christ, whereas we come after Him, the same faith is expressed in different words, by us and by them. For by them was it said: "Behold a virgin shall conceive and bear a son," where the verbs are in the future tense: whereas we express the same by means of verbs in the past tense, and say that she "conceived and bore." In like manner the ceremonies of the Old Law betokened Christ as having yet to be born and to suffer: whereas our sacraments signify Him as already born and having suffered. Consequently, just as it would be a mortal sin now for anyone, in making a profession of faith, to say that Christ is yet to be born, which the fathers of old said devoutly and truthfully; so too it would be a mortal sin now to observe those ceremonies which the fathers of old fulfilled with devotion and fidelity. Such is the teaching of Augustine (Contra Faust. xix, 16), who says: "It is no longer promised that He shall be born, shall suffer and rise again, truths of which their sacraments were a kind of image: but it is declared that He is already born, has suffered and risen again; of which our sacraments, in which Christians share, are the actual representation."

Reply Obj. 1: On this point there seems to have been a difference of opinion between Jerome and Augustine. For Jerome (Super Galat. ii, 11, seqq.) distinguished two periods of time. One was the time previous to Christ's Passion, during which the legal ceremonies were neither dead, since they were obligatory, and did expiate in their own fashion; nor deadly, because it was not sinful to observe them. But immediately after Christ's Passion they began to be not only dead, so as no longer to be either effectual or binding; but also deadly, so that whoever observed them was guilty of mortal sin. Hence he maintained that after the Passion the apostles never observed the legal ceremonies in real earnest; but only by a kind of pious pretense, lest, to wit, they should scandalize the Jews and hinder their conversion. This pretense, however, is to be understood, not as though they did not in reality perform those actions, but in the sense that they performed them without the mind to observe the ceremonies of the Law: thus a man might cut away his foreskin for health's sake, not with the intention of observing legal circumcision.

But since it seems unbecoming that the apostles, in order to avoid scandal, should have hidden things pertaining to the truth of life and doctrine, and that they should have made use of pretense, in things pertaining to the salvation of the faithful; therefore Augustine (Epist. lxxxii) more fittingly distinguished three periods of time. One was the time that preceded the Passion of Christ, during which the legal ceremonies were neither deadly nor dead: another period was after the publication of the Gospel, during which the legal ceremonies are both dead and deadly. The third is a middle period, viz. from the Passion of Christ until the publication of the Gospel, during which the legal ceremonies were dead indeed, because they had neither effect nor binding force; but were not deadly, because it was lawful for the Jewish converts to Christianity to observe them, provided they did not put their trust in them so as to hold them to be necessary unto salvation, as though faith in Christ could not justify without the legal observances. On the other hand, there was no reason why those who were converted from heathendom to Christianity should observe them. Hence Paul circumcised Timothy, who was born of a Jewish mother; but was unwilling to circumcise Titus, who was of heathen nationality.

The reason why the Holy Ghost did not wish the converted Jews to be debarred at once from observing the legal ceremonies, while converted heathens were forbidden to observe the rites of heathendom, was in order to show that there is a difference between these rites. For heathenish ceremonial was rejected as absolutely unlawful, and as prohibited by God for all time; whereas the legal ceremonial ceased as being fulfilled through Christ's Passion, being instituted by God as a figure of Christ.

Reply Obj. 2: According to Jerome, Peter withdrew himself from the Gentiles by pretense, in order to avoid giving scandal to the Jews, of whom he was the Apostle. Hence he did not sin at all in acting thus. On the other hand, Paul in like manner made a pretense of blaming him, in order to avoid scandalizing the Gentiles, whose Apostle he was. But Augustine disapproves of this solution: because in the canonical Scripture (viz. Gal. 2:11), wherein we must not hold anything to be false, Paul says that Peter "was to be blamed." Consequently it is true that Peter was at fault: and Paul blamed him in very truth and not with pretense. Peter, however, did not sin, by observing the legal ceremonial for the time being; because this was lawful for him who was a converted Jew. But he did sin by excessive minuteness in the observance of the legal rites lest he should scandalize the Jews, the result being that he gave scandal to the Gentiles.

Reply Obj. 3: Some have held that this prohibition of the apostles is not to be taken literally, but spiritually: namely, that the prohibition of blood signifies the prohibition of murder; the prohibition of things strangled, that of violence and rapine; the prohibition of things offered to idols, that of idolatry; while fornication is forbidden as being evil in itself: which opinion they gathered from certain glosses, which expound these prohibitions in a mystical sense. Since, however, murder and rapine were held to be unlawful even by the Gentiles, there would have been no need to give this special commandment to those who were converted to Christ from heathendom. Hence others maintain that those foods were forbidden literally, not to prevent the observance of legal ceremonies, but in order to prevent gluttony. Thus Jerome says on Ezech. 44:31 ("The priest shall not eat of anything that is dead"): "He condemns those priests who from gluttony did not keep these precepts."

But since certain foods are more delicate than these and more conducive to gluttony, there seems no reason why these should have been forbidden more than the others.

We must therefore follow the third opinion, and hold that these foods were forbidden literally, not with the purpose of enforcing compliance with the legal ceremonies, but in order to further the union of Gentiles and Jews living side by side. Because blood and things strangled were loathsome to the Jews by ancient custom; while the Jews might have suspected the Gentiles of relapse into idolatry if the latter had partaken of things offered to idols. Hence these things were prohibited for the time being, during which the Gentiles and Jews were to become united together. But as time went on, with the lapse of the cause, the effect lapsed also, when the truth of the Gospel teaching was divulged, wherein Our Lord taught that "not that which entereth into the mouth defileth a man" (Matt. 15:11); and that "nothing is to be rejected that is received with thanksgiving" (1 Tim. 4:4). With regard to fornication a special prohibition was made, because the Gentiles did not hold it to be sinful.

## QUESTION 104

OF THE JUDICIAL PRECEPTS (In Four Articles)

We must now consider the judicial precepts: and first of all we shall consider them in general; in the second place we shall consider their reasons. Under the first head there are four points of inquiry:

(1) What is meant by the judicial precepts?

(2) Whether they are figurative?

(3) Their duration;

(4) Their division.

FIRST ARTICLE [I-II, Q. 104, Art. 1]

Whether the Judicial Precepts Were Those Which Directed Man in Relation to His Neighbor?

Objection 1: It would seem that the judicial precepts were not those which directed man in his relations to his neighbor. For judicial precepts take their name from *judgment*. But there are many things that direct man as to his neighbor, which are not subordinate to judgment. Therefore the judicial precepts were not those which directed man in his relations to his neighbor.

Obj. 2: Further, the judicial precepts are distinct from the moral precepts, as stated above (Q. 99, A. 4). But there are many moral precepts which direct man as to his neighbor: as is evidently the case with the seven precepts of the second table. Therefore the judicial precepts are not so called from directing man as to his neighbor.

Obj. 3: Further, as the ceremonial precepts relate to God, so do the judicial precepts relate to one's neighbor, as stated above (Q. 99, A. 4; Q. 101, A. 1). But among the ceremonial precepts there are some which concern man himself, such as observances in matter of food and apparel, of which we have already spoken (Q. 102, A. 6, ad 1, 6). Therefore the judicial precepts are not so called from directing man as to his neighbor.

*On the contrary,* It is reckoned (Ezech. 18:8) among other works of a good and just man, that "he hath executed true judgment between man and man." But judicial precepts are so called from "judgment." Therefore it seems that the judicial precepts were those which directed the relations between man and man.

*I answer that,* As is evident from what we have stated above (Q. 95, A. 2; Q. 99, A. 4), in every law, some precepts derive their binding force from the dictate of reason itself, because natural reason dictates that something ought to be done or to be avoided. These are called "moral" precepts: since human morals are based on reason. At the same time there are other precepts which derive their binding force, not from the very dictate of reason (because, considered in themselves, they do not imply an obligation of something due or undue); but from some institution, Divine or human: and such are certain determinations of the moral precepts. When therefore the moral precepts are fixed by Divine institution in matters relating to man's subordination to God, they are called "ceremonial" precepts: but when they refer to man's relations to other men, they are called "judicial" precepts. Hence there are two conditions attached to the judicial precepts: viz. first, that they refer to man's relations to other men; secondly, that they derive their binding force not from reason alone, but in virtue of their institution.

Reply Obj. 1: Judgments emanate through the official pronouncement of certain men who are at the head of affairs, and in whom the judicial power is vested. Now it belongs to those who are at the head of affairs to regulate not only litigious matters, but also voluntary contracts which are concluded between man and man, and whatever matters concern the community at large and the government thereof. Consequently the judicial precepts are not only those which concern actions at law; but also all those that are directed to the ordering of one man in relation to another, which ordering is subject to the direction of the sovereign as supreme judge.

Reply Obj. 2: This argument holds in respect of those precepts which direct man in his relations to his neighbor, and derive their binding force from the mere dictate of reason.

Reply Obj. 3: Even in those precepts which direct us to God, some are moral precepts, which the reason itself dictates when it is quickened by faith; such as that God is to be loved and worshipped. There are also ceremonial precepts, which have no binding force except in virtue of their Divine institution. Now God is concerned not only with the sacrifices that are offered to Him, but also with whatever relates to the fitness of those who offer sacrifices to Him and worship Him. Because men are ordained to God as to their end; wherefore it concerns God and, consequently, is a matter of ceremonial precept, that man should show some fitness for the divine worship. On the other hand, man is not ordained to his neighbor as to his end, so as to need to be disposed in himself with regard to his neighbor, for such is the relationship of a slave to his master, since a slave "is his master's in all that he is," as the Philosopher says (Polit. i, 2). Hence there are no judicial precepts ordaining man in himself; all such precepts are moral: because the reason, which is the princip[le] in moral matters, holds the same position, in man, with regard to things that concern him, as a prince or judge holds in the state. Nevertheless we must take note that, since the relations of man to his neighbor are more subject to reason than the relations of man to God, there are more precepts whereby man is directed in his relations to his neighbor, than whereby he is directed to God. For the same reason there had to be more ceremonial than judicial precepts in the Law.

SECOND ARTICLE [I-II, Q. 104, Art. 2]

Whether the Judicial Precepts Were Figurative?

Objection 1: It would seem that the judicial precepts were not figurative. Because it seems proper to the ceremonial precepts to be instituted as figures of something else. Therefore, if the judicial precepts are figurative, there will be no difference between the judicial and ceremonial precepts.

Obj. 2: Further, just as certain judicial precepts were given to the Jewish people, so also were some given to other heathen peoples. But the judicial precepts given to other peoples were not figurative, but stated what had to be done. Therefore it seems that neither were the judicial precepts of the Old Law figures of anything.

Obj. 3: Further, those things which relate to the divine worship had to be taught under certain figures, because the things of God are above our reason, as stated above (Q. 101, A. 2, ad 2). But things concerning our neighbor are not above our reason. Therefore the judicial precepts which direct us in relation to our neighbor should not have been figurative.

*On the contrary,* The judicial precepts are expounded both in the allegorical and in the moral sense (Ex. 21).

*I answer that,* A precept may be figurative in two ways. First, primarily and in itself: because, to wit, it is instituted principally that it may be the figure of something. In this way the ceremonial precepts are figurative; since they were instituted for the very purpose that they might foreshadow something relating to the worship of God and the mystery of Christ. But some precepts are figurative, not primarily and in themselves, but consequently. In this way the judicial precepts of the Old Law are figurative. For they were not instituted for the purpose of being figurative, but in order that they might regulate the state of that people according to justice and equity. Nevertheless they did foreshadow something consequently: since, to wit, the entire state of that people, who were directed by these precepts, was figurative, according to 1 Cor. 10:11: "All ... things happened to them in figure."

Reply Obj. 1: The ceremonial precepts are not figurative in the same way as the judicial precepts, as explained above.

Reply Obj. 2: The Jewish people were chosen by God that Christ might be born of them. Consequently the entire state of that people had to be prophetic and figurative, as Augustine states (Contra Faust. xxii, 24). For this reason even the judicial precepts that were given to this people were more figurative that those which were given to other nations. Thus, too, the wars and deeds of this people are expounded in the mystical sense: but not the wars and deeds of the Assyrians or Romans, although the latter are more famous in the eyes of men.

Reply Obj. 3: In this people the direction of man in regard to his neighbor, considered in itself, was subject to reason. But in so far as it was referred to the worship of God, it was above reason: and in this respect it was figurative.

THIRD ARTICLE [I-II, Q. 104, Art. 3]

Whether the Judicial Precepts of the Old Law Bind for Ever?

Objection 1: It would seem that the judicial precepts of the Old Law bind for ever. Because the judicial precepts relate to the virtue of justice: since a judgment is an execution of the virtue of justice. Now "justice is perpetual and immortal" (Wis. 1:15). Therefore the judicial precepts bind for ever.

Obj. 2: Further, Divine institutions are more enduring than human institutions. But the judicial precepts of human laws bind for ever. Therefore much more do the judicial precepts of the Divine Law.

Obj. 3: Further, the Apostle says (Heb. 7:18) that "there is a setting aside of the former commandment, because of the weakness and unprofitableness thereof." Now this is true of the ceremonial precept, which "could [Vulg.: 'can'] not, as to the conscience, make him perfect that serveth only in meats and in drinks, and divers washings and justices of the flesh," as the Apostle declares (Heb. 9:9, 10). On the other hand, the judicial precepts were useful and efficacious in respect of the purpose for which they were instituted, viz. to establish justice and equity among men. Therefore the judicial precepts of the Old Law are not set aside, but still retain their efficacy.

*On the contrary,* The Apostle says (Heb. 7:12) that "the priesthood being translated it is necessary that a translation also be made of the Law." But the priesthood was transferred from Aaron to Christ. Therefore the entire Law was also transferred. Therefore the judicial precepts are no longer in force.

*I answer that,* The judicial precepts did not bind for ever, but were annulled by the coming of Christ: yet not in the same way as the ceremonial precepts. For the ceremonial precepts were annulled so far as to be not only "dead," but also deadly to those who observe them since the coming of Christ, especially since the promulgation of the Gospel. On the other hand, the judicial precepts are dead indeed, because they have no binding force: but they are not deadly. For if a sovereign were to order these judicial precepts to be observed in his kingdom, he would not sin: unless perchance they were observed, or ordered to be observed, as though they derived their binding force through being institutions of the Old Law: for it would be a deadly sin to intend to observe them thus.

The reason for this difference may be gathered from what has been said above (A. 2). For it has been stated that the ceremonial precepts are figurative primarily and in themselves, as being instituted chiefly for the purpose of foreshadowing the mysteries of Christ to come. On the other hand, the judicial precepts were not instituted that they might be figures, but that they might shape the state of that people who were directed to Christ. Consequently, when the state of that people changed with the coming of Christ, the judicial precepts lost their binding force: for the Law was a pedagogue, leading men to Christ, as stated in Gal. 3:24. Since, however, these judicial precepts are instituted, not for the purpose of being figures, but for the performance of certain deeds, the observance thereof is not prejudicial to the truth of faith. But the intention of observing them, as though one were bound by the Law, is prejudicial to the truth of faith: because it would follow that the former state of the people still lasts, and that Christ has not yet come.

Reply Obj. 1: The obligation of observing justice is indeed perpetual. But the determination of those things that are just, according to human or Divine institution, must needs be different, according to the different states of mankind.

Reply Obj. 2: The judicial precepts established by men retain their binding force for ever, so long as the state of government remains the same. But if the state or nation pass to another form of government, the laws must needs be changed. For democracy, which is government by the people, demands different laws from those of oligarchy, which is government by the rich, as the Philosopher shows (Polit. iv, 1). Consequently when the state of that people changed, the judicial precepts had to be changed also.

Reply Obj. 3: Those judicial precepts directed the people to justice and equity, in keeping with the demands of that state. But after the coming of Christ, there had to be a change in the state of that people, so that in Christ there was no distinction between Gentile and Jew, as there had been before. For this reason the judicial precepts needed to be changed also.

FOURTH ARTICLE [I-II, Q. 104, Art. 4]

Whether It Is Possible to Assign a Distinct Division of the Judicial Precepts?

Objection 1: It would seem that it is impossible to assign a distinct division of the judicial precepts. Because the judicial precepts direct men in their relations to one another. But those things which need to be directed, as pertaining to the relationship between man and man, and which are made use of by men, are not subject to division, since they are infinite in number. Therefore it is not possible to assign a distinct division of the judicial precepts.

Obj. 2: Further, the judicial precepts are decisions on moral matters. But moral precepts do not seem to be capable of division, except in so far as they are reducible to the precepts of the decalogue. Therefore there is no distinct division of the judicial precepts.

Obj. 3: Further, because there is a distinct division of the ceremonial precepts, the Law alludes to this division, by describing some as "sacrifices," others as "observances." But the Law contains no allusion to a division of the judicial precepts. Therefore it seems that they have no distinct division.

*On the contrary,* Wherever there is order there must needs be division. But the notion of order is chiefly applicable to the judicial precepts, since thereby that people was ordained. Therefore it is most necessary that they should have a distinct division.

*I answer that,* Since law is the art, as it were, of directing or ordering the life of man, as in every art there is a distinct division in the rules of art, so, in every law, there must be a distinct division of precepts: else the law would be rendered useless by confusion. We must therefore say that the judicial precepts of the Old Law, whereby men were directed in their relations to one another, are subject to division according to the divers ways in which man is directed.

Now in every people a fourfold order is to be found: one, of the people's sovereign to his subjects; a second of the subjects among themselves; a third, of the citizens to foreigners; a fourth, of members of the same household, such as the order of the father to his son; of the wife to her husband; of the master to his servant: and according to these four orders we may distinguish different kinds of judicial precepts in the Old Law. For certain precepts are laid down concerning the institution of the sovereign and relating to his office, and about the respect due to him: this is one part of the judicial precepts. Again, certain precepts are given in respect of a man to his fellow citizens: for instance, about buying and selling, judgments and penalties: this is the second part of the judicial precepts. Again, certain precepts are enjoined with regard to foreigners: for instance, about wars waged against their foes, and about the way to receive travelers and strangers: this is the third part of the judicial precepts. Lastly, certain precepts are given relating to home life: for instance, about servants, wives and children: this is the fourth part of the judicial precepts.

Reply Obj. 1: Things pertaining to the ordering of relations between one man and another are indeed infinite in number: yet they are reducible to certain distinct heads, according to the different relations in which one man stands to another, as stated above.

Reply Obj. 2: The precepts of the decalogue held the first place in the moral order, as stated above (Q. 100, A. 3): and consequently it is fitting that other moral precepts should be distinguished in relation to them. But the judicial and ceremonial precepts have a different binding force, derived, not from natural reason, but from their institution alone. Hence there is a distinct reason for distinguishing them.

Reply Obj. 3: The Law alludes to the division of the judicial precepts in the very things themselves which are prescribed by the judicial precepts of the Law.

## QUESTION 105

OF THE REASON FOR THE JUDICIAL PRECEPTS (In Four Articles)

We must now consider the reason for the judicial precepts: under which head there are four points of inquiry:

(1) Concerning the reason for the judicial precepts relating to the rulers;

(2) Concerning the fellowship of one man with another;

(3) Concerning matters relating to foreigners;

(4) Concerning things relating to domestic matters.

FIRST ARTICLE [I-II, Q. 105, Art. 1]

Whether the Old Law Enjoined Fitting Precepts Concerning Rulers?

Objection 1: It would seem that the Old Law made unfitting precepts concerning rulers. Because, as the Philosopher says (Polit. iii, 4), "the ordering of the people depends mostly on the chief ruler." But the Law contains no precept relating to the institution of the chief ruler; and yet we find therein prescriptions concerning the inferior rulers: firstly (Ex. 18:21): "Provide out of all the people wise [Vulg.: 'able'] men," etc.; again (Num. 11:16): "Gather unto Me seventy men of the ancients of Israel"; and again (Deut. 1:13): "Let Me have from among you wise and understanding men," etc. Therefore the Law provided insufficiently in regard to the rulers of the people.

Obj. 2: Further, "The best gives of the best," as Plato states (Tim. ii). Now the best ordering of a state or of any nation is to be ruled by a king: because this kind of government approaches nearest in resemblance to the Divine government, whereby God rules the world from the beginning. Therefore the Law should have set a king over the people, and they should not have been allowed a choice in the matter, as indeed they were allowed (Deut. 17:14, 15): "When thou ... shalt say: I will set a king over me ... thou shalt set him," etc.

Obj. 3: Further, according to Matt. 12:25: "Every kingdom divided against itself shall be made desolate": a saying which was verified in the Jewish people, whose destruction was brought about by the division of the kingdom. But the Law should aim chiefly at things pertaining to the general well-being of the people. Therefore it should have forbidden the kingdom to be divided under two kings: nor should this have been introduced even by Divine authority; as we read of its being introduced by the authority of the prophet Ahias the Silonite (3 Kings 11:29, seqq.).

Obj. 4: Further, just as priests are instituted for the benefit of the people in things concerning God, as stated in Heb. 5:1; so are rulers set up for the benefit of the people in human affairs. But certain things were allotted as a means of livelihood for the priests and Levites of the Law: such as the tithes and first-fruits, and many like things. Therefore in like manner certain things should have been determined for the livelihood of the rulers of the people: the more that they were forbidden to accept presents, as is clearly stated in Ex. 23:8: "You shall not [Vulg.: 'Neither shalt thou'] take bribes, which even blind the wise, and pervert the words of the just."

Obj. 5: Further, as a kingdom is the best form of government, so is tyranny the most corrupt. But when the Lord appointed the king, He established a tyrannical law; for it is written (1 Kings 8:11): "This will be the right of the king, that shall reign over you: He will take your sons," etc. Therefore the Law made unfitting provision with regard to the institution of rulers.

*On the contrary,* The people of Israel is commended for the beauty of its order (Num. 24:5): "How beautiful are thy tabernacles, O Jacob, and thy tents." But the beautiful ordering of a people depends on the right establishment of its rulers. Therefore the Law made right provision for the people with regard to its rulers.

*I answer that,* Two points are to be observed concerning the right ordering of rulers in a state or nation. One is that all should take some share in the government: for this form of constitution ensures peace among the people, commends itself to all, and is most enduring, as stated in *Polit.* ii, 6. The other point is to be observed in respect of the kinds of government, or the different ways in which the constitutions are established. For whereas these differ in kind, as the Philosopher states (Polit. iii, 5), nevertheless the first place is held by the *kingdom,* where the power of government is vested in one; and *aristocracy,* which signifies government by the best, where the power of government is vested in a few. Accordingly, the best form of government is in a state or kingdom, where one is given the power to preside over all; while under him are others having governing powers: and yet a government of this kind is shared by all, both because all are eligible to govern, and because the rules are chosen by all. For this is the best form of polity, being partly kingdom, since there is one at the head of all; partly aristocracy, in so far as a number of persons are set in authority; partly democracy, i.e. government by the people, in so far as the rulers can be chosen from the people, and the people have the right to choose their rulers.

Such was the form of government established by the Divine Law. For Moses and his successors governed the people in such a way that each of them was ruler over all; so that there was a kind of kingdom. Moreover, seventy-two men were chosen, who were elders in virtue: for it is written (Deut. 1:15): "I took out of your tribes wise and honorable, and appointed them rulers": so that there was an element of aristocracy. But it was a democratical government in so far as the rulers were chosen from all the people; for it is written (Ex. 18:21): "Provide out of all the people wise [Vulg.: 'able'] men," etc.; and, again, in so far as they were chosen by the people; wherefore it is written (Deut. 1:13): "Let me have from among you wise [Vulg.: 'able'] men," etc. Consequently it is evident that the ordering of the rulers was well provided for by the Law.

Reply Obj. 1: This people was governed under the special care of God: wherefore it is written (Deut. 7:6): "The Lord thy God hath chosen thee to be His peculiar people": and this is why the Lord reserved to Himself the institution of the chief ruler. For this too did Moses pray (Num. 27:16): "May the Lord the God of the spirits of all the flesh provide a man, that may be over this multitude." Thus by God's orders Josue was set at the head in place of Moses; and we read about each of the judges who succeeded Josue that God "raised ... up a saviour" for the people, and that "the spirit of the Lord was" in them (Judges 3:9, 10, 15). Hence the Lord did not leave the choice of a king to the people; but reserved this to Himself, as appears from Deut. 17:15: "Thou shalt set him whom the Lord thy God shall choose."

Reply Obj. 2: A kingdom is the best form of government of the people, so long as it is not corrupt. But since the power granted to a king is so great, it easily degenerates into tyranny, unless he to whom this power is given be a very virtuous man: for it is only the virtuous man that conducts himself well in the midst of prosperity, as the Philosopher observes (Ethic. iv, 3). Now perfect virtue is to be found in few: and especially were the Jews inclined to cruelty and avarice, which vices above all turn men into tyrants. Hence from the very first the Lord did not set up the kingly authority with full power, but gave them judges and governors to rule them. But afterwards when the people asked Him to do so, being indignant with them, so to speak, He granted them a king, as is clear from His words to Samuel (1 Kings 8:7): "They have not rejected thee, but Me, that I should not reign over them."

Nevertheless, as regards the appointment of a king, He did establish the manner of election from the very beginning (Deut. 17:14, seqq.): and then He determined two points: first, that in choosing a king they should wait for the Lord's decision; and that they should not make a man of another nation king, because such kings are wont to take little interest in the people they are set over, and consequently to have no care for their welfare: secondly, He prescribed how the king after his appointment should behave, in regard to himself; namely, that he should not accumulate chariots and horses, nor wives, nor immense wealth: because through craving for such things princes become tyrants and forsake justice. He also appointed the manner in which they were to conduct themselves towards God: namely, that they should continually read and ponder on God's Law, and should ever fear and obey God. Moreover, He decided how they should behave towards their subjects: namely, that they should not proudly despise them, or ill-treat them, and that they should not depart from the paths of justice.

Reply Obj. 3: The division of the kingdom, and a number of kings, was rather a punishment inflicted on that people for their many dissensions, specially against the just rule of David, than a benefit conferred on them for their profit. Hence it is written (Osee 13:11): "I will give thee a king in My wrath"; and (Osee 8:4): "They have reigned, but not by Me: they have been princes, and I knew not."

Reply Obj. 4: The priestly office was bequeathed by succession from father to son: and this, in order that it might be held in greater respect, if not any man from the people could become a priest: since honor was given to them out of reverence for the divine worship. Hence it was necessary to put aside certain things for them both as to tithes and as to first-fruits, and, again, as to oblations and sacrifices, that they might be afforded a means of livelihood. On the other hand, the rulers, as stated above, were chosen from the whole people; wherefore they had their own possessions, from which to derive a living: and so much the more, since the Lord forbade even a king to have superabundant wealth to make too much show of magnificence: both because he could scarcely avoid the excesses of pride and tyranny, arising from such things, and because, if the rulers were not very rich, and if their office involved much work and anxiety, it would not tempt the ambition of the common people; and would not become an occasion of sedition.

Reply Obj. 5: That right was not given to the king by Divine institution: rather was it foretold that kings would usurp that right, by framing unjust laws, and by degenerating into tyrants who preyed on their subjects. This is clear from the context that follows: "And you shall be his slaves [Douay: 'servants']": which is significative of tyranny, since a tyrant rules is subjects as though they were his slaves. Hence Samuel spoke these words to deter them from asking for a king; since the narrative continues: "But the people would not hear the voice of Samuel." It may happen, however, that even a good king, without being a tyrant, may take away the sons, and make them tribunes and centurions; and may take many things from his subjects in order to secure the common weal.

SECOND ARTICLE [I-II, Q. 105, Art. 2]

Whether the Judicial Precepts Were Suitably Framed As to the Relations of One Man with Another?

Objection 1: It would seem that the judicial precepts were not suitably framed as regards the relations of one man with another. Because men cannot live together in peace, if one man takes what belongs to another. But this seems to have been approved by the Law: since it is written (Deut. 23:24): "Going into thy neighbor's vineyard, thou mayest eat as many grapes as thou pleasest." Therefore the Old Law did not make suitable provisions for man's peace.

Obj. 2: Further, one of the chief causes of the downfall of states has been the holding of property by women, as the Philosopher says (Polit. ii, 6). But this was introduced by the Old Law; for it is written (Num. 27:8): "When a man dieth without a son, his inheritance shall pass to his daughter." Therefore the Law made unsuitable provision for the welfare of the people.

Obj. 3: Further, it is most conducive to the preservation of human society that men may provide themselves with necessaries by buying and selling, as stated in *Polit.* i. But the Old Law took away the force of sales; since it prescribes that in the 50th year of the jubilee all that is sold shall return to the vendor (Lev. 25:28). Therefore in this matter the Law gave the people an unfitting command.

Obj. 4: Further, man's needs require that men should be ready to lend: which readiness ceases if the creditors do not return the pledges: hence it is written (Ecclus. 29:10): "Many have refused to lend, not out of wickedness, but they were afraid to be defrauded without cause." And yet this was encouraged by the Law. First, because it prescribed (Deut. 15:2): "He to whom any thing is owing from his friend or neighbor or brother, cannot demand it again, because it is the year of remission of the Lord"; and (Ex. 22:15) it is stated that if a borrowed animal should die while the owner is present, the borrower is not bound to make restitution. Secondly, because the security acquired through the pledge is lost: for it is written (Deut. 24:10): "When thou shalt demand of thy neighbor any thing that he oweth thee, thou shalt not go into his house to take away a pledge"; and again (Deut. 24:12, 13): "The pledge shall not lodge with thee that night, but thou shalt restore it to him presently." Therefore the Law made insufficient provision in the matter of loans.

Obj. 5: Further, considerable risk attaches to goods deposited with a fraudulent depositary: wherefore great caution should be observed in such matters: hence it is stated in 2 Mac. 3:15 that "the priests ... called upon Him from heaven, Who made the law concerning things given to be kept, that He would preserve them safe, for them that had deposited them." But the precepts of the Old Law observed little caution in regard to deposits: since it is prescribed (Ex. 22:10, 11) that when goods deposited are lost, the owner is to stand by the oath of the depositary. Therefore the Law made unsuitable provision in this matter.

Obj. 6: Further, just as a workman offers his work for hire, so do men let houses and so forth. But there is no need for the tenant to pay his rent as soon as he takes a house. Therefore it seems an unnecessarily hard prescription (Lev. 19:13) that "the wages of him that hath been hired by thee shall not abide with thee until morning."

Obj. 7: Further, since there is often pressing need for a judge, it should be easy to gain access to one. It was therefore unfitting that the Law (Deut. 17:8, 9) should command them to go to a fixed place to ask for judgment on doubtful matters.

Obj. 8: Further, it is possible that not only two, but three or more, should agree to tell a lie. Therefore it is unreasonably stated (Deut. 19:15) that "in the mouth of two or three witnesses every word shall stand."

Objection 9: Further, punishment should be fixed according to the gravity of the fault: for which reason also it is written (Deut. 25:2): "According to the measure of the sin, shall the measure also of the stripes be." Yet the Law fixed unequal punishments for certain faults: for it is written (Ex. 22:1) that the thief "shall restore five oxen for one ox, and four sheep for one sheep." Moreover, certain slight offenses are severely punished: thus (Num. 15:32, seqq.) a man is stoned for gathering sticks on the sabbath day: and (Deut. 21:18, seqq.) the unruly son is commanded to be stoned on account of certain small transgressions, viz. because "he gave himself to revelling ... and banquetings." Therefore the Law prescribed punishments in an unreasonable manner.

Objection 10: Further, as Augustine says (De Civ. Dei xxi, 11), "Tully writes that the laws recognize eight forms of punishment, indemnity, prison, stripes, retaliation, public disgrace, exile, death, slavery." Now some of these were prescribed by the Law. "Indemnity," as when a thief was condemned to make restitution fivefold or fourfold. "Prison," as when (Num. 15:34) a certain man is ordered to be imprisoned. "Stripes"; thus (Deut. 25:2), "if they see that the offender be worthy of stripes; they shall lay him down, and shall cause him to be beaten before them." "Public disgrace" was brought on to him who refused to take to himself the wife of his deceased brother, for she took "off his shoe from his foot, and" did "spit in his face" (Deut. 25:9). It prescribed the "death" penalty, as is clear from (Lev. 20:9): "He that curseth his father, or mother, dying let him die." The Law also recognized the "lex talionis," by prescribing (Ex. 21:24): "Eye for eye, tooth for tooth." Therefore it seems unreasonable that the Law should not have inflicted the two other punishments, viz. "exile" and "slavery."

Objection 11: Further, no punishment is due except for a fault. But dumb animals cannot commit a fault. Therefore the Law is unreasonable in punishing them (Ex. 21:29): "If the ox … shall kill a man or a woman," it "shall be stoned": and (Lev. 20:16): "The woman that shall lie under any beast, shall be killed together with the same." Therefore it seems that matters pertaining to the relations of one man with another were unsuitably regulated by the Law.

Objection 12: Further, the Lord commanded (Ex. 21:12) a murderer to be punished with death. But the death of a dumb animal is reckoned of much less account than the slaying of a man. Hence murder cannot be sufficiently punished by the slaying of a dumb animal. Therefore it is unfittingly prescribed (Deut. 21:1, 4) that "when there shall be found … the corpse of a man slain, and it is not known who is guilty of the murder … the ancients" of the nearest city "shall take a heifer of the herd, that hath not drawn in the yoke, nor ploughed the ground, and they shall bring her into a rough and stony valley, that never was ploughed, nor sown; and there they shall strike off the head of the heifer."

*On the contrary,* It is recalled as a special blessing (Ps. 147:20) that "He hath not done in like manner to every nation; and His judgments He hath not made manifest to them."

*I answer that,* As Augustine says (De Civ. Dei ii, 21), quoting Tully, "a nation is a body of men united together by consent to the law and by community of welfare." Consequently it is of the essence of a nation that the mutual relations of the citizens be ordered by just laws. Now the relations of one man with another are twofold: some are effected under the guidance of those in authority: others are effected by the will of private individuals. And since whatever is subject to the power of an individual can be disposed of according to his will, hence it is that the decision of matters between one man and another, and the punishment of evildoers, depend on the direction of those in authority, to whom men are subject. On the other hand, the power of private persons is exercised over the things they possess: and consequently their dealings with one another, as regards such things, depend on their own will, for instance in buying, selling, giving, and so forth. Now the Law provided sufficiently in respect of each of these relations between one man and another. For it established judges, as is clearly indicated in Deut. 16:18: "Thou shalt appoint judges and magistrates in all its [Vulg.: 'thy'] gates … that they may judge the people with just judgment." It is also directed the manner of pronouncing just judgments, according to Deut. 1:16, 17: "Judge that which is just, whether he be one of your own country or a stranger: there shall be no difference of persons." It also removed an occasion of pronouncing unjust judgment, by forbidding judges to accept bribes (Ex. 23:8; Deut. 16:19). It prescribed the number of witnesses, viz. two or three: and it appointed certain punishments to certain crimes, as we shall state farther on (ad 10).

But with regard to possessions, it is a very good thing, says the Philosopher (Polit. ii, 2) that the things possessed should be distinct, and the use thereof should be partly common, and partly granted to others by the will of the possessors. These three points were provided for by the Law. Because, in the first place, the possessions themselves were divided among individuals: for it is written (Num. 33:53, 54): "I have given you" the land "for a possession: and you shall divide it among you by lot." And since many states have been ruined through want of regulations in the matter of possessions, as the Philosopher observes (Polit. ii, 6); therefore the Law provided a threefold remedy against the irregularity of possessions. The first was that they should be divided equally, wherefore it is written (Num. 33:54): "To the more you shall give a larger part, and to the fewer, a lesser." A second remedy was that possessions could not be alienated for ever, but after a certain lapse of time should return to their former owner, so as to avoid confusion of possessions (cf. ad 3). The third remedy aimed at the removal of this confusion, and provided that the dead should be succeeded by their next of kin: in the first place, the son; secondly, the daughter; thirdly, the brother; fourthly, the father's brother; fifthly, any other next of kin. Furthermore, in order to preserve the distinction of property, the Law enacted that heiresses should marry within their own tribe, as recorded in Num. 36:6.

Secondly, the Law commanded that, in some respects, the use of things should belong to all in common. Firstly, as regards the care of them; for it was prescribed (Deut. 22:1-4): "Thou shalt not pass by, if thou seest thy brother's ox or his sheep go astray; but thou shalt bring them back to thy brother," and in like manner as to other things. Secondly, as regards fruits. For all alike were allowed on entering a friend's vineyard to eat of the fruit, but not to take any away. And, specially, with respect to the poor, it was prescribed that the forgotten sheaves, and the bunches of grapes and fruit, should be left behind for them (Lev. 19:9; Deut. 24:19). Moreover, whatever grew in the seventh year was common property, as stated in Ex. 23:11 and Lev. 25:4.

Thirdly, the law recognized the transference of goods by the owner. There was a purely gratuitous transfer: thus it is written (Deut. 14:28, 29): "The third day thou shalt separate another tithe … and the Levite … and the stranger, and the fatherless, and the widow … shall come and shall eat and be filled." And there was a transfer for a consideration, for instance, by selling and buying, by letting out and hiring, by loan and also by deposit, concerning all of which we find that the Law made ample provision. Consequently it is clear that the Old Law provided sufficiently concerning the mutual relations of one man with another.

Reply Obj. 1: As the Apostle says (Rom. 13:8), "he that loveth his neighbor hath fulfilled the Law": because, to wit, all the precepts of the Law, chiefly those concerning our neighbor, seem to aim at the end that men should love one another. Now it is an effect of love that men give their own goods to others: because, as stated in 1 John 3:17: "He that … shall see his brother in need, and shall shut up his bowels from him: how doth the charity of God abide in him?" Hence the purpose of the Law was to accustom men to give of their own to others readily: thus the Apostle (1 Tim. 6:18) commands the rich "to give easily and to communicate to others." Now a man does not give easily to others if he will not suffer another man to take some little thing from him without any great injury to him. And so the Law laid down that it should be lawful for a man, on entering his neighbor's vineyard, to eat of the fruit there: but not to carry any away, lest this should lead to the infliction of a grievous harm, and cause a disturbance of the peace: for among well-behaved people, the taking of a little does not disturb the peace; in fact, it rather strengthens friendship and accustoms men to give things to one another.

Reply Obj. 2: The Law did not prescribe that women should succeed to their father's estate except in default of male issue: failing which it was necessary that succession should be granted to the female line in order to comfort the father, who would have been sad to think that his estate would pass to strangers. Nevertheless the Law observed due caution in the matter, by providing that those women who succeeded to their father's estate, should marry within their own tribe, in order to avoid confusion of tribal possessions, as stated in Num. 36:7, 8.

Reply Obj. 3: As the Philosopher says (Polit. ii, 4), the regulation of possessions conduces much to the preservation of a state or nation. Consequently, as he himself observes, it was forbidden by the law in some of the heathen states, "that anyone should sell his possessions, except to avoid a manifest loss." For if possessions were to be sold indiscriminately, they might happen to come into the hands of a few: so that it might become necessary for a state or country to become void of inhabitants. Hence the Old Law, in order to remove this danger, ordered things in such a way that while provision was made for men's needs, by allowing the sale of possessions to avail for a certain period, at the same time the said danger was removed, by prescribing the return of those possessions after that period had elapsed. The reason for this law was to prevent confusion of possessions, and to ensure the continuance of a definite distinction among the tribes.

But as the town houses were not allotted to distinct estates, therefore the Law allowed them to be sold in perpetuity, like movable goods. Because the number of houses in a town was not fixed, whereas there was a fixed limit to the amount of estates, which could not be exceeded, while the number of houses in a town could be increased. On the other hand, houses situated not in a town, but "in a village that hath no walls," could not be sold in perpetuity: because such houses are built merely with a view to the cultivation and care of possessions; wherefore the Law rightly made the same prescription in regard to both (Lev. 25).

Reply Obj. 4: As stated above (ad 1), the purpose of the Law was to accustom men to its precepts, so as to be ready to come to one another's assistance: because this is a very great incentive to friendship. The Law granted these facilities for helping others in the matter not only of gratuitous and absolute donations, but also of mutual transfers: because the latter kind of succor is more frequent and benefits the greater number: and it granted facilities for this purpose in many ways. First of all by prescribing that men should be ready to lend, and that they should not be less inclined to do so as the year of remission drew nigh, as stated in Deut. 15:7, seqq. Secondly, by forbidding them to burden a man to whom they might grant a loan, either by exacting usury, or by accepting necessities of life in security; and by prescribing that when this had been done they should be restored at once. For it is written (Deut. 23:19): "Thou shalt not lend to thy brother money to usury": and (Deut. 24:6): "Thou shalt not take the nether nor the upper millstone to pledge; for he hath pledged his life to thee": and (Ex. 22:26): "If thou take of thy neighbor a garment in pledge, thou shalt give it him again before sunset." Thirdly, by forbidding them to be importunate in exacting payment. Hence it is written (Ex. 22:25): "If thou lend money to any of my people that is poor that dwelleth with thee, thou shalt not be hard upon them as an extortioner." For this reason, too, it is enacted (Deut. 24:10, 11): "When thou shalt demand of thy neighbor anything that he oweth thee, thou shalt not go into his house to take away a pledge, but thou shalt stand without, and he shall bring out to thee what he hath": both because a man's house is his surest refuge, wherefore it is offensive to a man to be set upon in his own house; and because the Law does not allow the creditor to take away whatever he likes in security, but rather permits the debtor to give what he needs least. Fourthly, the Law prescribed that debts should cease together after the lapse of seven years. For it was probable that those who could conveniently pay their debts, would do so before the seventh year, and would not defraud the lender without cause. But if they were altogether insolvent, there was the same reason for remitting the debt from love for them, as there was for renewing the loan on account of their need.

As regards animals granted in loan, the Law enacted that if, through the neglect of the person to whom they were lent, they perished or deteriorated in his absence, he was bound to make restitution.

But if they perished or deteriorated while he was present and taking proper care of them, he was not bound to make restitution, especially if they were hired for a consideration: because they might have died or deteriorated in the same way if they had remained in possession of the lender, so that if the animal had been saved through being lent, the lender would have gained something by the loan which would no longer have been gratuitous. And especially was this to be observed when animals were hired for a consideration: because then the owner received a certain price for the use of the animals; wherefore he had no right to any profit, by receiving indemnity for the animal, unless the person who had charge of it were negligent. In the case, however, of animals not hired for a consideration, equity demanded that he should receive something by way of restitution at least to the value of the hire of the animal that had perished or deteriorated.

Reply Obj. 5: The difference between a loan and a deposit is that a loan is in respect of goods transferred for the use of the person to whom they are transferred, whereas a deposit is for the benefit of the depositor. Hence in certain cases there was a stricter obligation of returning a loan than of restoring goods held in deposit. Because the latter might be lost in two ways. First, unavoidably: i.e. either through a natural cause, for instance if an animal held in deposit were to die or depreciate in value; or through an extrinsic cause, for instance, if it were taken by an enemy, or devoured by a beast (in which case, however, a man was bound to restore to the owner what was left of the animal thus slain): whereas in the other cases mentioned above, he was not bound to make restitution; but only to take an oath in order to clear himself of suspicion. Secondly, the goods deposited might be lost through an avoidable cause, for instance by theft: and then the depositary was bound to restitution on account of his neglect. But, as stated above (ad 4), he who held an animal on loan, was bound to restitution, even if he were absent when it depreciated or died: because he was held responsible for less negligence than a depositary, who was only held responsible in case of theft.

Reply Obj. 6: Workmen who offer their labor for hire, are poor men who toil for their daily bread: and therefore the Law commanded wisely that they should be paid at once, lest they should lack food. But they who offer other commodities for hire, are wont to be rich: nor are they in such need of their price in order to gain a livelihood: and consequently the comparison does not hold.

Reply Obj. 7: The purpose for which judges are appointed among men, is that they may decide doubtful points in matters of justice. Now a matter may be doubtful in two ways. First, among simple-minded people: and in order to remove doubts of this kind, it was prescribed (Deut. 16:18) that "judges and magistrates" should be appointed in each tribe, "to judge the people with just judgment." Secondly, a matter may be doubtful even among experts: and therefore, in order to remove doubts of this kind, the Law prescribed that all should foregather in some chief place chosen by God, where there would be both the high-priest, who would decide doubtful matters relating to the ceremonies of divine worship; and the chief judge of the people, who would decide matters relating to the judgments of men: just as even now cases are taken from a lower to a higher court either by appeal or by consultation. Hence it is written (Deut. 17:8, 9): "If thou perceive that there be among you a hard and doubtful matter in judgment ... and thou see that the words of the judges within thy gates do vary; arise and go up to the place, which the Lord thy God shall choose; and thou shalt come to the priests of the Levitical race, and to the judge that shall be at that time." But such like doubtful matters did not often occur for judgment: wherefore the people were not burdened on this account.

Reply Obj. 8: In the business affairs of men, there is no such thing as demonstrative and infallible proof, and we must be content with a certain conjectural probability, such as that which an orator employs to persuade. Consequently, although it is quite possible for two or three witnesses to agree to a falsehood, yet it is neither easy nor probable that they succeed in so doing: wherefore their testimony is taken as being true, especially if they do not waver in giving it, or are not otherwise suspect. Moreover, in order that witnesses might not easily depart from the truth, the Law commanded that they should be most carefully examined, and that those who were found untruthful should be severely punished, as stated in Deut. 19:16, seqq.

There was, however, a reason for fixing on this particular number, in token of the unerring truth of the Divine Persons, Who are sometimes mentioned as two, because the Holy Ghost is the bond of the other two Persons; and sometimes as three: as Augustine observes on John 8:17: "In your law it is written that the testimony of two men is true."

Reply Obj. 9: A severe punishment is inflicted not only on account of the gravity of a fault, but also for other reasons. First, on account of the greatness of the sin, because a greater sin, other things being equal, deserves a greater punishment. Secondly, on account of a habitual sin, since men are not easily cured of habitual sin except by severe punishments. Thirdly, on account of a great desire for or a great pleasure in the sin: for men are not easily deterred from such sins unless they be severely punished. Fourthly, on account of the facility of committing a sin and of concealing it: for such like sins, when discovered, should be more severely punished in order to deter others from committing them.

Again, with regard to the greatness of a sin, four degrees may be observed, even in respect of one single deed. The first is when a sin is committed unwillingly; because then, if the sin be altogether involuntary, man is altogether excused from punishment; for it is written (Deut. 22:25, seqq.) that a damsel who suffers violence in a field is not guilty of death, because "she cried, and there was no man to help her." But if a man sinned in any way voluntarily, and yet through weakness, as for instance when a man sins from passion, the sin is diminished: and the punishment, according to true judgment, should be diminished also; unless perchance the common weal requires that the sin be severely punished in order to deter others from committing such sins, as stated above. The second degree is when a man sins through ignorance: and then he was held to be guilty to a certain extent, on account of his negligence in acquiring knowledge: yet he was not punished by the judges but expiated his sin by sacrifices. Hence it is written (Lev. 4:2): "The soul that sinneth through ignorance," etc. This is, however, to be taken as applying to ignorance of fact; and not to ignorance of the Divine precept, which all were bound to know. The third degree was when a man sinned from pride, i.e. through deliberate choice or malice: and then he was punished according to the greatness of the sin [*Cf. Deut. 25:2]. The fourth degree was when a man sinned from stubbornness or obstinacy: and then he was to be utterly cut off as a rebel and a destroyer of the commandment of the Law [*Cf. Num. 15:30, 31].

Accordingly we must say that, in appointing the punishment for theft, the Law considered what would be likely to happen most frequently (Ex. 22:1-9): wherefore, as regards theft of other things which can easily be safeguarded from a thief, the thief restored only twice their value. But sheep cannot be easily safeguarded from a thief, because they graze in the fields: wherefore it happened more frequently that sheep were stolen in the fields. Consequently the Law inflicted a heavier penalty, by ordering four sheep to be restored for the theft of one. As to cattle, they were yet more difficult to safeguard, because they are kept in the fields, and do not graze in flocks as sheep do; wherefore a yet more heavy penalty was inflicted in their regard, so that five oxen were to be restored for one ox. And this I say, unless perchance the animal itself were discovered in the thief's possession: because in that case he had to restore only twice the number, as in the case of other thefts: for there was reason to presume that he intended to restore the animal, since he kept it alive. Again, we might say, according to a gloss, that "a cow is useful in five ways: it may be used for sacrifice, for ploughing, for food, for milk, and its hide is employed for various purposes": and therefore for one cow five had to be restored. But the sheep was useful in four ways: "for sacrifice, for meat, for milk, and for its wool." The unruly son was slain, not because he ate and drank: but on account of his stubbornness and rebellion, which was always punished by death, as stated above. As to the man who gathered sticks on the sabbath, he was stoned as a breaker of the Law, which commanded the sabbath to be observed, to testify the belief in the newness of the world, as stated above (Q. 100, A. 5): wherefore he was slain as an unbeliever.

Reply Obj. 10: The Old Law inflicted the death penalty for the more grievous crimes, viz. for those which are committed against God, and for murder, for stealing a man, irreverence towards one's parents, adultery and incest. In the case of thief of other things it inflicted punishment by indemnification: while in the case of blows and mutilation it authorized punishment by retaliation; and likewise for the sin of bearing false witness. In other faults of less degree it prescribed the punishment of stripes or of public disgrace.

The punishment of slavery was prescribed by the Law in two cases. First, in the case of a slave who was unwilling to avail himself of the privilege granted by the Law, whereby he was free to depart in the seventh year of remission: wherefore he was punished by remaining a slave for ever. Secondly, in the case of a thief, who had not wherewith to make restitution, as stated in Ex. 22:3.

The punishment of absolute exile was not prescribed by the Law: because God was worshipped by that people alone, whereas all other nations were given to idolatry: wherefore if any man were exiled from that people absolutely, he would be in danger of falling into idolatry. For this reason it is related (1 Kings 26:19) that David said to Saul: "They are cursed in the sight of the Lord, who have cast me out this day, that I should not dwell in the inheritance of the Lord, saying: Go, serve strange gods." There was, however, a restricted sort of exile: for it is written in Deut. 19:4 [*Cf. Num. 35:25] that "he that striketh [Vulg.: 'killeth'] his neighbor ignorantly, and is proved to have had no hatred against him, shall flee to one of the cities" of refuge and "abide there until the death of the high-priest." For then it became lawful for him to return home, because when the whole people thus suffered a loss they forgot their private quarrels, so that the next of kin of the slain were not so eager to kill the slayer.

Reply Obj. 11: Dumb animals were ordered to be slain, not on account of any fault of theirs; but as a punishment to their owners, who had not safeguarded their beasts from these offenses. Hence the owner was more severely punished if his ox had butted anyone "yesterday or the day before" (in which case steps might have been taken to avoid the danger) than if it had taken to butting suddenly.—Or again, the animal was slain in detestation of the sin; and lest men should be horrified at the sight thereof.

Reply Obj. 12: The literal reason for this commandment, as Rabbi Moses declares (Doct. Perplex. iii), was because the slayer was frequently from the nearest city: wherefore the slaying of the calf was a means of investigating the hidden murder. This was brought about in three ways. In the first place the elders of the city swore that they had taken every measure for safeguarding the roads. Secondly, the owner of the heifer was indemnified for the slaying of his beast, and if the murder was previously discovered, the beast was not slain. Thirdly, the place, where the heifer was slain, remained uncultivated. Wherefore, in order to avoid this twofold loss, the men of the city would readily make known the murderer, if they knew who he was: and it would seldom happen but that some word or sign would escape about the matter. Or again, this was done in order to frighten people, in detestation of murder. Because the slaying of a heifer, which is a useful animal and full of strength, especially before it has been put under the yoke, signified that whoever committed murder, however useful and strong he might be, was to forfeit his life; and that, by a cruel death, which was implied by the striking off of its head; and that the murderer, as vile and abject, was to be cut off from the fellowship of men, which was betokened by the fact that the heifer after being slain was left to rot in a rough and uncultivated place.

Mystically, the heifer taken from the herd signifies the flesh of Christ; which had not drawn a yoke, since it had done no sin; nor did it plough the ground, i.e. it never knew the stain of revolt. The fact of the heifer being killed in an uncultivated valley signified the despised death of Christ, whereby all sins are washed away, and the devil is shown to be the arch-murderer.

THIRD ARTICLE [I-II, Q. 105, Art. 3]

Whether the Judicial Precepts Regarding Foreigners Were Framed in a Suitable Manner?

Objection 1: It would seem that the judicial precepts regarding foreigners were not suitably framed. For Peter said (Acts 10:34, 35): "In very deed I perceive that God is not a respecter of persons, but in every nation, he that feareth Him and worketh justice is acceptable to Him." But those who are acceptable to God should not be excluded from the Church of God. Therefore it is unsuitably commanded (Deut. 23:3) that "the Ammonite and the Moabite, even after the tenth generation, shall not enter into the church of the Lord for ever": whereas, on the other hand, it is prescribed (Deut. 23:7) to be observed with regard to certain other nations: "Thou shalt not abhor the Edomite, because he is thy brother; nor the Egyptian because thou wast a stranger in his land."

Obj. 2: Further, we do not deserve to be punished for those things which are not in our power. But it is not in man's power to be an eunuch, or born of a prostitute. Therefore it is unsuitably commanded (Deut. 23:1, 2) that "an eunuch and one born of a prostitute shalt not enter into the church of the Lord."

Obj. 3: Further, the Old Law mercifully forbade strangers to be molested: for it is written (Ex. 22:21): "Thou shalt not molest a stranger, nor afflict him; for yourselves also were strangers in the land of Egypt": and (Ex. 23:9): "Thou shalt not molest a stranger, for you know the hearts of strangers, for you also were strangers in the land of Egypt." But it is an affliction to be burdened with usury. Therefore the Law unsuitably permitted them (Deut. 23:19, 20) to lend money to the stranger for usury.

Obj. 4: Further, men are much more akin to us than trees. But we should show greater care and love for those things that are nearest to us, according to Ecclus. 13:19: "Every beast loveth its like: so also every man him that is nearest to himself." Therefore the Lord unsuitably commanded (Deut. 20:13-19) that all the inhabitants of a captured hostile city were to be slain, but that the fruit-trees should not be cut down.

Obj. 5: Further, every one should prefer the common good of virtue to the good of the individual. But the common good is sought in a war which men fight against their enemies. Therefore it is unsuitably commanded (Deut. 20:5-7) that certain men should be sent home, for instance a man that had built a new house, or who had planted a vineyard, or who had married a wife.

Obj. 6: Further, no man should profit by his own fault. But it is a man's fault if he be timid or faint-hearted: since this is contrary to the virtue of fortitude. Therefore the timid and faint-hearted are unfittingly excused from the toil of battle (Deut. 20:8).

*On the contrary,* Divine Wisdom declares (Prov. 8:8): "All my words are just, there is nothing wicked nor perverse in them."

*I answer that,* Man's relations with foreigners are twofold: peaceful, and hostile: and in directing both kinds of relation the Law contained suitable precepts. For the Jews were offered three opportunities of peaceful relations with foreigners. First, when foreigners passed through their land as travelers. Secondly, when they came to dwell in their land as newcomers. And in both these respects the Law made kind provision in its precepts: for it is written (Ex. 22:21): "Thou shalt not molest a stranger ( *advenam* )"; and again (Ex. 22:9): "Thou shalt not molest a stranger ( *peregrino* )." Thirdly, when any foreigners wished to be admitted entirely to their fellowship and mode of worship. With regard to these a certain order was observed. For they were not at once admitted to citizenship: just as it was law with some nations that no one was deemed a citizen except after two or three generations, as the Philosopher says (Polit. iii, 1). The reason for this was that if foreigners were allowed to meddle with the affairs of a nation as soon as they settled down in its midst, many dangers might occur, since the foreigners not yet having the common good firmly at heart might attempt something hurtful to the people. Hence it was that the Law prescribed in respect of certain nations that had close relations with the Jews (viz., the Egyptians among whom they were born and educated, and the Idumeans, the children of Esau, Jacob's brother), that they should be admitted to the fellowship of the people after the third generation; whereas others (with whom their relations had been hostile, such as the Ammonites and Moabites) were never to be admitted to citizenship; while the Amalekites, who were yet more hostile to them, and had no fellowship of kindred with them, were to be held as foes in perpetuity: for it is written (Ex. 17:16): "The war of the Lord shall be against Amalec from generation to generation."

In like manner with regard to hostile relations with foreigners, the Law contained suitable precepts. For, in the first place, it commanded that war should be declared for a just cause: thus it is commanded (Deut. 20:10) that when they advanced to besiege a city, they should at first make an offer of peace. Secondly, it enjoined that when once they had entered on a war they should undauntedly persevere in it, putting their trust in God. And in order that they might be the more heedful of this command, it ordered that on the approach of battle the priest should hearten them by promising them God's aid. Thirdly, it prescribed the removal of whatever might prove an obstacle to the fight, and that certain men, who might be in the way, should be sent home. Fourthly, it enjoined that they should use moderation in pursuing the advantage of victory, by sparing women and children, and by not cutting down fruit-trees of that country.

Reply Obj. 1: The Law excluded the men of no nation from the worship of God and from things pertaining to the welfare of the soul: for it is written (Ex. 12:48): "If any stranger be willing to dwell among you, and to keep the Phase of the Lord; all his males shall first be circumcised, and then shall he celebrate it according to the manner, and he shall be as that which is born in the land." But in temporal matters concerning the public life of the people, admission was not granted to everyone at once, for the reason given above: but to some, i.e. the Egyptians and Idumeans, in the third generation; while others were excluded in perpetuity, in detestation of their past offense, i.e. the peoples of Moab, Ammon, and Amalec. For just as one man is punished for a sin committed by him, in order that others seeing this may be deterred and refrain from sinning; so too may one nation or city be punished for a crime, that others may refrain from similar crimes.

Nevertheless it was possible by dispensation for a man to be admitted to citizenship on account of some act of virtue: thus it is related (Judith 14:6) that Achior, the captain of the children of Ammon, "was joined to the people of Israel, with all the succession of his kindred." The same applies to Ruth the Moabite who was "a virtuous woman" (Ruth 3:11): although it may be said that this prohibition regarded men and not women, who are not competent to be citizens absolutely speaking.

Reply Obj. 2: As the Philosopher says (Polit. iii, 3), a man is said to be a citizen in two ways: first, simply; secondly, in a restricted sense. A man is a citizen simply if he has all the rights of citizenship, for instance, the right of debating or voting in the popular assembly. On the other hand, any man may be called citizen, only in a restricted sense, if he dwells within the state, even common people or children or old men, who are not fit to enjoy power in matters pertaining to the common weal. For this reason bastards, by reason of their base origin, were excluded from the *ecclesia,* i.e. from the popular assembly, down to the tenth generation. The same applies to eunuchs, who were not competent to receive the honor due to a father, especially among the Jews, where the divine worship was continued through carnal generation: for even among the heathens, those who had many children were marked with special honor, as the Philosopher remarks (Polit. ii, 6). Nevertheless, in matters pertaining to the grace of God, eunuchs were not discriminated from others, as neither were strangers, as already stated: for it is written (Isa. 56:3): "Let not the son of the stranger that adhereth to the Lord speak, saying: The Lord will divide and separate me from His people. And let not the eunuch say: Behold I am a dry tree."

Reply Obj. 3: It was not the intention of the Law to sanction the acceptance of usury from strangers, but only to tolerate it on account of the proneness of the Jews to avarice; and in order to promote an amicable feeling towards those out of whom they made a profit.

Reply Obj. 4: A distinction was observed with regard to hostile cities. For some of them were far distant, and were not among those which had been promised to them. When they had taken these cities, they killed all the men who had fought against God's people; whereas the women and children were spared. But in the neighboring cities which had been promised to them, all were ordered to be slain, on account of their former crimes, to punish which God sent the Israelites as executor of Divine justice: for it is written (Deut. 9:5) "because they have done wickedly, they are destroyed at thy coming in." The fruit-trees were commanded to be left untouched, for the use of the people themselves, to whom the city with its territory was destined to be subjected.

Reply Obj. 5: The builder of a new house, the planter of a vineyard, the newly married husband, were excluded from fighting, for two reasons. First, because man is wont to give all his affection to those things which he has lately acquired, or is on the point of having, and consequently he is apt to dread the loss of these above other things. Wherefore it was likely enough that on account of this affection they would fear death all the more, and be so much the less brave in battle. Secondly, because, as the Philosopher says (Phys. ii, 5), "it is a misfortune for a man if he is prevented from obtaining something good when it is within his grasp." And so lest the surviving relations should be the more grieved at the death of these men who had not entered into the possession of the good things prepared for them; and also lest the people should be horror-stricken at the sight of their misfortune: these men were taken away from the danger of death by being removed from the battle.

Reply Obj. 6: The timid were sent back home, not that they might be the gainers thereby; but lest the people might be the losers by their presence, since their timidity and flight might cause others to be afraid and run away.

FOURTH ARTICLE [I-II, Q. 105, Art. 4]

Whether the Old Law Set Forth Suitable Precepts About the Members of the Household?

Objection 1: It would seem that the Old Law set forth unsuitable precepts about the members of the household. For a slave "is in every respect his master's property," as the Philosopher states (Polit. i, 2). But that which is a man's property should be his always. Therefore it was unfitting for the Law to command (Ex. 21:2) that slaves should "go out free" in the seventh year.

Obj. 2: Further, a slave is his master's property, just as an animal, e.g. an ass or an ox. But it is commanded (Deut. 22:1-3) with regard to animals, that they should be brought back to the owner if they be found going astray. Therefore it was unsuitably commanded (Deut. 23:15): "Thou shalt not deliver to his master the servant that is fled to thee."

Obj. 3: Further, the Divine Law should encourage mercy more even than the human law. But according to human laws those who ill-treat their servants and maidservants are severely punished: and the worse treatment of all seems to be that which results in death. Therefore it is unfittingly commanded (Ex. 21:20, 21) that "he that striketh his bondman or bondwoman with a rod, and they die under his hands ... if the party remain alive a day ... he shall not be subject to the punishment, because it is his money."

Obj. 4: Further, the dominion of a master over his slave differs from that of the father over his son (Polit. i, 3). But the dominion of master over slave gives the former the right to sell his servant or maidservant. Therefore it was unfitting for the Law to allow a man to sell his daughter to be a servant or handmaid (Ex. 21:7).

Obj. 5: Further, a father has power over his son. But he who has power over the sinner has the right to punish him for his offenses. Therefore it is unfittingly commanded (Deut. 21:18, seqq.) that a father should bring his son to the ancients of the city for punishment.

Obj. 6: Further, the Lord forbade them (Deut. 7:3, seqq.) to make marriages with strange nations; and commanded the dissolution of such as had been contracted (1 Esdras 10). Therefore it was unfitting to allow them to marry captive women from strange nations (Deut. 21:10, seqq.).

Obj. 7: Further, the Lord forbade them to marry within certain degrees of consanguinity and affinity, according to Lev. 18. Therefore it was unsuitably commanded (Deut. 25:5) that if any man died without issue, his brother should marry his wife.

Obj. 8: Further, as there is the greatest familiarity between man and wife, so should there be the staunchest fidelity. But this is impossible if the marriage bond can be sundered. Therefore it was unfitting for the Lord to allow (Deut. 24:1-4) a man to put his wife away, by writing a bill of divorce; and besides, that he could not take her again to wife.

Objection 9: Further, just as a wife can be faithless to her husband, so can a slave be to his master, and a son to his father. But the Law did not command any sacrifice to be offered in order to investigate the injury done by a servant to his master, or by a son to his father. Therefore it seems to have been superfluous for the Law to prescribe the "sacrifice of jealousy" in order to investigate a wife's adultery (Num. 5:12, seqq.). Consequently it seems that the Law put forth unsuitable judicial precepts about the members of the household.

*On the contrary,* It is written (Ps. 18:10): "The judgments of the Lord are true, justified in themselves."

*I answer that,* The mutual relations of the members of a household regard everyday actions directed to the necessities of life, as the Philosopher states (Polit. i, 1). Now the preservation of man's life may be considered from two points of view. First, from the point of view of the individual, i.e. in so far as man preserves his individuality: and for the purpose of the preservation of life, considered from this standpoint, man has at his service external goods, by means of which he provides himself with food and clothing and other such necessaries of life: in the handling of which he has need of servants. Secondly man's life is preserved from the point of view of the species, by means of generation, for which purpose man needs a wife, that she may bear him children. Accordingly the mutual relations of the members of a household admit of a threefold combination: viz. those of master and servant, those of husband and wife, and those of father and son: and in respect of all these relationships the Old Law contained fitting precepts. Thus, with regard to servants, it commanded them to be treated with moderation—both as to their work, lest, to wit, they should be burdened with excessive labor, wherefore the Lord commanded (Deut. 5:14) that on the Sabbath day "thy manservant and thy maidservant" should "rest even as thyself"—and also as to the infliction of punishment, for it ordered those who maimed their servants, to set them free (Ex. 21:26, 27). Similar provision was made in favor of a maidservant when married to anyone (Ex. 21:7, seqq.). Moreover, with regard to those servants in particular who were taken from among the people, the Law prescribed that they should go out free in the seventh year taking whatever they brought with them, even their clothes (Ex. 21:2, seqq.): and furthermore it was commanded (Deut. 15:13) that they should be given provision for the journey.

With regard to wives the Law made certain prescriptions as to those who were to be taken in marriage: for instance, that they should marry a wife from their own tribe (Num. 36:6): and this lest confusion should ensue in the property of various tribes. Also that a man should marry the wife of his deceased brother when the latter died without issue, as prescribed in Deut. 25:5, 6: and this in order that he who could not have successors according to carnal origin, might at least have them by a kind of adoption, and that thus the deceased might not be entirely forgotten. It also forbade them to marry certain women; to wit, women of strange nations, through fear of their losing their faith; and those of their near kindred, on account of the natural respect due to them. Furthermore it prescribed in what way wives were to be treated after marriage. To wit, that they should not be slandered without grave reason: wherefore it ordered punishment to be inflicted on the man who falsely accused his wife of a crime (Deut. 22:13, seqq.). Also that a man's hatred of his wife should not be detrimental to his son (Deut. 21:15, seqq.). Again, that a man should not ill-use his wife through hatred of her, but rather that he should write a bill of divorce and send her away (Deut. 24:1). Furthermore, in order to foster conjugal love from the very outset, it was prescribed that no public duties should be laid on a recently married man, so that he might be free to rejoice with his wife.

With regard to children, the Law commanded parents to educate them by instructing them in the faith: hence it is written (Ex. 12:26, seqq.): "When your children shall say to you: What is the meaning of this service? You shall say to them: It is the victim of the passage of the Lord." Moreover, they are commanded to teach them the rules of right conduct: wherefore it is written (Deut. 21:20) that the parents had to say: "He slighteth hearing our admonitions, he giveth himself to revelling and to debauchery."

Reply Obj. 1: As the children of Israel had been delivered by the Lord from slavery, and for this reason were bound to the service of God, He did not wish them to be slaves in perpetuity. Hence it is written (Lev. 25:39, seqq.): "If thy brother, constrained by poverty, sell himself to thee, thou shalt not oppress him with the service of bondservants: but he shall be as a hireling and a sojourner ... for they are My servants, and I brought them out of the land of Egypt: let them not be sold as bondmen": and consequently, since they were slaves, not absolutely but in a restricted sense, after a lapse of time they were set free.

Reply Obj. 2: This commandment is to be understood as referring to a servant whom his master seeks to kill, or to help him in committing some sin.

Reply Obj. 3: With regard to the ill-treatment of servants, the Law seems to have taken into consideration whether it was certain or not: since if it were certain, the Law fixed a penalty: for maiming, the penalty was forfeiture of the servant, who was ordered to be given his liberty: while for slaying, the punishment was that of a murderer, when the slave died under the blow of his master. If, however, the hurt was not certain, but only probable, the Law did not impose any penalty as regards a man's own servant: for instance if the servant did not die at once after being struck, but after some days: for it would be uncertain whether he died as a result of the blows he received. For when a man struck a free man, yet so that he did not die at once, but "walked abroad again upon his staff," he that struck him was quit of murder, even though afterwards he died. Nevertheless he was bound to pay the doctor's fees incurred by the victim of his assault. But this was not the case if a man killed his own servant: because whatever the servant had, even his very person, was the property of his master. Hence the reason for his not being subject to a pecuniary penalty is set down as being "because it is his money."

Reply Obj. 4: As stated above (ad 1), no Jew could own a Jew as a slave absolutely: but only in a restricted sense, as a hireling for a fixed time. And in this way the Law permitted that through stress of poverty a man might sell his son or daughter. This is shown by the very words of the Law, where we read: "If any man sell his daughter to be a servant, she shall not go out as bondwomen are wont to go out." Moreover, in this way a man might sell not only his son, but even himself, rather as a hireling than as a slave, according to Lev. 25:39, 40: "If thy brother, constrained by poverty, sell himself to thee, thou shalt not oppress him with the service of bondservants: but he shall be as a hireling and a sojourner."

Reply Obj. 5: As the Philosopher says (Ethic. x, 9), the paternal authority has the power only of admonition; but not that of coercion, whereby rebellious and headstrong persons can be compelled. Hence in this case the Lord commanded the stubborn son to be punished by the rulers of the city.

Reply Obj. 6: The Lord forbade them to marry strange women on account of the danger of seduction, lest they should be led astray into idolatry. And specially did this prohibition apply with respect to those nations who dwelt near them, because it was more probable that they would adopt their religious practices. When, however, the woman was willing to renounce idolatry, and become an adherent of the Law, it was lawful to take her in marriage: as was the case with Ruth whom Booz married. Wherefore she said to her mother-in-law (Ruth 1:16): "Thy people shall be my people, and thy God my God." Accordingly it was not permitted to marry a captive woman unless she first shaved her hair, and pared her nails, and put off the raiment wherein she was taken, and mourned for her father and mother, in token that she renounced idolatry for ever.

Reply Obj. 7: As Chrysostom says (Hom. xlviii super Matth.), "because death was an unmitigated evil for the Jews, who did everything with a view to the present life, it was ordained that children should be born to the dead man through his brother: thus affording a certain mitigation to his death. It was not, however, ordained that any other than his brother or one next of kin should marry the wife of the deceased, because" the offspring of this union "would not be looked upon as that of the deceased: and moreover, a stranger would not be under the obligation to support the household of the deceased, as his brother would be bound to do from motives of justice on account of his relationship." Hence it is evident that in marrying the wife of his dead brother, he took his dead brother's place.

Reply Obj. 8: The Law permitted a wife to be divorced, not as though it were just absolutely speaking, but on account of the Jews' hardness of heart, as Our Lord declared (Matt. 19:8). Of this, however, we must speak more fully in the treatise on Matrimony (Supp., Q. 67).

Reply Obj. 9: Wives break their conjugal faith by adultery, both easily, for motives of pleasure, and hiddenly, since "the eye of the adulterer observeth darkness" (Job 24:15). But this does not apply to a son in respect of his father, or to a servant in respect of his master: because the latter infidelity is not the result of the lust of pleasure, but rather of malice: nor can it remain hidden like the infidelity of an adulterous woman.

## QUESTION 106

OF THE LAW OF THE GOSPEL, CALLED THE NEW LAW, CONSIDERED IN ITSELF (In Four Articles)

In proper sequence we have to consider now the Law of the Gospel which is called the New Law: and in the first place we must consider it in itself; secondly, in comparison with the Old Law; thirdly, we shall treat of those things that are contained in the New Law. Under the first head there are four points of inquiry:

(1) What kind of law is it? i.e. Is it a written law or is it instilled in the heart?

(2) Of its efficacy, i.e. does it justify?

(3) Of its beginning: should it have been given at the beginning of the world?

(4) Of its end: i.e. whether it will last until the end, or will another law take its place?

FIRST ARTICLE [I-II, Q. 106, Art. 1]

Whether the New Law Is a Written Law?

Objection 1: It would seem that the New Law is a written law. For the New Law is just the same as the Gospel. But the Gospel is set forth in writing, according to John 20:31: "But these are written that you may believe." Therefore the New Law is a written law.

Obj. 2: Further, the law that is instilled in the heart is the natural law, according to Rom. 2:14, 15: "(The Gentiles) do by nature those things that are of the law ... who have [Vulg.: 'show'] the work of the law written in their hearts." If therefore the law of the Gospel were instilled in our hearts, it would not be distinct from the law of nature.

Obj. 3: Further, the law of the Gospel is proper to those who are in the state of the New Testament. But the law that is instilled in the heart is common to those who are in the New Testament and to those who are in the Old Testament: for it is written (Wis. 7:27) that Divine Wisdom "through nations conveyeth herself into holy souls, she maketh the friends of God and prophets." Therefore the New Law is not instilled in our hearts.

*On the contrary,* The New Law is the law of the New Testament. But the law of the New Testament is instilled in our hearts. For the Apostle, quoting the authority of Jeremiah 31:31, 33: "Behold the days shall come, saith the Lord; and I will perfect unto the house of Israel, and unto the house of Judah, a new testament," says, explaining what this statement is (Heb. 8:8, 10): "For this is the testament which I will make to the house of Israel ... by giving [Vulg.: 'I will give'] My laws into their mind, and in their heart will I write them." Therefore the New Law is instilled in our hearts.

*I answer that,* "Each thing appears to be that which preponderates in it," as the Philosopher states (Ethic. ix, 8). Now that which is preponderant in the law of the New Testament, and whereon all its efficacy is based, is the grace of the Holy Ghost, which is given through faith in Christ. Consequently the New Law is chiefly the grace itself of the Holy Ghost, which is given to those who believe in Christ. This is manifestly stated by the Apostle who says (Rom. 3:27): "Where is ... thy boasting? It is excluded. By what law? Of works? No, but by the law of faith": for he calls the grace itself of faith "a law." And still more clearly it is written (Rom. 8:2): "The law of the spirit of life, in Christ Jesus, hath delivered me from the law of sin and of death." Hence Augustine says (De Spir. et Lit. xxiv) that "as the law of deeds was written on tables of stone, so is the law of faith inscribed on the hearts of the faithful": and elsewhere, in the same book (xxi): "What else are the Divine laws written by God Himself on our hearts, but the very presence of His Holy Spirit?"

Nevertheless the New Law contains certain things that dispose us to receive the grace of the Holy Ghost, and pertaining to the use of that grace: such things are of secondary importance, so to speak, in the New Law; and the faithful need to be instructed concerning them, both by word and writing, both as to what they should believe and as to what they should do. Consequently we must say that the New Law is in the first place a law that is inscribed on our hearts, but that secondarily it is a written law.

Reply Obj. 1: The Gospel writings contain only such things as pertain to the grace of the Holy Ghost, either by disposing us thereto, or by directing us to the use thereof. Thus with regard to the intellect, the Gospel contains certain matters pertaining to the manifestation of Christ's Godhead or humanity, which dispose us by means of faith through which we receive the grace of the Holy Ghost: and with regard to the affections, it contains matters touching the contempt of the world, whereby man is rendered fit to receive the grace of the Holy Ghost: for "the world," i.e. worldly men, "cannot receive" the Holy Ghost (John 14:17). As to the use of spiritual grace, this consists in works of virtue to which the writings of the New Testament exhort men in divers ways.

Reply Obj. 2: There are two ways in which a thing may be instilled into man. First, through being part of his nature, and thus the natural law is instilled into man. Secondly, a thing is instilled into man by being, as it were, added on to his nature by a gift of grace. In this way the New Law is instilled into man, not only by indicating to him what he should do, but also by helping him to accomplish it.

Reply Obj. 3: No man ever had the grace of the Holy Ghost except through faith in Christ either explicit or implicit: and by faith in Christ man belongs to the New Testament. Consequently whoever had the law of grace instilled into them belonged to the New Testament.

SECOND ARTICLE [I-II, Q. 106, Art. 2]

Whether the New Law Justifies?

Objection 1: It would seem that the New Law does not justify. For no man is justified unless he obeys God's law, according to Heb. 5:9: "He," i.e. Christ, "became to all that obey Him the cause of eternal salvation." But the Gospel does not always cause men to believe in it: for it is written (Rom. 10:16): "All do not obey the Gospel." Therefore the New Law does not justify.

Obj. 2: Further, the Apostle proves in his epistle to the Romans that the Old Law did not justify, because transgression increased at its advent: for it is stated (Rom. 4:15): "The Law worketh wrath: for where there is no law, neither is there transgression." But much more did the New Law increase transgression: since he who sins after the giving of the New Law deserves greater punishment, according to Heb. 10:28, 29: "A man making void the Law of Moses dieth without any mercy under two or three witnesses. How much more, do you think, he deserveth worse punishments, who hath trodden underfoot the Son of God," etc.? Therefore the New Law, like the Old Law, does not justify.

Obj. 3: Further, justification is an effect proper to God, according to Rom. 8:33: "God that justifieth." But the Old Law was from God just as the New Law. Therefore the New Law does not justify any more than the Old Law.

*On the contrary,* The Apostle says (Rom. 1:16): "I am not ashamed of the Gospel: for it is the power of God unto salvation to everyone that believeth." But there is no salvation but to those who are justified. Therefore the Law of the Gospel justifies.

*I answer that,* As stated above (A. 1), there is a twofold element in the Law of the Gospel. There is the chief element, viz. the grace of the Holy Ghost bestowed inwardly. And as to this, the New Law justifies. Hence Augustine says (De Spir. et Lit. xvii): "There," i.e. in the Old Testament, "the Law was set forth in an outward fashion, that the ungodly might be afraid"; "here," i.e. in the New Testament, "it is given in an inward manner, that they may be justified." The other element of the Evangelical Law is secondary: namely, the teachings of faith, and those commandments which direct human affections and human actions. And as to this, the New Law does not justify. Hence the Apostle says (2 Cor. 3:6) "The letter killeth, but the spirit quickeneth": and Augustine explains this (De Spir. et Lit. xiv, xvii) by saying that the letter denotes any writing external to man, even that of the moral precepts such as are contained in the Gospel. Wherefore the letter, even of the Gospel would kill, unless there were the inward presence of the healing grace of faith.

Reply Obj. 1: This argument holds true of the New Law, not as to its principal, but as to its secondary element: i.e. as to the dogmas and precepts outwardly put before man either in words or in writing.

Reply Obj. 2: Although the grace of the New Testament helps man to avoid sin, yet it does not so confirm man in good that he cannot sin: for this belongs to the state of glory. Hence if a man sin after receiving the grace of the New Testament, he deserves greater punishment, as being ungrateful for greater benefits, and as not using the help given to him. And this is why the New Law is not said to "work wrath": because as far as it is concerned it gives man sufficient help to avoid sin.

Reply Obj. 3: The same God gave both the New and the Old Law, but in different ways. For He gave the Old Law written on tables of stone: whereas He gave the New Law written "in the fleshly tables of the heart," as the Apostle expresses it (2 Cor. 3:3). Wherefore, as Augustine says (De Spir. et Lit. xviii), "the Apostle calls this letter which is written outside man, a ministration of death and a ministration of condemnation: whereas he calls the other letter, i.e. the Law of the New Testament, the ministration of the spirit and the ministration of justice: because through the gift of the Spirit we work justice, and are delivered from the condemnation due to transgression."

THIRD ARTICLE [I-II, Q. 106, Art. 3]

Whether the New Law Should Have Been Given from the Beginning of the World?

Objection 1: It would seem that the New Law should have been given from the beginning of the world. "For there is no respect of persons with God" (Rom. 2:11). But "all" men "have sinned and do need the glory of God" (Rom. 3:23). Therefore the Law of the Gospel should have been given from the beginning of the world, in order that it might bring succor to all.

Obj. 2: Further, as men dwell in various places, so do they live in various times. But God, "Who will have all men to be saved" (1 Tim. 2:4), commanded the Gospel to be preached in all places, as may be seen in the last chapters of Matthew and Mark. Therefore the Law of the Gospel should have been at hand for all times, so as to be given from the beginning of the world.

Obj. 3: Further, man needs to save his soul, which is for all eternity, more than to save his body, which is a temporal matter. But God provided man from the beginning of the world with things that are necessary for the health of his body, by subjecting to his power whatever was created for the sake of man (Gen. 1:26-29). Therefore the New Law also, which is very necessary for the health of the soul, should have been given to man from the beginning of the world.

*On the contrary,* The Apostle says (1 Cor. 15:46): "That was not first which is spiritual, but that which is natural." But the New Law is highly spiritual. Therefore it was not fitting for it to be given from the beginning of the world.

*I answer that,* Three reasons may be assigned why it was not fitting for the New Law to be given from the beginning of the world. The first is because the New Law, as stated above (A. 1), consists chiefly in the grace of the Holy Ghost: which it behoved not to be given abundantly until sin, which is an obstacle to grace, had been cast out of man through the accomplishment of his redemption by Christ: wherefore it is written (John 7:39): "As yet the Spirit was not given, because Jesus was not yet glorified." This reason the Apostle states clearly (Rom. 8:2, seqq.) where, after speaking of "the Law of the Spirit of life," he adds: "God sending His own Son, in the likeness of sinful flesh, of sin* hath condemned sin in the flesh, that the justification of the Law might be fulfilled in us." [*St. Thomas, quoting perhaps from memory, omits the "et" (and), after "sinful flesh." The text quoted should read thus: "in the likeness of sinful flesh, and a sin offering ( *peri hamartias* ), hath," etc.]

A second reason may be taken from the perfection of the New Law. Because a thing is not brought to perfection at once from the outset, but through an orderly succession of time; thus one is at first a boy, and then a man. And this reason is stated by the Apostle (Gal. 3:24, 25): "The Law was our pedagogue in Christ that we might be justified by faith. But after the faith is come, we are no longer under a pedagogue."

The third reason is found in the fact that the New Law is the law of grace: wherefore it behoved man first of all to be left to himself under the state of the Old Law, so that through falling into sin, he might realize his weakness, and acknowledge his need of grace. This reason is set down by the Apostle (Rom. 5:20): "The Law entered in, that sin might abound: and when sin abounded grace did more abound."

Reply Obj. 1: Mankind on account of the sin of our first parents deserved to be deprived of the aid of grace: and so "from whom it is withheld it is justly withheld, and to whom it is given, it is mercifully given," as Augustine states (De Perfect. Justit. iv) [*Cf. Ep. ccvii; De Pecc. Mer. et Rem. ii, 19]. Consequently it does not follow that there is respect of persons with God, from the fact that He did not offer the Law of grace to all from the beginning of the world, which Law was to be published in due course of time, as stated above.

Reply Obj. 2: The state of mankind does not vary according to diversity of place, but according to succession of time. Hence the New Law avails for all places, but not for all times: although at all times there have been some persons belonging to the New Testament, as stated above (A. 1, ad 3).

Reply Obj. 3: Things pertaining to the health of the body are of service to man as regards his nature, which sin does not destroy: whereas things pertaining to the health of the soul are ordained to grace, which is forfeit through sin. Consequently the comparison will not hold.

FOURTH ARTICLE [I-II, Q. 106, Art. 4]

Whether the New Law Will Last Till the End of the World?

Objection 1: It would seem that the New Law will not last until the end of the world. Because, as the Apostle says (1 Cor. 13:10), "when that which is perfect is come, that which is in part shall be done away." But the New Law is "in part," since the Apostle says (1 Cor. 13:9): "We know in part and we prophesy in part." Therefore the New Law is to be done away, and will be succeeded by a more perfect state.

Obj. 2: Further, Our Lord (John 16:13) promised His disciples the knowledge of all truth when the Holy Ghost, the Comforter, should come. But the Church knows not yet all truth in the state of the New Testament. Therefore we must look forward to another state, wherein all truth will be revealed by the Holy Ghost.

Obj. 3: Further, just as the Father is distinct from the Son and the Son from the Father, so is the Holy Ghost distinct from the Father and the Son. But there was a state corresponding with the Person of the Father, viz. the state of the Old Law, wherein men were intent on begetting children: and likewise there is a state corresponding to the Person of the Son: viz. the state of the New Law, wherein the clergy who are intent on wisdom (which is appropriated to the Son) hold a prominent place. Therefore there will be a third state corresponding to the Holy Ghost, wherein spiritual men will hold the first place.

Obj. 4: Further, Our Lord said (Matt. 24:14): "This Gospel of the kingdom shall be preached in the whole world ... and then shall the consummation come." But the Gospel of Christ is already preached throughout the whole world: and yet the consummation has not yet come. Therefore the Gospel of Christ is not the Gospel of the kingdom, but another Gospel, that of the Holy Ghost, is to come yet, like unto another Law.

*On the contrary,* Our Lord said (Matt. 24:34): "I say to you that this generation shall not pass till all (these) things be done": which passage Chrysostom (Hom. lxxvii) explains as referring to "the generation of those that believe in Christ." Therefore the state of those who believe in Christ will last until the consummation of the world.

*I answer that,* The state of the world may change in two ways. In one way, according to a change of law: and thus no other state will succeed this state of the New Law. Because the state of the New Law succeeded the state of the Old Law, as a more perfect law a less perfect one. Now no state of the present life can be more perfect that the state of the New Law: since nothing can approach nearer to the last end than that which is the immediate cause of our being brought to the last end. But the New Law does this: wherefore the Apostle says (Heb. 10:19-22): "Having therefore, brethren, a confidence in the entering into the Holies by the blood of Christ, a new ... way which He hath dedicated for us ... let us draw near." Therefore no state of the present life can be more perfect than that of the New Law, since the nearer a thing is to the last end the more perfect it is.

In another way the state of mankind may change according as man stands in relation to one and the same law more or less perfectly. And thus the state of the Old Law underwent frequent changes, since at times the laws were very well kept, and at other times were altogether unheeded. Thus, too, the state of the New Law is subject to change with regard to various places, times, and persons, according as the grace of the Holy Ghost dwells in man more or less perfectly. Nevertheless we are not to look forward to a state wherein man is to possess the grace of the Holy Ghost more perfectly than he has possessed it hitherto, especially the apostles who "received the firstfruits of the Spirit, i.e. sooner and more abundantly than others," as a gloss expounds on Rom. 8:23.

Reply Obj. 1: As Dionysius says (Eccl. Hier. v), there is a threefold state of mankind; the first was under the Old Law; the second is that of the New Law; the third will take place not in this life, but in heaven. But as the first state is figurative and imperfect in comparison with the state of the Gospel; so is the present state figurative and imperfect in comparison with the heavenly state, with the advent of which the present state will be done away as expressed in that very passage (1 Cor. 13:12): "We see now through a glass in a dark manner; but then face to face."

Reply Obj. 2: As Augustine says (Contra Faust. xix, 31), Montanus and Priscilla pretended that Our Lord's promise to give the Holy Ghost was fulfilled, not in the apostles, but in themselves. In like manner the Manicheans maintained that it was fulfilled in Manes whom they held to be the Paraclete. Hence none of the above received the Acts of the Apostles, where it is clearly shown that the aforesaid promise was fulfilled in the apostles: just as Our Lord promised them a second time (Acts 1:5): "You shall be baptized with the Holy Ghost, not many days hence": which we read as having been fulfilled in Acts 2. However, these foolish notions are refuted by the statement (John 7:39) that "as yet the Spirit was not given, because Jesus was not yet glorified"; from which we gather that the Holy Ghost was given as soon as Christ was glorified in His Resurrection and Ascension. Moreover, this puts out of court the senseless idea that the Holy Ghost is to be expected to come at some other time.

Now the Holy Ghost taught the apostles all truth in respect of matters necessary for salvation; those things, to wit, that we are bound to believe and to do. But He did not teach them about all future events: for this did not regard them according to Acts 1:7: "It is not for you to know the times or moments which the Father hath put in His own power."

Reply Obj. 3: The Old Law corresponded not only to the Father, but also to the Son: because Christ was foreshadowed in the Old Law. Hence Our Lord said (John 5:46): "If you did believe Moses, you would perhaps believe me also; for he wrote of Me." In like manner the New Law corresponds not only to Christ, but also to the Holy Ghost; according to Rom. 8:2: "The Law of the Spirit of life in Christ Jesus," etc. Hence we are not to look forward to another law corresponding to the Holy Ghost.

Reply Obj. 4: Since Christ said at the very outset of the preaching of the Gospel: "The kingdom of heaven is at hand" (Matt. 4:17), it is most absurd to say that the Gospel of Christ is not the Gospel of the kingdom. But the preaching of the Gospel of Christ may be understood in two ways. First, as denoting the spreading abroad of the knowledge of Christ: and thus the Gospel was preached throughout the world even at the time of the apostles, as Chrysostom states (Hom. lxxv in Matth.). And in this sense the words that follow—"and then shall the consummation come," refer to the destruction of Jerusalem, of which He was speaking literally. Secondly, the preaching of the Gospel may be understood as extending throughout the world and producing its full effect, so that, to wit, the Church would be founded in every nation. And in these sense, as Augustine writes to Hesychius (Epist. cxcix), the Gospel is not preached to the whole world yet, but, when it is, the consummation of the world will come.

## QUESTION 107

OF THE NEW LAW AS COMPARED WITH THE OLD (In Four Articles)

We must now consider the New Law as compared with the Old: under which head there are four points of inquiry:

(1) Whether the New Law is distinct from the Old Law?

(2) Whether the New Law fulfils the Old?

(3) Whether the New Law is contained in the Old?

(4) Which is the more burdensome, the New or the Old Law?

FIRST ARTICLE [I-II, Q. 107, Art. 1]

Whether the New Law Is Distinct from the Old Law?

Objection 1: It would seem that the New Law is not distinct from the Old. Because both these laws were given to those who believe in God: since "without faith it is impossible to please God," according to Heb. 11:6. But the faith of olden times and of nowadays is the same, as the gloss says on Matt. 21:9. Therefore the law is the same also.

Obj. 2: Further, Augustine says (Contra Adamant. Manich. discip. xvii) that "there is little difference between the Law and Gospel" [*The 'little difference' refers to the Latin words 'timor' and 'amor']—"fear and love." But the New and Old Laws cannot be differentiated in respect of these two things: since even the Old Law comprised precepts of charity: "Thou shalt love thy neighbor" (Lev. 19:18), and: "Thou shalt love the Lord thy God" (Deut. 6:5). In like manner neither can they differ according to the other difference which Augustine assigns (Contra Faust. iv, 2), viz. that "the Old Testament contained temporal promises, whereas the New Testament contains spiritual and eternal promises": since even the New Testament contains temporal promises, according to Mk. 10:30: He shall receive "a hundred times as much ... in this time, houses and brethren," etc.: while in the Old Testament they hoped in promises spiritual and eternal, according to Heb. 11:16: "But now they desire a better, that is to say, a heavenly country," which is said of the patriarchs. Therefore it seems that the New Law is not distinct from the Old.

Obj. 3: Further, the Apostle seems to distinguish both laws by calling the Old Law "a law of works," and the New Law "a law of faith" (Rom. 3:27). But the Old Law was also a law of faith, according to Heb. 11:39: "All were [Vulg.: 'All these being'] approved by the testimony of faith," which he says of the fathers of the Old Testament. In like manner the New Law is a law of works: since it is written (Matt. 5:44): "Do good to them that hate you"; and (Luke 22:19): "Do this for a commemoration of Me." Therefore the New Law is not distinct from the Old.

*On the contrary,* the Apostle says (Heb. 7:12): "The priesthood being translated it is necessary that a translation also be made of the Law." But the priesthood of the New Testament is distinct from that of the Old, as the Apostle shows in the same place. Therefore the Law is also distinct.

*I answer that,* As stated above (Q. 90, A. 2; Q. 91, A. 4), every law ordains human conduct to some end. Now things ordained to an end may be divided in two ways, considered from the point of view of the end. First, through being ordained to different ends: and this difference will be specific, especially if such ends are proximate. Secondly, by reason of being closely or remotely connected with the end. Thus it is clear that movements differ in species through being directed to different terms: while according as one part of a movement is nearer to the term than another part, the difference of perfect and imperfect movement is assessed.

Accordingly then two laws may be distinguished from one another in two ways. First, through being altogether diverse, from the fact that they are ordained to diverse ends: thus a state-law ordained to democratic government, would differ specifically from a law ordained to government by the aristocracy. Secondly, two laws may be distinguished from one another, through one of them being more closely connected with the end, and the other more remotely: thus in one and the same state there is one law enjoined on men of mature age, who can forthwith accomplish that which pertains to the common good; and another law regulating the education of children who need to be taught how they are to achieve manly deeds later on.

We must therefore say that, according to the first way, the New Law is not distinct from the Old Law: because they both have the same end, namely, man's subjection to God; and there is but one God of the New and of the Old Testament, according to Rom. 3:30: "It is one God that justifieth circumcision by faith, and uncircumcision through faith." According to the second way, the New Law is distinct from the Old Law: because the Old Law is like a pedagogue of children, as the Apostle says (Gal. 3:24), whereas the New Law is the law of perfection, since it is the law of charity, of which the Apostle says (Col. 3:14) that it is "the bond of perfection."

Reply Obj. 1: The unity of faith under both Testaments witnesses to the unity of end: for it has been stated above (Q. 62, A. 2) that the object of the theological virtues, among which is faith, is the last end. Yet faith had a different state in the Old and in the New Law: since what they believed as future, we believe as fact.

Reply Obj. 2: All the differences assigned between the Old and New Laws are gathered from their relative perfection and imperfection. For the precepts of every law prescribe acts of virtue. Now the imperfect, who as yet are not possessed of a virtuous habit, are directed in one way to perform virtuous acts, while those who are perfected by the possession of virtuous habits are directed in another way. For those who as yet are not endowed with virtuous habits, are directed to the performance of virtuous acts by reason of some outward cause: for instance, by the threat of punishment, or the promise of some extrinsic rewards, such as honor, riches, or the like. Hence the Old Law, which was given to men who were imperfect, that is, who had not yet received spiritual grace, was called the "law of fear," inasmuch as it induced men to observe its commandments by threatening them with penalties; and is spoken of as containing temporal promises. On the other hand, those who are possessed of virtue, are inclined to do virtuous deeds through love of virtue, not on account of some extrinsic punishment or reward. Hence the New Law which derives its pre-eminence from the spiritual grace instilled into our hearts, is called the "Law of love": and it is described as containing spiritual and eternal promises, which are objects of the virtues, chiefly of charity. Accordingly such persons are inclined of themselves to those objects, not as to something foreign but as to something of their own. For this reason, too, the Old Law is described as "restraining the hand, not the will" [*Peter Lombard, Sent. iii, D, 40]; since when a man refrains from some sins through fear of being punished, his will does not shrink simply from sin, as does the will of a man who refrains from sin through love of righteousness: and hence the New Law, which is the Law of love, is said to restrain the will.

Nevertheless there were some in the state of the Old Testament who, having charity and the grace of the Holy Ghost, looked chiefly to spiritual and eternal promises: and in this respect they belonged to the New Law. In like manner in the New Testament there are some carnal men who have not yet attained to the perfection of the New Law; and these it was necessary, even under the New Testament, to lead to virtuous action by the fear of punishment and by temporal promises.

But although the Old Law contained precepts of charity, nevertheless it did not confer the Holy Ghost by Whom "charity ... is spread abroad in our hearts" (Rom. 5:5).

Reply Obj. 3: As stated above (Q. 106, AA. 1, 2), the New Law is called the law of faith, in so far as its pre-eminence is derived from that very grace which is given inwardly to believers, and for this reason is called the grace of faith. Nevertheless it consists secondarily in certain deeds, moral and sacramental: but the New Law does not consist chiefly in these latter things, as did the Old Law. As to those under the Old Testament who through faith were acceptable to God, in this respect they belonged to the New Testament: for they were not justified except through faith in Christ, Who is the Author of the New Testament. Hence of Moses the Apostle says (Heb. 11:26) that he esteemed "the reproach of Christ greater riches than the treasure of the Egyptians."

SECOND ARTICLE [I-II, Q. 107, Art. 2]

Whether the New Law Fulfils the Old?

Objection 1: It would seem that the New Law does not fulfil the Old. Because to fulfil and to void are contrary. But the New Law voids or excludes the observances of the Old Law: for the Apostle says (Gal. 5:2): "If you be circumcised, Christ shall profit you nothing." Therefore the New Law is not a fulfilment of the Old.

Obj. 2: Further, one contrary is not the fulfilment of another. But Our Lord propounded in the New Law precepts that were contrary to precepts of the Old Law. For we read (Matt. 5:27-32): "You have heard that it was said to them of old: ... 'Whosoever shall put away his wife, let him give her a bill of divorce. But I say to you that whosoever shall put away his wife ... maketh her to commit adultery.'" Furthermore, the same evidently applies to the prohibition against swearing, against retaliation, and against hating one's enemies. In like manner Our Lord seems to have done away with the precepts of the Old Law relating to the different kinds of foods (Matt. 15:11): "Not that which goeth into the mouth defileth the man: but what cometh out of the mouth, this defileth a man." Therefore the New Law is not a fulfilment of the Old.

Obj. 3: Further, whoever acts against a law does not fulfil the law. But Christ in certain cases acted against the Law. For He touched the leper (Matt. 8:3), which was contrary to the Law. Likewise He seems to have frequently broken the sabbath; since the Jews used to say of Him (John 9:16): "This man is not of God, who keepeth not the sabbath." Therefore Christ did not fulfil the Law: and so the New Law given by Christ is not a fulfilment of the Old.

Obj. 4: Further, the Old Law contained precepts, moral, ceremonial, and judicial, as stated above (Q. 99, A. 4). But Our Lord (Matt. 5) fulfilled the Law in some respects, but without mentioning the judicial and ceremonial precepts. Therefore it seems that the New Law is not a complete fulfilment of the Old.

*On the contrary,* Our Lord said (Matt. 5:17): "I am not come to destroy, but to fulfil": and went on to say (Matt. 5:18): "One jot or one tittle shall not pass of the Law till all be fulfilled."

*I answer that,* As stated above (A. 1), the New Law is compared to the Old as the perfect to the imperfect. Now everything perfect fulfils that which is lacking in the imperfect. And accordingly the New Law fulfils the Old by supplying that which was lacking in the Old Law.

Now two things in the Old Law offer themselves to our consideration: viz., the end, and the precepts contained in the Law.

Now the end of every law is to make men righteous and virtuous, as was stated above (Q. 92, A. 1): and consequently the end of the Old Law was the justification of men. The Law, however, could not accomplish this: but foreshadowed it by certain ceremonial actions, and promised it in words. And in this respect, the New Law fulfils the Old by justifying men through the power of Christ's Passion. This is what the Apostle says (Rom. 8:3, 4): "What the Law could not do ... God sending His own Son in the likeness of sinful flesh ... hath condemned sin in the flesh, that the justification of the Law might be fulfilled in us." And in this respect, the New Law gives what the Old Law promised, according to 2 Cor. 1:20: "Whatever are the promises of God, in Him," i.e. in Christ, "they are 'Yea.'" [*The Douay version reads thus: "All the promises of God are in Him, 'It is.'"] Again, in this respect, it also fulfils what the Old Law foreshadowed. Hence it is written (Col. 2:17) concerning the ceremonial precepts that they were "a shadow of things to come, but the body is of Christ"; in other words, the reality is found in Christ. Wherefore the New Law is called the law of reality; whereas the Old Law is called the law of shadow or of figure.

Now Christ fulfilled the precepts of the Old Law both in His works and in His doctrine. In His works, because He was willing to be circumcised and to fulfil the other legal observances, which were binding for the time being; according to Gal. 4:4: "Made under the Law." In His doctrine He fulfilled the precepts of the Law in three ways. First, by explaining the true sense of the Law. This is clear in the case of murder and adultery, the prohibition of which the Scribes and Pharisees thought to refer only to the exterior act: wherefore Our Lord fulfilled the Law by showing that the prohibition extended also to the interior acts of sins. Secondly, Our Lord fulfilled the precepts of the Law by prescribing the safest way of complying with the statutes of the Old Law. Thus the Old Law forbade perjury: and this is more safely avoided, by abstaining altogether from swearing, save in cases of urgency. Thirdly, Our Lord fulfilled the precepts of the Law, by adding some counsels of perfection: this is clearly seen in Matt. 19:21, where Our Lord said to the man who affirmed that he had kept all the precepts of the Old Law: "One thing is wanting to thee: If thou wilt be perfect, go, sell whatsoever thou hast," etc. [*St. Thomas combines Matt. 19:21 with Mk. 10:21].

Reply Obj. 1: The New Law does not void observance of the Old Law except in the point of ceremonial precepts, as stated above (Q. 103, AA. 3, 4). Now the latter were figurative of something to come. Wherefore from the very fact that the ceremonial precepts were fulfilled when those things were accomplished which they foreshadowed, it follows that they are no longer to be observed: for if they were to be observed, this would mean that something is still to be accomplished and is not yet fulfilled. Thus the promise of a future gift holds no longer when it has been fulfilled by the presentation of the gift. In this way the legal ceremonies are abolished by being fulfilled.

Reply Obj. 2: As Augustine says (Contra Faust. xix, 26), those precepts of Our Lord are not contrary to the precepts of the Old Law. For what Our Lord commanded about a man not putting away his wife, is not contrary to what the Law prescribed. "For the Law did not say: 'Let him that wills, put his wife away': the contrary of which would be not to put her away. *On the contrary,* the Law was unwilling that a man should put away his wife, since it prescribed a delay, so that excessive eagerness for divorce might cease through being weakened during the writing of the bill. Hence Our Lord, in order to impress the fact that a wife ought not easily to be put away, allowed no exception save in the case of fornication." The same applies to the prohibition about swearing, as stated above. The same is also clear with respect to the prohibition of retaliation. For the Law fixed a limit to revenge, by forbidding men to seek vengeance unreasonably: whereas Our Lord deprived them of vengeance more completely by commanding them to abstain from it altogether. With regard to the hatred of one's enemies, He dispelled the false interpretation of the Pharisees, by admonishing us to hate, not the person, but his sin. As to discriminating between various foods, which was a ceremonial matter, Our Lord did not forbid this to be observed: but He showed that no foods are naturally unclean, but only in token of something else, as stated above (Q. 102, A. 6, ad 1).

Reply Obj. 3: It was forbidden by the Law to touch a leper; because by doing so, man incurred a certain uncleanness of irregularity, as also by touching the dead, as stated above (Q. 102, A. 5, ad 4). But Our Lord, Who healed the leper, could not contract an uncleanness. By those things which He did on the sabbath, He did not break the sabbath in reality, as the Master Himself shows in the Gospel: both because He worked miracles by His Divine power, which is ever active among things; and because His works were concerned with the salvation of man, while the Pharisees were concerned for the well-being of animals even on the sabbath; and again because on account of urgency He excused His disciples for gathering the ears of corn on the sabbath. But He did seem to break the sabbath according to the superstitious interpretation of the Pharisees, who thought that man ought to abstain from doing even works of kindness on the sabbath; which was contrary to the intention of the Law.

Reply Obj. 4: The reason why the ceremonial precepts of the Law are not mentioned in Matt. 5 is because, as stated above (ad 1), their observance was abolished by their fulfilment. But of the judicial precepts He mentioned that of retaliation: so that what He said about it should refer to all the others. With regard to this precept, He taught that the intention of the Law was that retaliation should be sought out of love of justice, and not as a punishment out of revengeful spite, which He forbade, admonishing man to be ready to suffer yet greater insults; and this remains still in the New Law.

THIRD ARTICLE [I-II, Q. 107, Art. 3]

Whether the New Law Is Contained in the Old?

Objection 1: It would seem that the New Law is not contained in the Old. Because the New Law consists chiefly in faith: wherefore it is called the "law of faith" (Rom. 3:27). But many points of faith are set forth in the New Law, which are not contained in the Old. Therefore the New Law is not contained in the Old.

Obj. 2: Further, a gloss says on Matt. 5:19, "He that shall break one of these least commandments," that the lesser commandments are those of the Law, and the greater commandments, those contained in the Gospel. Now the greater cannot be contained in the lesser. Therefore the New Law is not contained in the Old.

Obj. 3: Further, who holds the container holds the contents. If, therefore, the New Law is contained in the Old, it follows that whoever had the Old Law had the New: so that it was superfluous to give men a New Law when once they had the Old. Therefore the New Law is not contained in the Old.

*On the contrary,* As expressed in Ezech. 1:16, there was "a wheel in the midst of a wheel," i.e. "the New Testament within the Old," according to Gregory's exposition.

*I answer that,* One thing may be contained in another in two ways. First, actually; as a located thing is in a place. Secondly, virtually; as an effect in its cause, or as the complement in that which is incomplete; thus a genus contains its species, and a seed contains the whole tree, virtually. It is in this way that the New Law is contained in the Old: for it has been stated (A. 1) that the New Law is compared to the Old as perfect to imperfect. Hence Chrysostom, expounding Mk. 4:28, "The earth of itself bringeth forth fruit, first the blade, then the ear, afterwards the full corn in the ear," expresses himself as follows: "He brought forth first the blade, i.e. the Law of Nature; then the ear, i.e. the Law of Moses; lastly, the full corn, i.e. the Law of the Gospel." Hence then the New Law is in the Old as the corn in the ear.

Reply Obj. 1: Whatsoever is set down in the New Testament explicitly and openly as a point of faith, is contained in the Old Testament as a matter of belief, but implicitly, under a figure. And accordingly, even as to those things which we are bound to believe, the New Law is contained in the Old.

Reply Obj. 2: The precepts of the New Law are said to be greater than those of the Old Law, in the point of their being set forth explicitly. But as to the substance itself of the precepts of the New Testament, they are all contained in the Old. Hence Augustine says (Contra Faust. xix, 23, 28) that "nearly all Our Lord's admonitions or precepts, where He expressed Himself by saying: 'But I say unto you,' are to be found also in those ancient books. Yet, since they thought that murder was only the slaying of the human body, Our Lord declared to them that every wicked impulse to hurt our brother is to be looked on as a kind of murder." And it is in the point of declarations of this kind that the precepts of the New Law are said to be greater than those of the Old. Nothing, however, prevents the greater from being contained in the lesser virtually; just as a tree is contained in the seed.

Reply Obj. 3: What is set forth implicitly needs to be declared explicitly. Hence after the publishing of the Old Law, a New Law also had to be given.

FOURTH ARTICLE [I-II, Q. 107, Art. 4]

Whether the New Law Is More Burdensome Than the Old?

Objection 1: It would seem that the New Law is more burdensome than the Old. For Chrysostom (Opus Imp. in Matth., Hom. x [*The work of an unknown author]) say: "The commandments given to Moses are easy to obey: Thou shalt not kill; Thou shalt not commit adultery: but the commandments of Christ are difficult to accomplish, for instance: Thou shalt not give way to anger, or to lust." Therefore the New Law is more burdensome than the Old.

Obj. 2: Further, it is easier to make use of earthly prosperity than to suffer tribulations. But in the Old Testament observance of the Law was followed by temporal prosperity, as may be gathered from Deut. 28:1-14; whereas many kinds of trouble ensue to those who observe the New Law, as stated in 2 Cor. 6:4-10: "Let us exhibit ourselves as the ministers of God, in much patience, in tribulation, in necessities, in distresses," etc. Therefore the New Law is more burdensome than the Old.

Obj. 3: The more one has to do, the more difficult it is. But the New Law is something added to the Old. For the Old Law forbade perjury, while the New Law proscribed even swearing: the Old Law forbade a man to cast off his wife without a bill of divorce, while the New Law forbade divorce altogether; as is clearly stated in Matt. 5:31, seqq., according to Augustine's expounding. Therefore the New Law is more burdensome than the Old.

*On the contrary,* It is written (Matt. 11:28): "Come to Me, all you that labor and are burdened": which words are expounded by Hilary thus: "He calls to Himself all those that labor under the difficulty of observing the Law, and are burdened with the sins of this world." And further on He says of the yoke of the Gospel: "For My yoke is sweet and My burden light." Therefore the New Law is a lighter burden than the Old.

*I answer that,* A twofold difficulty may attach to works of virtue with which the precepts of the Law are concerned. One is on the part of the outward works, which of themselves are, in a way, difficult and burdensome. And in this respect the Old Law is a much heavier burden than the New: since the Old Law by its numerous ceremonies prescribed many more outward acts than the New Law, which, in the teaching of Christ and the apostles, added very few precepts to those of the natural law; although afterwards some were added, through being instituted by the holy Fathers. Even in these Augustine says that moderation should be observed, lest good conduct should become a burden to the faithful. For he says in reply to the queries of Januarius (Ep. lv) that, "whereas God in His mercy wished religion to be a free service rendered by the public solemnization of a small number of most manifest sacraments, certain persons make it a slave's burden; so much so that the state of the Jews who were subject to the sacraments of the Law, and not to the presumptuous devices of man, was more tolerable."

The other difficulty attaches to works of virtue as to interior acts: for instance, that a virtuous deed be done with promptitude and pleasure. It is this difficulty that virtue solves: because to act thus is difficult for a man without virtue: but through virtue it becomes easy for him. In this respect the precepts of the New Law are more burdensome than those of the Old; because the New Law prohibits certain interior movements of the soul, which were not expressly forbidden in the Old Law in all cases, although they were forbidden in some, without, however, any punishment being attached to the prohibition. Now this is very difficult to a man without virtue: thus even the Philosopher states (Ethic. v, 9) that it is easy to do what a righteous man does; but that to do it in the same way, viz. with pleasure and promptitude, is difficult to a man who is not righteous. Accordingly we read also (1 John 5:3) that "His commandments are not heavy": which words Augustine expounds by saying that "they are not heavy to the man that loveth; whereas they are a burden to him that loveth not."

Reply Obj. 1: The passage quoted speaks expressly of the difficulty of the New Law as to the deliberate curbing of interior movements.

Reply Obj. 2: The tribulations suffered by those who observe the New Law are not imposed by the Law itself. Moreover they are easily borne, on account of the love in which the same Law consists: since, as Augustine says (De Verb. Dom., Serm. lxx), "love makes light and nothing of things that seem arduous and beyond our power."

Reply Obj. 3: The object of these additions to the precepts of the Old Law was to render it easier to do what it prescribed, as Augustine states [*De Serm. Dom. in Monte i, 17, 21; xix, 23, 26]. Accordingly this does not prove that the New Law is more burdensome, but rather that it is a lighter burden.

## QUESTION 108

OF THOSE THINGS THAT ARE CONTAINED IN THE NEW LAW (In Four Articles)

We must now consider those things that are contained in the New Law: under which head there are four points of inquiry:

(1) Whether the New Law ought to prescribe or to forbid any outward works?

(2) Whether the New Law makes sufficient provision in prescribing and forbidding external acts?

(3) Whether in the matter of internal acts it directs man sufficiently?

(4) Whether it fittingly adds counsels to precepts?

FIRST ARTICLE [I-II, Q. 108, Art. 1]

Whether the New Law Ought to Prescribe or Prohibit Any External Acts?

Objection 1: It would seem that the New Law should not prescribe or prohibit any external acts. For the New Law is the Gospel of the kingdom, according to Matt. 24:14: "This Gospel of the kingdom shall be preached in the whole world." But the kingdom of God consists not in exterior, but only in interior acts, according to Luke 17:21: "The kingdom of God is within you"; and Rom. 14:17: "The kingdom of God is not meat and drink; but justice and peace and joy in the Holy Ghost." Therefore the New Law should not prescribe or forbid any external acts.

Obj. 2: Further, the New Law is "the law of the Spirit" (Rom. 8:2). But "where the Spirit of the Lord is, there is liberty" (2 Cor. 3:17). Now there is no liberty when man is bound to do or avoid certain external acts. Therefore the New Law does not prescribe or forbid any external acts.

Obj. 3: Further, all external acts are understood as referable to the hand, just as interior acts belong to the mind. But this is assigned as the difference between the New and Old Laws that the "Old Law restrains the hand, whereas the New Law curbs the will" [*Peter Lombard, Sent. iii, D, 40]. Therefore the New Law should not contain prohibitions and commands about exterior deeds, but only about interior acts.

*On the contrary,* Through the New Law, men are made "children of light": wherefore it is written (John 12:36): "Believe in the light that you may be the children of light." Now it is becoming that children of the light should do deeds of light and cast aside deeds of darkness, according to Eph. 5:8: "You were heretofore darkness, but now light in the Lord. Walk ... as children of the light." Therefore the New Law had to forbid certain external acts and prescribe others.

*I answer that,* As stated above (Q. 106, AA. 1, 2), the New Law consists chiefly in the grace of the Holy Ghost, which is shown forth by faith that worketh through love. Now men become receivers of this grace through God's Son made man, Whose humanity grace filled first, and thence flowed forth to us. Hence it is written (John 1:14): "The Word was made flesh," and afterwards: "full of grace and truth"; and further on: "Of His fulness we all have received, and grace for grace." Hence it is added that "grace and truth came by Jesus Christ." Consequently it was becoming that the grace which flows from the incarnate Word should be given to us by means of certain external sensible objects; and that from this inward grace, whereby the flesh is subjected to the Spirit, certain external works should ensue.

Accordingly external acts may have a twofold connection with grace. In the first place, as leading in some way to grace. Such are the sacramental acts which are instituted in the New Law, e.g. Baptism, the Eucharist, and the like.

In the second place there are those external acts which ensue from the promptings of grace: and herein we must observe a difference. For there are some which are necessarily in keeping with, or in opposition to inward grace consisting in faith that worketh through love. Such external works are prescribed or forbidden in the New Law; thus confession of faith is prescribed, and denial of faith is forbidden; for it is written (Matt. 10:32, 33) "(Every one) that shall confess Me before men, I will also confess him before My Father ... But he that shall deny Me before men, I will also deny him before My Father." On the other hand, there are works which are not necessarily opposed to, or in keeping with faith that worketh through love. Such works are not prescribed or forbidden in the New Law, by virtue of its primitive institution; but have been left by the Lawgiver, i.e. Christ, to the discretion of each individual. And so to each one it is free to decide what he should do or avoid; and to each superior, to direct his subjects in such matters as regards what they must do or avoid. Wherefore also in this respect the Gospel is called the "law of liberty" [*Cf. Reply Obj. 2]: since the Old Law decided many points and left few to man to decide as he chose.

Reply Obj. 1: The kingdom of God consists chiefly in internal acts: but as a consequence all things that are essential to internal acts belong also to the kingdom of God. Thus if the kingdom of God is internal righteousness, peace, and spiritual joy, all external acts that are incompatible with righteousness, peace, and spiritual joy, are in opposition to the kingdom of God; and consequently should be forbidden in the Gospel of the kingdom. On the other hand, those things that are indifferent as regards the aforesaid, for instance, to eat of this or that food, are not part of the kingdom of God; wherefore the Apostle says before the words quoted: "The kingdom of God is not meat and drink."

Reply Obj. 2: According to the Philosopher (Metaph. i, 2), what is "free is cause of itself." Therefore he acts freely, who acts of his own accord. Now man does of his own accord that which he does from a habit that is suitable to his nature: since a habit inclines one as a second nature. If, however, a habit be in opposition to nature, man would not act according to his nature, but according to some corruption affecting that nature. Since then the grace of the Holy Ghost is like an interior habit bestowed on us and inclining us to act aright, it makes us do freely those things that are becoming to grace, and shun what is opposed to it.

Accordingly the New Law is called the law of liberty in two respects. First, because it does not bind us to do or avoid certain things, except such as are of themselves necessary or opposed to salvation, and come under the prescription or prohibition of the law. Secondly, because it also makes us comply freely with these precepts and prohibitions, inasmuch as we do so through the promptings of grace. It is for these two reasons that the New Law is called "the law of perfect liberty" (James 1:25).

Reply Obj. 3: The New Law, by restraining the mind from inordinate movements, must needs also restrain the hand from inordinate acts, which ensue from inward movements.

SECOND ARTICLE [I-II, Q. 108, Art. 2]

Whether the New Law Made Sufficient Ordinations About External Acts?

Objection 1: It would seem that the New Law made insufficient ordinations about external acts. Because faith that worketh through charity seems chiefly to belong to the New Law, according to Gal. 5:6: "In Christ Jesus neither circumcision availeth anything, nor uncircumcision: but faith that worketh through charity." But the New Law declared explicitly certain points of faith which were not set forth explicitly in the Old Law; for instance, belief in the Trinity. Therefore it should also have added certain outward moral deeds, which were not fixed in the Old Law.

Obj. 2: Further, in the Old Law not only were sacraments instituted, but also certain sacred things, as stated above (Q. 101, A. 4; Q. 102, A. 4). But in the New Law, although certain sacraments are instituted by Our Lord; for instance, pertaining either to the sanctification of a temple or of the vessels, or to the celebration of some particular feast.

Therefore the New Law made insufficient ordinations about external matters.

Obj. 3: Further, in the Old Law, just as there were certain observances pertaining to God's ministers, so also were there certain observances pertaining to the people: as was stated above when we were treating of the ceremonial of the Old Law (Q. 101, A. 4; Q. 102, A. 6). Now in the New Law certain observances seem to have been prescribed to the ministers of God; as may be gathered from Matt. 10:9: "Do not possess gold, nor silver, nor money in your purses," nor other things which are mentioned here and Luke 9, 10. Therefore certain observances pertaining to the faithful should also have been instituted in the New Law.

Obj. 4: Further, in the Old Law, besides moral and ceremonial precepts, there were certain judicial precepts. But in the New Law there are no judicial precepts. Therefore the New Law made insufficient ordinations about external works.

*On the contrary,* Our Lord said (Matt. 7:24): "Every one ... that heareth these My words, and doth them, shall be likened to a wise man that built his house upon a rock." But a wise builder leaves out nothing that is necessary to the building. Therefore Christ's words contain all things necessary for man's salvation.

*I answer that,* as stated above (A. 1), the New Law had to make such prescriptions or prohibitions alone as are essential for the reception or right use of grace. And since we cannot of ourselves obtain grace, but through Christ alone, hence Christ of Himself instituted the sacraments whereby we obtain grace: viz. Baptism, Eucharist, Orders of the ministers of the New Law, by the institution of the apostles and seventy-two disciples, Penance, and indissoluble Matrimony. He promised Confirmation through the sending of the Holy Ghost: and we read that by His institution the apostles healed the sick by anointing them with oil (Mk. 6:13). These are the sacraments of the New Law.

The right use of grace is by means of works of charity. These, in so far as they are essential to virtue, pertain to the moral precepts, which also formed part of the Old Law. Hence, in this respect, the New Law had nothing to add as regards external action. The determination of these works in their relation to the divine worship, belongs to the ceremonial precepts of the Law; and, in relation to our neighbor, to the judicial precepts, as stated above (Q. 99, A. 4). And therefore, since these determinations are not in themselves necessarily connected with inward grace wherein the Law consists, they do not come under a precept of the New Law, but are left to the decision of man; some relating to inferiors—as when a precept is given to an individual; others, relating to superiors, temporal or spiritual, referring, namely, to the common good.

Accordingly the New Law had no other external works to determine, by prescribing or forbidding, except the sacraments, and those moral precepts which have a necessary connection with virtue, for instance, that one must not kill, or steal, and so forth.

Reply Obj. 1: Matters of faith are above human reason, and so we cannot attain to them except through grace. Consequently, when grace came to be bestowed more abundantly, the result was an increase in the number of explicit points of faith. On the other hand, it is through human reason that we are directed to works of virtue, for it is the rule of human action, as stated above (Q. 19, A. 3; Q. 63, A. 2). Wherefore in such matters as these there was no need for any precepts to be given besides the moral precepts of the Law, which proceed from the dictate of reason.

Reply Obj. 2: In the sacraments of the New Law grace is bestowed, which cannot be received except through Christ: consequently they had to be instituted by Him. But in the sacred things no grace is given: for instance, in the consecration of a temple, an altar or the like, or, again, in the celebration of feasts. Wherefore Our Lord left the institution of such things to the discretion of the faithful, since they have not of themselves any necessary connection with inward grace.

Reply Obj. 3: Our Lord gave the apostles those precepts not as ceremonial observances, but as moral statutes: and they can be understood in two ways. First, following Augustine (De Consensu Evang. 30), as being not commands but permissions. For He permitted them to set forth to preach without scrip or stick, and so on, since they were empowered to accept their livelihood from those to whom they preached: wherefore He goes on to say: "For the laborer is worthy of his hire." Nor is it a sin, but a work of supererogation for a preacher to take means of livelihood with him, without accepting supplies from those to whom he preaches; as Paul did (1 Cor. 9:4, seqq.).

Secondly, according to the explanation of other holy men, they may be considered as temporal commands laid upon the apostles for the time during which they were sent to preach in Judea before Christ's Passion. For the disciples, being yet as little children under Christ's care, needed to receive some special commands from Christ, such as all subjects receive from their superiors: and especially so, since they were to be accustomed little by little to renounce the care of temporalities, so as to become fitted for the preaching of the Gospel throughout the whole world. Nor must we wonder if He established certain fixed modes of life, as long as the state of the Old Law endured and the people had not as yet achieved the perfect liberty of the Spirit. These statutes He abolished shortly before His Passion, as though the disciples had by their means become sufficiently practiced. Hence He said (Luke 22:35, 36) "When I sent you without purse and scrip and shoes, did you want anything? But they said: Nothing. Then said He unto them: But now, he that hath a purse, let him take it, and likewise a scrip." Because the time of perfect liberty was already at hand, when they would be left entirely to their own judgment in matters not necessarily connected with virtue.

Reply Obj. 4: Judicial precepts also, are not essential to virtue in respect of any particular determination, but only in regard to the common notion of justice. Consequently Our Lord left the judicial precepts to the discretion of those who were to have spiritual or temporal charge of others. But as regards the judicial precepts of the Old Law, some of them He explained, because they were misunderstood by the Pharisees, as we shall state later on (A. 3, ad 2).

THIRD ARTICLE [I-II, Q. 108, Art. 3]

Whether the New Law Directed Man Sufficiently As Regards Interior Actions?

Objection 1: It would seem that the New Law directed man insufficiently as regards interior actions. For there are ten commandments of the decalogue directing man to God and his neighbor. But Our Lord partly fulfilled only three of them: as regards, namely, the prohibition of murder, of adultery, and of perjury. Therefore it seems that, by omitting to fulfil the other precepts, He directed man insufficiently.

Obj. 2: Further, as regards the judicial precepts, Our Lord ordained nothing in the Gospel, except in the matter of divorcing a wife, of punishment by retaliation, and of persecuting one's enemies. But there are many other judicial precepts of the Old Law, as stated above (Q. 104, A. 4; Q. 105). Therefore, in this respect, He directed human life insufficiently.

Obj. 3: Further, in the Old Law, besides moral and judicial, there were ceremonial precepts about which Our Lord made no ordination. Therefore it seems that He ordained insufficiently.

Obj. 4: Further, in order that the mind be inwardly well disposed, man should do no good deed for any temporal end whatever. But there are many other temporal goods besides the favor of man: and there are many other good works besides fasting, alms-deeds, and prayer. Therefore Our Lord unbecomingly taught that only in respect of these three works, and of no other earthly goods ought we to shun the glory of human favor.

Obj. 5: Further, solicitude for the necessary means of livelihood is by nature instilled into man, and this solicitude even other animals share with man: wherefore it is written (Prov. 6:6, 8): "Go to the ant, O sluggard, and consider her ways ... she provideth her meat for herself in the summer, and gathereth her food in the harvest." But every command issued against the inclination of nature is an unjust command, forasmuch as it is contrary to the law of nature. Therefore it seems that Our Lord unbecomingly forbade solicitude about food and raiment.

Obj. 6: Further, no act of virtue should be the subject of a prohibition. Now judgment is an act of justice, according to Ps. 18:15: "Until justice be turned into judgment." Therefore it seems that Our Lord unbecomingly forbade judgment: and consequently that the New Law directed man insufficiently in the matter of interior acts.

*On the contrary,* Augustine says (De Serm. Dom. in Monte i, 1): We should take note that, when He said: "'He that heareth these My words,' He indicates clearly that this sermon of the Lord is replete with all the precepts whereby a Christian's life is formed."

*I answer that,* As is evident from Augustine's words just quoted, the sermon, which Our Lord delivered on the mountain, contains the whole process of forming the life of a Christian. Therein man's interior movements are ordered. Because after declaring that his end is Beatitude; and after commending the authority of the apostles, through whom the teaching of the Gospel was to be promulgated, He orders man's interior movements, first in regard to man himself, secondly in regard to his neighbor.

This he does in regard to man himself, in two ways, corresponding to man's two interior movements in respect of any prospective action, viz. volition of what has to be done, and intention of the end. Wherefore, in the first place, He directs man's will in respect of the various precepts of the Law: by prescribing that man should refrain not merely from those external works that are evil in themselves, but also from internal acts, and from the occasions of evil deeds. In the second place He directs man's intention, by teaching that in our good works, we should seek neither human praise, nor worldly riches, which is to lay up treasures on earth.

Afterwards He directs man's interior movement in respect of his neighbor, by forbidding us, on the one hand, to judge him rashly, unjustly, or presumptuously; and, on the other, to entrust him too readily with sacred things if he be unworthy.

Lastly, He teaches us how to fulfil the teaching of the Gospel; viz. by imploring the help of God; by striving to enter by the narrow door of perfect virtue; and by being wary lest we be led astray by evil influences. Moreover, He declares that we must observe His commandments, and that it is not enough to make profession of faith, or to work miracles, or merely to hear His words.

Reply Obj. 1: Our Lord explained the manner of fulfilling those precepts which the Scribes and Pharisees did not rightly understand: and this affected chiefly those precepts of the decalogue. For they thought that the prohibition of adultery and murder covered the external act only, and not the internal desire. And they held this opinion about murder and adultery rather than about theft and false witness, because the movement of anger tending to murder, and the movement of desire tending to adultery, seem to be in us from nature somewhat, but not the desire of stealing or bearing false witness. They held a false opinion about perjury, for they thought that perjury indeed was a sin; but that oaths were of themselves to be desired and to be taken frequently, since they seem to proceed from reverence to God. Hence Our Lord shows that an oath is not desirable as a good thing; and that it is better to speak without oaths, unless necessity forces us to have recourse to them.

Reply Obj. 2: The Scribes and Pharisees erred about the judicial precepts in two ways. First, because they considered certain matters contained in the Law of Moses by way of permission, to be right in themselves: namely, divorce of a wife, and the taking of usury from strangers. Wherefore Our Lord forbade a man to divorce his wife (Matt. 5:32); and to receive usury (Luke 6:35), when He said: "Lend, hoping for nothing thereby."

In another way they erred by thinking that certain things which the Old Law commanded to be done for justice's sake, should be done out of desire for revenge, or out of lust for temporal goods, or out of hatred of one's enemies; and this in respect of three precepts. For they thought that desire for revenge was lawful, on account of the precept concerning punishment by retaliation: whereas this precept was given that justice might be safeguarded, not that man might seek revenge. Wherefore, in order to do away with this, Our Lord teaches that man should be prepared in his mind to suffer yet more if necessary. They thought that movements of covetousness were lawful on account of those judicial precepts which prescribed restitution of what had been purloined, together with something added thereto, as stated above (Q. 105, A. 2, ad 9); whereas the Law commanded this to be done in order to safeguard justice, not to encourage covetousness. Wherefore Our Lord teaches that we should not demand our goods from motives of cupidity, and that we should be ready to give yet more if necessary. They thought that the movement of hatred was lawful, on account of the commandments of the Law about the slaying of one's enemies: whereas the Law ordered this for the fulfilment of justice, as stated above (Q. 105, A. 3, ad 4), not to satisfy hatred. Wherefore Our Lord teaches us that we ought to love our enemies, and to be ready to do good to them if necessary. For these precepts are to be taken as binding "the mind to be prepared to fulfil them," as Augustine says (De Serm. Dom. in Monte i, 19).

Reply Obj. 3: The moral precepts necessarily retained their force under the New Law, because they are of themselves essential to virtue: whereas the judicial precepts did not necessarily continue to bind in exactly the same way as had been fixed by the Law: this was left to man to decide in one way or another. Hence Our Lord directed us becomingly with regard to these two kinds of precepts. On the other hand, the observance of the ceremonial precepts was totally abolished by the advent of the reality; wherefore in regard to these precepts He commanded nothing on this occasion when He was giving the general points of His doctrine. Elsewhere, however, He makes it clear that the entire bodily worship which was fixed by the Law, was to be changed into spiritual worship: as is evident from John 4:21, 23, where He says: "The hour cometh when you shall neither on this mountain, nor in Jerusalem adore the Father ... but ... the true adorers shall adore the Father in spirit and in truth."

Reply Obj. 4: All worldly goods may be reduced to three—honors, riches, and pleasures; according to 1 John 2:16: "All that is in the world is the concupiscence of the flesh," which refers to pleasures of the flesh, "and the concupiscence of the eyes," which refers to riches, "and the pride of life," which refers to ambition for renown and honor. Now the Law did not promise an abundance of carnal pleasures; *on the contrary,* it forbade them. But it did promise exalted honors and abundant riches; for it is written in reference to the former (Deut. 28:1): "If thou wilt hear the voice of the Lord thy God ... He will make thee higher than all the nations"; and in reference to the latter, we read a little further on (Deut. 28:11): "He will make thee abound with all goods." But the Jews so distorted the true meaning of these promises, as to think that we ought to serve God, with these things as the end in view. Wherefore Our Lord set this aside by teaching, first of all, that works of virtue should not be done for human glory. And He mentions three works, to which all others may be reduced: since whatever a man does in order to curb his desires, comes under the head of fasting; and whatever a man does for the love of his neighbor, comes under the head of alms-deeds; and whatever a man does for the worship of God, comes under the head of prayer. And He mentions these three specifically, as they hold the principal place, and are most often used by men in order to gain glory. In the second place He taught us that we must not place our end in riches, when He said: "Lay not up to yourselves treasures on earth" (Matt. 6:19).

Reply Obj. 5: Our Lord forbade, not necessary, but inordinate solicitude. Now there is a fourfold solicitude to be avoided in temporal matters. First, we must not place our end in them, nor serve God for the sake of the necessities of food and raiment. Wherefore He says: "Lay not up for yourselves," etc. Secondly, we must not be so anxious about temporal things, as to despair of God's help: wherefore Our Lord says (Matt. 6:32): "Your Father knoweth that you have need of all these things." Thirdly, we must not add presumption to our solicitude; in other words, we must not be confident of getting the necessaries of life by our own efforts without God's help: such solicitude Our Lord sets aside by saying that a man cannot add anything to his stature (Matt. 6:27). We must not anticipate the time for anxiety; namely, by being solicitous now, for the needs, not of the present, but of a future time: wherefore He says (Matt. 6:34): "Be not ... solicitous for tomorrow."

Reply Obj. 6: Our Lord did not forbid the judgment of justice, without which holy things could not be withdrawn from the unworthy. But he forbade inordinate judgment, as stated above.

FOURTH ARTICLE [I-II, Q. 108, Art. 4]

Whether Certain Definite Counsels Are Fittingly Proposed in the New Law?

Objection 1: It would seem that certain definite counsels are not fittingly proposed in the New Law. For counsels are given about that which is expedient for an end, as we stated above, when treating of counsel (Q. 14, A. 2). But the same things are not expedient for all. Therefore certain definite counsels should not be proposed to all.

Obj. 2: Further, counsels regard a greater good. But there are no definite degrees to the greater good. Therefore definite counsels should not be given.

Obj. 3: Further, counsels pertain to the life of perfection. But obedience pertains to the life of perfection. Therefore it was unfitting that no counsel of obedience should be contained in the Gospel.

Obj. 4: Further, many matters pertaining to the life of perfection are found among the commandments, as, for instance, "Love your enemies" (Matt. 5:44), and those precepts which Our Lord gave His apostles (Matt. 10). Therefore the counsels are unfittingly given in the New Law: both because they are not all mentioned; and because they are not distinguished from the commandments.

*On the contrary,* The counsels of a wise friend are of great use, according to Prov. (27:9): "Ointment and perfumes rejoice the heart: and the good counsels of a friend rejoice the soul." But Christ is our wisest and greatest friend. Therefore His counsels are supremely useful and becoming.

*I answer that,* The difference between a counsel and a commandment is that a commandment implies obligation, whereas a counsel is left to the option of the one to whom it is given. Consequently in the New Law, which is the law of liberty, counsels are added to the commandments, and not in the Old Law, which is the law of bondage. We must therefore understand the commandments of the New Law to have been given about matters that are necessary to gain the end of eternal bliss, to which end the New Law brings us forthwith: but that the counsels are about matters that render the gaining of this end more assured and expeditious.

Now man is placed between the things of this world, and spiritual goods wherein eternal happiness consists: so that the more he cleaves to the one, the more he withdraws from the other, and conversely. Wherefore he that cleaves wholly to the things of this world, so as to make them his end, and to look upon them as the reason and rule of all he does, falls away altogether from spiritual goods. Hence this disorder is removed by the commandments. Nevertheless, for man to gain the end aforesaid, he does not need to renounce the things of the world altogether: since he can, while using the things of this world, attain to eternal happiness, provided he does not place his end in them: but he will attain more speedily thereto by giving up the goods of this world entirely: wherefore the evangelical counsels are given for this purpose.

Now the goods of this world which come into use in human life, consist in three things: viz. in external wealth pertaining to the "concupiscence of the eyes"; carnal pleasures pertaining to the "concupiscence of the flesh"; and honors, which pertain to the "pride of life," according to 1 John 2:16: and it is in renouncing these altogether, as far as possible, that the evangelical counsels consist. Moreover, every form of the religious life that professes the state of perfection is based on these three: since riches are renounced by poverty; carnal pleasures by perpetual chastity; and the pride of life by the bondage of obedience.

Now if a man observe these absolutely, this is in accordance with the counsels as they stand. But if a man observe any one of them in a particular case, this is taking that counsel in a restricted sense, namely, as applying to that particular case. For instance, when anyone gives an alms to a poor man, not being bound so to do, he follows the counsels in that particular case. In like manner, when a man for some fixed time refrains from carnal pleasures that he may give himself to prayer, he follows the counsel for that particular time. And again, when a man follows not his will as to some deed which he might do lawfully, he follows the counsel in that particular case: for instance, if he do good to his enemies when he is not bound to, or if he forgive an injury of which he might justly seek to be avenged. In this way, too, all particular counsels may be reduced to these three general and perfect counsels.

Reply Obj. 1: The aforesaid counsels, considered in themselves, are expedient to all; but owing to some people being ill-disposed, it happens that some of them are inexpedient, because their disposition is not inclined to such things. Hence Our Lord, in proposing the evangelical counsels, always makes mention of man's fitness for observing the counsels. For in giving the counsel of perpetual poverty (Matt. 19:21), He begins with the words: "If thou wilt be perfect," and then He adds: "Go, sell all [Vulg.: 'what'] thou hast." In like manner when He gave the counsel of perpetual chastity, saying (Matt. 19:12): "There are eunuchs who have made themselves eunuchs for the kingdom of heaven," He adds straightway: "He that can take, let him take it." And again, the Apostle (1 Cor. 7:35), after giving the counsel of virginity, says: "And this I speak for your profit; not to cast a snare upon you."

Reply Obj. 2: The greater goods are not definitely fixed in the individual; but those which are simply and absolutely the greater good in general are fixed: and to these all the above particular goods may be reduced, as stated above.

Reply Obj. 3: Even the counsel of obedience is understood to have been given by Our Lord in the words: "And [let him] follow Me." For we follow Him not only by imitating His works, but also by obeying His commandments, according to John 10:27: "My sheep hear My voice ... and they follow Me."

Reply Obj. 4: Those things which Our Lord prescribed about the true love of our enemies, and other similar sayings (Matt. 5; Luke 6), may be referred to the preparation of the mind, and then they are necessary for salvation; for instance, that man be prepared to do good to his enemies, and other similar actions, when there is need. Hence these things are placed among the precepts. But that anyone should actually and promptly behave thus towards an enemy when there is no special need, is to be referred to the particular counsels, as stated above. As to those matters which are set down in Matt. 10 and Luke 9 and 10, they were either disciplinary commands for that particular time, or concessions, as stated above (A. 2, ad 3). Hence they are not set down among the counsels.

TREATISE ON GRACE (QQ. 109-114)

## QUESTION 109

OF THE NECESSITY OF GRACE (In Ten Articles)

We must now consider the exterior principle of human acts, i.e. God, in so far as, through grace, we are helped by Him to do right: and, first, we must consider the grace of God; secondly, its cause; thirdly, its effects.

The first point of consideration will be threefold: for we shall consider (1) The necessity of grace; (2) grace itself, as to its essence; (3) its division.

Under the first head there are ten points of inquiry:

(1) Whether without grace man can know anything?

(2) Whether without God's grace man can do or wish any good?

(3) Whether without grace man can love God above all things?

(4) Whether without grace man can keep the commandments of the Law?

(5) Whether without grace he can merit eternal life?

(6) Whether without grace man can prepare himself for grace?

(7) Whether without grace he can rise from sin?

(8) Whether without grace man can avoid sin?

(9) Whether man having received grace can do good and avoid sin without any further Divine help?

(10) Whether he can of himself persevere in good?

FIRST ARTICLE [I-II, Q. 109, Art. 1]

Whether Without Grace Man Can Know Any Truth?

Objection 1: It would seem that without grace man can know no truth. For, on 1 Cor. 12:3: "No man can say, the Lord Jesus, but by the Holy Ghost," a gloss says: "Every truth, by whomsoever spoken is from the Holy Ghost." Now the Holy Ghost dwells in us by grace. Therefore we cannot know truth without grace.

Obj. 2: Further, Augustine says (Solil. i, 6) that "the most certain sciences are like things lit up by the sun so as to be seen. Now God Himself is He Who sheds the light. And reason is in the mind as sight is in the eye. And the eyes of the mind are the senses of the soul." Now the bodily senses, however pure, cannot see any visible object, without the sun's light. Therefore the human mind, however perfect, cannot, by reasoning, know any truth without Divine light: and this pertains to the aid of grace.

Obj. 3: Further, the human mind can only understand truth by thinking, as is clear from Augustine (De Trin. xiv, 7). But the Apostle says (2 Cor. 3:5): "Not that we are sufficient to think anything of ourselves, as of ourselves; but our sufficiency is from God." Therefore man cannot, of himself, know truth without the help of grace.

*On the contrary,* Augustine says (Retract. i, 4): "I do not approve having said in the prayer, O God, Who dost wish the sinless alone to know the truth; for it may be answered that many who are not sinless know many truths." Now man is cleansed from sin by grace, according to Ps. 50:12: "Create a clean heart in me, O God, and renew a right spirit within my bowels." Therefore without grace man of himself can know truth.

*I answer that,* To know truth is a use or act of intellectual light, since, according to the Apostle (Eph. 5:13): "All that is made manifest is light." Now every use implies movement, taking movement broadly, so as to call thinking and willing movements, as is clear from the Philosopher (De Anima iii, 4). Now in corporeal things we see that for movement there is required not merely the form which is the principle of the movement or action, but there is also required the motion of the first mover. Now the first mover in the order of corporeal things is the heavenly body. Hence no matter how perfectly fire has heat, it would not bring about alteration, except by the motion of the heavenly body. But it is clear that as all corporeal movements are reduced to the motion of the heavenly body as to the first corporeal mover, so all movements, both corporeal and spiritual, are reduced to the simple First Mover, Who is God. And hence no matter how perfect a corporeal or spiritual nature is supposed to be, it cannot proceed to its act unless it be moved by God; but this motion is according to the plan of His providence, and not by necessity of nature, as the motion of the heavenly body. Now not only is every motion from God as from the First Mover, but all formal perfection is from Him as from the First Act. And thus the act of the intellect or of any created being whatsoever depends upon God in two ways: first, inasmuch as it is from Him that it has the form whereby it acts; secondly, inasmuch as it is moved by Him to act.

Now every form bestowed on created things by God has power for a determined act, which it can bring about in proportion to its own proper endowment; and beyond which it is powerless, except by a superadded form, as water can only heat when heated by the fire. And thus the human understanding has a form, viz. intelligible light, which of itself is sufficient for knowing certain intelligible things, viz. those we can come to know through the senses. Higher intelligible things the human intellect cannot know, unless it be perfected by a stronger light, viz. the light of faith or prophecy which is called the "light of grace," inasmuch as it is added to nature.

Hence we must say that for the knowledge of any truth whatsoever man needs Divine help, that the intellect may be moved by God to its act. But he does not need a new light added to his natural light, in order to know the truth in all things, but only in some that surpass his natural knowledge. And yet at times God miraculously instructs some by His grace in things that can be known by natural reason, even as He sometimes brings about miraculously what nature can do.

Reply Obj. 1: Every truth by whomsoever spoken is from the Holy Ghost as bestowing the natural light, and moving us to understand and speak the truth, but not as dwelling in us by sanctifying grace, or as bestowing any habitual gift superadded to nature. For this only takes place with regard to certain truths that are known and spoken, and especially in regard to such as pertain to faith, of which the Apostle speaks.

Reply Obj. 2: The material sun sheds its light outside us; but the intelligible Sun, Who is God, shines within us. Hence the natural light bestowed upon the soul is God's enlightenment, whereby we are enlightened to see what pertains to natural knowledge; and for this there is required no further knowledge, but only for such things as surpass natural knowledge.

Reply Obj. 3: We always need God's help for every thought, inasmuch as He moves the understanding to act; for actually to understand anything is to think, as is clear from Augustine (De Trin. xiv, 7).

SECOND ARTICLE [I-II, Q. 109, Art. 2]

Whether Man Can Wish or Do Any Good Without Grace?

Objection 1: It would seem that man can wish and do good without grace. For that is in man's power, whereof he is master. Now man is master of his acts, and especially of his willing, as stated above (Q. 1, A. 1; Q. 13, A. 6). Hence man, of himself, can wish and do good without the help of grace.

Obj. 2: Further, man has more power over what is according to his nature than over what is beyond his nature. Now sin is against his nature, as Damascene says (De Fide Orth. ii, 30); whereas deeds of virtue are according to his nature, as stated above (Q. 71, A. 1). Therefore since man can sin of himself he can wish and do good.

Obj. 3: Further, the understanding's good is truth, as the Philosopher says (Ethic. vi, 2). Now the intellect can of itself know truth, even as every other thing can work its own operation of itself. Therefore, much more can man, of himself, do and wish good.

*On the contrary,* The Apostle says (Rom. 9:16): "It is not of him that willeth," namely, to will, "nor of him that runneth," namely to run, "but of God that showeth mercy." And Augustine says (De Corrept. et Gratia ii) that "without grace men do nothing good when they either think or wish or love or act."

*I answer that,* Man's nature may be looked at in two ways: first, in its integrity, as it was in our first parent before sin; secondly, as it is corrupted in us after the sin of our first parent. Now in both states human nature needs the help of God as First Mover, to do or wish any good whatsoever, as stated above (A. 1). But in the state of integrity, as regards the sufficiency of the operative power, man by his natural endowments could wish and do the good proportionate to his nature, such as the good of acquired virtue; but not surpassing good, as the good of infused virtue. But in the state of corrupt nature, man falls short of what he could do by his nature, so that he is unable to fulfil it by his own natural powers. Yet because human nature is not altogether corrupted by sin, so as to be shorn of every natural good, even in the state of corrupted nature it can, by virtue of its natural endowments, work some particular good, as to build dwellings, plant vineyards, and the like; yet it cannot do all the good natural to it, so as to fall short in nothing; just as a sick man can of himself make some movements, yet he cannot be perfectly moved with the movements of one in health, unless by the help of medicine he be cured.

And thus in the state of perfect nature man needs a gratuitous strength superadded to natural strength for one reason, viz. in order to do and wish supernatural good; but for two reasons, in the state of corrupt nature, viz. in order to be healed, and furthermore in order to carry out works of supernatural virtue, which are meritorious. Beyond this, in both states man needs the Divine help, that he may be moved to act well.

Reply Obj. 1: Man is master of his acts and of his willing or not willing, because of his deliberate reason, which can be bent to one side or another. And although he is master of his deliberating or not deliberating, yet this can only be by a previous deliberation; and since it cannot go on to infinity, we must come at length to this, that man's free-will is moved by an extrinsic principle, which is above the human mind, to wit by God, as the Philosopher proves in the chapter "On Good Fortune" (Ethic. Eudem. vii). Hence the mind of man still unweakened is not so much master of its act that it does not need to be moved by God; and much more the free-will of man weakened by sin, whereby it is hindered from good by the corruption of the nature.

Reply Obj. 2: To sin is nothing else than to fail in the good which belongs to any being according to its nature. Now as every created thing has its being from another, and, considered in itself, is nothing, so does it need to be preserved by another in the good which pertains to its nature. For it can of itself fail in good, even as of itself it can fall into non-existence, unless it is upheld by God.

Reply Obj. 3: Man cannot even know truth without Divine help, as stated above (A. 1). And yet human nature is more corrupt by sin in regard to the desire for good, than in regard to the knowledge of truth.

THIRD ARTICLE [I-II, Q. 109, Art. 3]

Whether by His Own Natural Powers and Without Grace Man Can Love God Above All Things?

Objection 1: It would seem that without grace man cannot love God above all things by his own natural powers. For to love God above all things is the proper and principal act of charity. Now man cannot of himself possess charity, since the "charity of God is poured forth in our hearts by the Holy Ghost Who is given to us," as is said Rom. 5:5. Therefore man by his natural powers alone cannot love God above all things.

Obj. 2: Further, no nature can rise above itself. But to love God above all things is to tend above oneself. Therefore without the help of grace no created nature can love God above itself.

Obj. 3: Further, to God, Who is the Highest Good, is due the best love, which is that He be loved above all things. Now without grace man is not capable of giving God the best love, which is His due; otherwise it would be useless to add grace. Hence man, without grace and with his natural powers alone, cannot love God above all things.

*On the contrary,* As some maintain, man was first made with only natural endowments; and in this state it is manifest that he loved God to some extent. But he did not love God equally with himself, or less than himself, otherwise he would have sinned. Therefore he loved God above himself. Therefore man, by his natural powers alone, can love God more than himself and above all things.

*I answer that,* As was said above (I, Q. 60, A. 5), where the various opinions concerning the natural love of the angels were set forth, man in a state of perfect nature, could by his natural power, do the good natural to him without the addition of any gratuitous gift, though not without the help of God moving him. Now to love God above all things is natural to man and to every nature, not only rational but irrational, and even to inanimate nature according to the manner of love which can belong to each creature. And the reason of this is that it is natural to all to seek and love things according as they are naturally fit (to be sought and loved) since "all things act according as they are naturally fit" as stated in *Phys.* ii, 8. Now it is manifest that the good of the part is for the good of the whole; hence everything, by its natural appetite and love, loves its own proper good on account of the common good of the whole universe, which is God. Hence Dionysius says (Div. Nom. iv) that "God leads everything to love of Himself." Hence in the state of perfect nature man referred the love of himself and of all other things to the love of God as to its end; and thus he loved God more than himself and above all things. But in the state of corrupt nature man falls short of this in the appetite of his rational will, which, unless it is cured by God's grace, follows its private good, on account of the corruption of nature. And hence we must say that in the state of perfect nature man did not need the gift of grace added to his natural endowments, in order to love God above all things naturally, although he needed God's help to move him to it; but in the state of corrupt nature man needs, even for this, the help of grace to heal his nature.

Reply Obj. 1: Charity loves God above all things in a higher way than nature does. For nature loves God above all things inasmuch as He is the beginning and the end of natural good; whereas charity loves Him, as He is the object of beatitude, and inasmuch as man has a spiritual fellowship with God. Moreover charity adds to natural love of God a certain quickness and joy, in the same way that every habit of virtue adds to the good act which is done merely by the natural reason of a man who has not the habit of virtue.

Reply Obj. 2: When it is said that nature cannot rise above itself, we must not understand this as if it could not be drawn to any object above itself, for it is clear that our intellect by its natural knowledge can know things above itself, as is shown in our natural knowledge of God. But we are to understand that nature cannot rise to an act exceeding the proportion of its strength. Now to love God above all things is not such an act; for it is natural to every creature, as was said above.

Reply Obj. 3: Love is said to be best, both with respect to degree of love, and with regard to the motive of loving, and the mode of love. And thus the highest degree of love is that whereby charity loves God as the giver of beatitude, as was said above.

FOURTH ARTICLE [I-II, Q. 109, Art. 4]

Whether Man Without Grace and by His Own Natural Powers Can Fulfil the Commandments of the Law?

Objection 1: It would seem that man without grace, and by his own natural powers, can fulfil the commandments of the Law. For the Apostle says (Rom. 2:14) that "the Gentiles who have not the law, do by nature those things that are of the Law." Now what a man does naturally he can do of himself without grace. Hence a man can fulfil the commandments of the Law without grace.

Obj. 2: Further, Jerome says (Expos. Cathol. Fide [*Symboli Explanatio ad Damasum, among the supposititious works of St. Jerome: now ascribed to Pelagius]) that "they are anathema who say God has laid impossibilities upon man." Now what a man cannot fulfil by himself is impossible to him. Therefore a man can fulfil all the commandments of himself.

Obj. 3: Further, of all the commandments of the Law, the greatest is this, "Thou shalt love the Lord thy God with thy whole heart" (Matt. 27:37). Now man with his natural endowments can fulfil this command by loving God above all things, as stated above (A. 3). Therefore man can fulfil all the commandments of the Law without grace.

*On the contrary,* Augustine says (De Haeres. lxxxviii) that it is part of the Pelagian heresy that "they believe that without grace man can fulfil all the Divine commandments."

*I answer that,* There are two ways of fulfilling the commandments of the Law. The first regards the substance of the works, as when a man does works of justice, fortitude, and of other virtues. And in this way man in the state of perfect nature could fulfil all the commandments of the Law; otherwise he would have been unable to sin in that state, since to sin is nothing else than to transgress the Divine commandments. But in the state of corrupted nature man cannot fulfil all the Divine commandments without healing grace. Secondly, the commandments of the law can be fulfilled, not merely as regards the substance of the act, but also as regards the mode of acting, i.e. their being done out of charity. And in this way, neither in the state of perfect nature, nor in the state of corrupt nature can man fulfil the commandments of the law without grace. Hence, Augustine (De Corrept. et Grat. ii) having stated that "without grace men can do no good whatever," adds: "Not only do they know by its light what to do, but by its help they do lovingly what they know." Beyond this, in both states they need the help of God's motion in order to fulfil the commandments, as stated above (AA. 2, 3).

Reply Obj. 1: As Augustine says (De Spir. et Lit. xxvii), "do not be disturbed at his saying that they do by nature those things that are of the Law; for the Spirit of grace works this, in order to restore in us the image of God, after which we were naturally made."

Reply Obj. 2: What we can do with the Divine assistance is not altogether impossible to us; according to the Philosopher (Ethic. iii, 3): "What we can do through our friends, we can do, in some sense, by ourselves." Hence Jerome [*Symboli Explanatio ad Damasum, among the supposititious works of St. Jerome: now ascribed to Pelagius] concedes that "our will is in such a way free that we must confess we still require God's help."

Reply Obj. 3: Man cannot, with his purely natural endowments, fulfil the precept of the love of God, as stated above (A. 3).

FIFTH ARTICLE [I-II, Q. 109, Art. 5]

Whether Man Can Merit Everlasting Life Without Grace?

Objection 1: It would seem that man can merit everlasting life without grace. For Our Lord says (Matt. 19:17): "If thou wilt enter into life, keep the commandments"; from which it would seem that to enter into everlasting life rests with man's will. But what rests with our will, we can do of ourselves. Hence it seems that man can merit everlasting life of himself.

Obj. 2: Further, eternal life is the wage of reward bestowed by God on men, according to Matt. 5:12: "Your reward is very great in heaven." But wage or reward is meted by God to everyone according to his works, according to Ps. 61:12: "Thou wilt render to every man according to his works." Hence, since man is master of his works, it seems that it is within his power to reach everlasting life.

Obj. 3: Further, everlasting life is the last end of human life. Now every natural thing by its natural endowments can attain its end. Much more, therefore, may man attain to life everlasting by his natural endowments, without grace.

*On the contrary,* The Apostle says (Rom. 6:23): "The grace of God is life everlasting." And as a gloss says, this is said "that we may understand that God, of His own mercy, leads us to everlasting life."

*I answer that,* Acts conducing to an end must be proportioned to the end. But no act exceeds the proportion of its active principle; and hence we see in natural things, that nothing can by its operation bring about an effect which exceeds its active force, but only such as is proportionate to its power. Now everlasting life is an end exceeding the proportion of human nature, as is clear from what we have said above (Q. 5, A. 5). Hence man, by his natural endowments, cannot produce meritorious works proportionate to everlasting life; and for this a higher force is needed, viz. the force of grace. And thus without grace man cannot merit everlasting life; yet he can perform works conducing to a good which is natural to man, as "to toil in the fields, to drink, to eat, or to have friends," and the like, as Augustine says in his third Reply to the Pelagians [*Hypognosticon iii, among the spurious works of St. Augustine].

Reply Obj. 1: Man, by his will, does works meritorious of everlasting life; but as Augustine says, in the same book, for this it is necessary that the will of man should be prepared with grace by God.

Reply Obj. 2: As the gloss upon Rom. 6:23, "The grace of God is life everlasting," says, "It is certain that everlasting life is meted to good works; but the works to which it is meted, belong to God's grace." And it has been said (A. 4), that to fulfil the commandments of the Law, in their due way, whereby their fulfilment may be meritorious, requires grace.

Reply Obj. 3: This objection has to do with the natural end of man. Now human nature, since it is nobler, can be raised by the help of grace to a higher end, which lower natures can nowise reach; even as a man who can recover his health by the help of medicines is better disposed to health than one who can nowise recover it, as the Philosopher observes (De Coelo ii, 12).

SIXTH ARTICLE [I, Q. 109, Art. 6]

Whether a Man, by Himself and Without the External Aid of Grace, Can Prepare Himself for Grace?

Objection 1: It would seem that man, by himself and without the external help of grace, can prepare himself for grace. For nothing impossible is laid upon man, as stated above (A. 4, ad 1). But it is written (Zech. 1:3): "Turn ye to Me ... and I will turn to you." Now to prepare for grace is nothing more than to turn to God. Therefore it seems that man of himself, and without the external help of grace, can prepare himself for grace.

Obj. 2: Further, man prepares himself for grace by doing what is in him to do, since if man does what is in him to do, God will not deny him grace, for it is written (Matt. 7:11) that God gives His good Spirit "to them that ask Him." But what is in our power is in us to do. Therefore it seems to be in our power to prepare ourselves for grace.

Obj. 3: Further, if a man needs grace in order to prepare for grace, with equal reason will he need grace to prepare himself for the first grace; and thus to infinity, which is impossible. Hence it seems that we must not go beyond what was said first, viz. that man, of himself and without grace, can prepare himself for grace.

Obj. 4: Further, it is written (Prov. 16:1) that "it is the part of man to prepare the soul." Now an action is said to be part of a man, when he can do it by himself. Hence it seems that man by himself can prepare himself for grace.

*On the contrary,* It is written (John 6:44): "No man can come to Me except the Father, Who hath sent Me, draw him." But if man could prepare himself, he would not need to be drawn by another. Hence man cannot prepare himself without the help of grace.

*I answer that,* The preparation of the human will for good is twofold: the first, whereby it is prepared to operate rightly and to enjoy God; and this preparation of the will cannot take place without the habitual gift of grace, which is the principle of meritorious works, as stated above (A. 5). There is a second way in which the human will may be taken to be prepared for the gift of habitual grace itself. Now in order that man prepare himself to receive this gift, it is not necessary to presuppose any further habitual gift in the soul, otherwise we should go on to infinity. But we must presuppose a gratuitous gift of God, Who moves the soul inwardly or inspires the good wish. For in these two ways do we need the Divine assistance, as stated above (AA. 2, 3). Now that we need the help of God to move us, is manifest. For since every agent acts for an end, every cause must direct is effect to its end, and hence since the order of ends is according to the order of agents or movers, man must be directed to the last end by the motion of the first mover, and to the proximate end by the motion of any of the subordinate movers; as the spirit of the soldier is bent towards seeking the victory by the motion of the leader of the army—and towards following the standard of a regiment by the motion of the standard-bearer. And thus since God is the First Mover, simply, it is by His motion that everything seeks to be likened to God in its own way. Hence Dionysius says (Div. Nom. iv) that "God turns all to Himself." But He directs righteous men to Himself as to a special end, which they seek, and to which they wish to cling, according to Ps. 72:28, "it is good for Me to adhere to my God." And that they are "turned" to God can only spring from God's having "turned" them. Now to prepare oneself for grace is, as it were, to be turned to God; just as, whoever has his eyes turned away from the light of the sun, prepares himself to receive the sun's light, by turning his eyes towards the sun. Hence it is clear that man cannot prepare himself to receive the light of grace except by the gratuitous help of God moving him inwardly.

Reply Obj. 1: Man's turning to God is by free-will; and thus man is bidden to turn himself to God. But free-will can only be turned to God, when God turns it, according to Jer. 31:18: "Convert me and I shall be converted, for Thou art the Lord, my God"; and Lam. 5:21: "Convert us, O Lord, to Thee, and we shall be converted."

Reply Obj. 2: Man can do nothing unless moved by God, according to John 15:5: "Without Me, you can do nothing." Hence when a man is said to do what is in him to do, this is said to be in his power according as he is moved by God.

Reply Obj. 3: This objection regards habitual grace, for which some preparation is required, since every form requires a disposition in that which is to be its subject. But in order that man should be moved by God, no further motion is presupposed since God is the First Mover. Hence we need not go to infinity.

Reply Obj. 4: It is the part of man to prepare his soul, since he does this by his free-will. And yet he does not do this without the help of God moving him, and drawing him to Himself, as was said above.

SEVENTH ARTICLE [I-II, Q. 109, Art. 7]

Whether Man Can Rise from Sin Without the Help of Grace?

Objection 1: It would seem that man can rise from sin without the help of grace. For what is presupposed to grace, takes place without grace. But to rise from sin is presupposed to the enlightenment of grace; since it is written (Eph. 5:14): "Arise from the dead and Christ shall enlighten thee." Therefore man can rise from sin without grace.

Obj. 2: Further, sin is opposed to virtue as illness to health, as stated above (Q. 71, A. 1, ad 3). Now, man, by force of his nature, can rise from illness to health, without the external help of medicine, since there still remains in him the principle of life, from which the natural operation proceeds. Hence it seems that, with equal reason, man may be restored by himself, and return from the state of sin to the state of justice without the help of external grace.

Obj. 3: Further, every natural thing can return by itself to the act befitting its nature, as hot water returns by itself to its natural coldness, and a stone cast upwards returns by itself to its natural movement. Now a sin is an act against nature, as is clear from Damascene (De Fide Orth. ii, 30). Hence it seems that man by himself can return from sin to the state of justice.

*On the contrary,* The Apostle says (Gal. 2:21; Cf. Gal. 3:21): "For if there had been a law given which could give life—then Christ died in vain," i.e. to no purpose. Hence with equal reason, if man has a nature, whereby he can he justified, "Christ died in vain," i.e. to no purpose. But this cannot fittingly be said. Therefore by himself he cannot be justified, i.e. he cannot return from a state of sin to a state of justice.

*I answer that,* Man by himself can no wise rise from sin without the help of grace. For since sin is transient as to the act and abiding in its guilt, as stated above (Q. 87, A. 6), to rise from sin is not the same as to cease the act of sin; but to rise from sin means that man has restored to him what he lost by sinning. Now man incurs a triple loss by sinning, as was clearly shown above (Q. 85, A. 1; Q. 86, A. 1; Q. 87, A. 1), viz. stain, corruption of natural good, and debt of punishment. He incurs a stain, inasmuch as he forfeits the lustre of grace through the deformity of sin. Natural good is corrupted, inasmuch as man's nature is disordered by man's will not being subject to God's; and this order being overthrown, the consequence is that the whole nature of sinful man remains disordered. Lastly, there is the debt of punishment, inasmuch as by sinning man deserves everlasting damnation.

Now it is manifest that none of these three can be restored except by God. For since the lustre of grace springs from the shedding of Divine light, this lustre cannot be brought back, except God sheds His light anew: hence a habitual gift is necessary, and this is the light of grace. Likewise, the order of nature can only be restored, i.e. man's will can only be subject to God when God draws man's will to Himself, as stated above (A. 6). So, too, the guilt of eternal punishment can be remitted by God alone, against Whom the offense was committed and Who is man's Judge. And thus in order that man rise from sin there is required the help of grace, both as regards a habitual gift, and as regards the internal motion of God.

Reply Obj. 1: To man is bidden that which pertains to the act of free-will, as this act is required in order that man should rise from sin. Hence when it is said, "Arise, and Christ shall enlighten thee," we are not to think that the complete rising from sin precedes the enlightenment of grace; but that when man by his free-will, moved by God, strives to rise from sin, he receives the light of justifying grace.

Reply Obj. 2: The natural reason is not the sufficient principle of the health that is in man by justifying grace. This principle is grace which is taken away by sin. Hence man cannot be restored by himself; but he requires the light of grace to be poured upon him anew, as if the soul were infused into a dead body for its resurrection.

Reply Obj. 3: When nature is perfect, it can be restored by itself to its befitting and proportionate condition; but without exterior help it cannot be restored to what surpasses its measure. And thus human nature undone by reason of the act of sin, remains no longer perfect, but corrupted, as stated above (Q. 85); nor can it be restored, by itself, to its connatural good, much less to the supernatural good of justice.

EIGHTH ARTICLE [I-II, Q. 109, Art. 8]

Whether Man Without Grace Can Avoid Sin?

Objection 1: It would seem that without grace man can avoid sin. Because "no one sins in what he cannot avoid," as Augustine says (De Duab. Anim. x, xi; De Libero Arbit. iii, 18). Hence if a man in mortal sin cannot avoid sin, it would seem that in sinning he does not sin, which is impossible.

Obj. 2: Further, men are corrected that they may not sin. If therefore a man in mortal sin cannot avoid sin, correction would seem to be given to no purpose; which is absurd.

Obj. 3: Further, it is written (Ecclus. 15:18): "Before man is life and death, good and evil; that which he shall choose shall be given him." But by sinning no one ceases to be a man. Hence it is still in his power to choose good or evil; and thus man can avoid sin without grace.

*On the contrary,* Augustine says (De Perfect Just.

xxi): "Whoever denies that we ought to say the prayer 'Lead us not into temptation' (and they deny it who maintain that the help of God's grace is not necessary to man for salvation, but that the gift of the law is enough for the human will) ought without doubt to be removed beyond all hearing, and to be anathematized by the tongues of all."

*I answer that,* We may speak of man in two ways: first, in the state of perfect nature; secondly, in the state of corrupted nature. Now in the state of perfect nature, man, without habitual grace, could avoid sinning either mortally or venially; since to sin is nothing else than to stray from what is according to our nature—and in the state of perfect nature man could avoid this. Nevertheless he could not have done it without God's help to uphold him in good, since if this had been withdrawn, even his nature would have fallen back into nothingness.

But in the state of corrupt nature man needs grace to heal his nature in order that he may entirely abstain from sin. And in the present life this healing is wrought in the mind—the carnal appetite being not yet restored. Hence the Apostle (Rom. 7:25) says in the person of one who is restored: "I myself, with the mind, serve the law of God, but with the flesh, the law of sin." And in this state man can abstain from all mortal sin, which takes its stand in his reason, as stated above (Q. 74, A. 5); but man cannot abstain from all venial sin on account of the corruption of his lower appetite of sensuality. For man can, indeed, repress each of its movements (and hence they are sinful and voluntary), but not all, because whilst he is resisting one, another may arise, and also because the reason is not always alert to avoid these movements, as was said above (Q. 74, A. 3, ad 2).

So, too, before man's reason, wherein is mortal sin, is restored by justifying grace, he can avoid each mortal sin, and for a time, since it is not necessary that he should be always actually sinning. But it cannot be that he remains for a long time without mortal sin. Hence Gregory says (Super Ezech. Hom. xi) that "a sin not at once taken away by repentance, by its weight drags us down to other sins": and this because, as the lower appetite ought to be subject to the reason, so should the reason be subject to God, and should place in Him the end of its will. Now it is by the end that all human acts ought to be regulated, even as it is by the judgment of the reason that the movements of the lower appetite should be regulated. And thus, even as inordinate movements of the sensitive appetite cannot help occurring since the lower appetite is not subject to reason, so likewise, since man's reason is not entirely subject to God, the consequence is that many disorders occur in the reason. For when man's heart is not so fixed on God as to be unwilling to be parted from Him for the sake of finding any good or avoiding any evil, many things happen for the achieving or avoiding of which a man strays from God and breaks His commandments, and thus sins mortally: especially since, when surprised, a man acts according to his preconceived end and his pre-existing habits, as the Philosopher says (Ethic. iii); although with premeditation of his reason a man may do something outside the order of his preconceived end and the inclination of his habit. But because a man cannot always have this premeditation, it cannot help occurring that he acts in accordance with his will turned aside from God, unless, by grace, he is quickly brought back to the due order.

Reply Obj. 1: Man can avoid each but not every act of sin, except by grace, as stated above. Nevertheless, since it is by his own shortcoming that he does not prepare himself to have grace, the fact that he cannot avoid sin without grace does not excuse him from sin.

Reply Obj. 2: Correction is useful "in order that out of the sorrow of correction may spring the wish to be regenerate; if indeed he who is corrected is a son of promise, in such sort that whilst the noise of correction is outwardly resounding and punishing, God by hidden inspirations is inwardly causing to will," as Augustine says (De Corr. et Gratia vi). Correction is therefore necessary, from the fact that man's will is required in order to abstain from sin; yet it is not sufficient without God's help. Hence it is written (Eccles. 7:14): "Consider the works of God that no man can correct whom He hath despised."

Reply Obj. 3: As Augustine says (Hypognosticon iii [*Among the spurious works of St. Augustine]), this saying is to be understood of man in the state of perfect nature, when as yet he was not a slave of sin. Hence he was able to sin and not to sin. Now, too, whatever a man wills, is given to him; but his willing good, he has by God's assistance.

NINTH ARTICLE [I-II, Q. 109, Art. 9]

Whether One Who Has Already Obtained Grace, Can, of Himself and Without Further Help of Grace, Do Good and Avoid Sin?

Objection 1: It would seem that whoever has already obtained grace, can by himself and without further help of grace, do good and avoid sin. For a thing is useless or imperfect, if it does not fulfil what it was given for. Now grace is given to us that we may do good and keep from sin. Hence if with grace man cannot do this, it seems that grace is either useless or imperfect.

Obj. 2: Further, by grace the Holy Spirit dwells in us, according to 1 Cor. 3:16: "Know you not that you are the temple of God, and that the Spirit of God dwelleth in you?" Now since the Spirit of God is omnipotent, He is sufficient to ensure our doing good and to keep us from sin. Hence a man who has obtained grace can do the above two things without any further assistance of grace.

Obj. 3: Further, if a man who has obtained grace needs further aid of grace in order to live righteously and to keep free from sin, with equal reason, will he need yet another grace, even though he has obtained this first help of grace. Therefore we must go on to infinity; which is impossible. Hence whoever is in grace needs no further help of grace in order to do righteously and to keep free from sin.

*On the contrary,* Augustine says (De Natura et Gratia xxvi) that "as the eye of the body though most healthy cannot see unless it is helped by the brightness of light, so, neither can a man, even if he is most righteous, live righteously unless he be helped by the eternal light of justice." But justification is by grace, according to Rom. 3:24: "Being justified freely by His grace." Hence even a man who already possesses grace needs a further assistance of grace in order to live righteously.

*I answer that,* As stated above (A. 5), in order to live righteously a man needs a twofold help of God—first, a habitual gift whereby corrupted human nature is healed, and after being healed is lifted up so as to work deeds meritorious of everlasting life, which exceed the capability of nature. Secondly, man needs the help of grace in order to be moved by God to act.

Now with regard to the first kind of help, man does not need a further help of grace, e.g. a further infused habit. Yet he needs the help of grace in another way, i.e. in order to be moved by God to act righteously, and this for two reasons: first, for the general reason that no created thing can put forth any act, unless by virtue of the Divine motion. Secondly, for this special reason—the condition of the state of human nature. For although healed by grace as to the mind, yet it remains corrupted and poisoned in the flesh, whereby it serves "the law of sin," Rom. 7:25. In the intellect, too, there remains the darkness of ignorance, whereby, as is written (Rom. 8:26): "We know not what we should pray for as we ought"; since on account of the various turns of circumstances, and because we do not know ourselves perfectly, we cannot fully know what is for our good, according to Wis. 9:14: "For the thoughts of mortal men are fearful and our counsels uncertain." Hence we must be guided and guarded by God, Who knows and can do all things. For which reason also it is becoming in those who have been born again as sons of God, to say: "Lead us not into temptation," and "Thy Will be done on earth as it is in heaven," and whatever else is contained in the Lord's Prayer pertaining to this.

Reply Obj. 1: The gift of habitual grace is not therefore given to us that we may no longer need the Divine help; for every creature needs to be preserved in the good received from Him. Hence if after having received grace man still needs the Divine help, it cannot be concluded that grace is given to no purpose, or that it is imperfect, since man will need the Divine help even in the state of glory, when grace shall be fully perfected. But here grace is to some extent imperfect, inasmuch as it does not completely heal man, as stated above.

Reply Obj. 2: The operation of the Holy Ghost, which moves and protects, is not circumscribed by the effect of habitual grace which it causes in us; but beyond this effect He, together with the Father and the Son, moves and protects us.

Reply Obj. 3: This argument merely proves that man needs no further habitual grace.

TENTH ARTICLE [I-II, Q. 109, Art. 10]

Whether Man Possessed of Grace Needs the Help of Grace in Order to Persevere?

Objection 1: It would seem that man possessed of grace needs no help to persevere. For perseverance is something less than virtue, even as continence is, as is clear from the Philosopher (Ethic. vii, 7, 9). Now since man is justified by grace, he needs no further help of grace in order to have the virtues. Much less, therefore, does he need the help of grace to have perseverance.

Obj. 2: Further, all the virtues are infused at once. But perseverance is put down as a virtue. Hence it seems that, together with grace, perseverance is given to the other infused virtues.

Obj. 3: Further, as the Apostle says (Rom. 5:20) more was restored to man by Christ's gift, than he had lost by Adam's sin. But Adam received what enabled him to persevere; and thus man does not need grace in order to persevere.

*On the contrary,* Augustine says (De Persev. ii): "Why is perseverance besought of God, if it is not bestowed by God? For is it not a mocking request to seek what we know He does not give, and what is in our power without His giving it?" Now perseverance is besought by even those who are hallowed by grace; and this is seen, when we say "Hallowed be Thy name," which Augustine confirms by the words of Cyprian (De Correp. et Grat. xii). Hence man, even when possessed of grace, needs perseverance to be given to him by God.

*I answer that,* Perseverance is taken in three ways. First, to signify a habit of the mind whereby a man stands steadfastly, lest he be moved by the assault of sadness from what is virtuous. And thus perseverance is to sadness as continence is to concupiscence and pleasure, as the Philosopher says (Ethic. vii, 7). Secondly, perseverance may be called a habit, whereby a man has the purpose of persevering in good unto the end. And in both these ways perseverance is infused together with grace, even as continence and the other virtues are. Thirdly, perseverance is called the abiding in good to the end of life. And in order to have this perseverance man does not, indeed, need another habitual grace, but he needs the Divine assistance guiding and guarding him against the attacks of the passions, as appears from the preceding article. And hence after anyone has been justified by grace, he still needs to beseech God for the aforesaid gift of perseverance, that he may be kept from evil till the end of his life. For to many grace is given to whom perseverance in grace is not given.

Reply Obj. 1: This objection regards the first mode of perseverance, as the second objection regards the second.

Hence the solution of the second objection is clear.

Reply Obj. 3: As Augustine says (De Natura et Gratia xliii) [*Cf. De Correp. et Grat. xii]: "in the original state man received a gift whereby he could persevere, but to persevere was not given him. But now, by the grace of Christ, many receive both the gift of grace whereby they may persevere, and the further gift of persevering," and thus Christ's gift is greater than Adam's fault. Nevertheless it was easier for man to persevere, with the gift of grace in the state of innocence in which the flesh was not rebellious against the spirit, than it is now. For the restoration by Christ's grace, although it is already begun in the mind, is not yet completed in the flesh, as it will be in heaven, where man will not merely be able to persevere but will be unable to sin.

## QUESTION 110

OF THE GRACE OF GOD AS REGARDS ITS ESSENCE (In Four Articles)

We must now consider the grace of God as regards its essence; and under this head there are four points of inquiry:

(1) Whether grace implies something in the soul?

(2) Whether grace is a quality?

(3) Whether grace differs from infused virtue?

(4) Of the subject of grace.

FIRST ARTICLE [I-II, Q. 110, Art. 1]

Whether Grace Implies Anything in the Soul?

Objection 1: It would seem that grace does not imply anything in the soul. For man is said to have the grace of God even as the grace of man. Hence it is written (Gen. 39:21) that the Lord gave to Joseph "grace [Douay: 'favor'] in the sight of the chief keeper of the prison." Now when we say that a man has the favor of another, nothing is implied in him who has the favor of the other, but an acceptance is implied in him whose favor he has. Hence when we say that a man has the grace of God, nothing is implied in his soul; but we merely signify the Divine acceptance.

Obj. 2: Further, as the soul quickens the body so does God quicken the soul; hence it is written (Deut. 30:20): "He is thy life." Now the soul quickens the body immediately. Therefore nothing can come as a medium between God and the soul. Hence grace implies nothing created in the soul.

Obj. 3: Further, on Rom. 1:7, "Grace to you and peace," the gloss says: "Grace, i.e. the remission of sins." Now the remission of sin implies nothing in the soul, but only in God, Who does not impute the sin, according to Ps. 31:2: "Blessed is the man to whom the Lord hath not imputed sin." Hence neither does grace imply anything in the soul.

*On the contrary,* Light implies something in what is enlightened. But grace is a light of the soul; hence Augustine says (De Natura et Gratia xxii): "The light of truth rightly deserts the prevaricator of the law, and those who have been thus deserted become blind." Therefore grace implies something in the soul.

*I answer that,* According to the common manner of speech, grace is usually taken in three ways. First, for anyone's love, as we are accustomed to say that the soldier is in the good graces of the king, i.e. the king looks on him with favor. Secondly, it is taken for any gift freely bestowed, as we are accustomed to say: I do you this act of grace. Thirdly, it is taken for the recompense of a gift given "gratis," inasmuch as we are said to be "grateful" for benefits. Of these three the second depends on the first, since one bestows something on another "gratis" from the love wherewith he receives him into his good "graces." And from the second proceeds the third, since from benefits bestowed "gratis" arises "gratitude."

Now as regards the last two, it is clear that grace implies something in him who receives grace: first, the gift given gratis; secondly, the acknowledgment of the gift. But as regards the first, a difference must be noted between the grace of God and the grace of man; for since the creature's good springs from the Divine will, some good in the creature flows from God's love, whereby He wishes the good of the creature. On the other hand, the will of man is moved by the good pre-existing in things; and hence man's love does not wholly cause the good of the thing, but pre-supposes it either in part or wholly. Therefore it is clear that every love of God is followed at some time by a good caused in the creature, but not co-eternal with the eternal love. And according to this difference of good the love of God to the creature is looked at differently. For one is common, whereby He loves "all things that are" (Wis. 11:25), and thereby gives things their natural being. But the second is a special love, whereby He draws the rational creature above the condition of its nature to a participation of the Divine good; and according to this love He is said to love anyone simply, since it is by this love that God simply wishes the eternal good, which is Himself, for the creature.

Accordingly when a man is said to have the grace of God, there is signified something bestowed on man by God. Nevertheless the grace of God sometimes signifies God's eternal love, as we say the grace of predestination, inasmuch as God gratuitously and not from merits predestines or elects some; for it is written (Eph. 1:5): "He hath predestinated us into the adoption of children ... unto the praise of the glory of His grace."

Reply Obj. 1: Even when a man is said to be in another's good graces, it is understood that there is something in him pleasing to the other; even as anyone is said to have God's grace—with this difference, that what is pleasing to a man in another is presupposed to his love, but whatever is pleasing to God in a man is caused by the Divine love, as was said above.

Reply Obj. 2: God is the life of the soul after the manner of an efficient cause; but the soul is the life of the body after the manner of a formal cause. Now there is no medium between form and matter, since the form, of itself, *informs* the matter or subject; whereas the agent *informs* the subject, not by its substance, but by the form, which it causes in the matter.

Reply Obj. 3: Augustine says (Retract. i, 25): "When I said that grace was for the remission of sins, and peace for our reconciliation with God, you must not take it to mean that peace and reconciliation do not pertain to general peace, but that the special name of grace signifies the remission of sins." Not only grace, therefore, but many other of God's gifts pertain to grace. And hence the remission of sins does not take place without some effect divinely caused in us, as will appear later (Q. 113, A. 2).

SECOND ARTICLE [I-II, Q. 110, Art. 2]

Whether Grace Is a Quality of the Soul?

Objection 1: It would seem that grace is not a quality of the soul. For no quality acts on its subject, since the action of a quality is not without the action of its subject, and thus the subject would necessarily act upon itself. But grace acts upon the soul, by justifying it. Therefore grace is not a quality.

Obj. 2: Furthermore, substance is nobler than quality. But grace is nobler than the nature of the soul, since we can do many things by grace, to which nature is not equal, as stated above (Q. 109, AA. 1, 2, 3). Therefore grace is not a quality.

Obj. 3: Furthermore, no quality remains after it has ceased to be in its subject. But grace remains; since it is not corrupted, for thus it would be reduced to nothing, since it was created from nothing; hence it is called a "new creature"(Gal. 6:15).

*On the contrary,* on Ps. 103:15: "That he may make the face cheerful with oil"; the gloss says: "Grace is a certain beauty of soul, which wins the Divine love." But beauty of soul is a quality, even as beauty of body. Therefore grace is a quality.

*I answer that,* As stated above (A. 1), there is understood to be an effect of God's gratuitous will in whoever is said to have God's grace. Now it was stated (Q. 109, A. 1) that man is aided by God's gratuitous will in two ways: first, inasmuch as man's soul is moved by God to know or will or do something, and in this way the gratuitous effect in man is not a quality, but a movement of the soul; for "motion is the act of the mover in the moved." Secondly, man is helped by God's gratuitous will, inasmuch as a habitual gift is infused by God into the soul; and for this reason, that it is not fitting that God should provide less for those He loves, that they may acquire supernatural good, than for creatures, whom He loves that they may acquire natural good. Now He so provides for natural creatures, that not merely does He move them to their natural acts, but He bestows upon them certain forms and powers, which are the principles of acts, in order that they may of themselves be inclined to these movements, and thus the movements whereby they are moved by God become natural and easy to creatures, according to Wis. 8:1: "she ... ordereth all things sweetly." Much more therefore does He infuse into such as He moves towards the acquisition of supernatural good, certain forms or supernatural qualities, whereby they may be moved by Him sweetly and promptly to acquire eternal good; and thus the gift of grace is a quality.

Reply Obj. 1: Grace, as a quality, is said to act upon the soul, not after the manner of an efficient cause, but after the manner of a formal cause, as whiteness makes a thing white, and justice, just.

Reply Obj. 2: Every substance is either the nature of the thing whereof it is the substance or is a part of the nature, even as matter and form are called substance. And because grace is above human nature, it cannot be a substance or a substantial form, but is an accidental form of the soul. Now what is substantially in God, becomes accidental in the soul participating the Divine goodness, as is clear in the case of knowledge. And thus because the soul participates in the Divine goodness imperfectly, the participation of the Divine goodness, which is grace, has its being in the soul in a less perfect way than the soul subsists in itself. Nevertheless, inasmuch as it is the expression or participation of the Divine goodness, it is nobler than the nature of the soul, though not in its mode of being.

Reply Obj. 3: As Boethius [*Pseudo-Bede, Sent. Phil. ex Artist.] says, the "being of an accident is to inhere." Hence no accident is called being as if it had being, but because by it something is; hence it is said to belong to a being rather to be a being (Metaph. vii, text. 2). And because to become and to be corrupted belong to what is, properly speaking, no accident comes into being or is corrupted, but is said to come into being and to be corrupted inasmuch as its subject begins or ceases to be in act with this accident. And thus grace is said to be created inasmuch as men are created with reference to it, i.e. are given a new being out of nothing, i.e. not from merits, according to Eph. 2:10, "created in Jesus Christ in good works."

THIRD ARTICLE [I-II, Q. 110, Art. 3]

Whether Grace Is the Same As Virtue?

Objection 1: It would seem that grace is the same as virtue. For Augustine says (De Spir. et Lit. xiv) that "operating grace is faith that worketh by charity." But faith that worketh by charity is a virtue. Therefore grace is a virtue.

Obj. 2: Further, what fits the definition, fits the defined. But the definitions of virtue given by saints and philosophers fit grace, since "it makes its subject good, and his work good," and "it is a good quality of the mind, whereby we live righteously," etc. Therefore grace is virtue.

Obj. 3: Further, grace is a quality. Now it is clearly not in the *fourth* species of quality; viz. form which is the "abiding figure of things," since it does not belong to bodies. Nor is it in the *third*, since it is not a "passion nor a passion-like quality," which is in the sensitive part of the soul, as is proved in *Physic.* viii; and grace is principally in the mind. Nor is it in the *second* species, which is "natural power" or "impotence"; since grace is above nature and does not regard good and evil, as does natural power. Therefore it must be in the *first* species which is "habit" or "disposition." Now habits of the mind are virtues; since even knowledge itself is a virtue after a manner, as stated above (Q. 57, AA. 1, 2). Therefore grace is the same as virtue.

*On the contrary,* If grace is a virtue, it would seem before all to be one of the three theological virtues. But grace is neither faith nor hope, for these can be without sanctifying grace. Nor is it charity, since "grace foreruns charity," as Augustine says in his book on the Predestination of the Saints (De Dono Persev. xvi). Therefore grace is not virtue.

*I answer that,* Some held that grace and virtue were identical in essence, and differed only logically—in the sense that we speak of grace inasmuch as it makes man pleasing to God, or is given gratuitously—and of virtue inasmuch as it empowers us to act rightly. And the Master seems to have thought this (Sent. ii, D 27).

But if anyone rightly considers the nature of virtue, this cannot hold, since, as the Philosopher says (Physic. vii, text. 17), "virtue is disposition of what is perfect—and I call perfect what is disposed according to its nature." Now from this it is clear that the virtue of a thing has reference to some pre-existing nature, from the fact that everything is disposed with reference to what befits its nature. But it is manifest that the virtues acquired by human acts of which we spoke above (Q. 55, seqq.) are dispositions, whereby a man is fittingly disposed with reference to the nature whereby he is a man; whereas infused virtues dispose man in a higher manner and towards a higher end, and consequently in relation to some higher nature, i.e. in relation to a participation of the Divine Nature, according to 2 Pet. 1:4: "He hath given us most great and most precious promises; that by these you may be made partakers of the Divine Nature." And it is in respect of receiving this nature that we are said to be born again sons of God.

And thus, even as the natural light of reason is something besides the acquired virtues, which are ordained to this natural light, so also the light of grace which is a participation of the Divine Nature is something besides the infused virtues which are derived from and are ordained to this light, hence the Apostle says (Eph. 5:8): "For you were heretofore darkness, but now light in the Lord. Walk then as children of the light." For as the acquired virtues enable a man to walk, in accordance with the natural light of reason, so do the infused virtues enable a man to walk as befits the light of grace.

Reply Obj. 1: Augustine calls "faith that worketh by charity" grace, since the act of faith of him that worketh by charity is the first act by which sanctifying grace is manifested.

Reply Obj. 2: Good is placed in the definition of virtue with reference to its fitness with some pre-existing nature essential or participated. Now good is not attributed to grace in this manner, but as to the root of goodness in man, as stated above.

Reply Obj. 3: Grace is reduced to the first species of quality; and yet it is not the same as virtue, but is a certain disposition which is presupposed to the infused virtues, as their principle and root.

FOURTH ARTICLE [I-II, Q. 110, Art. 4]

Whether Grace Is in the Essence of the Soul As in a Subject, or in One of the Powers?

Objection 1: It would seem that grace is not in the essence of the soul, as in a subject, but in one of the powers. For Augustine says (Hypognosticon iii [*Among the spurious works of St. Augustine]) that grace is related to the will or to the free will "as a rider to his horse." Now the will or the free will is a power, as stated above (I, Q. 83, A. 2). Hence grace is in a power of the soul, as in a subject.

Obj. 2: Further, "Man's merit springs from grace" as Augustine says (De Gratia et Lib. Arbit. vi). Now merit consists in acts, which proceed from a power. Hence it seems that grace is a perfection of a power of the soul.

Obj. 3: Further, if the essence of the soul is the proper subject of grace, the soul, inasmuch as it has an essence, must be capable of grace. But this is false; since it would follow that every soul would be capable of grace. Therefore the essence of the soul is not the proper subject of grace.

Obj. 4: Further, the essence of the soul is prior to its powers. Now what is prior may be understood without what is posterior. Hence it follows that grace may be taken to be in the soul, although we suppose no part or power of the soul—viz. neither the will, nor the intellect, nor anything else; which is impossible.

*On the contrary,* By grace we are born again sons of God. But generation terminates at the essence prior to the powers. Therefore grace is in the soul's essence prior to being in the powers.

*I answer that,* This question depends on the preceding. For if grace is the same as virtue, it must necessarily be in the powers of the soul as in a subject; since the soul's powers are the proper subject of virtue, as stated above (Q. 56, A. 1). But if grace differs from virtue, it cannot be said that a power of the soul is the subject of grace, since every perfection of the soul's powers has the nature of virtue, as stated above (Q. 55, A. 1; Q. 56, A. 1). Hence it remains that grace, as it is prior to virtue, has a subject prior to the powers of the soul, so that it is in the essence of the soul. For as man in his intellective powers participates in the Divine knowledge through the virtue of faith, and in his power of will participates in the Divine love through the virtue of charity, so also in the nature of the soul does he participate in the Divine Nature, after the manner of a likeness, through a certain regeneration or re-creation.

Reply Obj. 1: As from the essence of the soul flows its powers, which are the principles of deeds, so likewise the virtues, whereby the powers are moved to act, flow into the powers of the soul from grace. And thus grace is compared to the will as the mover to the moved, which is the same comparison as that of a horseman to the horse—but not as an accident to a subject.

And thereby is made clear the Reply to the Second Objection. For grace is the principle of meritorious works through the medium of virtues, as the essence of the soul is the principal of vital deeds through the medium of the powers.

Reply Obj. 3: The soul is the subject of grace, as being in the species of intellectual or rational nature. But the soul is not classed in a species by any of its powers, since the powers are natural properties of the soul following upon the species. Hence the soul differs specifically in its essence from other souls, viz. of dumb animals, and of plants. Consequently it does not follow that, if the essence of the human soul is the subject of grace, every soul may be the subject of grace; since it belongs to the essence of the soul, inasmuch as it is of such a species.

Reply Obj. 4: Since the powers of the soul are natural properties following upon the species, the soul cannot be without them. Yet, granted that it was without them, the soul would still be called intellectual or rational in its species, not that it would actually have these powers, but on account of the essence of such a species, from which these powers naturally flow.

# QUESTION 111

OF THE DIVISION OF GRACE (In Five Articles)

We must now consider the division of grace; under which head there are five points of inquiry:

(1) Whether grace is fittingly divided into gratuitous grace and sanctifying grace?

(2) Of the division into operating and cooperating grace;

(3) Of the division of it into prevenient and subsequent grace;

(4) Of the division of gratuitous grace;

(5) Of the comparison between sanctifying and gratuitous grace.

FIRST ARTICLE [I-II, Q. 111, Art. 1]

Whether Grace Is Fittingly Divided into Sanctifying Grace and Gratuitous Grace?

Objection 1: It would seem that grace is not fittingly divided into sanctifying grace and gratuitous grace. For grace is a gift of God, as is clear from what has been already stated (Q. 110, A. 1). But man is not therefore pleasing to God because something is given him by God, but rather on the contrary; since something is freely given by God, because man is pleasing to Him. Hence there is no sanctifying grace.

Obj. 2: Further, whatever is not given on account of preceding merits is given gratis. Now even natural good is given to man without preceding merit, since nature is presupposed to merit. Therefore nature itself is given gratuitously by God. But nature is condivided with grace. Therefore to be gratuitously given is not fittingly set down as a difference of grace, since it is found outside the genus of grace.

Obj. 3: Further, members of a division are mutually opposed. But even sanctifying grace, whereby we are justified, is given to us gratuitously, according to Rom. 3:24: "Being justified freely ( *gratis* ) by His grace." Hence sanctifying grace ought not to be divided against gratuitous grace.

*On the contrary,* The Apostle attributes both to grace, viz. to sanctify and to be gratuitously given. For with regard to the first he says (Eph. 1:6): "He hath graced us in His beloved son." And with regard to the second (Rom. 2:6): "And if by grace, it is not now by works, otherwise grace is no more grace." Therefore grace can be distinguished by its having one only or both.

*I answer that,* As the Apostle says (Rom. 13:1), "those things that are of God are well ordered [Vulg.: 'those that are, are ordained by God]." Now the order of things consists in this, that things are led to God by other things, as Dionysius says (Coel. Hier. iv). And hence since grace is ordained to lead men to God, this takes place in a certain order, so that some are led to God by others.

And thus there is a twofold grace: one whereby man himself is united to God, and this is called "sanctifying grace"; the other is that whereby one man cooperates with another in leading him to God, and this gift is called "gratuitous grace," since it is bestowed on a man beyond the capability of nature, and beyond the merit of the person. But whereas it is bestowed on a man, not to justify him, but rather that he may cooperate in the justification of another, it is not called sanctifying grace. And it is of this that the Apostle says (1 Cor. 12:7): "And the manifestation of the Spirit is given to every man unto utility," i.e. of others.

Reply Obj. 1: Grace is said to make pleasing, not efficiently but formally, i.e. because thereby a man is justified, and is made worthy to be called pleasing to God, according to Col. 1:21: "He hath made us worthy to be made partakers of the lot of the saints in light."

Reply Obj. 2: Grace, inasmuch as it is gratuitously given, excludes the notion of debt. Now debt may be taken in two ways: first, as arising from merit; and this regards the person whose it is to do meritorious works, according to Rom. 4:4: "Now to him that worketh, the reward is not reckoned according to grace, but according to debt." The second debt regards the condition of nature. Thus we say it is due to a man to have reason, and whatever else belongs to human nature. Yet in neither way is debt taken to mean that God is under an obligation to His creature, but rather that the creature ought to be subject to God, that the Divine ordination may be fulfilled in it, which is that a certain nature should have certain conditions or properties, and that by doing certain works it should attain to something further. And hence natural endowments are not a debt in the first sense but in the second. But supernatural gifts are due in neither sense. Hence they especially merit the name of grace.

Reply Obj. 3: Sanctifying grace adds to the notion of gratuitous grace something pertaining to the nature of grace, since it makes man pleasing to God. And hence gratuitous grace which does not do this keeps the common name, as happens in many other cases; and thus the two parts of the division are opposed as sanctifying and non-sanctifying grace.

SECOND ARTICLE [I-II, Q. 111, Art. 2]

Whether Grace Is Fittingly Divided into Operating and Cooperating Grace?

Objection 1: It would seem that grace is not fittingly divided into operating and cooperating grace. For grace is an accident, as stated above (Q. 110, A. 2). Now no accident can act upon its subject. Therefore no grace can be called operating.

Obj. 2: Further, if grace operates anything in us it assuredly brings about justification. But not only grace works this. For Augustine says, on John 14:12, "the works that I do he also shall do," says (Serm. clxix): "He Who created thee without thyself, will not justify thee without thyself." Therefore no grace ought to be called simply operating.

Obj. 3: Further, to cooperate seems to pertain to the inferior agent, and not to the principal agent. But grace works in us more than free-will, according to Rom. 9:16: "It is not of him that willeth, nor of him that runneth, but of God that sheweth mercy." Therefore no grace ought to be called cooperating.

Obj. 4: Further, division ought to rest on opposition. But to operate and to cooperate are not opposed; for one and the same thing can both operate and cooperate. Therefore grace is not fittingly divided into operating and cooperating.

*On the contrary,* Augustine says (De Gratia et Lib. Arbit. xvii): "God by cooperating with us, perfects what He began by operating in us, since He who perfects by cooperation with such as are willing, begins by operating that they may will." But the operations of God whereby He moves us to good pertain to grace. Therefore grace is fittingly divided into operating and cooperating.

*I answer that,* As stated above (Q. 110, A. 2) grace may be taken in two ways; first, as a Divine help, whereby God moves us to will and to act; secondly, as a habitual gift divinely bestowed on us.

Now in both these ways grace is fittingly divided into operating and cooperating. For the operation of an effect is not attributed to the thing moved but to the mover. Hence in that effect in which our mind is moved and does not move, but in which God is the sole mover, the operation is attributed to God, and it is with reference to this that we speak of "operating grace." But in that effect in which our mind both moves and is moved, the operation is not only attributed to God, but also to the soul; and it is with reference to this that we speak of "cooperating grace." Now there is a double act in us. First, there is the interior act of the will, and with regard to this act the will is a thing moved, and God is the mover; and especially when the will, which hitherto willed evil, begins to will good. And hence, inasmuch as God moves the human mind to this act, we speak of operating grace. But there is another, exterior act; and since it is commanded by the will, as was shown above (Q. 17, A. 9) the operation of this act is attributed to the will. And because God assists us in this act, both by strengthening our will interiorly so as to attain to the act, and by granting outwardly the capability of operating, it is with respect to this that we speak of cooperating grace. Hence after the aforesaid words Augustine subjoins: "He operates that we may will; and when we will, He cooperates that we may perfect." And thus if grace is taken for God's gratuitous motion whereby He moves us to meritorious good, it is fittingly divided into operating and cooperating grace.

But if grace is taken for the habitual gift, then again there is a double effect of grace, even as of every other form; the first of which is *being,* and the second, operation; thus the work of heat is to make its subject hot, and to give heat outwardly. And thus habitual grace, inasmuch as it heals and justifies the soul, or makes it pleasing to God, is called operating grace; but inasmuch as it is the principle of meritorious works, which spring from the free-will, it is called cooperating grace.

Reply Obj. 1: Inasmuch as grace is a certain accidental quality, it does not act upon the soul efficiently, but formally, as whiteness makes a surface white.

Reply Obj. 2: God does not justify us without ourselves, because whilst we are being justified we consent to God's justification ( *justitiae* ) by a movement of our free-will. Nevertheless this movement is not the cause of grace, but the effect; hence the whole operation pertains to grace.

Reply Obj. 3: One thing is said to cooperate with another not merely when it is a secondary agent under a principal agent, but when it helps to the end intended. Now man is helped by God to will the good, through the means of operating grace. And hence, the end being already intended, grace cooperates with us.

Reply Obj. 4: Operating and cooperating grace are the same grace; but are distinguished by their different effects, as is plain from what has been said.

THIRD ARTICLE [I-II, Q. 111, Art. 3]

Whether Grace Is Fittingly Divided into Prevenient and Subsequent Grace?

Objection 1: It would seem that grace is not fittingly divided into prevenient and subsequent. For grace is an effect of the Divine love. But God's love is never subsequent, but always prevenient, according to 1 John 4:10: "Not as though we had loved God, but because He hath first loved us." Therefore grace ought not to be divided into prevenient and subsequent.

Obj. 2: Further, there is but one sanctifying grace in man, since it is sufficient, according to 2 Cor. 12:9: "My grace is sufficient for thee." But the same thing cannot be before and after. Therefore grace is not fittingly divided into prevenient and subsequent.

Obj. 3: Further, grace is known by its effects. Now there are an infinite number of effects—one preceding another. Hence if with regard to these, grace must be divided into prevenient and subsequent, it would seem that there are infinite species of grace. Now no art takes note of the infinite in number. Hence grace is not fittingly divided into prevenient and subsequent.

*On the contrary,* God's grace is the outcome of His mercy. Now both are said in Ps. 58:11: "His mercy shall prevent me," and again, Ps. 22:6: "Thy mercy will follow me." Therefore grace is fittingly divided into prevenient and subsequent.

*I answer that,* As grace is divided into operating and cooperating, with regard to its diverse effects, so also is it divided into prevenient and subsequent, howsoever we consider grace. Now there are five effects of grace in us: of these, the first is, to heal the soul; the second, to desire good; the third, to carry into effect the good proposed; the fourth, to persevere in good; the fifth, to reach glory. And hence grace, inasmuch as it causes the first effect in us, is called prevenient with respect to the second, and inasmuch as it causes the second, it is called subsequent with respect to the first effect. And as one effect is posterior to this effect, and prior to that, so may grace be called prevenient and subsequent on account of the same effect viewed relatively to divers others. And this is what Augustine says (De Natura et Gratia xxxi): "It is prevenient, inasmuch as it heals, and subsequent, inasmuch as, being healed, we are strengthened; it is prevenient, inasmuch as we are called, and subsequent, inasmuch as we are glorified."

Reply Obj. 1: God's love signifies something eternal; and hence can never be called anything but prevenient. But grace signifies a temporal effect, which can precede and follow another; and thus grace may be both prevenient and subsequent.

Reply Obj. 2: The division into prevenient and subsequent grace does not divide grace in its essence, but only in its effects, as was already said of operating and cooperating grace. For subsequent grace, inasmuch as it pertains to glory, is not numerically distinct from prevenient grace whereby we are at present justified. For even as the charity of the earth is not voided in heaven, so must the same be said of the light of grace, since the notion of neither implies imperfection.

Reply Obj. 3: Although the effects of grace may be infinite in number, even as human acts are infinite, nevertheless all are reduced to some of a determinate species, and moreover all coincide in this—that one precedes another.

FOURTH ARTICLE [I-II, Q. 111, Art. 4]

Whether Gratuitous Grace Is Rightly Divided by the Apostle?

Objection 1: It would seem that gratuitous grace is not rightly divided by the Apostle. For every gift vouchsafed to us by God, may be called a gratuitous grace. Now there are an infinite number of gifts freely bestowed on us by God as regards both the good of the soul and the good of the body—and yet they do not make us pleasing to God. Hence gratuitous graces cannot be contained under any certain division.

Obj. 2: Further, gratuitous grace is distinguished from sanctifying grace. But faith pertains to sanctifying grace, since we are justified by it, according to Rom. 5:1: "Being justified therefore by faith." Hence it is not right to place faith amongst the gratuitous graces, especially since the other virtues are not so placed, as hope and charity.

Obj. 3: Further, the operation of healing, and speaking divers tongues are miracles. Again, the interpretation of speeches pertains either to wisdom or to knowledge, according to Dan. 1:17: "And to these children God gave knowledge and understanding in every book and wisdom." Hence it is not correct to divide the grace of healing and kinds of tongues against the working of miracles; and the interpretation of speeches against the word of wisdom and knowledge.

Obj. 4: Further, as wisdom and knowledge are gifts of the Holy Ghost, so also are understanding, counsel, piety, fortitude, and fear, as stated above (Q. 68, A. 4). Therefore these also ought to be placed amongst the gratuitous gifts.

*On the contrary,* The Apostle says (1 Cor. 12:8, 9, 10): "To one indeed by the Spirit is given the word of wisdom; and to another the word of knowledge, according to the same Spirit; to another, the working of miracles; to another, prophecy; to another, the discerning of spirits; to another divers kinds of tongues; to another interpretation of speeches."

*I answer that,* As was said above (A. 1), gratuitous grace is ordained to this, viz. that a man may help another to be led to God. Now no man can help in this by moving interiorly (for this belongs to God alone), but only exteriorly by teaching or persuading. Hence gratuitous grace embraces whatever a man needs in order to instruct another in Divine things which are above reason. Now for this three things are required: first, a man must possess the fullness of knowledge of Divine things, so as to be capable of teaching others. Secondly, he must be able to confirm or prove what he says, otherwise his words would have no weight. Thirdly, he must be capable of fittingly presenting to his hearers what he knows.

Now as regards the first, three things are necessary, as may be seen in human teaching. For whoever would teach another in any science must first be certain of the principles of the science, and with regard to this there is *faith,* which is certitude of invisible things, the principles of Catholic doctrine. Secondly, it behooves the teacher to know the principal conclusions of the science, and hence we have the word of *wisdom,* which is the knowledge of Divine things. Thirdly, he ought to abound with examples and a knowledge of effects, whereby at times he needs to manifest causes; and thus we have the word of *knowledge,* which is the knowledge of human things, since "the invisible things of Him ... are clearly seen, being understood by the things that are made" (Rom. 1:20).

Now the confirmation of such things as are within reason rests upon arguments; but the confirmation of what is above reason rests on what is proper to the Divine power, and this in two ways: first, when the teacher of sacred doctrine does what God alone can do, in miraculous deeds, whether with respect to bodily health—and thus there is the *grace of healing,* or merely for the purpose of manifesting the Divine power; for instance, that the sun should stand still or darken, or that the sea should be divided—and thus there is the *working of miracles.* Secondly, when he can manifest what God alone can know, and these are either future contingents—and thus there is *prophecy,* or also the secrets of hearts—and thus there is the *discerning of spirits.*

But the capability of speaking can regard either the idiom in which a person can be understood, and thus there is *kinds of tongues* ; or it can regard the sense of what is said, and thus there is the interpretation of speeches.

Reply Obj. 1: As stated above (A. 1), not all the benefits divinely conferred upon us are called gratuitous graces, but only those that surpass the power of nature—e.g. that a fisherman should be replete with the word of wisdom and of knowledge and the like; and such as these are here set down as gratuitous graces.

Reply Obj. 2: Faith is enumerated here under the gratuitous graces, not as a virtue justifying man in himself, but as implying a super-eminent certitude of faith, whereby a man is fitted for instructing others concerning such things as belong to the faith. With regard to hope and charity, they belong to the appetitive power, according as man is ordained thereby to God.

Reply Obj. 3: The grace of healing is distinguished from the general working of miracles because it has a special reason for inducing one to the faith, since a man is all the more ready to believe when he has received the gift of bodily health through the virtue of faith. So, too, to speak with divers tongues and to interpret speeches have special efficacy in bestowing faith. Hence they are set down as special gratuitous graces.

Reply Obj. 4: Wisdom and knowledge are not numbered among the gratuitous graces in the same way as they are reckoned among the gifts of the Holy Ghost, i.e. inasmuch as man's mind is rendered easily movable by the Holy Ghost to the things of wisdom and knowledge; for thus they are gifts of the Holy Ghost, as stated above (Q. 68, AA. 1, 4). But they are numbered amongst the gratuitous graces, inasmuch as they imply such a fullness of knowledge and wisdom that a man may not merely think aright of Divine things, but may instruct others and overpower adversaries. Hence it is significant that it is the "word" of wisdom and the "word" of knowledge that are placed in the gratuitous graces, since, as Augustine says (De Trin. xiv, 1), "It is one thing merely to know what a man must believe in order to reach everlasting life, and another thing to know how this may benefit the godly and may be defended against the ungodly."

FIFTH ARTICLE [I-II, Q. 111, Art. 5]

Whether Gratuitous Grace Is Nobler Than Sanctifying Grace?

Objection 1: It would seem that gratuitous grace is nobler than sanctifying grace. For "the people's good is better than the individual good," as the Philosopher says (Ethic. i, 2). Now sanctifying grace is ordained to the good of one man alone, whereas gratuitous grace is ordained to the common good of the whole Church, as stated above (AA. 1, 4). Hence gratuitous grace is nobler than sanctifying grace.

Obj. 2: Further, it is a greater power that is able to act upon another, than that which is confined to itself, even as greater is the brightness of the body that can illuminate other bodies, than of that which can only shine but cannot illuminate; and hence the Philosopher says (Ethic. v, 1) "that justice is the most excellent of the virtues," since by it a man bears himself rightly towards others. But by sanctifying grace a man is perfected only in himself; whereas by gratuitous grace a man works for the perfection of others. Hence gratuitous grace is nobler than sanctifying grace.

Obj. 3: Further, what is proper to the best is nobler than what is common to all; thus to reason, which is proper to man, is nobler than to feel, which is common to all animals. Now sanctifying grace is common to all members of the Church, but gratuitous grace is the proper gift of the more exalted members of the Church. Hence gratuitous grace is nobler than sanctifying grace.

*On the contrary,* The Apostle (1 Cor. 12:31), having enumerated the gratuitous graces, adds: "And I shew unto you yet a more excellent way"; and as the sequel proves he is speaking of charity, which pertains to sanctifying grace. Hence sanctifying grace is more noble than gratuitous grace.

*I answer that,* The higher the good to which a virtue is ordained, the more excellent is the virtue. Now the end is always greater than the means. But sanctifying grace ordains a man immediately to a union with his last end, whereas gratuitous grace ordains a man to what is preparatory to the end; i.e. by prophecy and miracles and so forth, men are induced to unite themselves to their last end. And hence sanctifying grace is nobler than gratuitous grace.

Reply Obj. 1: As the Philosopher says (Metaph. xii, text. 52), a multitude, as an army, has a double good; the first is in the multitude itself, viz. the order of the army; the second is separate from the multitude, viz. the good of the leader—and this is better good, since the other is ordained to it. Now gratuitous grace is ordained to the common good of the Church, which is ecclesiastical order, whereas sanctifying grace is ordained to the separate common good, which is God. Hence sanctifying grace is the nobler.

Reply Obj. 2: If gratuitous grace could cause a man to have sanctifying grace, it would follow that the gratuitous grace was the nobler; even as the brightness of the sun that enlightens is more excellent than that of an object that is lit up. But by gratuitous grace a man cannot cause another to have union with God, which he himself has by sanctifying grace; but he causes certain dispositions towards it. Hence gratuitous grace needs not to be the more excellent, even as in fire, the heat, which manifests its species whereby it produces heat in other things, is not more noble than its substantial form.

Reply Obj. 3: Feeling is ordained to reason, as to an end; and thus, to reason is nobler. But here it is the contrary; for what is proper is ordained to what is common as to an end. Hence there is no comparison.

# QUESTION 112

OF THE CAUSE OF GRACE (In Five Articles)

We must now consider the cause of grace; and under this head there are five points of inquiry:

(1) Whether God alone is the efficient cause of grace?

(2) Whether any disposition towards grace is needed on the part of the recipient, by an act of free-will?

(3) Whether such a disposition can make grace follow of necessity?

(4) Whether grace is equal in all?

(5) Whether anyone may know that he has grace?

FIRST ARTICLE [I-II, Q. 112, Art. 1]

Whether God Alone Is the Cause of Grace?

Objection 1: It would seem that God alone is not the cause of grace. For it is written (John 1:17): "Grace and truth came by Jesus Christ." Now, by the name of Jesus Christ is understood not merely the Divine Nature assuming, but the created nature assumed. Therefore a creature may be the cause of grace.

Obj. 2: Further, there is this difference between the sacraments of the New Law and those of the Old, that the sacraments of the New Law cause grace, whereas the sacraments of the Old Law merely signify it. Now the sacraments of the New Law are certain visible elements. Therefore God is not the only cause of grace.

Obj. 3: Further, according to Dionysius (Coel. Hier. iii, iv, vii, viii), "Angels cleanse, enlighten, and perfect both lesser angels and men." Now the rational creature is cleansed, enlightened, and perfected by grace. Therefore God is not the only cause of grace.

*On the contrary,* It is written (Ps. 83:12): "The Lord will give grace and glory."

*I answer that,* Nothing can act beyond its species, since the cause must always be more powerful than its effect. Now the gift of grace surpasses every capability of created nature, since it is nothing short of a partaking of the Divine Nature, which exceeds every other nature. And thus it is impossible that any creature should cause grace. For it is as necessary that God alone should deify, bestowing a partaking of the Divine Nature by a participated likeness, as it is impossible that anything save fire should enkindle.

Reply Obj. 1: Christ's humanity is an "organ of His Godhead," as Damascene says (De Fide Orth. iii, 19). Now an instrument does not bring forth the action of the principal agent by its own power, but in virtue of the principal agent. Hence Christ's humanity does not cause grace by its own power, but by virtue of the Divine Nature joined to it, whereby the actions of Christ's humanity are saving actions.

Reply Obj. 2: As in the person of Christ the humanity causes our salvation by grace, the Divine power being the principal agent, so likewise in the sacraments of the New Law, which are derived from Christ, grace is instrumentally caused by the sacraments, and principally by the power of the Holy Ghost working in the sacraments, according to John 3:5: "Unless a man be born again of water and the Holy Ghost he cannot enter into the kingdom of God."

Reply Obj. 3: Angels cleanse, enlighten, and perfect angels or men, by instruction, and not by justifying them through grace. Hence Dionysius says (Coel. Hier. vii) that "this cleansing and enlightenment and perfecting is nothing else than the assumption of Divine knowledge."

SECOND ARTICLE [I-II, Q. 112, Art. 2]

Whether Any Preparation and Disposition for Grace Is Required on Man's Part?

Objection 1: It would seem that no preparation or disposition for grace is required on man's part, since, as the Apostle says (Rom. 4:4), "To him that worketh, the reward is not reckoned according to grace, but according to debt." Now a man's preparation by free-will can only be through some operation. Hence it would do away with the notion of grace.

Obj. 2: Further, whoever is going on sinning, is not preparing himself to have grace. But to some who are going on sinning grace is given, as is clear in the case of Paul, who received grace whilst he was "breathing out threatenings and slaughter against the disciples of the Lord" (Act 9:1). Hence no preparation for grace is required on man's part.

Obj. 3: Further, an agent of infinite power needs no disposition in matter, since it does not even require matter, as appears in creation, to which grace is compared, which is called "a new creature" (Gal. 6:15). But only God, Who has infinite power, causes grace, as stated above (A. 1). Hence no preparation is required on man's part to obtain grace.

*On the contrary,* It is written (Amos 4:12): "Be prepared to meet thy God, O Israel," and (1 Kings 7:3): "Prepare your hearts unto the Lord."

*I answer that,* As stated above (Q. 111, A. 2), grace is taken in two ways: first, as a habitual gift of God. Secondly, as a help from God, Who moves the soul to good. Now taking grace in the first sense, a certain preparation of grace is required for it, since a form can only be in disposed matter. But if we speak of grace as it signifies a help from God to move us to good, no preparation is required on man's part, that, as it were, anticipates the Divine help, but rather, every preparation in man must be by the help of God moving the soul to good. And thus even the good movement of the free-will, whereby anyone is prepared for receiving the gift of grace, is an act of the free-will moved by God. And thus man is said to prepare himself, according to Prov. 16:1: "It is the part of man to prepare the soul"; yet it is principally from God, Who moves the free-will. Hence it is said that man's will is prepared by God, and that man's steps are guided by God.

Reply Obj. 1: A certain preparation of man for grace is simultaneous with the infusion of grace; and this operation is meritorious, not indeed of grace, which is already possessed—but of glory which is not yet possessed. But there is another imperfect preparation, which sometimes precedes the gift of sanctifying grace, and yet it is from God's motion. But it does not suffice for merit, since man is not yet justified by grace, and merit can only arise from grace, as will be seen further on (Q. 114, A. 2).

Reply Obj. 2: Since a man cannot prepare himself for grace unless God prevent and move him to good, it is of no account whether anyone arrive at perfect preparation instantaneously, or step by step. For it is written (Ecclus. 11:23): "It is easy in the eyes of God on a sudden to make the poor man rich." Now it sometimes happens that God moves a man to good, but not perfect good, and this preparation precedes grace. But He sometimes moves him suddenly and perfectly to good, and man receives grace suddenly, according to John 6:45: "Every one that hath heard of the Father, and hath learned, cometh to Me." And thus it happened to Paul, since, suddenly when he was in the midst of sin, his heart was perfectly moved by God to hear, to learn, to come; and hence he received grace suddenly.

Reply Obj. 3: An agent of infinite power needs no matter or disposition of matter, brought about by the action of something else; and yet, looking to the condition of the thing caused, it must cause, in the thing caused, both the matter and the due disposition for the form. So likewise, when God infuses grace into a soul, no preparation is required which He Himself does not bring about.

THIRD ARTICLE [I-II, Q. 112, Art. 3]

Whether Grace Is Necessarily Given to Whoever Prepares Himself for It, or to Whoever Does What He Can?

Objection 1: It would seem that grace is necessarily given to whoever prepares himself for grace, or to whoever does what he can, because, on Rom. 5:1, "Being justified ... by faith, let us have peace," etc. the gloss says: "God welcomes whoever flies to Him, otherwise there would be injustice with Him." But it is impossible for injustice to be with God. Therefore it is impossible for God not to welcome whoever flies to Him. Hence he receives grace of necessity.

Obj. 2: Further, Anselm says (De Casu Diaboli. iii) that the reason why God does not bestow grace on the devil, is that he did not wish, nor was he prepared, to receive it. But if the cause be removed, the effect must needs be removed also. Therefore, if anyone is willing to receive grace it is bestowed on them of necessity.

Obj. 3: Further, good is diffusive of itself, as appears from Dionysius (Div. Nom. iv). Now the good of grace is better than the good of nature. Hence, since natural forms necessarily come to disposed matter, much more does it seem that grace is necessarily bestowed on whoever prepares himself for grace.

*On the contrary,* Man is compared to God as clay to the potter, according to Jer. 18:6: "As clay is in the hand of the potter, so are you in My hand." But however much the clay is prepared, it does not necessarily receive its shape from the potter. Hence, however much a man prepares himself, he does not necessarily receive grace from God.

*I answer that,* As stated above (A. 2), man's preparation for grace is from God, as Mover, and from the free-will, as moved. Hence the preparation may be looked at in two ways: first, as it is from free-will, and thus there is no necessity that it should obtain grace, since the gift of grace exceeds every preparation of human power. But it may be considered, secondly, as it is from God the Mover, and thus it has a necessity—not indeed of coercion, but of infallibility—as regards what it is ordained to by God, since God's intention cannot fail, according to the saying of Augustine in his book on the *Predestination of the Saints* (De Dono Persev. xiv) that "by God's good gifts whoever is liberated, is most certainly liberated." Hence if God intends, while moving, that the one whose heart He moves should attain to grace, he will infallibly attain to it, according to John 6:45: "Every one that hath heard of the Father, and hath learned, cometh to Me."

Reply Obj. 1: This gloss is speaking of such as fly to God by a meritorious act of their free-will, already *informed* with grace; for if they did not receive grace, it would be against the justice which He Himself established. Or if it refers to the movement of free-will before grace, it is speaking in the sense that man's flight to God is by a Divine motion, which ought not, in justice, to fail.

Reply Obj. 2: The first cause of the defect of grace is on our part; but the first cause of the bestowal of grace is on God's according to Osee 13:9: "Destruction is thy own, O Israel; thy help is only in Me."

Reply Obj. 3: Even in natural things, the form does not necessarily ensue the disposition of the matter, except by the power of the agent that causes the disposition.

FOURTH ARTICLE [I-II, Q. 112, Art. 4]

Whether Grace Is Greater in One Than in Another?

Objection 1: It would seem that grace is not greater in one than in another. For grace is caused in us by the Divine love, as stated above (Q. 110, A. 1). Now it is written (Wis. 6:8): "He made the little and the great and He hath equally care of all." Therefore all obtain grace from Him equally.

Obj. 2: Further, whatever is the greatest possible, cannot be more or less. But grace is the greatest possible, since it joins us with our last end. Therefore there is no greater or less in it. Hence it is not greater in one than in another.

Obj. 3: Further, grace is the soul's life, as stated above (Q. 110, A. 1, ad 2). But there is no greater or less in life. Hence, neither is there in grace.

*On the contrary,* It is written (Eph. 4:7): "But to every one of us is given grace according to the measure of the giving of Christ." Now what is given in measure, is not given to all equally. Hence all have not an equal grace.

*I answer that,* As stated above (Q. 52, AA. 1, 2; Q. 56, AA. 1, 2), habits can have a double magnitude: one, as regards the end or object, as when a virtue is said to be more noble through being ordained to a greater good; the other on the part of the subject, which more or less participates in the habit inhering to it.

Now as regards the first magnitude, sanctifying grace cannot be greater or less, since, of its nature, grace joins man to the Highest Good, which is God. But as regards the subject, grace can receive more or less, inasmuch as one may be more perfectly enlightened by grace than another. And a certain reason for this is on the part of him who prepares himself for grace; since he who is better prepared for grace, receives more grace. Yet it is not here that we must seek the first cause of this diversity, since man prepares himself, only inasmuch as his free-will is prepared by God. Hence the first cause of this diversity is to be sought on the part of God, Who dispenses His gifts of grace variously, in order that the beauty and perfection of the Church may result from these various degrees; even as He instituted the various conditions of things, that the universe might be perfect. Hence after the Apostle had said (Eph. 4:7): "To every one of us is given grace according to the measure of the giving of Christ," having enumerated the various graces, he adds (Eph. 4:12): "For the perfecting of the saints ... for the edifying of the body of Christ."

Reply Obj. 1: The Divine care may be looked at in two ways: first, as regards the Divine act, which is simple and uniform; and thus His care looks equally to all, since by one simple act He administers great things and little. But, secondly, it may be considered in those things which come to be considered by the Divine care; and thus, inequality is found, inasmuch as God by His care provides greater gifts to some, and lesser gifts for others.

Reply Obj. 2: This objection is based on the first kind of magnitude of grace; since grace cannot be greater by ordaining to a greater good, but inasmuch as it more or less ordains to a greater or less participation of the same good. For there may be diversity of intensity and remissness, both in grace and in final glory as regards the subjects' participation.

Reply Obj. 3: Natural life pertains to man's substance, and hence cannot be more or less; but man partakes of the life of grace accidentally, and hence man may possess it more or less.

FIFTH ARTICLE [I-II, Q. 112, Art. 5]

Whether Man Can Know That He Has Grace?

Objection 1: It would seem that man can know

that he has grace. For grace by its physical reality is in the soul. Now the soul has most certain knowledge of those things that are in it by their physical reality, as appears from Augustine (Gen. ad lit. xii, 31). Hence grace may be known most certainly by one who has grace.

Obj. 2: Further, as knowledge is a gift of God, so is grace. But whoever receives knowledge from God, knows that he has knowledge, according to Wis. 7:17: The Lord "hath given me the true knowledge of the things that are." Hence, with equal reason, whoever receives grace from God, knows that he has grace.

Obj. 3: Further, light is more knowable than darkness, since, according to the Apostle (Eph. 5:13), "all that is made manifest is light." Now sin, which is spiritual darkness, may be known with certainty by one that is in sin. Much more, therefore, may grace, which is spiritual light, be known.

Obj. 4: Further, the Apostle says (1 Cor. 2:12): "Now we have received not the Spirit of this world, but the Spirit that is of God; that we may know the things that are given us from God." Now grace is God's first gift. Hence, the man who receives grace by the Holy Spirit, by the same Holy Spirit knows the grace given to him.

Obj. 5: Further, it was said by the Lord to Abraham (Gen. 22:12): "Now I know that thou fearest God," i.e. "I have made thee know." Now He is speaking there of chaste fear, which is not apart from grace. Hence a man may know that he has grace.

*On the contrary,* It is written (Eccles. 9:1): "Man knoweth not whether he be worthy of love or hatred." Now sanctifying grace maketh a man worthy of God's love. Therefore no one can know whether he has sanctifying grace.

*I answer that,* There are three ways of knowing a thing: first, by revelation, and thus anyone may know that he has grace, for God by a special privilege reveals this at times to some, in order that the joy of safety may begin in them even in this life, and that they may carry on toilsome works with greater trust and greater energy, and may bear the evils of this present life, as when it was said to Paul (2 Cor. 12:9): "My grace is sufficient for thee."

Secondly, a man may, of himself, know something, and with certainty; and in this way no one can know that he has grace. For certitude about a thing can only be had when we may judge of it by its proper principle. Thus it is by undemonstrable universal principles that certitude is obtained concerning demonstrative conclusions. Now no one can know he has the knowledge of a conclusion if he does not know its principle. But the principle of grace and its object is God, Who by reason of His very excellence is unknown to us, according to Job 36:26: "Behold God is great, exceeding our knowledge." And hence His presence in us and His absence cannot be known with certainty, according to Job 9:11: "If He come to me, I shall not see Him; if He depart I shall not understand." And hence man cannot judge with certainty that he has grace, according to 1 Cor. 4:3, 4: "But neither do I judge my own self ... but He that judgeth me is the Lord."

Thirdly, things are known conjecturally by signs; and thus anyone may know he has grace, when he is conscious of delighting in God, and of despising worldly things, and inasmuch as a man is not conscious of any mortal sin. And thus it is written (Apoc. 2:17): "To him that overcometh I will give the hidden manna ... which no man knoweth, but he that receiveth it," because whoever receives it knows, by experiencing a certain sweetness, which he who does not receive it, does not experience. Yet this knowledge is imperfect; hence the Apostle says (1 Cor. 4:4): "I am not conscious to myself of anything, yet am I not hereby justified," since, according to Ps. 18:13: "Who can understand sins? From my secret ones cleanse me, O Lord, and from those of others spare Thy servant."

Reply Obj. 1: Those things which are in the soul by their physical reality, are known through experimental knowledge; in so far as through acts man has experience of their inward principles: thus when we wish, we perceive that we have a will; and when we exercise the functions of life, we observe that there is life in us.

Reply Obj. 2: It is an essential condition of knowledge that a man should have certitude of the objects of knowledge; and again, it is an essential condition of faith that a man should be certain of the things of faith, and this, because certitude belongs to the perfection of the intellect, wherein these gifts exist. Hence, whoever has knowledge or faith is certain that he has them. But it is otherwise with grace and charity and such like, which perfect the appetitive faculty.

Reply Obj. 3: Sin has for its principal object commutable good, which is known to us. But the object or end of grace is unknown to us on account of the greatness of its light, according to 1 Tim. 6:16: "Who ... inhabiteth light inaccessible."

Reply Obj. 4: The Apostle is here speaking of the gifts of glory, which have been given to us in hope, and these we know most certainly by faith, although we do not know for certain that we have grace to enable us to merit them. Or it may be said that he is speaking of the privileged knowledge, which comes of revelation. Hence he adds (1 Cor. 2:10): "But to us God hath revealed them by His Spirit."

Reply Obj. 5: What was said to Abraham may refer to experimental knowledge which springs from deeds of which we are cognizant. For in the deed that Abraham had just wrought, he could know experimentally that he had the fear of God. Or it may refer to a revelation.

# QUESTION 113

OF THE EFFECTS OF GRACE (In Ten Articles)

We have now to consider the effect of grace; (1) the justification of the ungodly, which is the effect of operating grace; and (2) merit, which is the effect of cooperating grace. Under the first head there are ten points of inquiry:

(1) What is the justification of the ungodly?

(2) Whether grace is required for it?

(3) Whether any movement of the free-will is required?

(4) Whether a movement of faith is required?

(5) Whether a movement of the free-will against sin is required?

(6) Whether the remission of sins is to be reckoned with the foregoing?

(7) Whether the justification of the ungodly is a work of time or is sudden?

(8) Of the natural order of the things concurring to justification;

(9) Whether the justification of the ungodly is God's greatest work?

(10) Whether the justification of the ungodly is miraculous?

FIRST ARTICLE [I-II, Q. 113, Art. 1]

Whether the Justification of the Ungodly Is the Remission of Sins?

Objection 1: It would seem that the justification of the ungodly is not the remission of sins. For sin is opposed not only to justice, but to all the other virtues, as stated above (Q. 71, A. 1). Now justification signifies a certain movement towards justice. Therefore not even remission of sin is justification, since movement is from one contrary to the other.

Obj. 2: Further, everything ought to be named from what is predominant in it, according to *De Anima* ii, text. 49. Now the remission of sins is brought about chiefly by faith, according to Acts 15:9: "Purifying their hearts by faith"; and by charity, according to Prov. 10:12: "Charity covereth all sins." Therefore the remission of sins ought to be named after faith or charity rather than justice.

Obj. 3: Further, the remission of sins seems to be the same as being called, for whoever is called is afar off, and we are afar off from God by sin. But one is called before being justified according to Rom. 8:30: "And whom He called, them He also justified." Therefore justification is not the remission of sins.

*On the contrary,* On Rom. 8:30, "Whom He called, them He also justified," the gloss says i.e. "by the remission of sins." Therefore the remission of sins is justification.

*I answer that,* Justification taken passively implies a movement towards justice, as heating implies a movement towards heat. But since justice, by its nature, implies a certain rectitude of order, it may be taken in two ways: first, inasmuch as it implies a right order in man's act, and thus justice is placed amongst the virtues—either as particular justice, which directs a man's acts by regulating them in relation to his fellowman—or as legal justice, which directs a man's acts by regulating them in their relation to the common good of society, as appears from *Ethic.* v, 1.

Secondly, justice is so-called inasmuch as it implies a certain rectitude of order in the interior disposition of a man, in so far as what is highest in man is subject to God, and the inferior powers of the soul are subject to the superior, i.e. to the reason; and this disposition the Philosopher calls "justice metaphorically speaking" (Ethic. v, 11). Now this justice may be in man in two ways: first, by simple generation, which is from privation to form; and thus justification may belong even to such as are not in sin, when they receive this justice from God, as Adam is said to have received original justice. Secondly, this justice may be brought about in man by a movement from one contrary to the other, and thus justification implies a transmutation from the state of injustice to the aforesaid state of justice. And it is thus we are now speaking of the justification of the ungodly, according to the Apostle (Rom. 4:5): "But to him that worketh not, yet believeth in Him that justifieth the ungodly," etc. And because movement is named after its term *whereto* rather than from its term whence, the transmutation whereby anyone is changed by the remission of sins from the state of ungodliness to the state of justice, borrows its name from its term *whereto,* and is called "justification of the ungodly."

Reply Obj. 1: Every sin, inasmuch as it implies the disorder of a mind not subject to God, may be called injustice, as being contrary to the aforesaid justice, according to 1 John 3:4: "Whosoever committeth sin, committeth also iniquity; and sin is iniquity." And thus the removal of any sin is called the justification of the ungodly.

Reply Obj. 2: Faith and charity imply a special directing of the human mind to God by the intellect and will; whereas justice implies a general rectitude of order. Hence this transmutation is named after justice rather than after charity or faith.

Reply Obj. 3: Being called refers to God's help moving and exciting our mind to give up sin, and this motion of God is not the remission of sins, but its cause.

SECOND ARTICLE [I-II, Q. 113, Art. 2]

Whether the Infusion of Grace Is Required for the Remission of Guilt, i.e., for the Justification of the Ungodly?

Objection 1: It would seem that for the remission of guilt, which is the justification of the ungodly, no infusion of grace is required. For anyone may be moved from one contrary without being led to the other, if the contraries are not immediate. Now the state of guilt and the state of grace are not immediate contraries; for there is the middle state of innocence wherein a man has neither grace nor guilt. Hence a man may be pardoned his guilt without his being brought to a state of grace.

Obj. 2: Further, the remission of guilt consists in the Divine imputation, according to Ps. 31:2: "Blessed is the man to whom the Lord hath not imputed sin." Now the infusion of grace puts something into our soul, as stated above (Q. 110, A. 1). Hence the infusion of grace is not required for the remission of guilt.

Obj. 3: Further, no one can be subject to two contraries at once. Now some sins are contraries, as wastefulness and miserliness. Hence whoever is subject to the sin of wastefulness is not simultaneously subject to the sin of miserliness, yet it may happen that he has been subject to it hitherto. Hence by sinning with the vice of wastefulness he is freed from the sin of miserliness. And thus a sin is remitted without grace.

*On the contrary,* It is written (Rom. 3:24): "Justified freely by His grace."

*I answer that,* by sinning a man offends God as stated above (Q. 71, A. 5). Now an offense is remitted to anyone, only when the soul of the offender is at peace with the offended. Hence sin is remitted to us, when God is at peace with us, and this peace consists in the love whereby God loves us. Now God's love, considered on the part of the Divine act, is eternal and unchangeable; whereas, as regards the effect it imprints on us, it is sometimes interrupted, inasmuch as we sometimes fall short of it and once more require it. Now the effect of the Divine love in us, which is taken away by sin, is grace, whereby a man is made worthy of eternal life, from which sin shuts him out. Hence we could not conceive the remission of guilt, without the infusion of grace.

Reply Obj. 1: More is required for an offender to pardon an offense, than for one who has committed no offense, not to be hated. For it may happen amongst men that one man neither hates nor loves another. But if the other offends him, then the forgiveness of the offense can only spring from a special goodwill. Now God's goodwill is said to be restored to man by the gift of grace; and hence although a man before sinning may be without grace and without guilt, yet that he is without guilt after sinning can only be because he has grace.

Reply Obj. 2: As God's love consists not merely in the act of the Divine will but also implies a certain effect of grace, as stated above (Q. 110, A. 1), so likewise, when God does not impute sin to a man, there is implied a certain effect in him to whom the sin is not imputed; for it proceeds from the Divine love, that sin is not imputed to a man by God.

Reply Obj. 3: As Augustine says (De Nup. et Concup. i, 26), if to leave off sinning was the same as to have no sin, it would be enough if Scripture warned us thus: "'My son, hast thou sinned? do so no more?' Now this is not enough, but it is added: 'But for thy former sins also pray that they may be forgiven thee.'" For the act of sin passes, but the guilt remains, as stated above (Q. 87, A. 6). Hence when anyone passes from the sin of one vice to the sin of a contrary vice, he ceases to have the act of the former sin, but he does not cease to have the guilt, hence he may have the guilt of both sins at once. For sins are not contrary to each other on the part of their turning from God, wherein sin has its guilt.

THIRD ARTICLE [I-II, Q. 113, Art. 3]

Whether for the Justification of the Ungodly Is Required a Movement of the Free-will?

Objection 1: It would seem that no movement of the free-will is required for the justification of the ungodly. For we see that by the sacrament of Baptism, infants and sometimes adults are justified without a movement of their free-will: hence Augustine says (Confess. iv) that when one of his friends was taken with a fever, "he lay for a long time senseless and in a deadly sweat, and when he was despaired of, he was baptized without his knowing, and was regenerated"; which is effected by sanctifying grace. Now God does not confine His power to the sacraments. Hence He can justify a man without the sacraments, and without any movement of the free-will.

Obj. 2: Further, a man has not the use of reason when asleep, and without it there can be no movement of the free-will. But Solomon received from God the gift of wisdom when asleep, as related in 3 Kings 3 and 2 Paral 1. Hence with equal reason the gift of sanctifying grace is sometimes bestowed by God on man without the movement of his free-will.

Obj. 3: Further, grace is preserved by the same cause as brings it into being, for Augustine says (Gen. ad lit. viii, 12) that "so ought man to turn to God as he is ever made just by Him." Now grace is preserved in man without a movement of his free-will. Hence it can be infused in the beginning without a movement of the free-will.

*On the contrary,* It is written (John 6:45): "Every one that hath heard of the Father, and hath learned, cometh to Me." Now to learn cannot be without a movement of the free-will, since the learner assents to the teacher. Hence, no one comes to the Father by justifying grace without a movement of the free-will.

*I answer that,* The justification of the ungodly is brought about by God moving man to justice. For He it is "that justifieth the ungodly" according to Rom. 4:5. Now God moves everything in its own manner, just as we see that in natural things, what is heavy and what is light are moved differently, on account of their diverse natures. Hence He moves man to justice according to the condition of his human nature. But it is man's proper nature to have free-will. Hence in him who has the use of reason, God's motion to justice does not take place without a movement of the free-will; but He so infuses the gift of justifying grace that at the same time He moves the free-will to accept the gift of grace, in such as are capable of being moved thus.

Reply Obj. 1: Infants are not capable of the movement of their free-will; hence it is by the mere infusion of their souls that God moves them to justice. Now this cannot be brought about without a sacrament; because as original sin, from which they are justified, does not come to them from their own will, but by carnal generation, so also is grace given them by Christ through spiritual regeneration. And the same reason holds good with madmen and idiots that have never had the use of their free-will. But in the case of one who has had the use of his free-will and afterwards has lost it either through sickness or sleep, he does not obtain justifying grace by the exterior rite of Baptism, or of any other sacrament, unless he intended to make use of this sacrament, and this can only be by the use of his free-will. And it was in this way that he of whom Augustine speaks was regenerated, because both previously and afterwards he assented to the Baptism.

Reply Obj. 2: Solomon neither merited nor received wisdom whilst asleep; but it was declared to him in his sleep that on account of his previous desire wisdom would be infused into him by God. Hence it is said in his person (Wis. 7:7): "I wished, and understanding was given unto me."

Or it may be said that his sleep was not natural, but was the sleep of prophecy, according to Num. 12:6: "If there be among you a prophet of the Lord, I will appear to him in a vision, or I will speak to him in a dream." In such cases the use of free-will remains.

And yet it must be observed that the comparison between the gift of wisdom and the gift of justifying grace does not hold. For the gift of justifying grace especially ordains a man to good, which is the object of the will; and hence a man is moved to it by a movement of the will which is a movement of free-will. But wisdom perfects the intellect which precedes the will; hence without any complete movement of the free-will, the intellect can be enlightened with the gift of wisdom, even as we see that things are revealed to men in sleep, according to Job 33:15, 16: "When deep sleep falleth upon men and they are sleeping in their beds, then He openeth the ears of men, and teaching, instructeth them in what they are to learn."

Reply Obj. 3: In the infusion of justifying grace there is a certain transmutation of the human soul, and hence a proper movement of the human soul is required in order that the soul may be moved in its own manner. But the conservation of grace is without transmutation: no movement on the part of the soul is required but only a continuation of the Divine influx.

FOURTH ARTICLE [I-II, Q. 113, Art. 4]

Whether a Movement of Faith Is Required for the Justification of the Ungodly?

Objection 1: It would seem that no movement of faith is required for the justification of the ungodly. For as a man is justified by faith, so also by other things, viz. by fear, of which it is written (Ecclus. 1:27): "The fear of the Lord driveth out sin, for he that is without fear cannot be justified"; and again by charity, according to Luke 7:47: "Many sins are forgiven her because she hath loved much"; and again by humility, according to James 4:6: "God resisteth the proud and giveth grace to the humble"; and again by mercy, according to Prov. 15:27: "By mercy and faith sins are purged away." Hence the movement of faith is no more required for the justification of the ungodly, than the movements of the aforesaid virtues.

Obj. 2: Further, the act of faith is required for justification only inasmuch as a man knows God by faith. But a man may know God in other ways, viz. by natural knowledge, and by the gift of wisdom. Hence no act of faith is required for the justification of the ungodly.

Obj. 3: Further, there are several articles of faith. Therefore if the act of faith is required for the justification of the ungodly, it would seem that a man ought to think on every article of faith when he is first justified. But this seems inconvenient, since such thought would require a long delay of time. Hence it seems that an act of faith is not required for the justification of the ungodly.

*On the contrary,* It is written (Rom. 5:1): "Being justified therefore by faith, let us have peace with God."

*I answer that,* As stated above (A. 3) a movement of free-will is required for the justification of the ungodly, inasmuch as man's mind is moved by God. Now God moves man's soul by turning it to Himself according to Ps. 84:7 (Septuagint): "Thou wilt turn us, O God, and bring us to life." Hence for the justification of the ungodly a movement of the mind is required, by which it is turned to God. Now the first turning to God is by faith, according to Heb. 11:6: "He that cometh to God must believe that He is." Hence a movement of faith is required for the justification of the ungodly.

Reply Obj. 1: The movement of faith is not perfect unless it is quickened by charity; hence in the justification of the ungodly, a movement of charity is infused together with the movement of faith. Now free-will is moved to God by being subject to Him; hence an act of filial fear and an act of humility also concur. For it may happen that one and the same act of free-will springs from different virtues, when one commands and another is commanded, inasmuch as the act may be ordained to various ends. But the act of mercy counteracts sin either by way of satisfying for it, and thus it follows justification; or by way of preparation, inasmuch as the merciful obtain mercy; and thus it can either precede justification, or concur with the other virtues towards justification, inasmuch as mercy is included in the love of our neighbor.

Reply Obj. 2: By natural knowledge a man is not turned to God, according as He is the object of beatitude and the cause of justification. Hence such knowledge does not suffice for justification. But the gift of wisdom presupposes the knowledge of faith, as stated above (Q. 68, A. 4, ad 3).

Reply Obj. 3: As the Apostle says (Rom. 4:5), "to him that ... believeth in Him that justifieth the ungodly his faith is reputed to justice, according to the purpose of the grace of God." Hence it is clear that in the justification of the ungodly an act of faith is required in order that a man may believe that God justifies man through the mystery of Christ.

FIFTH ARTICLE [I-II, Q. 113, Art. 5]

Whether for the Justification of the Ungodly There Is Required a Movement of the Free-will Towards Sin?

Objection 1: It would seem that no movement of the free-will towards sin is required for the justification of the ungodly. For charity alone suffices to take away sin, according to Prov. 10:12: "Charity covereth all sins." Now the object of charity is not sin. Therefore for this justification of the ungodly no movement of the free-will towards sin is required.

Obj. 2: Further, whoever is tending onward, ought not to look back, according to Phil. 3:13, 14: "Forgetting the things that are behind, and stretching forth myself to those that are before, I press towards the mark, to the prize of the supernal vocation." But whoever is stretching forth to righteousness has his sins behind him. Hence he ought to forget them, and not stretch forth to them by a movement of his free-will.

Obj. 3: Further, in the justification of the ungodly one sin is not remitted without another, for "it is irreverent to expect half a pardon from God" [*Cap., Sunt. plures: Dist. iii, De Poenit.]. Hence, in the justification of the ungodly, if man's free-will must move against sin, he ought to think of all his sins. But this is unseemly, both because a great space of time would be required for such thought, and because a man could not obtain the forgiveness of such sins as he had forgotten. Hence for the justification of the ungodly no movement of the free-will is required.

*On the contrary,* It is written (Ps. 31:5): "I will confess against myself my injustice to the Lord; and Thou hast forgiven the wickedness of my sin."

*I answer that,* As stated above (A. 1), the justification of the ungodly is a certain movement whereby the human mind is moved by God from the state of sin to the state of justice. Hence it is necessary for the human mind to regard both extremes by an act of free-will, as a body in local movement is related to both terms of the movement. Now it is clear that in local movement the moving body leaves the term *whence* and nears the term whereto. Hence the human mind whilst it is being justified, must, by a movement of its free-will withdraw from sin and draw near to justice.

Now to withdraw from sin and to draw near to justice, in an act of free-will, means detestation and desire. For Augustine says on the words "the hireling fleeth," etc. (John 10:12): "Our emotions are the movements of our soul; joy is the soul's outpouring; fear is the soul's flight; your soul goes forward when you seek; your soul flees, when you are afraid." Hence in the justification of the ungodly there must be two acts of the free-will—one, whereby it tends to God's justice; the other whereby it hates sin.

Reply Obj. 1: It belongs to the same virtue to seek one contrary and to avoid the other; and hence, as it belongs to charity to love God, so likewise, to detest sin whereby the soul is separated from God.

Reply Obj. 2: A man ought not to return to those things that are behind, by loving them; but, for that matter, he ought to forget them, lest he be drawn to them. Yet he ought to recall them to mind, in order to detest them; for this is to fly from them.

Reply Obj. 3: Previous to justification a man must detest each sin he remembers to have committed, and from this remembrance the soul goes on to have a general movement of detestation with regard to all sins committed, in which are included such sins as have been forgotten. For a man is then in such a frame of mind that he would be sorry even for those he does not remember, if they were present to his memory; and this movement cooperates in his justification.

SIXTH ARTICLE [I-II, Q. 113, Art. 6]

Whether the Remission of Sins Ought to Be Reckoned Amongst the Things Required for Justification?

Objection 1: It would seem that the remission of sins ought not to be reckoned amongst the things required for justification. For the substance of a thing is not reckoned together with those that are required for a thing; thus a man is not reckoned together with his body and soul. But the justification of the ungodly is itself the remission of sins, as stated above (A. 1). Therefore the remission of sins ought not to be reckoned among the things required for the justification of the ungodly.

Obj. 2: Further, infusion of grace and remission of sins are the same; as illumination and expulsion of darkness are the same. But a thing ought not to be reckoned together with itself; for unity is opposed to multitude. Therefore the remission of sins ought not to be reckoned with the infusion of grace.

Obj. 3: Further, the remission of sin follows as effect from cause, from the free-will's movement towards God and sin; since it is by faith and contrition that sin is forgiven. But an effect ought not to be reckoned with its cause; since things thus enumerated together, and, as it were, condivided, are by nature simultaneous. Hence the remission of sins ought not to be reckoned with the things required for the justification of the ungodly.

*On the contrary,* In reckoning what is required for a thing we ought not to pass over the end, which is the chief part of everything. Now the remission of sins is the end of the justification of the ungodly; for it is written (Isa. 27:9): "This is all the fruit, that the sin thereof should be taken away." Hence the remission of sins ought to be reckoned amongst the things required for justification.

*I answer that,* There are four things which are accounted to be necessary for the justification of the ungodly, viz. the infusion of grace, the movement of the free-will towards God by faith, the movement of the free-will towards sin, and the remission of sins. The reason for this is that, as stated above (A. 1), the justification of the ungodly is a movement whereby the soul is moved by God from a state of sin to a state of justice. Now in the movement whereby one thing is moved by another, three things are required: first, the motion of the mover; secondly, the movement of the moved; thirdly, the consummation of the movement, or the attainment of the end. On the part of the Divine motion, there is the infusion of grace; on the part of the free-will which is moved, there are two movements—of departure from the term *whence,* and of approach to the term *whereto* ; but the consummation of the movement or the attainment of the end of the movement is implied in the remission of sins; for in this is the justification of the ungodly completed.

Reply Obj. 1: The justification of the ungodly is called the remission of sins, even as every movement has its species from its term. Nevertheless, many other things are required in order to reach the term, as stated above (A. 5).

Reply Obj. 2: The infusion of grace and the remission of sin may be considered in two ways: first, with respect to the substance of the act, and thus they are the same; for by the same act God bestows grace and remits sin. Secondly, they may be considered on the part of the objects; and thus they differ by the difference between guilt, which is taken away, and grace, which is infused; just as in natural things generation and corruption differ, although the generation of one thing is the corruption of another.

Reply Obj. 3: This enumeration is not the division of a genus into its species, in which the things enumerated must be simultaneous; but it is division of the things required for the completion of anything; and in this enumeration we may have what precedes and what follows, since some of the principles and parts of a composite thing may precede and some follow.

SEVENTH ARTICLE [I-II, Q. 113, Art. 7]

Whether the Justification of the Ungodly Takes Place in an Instant or Successively?

Objection 1: It would seem that the justification of the ungodly does not take place in an instant, but successively, since, as already stated (A. 3), for the justification of the ungodly, there is required a movement of free-will. Now the act of the free-will is choice, which requires the deliberation of counsel, as stated above (Q. 13, A. 1). Hence, since deliberation implies a certain reasoning process, and this implies succession, the justification of the ungodly would seem to be successive.

Obj. 2: Further, the free-will's movement is not without actual consideration. But it is impossible to understand many things actually and at once, as stated above (I, Q. 85, A. 4). Hence, since for the justification of the ungodly there is required a movement of the free-will towards several things, viz. towards God and towards sin, it would seem impossible for the justification of the ungodly to be in an instant.

Obj. 3: Further, a form that may be greater or less, e.g. blackness or whiteness, is received successively by its subject. Now grace may be greater or less, as stated above (Q. 112, A. 4). Hence it is not received suddenly by its subject. Therefore, seeing that the infusion of grace is required for the justification of the ungodly, it would seem that the justification of the ungodly cannot be in an instant.

Obj. 4: Further, the free-will's movement, which cooperates in justification, is meritorious; and hence it must proceed from grace, without which there is no merit, as we shall state further on (Q. 114, A. 2). Now a thing receives its form before operating by this form. Hence grace is first infused, and then the free-will is moved towards God and to detest sin. Hence justification is not all at once.

Obj. 5: Further, if grace is infused into the soul, there must be an instant when it first dwells in the soul; so, too, if sin is forgiven there must be a last instant that man is in sin. But it cannot be the same instant, otherwise opposites would be in the same simultaneously. Hence they must be two successive instants; between which there must be time, as the Philosopher says (Phys. vi, 1). Therefore the justification of the ungodly takes place not all at once, but successively.

*On the contrary,* The justification of the ungodly is caused by the justifying grace of the Holy Spirit. Now the Holy Spirit comes to men's minds suddenly, according to Acts 2:2: "And suddenly there came a sound from heaven as of a mighty wind coming," upon which the gloss says that "the grace of the Holy Ghost knows no tardy efforts." Hence the justification of the ungodly is not successive, but instantaneous.

*I answer that,* The entire justification of the ungodly consists as to its origin in the infusion of grace. For it is by grace that free-will is moved and sin is remitted. Now the infusion of grace takes place in an instant and without succession. And the reason of this is that if a form be not suddenly impressed upon its subject, it is either because that subject is not disposed, or because the agent needs time to dispose the subject. Hence we see that immediately the matter is disposed by a preceding alteration, the substantial form accrues to the matter; thus because the atmosphere of itself is disposed to receive light, it is suddenly illuminated by a body actually luminous. Now it was stated (Q. 112, A. 2) that God, in order to infuse grace into the soul, needs no disposition, save what He Himself has made. And sometimes this sufficient disposition for the reception of grace He makes suddenly, sometimes gradually and successively, as stated above (Q. 112, A. 2, ad 2). For the reason why a natural agent cannot suddenly dispose matter is that in the matter there is a resistant which has some disproportion with the power of the agent; and hence we see that the stronger the agent, the more speedily is the matter disposed. Therefore, since the Divine power is infinite, it can suddenly dispose any matter whatsoever to its form; and much more man's free-will, whose movement is by nature instantaneous. Therefore the justification of the ungodly by God takes place in an instant.

Reply Obj. 1: The movement of the free-will, which concurs in the justification of the ungodly, is a consent to detest sin, and to draw near to God; and this consent takes place suddenly. Sometimes, indeed, it happens that deliberation precedes, yet this is not of the substance of justification, but a way of justification; as local movement is a way of illumination, and alteration to generation.

Reply Obj. 2: As stated above (I, Q. 85, A. 5), there is nothing to prevent two things being understood at once, in so far as they are somehow one; thus we understand the subject and predicate together, inasmuch as they are united in the order of one affirmation. And in the same manner can the free-will be moved to two things at once in so far as one is ordained to the other. Now the free-will's movement towards sin is ordained to the free-will's movement towards God, since a man detests sin, as contrary to God, to Whom he wishes to cling. Hence in the justification of the ungodly the free-will simultaneously detests sin and turns to God, even as a body approaches one point and withdraws from another simultaneously.

Reply Obj. 3: The reason why a form is not received instantaneously in the matter is not the fact that it can inhere more or less; for thus the light would not be suddenly received in the air, which can be illumined more or less. But the reason is to be sought on the part of the disposition of the matter or subject, as stated above.

Reply Obj. 4: The same instant the form is acquired, the thing begins to operate with the form; as fire, the instant it is generated moves upwards, and if its movement was instantaneous, it would be terminated in the same instant. Now to will and not to will—the movements of the free-will—are not successive, but instantaneous. Hence the justification of the ungodly must not be successive.

Reply Obj. 5: The succession of opposites in the same subject must be looked at differently in the things that are subject to time and in those that are above time. For in those that are in time, there is no last instant in which the previous form inheres in the subject; but there is the last time, and the first instant that the subsequent form inheres in the matter or subject; and this for the reason, that in time we are not to consider one instant, since neither do instants succeed each other immediately in time, nor points in a line, as is proved in *Physic.* vi, 1. But time is terminated by an instant. Hence in the whole of the previous time wherein anything is moving towards its form, it is under the opposite form; but in the last instant of this time, which is the first instant of the subsequent time, it has the form which is the term of the movement.

But in those that are above time, it is otherwise. For if there be any succession of affections or intellectual conceptions in them (as in the angels), such succession is not measured by continuous time, but by discrete time, even as the things measured are not continuous, as stated above (I, Q. 53, AA. 2, 3). In these, therefore, there is a last instant in which the preceding is, and a first instant in which the subsequent is. Nor must there be time in between, since there is no continuity of time, which this would necessitate.

Now the human mind, which is justified, is, in itself, above time, but is subject to time accidentally, inasmuch as it understands with continuity and time, with respect to the phantasms in which it considers the intelligible species, as stated above (I, Q. 85, AA. 1, 2). We must, therefore, decide from this about its change as regards the condition of temporal movements, i.e. we must say that there is no last instant that sin inheres, but a last time; whereas there is a first instant that grace inheres; and in all the time previous sin inhered.

EIGHTH ARTICLE [I-II, Q. 113, Art. 8]

Whether the Infusion of Grace Is Naturally the First of the Things Required for the Justification of the Ungodly?

Objection 1: It would seem that the infusion of grace is not what is naturally required first for the justification of the ungodly. For we withdraw from evil before drawing near to good, according to Ps. 33:15: "Turn away from evil, and do good." Now the remission of sins regards the turning away from evil, and the infusion of grace regards the turning to good. Hence the remission of sin is naturally before the infusion of grace.

Obj. 2: Further, the disposition naturally precedes the form to which it disposes. Now the free-will's movement is a disposition for the reception of grace. Therefore it naturally precedes the infusion of grace.

Obj. 3: Further, sin hinders the soul from tending freely to God. Now a hindrance to movement must be removed before the movement takes place. Hence the remission of sin and the free-will's movement towards sin are naturally before the infusion of grace.

*On the contrary,* The cause is naturally prior to its effect. Now the infusion of grace is the cause of whatever is required for the justification of the ungodly, as stated above (A. 7). Therefore it is naturally prior to it.

*I answer that,* The aforesaid four things required for the justification of the ungodly are simultaneous in time, since the justification of the ungodly is not successive, as stated above (A. 7); but in the order of nature, one is prior to another; and in their natural order the first is the infusion of grace; the second, the free-will's movement towards God; the third, the free-will's movement towards sin; the fourth, the remission of sin.

The reason for this is that in every movement the motion of the mover is naturally first; the disposition of the matter, or the movement of the moved, is second; the end or term of the movement in which the motion of the mover rests, is last. Now the motion of God the Mover is the infusion of grace, as stated above (A. 6); the movement or disposition of the moved is the free-will's double movement; and the term or end of the movement is the remission of sin, as stated above (A. 6). Hence in their natural order the first in the justification of the ungodly is the infusion of grace; the second is the free-will's movement towards God; the third is the free-will's movement towards sin, for he who is being justified detests sin because it is against God, and thus the free-will's movement towards God naturally precedes the free-will's movement towards sin, since it is its cause and reason; the fourth and last is the remission of sin, to which this transmutation is ordained as to an end, as stated above (AA. 1, 6).

Reply Obj. 1: The withdrawal from one term and approach to another may be looked at in two ways: first, on the part of the thing moved, and thus the withdrawal from a term naturally precedes the approach to a term, since in the subject of movement the opposite which is put away is prior to the opposite which the subject moved attains to by its movement. But on the part of the agent it is the other way about, since the agent, by the form pre-existing in it, acts for the removal of the opposite form; as the sun by its light acts for the removal of darkness, and hence on the part of the sun, illumination is prior to the removal of darkness; but on the part of the atmosphere to be illuminated, to be freed from darkness is, in the order of nature, prior to being illuminated, although both are simultaneous in time. And since the infusion of grace and the remission of sin regard God Who justifies, hence in the order of nature the infusion of grace is prior to the freeing from sin. But if we look at what is on the part of the man justified, it is the other way about, since in the order of nature the being freed from sin is prior to the obtaining of justifying grace. Or it may be said that the term *whence* of justification is sin; and the term *whereto* is justice; and that grace is the cause of the forgiveness of sin and of obtaining of justice.

Reply Obj. 2: The disposition of the subject precedes the reception of the form, in the order of nature; yet it follows the action of the agent, whereby the subject is disposed. And hence the free-will's movement precedes the reception of grace in the order of nature, and follows the infusion of grace.

Reply Obj. 3: As the Philosopher says (Phys. ii, 9), in movements of the soul the movement toward the speculative principle or the practical end is the very first, but in exterior movements the removal of the impediment precedes the attainment of the end. And as the free-will's movement is a movement of the soul, in the order of nature it moves towards God as to its end, before removing the impediment of sin.

NINTH ARTICLE [I-II, Q. 113, Art. 9]

Whether the Justification of the Ungodly Is God's Greatest Work?

Objection 1: It would seem that the justification of the ungodly is not God's greatest work. For it is by the justification of the ungodly that we attain the grace of a wayfarer. Now by glorification we receive heavenly grace, which is greater. Hence the glorification of angels and men is a greater work than the justification of the ungodly.

Obj. 2: Further, the justification of the ungodly is ordained to the particular good of one man. But the good of the universe is greater than the good of one man, as is plain from *Ethic.* i, 2. Hence the creation of heaven and earth is a greater work than the justification of the ungodly.

Obj. 3: Further, to make something from nothing, where there is nought to cooperate with the agent, is greater than to make something with the cooperation of the recipient. Now in the work of creation something is made from nothing, and hence nothing can cooperate with the agent; but in the justification of the ungodly God makes something from something, i.e. a just man from a sinner, and there is a cooperation on man's part, since there is a movement of the free-will, as stated above (A. 3). Hence the justification of the ungodly is not God's greatest work.

*On the contrary,* It is written (Ps. 144:9): "His tender mercies are over all His works," and in a collect [*Tenth Sunday after Pentecost] we say: "O God, Who dost show forth Thine all-mightiness most by pardoning and having mercy," and Augustine, expounding the words, "greater than these shall he do" (John 14:12) says that "for a just man to be made from a sinner, is greater than to create heaven and earth."

*I answer that,* A work may be called great in two ways: first, on the part of the mode of action, and thus the work of creation is the greatest work, wherein something is made from nothing; secondly, a work may be called great on account of what is made, and thus the justification of the ungodly, which terminates at the eternal good of a share in the Godhead, is greater than the creation of heaven and earth, which terminates at the good of mutable nature. Hence, Augustine, after saying that "for a just man to be made from a sinner is greater than to create heaven and earth," adds, "for heaven and earth shall pass away, but the justification of the ungodly shall endure."

Again, we must bear in mind that a thing is called great in two ways: first, in an absolute quantity, and thus the gift of glory is greater than the gift of grace that sanctifies the ungodly; and in this respect the glorification of the just is greater than the justification of the ungodly. Secondly, a thing may be said to be great in proportionate quantity, and thus the gift of grace that justifies the ungodly is greater than the gift of glory that beatifies the just, for the gift of grace exceeds the worthiness of the ungodly, who are worthy of punishment, more than the gift of glory exceeds the worthiness of the just, who by the fact of their justification are worthy of glory. Hence Augustine says: "Let him that can, judge whether it is greater to create the angels just, than to justify the ungodly. Certainly, if they both betoken equal power, one betokens greater mercy."

And thus the reply to the first [objection] is clear.

Reply Obj. 2: The good of the universe is greater than the particular good of one, if we consider both in the same genus. But the good of grace in one is greater than the good of nature in the whole universe.

Reply Obj. 3: This objection rests on the manner of acting, in which way creation is God's greatest work.

TENTH ARTICLE [I-II, Q. 113, Art. 10]

Whether the Justification of the Ungodly Is a Miraculous Work?

Objection 1: It would seem that the justification of the ungodly is a miraculous work. For miraculous works are greater than non-miraculous. Now the justification of the ungodly is greater than the other miraculous works, as is clear from the quotation from Augustine (A. 9). Hence the justification of the ungodly is a miraculous work.

Obj. 2: Further, the movement of the will in the soul is like the natural inclination in natural things. But when God works in natural things against their inclination of their nature, it is a miraculous work, as when He gave sight to the blind or raised the dead. Now the will of the ungodly is bent on evil. Hence, since God in justifying a man moves him to good, it would seem that the justification of the ungodly is miraculous.

Obj. 3: Further, as wisdom is a gift of God, so also is justice. Now it is miraculous that anyone should suddenly obtain wisdom from God without study. Therefore it is miraculous that the ungodly should be justified by God.

*On the contrary,* Miraculous works are beyond natural power. Now the justification of the ungodly is not beyond natural power; for Augustine says (De Praed. Sanct. v) that "to be capable of having faith and to be capable of having charity belongs to man's nature; but to have faith and charity belongs to the grace of the faithful." Therefore the justification of the ungodly is not miraculous.

*I answer that,* In miraculous works it is usual to find three things: the first is on the part of the active power, because they can only be performed by Divine power; and they are simply wondrous, since their cause is hidden, as stated above (I, Q. 105, A. 7). And thus both the justification of the ungodly and the creation of the world, and, generally speaking, every work that can be done by God alone, is miraculous.

Secondly, in certain miraculous works it is found that the form introduced is beyond the natural power of such matter, as in the resurrection of the dead, life is above the natural power of such a body. And thus the justification of the ungodly is not miraculous, because the soul is naturally capable of grace; since from its having been made to the likeness of God, it is fit to receive God by grace, as Augustine says, in the above quotation.

Thirdly, in miraculous works something is found besides the usual and customary order of causing an effect, as when a sick man suddenly and beyond the wonted course of healing by nature or art, receives perfect health; and thus the justification of the ungodly is sometimes miraculous and sometimes not. For the common and wonted course of justification is that God moves the soul interiorly and that man is converted to God, first by an imperfect conversion, that it may afterwards become perfect; because "charity begun merits increase, and when increased merits perfection," as Augustine says (In Epist. Joan. Tract. v). Yet God sometimes moves the soul so vehemently that it reaches the perfection of justice at once, as took place in the conversion of Paul, which was accompanied at the same time by a miraculous external prostration. Hence the conversion of Paul is commemorated in the Church as miraculous.

Reply Obj. 1: Certain miraculous works, although they are less than the justification of the ungodly, as regards the good caused, are beyond the wonted order of such effects, and thus have more of the nature of a miracle.

Reply Obj. 2: It is not a miraculous work, whenever a natural thing is moved contrary to its inclination, otherwise it would be miraculous for water to be heated, or for a stone to be thrown upwards; but only whenever this takes place beyond the order of the proper cause, which naturally does this. Now no other cause save God can justify the ungodly, even as nothing save fire can heat water. Hence the justification of the ungodly by God is not miraculous in this respect.

Reply Obj. 3: A man naturally acquires wisdom and knowledge from God by his own talent and study. Hence it is miraculous when a man is made wise or learned outside this order. But a man does not naturally acquire justifying grace by his own action, but by God's. Hence there is no parity.

# QUESTION 114

OF MERIT (In Ten Articles)

We must now consider merit, which is the effect of cooperating grace; and under this head there are ten points of inquiry:

(1) Whether a man can merit anything from God?

(2) Whether without grace anyone can merit eternal life?

(3) Whether anyone with grace may merit eternal life condignly?

(4) Whether it is chiefly through the instrumentality of charity that grace is the principle of merit?

(5) Whether a man may merit the first grace for himself?

(6) Whether he may merit it for someone else?

(7) Whether anyone can merit restoration after sin?

(8) Whether he can merit for himself an increase of grace or charity?

(9) Whether he can merit final perseverance?

(10) Whether temporal goods fall under merit?

FIRST ARTICLE [I-II, Q. 114, Art. 1]

Whether a Man May Merit Anything from God?

Objection 1: It would seem that a man can merit nothing from God. For no one, it would seem, merits by giving another his due. But by all the good we do, we cannot make sufficient return to God, since yet more is His due, as also the Philosopher says (Ethic. viii, 14). Hence it is written (Luke 17:10): "When you have done all these things that are commanded you, say: We are unprofitable servants; we have done that which we ought to do." Therefore a man can merit nothing from God.

Obj. 2: Further, it would seem that a man merits nothing from God, by what profits himself only, and profits God nothing. Now by acting well, a man profits himself or another man, but not God, for it is written (Job 35:7): "If thou do justly, what shalt thou give Him, or what shall He receive of thy hand." Hence a man can merit nothing from God.

Obj. 3: Further, whoever merits anything from another makes him his debtor; for a man's wage is a debt due to him. Now God is no one's debtor; hence it is written (Rom. 11:35): "Who hath first given to Him, and recompense shall be made to him?" Hence no one can merit anything from God.

*On the contrary,* It is written (Jer. 31:16): "There is a reward for thy work." Now a reward means something bestowed by reason of merit. Hence it would seem that a man may merit from God.

*I answer that,* Merit and reward refer to the same, for a reward means something given anyone in return for work or toil, as a price for it. Hence, as it is an act of justice to give a just price for anything received from another, so also is it an act of justice to make a return for work or toil. Now justice is a kind of equality, as is clear from the Philosopher (Ethic. v, 3), and hence justice is simply between those that are simply equal; but where there is no absolute equality between them, neither is there absolute justice, but there may be a certain manner of justice, as when we speak of a father's or a master's right (Ethic. v, 6), as the Philosopher says. And hence where there is justice simply, there is the character of merit and reward simply. But where there is no simple right, but only relative, there is no character of merit simply, but only relatively, in so far as the character of justice is found there, since the child merits something from his father and the slave from his lord.

Now it is clear that between God and man there is the greatest inequality: for they are infinitely apart, and all man's good is from God. Hence there can be no justice of absolute equality between man and God, but only of a certain proportion, inasmuch as both operate after their own manner. Now the manner and measure of human virtue is in man from God. Hence man's merit with God only exists on the presupposition of the Divine ordination, so that man obtains from God, as a reward of his operation, what God gave him the power of operation for, even as natural things by their proper movements and operations obtain that to which they were ordained by God; differently, indeed, since the rational creature moves itself to act by its free-will, hence its action has the character of merit, which is not so in other creatures.

Reply Obj. 1: Man merits, inasmuch as he does what he ought, by his free-will; otherwise the act of justice whereby anyone discharges a debt would not be meritorious.

Reply Obj. 2: God seeks from our goods not profit, but glory, i.e. the manifestation of His goodness; even as He seeks it also in His own works. Now nothing accrues to Him, but only to ourselves, by our worship of Him. Hence we merit from God, not that by our works anything accrues to Him, but inasmuch as we work for His glory.

Reply Obj. 3: Since our action has the character of merit, only on the presupposition of the Divine ordination, it does not follow that God is made our debtor simply, but His own, inasmuch as it is right that His will should be carried out.

SECOND ARTICLE [I-II, Q. 114, Art. 2]

Whether Anyone Without Grace Can Merit Eternal Life?

Objection 1: It would seem that without grace anyone can merit eternal life. For man merits from

God what he is divinely ordained to, as stated above (A. 1). Now man by his nature is ordained to beatitude as his end; hence, too, he naturally wishes to be blessed. Hence man by his natural endowments and without grace can merit beatitude which is eternal life.

Obj. 2: Further, the less a work is due, the more meritorious it is. Now, less due is that work which is done by one who has received fewer benefits. Hence, since he who has only natural endowments has received fewer gifts from God, than he who has gratuitous gifts as well as nature, it would seem that his works are more meritorious with God. And thus if he who has grace can merit eternal life to some extent, much more may he who has no grace.

Obj. 3: Further, God's mercy and liberality infinitely surpass human mercy and liberality. Now a man may merit from another, even though he has not hitherto had his grace. Much more, therefore, would it seem that a man without grace may merit eternal life.

*On the contrary,* The Apostle says (Rom. 6:23): "The grace of God, life everlasting."

*I answer that,* Man without grace may be looked at in two states, as was said above (Q. 109, A. 2): the first, a state of perfect nature, in which Adam was before his sin; the second, a state of corrupt nature, in which we are before being restored by grace. Therefore, if we speak of man in the first state, there is only one reason why man cannot merit eternal life without grace, by his purely natural endowments, viz. because man's merit depends on the Divine pre-ordination. Now no act of anything whatsoever is divinely ordained to anything exceeding the proportion of the powers which are the principles of its act; for it is a law of Divine providence that nothing shall act beyond its powers. Now everlasting life is a good exceeding the proportion of created nature; since it exceeds its knowledge and desire, according to 1 Cor. 2:9: "Eye hath not seen, nor ear heard, neither hath it entered into the heart of man." And hence it is that no created nature is a sufficient principle of an act meritorious of eternal life, unless there is added a supernatural gift, which we call grace. But if we speak of man as existing in sin, a second reason is added to this, viz. the impediment of sin. For since sin is an offense against God, excluding us from eternal life, as is clear from what has been said above (Q. 71, A. 6; Q. 113, A. 2), no one existing in a state of mortal sin can merit eternal life unless first he be reconciled to God, through his sin being forgiven, which is brought about by grace. For the sinner deserves not life, but death, according to Rom. 6:23: "The wages of sin is death."

Reply Obj. 1: God ordained human nature to attain the end of eternal life, not by its own strength, but by the help of grace; and in this way its act can be meritorious of eternal life.

Reply Obj. 2: Without grace a man cannot have a work equal to a work proceeding from grace, since the more perfect the principle, the more perfect the action. But the objection would hold good, if we supposed the operations equal in both cases.

Reply Obj. 3: With regard to the first reason adduced, the case is different in God and in man. For a man receives all his power of well-doing from God, and not from man. Hence a man can merit nothing from God except by His gift, which the Apostle expresses aptly saying (Rom. 11:35): "Who hath first given to Him, and recompense shall be made to him?" But man may merit from man, before he has received anything from him, by what he has received from God.

But as regards the second proof taken from the impediment of sin, the case is similar with man and God, since one man cannot merit from another whom he has offended, unless he makes satisfaction to him and is reconciled.

THIRD ARTICLE [I-II, Q. 114, Art. 3]

Whether a Man in Grace Can Merit Eternal Life Condignly?

Objection 1: It would seem that a man in grace cannot merit eternal life condignly, for the Apostle says (Rom. 8:18): "The sufferings of this time are not worthy ( *condignae* ) to be compared with the glory to come, that shall be revealed in us." But of all meritorious works, the sufferings of the saints would seem the most meritorious. Therefore no works of men are meritorious of eternal life condignly.

Obj. 2: Further, on Rom. 6:23, "The grace of God, life everlasting," a gloss says: "He might have truly said: 'The wages of justice, life everlasting'; but He preferred to say 'The grace of God, life everlasting,' that we may know that God leads us to life everlasting of His own mercy and not by our merits." Now when anyone merits something condignly he receives it not from mercy, but from merit. Hence it would seem that a man with grace cannot merit life everlasting condignly.

Obj. 3: Further, merit that equals the reward, would seem to be condign. Now no act of the present life can equal everlasting life, which surpasses our knowledge and our desire, and moreover, surpasses the charity or love of the wayfarer, even as it exceeds nature. Therefore with grace a man cannot merit eternal life condignly.

*On the contrary,* What is granted in accordance with a fair judgment, would seem a condign reward. But life everlasting is granted by God, in accordance with the judgment of justice, according to 2 Tim. 4:8: "As to the rest, there is laid up for me a crown of justice, which the Lord, the just judge, will render to me in that day." Therefore man merits everlasting life condignly.

*I answer that,* Man's meritorious work may be considered in two ways: first, as it proceeds from free-will; secondly, as it proceeds from the grace of the Holy Ghost. If it is considered as regards the substance of the work, and inasmuch as it springs from the free-will, there can be no condignity because of the very great inequality. But there is congruity, on account of an equality of proportion: for it would seem congruous that, if a man does what he can, God should reward him according to the excellence of his power.

If, however, we speak of a meritorious work, inasmuch as it proceeds from the grace of the Holy Ghost moving us to life everlasting, it is meritorious of life everlasting condignly. For thus the value of its merit depends upon the power of the Holy Ghost moving us to life everlasting according to John 4:14: "Shall become in him a fount of water springing up into life everlasting." And the worth of the work depends on the dignity of grace, whereby a man, being made a partaker of the Divine Nature, is adopted as a son of God, to whom the inheritance is due by right of adoption, according to Rom. 8:17: "If sons, heirs also."

Reply Obj. 1: The Apostle is speaking of the substance of these sufferings.

Reply Obj. 2: This saying is to be understood of the first cause of our reaching everlasting life, viz. God's mercy. But our merit is a subsequent cause.

Reply Obj. 3: The grace of the Holy Ghost which we have at present, although unequal to glory in act, is equal to it virtually as the seed of a tree, wherein the whole tree is virtually. So likewise by grace of the Holy Ghost dwells in man; and He is a sufficient cause of life everlasting; hence, 2 Cor. 1:22, He is called the "pledge" of our inheritance.

FOURTH ARTICLE [I-II, Q. 114, Art. 4]

Whether Grace Is the Principle of Merit Through Charity Rather Than the Other Virtues?

Objection 1: It would seem that grace is not the principle of merit through charity rather than the other virtues. For wages are due to work, according to Matt. 20:8: "Call the laborers and pay them their hire." Now every virtue is a principle of some operation, since virtue is an operative habit, as stated above (Q. 55, A. 2). Hence every virtue is equally a principle of merit.

Obj. 2: Further, the Apostle says (1 Cor. 3:8): "Every man shall receive his own reward according to his labor." Now charity lessens rather than increases the labor, because as Augustine says (De Verbis Dom., Serm. lxx), "love makes all hard and repulsive tasks easy and next to nothing." Hence charity is no greater principle of merit than any other virtue.

Obj. 3: Further, the greatest principle of merit would seem to be the one whose acts are most meritorious. But the acts of faith and patience or fortitude would seem to be the most meritorious, as appears in the martyrs, who strove for the faith patiently and bravely even till death. Hence other virtues are a greater principle of merit than charity.

*On the contrary,* Our Lord said (John 14:21): "He that loveth Me, shall be loved of My Father; and I will love him and will manifest Myself to him." Now everlasting life consists in the manifest knowledge of God, according to John 17:3: "This is eternal life: that they may know Thee, the only true" and living "God." Hence the merit of eternal life rests chiefly with charity.

*I answer that,* As we may gather from what has been stated above (A. 1), human acts have the nature of merit from two causes: first and chiefly from the Divine ordination, inasmuch as acts are said to merit that good to which man is divinely ordained. Secondly, on the part of free-will, inasmuch as man, more than other creatures, has the power of voluntary acts by acting by himself. And in both these ways does merit chiefly rest with charity. For we must bear in mind that everlasting life consists in the enjoyment of God. Now the human mind's movement to the fruition of the Divine good is the proper act of charity, whereby all the acts of the other virtues are ordained to this end, since all the other virtues are commanded by charity. Hence the merit of life everlasting pertains first to charity, and secondly, to the other virtues, inasmuch as their acts are commanded by charity. So, likewise, is it manifest that what we do out of love we do most willingly. Hence, even inasmuch as merit depends on voluntariness, merit is chiefly attributed to charity.

Reply Obj. 1: Charity, inasmuch as it has the last end for object, moves the other virtues to act. For the habit to which the end pertains always commands the habits to which the means pertain, as was said above (Q. 9, A. 1).

Reply Obj. 2: A work can be toilsome and difficult in two ways: first, from the greatness of the work, and thus the greatness of the work pertains to the increase of merit; and thus charity does not lessen the toil—rather, it makes us undertake the greatest toils, "for it does great things, if it exists," as Gregory says (Hom. in Evang. xxx). Secondly, from the defect of the operator; for what is not done with a ready will is hard and difficult to all of us, and this toil lessens merit and is removed by charity.

Reply Obj. 3: The act of faith is not meritorious unless "faith ... worketh by charity" (Gal. 5:6). So, too, the acts of patience and fortitude are not meritorious unless a man does them out of charity, according to 1 Cor. 13:3: "If I should deliver my body to be burned, and have not charity, it profiteth me nothing."

FIFTH ARTICLE [I-II, Q. 114, Art. 5]

Whether a Man May Merit for Himself the First Grace?

Objection 1: It would seem that a man may merit for himself the first grace, because, as Augustine says (Ep. clxxxvi), "faith merits justification." Now a man is justified by the first grace. Therefore a man may merit the first grace.

Obj. 2: Further, God gives grace only to the worthy. Now, no one is said to be worthy of some good, unless he has merited it condignly. Therefore we may merit the first grace condignly.

Obj. 3: Further, with men we may merit a gift already received. Thus if a man receives a horse from his master, he merits it by a good use of it in his master's service. Now God is much more bountiful than man. Much more, therefore, may a man, by subsequent works, merit the first grace already received from God.

*On the contrary,* The nature of grace is repugnant to reward of works, according to Rom. 4:4: "Now to him that worketh, the reward is not reckoned according to grace but according to debt." Now a man merits what is reckoned to him according to debt, as the reward of his works. Hence a man may not merit the first grace.

*I answer that,* The gift of grace may be considered in two ways: first in the nature of a gratuitous gift, and thus it is manifest that all merit is repugnant to grace, since as the Apostle says (Rom. 11:6), "if by grace, it is not now by works." Secondly, it may be considered as regards the nature of the thing given, and thus, also, it cannot come under the merit of him who has not grace, both because it exceeds the proportion of nature, and because previous to grace a man in the state of sin has an obstacle to his meriting grace, viz. sin. But when anyone has grace, the grace already possessed cannot come under merit, since reward is the term of the work, but grace is the principle of all our good works, as stated above (Q. 109). But of anyone merits a further gratuitous gift by virtue of the preceding grace, it would not be the first grace. Hence it is manifest that no one can merit for himself the first grace.

Reply Obj. 1: As Augustine says (Retract. i, 23), he was deceived on this point for a time, believing the beginning of faith to be from us, and its consummation to be granted us by God; and this he here retracts. And seemingly it is in this sense that he speaks of faith as meriting justification. But if we suppose, as indeed it is a truth of faith, that the beginning of faith is in us from God, the first act must flow from grace; and thus it cannot be meritorious of the first grace. Therefore man is justified by faith, not as though man, by believing, were to merit justification, but that, he believes, whilst he is being justified; inasmuch as a movement of faith is required for the justification of the ungodly, as stated above (Q. 113, A. 4).

Reply Obj. 2: God gives grace to none but to the worthy, not that they were previously worthy, but that by His grace He makes them worthy, Who alone "can make him clean that is conceived of unclean seed" (Job 14:4).

Reply Obj. 3: Man's every good work proceeds from the first grace as from its principle; but not from any gift of man. Consequently, there is no comparison between gifts of grace and gifts of men.

SIXTH ARTICLE [I-II, Q. 114, Art. 6]

Whether a Man Can Merit the First Grace for Another?

Objection 1: It would seem that a man can merit the first grace for another. Because on Matt. 9:2: "Jesus seeing their faith," etc. a gloss says: "How much is our personal faith worth with God, Who set such a price on another's faith, as to heal the man both inwardly and outwardly!" Now inward healing is brought about by grace. Hence a man can merit the first grace for another.

Obj. 2: Further, the prayers of the just are not void, but efficacious, according to James 5:16: "The continued prayer of a just man availeth much." Now he had previously said: "Pray one for another, that you may be saved." Hence, since man's salvation can only be brought about by grace, it seems that one man may merit for another his first grace.

Obj. 3: Further, it is written (Luke 16:9): "Make unto you friends of the mammon of iniquity, that when you shall fail they may receive you into everlasting dwellings." Now it is through grace alone that anyone is received into everlasting dwellings, for by it alone does anyone merit everlasting life as stated above (A. 2; Q. 109, A. 5). Hence one man may by merit obtain for another his first grace.

*On the contrary,* It is written (Jer. 15:1): "If Moses and Samuel shall stand before Me, My soul is not towards this people"—yet they had great merit with God. Hence it seems that no one can merit the first grace for another.

*I answer that,* As shown above (AA. 1, 3, 4), our works are meritorious from two causes: first, by virtue of the Divine motion; and thus we merit condignly; secondly, according as they proceed from free-will in so far as we do them willingly, and thus they have congruous merit, since it is congruous that when a man makes good use of his power God should by His super-excellent power work still higher things. And therefore it is clear that no one can merit condignly for another his first grace, save Christ alone; since each one of us is moved by God to reach life everlasting through the gift of grace; hence condign merit does not reach beyond this motion. But Christ's soul is moved by God through grace, not only so as to reach the glory of life everlasting, but so as to lead others to it, inasmuch as He is the Head of the Church, and the Author of human salvation, according to Heb. 2:10: "Who hath brought many children into glory [to perfect] the Author of their salvation."

But one may merit the first grace for another congruously; because a man in grace fulfils God's will, and it is congruous and in harmony with friendship that God should fulfil man's desire for the salvation of another, although sometimes there may be an impediment on the part of him whose salvation the just man desires. And it is in this sense that the passage from Jeremias speaks.

Reply Obj. 1: A man's faith avails for another's salvation by congruous and not by condign merit.

Reply Obj. 2: The impetration of prayer rests on mercy, whereas condign merit rests on justice; hence a man may impetrate many things from the Divine mercy in prayer, which he does not merit in justice, according to Dan. 9:18: "For it is not for our justifications that we present our prayers before Thy face, but for the multitude of Thy tender mercies."

Reply Obj. 3: The poor who receive alms are said to receive others into everlasting dwellings, either by impetrating their forgiveness in prayer, or by meriting congruously by other good works, or materially speaking, inasmuch as by these good works of mercy, exercised towards the poor, we merit to be received into everlasting dwellings.

SEVENTH ARTICLE [I-II, Q. 114, Art. 7]

Whether a Man May Merit Restoration After a Fall?

Objection 1: It would seem that anyone may merit for himself restoration after a fall. For what a man may justly ask of God, he may justly merit. Now nothing may more justly be besought of God than to be restored after a fall, as Augustine says [*Cf. Ennar. i super Ps. lxx.], according to Ps. 70:9: "When my strength shall fail, do not Thou forsake me." Hence a man may merit to be restored after a fall.

Obj. 2: Further, a man's works benefit himself more than another. Now a man may, to some extent, merit for another his restoration after a fall, even as his first grace. Much more, therefore, may he merit for himself restoration after a fall.

Obj. 3: Further, when a man is once in grace he merits life everlasting by the good works he does, as was shown above (A. 2; Q. 109, A. 5). Now no one can attain life everlasting unless he is restored by grace. Hence it would seem that he merits for himself restoration.

*On the contrary,* It is written (Ezech. 18:24): "If the just man turn himself away from his justice and do iniquity ... all his justices which he hath done shall not be remembered." Therefore his previous merits will nowise help him to rise again. Hence no one can merit for himself restoration after a fall.

*I answer that,* No one can merit for himself restoration after a future fall, either condignly or congruously. He cannot merit for himself condignly, since the reason of this merit depends on the motion of Divine grace, and this motion is interrupted by the subsequent sin; hence all benefits which he afterwards obtains from God, whereby he is restored, do not fall under merit—the motion of the preceding grace not extending to them. Again, congruous merit, whereby one merits the first grace for another, is prevented from having its effect on account of the impediment of sin in the one for whom it is merited. Much more, therefore, is the efficacy of such merit impeded by the obstacle which is in him who merits, and in him for whom it is merited; for both these are in the same person. And therefore a man can nowise merit for himself restoration after a fall.

Reply Obj. 1: The desire whereby we seek for restoration after a fall is called just, and likewise the prayer whereby this restoration is besought is called just, because it tends to justice; and not that it depends on justice by way of merit, but only on mercy.

Reply Obj. 2: Anyone may congruously merit for another his first grace, because there is no impediment (at least, on the part of him who merits), such as is found when anyone recedes from justice after the merit of grace.

Reply Obj. 3: Some have said that no one *absolutely* merits life everlasting except by the act of final grace, but only *conditionally,* i.e. if he perseveres. But it is unreasonable to say this, for sometimes the act of the last grace is not more, but less meritorious than preceding acts, on account of the prostration of illness. Hence it must be said that every act of charity merits eternal life absolutely; but by subsequent sin, there arises an impediment to the preceding merit, so that it does not obtain its effect; just as natural causes fail of their effects on account of a supervening impediment.

EIGHTH ARTICLE [I-II, Q. 114, Art. 8]

Whether a Man May Merit the Increase of Grace or Charity?

Objection 1: It would seem that a man cannot merit an increase of grace or charity. For when anyone receives the reward he merited no other reward is due to him; thus it was said of some (Matt. 6:2): "They have received their reward." Hence, if anyone were to merit the increase of charity or grace, it would follow that, when his grace has been increased, he could not expect any further reward, which is unfitting.

Obj. 2: Further, nothing acts beyond its species. But the principle of merit is grace or charity, as was shown above (AA. 2, 4). Therefore no one can merit greater grace or charity than he has.

Obj. 3: Further, what falls under merit a man merits by every act flowing from grace or charity, as by every such act a man merits life everlasting. If, therefore, the increase of grace or charity falls under merit, it would seem that by every act quickened by charity a man would merit an increase of charity. But what a man merits, he infallibly receives from God, unless hindered by subsequent sin; for it is written (2 Tim. 1:12): "I know Whom I have believed, and I am certain that He is able to keep that which I have committed unto Him." Hence it would follow that grace or charity is increased by every meritorious act; and this would seem impossible since at times meritorious acts are not very fervent, and would not suffice for the increase of charity. Therefore the increase of charity does not come under merit.

*On the contrary,* Augustine says (super Ep. Joan.; cf. Ep. clxxxvi) that "charity merits increase, and being increased merits to be perfected." Hence the increase of grace or charity falls under merit.

*I answer that,* As stated above (AA. 6, 7), whatever the motion of grace reaches to, falls under condign merit. Now the motion of a mover extends not merely to the last term of the movement, but to the whole progress of the movement. But the term of the movement of grace is eternal life; and progress in this movement is by the increase of charity or grace according to Prov. 4:18: "But the path of the just as a shining light, goeth forward and increaseth even to perfect day," which is the day of glory. And thus the increase of grace falls under condign merit.

Reply Obj. 1: Reward is the term of merit. But there is a double term of movement, viz. the last, and the intermediate, which is both beginning and term; and this term is the reward of increase. Now the reward of human favor is as the last end to those who place their end in it; hence such as these receive no other reward.

Reply Obj. 2: The increase of grace is not above the virtuality of the pre-existing grace, although it is above its quantity, even as a tree is not above the virtuality of the seed, although above its quantity.

Reply Obj. 3: By every meritorious act a man merits the increase of grace, equally with the consummation of grace which is eternal life. But just as eternal life is not given at once, but in its own time, so neither is grace increased at once, but in its own time, viz. when a man is sufficiently disposed for the increase of grace.

NINTH ARTICLE [I-II, Q. 114, Art. 9]

Whether a Man May Merit Perseverance?

Objection 1: It would seem that anyone may merit perseverance. For what a man obtains by asking, can come under the merit of anyone that is in grace. Now men obtain perseverance by asking it of God; otherwise it would be useless to ask it of God in the petitions of the Lord's Prayer, as Augustine says (De Dono Persev. ii). Therefore perseverance may come under the merit of whoever has grace.

Obj. 2: Further, it is more not to be able to sin than not to sin. But not to be able to sin comes under merit, for we merit eternal life, of which impeccability is an essential part. Much more, therefore, may we merit not to sin, i.e. to persevere.

Obj. 3: Further, increase of grace is greater than perseverance in the grace we already possess. But a man may merit an increase of grace, as was stated above (A. 8). Much more, therefore, may he merit perseverance in the grace he has already.

*On the contrary,* What we merit, we obtain from God, unless it is hindered by sin. Now many have meritorious works, who do not obtain perseverance; nor can it be urged that this takes place because of the impediment of sin, since sin itself is opposed to perseverance; and thus if anyone were to merit perseverance, God would not permit him to fall into sin. Hence perseverance does not come under merit.

*I answer that,* Since man's free-will is naturally flexible towards good and evil, there are two ways of obtaining from God perseverance in good: first, inasmuch as free-will is determined to good by consummate grace, which will be in glory; secondly, on the part of the Divine motion, which inclines man to good unto the end. Now as explained above (AA. 6, 7, 8), that which is related as a term to the free-will's movement directed to God the mover, falls under human merit; and not what is related to the aforesaid movement as principle. Hence it is clear that the perseverance of glory which is the term of the aforesaid movement falls under merit; but perseverance of the wayfarer does not fall under merit, since it depends solely on the Divine motion, which is the principle of all merit. Now God freely bestows the good of perseverance, on whomsoever He bestows it.

Reply Obj. 1: We impetrate in prayer things that we do not merit, since God hears sinners who beseech the pardon of their sins, which they do not merit, as appears from Augustine [*Tract. xliv in Joan.] on John 11:31, "Now we know that God doth not hear sinners," otherwise it would have been useless for the publican to say: "O God, be merciful to me a sinner," Luke 18:13. So too may we impetrate of God in prayer the grace of perseverance either for ourselves or for others, although it does not fall under merit.

Reply Obj. 2: The perseverance which is in heaven is compared as term to the free-will's movement; not so, the perseverance of the wayfarer, for the reason given in the body of the article.

In the same way may we answer the third objection which concerns the increase of grace, as was explained above.

TENTH ARTICLE [I-II, Q. 114, Art. 10]

Whether Temporal Goods Fall Under Merit?

Objection 1: It would seem that temporal goods fall under merit. For what is promised to some as a reward of justice, falls under merit. Now, temporal goods were promised in the Old Law as the reward of justice, as appears from Deut. 28. Hence it seems that temporal goods fall under merit.

Obj. 2: Further, that would seem to fall under merit, which God bestows on anyone for a service done. But God sometimes bestows temporal goods on men for services done for Him. For it is written (Ex. 1:21): "And because the midwives feared God, He built them houses"; on which a gloss of Gregory (Moral. xviii, 4) says that "life everlasting might have been awarded them as the fruit of their goodwill, but on account of their sin of falsehood they received an earthly reward." And it is written (Ezech. 29:18): "The King of Babylon hath made his army to undergo hard service against Tyre ... and there hath been no reward given him," and further on: "And it shall be wages for his army ... I have given him the land of Egypt because he hath labored for me." Therefore temporal goods fall under merit.

Obj. 3: Further, as good is to merit so is evil to demerit. But on account of the demerit of sin some are punished by God with temporal punishments, as appears from the Sodomites, Gen. 19. Hence temporal goods fall under merit.

Obj. 4: *On the contrary,* What falls under merit does not come upon all alike. But temporal goods regard the good and the wicked alike; according to Eccles. 9:2: "All things equally happen to the just and the wicked, to the good and to the evil, to the clean and to the unclean, to him that offereth victims and to him that despiseth sacrifices." Therefore temporal goods do not fall under merit.

*I answer that,* What falls under merit is the reward or wage, which is a kind of good. Now man's good is twofold: the first, simply; the second, relatively. Now man's good simply is his last end (according to Ps. 72:27: "But it is good for men to adhere to my God") and consequently what is ordained and leads to this end; and these fall simply under merit. But the relative, not the simple, good of man is what is good to him now, or what is a good to him relatively; and this does not fall under merit simply, but relatively.

Hence we must say that if temporal goods are considered as they are useful for virtuous works, whereby we are led to heaven, they fall directly and simply under merit, even as increase of grace, and everything whereby a man is helped to attain beatitude after the first grace. For God gives men, both just and wicked, enough temporal goods to enable them to attain to everlasting life; and thus these temporal goods are simply good. Hence it is written (Ps. 33:10): "For there is no want to them that fear Him," and again, Ps. 36:25: "I have not seen the just forsaken," etc.

But if these temporal goods are considered in themselves, they are not man's good simply, but relatively, and thus they do not fall under merit simply, but relatively, inasmuch as men are moved by God to do temporal works, in which with God's help they reach their purpose. And thus as life everlasting is simply the reward of the works of justice in relation to the Divine motion, as stated above (AA. 3, 6), so have temporal goods, considered in themselves, the nature of reward, with respect to the Divine motion, whereby men's wills are moved to undertake these works, even though, sometimes, men have not a right intention in them.

Reply Obj. 1: As Augustine says (Contra Faust. iv, 2), "in these temporal promises were figures of spiritual things to come. For the carnal people were adhering to the promises of the present life; and not merely their speech but even their life was prophetic."

Reply Obj. 2: These rewards are said to have been divinely brought about in relation to the Divine motion, and not in relation to the malice of their wills, especially as regards the King of Babylon, since he did not besiege Tyre as if wishing to serve God, but rather in order to usurp dominion. So, too, although the midwives had a good will with regard to saving the children, yet their will was not right, inasmuch as they framed falsehoods.

Reply Obj. 3: Temporal evils are imposed as a punishment on the wicked, inasmuch as they are not thereby helped to reach life everlasting. But to the just who are aided by these evils they are not punishments but medicines as stated above (Q. 87, A. 8).

Reply Obj. 4: All things happen equally to the good and the wicked, as regards the substance of temporal good or evil; but not as regards the end, since the good and not the wicked are led to beatitude by them.

And now enough has been said regarding morals in general.

---

**The End**

# SUMMA THEOLOGICA PART II-II ("Secunda Secundae")

## QUESTION 1

OF FAITH (In Ten Articles)

Having to treat now of the theological virtues, we shall begin with Faith, secondly we shall speak of Hope, and thirdly, of Charity.

The treatise on Faith will be fourfold: (1) Of faith itself; (2) Of the corresponding gifts, knowledge and understanding; (3) Of the opposite vices; (4) Of the precepts pertaining to this virtue.

About faith itself we shall consider: (1) its object; (2) its act; (3) the habit of faith.

Under the first head there are ten points of inquiry:

(1) Whether the object of faith is the First Truth?

(2) Whether the object of faith is something complex or incomplex, i.e. whether it is a thing or a proposition?

(3) Whether anything false can come under faith?

(4) Whether the object of faith can be anything seen?

(5) Whether it can be anything known?

(6) Whether the things to be believed should be divided into a certain number of articles?

(7) Whether the same articles are of faith for all times?

(8) Of the number of articles;

(9) Of the manner of embodying the articles in a symbol;

(10) Who has the right to propose a symbol of faith?

FIRST ARTICLE [II-II, Q. 1, Art. 1]

Whether the Object of Faith Is the First Truth?

Objection 1: It would seem that the object of faith is not the First Truth. For it seems that the object of faith is that which is proposed to us to be believed. Now not only things pertaining to the Godhead, i.e. the First Truth, are proposed to us to be believed, but also things concerning Christ's human nature, and the sacraments of the Church, and the condition of creatures. Therefore the object of faith is not only the First Truth.

Obj. 2: Further, faith and unbelief have the same object since they are opposed to one another. Now unbelief can be about all things contained in Holy Writ, for whichever one of them a man denies, he is considered an unbeliever. Therefore faith also is about all things contained in Holy Writ. But there are many things therein, concerning man and other creatures. Therefore the object of faith is not only the First Truth, but also created truth.

Obj. 3: Further, faith is condivided with charity, as stated above (I-II, Q. 62, A. 3). Now by charity we love not only God, who is the sovereign Good, but also our neighbor. Therefore the object of Faith is not only the First Truth.

*On the contrary,* Dionysius says (Div. Nom. vii) that "faith is about the simple and everlasting truth." Now this is the First Truth. Therefore the object of faith is the First Truth.

*I answer that,* The object of every cognitive habit includes two things: first, that which is known materially, and is the material object, so to speak, and, secondly, that whereby it is known, which is the formal aspect of the object. Thus in the science of geometry, the conclusions are what is known materially, while the formal aspect of the science is the mean of demonstration, through which the conclusions are known.

Accordingly if we consider, in faith, the formal aspect of the object, it is nothing else than the First Truth. For the faith of which we are speaking, does not assent to anything, except because it is revealed by God. Hence the mean on which faith is based is the Divine Truth. If, however, we consider materially the things to which faith assents, they include not only God, but also many other things, which, nevertheless, do not come under the assent of faith, except as bearing some relation to God, in as much as, to wit, through certain effects of the Divine operation, man is helped on his journey towards the enjoyment of God. Consequently from this point of view also the object of faith is, in a way, the First Truth, in as much as nothing comes under faith except in relation to God, even as the object of the medical art is health, for it considers nothing save in relation to health.

Reply Obj. 1: Things concerning Christ's human nature, and the sacraments of the Church, or any creatures whatever, come under faith, in so far as by them we are directed to God, and in as much as we assent to them on account of the Divine Truth.

The same answer applies to the Second Objection, as regards all things contained in Holy Writ.

Reply Obj. 3: Charity also loves our neighbor on account of God, so that its object, properly speaking, is God, as we shall show further on (Q. 25, A. 1).

SECOND ARTICLE [II-II, Q. 1, Art. 2]

Whether the Object of Faith Is Something Complex, by Way of a Proposition?

Objection 1: It would seem that the object of faith is not something complex by way of a proposition. For the object of faith is the First Truth, as stated above (A. 1). Now the First Truth is something simple. Therefore the object of faith is not something complex.

Obj. 2: Further, the exposition of faith is contained in the symbol. Now the symbol does not contain propositions, but things: for it is not stated therein that God is almighty, but: "I believe in God ... almighty." Therefore the object of faith is not a proposition but a thing.

Obj. 3: Further, faith is succeeded by vision, according to 1 Cor. 13:12: "We see now through a glass in a dark manner; but then face to face. Now I know in part; but then I shall know even as I am known." But the object of the heavenly vision is something simple, for it is the Divine Essence. Therefore the faith of the wayfarer is also.

*On the contrary,* Faith is a mean between science and opinion. Now the mean is in the same genus as the extremes. Since, then, science and opinion are about propositions, it seems that faith is likewise about propositions; so that its object is something complex.

*I answer that,* The thing known is in the knower according to the mode of the knower. Now the mode proper to the human intellect is to know the truth by synthesis and analysis, as stated in the First Part (Q. 85, A. 5). Hence things that are simple in themselves, are known by the intellect with a certain amount of complexity, just as on the other hand, the Divine intellect knows, without any complexity, things that are complex in themselves.

Accordingly the object of faith may be considered in two ways. First, as regards the thing itself which is believed, and thus the object of faith is something simple, namely the thing itself about which we have faith. Secondly, on the part of the believer, and in this respect the object of faith is something complex by way of a proposition.

Hence in the past both opinions have been held with a certain amount of truth.

Reply Obj. 1: This argument considers the object of faith on the part of the thing believed.

Reply Obj. 2: The symbol mentions the things about which faith is, in so far as the act of the believer is terminated in them, as is evident from the manner of speaking about them. Now the act of the believer does not terminate in a proposition, but in a thing. For as in science we do not form propositions, except in order to have knowledge about things through their means, so is it in faith.

Reply Obj. 3: The object of the heavenly vision will be the First Truth seen in itself, according to 1 John 3:2: "We know that when He shall appear, we shall be like to Him: because we shall see Him as He is": hence that vision will not be by way of a proposition but by way of a simple understanding. On the other hand, by faith, we do not apprehend the First Truth as it is in itself. Hence the comparison fails.

THIRD ARTICLE [II-II, Q. 1, Art. 3]

Whether Anything False Can Come Under Faith?

Objection 1: It would seem that something false can come under faith. For faith is condivided with hope and charity. Now something false can come under hope, since many hope to have eternal life, who will not obtain it. The same may be said of charity, for many are loved as being good, who, nevertheless, are not good. Therefore something false can be the object of faith.

Obj. 2: Further, Abraham believed that Christ would be born, according to John 8:56: "Abraham your father rejoiced that he might see My day: he saw it, and was glad." But after the time of Abraham, God might not have taken flesh, for it was merely because He willed that He did, so that what Abraham believed about Christ would have been false. Therefore the object of faith can be something false.

Obj. 3: Further, the ancients believed in the future birth of Christ, and many continued so to believe, until they heard the preaching of the Gospel. Now, when once Christ was born, even before He began to preach, it was false that Christ was yet to be born. Therefore something false can come under faith.

Obj. 4: Further, it is a matter of faith, that one should believe that the true Body of Christ is contained in the Sacrament of the altar. But it might happen that the bread was not rightly consecrated, and that there was not Christ's true Body there, but only bread. Therefore something false can come under faith.

*On the contrary,* No virtue that perfects the intellect is related to the false, considered as the evil of the intellect, as the Philosopher declares (Ethic. vi, 2). Now faith is a virtue that perfects the intellect, as we shall show further on (Q. 4, AA. 2, 5). Therefore nothing false can come under it.

*I answer that,* Nothing comes under any power, habit or act, except by means of the formal aspect of the object: thus color cannot be seen except by means of light, and a conclusion cannot be known save through the mean of demonstration. Now it has been stated (A. 1) that the formal aspect of the object of faith is the First Truth; so that nothing can come under faith, save in so far as it stands under the First Truth, under which nothing false can stand, as neither can non-being stand under being, nor evil under goodness. It follows therefore that nothing false can come under faith.

Reply Obj. 1: Since the true is the good of the intellect, but not of the appetitive power, it follows that all virtues which perfect the intellect, exclude the false altogether, because it belongs to the nature of a virtue to bear relation to the good alone. On the other hand those virtues which perfect the appetitive faculty, do not entirely exclude the false, for it is possible to act in accordance with justice or temperance, while having a false opinion about what one is doing. Therefore, as faith perfects the intellect, whereas hope and charity perfect the appetitive part, the comparison between them fails.

Nevertheless neither can anything false come under hope, for a man hopes to obtain eternal life, not by his own power (since this would be an act of presumption), but with the help of grace; and if he perseveres therein he will obtain eternal life surely and infallibly.

In like manner it belongs to charity to love God, wherever He may be; so that it matters not to charity, whether God be in the individual whom we love for God's sake.

Reply Obj. 2: That "God would not take flesh," considered in itself was possible even after Abraham's time, but in so far as it stands in God's foreknowledge, it has a certain necessity of infallibility, as explained in the First Part (Q. 14, AA. 13, 15): and it is thus that it comes under faith. Hence in so far as it comes under faith, it cannot be false.

Reply Obj. 3: After Christ's birth, to believe in Him, was to believe in Christ's birth at some time or other. The fixing of the time, wherein some were deceived was not due to their faith, but to a human conjecture. For it is possible for a believer to have a false opinion through a human conjecture, but it is quite impossible for a false opinion to be the outcome of faith.

Reply Obj. 4: The faith of the believer is not directed to such and such accidents of bread, but to the fact that the true body of Christ is under the appearances of sensible bread, when it is rightly consecrated. Hence if it be not rightly consecrated, it does not follow that anything false comes under faith.

FOURTH ARTICLE [II-II, Q. 1, Art. 4]

Whether the Object of Faith Can Be Something Seen?

Objection 1: It would seem that the object of faith is something seen. For Our Lord said to Thomas (John 20:29): "Because thou hast seen Me, Thomas, thou hast believed." Therefore vision and faith regard the same object.

Obj. 2: Further, the Apostle, while speaking of the knowledge of faith, says (1 Cor. 13:12): "We see now through a glass in a dark manner." Therefore what is believed is seen.

Obj. 3: Further, faith is a spiritual light. Now something is seen under every light. Therefore faith is of things seen.

Obj. 4: Further, "Every sense is a kind of sight," as Augustine states (De Verb. Domini, Serm. xxxiii). But faith is of things heard, according to Rom. 10:17: "Faith ... cometh by hearing." Therefore faith is of things seen.

*On the contrary,* The Apostle says (Heb. 11:1) that "faith is the evidence of things that appear not."

*I answer that,* Faith implies assent of the intellect to that which is believed. Now the intellect assents to a thing in two ways. First, through being moved to assent by its very object, which is known either by itself (as in the case of first principles, which are held by the habit of understanding), or through something else already known (as in the case of conclusions which are held by the habit of science). Secondly the intellect assents to something, not through being sufficiently moved to this assent by its proper object, but through an act of choice, whereby it turns voluntarily to one side rather than to the other: and if this be accompanied by doubt or fear of the opposite side, there will be opinion, while, if there be certainty and no fear of the other side, there will be faith.

Now those things are said to be seen which, of themselves, move the intellect or the senses to knowledge of them. Wherefore it is evident that neither faith nor opinion can be of things seen either by the senses or by the intellect.

Reply Obj. 1: Thomas "saw one thing, and believed another" [*St. Gregory: Hom. xxvi in Evang.]: he saw the Man, and believing Him to be God, he made profession of his faith, saying: "My Lord and my God."

Reply Obj. 2: Those things which come under faith can be considered in two ways. First, in particular; and thus they cannot be seen and believed at the same time, as shown above. Secondly, in general, that is, under the common aspect of credibility; and in this way they are seen by the believer. For he would not believe unless, on the evidence of signs, or of something similar, he saw that they ought to be believed.

Reply Obj. 3: The light of faith makes us see what we believe. For just as, by the habits of the other virtues, man sees what is becoming to him in respect of that habit, so, by the habit of faith, the human mind is directed to assent to such things as are becoming to a right faith, and not to assent to others.

Reply Obj. 4: Hearing is of words signifying what is of faith, but not of the things themselves that are believed; hence it does not follow that these things are seen.

FIFTH ARTICLE [II-II, Q. 1, Art. 5]

Whether Those Things That Are of Faith Can Be an Object of Science [*Science is certain knowledge of a demonstrated conclusion through its demonstration]?

Objection 1: It would seem that those things that are of faith can be an object of science. For where science is lacking there is ignorance, since ignorance is the opposite of science. Now we are not in ignorance of those things we have to believe, since ignorance of such things savors of unbelief, according to 1 Tim. 1:13: "I did it ignorantly in unbelief." Therefore things that are of faith can be an object of science.

Obj. 2: Further, science is acquired by reasons. Now sacred writers employ reasons to inculcate things that are of faith. Therefore such things can be an object of science.

Obj. 3: Further, things which are demonstrated are an object of science, since a "demonstration is a syllogism that produces science." Now certain matters of faith have been demonstrated by the philosophers, such as the Existence and Unity of God, and so forth. Therefore things that are of faith can be an object of science.

Obj. 4: Further, opinion is further from science than faith is, since faith is said to stand between opinion and science. Now opinion and science can, in a way, be about the same object, as stated in Poster. i. Therefore faith and science can be about the same object also.

*On the contrary,* Gregory says (Hom. xxvi in Evang.) that "when a thing is manifest, it is the object, not of faith, but of perception." Therefore things that are of faith are not the object of perception, whereas what is an object of science is the object of perception. Therefore there can be no faith about things which are an object of science.

*I answer that,* All science is derived from self-evident and therefore "seen" principles; wherefore all objects of science must needs be, in a fashion, seen.

Now as stated above (A. 4), it is impossible that one and the same thing should be believed and seen by the same person. Hence it is equally impossible for one and the same thing to be an object of science and of belief for the same person. It may happen, however, that a thing which is an object of vision or science for one, is believed by another: since we hope to see some day what we now believe about the Trinity, according to 1 Cor. 13:12: "We see now through a glass in a dark manner; but then face to face": which vision the angels possess already; so that what we believe, they see. In like manner it may happen that what is an object of vision or scientific knowledge for one man, even in the state of a wayfarer, is, for another man, an object of faith, because he does not know it by demonstration.

Nevertheless that which is proposed to be believed equally by all, is equally unknown by all as an object of science: such are the things which are of faith simply. Consequently faith and science are not about the same things.

Reply Obj. 1: Unbelievers are in ignorance of things that are of faith, for neither do they see or know them in themselves, nor do they know them to be credible. The faithful, on the other hand, know them, not as by demonstration, but by the light of faith which makes them see that they ought to believe them, as stated above (A. 4, ad 2, 3).

Reply Obj. 2: The reasons employed by holy men to prove things that are of faith, are not demonstrations; they are either persuasive arguments showing that what is proposed to our faith is not impossible, or else they are proofs drawn from the principles of faith, i.e. from the authority of Holy Writ, as Dionysius declares (Div. Nom. ii). Whatever is based on these principles is as well proved in the eyes of the faithful, as a conclusion drawn from self-evident principles is in the eyes of all. Hence again, theology is a science, as we stated at the outset of this work (P. I, Q. 1, A. 2).

Reply Obj. 3: Things which can be proved by demonstration are reckoned among the articles of faith, not because they are believed simply by all, but because they are a necessary presupposition to matters of faith, so that those who do not known them by demonstration must know them first of all by faith.

Reply Obj. 4: As the Philosopher says (Poster. i), "science and opinion about the same object can certainly be in different men," as we have stated above about science and faith; yet it is possible for one and the same man to have science and faith about the same thing relatively, i.e. in relation to the object, but not in the same respect. For it is possible for the same person, about one and the same object, to know one thing and to think another: and, in like manner, one may know by demonstration the unity of the Godhead, and, by faith, the Trinity. On the other hand, in one and the same man, about the same object, and in the same respect, science is incompatible with either opinion or faith, yet for different reasons. Because science is incompatible with opinion about the same object simply, for the reason that science demands that its object should be deemed impossible to be otherwise, whereas it is essential to opinion, that its object should be deemed possible to be otherwise. Yet that which is the object of faith, on account of the certainty of faith, is also deemed impossible to be otherwise; and the reason why science and faith cannot be about the same object and in the same respect is because the object of science is something seen whereas the object of faith is the unseen, as stated above.

SIXTH ARTICLE [II-II, Q. 1, Art. 6]

Whether Those Things That Are of Faith Should Be Divided into Certain Articles?

Objection 1: It would seem that those things that are of faith should not be divided into certain articles. For all things contained in Holy Writ are matters of faith. But these, by reason of their multitude, cannot be reduced to a certain number. Therefore it seems superfluous to distinguish certain articles of faith.

Obj. 2: Further, material differences can be multiplied indefinitely, and therefore art should take no notice of them. Now the formal aspect of the object of faith is one and indivisible, as stated above (A. 1), viz. the First Truth, so that matters of faith cannot be distinguished in respect of their formal object. Therefore no notice should be taken of a material division of matters of faith into articles.

Obj. 3: Further, it has been said by some [*Cf. William of Auxerre, Summa Aurea] that "an article is an indivisible truth concerning God, exacting [arctans] our belief." Now belief is a voluntary act, since, as Augustine says (Tract. xxvi in Joan.), "no man believes against his will." Therefore it seems that matters of faith should not be divided into articles.

*On the contrary,* Isidore says: "An article is a glimpse of Divine truth, tending thereto." Now we can only get a glimpse of Divine truth by way of analysis, since things which in God are one, are manifold in our intellect. Therefore matters of faith should be divided into articles.

*I answer that,* the word "article" is apparently derived from the Greek; for the Greek *arthron* [*Cf. William of Auxerre, Summa Aurea] which the Latin renders "articulus," signifies a fitting together of distinct parts: wherefore the small parts of the body which fit together are called the articulations of the limbs. Likewise, in the Greek grammar, articles are parts of speech which are affixed to words to show their gender, number or case. Again in rhetoric, articles are parts that fit together in a sentence, for Tully says (Rhet. iv) that an article is composed of words each pronounced singly and separately, thus: "Your passion, your voice, your look, have struck terror into your foes."

Hence matters of Christian faith are said to contain distinct articles, in so far as they are divided into parts, and fit together. Now the object of faith is something unseen in connection with God, as stated above (A. 4). Consequently any matter that, for a special reason, is unseen, is a special article; whereas when several matters are known or not known, under the same aspect, we are not to distinguish various articles. Thus one encounters one difficulty in seeing that God suffered, and another in seeing that He rose again from the dead, wherefore the article of the Resurrection is distinct from the article of the Passion. But that He suffered, died and was buried, present the same difficulty, so that if one be accepted, it is not difficult to accept the others; wherefore all these belong to one article.

Reply Obj. 1: Some things are proposed to our belief are in themselves of faith, while others are of faith, not in themselves but only in relation to others: even as in sciences certain propositions are put forward on their own account, while others are put forward in order to manifest others. Now, since the chief object of faith consists in those things which we hope to see, according to Heb. 11:2: "Faith is the substance of things to be hoped for," it follows that those things are in themselves of faith, which order us directly to eternal life. Such are the Trinity of Persons in Almighty God [*The Leonine Edition reads: The Three Persons, the omnipotence of God, etc.], the mystery of Christ's Incarnation, and the like: and these are distinct articles of faith. On the other hand certain things in Holy Writ are proposed to our belief, not chiefly on their own account, but for the manifestation of those mentioned above: for instance, that Abraham had two sons, that a dead man rose again at the touch of Eliseus' bones, and the like, which are related in Holy Writ for the purpose of manifesting the Divine mystery or the Incarnation of Christ: and such things should not form distinct articles.

Reply Obj. 2: The formal aspect of the object of faith can be taken in two ways: first, on the part of the thing believed, and thus there is one formal aspect of all matters of faith, viz. the First Truth: and from this point of view there is no distinction of articles. Secondly, the formal aspect of matters of faith, can be considered from our point of view; and thus the formal aspect of a matter of faith is that it is something unseen; and from this point of view there are various distinct articles of faith, as we saw above.

Reply Obj. 3: This definition of an article is taken from an etymology of the word as derived from the Latin, rather than in accordance with its real meaning, as derived from the Greek: hence it does not carry much weight. Yet even then it could be said that although faith is exacted of no man by a necessity of coercion, since belief is a voluntary act, yet it is exacted of him by a necessity of end, since "he that cometh to God must believe that He is," and "without faith it is impossible to please God," as the Apostle declares (Heb. 11:6).

SEVENTH ARTICLE [II-II, Q. 1, Art. 7]

Whether the Articles of Faith Have Increased in Course of Time?

Objection 1: It would seem that the articles of faith have not increased in course of time. Because, as the Apostle says (Heb. 11:1), "faith is the substance of things to be hoped for." Now the same things are to be hoped for at all times. Therefore, at all times, the same things are to be believed.

Obj. 2: Further, development has taken place, in sciences devised by man, on account of the lack of knowledge in those who discovered them, as the Philosopher observes (Metaph. ii). Now the doctrine of faith was not devised by man, but was delivered to us by God, as stated in Eph. 2:8: "It is the gift of God." Since then there can be no lack of knowledge in God, it seems that knowledge of matters of faith was perfect from the beginning and did not increase as time went on.

Obj. 3: Further, the operation of grace proceeds in orderly fashion no less than the operation of nature. Now nature always makes a beginning with perfect things, as Boethius states (De Consol. iii). Therefore it seems that the operation of grace also began with perfect things, so that those who were the first to deliver the faith, knew it most perfectly.

Obj. 4: Further, just as the faith of Christ was delivered to us through the apostles, so too, in the Old Testament, the knowledge of faith was delivered by the early fathers to those who came later, according to Deut. 32:7: "Ask thy father, and he will declare to thee." Now the apostles were most fully instructed about the mysteries, for "they received them more fully than others, even as they received them earlier," as a gloss says on Rom. 8:23: "Ourselves also who have the first fruits of the Spirit." Therefore it seems that knowledge of matters of faith has not increased as time went on.

*On the contrary,* Gregory says (Hom. xvi in Ezech.) that "the knowledge of the holy fathers increased as time went on ... and the nearer they were to Our Savior's coming, the more fully did they receive the mysteries of salvation."

*I answer that,* The articles of faith stand in the same relation to the doctrine of faith, as self-evident principles to a teaching based on natural reason. Among these principles there is a certain order, so that some are contained implicitly in others; thus all principles are reduced, as to their first principle, to this one: "The same thing cannot be affirmed and denied at the same time," as the Philosopher states (Metaph. iv, text. 9). In like manner all the articles are contained implicitly in certain primary matters of faith, such as God's existence, and His providence over the salvation of man, according to Heb. 11: "He that cometh to God, must believe that He is, and is a rewarder to them that seek Him." For the existence of God includes all that we believe to exist in God eternally, and in these our happiness consists; while belief in His providence includes all those things which God dispenses in time, for man's salvation, and which are the way to that happiness: and in this way, again, some of those articles which follow from these are contained in others: thus faith in the Redemption of mankind includes belief in the Incarnation of Christ, His Passion and so forth.

Accordingly we must conclude that, as regards the substance of the articles of faith, they have not received any increase as time went on: since whatever those who lived later have believed, was contained, albeit implicitly, in the faith of those Fathers who preceded them. But there was an increase in the number of articles believed explicitly, since to those who lived in later times some were known explicitly which were not known explicitly by those who lived before them. Hence the Lord said to Moses (Ex. 6:2, 3): "I am the God of Abraham, the God of Isaac, the God of Jacob [*Vulg.: 'I am the Lord that appeared to Abraham, to Isaac, and to Jacob'] ... and My name Adonai I did not show them": David also said (Ps. 118:100): "I have had understanding above ancients": and the Apostle says (Eph. 3:5) that the mystery of Christ, "in other generations was not known, as it is now revealed to His holy apostles and prophets."

Reply Obj. 1: Among men the same things were always to be hoped for from Christ. But as they did not acquire this hope save through Christ, the further they were removed from Christ in point of time, the further they were from obtaining what they hoped for. Hence the Apostle says (Heb. 11:13): "All these died according to faith, not having received the promises, but beholding them afar off." Now the further off a thing is the less distinctly is it seen; wherefore those who were nigh to Christ's advent had a more distinct knowledge of the good things to be hoped for.

Reply Obj. 2: Progress in knowledge occurs in two ways. First, on the part of the teacher, be he one or many, who makes progress in knowledge as time goes on: and this is the kind of progress that takes place in sciences devised by man. Secondly, on the part of the learner; thus the master, who has perfect knowledge of the art, does not deliver it all at once to his disciple from the very outset, for he would not be able to take it all in, but he condescends to the disciple's capacity and instructs him little by little. It is in this way that men made progress in the knowledge of faith as time went on. Hence the Apostle (Gal. 3:24) compares the state of the Old Testament to childhood.

Reply Obj. 3: Two causes are requisite before actual generation can take place, an agent, namely, and matter. In the order of the active cause, the more perfect is naturally first; and in this way nature makes a beginning with perfect things, since the imperfect is not brought to perfection, except by something perfect already in existence. On the other hand, in the order of the material cause, the imperfect comes first, and in this way nature proceeds from the imperfect to the perfect. Now in the manifestation of faith, God is the active cause, having perfect knowledge from all eternity; while man is likened to matter in receiving the influx of God's action. Hence, among men, the knowledge of faith had to proceed from imperfection to perfection; and, although some men have been after the manner of active causes, through being doctors of faith, nevertheless the manifestation of the Spirit is given to such men for the common good, according to 1 Cor. 12:7; so that the knowledge of faith was imparted to the Fathers who were instructors in the faith, so far as was necessary at the time for the instruction of the people, either openly or in figures.

Reply Obj. 4: The ultimate consummation of grace was effected by Christ, wherefore the time of His coming is called the "time of fulness [*Vulg.: 'fulness of time']" (Gal. 4:4). Hence those who were nearest to Christ, whether before, like John the Baptist, or after, like the apostles, had a fuller knowledge of the mysteries of faith; for even with regard to man's state we find that the perfection of manhood comes in youth, and that a man's state is all the more perfect, whether before or after, the nearer it is to the time of his youth.

EIGHTH ARTICLE [II-II, Q. 1, Art. 8]

Whether the Articles of Faith Are Suitably Formulated?

Objection 1: It would seem that the articles of faith are unsuitably formulated. For those things, which can be known by demonstration, do not belong to faith as to an object of belief for all, as stated above (A. 5). Now it can be known by demonstration that there is one God; hence the Philosopher proves this (Metaph. xii, text. 52) and many other philosophers demonstrated the same truth. Therefore that "there is one God" should not be set down as an article of faith.

Obj. 2: Further, just as it is necessary to faith that we should believe God to be almighty, so is it too that we should believe Him to be "all-knowing" and "provident for all," about both of which points some have erred. Therefore, among the articles of faith, mention should have been made of God's wisdom and providence, even as of His omnipotence.

Obj. 3: Further, to know the Father is the same things as to know the Son, according to John 14:9: "He that seeth Me, seeth the Father also." Therefore there ought to be but one article about the Father and Son, and, for the same reason, about the Holy Ghost.

Obj. 4: Further, the Person of the Father is no less than the Person of the Son, and of the Holy Ghost. Now there are several articles about the Person of the Holy Ghost, and likewise about the Person of the Son. Therefore there should be several articles about the Person of the Father.

Obj. 5: Further, just as certain things are said by appropriation, of the Person of the Father and of the Person of the Holy Ghost, so too is something appropriated to the Person of the Son, in respect of His Godhead. Now, among the articles of faith, a place is given to a work appropriated to the Father, viz. the creation, and likewise, a work appropriated to the Holy Ghost, viz. that "He spoke by the prophets." Therefore the articles of faith should contain some work appropriated to the Son in respect of His Godhead.

Obj. 6: Further, the sacrament of the Eucharist presents a special difficulty over and above the other articles. Therefore it should have been mentioned in a special article: and consequently it seems that there is not a sufficient number of articles.

On the contrary stands the authority of the Church who formulates the articles thus.

*I answer that,* As stated above (AA. 4, 6), to faith those things in themselves belong, the sight of which we shall enjoy in eternal life, and by which we are brought to eternal life. Now two things are proposed to us to be seen in eternal life: viz. the secret of the Godhead, to see which is to possess happiness; and the mystery of Christ's Incarnation, "by Whom we have access" to the glory of the sons of God, according to Rom. 5:2. Hence it is written (John 17:3): "This is eternal life: that they may know Thee, the ... true God, and Jesus Christ Whom Thou hast sent." Wherefore the first distinction in matters of faith is that some concern the majesty of the Godhead, while others pertain to the mystery of Christ's human nature, which is the "mystery of godliness" (1 Tim. 3:16).

Now with regard to the majesty of the Godhead, three things are proposed to our belief: first, the unity of the Godhead, to which the first article refers; secondly, the trinity of the Persons, to which three articles refer, corresponding to the three Persons; and thirdly, the works proper to the Godhead, the first of which refers to the order of nature, in relation to which the article about the creation is proposed to us; the second refers to the order of grace, in relation to which all matters concerning the sanctification of man are included in one article; while the third refers to the order of glory, and in relation to this another article is proposed to us concerning the resurrection of the dead and life everlasting. Thus there are seven articles referring to the Godhead.

In like manner, with regard to Christ's human nature, there are seven articles, the first of which refers to Christ's incarnation or conception; the second, to His virginal birth; the third, to His Passion, death and burial; the fourth, to His descent into hell; the fifth, to His resurrection; the sixth, to His ascension; the seventh, to His coming for the judgment, so that in all there are fourteen articles.

Some, however, distinguish twelve articles, six pertaining to the Godhead, and six to the humanity. For they include in one article the three about the three Persons; because we have one knowledge of the three Persons: while they divide the article referring to the work of glorification into two, viz. the resurrection of the body, and the glory of the soul. Likewise they unite the conception and nativity into one article.

Reply Obj. 1: By faith we hold many truths about God, which the philosophers were unable to discover by natural reason, for instance His providence and omnipotence, and that He alone is to be worshiped, all of which are contained in the one article of the unity of God.

Reply Obj. 2: The very name of the Godhead implies a kind of watching over things, as stated in the First Part (Q. 13, A. 8). Now in beings having an intellect, power does not work save by the will and knowledge. Hence God's omnipotence includes, in a way, universal knowledge and providence. For He would not be able to do all He wills in things here below, unless He knew them, and exercised His providence over them.

Reply Obj. 3: We have but one knowledge of the Father, Son, and Holy Ghost, as to the unity of the Essence, to which the first article refers: but, as to the distinction of the Persons, which is by the relations of origin, knowledge of the Father does indeed, in a way, include knowledge of the Son, for He would not be Father, had He not a Son; the bond whereof being the Holy Ghost. From this point of view, there was a sufficient motive for those who referred one article to the three Persons. Since, however, with regard to each Person, certain points have to be observed, about which some happen to fall into error, looking at it in this way, we may distinguish three articles about the three Persons. For Arius believed in the omnipotence and eternity of the Father, but did not believe the Son to be co-equal and consubstantial with the Father; hence the need for an article about the Person of the Son in order to settle this point. In like manner it was necessary to appoint a third article about the Person of the Holy Ghost, against Macedonius. In the same way Christ's conception and birth, just as the resurrection and life everlasting, can from one point of view be united together in one article, in so far as they are ordained to one end; while, from another point of view, they can be distinct articles, in as much as each one separately presents a special difficulty.

Reply Obj. 4: It belongs to the Son and Holy Ghost to be sent to sanctify the creature; and about this several things have to be believed. Hence it is that there are more articles about the Persons of the Son and Holy Ghost than about the Person of the Father, Who is never sent, as we stated in the First Part (Q. 43, A. 4).

Reply Obj. 5: The sanctification of a creature by grace, and its consummation by glory, is also effected by the gift of charity, which is appropriated to the Holy Ghost, and by the gift of wisdom, which is appropriated to the Son: so that each work belongs by appropriation, but under different aspects, both to the Son and to the Holy Ghost.

Reply Obj. 6: Two things may be considered in the sacrament of the Eucharist. One is the fact that it is a sacrament, and in this respect it is like the other effects of sanctifying grace. The other is that Christ's body is miraculously contained therein and thus it is included under God's omnipotence, like all other miracles which are ascribed to God's almighty power.

NINTH ARTICLE [II-II, Q. 1, Art. 9]

Whether It Is Suitable for the Articles of Faith to Be Embodied in a Symbol?

Objection 1: It would seem that it is unsuitable for the articles of faith to be embodied in a symbol. Because Holy Writ is the rule of faith, to which no addition or subtraction can lawfully be made, since it is written (Deut. 4:2): "You shall not add to the word that I speak to you, neither shall you take away from it." Therefore it was unlawful to make a symbol as a rule of faith, after the Holy Writ had once been published.

Obj. 2: Further, according to the Apostle (Eph. 4:5) there is but "one faith." Now the symbol is a profession of faith. Therefore it is not fitting that there should be more than one symbol.

Obj. 3: Further, the confession of faith, which is contained in the symbol, concerns all the faithful. Now the faithful are not all competent to believe in God, but only those who have living faith. Therefore it is unfitting for the symbol of faith to be expressed in the words: "I believe in one God."

Obj. 4: Further, the descent into hell is one of the articles of faith, as stated above (A. 8). But the descent into hell is not mentioned in the symbol of the Fathers. Therefore the latter is expressed inadequately.

Obj. 5: Further, Augustine (Tract. xxix in Joan.) expounding the passage, "You believe in God, believe also in Me" (John 14:1) says: "We believe Peter or Paul, but we speak only of believing 'in' God." Since then the Catholic Church is merely a created being, it seems unfitting to say: "In the One, Holy, Catholic and Apostolic Church."

Obj. 6: Further, a symbol is drawn up that it may be a rule of faith. Now a rule of faith ought to be proposed to all, and that publicly. Therefore every symbol, besides the symbol of the Fathers, should be sung at Mass. Therefore it seems unfitting to publish the articles of faith in a symbol.

*On the contrary,* The universal Church cannot err, since she is governed by the Holy Ghost, Who is the Spirit of truth: for such was Our Lord's promise to His disciples (John 16:13): "When He, the Spirit of truth, is come, He will teach you all truth." Now the symbol is published by the authority of the universal Church. Therefore it contains nothing defective.

*I answer that,* As the Apostle says (Heb. 11:6), "he that cometh to God, must believe that He is." Now a man cannot believe, unless the truth be proposed to him that he may believe it. Hence the need for the truth of faith to be collected together, so that it might the more easily be proposed to all, lest anyone might stray from the truth through ignorance of the faith. It is from its being a collection of maxims of faith that the symbol [*The Greek *symballein* ] takes its name.

Reply Obj. 1: The truth of faith is contained in Holy Writ, diffusely, under various modes of expression, and sometimes obscurely, so that, in order to gather the truth of faith from Holy Writ, one needs long study and practice, which are unattainable by all those who require to know the truth of faith, many of whom have no time for study, being busy with other affairs. And so it was necessary to gather together a clear summary from the sayings of Holy Writ, to be proposed to the belief of all. This indeed was no addition to Holy Writ, but something taken from it.

Reply Obj. 2: The same doctrine of faith is taught in all the symbols. Nevertheless, the people need more careful instruction about the truth of faith, when errors arise, lest the faith of simple-minded persons be corrupted by heretics. It was this that gave rise to the necessity of formulating several symbols, which nowise differ from one another, save that on account of the obstinacy of heretics, one contains more explicitly what another contains implicitly.

Reply Obj. 3: The confession of faith is drawn up in a symbol in the person, as it were, of the whole Church, which is united together by faith. Now the faith of the Church is living faith; since such is the faith to be found in all those who are of the Church not only outwardly but also by merit. Hence the confession of faith is expressed in a symbol, in a manner that is in keeping with living faith, so that even if some of the faithful lack living faith, they should endeavor to acquire it.

Reply Obj. 4: No error about the descent into hell had arisen among heretics, so that there was no need to be more explicit on that point. For this reason it is not repeated in the symbol of the Fathers, but is supposed as already settled in the symbol of the Apostles. For a subsequent symbol does not cancel a preceding one; rather does it expound it, as stated above (ad 2).

Reply Obj. 5: If we say: "'In' the holy Catholic Church," this must be taken as verified in so far as our faith is directed to the Holy Ghost, Who sanctifies the Church; so that the sense is: "I believe in the Holy Ghost sanctifying the Church." But it is better and more in keeping with the common use, to omit the 'in,' and say simply, "the holy Catholic Church," as Pope Leo [*Rufinus, Comm. in Sym. Apost.] observes.

Reply Obj. 6: Since the symbol of the Fathers is an explanation of the symbol of the Apostles, and was drawn up after the faith was already spread abroad, and when the Church was already at peace, it is sung publicly in the Mass. On the other hand the symbol of the Apostles, which was drawn up at the time of persecution, before the faith was made public, is said secretly at Prime and Compline, as though it were against the darkness of past and future errors.

TENTH ARTICLE [II-II, Q. 1, Art. 10]

Whether It Belongs to the Sovereign Pontiff to Draw Up a Symbol of Faith?

Objection 1: It would seem that it does not belong to the Sovereign Pontiff to draw up a symbol of faith. For a new edition of the symbol becomes necessary in order to explain the articles of faith, as stated above (A. 9). Now, in the Old Testament, the articles of faith were more and more explained as time went on, by reason of the truth of faith becoming clearer through greater nearness to Christ, as stated above (A. 7). Since then this reason ceased with the advent of the New Law, there is no need for the articles of faith to be more and more explicit. Therefore it does not seem to belong to the authority of the Sovereign Pontiff to draw up a new edition of the symbol.

Obj. 2: Further, no man has the power to do what is forbidden under pain of anathema by the universal Church. Now it was forbidden under pain of anathema by the universal Church, to make a new edition of the symbol. For it is stated in the acts of the first* council of Ephesus (P. ii, Act. 6) that "after the symbol of the Nicene council had been read through, the holy synod decreed that it was unlawful to utter, write or draw up any other creed, than that which was defined by the Fathers assembled at Nicaea together with the Holy Ghost," and this under pain of anathema. [*St. Thomas wrote 'first' (expunged by Nicolai) to distinguish it from the other council, A.D. 451, known as the "Latrocinium" and condemned by the Pope.] The same was repeated in the acts of the council of Chalcedon (P. ii, Act. 5). Therefore it seems that the Sovereign Pontiff has no authority to publish a new edition of the symbol.

Obj. 3: Further, Athanasius was not the Sovereign Pontiff, but patriarch of Alexandria, and yet he published a symbol which is sung in the Church. Therefore it does not seem to belong to the Sovereign Pontiff any more than to other bishops, to publish a new edition of the symbol.

*On the contrary,* The symbol was drawn up by a general council. Now such a council cannot be convoked otherwise than by the authority of the Sovereign Pontiff, as stated in the Decretals [*Dist. xvii, Can. 4, 5]. Therefore it belongs to the authority of the Sovereign Pontiff to draw up a symbol.

*I answer that,* As stated above (Obj. 1), a new edition of the symbol becomes necessary in order to set aside the errors that may arise. Consequently to publish a new edition of the symbol belongs to that authority which is empowered to decide matters of faith finally, so that they may be held by all with unshaken faith. Now this belongs to the authority of the Sovereign Pontiff, "to whom the more important and more difficult questions that arise in the Church are referred," as stated in the Decretals [*Dist. xvii, Can. 5]. Hence our Lord said to Peter whom he made Sovereign Pontiff (Luke 22:32): "I have prayed for thee," Peter, "that thy faith fail not, and thou, being once converted, confirm thy brethren." The reason of this is that there should be but one faith of the whole Church, according to 1 Cor. 1:10: "That you all speak the same thing, and that there be no schisms among you": and this could not be secured unless any question of faith that may arise be decided by him who presides over the whole Church, so that the whole Church may hold firmly to his decision. Consequently it belongs to the sole authority of the Sovereign Pontiff to publish a new edition of the symbol, as do all other matters which concern the whole Church, such as to convoke a general council and so forth.

Reply Obj. 1: The truth of faith is sufficiently explicit in the teaching of Christ and the apostles. But since, according to 2 Pet. 3:16, some men are so evil-minded as to pervert the apostolic teaching and other doctrines and Scriptures to their own destruction, it was necessary as time went on to express the faith more explicitly against the errors which arose.

Reply Obj. 2: This prohibition and sentence of the council was intended for private individuals, who have no business to decide matters of faith: for this decision of the general council did not take away from a subsequent council the power of drawing up a new edition of the symbol, containing not indeed a new faith, but the same faith with greater explicitness. For every council has taken into account that a subsequent council would expound matters more fully than the preceding council, if this became necessary through some heresy arising. Consequently this belongs to the Sovereign Pontiff, by whose authority the council is convoked, and its decision confirmed.

Reply Obj. 3: Athanasius drew up a declaration of faith, not under the form of a symbol, but rather by way of an exposition of doctrine, as appears from his way of speaking. But since it contained briefly the whole truth of faith, it was accepted by the authority of the Sovereign Pontiff, so as to be considered as a rule of faith. Since it contained briefly the whole truth of faith, it was accepted by the authority of the Sovereign Pontiff, so as to be considered as a rule of faith.

# QUESTION 2

OF THE ACT OF FAITH (In Ten Articles)

We must now consider the act of faith, and (1) the internal act; (2) the external act.

Under the first head there are ten points of inquiry:

(1) What is "to believe," which is the internal act of faith?

(2) In how many ways is it expressed?

(3) Whether it is necessary for salvation to believe in anything above natural reason?

(4) Whether it is necessary to believe those things that are attainable by natural reason?

(5) Whether it is necessary for salvation to believe certain things explicitly?

(6) Whether all are equally bound to explicit faith?

(7) Whether explicit faith in Christ is always necessary for salvation?

(8) Whether it is necessary for salvation to believe in the Trinity explicitly?

(9) Whether the act of faith is meritorious?

(10) Whether human reason diminishes the merit of faith?

FIRST ARTICLE [II-II, Q. 2, Art. 1]

Whether to Believe Is to Think with Assent?

Objection 1: It would seem that to believe is not to think with assent. Because the Latin word "cogitatio" [thought] implies a research, for "cogitare" [to think] seems to be equivalent to "coagitare," i.e. "to discuss together." Now Damascene says (De Fide Orth. iv) that faith is "an assent without research." Therefore thinking has no place in the act of faith.

Obj. 2: Further, faith resides in the reason, as we shall show further on (Q. 4, A. 2). Now to think is an act of the cogitative power, which belongs to the sensitive faculty, as stated in the First Part (Q. 78, A. 4). Therefore thought has nothing to do with faith.

Obj. 3: Further, to believe is an act of the intellect, since its object is truth. But assent seems to be an act not of the intellect, but of the will, even as consent is, as stated above (I-II, Q. 15, A. 1, ad 3). Therefore to believe is not to think with assent.

*On the contrary,* This is how "to believe" is defined by Augustine (De Praedest. Sanct. ii).

*I answer that,* "To think" can be taken in three ways. First, in a general way for any kind of actual consideration of the intellect, as Augustine observes (De Trin. xiv, 7): "By understanding I mean now the faculty whereby we understand when thinking." Secondly, "to think" is more strictly taken for that consideration of the intellect, which is accompanied by some kind of inquiry, and which precedes the intellect's arrival at the stage of perfection that comes with the certitude of sight. In this sense Augustine says (De Trin. xv, 16) that "the Son of God is not called the Thought, but the Word of God. When our thought realizes what we know and takes form therefrom, it becomes our word. Hence the Word of God must be understood without any thinking on the part of God, for there is nothing there that can take form, or be unformed." In this way thought is, properly speaking, the movement of the mind while yet deliberating, and not yet perfected by the clear sight of truth. Since, however, such a movement of the mind may be one of deliberation either about universal notions, which belongs to the intellectual faculty, or about particular matters, which belongs to the sensitive part, hence it is that "to think" is taken secondly for an act of the deliberating intellect, and thirdly for an act of the cogitative power.

Accordingly, if "to think" be understood broadly according to the first sense, then "to think with assent," does not express completely what is meant by "to believe": since, in this way, a man thinks with assent even when he considers what he knows by science [*Science is certain knowledge of a demonstrated conclusion through its demonstration.], or understands. If, on the other hand, "to think" be understood in the second way, then this expresses completely the nature of the act of believing. For among the acts belonging to the intellect, some have a firm assent without any such kind of thinking, as when a man considers the things that he knows by science, or understands, for this consideration is already formed. But some acts of the intellect have unformed thought devoid of a firm assent, whether they incline to neither side, as in one who "doubts"; or incline to one side rather than the other, but on account of some slight motive, as in one who "suspects"; or incline to one side yet with fear of the other, as in one who "opines." But this act "to believe," cleaves firmly to one side, in which respect belief has something in common with science and understanding; yet its knowledge does not attain the perfection of clear sight, wherein it agrees with doubt, suspicion and opinion. Hence it is proper to the believer to think with assent: so that the act of believing is distinguished from all the other acts of the intellect, which are about the true or the false.

Reply Obj. 1: Faith has not that research of natural reason which demonstrates what is believed, but a research into those things whereby a man is induced to believe, for instance that such things have been uttered by God and confirmed by miracles.

Reply Obj. 2: "To think" is not taken here for the

act of the cogitative power, but for an act of the intellect, as explained above.

Reply Obj. 3: The intellect of the believer is determined to one object, not by the reason, but by the will, wherefore assent is taken here for an act of the intellect as determined to one object by the will.

SECOND ARTICLE [II-II, Q. 2, Art. 2]

Whether the Act of Faith Is Suitably Distinguished As Believing God, Believing in a God and Believing in God?

Objection 1: It would seem that the act of faith is unsuitably distinguished as believing God, believing in a God, and believing in God. For one habit has but one act. Now faith is one habit since it is one virtue. Therefore it is unreasonable to say that there are three acts of faith.

Obj. 2: Further, that which is common to all acts of faith should not be reckoned as a particular kind of act of faith. Now "to believe God" is common to all acts of faith, since faith is founded on the First Truth. Therefore it seems unreasonable to distinguish it from certain other acts of faith.

Obj. 3: Further, that which can be said of unbelievers, cannot be called an act of faith. Now unbelievers can be said to believe in a God. Therefore it should not be reckoned an act of faith.

Obj. 4: Further, movement towards the end belongs to the will, whose object is the good and the end. Now to believe is an act, not of the will, but of the intellect. Therefore "to believe in God," which implies movement towards an end, should not be reckoned as a species of that act.

*On the contrary* is the authority of Augustine who makes this distinction (De Verb. Dom., Serm. lxi—Tract. xxix in Joan.).

*I answer that,* The act of any power or habit depends on the relation of that power or habit to its object. Now the object of faith can be considered in three ways. For, since "to believe" is an act of the intellect, in so far as the will moves it to assent, as stated above (A. 1, ad 3), the object of faith can be considered either on the part of the intellect, or on the part of the will that moves the intellect.

If it be considered on the part of the intellect, then two things can be observed in the object of faith, as stated above (Q. 1, A. 1). One of these is the material object of faith, and in this way an act of faith is "to believe in a God"; because, as stated above (ibid.) nothing is proposed to our belief, except in as much as it is referred to God. The other is the formal aspect of the object, for it is the medium on account of which we assent to such and such a point of faith; and thus an act of faith is "to believe God," since, as stated above (ibid.) the formal object of faith is the First Truth, to Which man gives his adhesion, so as to assent for Its sake to whatever he believes.

Thirdly, if the object of faith be considered in so far as the intellect is moved by the will, an act of faith is "to believe in God." For the First Truth is referred to the will, through having the aspect of an end.

Reply Obj. 1: These three do not denote different acts of faith, but one and the same act having different relations to the object of faith.

This suffices for the Reply to the Second Objection.

Reply Obj. 3: Unbelievers cannot be said "to believe in a God" as we understand it in relation to the act of faith. For they do not believe that God exists under the conditions that faith determines; hence they do not truly imply believe in a God, since, as the Philosopher observes (Metaph. ix, text. 22) "to know simple things defectively is not to know them at all."

Reply Obj. 4: As stated above (I-II, Q. 9, A. 1) the will moves the intellect and the other powers of the soul to the end: and in this respect an act of faith is "to believe in God."

THIRD ARTICLE [II-II, Q. 2, Art. 3]

Whether It Is Necessary for Salvation to Believe Anything Above the Natural Reason?

Objection 1: It would seem unnecessary for salvation to believe anything above the natural reason. For the salvation and perfection of a thing seem to be sufficiently insured by its natural endowments. Now matters of faith, surpass man's natural reason, since they are things unseen as stated above (Q. 1, A. 4). Therefore to believe seems unnecessary for salvation.

Obj. 2: Further, it is dangerous for man to assent to matters, wherein he cannot judge whether that which is proposed to him be true or false, according to Job 12:11: "Doth not the ear discern words?" Now a man cannot form a judgment of this kind in matters of faith, since he cannot trace them back to first principles, by which all our judgments are guided. Therefore it is dangerous to believe in such matters. Therefore to believe is not necessary for salvation.

Obj. 3: Further, man's salvation rests on God, according to Ps. 36:39: "But the salvation of the just is from the Lord." Now "the invisible things" of God "are clearly seen, being understood by the things that are made; His eternal power also and Divinity," according to Rom. 1:20: and those things which are clearly seen by the understanding are not an object of belief. Therefore it is not necessary for man's salvation, that he should believe certain things.

*On the contrary,* It is written (Heb. 11:6): "Without faith it is impossible to please God."

*I answer that,* Wherever one nature is subordinate to another, we find that two things concur towards the perfection of the lower nature, one of which is in respect of that nature's proper movement, while the other is in respect of the movement of the higher nature. Thus water by its proper movement moves towards the centre (of the earth), while according to the movement of the moon, it moves round the centre by ebb and flow. In like manner the planets have their proper movements from west to east, while in accordance with the movement of the first heaven, they have a movement from east to west. Now the created rational nature alone is immediately subordinate to God, since other creatures do not attain to the universal, but only to something particular, while they partake of the Divine goodness either in *being* only, as inanimate things, or also in living, and in *knowing singulars,* as plants and animals; whereas the rational nature, in as much as it apprehends the universal notion of good and being, is immediately related to the universal principle of being.

Consequently the perfection of the rational creature consists not only in what belongs to it in respect of its nature, but also in that which it acquires through a supernatural participation of Divine goodness. Hence it was said above (I-II, Q. 3, A. 8) that man's ultimate happiness consists in a supernatural vision of God: to which vision man cannot attain unless he be taught by God, according to John 6:45: "Every one that hath heard of the Father and hath learned cometh to Me." Now man acquires a share of this learning, not indeed all at once, but by little and little, according to the mode of his nature: and every one who learns thus must needs believe, in order that he may acquire science in a perfect degree; thus also the Philosopher remarks (De Soph. Elench. i, 2) that "it behooves a learner to believe."

Hence in order that a man arrive at the perfect vision of heavenly happiness, he must first of all believe God, as a disciple believes the master who is teaching him.

Reply Obj. 1: Since man's nature is dependent on a higher nature, natural knowledge does not suffice for its perfection, and some supernatural knowledge is necessary, as stated above.

Reply Obj. 2: Just as man assents to first principles, by the natural light of his intellect, so does a virtuous man, by the habit of virtue, judge aright of things concerning that virtue; and in this way, by the light of faith which God bestows on him, a man assents to matters of faith and not to those which are against faith. Consequently "there is no" danger or "condemnation to them that are in Christ Jesus," and whom He has enlightened by faith.

Reply Obj. 3: In many respects faith perceives the invisible things of God in a higher way than natural reason does in proceeding to God from His creatures. Hence it is written (Ecclus. 3:25): "Many things are shown to thee above the understandings of man."

FOURTH ARTICLE [II-II, Q. 2, Art. 4]

Whether It Is Necessary to Believe Those Things Which Can Be Proved by Natural Reason?

Objection 1: It would seem unnecessary to believe those things which can be proved by natural reason. For nothing is superfluous in God's works, much less even than in the works of nature. Now it is superfluous to employ other means, where one already suffices. Therefore it would be superfluous to receive by faith, things that can be known by natural reason.

Obj. 2: Further, those things must be believed, which are the object of faith. Now science and faith are not about the same object, as stated above (Q. 1, AA. 4, 5). Since therefore all things that can be known by natural reason are an object of science, it seems that there is no need to believe what can be proved by natural reason.

Obj. 3: Further, all things knowable scientifically [*Science is certain knowledge of a demonstrated conclusion through its demonstration] would seem to come under one head: so that if some of them are proposed to man as objects of faith, in like manner the others should also be believed. But this is not true. Therefore it is not necessary to believe those things which can be proved by natural reason.

*On the contrary,* It is necessary to believe that God is one and incorporeal: which things philosophers prove by natural reason.

*I answer that,* It is necessary for man to accept by faith not only things which are above reason, but also those which can be known by reason: and this for three motives. First, in order that man may arrive more quickly at the knowledge of Divine truth. Because the science to whose province it belongs to prove the existence of God, is the last of all to offer itself to human research, since it presupposes many other sciences: so that it would not by until late in life that man would arrive at the knowledge of God. The second reason is, in order that the knowledge of God may be more general. For many are unable to make progress in the study of science, either through dullness of mind, or through having a number of occupations, and temporal needs, or even through laziness in learning, all of whom would be altogether deprived of the knowledge of God, unless Divine things were brought to their knowledge under the guise of faith. The third reason is for the sake of certitude. For human reason is very deficient in things concerning God. A sign of this is that philosophers in their researches, by natural investigation, into human affairs, have fallen into many errors, and have disagreed among themselves. And consequently, in order that men might have knowledge of God, free of doubt and uncertainty, it was necessary for Divine matters to be delivered to them by way of faith, being told to them, as it were, by God Himself Who cannot lie.

Reply Obj. 1: The researches of natural reason do not suffice mankind for the knowledge of Divine matters, even of those that can be proved by reason: and so it is not superfluous if these others be believed.

Reply Obj. 2: Science and faith cannot be in the same subject and about the same object: but what is an object of science for one, can be an object of faith for another, as stated above (Q. 1, A. 5).

Reply Obj. 3: Although all things that can be known by science are of one common scientific aspect, they do not all alike lead man to beatitude: hence they are not all equally proposed to our belief.

FIFTH ARTICLE [II-II, Q. 2, Art. 5]

Whether Man Is Bound to Believe Anything Explicitly?

Objection 1: It would seem that man is not bound to believe anything explicitly. For no man is bound to do what is not in his power. Now it is not in man's power to believe a thing explicitly, for it is written (Rom. 10:14, 15): "How shall they believe Him, of whom they have not heard? And how shall they hear without a preacher? And how shall they preach unless they be sent?" Therefore man is not bound to believe anything explicitly.

Obj. 2: Further, just as we are directed to God by faith, so are we by charity. Now man is not bound to keep the precepts of charity, and it is enough if he be ready to fulfil them: as is evidenced by the precept of Our Lord (Matt. 5:39): "If one strike thee on one [Vulg.: 'thy right'] cheek, turn to him also the other"; and by others of the same kind, according to Augustine's exposition (De Serm. Dom. in Monte xix). Therefore neither is man bound to believe anything explicitly, and it is enough if he be ready to believe whatever God proposes to be believed.

Obj. 3: Further, the good of faith consists in obedience, according to Rom. 1:5: "For obedience to the faith in all nations." Now the virtue of obedience does not require man to keep certain fixed precepts, but it is enough that his mind be ready to obey, according to Ps. 118:60: "I am ready and am not troubled; that I may keep Thy commandments." Therefore it seems enough for faith, too, that man should be ready to believe whatever God may propose, without his believing anything explicitly.

*On the contrary,* It is written (Heb. 11:6): "He that cometh to God, must believe that He is, and is a rewarder to them that seek Him."

*I answer that,* The precepts of the Law, which man is bound to fulfil, concern acts of virtue which are the means of attaining salvation. Now an act of virtue, as stated above (I-II, Q. 60, A. 5) depends on the relation of the habit to its object. Again two things may be considered in the object of any virtue; namely, that which is the proper and direct object of that virtue, and that which is accidental and consequent to the object properly so called. Thus it belongs properly and directly to the object of fortitude, to face the dangers of death, and to charge at the foe with danger to oneself, for the sake of the common good: yet that, in a just war, a man be armed, or strike another with his sword, and so forth, is reduced to the object of fortitude, but indirectly.

Accordingly, just as a virtuous act is required for the fulfilment of a precept, so is it necessary that the virtuous act should terminate in its proper and direct object: but, on the other hand, the fulfilment of the precept does not require that a virtuous act should terminate in those things which have an accidental or secondary relation to the proper and direct object of that virtue, except in certain places and at certain times. We must, therefore, say that the direct object of faith is that whereby man is made one of the Blessed, as stated above (Q. 1, A. 8): while the indirect and secondary object comprises all things delivered by God to us in Holy Writ, for instance that Abraham had two sons, that David was the son of Jesse, and so forth.

Therefore, as regards the primary points or articles of faith, man is bound to believe them, just as he is bound to have faith; but as to other points of faith, man is not bound to believe them explicitly, but only implicitly, or to be ready to believe them, in so far as he is prepared to believe whatever is contained in the Divine Scriptures. Then alone is he bound to believe such things explicitly, when it is clear to him that they are contained in the doctrine of faith.

Reply Obj. 1: If we understand those things alone to be in a man's power, which we can do without the help of grace, then we are bound to do many things which we cannot do without the aid of healing grace, such as to love God and our neighbor, and likewise to believe the articles of faith. But with the help of grace we can do this, for this help "to whomsoever it is given from above it is mercifully given; and from whom it is withheld it is justly withheld, as a punishment of a previous, or at least of original, sin," as Augustine states (De Corr. et Grat. v, vi [*Cf. Ep. cxc; De Praed. Sanct. viii.]).

Reply Obj. 2: Man is bound to love definitely those lovable things which are properly and directly the objects of charity, namely, God and our neighbor. The objection refers to those precepts of charity which belong, as a consequence, to the objects of charity.

Reply Obj. 3: The virtue of obedience is seated, properly speaking, in the will; hence promptness of the will subject to authority, suffices for the act of obedience, because it is the proper and direct object of obedience. But this or that precept is accidental or consequent to that proper and direct object.

SIXTH ARTICLE [II-II, Q. 2, Art. 6]

Whether All Are Equally Bound to Have Explicit Faith?

Objection 1: It would seem that all are equally bound to have explicit faith. For all are bound to those things which are necessary for salvation, as is evidenced by the precepts of charity. Now it is necessary for salvation that certain things should be believed explicitly. Therefore all are equally bound to have explicit faith.

Obj. 2: Further, no one should be put to test in matters that he is not bound to believe. But simple persons are sometimes tested in reference to the slightest articles of faith. Therefore all are bound to believe everything explicitly.

Obj. 3: Further, if the simple are bound to have, not explicit but only implicit faith, their faith must needs be implied in the faith of the learned. But this seems unsafe, since it is possible for the learned to err. Therefore it seems that the simple should also have explicit faith; so that all are, therefore, equally bound to have explicit faith.

*On the contrary,* It is written (Job 1:14): "The oxen were ploughing, and the asses feeding beside them," because, as Gregory expounds this passage (Moral. ii, 17), the simple, who are signified by the asses, ought, in matters of faith, to stay by the learned, who are denoted by the oxen.

*I answer that,* The unfolding of matters of faith is the result of Divine revelation: for matters of faith surpass natural reason. Now Divine revelation reaches those of lower degree through those who are over them, in a certain order; to men, for instance, through the angels, and to the lower angels through the higher, as Dionysius explains (Coel. Hier. iv, vii). In like manner therefore the unfolding of faith must needs reach men of lower degree through those of higher degree. Consequently, just as the higher angels, who enlighten those who are below them, have a fuller knowledge of Divine things than the lower angels, as Dionysius states (Coel. Hier. xii), so too, men of higher degree, whose business it is to teach others, are under obligation to have fuller knowledge of matters of faith, and to believe them more explicitly.

Reply Obj. 1: The unfolding of the articles of faith is not equally necessary for the salvation of all, since those of higher degree, whose duty it is to teach others, are bound to believe explicitly more things than others are.

Reply Obj. 2: Simple persons should not be put to the test about subtle questions of faith, unless they be suspected of having been corrupted by heretics, who are wont to corrupt the faith of simple people in such questions. If, however, it is found that they are free from obstinacy in their heterodox sentiments, and that it is due to their simplicity, it is no fault of theirs.

Reply Obj. 3: The simple have no faith implied in that of the learned, except in so far as the latter adhere to the Divine teaching. Hence the Apostle says (1 Cor. 4:16): "Be ye followers of me, as I also am of Christ." Hence it is not human knowledge, but the Divine truth that is the rule of faith: and if any of the learned stray from this rule, he does not harm the faith of the simple ones, who think that the learned believe aright; unless the simple hold obstinately to their individual errors, against the faith of the universal Church, which cannot err, since Our Lord said (Luke 22:32): "I have prayed for thee," Peter, "that thy faith fail not."

SEVENTH ARTICLE [II-II, Q. 2, Art. 7]

Whether It Is Necessary for the Salvation of All, That They Should Believe Explicitly in the Mystery of Christ?

Objection 1: It would seem that it is not necessary for the salvation of all that they should believe explicitly in the mystery of Christ. For man is not bound to believe explicitly what the angels are ignorant about: since the unfolding of faith is the result of Divine revelation, which reaches man by means of the angels, as stated above (A. 6; I, Q. 111, A. 1). Now even the angels were in ignorance of the mystery of the Incarnation: hence, according to the commentary of Dionysius (Coel. Hier. vii), it is they who ask (Ps. 23:8): "Who is this king of glory?" and (Isa. 63:1): "Who is this that cometh from Edom?" Therefore men were not bound to believe explicitly in the mystery of Christ's Incarnation.

Obj. 2: Further, it is evident that John the Baptist was one of the teachers, and most nigh to Christ, Who said of him (Matt. 11:11) that "there hath not risen among them that are born of women, a greater than" he. Now John the Baptist does not appear to have known the mystery of Christ explicitly, since he asked Christ (Matt. 11:3): "Art Thou He that art to come, or look we for another?" Therefore even the teachers were not bound to explicit faith in Christ.

Obj. 3: Further, many gentiles obtained salvation through the ministry of the angels, as Dionysius states (Coel. Hier. ix). Now it would seem that the gentiles had neither explicit nor implicit faith in Christ, since they received no revelation. Therefore it seems that it was not necessary for the salvation of all to believe explicitly in the mystery of Christ.

*On the contrary,* Augustine says (De Corr. et Gratia vii; Ep. cxc): "Our faith is sound if we believe that no man, old or young is delivered from the contagion of death and the bonds of sin, except by the one Mediator of God and men, Jesus Christ."

*I answer that,* As stated above (A. 5; Q. 1, A. 8), the object of faith includes, properly and directly, that thing through which man obtains beatitude. Now the mystery of Christ's Incarnation and Passion is the way by which men obtain beatitude; for it is written (Acts 4:12): "There is no other name under heaven given to men, whereby we must be saved." Therefore belief of some kind in the mystery of Christ's Incarnation was necessary at all times and for all persons, but this belief differed according to differences of times and persons. The reason of this is that before the state of sin, man believed, explicitly in Christ's Incarnation, in so far as it was intended for the consummation of glory, but not as it was intended to deliver man from sin by the Passion and Resurrection, since man had no foreknowledge of his future sin. He does, however, seem to have had foreknowledge of the Incarnation of Christ, from the fact that he said (Gen. 2:24): "Wherefore a man shall leave father and mother, and shall cleave to his wife," of which the Apostle says (Eph. 5:32) that "this is a great sacrament ... in Christ and the Church," and it is incredible that the first man was ignorant about this sacrament.

But after sin, man believed explicitly in Christ, not only as to the Incarnation, but also as to the Passion and Resurrection, whereby the human race is delivered from sin and death: for they would not, else, have foreshadowed Christ's Passion by certain sacrifices both before and after the Law, the meaning of which sacrifices was known by the learned explicitly, while the simple folk, under the veil of those sacrifices, believed them to be ordained by God in reference to Christ's coming, and thus their knowledge was covered with a veil, so to speak. And, as stated above (Q. 1, A. 7), the nearer they were to Christ, the more distinct was their knowledge of Christ's mysteries.

After grace had been revealed, both learned and simple folk are bound to explicit faith in the mysteries of Christ, chiefly as regards those which are observed throughout the Church, and publicly proclaimed, such as the articles which refer to the Incarnation, of which we have spoken above (Q. 1, A. 8). As to other minute points in reference to the articles of the Incarnation, men have been bound to believe them more or less explicitly according to each one's state and office.

Reply Obj. 1: The mystery of the Kingdom of God was not entirely hidden from the angels, as Augustine observes (Gen. ad lit. v, 19), yet certain aspects thereof were better known to them when Christ revealed them to them.

Reply Obj. 2: It was not through ignorance that John the Baptist inquired of Christ's advent in the flesh, since he had clearly professed his belief therein, saying: "I saw, and I gave testimony, that this is the Son of God" (John 1:34). Hence he did not say: "Art Thou He that hast come?" but "Art Thou He that art to come?" thus saying about the future, not about the past. Likewise it is not to be believed that he was ignorant of Christ's future Passion, for he had already said (John 1:39): "Behold the Lamb of God, behold Him who taketh away the sins [Vulg.: 'sin'] of the world," thus foretelling His future immolation; and since other prophets had foretold it, as may be seen especially in Isaias 53. We may therefore say with Gregory (Hom. xxvi in Evang.) that he asked this question, being in ignorance as to whether Christ would descend into hell in His own Person. But he did not ignore the fact that the power of Christ's Passion would be extended to those who were detained in Limbo, according to Zech. 9:11: "Thou also, by the blood of Thy testament hast sent forth Thy prisoners out of the pit, wherein there is no water"; nor was he bound to believe explicitly, before its fulfilment, that Christ was to descend thither Himself.

It may also be replied that, as Ambrose observes in his commentary on Luke 7:19, he made this inquiry, not from doubt or ignorance but from devotion: or again, with Chrysostom (Hom. xxxvi in Matth.), that he inquired, not as though ignorant himself, but because he wished his disciples to be satisfied on that point, through Christ: hence the latter framed His answer so as to instruct the disciples, by pointing to the signs of His works.

Reply Obj. 3: Many of the gentiles received revelations of Christ, as is clear from their predictions. Thus we read (Job 19:25): "I know that my Redeemer liveth." The Sibyl too foretold certain things about Christ, as Augustine states (Contra Faust. xiii, 15). Moreover, we read in the history of the Romans, that at the time of Constantine Augustus and his mother Irene a tomb was discovered, wherein lay a man on whose breast was a golden plate with the inscription: "Christ shall be born of a virgin, and in Him, I believe. O sun, during the lifetime of Irene and Constantine, thou shalt see me again" [*Cf. Baron, Annal., A.D. 780]. If, however, some were saved without receiving any revelation, they were not saved without faith in a Mediator, for, though they did not believe in Him explicitly, they did, nevertheless, have implicit faith through believing in Divine providence, since they believed that God would deliver mankind in whatever way was pleasing to Him, and according to the revelation of the Spirit to those who knew the truth, as stated in Job 35:11: "Who teacheth us more than the beasts of the earth."

EIGHTH ARTICLE [II-II, Q. 2, Art. 8]

Whether It Is Necessary for Salvation to Believe Explicitly in the Trinity?

Objection 1: It would seem that it was not necessary for salvation to believe explicitly in the Trinity. For the Apostle says (Heb. 11:6): "He that cometh to God must believe that He is, and is a rewarder to them that seek Him." Now one can believe this without believing in the Trinity. Therefore it was not necessary to believe explicitly in the Trinity.

Obj. 2: Further our Lord said (John 17:5, 6): "Father, I have manifested Thy name to men," which words Augustine expounds (Tract. cvi) as follows: "Not the name by which Thou art called God, but the name whereby Thou art called My Father," and further on he adds: "In that He made this world, God is known to all nations; in that He is not to be worshipped together with false gods, 'God is known in Judea'; but, in that He is the Father of this Christ, through Whom He takes away the sin of the world, He now makes known to men this name of His, which hitherto they knew not." Therefore before the coming of Christ it was not known that Paternity and Filiation were in the Godhead: and so the Trinity was not believed explicitly.

Obj. 3: Further, that which we are bound to believe explicitly of God is the object of heavenly happiness. Now the object of heavenly happiness is the sovereign good, which can be understood to be in God, without any distinction of Persons. Therefore it was not necessary to believe explicitly in the Trinity.

*On the contrary,* In the Old Testament the Trinity of Persons is expressed in many ways; thus at the very outset of Genesis it is written in manifestation of the Trinity: "Let us make man to Our image and likeness" (Gen. 1:26). Therefore from the very beginning it was necessary for salvation to believe in the Trinity.

*I answer that,* It is impossible to believe explicitly in the mystery of Christ, without faith in the Trinity, since the mystery of Christ includes that the Son of God took flesh; that He renewed the world through the grace of the Holy Ghost; and again, that He was conceived by the Holy Ghost. Wherefore just as, before Christ, the mystery of Christ was believed explicitly by the learned, but implicitly and under a veil, so to speak, by the simple, so too was it with the mystery of the Trinity. And consequently, when once grace had been revealed, all were bound to explicit faith in the mystery of the Trinity: and all who are born again in Christ, have this bestowed on them by the invocation of the Trinity, according to Matt. 28:19: "Going therefore teach ye all nations, baptizing them in the name of the Father, and of the Son and of the Holy Ghost."

Reply Obj. 1: Explicit faith in those two things was necessary at all times and for all people: but it was not sufficient at all times and for all people.

Reply Obj. 2: Before Christ's coming, faith in the Trinity lay hidden in the faith of the learned, but through Christ and the apostles it was shown to the world.

Reply Obj. 3: God's sovereign goodness as we understand it now through its effects, can be understood without the Trinity of Persons: but as understood in itself, and as seen by the Blessed, it cannot be understood without the Trinity of Persons. Moreover the mission of the Divine Persons brings us to heavenly happiness.

NINTH ARTICLE [II-II, Q. 2, Art. 9]

Whether to Believe Is Meritorious?

Objection 1: It would seem that to believe is not meritorious. For the principle of all merit is charity, as stated above (I-II, Q. 114, A. 4). Now faith, like nature, is a preamble to charity. Therefore, just as an act of nature is not meritorious, since we do not merit by our natural gifts, so neither is an act of faith.

Obj. 2: Further, belief is a mean between opinion and scientific knowledge or the consideration of things scientifically known [*Science is a certain knowledge of a demonstrated conclusion through its demonstration.]. Now the considerations of science are not meritorious, nor on the other hand is opinion. Therefore belief is not meritorious.

Obj. 3: Further, he who assents to a point of faith, either has a sufficient motive for believing, or he has not. If he has a sufficient motive for his belief, this does not seem to imply any merit on his part, since he is no longer free to believe or not to believe: whereas if he has not a sufficient motive for believing, this is a mark of levity, according to Ecclus. 19:4: "He that is hasty to give credit, is light of heart," so that, seemingly, he gains no merit thereby. Therefore to believe is by no means meritorious.

*On the contrary,* It is written (Heb. 11:33) that the saints "by faith ... obtained promises," which would not be the case if they did not merit by believing. Therefore to believe is meritorious.

*I answer that,* As stated above (I-II, Q. 114, AA. 3, 4), our actions are meritorious in so far as they proceed from the free-will moved with grace by God. Therefore every human act proceeding from the free-will, if it be referred to God, can be meritorious. Now the act of believing is an act of the intellect assenting to the Divine truth at the command of the will moved by the grace of God, so that it is subject to the free-will in relation to God; and consequently the act of faith can be meritorious.

Reply Obj. 1: Nature is compared to charity which is the principle of merit, as matter to form: whereas faith is compared to charity as the disposition which precedes the ultimate form. Now it is evident that the subject or the matter cannot act save by virtue of the form, nor can a preceding disposition, before the advent of the form: but after the advent of the form, both the subject and the preceding disposition act by virtue of the form, which is the chief principle of action, even as the heat of fire acts by virtue of the substantial form of fire. Accordingly neither nature nor faith can, without charity, produce a meritorious act; but, when accompanied by charity, the act of faith is made meritorious thereby, even as an act of nature, and a natural act of the free-will.

Reply Obj. 2: Two things may be considered in science: namely the scientist's assent to a scientific fact and his consideration of that fact. Now the assent of science is not subject to free-will, because the scientist is obliged to assent by force of the demonstration, wherefore scientific assent is not meritorious. But the actual consideration of what a man knows scientifically is subject to his free-will, for it is in his power to consider or not to consider. Hence scientific consideration may be meritorious if it be referred to the end of charity, i.e. to the honor of God or the good of our neighbor. On the other hand, in the case of faith, both these things are subject to the free-will so that in both respects the act of faith can be meritorious: whereas in the case of opinion, there is no firm assent, since it is weak and infirm, as the Philosopher observes (Poster. i, 33), so that it does not seem to proceed from a perfect act of the will: and for this reason, as regards the assent, it does not appear to be very meritorious, though it can be as regards the actual consideration.

Reply Obj. 3: The believer has sufficient motive for believing, for he is moved by the authority of Divine teaching confirmed by miracles, and, what is more, by the inward instinct of the Divine invitation: hence he does not believe lightly. He has not, however, sufficient reason for scientific knowledge, hence he does not lose the merit.

TENTH ARTICLE [II-II, Q. 2, Art. 10]

Whether Reasons in Support of What We Believe Lessen the Merit of Faith?

Objection 1: It would seem that reasons in support of what we believe lessen the merit of faith. For Gregory says (Hom. xxvi in Evang.) that "there is no merit in believing what is shown by reason." If, therefore, human reason provides sufficient proof, the merit of faith is altogether taken away. Therefore it seems that any kind of human reasoning in support of matters of faith, diminishes the merit of believing.

Obj. 2: Further, whatever lessens the measure of virtue, lessens the amount of merit, since "happiness is the reward of virtue," as the Philosopher states (Ethic. i, 9). Now human reasoning seems to diminish the measure of the virtue of faith, since it is essential to faith to be about the unseen, as stated above (Q. 1, AA. 4, 5). Now the more a thing is supported by reasons the less is it unseen. Therefore human reasons in support of matters of faith diminish the merit of faith.

Obj. 3: Further, contrary things have contrary causes. Now an inducement in opposition to faith increases the merit of faith whether it consist in persecution inflicted by one who endeavors to force a man to renounce his faith, or in an argument persuading him to do so. Therefore reasons in support of faith diminish the merit of faith.

*On the contrary,* It is written (1 Pet. 3:15): "Being ready always to satisfy every one that asketh you a reason of that faith [*Vulg.: 'Of that hope which is in you.' St. Thomas' reading is apparently taken from Bede.] and hope which is in you." Now the Apostle would not give this advice, if it would imply a diminution in the merit of faith. Therefore reason does not diminish the merit of faith.

*I answer that,* As stated above (A. 9), the act of faith can be meritorious, in so far as it is subject to the will, not only as to the use, but also as to the assent. Now human reason in support of what we believe, may stand in a twofold relation to the will of the believer. First, as preceding the act of the will; as, for instance, when a man either has not the will, or not a prompt will, to believe, unless he be moved by human reasons: and in this way human reason diminishes the merit of faith. In this sense it has been said above (I-II, Q. 24, A. 3, ad 1; Q. 77, A. 6, ad 2) that, in moral virtues, a passion which precedes choice makes the virtuous act less praiseworthy. For just as a man ought to perform acts of moral virtue, on account of the judgment of his reason, and not on account of a passion, so ought he to believe matters of faith, not on account of human reason, but on account of the Divine authority. Secondly, human reasons may be consequent to the will of the believer. For when a man's will is ready to believe, he loves the truth he believes, he thinks out and takes to heart whatever reasons he can find in support thereof; and in this way human reason does not exclude the merit of faith but is a sign of greater merit. Thus again, in moral virtues a consequent passion is the sign of a more prompt will, as stated above (I-II, Q. 24, A. 3, ad 1). We have an indication of this in the words of the Samaritans to the woman, who is a type of human reason: "We now believe, not for thy saying" (John 4:42).

Reply Obj. 1: Gregory is referring to the case of a man who has no will to believe what is of faith, unless he be induced by reasons. But when a man has the will to believe what is of faith on the authority of God alone, although he may have reasons in demonstration of some of them, e.g. of the existence of God, the merit of his faith is not, for that reason, lost or diminished.

Reply Obj. 2: The reasons which are brought forward in support of the authority of faith, are not demonstrations which can bring intellectual vision to the human intellect, wherefore they do not cease to be unseen. But they remove obstacles to faith, by showing that what faith proposes is not impossible; wherefore such reasons do not diminish the merit or the measure of faith. On the other hand, though demonstrative reasons in support of the preambles of faith [*The Leonine Edition reads: 'in support of matters of faith which are however, preambles to the articles of faith, diminish,' etc.], but not of the articles of faith, diminish the measure of faith, since they make the thing believed to be seen, yet they do not diminish the measure of charity, which makes the will ready to believe them, even if they were unseen; and so the measure of merit is not diminished.

Reply Obj. 3: Whatever is in opposition to faith, whether it consist in a man's thoughts, or in outward persecution, increases the merit of faith, in so far as the will is shown to be more prompt and firm in believing. Hence the martyrs had more merit of faith, through not renouncing faith on account of persecution; and even the wise have greater merit of faith, through not renouncing their faith on account of the reasons brought forward by philosophers or heretics in opposition to faith. On the other hand things that are favorable to faith, do not always diminish the promptness of the will to believe, and therefore they do not always diminish the merit of faith.

# QUESTION 3

OF THE OUTWARD ACT OF FAITH (In Two Articles)

We must now consider the outward act, viz. the confession of faith: under which head there are two points of inquiry:

(1) Whether confession is an act of faith?

(2) Whether confession of faith is necessary for salvation?

FIRST ARTICLE [II-II, Q. 3, Art. 1]

Whether Confession Is an Act of Faith?

Objection 1: It would seem that confession is not an act of faith. For the same act does not belong to different virtues. Now confession belongs to penance of which it is a part. Therefore it is not an act of faith.

Obj. 2: Further, man is sometimes deterred by fear or some kind of confusion, from confessing his faith: wherefore the Apostle (Eph. 6:19) asks for prayers that it may be granted him "with confidence, to make known the mystery of the gospel." Now it belongs to fortitude, which moderates daring and fear, not to be deterred from doing good on account of confusion or fear. Therefore it seems that confession is not an act of faith, but rather of fortitude or constancy.

Obj. 3: Further, just as the ardor of faith makes one confess one's faith outwardly, so does it make one do other external good works, for it is written (Gal. 5:6) that "faith ... worketh by charity." But other external works are not reckoned acts of faith. Therefore neither is confession an act of faith.

*On the contrary,* A gloss explains the words of 2 Thess. 1:11, "and the work of faith in power" as referring to "confession which is a work proper to faith."

*I answer that,* Outward actions belong properly to the virtue to whose end they are specifically referred: thus fasting is referred specifically to the end of abstinence, which is to tame the flesh, and consequently it is an act of abstinence.

Now confession of those things that are of faith is referred specifically as to its end, to that which concerns faith, according to 2 Cor. 4:13: "Having the same spirit of faith ... we believe, and therefore we speak also." For the outward utterance is intended to signify the inward thought. Wherefore, just as the inward thought of matters of faith is properly an act of faith, so too is the outward confession of them.

Reply Obj. 1: A threefold confession is commended by the Scriptures. One is the confession of matters of faith, and this is a proper act of faith, since it is referred to the end of faith as stated above. Another is the confession of thanksgiving or praise, and this is an act of "latria," for its purpose is to give outward honor to God, which is the end of "latria." The third is the confession of sins, which is ordained to the blotting out of sins, which is the end of penance, to which virtue it therefore belongs.

Reply Obj. 2: That which removes an obstacle is not a direct, but an indirect, cause, as the Philosopher proves (Phys. viii, 4). Hence fortitude which removes an obstacle to the confession of faith, viz. fear or shame, is not the proper and direct cause of confession, but an indirect cause so to speak.

Reply Obj. 3: Inward faith, with the aid of charity, causes all outward acts of virtue, by means of the other virtues, commanding, but not eliciting them; whereas it produces the act of confession as its proper act, without the help of any other virtue.

SECOND ARTICLE [II-II, Q. 3, Art. 2]

Whether Confession of Faith Is Necessary for Salvation?

Objection 1: It would seem that confession of faith is not necessary for salvation. For, seemingly, a thing is sufficient for salvation, if it is a means of attaining the end of virtue. Now the proper end of faith is the union of the human mind with Divine truth, and this can be realized without any outward confession. Therefore confession of faith is not necessary for salvation.

Obj. 2: Further, by outward confession of faith, a man reveals his faith to another man. But this is unnecessary save for those who have to instruct others in the faith. Therefore it seems that the simple folk are not bound to confess the faith.

Obj. 3: Further, whatever may tend to scandalize and disturb others, is not necessary for salvation, for the Apostle says (1 Cor. 10:32): "Be without offense to the Jews and to the gentiles and to the Church of God." Now confession of faith sometimes causes a disturbance among unbelievers. Therefore it is not necessary for salvation.

*On the contrary,* The Apostle says (Rom. 10:10): "With the heart we believe unto justice; but with the mouth, confession is made unto salvation."

*I answer that,* Things that are necessary for salvation come under the precepts of the Divine law. Now since confession of faith is something affirmative, it can only fall under an affirmative precept. Hence its necessity for salvation depends on how it falls under an affirmative precept of the Divine law. Now affirmative precepts as stated above (I-II, Q. 71, A. 5, ad 3; I-II, Q. 88, A. 1, ad 2) do not bind for always, although they are always binding; but they bind as to place and time according to other due circumstances, in respect of which human acts have to be regulated in order to be acts of virtue.

Thus then it is not necessary for salvation to confess one's faith at all times and in all places, but in certain places and at certain times, when, namely, by omitting to do so, we would deprive God of due honor, or our neighbor of a service that we ought to render him: for instance, if a man, on being asked about his faith, were to remain silent, so as to make people believe either that he is without faith, or that the faith is false, or so as to turn others away from the faith; for in such cases as these, confession of faith is necessary for salvation.

Reply Obj. 1: The end of faith, even as of the other virtues, must be referred to the end of charity, which is the love of God and our neighbor. Consequently when God's honor and our neighbor's good demand, man should not be contented with being united by faith to God's truth, but ought to confess his faith outwardly.

Reply Obj. 2: In cases of necessity where faith is in danger, every one is bound to proclaim his faith to others, either to give good example and encouragement to the rest of the faithful, or to check the attacks of unbelievers: but at other times it is not the duty of all the faithful to instruct others in the faith.

Reply Obj. 3: There is nothing commendable in making a public confession of one's faith, if it causes a disturbance among unbelievers, without any profit either to the faith or to the faithful. Hence Our Lord said (Matt. 7:6): "Give not that which is holy to dogs, neither cast ye your pearls before swine ... lest turning upon you, they tear you." Yet, if there is hope of profit to the faith, or if there be urgency, a man should disregard the disturbance of unbelievers, and confess his faith in public. Hence it is written (Matt. 15:12) that when the disciples had said to Our Lord that "the Pharisee, when they heard this word, were scandalized," He answered: "Let them alone, they are blind, and leaders of the blind."

## QUESTION 4

OF THE VIRTUE ITSELF OF FAITH (In Eight Articles)

We must now consider the virtue itself of faith, and, in the first place, faith itself; secondly, those who have faith; thirdly, the cause of faith; fourthly, its effects.

Under the first head there are eight points of inquiry:

(1) What is faith?

(2) In what power of the soul does it reside?

(3) Whether its form is charity?

(4) Whether living ( *formata* ) faith and lifeless ( informis ) faith are one identically?

(5) Whether faith is a virtue?

(6) Whether it is one virtue?

(7) Of its relation to the other virtues;

(8) Of its certitude as compared with the certitude of the intellectual virtues.

FIRST ARTICLE [II-II, Q. 4, Art. 1]

Whether This Is a Fitting Definition of Faith: "Faith Is the Substance of Things to Be Hoped For, the Evidence of Things That Appear Not?"

Objection 1: It would seem that the Apostle gives an unfitting definition of faith (Heb. 11:1) when he says: "Faith is the substance of things to be hoped for, the evidence of things that appear not." For no quality is a substance: whereas faith is a quality, since it is a theological virtue, as stated above (I-II, Q. 62, A. 3). Therefore it is not a substance.

Obj. 2: Further, different virtues have different objects. Now things to be hoped for are the object of hope. Therefore they should not be included in a definition of faith, as though they were its object.

Obj. 3: Further, faith is perfected by charity rather than by hope, since charity is the form of faith, as we shall state further on (A. 3). Therefore the definition of faith should have included the thing to be loved rather than the thing to be hoped for.

Obj. 4: Further, the same thing should not be placed in different genera. Now "substance" and "evidence" are different genera, and neither is subalternate to the other. Therefore it is unfitting to state that faith is both "substance" and "evidence."

Obj. 5: Further, evidence manifests the truth of the matter for which it is adduced. Now a thing is said to be apparent when its truth is already manifest. Therefore it seems to imply a contradiction to speak of "evidence of things that appear not": and so faith is unfittingly defined.

*On the contrary,* The authority of the Apostle suffices.

*I answer that,* Though some say that the above words of the Apostle are not a definition of faith, yet if we consider the matter aright, this definition overlooks none of the points in reference to which faith can be defined, albeit the words themselves are not arranged in the form of a definition, just as the philosophers touch on the principles of the syllogism, without employing the syllogistic form.

In order to make this clear, we must observe that since habits are known by their acts, and acts by their objects, faith, being a habit, should be defined by its proper act in relation to its proper object. Now the act of faith is to believe, as stated above (Q. 2, AA. 2, 3), which is an act of the intellect determinate to one object of the will's command. Hence an act of faith is related both to the object of the will, i.e. to the good and the end, and to the object of the intellect, i.e. to the true. And since faith, through being a theological virtue, as stated above (I-II, Q. 62, A. 2), has one same thing for object and end, its object and end must, of necessity, be in proportion to one another. Now it has been already stated (Q. 1, AA. 1, 4) that the object of faith is the First Truth, as unseen, and whatever we hold on account thereof: so that it must needs be under the aspect of something unseen that the First Truth is the end of the act of faith, which aspect is that of a thing hoped for, according to the Apostle (Rom. 8:25): "We hope for that which we see not": because to see the truth is to possess it. Now one hopes not for what one has already, but for what one has not, as stated above (I-II, Q. 67, A. 4). Accordingly the relation of the act of faith to its end which is the object of the will, is indicated by the words: "Faith is the substance of things to be hoped for." For we are wont to call by the name of substance, the first beginning of a thing, especially when the whole subsequent thing is virtually contained in the first beginning; for instance, we might say that the first self-evident principles are the substance of science, because, to wit, these principles are in us the first beginnings of science, the whole of which is itself contained in them virtually. In this way then faith is said to be the "substance of things to be hoped for," for the reason that in us the first beginning of things to be hoped for is brought about by the assent of faith, which contains virtually all things to be hoped for. Because we hope to be made happy through seeing the unveiled truth to which our faith cleaves, as was made evident when we were speaking of happiness (I-II, Q. 3, A. 8; I-II, Q. 4, A. 3).

The relationship of the act of faith to the object of the intellect, considered as the object of faith, is indicated by the words, "evidence of things that appear not," where "evidence" is taken for the result of evidence. For evidence induces the intellect to adhere to a truth, wherefore the firm adhesion of the intellect to the non-apparent truth of faith is called "evidence" here. Hence another reading has "conviction," because to wit, the intellect of the believer is convinced by Divine authority, so as to assent to what it sees not. Accordingly if anyone would reduce the foregoing words to the form of a definition, he may say that "faith is a habit of the mind, whereby eternal life is begun in us, making the intellect assent to what is non-apparent."

In this way faith is distinguished from all other things pertaining to the intellect. For when we describe it as "evidence," we distinguish it from opinion, suspicion, and doubt, which do not make the intellect adhere to anything firmly; when we go on to say, "of things that appear not," we distinguish it from science and understanding, the object of which is something apparent; and when we say that it is "the substance of things to be hoped for," we distinguish the virtue of faith from faith commonly so called, which has no reference to the beatitude we hope for.

Whatever other definitions are given of faith, are explanations of this one given by the Apostle. For when Augustine says (Tract. xl in Joan.: QQ. Evang. ii, qu. 39) that "faith is a virtue whereby we believe what we do not see," and when Damascene says (De Fide Orth. iv, 11) that "faith is an assent without research," and when others say that "faith is that certainty of the mind about absent things which surpasses opinion but falls short of science," these all amount to the same as the Apostle's words: "Evidence of things that appear not"; and when Dionysius says (Div. Nom. vii) that "faith is the solid foundation of the believer, establishing him in the truth, and showing forth the truth in him," comes to the same as "substance of things to be hoped for."

Reply Obj. 1: "Substance" here does not stand for the supreme genus condivided with the other genera, but for that likeness to substance which is found in each genus, inasmuch as the first thing in a genus contains the others virtually and is said to be the substance thereof.

Reply Obj. 2: Since faith pertains to the intellect as commanded by the will, it must needs be directed, as to its end, to the objects of those virtues which perfect the will, among which is hope, as we shall prove further on (Q. 18, A. 1). For this reason the definition of faith includes the object of hope.

Reply Obj. 3: Love may be of the seen and of the unseen, of the present and of the absent. Consequently a thing to be loved is not so adapted to faith, as a thing to be hoped for, since hope is always of the absent and the unseen.

Reply Obj. 4: "Substance" and "evidence" as included in the definition of faith, do not denote various genera of faith, nor different acts, but different relationships of one act to different objects, as is clear from what has been said.

Reply Obj. 5: Evidence taken from the proper principles of a thing, make[s] it apparent, whereas evidence taken from Divine authority does not make a thing apparent in itself, and such is the evidence referred to in the definition of faith.

SECOND ARTICLE [II-II, Q. 4, Art. 2]

Whether Faith Resides in the Intellect?

Objection 1: It would seem that faith does not reside in the intellect. For Augustine says (De Praedest. Sanct. v) that "faith resides in the believer's will." Now the will is a power distinct from the intellect. Therefore faith does not reside in the intellect.

Obj. 2: Further, the assent of faith to believe anything, proceeds from the will obeying God. Therefore it seems that faith owes all its praise to obedience. Now obedience is in the will. Therefore faith is in the will, and not in the intellect.

Obj. 3: Further, the intellect is either speculative or practical. Now faith is not in the speculative intellect, since this is not concerned with things to be sought or avoided, as stated in De Anima iii, 9, so that it is not a principle of operation, whereas "faith ... worketh by charity" (Gal. 5:6). Likewise, neither is it in the practical intellect, the object of which is some true, contingent thing, that can be made or done. For the object of faith is the Eternal Truth, as was shown above (Q. 1, A. 1). Therefore faith does not reside in the intellect.

*On the contrary,* Faith is succeeded by the heavenly vision, according to 1 Cor. 13:12: "We see now through a glass in a dark manner; but then face to face." Now vision is in the intellect. Therefore faith is likewise.

*I answer that,* Since faith is a virtue, its act must needs be perfect. Now, for the perfection of an act proceeding from two active principles, each of these principles must be perfect: for it is not possible for a thing to be sawn well, unless the sawyer possess the art, and the saw be well fitted for sawing. Now, in a power of the soul, which is related to opposite objects, a disposition to act well is a habit, as stated above (I-II, Q. 49, A. 4, ad 1, 2, 3). Wherefore an act that proceeds from two such powers must be perfected by a habit residing in each of them. Again, it has been stated above (Q. 2, AA. 1, 2) that to believe is an act of the intellect inasmuch as the will moves it to assent. And this act proceeds from the will and the intellect, both of which have a natural aptitude to be perfected in this way. Consequently, if the act of faith is to be perfect, there needs to be a habit in the will as well as in the intellect: even as there needs to be the habit of prudence in the reason, besides the habit of temperance in the concupiscible faculty, in order that the act of that faculty be perfect. Now, to believe is immediately an act of the intellect, because the object of that act is "the true," which pertains properly to the intellect. Consequently faith, which is the proper principle of that act, must needs reside in the intellect.

Reply Obj. 1: Augustine takes faith for the act of faith, which is described as depending on the believer's will, in so far as his intellect assents to matters of faith at the command of the will.

Reply Obj. 2: Not only does the will need to be ready to obey but also the intellect needs to be well disposed to follow the command of the will, even as the concupiscible faculty needs to be well disposed in order to follow the command of reason; hence there needs to be a habit of virtue not only in the commanding will but also in the assenting intellect.

Reply Obj. 3: Faith resides in the speculative intellect, as evidenced by its object. But since this object, which is the First Truth, is the end of all our desires and actions, as Augustine proves (De Trin. i, 8), it follows that faith worketh by charity just as "the speculative intellect becomes practical by extension" (De Anima iii, 10).

THIRD ARTICLE [II-II, Q. 4, Art. 3]

Whether Charity Is the Form of Faith?

Objection 1: It would seem that charity is not the form of faith. For each thing derives its species from its form. When therefore two things are opposite members of a division, one cannot be the form of the other. Now faith and charity are stated to be opposite members of a division, as different species of virtue (1 Cor. 13:13). Therefore charity is not the form of faith.

Obj. 2: Further, a form and the thing of which it is the form are in one subject, since together they form one simply. Now faith is in the intellect, while charity is in the will. Therefore charity is not the form of faith.

Obj. 3: Further, the form of a thing is a principle thereof. Now obedience, rather than charity, seems to be the principle of believing, on the part of the will, according to Rom. 1:5: "For obedience to the faith in all nations." Therefore obedience rather than charity, is the form of faith.

*On the contrary,* Each thing works through its form. Now faith works through charity. Therefore the love of charity is the form of faith.

*I answer that,* As appears from what has been said above (I-II, Q. 1, A. 3; I-II, Q. 18, A. 6), voluntary acts take their species from their end which is the will's object. Now that which gives a thing its species, is after the manner of a form in natural things. Wherefore the form of any voluntary act is, in a manner, the end to which that act is directed, both because it takes its species therefrom, and because the mode of an action should correspond proportionately to the end. Now it is evident from what has been said (A. 1), that the act of faith is directed to the object of the will, i.e. the good, as to its end: and this good which is the end of faith, viz. the Divine Good, is the proper object of charity. Therefore charity is called the form of faith in so far as the act of faith is perfected and formed by charity.

Reply Obj. 1: Charity is called the form of faith because it quickens the act of faith. Now nothing hinders one act from being quickened by different habits, so as to be reduced to various species in a certain order, as stated above (I-II, Q. 18, AA. 6, 7; I-II, Q. 61, A. 2) when we were treating of human acts in general.

Reply Obj. 2: This objection is true of an intrinsic form. But it is not thus that charity is the form of faith, but in the sense that it quickens the act of faith, as explained above.

Reply Obj. 3: Even obedience, and hope likewise, and whatever other virtue might precede the act of faith, is quickened by charity, as we shall show further on (Q. 23, A. 8), and consequently charity is spoken of as the form of faith.

FOURTH ARTICLE [II-II, Q. 4, Art. 4]

Whether Lifeless Faith Can Become Living, or Living Faith, Lifeless?

Objection 1: It would seem that lifeless faith does not become living, or living faith lifeless. For, according to 1 Cor. 13:10, "when that which is perfect is come, that which is in part shall be done away." Now lifeless faith is imperfect in comparison with living faith. Therefore when living faith comes, lifeless faith is done away, so that they are not one identical habit.

Obj. 2: Further, a dead thing does not become a living thing. Now lifeless faith is dead, according to James 2:20: "Faith without works is dead." Therefore lifeless faith cannot become living.

Obj. 3: Further, God's grace, by its advent, has no less effect in a believer than in an unbeliever. Now by coming to an unbeliever it causes the habit of faith. Therefore when it comes to a believer, who hitherto had the habit of lifeless faith, it causes another habit of faith in him.

Obj. 4: Further, as Boethius says (In Categ. Arist. i), "accidents cannot be altered." Now faith is an accident. Therefore the same faith cannot be at one time living, and at another, lifeless.

*On the contrary,* A gloss on the words, "Faith without works is dead" (James 2:20) adds, "by which it lives once more." Therefore faith which was lifeless and without form hitherto, becomes formed and living.

*I answer that,* There have been various opinions on this question. For some [*William of Auxerre, Sum. Aur. III, iii, 15] have said that living and lifeless faith are distinct habits, but that when living faith comes, lifeless faith is done away, and that, in like manner, when a man sins mortally after having living faith, a new habit of lifeless faith is infused into him by God. But it seems unfitting that grace should deprive man of a gift of God by coming to him, and that a gift of God should be infused into man, on account of a mortal sin.

Consequently others [*Alexander of Hales, Sum. Theol. iii, 64] have said that living and lifeless faith are indeed distinct habits, but that, all the same, when living faith comes the habit of lifeless faith is not taken away, and that it remains together with the habit of living faith in the same subject. Yet again it seems unreasonable that the habit of lifeless faith should remain inactive in a person having living faith.

We must therefore hold differently that living and lifeless faith are one and the same habit. The reason is that a habit is differentiated by that which directly pertains to that habit. Now since faith is a perfection of the intellect, that pertains directly to faith, which pertains to the intellect. Again, what pertains to the will, does not pertain directly to faith, so as to be able to differentiate the habit of faith. But the distinction of living from lifeless faith is in respect of something pertaining to the will, i.e. charity, and not in respect of something pertaining to the intellect. Therefore living and lifeless faith are not distinct habits.

Reply Obj. 1: The saying of the Apostle refers to those imperfect things from which imperfection is inseparable, for then, when the perfect comes the imperfect must needs be done away. Thus with the advent of clear vision, faith is done away, because it is essentially "of the things that appear not." When, however, imperfection is not inseparable from the imperfect thing, the same identical thing which was imperfect becomes perfect. Thus childhood is not essential to man and consequently the same identical subject who was a child, becomes a man. Now lifelessness is not essential to faith, but is accidental thereto as stated above. Therefore lifeless faith itself becomes living.

Reply Obj. 2: That which makes an animal live is inseparable from an animal, because it is its substantial form, viz. the soul: consequently a dead thing cannot become a living thing, and a living and a dead thing differ specifically. On the other hand that which gives faith its form, or makes it live, is not essential to faith. Hence there is no comparison.

Reply Obj. 3: Grace causes faith not only when faith begins anew to be in a man, but also as long as faith lasts. For it has been said above (I, Q. 104, A. 1; I-II, Q. 109, A. 9) that God is always working man's justification, even as the sun is always lighting up the air. Hence grace is not less effective when it comes to a believer than when it comes to an unbeliever: since it causes faith in both, in the former by confirming and perfecting it, in the latter by creating it anew.

We might also reply that it is accidental, namely on account of the disposition of the subject, that grace does not cause faith in one who has it already: just as, on the other hand, a second mortal sin does not take away grace from one who has already lost it through a previous mortal sin.

Reply Obj. 4: When living faith becomes lifeless, faith is not changed, but its subject, the soul, which at one time has faith without charity, and at another time, with charity.

FIFTH ARTICLE [II-II, Q. 4, Art. 5]

Whether Faith Is a Virtue?

Objection 1: It would seem that faith is not a virtue. For virtue is directed to the good, since "it is virtue that makes its subject good," as the Philosopher states (Ethic. ii, 6). But faith is directed to the true. Therefore faith is not a virtue.

Obj. 2: Further, infused virtue is more perfect than acquired virtue. Now faith, on account of its imperfection, is not placed among the acquired intellectual virtues, as the Philosopher states (Ethic. vi, 3). Much less, therefore, can it be considered an infused virtue.

Obj. 3: Further, living and lifeless faith are the same species, as stated above (A. 4). Now lifeless faith is not a virtue, since it is not connected with the other virtues. Therefore neither is living faith a virtue.

Obj. 4: Further, the gratuitous graces and the fruits are distinct from the virtues. But faith is numbered among the gratuitous graces (1 Cor. 12:9) and likewise among the fruits (Gal. 5:23). Therefore faith is not a virtue.

*On the contrary,* Man is justified by the virtues, since "justice is all virtue," as the Philosopher states (Ethic. v, 1). Now man is justified by faith according to Rom. 5:1: "Being justified therefore by faith let us have peace," etc. Therefore faith is a virtue.

*I answer that,* As shown above, it is by human virtue that human acts are rendered good; hence, any habit that is always the principle of a good act, may be called a human virtue. Such a habit is living faith. For since to believe is an act of the intellect assenting to the truth at the command of the will, two things are required that this act may be perfect: one of which is that the intellect should infallibly tend to its object, which is the true; while the other is that the will should be infallibly directed to the last end, on account of which it assents to the true: and both of these are to be found in the act of living faith. For it belongs to the very essence of faith that the intellect should ever tend to the true, since nothing false can be the object of faith, as proved above (Q. 1, A. 3): while the effect of charity, which is the form of faith, is that the soul ever has its will directed to a good end. Therefore living faith is a virtue.

On the other hand, lifeless faith is not a virtue, because, though the act of lifeless faith is duly perfect on the part of the intellect, it has not its due perfection as regards the will: just as if temperance be in the concupiscible, without prudence being in the rational part, temperance is not a virtue, as stated above (I-II, Q. 65, A. 1), because the act of temperance requires both an act of reason, and an act of the concupiscible faculty, even as the act of faith requires an act of the will, and an act of the intellect.

Reply Obj. 1: The truth is itself the good of the intellect, since it is its perfection: and consequently faith has a relation to some good in so far as it directs the intellect to the true. Furthermore, it has a relation to the good considered as the object of the will, inasmuch as it is formed by charity.

Reply Obj. 2: The faith of which the Philosopher speaks is based on human reasoning in a conclusion which does not follow, of necessity, from its premisses; and which is subject to be false: hence such like faith is not a virtue. On the other hand, the faith of which we are speaking is based on the Divine Truth, which is infallible, and consequently its object cannot be anything false; so that faith of this kind can be a virtue.

Reply Obj. 3: Living and lifeless faith do not differ specifically, as though they belonged to different species. But they differ as perfect and imperfect within the same species. Hence lifeless faith, being imperfect, does not satisfy the conditions of a perfect virtue, for "virtue is a kind of perfection" (Phys. vii, text. 18).

Reply Obj. 4: Some say that faith which is numbered among the gratuitous graces is lifeless faith. But this is said without reason, since the gratuitous graces, which are mentioned in that passage, are not common to all the members of the Church: wherefore the Apostle says: "There are diversities of graces," and again, "To one is given" this grace and "to another" that. Now lifeless faith is common to all members of the Church, because its lifelessness is not part of its substance, if we consider it as a gratuitous gift. We must, therefore, say that in that passage, faith denotes a certain excellency of faith, for instance, "constancy in faith," according to a gloss, or the "word of faith."

Faith is numbered among the fruits, in so far as it gives a certain pleasure in its act by reason of its certainty, wherefore the gloss on the fifth chapter to the Galatians, where the fruits are enumerated, explains faith as being "certainty about the unseen."

SIXTH ARTICLE [II-II, Q. 4, Art. 6]

Whether Faith Is One Virtue?

Objection 1: It would seem that faith is not one. For just as faith is a gift of God according to Eph. 2:8, so also wisdom and knowledge are numbered among God's gifts according to Isa. 11:2. Now wisdom and knowledge differ in this, that wisdom is about eternal things, and knowledge about temporal things, as Augustine states (De Trin. xii, 14, 15). Since, then, faith is about eternal things, and also about some temporal things, it seems that faith is not one virtue, but divided into several parts.

Obj. 2: Further, confession is an act of faith, as stated above (Q. 3, A. 1). Now confession of faith is not one and the same for all: since what we confess as past, the fathers of old confessed as yet to come, as appears from Isa. 7:14: "Behold a virgin shall conceive." Therefore faith is not one.

Obj. 3: Further, faith is common to all believers in Christ. But one accident cannot be in many subjects. Therefore all cannot have one faith.

*On the contrary,* The Apostle says (Eph. 4:5): "One Lord, one faith."

*I answer that,* If we take faith as a habit, we can consider it in two ways. First on the part of the object, and thus there is one faith. Because the formal object of faith is the First Truth, by adhering to which we believe whatever is contained in the faith. Secondly, on the part of the subject, and thus faith is differentiated according as it is in various subjects. Now it is evident that faith, just as any other habit, takes its species from the formal aspect of its object, but is individualized by its subject. Hence if we take faith for the habit whereby we believe, it is one specifically, but differs numerically according to its various subjects.

If, on the other hand, we take faith for that which is believed, then, again, there is one faith, since what is believed by all is one same thing: for though the things believed, which all agree in believing, be diverse from one another, yet they are all reduced to one.

Reply Obj. 1: Temporal matters which are proposed to be believed, do not belong to the object of faith, except in relation to something eternal, viz. the First Truth, as stated above (Q. 1, A. 1). Hence there is one faith of things both temporal and eternal. It is different with wisdom and knowledge, which consider temporal and eternal matters under their respective aspects.

Reply Obj. 2: This difference of past and future arises, not from any difference in the thing believed, but from the different relationships of believers to the one thing believed, as also we have mentioned above (I-II, Q. 103, A. 4; I-II, Q. 107, A. 1, ad 1).

Reply Obj. 3: This objection considers numerical diversity of faith.

SEVENTH ARTICLE [II-II, Q. 4, Art. 7]

Whether Faith Is the First of the Virtues?

Objection 1: It would seem that faith is not the first of the virtues. For a gloss on Luke 12:4, "I say to you My friends," says that fortitude is the foundation of faith. Now the foundation precedes that which is founded thereon. Therefore faith is not the first of the virtues.

Obj. 2: Further, a gloss on Ps. 36, "Be not emulous," says that hope "leads on to faith." Now hope is a virtue, as we shall state further on (Q. 17, A. 1). Therefore faith is not the first of the virtues.

Obj. 3: Further, it was stated above (A. 2) that the intellect of the believer is moved, out of obedience to God, to assent to matters of faith. Now obedience also is a virtue. Therefore faith is not the first virtue.

Obj. 4: Further, not lifeless but living faith is the foundation, as a gloss remarks on 1 Cor. 3:11 [*Augustine, De Fide et Oper. xvi.]. Now faith is formed by charity, as stated above (A. 3). Therefore it is owing to charity that faith is the foundation: so that charity is the foundation yet more than faith is (for the foundation is the first part of a building) and consequently it seems to precede faith.

Obj. 5: Further, the order of habits is taken from the order of acts. Now, in the act of faith, the act of the will which is perfected by charity, precedes the act of the intellect, which is perfected by faith, as the cause which precedes its effect. Therefore charity precedes faith. Therefore faith is not the first of the virtues.

*On the contrary,* The Apostle says (Heb. 11:1) that "faith is the substance of things to be hoped for." Now the substance of a thing is that which comes first. Therefore faith is first among the virtues.

*I answer that,* One thing can precede another in two ways: first, by its very nature; secondly, by accident. Faith, by its very nature, precedes all other virtues. For since the end is the principle in matters of action, as stated above (I-II, Q. 13, A. 3; I-II, Q. 34, A. 4, ad 1), the theological virtues, the object of which is the last end, must needs precede all the others. Again, the last end must of necessity be present to the intellect before it is present to the will, since the will has no inclination for anything except in so far as it is apprehended by the intellect. Hence, as the last end is present in the will by hope and charity, and in the intellect, by faith, the first of all the virtues must, of necessity, be faith, because natural knowledge cannot reach God as the object of heavenly bliss, which is the aspect under which hope and charity tend towards Him.

On the other hand, some virtues can precede faith accidentally. For an accidental cause precedes its effect accidentally. Now that which removes an obstacle is a kind of accidental cause, according to the Philosopher (Phys. viii, 4): and in this sense certain virtues may be said to precede faith accidentally, in so far as they remove obstacles to belief. Thus fortitude removes the inordinate fear that hinders faith; humility removes pride, whereby a man refuses to submit himself to the truth of faith. The same may be said of some other virtues, although there are no real virtues, unless faith be presupposed, as Augustine states (Contra Julian. iv, 3).

This suffices for the Reply to the First Objection.

Reply Obj. 2: Hope cannot lead to faith absolutely. For one cannot hope to obtain eternal happiness, unless one believes this possible, since hope does not tend to the impossible, as stated above (I-II, Q. 40, A. 1). It is, however, possible for one to be led by hope to persevere in faith, or to hold firmly to faith; and it is in this sense that hope is said to lead to faith.

Reply Obj. 3: Obedience is twofold: for sometimes it denotes the inclination of the will to fulfil God's commandments. In this way it is not a special virtue, but is a general condition of every virtue; since all acts of virtue come under the precepts of the Divine law, as stated above (I-II, Q. 100, A. 2); and thus it is requisite for faith. In another way, obedience denotes an inclination to fulfil the commandments considered as a duty. In this way it is a special virtue, and a part of justice: for a man does his duty by his superior when he obeys him: and thus obedience follows faith, whereby man knows that God is his superior, Whom he must obey.

Reply Obj. 4: To be a foundation a thing requires not only to come first, but also to be connected with the other parts of the building: since the building would not be founded on it unless the other parts adhered to it. Now the connecting bond of the spiritual edifice is charity, according to Col. 3:14: "Above all ... things have charity which is the bond of perfection." Consequently faith without charity cannot be the foundation: and yet it does not follow that charity precedes faith.

Reply Obj. 5: Some act of the will is required before faith, but not an act of the will quickened by charity. This latter act presupposes faith, because the will cannot tend to God with perfect love, unless the intellect possesses right faith about Him.

EIGHTH ARTICLE [II-II, Q. 4, Art. 8]

Whether Faith Is More Certain Than Science and the Other Intellectual Virtues?

Objection 1: It would seem that faith is not more certain than science and the other intellectual virtues. For doubt is opposed to certitude, wherefore a thing would seem to be the more certain, through being less doubtful, just as a thing is the whiter, the less it has of an admixture of black. Now understanding, science and also wisdom are free of any doubt about their objects; whereas the believer may sometimes suffer a movement of doubt, and doubt about matters of faith. Therefore faith is no more certain than the intellectual virtues.

Obj. 2: Further, sight is more certain than hearing. But "faith is through hearing" according to Rom. 10:17; whereas understanding, science and wisdom imply some kind of intellectual sight. Therefore science and understanding are more certain than faith.

Obj. 3: Further, in matters concerning the intellect, the more perfect is the more certain. Now understanding is more perfect than faith, since faith is the way to understanding, according to another version [*The Septuagint] of Isa. 7:9: "If you will not believe, you shall not understand [Vulg.: 'continue']": and Augustine says (De Trin. xiv, 1) that "faith is strengthened by science." Therefore it seems that science or understanding is more certain than faith.

*On the contrary,* The Apostle says (1 Thess. 2:15): "When you had received of us the word of the hearing," i.e. by faith ... "you received it not as the word of men, but, as it is indeed, the word of God." Now nothing is more certain than the word of God. Therefore science is not more certain than faith; nor is anything else.

*I answer that,* As stated above (I-II, Q. 57, A. 4, ad 2) two of the intellectual virtues are about contingent matter, viz. prudence and art; to which faith is preferable in point of certitude, by reason of its matter, since it is about eternal things, which never change, whereas the other three intellectual virtues, viz. wisdom, science [*In English the corresponding 'gift' is called knowledge] and understanding, are about necessary things, as stated above (I-II, Q. 57, A. 5, ad 3). But it must be observed that wisdom, science and understanding may be taken in two ways: first, as intellectual virtues, according to the Philosopher (Ethic. vi, 2, 3); secondly, for the gifts of the Holy Ghost. If we consider them in the first way, we must note that certitude can be looked at in two ways. First, on the part of its cause, and thus a thing which has a more certain cause, is itself more certain. In this way faith is more certain than those three virtues, because it is founded on the Divine truth, whereas the aforesaid three virtues are based on human reason. Secondly, certitude may be considered on the part of the subject, and thus the more a man's intellect lays hold of a thing, the more certain it is. In this way, faith is less certain, because matters of faith are above the human intellect, whereas the objects of the aforesaid three virtues are not. Since, however, a thing is judged simply with regard to its cause, but relatively, with respect to a disposition on the part of the subject, it follows that faith is more certain simply, while the others are more certain relatively, i.e. for us. Likewise if these three be taken as gifts received in this present life, they are related to faith as to their principle which they presuppose: so that again, in this way, faith is more certain.

Reply Obj. 1: This doubt is not on the side of the cause of faith, but on our side, in so far as we do not fully grasp matters of faith with our intellect.

Reply Obj. 2: Other things being equal sight is more certain than hearing; but if (the authority of) the person from whom we hear greatly surpasses that of the seer's sight, hearing is more certain than sight: thus a man of little science is more certain about what he hears on the authority of an expert in science, than about what is apparent to him according to his own reason: and much more is a man certain about what he hears from God, Who cannot be deceived, than about what he sees with his own reason, which can be mistaken.

Reply Obj. 3: The gifts of understanding and knowledge are more perfect than the knowledge of faith in the point of their greater clearness, but not in regard to more certain adhesion: because the whole certitude of the gifts of understanding and knowledge, arises from the certitude of faith, even as the certitude of the knowledge of conclusions arises from the certitude of premisses. But in so far as science, wisdom and understanding are intellectual virtues, they are based upon the natural light of reason, which falls short of the certitude of God's word, on which faith is founded.

# QUESTION 5

OF THOSE WHO HAVE FAITH (In Four Articles)

We must now consider those who have faith: under which head there are four points of inquiry:

(1) Whether there was faith in the angels, or in man, in their original state?

(2) Whether the demons have faith?

(3) Whether those heretics who err in one article, have faith in others?

(4) Whether among those who have faith, one has it more than another?

FIRST ARTICLE [II-II, Q. 5, Art. 1]

Whether There Was Faith in the Angels, or in Man, in Their Original State?

Objection 1: It would seem that there was no faith, either in the angels, or in man, in their original state. For Hugh of S. Victor says in his Sentences (De Sacram. i, 10) that "man cannot see God or things that are in God, because he closes his eyes to contemplation." Now the angels, in their original state, before they were either confirmed in grace, or had fallen from it, had their eyes opened to contemplation, since "they saw things in the Word," according to Augustine (Gen. ad lit. ii, 8). Likewise the first man, while in the state of innocence, seemingly had his eyes open to contemplation; for Hugh St. Victor says (De Sacram. i, 6) that "in his original state man knew his Creator, not by the mere outward perception of hearing, but by inward inspiration, not as now believers seek an absent God by faith, but by seeing Him clearly present to their contemplation." Therefore there was no faith in the angels and man in their original state.

Obj. 2: Further, the knowledge of faith is dark and obscure, according to 1 Cor. 13:13: "We see now through a glass in a dark manner." Now in their original state there was not obscurity either in the angels or in man, because it is a punishment of sin. Therefore there could be no faith in the angels or in man, in their original state.

Obj. 3: Further, the Apostle says (Rom. 10:17) that "faith ... cometh by hearing." Now this could not apply to angels and man in their original state; for then they could not hear anything from another. Therefore, in that state, there was no faith either in man or in the angels.

*On the contrary,* It is written (Heb. 11:6): "He that cometh to God, must believe." Now the original state of angels and man was one of approach to God. Therefore they had need of faith.

*I answer that,* Some say that there was no faith in the angels before they were confirmed in grace or fell from it, and in man before he sinned, by reason of the manifest contemplation that they had of Divine things. Since, however, "faith is the evidence of things that appear not," according to the Apostle (Heb. 11:2), and since "by faith we believe what we see not," according to Augustine (Tract. xl in Joan.; QQ. Evang. ii, qu. 39), that manifestation alone excludes faith, which renders apparent or seen the principal object of faith. Now the principal object of faith is the First Truth, the sight of which gives the happiness of heaven and takes the place of faith. Consequently, as the angels before their confirmation in grace, and man before sin, did not possess the happiness whereby God is seen in His Essence, it is evident that the knowledge they possessed was not such as to exclude faith.

It follows then, that the absence of faith in them could only be explained by their being altogether ignorant of the object of faith. And if man and the angels were created in a purely natural state, as some [*St. Bonaventure, Sent. ii, D, 29] hold, perhaps one might hold that there was no faith in the angels before their confirmation in grace, or in man before sin, because the knowledge of faith surpasses not only a man's but even an angel's natural knowledge about God.

Since, however, we stated in the First Part (Q. 62, A. 3; Q. 95, A. 1) that man and the angels were created with the gift of grace, we must needs say that there was in them a certain beginning of hoped-for happiness, by reason of grace received but not yet consummated, which happiness was begun in their will by hope and charity, and in the intellect by faith, as stated above (Q. 4, A. 7). Consequently we must hold that the angels had faith before they were confirmed, and man, before he sinned. Nevertheless we must observe that in the object of faith, there is something formal, as it were, namely the First Truth surpassing all the natural knowledge of a creature, and something material, namely, the thing to which we assent while adhering to the First Truth. With regard to the former, before obtaining the happiness to come, faith is common to all who have knowledge of God, by adhering to the First Truth: whereas with regard to the things which are proposed as the material object of faith, some are believed by one, and known manifestly by another, even in the present state, as we have shown above (Q. 1, A. 5; Q. 2, A. 4, ad 2). In this respect, too, it may be said that the angels before being confirmed, and man, before sin, possessed manifest knowledge about certain points in the Divine mysteries, which now we cannot know except by believing them.

Reply Obj. 1: Although the words of Hugh of S. Victor are those of a master, and have the force of an authority, yet it may be said that the contemplation which removes the need of faith is heavenly contemplation, whereby the supernatural truth is seen in its essence. Now the angels did not possess this contemplation before they were confirmed, nor did man before he sinned: yet their contemplation was of a higher order than ours, for by its means they approached nearer to God, and had manifest knowledge of more of the Divine effects and mysteries than we can have knowledge of. Hence faith was not in them so that they sought an absent God as we seek Him: since by the light of wisdom He was more present to them than He is to us, although He was not so present to them as He is to the Blessed by the light of glory.

Reply Obj. 2: There was no darkness of sin or punishment in the original state of man and the angels, but there was a certain natural obscurity in the human and angelic intellect, in so far as every creature is darkness in comparison with the immensity of the Divine light: and this obscurity suffices for faith.

Reply Obj. 3: In the original state there was no hearing anything from man speaking outwardly, but there was from God inspiring inwardly: thus the prophets heard, as expressed by the Ps. 84:9: "I will hear what the Lord God will speak in me."

SECOND ARTICLE [II-II, Q. 5, Art. 2]

Whether in the Demons There Is Faith?

Objection 1: It would seem that the demons have no faith. For Augustine says (De Praedest. Sanct. v) that "faith depends on the believer's will": and this is a good will, since by it man wishes to believe in God. Since then no deliberate will of the demons is good, as stated above (I, Q. 64, A. 2, ad 5), it seems that in the demons there is no faith.

Obj. 2: Further, faith is a gift of Divine grace, according to Eph. 2:8: "By grace you are saved through faith ... for it is the gift of God." Now, according to a gloss on Osee 3:1, "They look to strange gods, and love the husks of the grapes," the demons lost their gifts of grace by sinning. Therefore faith did not remain in the demons after they sinned.

Obj. 3: Further, unbelief would seem to be graver than other sins, as Augustine observes (Tract. lxxxix in Joan.) on John 15:22, "If I had not come and spoken to them, they would not have sin: but now they have no excuse for their sin." Now the sin of unbelief is in some men. Consequently, if the demons have faith, some men would be guilty of a sin graver than that of the demons, which seems unreasonable. Therefore in the demons there is no faith.

*On the contrary,* It is written (James 2:19): "The devils ... believe and tremble."

*I answer that,* As stated above (Q. 1, A. 4; Q. 2, A. 1), the believer's intellect assents to that which he believes, not because he sees it either in itself, or by resolving it to first self-evident principles, but because his will commands his intellect to assent. Now, that the will moves the intellect to assent, may be due to two causes. First, through the will being directed to the good, and in this way, to believe is a praiseworthy action. Secondly, because the intellect is convinced that it ought to believe what is said, though that conviction is not based on objective evidence. Thus if a prophet, while preaching the word of God, were to foretell something, and were to give a sign, by raising a dead person to life, the intellect of a witness would be convinced so as to recognize clearly that God, Who lieth not, was speaking, although the thing itself foretold would not be evident in itself, and consequently the essence of faith would not be removed.

Accordingly we must say that faith is commended in the first sense in the faithful of Christ: and in this way faith is not in the demons, but only in the second way, for they see many evident signs, whereby they recognize that the teaching of the Church is from God, although they do not see the things themselves that the Church teaches, for instance that there are three Persons in God, and so forth.

Reply Obj. 1: The demons are, in a way, compelled to believe, by the evidence of signs, and so their will deserves no praise for their belief.

Reply Obj. 2: Faith, which is a gift of grace, inclines man to believe, by giving him a certain affection for the good, even when that faith is lifeless. Consequently the faith which the demons have, is not a gift of grace. Rather are they compelled to believe through their natural intellectual acumen.

Reply Obj. 3: The very fact that the signs of faith are so evident, that the demons are compelled to believe, is displeasing to them, so that their malice is by no means diminished by their belief.

THIRD ARTICLE [II-II, Q. 5, Art. 3]

Whether a Man Who Disbelieves One Article of Faith, Can Have Lifeless Faith in the Other Articles?

Objection 1: It would seem that a heretic who disbelieves one article of faith, can have lifeless faith in the other articles. For the natural intellect of a heretic is not more able than that of a catholic. Now a catholic's intellect needs the aid of the gift of faith in order to believe any article whatever of faith. Therefore it seems that heretics cannot believe any articles of faith without the gift of lifeless faith.

Obj. 2: Further, just as faith contains many articles, so does one science, viz. geometry, contain many conclusions. Now a man may possess the science of geometry as to some geometrical conclusions, and yet be ignorant of other conclusions. Therefore a man can believe some articles of faith without believing the others.

Obj. 3: Further, just as man obeys God in believing the articles of faith, so does he also in keeping the commandments of the Law. Now a man can obey some commandments, and disobey others. Therefore he can believe some articles, and disbelieve others.

*On the contrary,* Just as mortal sin is contrary to charity, so is disbelief in one article of faith contrary to faith. Now charity does not remain in a man after one mortal sin. Therefore neither does faith, after a man disbelieves one article.

*I answer that,* Neither living nor lifeless faith remains in a heretic who disbelieves one article of faith.

The reason of this is that the species of every habit depends on the formal aspect of the object, without which the species of the habit cannot remain. Now the formal object of faith is the First Truth, as manifested in Holy Writ and the teaching of the Church, which proceeds from the First Truth. Consequently whoever does not adhere, as to an infallible and Divine rule, to the teaching of the Church, which proceeds from the First Truth manifested in Holy Writ, has not the habit of faith, but holds that which is of faith otherwise than by faith. Even so, it is evident that a man whose mind holds a conclusion without knowing how it is proved, has not scientific knowledge, but merely an opinion about it. Now it is manifest that he who adheres to the teaching of the Church, as to an infallible rule, assents to whatever the Church teaches; otherwise, if, of the things taught by the Church, he holds what he chooses to hold, and rejects what he chooses to reject, he no longer adheres to the teaching of the Church as to an infallible rule, but to his own will. Hence it is evident that a heretic who obstinately disbelieves one article of faith, is not prepared to follow the teaching of the Church in all things; but if he is not obstinate, he is no longer in heresy but only in error. Therefore it is clear that such a heretic with regard to one article has no faith in the other articles, but only a kind of opinion in accordance with his own will.

Reply Obj. 1: A heretic does not hold the other articles of faith, about which he does not err, in the same way as one of the faithful does, namely by adhering simply to the Divine Truth, because in order to do so, a man needs the help of the habit of faith; but he holds the things that are of faith, by his own will and judgment.

Reply Obj. 2: The various conclusions of a science have their respective means of demonstration, one of which may be known without another, so that we may know some conclusions of a science without knowing the others. On the other hand faith adheres to all the articles of faith by reason of one mean, viz. on account of the First Truth proposed to us in Scriptures, according to the teaching of the Church who has the right understanding of them. Hence whoever abandons this mean is altogether lacking in faith.

Reply Obj. 3: The various precepts of the Law may be referred either to their respective proximate motives, and thus one can be kept without another; or to their primary motive, which is perfect obedience to God, in which a man fails whenever he breaks one commandment, according to James 2:10: "Whosoever shall ... offend in one point is become guilty of all."

FOURTH ARTICLE [II-II, Q. 5, Art. 4]

Whether Faith Can Be Greater in One Man Than in Another?

Objection 1: It would seem that faith cannot be greater in one man than in another. For the quantity of a habit is taken from its object. Now whoever has faith believes everything that is of faith, since by failing in one point, a man loses his faith altogether, as stated above (A. 3). Therefore it seems that faith cannot be greater in one than in another.

Obj. 2: Further, those things which consist in something supreme cannot be "more" or "less." Now faith consists in something supreme, because it requires that man should adhere to the First Truth above all things. Therefore faith cannot be "more" or "less."

Obj. 3: Further, faith is to knowledge by grace, as the understanding of principles is to natural knowledge, since the articles of faith are the first principles of knowledge by grace, as was shown above (Q. 1, A. 7). Now the understanding of principles is possessed in equal degree by all men. Therefore faith is possessed in equal degree by all the faithful.

*On the contrary,* Wherever we find great and little, there we find more or less. Now in the matter of faith we find great and little, for Our Lord said to Peter (Matt. 14:31): "O thou of little faith, why didst thou doubt?" And to the woman he said (Matt. 15: 28): "O woman, great is thy faith!" Therefore faith can be greater in one than in another.

*I answer that,* As stated above (I-II, Q. 52, AA. 1, 2; I-II, Q. 112, A. 4), the quantity of a habit may be considered from two points of view: first, on the part of the object; secondly, on the part of its participation by the subject.

Now the object of faith may be considered in two ways: first, in respect of its formal aspect; secondly, in respect of the material object which is proposed to be believed. Now the formal object of faith is one and simple, namely the First Truth, as stated above (Q. 1, A. 1). Hence in this respect there is no diversity of faith among believers, but it is specifically one in all, as stated above (Q. 4, A. 6). But the things which are proposed as the matter of our belief are many and can be received more or less explicitly; and in this respect one man can believe explicitly more things than another, so that faith can be greater in one man on account of its being more explicit.

If, on the other hand, we consider faith from the point of view of its participation by the subject, this happens in two ways, since the act of faith proceeds both from the intellect and from the will, as stated above (Q. 2, AA. 1, 2; Q. 4, A. 2). Consequently a man's faith may be described as being greater, in one way, on the part of his intellect, on account of its greater certitude and firmness, and, in another way, on the part of his will, on account of his greater promptitude, devotion, or confidence.

Reply Obj. 1: A man who obstinately disbelieves a thing that is of faith, has not the habit of faith, and yet he who does not explicitly believe all, while he is prepared to believe all, has that habit. In this respect, one man has greater faith than another, on the part of the object, in so far as he believes more things, as stated above.

Reply Obj. 2: It is essential to faith that one should give the first place to the First Truth. But among those who do this, some submit to it with greater certitude and devotion than others; and in this way faith is greater in one than in another.

Reply Obj. 3: The understanding of principles results from man's very nature, which is equally shared by all: whereas faith results from the gift of grace, which is not equally in all, as explained above (I-II, Q. 112, A. 4). Hence the comparison fails.

Nevertheless the truth of principles is more known to one than to another, according to the greater capacity of intellect.

## QUESTION 6

OF THE CAUSE OF FAITH (In Two Articles)

We must now consider the cause of faith, under which head there are two points of inquiry:

(1) Whether faith is infused into man by God?

(2) Whether lifeless faith is a gift of God?

FIRST ARTICLE [II-II, Q. 6, Art. 1]

Whether Faith Is Infused into Man by God?

Objection 1: It would seem that faith is not infused into man by God. For Augustine says (De Trin. xiv) that "science begets faith in us, and nourishes, defends and strengthens it." Now those things which science begets in us seem to be acquired rather than infused. Therefore faith does not seem to be in us by Divine infusion.

Obj. 2: Further, that to which man attains by hearing and seeing, seems to be acquired by him. Now man attains to belief, both by seeing miracles, and by hearing the teachings of faith: for it is written (John 4:53): "The father ... knew that it was at the same hour, that Jesus said to him, Thy son liveth; and himself believed, and his whole house"; and (Rom. 10:17) it is said that "faith is through hearing." Therefore man attains to faith by acquiring it.

Obj. 3: Further, that which depends on a man's

will can be acquired by him. But "faith depends on the believer's will," according to Augustine (De Praedest. Sanct. v). Therefore faith can be acquired by man.

*On the contrary,* It is written (Eph. 2:8, 9): "By grace you are saved through faith, and that not of yourselves ... that no man may glory ... for it is the gift of God."

*I answer that,* Two things are requisite for faith. First, that the things which are of faith should be proposed to man: this is necessary in order that man believe anything explicitly. The second thing requisite for faith is the assent of the believer to the things which are proposed to him. Accordingly, as regards the first of these, faith must needs be from God. Because those things which are of faith surpass human reason, hence they do not come to man's knowledge, unless God reveal them. To some, indeed, they are revealed by God immediately, as those things which were revealed to the apostles and prophets, while to some they are proposed by God in sending preachers of the faith, according to Rom. 10:15: "How shall they preach, unless they be sent?"

As regards the second, viz. man's assent to the things which are of faith, we may observe a twofold cause, one of external inducement, such as seeing a miracle, or being persuaded by someone to embrace the faith: neither of which is a sufficient cause, since of those who see the same miracle, or who hear the same sermon, some believe, and some do not. Hence we must assert another internal cause, which moves man inwardly to assent to matters of faith.

The Pelagians held that this cause was nothing else than man's free-will: and consequently they said that the beginning of faith is from ourselves, inasmuch as, to wit, it is in our power to be ready to assent to things which are of faith, but that the consummation of faith is from God, Who proposes to us the things we have to believe. But this is false, for, since man, by assenting to matters of faith, is raised above his nature, this must needs accrue to him from some supernatural principle moving him inwardly; and this is God. Therefore faith, as regards the assent which is the chief act of faith, is from God moving man inwardly by grace.

Reply Obj. 1: Science begets and nourishes faith, by way of external persuasion afforded by science; but the chief and proper cause of faith is that which moves man inwardly to assent.

Reply Obj. 2: This argument again refers to the cause that proposes outwardly the things that are of faith, or persuades man to believe by words or deeds.

Reply Obj. 3: To believe does indeed depend on the will of the believer: but man's will needs to be prepared by God with grace, in order that he may be raised to things which are above his nature, as stated above (Q. 2, A. 3).

SECOND ARTICLE [II-II, Q. 6, Art. 2]

Whether Lifeless Faith Is a Gift of God?

Objection 1: It would seem that lifeless faith is not a gift of God. For it is written (Deut. 32:4) that "the works of God are perfect." Now lifeless faith is something imperfect. Therefore it is not the work of God.

Obj. 2: Further, just as an act is said to be deformed through lacking its due form, so too is faith called lifeless ( *informis* ) when it lacks the form due to it. Now the deformed act of sin is not from God, as stated above (I-II, Q. 79, A. 2, ad 2). Therefore neither is lifeless faith from God.

Obj. 3: Further, whomsoever God heals, He heals wholly: for it is written (John 7:23): "If a man receive circumcision on the sabbath-day, that the law of Moses may not be broken; are you angry at Me because I have healed the whole man on the sabbath-day?" Now faith heals man from unbelief. Therefore whoever receives from God the gift of faith, is at the same time healed from all his sins. But this is not done except by living faith. Therefore living faith alone is a gift of God: and consequently lifeless faith is not from God.

*On the contrary,* A gloss on 1 Cor. 13:2 says that "the faith which lacks charity is a gift of God." Now this is lifeless faith. Therefore lifeless faith is a gift of God.

*I answer that,* Lifelessness is a privation. Now it must be noted that privation is sometimes essential to the species, whereas sometimes it is not, but supervenes in a thing already possessed of its proper species: thus privation of the due equilibrium of the humors is essential to the species of sickness, while darkness is not essential to a diaphanous body, but supervenes in it. Since, therefore, when we assign the cause of a thing, we intend to assign the cause of that thing as existing in its proper species, it follows that what is not the cause of privation, cannot be assigned as the cause of the thing to which that privation belongs as being essential to its species. For we cannot assign as the cause of a sickness, something which is not the cause of a disturbance in the humors: though we can assign as cause of a diaphanous body, something which is not the cause of the darkness, which is not essential to the diaphanous body.

Now the lifelessness of faith is not essential to the species of faith, since faith is said to be lifeless through lack of an extrinsic form, as stated above (Q. 4, A. 4). Consequently the cause of lifeless faith is that which is the cause of faith strictly so called: and this is God, as stated above (A. 1). It follows, therefore, that lifeless faith is a gift of God.

Reply Obj. 1: Lifeless faith, though it is not simply perfect with the perfection of a virtue, is, nevertheless, perfect with a perfection that suffices for the essential notion of faith.

Reply Obj. 2: The deformity of an act is essential to the act's species, considered as a moral act, as stated above (I, Q. 48, A. 1, ad 2; I-II, Q. 18, A. 5): for an act is said to be deformed through being deprived of an intrinsic form, viz. the due commensuration of the act's circumstances. Hence we cannot say that God is the cause of a deformed act, for He is not the cause of its deformity, though He is the cause of the act as such.

We may also reply that deformity denotes not only privation of a due form, but also a contrary disposition, wherefore deformity is compared to the act, as falsehood is to faith. Hence, just as the deformed act is not from God, so neither is a false faith; and as lifeless faith is from God, so too, acts that are good generically, though not quickened by charity, as is frequently the case in sinners, are from God.

Reply Obj. 3: He who receives faith from God without charity, is healed from unbelief, not entirely (because the sin of his previous unbelief is not removed) but in part, namely, in the point of ceasing from committing such and such a sin. Thus it happens frequently that a man desists from one act of sin, through God causing him thus to desist, without desisting from another act of sin, through the instigation of his own malice. And in this way sometimes it is granted by God to a man to believe, and yet he is not granted the gift of charity: even so the gift of prophecy, or the like, is given to some without charity.

## QUESTION 7

OF THE EFFECTS OF FAITH (In Two Articles)

We must now consider the effects of faith: under which head there are two points of inquiry:

(1) Whether fear is an effect of faith?

(2) Whether the heart is purified by faith?

FIRST ARTICLE [II-II, Q. 7, Art. 1]

Whether Fear Is an Effect of Faith?

Objection 1: It would seem that fear is not an effect of faith. For an effect does not precede its cause. Now fear precedes faith: for it is written (Ecclus. 2:8): "Ye that fear the Lord, believe in Him." Therefore fear is not an effect of faith.

Obj. 2: Further, the same thing is not the cause of contraries. Now fear and hope are contraries, as stated above (I-II, Q. 23, A. 2): and faith begets hope, as a gloss observes on Matt. 1:2. Therefore fear is not an effect of faith.

Obj. 3: Further, one contrary does not cause another. Now the object of faith is a good, which is the First Truth, while the object of fear is an evil, as stated above (I-II, Q. 42, A. 1). Again, acts take their species from the object, according to what was stated above (I-II, Q. 18, A. 2). Therefore faith is not a cause of fear.

*On the contrary,* It is written (James 2:19): "The devils ... believe and tremble."

*I answer that,* Fear is a movement of the appetitive power, as stated above (I-II, Q. 41, A. 1). Now the principle of all appetitive movements is the good or evil apprehended: and consequently the principle of fear and of every appetitive movement must be an apprehension. Again, through faith there arises in us an apprehension of certain penal evils, which are inflicted in accordance with the Divine judgment. In this way, then, faith is a cause of the fear whereby one dreads to be punished by God; and this is servile fear.

It is also the cause of filial fear, whereby one dreads to be separated from God, or whereby one shrinks from equalling oneself to Him, and holds Him in reverence, inasmuch as faith makes us appreciate God as an unfathomable and supreme good, separation from which is the greatest evil, and to which it is wicked to wish to be equalled. Of the first fear, viz. servile fear, lifeless faith is the cause, while living faith is the cause of the second, viz. filial fear, because it makes man adhere to God and to be subject to Him by charity.

Reply Obj. 1: Fear of God cannot altogether precede faith, because if we knew nothing at all about Him, with regard to rewards and punishments, concerning which faith teaches us, we should nowise fear Him. If, however, faith be presupposed in reference to certain articles of faith, for example the Divine excellence, then reverential fear follows, the result of which is that man submits his intellect to God, so as to believe in all the Divine promises. Hence the text quoted continues: "And your reward shall not be made void."

Reply Obj. 2: The same thing in respect of contraries can be the cause of contraries, but not under the same aspect. Now faith begets hope, in so far as it enables us to appreciate the prize which God awards to the just, while it is the cause of fear, in so far as it makes us appreciate the punishments which He intends to inflict on sinners.

Reply Obj. 3: The primary and formal object of faith is the good which is the First Truth; but the material object of faith includes also certain evils; for instance, that it is an evil either not to submit to God, or to be separated from Him, and that sinners will suffer penal evils from God: in this way faith can be the cause of fear.

SECOND ARTICLE [II-II, Q. 7, Art. 2]

Whether Faith Has the Effect of Purifying the Heart?

Objection 1: It would seem that faith does not purify the heart. For purity of the heart pertains chiefly to the affections, whereas faith is in the intellect. Therefore faith has not the effect of purifying the heart.

Obj. 2: Further, that which purifies the heart is incompatible with impurity. But faith is compatible with the impurity of sin, as may be seen in those who have lifeless faith. Therefore faith does not purify the heart.

Obj. 3: Further, if faith were to purify the human heart in any way, it would chiefly purify the intellect of man. Now it does not purify the intellect from obscurity, since it is a veiled knowledge. Therefore faith nowise purifies the heart.

*On the contrary,* Peter said (Acts 15:9): "Purifying their hearts by faith."

*I answer that,* A thing is impure through being mixed with baser things: for silver is not called impure, when mixed with gold, which betters it, but when mixed with lead or tin. Now it is evident that the rational creature is more excellent than all transient and corporeal creatures; so that it becomes impure through subjecting itself to transient things by loving them. From this impurity the rational creature is purified by means of a contrary movement, namely, by tending to that which is above it, viz. God. The first beginning of this movement is faith: since "he that cometh to God must believe that He is," according to Heb. 11:6. Hence the first beginning of the heart's purifying is faith; and if this be perfected through being quickened by charity, the heart will be perfectly purified thereby.

Reply Obj. 1: Things that are in the intellect are the principles of those which are in the appetite, in so far as the apprehended good moves the appetite.

Reply Obj. 2: Even lifeless faith excludes a certain impurity which is contrary to it, viz. that of error, and which consists in the human intellect, adhering inordinately to things below itself, through wishing to measure Divine things by the rule of sensible objects. But when it is quickened by charity, then it is incompatible with any kind of impurity, because "charity covereth all sins" (Prov. 10:12).

Reply Obj. 3: The obscurity of faith does not pertain to the impurity of sin, but rather to the natural defect of the human intellect, according to the present state of life.

# QUESTION 8

OF THE GIFT OF UNDERSTANDING (In Eight Articles)

We must now consider the gifts of understanding and knowledge, which respond to the virtue of faith. With regard to the gift of understanding there are eight points of inquiry:

(1) Whether understanding is a gift of the Holy Ghost?

(2) Whether it can be together with faith in the same person?

(3) Whether the understanding which is a gift of the Holy Ghost, is only speculative, or practical also?

(4) Whether all who are in a state of grace have the gift of understanding?

(5) Whether this gift is to be found in those who are without grace?

(6) Of the relationship of the gift of understanding to the other gifts.

(7) Which of the beatitudes corresponds to this gift?

(8) Which of the fruits?

FIRST ARTICLE [II-II, Q. 8, Art. 1]

Whether Understanding Is a Gift of the Holy Ghost?

Objection 1: It would seem that understanding is not a gift of the Holy Ghost. For the gifts of grace are distinct from the gifts of nature, since they are given in addition to the latter. Now understanding is a natural habit of the soul, whereby self-evident principles are known, as stated in *Ethic.* vi, 6. Therefore it should not be reckoned among the gifts of the Holy Ghost.

Obj. 2: Further, the Divine gifts are shared by creatures according to their capacity and mode, as Dionysius states (Div. Nom. iv). Now the mode of human nature is to know the truth, not simply (which is a sign of understanding), but discursively (which is a sign of reason), as Dionysius explains (Div. Nom. vii). Therefore the Divine knowledge which is bestowed on man, should be called a gift of reason rather than a gift of understanding.

Obj. 3: Further, in the powers of the soul the understanding is condivided with the will (De Anima iii, 9, 10). Now no gift of the Holy Ghost is called after the will. Therefore no gift of the Holy Ghost should receive the name of understanding.

*On the contrary,* It is written (Isa. 11:2): "The Spirit of the Lord shall rest upon him, the Spirit of wisdom of understanding."

*I answer that,* Understanding implies an intimate knowledge, for "intelligere" [to understand] is the same as "intus legere" [to read inwardly]. This is clear to anyone who considers the difference between intellect and sense, because sensitive knowledge is concerned with external sensible qualities, whereas intellective knowledge penetrates into the very essence of a thing, because the object of the intellect is "what a thing is," as stated in *De Anima* iii, 6.

Now there are many kinds of things that are hidden within, to find which human knowledge has to penetrate within so to speak. Thus, under the accidents lies hidden the nature of the substantial reality, under words lies hidden their meaning; under likenesses and figures the truth they denote lies hidden (because the intelligible world is enclosed within as compared with the sensible world, which is perceived externally), and effects lie hidden in their causes, and vice versa. Hence we may speak of understanding with regard to all these things.

Since, however, human knowledge begins with the outside of things as it were, it is evident that the stronger the light of the understanding, the further can it penetrate into the heart of things. Now the natural light of our understanding is of finite power; wherefore it can reach to a certain fixed point. Consequently man needs a supernatural light in order to penetrate further still so as to know what it cannot know by its natural light: and this supernatural light which is bestowed on man is called the gift of understanding.

Reply Obj. 1: The natural light instilled within us, manifests only certain general principles, which are known naturally. But since man is ordained to supernatural happiness, as stated above (Q. 2, A. 3; I-II, Q. 3, A. 8), man needs to reach to certain higher truths, for which he requires the gift of understanding.

Reply Obj. 2: The discourse of reason always begins from an understanding and ends at an understanding; because we reason by proceeding from certain understood principles, and the discourse of reason is perfected when we come to understand what hitherto we ignored. Hence the act of reasoning proceeds from something previously understood. Now a gift of grace does not proceed from the light of nature, but is added thereto as perfecting it. Wherefore this addition is not called "reason" but "understanding," since the additional light is in comparison with what we know supernaturally, what the natural light is in regard to those things which we know from the first.

Reply Obj. 3: "Will" denotes simply a movement of the appetite without indicating any excellence; whereas "understanding" denotes a certain excellence of a knowledge that penetrates into the heart of things. Hence the supernatural gift is called after the understanding rather than after the will.

SECOND ARTICLE [II-II, Q. 8, Art. 2]

Whether the Gift of Understanding Is Compatible with Faith?

Objection 1: It would seem that the gift of understanding is incompatible with faith. For Augustine says (QQ. lxxxiii, qu. 15) that "the thing which is understood is bounded by the comprehension of him who understands it." But the thing which is believed is not comprehended, according to the word of the Apostle to the Philippians 3:12: "Not as though I had already comprehended [Douay: 'attained'], or were already perfect." Therefore it seems that faith and understanding are incompatible in the same subject.

Obj. 2: Further, whatever is understood is seen by the understanding. But faith is of things that appear not, as stated above (Q. 1, A. 4; Q. 4, A. 1). Therefore faith is incompatible with understanding in the same subject.

Obj. 3: Further, understanding is more certain than science. But science and faith are incompatible in the same subject, as stated above (Q. 1, AA. 4, 5). Much less, therefore, can understanding and faith be in the same subject.

*On the contrary,* Gregory says (Moral. i, 15) that "understanding enlightens the mind concerning the things it has heard." Now one who has faith can be enlightened in his mind concerning what he has heard; thus it is written (Luke 24:27, 32) that Our Lord opened the scriptures to His disciples, that they might understand them. Therefore understanding is compatible with faith.

*I answer that,* We need to make a twofold distinction here: one on the side of faith, the other on the part of understanding.

On the side of faith the distinction to be made is that certain things, of themselves, come directly under faith, such as the mystery to three Persons in one God, and the incarnation of God the Son; whereas other things come under faith, through being subordinate, in one way or another, to those just mentioned, for instance, all that is contained in the Divine Scriptures.

On the part of understanding the distinction to be observed is that there are two ways in which we may be said to understand. In one way, we understand a thing perfectly, when we arrive at knowing the essence of the thing we understand, and the very truth considered in itself of the proposition understood. In this way, so long as the state of faith lasts, we cannot understand those things which are the direct object of faith: although certain other things that are subordinate to faith can be understood even in this way.

In another way we understand a thing imperfectly, when the essence of a thing or the truth of a proposition is not known as to its quiddity or mode of being, and yet we know that whatever be the outward appearances, they do not contradict the truth, in so far as we understand that we ought not to depart from matters of faith, for the sake of things that appear externally. In this way, even during the state of faith, nothing hinders us from understanding even those things which are the direct object of faith.

This suffices for the Replies to the Objections: for the first three argue in reference to perfect understanding, while the last refers to the understanding of matters subordinate to faith.

THIRD ARTICLE [II-II, Q. 8, Art. 3]

Whether the Gift of Understanding Is Merely Speculative or Also Practical?

Objection 1: It would seem that understanding, considered as a gift of the Holy Ghost, is not practical, but only speculative. For, according to Gregory (Moral. i, 32), "understanding penetrates certain more exalted things." But the practical intellect is occupied, not with exalted, but with inferior things, viz. singulars, about which actions are concerned. Therefore understanding, considered as a gift, is not practical.

Obj. 2: Further, the gift of understanding is something more excellent than the intellectual virtue of understanding. But the intellectual virtue of understanding is concerned with none but necessary things, according to the Philosopher (Ethic. vi, 6). Much more, therefore, is the gift of understanding concerned with none but necessary matters.

Now the practical intellect is not about necessary things, but about things which may be otherwise than they are, and which may result from man's activity. Therefore the gift of understanding is not practical.

Obj. 3: Further, the gift of understanding enlightens the mind in matters which surpass natural reason. Now human activities, with which the practical intellect is concerned, do not surpass natural reason, which is the directing principle in matters of action, as was made clear above (I-II, Q. 58, A. 2; I-II, Q. 71, A. 6). Therefore the gift of understanding is not practical.

*On the contrary,* It is written (Ps. 110:10): "A good understanding to all that do it."

*I answer that,* As stated above (A. 2), the gift of understanding is not only about those things which come under faith first and principally, but also about all things subordinate to faith. Now good actions have a certain relationship to faith: since "faith worketh through charity," according to the Apostle (Gal. 5:6). Hence the gift of understanding extends also to certain actions, not as though these were its principal object, but in so far as the rule of our actions is the eternal law, to which the higher reason, which is perfected by the gift of understanding, adheres by contemplating and consulting it, as Augustine states (De Trin. xii, 7).

Reply Obj. 1: The things with which human actions are concerned are not surpassingly exalted considered in themselves, but, as referred to the rule of the eternal law, and to the end of Divine happiness, they are exalted so that they can be the matter of understanding.

Reply Obj. 2: The excellence of the gift of understanding consists precisely in its considering eternal or necessary matters, not only as they are rules of human actions, because a cognitive virtue is the more excellent, according to the greater extent of its object.

Reply Obj. 3: The rule of human actions is the human reason and the eternal law, as stated above (I-II, Q. 71, A. 6). Now the eternal law surpasses human reason: so that the knowledge of human actions, as ruled by the eternal law, surpasses the natural reason, and requires the supernatural light of a gift of the Holy Ghost.

FOURTH ARTICLE [II-II, Q. 8, Art. 4]

Whether the Gift of Understanding Is in All Who Are in a State of Grace?

Objection 1: It would seem that the gift of understanding is not in all who are in a state of grace. For Gregory says (Moral. ii, 49) that "the gift of understanding is given as a remedy against dulness of mind." Now many who are in a state of grace suffer from dulness of mind. Therefore the gift of understanding is not in all who are in a state of grace.

Obj. 2: Further, of all the things that are connected with knowledge, faith alone seems to be necessary for salvation, since by faith Christ dwells in our hearts, according to Eph. 3:17. Now the gift of understanding is not in everyone that has faith; indeed, those who have faith ought to pray that they may understand, as Augustine says (De Trin. xv, 27). Therefore the gift of understanding is not necessary for salvation: and, consequently, is not in all who are in a state of grace.

Obj. 3: Further, those things which are common to all who are in a state of grace, are never withdrawn from them. Now the grace of understanding and of the other gifts sometimes withdraws itself profitably, for, at times, "when the mind is puffed up with understanding sublime things, it becomes sluggish and dull in base and vile things," as Gregory observes (Moral. ii, 49). Therefore the gift of understanding is not in all who are in a state of grace.

*On the contrary,* It is written (Ps. 81:5): "They have not known or understood, they walk on in darkness." But no one who is in a state of grace walks in darkness, according to John 8:12: "He that followeth Me, walketh not in darkness." Therefore no one who is in a state of grace is without the gift of understanding.

*I answer that,* In all who are in a state of grace, there must needs be rectitude of the will, since grace prepares man's will for good, according to Augustine (Contra Julian. Pelag. iv, 3). Now the will cannot be rightly directed to good, unless there be already some knowledge of the truth, since the object of the will is good understood, as stated in *De Anima* iii, 7. Again, just as the Holy Ghost directs man's will by the gift of charity, so as to move it directly to some supernatural good; so also, by the gift of understanding, He enlightens the human mind, so that it knows some supernatural truth, to which the right will needs to tend.

Therefore, just as the gift of charity is in all of those who have sanctifying grace, so also is the gift of understanding.

Reply Obj. 1: Some who have sanctifying grace may suffer dulness of mind with regard to things that are not necessary for salvation; but with regard to those that are necessary for salvation, they are sufficiently instructed by the Holy Ghost, according to 1 John 2:27: "His unction teacheth you of all things."

Reply Obj. 2: Although not all who have faith understand fully the things that are proposed to be believed, yet they understand that they ought to believe them, and that they ought nowise to deviate from them.

Reply Obj. 3: With regard to things necessary for salvation, the gift of understanding never withdraws from holy persons: but, in order that they may have no incentive to pride, it does withdraw sometimes with regard to other things, so that their mind is unable to penetrate all things clearly.

FIFTH ARTICLE [II-II, Q. 8, Art. 5]

Whether the Gift of Understanding Is Found Also in Those Who Have Not Sanctifying Grace?

Objection 1: It would seem that the gift of understanding is found also in those who have not sanctifying grace. For Augustine, in expounding the words of Ps. 118:20: "My soul hath coveted to long for Thy justifications," says: "Understanding flies ahead, and man's will is weak and slow to follow." But in all who have sanctifying grace, the will is prompt on account of charity. Therefore the gift of understanding can be in those who have not sanctifying grace.

Obj. 2: Further, it is written (Dan. 10:1) that "there is need of understanding in a" prophetic "vision," so that, seemingly, there is no prophecy without the gift of understanding. But there can be prophecy without sanctifying grace, as evidenced by Matt. 7:22, where those who say: "We have prophesied in Thy name [*Vulg.: 'Have we not prophesied in Thy name?']," are answered with the words: "I never knew you." Therefore the gift of understanding can be without sanctifying grace.

Obj. 3: Further, the gift of understanding responds to the virtue of faith, according to Isa. 7:9, following another reading [*The Septuagint]: "If you will not believe you shall not understand." Now faith can be without sanctifying grace. Therefore the gift of understanding can be without it.

*On the contrary,* Our Lord said (John 6:45): "Every one that hath heard of the Father, and hath learned, cometh to Me." Now it is by the intellect, as Gregory observes (Moral. i, 32), that we learn or understand what we hear. Therefore whoever has the gift of understanding, cometh to Christ, which is impossible without sanctifying grace. Therefore the gift of understanding cannot be without sanctifying grace.

*I answer that,* As stated above (I-II, Q. 68, AA. 1, 2) the gifts of the Holy Ghost perfect the soul, according as it is amenable to the motion of the Holy Ghost. Accordingly then, the intellectual light of grace is called the gift of understanding, in so far as man's understanding is easily moved by the Holy Ghost, the consideration of which movement depends on a true apprehension of the end. Wherefore unless the human intellect be moved by the Holy Ghost so far as to have a right estimate of the end, it has not yet obtained the gift of understanding, however much the Holy Ghost may have enlightened it in regard to other truths that are preambles to the faith.

Now to have a right estimate about the last end one must not be in error about the end, and must adhere to it firmly as to the greatest good: and no one can do this without sanctifying grace; even as in moral matters a man has a right estimate about the end through a habit of virtue. Therefore no one has the gift of understanding without sanctifying grace.

Reply Obj. 1: By understanding Augustine means any kind of intellectual light, that, however, does not fulfil all the conditions of a gift, unless the mind of man be so far perfected as to have a right estimate about the end.

Reply Obj. 2: The understanding that is requisite for prophecy, is a kind of enlightenment of the mind with regard to the things revealed to the prophet: but it is not an enlightenment of the mind with regard to a right estimate about the last end, which belongs to the gift of understanding.

Reply Obj. 3: Faith implies merely assent to what is proposed but understanding implies a certain perception of the truth, which perception, except in one who has sanctifying grace, cannot regard the end, as stated above. Hence the comparison fails between understanding and faith.

SIXTH ARTICLE [II-II, Q. 8, Art. 6]

Whether the Gift of Understanding Is Distinct from the Other Gifts?

Objection 1: It would seem that the gift of understanding is not distinct from the other gifts. For there is no distinction between things whose opposites are not distinct. Now "wisdom is contrary to folly, understanding is contrary to dulness, counsel is contrary to rashness, knowledge is contrary to ignorance," as Gregory states (Moral. ii, 49). But there would seem to be no difference between folly, dulness, ignorance and rashness. Therefore neither does understanding differ from the other gifts.

Obj. 2: Further, the intellectual virtue of understanding differs from the other intellectual virtues in that it is proper to it to be about self-evident principles. But the gift of understanding is not about any self-evident principles, since the natural habit of first principles suffices in respect of those matters which are naturally self-evident: while faith is sufficient in respect of such things as are supernatural, since the articles of faith are like first principles in supernatural knowledge, as stated above (Q. 1, A. 7). Therefore the gift of understanding does not differ from the other intellectual gifts.

Obj. 3: Further, all intellectual knowledge is either speculative or practical. Now the gift of understanding is related to both, as stated above (A. 3). Therefore it is not distinct from the other intellectual gifts, but comprises them all.

*On the contrary,* When several things are enumerated together they must be, in some way, distinct from one another, because distinction is the origin of number. Now the gift of understanding is enumerated together with the other gifts, as appears from Isa. 11:2. Therefore the gift of understanding is distinct from the other gifts.

*I answer that,* The difference between the gift of understanding and three of the others, viz. piety, fortitude, and fear, is evident, since the gift of understanding belongs to the cognitive power, while the three belong to the appetitive power.

But the difference between this gift of understanding and the remaining three, viz. wisdom, knowledge, and counsel, which also belong to the cognitive power, is not so evident. To some [*William of Auxerre, Sum. Aur. III, iii, 8], it seems that the gift of understanding differs from the gifts of knowledge and counsel, in that these two belong to practical knowledge, while the gift of understanding belongs to speculative knowledge; and that it differs from the gift of wisdom, which also belongs to speculative knowledge, in that wisdom is concerned with judgment, while understanding renders the mind apt to grasp the things that are proposed, and to penetrate into their very heart. And in this sense we have assigned the number of the gifts, above (I-II, Q. 68, A. 4).

But if we consider the matter carefully, the gift of understanding is concerned not only with speculative, but also with practical matters, as stated above (A. 3), and likewise, the gift of knowledge regards both matters, as we shall show further on (Q. 9, A. 3), and consequently, we must take their distinction in some other way. For all these four gifts are ordained to supernatural knowledge, which, in us, takes its foundation from faith. Now "faith is through hearing" (Rom. 10:17). Hence some things must be proposed to be believed by man, not as seen, but as heard, to which he assents by faith. But faith, first and principally, is about the First Truth, secondarily, about certain considerations concerning creatures, and furthermore extends to the direction of human actions, in so far as it works through charity, as appears from what has been said above (Q. 4, A. 2, ad 3).

Accordingly on the part of the things proposed to faith for belief, two things are requisite on our part: first that they be penetrated or grasped by the intellect, and this belongs to the gift of understanding. Secondly, it is necessary that man should judge these things aright, that he should esteem that he ought to adhere to these things, and to withdraw from their opposites: and this judgment, with regard to Divine things belong to the gift of wisdom, but with regard to created things, belongs to the gift of knowledge, and as to its application to individual actions, belongs to the gift of counsel.

Reply Obj. 1: The foregoing difference between those four gifts is clearly in agreement with the distinction of those things which Gregory assigns as their opposites. For dulness is contrary to sharpness, since an intellect is said, by comparison, to be sharp, when it is able to penetrate into the heart of the things that are proposed to it. Hence it is dulness of mind that renders the mind unable to pierce into the heart of a thing. A man is said to be a fool if he judges wrongly about the common end of life, wherefore folly is properly opposed to wisdom, which makes us judge aright about the universal cause. Ignorance implies a defect in the mind, even about any particular things whatever, so that it is contrary to knowledge, which gives man a right judgment about particular causes, viz. about creatures. Rashness is clearly opposed to counsel, whereby man does not proceed to action before deliberating with his reason.

Reply Obj. 2: The gift of understanding is about the first principles of that knowledge which is conferred by grace; but otherwise than faith, because it belongs to faith to assent to them, while it belongs to the gift of understanding to pierce with the mind the things that are said.

Reply Obj. 3: The gift of understanding is related to both kinds of knowledge, viz. speculative and practical, not as to the judgment, but as to apprehension, by grasping what is said.

SEVENTH ARTICLE [II-II, Q. 8, Art. 7]

Whether the Sixth Beatitude, "Blessed Are the Clean of Heart," etc., Responds to the Gift of Understanding?

Objection 1: It would seem that the sixth beatitude, "Blessed are the clean of heart, for they shall see God," does not respond to the gift of understanding. Because cleanness of heart seems to belong chiefly to the appetite. But the gift of understanding belongs, not to the appetite, but rather to the intellectual power. Therefore the aforesaid beatitude does not respond to the gift of understanding.

Obj. 2: Further, it is written (Acts 15:9): "Purifying their hearts by faith." Now cleanness of heart is acquired by the heart being purified. Therefore the aforesaid beatitude is related to the virtue of faith rather than to the gift of understanding.

Obj. 3: Further, the gifts of the Holy Ghost perfect man in the present state of life. But the sight of God does not belong to the present life, since it is that which gives happiness to the Blessed, as stated above (I-II, Q. 3, A. 8). Therefore the sixth beatitude which comprises the sight of God, does not respond to the gift of understanding.

*On the contrary,* Augustine says (De Serm. Dom. in Monte i, 4): "The sixth work of the Holy Ghost which is understanding, is applicable to the clean of heart, whose eye being purified, they can see what eye hath not seen."

*I answer that,* Two things are contained in the sixth beatitude, as also in the others, one by way of merit, viz. cleanness of heart; the other by way of reward, viz. the sight of God, as stated above (I-II, Q. 69, AA. 2, 4), and each of these, in some way, responds to the gift of understanding.

For cleanness is twofold. One is a preamble and a disposition to seeing God, and consists in the heart being cleansed of inordinate affections: and this cleanness of heart is effected by the virtues and gifts belonging to the appetitive power. The other cleanness of heart is a kind of complement to the sight of God; such is the cleanness of the mind that is purged of phantasms and errors, so as to receive the truths which are proposed to it about God, no longer by way of corporeal phantasms, nor infected with heretical misrepresentations: and this cleanness is the result of the gift of understanding.

Again, the sight of God is twofold. One is perfect, whereby God's Essence is seen: the other is imperfect, whereby, though we see not what God is, yet we see what He is not; and whereby, the more perfectly do we know God in this life, the more we understand that He surpasses all that the mind comprehends. Each of these visions of God belongs to the gift of understanding; the first, to the gift of understanding in its state of perfection, as possessed in heaven; the second, to the gift of understanding in its state of inchoation, as possessed by wayfarers.

This suffices for the Replies to the Objections: for the first two arguments refer to the first kind of cleanness; while the third refers to the perfect vision of God. Moreover the gifts both perfect us in this life by way of inchoation, and will be fulfilled, as stated above (I-II, Q. 69, A. 2).

EIGHTH ARTICLE [II-II, Q. 8, Art. 8]

Whether Faith, Among the Fruits, Responds to the Gift of Understanding?

Objection 1: It would seem that, among the fruits, faith does not respond to the gift of understanding. For understanding is the fruit of faith, since it is written (Isa. 7:9) according to another reading [*The Septuagint]: "If you will not believe you shall not understand," where our version has: "If you will not believe, you shall not continue." Therefore fruit is not the fruit of understanding.

Obj. 2: Further, that which precedes is not the fruit of what follows. But faith seems to precede understanding, since it is the foundation of the entire spiritual edifice, as stated above (Q. 4, AA. 1, 7). Therefore faith is not the fruit of understanding.

Obj. 3: Further, more gifts pertain to the intellect than to the appetite. Now, among the fruits, only one pertains to the intellect; namely, faith, while all the others pertain to the appetite. Therefore faith, seemingly, does not pertain to understanding more than to wisdom, knowledge or counsel.

*On the contrary,* The end of a thing is its fruit. Now the gift of understanding seems to be ordained chiefly to the certitude of faith, which certitude is reckoned a fruit. For a gloss on Gal. 5:22 says that the "faith which is a fruit, is certitude about the unseen." Therefore faith, among the fruits, responds to the gift of understanding.

*I answer that,* The fruits of the Spirit, as stated above (I-II, Q. 70, A. 1), when we were discussing them, are so called because they are something ultimate and delightful, produced in us by the power of the Holy Ghost. Now the ultimate and delightful has the nature of an end, which is the proper object of the will: and consequently that which is ultimate and delightful with regard to the will, must be, after a fashion, the fruit of all the other things that pertain to the other powers.

Accordingly, therefore, to this kind of gift of virtue that perfects a power, we may distinguish a double fruit: one, belonging to the same power; the other, the last of all as it were, belonging to the will. In this way we must conclude that the fruit which properly responds to the gift of understanding is faith, i.e. the certitude of faith; while the fruit that responds to it last of all is joy, which belongs to the will.

Reply Obj. 1: Understanding is the fruit of faith, taken as a virtue. But we are not taking faith in this sense here, but for a kind of certitude of faith, to which man attains by the gift of understanding.

Reply Obj. 2: Faith cannot altogether precede understanding, for it would be impossible to assent by believing what is proposed to be believed, without understanding it in some way. However, the perfection of understanding follows the virtue of faith: which perfection of understanding is itself followed by a kind of certainty of faith.

Reply Obj. 3: The fruit of practical knowledge cannot consist in that very knowledge, since knowledge of that kind is known not for its own sake, but for the sake of something else. On the other hand, speculative knowledge has its fruit in its very self, which fruit is the certitude about the thing known. Hence the gift of counsel, which belongs only to practical knowledge, has no corresponding fruit of its own: while the gifts of wisdom, understanding and knowledge, which can belongs also to speculative knowledge, have but one corresponding fruit, which is certainly denoted by the name of faith. The reason why there are several fruits pertaining to the appetitive faculty, is because, as already stated, the character of end, which the word fruit implies, pertains to the appetitive rather than to the intellective part.

## QUESTION 9

OF THE GIFT OF KNOWLEDGE (In Four Articles)

We must now consider the gift of knowledge, under which head there are four points of inquiry:

(1) Whether knowledge is a gift?

(2) Whether it is about Divine things?

(3) Whether it is speculative or practical?

(4) Which beatitude responds to it?

FIRST ARTICLE [II-II, Q. 9, Art. 1]

Whether Knowledge Is a Gift?

Objection 1: It would seem that knowledge is not a gift. For the gifts of the Holy Ghost surpass the natural faculty. But knowledge implies an effect of natural reason: for the Philosopher says (Poster. i, 2) that a "demonstration is a syllogism which produces knowledge." Therefore knowledge is not a gift of the Holy Ghost.

Obj. 2: Further, the gifts of the Holy Ghost are common to all holy persons, as stated above (Q. 8, A. 4; I-II, Q. 68, A. 5). Now Augustine says (De Trin. xiv, 1) that "many of the faithful lack knowledge though they have faith." Therefore knowledge is not a gift.

Obj. 3: Further, the gifts are more perfect than the virtues, as stated above (I-II, Q. 68, A. 8). Therefore one gift suffices for the perfection of one virtue. Now the gift of understanding responds to the virtue of faith, as stated above (Q. 8, A. 2). Therefore the gift of knowledge does not respond to that virtue, nor does it appear to which other virtue it can respond. Since, then, the gifts are perfections of virtues, as stated above (I-II, Q. 68, AA. 1, 2), it seems that knowledge is not a gift.

*On the contrary,* Knowledge is reckoned among the seven gifts (Isa. 11:2).

*I answer that,* Grace is more perfect than nature, and, therefore, does not fail in those things wherein man can be perfected by nature. Now, when a man, by his natural reason, assents by his intellect to some truth, he is perfected in two ways in respect of that truth: first, because he grasps it; secondly, because he forms a sure judgment on it.

Accordingly, two things are requisite in order that the human intellect may perfectly assent to the truth of the faith: one of these is that he should have a sound grasp of the things that are proposed to be believed, and this pertains to the gift of understanding, as stated above (Q. 8, A. 6): while the other is that he should have a sure and right judgment on them, so as to discern what is to be believed, from what is not to be believed, and for this the gift of knowledge is required.

Reply Obj. 1: Certitude of knowledge varies in various natures, according to the various conditions of each nature. Because man forms a sure judgment about a truth by the discursive process of his reason: and so human knowledge is acquired by means of demonstrative reasoning. On the other hand, in God, there is a sure judgment of truth, without any discursive process, by simple intuition, as was stated in the First Part (Q. 14, A. 7); wherefore God's knowledge is not discursive, or argumentative, but absolute and simple, to which that knowledge is likened which is a gift of the Holy Ghost, since it is a participated likeness thereof.

Reply Obj. 2: A twofold knowledge may be had about matters of belief. One is the knowledge of what one ought to believe by discerning things to be believed from things not to be believed: in this way knowledge is a gift and is common to all holy persons. The other is a knowledge about matters of belief, whereby one knows not only what one ought to believe, but also how to make the faith known, how to induce others to believe, and confute those who deny the faith. This knowledge is numbered among the gratuitous graces, which are not given to all, but to some. Hence Augustine, after the words quoted, adds: "It is one thing for a man merely to know what he ought to believe, and another to know how to dispense what he believes to the godly, and to defend it against the ungodly."

Reply Obj. 3: The gifts are more perfect than the moral and intellectual virtues; but they are not more perfect than the theological virtues; rather are all the gifts ordained to the perfection of the theological virtues, as to their end. Hence it is not unreasonable if several gifts are ordained to one theological virtue.

SECOND ARTICLE [II-II, Q. 9, Art. 2]

Whether the Gift of Knowledge Is About Divine Things?

Objection 1: It would seem that the gift of knowledge is about Divine things. For Augustine says (De Trin. xiv, 1) that "knowledge begets, nourishes and strengthens faith." Now faith is about Divine things, because its object is the First Truth, as stated above (Q. 1, A. 1). Therefore the gift of knowledge also is about Divine things.

Obj. 2: Further, the gift of knowledge is more excellent than acquired knowledge. But there is an acquired knowledge about Divine things, for instance, the science of metaphysics. Much more therefore is the gift of knowledge about Divine things.

Obj. 3: Further, according to Rom. 1:20, "the invisible things of God ... are clearly seen, being understood by the things that are made." If therefore there is knowledge about created things, it seems that there is also knowledge of Divine things.

*On the contrary,* Augustine says (De Trin. xiv, 1): "The knowledge of Divine things may be properly called wisdom, and the knowledge of human affairs may properly receive the name of knowledge."

*I answer that,* A sure judgment about a thing is formed chiefly from its cause, and so the order of judgments should be according to the order of causes. For just as the first cause is the cause of the second, so ought the judgment about the second cause to be formed through the first cause: nor is it possible to judge of the first cause through any other cause; wherefore the judgment which is formed through the first cause, is the first and most perfect judgment.

Now in those things where we find something most perfect, the common name of the genus is appropriated for those things which fall short of the most perfect, and some special name is adapted to the most perfect thing, as is the case in Logic. For in the genus of convertible terms, that which signifies "what a thing is," is given the special name of "definition," but the convertible terms which fall short of this, retain the common name, and are called "proper" terms.

Accordingly, since the word knowledge implies certitude of judgment as stated above (A. 1), if this certitude of the judgment is derived from the highest cause, the knowledge has a special name, which is wisdom: for a wise man in any branch of knowledge is one who knows the highest cause of that kind of knowledge, and is able to judge of all matters by that cause: and a wise man "absolutely," is one who knows the cause which is absolutely highest, namely God. Hence the knowledge of Divine things is called "wisdom," while the knowledge of human things is called "knowledge," this being the common name denoting certitude of judgment, and appropriated to the judgment which is formed through second causes. Accordingly, if we take knowledge in this way, it is a distinct gift from the gift of wisdom, so that the gift of knowledge is only about human or created things.

Reply Obj. 1: Although matters of faith are Divine and eternal, yet faith itself is something temporal in the mind of the believer. Hence to know what one ought to believe, belongs to the gift of knowledge, but to know in themselves the very things we believe, by a kind of union with them, belongs to the gift of wisdom. Therefore the gift of wisdom corresponds more to charity which unites man's mind to God.

Reply Obj. 2: This argument takes knowledge in the generic acceptation of the term: it is not thus that knowledge is a special gift, but according as it is restricted to judgments formed through created things.

Reply Obj. 3: As stated above (Q. 1, A. 1), every cognitive habit regards formally the mean through which things are known, and materially, the things that are known through the mean. And since that which is formal, is of most account, it follows that those sciences which draw conclusions about physical matter from mathematical principles, are reckoned rather among the mathematical sciences, though, as to their matter they have more in common with physical sciences: and for this reason it is stated in *Phys.* ii, 2 that they are more akin to physics. Accordingly, since man knows God through His creatures, this seems to pertain to "knowledge," to which it belongs formally, rather than to "wisdom," to which it belongs materially: and, conversely, when we judge of creatures according to Divine things, this pertains to "wisdom" rather than to "knowledge."

THIRD ARTICLE [II-II, Q. 9, Art. 3]

Whether the Gift of Knowledge Is Practical Knowledge?

Objection 1: It would seem that the knowledge, which is numbered among the gifts, is practical knowledge. For Augustine says (De Trin. xii, 14) that "knowledge is concerned with the actions in which we make use of external things." But the knowledge which is concerned about actions is practical. Therefore the gift of knowledge is practical.

Obj. 2: Further, Gregory says (Moral. i, 32): "Knowledge is nought if it hath not its use for piety ... and piety is very useless if it lacks the discernment of knowledge." Now it follows from this authority that knowledge directs piety. But this cannot apply to a speculative science. Therefore the gift of knowledge is not speculative but practical.

Obj. 3: Further, the gifts of the Holy Ghost are only in the righteous, as stated above (Q. 9, A. 5). But speculative knowledge can be also in the unrighteous, according to James 4:17: "To him ... who knoweth to do good, and doth it not, to him it is a sin." Therefore the gift of knowledge is not speculative but practical.

*On the contrary,* Gregory says (Moral. i, 32): "Knowledge on her own day prepares a feast, because she overcomes the fast of ignorance in the mind." Now ignorance is not entirely removed, save by both kinds of knowledge, viz. speculative and practical. Therefore the gift of knowledge is both speculative and practical.

*I answer that,* As stated above (Q. 9, A. 8), the gift of knowledge, like the gift of understanding, is ordained to the certitude of faith. Now faith consists primarily and principally in speculation, in as much as it is founded on the First Truth. But since the First Truth is also the last end for the sake of which our works are done, hence it is that faith extends to works, according to Gal. 5:6: "Faith ... worketh by charity."

The consequence is that the gift of knowledge also, primarily and principally indeed, regards speculation, in so far as man knows what he ought to hold by faith; yet, secondarily, it extends to works, since we are directed in our actions by the knowledge of matters of faith, and of conclusions drawn therefrom.

Reply Obj. 1: Augustine is speaking of the gift of knowledge, in so far as it extends to works; for action is ascribed to knowledge, yet not action solely, nor primarily: and in this way it directs piety.

Hence the Reply to the Second Objection is clear.

Reply Obj. 3: As we have already stated (Q. 8, A. 5) about the gift of understanding, not everyone who understands, has the gift of understanding, but only he that understands through a habit of grace: and so we must take note, with regard to the gift of knowledge, that they alone have the gift of knowledge, who judge aright about matters of faith and action, through the grace bestowed on them, so as never to wander from the straight path of justice. This is the knowledge of holy things, according to Wis. 10:10: "She conducted the just ... through the right ways ... and gave him the knowledge of holy things."

FOURTH ARTICLE [II-II, Q. 9, Art. 4]

Whether the Third Beatitude, "Blessed Are They That Mourn," etc. Corresponds to the Gift of Knowledge?

Objection 1: It would seem that the third beatitude, "Blessed are they that mourn," does not correspond to the gift of knowledge. For, even as evil is the cause of sorrow and grief, so is good the cause of joy. Now knowledge brings good to light rather than evil, since the latter is known through evil: for "the straight line rules both itself and the crooked line" (De Anima i, 5). Therefore the aforesaid beatitude does not suitably correspond to the gift of knowledge.

Obj. 2: Further, consideration of truth is an

act of knowledge. Now there is no sorrow in the consideration of truth; rather is there joy, since it is written (Wis. 8:16): "Her conversation hath no bitterness, nor her company any tediousness, but joy and gladness." Therefore the aforesaid beatitude does not suitably correspond with the gift of knowledge.

Obj. 3: Further, the gift of knowledge consists in speculation, before operation. Now, in so far as it consists in speculation, sorrow does not correspond to it, since "the speculative intellect is not concerned about things to be sought or avoided" (De Anima iii, 9). Therefore the aforesaid beatitude is not suitably reckoned to correspond with the gift of knowledge.

*On the contrary,* Augustine says (De Serm. Dom. in Monte iv): "Knowledge befits the mourner, who has discovered that he has been mastered by the evil which he coveted as though it were good."

*I answer that,* Right judgment about creatures belongs properly to knowledge. Now it is through creatures that man's aversion from God is occasioned, according to Wis. 14:11: "Creatures ... are turned to an abomination ... and a snare to the feet of the unwise," of those, namely, who do not judge aright about creatures, since they deem the perfect good to consist in them. Hence they sin by placing their last end in them, and lose the true good. It is by forming a right judgment of creatures that man becomes aware of the loss (of which they may be the occasion), which judgment he exercises through the gift of knowledge.

Hence the beatitude of sorrow is said to correspond to the gift of knowledge.

Reply Obj. 1: Created goods do not cause spiritual joy, except in so far as they are referred to the Divine good, which is the proper cause of spiritual joy. Hence spiritual peace and the resulting joy correspond directly to the gift of wisdom: but to the gift of knowledge there corresponds, in the first place, sorrow for past errors, and, in consequence, consolation, since, by his right judgment, man directs creatures to the Divine good. For this reason sorrow is set forth in this beatitude, as the merit, and the resulting consolation, as the reward; which is begun in this life, and is perfected in the life to come.

Reply Obj. 2: Man rejoices in the very consideration of truth; yet he may sometimes grieve for the thing, the truth of which he considers: it is thus that sorrow is ascribed to knowledge.

Reply Obj. 3: No beatitude corresponds to knowledge, in so far as it consists in speculation, because man's beatitude consists, not in considering creatures, but in contemplating God. But man's beatitude does consist somewhat in the right use of creatures, and in well-ordered love of them: and this I say with regard to the beatitude of a wayfarer. Hence beatitude relating to contemplation is not ascribed to knowledge, but to understanding and wisdom, which are about Divine things.

## QUESTION 10

OF UNBELIEF IN GENERAL (In Twelve Articles)

In due sequence we must consider the contrary vices: first, unbelief, which is contrary to faith; secondly, blasphemy, which is opposed to confession of faith; thirdly, ignorance and dulness of mind, which are contrary to knowledge and understanding.

As to the first, we must consider (1) unbelief in general; (2) heresy; (3) apostasy from the faith.

Under the first head there are twelve points of inquiry:

(1) Whether unbelief is a sin?

(2) What is its subject?

(3) Whether it is the greatest of sins?

(4) Whether every action of unbelievers is a sin?

(5) Of the species of unbelief;

(6) Of their comparison, one with another;

(7) Whether we ought to dispute about faith with unbelievers?

(8) Whether they ought to be compelled to the faith?

(9) Whether we ought to have communications with them?

(10) Whether unbelievers can have authority over Christians?

(11) Whether the rites of unbelievers should be tolerated?

(12) Whether the children of unbelievers are to be baptized against their parents' will?

FIRST ARTICLE [II-II, Q. 10, Art. 1]

Whether Unbelief Is a Sin?

Objection 1: It would seem that unbelief is not a sin. For every sin is contrary to nature, as Damascene proves (De Fide Orth. ii, 4). Now unbelief seems not to be contrary to nature; for Augustine says (De Praedest. Sanct. v) that "to be capable to having faith, just as to be capable of having charity, is natural to all men; whereas to have faith, even as to have charity, belongs to the grace of the faithful." Therefore not to have faith, which is to be an unbeliever, is not a sin.

Obj. 2: Further, no one sins that which he cannot avoid, since every sin is voluntary. Now it is not in a man's power to avoid unbelief, for he cannot avoid it unless he have faith, because the Apostle says (Rom. 10:14): "How shall they believe in Him, of Whom they have not heard? And how shall they hear without a preacher?" Therefore unbelief does not seem to be a sin.

Obj. 3: Further, as stated above (I-II, Q. 84, A. 4), there are seven capital sins, to which all sins are reduced. But unbelief does not seem to be comprised under any of them. Therefore unbelief is not a sin.

*On the contrary,* Vice is opposed to virtue. Now faith is a virtue, and unbelief is opposed to it. Therefore unbelief is a sin.

*I answer that,* Unbelief may be taken in two ways: first, by way of pure negation, so that a man be called an unbeliever, merely because he has not the faith. Secondly, unbelief may be taken by way of opposition to the faith; in which sense a man refuses to hear the faith, or despises it, according to Isa. 53:1: "Who hath believed our report?" It is this that completes the notion of unbelief, and it is in this sense that unbelief is a sin.

If, however, we take it by way of pure negation, as we find it in those who have heard nothing about the faith, it bears the character, not of sin, but of punishment, because such like ignorance of Divine things is a result of the sin of our first parent. If such like unbelievers are damned, it is on account of other sins, which cannot be taken away without faith, but not on account of their sin of unbelief. Hence Our Lord said (John 15:22) "If I had not come, and spoken to them, they would not have sin"; which Augustine expounds (Tract. lxxxix in Joan.) as "referring to the sin whereby they believed not in Christ."

Reply Obj. 1: To have the faith is not part of human nature, but it is part of human nature that man's mind should not thwart his inner instinct, and the outward preaching of the truth. Hence, in this way, unbelief is contrary to nature.

Reply Obj. 2: This argument takes unbelief as denoting a pure negation.

Reply Obj. 3: Unbelief, in so far as it is a sin, arises from pride, through which man is unwilling to subject his intellect to the rules of faith, and to the sound interpretation of the Fathers. Hence Gregory says (Moral. xxxi, 45) that "presumptuous innovations arise from vainglory."

It might also be replied that just as the theological virtues are not reduced to the cardinal virtues, but precede them, so too, the vices opposed to the theological virtues are not reduced to the capital vices.

SECOND ARTICLE [II-II, Q. 10, Art. 2]

Whether Unbelief Is in the Intellect As Its Subject?

Objection 1: It would seem that unbelief is not in the intellect as its subject. For every sin is in the will, according to Augustine (De Duabus Anim. x, xi). Now unbelief is a sin, as stated above (A. 1). Therefore unbelief resides in the will and not in the intellect.

Obj. 2: Further, unbelief is sinful through contempt of the preaching of the faith. But contempt pertains to the will. Therefore unbelief is in the will.

Obj. 3: Further, a gloss [*Augustine, Enchiridion lx.] on 2 Cor. 11:14 "Satan ... transformeth himself into an angel of light," says that if "a wicked angel pretend to be a good angel, and be taken for a good angel, it is not a dangerous or an unhealthy error, if he does or says what is becoming to a good angel." This seems to be because of the rectitude of the will of the man who adheres to the angel, since his intention is to adhere to a good angel. Therefore the sin of unbelief seems to consist entirely in a perverse will: and, consequently, it does not reside in the intellect.

*On the contrary,* Things which are contrary to one another are in the same subject. Now faith, to which unbelief is opposed, resides in the intellect. Therefore unbelief also is in the intellect.

*I answer that,* As stated above (I-II, Q. 74, AA. 1, 2), sin is said to be in the power which is the principle of the sinful act. Now a sinful act may have two principles: one is its first and universal principle, which commands all acts of sin; and this is the will, because every sin is voluntary. The other principle of the sinful act is the proper and proximate principle which elicits the sinful act: thus the concupiscible is the principle of gluttony and lust, wherefore these sins are said to be in the concupiscible. Now dissent, which is the act proper to unbelief, is an act of the intellect, moved, however, by the will, just as assent is.

Therefore unbelief, like faith, is in the intellect as its proximate subject. But it is in the will as its first moving principle, in which way every sin is said to be in the will.

Hence the Reply to the First Objection is clear.

Reply Obj. 2: The will's contempt causes the intellect's dissent, which completes the notion of unbelief. Hence the cause of unbelief is in the will, while unbelief itself is in the intellect.

Reply Obj. 3: He that believes a wicked angel to be a good one, does not dissent from a matter of faith, because "his bodily senses are deceived, while his mind does not depart from a true and right judgment" as the gloss observes [*Augustine, Enchiridion lx]. But, according to the same authority, to adhere to Satan when he begins to invite one to his abode, i.e. wickedness and error, is not without sin.

THIRD ARTICLE [II-II, Q. 10, Art. 3]

Whether Unbelief Is the Greatest of Sins?

Objection 1: It would seem that unbelief is not the greatest of sins. For Augustine says (De Bapt. contra Donat. iv, 20): "I should hesitate to decide whether a very wicked Catholic ought to be preferred to a heretic, in whose life one finds nothing reprehensible beyond the fact that he is a heretic." But a heretic is an unbeliever. Therefore we ought not to say absolutely that unbelief is the greatest of sins.

Obj. 2: Further, that which diminishes or excuses a sin is not, seemingly, the greatest of sins. Now unbelief excuses or diminishes sin: for the Apostle says (1 Tim. 1:12, 13): "I ... before was a blasphemer, and a persecutor and contumelious; but I obtained ... mercy ... because I did it ignorantly in unbelief." Therefore unbelief is not the greatest of sins.

Obj. 3: Further, the greater sin deserves the greater punishment, according to Deut. 25:2: "According to the measure of the sin shall the measure also of the stripes be." Now a greater punishment is due to believers than to unbelievers, according to Heb. 10:29: "How much more, do you think, he deserveth worse punishments, who hath trodden under foot the Son of God, and hath esteemed the blood of the testament unclean, by which he was sanctified?" Therefore unbelief is not the greatest of sins.

*On the contrary,* Augustine, commenting on John 15:22, "If I had not come, and spoken to them, they would not have sin," says (Tract. lxxxix in Joan.): "Under the general name, He refers to a singularly great sin. For this," viz. infidelity, "is the sin to which all others may be traced." Therefore unbelief is the greatest of sins.

*I answer that,* Every sin consists formally in aversion from God, as stated above (I-II, Q. 71, A. 6; I-II, Q. 73, A. 3). Hence the more a sin severs man from God, the graver it is. Now man is more than ever separated from God by unbelief, because he has not even true knowledge of God: and by false knowledge of God, man does not approach Him, but is severed from Him.

Nor is it possible for one who has a false opinion of God, to know Him in any way at all, because the object of his opinion is not God. Therefore it is clear that the sin of unbelief is greater than any sin that occurs in the perversion of morals. This does not apply to the sins that are opposed to the theological virtues, as we shall state further on (Q. 20, A. 3; Q. 34, A. 2, ad 2; Q. 39, A. 2, ad 3).

Reply Obj. 1: Nothing hinders a sin that is more grave in its genus from being less grave in respect of some circumstances. Hence Augustine hesitated to decide between a bad Catholic, and a heretic not sinning otherwise, because although the heretic's sin is more grave generically, it can be lessened by a circumstance, and conversely the sin of the Catholic can, by some circumstance, be aggravated.

Reply Obj. 2: Unbelief includes both ignorance, as an accessory thereto, and resistance to matters of faith, and in the latter respect it is a most grave sin. In respect, however, of this ignorance, it has a certain reason for excuse, especially when a man sins not from malice, as was the case with the Apostle.

Reply Obj. 3: An unbeliever is more severely punished for his sin of unbelief than another sinner is for any sin whatever, if we consider the kind of sin. But in the case of another sin, e.g. adultery, committed by a believer, and by an unbeliever, the believer, other things being equal, sins more gravely than the unbeliever, both on account of his knowledge of the truth through faith, and on account of the sacraments of faith with which he has been satiated, and which he insults by committing sin.

FOURTH ARTICLE [II-II, Q. 10, Art. 4]

Whether Every Act of an Unbeliever Is a Sin?

Objection 1: It would seem that each act of an unbeliever is a sin. Because a gloss on Rom. 14:23, "All that is not of faith is sin," says: "The whole life of unbelievers is a sin." Now the life of unbelievers consists of their actions. Therefore every action of an unbeliever is a sin.

Obj. 2: Further, faith directs the intention. Now there can be no good save what comes from a right intention. Therefore, among unbelievers, no action can be good.

Obj. 3: Further, when that which precedes is corrupted, that which follows is corrupted also. Now an act of faith precedes the acts of all the virtues. Therefore, since there is no act of faith in unbelievers, they can do no good work, but sin in every action of theirs.

*On the contrary,* It is said of Cornelius, while yet an unbeliever (Acts 10:4, 31), that his alms were acceptable to God. Therefore not every action of an unbeliever is a sin, but some of his actions are good.

*I answer that,* As stated above (I-II, Q. 85, AA. 2, 4) mortal sin takes away sanctifying grace, but does not wholly corrupt the good of nature. Since therefore, unbelief is a mortal sin, unbelievers are without grace indeed, yet some good of nature remains in them. Consequently it is evident that unbelievers cannot do those good works which proceed from grace, viz. meritorious works; yet they can, to a certain extent, do those good works for which the good of nature suffices.

Hence it does not follow that they sin in everything they do; but whenever they do anything out of their unbelief, then they sin. For even as one who has the faith, can commit an actual sin, venial or even mortal, which he does not refer to the end of faith, so too, an unbeliever can do a good deed in a matter which he does not refer to the end of his unbelief.

Reply Obj. 1: The words quoted must be taken to mean either that the life of unbelievers cannot be sinless, since without faith no sin is taken away, or that whatever they do out of unbelief, is a sin. Hence the same authority adds: "Because every one that lives or acts according to his unbelief, sins grievously."

Reply Obj. 2: Faith directs the intention with regard to the supernatural last end: but even the light of natural reason can direct the intention in respect of a connatural good.

Reply Obj. 3: Unbelief does not so wholly destroy natural reason in unbelievers, but that some knowledge of the truth remains in them, whereby they are able to do deeds that are generically good. With regard, however, to Cornelius, it is to be observed that he was not an unbeliever, else his works would not have been acceptable to God, whom none can please without faith. Now he had implicit faith, as the truth of the Gospel was not yet made manifest: hence Peter was sent to him to give him fuller instruction in the faith.

FIFTH ARTICLE [II-II, Q. 10, Art. 5]

Whether There Are Several Species of Unbelief?

Objection 1: It would seem that there are not several species of unbelief. For, since faith and unbelief are contrary to one another, they must be about the same thing. Now the formal object of faith is the First Truth, whence it derives its unity, although its matter contains many points of belief. Therefore the object of unbelief also is the First Truth; while the things which an unbeliever disbelieves are the matter of his unbelief. Now the specific difference depends not on material but on formal principles. Therefore there are not several species of unbelief, according to the various points which the unbeliever disbelieves.

Obj. 2: Further, it is possible to stray from the truth of faith in an infinite number of ways. If therefore the various species of unbelief correspond to the number of various errors, it would seem to follow that there is an infinite number of species of unbelief, and consequently, that we ought not to make these species the object of our consideration.

Obj. 3: Further, the same thing does not belong to different species. Now a man may be an unbeliever through erring about different points of truth. Therefore diversity of errors does not make a diversity of species of unbelief: and so there are not several species of unbelief.

*On the contrary,* Several species of vice are opposed to each virtue, because "good happens in one way, but evil in many ways," according to Dionysius (Div. Nom. iv) and the Philosopher (Ethic. ii, 6). Now faith is a virtue. Therefore several species of vice are opposed to it.

*I answer that,* As stated above (I-II, Q. 55, A. 4; I-II, Q. 64, A. 1), every virtue consists in following some rule of human knowledge or operation. Now conformity to a rule happens one way in one matter, whereas a breach of the rule happens in many ways, so that many vices are opposed to one virtue. The diversity of the vices that are opposed to each virtue may be considered in two ways, first, with regard to their different relations to the virtue: and in this way there are determinate species of vices contrary to a virtue: thus to a moral virtue one vice is opposed by exceeding the virtue, and another, by falling short of the virtue. Secondly, the diversity of vices opposed to one virtue may be considered in respect of the corruption of the various conditions required for that virtue. In this way an infinite number of vices are opposed to one virtue, e.g. temperance or fortitude, according to the infinite number of ways in which the various circumstances of a virtue may be corrupted, so that the rectitude of virtue is forsaken. For this reason the Pythagoreans held evil to be infinite.

Accordingly we must say that if unbelief be considered in comparison to faith, there are several species of unbelief, determinate in number. For, since the sin of unbelief consists in resisting the faith, this may happen in two ways: either the faith is resisted before it has been accepted, and such is the unbelief of pagans or heathens; or the Christian faith is resisted after it has been accepted, and this either in the figure, and such is the unbelief of the Jews, or in the very manifestation of truth, and such is the unbelief of heretics. Hence we may, in a general way, reckon these three as species of unbelief.

If, however, the species of unbelief be distinguished according to the various errors that occur in matters of faith, there are not determinate species of unbelief: for errors can be multiplied indefinitely, as Augustine observes (De Haeresibus).

Reply Obj. 1: The formal aspect of a sin can be considered in two ways. First, according to the intention of the sinner, in which case the thing to which the sinner turns is the formal object of his sin, and determines the various species of that sin. Secondly, it may be considered as an evil, and in this case the good which is forsaken is the formal object of the sin; which however does not derive its species from this point of view, in fact it is a privation. We must therefore reply that the object of unbelief is the First Truth considered as that which unbelief forsakes, but its formal aspect, considered as that to which unbelief turns, is the false opinion that it follows: and it is from this point of view that unbelief derives its various species. Hence, even as charity is one, because it adheres to the Sovereign Good, while there are various species of vice opposed to charity, which turn away from the Sovereign Good by turning to various temporal goods, and also in respect of various inordinate relations to God, so too, faith is one virtue through adhering to the one First Truth, yet there are many species of unbelief, because unbelievers follow many false opinions.

Reply Obj. 2: This argument considers the various species of unbelief according to various points in which errors occur.

Reply Obj. 3: Since faith is one because it believes in many things in relation to one, so may unbelief, although it errs in many things, be one in so far as all those things are related to one. Yet nothing hinders one man from erring in various species of unbelief, even as one man may be subject to various vices, and to various bodily diseases.

SIXTH ARTICLE [II-II, Q. 10, Art. 6]

Whether the Unbelief of Pagans or Heathens Is Graver Than Other Kinds?

Objection 1: It would seem that the unbelief of heathens or pagans is graver than other kinds. For just as bodily disease is graver according as it endangers the health of a more important member of the body, so does sin appear to be graver, according as it is opposed to that which holds a more important place in virtue. Now that which is most important in faith, is belief in the unity of God, from which the heathens deviate by believing in many gods. Therefore their unbelief is the gravest of all.

Obj. 2: Further, among heresies, the more detestable are those which contradict the truth of faith in more numerous and more important points: thus, the heresy of Arius, who severed the Godhead, was more detestable than that of Nestorius who severed the humanity of Christ from the Person of God the Son. Now the heathens deny the faith in more numerous and more important points than Jews and heretics; since they do not accept the faith at all. Therefore their unbelief is the gravest.

Obj. 3: Further, every good diminishes evil. Now there is some good in the Jews, since they believe in the Old Testament as being from God, and there is some good in heretics, since they venerate the New Testament. Therefore they sin less grievously than heathens, who receive neither Testament.

*On the contrary,* It is written (2 Pet. 2:21): "It had been better for them not to have known the way of justice, than after they have known it, to turn back." Now the heathens have not known the way of justice, whereas heretics and Jews have abandoned it after knowing it in some way. Therefore theirs is the graver sin.

*I answer that,* As stated above (A. 5), two things may be considered in unbelief. One of these is its relation to faith: and from this point of view, he who resists the faith after accepting it, sins more grievously against faith, than he who resists it without having accepted it, even as he who fails to fulfil what he has promised, sins more grievously than if he had never promised it. In this way the unbelief of heretics, who confess their belief in the Gospel, and resist that faith by corrupting it, is a more grievous sin than that of the Jews, who have never accepted the Gospel faith. Since, however, they accepted the figure of that faith in the Old Law, which they corrupt by their false interpretations, their unbelief is a more grievous sin than that of the heathens, because the latter have not accepted the Gospel faith in any way at all.

The second thing to be considered in unbelief is the corruption of matters of faith. In this respect, since heathens err on more points than Jews, and these in more points than heretics, the unbelief of heathens is more grievous than the unbelief of the Jews, and that of the Jews than that of the heretics, except in such cases as that of the Manichees, who, in matters of faith, err even more than heathens do.

Of these two gravities the first surpasses the second from the point of view of guilt; since, as stated above (A. 1) unbelief has the character of guilt, from its resisting faith rather than from the mere absence of faith, for the latter as was stated (A. 1) seems rather to bear the character of punishment. Hence, speaking absolutely, the unbelief of heretics is the worst.

This suffices for the Replies to the Objections.

SEVENTH ARTICLE [II-II, Q. 10, Art. 7]

Whether One Ought to Dispute with Unbelievers in Public?

Objection 1: It would seem that one ought not to dispute with unbelievers in public. For the Apostle says (2 Tim. 2:14): "Contend not in words, for it is to no profit, but to the subverting of the hearers." But it is impossible to dispute with unbelievers publicly without contending in words. Therefore one ought not to dispute publicly with unbelievers.

Obj. 2: Further, the law of Martianus Augustus confirmed by the canons [*De Sum. Trin. Cod. lib. i, leg. Nemo] expresses itself thus: "It is an insult to the judgment of the most religious synod, if anyone ventures to debate or dispute in public about matters which have once been judged and disposed of." Now all matters of faith have been decided by the holy councils. Therefore it is an insult to the councils, and consequently a grave sin to presume to dispute in public about matters of faith.

Obj. 3: Further, disputations are conducted by means of arguments. But an argument is a reason in settlement of a dubious matter: whereas things that are of faith, being most certain, ought not to be a matter of doubt. Therefore one ought not to dispute in public about matters of faith.

*On the contrary,* It is written (Acts 9:22, 29) that "Saul increased much more in strength, and confounded the Jews," and that "he spoke ... to the gentiles and disputed with the Greeks."

*I answer that,* In disputing about the faith, two things must be observed: one on the part of the disputant; the other on the part of his hearers. On the part of the disputant, we must consider his intention. For if he were to dispute as though he had doubts about the faith, and did not hold the truth of faith for certain, and as though he intended to probe it with arguments, without doubt he would sin, as being doubtful of the faith and an unbeliever. On the other hand, it is praiseworthy to dispute about the faith in order to confute errors, or for practice.

On the part of the hearers we must consider whether those who hear the disputation are instructed and firm in the faith, or simple and wavering. As to those who are well instructed and firm in the faith, there can be no danger in disputing about the faith in their presence. But as to simple-minded people, we must make a distinction; because either they are provoked and molested by unbelievers, for instance, Jews or heretics, or pagans who strive to corrupt the faith in them, or else they are not subject to provocation in this matter, as in those countries where there are no unbelievers. In the first case it is necessary to dispute in public about the faith, provided there be those who are equal and adapted to the task of confuting errors; since in this way simple people are strengthened in the faith, and unbelievers are deprived of the opportunity to deceive, while if those who ought to withstand the perverters of the truth of faith were silent, this would tend to strengthen error. Hence Gregory says (Pastor. ii, 4): "Even as a thoughtless speech gives rise to error, so does an indiscreet silence leave those in error who might have been instructed." On the other hand, in the second case it is dangerous to dispute in public about the faith, in the presence of simple people, whose faith for this very reason is more firm, that they have never heard anything differing from what they believe. Hence it is not expedient for them to hear what unbelievers have to say against the faith.

Reply Obj. 1: The Apostle does not entirely forbid disputations, but such as are inordinate, and consist of contentious words rather than of sound speeches.

Reply Obj. 2: That law forbade those public disputations about the faith, which arise from doubting the faith, but not those which are for the safeguarding thereof.

Reply Obj. 3: One ought to dispute about matters of faith, not as though one doubted about them, but in order to make the truth known, and to confute errors. For, in order to confirm the faith, it is necessary sometimes to dispute with unbelievers, sometimes by defending the faith, according to 1 Pet. 3:15: "Being ready always to satisfy everyone that asketh you a reason of that hope and faith which is in you [*Vulg.: 'Of that hope which is in you'; St. Thomas' reading is apparently taken from Bede]." Sometimes again, it is necessary, in order to convince those who are in error, according to Titus 1:9: "That he may be able to exhort in sound doctrine and to convince the gainsayers."

EIGHTH ARTICLE [II-II, Q. 10, Art. 8]

Whether Unbelievers Ought to Be Compelled to the Faith?

Objection 1: It would seem that unbelievers ought by no means to be compelled to the faith. For it is written (Matt. 13:28) that the servants of the householder, in whose field cockle had been sown, asked him: "Wilt thou that we go and gather it up?" and that he answered: "No, lest perhaps gathering up the cockle, you root up the wheat also together with it": on which passage Chrysostom says (Hom. xlvi in Matth.): "Our Lord says this so as to forbid the slaying of men. For it is not right to slay heretics, because if you do you will necessarily slay many innocent persons." Therefore it seems that for the same reason unbelievers ought not to be compelled to the faith.

Obj. 2: Further, we read in the Decretals (Dist. xlv can., De Judaeis): "The holy synod prescribes, with regard to the Jews, that for the future, none are to be compelled to believe." Therefore, in like manner, neither should unbelievers be compelled to the faith.

Obj. 3: Further, Augustine says (Tract. xxvi in Joan.) that "it is possible for a man to do other things against his will, but he cannot believe unless he is willing." Therefore it seems that unbelievers ought not to be compelled to the faith.

Obj. 4: It is said in God's person (Ezech. 18:32 [*Ezech. 33:11]): "I desire not the death of the sinner [Vulg.: 'of him that dieth']." Now we ought to conform our will to the Divine will, as stated above (I-II, Q. 19, AA. 9, 10). Therefore we should not even wish unbelievers to be put to death.

*On the contrary,* It is written (Luke 14:23): "Go out into the highways and hedges; and compel them to come in." Now men enter into the house of God, i.e. into Holy Church, by faith. Therefore some ought to be compelled to the faith.

*I answer that,* Among unbelievers there are some who have never received the faith, such as the heathens and the Jews: and these are by no means to be compelled to the faith, in order that they may believe, because to believe depends on the will: nevertheless they should be compelled by the faithful, if it be possible to do so, so that they do not hinder the faith, by their blasphemies, or by their evil persuasions, or even by their open persecutions. It is for this reason that Christ's faithful often wage war with unbelievers, not indeed for the purpose of forcing them to believe, because even if they were to conquer them, and take them prisoners, they should still leave them free to believe, if they will, but in order to prevent them from hindering the faith of Christ.

On the other hand, there are unbelievers who at some time have accepted the faith, and professed it, such as heretics and all apostates: such should be submitted even to bodily compulsion, that they may fulfil what they have promised, and hold what they, at one time, received.

Reply Obj. 1: Some have understood the authority quoted to forbid, not the excommunication but the slaying of heretics, as appears from the words of Chrysostom. Augustine too, says (Ep. ad Vincent. xciii) of himself: "It was once my opinion that none should be compelled to union with Christ, that we should deal in words, and fight with arguments. However this opinion of mine is undone, not by words of contradiction, but by convincing examples. Because fear of the law was so profitable, that many say: Thanks be to the Lord Who has broken our chains asunder." Accordingly the meaning of Our Lord's words, "Suffer both to grow until the harvest," must be gathered from those which precede, "lest perhaps gathering up the cockle, you root the wheat also together with it." For, Augustine says (Contra Ep. Parmen. iii, 2) "these words show that when this is not to be feared, that is to say, when a man's crime is so publicly known, and so hateful to all, that he has no defenders, or none such as might cause a schism, the severity of discipline should not slacken."

Reply Obj. 2: Those Jews who have in no way received the faith, ought not by no means to be compelled to the faith: if, however, they have received it, they ought to be compelled to keep it, as is stated in the same chapter.

Reply Obj. 3: Just as taking a vow is a matter

of will, and keeping a vow, a matter of obligation, so acceptance of the faith is a matter of the will, whereas keeping the faith, when once one has received it, is a matter of obligation. Wherefore heretics should be compelled to keep the faith. Thus Augustine says to the Count Boniface (Ep. clxxxv): "What do these people mean by crying out continually: 'We may believe or not believe just as we choose. Whom did Christ compel?' They should remember that Christ at first compelled Paul and afterwards taught Him."

Reply Obj. 4: As Augustine says in the same letter, "none of us wishes any heretic to perish. But the house of David did not deserve to have peace, unless his son Absalom had been killed in the war which he had raised against his father. Thus if the Catholic Church gathers together some of the perdition of others, she heals the sorrow of her maternal heart by the delivery of so many nations."

NINTH ARTICLE [II-II, Q. 10, Art. 9]

Whether It Is Lawful to Communicate with Unbelievers?

Objection 1: It would seem that it is lawful to communicate with unbelievers. For the Apostle says (1 Cor. 10:27): "If any of them that believe not, invite you, and you be willing to go, eat of anything that is set before you." And Chrysostom says (Hom. xxv super Epist. ad Heb.): "If you wish to go to dine with pagans, we permit it without any reservation." Now to sit at table with anyone is to communicate with him. Therefore it is lawful to communicate with unbelievers.

Obj. 2: Further, the Apostle says (1 Cor. 5:12): "What have I to do to judge them that are without?" Now unbelievers are without. When, therefore, the Church forbids the faithful to communicate with certain people, it seems that they ought not to be forbidden to communicate with unbelievers.

Obj. 3: Further, a master cannot employ his servant, unless he communicate with him, at least by word, since the master moves his servant by command. Now Christians can have unbelievers, either Jews, or pagans, or Saracens, for servants. Therefore they can lawfully communicate with them.

*On the contrary,* It is written (Deut. 7:2, 3): "Thou shalt make no league with them, nor show mercy to them; neither shalt thou make marriages with them": and a gloss on Lev. 15:19, "The woman who at the return of the month," etc. says: "It is so necessary to shun idolatry, that we should not come in touch with idolaters or their disciples, nor have any dealings with them."

*I answer that,* Communication with a particular person is forbidden to the faithful, in two ways: first, as a punishment of the person with whom they are forbidden to communicate; secondly, for the safety of those who are forbidden to communicate with others. Both motives can be gathered from the Apostle's words (1 Cor. 5:6). For after he had pronounced sentence of excommunication, he adds as his reason: "Know you not that a little leaven corrupts the whole lump?" and afterwards he adds the reason on the part of the punishment inflicted by the sentence of the Church when he says (1 Cor. 5:12): "Do not you judge them that are within?"

Accordingly, in the first way the Church does not forbid the faithful to communicate with unbelievers, who have not in any way received the Christian faith, viz. with pagans and Jews, because she has not the right to exercise spiritual judgment over them, but only temporal judgment, in the case when, while dwelling among Christians they are guilty of some misdemeanor, and are condemned by the faithful to some temporal punishment. On the other hand, in this way, i.e. as a punishment, the Church forbids the faithful to communicate with those unbelievers who have forsaken the faith they once received, either by corrupting the faith, as heretics, or by entirely renouncing the faith, as apostates, because the Church pronounces sentence of excommunication on both.

With regard to the second way, it seems that one ought to distinguish according to the various conditions of persons, circumstances and time. For some are firm in the faith; and so it is to be hoped that their communicating with unbelievers will lead to the conversion of the latter rather than to the aversion of the faithful from the faith. These are not to be forbidden to communicate with unbelievers who have not received the faith, such as pagans or Jews, especially if there be some urgent necessity for so doing. But in the case of simple people and those who are weak in the faith, whose perversion is to be feared as a probable result, they should be forbidden to communicate with unbelievers, and especially to be on very familiar terms with them, or to communicate with them without necessity.

This suffices for the Reply to the First Objection.

Reply Obj. 2: The Church does not exercise judgment against unbelievers in the point of inflicting spiritual punishment on them: but she does exercise judgment over some of them in the matter of temporal punishment. It is under this head that sometimes the Church, for certain special sins, withdraws the faithful from communication with certain unbelievers.

Reply Obj. 3: There is more probability that a servant who is ruled by his master's commands, will be converted to the faith of his master who is a believer, than if the case were the reverse: and so the faithful are not forbidden to have unbelieving servants. If, however, the master were in danger, through communicating with such a servant, he should send him away, according to Our Lord's command (Matt. 18:8): "If ... thy foot scandalize thee, cut it off, and cast it from thee."

With regard to the argument in the contrary [*The Leonine Edition gives this solution before the Reply Obj. 2] sense the reply is that the Lord gave this command in reference to those nations into whose territory the Jews were about to enter. For the latter were inclined to idolatry, so that it was to be feared lest, through frequent dealings with those nations, they should be estranged from the faith: hence the text goes on (Deut. 7:4): "For she will turn away thy son from following Me."

TENTH ARTICLE [II-II, Q. 10, Art. 10]

Whether Unbelievers May Have Authority or Dominion Over the Faithful?

Objection 1: It would seem that unbelievers may have authority or dominion over the faithful. For the Apostle says (1 Tim. 6:1): "Whosoever are servants under the yoke, let them count their masters worthy of all honor": and it is clear that he is speaking of unbelievers, since he adds (1 Tim. 6:2): "But they that have believing masters, let them not despise them." Moreover it is written (1 Pet. 2:18): "Servants be subject to your masters with all fear, not only to the good and gentle, but also to the froward." Now this command would not be contained in the apostolic teaching unless unbelievers could have authority over the faithful. Therefore it seems that unbelievers can have authority over the faithful.

Obj. 2: Further, all the members of a prince's household are his subjects. Now some of the faithful were members of unbelieving princes' households, for we read in the Epistle to the Philippians (4:22): "All the saints salute you, especially they that are of Caesar's household," referring to Nero, who was an unbeliever. Therefore unbelievers can have authority over the faithful.

Obj. 3: Further, according to the Philosopher (Polit. i, 2) a slave is his master's instrument in matters concerning everyday life, even as a craftsman's laborer is his instrument in matters concerning the working of his art. Now, in such matters, a believer can be subject to an unbeliever, for he may work on an unbeliever's farm. Therefore unbelievers may have authority over the faithful even as to dominion.

*On the contrary,* Those who are in authority can pronounce judgment on those over whom they are placed. But unbelievers cannot pronounce judgment on the faithful, for the Apostle says (1 Cor. 6:1): "Dare any of you, having a matter against another, go to be judged before the unjust," i.e. unbelievers, "and not before the saints?" Therefore it seems that unbelievers cannot have authority over the faithful.

*I answer that,* That this question may be considered in two ways. First, we may speak of dominion or authority of unbelievers over the faithful as of a thing to be established for the first time. This ought by no means to be allowed, since it would provoke scandal and endanger the faith, for subjects are easily influenced by their superiors to comply with their commands, unless the subjects are of great virtue: moreover unbelievers hold the faith in contempt, if they see the faithful fall away. Hence the Apostle forbade the faithful to go to law before an unbelieving judge. And so the Church altogether forbids unbelievers to acquire dominion over believers, or to have authority over them in any capacity whatever.

Secondly, we may speak of dominion or authority, as already in force: and here we must observe that dominion and authority are institutions of human law, while the distinction between faithful and unbelievers arises from the Divine law. Now the Divine law which is the law of grace, does not do away with human law which is the law of natural reason. Wherefore the distinction between faithful and unbelievers, considered in itself, does not do away with dominion and authority of unbelievers over the faithful.

Nevertheless this right of dominion or authority can be justly done away with by the sentence or ordination of the Church who has the authority of God: since unbelievers in virtue of their unbelief deserve to forfeit their power over the faithful who are converted into children of God.

This the Church does sometimes, and sometimes not. For among those unbelievers who are subject, even in temporal matters, to the Church and her members, the Church made the law that if the slave of a Jew became a Christian, he should forthwith receive his freedom, without paying any price, if he should be a "vernaculus," i.e. born in slavery; and likewise if, when yet an unbeliever, he had been bought for his service: if, however, he had been bought for sale, then he should be offered for sale within three months. Nor does the Church harm them in this, because since those Jews themselves are subject to the Church, she can dispose of their possessions, even as secular princes have enacted many laws to be observed by their subjects, in favor of liberty. On the other hand, the Church has not applied the above law to those unbelievers who are not subject to her or her members, in temporal matters, although she has the right to do so: and this, in order to avoid scandal, for as Our Lord showed (Matt. 17:25, 26) that He could be excused from paying the tribute, because "the children are free," yet He ordered the tribute to be paid in order to avoid giving scandal. Thus Paul too, after saying that servants should honor their masters, adds, "lest the name of the Lord and His doctrine be blasphemed."

This suffices for the Reply to the First Objection.

Reply Obj. 2: The authority of Caesar preceded the distinction of faithful from unbelievers. Hence it was not cancelled by the conversion of some to the faith. Moreover it was a good thing that there should be a few of the faithful in the emperor's household, that they might defend the rest of the faithful. Thus the Blessed Sebastian encouraged those whom he saw faltering under torture, and, the while, remained hidden under the military cloak in the palace of Diocletian.

Reply Obj. 3: Slaves are subject to their masters for their whole lifetime, and are subject to their overseers in everything: whereas the craftsman's laborer is subject to him for certain special works. Hence it would be more dangerous for unbelievers to have dominion or authority over the faithful, than that they should be allowed to employ them in some craft. Wherefore the Church permits Christians to work on the land of Jews, because this does not entail their living together with them. Thus Solomon besought the King of Tyre to send master workmen to hew the trees, as related in 3 Kings 5:6. Yet, if there be reason to fear that the faithful will be perverted by such communications and dealings, they should be absolutely forbidden.

ELEVENTH ARTICLE [II-II, Q. 10, Art. 11]

Whether the Rites of Unbelievers Ought to Be Tolerated?

Objection 1: It would seem that rites of unbelievers ought not to be tolerated. For it is evident that unbelievers sin in observing their rites: and not to prevent a sin, when one can, seems to imply consent therein, as a gloss observes on Rom. 1:32: "Not only they that do them, but they also that consent to them that do them." Therefore it is a sin to tolerate their rites.

Obj. 2: Further, the rites of the Jews are compared to idolatry, because a gloss on Gal. 5:1, "Be not held again under the yoke of bondage," says: "The bondage of that law was not lighter than that of idolatry." But it would not be allowable for anyone to observe the rites of idolatry, in fact Christian princes at first caused the temples of idols to be closed, and afterwards, to be destroyed, as Augustine relates (De Civ. Dei xviii, 54). Therefore it follows that even the rites of Jews ought not to be tolerated.

Obj. 3: Further, unbelief is the greatest of sins, as stated above (A. 3). Now other sins such as adultery, theft and the like, are not tolerated, but are punishable by law. Therefore neither ought the rites of unbelievers to be tolerated.

*On the contrary,* Gregory [*Regist. xi, Ep. 15: cf. Decret., dist. xlv, can., Qui sincera] says, speaking of the Jews: "They should be allowed to observe all their feasts, just as hitherto they and their fathers have for ages observed them."

*I answer that,* Human government is derived from the Divine government, and should imitate it. Now although God is all-powerful and supremely good, nevertheless He allows certain evils to take place in the universe, which He might prevent, lest, without them, greater goods might be forfeited, or greater evils ensue. Accordingly in human government also, those who are in authority, rightly tolerate certain evils, lest certain goods be lost, or certain greater evils be incurred: thus Augustine says (De Ordine ii, 4): "If you do away with harlots, the world will be convulsed with lust." Hence, though unbelievers sin in their rites, they may be tolerated, either on account of some good that ensues therefrom, or because of some evil avoided. Thus from the fact that the Jews observe their rites, which, of old, foreshadowed the truth of the faith which we hold, there follows this good—that our very enemies bear witness to our faith, and that our faith is represented in a figure, so to speak. For this reason they are tolerated in the observance of their rites.

On the other hand, the rites of other unbelievers, which are neither truthful nor profitable are by no means to be tolerated, except perchance in order to avoid an evil, e.g. the scandal or disturbance that might ensue, or some hindrance to the salvation of those who if they were unmolested might gradually be converted to the faith. For this reason the Church, at times, has tolerated the rites even of heretics and pagans, when unbelievers were very numerous.

This suffices for the Replies to the Objections.

TWELFTH ARTICLE [II-II, Q. 10, Art. 12]

Whether the Children of Jews and Other Unbelievers Ought to Be Baptized Against Their Parents' Will?

Objection 1: It would seem that the children of Jews and of other unbelievers ought to be baptized against their parents' will. For the bond of marriage is stronger than the right of parental authority over children, since the right of parental authority can be made to cease, when a son is set at liberty; whereas the marriage bond cannot be severed by man, according to Matt. 19:6: "What ... God hath joined together let no man put asunder." And yet the marriage bond is broken on account of unbelief: for the Apostle says (1 Cor. 7:15): "If the unbeliever depart, let him depart. For a brother or sister is not under servitude in such cases": and a canon [*Can. Uxor legitima, and Idololatria, qu. i] says that "if the unbelieving partner is unwilling to abide with the other, without insult to their Creator, then the other partner is not bound to cohabitation." Much more, therefore, does unbelief abrogate the right of unbelieving parents' authority over their children: and consequently their children may be baptized against their parents' will.

Obj. 2: Further, one is more bound to succor a man who is in danger of everlasting death, than one who is in danger of temporal death. Now it would be a sin, if one saw a man in danger of temporal death and failed to go to his aid. Since, then, the children of Jews and other unbelievers are in danger of everlasting death, should they be left to their parents who would imbue them with their unbelief, it seems that they ought to be taken away from them and baptized, and instructed in the faith.

Obj. 3: Further, the children of a bondsman are themselves bondsmen, and under the power of his master. Now the Jews are bondsmen of kings and princes: therefore their children are also. Consequently kings and princes have the power to do what they will with Jewish children. Therefore no injustice is committed if they baptize them against their parents' wishes.

Obj. 4: Further, every man belongs more to God, from Whom he has his soul, than to his carnal father, from whom he has his body. Therefore it is not unjust if Jewish children be taken away from their parents, and consecrated to God in Baptism.

Obj. 5: Further, Baptism avails for salvation more than preaching does, since Baptism removes forthwith the stain of sin and the debt of punishment, and opens the gate of heaven. Now if danger ensue through not preaching, it is imputed to him who omitted to preach, according to the words of Ezech. 33:6 about the man who "sees the sword coming and sounds not the trumpet." Much more therefore, if Jewish children are lost through not being baptized are they accounted guilty of sin, who could have baptized them and did not.

*On the contrary,* Injustice should be done to no man. Now it would be an injustice to Jews if their children were to be baptized against their will, since they would lose the rights of parental authority over their children as soon as these were Christians. Therefore these should not be baptized against their parents' will.

*I answer that,* The custom of the Church has very great authority and ought to be jealously observed in all things, since the very doctrine of catholic doctors derives its authority from the Church. Hence we ought to abide by the authority of the Church rather than by that of an Augustine or a Jerome or of any doctor whatever. Now it was never the custom of the Church to baptize the children of the Jews against the will of their parents, although at times past there have been many very powerful catholic princes like Constantine and Theodosius, with whom most holy bishops have been on most friendly terms, as Sylvester with Constantine, and Ambrose with Theodosius, who would certainly not have failed to obtain this favor from them if it had been at all reasonable. It seems therefore hazardous to repeat this assertion, that the children of Jews should be baptized against their parents' wishes, in contradiction to the Church's custom observed hitherto.

There are two reasons for this custom. One is on account of the danger to the faith. For children baptized before coming to the use of reason, afterwards when they come to perfect age, might easily be persuaded by their parents to renounce what they had unknowingly embraced; and this would be detrimental to the faith.

The other reason is that it is against natural justice. For a child is by nature part of its father: thus, at first, it is not distinct from its parents as to its body, so long as it is enfolded within its mother's womb; and later on after birth, and before it has the use of its free-will, it is enfolded in the care of its parents, which is like a spiritual womb, for so long as man has not the use of reason, he differs not from an irrational animal; so that even as an ox or a horse belongs to someone who, according to the civil law, can use them when he likes, as his own instrument, so, according to the natural law, a son, before coming to the use of reason, is under his father's care. Hence it would be contrary to natural justice, if a child, before coming to the use of reason, were to be taken away from its parents' custody, or anything done to it against its parents' wish. As soon, however, as it begins to have the use of its free-will, it begins to belong to itself, and is able to look after itself, in matters concerning the Divine or the natural law, and then it should be induced, not by compulsion but by persuasion, to embrace the faith: it can then consent to the faith, and be baptized, even against its parents' wish; but not before it comes to the use of reason. Hence it is said of the children of the fathers of old that they were saved in the faith of their parents; whereby we are given to understand that it is the parents' duty to look after the salvation of their children, especially before they come to the use of reason.

Reply Obj. 1: In the marriage bond, both husband and wife have the use of the free-will, and each can assent to the faith without the other's consent. But this does not apply to a child before it comes to the use of reason: yet the comparison holds good after the child has come to the use of reason, if it is willing to be converted.

Reply Obj. 2: No one should be snatched from natural death against the order of civil law: for instance, if a man were condemned by the judge to temporal death, nobody ought to rescue him by violence: hence no one ought to break the order of the natural law, whereby a child is in the custody of its father, in order to rescue it from the danger of everlasting death.

Reply Obj. 3: Jews are bondsmen of princes by civil bondage, which does not exclude the order of natural or Divine law.

Reply Obj. 4: Man is directed to God by his reason, whereby he can know Him. Hence a child before coming to the use of reason, in the natural order of things, is directed to God by its parents' reason, under whose care it lies by nature: and it is for them to dispose of the child in all matters relating to God.

Reply Obj. 5: The peril that ensues from the omission of preaching, threatens only those who are entrusted with the duty of preaching. Hence it had already been said (Ezech. 3:17): "I have made thee a watchman to the children [Vulg.: 'house'] of Israel." On the other hand, to provide the sacraments of salvation for the children of unbelievers is the duty of their parents. Hence it is they whom the danger threatens, if through being deprived of the sacraments their children fail to obtain salvation.

# QUESTION 11

OF HERESY (In Four Articles)

We must now consider heresy: under which head there are four points of inquiry:

(1) Whether heresy is a kind of unbelief?

(2) Of the matter about which it is;

(3) Whether heretics should be tolerated?

(4) Whether converts should be received?

FIRST ARTICLE [II-II, Q. 11, Art. 1]

Whether Heresy Is a Species of Unbelief?

Objection 1: It would seem that heresy is not a species of unbelief. For unbelief is in the understanding, as stated above (Q. 10, A. 2). Now heresy would seem not to pertain to the understanding, but rather to the appetitive power; for Jerome says on Gal. 5:19: [*Cf. Decretals xxiv, qu. iii, cap. 27] "The works of the flesh are manifest: Heresy is derived from a Greek word meaning choice, whereby a man makes choice of that school which he deems best." But choice is an act of the appetitive power, as stated above (I-II, Q. 13, A. 1). Therefore heresy is not a species of unbelief.

Obj. 2: Further, vice takes its species chiefly from its end; hence the Philosopher says (Ethic. v, 2) that "he who commits adultery that he may steal, is a thief rather than an adulterer." Now the end of heresy is temporal profit, especially lordship and glory, which belong to the vice of pride or covetousness: for Augustine says (De Util. Credendi i) that "a heretic is one who either devises or follows false and new opinions, for the sake of some temporal profit, especially that he may lord and be honored above others." Therefore heresy is a species of pride rather than of unbelief.

Obj. 3: Further, since unbelief is in the understanding, it would seem not to pertain to the flesh. Now heresy belongs to the works of the flesh, for the Apostle says (Gal. 5:19): "The works of the flesh are manifest, which are fornication, uncleanness," and among the others, he adds, "dissensions, sects," which are the same as heresies. Therefore heresy is not a species of unbelief.

*On the contrary,* Falsehood is contrary to truth. Now a heretic is one who devises or follows false or new opinions. Therefore heresy is opposed to the truth, on which faith is founded; and consequently it is a species of unbelief.

*I answer that,* The word heresy as stated in the first objection denotes a choosing. Now choice as stated above (I-II, Q. 13, A. 3) is about things directed to the end, the end being presupposed. Now, in matters of faith, the will assents to some truth, as to its proper good, as was shown above (Q. 4, A. 3): wherefore that which is the chief truth, has the character of last end, while those which are secondary truths, have the character of being directed to the end.

Now, whoever believes, assents to someone's words; so that, in every form of unbelief, the person to whose words assent is given seems to hold the chief place and to be the end as it were; while the things by holding which one assents to that person hold a secondary place. Consequently he that holds the Christian faith aright, assents, by his will, to Christ, in those things which truly belong to His doctrine.

Accordingly there are two ways in which a man may deviate from the rectitude of the Christian faith. First, because he is unwilling to assent to Christ: and such a man has an evil will, so to say, in respect of the very end. This belongs to the species of unbelief in pagans and Jews. Secondly, because, though he intends to assent to Christ, yet he fails in his choice of those things wherein he assents to Christ, because he chooses not what Christ really taught, but the suggestions of his own mind.

Therefore heresy is a species of unbelief, belonging to those who profess the Christian faith, but corrupt its dogmas.

Reply Obj. 1: Choice regards unbelief in the same way as the will regards faith, as stated above.

Reply Obj. 2: Vices take their species from their proximate end, while, from their remote end, they take their genus and cause. Thus in the case of adultery committed for the sake of theft, there is the species of adultery taken from its proper end and object; but the ultimate end shows that the act of adultery is both the result of the theft, and is included under it, as an effect under its cause, or a species under its genus, as appears from what we have said about acts in general (I-II, Q. 18, A. 7). Wherefore, as to the case in point also, the proximate end of heresy is adherence to one's own false opinion, and from this it derives its species, while its remote end reveals its cause, viz. that it arises from pride or covetousness.

Reply Obj. 3: Just as heresy is so called from its being a choosing [*From the Greek *hairein* , to cut off], so does sect derive its name from its being a cutting off ( *secando* ), as Isidore states (Etym. viii, 3). Wherefore heresy and sect are the same thing, and each belongs to the works of the flesh, not indeed by reason of the act itself of unbelief in respect of its proximate object, but by reason of its cause, which is either the desire of an undue end in which way it arises from pride or covetousness, as stated in the second objection, or some illusion of the imagination (which gives rise to error, as the Philosopher states in *Metaph.* iv; Ed. Did. iii, 5), for this faculty has a certain connection with the flesh, in as much as its act is independent on a bodily organ.

SECOND ARTICLE [II-II, Q. 11, Art. 2]

Whether Heresy Is Properly About Matters of Faith?

Objection 1: It would seem that heresy is not properly about matters of faith. For just as there are heresies and sects among Christians, so were there among the Jews, and Pharisees, as Isidore observes (Etym. viii, 3, 4, 5). Now their dissensions were not about matters of faith. Therefore heresy is not about matters of faith, as though they were its proper matter.

Obj. 2: Further, the matter of faith is the thing believed. Now heresy is not only about things, but also about works, and about interpretations of Holy Writ. For Jerome says on Gal. 5:20 that "whoever expounds the Scriptures in any sense but that of the Holy Ghost by Whom they were written, may be called a heretic, though he may not have left the Church": and elsewhere he says that "heresies spring up from words spoken amiss." [*St. Thomas quotes this saying elsewhere, in Sent. iv, D, 13, and III, Q. 16, A. 8, but it is not to be found in St. Jerome's works.] Therefore heresy is not properly about the matter of faith.

Obj. 3: Further, we find the holy doctors differing even about matters pertaining to the faith, for example Augustine and Jerome, on the question about the cessation of the legal observances: and yet this was without any heresy on their part. Therefore heresy is not properly about the matter of faith.

*On the contrary,* Augustine says against the Manichees [*Cf. De Civ. Dei xviii, 51]: "In Christ's Church, those are heretics, who hold mischievous and erroneous opinions, and when rebuked that they may think soundly and rightly, offer a stubborn resistance, and, refusing to mend their pernicious and deadly doctrines, persist in defending them." Now pernicious and deadly doctrines are none but those which are contrary to the dogmas of faith, whereby "the just man liveth" (Rom. 1:17). Therefore heresy is about matters of faith, as about its proper matter.

*I answer that,* We are speaking of heresy now as denoting a corruption of the Christian faith. Now it does not imply a corruption of the Christian faith, if a man has a false opinion in matters that are not of faith, for instance, in questions of geometry and so forth, which cannot belong to the faith by any means; but only when a person has a false opinion about things belonging to the faith.

Now a thing may be of the faith in two ways, as stated above (I, Q. 32, A. 4; I-II, Q. 1, A. 6, ad 1; I-II, Q. 2, A. 5), in one way, directly and principally, e.g. the articles of faith; in another way, indirectly and secondarily, e.g. those matters, the denial of which leads to the corruption of some article of faith; and there may be heresy in either way, even as there can be faith.

Reply Obj. 1: Just as the heresies of the Jews and Pharisees were about opinions relating to Judaism or Pharisaism, so also heresies among Christians are about matter touching the Christian faith.

Reply Obj. 2: A man is said to expound Holy Writ in another sense than that required by the Holy Ghost, when he so distorts the meaning of Holy Writ, that it is contrary to what the Holy Ghost has revealed. Hence it is written (Ezech. 13:6) about the false prophets: "They have persisted to confirm what they have said," viz. by false interpretations of Scripture. Moreover a man professes his faith by the words that he utters, since confession is an act of faith, as stated above (Q. 3, A. 1). Wherefore inordinate words about matters of faith may lead to corruption of the faith; and hence it is that Pope Leo says in a letter to Proterius, Bishop of Alexandria: "The enemies of Christ's cross lie in wait for our every deed and word, so that, if we but give them the slightest pretext, they may accuse us mendaciously of agreeing with Nestorius."

Reply Obj. 3: As Augustine says (Ep. xliii) and we find it stated in the Decretals (xxiv, qu. 3, can. Dixit Apostolus): "By no means should we accuse of heresy those who, however false and perverse their opinion may be, defend it without obstinate fervor, and seek the truth with careful anxiety, ready to mend their opinion, when they have found the truth," because, to wit, they do not make a choice in contradiction to the doctrine of the Church. Accordingly, certain doctors seem to have differed either in matters the holding of which in this or that way is of no consequence, so far as faith is concerned, or even in matters of faith, which were not as yet defined by the Church; although if anyone were obstinately to deny them after they had been defined by the authority of the universal Church, he would be deemed a heretic. This authority resides chiefly in the Sovereign Pontiff. For we read [*Decret. xxiv, qu. 1, can. Quoties]: "Whenever a question of faith is in dispute, I think, that all our brethren and fellow bishops ought to refer the matter to none other than Peter, as being the source of their name and honor, against whose authority neither Jerome nor Augustine nor any of the holy doctors defended their opinion." Hence Jerome says (Exposit. Symbol [*Among the supposititious works of St. Jerome]): "This, most blessed Pope, is the faith that we have been taught in the Catholic Church. If anything therein has been incorrectly or carelessly expressed, we beg that it may be set aright by you who hold the faith and see of Peter. If however this, our profession, be approved by the judgment of your apostleship, whoever may blame me, will prove that he himself is ignorant, or malicious, or even not a catholic but a heretic."

THIRD ARTICLE [II-II, Q. 11, Art. 3]

Whether Heretics Ought to Be Tolerated?

Objection 1: It seems that heretics ought to be tolerated. For the Apostle says (2 Tim. 2:24, 25): "The servant of the Lord must not wrangle ... with modesty admonishing them that resist the truth, if peradventure God may give them repentance to know the truth, and they may recover themselves from the snares of the devil." Now if heretics are not tolerated but put to death, they lose the opportunity of repentance. Therefore it seems contrary to the Apostle's command.

Obj. 2: Further, whatever is necessary in the Church should be tolerated. Now heresies are necessary in the Church, since the Apostle says (1 Cor. 11:19): "There must be ... heresies, that they ... who are reproved, may be manifest among you." Therefore it seems that heretics should be tolerated.

Obj. 3: Further, the Master commanded his servants (Matt. 13:30) to suffer the cockle "to grow until the harvest," i.e. the end of the world, as a gloss explains it. Now holy men explain that the cockle denotes heretics. Therefore heretics should be tolerated.

*On the contrary,* The Apostle says (Titus 3:10, 11): "A man that is a heretic, after the first and second admonition, avoid: knowing that he, that is such an one, is subverted."

*I answer that,* With regard to heretics two points must be observed: one, on their own side; the other, on the side of the Church. On their own side there is the sin, whereby they deserve not only to be separated from the Church by excommunication, but also to be severed from the world by death. For it is a much graver matter to corrupt the faith which quickens the soul, than to forge money, which supports temporal life. Wherefore if forgers of money and other evil-doers are forthwith condemned to death by the secular authority, much more reason is there for heretics, as soon as they are convicted of heresy, to be not only excommunicated but even put to death.

On the part of the Church, however, there is mercy which looks to the conversion of the wanderer, wherefore she condemns not at once, but "after the first and second admonition," as the Apostle directs: after that, if he is yet stubborn, the Church no longer hoping for his conversion, looks to the salvation of others, by excommunicating him and separating him from the Church, and furthermore delivers him to the secular tribunal to be exterminated thereby from the world by death. For Jerome commenting on Gal. 5:9, "A little leaven," says: "Cut off the decayed flesh, expel the mangy sheep from the fold, lest the whole house, the whole paste, the whole body, the whole flock, burn, perish, rot, die. Arius was but one spark in Alexandria, but as that spark was not at once put out, the whole earth was laid waste by its flame."

Reply Obj. 1: This very modesty demands that the heretic should be admonished a first and second time: and if he be unwilling to retract, he must be reckoned as already "subverted," as we may gather from the words of the Apostle quoted above.

Reply Obj. 2: The profit that ensues from heresy is beside the intention of heretics, for it consists in the constancy of the faithful being put to the test, and "makes us shake off our sluggishness, and search the Scriptures more carefully," as Augustine states (De Gen. cont. Manich. i, 1). What they really intend is the corruption of the faith, which is to inflict very great harm indeed. Consequently we should consider what they directly intend, and expel them, rather than what is beside their intention, and so, tolerate them.

Reply Obj. 3: According to Decret. (xxiv, qu. iii, can. Notandum), "to be excommunicated is not to be uprooted." A man is excommunicated, as the Apostle says (1 Cor. 5:5) that his "spirit may be saved in the day of Our Lord." Yet if heretics be altogether uprooted by death, this is not contrary to Our Lord's command, which is to be understood as referring to the case when the cockle cannot be plucked up without plucking up the wheat, as we explained above (Q. 10, A. 8, ad 1), when treating of unbelievers in general.

FOURTH ARTICLE [II-II, Q. 11, Art. 4]

Whether the Church Should Receive Those Who Return from Heresy?

Objection 1: It would seem that the Church ought in all cases to receive those who return from heresy. For it is written (Jer. 3:1) in the person of the Lord: "Thou hast prostituted thyself to many lovers; nevertheless return to Me saith the Lord." Now the sentence of the Church is God's sentence, according to Deut. 1:17: "You shall hear the little as well as the great: neither shall you respect any man's person, because it is the judgment of God." Therefore even those who are guilty of the prostitution of unbelief which is spiritual prostitution, should be received all the same.

Obj. 2: Further, Our Lord commanded Peter (Matt. 18:22) to forgive his offending brother "not" only "till seven times, but till seventy times seven times," which Jerome expounds as meaning that "a man should be forgiven, as often as he has sinned." Therefore he ought to be received by the Church as often as he has sinned by falling back into heresy.

Obj. 3: Further, heresy is a kind of unbelief. Now other unbelievers who wish to be converted are received by the Church. Therefore heretics also should be received.

*On the contrary,* The Decretal Ad abolendam (De Haereticis, cap. ix) says that "those who are found to have relapsed into the error which they had already abjured, must be left to the secular tribunal." Therefore they should not be received by the Church.

*I answer that,* In obedience to Our Lord's institution, the Church extends her charity to all, not only to friends, but also to foes who persecute her, according to Matt. 5:44: "Love your enemies; do good to them that hate you." Now it is part of charity that we should both wish and work our neighbor's good. Again, good is twofold: one is spiritual, namely the health of the soul, which good is chiefly the object of charity, since it is this chiefly that we should wish for one another. Consequently, from this point of view, heretics who return after falling no matter how often, are admitted by the Church to Penance whereby the way of salvation is opened to them.

The other good is that which charity considers secondarily, viz. temporal good, such as life of the body, worldly possessions, good repute, ecclesiastical or secular dignity, for we are not bound by charity to wish others this good, except in relation to the eternal salvation of them and of others. Hence if the presence of one of these goods in one individual might be an obstacle to eternal salvation in many, we are not bound out of charity to wish such a good to that person, rather should we desire him to be without it, both because eternal salvation takes precedence of temporal good, and because the good of the many is to be preferred to the good of one. Now if heretics were always received on their return, in order to save their lives and other temporal goods, this might be prejudicial to the salvation of others, both because they would infect others if they relapsed again, and because, if they escaped without punishment, others would feel more assured in lapsing into heresy. For it is written (Eccles. 8:11): "For because sentence is not speedily pronounced against the evil, the children of men commit evils without any fear."

For this reason the Church not only admits to Penance those who return from heresy for the first time, but also safeguards their lives, and sometimes by dispensation, restores them to the ecclesiastical dignities which they may have had before, should their conversion appear to be sincere: we read of this as having frequently been done for the good of peace. But when they fall again, after having been received, this seems to prove them to be inconstant in faith, wherefore when they return again, they are admitted to Penance, but are not delivered from the pain of death.

Reply Obj. 1: In God's tribunal, those who return are always received, because God is a searcher of hearts, and knows those who return in sincerity. But the Church cannot imitate God in this, for she presumes that those who relapse after being once received, are not sincere in their return; hence she does not debar them from the way of salvation, but neither does she protect them from the sentence of death.

Reply Obj. 2: Our Lord was speaking to Peter of sins committed against oneself, for one should always forgive such offenses and spare our brother when he repents. These words are not to be applied to sins committed against one's neighbor or against God, for it is not left to our discretion to forgive such offenses, as Jerome says on Matt. 18:15, "If thy brother shall offend against thee." Yet even in this matter the law prescribes limits according as God's honor or our neighbor's good demands.

Reply Obj. 3: When other unbelievers, who have never received the faith are converted, they do not as yet show signs of inconstancy in faith, as relapsed heretics do; hence the comparison fails.

## QUESTION 12

OF APOSTASY (In Two Articles)

We must now consider apostasy: about which there are two points of inquiry:

(1) Whether apostasy pertains to unbelief?

(2) Whether, on account of apostasy from the faith, subjects are absolved from allegiance to an apostate prince?

FIRST ARTICLE [II-II, Q. 12, Art. 1]

Whether Apostasy Pertains to Unbelief?

Objection 1: It would seem that apostasy does not pertain to unbelief. For that which is the origin of all sins, does not, seemingly, pertain to unbelief, since many sins there are without unbelief. Now apostasy seems to be the origin of every sin, for it is written (Ecclus. 10:14): "The beginning of the pride of man is apostasy [Douay: 'to fall off'] from God," and further on, (Ecclus. 10:15): "Pride is the beginning of all sin." Therefore apostasy does not pertain to unbelief.

Obj. 2: Further, unbelief is an act of the understanding: whereas apostasy seems rather to consist in some outward deed or utterance, or even in some inward act of the will, for it is written (Prov. 6:12-14): "A man that is an apostate, an unprofitable man walketh with a perverse mouth. He winketh with the eyes, presseth with the foot, speaketh with the finger. With a wicked heart he deviseth evil, and at all times he soweth discord." Moreover if anyone were to have himself circumcised, or to worship at the tomb of Mahomet, he would be deemed an apostate. Therefore apostasy does not pertain to unbelief.

Obj. 3: Further, heresy, since it pertains to unbelief, is a determinate species of unbelief. If then, apostasy pertained to unbelief, it would follow that it is a determinate species of unbelief, which does not seem to agree with what has been said (Q. 10, A. 5). Therefore apostasy does not pertain to unbelief.

*On the contrary,* It is written (John 6:67): "Many of his disciples went back," i.e. apostatized, of whom Our Lord had said previously (John 6:65): "There are some of you that believe not." Therefore apostasy pertains to unbelief.

*I answer that,* Apostasy denotes a backsliding from God. This may happen in various ways according to the different kinds of union between man and God. For, in the first place, man is united to God by faith; secondly, by having his will duly submissive in obeying His commandments; thirdly, by certain special things pertaining to supererogation such as the religious life, the clerical state, or Holy Orders. Now if that which follows be removed, that which precedes, remains, but the converse does not hold. Accordingly a man may apostatize from God, by withdrawing from the religious life to which he was bound by profession, or from the Holy Order which he had received: and this is called "apostasy from religious life" or "Orders." A man may also apostatize from God, by rebelling in his mind against the Divine commandments: and though man may apostatize in both the above ways, he may still remain united to God by faith.

But if he give up the faith, then he seems to turn away from God altogether: and consequently, apostasy simply and absolutely is that whereby a man withdraws from the faith, and is called "apostasy of perfidy." In this way apostasy, simply so called, pertains to unbelief.

Reply Obj. 1: This objection refers to the second kind of apostasy, which denotes an act of the will in rebellion against God's commandments, an act that is to be found in every mortal sin.

Reply Obj. 2: It belongs to faith not only that the heart should believe, but also that external words and deeds should bear witness to the inward faith, for confession is an act of faith. In this way too, certain external words or deeds pertain to unbelief, in so far as they are signs of unbelief, even as a sign of health is said itself to be healthy. Now although the authority quoted may be understood as referring to every kind of apostate, yet it applies most truly to an apostate from the faith. For since faith is the first foundation of things to be hoped for, and since, without faith it is "impossible to please God"; when once faith is removed, man retains nothing that may be useful for the obtaining of eternal salvation, for which reason it is written (Prov. 6:12): "A man that is an apostate, an unprofitable man": because faith is the life of the soul, according to Rom. 1:17: "The just man liveth by faith." Therefore, just as when the life of the body is taken away, man's every member and part loses its due disposition, so when the life of justice, which is by faith, is done away, disorder appears in all his members. First, in his mouth, whereby chiefly his mind stands revealed; secondly, in his eyes; thirdly, in the instrument of movement; fourthly, in his will, which tends to evil. The result is that "he sows discord," endeavoring to sever others from the faith even as he severed himself.

Reply Obj. 3: The species of a quality or form are not diversified by the fact of its being the term *wherefrom* or whereto of movement: *on the contrary,* it is the movement that takes its species from the terms. Now apostasy regards unbelief as the term *whereto* of the movement of withdrawal from the faith; wherefore apostasy does not imply a special kind of unbelief, but an aggravating circumstance thereof, according to 2 Pet. 2:21: "It had been better for them not to know the truth [Vulg.: 'the way of justice'], than after they had known it, to turn back."

SECOND ARTICLE [II-II, Q. 12, Art. 2]

Whether a Prince Forfeits His Dominion Over His Subjects, on Account of Apostasy from the Faith, So That They No Longer Owe Him Allegiance?

Objection 1: It would seem that a prince does not so forfeit his dominion over his subjects, on account of apostasy from the faith, that they no longer owe him allegiance. For Ambrose [*St. Augustine, Super Ps. 124:3] says that the Emperor Julian, though an apostate, nevertheless had under him Christian soldiers, who when he said to them, "Fall into line for the defense of the republic," were bound to obey. Therefore subjects are not absolved from their allegiance to their prince on account of his apostasy.

Obj. 2: Further, an apostate from the faith is an unbeliever. Now we find that certain holy men served unbelieving masters; thus Joseph served Pharaoh, Daniel served Nabuchodonosor, and Mardochai served Assuerus. Therefore apostasy from the faith does not release subjects from allegiance to their sovereign.

Obj. 3: Further, just as by apostasy from the faith, a man turns away from God, so does every sin. Consequently if, on account of apostasy from the faith, princes were to lose their right to command those of their subjects who are believers, they would equally lose it on account of other sins: which is evidently not the case. Therefore we ought not to refuse allegiance to a sovereign on account of his apostatizing from the faith.

*On the contrary,* Gregory VII says (Council, Roman V): "Holding to the institutions of our holy predecessors, we, by our apostolic authority, absolve from their oath those who through loyalty or through the sacred bond of an oath owe allegiance to excommunicated persons: and we absolutely forbid them to continue their allegiance to such persons, until these shall have made amends." Now apostates from the faith, like heretics, are excommunicated, according to the Decretal [*Extra, De Haereticis, cap. Ad abolendam]. Therefore princes should not be obeyed when they have apostatized from the faith.

*I answer that,* As stated above (Q. 10, A. 10), unbelief, in itself, is not inconsistent with dominion, since dominion is a device of the law of nations which is a human law: whereas the distinction between believers and unbelievers is of Divine right, which does not annul human right. Nevertheless a man who sins by unbelief may be sentenced to the loss of his right of dominion, as also, sometimes, on account of other sins.

Now it is not within the competency of the Church to punish unbelief in those who have never received the faith, according to the saying of the Apostle (1 Cor. 5:12): "What have I to do to judge them that are without?" She can, however, pass sentence of punishment on the unbelief of those who have received the faith: and it is fitting that they should be punished by being deprived of the allegiance of their subjects: for this same allegiance might conduce to great corruption of the faith, since, as was stated above (A. 1, Obj. 2), "a man that is an apostate ... with a wicked heart deviseth evil, and ... soweth discord," in order to sever others from the faith. Consequently, as soon as sentence of excommunication is passed on a man on account of apostasy from the faith, his subjects are "ipso facto" absolved from his authority and from the oath of allegiance whereby they were bound to him.

Reply Obj. 1: At that time the Church was but recently instituted, and had not, as yet, the power of curbing earthly princes; and so she allowed the faithful to obey Julian the apostate, in matters that were not contrary to the faith, in order to avoid incurring a yet greater danger.

Reply Obj. 2: As stated in the article, it is not a question of those unbelievers who have never received the faith.

Reply Obj. 3: Apostasy from the faith severs man from God altogether, as stated above (A. 1), which is not the case in any other sin.

# QUESTION 13

OF THE SIN OF BLASPHEMY, IN GENERAL (In Four Articles)

We must now consider the sin of blasphemy, which is opposed to the confession of faith; and (1) blasphemy in general, (2) that blasphemy which is called the sin against the Holy Ghost.

Under the first head there are four points of inquiry:

(1) Whether blasphemy is opposed to the confession of faith?

(2) Whether blasphemy is always a mortal sin?

(3) Whether blasphemy is the most grievous sin?

(4) Whether blasphemy is in the damned?

FIRST ARTICLE [II-II, Q. 13, Art. 1]

Whether Blasphemy Is Opposed to the Confession of Faith?

Objection 1: It would seem that blasphemy is not opposed to the confession of faith. Because to blaspheme is to utter an affront or insult against the Creator. Now this pertains to ill-will against God rather than to unbelief. Therefore blasphemy is not opposed to the confession of faith.

Obj. 2: Further, on Eph. 4:31, "Let blasphemy ... be put away from you," a gloss says, "that which is committed against God or the saints." But confession of faith, seemingly, is not about other things than those pertaining to God, Who is the object of faith. Therefore blasphemy is not always opposed to the confession of faith.

Obj. 3: Further, according to some, there are three kinds of blasphemy. The first of these is when something unfitting is affirmed of God; the second is when something fitting is denied of Him; and the third, when something proper to God is ascribed to a creature, so that, seemingly, blasphemy is not only about God, but also about His creatures. Now the object of faith is God. Therefore blasphemy is not opposed to confession of faith.

*On the contrary,* The Apostle says (1 Tim. 1:12, 13): "I ... before was a blasphemer and a persecutor," and afterwards, "I did it ignorantly in" my "unbelief." Hence it seems that blasphemy pertains to unbelief.

*I answer that,* The word blasphemy seems to denote the disparagement of some surpassing goodness, especially that of God. Now God, as Dionysius says (Div. Nom. i), is the very essence of true goodness. Hence whatever befits God, pertains to His goodness, and whatever does not befit Him, is far removed from the perfection of goodness which is His Essence. Consequently whoever either denies anything befitting God, or affirms anything unbefitting Him, disparages the Divine goodness.

Now this may happen in two ways. In the first way it may happen merely in respect of the opinion in the intellect; in the second way this opinion is united to a certain detestation in the affections, even as, on the other hand, faith in God is perfected by love of Him. Accordingly this disparagement of the Divine goodness is either in the intellect alone, or in the affections also. If it is in thought only, it is blasphemy of the heart, whereas if it betrays itself outwardly in speech it is blasphemy of the tongue. It is in this sense that blasphemy is opposed to confession of faith.

Reply Obj. 1: He that speaks against God, with the intention of reviling Him, disparages the Divine goodness, not only in respect of the falsehood in his intellect, but also by reason of the wickedness of his will, whereby he detests and strives to hinder the honor due to God, and this is perfect blasphemy.

Reply Obj. 2: Even as God is praised in His saints, in so far as praise is given to the works which God does in His saints, so does blasphemy against the saints, redound, as a consequence, against God.

Reply Obj. 3: Properly speaking, the sin of blasphemy is not in this way divided into three species: since to affirm unfitting things, or to deny fitting things of God, differ merely as affirmation and negation. For this diversity does not cause distinct species of habits, since the falsehood of affirmations and negations is made known by the same knowledge, and it is the same ignorance which errs in either way, since negatives are proved by affirmatives, according to Poster. i, 25. Again to ascribe to creatures things that are proper to God, seems to amount to the same as affirming something unfitting of Him, since whatever is proper to God is God Himself: and to ascribe to a creature, that which is proper to God, is to assert that God is the same as a creature.

SECOND ARTICLE [II-II, Q. 13, Art. 2]

Whether Blasphemy Is Always a Mortal Sin?

Objection 1: It would seem that blasphemy is not always a mortal sin. Because a gloss on the words, "Now lay you also all away," etc. (Col. 3:8) says:

"After prohibiting greater crimes he forbids lesser sins": and yet among the latter he includes blasphemy. Therefore blasphemy is comprised among the lesser, i.e. venial, sins.

Obj. 2: Further, every mortal sin is opposed to one of the precepts of the decalogue. But, seemingly, blasphemy is not contrary to any of them. Therefore blasphemy is not a mortal sin.

Obj. 3: Further, sins committed without deliberation, are not mortal: hence first movements are not mortal sins, because they precede the deliberation of the reason, as was shown above (I-II, Q. 74, AA. 3, 10). Now blasphemy sometimes occurs without deliberation of the reason. Therefore it is not always a mortal sin.

*On the contrary,* It is written (Lev. 24:16): "He that blasphemeth the name of the Lord, dying let him die." Now the death punishment is not inflicted except for a mortal sin. Therefore blasphemy is a mortal sin.

*I answer that,* As stated above (I-II, Q. 72, A. 5), a mortal sin is one whereby a man is severed from the first principle of spiritual life, which principle is the charity of God. Therefore whatever things are contrary to charity, are mortal sins in respect of their genus. Now blasphemy, as to its genus, is opposed to Divine charity, because, as stated above (A. 1), it disparages the Divine goodness, which is the object of charity. Consequently blasphemy is a mortal sin, by reason of its genus.

Reply Obj. 1: This gloss is not to be understood as meaning that all the sins which follow, are mortal, but that whereas all those mentioned previously are more grievous sins, some of those mentioned afterwards are less grievous; and yet among the latter some more grievous sins are included.

Reply Obj. 2: Since, as stated above (A. 1), blasphemy is contrary to the confession of faith, its prohibition is comprised under the prohibition of unbelief, expressed by the words: "I am the Lord thy God," etc. (Ex. 20:1). Or else, it is forbidden by the words: "Thou shalt not take the name of ... God in vain" (Ex. 20:7). Because he who asserts something false about God, takes His name in vain even more than he who uses the name of God in confirmation of a falsehood.

Reply Obj. 3: There are two ways in which blasphemy may occur unawares and without deliberation. In the first way, by a man failing to advert to the blasphemous nature of his words, and this may happen through his being moved suddenly by passion so as to break out into words suggested by his imagination, without heeding to the meaning of those words: this is a venial sin, and is not a blasphemy properly so called. In the second way, by adverting to the meaning of his words, and to their blasphemous nature: in which case he is not excused from mortal sin, even as neither is he who, in a sudden movement of anger, kills one who is sitting beside him.

THIRD ARTICLE [II-II, Q. 13, Art. 3]

Whether the Sin of Blasphemy Is the Greatest Sin?

Objection 1: It would seem that the sin of blasphemy is not the greatest sin. For, according to Augustine (Enchiridion xii), a thing is said to be evil because it does harm. Now the sin of murder, since it destroys a man's life, does more harm than the sin of blasphemy, which can do no harm to God. Therefore the sin of murder is more grievous than that of blasphemy.

Obj. 2: Further, a perjurer calls upon God to witness to a falsehood, and thus seems to assert that God is false. But not every blasphemer goes so far as to say that God is false. Therefore perjury is a more grievous sin than blasphemy.

Obj. 3: Further, on Ps. 74:6, "Lift not up your horn on high," a gloss says: "To excuse oneself for sin is the greatest sin of all." Therefore blasphemy is not the greatest sin.

*On the contrary,* On Isa. 18:2, "To a terrible people," etc. a gloss says: "In comparison with blasphemy, every sin is slight."

*I answer that,* As stated above (A. 1), blasphemy is opposed to the confession of faith, so that it contains the gravity of unbelief: while the sin is aggravated if the will's detestation is added thereto, and yet more, if it breaks out into words, even as love and confession add to the praise of faith.

Therefore, since, as stated above (Q. 10, A. 3), unbelief is the greatest of sins in respect of its genus, it follows that blasphemy also is a very great sin, through belonging to the same genus as unbelief and being an aggravated form of that sin.

Reply Obj. 1: If we compare murder and blasphemy as regards the objects of those sins, it is clear that blasphemy, which is a sin committed directly against God, is more grave than murder, which is a sin against one's neighbor. On the other hand, if we compare them in respect of the harm wrought by them, murder is the graver sin, for murder does more harm to one's neighbor, than blasphemy does to God. Since, however, the gravity of a sin depends on the intention of the evil will, rather than on the effect of the deed, as was shown above (I-II, Q. 73, A. 8), it follows that, as the blasphemer intends to do harm to God's honor, absolutely speaking, he sins more grievously that the murderer. Nevertheless murder takes precedence, as to punishment, among sins committed against our neighbor.

Reply Obj. 2: A gloss on the words, "Let ... blasphemy be put away from you" (Eph. 4:31) says: "Blasphemy is worse than perjury." The reason is that the perjurer does not say or think something false about God, as the blasphemer does: but he calls God to witness to a falsehood, not that he deems God a false witness, but in the hope, as it were, that God will not testify to the matter by some evident sign.

Reply Obj. 3: To excuse oneself for sin is a circumstance that aggravates every sin, even blasphemy itself: and it is called the most grievous sin, for as much as it makes every sin more grievous.

FOURTH ARTICLE [II-II, Q. 13, Art. 4]

Whether the Damned Blaspheme?

Objection 1: It would seem that the damned do not blaspheme. Because some wicked men are deterred from blaspheming now, on account of the fear of future punishment. But the damned are undergoing these punishments, so that they abhor them yet more. Therefore, much more are they restrained from blaspheming.

Obj. 2: Further, since blasphemy is a most grievous sin, it is most demeritorious. Now in the life to come there is no state of meriting or demeriting. Therefore there will be no place for blasphemy.

Obj. 3: Further, it is written (Eccles. 11:3) that "the tree ... in what place soever it shall fall, there shall it be": whence it clearly follows that, after this life, man acquires neither merit nor sin, which he did not already possess in this life. Now many will be damned who were not blasphemous in this life. Neither, therefore, will they blaspheme in the life to come.

*On the contrary,* It is written (Apoc. 16:9): "The men were scorched with great heat, and they blasphemed the name of God, Who hath power over these plagues," and a gloss on these words says that "those who are in hell, though aware that they are deservedly punished, will nevertheless complain that God is so powerful as to torture them thus." Now this would be blasphemy in their present state: and consequently it will also be in their future state.

*I answer that,* As stated above (AA. 1, 3), detestation of the Divine goodness is a necessary condition of blasphemy. Now those who are in hell retain their wicked will which is turned away from God's justice, since they love the things for which they are punished, would wish to use them if they could, and hate the punishments inflicted on them for those same sins. They regret indeed the sins which they have committed, not because they hate them, but because they are punished for them. Accordingly this detestation of the Divine justice is, in them, the interior blasphemy of the heart: and it is credible that after the resurrection they will blaspheme God with the tongue, even as the saints will praise Him with their voices.

Reply Obj. 1: In the present life men are deterred from blasphemy through fear of punishment which they think they can escape: whereas, in hell, the damned have no hope of escape, so that, in despair, they are borne towards whatever their wicked will suggests to them.

Reply Obj. 2: Merit and demerit belong to the state of a wayfarer, wherefore good is meritorious in them, while evil is demeritorious. In the blessed, on the other hand, good is not meritorious, but is part of their blissful reward, and, in like manner, in the damned, evil is not demeritorious, but is part of the punishment of damnation.

Reply Obj. 3: Whoever dies in mortal sin, bears with him a will that detests the Divine justice with regard to a certain thing, and in this respect there can be blasphemy in him.

## QUESTION 14

OF BLASPHEMY AGAINST THE HOLY GHOST (In Four Articles)

We must now consider in particular blasphemy against the Holy Ghost: under which head there are four points of inquiry:

(1) Whether blasphemy or the sin against the Holy Ghost is the same as the sin committed through certain malice?

(2) Of the species of this sin;

(3) Whether it can be forgiven?

(4) Whether it is possible to begin by sinning against the Holy Ghost before committing other sins?

FIRST ARTICLE [II-II, Q. 14, Art. 1]

Whether the Sin Against the Holy Ghost Is the Same As the Sin Committed Through Certain Malice?

Objection 1: It would seem that the sin against the Holy Ghost is not the same as the sin committed through certain malice. Because the sin against the Holy Ghost is the sin of blasphemy, according to Matt. 12:32. But not every sin committed through certain malice is a sin of blasphemy: since many other kinds of sin may be committed through certain malice. Therefore the sin against the Holy Ghost is not the same as the sin committed through certain malice.

Obj. 2: Further, the sin committed through certain malice is condivided with sin committed through ignorance, and sin committed through weakness: whereas the sin against the Holy Ghost is condivided with the sin against the Son of Man (Matt. 12:32). Therefore the sin against the Holy Ghost is not the same as the sin committed through certain malice, since things whose opposites differ, are themselves different.

Obj. 3: Further, the sin against the Holy Ghost is itself a generic sin, having its own determinate species: whereas sin committed through certain malice is not a special kind of sin, but a condition or general circumstance of sin, which can affect any kind of sin at all. Therefore the sin against the Holy Ghost is not the same as the sin committed through certain malice.

*On the contrary,* The Master says (Sent. ii, D, 43) that "to sin against the Holy Ghost is to take pleasure in the malice of sin for its own sake." Now this is to sin through certain malice. Therefore it seems that the sin committed through certain malice is the same as the sin against the Holy Ghost.

*I answer that,* Three meanings have been given to the sin against the Holy Ghost. For the earlier doctors, viz. Athanasius (Super Matth. xii, 32), Hilary (Can. xii in Matth.), Ambrose (Super Luc. xii, 10), Jerome (Super Matth. xii), and Chrysostom (Hom. xli in Matth.), say that the sin against the Holy Ghost is literally to utter a blasphemy against the Holy Spirit, whether by Holy Spirit we understand the essential name applicable to the whole Trinity, each Person of which is a Spirit and is holy, or the personal name of one of the Persons of the Trinity, in which sense blasphemy against the Holy Ghost is distinct from the blasphemy against the Son of Man (Matt. 12:32), for Christ did certain things in respect of His human nature, by eating, drinking, and such like actions, while He did others in respect of His Godhead, by casting out devils, raising the dead, and the like: which things He did both by the power of His own Godhead and by the operation of the Holy Ghost, of Whom He was full, according to his human nature. Now the Jews began by speaking blasphemy against the Son of Man, when they said (Matt. 11:19) that He was "a glutton ... a wine drinker," and a "friend of publicans": but afterwards they blasphemed against the Holy Ghost, when they ascribed to the prince of devils those works which Christ did by the power of His own Divine Nature and by the operation of the Holy Ghost.

Augustine, however (De Verb. Dom., Serm. lxxi), says that blasphemy or the sin against the Holy Ghost, is final impenitence when, namely, a man perseveres in mortal sin until death, and that it is not confined to utterance by word of mouth, but extends to words in thought and deed, not to one word only, but to many. Now this word, in this sense, is said to be uttered against the Holy Ghost, because it is contrary to the remission of sins, which is the work of the Holy Ghost, Who is the charity both of the Father and of the Son. Nor did Our Lord say this to the Jews, as though they had sinned against the Holy Ghost, since they were not yet guilty of final impenitence, but He warned them, lest by similar utterances they should come to sin against the Holy Ghost: and it is in this sense that we are to understand Mark 3:29, 30, where after Our Lord had said: "But he that shall blaspheme against the Holy Ghost," etc. the Evangelist adds, "because they said: He hath an unclean spirit."

But others understand it differently, and say that the sin of blasphemy against the Holy Ghost, is a sin committed against that good which is appropriated to the Holy Ghost: because goodness is appropriated to the Holy Ghost, just a power is appropriated to the Father, and wisdom to the Son. Hence they say that when a man sins through weakness, it is a sin "against the Father"; that when he sins through ignorance, it is a sin "against the Son"; and that when he sins through certain malice, i.e. through the very choosing of evil, as explained above (I-II, Q. 78, AA. 1, 3), it is a sin "against the Holy Ghost."

Now this may happen in two ways. First by reason of the very inclination of a vicious habit which we call malice, and, in this way, to sin through malice is not the same as to sin against the Holy Ghost. In another way it happens that by reason of contempt, that which might have prevented the choosing of evil, is rejected or removed; thus hope is removed by despair, and fear by presumption, and so on, as we shall explain further on (QQ. 20, 21). Now all these things which prevent the choosing of sin are effects of the Holy Ghost in us; so that, in this sense, to sin through malice is to sin against the Holy Ghost.

Reply Obj. 1: Just as the confession of faith consists in a protestation not only of words but also of deeds, so blasphemy against the Holy Ghost can be uttered in word, thought and deed.

Reply Obj. 2: According to the third interpretation, blasphemy against the Holy Ghost is condivided with blasphemy against the Son of Man, forasmuch as He is also the Son of God, i.e. the "power of God and the wisdom of God" (1 Cor. 1:24). Wherefore, in this sense, the sin against the Son of Man will be that which is committed through ignorance, or through weakness.

Reply Obj. 3: Sin committed through certain malice, in so far as it results from the inclination of a habit, is not a special sin, but a general condition of sin: whereas, in so far as it results from a special contempt of an effect of the Holy Ghost in us, it has the character of a special sin. According to this interpretation the sin against the Holy Ghost is a special kind of sin, as also according to the first interpretation: whereas according to the second, it is not a species of sin, because final impenitence may be a circumstance of any kind of sin.

SECOND ARTICLE [II-II, Q. 14, Art. 2]

Whether It Is Fitting to Distinguish Six Kinds of Sin Against the Holy Ghost?

Objection 1: It would seem unfitting to distinguish six kinds of sin against the Holy Ghost, viz. despair, presumption, impenitence, obstinacy, resisting the known truth, envy of our brother's spiritual good, which are assigned by the Master (Sent. ii, D, 43). For to deny God's justice or mercy belongs to unbelief. Now, by despair, a man rejects God's mercy, and by presumption, His justice. Therefore each of these is a kind of unbelief rather than of the sin against the Holy Ghost.

Obj. 2: Further, impenitence, seemingly, regards past sins, while obstinacy regards future sins. Now past and future time do not diversify the species of virtues or vices, since it is the same faith whereby we believe that Christ was born, and those of old believed that He would be born. Therefore obstinacy and impenitence should not be reckoned as two species of sin against the Holy Ghost.

Obj. 3: Further, "grace and truth came by Jesus Christ" (John 1:17). Therefore it seem that resistance of the known truth, and envy of a brother's spiritual good, belong to blasphemy against the Son rather than against the Holy Ghost.

Obj. 4: Further, Bernard says (De Dispens. et Praecept. xi) that "to refuse to obey is to resist the Holy Ghost." Moreover a gloss on Lev. 10:16, says that "a feigned repentance is a blasphemy against the Holy Ghost." Again, schism is, seemingly, directly opposed to the Holy Ghost by Whom the Church is united together. Therefore it seems that the species of sins against the Holy Ghost are insufficiently enumerated.

*On the contrary,* Augustine [*Fulgentius] (De Fide ad Petrum iii) says that "those who despair of pardon for their sins, or who without merits presume on God's mercy, sin against the Holy Ghost," and (Enchiridion lxxxiii) that "he who dies in a state of obstinacy is guilty of the sin against the Holy Ghost," and (De Verb. Dom., Serm. lxxi) that "impenitence is a sin against the Holy Ghost," and (De Serm. Dom. in Monte xxii), that "to resist fraternal goodness with the brands of envy is to sin against the Holy Ghost," and in his book De unico Baptismo (De Bap. contra Donat. vi, 35) he says that "a man who spurns the truth, is either envious of his brethren to whom the truth is revealed, or ungrateful to God, by Whose inspiration the Church is taught," and therefore, seemingly, sins against the Holy Ghost.

*I answer that,* The above species are fittingly assigned to the sin against the Holy Ghost taken in the third sense, because they are distinguished in respect of the removal or contempt of those things whereby a man can be prevented from sinning through choice. These things are either on the part of God's judgment, or on the part of His gifts, or on the part of sin. For, by consideration of the Divine judgment, wherein justice is accompanied with mercy, man is hindered from sinning through choice, both by hope, arising from the consideration of the mercy that pardons sins and rewards good deeds, which hope is removed by "despair"; and by fear, arising from the consideration of the Divine justice that punishes sins, which fear is removed by "presumption," when, namely, a man presumes that he can obtain glory without merits, or pardon without repentance.

God's gifts whereby we are withdrawn from sin, are two: one is the acknowledgment of the truth, against which there is the "resistance of the known truth," when, namely, a man resists the truth which he has acknowledged, in order to sin more freely: while the other is the assistance of inward grace, against which there is "envy of a brother's spiritual good," when, namely, a man is envious not only of his brother's person, but also of the increase of Divine grace in the world.

On the part of sin, there are two things which may withdraw man therefrom: one is the inordinateness and shamefulness of the act, the consideration of which is wont to arouse man to repentance for the sin he has committed, and against this there is "impenitence," not as denoting permanence in sin until death, in which sense it was taken above (for thus it would not be a special sin, but a circumstance of sin), but as denoting the purpose of not repenting. The other thing is the smallness or brevity of the good which is sought in sin, according to Rom. 6:21: "What fruit had you therefore then in those things, of which you are now ashamed?" The consideration of this is wont to prevent man's will from being hardened in sin, and this is removed by "obstinacy," whereby man hardens his purpose by clinging to sin. Of these two it is written (Jer. 8:6): "There is none that doth penance for his sin, saying: What have I done?" as regards the first; and, "They are all turned to their own course, as a horse rushing to the battle," as regards the second.

Reply Obj. 1: The sins of despair and presumption consist, not in disbelieving in God's justice and mercy, but in contemning them.

Reply Obj. 2: Obstinacy and impenitence differ not only in respect of past and future time, but also in respect of certain formal aspects by reason of the diverse consideration of those things which may be considered in sin, as explained above.

Reply Obj. 3: Grace and truth were the work of Christ through the gifts of the Holy Ghost which He gave to men.

Reply Obj. 4: To refuse to obey belongs to obstinacy, while a feigned repentance belongs to impenitence, and schism to the envy of a brother's spiritual good, whereby the members of the Church are united together.

THIRD ARTICLE [II-II, Q. 14, Art. 3]

Whether the Sin Against the Holy Ghost Can Be Forgiven?

Objection 1: It would seem that the sin against the Holy Ghost can be forgiven. For Augustine says (De Verb. Dom., Serm. lxxi): "We should despair of no man, so long as Our Lord's patience brings him back to repentance." But if any sin cannot be forgiven, it would be possible to despair of some sinners. Therefore the sin against the Holy Ghost can be forgiven.

Obj. 2: Further, no sin is forgiven, except through the soul being healed by God. But "no disease is incurable to an all-powerful physician," as a gloss says on Ps. 102:3, "Who healeth all thy diseases." Therefore the sin against the Holy Ghost can be forgiven.

Obj. 3: Further, the free-will is indifferent to either good or evil. Now, so long as man is a wayfarer, he can fall away from any virtue, since even an angel fell from heaven, wherefore it is written (Job 4:18, 19): "In His angels He found wickedness: how much more shall they that dwell in houses of clay?" Therefore, in like manner, a man can return from any sin to the state of justice. Therefore the sin against the Holy Ghost can be forgiven.

*On the contrary,* It is written (Matt. 12:32): "He

that shall speak against the Holy Ghost, it shall not be forgiven him, neither in this world, nor in the world to come": and Augustine says (De Serm. Dom. in Monte i, 22) that "so great is the downfall of this sin that it cannot submit to the humiliation of asking for pardon."

*I answer that,* According to the various interpretations of the sin against the Holy Ghost, there are various ways in which it may be said that it cannot be forgiven. For if by the sin against the Holy Ghost we understand final impenitence, it is said to be unpardonable, since in no way is it pardoned: because the mortal sin wherein a man perseveres until death will not be forgiven in the life to come, since it was not remitted by repentance in this life.

According to the other two interpretations, it is said to be unpardonable, not as though it is nowise forgiven, but because, considered in itself, it deserves not to be pardoned: and this in two ways. First, as regards the punishment, since he that sins through ignorance or weakness, deserves less punishment, whereas he that sins through certain malice, can offer no excuse in alleviation of his punishment. Likewise those who blasphemed against the Son of Man before His Godhead was revealed, could have some excuse, on account of the weakness of the flesh which they perceived in Him, and hence, they deserved less punishment; whereas those who blasphemed against His very Godhead, by ascribing to the devil the works of the Holy Ghost, had no excuse in diminution of their punishment. Wherefore, according to Chrysostom's commentary (Hom. xlii in Matth.), the Jews are said not to be forgiven this sin, neither in this world nor in the world to come, because they were punished for it, both in the present life, through the Romans, and in the life to come, in the pains of hell. Thus also Athanasius adduces the example of their forefathers who, first of all, wrangled with Moses on account of the shortage of water and bread; and this the Lord bore with patience, because they were to be excused on account of the weakness of the flesh: but afterwards they sinned more grievously when, by ascribing to an idol the favors bestowed by God Who had brought them out of Egypt, they blasphemed, so to speak, against the Holy Ghost, saying (Ex. 32:4): "These are thy gods, O Israel, that have brought thee out of the land of Egypt." Therefore the Lord both inflicted temporal punishment on them, since "there were slain on that day about three and twenty thousand men" (Ex. 32:28), and threatened them with punishment in the life to come, saying, (Ex. 32:34): "I, in the day of revenge, will visit this sin … of theirs."

Secondly, this may be understood to refer to the guilt: thus a disease is said to be incurable in respect of the nature of the disease, which removes whatever might be a means of cure, as when it takes away the power of nature, or causes loathing for food and medicine, although God is able to cure such a disease. So too, the sin against the Holy Ghost is said to be unpardonable, by reason of its nature, in so far as it removes those things which are a means towards the pardon of sins. This does not, however, close the way of forgiveness and healing to an all-powerful and merciful God, Who, sometimes, by a miracle, so to speak, restores spiritual health to such men.

Reply Obj. 1: We should despair of no man in this life, considering God's omnipotence and mercy. But if we consider the circumstances of sin, some are called (Eph. 2:2) "children of despair" [* *Filios diffidentiae,* which the Douay version renders "children of unbelief."].

Reply Obj. 2: This argument considers the question on the part of God's omnipotence, not on that of the circumstances of sin.

Reply Obj. 3: In this life the free-will does indeed ever remain subject to change: yet sometimes it rejects that whereby, so far as it is concerned, it can be turned to good. Hence considered in itself this sin is unpardonable, although God can pardon it.

FOURTH ARTICLE [II-II, Q. 14, Art. 4]

Whether a Man Can Sin First of All Against the Holy Ghost?

Objection 1: It would seem that a man cannot sin first of all against the Holy Ghost, without having previously committed other sins. For the natural order requires that one should be moved to perfection from imperfection. This is evident as regards good things, according to Prov. 4:18: "The path of the just, as a shining light, goeth forwards and increases even to perfect day." Now, in evil things, the perfect is the greatest evil, as the Philosopher states (Metaph. v, text. 21). Since then the sin against the Holy Ghost is the most grievous sin, it seems that man comes to commit this sin through committing lesser sins.

Obj. 2: Further, to sin against the Holy Ghost is to sin through certain malice, or through choice. Now man cannot do this until he has sinned many times; for the Philosopher says (Ethic. v, 6, 9) that "although a man is able to do unjust deeds, yet he cannot all at once do them as an unjust man does," viz. from choice. Therefore it seems that the sin against the Holy Ghost cannot be committed except after other sins.

Obj. 3: Further, repentance and impenitence are about the same object. But there is no repentance, except about past sins. Therefore the same applies to impenitence which is a species of the sin against the Holy Ghost. Therefore the sin against the Holy Ghost presupposes other sins.

*On the contrary,* "It is easy in the eyes of God on a sudden to make a poor man rich" (Ecclus. 11:23). Therefore, conversely, it is possible for a man, according to the malice of the devil who tempts him, to be led to commit the most grievous of sins which is that against the Holy Ghost.

*I answer that,* As stated above (A. 1), in one way, to sin against the Holy Ghost is to sin through certain malice. Now one may sin through certain malice in two ways, as stated in the same place: first, through the inclination of a habit; but this is not, properly speaking, to sin against the Holy Ghost, nor does a man come to commit this sin all at once, in as much as sinful acts must precede so as to cause the habit that induces to sin. Secondly, one may sin through certain malice, by contemptuously rejecting the things whereby a man is withdrawn from sin. This is, properly speaking, to sin against the Holy Ghost, as stated above (A. 1); and this also, for the most part, presupposes other sins, for it is written (Prov. 18:3) that "the wicked man, when he is come into the depth of sins, contemneth."

Nevertheless it is possible for a man, in his first sinful act, to sin against the Holy Ghost by contempt, both on account of his free-will, and on account of the many previous dispositions, or again, through being vehemently moved to evil, while but feebly attached to good. Hence never or scarcely ever does it happen that the perfect sin all at once against the Holy Ghost: wherefore Origen says (Peri Archon. i, 3): "I do not think that anyone who stands on the highest step of perfection, can fail or fall suddenly; this can only happen by degrees and bit by bit."

The same applies, if the sin against the Holy Ghost be taken literally for blasphemy against the Holy Ghost. For such blasphemy as Our Lord speaks of, always proceeds from contemptuous malice.

If, however, with Augustine (De Verb. Dom., Serm. lxxi) we understand the sin against the Holy Ghost to denote final impenitence, it does not regard the question in point, because this sin against the Holy Ghost requires persistence in sin until the end of life.

Reply Obj. 1: Movement both in good and in evil is made, for the most part, from imperfect to perfect, according as man progresses in good or evil: and yet in both cases, one man can begin from a greater (good or evil) than another man does. Consequently, that from which a man begins can be perfect in good or evil according to its genus, although it may be imperfect as regards the series of good or evil actions whereby a man progresses in good or evil.

Reply Obj. 2: This argument considers the sin which is committed through certain malice, when it proceeds from the inclination of a habit.

Reply Obj. 3: If by impenitence we understand with Augustine (De Verb. Dom., Serm. lxxi) persistence in sin until the end, it is clear that it presupposes sin, just as repentance does. If, however, we take it for habitual impenitence, in which sense it is a sin against the Holy Ghost, it is evident that it can precede sin: for it is possible for a man who has never sinned to have the purpose either of repenting or of not repenting, if he should happen to sin.

## QUESTION 15

OF THE VICES OPPOSED TO KNOWLEDGE AND UNDERSTANDING (In Three Articles)

We must now consider the vices opposed to knowledge and understanding. Since, however, we have treated of ignorance which is opposed to knowledge, when we were discussing the causes of sins (I-II, Q. 76), we must now inquire about blindness of mind and dulness of sense, which are opposed to the gift of understanding; and under this head there are three points of inquiry:

(1) Whether blindness of mind is a sin?

(2) Whether dulness of sense is a sin distinct from blindness of mind?

(3) Whether these vices arise from sins of the flesh?

FIRST ARTICLE [II-II, Q. 15, Art. 1]

Whether Blindness of Mind Is a Sin?

Objection 1: It would seem that blindness of mind is not a sin. Because, seemingly, that which excuses from sin is not itself a sin. Now blindness of mind excuses from sin; for it is written (John 9:41): "If you were blind, you should not have sin." Therefore blindness of mind is not a sin.

Obj. 2: Further, punishment differs from guilt. But blindness of mind is a punishment as appears from Isa. 6:10, "Blind the heart of this people," for, since it is an evil, it could not be from God, were it not a punishment. Therefore blindness of mind is not a sin.

Obj. 3: Further, every sin is voluntary, according to Augustine (De Vera Relig. xiv). Now blindness of mind is not voluntary, since, as Augustine says (Confess. x), "all love to know the resplendent truth," and as we read in Eccles. 11:7, "the light is sweet and it is delightful for the eyes to see the sun." Therefore blindness of mind is not a sin.

*On the contrary,* Gregory (Moral. xxxi, 45) reckons blindness of mind among the vices arising from lust.

*I answer that,* Just as bodily blindness is the privation of the principle of bodily sight, so blindness of mind is the privation of the principle of mental or intellectual sight. Now this has a threefold principle. One is the light of natural reason, which light, since it pertains to the species of the rational soul, is never forfeit from the soul, and yet, at times, it is prevented from exercising its proper act, through being hindered by the lower powers which the human intellect needs in order to understand, for instance in the case of imbeciles and madmen, as stated in the First Part (Q. 84, AA. 7, 8).

Another principle of intellectual sight is a certain habitual light superadded to the natural light of reason, which light is sometimes forfeit from the soul. This privation is blindness, and is a punishment, in so far as the privation of the light of grace is a punishment. Hence it is written concerning some (Wis. 2:21): "Their own malice blinded them."

A third principle of intellectual sight is an intelligible principle, through which a man understands other things; to which principle a man may attend or not attend. That he does not attend thereto happens in two ways. Sometimes it is due to the fact that a man's will is deliberately turned away from the consideration of that principle, according to Ps. 35:4, "He would not understand, that he might do well": whereas sometimes it is due to the mind being more busy about things which it loves more, so as to be hindered thereby from considering this principle, according to Ps. 57:9, "Fire," i.e. of concupiscence, "hath fallen on them and they shall not see the sun." In either of these ways blindness of mind is a sin.

Reply Obj. 1: The blindness that excuses from sin is that which arises from the natural defect of one who cannot see.

Reply Obj. 2: This argument considers the second kind of blindness which is a punishment.

Reply Obj. 3: To understand the truth is, in itself, beloved by all; and yet, accidentally it may be hateful to someone, in so far as a man is hindered thereby from having what he loves yet more.

SECOND ARTICLE [II-II, Q. 15, Art. 2]

Whether Dulness of Sense Is a Sin Distinct from Blindness of Mind?

Objection 1: It seems that dulness of sense is not a distinct sin from blindness of mind. Because one thing has one contrary. Now dulness is opposed to the gift of understanding, according to Gregory (Moral. ii, 49); and so is blindness of mind, since understanding denotes a principle of sight. Therefore dulness of sense is the same as blindness of mind.

Obj. 2: Further, Gregory (Moral. xxxi, 45) in speaking of dulness describes it as "dulness of sense in respect of understanding." Now dulness of sense in respect of understanding seems to be the same as a defect in understanding, which pertains to blindness of mind. Therefore dulness of sense is the same as blindness of mind.

Obj. 3: Further, if they differ at all, it seems to be chiefly in the fact that blindness of mind is voluntary, as stated above (A. 1), while dulness of sense is a natural defect. But a natural defect is not a sin: so that, accordingly, dulness of sense would not be a sin, which is contrary to what Gregory says (Moral. xxxi, 45), where he reckons it among the sins arising from gluttony.

*On the contrary,* Different causes produce different effects. Now Gregory says (Moral. xxxi, 45) that dulness of sense arises from gluttony, and that blindness of mind arises from lust. Now these others are different vices. Therefore those are different vices also.

*I answer that,* Dull is opposed to sharp: and a thing is said to be sharp because it can pierce; so that a thing is called dull through being obtuse and unable to pierce. Now a bodily sense, by a kind of metaphor, is said to pierce the medium, in so far as it perceives its object from a distance or is able by penetration as it were to perceive the smallest details or the inmost parts of a thing. Hence in corporeal things the senses are said to be acute when they can perceive a sensible object from afar, by sight, hearing, or scent, while on the other hand they are said to be dull, through being unable to perceive, except sensible objects that are near at hand, or of great power.

Now, by way of similitude to bodily sense, we speak of sense in connection with the intellect; and this latter sense is in respect of certain primals and extremes, as stated in *Ethic.* vi, even as the senses are cognizant of sensible objects as of certain principles of knowledge. Now this sense which is connected with understanding, does not perceive its object through a medium of corporeal distance, but through certain other media, as, for instance, when it perceives a thing's essence through a property thereof, and the cause through its effect. Consequently a man is said to have an acute sense in connection with his understanding, if, as soon as he apprehends a property or effect of a thing, he understands the nature or the thing itself, and if he can succeed in perceiving its slightest details: whereas a man is said to have a dull sense in connection with his understanding, if he cannot arrive at knowing the truth about a thing, without many explanations; in which case, moreover, he is unable to obtain a perfect perception of everything pertaining to the nature of that thing.

Accordingly dulness of sense in connection with understanding denotes a certain weakness of the mind as to the consideration of spiritual goods; while blindness of mind implies the complete privation of the knowledge of such things. Both are opposed to the gift of understanding, whereby a man knows spiritual goods by apprehending them, and has a subtle penetration of their inmost nature. This dulness has the character of sin, just as blindness of mind has, that is, in so far as it is voluntary, as evidenced in one who, owing to his affection for carnal things, dislikes or neglects the careful consideration of spiritual things.

This suffices for the Replies to the Objections.

THIRD ARTICLE [II-II, Q. 15, Art. 3]

Whether Blindness of Mind and Dulness of Sense Arise from Sins of the Flesh?

Objection 1: It would seem that blindness of mind and dulness of sense do not arise from sins of the flesh. For Augustine (Retract. i, 4) retracts what he had said in his Soliloquies i, 1, "God Who didst wish none but the clean to know the truth," and says that one might reply that "many, even those who are unclean, know many truths." Now men become unclean chiefly by sins of the flesh. Therefore blindness of mind and dulness of sense are not caused by sins of the flesh.

Obj. 2: Further, blindness of mind and dulness of sense are defects in connection with the intellective part of the soul: whereas carnal sins pertain to the corruption of the flesh. But the flesh does not act on the soul, but rather the reverse. Therefore the sins of the flesh do not cause blindness of mind and dulness of sense.

Obj. 3: Further, all things are more passive to what is near them than to what is remote. Now spiritual vices are nearer the mind than carnal vices are. Therefore blindness of mind and dulness of sense are caused by spiritual rather than by carnal vices.

*On the contrary,* Gregory says (Moral. xxxi, 45) that dulness of sense arises from gluttony and blindness of mind from lust.

*I answer that,* The perfect intellectual operation in man consists in an abstraction from sensible phantasms, wherefore the more a man's intellect is freed from those phantasms, the more thoroughly will it be able to consider things intelligible, and to set in order all things sensible. Thus Anaxagoras stated that the intellect requires to be "detached" in order to command, and that the agent must have power over matter, in order to be able to move it. Now it is evident that pleasure fixes a man's attention on that which he takes pleasure in: wherefore the Philosopher says (Ethic. x, 4, 5) that we all do best that which we take pleasure in doing, while as to other things, we do them either not at all, or in a faint-hearted fashion.

Now carnal vices, namely gluttony and lust, are concerned with pleasures of touch in matters of food and sex; and these are the most impetuous of all pleasures of the body. For this reason these vices cause man's attention to be very firmly fixed on corporeal things, so that in consequence man's operation in regard to intelligible things is weakened, more, however, by lust than by gluttony, forasmuch as sexual pleasures are more vehement than those of the table. Wherefore lust gives rise to blindness of mind, which excludes almost entirely the knowledge of spiritual things, while dulness of sense arises from gluttony, which makes a man weak in regard to the same intelligible things. On the other hand, the contrary virtues, viz. abstinence and chastity, dispose man very much to the perfection of intellectual operation. Hence it is written (Dan. 1:17) that "to these children" on account of their abstinence and continency, "God gave knowledge and understanding in every book, and wisdom."

Reply Obj. 1: Although some who are the slaves of carnal vices are at times capable of subtle considerations about intelligible things, on account of the perfection of their natural genius, or of some habit superadded thereto, nevertheless, on account of the pleasures of the body, it must needs happen that their attention is frequently withdrawn from this subtle contemplation: wherefore the unclean can know some truths, but their uncleanness is a clog on their knowledge.

Reply Obj. 2: The flesh acts on the intellective faculties, not by altering them, but by impeding their operation in the aforesaid manner.

Reply Obj. 3: It is owing to the fact that the carnal vices are further removed from the mind, that they distract the mind's attention to more remote things, so that they hinder the mind's contemplation all the more.

# QUESTION 16

OF THE PRECEPTS OF FAITH, KNOWLEDGE AND UNDERSTANDING (In Two Articles)

We must now consider the precepts pertaining to the aforesaid, and under this head there are two points of inquiry:

(1) The precepts concerning faith;

(2) The precepts concerning the gifts of knowledge and understanding.

FIRST ARTICLE [II-II, Q. 16, Art. 1]

Whether in the Old Law There Should Have Been Given Precepts of Faith?

Objection 1: It would seem that, in the Old Law, there should have been given precepts of faith. Because a precept is about something due and necessary. Now it is most necessary for man that he should believe, according to Heb. 11:6, "Without faith it is impossible to please God." Therefore there was very great need for precepts of faith to be given.

Obj. 2: Further, the New Testament is contained in the Old, as the reality in the figure, as stated above (I-II, Q. 107, A. 3). Now the New Testament contains explicit precepts of faith, for instance John 14:1: "You believe in God; believe also in Me." Therefore it seems that some precepts of faith ought to have been given in the Old Law also.

Obj. 3: Further, to prescribe the act of a virtue comes to the same as to forbid the opposite vices. Now the Old Law contained many precepts forbidding unbelief: thus (Ex. 20:3): "Thou shalt not have strange gods before Me," and (Deut. 13:1-3) they were forbidden to hear the words of the prophet or dreamer who might wish to turn them away from their faith in God. Therefore precepts of faith should have been given in the Old Law also.

Obj. 4: Further, confession is an act of faith, as stated above (Q. 3, A. 1). Now the Old Law contained precepts about the confession and the promulgation of faith: for they were commanded (Ex. 12:27) that, when their children should ask them, they should tell them the meaning of the paschal observance, and (Deut. 13:9) they were commanded to slay anyone who disseminated doctrine contrary to faith. Therefore the Old Law should have contained precepts of faith.

Obj. 5: Further, all the books of the Old Testament are contained in the Old Law; wherefore Our Lord said (John 15:25) that it was written in the Law: "They have hated Me without cause," although this is found written in Ps. 34 and 68. Now it is written (Ecclus. 2:8): "Ye that fear the Lord, believe Him." Therefore the Old Law should have contained precepts of faith.

*On the contrary,* The Apostle (Rom. 3:27) calls the Old Law the "law of works" which he contrasts with the "law of faith." Therefore the Old Law ought not to have contained precepts of faith.

*I answer that,* A master does not impose laws on others than his subjects; wherefore the precepts of a law presuppose that everyone who receives the law is subject to the giver of the law. Now the primary subjection of man to God is by faith, according to Heb. 11:6: "He that cometh to God, must believe that He is." Hence faith is presupposed to the precepts of the Law: for which reason (Ex. 20:2) that which is of faith, is set down before the legal precepts, in the words, "I am the Lord thy God, Who brought thee out of the land of Egypt," and, likewise (Deut. 6:4), the words, "Hear, O Israel, the Lord thy [Vulg.: 'our'] God is one," precede the recording of the precepts.

Since, however, faith contains many things subordinate to the faith whereby we believe that God is, which is the first and chief of all articles of faith, as stated above (Q. 1, AA. 1, 7), it follows that, if we presuppose faith in God, whereby man's mind is subjected to Him, it is possible for precepts to be given about other articles of faith. Thus Augustine expounding the words: "This is My commandment" (John 15:12) says (Tract. lxxxiii in Joan.) that we have received many precepts of faith. In the Old Law, however, the secret things of faith were not to be set before the people, wherefore, presupposing their faith in one God, no other precepts of faith were given in the Old Law.

Reply Obj. 1: Faith is necessary as being the principle of spiritual life, wherefore it is presupposed before the receiving of the Law.

Reply Obj. 2: Even then Our Lord both presupposed something of faith, namely belief in one God, when He said: "You believe in God," and commanded something, namely, belief in the Incarnation whereby one Person is God and man. This explanation of faith belongs to the faith of the New Testament, wherefore He added: "Believe also in Me."

Reply Obj. 3: The prohibitive precepts regard sins, which corrupt virtue. Now virtue is corrupted by any particular defect, as stated above (I-II, Q. 18, A. 4, ad 3; I-II, Q. 19, A. 6, ad 1, A. 7, ad 3). Therefore faith in one God being presupposed, prohibitive precepts had to be given in the Old Law, so that men might be warned off those particular defects whereby their faith might be corrupted.

Reply Obj. 4: Confession of faith and the teaching thereof also presuppose man's submission to God by faith: so that the Old Law could contain precepts relating to the confession and teaching of faith, rather than to faith itself.

Reply Obj. 5: In this passage again that faith is presupposed whereby we believe that God is; hence it begins, "Ye that fear the Lord," which is not possible without faith. The words which follow—"believe Him"—must be referred to certain special articles of faith, chiefly to those things which God promises to them that obey Him, wherefore the passage concludes—"and your reward shall not be made void."

SECOND ARTICLE [II-II, Q. 16, Art. 2]

Whether the Precepts Referring to Knowledge and Understanding Were Fittingly Set Down in the Old Law?

Objection 1: It would seem that the precepts referring to knowledge and understanding were unfittingly set down in the Old Law. For knowledge and understanding pertain to cognition. Now cognition precedes and directs action. Therefore the precepts referring to knowledge and understanding should precede the precepts of the Law referring to action. Since, then, the first precepts of the Law are those of the decalogue, it seems that precepts of knowledge and understanding should have been given a place among the precepts of the decalogue.

Obj. 2: Further, learning precedes teaching, for a man must learn from another before he teaches another. Now the Old Law contains precepts about teaching—both affirmative precepts as, for example, (Deut. 4:9), "Thou shalt teach them to thy sons"—and prohibitive precepts, as, for instance, (Deut. 4:2), "You shall not add to the word that I speak to you, neither shall you take away from it." Therefore it seems that man ought to have been given also some precepts directing him to learn.

Obj. 3: Further, knowledge and understanding seem more necessary to a priest than to a king, wherefore it is written (Malachi 2:7): "The lips of the priest shall keep knowledge, and they shall seek the law at his mouth," and (Osee 4:6): "Because thou hast rejected knowledge, I will reject thee, that thou shalt not do the office of priesthood to Me." Now the king is commanded to learn knowledge of the Law (Deut. 17:18, 19). Much more therefore should the Law have commanded the priests to learn the Law.

Obj. 4: Further, it is not possible while asleep to meditate on things pertaining to knowledge and understanding: moreover it is hindered by extraneous occupations. Therefore it is unfittingly commanded (Deut. 6:7): "Thou shalt meditate upon them sitting in thy house, and walking on thy journey, sleeping and rising." Therefore the precepts relating to knowledge and understanding are unfittingly set down in the Law.

*On the contrary,* It is written (Deut. 4:6): "That, hearing all these precepts, they may say, Behold a wise and understanding people."

*I answer that,* Three things may be considered in relation to knowledge and understanding: first, the reception thereof; secondly, the use; and thirdly, their preservation. Now the reception of knowledge or understanding, is by means of teaching and learning, and both are prescribed in the Law. For it is written (Deut. 6:6): "These words which I command thee ... shall be in thy heart." This refers to learning, since it is the duty of a disciple to apply his mind to what is said, while the words that follow—"and thou shalt tell them to thy children"—refer to teaching.

The use of knowledge and understanding is the meditation on those things which one knows or understands. In reference to this, the text goes on: "thou shalt meditate upon them sitting in thy house," etc.

Their preservation is effected by the memory, and, as regards this, the text continues—"and thou shalt bind them as a sign on thy hand, and they shall be and shall move between thy eyes. And thou shalt write them in the entry, and on the doors of thy house." Thus the continual remembrance of God's commandments is signified, since it is impossible for us to forget those things which are continually attracting the notice of our senses, whether by touch, as those things we hold in our hands, or by sight, as those things which are ever before our eyes, or to which we are continually returning, for instance, to the house door. Moreover it is clearly stated (Deut. 4:9): "Forget not the words that thy eyes have seen and let them not go out of thy heart all the days of thy life."

We read of these things also being commanded more notably in the New Testament, both in the teaching of the Gospel and in that of the apostles.

Reply Obj. 1: According to Deut. 4:6, "this is your wisdom and understanding in the sight of the nations." By this we are given to understand that the wisdom and understanding of those who believe in God consist in the precepts of the Law. Wherefore the precepts of the Law had to be given first, and afterwards men had to be led to know and understand them, and so it was not fitting that the aforesaid precepts should be placed among the precepts of the decalogue which take the first place.

Reply Obj. 2: There are also in the Law precepts relating to learning, as stated above. Nevertheless teaching was commanded more expressly than learning, because it concerned the learned, who were not under any other authority, but were immediately under the law, and to them the precepts of the Law were given. On the other hand learning concerned the people of lower degree, and these the precepts of the Law have to reach through the learned.

Reply Obj. 3: Knowledge of the Law is so closely bound up with the priestly office that being charged with the office implies being charged to know the Law: hence there was no need for special precepts to be given about the training of the priests. On the other hand, the doctrine of God's law is not so bound up with the kingly office, because a king is placed over his people in temporal matters: hence it is especially commanded that the king should be instructed by the priests about things pertaining to the law of God.

Reply Obj. 4: That precept of the Law does not mean that man should meditate on God's law by sleeping, but during sleep, i.e. that he should meditate on the law of God when he is preparing to sleep, because this leads to his having better phantasms while asleep, in so far as our movements pass from the state of vigil to the state of sleep, as the Philosopher explains (Ethic. i, 13). In like manner we are commanded to meditate on the Law in every action of ours, not that we are bound to be always actually thinking about the Law, but that we should regulate all our actions according to it.

## QUESTION 17

OF HOPE, CONSIDERED IN ITSELF (In Eight Articles)

After treating of faith, we must consider hope and (1) hope itself; (2) the gift of fear; (3) the contrary vices; (4) the corresponding precepts. The first of these points gives rise to a twofold consideration: (1) hope, considered in itself; (2) its subject.

Under the first head there are eight points of inquiry:

(1) Whether hope is a virtue?

(2) Whether its object is eternal happiness?

(3) Whether, by the virtue of hope, one man may hope for another's happiness?

(4) Whether a man may lawfully hope in man?

(5) Whether hope is a theological virtue?

(6) Of its distinction from the other theological virtues?

(7) Of its relation to faith;

(8) Of its relation to charity.

FIRST ARTICLE [II-II, Q. 17, Art. 1]

Whether Hope Is a Virtue?

Objection 1: It would seem that hope is not a virtue. For "no man makes ill use of a virtue," as Augustine states (De Lib. Arb. ii, 18). But one may make ill use of hope, since the passion of hope, like the other passions, is subject to a mean and extremes. Therefore hope is not a virtue.

Obj. 2: Further, no virtue results from merits, since "God works virtue in us without us," as Augustine states (De Grat. et Lib. Arb. xvii). But hope is caused by grace and merits, according to the Master (Sent. iii, D, 26). Therefore hope is not a virtue.

Obj. 3: Further, "virtue is the disposition of a perfect thing" (Phys. vii, text. 17, 18). But hope is the disposition of an imperfect thing, of one, namely, that lacks what it hopes to have. Therefore hope is not a virtue.

*On the contrary,* Gregory says (Moral. i, 33) that the three daughters of Job signify these three virtues, faith, hope and charity. Therefore hope is a virtue.

*I answer that,* According to the Philosopher (Ethic. ii, 6) "the virtue of a thing is that which makes its subject good, and its work good likewise." Consequently wherever we find a good human act, it must correspond to some human virtue. Now in all things measured and ruled, the good is that which attains its proper rule: thus we say that a coat is good if it neither exceeds nor falls short of its proper measurement. But, as we stated above (Q. 8, A. 3, ad 3) human acts have a twofold measure; one is proximate and homogeneous, viz. the reason, while the other is remote and excelling, viz. God: wherefore every human act is good, which attains reason or God Himself. Now the act of hope, whereof we speak now, attains God. For, as we have already stated (I-II, Q. 40, A. 1), when we were treating of the passion of hope, the object of hope is a future good, difficult but possible to obtain. Now a thing is possible to us in two ways: first, by ourselves; secondly, by means of others, as stated in *Ethic.* iii. Wherefore, in so far as we hope for anything as being possible to us by means of the Divine assistance, our hope attains God Himself, on Whose help it leans. It is therefore evident that hope is a virtue, since it causes a human act to be good and to attain its due rule.

Reply Obj. 1: In the passions, the mean of virtue depends on right reason being attained, wherein also consists the essence of virtue. Wherefore in hope too, the good of virtue depends on a man's attaining, by hoping, the due rule, viz. God. Consequently man cannot make ill use of hope which attains God, as neither can he make ill use of moral virtue which attains the reason, because to attain thus is to make good use of virtue. Nevertheless, the hope of which we speak now, is not a passion but a habit of the mind, as we shall show further on (A. 5; Q. 18, A. 1).

Reply Obj. 2: Hope is said to arise from merits, as regards the thing hoped for, in so far as we hope to obtain happiness by means of grace and merits; or as regards the act of living hope. The habit itself of hope, whereby we hope to obtain happiness, does not flow from our merits, but from grace alone.

Reply Obj. 3: He who hopes is indeed imperfect in relation to that which he hopes to obtain, but has not as yet; yet he is perfect, in so far as he already attains his proper rule, viz. God, on Whose help he leans.

SECOND ARTICLE [II-II, Q. 17, Art. 2]

Whether Eternal Happiness Is the Proper Object of Hope?

Objection 1: It would seem that eternal happiness is not the proper object of hope. For a man does not hope for that which surpasses every movement of the soul, since hope itself is a movement of the soul. Now eternal happiness surpasses every movement of the human soul, for the Apostle says (1 Cor. 2:9) that it hath not "entered into the heart of man." Therefore happiness is not the proper object of hope.

Obj. 2: Further, prayer is an expression of hope, for it is written (Ps. 36:5): "Commit thy way to the Lord, and trust in Him, and He will do it." Now it is lawful for man to pray God not only for eternal happiness, but also for the goods, both temporal and spiritual, of the present life, and, as evidenced by the Lord's Prayer, to be delivered from evils which will no longer be in eternal happiness. Therefore eternal happiness is not the proper object of hope.

Obj. 3: Further, the object of hope is something difficult. Now many things besides eternal happiness are difficult to man. Therefore eternal happiness is not the proper object of hope.

*On the contrary,* The Apostle says (Heb. 6:19) that we have hope "which entereth in," i.e. maketh us to enter ... "within the veil," i.e. into the happiness of heaven, according to the interpretation of a gloss on these words. Therefore the object of hope is eternal happiness.

*I answer that,* As stated above (A. 1), the hope of which we speak now, attains God by leaning on His help in order to obtain the hoped for good. Now an effect must be proportionate to its cause. Wherefore the good which we ought to hope for from God properly and chiefly is the infinite good, which is proportionate to the power of our divine helper, since it belongs to an infinite power to lead anyone to an infinite good. Such a good is eternal life, which consists in the enjoyment of God Himself. For we should hope from Him for nothing less than Himself, since His goodness, whereby He imparts good things to His creature, is no less than His Essence. Therefore the proper and principal object of hope is eternal happiness.

Reply Obj. 1: Eternal happiness does not enter into the heart of man perfectly, i.e. so that it be possible for a wayfarer to know its nature and quality; yet, under the general notion of the perfect good, it is possible for it to be apprehended by a man, and it is in this way that the movement of hope towards it arises. Hence the Apostle says pointedly (Heb. 6:19) that hope "enters in, even within the veil," because that which we hope for is as yet veiled, so to speak.

Reply Obj. 2: We ought not to pray God for any other goods, except in reference to eternal happiness. Hence hope regards eternal happiness chiefly, and other things, for which we pray God, it regards secondarily and as referred to eternal happiness: just as faith regards God principally, and, secondarily, those things which are referred to God, as stated above (Q. 1, A. 1).

Reply Obj. 3: To him that longs for something great, all lesser things seem small; wherefore to him that hopes for eternal happiness, nothing else appears arduous, as compared with that hope; although, as compared with the capability of the man who hopes, other things besides may be arduous to him, so that he may have hope for such things in reference to its principal object.

THIRD ARTICLE [II-II, Q. 17, Art. 3]

Whether One Man May Hope for Another's Eternal Happiness?

Objection 1: It would seem that one may hope for another's eternal happiness. For the Apostle says (Phil. 1:6): "Being confident of this very thing, that He Who hath begun a good work in you, will perfect it unto the day of Jesus Christ." Now the perfection of that day will be eternal happiness. Therefore one man may hope for another's eternal happiness.

Obj. 2: Further, whatever we ask of God, we hope to obtain from Him. But we ask God to bring others to eternal happiness, according to James 5:16: "Pray for one another that you may be saved." Therefore we can hope for another's eternal happiness.

Obj. 3: Further, hope and despair are about the same object. Now it is possible to despair of another's eternal happiness, else Augustine would have no reason for saying (De Verb. Dom., Serm. lxxi) that we should not despair of anyone so long as he lives. Therefore one can also hope for another's eternal salvation.

*On the contrary,* Augustine says (Enchiridion viii) that "hope is only of such things as belong to him who is supposed to hope for them."

*I answer that,* We can hope for something in two ways: first, absolutely, and thus the object of hope is always something arduous and pertaining to the person who hopes. Secondly, we can hope for something, through something else being presupposed, and in this way its object can be something pertaining to someone else. In order to explain this we must observe that love and hope differ in this, that love denotes union between lover and beloved, while hope denotes a movement or a stretching forth of the appetite towards an arduous good. Now union is of things that are distinct, wherefore love can directly regard the other whom a man unites to himself by love, looking upon him as his other self: whereas movement is always towards its own term which is proportionate to the subject moved. Therefore hope regards directly one's own good, and not that which pertains to another. Yet if we presuppose the union of love with another, a man can hope for and desire something for another man, as for himself; and, accordingly, he can hope for another's eternal life, inasmuch as he is united to him by love, and just as it is the same virtue of charity whereby a man loves God, himself, and his neighbor, so too it is the same virtue of hope, whereby a man hopes for himself and for another.

This suffices for the Replies to the Objections.

FOURTH ARTICLE [II-II, Q. 17, Art. 4]

Whether a Man Can Lawfully Hope in Man?

Objection 1: It would seem that one may lawfully hope in man. For the object of hope is eternal happiness. Now we are helped to obtain eternal happiness by the patronage of the saints, for Gregory says (Dial. i, 8) that "predestination is furthered by the saints' prayers." Therefore one may hope in man.

Obj. 2: Further, if a man may not hope in another man, it ought not to be reckoned a sin in a man, that one should not be able to hope in him. Yet this is reckoned a vice in some, as appears from Jer. 9:4: "Let every man take heed of his neighbor, and let him not trust in any brother of his." Therefore it is lawful to trust in a man.

Obj. 3: Further, prayer is the expression of hope, as stated above (A. 2, Obj. 2). But it is lawful to pray to a man for something. Therefore it is lawful to trust in him.

*On the contrary,* It is written (Jer. 17:5): "Cursed be the man that trusteth in man."

*I answer that,* Hope, as stated above (A. 1; I-II, Q. 40, A. 7), regards two things, viz. the good which it intends to obtain, and the help by which that good is obtained. Now the good which a man hopes to obtain, has the aspect of a final cause, while the help by which one hopes to obtain that good, has the character of an efficient cause. Now in each of these kinds of cause we find a principal and a secondary cause. For the principal end is the last end, while the secondary end is that which is referred to an end. In like manner the principal efficient cause is the first agent, while the secondary efficient cause is the secondary and instrumental agent. Now hope regards eternal happiness as its last end, and the Divine assistance as the first cause leading to happiness.

Accordingly, just as it is not lawful to hope for any good save happiness, as one's last end, but only as something referred to final happiness, so too, it is unlawful to hope in any man, or any creature, as though it were the first cause of movement towards happiness. It is, however, lawful to hope in a man or a creature as being the secondary and instrumental agent through whom one is helped to obtain any goods that are ordained to happiness. It is in this way that we turn to the saints, and that we ask men also for certain things; and for this reason some are blamed in that they cannot be trusted to give help.

This suffices for the Replies to the Objections.

FIFTH ARTICLE [II-II, Q. 17, Art. 5]

Whether Hope Is a Theological Virtue?

Objection 1: It would seem that hope is not a theological virtue. For a theological virtue is one that has God for its object. Now hope has for its object not only God but also other goods which we hope to obtain from God. Therefore hope is not a theological virtue.

Obj. 2: Further, a theological virtue is not a mean between two vices, as stated above (I-II, Q. 64, A. 4). But hope is a mean between presumption and despair. Therefore hope is not a theological virtue.

Obj. 3: Further, expectation belongs to longanimity which is a species of fortitude. Since, then, hope is a kind of expectation, it seems that hope is not a theological, but a moral virtue.

Obj. 4: Further, the object of hope is something arduous. But it belongs to magnanimity, which is a moral virtue, to tend to the arduous. Therefore hope is a moral, and not a theological virtue.

*On the contrary,* Hope is enumerated (1 Cor. 13) together with faith and charity, which are theological virtues.

*I answer that,* Since specific differences, by their very nature, divide a genus, in order to decide under what division we must place hope, we must observe whence it derives its character of virtue.

Now it has been stated above (A. 1) that hope has the character of virtue from the fact that it attains the supreme rule of human actions: and this it attains both as its first efficient cause, in as much as it leans on its assistance, and as its last final cause, in as much as it expects happiness in the enjoyment thereof. Hence it is evident that God is the principal object of hope, considered as a virtue. Since, then, the very idea of a theological virtue is one that has God for its object, as stated above (I-II, Q. 62, A. 1), it is evident that hope is a theological virtue.

Reply Obj. 1: Whatever else hope expects to obtain, it hopes for it in reference to God as the last end, or as the first efficient cause, as stated above (A. 4).

Reply Obj. 2: In things measured and ruled the mean consists in the measure or rule being attained; if we go beyond the rule, there is excess, if we fall short of the rule, there is deficiency. But in the rule or measure itself there is no such thing as a mean or extremes. Now a moral virtue is concerned with things ruled by reason, and these things are its proper object; wherefore it is proper to it to follow the mean as regards its proper object. On the other hand, a theological virtue is concerned with the First Rule not ruled by another rule, and that Rule is its proper object. Wherefore it is not proper for a theological virtue, with regard to its proper object, to follow the mean, although this may happen to it accidentally with regard to something that is referred to its principal object. Thus faith can have no mean or extremes in the point of trusting to the First Truth, in which it is impossible to trust too much; whereas on the part of the things believed, it may have a mean and extremes; for instance one truth is a mean between two falsehoods. So too, hope has no mean or extremes, as regards its principal object, since it is impossible to trust too much in the Divine assistance; yet it may have a mean and extremes, as regards those things a man trusts to obtain, in so far as he either presumes above his capability, or despairs of things of which he is capable.

Reply Obj. 3: The expectation which is mentioned in the definition of hope does not imply delay, as does the expectation which belongs to longanimity. It implies a reference to the Divine assistance, whether that which we hope for be delayed or not.

Reply Obj. 4: Magnanimity tends to something arduous in the hope of obtaining something that is within one's power, wherefore its proper object is the doing of great things. On the other hand hope, as a theological virtue, regards something arduous, to be obtained by another's help, as stated above (A. 1).

SIXTH ARTICLE [II-II, Q. 17, Art. 6]

Whether Hope Is Distinct from the Other Theological Virtues?

Objection 1: It would seem that hope is not distinct from the other theological virtues. For habits are distinguished by their objects, as stated above (I-II, Q. 54, A. 2). Now the object of hope is the same as of the other theological virtues. Therefore hope is not distinct from the other theological virtues.

Obj. 2: Further, in the symbol of faith, whereby we make profession of faith, we say: "I expect the resurrection of the dead and the life of the world to come." Now expectation of future happiness belongs to hope, as stated above (A. 5). Therefore hope is not distinct from faith.

Obj. 3: Further, by hope man tends to God. But this belongs properly to charity. Therefore hope is not distinct from charity.

*On the contrary,* There cannot be number without distinction. Now hope is numbered with the other theological virtues: for Gregory says (Moral. i, 16) that the three virtues are faith, hope, and charity. Therefore hope is distinct from the theological virtues.

*I answer that,* A virtue is said to be theological from having God for the object to which it adheres. Now one may adhere to a thing in two ways: first, for its own sake; secondly, because something else is attained thereby. Accordingly charity makes us adhere to God for His own sake, uniting our minds to God by the emotion of love.

On the other hand, hope and faith make man adhere to God as to a principle wherefrom certain things accrue to us. Now we derive from God both knowledge of truth and the attainment of perfect goodness. Accordingly faith makes us adhere to God, as the source whence we derive the knowledge of truth, since we believe that what God tells us is true: while hope makes us adhere to God, as the source whence we derive perfect goodness, i.e. in so far as, by hope, we trust to the Divine assistance for obtaining happiness.

Reply Obj. 1: God is the object of these virtues under different aspects, as stated above: and a different aspect of the object suffices for the distinction of habits, as stated above (I-II, Q. 54, A. 2).

Reply Obj. 2: Expectation is mentioned in the symbol of faith, not as though it were the proper act of faith, but because the act of hope presupposes the act of faith, as we shall state further on (A. 7). Hence an act of faith is expressed in the act of hope.

Reply Obj. 3: Hope makes us tend to God, as to a good to be obtained finally, and as to a helper strong to assist: whereas charity, properly speaking, makes us tend to God, by uniting our affections to Him, so that we live, not for ourselves, but for God.

SEVENTH ARTICLE [II-II, Q. 17, Art. 7]

Whether Hope Precedes Faith?

Objection 1: It would seem that hope precedes faith. Because a gloss on Ps. 36:3, "Trust in the Lord, and do good," says: "Hope is the entrance to faith and the beginning of salvation." But salvation is by faith whereby we are justified. Therefore hope precedes faith.

Obj. 2: Further, that which is included in a definition should precede the thing defined and be more known. But hope is included in the definition of faith (Heb. 11:1): "Faith is the substance of things to be hoped for." Therefore hope precedes faith.

Obj. 3: Further, hope precedes a meritorious act, for the Apostle says (1 Cor. 9:10): "He that plougheth should plough in hope ... to receive fruit." But the act of faith is meritorious. Therefore hope precedes faith.

*On the contrary,* It is written (Matt. 1:2): "Abraham begot Isaac," i.e. "Faith begot hope," according to a gloss.

*I answer that,* Absolutely speaking, faith precedes hope. For the object of hope is a future good, arduous but possible to obtain. In order, therefore, that we may hope, it is necessary for the object of hope to be proposed to us as possible. Now the object of hope is, in one way, eternal happiness, and in another way, the Divine assistance, as explained above (A. 2; A. 6, ad 3): and both of these are proposed to us by faith, whereby we come to know that we are able to obtain eternal life, and that for this purpose the Divine assistance is ready for us, according to Heb. 11:6: "He that cometh to God, must believe that He is, and is a rewarder to them that seek Him." Therefore it is evident that faith precedes hope.

Reply Obj. 1: As the same gloss observes further on, "hope" is called "the entrance" to faith, i.e. of the thing believed, because by hope we enter in to see what we believe. Or we may reply that it is called the "entrance to faith," because thereby man begins to be established and perfected in faith.

Reply Obj. 2: The thing to be hoped for is included in the definition of faith, because the proper object of faith, is something not apparent in itself. Hence it was necessary to express it in a circumlocution by something resulting from faith.

Reply Obj. 3: Hope does not precede every meritorious act; but it suffices for it to accompany or follow it.

EIGHTH ARTICLE [II-II, Q. 17, Art. 8]

Whether Charity Precedes Hope?

Objection 1: It would seem that charity precedes hope. For Ambrose says on Luke 27:6, "If you had faith like to a grain of mustard seed," etc.: "Charity flows from faith, and hope from charity." But faith precedes charity. Therefore charity precedes hope.

Obj. 2: Further, Augustine says (De Civ. Dei xiv, 9) that "good emotions and affections proceed from love and holy charity." Now to hope, considered as an act of hope, is a good emotion of the soul. Therefore it flows from charity.

Obj. 3: Further, the Master says (Sent. iii, D, 26) that hope proceeds from merits, which precede not only the thing hoped for, but also hope itself, which, in the order of nature, is preceded by charity. Therefore charity precedes hope.

*On the contrary,* The Apostle says (1 Tim. 1:5): "The end of the commandment is charity from a pure heart, and a good conscience," i.e. "from hope," according to a gloss. Therefore hope precedes charity.

*I answer that,* Order is twofold. One is the order of generation and of matter, in respect of which the imperfect precedes the perfect: the other is the order of perfection and form, in respect of which the perfect naturally precedes the imperfect. In respect of the first order hope precedes charity: and this is clear from the fact that hope and all movements of the appetite flow from love, as stated above (I-II, Q. 27, A. 4; I-II, Q. 28, A. 6, ad 2; I-II, Q. 40, A. 7) in the treatise on the passions.

Now there is a perfect, and an imperfect love. Perfect love is that whereby a man is loved in himself, as when someone wishes a person some good for his own sake; thus a man loves his friend. Imperfect love is that whereby a man love something, not for its own sake, but that he may obtain that good for himself; thus a man loves what he desires. The first love of God pertains to charity, which adheres to God for His own sake; while hope pertains to the second love, since he that hopes, intends to obtain possession of something for himself.

Hence in the order of generation, hope precedes charity. For just as a man is led to love God, through fear of being punished by Him for his sins, as Augustine states (In primam canon. Joan. Tract. ix), so too, hope leads to charity, in as much as a man through hoping to be rewarded by God, is encouraged to love God and obey His commandments. On the other hand, in the order of perfection charity naturally precedes hope, wherefore, with the advent of charity, hope is made more perfect, because we hope chiefly in our friends. It is in this sense that Ambrose states (Obj. 1) that charity flows from hope: so that this suffices for the Reply to the First Objection.

Reply Obj. 2: Hope and every movement of the appetite proceed from some kind of love, whereby the expected good is loved. But not every kind of hope proceeds from charity, but only the movement of living hope, viz. that whereby man hopes to obtain good from God, as from a friend.

Reply Obj. 3: The Master is speaking of living hope, which is naturally preceded by charity and the merits caused by charity.

# QUESTION 18

OF THE SUBJECT OF HOPE (In Four Articles)

We must now consider the subject of hope, under which head there are four points of inquiry:

(1) Whether the virtue of hope is in the will as its subject?

(2) Whether it is in the blessed?

(3) Whether it is in the damned?

(4) Whether there is certainty in the hope of the wayfarer?

FIRST ARTICLE [II-II, Q. 18, Art. 1]

Whether Hope Is in the Will As Its Subject?

Objection 1: It would seem that hope is not in the will as its subject. For the object of hope is an arduous good, as stated above (Q. 17, A. 1; I-II, Q. 40, A. 1). Now the arduous is the object, not of the will, but of the irascible. Therefore hope is not in the will but in the irascible.

Obj. 2: Further, where one suffices it is superfluous to add another. Now charity suffices for the perfecting of the will, which is the most perfect of the virtues. Therefore hope is not in the will.

Obj. 3: Further, the one same power cannot exercise two acts at the same time; thus the intellect cannot understand many things simultaneously. Now the act of hope can be at the same time as an act of charity. Since, then, the act of charity evidently belongs to the will, it follows that the act of hope does not belong to that power: so that, therefore, hope is not in the will.

*On the contrary,* The soul is not apprehensive of God save as regards the mind in which is memory, intellect and will, as Augustine declares (De Trin. xiv, 3, 6). Now hope is a theological virtue having God for its object. Since therefore it is neither in the memory, nor in the intellect, which belong to the cognitive faculty, it follows that it is in the will as its subject.

*I answer that,* As shown above (I, Q. 87, A. 2), habits are known by their acts. Now the act of hope is a movement of the appetitive faculty, since its object is a good. And, since there is a twofold appetite in man, namely, the sensitive which is divided into irascible and concupiscible, and the intellective appetite, called the will, as stated in the First Part (Q. 82, A. 5), those movements which occur in the lower appetite, are with passion, while those in the higher appetite are without passion, as shown above (I, Q. 87, A. 2, ad 1; I-II, Q. 22, A. 3, ad 3). Now the act of the virtue of hope cannot belong to the sensitive appetite, since the good which is the principal object of this virtue, is not a sensible but a Divine good. Therefore hope resides in the higher appetite called the will, and not in the lower appetite, of which the irascible is a part.

Reply Obj. 1: The object of the irascible is an arduous sensible: whereas the object of the virtue of hope is an arduous intelligible, or rather superintelligible.

Reply Obj. 2: Charity perfects the will sufficiently with regard to one act, which is the act of loving: but another virtue is required in order to perfect it with regard to its other act, which is that of hoping.

Reply Obj. 3: The movement of hope and the movement of charity are mutually related, as was shown above (Q. 17, A. 8). Hence there is no reason why both movements should not belong at the same time to the same power: even as the intellect can understand many things at the same time if they be related to one another, as stated in the First Part (Q. 85, A. 4).

SECOND ARTICLE [II-II, Q. 18, Art. 2]

Whether in the Blessed There Is Hope?

Objection 1: It would seem that in the blessed there is hope. For Christ was a perfect comprehensor from the first moment of His conception. Now He had hope, since, according to a gloss, the words of Ps. 30:2, "In Thee, O Lord, have I hoped," are said in His person. Therefore in the blessed there can be hope.

Obj. 2: Further, even as the obtaining of happiness is an arduous good, so is its continuation. Now, before they obtain happiness, men hope to obtain it. Therefore, after they have obtained it, they can hope to continue in its possession.

Obj. 3: Further, by the virtue of hope, a man can hope for happiness, not only for himself, but also for others, as stated above (Q. 17, A. 3). But the blessed who are in heaven hope for the happiness of others, else they would not pray for them. Therefore there can be hope in them.

Obj. 4: Further, the happiness of the saints implies not only glory of the soul but also glory of the body. Now the souls of the saints in heaven, look yet for the glory of their bodies (Apoc. 6:10; Augustine, Gen. ad lit. xii, 35). Therefore in the blessed there can be hope.

*On the contrary,* The Apostle says (Rom. 8:24): "What a man seeth, why doth he hope for?" Now the blessed enjoy the sight of God. Therefore hope has no place in them.

*I answer that,* If what gives a thing its species be removed, the species is destroyed, and that thing cannot remain the same; just as when a natural body loses its form, it does not remain the same specifically. Now hope takes its species from its principal object, even as the other virtues do, as was shown above (Q. 17, AA. 5, 6; I-II, Q. 54, A. 2): and its principal object is eternal happiness as being possible to obtain by the assistance of God, as stated above (Q. 17, A. 2).

Since then the arduous possible good cannot be an object of hope except in so far as it is something future, it follows that when happiness is no longer future, but present, it is incompatible with the virtue of hope. Consequently hope, like faith, is voided in heaven, and neither of them can be in the blessed.

Reply Obj. 1: Although Christ was a comprehensor and therefore blessed as to the enjoyment of God, nevertheless He was, at the same time, a wayfarer, as regards the passibility of nature, to which He was still subject. Hence it was possible for Him to hope for the glory of impassibility and immortality, yet not so as to have the virtue of hope, the principal object of which is not the glory of the body but the enjoyment of God.

Reply Obj. 2: The happiness of the saints is called eternal life, because through enjoying God they become partakers, as it were, of God's eternity which surpasses all time: so that the continuation of happiness does not differ in respect of present, past and future. Hence the blessed do not hope for the continuation of their happiness (for as regards this there is no future), but are in actual possession thereof.

Reply Obj. 3: So long as the virtue of hope lasts, it is by the same hope that one hopes for one's own happiness, and for that of others. But when hope is voided in the blessed, whereby they hoped for their own happiness, they hope for the happiness of others indeed, yet not by the virtue of hope, but rather by the love of charity. Even so, he that has Divine charity, by that same charity loves his neighbor, without having the virtue of charity, but by some other love.

Reply Obj. 4: Since hope is a theological virtue having God for its object, its principal object is the glory of the soul, which consists in the enjoyment of God, and not the glory of the body. Moreover, although the glory of the body is something arduous in comparison with human nature, yet it is not so for one who has the glory of the soul; both because the glory of the body is a very small thing as compared with the glory of the soul, and because one who has the glory of the soul has already the sufficient cause of the glory of the body.

THIRD ARTICLE [II-II, Q. 18, Art. 3]

Whether Hope Is in the Damned?

Objection 1: It would seem that there is hope in the damned. For the devil is damned and prince of the damned, according to Matt. 25:41: "Depart ... you cursed, into everlasting fire, which was prepared for the devil and his angels." But the devil has hope, according to Job 40:28, "Behold his hope shall fail him." Therefore it seems that the damned have hope.

Obj. 2: Further, just as faith is either living or dead, so is hope. But lifeless faith can be in the devils and the damned, according to James 2:19: "The devils ... believe and tremble." Therefore it seems that lifeless hope also can be in the damned.

Obj. 3: Further, after death there accrues to man no merit or demerit that he had not before, according to Eccles. 11:3, "If the tree fall to the south, or to the north, in what place soever it shall fall, there shall it be." Now many who are damned, in this life hoped and never despaired. Therefore they will hope in the future life also.

*On the contrary,* Hope causes joy, according to Rom. 12:12, "Rejoicing in hope." Now the damned have no joy, but sorrow and grief, according to Isa. 65:14, "My servants shall praise for joyfulness of heart, and you shall cry for sorrow of heart, and shall howl for grief of spirit." Therefore no hope is in the damned.

*I answer that,* Just as it is a condition of happiness that the will should find rest therein, so is it a condition of punishment, that what is inflicted in punishment, should go against the will. Now that which is not known can neither be restful nor repugnant to the will: wherefore Augustine says (Gen. ad lit. xi, 17) that the angels could not be perfectly happy in their first state before their confirmation, or unhappy before their fall, since they had no foreknowledge of what would happen to them. For perfect and true happiness requires that one should be certain of being happy for ever, else the will would not rest.

In like manner, since the everlastingness of damnation is a necessary condition of the punishment of the damned, it would not be truly penal unless it went against the will; and this would be impossible if they were ignorant of the everlastingness of their damnation. Hence it belongs to the unhappy state of the damned, that they should know that they cannot by any means escape from damnation and obtain happiness. Wherefore it is written (Job 15:22): "He believeth not that he may return from darkness to light." It is, therefore, evident that they cannot apprehend happiness as a possible good, as neither can the blessed apprehend it as a future good. Consequently there is no hope either in the blessed or in the damned. On the other hand, hope can be in wayfarers, whether of this life or in purgatory, because in either case they apprehend happiness as a future possible thing.

Reply Obj. 1: As Gregory says (Moral. xxxiii, 20) this is said of the devil as regards his members, whose hope will fail utterly: or, if it be understood of the devil himself, it may refer to the hope whereby he expects to vanquish the saints, in which sense we read just before (Job 40:18): "He trusteth that the Jordan may run into his mouth": this is not, however, the hope of which we are speaking.

Reply Obj. 2: As Augustine says (Enchiridion

viii), "faith is about things, bad or good, past, present, or future, one's own or another's; whereas hope is only about good things, future and concerning oneself." Hence it is possible for lifeless faith to be in the damned, but not hope, since the Divine goods are not for them future possible things, but far removed from them.

Reply Obj. 3: Lack of hope in the damned does not change their demerit, as neither does the voiding of hope in the blessed increase their merit: but both these things are due to the change in their respective states.

FOURTH ARTICLE [II-II, Q. 18, Art. 4]

Whether There Is Certainty in the Hope of a Wayfarer?

Objection 1: It would seem that there is no certainty in the hope of a wayfarer. For hope resides in the will. But certainty pertains not to the will but to the intellect. Therefore there is no certainty in hope.

Obj. 2: Further, hope is based on grace and merits, as stated above (Q. 17, A. 1). Now it is impossible in this life to know for certain that we are in a state of grace, as stated above (I-II, Q. 112, A. 5). Therefore there is no certainty in the hope of a wayfarer.

Obj. 3: Further, there can be no certainty about that which may fail. Now many a hopeful wayfarer fails to obtain happiness. Therefore wayfarer's hope has no certainty.

*On the contrary,* "Hope is the certain expectation of future happiness," as the Master states (Sent. iii, D, 26): and this may be gathered from 2 Tim. 1:12, "I know Whom I have believed, and I am certain that He is able to keep that which I have committed to Him."

*I answer that,* Certainty is found in a thing in two ways, essentially and by participation. It is found essentially in the cognitive power; by participation in whatever is moved infallibly to its end by the cognitive power. In this way we say that nature works with certainty, since it is moved by the Divine intellect which moves everything with certainty to its end. In this way too, the moral virtues are said to work with greater certainty than art, in as much as, like a second nature, they are moved to their acts by the reason: and thus too, hope tends to its end with certainty, as though sharing in the certainty of faith which is in the cognitive faculty.

This suffices for the Reply to the First Objection.

Reply Obj. 2: Hope does not trust chiefly in grace already received, but on God's omnipotence and mercy, whereby even he that has not grace, can obtain it, so as to come to eternal life. Now whoever has faith is certain of God's omnipotence and mercy.

Reply Obj. 3: That some who have hope fail to obtain happiness, is due to a fault of the free will in placing the obstacle of sin, but not to any deficiency in God's power or mercy, in which hope places its trust. Hence this does not prejudice the certainty of hope.

## QUESTION 19

OF THE GIFT OF FEAR (In Twelve Articles)

We must now consider the gift of fear, about which there are twelve points of inquiry:

(1) Whether God is to be feared?

(2) Of the division of fear into filial, initial, servile and worldly;

(3) Whether worldly fear is always evil?

(4) Whether servile fear is good?

(5) Whether it is substantially the same as filial fear?

(6) Whether servile fear departs when charity comes?

(7) Whether fear is the beginning of wisdom?

(8) Whether initial fear is substantially the same as filial fear?

(9) Whether fear is a gift of the Holy Ghost?

(10) Whether it grows when charity grows?

(11) Whether it remains in heaven?

(12) Which of the beatitudes and fruits correspond to it?

FIRST ARTICLE [II-II, Q. 19, Art. 1]

Whether God Can Be Feared?

Objection 1: It would seem that God cannot be feared. For the object of fear is a future evil, as stated above (I-II, Q. 41, AA. 2, 3). But God is free of all evil, since He is goodness itself. Therefore God cannot be feared.

Obj. 2: Further, fear is opposed to hope. Now we hope in God. Therefore we cannot fear Him at the same time.

Obj. 3: Further, as the Philosopher states (Rhet. ii, 5), "we fear those things whence evil comes to us." But evil comes to us, not from God, but from ourselves, according to Osee 13:9: "Destruction is thy own, O Israel: thy help is ... in Me." Therefore God is not to be feared.

*On the contrary,* It is written (Jer. 10:7): "Who shall not fear Thee, O King of nations?" and (Malachi 1:6): "If I be a master, where is My fear?"

*I answer that,* Just as hope has two objects, one of which is the future good itself, that one expects to obtain, while the other is someone's help, through whom one expects to obtain what one hopes for, so, too, fear may have two objects, one of which is the very evil which a man shrinks from, while the other is that from which the evil may come. Accordingly, in the first way God, Who is goodness itself, cannot be an object of fear; but He can be an object of fear in the second way, in so far as there may come to us some evil either from Him or in relation to Him.

From Him there comes the evil of punishment, but this is evil not absolutely but relatively, and, absolutely speaking, is a good. Because, since a thing is said to be good through being ordered to an end, while evil implies lack of this order, that which excludes the order to the last end is altogether evil, and such is the evil of fault. On the other hand the evil of punishment is indeed an evil, in so far as it is the privation of some particular good, yet absolutely speaking, it is a good, in so far as it is ordained to the last end.

In relation to God the evil of fault can come to us, if we be separated from Him: and in this way God can and ought to be feared.

Reply Obj. 1: This objection considers the object of fear as being the evil which a man shuns.

Reply Obj. 2: In God, we may consider both His justice, in respect of which He punishes those who sin, and His mercy, in respect of which He sets us free: in us the consideration of His justice gives rise to fear, but the consideration of His mercy gives rise to hope, so that, accordingly, God is the object of both hope and fear, but under different aspects.

Reply Obj. 3: The evil of fault is not from God as its author but from us, in for far as we forsake God: while the evil of punishment is from God as its author, in so far as it has character of a good, since it is something just, through being inflicted on us justly; although originally this is due to the demerit of sin: thus it is written (Wis. 1:13, 16): "God made not death ... but the wicked with works and words have called it to them."

SECOND ARTICLE [II-II, Q. 19, Art. 2]

Whether Fear Is Fittingly Divided into Filial, Initial, Servile and Worldly Fear?

Objection 1: It would seem that fear is unfittingly divided into filial, initial, servile and worldly fear. For Damascene says (De Fide Orth. ii, 15) that there are six kinds of fear, viz. "laziness, shamefacedness," etc. of which we have treated above (I-II, Q. 41, A. 4), and which are not mentioned in the division in question. Therefore this division of fear seems unfitting.

Obj. 2: Further, each of these fears is either good or evil. But there is a fear, viz. natural fear, which is neither morally good, since it is in the demons, according to James 2:19, "The devils ... believe and tremble," nor evil, since it is in Christ, according to Mk. 14:33, Jesus "began to fear and be heavy." Therefore the aforesaid division of fear is insufficient.

Obj. 3: Further, the relation of son to father differs from that of wife to husband, and this again from that of servant to master. Now filial fear, which is that of the son in comparison with his father, is distinct from servile fear, which is that of the servant in comparison with his master. Therefore chaste fear, which seems to be that of the wife in comparison with her husband, ought to be distinguished from all these other fears.

Obj. 4: Further, even as servile fear fears punishment, so do initial and worldly fear. Therefore no distinction should be made between them.

Obj. 5: Further, even as concupiscence is about some good, so is fear about some evil. Now "concupiscence of the eyes," which is the desire for things of this world, is distinct from "concupiscence of the flesh," which is the desire for one's own pleasure. Therefore "worldly fear," whereby one fears to lose external goods, is distinct from "human fear," whereby one fears harm to one's own person.

On the contrary stands the authority of the Master (Sent. iii, D, 34).

*I answer that,* We are speaking of fear now, in so far as it makes us turn, so to speak, to God or away from Him. For, since the object of fear is an evil, sometimes, on account of the evils he fears, man withdraws from God, and this is called human fear; while sometimes, on account of the evils he fears, he turns to God and adheres to Him. This latter evil is twofold, viz. evil of punishment, and evil of fault.

Accordingly if a man turn to God and adhere to Him, through fear of punishment, it will be servile fear; but if it be on account of fear of committing a fault, it will be filial fear, for it becomes a child to fear offending its father. If, however, it be on account of both, it will be initial fear, which is between both these fears. As to whether it is possible to fear the evil of fault, the question has been treated above (I-II, Q. 42, A. 3) when we were considering the passion of fear.

Reply Obj. 1: Damascene divides fear as a passion of the soul: whereas this division of fear is taken from its relation to God, as explained above.

Reply Obj. 2: Moral good consists chiefly in turning to God, while moral evil consists chiefly in turning away from Him: wherefore all the fears mentioned above imply either moral evil or moral good. Now natural fear is presupposed to moral good and evil, and so it is not numbered among these kinds of fear.

Reply Obj. 3: The relation of servant to master is based on the power which the master exercises over the servant; whereas, *on the contrary,* the relation of a son to his father or of a wife to her husband is based on the son's affection towards his father to whom he submits himself, or on the wife's affection towards her husband to whom she binds herself in the union of love. Hence filial and chaste fear amount to the same, because by the love of charity God becomes our Father, according to Rom. 8:15, "You have received the spirit of adoption of sons, whereby we cry: Abba (Father)"; and by this same charity He is called our spouse, according to 2 Cor. 11:2, "I have espoused you to one husband, that I may present you as a chaste virgin to Christ": whereas servile fear has no connection with these, since it does not include charity in its definition.

Reply Obj. 4: These three fears regard punishment but in different ways. For worldly or human fear regards a punishment which turns man away from God, and which God's enemies sometimes inflict or threaten: whereas servile and initial fear regard a punishment whereby men are drawn to God, and which is inflicted or threatened by God. Servile fear regards this punishment chiefly, while initial fear regards it secondarily.

Reply Obj. 5: It amounts to the same whether man turns away from God through fear of losing his worldly goods, or through fear of forfeiting the well-being of his body, since external goods belong to the body. Hence both these fears are reckoned as one here, although they fear different evils, even as they correspond to the desire of different goods. This diversity causes a specific diversity of sins, all of which alike however lead man away from God.

THIRD ARTICLE [II-II, Q. 19, Art. 3]

Whether Worldly Fear Is Always Evil?

Objection 1: It would seem that worldly fear is not always evil. Because regard for men seems to be a kind of human fear. Now some are blamed for having no regard for man, for instance, the unjust judge of whom we read (Luke 18:2) that he "feared not God, nor regarded man." Therefore it seems that worldly fear is not always evil.

Obj. 2: Further, worldly fear seems to have reference to the punishments inflicted by the secular power. Now such like punishments incite us to good actions, according to Rom. 13:3, "Wilt thou not be afraid of the power? Do that which is good, and thou shalt have praise from the same." Therefore worldly fear is not always evil.

Obj. 3: Further, it seems that what is in us naturally, is not evil, since our natural gifts are from God. Now it is natural to man to fear detriment to his body, and loss of his worldly goods, whereby the present life is supported. Therefore it seems that worldly fear is not always evil.

*On the contrary,* Our Lord said (Matt. 10:28): "Fear ye not them that kill the body," thus forbidding worldly fear. Now nothing but what is evil is forbidden by God. Therefore worldly fear is evil.

*I answer that,* As shown above (I-II, Q. 1, A. 3; I-II, Q. 18, A. 1; I-II, Q. 54, A. 2) moral acts and habits take their name and species from their objects. Now the proper object of the appetite's movement is the final good: so that, in consequence, every appetitive movement is both specified and named from its proper end. For if anyone were to describe covetousness as love of work because men work on account of covetousness, this description would be incorrect, since the covetous man seeks work not as end but as a means: the end that he seeks is wealth, wherefore covetousness is rightly described as the desire or the love of wealth, and this is evil. Accordingly worldly love is, properly speaking, the love whereby a man trusts in the world as his end, so that worldly love is always evil. Now fear is born of love, since man fears the loss of what he loves, as Augustine states (Qq. lxxxiii, qu. 33). Now worldly fear is that which arises from worldly love as from an evil root, for which reason worldly fear is always evil.

Reply Obj. 1: One may have regard for men in two ways. First in so far as there is in them something divine, for instance, the good of grace or of virtue, or at least of the natural image of God: and in this way those are blamed who have no regard for man. Secondly, one may have regard for men as being in opposition to God, and thus it is praiseworthy to have no regard for men, according as we read of Elias or Eliseus (Ecclus. 48:13): "In his days he feared not the prince."

Reply Obj. 2: When the secular power inflicts punishment in order to withdraw men from sin, it is acting as God's minister, according to Rom. 13:4, "For he is God's minister, an avenger to execute wrath upon him that doth evil." To fear the secular power in this way is part, not of worldly fear, but of servile or initial fear.

Reply Obj. 3: It is natural for man to shrink from detriment to his own body and loss of worldly goods, but to forsake justice on that account is contrary to natural reason. Hence the Philosopher says (Ethic. iii, 1) that there are certain things, viz. sinful deeds, which no fear should drive us to do, since to do such things is worse than to suffer any punishment whatever.

FOURTH ARTICLE [II-II, Q. 19, Art. 4]

Whether Servile Fear Is Good?

Objection 1: It would seem that servile fear is not good. For if the use of a thing is evil, the thing itself is evil. Now the use of servile fear is evil, for according to a gloss on Rom. 8:15, "if a man do anything through fear, although the deed be good, it is not well done." Therefore servile fear is not good.

Obj. 2: Further, no good grows from a sinful root. Now servile fear grows from a sinful root, because when commenting on Job 3:11, "Why did I not die in the womb?" Gregory says (Moral. iv, 25): "When a man dreads the punishment which confronts him for his sin and no longer loves the friendship of God which he has lost, his fear is born of pride, not of humility." Therefore servile fear is evil.

Obj. 3: Further, just as mercenary love is opposed to the love of charity, so is servile fear, apparently, opposed to chaste fear. But mercenary love is always evil. Therefore servile fear is also.

*On the contrary,* Nothing evil is from the Holy Ghost. But servile fear is from the Holy Ghost, since a gloss on Rom. 8:15, "You have not received the spirit of bondage," etc. says: "It is the one same spirit that bestows two fears, viz. servile and chaste fear." Therefore servile fear is not evil.

*I answer that,* It is owing to its servility that servile fear may be evil. For servitude is opposed to freedom. Since, then, "what is free is cause of itself" (Metaph. i, 2), a slave is one who does not act as cause of his own action, but as though moved from without. Now whoever does a thing through love, does it of himself so to speak, because it is by his own inclination that he is moved to act: so that it is contrary to the very notion of servility that one should act from love. Consequently servile fear as such is contrary to charity: so that if servility were essential to fear, servile fear would be evil simply, even as adultery is evil simply, because that which makes it contrary to charity belongs to its very species.

This servility, however, does not belong to the species of servile fear, even as neither does lifelessness to the species of lifeless faith. For the species of a moral habit or act is taken from the object. Now the object of servile fear is punishment, and it is by accident that, either the good to which the punishment is contrary, is loved as the last end, and that consequently the punishment is feared as the greatest evil, which is the case with one who is devoid of charity, or that the punishment is directed to God as its end, and that, consequently, it is not feared as the greatest evil, which is the case with one who has charity. For the species of a habit is not destroyed through its object or end being directed to a further end. Consequently servile fear is substantially good, but is servility is evil.

Reply Obj. 1: This saying of Augustine is to be applied to a man who does something through servile fear as such, so that he loves not justice, and fears nothing but the punishment.

Reply Obj. 2: Servile fear as to its substance is not born of pride, but its servility is, inasmuch as man is unwilling, by love, to subject his affections to the yoke of justice.

Reply Obj. 3: Mercenary love is that whereby God is loved for the sake of worldly goods, and this is, of itself, contrary to charity, so that mercenary love is always evil. But servile fear, as to its substance, implies merely fear of punishment, whether or not this be feared as the principal evil.

FIFTH ARTICLE [II-II, Q. 19, Art. 5]

Whether Servile Fear Is Substantially the Same As Filial Fear?

Objection 1: It would seem that servile fear is substantially the same as filial fear. For filial fear is to servile fear the same apparently as living faith is to lifeless faith, since the one is accompanied by mortal sin and the other not. Now living faith and lifeless faith are substantially the same. Therefore servile and filial fear are substantially the same.

Obj. 2: Further, habits are diversified by their objects. Now the same thing is the object of servile and of filial fear, since they both fear God. Therefore servile and filial fear are substantially the same.

Obj. 3: Further, just as man hopes to enjoy God and to obtain favors from Him, so does he fear to be separated from God and to be punished by Him. Now it is the same hope whereby we hope to enjoy God, and to receive other favors from Him, as stated above (Q. 17, A. 2, ad 2). Therefore filial fear, whereby we fear separation from God, is the same as servile fear whereby we fear His punishments.

*On the contrary,* Augustine (In prim. canon. Joan. Tract. ix) says that there are two fears, one servile, another filial or chaste fear.

*I answer that,* The proper object of fear is evil. And since acts and habits are diversified by their objects, as shown above (I-II, Q. 54, A. 2), it follows of necessity that different kinds of fear correspond to different kinds of evil.

Now the evil of punishment, from which servile fear shrinks, differs specifically from evil of fault, which filial fear shuns, as shown above (A. 2). Hence it is evident that servile and filial fear are not the same substantially but differ specifically.

Reply Obj. 1: Living and lifeless faith differ, not as regards the object, since each of them believes God and believes in a God, but in respect of something extrinsic, viz. the presence or absence of charity, and so they do not differ substantially. On the other hand, servile and filial fear differ as to their objects: and hence the comparison fails.

Reply Obj. 2: Servile fear and filial fear do not regard God in the same light. For servile fear looks upon God as the cause of the infliction of punishment, whereas filial fear looks upon Him, not as the active cause of guilt, but rather as the term wherefrom it shrinks to be separated by guilt. Consequently the identity of object, viz. God, does not prove a specific identity of fear, since also natural movements differ specifically according to their different relationships to some one term, for movement from whiteness is not specifically the same as movement towards whiteness.

Reply Obj. 3: Hope looks upon God as the principle not only of the enjoyment of God, but also of any other favor whatever. This cannot be said of fear; and so there is no comparison.

SIXTH ARTICLE [II-II, Q. 19, Art. 6]

Whether Servile Fear Remains with Charity?

Objection 1: It would seem that servile fear does not remain with charity. For Augustine says (In prim. canon. Joan. Tract. ix) that "when charity takes up its abode, it drives away fear which had prepared a place for it."

Obj. 2: Further, "The charity of God is poured forth in our hearts, by the Holy Ghost, Who is given to us" (Rom. 5:5). Now "where the Spirit of the Lord is, there is liberty" (2 Cor. 3:17). Since then freedom excludes servitude, it seems that servile fear is driven away when charity comes.

Obj. 3: Further, servile fear is caused by self-love, in so far as punishment diminishes one's own good. Now love of God drives away self-love, for it makes us despise ourselves: thus Augustine testifies (De Civ. Dei xiv, 28) that "the love of God unto the contempt of self builds up the city of God." Therefore it seems that servile fear is driven out when charity comes.

*On the contrary,* Servile fear is a gift of the Holy Ghost, as stated above (A. 4). Now the gifts of the Holy Ghost are not forfeited through the advent of charity, whereby the Holy Ghost dwells in us.

Therefore servile fear is not driven out when charity comes.

*I answer that,* Servile fear proceeds from self-love, because it is fear of punishment which is detrimental to one's own good. Hence the fear of punishment is consistent with charity, in the same way as self-love is: because it comes to the same that a man love his own good and that he fear to be deprived of it.

Now self-love may stand in a threefold relationship to charity. In one way it is contrary to charity, when a man places his end in the love of his own good. In another way it is included in charity, when a man loves himself for the sake of God and in God. In a third way, it is indeed distinct from charity, but is not contrary thereto, as when a man loves himself from the point of view of his own good, yet not so as to place his end in this his own good: even as one may have another special love for one's neighbor, besides the love of charity which is founded on God, when we love him by reason of usefulness, consanguinity, or some other human consideration, which, however, is referable to charity.

Accordingly fear of punishment is, in one way, included in charity, because separation from God is a punishment, which charity shuns exceedingly; so that this belongs to chaste fear. In another way, it is contrary to charity, when a man shrinks from the punishment that is opposed to his natural good, as being the principal evil in opposition to the good which he loves as an end; and in this way fear of punishment is not consistent with charity. In another way fear of punishment is indeed substantially distinct from chaste fear, when, to wit, a man fears a penal evil, not because it separates him from God, but because it is hurtful to his own good, and yet he does not place his end in this good, so that neither does he dread this evil as being the principal evil. Such fear of punishment is consistent with charity; but it is not called servile, except when punishment is dreaded as a principal evil, as explained above (AA. 2, 4). Hence fear considered as servile, does not remain with charity, but the substance of servile fear can remain with charity, even as self-love can remain with charity.

Reply Obj. 1: Augustine is speaking of fear considered as servile: and such is the sense of the two other objections.

SIXTH ARTICLE [II-II, Q. 19, Art. 6]

Whether Fear Is the Beginning of Wisdom?

Objection 1: It would seem that fear is not the beginning of wisdom. For the beginning of a thing is a part thereof. But fear is not a part of wisdom, since fear is seated in the appetitive faculty, while wisdom is in the intellect. Therefore it seems that fear is not the beginning of wisdom.

Obj. 2: Further, nothing is the beginning of itself. "Now fear of the Lord, that is wisdom," according to Job 28:28. Therefore it seems that fear of God is not the beginning of wisdom.

Obj. 3: Further, nothing is prior to the beginning. But something is prior to fear, since faith precedes fear. Therefore it seems that fear is not the beginning of wisdom.

*On the contrary,* It is written in the Ps. 110:10: "The fear of the Lord is the beginning of wisdom."

*I answer that,* A thing may be called the beginning of wisdom in two ways: in one way because it is the beginning of wisdom itself as to its essence; in another way, as to its effect. Thus the beginning of an art as to its essence consists in the principles from which that art proceeds, while the beginning of an art as to its effect is that wherefrom it begins to operate: for instance we might say that the beginning of the art of building is the foundation because that is where the builder begins his work.

Now, since wisdom is the knowledge of Divine things, as we shall state further on (Q. 45, A. 1), it is considered by us in one way, and in another way by philosophers. For, seeing that our life is ordained to the enjoyment of God, and is directed thereto according to a participation of the Divine Nature, conferred on us through grace, wisdom, as we look at it, is considered not only as being cognizant of God, as it is with the philosophers, but also as directing human conduct; since this is directed not only by the human law, but also by the Divine law, as Augustine shows (De Trin. xii, 14). Accordingly the beginning of wisdom as to its essence consists in the first principles of wisdom, i.e. the articles of faith, and in this sense faith is said to be the beginning of wisdom. But as regards the effect, the beginning of wisdom is the point where wisdom begins to work, and in this way fear is the beginning of wisdom, yet servile fear in one way, and filial fear, in another. For servile fear is like a principle disposing a man to wisdom from without, in so far as he refrains from sin through fear of punishment, and is thus fashioned for the effect of wisdom, according to Ecclus. 1:27, "The fear of the Lord driveth out sin." On the other hand, chaste or filial fear is the beginning of wisdom, as being the first effect of wisdom. For since the regulation of human conduct by the Divine law belongs to wisdom, in order to make a beginning, man must first of all fear God and submit himself to Him: for the result will be that in all things he will be ruled by God.

Reply Obj. 1: This argument proves that fear is not the beginning of wisdom as to the essence of wisdom.

Reply Obj. 2: The fear of God is compared to a man's whole life that is ruled by God's wisdom, as the root to the tree: hence it is written (Ecclus. 1:25): "The root of wisdom is to fear the Lord, for [Vulg.: 'and'] the branches thereof are longlived." Consequently, as the root is said to be virtually the tree, so the fear of God is said to be wisdom.

Reply Obj. 3: As stated above, faith is the beginning of wisdom in one way, and fear, in another. Hence it is written (Ecclus. 25:16): "The fear of God is the beginning of love: and the beginning of faith is to be fast joined to it."

SEVENTH ARTICLE [II-II, Q. 19, Art. 7]

Whether Initial Fear Differs Substantially from Filial Fear?

Objection 1: It would seem that initial fear differs substantially from filial fear. For filial fear is caused by love. Now initial fear is the beginning of love, according to Ecclus. 25:16, "The fear of God is the beginning of love." Therefore initial fear is distinct from filial fear.

Obj. 2: Further, initial fear dreads punishment, which is the object of servile fear, so that initial and servile fear would seem to be the same. But servile fear is distinct from filial fear. Therefore initial fear also is substantially distinct from initial fear.

Obj. 3: Further, a mean differs in the same ratio from both the extremes. Now initial fear is the mean between servile and filial fear. Therefore it differs from both filial and servile fear.

*On the contrary,* Perfect and imperfect do not diversify the substance of a thing. Now initial and filial fear differ in respect of perfection and imperfection of charity, as Augustine states (In prim. canon. Joan. Tract. ix). Therefore initial fear does not differ substantially from filial fear.

*I answer that,* Initial fear is so called because it is a beginning ( initium ). Since, however, both servile and filial fear are, in some way, the beginning of wisdom, each may be called in some way, initial.

It is not in this sense, however, that we are to understand initial fear in so far as it is distinct from servile and filial fear, but in the sense according to which it belongs to the state of beginners, in whom there is a beginning of filial fear resulting from a beginning of charity, although they do not possess the perfection of filial fear, because they have not yet attained to the perfection of charity. Consequently initial fear stands in the same relation to filial fear as imperfect to perfect charity. Now perfect and imperfect charity differ, not as to essence but as to state. Therefore we must conclude that initial fear, as we understand it here, does not differ essentially from filial fear.

Reply Obj. 1: The fear which is a beginning of love is servile fear, which is the herald of charity, just as the bristle introduces the thread, as Augustine states (Tract. ix in Ep. i Joan.). Or else, if it be referred to initial fear, this is said to be the beginning of love, not absolutely, but relatively to the state of perfect charity.

Reply Obj. 2: Initial fear does not dread punishment as its proper object, but as having something of servile fear connected with it: for this servile fear, as to its substance, remains indeed, with charity, its servility being cast aside; whereas its act remains with imperfect charity in the man who is moved to perform good actions not only through love of justice, but also through fear of punishment, though this same act ceases in the man who has perfect charity, which "casteth out fear," according to 1 John 4:18.

Reply Obj. 3: Initial fear is a mean between servile and filial fear, not as between two things of the same genus, but as the imperfect is a mean between a perfect being and a non-being, as stated in *Metaph.* ii, for it is the same substantially as the perfect being, while it differs altogether from non-being.

NINTH ARTICLE [II-II, Q. 19, Art. 9]

Whether Fear Is a Gift of the Holy Ghost?

Objection 1: It would seem that fear is not a gift of the Holy Ghost. For no gift of the Holy Ghost is opposed to a virtue, which is also from the Holy Ghost; else the Holy Ghost would be in opposition to Himself. Now fear is opposed to hope, which is a virtue. Therefore fear is not a gift of the Holy Ghost.

Obj. 2: Further, it is proper to a theological virtue to have God for its object. But fear has God for its object, in so far as God is feared. Therefore fear is not a gift, but a theological virtue.

Obj. 3: Further, fear arises from love. But love is reckoned a theological virtue. Therefore fear also is a theological virtue, being connected with the same matter, as it were.

Obj. 4: Further, Gregory says (Moral. ii, 49) that "fear is bestowed as a remedy against pride." But the virtue of humility is opposed to pride. Therefore again, fear is a kind of virtue.

Obj. 5: Further, the gifts are more perfect than the virtues, since they are bestowed in support of the virtues as Gregory says (Moral. ii, 49). Now hope is more perfect than fear, since hope regards good, while fear regards evil. Since, then, hope is a virtue, it should not be said that fear is a gift.

*On the contrary,* The fear of the Lord is numbered among the seven gifts of the Holy Ghost (Isa. 11:3).

*I answer that,* Fear is of several kinds, as stated above (A. 2). Now it is not "human fear," according to Augustine (De Gratia et Lib. Arb. xviii), "that is a gift of God"—for it was by this fear that Peter denied Christ—but that fear of which it was said (Matt. 10:28): "Fear Him that can destroy both soul and body into hell."

Again servile fear is not to be reckoned among the seven gifts of the Holy Ghost, though it is from Him, because according to Augustine (De Nat. et Grat. lvii) it is compatible with the will to sin: whereas the gifts of the Holy Ghost are incompatible with the will to sin, as they are inseparable from charity, as stated above (I-II, Q. 68, A. 5).

It follows, therefore, that the fear of God, which is numbered among the seven gifts of the Holy Ghost, is filial or chaste fear. For it was stated above (I-II, Q. 68, AA. 1, 3) that the gifts of the Holy Ghost are certain habitual perfections of the soul's powers, whereby these are rendered amenable to the motion of the Holy Ghost, just as, by the moral virtues, the appetitive powers are rendered amenable to the motion of reason. Now for a thing to be amenable to the motion of a certain mover, the first condition required is that it be a non-resistant subject of that mover, because resistance of the movable subject to the mover hinders the movement. This is what filial or chaste fear does, since thereby we revere God and avoid separating ourselves from Him. Hence, according to Augustine (De Serm. Dom. in Monte i, 4) filial fear holds the first place, as it were, among the gifts of the Holy Ghost, in the ascending order, and the last place, in the descending order.

Reply Obj. 1: Filial fear is not opposed to the virtue of hope: since thereby we fear, not that we may fail of what we hope to obtain by God's help, but lest we withdraw ourselves from this help. Wherefore filial fear and hope cling together, and perfect one another.

Reply Obj. 2: The proper and principal object of fear is the evil shunned, and in this way, as stated above (A. 1), God cannot be an object of fear. Yet He is, in this way, the object of hope and the other theological virtues, since, by the virtue of hope, we trust in God's help, not only to obtain any other goods, but, chiefly, to obtain God Himself, as the principal good. The same evidently applies to the other theological virtues.

Reply Obj. 3: From the fact that love is the origin of fear, it does not follow that the fear of God is not a distinct habit from charity which is the love of God, since love is the origin of all the emotions, and yet we are perfected by different habits in respect of different emotions. Yet love is more of a virtue than fear is, because love regards good, to which virtue is principally directed by reason of its own nature, as was shown above (I-II, Q. 55, AA. 3, 4); for which reason hope is also reckoned as a virtue; whereas fear principally regards evil, the avoidance of which it denotes, wherefore it is something less than a theological virtue.

Reply Obj. 4: According to Ecclus. 10:14, "the beginning of the pride of man is to fall off from God," that is to refuse submission to God, and this is opposed to filial fear, which reveres God. Thus fear cuts off the source of pride for which reason it is bestowed as a remedy against pride. Yet it does not follow that it is the same as the virtue of humility, but that it is its origin. For the gifts of the Holy Ghost are the origin of the intellectual and moral virtues, as stated above (I-II, Q. 68, A. 4), while the theological virtues are the origin of the gifts, as stated above (I-II, Q. 69, A. 4, ad 3).

This suffices for the Reply to the Fifth Objection.

TENTH ARTICLE [II-II, Q. 19, Art. 10]

Whether Fear Decreases When Charity Increases?

Objection 1: It seems that fear decreases when charity increases. For Augustine says (In prim. canon. Joan. Tract. ix): "The more charity increases, the more fear decreases."

Obj. 2: Further, fear decreases when hope increases. But charity increases when hope increases, as stated above (Q. 17, A. 8). Therefore fear decreases when charity increases.

Obj. 3: Further, love implies union, whereas fear implies separation. Now separation decreases when union increases. Therefore fear decreases when the love of charity increases.

*On the contrary,* Augustine says (Qq. lxxxiii, qu. 36) that "the fear of God not only begins but also perfects wisdom, whereby we love God above all things, and our neighbor as ourselves."

*I answer that,* Fear is twofold, as stated above (AA. 2, 4); one is filial fear, whereby a son fears to offend his father or to be separated from him; the other is servile fear, whereby one fears punishment.

Now filial fear must needs increase when charity increases, even as an effect increases with the increase of its cause. For the more one loves a man, the more one fears to offend him and to be separated from him.

On the other hand servile fear, as regards its servility, is entirely cast out when charity comes, although the fear of punishment remains as to its substance, as stated above (A. 6). This fear decreases as charity increases, chiefly as regards its act, since the more a man loves God, the less he fears punishment; first, because he thinks less of his own good, to which punishment is opposed; secondly, because, the faster he clings, the more confident he is of the reward, and, consequently the less fearful of punishment.

Reply Obj. 1: Augustine speaks there of the fear of punishment.

Reply Obj. 2: It is fear of punishment that decreases when hope increases; but with the increase of the latter filial fear increases, because the more certainly a man expects to obtain a good by another's help, the more he fears to offend him or to be separated from him.

Reply Obj. 3: Filial fear does not imply separation from God, but submission to Him, and shuns separation from that submission. Yet, in a way, it implies separation, in the point of not presuming to equal oneself to Him, and of submitting to Him, which separation is to be observed even in charity, in so far as a man loves God more than himself and more than aught else. Hence the increase of the love of charity implies not a decrease but an increase in the reverence of fear.

ELEVENTH ARTICLE [II-II, Q. 19, Art. 11]

Whether Fear Remains in Heaven?

Objection 1: It would seem that fear does not remain in heaven. For it is written (Prov. 1:33): "He ... shall enjoy abundance, without fear of evils," which is to be understood as referring to those who already enjoy wisdom in everlasting happiness. Now every fear is about some evil, since evil is the object of fear, as stated above (AA. 2, 5; I-II, Q. 42, A. 1). Therefore there will be no fear in heaven.

Obj. 2: Further, in heaven men will be conformed to God, according to 1 John 3:2, "When He shall appear, we shall be like to Him." But God fears nothing. Therefore, in heaven, men will have no fear.

Obj. 3: Further, hope is more perfect than fear, since hope regards good, and fear, evil. Now hope will not be in heaven. Therefore neither will there be fear in heaven.

*On the contrary,* It is written (Ps. 18:10): "The fear of the Lord is holy, enduring for ever and ever."

*I answer that,* Servile fear, or fear of punishment, will by no means be in heaven, since such a fear is excluded by the security which is essential to everlasting happiness, as stated above (I-II, Q. 5, A. 4).

But with regard to filial fear, as it increases with the increase of charity, so is it perfected when charity is made perfect; hence, in heaven, it will not have quite the same act as it has now.

In order to make this clear, we must observe that the proper object of fear is a possible evil, just as the proper object of hope is a possible good: and since the movement of fear is like one of avoidance, fear implies avoidance of a possible arduous evil, for little evils inspire no fear. Now as a thing's good consists in its staying in its own order, so a thing's evil consists in forsaking its order. Again, the order of a rational creature is that it should be under God and above other creatures. Hence, just as it is an evil for a rational creature to submit, by love, to a lower creature, so too is it an evil for it, if it submit not to God, but presumptuously revolt against Him or contemn Him. Now this evil is possible to a rational creature considered as to its nature on account of the natural flexibility of the free-will; whereas in the blessed, it becomes impossible, by reason of the perfection of glory. Therefore the avoidance of this evil that consists in non-subjection to God, and is possible to nature, but impossible in the state of bliss, will be in heaven; while in this life there is avoidance of this evil as of something altogether possible. Hence Gregory, expounding the words of Job (26:11), "The pillars of heaven tremble, and dread at His beck," says (Moral. xvii, 29): "The heavenly powers that gaze on Him without ceasing, tremble while contemplating: but their awe, lest it should be of a penal nature, is one not of fear but of wonder," because, to wit, they wonder at God's supereminence and incomprehensibility. Augustine also (De Civ. Dei xiv, 9) in this sense, admits fear in heaven, although he leaves the question doubtful. "If," he says, "this chaste fear that endureth for ever and ever is to be in the future life, it will not be a fear that is afraid of an evil which might possibly occur, but a fear that holds fast to a good which we cannot lose. For when we love the good which we have acquired, with an unchangeable love, without doubt, if it is allowable to say so, our fear is sure of avoiding evil. Because chaste fear denotes a will that cannot consent to sin, and whereby we avoid sin without trembling lest, in our weakness, we fall, and possess ourselves in the tranquillity born of charity. Else, if no kind of fear is possible there, perhaps fear is said to endure for ever and ever, because that which fear will lead us to, will be everlasting."

Reply Obj. 1: The passage quoted excludes from the blessed, the fear that denotes solicitude, and anxiety about evil, but not the fear which is accompanied by security.

Reply Obj. 2: As Dionysius says (Div. Nom. ix) "the same things are both like and unlike God. They are like by reason of a variable imitation of the Inimitable"—that is, because, so far as they can, they imitate God Who cannot be imitated perfectly—"they are unlike because they are the effects of a Cause of Whom they fall short infinitely and immeasurably." Hence, if there be no fear in God (since there is none above Him to whom He may be subject) it does not follow that there is none in the blessed, whose happiness consists in perfect subjection to God.

Reply Obj. 3: Hope implies a certain defect, namely the futurity of happiness, which ceases when happiness is present: whereas fear implies a natural defect in a creature, in so far as it is infinitely distant from God, and this defect will remain even in heaven. Hence fear will not be cast out altogether.

TWELFTH ARTICLE [II-II, Q. 19, Art. 12]

Whether Poverty of Spirit Is the Beatitude Corresponding to the Gift of Fear?

Objection 1: It would seem that poverty of spirit is not the beatitude corresponding to the gift of fear. For fear is the beginning of the spiritual life, as explained above (A. 7): whereas poverty belongs to the perfection of the spiritual life, according to Matt. 19:21, "If thou wilt be perfect, go sell what thou hast, and give to the poor." Therefore poverty of spirit does not correspond to the gift of fear.

Obj. 2: Further, it is written (Ps. 118:120): "Pierce Thou my flesh with Thy fear," whence it seems to follow that it belongs to fear to restrain the flesh. But the curbing of the flesh seems to belong rather to the beatitude of mourning. Therefore the beatitude of mourning corresponds to the gift of fear, rather than the beatitude of poverty.

Obj. 3: Further, the gift of fear corresponds to the virtue of hope, as stated above (A. 9, ad 1). Now the last beatitude which is, "Blessed are the peacemakers, for they shall be called the children of God," seems above all to correspond to hope, because according to Rom. 5:2, "we ... glory in the hope of the glory of the sons of God." Therefore that beatitude corresponds to the gift of fear, rather than poverty of spirit.

Obj. 4: Further, it was stated above (I-II, Q. 70, A. 2) that the fruits correspond to the beatitudes. Now none of the fruits correspond to the gift of fear. Neither, therefore, does any of the beatitudes.

*On the contrary,* Augustine says (De Serm. Dom.

in Monte i, 4): "The fear of the Lord is befitting the humble of whom it is said: Blessed are the poor in spirit."

*I answer that,* Poverty of spirit properly corresponds to fear. Because, since it belongs to filial fear to show reverence and submission to God, whatever results from this submission belongs to the gift of fear. Now from the very fact that a man submits to God, it follows that he ceases to seek greatness either in himself or in another but seeks it only in God. For that would be inconsistent with perfect subjection to God, wherefore it is written (Ps. 19:8): "Some trust in chariots and some in horses; but we will call upon the name of ... our God." It follows that if a man fear God perfectly, he does not, by pride, seek greatness either in himself or in external goods, viz. honors and riches. In either case, this proceeds from poverty of spirit, in so far as the latter denotes either the voiding of a puffed up and proud spirit, according to Augustine's interpretation (De Serm. Dom. in Monte i, 4), or the renunciation of worldly goods which is done in spirit, i.e. by one's own will, through the instigation of the Holy Spirit, according to the expounding of Ambrose on Luke 6:20 and Jerome on Matt. 5:3.

Reply Obj. 1: Since a beatitude is an act of perfect virtue, all the beatitudes belong to the perfection of spiritual life. And this perfection seems to require that whoever would strive to obtain a perfect share of spiritual goods, needs to begin by despising earthly goods, wherefore fear holds the first place among the gifts. Perfection, however, does not consist in the renunciation itself of temporal goods; since this is the way to perfection: whereas filial fear, to which the beatitude of poverty corresponds, is consistent with the perfection of wisdom, as stated above (AA. 7, 10).

Reply Obj. 2: The undue exaltation of man either in himself or in another is more directly opposed to that submission to God which is the result of filial fear, than is external pleasure. Yet this is, in consequence, opposed to fear, since whoever fears God and is subject to Him, takes no delight in things other than God. Nevertheless, pleasure is not concerned, as exaltation is, with the arduous character of a thing which fear regards: and so the beatitude of poverty corresponds to fear directly, and the beatitude of mourning, consequently.

Reply Obj. 3: Hope denotes a movement by way of a relation of tendency to a term, whereas fear implies movement by way of a relation of withdrawal from a term: wherefore the last beatitude which is the term of spiritual perfection, fittingly corresponds to hope, by way of ultimate object; while the first beatitude, which implies withdrawal from external things which hinder submission to God, fittingly corresponds to fear.

Reply Obj. 4: As regards the fruits, it seems that those things correspond to the gift of fear, which pertain to the moderate use of temporal things or to abstinence therefrom; such are modesty, continency and chastity.

## QUESTION 20

OF DESPAIR (In Four Articles)

We must now consider the contrary vices; (1) despair; (2) presumption. Under the first head there are four points of inquiry:

(1) Whether despair is a sin?

(2) Whether it can be without unbelief?

(3) Whether it is the greatest of sins?

(4) Whether it arises from sloth?

FIRST ARTICLE [II-II, Q. 20, Art. 1]

Whether Despair Is a Sin?

Objection 1: It would seem that despair is not a sin. For every sin includes conversion to a mutable good, together with aversion from the immutable good, as Augustine states (De Lib. Arb. ii, 19). But despair includes no conversion to a mutable good. Therefore it is not a sin.

Obj. 2: Further, that which grows from a good root, seems to be no sin, because "a good tree cannot bring forth evil fruit" (Matt. 7:18). Now despair seems to grow from a good root, viz. fear of God, or from horror at the greatness of one's own sins. Therefore despair is not a sin.

Obj. 3: Further, if despair were a sin, it would be a sin also for the damned to despair. But this is not imputed to them as their fault but as part of their damnation. Therefore neither is it imputed to wayfarers as their fault, so that it is not a sin.

*On the contrary,* That which leads men to sin, seems not only to be a sin itself, but a source of sins. Now such is despair, for the Apostle says of certain men (Eph. 4:19): "Who, despairing, have given themselves up to lasciviousness, unto the working of all uncleanness and [Vulg.: 'unto'] covetousness." Therefore despair is not only a sin but also the origin of other sins.

*I answer that,* According to the Philosopher (Ethic. vi, 2) affirmation and negation in the intellect correspond to search and avoidance in the appetite; while truth and falsehood in the intellect correspond to good and evil in the appetite. Consequently every appetitive movement which is conformed to a true intellect, is good in itself, while every appetitive movement which is conformed to a false intellect is evil in itself and sinful. Now the true opinion of the intellect about God is that from Him comes salvation to mankind, and pardon to sinners, according to Ezech. 18:23, "I desire not the death of the sinner, but that he should be converted, and live" [*Vulg.: 'Is it My will that a sinner should die ... and not that he should be converted and live?' Cf. Ezech. 33:11]: while it is a false opinion that He refuses pardon to the repentant sinner, or that He does not turn sinners to Himself by sanctifying grace. Therefore, just as the movement of hope, which is in conformity with the true opinion, is praiseworthy and virtuous, so the contrary movement of despair, which is in conformity with the false opinion about God, is vicious and sinful.

Reply Obj. 1: In every mortal sin there is, in some way, aversion from the immutable good, and conversion to a mutable good, but not always in the same way. Because, since the theological virtues have God for their object, the sins which are contrary to them, such as hatred of God, despair and unbelief, consist principally in aversion from the immutable good; but, consequently, they imply conversion to a mutable good, in so far as the soul that is a deserter from God, must necessarily turn to other things. Other sins, however, consist principally in conversion to a mutable good, and, consequently, in aversion from the immutable good: because the fornicator intends, not to depart from God, but to enjoy carnal pleasure, the result of which is that he departs from God.

Reply Obj. 2: A thing may grow from a virtuous root in two ways: first, directly and on the part of the virtue itself; even as an act proceeds from a habit: and in this way no sin can grow from a virtuous root, for in this sense Augustine declared (De Lib. Arb. ii, 18, 19) that "no man makes evil use of virtue." Secondly, a thing proceeds from a virtue indirectly, or is occasioned by a virtue, and in this way nothing hinders a sin proceeding from a virtue: thus sometimes men pride themselves of their virtues, according to Augustine (Ep. ccxi): "Pride lies in wait for good works that they may die." In this way fear of God or horror of one's own sins may lead to despair, in so far as man makes evil use of those good things, by allowing them to be an occasion of despair.

Reply Obj. 3: The damned are outside the pale of hope on account of the impossibility of returning to happiness: hence it is not imputed to them that they hope not, but it is a part of their damnation. Even so, it would be no sin for a wayfarer to despair of obtaining that which he had no natural capacity for obtaining, or which was not due to be obtained by him; for instance, if a physician were to despair of healing some sick man, or if anyone were to despair of ever becoming rich.

SECOND ARTICLE [II-II, Q. 20, Art. 2]

Whether There Can Be Despair Without Unbelief?

Objection 1: It would seem that there can be no despair without unbelief. For the certainty of hope is derived from faith; and so long as the cause remains the effect is not done away. Therefore a man cannot lose the certainty of hope, by despairing, unless his faith be removed.

Obj. 2: Further, to prefer one's own guilt to God's mercy and goodness, is to deny the infinity of God's goodness and mercy, and so savors of unbelief. But whoever despairs, prefers his own guilt to the Divine mercy and goodness, according to Gen. 4:13: "My iniquity is greater than that I may deserve pardon." Therefore whoever despairs, is an unbeliever.

Obj. 3: Further, whoever falls into a condemned heresy, is an unbeliever. But he that despairs seems to fall into a condemned heresy, viz. that of the Novatians, who say that there is no pardon for sins after Baptism. Therefore it seems that whoever despairs, is an unbeliever.

*On the contrary,* If we remove that which follows, that which precedes remains. But hope follows faith, as stated above (Q. 17, A. 7). Therefore when hope is removed, faith can remain; so that, not everyone who despairs, is an unbeliever.

*I answer that,* Unbelief pertains to the intellect, but despair, to the appetite: and the intellect is about universals, while the appetite is moved in connection with particulars, since the appetitive movement is from the soul towards things, which, in themselves, are particular. Now it may happen that a man, while having a right opinion in the universal, is not rightly disposed as to his appetitive movement, his estimate being corrupted in a particular matter, because, in order to pass from the universal opinion to the appetite for a particular thing, it is necessary to have a particular estimate (De Anima iii, 2), just as it is impossible to infer a particular conclusion from an universal proposition, except through the holding of a particular proposition. Hence it is that a man, while having right faith, in the universal, fails in an appetitive movement, in regard to some particular, his particular estimate being corrupted by a habit or a passion, just as the fornicator, by choosing fornication as a good for himself at this particular moment, has a corrupt estimate in a particular matter, although he retains the true universal estimate according to faith, viz. that fornication is a mortal sin. In the same way, a man while retaining in the universal, the true estimate of faith, viz. that there is in the Church the power of forgiving sins, may suffer a movement of despair, to wit, that for him, being in such a state, there is no hope of pardon, his estimate being corrupted in a particular matter. In this way there can be despair, just as there can be other mortal sins, without belief.

Reply Obj. 1: The effect is done away, not only when the first cause is removed, but also when the secondary cause is removed. Hence the movement of hope can be done away, not only by the removal of the universal estimate of faith, which is, so to say, the first cause of the certainty of hope, but also by the removal of the particular estimate, which is the secondary cause, as it were.

Reply Obj. 2: If anyone were to judge, in universal, that God's mercy is not infinite, he would be an unbeliever. But he who despairs judges not thus, but that, for him in that state, on account of some particular disposition, there is no hope of the Divine mercy.

The same answer applies to the Third Objection, since the Novatians denied, in universal, that there is remission of sins in the Church.

THIRD ARTICLE [II-II, Q. 20, Art. 3]

Whether Despair Is the Greatest of Sins?

Objection 1: It would seem that despair is not the greatest of sins. For there can be despair without unbelief, as stated above (A. 2). But unbelief is the greatest of sins because it overthrows the foundation of the spiritual edifice. Therefore despair is not the greatest of sins.

Obj. 2: Further, a greater evil is opposed to a greater good, as the Philosopher states (Ethic. viii, 10). But charity is greater than hope, according to 1 Cor. 13:13. Therefore hatred of God is a greater sin than despair.

Obj. 3: Further, in the sin of despair there is nothing but inordinate aversion from God: whereas in other sins there is not only inordinate aversion from God, but also an inordinate conversion. Therefore the sin of despair is not more but less grave than other sins.

*On the contrary,* An incurable sin seems to be most grievous, according to Jer. 30:12: "Thy bruise is incurable, thy wound is very grievous." Now the sin of despair is incurable, according to Jer. 15:18: "My wound is desperate so as to refuse to be healed." [*Vulg.: "Why is my wound," etc.] Therefore despair is a most grievous sin.

*I answer that,* Those sins which are contrary to the theological virtues are in themselves more grievous than others: because, since the theological virtues have God for their object, the sins which are opposed to them imply aversion from God directly and principally. Now every mortal sin takes its principal malice and gravity from the fact of its turning away from God, for if it were possible to turn to a mutable good, even inordinately, without turning away from God, it would not be a mortal sin. Consequently a sin which, first and of its very nature, includes aversion from God, is most grievous among mortal sins.

Now unbelief, despair and hatred of God are opposed to the theological virtues: and among them, if we compare hatred of God and unbelief to despair, we shall find that, in themselves, that is, in respect of their proper species, they are more grievous. For unbelief is due to a man not believing God's own truth; while the hatred of God arises from man's will being opposed to God's goodness itself; whereas despair consists in a man ceasing to hope for a share of God's goodness. Hence it is clear that unbelief and hatred of God are against God as He is in Himself, while despair is against Him, according as His good is partaken of by us. Wherefore strictly speaking it is a more grievous sin to disbelieve God's truth, or to hate God, than not to hope to receive glory from Him.

If, however, despair be compared to the other two sins from our point of view, then despair is more dangerous, since hope withdraws us from evils and induces us to seek for good things, so that when hope is given up, men rush headlong into sin, and are drawn away from good works. Wherefore a gloss on Prov. 24:10, "If thou lose hope being weary in the day of distress, thy strength shall be diminished," says: "Nothing is more hateful than despair, for the man that has it loses his constancy both in the every day toils of this life, and, what is worse, in the battle of faith." And Isidore says (De Sum. Bono ii, 14): "To commit a crime is to kill the soul, but to despair is to fall into hell."

[And from this the response to the objections is evident.]

FOURTH ARTICLE [II-II, Q. 20, Art. 4]

Whether Despair Arises from Sloth?

Objection 1: It would seem that despair does not arise from sloth. Because different causes do not give rise to one same effect. Now despair of the future life arises from lust, according to Gregory (Moral. xxxi, 45). Therefore it does not arise from sloth.

Obj. 2: Further, just as despair is contrary to hope, so is sloth contrary to spiritual joy. But spiritual joy arises from hope, according to Rom. 12:12, "rejoicing in hope." Therefore sloth arises from despair, and not vice versa.

Obj. 3: Further, contrary effects have contrary causes. Now hope, the contrary of which is despair, seems to proceed from the consideration of Divine favors, especially the Incarnation, for Augustine says (De Trin. xiii, 10): "Nothing was so necessary to raise our hope, than that we should be shown how much God loves us. Now what greater proof could we have of this than that God's Son should deign to unite Himself to our nature?" Therefore despair arises rather from the neglect of the above consideration than from sloth.

*On the contrary,* Gregory (Moral. xxxi, 45) reckons despair among the effects of sloth.

*I answer that,* As stated above (Q. 17, A. 1; I-II, Q. 40, A. 1), the object of hope is a good, difficult but possible to obtain by oneself or by another. Consequently the hope of obtaining happiness may be lacking in a person in two ways: first, through his not deeming it an arduous good; secondly, through his deeming it impossible to obtain either by himself, or by another. Now, the fact that spiritual goods taste good to us no more, or seem to be goods of no great account, is chiefly due to our affections being infected with the love of bodily pleasures, among which, sexual pleasures hold the first place: for the love of those pleasures leads man to have a distaste for spiritual things, and not to hope for them as arduous goods. In this way despair is caused by lust.

On the other hand, the fact that a man deems an arduous good impossible to obtain, either by himself or by another, is due to his being over downcast, because when this state of mind dominates his affections, it seems to him that he will never be able to rise to any good. And since sloth is a sadness that casts down the spirit, in this way despair is born of sloth.

Now this is the proper object of hope—that the thing is possible, because the good and the arduous regard other passions also. Hence despair is born of sloth in a more special way: though it may arise from lust, for the reason given above.

This suffices for the Reply to the First Objection.

Reply Obj. 2: According to the Philosopher (Rhet. i, 11), just as hope gives rise to joy, so, when a man is joyful he has greater hope: and, accordingly, those who are sorrowful fall the more easily into despair, according to 2 Cor. 2:7: "Lest ... such an one be swallowed up by overmuch sorrow." Yet, since the object of hope is good, to which the appetite tends naturally, and which it shuns, not naturally but only on account of some supervening obstacle, it follows that, more directly, hope gives birth to joy, while on the contrary despair is born of sorrow.

Reply Obj. 3: This very neglect to consider the Divine favors arises from sloth. For when a man is influenced by a certain passion he considers chiefly the things which pertain to that passion: so that a man who is full of sorrow does not easily think of great and joyful things, but only of sad things, unless by a great effort he turn his thoughts away from sadness.

## QUESTION 21

OF PRESUMPTION (In Four Articles)

We must now consider presumption, under which head there are four points of inquiry:

(1) What is the object in which presumption trusts?

(2) Whether presumption is a sin?

(3) To what is it opposed?

(4) From what vice does it arise?

FIRST ARTICLE [II-II, Q. 21, Art. 1]

Whether Presumption Trusts in God or in Our Own Power?

Objection 1: It would seem that presumption, which is a sin against the Holy Ghost, trusts, not in God, but in our own power. For the lesser the power, the more grievously does he sin who trusts in it too much. But man's power is less than God's. Therefore it is a more grievous sin to presume on human power than to presume on the power of God. Now the sin against the Holy Ghost is most grievous. Therefore presumption, which is reckoned a species of sin against the Holy Ghost, trusts to human rather than to Divine power.

Obj. 2: Further, other sins arise from the sin against the Holy Ghost, for this sin is called malice which is a source from which sins arise. Now other sins seem to arise from the presumption whereby man presumes on himself rather than from the presumption whereby he presumes on God, since self-love is the origin of sin, according to Augustine (De Civ. Dei xiv, 28). Therefore it seems that presumption which is a sin against the Holy Ghost, relies chiefly on human power.

Obj. 3: Further, sin arises from the inordinate conversion to a mutable good. Now presumption is a sin. Therefore it arises from turning to human power, which is a mutable good, rather than from turning to the power of God, which is an immutable good.

*On the contrary,* Just as, through despair, a man despises the Divine mercy, on which hope relies, so, through presumption, he despises the Divine justice, which punishes the sinner. Now justice is in God even as mercy is. Therefore, just as despair consists in aversion from God, so presumption consists in inordinate conversion to Him.

*I answer that,* Presumption seems to imply immoderate hope. Now the object of hope is an arduous possible good: and a thing is possible to a man in two ways: first by his own power; secondly, by the power of God alone. With regard to either hope there may be presumption owing to lack of moderation. As to the hope whereby a man relies on his own power, there is presumption if he tends to a good as though it were possible to him, whereas it surpasses his powers, according to Judith 6:15: "Thou humblest them that presume of themselves." This presumption is contrary to the virtue of magnanimity which holds to the mean in this kind of hope.

But as to the hope whereby a man relies on the power of God, there may be presumption through immoderation, in the fact that a man tends to some good as though it were possible by the power and mercy of God, whereas it is not possible, for instance, if a man hope to obtain pardon without repenting, or glory without merits. This presumption is, properly, the sin against the Holy Ghost, because, to wit, by presuming thus a man removes or despises the assistance of the Holy Spirit, whereby he is withdrawn from sin.

Reply Obj. 1: As stated above (Q. 20, A. 3; I-II, Q. 73, A. 3) a sin which is against God is, in its genus, graver than other sins. Hence presumption whereby a man relies on God inordinately, is a more grievous sin than the presumption of trusting in one's own power, since to rely on the Divine power for obtaining what is unbecoming to God, is to depreciate the Divine power, and it is evident that it is a graver sin to detract from the Divine power than to exaggerate one's own.

Reply Obj. 2: The presumption whereby a man presumes inordinately on God, includes self-love, whereby he loves his own good inordinately. For when we desire a thing very much, we think we can easily procure it through others, even though we cannot.

Reply Obj. 3: Presumption on God's mercy implies both conversion to a mutable good, in so far as it arises from an inordinate desire of one's own good, and aversion from the immutable good, in as much as it ascribes to the Divine power that which is unbecoming to it, for thus man turns away from God's power.

SECOND ARTICLE [II-II, Q. 21, Art. 2]

Whether Presumption Is a Sin?

Objection 1: It would seem that presumption is not a sin. For no sin is a reason why man should be heard by God. Yet, through presumption some are heard by God, for it is written (Judith 9:17): "Hear me a poor wretch making supplication to Thee, and presuming of Thy mercy." Therefore presumption on God's mercy is not a sin.

Obj. 2: Further, presumption denotes excessive hope. But there cannot be excess of that hope which is in God, since His power and mercy are infinite. Therefore it seems that presumption is not a sin.

Obj. 3: Further, that which is a sin does not excuse from sin: for the Master says (Sent. ii, D, 22) that "Adam sinned less, because he sinned in the hope of pardon," which seems to indicate presumption. Therefore presumption is not a sin.

*On the contrary,* It is reckoned a species of sin against the Holy Ghost.

*I answer that,* As stated above (Q. 20, A. 1) with regard to despair, every appetitive movement that is conformed to a false intellect, is evil in itself and sinful. Now presumption is an appetitive movement, since it denotes an inordinate hope. Moreover it is conformed to a false intellect, just as despair is: for just as it is false that God does not pardon the repentant, or that He does not turn sinners to repentance, so is it false that He grants forgiveness to those who persevere in their sins, and that He gives glory to those who cease from good works: and it is to this estimate that the movement of presumption is conformed.

Consequently presumption is a sin, but less grave than despair, since, on account of His infinite goodness, it is more proper to God to have mercy and to spare, than to punish: for the former becomes God in Himself, the latter becomes Him by reason of our sins.

Reply Obj. 1: Presumption sometimes stands for hope, because even the right hope which we have in God seems to be presumption, if it be measured according to man's estate: yet it is not, if we look at the immensity of the goodness of God.

Reply Obj. 2: Presumption does not denote excessive hope, as though man hoped too much in God; but through man hoping to obtain from God something unbecoming to Him; which is the same as to hope too little in Him, since it implies a depreciation of His power; as stated above (A. 1, ad 1).

Reply Obj. 3: To sin with the intention of persevering in sin and through the hope of being pardoned, is presumptuous, and this does not diminish, but increases sin. To sin, however, with the hope of obtaining pardon some time, and with the intention of refraining from sin and of repenting of it, is not presumptuous, but diminishes sin, because this seems to indicate a will less hardened in sin.

THIRD ARTICLE [II-II, Q. 21, Art. 3]

Whether Presumption Is More Opposed to Fear Than to Hope?

Objection 1: It would seem that presumption is more opposed to fear than to hope. Because inordinate fear is opposed to right fear. Now presumption seems to pertain to inordinate fear, for it is written (Wis. 17:10): "A troubled conscience always presumes [Douay: 'forecasteth'] grievous things," and (Wis. 17:11) that "fear is a help to presumption [*Vulg.: 'Fear is nothing else but a yielding up of the succours from thought.']." Therefore presumption is opposed to fear rather than to hope.

Obj. 2: Further, contraries are most distant from one another. Now presumption is more distant from fear than from hope, because presumption implies movement to something, just as hope does, whereas fear denotes movement from a thing. Therefore presumption is contrary to fear rather than to hope.

Obj. 3: Further, presumption excludes fear altogether, whereas it does not exclude hope altogether, but only the rectitude of hope. Since therefore contraries destroy one another, it seems that presumption is contrary to fear rather than to hope.

*On the contrary,* When two vices are opposed to one another they are contrary to the same virtue, as timidity and audacity are opposed to fortitude. Now the sin of presumption is contrary to the sin of despair, which is directly opposed to hope. Therefore it seems that presumption also is more directly opposed to hope.

*I answer that,* As Augustine states (Contra Julian. iv, 3), "every virtue not only has a contrary vice manifestly distinct from it, as temerity is opposed to prudence, but also a sort of kindred vice, alike, not in truth but only in its deceitful appearance, as cunning is opposed to prudence." This agrees with the Philosopher who says (Ethic. ii, 8) that a virtue seems to have more in common with one of the contrary vices than with the other, as temperance with insensibility, and fortitude with audacity.

Accordingly presumption appears to be manifestly opposed to fear, especially servile fear, which looks at the punishment arising from God's justice, the remission of which presumption hopes for; yet by a kind of false likeness it is more opposed to hope, since it denotes an inordinate hope in God. And since things are more directly opposed when they belong to the same genus, than when they belong to different genera, it follows that presumption is more directly opposed to hope than to fear. For they both regard and rely on the same object, hope inordinately, presumption inordinately.

Reply Obj. 1: Just as hope is misused in speaking of evils, and properly applied in speaking of good, so is presumption: it is in this way that inordinate fear is called presumption.

Reply Obj. 2: Contraries are things that are most distant from one another within the same genus. Now presumption and hope denote a movement of the same genus, which can be either ordinate or inordinate. Hence presumption is more directly opposed to hope than to fear, since it is opposed to hope in respect of its specific difference, as an inordinate thing to an ordinate one, whereas it is opposed to fear, in respect of its generic difference, which is the movement of hope.

Reply Obj. 3: Presumption is opposed to fear by a generic contrariety, and to the virtue of hope by a specific contrariety. Hence presumption excludes fear altogether even generically, whereas it does not exclude hope except by reason of its difference, by excluding its ordinateness.

FOURTH ARTICLE [II-II, Q. 21, Art. 4]

Whether Presumption Arises from Vainglory?

Objection 1: It would seem that presumption does not arise from vainglory. For presumption seems to rely most of all on the Divine mercy. Now mercy ( *misericordia* ) regards unhappiness ( *miseriam* ) which is contrary to glory. Therefore presumption does not arise from vainglory.

Obj. 2: Further, presumption is opposed to despair. Now despair arises from sorrow, as stated above (Q. 20, A. 4, ad 2). Since therefore opposites have opposite causes, presumption would seem to arise from pleasure, and consequently from sins of the flesh, which give the most absorbing pleasure.

Obj. 3: Further, the vice of presumption consists in tending to some impossible good, as though it were possible. Now it is owing to ignorance that one deems an impossible thing to be possible. Therefore presumption arises from ignorance rather than from vainglory.

*On the contrary,* Gregory says (Moral. xxxi, 45) that "presumption of novelties is a daughter of vainglory."

*I answer that,* As stated above (A. 1), presumption is twofold; one whereby a man relies on his own power, when he attempts something beyond his power, as though it were possible to him. Such like presumption clearly arises from vainglory; for it is owing to a great desire for glory, that a man attempts things beyond his power, and especially novelties which call for greater admiration. Hence Gregory states explicitly that presumption of novelties is a daughter of vainglory.

The other presumption is an inordinate trust in the Divine mercy or power, consisting in the hope of obtaining glory without merits, or pardon without repentance. Such like presumption seems to arise directly from pride, as though man thought so much of himself as to esteem that God would not punish him or exclude him from glory, however much he might be a sinner.

This suffices for the Replies to the Objections.

## QUESTION 22

OF THE PRECEPTS RELATING TO HOPE AND FEAR (In Two Articles)

We must now consider the precepts relating to hope and fear: under which head there are two points of inquiry:

(1) The precepts relating to hope;

(2) The precepts relating to fear.

FIRST ARTICLE [II-II, Q. 22, Art. 1]

Whether There Should Be a Precept of Hope?

Objection 1: It would seem that no precept should be given relating to the virtue of hope. For when an effect is sufficiently procured by one cause, there is no need to induce it by another. Now man is sufficiently induced by his natural inclination to hope for good. Therefore there is no need of a precept of the Law to induce him to do this.

Obj. 2: Further, since precepts are given about acts of virtue, the chief precepts are about the acts of the chief virtues. Now the chief of all the virtues are the three theological virtues, viz. hope, faith and charity. Consequently, as the chief precepts of the Law are those of the decalogue, to which all others may be reduced, as stated above (I-II, Q. 100, A. 3), it seems that if any precept of hope were given, it should be found among the precepts of the decalogue. But it is not to be found there. Therefore it seems that the Law should contain no precept of hope.

Obj. 3: Further, to prescribe an act of virtue is equivalent to a prohibition of the act of the opposite vice. Now no precept is to be found forbidding despair which is contrary to hope. Therefore it seems that the Law should contain no precept of hope.

*On the contrary,* Augustine says on John 15:12, "This is My commandment, that you love one another" (Tract. lxxxiii in Joan.): "How many things are commanded us about faith! How many relating to hope!" Therefore it is fitting that some precepts should be given about hope.

*I answer that,* Among the precepts contained in Holy Writ, some belong to the substance of the Law, others are preambles to the Law. The preambles to the Law are those without which no law is possible: such are the precepts relating to the act of faith and the act of hope, because the act of faith inclines man's mind so that he believes the Author of the Law to be One to Whom he owes submission, while, by the hope of a reward, he is induced to observe the precepts. The precepts that belong to the substance of the Law are those which relate to right conduct and are imposed on man already subject and ready to obey: wherefore when the Law was given these precepts were set forth from the very outset under the form of a command.

Yet the precepts of hope and faith were not to be given under the form of a command, since, unless man already believed and hoped, it would be useless to give him the Law: but, just as the precept of faith had to be given under the form of an announcement or reminder, as stated above (Q. 16, A. 1), so too, the precept of hope, in the first promulgation of the Law, had to be given under the form of a promise. For he who promises rewards to them that obey him, by that very fact, urges them to hope: hence all the promises contained in the Law are incitements to hope.

Since, however, when once the Law has been given, it is for a wise man to induce men not only to observe the precepts, but also, and much more, to safeguard the foundation of the Law, therefore, after the first promulgation of the Law, Holy Writ holds out to man many inducements to hope, even by way of warning or command, and not merely by way of promise, as in the Law; for instance, in the Ps. 61:9: "Hope [Douay: 'Trust'] in Him all ye congregation of the people," and in many other passages of the Scriptures.

Reply Obj. 1: Nature inclines us to hope for the good which is proportionate to human nature; but for man to hope for a supernatural good he had to be induced by the authority of the Divine law, partly by promises, partly by admonitions and commands. Nevertheless there was need for precepts of the Divine law to be given even for those things to which natural reason inclines us, such as the acts of the moral virtues, for sake of insuring a greater stability, especially since the natural reason of man was clouded by the lusts of sin.

Reply Obj. 2: The precepts of the law of the decalogue belong to the first promulgation of the Law: hence there was no need for a precept of hope among the precepts of the decalogue, and it was enough to induce men to hope by the inclusion of certain promises, as in the case of the first and fourth commandments.

Reply Obj. 3: In those observances to which man is bound as under a duty, it is enough that he receive an affirmative precept as to what he has to do, wherein is implied the prohibition of what he must avoid doing: thus he is given a precept concerning the honor due to parents, but not a prohibition against dishonoring them, except by the law inflicting punishment on those who dishonor their parents. And since in order to be saved it is man's duty to hope in God, he had to be induced to do so by one of the above ways, affirmatively, so to speak, wherein is implied the prohibition of the opposite.

SECOND ARTICLE [II-II, Q. 22, Art. 2]

Whether There Should Have Been Given a Precept of Fear?

Objection 1: It would seem that, in the Law, there should not have been given a precept of fear. For the fear of God is about things which are a preamble to the Law, since it is the "beginning of wisdom." Now things which are a preamble to the Law do not come under a precept of the Law. Therefore no precept of fear should be given in the Law.

Obj. 2: Further, given the cause, the effect is also given. Now love is the cause of fear, since "every fear proceeds from some kind of love," as Augustine states (Qq. lxxxiii, qu. 33). Therefore given the precept of love, it would have been superfluous to command fear.

Obj. 3: Further, presumption, in a way, is opposed to fear. But the Law contains no prohibition against presumption. Therefore it seems that neither should any precept of fear have been given.

*On the contrary,* It is written (Deut. 10:12): "And now, Israel, what doth the Lord thy God require of thee, but that thou fear the Lord thy God?" But He requires of us that which He commands us to do. Therefore it is a matter of precept that man should fear God.

*I answer that,* Fear is twofold, servile and filial. Now just as man is induced, by the hope of rewards, to observe precepts of law, so too is he induced thereto by the fear of punishment, which fear is servile.

And just as according to what has been said (A. 1), in the promulgation of the Law there was no need for a precept of the act of hope, and men were to be induced thereto by promises, so neither was there need for a precept, under form of command, of fear which regards punishment, and men were to be induced thereto by the threat of punishment: and this was realized both in the precepts of the decalogue, and afterwards, in due sequence, in the secondary precepts of the Law.

Yet, just as wise men and the prophets who, consequently, strove to strengthen man in the observance of the Law, delivered their teaching about hope under the form of admonition or command, so too did they in the matter of fear.

On the other hand filial fear which shows reverence to God, is a sort of genus in respect of the love of God, and a kind of principle of all observances connected with reverence for God. Hence precepts of filial fear are given in the Law, even as precepts of love, because each is a preamble to the external acts prescribed by the Law and to which the precepts of the decalogue refer. Hence in the passage quoted in the argument *On the contrary,* man is required "to have fear, to walk in God's ways," by worshipping Him, and "to love Him."

Reply Obj. 1: Filial fear is a preamble to the Law, not as though it were extrinsic thereto, but as being the beginning of the Law, just as love is. Hence precepts are given of both, since they are like general principles of the whole Law.

Reply Obj. 2: From love proceeds filial fear as also other good works that are done from charity. Hence, just as after the precept of charity, precepts are given of the other acts of virtue, so at the same time precepts are given of fear and of the love of charity, just as, in demonstrative sciences, it is not enough to lay down the first principles, unless the conclusions also are given which follow from them proximately or remotely.

Reply Obj. 3: Inducement to fear suffices to exclude presumption, even as inducement to hope suffices to exclude despair, as stated above (A. 1, ad 3).

# QUESTION 23

OF CHARITY, CONSIDERED IN ITSELF (In Eight Articles)

In proper sequence, we must consider charity; and (1) charity itself; (2) the corresponding gift of wisdom. The first consideration will be fivefold: (1) Charity itself; (2) The object of charity; (3) Its acts; (4) The opposite vices; (5) The precepts relating thereto.

The first of these considerations will be twofold: (1) Charity, considered as regards itself; (2) Charity, considered in its relation to its subject. Under the first head there are eight points of inquiry:

(1) Whether charity is friendship?

(2) Whether it is something created in the soul?

(3) Whether it is a virtue?

(4) Whether it is a special virtue?

(5) Whether it is one virtue?

(6) Whether it is the greatest of the virtues?

(7) Whether any true virtue is possible without it?

(8) Whether it is the form of the virtues?

FIRST ARTICLE [II-II, Q. 23, Art. 1]

Whether Charity Is Friendship?

Objection 1: It would seem that charity is not friendship. For nothing is so appropriate to friendship as to dwell with one's friend, according to the Philosopher (Ethic. viii, 5). Now charity is of man towards God and the angels, "whose dwelling [Douay: 'conversation'] is not with men" (Dan. 2:11). Therefore charity is not friendship.

Obj. 2: Further, there is no friendship without return of love (Ethic. viii, 2). But charity extends even to one's enemies, according to Matt. 5:44: "Love your enemies." Therefore charity is not friendship.

Obj. 3: Further, according to the Philosopher (Ethic. viii, 3) there are three kinds of friendship, directed respectively towards the delightful, the useful, or the virtuous. Now charity is not the friendship for the useful or delightful; for Jerome says in his letter to Paulinus which is to be found at the beginning of the Bible: "True friendship cemented by Christ, is where men are drawn together, not by household interests, not by mere bodily presence, not by crafty and cajoling flattery, but by the fear of God, and the study of the Divine Scriptures." No more is it friendship for the virtuous, since by charity we love even sinners, whereas friendship based on the virtuous is only for virtuous men (Ethic. viii). Therefore charity is not friendship.

*On the contrary,* It is written (John 15:15): "I will not now call you servants ... but My friends." Now this was said to them by reason of nothing else than charity. Therefore charity is friendship.

*I answer that,* According to the Philosopher (Ethic. viii, 2, 3) not every love has the character of friendship, but that love which is together with benevolence, when, to wit, we love someone so as to wish good to him. If, however, we do not wish good to what we love, but wish its good for ourselves, (thus we are said to love wine, or a horse, or the like), it is love not of friendship, but of a kind of concupiscence. For it would be absurd to speak of having friendship for wine or for a horse.

Yet neither does well-wishing suffice for friendship, for a certain mutual love is requisite, since friendship is between friend and friend: and this well-wishing is founded on some kind of communication.

Accordingly, since there is a communication between man and God, inasmuch as He communicates His happiness to us, some kind of friendship must needs be based on this same communication, of which it is written (1 Cor. 1:9): "God is faithful: by Whom you are called unto the fellowship of His Son." The love which is based on this communication, is charity: wherefore it is evident that charity is the friendship of man for God.

Reply Obj. 1: Man's life is twofold. There is his outward life in respect of his sensitive and corporeal nature: and with regard to this life there is no communication or fellowship between us and God or the angels. The other is man's spiritual life in respect of his mind, and with regard to this life there is fellowship between us and both God and the angels, imperfectly indeed in this present state of life, wherefore it is written (Phil. 3:20): "Our conversation is in heaven." But this "conversation" will be perfected in heaven, when "His servants shall serve Him, and they shall see His face" (Apoc. 22:3, 4). Therefore charity is imperfect here, but will be perfected in heaven.

Reply Obj. 2: Friendship extends to a person in two ways: first in respect of himself, and in this way friendship never extends but to one's friends: secondly, it extends to someone in respect of another, as, when a man has friendship for a certain person, for his sake he loves all belonging to him, be they children, servants, or connected with him in any way. Indeed so much do we love our friends, that for their sake we love all who belong to them, even if they hurt or hate us; so that, in this way, the friendship of charity extends even to our enemies, whom we love out of charity in relation to God, to Whom the friendship of charity is chiefly directed.

Reply Obj. 3: The friendship that is based on the virtuous is directed to none but a virtuous man as the principal person, but for his sake we love those who belong to him, even though they be not virtuous: in this way charity, which above all is friendship based on the virtuous, extends to sinners, whom, out of charity, we love for God's sake.

SECOND ARTICLE [II-II, Q. 23, Art. 2]

Whether Charity Is Something Created in the Soul?

Objection 1: It would seem that charity is not something created in the soul. For Augustine says (De Trin. viii, 7): "He that loveth his neighbor, consequently, loveth love itself." Now God is love. Therefore it follows that he loves God in the first place. Again he says (De Trin. xv, 17): "It was said: God is Charity, even as it was said: God is a Spirit." Therefore charity is not something created in the soul, but is God Himself.

Obj. 2: Further, God is the life of the soul spiritually just as the soul is the life of the body, according to Deut. 30:20: "He is thy life." Now the soul by itself quickens the body. Therefore God quickens the soul by Himself. But He quickens it by charity, according to 1 John 3:14: "We know that we have passed from death to life, because we love the brethren." Therefore God is charity itself.

Obj. 3: Further, no created thing is of infinite power; on the contrary every creature is vanity. But charity is not vanity, indeed it is opposed to vanity; and it is of infinite power, since it brings the human soul to the infinite good. Therefore charity is not something created in the soul.

On the charity, Augustine says (De Doctr. Christ. iii, 10): "By charity I mean the movement of the soul towards the enjoyment of God for His own sake." But a movement of the soul is something created in the soul. Therefore charity is something created in the soul.

*I answer that,* The Master looks thoroughly into this question in Q. 17 of the First Book, and concludes that charity is not something created in the soul, but is the Holy Ghost Himself dwelling in the mind. Nor does he mean to say that this movement of love whereby we love God is the Holy Ghost Himself, but that this movement is from the Holy Ghost without any intermediary habit, whereas other virtuous acts are from the Holy Ghost by means of the habits of other virtues, for instance the habit of faith or hope or of some other virtue: and this he said on account of the excellence of charity.

But if we consider the matter aright, this would be, *on the contrary,* detrimental to charity. For when the Holy Ghost moves the human mind the movement of charity does not proceed from this motion in such a way that the human mind be merely moved, without being the principle of this movement, as when a body is moved by some extrinsic motive power. For this is contrary to the nature of a voluntary act, whose principle needs to be in itself, as stated above (I-II, Q. 6, A. 1): so that it would follow that to love is not a voluntary act, which involves a contradiction, since love, of its very nature, implies an act of the will.

Likewise, neither can it be said that the Holy Ghost moves the will in such a way to the act of loving, as though the will were an instrument, for an instrument, though it be a principle of action, nevertheless has not the power to act or not to act, for then again the act would cease to be voluntary and meritorious, whereas it has been stated above (I-II, Q. 114, A. 4) that the love of charity is the root of merit: and, given that the will is moved by the Holy Ghost to the act of love, it is necessary that the will also should be the efficient cause of that act.

Now no act is perfectly produced by an active power, unless it be connatural to that power by reason of some form which is the principle of that action. Wherefore God, Who moves all things to their due ends, bestowed on each thing the form whereby it is inclined to the end appointed to it by Him; and in this way He "ordereth all things sweetly" (Wis. 8:1). But it is evident that the act of charity surpasses the nature of the power of the will, so that, therefore, unless some form be superadded to the natural power, inclining it to the act of love, this same act would be less perfect than the natural acts and the acts of the other powers; nor would it be easy and pleasurable to perform. And this is evidently untrue, since no virtue has such a strong inclination to its act as charity has, nor does any virtue perform its act with so great pleasure. Therefore it is most necessary that, for us to perform the act of charity, there should be in us some habitual form superadded to the natural power, inclining that power to the act of charity, and causing it to act with ease and pleasure.

Reply Obj. 1: The Divine Essence Itself is charity, even as It is wisdom and goodness. Wherefore just as we are said to be good with the goodness which is God, and wise with the wisdom which is God (since the goodness whereby we are formally good is a participation of Divine goodness, and the wisdom whereby we are formally wise, is a share of Divine wisdom), so too, the charity whereby formally we love our neighbor is a participation of Divine charity. For this manner of speaking is common among the Platonists, with whose doctrines Augustine was imbued; and the lack of adverting to this has been to some an occasion of error.

Reply Obj. 2: God is effectively the life both of the soul by charity, and of the body by the soul: but formally charity is the life of the soul, even as the soul is the life of the body. Consequently we may conclude from this that just as the soul is immediately united to the body, so is charity to the soul.

Reply Obj. 3: Charity works formally. Now the efficacy of a form depends on the power of the agent, who instills the form, wherefore it is evident that charity is not vanity. But because it produces an infinite effect, since, by justifying the soul, it unites it to God, this proves the infinity of the Divine power, which is the author of charity.

THIRD ARTICLE [II-II, Q. 23, Art. 3]

Whether Charity Is a Virtue?

Objection 1: It would seem that charity is not a virtue. For charity is a kind of friendship. Now philosophers do not reckon friendship a virtue, as may be gathered from *Ethic.* viii, 1; nor is it numbered among the virtues whether moral or intellectual. Neither, therefore, is charity a virtue.

Obj. 2: Further, "virtue is the ultimate limit of power" (De Coelo et Mundo i, 11). But charity is not something ultimate, this applies rather to joy and peace. Therefore it seems that charity is not a virtue, and that this should be said rather of joy and peace.

Obj. 3: Further, every virtue is an accidental habit. But charity is not an accidental habit, since it is a more excellent thing than the soul itself: whereas no accident is more excellent than its subject. Therefore charity is not a virtue.

*On the contrary,* Augustine says (De Moribus Eccl. xi): "Charity is a virtue which, when our affections are perfectly ordered, unites us to God, for by it we love Him."

*I answer that,* Human acts are good according as they are regulated by their due rule and measure. Wherefore human virtue which is the principle of all man's good acts consists in following the rule of human acts, which is twofold, as stated above (Q. 17, A. 1), viz. human reason and God.

Consequently just as moral virtue is defined as being "in accord with right reason," as stated in *Ethic.* ii, 6, so too, the nature of virtue consists in attaining God, as also stated above with regard to faith, (Q. 4, A. 5) and hope (Q. 17, A. 1). Wherefore, it follows that charity is a virtue, for, since charity attains God, it unites us to God, as evidenced by the authority of Augustine quoted above.

Reply Obj. 1: The Philosopher (Ethic. viii) does not deny that friendship is a virtue, but affirms that it is "either a virtue or with a virtue." For we might say that it is a moral virtue about works done in respect of another person, but under a different aspect from justice. For justice is about works done in respect of another person, under the aspect of the legal due, whereas friendship considers the aspect of a friendly and moral duty, or rather that of a gratuitous favor, as the Philosopher explains (Ethic. viii, 13). Nevertheless it may be admitted that it is not a virtue distinct of itself from the other virtues. For its praiseworthiness and virtuousness are derived merely from its object, in so far, to wit, as it is based on the moral goodness of the virtues. This is evident from the fact that not every friendship is praiseworthy and virtuous, as in the case of friendship based on pleasure or utility. Wherefore friendship for the virtuous is something consequent to virtue rather than a virtue. Moreover there is no comparison with charity since it is not founded principally on the virtue of a man, but on the goodness of God.

Reply Obj. 2: It belongs to the same virtue to love a man and to rejoice about him, since joy results from love, as stated above (I-II, Q. 25, A. 2) in the treatise on the passions: wherefore love is reckoned a virtue, rather than joy, which is an effect of love. And when virtue is described as being something ultimate, we mean that it is last, not in the order of effect, but in the order of excess, just as one hundred pounds exceed sixty.

Reply Obj. 3: Every accident is inferior to substance if we consider its being, since substance has being in itself, while an accident has its being in another: but considered as to its species, an accident which results from the principles of its subject is inferior to its subject, even as an effect is inferior to its cause; whereas an accident that results from a participation of some higher nature is superior to its subject, in so far as it is a likeness of that higher nature, even as light is superior to the diaphanous body. In this way charity is superior to the soul, in as much as it is a participation of the Holy Ghost.

FOURTH ARTICLE [II-II, Q. 23, Art. 4]

Whether Charity Is a Special Virtue?

Objection 1: It would seem that charity is not a special virtue. For Jerome says: "Let me briefly define all virtue as the charity whereby we love God" [*The reference should be to Augustine, Ep. clxvii]: and Augustine says (De Moribus Eccl. xv) [*De Civ. Dei xv, 22] that "virtue is the order of love." Now no special virtue is included in the definition of virtue in general. Therefore charity is not a special virtue.

Obj. 2: Further, that which extends to all works of virtue, cannot be a special virtue. But charity extends to all works of virtue, according to 1 Cor. 13:4: "Charity is patient, is kind," etc.; indeed it extends to all human actions, according to 1 Cor. 16:14: "Let all your things be done in charity." Therefore charity is not a special virtue.

Obj. 3: Further, the precepts of the Law refer to acts of virtue. Now Augustine says (De Perfect. Human. Justit. v) that, "Thou shalt love" is "a general commandment," and "Thou shalt not covet," "a general prohibition." Therefore charity is a general virtue.

*On the contrary,* Nothing general is enumerated together with what is special. But charity is enumerated together with special virtues, viz. hope and faith, according to 1 Cor. 13:13: "And now there remain faith, hope, charity, these three." Therefore charity is a special virtue.

*I answer that,* Acts and habits are specified by their objects, as shown above (I-II, Q. 18, A. 2; I-II, Q. 54, A. 2). Now the proper object of love is the good, as stated above (I-II, Q. 27, A. 1), so that wherever there is a special aspect of good, there is a special kind of love. But the Divine good, inasmuch as it is the object of happiness, has a special aspect of good, wherefore the love of charity, which is the love of that good, is a special kind of love. Therefore charity is a special virtue.

Reply Obj. 1: Charity is included in the definition of every virtue, not as being essentially every virtue, but because every virtue depends on it in a way, as we shall state further on (AA. 7, 8). In this way prudence is included in the definition of the moral virtues, as explained in *Ethic.* ii, vi, from the fact that they depend on prudence.

Reply Obj. 2: The virtue or art which is concerned about the last end, commands the virtues or arts which are concerned about other ends which are secondary, thus the military art commands the art of horse-riding (Ethic. i). Accordingly since charity has for its object the last end of human life, viz. everlasting happiness, it follows that it extends to the acts of a man's whole life, by commanding them, not by eliciting immediately all acts of virtue.

Reply Obj. 3: The precept of love is said to be a general command, because all other precepts are reduced thereto as to their end, according to 1 Tim. 1:5: "The end of the commandment is charity."

FIFTH ARTICLE [II-II, Q. 23, Art. 5]

Whether Charity Is One Virtue?

Objection 1: It would seem that charity is not one virtue. For habits are distinct according to their objects. Now there are two objects of charity—God and our neighbor—which are infinitely distant from one another. Therefore charity is not one virtue.

Obj. 2: Further, different aspects of the object diversify a habit, even though that object be one in reality, as shown above (Q. 17, A. 6; I-II, Q. 54, A. 2, ad 1). Now there are many aspects under which God is an object of love, because we are debtors to His love by reason of each one of His favors. Therefore charity is not one virtue.

Obj. 3: Further, charity comprises friendship for our neighbor. But the Philosopher reckons several species of friendship (Ethic. viii, 3, 11, 12). Therefore charity is not one virtue, but is divided into a number of various species.

*On the contrary,* Just as God is the object of faith, so is He the object of charity. Now faith is one virtue by reason of the unity of the Divine truth, according to Eph. 4:5: "One faith." Therefore charity also is one virtue by reason of the unity of the Divine goodness.

*I answer that,* Charity, as stated above (A. 1) is a kind of friendship of man for God. Now the different species of friendship are differentiated, first of all, in respect of a diversity of end, and in this way there are three species of friendship, namely friendship for the useful, for the delightful, and for the virtuous; secondly, in respect of the different kinds of communion on which friendships are based; thus there is one species of friendship between kinsmen, and another between fellow citizens or fellow travellers, the former being based on natural communion, the latter on civil communion or on the comradeship of the road, as the Philosopher explains (Ethic. viii, 12).

Now charity cannot be differentiated in either of these ways: for its end is one, namely, the goodness of God; and the fellowship of everlasting happiness, on which this friendship is based, is also one. Hence it follows that charity is simply one virtue, and not divided into several species.

Reply Obj. 1: This argument would hold, if God and our neighbor were equally objects of charity. But this is not true: for God is the principal object of charity, while our neighbor is loved out of charity for God's sake.

Reply Obj. 2: God is loved by charity for His own sake: wherefore charity regards principally but one aspect of lovableness, namely God's goodness, which is His substance, according to Ps. 105:1: "Give glory to the Lord for He is good." Other reasons that inspire us with love for Him, or which make it our duty to love Him, are secondary and result from the first.

Reply Obj. 3: Human friendship of which the Philosopher treats has various ends and various forms of fellowship. This does not apply to charity, as stated above: wherefore the comparison fails.

SIXTH ARTICLE [II-II, Q. 23, Art. 6]

Whether Charity Is the Most Excellent of the Virtues?

Objection 1: It would seem that charity is not the most excellent of the virtues. Because the higher power has the higher virtue even as it has a higher operation. Now the intellect is higher than the will, since it directs the will. Therefore, faith, which is in the intellect, is more excellent than charity which is in the will.

Obj. 2: Further, the thing by which another works seems the less excellent of the two, even as a servant, by whom his master works, is beneath his master. Now "faith ... worketh by charity," according to Gal. 5:6. Therefore faith is more excellent than charity.

Obj. 3: Further, that which is by way of addition to another seems to be the more perfect of the two. Now hope seems to be something additional to charity: for the object of charity is good, whereas the object of hope is an arduous good. Therefore hope is more excellent than charity.

*On the contrary,* It is written (1 Cor. 13:13): "The greater of these is charity."

*I answer that,* Since good, in human acts, depends on their being regulated by the due rule, it must needs be that human virtue, which is a principle of good acts, consists in attaining the rule of human acts. Now the rule of human acts is twofold, as stated above (A. 3), namely, human reason and God: yet God is the first rule, whereby, even human reason must be regulated. Consequently the theological virtues, which consist in attaining this first rule, since their object is God, are more excellent than the moral, or the intellectual virtues, which consist in attaining human reason: and it follows that among the theological virtues themselves, the first place belongs to that which attains God most.

Now that which is of itself always ranks before that which is by another. But faith and hope attain God indeed in so far as we derive from Him the knowledge of truth or the acquisition of good, whereas charity attains God Himself that it may rest in Him, but not that something may accrue to us from Him. Hence charity is more excellent than faith or hope, and, consequently, than all the other virtues, just as prudence, which by itself attains reason, is more excellent than the other moral virtues, which attain reason in so far as it appoints the mean in human operations or passions.

Reply Obj. 1: The operation of the intellect is completed by the thing understood being in the intellectual subject, so that the excellence of the intellectual operation is assessed according to the measure of the intellect. On the other hand, the operation of the will and of every appetitive power is completed in the tendency of the appetite towards a thing as its term, wherefore the excellence of the appetitive operation is gauged according to the thing which is the object of the operation. Now those things which are beneath the soul are more excellent in the soul than they are in themselves, because a thing is contained according to the mode of the container (De Causis xii). On the other hand, things that are above the soul, are more excellent in themselves than they are in the soul. Consequently it is better to know than to love the things that are beneath us; for which reason the Philosopher gave the preference to the intellectual virtues over the moral virtues (Ethic. x, 7, 8): whereas the love of the things that are above us, especially of God, ranks before the knowledge of such things. Therefore charity is more excellent than faith.

Reply Obj. 2: Faith works by love, not instrumentally, as a master by his servant, but as by its proper form: hence the argument does not prove.

Reply Obj. 3: The same good is the object of charity and of hope: but charity implies union with that good, whereas hope implies distance therefrom. Hence charity does not regard that good as being arduous, as hope does, since what is already united has not the character of arduous: and this shows that charity is more perfect than hope.

SEVENTH ARTICLE [II-II, Q. 23, Art. 7]

Whether Any True Virtue Is Possible Without Charity?

Objection 1: It would seem that there can be true virtue without charity. For it is proper to virtue to produce a good act. Now those who have not charity, do some good actions, as when they clothe the naked, or feed the hungry and so forth. Therefore true virtue is possible without charity.

Obj. 2: Further, charity is not possible without faith, since it comes of "an unfeigned faith," as the Apostle says (1 Tim. 1:5). Now, in unbelievers, there can be true chastity, if they curb their concupiscences, and true justice, if they judge rightly. Therefore true virtue is possible without charity.

Obj. 3: Further, science and art are virtues, according to *Ethic.* vi. But they are to be found in sinners who lack charity. Therefore true virtue can be without charity.

*On the contrary,* The Apostle says (1 Cor. 13:3): "If I should distribute all my goods to the poor, and if I should deliver my body to be burned, and have not charity, it profiteth me nothing." And yet true virtue is very profitable, according to Wis. 8:7: "She teacheth temperance, and prudence, and justice, and fortitude, which are such things as men can have nothing more profitable in life." Therefore no true virtue is possible without charity.

*I answer that,* Virtue is ordered to the good, as stated above (I-II, Q. 55, A. 4). Now the good is chiefly an end, for things directed to the end are not said to be good except in relation to the end. Accordingly, just as the end is twofold, the last end, and the proximate end, so also, is good twofold, one, the ultimate and universal good, the other proximate and particular. The ultimate and principal good of man is the enjoyment of God, according to Ps. 72:28: "It is good for me to adhere to God," and to this good man is ordered by charity. Man's secondary and, as it were, particular good may be twofold: one is truly good, because, considered in itself, it can be directed to the principal good, which is the last end; while the other is good apparently and not truly, because it leads us away from the final good. Accordingly it is evident that simply true virtue is that which is directed to man's principal good; thus also the Philosopher says (Phys. vii, text. 17) that "virtue is the disposition of a perfect thing to that which is best": and in this way no true virtue is possible without charity.

If, however, we take virtue as being ordered to some particular end, then we speak of virtue being where there is no charity, in so far as it is directed to some particular good. But if this particular good is not a true, but an apparent good, it is not a true virtue that is ordered to such a good, but a counterfeit virtue. Even so, as Augustine says (Contra Julian. iv, 3), "the prudence of the miser, whereby he devises various roads to gain, is no true virtue; nor the miser's justice, whereby he scorns the property of another through fear of severe punishment; nor the miser's temperance, whereby he curbs his desire for expensive pleasures; nor the miser's fortitude, whereby as Horace, says, 'he braves the sea, he crosses mountains, he goes through fire, in order to avoid poverty'" (Epis. lib, 1; Ep. i, 45). If, on the other hand, this particular good be a true good, for instance the welfare of the state, or the like, it will indeed be a true virtue, imperfect, however, unless it be referred to the final and perfect good. Accordingly no strictly true virtue is possible without charity.

Reply Obj. 1: The act of one lacking charity may be of two kinds; one is in accordance with his lack of charity, as when he does something that is referred to that whereby he lacks charity. Such an act is always evil: thus Augustine says (Contra Julian. iv, 3) that the actions which an unbeliever performs as an unbeliever, are always sinful, even when he clothes the naked, or does any like thing, and directs it to his unbelief as end.

There is, however, another act of one lacking charity, not in accordance with his lack of charity, but in accordance with his possession of some other gift of God, whether faith, or hope, or even his natural good, which is not completely taken away by sin, as stated above (Q. 10, A. 4; I-II, Q. 85, A. 2). In this way it is possible for an act, without charity, to be generically good, but not perfectly good, because it lacks its due order to the last end.

Reply Obj. 2: Since the end is in practical matters, what the principle is in speculative matters, just as there can be no strictly true science, if a right estimate of the first indemonstrable principle be lacking, so, there can be no strictly true justice, or chastity, without that due ordering to the end, which is effected by charity, however rightly a man may be affected about other matters.

Reply Obj. 3: Science and art of their very nature imply a relation to some particular good, and not to the ultimate good of human life, as do the moral virtues, which make man good simply, as stated above (I-II, Q. 56, A. 3). Hence the comparison fails.

EIGHTH ARTICLE [II-II, Q. 23, Art. 8]

Whether Charity Is the Form of the Virtues?

Objection 1: It would seem that charity is not the true form of the virtues. Because the form of a thing is either exemplar or essential. Now charity is not the exemplar form of the other virtues, since it would follow that the other virtues are of the same species as charity: nor is it the essential form of the other virtues, since then it would not be distinct from them. Therefore it is in no way the form of the virtues.

Obj. 2: Further, charity is compared to the other virtues as their root and foundation, according to Eph. 3:17: "Rooted and founded in charity." Now a root or foundation is not the form, but rather the matter of a thing, since it is the first part in the making. Therefore charity is not the form of the virtues.

Obj. 3: Further, formal, final, and efficient causes do not coincide with one another (Phys. ii, 7). Now charity is called the end and the mother of the virtues. Therefore it should not be called their form.

*On the contrary,* Ambrose [*Lombard, Sent. iii, D, 23] says that charity is the form of the virtues.

*I answer that,* In morals the form of an act is taken chiefly from the end. The reason of this is that the principal of moral acts is the will, whose object and form, so to speak, are the end. Now the form of an act always follows from a form of the agent. Consequently, in morals, that which gives an act its order to the end, must needs give the act its form. Now it is evident, in accordance with what has been said (A. 7), that it is charity which directs the acts of all other virtues to the last end, and which, consequently, also gives the form to all other acts of virtue: and it is precisely in this sense that charity is called the form of the virtues, for these are called virtues in relation to "informed" acts.

Reply Obj. 1: Charity is called the form of the other virtues not as being their exemplar or their essential form, but rather by way of efficient cause, in so far as it sets the form on all, in the aforesaid manner.

Reply Obj. 2: Charity is compared to the foundation or root in so far as all other virtues draw their sustenance and nourishment therefrom, and not in the sense that the foundation and root have the character of a material cause.

Reply Obj. 3: Charity is said to be the end of other virtues, because it directs all other virtues to its own end. And since a mother is one who conceives within herself and by another, charity is called the mother of the other virtues, because, by commanding them, it conceives the acts of the other virtues, by the desire of the last end.

# QUESTION 24

OF THE SUBJECT OF CHARITY (In Twelve Articles)

We must now consider charity in relation to its subject, under which head there are twelve points of inquiry:

(1) Whether charity is in the will as its subject?

(2) Whether charity is caused in man by preceding acts or by a Divine infusion?

(3) Whether it is infused according to the capacity of our natural gifts?

(4) Whether it increases in the person who has it?

(5) Whether it increases by addition?

(6) Whether it increases by every act?

(7) Whether it increases indefinitely?

(8) Whether the charity of a wayfarer can be perfect?

(9) Of the various degrees of charity;

(10) Whether charity can diminish?

(11) Whether charity can be lost after it has been possessed?

(12) Whether it is lost through one mortal sin?

FIRST ARTICLE [II-II, Q. 24, Art. 1]

Whether the Will Is the Subject of Charity?

Objection 1: It would seem that the will is not the subject of charity. For charity is a kind of love. Now, according to the Philosopher (Topic. ii, 3) love is in the concupiscible part. Therefore charity is also in the concupiscible and not in the will.

Obj. 2: Further, charity is the foremost of the virtues, as stated above (Q. 23, A. 6). But the reason is the subject of virtue. Therefore it seems that charity is in the reason and not in the will.

Obj. 3: Further, charity extends to all human acts, according to 1 Cor. 16:14: "Let all your things be done in charity." Now the principle of human acts is the free-will. Therefore it seems that charity is chiefly in the free-will as its subject and not in the will.

*On the contrary,* The object of charity is the good, which is also the object of the will. Therefore charity is in the will as its subject.

*I answer that,* Since, as stated in the First Part (Q. 80, A. 2), the appetite is twofold, namely the sensitive, and the intellective which is called the will, the object of each is the good, but in different ways: for the object of the sensitive appetite is a good apprehended by sense, whereas the object of the intellective appetite or will is good under the universal aspect of good, according as it can be apprehended by the intellect. Now the object of charity is not a sensible good, but the Divine good which is known by the intellect alone. Therefore the subject of charity is not the sensitive, but the intellective appetite, i.e. the will.

Reply Obj. 1: The concupiscible is a part of the sensitive, not of the intellective appetite, as proved in the First Part (Q. 81, A. 2): wherefore the love which is in the concupiscible, is the love of sensible good: nor can the concupiscible reach to the Divine good which is an intelligible good; the will alone can. Consequently the concupiscible cannot be the subject of charity.

Reply Obj. 2: According to the Philosopher (De Anima iii, 9), the will also is in the reason: wherefore charity is not excluded from the reason through being in the will. Yet charity is regulated, not by the reason, as human virtues are, but by God's wisdom, and transcends the rule of human reason, according to Eph. 3:19: "The charity of Christ, which surpasseth all knowledge." Hence it is not in the reason, either as its subject, like prudence is, or as its rule, like justice and temperance are, but only by a certain kinship of the will to the reason.

Reply Obj. 3: As stated in the First Part (Q. 83, A. 4), the free-will is not a distinct power from the will. Yet charity is not in the will considered as free-will, the act of which is to choose. For choice is of things directed to the end, whereas the will is of the end itself (Ethic. iii, 2). Hence charity, whose object is the last end, should be described as residing in the will rather than in the free-will.

SECOND ARTICLE [II-II, Q. 24, Art. 2]

Whether Charity Is Caused in Us by Infusion?

Objection 1: It would seem that charity is not caused in us by infusion. For that which is common to all creatures, is in man naturally. Now, according to Dionysius (Div. Nom. iv), the "Divine good," which is the object of charity, "is for all an object of dilection and love." Therefore charity is in us naturally, and not by infusion.

Obj. 2: Further, the more lovable a thing is the easier it is to love it. Now God is supremely lovable, since He is supremely good. Therefore it is easier to love Him than other things. But we need no infused habit in order to love other things. Neither, therefore, do we need one in order to love God.

Obj. 3: Further, the Apostle says (1 Tim. 1:5): "The end of the commandment is charity from a pure heart, and a good conscience, and an unfeigned faith." Now these three have reference to human acts. Therefore charity is caused in us from preceding acts, and not from infusion.

*On the contrary,* The Apostle says (Rom. 5:5): "The charity of God is poured forth in our hearts by the Holy Ghost, Who is given to us."

*I answer that,* As stated above (Q. 23, A. 1), charity is a friendship of man for God, founded upon the fellowship of everlasting happiness. Now this fellowship is in respect, not of natural, but of gratuitous gifts, for, according to Rom. 6:23, "the grace of God is life everlasting": wherefore charity itself surpasses our natural facilities. Now that which surpasses the faculty of nature, cannot be natural or acquired by the natural powers, since a natural effect does not transcend its cause.

Therefore charity can be in us neither naturally, nor through acquisition by the natural powers, but by the infusion of the Holy Ghost, Who is the love of the Father and the Son, and the participation of Whom in us is created charity, as stated above (Q. 23, A. 2).

Reply Obj. 1: Dionysius is speaking of the love of God, which is founded on the fellowship of natural goods, wherefore it is in all naturally. On the other hand, charity is founded on a supernatural fellowship, so the comparison fails.

Reply Obj. 2: Just as God is supremely knowable in Himself yet not to us, on account of a defect in our knowledge which depends on sensible things, so too, God is supremely lovable in Himself, in as much as He is the object of happiness. But He is not supremely lovable to us in this way, on account of the inclination of our appetite towards visible goods. Hence it is evident that for us to love God above all things in this way, it is necessary that charity be infused into our hearts.

Reply Obj. 3: When it is said that in us charity proceeds from "a pure heart, and a good conscience, and an unfeigned faith," this must be referred to the act of charity which is aroused by these things. Or again, this is said because the aforesaid acts dispose man to receive the infusion of charity. The same remark applies to the saying of Augustine (Tract. ix in prim. canon. Joan.): "Fear leads to charity," and of a gloss on Matt. 1:2: "Faith begets hope, and hope charity."

THIRD ARTICLE [II-II, Q. 24, Art. 3]

Whether Charity Is Infused According to the Capacity of Our Natural Gifts?

Objection 1: It would seem that charity is infused according to the capacity of our natural gifts. For it is written (Matt. 25:15) that "He gave to every one according to his own virtue [Douay: 'proper ability']." Now, in man, none but natural virtue precedes charity, since there is no virtue without charity, as stated above (Q. 23, A. 7). Therefore God infuses charity into man according to the measure of his natural virtue.

Obj. 2: Further, among things ordained towards one another, the second is proportionate to the first: thus we find in natural things that the form is proportionate to the matter, and in gratuitous gifts, that glory is proportionate to grace. Now, since charity is a perfection of nature, it is compared to the capacity of nature as second to first. Therefore it seems that charity is infused according to the capacity of nature.

Obj. 3: Further, men and angels partake of happiness according to the same measure, since happiness is alike in both, according to Matt. 22:30 and Luke 20:36. Now charity and other gratuitous gifts are bestowed on the angels, according to their natural capacity, as the Master teaches (Sent. ii, D, 3). Therefore the same apparently applies to man.

*On the contrary,* It is written (John 3:8): "The Spirit breatheth where He will," and (1 Cor. 12:11): "All these things one and the same Spirit worketh, dividing to every one according as He will." Therefore charity is given, not according to our natural capacity, but according as the Spirit wills to distribute His gifts.

*I answer that,* The quantity of a thing depends on the proper cause of that thing, since the more universal cause produces a greater effect. Now, since charity surpasses the proportion of human nature, as stated above (A. 2) it depends, not on any natural virtue, but on the sole grace of the Holy Ghost Who infuses charity. Wherefore the quantity of charity depends neither on the condition of nature nor on the capacity of natural virtue, but only on the will of the Holy Ghost Who "divides" His gifts "according as He will." Hence the Apostle says (Eph. 4:7): "To every one of us is given grace according to the measure of the giving of Christ."

Reply Obj. 1: The virtue in accordance with which God gives His gifts to each one, is a disposition or previous preparation or effort of the one who receives grace. But the Holy Ghost forestalls even this disposition or effort, by moving man's mind either more or less, according as He will. Wherefore the Apostle says (Col. 1:12): "Who hath made us worthy to be partakers of the lot of the saints in light."

Reply Obj. 2: The form does not surpass the proportion of the matter. In like manner grace and glory are referred to the same genus, for grace is nothing else than a beginning of glory in us. But charity and nature do not belong to the same genus, so that the comparison fails.

Reply Obj. 3: The angel's is an intellectual nature, and it is consistent with his condition that he should be borne wholly whithersoever he is borne, as stated in the First Part (Q. 61, A. 6). Hence there was a greater effort in the higher angels, both for good in those who persevered, and for evil in those who fell, and consequently those of the higher angels who remained steadfast became better than the others, and those who fell became worse. But man's is a rational nature, with which it is consistent to be sometimes in potentiality and sometimes in act: so that it is not necessarily borne wholly whithersoever it is borne, and where there are greater natural gifts there may be less effort, and vice versa. Thus the comparison fails.

FOURTH ARTICLE [II-II, Q. 24, Art. 4]

Whether Charity Can Increase?

Objection 1: It would seem that charity cannot increase. For nothing increases save what has quantity. Now quantity is twofold, namely dimensive and virtual. The former does not befit charity which is a spiritual perfection, while virtual quantity regards the objects in respect of which charity does not increase, since the slightest charity loves all that is to be loved out of charity. Therefore charity does not increase.

Obj. 2: Further, that which consists in something extreme receives no increase. But charity consists in something extreme, being the greatest of the virtues, and the supreme love of the greatest good. Therefore charity cannot increase.

Obj. 3: Further, increase is a kind of movement. Therefore wherever there is increase there is movement, and if there be increase of essence there is movement of essence. Now there is no movement of essence save either by corruption or generation. Therefore charity cannot increase essentially, unless it happen to be generated anew or corrupted, which is unreasonable.

*On the contrary,* Augustine says (Tract. lxxiv in Joan.) [*Cf. Ep. clxxxv.] that "charity merits increase that by increase it may merit perfection."

*I answer that,* The charity of a wayfarer can increase. For we are called wayfarers by reason of our being on the way to God, Who is the last end of our happiness. In this way we advance as we get nigh to God, Who is approached, "not by steps of the body but by the affections of the soul" [*St. Augustine, Tract. in Joan. xxxii]: and this approach is the result of charity, since it unites man's mind to God. Consequently it is essential to the charity of a wayfarer that it can increase, for if it could not, all further advance along the way would cease. Hence the Apostle calls charity the way, when he says (1 Cor. 12:31): "I show unto you yet a more excellent way."

Reply Obj. 1: Charity is not subject to dimensive, but only to virtual quantity: and the latter depends not only on the number of objects, namely whether they be in greater number or of greater excellence, but also on the intensity of the act, namely whether a thing is loved more, or less; it is in this way that the virtual quantity of charity increases.

Reply Obj. 2: Charity consists in an extreme with regard to its object, in so far as its object is the Supreme Good, and from this it follows that charity is the most excellent of the virtues. Yet not every charity consists in an extreme, as regards the intensity of the act.

Reply Obj. 3: Some have said that charity does not increase in its essence, but only as to its radication in its subject, or according to its fervor.

But these people did not know what they were talking about. For since charity is an accident, its being is to be in something. So that an essential increase of charity means nothing else but that it is yet more in its subject, which implies a greater radication in its subject. Furthermore, charity is essentially a virtue ordained to act, so that an essential increase of charity implies ability to produce an act of more fervent love. Hence charity increases essentially, not by beginning anew, or ceasing to be in its subject, as the objection imagines, but by beginning to be more and more in its subject.

FIFTH ARTICLE [II-II, Q. 24, Art. 5]

Whether Charity Increases by Addition?

Objection 1: It would seem that charity increases by addition. For just as increase may be in respect of bodily quantity, so may it be according to virtual quantity. Now increase in bodily quantity results from addition; for the Philosopher says (De Gener. i, 5) that "increase is addition to pre-existing magnitude." Therefore the increase of charity which is according to virtual quantity is by addition.

Obj. 2: Further, charity is a kind of spiritual light in the soul, according to 1 John 2:10: "He that loveth his brother abideth in the light." Now light increases in the air by addition; thus the light in a house increases when another candle is lit. Therefore charity also increases in the soul by addition.

Obj. 3: Further, the increase of charity is God's work, even as the causing of it, according to 2 Cor. 9:10: "He will increase the growth of the fruits of your justice." Now when God first infuses charity, He puts something in the soul that was not there before. Therefore also, when He increases charity, He puts something there which was not there before. Therefore charity increases by addition.

*On the contrary,* Charity is a simple form. Now nothing greater results from the addition of one simple thing to another, as proved in Phys. iii, text. 59, and Metaph. ii, 4. Therefore charity does not increase by addition.

*I answer that,* Every addition is of something to something else: so that in every addition we must at least presuppose that the things added together are distinct before the addition. Consequently if charity be added to charity, the added charity must be presupposed as distinct from charity to which it is added, not necessarily by a distinction of reality, but at least by a distinction of thought. For God is able to increase a bodily quantity by adding a magnitude which did not exist before, but was created at that very moment; which magnitude, though not pre-existent in reality, is nevertheless capable of being distinguished from the quantity to which it is added. Wherefore if charity be added to charity we must presuppose the distinction, at least logical, of the one charity from the other.

Now distinction among forms is twofold: specific and numeric. Specific distinction of habits follows diversity of objects, while numeric distinction follows distinction of subjects. Consequently a habit may receive increase through extending to objects to which it did not extend before: thus the science of geometry increases in one who acquires knowledge of geometrical matters which he ignored hitherto. But this cannot be said of charity, for even the slightest charity extends to all that we have to love by charity. Hence the addition which causes an increase of charity cannot be understood, as though the added charity were presupposed to be distinct specifically from that to which it is added.

It follows therefore that if charity be added to charity, we must presuppose a numerical distinction between them, which follows a distinction of subjects: thus whiteness receives an increase when one white thing is added to another, although such an increase does not make a thing whiter. This, however, does not apply to the case in point, since the subject of charity is none other than the rational mind, so that such like an increase of charity could only take place by one rational mind being added to another; which is impossible. Moreover, even if it were possible, the result would be a greater lover, but not a more loving one. It follows, therefore, that charity can by no means increase by addition of charity to charity, as some have held to be the case.

Accordingly charity increases only by its subject partaking of charity more and more subject thereto. For this is the proper mode of increase in a form that is intensified, since the being of such a form consists wholly in its adhering to its subject. Consequently, since the magnitude of a thing follows on its being, to say that a form is greater is the same as to say that it is more in its subject, and not that another form is added to it: for this would be the case if the form, of itself, had any quantity, and not in comparison with its subject. Therefore charity increases by being intensified in its subject, and this is for charity to increase in its essence; and not by charity being added to charity.

Reply Obj. 1: Bodily quantity has something as quantity, and something else, in so far as it is an accidental form. As quantity, it is distinguishable in respect of position or number, and in this way we have the increase of magnitude by addition, as may be seen in animals. But in so far as it is an accidental form, it is distinguishable only in respect of its subject, and in this way it has its proper increase, like other accidental forms, by way of intensity in its subject, for instance in things subject to rarefaction, as is proved in *Phys.* iv, 9. In like manner science, as a habit, has its quantity from its objects, and accordingly it increases by addition, when a man knows more things; and again, as an accidental form, it has a certain quantity through being in its subject, and in this way it increases in a man who knows the same scientific truths with greater certainty now than before. In the same way charity has a twofold quantity; but with regard to that which it has from its object, it does not increase, as stated above: hence it follows that it increases solely by being intensified.

Reply Obj. 2: The addition of light to light can be understood through the light being intensified in the air on account of there being several luminaries giving light: but this distinction does not apply to the case in point, since there is but one luminary shedding forth the light of charity.

Reply Obj. 3: The infusion of charity denotes a change to the state of *having* charity from the state of not having it, so that something must needs come which was not there before. On the other hand, the increase of charity denotes a change to *more having* from *less having,* so that there is need, not for anything to be there that was not there before, but for something to be more there that previously was less there. This is what God does when He increases charity, that is He makes it to have a greater hold on the soul, and the likeness of the Holy Ghost to be more perfectly participated by the soul.

SIXTH ARTICLE

Whether Charity Increases Through Every Act of Charity?

Objection 1: It would seem that charity increases through every act of charity. For that which can do what is more, can do what is less. But every act of charity can merit everlasting life; and this is more than a simple addition of charity, since it includes the perfection of charity. Much more, therefore, does every act of charity increase charity.

Obj. 2: Further, just as the habits of acquired virtue are engendered by acts, so too an increase of charity is caused by an act of charity. Now each virtuous act conduces to the engendering of virtue. Therefore also each virtuous act of charity conduces to the increase of charity.

Obj. 3: Further, Gregory [*St. Bernard, Serm. ii in Festo Purif.] says that "to stand still in the way to God is to go back." Now no man goes back when he is moved by an act of charity. Therefore whoever is moved by an act of charity goes forward in the way to God. Therefore charity increases through every act of charity.

*On the contrary,* The effect does not surpass the power of its cause. But an act of charity is sometimes done with tepidity or slackness. Therefore it does not conduce to a more excellent charity, rather does it dispose one to a lower degree.

*I answer that,* The spiritual increase of charity is somewhat like the increase of a body. Now bodily increase in animals and plants is not a continuous movement, so that, to wit, if a thing increase so much in so much time, it need to increase proportionally in each part of that time, as happens in local movement; but for a certain space of time nature works by disposing for the increase, without causing any actual increase, and afterwards brings into effect that to which it had disposed, by giving the animal or plant an actual increase. In like manner charity does not actually increase through every act of charity, but each act of charity disposes to an increase of charity, in so far as one act of charity makes man more ready to act again according to charity, and this readiness increasing, man breaks out into an act of more fervent love, and strives to advance in charity, and then his charity increases actually.

Reply Obj. 1: Every act of charity merits everlasting life, which, however, is not to be bestowed then and there, but at its proper time. In like manner every act of charity merits an increase of charity; yet this increase does not take place at once, but when we strive for that increase.

Reply Obj. 2: Even when an acquired virtue is being engendered, each act does not complete the formation of the virtue, but conduces towards that effect by disposing to it, while the last act, which is the most perfect, and acts in virtue of all those that preceded it, reduces the virtue into act, just as when many drops hollow out a stone.

Reply Obj. 3: Man advances in the way to God, not merely by actual increase of charity, but also by being disposed to that increase.

SEVENTH ARTICLE [II-II, Q. 24, Art. 7]

Whether Charity Increases Indefinitely?

Objection 1: It would seem that charity does not increase indefinitely. For every movement is towards some end and term, as stated in *Metaph.* ii, text. 8, 9. But the increase of charity is a movement. Therefore it tends to an end and term. Therefore charity does not increase indefinitely.

Obj. 2: Further, no form surpasses the capacity of its subject. But the capacity of the rational creature who is the subject of charity is finite. Therefore charity cannot increase indefinitely.

Obj. 3: Further, every finite thing can, by continual increase, attain to the quantity of another finite thing however much greater, unless the amount of its increase be ever less and less. Thus the Philosopher states (Phys. iii, 6) that if we divide a line into an indefinite number of parts, and take these parts away and add them indefinitely to another line, we shall never arrive at any definite quantity resulting from those two lines, viz. the one from which we subtracted and the one to which we added what was subtracted. But this does not occur in the case in point: because there is no need for the second increase of charity to be less than the first, since rather is it probable that it would be equal or greater. As, therefore, the charity of the blessed is something finite, if the charity of the wayfarer can increase indefinitely, it would follow that the charity of the way can equal the charity of heaven; which is absurd. Therefore the wayfarer's charity cannot increase indefinitely.

*On the contrary,* The Apostle says (Phil. 3:12): "Not as though I had already attained, or were already perfect; but I follow after, if I may, by any means apprehend," on which words a gloss says: "Even if he has made great progress, let none of the faithful say: 'Enough.' For whosoever says this, leaves the road before coming to his destination." Therefore the wayfarer's charity can ever increase more and more.

*I answer that,* A term to the increase of a form may be fixed in three ways: first by reason of the form itself having a fixed measure, and when this has been reached it is no longer possible to go any further in that form, but if any further advance is made, another form is attained. An example of this is paleness, the bounds of which may, by continual alteration, be passed, either so that whiteness ensues, or so that blackness results. Secondly, on the part of the agent, whose power does not extend to a further increase of the form in its subject. Thirdly, on the part of the subject, which is not capable of ulterior perfection.

Now, in none of these ways, is a limit imposed to the increase of man's charity, while he is in the state of the wayfarer. For charity itself considered as such has no limit to its increase, since it is a participation of the infinite charity which is the Holy Ghost. In like manner the cause of the increase of charity, viz. God, is possessed of infinite power. Furthermore, on the part of its subject, no limit to this increase can be determined, because whenever charity increases, there is a corresponding increased ability to receive a further increase. It is therefore evident that it is not possible to fix any limits to the increase of charity in this life.

Reply Obj. 1: The increase of charity is directed to an end, which is not in this, but in a future life.

Reply Obj. 2: The capacity of the rational creature is increased by charity, because the heart is enlarged thereby, according to 2 Cor. 6:11: "Our heart is enlarged"; so that it still remains capable of receiving a further increase.

Reply Obj. 3: This argument holds good in those things which have the same kind of quantity, but not in those which have different kinds: thus however much a line may increase it does not reach the quantity of a superficies. Now the quantity of a wayfarer's charity which follows the knowledge of faith is not of the same kind as the quantity of the charity of the blessed, which follows open vision. Hence the argument does not prove.

EIGHTH ARTICLE [II-II, Q. 24, Art. 8]

Whether Charity Can Be Perfect in This Life?

Objection 1: It would seem that charity cannot be perfect in this life. For this would have been the case with the apostles before all others. Yet it was not so, since the Apostle says (Phil. 3:12): "Not as though I had already attained, or were already perfect." Therefore charity cannot be perfect in this life.

Obj. 2: Further, Augustine says (Qq. lxxxiii, qu. 36) that "whatever kindles charity quenches cupidity, but where charity is perfect, cupidity is done away altogether." But this cannot be in this world, wherein it is impossible to live without sin, according to 1 John 1:8: "If we say that we have no sin, we deceive ourselves." Now all sin arises from some inordinate cupidity. Therefore charity cannot be perfect in this life.

Obj. 3: Further, what is already perfect cannot be perfected any more. But in this life charity can always increase, as stated above (A. 7). Therefore charity cannot be perfect in this life.

*On the contrary,* Augustine says (In prim. canon. Joan. Tract. v) "Charity is perfected by being strengthened; and when it has been brought to perfection, it exclaims, 'I desire to be dissolved and to be with Christ.'" Now this is possible in this life, as in the case of Paul. Therefore charity can be perfect in this life.

*I answer that,* The perfection of charity may be understood in two ways: first with regard to the object loved, secondly with regard to the person who loves. With regard to the object loved, charity is perfect, if the object be loved as much as it is lovable. Now God is as lovable as He is good, and His goodness is infinite, wherefore He is infinitely lovable. But no creature can love Him infinitely since all created power is finite. Consequently no creature's charity can be perfect in this way; the charity of God alone can, whereby He loves Himself.

On the part of the person who loves, charity is perfect, when he loves as much as he can. This happens in three ways. First, so that a man's whole heart is always actually borne towards God: this is the perfection of the charity of heaven, and is not possible in this life, wherein, by reason of the weakness of human life, it is impossible to think always actually of God, and to be moved by love towards Him. Secondly, so that man makes an earnest endeavor to give his time to God and Divine things, while scorning other things except in so far as the needs of the present life demand. This is the perfection of charity that is possible to a wayfarer; but is not common to all who have charity. Thirdly, so that a man gives his whole heart to God habitually, viz. by neither thinking nor desiring anything contrary to the love of God; and this perfection is common to all who have charity.

Reply Obj. 1: The Apostle denies that he has the perfection of heaven, wherefore a gloss on the same passage says that "he was a perfect wayfarer, but had not yet achieved the perfection to which the way leads."

Reply Obj. 2: This is said on account of venial sins, which are contrary, not to the habit, but to the act of charity: hence they are incompatible, not with the perfection of the way, but with that of heaven.

Reply Obj. 3: The perfection of the way is not perfection simply, wherefore it can always increase.

NINTH ARTICLE [II-II, Q. 24, Art. 9]

Whether Charity Is Rightly Distinguished into Three Degrees, Beginning, Progress, and Perfection?

Objection 1: It would seem unfitting to distinguish three degrees of charity, beginning, progress, and perfection. For there are many degrees between the beginning of charity and its ultimate perfection. Therefore it is not right to put only one.

Obj. 2: Further, charity begins to progress as soon as it begins to be. Therefore we ought not to distinguish between charity as progressing and as beginning.

Obj. 3: Further, in this world, however perfect a man's charity may be, it can increase, as stated above (A. 7). Now for charity to increase is to progress. Therefore perfect charity ought not to be distinguished from progressing charity: and so the aforesaid degrees are unsuitably assigned to charity.

*On the contrary,* Augustine says (In prim. canon. Joan. Tract. v) "As soon as charity is born it takes food," which refers to beginners, "after taking food, it waxes strong," which refers to those who are progressing, "and when it has become strong it is perfected," which refers to the perfect. Therefore there are three degrees of charity.

*I answer that,* The spiritual increase of charity may be considered in respect of a certain likeness to the growth of the human body. For although this latter growth may be divided into many parts, yet it has certain fixed divisions according to those particular actions or pursuits to which man is brought by this same growth. Thus we speak of a man being an infant until he has the use of reason, after which we distinguish another state of man wherein he begins to speak and to use his reason, while there is again a third state, that of puberty when he begins to acquire the power of generation, and so on until he arrives at perfection.

In like manner the divers degrees of charity are distinguished according to the different pursuits to which man is brought by the increase of charity. For at first it is incumbent on man to occupy himself chiefly with avoiding sin and resisting his concupiscences, which move him in opposition to charity: this concerns beginners, in whom charity has to be fed or fostered lest it be destroyed: in the second place man's chief pursuit is to aim at progress in good, and this is the pursuit of the proficient, whose chief aim is to strengthen their charity by adding to it: while man's third pursuit is to aim chiefly at union with and enjoyment of God: this belongs to the perfect who "desire to be dissolved and to be with Christ."

In like manner we observe in local motion that at first there is withdrawal from one term, then approach to the other term, and thirdly, rest in this term.

Reply Obj. 1: All these distinct degrees which can be discerned in the increase of charity, are comprised in the aforesaid three, even as every division of continuous things is included in these three—the beginning, the middle, and the end, as the Philosopher states (De Coelo i, 1).

Reply Obj. 2: Although those who are beginners in charity may progress, yet the chief care that besets them is to resist the sins which disturb them by their onslaught. Afterwards, however, when they come to feel this onslaught less, they begin to tend to perfection with greater security; yet with one hand doing the work, and with the other holding the sword as related in 2 Esdr. 4:17 about those who built up Jerusalem.

Reply Obj. 3: Even the perfect make progress in charity: yet this is not their chief care, but their aim is principally directed towards union with God. And though both the beginner and the proficient seek this, yet their solicitude is chiefly about other things, with the beginner, about avoiding sin, with the proficient, about progressing in virtue.

TENTH ARTICLE [II-II, Q. 24, Art. 10]

Whether Charity Can Decrease?

Objection 1: It would seem that charity can decrease. For contraries by their nature affect the same subject. Now increase and decrease are contraries. Since then charity increases, as stated above (A. 4), it seems that it can also decrease.

Obj. 2: Further, Augustine, speaking to God, says (Confess. x) "He loves Thee less, who loves aught besides Thee": and (Qq. lxxxiii, qu. 36) he says that "what kindles charity quenches cupidity." From this it seems to follow that, *on the contrary,* what arouses cupidity quenches charity. But cupidity, whereby a man loves something besides God, can increase in man. Therefore charity can decrease.

Obj. 3: Further, as Augustine says (Gen. ad lit. viii, 12) "God makes the just man, by justifying him, but in such a way, that if the man turns away from God, he no longer retains the effect of the Divine operation." From this we may gather that when God preserves charity in man, He works in the same way as when He first infuses charity into him. Now at the first infusion of charity God infuses less charity into him that prepares himself less. Therefore also in preserving charity, He preserves less charity in him that prepares himself less. Therefore charity can decrease.

*On the contrary,* In Scripture, charity is compared to fire, according to Cant 8:6: "The lamps thereof," i.e. of charity, "are fire and flames." Now fire ever mounts upward so long as it lasts. Therefore as long as charity endures, it can ascend, but cannot descend, i.e. decrease.

*I answer that,* The quantity which charity has in comparison with its proper object, cannot decrease, even as neither can it increase, as stated above (A. 4, ad 2).

Since, however, it increases in that quantity which it has in comparison with its subject, here is the place to consider whether it can decrease in this way. Now, if it decrease, this must needs be either through an act, or by the mere cessation from act. It is true that virtues acquired through acts decrease and sometimes cease altogether through cessation from act, as stated above (I-II, Q. 53, A. 3). Wherefore the Philosopher says, in reference to friendship (Ethic. viii, 5) "that want of intercourse," i.e. the neglect to call upon or speak with one's friends, "has destroyed many a friendship." Now this is because the safe-keeping of a thing depends on its cause, and the cause of human virtue is a human act, so that when human acts cease, the virtue acquired thereby decreases and at last ceases altogether. Yet this does not occur to charity, because it is not the result of human acts, but is caused by God alone, as stated above (A. 2). Hence it follows that even when its act ceases, it does not for this reason decrease, or cease altogether, unless the cessation involves a sin.

The consequence is that a decrease of charity cannot be caused except either by God or by some sinful act. Now no defect is caused in us by God, except by way of punishment, in so far as He withdraws His grace in punishment of sin. Hence He does not diminish charity except by way of punishment: and this punishment is due on account of sin.

It follows, therefore, that if charity decrease, the cause of this decrease must be sin either effectively or by way of merit. But mortal sin does not diminish charity, in either of these ways, but destroys it entirely, both effectively, because every mortal sin is contrary to charity, as we shall state further on (A. 12), and by way of merit, since when, by sinning mortally, a man acts against charity, he deserves that God should withdraw charity from him.

In like manner, neither can venial sin diminish charity either effectively or by way of merit. Not effectively, because it does not touch charity, since charity is about the last end, whereas venial sin is a disorder about things directed to the end: and a man's love for the end is none the less through his committing an inordinate act as regards the things directed to the end. Thus sick people sometimes, though they love health much, are irregular in keeping to their diet: and thus again, in speculative sciences, the false opinions that are derived from the principles, do not diminish the certitude of the principles. So too, venial sin does not merit diminution of charity; for when a man offends in a small matter he does not deserve to be mulcted in a great matter. For God does not turn away from man, more than man turns away from Him: wherefore he that is out of order in respect of things directed to the end, does not deserve to be mulcted in charity whereby he is ordered to the last end.

The consequence is that charity can by no means be diminished, if we speak of direct causality, yet whatever disposes to its corruption may be said to conduce indirectly to its diminution, and such are venial sins, or even the cessation from the practice of works of charity.

Reply Obj. 1: Contraries affect the same subject when that subject stands in equal relation to both. But charity does not stand in equal relation to increase and decrease. For it can have a cause of increase, but not of decrease, as stated above. Hence the argument does not prove.

Reply Obj. 2: Cupidity is twofold, one whereby man places his end in creatures, and this kills charity altogether, since it is its poison, as Augustine states (Confess. x). This makes us love God less (i.e. less than we ought to love Him by charity), not indeed by diminishing charity but by destroying it altogether. It is thus that we must understand the saying: "He loves Thee less, who loves aught beside Thee," for he adds these words, "which he loveth not for Thee." This does not apply to venial sin, but only to mortal sin: since that which we love in venial sin, is loved for God's sake habitually though not actually. There is another cupidity, that of venial sin, which is always diminished by charity: and yet this cupidity cannot diminish charity, for the reason given above.

Reply Obj. 3: A movement of the free-will is requisite in the infusion of charity, as stated above (I-II, Q. 113, A. 3). Wherefore that which diminishes the intensity of the free-will conduces dispositively to a diminution in the charity to be infused. On the other hand, no movement of the free-will is required for the safe-keeping of charity, else it would not remain in us while we sleep. Hence charity does not decrease on account of an obstacle on the part of the intensity of the free-will's movement.

ELEVENTH ARTICLE [II-II, Q. 24, Art. 11]

Whether We Can Lose Charity When Once We Have It?

Objection 1: It would seem that we cannot lose charity when once we have it. For if we lose it, this can only be through sin. Now he who has charity cannot sin, for it is written (1 John 3:9): "Whosoever is born of God, committeth not sin; for His seed abideth in him, and he cannot sin, because he is born of God." But none save the children of God have charity, for it is this which distinguishes "the children of God from the children of perdition," as Augustine says (De Trin. xv, 17). Therefore he that has charity cannot lose it.

Obj. 2: Further, Augustine says (De Trin. viii, 7) that "if love be not true, it should not be called love." Now, as he says again in a letter to Count Julian, "charity which can fail was never true." [*The quotation is from De Salutaribus Documentis ad quemdam comitem, vii., among the works of Paul of Friuli, more commonly known as Paul the Deacon, a monk of Monte Cassino.] Therefore it was no charity at all. Therefore, when once we have charity, we cannot lose it.

Obj. 3: Further, Gregory says in a homily for Pentecost (In Evang. xxx) that "God's love works great things where it is; if it ceases to work it is not charity." Now no man loses charity by doing great things. Therefore if charity be there, it cannot be lost.

Obj. 4: Further, the free-will is not inclined to sin unless by some motive for sinning. Now charity excludes all motives for sinning, both self-love and cupidity, and all such things. Therefore charity cannot be lost.

*On the contrary,* It is written (Apoc. 2:4): "I have somewhat against thee, because thou hast left thy first charity."

*I answer that,* The Holy Ghost dwells in us by charity, as shown above (A. 2; QQ. 23, 24). We can, accordingly, consider charity in three ways: first on the part of the Holy Ghost, Who moves the soul to love God, and in this respect charity is incompatible with sin through the power of the Holy Ghost, Who does unfailingly whatever He wills to do. Hence it is impossible for these two things to be true at the same time—that the Holy Ghost should will to move a certain man to an act of charity, and that this man, by sinning, should lose charity. For the gift of perseverance is reckoned among the blessings of God whereby "whoever is delivered, is most certainly delivered," as Augustine says in his book on the Predestination of the saints (De Dono Persev. xiv).

Secondly, charity may be considered as such, and thus it is incapable of anything that is against its nature. Wherefore charity cannot sin at all, even as neither can heat cool, nor unrighteousness do good, as Augustine says (De Serm. Dom. in Monte ii, 24).

Thirdly, charity can be considered on the part of its subject, which is changeable on account of the free-will. Moreover charity may be compared with this subject, both from the general point of view of form in comparison with matter, and from the specific point of view of habit as compared with power. Now it is natural for a form to be in its subject in such a way that it can be lost, when it does not entirely fill the potentiality of matter: this is evident in the forms of things generated and corrupted, because the matter of such things receives one form in such a way, that it retains the potentiality to another form, as though its potentiality were not completely satisfied with the one form. Hence the one form may be lost by the other being received. On the other hand the form of a celestial body which entirely fills the potentiality of its matter, so that the latter does not retain the potentiality to another form, is in its subject inseparably. Accordingly the charity of the blessed, because it entirely fills the potentiality of the rational mind, since every actual movement of that mind is directed to God, is possessed by its subject inseparably: whereas the charity of the wayfarer does not so fill the potentiality of its subject, because the latter is not always actually directed to God: so that when it is not actually directed to God, something may occur whereby charity is lost.

It is proper to a habit to incline a power to act, and this belongs to a habit, in so far as it makes whatever is suitable to it, to seem good, and whatever is unsuitable, to seem evil. For as the taste judges of savors according to its disposition, even so does the human mind judge of things to be done, according to its habitual disposition. Hence the Philosopher says (Ethic. iii, 5) that "such as a man is, so does the end appear to him." Accordingly charity is inseparable from its possessor, where that which pertains to charity cannot appear otherwise than good, and that is in heaven, where God is seen in His Essence, which is the very essence of goodness. Therefore the charity of heaven cannot be lost, whereas the charity of the way can, because in this state God is not seen in His Essence, which is the essence of goodness.

Reply Obj. 1: The passage quoted speaks from the point of view of the power of the Holy Ghost, by Whose safeguarding, those whom He wills to move are rendered immune from sin, as much as He wills.

Reply Obj. 2: The charity which can fail by reason of itself is no true charity; for this would be the case, were its love given only for a time, and afterwards were to cease, which would be inconsistent with true love. If, however, charity be lost through the changeableness of the subject, and against the purpose of charity included in its act, this is not contrary to true charity.

Reply Obj. 3: The love of God ever works great things in its purpose, which is essential to charity; but it does not always work great things in its act, on account of the condition of its subject.

Reply Obj. 4: Charity by reason of its act excludes every motive for sinning. But it happens sometimes that charity is not acting actually, and then it is possible for a motive to intervene for sinning, and if we consent to this motive, we lose charity.

TWELFTH ARTICLE [II-II, Q. 24, Art. 12]

Whether Charity Is Lost Through One Mortal Sin?

Objection 1: It would seem that charity is not lost through one mortal sin. For Origen says (Peri Archon i): "When a man who has mounted to the stage of perfection, is satiated, I do not think that he will become empty or fall away suddenly; but he must needs do so gradually and by little and little." But man falls away by losing charity. Therefore charity is not lost through only one mortal sin.

Obj. 2: Further, Pope Leo in a sermon on the Passion (lx) addresses Peter thus: "Our Lord saw in thee not a conquered faith, not an averted love, but constancy shaken. Tears abounded where love never failed, and the words uttered in trepidation were washed away by the fount of charity." From this Bernard [*William of St. Thierry, De Nat. et Dig. Amoris. vi.] drew his assertion that "charity in Peter was not quenched, but cooled." But Peter sinned mortally in denying Christ. Therefore charity is not lost through one mortal sin.

Obj. 3: Further, charity is stronger than an acquired virtue. Now a habit of acquired virtue is not destroyed by one contrary sinful act. Much less, therefore, is charity destroyed by one contrary mortal sin.

Obj. 4: Further, charity denotes love of God and our neighbor. Now, seemingly, one may commit a mortal sin, and yet retain the love of God and one's neighbor; because an inordinate affection for things directed to the end, does not remove the love for the end, as stated above (A. 10). Therefore charity towards God can endure, though there be a mortal sin through an inordinate affection for some temporal good.

Obj. 5: Further, the object of a theological virtue is the last end. Now the other theological virtues, namely faith and hope, are not done away by one mortal sin, in fact they remain though lifeless. Therefore charity can remain without a form, even when a mortal sin has been committed.

*On the contrary,* By mortal sin man becomes deserving of eternal death, according to Rom. 6:23: "The wages of sin is death." On the other hand whoever has charity is deserving of eternal life, for it is written (John 14:21): "He that loveth Me, shall be loved by My Father: and I will love Him, and will manifest Myself to him," in which manifestation everlasting life consists, according to John 17:3: "This is eternal life; that they may know Thee the ... true God, and Jesus Christ Whom Thou hast sent." Now no man can be worthy, at the same time, of eternal life and of eternal death. Therefore it is impossible for a man to have charity with a mortal sin. Therefore charity is destroyed by one mortal sin.

*I answer that,* That one contrary is removed by the other contrary supervening. Now every mortal sin is contrary to charity by its very nature, which consists in man's loving God above all things, and subjecting himself to Him entirely, by referring all that is his to God. It is therefore essential to charity that man should so love God as to wish to submit to Him in all things, and always to follow the rule of His commandments; since whatever is contrary to His commandments is manifestly contrary to charity, and therefore by its very nature is capable of destroying charity.

If indeed charity were an acquired habit dependent on the power of its subject, it would not necessarily be removed by one mortal sin, for act is directly contrary, not to habit but to act. Now the endurance of a habit in its subject does not require the endurance of its act, so that when a contrary act supervenes the acquired habit is not at once done away. But charity, being an infused habit, depends on the action of God Who infuses it, Who stands in relation to the infusion and safekeeping of charity, as the sun does to the diffusion of light in the air, as stated above (A. 10, Obj. 3). Consequently, just as the light would cease at once in the air, were an obstacle placed to its being lit up by the sun, even so charity ceases at once to be in the soul through the placing of an obstacle to the outpouring of charity by God into the soul.

Now it is evident that through every mortal sin which is contrary to God's commandments, an obstacle is placed to the outpouring of charity, since from the very fact that a man chooses to prefer sin to God's friendship, which requires that we should obey His will, it follows that the habit of charity is lost at once through one mortal sin. Hence Augustine says (Gen. ad lit. viii, 12) that "man is enlightened by God's presence, but he is darkened at once by God's absence, because distance from Him is effected not by change of place but by aversion of the will."

Reply Obj. 1: This saying of Origen may be understood, in one way, that a man who is in the state of perfection, does not suddenly go so far as to commit a mortal sin, but is disposed thereto by some previous negligence, for which reason venial sins are said to be dispositions to mortal sin, as stated above (I-II, Q. 88, A. 3). Nevertheless he falls, and loses charity through the one mortal sin if he commits it.

Since, however, he adds: "If some slight slip should occur, and he recover himself quickly he does not appear to fall altogether," we may reply in another way, that when he speaks of a man being emptied and falling away altogether, he means one who falls so as to sin through malice; and this does not occur in a perfect man all at once.

Reply Obj. 2: Charity may be lost in two ways; first, directly, by actual contempt, and, in this way, Peter did not lose charity. Secondly, indirectly, when a sin is committed against charity, through some passion of desire or fear; it was by sinning against charity in this way, that Peter lost charity; yet he soon recovered it.

The Reply to the Third Objection is evident from what has been said.

Reply Obj. 4: Not every inordinate affection for things directed to the end, i.e., for created goods, constitutes a mortal sin, but only such as is directly contrary to the Divine will; and then the inordinate affection is contrary to charity, as stated.

Reply Obj. 5: Charity denotes union with God, whereas faith and hope do not. Now every mortal sin consists in aversion from God, as stated above (Gen. ad lit. viii, 12). Consequently every mortal sin is contrary to charity, but not to faith and hope, but only certain determinate sins, which destroy the habit of faith or of hope, even as charity is destroyed by every moral sin. Hence it is evident that charity cannot remain lifeless, since it is itself the ultimate form regarding God under the aspect of last end as stated above (Q. 23, A. 8).

## QUESTION 25

OF THE OBJECT OF CHARITY (TWELVE ARTICLES)

We must now consider the object of charity; which consideration will be twofold: (1) The things we ought to love out of charity: (2) The order in which they ought to be loved. Under the first head there are twelve points of inquiry:

(1) Whether we should love God alone, out of charity, or should we love our neighbor also?

(2) Whether charity should be loved out of charity?

(3) Whether irrational creatures ought to be loved out of charity?

(4) Whether one may love oneself out of charity?

(5) Whether one's own body?

(6) Whether sinners should be loved out of charity?

(7) Whether sinners love themselves?

(8) Whether we should love our enemies out of charity?

(9) Whether we are bound to show them tokens of friendship?

(10) Whether we ought to love the angels out of charity?

(11) Whether we ought to love the demons?

(12) How to enumerate the things we are bound to love out of charity.

FIRST ARTICLE [II-II, Q. 25, Art. 1]

Whether the Love of Charity Stops at God, or Extends to Our Neighbor?

Objection 1: It would seem that the love of charity stops at God and does not extend to our neighbor. For as we owe God love, so do we owe Him fear, according Deut. 10:12: "And now Israel, what doth the Lord thy God require of thee, but that thou fear ... and love Him?" Now the fear with which we fear man, and which is called human fear, is distinct from the fear with which we fear God, and which is either servile or filial, as is evident from what has been stated above (Q. 10, A. 2). Therefore also the love with which we love God, is distinct from the love with which we love our neighbor.

Obj. 2: Further, the Philosopher says (Ethic. viii, 8) that "to be loved is to be honored." Now the honor due to God, which is known as *latria*, is distinct from the honor due to a creature, and known as dulia. Therefore again the love wherewith we love God, is distinct from that with which we love our neighbor.

Obj. 3: Further, hope begets charity, as a gloss states on Matt. 1:2. Now hope is so due to God that it is reprehensible to hope in man, according to Jer. 17:5: "Cursed be the man that trusteth in man." Therefore charity is so due to God, as not to extend to our neighbor.

*On the contrary,* It is written (1 John 4:21): "This commandment we have from God, that he, who loveth God, love also his brother."

*I answer that,* As stated above (Q. 17, A. 6; Q. 19, A. 3; I-II, Q. 54, A. 3) habits are not differentiated except their acts be of different species. For every act of the one species belongs to the same habit. Now since the species of an act is derived from its object, considered under its formal aspect, it follows of necessity that it is specifically the same act that tends to an aspect of the object, and that tends to the object under that aspect: thus it is specifically the same visual act whereby we see the light, and whereby we see the color under the aspect of light.

Now the aspect under which our neighbor is to be loved, is God, since what we ought to love in our neighbor is that he may be in God. Hence it is clear that it is specifically the same act whereby we love God, and whereby we love our neighbor. Consequently the habit of charity extends not only to the love of God, but also to the love of our neighbor.

Reply Obj. 1: We may fear our neighbor, even as we may love him, in two ways: first, on account of something that is proper to him, as when a man fears a tyrant on account of his cruelty, or loves him by reason of his own desire to get something from him. Such like human fear is distinct from the fear of God, and the same applies to love. Secondly, we fear a man, or love him on account of what he has of God; as when we fear the secular power by reason of its exercising the ministry of God for the punishment of evildoers, and love it for its justice: such like fear of man is not distinct from fear of God, as neither is such like love.

Reply Obj. 2: Love regards good in general, whereas honor regards the honored person's own good, for it is given to a person in recognition of his own virtue. Hence love is not differentiated specifically on account of the various degrees of goodness in various persons, so long as it is referred to one good common to all, whereas honor is distinguished according to the good belonging to individuals. Consequently we love all our neighbors with the same love of charity, in so far as they are referred to one good common to them all, which is God; whereas we give various honors to various people, according to each one's own virtue, and likewise to God we give the singular honor of latria on account of His singular virtue.

Reply Obj. 3: It is wrong to hope in man as though he were the principal author of salvation, but not, to hope in man as helping us ministerially under God. In like manner it would be wrong if a man loved his neighbor as though he were his last end, but not, if he loved him for God's sake; and this is what charity does.

SECOND ARTICLE [II-II, Q. 25, Art. 2]

Whether We Should Love Charity Out of Charity?

Objection 1: It would seem that charity need not be loved out of charity. For the things to be loved out of charity are contained in the two precepts of charity (Matt. 22:37-39): and neither of them includes charity, since charity is neither God nor our neighbor. Therefore charity need not be loved out of charity.

Obj. 2: Further, charity is founded on the fellowship of happiness, as stated above (Q. 23, A. 1). But charity cannot participate in happiness. Therefore charity need not be loved out of charity.

Obj. 3: Further, charity is a kind of friendship, as stated above (Q. 23, A. 1). But no man can have friendship for charity or for an accident, since such things cannot return love for love, which is essential to friendship, as stated in *Ethic.* viii. Therefore charity need not be loved out of charity.

*On the contrary,* Augustine says (De Trin. viii, 8): "He that loves his neighbor, must, in consequence, love love itself." But we love our neighbor out of charity. Therefore it follows that charity also is loved out of charity.

*I answer that,* Charity is love. Now love, by reason of the nature of the power whose act it is, is capable of reflecting on itself; for since the object of the will is the universal good, whatever has the aspect of good, can be the object of an act of the will: and since to will is itself a good, man can will himself to will. Even so the intellect, whose object is the true, understands that it understands, because this again is something true. Love, however, even by reason of its own species, is capable of reflecting on itself, because it is a spontaneous movement of the lover towards the beloved, wherefore from the moment a man loves, he loves himself to love.

Yet charity is not love simply, but has the nature of friendship, as stated above (Q. 23, A. 1). Now by friendship a thing is loved in two ways: first, as the friend for whom we have friendship, and to whom we wish good things: secondly, as the good which we wish to a friend. It is in the latter and not in the former way that charity is loved out of charity, because charity is the good which we desire for all those whom we love out of charity. The same applies to happiness, and to the other virtues.

Reply Obj. 1: God and our neighbor are those with whom we are friends, but love of them includes the loving of charity, since we love both God and our neighbor, in so far as we love ourselves and our neighbor to love God, and this is to love charity.

Reply Obj. 2: Charity is itself the fellowship of the spiritual life, whereby we arrive at happiness: hence it is loved as the good which we desire for all whom we love out of charity.

Reply Obj. 3: This argument considers friendship as referred to those with whom we are friends.

THIRD ARTICLE [II-II, Q. 25, Art. 3]

Whether Irrational Creatures Also Ought to Be Loved Out of Charity?

Objection 1: It would seem that irrational creatures also ought to be loved out of charity. For it is chiefly by charity that we are conformed to God. Now God loves irrational creatures out of charity, for He loves "all things that are" (Wis. 11:25), and whatever He loves, He loves by Himself Who is charity. Therefore we also should love irrational creatures out of charity.

Obj. 2: Further, charity is referred to God principally, and extends to other things as referable to God. Now just as the rational creature is referable to God, in as much as it bears the resemblance of image, so too, are the irrational creatures, in as much as they bear the resemblance of a trace [*Cf. I, Q. 45, A. 7]. Therefore charity extends also to irrational creatures.

Obj. 3: Further, just as the object of charity is God. so is the object of faith. Now faith extends to irrational creatures, since we believe that heaven and earth were created by God, that the fishes and birds were brought forth out of the waters, and animals that walk, and plants, out of the earth. Therefore charity extends also to irrational creatures.

*On the contrary,* The love of charity extends to none but God and our neighbor. But the word neighbor cannot be extended to irrational creatures, since they have no fellowship with man in the rational life. Therefore charity does not extend to irrational creatures.

*I answer that,* According to what has been stated above (Q. 13, A. 1) charity is a kind of friendship. Now the love of friendship is twofold: first, there is the love for the friend to whom our friendship is given, secondly, the love for those good things which we desire for our friend. With regard to the first, no irrational creature can be loved out of charity; and for three reasons. Two of these reasons refer in a general way to friendship, which cannot have an irrational creature for its object: first because friendship is towards one to whom we wish good things, while, properly speaking, we cannot wish good things to an irrational creature, because it is not competent, properly speaking, to possess good, this being proper to the rational creature which, through its free-will, is the master of its disposal of the good it possesses. Hence the Philosopher says (Phys. ii, 6) that we do not speak of good or evil befalling such like things, except metaphorically. Secondly, because all friendship is based on some fellowship in life; since "nothing is so proper to friendship as to live together," as the Philosopher proves (Ethic. viii, 5). Now irrational creatures can have no fellowship in human life which is regulated by reason. Hence friendship with irrational creatures is impossible, except metaphorically speaking. The third reason is proper to charity, for charity is based on the fellowship of everlasting happiness, to which the irrational creature cannot attain. Therefore we cannot have the friendship of charity towards an irrational creature.

Nevertheless we can love irrational creatures out of charity, if we regard them as the good things that we desire for others, in so far, to wit, as we wish for their preservation, to God's honor and man's use; thus too does God love them out of charity.

Wherefore the Reply to the First Objection is evident.

Reply Obj. 2: The likeness by way of trace does not confer the capacity for everlasting life, whereas the likeness of image does: and so the comparison fails.

Reply Obj. 3: Faith can extend to all that is in any way true, whereas the friendship of charity extends only to such things as have a natural capacity for everlasting life; wherefore the comparison fails.

FOURTH ARTICLE [II-II, Q. 25, Art. 4]

Whether a Man Ought to Love Himself Out of Charity?

Objection 1: It would seem that a man is [not] bound to love himself out of charity. For Gregory says in a homily (In Evang. xvii) that there "can be no charity between less than two." Therefore no man has charity towards himself.

Obj. 2: Further, friendship, by its very nature, implies mutual love and equality (Ethic. viii, 2, 7), which cannot be of one man towards himself. But charity is a kind of friendship, as stated above (Q. 23, A. 1). Therefore a man cannot have charity towards himself.

Obj. 3: Further, anything relating to charity cannot be blameworthy, since charity "dealeth not perversely" (1 Cor. 23:4). Now a man deserves to be blamed for loving himself, since it is written (2 Tim. 3:1, 2): "In the last days shall come dangerous times, men shall be lovers of themselves." Therefore a man cannot love himself out of charity.

*On the contrary,* It is written (Lev. 19:18): "Thou shalt love thy friend as thyself." Now we love our friends out of charity. Therefore we should love ourselves too out of charity.

*I answer that,* Since charity is a kind of friendship, as stated above (Q. 23, A. 1), we may consider charity from two standpoints: first, under the general notion of friendship, and in this way we must hold that, properly speaking, a man is not a friend to himself, but something more than a friend, since friendship implies union, for Dionysius says (Div. Nom. iv) that "love is a unitive force," whereas a man is one with himself which is more than being united to another. Hence, just as unity is the principle of union, so the love with which a man loves himself is the form and root of friendship. For if we have friendship with others it is because we do unto them as we do unto ourselves, hence we read in *Ethic.* ix, 4, 8, that "the origin of friendly relations with others lies in our relations to ourselves." Thus too with regard to principles we have something greater than science, namely understanding.

Secondly, we may speak of charity in respect of its specific nature, namely as denoting man's friendship with God in the first place, and, consequently, with the things of God, among which things is man himself who has charity. Hence, among these other things which he loves out of charity because they pertain to God, he loves also himself out of charity.

Reply Obj. 1: Gregory speaks there of charity under the general notion of friendship: and the Second Objection is to be taken in the same sense.

Reply Obj. 3: Those who love themselves are to be blamed, in so far as they love themselves as regards their sensitive nature, which they humor. This is not to love oneself truly according to one's rational nature, so as to desire for oneself the good things which pertain to the perfection of reason: and in this way chiefly it is through charity that a man loves himself.

FIFTH ARTICLE [II-II, Q. 25, Art. 5]

Whether a Man Ought to Love His Body Out of Charity?

Objection 1: It would seem that a man ought not to love his body out of charity. For we do not love one with whom we are unwilling to associate. But those who have charity shun the society of the body, according to Rom. 7:24: "Who shall deliver me from the body of this death?" and Phil. 1:23: "Having a desire to be dissolved and to be with Christ." Therefore our bodies are not to be loved out of charity.

Obj. 2: Further, the friendship of charity is based on fellowship in the enjoyment of God. But the body can have no share in that enjoyment. Therefore the body is not to be loved out of charity.

Obj. 3: Further, since charity is a kind of friendship it is towards those who are capable of loving in return. But our body cannot love us out of charity. Therefore it should not be loved out of charity.

*On the contrary,* Augustine says (De Doctr. Christ. i, 23, 26) that there are four things that we should love out of charity, and among them he reckons our own body.

*I answer that,* Our bodies can be considered in two ways: first, in respect of their nature, secondly, in respect of the corruption of sin and its punishment.

Now the nature of our body was created, not by an evil principle, as the Manicheans pretend, but by God. Hence we can use it for God's service, according to Rom. 6:13: "Present ... your members as instruments of justice unto God." Consequently, out of the love of charity with which we love God, we ought to love our bodies also, but we ought not to love the evil effects of sin and the corruption of punishment; we ought rather, by the desire of charity, to long for the removal of such things.

Reply Obj. 1: The Apostle did not shrink from the society of his body, as regards the nature of the body, in fact in this respect he was loth to be deprived thereof, according to 2 Cor. 5:4: "We would not be unclothed, but clothed over." He did, however, wish to escape from the taint of concupiscence, which remains in the body, and from the corruption of the body which weighs down the soul, so as to hinder it from seeing God. Hence he says expressly: "From the body of this death."

Reply Obj. 2: Although our bodies are unable to enjoy God by knowing and loving Him, yet by the works which we do through the body, we are able to attain to the perfect knowledge of God. Hence from the enjoyment in the soul there overflows a certain happiness into the body, viz., "the flush of health and incorruption," as Augustine states (Ep. ad Dioscor. cxviii). Hence, since the body has, in a fashion, a share of happiness, it can be loved with the love of charity.

Reply Obj. 3: Mutual love is found in the friendship which is for another, but not in that which a man has for himself, either in respect of his soul, or in respect of his body.

SIXTH ARTICLE [II-II, Q. 25, Art. 6]

Whether We Ought to Love Sinners Out of Charity?

Objection 1: It would seem that we ought not to love sinners out of charity. For it is written (Ps. 118:113): "I have hated the unjust." But David had perfect charity. Therefore sinners should be hated rather than loved, out of charity.

Obj. 2: Further, "love is proved by deeds" as Gregory says in a homily for Pentecost (In Evang. xxx). But good men do no works of the unjust: *on the contrary,* they do such as would appear to be works of hate, according to Ps. 100:8: "In the morning I put to death all the wicked of the land": and God commanded (Ex. 22:18): "Wizards thou shalt not suffer to live." Therefore sinners should not be loved out of charity.

Obj. 3: Further, it is part of friendship that one should desire and wish good things for one's friends. Now the saints, out of charity, desire evil things for the wicked, according to Ps. 9:18: "May the wicked be turned into hell [*Douay and A. V.: 'The wicked shall be,' etc. See Reply to this Objection.]." Therefore sinners should not be loved out of charity.

Obj. 4: Further, it is proper to friends to rejoice in, and will the same things. Now charity does not make us will what sinners will, nor to rejoice in what gives them joy, but rather the contrary. Therefore sinners should not be loved out of charity.

Obj. 5: Further, it is proper to friends to associate together, according to *Ethic.* viii. But we ought not to associate with sinners, according to 2 Cor. 6:17: "Go ye out from among them." Therefore we should not love sinners out of charity.

*On the contrary,* Augustine says (De Doctr. Christ. i, 30) that "when it is said: 'Thou shalt love thy neighbor,' it is evident that we ought to look upon every man as our neighbor." Now sinners do not cease to be men, for sin does not destroy nature. Therefore we ought to love sinners out of charity.

*I answer that,* Two things may be considered in the sinner: his nature and his guilt. According to his nature, which he has from God, he has a capacity for happiness, on the fellowship of which charity is based, as stated above (A. 3; Q. 23, AA. 1, 5), wherefore we ought to love sinners, out of charity, in respect of their nature.

On the other hand their guilt is opposed to God, and is an obstacle to happiness. Wherefore, in respect of their guilt whereby they are opposed to God, all sinners are to be hated, even one's father or mother or kindred, according to Luke 12:26. For it is our duty to hate, in the sinner, his being a sinner, and to love in him, his being a man capable of bliss; and this is to love him truly, out of charity, for God's sake.

Reply Obj. 1: The prophet hated the unjust, as such, and the object of his hate was their injustice, which was their evil. Such hatred is perfect, of which he himself says (Ps. 138:22): "I have hated them with a perfect hatred." Now hatred of a person's evil is equivalent to love of his good. Hence also this perfect hatred belongs to charity.

Reply Obj. 2: As the Philosopher observes (Ethic. ix, 3), when our friends fall into sin, we ought not to deny them the amenities of friendship, so long as there is hope of their mending their ways, and we ought to help them more readily to regain virtue than to recover money, had they lost it, for as much as virtue is more akin than money to friendship. When, however, they fall into very great wickedness, and become incurable, we ought no longer to show them friendliness. It is for this reason that both Divine and human laws command such like sinners to be put to death, because there is greater likelihood of their harming others than of their mending their ways. Nevertheless the judge puts this into effect, not out of hatred for the sinners, but out of the love of charity, by reason of which he prefers the public good to the life of the individual. Moreover the death inflicted by the judge profits the sinner, if he be converted, unto the expiation of his crime; and, if he be not converted, it profits so as to put an end to the sin, because the sinner is thus deprived of the power to sin any more.

Reply Obj. 3: Such like imprecations which we come across in Holy Writ, may be understood in three ways: first, by way of prediction, not by way of wish, so that the sense is: "May the wicked be," that is, "The wicked shall be, turned into hell." Secondly, by way of wish, yet so that the desire of the wisher is not referred to the man's punishment, but to the justice of the punisher, according to Ps. 57:11: "The just shall rejoice when he shall see the revenge," since, according to Wis. 1:13, not even God "hath pleasure in the destruction of the wicked [Vulg.:

'living']" when He punishes them, but He rejoices in His justice, according to Ps. 10:8: "The Lord is just and hath loved justice." Thirdly, so that this desire is referred to the removal of the sin, and not to the punishment itself, to the effect, namely, that the sin be destroyed, but that the man may live.

Reply Obj. 4: We love sinners out of charity, not so as to will what they will, or to rejoice in what gives them joy, but so as to make them will what we will, and rejoice in what rejoices us. Hence it is written (Jer. 15:19): "They shall be turned to thee, and thou shalt not to be turned to them."

Reply Obj. 5: The weak should avoid associating with sinners, on account of the danger in which they stand of being perverted by them. But it is commendable for the perfect, of whose perversion there is no fear, to associate with sinners that they may convert them. For thus did Our Lord eat and drink with sinners as related by Matt. 9:11-13. Yet all should avoid the society of sinners, as regards fellowship in sin; in this sense it is written (2 Cor. 6:17): "Go out from among them ... and touch not the unclean thing," i.e. by consenting to sin.

SEVENTH ARTICLE [II-II, Q. 25, Art. 7]

Whether Sinners Love Themselves?

Objection 1: It would seem that sinners love themselves. For that which is the principle of sin, is most of all in the sinner. Now love of self is the principle of sin, since Augustine says (De Civ. Dei xiv, 28) that it "builds up the city of Babylon." Therefore sinners most of all love themselves.

Obj. 2: Further, sin does not destroy nature. Now it is in keeping with nature that every man should love himself: wherefore even irrational creatures naturally desire their own good, for instance, the preservation of their being, and so forth. Therefore sinners love themselves.

Obj. 3: Further, good is beloved by all, as Dionysius states (Div. Nom. iv). Now many sinners reckon themselves to be good. Therefore many sinners love themselves.

*On the contrary,* It is written (Ps. 10:6): "He that loveth iniquity, hateth his own soul."

*I answer that,* Love of self is common to all, in one way; in another way it is proper to the good; in a third way, it is proper to the wicked. For it is common to all for each one to love what he thinks himself to be. Now a man is said to be a thing, in two ways: first, in respect of his substance and nature, and, this way all think themselves to be what they are, that is, composed of a soul and body. In this way too, all men, both good and wicked, love themselves, in so far as they love their own preservation.

Secondly, a man is said to be something in respect of some predominance, as the sovereign of a state is spoken of as being the state, and so, what the sovereign does, the state is said to do. In this way, all do not think themselves to be what they are. For the reasoning mind is the predominant part of man, while the sensitive and corporeal nature takes the second place, the former of which the Apostle calls the "inward man," and the latter, the "outward man" (2 Cor. 4:16). Now the good look upon their rational nature or the inward man as being the chief thing in them, wherefore in this way they think themselves to be what they are. On the other hand, the wicked reckon their sensitive and corporeal nature, or the outward man, to hold the first place. Wherefore, since they know not themselves aright, they do not love themselves aright, but love what they think themselves to be. But the good know themselves truly, and therefore truly love themselves.

The Philosopher proves this from five things that are proper to friendship. For in the first place, every friend wishes his friend to be and to live; secondly, he desires good things for him; thirdly, he does good things to him; fourthly, he takes pleasure in his company; fifthly, he is of one mind with him, rejoicing and sorrowing in almost the same things. In this way the good love themselves, as to the inward man, because they wish the preservation thereof in its integrity, they desire good things for him, namely spiritual goods, indeed they do their best to obtain them, and they take pleasure in entering into their own hearts, because they find there good thoughts in the present, the memory of past good, and the hope of future good, all of which are sources of pleasure. Likewise they experience no clashing of wills, since their whole soul tends to one thing.

On the other hand, the wicked have no wish to be preserved in the integrity of the inward man, nor do they desire spiritual goods for him, nor do they work for that end, nor do they take pleasure in their own company by entering into their own hearts, because whatever they find there, present, past and future, is evil and horrible; nor do they agree with themselves, on account of the gnawings of conscience, according to Ps. 49:21: "I will reprove thee and set before thy face."

In the same manner it may be shown that the wicked love themselves, as regards the corruption of the outward man, whereas the good do not love themselves thus.

Reply Obj. 1: The love of self which is the principle of sin is that which is proper to the wicked, and reaches "to the contempt of God," as stated in the passage quoted, because the wicked so desire external goods as to despise spiritual goods.

Reply Obj. 2: Although natural love is not altogether forfeited by wicked men, yet it is perverted in them, as explained above.

Reply Obj. 3: The wicked have some share of self-love, in so far as they think themselves good. Yet such love of self is not true but apparent: and even this is not possible in those who are very wicked.

EIGHTH ARTICLE [II-II, Q. 25, Art. 8]

Whether Charity Requires That We Should Love Our Enemies?

Objection 1: It would seem that charity does not require us to love our enemies. For Augustine says (Enchiridion lxxiii) that "this great good," namely, the love of our enemies, is "not so universal in its application, as the object of our petition when we say: Forgive us our trespasses." Now no one is forgiven sin without he have charity, because, according to Prov. 10:12, "charity covereth all sins." Therefore charity does not require that we should love our enemies.

Obj. 2: Further, charity does not do away with nature. Now everything, even an irrational being, naturally hates its contrary, as a lamb hates a wolf, and water fire. Therefore charity does not make us love our enemies.

Obj. 3: Further, charity "doth nothing perversely" (1 Cor. 13:4). Now it seems perverse to love one's enemies, as it would be to hate one's friends: hence Joab upbraided David by saying (2 Kings 19:6): "Thou lovest them that hate thee, and thou hatest them that love thee." Therefore charity does not make us love our enemies.

*On the contrary,* Our Lord said (Matt. 4:44): "Love your enemies."

*I answer that,* Love of one's enemies may be understood in three ways. First, as though we were to love our enemies as such: this is perverse, and contrary to charity, since it implies love of that which is evil in another.

Secondly love of one's enemies may mean that we love them as to their nature, but in general: and in this sense charity requires that we should love our enemies, namely, that in loving God and our neighbor, we should not exclude our enemies from the love given to our neighbor in general.

Thirdly, love of one's enemies may be considered as specially directed to them, namely, that we should have a special movement of love towards our enemies. Charity does not require this absolutely, because it does not require that we should have a special movement of love to every individual man, since this would be impossible. Nevertheless charity does require this, in respect of our being prepared in mind, namely, that we should be ready to love our enemies individually, if the necessity were to occur. That man should actually do so, and love his enemy for God's sake, without it being necessary for him to do so, belongs to the perfection of charity. For since man loves his neighbor, out of charity, for God's sake, the more he loves God, the more does he put enmities aside and show love towards his neighbor: thus if we loved a certain man very much, we would love his children though they were unfriendly towards us. This is the sense in which Augustine speaks in the passage quoted in the First Objection, the Reply to which is therefore evident.

Reply Obj. 2: Everything naturally hates its contrary as such. Now our enemies are contrary to us, as enemies, wherefore this itself should be hateful to us, for their enmity should displease us. They are not, however, contrary to us, as men and capable of happiness: and it is as such that we are bound to love them.

Reply Obj. 3: It is wrong to love one's enemies as such: charity does not do this, as stated above.

NINTH ARTICLE [II-II, Q. 25, Art. 9]

Whether It Is Necessary for Salvation That We Should Show Our Enemies the Signs and Effects of Love?

Objection 1: It would seem that charity demands of a man to show his enemy the signs or effects of love. For it is written (1 John 3:18): "Let us not love in word nor in tongue, but in deed and in truth." Now a man loves in deed by showing the one he loves signs and effects of love. Therefore charity requires that a man show his enemies such signs and effects of love.

Obj. 2: Further, Our Lord said in the same breath (Matt. 5:44): "Love your enemies," and, "Do good to them that hate you." Now charity demands that we love our enemies. Therefore it demands also that we should "do good to them."

Obj. 3: Further, not only God but also our neighbor is the object of charity. Now Gregory says in a homily for Pentecost (In Evang. xxx), that "love of God cannot be idle for wherever it is it does great things, and if it ceases to work, it is no longer love." Hence charity towards our neighbor cannot be without producing works. But charity requires us to love our neighbor without exception, though he be an enemy. Therefore charity requires us to show the signs and effects of love towards our enemies.

*On the contrary,* A gloss on Matt. 5:44, "Do good to them that hate you," says: "To do good to one's enemies is the height of perfection" [*Augustine, Enchiridion lxxiii]. Now charity does not require us to do that which belongs to its perfection. Therefore charity does not require us to show the signs and effects of love to our enemies.

*I answer that,* The effects and signs of charity are the result of inward love, and are in proportion with it. Now it is absolutely necessary, for the fulfilment of the precept, that we should inwardly love our enemies in general, but not individually, except as regards the mind being prepared to do so, as explained above (A. 8).

We must accordingly apply this to the showing of the effects and signs of love. For some of the signs and favors of love are shown to our neighbors in general, as when we pray for all the faithful, or for a whole people, or when anyone bestows a favor on a whole community: and the fulfilment of the precept requires that we should show such like favors or signs of love towards our enemies. For if we did not so, it would be a proof of vengeful spite, and contrary to what is written (Lev. 19:18): "Seek not revenge, nor be mindful of the injury of thy citizens." But there are other favors or signs of love, which one shows to certain persons in particular: and it is not necessary for salvation that we show our enemies such like favors and signs of love, except as regards being ready in our minds, for instance to come to their assistance in a case of urgency, according to Prov. 25:21: "If thy enemy be hungry, give him to eat; if he thirst, give him ... drink." Outside cases of urgency, to show such like favors to an enemy belongs to the perfection of charity, whereby we not only beware, as in duty bound, of being overcome by evil, but also wish to overcome evil by good [*Rom. 12:21], which belongs to perfection: for then we not only beware of being drawn into hatred on account of the hurt done to us, but purpose to induce our enemy to love us on account of our kindliness.

This suffices for the Replies to the Objections.

TENTH ARTICLE [II-II, Q. 25, Art. 10]

Whether We Ought to Love the Angels Out of Charity?

Objection 1: It would seem that we are not bound to love the angels out of charity. For, as Augustine says (De Doctr. Christ. i), charity is a twofold love: the love of God and of our neighbor. Now love of the angels is not contained in the love of God, since they are created substances; nor is it, seemingly, contained in the love of our neighbor, since they do not belong with us to a common species. Therefore we are not bound to love them out of charity.

Obj. 2: Further, dumb animals have more in common with us than the angels have, since they belong to the same proximate genus as we do. But we have not charity towards dumb animals, as stated above (A. 3). Neither, therefore, have we towards the angels.

Obj. 3: Further, nothing is so proper to friends as companionship with one another (Ethic. viii, 5). But the angels are not our companions; we cannot even see them. Therefore we are unable to give them the friendship of charity.

*On the contrary,* Augustine says (De Doctr. Christ. i, 30): "If the name of neighbor is given either to those whom we pity, or to those who pity us, it is evident that the precept binding us to love our neighbor includes also the holy angels from whom we receive many merciful favors."

*I answer that,* As stated above (Q. 23, A. 1), the friendship of charity is founded upon the fellowship of everlasting happiness, in which men share in common with the angels. For it is written (Matt. 22:30) that "in the resurrection ... men shall be as the angels of God in heaven." It is therefore evident that the friendship of charity extends also to the angels.

Reply Obj. 1: Our neighbor is not only one who is united to us in a common species, but also one who is united to us by sharing in the blessings pertaining to everlasting life, and it is on the latter fellowship that the friendship of charity is founded.

Reply Obj. 2: Dumb animals are united to us in the proximate genus, by reason of their sensitive nature; whereas we are partakers of everlasting happiness, by reason not of our sensitive nature but of our rational mind wherein we associate with the angels.

Reply Obj. 3: The companionship of the angels does not consist in outward fellowship, which we have in respect of our sensitive nature; it consists in a fellowship of the mind, imperfect indeed in this life, but perfect in heaven, as stated above (Q. 23, A. 1, ad 1).

ELEVENTH ARTICLE [II-II, Q. 25, Art. 11]

Whether We Are Bound to Love the Demons Out of Charity?

Objection 1: It would seem that we ought to love the demons out of charity. For the angels are our neighbors by reason of their fellowship with us in a rational mind. But the demons also share in our fellowship thus, since natural gifts, such as life and understanding, remain in them unimpaired, as Dionysius states (Div. Nom. iv). Therefore we ought to love the demons out of charity.

Obj. 2: Further, the demons differ from the blessed angels in the matter of sin, even as sinners from just men. Now the just man loves the sinner out of charity. Therefore he ought to love the demons also out of charity.

Obj. 3: Further, we ought, out of charity, to love, as being our neighbors, those from whom we receive favors, as appears from the passage of Augustine quoted above (A. 9). Now the demons are useful to us in many things, for "by tempting us they work crowns for us," as Augustine says (De Civ. Dei xi, 17). Therefore we ought to love the demons out of charity.

*On the contrary,* It is written (Isa. 28:18): "Your league with death shall be abolished, and your covenant with hell shall not stand." Now the perfection of a peace and covenant is through charity. Therefore we ought not to have charity for the demons who live in hell and compass death.

*I answer that,* As stated above (A. 6), in the sinner, we are bound, out of charity, to love his nature, but to hate his sin. But the name of demon is given to designate a nature deformed by sin, wherefore demons should not be loved out of charity. Without however laying stress on the word, the question as to whether the spirits called demons ought to be loved out of charity, must be answered in accordance with the statement made above (AA. 2, 3), that a thing may be loved out of charity in two ways. First, a thing may be loved as the person who is the object of friendship, and thus we cannot have the friendship of charity towards the demons. For it is an essential part of friendship that one should be a well-wisher towards one's friend; and it is impossible for us, out of charity, to desire the good of everlasting life, to which charity is referred, for those spirits whom God has condemned eternally, since this would be in opposition to our charity towards God whereby we approve of His justice.

Secondly, we love a thing as being that which we desire to be enduring as another's good. In this way we love irrational creatures out of charity, in as much as we wish them to endure, to give glory to God and be useful to man, as stated above (A. 3): and in this way too we can love the nature of the demons even out of charity, in as much as we desire those spirits to endure, as to their natural gifts, unto God's glory.

Reply Obj. 1: The possession of everlasting happiness is not impossible for the angelic mind as it is for the mind of a demon; consequently the friendship of charity which is based on the fellowship of everlasting life, rather than on the fellowship of nature, is possible towards the angels, but not towards the demons.

Reply Obj. 2: In this life, men who are in sin retain the possibility of obtaining everlasting happiness: not so those who are lost in hell, who, in this respect, are in the same case as the demons.

Reply Obj. 3: That the demons are useful to us is due not to their intention but to the ordering of Divine providence; hence this leads us to be friends, not with them, but with God, Who turns their perverse intention to our profit.

TWELFTH ARTICLE [II-II, Q. 25, Art. 12]

Whether Four Things Are Rightly Reckoned As to Be Loved Out of Charity, Viz. God, Our Neighbor, Our Body and Ourselves?

Objection 1: It would seem that these four things are not rightly reckoned as to be loved out of charity, to wit: God, our neighbor, our body, and ourselves. For, as Augustine states (Tract. super Joan. lxxxiii), "he that loveth not God, loveth not himself." Hence love of oneself is included in the love of God. Therefore love of oneself is not distinct from the love of God.

Obj. 2: Further, a part ought not to be condivided with the whole. But our body is part of ourselves. Therefore it ought not to be condivided with ourselves as a distinct object of love.

Obj. 3: Further, just as a man has a body, so has his neighbor. Since then the love with which a man loves his neighbor, is distinct from the love with which a man loves himself, so the love with which a man loves his neighbor's body, ought to be distinct from the love with which he loves his own body. Therefore these four things are not rightly distinguished as objects to be loved out of charity.

*On the contrary,* Augustine says (De Doctr. Christ. i, 23): "There are four things to be loved; one which is above us," namely God, "another, which is ourselves, a third which is nigh to us," namely our neighbor, "and a fourth which is beneath us," namely our own body.

*I answer that,* As stated above (Q. 23, AA. 1, 5), the friendship of charity is based on the fellowship of happiness. Now, in this fellowship, one thing is considered as the principle from which happiness flows, namely God; a second is that which directly partakes of happiness, namely men and angels; a third is a thing to which happiness comes by a kind of overflow, namely the human body.

Now the source from which happiness flows is lovable by reason of its being the cause of happiness: that which is a partaker of happiness, can be an object of love for two reasons, either through being identified with ourselves, or through being associated with us in partaking of happiness, and in this respect, there are two things to be loved out of charity, in as much as man loves both himself and his neighbor.

Reply Obj. 1: The different relations between a lover and the various things loved make a different kind of lovableness. Accordingly, since the relation between the human lover and God is different from his relation to himself, these two are reckoned as distinct objects of love, for the love of the one is the cause of the love of the other, so that the former love being removed the latter is taken away.

Reply Obj. 2: The subject of charity is the rational mind that can be capable of obtaining happiness, to which the body does not reach directly, but only by a kind of overflow. Hence, by his reasonable mind which holds the first place in him, man, out of charity, loves himself in one way, and his own body in another.

Reply Obj. 3: Man loves his neighbor, both as to his soul and as to his body, by reason of a certain fellowship in happiness. Wherefore, on the part of his neighbor, there is only one reason for loving him; and our neighbor's body is not reckoned as a special object of love.

## QUESTION 26

OF THE ORDER OF CHARITY (In Thirteen Articles)

We must now consider the order of charity, under which head there are thirteen points of inquiry:

(1) Whether there is an order in charity?

(2) Whether man ought to love God more than his neighbor?

(3) Whether more than himself?

(4) Whether he ought to love himself more than his neighbor?

(5) Whether man ought to love his neighbor more than his own body?

(6) Whether he ought to love one neighbor more than another?

(7) Whether he ought to love more, a neighbor who is better, or one who is more closely united to him?

(8) Whether he ought to love more, one who is akin to him by blood, or one who is united to him by other ties?

(9) Whether, out of charity, a man ought to love his son more than his father?

(10) Whether he ought to love his mother more than his father?

(11) Whether he ought to love his wife more than his father or mother?

(12) Whether we ought to love those who are kind to us more than those whom we are kind to?

(13) Whether the order of charity endures in heaven?

FIRST ARTICLE [II-II, Q. 26, Art. 1]

Whether There Is Order in Charity?

Objection 1: It would seem that there is no order in charity. For charity is a virtue. But no order is assigned to the other virtues. Neither, therefore, should any order be assigned to charity.

Obj. 2: Further, just as the object of faith is the First Truth, so is the object of charity the Sovereign Good. Now no order is appointed for faith, but all things are believed equally. Neither, therefore, ought there to be any order in charity.

Obj. 3: Further, charity is in the will: whereas ordering belongs, not to the will, but to the reason. Therefore no order should be ascribed to charity.

*On the contrary,* It is written (Cant 2:4): "He brought me into the cellar of wine, he set in order charity in me."

*I answer that,* As the Philosopher says (Metaph. v, text. 16), the terms "before" and "after" are used in reference to some principle. Now order implies that certain things are, in some way, before or after. Hence wherever there is a principle, there must needs be also order of some kind. But it has been said above (Q. 23, A. 1; Q. 25, A. 12) that the love of charity tends to God as to the principle of happiness, on the fellowship of which the friendship of charity is based. Consequently there must needs be some order in things loved out of charity, which order is in reference to the first principle of that love, which is God.

Reply Obj. 1: Charity tends towards the last end considered as last end: and this does not apply to any other virtue, as stated above (Q. 23, A. 6). Now the end has the character of principle in matters of appetite and action, as was shown above (Q. 23, A. 7, ad 2; I-II, A. 1, ad 1). Wherefore charity, above all, implies relation to the First Principle, and consequently, in charity above all, we find an order in reference to the First Principle.

Reply Obj. 2: Faith pertains to the cognitive power, whose operation depends on the thing known being in the knower. On the other hand, charity is in an appetitive power, whose operation consists in the soul tending to things themselves. Now order is to be found in things themselves, and flows from them into our knowledge. Hence order is more appropriate to charity than to faith.

And yet there is a certain order in faith, in so far as it is chiefly about God, and secondarily about things referred to God.

Reply Obj. 3: Order belongs to reason as the faculty that orders, and to the appetitive power as to the faculty which is ordered. It is in this way that order is stated to be in charity.

SECOND ARTICLE [II-II, Q. 26, Art. 2]

Whether God Ought to Be Loved More Than Our Neighbor?

Objection 1: It would seem that God ought not to be loved more than our neighbor. For it is written (1 John 4:20): "He that loveth not his brother whom he seeth, how can he love God, Whom he seeth not?" Whence it seems to follow that the more a thing is visible the more lovable it is, since loving begins with seeing, according to *Ethic.* ix, 5, 12. Now God is less visible than our neighbor. Therefore He is less lovable, out of charity, than our neighbor.

Obj. 2: Further, likeness causes love, according to Ecclus. 13:19: "Every beast loveth its like." Now man bears more likeness to his neighbor than to God. Therefore man loves his neighbor, out of charity, more than he loves God.

Obj. 3: Further, what charity loves in a neighbor, is God, according to Augustine (De Doctr. Christ. i, 22, 27). Now God is not greater in Himself than He is in our neighbor. Therefore He is not more to be loved in Himself than in our neighbor. Therefore we ought not to love God more than our neighbor.

*On the contrary,* A thing ought to be loved more, if others ought to be hated on its account. Now we ought to hate our neighbor for God's sake, if, to wit, he leads us astray from God, according to Luke 14:26: "If any man come to Me and hate not his father, and mother, and wife, end children, and brethren, and sisters ... he cannot be My disciple." Therefore we ought to love God, out of charity, more than our neighbor.

*I answer that,* Each kind of friendship regards chiefly the subject in which we chiefly find the good on the fellowship of which that friendship is based: thus civil friendship regards chiefly the ruler of the state, on whom the entire common good of the state depends; hence to him before all, the citizens owe fidelity and obedience. Now the friendship of charity is based on the fellowship of happiness, which consists essentially in God, as the First Principle, whence it flows to all who are capable of happiness.

Therefore God ought to be loved chiefly and before all out of charity: for He is loved as the cause of happiness, whereas our neighbor is loved as receiving together with us a share of happiness from Him.

Reply Obj. 1: A thing is a cause of love in two ways: first, as being the reason for loving. In this way good is the cause of love, since each thing is loved according to its measure of goodness. Secondly, a thing causes love, as being a way to acquire love. It is in this way that seeing is the cause of loving, not as though a thing were lovable according as it is visible, but because by seeing a thing we are led to love it. Hence it does not follow that what is more visible is more lovable, but that as an object of love we meet with it before others: and that is the sense of the Apostle's argument. For, since our neighbor is more visible to us, he is the first lovable object we meet with, because "the soul learns, from those things it knows, to love what it knows not," as Gregory says in a homily (In Evang. xi). Hence it can be argued that, if any man loves not his neighbor, neither does he love God, not because his neighbor is more lovable, but because he is the first thing to demand our love: and God is more lovable by reason of His greater goodness.

Reply Obj. 2: The likeness we have to God precedes and causes the likeness we have to our neighbor: because from the very fact that we share along with our neighbor in something received from God, we become like to our neighbor. Hence by reason of this likeness we ought to love God more than we love our neighbor.

Reply Obj. 3: Considered in His substance, God is equally in all, in whomsoever He may be, for He is not lessened by being in anything. And yet our neighbor does not possess God's goodness equally with God, for God has it essentially, and our neighbor by participation.

THIRD ARTICLE [II-II, Q. 26, Art. 3]

Whether Out of Charity, Man Is Bound to Love God More Than Himself?

Objection 1: It would seem that man is not bound, out of charity, to love God more than himself. For the Philosopher says (Ethic. ix, 8) that "a man's friendly relations with others arise from his friendly relations with himself." Now the cause is stronger than its effect. Therefore man's friendship towards himself is greater than his friendship for anyone else. Therefore he ought to love himself more than God.

Obj. 2: Further, one loves a thing in so far as it is one's own good. Now the reason for loving a thing is more loved than the thing itself which is loved for that reason, even as the principles which are the reason for knowing a thing are more known. Therefore man loves himself more than any other good loved by him. Therefore he does not love God more than himself.

Obj. 3: Further, a man loves God as much as he loves to enjoy God. But a man loves himself as much as he loves to enjoy God; since this is the highest good a man can wish for himself. Therefore man is not bound, out of charity, to love God more than himself.

*On the contrary,* Augustine says (De Doctr. Christ. i, 22): "If thou oughtest to love thyself, not for thy own sake, but for the sake of Him in Whom is the rightest end of thy love, let no other man take offense if him also thou lovest for God's sake." Now "the cause of a thing being such is yet more so." Therefore man ought to love God more than himself.

*I answer that,* The good we receive from God is twofold, the good of nature, and the good of grace. Now the fellowship of natural goods bestowed on us by God is the foundation of natural love, in virtue of which not only man, so long as his nature remains unimpaired, loves God above all things and more than himself, but also every single creature, each in its own way, i.e. either by an intellectual, or by a rational, or by an animal, or at least by a natural love, as stones do, for instance, and other things bereft of knowledge, because each part naturally loves the common good of the whole more than its own particular good. This is evidenced by its operation, since the principal inclination of each part is towards common action conducive to the good of the whole. It may also be seen in civic virtues whereby sometimes the citizens suffer damage even to their own property and persons for the sake of the common good. Wherefore much more is this realized with regard to the friendship of charity which is based on the fellowship of the gifts of grace.

Therefore man ought, out of charity, to love God, Who is the common good of all, more than himself: since happiness is in God as in the universal and fountain principle of all who are able to have a share of that happiness.

Reply Obj. 1: The Philosopher is speaking of friendly relations towards another person in whom the good, which is the object of friendship, resides in some restricted way; and not of friendly relations with another in whom the aforesaid good resides in totality.

Reply Obj. 2: The part does indeed love the good of the whole, as becomes a part, not however so as to refer the good of the whole to itself, but rather itself to the good of the whole.

Reply Obj. 3: That a man wishes to enjoy God pertains to that love of God which is love of concupiscence. Now we love God with the love of friendship more than with the love of concupiscence, because the Divine good is greater in itself, than our share of good in enjoying Him. Hence, out of charity, man simply loves God more than himself.

FOURTH ARTICLE [II-II, Q. 26, Art. 4]

Whether Out of Charity, Man Ought to Love Himself More Than His Neighbor?

Objection 1: It would seem that a man ought not, out of charity, to love himself more than his neighbor. For the principal object of charity is God, as stated above (A. 2; Q. 25, AA. 1, 12). Now sometimes our neighbor is more closely united to God than we are ourselves. Therefore we ought to love such a one more than ourselves.

Obj. 2: Further, the more we love a person, the more we avoid injuring him. Now a man, out of charity, submits to injury for his neighbor's sake, according to Prov. 12:26: "He that neglecteth a loss for the sake of a friend, is just." Therefore a man ought, out of charity, to love his neighbor more than himself.

Obj. 3: Further, it is written (1 Cor. 13:5) "charity seeketh not its own." Now the thing we love most is the one whose good we seek most. Therefore a man does not, out of charity, love himself more than his neighbor.

*On the contrary,* It is written (Lev. 19:18, Matt. 22:39): "Thou shalt love thy neighbor (Lev. 19:18: 'friend') as thyself." Whence it seems to follow that man's love for himself is the model of his love for another. But the model exceeds the copy. Therefore, out of charity, a man ought to love himself more than his neighbor.

*I answer that,* There are two things in man, his spiritual nature and his corporeal nature. And a man is said to love himself by reason of his loving himself with regard to his spiritual nature, as stated above (Q. 25, A. 7): so that accordingly, a man ought, out of charity, to love himself more than he loves any other person.

This is evident from the very reason for loving: since, as stated above (Q. 25, AA. 1, 12), God is loved as the principle of good, on which the love of charity is founded; while man, out of charity, loves himself by reason of his being a partaker of the aforesaid good, and loves his neighbor by reason of his fellowship in that good. Now fellowship is a reason for love according to a certain union in relation to God. Wherefore just as unity surpasses union, the fact that man himself has a share of the Divine good, is a more potent reason for loving than that another should be a partner with him in that share. Therefore man, out of charity, ought to love himself more than his neighbor: in sign whereof, a man ought not to give way to any evil of sin, which counteracts his share of happiness, not even that he may free his neighbor from sin.

Reply Obj. 1: The love of charity takes its quantity not only from its object which is God, but also from the lover, who is the man that has charity, even as the quantity of any action depends in some way on the subject. Wherefore, though a better neighbor is nearer to God, yet because he is not as near to the man who has charity, as this man is to himself, it does not follow that a man is bound to love his neighbor more than himself.

Reply Obj. 2: A man ought to bear bodily injury for his friend's sake, and precisely in so doing he loves himself more as regards his spiritual mind, because it pertains to the perfection of virtue, which is a good of the mind. In spiritual matters, however, man ought not to suffer injury by sinning, in order to free his neighbor from sin, as stated above.

Reply Obj. 3: As Augustine says in his Rule (Ep. ccxi), the saying, "'charity seeks not her own,' means that it prefers the common to the private good." Now the common good is always more lovable to the individual than his private good, even as the good of the whole is more lovable to the part, than the latter's own partial good, as stated above (A. 3).

FIFTH ARTICLE [II-II, Q. 26, Art. 5]

Whether a Man Ought to Love His Neighbor More Than His Own Body?

Objection 1: It would seem that a man is not bound to love his neighbor more than his own body. For his neighbor includes his neighbor's body. If therefore a man ought to love his neighbor more than his own body, it follows that he ought to love his neighbor's body more than his own.

Obj. 2: Further, a man ought to love his own soul more than his neighbor's, as stated above (A. 4). Now a man's own body is nearer to his soul than his neighbor. Therefore we ought to love our body more than our neighbor.

Obj. 3: Further, a man imperils that which he loves less for the sake of what he loves more. Now every man is not bound to imperil his own body for his neighbor's safety: this belongs to the perfect, according to John 15:13: "Greater love than this no man hath, that a man lay down his life for his friends." Therefore a man is not bound, out of charity, to love his neighbor more than his own body.

*On the contrary,* Augustine says (De Doctr. Christ. i, 27) that "we ought to love our neighbor more than our own body."

*I answer that,* Out of charity we ought to love more that which has more fully the reason for being loved out of charity, as stated above (A. 2; Q. 25, A. 12). Now fellowship in the full participation of happiness which is the reason for loving one's neighbor, is a greater reason for loving, than the participation of happiness by way of overflow, which is the reason for loving one's own body. Therefore, as regards the welfare of the soul we ought to love our neighbor more than our own body.

Reply Obj. 1: According to the Philosopher (Ethic. ix, 8) a thing seems to be that which is predominant in it: so that when we say that we ought to love our neighbor more than our own body, this refers to his soul, which is his predominant part.

Reply Obj. 2: Our body is nearer to our soul than our neighbor, as regards the constitution of our own nature: but as regards the participation of happiness, our neighbor's soul is more closely associated with our own soul, than even our own body is.

Reply Obj. 3: Every man is immediately concerned with the care of his own body, but not with his neighbor's welfare, except perhaps in cases of urgency: wherefore charity does not necessarily require a man to imperil his own body for his neighbor's welfare, except in a case where he is under obligation to do so; and if a man of his own accord offer himself for that purpose, this belongs to the perfection of charity.

SIXTH ARTICLE [II-II, Q. 26, Art. 6]

Whether We Ought to Love One Neighbor More Than Another?

Objection 1: It would seem that we ought not to love one neighbor more than another. For Augustine says (De Doctr. Christ. i, 28): "One ought to love all men equally. Since, however, one cannot do good to all, we ought to consider those chiefly who by reason of place, time or any other circumstance, by a kind of chance, are more closely united to us." Therefore one neighbor ought not to be loved more than another.

Obj. 2: Further, where there is one and the same reason for loving several, there should be no inequality of love. Now there is one and the same reason for loving all one's neighbors, which reason is God, as Augustine states (De Doctr. Christ. i, 27). Therefore we ought to love all our neighbors equally.

Obj. 3: Further, to love a man is to wish him good things, as the Philosopher states (Rhet. ii, 4). Now to all our neighbors we wish an equal good, viz. everlasting life. Therefore we ought to love all our neighbors equally.

*On the contrary,* One's obligation to love a person is proportionate to the gravity of the sin one commits in acting against that love. Now it is a more grievous sin to act against the love of certain neighbors, than against the love of others. Hence the commandment (Lev. 10:9), "He that curseth his father or mother, dying let him die," which does not apply to those who cursed others than the above. Therefore we ought to love some neighbors more than others.

*I answer that,* There have been two opinions on this question: for some have said that we ought, out of charity, to love all our neighbors equally, as regards our affection, but not as regards the outward effect. They held that the order of love is to be understood as applying to outward favors, which we ought to confer on those who are connected with us in preference to those who are unconnected, and not to the inward affection, which ought to be given equally to all including our enemies.

But this is unreasonable. For the affection of charity, which is the inclination of grace, is not less orderly than the natural appetite, which is the inclination of nature, for both inclinations flow from Divine wisdom. Now we observe in the physical order that the natural inclination in each thing is proportionate to the act or movement that is becoming to the nature of that thing: thus in earth the inclination of gravity is greater than in water, because it is becoming to earth to be beneath water. Consequently the inclination also of grace which is the effect of charity, must needs be proportionate to those actions which have to be performed outwardly, so that, to wit, the affection of our charity be more intense towards those to whom we ought to behave with greater kindness.

We must, therefore, say that, even as regards the affection we ought to love one neighbor more than another. The reason is that, since the principle of love is God, and the person who loves, it must needs be that the affection of love increases in proportion to the nearness to one or the other of those principles. For as we stated above (A. 1), wherever we find a principle, order depends on relation to that principle.

Reply Obj. 1: Love can be unequal in two ways: first on the part of the good we wish our friend. In this respect we love all men equally out of charity: because we wish them all one same generic good, namely everlasting happiness. Secondly love is said to be greater through its action being more intense: and in this way we ought not to love all equally.

Or we may reply that we have unequal love for certain persons in two ways: first, through our loving some and not loving others. As regards beneficence we are bound to observe this inequality, because we cannot do good to all: but as regards benevolence, love ought not to be thus unequal. The other inequality arises from our loving some more than others: and Augustine does not mean to exclude the latter inequality, but the former, as is evident from what he says of beneficence.

Reply Obj. 2: Our neighbors are not all equally related to God; some are nearer to Him, by reason of their greater goodness, and those we ought, out of charity, to love more than those who are not so near to Him.

Reply Obj. 3: This argument considers the quantity of love on the part of the good which we wish our friends.

SEVENTH ARTICLE [II-II, Q. 26, Art. 7]

Whether We Ought to Love Those Who Are Better More Than Those Who Are More Closely United Us?

Objection 1: It would seem that we ought to love those who are better more than those who are more closely united to us. For that which is in no way hateful seems more lovable than that which is hateful for some reason: just as a thing is all the whiter for having less black mixed with it. Now those who are connected with us are hateful for some reason, according to Luke 14:26: "If any man come to Me, and hate not his father," etc. On the other hand good men are not hateful for any reason. Therefore it seems that we ought to love those who are better more than those who are more closely connected with us.

Obj. 2: Further, by charity above all, man is likened to God. But God loves more the better man. Therefore man also, out of charity, ought to love the better man more than one who is more closely united to him.

Obj. 3: Further, in every friendship, that ought to be loved most which has most to do with the foundation of that friendship: for, by natural friendship we love most those who are connected with us by nature, our parents for instance, or our children. Now the friendship of charity is founded upon the fellowship of happiness, which has more to do with better men than with those who are more closely united to us. Therefore, out of charity, we ought to love better men more than those who are more closely connected with us.

*On the contrary,* It is written (1 Tim. 5:8): "If

any man have not care of his own and especially of those of his house, he hath denied the faith, and is worse than an infidel." Now the inward affection of charity ought to correspond to the outward effect. Therefore charity regards those who are nearer to us before those who are better.

*I answer that,* Every act should be proportionate both to its object and to the agent. But from its object it takes its species, while, from the power of the agent it takes the mode of its intensity: thus movement has its species from the term to which it tends, while the intensity of its speed arises from the disposition of the thing moved and the power of the mover. Accordingly love takes its species from its object, but its intensity is due to the lover.

Now the object of charity's love is God, and man is the lover. Therefore the specific diversity of the love which is in accordance with charity, as regards the love of our neighbor, depends on his relation to God, so that, out of charity, we should wish a greater good to one who is nearer to God; for though the good which charity wishes to all, viz. everlasting happiness, is one in itself, yet it has various degrees according to various shares of happiness, and it belongs to charity to wish God's justice to be maintained, in accordance with which better men have a fuller share of happiness. And this regards the species of love; for there are different species of love according to the different goods that we wish for those whom we love.

On the other hand, the intensity of love is measured with regard to the man who loves, and accordingly man loves those who are more closely united to him, with more intense affection as to the good he wishes for them, than he loves those who are better as to the greater good he wishes for them.

Again a further difference must be observed here: for some neighbors are connected with us by their natural origin, a connection which cannot be severed, since that origin makes them to be what they are. But the goodness of virtue, wherein some are close to God, can come and go, increase and decrease, as was shown above (Q. 24, AA. 4, 10, 11). Hence it is possible for one, out of charity, to wish this man who is more closely united to one, to be better than another, and so reach a higher degree of happiness.

Moreover there is yet another reason for which, out of charity, we love more those who are more nearly connected with us, since we love them in more ways. For, towards those who are not connected with us we have no other friendship than charity, whereas for those who are connected with us, we have certain other friendships, according to the way in which they are connected. Now since the good on which every other friendship of the virtuous is based, is directed, as to its end, to the good on which charity is based, it follows that charity commands each act of another friendship, even as the art which is about the end commands the art which is about the means. Consequently this very act of loving someone because he is akin or connected with us, or because he is a fellow-countryman or for any like reason that is referable to the end of charity, can be commanded by charity, so that, out of charity both eliciting and commanding, we love in more ways those who are more nearly connected with us.

Reply Obj. 1: We are commanded to hate, in our kindred, not their kinship, but only the fact of their being an obstacle between us and God. In this respect they are not akin but hostile to us, according to Micah 7:6: "A men's enemies are they of his own household."

Reply Obj. 2: Charity conforms man to God proportionately, by making man comport himself towards what is his, as God does towards what is His. For we may, out of charity, will certain things as becoming to us which God does not will, because it becomes Him not to will them, as stated above (I-II, Q. 19, A. 10), when we were treating of the goodness of the will.

Reply Obj. 3: Charity elicits the act of love not only as regards the object, but also as regards the lover, as stated above. The result is that the man who is more nearly united to us is more loved.

EIGHTH ARTICLE [II-II, Q. 26, Art. 8]

Whether We Ought to Love More Those Who Are Connected with Us by Ties of Blood?

Objection 1: It would seem that we ought not to love more those who are more closely united to us by ties of blood. For it is written (Prov. 18:24): "A man amiable in society, shall be more friendly than a brother." Again, Valerius Maximus says (Fact. et Dict. Memor. iv 7): "The ties of friendship are most strong and in no way yield to the ties of blood." Moreover it is quite certain and undeniable, that as to the latter, the lot of birth is fortuitous, whereas we contract the former by an untrammelled will, and a solid pledge. Therefore we ought not to love more than others those who are united to us by ties of blood.

Obj. 2: Further, Ambrose says (De Officiis i, 7): "I love not less you whom I have begotten in the Gospel, than if I had begotten you in wedlock, for nature is no more eager to love than grace." Surely we ought to love those whom we expect to be with us for ever more than those who will be with us only in this world. Therefore we should not love our kindred more than those who are otherwise connected with us.

Obj. 3: Further, "Love is proved by deeds," as Gregory states (Hom. in Evang. xxx). Now we are bound to do acts of love to others than our kindred: thus in the army a man must obey his officer rather than his father. Therefore we are not bound to love our kindred most of all.

*On the contrary,* The commandments of the decalogue contain a special precept about the honor due to our parents (Ex. 20:12). Therefore we ought to love more specially those who are united to us by ties of blood.

*I answer that,* As stated above (A. 7), we ought out of charity to love those who are more closely united to us more, both because our love for them is more intense, and because there are more reasons for loving them. Now intensity of love arises from the union of lover and beloved: and therefore we should measure the love of different persons according to the different kinds of union, so that a man is more loved in matters touching that particular union in respect of which he is loved. And, again, in comparing love to love we should compare one union with another. Accordingly we must say that friendship among blood relations is based upon their connection by natural origin, the friendship of fellow-citizens on their civic fellowship, and the friendship of those who are fighting side by side on the comradeship of battle. Wherefore in matters pertaining to nature we should love our kindred most, in matters concerning relations between citizens, we should prefer our fellow-citizens, and on the battlefield our fellow-soldiers. Hence the Philosopher says (Ethic. ix, 2) that "it is our duty to render to each class of people such respect as is natural and appropriate. This is in fact the principle upon which we seem to act, for we invite our relations to a wedding ... It would seem to be a special duty to afford our parents the means of living ... and to honor them."

The same applies to other kinds of friendship.

If however we compare union with union, it is evident that the union arising from natural origin is prior to, and more stable than, all others, because it is something affecting the very substance, whereas other unions supervene and may cease altogether. Therefore the friendship of kindred is more stable, while other friendships may be stronger in respect of that which is proper to each of them.

Reply Obj. 1: In as much as the friendship of comrades originates through their own choice, love of this kind takes precedence of the love of kindred in matters where we are free to do as we choose, for instance in matters of action. Yet the friendship of kindred is more stable, since it is more natural, and preponderates over others in matters touching nature: consequently we are more beholden to them in the providing of necessaries.

Reply Obj. 2: Ambrose is speaking of love with regard to favors respecting the fellowship of grace, namely, moral instruction. For in this matter, a man ought to provide for his spiritual children whom he has begotten spiritually, more than for the sons of his body, whom he is bound to support in bodily sustenance.

Reply Obj. 3: The fact that in the battle a man obeys his officer rather than his father proves, that he loves his father less, not simply [but] relatively, i.e. as regards the love which is based on fellowship in battle.

NINTH ARTICLE [II-II, Q. 26, Art. 9]

Whether a Man Ought, Out of Charity, to Love His Children More Than His Father?

Objection 1: It seems that a man ought, out of charity, to love his children more than his father. For we ought to love those more to whom we are more bound to do good. Now we are more bound to do good to our children than to our parents, since the Apostle says (2 Cor. 12:14): "Neither ought the children to lay up for the parents, but the parents for the children." Therefore a man ought to love his children more than his parents.

Obj. 2: Further, grace perfects nature. But parents naturally love their children more than these love them, as the Philosopher states (Ethic. viii, 12). Therefore a man ought to love his children more than his parents.

Obj. 3: Further, man's affections are conformed to God by charity. But God loves His children more than they love Him. Therefore we also ought to love our children more than our parents.

*On the contrary,* Ambrose [*Origen, Hom. ii in Cant.] says: "We ought to love God first, then our parents, then our children, and lastly those of our household."

*I answer that,* As stated above (A. 4, ad 1; A. 7), the degrees of love may be measured from two standpoints. First, from that of the object. In this respect the better a thing is, and the more like to God, the more is it to be loved: and in this way a man ought to love his father more than his children, because, to wit, he loves his father as his principle, in which respect he is a more exalted good and more like God.

Secondly, the degrees of love may be measured from the standpoint of the lover, and in this respect a man loves more that which is more closely connected with him, in which way a man's children are more lovable to him than his father, as the Philosopher states (Ethic. viii). First, because parents love their children as being part of themselves, whereas the father is not part of his son, so that the love of a father for his children, is more like a man's love for himself. Secondly, because parents know better that so and so is their child than vice versa. Thirdly, because children are nearer to their parents, as being part of them, than their parents are to them to whom they stand in the relation of a principle. Fourthly, because parents have loved longer, for the father begins to love his child at once, whereas the child begins to love his father after a lapse of time; and the longer love lasts, the stronger it is, according to Ecclus. 9:14: "Forsake not an old friend, for the new will not be like to him."

Reply Obj. 1: The debt due to a principle is submission of respect and honor, whereas that due to the effect is one of influence and care. Hence the duty of children to their parents consists chiefly in honor: while that of parents to their children is especially one of care.

Reply Obj. 2: It is natural for a man as father to love his children more, if we consider them as closely connected with him: but if we consider which is the more exalted good, the son naturally loves his father more.

Reply Obj. 3: As Augustine says (De Doctr. Christ. i, 32), God loves us for our good and for His honor. Wherefore since our father is related to us as principle, even as God is, it belongs properly to the father to receive honor from his children, and to the children to be provided by their parents with what is good for them. Nevertheless in cases of necessity the child is bound out of the favors received to provide for his parents before all.

TENTH ARTICLE [II-II, Q. 26, Art. 10]

Whether a Man Ought to Love His Mother More Than His Father?

Objection 1: It would seem that a man ought to love his mother more than his father. For, as the Philosopher says (De Gener. Animal. i, 20), "the female produces the body in generation." Now man receives his soul, not from his father, but from God by creation, as stated in the First Part (Q. 90, A. 2; Q. 118). Therefore a man receives more from his mother than from his father: and consequently he ought to love her more than him.

Obj. 2: Further, where greater love is given, greater love is due. Now a mother loves her child more than the father does: for the Philosopher says (Ethic. ix, 7) that "mothers have greater love for their children. For the mother labors more in child-bearing, and she knows more surely than the father who are her children."

Obj. 3: Further, love should be more fond towards those who have labored for us more, according to Rom. 16:6: "Salute Mary, who hath labored much among you." Now the mother labors more than the father in giving birth and education to her child; wherefore it is written (Ecclus. 7:29): "Forget not the groanings of thy mother." Therefore a man ought to love his mother more than his father.

*On the contrary,* Jerome says on Ezech. 44:25 that "man ought to love God the Father of all, and then his own father," and mentions the mother afterwards.

*I answer that,* In making such comparisons as this, we must take the answer in the strict sense, so that the present question is whether the father as father, ought to be loved more than the mother as mother. The reason is that virtue and vice may make such a difference in such like matters, that friendship may be diminished or destroyed, as the Philosopher remarks (Ethic. viii, 7). Hence Ambrose [*Origen, Hom. ii in Cant.] says: "Good servants should be preferred to wicked children."

Strictly speaking, however, the father should be loved more than the mother. For father and mother are loved as principles of our natural origin. Now the father is principle in a more excellent way than the mother, because he is the active principle, while the mother is a passive and material principle. Consequently, strictly speaking, the father is to be loved more.

Reply Obj. 1: In the begetting of man, the mother supplies the formless matter of the body; and the latter receives its form through the formative power that is in the semen of the father. And though this power cannot create the rational soul, yet it disposes the matter of the body to receive that form.

Reply Obj. 2: This applies to another kind of love. For the friendship between lover and lover differs specifically from the friendship between child and parent: while the friendship we are speaking of here, is that which a man owes his father and mother through being begotten of them.

The Reply to the Third Objection is evident.

ELEVENTH ARTICLE [II-II, Q. 26, Art. 11]

Whether a Man Ought to Love His Wife More Than His Father and Mother?

Objection 1: It would seem that a man ought to love his wife more than his father and mother. For no man leaves a thing for another unless he love the latter more. Now it is written (Gen. 2:24) that "a man shell leave father and mother" on account of his wife. Therefore a man ought to love his wife more than his father and mother.

Obj. 2: Further, the Apostle says (Eph. 5:33) that a husband should "love his wife as himself." Now a man ought to love himself more than his parents. Therefore he ought to love his wife also more than his parents.

Obj. 2: Further, love should be greater where there are more reasons for loving. Now there are more reasons for love in the friendship of a man towards his wife. For the Philosopher says (Ethic. viii, 12) that "in this friendship there are the motives of utility, pleasure, and also of virtue, if husband and wife are virtuous." Therefore a man's love for his wife ought to be greater than his love for his parents.

*On the contrary,* According to Eph. 5:28, "men ought to love their wives as their own bodies." Now a man ought to love his body less than his neighbor, as stated above (A. 5): and among his neighbors he should love his parents most. Therefore he ought to love his parents more than his wife.

*I answer that,* As stated above (A. 9), the degrees of love may be taken from the good (which is loved), or from the union between those who love. On the part of the good which is the object loved, a man should love his parents more than his wife, because he loves them as his principles and considered as a more exalted good.

But on the part of the union, the wife ought to be loved more, because she is united with her husband, as one flesh, according to Matt. 19:6: "Therefore now they are not two, but one flesh." Consequently a man loves his wife more intensely, but his parents with greater reverence.

Reply Obj. 1: A man does not in all respects leave his father and mother for the sake of his wife: for in certain cases a man ought to succor his parents rather than his wife. He does however leave all his kinsfolk, and cleaves to his wife as regards the union of carnal connection and co-habitation.

Reply Obj. 2: The words of the Apostle do not mean that a man ought to love his wife equally with himself, but that a man's love for himself is the reason for his love of his wife, since she is one with him.

Reply Obj. 3: There are also several reasons for a man's love for his father; and these, in a certain respect, namely, as regards good, are more weighty than those for which a man loves his wife; although the latter outweigh the former as regards the closeness of the union.

As to the argument in the contrary sense, it must be observed that in the words quoted, the particle "as" denotes not equality of love but the motive of love. For the principal reason why a man loves his wife is her being united to him in the flesh.

TWELFTH ARTICLE [II-II, Q. 26, Art. 12]

Whether a Man Ought to Love More His Benefactor Than One He Has Benefited?

Objection 1: It would seem that a man ought to love his benefactor more than one he has benefited. For Augustine says (De Catech. Rud. iv): "Nothing will incite another more to love you than that you love him first: for he must have a hard heart indeed, who not only refuses to love, but declines to return love already given." Now a man's benefactor forestalls him in the kindly deeds of charity. Therefore we ought to love our benefactors above all.

Obj. 2: Further, the more grievously we sin by ceasing to love a man or by working against him, the more ought we to love him. Now it is a more grievous sin to cease loving a benefactor or to work against him, than to cease loving one to whom one has hitherto done kindly actions. Therefore we ought to love our benefactors more than those to whom we are kind.

Obj. 3: Further, of all things lovable, God is to be loved most, and then one's father, as Jerome says [*Comment. in Ezechiel xliv, 25]. Now these are our greatest benefactors. Therefore a benefactor should be loved above all others.

*On the contrary,* The Philosopher says (Ethic. ix, 7), that "benefactors seem to love recipients of their benefactions, rather than vice versa."

*I answer that,* As stated above (AA. 9, 11), a thing is loved more in two ways: first because it has the character of a more excellent good, secondly by reason of a closer connection. In the first way we ought to love our benefactor most, because, since he is a principle of good to the man he has benefited, he has the character of a more excellent good, as stated above with regard to one's father (A. 9).

In the second way, however, we love those more who have received benefactions from us, as the Philosopher proves (Ethic. ix, 7) by four arguments. First because the recipient of benefactions is the handiwork of the benefactor, so that we are wont to say of a man: "He was made by so and so." Now it is natural to a man to love his own work (thus it is to be observed that poets love their own poems): and the reason is that we love *to be* and to live, and these are made manifest in our *action.* Secondly, because we all naturally love that in which we see our own good. Now it is true that the benefactor has some good of his in the recipient of his benefaction, and the recipient some good in the benefactor; but the benefactor sees his virtuous good in the recipient, while the recipient sees his useful good in the benefactor. Now it gives more pleasure to see one's virtuous good than one's useful good, both because it is more enduring,—for usefulness quickly flits by, and the pleasure of calling a thing to mind is not like the pleasure of having it present—and because it is more pleasant to recall virtuous goods than the profit we have derived from others. Thirdly, because is it the lover's part to act, since he wills and works the good of the beloved, while the beloved takes a passive part in receiving good, so that to love surpasses being loved, for which reason the greater love is on the part of the benefactor. Fourthly because it is more difficult to give than to receive favors: and we are most fond of things which have cost us most trouble, while we almost despise what comes easy to us.

Reply Obj. 1: It is some thing in the benefactor that incites the recipient to love him: whereas the benefactor loves the recipient, not through being incited by him, but through being moved thereto of his own accord: and what we do of our own accord surpasses what we do through another.

Reply Obj. 2: The love of the beneficiary for the benefactor is more of a duty, wherefore the contrary is the greater sin. On the other hand, the love of the benefactor for the beneficiary is more spontaneous, wherefore it is quicker to act.

Reply Obj. 3: God also loves us more than we love Him, and parents love their children more than these love them. Yet it does not follow that we love all who have received good from us, more than any of our benefactors. For we prefer such benefactors as God and our parents, from whom we have received the greatest favors, to those on whom we have bestowed lesser benefits.

THIRTEENTH ARTICLE [II-II, Q. 26, Art. 13]

Whether the Order of Charity Endures in Heaven?

Objection 1: It would seem that the order of charity does not endure in heaven. For Augustine says (De Vera Relig. xlviii): "Perfect charity consists in loving greater goods more, and lesser goods less." Now charity will be perfect in heaven. Therefore a man will love those who are better more than either himself or those who are connected with him.

Obj. 2: Further, we love more him to whom we wish a greater good. Now each one in heaven wishes a greater good for those who have more good, else his will would not be conformed in all things to God's will: and there to be better is to have more good. Therefore in heaven each one loves more those who are better, and consequently he loves others more than himself, and one who is not connected with him, more than one who is.

Obj. 3: Further, in heaven love will be entirely for God's sake, for then will be fulfilled the words of 1 Cor. 15:28: "That God may be all in all." Therefore he who is nearer God will be loved more, so that a man will love a better man more than himself, and one who is not connected with him, more than one who is.

*On the contrary,* Nature is not done away, but perfected, by glory. Now the order of charity given above (AA. 2, 3, 4) is derived from nature: since all things naturally love themselves more than others. Therefore this order of charity will endure in heaven.

*I answer that,* The order of charity must needs remain in heaven, as regards the love of God above all things. For this will be realized simply when man shall enjoy God perfectly. But, as regards the order between man himself and other men, a distinction would seem to be necessary, because, as we stated above (AA. 7, 9), the degrees of love may be distinguished either in respect of the good which a man desires for another, or according to the intensity of love itself. In the first way a man will love better men more than himself, and those who are less good, less than himself: because, by reason of the perfect conformity of the human to the Divine will, each of the blessed will desire everyone to have what is due to him according to Divine justice. Nor will that be a time for advancing by means of merit to a yet greater reward, as happens now while it is possible for a man to desire both the virtue and the reward of a better man, whereas then the will of each one will rest within the limits determined by God. But in the second way a man will love himself more than even his better neighbors, because the intensity of the act of love arises on the part of the person who loves, as stated above (AA. 7, 9). Moreover it is for this that the gift of charity is bestowed by God on each one, namely, that he may first of all direct his mind to God, and this pertains to a man's love for himself, and that, in the second place, he may wish other things to be directed to God, and even work for that end according to his capacity.

As to the order to be observed among our neighbors, a man will simply love those who are better, according to the love of charity. Because the entire life of the blessed consists in directing their minds to God, wherefore the entire ordering of their love will be ruled with respect to God, so that each one will love more and reckon to be nearer to himself those who are nearer to God. For then one man will no longer succor another, as he needs to in the present life, wherein each man has to succor those who are closely connected with him rather than those who are not, no matter what be the nature of their distress: hence it is that in this life, a man, by the inclination of charity, loves more those who are more closely united to him, for he is under a greater obligation to bestow on them the effect of charity. It will however be possible in heaven for a man to love in several ways one who is connected with him, since the causes of virtuous love will not be banished from the mind of the blessed. Yet all these reasons are incomparably surpassed by that which is taken from nighness to God.

Reply Obj. 1: This argument should be granted as to those who are connected together; but as regards man himself, he ought to love himself so much the more than others, as his charity is more perfect, since perfect entire reason of his love, for God is man's charity directs man to God perfectly, and this belongs to love of oneself, as stated above.

Reply Obj. 2: This argument considers the order of charity in respect of the degree of good one wills the person one loves.

Reply Obj. 3: God will be to each one the entire reason of his love, for God is man's entire good. For if we make the impossible supposition that God were not man's good, He would not be man's reason for loving. Hence it is that in the order of love man should love himself more than all else after God.

# QUESTION 27

OF THE PRINCIPAL ACT OF CHARITY, WHICH IS TO LOVE (In Eight Articles)

We must now consider the act of charity, and (1) the principal act of charity, which is to love, (2) the other acts or effects which follow from that act.

Under the first head there are eight points of inquiry:

(1) Which is the more proper to charity, to love or to be loved?

(2) Whether to love considered as an act of charity is the same as goodwill?

(3) Whether God should be loved for His own sake?

(4) Whether God can be loved immediately in this life?

(5) Whether God can be loved wholly?

(6) Whether the love of God is according to measure?

(7) Which is the better, to love one's friend, or one's enemy?

(8) Which is the better, to love God, or one's neighbor?

FIRST ARTICLE [II-II, Q. 27, Art. 1]

Whether to Be Loved Is More Proper to Charity Than to Love?

Objection 1: It would seem that it is more proper to charity to be loved than to love. For the better charity is to be found in those who are themselves better. But those who are better should be more loved. Therefore to be loved is more proper to charity.

Obj. 2: Further, that which is to be found in more subjects seems to be more in keeping with nature, and, for that reason, better. Now, as the Philosopher says (Ethic. viii, 8), "many would rather be loved than love, and lovers of flattery always abound." Therefore it is better to be loved than to love, and consequently it is more in keeping with charity.

Obj. 3: Further, "the cause of anything being such is yet more so." Now men love because they are loved, for Augustine says (De Catech. Rud. iv) that "nothing incites another more to love you than that you love him first." Therefore charity consists in being loved rather than in loving.

*On the contrary,* The Philosopher says (Ethic. viii, 8) that friendship consists in loving rather than in being loved. Now charity is a kind of friendship. Therefore it consists in loving rather than in being loved.

*I answer that,* To love belongs to charity as charity. For, since charity is a virtue, by its very essence it has an inclination to its proper act. Now to be loved is not the act of the charity of the person loved; for this act is to love: and to be loved is competent to him as coming under the common notion of good, in so far as another tends towards his good by an act of charity. Hence it is clear that to love is more proper to charity than to be loved: for that which befits a thing by reason of itself and its essence is more competent to it than that which is befitting to it by reason of something else. This can be exemplified in two ways. First, in the fact that friends are more commended for loving than for being loved, indeed, if they be loved and yet love not, they are blamed. Secondly, because a mother, whose love is the greatest, seeks rather to love than to be loved: for "some women," as the Philosopher observes (Ethic. viii, 8) "entrust their children to a nurse; they do love them indeed, yet seek not to be loved in return, if they happen not to be loved."

Reply Obj. 1: A better man, through being better, is more lovable; but through having more perfect charity, loves more. He loves more, however, in proportion to the person he loves. For a better man does not love that which is beneath him less than it ought to be loved: whereas he who is less good fails to love one who is better, as much as he ought to be loved.

Reply Obj. 2: As the Philosopher says (Ethic. viii, 8), "men wish to be loved in as much as they wish to be honored." For just as honor is bestowed on a man in order to bear witness to the good which is in him, so by being loved a man is shown to have some good, since good alone is lovable. Accordingly men seek to be loved and to be honored, for the sake of something else, viz. to make known the good which is in the person loved. On the other hand, those who have charity seek to love for the sake of loving, as though this were itself the good of charity, even as the act of any virtue is that virtue's good. Hence it is more proper to charity to wish to love than to wish to be loved.

Reply Obj. 3: Some love on account of being loved, not so that to be loved is the end of their loving, but because it is a kind of way leading a man to love.

SECOND ARTICLE [II-II, Q. 27, Art. 2]

Whether to Love Considered As an Act of Charity Is the Same As Goodwill?

Objection 1: It would seem that to love, considered as an act of charity, is nothing else than goodwill. For the Philosopher says (Rhet. ii, 4) that "to love is to wish a person well"; and this is goodwill. Therefore the act of charity is nothing but goodwill.

Obj. 2: Further, the act belongs to the same subject as the habit. Now the habit of charity is in the power of the will, as stated above (Q. 24, A. 1). Therefore the act of charity is also an act of the will. But it tends to good only, and this is goodwill. Therefore the act of charity is nothing else than goodwill.

Obj. 3: Further, the Philosopher reckons five things pertaining to friendship (Ethic. ix, 4), the first of which is that a man should wish his friend well; the second, that he should wish him to be and to live; the third, that he should take pleasure in his company; the fourth, that he should make choice of the same things; the fifth, that he should grieve and rejoice with him. Now the first two pertain to goodwill. Therefore goodwill is the first act of charity.

*On the contrary,* The Philosopher says (Ethic. ix, 5) that "goodwill is neither friendship nor love, but the beginning of friendship." Now charity is friendship, as stated above (Q. 23, A. 1). Therefore goodwill is not the same as to love considered as an act of charity.

*I answer that,* Goodwill properly speaking is that act of the will whereby we wish well to another. Now this act of the will differs from actual love, considered not only as being in the sensitive appetite but also as being in the intellective appetite or will. For the love which is in the sensitive appetite is a passion. Now every passion seeks its object with a certain eagerness. And the passion of love is not aroused suddenly, but is born of an earnest consideration of the object loved; wherefore the Philosopher, showing the difference between goodwill and the love which is a passion, says (Ethic. ix, 5) that goodwill does not imply impetuosity or desire, that is to say, has not an eager inclination, because it is by the sole judgment of his reason that one man wishes another well. Again such like love arises from previous acquaintance, whereas goodwill sometimes arises suddenly, as happens to us if we look on at a boxing-match, and we wish one of the boxers to win. But the love, which is in the intellective appetite, also differs from goodwill, because it denotes a certain union of affections between the lover and the beloved, in as much as the lover deems the beloved as somewhat united to him, or belonging to him, and so tends towards him. On the other hand, goodwill is a simple act of the will, whereby we wish a person well, even without presupposing the aforesaid union of the affections with him. Accordingly, to love, considered as an act of charity, includes goodwill, but such dilection or love adds union of affections, wherefore the Philosopher says (Ethic. ix, 5) that "goodwill is a beginning of friendship."

Reply Obj. 1: The Philosopher, by thus defining "to love," does not describe it fully, but mentions only that part of its definition in which the act of love is chiefly manifested.

Reply Obj. 2: To love is indeed an act of the will tending to the good, but it adds a certain union with the beloved, which union is not denoted by goodwill.

Reply Obj. 3: These things mentioned by the Philosopher belong to friendship because they arise from a man's love for himself, as he says in the same passage, in so far as a man does all these things in respect of his friend, even as he does them to himself: and this belongs to the aforesaid union of the affections.

THIRD ARTICLE [II-II, Q. 27, Art. 3]

Whether Out of Charity God Ought to Be Loved for Himself?

Objection 1: It would seem that God is loved out of charity, not for Himself but for the sake of something else. For Gregory says in a homily (In Evang. xi): "The soul learns from the things it knows, to love those it knows not," where by things unknown he means the intelligible and the Divine, and by things known he indicates the objects of the senses. Therefore God is to be loved for the sake of something else.

Obj. 2: Further, love follows knowledge. But God is known through something else, according to Rom. 1:20: "The invisible things of God are clearly seen, being understood by the things that are made." Therefore He is also loved on account of something else and not for Himself.

Obj. 3: Further, "hope begets charity" as a gloss says on Matt. 1:1, and "fear leads to charity," according to Augustine in his commentary on the First Canonical Epistle of John (In prim. canon. Joan. Tract. ix). Now hope looks forward to obtain something from God, while fear shuns something which can be inflicted by God. Therefore it seems that God is to be loved on account of some good we hope for, or some evil to be feared. Therefore He is not to be loved for Himself.

*On the contrary,* According to Augustine (De Doctr. Christ. i), to enjoy is to cleave to something for its own sake. Now "God is to be enjoyed" as he says in the same book. Therefore God is to be loved for Himself.

*I answer that,* The preposition "for" denotes a relation of causality. Now there are four kinds of cause, viz., final, formal, efficient, and material, to which a material disposition also is to be reduced, though it is not a cause simply but relatively. According to these four different causes one thing is said to be loved for another. In respect of the final cause, we love medicine, for instance, for health; in respect of the formal cause, we love a man for his virtue, because, to wit, by his virtue he is formally good and therefore lovable; in respect of the efficient cause, we love certain men because, for instance, they are the sons of such and such a father; and in respect of the disposition which is reducible to the genus of a material cause, we speak of loving something for that which disposed us to love it, e.g. we love a man for the favors received from him, although after we have begun to love our friend, we no longer love him for his favors, but for his virtue. Accordingly, as regards the first three ways, we love God, not for anything else, but for Himself. For He is not directed to anything else as to an end, but is Himself the last end of all things; nor does He require to receive any form in order to be good, for His very substance is His goodness, which is itself the exemplar of all other good things; nor again does goodness accrue to Him from aught else, but from Him to all other things. In the fourth way, however, He can be loved for something else, because we are disposed by certain things to advance in His love, for instance, by favors bestowed by Him, by the rewards we hope to receive from Him, or even by the punishments which we are minded to avoid through Him.

Reply Obj. 1: From the things it knows the soul learns to love what it knows not, not as though the things it knows were the reason for its loving things it knows not, through being the formal, final, or efficient cause of this love, but because this knowledge disposes man to love the unknown.

Reply Obj. 2: Knowledge of God is indeed acquired through other things, but after He is known, He is no longer known through them, but through Himself, according to John 4:42: "We now believe, not for thy saying: for we ourselves have heard Him, and know that this is indeed the Saviour of the world."

Reply Obj. 3: Hope and fear lead to charity by way of a certain disposition, as was shown above (Q. 17, A. 8; Q. 19, AA. 4, 7, 10).

FOURTH ARTICLE [II-II, Q. 27, Art. 4]

Whether God Can Be Loved Immediately in This Life?

Objection 1: It would seem that God cannot be loved immediately in this life. For the "unknown cannot be loved" as Augustine says (De Trin. x, 1). Now we do not know God immediately in this life, since "we see now through a glass, in a dark manner" (1 Cor. 13:12). Neither, therefore, do we love Him immediately.

Obj. 2: Further, he who cannot do what is less, cannot do what is more. Now it is more to love God than to know Him, since "he who is joined" to God by love, is "one spirit with Him" (1 Cor. 6:17). But man cannot know God immediately. Therefore much less can he love Him immediately.

Obj. 3: Further, man is severed from God by sin, according to Isa. 59:2: "Your iniquities have divided between you and your God." Now sin is in the will rather than in the intellect. Therefore man is less able to love God immediately than to know Him immediately.

*On the contrary,* Knowledge of God, through being mediate, is said to be "enigmatic," and "falls away" in heaven, as stated in 1 Cor. 13:12. But charity "does not fall away" as stated in the same passage (1 Cor. 13:12). Therefore the charity of the way adheres to God immediately.

*I answer that,* As stated above (I, Q. 82, A. 3; Q. 84, A. 7), the act of a cognitive power is completed by the thing known being in the knower, whereas the act of an appetitive power consists in the appetite being inclined towards the thing in itself. Hence it follows that the movement of the appetitive power is towards things in respect of their own condition, whereas the act of a cognitive power follows the mode of the knower.

Now in itself the very order of things is such, that God is knowable and lovable for Himself, since He is essentially truth and goodness itself, whereby other things are known and loved: but with regard to us, since our knowledge is derived through the senses, those things are knowable first which are nearer to our senses, and the last term of knowledge is that which is most remote from our senses.

Accordingly, we must assert that to love which is an act of the appetitive power, even in this state of life, tends to God first, and flows on from Him to other things, and in this sense charity loves God immediately, and other things through God. On the other hand, with regard to knowledge, it is the reverse, since we know God through other things, either as a cause through its effects, or by way of pre-eminence or negation as Dionysius states (Div. Nom. i; cf. I, Q. 12, A. 12).

Reply Obj. 1: Although the unknown cannot be loved, it does not follow that the order of knowledge is the same as the order of love, since love is the term of knowledge, and consequently, love can begin at once where knowledge ends, namely in the thing itself which is known through another thing.

Reply Obj. 2: Since to love God is something greater than to know Him, especially in this state of life, it follows that love of God presupposes knowledge of God. And because this knowledge does not rest in creatures, but, through them, tends to something else, love begins there, and thence goes on to other things by a circular movement so to speak; for knowledge begins from creatures, tends to God, and love begins with God as the last end, and passes on to creatures.

Reply Obj. 3: Aversion from God, which is brought about by sin, is removed by charity, but not by knowledge alone: hence charity, by loving God, unites the soul immediately to Him with a chain of spiritual union.

FIFTH ARTICLE [II-II, Q. 27, Art. 5]

Whether God can be loved wholly? [*Cf. Q. 184, A. 2]

Objection 1: It would seem that God cannot be loved wholly. For love follows knowledge. Now God cannot be wholly known by us, since this would imply comprehension of Him. Therefore He cannot be wholly loved by us.

Obj. 2: Further, love is a kind of union, as Dionysius shows (Div. Nom. iv). But the heart of man cannot be wholly united to God, because "God is greater than our heart" (1 John 3:20). Therefore God cannot be loved wholly.

Obj. 3: Further, God loves Himself wholly. If therefore He be loved wholly by another, this one will love Him as much as God loves Himself. But this is unreasonable. Therefore God cannot be wholly loved by a creature.

*On the contrary,* It is written (Deut. 6:5): "Thou shalt love the Lord thy God with thy whole heart."

*I answer that,* Since love may be considered as something between lover and beloved, when we ask whether God can be wholly loved, the question may be understood in three ways, first so that the qualification "wholly" be referred to the thing loved, and thus God is to be loved wholly, since man should love all that pertains to God.

Secondly, it may be understood as though "wholly" qualified the lover: and thus again God ought to be loved wholly, since man ought to love God with all his might, and to refer all he has to the love of God, according to Deut. 6:5: "Thou shalt love the Lord thy God with thy whole heart."

Thirdly, it may be understood by way of comparison of the lover to the thing loved, so that the mode of the lover equal the mode of the thing loved. This is impossible: for, since a thing is lovable in proportion to its goodness, God is infinitely lovable, since His goodness is infinite. Now no creature can love God infinitely, because all power of creatures, whether it be natural or infused, is finite.

This suffices for the Replies to the Objections, because the first three objections consider the question in this third sense, while the last takes it in the second sense.

SIXTH ARTICLE [II-II, Q. 27, Art. 6]

Whether in Loving God We Ought to Observe Any Mode?

Objection 1: It would seem that we ought to observe some mode in loving God. For the notion of good consists in mode, species and order, as Augustine states (De Nat. Boni iii, iv). Now the love of God is the best thing in man, according to Col.

3:14: "Above all ... things, have charity." Therefore there ought to be a mode of the love of God.

Obj. 2: Further, Augustine says (De Morib. Eccl. viii): "Prithee, tell me which is the mode of love. For I fear lest I burn with the desire and love of my Lord, more or less than I ought." But it would be useless to seek the mode of the Divine love, unless there were one. Therefore there is a mode of the love of God.

Obj. 3: Further, as Augustine says (Gen. ad lit. iv, 3), "the measure which nature appoints to a thing, is its mode." Now the measure of the human will, as also of external action, is the reason. Therefore just as it is necessary for the reason to appoint a mode to the exterior effect of charity, according to Rom. 12:1: "Your reasonable service," so also the interior love of God requires a mode.

*On the contrary,* Bernard says (De Dilig. Deum 1) that "God is the cause of our loving God; the measure is to love Him without measure."

*I answer that,* As appears from the words of Augustine quoted above (Obj. 3) mode signifies a determination of measure; which determination is to be found both in the measure and in the thing measured, but not in the same way. For it is found in the measure essentially, because a measure is of itself the determining and modifying rule of other things; whereas in the things measured, it is found relatively, that is in so far as they attain to the measure. Hence there can be nothing unmodified in the measure whereas the thing measured is unmodified if it fails to attain to the measure, whether by deficiency or by excess.

Now in all matters of appetite and action the measure is the end, because the proper reason for all that we desire or do should be taken from the end, as the Philosopher proves (Phys. ii, 9). Therefore the end has a mode by itself, while the means take their mode from being proportionate to the end. Hence, according to the Philosopher (Polit. i, 3), "in every art, the desire for the end is endless and unlimited," whereas there is a limit to the means: thus the physician does not put limits to health, but makes it as perfect as he possibly can; but he puts a limit to medicine, for he does not give as much medicine as he can, but according as health demands so that if he give too much or too little, the medicine would be immoderate.

Again, the end of all human actions and affections is the love of God, whereby principally we attain to our last end, as stated above (Q. 23, A. 6), wherefore the mode in the love of God, must not be taken as in a thing measured where we find too much or too little, but as in the measure itself, where there cannot be excess, and where the more the rule is attained the better it is, so that the more we love God the better our love is.

Reply Obj. 1: That which is so by its essence takes precedence of that which is so through another, wherefore the goodness of the measure which has the mode essentially, takes precedence of the goodness of the thing measured, which has its mode through something else; and so too, charity, which has a mode as a measure has, stands before the other virtues, which have a mode through being measured.

Reply Obj. 2: As Augustine adds in the same passage, "the measure of our love for God is to love Him with our whole heart," that is to love Him as much as He can be loved, and this belongs to the mode which is proper to the measure.

Reply Obj. 3: An affection, whose object is subject to reason's judgment, should be measured by reason. But the object of the Divine love which is God surpasses the judgment of reason, wherefore it is not measured by reason but transcends it. Nor is there parity between the interior act and external acts of charity. For the interior act of charity has the character of an end, since man's ultimate good consists in his soul cleaving to God, according to Ps. 72:28: "It is good for me to adhere to my God"; whereas the exterior acts are as means to the end, and so have to be measured both according to charity and according to reason.

SEVENTH ARTICLE [II-II, Q. 27, Art. 7]

Whether It Is More Meritorious to Love an Enemy Than to Love a Friend?

Objection 1: It would seem more meritorious to love an enemy than to love a friend. For it is written (Matt. 5:46): "If you love them that love you, what reward shall you have?" Therefore it is not deserving of reward to love one's friend: whereas, as the same passage proves, to love one's enemy is deserving of a reward. Therefore it is more meritorious to love one's enemy than to love one's friend.

Obj. 2: Further, an act is the more meritorious through proceeding from a greater charity. But it belongs to the perfect children of God to love their enemies, whereas those also who have imperfect charity love their friends. Therefore it is more meritorious to love one's enemy than to love one's friend.

Obj. 3: Further, where there is more effort for good, there seems to be more merit, since "every man shall receive his own reward according to his own labor" (1 Cor. 3:8). Now a man has to make a greater effort to love his enemy than to love his friend, because it is more difficult. Therefore it seems more meritorious to love one's enemy than to love one's friend.

*On the contrary,* The better an action is, the more meritorious it is. Now it is better to love one's friend, since it is better to love a better man, and the friend who loves you is better than the enemy who hates you. Therefore it is more meritorious to love one's friend than to love one's enemy.

*I answer that,* God is the reason for our loving our neighbor out of charity, as stated above (Q. 25, A. 1). When therefore it is asked which is better or more meritorious, to love one's friend or one's enemy, these two loves may be compared in two ways, first, on the part of our neighbor whom we love, secondly, on the part of the reason for which we love him.

In the first way, love of one's friend surpasses love of one's enemy, because a friend is both better and more closely united to us, so that he is a more suitable matter of love and consequently the act of love that passes over this matter, is better, and therefore its opposite is worse, for it is worse to hate a friend than an enemy.

In the second way, however, it is better to love one's enemy than one's friend, and this for two reasons. First, because it is possible to love one's friend for another reason than God, whereas God is the only reason for loving one's enemy. Secondly, because if we suppose that both are loved for God, our love for God is proved to be all the stronger through carrying a man's affections to things which are furthest from him, namely, to the love of his enemies, even as the power of a furnace is proved to be the stronger, according as it throws its heat to more distant objects. Hence our love for God is proved to be so much the stronger, as the more difficult are the things we accomplish for its sake, just as the power of fire is so much the stronger, as it is able to set fire to a less inflammable matter.

Yet just as the same fire acts with greater force on what is near than on what is distant, so too, charity loves with greater fervor those who are united to us than those who are far removed; and in this respect the love of friends, considered in itself, is more ardent and better than the love of one's enemy.

Reply Obj. 1: The words of Our Lord must be taken in their strict sense: because the love of one's friends is not meritorious in God's sight when we love them merely because they are our friends: and this would seem to be the case when we love our friends in such a way that we love not our enemies. On the other hand the love of our friends is meritorious, if we love them for God's sake, and not merely because they are our friends.

The Reply to the other Objections is evident from what has been said in the article, because the two arguments that follow consider the reason for loving, while the last considers the question on the part of those who are loved.

EIGHTH ARTICLE [II-II, Q. 27, Art. 8]

Whether It Is More Meritorious to Love One's Neighbor Than to Love God?

Objection 1: It would seem that it is more meritorious to love one's neighbor than to love God. For the more meritorious thing would seem to be what the Apostle preferred. Now the Apostle preferred the love of our neighbor to the love of God, according to Rom. 9:3: "I wished myself to be an anathema from Christ for my brethren." Therefore it is more meritorious to love one's neighbor than to love God.

Obj. 2: Further, in a certain sense it seems to be less meritorious to love one's friend, as stated above (A. 7). Now God is our chief friend, since "He hath first loved us" (1 John 4:10). Therefore it seems less meritorious to love God.

Obj. 3: Further, whatever is more difficult seems to be more virtuous and meritorious since "virtue is about that which is difficult and good" (Ethic. ii, 3). Now it is easier to love God than to love one's neighbor, both because all things love God naturally, and because there is nothing unlovable in God, and this cannot be said of one's neighbor. Therefore it is more meritorious to love one's neighbor than to love God.

*On the contrary,* That on account of which a thing is such, is yet more so. Now the love of one's neighbor is not meritorious, except by reason of his being loved for God's sake. Therefore the love of God is more meritorious than the love of our neighbor.

*I answer that,* This comparison may be taken in two ways. First, by considering both loves separately: and then, without doubt, the love of God is the more meritorious, because a reward is due to it for its own sake, since the ultimate reward is the enjoyment of God, to Whom the movement of the Divine love tends: hence a reward is promised to him that loves God (John 14:21): "He that loveth Me, shall be loved of My Father, and I will ... manifest Myself to him." Secondly, the comparison may be understood to be between the love of God alone on the one side, and the love of one's neighbor for God's sake, on the other. In this way love of our neighbor includes love of God, while love of God does not include love of our neighbor. Hence the comparison will be between perfect love of God, extending also to our neighbor, and inadequate and imperfect love of God, for "this commandment we have from God, that he, who loveth God, love also his brother" (1 John 4:21).

Reply Obj. 1: According to one gloss, the Apostle did not desire this, viz. to be severed from Christ for his brethren, when he was in a state of grace, but had formerly desired it when he was in a state of unbelief, so that we should not imitate him in this respect.

We may also reply, with Chrysostom (De Compunct. i, 8) [*Hom. xvi in Ep. ad Rom.] that this does not prove the Apostle to have loved his neighbor more than God, but that he loved God more than himself. For he wished to be deprived for a time of the Divine fruition which pertains to love of one self, in order that God might be honored in his neighbor, which pertains to the love of God.

Reply Obj. 2: A man's love for his friends is sometimes less meritorious in so far as he loves them for their sake, so as to fall short of the true reason for the friendship of charity, which is God. Hence that God be loved for His own sake does not diminish the merit, but is the entire reason for merit.

Reply Obj. 3: The *good* has, more than the difficult, to do with the reason of merit and virtue. Therefore it does not follow that whatever is more difficult is more meritorious, but only what is more difficult, and at the same time better.

## QUESTION 28

OF JOY (In Four Articles)

We must now consider the effects which result from the principal act of charity which is love, and (1) the interior effects, (2) the exterior effects. As to the first, three things have to be considered: (1) Joy, (2) Peace, (3) Mercy.

Under the first head there are four points of inquiry:

(1) Whether joy is an effect of charity?

(2) Whether this kind of joy is compatible with sorrow?

(3) Whether this joy can be full?

(4) Whether it is a virtue?

FIRST ARTICLE [II-II, Q. 28, Art. 1]

Whether Joy Is Effected in Us by Charity?

Objection 1: It would seem that joy is not effected in us by charity. For the absence of what we love causes sorrow rather than joy. But God, Whom we love by charity, is absent from us, so long as we are in this state of life, since "while we are in the body, we are absent from the Lord" (2 Cor. 5:6). Therefore charity causes sorrow in us rather than joy.

Obj. 2: Further, it is chiefly through charity that we merit happiness. Now mourning, which pertains to sorrow, is reckoned among those things whereby we merit happiness, according to Matt. 5:5: "Blessed are they that mourn, for they shall be comforted." Therefore sorrow, rather than joy, is an effect of charity.

Obj. 3: Further, charity is a virtue distinct from hope, as shown above (Q. 17, A. 6). Now joy is the effect of hope, according to Rom. 12:12: "Rejoicing in hope." Therefore it is not the effect of charity.

*On the contrary,* It is written (Rom. 5:5): "The charity of God is poured forth in our hearts by the Holy Ghost, Who is given to us." But joy is caused in us by the Holy Ghost according to Rom. 14:17: "The kingdom of God is not meat and drink, but justice and peace, and joy in the Holy Ghost." Therefore charity is a cause of joy.

*I answer that,* As stated above (I-II, Q. 25, AA. 1, 2, 3), when we were treating of the passions, joy and sorrow proceed from love, but in contrary ways. For joy is caused by love, either through the presence of the thing loved, or because the proper good of the thing loved exists and endures in it; and the latter is the case chiefly in the love of benevolence, whereby a man rejoices in the well-being of his friend, though he be absent. On the other hand sorrow arises from love, either through the absence of the thing loved, or because the loved object to which we wish well, is deprived of its good or afflicted with some evil. Now charity is love of God, Whose good is unchangeable, since He is His goodness, and from the very fact that He is loved, He is in those who love Him by His most excellent effect, according to 1 John 4:16: "He that abideth in charity, abideth in God, and God in him." Therefore spiritual joy, which is about God, is caused by charity.

Reply Obj. 1: So long as we are in the body, we are said to be "absent from the Lord," in comparison with that presence whereby He is present to some by the vision of "sight"; wherefore the Apostle goes on to say (2 Cor. 5:6): "For we walk by faith and not by sight." Nevertheless, even in this life, He is present to those who love Him, by the indwelling of His grace.

Reply Obj. 2: The mourning that merits happiness, is about those things that are contrary to happiness. Wherefore it amounts to the same that charity causes this mourning, and this spiritual joy about God, since to rejoice in a certain good amounts to the same as to grieve for things that are contrary to it.

Reply Obj. 3: There can be spiritual joy about God in two ways. First, when we rejoice in the Divine good considered in itself; secondly, when we rejoice in the Divine good as participated by us. The former joy is the better, and proceeds from charity chiefly: while the latter joy proceeds from hope also, whereby we look forward to enjoy the Divine good, although this enjoyment itself, whether perfect or imperfect, is obtained according to the measure of one's charity.

SECOND ARTICLE [II-II, Q. 28, Art. 2]

Whether the Spiritual Joy, Which Results from Charity, Is Compatible with an Admixture of Sorrow?

Objection 1: It would seem that the spiritual joy that results from charity is compatible with an admixture of sorrow. For it belongs to charity to rejoice in our neighbor's good, according to 1 Cor. 13:4, 6: "Charity ... rejoiceth not in iniquity, but rejoiceth with the truth." But this joy is compatible with an admixture of sorrow, according to Rom. 12:15: "Rejoice with them that rejoice, weep with them that weep." Therefore the spiritual joy of charity is compatible with an admixture of sorrow.

Obj. 2: Further, according to Gregory (Hom. in Evang. xxxiv), "penance consists in deploring past sins, and in not committing again those we have deplored." But there is no true penance without charity. Therefore the joy of charity has an admixture of sorrow.

Obj. 3: Further, it is through charity that man desires to be with Christ according to Phil. 1:23: "Having a desire to be dissolved and to be with Christ." Now this desire gives rise, in man, to a certain sadness, according to Ps. 119:5: "Woe is me that my sojourning is prolonged!" Therefore the joy of charity admits of a seasoning of sorrow.

*On the contrary,* The joy of charity is joy about the Divine wisdom. Now such like joy has no admixture of sorrow, according to Wis. 8:16: "Her conversation hath no bitterness." Therefore the joy of charity is incompatible with an admixture of sorrow.

*I answer that,* As stated above (A. 1, ad 3), a twofold joy in God arises from charity. One, the more excellent, is proper to charity; and with this joy we rejoice in the Divine good considered in itself. This joy of charity is incompatible with an admixture of sorrow, even as the good which is its object is incompatible with any admixture of evil: hence the Apostle says (Phil. 4:4): "Rejoice in the Lord always."

The other is the joy of charity whereby we rejoice in the Divine good as participated by us. This participation can be hindered by anything contrary to it, wherefore, in this respect, the joy of charity is compatible with an admixture of sorrow, in so far as a man grieves for that which hinders the participation of the Divine good, either in us or in our neighbor, whom we love as ourselves.

Reply Obj. 1: Our neighbor does not weep save on account of some evil. Now every evil implies lack of participation in the sovereign good: hence charity makes us weep with our neighbor in so far as he is hindered from participating in the Divine good.

Reply Obj. 2: Our sins divide between us and God, according to Isa. 59:2; wherefore this is the reason why we grieve for our past sins, or for those of others, in so far as they hinder us from participating in the Divine good.

Reply Obj. 3: Although in this unhappy abode we participate, after a fashion, in the Divine good, by knowledge and love, yet the unhappiness of this life is an obstacle to a perfect participation in the Divine good: hence this very sorrow, whereby a man grieves for the delay of glory, is connected with the hindrance to a participation of the Divine good.

THIRD ARTICLE [II-II, Q. 28, Art. 3]

Whether the Spiritual Joy Which Proceeds from Charity, Can Be Filled?

Objection 1: It would seem that the spiritual joy which proceeds from charity cannot be filled. For the more we rejoice in God, the more is our joy in Him filled. But we can never rejoice in Him as much as it is meet that we should rejoice in God, since His goodness which is infinite, surpasses the creature's joy which is finite. Therefore joy in God can never be filled.

Obj. 2: Further, that which is filled cannot be increased. But the joy, even of the blessed, can be increased, since one's joy is greater than another's. Therefore joy in God cannot be filled in a creature.

Obj. 3: Further, comprehension seems to be nothing else than the fulness of knowledge. Now, just as the cognitive power of a creature is finite, so is its appetitive power. Since therefore God cannot be comprehended by any creature, it seems that no creature's joy in God can be filled.

*On the contrary,* Our Lord said to His disciples (John 15:11): "That My joy may be in you, and your joy may be filled."

*I answer that,* Fulness of joy can be understood in two ways; first, on the part of the thing rejoiced in, so that one rejoice in it as much as it is meet that one should rejoice in it, and thus God's joy alone in Himself is filled, because it is infinite; and this is condignly due to the infinite goodness of God: but the joy of any creature must needs be finite. Secondly, fulness of joy may be understood on the part of the one who rejoices. Now joy is compared to desire, as rest to movement, as stated above (I-II, Q. 25, AA. 1, 2), when we were treating of the passions: and rest is full when there is no more movement. Hence joy is full, when there remains nothing to be desired. But as long as we are in this world, the movement of desire does not cease in us, because it still remains possible for us to approach nearer to God by grace, as was shown above (Q. 24, AA. 4, 7). When once, however, perfect happiness has been attained, nothing will remain to be desired, because then there will be full enjoyment of God, wherein man will obtain whatever he had desired, even with regard to other goods, according to Ps. 102:5: "Who satisfieth thy desire with good things." Hence desire will be at rest, not only our desire for God, but all our desires: so that the joy of the blessed is full to perfection—indeed over-full, since they will obtain more than they were capable of desiring: for "neither hath it entered into the heart of man, what things God hath prepared for them that love Him" (1 Cor. 2:9). This is what is meant by the words of Luke 6:38: "Good measure and pressed down, and shaken together, and running over shall they give into your bosom." Yet, since no creature is capable of the joy condignly due to God, it follows that this perfectly full joy is not taken into man, but, *on the contrary,* man enters into it, according to Matt. 25:21: "Enter into the joy of thy Lord."

Reply Obj. 1: This argument takes the fulness of joy in reference to the thing in which we rejoice.

Reply Obj. 2: When each one attains to happiness he will reach the term appointed to him by Divine predestination, and nothing further will remain to which he may tend, although by reaching that term, some will approach nearer to God than others. Hence each one's joy will be full with regard to himself, because his desire will be fully set at rest; yet one's joy will be greater than another's, on account of a fuller participation of the Divine happiness.

Reply Obj. 3: Comprehension denotes fulness of knowledge in respect of the thing known, so that it is known as much as it can be. There is however a fulness of knowledge in respect of the knower, just as we have said of joy. Wherefore the Apostle says (Col. 1:9): "That you may be filled with the knowledge of His will, in all wisdom and spiritual understanding."

FOURTH ARTICLE [II-II, Q. 28, Art. 4]

Whether Joy Is a Virtue?

Objection 1: It would seem that joy is a virtue. For vice is contrary to virtue. Now sorrow is set down as a vice, as in the case of sloth and envy. Therefore joy also should be accounted a virtue.

Obj. 2: Further, as love and hope are passions, the object of which is *good*, so also is joy. Now love and hope are reckoned to be virtues. Therefore joy also should be reckoned a virtue.

Obj. 3: Further, the precepts of the Law are about acts of virtue. But we are commanded to rejoice in the Lord, according to Phil. 4:4: "Rejoice in the Lord always." Therefore joy is a virtue.

*On the contrary,* It is not numbered among the theological virtues, nor among the moral, nor among the intellectual virtues, as is evident from what has been said above (I-II, QQ. 57, 60, 62).

*I answer that,* As stated above (I-II, Q. 55, AA. 2, 4), virtue is an operative habit, wherefore by its very nature it has an inclination to a certain act. Now it may happen that from the same habit there proceed several ordinate and homogeneous acts, each of which follows from another. And since the subsequent acts do not proceed from the virtuous habit except through the preceding act, hence it is that the virtue is defined and named in reference to that preceding act, although those other acts also proceed from the virtue. Now it is evident from what we have said about the passions (I-II, Q. 25, AA. 2, 4) that love is the first affection of the appetitive power, and that desire and joy follow from it. Hence the same virtuous habit inclines us to love and desire the beloved good, and to rejoice in it. But in as much as love is the first of these acts, that virtue takes its name, not from joy, nor from desire, but from love, and is called charity. Hence joy is not a virtue distinct from charity, but an act, or effect, of charity: for which reason it is numbered among the Fruits (Gal. 5:22).

Reply Obj. 1: The sorrow which is a vice is caused by inordinate self-love, and this is not a special vice, but a general source of the vices, as stated above (I-II, Q. 77, A. 4); so that it was necessary to account certain particular sorrows as special vices, because they do not arise from a special, but from a general vice. On the other hand love of God is accounted a special virtue, namely charity, to which joy must be referred, as its proper act, as stated above (here and A. 2).

Reply Obj. 2: Hope proceeds from love even as joy does, but hope adds, on the part of the object, a special character, viz. *difficult,* and possible to obtain; for which reason it is accounted a special virtue. On the other hand joy does not add to love any special aspect, that might cause a special virtue.

Reply Obj. 3: The Law prescribes joy, as being an act of charity, albeit not its first act.

## QUESTION 29

OF PEACE (Four Articles)

We must now consider Peace, under which head there are four points of inquiry:

(1) Whether peace is the same as concord?

(2) Whether all things desire peace?

(3) Whether peace is an effect of charity?

(4) Whether peace is a virtue?

FIRST ARTICLE [II-II, Q. 29, Art. 1]

Whether Peace Is the Same As Concord?

Objection 1: It would seem that peace is the same as concord. For Augustine says (De Civ. Dei xix, 13): "Peace among men is well ordered concord." Now we are speaking here of no other peace than that of men. Therefore peace is the same as concord.

Obj. 2: Further, concord is union of wills. Now the nature of peace consists in such like union, for Dionysius says (Div. Nom. xi) that peace unites all, and makes them of one mind. Therefore peace is the same as concord.

Obj. 3: Further, things whose opposites are identical are themselves identical. Now the one same thing is opposed to concord and peace, viz. dissension; hence it is written (1 Cor. 16:33): "God is not the God of dissension but of peace." Therefore peace is the same as concord.

*On the contrary,* There can be concord in evil between wicked men. But "there is no peace to the wicked" (Isa. 48:22). Therefore peace is not the same as concord.

*I answer that,* Peace includes concord and adds something thereto. Hence wherever peace is, there is concord, but there is not peace, wherever there is concord, if we give peace its proper meaning.

For concord, properly speaking, is between one man and another, in so far as the wills of various hearts agree together in consenting to the same thing. Now the heart of one man may happen to tend to diverse things, and this in two ways. First, in respect of the diverse appetitive powers: thus the sensitive appetite tends sometimes to that which is opposed to the rational appetite, according to Gal. 5:17: "The flesh lusteth against the spirit." Secondly, in so far as one and the same appetitive power tends to diverse objects of appetite, which it cannot obtain all at the same time: so that there must needs be a clashing of the movements of the appetite. Now the union of such movements is essential to peace, because man's heart is not at peace, so long as he has not what he wants, or if, having what he wants, there still remains something for him to want, and which he cannot have at the same time. On the other hand this union is not essential to concord: wherefore concord denotes union of appetites among various persons, while peace denotes, in addition to this union, the union of the appetites even in one man.

Reply Obj. 1: Augustine is speaking there of that peace which is between one man and another, and he says that this peace is concord, not indeed any kind of concord, but that which is well ordered, through one man agreeing with another in respect of something befitting to both of them. For if one man concord with another, not of his own accord, but through being forced, as it were, by the fear of some evil that besets him, such concord is not really peace, because the order of each concordant is not observed, but is disturbed by some fear-inspiring cause. For this reason he premises that "peace is tranquillity of order," which tranquillity consists in all the appetitive movements in one man being set at rest together.

Reply Obj. 2: If one man consent to the same thing together with another man, his consent is nevertheless not perfectly united to himself, unless at the same time all his appetitive movements be in agreement.

Reply Obj. 3: A twofold dissension is opposed to peace, namely dissension between a man and himself, and dissension between one man and another. The latter alone is opposed to concord.

SECOND ARTICLE [II-II, Q. 29, Art. 2]

Whether All Things Desire Peace?

Objection 1: It would seem that not all things desire peace. For, according to Dionysius (Div. Nom. xi), peace "unites consent." But there cannot be unity of consent in things which are devoid of knowledge. Therefore such things cannot desire peace.

Obj. 2: Further, the appetite does not tend to opposite things at the same time. Now many desire war and dissension. Therefore all men do not desire peace.

Obj. 3: Further, good alone is an object of appetite. But a certain peace is, seemingly, evil, else Our Lord would not have said (Matt. 10:34): "I came not to send peace." Therefore all things do not desire peace.

Obj. 4: Further, that which all desire is, seemingly, the sovereign good which is the last end. But this is not true of peace, since it is attainable even by a wayfarer; else Our Lord would vainly command (Mk. 9:49): "Have peace among you." Therefore all things do not desire peace.

*On the contrary,* Augustine says (De Civ. Dei xix, 12, 14) that "all things desire peace": and Dionysius says the same (Div. Nom. xi).

*I answer that,* From the very fact that a man desires a certain thing it follows that he desires to obtain what he desires, and, in consequence, to remove whatever may be an obstacle to his obtaining it. Now a man may be hindered from obtaining the good he desires, by a contrary desire either of his own or of some other, and both are removed by peace, as stated above. Hence it follows of necessity that whoever desires anything desires peace, in so far as he who desires anything, desires to attain, with tranquillity and without hindrance, to that which he desires: and this is what is meant by peace which Augustine defines (De Civ. Dei xix, 13) "the tranquillity of order."

Reply Obj. 1: Peace denotes union not only of the intellective or rational appetite, or of the animal appetite, in both of which consent may be found, but also of the natural appetite. Hence Dionysius says that "peace is the cause of consent and of connaturalness," where "consent" denotes the union of appetites proceeding from knowledge, and "connaturalness," the union of natural appetites.

Reply Obj. 2: Even those who seek war and dissension, desire nothing but peace, which they deem themselves not to have. For as we stated above, there is no peace when a man concords with another man counter to what he would prefer. Consequently men seek by means of war to break this concord, because it is a defective peace, in order that they may obtain peace, where nothing is contrary to their will. Hence all wars are waged that men may find a more perfect peace than that which they had heretofore.

Reply Obj. 3: Peace gives calm and unity to the appetite. Now just as the appetite may tend to what is good simply, or to what is good apparently, so too, peace may be either true or apparent. There can be no true peace except where the appetite is directed to what is truly good, since every evil, though it may appear good in a way, so as to calm the appetite in some respect, has, nevertheless many defects, which cause the appetite to remain restless and disturbed. Hence true peace is only in good men and about good things. The peace of the wicked is not a true peace but a semblance thereof, wherefore it is written (Wis. 14:22): "Whereas they lived in a great war of ignorance, they call so many and so great evils peace."

Reply Obj. 4: Since true peace is only about good things, as the true good is possessed in two ways, perfectly and imperfectly, so there is a twofold true peace. One is perfect peace. It consists in the perfect enjoyment of the sovereign good, and unites all one's desires by giving them rest in one object. This is the last end of the rational creature, according to Ps. 147:3: "Who hath placed peace in thy borders." The other is imperfect peace, which may be had in this world, for though the chief movement of the soul finds rest in God, yet there are certain things within and without which disturb the peace.

THIRD ARTICLE [II-II, Q. 29, Art. 3]

Whether Peace Is the Proper Effect of Charity?

Objection 1: It would seem that peace is not the proper effect of charity. For one cannot have charity without sanctifying grace. But some have peace who have not sanctifying grace, thus heathens sometimes have peace. Therefore peace is not the effect of charity.

Obj. 2: Further, if a certain thing is caused by

charity, its contrary is not compatible with charity. But dissension, which is contrary to peace, is compatible with charity, for we find that even holy doctors, such as Jerome and Augustine, dissented in some of their opinions. We also read that Paul and Barnabas dissented from one another (Acts 15). Therefore it seems that peace is not the effect of charity.

Obj. 3: Further, the same thing is not the proper effect of different things. Now peace is the effect of justice, according to Isa. 32:17: "And the work of justice shall be peace." Therefore it is not the effect of charity.

*On the contrary,* It is written (Ps. 118:165): "Much peace have they that love Thy Law."

*I answer that,* Peace implies a twofold union, as stated above (A. 1). The first is the result of one's own appetites being directed to one object; while the other results from one's own appetite being united with the appetite of another: and each of these unions is effected by charity—the first, in so far as man loves God with his whole heart, by referring all things to Him, so that all his desires tend to one object—the second, in so far as we love our neighbor as ourselves, the result being that we wish to fulfil our neighbor's will as though it were ours: hence it is reckoned a sign of friendship if people "make choice of the same things" (Ethic. ix, 4), and Tully says (De Amicitia) that friends "like and dislike the same things" (Sallust, Catilin.)

Reply Obj. 1: Without sin no one falls from a state of sanctifying grace, for it turns man away from his due end by making him place his end in something undue: so that his appetite does not cleave chiefly to the true final good, but to some apparent good. Hence, without sanctifying grace, peace is not real but merely apparentapparent.

Reply Obj. 2: As the Philosopher says (Ethic. ix, 6) friends need not agree in opinion, but only upon such goods as conduce to life, and especially upon such as are important; because dissension in small matters is scarcely accounted dissension. Hence nothing hinders those who have charity from holding different opinions. Nor is this an obstacle to peace, because opinions concern the intellect, which precedes the appetite that is united by peace. In like manner if there be concord as to goods of importance, dissension with regard to some that are of little account is not contrary to charity: for such a dissension proceeds from a difference of opinion, because one man thinks that the particular good, which is the object of dissension, belongs to the good about which they agree, while the other thinks that it does not. Accordingly such like dissension about very slight matters and about opinions is inconsistent with a state of perfect peace, wherein the truth will be known fully, and every desire fulfilled; but it is not inconsistent with the imperfect peace of the wayfarer.

Reply Obj. 3: Peace is the "work of justice" indirectly, in so far as justice removes the obstacles to peace: but it is the work of charity directly, since charity, according to its very nature, causes peace. For love is "a unitive force" as Dionysius says (Div. Nom. iv): and peace is the union of the appetite's inclinations.

FOURTH ARTICLE [II-II, Q. 29, Art. 4]

Whether Peace Is a Virtue?

Objection 1: It would seem that peace is a virtue. For nothing is a matter of precept, unless it be an act of virtue. But there are precepts about keeping peace, for example: "Have peace among you" (Mk. 9:49). Therefore peace is a virtue.

Obj. 2: Further, we do not merit except by acts of virtue. Now it is meritorious to keep peace, according to Matt. 5:9: "Blessed are the peacemakers, for they shall be called the children of God." Therefore peace is a virtue.

Obj. 3: Further, vices are opposed to virtues. But dissensions, which are contrary to peace, are numbered among the vices (Gal. 5:20). Therefore peace is a virtue.

*On the contrary,* Virtue is not the last end, but the way thereto. But peace is the last end, in a sense, as Augustine says (De Civ. Dei xix, 11). Therefore peace is not a virtue.

*I answer that,* As stated above (Q. 28, A. 4), when a number of acts all proceeding uniformly from an agent, follow one from the other, they all arise from the same virtue, nor do they each have a virtue from which they proceed, as may be seen in corporeal things. For, though fire by heating, both liquefies and rarefies, there are not two powers in fire, one of liquefaction, the other of rarefaction: and fire produces all such actions by its own power of calefaction.

Since then charity causes peace precisely because it is love of God and of our neighbor, as shown above (A. 3), there is no other virtue except charity whose proper act is peace, as we have also said in reference to joy (Q. 28, A. 4).

Reply Obj. 1: We are commanded to keep peace because it is an act of charity; and for this reason too it is a meritorious act. Hence it is placed among the beatitudes, which are acts of perfect virtue, as stated above (I-II, Q. 69, AA. 1, 3). It is also numbered among the fruits, in so far as it is a final good, having spiritual sweetness.

This suffices for the Reply to the Second Objection.

Reply Obj. 3: Several vices are opposed to one virtue in respect of its various acts: so that not only is hatred opposed to charity, in respect of its act which is love, but also sloth and envy, in respect of joy, and dissension in respect of peace.

## QUESTION 30

OF MERCY* [*The one Latin word "misericordia" signifies either pity or mercy. The distinction between these two is that pity may stand either for the act or for the virtue, whereas mercy stands only for the virtue.] (In Four Articles)

We must now go on to consider Mercy, under which head there are four points of inquiry:

(1) Whether evil is the cause of mercy on the part of the person pitied?

(2) To whom does it belong to pity?

(3) Whether mercy is a virtue?

(4) Whether it is the greatest of virtues?

FIRST ARTICLE [II-II, Q. 30, Art. 1]

Whether Evil Is Properly the Motive of Mercy?

Objection 1: It would seem that, properly speaking, evil is not the motive of mercy. For, as shown above (Q. 19, A. 1; I-II, Q. 79, A. 1, ad 4; I, Q. 48, A. 6), fault is an evil rather than punishment. Now fault provokes indignation rather than mercy. Therefore evil does not excite mercy.

Obj. 2: Further, cruelty and harshness seem to excel other evils. Now the Philosopher says (Rhet. ii, 8) that "harshness does not call for pity but drives it away." Therefore evil, as such, is not the motive of mercy.

Obj. 3: Further, signs of evils are not true evils. But signs of evils excite one to mercy, as the Philosopher states (Rhet. ii, 8). Therefore evil, properly speaking, is not an incentive to mercy.

*On the contrary,* Damascene says (De Fide Orth. ii, 2) that mercy is a kind of sorrow. Now evil is the motive of sorrow. Therefore it is the motive of mercy.

*I answer that,* As Augustine says (De Civ. Dei ix, 5), mercy is heartfelt sympathy for another's distress, impelling us to succor him if we can. For mercy takes its name *misericordia* from denoting a man's compassionate heart ( *miserum cor* ) for another's unhappiness. Now unhappiness is opposed to happiness: and it is essential to beatitude or happiness that one should obtain what one wishes; for, according to Augustine (De Trin. xiii, 5), "happy is he who has whatever he desires, and desires nothing amiss." Hence, on the other hand, it belongs to unhappiness that a man should suffer what he wishes not.

Now a man wishes a thing in three ways: first, by his natural appetite; thus all men naturally wish to be and to live: secondly, a man wishes a thing from deliberate choice: thirdly, a man wishes a thing, not in itself, but in its cause, thus, if a man wishes to eat what is bad for him, we say that, in a way, he wishes to be ill.

Accordingly the motive of *mercy,* being something pertaining to *misery,* is, in the first way, anything contrary to the will's natural appetite, namely corruptive or distressing evils, the contrary of which man desires naturally, wherefore the Philosopher says (Rhet. ii, 8) that "pity is sorrow for a visible evil, whether corruptive or distressing." Secondly, such like evils are yet more provocative of pity if they are contrary to deliberate choice, wherefore the Philosopher says (Rhet. ii, 8) that evil excites our pity "when it is the result of an accident, as when something turns out ill, whereas we hoped well of it." Thirdly, they cause yet greater pity, if they are entirely contrary to the will, as when evil befalls a man who has always striven to do well: wherefore the Philosopher says (Rhet. ii, 8) that "we pity most the distress of one who suffers undeservedly."

Reply Obj. 1: It is essential to fault that it be voluntary; and in this respect it deserves punishment rather than mercy. Since, however, fault may be, in a way, a punishment, through having something connected with it that is against the sinner's will, it may, in this respect, call for mercy. It is in this sense that we pity and commiserate sinners. Thus Gregory says in a homily (Hom. in Evang. xxxiv) that "true godliness is not disdainful but compassionate," and again it is written (Matt. 9:36) that Jesus "seeing the multitudes, had compassion on them: because they were distressed, and lying like sheep that have no shepherd."

Reply Obj. 2: Since pity is sympathy for another's distress, it is directed, properly speaking, towards another, and not to oneself, except figuratively, like justice, according as a man is considered to have various parts (Ethic. v, 11). Thus it is written (Ecclus. 30:24): "Have pity on thy own soul, pleasing God" [*Cf. Q. 106, A. 3, ad 1].

Accordingly just as, properly speaking, a man does not pity himself, but suffers in himself, as when we suffer cruel treatment in ourselves, so too, in the case of those who are so closely united to us, as to be part of ourselves, such as our children or our parents, we do not pity their distress, but suffer as for our own sores; in which sense the Philosopher says that "harshness drives pity away."

Reply Obj. 3: Just as pleasure results from hope and memory of good things, so does sorrow arise from the prospect or the recollection of evil things; though not so keenly as when they are present to the senses. Hence the signs of evil move us to pity, in so far as they represent as present, the evil that excites our pity.

SECOND ARTICLE [II-II, Q. 30, Art. 2]

Whether the Reason for Taking Pity Is a Defect in the Person Who Pities?

Objection 1: It would seem that the reason for taking pity is not a defect in the person who takes pity. For it is proper to God to be merciful, wherefore it is written (Ps. 144:9): "His tender mercies are over all His works." But there is no defect in God. Therefore a defect cannot be the reason for taking pity.

Obj. 2: Further, if a defect is the reason for taking pity, those in whom there is most defect, must needs take most pity. But this is false: for the Philosopher says (Rhet. ii, 8) that "those who are in a desperate state are pitiless." Therefore it seems that the reason for taking pity is not a defect in the person who pities.

Obj. 3: Further, to be treated with contempt is to be defective. But the Philosopher says (Rhet. ii, 8) that "those who are disposed to contumely are pitiless." Therefore the reason for taking pity, is not a defect in the person who pities.

*On the contrary,* Pity is a kind of sorrow. But a defect is the reason of sorrow, wherefore those who are in bad health give way to sorrow more easily, as we shall say further on (Q. 35, A. 1, ad 2). Therefore the reason why one takes pity is a defect in oneself.

*I answer that,* Since pity is grief for another's distress, as stated above (A. 1), from the very fact that a person takes pity on anyone, it follows that another's distress grieves him. And since sorrow or grief is about one's own ills, one grieves or sorrows for another's distress, in so far as one looks upon another's distress as one's own.

Now this happens in two ways: first, through union of the affections, which is the effect of love. For, since he who loves another looks upon his friend as another self, he counts his friend's hurt as his own, so that he grieves for his friend's hurt as though he were hurt himself. Hence the Philosopher (Ethic. ix, 4) reckons "grieving with one's friend" as being one of the signs of friendship, and the Apostle says (Rom. 12:15): "Rejoice with them that rejoice, weep with them that weep."

Secondly, it happens through real union, for instance when another's evil comes near to us, so as to pass to us from him. Hence the Philosopher says (Rhet. ii, 8) that men pity such as are akin to them, and the like, because it makes them realize that the same may happen to themselves. This also explains why the old and the wise who consider that they may fall upon evil times, as also feeble and timorous persons, are more inclined to pity: whereas those who deem themselves happy, and so far powerful as to think themselves in no danger of suffering any hurt, are not so inclined to pity.

Accordingly a defect is always the reason for taking pity, either because one looks upon another's defect as one's own, through being united to him by love, or on account of the possibility of suffering in the same way.

Reply Obj. 1: God takes pity on us through love alone, in as much as He loves us as belonging to Him.

Reply Obj. 2: Those who are already in infinite distress, do not fear to suffer more, wherefore they are without pity. In like manner this applies to those also who are in great fear, for they are so intent on their own passion, that they pay no attention to the suffering of others.

Reply Obj. 3: Those who are disposed to contumely, whether through having been contemned, or because they wish to contemn others, are incited to anger and daring, which are manly passions and arouse the human spirit to attempt difficult things. Hence they make a man think that he is going to suffer something in the future, so that while they are disposed in that way they are pitiless, according to Prov. 27:4: "Anger hath no mercy, nor fury when it breaketh forth." For the same reason the proud are without pity, because they despise others, and think them wicked, so that they account them as suffering deservedly whatever they suffer. Hence Gregory says (Hom. in Evang. xxxiv) that "false godliness," i.e. of the proud, "is not compassionate but disdainful."

THIRD ARTICLE [II-II, Q. 30, Art. 3]

Whether Mercy Is a Virtue?

Objection 1: It would seem that mercy is not a virtue. For the chief part of virtue is choice as the Philosopher states (Ethic. ii, 5). Now choice is "the desire of what has been already counselled" (Ethic. iii, 2). Therefore whatever hinders counsel cannot be called a virtue. But mercy hinders counsel, according to the saying of Sallust (Catilin.): "All those that take counsel about matters of doubt, should be free from ... anger ... and mercy, because the mind does not easily see aright, when these things stand in the way." Therefore mercy is not a virtue.

Obj. 2: Further, nothing contrary to virtue is praiseworthy. But nemesis is contrary to mercy, as the Philosopher states (Rhet. ii, 9), and yet it is a praiseworthy passion (Rhet. ii, 9). Therefore mercy is not a virtue.

Obj. 3: Further, joy and peace are not special virtues, because they result from charity, as stated above (Q. 28, A. 4; Q. 29, A. 4). Now mercy, also, results from charity; for it is out of charity that we weep with them that weep, as we rejoice with them that rejoice. Therefore mercy is not a special virtue.

Obj. 4: Further, since mercy belongs to the appetitive power, it is not an intellectual virtue, and, since it has not God for its object, neither is it a theological virtue. Moreover it is not a moral virtue, because neither is it about operations, for this belongs to justice; nor is it about passions, since it is not reduced to one of the twelve means mentioned by the Philosopher (Ethic. ii, 7). Therefore mercy is not a virtue.

*On the contrary,* Augustine says (De Civ. Dei ix, 5): "Cicero in praising Caesar expresses himself much better and in a fashion at once more humane and more in accordance with religious feeling, when he says: 'Of all thy virtues none is more marvelous or more graceful than thy mercy.'" Therefore mercy is a virtue.

*I answer that,* Mercy signifies grief for another's distress. Now this grief may denote, in one way, a movement of the sensitive appetite, in which case mercy is not a virtue but a passion; whereas, in another way, it may denote a movement of the intellective appetite, in as much as one person's evil is displeasing to another. This movement may be ruled in accordance with reason, and in accordance with this movement regulated by reason, the movement of the lower appetite may be regulated. Hence Augustine says (De Civ. Dei ix, 5) that "this movement of the mind" (viz. mercy) "obeys the reason, when mercy is vouchsafed in such a way that justice is safeguarded, whether we give to the needy or forgive the repentant." And since it is essential to human virtue that the movements of the soul should be regulated by reason, as was shown above (I-II, Q. 59, AA. 4, 5), it follows that mercy is a virtue.

Reply Obj. 1: The words of Sallust are to be understood as applying to the mercy which is a passion unregulated by reason: for thus it impedes the counselling of reason, by making it wander from justice.

Reply Obj. 2: The Philosopher is speaking there of pity and nemesis, considered, both of them, as passions. They are contrary to one another on the part of their respective estimation of another's evils, for which pity grieves, in so far as it esteems someone to suffer undeservedly, whereas nemesis rejoices, in so far as it esteems someone to suffer deservedly, and grieves, if things go well with the undeserving: "both of these are praiseworthy and come from the same disposition of character" (Rhet. ii, 9). Properly speaking, however, it is envy which is opposed to pity, as we shall state further on (Q. 36, A. 3).

Reply Obj. 3: Joy and peace add nothing to the aspect of good which is the object of charity, wherefore they do not require any other virtue besides charity. But mercy regards a certain special aspect, namely the misery of the person pitied.

Reply Obj. 4: Mercy, considered as a virtue, is a moral virtue having relation to the passions, and it is reduced to the mean called nemesis, because "they both proceed from the same character" (Rhet. ii, 9). Now the Philosopher proposes these means not as virtues, but as passions, because, even as passions, they are praiseworthy. Yet nothing prevents them from proceeding from some elective habit, in which case they assume the character of a virtue.

FOURTH ARTICLE [II-II, Q. 30, Art. 4]

Whether Mercy Is the Greatest of the Virtues?

Objection 1: It would seem that mercy is the greatest of the virtues. For the worship of God seems a most virtuous act. But mercy is preferred before the worship of God, according to Osee 6:6 and Matt. 12:7: "I have desired mercy and not sacrifice." Therefore mercy is the greatest virtue.

Obj. 2: Further, on the words of 1 Tim. 4:8: "Godliness is profitable to all things," a gloss says: "The sum total of a Christian's rule of life consists in mercy and godliness." Now the Christian rule of life embraces every virtue. Therefore the sum total of all virtues is contained in mercy.

Obj. 3: Further, "Virtue is that which makes its subject good," according to the Philosopher. Therefore the more a virtue makes a man like God, the better is that virtue: since man is the better for being more like God. Now this is chiefly the result of mercy, since of God is it said (Ps. 144:9) that "His tender mercies are over all His works," and (Luke 6:36) Our Lord said: "Be ye ... merciful, as your Father also is merciful." Therefore mercy is the greatest of virtues.

*On the contrary,* The Apostle after saying (Col. 3:12): "Put ye on ... as the elect of God ... the bowels of mercy," etc., adds (Col. 3:14): "Above all things have charity." Therefore mercy is not the greatest of virtues.

*I answer that,* A virtue may take precedence of others in two ways: first, in itself; secondly, in comparison with its subject. In itself, mercy takes precedence of other virtues, for it belongs to mercy to be bountiful to others, and, what is more, to succor others in their wants, which pertains chiefly to one who stands above. Hence mercy is accounted as being proper to God: and therein His omnipotence is declared to be chiefly manifested [*Collect, Tenth Sunday after Pentecost].

On the other hand, with regard to its subject, mercy is not the greatest virtue, unless that subject be greater than all others, surpassed by none and excelling all: since for him that has anyone above him it is better to be united to that which is above than to supply the defect of that which is beneath. [*"The quality of mercy is not strained./'Tis mightiest in the mightiest: it becomes/The throned monarch better than his crown." Merchant of Venice, Act IV, Scene i.]. Hence, as regards man, who has God above him, charity which unites him to God, is greater than mercy, whereby he supplies the defects of his neighbor. But of all the virtues which relate to our neighbor, mercy is the greatest, even as its act surpasses all others, since it belongs to one who is higher and better to supply the defect of another, in so far as the latter is deficient.

Reply Obj. 1: We worship God by external sacrifices and gifts, not for His own profit, but for that of ourselves and our neighbor. For He needs not our sacrifices, but wishes them to be offered to Him, in order to arouse our devotion and to profit our neighbor. Hence mercy, whereby we supply others' defects is a sacrifice more acceptable to Him, as conducing more directly to our neighbor's well-being, according to Heb. 13:16: "Do not forget to do good and to impart, for by such sacrifices God's favor is obtained."

Reply Obj. 2: The sum total of the Christian religion consists in mercy, as regards external works: but the inward love of charity, whereby we are united to God preponderates over both love and mercy for our neighbor.

Reply Obj. 3: Charity likens us to God by uniting us to Him in the bond of love: wherefore it surpasses mercy, which likens us to God as regards similarity of works.

# QUESTION 31

OF BENEFICENCE (In Four Articles)

We must now consider the outward acts or effects of charity, (1) Beneficence, (2) Almsdeeds, which are a part of beneficence, (3) Fraternal correction, which is a kind of alms.

Under the first head there are four points of inquiry:

(1) Whether beneficence is an act of charity?

(2) Whether we ought to be beneficent to all?

(3) Whether we ought to be more beneficent to those who are more closely united to us?

(4) Whether beneficence is a special virtue?

FIRST ARTICLE [II-II, Q. 31, Art. 1]

Whether Beneficence Is an Act of Charity?

Objection 1: It would seem that beneficence is not an act of charity. For charity is chiefly directed to God. Now we cannot benefit God, according to Job 35:7: "What shalt thou give Him? or what shall He receive of thy hand?" Therefore beneficence is not an act of charity.

Obj. 2: Further, beneficence consists chiefly in making gifts. But this belongs to liberality. Therefore beneficence is an act of liberality and not of charity.

Obj. 3: Further, what a man gives, he gives either as being due, or as not due. But a benefit conferred as being due belongs to justice while a benefit conferred as not due, is gratuitous, and in this respect is an act of mercy. Therefore every benefit conferred is either an act of justice, or an act of mercy. Therefore it is not an act of charity.

*On the contrary,* Charity is a kind of friendship, as stated above (Q. 23, A. 1). Now the Philosopher reckons among the acts of friendship (Ethic. ix, 1) "doing good," i.e. being beneficent, "to one's friends." Therefore it is an act of charity to do good to others.

*I answer that,* Beneficence simply means doing good to someone. This good may be considered in two ways, first under the general aspect of good, and this belongs to beneficence in general, and is an act of friendship, and, consequently, of charity: because the act of love includes goodwill whereby a man wishes his friend well, as stated above (Q. 23, A. 1; Q. 27, A. 2). Now the will carries into effect if possible, the things it wills, so that, consequently, the result of an act of love is that a man is beneficent to his friend. Therefore beneficence in its general acceptation is an act of friendship or charity.

But if the good which one man does another, be considered under some special aspect of good, then beneficence will assume a special character and will belong to some special virtue.

Reply Obj. 1: According to Dionysius (Div. Nom. iv), "love moves those, whom it unites, to a mutual relationship: it turns the inferior to the superior to be perfected thereby; it moves the superior to watch over the inferior:" and in this respect beneficence is an effect of love. Hence it is not for us to benefit God, but to honor Him by obeying Him, while it is for Him, out of His love, to bestow good things on us.

Reply Obj. 2: Two things must be observed in the bestowal of gifts. One is the thing given outwardly, while the other is the inward passion that a man has in the delight of riches. It belongs to liberality to moderate this inward passion so as to avoid excessive desire and love for riches; for this makes a man more ready to part with his wealth. Hence, if a man makes some great gift, while yet desiring to keep it for himself, his is not a liberal giving. On the other hand, as regards the outward gift, the act of beneficence belongs in general to friendship or charity. Hence it does not detract from a man's friendship, if, through love, he give his friend something he would like to keep for himself; rather does this prove the perfection of his friendship.

Reply Obj. 3: Just as friendship or charity sees, in the benefit bestowed, the general aspect of good, so does justice see therein the aspect of debt, while pity considers the relieving of distress or defect.

SECOND ARTICLE [II-II, Q. 31, Art. 2]

Whether We Ought to Do Good to All?

Objection 1: It would seem that we are not bound to do good to all. For Augustine says (De Doctr. Christ. i, 28) that we "are unable to do good to everyone." Now virtue does not incline one to the impossible. Therefore it is not necessary to do good to all.

Obj. 2: Further, it is written (Ecclus. 12:5) "Give to the good, and receive not a sinner." But many men are sinners. Therefore we need not do good to all.

Obj. 3: Further, "Charity dealeth not perversely" (1 Cor. 13:4). Now to do good to some is to deal perversely: for instance if one were to do good to an enemy of the common weal, or if one were to do good to an excommunicated person, since, by doing so, he would be holding communion with him. Therefore, since beneficence is an act of charity, we ought not to do good to all.

*On the contrary,* The Apostle says (Gal. 6:10): "Whilst we have time, let us work good to all men."

*I answer that,* As stated above (A. 1, ad 1), beneficence is an effect of love in so far as love moves the superior to watch over the inferior. Now degrees among men are not unchangeable as among angels, because men are subject to many failings, so that he who is superior in one respect, is or may be inferior in another. Therefore, since the love of charity extends to all, beneficence also should extend to all, but according as time and place require: because all acts of virtue must be modified with a view to their due circumstances.

Reply Obj. 1: Absolutely speaking it is impossible to do good to every single one: yet it is true of each individual that one may be bound to do good to him in some particular case. Hence charity binds us, though not actually doing good to someone, to be prepared in mind to do good to anyone if we have time to spare. There is however a good that we can do to all, if not to each individual, at least to all in general, as when we pray for all, for unbelievers as well as for the faithful.

Reply Obj. 2: In a sinner there are two things, his guilt and his nature. Accordingly we are bound to succor the sinner as to the maintenance of his nature, but not so as to abet his sin, for this would be to do evil rather than good.

Reply Obj. 3: The excommunicated and the enemies of the common weal are deprived of all beneficence, in so far as this prevents them from doing evil deeds. Yet if their nature be in urgent need of succor lest it fail, we are bound to help them: for instance, if they be in danger of death through hunger or thirst, or suffer some like distress, unless this be according to the order of justice.

THIRD ARTICLE [II-II, Q. 31, Art. 3]

Whether We Ought to Do Good to Those Rather Who Are More Closely United to Us?

Objection 1: It would seem that we are not bound to do good to those rather who are more closely united to us. For it is written (Luke 14:12): "When thou makest a dinner or a supper, call not thy friends, nor thy brethren, nor thy kinsmen." Now these are the most closely united to us. Therefore we are not bound to do good to those rather who are more closely united to us, but preferably to strangers and to those who are in want: hence the text goes on: "But, when thou makest a feast, call the poor, the maimed," etc.

.Obj. 3: Further, we should pay what is due before conferring gratuitous favors. But it is a man's duty to be good to those who have been good to him. Therefore we ought to do good to our benefactors rather than to those who are closely united to us.

Obj. 4: Further, a man ought to love his parents more than his children, as stated above (Q. 26, A. 9). Yet a man ought to be more beneficent to his children, since "neither ought the children to lay up for the parents," according to 2 Cor. 12:14. Therefore we are not bound to be more beneficent to those who are more closely united to us.

*On the contrary,* Augustine says (De Doctr. Christ. i, 28): "Since one cannot do good to all, we ought to consider those chiefly who by reason of place, time or any other circumstance, by a kind of chance are more closely united to us."

*I answer that,* Grace and virtue imitate the order of nature, which is established by Divine wisdom. Now the order of nature is such that every natural agent pours forth its activity first and most of all on the things which are nearest to it: thus fire heats most what is next to it. In like manner God pours forth the gifts of His goodness first and most plentifully on the substances which are nearest to Him, as Dionysius declares (Coel. Hier. vii). But the bestowal of benefits is an act of charity towards others. Therefore we ought to be most beneficent towards those who are most closely connected with us.

Now one man's connection with another may be measured in reference to the various matters in which men are engaged together; (thus the intercourse of kinsmen is in natural matters, that of fellow-citizens is in civic matters, that of the faithful is in spiritual matters, and so forth): and various benefits should be conferred in various ways according to these various connections, because we ought in preference to bestow on each one such benefits as pertain to the matter in which, speaking simply, he is most closely connected with us. And yet this may vary according to the various requirements of time, place, or matter in hand: because in certain cases one ought, for instance, to succor a stranger, in extreme necessity, rather than one's own father, if he is not in such urgent need.

Reply Obj. 1: Our Lord did not absolutely forbid us to invite our friends and kinsmen to eat with us, but to invite them so that they may invite us in return, since that would be an act not of charity but of cupidity. The case may occur, however, that one ought rather to invite strangers, on account of their greater want. For it must be understood that, other things being equal, one ought to succor those rather who are most closely connected with us. And if of two, one be more closely connected, and the other in greater want, it is not possible to decide, by any general rule, which of them we ought to help rather than the other, since there are various degrees of want as well as of connection: and the matter requires the judgment of a prudent man.

Reply Obj. 2: The common good of many is more Godlike than the good of an individual. Wherefore it is a virtuous action for a man to endanger even his own life, either for the spiritual or for the temporal common good of his country. Since therefore men engage together in warlike acts in order to safeguard the common weal, the soldier who with this in view succors his comrade, succors him not as a private individual, but with a view to the welfare of his country as a whole: wherefore it is not a matter for wonder if a stranger be preferred to one who is a blood relation.

Reply Obj. 3: A thing may be due in two ways. There is one which should be reckoned, not among the goods of the debtor, but rather as belonging to the person to whom it is due: for instance, a man may have another's goods, whether in money or in kind, either because he has stolen them, or because he has received them on loan or in deposit or in some other way. In this case a man ought to pay what he owes, rather than benefit his connections out of it, unless perchance the case be so urgent that it would be lawful for him to take another's property in order to relieve the one who is in need. Yet, again, this would not apply if the creditor were in equal distress: in which case, however, the claims on either side would have to be weighed with regard to such other conditions as a prudent man would take into consideration, because, on account of the different particular cases, as the Philosopher states (Ethic. ix, 2), it is impossible to lay down a general rule.

The other kind of due is one which is reckoned among the goods of the debtor and not of the creditor; for instance, a thing may be due, not because justice requires it, but on account of a certain moral equity, as in the case of benefits received gratis. Now no benefactor confers a benefit equal to that which a man receives from his parents: wherefore in paying back benefits received, we should give the first place to our parents before all others, unless, on the other side, there be such weightier motives, as need or some other circumstance, for instance the common good of the Church or state. In other cases we must take to account the connection and the benefit received; and here again no general rule can laid down.

Reply Obj. 4: Parents are like superiors, and so a parent's love tends to conferring benefits, while the children's love tends to honor their parents. Nevertheless in a case of extreme urgency it would be lawful to abandon one's children rather than one's parents, to abandon whom it is by no means lawful, on account of the obligation we lie under towards them for the benefits we have received from them, as the Philosopher states (Ethic. iii, 14).

FOURTH ARTICLE [II-II, Q. 31, Art. 4]

Whether Beneficence Is a Special Virtue?

Objection 1: It would seem that beneficence is a special virtue. For precepts are directed to virtue, since lawgivers purpose to make men virtuous (Ethic. i 9, 13; ii, 1). Now beneficence and love are prescribed as distinct from one another, for it is written (Matt. 4:44): "Love your enemies, do good to them that hate you." Therefore beneficence is a virtue distinct from charity.

Obj. 2: Further, vices are opposed to virtues. Now there are opposed to beneficence certain vices whereby a hurt is inflicted on our neighbor, for instance, rapine, theft and so forth. Therefore beneficence is a special virtue.

Obj. 3: Further, charity is not divided into several species: whereas there would seem to be several kinds of beneficence, according to the various kinds of benefits. Therefore beneficence is a distinct virtue from charity.

*On the contrary,* The internal and the external act do not require different virtues. Now beneficence and goodwill differ only as external and internal act, since beneficence is the execution of goodwill. Therefore as goodwill is not a distinct virtue from charity, so neither is beneficence.

*I answer that,* Virtues differ according to the different aspects of their objects. Now the formal aspect of the object of charity and of beneficence is the same, since both virtues regard the common aspect of good, as explained above (A. 1). Wherefore beneficence is not a distinct virtue from charity, but denotes an act of charity.

Reply Obj. 1: Precepts are given, not about habits but about acts of virtue: wherefore distinction of precept denotes distinction, not of habits, but of acts.

Reply Obj. 2: Even as all benefits conferred on our neighbor, if we consider them under the common aspect of good, are to be traced to love, so all hurts considered under the common aspect of evil, are to be traced to hatred. But if we consider these same things under certain special aspects of good or of evil, they are to be traced to certain special virtues or vices, and in this way also there are various kinds of benefits.

Hence the Reply to the Third Objection is evident.

# QUESTION 32

OF ALMSDEEDS (In Ten Articles)

We must now consider almsdeeds, under which head there are ten points of inquiry:

(1) Whether almsgiving is an act of charity?

(2) Of the different kinds of alms;

(3) Which alms are of greater account, spiritual or corporal?

(4) Whether corporal alms have a spiritual effect?

(5) Whether the giving of alms is a matter of precept?

(6) Whether corporal alms should be given out of the things we need?

(7) Whether corporal alms should be given out of ill-gotten goods?

(8) Who can give alms?

(9) To whom should we give alms?

(10) How should alms be given?

FIRST ARTICLE [II-II, Q. 32, Art. 1]

Whether Almsgiving Is an Act of Charity?

Objection 1: It would seem that almsgiving is not an act of charity. For without charity one cannot do acts of charity. Now it is possible to give alms without having charity, according to 1 Cor. 13:3: "If I should distribute all my goods to feed the poor ... and have not charity, it profiteth me nothing." Therefore almsgiving is not an act of charity.

Obj. 2: Further, almsdeeds are reckoned among works of satisfaction, according to Dan. 4:24: "Redeem thou thy sins with alms." Now satisfaction is an act of justice. Therefore almsgiving is an act of justice and not of charity.

Obj. 3: Further, the offering of sacrifices to God is an act of religion. But almsgiving is offering a sacrifice to God, according to Heb. 13:16: "Do not forget to do good and to impart, for by such sacrifices God's favor is obtained." Therefore almsgiving is not an act of charity, but of religion.

Obj. 4: Further, the Philosopher says (Ethic. iv, 1) that to give for a good purpose is an act of liberality. Now this is especially true of almsgiving. Therefore almsgiving is not an act of charity.

*On the contrary,* It is written 2 John 3:17: "He that hath the substance of this world, and shall see his brother in need, and shall put up his bowels from him, how doth the charity of God abide in him?"

*I answer that,* External acts belong to that virtue which regards the motive for doing those acts. Now the motive for giving alms is to relieve one who is in need. Wherefore some have defined alms as being "a deed whereby something is given to the needy, out of compassion and for God's sake," which motive belongs to mercy, as stated above (Q. 30, AA. 1, 2). Hence it is clear that almsgiving is, properly speaking, an act of mercy. This appears in its very name, for in Greek ( *eleemosyne* ) it is derived from having mercy ( eleein ) even as the Latin *miseratio* is. And since mercy is an effect of charity, as shown above (Q. 30, A. 2, A. 3, Obj. 3), it follows that almsgiving is an act of charity through the medium of mercy.

Reply Obj. 1: An act of virtue may be taken in two ways: first materially, thus an act of justice is to do what is just; and such an act of virtue can be without the virtue, since many, without having the habit of justice, do what is just, led by the natural light of reason, or through fear, or in the hope of gain. Secondly, we speak of a thing being an act of justice formally, and thus an act of justice is to do what is just, in the same way as a just man, i.e. with readiness and delight, and such an act of virtue cannot be without the virtue.

Accordingly almsgiving can be materially without charity, but to give alms formally, i.e. for God's sake, with delight and readiness, and altogether as one ought, is not possible without charity.

Reply Obj. 2: Nothing hinders the proper elicited act of one virtue being commanded by another virtue as commanding it and directing it to this other virtue's end. It is in this way that almsgiving is reckoned among works of satisfaction in so far as pity for the one in distress is directed to the satisfaction for his sin; and in so far as it is directed to placate God, it has the character of a sacrifice, and thus it is commanded by religion.

Wherefore the Reply to the Third Objection is evident.

Reply Obj. 4: Almsgiving belongs to liberality, in so far as liberality removes an obstacle to that act, which might arise from excessive love of riches, the result of which is that one clings to them more than one ought.

SECOND ARTICLE [II-II, Q. 32, Art. 2]

Whether the Different Kinds of Almsdeeds Are Suitably Enumerated?

Objection 1: It would seem that the different kinds of almsdeeds are unsuitably enumerated. For we reckon seven corporal almsdeeds, namely, to feed the hungry, to give drink to the thirsty, to clothe the naked, to harbor the harborless, to visit the sick, to ransom the captive, to bury the dead; all of which are expressed in the following verse: "To visit, to quench, to feed, to ransom, clothe, harbor or bury."

Again we reckon seven spiritual alms, namely, to instruct the ignorant, to counsel the doubtful, to comfort the sorrowful, to reprove the sinner, to forgive injuries, to bear with those who trouble and annoy us, and to pray for all, which are all contained in the following verse: "To counsel, reprove, console, to pardon, forbear, and to pray," yet so that counsel includes both advice and instruction.

And it seems that these various almsdeeds are unsuitably enumerated. For the purpose of almsdeeds is to succor our neighbor. But a dead man profits nothing by being buried, else Our Lord would not have spoken truly when He said (Matt. 10:28): "Be not afraid of them who kill the body, and after that have no more that they can do." [*The quotation is from Luke 12:4.] This explains why Our Lord, in enumerating the works of mercy, made no mention of the burial of the dead (Matt. 25:35, 36). Therefore it seems that these almsdeeds are unsuitably enumerated.

Obj. 2: Further, as stated above (A. 1), the purpose of giving alms is to relieve our neighbor's need. Now there are many needs of human life other than those mentioned above, for instance, a blind man needs a leader, a lame man needs someone to lean on, a poor man needs riches. Therefore these almsdeeds are unsuitably enumerated.

Obj. 3: Further, almsgiving is a work of mercy. But the reproof of the wrong-doer savors, apparently, of severity rather than of mercy. Therefore it ought not to be reckoned among the spiritual almsdeeds.

Obj. 4: Further, almsgiving is intended for the supply of a defect. But no man is without the defect of ignorance in some matter or other. Therefore, apparently, each one ought to instruct anyone who is ignorant of what he knows himself.

*On the contrary,* Gregory says (Nom. in Evang. ix): "Let him that hath understanding beware lest he withhold his knowledge; let him that hath abundance of wealth, watch lest he slacken his merciful bounty; let him who is a servant to art be most solicitous to share his skill and profit with his neighbor; let him who has an opportunity of speaking with the wealthy, fear lest he be condemned for retaining his talent, if when he has the chance he plead not with him the cause of the poor." Therefore the aforesaid almsdeeds are suitably enumerated in respect of those things whereof men have abundance or insufficiency.

*I answer that,* The aforesaid distinction of almsdeeds is suitably taken from the various needs of our neighbor: some of which affect the soul, and are relieved by spiritual almsdeeds, while others affect the body, and are relieved by corporal almsdeeds. For corporal need occurs either during this life or afterwards. If it occurs during this life, it is either a common need in respect of things needed by all, or it is a special need occurring through some accident supervening. In the first case, the need is either internal or external. Internal need is twofold: one which is relieved by solid food, viz. hunger, in respect of which we have *to feed the hungry;* while the other is relieved by liquid food, viz. thirst, and in respect of this we have *to give drink to the thirsty.* The common need with regard to external help is twofold; one in respect of clothing, and as to this we have *to clothe the naked:* while the other is in respect of a dwelling place, and as to this we have to harbor the harborless. Again if the need be special, it is either the result of an internal cause, like sickness, and then we have to visit the sick, or it results from an external cause, and then we have *to ransom the captive.* After this life we give burial to the dead.

In like manner spiritual needs are relieved by spiritual acts in two ways, first by asking for help from God, and in this respect we have *prayer,* whereby one man prays for others; secondly, by giving human assistance, and this in three ways. First, in order to relieve a deficiency on the part of the intellect, and if this deficiency be in the speculative intellect, the remedy is applied by *instructing,* and if in the practical intellect, the remedy is applied by *counselling.* Secondly, there may be a deficiency on the part of the appetitive power, especially by way of sorrow, which is remedied by *comforting.* Thirdly, the deficiency may be due to an inordinate act; and this may be the subject of a threefold consideration. First, in respect of the sinner, inasmuch as the sin proceeds from his inordinate will, and thus the remedy takes the form of *reproof.* Secondly, in respect of the person sinned against; and if the sin be committed against ourselves, we apply the remedy by pardoning the injury, while, if it be committed against God or our neighbor, it is not in our power to pardon, as Jerome observes (Super Matth. xviii, 15). Thirdly, in respect of the result of the inordinate act, on account of which the sinner is an annoyance to those who live with him, even beside his intention; in which case the remedy is applied by *bearing with him,* especially with regard to those who sin out of weakness, according to Rom. 15:1: "We that are stronger, ought to bear the infirmities of the weak," and not only as regards their being infirm and consequently troublesome on account of their unruly actions, but also by bearing any other burdens of theirs with them, according to Gal. 6:2: "Bear ye one another's burdens."

Reply Obj. 1: Burial does not profit a dead man as though his body could be capable of perception after death. In this sense Our Lord said that those who kill the body "have no more that they can do"; and for this reason He did not mention the burial of the dead with the other works of mercy, but those only which are more clearly necessary. Nevertheless it does concern the deceased what is done with his body: both that he may live in the memory of man whose respect he forfeits if he remain without burial, and as regards a man's fondness for his own body while he was yet living, a fondness which kindly persons should imitate after his death. It is thus that some are praised for burying the dead, as Tobias, and those who buried Our Lord; as Augustine says (De Cura pro Mort. iii).

Reply Obj. 2: All other needs are reduced to these, for blindness and lameness are kinds of sickness, so that to lead the blind, and to support the lame, come to the same as visiting the sick. In like manner to assist a man against any distress that is due to an extrinsic cause comes to the same as the ransom of captives. And the wealth with which we relieve the poor is sought merely for the purpose of relieving the aforesaid needs: hence there was no reason for special mention of this particular need.

Reply Obj. 3: The reproof of the sinner, as to the exercise of the act of reproving, seems to imply the severity of justice, but, as to the intention of the reprover, who wishes to free a man from the evil of sin, it is an act of mercy and lovingkindness, according to Prov. 27:6: "Better are the wounds of a friend, than the deceitful kisses of an enemy."

Reply Obj. 4: Nescience is not always a defect, but only when it is about what one ought to know, and it is a part of almsgiving to supply this defect by instruction. In doing this however we should observe the due circumstances of persons, place and time, even as in other virtuous acts.

THIRD ARTICLE [II-II, Q. 32, Art. 3]

Whether Corporal Alms Are of More Account Than Spiritual Alms?

Objection 1: It would seem that corporal alms are of more account than spiritual alms. For it is more praiseworthy to give an alms to one who is in greater want, since an almsdeed is to be praised because it relieves one who is in need. Now the body which is relieved by corporal alms, is by nature more needy than the spirit which is relieved by spiritual alms. Therefore corporal alms are of more account.

Obj. 2: Further, an alms is less praiseworthy and meritorious if the kindness is compensated, wherefore Our Lord says (Luke 14:12): "When thou makest a dinner or a supper, call not thy neighbors who are rich, lest perhaps they also invite thee again." Now there is always compensation in spiritual almsdeeds, since he who prays for another, profits thereby, according to Ps. 34:13: "My prayer shall be turned into my bosom": and he who teaches another, makes progress in knowledge, which cannot be said of corporal almsdeeds. Therefore corporal almsdeeds are of more account than spiritual almsdeeds.

Obj. 3: Further, an alms is to be commended if the needy one is comforted by it: wherefore it is written (Job 31:20): "If his sides have not blessed me," and the Apostle says to Philemon (verse 7): "The bowels of the saints have been refreshed by thee, brother." Now a corporal alms is sometimes more welcome to a needy man than a spiritual alms. Therefore bodily almsdeeds are of more account than spiritual almsdeeds.

*On the contrary,* Augustine says (De Serm. Dom. in Monte i, 20) on the words, "Give to him that asketh of thee" (Matt. 5:42): "You should give so as to injure neither yourself nor another, and when you refuse what another asks you must not lose sight of the claims of justice, and send him away empty; at times indeed you will give what is better than what is asked for, if you reprove him that asks unjustly." Now reproof is a spiritual alms. Therefore spiritual almsdeeds are preferable to corporal almsdeeds.

*I answer that,* There are two ways of comparing these almsdeeds. First, simply; and in this respect, spiritual almsdeeds hold the first place, for three reasons. First, because the offering is more excellent, since it is a spiritual gift, which surpasses a corporal gift, according to Prov. 4:2: "I will give you a good gift, forsake not My Law." Secondly, on account of the object succored, because the spirit is more excellent than the body, wherefore, even as a man in looking after himself, ought to look to his soul more than to his body, so ought he in looking after his neighbor, whom he ought to love as himself. Thirdly, as regards the acts themselves by which our neighbor is succored, because spiritual acts are more excellent than corporal acts, which are, in a fashion, servile.

Secondly, we may compare them with regard to some particular case, when some corporal alms excels some spiritual alms: for instance, a man in hunger is to be fed rather than instructed, and as the Philosopher observes (Topic. iii, 2), for a needy man "money is better than philosophy," although the latter is better simply.

Reply Obj. 1: It is better to give to one who is in greater want, other things being equal, but if he who is less needy is better, and is in want of better things, it is better to give to him: and it is thus in the case in point.

Reply Obj. 2: Compensation does not detract from merit and praise if it be not intended, even as human glory, if not intended, does not detract from virtue. Thus Sallust says of Cato (Catilin.), that "the less he sought fame, the more he became famous": and thus it is with spiritual almsdeeds.

Nevertheless the intention of gaining spiritual goods does not detract from merit, as the intention of gaining corporal goods.

Reply Obj. 3: The merit of an almsgiver depends on that in which the will of the recipient rests reasonably, and not on that in which it rests when it is inordinate.

FOURTH ARTICLE [II-II, Q. 32, Art. 4]

Whether Corporal Almsdeeds Have a Spiritual Effect?

Objection 1: It would seem that corporal almsdeeds have not a spiritual effect. For no effect exceeds its cause. But spiritual goods exceed corporal goods. Therefore corporal almsdeeds have no spiritual effect.

Obj. 2: Further, the sin of simony consists in giving the corporal for the spiritual, and it is to be utterly avoided. Therefore one ought not to give alms in order to receive a spiritual effect.

Obj. 3: Further, to multiply the cause is to multiply the effect. If therefore corporal almsdeeds cause a spiritual effect, the greater the alms, the greater the spiritual profit, which is contrary to what we read (Luke 21:3) of the widow who cast two brass mites into the treasury, and in Our Lord's own words "cast in more than ... all." Therefore bodily almsdeeds have no spiritual effect.

*On the contrary,* It is written (Ecclus. 17:18): "The alms of a man ... shall preserve the grace of a man as the apple of the eye."

*I answer that,* Corporal almsdeeds may be considered in three ways. First, with regard to their substance, and in this way they have merely a corporal effect, inasmuch as they supply our neighbor's corporal needs. Secondly, they may be considered with regard to their cause, in so far as a man gives a corporal alms out of love for God and his neighbor, and in this respect they bring forth a spiritual fruit, according to Ecclus. 29:13, 14: "Lose thy money for thy brother ... place thy treasure in the commandments of the Most High, and it shall bring thee more profit than gold."

Thirdly, with regard to the effect, and in this way again, they have a spiritual fruit, inasmuch as our neighbor, who is succored by a corporal alms, is moved to pray for his benefactor; wherefore the above text goes on (Ecclus. 29:15): "Shut up alms in the heart of the poor, and it shall obtain help for thee from all evil."

Reply Obj. 1: This argument considers corporal almsdeeds as to their substance.

Reply Obj. 2: He who gives an alms does not intend to buy a spiritual thing with a corporal thing, for he knows that spiritual things infinitely surpass corporal things, but he intends to merit a spiritual fruit through the love of charity.

Reply Obj. 3: The widow who gave less in quantity, gave more in proportion; and thus we gather that the fervor of her charity, whence corporal almsdeeds derive their spiritual efficacy, was greater.

FIFTH ARTICLE [II-II, Q. 32, Art. 5]

Whether Almsgiving Is a Matter of Precept?

Objection 1: It would seem that almsgiving is not a matter of precept. For the counsels are distinct from the precepts. Now almsgiving is a matter of counsel, according to Dan. 4:24: "Let my counsel be acceptable to the King; [Vulg.: 'to thee, and'] redeem thou thy sins with alms." Therefore almsgiving is not a matter of precept.

Obj. 2: Further, it is lawful for everyone to use and to keep what is his own. Yet by keeping it he will not give alms. Therefore it is lawful not to give alms: and consequently almsgiving is not a matter of precept.

Obj. 3: Further, whatever is a matter of precept binds the transgressor at some time or other under pain of mortal sin, because positive precepts are binding for some fixed time. Therefore, if almsgiving were a matter of precept, it would be possible to point to some fixed time when a man would commit a mortal sin unless he gave an alms. But it does not appear how this can be so, because it can always be deemed probable that the person in need can be relieved in some other way, and that what we would spend in almsgiving might be needful to ourselves either now or in some future time. Therefore it seems that almsgiving is not a matter of precept.

Obj. 4: Further, every commandment is reducible to the precepts of the Decalogue. But these precepts contain no reference to almsgiving. Therefore almsgiving is not a matter of precept.

*On the contrary,* No man is punished eternally for omitting to do what is not a matter of precept. But some are punished eternally for omitting to give alms, as is clear from Matt. 25:41-43. Therefore almsgiving is a matter of precept.

*I answer that,* As love of our neighbor is a matter of precept, whatever is a necessary condition to the love of our neighbor is a matter of precept also. Now the love of our neighbor requires that not only should we be our neighbor's well-wishers, but also his well-doers, according to 1 John 3:18: "Let us not love in word, nor in tongue, but in deed, and in truth." And in order to be a person's well-wisher and well-doer, we ought to succor his needs: this is done by almsgiving. Therefore almsgiving is a matter of precept.

Since, however, precepts are about acts of virtue, it follows that all almsgiving must be a matter of precept, in so far as it is necessary to virtue, namely, in so far as it is demanded by right reason. Now right reason demands that we should take into consideration something on the part of the giver, and something on the part of the recipient. On the part of the giver, it must be noted that he should give of his surplus, according to Luke 11:41: "That which remaineth, give alms." This surplus is to be taken in reference not only to himself, so as to denote what is unnecessary to the individual, but also in reference to those of whom he has charge (in which case we have the expression "necessary to the person" [*The official necessities of a person in position] taking the word "person" as expressive of dignity). Because each one must first of all look after himself and then after those over whom he has charge, and afterwards with what remains relieve the needs of others. Thus nature first, by its nutritive power, takes what it requires for the upkeep of one's own body, and afterwards yields the residue for the formation of another by the power of generation.

On the part of the recipient it is requisite that he should be in need, else there would be no reason for giving him alms: yet since it is not possible for one individual to relieve the needs of all, we are not bound to relieve all who are in need, but only those who could not be succored if we not did succor them. For in such cases the words of Ambrose apply, "Feed him that dies of hunger: if thou hast not fed him, thou hast slain him" [*Cf. Canon *Pasce,* dist. lxxxvi, whence the words, as quoted, are taken]. Accordingly we are bound to give alms of our surplus, as also to give alms to one whose need is extreme: otherwise almsgiving, like any other greater good, is a matter of counsel.

Reply Obj. 1: Daniel spoke to a king who was not subject to God's Law, wherefore such things as were prescribed by the Law which he did not profess, had to be counselled to him. Or he may have been speaking in reference to a case in which almsgiving was not a matter of precept.

Reply Obj. 2: The temporal goods which God grants us, are ours as to the ownership, but as to the use of them, they belong not to us alone but also to such others as we are able to succor out of what we have over and above our needs. Hence Basil says [*Hom. super Luc. xii, 18]: "If you acknowledge them," viz. your temporal goods, "as coming from God, is He unjust because He apportions them unequally? Why are you rich while another is poor, unless it be that you may have the merit of a good stewardship, and he the reward of patience? It is the hungry man's bread that you withhold, the naked man's cloak that you have stored away, the shoe of the barefoot that you have left to rot, the money of the needy that you have buried underground: and so you injure as many as you might help." Ambrose expresses himself in the same way.

Reply Obj. 3: There is a time when we sin mortally if we omit to give alms; on the part of the recipient when we see that his need is evident and urgent, and that he is not likely to be succored otherwise—on the part of the giver, when he has superfluous goods, which he does not need for the time being, as far as he can judge with probability. Nor need he consider every case that may possibly occur in the future, for this would be to think about the morrow, which Our Lord forbade us to do (Matt. 6:34), but he should judge what is superfluous and what necessary, according as things probably and generally occur.

Reply Obj. 4: All succor given to our neighbor is reduced to the precept about honoring our parents. For thus does the Apostle interpret it (1 Tim. 4:8) where he says: "Dutifulness* [Douay: 'Godliness'] is profitable to all things, having promise of the life that now is, and of that which is to come," and he says this because the precept about honoring our parents contains the promise, "that thou mayest be longlived upon the land" (Ex. 20:12): and dutifulness comprises all kinds of almsgiving. [* *Pietas,* whence our English word "Piety." Cf. also inf. Q. 101, A. 2.]

SIXTH ARTICLE [II-II, Q. 32, Art. 6]

Whether One Ought to Give Alms Out of What One Needs?

Objection 1: It would seem that one ought not to give alms out of what one needs. For the order of charity should be observed not only as regards the effect of our benefactions but also as regards our interior affections. Now it is a sin to contravene the order of charity, because this order is a matter of precept. Since, then, the order of charity requires that a man should love himself more than his neighbor, it seems that he would sin if he deprived himself of what he needed, in order to succor his neighbor.

Obj. 2: Further, whoever gives away what he needs himself, squanders his own substance, and that is to be a prodigal, according to the Philosopher (Ethic. iv, 1). But no sinful deed should be done. Therefore we should not give alms out of what we need.

Obj. 3: Further, the Apostle says (1 Tim. 5:8): "If any man have not care of his own, and especially of those of his house, he hath denied the faith, and is worse than an infidel." Now if a man gives of what he needs for himself or for his charge, he seems to detract from the care he should have for himself or his charge. Therefore it seems that whoever gives alms from what he needs, sins gravely.

*On the contrary,* Our Lord said (Matt. 19:21): "If thou wilt be perfect, go, sell what thou hast, and give to the poor." Now he that gives all he has to the poor, gives not only what he needs not, but also what he needs. Therefore a man may give alms out of what he needs.

*I answer that,* A thing is necessary in two ways: first, because without it something is impossible, and it is altogether wrong to give alms out of what is necessary to us in this sense; for instance, if a man found himself in the presence of a case of urgency, and had merely sufficient to support himself and his children, or others under his charge, he would be throwing away his life and that of others if he were to give away in alms, what was then necessary to him. Yet I say this without prejudice to such a case as might happen, supposing that by depriving himself of necessaries a man might help a great personage, and a support of the Church or State, since it would be a praiseworthy act to endanger one's life and the lives of those who are under our charge for the delivery of such a person, since the common good is to be preferred to one's own.

Secondly, a thing is said to be necessary, if a man cannot without it live in keeping with his social station, as regards either himself or those of whom he has charge. The "necessary" considered thus is not an invariable quantity, for one might add much more to a man's property, and yet not go beyond what he needs in this way, or one might take much from him, and he would still have sufficient for the decencies of life in keeping with his own position. Accordingly it is good to give alms of this kind of "necessary"; and it is a matter not of precept but of counsel. Yet it would be inordinate to deprive oneself of one's own, in order to give to others to such an extent that the residue would be insufficient for one to live in keeping with one's station and the ordinary occurrences of life: for no man ought to live unbecomingly. There are, however, three exceptions to the above rule. The first is when a man changes his state of life, for instance, by entering religion, for then he gives away all his possessions for Christ's sake, and does the deed of perfection by transferring himself to another state. Secondly, when that which he deprives himself of, though it be required for the decencies of life, can nevertheless easily be recovered, so that he does not suffer extreme inconvenience. Thirdly, when he is in presence of extreme indigence in an individual, or great need on the part of the common weal. For in such cases it would seem praiseworthy to forego the requirements of one's station, in order to provide for a greater need.

The objections may be easily solved from what has been said.

SEVENTH ARTICLE [II-II, Q. 32, Art. 7]

Whether One May Give Alms Out of Ill-gotten Goods?

Objection 1: It would seem that one may give alms out of ill-gotten goods. For it is written (Luke 16:9): "Make unto you friends of the mammon of iniquity." Now mammon signifies riches. Therefore it is lawful to make unto oneself spiritual friends by giving alms out of ill-gotten riches.

Obj. 2: Further, all filthy lucre seems to be ill-gotten. But the profits from whoredom are filthy lucre; wherefore it was forbidden (Deut. 23:18) to offer therefrom sacrifices or oblations to God: "Thou shalt not offer the hire of a strumpet ... in the house of ... thy God." In like manner gains from games of chance are ill-gotten, for, as the Philosopher says (Ethic. iv, 1), "we take such like gains from our friends to whom we ought rather to give." And most of all are the profits from simony ill-gotten, since thereby the Holy Ghost is wronged. Nevertheless out of such gains it is lawful to give alms. Therefore one may give alms out of ill-gotten goods.

Obj. 3: Further, greater evils should be avoided more than lesser evils. Now it is less sinful to keep back another's property than to commit murder, of which a man is guilty if he fails to succor one who is in extreme need, as appears from the words of Ambrose who says (Cf. Canon *Pasce* dist. lxxxvi, whence the words, as quoted, are taken): "Feed him that dies of hunger, if thou hast not fed him, thou hast slain him". Therefore, in certain cases, it is lawful to give alms of ill-gotten goods.

*On the contrary,* Augustine says (De Verb. Dom. xxxv, 2): "Give alms from your just labors. For you will not bribe Christ your judge, not to hear you with the poor whom you rob ... Give not alms from interest and usury: I speak to the faithful to whom we dispense the Body of Christ."

*I answer that,* A thing may be ill-gotten in three ways. In the first place a thing is ill-gotten if it be due to the person from whom it is gotten, and may not be kept by the person who has obtained possession of it; as in the case of rapine, theft and usury, and of such things a man may not give alms since he is bound to restore them.

Secondly, a thing is ill-gotten, when he that has it may not keep it, and yet he may not return it to the person from whom he received it, because he received it unjustly, while the latter gave it unjustly. This happens in simony, wherein both giver and receiver contravene the justice of the Divine Law, so that restitution is to be made not to the giver, but by giving alms. The same applies to all similar cases of illegal giving and receiving.

Thirdly, a thing is ill-gotten, not because the taking was unlawful, but because it is the outcome of something unlawful, as in the case of a woman's profits from whoredom. This is filthy lucre properly so called, because the practice of whoredom is filthy and against the Law of God, yet the woman does not act unjustly or unlawfully in taking the money. Consequently it is lawful to keep and to give in alms what is thus acquired by an unlawful action.

Reply Obj. 1: As Augustine says (De Verb. Dom. 2), "Some have misunderstood this saying of Our Lord, so as to take another's property and give thereof to the poor, thinking that they are fulfilling the commandment by so doing. This interpretation must be amended. Yet all riches are called riches of iniquity, as stated in *De Quaest. Ev.* ii, 34, because "riches are not unjust save for those who are themselves unjust, and put all their trust in them. Or, according to Ambrose in his commentary on Luke 16:9, "Make unto yourselves friends," etc., "He calls mammon unjust, because it draws our affections by the various allurements of wealth." Or, because "among the many ancestors whose property you inherit, there is one who took the property of others unjustly, although you know nothing about it," as Basil says in a homily (Hom. super Luc. A, 5). Or, all riches are styled riches "of iniquity," i.e., of "inequality," because they are not distributed equally among all, one being in need, and another in affluence.

Reply Obj. 2: We have already explained how alms may be given out of the profits of whoredom. Yet sacrifices and oblations were not made therefrom at the altar, both on account of the scandal, and through reverence for sacred things. It is also lawful to give alms out of the profits of simony, because they are not due to him who paid, indeed he deserves to lose them. But as to the profits from games of chance, there would seem to be something unlawful as being contrary to the Divine Law, when a man wins from one who cannot alienate his property, such as minors, lunatics and so forth, or when a man, with the desire of making money out of another man, entices him to play, and wins from him by cheating. In these cases he is bound to restitution, and consequently cannot give away his gains in alms. Then again there would seem to be something unlawful as being against the positive civil law, which altogether forbids any such profits. Since, however, a civil law does not bind all, but only those who are subject to that law, and moreover may be abrogated through desuetude, it follows that all such as are bound by these laws are bound to make restitution of such gains, unless perchance the contrary custom prevail, or unless a man win from one who enticed him to play, in which case he is not bound to restitution, because the loser does not deserve to be paid back: and yet he cannot lawfully keep what he has won, so long as that positive law is in force, wherefore in this case he ought to give it away in alms.

Reply Obj. 3: All things are common property in a case of extreme necessity. Hence one who is in such dire straits may take another's goods in order to succor himself, if he can find no one who is willing to give him something. For the same reason a man may retain what belongs to another, and give alms thereof; or even take something if there be no other way of succoring the one who is in need. If however this be possible without danger, he must ask the owner's consent, and then succor the poor man who is in extreme necessity.

EIGHTH ARTICLE [II-II, Q. 32, Art. 8]

Whether One Who Is Under Another's Power Can Give Alms?

Objection 1: It would seem that one who is under another's power can give alms. For religious are under the power of their prelates to whom they have vowed obedience. Now if it were unlawful for them to give alms, they would lose by entering the state of religion, for as Ambrose [*The quotation is from the works of Ambrosiaster. Cf. Index to ecclesiastical authorities quoted by St. Thomas] says on 1 Tim. 4:8: "'Dutifulness [Douay: 'godliness'] is profitable to all things': The sum total of the Christian religion consists in doing one's duty by all," and the most creditable way of doing this is to give alms. Therefore those who are in another's power can give alms.

Obj. 2: Further, a wife is under her husband's power (Gen. 3:16). But a wife can give alms since she is her husband's partner; hence it is related of the Blessed Lucy that she gave alms without the knowledge of her betrothed [* *Sponsus.* The matrimonial institutions of the Romans were so entirely different from ours that *sponsus* is no longer accurately rendered either "husband" or "betrothed."] Therefore a person is not prevented from giving alms, by being under another's power.

Obj. 3: Further, the subjection of children to their parents is founded on nature, wherefore the Apostle says (Eph. 6:1): "Children, obey your parents in the Lord." But, apparently, children may give alms out of their parents' property. For it is their own, since they are the heirs; wherefore, since they can employ it for some bodily use, it seems that much more can they use it in giving alms so as to profit their souls. Therefore those who are under another's power can give alms.

Obj. 4: Further, servants are under their master's power, according to Titus 2:9: "Exhort servants to be obedient to their masters." Now they may lawfully do anything that will profit their masters: and this would be especially the case if they gave alms for them. Therefore those who are under another's power can give alms.

*On the contrary,* Alms should not be given out of another's property; and each one should give alms out of the just profit of his own labor as Augustine says (De Verb. Dom. xxxv, 2). Now if those who are subject to anyone were to give alms, this would be out of another's property. Therefore those who are under another's power cannot give alms.

*I answer that,* Anyone who is under another's power must, as such, be ruled in accordance with the power of his superior: for the natural order demands that the inferior should be ruled according to its superior. Therefore in those matters in which the inferior is subject to his superior, his ministrations must be subject to the superior's permission.

Accordingly he that is under another's power must not give alms of anything in respect of which he is subject to that other, except in so far as he has been commissioned by his superior. But if he has something in respect of which he is not under the power of his superior, he is no longer subject to another in its regard, being independent in respect of that particular thing, and he can give alms therefrom.

Reply Obj. 1: If a monk be dispensed through being commissioned by his superior, he can give alms from the property of his monastery, in accordance with the terms of his commission; but if he has no such dispensation, since he has nothing of his own, he cannot give alms without his abbot's permission either express or presumed for some probable reason: except in a case of extreme necessity, when it would be lawful for him to commit a theft in order to give an alms. Nor does it follow that he is worse off than before, because, as stated in *De Eccles. Dogm.* lxxi, "it is a good thing to give one's property to the poor little by little, but it is better still to give all at once in order to follow Christ, and being freed from care, to be needy with Christ."

Reply Obj. 2: A wife, who has other property besides her dowry which is for the support of the burdens of marriage, whether that property be gained by her own industry or by any other lawful means, can give alms, out of that property, without asking her husband's permission: yet such alms should be moderate, lest through giving too much she impoverish her husband. Otherwise she ought not to give alms without the express or presumed consent of her husband, except in cases of necessity as stated, in the case of a monk, in the preceding Reply. For though the wife be her husband's equal in the marriage act, yet in matters of housekeeping, the head of the woman is the man, as the Apostle says (1 Cor. 11:3). As regards Blessed Lucy, she had a betrothed, not a husband, wherefore she could give alms with her mother's consent.

Reply Obj. 3: What belongs to the children belongs also to the father: wherefore the child cannot give alms, except in such small quantity that one may presume the father to be willing: unless, perchance, the father authorize his child to dispose of any particular property. The same applies to servants. Hence the Reply to the Fourth Objection is clear.

NINTH ARTICLE [II-II, Q. 32, Art. 9]

Whether One Ought to Give Alms to Those Rather Who Are More Closely United to Us?

Objection 1: It would seem that one ought not to give alms to those rather who are more closely united to us. For it is written (Ecclus. 12:4, 6): "Give to the merciful and uphold not the sinner ... Do good to the humble and give not to the ungodly." Now it happens sometimes that those who are closely united to us are sinful and ungodly. Therefore we ought not to give alms to them in preference to others.

Obj. 2: Further, alms should be given that we may receive an eternal reward in return, according to Matt. 6:18: "And thy Father Who seeth in secret, will repay thee." Now the eternal reward is gained chiefly by the alms which are given to the saints, according to Luke 16:9: "Make unto you friends of the mammon of iniquity, that when you shall fail, they may receive you into everlasting dwellings," which passage Augustine expounds (De Verb. Dom. xxxv, 1): "Who shall have everlasting dwellings unless the saints of God? And who are they that shall be received by them into their dwellings, if not those who succor them in their needs?" Therefore alms should be given to the more holy persons rather than to those who are more closely united to us.

Obj. 3: Further, man is more closely united to himself. But a man cannot give himself an alms. Therefore it seems that we are not bound to give alms to those who are most closely united to us.

*On the contrary,* The Apostle says (1 Tim. 5:8): "If any man have not care of his own, and especially of those of his house, he hath denied the faith, and is worse than an infidel."

*I answer that,* As Augustine says (De Doctr.

Christ. i, 28), "it falls to us by lot, as it were, to have to look to the welfare of those who are more closely united to us." Nevertheless in this matter we must employ discretion, according to the various degrees of connection, holiness and utility. For we ought to give alms to one who is much holier and in greater want, and to one who is more useful to the common weal, rather than to one who is more closely united to us, especially if the latter be not very closely united, and has no special claim on our care then and there, and who is not in very urgent need.

Reply Obj. 1: We ought not to help a sinner as such, that is by encouraging him to sin, but as man, that is by supporting his nature.

Reply Obj. 2: Almsdeeds deserve on two counts to receive an eternal reward. First because they are rooted in charity, and in this respect an almsdeed is meritorious in so far as it observes the order of charity, which requires that, other things being equal, we should, in preference, help those who are more closely connected with us. Wherefore Ambrose says (De Officiis i, 30): "It is with commendable liberality that you forget not your kindred, if you know them to be in need, for it is better that you should yourself help your own family, who would be ashamed to beg help from others." Secondly, almsdeeds deserve to be rewarded eternally, through the merit of the recipient, who prays for the giver, and it is in this sense that Augustine is speaking.

Reply Obj. 3: Since almsdeeds are works of mercy, just as a man does not, properly speaking, pity himself, but only by a kind of comparison, as stated above (Q. 30, AA. 1, 2), so too, properly speaking, no man gives himself an alms, unless he act in another's person; thus when a man is appointed to distribute alms, he can take something for himself, if he be in want, on the same ground as when he gives to others.

TENTH ARTICLE [II-II, Q. 32, Art. 10]

Whether Alms Should Be Given in Abundance?

Objection 1: It would seem that alms should not be given in abundance. For we ought to give alms to those chiefly who are most closely connected with us. But we ought not to give to them in such a way that they are likely to become richer thereby, as Ambrose says (De Officiis i, 30). Therefore neither should we give abundantly to others.

Obj. 2: Further, Ambrose says (De Officiis i, 30): "We should not lavish our wealth on others all at once, we should dole it out by degrees." But to give abundantly is to give lavishly. Therefore alms should not be given in abundance.

Obj. 3: Further, the Apostle says (2 Cor. 8:13): "Not that others should be eased," i.e. should live on you without working themselves, "and you burthened," i.e. impoverished. But this would be the result if alms were given in abundance. Therefore we ought not to give alms abundantly.

*On the contrary,* It is written (Tob. 4:93): "If thou have much, give abundantly."

*I answer that,* Alms may be considered abundant in relation either to the giver, or to the recipient: in relation to the giver, when that which a man gives is great as compared with his means. To give thus is praiseworthy, wherefore Our Lord (Luke 21:3, 4) commended the widow because "of her want, she cast in all the living that she had." Nevertheless those conditions must be observed which were laid down when we spoke of giving alms out of one's necessary goods (A. 9).

On the part of the recipient, an alms may be abundant in two ways; first, by relieving his need sufficiently, and in this sense it is praiseworthy to give alms: secondly, by relieving his need more than sufficiently; this is not praiseworthy, and it would be better to give to several that are in need, wherefore the Apostle says (1 Cor. 13:3): "If I should distribute ... to feed the poor," on which words a gloss comments: "Thus we are warned to be careful in giving alms, and to give, not to one only, but to many, that we may profit many."

Reply Obj. 1: This argument considers abundance of alms as exceeding the needs of the recipient.

Reply Obj. 2: The passage quoted considers abundance of alms on the part of the giver; but the sense is that God does not wish a man to lavish all his wealth at once, except when he changes his state of life, wherefore he goes on to say: "Except we imitate Eliseus who slew his oxen and fed the poor with what he had, so that no household cares might keep him back" (3 Kings 19:21).

Reply Obj. 3: In the passage quoted the words, "not that others should be eased or refreshed," refer to that abundance of alms which surpasses the need of the recipient, to whom one should give alms not that he may have an easy life, but that he may have relief. Nevertheless we must bring discretion to bear on the matter, on account of the various conditions of men, some of whom are more daintily nurtured, and need finer food and clothing. Hence Ambrose says (De Officiis i, 30): "When you give an alms to a man, you should take into consideration his age and his weakness; and sometimes the shame which proclaims his good birth; and again that perhaps he has fallen from riches to indigence through no fault of his own."

With regard to the words that follow, "and you burdened," they refer to abundance on the part of the giver. Yet, as a gloss says on the same passage, "he says this, not because it would be better to give in abundance, but because he fears for the weak, and he admonishes them so to give that they lack not for themselves."

# QUESTION 33

OF FRATERNAL CORRECTION (In Eight Articles)

We must now consider Fraternal Correction, under which head there are eight points of inquiry:

(1) Whether fraternal correction is an act of charity?

(2) Whether it is a matter of precept?

(3) Whether this precept binds all, or only superiors?

(4) Whether this precept binds the subject to correct his superior?

(5) Whether a sinner may correct anyone?

(6) Whether one ought to correct a person who becomes worse through being corrected?

(7) Whether secret correction should precede denouncement?

(8) Whether witnesses should be called before denouncement?

FIRST ARTICLE [II-II, Q. 33, Art. 1]

Whether Fraternal Correction Is an Act of Charity?

Objection 1: It would seem that fraternal correction is not an act of charity. For a gloss on Matt. 18:15, "If thy brother shall offend against thee," says that "a man should reprove his brother out of zeal for justice." But justice is a distinct virtue from charity. Therefore fraternal correction is an act, not of charity, but of justice.

Obj. 2: Further, fraternal correction is given by secret admonition. Now admonition is a kind of counsel, which is an act of prudence, for a prudent man is one who is of good counsel (Ethic. vi, 5). Therefore fraternal correction is an act, not of charity, but of prudence.

Obj. 3: Further, contrary acts do not belong to the same virtue. Now it is an act of charity to bear with a sinner, according to Gal. 6:2: "Bear ye one another's burdens, and so you shall fulfil the law of Christ," which is the law of charity. Therefore it seems that the correction of a sinning brother, which is contrary to bearing with him, is not an act of charity.

*On the contrary,* To correct the wrongdoer is a spiritual almsdeed. But almsdeeds are works of charity, as stated above (Q. 32, A. 1). Therefore fraternal correction is an act of charity.

*I answer that,* The correction of the wrongdoer is a remedy which should be employed against a man's sin. Now a man's sin may be considered in two ways, first as being harmful to the sinner, secondly as conducing to the harm of others, by hurting or scandalizing them, or by being detrimental to the common good, the justice of which is disturbed by that man's sin.

Consequently the correction of a wrongdoer is twofold, one which applies a remedy to the sin considered as an evil of the sinner himself. This is fraternal correction properly so called, which is directed to the amendment of the sinner. Now to do away with anyone's evil is the same as to procure his good: and to procure a person's good is an act of charity, whereby we wish and do our friend well. Consequently fraternal correction also is an act of charity, because thereby we drive out our brother's evil, viz. sin, the removal of which pertains to charity rather than the removal of an external loss, or of a bodily injury, in so much as the contrary good of virtue is more akin to charity than the good of the body or of external things. Therefore fraternal correction is an act of charity rather than the healing of a bodily infirmity, or the relieving of an external bodily need. There is another correction which applies a remedy to the sin of the wrongdoer, considered as hurtful to others, and especially to the common good. This correction is an act of justice, whose concern it is to safeguard the rectitude of justice between one man and another.

Reply Obj. 1: This gloss speaks of the second correction which is an act of justice. Or if it speaks of the first correction, then it takes justice as denoting a general virtue, as we shall state further on (Q. 58, A. 5), in which sense again all "sin is iniquity" (1 John 3:4), through being contrary to justice.

Reply Obj. 2: According to the Philosopher (Ethic. vi, 12), prudence regulates whatever is directed to the end, about which things counsel and choice are concerned. Nevertheless when, guided by prudence, we perform some action aright which is directed to the end of some virtue, such as temperance or fortitude, that action belongs chiefly to the virtue to whose end it is directed. Since, then, the admonition which is given in fraternal correction is directed to the removal of a brother's sin, which removal pertains to charity, it is evident that this admonition is chiefly an act of charity, which virtue commands it, so to speak, but secondarily an act of prudence, which executes and directs the action.

Reply Obj. 3: Fraternal correction is not opposed to forbearance with the weak, on the contrary it results from it. For a man bears with a sinner, in so far as he is not disturbed against him, and retains his goodwill towards him: the result being that he strives to make him do better.

SECOND ARTICLE [II-II, Q. 33, Art. 2]

Whether Fraternal Correction Is a Matter of Precept?

Objection 1: It would seem that fraternal correction is not a matter of precept. For nothing impossible is a matter of precept, according to the saying of Jerome [*Pelagius, Expos. Symb. ad Damas]: "Accursed be he who says that God has commanded anything impossible." Now it is written (Eccles. 7:14): "Consider the works of God, that no man can correct whom He hath despised." Therefore fraternal correction is not a matter of precept.

Obj. 2: Further, all the precepts of the Divine Law are reduced to the precepts of the Decalogue. But fraternal correction does not come under any precept of the Decalogue. Therefore it is not a matter of precept.

Obj. 3: Further, the omission of a Divine precept is a mortal sin, which has no place in a holy man. Yet holy and spiritual men are found to omit fraternal correction: since Augustine says (De Civ. Dei i, 9): "Not only those of low degree, but also those of high position, refrain from reproving others, moved by a guilty cupidity, not by the claims of charity." Therefore fraternal correction is not a matter of precept.

Obj. 4: Further, whatever is a matter of precept is something due. If, therefore, fraternal correction is a matter of precept, it is due to our brethren that we correct them when they sin. Now when a man owes anyone a material due, such as the payment of a sum of money, he must not be content that his creditor come to him, but he should seek him out, that he may pay him his due. Hence we should have to go seeking for those who need correction, in order that we might correct them; which appears to be inconvenient, both on account of the great number of sinners, for whose correction one man could not suffice, and because religious would have to leave the cloister in order to reprove men, which would be unbecoming. Therefore fraternal correction is not a matter of precept.

*On the contrary,* Augustine says (De Verb. Dom. xvi, 4): "You become worse than the sinner if you fail to correct him." But this would not be so unless, by this neglect, one omitted to observe some precept. Therefore fraternal correction is a matter of precept.

*I answer that,* Fraternal correction is a matter of precept. We must observe, however, that while the negative precepts of the Law forbid sinful acts, the positive precepts inculcate acts of virtue. Now sinful acts are evil in themselves, and cannot become good, no matter how, or when, or where, they are done, because of their very nature they are connected with an evil end, as stated in *Ethic.* ii, 6: wherefore negative precepts bind always and for all times. On the other hand, acts of virtue must not be done anyhow, but by observing the due circumstances, which are requisite in order that an act be virtuous; namely, that it be done where, when, and how it ought to be done. And since the disposition of whatever is directed to the end depends on the formal aspect of the end, the chief of these circumstances of a virtuous act is this aspect of the end, which in this case is the good of virtue. If therefore such a circumstance be omitted from a virtuous act, as entirely takes away the good of virtue, such an act is contrary to a precept. If, however, the circumstance omitted from a virtuous act be such as not to destroy the virtue altogether, though it does not perfectly attain the good of virtue, it is not against a precept. Hence the Philosopher (Ethic. ii, 9) says that if we depart but little from the mean, it is not contrary to the virtue, whereas if we depart much from the mean virtue is destroyed in its act. Now fraternal correction is directed to a brother's amendment: so that it is a matter of precept, in so far as it is necessary for that end, but not so as we have to correct our erring brother at all places and times.

Reply Obj. 1: In all good deeds man's action is not efficacious without the Divine assistance: and yet man must do what is in his power. Hence Augustine says (De Correp. et Gratia xv): "Since we ignore who is predestined and who is not, charity should so guide our feelings, that we wish all to be saved." Consequently we ought to do our brethren the kindness of correcting them, with the hope of God's help.

Reply Obj. 2: As stated above (Q. 32, A. 5, ad 4), all the precepts about rendering service to our neighbor are reduced to the precept about the honor due to parents.

Reply Obj. 3: Fraternal correction may be omitted in three ways.

First, meritoriously, when out of charity one omits to correct someone. For Augustine says (De Civ. Dei i, 9): "If a man refrains from chiding and reproving wrongdoers, because he awaits a suitable time for so doing, or because he fears lest, if he does so, they may become worse, or hinder, oppress, or turn away from the faith, others who are weak and need to be instructed in a life of goodness and virtue, this does not seem to result from covetousness, but to be counselled by charity."

Secondly, fraternal correction may be omitted in such a way that one commits a mortal sin, namely, "when" (as he says in the same passage) "one fears what people may think, or lest one may suffer grievous pain or death; provided, however, that the mind is so dominated by such things, that it gives them the preference to fraternal charity." This would seem to be the case when a man reckons that he might probably withdraw some wrongdoer from sin, and yet omits to do so, through fear or covetousness.

Thirdly, such an omission is a venial sin, when through fear or covetousness, a man is loth to correct his brother's faults, and yet not to such a degree, that if he saw clearly that he could withdraw him from sin, he would still forbear from so doing, through fear or covetousness, because in his own mind he prefers fraternal charity to these things. It is in this way that holy men sometimes omit to correct wrongdoers.

Reply Obj. 4: We are bound to pay that which is due to some fixed and certain person, whether it be a material or a spiritual good, without waiting for him to come to us, but by taking proper steps to find him. Wherefore just as he that owes money to a creditor should seek him, when the time comes, so as to pay him what he owes, so he that has spiritual charge of some person is bound to seek him out, in order to reprove him for a sin. On the other hand, we are not bound to seek someone on whom to bestow such favors as are due, not to any certain person, but to all our neighbors in general, whether those favors be material or spiritual goods, but it suffices that we bestow them when the opportunity occurs; because, as Augustine says (De Doctr. Christ. i, 28), we must look upon this as a matter of chance. For this reason he says (De Verb. Dom. xvi, 1) that "Our Lord warns us not to be listless in regard of one another's sins: not indeed by being on the lookout for something to denounce, but by correcting what we see": else we should become spies on the lives of others, which is against the saying of Prov. 24:19: "Lie not in wait, nor seek after wickedness in the house of the just, nor spoil his rest." It is evident from this that there is no need for religious to leave their cloister in order to rebuke evil-doers.

THIRD ARTICLE [II-II, Q. 33, Art. 3]

Whether Fraternal Correction Belongs Only to Prelates?

Objection 1: It would seem that fraternal correction belongs to prelates alone. For Jerome [*Origen, Hom. vii in Joan.] says: "Let priests endeavor to fulfil this saying of the Gospel: 'If thy brother sin against thee,'" etc. Now prelates having charge of others were usually designated under the name of priests. Therefore it seems that fraternal correction belongs to prelates alone.

Obj. 2: Further, fraternal correction is a spiritual alms. Now corporal almsgiving belongs to those who are placed above others in temporal matters, i.e. to the rich. Therefore fraternal correction belongs to those who are placed above others in spiritual matters, i.e. to prelates.

Obj. 3: Further, when one man reproves another he moves him by his rebuke to something better. Now in the physical order the inferior is moved by the superior. Therefore in the order of virtue also, which follows the order of nature, it belongs to prelates alone to correct inferiors.

*On the contrary,* It is written (Dist. xxiv, qu. 3, Can. Tam Sacerdotes): "Both priests and all the rest of the faithful should be most solicitous for those who perish, so that their reproof may either correct their sinful ways, or, if they be incorrigible, cut them off from the Church."

*I answer that,* As stated above (A. 1), correction is twofold. One is an act of charity, which seeks in a special way the recovery of an erring brother by means of a simple warning: such like correction belongs to anyone who has charity, be he subject or prelate.

But there is another correction which is an act of justice purposing the common good, which is procured not only by warning one's brother, but also, sometimes, by punishing him, that others may, through fear, desist from sin. Such a correction belongs only to prelates, whose business it is not only to admonish, but also to correct by means of punishments.

Reply Obj. 1: Even as regards that fraternal correction which is common to all, prelates have a grave responsibility, as Augustine says (De Civ. Dei i, 9): "for just as a man ought to bestow temporal favors on those especially of whom he has temporal care, so too ought he to confer spiritual favors, such as correction, teaching and the like, on those who are entrusted to his spiritual care." Therefore Jerome does not mean that the precept of fraternal correction concerns priests only, but that it concerns them chiefly.

Reply Obj. 2: Just as he who has the means wherewith to give corporal assistance is rich in this respect, so he whose reason is gifted with a sane judgment, so as to be able to correct another's wrong-doing, is, in this respect, to be looked on as a superior.

Reply Obj. 3: Even in the physical order certain things act mutually on one another, through being in some respect higher than one another, in so far as each is somewhat in act, and somewhat in potentiality with regard to another. In like manner one man can correct another in so far as he has a sane judgment in a matter wherein the other sins, though he is not his superior simply.

FOURTH ARTICLE [II-II, Q. 33, Art. 4]

Whether a Man Is Bound to Correct His Prelate?

Objection 1: It would seem that no man is bound to correct his prelate. For it is written (Ex. 19:12): "The beast that shall touch the mount shall be stoned," [*Vulg.: 'Everyone that shall touch the mount, dying he shall die.'] and (2 Kings 6:7) it is related that the Lord struck Oza for touching the ark. Now the mount and the ark signify our prelates. Therefore prelates should not be corrected by their subjects.

Obj. 2: Further, a gloss on Gal. 2:11, "I withstood him to the face," adds: "as an equal." Therefore, since a subject is not equal to his prelate, he ought not to correct him.

Obj. 3: Further, Gregory says (Moral. xxiii, 8) that "one ought not to presume to reprove the conduct of holy men, unless one thinks better of oneself." But one ought not to think better of oneself than of one's prelate. Therefore one ought not to correct one's prelate.

*On the contrary,* Augustine says in his Rule: "Show mercy not only to yourselves, but also to him who, being in the higher position among you, is therefore in greater danger." But fraternal correction is a work of mercy. Therefore even prelates ought to be corrected.

*I answer that,* A subject is not competent to administer to his prelate the correction which is an act of justice through the coercive nature of punishment: but the fraternal correction which is an act of charity is within the competency of everyone in respect of any person towards whom he is bound by charity, provided there be something in that person which requires correction.

Now an act which proceeds from a habit or power extends to whatever is contained under the object of that power or habit: thus vision extends to all things comprised in the object of sight. Since, however, a virtuous act needs to be moderated by due circumstances, it follows that when a subject corrects his prelate, he ought to do so in a becoming manner, not with impudence and harshness, but with gentleness and respect. Hence the Apostle says (1 Tim. 5:1): "An ancient man rebuke not, but entreat him as a father." Wherefore Dionysius finds fault with the monk Demophilus (Ep. viii), for rebuking a priest with insolence, by striking and turning him out of the church.

Reply Obj. 1: It would seem that a subject touches his prelate inordinately when he upbraids him with insolence, as also when he speaks ill of him: and this is signified by God's condemnation of those who touched the mount and the ark.

Reply Obj. 2: To withstand anyone in public exceeds the mode of fraternal correction, and so Paul would not have withstood Peter then, unless he were in some way his equal as regards the defense of the faith. But one who is not an equal can reprove privately and respectfully. Hence the Apostle in writing to the Colossians (4:17) tells them to admonish their prelate: "Say to Archippus: Fulfil thy ministry [*Vulg.: 'Take heed to the ministry which thou hast received in the Lord, that thou fulfil it.' Cf. 2 Tim. 4:5]." It must be observed, however, that if the faith were endangered, a subject ought to rebuke his prelate even publicly. Hence Paul, who was Peter's subject, rebuked him in public, on account of the imminent danger of scandal concerning faith, and, as the gloss of Augustine says on Gal. 2:11, "Peter gave an example to superiors, that if at any time they should happen to stray from the straight path, they should not disdain to be reproved by their subjects."

Reply Obj. 3: To presume oneself to be simply better than one's prelate, would seem to savor of presumptuous pride; but there is no presumption in thinking oneself better in some respect, because, in this life, no man is without some fault. We must also remember that when a man reproves his prelate charitably, it does not follow that he thinks himself any better, but merely that he offers his help to one who, "being in the higher position among you, is therefore in greater danger," as Augustine observes in his Rule quoted above.

FIFTH ARTICLE [II-II, Q. 33, Art. 5]

Whether a Sinner Ought to Reprove a Wrongdoer?

Objection 1: It would seem that a sinner ought to reprove a wrongdoer. For no man is excused from obeying a precept by having committed a sin. But fraternal correction is a matter of precept, as stated above (A. 2). Therefore it seems that a man ought not to forbear from such like correction for the reason that he has committed a sin.

Obj. 2: Further, spiritual almsdeeds are of more account than corporal almsdeeds. Now one who is in sin ought not to abstain from administering corporal alms. Much less therefore ought he, on account of a previous sin, to refrain from correcting wrongdoers.

Obj. 3: Further, it is written (1 John 1:8): "If we say that we have no sin, we deceive ourselves." Therefore if, on account of a sin, a man is hindered from reproving his brother, there will be none to reprove the wrongdoer. But the latter proposition is unreasonable: therefore the former is also.

*On the contrary,* Isidore says (De Summo Bono iii, 32): "He that is subject to vice should not correct the vices of others." Again it is written (Rom. 2:1): "Wherein thou judgest another, thou condemnest thyself. For thou dost the same things which thou judgest."

*I answer that,* As stated above (A. 3, ad 2), to correct a wrongdoer belongs to a man, in so far as his reason is gifted with right judgment. Now sin, as stated above (I-II, Q. 85, AA. 1, 2), does not destroy the good of nature so as to deprive the sinner's reason of all right judgment, and in this respect he may be competent to find fault with others for committing sin. Nevertheless a previous sin proves somewhat of a hindrance to this correction, for three reasons. First because this previous sin renders a man unworthy to rebuke another; and especially is he unworthy to correct another for a lesser sin, if he himself has committed a greater. Hence Jerome says on the words, "Why seest thou the mote?" etc. (Matt. 7:3): "He is speaking of those who, while they are themselves guilty of mortal sin, have no patience with the lesser sins of their brethren."

Secondly, such like correction becomes unseemly, on account of the scandal which ensues therefrom, if the corrector's sin be well known, because it would seem that he corrects, not out of charity, but more for the sake of ostentation. Hence the words of Matt. 7:4, "How sayest thou to thy brother?" etc. are expounded by Chrysostom [*Hom. xvii in the Opus Imperfectum falsely ascribed to St. John Chrysostom] thus: "That is—'With what object?' Out of charity, think you, that you may save your neighbor?" No, "because you would look after your own salvation first. What you want is, not to save others, but to hide your evil deeds with good teaching, and to seek to be praised by men for your knowledge."

Thirdly, on account of the rebuker's pride; when, for instance, a man thinks lightly of his own sins, and, in his own heart, sets himself above his neighbor, judging the latter's sins with harsh severity, as though he himself were a just man. Hence Augustine says (De Serm. Dom. in Monte ii, 19): "To reprove the faults of others is the duty of good and kindly men: when a wicked man rebukes anyone, his rebuke is the latter's acquittal." And so, as Augustine says (De Serm. Dom. in Monte ii, 19): "When we have to find fault with anyone, we should think whether we were never guilty of his sin; and then we must remember that we are men, and might have been guilty of it; or that we once had it on our conscience, but have it no longer: and then we should bethink ourselves that we are all weak, in order that our reproof may be the outcome, not of hatred, but of pity. But if we find that we are guilty of the same sin, we must not rebuke him, but groan with him, and invite him to repent with us." It follows from this that, if a sinner reprove a wrongdoer with humility, he does not sin, nor does he bring a further condemnation on himself, although thereby he proves himself deserving of condemnation, either in his brother's or in his own conscience, on account of his previous sin.

Hence the Replies to the Objections are clear.

SIXTH ARTICLE [II-II, Q. 33, Art. 6]

Whether One Ought to Forbear from Correcting Someone, Through Fear Lest He Become Worse?

Objection 1: It would seem that one ought not to forbear from correcting someone through fear lest he become worse. For sin is weakness of the soul, according to Ps. 6:3: "Have mercy on me, O Lord, for I am weak." Now he that has charge of a sick person, must not cease to take care of him, even if he be fractious or contemptuous, because then the danger is greater, as in the case of madmen. Much more, therefore should one correct a sinner, no matter how badly he takes it.

Obj. 2: Further, according to Jerome vital truths are not to be foregone on account of scandal. Now God's commandments are vital truths. Since, therefore, fraternal correction is a matter of precept, as stated above (A. 2), it seems that it should not be foregone for fear of scandalizing the person to be corrected.

Obj. 3: Further, according to the Apostle (Rom. 3:8) we should not do evil that good may come of it. Therefore, in like manner, good should not be omitted lest evil befall. Now fraternal correction is a good thing. Therefore it should not be omitted for fear lest the person corrected become worse.

*On the contrary,* It is written (Prov. 9:8): "Rebuke not a scorner lest he hate thee," where a gloss remarks: "You must not fear lest the scorner insult you when you rebuke him: rather should you bear in mind that by making him hate you, you may make him worse." Therefore one ought to forego fraternal correction, when we fear lest we may make a man worse.

*I answer that,* As stated above (A. 3) the correction of the wrongdoer is twofold. One, which belongs to prelates, and is directed to the common good, has coercive force. Such correction should not be omitted lest the person corrected be disturbed, both because if he is unwilling to amend his ways of his own accord, he should be made to cease sinning by being punished, and because, if he be incorrigible, the common good is safeguarded in this way, since the order of justice is observed, and others are deterred by one being made an example of. Hence a judge does not desist from pronouncing sentence of condemnation against a sinner, for fear of disturbing him or his friends.

The other fraternal correction is directed to the amendment of the wrongdoer, whom it does not coerce, but merely admonishes. Consequently when it is deemed probable that the sinner will not take the warning, and will become worse, such fraternal correction should be foregone, because the means should be regulated according to the requirements of the end.

Reply Obj. 1: The doctor uses force towards a madman, who is unwilling to submit to his treatment; and this may be compared with the correction administered by prelates, which has coercive power, but not with simple fraternal correction.

Reply Obj. 2: Fraternal correction is a matter of precept, in so far as it is an act of virtue, and it will be a virtuous act in so far as it is proportionate to the end. Consequently whenever it is a hindrance to the end, for instance when a man becomes worse through it, it is longer a vital truth, nor is it a matter of precept.

Reply Obj. 3: Whatever is directed to an end, becomes good through being directed to the end. Hence whenever fraternal correction hinders the end, namely the amendment of our brother, it is no longer good, so that when such a correction is omitted, good is not omitted lest evil should befall.

SEVENTH ARTICLE [II-II, Q. 33, Art. 7]

Whether the Precept of Fraternal Correction Demands That a Private Admonition Should Precede Denunciation?

Objection 1: It would seem that the precept of fraternal correction does not demand that a private admonition should precede denunciation. For, in works of charity, we should above all follow the example of God, according to Eph. 5:1, 2: "Be ye followers of God, as most dear children, and walk in love." Now God sometimes punishes a man for a sin, without previously warning him in secret. Therefore it seems that there is no need for a private admonition to precede denunciation.

Obj. 2: Further, according to Augustine (De Mendacio xv), we learn from the deeds of holy men how we ought to understand the commandments of Holy Writ. Now among the deeds of holy men we find that a hidden sin is publicly denounced, without any previous admonition in private. Thus we read (Gen. 37:2) that "Joseph accused his brethren to his father of a most wicked crime": and (Acts 5:4, 9) that Peter publicly denounced Ananias and Saphira who had secretly "by fraud kept back the price of the land," without beforehand admonishing them in private: nor do we read that Our Lord admonished Judas in secret before denouncing him. Therefore the precept does not require that secret admonition should precede public denunciation.

Obj. 3: Further, it is a graver matter to accuse than to denounce. Now one may go to the length of accusing a person publicly, without previously admonishing him in secret: for it is decided in the Decretal (Cap. Qualiter, xiv, De Accusationibus) that "nothing else need precede accusation except inscription." [*The accuser was bound by Roman Law to endorse (se inscribere) the writ of accusation. The effect of this endorsement or inscription was that the accuser bound himself, if he failed to prove the accusation, to suffer the same punishment as the accused would have to suffer if proved guilty.] Therefore it seems that the precept does not require that a secret admonition should precede public denunciation.

Obj. 4: Further, it does not seem probable that the customs observed by religious in general are contrary to the precepts of Christ. Now it is customary among religious orders to proclaim this or that one for a fault, without any previous secret admonition. Therefore it seems that this admonition is not required by the precept.

Obj. 5: Further, religious are bound to obey their prelates. Now a prelate sometimes commands either all in general, or someone in particular, to tell him if they know of anything that requires correction. Therefore it would seem that they are bound to tell them this, even before any secret admonition. Therefore the precept does not require secret admonition before public denunciation.

*On the contrary,* Augustine says (De Verb. Dom. xvi, 4) on the words, "Rebuke him between thee and him alone" (Matt. 18:15): "Aiming at his amendment, while avoiding his disgrace: since perhaps from shame he might begin to defend his sin; and him whom you thought to make a better man, you make worse." Now we are bound by the precept of charity to beware lest our brother become worse. Therefore the order of fraternal correction comes under the precept.

*I answer that,* With regard to the public denunciation of sins it is necessary to make a distinction: because sins may be either public or secret. In the case of public sins, a remedy is required not only for the sinner, that he may become better, but also for others, who know of his sin, lest they be scandalized. Wherefore such like sins should be denounced in public, according to the saying of the Apostle (1 Tim. 5:20): "Them that sin reprove before all, that the rest also may have fear," which is to be understood as referring to public sins, as Augustine states (De Verb. Dom. xvi, 7).

On the other hand, in the case of secret sins, the words of Our Lord seem to apply (Matt. 18:15): "If thy brother shall offend against thee," etc. For if he offend thee publicly in the presence of others, he no longer sins against thee alone, but also against others whom he disturbs. Since, however, a man's neighbor may take offense even at his secret sins, it seems that we must make yet a further distinction. For certain secret sins are hurtful to our neighbor either in his body or in his soul, as, for instance, when a man plots secretly to betray his country to its enemies, or when a heretic secretly turns other men away from the faith. And since he that sins thus in secret, sins not only against you in particular, but also against others, it is necessary to take steps to denounce him at once, in order to prevent him doing such harm, unless by chance you were firmly persuaded that this evil result would be prevented by admonishing him secretly. On the other hand there are other sins which injure none but the sinner, and the person sinned against, either because he alone is hurt by the sinner, or at least because he alone knows about his sin, and then our one purpose should be to succor our sinning brother: and just as the physician of the body restores the sick man to health, if possible, without cutting off a limb, but, if this be unavoidable, cuts off a limb which is least indispensable, in order to preserve the life of the whole body, so too he who desires his brother's amendment should, if possible, so amend him as regards his conscience, that he keep his good name.

For a good name is useful, first of all to the sinner himself, not only in temporal matters wherein a man suffers many losses, if he lose his good name, but also in spiritual matters, because many are restrained from sinning, through fear of dishonor, so that when a man finds his honor lost, he puts no curb on his sinning. Hence Jerome says on Matt. 18:15: "If he sin against thee, thou shouldst rebuke him in private, lest he persist in his sin if he should once become shameless or unabashed." Secondly, we ought to safeguard our sinning brother's good name, both because the dishonor of one leads to the dishonor of others, according to the saying of Augustine (Ep. ad pleb. Hipponens. lxxviii): "When a few of those who bear a name for holiness are reported falsely or proved in truth to have done anything wrong, people will seek by busily repeating it to make it believed of all": and also because when one man's sin is made public others are incited to sin likewise.

Since, however, one's conscience should be preferred to a good name, Our Lord wished that we should publicly denounce our brother and so deliver his conscience from sin, even though he should forfeit his good name. Therefore it is evident that the precept requires a secret admonition to precede public denunciation.

Reply Obj. 1: Whatever is hidden, is known to God, wherefore hidden sins are to the judgment of God, just what public sins are to the judgment of man. Nevertheless God does rebuke sinners sometimes by secretly admonishing them, so to speak, with an inward inspiration, either while they wake or while they sleep, according to Job 33:15-17: "By a dream in a vision by night, when deep sleep falleth upon men ... then He openeth the ears of men, and teaching instructeth them in what they are to learn, that He may withdraw a man from the things he is doing."

Reply Obj. 2: Our Lord as God knew the sin of Judas as though it were public, wherefore He could have made it known at once. Yet He did not, but warned Judas of his sin in words that were obscure. The sin of Ananias and Saphira was denounced by Peter acting as God's executor, by Whose revelation he knew of their sin. With regard to Joseph it is probable that he warned his brethren, though Scripture does not say so. Or we may say that the sin was public with regard to his brethren, wherefore it is stated in the plural that he accused "his brethren."

Reply Obj. 3: When there is danger to a great number of people, those words of Our Lord do not apply, because then thy brother does not sin against thee alone.

Reply Obj. 4: Proclamations made in the chapter of religious are about little faults which do not affect a man's good name, wherefore they are reminders of forgotten faults rather than accusations or denunciations. If, however, they should be of such a nature as to injure our brother's good name, it would be contrary to Our Lord's precept, to denounce a brother's fault in this manner.

Reply Obj. 5: A prelate is not to be obeyed contrary to a Divine precept, according to Acts 5:29: "We ought to obey God rather then men." Therefore when a prelate commands anyone to tell him anything that he knows to need correction, the command rightly understood supports the safeguarding of the order of fraternal correction, whether the command be addressed to all in general, or to some particular individual. If, on the other hand, a prelate were to issue a command in express opposition to this order instituted by Our Lord, both would sin, the one commanding, and the one obeying him, as disobeying Our Lord's command. Consequently he ought not to be obeyed, because a prelate is not the judge of secret things, but God alone is, wherefore he has no power to command anything in respect of hidden matters, except in so far as they are made known through certain signs, as by ill-repute or suspicion; in which cases a prelate can command just as a judge, whether secular or ecclesiastical, can bind a man under oath to tell the truth.

EIGHTH ARTICLE [II-II, Q. 33, Art. 8]

Whether Before the Public Denunciation Witnesses Ought to Be Brought Forward?

Objection 1: It would seem that before the public denunciation witnesses ought not to be brought forward. For secret sins ought not to be made known to others, because by so doing "a man would betray his brother's sins instead of correcting them," as Augustine says (De Verb. Dom. xvi, 7). Now by bringing forward witnesses one makes known a brother's sin to others. Therefore in the case of secret sins one ought not to bring witnesses forward before the public denunciation.

Obj. 2: Further, man should love his neighbor as himself. Now no man brings in witnesses to prove his own secret sin. Neither therefore ought one to bring forward witnesses to prove the secret sin of our brother.

Obj. 3: Further, witnesses are brought forward to prove something. But witnesses afford no proof in secret matters. Therefore it is useless to bring witnesses forward in such cases.

Obj. 4: Further, Augustine says in his Rule that "before bringing it to the notice of witnesses ... it should be put before the superior." Now to bring a matter before a superior or a prelate is to tell the Church. Therefore witnesses should not be brought forward before the public denunciation.

*On the contrary,* Our Lord said (Matt. 18:16): "Take with thee one or two more, that in the mouth of two," etc.

*I answer that,* The right way to go from one extreme to another is to pass through the middle space. Now Our Lord wished the beginning of fraternal correction to be hidden, when one brother corrects another between this one and himself alone, while He wished the end to be public, when such a one would be denounced to the Church. Consequently it is befitting that a citation of witnesses should be placed between the two extremes, so that at first the brother's sin be indicated to a few, who will be of use without being a hindrance, and thus his sin be amended without dishonoring him before the public.

Reply Obj. 1: Some have understood the order of fraternal correction to demand that we should first of all rebuke our brother secretly, and that if he listens, it is well; but if he listen not, and his sin be altogether hidden, they say that we should go no further in the matter, whereas if it has already begun to reach the ears of several by various signs, we ought to prosecute the matter, according to Our Lord's command. But this is contrary to what Augustine says in his Rule that "we are bound to reveal" a brother's sin, if it "will cause a worse corruption in the heart." Wherefore we must say otherwise that when the secret admonition has been given once or several times, as long as there is probable hope of his amendment, we must continue to admonish him in private, but as soon as we are able to judge with any probability that the secret admonition is of no avail, we must take further steps, however secret the sin may be, and call witnesses, unless perhaps it were thought probable that this would not conduce to our brother's amendment, and that he would become worse: because on that account one ought to abstain altogether from correcting him, as stated above (A. 6).

Reply Obj. 2: A man needs no witnesses that he may amend his own sin: yet they may be necessary that we may amend a brother's sin. Hence the comparison fails.

Reply Obj. 3: There may be three reasons for

citing witnesses. First, to show that the deed in question is a sin, as Jerome says: secondly, to prove that the deed was done, if repeated, as Augustine says (loc. cit.): thirdly, "to prove that the man who rebuked his brother, has done what he could," as Chrysostom says (Hom. in Matth. lx).

Reply Obj. 4: Augustine means that the matter ought to be made known to the prelate before it is stated to the witnesses, in so far as the prelate is a private individual who is able to be of more use than others, but not that it is to be told him as to the Church, i.e. as holding the position of judge.

# QUESTION 34

OF HATRED (In Six Articles)

We must now consider the vices opposed to charity: (1) hatred, which is opposed to love; (2) sloth and envy, which are opposed to the joy of charity; (3) discord and schism, which are contrary to peace; (4) offense and scandal, which are contrary to beneficence and fraternal correction.

Under the first head there are six points of inquiry:

(1) Whether it is possible to hate God?

(2) Whether hatred of God is the greatest of sins?

(3) Whether hatred of one's neighbor is always a sin?

(4) Whether it is the greatest of all sins against our neighbor?

(5) Whether it is a capital sin?

(6) From what capital sin does it arise?

FIRST ARTICLE [II-II, Q. 34, Art. 1]

Whether It Is Possible for Anyone to Hate God?

Objection 1: It would seem that no man can hate God. For Dionysius says (Div. Nom. iv) that "the first good and beautiful is an object of love and dilection to all." But God is goodness and beauty itself. Therefore He is hated by none.

Obj. 2: Further, in the Apocryphal books of 3 Esdras 4:36, 39 it is written that "all things call upon truth ... and (all men) do well like of her works." Now God is the very truth according to John 14:6. Therefore all love God, and none can hate Him.

Obj. 3: Further, hatred is a kind of aversion. But according to Dionysius (Div. Nom. i) God draws all things to Himself. Therefore none can hate Him.

*On the contrary,* It is written (Ps. 73:23): "The pride of them that hate Thee ascendeth continually," and (John 15:24): "But now they have both seen and hated both Me and My Father."

*I answer that,* As shown above (I-II, Q. 29, A. 1), hatred is a movement of the appetitive power, which power is not set in motion save by something apprehended. Now God can be apprehended by man in two ways; first, in Himself, as when He is seen in His Essence; secondly, in His effects, when, to wit, "the invisible things" of God ... "are clearly seen, being understood by the things that are made" (Rom. 1:20). Now God in His Essence is goodness itself, which no man can hate—for it is natural to good to be loved. Hence it is impossible for one who sees God in His Essence, to hate Him.

Moreover some of His effects are such that they can nowise be contrary to the human will, since *to be, to live, to understand,* which are effects of God, are desirable and lovable to all. Wherefore again God cannot be an object of hatred if we consider Him as the Author of such like effects. Some of God's effects, however, are contrary to an inordinate will, such as the infliction of punishment, and the prohibition of sin by the Divine Law. Such like effects are repugnant to a will debased by sin, and as regards the consideration of them, God may be an object of hatred to some, in so far as they look upon Him as forbidding sin, and inflicting punishment.

Reply Obj. 1: This argument is true of those who see God's Essence, which is the very essence of goodness.

Reply Obj. 2: This argument is true in so far as God is apprehended as the cause of such effects as are naturally beloved of all, among which are the works of Truth who reveals herself to men.

Reply Obj. 3: God draws all things to Himself, in so far as He is the source of being, since all things, in as much as they are, tend to be like God, Who is Being itself.

SECOND ARTICLE [II-II, Q. 34, Art. 2]

Whether Hatred of God Is the Greatest of Sins?

Objection 1: It would seem that hatred of God is not the greatest of sins. For the most grievous sin is the sin against the Holy Ghost, since it cannot be forgiven, according to Matt. 12:32. Now hatred of God is not reckoned among the various kinds of sin against the Holy Ghost, as may be seen from what has been said above (Q. 14, A. 2). Therefore hatred of God is not the most grievous sin.

Obj. 2: Further, sin consists in withdrawing oneself from God. Now an unbeliever who has not even knowledge of God seems to be further away from Him than a believer, who though he hate God, nevertheless knows Him. Therefore it seems that the sin of unbelief is graver than the sin of hatred against God.

Obj. 3: Further, God is an object of hatred, only by reason of those of His effects that are contrary to the will: the chief of which is punishment. But hatred of punishment is not the most grievous sin. Therefore hatred of God is not the most grievous sin.

*On the contrary,* The best is opposite to the worst, according to the Philosopher (Ethic. viii, 10). But hatred of God is contrary to the love of God, wherein man's best consists. Therefore hatred of God is man's worst sin.

*I answer that,* The defect in sin consists in its aversion from God, as stated above (Q. 10, A. 3): and this aversion would not have the character of guilt, were it not voluntary. Hence the nature of guilt consists in a voluntary aversion from God.

Now this voluntary aversion from God is directly implied in the hatred of God, but in other sins, by participation and indirectly. For just as the will cleaves directly to what it loves, so does it directly shun what it hates. Hence when a man hates God, his will is directly averted from God, whereas in other sins, fornication for instance, a man turns away from God, not directly, but indirectly, in so far, namely, as he desires an inordinate pleasure, to which aversion from God is connected. Now that which is so by itself, always takes precedence of that which is so by another. Wherefore hatred of God is more grievous than other sins.

Reply Obj. 1: According to Gregory (Moral. xxv, 11), "it is one thing not to do good things, and another to hate the giver of good things, even as it is one thing to sin indeliberately, and another to sin deliberately." This implies that to hate God, the giver of all good things, is to sin deliberately, and this is a sin against the Holy Ghost. Hence it is evident that hatred of God is chiefly a sin against the Holy Ghost, in so far as the sin against the Holy Ghost denotes a special kind of sin: and yet it is not reckoned among the kinds of sin against the Holy Ghost, because it is universally found in every kind of that sin.

Reply Obj. 2: Even unbelief is not sinful unless it be voluntary: wherefore the more voluntary it is, the more it is sinful. Now it becomes voluntary by the fact that a man hates the truth that is proposed to him. Wherefore it is evident that unbelief derives its sinfulness from hatred of God, Whose truth is the object of faith; and hence just as a cause is greater than its effect, so hatred of God is a greater sin than unbelief.

Reply Obj. 3: Not everyone who hates his punishment, hates God the author of punishments. For many hate the punishments inflicted on them, and yet they bear them patiently out of reverence for the Divine justice. Wherefore Augustine says (Confess. x) that God commands us to bear with penal evils, not to love them. On the other hand, to break out into hatred of God when He inflicts those punishments, is to hate God's very justice, and that is a most grievous sin. Hence Gregory says (Moral. xxv, 11): "Even as sometimes it is more grievous to love sin than to do it, so is it more wicked to hate justice than not to have done it."

THIRD ARTICLE [II-II, Q. 34, Art. 3]

Whether hatred of one's neighbor is always a sin?

Objection 1: It would seem that hatred of one's neighbor is not always a sin. For no sin is commanded or counselled by God, according to Prov. 8:8: "All My words are just, there is nothing wicked nor perverse in them." Now, it is written (Luke 14:26): "If any man come to Me, and hate not his father and mother ... he cannot be My disciple." Therefore hatred of one's neighbor is not always a sin.

Obj. 2: Further, nothing wherein we imitate God can be a sin. But it is in imitation of God that we hate certain people: for it is written (Rom. 1:30): "Detractors, hateful to God." Therefore it is possible to hate certain people without committing a sin.

Obj. 3: Further, nothing that is natural is a sin, for sin is a "wandering away from what is according to nature," according to Damascene (De Fide Orth. ii, 4, 30; iv, 20). Now it is natural to a thing to hate whatever is contrary to it, and to aim at its undoing. Therefore it seems that it is not a sin to hate one's I enemy.

*On the contrary,* It is written (1 John 2:9): "He that ... hateth his brother, is in darkness." Now spiritual darkness is sin. Therefore there cannot be hatred of one's neighbor without sin.

*I answer that,* Hatred is opposed to love, as stated above (I-II, Q. 29, A. 2); so that hatred of a thing is evil according as the love of that thing is good. Now love is due to our neighbor in respect of what he holds from God, i.e. in respect of nature and grace, but not in respect of what he has of himself and from the devil, i.e. in respect of sin and lack of justice.

Consequently it is lawful to hate the sin in one's brother, and whatever pertains to the defect of Divine justice, but we cannot hate our brother's nature and grace without sin. Now it is part of our love for our brother that we hate the fault and the lack of good in him, since desire for another's good is equivalent to hatred of his evil. Consequently the hatred of one's brother, if we consider it simply, is always sinful.

Reply Obj. 1: By the commandment of God (Ex. 20:12) we must honor our parents—as united to us in nature and kinship. But we must hate them in so far as they prove an obstacle to our attaining the perfection of Divine justice.

Reply Obj. 2: God hates the sin which is in the detractor, not his nature: so that we can hate detractors without committing a sin.

Reply Obj. 3: Men are not opposed to us in respect of the goods which they have received from God: wherefore, in this respect, we should love them. But they are opposed to us, in so far as they show hostility towards us, and this is sinful in them. In this respect we should hate them, for we should hate in them the fact that they are hostile to us.

FOURTH ARTICLE [II-II, Q. 34, Art. 4]

Whether Hatred of Our Neighbor Is the Most Grievous Sin Against Our Neighbor?

Objection 1: It would seem that hatred of our neighbor is the most grievous sin against our neighbor. For it is written (1 John 3:15): "Whosoever hateth his brother is a murderer." Now murder is the most grievous of sins against our neighbor. Therefore hatred is also.

Obj. 2: Further, worst is opposed to best. Now

the best thing we give our neighbor is love, since all other things are referable to love. Therefore hatred is the worst.

*On the contrary,* A thing is said to be evil, because it hurts, as Augustine observes (Enchiridion xii). Now there are sins by which a man hurts his neighbor more than by hatred, e.g. theft, murder and adultery. Therefore hatred is not the most grievous sin.

Moreover, Chrysostom [*Hom. x in the Opus Imperfectum, falsely ascribed to St. John Chrysostom] commenting on Matt. 5:19, "He that shall break one of these least commandments," says: "The commandments of Moses, Thou shalt not kill, Thou shalt not commit adultery, count for little in their reward, but they count for much if they be disobeyed. On the other hand the commandments of Christ such as, Thou shalt not be angry, Thou shalt not desire, are reckoned great in their reward, but little in the transgression." Now hatred is an internal movement like anger and desire. Therefore hatred of one's brother is a less grievous sin than murder.

*I answer that,* Sins committed against our neighbor are evil on two counts; first by reason of the disorder in the person who sins, secondly by reason of the hurt inflicted on the person sinned against. On the first count, hatred is a more grievous sin than external actions that hurt our neighbor, because hatred is a disorder of man's will, which is the chief part of man, and wherein is the root of sin, so that if a man's outward actions were to be inordinate, without any disorder in his will, they would not be sinful, for instance, if he were to kill a man, through ignorance or out of zeal for justice: and if there be anything sinful in a man's outward sins against his neighbor, it is all to be traced to his inward hatred.

On the other hand, as regards the hurt inflicted on his neighbor, a man's outward sins are worse than his inward hatred. This suffices for the Replies to the Objections.

FIFTH ARTICLE [II-II, Q. 34, Art. 5]

Whether Hatred Is a Capital Sin?

Objection 1: It would seem that hatred is a capital sin. For hatred is directly opposed to charity. Now charity is the foremost among the virtues, and the mother of all others. Therefore hatred is the chief of the capital sins, and the origin of all others.

Obj. 2: Further, sins arise in us on account of the inclinations of our passions, according to Rom. 7:5: "The passions of sins ... did work in our members to bring forth fruit unto death." Now all other passions of the soul seem to arise from love and hatred, as was shown above (I-II, Q. 25, AA. 1, 2). Therefore hatred should be reckoned one of the capital sins.

Obj. 3: Further, vice is a moral evil. Now hatred regards evil more than any other passion does. Therefore it seems that hatred should be reckoned a capital sin.

*On the contrary,* Gregory (Moral. xxxi) does not reckon hatred among the seven capital sins.

*I answer that,* As stated above (I-II, Q. 84, AA. 3, 4), a capital vice is one from which other vices arise most frequently. Now vice is contrary to man's nature, in as much as he is a rational animal: and when a thing acts contrary to its nature, that which is natural to it is corrupted little by little. Consequently it must first of all fail in that which is less in accordance with its nature, and last of all in that which is most in accordance with its nature, since what is first in construction is last in destruction. Now that which, first and foremost, is most natural to man, is the love of what is good, and especially love of the Divine good, and of his neighbor's good. Wherefore hatred, which is opposed to this love, is not the first but the last thing in the downfall of virtue resulting from vice: and therefore it is not a capital vice.

Reply Obj. 1: As stated in *Phys.* vii, text. 18, "the virtue of a thing consists in its being well disposed in accordance with its nature." Hence what is first and foremost in the virtues must be first and foremost in the natural order. Hence charity is reckoned the foremost of the virtues, and for the same reason hatred cannot be first among the vices, as stated above.

Reply Obj. 2: Hatred of the evil that is contrary to one's natural good, is the first of the soul's passions, even as love of one's natural good is. But hatred of one's connatural good cannot be first, but is something last, because such like hatred is a proof of an already corrupted nature, even as love of an extraneous good.

Reply Obj. 3: Evil is twofold. One is a true evil, for the reason that it is incompatible with one's natural good, and the hatred of such an evil may have priority over the other passions. There is, however, another which is not a true, but an apparent evil, which, namely, is a true and connatural good, and yet is reckoned evil on account of the corruption of nature: and the hatred of such an evil must needs come last. This hatred is vicious, but the former is not.

SIXTH ARTICLE [II-II, Q. 34, Art. 6]

Whether Hatred Arises from Envy?

Objection 1: It seems that hatred does not arise from envy. For envy is sorrow for another's good. Now hatred does not arise from sorrow, for, *on the contrary,* we grieve for the presence of the evil we hate. Therefore hatred does not arise from envy.

Obj. 2: Further, hatred is opposed to love. Now love of our neighbor is referred to our love of God, as stated above (Q. 25, A. 1; Q. 26, A. 2). Therefore hatred of our neighbor is referred to our hatred of God. But hatred of God does not arise from envy, for we do not envy those who are very far removed from us, but rather those who seem to be near us, as the Philosopher states (Rhet. ii). Therefore hatred does not arise from envy.

Obj. 3: Further, to one effect there is one cause. Now hatred is caused by anger, for Augustine says in his Rule that "anger grows into hatred." Therefore hatred does not arise from envy.

*On the contrary,* Gregory says (Moral. xxxi, 45) that "out of envy cometh hatred."

*I answer that,* As stated above (A. 5), hatred of his neighbor is a man's last step in the path of sin, because it is opposed to the love which he naturally has for his neighbor. Now if a man declines from that which is natural, it is because he intends to avoid that which is naturally an object to be shunned. Now every animal naturally avoids sorrow, just as it desires pleasure, as the Philosopher states (Ethic. vii, x). Accordingly just as love arises from pleasure, so does hatred arise from sorrow. For just as we are moved to love whatever gives us pleasure, in as much as for that very reason it assumes the aspect of good; so we are moved to hate whatever displeases us, in so far as for this very reason it assumes the aspect of evil. Wherefore, since envy is sorrow for our neighbor's good, it follows that our neighbor's good becomes hateful to us, so that "out of envy cometh hatred."

Reply Obj. 1: Since the appetitive power, like the apprehensive power, reflects on its own acts, it follows that there is a kind of circular movement in the actions of the appetitive power. And so according to the first forward course of the appetitive movement, love gives rise to desire, whence follows pleasure when one has obtained what one desired. And since the very fact of taking pleasure in the good one loves is a kind of good, it follows that pleasure causes love. And in the same way sorrow causes hatred.

Reply Obj. 2: Love and hatred are essentially different, for the object of love is good, which flows from God to creatures, wherefore love is due to God in the first place, and to our neighbor afterwards. On the other hand, hatred is of evil, which has no place in God Himself, but only in His effects, for which reason it has been stated above (A. 1), that God is not an object of hatred, except in so far as He is considered in relation to His effects, and consequently hatred is directed to our neighbor before being directed to God. Therefore, since envy of our neighbor is the mother of hatred of our neighbor, it becomes, in consequence, the cause of hatred towards God.

Reply Obj. 3: Nothing prevents a thing arising from various causes in various respects, and accordingly hatred may arise both from anger and from envy. However it arises more directly from envy, which looks upon the very good of our neighbor as displeasing and therefore hateful, whereas hatred arises from anger by way of increase. For at first, through anger, we desire our neighbor's evil according to a certain measure, that is in so far as that evil has the aspect of vengeance: but afterwards, through the continuance of anger, man goes so far as absolutely to desire his neighbor's evil, which desire is part of hatred. Wherefore it is evident that hatred is caused by envy formally as regards the aspect of the object, but dispositively by anger.

## QUESTION 35

OF SLOTH (In Four Articles)

We must now consider the vices opposed to the joy of charity. This joy is either about the Divine good, and then its contrary is sloth, or about our neighbor's good, and then its contrary is envy. Wherefore we must consider (1) Sloth and (2) Envy.

Under the first head there are four points of inquiry:

(1) Whether sloth is a sin?

(2) Whether it is a special vice?

(3) Whether it is a mortal sin?

(4) Whether it is a capital sin?

FIRST ARTICLE [II-II, Q. 35, Art. 1]

Whether Sloth Is a Sin?

Objection 1: It would seem that sloth is not a sin. For we are neither praised nor blamed for our passions, according to the Philosopher (Ethic. ii, 5). Now sloth is a passion, since it is a kind of sorrow, according to Damascene (De Fide Orth. ii, 14), and as we stated above (I-II, Q. 35, A. 8). Therefore sloth is not a sin.

Obj. 2: Further, no bodily failing that occurs at fixed times is a sin. But sloth is like this, for Cassian says (De Instit. Monast. x, [*De Institutione Caenobiorum]): "The monk is troubled with sloth chiefly about the sixth hour: it is like an intermittent fever, and inflicts the soul of the one it lays low with burning fires at regular and fixed intervals." Therefore sloth is not a sin.

Obj. 3: Further, that which proceeds from a good root is, seemingly, no sin. Now sloth proceeds from a good root, for Cassian says (De Instit. Monast. x) that "sloth arises from the fact that we sigh at being deprived of spiritual fruit, and think that other monasteries and those which are a long way off are much better than the one we dwell in": all of which seems to point to humility. Therefore sloth is not a sin.

Obj. 4: Further, all sin is to be avoided, according to Ecclus. 21:2: "Flee from sins as from the face of a serpent." Now Cassian says (De Instit. Monast. x): "Experience shows that the onslaught of sloth is not to be evaded by flight but to be conquered by resistance." Therefore sloth is not a sin.

*On the contrary,* Whatever is forbidden in Holy Writ is a sin. Now such is sloth ( acedia ): for it is written (Ecclus. 6:26): "Bow down thy shoulder, and bear her," namely spiritual wisdom, "and be not grieved ( acedieris ) with her bands." Therefore sloth is a sin.

*I answer that,* Sloth, according to Damascene (De Fide Orth. ii, 14) is an oppressive sorrow, which, to wit, so weighs upon man's mind, that he wants to do nothing; thus acid things are also cold. Hence sloth implies a certain weariness of work, as appears from a gloss on Ps. 106:18, "Their soul abhorred all manner of meat," and from the definition of some who say that sloth is a "sluggishness of the mind which neglects to begin good."

Now this sorrow is always evil, sometimes in itself, sometimes in its effect. For sorrow is evil in itself when it is about that which is apparently evil but good in reality, even as, on the other hand, pleasure is evil if it is about that which seems to be good but is, in truth, evil. Since, then, spiritual good is a good in very truth, sorrow about spiritual good is evil in itself. And yet that sorrow also which is about a real evil, is evil in its effect, if it so oppresses man as to draw him away entirely from good deeds. Hence the Apostle (2 Cor. 2:7) did not wish those who repented to be "swallowed up with overmuch sorrow."

Accordingly, since sloth, as we understand it here, denotes sorrow for spiritual good, it is evil on two counts, both in itself and in point of its effect. Consequently it is a sin, for by sin we mean an evil movement of the appetite, as appears from what has been said above (Q. 10, A. 2; I-II, Q. 74, A. 4).

Reply Obj. 1: Passions are not sinful in themselves; but they are blameworthy in so far as they are applied to something evil, just as they deserve praise in so far as they are applied to something good. Wherefore sorrow, in itself, calls neither for praise nor for blame: whereas moderate sorrow for evil calls for praise, while sorrow for good, and again immoderate sorrow for evil, call for blame. It is in this sense that sloth is said to be a sin.

Reply Obj. 2: The passions of the sensitive appetite may either be venial sins in themselves, or incline the soul to mortal sin. And since the sensitive appetite has a bodily organ, it follows that on account of some bodily transmutation a man becomes apt to commit some particular sin. Hence it may happen that certain sins may become more insistent, through certain bodily transmutations occurring at certain fixed times. Now all bodily effects, of themselves, dispose one to sorrow; and thus it is that those who fast are harassed by sloth towards mid-day, when they begin to feel the want of food, and to be parched by the sun's heat.

Reply Obj. 3: It is a sign of humility if a man does not think too much of himself, through observing his own faults; but if a man contemns the good things he has received from God, this, far from being a proof of humility, shows him to be ungrateful: and from such like contempt results sloth, because we sorrow for things that we reckon evil and worthless. Accordingly we ought to think much of the goods of others, in such a way as not to disparage those we have received ourselves, because if we did they would give us sorrow.

Reply Obj. 4: Sin is ever to be shunned, but the assaults of sin should be overcome, sometimes by flight, sometimes by resistance; by flight when a continued thought increases the incentive to sin, as in lust; for which reason it is written (1 Cor. 6:18): "Fly fornication"; by resistance, when perseverance in the thought diminishes the incentive to sin, which incentive arises from some trivial consideration. This is the case with sloth, because the more we think about spiritual goods, the more pleasing they become to us, and forthwith sloth dies away.

SECOND ARTICLE [II-II, Q. 35, Art. 2]

Whether Sloth Is a Special Vice?

Objection 1: It would seem that sloth is not a special vice. For that which is common to all vices does not constitute a special kind of vice. But every vice makes a man sorrowful about the opposite spiritual good: for the lustful man is sorrowful about the good of continence, and the glutton about the good of abstinence. Since then sloth is sorrow for spiritual good, as stated above (A. 1), it seems that sloth is not a special sin.

Obj. 2: Further, sloth, through being a kind of sorrow, is opposed to joy. Now joy is not accounted one special virtue. Therefore sloth should not be reckoned a special vice.

Obj. 3: Further, since spiritual good is a general kind of object, which virtue seeks, and vice shuns, it does not constitute a special virtue or vice, unless it be determined by some addition. Now nothing, seemingly, except toil, can determine it to sloth, if this be a special vice; because the reason why a man shuns spiritual goods, is that they are toilsome, wherefore sloth is a kind of weariness: while dislike of toil, and love of bodily repose seem to be due to the same cause, viz. idleness. Hence sloth would be nothing but laziness, which seems untrue, for idleness is opposed to carefulness, whereas sloth is opposed to joy. Therefore sloth is not a special vice.

*On the contrary,* Gregory (Moral. xxxi, 45) distinguishes sloth from the other vices. Therefore it is a special vice.

*I answer that,* Since sloth is sorrow for spiritual good, if we take spiritual good in a general way, sloth will not be a special vice, because, as stated above (I-II, Q. 71, A. 1), every vice shuns the spiritual good of its opposite virtue. Again it cannot be said that sloth is a special vice, in so far as it shuns spiritual good, as toilsome, or troublesome to the body, or as a hindrance to the body's pleasure, for this again would not sever sloth from carnal vices, whereby a man seeks bodily comfort and pleasure.

Wherefore we must say that a certain order exists among spiritual goods, since all the spiritual goods that are in the acts of each virtue are directed to one spiritual good, which is the Divine good, about which there is a special virtue, viz. charity. Hence it is proper to each virtue to rejoice in its own spiritual good, which consists in its own act, while it belongs specially to charity to have that spiritual joy whereby one rejoices in the Divine good. In like manner the sorrow whereby one is displeased at the spiritual good which is in each act of virtue, belongs, not to any special vice, but to every vice, but sorrow in the Divine good about which charity rejoices, belongs to a special vice, which is called sloth. This suffices for the Replies to the Objections.

THIRD ARTICLE [II-II, Q. 35, Art. 3]

Whether Sloth Is a Mortal Sin?

Objection 1: It would seem that sloth is not a mortal sin. For every mortal sin is contrary to a precept of the Divine Law. But sloth seems contrary to no precept, as one may see by going through the precepts of the Decalogue. Therefore sloth is not a mortal sin.

Obj. 2: Further, in the same genus, a sin of deed is no less grievous than a sin of thought. Now it is not a mortal sin to refrain in deed from some spiritual good which leads to God, else it would be a mortal sin not to observe the counsels. Therefore it is not a mortal sin to refrain in thought from such like spiritual works. Therefore sloth is not a mortal sin.

Obj. 3: Further, no mortal sin is to be found in a perfect man. But sloth is to be found in a perfect man: for Cassian says (De Instit. Caenob. x, l) that "sloth is well known to the solitary, and is a most vexatious and persistent foe to the hermit." Therefore sloth is not always a mortal sin.

*On the contrary,* It is written (2 Cor. 7:20): "The sorrow of the world worketh death." But such is sloth; for it is not sorrow "according to God," which is contrasted with sorrow of the world. Therefore it is a mortal sin.

*I answer that,* As stated above (I-II, Q. 88, AA. 1, 2), mortal sin is so called because it destroys the spiritual life which is the effect of charity, whereby God dwells in us. Wherefore any sin which by its very nature is contrary to charity is a mortal sin by reason of its genus. And such is sloth, because the proper effect of charity is joy in God, as stated above (Q. 28, A. 1), while sloth is sorrow about spiritual good in as much as it is a Divine good. Therefore sloth is a mortal sin in respect of its genus. But it must be observed with regard to all sins that are mortal in respect of their genus, that they are not mortal, save when they attain to their perfection. Because the consummation of sin is in the consent of reason: for we are speaking now of human sins consisting in human acts, the principle of which is the reason. Wherefore if the sin be a mere beginning of sin in the sensuality alone, without attaining to the consent of reason, it is a venial sin on account of the imperfection of the act. Thus in the genus of adultery, the concupiscence that goes no further than the sensuality is a venial sin, whereas if it reach to the consent of reason, it is a mortal sin. So too, the movement of sloth is sometimes in the sensuality alone, by reason of the opposition of the flesh to the spirit, and then it is a venial sin; whereas sometimes it reaches to the reason, which consents in the dislike, horror and detestation of the Divine good, on account of the flesh utterly prevailing over the spirit. In this case it is evident that sloth is a mortal sin.

Reply Obj. 1: Sloth is opposed to the precept about hallowing the Sabbath day. For this precept, in so far as it is a moral precept, implicitly commands the mind to rest in God: and sorrow of the mind about the Divine good is contrary thereto.

Reply Obj. 2: Sloth is not an aversion of the mind from any spiritual good, but from the Divine good, to which the mind is obliged to adhere. Wherefore if a man is sorry because someone forces him to do acts of virtue that he is not bound to do, this is not a sin of sloth; but when he is sorry to have to do something for God's sake.

Reply Obj. 3: Imperfect movements of sloth are to be found in holy men, but they do not reach to the consent of reason.

FOURTH ARTICLE [II-II, Q. 35, Art. 4]

Whether Sloth Should Be Accounted a Capital Vice?

Objection 1: It would seem that sloth ought not to be accounted a capital vice. For a capital vice is one that moves a man to sinful acts, as stated above (Q. 34, A. 5). Now sloth does not move one to action, but on the contrary withdraws one from it. Therefore it should not be accounted a capital sin.

Obj. 2: Further, a capital sin is one to which daughters are assigned. Now Gregory (Moral. xxxi, 45) assigns six daughters to sloth, viz. "malice, spite, faint-heartedness, despair, sluggishness in regard to the commandments, wandering of the mind after unlawful things." Now these do not seem in reality to arise from sloth. For "spite" is, seemingly the same as hatred, which arises from envy, as stated above (Q. 34, A. 6); "malice" is a genus which contains all vices, and, in like manner, a "wandering" of the mind after unlawful things is to be found in every vice; "sluggishness" about the commandments seems to be the same as sloth, while "faint-heartedness" and "despair" may arise from any sin. Therefore sloth is not rightly accounted a capital sin.

Obj. 3: Further, Isidore distinguishes the vice of sloth from the vice of sorrow, saying (De Summo Bono ii, 37) that in so far as a man shirks his duty because it is distasteful and burdensome, it is sorrow, and in so far as he is inclined to undue repose, it is sloth: and of sorrow he says that it gives rise to "spite, faint-heartedness, bitterness, despair," whereas he states that from sloth seven things arise, viz. "idleness, drowsiness, uneasiness of the mind, restlessness of the body, instability, loquacity, curiosity." Therefore it seems that either Gregory or Isidore has wrongly assigned sloth as a capital sin together with its daughters.

*On the contrary,* The same Gregory (Moral. xxxi,

45) states that sloth is a capital sin, and has the daughters aforesaid.

*I answer that,* As stated above (I-II, Q. 84, AA. 3, 4), a capital vice is one which easily gives rise to others as being their final cause. Now just as we do many things on account of pleasure, both in order to obtain it, and through being moved to do something under the impulse of pleasure, so again we do many things on account of sorrow, either that we may avoid it, or through being exasperated into doing something under pressure thereof. Wherefore, since sloth is a kind of sorrow, as stated above (A. 2; I-II, Q. 85, A. 8), it is fittingly reckoned a capital sin.

Reply Obj. 1: Sloth by weighing on the mind, hinders us from doing things that cause sorrow: nevertheless it induces the mind to do certain things, either because they are in harmony with sorrow, such as weeping, or because they are a means of avoiding sorrow.

Reply Obj. 2: Gregory fittingly assigns the daughters of sloth. For since, according to the Philosopher (Ethic. viii, 5, 6) "no man can be a long time in company with what is painful and unpleasant," it follows that something arises from sorrow in two ways: first, that man shuns whatever causes sorrow; secondly, that he passes to other things that give him pleasure: thus those who find no joy in spiritual pleasures, have recourse to pleasures of the body, according to the Philosopher (Ethic. x, 6). Now in the avoidance of sorrow the order observed is that man at first flies from unpleasant objects, and secondly he even struggles against such things as cause sorrow. Now spiritual goods which are the object of the sorrow of sloth, are both end and means. Avoidance of the end is the result of "despair," while avoidance of those goods which are the means to the end, in matters of difficulty which come under the counsels, is the effect of "faint-heartedness," and in matters of common righteousness, is the effect of "sluggishness about the commandments." The struggle against spiritual goods that cause sorrow is sometimes with men who lead others to spiritual goods, and this is called "spite"; and sometimes it extends to the spiritual goods themselves, when a man goes so far as to detest them, and this is properly called "malice." In so far as a man has recourse to eternal objects of pleasure, the daughter of sloth is called "wandering after unlawful things." From this it is clear how to reply to the objections against each of the daughters: for "malice" does not denote here that which is generic to all vices, but must be understood as explained. Nor is "spite" taken as synonymous with hatred, but for a kind of indignation, as stated above: and the same applies to the others.

Reply Obj. 3: This distinction between sorrow and sloth is also given by Cassian (De Instit. Caenob. x, 1). But Gregory more fittingly (Moral. xxxi, 45) calls sloth a kind of sorrow, because, as stated above (A. 2), sorrow is not a distinct vice, in so far as a man shirks a distasteful and burdensome work, or sorrows on account of any other cause whatever, but only in so far as he is sorry on account of the Divine good, which sorrow belongs essentially to sloth; since sloth seeks undue rest in so far as it spurns the Divine good. Moreover the things which Isidore reckons to arise from sloth and sorrow, are reduced to those mentioned by Gregory: for "bitterness" which Isidore states to be the result of sorrow, is an effect of "spite." "Idleness" and "drowsiness" are reduced to "sluggishness about the precepts": for some are idle and omit them altogether, while others are drowsy and fulfil them with negligence. All the other five which he reckons as effects of sloth, belong to the "wandering of the mind after unlawful things." This tendency to wander, if it reside in the mind itself that is desirous of rushing after various things without rhyme or reason, is called "uneasiness of the mind," but if it pertains to the imaginative power, it is called "curiosity"; if it affect the speech it is called "loquacity"; and in so far as it affects a body that changes place, it is called "restlessness of the body," when, to wit, a man shows the unsteadiness of his mind, by the inordinate movements of members of his body; while if it causes the body to move from one place to another, it is called "instability"; or "instability" may denote changeableness of purpose.

# QUESTION 36

OF ENVY (FOUR ARTICLES)

We must now consider envy, and under this head there are four points of inquiry:

(1) What is envy?

(2) Whether it is a sin?

(3) Whether it is a mortal sin?

(4) Whether it is a capital sin, and which are its daughters?

FIRST ARTICLE [II-II, Q. 36, Art. 1]

Whether Envy Is a Kind of Sorrow?

Objection 1: It would seem that envy is not a kind of sorrow. For the object of envy is a good, for Gregory says (Moral. v, 46) of the envious man that "self-inflicted pain wounds the pining spirit, which is racked by the prosperity of another." Therefore envy is not a kind of sorrow.

Obj. 2: Further, likeness is a cause, not of sorrow but rather of pleasure. But likeness is a cause of envy: for the Philosopher says (Rhet. ii, 10): "Men are envious of such as are like them in genus, in knowledge, in stature, in habit, or in reputation." Therefore envy is not a kind of sorrow.

Obj. 3: Further, sorrow is caused by a defect, wherefore those who are in great defect are inclined to sorrow, as stated above (I-II, Q. 47, A. 3) when we were treating of the passions. Now those who lack little, and who love honors, and who are considered wise, are envious, according to the Philosopher (Rhet. ii, 10). Therefore envy is not a kind of sorrow.

Obj. 4: Further, sorrow is opposed to pleasure. Now opposite effects have not one and the same cause. Therefore, since the recollection of goods once possessed is a cause of pleasure, as stated above (I-II, Q. 32, A. 3) it will not be a cause of sorrow. But it is a cause of envy; for the Philosopher says (Rhet. ii, 10) that "we envy those who have or have had things that befitted ourselves, or which we possessed at some time." Therefore sloth is not a kind of sorrow.

*On the contrary,* Damascene (De Fide Orth. ii, 14) calls envy a species of sorrow, and says that "envy is sorrow for another's good."

*I answer that,* The object of a man's sorrow is his own evil. Now it may happen that another's good is apprehended as one's own evil, and in this way sorrow can be about another's good. But this happens in two ways: first, when a man is sorry about another's good, in so far as it threatens to be an occasion of harm to himself, as when a man grieves for his enemy's prosperity, for fear lest he may do him some harm: such like sorrow is not envy, but rather an effect of fear, as the Philosopher states (Rhet. ii, 9).

Secondly, another's good may be reckoned as being one's own evil, in so far as it conduces to the lessening of one's own good name or excellence. It is in this way that envy grieves for another's good: and consequently men are envious of those goods in which a good name consists, and about which men like to be honored and esteemed, as the Philosopher remarks (Rhet. ii, 10).

Reply Obj. 1: Nothing hinders what is good for one from being reckoned as evil for another: and in this way it is possible for sorrow to be about good, as stated above.

Reply Obj. 2: Since envy is about another's good name in so far as it diminishes the good name a man desires to have, it follows that a man is envious of those only whom he wishes to rival or surpass in reputation. But this does not apply to people who are far removed from one another: for no man, unless he be out of his mind, endeavors to rival or surpass in reputation those who are far above him. Thus a commoner does not envy the king, nor does the king envy a commoner whom he is far above. Wherefore a man envies not those who are far removed from him, whether in place, time, or station, but those who are near him, and whom he strives to rival or surpass. For it is against our will that these should be in better repute than we are, and that gives rise to sorrow. On the other hand, likeness causes pleasure in so far as it is in agreement with the will.

Reply Obj. 3: A man does not strive for mastery in matters where he is very deficient; so that he does not envy one who surpasses him in such matters, unless he surpass him by little, for then it seems to him that this is not beyond him, and so he makes an effort; wherefore, if his effort fails through the other's reputation surpassing his, he grieves. Hence it is that those who love to be honored are more envious; and in like manner the faint-hearted are envious, because all things are great to them, and whatever good may befall another, they reckon that they themselves have been bested in something great. Hence it is written (Job 5:2): "Envy slayeth the little one," and Gregory says (Moral. v, 46) that "we can envy those only whom we think better in some respect than ourselves."

Reply Obj. 4: Recollection of past goods in so far as we have had them, causes pleasure; in so far as we have lost them, causes sorrow; and in so far as others have them, causes envy, because that, above all, seems to belittle our reputation. Hence the Philosopher says (Rhet. ii) that the old envy the young, and those who have spent much in order to get something, envy those who have got it by spending little, because they grieve that they have lost their goods, and that others have acquired goods.

SECOND ARTICLE [II-II, Q. 36, Art. 2]

Whether Envy Is a Sin?

Objection 1: It would seem that envy is not a sin. For Jerome says to Laeta about the education of her daughter (Ep. cvii): "Let her have companions, so that she may learn together with them, envy them, and be nettled when they are praised." But no one should be advised to commit a sin. Therefore envy is not a sin.

Objection 2: Further, "Envy is sorrow for another's good," as Damascene says (De Fide Orth. ii, 14). But this is sometimes praiseworthy: for it is written (Prov. 29:2): "When the wicked shall bear rule, the people shall mourn." Therefore envy is not always a sin.

Obj. 3: Further, envy denotes a kind of zeal. But there is a good zeal, according to Ps. 68:10: "The zeal of Thy house hath eaten me up." Therefore envy is not always a sin.

Obj. 4: Further, punishment is condivided with fault. But envy is a kind of punishment: for Gregory says (Moral. v, 46): "When the foul sore of envy corrupts the vanquished heart, the very exterior itself shows how forcibly the mind is urged by madness. For paleness seizes the complexion, the eyes are weighed down, the spirit is inflamed, while the limbs are chilled, there is frenzy in the heart, there is gnashing with the teeth." Therefore envy is not a sin.

*On the contrary,* It is written (Gal. 5:26): "Let us not be made desirous of vainglory, provoking one another, envying one another."

*I answer that,* As stated above (A. 1), envy is sorrow for another's good. Now this sorrow may come about in four ways. First, when a man grieves for another's good, through fear that it may cause harm either to himself, or to some other goods. This sorrow is not envy, as stated above (A. 1), and may be void of sin. Hence Gregory says (Moral. xxii, 11): "It very often happens that without charity being lost, both the destruction of an enemy rejoices us, and again his glory, without any sin of envy, saddens us, since, when he falls, we believe that some are deservedly set up, and when he prospers, we dread lest many suffer unjustly."

Secondly, we may grieve over another's good, not because he has it, but because the good which he has, we have not: and this, properly speaking, is zeal, as the Philosopher says (Rhet. ii, 9). And if this zeal be about virtuous goods, it is praiseworthy, according to 1 Cor. 14:1: "Be zealous for spiritual gifts": while, if it be about temporal goods, it may be either sinful or sinless. Thirdly, one may grieve over another's good, because he who happens to have that good is unworthy of it. Such sorrow as this cannot be occasioned by virtuous goods, which make a man righteous, but, as the Philosopher states, is about riches, and those things which can accrue to the worthy and the unworthy; and he calls this sorrow *nemesis* [*The nearest equivalent is "indignation." The use of the word "nemesis" to signify "revenge" does not represent the original Greek.], saying that it belongs to good morals. But he says this because he considered temporal goods in themselves, in so far as they may seem great to those who look not to eternal goods: whereas, according to the teaching of faith, temporal goods that accrue to those who are unworthy, are so disposed according to God's just ordinance, either for the correction of those men, or for their condemnation, and such goods are as nothing in comparison with the goods to come, which are prepared for good men. Wherefore sorrow of this kind is forbidden in Holy Writ, according to Ps. 36:1: "Be not emulous of evil doers, nor envy them that work iniquity," and elsewhere (Ps. 72:2, 3): "My steps had well nigh slipped, for I was envious of the wicked, when I saw the prosperity of sinners [*Douay: 'because I had a zeal on occasion of the wicked, seeing the prosperity of sinners']." Fourthly, we grieve over a man's good, in so far as his good surpasses ours; this is envy properly speaking, and is always sinful, as also the Philosopher states (Rhet. ii, 10), because to do so is to grieve over what should make us rejoice, viz. over our neighbor's good.

Reply Obj. 1: Envy there denotes the zeal with which we ought to strive to progress with those who are better than we are.

Reply Obj. 2: This argument considers sorrow for another's good in the first sense given above.

Reply Obj. 3: Envy differs from zeal, as stated above. Hence a certain zeal may be good, whereas envy is always evil.

Reply Obj. 4: Nothing hinders a sin from being penal accidentally, as stated above (I-II, Q. 87, A. 2) when we were treating of sins.

THIRD ARTICLE [II-II, Q. 36, Art. 3]

Whether Envy Is a Mortal Sin?

Objection 1: It would seem that envy is not a mortal sin. For since envy is a kind of sorrow, it is a passion of the sensitive appetite. Now there is no mortal sin in the sensuality, but only in the reason, as Augustine declares (De Trin. xii, 12) [*Cf. I-II, Q. 74, A. 4]. Therefore envy is not a mortal sin.

Obj. 2: Further, there cannot be mortal sin in infants. But envy can be in them, for Augustine says (Confess. i): "I myself have seen and known even a baby envious, it could not speak, yet it turned pale and looked bitterly on its foster-brother." Therefore envy is not a mortal sin.

Obj. 3: Further, every mortal sin is contrary to some virtue. But envy is contrary, not to a virtue but to *nemesis* , which is a passion, according to the Philosopher (Rhet. ii, 9). Therefore envy is not a mortal sin.

*On the contrary,* It is written (Job 5:2): "Envy slayeth the little one." Now nothing slays spiritually, except mortal sin. Therefore envy is a mortal sin.

*I answer that,* Envy is a mortal sin, in respect of its genus. For the genus of a sin is taken from its object; and envy according to the aspect of its object is contrary to charity, whence the soul derives its spiritual life, according to 1 John 3:14: "We know that we have passed from death to life, because we love the brethren." Now the object both of charity and of envy is our neighbor's good, but by contrary movements, since charity rejoices in our neighbor's good, while envy grieves over it, as stated above (A. 1). Therefore it is evident that envy is a mortal sin in respect of its genus.

Nevertheless, as stated above (Q. 35, A. 4; I-II, Q. 72, A. 5, ad 1), in every kind of mortal sin we find certain imperfect movements in the sensuality, which are venial sins: such are the first movement of concupiscence, in the genus of adultery, and the first movement of anger, in the genus of murder, and so in the genus of envy we find sometimes even in perfect men certain first movements, which are venial sins.

Reply Obj. 1: The movement of envy in so far as it is a passion of the sensuality, is an imperfect thing in the genus of human acts, the principle of which is the reason, so that envy of that kind is not a mortal sin. The same applies to the envy of little children who have not the use of reason: wherefore the Reply to the Second Objection is manifest.

Reply Obj. 3: According to the Philosopher (Rhet. ii, 9), envy is contrary both to *nemesis* and to pity, but for different reasons. For it is directly contrary to pity, their principal objects being contrary to one another, since the envious man grieves over his neighbor's good, whereas the pitiful man grieves over his neighbor's evil, so that the envious have no pity, as he states in the same passage, nor is the pitiful man envious. On the other hand, envy is contrary to *nemesis* on the part of the man whose good grieves the envious man, for *nemesis* is sorrow for the good of the undeserving according to Ps. 72:3: "I was envious of the wicked, when I saw the prosperity of sinners" [*Douay: "because I had a zeal on occasion of the wicked, seeing the prosperity of sinners"], whereas the envious grieves over the good of those who are deserving of it. Hence it is clear that the former contrariety is more direct than the latter. Now pity is a virtue, and an effect proper to charity: so that envy is contrary to pity and charity.

FOURTH ARTICLE [II-II, Q. 36, Art. 4]

Whether Envy Is a Capital Vice?

Objection 1: It would seem that envy is not a capital vice. For the capital vices are distinct from their daughters. Now envy is the daughter of vainglory; for the Philosopher says (Rhet. ii, 10) that "those who love honor and glory are more envious." Therefore envy is not a capital vice.

Obj. 2: Further, the capital vices seem to be less grave than the other vices which arise from them. For Gregory says (Moral. xxxi, 45): "The leading vices seem to worm their way into the deceived mind under some kind of pretext, but those which follow them provoke the soul to all kinds of outrage, and confuse the mind with their wild outcry." Now envy is seemingly a most grave sin, for Gregory says (Moral. v, 46): "Though in every evil thing that is done, the venom of our old enemy is infused into the heart of man, yet in this wickedness the serpent stirs his whole bowels and discharges the bane of spite fitted to enter deep into the mind." Therefore envy is not a capital sin.

Obj. 3: Further, it seems that its daughters are unfittingly assigned by Gregory (Moral. xxxi, 45), who says that from envy arise "hatred, tale-bearing, detraction, joy at our neighbor's misfortunes, and grief for his prosperity." For joy at our neighbor's misfortunes and grief for his prosperity seem to be the same as envy, as appears from what has been said above (A. 3). Therefore these should not be assigned as daughters of envy.

On the contrary stands the authority of Gregory (Moral. xxxi, 45) who states that envy is a capital sin and assigns the aforesaid daughters thereto.

*I answer that,* Just as sloth is grief for a Divine spiritual good, so envy is grief for our neighbor's good. Now it has been stated above (Q. 35, A. 4) that sloth is a capital vice for the reason that it incites man to do certain things, with the purpose either of avoiding sorrow or of satisfying its demands. Wherefore envy is accounted a capital vice for the same reason.

Reply Obj. 1: As Gregory says (Moral. xxxi, 45), "the capital vices are so closely akin to one another that one springs from the other. For the first offspring of pride is vainglory, which by corrupting the mind it occupies begets envy, since while it craves for the power of an empty name, it repines for fear lest another should acquire that power." Consequently the notion of a capital vice does not exclude its originating from another vice, but it demands that it should have some principal reason for being itself the origin of several kinds of sin. However it is perhaps because envy manifestly arises from vainglory, that it is not reckoned a capital sin, either by Isidore (De Summo Bono) or by Cassian (De Instit. Caenob. v, 1).

Reply Obj. 2: It does not follow from the passage quoted that envy is the greatest of sins, but that when the devil tempts us to envy, he is enticing us to that which has its chief place in his heart, for as quoted further on in the same passage, "by the envy of the devil, death came into the world" (Wis. 2:24).

There is, however, a kind of envy which is accounted among the most grievous sins, viz. envy of another's spiritual good, which envy is a sorrow for the increase of God's grace, and not merely for our neighbor's good. Hence it is accounted a sin against the Holy Ghost, because thereby a man envies, as it were, the Holy Ghost Himself, Who is glorified in His works.

Reply Obj. 3: The number of envy's daughters may be understood for the reason that in the struggle aroused by envy there is something by way of beginning, something by way of middle, and something by way of term. The beginning is that a man strives to lower another's reputation, and this either secretly, and then we have *tale-bearing,* or openly, and then we have detraction. The middle consists in the fact that when a man aims at defaming another, he is either able to do so, and then we have *joy at another's misfortune,* or he is unable, and then we have *grief at another's prosperity.* The term is hatred itself, because just as good which delights causes love, so does sorrow cause hatred, as stated above (Q. 34, A. 6). Grief at another's prosperity is in one way the very same as envy, when, to Wit, a man grieves over another's prosperity, in so far as it gives the latter a good name, but in another way it is a daughter of envy, in so far as the envious man sees his neighbor prosper notwithstanding his efforts to prevent it. On the other hand, joy at another's misfortune is not directly the same as envy, but is a result thereof, because grief over our neighbor's good which is envy, gives rise to joy in his evil.

## QUESTION 37

OF DISCORD, WHICH IS CONTRARY TO PEACE (In Two Articles)

We must now consider the sins contrary to peace, and first we shall consider discord which is in the heart, secondly contention, which is on the lips, thirdly, those things which consist in deeds, viz. schism, quarrelling, war, and sedition. Under the first head there are two points of inquiry:

(1) Whether discord is a sin?

(2) Whether it is a daughter of vainglory?

FIRST ARTICLE [II-II, Q. 37, Art. 1]

Whether Discord Is a Sin?

Objection 1: It would seem that discord is not a sin. For to disaccord with man is to sever oneself from another's will. But this does not seem to be a sin, because God's will alone, and not our neighbor's, is the rule of our own will. Therefore discord is not a sin.

Obj. 2: Further, whoever induces another to sin, sins also himself. But it appears not to be a sin to incite others to discord, for it is written (Acts 23:6) that Paul, knowing that the one part were Sadducees, and the other Pharisees, cried out in the council: "Men brethren, I am a Pharisee, the son of Pharisees, concerning the hope and resurrection of the dead I am called in question. And when he had so said, there arose a dissension between the Pharisees and the Sadducees." Therefore discord is not a sin.

Obj. 3: Further, sin, especially mortal sin, is not to be found in a holy man. But discord is to be found even among holy men, for it is written (Acts 15:39): "There arose a dissension" between Paul and Barnabas, "so that they departed one from another." Therefore discord is not a sin, and least of all a mortal sin.

*On the contrary,* "Dissensions," that is, discords, are reckoned among the works of the flesh (Gal. 5:20), of which it is said afterwards (Gal. 5:21) that "they who do such things shall not obtain the kingdom of God." Now nothing, save mortal sin, excludes man from the kingdom of God. Therefore discord is a mortal sin.

*I answer that,* Discord is opposed to concord. Now, as stated above (Q. 29, AA. 1, 3) concord results from charity, in as much as charity directs many hearts together to one thing, which is chiefly the Divine good, secondarily, the good of our neighbor. Wherefore discord is a sin, in so far as it is opposed to this concord.

But it must be observed that this concord is destroyed by discord in two ways: first, directly; secondly, accidentally. Now, human acts and movements are said to be direct when they are according to one's intention. Wherefore a man directly disaccords with his neighbor, when he knowingly and intentionally dissents from the Divine good and his neighbor's good, to which he ought to consent. This is a mortal sin in respect of its genus, because it is contrary to charity, although the first movements of such discord are venial sins by reason of their being imperfect acts.

The accidental in human acts is that which occurs beside the intention. Hence when several intend a good pertaining to God's honor, or our neighbor's profit, while one deems a certain thing good, and another thinks contrariwise, the discord is in this case accidentally contrary to the Divine good or that of our neighbor. Such like discord is neither sinful nor against charity, unless it be accompanied by an error about things necessary to salvation, or by undue obstinacy, since it has also been stated above (Q. 29, AA. 1, 3, ad 2) that the concord which is an effect of charity, is union of wills not of opinions. It follows from this that discord is sometimes the sin of one party only, for instance, when one wills a good which the other knowingly resists; while sometimes it implies sin in both parties, as when each dissents from the other's good, and loves his own.

Reply Obj. 1: One man's will considered in itself is not the rule of another man's will; but in so far as our neighbor's will adheres to God's will, it becomes in consequence, a rule regulated according to its proper measure. Wherefore it is a sin to disaccord with such a will, because by that very fact one disaccords with the Divine rule.

Reply Obj. 2: Just as a man's will that adheres to God is a right rule, to disaccord with which is a sin, so too a man's will that is opposed to God is a perverse rule, to disaccord with which is good. Hence to cause a discord, whereby a good concord resulting from charity is destroyed, is a grave sin: wherefore it is written (Prov. 6:16): "Six things there are, which the Lord hateth, and the seventh His soul detesteth," which seventh is stated (Prov. 6:19) to be "him that soweth discord among brethren." On the other hand, to arouse a discord whereby an evil concord (i.e. concord in an evil will) is destroyed, is praiseworthy. In this way Paul was to be commended for sowing discord among those who concorded together in evil, because Our Lord also said of Himself (Matt. 10:34): "I came not to send peace, but the sword."

Reply Obj. 3: The discord between Paul and Barnabas was accidental and not direct: because each intended some good, yet the one thought one thing good, while the other thought something else, which was owing to human deficiency: for that controversy was not about things necessary to salvation. Moreover all this was ordained by Divine providence, on account of the good which would ensue.

SECOND ARTICLE [II-II, Q. 37, Art. 2]

Whether Discord Is a Daughter of Vainglory?

Objection 1: It would seem that discord is not a daughter of vainglory. For anger is a vice distinct from vainglory. Now discord is apparently the daughter of anger, according to Prov. 15:18: "A passionate man stirreth up strifes." Therefore it is not a daughter of vainglory.

Obj. 2: Further, Augustine expounding the words of John 7:39, "As yet the Spirit was not given," says (Tract. xxxii) "Malice severs, charity unites." Now discord is merely a separation of wills. Therefore discord arises from malice, i.e. envy, rather than from vainglory.

Obj. 3: Further, whatever gives rise to many evils, would seem to be a capital vice. Now such is discord, because Jerome in commenting on Matt. 12:25, "Every kingdom divided against itself shall be made desolate," says: "Just as concord makes small things thrive, so discord brings the greatest things to ruin." Therefore discord should itself be reckoned a capital vice, rather than a daughter of vainglory.

On the contrary stands the authority of Gregory (Moral. xxxi, 45).

*I answer that,* Discord denotes a certain disunion of wills, in so far, to wit, as one man's will holds fast to one thing, while the other man's will holds fast to something else. Now if a man's will holds fast to its own ground, this is due to the act that he prefers what is his own to that which belongs to others, and if he do this inordinately, it is due to pride and vainglory. Therefore discord, whereby a man holds to his own way of thinking, and departs from that of others, is reckoned to be a daughter of vainglory.

Reply Obj. 1: Strife is not the same as discord, for strife consists in external deeds, wherefore it is becoming that it should arise from anger, which incites the mind to hurt one's neighbor; whereas discord consists in a divergence in the movements of wills, which arises from pride or vainglory, for the reason given above.

Reply Obj. 2: In discord we may consider that which is the term *wherefrom,* i.e. another's will from which we recede, and in this respect it arises from envy; and again we may consider that which is the term *whither,* i.e. something of our own to which we cling, and in this respect it is caused by vainglory. And since in every moment the term *whither* is more important than the term wherefrom (because the end is of more account than the beginning), discord is accounted a daughter of vainglory rather than of envy, though it may arise from both for different reasons, as stated.

Reply Obj. 3: The reason why concord makes small things thrive, while discord brings the greatest to ruin, is because "the more united a force is, the stronger it is, while the more disunited it is the weaker it becomes" (De Causis xvii). Hence it is evident that this is part of the proper effect of discord which is a disunion of wills, and in no way indicates that other vices arise from discord, as though it were a capital vice.

## QUESTION 38

OF CONTENTION (In Two Articles)

We must now consider contention, in respect of which there are two points of inquiry:

(1) Whether contention is a mortal sin?

(2) Whether it is a daughter of vainglory?

FIRST ARTICLE [II-II, Q. 38, Art. 1]

Whether Contention Is a Mortal Sin?

Objection 1: It would seem that contention is not a mortal sin. For there is no mortal sin in spiritual men: and yet contention is to be found in them, according to Luke 22:24: "And there was also a strife amongst" the disciples of Jesus, "which of them should ... be the greatest." Therefore contention is not a mortal sin.

Obj. 2: Further, no well disposed man should be pleased that his neighbor commit a mortal sin. But the Apostle says (Phil. 1:17): "Some out of contention preach Christ," and afterwards he says (Phil. 1:18): "In this also I rejoice, yea, and will rejoice." Therefore contention is not a mortal sin.

Obj. 3: Further, it happens that people contend either in the courts or in disputations, without any spiteful purpose, and with a good intention, as, for example, those who contend by disputing with heretics. Hence a gloss on 1 Kings 14:1, "It came to pass one day," etc. says: "Catholics do not raise contentions with heretics, unless they are first challenged to dispute." Therefore contention is not a mortal sin.

Obj. 4: Further, Job seems to have contended with God, according to Job 39:32: "Shall he that contendeth with God be so easily silenced?" And yet Job was not guilty of mortal sin, since the Lord said of him (Job 42:7): "You have not spoken the thing that is right before me, as my servant Job hath." Therefore contention is not always a mortal sin.

*On the contrary,* It is against the precept of the Apostle who says (2 Tim. 2:14): "Contend not in words." Moreover (Gal. 5:20) contention is included among the works of the flesh, and as stated there (Gal. 5:21) "they who do such things shall not obtain the kingdom of God." Now whatever excludes a man from the kingdom of God and is against a precept, is a mortal sin. Therefore contention is a mortal sin.

*I answer that,* To contend is to tend against some one. Wherefore just as discord denotes a contrariety of wills, so contention signifies contrariety of speech. For this reason when a man contrasts various contrary things in a speech, this is called *contentio,* which Tully calls one of the rhetorical colors (De Rhet. ad Heren. iv), where he says that "it consists in developing a speech from contrary things," for instance: "Adulation has a pleasant beginning, and a most bitter end."

Now contrariety of speech may be looked at in two ways: first with regard to the intention of the contentious party, secondly, with regard to the manner of contending. As to the intention, we must consider whether he contends against the truth, and then he is to be blamed, or against falsehood, and then he should be praised. As to the manner, we must consider whether his manner of contending is in keeping with the persons and the matter in dispute, for then it would be praiseworthy, hence Tully says (De Rhet. ad Heren. iii) that "contention is a sharp speech suitable for proof and refutation"—or whether it exceeds the demands of the persons and matter in dispute, in which case it is blameworthy.

Accordingly if we take contention as denoting a disclaimer of the truth and an inordinate manner, it is a mortal sin. Thus Ambrose [*Cf. Gloss. Ord. in Rom. i, 29] defines contention: "Contention is a disclaimer of the truth with clamorous confidence." If, however, contention denote a disavowal of what is false, with the proper measure of acrimony, it is praiseworthy: whereas, if it denote a disavowal of falsehood, together with an inordinate manner, it can be a venial sin, unless the contention be conducted so inordinately, as to give scandal to others. Hence the Apostle after saying (2 Tim. 2:14): "Contend not in words," adds, "for it is to no profit, but to the subverting of the hearers."

Reply Obj. 1: The disciples of Christ contended together, not with the intention of disclaiming the truth, since each one stood up for what he thought was true. Yet there was inordinateness in their contention, because they contended about a matter which they ought not to have contended about, viz. the primacy of honor; for they were not spiritual men as yet, as a gloss says on the same passage; and for this reason Our Lord checked them.

Reply Obj. 2: Those who preached Christ "out of contention," were to be blamed, because, although they did not gainsay the truth of faith, but preached it, yet they did gainsay the truth, by the fact that they thought they would "raise affliction" to the Apostle who was preaching the truth of faith. Hence the Apostle rejoiced not in their contention, but in the fruit that would result therefrom, namely that Christ would be made known—since evil is sometimes the occasion of good results.

Reply Obj. 3: Contention is complete and is a mortal sin when, in contending before a judge, a man gainsays the truth of justice, or in a disputation, intends to impugn the true doctrine. In this sense Catholics do not contend against heretics, but the reverse. But when, whether in court or in a disputation, it is incomplete, i.e. in respect of the acrimony of speech, it is not always a mortal sin.

Reply Obj. 4: Contention here denotes an ordinary dispute. For Job had said (13:3): "I will speak to the Almighty, and I desire to reason with God": yet he intended not to impugn the truth, but to defend it, and in seeking the truth thus, he had no wish to be inordinate in mind or in speech.

SECOND ARTICLE [II-II, Q. 38, Art. 2]

Whether Contention Is a Daughter of Vainglory?

Objection 1: It would seem that contention is not a daughter of vainglory. For contention is akin to zeal, wherefore it is written (1 Cor. 3:3): "Whereas there is among you zeal [Douay: 'envying'] and contention, are you not carnal, and walk according to men?" Now zeal pertains to envy. Therefore contention arises rather from envy.

Obj. 2: Further, contention is accompanied by raising of the voice. But the voice is raised on account of anger, as Gregory declares (Moral. xxxi, 14). Therefore contention too arises from anger.

Obj. 3: Further, among other things knowledge seems to be the matter of pride and vainglory, according to 1 Cor. 8:1: "Knowledge puffeth up." Now contention is often due to lack of knowledge, and by knowledge we do not impugn the truth, we know it. Therefore contention is not a daughter of vainglory.

On the contrary stands the authority of Gregory (Moral. xxxi, 14).

*I answer that,* As stated above (Q. 37, A. 2), discord is a daughter of vainglory, because each of the disaccording parties clings to his own opinion, rather than acquiesce with the other. Now it is proper to pride and vainglory to seek one's own glory. And just as people are discordant when they hold to their own opinion in their hearts, so are they contentious when each defends his own opinion by words. Consequently contention is reckoned a daughter of vainglory for the same reason as discord.

Reply Obj. 1: Contention, like discord, is akin to envy in so far as a man severs himself from the one with whom he is discordant, or with whom he contends, but in so far as a contentious man holds to something, it is akin to pride and vainglory, because, to wit, he clings to his own opinion, as stated above (Q. 37, A. 2, ad 1).

Reply Obj. 2: The contention of which we are speaking puts on a loud voice, for the purpose of impugning the truth, so that it is not the chief part of contention. Hence it does not follow that contention arises from the same source as the raising of the voice.

Reply Obj. 3: Pride and vainglory are occasioned chiefly by goods even those that are contrary to them, for instance, when a man is proud of his humility: for when a thing arises in this way, it does so not directly but accidentally, in which way nothing hinders one contrary from arising out of another. Hence there is no reason why the *per se* and direct effects of pride or vainglory, should not result from the contraries of those things which are the occasion of pride.

# QUESTION 39

OF SCHISM (In Four Articles)

We must now consider the vices contrary to peace, which belong to deeds: such are schism, strife, sedition, and war. In the first place, then, about schism, there are four points of inquiry:

(1) Whether schism is a special sin?

(2) Whether it is graver than unbelief?

(3) Of the power exercised by schismatics;

(4) Of the punishment inflicted on them.

FIRST ARTICLE [II-II, Q. 39, Art. 1]

Whether Schism Is a Special Sin?

Objection 1: It would seem that schism is not a special sin. For "schism," as Pope Pelagius I says (Epist. ad Victor. et Pancrat.), "denotes a division." But every sin causes a division, according to Isa. 59: "Your sins have divided between you and your God." Therefore schism is not a special sin.

Obj. 2: Further, a man is apparently a schismatic if he disobeys the Church. But every sin makes a man disobey the commandments of the Church, because sin, according to Ambrose (De Parad. viii) "is disobedience against the heavenly commandments." Therefore every sin is a schism.

Obj. 3: Further, heresy also divides a man from the unity of faith. If, therefore, the word schism denotes a division, it would seem not to differ, as a special sin, from the sin of unbelief.

*On the contrary,* Augustine (Contra Faust. xx, 3; Contra Crescon. ii, 4) distinguishes between schism and heresy, for he says that a "schismatic is one who holds the same faith, and practises the same worship, as others, and takes pleasure in the mere disunion of the community, whereas a heretic is one who holds another faith from that of the Catholic Church." Therefore schism is not a generic sin.

*I answer that,* As Isidore says (Etym. viii, 3), schism takes its name "from being a scission of minds," and scission is opposed to unity. Wherefore the sin of schism is one that is directly and essentially opposed to unity. For in the moral, as in the physical order, the species is not constituted by that which is accidental. Now, in the moral order, the essential is that which is intended, and that which results beside the intention, is, as it were, accidental. Hence the sin of schism is, properly speaking, a special sin, for the reason that the schismatic intends to sever himself from that unity which is the effect of charity: because charity unites not only one person to another with the bond of spiritual love, but also the whole Church in unity of spirit.

Accordingly schismatics properly so called are those who, wilfully and intentionally separate themselves from the unity of the Church; for this is the chief unity, and the particular unity of several individuals among themselves is subordinate to the unity of the Church, even as the mutual adaptation of each member of a natural body is subordinate to the unity of the whole body. Now the unity of the Church consists in two things; namely, in the mutual connection or communion of the members of the Church, and again in the subordination of all the members of the Church to the one head, according to Col. 2:18, 19: "Puffed up by the sense of his flesh, and not holding the Head, from which the whole body, by joints and bands, being supplied with nourishment and compacted, groweth unto the increase of God." Now this Head is Christ Himself, Whose viceregent in the Church is the Sovereign Pontiff. Wherefore schismatics are those who refuse to submit to the Sovereign Pontiff, and to hold communion with those members of the Church who acknowledge his supremacy.

Reply Obj. 1: The division between man and God that results from sin is not intended by the sinner: it happens beside his intention as a result of his turning inordinately to a mutable good, and so it is not schism properly so called.

Reply Obj. 2: The essence of schism consists in rebelliously disobeying the commandments: and I say "rebelliously," since a schismatic both obstinately scorns the commandments of the Church, and refuses to submit to her judgment. But every sinner does not do this, wherefore not every sin is a schism.

Reply Obj. 3: Heresy and schism are distinguished in respect of those things to which each is opposed essentially and directly. For heresy is essentially opposed to faith, while schism is essentially opposed to the unity of ecclesiastical charity. Wherefore just as faith and charity are different virtues, although whoever lacks faith lacks charity, so too schism and heresy are different vices, although whoever is a heretic is also a schismatic, but not conversely. This is what Jerome says in his commentary on the Epistle to the Galatians [*In Ep. ad Tit. iii, 10]: "I consider the difference between schism and heresy to be that heresy holds false doctrine while schism severs a man from the Church." Nevertheless, just as the loss of charity is the road to the loss of faith, according to 1 Tim. 1:6: "From which things," i.e. charity and the like, "some going astray, are turned aside into vain babbling," so too, schism is the road to heresy. Wherefore Jerome adds (In Ep. ad Tit. iii, 10) that "at the outset it is possible, in a certain respect, to find a difference between schism and heresy: yet there is no schism that does not devise some heresy for itself, that it may appear to have had a reason for separating from the Church."

SECOND ARTICLE [II-II, Q. 39, Art. 2]

Whether Schism Is a Graver Sin Than Unbelief?

Objection 1: It would seem that schism is a graver sin than unbelief. For the graver sin meets with a graver punishment, according to Deut. 25:2: "According to the measure of the sin shall the measure also of the stripes be." Now we find the sin of schism punished more severely than even the sin of unbelief or idolatry: for we read (Ex. 32:28) that some were slain by the swords of their fellow men on account of idolatry: whereas of the sin of schism we read (Num. 16:30): "If the Lord do a new thing, and the earth opening her mouth swallow them down, and all things that belong to them, and they go down alive into hell, you shall know that they have blasphemed the Lord God." Moreover the ten tribes who were guilty of schism in revolting from the rule of David were most severely punished (4

Kings 17). Therefore the sin of schism is graver than the sin of unbelief.

Obj. 2: Further, "The good of the multitude is greater and more godlike than the good of the individual," as the Philosopher states (Ethic. i, 2). Now schism is opposed to the good of the multitude, namely, ecclesiastical unity, whereas unbelief is contrary to the particular good of one man, namely the faith of an individual. Therefore it seems that schism is a graver sin than unbelief.

Obj. 3: Further, a greater good is opposed to a greater evil, according to the Philosopher (Ethic. viii, 10). Now schism is opposed to charity, which is a greater virtue than faith to which unbelief is opposed, as shown above (Q. 10, A. 2; Q. 23, A. 6). Therefore schism is a graver sin than unbelief.

*On the contrary,* That which results from an addition to something else surpasses that thing either in good or in evil. Now heresy results from something being added to schism, for it adds corrupt doctrine, as Jerome declares in the passage quoted above (A. 1, ad 3). Therefore schism is a less grievous sin than unbelief.

*I answer that,* The gravity of a sin can be considered in two ways: first, according to the species of that sin, secondly, according to its circumstances. And since particular circumstances are infinite in number, so too they can be varied in an infinite number of ways: wherefore if one were to ask in general which of two sins is the graver, the question must be understood to refer to the gravity derived from the sin's genus. Now the genus or species of a sin is taken from its object, as shown above (I-II, Q. 72, A. 1; I-II, Q. 73, A. 3). Wherefore the sin which is opposed to the greater good is, in respect of its genus, more grievous, for instance a sin committed against God is graver than a sin committed against one's neighbor.

Now it is evident that unbelief is a sin committed against God Himself, according as He is Himself the First Truth, on which faith is founded; whereas schism is opposed to ecclesiastical unity, which is a participated good, and a lesser good than God Himself. Wherefore it is manifest that the sin of unbelief is generically more grievous than the sin of schism, although it may happen that a particular schismatic sins more grievously than a particular unbeliever, either because his contempt is greater, or because his sin is a source of greater danger, or for some similar reason.

Reply Obj. 1: It had already been declared to that people by the law which they had received that there was one God, and that no other God was to be worshipped by them; and the same had been confirmed among them by many kinds of signs. Consequently there was no need for those who sinned against this faith by falling into idolatry, to be punished in an unwonted manner: it was enough that they should be punished in the usual way. On the other hand, it was not so well known among them that Moses was always to be their ruler, and so it behooved those who rebelled against his authority to be punished in a miraculous and unwonted manner.

We may also reply by saying that the sin of schism was sometimes more severely punished in that people, because they were inclined to seditions and schisms. For it is written (1 Esdra 4:15): "This city since days gone by has rebelled against its kings: and seditions and wars were raised therein [*Vulg.: 'This city is a rebellious city, and hurtful to the kings and provinces, and ... wars were raised therein of old']." Now sometimes a more severe punishment is inflicted for an habitual sin (as stated above, I-II, Q. 105, A. 2, ad 9), because punishments are medicines intended to keep man away from sin: so that where there is greater proneness to sin, a more severe punishment ought to be inflicted. As regards the ten tribes, they were punished not only for the sin of schism, but also for that of idolatry as stated in the passage quoted.

Reply Obj. 2: Just as the good of the multitude is greater than the good of a unit in that multitude, so is it less than the extrinsic good to which that multitude is directed, even as the good of a rank in the army is less than the good of the commander-in-chief. In like manner the good of ecclesiastical unity, to which schism is opposed, is less than the good of Divine truth, to which unbelief is opposed.

Reply Obj. 3: Charity has two objects; one is its principal object and is the Divine goodness, the other is its secondary object and is our neighbor's good. Now schism and other sins against our neighbor, are opposed to charity in respect of its secondary good, which is less than the object of faith, for this is God Himself; and so these sins are less grievous than unbelief. On the other hand, hatred of God, which is opposed to charity in respect of its principal object, is not less grievous than unbelief. Nevertheless of all sins committed by man against his neighbor, the sin of schism would seem to be the greatest, because it is opposed to the spiritual good of the multitude.

THIRD ARTICLE [II-II, Q. 39, Art. 3]

Whether Schismatics Have Any Power?

Objection 1: It would seem that schismatics have some power. For Augustine says (Contra Donat. i, 1): "Just as those who come back to the Church after being baptized, are not baptized again, so those who return after being ordained, are not ordained again." Now Order is a kind of power. Therefore schismatics have some power since they retain their Orders.

Obj. 2: Further, Augustine says (De Unico Bapt. [*De Bap. contra Donat. vi, 5]): "One who is separated can confer a sacrament even as he can have it." But the power of conferring a sacrament is a very great power. Therefore schismatics who are separated from the Church, have a spiritual power.

Obj. 3: Further, Pope Urban II [*Council of Piacenza, cap. x; cf. Can. Ordinationes, ix, qu. 1] says: "We command that persons consecrated by bishops who were themselves consecrated according to the Catholic rite, but have separated themselves by schism from the Roman Church, should be received mercifully and that their Orders should be acknowledged, when they return to the unity of the Church, provided they be of commendable life and knowledge." But this would not be so, unless spiritual power were retained by schismatics. Therefore schismatics have spiritual power.

*On the contrary,* Cyprian says in a letter (Ep. lii, quoted vii, qu. 1, can. Novatianus): "He who observes neither unity of spirit nor the concord of peace, and severs himself from the bonds of the Church, and from the fellowship of her priests, cannot have episcopal power or honor."

*I answer that,* Spiritual power is twofold, the one sacramental, the other a power of jurisdiction. The sacramental power is one that is conferred by some kind of consecration. Now all the consecrations of the Church are immovable so long as the consecrated thing remains: as appears even in inanimate things, since an altar, once consecrated, is not consecrated again unless it has been broken up. Consequently such a power as this remains, as to its essence, in the man who has received it by consecration, as long as he lives, even if he fall into schism or heresy: and this is proved from the fact that if he come back to the Church, he is not consecrated anew. Since, however, the lower power ought not to exercise its act, except in so far as it is moved by the higher power, as may be seen also in the physical order, it follows that such persons lose the use of their power, so that it is not lawful for them to use it. Yet if they use it, this power has its effect in sacramental acts, because therein man acts only as God's instrument, so that sacramental effects are not precluded on account of any fault whatever in the person who confers the sacrament.

On the other hand, the power of jurisdiction is that which is conferred by a mere human appointment. Such a power as this does not adhere to the recipient immovably: so that it does not remain in heretics and schismatics; and consequently they neither absolve nor excommunicate, nor grant indulgence, nor do anything of the kind, and if they do, it is invalid.

Accordingly when it is said that such like persons have no spiritual power, it is to be understood as referring either to the second power, or if it be referred to the first power, not as referring to the essence of the power, but to its lawful use.

This suffices for the Replies to the Objections.

FOURTH ARTICLE [II-II, Q. 39, Art. 4]

Whether It Is Right That Schismatics Should Be Punished with Excommunication?

Objection 1: It would seem that schismatics are not rightly punished with excommunication. For excommunication deprives a man chiefly of a share in the sacraments. But Augustine says (Contra Donat. vi, 5) that "Baptism can be received from a schismatic." Therefore it seems that excommunication is not a fitting punishment for schismatics.

Obj. 2: Further, it is the duty of Christ's faithful to lead back those who have gone astray, wherefore it is written against certain persons (Ezech. 34:4): "That which was driven away you have not brought again, neither have you sought that which was lost." Now schismatics are more easily brought back by such as may hold communion with them. Therefore it seems that they ought not to be excommunicated.

Obj. 3: Further, a double punishment is not inflicted for one and the same sin, according to Nahum 1:9: "God will not judge the same twice" [*Septuagint version]. Now some receive a temporal punishment for the sin of schism, according to 23, qu. 5 [*Gratianus, Decretum, P. II, causa XXIII, qu. 5, can. 44, Quali nos (RP I, 943)], where it is stated: "Both divine and earthly laws have laid down that those who are severed from the unity of the Church, and disturb her peace, must be punished by the secular power." Therefore they ought not to be punished with excommunication.

*On the contrary,* It is written (Num. 16:26): "Depart from the tents of these wicked men," those, to wit, who had caused the schism, "and touch nothing of theirs, lest you be involved in their sins."

*I answer that,* According to Wis. 11:11, "By what things a man sinneth, by the same also he should be punished" [Vulg.: 'he is tormented']. Now a schismatic, as shown above (A. 1), commits a twofold sin: first by separating himself from communion with the members of the Church, and in this respect the fitting punishment for schismatics is that they be excommunicated. Secondly, they refuse submission to the head of the Church, wherefore, since they are unwilling to be controlled by the Church's spiritual power, it is just that they should be compelled by the secular power.

Reply Obj. 1: It is not lawful to receive Baptism from a schismatic, save in a case of necessity, since it is better for a man to quit this life, marked with the sign of Christ, no matter from whom he may receive it, whether from a Jew or a pagan, than deprived of that mark, which is bestowed in Baptism.

Reply Obj. 2: Excommunication does not forbid the intercourse whereby a person by salutary admonitions leads back to the unity of the Church those who are separated from her. Indeed this very separation brings them back somewhat, because through confusion at their separation, they are sometimes led to do penance.

Reply Obj. 3: The punishments of the present life are medicinal, and therefore when one punishment does not suffice to compel a man, another is added: just as physicians employ several bod[il]y medicines when one has no effect. In like manner the Church, when excommunication does not sufficiently restrain certain men, employs the compulsion of the secular arm. If, however, one punishment suffices, another should not be employed.

## QUESTION 40

OF WAR (In Four Articles)

We must now consider war, under which head there are four points of inquiry:

(1) Whether some kind of war is lawful?

(2) Whether it is lawful for clerics to fight?

(3) Whether it is lawful for belligerents to lay ambushes?

(4) Whether it is lawful to fight on holy days?

FIRST ARTICLE [II-II, Q. 40, Art. 1]

Whether It Is Always Sinful to Wage War?

Objection 1: It would seem that it is always sinful to wage war. Because punishment is not inflicted except for sin. Now those who wage war are threatened by Our Lord with punishment, according to Matt. 26:52: "All that take the sword shall perish with the sword." Therefore all wars are unlawful.

Obj. 2: Further, whatever is contrary to a Divine precept is a sin. But war is contrary to a Divine precept, for it is written (Matt. 5:39): "But I say to you not to resist evil"; and (Rom. 12:19): "Not revenging yourselves, my dearly beloved, but give place unto wrath." Therefore war is always sinful.

Obj. 3: Further, nothing, except sin, is contrary to an act of virtue. But war is contrary to peace. Therefore war is always a sin.

Obj. 4: Further, the exercise of a lawful thing is itself lawful, as is evident in scientific exercises. But warlike exercises which take place in tournaments are forbidden by the Church, since those who are slain in these trials are deprived of ecclesiastical burial. Therefore it seems that war is a sin in itself.

*On the contrary,* Augustine says in a sermon on the son of the centurion [*Ep. ad Marcel. cxxxviii]: "If the Christian Religion forbade war altogether, those who sought salutary advice in the Gospel would rather have been counselled to cast aside their arms, and to give up soldiering altogether. *On the contrary,* they were told: 'Do violence to no man ... and be content with your pay' [*Luke 3:14]. If he commanded them to be content with their pay, he did not forbid soldiering."

*I answer that,* In order for a war to be just, three things are necessary. First, the authority of the sovereign by whose command the war is to be waged. For it is not the business of a private individual to declare war, because he can seek for redress of his rights from the tribunal of his superior. Moreover it is not the business of a private individual to summon together the people, which has to be done in wartime. And as the care of the common weal is committed to those who are in authority, it is their business to watch over the common weal of the city, kingdom or province subject to them. And just as it is lawful for them to have recourse to the sword in defending that common weal against internal disturbances, when they punish evil-doers, according to the words of the Apostle (Rom. 13:4): "He beareth not the sword in vain: for he is God's minister, an avenger to execute wrath upon him that doth evil"; so too, it is their business to have recourse to the sword of war in defending the common weal against external enemies. Hence it is said to those who are in authority (Ps. 81:4): "Rescue the poor: and deliver the needy out of the hand of the sinner"; and for this reason Augustine says (Contra Faust. xxii, 75): "The natural order conducive to peace among mortals demands that the power to declare and counsel war should be in the hands of those who hold the supreme authority."

Secondly, a just cause is required, namely that those who are attacked, should be attacked because they deserve it on account of some fault. Wherefore Augustine says (QQ. in Hept., qu. x, super Jos.): "A just war is wont to be described as one that avenges wrongs, when a nation or state has to be punished, for refusing to make amends for the wrongs inflicted by its subjects, or to restore what it has seized unjustly."

Thirdly, it is necessary that the belligerents should have a rightful intention, so that they intend the advancement of good, or the avoidance of evil. Hence Augustine says (De Verb. Dom. [*The words quoted are to be found not in St. Augustine's works, but Can. Apud. Caus. xxiii, qu. 1]): "True religion looks upon as peaceful those wars that are waged not for motives of aggrandizement, or cruelty, but with the object of securing peace, of punishing evil-doers, and of uplifting the good." For it may happen that the war is declared by the legitimate authority, and for a just cause, and yet be rendered unlawful through a wicked intention. Hence Augustine says (Contra Faust. xxii, 74): "The passion for inflicting harm, the cruel thirst for vengeance, an unpacific and relentless spirit, the fever of revolt, the lust of power, and such like things, all these are rightly condemned in war."

Reply Obj. 1: As Augustine says (Contra Faust. xxii, 70): "To take the sword is to arm oneself in order to take the life of anyone, without the command or permission of superior or lawful authority." On the other hand, to have recourse to the sword (as a private person) by the authority of the sovereign or judge, or (as a public person) through zeal for justice, and by the authority, so to speak, of God, is not to "take the sword," but to use it as commissioned by another, wherefore it does not deserve punishment. And yet even those who make sinful use of the sword are not always slain with the sword, yet they always perish with their own sword, because, unless they repent, they are punished eternally for their sinful use of the sword.

Reply Obj. 2: Such like precepts, as Augustine observes (De Serm. Dom. in Monte i, 19), should always be borne in readiness of mind, so that we be ready to obey them, and, if necessary, to refrain from resistance or self-defense. Nevertheless it is necessary sometimes for a man to act otherwise for the common good, or for the good of those with whom he is fighting. Hence Augustine says (Ep. ad Marcellin. cxxxviii): "Those whom we have to punish with a kindly severity, it is necessary to handle in many ways against their will. For when we are stripping a man of the lawlessness of sin, it is good for him to be vanquished, since nothing is more hopeless than the happiness of sinners, whence arises a guilty impunity, and an evil will, like an internal enemy."

Reply Obj. 3: Those who wage war justly aim at peace, and so they are not opposed to peace, except to the evil peace, which Our Lord "came not to send upon earth" (Matt. 10:34). Hence Augustine says (Ep. ad Bonif. clxxxix): "We do not seek peace in order to be at war, but we go to war that we may have peace. Be peaceful, therefore, in warring, so that you may vanquish those whom you war against, and bring them to the prosperity of peace."

Reply Obj. 4: Manly exercises in warlike feats of arms are not all forbidden, but those which are inordinate and perilous, and end in slaying or plundering. In olden times warlike exercises presented no such danger, and hence they were called "exercises of arms" or "bloodless wars," as Jerome states in an epistle [*Reference incorrect: cf. Veget., De Re Milit. i].

SECOND ARTICLE [II-II, Q. 40, Art. 2]

Whether It Is Lawful for Clerics and Bishops to Fight?

Objection 1: It would seem lawful for clerics and bishops to fight. For, as stated above (A. 1), wars are lawful and just in so far as they protect the poor and the entire common weal from suffering at the hands of the foe. Now this seems to be above all the duty of prelates, for Gregory says (Hom. in Ev. xiv): "The wolf comes upon the sheep, when any unjust and rapacious man oppresses those who are faithful and humble. But he who was thought to be the shepherd, and was not, leaveth the sheep, and flieth, for he fears lest the wolf hurt him, and dares not stand up against his injustice." Therefore it is lawful for prelates and clerics to fight.

Obj. 2: Further, Pope Leo IV writes (xxiii, qu. 8, can. Igitur): "As untoward tidings had frequently come from the Saracen side, some said that the Saracens would come to the port of Rome secretly and covertly; for which reason we commanded our people to gather together, and ordered them to go down to the seashore." Therefore it is lawful for bishops to fight.

Obj. 3: Further, apparently, it comes to the same whether a man does a thing himself, or consents to its being done by another, according to Rom. 1:32: "They who do such things, are worthy of death, and not only they that do them, but they also that consent to them that do them." Now those, above all, seem to consent to a thing, who induce others to do it. But it is lawful for bishops and clerics to induce others to fight: for it is written (xxiii, qu. 8, can. Hortatu) that Charles went to war with the Lombards at the instance and entreaty of Adrian, bishop of Rome. Therefore they also are allowed to fight.

Obj. 4: Further, whatever is right and meritorious in itself, is lawful for prelates and clerics. Now it is sometimes right and meritorious to make war, for it is written (xxiii, qu. 8, can. Omni timore) that if "a man die for the true faith, or to save his country, or in defense of Christians, God will give him a heavenly reward." Therefore it is lawful for bishops and clerics to fight.

*On the contrary,* It was said to Peter as representing bishops and clerics (Matt. 16:52): "Put up again thy sword into the scabbard [Vulg.: 'its place'] [*"Scabbard" is the reading in John 18:11]." Therefore it is not lawful for them to fight.

*I answer that,* Several things are requisite for the good of a human society: and a number of things are done better and quicker by a number of persons than by one, as the Philosopher observes (Polit. i, 1), while certain occupations are so inconsistent with one another, that they cannot be fittingly exercised at the same time; wherefore those who are deputed to important duties are forbidden to occupy themselves with things of small importance. Thus according to human laws, soldiers who are deputed to warlike pursuits are forbidden to engage in commerce [*Cod. xii, 35, De Re Milit.].

Now warlike pursuits are altogether incompatible with the duties of a bishop and a cleric, for two reasons. The first reason is a general one, because, to wit, warlike pursuits are full of unrest, so that they hinder the mind very much from the contemplation of Divine things, the praise of God, and prayers for the people, which belong to the duties of a cleric. Wherefore just as commercial enterprises are forbidden to clerics, because they unsettle the mind too much, so too are warlike pursuits, according to 2 Tim. 2:4: "No man being a soldier to God, entangleth himself with secular business." The second reason is a special one, because, to wit, all the clerical Orders are directed to the ministry of the altar, on which the Passion of Christ is represented sacramentally, according to 1 Cor. 11:26: "As often as you shall eat this bread, and drink the chalice, you shall show the death of the Lord, until He come." Wherefore it is unbecoming for them to slay or shed blood, and it is more fitting that they should be ready to shed their own blood for Christ, so as to imitate in deed what they portray in their ministry. For this reason it has been decreed that those who shed blood, even without sin, become irregular. Now no man who has a certain duty to perform, can lawfully do that which renders him unfit for that duty. Wherefore it is altogether unlawful for clerics to fight, because war is directed to the shedding of blood.

Reply Obj. 1: Prelates ought to withstand not only the wolf who brings spiritual death upon the flock, but also the pillager and the oppressor who work bodily harm; not, however, by having recourse themselves to material arms, but by means of spiritual weapons, according to the saying of the Apostle (2 Cor. 10:4): "The weapons of our warfare are not carnal, but mighty through God." Such are salutary warnings, devout prayers, and, for those who are obstinate, the sentence of excommunication.

Reply Obj. 2: Prelates and clerics may, by the authority of their superiors, take part in wars, not indeed by taking up arms themselves, but by affording spiritual help to those who fight justly, by exhorting and absolving them, and by other like spiritual helps. Thus in the Old Testament (Joshua 6:4) the priests were commanded to sound the sacred trumpets in the battle. It was for this purpose that bishops or clerics were first allowed to go to the front: and it is an abuse of this permission, if any of them take up arms themselves.

Reply Obj. 3: As stated above (Q. 23, A. 4, ad 2) every power, art or virtue that regards the end, has to dispose that which is directed to the end. Now, among the faithful, carnal wars should be considered as having for their end the Divine spiritual good to which clerics are deputed. Wherefore it is the duty of clerics to dispose and counsel other men to engage in just wars. For they are forbidden to take up arms, not as though it were a sin, but because such an occupation is unbecoming their personality.

Reply Obj. 4: Although it is meritorious to wage a just war, nevertheless it is rendered unlawful for clerics, by reason of their being deputed to works more meritorious still. Thus the marriage act may be meritorious; and yet it becomes reprehensible in those who have vowed virginity, because they are bound to a yet greater good.

THIRD ARTICLE [II-II, Q., 40, Art. 3]

Whether It Is Lawful to Lay Ambushes in War?

Objection 1: It would seem that it is unlawful to lay ambushes in war. For it is written (Deut. 16:20): "Thou shalt follow justly after that which is just." But ambushes, since they are a kind of deception, seem to pertain to injustice. Therefore it is unlawful to lay ambushes even in a just war.

Obj. 2: Further, ambushes and deception seem to be opposed to faithfulness even as lies are. But since we are bound to keep faith with all men, it is wrong to lie to anyone, as Augustine states (Contra Mend. xv). Therefore, as one is bound to keep faith with one's enemy, as Augustine states (Ep. ad Bonif. clxxxix), it seems that it is unlawful to lay ambushes for one's enemies.

Obj. 3: Further, it is written (Matt. 7:12): "Whatsoever you would that men should do to you, do you also to them": and we ought to observe this in all our dealings with our neighbor. Now our enemy is our neighbor. Therefore, since no man wishes ambushes or deceptions to be prepared for himself, it seems that no one ought to carry on war by laying ambushes.

*On the contrary,* Augustine says (QQ. in Hept. qu. x super Jos): "Provided the war be just, it is no concern of justice whether it be carried on openly or by ambushes": and he proves this by the authority of the Lord, Who commanded Joshua to lay ambushes for the city of Hai (Joshua 8:2).

*I answer that,* The object of laying ambushes is in order to deceive the enemy. Now a man may be deceived by another's word or deed in two ways. First, through being told something false, or through the breaking of a promise, and this is always unlawful. No one ought to deceive the enemy in this way, for there are certain "rights of war and covenants, which ought to be observed even among enemies," as Ambrose states (De Officiis i).

Secondly, a man may be deceived by what we say or do, because we do not declare our purpose or meaning to him. Now we are not always bound to do this, since even in the Sacred Doctrine many things have to be concealed, especially from unbelievers, lest they deride it, according to Matt. 7:6: "Give not that which is holy, to dogs." Wherefore much more ought the plan of campaign to be hidden from the enemy. For this reason among other things that a soldier has to learn is the art of concealing his purpose lest it come to the enemy's knowledge, as stated in the Book on *Strategy* [*Stratagematum i, 1] by Frontinus. Such like concealment is what is meant by an ambush which may be lawfully employed in a just war.

Nor can these ambushes be properly called deceptions, nor are they contrary to justice or to a well-ordered will. For a man would have an inordinate will if he were unwilling that others should hide anything from him.

This suffices for the Replies to the Objections.

FOURTH ARTICLE [II-II, Q. 40, Art. 4]

Whether It Is Lawful to Fight on Holy Days?

Objection 1: It would seem unlawful to fight on holy days. For holy days are instituted that we may give our time to the things of God. Hence they are included in the keeping of the Sabbath prescribed Ex. 20:8: for "sabbath" is interpreted "rest." But wars are full of unrest. Therefore by no means is it lawful to fight on holy days.

Obj. 2: Further, certain persons are reproached (Isa. 58:3) because on fast-days they exacted what was owing to them, were guilty of strife, and of smiting with the fist. Much more, therefore, is it unlawful to fight on holy days.

Obj. 3: Further, no ill deed should be done to avoid temporal harm. But fighting on a holy day seems in itself to be an ill deed. Therefore no one should fight on a holy day even through the need of avoiding temporal harm.

*On the contrary,* It is written (1 Mac. 2:41): The Jews rightly determined ... saying: "Whosoever shall come up against us to fight on the Sabbath-day, we will fight against him."

*I answer that,* The observance of holy days is no hindrance to those things which are ordained to man's safety, even that of his body. Hence Our Lord argued with the Jews, saying (John 7:23): "Are you angry at Me because I have healed the whole man on the Sabbath-day?" Hence physicians may lawfully attend to their patients on holy days. Now there is much more reason for safeguarding the common weal (whereby many are saved from being slain, and innumerable evils both temporal and spiritual prevented), than the bodily safety of an individual. Therefore, for the purpose of safeguarding the common weal of the faithful, it is lawful to carry on a war on holy days, provided there be need for doing so: because it would be to tempt God, if notwithstanding such a need, one were to choose to refrain from fighting.

However, as soon as the need ceases, it is no longer lawful to fight on a holy day, for the reasons given: wherefore this suffices for the Replies to the Objections.

# QUESTION 41

OF STRIFE (In Two Articles) [*Strife here denotes fighting between individuals]

We must now consider strife, under which head there are two points of inquiry:

(1) Whether strife is a sin?

(2) Whether it is a daughter of anger?

FIRST ARTICLE [II-II, Q. 41, Art. 1]

Whether Strife Is Always a Sin?

Objection 1: It would seem that strife is not always a sin. For strife seems a kind of contention: hence Isidore says (Etym. x) that the word "rixosus [quarrelsome] is derived from the snarling [rictu] of a dog, because the quarrelsome man is ever ready to contradict; he delights in brawling, and provokes contention." Now contention is not always a sin. Neither, therefore, is strife.

Obj. 2: Further, it is related (Gen. 26:21) that the servants of Isaac "digged" another well, "and for that they quarrelled likewise." Now it is not credible that the household of Isaac quarrelled publicly, without being reproved by him, supposing it were a sin. Therefore strife is not a sin.

Obj. 3: Further, strife seems to be a war between individuals. But war is not always sinful. Therefore strife is not always a sin.

*On the contrary,* Strifes [*The Douay version has 'quarrels'] are reckoned among the works of the flesh (Gal. 5:20), and "they who do such things shall not obtain the kingdom of God." Therefore strifes are not only sinful, but they are even mortal sins.

*I answer that,* While contention implies a contradiction of words, strife denotes a certain contradiction of deeds. Wherefore a gloss on Gal. 5:20 says that "strifes are when persons strike one another through anger." Hence strife is a kind of private war, because it takes place between private persons, being declared not by public authority, but rather by an inordinate will. Therefore strife is always sinful. In fact it is a mortal sin in the man who attacks another unjustly, for it is not without mortal sin that one inflicts harm on another even if the deed be done by the hands. But in him who defends himself, it may be without sin, or it may sometimes involve a venial sin, or sometimes a mortal sin; and this depends on his intention and on his manner of defending himself. For if his sole intention be to withstand the injury done to him, and he defend himself with due moderation, it is no sin, and one cannot say properly that there is strife on his part. But if, on the other hand, his self-defense be inspired by vengeance and hatred, it is always a sin. It is a venial sin, if a slight movement of hatred or vengeance obtrude itself, or if he does not much exceed moderation in defending himself: but it is a mortal sin if he makes for his assailant with the fixed intention of killing him, or inflicting grievous harm on him.

Reply Obj. 1: Strife is not just the same as contention: and there are three things in the passage quoted from Isidore, which express the inordinate nature of strife. First, the quarrelsome man is always ready to fight, and this is conveyed by the words, "ever ready to contradict," that is to say, whether the other man says or does well or ill. Secondly, he delights in quarrelling itself, and so the passage proceeds, "and delights in brawling." Thirdly, "he" provokes others to quarrel, wherefore it goes on, "and provokes contention."

Reply Obj. 1: The sense of the text is not that the servants of Isaac quarrelled, but that the inhabitants of that country quarrelled with them: wherefore these sinned, and not the servants of Isaac, who bore the calumny [*Cf. Gen. 26:20].

Reply Obj. 3: In order for a war to be just it must be declared by authority of the governing power, as stated above (Q. 40, A. 1); whereas strife proceeds from a private feeling of anger or hatred. For if the servants of a sovereign or judge, in virtue of their public authority, attack certain men and these defend themselves, it is not the former who are said to be guilty of strife, but those who resist the public authority. Hence it is not the assailants in this case who are guilty of strife and commit sin, but those who defend themselves inordinately.

SECOND ARTICLE [II-II, Q. 41, Art. 2]

Whether Strife Is a Daughter of Anger?

Objection 1: It would seem that strife is not a daughter of anger. For it is written (James 4:1): "Whence are wars and contentions? Are they not

... from your concupiscences, which war in your members?" But anger is not in the concupiscible faculty. Therefore strife is a daughter, not of anger, but of concupiscence.

Obj. 2: Further, it is written (Prov. 28:25): "He that boasteth and puffeth up himself, stirreth up quarrels." Now strife is apparently the same as quarrel. Therefore it seems that strife is a daughter of pride or vainglory which makes a man boast and puff himself up.

Obj. 3: Further, it is written (Prov. 18:6): "The lips of a fool intermeddle with strife." Now folly differs from anger, for it is opposed, not to meekness, but to wisdom or prudence. Therefore strife is not a daughter of anger.

Obj. 4: Further, it is written (Prov. 10:12): "Hatred stirreth up strifes." But hatred arises from envy, according to Gregory (Moral. xxxi, 17). Therefore strife is not a daughter of anger, but of envy.

Obj. 5: Further, it is written (Prov. 17:19): "He that studieth discords, soweth [Vulg.: 'loveth'] quarrels." But discord is a daughter of vainglory, as stated above (Q. 37, A. 2). Therefore strife is also.

*On the contrary,* Gregory says (Moral. xxxi, 17) that "anger gives rise to strife"; and it is written (Prov. 15:18; 29:22): "A passionate man stirreth up strifes."

*I answer that,* As stated above (A. 1), strife denotes an antagonism extending to deeds, when one man designs to harm another. Now there are two ways in which one man may intend to harm another. In one way it is as though he intended absolutely the other's hurt, which in this case is the outcome of hatred, for the intention of hatred is directed to the hurt of one's enemy either openly or secretly. In another way a man intends to hurt another who knows and withstands his intention. This is what we mean by strife, and belongs properly to anger which is the desire of vengeance: for the angry man is not content to hurt secretly the object of his anger, he even wishes him to feel the hurt and know that what he suffers is in revenge for what he has done, as may be seen from what has been said above about the passion of anger (I-II, Q. 46, A. 6, ad 2). Therefore, properly speaking, strife arises from anger.

Reply Obj. 1: As stated above (I-II, Q. 25, AA. 1, 2), all the irascible passions arise from those of the concupiscible faculty, so that whatever is the immediate outcome of anger, arises also from concupiscence as from its first root.

Reply Obj. 2: Boasting and puffing up of self which are the result of anger or vainglory, are not the direct but the occasional cause of quarrels or strife, because, when a man resents another being preferred to him, his anger is aroused, and then his anger results in quarrel and strife.

Reply Obj. 3: Anger, as stated above (I-II, Q. 48, A. 3) hinders the judgment of the reason, so that it bears a likeness to folly. Hence they have a common effect, since it is due to a defect in the reason that a man designs to hurt another inordinately.

Reply Obj. 4: Although strife sometimes arises from hatred, it is not the proper effect thereof, because when one man hates another it is beside his intention to hurt him in a quarrelsome and open manner, since sometimes he seeks to hurt him secretly. When, however, he sees himself prevailing, he endeavors to harm him with strife and quarrel. But to hurt a man in a quarrel is the proper effect of anger, for the reason given above.

Reply Obj. 5: Strifes give rise to hatred and discord in the hearts of those who are guilty of strife, and so he that "studies," i.e., intends to sow discord among others, causes them to quarrel among themselves. Even so any sin may command the act of another sin, by directing it to its own end. This does not, however, prove that strife is the daughter of vainglory properly and directly.

## QUESTION 42

OF SEDITION (In Two Articles)

We must now consider sedition, under which head there are two points of inquiry:

(1) Whether it is a special sin?

(2) Whether it is a mortal sin?

FIRST ARTICLE [II-II, Q. 42, Art. 1]

Whether Sedition Is a Special Sin Distinct from Other Sins?

Objection 1: It would seem that sedition is not a special sin distinct from other sins. For, according to Isidore (Etym. x), "a seditious man is one who sows dissent among minds, and begets discord." Now, by provoking the commission of a sin, a man sins by no other kind of sin than that which he provoked. Therefore it seems that sedition is not a special sin distinct from discord.

Obj. 2: Further, sedition denotes a kind of division. Now schism takes its name from scission, as stated above (Q. 39, A. 1). Therefore, seemingly, the sin of sedition is not distinct from that of schism.

Obj. 3: Further, every special sin that is distinct from other sins, is either a capital vice, or arises from some capital vice. Now sedition is reckoned neither among the capital vices, nor among those vices which arise from them, as appears from Moral. xxxi, 45, where both kinds of vice are enumerated. Therefore sedition is not a special sin, distinct from other sins.

*On the contrary,* Seditions are mentioned as distinct from other sins (2 Cor. 12:20).

*I answer that,* Sedition is a special sin, having something in common with war and strife, and differing somewhat from them. It has something in common with them, in so far as it implies a certain antagonism, and it differs from them in two points. First, because war and strife denote actual aggression on either side, whereas sedition may be said to denote either actual aggression, or the preparation for such aggression. Hence a gloss on 2 Cor. 12:20 says that "seditions are tumults tending to fight," when, to wit, a number of people make preparations with the intention of fighting. Secondly, they differ in that war is, properly speaking, carried on against external foes, being as it were between one people and another, whereas strife is between one individual and another, or between few people on one side and few on the other side, while sedition, in its proper sense, is between mutually dissentient parts of one people, as when one part of the state rises in tumult against another part. Wherefore, since sedition is opposed to a special kind of good, namely the unity and peace of a people, it is a special kind of sin.

Reply Obj. 1: A seditious man is one who incites others to sedition, and since sedition denotes a kind of discord, it follows that a seditious man is one who creates discord, not of any kind, but between the parts of a multitude. And the sin of sedition is not only in him who sows discord, but also in those who dissent from one another inordinately.

Reply Obj. 2: Sedition differs from schism in two respects. First, because schism is opposed to the spiritual unity of the multitude, viz. ecclesiastical unity, whereas sedition is contrary to the temporal or secular unity of the multitude, for instance of a city or kingdom. Secondly, schism does not imply any preparation for a material fight as sedition does, but only for a spiritual dissent.

Reply Obj. 3: Sedition, like schism, is contained under discord, since each is a kind of discord, not between individuals, but between the parts of a multitude.

SECOND ARTICLE [II-II, Q. 42, Art. 2]

Whether Sedition Is Always a Mortal Sin?

Objection 1: It would seem that sedition is not always a mortal sin. For sedition denotes "a tumult tending to fight," according to the gloss quoted above (A. 1). But fighting is not always a mortal sin, indeed it is sometimes just and lawful, as stated above (Q. 40, A. 1). Much more, therefore, can sedition be without a mortal sin.

Obj. 2: Further, sedition is a kind of discord, as stated above (A. 1, ad 3). Now discord can be without mortal sin, and sometimes without any sin at all. Therefore sedition can be also.

Obj. 3: Further, it is praiseworthy to deliver a multitude from a tyrannical rule. Yet this cannot easily be done without some dissension in the multitude, if one part of the multitude seeks to retain the tyrant, while the rest strive to dethrone him. Therefore there can be sedition without mortal sin.

*On the contrary,* The Apostle forbids seditions together with other things that are mortal sins (2 Cor. 12:20).

*I answer that,* As stated above (A. 1, ad 2), sedition is contrary to the unity of the multitude, viz. the people of a city or kingdom. Now Augustine says (De Civ. Dei ii, 21) that "wise men understand the word people to designate not any crowd of persons, but the assembly of those who are united together in fellowship recognized by law and for the common good." Wherefore it is evident that the unity to which sedition is opposed is the unity of law and common good: whence it follows manifestly that sedition is opposed to justice and the common good. Therefore by reason of its genus it is a mortal sin, and its gravity will be all the greater according as the common good which it assails surpasses the private good which is assailed by strife.

Accordingly the sin of sedition is first and chiefly in its authors, who sin most grievously; and secondly it is in those who are led by them to disturb the common good. Those, however, who defend the common good, and withstand the seditious party, are not themselves seditious, even as neither is a man to be called quarrelsome because he defends himself, as stated above (Q. 41, A. 1).

Reply Obj. 1: It is lawful to fight, provided it be for the common good, as stated above (Q. 40, A. 1). But sedition runs counter to the common good of the multitude, so that it is always a mortal sin.

Reply Obj. 2: Discord from what is not evidently good, may be without sin, but discord from what is evidently good, cannot be without sin: and sedition is discord of this kind, for it is contrary to the unity of the multitude, which is a manifest good.

Reply Obj. 3: A tyrannical government is not just, because it is directed, not to the common good, but to the private good of the ruler, as the Philosopher states (Polit. iii, 5; *Ethic.* viii, 10). Consequently there is no sedition in disturbing a government of this kind, unless indeed the tyrant's rule be disturbed so inordinately, that his subjects suffer greater harm from the consequent disturbance than from the tyrant's government. Indeed it is the tyrant rather that is guilty of sedition, since he encourages discord and sedition among his subjects, that he may lord over them more securely; for this is tyranny, being conducive to the private good of the ruler, and to the injury of the multitude.

## QUESTION 43

OF SCANDAL (In Eight Articles)

It remains for us to consider the vices which are opposed to beneficence, among which some come under the head of injustice, those, to wit, whereby one harms one's neighbor unjustly. But scandal seems to be specially opposed to charity. Accordingly we must here consider scandal, under which head there are eight points of inquiry:

(1) What is scandal?

(2) Whether scandal is a sin?

(3) Whether it is a special sin?

(4) Whether it is a mortal sin?

(5) Whether the perfect can be scandalized?

(6) Whether they can give scandal?

(7) Whether spiritual goods are to be foregone on account of scandal?

(8) Whether temporal things are to be foregone on account of scandal?

FIRST ARTICLE [II-II, Q. 43, Art. 1]

Whether Scandal Is Fittingly Defined As Being Something Less Rightly Said or Done That Occasions Spiritual Downfall?

Objection 1: It would seem that scandal is unfittingly defined as "something less rightly said or done that occasions spiritual downfall." For scandal is a sin as we shall state further on (A. 2). Now, according to Augustine (Contra Faust. xxii, 27), a sin is a "word, deed, or desire contrary to the law of God." Therefore the definition given above is insufficient, since it omits "thought" or "desire."

Obj. 2: Further, since among virtuous or right acts one is more virtuous or more right than another, that one alone which has perfect rectitude would not seem to be a "less" right one. If, therefore, scandal is something "less" rightly said or done, it follows that every virtuous act except the best of all, is a scandal.

Obj. 3: Further, an occasion is an accidental cause. But nothing accidental should enter a definition, because it does not specify the thing defined. Therefore it is unfitting, in defining scandal, to say that it is an "occasion."

Obj. 4: Further, whatever a man does may be the occasion of another's spiritual downfall, because accidental causes are indeterminate. Consequently, if scandal is something that occasions another's spiritual downfall, any deed or word can be a scandal: and this seems unreasonable.

Obj. 5: Further, a man occasions his neighbor's spiritual downfall when he offends or weakens him. Now scandal is condivided with offense and weakness, for the Apostle says (Rom. 14:21): "It is good not to eat flesh, and not to drink wine, nor anything whereby thy brother is offended or scandalized, or weakened." Therefore the aforesaid definition of scandal is unfitting.

*On the contrary,* Jerome in expounding Matt. 15:12, "Dost thou know that the Pharisees, when they heard this word," etc. says: "When we read 'Whosoever shall scandalize,' the sense is 'Whosoever shall, by deed or word, occasion another's spiritual downfall.'"

*I answer that,* As Jerome observes the Greek skandalon may be rendered offense, downfall, or a stumbling against something. For when a body, while moving along a path, meets with an obstacle, it may happen to stumble against it, and be disposed to fall down: such an obstacle is a skandalon .

In like manner, while going along the spiritual way, a man may be disposed to a spiritual downfall by another's word or deed, in so far, to wit, as one man by his injunction, inducement or example, moves another to sin; and this is scandal properly so called.

Now nothing by its very nature disposes a man to spiritual downfall, except that which has some lack of rectitude, since what is perfectly right, secures man against a fall, instead of conducing to his downfall. Scandal is, therefore, fittingly defined as "something less rightly done or said, that occasions another's spiritual downfall."

Reply Obj. 1: The thought or desire of evil lies hidden in the heart, wherefore it does not suggest itself to another man as an obstacle conducing to his spiritual downfall: hence it cannot come under the head of scandal.

Reply Obj. 2: A thing is said to be less right, not because something else surpasses it in rectitude, but because it has some lack of rectitude, either through being evil in itself, such as sin, or through having an appearance of evil. Thus, for instance, if a man were to "sit at meat in the idol's temple" (1 Cor. 8:10), though this is not sinful in itself, provided it be done with no evil intention, yet, since it has a certain appearance of evil, and a semblance of worshipping the idol, it might occasion another man's spiritual downfall. Hence the Apostle says (1 Thess. 5:22): "From all appearance of evil refrain yourselves." Scandal is therefore fittingly described as something done "less rightly," so as to comprise both whatever is sinful in itself, and all that has an appearance of evil.

Reply Obj. 3: As stated above (I-II, Q. 75, AA. 2, 3; I-II, Q. 80, A. 1), nothing can be a sufficient cause of a man's spiritual downfall, which is sin, save his own will. Wherefore another man's words or deeds can only be an imperfect cause, conducing somewhat to that downfall. For this reason scandal is said to afford not a cause, but an occasion, which is an imperfect, and not always an accidental cause. Nor is there any reason why certain definitions should not make mention of things that are accidental, since what is accidental to one, may be proper to something else: thus the accidental cause is mentioned in the definition of chance (Phys. ii, 5).

Reply Obj. 4: Another's words or deed may be the cause of another's sin in two ways, directly and accidentally. Directly, when a man either intends, by his evil word or deed, to lead another man into sin, or, if he does not so intend, when his deed is of such a nature as to lead another into sin: for instance, when a man publicly commits a sin or does something that has an appearance of sin. In this case he that does such an act does, properly speaking, afford an occasion of another's spiritual downfall, wherefore his act is called "active scandal." One man's word or deed is the accidental cause of another's sin, when he neither intends to lead him into sin, nor does what is of a nature to lead him into sin, and yet this other one, through being ill-disposed, is led into sin, for instance, into envy of another's good, and then he who does this righteous act, does not, so far as he is concerned, afford an occasion of the other's downfall, but it is this other one who takes the occasion according to Rom. 7:8: "Sin taking occasion by the commandment wrought in me all manner of concupiscence." Wherefore this is "passive," without "active scandal," since he that acts rightly does not, for his own part, afford the occasion of the other's downfall. Sometimes therefore it happens that there is active scandal in the one together with passive scandal in the other, as when one commits a sin being induced thereto by another; sometimes there is active without passive scandal, for instance when one, by word or deed, provokes another to sin, and the latter does not consent; and sometimes there is passive without active scandal, as we have already said.

Reply Obj. 5: "Weakness" denotes proneness to scandal; while "offense" signifies resentment against the person who commits a sin, which resentment may be sometimes without spiritual downfall; and "scandal" is the stumbling that results in downfall.

SECOND ARTICLE [II-II, Q. 43, Art. 2]

Whether Scandal Is a Sin?

Objection 1: It would seem that scandal is not a sin. For sins do not occur from necessity, since all sin is voluntary, as stated above (I-II, Q. 74, AA. 1, 2). Now it is written (Matt. 18:7): "It must needs be that scandals come." Therefore scandal is not a sin.

Obj. 2: Further, no sin arises from a sense of dutifulness, because "a good tree cannot bring forth evil fruit" (Matt. 7:18). But scandal may come from a sense of dutifulness, for Our Lord said to Peter (Matt. 16:23): "Thou art a scandal unto Me," in reference to which words Jerome says that "the Apostle's error was due to his sense of dutifulness, and such is never inspired by the devil." Therefore scandal is not always a sin.

Obj. 3: Further, scandal denotes a stumbling. But he that stumbles does not always fall. Therefore scandal, which is a spiritual fall, can be without sin.

*On the contrary,* Scandal is "something less rightly said or done." Now anything that lacks rectitude is a sin. Therefore scandal is always with sin.

*I answer that,* As already said (A. 1, ad 4), scandal is of two kinds, passive scandal in the person scandalized, and active scandal in the person who gives scandal, and so occasions a spiritual downfall. Accordingly passive scandal is always a sin in the person scandalized; for he is not scandalized except in so far as he succumbs to a spiritual downfall, and that is a sin.

Yet there can be passive scandal, without sin on the part of the person whose action has occasioned the scandal, as for instance, when a person is scandalized at another's good deed. In like manner active scandal is always a sin in the person who gives scandal, since either what he does is a sin, or if it only have the appearance of sin, it should always be left undone out of that love for our neighbor which binds each one to be solicitous for his neighbor's spiritual welfare; so that if he persist in doing it he acts against charity.

Yet there can be active scandal without sin on the part of the person scandalized, as stated above (A. 1, ad 4).

Reply Obj. 1: These words, "It must needs be that scandals come," are to be understood to convey, not the absolute, but the conditional necessity of scandal; in which sense it is necessary that whatever God foresees or foretells must happen, provided it be taken conjointly with such foreknowledge, as explained in the First Part (Q. 14, A. 13, ad 3; Q. 23, A. 6, ad 2).

Or we may say that the necessity of scandals occurring is a necessity of end, because they are useful in order that "they ... who are reproved may be made manifest" (1 Cor. 11:19).

Or scandals must needs occur, seeing the condition of man who fails to shield himself from sin. Thus a physician on seeing a man partaking of unsuitable food might say that such a man must needs injure his health, which is to be understood on the condition that he does not change his diet. In like manner it must needs be that scandals come, so long as men fail to change their evil mode of living.

Reply Obj. 2: In that passage scandal denotes any kind of hindrance: for Peter wished to hinder Our Lord's Passion out of a sense of dutifulness towards Christ.

Reply Obj. 3: No man stumbles spiritually, without being kept back somewhat from advancing in God's way, and that is at least a venial sin.

THIRD ARTICLE [II-II, Q. 43, Art. 3]

Whether Scandal Is a Special Sin?

Objection 1: It would seem that scandal is not a special sin. For scandal is "something said or done less rightly." But this applies to every kind of sin. Therefore every sin is a scandal, and consequently, scandal is not a special sin.

Obj. 2: Further, every special kind of sin, or every special kind of injustice, may be found separately from other kinds, as stated in *Ethic.* v, 3, 5. But scandal is not to be found separately from other sins. Therefore it is not a special kind of sin.

Obj. 3: Further, every special sin is constituted by something which specifies the moral act. But the notion of scandal consists in its being something done in the presence of others: and the fact of a sin being committed openly, though it is an aggravating circumstance, does not seem to constitute the species of a sin. Therefore scandal is not a special sin.

*On the contrary,* A special virtue has a special sin opposed to it. But scandal is opposed to a special virtue, viz. charity. For it is written (Rom. 14:15): "If, because of thy meat, thy brother be grieved, thou walkest not now according to charity." Therefore scandal is a special sin.

*I answer that,* As stated above (A. 2), scandal is twofold, active and passive. Passive scandal cannot be a special sin, because through another's word or deed a man may fall into any kind of sin: and the fact that a man takes occasion to sin from another's word or deed, does not constitute a special kind of sin, because it does not imply a special deformity in opposition to a special virtue.

On the other hand, active scandal may be understood in two ways, directly and accidentally. The scandal is accidental when it is beside the agent's intention, as when a man does not intend, by his inordinate deed or word, to occasion another's spiritual downfall, but merely to satisfy his own will. In such a case even active scandal is not a special sin, because a species is not constituted by that which is accidental.

Active scandal is direct when a man intends, by his inordinate word or deed, to draw another into sin, and then it becomes a special kind of sin on account of the intention of a special kind of end, because moral actions take their species from their end, as stated above (I-II, Q. 1, A. 3; Q. 18, AA. 4, 6). Hence, just as theft and murder are special kinds of sin, on account of their denoting the intention of doing a special injury to one's neighbor: so too, scandal is a special kind of sin, because thereby a man intends a special harm to his neighbor, and it is directly opposed to fraternal correction, whereby a man intends the removal of a special kind of harm.

Reply Obj. 1: Any sin may be the matter of active scandal, but it may derive the formal aspect of a special sin from the end intended, as stated above.

Reply Obj. 2: Active scandal can be found separate from other sins, as when a man scandalizes his neighbor by a deed which is not a sin in itself, but has an appearance of evil.

Reply Obj. 3: Scandal does not derive the species of a special sin from the circumstance in question, but from the intention of the end, as stated above.

FOURTH ARTICLE [II-II, Q. 43, Art. 4]

Whether Scandal Is a Mortal Sin?

Objection 1: It would seem that scandal is a mortal sin. For every sin that is contrary to charity is a mortal sin, as stated above (Q. 24, A. 12; Q. 35, A. 3). But scandal is contrary to charity, as stated above (AA. 2, 3). Therefore scandal is a mortal sin.

Obj. 2: Further, no sin, save mortal sin, deserves the punishment of eternal damnation. But scandal deserves the punishment of eternal damnation, according to Matt. 18:6: "He that shall scandalize one of these little ones, that believe in Me, it were better for him that a mill-stone should be hanged about his neck, and that he should be drowned in the depth of the sea." For, as Jerome says on this passage, "it is much better to receive a brief punishment for a fault, than to await everlasting torments." Therefore scandal is a mortal sin.

Obj. 3: Further, every sin committed against God is a mortal sin, because mortal sin alone turns man away from God. Now scandal is a sin against God, for the Apostle says (1 Cor. 8:12): "When you wound the weak conscience of the brethren [*Vulg.: 'When you sin thus against the brethren and wound their weak conscience'], you sin against Christ." Therefore scandal is always a mortal sin.

*On the contrary,* It may be a venial sin to lead a person into venial sin: and yet this would be to give scandal. Therefore scandal may be a venial sin.

*I answer that,* As stated above (A. 1), scandal denotes a stumbling whereby a person is disposed to a spiritual downfall. Consequently passive scandal may sometimes be a venial sin, when it consists in a stumbling and nothing more; for instance, when a person is disturbed by a movement of venial sin occasioned by another's inordinate word or deed: while sometimes it is a mortal sin, when the stumbling results in a downfall, for instance, when a person goes so far as to commit a mortal sin through another's inordinate word or deed.

Active scandal, if it be accidental, may sometimes be a venial sin; for instance, when, through a slight indiscretion, a person either commits a venial sin, or does something that is not a sin in itself, but has some appearance of evil. On the other hand, it is sometimes a mortal sin, either because a person commits a mortal sin, or because he has such contempt for his neighbor's spiritual welfare that he declines, for the sake of procuring it, to forego doing what he wishes to do. But in the case of active direct scandal, as when a person intends to lead another into sin, if he intends to lead him into mortal sin, his own sin will be mortal; and in like manner if he intends by committing a mortal sin himself, to lead another into venial sin; whereas if he intends, by committing a venial sin, to lead another into venial sin, there will be a venial sin of scandal.

And this suffices for the Replies to the Objections.

FIFTH ARTICLE [II-II, Q. 43, Art. 5]

Whether Passive Scandal May Happen Even to the Perfect?

Objection 1: It would seem that passive scandal may happen even to the perfect. For Christ was supremely perfect: and yet He said to Peter (Matt. 16:23): "Thou art a scandal to Me." Much more therefore can other perfect men suffer scandal.

Obj. 2: Further, scandal denotes an obstacle which is put in a person's spiritual way. Now even perfect men can be hindered in their progress along the spiritual way, according to 1 Thess. 2:18: "We would have come to you, I Paul indeed, once and again; but Satan hath hindered us." Therefore even perfect men can suffer scandal.

Obj. 3: Further, even perfect men are liable to venial sins, according to 1 John 1:8: "If we say that we have no sin, we deceive ourselves." Now passive scandal is not always a mortal sin, but is sometimes venial, as stated above (A. 4). Therefore passive scandal may be found in perfect men.

*On the contrary,* Jerome, in commenting on Matt. 18:6, "He that shall scandalize one of these little ones," says: "Observe that it is the little one that is scandalized, for the elders do not take scandal."

*I answer that,* Passive scandal implies that the mind of the person who takes scandal is unsettled in its adherence to good. Now no man can be unsettled, who adheres firmly to something immovable. The elders, i.e. the perfect, adhere to God alone, Whose goodness is unchangeable, for though they adhere to their superiors, they do so only in so far as these adhere to Christ, according to 1 Cor. 4:16: "Be ye followers of me, as I also am of Christ." Wherefore, however much others may appear to them to conduct themselves ill in word or deed, they themselves do not stray from their righteousness, according to Ps. 124:1: "They that trust in the Lord shall be as Mount Sion: he shall not be moved for ever that dwelleth in Jerusalem." Therefore scandal is not found in those who adhere to God perfectly by love, according to Ps. 118:165: "Much peace have they that love Thy law, and to them there is no stumbling-block ( *scandalum* )."

Reply Obj. 1: As stated above (A. 2, ad 2), in this passage, scandal is used in a broad sense, to denote any kind of hindrance. Hence Our Lord said to Peter: "Thou art a scandal to Me," because he was endeavoring to weaken Our Lord's purpose of undergoing His Passion.

Reply Obj. 2: Perfect men may be hindered in the performance of external actions. But they are not hindered by the words or deeds of others, from tending to God in the internal acts of the will, according to Rom. 8:38, 39: "Neither death, nor life ... shall be able to separate us from the love of God."

Reply Obj. 3: Perfect men sometimes fall into venial sins through the weakness of the flesh; but they are not scandalized (taking scandal in its true sense), by the words or deeds of others, although there can be an approach to scandal in them, according to Ps. 72:2: "My feet were almost moved."

SIXTH ARTICLE [II-II, Q. 43, Art. 6]

Whether Active Scandal Can Be Found in the Perfect?

Objection 1: It would seem that active scandal can be found in the perfect. For passion is the effect of action. Now some are scandalized passively by the words or deeds of the perfect, according to Matt. 15:12: "Dost thou know that the Pharisees, when they heard this word, were scandalized?" Therefore active scandal can be found in the perfect.

Obj. 2: Further, Peter, after receiving the Holy Ghost, was in the state of the perfect. Yet afterwards he scandalized the gentiles: for it is written (Gal. 2:14): "When I saw that they walked not uprightly unto the truth of the Gospel, I said to Cephas," i.e. Peter, "before them all: If thou being a Jew, livest after the manner of the gentiles, and not as the Jews do, how dost thou compel the gentiles to live as do the Jews?" Therefore active scandal can be in the perfect.

Obj. 3: Further, active scandal is sometimes a venial sin. But venial sins may be in perfect men. Therefore active scandal may be in perfect men.

*On the contrary,* Active scandal is more opposed to perfection, than passive scandal. But passive scandal cannot be in the perfect. Much less, therefore, can active scandal be in them.

*I answer that,* Active scandal, properly so called, occurs when a man says or does a thing which in itself is of a nature to occasion another's spiritual downfall, and that is only when what he says or does is inordinate. Now it belongs to the perfect to direct all their actions according to the rule of reason, as stated in 1 Cor. 14:40: "Let all things be done decently and according to order"; and they are careful to do this in those matters chiefly wherein not only would they do wrong, but would also be to others an occasion of wrongdoing. And if indeed they fail in this moderation in such words or deeds as come to the knowledge of others, this has its origin in human weakness wherein they fall short of perfection. Yet they do not fall short so far as to stray far from the order of reason, but only a little and in some slight matter: and this is not so grave that anyone can reasonably take therefrom an occasion for committing sin.

Reply Obj. 1: Passive scandal is always due to some active scandal; yet this active scandal is not always in another, but in the very person who is scandalized, because, to wit, he scandalizes himself.

Reply Obj. 2: In the opinion of Augustine (Ep. xxviii, xl, lxxxii) and of Paul also, Peter sinned and was to be blamed, in withdrawing from the gentiles in order to avoid the scandal of the Jews, because he did this somewhat imprudently, so that the gentiles who had been converted to the faith were scandalized. Nevertheless Peter's action was not so grave a sin as to give others sufficient ground for scandal. Hence they were guilty of passive scandal, while there was no active scandal in Peter.

Reply Obj. 3: The venial sins of the perfect consist chiefly in sudden movements, which being hidden cannot give scandal. If, however, they commit any venial sins even in their external words or deeds, these are so slight as to be insufficient in themselves to give scandal.

SEVENTH ARTICLE [II-II, Q. 43, Art. 7]

Whether Spiritual Goods Should Be Foregone on Account of Scandal?

Objection 1: It would seem that spiritual goods ought to be foregone on account of scandal. For Augustine (Contra Ep. Parmen. iii, 2) teaches that "punishment for sin should cease, when the peril of schism is feared." But punishment of sins is a spiritual good, since it is an act of justice. Therefore a spiritual good is to be foregone on account of scandal.

Obj. 2: Further, the Sacred Doctrine is a most

spiritual thing. Yet one ought to desist therefrom on account of scandal, according to Matt. 7:6: "Give not that which is holy to dogs, neither cast ye your pearls before swine lest … turning upon you, they tear you." Therefore a spiritual good should be foregone on account of scandal.

Obj. 3: Further, since fraternal correction is an act of charity, it is a spiritual good. Yet sometimes it is omitted out of charity, in order to avoid giving scandal to others, as Augustine observes (De Civ. Dei i, 9). Therefore a spiritual good should be foregone on account of scandal.

Obj. 4: Further, Jerome [*Hugh de S. Cher., In Matth. xviii; in Luc. xvii, 2] says that in order to avoid scandal we should forego whatever it is possible to omit without prejudice to the threefold truth, i.e. "the truth of life, of justice and of doctrine." Now the observance of the counsels, and the bestowal of alms may often be omitted without prejudice to the aforesaid threefold truth, else whoever omitted them would always be guilty of sin, and yet such things are the greatest of spiritual works. Therefore spiritual works should be omitted on account of scandal.

Obj. 5: Further, the avoidance of any sin is a spiritual good, since any sin brings spiritual harm to the sinner. Now it seems that one ought sometimes to commit a venial sin in order to avoid scandalizing one's neighbor, for instance, when by sinning venially, one would prevent someone else from committing a mortal sin: because one is bound to hinder the damnation of one's neighbor as much as one can without prejudice to one's own salvation, which is not precluded by a venial sin. Therefore one ought to forego a spiritual good in order to avoid scandal.

*On the contrary,* Gregory says (Hom. Super Ezech. vii): "If people are scandalized at the truth, it is better to allow the birth of scandal, than to abandon the truth." Now spiritual goods belong, above all others, to the truth. Therefore spiritual goods are not to be foregone on account of scandal.

*I answer that,* Whereas scandal is twofold, active and passive, the present question does not apply to active scandal, for since active scandal is "something said or done less rightly," nothing ought to be done that implies active scandal. The question does, however, apply to passive scandal, and accordingly we have to see what ought to be foregone in order to avoid scandal. Now a distinction must be made in spiritual goods. For some of them are necessary for salvation, and cannot be foregone without mortal sin: and it is evident that no man ought to commit a mortal sin, in order to prevent another from sinning, because according to the order of charity, a man ought to love his own spiritual welfare more than another's. Therefore one ought not to forego that which is necessary for salvation, in order to avoid giving scandal.

Again a distinction seems necessary among spiritual things which are not necessary for salvation: because the scandal which arises from such things sometimes proceeds from malice, for instance when a man wishes to hinder those spiritual goods by stirring up scandal. This is the "scandal of the Pharisees," who were scandalized at Our Lord's teaching: and Our Lord teaches (Matt. 15:14) that we ought to treat such like scandal with contempt. Sometimes scandal proceeds from weakness or ignorance, and such is the "scandal of little ones." In order to avoid this kind of scandal, spiritual goods ought to be either concealed, or sometimes even deferred (if this can be done without incurring immediate danger), until the matter being explained the scandal cease. If, however, the scandal continue after the matter has been explained, it would seem to be due to malice, and then it would no longer be right to forego that spiritual good in order to avoid such like scandal.

Reply Obj. 1: In the infliction of punishment it is not the punishment itself that is the end in view, but its medicinal properties in checking sin; wherefore punishment partakes of the nature of justice, in so far as it checks sin. But if it is evident that the infliction of punishment will result in more numerous and more grievous sins being committed, the infliction of punishment will no longer be a part of justice. It is in this sense that Augustine is speaking, when, to wit, the excommunication of a few threatens to bring about the danger of a schism, for in that case it would be contrary to the truth of justice to pronounce excommunication.

Reply Obj. 2: With regard to a man's doctrine two points must be considered, namely, the truth which is taught, and the act of teaching. The first of these is necessary for salvation, to wit, that he whose duty it is to teach should not teach what is contrary to the truth, and that he should teach the truth according to the requirements of times and persons: wherefore on no account ought he to suppress the truth and teach error in order to avoid any scandal that might ensue. But the act itself of teaching is one of the spiritual almsdeeds, as stated above (Q. 32, A. 2), and so the same is to be said of it as of the other works of mercy, of which we shall speak further on (ad 4).

Reply Obj. 3: As stated above (Q. 33, A. 1), fraternal correction aims at the correction of a brother, wherefore it is to be reckoned among spiritual goods in so far as this end can be obtained, which is not the case if the brother be scandalized through being corrected. And so, if the correction be omitted in order to avoid scandal, no spiritual good is foregone.

Reply Obj. 4: The truth of life, of doctrine, and of justice comprises not only whatever is necessary for salvation, but also whatever is a means of obtaining salvation more perfectly, according to 1 Cor. 12:31: "Be zealous for the better gifts." Wherefore neither the counsels nor even the works of mercy are to be altogether omitted in order to avoid scandal; but sometimes they should be concealed or deferred, on account of the scandal of the little ones, as stated above. Sometimes, however, the observance of the counsels and the fulfilment of the works of mercy are necessary for salvation. This may be seen in the case of those who have vowed to keep the counsels, and of those whose duty it is to relieve the wants of others, either in temporal matters (as by feeding the hungry), or in spiritual matters (as by instructing the ignorant), whether such duties arise from their being enjoined as in the case of prelates, or from the need on the part of the person in want; and then the same applies to these things as to others that are necessary for salvation.

Reply Obj. 5: Some have said that one ought to commit a venial sin in order to avoid scandal. But this implies a contradiction, since if it ought to be done, it is no longer evil or sinful, for a sin cannot be a matter of choice. It may happen however that, on account of some circumstance, something is not a venial sin, though it would be were it not for that circumstance: thus an idle word is a venial sin, when it is uttered uselessly; yet if it be uttered for a reasonable cause, it is neither idle nor sinful. And though venial sin does not deprive a man of grace which is his means of salvation, yet, in so far as it disposes him to mortal sin, it tends to the loss of salvation.

EIGHTH ARTICLE [II-II, Q. 43, Art. 8]

Whether Temporal Goods Should Be Foregone on Account of Scandal?

Objection 1: It would seem that temporal goods should be foregone on account of scandal. For we ought to love our neighbor's spiritual welfare which is hindered by scandal, more than any temporal goods whatever. But we forego what we love less for the sake of what we love more. Therefore we should forego temporal goods in order to avoid scandalizing our neighbor.

Obj. 2: Further, according to Jerome's rule [*Cf. A. 7, Obj. 4], whatever can be foregone without prejudice to the threefold truth, should be omitted in order to avoid scandal. Now temporal goods can be foregone without prejudice to the threefold truth. Therefore they should be foregone in order to avoid scandal.

Obj. 3: Further, no temporal good is more necessary than food. But we ought to forego taking food on account of scandal, according to Rom. 14:15: "Destroy not him with thy meat for whom Christ died." Much more therefore should all other temporal goods be foregone on account of scandal.

Obj. 4: Further, the most fitting way of safeguarding and recovering temporal goods is the court of justice. But it is unlawful to have recourse to justice, especially if scandal ensues: for it is written (Matt. 5:40): "If a man will contend with thee in judgment, and take away thy coat, let go thy cloak also unto him"; and (1 Cor. 6:7): "Already indeed there is plainly a fault among you, that you have lawsuits one with another. Why do you not rather take wrong? why do you not rather suffer yourselves to be defrauded?" Therefore it seems that we ought to forego temporal goods on account of scandal.

Obj. 5: Further, we ought, seemingly, to forego least of all those temporal goods which are connected with spiritual goods: and yet we ought to forego them on account of scandal. For the Apostle while sowing spiritual things did not accept a temporal stipend lest he "should give any hindrance to the Gospel of Christ" as we read 1 Cor. 9:12. For a like reason the Church does not demand tithes in certain countries, in order to avoid scandal. Much more, therefore, ought we to forego other temporal goods in order to avoid scandal.

*On the contrary,* Blessed Thomas of Canterbury demanded the restitution of Church property, notwithstanding that the king took scandal from his doing so.

*I answer that,* A distinction must be made in temporal goods: for either they are ours, or they are consigned to us to take care of them for someone else; thus the goods of the Church are consigned to prelates, and the goods of the community are entrusted to all such persons as have authority over the common weal. In this latter case the care of such things (as of things held in deposit) devolves of necessity on those persons to whom they are entrusted, wherefore, even as other things that are necessary for salvation, they are not to be foregone on account of scandal. On the other hand, as regards those temporalities of which we have the dominion, sometimes, on account of scandal, we are bound to forego them, and sometimes we are not so bound, whether we forego them by giving them up, if we have them in our possession, or by omitting to claim them, if they are in the possession of others. For if the scandal arise therefrom through the ignorance or weakness of others (in which case, as stated above, A. 7, it is scandal of the little ones) we must either forego such temporalities altogether, or the scandal must be abated by some other means, namely, by some kind of admonition. Hence Augustine says (De Serm. Dom. in Monte i, 20): "Thou shouldst give so as to injure neither thyself nor another, as much as thou canst lend, and if thou refusest what is asked, thou must yet be just to him, indeed thou wilt give him something better than he asks, if thou reprove him that asks unjustly." Sometimes, however, scandal arises from malice. This is scandal of the Pharisees: and we ought not to forego temporal goods for the sake of those who stir up scandals of this kind, for this would both be harmful to the common good, since it would give wicked men an opportunity of plunder, and would be injurious to the plunderers themselves, who would remain in sin as long as they were in possession of another's property.

Hence Gregory says (Moral. xxxi, 13): "Sometimes we ought to suffer those who rob us of our temporalities, while sometimes we should resist them, as far as equity allows, in the hope not only that we may safeguard our property, but also lest those who take what is not theirs may lose themselves."

This suffices for the Reply to the First Objection.

Reply Obj. 2: If it were permissible for wicked men to rob other people of their property, this would tend to the detriment of the truth of life and justice. Therefore we are not always bound to forego our temporal goods in order to avoid scandal.

Reply Obj. 3: The Apostle had no intention of counselling total abstinence from food on account of scandal, because our welfare requires that we should take food: but he intended to counsel abstinence from a particular kind of food, in order to avoid scandal, according to 1 Cor. 8:13: "I will never eat flesh, lest I should scandalize my brother."

Reply Obj. 4: According to Augustine (De Serm. Dom. in Monte i, 19) this precept of Our Lord is to be understood of the preparedness of the mind, namely, that man should be prepared, if it be expedient, to suffer being harmed or defrauded, rather than go to law. But sometimes it is not expedient, as stated above (ad 2). The same applies to the saying of the Apostle.

Reply Obj. 5: The scandal which the Apostle avoided, arose from an error of the gentiles who were not used to this payment. Hence it behooved him to forego it for the time being, so that they might be taught first of all that such a payment was a duty. For a like reason the Church refrains from demanding tithes in those countries where it is not customary to pay them.

## QUESTION 44

OF THE PRECEPTS OF CHARITY (In Eight Articles)

We must now consider the Precepts of Charity, under which there are eight points of inquiry:

(1) Whether precepts should be given about charity?

(2) Whether there should be one or two?

(3) Whether two suffice?

(4) Whether it is fittingly prescribed that we should love God, "with thy whole heart"?

(5) Whether it is fittingly added: "With thy whole mind," etc.?

(6) Whether it is possible to fulfil this precept in this life?

(7) Of the precept: "Thou shalt love thy neighbor as thyself";

(8) Whether the order of charity is included in the precept?

FIRST ARTICLE [II-II, Q. 44, Art. 1]

Whether Any Precept Should Be Given About Charity?

Objection 1: It would seem that no precept should be given about charity. For charity imposes the mode on all acts of virtue, since it is the form of the virtues as stated above (Q. 23, A. 8), while the precepts are about the virtues themselves. Now, according to the common saying, the mode is not included in the precept. Therefore no precepts should be given about charity.

Obj. 2: Further, charity, which "is poured forth in our hearts by the Holy Ghost" (Rom. 5:5), makes us free, since "where the Spirit of the Lord is, there is liberty" (2 Cor. 3:17). Now the obligation that arises from a precept is opposed to liberty, since it imposes a necessity. Therefore no precept should be given about charity.

Obj. 3: Further, charity is the foremost among all the virtues, to which the precepts are directed, as shown above (I-II, Q. 90, A. 2; Q. 100, A. 9). If, therefore, any precepts were given about charity, they should have a place among the chief precepts which are those of the decalogue. But they have no place there. Therefore no precepts should be given about charity.

*On the contrary,* Whatever God requires of us is included in a precept. Now God requires that man should love Him, according to Deut. 10:12. Therefore it behooved precepts to be given about the love of charity, which is the love of God.

*I answer that,* As stated above (Q. 16, A. 1; I-II, Q. 99, A. 1), a precept implies the notion of something due. Hence a thing is a matter of precept, in so far as it is something due. Now a thing is due in two ways, for its own sake, and for the sake of something else. In every affair, it is the end that is due for its own sake, because it has the character of a good for its own sake: while that which is directed to the end is due for the sake of something else: thus for a physician, it is due for its own sake, that he should heal, while it is due for the sake of something else that he should give a medicine in order to heal. Now the end of the spiritual life is that man be united to God, and this union is effected by charity, while all things pertaining to the spiritual life are ordained to this union, as to their end. Hence the Apostle says (1 Tim. 1:5): "The end of the commandment is charity from a pure heart, and a good conscience, and an unfeigned faith." For all the virtues, about whose acts the precepts are given, are directed either to the freeing of the heart from the whirl of the passions—such are the virtues that regulate the passions—or at least to the possession of a good conscience—such are the virtues that regulate operations—or to the having of a right faith—such are those which pertain to the worship of God: and these three things are required of man that he may love God. For an impure heart is withdrawn from loving God, on account of the passion that inclines it to earthly things; an evil conscience gives man a horror for God's justice, through fear of His punishments; and an untrue faith draws man's affections to an untrue representation of God, and separates him from the truth of God. Now in every genus that which is for its own sake takes precedence of that which is for the sake of another, wherefore the greatest precept is that of charity, as stated in Matt. 22:39.

Reply Obj. 1: As stated above (I-II, Q. 100, A. 10) when we were treating of the commandments, the mode of love does not come under those precepts which are about the other acts of virtue: for instance, this precept, "Honor thy father and thy mother," does not prescribe that this should be done out of charity. The act of love does, however, fall under special precepts.

Reply Obj. 2: The obligation of a precept is not opposed to liberty, except in one whose mind is averted from that which is prescribed, as may be seen in those who keep the precepts through fear alone. But the precept of love cannot be fulfilled save of one's own will, wherefore it is not opposed to charity.

Reply Obj. 3: All the precepts of the decalogue are directed to the love of God and of our neighbor: and therefore the precepts of charity had not to be enumerated among the precepts of the decalogue, since they are included in all of them.

SECOND ARTICLE [II-II, Q. 44, Art. 2]

Whether There Should Have Been Given Two Precepts of Charity?

Objection 1: It would seem that there should not have been given two precepts of charity. For the precepts of the Law are directed to virtue, as stated above (A. 1, Obj. 3). Now charity is one virtue, as shown above (Q. 33, A. 5). Therefore only one precept of charity should have been given.

Obj. 2: Further, as Augustine says (De Doctr. Christ. i, 22, 27), charity loves none but God in our neighbor. Now we are sufficiently directed to love God by the precept, "Thou shalt love the Lord thy God." Therefore there was no need to add the precept about loving our neighbor.

Obj. 3: Further, different sins are opposed to different precepts. But it is not a sin to put aside the love of our neighbor, provided we put not aside the love of God; indeed, it is written (Luke 15:26): "If any man come to Me, and hate not his father, and mother ... he cannot be My disciple." Therefore the precept of the love of God is not distinct from the precept of the love of our neighbor.

Obj. 4: Further, the Apostle says (Rom. 13:8): "He that loveth his neighbor hath fulfilled the Law." But a law is not fulfilled unless all its precepts be observed. Therefore all the precepts are included in the love of our neighbor: and consequently the one precept of the love of our neighbor suffices. Therefore there should not be two precepts of charity.

*On the contrary,* It is written (1 John 4:21): "This commandment we have from God, that he who loveth God, love also his brother."

*I answer that,* As stated above (I-II, Q. 91, A. 3; Q. 94, A. 2) when we were treating of the commandments, the precepts are to the Law what propositions are to speculative sciences, for in these latter, the conclusions are virtually contained in the first principles. Hence whoever knows the principles as to their entire virtual extent has no need to have the conclusions put separately before him. Since, however, some who know the principles are unable to consider all that is virtually contained therein, it is necessary, for their sake, that scientific conclusions should be traced to their principles. Now in practical matters wherein the precepts of the Law direct us, the end has the character of principle, as stated above (Q. 23, A. 7, ad 2; Q. 26, A. 1, ad 1): and the love of God is the end to which the love of our neighbor is directed. Therefore it behooved us to receive precepts not only of the love of God but also of the love of our neighbor, on account of those who are less intelligent, who do not easily understand that one of these precepts is included in the other.

Reply Obj. 1: Although charity is one virtue, yet it has two acts, one of which is directed to the other as to its end. Now precepts are given about acts of virtue, and so there had to be several precepts of charity.

Reply Obj. 2: God is loved in our neighbor, as the end is loved in that which is directed to the end; and yet there was need for an explicit precept about both, for the reason given above.

Reply Obj. 3: The means derive their goodness from their relation to the end, and accordingly aversion from the means derives its malice from the same source and from no other.

Reply Obj. 4: Love of our neighbor includes love of God, as the end is included in the means, and vice versa: and yet it behooved each precept to be given explicitly, for the reason given above.

THIRD ARTICLE [II-II, Q. 44, Art. 3]

Whether Two Precepts of Charity Suffice?

Objection 1: It would seem that two precepts of charity do not suffice. For precepts are given about acts of virtue. Now acts are distinguished by their objects. Since, then, man is bound to love four things out of charity, namely, God, himself, his neighbor and his own body, as shown above (Q. 25, A. 12; Q. 26), it seems that there ought to be four precepts of charity, so that two are not sufficient.

Obj. 2: Further, love is not the only act of charity, but also joy, peace and beneficence. But precepts should be given about the acts of the virtues. Therefore two precepts of charity do not suffice.

Obj. 3: Further, virtue consists not only in doing good but also in avoiding evil. Now we are led by the positive precepts to do good, and by the negative precepts to avoid evil. Therefore there ought to have been not only positive, but also negative precepts about charity; and so two precepts of charity are not sufficient.

*On the contrary,* Our Lord said (Matt. 22:40): "On these two commandments dependeth the whole Law and the prophets."

*I answer that,* Charity, as stated above (Q. 23, A. 1), is a kind of friendship. Now friendship is between one person and another, wherefore Gregory says (Hom. in Ev. xvii): "Charity is not possible between less than two": and it has been explained how one may love oneself out of charity (Q. 25, A. 4). Now since good is the object of dilection and love, and since good is either an end or a means, it is fitting that there should be two precepts of charity, one whereby we are induced to love God as our end, and another whereby we are led to love our neighbor for God's sake, as for the sake of our end.

Reply Obj. 1: As Augustine says (De Doctr. Christ. i, 23), "though four things are to be loved out of charity, there was no need of a precept as regards the second and fourth," i.e. love of oneself and of one's own body. "For however much a man may stray from the truth, the love of himself and of his own body always remains in him." And yet the mode of this love had to be prescribed to man, namely, that he should love himself and his own body in an ordinate manner, and this is done by his loving God and his neighbor.

Reply Obj. 2: As stated above (Q. 28, A. 4; Q. 29, A. 3), the other acts of charity result from the act of love as effects from their cause. Hence the precepts of love virtually include the precepts about the other acts. And yet we find that, for the sake of the laggards, special precepts were given about each act—about joy (Phil. 4:4): "Rejoice in the Lord always"—about peace (Heb. 12:14): "Follow peace with all men"—about beneficence (Gal. 6:10): "Whilst we have time, let us work good to all men"—and Holy Writ contains precepts about each of the parts of beneficence, as may be seen by anyone who considers the matter carefully.

Reply Obj. 3: To do good is more than to avoid evil, and therefore the positive precepts virtually include the negative precepts. Nevertheless we find explicit precepts against the vices contrary to charity: for, against hatred it is written (Lev. 12:17): "Thou shalt not hate thy brother in thy heart"; against sloth (Ecclus. 6:26): "Be not grieved with her bands"; against envy (Gal. 5:26): "Let us not be made desirous of vainglory, provoking one another, envying one another"; against discord (1 Cor. 1:10): "That you all speak the same thing, and that there be no schisms among you"; and against scandal (Rom. 14:13): "That you put not a stumbling-block or a scandal in your brother's way."

FOURTH ARTICLE [II-II, Q. 44, Art. 4]

Whether It Is Fittingly Commanded That Man Should Love God with His Whole Heart?

Objection 1: It would seem that it is unfittingly commanded that man should love God with his whole heart. For the mode of a virtuous act is not a matter of precept, as shown above (A. 1, ad 1; I-II, Q. 100, A. 9). Now the words "with thy whole heart" signify the mode of the love of God. Therefore it is unfittingly commanded that man should love God with his whole heart.

Obj. 2: Further, "A thing is whole and perfect when it lacks nothing" (Phys. iii, 6). If therefore it is a matter of precept that God be loved with the whole heart, whoever does something not pertaining to the love of God, acts counter to the precept, and consequently sins mortally. Now a venial sin does not pertain to the love of God. Therefore a venial sin is a mortal sin, which is absurd.

Obj. 3: Further, to love God with one's whole heart belongs to perfection, since according to the Philosopher (Phys. iii, text. 64), "to be whole is to be perfect." But that which belongs to perfection is not a matter of precept, but a matter of counsel. Therefore we ought not to be commanded to love God with our whole heart.

*On the contrary,* It is written (Deut. 6:5): "Thou shalt love the Lord thy God with thy whole heart."

*I answer that,* Since precepts are given about acts of virtue, an act is a matter of precept according as it is an act of virtue. Now it is requisite for an act of virtue that not only should it fall on its own matter, but also that it should be endued with its due circumstances, whereby it is adapted to that matter. But God is to be loved as the last end, to which all things are to be referred. Therefore some kind of totality was to be indicated in connection with the precept of the love of God.

Reply Obj. 1: The commandment that prescribes an act of virtue does not prescribe the mode which that virtue derives from another and higher virtue, but it does prescribe the mode which belongs to its own proper virtue, and this mode is signified in the words "with thy whole heart."

Reply Obj. 2: To love God with one's whole heart has a twofold signification. First, actually, so that a man's whole heart be always actually directed to God: this is the perfection of heaven. Secondly, in the sense that a man's whole heart be habitually directed to God, so that it consent to nothing contrary to the love of God, and this is the perfection of the way. Venial sin is not contrary to this latter perfection, because it does not destroy the habit of charity, since it does not tend to a contrary object, but merely hinders the use of charity.

Reply Obj. 3: That perfection of charity to which the counsels are directed, is between the two perfections mentioned in the preceding reply: and it consists in man renouncing, as much as possible, temporal things, even such as are lawful, because they occupy the mind and hinder the actual movement of the heart towards God.

FIFTH ARTICLE [II-II, Q. 44, Art. 5]

Whether to the Words, "Thou Shalt Love the Lord Thy God with Thy Whole Heart," It Was Fitting to Add "and with Thy Whole Soul, and with Thy Whole Strength"?

Objection 1: It would seem that it was unfitting to the words, "Thou shalt love the Lord thy God, with thy whole heart," to add, "and with thy whole soul, and with thy whole strength" (Deut. 6:5). For heart does not mean here a part of the body, since to love God is not a bodily action: and therefore heart is to be taken here in a spiritual sense. Now the heart understood spiritually is either the soul itself or part of the soul. Therefore it is superfluous to mention both heart and soul.

Obj. 2: Further, a man's strength whether spiritual or corporal depends on the heart. Therefore after the words, "Thou shalt love the Lord thy God with thy whole heart," it was unnecessary to add, "with all thy strength."

Obj. 3: Further, in Matt. 22:37 we read: "With all thy mind," which words do not occur here. Therefore it seems that this precept is unfittingly worded in Deut. 6.

On the contrary stands the authority of Scripture.

*I answer that,* This precept is differently worded in various places: for, as we said in the first objection, in Deut. 6 three points are mentioned: "with thy whole heart," and "with thy whole soul," and "with thy whole strength." In Matt. 22 we find two of these mentioned, viz. "with thy whole heart" and "with thy whole soul," while "with thy whole strength" is omitted, but "with thy whole mind" is added. Yet in Mark 12 we find all four, viz. "with thy whole heart," and "with thy whole soul," and "with thy whole mind," and "with thy whole force" which is the same as "strength." Moreover, these four are indicated in Luke 10, where in place of "strength" or "force" we read "with all thy might." [*St. Thomas is explaining the Latin text which reads "ex tota fortitudine tua" (Deut.), "ex tota virtue tua" (Mk.), and "ex omnibus viribus tuis" (Luke), although the Greek in all three cases has *ex holes tes ischyos* , which the Douay renders "with thy whole strength."]

Accordingly these four have to be explained, since the fact that one of them is omitted here or there is due to one implying another. We must therefore observe that love is an act of the will which is here denoted by the "heart," because just as the bodily heart is the principle of all the movements of the body, so too the will, especially as regards the intention of the last end which is the object of charity, is the principle of all the movements of the soul. Now there are three principles of action that are moved by the will, namely, the intellect which is signified by "the mind," the lower appetitive power, signified by "the soul"; and the exterior executive power signified by "strength," "force" or "might." Accordingly we are commanded to direct our whole intention to God, and this is signified by the words "with thy whole heart"; to submit our intellect to God, and this is expressed in the words "with thy whole mind"; to regulate our appetite according to God, in the words "with thy whole soul"; and to obey God in our external actions, and this is to love God with our whole "strength," "force" or "might."

Chrysostom [*The quotation is from an anonymous author's unfinished work (Opus imperf. Hom. xlii, in Matth.) which is included in Chrysostom's works], on the other hand, takes "heart" and "soul" in the contrary sense; and Augustine (De Doctr. Christ. i, 22) refers "heart" to the thought, "soul" to the manner of life, and "mind" to the intellect. Again some explain "with thy whole heart" as denoting the intellect, "with thy whole soul" as signifying the will, "with thy mind" as pointing to the memory. And again, according to Gregory of Nyssa (De Hom. Opif. viii), "heart" signifies the vegetative soul, "soul" the sensitive, and "mind" the intellective soul, because our nourishment, sensation, and understanding ought all to be referred by us to God.

This suffices for the Replies to the Objections.

SIXTH ARTICLE [II-II, Q. 44, Art. 6]

Whether It Is Possible in This Life to Fulfil This Precept of the Love of God?

Objection 1: It would seem that in this life it is possible to fulfil this precept of the love of God. For according to Jerome [*Pelagius, Exposit. Cath. Fid.] "accursed is he who says that Cod has commanded anything impossible." But God gave this commandment, as is clear from Deut. 6:5. Therefore it is possible to fulfil this precept in this life.

Obj. 2: Further, whoever does not fulfil a precept sins mortally, since according to Ambrose (De Parad. viii) sin is nothing else than "a transgression of the Divine Law, and disobedience of the heavenly commandments." If therefore this precept cannot be fulfilled by wayfarers, it follows that in this life no man can be without mortal sin, and this is against the saying of the Apostle (1 Cor. 1:8): "(Who also) will confirm you unto the end without crime," and (1 Tim. 3:10): "Let them minister, having no crime."

Obj. 3: Further, precepts are given in order to direct man in the way of salvation, according to Ps. 18:9: "The commandment of the Lord is lightsome, enlightening the eyes." Now it is useless to direct anyone to what is impossible. Therefore it is not impossible to fulfill this precept in this life.

*On the contrary,* Augustine says (De Perfect. Justit. viii): "In the fulness of heavenly charity this precept will be fulfilled: Thou shalt love the Lord thy God," etc. For as long as any carnal concupiscence remains, that can be restrained by continence, man cannot love God with all his heart.

*I answer that,* A precept can be fulfilled in two ways; perfectly, and imperfectly. A precept is fulfilled perfectly, when the end intended by the author of the precept is reached; yet it is fulfilled, imperfectly however, when although the end intended by its author is not reached, nevertheless the order to that end is not departed from. Thus if the commander of an army order his soldiers to fight, his command will be perfectly obeyed by those who fight and conquer the foe, which is the commander's intention; yet it is fulfilled, albeit imperfectly, by those who fight without gaining the victory, provided they do nothing contrary to military discipline. Now God intends by this precept that man should be entirely united to Him, and this will be realized in heaven, when God will be "all in all," according to 1 Cor. 15:28. Hence this precept will be observed fully and perfectly in heaven; yet it is fulfilled, though imperfectly, on the way. Nevertheless on the way one man will fulfil it more perfectly than another, and so much the more, as he approaches by some kind of likeness to the perfection of heaven.

Reply Obj. 1: This argument proves that the precept can be fulfilled after a fashion on the way, but not perfectly.

Reply Obj. 2: Even as the soldier who fights legitimately without conquering is not blamed nor deserves to be punished for this, so too he that does not fulfil this precept on the way, but does nothing against the love of God, does not sin mortally.

Reply Obj. 3: As Augustine says (De Perfect. Justit. viii), "why should not this perfection be prescribed to man, although no man attains it in this life? For one cannot run straight unless one knows whither to run. And how would one know this if no precept pointed it out."

SEVENTH ARTICLE [II-II, Q. 44, Art. 7]

Whether the Precept of Love of Our Neighbor Is Fittingly Expressed?

Objection 1: It would seem that the precept of the love of our neighbor is unfittingly expressed. For the love of charity extends to all men, even to our enemies, as may be seen in Matt. 5:44. But the word "neighbor" denotes a kind of "nighness" which does not seem to exist towards all men. Therefore it seems that this precept is unfittingly expressed.

Obj. 2: Further, according to the Philosopher (Ethic. ix, 8) "the origin of our friendly relations with others lies in our relation to ourselves," whence it seems to follow that love of self is the origin of one's love for one's neighbor. Now the principle is greater than that which results from it. Therefore man ought not to love his neighbor as himself.

Obj. 3: Further, man loves himself, but not his neighbor, naturally. Therefore it is unfitting that he should be commanded to love his neighbor as himself.

*On the contrary,* It is written (Matt. 22:39): "The second" commandment "is like to this: Thou shalt love thy neighbor as thyself."

*I answer that,* This precept is fittingly expressed, for it indicates both the reason for loving and the mode of love. The reason for loving is indicated in the word "neighbor," because the reason why we ought to love others out of charity is because they are nigh to us, both as to the natural image of God, and as to the capacity for glory. Nor does it matter whether we say "neighbor," or "brother" according to 1 John 4:21, or "friend," according to Lev. 19:18, because all these words express the same affinity.

The mode of love is indicated in the words "as thyself." This does not mean that a man must love his neighbor equally as himself, but in like manner as himself, and this in three ways. First, as regards the end, namely, that he should love his neighbor for God's sake, even as he loves himself for God's sake, so that his love for his neighbor is a *holy* love. Secondly, as regards the rule of love, namely, that a man should not give way to his neighbor in evil, but only in good things, even as he ought to gratify his will in good things alone, so that his love for his neighbor may be a *righteous* love. Thirdly, as regards the reason for loving, namely, that a man should love his neighbor, not for his own profit, or pleasure, but in the sense of wishing his neighbor well, even as he wishes himself well, so that his love for his neighbor may be a *true* love: since when a man loves his neighbor for his own profit or pleasure, he does not love his neighbor truly, but loves himself.

This suffices for the Replies to the Objections.

EIGHTH ARTICLE [II-II, Q. 44, Art. 8]

Whether the Order of Charity Is Included in the Precept?

Objection 1: It would seem that the order of charity is not included in the precept. For whoever transgresses a precept does a wrong. But if man loves some one as much as he ought, and loves any other man more, he wrongs no man. Therefore he does not transgress the precept. Therefore the order of charity is not included in the precept.

Obj. 2: Further, whatever is a matter of precept is sufficiently delivered to us in Holy Writ. Now the order of charity which was given above (Q. 26) is nowhere indicated in Holy Writ. Therefore it is not included in the precept.

Obj. 3: Further, order implies some kind of distinction. But the love of our neighbor is prescribed without any distinction, in the words, "Thou shalt love thy neighbor as thyself." Therefore the order of charity is not included in the precept.

*On the contrary,* Whatever God works in us by His grace, He teaches us first of all by His Law, according to Jer. 31:33: "I will give My Law in their heart [*Vulg.: 'in their bowels, and I will write it in their heart']." Now God causes in us the order of charity, according to Cant. 2:4: "He set in order charity in me." Therefore the order of charity comes under the precept of the Law.

*I answer that,* As stated above (A. 4, ad 1), the mode which is essential to an act of virtue comes under the precept which prescribes that virtuous act. Now the order of charity is essential to the virtue, since it is based on the proportion of love to the thing beloved, as shown above (Q. 25, A. 12; Q. 26, AA. 1, 2). It is therefore evident that the order of charity must come under the precept.

Reply Obj. 1: A man gratifies more the person he loves more, so that if he loved less one whom he ought to love more, he would wish to gratify more one whom he ought to gratify less, and so he would do an injustice to the one he ought to love more.

Reply Obj. 2: The order of those four things we have to love out of charity is expressed in Holy Writ. For when we are commanded to love God with our "whole heart," we are given to understand that we must love Him above all things. When we are commanded to love our neighbor "as ourselves," the love of self is set before love of our neighbor. In like manner where we are commanded (1 John 3:16) "to lay down our souls," i.e. the life of our bodies, "for the brethren," we are given to understand that a man ought to love his neighbor more than his own body; and again when we are commanded (Gal. 6:10) to "work good ... especially to those who are of the household of the faith," and when a man is blamed (1 Tim. 5:8) if he "have not care of his own, and especially of those of his house," it means that we ought to love most those of our neighbors who are more virtuous or more closely united to us.

Reply Obj. 3: It follows from the very words, "Thou shalt love thy neighbor" that those who are nearer to us are to be loved more.

## QUESTION 45

OF THE GIFT OF WISDOM (In Six Articles)

We must now consider the gift of wisdom which corresponds to charity; and firstly, wisdom itself, secondly, the opposite vice. Under the first head there are six points of inquiry:

(1) Whether wisdom should be reckoned among the gifts of the Holy Ghost?

(2) What is its subject?

(3) Whether wisdom is only speculative or also practical?

(4) Whether the wisdom that is a gift is compatible with mortal sin?

(5) Whether it is in all those who have sanctifying grace?

(6) Which beatitude corresponds to it?

FIRST ARTICLE [II-II, Q. 45, Art. 1]

Whether Wisdom Should Be Reckoned Among the Gifts of the Holy Ghost?

Objection 1: It would seem that wisdom ought not to be reckoned among the gifts of the Holy Ghost. For the gifts are more perfect than the virtues, as stated above (I-II, Q. 68, A. 8). Now virtue is directed to the good alone, wherefore Augustine says (De Lib. Arb. ii, 19) that "no man makes bad use of the virtues." Much more therefore are the gifts of the Holy Ghost directed to the good alone. But wisdom is directed to evil also, for it is written (James 3:15) that a certain wisdom is "earthly, sensual, devilish." Therefore wisdom should not be reckoned among the gifts of the Holy Ghost.

Obj. 2: Further, according to Augustine (De Trin. xii, 14) "wisdom is the knowledge of Divine things." Now that knowledge of Divine things which man can acquire by his natural endowments, belongs to the wisdom which is an intellectual virtue, while the supernatural knowledge of Divine things belongs to faith which is a theological virtue, as explained above (Q. 4, A. 5; I-II, Q. 62, A. 3). Therefore wisdom should be called a virtue rather than a gift.

Obj. 3: Further, it is written (Job 28:28): "Behold the fear of the Lord, that is wisdom, and to depart from evil, that is understanding." And in this passage according to the rendering of the Septuagint which Augustine follows (De Trin. xii, 14; xiv, 1) we read: "Behold piety, that is wisdom." Now both fear and piety are gifts of the Holy Ghost. Therefore wisdom should not be reckoned among the gifts of the Holy Ghost, as though it were distinct from the others.

*On the contrary,* It is written (Isa. 11:2): "The Spirit of the Lord shall rest upon Him; the spirit of wisdom and of understanding."

*I answer that,* According to the Philosopher (Metaph. i: 2), it belongs to wisdom to consider the highest cause. By means of that cause we are able to form a most certain judgment about other causes, and according thereto all things should be set in order. Now the highest cause may be understood in two ways, either simply or in some particular genus. Accordingly he that knows the highest cause in any particular genus, and by its means is able to judge and set in order all the things that belong to that genus, is said to be wise in that genus, for instance in medicine or architecture, according to 1 Cor. 3:10: "As a wise architect, I have laid a foundation." On the other hand, he who knows the cause that is simply the highest, which is God, is said to be wise simply, because he is able to judge and set in order all things according to Divine rules.

Now man obtains this judgment through the Holy Ghost, according to 1 Cor. 2:15: "The spiritual man judgeth all things," because as stated in the same chapter (1 Cor. 2:10), "the Spirit searcheth all things, yea the deep things of God." Wherefore it is evident that wisdom is a gift of the Holy Ghost.

Reply Obj. 1: A thing is said to be good in two senses: first in the sense that it is truly good and simply perfect, secondly, by a kind of likeness, being perfect in wickedness; thus we speak of a good or a perfect thief, as the Philosopher observes (Metaph. v, text. 21). And just as with regard to those things which are truly good, we find a highest cause, namely the sovereign good which is the last end, by knowing which, man is said to be truly wise, so too in evil things something is to be found to which all others are to be referred as to a last end, by knowing which, man is said to be wise unto evil doing, according to Jer. 4:22: "They are wise to do evils, but to do good they have no knowledge." Now whoever turns away from his due end, must needs fix on some undue end, since every agent acts for an end. Wherefore, if he fixes his end in external earthly things, his "wisdom" is called "earthly," if in the goods of the body, it is called "sensual wisdom," if in some excellence, it is called "devilish wisdom" because it imitates the devil's pride, of which it is written (Job 41:25): "He is king over all the children of pride."

Reply Obj. 2: The wisdom which is called a gift of the Holy Ghost, differs from that which is an acquired intellectual virtue, for the latter is attained by human effort, whereas the latter is "descending from above" (James 3:15). In like manner it differs from faith, since faith assents to the Divine truth in itself, whereas it belongs to the gift of wisdom to judge according to the Divine truth. Hence the gift of wisdom presupposes faith, because "a man judges well what he knows" (Ethic. i, 3).

Reply Obj. 3: Just as piety which pertains to the worship of God is a manifestation of faith, in so far as we make profession of faith by worshipping God, so too, piety manifests wisdom. For this reason piety is stated to be wisdom, and so is fear, for the same reason, because if a man fear and worship God, this shows that he has a right judgment about Divine things.

SECOND ARTICLE [II-II, Q. 45, Art. 2]

Whether Wisdom Is in the Intellect As Its Subject?

Objection 1: It would seem that wisdom is not in the intellect as its subject. For Augustine says (Ep. cxx) that "wisdom is the charity of God." Now charity is in the will as its subject, and not in the intellect, as stated above (Q. 24, A. 1). Therefore wisdom is not in the intellect as its subject.

Obj. 2: Further, it is written (Ecclus. 6:23): "The wisdom of doctrine is according to her name," for wisdom ( *sapientia* ) may be described as "sweet-tasting science ( sapida scientia )," and this would seem to regard the appetite, to which it belongs to taste spiritual pleasure or sweetness. Therefore wisdom is in the appetite rather than in the intellect.

Obj. 3: Further, the intellective power is sufficiently perfected by the gift of understanding. Now it is superfluous to require two things where one suffices for the purpose. Therefore wisdom is not in the intellect.

*On the contrary,* Gregory says (Moral. ii, 49) that "wisdom is contrary to folly." But folly is in the intellect. Therefore wisdom is also.

*I answer that,* As stated above (A. 1), wisdom denotes a certain rectitude of judgment according to the Eternal Law. Now rectitude of judgment is twofold: first, on account of perfect use of reason, secondly, on account of a certain connaturality with the matter about which one has to judge. Thus, about matters of chastity, a man after inquiring with his reason forms a right judgment, if he has learnt the science of morals, while he who has the habit of chastity judges of such matters by a kind of connaturality.

Accordingly it belongs to the wisdom that is an intellectual virtue to pronounce right judgment about Divine things after reason has made its inquiry, but it belongs to wisdom as a gift of the Holy Ghost to judge aright about them on account of connaturality with them: thus Dionysius says (Div. Nom. ii) that "Hierotheus is perfect in Divine things, for he not only learns, but is patient of, Divine things."

Now this sympathy or connaturality for Divine things is the result of charity, which unites us to God, according to 1 Cor. 6:17: "He who is joined to the Lord, is one spirit." Consequently wisdom which is a gift, has its cause in the will, which cause is charity, but it has its essence in the intellect, whose act is to judge aright, as stated above (I-II, Q. 14, A. 1).

Reply Obj. 1: Augustine is speaking of wisdom as to its cause, whence also wisdom ( *sapientia* ) takes its name, in so far as it denotes a certain sweetness ( *saporem* ). Hence the Reply to the Second Objection is evident, that is if this be the true meaning of the text quoted. For, apparently this is not the case, because such an exposition of the text would only fit the Latin word for wisdom, whereas it does not apply to the Greek and perhaps not in other languages. Hence it would seem that in the text quoted wisdom stands for the renown of doctrine, for which it is praised by all.

Reply Obj. 3: The intellect exercises a twofold act, perception and judgment. The gift of understanding regards the former; the gift of wisdom regards the latter according to the Divine ideas, the gift of knowledge, according to human ideas.

THIRD ARTICLE [II-II, Q. 45, Art. 3]

Whether Wisdom Is Merely Speculative, or Practical Also?

Objection 1: It would seem that wisdom is not practical but merely speculative. For the gift of wisdom is more excellent than the wisdom which is an intellectual virtue. But wisdom, as an intellectual virtue, is merely speculative. Much more therefore is wisdom, as a gift, speculative and not practical.

Obj. 2: Further, the practical intellect is about matters of operation which are contingent. But wisdom is about Divine things which are eternal and necessary. Therefore wisdom cannot be practical.

Obj. 3: Further, Gregory says (Moral. vi, 37) that "in contemplation we seek the Beginning which is God, but in action we labor under a mighty bundle of wants." Now wisdom regards the vision of Divine things, in which there is no toiling under a load, since according to Wis. 8:16, "her conversation hath no bitterness, nor her company any tediousness." Therefore wisdom is merely contemplative, and not practical or active.

*On the contrary,* It is written (Col. 4:5): "Walk with wisdom towards them that are without." Now this pertains to action. Therefore wisdom is not merely speculative, but also practical.

*I answer that,* As Augustine says (De Trin. xii, 14), the higher part of the reason is the province of wisdom, while the lower part is the domain of knowledge. Now the higher reason according to the same authority (De Trin. xii, 7) "is intent on the consideration and consultation of the heavenly," i.e. Divine, "types" [*Cf. I, Q. 79, A. 9; I-II, Q. 74, A. 7]; it considers them, in so far as it contemplates Divine things in themselves, and it consults them, in so far as it judges of human acts by Divine things, and directs human acts according to Divine rules.

Accordingly wisdom as a gift, is not merely speculative but also practical.

Reply Obj. 1: The higher a virtue is, the greater the number of things to which it extends, as stated in *De Causis,* prop. x, xvii. Wherefore from the very fact that wisdom as a gift is more excellent than wisdom as an intellectual virtue, since it attains to God more intimately by a kind of union of the soul with Him, it is able to direct us not only in contemplation but also in action.

Reply Obj. 2: Divine things are indeed necessary and eternal in themselves, yet they are the rules of the contingent things which are the subject-matter of human actions.

Reply Obj. 3: A thing is considered in itself before being compared with something else. Wherefore to wisdom belongs first of all contemplation which is the vision of the Beginning, and afterwards the direction of human acts according to the Divine rules. Nor from the direction of wisdom does there result any bitterness or toil in human acts; on the contrary the result of wisdom is to make the bitter sweet, and labor a rest.

FOURTH ARTICLE [II-II, Q. 45, Art. 4]

Whether Wisdom Can Be Without Grace, and with Mortal Sin?

Objection 1: It would seem that wisdom can be without grace and with mortal sin. For saints glory chiefly in such things as are incompatible with mortal sin, according to 2 Cor. 1:12: "Our glory is this, the testimony of our conscience." Now one ought not to glory in one's wisdom, according to Jer. 9:23: "Let not the wise man glory in his wisdom." Therefore wisdom can be without grace and with mortal sin.

Obj. 2: Further, wisdom denotes knowledge of Divine things, as stated above (A. 1). Now one in mortal sin may have knowledge of the Divine truth, according to Rom. 1:18: "(Those men that) detain the truth of God in injustice." Therefore wisdom is compatible with mortal sin.

Obj. 3: Further, Augustine says (De Trin. xv, 18) while speaking of charity: "Nothing surpasses this gift of God, it is this alone that divides the children of the eternal kingdom from the children of eternal perdition." But wisdom is distinct from charity. Therefore it does not divide the children of the kingdom from the children of perdition. Therefore it is compatible with mortal sin.

*On the contrary,* It is written (Wis. 1:4): "Wisdom will not enter into a malicious soul, nor dwell in a body subject to sins."

*I answer that,* The wisdom which is a gift of the Holy Ghost, as stated above (A. 1), enables us to judge aright of Divine things, or of other things according to Divine rules, by reason of a certain connaturalness or union with Divine things, which is the effect of charity, as stated above (A. 2; Q. 23, A. 5). Hence the wisdom of which we are speaking presupposes charity. Now charity is incompatible with mortal sin, as shown above (Q. 24, A. 12). Therefore it follows that the wisdom of which we are speaking cannot be together with mortal sin.

Reply Obj. 1: These words are to be understood as referring to worldly wisdom, or to wisdom in Divine things acquired through human reasons. In such wisdom the saints do not glory, according to Prov. 30:2: "The wisdom of men is not with Me": But they do glory in Divine wisdom according to 1 Cor. 1:30: "(Who) of God is made unto us wisdom."

Reply Obj. 2: This argument considers, not the wisdom of which we speak but that which is acquired by the study and research of reason, and is compatible with mortal sin.

Reply Obj. 3: Although wisdom is distinct from charity, it presupposes it, and for that very reason divides the children of perdition from the children of the kingdom.

FIFTH ARTICLE [II-II, Q. 45, Art. 5]

Whether Wisdom Is in All Who Have Grace?

Objection 1: It would seem that wisdom is not in all who have grace. For it is more to have wisdom than to hear wisdom. Now it is only for the perfect to hear wisdom, according to 1 Cor. 2:6: "We speak wisdom among the perfect." Since then not all who have grace are perfect, it seems that much less all who have grace have wisdom.

Obj. 2: Further, "The wise man sets things in order," as the Philosopher states (Metaph. i, 2): and it is written (James 3:17) that the wise man "judges without dissimulation [*Vulg.: 'The wisdom that is from above ... is ... without judging, without dissimulation']". Now it is not for all that have grace, to judge, or put others in order, but only for those in authority. Therefore wisdom is not in all that have grace.

Obj. 3: Further, "Wisdom is a remedy against folly," as Gregory says (Moral. ii, 49). Now many that have grace are naturally foolish, for instance madmen who are baptized or those who without being guilty of mortal sin have become insane. Therefore wisdom is not in all that have grace.

*On the contrary,* Whoever is without mortal sin, is beloved of God; since he has charity, whereby he loves God, and God loves them that love Him (Prov. 8:17). Now it is written (Wis. 7:28) that "God loveth none but him that dwelleth with wisdom." Therefore wisdom is in all those who have charity and are without mortal sin.

*I answer that,* The wisdom of which we are speaking, as stated above (A. 4), denotes a certain rectitude of judgment in the contemplation and consultation of Divine things, and as to both of these men obtain various degrees of wisdom through union with Divine things. For the measure of right judgment attained by some, whether in the contemplation of Divine things or in directing human affairs according to Divine rules, is no more than suffices for their salvation. This measure is wanting to none who is without mortal sin through having sanctifying grace, since if nature does not fail in necessaries, much less does grace fail: wherefore it is written (1 John 2:27): "(His) unction teacheth you of all things."

Some, however, receive a higher degree of the gift of wisdom, both as to the contemplation of Divine things (by both knowing more exalted mysteries and being able to impart this knowledge to others) and as to the direction of human affairs according to Divine rules (by being able to direct not only themselves but also others according to those rules). This degree of wisdom is not common to all that have sanctifying grace, but belongs rather to the gratuitous graces, which the Holy Ghost dispenses as He will, according to 1 Cor. 12:8: "To one indeed by the Spirit is given the word of wisdom," etc.

Reply Obj. 1: The Apostle speaks there of wisdom, as extending to the hidden mysteries of Divine things, as indeed he says himself (2 Cor. 1:7): "We speak the wisdom of God in a mystery, a wisdom which is hidden."

Reply Obj. 2: Although it belongs to those alone who are in authority to direct and judge other men, yet every man is competent to direct and judge his own actions, as Dionysius declares (Ep. ad Demophil.).

Reply Obj. 3: Baptized idiots, like little children, have the habit of wisdom, which is a gift of the Holy Ghost, but they have not the act, on account of the bodily impediment which hinders the use of reason in them.

SIXTH ARTICLE [II-II, Q. 45, Art. 6]

Whether the Seventh Beatitude Corresponds to the Gift of Wisdom?

Objection 1: It seems that the seventh beatitude does not correspond to the gift of wisdom. For the seventh beatitude is: "Blessed are the peacemakers, for they shall be called the children of God." Now both these things belong to charity: since of peace it is written (Ps. 118:165): "Much peace have they that love Thy law," and, as the Apostle says (Rom. 5:5), "the charity of God is poured forth in our hearts by the Holy Ghost Who is given to us," and Who is "the Spirit of adoption of sons, whereby we cry: Abba [Father]" (Rom. 8:15). Therefore the seventh beatitude ought to be ascribed to charity rather than to wisdom.

Obj. 2: Further, a thing is declared by its proximate effect rather than by its remote effect. Now the proximate effect of wisdom seems to be charity, according to Wis. 7:27: "Through nations she conveyeth herself into holy souls; she maketh the friends of God and prophets": whereas peace and the adoption of sons seem to be remote effects, since they result from charity, as stated above (Q. 29, A. 3). Therefore the beatitude corresponding to wisdom should be determined in respect of the love of charity rather than in respect of peace.

Obj. 3: Further, it is written (James 3:17): "The wisdom, that is from above, first indeed is chaste, then peaceable, modest, easy to be persuaded, consenting to the good, full of mercy and good fruits, judging without dissimulation [*Vulg.: 'without judging, without dissimulation']." Therefore the beatitude corresponding to wisdom should not refer to peace rather than to the other effects of heavenly wisdom.

*On the contrary,* Augustine says (De Serm. Dom. in Monte i, 4) that "wisdom is becoming to peacemakers, in whom there is no movement of rebellion, but only obedience to reason."

*I answer that,* The seventh beatitude is fittingly ascribed to the gift of wisdom, both as to the merit and as to the reward. The merit is denoted in the words, "Blessed are the peacemakers." Now a peacemaker is one who makes peace, either in himself, or in others: and in both cases this is the result of setting in due order those things in which peace is established, for "peace is the tranquillity of order," according to Augustine (De Civ. Dei xix, 13). Now it belongs to wisdom to set things in order, as the Philosopher declares (Metaph. i, 2), wherefore peaceableness is fittingly ascribed to wisdom. The reward is expressed in the words, "they shall be called the children of God." Now men are called the children of God in so far as they participate in the likeness of the only-begotten and natural Son of God, according to Rom. 8:29, "Whom He foreknew ... to be made conformable to the image of His Son," Who is Wisdom Begotten. Hence by participating in the gift of wisdom, man attains to the sonship of God.

Reply Obj. 1: It belongs to charity to be at peace, but it belongs to wisdom to make peace by setting things in order. Likewise the Holy Ghost is called the "Spirit of adoption" in so far as we receive from Him the likeness of the natural Son, Who is the Begotten Wisdom.

Reply Obj. 2: These words refer to the Uncreated Wisdom, which in the first place unites itself to us by the gift of charity, and consequently reveals to us the mysteries the knowledge of which is infused wisdom. Hence, the infused wisdom which is a gift, is not the cause but the effect of charity.

Reply Obj. 3: As stated above (A. 3) it belongs to wisdom, as a gift, not only to contemplate Divine things, but also to regulate human acts. Now the first thing to be effected in this direction of human acts is the removal of evils opposed to wisdom: wherefore fear is said to be "the beginning of wisdom," because it makes us shun evil, while the last thing is like an end, whereby all things are reduced to their right order; and it is this that constitutes peace. Hence James said with reason that "the wisdom that is from above" (and this is the gift of the Holy Ghost) "first indeed is chaste," because it avoids the corruption of sin, and "then peaceable," wherein lies the ultimate effect of wisdom, for which reason peace is numbered among the beatitudes. As to the things that follow, they declare in becoming order the means whereby wisdom leads to peace. For when a man, by chastity, avoids the corruption of sin, the first thing he has to do is, as far as he can, to be moderate in all things, and in this respect wisdom is said to be modest. Secondly, in those matters in which he is not sufficient by himself, he should be guided by the advice of others, and as to this we are told further that wisdom is "easy to be persuaded." These two are conditions required that man may be at peace with himself. But in order that man may be at peace with others it is furthermore required, first that he should not be opposed to their good; this is what is meant by "consenting to the good." Secondly, that he should bring to his neighbor's deficiencies, sympathy in his heart, and succor in his actions, and this is denoted by the words "full of mercy and good fruits." Thirdly, he should strive in all charity to correct the sins of others, and this is indicated by the words "judging without dissimulation [*Vulg.: 'The wisdom that is from above ... is ... without judging, without dissimulation']" lest he should purpose to sate his hatred under cover of correction.

# QUESTION 46

OF FOLLY WHICH IS OPPOSED TO WISDOM (In Three Articles)

We must now consider folly which is opposed to wisdom; and under this head there are three points of inquiry:

(1) Whether folly is contrary to wisdom?

(2) Whether folly is a sin?

(3) To which capital sin is it reducible?

FIRST ARTICLE [II-II, Q. 46, Art. 1]

Whether Folly Is Contrary to Wisdom?

Objection 1: It would seem that folly is not contrary to wisdom. For seemingly unwisdom is directly opposed to wisdom. But folly does not seem to be the same as unwisdom, for the latter is apparently about Divine things alone, whereas folly is about both Divine and human things. Therefore folly is not contrary to wisdom.

Obj. 2: Further, one contrary is not the way to arrive at the other. But folly is the way to arrive at wisdom, for it is written (1 Cor. 3:18): "If any man among you seem to be wise in this world, let him become a fool, that he may be wise." Therefore folly is not opposed to wisdom.

Obj. 3: Further, one contrary is not the cause of the other. But wisdom is the cause of folly; for it is written (Jer. 10:14): "Every man is become a fool for knowledge," and wisdom is a kind of knowledge. Moreover, it is written (Isa. 47:10): "Thy wisdom and thy knowledge, this hath deceived thee." Now it belongs to folly to be deceived. Therefore folly is not contrary to wisdom.

Obj. 4: Further, Isidore says (Etym. x, under the letter S) that "a fool is one whom shame does not incite to sorrow, and who is unconcerned when he is injured." But this pertains to spiritual wisdom, according to Gregory (Moral. x, 49). Therefore folly is not opposed to wisdom.

*On the contrary,* Gregory says (Moral. ii, 26) that "the gift of wisdom is given as a remedy against folly."

*I answer that,* Stultitia (Folly) seems to take its name from *stupor;* wherefore Isidore says (loc. cit.): "A fool is one who through dullness ( *stuporem* ) remains unmoved." And folly differs from fatuity, according to the same authority (Etym. x), in that folly implies apathy in the heart and dullness in the senses, while fatuity denotes entire privation of the spiritual sense. Therefore folly is fittingly opposed to wisdom.

For "sapiens" ( *wise* ) as Isidore says (Etym. x) "is so named from *sapor* (savor), because just as the taste is quick to distinguish between savors of meats, so is a wise man in discerning things and causes." Wherefore it is manifest that *folly* is opposed to wisdom as its contrary, while *fatuity* is opposed to it as a pure negation: since the fatuous man lacks the sense of judgment, while the fool has the sense, though dulled, whereas the wise man has the sense acute and penetrating.

Reply Obj. 1: According to Isidore (Etym. x), "unwisdom is contrary to wisdom because it lacks the savor of discretion and sense"; so that unwisdom is seemingly the same as folly. Yet a man would appear to be a fool chiefly through some deficiency in the verdict of that judgment, which is according to the highest cause, for if a man fails in judgment about some trivial matter, he is not for that reason called a fool.

Reply Obj. 2: Just as there is an evil wisdom, as stated above (Q. 45, A. 1, ad 1), called "worldly wisdom," because it takes for the highest cause and last end some worldly good, so too there is a good folly opposed to this evil wisdom, whereby man despises worldly things: and it is of this folly that the Apostle speaks.

Reply Obj. 3: It is the wisdom of the world that deceives and makes us foolish in God's sight, as is evident from the Apostle's words (1 Cor. 3:19).

Reply Obj. 4: To be unconcerned when one is injured is sometimes due to the fact that one has no taste for worldly things, but only for heavenly things. Hence this belongs not to worldly but to Divine wisdom, as Gregory declares (Moral. x, 49). Sometimes however it is the result of a man's being simply stupid about everything, as may be seen in idiots, who do not discern what is injurious to them, and this belongs to folly simply.

SECOND ARTICLE [II-II, Q. 45, Art. 2]

Whether Folly Is a Sin?

Objection 1: It would seem that folly is not a sin. For no sin arises in us from nature. But some are fools naturally. Therefore folly is not a sin.

Obj. 2: Further, "Every sin is voluntary," according to Augustine (De Vera Relig. xiv). But folly is not voluntary. Therefore it is not a sin.

Obj. 3: Further, every sin is contrary to a Divine precept. But folly is not contrary to any precept. Therefore folly is not a sin.

*On the contrary,* It is written (Prov. 1:32): "The prosperity of fools shall destroy them." But no man is destroyed save for sin. Therefore folly is a sin.

*I answer that,* Folly, as stated above (A. 1), denotes dullness of sense in judging, and chiefly as regards the highest cause, which is the last end and the sovereign good. Now a man may in this respect contract dullness in judgment in two ways. First, from a natural indisposition, as in the case of idiots, and such like folly is no sin. Secondly, by plunging his sense into earthly things, whereby his sense is rendered incapable of perceiving Divine things, according to 1 Cor. 2:14, "The sensual man perceiveth not these things that are of the Spirit of God," even as sweet things have no savor for a man whose taste is infected with an evil humor: and such like folly is a sin.

This suffices for the Reply to the First Objection.

Reply Obj. 2: Though no man wishes to be a fool, yet he wishes those things of which folly is a consequence, viz. to withdraw his sense from spiritual things and to plunge it into earthly things. The same thing happens in regard to other sins; for the lustful man desires pleasure, without which there is no sin, although he does not desire sin simply, for he would wish to enjoy the pleasure without sin.

Reply Obj. 3: Folly is opposed to the precepts about the contemplation of truth, of which we have spoken above (Q. 16) when we were treating of knowledge and understanding.

THIRD ARTICLE [II-II, Q. 46, Art. 3]

Whether Folly Is a Daughter of Lust?

Objection 1: It would seem that folly is not a daughter of lust. For Gregory (Moral. xxxi, 45) enumerates the daughters of lust, among which however he makes no mention of folly. Therefore folly does not proceed from lust.

Obj. 2: Further, the Apostle says (1 Cor. 3:19): "The wisdom of this world is foolishness with God." Now, according to Gregory (Moral. x, 29) "the wisdom of this world consists in covering the heart with crafty devices;" and this savors of duplicity. Therefore folly is a daughter of duplicity rather than of lust.

Obj. 3: Further, anger especially is the cause of fury and madness in some persons; and this pertains to folly. Therefore folly arises from anger rather than from lust.

*On the contrary,* It is written (Prov. 7:22): "Immediately he followeth her," i.e. the harlot ... "not knowing that he is drawn like a fool to bonds."

*I answer that,* As already stated (A. 2), folly, in so far as it is a sin, is caused by the spiritual sense being dulled, so as to be incapable of judging spiritual things. Now man's sense is plunged into earthly things chiefly by lust, which is about the greatest of pleasures; and these absorb the mind more than any others. Therefore the folly which is a sin, arises chiefly from lust.

Reply Obj. 1: It is part of folly that a man should have a distaste for God and His gifts. Hence Gregory mentions two daughters of lust, pertaining to folly, namely, "hatred of God" and "despair of the life to come"; thus he divides folly into two parts as it were.

Reply Obj. 2: These words of the Apostle are to be understood, not causally but essentially, because, to wit, worldly wisdom itself is folly with God. Hence it does not follow that whatever belongs to worldly wisdom, is a cause of this folly.

Reply Obj. 3: Anger by reason of its keenness, as stated above (I-II, Q. 48, AA. 2, 3, 4), produces a great change in the nature of the body, wherefore it conduces very much to the folly which results from a bodily impediment. On the other hand the folly which is caused by a spiritual impediment, viz. by the mind being plunged into earthly things, arises chiefly from lust, as stated above.

TREATISE ON THE CARDINAL VIRTUES (QQ. 47-170)

## QUESTION 47

OF PRUDENCE, CONSIDERED IN ITSELF (In Sixteen Articles)

After treating of the theological virtues, we must in due sequence consider the cardinal virtues. In the first place we shall consider prudence in itself; secondly, its parts; thirdly, the corresponding gift; fourthly, the contrary vices; fifthly, the precepts concerning prudence.

Under the first head there are sixteen points of inquiry:

(1) Whether prudence is in the will or in the reason?

(2) If in the reason, whether it is only in the practical, or also in the speculative reason?

(3) Whether it takes cognizance of singulars?

(4) Whether it is virtue?

(5) Whether it is a special virtue?

(6) Whether it appoints the end to the moral virtues?

(7) Whether it fixes the mean in the moral virtues?

(8) Whether its proper act is command?

(9) Whether solicitude or watchfulness belongs to prudence?

(10) Whether prudence extends to the governing of many?

(11) Whether the prudence which regards private good is the same in species as that which regards the common good?

(12) Whether prudence is in subjects, or only in their rulers?

(13) Whether prudence is in the wicked?

(14) Whether prudence is in all good men?

(15) Whether prudence is in us naturally?

(16) Whether prudence is lost by forgetfulness?

FIRST ARTICLE [II-II, Q. 47, Art. 1]

Whether Prudence Is in the Cognitive or in the Appetitive Faculty?

Objection 1: It would seem that prudence is not in the cognitive but in the appetitive faculty. For Augustine says (De Morib. Eccl. xv): "Prudence is love choosing wisely between the things that help and those that hinder." Now love is not in the cognitive, but in the appetitive faculty. Therefore prudence is in the appetitive faculty.

Obj. 2: Further, as appears from the foregoing definition it belongs to prudence "to choose wisely." But choice is an act of the appetitive faculty, as stated above (I-II, Q. 13, A. 1). Therefore prudence is not in the cognitive but in the appetitive faculty.

Obj. 3: Further, the Philosopher says (Ethic. vi, 5) that "in art it is better to err voluntarily than involuntarily, whereas in the case of prudence, as of the virtues, it is worse." Now the moral virtues, of which he is treating there, are in the appetitive faculty, whereas art is in the reason. Therefore prudence is in the appetitive rather than in the rational faculty.

*On the contrary,* Augustine says (QQ. lxxxiii, qu. 61): "Prudence is the knowledge of what to seek and what to avoid."

*I answer that,* As Isidore says (Etym. x): "A prudent man is one who sees as it were from afar, for his sight is keen, and he foresees the event of uncertainties." Now sight belongs not to the appetitive but to the cognitive faculty. Wherefore it is manifest that prudence belongs directly to the cognitive, and not to the sensitive faculty, because by the latter we know nothing but what is within reach and offers itself to the senses: while to obtain knowledge of the future from knowledge of the present or past, which pertains to prudence, belongs properly to the reason, because this is done by a process of comparison. It follows therefore that prudence, properly speaking, is in the reason.

Reply Obj. 1: As stated above (I, Q. 82, A. 4) the will moves all the faculties to their acts. Now the first act of the appetitive faculty is love, as stated above (I-II, Q. 25, AA. 1, 2). Accordingly prudence is said to be love, not indeed essentially, but in so far as love moves to the act of prudence. Wherefore Augustine goes on to say that "prudence is love discerning aright that which helps from that which hinders us in tending to God." Now love is said to discern because it moves the reason to discern.

Reply Obj. 2: The prudent man considers things afar off, in so far as they tend to be a help or a hindrance to that which has to be done at the present time. Hence it is clear that those things which prudence considers stand in relation to this other, as in relation to the end. Now of those things that are directed to the end there is counsel in the reason, and choice in the appetite, of which two, counsel belongs more properly to prudence, since the Philosopher states (Ethic. vi, 5, 7, 9) that a prudent man "takes good counsel." But as choice presupposes counsel, since it is "the desire for what has been already counselled" (Ethic. iii, 2), it follows that choice can also be ascribed to prudence indirectly, in so far, to wit, as prudence directs the choice by means of counsel.

Reply Obj. 3: The worth of prudence consists not in thought merely, but in its application to action, which is the end of the practical reason. Wherefore if any defect occur in this, it is most contrary to prudence, since, the end being of most import in everything, it follows that a defect which touches the end is the worst of all. Hence the Philosopher goes on to say (Ethic. vi, 5) that prudence is "something more than a merely rational habit," such as art is, since, as stated above (I-II, Q. 57, A. 4) it includes application to action, which application is an act of the will.

SECOND ARTICLE [II-II, Q. 47, Art. 2]

Whether Prudence Belongs to the Practical Reason Alone or Also to the Speculative Reason?

Objection 1: It would seem that prudence belongs not only to the practical, but also to the speculative reason. For it is written (Prov. 10:23): "Wisdom is prudence to a man." Now wisdom consists chiefly in contemplation. Therefore prudence does also.

Obj. 2: Further, Ambrose says (De Offic. i, 24): "Prudence is concerned with the quest of truth, and fills us with the desire of fuller knowledge." Now this belongs to the speculative reason. Therefore prudence resides also in the speculative reason.

Obj. 3: Further, the Philosopher assigns art and prudence to the same part of the soul (Ethic. vi, 1). Now art may be not only practical but also speculative, as in the case of the liberal arts. Therefore prudence also is both practical and speculative.

*On the contrary,* The Philosopher says (Ethic. vi, 5) that prudence is right reason applied to action. Now this belongs to none but the practical reason. Therefore prudence is in the practical reason only.

*I answer that,* According to the Philosopher (Ethic. vi, 5) "a prudent man is one who is capable of taking good counsel." Now counsel is about things that we have to do in relation to some end: and the reason that deals with things to be done for an end is the practical reason. Hence it is evident that prudence resides only in the practical reason.

Reply Obj. 1: As stated above (Q. 45, AA. 1, 3), wisdom considers the absolutely highest cause: so that the consideration of the highest cause in any particular genus belongs to wisdom in that genus. Now in the genus of human acts the highest cause is the common end of all human life, and it is this end that prudence intends. For the Philosopher says (Ethic. vi, 5) that just as he who reasons well for the realization of a particular end, such as victory, is said to be prudent, not absolutely, but in a particular genus, namely warfare, so he that reasons well with regard to right conduct as a whole, is said to be prudent absolutely. Wherefore it is clear that prudence is wisdom about human affairs: but not wisdom absolutely, because it is not about the absolutely highest cause, for it is about human good, and this is not the best thing of all. And so it is stated significantly that "prudence is wisdom for man," but not wisdom absolutely.

Reply Obj. 2: Ambrose, and Tully also (De Invent. ii, 53) take the word prudence in a broad sense for any human knowledge, whether speculative or practical. And yet it may also be replied that the act itself of the speculative reason, in so far as it is voluntary, is a matter of choice and counsel as to its exercise; and consequently comes under the direction of prudence. On the other hand, as regards its specification in relation to its object which is the "necessary true," it comes under neither counsel nor prudence.

Reply Obj. 3: Every application of right reason in the work of production belongs to art: but to prudence belongs only the application of right reason in matters of counsel, which are those wherein there is no fixed way of obtaining the end, as stated in *Ethic.* iii, 3. Since then, the speculative reason makes things such as syllogisms, propositions and the like, wherein the process follows certain and fixed rules, consequently in respect of such things it is possible to have the essentials of art, but not of prudence; and so we find such a thing as a speculative art, but not a speculative prudence.

THIRD ARTICLE [II-II, Q. 47, Art. 3]

Whether Prudence Takes Cognizance of Singulars?

Objection 1: It would seem that prudence does not take cognizance of singulars. For prudence is in the reason, as stated above (AA. 1, 2). But "reason deals with universals," according to *Phys.* i, 5. Therefore prudence does not take cognizance except of universals.

Obj. 2: Further, singulars are infinite in number. But the reason cannot comprehend an infinite number of things. Therefore prudence which is right reason, is not about singulars.

Obj. 3: Further, particulars are known by the senses. But prudence is not in a sense, for many persons who have keen outward senses are devoid of prudence. Therefore prudence does not take cognizance of singulars.

*On the contrary,* The Philosopher says (Ethic. vi, 7) that "prudence does not deal with universals only, but needs to take cognizance of singulars also."

*I answer that,* As stated above (A. 1, ad 3), to prudence belongs not only the consideration of the reason, but also the application to action, which is the end of the practical reason. But no man can conveniently apply one thing to another, unless he knows both the thing to be applied, and the thing to which it has to be applied. Now actions are in singular matters: and so it is necessary for the prudent man to know both the universal principles of reason, and the singulars about which actions are concerned.

Reply Obj. 1: Reason first and chiefly is concerned with universals, and yet it is able to apply universal rules to particular cases: hence the conclusions of syllogisms are not only universal, but also particular, because the intellect by a kind of reflection extends to matter, as stated in *De Anima* iii.

Reply Obj. 2: It is because the infinite number of singulars cannot be comprehended by human reason, that "our counsels are uncertain" (Wis. 9:14). Nevertheless experience reduces the infinity of singulars to a certain finite number which occur as a general rule, and the knowledge of these suffices for human prudence.

Reply Obj. 3: As the Philosopher says (Ethic. vi, 8), prudence does not reside in the external senses whereby we know sensible objects, but in the interior sense, which is perfected by memory and experience so as to judge promptly of particular cases. This does not mean however that prudence is in the interior sense as in its princip[al] subject, for it is chiefly in the reason, yet by a kind of application it extends to this sense.

FOURTH ARTICLE [II-II, Q. 47, Art. 4]

Whether Prudence Is a Virtue?

Objection 1: It would seem that prudence is not a virtue. For Augustine says (De Lib. Arb. i, 13) that "prudence is the science of what to desire and what to avoid." Now science is condivided with virtue, as appears in the *Predicaments* (vi). Therefore prudence is not a virtue.

Obj. 2: Further, there is no virtue of a virtue: but "there is a virtue of art," as the Philosopher states (Ethic. vi, 5): wherefore art is not a virtue. Now there is prudence in art, for it is written (2 Paralip. ii, 14) concerning Hiram, that he knew "to grave all sort of graving, and to devise ingeniously ( *prudenter* ) all that there may be need of in the work." Therefore prudence is not a virtue.

Obj. 3: Further, no virtue can be immoderate. But prudence is immoderate, else it would be useless to say (Prov. 23:4): "Set bounds to thy prudence." Therefore prudence is not a virtue.

*On the contrary,* Gregory states (Moral. ii, 49) that prudence, temperance, fortitude and justice are four virtues.

*I answer that,* As stated above (I-II, Q. 55, A. 3; Q. 56, A. 1) when we were treating of virtues in general, "virtue is that which makes its possessor good, and his work good likewise." Now good may be understood in a twofold sense: first, materially, for the thing that is good, secondly, formally, under the aspect of good. Good, under the aspect of good, is the object of the appetitive power. Hence if any habits rectify the consideration of reason, without regarding the rectitude of the appetite, they have less of the nature of a virtue since they direct man to good materially, that is to say, to the thing which is good, but without considering it under the aspect of good. On the other hand those virtues which regard the rectitude of the appetite, have more of the nature of virtue, because they consider the good not only materially, but also formally, in other words, they consider that which is good under the aspect of good.

Now it belongs to prudence, as stated above (A. 1, ad 3; A. 3) to apply right reason to action, and this is not done without a right appetite. Hence prudence has the nature of virtue not only as the other intellectual virtues have it, but also as the moral virtues have it, among which virtues it is enumerated.

Reply Obj. 1: Augustine there takes science in the broad sense for any kind of right reason.

Reply Obj. 2: The Philosopher says that there is a virtue of art, because art does not require rectitude of the appetite; wherefore in order that a man may make right use of his art, he needs to have a virtue which will rectify his appetite. Prudence however has nothing to do with the matter of art, because art is both directed to a particular end, and has fixed means of obtaining that end. And yet, by a kind of comparison, a man may be said to act prudently in matters of art. Moreover in certain arts, on account of the uncertainty of the means for obtaining the end, there is need for counsel, as for instance in the arts of medicine and navigation, as stated in *Ethic.* iii, 3.

Reply Obj. 3: This saying of the wise man does not mean that prudence itself should be moderate, but that moderation must be imposed on other things according to prudence.

FIFTH ARTICLE [II-II, Q. 47, Art. 5]

Whether Prudence Is a Special Virtue?

Objection 1: It would seem that prudence is not a special virtue. For no special virtue is included in the definition of virtue in general, since virtue is defined (Ethic. ii, 6) "an elective habit that follows a mean appointed by reason in relation to ourselves, even as a wise man decides." Now right reason is reason in accordance with prudence, as stated in *Ethic.* vi, 13. Therefore prudence is not a special virtue.

Obj. 2: Further, the Philosopher says (Ethic. vi, 13) that "the effect of moral virtue is right action as regards the end, and that of prudence, right action as regards the means." Now in every virtue certain things have to be done as means to the end. Therefore prudence is in every virtue, and consequently is not a special virtue.

Obj. 3: Further, a special virtue has a special object. But prudence has not a special object, for it is right reason "applied to action" (Ethic. vi, 5); and all works of virtue are actions. Therefore prudence is not a special virtue.

*On the contrary,* It is distinct from and numbered among the other virtues, for it is written (Wis. 8:7): "She teacheth temperance and prudence, justice and fortitude."

*I answer that,* Since acts and habits take their species from their objects, as shown above (I-II, Q. 1, A. 3; Q. 18, A. 2; Q. 54, A. 2), any habit that has a corresponding special object, distinct from other objects, must needs be a special habit, and if it be a good habit, it must be a special virtue. Now an object is called special, not merely according to the consideration of its matter, but rather according to its formal aspect, as explained above (I-II, Q. 54, A. 2, ad 1). Because one and the same thing is the subject matter of the acts of different habits, and also of different powers, according to its different formal aspects. Now a yet greater difference of object is requisite for a difference of powers than for a difference of habits, since several habits are found in the same power, as stated above (I-II, Q. 54, A. 1). Consequently any difference in the aspect of an object, that requires a difference of powers, will *a fortiori* require a difference of habits.

Accordingly we must say that since prudence is in the reason, as stated above (A. 2), it is differentiated from the other intellectual virtues by a material difference of objects. *Wisdom,* knowledge and *understanding* are about necessary things, whereas art and *prudence* are about contingent things, art being concerned with *things made,* that is, with things produced in external matter, such as a house, a knife and so forth; and prudence, being concerned with *things done,* that is, with things that have their being in the doer himself, as stated above (I-II, Q. 57, A. 4). On the other hand prudence is differentiated from the moral virtues according to a formal aspect distinctive of powers, i.e. the intellective power, wherein is prudence, and the appetitive power, wherein is moral virtue. Hence it is evident that prudence is a special virtue, distinct from all other virtues.

Reply Obj. 1: This is not a definition of virtue in general, but of moral virtue, the definition of which fittingly includes an intellectual virtue, viz., prudence, which has the same matter in common with moral virtue; because, just as the subject of moral virtue is something that partakes of reason, so moral virtue has the aspect of virtue, in so far as it partakes of intellectual virtue.

Reply Obj. 2: This argument proves that prudence helps all the virtues, and works in all of them; but this does not suffice to prove that it is not a special virtue; for nothing prevents a certain genus from containing a species which is operative in every other species of that same genus, even as the sun has an influence over all bodies.

Reply Obj. 3: Things done are indeed the matter of prudence, in so far as they are the object of reason, that is, considered as true: but they are the matter of the moral virtues, in so far as they are the object of the appetitive power, that is, considered as good.

SIXTH ARTICLE [II-II, Q. 47, Art. 6]

Whether Prudence Appoints the End to Moral Virtues?

Objection 1: It would seem that prudence appoints the end to moral virtues. Since prudence is in the reason, while moral virtue is in the appetite, it seems that prudence stands in relation to moral virtue, as reason to the appetite. Now reason appoints the end to the appetitive power. Therefore prudence appoints the end to the moral virtues.

Obj. 2: Further, man surpasses irrational beings by his reason, but he has other things in common with them. Accordingly the other parts of man are in relation to his reason, what man is in relation to irrational creatures. Now man is the end of irrational creatures, according to *Polit.* i, 3. Therefore all the other parts of man are directed to reason as to their end. But prudence is "right reason applied to action," as stated above (A. 2). Therefore all actions are directed to prudence as their end. Therefore prudence appoints the end to all moral virtues.

Obj. 3: Further, it belongs to the virtue, art, or power that is concerned about the end, to command the virtues or arts that are concerned about the means. Now prudence disposes of the other moral virtues, and commands them. Therefore it appoints their end to them.

*On the contrary,* The Philosopher says (Ethic. vi, 12) that "moral virtue ensures the rectitude of the intention of the end, while prudence ensures the rectitude of the means." Therefore it does not belong to prudence to appoint the end to moral virtues, but only to regulate the means.

*I answer that,* The end of moral virtues is human good. Now the good of the human soul is to be in accord with reason, as Dionysius declares (Div. Nom. iv). Wherefore the ends of moral virtue must of necessity pre-exist in the reason.

Now, just as, in the speculative reason, there are certain things naturally known, about which is *understanding,* and certain things of which we obtain knowledge through them, viz. conclusions, about which is *science,* so in the practical reason, certain things pre-exist, as naturally known principles, and such are the ends of the moral virtues, since the end is in practical matters what principles are in speculative matters, as stated above (Q. 23, A. 7, ad 2; I-II, Q. 13, A. 3); while certain things are in the practical reason by way of conclusions, and such are the means which we gather from the ends themselves. About these is prudence, which applies universal principles to the particular conclusions of practical matters. Consequently it does not belong to prudence to appoint the end to moral virtues, but only to regulate the means.

Reply Obj. 1: Natural reason known by the name of *synderesis* appoints the end to moral virtues, as stated above (I, Q. 79, A. 12): but prudence does not do this for the reason given above.

This suffices for the Reply to the Second Objection.

Reply Obj. 3: The end concerns the moral virtues, not as though they appointed the end, but because they tend to the end which is appointed by natural reason. In this they are helped by prudence, which prepares the way for them, by disposing the means. Hence it follows that prudence is more excellent than the moral virtues, and moves them: yet *synderesis* moves prudence, just as the understanding of principles moves science.

SEVENTH ARTICLE [II-II, Q. 47, Art. 7]

Whether It Belongs to Prudence to Find the Mean in Moral Virtues?

Objection 1: It would seem that it does not belong to prudence to find the mean in moral virtues. For the achievement of the mean is the end of moral virtues. But prudence does not appoint the end to moral virtues, as shown above (A. 6). Therefore it does not find the mean in them.

Obj. 2: Further, that which of itself has being, would seem to have no cause, but its very being is its cause, since a thing is said to have being by reason of its cause. Now "to follow the mean" belongs to moral virtue by reason of itself, as part of its definition, as shown above (A. 5, Obj. 1). Therefore prudence does not cause the mean in moral virtues.

Obj. 3: Further, prudence works after the manner of reason. But moral virtue tends to the mean after the manner of nature, because, as Tully states (De Invent. Rhet. ii, 53), "virtue is a habit like a second nature in accord with reason." Therefore prudence does not appoint the mean to moral virtues.

*On the contrary,* In the foregoing definition of moral virtue (A. 5, Obj. 1) it is stated that it "follows a mean appointed by reason ... even as a wise man decides."

*I answer that,* The proper end of each moral virtue consists precisely in conformity with right reason. For temperance intends that man should not stray from reason for the sake of his concupiscences; fortitude, that he should not stray from the right judgment of reason through fear or daring. Moreover this end is appointed to man according to natural reason, since natural reason dictates to each one that he should act according to reason.

But it belongs to the ruling of prudence to decide in what manner and by what means man shall obtain the mean of reason in his deeds. For though the attainment of the mean is the end of a moral virtue, yet this mean is found by the right disposition of these things that are directed to the end.

This suffices for the Reply to the First Objection.

Reply Obj. 2: Just as a natural agent makes form to be in matter, yet does not make that which is essential to the form to belong to it, so too, prudence appoints the mean in passions and operations, and yet does not make the searching of the mean to belong to virtue.

Reply Obj. 3: Moral virtue after the manner of nature intends to attain the mean. Since, however, the mean as such is not found in all matters after the same manner, it follows that the inclination of nature which ever works in the same manner, does not suffice for this purpose, and so the ruling of prudence is required.

EIGHTH ARTICLE [II-II, Q. 47, Art. 8]

Whether Command Is the Chief Act of Prudence?

Objection 1: It would seem that command is not the chief act of prudence. For command regards the good to be ensued. Now Augustine (De Trin. xiv, 9) states that it is an act of prudence "to avoid ambushes." Therefore command is not the chief act of prudence.

Obj. 2: Further, the Philosopher says (Ethic. vi, 5) that "the prudent man takes good counsel." Now "to take counsel" and "to command" seem to be different acts, as appears from what has been said above (I-II, Q. 57, A. 6). Therefore command is not the chief act of prudence.

Obj. 3: Further, it seems to belong to the will to command and to rule, since the will has the end for its object, and moves the other powers of the soul. Now prudence is not in the will, but in the reason. Therefore command is not an act of prudence.

*On the contrary,* The Philosopher says (Ethic. vi, 10) that "prudence commands."

*I answer that,* Prudence is "right reason applied to action," as stated above (A. 2). Hence that which is the chief act of reason in regard to action must needs be the chief act of prudence. Now there are three such acts. The first is *to take counsel,* which belongs to discovery, for counsel is an act of inquiry, as stated above (I-II, Q. 14, A. 1). The second act is to judge of what one has discovered, and this is an act of the speculative reason. But the practical reason, which is directed to action, goes further, and its third act is *to command,* which act consists in applying to action the things counselled and judged. And since this act approaches nearer to the end of the practical reason, it follows that it is the chief act of the practical reason, and consequently of prudence.

In confirmation of this we find that the perfection of art consists in judging and not in commanding: wherefore he who sins voluntarily against his craft is reputed a better craftsman than he who does so involuntarily, because the former seems to do so from right judgment, and the latter from a defective judgment. On the other hand it is the reverse in prudence, as stated in *Ethic.* vi, 5, for it is more imprudent to sin voluntarily, since this is to be lacking in the chief act of prudence, viz. command, than to sin involuntarily.

Reply Obj. 1: The act of command extends both to the ensuing of good and to the avoidance of evil. Nevertheless Augustine ascribes "the avoidance of ambushes" to prudence, not as its chief act, but as an act of prudence that does not continue in heaven.

Reply Obj. 2: Good counsel is required in order that the good things discovered may be applied to action: wherefore command belongs to prudence which takes good counsel.

Reply Obj. 3: Simply to move belongs to the will: but command denotes motion together with a kind of ordering, wherefore it is an act of the reason, as stated above (I-II, Q. 17, A. 1).

NINTH ARTICLE [II-II, Q. 47, Art. 9]

Whether Solicitude Belongs to Prudence?

Objection 1: It would seem that solicitude does not belong to prudence. For solicitude implies disquiet, wherefore Isidore says (Etym. x) that "a solicitous man is a restless man." Now motion belongs chiefly to the appetitive power: wherefore solicitude does also. But prudence is not in the appetitive power, but in the reason, as stated above (A. 1). Therefore solicitude does not belong to prudence.

Obj. 2: Further, the certainty of truth seems opposed to solicitude, wherefore it is related (1 Kings 9:20) that Samuel said to Saul: "As for the asses which were lost three days ago, be not solicitous, because they are found." Now the certainty of truth belongs to prudence, since it is an intellectual virtue. Therefore solicitude is in opposition to prudence rather than belonging to it.

Obj. 3: Further, the Philosopher says (Ethic. iv, 3) the "magnanimous man is slow and leisurely." Now slowness is contrary to solicitude. Since then prudence is not opposed to magnanimity, for "good is not opposed to good," as stated in the *Predicaments* (viii) it would seem that solicitude does not belong to prudence.

*On the contrary,* It is written (1 Pet. 4:7): "Be prudent ... and watch in prayers." But watchfulness is the same as solicitude. Therefore solicitude belongs to prudence.

*I answer that,* According to Isidore (Etym. x), a man is said to be solicitous through being shrewd ( *solers* ) and alert ( citus ), in so far as a man through a certain shrewdness of mind is on the alert to do whatever has to be done. Now this belongs to prudence, whose chief act is a command about what has been already counselled and judged in matters of action. Hence the Philosopher says (Ethic. vi, 9) that "one should be quick in carrying out the counsel taken, but slow in taking counsel." Hence it is that solicitude belongs properly to prudence, and for this reason Augustine says (De Morib. Eccl. xxiv) that "prudence keeps most careful watch and ward, lest by degrees we be deceived unawares by evil counsel."

Reply Obj. 1: Movement belongs to the appetitive power as to the principle of movement, in accordance however, with the direction and command of reason, wherein solicitude consists.

Reply Obj. 2: According to the Philosopher (Ethic. i, 3), "equal certainty should not be sought in all things, but in each matter according to its proper mode." And since the matter of prudence is the contingent singulars about which are human actions, the certainty of prudence cannot be so great as to be devoid of all solicitude.

Reply Obj. 3: The magnanimous man is said to be "slow and leisurely" not because he is solicitous about nothing, but because he is not over-solicitous about many things, and is trustful in matters where he ought to have trust, and is not over-solicitous about them: for over-much fear and distrust are the cause of over-solicitude, since fear makes us take counsel, as stated above (I-II, Q. 44, A. 2) when we were treating of the passion of fear.

TENTH ARTICLE [II-II, Q. 47, Art. 10]

Whether Solicitude Belongs to Prudence?

Objection 1: It would seem that prudence does not extend to the governing of many, but only to the government of oneself. For the Philosopher says (Ethic. v, 1) that virtue directed to the common good is justice. But prudence differs from justice. Therefore prudence is not directed to the common good.

Obj. 2: Further, he seems to be prudent, who seeks and does good for himself. Now those who seek the common good often neglect their own. Therefore they are not prudent.

Obj. 3: Further, prudence is specifically distinct from temperance and fortitude. But temperance and fortitude seem to be related only to a man's own good. Therefore the same applies to prudence.

*On the contrary,* Our Lord said (Matt. 24:45): "Who, thinkest thou, is a faithful and prudent [Douay: 'wise'] servant whom his lord hath appointed over his family?"

*I answer that,* According to the Philosopher (Ethic. vi, 8) some have held that prudence does not extend to the common good, but only to the good of the individual, and this because they thought that man is not bound to seek other than his own good. But this opinion is opposed to charity, which "seeketh not her own" (1 Cor. 13:5): wherefore the Apostle says of himself (1 Cor. 10:33): "Not seeking that which is profitable to myself, but to many, that they may be saved." Moreover it is contrary to right reason, which judges the common good to be better than the good of the individual.

Accordingly, since it belongs to prudence rightly to counsel, judge, and command concerning the means of obtaining a due end, it is evident that prudence regards not only the private good of the individual, but also the common good of the multitude.

Reply Obj. 1: The Philosopher is speaking there of moral virtue. Now just as every moral virtue that is directed to the common good is called "legal" justice, so the prudence that is directed to the common good is called "political" prudence, for the latter stands in the same relation to legal justice, as prudence simply so called to moral virtue.

Reply Obj. 2: He that seeks the good of the many, seeks in consequence his own good, for two reasons. First, because the individual good is impossible without the common good of the family, state, or kingdom. Hence Valerius Maximus says [*Fact. et Dict. Memor. iv, 6] of the ancient Romans that "they would rather be poor in a rich empire than rich in a poor empire." Secondly, because, since man is a part of the home and state, he must needs consider what is good for him by being prudent about the good of the many. For the good disposition of parts depends on their relation to the whole; thus Augustine says (Confess. iii, 8) that "any part which does not harmonize with its whole, is offensive."

Reply Obj. 3: Even temperance and fortitude can be directed to the common good, hence there are precepts of law concerning them as stated in *Ethic.* v, 1: more so, however, prudence and justice, since these belong to the rational faculty which directly regards the universal, just as the sensitive part regards singulars.

ELEVENTH ARTICLE [II-II, Q. 47, Art. 11]

Whether Prudence About One's Own Good Is Specifically the Same As That Which Extends to the Common Good?

Objection 1: It seems that prudence about one's own good is the same specifically as that which extends to the common good. For the Philosopher says (Ethic. vi, 8) that "political prudence, and prudence are the same habit, yet their essence is not the same."

Obj. 2: Further, the Philosopher says (Polit. iii, 2) that "virtue is the same in a good man and in a good ruler." Now political prudence is chiefly in the ruler, in whom it is architectonic, as it were. Since then prudence is a virtue of a good man, it seems that prudence and political prudence are the same habit.

Obj. 3: Further, a habit is not diversified in species or essence by things which are subordinate to one another. But the particular good, which belongs to prudence simply so called, is subordinate to the common good, which belongs to political prudence. Therefore prudence and political prudence differ neither specifically nor essentially.

*On the contrary,* "Political prudence," which is directed to the common good of the state, "domestic economy" which is of such things as relate to the common good of the household or family, and "monastic economy" which is concerned with things affecting the good of one person, are all distinct sciences. Therefore in like manner there are different kinds of prudence, corresponding to the above differences of matter.

*I answer that,* As stated above (A. 5; Q. 54, A. 2, ad 1), the species of habits differ according to the difference of object considered in its formal aspect. Now the formal aspect of all things directed to the end, is taken from the end itself, as shown above (I-II, Prolog.; Q. 102, A. 1), wherefore the species of habits differ by their relation to different ends. Again the individual good, the good of the family, and the good of the city and kingdom are different ends. Wherefore there must needs be different species of prudence corresponding to these different ends, so that one is "prudence" simply so called, which is directed to one's own good; another, "domestic prudence" which is directed to the common good of the home; and a third, "political prudence," which is directed to the common good of the state or kingdom.

Reply Obj. 1: The Philosopher means, not that political prudence is substantially the same habit as any kind of prudence, but that it is the same as the prudence which is directed to the common good. This is called "prudence" in respect of the common notion of prudence, i.e. as being right reason applied to action, while it is called "political," as being directed to the common good.

Reply Obj. 2: As the Philosopher declares (Polit. iii, 2), "it belongs to a good man to be able to rule well and to obey well," wherefore the virtue of a good man includes also that of a good ruler. Yet the virtue of the ruler and of the subject differs specifically, even as the virtue of a man and of a woman, as stated by the same authority (Polit. iii, 2).

Reply Obj. 3: Even different ends, one of which is subordinate to the other, diversify the species of a habit, thus for instance, habits directed to riding, soldiering, and civic life, differ specifically although their ends are subordinate to one another. In like manner, though the good of the individual is subordinate to the good of the many, that does not prevent this difference from making the habits differ specifically; but it follows that the habit which is directed to the last end is above the other habits and commands them.

TWELFTH ARTICLE [II-II, Q. 47, Art. 12]

Whether Prudence Is in Subjects, or Only in Their Rulers?

Objection 1: It would seem that prudence is not in subjects but only in their rulers. For the Philosopher says (Polit. iii, 2) that "prudence alone is the virtue proper to a ruler, while other virtues are common to subjects and rulers, and the prudence of the subject is not a virtue but a true opinion."

Obj. 2: Further, it is stated in *Polit.* i, 5 that "a slave is not competent to take counsel." But prudence makes a man take good counsel (Ethic. vi, 5). Therefore prudence is not befitting slaves or subjects.

Obj. 3: Further, prudence exercises command, as stated above (A. 8). But command is not in the competency of slaves or subjects but only of rulers. Therefore prudence is not in subjects but only in rulers.

*On the contrary,* The Philosopher says (Ethic. vi, 8) that there are two kinds of political prudence, one of which is "legislative" and belongs to rulers, while the other "retains the common name political," and is about "individual actions." Now it belongs also to subjects to perform these individual actions. Therefore prudence is not only in rulers but also in subjects.

*I answer that,* Prudence is in the reason. Now ruling and governing belong properly to the reason; and therefore it is proper to a man to reason and be prudent in so far as he has a share in ruling and governing. But it is evident that the subject as subject, and the slave as slave, are not competent to rule and govern, but rather to be ruled and governed. Therefore prudence is not the virtue of a slave as slave, nor of a subject as subject.

Since, however, every man, for as much as he is rational, has a share in ruling according to the judgment of reason, he is proportionately competent to have prudence. Wherefore it is manifest that prudence is in the ruler "after the manner of a mastercraft" (Ethic. vi, 8), but in the subjects, "after the manner of a handicraft."

Reply Obj. 1: The saying of the Philosopher is to be understood strictly, namely, that prudence is not the virtue of a subject as such.

Reply Obj. 2: A slave is not capable of taking counsel, in so far as he is a slave (for thus he is the instrument of his master), but he does take counsel in so far as he is a rational animal.

Reply Obj. 3: By prudence a man commands not only others, but also himself, in so far as the reason is said to command the lower powers.

THIRTEENTH ARTICLE [II-II, Q. 47, Art. 13]

Whether Prudence Can Be in Sinners?

Objection 1: It would seem that there can be prudence in sinners. For our Lord said (Luke 16:8): "The children of this world are more prudent [Douay: 'wiser'] in their generation than the children of light." Now the children of this world are sinners. Therefore there be prudence in sinners.

Obj. 2: Further, faith is a more excellent virtue

than prudence. But there can be faith in sinners. Therefore there can be prudence also.

Obj. 3: Further, according to *Ethic.* vi, 7, "we say that to be of good counsel is the work of prudent man especially." Now many sinners can take good counsel. Therefore sinners can have prudence.

*On the contrary,* The Philosopher declares (Ethic. vi, 12) that "it is impossible for a man be prudent unless he be good." Now no sinner is a good man. Therefore no sinner is prudent.

*I answer that,* Prudence is threefold. There is a false prudence, which takes its name from its likeness to true prudence. For since a prudent man is one who disposes well of the things that have to be done for a good end, whoever disposes well of such things as are fitting for an evil end, has false prudence, in far as that which he takes for an end, is good, not in truth but in appearance. Thus man is called "a good robber," and in this way may speak of "a prudent robber," by way of similarity, because he devises fitting ways of committing robbery. This is the prudence of which the Apostle says (Rom. 8:6): "The prudence [Douay: 'wisdom'] of the flesh is death," because, to wit, it places its ultimate end in the pleasures of the flesh.

The second prudence is indeed true prudence, because it devises fitting ways of obtaining a good end; and yet it is imperfect, from a twofold source. First, because the good which it takes for an end, is not the common end of all human life, but of some particular affair; thus when a man devises fitting ways of conducting business or of sailing a ship, he is called a prudent businessman, or a prudent sailor; secondly, because he fails in the chief act of prudence, as when a man takes counsel aright, and forms a good judgment, even about things concerning life as a whole, but fails to make an effective command.

The third prudence is both true and perfect, for it takes counsel, judges and commands aright in respect of the good end of man's whole life: and this alone is prudence simply so-called, and cannot be in sinners, whereas the first prudence is in sinners alone, while imperfect prudence is common to good and wicked men, especially that which is imperfect through being directed to a particular end, since that which is imperfect on account of a failing in the chief act, is only in the wicked.

Reply Obj. 1: This saying of our Lord is to be understood of the first prudence, wherefore it is not said that they are prudent absolutely, but that they are prudent in "their generation."

Reply Obj. 2: The nature of faith consists not in conformity with the appetite for certain right actions, but in knowledge alone. On the other hand prudence implies a relation to a right appetite. First because its principles are the ends in matters of action; and of such ends one forms a right estimate through the habits of moral virtue, which rectify the appetite: wherefore without the moral virtues there is no prudence, as shown above (I-II, Q. 58, A. 5); secondly because prudence commands right actions, which does not happen unless the appetite be right. Wherefore though faith on account of its object is more excellent than prudence, yet prudence, by its very nature, is more opposed to sin, which arises from a disorder of the appetite.

Reply Obj. 3: Sinners can take good counsel for an evil end, or for some particular good, but they do not perfectly take good counsel for the end of their whole life, since they do not carry that counsel into effect. Hence they lack prudence which is directed to the good only; and yet in them, according to the Philosopher (Ethic. vi, 12) there is "cleverness," [* *deinotike* ] i.e. natural diligence which may be directed to both good and evil; or "cunning," [* *panourgia* ] which is directed only to evil, and which we have stated above, to be "false prudence" or "prudence of the flesh."

FOURTEENTH ARTICLE [II-II, Q. 47, Art. 14]

Whether Prudence Is in All Who Have Grace?

Objection 1: It would seem that prudence is not in all who have grace. Prudence requires diligence, that one may foresee aright what has to be done. But many who have grace have not this diligence. Therefore not all who have grace have prudence.

Obj. 2: Further, a prudent man is one who takes good counsel, as stated above (A. 8, Obj. 2; A. 13, Obj. 3). Yet many have grace who do not take good counsel, and need to be guided by the counsel of others. Therefore not all who have grace, have prudence.

Obj. 3: Further, the Philosopher says (Topic. iii, 2) that "young people are not obviously prudent." Yet many young people have grace. Therefore prudence is not to be found in all who have grace.

*On the contrary,* No man has grace unless he be virtuous. Now no man can be virtuous without prudence, for Gregory says (Moral. ii, 46) that "the other virtues cannot be virtues at all unless they effect prudently what they desire to accomplish." Therefore all who have grace have prudence.

*I answer that,* The virtues must needs be connected together, so that whoever has one has all, as stated above (I-II, Q. 65, A. 1). Now whoever has grace has charity, so that he must needs have all the other virtues, and hence, since prudence is a virtue, as shown above (A. 4), he must, of necessity, have prudence also.

Reply Obj. 1: Diligence is twofold: one is merely sufficient with regard to things necessary for salvation; and such diligence is given to all who have grace, whom "His unction teacheth of all things" (1 John 2:27). There is also another diligence which is more than sufficient, whereby a man is able to make provision both for himself and for others, not only in matters necessary for salvation, but also in all things relating to human life; and such diligence as this is not in all who have grace.

Reply Obj. 2: Those who require to be guided by the counsel of others, are able, if they have grace, to take counsel for themselves in this point at least, that they require the counsel of others and can discern good from evil counsel.

Reply Obj. 3: Acquired prudence is caused by the exercise of acts, wherefore "its acquisition demands experience and time" (Ethic. ii, 1), hence it cannot be in the young, neither in habit nor in act. On the other hand gratuitous prudence is caused by divine infusion. Wherefore, in children who have been baptized but have not come to the use of reason, there is prudence as to habit but not as to act, even as in idiots; whereas in those who have come to the use of reason, it is also as to act, with regard to things necessary for salvation. This by practice merits increase, until it becomes perfect, even as the other virtues. Hence the Apostle says (Heb. 5:14) that "strong meat is for the perfect, for them who by custom have their senses exercised to the discerning of good and evil."

FIFTEENTH ARTICLE [II-II, Q. 47, Art. 15]

Whether Prudence Is in Us by Nature?

Objection 1: It would seem that prudence is in us by nature. The Philosopher says that things connected with prudence "seem to be natural," namely "synesis, gnome" [* *synesis* and gnome , Cf. I-II, Q. 57, A. 6] and the like, but not those which are connected with speculative wisdom. Now things belonging to the same genus have the same kind of origin. Therefore prudence also is in us from nature.

Obj. 2: Further, the changes of age are according to nature. Now prudence results from age, according to Job 12:12: "In the ancient is wisdom, and in length of days prudence." Therefore prudence is natural.

Obj. 3: Further, prudence is more consistent with human nature than with that of dumb animals. Now there are instances of a certain natural prudence in dumb animals, according to the Philosopher (De Hist. Anim. viii, 1). Therefore prudence is natural.

*On the contrary,* The Philosopher says (Ethic. ii, 1) that "intellectual virtue is both originated and fostered by teaching; it therefore demands experience and time." Now prudence is an intellectual virtue, as stated above (A. 4). Therefore prudence is in us, not by nature, but by teaching and experience.

*I answer that,* As shown above (A. 3), prudence includes knowledge both of universals, and of the singular matters of action to which prudence applies the universal principles. Accordingly, as regards the knowledge of universals, the same is to be said of prudence as of speculative science, because the primary universal principles of either are known naturally, as shown above (A. 6): except that the common principles of prudence are more connatural to man; for as the Philosopher remarks (Ethic. x, 7) "the life which is according to the speculative reason is better than that which is according to man": whereas the secondary universal principles, whether of the speculative or of the practical reason, are not inherited from nature, but are acquired by discovery through experience, or through teaching.

On the other hand, as regards the knowledge of particulars which are the matter of action, we must make a further distinction, because this matter of action is either an end or the means to an end. Now the right ends of human life are fixed; wherefore there can be a natural inclination in respect of these ends; thus it has been stated above (I-II, Q. 51, A. 1; Q. 63, A. 1) that some, from a natural inclination, have certain virtues whereby they are inclined to right ends; and consequently they also have naturally a right judgment about such like ends.

But the means to the end, in human concerns, far from being fixed, are of manifold variety according to the variety of persons and affairs. Wherefore since the inclination of nature is ever to something fixed, the knowledge of those means cannot be in man naturally, although, by reason of his natural disposition, one man has a greater aptitude than another in discerning them, just as it happens with regard to the conclusions of speculative sciences. Since then prudence is not about the ends, but about the means, as stated above (A. 6; I-II, Q. 57, A. 5), it follows that prudence is not from nature.

Reply Obj. 1: The Philosopher is speaking there of things relating to prudence, in so far as they are directed to ends. Wherefore he had said before (Ethic. vi, 5, 11) that "they are the principles of the *ou heneka* " [*Literally, 'for the sake of which' (are the means)], namely, the end; and so he does not mention euboulia among them, because it takes counsel about the means.

Reply Obj. 2: Prudence is rather in the old, not only because their natural disposition calms the movement of the sensitive passions, but also because of their long experience.

Reply Obj. 3: Even in dumb animals there are fixed ways of obtaining an end, wherefore we observe that all the animals of a same species act in like manner. But this is impossible in man, on account of his reason, which takes cognizance of universals, and consequently extends to an infinity of singulars.

SIXTEENTH ARTICLE [II-II, Q. 47, Art. 16]

Whether Prudence Can Be Lost Through Forgetfulness?

Objection 1: It would seem that prudence can be lost through forgetfulness. For since science is about necessary things, it is more certain than prudence which is about contingent matters of action. But science is lost by forgetfulness. Much more therefore is prudence.

Obj. 2: Further, as the Philosopher says (Ethic. ii, 3) "the same things, but by a contrary process, engender and corrupt virtue." Now the engendering of prudence requires experience which is made up "of many memories," as he states at the beginning of his *Metaphysics* (i, 1). Therefore since forgetfulness is contrary to memory, it seems that prudence can be lost through forgetfulness.

Obj. 3: Further, there is no prudence without knowledge of universals. But knowledge of universals can be lost through forgetfulness. Therefore prudence can also.

*On the contrary,* The Philosopher says (Ethic. vi, 5) that "forgetfulness is possible to art but not to prudence."

*I answer that,* Forgetfulness regards knowledge only, wherefore one can forget art and science, so as to lose them altogether, because they belong to the reason. But prudence consists not in knowledge alone, but also in an act of the appetite, because as stated above (A. 8), its principal act is one of command, whereby a man applies the knowledge he has, to the purpose of appetition and operation. Hence prudence is not taken away directly by forgetfulness, but rather is corrupted by the passions. For the Philosopher says (Ethic. vi, 5) that "pleasure and sorrow pervert the estimate of prudence": wherefore it is written (Dan. 13:56): "Beauty hath deceived thee, and lust hath subverted thy heart," and (Ex. 23:8): "Neither shalt thou take bribes which blind even the prudent [Douay: 'wise']."

Nevertheless forgetfulness may hinder prudence, in so far as the latter's command depends on knowledge which may be forgotten.

Reply Obj. 1: Science is in the reason only: hence the comparison fails, as stated above [*Cf. I-II, Q. 53, A. 1].

Reply Obj. 2: The experience required by prudence results not from memory alone, but also from the practice of commanding aright.

Reply Obj. 3: Prudence consists chiefly, not in the knowledge of universals, but in applying them to action, as stated above (A. 3). Wherefore forgetting the knowledge of universals does not destroy the principal part of prudence, but hinders it somewhat, as stated above.

# QUESTION 48

OF THE PARTS OF PRUDENCE (In One Article)

We must now consider the parts of prudence, under which head there are four points of inquiry:

(1) Which are the parts of prudence?

(2) Of its integral parts;

(3) Of its subjective parts;

(4) Of its potential parts.

ARTICLE [II-II, Q. 48, Art.]

Whether Three Parts of Prudence Are Fittingly Assigned?

Objection 1: It would seem that the parts of prudence are assigned unfittingly. Tully (De Invent. Rhet. ii, 53) assigns three parts of prudence, namely, "memory," "understanding" and "foresight." Macrobius (In Somn. Scip. i) following the opinion of Plotinus ascribes to prudence six parts, namely, "reasoning," "understanding," "circumspection," "foresight," "docility" and "caution." Aristotle says (Ethic. vi, 9, 10, 11) that "good counsel," "synesis" and "gnome" belong to prudence. Again under the head of prudence he mentions "conjecture," "shrewdness," "sense" and "understanding." And another Greek philosopher [*Andronicus; Cf. Q. 80, Obj. 4] says that ten things are connected with prudence, namely, "good counsel," "shrewdness," "foresight," "regnative [*Regnativa]," "military," "political" and "domestic prudence," "dialectics," "rhetoric" and "physics." Therefore it seems that one or the other enumeration is either excessive or deficient.

Obj. 2: Further, prudence is specifically distinct from science. But politics, economics, logic, rhetoric, physics are sciences. Therefore they are not parts of prudence.

Obj. 3: Further, the parts do not exceed the whole. Now the intellective memory or intelligence, reason, sense and docility, belong not only to prudence but also to all the cognitive habits. Therefore they should not be set down as parts of prudence.

Obj. 4: Further, just as counselling, judging and commanding are acts of the practical reason, so also is using, as stated above (I-II, Q. 16, A. 1). Therefore, just as "eubulia" which refers to counsel, is connected with prudence, and "synesis" and "gnome" which refer to judgment, so also ought something to have been assigned corresponding to use.

Obj. 5: Further, solicitude pertains to prudence, as stated above (Q. 47, A. 9). Therefore solicitude also should have been mentioned among the parts of prudence.

*I answer that,* Parts are of three kinds, namely, integral, as wall, roof, and foundations are parts of a house; *subjective,* as ox and lion are parts of animal; and *potential,* as the nutritive and sensitive powers are parts of the soul. Accordingly, parts can be assigned to a virtue in three ways. First, in likeness to integral parts, so that the things which need to concur for the perfect act of a virtue, are called the parts of that virtue. In this way, out of all the things mentioned above, eight may be taken as parts of prudence, namely, the six assigned by Macrobius; with the addition of a seventh, viz. *memory* mentioned by Tully; and eustochia or *shrewdness* mentioned by Aristotle. For the sense of prudence is also called *understanding* : wherefore the Philosopher says (Ethic. vi, 11): "Of such things one needs to have the sense, and this is understanding." Of these eight, five belong to prudence as a cognitive virtue, namely, memory, reasoning, understanding, *docility* and shrewdness: while the three others belong thereto, as commanding and applying knowledge to action, namely, foresight, circumspection*and*caution. The reason of their difference is seen from the fact that three things may be observed in reference to knowledge. In the first place, knowledge itself, which, if it be of the past, is called *memory,* if of the present, whether contingent or necessary, is called *understanding* or intelligence. Secondly, the acquiring of knowledge, which is caused either by teaching, to which pertains *docility,* or by discovery, and to this belongs to *eustochia* , i.e. "a happy conjecture," of which shrewdness is a part, which is a "quick conjecture of the middle term," as stated in Poster. i, 9. Thirdly, the use of knowledge, in as much as we proceed from things known to knowledge or judgment of other things, and this belongs to *reasoning.* And the reason, in order to command aright, requires to have three conditions. First, to order that which is befitting the end, and this belongs to *foresight;* secondly, to attend to the circumstances of the matter in hand, and this belongs to *circumspection;* thirdly, to avoid obstacles, and this belongs to *caution.*

The subjective parts of a virtue are its various species. In this way the parts of prudence, if we take them properly, are the prudence whereby a man rules himself, and the prudence whereby a man governs a multitude, which differ specifically as stated above (Q. 47, A. 11). Again, the prudence whereby a multitude is governed, is divided into various species according to the various kinds of multitude. There is the multitude which is united together for some particular purpose; thus an army is gathered together to fight, and the prudence that governs this is called *military.* There is also the multitude that is united together for the whole of life; such is the multitude of a home or family, and this is ruled by *domestic prudence* : and such again is the multitude of a city or kingdom, the ruling principle of which is *regnative prudence* in the ruler, and political prudence, simply so called, in the subjects.

If, however, prudence be taken in a wide sense, as including also speculative knowledge, as stated above (Q. 47, A. 2, ad 2) then its parts include *dialectics,* rhetoric and physics, according to three methods of prudence in the sciences. The first of these is the attaining of science by demonstration, which belongs to *physics* (if physics be understood to comprise all demonstrative sciences). The second method is to arrive at an opinion through probable premises, and this belongs to *dialectics.* The third method is to employ conjectures in order to induce a certain suspicion, or to persuade somewhat, and this belongs to *rhetoric.* It may be said, however, that these three belong also to prudence properly so called, since it argues sometimes from necessary premises, sometimes from probabilities, and sometimes from conjectures.

The potential parts of a virtue are the virtues connected with it, which are directed to certain secondary acts or matters, not having, as it were, the whole power of the principal virtue. In this way the parts of prudence are *good counsel,* which concerns counsel, *synesis,* which concerns judgment in matters of ordinary occurrence, and *gnome,* which concerns judgment in matters of exception to the law: while *prudence* is about the chief act, viz. that of commanding.

Reply Obj. 1: The various enumerations differ, either because different kinds of parts are assigned, or because that which is mentioned in one enumeration includes several mentioned in another enumeration. Thus Tully includes "caution" and "circumspection" under "foresight," and "reasoning," "docility" and "shrewdness" under "understanding."

Reply Obj. 2: Here domestic and civic prudence are not to be taken as sciences, but as kinds of prudence. As to the other three, the reply may be gathered from what has been said.

Reply Obj. 3: All these things are reckoned parts of prudence, not by taking them altogether, but in so far as they are connected with things pertaining to prudence.

Reply Obj. 4: Right command and right use always go together, because the reason's command is followed by obedience on the part of the lower powers, which pertain to use.

Reply Obj. 5: Solicitude is included under foresight.

# QUESTION 49

OF EACH QUASI-INTEGRAL PART OF PRUDENCE (In Eight Articles)

We must now consider each quasi-integral part of prudence, and under this head there are eight points of inquiry:

(1) Memory;

(2) Understanding or Intelligence;

(3) Docility;

(4) Shrewdness;

(5) Reason;

(6) Foresight;

(7) Circumspection;

(8) Caution.

FIRST ARTICLE [II-II, Q. 49, Art. 1]

Whether Memory Is a Part of Prudence?

Objection 1: It would seem that memory is not a part of prudence. For memory, as the Philosopher proves (De Memor. et Remin. i), is in the sensitive part of the soul: whereas prudence is in the rational part (Ethic. vi, 5). Therefore memory is not a part of prudence.

Obj. 2: Further, prudence is acquired and perfected by experience, whereas memory is in us from nature. Therefore memory is not a part of prudence.

Obj. 3: Further, memory regards the past, whereas prudence regards future matters of action, about which counsel is concerned, as stated in *Ethic.* vi, 2, 7. Therefore memory is not a part of prudence.

*On the contrary,* Tully (De Invent. Rhet. ii, 53) places memory among the parts of prudence.

*I answer that,* Prudence regards contingent matters of action, as stated above (Q. 47, A. 5). Now in such like matters a man can be directed, not by those things that are simply and necessarily true, but by those which occur in the majority of cases: because principles must be proportionate to their conclusions, and "like must be concluded from like" (Ethic. vi [*Anal. Post. i. 32]). But we need experience to discover what is true in the majority of cases: wherefore the Philosopher says (Ethic. ii, 1) that "intellectual virtue is engendered and fostered by experience and time." Now experience is the result of many memories as stated in *Metaph.* i, 1, and therefore prudence requires the memory of many things. Hence memory is fittingly accounted a part of prudence.

Reply Obj. 1: As stated above (Q. 47, AA. 3, 6), prudence applies universal knowledge to particulars which are objects of sense: hence many things belonging to the sensitive faculties are requisite for prudence, and memory is one of them.

Reply Obj. 2: Just as aptitude for prudence is in our nature, while its perfection comes through practice or grace, so too, as Tully says in his Rhetoric [*Ad Herenn. de Arte Rhet. iii, 16, 24], memory not only arises from nature, but is also aided by art and diligence.

There are four things whereby a man perfects his memory. First, when a man wishes to remember a thing, he should take some suitable yet somewhat unwonted illustration of it, since the unwonted strikes us more, and so makes a greater and stronger impression on the mind; the mind; and this explains why we remember better what we saw when we were children. Now the reason for the necessity of finding these illustrations or images, is that simple and spiritual impressions easily slip from the mind, unless they be tied as it were to some corporeal image, because human knowledge has a greater hold on sensible objects. For this reason memory is assigned to the sensitive part of the soul. Secondly, whatever a man wishes to retain in his memory he must carefully consider and set in order, so that he may pass easily from one memory to another. Hence the Philosopher says (De Memor. et Remin. ii): "Sometimes a place brings memories back to us: the reason being that we pass quickly from the one to the other." Thirdly, we must be anxious and earnest about the things we wish to remember, because the more a thing is impressed on the mind, the less it is liable to slip out of it. Wherefore Tully says in his Rhetoric [*Ad Herenn. de Arte Rhet. iii.] that "anxiety preserves the figures of images entire." Fourthly, we should often reflect on the things we wish to remember. Hence the Philosopher says (De Memoria i) that "reflection preserves memories," because as he remarks (De Memoria ii) "custom is a second nature": wherefore when we reflect on a thing frequently, we quickly call it to mind, through passing from one thing to another by a kind of natural order.

Reply Obj. 3: It behooves us to argue, as it were, about the future from the past; wherefore memory of the past is necessary in order to take good counsel for the future.

SECOND ARTICLE [II-II, Q. 49, Art. 2]

Whether Understanding* Is a Part of Prudence? [*Otherwise intuition; Aristotle's word is *nous* ]

Objection 1: It would seem that understanding is not a part of prudence. When two things are members of a division, one is not part of the other. But intellectual virtue is divided into understanding and prudence, according to *Ethic.* vi, 3. Therefore understanding should not be reckoned a part of prudence.

Obj. 2: Further, understanding is numbered among the gifts of the Holy Ghost, and corresponds to faith, as stated above (Q. 8, AA. 1, 8). But prudence is a virtue other than faith, as is clear from what has been said above (Q. 4, A. 8; I-II, Q. 62, A. 2). Therefore understanding does not pertain to prudence.

Obj. 3: Further, prudence is about singular matters of action (Ethic. vi, 7): whereas understanding takes cognizance of universal and immaterial objects (De Anima iii, 4). Therefore understanding is not a part of prudence.

*On the contrary,* Tully [*De Invent. Rhet. ii, 53] accounts "intelligence" a part of prudence, and Macrobius [*In Somn. Scip. i, 8] mentions "understanding," which comes to the same.

*I answer that,* Understanding denotes here, not the intellectual power, but the right estimate about some final principle, which is taken as self-evident: thus we are said to understand the first principles of demonstrations. Now every deduction of reason proceeds from certain statements which are taken as primary: wherefore every process of reasoning must needs proceed from some understanding. Therefore since prudence is right reason applied to action, the whole process of prudence must needs have its source in understanding. Hence it is that understanding is reckoned a part of prudence.

Reply Obj. 1: The reasoning of prudence terminates, as in a conclusion, in the particular matter of action, to which, as stated above (Q. 47, AA. 3, 6), it applies the knowledge of some universal principle. Now a singular conclusion is argued from a universal and a singular proposition. Wherefore the reasoning of prudence must proceed from a twofold understanding. The one is cognizant of universals, and this belongs to the understanding which is an intellectual virtue, whereby we know naturally not only speculative principles, but also practical universal principles, such as "One should do evil to no man," as shown above (Q. 47, A. 6). The other understanding, as stated in *Ethic.* vi, 11, is cognizant of an extreme, i.e. of some primary singular and contingent practical matter, viz. the minor premiss, which must needs be singular in the syllogism of prudence, as stated above (Q. 47, AA. 3, 6). Now this primary singular is some singular end, as stated in the same place. Wherefore the understanding which is a part of prudence is a right estimate of some particular end.

Reply Obj. 2: The understanding which is a gift of the Holy Ghost, is a quick insight into divine things, as shown above (Q. 8, AA. 1, 2). It is in another sense that it is accounted a part of prudence, as stated above.

Reply Obj. 3: The right estimate about a particular end is called both "understanding," in so far as its object is a principle, and "sense," in so far as its object is a particular. This is what the Philosopher means when he says (Ethic. v, 11): "Of such things we need to have the sense, and this is understanding." But this is to be understood as referring, not to the particular sense whereby we know proper sensibles, but to the interior sense, whereby we judge of a particular.

THIRD ARTICLE [II-II, Q. 49, Art. 3]

Whether Docility Should Be Accounted a Part of Prudence?

Objection 1: It would seem that docility should not be accounted a part of prudence. For that which is a necessary condition of every intellectual virtue, should not be appropriated to one of them. But docility is requisite for every intellectual virtue. Therefore it should not be accounted a part of prudence.

Obj. 2: Further, that which pertains to a human virtue is in our power, since it is for things that are in our power that we are praised or blamed. Now it is not in our power to be docile, for this is befitting to some through their natural disposition. Therefore it is not a part of prudence.

Obj. 3: Further, docility is in the disciple: whereas prudence, since it makes precepts, seems rather to belong to teachers, who are also called "preceptors." Therefore docility is not a part of prudence.

*On the contrary,* Macrobius [*In Somn. Scip. i, 8] following the opinion of Plotinus places docility among the parts of prudence.

*I answer that,* As stated above (A. 2, ad 1; Q. 47, A. 3) prudence is concerned with particular matters of action, and since such matters are of infinite variety, no one man can consider them all sufficiently; nor can this be done quickly, for it requires length of time. Hence in matters of prudence man stands in very great need of being taught by others, especially by old folk who have acquired a sane understanding of the ends in practical matters. Wherefore the Philosopher says (Ethic. vi, 11): "It is right to pay no less attention to the undemonstrated assertions and opinions of such persons as are experienced, older than we are, and prudent, than to their demonstrations, for their experience gives them an insight into principles." Thus it is written (Prov. 3:5): "Lean not on thy own prudence," and (Ecclus. 6:35): "Stand in the multitude of the ancients" (i.e. the old men), "that are wise, and join thyself from thy heart to their wisdom." Now it is a mark of docility to be ready to be taught: and consequently docility is fittingly reckoned a part of prudence.

Reply Obj. 1: Although docility is useful for every intellectual virtue, yet it belongs to prudence chiefly, for the reason given above.

Reply Obj. 2: Man has a natural aptitude for docility even as for other things connected with prudence. Yet his own efforts count for much towards the attainment of perfect docility: and he must carefully, frequently and reverently apply his mind to the teachings of the learned, neither neglecting them through laziness, nor despising them through pride.

Reply Obj. 3: By prudence man makes precepts not only for others, but also for himself, as stated above (Q. 47, A. 12, ad 3). Hence as stated (Ethic. vi, 11), even in subjects, there is place for prudence; to which docility pertains. And yet even the learned should be docile in some respects, since no man is altogether self-sufficient in matters of prudence, as stated above.

FOURTH ARTICLE [II-II, Q. 49, Art. 4]

Whether Shrewdness Is Part of Prudence?

Objection 1: It would seem that shrewdness is not a part of prudence. For shrewdness consists in easily finding the middle term for demonstrations, as stated in *Poster.* i, 34. Now the reasoning of prudence is not a demonstration since it deals with contingencies. Therefore shrewdness does not pertain to prudence.

Obj. 2: Further, good counsel pertains to prudence according to *Ethic.* vi, 5, 7, 9. Now there is no place in good counsel for shrewdness [*Ethic. vi, 9; Poster. i, 34] which is a kind of *eustochia* , i.e. "a happy conjecture": for the latter is "unreasoning and rapid," whereas counsel needs to be slow, as stated in *Ethic.* vi, 9. Therefore shrewdness should not be accounted a part of prudence.

Obj. 3: Further, shrewdness as stated above (Q. 48) is a "happy conjecture." Now it belongs to rhetoricians to make use of conjectures. Therefore shrewdness belongs to rhetoric rather than to prudence.

*On the contrary,* Isidore says (Etym. x): "A solicitous man is one who is shrewd and alert ( solers citus )." But solicitude belongs to prudence, as stated above (Q. 47, A. 9). Therefore shrewdness does also.

*I answer that,* Prudence consists in a right estimate about matters of action. Now a right estimate or opinion is acquired in two ways, both in practical and in speculative matters, first by discovering it oneself, secondly by learning it from others.

Now just as docility consists in a man being well disposed to acquire a right opinion from another man, so shrewdness is an apt disposition to acquire a right estimate by oneself, yet so that shrewdness be taken for *eustochia* , of which it is a part. For *eustochia* is a happy conjecture about any matter, while shrewdness is "an easy and rapid conjecture in finding the middle term" (Poster. i, 34). Nevertheless the philosopher [*Andronicus; Cf. Q. 48, Obj. 1] who calls shrewdness a part of prudence, takes it for *eustochia* , in general, hence he says: "Shrewdness is a habit whereby congruities are discovered rapidly."

Reply Obj. 1: Shrewdness is concerned with the discovery of the middle term not only in demonstrative, but also in practical syllogisms, as, for instance, when two men are seen to be friends they are reckoned to be enemies of a third one, as the Philosopher says (Poster. i, 34). In this way shrewdness belongs to prudence.

Reply Obj. 2: The Philosopher adduces the true reason (Ethic. vi, 9) to prove that *euboulia* , i.e. good counsel, is not eustochia , which is commended for grasping quickly what should be done. Now a man may take good counsel, though he be long and slow in so doing, and yet this does not discount the utility of a happy conjecture in taking good counsel: indeed it is sometimes a necessity, when, for instance, something has to be done without warning. It is for this reason that shrewdness is fittingly reckoned a part of prudence.

Reply Obj. 3: Rhetoric also reasons about practical matters, wherefore nothing hinders the same thing belonging both to rhetoric and prudence. Nevertheless, conjecture is taken here not only in the sense in which it is employed by rhetoricians, but also as applicable to all matters whatsoever wherein man is said to conjecture the truth.

FIFTH ARTICLE [II-II, Q. 49, Art. 5]

Whether Reason Should Be Reckoned a Part of Prudence?

Objection 1: It would seem that reason should not be reckoned a part of prudence. For the subject of an accident is not a part thereof. But prudence is in the reason as its subject (Ethic. vi, 5). Therefore reason should not be reckoned a part of prudence.

Obj. 2: Further, that which is common to many, should not be reckoned a part of any one of them; or if it be so reckoned, it should be reckoned a part of that one to which it chiefly belongs. Now reason is necessary in all the intellectual virtues, and chiefly in wisdom and science, which employ a demonstrative reason. Therefore reason should not be reckoned a part of prudence

Obj. 3: Further, reason as a power does not differ essentially from the intelligence, as stated above (I, Q. 79, A. 8). If therefore intelligence be reckoned a part of prudence, it is superfluous to add reason.

*On the contrary,* Macrobius [*In Somn. Scip. i], following the opinion of Plotinus, numbers reason among the parts of prudence.

*I answer that,* The work of prudence is to take good counsel, as stated in *Ethic.* vi, 7. Now counsel is a research proceeding from certain things to others. But this is the work of reason. Wherefore it is requisite for prudence that man should be an apt reasoner. And since the things required for the perfection of prudence are called requisite or quasi-integral parts of prudence, it follows that reason should be numbered among these parts.

Reply Obj. 1: Reason denotes here, not the power of reason, but its good use.

Reply Obj. 2: The certitude of reason comes from the intellect. Yet the need of reason is from a defect in the intellect, since those things in which the intellective power is in full vigor, have no need for reason, for they comprehend the truth by their simple insight, as do God and the angels. On the other hand particular matters of action, wherein prudence guides, are very far from the condition of things intelligible, and so much the farther, as they are less certain and fixed. Thus matters of art, though they are singular, are nevertheless more fixed and certain, wherefore in many of them there is no room for counsel on account of their certitude, as stated in *Ethic.* iii, 3. Hence, although in certain other intellectual virtues reason is more certain than in prudence, yet prudence above all requires that man be an apt reasoner, so that he may rightly apply universals to particulars, which latter are various and uncertain.

Reply Obj. 3: Although intelligence and reason are not different powers, yet they are named after different acts. For intelligence takes its name from being an intimate penetration of the truth [*Cf. II-II, Q. 8, A. 1], while reason is so called from being inquisitive and discursive. Hence each is accounted a part of reason as explained above (A. 2; Q. 47, A. 2, 3).

SIXTH ARTICLE [II-II, Q. 49, Art. 6]

Whether Foresight* Should Be Accounted a Part of Prudence? [*"Providentia," which may be translated either "providence" or "foresight."]

Objection 1: It would seem that foresight should not be accounted a part of prudence. For nothing is part of itself. Now foresight seems to be the same as prudence, because according to Isidore (Etym. x), "a prudent man is one who sees from afar ( *porro videns* )": and this is also the derivation of *providentia* (foresight), according to Boethius (De Consol. v). Therefore foresight is not a part of prudence.

Obj. 2: Further, prudence is only practical, whereas foresight may be also speculative, because *seeing,* whence we have the word "to foresee," has more to do with speculation than operation. Therefore foresight is not a part of prudence.

Obj. 3: Further, the chief act of prudence is to command, while its secondary act is to judge and to take counsel. But none of these seems to be properly implied by foresight. Therefore foresight is not part of prudence.

On the contrary stands the authority of Tully and Macrobius, who number foresight among the parts of prudence, as stated above (Q. 48).

*I answer that,* As stated above (Q. 47, A. 1, ad 2, AA. 6, 13), prudence is properly about the means to an end, and its proper work is to set them in due order to the end. And although certain things are necessary for an end, which are subject to divine providence, yet nothing is subject to human providence except the contingent matters of actions which can be done by man for an end. Now the past has become a kind of necessity, since what has been done cannot be undone. In like manner, the present as such, has a kind of necessity, since it is necessary that Socrates sit, so long as he sits.

Consequently, future contingents, in so far as they can be directed by man to the end of human life, are the matter of prudence: and each of these things is implied in the word foresight, for it implies the notion of something distant, to which that which occurs in the present has to be directed. Therefore foresight is part of prudence.

Reply Obj. 1: Whenever many things are requisite for a unity, one of them must needs be the principal to which all the others are subordinate. Hence in every whole one part must be formal and predominant, whence the whole has unity. Accordingly foresight is the principal of all the parts of prudence, since whatever else is required for prudence, is necessary precisely that some particular thing may be rightly directed to its end. Hence it is that the very name of prudence is taken from foresight ( *providentia* ) as from its principal part.

Reply Obj. 2: Speculation is about universal and necessary things, which, in themselves, are not distant, since they are everywhere and always, though they are distant from us, in so far as we fail to know them. Hence foresight does not apply properly to speculative, but only to practical matters.

Reply Obj. 3: Right order to an end which is included in the notion of foresight, contains rectitude of counsel, judgment and command, without which no right order to the end is possible.

SEVENTH ARTICLE [II-II, Q. 49, Art. 7]

Whether Circumspection Can Be a Part of Prudence?

Objection 1: It would seem that circumspection cannot be a part of prudence. For circumspection seems to signify looking at one's surroundings. But these are of infinite number, and cannot be considered by the reason wherein is prudence. Therefore circumspection should not be reckoned a part of prudence.

Obj. 2: Further, circumstances seem to be the concern of moral virtues rather than of prudence. But circumspection seems to denote nothing but attention to circumstances. Therefore circumspection apparently belongs to the moral virtues rather than to prudence.

Obj. 3: Further, whoever can see things afar off can much more see things that are near. Now foresight enables a man to look on distant things. Therefore there is no need to account circumspection a part of prudence in addition to foresight.

On the contrary stands the authority of Macrobius, quoted above (Q. 48).

*I answer that,* As stated above (A. 6), it belongs to prudence chiefly to direct something aright to an end; and this is not done aright unless both the end be good, and the means good and suitable.

Since, however, prudence, as stated above (Q. 47, A. 3) is about singular matters of action, which contain many combinations of circumstances, it happens that a thing is good in itself and suitable to the end, and nevertheless becomes evil or unsuitable to the end, by reason of some combination of circumstances. Thus to show signs of love to someone seems, considered in itself, to be a fitting way to arouse love in his heart, yet if pride or suspicion of flattery arise in his heart, it will no longer be a means suitable to the end. Hence the need of circumspection in prudence, viz. of comparing the means with the circumstances.

Reply Obj. 1: Though the number of possible circumstances be infinite, the number of actual circumstances is not; and the judgment of reason in matters of action is influenced by things which are few in number.

Reply Obj. 2: Circumstances are the concern of prudence, because prudence has to fix them; on the other hand they are the concern of moral virtues, in so far as moral virtues are perfected by the fixing of circumstances.

Reply Obj. 3: Just as it belongs to foresight to look on that which is by its nature suitable to an end, so it belongs to circumspection to consider whether it be suitable to the end in view of the circumstances. Now each of these presents a difficulty of its own, and therefore each is reckoned a distinct part of prudence.

EIGHTH ARTICLE [II-II, Q. 49, Art. 8]

Whether Caution Should Be Reckoned a Part of Prudence?

Objection 1: It would seem that caution should not be reckoned a part of prudence. For when no evil is possible, no caution is required. Now no man makes evil use of virtue, as Augustine declares (De Lib. Arb. ii, 19). Therefore caution does not belong to prudence which directs the virtues.

Obj. 2: Further, to foresee good and to avoid evil belong to the same faculty, just as the same art gives health and cures ill-health. Now it belongs to foresight to foresee good, and consequently, also to avoid evil. Therefore caution should not be accounted a part of prudence, distinct from foresight.

Obj. 3: Further, no prudent man strives for the impossible. But no man can take precautions against all possible evils. Therefore caution does not belong to prudence.

*On the contrary,* The Apostle says (Eph. 5:15): "See how you walk cautiously [Douay: 'circumspectly']."

*I answer that,* The things with which prudence is concerned, are contingent matters of action, wherein, even as false is found with true, so is evil mingled with good, on account of the great variety of these matters of action, wherein good is often hindered by evil, and evil has the appearance of good. Wherefore prudence needs caution, so that we may have such a grasp of good as to avoid evil.

Reply Obj. 1: Caution is required in moral acts, that we may be on our guard, not against acts of virtue, but against the hindrance of acts of virtue.

Reply Obj. 2: It is the same in idea, to ensue good and to avoid the opposite evil, but the avoidance of outward hindrances is different in idea. Hence caution differs from foresight, although they both belong to the one virtue of prudence.

Reply Obj. 3: Of the evils which man has to avoid, some are of frequent occurrence; the like can be grasped by reason, and against them caution is directed, either that they may be avoided altogether, or that they may do less harm. Others there are that occur rarely and by chance, and these, since they are infinite in number, cannot be grasped by reason, nor is man able to take precautions against them, although by exercising prudence he is able to prepare against all the surprises of chance, so as to suffer less harm thereby.

## QUESTION 50

OF THE SUBJECTIVE PARTS OF PRUDENCE (In Four Articles)

We must, in due sequence, consider the subjective parts of prudence. And since we have already spoken of the prudence with which a man rules himself (Q. 47, seqq.), it remains for us to discuss the species of prudence whereby a multitude is governed. Under this head there are four points of inquiry:

(1) Whether a species of prudence is regnative?

(2) Whether political and (3) domestic economy are species of prudence?

(4) Whether military prudence is?

FIRST ARTICLE [II-II, Q. 50, Art. 1]

Whether a Species of Prudence Is Regnative?

Objection 1: It would seem that regnative should not be reckoned a species of prudence. For regnative prudence is directed to the preservation of justice, since according to *Ethic.* v, 6 the prince is the guardian of justice. Therefore regnative prudence belongs to justice rather than to prudence.

Obj. 2: Further, according to the Philosopher (Polit. iii, 5) a kingdom ( *regnum* ) is one of six species of government. But no species of prudence is ascribed to the other five forms of government, which are "aristocracy," "polity," also called "timocracy" [*Cf. *Ethic.* viii, 10], "tyranny," "oligarchy" and "democracy." Therefore neither should a regnative species be ascribed to a kingdom.

Obj. 3: Further, lawgiving belongs not only to kings, but also to certain others placed in authority, and even to the people, according to Isidore (Etym. v). Now the Philosopher (Ethic. vi, 8) reckons a part of prudence to be "legislative." Therefore it is not becoming to substitute regnative prudence in its place.

*On the contrary,* The Philosopher says (Polit. iii, 11) that "prudence is a virtue which is proper to the prince." Therefore a special kind of prudence is regnative.

*I answer that,* As stated above (Q. 47, AA. 8, 10), it belongs to prudence to govern and command, so that wherever in human acts we find a special kind of governance and command, there must be a special kind of prudence. Now it is evident that there is a special and perfect kind of governance in one who has to govern not only himself but also the perfect community of a city or kingdom; because a government is the more perfect according as it is more universal, extends to more matters, and attains a higher end. Hence prudence in its special and most perfect sense, belongs to a king who is charged with the government of a city or kingdom: for which reason a species of prudence is reckoned to be regnative.

Reply Obj. 1: All matters connected with moral virtue belong to prudence as their guide, wherefore "right reason in accord with prudence" is included in the definition of moral virtue, as stated above (Q. 47, A. 5, ad 1; I-II, Q. 58, A. 2, ad 4). For this reason also the execution of justice in so far as it is directed to the common good, which is part of the kingly office, needs the guidance of prudence. Hence these two virtues—prudence and justice—belong most properly to a king, according to Jer. 23:5: "A king shall reign and shall be wise, and shall execute justice and judgment in the earth." Since, however, direction belongs rather to the king, and execution to his subjects, regnative prudence is reckoned a species of prudence which is directive, rather than to justice which is executive.

Reply Obj. 2: A kingdom is the best of all governments, as stated in *Ethic.* viii, 10: wherefore the species of prudence should be denominated rather from a kingdom, yet so as to comprehend under regnative all other rightful forms of government, but not perverse forms which are opposed to virtue, and which, accordingly, do not pertain to prudence.

Reply Obj. 3: The Philosopher names regnative prudence after the principal act of a king which is to make laws, and although this applies to the other forms of government, this is only in so far as they have a share of kingly government.

SECOND ARTICLE [II-II, Q. 50, Art. 2]

Whether Political Prudence Is Fittingly Accounted a Part of Prudence?

Objection 1: It would seem that political prudence is not fittingly accounted a part of prudence. For regnative is a part of political prudence, as stated above (A. 1). But a part should not be reckoned a species with the whole. Therefore political prudence should not be reckoned a part of prudence.

Obj. 2: Further, the species of habits are distinguished by their various objects. Now what the ruler has to command is the same as what the subject has to execute. Therefore political prudence as regards the subjects, should not be reckoned a species of prudence distinct from regnative prudence.

Obj. 3: Further, each subject is an individual person. Now each individual person can direct himself sufficiently by prudence commonly so called. Therefore there is no need of a special kind of prudence called political.

*On the contrary,* The Philosopher says (Ethic. vi, 8) that "of the prudence which is concerned with the state one kind is a master-prudence and is called legislative; another kind bears the common name political, and deals with individuals."

*I answer that,* A slave is moved by his master, and a subject by his ruler, by command, but otherwise than as irrational and inanimate beings are set in motion by their movers. For irrational and inanimate beings are moved only by others and do not put themselves in motion, since they have no free-will whereby to be masters of their own actions, wherefore the rectitude of their government is not in their power but in the power of their movers. On the other hand, men who are slaves or subjects in any sense, are moved by the commands of others in such a way that they move themselves by their free-will; wherefore some kind of rectitude of government is required in them, so that they may direct themselves in obeying their superiors; and to this belongs that species of prudence which is called political.

Reply Obj. 1: As stated above, regnative is the most perfect species of prudence, wherefore the prudence of subjects, which falls short of regnative prudence, retains the common name of political prudence, even as in logic a convertible term which does not denote the essence of a thing retains the name of "proper."

Reply Obj. 2: A different aspect of the object diversifies the species of a habit, as stated above (Q. 47, A. 5). Now the same actions are considered by the king, but under a more general aspect, as by his subjects who obey: since many obey one king in various departments. Hence regnative prudence is compared to this political prudence of which we are speaking, as mastercraft to handicraft.

Reply Obj. 3: Man directs himself by prudence commonly so called, in relation to his own good, but by political prudence, of which we speak, he directs himself in relation to the common good.

THIRD ARTICLE [II-II, Q. 50, Art. 3]

Whether a Part of Prudence Should Be Reckoned to Be Domestic?

Objection 1: It would seem that domestic should not be reckoned a part of prudence. For, according to the Philosopher (Ethic. vi, 5) "prudence is directed to a good life in general": whereas domestic prudence is directed to a particular end, viz. wealth, according to *Ethic.* i, 1. Therefore a species of prudence is not domestic.

Obj. 2: Further, as stated above (Q. 47, A. 13) prudence is only in good people. But domestic prudence may be also in wicked people, since many sinners are provident in governing their household. Therefore domestic prudence should not be reckoned a species of prudence.

Obj. 3: Further, just as in a kingdom there is a ruler and subject, so also is there in a household. If therefore domestic like political is a species of prudence, there should be a paternal corresponding to regnative prudence. Now there is no such prudence. Therefore neither should domestic prudence be accounted a species of prudence.

*On the contrary,* The Philosopher states (Ethic. vi, 8) that there are various kinds of prudence in the government of a multitude, "one of which is domestic, another legislative, and another political."

*I answer that,* Different aspects of an object, in respect of universality and particularity, or of totality and partiality, diversify arts and virtues; and in respect of such diversity one act of virtue is principal as compared with another. Now it is evident that a household is a mean between the individual and the city or kingdom, since just as the individual is part of the household, so is the household part of the city or kingdom. And therefore, just as prudence commonly so called which governs the individual, is distinct from political prudence, so must domestic prudence be distinct from both.

Reply Obj. 1: Riches are compared to domestic prudence, not as its last end, but as its instrument, as stated in *Polit. i, 3. On the other hand, the end of political prudence is "a good life in general" as regards the conduct of the household. In*Ethic. i, 1 the Philosopher speaks of riches as the end of political prudence, by way of example and in accordance with the opinion of many.

Reply Obj. 2: Some sinners may be provident in certain matters of detail concerning the disposition of their household, but not in regard to "a good life in general" as regards the conduct of the household, for which above all a virtuous life is required.

Reply Obj. 3: The father has in his household an authority like that of a king, as stated in *Ethic.* viii, 10, but he has not the full power of a king, wherefore paternal government is not reckoned a distinct species of prudence, like regnative prudence.

FOURTH ARTICLE [II-II, Q. 50, Art. 4]

Whether Military Prudence Should Be Reckoned a Part of Prudence?

Objection 1: It would seem that military prudence should not be reckoned a part of prudence. For prudence is distinct from art, according to *Ethic.* vi, 3. Now military prudence seems to be the art of warfare, according to the Philosopher (Ethic. iii, 8). Therefore military prudence should not be accounted a species of prudence.

Obj. 2: Further, just as military business is contained under political affairs, so too are many other matters, such as those of tradesmen, craftsmen, and so forth. But there are no species of prudence corresponding to other affairs in the state. Neither therefore should any be assigned to military business.

Obj. 3: Further, the soldiers' bravery counts for a great deal in warfare. Therefore military prudence pertains to fortitude rather than to prudence.

*On the contrary,* It is written (Prov. 24:6): "War is managed by due ordering, and there shall be safety where there are many counsels." Now it belongs to prudence to take counsel. Therefore there is great need in warfare for that species of prudence which is called "military."

*I answer that,* Whatever things are done according to art or reason, should be made to conform to those which are in accordance with nature, and are established by the Divine Reason. Now nature has a twofold tendency: first, to govern each thing in itself, secondly, to withstand outward assailants and corruptives: and for this reason she has provided animals not only with the concupiscible faculty, whereby they are moved to that which is conducive to their well-being, but also with the irascible power, whereby the animal withstands an assailant. Therefore in those things also which are in accordance with reason, there should be not only "political" prudence, which disposes in a suitable manner such things as belong to the common good, but also a "military" prudence, whereby hostile attacks are repelled.

Reply Obj. 1: Military prudence may be an art, in so far as it has certain rules for the right use of certain external things, such as arms and horses, but in so far as it is directed to the common good, it belongs rather to prudence.

Reply Obj. 2: Other matters in the state are directed to the profit of individuals, whereas the business of soldiering is directed to the service belongs to fortitude, but the direction, protection of the entire common good.

Reply Obj. 3: The execution of military service belongs to fortitude, but the direction, especially in so far as it concerns the commander-in-chief, belongs to prudence.

## QUESTION 51

OF THE VIRTUES WHICH ARE CONNECTED WITH PRUDENCE (In Four Articles)

In due sequence, we must consider the virtues that are connected with prudence, and which are its quasi-potential parts. Under this head there are four points of inquiry:

(1) Whether *euboulia* is a virtue?

(2) Whether it is a special virtue, distinct from prudence?

(3) Whether *synesis* is a special virtue?

(4) Whether *gnome* is a special virtue?

[*These three Greek words may be rendered as the faculties of deliberating well ( *euboulia* ), of judging well according to common law ( synesis ), and of judging well according to general law ( gnome ), respectively.]

FIRST ARTICLE [II-II, Q. 51, Art. 1]

Whether *Euboulia* Is a Virtue?

Objection 1: It would seem that *euboulia* is not a virtue. For, according to Augustine (De Lib. Arb. ii, 18, 19) "no man makes evil use of virtue." Now some make evil use of *euboulia* or good counsel, either through devising crafty counsels in order to achieve evil ends, or through committing sin in order that they may achieve good ends, as those who rob that they may give alms. Therefore *euboulia* is not a virtue.

Obj. 2: Further, virtue is a perfection, according to *Phys.* vii. But euboulia is concerned with counsel, which implies doubt and research, and these are marks of imperfection. Therefore euboulia is not a virtue.

Obj. 3: Further, virtues are connected with one another, as stated above (I-II, Q. 65). Now *euboulia* is not connected with the other virtues, since many sinners take good-counsel, and many godly men are slow in taking counsel. Therefore *euboulia* is not a virtue.

*On the contrary,* According to the Philosopher (Ethic. vi, 9) euboulia "is a right counselling." Now the perfection of virtue consists in right reason. Therefore euboulia is a virtue.

*I answer that,* As stated above (Q. 47, A. 4) the nature of a human virtue consists in making a human act good. Now among the acts of man, it is proper to him to take counsel, since this denotes a research of the reason about the actions he has to perform and whereof human life consists, for the speculative life is above man, as stated in *Ethic.* x. But euboulia signifies goodness of counsel, for it is derived from the *eu* , good, and boule , counsel, being "a good counsel" or rather "a disposition to take good counsel." Hence it is evident that *euboulia* is a human virtue.

Reply Obj. 1: There is no good counsel either in deliberating for an evil end, or in discovering evil means for attaining a good end, even as in speculative matters, there is no good reasoning either in coming to a false conclusion, or in coming to a true conclusion from false premisses through employing an unsuitable middle term. Hence both the aforesaid processes are contrary to *euboulia,* as the Philosopher declares (Ethic. vi, 9).

Reply Obj. 2: Although virtue is essentially a perfection, it does not follow that whatever is the matter of a virtue implies perfection. For man needs to be perfected by virtues in all his parts, and this not only as regards the acts of reason, of which counsel is one, but also as regards the passions of the sensitive appetite, which are still more imperfect.

It may also be replied that human virtue is a perfection according to the mode of man, who is unable by simple insight to comprehend with certainty the truth of things, especially in matters of action which are contingent.

Reply Obj. 3: In no sinner as such is *euboulia* to be found: since all sin is contrary to taking good counsel. For good counsel requires not only the discovery or devising of fit means for the end, but also other circumstances. Such are suitable time, so that one be neither too slow nor too quick in taking counsel, and the mode of taking counsel, so that one be firm in the counsel taken, and other like due circumstances, which sinners fail to observe when they sin. On the other hand, every virtuous man takes good counsel in those things which are directed to the end of virtue, although perhaps he does not take good counsel in other particular matters, for instance in matters of trade, or warfare, or the like.

SECOND ARTICLE [II-II, Q. 51, Art. 2]

Whether *Euboulia* Is a Special Virtue, Distinct from Prudence?

Objection 1: It would seem that *euboulia* is not a distinct virtue from prudence. For, according to the Philosopher (Ethic. vi, 5), the "prudent man is, seemingly, one who takes good counsel." Now this belongs to *euboulia* as stated above. Therefore *euboulia* is not distinct from prudence.

Obj. 2: Further, human acts to which human virtues are directed, are specified chiefly by their end, as stated above (I-II, Q. 1, A. 3; Q. 18, AA. 4, 6). Now *euboulia* and prudence are directed to the same end, as stated in Ethic. vi, 9, not indeed to some particular end, but to the common end of all life. Therefore *euboulia* is not a distinct virtue from prudence.

Obj. 3: Further, in speculative sciences, research and decision belong to the same science. Therefore in like manner these belong to the same virtue in practical matters. Now research belongs to *euboulia,* while decision belongs to prudence. There euboulia is not a distinct virtue from prudence.

*On the contrary,* Prudence is preceptive, according to Ethic. vi, 10. But this does not apply to euboulia . Therefore euboulia is a distinct virtue from prudence.

*I answer that,* As stated above (A. 1), virtue is properly directed to an act which it renders good; and consequently virtues must differ according to different acts, especially when there is a different kind of goodness in the acts. For, if various acts contained the same kind of goodness, they would belong to the same virtue: thus the goodness of love, desire and joy depends on the same, wherefore all these belong to the same virtue of charity.

Now acts of the reason that are ordained to action are diverse, nor have they the same kind of goodness: since it is owing to different causes that a man acquires good counsel, good judgment, or good command, inasmuch as these are sometimes separated from one another. Consequently *euboulia* which makes man take good counsel must needs be a distinct virtue from prudence, which makes man command well. And since counsel is directed to command as to that which is principal, so *euboulia* is directed to prudence as to a principal virtue, without which it would be no virtue at all, even as neither are the moral virtues without prudence, nor the other virtues without charity.

Reply Obj. 1: It belongs to prudence to take good counsel by commanding it, to *euboulia* by eliciting it.

Reply Obj. 2: Different acts are directed in different degrees to the one end which is "a good life in general" [*Ethic. vi, 5]: for counsel comes first, judgment follows, and command comes last. The last named has an immediate relation to the last end: whereas the other two acts are related thereto remotely. Nevertheless these have certain proximate ends of their own, the end of counsel being the discovery of what has to be done, and the end of judgment, certainty. Hence this proves not that *euboulia* is not a distinct virtue from prudence, but that it is subordinate thereto, as a secondary to a principal virtue.

Reply Obj. 3: Even in speculative matters the rational science of dialectics, which is directed to research and discovery, is distinct from demonstrative science, which decides the truth.

THIRD ARTICLE [II-II, Q. 51, Art. 3]

Whether *Synesis* Is a Virtue?

Objection 1: It would seem that *synesis* is not a virtue. Virtues are not in us by nature, according to Ethic. ii, 1. But *synesis* is natural to some, as the Philosopher states (Ethic. vi, 11). Therefore *synesis* is not a virtue.

Obj. 2: Further, as stated in the same book (10), *synesis* is nothing but "a faculty of judging." But judgment without command can be even in the wicked. Since then virtue is only in the good, it seems that *synesis* is not a virtue.

Obj. 3: Further, there is never a defective command, unless there be a defective judgment, at least in a particular matter of action; for it is in this that every wicked man errs. If therefore *synesis* be reckoned a virtue directed to good judgment, it seems that there is no need for any other virtue directed to good command: and consequently prudence would be superfluous, which is not reasonable. Therefore *synesis* is not a virtue.

*On the contrary,* Judgment is more perfect than

counsel. But euboulia , or good counsel, is a virtue. Much more, therefore, is synesis a virtue, as being good judgment.

*I answer that,* synesis signifies a right judgment, not indeed about speculative matters, but about particular practical matters, about which also is prudence. Hence in Greek some, in respect of synesis are said to be synetoi, i.e. "persons of sense," or eusynetoi, i.e. "men of good sense," just as on the other hand, those who lack this virtue are called asynetoi, i.e. "senseless."

Now, different acts which cannot be ascribed to the same cause, must correspond to different virtues. And it is evident that goodness of counsel and goodness of judgment are not reducible to the same cause, for many can take good counsel, without having good sense so as to judge well. Even so, in speculative matters some are good at research, through their reason being quick at arguing from one thing to another (which seems to be due to a disposition of their power of imagination, which has a facility in forming phantasms), and yet such persons sometimes lack good judgment (and this is due to a defect in the intellect arising chiefly from a defective disposition of the common sense which fails to judge aright). Hence there is need, besides *euboulia* , for another virtue, which judges well, and this is called *synesis.*

Reply Obj. 1: Right judgment consists in the cognitive power apprehending a thing just as it is in reality, and this is due to the right disposition of the apprehensive power. Thus if a mirror be well disposed the forms of bodies are reflected in it just as they are, whereas if it be ill disposed, the images therein appear distorted and misshapen. Now that the cognitive power be well disposed to receive things just as they are in reality, is radically due to nature, but, as to its consummation, is due to practice or to a gift of grace, and this in two ways. First directly, on the part of the cognitive power itself, for instance, because it is imbued, not with distorted, but with true and correct ideas: this belongs to *synesis* which in this respect is a special virtue. Secondly indirectly, through the good disposition of the appetitive power, the result being that one judges well of the objects of appetite: and thus a good judgment of virtue results from the habits of moral virtue; but this judgment is about the ends, whereas *synesis* is rather about the means.

Reply Obj. 2: In wicked men there may be right judgment of a universal principle, but their judgment is always corrupt in the particular matter of action, as stated above (Q. 47, A. 13).

Reply Obj. 3: Sometimes after judging aright we delay to execute or execute negligently or inordinately. Hence after the virtue which judges aright there is a further need of a final and principal virtue, which commands aright, and this is prudence.

FOURTH ARTICLE [II-II, Q. 51, Art. 4]

Whether *Gnome* Is a Special Virtue?

Objection 1: It would seem that *gnome* is not a special virtue distinct from synesis. For a man is said, in respect of synesis, to have good judgment. Now no man can be said to have good judgment, unless he judge aright in all things. Therefore synesis extends to all matters of judgment, and consequently there is no other virtue of good judgment called gnome.

Obj. 2: Further, judgment is midway between counsel and precept. Now there is only one virtue of good counsel, viz. *euboulia,* and only one virtue of good command, viz. prudence. Therefore there is only one virtue of good judgment, viz. synesis.

Obj. 3: Further, rare occurrences wherein there is need to depart from the common law, seem for the most part to happen by chance, and with such things reason is not concerned, as stated in *Phys.* ii, 5. Now all the intellectual virtues depend on right reason. Therefore there is no intellectual virtue about such matters.

*On the contrary,* The Philosopher concludes (Ethic. vi, 11) that gnome is a special virtue.

*I answer that* cognitive habits differ according to higher and lower principles: thus in speculative matters wisdom considers higher principles than science does, and consequently is distinguished from it; and so must it be also in practical matters. Now it is evident that what is beside the order of a lower principle or cause, is sometimes reducible to the order of a higher principle; thus monstrous births of animals are beside the order of the active seminal force, and yet they come under the order of a higher principle, namely, of a heavenly body, or higher still, of Divine Providence. Hence by considering the active seminal force one could not pronounce a sure judgment on such monstrosities, and yet this is possible if we consider Divine Providence.

Now it happens sometimes that something has to be done which is not covered by the common rules of actions, for instance in the case of the enemy of one's country, when it would be wrong to give him back his deposit, or in other similar cases. Hence it is necessary to judge of such matters according to higher principles than the common laws, according to which *synesis* judges: and corresponding to such higher principles it is necessary to have a higher virtue of judgment, which is called *gnome,* and which denotes a certain discrimination in judgment.

Reply Obj. 1: *Synesis* judges rightly about all actions that are covered by the common rules: but certain things have to be judged beside these common rules, as stated above.

Reply Obj. 2: Judgment about a thing should be formed from the proper principles thereof, whereas research is made by employing also common principles. Wherefore also in speculative matters, dialectics which aims at research proceeds from common principles; while demonstration which tends to judgment, proceeds from proper principles. Hence *euboulia* to which the research of counsel belongs is one for all, but not so *synesis* whose act is judicial. Command considers in all matters the one aspect of good, wherefore prudence also is only one.

Reply Obj. 3: It belongs to Divine Providence alone to consider all things that may happen beside the common course. On the other hand, among men, he who is most discerning can judge a greater number of such things by his reason: this belongs to *gnome,* which denotes a certain discrimination in judgment.

## QUESTION 52

OF THE GIFT OF COUNSEL (In Four Articles)

We must now consider the gift of counsel which corresponds to prudence. Under this head there are four points of inquiry:

(1) Whether counsel should be reckoned among the seven gifts of the Holy Ghost?

(2) Whether the gift of counsel corresponds to prudence?

(3) Whether the gift of counsel remains in heaven?

(4) Whether the fifth beatitude, "Blessed are the merciful," etc. corresponds to the gift of counsel?

FIRST ARTICLE [II-II, Q. 52, Art. 1]

Whether Counsel Should Be Reckoned Among the Gifts of the Holy Ghost?

Objection 1: It would seem that counsel should not be reckoned among the gifts of the Holy Ghost. The gifts of the Holy Ghost are given as a help to the virtues, according to Gregory (Moral. ii, 49). Now for the purpose of taking counsel, man is sufficiently perfected by the virtue of prudence, or even of *euboulia* , as is evident from what has been said (Q. 47, A. 1, ad 2; Q. 51, AA. 1, 2). Therefore counsel should not be reckoned among the gifts of the Holy Ghost.

Obj. 2: Further, the difference between the seven gifts of the Holy Ghost and the gratuitous graces seems to be that the latter are not given to all, but are divided among various people, whereas the gifts of the Holy Ghost are given to all who have the Holy Ghost. But counsel seems to be one of those things which are given by the Holy Ghost specially to certain persons, according to 1 Macc. 2:65: "Behold ... your brother Simon is a man of counsel." Therefore counsel should be numbered among the gratuitous graces rather than among the seven gifts of the Holy Ghost.

Obj. 3: Further, it is written (Rom. 8:14): "Whosoever are led by the Spirit of God, they are the sons of God." But counselling is not consistent with being led by another. Since then the gifts of the Holy Ghost are most befitting the children of God, who "have received the spirit of adoption of sons," it would seem that counsel should not be numbered among the gifts of the Holy Ghost.

*On the contrary,* It is written (Isa. 11:2): "(The Spirit of the Lord) shall rest upon him ... the spirit of counsel, and of fortitude."

*I answer that,* As stated above (I-II, Q. 68, A. 1), the gifts of the Holy Ghost are dispositions whereby the soul is rendered amenable to the motion of the Holy Ghost. Now God moves everything according to the mode of the thing moved: thus He moves the corporeal creature through time and place, and the spiritual creature through time, but not through place, as Augustine declares (Gen. ad lit. viii, 20, 22). Again, it is proper to the rational creature to be moved through the research of reason to perform any particular action, and this research is called counsel. Hence the Holy Ghost is said to move the rational creature by way of counsel, wherefore counsel is reckoned among the gifts of the Holy Ghost.

Reply Obj. 1: Prudence or *euboulia* , whether acquired or infused, directs man in the research of counsel according to principles that the reason can grasp; hence prudence or *euboulia* makes man take good counsel either for himself or for another. Since, however, human reason is unable to grasp the singular and contingent things which may occur, the result is that "the thoughts of mortal men are fearful, and our counsels uncertain" (Wis. 9:14). Hence in the research of counsel, man requires to be directed by God who comprehends all things: and this is done through the gift of counsel, whereby man is directed as though counseled by God, just as, in human affairs, those who are unable to take counsel for themselves, seek counsel from those who are wiser.

Reply Obj. 2: That a man be of such good counsel as to counsel others, may be due to a gratuitous grace; but that a man be counselled by God as to what he ought to do in matters necessary for salvation is common to all holy persons.

Reply Obj. 3: The children of God are moved by the Holy Ghost according to their mode, without prejudice to their free-will which is the "faculty of will and reason" [*Sent. iii, D, 24]. Accordingly the gift of counsel is befitting the children of God in so far as the reason is instructed by the Holy Ghost about what we have to do.

SECOND ARTICLE [II-II, Q. 52, Art. 2]

Whether the Gift of Counsel Corresponds to the Virtue of Prudence?

Objection 1: It would seem that the gift of counsel does not fittingly correspond to the virtue of prudence. For "the highest point of that which is underneath touches that which is above," as Dionysius observes (Div. Nom. vii), even as a man comes into contact with the angel in respect of his intellect. Now cardinal virtues are inferior to the gifts, as stated above (I-II, Q. 68, A. 8). Since, then, counsel is the first and lowest act of prudence, while command is its highest act, and judgment comes between, it seems that the gift corresponding to prudence is not counsel, but rather a gift of judgment or command.

Obj. 2: Further, one gift suffices to help one virtue, since the higher a thing is the more one it is, as proved in *De Causis.* Now prudence is helped by the gift of knowledge, which is not only speculative but also practical, as shown above (Q. 9, A. 3). Therefore the gift of counsel does not correspond to the virtue of prudence.

Obj. 3: Further, it belongs properly to prudence to direct, as stated above (Q. 47, A. 8). But it belongs to the gift of counsel that man should be directed by God, as stated above (A. 1). Therefore the gift of counsel does not correspond to the virtue of prudence.

*On the contrary,* The gift of counsel is about what has to be done for the sake of the end. Now prudence is about the same matter. Therefore they correspond to one another.

*I answer that,* A lower principle of movement is helped chiefly, and is perfected through being moved by a higher principle of movement, as a body through being moved by a spirit. Now it is evident that the rectitude of human reason is compared to the Divine Reason, as a lower motive principle to a higher: for the Eternal Reason is the supreme rule of all human rectitude. Consequently prudence, which denotes rectitude of reason, is chiefly perfected and helped through being ruled and moved by the Holy Ghost, and this belongs to the gift of counsel, as stated above (A. 1). Therefore the gift of counsel corresponds to prudence, as helping and perfecting it.

Reply Obj. 1: To judge and command belongs not to the thing moved, but to the mover. Wherefore, since in the gifts of the Holy Ghost, the position of the human mind is of one moved rather than of a mover, as stated above (A. 1; I-II, Q. 68, A. 1), it follows that it would be unfitting to call the gift corresponding to prudence by the name of command or judgment rather than of counsel whereby it is possible to signify that the counselled mind is moved by another counselling it.

Reply Obj. 2: The gift of knowledge does not directly correspond to prudence, since it deals with speculative matters: yet by a kind of extension it helps it. On the other hand the gift of counsel corresponds to prudence directly, because it is concerned about the same things.

Reply Obj. 3: The mover that is moved, moves through being moved. Hence the human mind, from the very fact that it is directed by the Holy Ghost, is enabled to direct itself and others.

THIRD ARTICLE [II-II, Q. 52, Art. 3]

Whether the Gift of Counsel Remains in Heaven?

Objection 1: It would seem that the gift of counsel does not remain in heaven. For counsel is about what has to be done for the sake of an end. But in heaven nothing will have to be done for the sake of an end, since there man possesses the last end. Therefore the gift of counsel is not in heaven.

Obj. 2: Further, counsel implies doubt, for it is absurd to take counsel in matters that are evident, as the Philosopher observes (Ethic. iii, 3). Now all doubt will cease in heaven. Therefore there is no counsel in heaven.

Obj. 3: Further, the saints in heaven are most conformed to God, according to 1 John 3:2, "When He shall appear, we shall be like to Him." But counsel is not becoming to God, according to Rom. 11:34, "Who hath been His counsellor?" Therefore neither to the saints in heaven is the gift of counsel becoming.

*On the contrary,* Gregory says (Moral. xvii, 12): "When either the guilt or the righteousness of each nation is brought into the debate of the heavenly Court, the guardian of that nation is said to have won in the conflict, or not to have won."

*I answer that,* As stated above (A. 2; I-II, Q. 68, A. 1), the gifts of the Holy Ghost are connected with the motion of the rational creature by God. Now we must observe two points concerning the motion of the human mind by God. First, that the disposition of that which is moved, differs while it is being moved from its disposition when it is in the term of movement. Indeed if the mover is the principle of the movement alone, when the movement ceases, the action of the mover ceases as regards the thing moved, since it has already reached the term of movement, even as a house, after it is built, ceases being built by the builder. On the other hand, when the mover is cause not only of the movement, but also of the form to which the movement tends, then the action of the mover does not cease even after the form has been attained: thus the sun lightens the air even after it is lightened. In this way, then, God causes in us virtue and knowledge, not only when we first acquire them, but also as long as we persevere in them: and it is thus that God causes in the blessed a knowledge of what is to be done, not as though they were ignorant, but by continuing that knowledge in them.

Nevertheless there are things which the blessed, whether angels or men, do not know: such things are not essential to blessedness, but concern the government of things according to Divine Providence. As regards these, we must make a further observation, namely, that God moves the mind of the blessed in one way, and the mind of the wayfarer, in another. For God moves the mind of the wayfarer in matters of action, by soothing the pre-existing anxiety of doubt; whereas there is simple nescience in the mind of the blessed as regards the things they do not know. From this nescience the angel's mind is cleansed, according to Dionysius (Coel. Hier. vii), nor does there precede in them any research of doubt, for they simply turn to God; and this is to take counsel of God, for as Augustine says (Gen. ad lit. v, 19) "the angels take counsel of God about things beneath them": wherefore the instruction which they receive from God in such matters is called "counsel."

Accordingly the gift of counsel is in the blessed, in so far as God preserves in them the knowledge that they have, and enlightens them in their nescience of what has to be done.

Reply Obj. 1: Even in the blessed there are acts directed to an end, or resulting, as it were, from their attainment of the end, such as the acts of praising God, or of helping on others to the end which they themselves have attained, for example the ministrations of the angels, and the prayers of the saints. In this respect the gift of counsel finds a place in them.

Reply Obj. 2: Doubt belongs to counsel according to the present state of life, but not to that counsel which takes place in heaven. Even so neither have the theological virtues quite the same acts in heaven as on the way thither.

Reply Obj. 3: Counsel is in God, not as receiving but as giving it: and the saints in heaven are conformed to God, as receivers to the source whence they receive.

FOURTH ARTICLE [II-II, Q. 52, Art. 4]

Whether the Fifth Beatitude, Which Is That of Mercy, Corresponds to the Gift of Counsel?

Objection 1: It would seem that the fifth beatitude, which is that of mercy, does not correspond to the gift of counsel. For all the beatitudes are acts of virtue, as stated above (I-II, Q. 69, A. 1). Now we are directed by counsel in all acts of virtue. Therefore the fifth beatitude does not correspond more than any other to counsel.

Obj. 2: Further, precepts are given about matters necessary for salvation, while counsel is given about matters which are not necessary for salvation. Now mercy is necessary for salvation, according to James 2:13, "Judgment without mercy to him that hath not done mercy." On the other hand poverty is not necessary for salvation, but belongs to the life of perfection, according to Matt. 19:21. Therefore the beatitude of poverty corresponds to the gift of counsel, rather than to the beatitude of mercy.

Obj. 3: Further, the fruits result from the beatitudes, for they denote a certain spiritual delight resulting from perfect acts of virtue. Now none of the fruits correspond to the gift of counsel, as appears from Gal. 5:22, 23. Therefore neither does the beatitude of mercy correspond to the gift of counsel.

*On the contrary,* Augustine says (De Serm. Dom. iv): "Counsel is befitting the merciful, because the one remedy is to be delivered from evils so great, to pardon, and to give."

*I answer that,* Counsel is properly about things useful for an end. Hence such things as are of most use for an end, should above all correspond to the gift of counsel. Now such is mercy, according to 1 Tim. 4:8, "Godliness [* *Pietas,* whence our English word pity, which is the same as mercy; see note on II-II, Q. 30, A. 1] is profitable to all things." Therefore the beatitude of mercy specially corresponds to the gift of counsel, not as eliciting but as directing mercy.

Reply Obj. 1: Although counsel directs in all the acts of virtue, it does so in a special way in works of mercy, for the reason given above.

Reply Obj. 2: Counsel considered as a gift of the Holy Ghost guides us in all matters that are directed to the end of eternal life whether they be necessary for salvation or not, and yet not every work of mercy is necessary for salvation.

Reply Obj. 3: Fruit denotes something ultimate. Now the ultimate in practical matters consists not in knowledge but in an action which is the end. Hence nothing pertaining to practical knowledge is numbered among the fruits, but only such things as pertain to action, in which practical knowledge is the guide. Among these we find "goodness" and "benignity" which correspond to mercy.

# QUESTION 53

OF IMPRUDENCE (In Six Articles)

We must now consider the vices opposed to prudence. For Augustine says (Contra Julian. iv, 3): "There are vices opposed to every virtue, not only vices that are in manifest opposition to virtue, as temerity is opposed to prudence, but also vices which have a kind of kinship and not a true but a spurious likeness to virtue; thus in opposition to prudence we have craftiness."

Accordingly we must consider first of all those vices which are in evident opposition to prudence, those namely which are due to a defect either of prudence or of those things which are requisite for prudence, and secondly those vices which have a false resemblance to prudence, those namely which are due to abuse of the things required for prudence. And since solicitude pertains to prudence, the first of these considerations will be twofold: (1) Of imprudence; (2) Of negligence which is opposed to solicitude.

Under the first head there are six points of inquiry:

(1) Concerning imprudence, whether it is a sin?
(2) Whether it is a special sin?
(3) Of precipitation or temerity;
(4) Of thoughtlessness;
(5) Of inconstancy;
(6) Concerning the origin of these vices.

FIRST ARTICLE [II-II, Q. 53, Art. 1]

Whether Imprudence Is a Sin?

Objection 1: It would seem that imprudence is not a sin. For every sin is voluntary, according to

Augustine [*De Vera Relig. xiv]; whereas imprudence is not voluntary, since no man wishes to be imprudent. Therefore imprudence is not a sin.

Obj. 2: Further, none but original sin comes to man with his birth. But imprudence comes to man with his birth, wherefore the young are imprudent; and yet it is not original sin which is opposed to original justice. Therefore imprudence is not a sin.

Obj. 3: Further, every sin is taken away by repentance. But imprudence is not taken away by repentance. Therefore imprudence is not a sin.

*On the contrary,* The spiritual treasure of grace is not taken away save by sin. But it is taken away by imprudence, according to Prov. 21:20, "There is a treasure to be desired, and oil in the dwelling of the just, and the imprudent [Douay: 'foolish'] man shall spend it." Therefore imprudence is a sin.

*I answer that,* Imprudence may be taken in two ways, first, as a privation, secondly, as a contrary. Properly speaking it is not taken as a negation, so as merely to signify the absence of prudence, for this can be without any sin. Taken as a privation, imprudence denotes lack of that prudence which a man can and ought to have, and in this sense imprudence is a sin by reason of a man's negligence in striving to have prudence.

Imprudence is taken as a contrary, in so far as the movement or act of reason is in opposition to prudence: for instance, whereas the right reason of prudence acts by taking counsel, the imprudent man despises counsel, and the same applies to the other conditions which require consideration in the act of prudence. In this way imprudence is a sin in respect of prudence considered under its proper aspect, since it is not possible for a man to act against prudence, except by infringing the rules on which the right reason of prudence depends. Wherefore, if this should happen through aversion from the Divine Law, it will be a mortal sin, as when a man acts precipitately through contempt and rejection of the Divine teaching: whereas if he act beside the Law and without contempt, and without detriment to things necessary for salvation, it will be a venial sin.

Reply Obj. 1: No man desires the deformity of imprudence, but the rash man wills the act of imprudence, because he wishes to act precipitately. Hence the Philosopher says (Ethic. vi, 5) that "he who sins willingly against prudence is less to be commended."

Reply Obj. 2: This argument takes imprudence in the negative sense. It must be observed however that lack of prudence or of any other virtue is included in the lack of original justice which perfected the entire soul. Accordingly all such lack of virtue may be ascribed to original sin.

Reply Obj. 3: Repentance restores infused prudence, and thus the lack of this prudence ceases; but acquired prudence is not restored as to the habit, although the contrary act is taken away, wherein properly speaking the sin of imprudence consists.

SECOND ARTICLE [II-II, Q. 53, Art. 2]

Whether Imprudence Is a Special Sin?

Objection 1: It would seem that imprudence is not a special sin. For whoever sins, acts against right reason, i.e. against prudence. But imprudence consists in acting against prudence, as stated above (A. 1). Therefore imprudence is not a special sin.

Obj. 2: Further, prudence is more akin to moral action than knowledge is. But ignorance which is opposed to knowledge, is reckoned one of the general causes of sin. Much more therefore should imprudence be reckoned among those causes.

Obj. 3: Further, sin consists in the corruption of the circumstances of virtue, wherefore Dionysius says (Div. Nom. iv) that "evil results from each single defect." Now many things are requisite for prudence; for instance, reason, intelligence, docility, and so on, as stated above (QQ. 48, 49). Therefore there are many species of imprudence, so that it is not a special sin.

*On the contrary,* Imprudence is opposed to prudence, as stated above (A. 1). Now prudence is a special virtue. Therefore imprudence too is one special vice.

*I answer that,* A vice or sin may be styled general in two ways; first, absolutely, because, to wit, it is general in respect of all sins; secondly, because it is general in respect of certain vices, which are its species. In the first way, a vice may be said to be general on two counts: first, essentially, because it is predicated of all sins: and in this way imprudence is not a general sin, as neither is prudence a general virtue: since it is concerned with special acts, namely the very acts of reason: secondly, by participation; and in this way imprudence is a general sin: for, just as all the virtues have a share of prudence, in so far as it directs them, so have all vices and sins a share of imprudence, because no sin can occur, without some defect in an act of the directing reason, which defect belongs to imprudence.

If, on the other hand, a sin be called general, not simply but in some particular genus, that is, as containing several species of sin, then imprudence is a general sin. For it contains various species in three ways. First, by opposition to the various subjective parts of prudence, for just as we distinguish the prudence that guides the individual, from other kinds that govern communities, as stated above (Q. 48; Q. 50, A. 7), so also we distinguish various kinds of imprudence. Secondly, in respect of the quasi-potential parts of prudence, which are virtues connected with it, and correspond to the several acts of reason. Thus, by defect of "counsel" to which *euboulia* corresponds, "precipitation" or "temerity" is a species of imprudence; by defect of "judgment," to which *synesis* (judging well according to common law) and *gnome* (judging well according to general law) refer, there is "thoughtlessness"; while "inconstancy" and "negligence" correspond to the "command" which is the proper act of prudence. Thirdly, this may be taken by opposition to those things which are requisite for prudence, which are the quasi-integral parts of prudence. Since however all these things are intended for the direction of the aforesaid three acts of reason, it follows that all the opposite defects are reducible to the four parts mentioned above. Thus incautiousness and incircumspection are included in "thoughtlessness"; lack of docility, memory, or reason is referable to "precipitation"; improvidence, lack of intelligence and of shrewdness, belong to "negligence" and "inconstancy."

Reply Obj. 1: This argument considers generality by participation.

Reply Obj. 2: Since knowledge is further removed from morality than prudence is, according to their respective proper natures, it follows that ignorance has the nature of mortal sin, not of itself, but on account either of a preceding negligence, or of the consequent result, and for this reason it is reckoned one of the general causes of sin. On the other hand imprudence, by its very nature, denotes a moral vice; and for this reason it can be called a special sin.

Reply Obj. 3: When various circumstances are corrupted for the same motive, the species of sin is not multiplied: thus it is the same species of sin to take what is not one's own, where one ought not, and when one ought not. If, however, there be various motives, there are various species: for instance, if one man were to take another's property from where he ought not, so as to wrong a sacred place, this would constitute the species called sacrilege, while if another were to take another's property when he ought not, merely through the lust of possession, this would be a case of simple avarice. Hence the lack of those things which are requisite for prudence, does not constitute a diversity of species, except in so far as they are directed to different acts of reason, as stated above.

THIRD ARTICLE [II-II, Q. 53, Art. 3]

Whether Precipitation Is a Sin Included in Imprudence?

Objection 1: It would seem that precipitation is not a sin included in imprudence. Imprudence is opposed to the virtue of prudence; whereas precipitation is opposed to the gift of counsel, according to Gregory, who says (Moral. ii, 49) that the gift of "counsel is given as a remedy to precipitation." Therefore precipitation is not a sin contained under imprudence.

Obj. 2: Further, precipitation seemingly pertains to rashness. Now rashness implies presumption, which pertains to pride. Therefore precipitation is not a vice contained under imprudence.

Obj. 3: Further, precipitation seems to denote inordinate haste. Now sin happens in counselling not only through being over hasty but also through being over slow, so that the opportunity for action passes by, and through corruption of other circumstances, as stated in *Ethic.* vi, 9. Therefore there is no reason for reckoning precipitation as a sin contained under imprudence, rather than slowness, or something else of the kind pertaining to inordinate counsel.

*On the contrary,* It is written (Prov. 4:19): "The way of the wicked is darksome, they know not where they fall." Now the darksome ways of ungodliness belong to imprudence. Therefore imprudence leads a man to fall or to be precipitate.

*I answer that,* Precipitation is ascribed metaphorically to acts of the soul, by way of similitude to bodily movement. Now a thing is said to be precipitated as regards bodily movement, when it is brought down from above by the impulse either of its own movement or of another's, and not in orderly fashion by degrees. Now the summit of the soul is the reason, and the base is reached in the action performed by the body; while the steps that intervene by which one ought to descend in orderly fashion are *memory* of the past, *intelligence* of the present, shrewdness in considering the future outcome, *reasoning* which compares one thing with another, *docility* in accepting the opinions of others. He that takes counsel descends by these steps in due order, whereas if a man is rushed into action by the impulse of his will or of a passion, without taking these steps, it will be a case of precipitation. Since then inordinate counsel pertains to imprudence, it is evident that the vice of precipitation is contained under imprudence.

Reply Obj. 1: Rectitude of counsel belongs to the gift of counsel and to the virtue of prudence; albeit in different ways, as stated above (Q. 52, A. 2), and consequently precipitation is opposed to both.

Reply Obj. 2: Things are said to be done rashly when they are not directed by reason: and this may happen in two ways; first through the impulse of the will or of a passion, secondly through contempt of the directing rule; and this is what is meant by rashness properly speaking, wherefore it appears to proceed from that root of pride, which refuses to submit to another's ruling. But precipitation refers to both, so that rashness is contained under precipitation, although precipitation refers rather to the first.

Reply Obj. 3: Many things have to be considered in the research of reason; hence the Philosopher declares (Ethic. vi, 9) that "one should be slow in taking counsel." Hence precipitation is more directly opposed to rectitude of counsel than over slowness is, for the latter bears a certain likeness to right counsel.

FOURTH ARTICLE [II-II, Q. 53, Art. 4]

Whether Thoughtlessness Is a Special Sin Included in Imprudence?

Objection 1: It would seem that thoughtlessness is not a special sin included in imprudence. For the Divine law does not incite us to any sin, according to Ps. 18:8, "The law of the Lord is unspotted";

and yet it incites us to be thoughtless, according to Matt. 10:19, "Take no thought how or what to speak." Therefore thoughtlessness is not a sin.

Obj. 2: Further, whoever takes counsel must needs give thought to many things. Now precipitation is due to a defect of counsel and therefore to a defect of thought. Therefore precipitation is contained under thoughtlessness: and consequently thoughtlessness is not a special sin.

Obj. 3: Further, prudence consists in acts of the practical reason, viz. *counsel*, judgment about what has been counselled, and command [*Cf. Q. 47, A. 8]. Now thought precedes all these acts, since it belongs also to the speculative intellect. Therefore thoughtlessness is not a special sin contained under imprudence.

*On the contrary,* It is written (Prov. 4:25): "Let thy eyes look straight on, and let thine eye-lids go before thy steps." Now this pertains to prudence, while the contrary pertains to thoughtlessness. Therefore thoughtlessness is a special sin contained under imprudence.

*I answer that,* Thought signifies the act of the intellect in considering the truth about something. Now just as research belongs to the reason, so judgment belongs to the intellect. Wherefore in speculative matters a demonstrative science is said to exercise judgment, in so far as it judges the truth of the results of research by tracing those results back to the first indemonstrable principles. Hence thought pertains chiefly to judgment; and consequently the lack of right judgment belongs to the vice of thoughtlessness, in so far, to wit, as one fails to judge rightly through contempt or neglect of those things on which a right judgment depends. It is therefore evident that thoughtlessness is a sin.

Reply Obj. 1: Our Lord did not forbid us to take thought, when we have the opportunity, about what we ought to do or say, but, in the words quoted, He encourages His disciples, so that when they had no opportunity of taking thought, either through lack of knowledge or through a sudden call, they should trust in the guidance of God alone, because "as we know not what to do, we can only turn our eyes to God," according to 2 Paral. 20:12: else if man, instead of doing what he can, were to be content with awaiting God's assistance, he would seem to tempt God.

Reply Obj. 2: All thought about those things of which counsel takes cognizance, is directed to the formation of a right judgment, wherefore this thought is perfected in judgment. Consequently thoughtlessness is above all opposed to the rectitude of judgment.

Reply Obj. 3: Thoughtlessness is to be taken here in relation to a determinate matter, namely, that of human action, wherein more things have to be thought about for the purpose of right judgment, than in speculative matters, because actions are about singulars.

FIFTH ARTICLE [II-II, Q. 53, Art. 5]

Whether Inconstancy Is a Vice Contained Under Imprudence?

Objection 1: It would seem that inconstancy is not a vice contained under imprudence. For inconstancy consists seemingly in a lack of perseverance in matters of difficulty. But perseverance in difficult matters belongs to fortitude. Therefore inconstancy is opposed to fortitude rather than to prudence.

Obj. 2: Further, it is written (James 3:16): "Where jealousy [Douay: 'envy'] and contention are, there are inconstancy and every evil work." But jealousy pertains to envy. Therefore inconstancy pertains not to imprudence but to envy.

Obj. 3: Further, a man would seem to be inconstant who fails to persevere in what he has proposed to do. Now this is a mark of "incontinency" in pleasurable matters, and of "effeminacy" or "squeamishness" in unpleasant matters, according to *Ethic.* vii, 1. Therefore inconstancy does not pertain to imprudence.

*On the contrary,* It belongs to prudence to prefer the greater good to the lesser. Therefore to forsake the greater good belongs to imprudence. Now this is inconstancy. Therefore inconstancy belongs to imprudence.

*I answer that,* Inconstancy denotes withdrawal from a definite good purpose. Now the origin of this withdrawal is in the appetite, for a man does not withdraw from a previous good purpose, except on account of something being inordinately pleasing to him: nor is this withdrawal completed except through a defect of reason, which is deceived in rejecting what before it had rightly accepted. And since it can resist the impulse of the passions, if it fail to do this, it is due to its own weakness in not standing to the good purpose it has conceived; hence inconstancy, as to its completion, is due to a defect in the reason. Now just as all rectitude of the practical reason belongs in some degree to prudence, so all lack of that rectitude belongs to imprudence. Consequently inconstancy, as to its completion, belongs to imprudence. And just as precipitation is due to a defect in the act of counsel, and thoughtlessness to a defect in the act of judgment, so inconstancy arises from a defect in the act of command. For a man is stated to be inconstant because his reason fails in commanding what has been counselled and judged.

Reply Obj. 1: The good of prudence is shared by all the moral virtues, and accordingly perseverance in good belongs to all moral virtues, chiefly, however, to fortitude, which suffers a greater impulse to the contrary.

Reply Obj. 2: Envy and anger, which are the source of contention, cause inconstancy on the part of the appetite, to which power the origin of inconstancy is due, as stated above.

Reply Obj. 3: Continency and perseverance seem to be not in the appetitive power, but in the reason. For the continent man suffers evil concupiscences, and the persevering man suffers grievous sorrows (which points to a defect in the appetitive power); but reason stands firm, in the continent man, against concupiscence, and in the persevering man, against sorrow. Hence continency and perseverance seem to be species of constancy which pertains to reason; and to this power inconstancy pertains also.

SIXTH ARTICLE [II-II, Q. 53, Art. 6]

Whether the Aforesaid Vices Arise from Lust?

Objection 1: It would seem that the aforesaid vices do not arise from lust. For inconstancy arises from envy, as stated above (A. 5, ad 2). But envy is a distinct vice from lust.

Obj. 2: Further, it is written (James 1:8): "A double-minded man is inconstant in all his ways." Now duplicity does not seem to pertain to lust, but rather to deceitfulness, which is a daughter of covetousness, according to Gregory (Moral. xxxi, 45). Therefore the aforesaid vices do not arise from lust.

Obj. 3: Further, the aforesaid vices are connected with some defect of reason. Now spiritual vices are more akin to the reason than carnal vices. Therefore the aforesaid vices arise from spiritual vices rather than from carnal vices.

*On the contrary,* Gregory declares (Moral. xxxi, 45) that the aforesaid vices arise from lust.

*I answer that,* As the Philosopher states (Ethic. vi, 5) "pleasure above all corrupts the estimate of prudence," and chiefly sexual pleasure which absorbs the mind, and draws it to sensible delight. Now the perfection of prudence and of every intellectual virtue consists in abstraction from sensible objects. Wherefore, since the aforesaid vices involve a defect of prudence and of the practical reason, as stated above (AA. 2, 5), it follows that they arise chiefly from lust.

Reply Obj. 1: Envy and anger cause inconstancy by drawing away the reason to something else; whereas lust causes inconstancy by destroying the judgment of reason entirely. Hence the Philosopher says (Ethic. vii, 6) that "the man who is incontinent through anger listens to reason, yet not perfectly, whereas he who is incontinent through lust does not listen to it at all."

Reply Obj. 2: Duplicity also is something resulting from lust, just as inconstancy is, if by duplicity we understand fluctuation of the mind from one thing to another. Hence Terence says (Eunuch. act 1, sc. 1) that "love leads to war, and likewise to peace and truce."

Reply Obj. 3: Carnal vices destroy the judgment of reason so much the more as they lead us away from reason.

# QUESTION 54

OF NEGLIGENCE (In Three Articles)

We must now consider negligence, under which head there are three points of inquiry:

(1) Whether negligence is a special sin?

(2) To which virtue is it opposed?

(3) Whether negligence is a mortal sin?

FIRST ARTICLE [II-II, Q. 54, Art. 1]

Whether Negligence Is a Special Sin?

Objection 1: It would seem that negligence is not a special sin. For negligence is opposed to diligence. But diligence is required in every virtue. Therefore negligence is not a special sin.

Obj. 2: Further, that which is common to every sin is not a special sin. Now negligence is common to every sin, because he who sins neglects that which withdraws him from sin, and he who perseveres in sin neglects to be contrite for his sin. Therefore negligence is not a special sin.

Obj. 3: Further, every special sin has a determinate matter. But negligence seems to have no determinate matter: since it is neither about evil or indifferent things (for no man is accused of negligence if he omit them), nor about good things, for if these be done negligently, they are no longer good. Therefore it seems that negligence is not a special vice.

*On the contrary,* Sins committed through negligence, are distinguished from those which are committed through contempt.

*I answer that,* Negligence denotes lack of due solicitude. Now every lack of a due act is sinful: wherefore it is evident that negligence is a sin, and that it must needs have the character of a special sin according as solicitude is the act of a special virtue. For certain sins are special through being about a special matter, as lust is about sexual matters, while some vices are special on account of their having a special kind of act which extends to all kinds of matter, and such are all vices affecting an act of reason, since every act of reason extends to any kind of moral matter. Since then solicitude is a special act of reason, as stated above (Q. 47, A. 9), it follows that negligence, which denotes lack of solicitude, is a special sin.

Reply Obj. 1: Diligence seems to be the same as solicitude, because the more we love ( *diligimus* ) a thing the more solicitous are we about it. Hence diligence, no less than solicitude, is required for every virtue, in so far as due acts of reason are requisite for every virtue.

Reply Obj. 2: In every sin there must needs be a defect affecting an act of reason, for instance a defect in counsel or the like. Hence just as precipitation is a special sin on account of a special act of reason which is omitted, namely counsel, although it may be found in any kind of sin; so negligence is a special sin on account of the lack of a special act of reason, namely solicitude, although it is found more or less in all sins.

Reply Obj. 3: Properly speaking the matter of negligence is a good that one ought to do, not that it is a good when it is done negligently, but because on account of negligence it incurs a lack of goodness, whether a due act be entirely omitted through lack of solicitude, or some due circumstance be omitted.

SECOND ARTICLE [II-II, Q. 54, Art. 2]

Whether Negligence Is Opposed to Prudence?

Objection 1: It would seem that negligence is not opposed to prudence. For negligence seems to be the same as idleness or laziness, which belongs to sloth, according to Gregory (Moral. xxxi, 45). Now sloth is not opposed to prudence, but to charity, as stated above (Q. 35, A. 3). Therefore negligence is not opposed to prudence.

Obj. 2: Further, every sin of omission seems to be due to negligence. But sins of omission are not opposed to prudence, but to the executive moral virtues. Therefore negligence is not opposed to prudence.

Obj. 3: Further, imprudence relates to some act of reason. But negligence does not imply a defect of counsel, for that is *precipitation,* nor a defect of judgment, since that is thoughtlessness, nor a defect of command, because that is inconstancy. Therefore negligence does not pertain to imprudence.

Obj. 4: Further, it is written (Eccles. 7:19): "He that feareth God, neglecteth nothing." But every sin is excluded by the opposite virtue. Therefore negligence is opposed to fear rather than to prudence.

*On the contrary,* It is written (Ecclus. 20:7): "A babbler and a fool ( imprudens ) will regard no time." Now this is due to negligence. Therefore negligence is opposed to prudence.

*I answer that,* Negligence is directly opposed to solicitude. Now solicitude pertains to the reason, and rectitude of solicitude to prudence. Hence, on the other hand, negligence pertains to imprudence. This appears from its very name, because, as Isidore observes (Etym. x) "a negligent man is one who fails to choose ( nec eligens )": and the right choice of the means belongs to prudence. Therefore negligence pertains to imprudence.

Reply Obj. 1: Negligence is a defect in the internal act, to which choice also belongs: whereas idleness and laziness denote slowness of execution, yet so that idleness denotes slowness in setting about the execution, while laziness denotes remissness in the execution itself. Hence it is becoming that laziness should arise from sloth, which is "an oppressive sorrow," i.e. hindering, the mind from action [*Cf. Q. 35, A. 1; I-II, Q. 35, A. 8].

Reply Obj. 2: Omission regards the external act, for it consists in failing to perform an act which is due. Hence it is opposed to justice, and is an effect of negligence, even as the execution of a just deed is the effect of right reason.

Reply Obj. 3: Negligence regards the act of command, which solicitude also regards. Yet the negligent man fails in regard to this act otherwise than the inconstant man: for the inconstant man fails in commanding, being hindered as it were, by something, whereas the negligent man fails through lack of a prompt will.

Reply Obj. 4: The fear of God helps us to avoid all sins, because according to Prov. 15:27, "by the fear of the Lord everyone declineth from evil." Hence fear makes us avoid negligence, yet not as though negligence were directly opposed to fear, but because fear incites man to acts of reason. Wherefore also it has been stated above (I-II, Q. 44, A. 2) when we were treating of the passions, that "fear makes us take counsel."

THIRD ARTICLE [II-II, Q. 54, Art. 3]

Whether Negligence Can Be a Mortal Sin?

Objection 1: It would seem that negligence cannot be a mortal sin. For a gloss of Gregory [*Moral. ix. 34] on Job 9:28, "I feared all my works," etc. says that "too little love of God aggravates the former," viz. negligence. But wherever there is mortal sin, the love of God is done away with altogether. Therefore negligence is not a mortal sin.

Obj. 2: Further, a gloss on Ecclus. 7:34, "For thy negligences purify thyself with a few," says: "Though the offering be small it cleanses the negligences of many sins." Now this would not be, if negligence were a mortal sin. Therefore negligence is not a mortal sin.

Obj. 3: Further, under the law certain sacrifices were prescribed for mortal sins, as appears from the book of Leviticus. Yet no sacrifice was prescribed for negligence. Therefore negligence is not a mortal sin.

*On the contrary,* It is written (Prov. 19:16): "He that neglecteth his own life [Vulg.: 'way'] shall die."

*I answer that,* As stated above (A. 2, ad 3), negligence arises out of a certain remissness of the will, the result being a lack of solicitude on the part of the reason in commanding what it should command, or as it should command. Accordingly negligence may happen to be a mortal sin in two ways. First on the part of that which is omitted through negligence. If this be either an act or a circumstance necessary for salvation, it will be a mortal sin. Secondly on the part of the cause: for if the will be so remiss about Divine things, as to fall away altogether from the charity of God, such negligence is a mortal sin, and this is the case chiefly when negligence is due to contempt.

But if negligence consists in the omission of an act or circumstance that is not necessary for salvation, it is not a mortal but a venial sin, provided the negligence arise, not from contempt, but from some lack of fervor, to which venial sin is an occasional obstacle.

Reply Obj. 1: Man may be said to love God less in two ways. First through lack of the fervor of charity, and this causes the negligence that is a venial sin: secondly through lack of charity itself, in which sense we say that a man loves God less when he loves Him with a merely natural love; and this causes the negligence that is a mortal sin.

Reply Obj. 2: According to the same authority (gloss), a small offering made with a humble mind and out of pure love, cleanses man not only from venial but also from mortal sin.

Reply Obj. 3: When negligence consists in the omission of that which is necessary for salvation, it is drawn to the other more manifest genus of sin. Because those sins that consist of inward actions, are more hidden, wherefore no special sacrifices were prescribed for them in the Law, since the offering of sacrifices was a kind of public confession of sin, whereas hidden sins should not be confessed in public.

## QUESTION 55

OF VICES OPPOSED TO PRUDENCE BY WAY OF RESEMBLANCE (In Eight Articles)

We must now consider those vices opposed to prudence, which have a resemblance thereto. Under this head there are eight points of inquiry:

(1) Whether prudence of the flesh is a sin?
(2) Whether it is a mortal sin?
(3) Whether craftiness is a special sin?
(4) Of guile;
(5) Of fraud;
(6) Of solicitude about temporal things;
(7) Of solicitude about the future;
(8) Of the origin of these vices.

FIRST ARTICLE [II-II, Q. 55, Art. 1]

Whether Prudence of the Flesh Is a Sin?

Objection 1: It would seem that prudence of the flesh is not a sin. For prudence is more excellent than the other moral virtues, since it governs them all. But no justice or temperance is sinful. Neither therefore is any prudence a sin.

Obj. 2: Further, it is not a sin to act prudently for an end which it is lawful to love. But it is lawful to love the flesh, "for no man ever hated his own flesh" (Eph. 5:29). Therefore prudence of the flesh is not a sin.

Obj. 3: Further, just as man is tempted by the flesh, so too is he tempted by the world and the devil. But no prudence of the world, or of the devil is accounted a sin. Therefore neither should any prudence of the flesh be accounted among sins.

*On the contrary,* No man is an enemy to God save for wickedness according to Wis. 14:9, "To God the wicked and his wickedness are hateful alike." Now it is written (Rom. 8:7): "The prudence [Vulg.: 'wisdom'] of the flesh is an enemy to God." Therefore prudence of the flesh is a sin.

*I answer that,* As stated above (Q. 47, A. 13), prudence regards things which are directed to the end of life as a whole. Hence prudence of the flesh signifies properly the prudence of a man who looks upon carnal goods as the last end of his life. Now it is evident that this is a sin, because it involves a disorder in man with respect to his last end, which does not consist in the goods of the body, as stated above (I-II, Q. 2, A. 5). Therefore prudence of the flesh is a sin.

Reply Obj. 1: Justice and temperance include in their very nature that which ranks them among the virtues, viz. equality and the curbing of concupiscence; hence they are never taken in a bad sense. On the other hand prudence is so called from foreseeing ( *providendo* ), as stated above (Q. 47, A. 1; Q. 49, A. 6), which can extend to evil things also. Therefore, although prudence is taken simply in a good sense, yet, if something be added, it may be taken in a bad sense: and it is thus that prudence of the flesh is said to be a sin.

Reply Obj. 2: The flesh is on account of the soul, as matter is on account of the form, and the instrument on account of the principal agent. Hence the flesh is loved lawfully, if it be directed to the good of the soul as its end. If, however, a man place his last end in a good of the flesh, his love will be inordinate and unlawful, and it is thus that the prudence of the flesh is directed to the love of the flesh.

Reply Obj. 3: The devil tempts us, not through the good of the appetible object, but by way of suggestion. Wherefore, since prudence implies direction to some appetible end, we do not speak of "prudence of the devil," as of a prudence directed to some evil end, which is the aspect under which the world and the flesh tempt us, in so far as worldly or carnal goods are proposed to our appetite. Hence we speak of "carnal" and again of "worldly" prudence, according to Luke 16:8, "The children of this world are more prudent [Douay: 'wiser'] in their generation," etc. The Apostle includes all in the "prudence of the flesh," because we covet the external things of the world on account of the flesh.

We may also reply that since prudence is in a certain sense called "wisdom," as stated above (Q. 47, A. 2, ad 1), we may distinguish a threefold prudence corresponding to the three kinds of temptation. Hence it is written (James 3:15) that there is a wisdom which is "earthly, sensual and devilish," as explained above (Q. 45, A. 1, ad 1), when we were treating of wisdom.

SECOND ARTICLE [II-II, Q. 55, Art. 2]

Whether Prudence of the Flesh Is a Mortal Sin?

Objection 1: It would seem that prudence of the flesh is a mortal sin. For it is a mortal sin to rebel against the Divine law, since this implies contempt of God. Now "the prudence [Douay: 'wisdom'] of the flesh ... is not subject to the law of God" (Rom. 8:7). Therefore prudence of the flesh is a mortal sin.

Obj. 2: Further, every sin against the Holy Ghost is a mortal sin. Now prudence of the flesh seems to be a sin against the Holy Ghost, for "it cannot be subject to the law of God" (Rom. 8:7), and so it seems to be an unpardonable sin, which is proper to the sin against the Holy Ghost. Therefore prudence of the flesh is a mortal sin.

Obj. 3: Further, the greatest evil is opposed to the greatest good, as stated in *Ethic.* viii, 10. Now prudence of the flesh is opposed to that prudence which is the chief of the moral virtues. Therefore prudence of the flesh is chief among mortal sins, so that it is itself a mortal sin.

*On the contrary,* That which diminishes a sin has not of itself the nature of a mortal sin. Now the thoughtful quest of things pertaining to the care of the flesh, which seems to pertain to carnal prudence, diminishes sin [*Cf. Prov. 6:30]. Therefore prudence of the flesh has not of itself the nature of a mortal sin.

*I answer that,* As stated above (Q. 47, A. 2, ad 1; A. 13), a man is said to be prudent in two ways. First, simply, i.e. in relation to the end of life as a whole. Secondly, relatively, i.e. in relation to some particular end; thus a man is said to be prudent in business or something else of the kind. Accordingly if prudence of the flesh be taken as corresponding to prudence in its absolute signification, so that a man place the last end of his whole life in the care of the flesh, it is a mortal sin, because he turns away from God by so doing, since he cannot have several last ends, as stated above (I-II, Q. 1, A. 5).

If, on the other hand, prudence of the flesh be taken as corresponding to particular prudence, it is a venial sin. For it happens sometimes that a man has an inordinate affection for some pleasure of the flesh, without turning away from God by a mortal sin; in which case he does not place the end of his whole life in carnal pleasure. To apply oneself to obtain this pleasure is a venial sin and pertains to prudence of the flesh. But if a man actually refers the care of the flesh to a good end, as when one is careful about one's food in order to sustain one's body, this is no longer prudence of the flesh, because then one uses the care of the flesh as a means to an end.

Reply Obj. 1: The Apostle is speaking of that carnal prudence whereby a man places the end of his whole life in the goods of the flesh, and this is a mortal sin.

Reply Obj. 2: Prudence of the flesh does not imply a sin against the Holy Ghost. For when it is stated that "it cannot be subject to the law of God," this does not mean that he who has prudence of the flesh, cannot be converted and submit to the law of God, but that carnal prudence itself cannot be subject to God's law, even as neither can injustice be just, nor heat cold, although that which is hot may become cold.

Reply Obj. 3: Every sin is opposed to prudence, just as prudence is shared by every virtue. But it does not follow that every sin opposed to prudence is most grave, but only when it is opposed to prudence in some very grave matter.

THIRD ARTICLE [II-II, Q. 55, Art. 3]

Whether Craftiness Is a Special Sin?

Objection 1: It would seem that craftiness is not a special sin. For the words of Holy Writ do not induce anyone to sin; and yet they induce us to be crafty, according to Prov. 1:4, "To give craftiness [Douay: 'subtlety'] to little ones." Therefore craftiness is not a sin.

Obj. 2: Further, it is written (Prov. 13:16): "The crafty [Douay: 'prudent'] man doth all things with counsel." Therefore, he does so either for a good or for an evil end. If for a good end, there is no sin seemingly, and if for an evil end, it would seem to pertain to carnal or worldly prudence. Therefore craftiness is not a special sin distinct from prudence of the flesh.

Obj. 3: Further, Gregory expounding the words of Job 12, "The simplicity of the just man is laughed to scorn," says (Moral. x, 29): "The wisdom of this world is to hide one's thoughts by artifice, to conceal one's meaning by words, to represent error as truth, to make out the truth to be false," and further on he adds: "This prudence is acquired by the young, it is learnt at a price by children." Now the above things seem to belong to craftiness. Therefore craftiness is not distinct from carnal or worldly prudence, and consequently it seems not to be a special sin.

*On the contrary,* The Apostle says (2 Cor. 4:2): "We renounce the hidden things of dishonesty, not walking in craftiness, nor adulterating the word of God." Therefore craftiness is a sin.

*I answer that,* Prudence is right reason applied to action, just as science is *right reason applied to knowledge.* In speculative matters one may sin against rectitude of knowledge in two ways: in one way when the reason is led to a false conclusion that appears to be true; in another way when the reason proceeds from false premises, that appear to be true, either to a true or to a false conclusion. Even so a sin may be against prudence, through having some resemblance thereto, in two ways. First, when the purpose of the reason is directed to an end which is good not in truth but in appearance, and this pertains to prudence of the flesh; secondly, when, in order to obtain a certain end, whether good or evil, a man uses means that are not true but fictitious and counterfeit, and this belongs to the sin of craftiness. This is consequently a sin opposed to prudence, and distinct from prudence of the flesh.

Reply Obj. 1: As Augustine observes (Contra Julian. iv, 3) just as prudence is sometimes improperly taken in a bad sense, so is craftiness sometimes taken in a good sense, and this on account of their mutual resemblance. Properly speaking, however, craftiness is taken in a bad sense, as the Philosopher states in *Ethic.* vi, 12.

Reply Obj. 2: Craftiness can take counsel both for a good end and for an evil end: nor should a good end be pursued by means that are false and counterfeit but by such as are true. Hence craftiness is a sin if it be directed to a good end.

Reply Obj. 3: Under "worldly prudence" Gregory included everything that can pertain to false prudence, so that it comprises craftiness also.

FOURTH ARTICLE [II-II, Q. 55, Art. 4]

Whether Guile Is a Sin Pertaining to Craftiness?

Objection 1: It would seem that guile is not a sin pertaining to craftiness. For sin, especially mortal, has no place in perfect men. Yet a certain guile is to be found in them, according to 2 Cor. 12:16, "Being crafty I caught you by guile." Therefore guile is not always a sin.

Obj. 2: Further, guile seems to pertain chiefly to the tongue, according to Ps. 5:11, "They dealt deceitfully with their tongues." Now craftiness like prudence is in the very act of reason. Therefore guile does not pertain to craftiness.

Obj. 3: Further, it is written (Prov. 12:20): "Guile [Douay: 'Deceit'] is in the heart of them that think evil things." But the thought of evil things does not always pertain to craftiness. Therefore guile does not seem to belong to craftiness.

*On the contrary,* Craftiness aims at lying in wait, according to Eph. 4:14, "By cunning craftiness by which they lie in wait to deceive": and guile aims at this also. Therefore guile pertains to craftiness.

*I answer that,* As stated above (A. 3), it belongs to craftiness to adopt ways that are not true but counterfeit and apparently true, in order to attain some end either good or evil. Now the adopting of such ways may be subjected to a twofold consideration; first, as regards the process of thinking them out, and this belongs properly to craftiness, even as thinking out right ways to a due end belongs to prudence. Secondly the adopting of such like ways may be considered with regard to their actual execution, and in this way it belongs to guile. Hence guile denotes a certain execution of craftiness, and accordingly belongs thereto.

Reply Obj. 1: Just as craftiness is taken properly in a bad sense, and improperly in a good sense, so too is guile which is the execution of craftiness.

Reply Obj. 2: The execution of craftiness with the purpose of deceiving, is effected first and foremost by words, which hold the chief place among those signs whereby a man signifies something to another man, as Augustine states (De Doctr. Christ. ii, 3), hence guile is ascribed chiefly to speech. Yet guile may happen also in deeds, according to Ps. 104:25, "And to deal deceitfully with his servants." Guile is also in the heart, according to Ecclus. 19:23, "His interior is full of deceit," but this is to devise deceits, according to Ps. 37:13: "They studied deceits all the day long."

Reply Obj. 3: Whoever purposes to do some evil deed, must needs devise certain ways of attaining his purpose, and for the most part he devises deceitful ways, whereby the more easily to obtain his end. Nevertheless it happens sometimes that evil is done openly and by violence without craftiness and guile; but as this is more difficult, it is of less frequent occurrence.

FIFTH ARTICLE [II-II, Q. 55, Art. 5]

Whether Fraud Pertains to Craftiness?

Objection 1: It would seem that fraud does not pertain to craftiness. For a man does not deserve praise if he allows himself to be deceived, which is the object of craftiness; and yet a man deserves praise for allowing himself to be defrauded, according to 1 Cor. 6:1, "Why do you not rather suffer yourselves to be defrauded?" Therefore fraud does not belong to craftiness.

Obj. 2: Further, fraud seems to consist in unlawfully taking or receiving external things, for it is written (Acts 5:1) that "a certain man named Ananias with Saphira his wife, sold a piece of land, and by fraud kept back part of the price of the land." Now it pertains to injustice or illiberality to take possession of or retain external things unjustly. Therefore fraud does not belong to craftiness which is opposed to prudence.

Obj. 3: Further, no man employs craftiness against himself. But the frauds of some are against themselves, for it is written (Prov. 1:18) concerning some "that they practice frauds [Douay: 'deceits'] against their own souls." Therefore fraud does not belong to craftiness.

*On the contrary,* The object of fraud is to deceive, according to Job 13:9, "Shall he be deceived as a man, with your fraudulent [Douay: 'deceitful'] dealings?" Now craftiness is directed to the same object. Therefore fraud pertains to craftiness.

*I answer that,* Just as guile consists in the execution of craftiness, so also does fraud. But they seem to differ in the fact that guile belongs in general to the execution of craftiness, whether this be effected by words, or by deeds, whereas fraud belongs more properly to the execution of craftiness by deeds.

Reply Obj. 1: The Apostle does not counsel the faithful to be deceived in their knowledge, but to bear patiently the effect of being deceived, and to endure wrongs inflicted on them by fraud.

Reply Obj. 2: The execution of craftiness may be carried out by another vice, just as the execution of prudence by the virtues: and accordingly nothing hinders fraud from pertaining to covetousness or illiberality.

Reply Obj. 3: Those who commit frauds, do not design anything against themselves or their own souls; it is through God's just judgment that what they plot against others, recoils on themselves, according to Ps. 7:16, "He is fallen into the hole he made."

SIXTH ARTICLE [II-II, Q. 55, Art. 6]

Whether It Is Lawful to Be Solicitous About Temporal Matters?

Objection 1: It would seem lawful to be solicitous about temporal matters. Because a superior should be solicitous for his subjects, according to Rom. 12:8, "He that ruleth, with solicitude." Now according to the Divine ordering, man is placed over temporal things, according to Ps. 8:8, "Thou hast subjected all things under his feet," etc. Therefore man should be solicitous about temporal things.

Obj. 2: Further, everyone is solicitous about the end for which he works. Now it is lawful for a man to work for the temporal things whereby he sustains life, wherefore the Apostle says (2 Thess. 3:10): "If any man will not work, neither let him eat." Therefore it is lawful to be solicitous about temporal things.

Obj. 3: Further, solicitude about works of mercy is praiseworthy, according to 2 Tim. 1:17, "When he was come to Rome, he carefully sought me." Now solicitude about temporal things is sometimes connected with works of mercy; for instance, when a man is solicitous to watch over the interests of orphans and poor persons. Therefore solicitude about temporal things is not unlawful.

*On the contrary,* Our Lord said (Matt. 6:31): "Be not solicitous ... saying, What shall we eat, or what shall we drink, or wherewith shall we be clothed?" And yet such things are very necessary.

*I answer that,* Solicitude denotes an earnest endeavor to obtain something. Now it is evident that the endeavor is more earnest when there is fear of failure, so that there is less solicitude when success is assured. Accordingly solicitude about temporal things may be unlawful in three ways. First on the part of the object of solicitude; that is, if we seek temporal things as an end. Hence Augustine says (De Operibus Monach. xxvi): "When Our Lord said: 'Be not solicitous, ' etc... . He intended to forbid them either to make such things their end, or for the sake of these things to do whatever they were commanded to do in preaching the Gospel." Secondly, solicitude about temporal things may be unlawful, through too much earnestness in endeavoring to obtain temporal things, the result being that a man is drawn away from spiritual things which ought to be the chief object of his search, wherefore it is written (Matt. 13:22) that "the care of this world ... chokes up the word." Thirdly, through over much fear, when, to wit, a man fears to lack necessary things if he do what he ought to do. Now our Lord gives three motives for laying aside this fear. First, on account of the yet greater favors bestowed by God on man, independently of his solicitude, viz. his body and soul (Matt. 6:26); secondly, on account of the care with which God watches over animals and plants without the assistance of man, according to the requirements of their nature; thirdly, because of Divine providence, through ignorance of which the gentiles are solicitous in seeking temporal goods before all others. Consequently He concludes that we should be solicitous most of all about spiritual goods, hoping that temporal goods also may be granted us according to our needs, if we do what we ought to do.

Reply Obj. 1: Temporal goods are subjected to man that he may use them according to his needs, not that he may place his end in them and be over solicitous about them.

Reply Obj. 2: The solicitude of a man who gains his bread by bodily labor is not superfluous but proportionate; hence Jerome says on Matt. 6:31, "Be not solicitous," that "labor is necessary, but solicitude must be banished," namely superfluous solicitude which unsettles the mind.

Reply Obj. 3: In the works of mercy solicitude about temporal things is directed to charity as its end, wherefore it is not unlawful, unless it be superfluous.

SEVENTH ARTICLE [II-II, Q. 55, Art. 7]

Whether We Should Be Solicitous About the Future?

Objection 1: It would seem that we should be solicitous about the future. For it is written (Prov. 6:6-8): "Go to the ant, O sluggard, and consider her ways and learn wisdom; which, although she hath no guide, nor master ... provideth her meat for herself in the summer, and gathereth her food in the harvest." Now this is to be solicitous about the future. Therefore solicitude about the future is praiseworthy.

Obj. 2: Further, solicitude pertains to prudence. But prudence is chiefly about the future, since its principal part is *foresight of future things,* as stated above (Q. 49, A. 6, ad 1). Therefore it is virtuous to be solicitous about the future.

Obj. 3: Further, whoever puts something by that he may keep it for the morrow, is solicitous about the future. Now we read (John 12:6) that Christ had a bag for keeping things in, which Judas carried, and (Acts 4:34-37) that the Apostles kept the price of the land, which had been laid at their feet. Therefore it is lawful to be solicitous about the future.

*On the contrary,* Our Lord said (Matt. 6:34): "Be not ... solicitous for tomorrow"; where "tomorrow" stands for the future, as Jerome says in his commentary on this passage.

*I answer that,* No work can be virtuous, unless it be vested with its due circumstances, and among these is the due time, according to Eccles. 8:6, "There is a time and opportunity for every business"; which applies not only to external deeds but also to internal solicitude. For every time has its own fitting proper solicitude; thus solicitude about the crops belongs to the summer time, and solicitude about the vintage to the time of autumn. Accordingly if a man were solicitous about the vintage during the summer, he would be needlessly forestalling the solicitude belonging to a future time. Hence Our Lord forbids such like excessive solicitude, saying: "Be ... not solicitous for tomorrow," wherefore He adds, "for the morrow will be solicitous for itself," that is to say, the morrow will have its own solicitude, which will be burden enough for the soul. This is what He means by adding: "Sufficient for the day is the evil thereof," namely, the burden of solicitude.

Reply Obj. 1: The ant is solicitous at a befitting time, and it is this that is proposed for our example.

Reply Obj. 2: Due foresight of the future belongs to prudence. But it would be an inordinate foresight or solicitude about the future, if a man were to seek temporal things, to which the terms "past" and "future" apply, as ends, or if he were to seek them in excess of the needs of the present life, or if he were to forestall the time for solicitude.

Reply Obj. 3: As Augustine says (De Serm. Dom. in Monte ii, 17), "when we see a servant of God taking thought lest he lack these needful things, we must not judge him to be solicitous for the morrow, since even Our Lord deigned for our example to have a purse, and we read in the Acts of the Apostles that they procured the necessary means of livelihood in view of the future on account of a threatened famine. Hence Our Lord does not condemn those who according to human custom, provide themselves with such things, but those who oppose themselves to God for the sake of these things."

EIGHTH ARTICLE [II-II, Q. 55, Art. 8]

Whether These Vices Arise from Covetousness?

Objection 1: It would seem that these vices do not arise from covetousness. As stated above (Q. 43, A. 6) lust is the chief cause of lack of rectitude in the reason. Now these vices are opposed to right reason, i.e. to prudence. Therefore they arise chiefly from lust; especially since the Philosopher says (Ethic. vii, 6) that "Venus is full of guile and her girdle is many colored" and that "he who is incontinent in desire acts with cunning."

Obj. 2: Further, these vices bear a certain resemblance to prudence, as stated above (Q. 47, A. 13). Now, since prudence is in the reason, the more spiritual vices seem to be more akin thereto, such as pride and vainglory. Therefore the aforesaid vices seem to arise from pride rather than from covetousness.

Obj. 3: Further, men make use of stratagems not only in laying hold of other people's goods, but also in plotting murders, the former of which pertains to covetousness, and the latter to anger. Now the use of stratagems pertains to craftiness, guile, and fraud. Therefore the aforesaid vices arise not only from covetousness, but also from anger.

*On the contrary,* Gregory (Moral. xxxi, 45) states that fraud is a daughter of covetousness.

*I answer that,* As stated above (A. 3; Q. 47, A. 13), carnal prudence and craftiness, as well as guile and fraud, bear a certain resemblance to prudence in some kind of use of the reason. Now among all the moral virtues it is justice wherein the use of right reason appears chiefly, for justice is in the rational appetite. Hence the undue use of reason appears chiefly in the vices opposed to justice, the chief of which is covetousness. Therefore the aforesaid vices arise chiefly from covetousness.

Reply Obj. 1: On account of the vehemence of pleasure and of concupiscence, lust entirely suppresses the reason from exercising its act: whereas in the aforesaid vices there is some use of reason, albeit inordinate. Hence these vices do not arise directly from lust. When the Philosopher says that "Venus is full of guile," he is referring to a certain resemblance, in so far as she carries man away suddenly, just as he is moved in deceitful actions, yet not by means of craftiness but rather by the vehemence of concupiscence and pleasure; wherefore he adds that "Venus doth cozen the wits of the wisest man" [*Cf. Iliad xiv, 214-217].

Reply Obj. 2: To do anything by stratagem seems to be due to pusillanimity: because a magnanimous man wishes to act openly, as the Philosopher says (Ethic. iv, 3). Wherefore, as pride resembles or apes magnanimity, it follows that the aforesaid vices which make use of fraud and guile, do not arise directly from pride, but rather from covetousness, which seeks its own profit and sets little by excellence.

Reply Obj. 3: Anger's movement is sudden, hence it acts with precipitation, and without counsel, contrary to the use of the aforesaid vices, though these use counsel inordinately. That men use stratagems in plotting murders, arises not from anger but rather from hatred, because the angry man desires to harm manifestly, as the Philosopher states (Rhet. ii, 2, 3) [*Cf. *Ethic.* vii, 6].

## QUESTION 56

OF THE PRECEPTS RELATING TO PRUDENCE (In Two Articles)

We must now consider the precepts relating to prudence, under which head there are two points of inquiry:

(1) The precepts of prudence;

(2) The precepts relating to the opposite vices.

FIRST ARTICLE [II-II, Q. 56, Art. 1]

Whether the Precepts of the Decalogue Should Have Included a Precept of Prudence?

Objection 1: It would seem that the precepts of the decalogue should have included a precept of prudence. For the chief precepts should include a precept of the chief virtue. Now the chief precepts are those of the decalogue. Since then prudence is the chief of the moral virtues, it seems that the precepts of the decalogue should have included a precept of prudence.

Obj. 2: Further, the teaching of the Gospel contains the Law especially with regard to the precepts of the decalogue. Now the teaching of the Gospel contains a precept of prudence (Matt. 10:16): "Be ye ... prudent [Douay: 'wise'] as serpents." Therefore the precepts of the decalogue should have included a precept of prudence.

Obj. 3: Further, the other lessons of the Old Testament are directed to the precepts of the decalogue: wherefore it is written (Malach. 4:4): "Remember the law of Moses My servant, which I commanded him in Horeb." Now the other lessons of the Old Testament include precepts of prudence; for instance (Prov. 3:5): "Lean not upon thy own prudence"; and further on (Prov. 4:25): "Let thine eyelids go before thy steps." Therefore the Law also should have contained a precept of prudence, especially among the precepts of the decalogue.

The contrary however appears to anyone who goes through the precepts of the decalogue.

*I answer that,* As stated above (I-II, Q. 100, A. 3; A. 5, ad 1) when we were treating of precepts, the commandments of the decalogue being given to the whole people, are a matter of common knowledge to all, as coming under the purview of natural reason. Now foremost among the things dictated by natural reason are the ends of human life, which are to the practical order what naturally known principles are to the speculative order, as shown above (Q. 47, A. 6). Now prudence is not about the end, but about the means, as stated above (Q. 47, A. 6). Hence it was not fitting that the precepts of the decalogue should include a precept relating directly to prudence. And yet all the precepts of the decalogue are related to prudence, in so far as it directs all virtuous acts.

Reply Obj. 1: Although prudence is simply foremost among all the moral virtues, yet justice, more than any other virtue, regards its object under the aspect of something due, which is a necessary condition for a precept, as stated above (Q. 44, A. 1; I-II, Q. 99, AA. 1, 5). Hence it behooved the chief precepts of the Law, which are those of the decalogue, to refer to justice rather than to prudence.

Reply Obj. 2: The teaching of the Gospel is the doctrine of perfection. Therefore it needed to instruct man perfectly in all matters relating to right conduct, whether ends or means: wherefore it behooved the Gospel teaching to contain precepts also of prudence.

Reply Obj. 3: Just as the rest of the teaching of the Old Testament is directed to the precepts of the decalogue as its end, so it behooved man to be instructed by the subsequent lessons of the Old Testament about the act of prudence which is directed to the means.

SECOND ARTICLE [II-II, Q. 56, Art. 2]

Whether the Prohibitive Precepts Relating to the Vices Opposed to Prudence Are Fittingly Propounded in the Old Law?

Objection 1: It would seem that the prohibitive precepts relating to the vices opposed to prudence are unfittingly propounded in the Old Law. For such vices as imprudence and its parts which are directly opposed to prudence are not less opposed thereto, than those which bear a certain resemblance to prudence, such as craftiness and vices connected with it. Now the latter vices are forbidden in the Law: for it is written (Lev. 19:13): "Thou shalt not calumniate thy neighbor," and (Deut. 25:13): "Thou shalt not have divers weights in thy bag, a greater and a less." Therefore there should have also been prohibitive precepts about the vices directly opposed to prudence.

Obj. 2: Further, there is room for fraud in other things than in buying and selling. Therefore the Law unfittingly forbade fraud solely in buying and selling.

Obj. 3: Further, there is the same reason for prescribing an act of virtue as for prohibiting the act of a contrary vice. But acts of prudence are not prescribed in the Law. Therefore neither should any contrary vices have been forbidden in the Law.

The contrary, however, appears from the precepts of the Law which are quoted in the first objection.

*I answer that,* As stated above (A. 1), justice, above all, regards the aspect of something due, which is a necessary condition for a precept, because justice tends to render that which is due to another, as we shall state further on (Q. 58, A. 2). Now craftiness, as to its execution, is committed chiefly in matters of justice, as stated above (Q. 55, A. 8): and so it was fitting that the Law should contain precepts forbidding the execution of craftiness, in so far as this pertains to injustice, as when a man uses guile and fraud in calumniating another or in stealing his goods.

Reply Obj. 1: Those vices that are manifestly opposed to prudence, do not pertain to injustice in the same way as the execution of craftiness, and so they are not forbidden in the Law, as fraud and guile are, which latter pertain to injustice.

Reply Obj. 2: All guile and fraud committed in matters of injustice, can be understood to be forbidden in the prohibition of calumny (Lev. 19:13). Yet fraud and guile are wont to be practiced chiefly in buying and selling, according to Ecclus. 26:28, "A huckster shall not be justified from the sins of the lips": and it is for this reason that the Law contained a special precept forbidding fraudulent buying and selling.

Reply Obj. 3: All the precepts of the Law that relate to acts of justice pertain to the execution of prudence, even as the precepts prohibitive of stealing, calumny and fraudulent selling pertain to the execution of craftiness.

# QUESTION 57

OF RIGHT (In Four Articles)

After considering prudence we must in due sequence consider justice, the consideration of which will be fourfold:

(1) Of justice;

(2) Of its parts;

(3) Of the corresponding gift;

(4) Of the precepts relating to justice.

Four points will have to be considered about justice: (1) Right; (2) Justice itself; (3) Injustice; (4) Judgment.

Under the first head there are four points of inquiry:

(1) Whether right is the object of justice?

(2) Whether right is fittingly divided into natural and positive right?

(3) Whether the right of nations is the same as natural right?

(4) Whether right of dominion and paternal right are distinct species?

FIRST ARTICLE [II-II, Q. 57, Art. 1]

Whether Right Is the Object of Justice?

Objection 1: It would seem that right is not the object of justice. For the jurist Celsus says [*Digest. i, 1; De Just. et Jure 1] that "right is the art of goodness and equality." Now art is not the object of justice, but is by itself an intellectual virtue. Therefore right is not the object of justice.

Obj. 2: Further, "Law," according to Isidore (Etym. v, 3), "is a kind of right." Now law is the object not of justice but of prudence, wherefore the Philosopher [*Ethic. vi, 8] reckons "legislative" as one of the parts of prudence. Therefore right is not the object of justice.

Obj. 3: Further, justice, before all, subjects man to God: for Augustine says (De Moribus Eccl. xv) that "justice is love serving God alone, and consequently governing aright all things subject to man." Now right ( *jus* ) does not pertain to Divine things, but only to human affairs, for Isidore says (Etym. v, 2) that " *fas* is the Divine law, and *jus,* the human law." Therefore right is not the object of justice.

*On the contrary,* Isidore says (Etym. v, 2) that " jus (right) is so called because it is just." Now the just is the object of justice, for the Philosopher declares (Ethic. v, 1) that "all are agreed in giving the name of justice to the habit which makes men capable of doing just actions."

*I answer that,* It is proper to justice, as compared with the other virtues, to direct man in his relations with others: because it denotes a kind of equality, as its very name implies; indeed we are wont to say that things are adjusted when they are made equal, for equality is in reference of one thing to some other. On the other hand the other virtues perfect man in those matters only which befit him in relation to himself. Accordingly that which is right in the works of the other virtues, and to which the intention of the virtue tends as to its proper object, depends on its relation to the agent only, whereas the right in a work of justice, besides its relation to the agent, is set up by its relation to others. Because a man's work is said to be just when it is related to some other by way of some kind of equality, for instance the payment of the wage due for a service rendered. And so a thing is said to be just, as having the rectitude of justice, when it is the term of an act of justice, without taking into account the way in which it is done by the agent: whereas in the other virtues nothing is declared to be right unless it is done in a certain way by the agent. For this reason justice has its own special proper object over and above the other virtues, and this object is called the just, which is the same as *right.* Hence it is evident that right is the object of justice.

Reply Obj. 1: It is usual for words to be distorted from their original signification so as to mean something else: thus the word "medicine" was first employed to signify a remedy used for curing a sick person, and then it was drawn to signify the art by which this is done. In like manner the word *jus* (right) was first of all used to denote the just thing itself, but afterwards it was transferred to designate the art whereby it is known what is just, and further to denote the place where justice is administered, thus a man is said to appear *in jure* [*In English we speak of a court of law, a barrister at law, etc.], and yet further, we say even that a man, who has the office of exercising justice, administers the *jus* even if his sentence be unjust.

Reply Obj. 2: Just as there pre-exists in the mind of the craftsman an expression of the things to be made externally by his craft, which expression is called the rule of his craft, so too there pre-exists in the mind an expression of the particular just work which the reason determines, and which is a kind of rule of prudence. If this rule be expressed in writing it is called a "law," which according to Isidore (Etym. v, 1) is "a written decree": and so law is not the same as right, but an expression of right.

Reply Obj. 3: Since justice implies equality, and since we cannot offer God an equal return, it follows that we cannot make Him a perfectly just repayment. For this reason the Divine law is not properly called *jus* but fas, because, to wit, God is satisfied if we accomplish what we can. Nevertheless justice tends to make man repay God as much as he can, by subjecting his mind to Him entirely.

SECOND ARTICLE [II-II, Q. 57, Art. 2]

Whether Right Is Fittingly Divided into Natural Right and Positive Right?

Objection 1: It would seem that right is not fittingly divided into natural right and positive right. For that which is natural is unchangeable, and is the same for all. Now nothing of the kind is to be found in human affairs, since all the rules of human right fail in certain cases, nor do they obtain force everywhere. Therefore there is no such thing as natural right.

Obj. 2: Further, a thing is called "positive" when it proceeds from the human will. But a thing is not just, simply because it proceeds from the human will, else a man's will could not be unjust. Since then the "just" and the "right" are the same, it seems that there is no positive right.

Obj. 3: Further, Divine right is not natural right, since it transcends human nature. In like manner, neither is it positive right, since it is based not on human, but on Divine authority. Therefore right is unfittingly divided into natural and positive.

*On the contrary,* The Philosopher says (Ethic. v, 7) that "political justice is partly natural and partly legal," i.e. established by law.

*I answer that,* As stated above (A. 1) the "right" or the "just" is a work that is adjusted to another person according to some kind of equality. Now a thing can be adjusted to a man in two ways: first by its very nature, as when a man gives so much that he may receive equal value in return, and this is called "natural right." In another way a thing is adjusted or commensurated to another person, by agreement, or by common consent, when, to wit, a man deems himself satisfied, if he receive so much. This can be done in two ways: first by private agreement, as that which is confirmed by an agreement between private individuals; secondly, by public agreement, as when the whole community agrees that something should be deemed as though it were adjusted and commensurated to another person, or when this is decreed by the prince who is placed over the people, and acts in its stead, and this is called "positive right."

Reply Obj. 1: That which is natural to one whose nature is unchangeable, must needs be such always and everywhere. But man's nature is changeable, wherefore that which is natural to man may sometimes fail. Thus the restitution of a deposit to the depositor is in accordance with natural equality, and if human nature were always right, this would always have to be observed; but since it happens sometimes that man's will is unrighteous there are cases in which a deposit should not be restored, lest a man of unrighteous will make evil use of the thing deposited: as when a madman or an enemy of the common weal demands the return of his weapons.

Reply Obj. 2: The human will can, by common agreement, make a thing to be just provided it be not, of itself, contrary to natural justice, and it is in such matters that positive right has its place. Hence the Philosopher says (Ethic. v, 7) that "in the case of the legal just, it does not matter in the first instance whether it takes one form or another, it only matters when once it is laid down." If, however, a thing is, of itself, contrary to natural right, the human will cannot make it just, for instance by decreeing that it is lawful to steal or to commit adultery. Hence it is written (Isa. 10:1): "Woe to them that make wicked laws."

Reply Obj. 3: The Divine right is that which is promulgated by God. Such things are partly those that are naturally just, yet their justice is hidden to man, and partly are made just by God's decree. Hence also Divine right may be divided in respect of these two things, even as human right is. For the Divine law commands certain things because they are good, and forbids others, because they are evil, while others are good because they are prescribed, and others evil because they are forbidden.

THIRD ARTICLE [II-II, Q. 57, Art. 3]

Whether the Right of Nations Is the Same As the Natural Right?

Objection 1: It would seem that the right of nations is the same as the natural right. For all men do not agree save in that which is natural to them. Now all men agree in the right of nations; since the jurist [*Ulpian: Digest. i, 1; De Just. et Jure i] "the right of nations is that which is in use among all nations." Therefore the right of nations is the natural right.

Obj. 2: Further, slavery among men is natural, for some are naturally slaves according to the Philosopher (Polit. i, 2). Now "slavery belongs to the right of nations," as Isidore states (Etym. v, 4). Therefore the right of nations is a natural right.

Obj. 3: Further, right as stated above (A. 2) is divided into natural and positive. Now the right of nations is not a positive right, since all nations never agreed to decree anything by common agreement. Therefore the right of nations is a natural right.

*On the contrary,* Isidore says (Etym. v, 4) that "right is either natural, or civil, or right of nations," and consequently the right of nations is distinct from natural right.

*I answer that,* As stated above (A. 2), the natural right or just is that which by its very nature is adjusted to or commensurate with another person. Now this may happen in two ways; first, according as it is considered absolutely: thus a male by [his] very nature is commensurate with the female to beget offspring by her, and a parent is commensurate with the offspring to nourish it. Secondly a thing is naturally commensurate with another person, not according as it is considered absolutely, but according to something resultant from it, for instance the possession of property. For if a particular piece of land be considered absolutely, it contains no reason why it should belong to one man more than to another, but if it be considered in respect of its adaptability to cultivation, and the unmolested use of the land, it has a certain commensuration to be the property of one and not of another man, as the Philosopher shows (Polit. ii, 2).

Now it belongs not only to man but also to other animals to apprehend a thing absolutely: wherefore the right which we call natural, is common to us and other animals according to the first kind of commensuration. But the right of nations falls short of natural right in this sense, as the jurist [*Digest. i, 1; De Just. et Jure i] says because "the latter is common to all animals, while the former is common to men only." On the other hand to consider a thing by comparing it with what results from it, is proper to reason, wherefore this same is natural to man in respect of natural reason which dictates it. Hence the jurist Gaius says (Digest. i, 1; De Just. et Jure i, 9): "whatever natural reason decrees among all men, is observed by all equally, and is called the right of nations." This suffices for the Reply to the First Objection.

Reply Obj. 2: Considered absolutely, the fact that this particular man should be a slave rather than another man, is based, not on natural reason, but on some resultant utility, in that it is useful to this man to be ruled by a wiser man, and to the latter to be helped by the former, as the Philosopher states (Polit. i, 2). Wherefore slavery which belongs to the right of nations is natural in the second way, but not in the first.

Reply Obj. 3: Since natural reason dictates matters which are according to the right of nations, as implying a proximate equality, it follows that they need no special institution, for they are instituted by natural reason itself, as stated by the authority quoted above.

FOURTH ARTICLE [II-II, Q. 57, Art. 4]

Whether Paternal Right and Right of Dominion Should Be Distinguished As Special Species?

Objection 1: It would seem that "paternal right" and "right of dominion" should not be distinguished as special species. For it belongs to justice to render to each one what is his, as Ambrose states (De Offic. i, 24). Now right is the object of justice, as stated above (A. 1). Therefore right belongs to each one equally; and we ought not to distinguish the rights of fathers and masters as distinct species.

Obj. 2: Further, the law is an expression of what is just, as stated above (A. 1, ad 2). Now a law looks to the common good of a city or kingdom, as stated above (I-II, Q. 90, A. 2), but not to the private good of an individual or even of one household. Therefore there is no need for a special right of dominion or paternal right, since the master and the father pertain to a household, as stated in *Polit.* i, 2.

Obj. 3: Further, there are many other differences of degrees among men, for instance some are soldiers, some are priests, some are princes. Therefore some special kind of right should be allotted to them.

*On the contrary,* The Philosopher (Ethic. v, 6) distinguishes right of dominion, paternal right and so on as species distinct from civil right.

*I answer that,* Right or just depends on commensuration with another person. Now "another" has a twofold signification. First, it may denote something that is other simply, as that which is altogether distinct; as, for example, two men neither of whom is subject to the other, and both of whom are subjects of the ruler of the state; and between these according to the Philosopher (Ethic. v, 6) there is the "just" simply. Secondly a thing is said to be other from something else, not simply, but as belonging in some way to that something else: and in this way, as regards human affairs, a son belongs to his father, since he is part of him somewhat, as stated in *Ethic.* viii, 12, and a slave belongs to his master, because he is his instrument, as stated in *Polit.* i, 2 [*Cf. Ethic. viii, 11]. Hence a father is not compared to his son as to another simply, and so between them there is not the just simply, but a kind of just, called "paternal." In like manner neither is there the just simply, between master and servant, but that which is called "dominative." A wife, though she is something belonging to the husband, since she stands related to him as to her own body, as the Apostle declares (Eph. 5:28), is nevertheless more distinct from her husband, than a son from his father, or a slave from his master: for she is received into a kind of social life, that of matrimony, wherefore according to the Philosopher (Ethic. v, 6) there is more scope for justice between husband and wife than between father and son, or master and slave, because, as husband and wife have an immediate relation to the community of the household, as stated in *Polit.* i, 2, 5, it follows that between them there is "domestic justice" rather than "civic."

Reply Obj. 1: It belongs to justice to render to each one his right, the distinction between individuals being presupposed: for if a man gives himself his due, this is not strictly called "just." And since what belongs to the son is his father's, and what belongs to the slave is his master's, it follows that properly speaking there is not justice of father to son, or of master to slave.

Reply Obj. 2: A son, as such, belongs to his father, and a slave, as such, belongs to his master; yet each, considered as a man, is something having separate existence and distinct from others. Hence in so far as each of them is a man, there is justice towards them in a way: and for this reason too there are certain laws regulating the relations of father to his son, and of a master to his slave; but in so far as each is something belonging to another, the perfect idea of "right" or "just" is wanting to them.

Reply Obj. 3: All other differences between one person and another in a state, have an immediate relation to the community of the state and to its ruler, wherefore there is just towards them in the perfect sense of justice. This "just" however is distinguished according to various offices, hence when we speak of "military," or "magisterial," or "priestly" right, it is not as though such rights fell short of the simply right, as when we speak of "paternal" right, or right of "dominion," but for the reason that something proper is due to each class of person in respect of his particular office.

## QUESTION 58

OF JUSTICE (In Twelve Articles)

We must now consider justice. Under this head there are twelve points of inquiry:

(1) What is justice?

(2) Whether justice is always towards another?

(3) Whether it is a virtue?
(4) Whether it is in the will as its subject?
(5) Whether it is a general virtue?
(6) Whether, as a general virtue, it is essentially the same as every virtue?
(7) Whether there is a particular justice?
(8) Whether particular justice has a matter of its own?
(9) Whether it is about passions, or about operations only?
(10) Whether the mean of justice is the real mean?
(11) Whether the act of justice is to render to everyone his own?
(12) Whether justice is the chief of the moral virtues?

FIRST ARTICLE [II-II, Q. 58, Art. 1]

Whether Justice Is Fittingly Defined As Being the Perpetual and Constant Will to Render to Each One His Right?

Objection 1: It would seem that lawyers have unfittingly defined justice as being "the perpetual and constant will to render to each one his right" [*Digest. i, 1; De Just. et Jure 10]. For, according to the Philosopher (Ethic. v, 1), justice is a habit which makes a man "capable of doing what is just, and of being just in action and in intention." Now "will" denotes a power, or also an act. Therefore justice is unfittingly defined as being a will.

Obj. 2: Further, rectitude of the will is not the will; else if the will were its own rectitude, it would follow that no will is unrighteous. Yet, according to Anselm (De Veritate xii), justice is rectitude. Therefore justice is not the will.

Obj. 3: Further, no will is perpetual save God's. If therefore justice is a perpetual will, in God alone will there be justice.

Obj. 4: Further, whatever is perpetual is constant, since it is unchangeable. Therefore it is needless in defining justice, to say that it is both "perpetual" and "constant."

Obj. 5: Further, it belongs to the sovereign to give each one his right. Therefore, if justice gives each one his right, it follows that it is in none but the sovereign: which is absurd.

Obj. 6: Further, Augustine says (De Moribus Eccl. xv) that "justice is love serving God alone." Therefore it does not render to each one his right.

*I answer that,* The aforesaid definition of justice is fitting if understood aright. For since every virtue is a habit that is the principle of a good act, a virtue must needs be defined by means of the good act bearing on the matter proper to that virtue. Now the proper matter of justice consists of those things that belong to our intercourse with other men, as shall be shown further on (A. 2). Hence the act of justice in relation to its proper matter and object is indicated in the words, "Rendering to each one his right," since, as Isidore says (Etym. x), "a man is said to be just because he respects the rights ( *jus* ) of others."

Now in order that an act bearing upon any matter whatever be virtuous, it requires to be voluntary, stable, and firm, because the Philosopher says (Ethic. ii, 4) that in order for an act to be virtuous it needs first of all to be done "knowingly," secondly to be done "by choice," and "for a due end," thirdly to be done "immovably." Now the first of these is included in the second, since "what is done through ignorance is involuntary" (Ethic. iii, 1). Hence the definition of justice mentions first the "will," in order to show that the act of justice must be voluntary; and mention is made afterwards of its "constancy" and "perpetuity" in order to indicate the firmness of the act.

Accordingly, this is a complete definition of justice; save that the act is mentioned instead of the habit, which takes its species from that act, because habit implies relation to act. And if anyone would reduce it to the proper form of a definition, he might say that "justice is a habit whereby a man renders to each one his due by a constant and perpetual will": and this is about the same definition as that given by the Philosopher (Ethic. v, 5) who says that "justice is a habit whereby a man is said to be capable of doing just actions in accordance with his choice."

Reply Obj. 1: Will here denotes the act, not the power: and it is customary among writers to define habits by their acts: thus Augustine says (Tract. in Joan. xl) that "faith is to believe what one sees not."

Reply Obj. 2: Justice is the same as rectitude, not essentially but causally; for it is a habit which rectifies the deed and the will.

Reply Obj. 3: The will may be called perpetual in two ways. First on the part of the will's act which endures for ever, and thus God's will alone is perpetual. Secondly on the part of the subject, because, to wit, a man wills to do a certain thing always, and this is a necessary condition of justice. For it does not satisfy the conditions of justice that one wish to observe justice in some particular matter for the time being, because one could scarcely find a man willing to act unjustly in every case; and it is requisite that one should have the will to observe justice at all times and in all cases.

Reply Obj. 4: Since "perpetual" does not imply perpetuity of the act of the will, it is not superfluous to add "constant": for while the "perpetual will" denotes the purpose of observing justice always, "constant" signifies a firm perseverance in this purpose.

Reply Obj. 5: A judge renders to each one what belongs to him, by way of command and direction, because a judge is the "personification of justice," and "the sovereign is its guardian" (Ethic. v, 4). On the other hand, the subjects render to each one what belongs to him, by way of execution.

Reply Obj. 6: Just as love of God includes love of our neighbor, as stated above (Q. 25, A. 1), so too the service of God includes rendering to each one his due.

SECOND ARTICLE [II-II, Q. 58, Art. 2]

Whether Justice Is Always Towards Another?

Objection 1: It would seem that justice is not always towards another. For the Apostle says (Rom. 3:22) that "the justice of God is by faith of Jesus Christ." Now faith does not concern the dealings of one man with another. Neither therefore does justice.

Obj. 2: Further, according to Augustine (De Moribus Eccl. xv), "it belongs to justice that man should direct to the service of God his authority over the things that are subject to him." Now the sensitive appetite is subject to man, according to Gen. 4:7, where it is written: "The lust thereof," viz. of sin, "shall be under thee, and thou shalt have dominion over it." Therefore it belongs to justice to have dominion over one's own appetite: so that justice is towards oneself.

Obj. 3: Further, the justice of God is eternal. But nothing else is co-eternal with God. Therefore justice is not essentially towards another.

Obj. 4: Further, man's dealings with himself need to be rectified no less than his dealings with another. Now man's dealings are rectified by justice, according to Prov. 11:5, "The justice of the upright shall make his way prosperous." Therefore justice is about our dealings not only with others, but also with ourselves.

*On the contrary,* Tully says (De Officiis i, 7) that "the object of justice is to keep men together in society and mutual intercourse." Now this implies relationship of one man to another. Therefore justice is concerned only about our dealings with others.

*I answer that,* As stated above (Q. 57, A. 1) since justice by its name implies equality, it denotes essentially relation to another, for a thing is equal, not to itself, but to another. And forasmuch as it belongs to justice to rectify human acts, as stated above (Q. 57, A. 1; I-II, Q. 113, A. 1) this otherness which justice demands must needs be between beings capable of action. Now actions belong to supposits [*Cf. I, Q. 29, A. 2] and wholes and, properly speaking, not to parts and forms or powers, for we do not say properly that the hand strikes, but a man with his hand, nor that heat makes a thing hot, but fire by heat, although such expressions may be employed metaphorically. Hence, justice properly speaking demands a distinction of supposits, and consequently is only in one man towards another. Nevertheless in one and the same man we may speak metaphorically of his various principles of action such as the reason, the irascible, and the concupiscible, as though they were so many agents: so that metaphorically in one and the same man there is said to be justice in so far as the reason commands the irascible and concupiscible, and these obey reason; and in general in so far as to each part of man is ascribed what is becoming to it. Hence the Philosopher (Ethic. v, 11) calls this "metaphorical justice."

Reply Obj. 1: The justice which faith works in us, is that whereby the ungodly is justified: it consists in the due coordination of the parts of the soul, as stated above (I-II, Q. 113, A. 1) where we were treating of the justification of the ungodly. Now this belongs to metaphorical justice, which may be found even in a man who lives all by himself.

This suffices for the Reply to the Second Objection.

Reply Obj. 3: God's justice is from eternity in respect of the eternal will and purpose (and it is chiefly in this that justice consists); although it is not eternal as regards its effect, since nothing is co-eternal with God.

Reply Obj. 4: Man's dealings with himself are sufficiently rectified by the rectification of the passions by the other moral virtues. But his dealings with others need a special rectification, not only in relation to the agent, but also in relation to the person to whom they are directed. Hence about such dealings there is a special virtue, and this is justice.

THIRD ARTICLE [II-II, Q. 58, Art. 3]

Whether Justice Is a Virtue?

Objection 1: It would seem that justice is not a virtue. For it is written (Luke 17:10): "When you shall have done all these things that are commanded you, say: We are unprofitable servants; we have done that which we ought to do." Now it is not unprofitable to do a virtuous deed: for Ambrose says (De Officiis ii, 6): "We look to a profit that is estimated not by pecuniary gain but by the acquisition of godliness." Therefore to do what one ought to do, is not a virtuous deed. And yet it is an act of justice. Therefore justice is not a virtue.

Obj. 2: Further, that which is done of necessity, is not meritorious. But to render to a man what belongs to him, as justice requires, is of necessity. Therefore it is not meritorious. Yet it is by virtuous actions that we gain merit. Therefore justice is not a virtue.

Obj. 3: Further, every moral virtue is about matters of action. Now those things which are wrought externally are not things concerning behavior but concerning handicraft, according to the Philosopher (Metaph. ix) [*Didot ed., viii, 8]. Therefore since it belongs to justice to produce externally a deed that is just in itself, it seems that justice is not a moral virtue.

*On the contrary,* Gregory says (Moral. ii, 49) that "the entire structure of good works is built on four virtues," viz. temperance, prudence, fortitude and justice.

*I answer that,* A human virtue is one "which renders a human act and man himself good" [*Ethic. ii, 6], and this can be applied to justice. For a man's act is made good through attaining the rule of reason, which is the rule whereby human acts are regulated. Hence, since justice regulates human operations, it is evident that it renders man's operations good, and, as Tully declares (De Officiis i, 7), good men are so called chiefly from their justice, wherefore, as he says again (De Officiis i, 7) "the luster of virtue appears above all in justice."

Reply Obj. 1: When a man does what he ought, he brings no gain to the person to whom he does what he ought, but only abstains from doing him a harm. He does however profit himself, in so far as he does what he ought, spontaneously and readily, and this is to act virtuously. Hence it is written (Wis. 8:7) that Divine wisdom "teacheth temperance, and prudence, and justice, and fortitude, which are such things as men (i.e. virtuous men) can have nothing more profitable in life."

Reply Obj. 2: Necessity is twofold. One arises from *constraint,* and this removes merit, since it runs counter to the will. The other arises from the obligation of a *command,* or from the necessity of obtaining an end, when, to wit, a man is unable to achieve the end of virtue without doing some particular thing. The latter necessity does not remove merit, when a man does voluntarily that which is necessary in this way. It does however exclude the credit of supererogation, according to 1 Cor. 9:16, "If I preach the Gospel, it is no glory to me, for a necessity lieth upon me."

Reply Obj. 3: Justice is concerned about external things, not by making them, which pertains to art, but by using them in our dealings with other men.

FOURTH ARTICLE [II-II, Q. 58, Art. 4]

Whether Justice Is in the Will As Its Subject?

Objection 1: It would seem that justice is not in the will as its subject. For justice is sometimes called truth. But truth is not in the will, but in the intellect. Therefore justice is not in the will as its subject.

Obj. 2: Further, justice is about our dealings with others. Now it belongs to the reason to direct one thing in relation to another. Therefore justice is not in the will as its subject but in the reason.

Obj. 3: Further, justice is not an intellectual virtue, since it is not directed to knowledge; wherefore it follows that it is a moral virtue. Now the subject of moral virtue is the faculty which is "rational by participation," viz. the irascible and the concupiscible, as the Philosopher declares (Ethic. i, 13). Therefore justice is not in the will as its subject, but in the irascible and concupiscible.

*On the contrary,* Anselm says (De Verit. xii) that "justice is rectitude of the will observed for its own sake."

*I answer that,* The subject of a virtue is the power whose act that virtue aims at rectifying. Now justice does not aim at directing an act of the cognitive power, for we are not said to be just through knowing something aright. Hence the subject of justice is not the intellect or reason which is a cognitive power. But since we are said to be just through doing something aright, and because the proximate principle of action is the appetitive power, justice must needs be in some appetitive power as its subject.

Now the appetite is twofold; namely, the will which is in the reason and the sensitive appetite which follows on sensitive apprehension, and is divided into the irascible and the concupiscible, as stated in the First Part (Q. 81, A. 2). Again the act of rendering his due to each man cannot proceed from the sensitive appetite, because sensitive apprehension does not go so far as to be able to consider the relation of one thing to another; but this is proper to the reason. Therefore justice cannot be in the irascible or concupiscible as its subject, but only in the will: hence the Philosopher (Ethic. v, 1) defines justice by an act of the will, as may be seen above (A. 1).

Reply Obj. 1: Since the will is the rational appetite, when the rectitude of the reason which is called truth is imprinted on the will on account of its nighness to the reason, this imprint retains the name of truth; and hence it is that justice sometimes goes by the name of truth.

Reply Obj. 2: The will is borne towards its object consequently on the apprehension of reason: wherefore, since the reason directs one thing in relation to another, the will can will one thing in relation to another, and this belongs to justice.

Reply Obj. 3: Not only the irascible and concupiscible parts are *rational by participation,* but the entire appetitive faculty, as stated in Ethic. i, 13, because all appetite is subject to reason. Now the will is contained in the appetitive faculty, wherefore it can be the subject of moral virtue.

FIFTH ARTICLE [II-II, Q. 58, Art. 5]

Whether Justice Is a General Virtue?

Objection 1: It would seem that justice is not a general virtue. For justice is specified with the other virtues, according to Wis. 8:7, "She teacheth temperance and prudence, and justice, and fortitude." Now the "general" is not specified or reckoned together with the species contained under the same "general." Therefore justice is not a general virtue.

Obj. 2: Further, as justice is accounted a cardinal virtue, so are temperance and fortitude. Now neither temperance nor fortitude is reckoned to be a general virtue. Therefore neither should justice in any way be reckoned a general virtue.

Obj. 3: Further, justice is always towards others, as stated above (A. 2). But a sin committed against one's neighbor cannot be a general sin, because it is condivided with sin committed against oneself. Therefore neither is justice a general virtue.

*On the contrary,* The Philosopher says (Ethic. v, 1) that "justice is every virtue."

*I answer that,* Justice, as stated above (A. 2) directs man in his relations with other men. Now this may happen in two ways: first as regards his relation with individuals, secondly as regards his relations with others in general, in so far as a man who serves a community, serves all those who are included in that community. Accordingly justice in its proper acceptation can be directed to another in both these senses. Now it is evident that all who are included in a community, stand in relation to that community as parts to a whole; while a part, as such, belongs to a whole, so that whatever is the good of a part can be directed to the good of the whole. It follows therefore that the good of any virtue, whether such virtue direct man in relation to himself, or in relation to certain other individual persons, is referable to the common good, to which justice directs: so that all acts of virtue can pertain to justice, in so far as it directs man to the common good. It is in this sense that justice is called a general virtue. And since it belongs to the law to direct to the common good, as stated above (I-II, Q. 90, A. 2), it follows that the justice which is in this way styled general, is called "legal justice," because thereby man is in harmony with the law which directs the acts of all the virtues to the common good.

Reply Obj. 1: Justice is specified or enumerated with the other virtues, not as a general but as a special virtue, as we shall state further on (AA. 7, 12).

Reply Obj. 2: Temperance and fortitude are in the sensitive appetite, viz. in the concupiscible and irascible. Now these powers are appetitive of certain particular goods, even as the senses are cognitive of particulars. On the other hand justice is in the intellective appetite as its subject, which can have the universal good as its object, knowledge whereof belongs to the intellect. Hence justice can be a general virtue rather than temperance or fortitude.

Reply Obj. 3: Things referable to oneself are referable to another, especially in regard to the common good. Wherefore legal justice, in so far as it directs to the common good, may be called a general virtue: and in like manner injustice may be called a general sin; hence it is written (1 John 3:4) that all "sin is iniquity."

SIXTH ARTICLE [II-II, Q. 58, Art. 6]

Whether Justice, As a General Virtue, Is Essentially the Same As All Virtue?

Objection 1: It would seem that justice, as a general virtue, is essentially the same as all virtue. For the Philosopher says (Ethic. v, 1) that "virtue and legal justice are the same as all virtue, but differ in their mode of being." Now things that differ merely in their mode of being or logically do not differ essentially. Therefore justice is essentially the same as every virtue.

Obj. 2: Further, every virtue that is not essentially the same as all virtue is a part of virtue. Now the aforesaid justice, according to the Philosopher (Ethic. v. 1) "is not a part but the whole of virtue." Therefore the aforesaid justice is essentially the same as all virtue.

Obj. 3: Further, the essence of a virtue does not change through that virtue directing its act to some higher end even as the habit of temperance remains essentially the same even though its act be directed to a Divine good. Now it belongs to legal justice that the acts of all the virtues are directed to a higher end, namely the common good of the multitude, which transcends the good of one single individual. Therefore it seems that legal justice is essentially all virtue.

Obj. 4: Further, every good of a part can be directed to the good of the whole, so that if it be not thus directed it would seem without use or purpose. But that which is in accordance with virtue cannot be so. Therefore it seems that there can be no act of any virtue, that does not belong to general justice, which directs to the common good; and so it seems that general justice is essentially the same as all virtue.

*On the contrary,* The Philosopher says (Ethic. v, 1) that "many are able to be virtuous in matters affecting themselves, but are unable to be virtuous in matters relating to others," and (Polit. iii, 2) that "the virtue of the good man is not strictly the same as the virtue of the good citizen." Now the virtue of a good citizen is general justice, whereby a man is directed to the common good. Therefore general justice is not the same as virtue in general, and it is possible to have one without the other.

*I answer that,* A thing is said to be "general" in two ways. First, by *predication:* thus "animal" is general in relation to man and horse and the like: and in this sense that which is general must needs be essentially the same as the things in relation to which it is general, for the reason that the genus belongs to the essence of the species, and forms part of its definition. Secondly a thing is said to be general *virtually;* thus a universal cause is general in relation to all its effects, the sun, for instance, in relation to all bodies that are illumined, or transmuted by its power; and in this sense there is no need for that which is "general" to be essentially the same as those things in relation to which it is general, since cause and effect are not essentially the same. Now it is in the latter sense that, according to what has been said (A. 5), legal justice is said to be a general virtue, in as much, to wit, as it directs the acts of the other virtues to its own end, and this is to move all the other virtues by its command; for just as charity may be called a general virtue in so far as it directs the acts of all the virtues to the Divine good, so too is legal justice, in so far as it directs the acts of all the virtues to the common good. Accordingly, just as charity which regards the Divine good as its proper object, is a special virtue in respect of its essence, so too legal justice is a special virtue in respect of its essence, in so far as it regards the common good as its proper object. And thus it is in the sovereign principally and by way of a mastercraft, while it is secondarily and administratively in his subjects.

However the name of legal justice can be given to every virtue, in so far as every virtue is directed to the common good by the aforesaid legal justice, which though special essentially is nevertheless virtually general. Speaking in this way, legal justice is essentially the same as all virtue, but differs therefrom logically: and it is in this sense that the Philosopher speaks.

Wherefore the Replies to the First and Second Objections are manifest.

Reply Obj. 3: This argument again takes legal justice for the virtue commanded by legal justice.

Reply Obj. 4: Every virtue strictly speaking directs its act to that virtue's proper end: that it should happen to be directed to a further end either always or sometimes, does not belong to that virtue considered strictly, for it needs some higher virtue to direct it to that end. Consequently there must be one supreme virtue essentially distinct from every other virtue, which directs all the virtues to the common good; and this virtue is legal justice.

SEVENTH ARTICLE [II-II, Q. 58, Art. 7]

Whether There Is a Particular Besides a General Justice?

Objection 1: It would seem that there is not a particular besides a general justice. For there is nothing superfluous in the virtues, as neither is there in nature. Now general justice directs man sufficiently in all his relations with other men. Therefore there is no need for a particular justice.

Obj. 2: Further, the species of a virtue does not vary according to "one" and "many." But legal justice directs one man to another in matters relating to the multitude, as shown above (AA. 5, 6). Therefore there is not another species of justice directing one man to another in matters relating to the individual.

Obj. 3: Further, between the individual and the general public stands the household community. Consequently, if in addition to general justice there is a particular justice corresponding to the individual, for the same reason there should be a domestic justice directing man to the common good of a household: and yet this is not the case. Therefore neither should there be a particular besides a legal justice.

*On the contrary,* Chrysostom in his commentary on Matt. 5:6, "Blessed are they that hunger and thirst after justice," says (Hom. xv in Matth.): "By justice He signifies either the general virtue, or the particular virtue which is opposed to covetousness."

*I answer that,* As stated above (A. 6), legal justice is not essentially the same as every virtue, and besides legal justice which directs man immediately to the common good, there is a need for other virtues to direct him immediately in matters relating to particular goods: and these virtues may be relative to himself or to another individual person. Accordingly, just as in addition to legal justice there is a need for particular virtues to direct man in relation to himself, such as temperance and fortitude, so too besides legal justice there is need for particular justice to direct man in his relations to other individuals.

Reply Obj. 1: Legal justice does indeed direct man sufficiently in his relations towards others. As regards the common good it does so immediately, but as to the good of the individual, it does so mediately. Wherefore there is need for particular justice to direct a man immediately to the good of another individual.

Reply Obj. 2: The common good of the realm and the particular good of the individual differ not only in respect of the *many* and the *few,* but also under a formal aspect. For the aspect of the common good differs from the aspect of the *individual* good, even as the aspect of *whole* differs from that of part. Wherefore the Philosopher says (Polit. i, 1) that "they are wrong who maintain that the State and the home and the like differ only as many and few and not specifically."

Reply Obj. 3: The household community, according to the Philosopher (Polit. i, 2), differs in respect of a threefold fellowship; namely "of husband and wife, father and son, master and slave," in each of which one person is, as it were, part of the other. Wherefore between such persons there is not justice simply, but a species of justice, viz. *domestic* justice, as stated in Ethic. v, 6.

EIGHTH ARTICLE [II-II, Q. 58, Art. 8]

Whether Particular Justice Has a Special Matter?

Objection 1: It would seem that particular justice has no special matter. Because a gloss on Gen. 2:14, "The fourth river is Euphrates," says: "Euphrates signifies 'fruitful'; nor is it stated through what country it flows, because justice pertains to all the parts of the soul." Now this would not be the case, if justice had a special matter, since every special matter belongs to a special power. Therefore particular justice has no special matter.

Obj. 2: Further, Augustine says (QQ. lxxxiii, qu. 61) that "the soul has four virtues whereby, in this life, it lives spiritually, viz. temperance, prudence, fortitude and justice;" and he says that "the fourth is justice, which pervades all the virtues." Therefore particular justice, which is one of the four cardinal virtues, has no special matter.

Obj. 3: Further, justice directs man sufficiently in matters relating to others. Now a man can be directed to others in all matters relating to this life. Therefore the matter of justice is general and not special.

*On the contrary,* The Philosopher reckons (Ethic. v, 2) particular justice to be specially about those things which belong to social life.

*I answer that,* Whatever can be rectified by reason is the matter of moral virtue, for this is defined in reference to right reason, according to the Philosopher (Ethic. ii, 6). Now the reason can rectify not only the internal passions of the soul, but also external actions, and also those external things of which man can make use. And yet it is in respect of external actions and external things by means of which men can communicate with one another, that the relation of one man to another is to be considered; whereas it is in respect of internal passions that we consider man's rectitude in himself. Consequently, since justice is directed to others, it is not about the entire matter of moral virtue, but only about external actions and things, under a certain special aspect of the object, in so far as one man is related to another through them.

Reply Obj. 1: It is true that justice belongs essentially to one part of the soul, where it resides as in its subject; and this is the will which moves by its command all the other parts of the soul; and accordingly justice belongs to all the parts of the soul, not directly but by a kind of diffusion.

Reply Obj. 2: As stated above (I-II, Q. 61, AA. 3, 4), the cardinal virtues may be taken in two ways: first as special virtues, each having a determinate matter; secondly, as certain general modes of virtue. In this latter sense Augustine speaks in the passage quoted: for he says that "prudence is knowledge of what we should seek and avoid, temperance is the curb on the lust for fleeting pleasures, fortitude is strength of mind in bearing with passing trials, justice is the love of God and our neighbor which pervades the other virtues, that is to say, is the common principle of the entire order between one man and another."

Reply Obj. 3: A man's internal passions which are a part of moral matter, are not in themselves directed to another man, which belongs to the specific nature of justice; yet their effects, i.e. external actions, are capable of being directed to another man. Consequently it does not follow that the matter of justice is general.

NINTH ARTICLE [II-II, Q. 58, Art. 9]

Whether Justice Is About the Passions?

Objection 1: It would seem that justice is about the passions. For the Philosopher says (Ethic. ii, 3) that "moral virtue is about pleasure and pain." Now pleasure or delight, and pain are passions, as stated above [*I-II, Q. 23, A. 4; Q. 31, A. 1; Q. 35, A. 1] when we were treating of the passions. Therefore justice, being a moral virtue, is about the passions.

Obj. 2: Further, justice is the means of rectifying a man's operations in relation to another man. Now such like operations cannot be rectified unless the passions be rectified, because it is owing to disorder of the passions that there is disorder in the aforesaid operations: thus sexual lust leads to adultery, and overmuch love of money leads to theft. Therefore justice must needs be about the passions.

Obj. 3: Further, even as particular justice is towards another person so is legal justice. Now legal justice is about the passions, else it would not extend to all the virtues, some of which are evidently about the passions. Therefore justice is about the passions.

*On the contrary,* The Philosopher says (Ethic. v, 1) that justice is about operations.

*I answer that,* The true answer to this question may be gathered from a twofold source. First from the subject of justice, i.e. from the will, whose movements or acts are not passions, as stated above (I-II, Q. 22, A. 3; Q. 59, A. 4), for it is only the sensitive appetite whose movements are called passions. Hence justice is not about the passions, as are temperance and fortitude, which are in the irascible and concupiscible parts. Secondly, on he part of the matter, because justice is about man's relations with another, and we are not directed immediately to another by the internal passions. Therefore justice is not about the passions.

Reply Obj. 1: Not every moral virtue is about pleasure and pain as its proper matter, since fortitude is about fear and daring: but every moral virtue is directed to pleasure and pain, as to ends to be acquired, for, as the Philosopher says (Ethic. vii, 11), "pleasure and pain are the principal end in respect of which we say that this is an evil, and that a good": and in this way too they belong to justice, since "a man is not just unless he rejoice in just actions" (Ethic. i, 8).

Reply Obj. 2: External operations are as it were between external things, which are their matter, and internal passions, which are their origin. Now it happens sometimes that there is a defect in one of these, without there being a defect in the other. Thus a man may steal another's property, not through the desire to have the thing, but through the will to hurt the man; or vice versa, a man may covet another's property without wishing to steal it. Accordingly the directing of operations in so far as they tend towards external things, belongs to justice, but in so far as they arise from the passions, it belongs to the other moral virtues which are about the passions. Hence justice hinders theft of another's property, in so far as stealing is contrary to the equality that should be maintained in external things, while liberality hinders it as resulting from an immoderate desire for wealth. Since, however, external operations take their species, not from the internal passions but from external things as being their objects, it follows that, external operations are essentially the matter of justice rather than of the other moral virtues.

Reply Obj. 3: The common good is the end of each individual member of a community, just as the good of the whole is the end of each part. On the other hand the good of one individual is not the end of another individual: wherefore legal justice which is directed to the common good, is more capable of extending to the internal passions whereby man is disposed in some way or other in himself, than particular justice which is directed to the good of another individual: although legal justice extends chiefly to other virtues in the point of their external operations, in so far, to wit, as "the law commands us to perform the actions of a courageous person ... the actions of a temperate person ... and the actions of a gentle person" (Ethic. v, 5).

TENTH ARTICLE [II-II, Q. 58, Art. 10]

Whether the Mean of Justice Is the Real Mean?

Objection 1: It would seem that the mean of justice is not the real mean. For the generic nature remains entire in each species. Now moral virtue is defined (Ethic. ii, 6) to be "an elective habit which observes the mean fixed, in our regard, by reason." Therefore justice observes the rational and not the real mean.

Obj. 2: Further, in things that are good simply, there is neither excess nor defect, and consequently neither is there a mean; as is clearly the case with the virtues, according to *Ethic.* ii, 6. Now justice is about things that are good simply, as stated in *Ethic.* v. Therefore justice does not observe the real mean.

Obj. 3: Further, the reason why the other virtues are said to observe the rational and not the real mean, is because in their case the mean varies according to different persons, since what is too much for one is too little for another (Ethic. ii, 6). Now this is also the case in justice: for one who strikes a prince does not receive the same punishment as one who strikes a private individual. Therefore justice also observes, not the real, but the rational mean.

*On the contrary,* The Philosopher says (Ethic. ii, 6; v, 4) that the mean of justice is to be taken according to "arithmetical" proportion, so that it is the real mean.

*I answer that,* As stated above (A. 9; I-II, Q. 59, A. 4), the other moral virtues are chiefly concerned with the passions, the regulation of which is gauged entirely by a comparison with the very man who is the subject of those passions, in so far as his anger and desire are vested with their various due circumstances. Hence the mean in such like virtues is measured not by the proportion of one thing to another, but merely by comparison with the virtuous man himself, so that with them the mean is only that which is fixed by reason in our regard.

On the other hand, the matter of justice is external operation, in so far as an operation or the thing used in that operation is duly proportionate to another person, wherefore the mean of justice consists in a certain proportion of equality between the external thing and the external person. Now equality is the real mean between greater and less, as stated in *Metaph.* x [*Didot ed., ix, 5; Cf. *Ethic.* v, 4]: wherefore justice observes the real mean.

Reply Obj. 1: This real mean is also the rational mean, wherefore justice satisfies the conditions of a moral virtue.

Reply Obj. 2: We may speak of a thing being good simply in two ways. First a thing may be good in every way: thus the virtues are good; and there is neither mean nor extremes in things that are good simply in this sense. Secondly a thing is said to be good simply through being good absolutely i.e. in its nature, although it may become evil through being abused. Such are riches and honors; and in the like it is possible to find excess, deficiency and mean, as regards men who can use them well or ill: and it is in this sense that justice is about things that are good simply.

Reply Obj. 3: The injury inflicted bears a different proportion to a prince from that which it bears to a private person: wherefore each injury requires to be equalized by vengeance in a different way: and this implies a real and not merely a rational diversity.

ELEVENTH ARTICLE [II-II, Q. 58, Art. 11]

Whether the Act of Justice Is to Render to Each One His Own?

Objection 1: It would seem that the act of justice is not to render to each one his own. For Augustine (De Trin. xiv, 9) ascribes to justice the act of succoring the needy. Now in succoring the needy we give them what is not theirs but ours. Therefore the act of justice does not consist in rendering to each one his own.

Obj. 2: Further, Tully says (De Offic. i, 7) that "beneficence which we may call kindness or liberality, belongs to justice." Now it pertains to liberality to give to another of one's own, not of what is his. Therefore the act of justice does not consist in rendering to each one his own.

Obj. 3: Further, it belongs to justice not only to distribute things duly, but also to repress injurious actions, such as murder, adultery and so forth. But the rendering to each one of what is his seems to belong solely to the distribution of things. Therefore the act of justice is not sufficiently described by saying that it consists in rendering to each one his own.

*On the contrary,* Ambrose says (De Offic. i, 24): "It is justice that renders to each one what is his, and claims not another's property; it disregards its own profit in order to preserve the common equity."

*I answer that,* As stated above (AA. 8, 10), the matter of justice is an external operation in so far as either it or the thing we use by it is made proportionate to some other person to whom we are related by justice. Now each man's own is that which is due to him according to equality of proportion. Therefore the proper act of justice is nothing else than to render to each one his own.

Reply Obj. 1: Since justice is a cardinal virtue, other secondary virtues, such as mercy, liberality and the like are connected with it, as we shall state further on (Q. 80, A. 1). Wherefore to succor the needy, which belongs to mercy or pity, and to be liberally beneficent, which pertains to liberality, are by a kind of reduction ascribed to justice as to their principal virtue.

This suffices for the Reply to the Second Objection.

Reply Obj. 3: As the Philosopher states (Ethic. v, 4), in matters of justice, the name of "profit" is extended to whatever is excessive, and whatever is deficient is called "loss." The reason for this is that justice is first of all and more commonly exercised in voluntary interchanges of things, such as buying and selling, wherein those expressions are properly employed; and yet they are transferred to all other matters of justice. The same applies to the rendering to each one of what is his own.

TWELFTH ARTICLE [II-II, Q. 58, Art. 12]

Whether Justice Stands Foremost Among All Moral Virtues?

Objection 1: It would seem that justice does not stand foremost among all the moral virtues. Because it belongs to justice to render to each one what is his, whereas it belongs to liberality to give of one's own, and this is more virtuous. Therefore liberality is a greater virtue than justice.

Obj. 2: Further, nothing is adorned by a less excellent thing than itself. Now magnanimity is the ornament both of justice and of all the virtues, according to *Ethic.* iv, 3. Therefore magnanimity is more excellent than justice.

Obj. 3: Further, virtue is about that which is "difficult" and "good," as stated in *Ethic.* ii, 3. But fortitude is about more difficult things than justice is, since it is about dangers of death, according to *Ethic.* iii, 6. Therefore fortitude is more excellent than justice.

*On the contrary,* Tully says (De Offic. i, 7): "Justice is the most resplendent of the virtues, and gives its name to a good man."

*I answer that,* If we speak of legal justice, it is evident that it stands foremost among all the moral virtues, for as much as the common good transcends the individual good of one person. In this sense the Philosopher declares (Ethic. v, 1) that "the most excellent of the virtues would seem to be justice, and more glorious than either the evening or the morning star." But, even if we speak of particular justice, it excels the other moral virtues for two reasons. The first reason may be taken from the subject, because justice is in the more excellent part of the soul, viz. the rational appetite or will, whereas the other moral virtues are in the sensitive appetite, whereunto appertain the passions which are the matter of the other moral virtues. The second reason is taken from the object, because the other virtues are commendable in respect of the sole good of the virtuous person himself, whereas justice is praiseworthy in respect of the virtuous person being well disposed towards another, so that justice is somewhat the good of another person, as stated in *Ethic.* v, 1. Hence the Philosopher says (Rhet. i, 9): "The greatest virtues must needs be those which are most profitable to other persons, because virtue is a faculty of doing good to others. For this reason the greatest honors are accorded the brave and the just, since bravery is useful to others in warfare, and justice is useful to others both in warfare and in time of peace."

Reply Obj. 1: Although the liberal man gives of his own, yet he does so in so far as he takes into consideration the good of his own virtue, while the just man gives to another what is his, through consideration of the common good. Moreover justice is observed towards all, whereas liberality cannot extend to all. Again liberality which gives of a man's own is based on justice, whereby one renders to each man what is his.

Reply Obj. 2: When magnanimity is added to justice it increases the latter's goodness; and yet without justice it would not even be a virtue.

Reply Obj. 3: Although fortitude is about the most difficult things, it is not about the best, for it is only useful in warfare, whereas justice is useful both in war and in peace, as stated above.

## QUESTION 59

OF INJUSTICE (In Four Articles)

We must now consider injustice, under which head there are four points of inquiry:

(1) Whether injustice is a special vice?

(2) Whether it is proper to the unjust man to do unjust deeds?

(3) Whether one can suffer injustice willingly?

(4) Whether injustice is a mortal sin according to its genus?

FIRST ARTICLE [II-II, Q. 59, Art. 1]

Whether Injustice Is a Special Virtue?

Objection 1: It would seem that injustice is not a special vice. For it is written (1 John 3:4): "All sin is iniquity [*Vulg.: 'Whosoever committeth sin, committeth also iniquity; and sin is iniquity']." Now iniquity would seem to be the same as injustice, because justice is a kind of equality, so that injustice is apparently the same as inequality or iniquity. Therefore injustice is not a special sin.

Obj. 2: Further, no special sin is contrary to all the virtues. But injustice is contrary to all the virtues: for as regards adultery it is opposed to chastity, as regards murder it is opposed to meekness, and in like manner as regards the other sins. Therefore injustice is not a special sin.

Obj. 3: Further, injustice is opposed to justice which is in the will. But every sin is in the will, as Augustine declares (De Duabus Anim. x). Therefore injustice is not a special sin.

*On the contrary,* Injustice is contrary to justice. But justice is a special virtue. Therefore injustice is a special vice.

*I answer that,* Injustice is twofold. First there is illegal injustice which is opposed to legal justice: and this is essentially a special vice, in so far as it regards a special object, namely the common good which it contemns; and yet it is a general vice, as regards the intention, since contempt of the common good may lead to all kinds of sin. Thus too all vices, as being repugnant to the common good, have the character of injustice, as though they arose from injustice, in accord with what has been said above about justice (Q. 58, AA. 5, 6). Secondly we speak of injustice in reference to an inequality between one person and another, when one man wishes to have more goods, riches for example, or honors, and less evils, such as toil and losses, and thus injustice has a special matter and is a particular vice opposed to particular justice.

Reply Obj. 1: Even as legal justice is referred to human common good, so Divine justice is referred to the Divine good, to which all sin is repugnant, and in this sense all sin is said to be iniquity.

Reply Obj. 2: Even particular justice is indirectly opposed to all the virtues; in so far, to wit, as even external acts pertain both to justice and to the other moral virtues, although in different ways as stated above (Q. 58, A. 9, ad 2).

Reply Obj. 3: The will, like the reason, extends to all moral matters, i.e. passions and those external operations that relate to another person. On the other hand justice perfects the will solely in the point of its extending to operations that relate to another: and the same applies to injustice.

SECOND ARTICLE [II-II, Q. 59, Art. 2]

Whether a Man Is Called Unjust Through Doing an Unjust Thing?

Objection 1: It would seem that a man is called unjust through doing an unjust thing. For habits are specified by their objects, as stated above (I-II, Q. 54, A. 2). Now the proper object of justice is the just, and the proper object of injustice is the unjust. Therefore a man should be called just through doing a just thing, and unjust through doing an unjust thing.

Obj. 2: Further, the Philosopher declares (Ethic. v, 9) that they hold a false opinion who maintain that it is in a man's power to do suddenly an unjust thing, and that a just man is no less capable of doing what is unjust than an unjust man. But this opinion would not be false unless it were proper to the unjust man to do what is unjust. Therefore a man is to be deemed unjust from the fact that he does an unjust thing.

Obj. 3: Further, every virtue bears the same relation to its proper act, and the same applies to the contrary vices. But whoever does what is intemperate, is said to be intemperate. Therefore whoever does an unjust thing, is said to be unjust.

*On the contrary,* The Philosopher says (Ethic. v, 6) that "a man may do an unjust thing without being unjust."

*I answer that,* Even as the object of justice is something equal in external things, so too the object of injustice is something unequal, through more or less being assigned to some person than is due to him. To this object the habit of injustice is compared by means of its proper act which is called an injustice. Accordingly it may happen in two ways that a man who does an unjust thing, is not unjust: first, on account of a lack of correspondence between the operation and its proper object. For the operation takes its species and name from its direct and not from its indirect object: and in things directed to an end the direct is that which is intended, and the indirect is what is beside the intention. Hence if a man do that which is unjust, without intending to do an unjust thing, for instance if he do it through ignorance, being unaware that it is unjust, properly speaking he does an unjust thing, not directly, but only indirectly, and, as it were, doing materially that which is unjust: hence such an operation is not called an injustice. Secondly, this may happen on account of a lack of proportion between the operation and the habit. For an injustice may sometimes arise from a passion, for instance, anger or desire, and sometimes from choice, for instance when the injustice itself is the direct object of one's complacency. In the latter case properly speaking it arises from a habit, because whenever a man has a habit, whatever befits that habit is, of itself, pleasant to him. Accordingly, to do what is unjust intentionally and by choice is proper to the unjust man, in which sense the unjust man is one who has the habit of injustice: but a man may do what is unjust, unintentionally or through passion, without having the habit of injustice.

Reply Obj. 1: A habit is specified by its object in its direct and formal acceptation, not in its material and indirect acceptation.

Reply Obj. 2: It is not easy for any man to do an unjust thing from choice, as though it were pleasing for its own sake and not for the sake of something else: this is proper to one who has the habit, as the Philosopher declares (Ethic. v, 9).

Reply Obj. 3: The object of temperance is not something established externally, as is the object of justice: the object of temperance, i.e. the temperate thing, depends entirely on proportion to the man himself. Consequently what is accidental and unintentional cannot be said to be temperate either materially or formally. In like manner neither can it be called intemperate: and in this respect there is dissimilarity between justice and the other moral virtues; but as regards the proportion between operation and habit, there is similarity in all respects.

THIRD ARTICLE [II-II, Q. 59, Art. 3]

Whether We Can Suffer Injustice Willingly?

Objection 1: It would seem that one can suffer injustice willingly. For injustice is inequality, as stated above (A. 2). Now a man by injuring himself, departs from equality, even as by injuring another. Therefore a man can do an injustice to himself, even as to another. But whoever does himself an injustice, does so involuntarily. Therefore a man can voluntarily suffer injustice especially if it be inflicted by himself.

Obj. 2: Further, no man is punished by the civil law, except for having committed some injustice. Now suicides were formerly punished according to the law of the state by being deprived of an honorable burial, as the Philosopher declares (Ethic. v, 11). Therefore a man can do himself an injustice, and consequently it may happen that a man suffers injustice voluntarily.

Obj. 3: Further, no man does an injustice save to one who suffers that injustice. But it may happen that a man does an injustice to one who wishes it, for instance if he sell him a thing for more than it is worth. Therefore a man may happen to suffer an injustice voluntarily.

*On the contrary,* To suffer an injustice and to do an injustice are contraries. Now no man does an injustice against his will. Therefore on the other hand no man suffers an injustice except against his will.

*I answer that,* Action by its very nature proceeds from an agent, whereas passion as such is from another: wherefore the same thing in the same respect cannot be both agent and patient, as stated in *Phys.* iii, 1; viii, 5. Now the proper principle of action in man is the will, wherefore man does properly and essentially what he does voluntarily, and on the other hand a man suffers properly what he suffers against his will, since in so far as he is willing, he is a principle in himself, and so, considered thus, he is active rather than passive. Accordingly we must conclude that properly and strictly speaking no man can do an injustice except voluntarily, nor suffer an injustice save involuntarily; but that accidentally and materially so to speak, it is possible for that which is unjust in itself either to be done involuntarily (as when a man does anything unintentionally), or to be suffered voluntarily (as when a man voluntarily gives to another more than he owes him).

Reply Obj. 1: When one man gives voluntarily to another that which he does not owe him, he causes neither injustice nor inequality. For a man's ownership depends on his will, so there is no disproportion if he forfeit something of his own free-will, either by his own or by another's action.

Reply Obj. 2: An individual person may be considered in two ways. First, with regard to himself; and thus, if he inflict an injury on himself, it may come under the head of some other kind of sin, intemperance for instance or imprudence, but not injustice; because injustice no less than justice, is always referred to another person. Secondly, this or that man may be considered as belonging to the State as part thereof, or as belonging to God, as His creature and image; and thus a man who kills himself, does an injury not indeed to himself, but to the State and to God. Wherefore he is punished in accordance with both Divine and human law, even as the Apostle declares in respect of the fornicator (1 Cor. 3:17): "If any man violate the temple of God, him shall God destroy."

Reply Obj. 3: Suffering is the effect of external action. Now in the point of doing and suffering injustice, the material element is that which is done externally, considered in itself, as stated above (A. 2), and the formal and essential element is on the part of the will of agent and patient, as stated above (A. 2). Accordingly we must reply that injustice suffered by one man and injustice done by another man always accompany one another, in the material sense. But if we speak in the formal sense a man can do an injustice with the intention of doing an injustice, and yet the other man does not suffer an injustice, because he suffers voluntarily; and on the other hand a man can suffer an injustice if he suffer an injustice against his will, while the man who does the injury unknowingly, does an injustice, not formally but only materially.

FOURTH ARTICLE [II-II, Q. 59, Art. 4]

Whether Whoever Does an Injustice Sins Mortally?

Objection 1: It would seem that not everyone who does an injustice sins mortally. For venial sin is opposed to mortal sin. Now it is sometimes a venial sin to do an injury: for the Philosopher says (Ethic. v, 8) in reference to those who act unjustly: "Whatever they do not merely in ignorance but through ignorance is a venial matter." Therefore not everyone that does an injustice sins mortally.

Obj. 2: Further, he who does an injustice in a small matter, departs but slightly from the mean. Now this seems to be insignificant and should be accounted among the least of evils, as the Philosopher declares (Ethic. ii, 9). Therefore not everyone that does an injustice sins mortally.

Obj. 3: Further, charity is the "mother of all the virtues" [*Peter Lombard, Sent. iii, D. 23], and it is through being contrary thereto that a sin is called mortal. But not all the sins contrary to the other virtues are mortal. Therefore neither is it always a mortal sin to do an injustice.

*On the contrary,* Whatever is contrary to the law of God is a mortal sin. Now whoever does an injustice does that which is contrary to the law of God, since it amounts either to theft, or to adultery, or to murder, or to something of the kind, as will be shown further on (Q. 64, seqq.). Therefore whoever does an injustice sins mortally.

*I answer that,* As stated above (I-II, Q. 12, A. 5), when we were treating of the distinction of sins, a mortal sin is one that is contrary to charity which gives life to the soul. Now every injury inflicted on another person is of itself contrary to charity, which moves us to will the good of another. And so since injustice always consists in an injury inflicted on another person, it is evident that to do an injustice is a mortal sin according to its genus.

Reply Obj. 1: This saying of the Philosopher is to be understood as referring to ignorance of fact, which he calls "ignorance of particular circumstances" [*Ethic. iii, 1], and which deserves pardon, and not to ignorance of the law which does not excuse: and he who does an injustice through ignorance, does no injustice except accidentally, as stated above (A. 2)

Reply Obj. 2: He who does an injustice in small matters falls short of the perfection of an unjust deed, in so far as what he does may be deemed not altogether contrary to the will of the person who suffers therefrom: for instance, if a man take an apple or some such thing from another man, in which case it is probable that the latter is not hurt or displeased.

Reply Obj. 3: The sins which are contrary to the other virtues are not always hurtful to another person, but imply a disorder affecting human passions; hence there is no comparison.

# QUESTION 60

OF JUDGMENT (In Six Articles)

In due sequence we must consider judgment, under which head there are six points of inquiry:

(1) Whether judgment is an act of justice?

(2) Whether it is lawful to judge?

(3) Whether judgment should be based on suspicions?

(4) Whether doubts should be interpreted favorably?

(5) Whether judgment should always be given according to the written law?

(6) Whether judgment is perverted by being usurped?

FIRST ARTICLE [II-II, Q. 60, Art. 1]

Whether Judgment Is an Act of Justice?

Objection 1: It would seem that judgment is not an act of justice. The Philosopher says (Ethic. i, 3) that "everyone judges well of what he knows," so that judgment would seem to belong to the cognitive faculty. Now the cognitive faculty is perfected by prudence. Therefore judgment belongs to prudence rather than to justice, which is in the will, as stated above (Q. 58, A. 4).

Obj. 2: Further, the Apostle says (1 Cor. 2:15): "The spiritual man judgeth all things." Now man is made spiritual chiefly by the virtue of charity, which "is poured forth in our hearts by the Holy Ghost Who is given to us" (Rom. 5:5). Therefore judgment belongs to charity rather than to justice.

Obj. 3: Further, it belongs to every virtue to judge aright of its proper matter, because "the virtuous man is the rule and measure in everything," according to the Philosopher (Ethic. iii, 4). Therefore judgment does not belong to justice any more than to the other moral virtues.

Obj. 4: Further, judgment would seem to belong only to judges. But the act of justice is to be found in every just man. Since then judges are not the only just men, it seems that judgment is not the proper act of justice.

*On the contrary,* It is written (Ps. 93:15): "Until justice be turned into judgment."

*I answer that,* Judgment properly denotes the act of a judge as such. Now a judge ( *judex* ) is so called because he asserts the right ( *jus dicens* ) and right is the object of justice, as stated above (Q. 57, A. 1). Consequently the original meaning of the word "judgment" is a statement or decision of the just or right. Now to decide rightly about virtuous deeds proceeds, properly speaking, from the virtuous habit; thus a chaste person decides rightly about matters relating to chastity. Therefore judgment, which denotes a right decision about what is just, belongs properly to justice. For this reason the Philosopher says (Ethic. v, 4) that "men have recourse to a judge as to one who is the personification of justice."

Reply Obj. 1: The word "judgment," from its original meaning of a right decision about what is just, has been extended to signify a right decision in any matter whether speculative or practical. Now a right judgment in any matter requires two things. The first is the virtue itself that pronounces judgment: and in this way, judgment is an act of reason, because it belongs to the reason to pronounce or define. The other is the disposition of the one who judges, on which depends his aptness for judging aright. In this way, in matters of justice, judgment proceeds from justice, even as in matters of fortitude, it proceeds from fortitude. Accordingly judgment is an act of justice in so far as justice inclines one to judge aright, and of prudence in so far as prudence pronounces judgment: wherefore *synesis* which belongs to prudence is said to "judge rightly," as stated above (Q. 51, A. 3).

Reply Obj. 2: The spiritual man, by reason of the habit of charity, has an inclination to judge aright of all things according to the Divine rules; and it is in conformity with these that he pronounces judgment through the gift of wisdom: even as the just man pronounces judgment through the virtue of prudence conformably with the ruling of the law.

Reply Obj. 3: The other virtues regulate man in himself, whereas justice regulates man in his dealings with others, as shown above (Q. 58, A. 2). Now man is master in things concerning himself, but not in matters relating to others. Consequently where the other virtues are in question, there is no need for judgment other than that of a virtuous man, taking judgment in its broader sense, as explained above (ad 1). But in matters of justice, there is further need for the judgment of a superior, who is "able to reprove both, and to put his hand between both" [*Job 9:33]. Hence judgment belongs more specifically to justice than to any other virtue.

Reply Obj. 4: Justice is in the sovereign as a master-virtue [*Cf. Q. 58, A. 6], commanding and prescribing what is just; while it is in the subjects as an executive and administrative virtue. Hence judgment, which denotes a decision of what is just, belongs to justice, considered as existing chiefly in one who has authority.

SECOND ARTICLE [II-II, Q. 60, Art. 2]

Whether It Is Lawful to Judge?

Objection 1: It would seem unlawful to judge. For nothing is punished except what is unlawful. Now those who judge are threatened with punishment, which those who judge not will escape, according to Matt. 7:1, "Judge not, and ye shall not be judged." Therefore it is unlawful to judge.

Obj. 2: Further, it is written (Rom. 14:4): "Who art thou that judgest another man's servant[?] To his own lord he standeth or falleth." Now God is the Lord of all. Therefore to no man is it lawful to judge.

Obj. 3: Further, no man is sinless, according to 1 John 1:8, "If we say that we have no sin, we deceive ourselves." Now it is unlawful for a sinner to judge, according to Rom. 2:1, "Thou art inexcusable, O man, whosoever thou art, that judgest; for wherein thou judgest another, thou condemnest thyself, for thou dost the same things which thou judgest." Therefore to no man is it lawful to judge.

*On the contrary,* It is written (Deut. 16:18): "Thou shalt appoint judges and magistrates in all thy gates ... that they may judge the people with just judgment."

*I answer that,* Judgment is lawful in so far as it is an act of justice. Now it follows from what has been stated above (A. 1, ad 1, 3) that three conditions are requisite for a judgment to be an act of justice: first, that it proceed from the inclination of justice; secondly, that it come from one who is in authority; thirdly, that it be pronounced according to the right ruling of prudence. If any one of these be lacking, the judgment will be faulty and unlawful. First, when it is contrary to the rectitude of justice, and then it is called "perverted" or "unjust": secondly, when a man judges about matters wherein he has no authority, and this is called judgment "by usurpation": thirdly, when the reason lacks certainty, as when a man, without any solid motive, forms a judgment on some doubtful or hidden matter, and then it is called judgment by "suspicion" or "rash" judgment.

Reply Obj. 1: In these words our Lord forbids rash judgment which is about the inward intention, or other uncertain things, as Augustine states (De Serm. Dom. in Monte ii, 18). Or else He forbids judgment about Divine things, which we ought not to judge, but simply believe, since they are above us, as Hilary declares in his commentary on Matt. 5. Or again according to Chrysostom [*Hom. xvii in Matth. in the Opus Imperfectum falsely ascribed to St. John Chrysostom], He forbids the judgment which proceeds not from benevolence but from bitterness of heart.

Reply Obj. 2: A judge is appointed as God's servant; wherefore it is written (Deut. 1:16): "Judge that which is just," and further on (Deut. 1:17), "because it is the judgment of God."

Reply Obj. 3: Those who stand guilty of grievous sins should not judge those who are guilty of the same or lesser sins, as Chrysostom [*Hom. xxiv] says on the words of Matt. 7:1, "Judge not." Above all does this hold when such sins are public, because there would be an occasion of scandal arising in the hearts of others. If however they are not public but hidden, and there be an urgent necessity for the judge to pronounce judgment, because it is his duty, he can reprove or judge with humility and fear. Hence Augustine says (De Serm. Dom. in Monte ii, 19): "If we find that we are guilty of the same sin as another man, we should groan together with him, and invite him to strive against it together with us." And yet it is not through acting thus that a man condemns himself so as to deserve to be condemned once again, but when, in condemning another, he shows himself to be equally deserving of condemnation on account of another or a like sin.

THIRD ARTICLE [II-II, Q. 60, Art. 3]

Whether It Is Unlawful to Form a Judgment from Suspicions?

Objection 1: It would seem that it is not unlawful to form a judgment from suspicions. For suspicion is seemingly an uncertain opinion about an evil, wherefore the Philosopher states (Ethic. vi, 3) that suspicion is about both the true and the false. Now it is impossible to have any but an uncertain opinion about contingent singulars. Since then human judgment is about human acts, which are about singular and contingent matters, it seems that no judgment would be lawful, if it were not lawful to judge from suspicions.

Obj. 2: Further, a man does his neighbor an injury by judging him unlawfully. But an evil suspicion consists in nothing more than a man's opinion, and consequently does not seem to pertain to the injury of another man. Therefore judgment based on suspicion is not unlawful.

Obj. 3: Further, if it is unlawful, it must needs be reducible to an injustice, since judgment is an act of justice, as stated above (A. 1). Now an injustice is always a mortal sin according to its genus, as stated above (Q. 59, A. 4). Therefore a judgment based on suspicion would always be a mortal sin, if it were unlawful. But this is false, because "we cannot avoid suspicions," according to a gloss of Augustine (Tract. xc in Joan.) on 1 Cor. 4:5, "Judge not before the time." Therefore a judgment based on suspicion would seem not to be unlawful.

*On the contrary,* Chrysostom [*Hom. xvii in Matth. in the Opus Imperfectum falsely ascribed to St. John Chrysostom] in comment on the words of Matt. 7:1, "Judge not," etc., says: "By this commandment our Lord does not forbid Christians to reprove others from kindly motives, but that Christian should despise Christian by boasting his own righteousness, by hating and condemning others for the most part on mere suspicion."

*I answer that,* As Tully says (De Invent. Rhet. ii), suspicion denotes evil thinking based on slight indications, and this is due to three causes. First, from a man being evil in himself, and from this very fact, as though conscious of his own wickedness, he is prone to think evil of others, according to Eccles. 10:3, "The fool when he walketh in the way, whereas he himself is a fool, esteemeth all men fools." Secondly, this is due to a man being ill-disposed towards another: for when a man hates or despises another, or is angry with or envious of him, he is led by slight indications to think evil of him, because everyone easily believes what he desires. Thirdly, this is due to long experience: wherefore the Philosopher says (Rhet. ii, 13) that "old people are very suspicious, for they have often experienced the faults of others." The first two causes of suspicion evidently connote perversity of the affections, while the third diminishes the nature of suspicion, in as much as experience leads to certainty which is contrary to the nature of suspicion. Consequently suspicion denotes a certain amount of vice, and the further it goes, the more vicious it is.

Now there are three degrees of suspicion. The first degree is when a man begins to doubt of another's goodness from slight indications. This is a venial and a light sin; for "it belongs to human temptation without which no man can go through this life," according to a gloss on 1 Cor. 4:5, "Judge not before the time." The second degree is when a man, from slight indications, esteems another man's wickedness as certain. This is a mortal sin, if it be about a grave matter, since it cannot be without contempt of one's neighbor. Hence the same gloss goes on to say: "If then we cannot avoid suspicions, because we are human, we must nevertheless restrain our judgment, and refrain from forming a definite and fixed opinion." The third degree is when a judge goes so far as to condemn a man on suspicion: this pertains directly to injustice, and consequently is a mortal sin.

Reply Obj. 1: Some kind of certainty is found in human acts, not indeed the certainty of a demonstration, but such as is befitting the matter in point, for instance when a thing is proved by suitable witnesses.

Reply Obj. 2: From the very fact that a man thinks evil of another without sufficient cause, he despises him unduly, and therefore does him an injury.

Reply Obj. 3: Since justice and injustice are about external operations, as stated above (Q. 58, AA. 8, 10, 11; Q. 59, A. 1, ad 3), the judgment of suspicion pertains directly to injustice when it is betrayed by external action, and then it is a mortal sin, as stated above. The internal judgment pertains to justice, in so far as it is related to the external judgment, even as the internal to the external act, for instance as desire is related to fornication, or anger to murder.

FOURTH ARTICLE [II-II, Q. 60, Art. 4]

Whether Doubts Should Be Interpreted for the Best?

Objection 1: It would seem that doubts should not be interpreted for the best. Because we should judge from what happens for the most part. But it happens for the most part that evil is done, since "the number of fools is infinite" (Eccles. 1:15), "for the imagination and thought of man's heart are prone to evil from his youth" (Gen. 8:21). Therefore doubts should be interpreted for the worst rather than for the best.

Obj. 2: Further, Augustine says (De Doctr. Christ. i, 27) that "he leads a godly and just life who is sound in his estimate of things, and turns neither to this side nor to that." Now he who interprets a doubtful point for the best, turns to one side. Therefore this should not be done.

Obj. 3: Further, man should love his neighbor as himself. Now with regard to himself, a man should interpret doubtful matters for the worst, according to Job 9:28, "I feared all my works." Therefore it seems that doubtful matters affecting one's neighbor should be interpreted for the worst.

*On the contrary,* A gloss on Rom. 14:3, "He that eateth not, let him not judge him that eateth," says: "Doubts should be interpreted in the best sense."

*I answer that,* As stated above (A. 3, ad 2), from the very fact that a man thinks ill of another without sufficient cause, he injures and despises him. Now no man ought to despise or in any way injure another man without urgent cause: and, consequently, unless we have evident indications of a person's wickedness, we ought to deem him good, by interpreting for the best whatever is doubtful about him.

Reply Obj. 1: He who interprets doubtful matters for the best, may happen to be deceived more often than not; yet it is better to err frequently through thinking well of a wicked man, than to err less frequently through having an evil opinion of a good man, because in the latter case an injury is inflicted, but not in the former.

Reply Obj. 2: It is one thing to judge of things and another to judge of men. For when we judge of things, there is no question of the good or evil of the thing about which we are judging, since it will take no harm no matter what kind of judgment we form about it; but there is question of the good of the person who judges, if he judge truly, and of his evil if he judge falsely because "the true is the good of the intellect, and the false is its evil," as stated in *Ethic.* vi, 2, wherefore everyone should strive to make his judgment accord with things as they are. On the other hand when we judge of men, the good and evil in our judgment is considered chiefly on the part of the person about whom judgment is being formed; for he is deemed worthy of honor from the very fact that he is judged to be good, and deserving of contempt if he is judged to be evil. For this reason we ought, in this kind of judgment, to aim at judging a man good, unless there is evident proof of the contrary. And though we may judge falsely, our judgment in thinking well of another pertains to our good feeling and not to the evil of the intellect, even as neither does it pertain to the intellect's perfection to know the truth of contingent singulars in themselves.

Reply Obj. 3: One may interpret something for the worst or for the best in two ways. First, by a kind of supposition; and thus, when we have to apply a remedy to some evil, whether our own or another's, in order for the remedy to be applied with greater certainty of a cure, it is expedient to take the worst for granted, since if a remedy be efficacious against a worse evil, much more is it efficacious against a lesser evil. Secondly we may interpret something for the best or for the worst, by deciding or determining, and in this case when judging of things we should try to interpret each thing according as it is, and when judging of persons, to interpret things for the best as stated above.

FIFTH ARTICLE [II-II, Q. 60, Art. 5]

Whether We Should Always Judge According to the Written Law?

Objection 1: It would seem that we ought not always to judge according to the written law. For we ought always to avoid judging unjustly. But written laws sometimes contain injustice, according to Isa. 10:1, "Woe to them that make wicked laws, and when they write, write injustice." Therefore we ought not always to judge according to the written law.

Obj. 2: Further, judgment has to be formed about individual happenings. But no written law can cover each and every individual happening, as the Philosopher declares (Ethic. v, 10). Therefore it seems that we are not always bound to judge according to the written law.

Obj. 3: Further, a law is written in order that the lawgiver's intention may be made clear. But it happens sometimes that even if the lawgiver himself were present he would judge otherwise. Therefore we ought not always to judge according to the written law.

*On the contrary,* Augustine says (De Vera Relig. xxxi): "In these earthly laws, though men judge about them when they are making them, when once they are established and passed, the judges may judge no longer of them, but according to them."

*I answer that,* As stated above (A. 1), judgment is nothing else but a decision or determination of what is just. Now a thing becomes just in two ways: first by the very nature of the case, and this is called "natural right," secondly by some agreement between men, and this is called "positive right," as stated above (Q. 57, A. 2). Now laws are written for the purpose of manifesting both these rights, but in different ways. For the written law does indeed contain natural right, but it does not establish it, for the latter derives its force, not from the law but from nature: whereas the written law both contains positive right, and establishes it by giving it force of authority.

Hence it is necessary to judge according to the written law, else judgment would fall short either of the natural or of the positive right.

Reply Obj. 1: Just as the written law does not give force to the natural right, so neither can it diminish or annul its force, because neither can man's will change nature. Hence if the written law contains anything contrary to the natural right, it is unjust and has no binding force. For positive right has no place except where "it matters not," according to the natural right, "whether a thing be done in one way or in another"; as stated above (Q. 57, A. 2, ad 2). Wherefore such documents are to be called, not laws, but rather corruptions of law, as stated above (I-II, Q. 95, A. 2): and consequently judgment should not be delivered according to them.

Reply Obj. 2: Even as unjust laws by their very nature are, either always or for the most part, contrary to the natural right, so too laws that are rightly established, fail in some cases, when if they were observed they would be contrary to the natural right. Wherefore in such cases judgment should be delivered, not according to the letter of the law, but according to equity which the lawgiver has in view. Hence the jurist says [*Digest. i, 3; De leg. senatusque consult. 25]: "By no reason of law, or favor of equity, is it allowable for us to interpret harshly, and render burdensome, those useful measures which have been enacted for the welfare of man." In such cases even the lawgiver himself would decide otherwise; and if he had foreseen the case, he might have provided for it by law.

This suffices for the Reply to the Third Objection.

SIXTH ARTICLE [II-II, Q. 60, Art. 6]

Whether Judgment Is Rendered Perverse by Being Usurped?

Objection 1: It would seem that judgment is not rendered perverse by being usurped. For justice is rectitude in matters of action. Now truth is not impaired, no matter who tells it, but it may suffer from the person who ought to accept it. Therefore again justice loses nothing, no matter who declares what is just, and this is what is meant by judgment.

Obj. 2: Further, it belongs to judgment to punish sins. Now it is related to the praise of some that they punished sins without having authority over those whom they punished; such as Moses in slaying the Egyptian (Ex. 2:12), and Phinees the son of Eleazar in slaying Zambri the son of Salu (Num. 25:7-14), and "it was reputed to him unto justice" (Ps. 105:31). Therefore usurpation of judgment pertains not to injustice.

Obj. 3: Further, spiritual power is distinct from temporal. Now prelates having spiritual power sometimes interfere in matters concerning the secular power. Therefore usurped judgment is not unlawful.

Obj. 4: Further, even as the judge requires authority in order to judge aright, so also does he need justice and knowledge, as shown above (A. 1, ad 1, 3; A. 2). But a judgment is not described as unjust, if he who judges lacks the habit of justice or the knowledge of the law. Neither therefore is it always unjust to judge by usurpation, i.e. without authority.

*On the contrary,* It is written (Rom. 14:4): "Who art thou that judgest another man's servant?"

*I answer that,* Since judgment should be pronounced according to the written law, as stated above (A. 5), he that pronounces judgment, interprets, in a way, the letter of the law, by applying it to some particular case. Now since it belongs to the same authority to interpret and to make a law, just as a law cannot be made save by public authority, so neither can a judgment be pronounced except by public authority, which extends over those who are subject to the community. Wherefore even as it would be unjust for one man to force another to observe a law that was not approved by public authority, so too it is unjust, if a man compels another to submit to a judgment that is pronounced by other than the public authority.

Reply Obj. 1: When the truth is declared there is no obligation to accept it, and each one is free to receive it or not, as he wishes. On the other hand judgment implies an obligation, wherefore it is unjust for anyone to be judged by one who has no public authority.

Reply Obj. 2: Moses seems to have slain the Egyptian by authority received as it were, by divine inspiration; this seems to follow from Acts 7:24, 25, where it is said that "striking the Egyptian ... he thought that his brethren understood that God by his hand would save Israel [Vulg.: 'them']." Or it may be replied that Moses slew the Egyptian in order to defend the man who was unjustly attacked, without himself exceeding the limits of a blameless defence. Wherefore Ambrose says (De Offic. i, 36) that "whoever does not ward off a blow from a fellow man when he can, is as much in fault as the striker"; and he quotes the example of Moses. Again we may reply with Augustine (QQ. Exod. qu. 2) [*Cf. Contra Faust. xxii, 70] that just as "the soil gives proof of its fertility by producing useless herbs before the useful seeds have grown, so this deed of Moses was sinful although it gave a sign of great fertility," in so far, to wit, as it was a sign of the power whereby he was to deliver his people.

With regard to Phinees the reply is that he did this out of zeal for God by Divine inspiration; or because though not as yet high-priest, he was nevertheless the high-priest's son, and this judgment was his concern as of the other judges, to whom this was commanded [*Ex. 22:20; Lev. 20; Deut. 13, 17].

Reply Obj. 3: The secular power is subject to the spiritual, even as the body is subject to the soul. Consequently the judgment is not usurped if the spiritual authority interferes in those temporal matters that are subject to the spiritual authority or which have been committed to the spiritual by the temporal authority.

Reply Obj. 4: The habits of knowledge and justice are perfections of the individual, and consequently their absence does not make a judgment to be usurped, as in the absence of public authority which gives a judgment its coercive force.

## QUESTION 61

OF THE PARTS OF JUSTICE (In Four Articles)

We must now consider the parts of justice; (1) the subjective parts, which are the species of justice, i.e. distributive and commutative justice; (2) the quasi-integral parts; (3) the quasi-potential parts, i.e. the virtues connected with justice. The first consideration will be twofold: (1) The parts of justice; (2) their opposite vices. And since restitution would seem to be an act of commutative justice, we must consider (1) the distinction between commutative and distributive justice; (2) restitution.

Under the first head there are four points of inquiry:

(1) Whether there are two species of justice, viz. distributive and commutative?

(2) Whether in either case the mean is take in the same way?

(3) Whether their matter is uniform or manifold?

(4) Whether in any of these species the just is the same as counter-passion?

FIRST ARTICLE [II-II, Q. 61, Art. 1]

Whether Two Species of Justice Are Suitably Assigned, Viz. Commutative and Distributive?

Objection 1: It would seem that the two species of justice are unsuitably assigned, viz. distributive and commutative. That which is hurtful to the many cannot be a species of justice, since justice is directed to the common good. Now it is hurtful to the common good of the many, if the goods of the community are distributed among many, both because the goods of the community would be exhausted, and because the morals of men would be corrupted. For Tully says (De Offic. ii, 15): "He who receives becomes worse, and the more ready to expect that he will receive again." Therefore distribution does not belong to any species of justice.

Obj. 2: Further, the act of justice is to render to each one what is his own, as stated above (Q. 58, A. 2). But when things are distributed, a man does not receive what was his, but becomes possessed of something which belonged to the community. Therefore this does not pertain to justice.

Obj. 3: Further, justice is not only in the sovereign, but also in the subject, as stated above (Q. 58, A. 6). But it belongs exclusively to the sovereign to distribute. Therefore distribution does not always belong to justice.

Obj. 4: Further, "Distributive justice regards common goods" (Ethic. v, 4). Now matters regarding the community pertain to legal justice. Therefore distributive justice is a part, not of particular, but of legal justice.

Obj. 5: Further, unity or multitude do not change the species of a virtue. Now commutative justice consists in rendering something to one person, while distributive justice consists in giving something to many. Therefore they are not different species of justice.

*On the contrary,* The Philosopher assigns two parts to justice and says (Ethic. v, 2) that "one directs distributions, the other, commutations."

*I answer that,* As stated above (Q. 58, AA. 7, 8), particular justice is directed to the private individual, who is compared to the community as a part to the whole. Now a twofold order may be considered in relation to a part. In the first place there is the order of one part to another, to which corresponds the order of one private individual to another. This order is directed by commutative justice, which is concerned about the mutual dealings between two persons. In the second place there is the order of the whole towards the parts, to which corresponds the order of that which belongs to the community in relation to each single person. This order is directed by distributive justice, which distributes common goods proportionately. Hence there are two species of justice, distributive and commutative.

Reply Obj. 1: Just as a private individual is praised for moderation in his bounty, and blamed for excess therein, so too ought moderation to be observed in the distribution of common goods, wherein distributive justice directs.

Reply Obj. 2: Even as part and whole are somewhat the same, so too that which pertains to the whole, pertains somewhat to the part also: so that when the goods of the community are distributed among a number of individuals each one receives that which, in a way, is his own.

Reply Obj. 3: The act of distributing the goods of the community, belongs to none but those who exercise authority over those goods; and yet distributive justice is also in the subjects to whom those goods are distributed in so far as they are contented by a just distribution. Moreover distribution of common goods is sometimes made not to the state but to the members of a family, and such distribution can be made by authority of a private individual.

Reply Obj. 4: Movement takes its species from the term *whereunto.* Hence it belongs to legal justice to direct to the common good those matters which concern private individuals: whereas on the contrary it belongs to particular justice to direct the common good to particular individuals by way of distribution.

Reply Obj. 5: Distributive and commutative justice differ not only in respect of unity and multitude, but also in respect of different kinds of due: because common property is due to an individual in one way, and his personal property in another way.

SECOND ARTICLE [II-II, Q. 61, Art. 2]

Whether the Mean Is to Be Observed in the Same Way in Distributive As in Commutative Justice?

Objection 1: It would seem that the mean in distributive justice is to be observed in the same way as in commutative justice. For each of these is a kind of particular justice, as stated above (A. 1). Now the mean is taken in the same way in all the parts of temperance or fortitude. Therefore the mean should also be observed in the same way in both distributive and commutative justice.

Obj. 2: Further, the form of a moral virtue consists in observing the mean which is determined in accordance with reason. Since, then, one virtue has one form, it seems that the mean for both should be the same.

Obj. 3: Further, in order to observe the mean in distributive justice we have to consider the various deserts of persons. Now a person's deserts are considered also in commutative justice, for instance, in punishments; thus a man who strikes a prince is punished more than one who strikes a private individual. Therefore the mean is observed in the same way in both kinds of justice.

*On the contrary,* The Philosopher says (Ethic. v, 3, 4) that the mean in distributive justice is observed according to "geometrical proportion," whereas in commutative justice it follows "arithmetical proportion."

*I answer that,* As stated above (A. 1), in distributive justice something is given to a private individual, in so far as what belongs to the whole is due to the part, and in a quantity that is proportionate to the importance of the position of that part in respect of the whole. Consequently in distributive justice a person receives all the more of the common goods, according as he holds a more prominent position in the community. This prominence in an aristocratic community is gauged according to virtue, in an oligarchy according to wealth, in a democracy according to liberty, and in various ways according to various forms of community. Hence in distributive justice the mean is observed, not according to equality between thing and thing, but according to proportion between things and persons: in such a way that even as one person surpasses another, so that which is given to one person surpasses that which is allotted to another. Hence the Philosopher says (Ethic. v, 3, 4) that the mean in the latter case follows "geometrical proportion," wherein equality depends not on quantity but on proportion. For example we say that 6 is to 4 as 3 is to 2, because in either case the proportion equals

11/2; since the greater number is the sum of the lesser plus its half: whereas the equality of excess is not one of quantity, because 6 exceeds 4 by 2, while 3 exceeds 2 by 1.

On the other hand in commutations something is paid to an individual on account of something of his that has been received, as may be seen chiefly in selling and buying, where the notion of commutation is found primarily. Hence it is necessary to equalize thing with thing, so that the one person should pay back to the other just so much as he has become richer out of that which belonged to the other. The result of this will be equality according to the "arithmetical mean" which is gauged according to equal excess in quantity. Thus 5 is the mean between 6 and 4, since it exceeds the latter and is exceeded by the former, by 1. Accordingly if, at the start, both persons have 5, and one of them receives 1 out of the other's belongings, the one that is the receiver, will have 6, and the other will be left with 4: and so there will be justice if both be brought back to the mean, 1 being taken from him that has 6, and given to him that has 4, for then both will have 5 which is the mean.

Reply Obj. 1: In the other moral virtues the rational, not the real mean, is to be followed: but justice follows the real mean; wherefore the mean, in justice, depends on the diversity of things.

Reply Obj. 2: Equality is the general form of justice, wherein distributive and commutative justice agree: but in one we find equality of geometrical proportion, whereas in the other we find equality of arithmetical proportion.

Reply Obj. 3: In actions and passions a person's station affects the quantity of a thing: for it is a greater injury to strike a prince than a private person. Hence in distributive justice a person's station is considered in itself, whereas in commutative justice it is considered in so far as it causes a diversity of things.

THIRD ARTICLE [II-II, Q. 61, Art. 3]

Whether There Is a Different Matter for Both Kinds of Justice?

Objection 1: It would seem that there is not a different matter for both kinds of justice. Diversity of matter causes diversity of virtue, as in the case of fortitude and temperance. Therefore, if distributive and commutative justice have different matters, it would seem that they are not comprised under the same virtue, viz. justice.

Obj. 2: Further, the distribution that has to do with distributive justice is one of "wealth or of honors, or of whatever can be distributed among the members of the community" (Ethic. v, 2), which very things are the subject matter of commutations between one person and another, and this belongs to commutative justice. Therefore the matters of distributive and commutative justice are not distinct.

Obj. 3: Further, if the matter of distributive justice differs from that of commutative justice, for the reason that they differ specifically, where there is no specific difference, there ought to be no diversity of matter. Now the Philosopher (Ethic. v, 2) reckons commutative justice as one species, and yet this has many kinds of matter. Therefore the matter of these species of justice is, seemingly, not of many kinds.

*On the contrary,* It is stated in Ethic. v, 2 that "one kind of justice directs distributions, and another commutations."

*I answer that,* As stated above (Q. 51, AA. 8, 10), justice is about certain external operations, namely distribution and commutation. These consist in the use of certain externals, whether things, persons or even works: of things, as when one man takes from or restores to another that which is his; of persons, as when a man does an injury to the very person of another, for instance by striking or insulting him, or even by showing respect for him; and of works, as when a man justly exacts a work of another, or does a work for him. Accordingly, if we take for the matter of each kind of justice the things themselves of which the operations are the use, the matter of distributive and commutative justice is the same, since things can be distributed out of the common property to individuals, and be the subject of commutation between one person and another; and again there is a certain distribution and payment of laborious works.

If, however, we take for the matter of both kinds of justice the principal actions themselves, whereby we make use of persons, things, and works, there is then a difference of matter between them. For distributive justice directs distributions, while commutative justice directs commutations that can take place between two persons. Of these some are involuntary, some voluntary. They are involuntary when anyone uses another man's chattel, person, or work against his will, and this may be done secretly by fraud, or openly by violence. In either case the offence may be committed against the other man's chattel or person, or against a person connected with him. If the offence is against his chattel and this be taken secretly, it is called "theft," if openly, it is called "robbery." If it be against another man's person, it may affect either the very substance of his person, or his dignity. If it be against the substance of his person, a man is injured secretly if he is treacherously slain, struck or poisoned, and openly, if he is publicly slain, imprisoned, struck or maimed. If it be against his personal dignity, a man is injured secretly by false witness, detractions and so forth, whereby he is deprived of his good name, and openly, by being accused in a court of law, or by public insult. If it be against a personal connection, a man is injured in the person of his wife, secretly (for the most part) by adultery, in the person of his slave, if the latter be induced to leave his master: which things can also be done openly. The same applies to other personal connections, and whatever injury may be committed against the principal, may be committed against them also. Adultery, however, and inducing a slave to leave his master are properly injuries against the person; yet the latter, since a slave is his master's chattel, is referred to theft. Voluntary commutations are when a man voluntarily transfers his chattel to another person. And if he transfer it simply so that the recipient incurs no debt, as in the case of gifts, it is an act, not of justice but of liberality. A voluntary transfer belongs to justice in so far as it includes the notion of debt, and this may occur in many ways. First when one man simply transfers his thing to another in exchange for another thing, as happens in selling and buying. Secondly when a man transfers his thing to another, that the latter may have the use of it with the obligation of returning it to its owner. If he grant the use of a thing gratuitously, it is called "usufruct" in things that bear fruit; and simply "borrowing" on "loan" in things that bear no fruit, such as money, pottery, etc.; but if not even the use is granted gratis, it is called "letting" or "hiring." Thirdly, a man transfers his thing with the intention of recovering it, not for the purpose of its use, but that it may be kept safe, as in a "deposit," or under some obligation, as when a man pledges his property, or when one man stands security for another. In all these actions, whether voluntary or involuntary, the mean is taken in the same way according to the equality of repayment. Hence all these actions belong to the one same species of justice, namely commutative justice. And this suffices for the Replies to the Objections.

FOURTH ARTICLE [II-II, Q. 61, Art. 4]

Whether the Just Is Absolutely the Same As Retaliation?

Objection 1: It would seem that the just is absolutely the same as retaliation. For the judgment of God is absolutely just. Now the judgment of God is such that a man has to suffer in proportion with his deeds, according to Matt. 7:2: "With what measure you judge, you shall be judged: and with what measure you mete, it shall be measured to you again." Therefore the just is absolutely the same as retaliation.

Obj. 2: Further, in either kind of justice something is given to someone according to a kind of equality. In distributive justice this equality regards personal dignity, which would seem to depend chiefly on what a person has done for the good of the community; while in commutative justice it regards the thing in which a person has suffered loss. Now in respect of either equality there is retaliation in respect of the deed committed. Therefore it would seem that the just is absolutely the same as retaliation.

Obj. 3: Further, the chief argument against retaliation is based on the difference between the voluntary and the involuntary; for he who does an injury involuntarily is less severely punished. Now voluntary and involuntary taken in relation to ourselves, do not diversify the mean of justice since this is the real mean and does not depend on us. Therefore it would seem that the just is absolutely the same as retaliation.

*On the contrary,* The Philosopher proves (Ethic. v, 5) that the just is not always the same as retaliation.

*I answer that,* Retaliation ( contrapassum ) denotes equal passion repaid for previous action; and the expression applies most properly to injurious passions and actions, whereby a man harms the person of his neighbor; for instance if a man strike, that he be struck back. This kind of just is laid down in the Law (Ex. 21:23, 24): "He shall render life for life, eye for eye," etc. And since also to take away what belongs to another is to do an unjust thing, it follows that secondly retaliation consists in this also, that whosoever causes loss to another, should suffer loss in his belongings. This just loss is also found in the Law (Ex. 22:1): "If any man steal an ox or a sheep, and kill or sell it, he shall restore five oxen for one ox and four sheep for one sheep." Thirdly retaliation is transferred to voluntary commutations, where action and passion are on both sides, although voluntariness detracts from the nature of passion, as stated above (Q. 59, A. 3).

In all these cases, however, repayment must be made on a basis of equality according to the requirements of commutative justice, namely that the meed of passion be equal to the action. Now there would not always be equality if passion were in the same species as the action. Because, in the first place, when a person injures the person of one who is greater, the action surpasses any passion of the same species that he might undergo, wherefore he that strikes a prince, is not only struck back, but is much more severely punished. In like manner when a man despoils another of his property against the latter's will, the action surpasses the passion if he be merely deprived of that thing, because the man who caused another's loss, himself would lose nothing, and so he is punished by making restitution several times over, because not only did he injure a private individual, but also the common weal, the security of whose protection he has infringed. Nor again would there be equality of passion in voluntary commutations, were one always to exchange one's chattel for another man's, because it might happen that the other man's chattel is much greater than our own: so that it becomes necessary to equalize passion and action in commutations according to a certain proportionate commensuration, for which purpose money was invented. Hence retaliation is in accordance with commutative justice: but there is no place for it in distributive justice, because in distributive justice we do not consider the equality between thing and thing or between passion and action (whence the expression *contrapassum* ), but according to proportion between things and persons, as stated above (A. 2).

Reply Obj. 1: This form of the Divine judgment is in accordance with the conditions of commutative justice, in so far as rewards are apportioned to merits, and punishments to sins.

Reply Obj. 2: When a man who has served the community is paid for his services, this is to be referred to commutative, not distributive, justice. Because distributive justice considers the equality, not between the thing received and the thing done, but between the thing received by one person and the thing received by another according to the respective conditions of those persons.

Reply Obj. 3: When the injurious action is voluntary, the injury is aggravated and consequently is considered as a greater thing. Hence it requires a greater punishment in repayment, by reason of a difference, not on our part, but on the part of the thing.

## QUESTION 62

OF RESTITUTION (In Eight Articles)

We must now consider restitution, under which head there are eight points of inquiry:

(1) Of what is it an act?

(2) Whether it is always of necessity for salvation to restore what one has taken away?

(3) Whether it is necessary to restore more than has been taken away?

(4) Whether it is necessary to restore what one has not taken away?

(5) Whether it is necessary to make restitution to the person from whom something has been taken?

(6) Whether the person who has taken something away is bound to restore it?

(7) Whether any other person is bound to restitution?

(8) Whether one is bound to restore at once?

FIRST ARTICLE [II-II, Q. 62, Art. 1]

Whether Restitution Is an Act of Commutative Justice?

Objection 1: It would seem that restitution is not an act of commutative justice. For justice regards the notion of what is due. Now one may restore, even as one may give, that which is not due. Therefore restitution is not the act of any part of justice.

Obj. 2: Further, that which has passed away and is no more cannot be restored. Now justice and injustice are about certain actions and passions, which are unenduring and transitory. Therefore restitution would not seem to be the act of a part of justice.

Obj. 3: Further, restitution is repayment of something taken away. Now something may be taken away from a man not only in commutation, but also in distribution, as when, in distributing, one gives a man less than his due. Therefore restitution is not more an act of commutative than of distributive justice.

*On the contrary,* Restitution is opposed to taking away. Now it is an act of commutative injustice to take away what belongs to another. Therefore to restore it is an act of that justice which directs commutations.

*I answer that,* To restore is seemingly the same as to reinstate a person in the possession or dominion of his thing, so that in restitution we consider the equality of justice attending the payment of one thing for another, and this belongs to commutative justice. Hence restitution is an act of commutative justice, occasioned by one person having what belongs to another, either with his consent, for instance on loan or deposit, or against his will, as in robbery or theft.

Reply Obj. 1: That which is not due to another is not his properly speaking, although it may have been his at some time: wherefore it is a mere gift rather than a restitution, when anyone renders to another what is not due to him. It is however somewhat like a restitution, since the thing itself is materially the same; yet it is not the same in respect of the formal aspect of justice, which considers that thing as belonging to this particular man: and so it is not restitution properly so called.

Reply Obj. 2: In so far as the word restitution denotes something done over again, it implies identity of object. Hence it would seem originally to have applied chiefly to external things, which can pass from one person to another, since they remain the same both substantially and in respect of the right of dominion. But, even as the term "commutation" has passed from such like things to those actions and passions which confer reverence or injury, harm or profit on another person, so too the term "restitution" is applied, to things which though they be transitory in reality, yet remain in their effect; whether this touch his body, as when the body is hurt by being struck, or his reputation, as when a man remains defamed or dishonored by injurious words.

Reply Obj. 3: Compensation is made by the distributor to the man to whom less was given than his due, by comparison of thing with thing, when the latter receives so much the more according as he received less than his due: and consequently it pertains to commutative justice.

SECOND ARTICLE [II-II, Q. 62, Art. 2]

Whether Restitution of What Has Been Taken Away Is Necessary for Salvation?

Objection 1: It would seem that it is not necessary to restore what has been taken away. For that which is impossible is not necessary for salvation. But sometimes it is impossible to restore what has been taken, as when a man has taken limb or life. Therefore it does not seem necessary for salvation to restore what one has taken from another.

Obj. 2: Further, the commission of a sin is not necessary for salvation, for then a man would be in a dilemma. But sometimes it is impossible, without sin, to restore what has been taken, as when one has taken away another's good name by telling the truth. Therefore it is not necessary for salvation to restore what one has taken from another.

Obj. 3: Further, what is done cannot be undone. Now sometimes a man loses his personal honor by being unjustly insulted. Therefore that which has been taken from him cannot be restored to him: so that it is not necessary for salvation to restore what one has taken.

Obj. 4: Further, to prevent a person from obtaining a good thing is seemingly the same as to take it away from him, since "to lack little is almost the same as to lack nothing at all," as the Philosopher says (Phys. ii, 5). Now when anyone prevents a man from obtaining a benefice or the like, seemingly he is not bound to restore the benefice, since this would be sometimes impossible. Therefore it is not necessary for salvation to restore what one has taken.

*On the contrary,* Augustine says (Ep. ad Maced. cxliii): "Unless a man restore what he has purloined, his sin is not forgiven."

*I answer that,* Restitution as stated above (A. 1) is an act of commutative justice, and this demands a certain equality. Wherefore restitution denotes the return of the thing unjustly taken; since it is by giving it back that equality is reestablished. If, however, it be taken away justly, there will be equality, and so there will be no need for restitution, for justice consists in equality. Since therefore the safeguarding of justice is necessary for salvation, it follows that it is necessary for salvation to restore what has been taken unjustly.

Reply Obj. 1: When it is impossible to repay the equivalent, it suffices to repay what one can, as in the case of honor due to God and our parents, as the Philosopher states (Ethic. viii, 14). Wherefore when that which has been taken cannot be restored in equivalent, compensation should be made as far as possible: for instance if one man has deprived another of a limb, he must make compensation either in money or in honor, the condition of either party being duly considered according to the judgment of a good man.

Reply Obj. 2: There are three ways in which one may take away another's good name. First, by saying what is true, and this justly, as when a man reveals another's sin, while observing the right order of so doing, and then he is not bound to restitution. Secondly, by saying what is untrue and unjustly, and then he is bound to restore that man's good name, by confessing that he told an untruth. Thirdly, by saying what is true, but unjustly, as when a man reveals another's sin contrarily to the right order of so doing, and then he is bound to restore his good name as far as he can, and yet without telling an untruth; for instance by saying that he spoke ill, or that he defamed him unjustly; or if he be unable to restore his good name, he must compensate him otherwise, the same as in other cases, as stated above (ad 1).

Reply Obj. 3: The action of the man who has defamed another cannot be undone, but it is possible, by showing him deference, to undo its effect, viz. the lowering of the other man's personal dignity in the opinion of other men.

Reply Obj. 4: There are several ways of preventing a man from obtaining a benefice. First, justly: for instance, if having in view the honor of God or the good of the Church, one procures its being conferred on a more worthy subject, and then there is no obligation whatever to make restitution or compensation. Secondly, unjustly, if the intention is to injure the person whom one hinders, through hatred, revenge or the like. In this case, if before the benefice has been definitely assigned to anyone, one prevents its being conferred on a worthy subject by counseling that it be not conferred on him, one is bound to make some compensation, after taking account of the circumstances of persons and things according to the judgment of a prudent person: but one is not bound in equivalent, because that man had not obtained the benefice and might have been prevented in many ways from obtaining it. If, on the other hand, the benefice had already been assigned to a certain person, and someone, for some undue cause procures its revocation, it is the same as though he had deprived a man of what he already possessed, and consequently he would be bound to compensation in equivalent, in proportion, however, to his means.

THIRD ARTICLE [II-II, Q. 62, Art. 3]

Whether It Suffices to Restore the Exact Amount Taken?

Objection 1: It would seem that it is not sufficient to restore the exact amount taken. For it is written (Ex. 22:1): "If a man shall steal an ox or a sheep and kill or sell it, he shall restore five oxen for one ox, and four sheep for one sheep." Now everyone is bound to keep the commandments of the Divine law. Therefore a thief is bound to restore four- or fivefold.

Obj. 2: Further, "What things soever were written, were written for our learning" (Rom. 15:4). Now Zachaeus said (Luke 19:8) to our Lord: "If I have wronged any man of any thing, I restore him fourfold." Therefore a man is bound to restore several times over the amount he has taken unjustly.

Obj. 3: Further, no one can be unjustly deprived of what he is not bound to give. Now a judge justly deprives a thief of more than the amount of his theft, under the head of damages. Therefore a man is bound to pay it, and consequently it is not sufficient to restore the exact amount.

*On the contrary,* Restitution re-establishes equality where an unjust taking has caused inequality. Now equality is restored by repaying the exact amount taken. Therefore there is no obligation to restore more than the exact amount taken.

*I answer that,* When a man takes another's thing unjustly, two things must be considered. One is the inequality on the part of the thing, which inequality is sometimes void of injustice, as is the case in loans. The other is the sin of injustice, which is consistent with equality on the part of the thing, as when a person intends to use violence but fails.

As regards the first, the remedy is applied by making restitution, since thereby equality is re-established; and for this it is enough that a man restore just so much as he has belonging to another. But as regards the sin, the remedy is applied by punishment, the infliction of which belongs to the judge: and so, until a man is condemned by the judge, he is not bound to restore more than he took, but when once he is condemned, he is bound to pay the penalty.

Hence it is clear how to answer the First Objection: because this law fixes the punishment to be inflicted by the judge. Nor is this commandment to be kept now, because since the coming of Christ no man is bound to keep the judicial precepts, as stated above (I-II, Q. 104, A. 3). Nevertheless the same might be determined by human law, and then the same answer would apply.

Reply Obj. 2: Zachaeus said this being willing to do more than he was bound to do; hence he had said already: "Behold ... the half of my goods I give to the poor."

Reply Obj. 3: By condemning the man justly, the judge can exact more by way of damages; and yet this was not due before the sentence.

FOURTH ARTICLE [II-II, Q. 62, Art. 4]

Whether a Man Is Bound to Restore What He Has Not Taken?

Objection 1: It would seem that a man is bound to restore what he has not taken. For he that has inflicted a loss on a man is bound to remove that loss. Now it happens sometimes that the loss sustained is greater than the thing taken: for instance, if you dig up a man's seeds, you inflict on the sower a loss equal to the coming harvest, and thus you would seem to be bound to make restitution accordingly. Therefore a man is bound to restore what he has not taken.

Obj. 2: Further, he who retains his creditor's money beyond the stated time, would seem to occasion his loss of all his possible profits from that money, and yet he does not really take them. Therefore it seems that a man is bound to restore what he did not take.

Obj. 3: Further, human justice is derived from Divine justice. Now a man is bound to restore to God more than he has received from Him, according to Matt. 25:26, "Thou knewest that I reap where I sow not, and gather where I have not strewed." Therefore it is just that one should restore to a man also, something that one has not taken.

*On the contrary,* Restitution belongs to justice, because it re-establishes equality. But if one were to restore what one did not take, there would not be equality. Therefore it is not just to make such a restitution.

*I answer that,* Whoever brings a loss upon another person, seemingly, takes from him the amount of the loss, since, according to the Philosopher (Ethic. v, 4) loss is so called from a man having *less* * than his due. [*The derivation is more apparent in English than in Latin, where *damnum* stands for loss, and minus for *less.* Aristotle merely says that to have more than your own is called "gain," and to have less than you started with is called "loss."] Therefore a man is bound to make restitution according to the loss he has brought upon another.

Now a man suffers a loss in two ways. First, by being deprived of what he actually has; and a loss of this kind is always to be made good by repayment in equivalent: for instance if a man damnifies another by destroying his house he is bound to pay him the value of the house. Secondly, a man may damnify another by preventing him from obtaining what he was on the way to obtain. A loss of this kind need not be made good in equivalent; because to have a thing virtually is less than to have it actually, and to be on the way to obtain a thing is to have it merely virtually or potentially, and so were he to be indemnified by receiving the thing actually, he would be paid, not the exact value taken from him, but more, and this is not necessary for salvation, as stated above. However he is bound to make some compensation, according to the condition of persons and things.

From this we see how to answer the First and Second Objections: because the sower of the seed in the field, has the harvest, not actually but only virtually. In like manner he that has money has the profit not yet actually but only virtually: and both may be hindered in many ways.

Reply Obj. 3: God requires nothing from us but what He Himself has sown in us. Hence this saying is to be understood as expressing either the shameful thought of the lazy servant, who deemed that he had received nothing from the other, or the fact that God expects from us the fruit of His gifts, which fruit is from Him and from us, although the gifts themselves are from God without us.

FIFTH ARTICLE [II-II, Q. 62, Art. 5]

Whether Restitution Must Always Be Made to the Person from Whom a Thing Has Been Taken?

Objection 1: It would seem that restitution need not always be made to the person from whom a thing has been taken. For it is not lawful to injure anyone. Now it would sometimes be injurious to the man himself, or to others, were one to restore to him what has been taken from him; if, for instance, one were to return a madman his sword. Therefore restitution need not always be made to the person from whom a thing has been taken.

Obj. 2: Further, if a man has given a thing unlawfully, he does not deserve to recover it. Now sometimes a man gives unlawfully that which another accepts unlawfully, as in the case of the giver and receiver who are guilty of simony. Therefore it is not always necessary to make restitution to the person from whom one has taken something.

Obj. 3: Further, no man is bound to do what is impossible. Now it is sometimes impossible to make restitution to the person from whom a thing has been taken, either because he is dead, or because he is too far away, or because he is unknown to us. Therefore restitution need not always be made to the person from whom a thing has been taken.

Obj. 4: Further, we owe more compensation to one from whom we have received a greater favor. Now we have received greater favors from others (our parents for instance) than from a lender or depositor. Therefore sometimes we ought to succor some other person rather than make restitution to one from whom we have taken something.

Obj. 5: Further, it is useless to restore a thing which reverts to the restorer by being restored. Now if a prelate has unjustly taken something from the Church and makes restitution to the Church, it reverts into his hands, since he is the guardian of the Church's property. Therefore he ought not to restore to the Church from whom he has taken: and so restitution should not always be made to the person from whom something has been taken away.

*On the contrary,* It is written (Rom. 13:7): "Render ... to all men their dues; tribute to whom tribute is due, custom to whom custom."

*I answer that,* Restitution re-establishes the equality of commutative justice, which equality consists in the equalizing of thing to thing, as stated above (A. 2; Q. 58, A. 10). Now this equalizing of things is impossible, unless he that has less than his due receive what is lacking to him: and for this to be done, restitution must be made to the person from whom a thing has been taken.

Reply Obj. 1: When the thing to be restored appears to be grievously injurious to the person to whom it is to be restored, or to some other, it should not be restored to him there and then, because restitution is directed to the good of the person to whom it is made, since all possessions come under the head of the useful. Yet he who retains another's property must not appropriate it, but must either reserve it, that he may restore it at a fitting time, or hand it over to another to keep it more securely.

Reply Obj. 2: A person may give a thing unlawfully in two ways. First through the giving itself being illicit and against the law, as is the case when a man gives a thing simoniacally. Such a man deserves to lose what he gave, wherefore restitution should not be made to him: and, since the receiver acted against the law in receiving, he must not retain the price, but must use it for some pious object. Secondly a man gives unlawfully, through giving for an unlawful purpose, albeit the giving itself is not unlawful, as when a woman receives payment for fornication: wherefore she may keep what she has received. If, however, she has extorted overmuch by fraud or deceit, she would be bound to restitution.

Reply Obj. 3: If the person to whom restitution is due is unknown altogether, restitution must be made as far as possible, for instance by giving an alms for his spiritual welfare (whether he be dead or living): but not without previously making a careful inquiry about his person. If the person to whom restitution is due be dead, restitution should be made to his heir, who is looked upon as one with him. If he be very far away, what is due to him should be sent to him, especially if it be of great value and can easily be sent: else it should be deposited in a safe place to be kept for him, and the owner should be advised of the fact.

Reply Obj. 4: A man is bound, out of his own property, to succor his parents, or those from whom he has received greater benefits; but he ought not to compensate a benefactor out of what belongs to others; and he would be doing this if he were to compensate one with what is due to another. Exception must be made in cases of extreme need, for then he could and should even take what belongs to another in order to succor a parent.

Reply Obj. 5: There are three ways in which a prelate can rob the Church of her property. First by laying hands on Church property which is committed, not to him but to another; for instance, if a bishop appropriates the property of the chapter. In such a case it is clear that he is bound to restitution, by handing it over to those who are its lawful owners. Secondly by transferring to another person (for instance a relative or a friend) Church property committed to himself: in which case he must make restitution to the Church, and have it under his own care, so as to hand it over to his successor. Thirdly, a prelate may lay hands on Church property, merely in intention, when, to wit, he begins to have a mind to hold it as his own and not in the name of the Church: in which case he must make restitution by renouncing his intention.

SIXTH ARTICLE [II-II, Q. 62, Art. 6]

Whether He That Has Taken a Thing Is Always Bound to Restitution?

Objection 1: It would seem that he who has taken a thing is not always bound to restore it. Restitution re-establishes the equality of justice, by taking away from him that has more and giving to him that has less. Now it happens sometimes that he who has taken that which belongs to another, no longer has it, through its having passed into another's hands. Therefore it should be restored, not by the person that took it, but by the one that has it.

Obj. 2: Further, no man is bound to reveal his own crime. But by making restitution a man would sometimes reveal his crime, as in the case of theft.

Therefore he that has taken a thing is not always bound to restitution.

Obj. 3: Further, the same thing should not be restored several times. Now sometimes several persons take a thing at the same time, and one of them restores it in its entirety. Therefore he that takes a thing is not always bound to restitution.

*On the contrary,* He that has sinned is bound to satisfaction. Now restitution belongs to satisfaction. Therefore he that has taken a thing is bound to restore it.

*I answer that,* With regard to a man who has taken another's property, two points must be considered: the thing taken, and the taking. By reason of the thing taken, he is bound to restore it as long as he has it in his possession, since the thing that he has in addition to what is his, should be taken away from him, and given to him who lacks it according to the form of commutative justice. On the other hand, the taking of the thing that is another's property, may be threefold. For sometimes it is injurious, i.e. against the will of the owner, as in theft and robbery: in which case the thief is bound to restitution not only by reason of the thing, but also by reason of the injurious action, even though the thing is no longer in his possession. For just as a man who strikes another, though he gain nothing thereby, is bound to compensate the injured person, so too he that is guilty of theft or robbery, is bound to make compensation for the loss incurred, although he be no better off; and in addition he must be punished for the injustice committed. Secondly, a man takes another's property for his own profit but without committing an injury, i.e. with the consent of the owner, as in the case of a loan: and then, the taker is bound to restitution, not only by reason of the thing, but also by reason of the taking, even if he has lost the thing: for he is bound to compensate the person who has done him a favor, and he would not be doing so if the latter were to lose thereby. Thirdly, a man takes another's property without injury to the latter or profit to himself, as in the case of a deposit; wherefore he that takes a thing thus, incurs no obligation on account of the taking, in fact by taking he grants a favor; but he is bound to restitution on account of the thing taken. Consequently if this thing be taken from him without any fault on his part, he is not bound to restitution, although he would be, if he were to lose the thing through a grievous fault on his part.

Reply Obj. 1: The chief end of restitution is, not that he who has more than his due may cease to have it, but that he who has less than his due may be compensated. Wherefore there is no place for restitution in those things which one man may receive from another without loss to the latter, as when a person takes a light from another's candle. Consequently although he that has taken something from another, may have ceased to have what he took, through having transferred it to another, yet since that other is deprived of what is his, both are bound to restitution, he that took the thing, on account of the injurious taking, and he that has it, on account of the thing.

Reply Obj. 2: Although a man is not bound to reveal his crime to other men, yet is he bound to reveal it to God in confession; and so he may make restitution of another's property through the priest to whom he confesses.

Reply Obj. 3: Since restitution is chiefly directed to the compensation for the loss incurred by the person from whom a thing has been taken unjustly, it stands to reason that when he has received sufficient compensation from one, the others are not bound to any further restitution in his regard: rather ought they to refund the person who has made restitution, who, nevertheless, may excuse them from so doing.

SEVENTH ARTICLE [II-II, Q. 62, Art. 7]

Whether Restitution Is Binding on Those Who Have Not Taken?

Objection 1: It would seem that restitution is not binding on those who have not taken. For restitution is a punishment of the taker. Now none should be punished except the one who sinned. Therefore none are bound to restitution save the one who has taken.

Obj. 2: Further, justice does not bind one to increase another's property. Now if restitution were binding not only on the man who takes a thing but also on all those who cooperate with him in any way whatever, the person from whom the thing was taken would be the gainer, both because he would receive restitution many times over, and because sometimes a person cooperates towards a thing being taken away from someone, without its being taken away in effect. Therefore the others are not bound to restitution.

Obj. 3: Further, no man is bound to expose himself to danger, in order to safeguard another's property. Now sometimes a man would expose himself to the danger of death, were he to betray a thief, or withstand him. Therefore one is not bound to restitution, through not betraying or withstanding a thief.

*On the contrary,* It is written (Rom. 1:32): "They who do such things are worthy of death, and not only they that do them, but also they that consent to them that do them." Therefore in like manner they that consent are bound to restitution.

*I answer that,* As stated above (A. 6), a person is bound to restitution not only on account of someone else's property which he has taken, but also on account of the injurious taking. Hence whoever is cause of an unjust taking is bound to restitution. This happens in two ways, directly and indirectly. Directly, when a man induces another to take, and this in three ways. First, on the part of the taking, by moving a man to take, either by express command, counsel, or consent, or by praising a man for his courage in thieving. Secondly, on the part of the taker, by giving him shelter or any other kind of assistance. Thirdly, on the part of the thing taken, by taking part in the theft or robbery, as a fellow evil-doer. Indirectly, when a man does not prevent another from evil-doing (provided he be able and bound to prevent him), either by omitting the command or counsel which would hinder him from thieving or robbing, or by omitting to do what would have hindered him, or by sheltering him after the deed. All these are expressed as follows:

"By command, by counsel, by consent, by flattery, by receiving, by participation, by silence, by not preventing, by not denouncing."

It must be observed, however, that in five of these cases the cooperator is always bound to restitution. First, in the case of command: because he that commands is the chief mover, wherefore he is bound to restitution principally. Secondly, in the case of consent; namely of one without whose consent the robbery cannot take place. Thirdly, in the case of receiving; when, to wit, a man is a receiver of thieves, and gives them assistance. Fourthly, in the case of participation; when a man takes part in the theft and in the booty. Fifthly, he who does not prevent the theft, whereas he is bound to do so; for instance, persons in authority who are bound to safeguard justice on earth, are bound to restitution, if by their neglect thieves prosper, because their salary is given to them in payment of their preserving justice here below.

In the other cases mentioned above, a man is not always bound to restitution: because counsel and flattery are not always the efficacious cause of robbery. Hence the counsellor or flatterer is bound to restitution, only when it may be judged with probability that the unjust taking resulted from such causes.

Reply Obj. 1: Not only is he bound to restitution who commits the sin, but also he who is in any way cause of the sin, whether by counselling, or by commanding, or in any other way whatever.

Reply Obj. 2: He is bound chiefly to restitution, who is the principal in the deed; first of all, the *commander;* secondly, the *executor,* and in due sequence, the others: yet so that, if one of them make restitution, another is not bound to make restitution to the same person. Yet those who are principals in the deed, and who took possession of the thing, are bound to compensate those who have already made restitution. When a man commands an unjust taking that does not follow, no restitution has to be made, since its end is chiefly to restore the property of the person who has been unjustly injured.

Reply Obj. 3: He that fails to denounce a thief or does not withstand or reprehend him is not always bound to restitution, but only when he is obliged, in virtue of his office, to do so: as in the case of earthly princes who do not incur any great danger thereby; for they are invested with public authority, in order that they may maintain justice.

EIGHTH ARTICLE [II-II, Q. 62, Art. 8]

Whether a Man Is Bound to Immediate Restitution, or May He Put It Off?

Objection 1: It would seem that a man is not bound to immediate restitution, and can lawfully delay to restore. For affirmative precepts do not bind for always. Now the necessity of making restitution is binding through an affirmative precept. Therefore a man is not bound to immediate restitution.

Obj. 2: Further, no man is bound to do what is impossible. But it is sometimes impossible to make restitution at once. Therefore no man is bound to immediate restitution.

Obj. 3: Further, restitution is an act of virtue, viz. of justice. Now time is one of the circumstances requisite for virtuous acts. Since then the other circumstances are not determinate for acts of virtue, but are determinable according to the dictate of prudence, it seems that neither in restitution is there any fixed time, so that a man be bound to restore at once.

*On the contrary,* All matters of restitution seem to come under one head. Now a man who hires the services of a wage-earner, must not delay compensation, as appears from Lev. 19:13, "The wages of him that hath been hired by thee shall not abide with thee until the morning." Therefore neither is it lawful, in other cases of restitution, to delay, and restitution should be made at once.

*I answer that,* Even as it is a sin against justice to take another's property, so also is it to withhold it, since, to withhold the property of another against the owner's will, is to deprive him of the use of what belongs to him, and to do him an injury. Now it is clear that it is wrong to remain in sin even for a short time; and one is bound to renounce one's sin at once, according to Ecclus. 21:2, "Flee from sin as from the face of a serpent." Consequently one is bound to immediate restitution, if possible, or to ask for a respite from the person who is empowered to grant the use of the thing.

Reply Obj. 1: Although the precept about the making of restitution is affirmative in form, it implies a negative precept forbidding us to withhold another's property.

Reply Obj. 2: When one is unable to restore at once, this very inability excuses one from immediate restitution: even as a person is altogether excused from making restitution if he is altogether unable to make it. He is, however, bound either himself or through another to ask the person to whom he owes compensation to grant him a remission or a respite.

Reply Obj. 3: Whenever the omission of a circumstance is contrary to virtue that circumstance must be looked upon as determinate, and we are bound to observe it: and since delay of restitution involves a sin of unjust detention which is opposed to just detention, it stands to reason that the time is determinate in the point of restitution being immediate.

## QUESTION 63

OF RESPECT OF PERSONS (In Four Articles)

We must now consider the vices opposed to the aforesaid parts of justice. First we shall consider respect of persons which is opposed to distributive justice; secondly we shall consider the vices opposed to commutative justice.

Under the first head there are four points of inquiry:

(1) Whether respect of persons is a sin?

(2) Whether it takes place in the dispensation of spiritualities?

(3) Whether it takes place in showing honor?

(4) Whether it takes place in judicial sentences?

FIRST ARTICLE [II-II, Q. 63, Art. 1]

Whether Respect of Persons Is a Sin?

Objection 1: It would seem that respect of persons is not a sin. For the word "person" includes a reference to personal dignity [*Cf. I, Q. 29, A. 3, ad 2]. Now it belongs to distributive justice to consider personal dignity. Therefore respect of persons is not a sin.

Obj. 2: Further, in human affairs persons are of more importance than things, since things are for the benefit of persons and not conversely. But respect of things is not a sin. Much less, therefore, is respect of persons.

Obj. 3: Further, no injustice or sin can be in God. Yet God seems to respect persons, since of two men circumstanced alike He sometimes upraises one by grace, and leaves the other in sin, according to Matt. 24:40: "Two shall be in a bed [Vulg.: 'field'] [*'Bed' is the reading of Luke 17:34], one shall be taken, and one shall be left." Therefore respect of persons is not a sin.

*On the contrary,* Nothing but sin is forbidden in the Divine law. Now respect of persons is forbidden, Deut. 1:17: "Neither shall you respect any man's person." Therefore respect of persons is a sin.

*I answer that,* Respect of persons is opposed to distributive justice. For the equality of distributive justice consists in allotting various things to various persons in proportion to their personal dignity. Accordingly, if one considers that personal property by reason of which the thing allotted to a particular person is due to him, this is respect not of the person but of the cause. Hence a gloss on Eph. 6:9, "There is no respect of persons with God [Vulg.: 'Him']," says that "a just judge regards causes, not persons." For instance if you promote a man to a professorship on account of his having sufficient knowledge, you consider the due cause, not the person; but if, in conferring something on someone, you consider in him not the fact that what you give him is proportionate or due to him, but the fact that he is this particular man (e.g. Peter or Martin), then there is respect of the person, since you give him something not for some cause that renders him worthy of it, but simply because he is this person. And any circumstance that does not amount to a reason why this man be worthy of this gift, is to be referred to his person: for instance if a man promote someone to a prelacy or a professorship, because he is rich or because he is a relative of his, it is respect of persons. It may happen, however, that a circumstance of person makes a man worthy as regards one thing, but not as regards another: thus consanguinity makes a man worthy to be appointed heir to an estate, but not to be chosen for a position of ecclesiastical authority: wherefore consideration of the same circumstance of person will amount to respect of persons in one matter and not in another. It follows, accordingly, that respect of persons is opposed to distributive justice in that it fails to observe due proportion. Now nothing but sin is opposed to virtue: and therefore respect of persons is a sin.

Reply Obj. 1: In distributive justice we consider those circumstances of a person which result in dignity or right, whereas in respect of persons we consider circumstances that do not so result.

Reply Obj. 2: Persons are rendered proportionate to and worthy of things which are distributed among them, by reason of certain things pertaining to circumstances of person, wherefore such conditions ought to be considered as the proper cause. But when we consider the persons themselves, that which is not a cause is considered as though it were; and so it is clear that although persons are more worthy, absolutely speaking, yet they are not more worthy in this regard.

Reply Obj. 3: There is a twofold giving. One belongs to justice, and occurs when we give a man his due: in such like givings respect of persons takes place. The other giving belongs to liberality, when one gives gratis that which is not a man's due: such is the bestowal of the gifts of grace, whereby sinners are chosen by God. In such a giving there is no place for respect of persons, because anyone may, without injustice, give of his own as much as he will, and to whom he will, according to Matt. 20:14, 15, "Is it not lawful for me to do what I will? ... Take what is thine, and go thy way."

SECOND ARTICLE [II-II, Q. 63, Art. 2]

Whether Respect of Persons Takes Place in the Dispensation of Spiritual Goods?

Objection 1: It would seem that respect of persons does not take place in the dispensation of spiritual goods. For it would seem to savor of respect of persons if a man confers ecclesiastical dignity or benefice on account of consanguinity, since consanguinity is not a cause whereby a man is rendered worthy of an ecclesiastical benefice. Yet this apparently is not a sin, for ecclesiastical prelates are wont to do so. Therefore the sin of respect of persons does not take place in the conferring of spiritual goods.

Obj. 2: Further, to give preference to a rich man rather than to a poor man seems to pertain to respect of persons, according to James 2:2, 3. Nevertheless dispensations to marry within forbidden degrees are more readily granted to the rich and powerful than to others. Therefore the sin of respect of persons seems not to take place in the dispensation of spiritual goods.

Obj. 3: Further, according to jurists [*Cap. Cum dilectus.] it suffices to choose a good man, and it is not requisite that one choose the better man. But it would seem to savor of respect of persons to choose one who is less good for a higher position. Therefore respect of persons is not a sin in spiritual matters.

Obj. 4: Further, according to the law of the Church (Cap. Cum dilectus.) the person to be chosen should be "a member of the flock." Now this would seem to imply respect of persons, since sometimes more competent persons would be found elsewhere. Therefore respect of persons is not a sin in spiritual matters.

*On the contrary,* It is written (James 2:1): "Have not the faith of our Lord Jesus Christ ... with respect of persons." On these words a gloss of Augustine says: "Who is there that would tolerate the promotion of a rich man to a position of honor in the Church, to the exclusion of a poor man more learned and holier?" [*Augustine, Ep. ad Hieron. clxvii.]

*I answer that,* As stated above (A. 1), respect of persons is a sin, in so far as it is contrary to justice. Now the graver the matter in which justice is transgressed, the more grievous the sin: so that, spiritual things being of greater import than temporal, respect of persons is a more grievous sin in dispensing spiritualities than in dispensing temporalities. And since it is respect of persons when something is allotted to a person out of proportion to his deserts, it must be observed that a person's worthiness may be considered in two ways. First, simply and absolutely: and in this way the man who abounds the more in the spiritual gifts of grace is the more worthy. Secondly, in relation to the common good; for it happens at times that the less holy and less learned man may conduce more to the common good, on account of worldly authority or activity, or something of the kind. And since the dispensation of spiritualities is directed chiefly to the common good, according to 1 Cor. 12:7, "The manifestation of the Spirit is given to every man unto profit," it follows that in the dispensation of spiritualities the simply less good are sometimes preferred to the better, without respect of persons, just as God sometimes bestows gratuitous graces on the less worthy.

Reply Obj. 1: We must make a distinction with regard to a prelate's kinsfolk: for sometimes they are less worthy, both absolutely speaking, and in relation to the common good: and then if they are preferred to the more worthy, there is a sin of respect of persons in the dispensation of spiritual goods, whereof the ecclesiastical superior is not the owner, with power to give them away as he will, but the dispenser, according to 1 Cor. 4:1, "Let a man so account of us as of the ministers of Christ, and the dispensers of the mysteries of God." Sometimes however the prelate's kinsfolk are as worthy as others, and then without respect of persons he can lawfully give preference to his kindred since there is at least this advantage, that he can trust the more in their being of one mind with him in conducting the business of the Church. Yet he would have to forego so doing for fear of scandal, if anyone might take an example from him and give the goods of the Church to their kindred without regard to their deserts.

Reply Obj. 2: Dispensations for contracting marriage came into use for the purpose of strengthening treaties of peace: and this is more necessary for the common good in relation to persons of standing, so that there is no respect of persons in granting dispensations more readily to such persons.

Reply Obj. 3: In order that an election be not rebutted in a court of law, it suffices to elect a good man, nor is it necessary to elect the better man, because otherwise every election might have a flaw. But as regards the conscience of an elector, it is necessary to elect one who is better, either absolutely speaking, or in relation to the common good. For if it is possible to have one who is more competent for a post, and yet another be preferred, it is necessary to have some cause for this. If this cause have anything to do with the matter in point, he who is elected will, in this respect, be more competent; and if that which is taken for cause have nothing to do with the matter, it will clearly be respect of persons.

Reply Obj. 4: The man who is taken from among the members of a particular Church, is generally speaking more useful as regards the common good, since he loves more the Church wherein he was brought up. For this reason it was commanded (Deut. 17:15): "Thou mayest not make a man of another nation king, who is not thy brother."

THIRD ARTICLE [II-II, Q. 63, Art. 3]

Whether Respect of Persons Takes Place in Showing Honor and Respect?

Objection 1: It would seem that respect of persons does not take place in showing honor and respect. For honor is apparently nothing else than "reverence shown to a person in recognition of his virtue," as the Philosopher states (Ethic. i, 5). Now prelates and princes should be honored although they be wicked, even as our parents, of whom it is written (Ex. 20:12): "Honor thy father and thy mother." Again masters, though they be wicked, should be honored by their servants, according to 1 Tim. 6:1: "Whoever are servants under the yoke, let them count their masters worthy of all honor." Therefore it seems that it is not a sin to respect persons in showing honor.

Obj. 2: Further, it is commanded (Lev. 19:32): "Rise up before the hoary head, and, honor the person of the aged man." But this seems to savor of respect of persons, since sometimes old men are not virtuous; according to Dan. 13:5: "Iniquity came out from the ancients of the people [*Vulg.: 'Iniquity came out of Babylon from the ancient judges, that seemed to govern the people.']." Therefore it is not a sin to respect persons in showing honor.

Obj. 3: Further, on the words of James 2:1, "Have not the faith ... with respect of persons," a gloss of Augustine [*Ep. ad Hieron. clxvii.] says: "If the saying of James, 'If there shall come into your assembly a man having a golden ring,' etc., refer to our daily meetings, who sins not here, if however he sin at all?" Yet it is respect of persons to honor the rich for their riches, for Gregory says in a homily (xxviii in Evang.): "Our pride is blunted, since in men we honor, not the nature wherein they are made to God's image, but wealth," so that, wealth not being a due cause of honor, this will savor of respect of persons. Therefore it is not a sin to respect persons in showing honor.

*On the contrary,* A gloss on James 2:1, says: "Whoever honors the rich for their riches, sins," and in like manner, if a man be honored for other causes that do not render him worthy of honor. Now this savors of respect of persons. Therefore it is a sin to respect persons in showing honor.

*I answer that,* To honor a person is to recognize him as having virtue, wherefore virtue alone is the due cause of a person being honored. Now it is to be observed that a person may be honored not only for his own virtue, but also for another's: thus princes and prelates, although they be wicked, are honored as standing in God's place, and as representing the community over which they are placed, according to Prov. 26:8, "As he that casteth a stone into the heap of Mercury, so is he that giveth honor to a fool." For, since the gentiles ascribed the keeping of accounts to Mercury, "the heap of Mercury" signifies the casting up of an account, when a merchant sometimes substitutes a pebble [* *Lapillus* or calculus whence the English word 'calculate'] for one hundred marks. So too, is a fool honored if he stand in God's place or represent the whole community: and in the same way parents and masters should be honored, on account of their having a share of the dignity of God Who is the Father and Lord of all. The aged should be honored, because old age is a sign of virtue, though this sign fail at times: wherefore, according to Wis. 4:8, 9, "venerable old age is not that of long time, nor counted by the number of years; but the understanding of a man is gray hairs, and a spotless life is old age." The rich ought to be honored by reason of their occupying a higher position in the community: but if they be honored merely for their wealth, it will be the sin of respect of persons.

Hence the Replies to the Objections are clear.

FOURTH ARTICLE [II-II, Q. 63, Art. 4]

Whether the Sin of Respect of Persons Takes Place in Judicial Sentences?

Objection 1: It would seem that the sin of respect of persons does not take place in judicial sentences. For respect of persons is opposed to distributive justice, as stated above (A. 1): whereas judicial sentences seem to pertain chiefly to commutative justice. Therefore respect of persons does not take place in judicial sentences.

Obj. 2: Further, penalties are inflicted according to a sentence. Now it is not a sin to respect persons in pronouncing penalties, since a heavier punishment is inflicted on one who injures the person of a prince than on one who injures the person of others. Therefore respect of persons does not take place in judicial sentences.

Obj. 3: Further, it is written (Ecclus. 4:10): "In judging be merciful to the fatherless." But this seems to imply respect of the person of the needy. Therefore in judicial sentences respect of persons is not a sin.

*On the contrary,* It is written (Prov. 18:5): "It is not good to accept the person in judgment [*Vulg.: 'It is not good to accept the person of the wicked, to decline from the truth of judgment.']."

*I answer that,* As stated above (Q. 60, A. 1), judgment is an act of justice, in as much as the judge restores to the equality of justice, those things which may cause an opposite inequality. Now respect of persons involves a certain inequality, in so far as something is allotted to a person out of that proportion to him in which the equality of justice consists. Wherefore it is evident that judgment is rendered corrupt by respect of persons.

Reply Obj. 1: A judgment may be looked at in two ways. First, in view of the thing judged, and in this way judgment is common to commutative and distributive justice: because it may be decided by judgment how some common good is to be distributed among many, and how one person is to restore to another what he has taken from him. Secondly, it may be considered in view of the form of judgment, in as much as, even in commutative justice, the judge takes from one and gives to another, and this belongs to distributive justice. In this way respect of persons may take place in any judgment.

Reply Obj. 2: When a person is more severely punished on account of a crime committed against a greater person, there is no respect of persons, because the very difference of persons causes, in that case, a diversity of things, as stated above (Q. 58, A. 10, ad 3; Q. 61, A. 2, ad 3).

Reply Obj. 3: In pronouncing judgment one ought to succor the needy as far as possible, yet without prejudice to justice: else the saying of Ex. 23:3 would apply: "Neither shalt thou favor a poor man in judgment."

## QUESTION 64

OF MURDER (In Eight Articles)

In due sequence we must consider the vices opposed to commutative justice. We must consider (1) those sins that are committed in relation to involuntary commutations; (2) those that are committed with regard to voluntary commutations. Sins are committed in relation to involuntary commutations by doing an injury to one's neighbor against his will: and this can be done in two ways, namely by deed or by word. By deed when one's neighbor is injured either in his own person, or in a person connected with him, or in his possessions.

We must therefore consider these points in due order, and in the first place we shall consider murder whereby a man inflicts the greatest injury on his neighbor. Under this head there are eight points of inquiry:

(1) Whether it is a sin to kill dumb animals or even plants?

(2) Whether it is lawful to kill a sinner?

(3) Whether this is lawful to a private individual, or to a public person only?

(4) Whether this is lawful to a cleric?

(5) Whether it is lawful to kill oneself?

(6) Whether it is lawful to kill a just man?

(7) Whether it is lawful to kill a man in self-defense?

(8) Whether accidental homicide is a mortal sin?

FIRST ARTICLE [II-II, Q. 64, Art. 1]

Whether It Is Unlawful to Kill Any Living Thing?

Objection 1: It would seem unlawful to kill any living thing. For the Apostle says (Rom. 13:2): "They that resist the ordinance of God purchase to themselves damnation [*Vulg.: 'He that resisteth the power, resisteth the ordinance of God: and they that resist, purchase themselves damnation.']." Now Divine providence has ordained that all living things should be preserved, according to Ps. 146:8, 9, "Who maketh grass to grow on the mountains ... Who giveth to beasts their food." Therefore it seems unlawful to take the life of any living thing.

Obj. 2: Further, murder is a sin because it deprives a man of life. Now life is common to all animals and plants. Hence for the same reason it is apparently a sin to slay dumb animals and plants.

Obj. 3: Further, in the Divine law a special punishment is not appointed save for a sin. Now a special punishment had to be inflicted, according to the Divine law, on one who killed another man's ox or sheep (Ex. 22:1). Therefore the slaying of dumb animals is a sin.

*On the contrary,* Augustine says (De Civ. Dei i, 20): "When we hear it said, 'Thou shalt not kill,' we do not take it as referring to trees, for they have no sense, nor to irrational animals, because they have no fellowship with us. Hence it follows that the words, 'Thou shalt not kill' refer to the killing of a man."

*I answer that,* There is no sin in using a thing for the purpose for which it is. Now the order of things is such that the imperfect are for the perfect, even as in the process of generation nature proceeds from imperfection to perfection. Hence it is that just as in the generation of a man there is first a living thing, then an animal, and lastly a man, so too things, like the plants, which merely have life, are all alike for animals, and all animals are for man. Wherefore it is not unlawful if man use plants for the good of animals, and animals for the good of man, as the Philosopher states (Polit. i, 3).

Now the most necessary use would seem to consist in the fact that animals use plants, and men use animals, for food, and this cannot be done unless these be deprived of life: wherefore it is lawful both to take life from plants for the use of animals, and from animals for the use of men. In fact this is in keeping with the commandment of God Himself: for it is written (Gen. 1:29, 30): "Behold I have given you every herb ... and all trees ... to be your meat, and to all beasts of the earth": and again (Gen. 9:3): "Everything that moveth and liveth shall be meat to you."

Reply Obj. 1: According to the Divine ordinance the life of animals and plants is preserved not for themselves but for man. Hence, as Augustine says (De Civ. Dei i, 20), "by a most just ordinance of the Creator, both their life and their death are subject to our use."

Reply Obj. 2: Dumb animals and plants are devoid of the life of reason whereby to set themselves in motion; they are moved, as it were by another, by a kind of natural impulse, a sign of which is that they are naturally enslaved and accommodated to the uses of others.

Reply Obj. 3: He that kills another's ox, sins, not through killing the ox, but through injuring another man in his property. Wherefore this is not a species of the sin of murder but of the sin of theft or robbery.

SECOND ARTICLE [II-II, Q. 64, Art. 2]

Whether It Is Lawful to Kill Sinners?

Objection 1: It would seem unlawful to kill men who have sinned. For our Lord in the parable (Matt. 13) forbade the uprooting of the cockle which denotes wicked men according to a gloss. Now whatever is forbidden by God is a sin. Therefore it is a sin to kill a sinner.

Obj. 2: Further, human justice is conformed to Divine justice. Now according to Divine justice sinners are kept back for repentance, according to

Ezech. 33:11, "I desire not the death of the wicked, but that the wicked turn from his way and live." Therefore it seems altogether unjust to kill sinners.

Obj. 3: Further, it is not lawful, for any good end whatever, to do that which is evil in itself, according to Augustine (Contra Mendac. vii) and the Philosopher (Ethic. ii, 6). Now to kill a man is evil in itself, since we are bound to have charity towards all men, and "we wish our friends to live and to exist," according to *Ethic.* ix, 4. Therefore it is nowise lawful to kill a man who has sinned.

*On the contrary,* It is written (Ex. 22:18): "Wizards thou shalt not suffer to live"; and (Ps. 100:8): "In the morning I put to death all the wicked of the land."

*I answer that,* As stated above (A. 1), it is lawful to kill dumb animals, in so far as they are naturally directed to man's use, as the imperfect is directed to the perfect. Now every part is directed to the whole, as imperfect to perfect, wherefore every part is naturally for the sake of the whole. For this reason we observe that if the health of the whole body demands the excision of a member, through its being decayed or infectious to the other members, it will be both praiseworthy and advantageous to have it cut away. Now every individual person is compared to the whole community, as part to whole. Therefore if a man be dangerous and infectious to the community, on account of some sin, it is praiseworthy and advantageous that he be killed in order to safeguard the common good, since "a little leaven corrupteth the whole lump" (1 Cor. 5:6).

Reply Obj. 1: Our Lord commanded them to forbear from uprooting the cockle in order to spare the wheat, i.e. the good. This occurs when the wicked cannot be slain without the good being killed with them, either because the wicked lie hidden among the good, or because they have many followers, so that they cannot be killed without danger to the good, as Augustine says (Contra Parmen. iii, 2). Wherefore our Lord teaches that we should rather allow the wicked to live, and that vengeance is to be delayed until the last judgment, rather than that the good be put to death together with the wicked. When, however, the good incur no danger, but rather are protected and saved by the slaying of the wicked, then the latter may be lawfully put to death.

Reply Obj. 2: According to the order of His wisdom, God sometimes slays sinners forthwith in order to deliver the good, whereas sometimes He allows them time to repent, according as He knows what is expedient for His elect. This also does human justice imitate according to its powers; for it puts to death those who are dangerous to others, while it allows time for repentance to those who sin without grievously harming others.

Reply Obj. 3: By sinning man departs from the order of reason, and consequently falls away from the dignity of his manhood, in so far as he is naturally free, and exists for himself, and he falls into the slavish state of the beasts, by being disposed of according as he is useful to others. This is expressed in Ps. 48:21: "Man, when he was in honor, did not understand; he hath been compared to senseless beasts, and made like to them," and Prov. 11:29: "The fool shall serve the wise." Hence, although it be evil in itself to kill a man so long as he preserve his dignity, yet it may be good to kill a man who has sinned, even as it is to kill a beast. For a bad man is worse than a beast, and is more harmful, as the Philosopher states (Polit. i, 1 and *Ethic.* vii, 6).

THIRD ARTICLE [II-II, Q. 64, Art. 3]

Whether It Is Lawful for a Private Individual to Kill a Man Who Has Sinned?

Objection 1: It would seem lawful for a private individual to kill a man who has sinned. For nothing unlawful is commanded in the Divine law. Yet, on account of the sin of the molten calf, Moses commanded (Ex. 32:27): "Let every man kill his brother, and friend, and neighbor." Therefore it is lawful for private individuals to kill a sinner.

Obj. 2: Further, as stated above (A. 2, ad 3), man, on account of sin, is compared to the beasts. Now it is lawful for any private individual to kill a wild beast, especially if it be harmful. Therefore for the same reason, it is lawful for any private individual to kill a man who has sinned.

Obj. 3: Further, a man, though a private individual, deserves praise for doing what is useful for the common good. Now the slaying of evildoers is useful for the common good, as stated above (A. 2). Therefore it is deserving of praise if even private individuals kill evil-doers.

*On the contrary,* Augustine says (De Civ. Dei i) [*Can. Quicumque percutit, caus. xxiii, qu. 8]: "A man who, without exercising public authority, kills an evil-doer, shall be judged guilty of murder, and all the more, since he has dared to usurp a power which God has not given him."

*I answer that,* As stated above (A. 2), it is lawful to kill an evildoer in so far as it is directed to the welfare of the whole community, so that it belongs to him alone who has charge of the community's welfare. Thus it belongs to a physician to cut off a decayed limb, when he has been entrusted with the care of the health of the whole body. Now the care of the common good is entrusted to persons of rank having public authority: wherefore they alone, and not private individuals, can lawfully put evildoers to death.

Reply Obj. 1: The person by whose authority a thing is done really does the thing as Dionysius declares (Coel. Hier. iii). Hence according to Augustine (De Civ. Dei i, 21), "He slays not who owes his service to one who commands him, even as a sword is merely the instrument to him that wields it." Wherefore those who, at the Lord's command, slew their neighbors and friends, would seem not to have done this themselves, but rather He by whose authority they acted thus: just as a soldier slays the foe by the authority of his sovereign, and the executioner slays the robber by the authority of the judge.

Reply Obj. 2: A beast is by nature distinct from man, wherefore in the case of a wild beast there is no need for an authority to kill it; whereas, in the case of domestic animals, such authority is required, not for their sake, but on account of the owner's loss. On the other hand a man who has sinned is not by nature distinct from good men; hence a public authority is requisite in order to condemn him to death for the common good.

Reply Obj. 3: It is lawful for any private individual to do anything for the common good, provided it harm nobody: but if it be harmful to some other, it cannot be done, except by virtue of the judgment of the person to whom it pertains to decide what is to be taken from the parts for the welfare of the whole.

FOURTH ARTICLE [II-II, Q. 64, Art. 4]

Whether It Is Lawful for Clerics to Kill Evil-doers?

Objection 1: It would seem lawful for clerics to kill evil-doers. For clerics especially should fulfil the precept of the Apostle (1 Cor. 4:16): "Be ye followers of me as I also am of Christ," whereby we are called upon to imitate God and His saints. Now the very God whom we worship puts evildoers to death, according to Ps. 135:10, "Who smote Egypt with their firstborn." Again Moses made the Levites slay twenty-three thousand men on account of the worship of the calf (Ex. 32), the priest Phinees slew the Israelite who went in to the woman of Madian (Num. 25), Samuel killed Agag king of Amalec (1 Kings 15), Elias slew the priests of Baal (3 Kings 18), Mathathias killed the man who went up to the altar to sacrifice (1 Mac. 2); and, in the New Testament, Peter killed Ananias and Saphira (Acts 5). Therefore it seems that even clerics may kill evil-doers.

Obj. 2: Further, spiritual power is greater than the secular and is more united to God. Now the secular power as "God's minister" lawfully puts evil-doers to death, according to Rom. 13:4. Much more therefore may clerics, who are God's ministers and have spiritual power, put evil-doers to death.

Obj. 3: Further, whosoever lawfully accepts an office, may lawfully exercise the functions of that office. Now it belongs to the princely office to slay evildoers, as stated above (A. 3). Therefore those clerics who are earthly princes may lawfully slay malefactors.

*On the contrary,* It is written (1 Tim. 3:2, 3): "It behooveth ... a bishop to be without crime [*Vulg.: 'blameless.' 'Without crime' is the reading in Tit. 1:7] ... not given to wine, no striker."

*I answer that,* It is unlawful for clerics to kill, for two reasons. First, because they are chosen for the ministry of the altar, whereon is represented the Passion of Christ slain "Who, when He was struck did not strike [Vulg.: 'When He suffered, He threatened not']" (1 Pet. 2:23). Therefore it becomes not clerics to strike or kill: for ministers should imitate their master, according to Ecclus. 10:2, "As the judge of the people is himself, so also are his ministers." The other reason is because clerics are entrusted with the ministry of the New Law, wherein no punishment of death or of bodily maiming is appointed: wherefore they should abstain from such things in order that they may be fitting ministers of the New Testament.

Reply Obj. 1: God works in all things without exception whatever is right, yet in each one according to its mode. Wherefore everyone should imitate God in that which is specially becoming to him. Hence, though God slays evildoers even corporally, it does not follow that all should imitate Him in this. As regards Peter, he did not put Ananias and Saphira to death by his own authority or with his own hand, but published their death sentence pronounced by God. The Priests or Levites of the Old Testament were the ministers of the Old Law, which appointed corporal penalties, so that it was fitting for them to slay with their own hands.

Reply Obj. 2: The ministry of clerics is concerned with better things than corporal slayings, namely with things pertaining to spiritual welfare, and so it is not fitting for them to meddle with minor matters.

Reply Obj. 3: Ecclesiastical prelates accept the office of earthly princes, not that they may inflict capital punishment themselves, but that this may be carried into effect by others in virtue of their authority.

FIFTH ARTICLE [II-II, Q. 64, Art. 5]

Whether It Is Lawful to Kill Oneself?

Objection 1: It would seem lawful for a man to kill himself. For murder is a sin in so far as it is contrary to justice. But no man can do an injustice to himself, as is proved in *Ethic.* v, 11. Therefore no man sins by killing himself.

Obj. 2: Further, it is lawful, for one who exercises public authority, to kill evil-doers. Now he who exercises public authority is sometimes an evil-doer. Therefore he may lawfully kill himself.

Obj. 3: Further, it is lawful for a man to suffer spontaneously a lesser danger that he may avoid a greater: thus it is lawful for a man to cut off a decayed limb even from himself, that he may save his whole body. Now sometimes a man, by killing himself, avoids a greater evil, for example an unhappy life, or the shame of sin. Therefore a man may kill himself.

Obj. 4: Further, Samson killed himself, as related in Judges 16, and yet he is numbered among the saints (Heb. 11). Therefore it is lawful for a man to kill himself.

Obj. 5: Further, it is related (2 Mac. 14:42) that a certain Razias killed himself, "choosing to die nobly rather than to fall into the hands of the wicked, and to suffer abuses unbecoming his noble birth." Now nothing that is done nobly and bravely is unlawful. Therefore suicide is not unlawful.

*On the contrary,* Augustine says (De Civ. Dei i, 20): "Hence it follows that the words 'Thou shalt not kill' refer to the killing of a man—not another man; therefore, not even thyself. For he who kills himself, kills nothing else than a man."

*I answer that,* It is altogether unlawful to kill oneself, for three reasons. First, because everything naturally loves itself, the result being that everything naturally keeps itself in being, and resists corruptions so far as it can. Wherefore suicide is contrary to the inclination of nature, and to charity whereby every man should love himself. Hence suicide is always a mortal sin, as being contrary to the natural law and to charity. Secondly, because every part, as such, belongs to the whole. Now every man is part of the community, and so, as such, he belongs to the community. Hence by killing himself he injures the community, as the Philosopher declares (Ethic. v, 11). Thirdly, because life is God's gift to man, and is subject to His power, Who kills and makes to live. Hence whoever takes his own life, sins against God, even as he who kills another's slave, sins against that slave's master, and as he who usurps to himself judgment of a matter not entrusted to him. For it belongs to God alone to pronounce sentence of death and life, according to Deut. 32:39, "I will kill and I will make to live."

Reply Obj. 1: Murder is a sin, not only because it is contrary to justice, but also because it is opposed to charity which a man should have towards himself: in this respect suicide is a sin in relation to oneself. In relation to the community and to God, it is sinful, by reason also of its opposition to justice.

Reply Obj. 2: One who exercises public authority may lawfully put to death an evil-doer, since he can pass judgment on him. But no man is judge of himself. Wherefore it is not lawful for one who exercises public authority to put himself to death for any sin whatever: although he may lawfully commit himself to the judgment of others.

Reply Obj. 3: Man is made master of himself through his free-will: wherefore he can lawfully dispose of himself as to those matters which pertain to this life which is ruled by man's free-will. But the passage from this life to another and happier one is subject not to man's free-will but to the power of God. Hence it is not lawful for man to take his own life that he may pass to a happier life, nor that he may escape any unhappiness whatsoever of the present life, because the ultimate and most fearsome evil of this life is death, as the Philosopher states (Ethic. iii, 6). Therefore to bring death upon oneself in order to escape the other afflictions of this life, is to adopt a greater evil in order to avoid a lesser. In like manner it is unlawful to take one's own life on account of one's having committed a sin, both because by so doing one does oneself a very great injury, by depriving oneself of the time needful for repentance, and because it is not lawful to slay an evildoer except by the sentence of the public authority. Again it is unlawful for a woman to kill herself lest she be violated, because she ought not to commit on herself the very great sin of suicide, to avoid the lesser sin of another. For she commits no sin in being violated by force, provided she does not consent, since "without consent of the mind there is no stain on the body," as the Blessed Lucy declared. Now it is evident that fornication and adultery are less grievous sins than taking a man's, especially one's own, life: since the latter is most grievous, because one injures oneself, to whom one owes the greatest love. Moreover it is most dangerous since no time is left wherein to expiate it by repentance. Again it is not lawful for anyone to take his own life for fear he should consent to sin, because "evil must not be done that good may come" (Rom. 3:8) or that evil may be avoided especially if the evil be of small account and an uncertain event, for it is uncertain whether one will at some future time consent to a sin, since God is able to deliver man from sin under any temptation whatever.

Reply Obj. 4: As Augustine says (De Civ. Dei i, 21), "not even Samson is to be excused that he crushed himself together with his enemies under the ruins of the house, except the Holy Ghost, Who had wrought many wonders through him, had secretly commanded him to do this." He assigns the same reason in the case of certain holy women, who at the time of persecution took their own lives, and who are commemorated by the Church.

Reply Obj. 5: It belongs to fortitude that a man does not shrink from being slain by another, for the sake of the good of virtue, and that he may avoid sin. But that a man take his own life in order to avoid penal evils has indeed an appearance of fortitude (for which reason some, among whom was Razias, have killed themselves thinking to act from fortitude), yet it is not true fortitude, but rather a weakness of soul unable to bear penal evils, as the Philosopher (Ethic. iii, 7) and Augustine (De Civ. Dei 22, 23) declare.

SIXTH ARTICLE [II-II, Q. 64, Art. 6]

Whether It Is Lawful to Kill the Innocent?

Objection 1: It would seem that in some cases it is lawful to kill the innocent. The fear of God is never manifested by sin, since on the contrary "the fear of the Lord driveth out sin" (Ecclus. 1:27). Now Abraham was commended in that he feared the Lord, since he was willing to slay his innocent son. Therefore one may, without sin, kill an innocent person.

Obj. 2: Further, among those sins that are committed against one's neighbor, the more grievous seem to be those whereby a more grievous injury is inflicted on the person sinned against. Now to be killed is a greater injury to a sinful than to an innocent person, because the latter, by death, passes forthwith from the unhappiness of this life to the glory of heaven. Since then it is lawful in certain cases to kill a sinful man, much more is it lawful to slay an innocent or a righteous person.

Obj. 3: Further, what is done in keeping with the order of justice is not a sin. But sometimes a man is forced, according to the order of justice, to slay an innocent person: for instance, when a judge, who is bound to judge according to the evidence, condemns to death a man whom he knows to be innocent but who is convicted by false witnesses; and again the executioner, who in obedience to the judge puts to death the man who has been unjustly sentenced.

*On the contrary,* It is written (Ex. 23:7): "The innocent and just person thou shalt not put to death."

*I answer that,* An individual man may be considered in two ways: first, in himself; secondly, in relation to something else. If we consider a man in himself, it is unlawful to kill any man, since in every man though he be sinful, we ought to love the nature which God has made, and which is destroyed by slaying him. Nevertheless, as stated above (A. 2) the slaying of a sinner becomes lawful in relation to the common good, which is corrupted by sin. On the other hand the life of righteous men preserves and forwards the common good, since they are the chief part of the community. Therefore it is in no way lawful to slay the innocent.

Reply Obj. 1: God is Lord of death and life, for by His decree both the sinful and the righteous die. Hence he who at God's command kills an innocent man does not sin, as neither does God Whose behest he executes: indeed his obedience to God's commands is a proof that he fears Him.

Reply Obj. 2: In weighing the gravity of a sin we must consider the essential rather than the accidental. Wherefore he who kills a just man, sins more grievously than he who slays a sinful man: first, because he injures one whom he should love more, and so acts more in opposition to charity: secondly, because he inflicts an injury on a man who is less deserving of one, and so acts more in opposition to justice: thirdly, because he deprives the community of a greater good: fourthly, because he despises God more, according to Luke 10:16, "He that despiseth you despiseth Me." On the other hand it is accidental to the slaying that the just man whose life is taken be received by God into glory.

Reply Obj. 3: If the judge knows that a man who has been convicted by false witnesses, is innocent he must, like Daniel, examine the witnesses with great care, so as to find a motive for acquitting the innocent: but if he cannot do this he should remit him for judgment by a higher tribunal. If even this is impossible, he does not sin if he pronounce sentence in accordance with the evidence, for it is not he that puts the innocent man to death, but they who stated him to be guilty. He that carries out the sentence of the judge who has condemned an innocent man, if the sentence contains an inexcusable error, he should not obey, else there would be an excuse for the executions of the martyrs: if however it contain no manifest injustice, he does not sin by carrying out the sentence, because he has no right to discuss the judgment of his superior; nor is it he who slays the innocent man, but the judge whose minister he is.

SEVENTH ARTICLE [II-II, Q. 64, Art. 7]

Whether It Is Lawful to Kill a Man in Self-defense?

Objection 1: It would seem that nobody may lawfully kill a man in self-defense. For Augustine says to Publicola (Ep. xlvii): "I do not agree with the opinion that one may kill a man lest one be killed by him; unless one be a soldier, exercise a public office, so that one does it not for oneself but for others, having the power to do so, provided it be in keeping with one's person." Now he who kills a man in self-defense, kills him lest he be killed by him. Therefore this would seem to be unlawful.

Obj. 2: Further, he says (De Lib. Arb. i, 5): "How are they free from sin in sight of Divine providence, who are guilty of taking a man's life for the sake of these contemptible things?" Now among contemptible things he reckons "those which men may forfeit unwillingly," as appears from the context (De Lib. Arb. i, 5): and the chief of these is the life of the body. Therefore it is unlawful for any man to take another's life for the sake of the life of his own body.

Obj. 3: Further, Pope Nicolas [*Nicolas I, Dist. 1, can. De his clericis] says in the Decretals: "Concerning the clerics about whom you have consulted Us, those, namely, who have killed a pagan in self-defense, as to whether, after making amends by repenting, they may return to their former state, or rise to a higher degree; know that in no case is it lawful for them to kill any man under any circumstances whatever." Now clerics and laymen are alike bound to observe the moral precepts. Therefore neither is it lawful for laymen to kill anyone in self-defense.

Obj. 4: Further, murder is a more grievous sin than fornication or adultery. Now nobody may lawfully commit simple fornication or adultery or any other mortal sin in order to save his own life; since the spiritual life is to be preferred to the life of the body. Therefore no man may lawfully take another's life in self-defense in order to save his own life.

Obj. 5: Further, if the tree be evil, so is the fruit, according to Matt. 7:17. Now self-defense itself seems to be unlawful, according to Rom. 12:19: "Not defending [Douay: 'revenging'] yourselves, my dearly beloved." Therefore its result, which is the slaying of a man, is also unlawful.

*On the contrary,* It is written (Ex. 22:2): "If a thief be found breaking into a house or undermining it, and be wounded so as to die; he that slew him shall not be guilty of blood." Now it is much more lawful to defend one's life than one's house. Therefore neither is a man guilty of murder if he kill another in defense of his own life.

*I answer that,* Nothing hinders one act from having two effects, only one of which is intended, while the other is beside the intention. Now moral acts take their species according to what is intended, and not according to what is beside the intention, since this is accidental as explained above (Q. 43, A. 3; I-II, Q. 12, A. 1). Accordingly the act of self-defense may have two effects, one is the saving of one's life, the other is the slaying of the aggressor. Therefore this act, since one's intention is to save one's own life, is not unlawful, seeing that it is natural to everything to keep itself in *being,* as far as possible. And yet, though proceeding from a good intention, an act may be rendered unlawful, if it be out of proportion to the end. Wherefore if a man, in self-defense, uses more than necessary violence, it will be unlawful: whereas if he repel force with moderation his defense will be lawful, because according to the jurists [*Cap. Significasti, De Homicid. volunt. vel casual.], "it is lawful to repel force by force, provided one does not exceed the limits of a blameless defense." Nor is it necessary for salvation that a man omit the act of moderate self-defense in order to avoid killing the other man, since one is bound to take more care of one's own life than of another's. But as it is unlawful to take a man's life, except for the public authority acting for the common good, as stated above (A. 3), it is not lawful for a man to intend killing a man in self-defense, except for such as have public authority, who while intending to kill a man in self-defense, refer this to the public good, as in the case of a soldier fighting against the foe, and in the minister of the judge struggling with robbers, although even these sin if they be moved by private animosity.

Reply Obj. 1: The words quoted from Augustine refer to the case when one man intends to kill another to save himself from death. The passage quoted in the Second Objection is to be understood in the same sense. Hence he says pointedly, "for the sake of these things," whereby he indicates the intention. This suffices for the Reply to the Second Objection.

Reply Obj. 3: Irregularity results from the act though sinless of taking a man's life, as appears in the case of a judge who justly condemns a man to death. For this reason a cleric, though he kill a man in self-defense, is irregular, albeit he intends not to kill him, but to defend himself.

Reply Obj. 4: The act of fornication or adultery is not necessarily directed to the preservation of one's own life, as is the act whence sometimes results the taking of a man's life.

Reply Obj. 5: The defense forbidden in this passage is that which comes from revengeful spite. Hence a gloss says: "Not defending yourselves—that is, not striking your enemy back."

EIGHTH ARTICLE [II-II, Q. 64, Art. 8]

Whether One Is Guilty of Murder Through Killing Someone by Chance?

Objection 1: It would seem that one is guilty of murder through killing someone by chance. For we read (Gen. 4:23, 24) that Lamech slew a man in mistake for a wild beast [*The text of the Bible does not say so, but this was the Jewish traditional commentary on Gen. 4:23], and that he was accounted guilty of murder. Therefore one incurs the guilt of murder through killing a man by chance.

Obj. 2: Further, it is written (Ex. 21:22): "If ... one strike a woman with child, and she miscarry indeed ... if her death ensue thereupon, he shall render life for life." Yet this may happen without any intention of causing her death. Therefore one is guilty of murder through killing someone by chance.

Obj. 3: Further, the Decretals [*Dist. 1] contain several canons prescribing penalties for unintentional homicide. Now penalty is not due save for guilt. Therefore he who kills a man by chance, incurs the guilt of murder.

*On the contrary,* Augustine says to Publicola (Ep. xlvii): "When we do a thing for a good and lawful purpose, if thereby we unintentionally cause harm to anyone, it should by no means be imputed to us." Now it sometimes happens by chance that a person is killed as a result of something done for a good purpose. Therefore the person who did it is not accounted guilty.

*I answer that,* According to the Philosopher (Phys. ii, 6) "chance is a cause that acts beside one's intention." Hence chance happenings, strictly speaking, are neither intended nor voluntary. And since every sin is voluntary, according to Augustine (De Vera Relig. xiv) it follows that chance happenings, as such, are not sins.

Nevertheless it happens that what is not actually and directly voluntary and intended, is voluntary and intended accidentally, according as that which removes an obstacle is called an accidental cause. Wherefore he who does not remove something whence homicide results whereas he ought to remove it, is in a sense guilty of voluntary homicide. This happens in two ways: first when a man causes another's death through occupying himself with unlawful things which he ought to avoid: secondly, when he does not take sufficient care. Hence, according to jurists, if a man pursue a lawful occupation and take due care, the result being that a person loses his life, he is not guilty of that person's death: whereas if he be occupied with something unlawful, or even with something lawful, but without due care, he does not escape being guilty of murder, if his action results in someone's death.

Reply Obj. 1: Lamech did not take sufficient care to avoid taking a man's life: and so he was not excused from being guilty of homicide.

Reply Obj. 2: He that strikes a woman with child does something unlawful: wherefore if there results the death either of the woman or of the animated fetus, he will not be excused from homicide, especially seeing that death is the natural result of such a blow.

Reply Obj. 3: According to the canons a penalty is inflicted on those who cause death unintentionally, through doing something unlawful, or failing to take sufficient care.

# QUESTION 65

OF OTHER INJURIES COMMITTED ON THE PERSON (In Four Articles)

We must now consider other sinful injuries committed on the person. Under this head there are four points of inquiry:

(1) The mutilation of members;

(2) Blows;

(3) Imprisonment;

(4) Whether the sins that consist in inflicting such like injuries are aggravated through being perpetrated on persons connected with others?

FIRST ARTICLE [II-II, Q. 65, Art. 1]

Whether in Some Cases It May Be Lawful to Maim Anyone?

Objection 1: It would seem that in no case can it be lawful to maim anyone. For Damascene says (De Fide Orth. iv, 20) that "sin consists in departing from what is according to nature, towards that which is contrary to nature." Now according to nature it is appointed by God that a man's body should be entire in its members, and it is contrary to nature that it should be deprived of a member. Therefore it seems that it is always a sin to maim a person.

Obj. 2: Further, as the whole soul is to the whole body, so are the parts of the soul to the parts of the body (De Anima ii, 1). But it is unlawful to deprive a man of his soul by killing him, except by public authority. Therefore neither is it lawful to maim anyone, except perhaps by public authority.

Obj. 3: Further, the welfare of the soul is to be preferred to the welfare of the body. Now it is not lawful for a man to maim himself for the sake of the soul's welfare: since the council of Nicea [*P. I, sect. 4, can. i] punished those who castrated themselves that they might preserve chastity. Therefore it is not lawful for any other reason to maim a person.

*On the contrary,* It is written (Ex. 21:24): "Eye for eye, tooth for tooth, hand for hand, foot for foot."

*I answer that,* Since a member is part of the whole human body, it is for the sake of the whole, as the imperfect for the perfect. Hence a member of the human body is to be disposed of according as it is expedient for the body. Now a member of the human body is of itself useful to the good of the whole body, yet, accidentally it may happen to be hurtful, as when a decayed member is a source of corruption to the whole body. Accordingly so long as a member is healthy and retains its natural disposition, it cannot be cut off without injury to the whole body. But as the whole of man is directed as to his end to the whole of the community of which he is a part, as stated above (Q. 61, A. 1; Q. 64, AA. 2, 5), it may happen that although the removal of a member may be detrimental to the whole body, it may nevertheless be directed to the good of the community, in so far as it is applied to a person as a punishment for the purpose of restraining sin. Hence just as by public authority a person is lawfully deprived of life altogether on account of certain more heinous sins, so is he deprived of a member on account of certain lesser sins. But this is not lawful for a private individual, even with the consent of the owner of the member, because this would involve an injury to the community, to whom the man and all his parts belong. If, however, the member be decayed and therefore a source of corruption to the whole body, then it is lawful with the consent of the owner of the member, to cut away the member for the welfare of the whole body, since each one is entrusted with the care of his own welfare. The same applies if it be done with the consent of the person whose business it is to care for the welfare of the person who has a decayed member: otherwise it is altogether unlawful to maim anyone.

Reply Obj. 1: Nothing prevents that which is contrary to a particular nature from being in harmony with universal nature: thus death and corruption, in the physical order, are contrary to the particular nature of the thing corrupted, although they are in keeping with universal nature. In like manner to maim anyone, though contrary to the particular nature of the body of the person maimed, is nevertheless in keeping with natural reason in relation to the common good.

Reply Obj. 2: The life of the entire man is not directed to something belonging to man; on the contrary whatever belongs to man is directed to his life. Hence in no case does it pertain to a person to take anyone's life, except to the public authority to whom is entrusted the procuring of the common good. But the removal of a member can be directed to the good of one man, and consequently in certain cases can pertain to him.

Reply Obj. 3: A member should not be removed for the sake of the bodily health of the whole, unless otherwise nothing can be done to further the good of the whole. Now it is always possible to further one's spiritual welfare otherwise than by cutting off a member, because sin is always subject to the will: and consequently in no case is it allowable to maim oneself, even to avoid any sin whatever. Hence Chrysostom, in his exposition on Matt. 19:12 (Hom. lxii in Matth.), "There are eunuchs who have made themselves eunuchs for the kingdom of heaven," says: "Not by maiming themselves, but by destroying evil thoughts, for a man is accursed who maims himself, since they are murderers who do such things." And further on he says: "Nor is lust tamed thereby, on the contrary it becomes more importunate, for the seed springs in us from other sources, and chiefly from an incontinent purpose and a careless mind: and temptation is curbed not so much by cutting off a member as by curbing one's thoughts."

SECOND ARTICLE [II-II, Q. 65, Art. 2]

Whether It Is Lawful for Parents to Strike Their Children, or Masters Their Slaves?

Objection 1: It would seem unlawful for parents to strike their children, or masters their slaves. For the Apostle says (Eph. 6:4): "You, fathers, provoke not your children to anger"; and further on (Eph. 9:6): "And you, masters, do the same thing to your slaves [Vulg.: 'to them'] forbearing threatenings." Now some are provoked to anger by blows, and become more troublesome when threatened. Therefore neither should parents strike their children, nor masters their slaves.

Obj. 2: Further, the Philosopher says (Ethic. x, 9) that "a father's words are admonitory and not coercive." Now blows are a kind of coercion. Therefore it is unlawful for parents to strike their children.

Obj. 3: Further, everyone is allowed to impart correction, for this belongs to the spiritual almsdeeds, as stated above (Q. 32, A. 2). If, therefore, it is lawful for parents to strike their children for the sake of correction, for the same reason it will be lawful for any person to strike anyone, which is clearly false. Therefore the same conclusion follows.

*On the contrary,* It is written (Prov. 13:24): "He that spareth the rod hateth his son," and further on (Prov. 23:13): "Withhold not correction from a child, for if thou strike him with the rod, he shall not die. Thou shalt beat him with the rod, and deliver his soul from hell." Again it is written (Ecclus. 33:28): "Torture and fetters are for a malicious slave."

*I answer that,* Harm is done a body by striking it, yet not so as when it is maimed: since maiming destroys the body's integrity, while a blow merely affects the sense with pain, wherefore it causes much less harm than cutting off a member. Now it is unlawful to do a person a harm, except by way of punishment in the cause of justice. Again, no man justly punishes another, except one who is subject to his jurisdiction. Therefore it is not lawful for a man to strike another, unless he have some power over the one whom he strikes. And since the child is subject to the power of the parent, and the slave to the power of his master, a parent can lawfully strike his child, and a master his slave that instruction may be enforced by correction.

Reply Obj. 1: Since anger is a desire for vengeance, it is aroused chiefly when a man deems himself unjustly injured, as the Philosopher states (Rhet. ii). Hence when parents are forbidden to provoke their children to anger, they are not prohibited from striking their children for the purpose of correction, but from inflicting blows on them without moderation. The command that masters should forbear from threatening their slaves may be understood in two ways. First that they should be slow to threaten, and this pertains to the moderation of correction; secondly, that they should not always carry out their threats, that is that they should sometimes by a merciful forgiveness temper the judgment whereby they threatened punishment.

Reply Obj. 2: The greater power should exercise the greater coercion. Now just as a city is a perfect community, so the governor of a city has perfect coercive power: wherefore he can inflict irreparable punishments such as death and mutilation. On the other hand the father and the master who preside over the family household, which is an imperfect community, have imperfect coercive power, which is exercised by inflicting lesser punishments, for instance by blows, which do not inflict irreparable harm.

Reply Obj. 3: It is lawful for anyone to impart correction to a willing subject. But to impart it to an unwilling subject belongs to those only who have charge over him. To this pertains chastisement by blows.

THIRD ARTICLE [II-II, Q. 65, Art. 3]

Whether It Is Lawful to Imprison a Man?

Objection 1: It would seem unlawful to imprison a man. An act which deals with undue matter is evil in its genus, as stated above (I-II, Q. 18, A. 2). Now man, having a free-will, is undue matter for imprisonment which is inconsistent with free-will. Therefore it is unlawful to imprison a man.

Obj. 2: Further, human justice should be ruled by Divine justice. Now according to Ecclus. 15:14, "God left man in the hand of his own counsel." Therefore it seems that a man ought not to be coerced by chains or prisons.

Obj. 3: Further, no man should be forcibly prevented except from doing an evil deed; and any man can lawfully prevent another from doing this. If, therefore, it were lawful to imprison a man, in order to restrain him from evil deeds, it would be lawful for anyone to put a man in prison; and this is clearly false. Therefore the same conclusion follows.

*On the contrary,* We read in Lev. 24 that a man was imprisoned for the sin of blasphemy.

*I answer that,* In the goods of the body three things may be considered in due order. First, the substantial integrity of the body, and this is injured by death or maiming. Secondly, pleasure or rest of the senses, and to this striking or anything causing a sense of pain is opposed. Thirdly, the movement or use of the members, and this is hindered by binding or imprisoning or any kind of detention.

Therefore it is unlawful to imprison or in any way detain a man, unless it be done according to the order of justice, either in punishment, or as a measure of precaution against some evil.

Reply Obj. 1: A man who abuses the power entrusted to him deserves to lose it, and therefore when a man by sinning abuses the free use of his members, he becomes a fitting matter for imprisonment.

Reply Obj. 2: According to the order of His wisdom God sometimes restrains a sinner from accomplishing a sin, according to Job 5:12: "Who bringeth to nought the designs of the malignant, so that their hand cannot accomplish what they had begun, while sometimes He allows them to do what they will." In like manner, according to human justice, men are imprisoned, not for every sin but for certain ones.

Reply Obj. 3: It is lawful for anyone to restrain a man for a time from doing some unlawful deed there and then: as when a man prevents another from throwing himself over a precipice, or from striking another. But to him alone who has the right of disposing in general of the actions and of the life of another does it belong primarily to imprison or fetter, because by so doing he hinders him from doing not only evil but also good deeds.

FOURTH ARTICLE [II-II, Q. 65, Art. 4]

Whether the Sin Is Aggravated by the Fact That the Aforesaid Injuries Are Perpetrated on Those Who Are Connected with Others?

Objection 1: It would seem that the sin is not aggravated by the fact that the aforesaid injuries are perpetrated on those who are connected with others. Such like injuries take their sinful character from inflicting an injury on another against his will. Now the evil inflicted on a man's own person is more against his will than that which is inflicted on a person connected with him. Therefore an injury inflicted on a person connected with another is less grievous.

Obj. 2: Further, Holy Writ reproves those especially who do injuries to orphans and widows: hence it is written (Ecclus. 35:17): "He will not despise the prayers of the fatherless, nor the widow when she poureth out her complaint." Now the widow and the orphan are not connected with other persons. Therefore the sin is not aggravated through an injury being inflicted on one who is connected with others.

Obj. 3: Further, the person who is connected has a will of his own just as the principal person has, so that something may be voluntary for him and yet against the will of the principal person, as in the case of adultery which pleases the woman but not the husband. Now these injuries are sinful in so far as they consist in an involuntary commutation. Therefore such like injuries are of a less sinful nature.

*On the contrary,* It is written (Deut. 28:32) as though indicating an aggravating circumstance: "Thy sons and thy daughters shall be given to another people, thy eyes looking on [*Vulg.: 'May thy sons and thy daughters be given,' etc.]."

*I answer that,* Other things being equal, an injury is a more grievous sin according as it affects more persons; and hence it is that it is a more grievous sin to strike or injure a person in authority than a private individual, because it conduces to the injury of the whole community, as stated above (I-II, Q. 73, A. 9). Now when an injury is inflicted on one who is connected in any way with another, that injury affects two persons, so that, other things being equal, the sin is aggravated by this very fact. It may happen, however, that in view of certain circumstances, a sin committed against one who is not connected with any other person, is more grievous, on account of either the dignity of the person, or the greatness of the injury.

Reply Obj. 1: An injury inflicted on a person connected with others is less harmful to the persons with whom he is connected, than if it were perpetrated immediately on them, and from this point of view it is a less grievous sin. But all that belongs to the injury of the person with whom he is connected, is added to the sin of which a man is guilty through injuring the other one in himself.

Reply Obj. 2: Injuries done to widows and orphans are more insisted upon both through being more opposed to mercy, and because the same injury done to such persons is more grievous to them since they have no one to turn to for relief.

Reply Obj. 3: The fact that the wife voluntarily consents to the adultery, lessens the sin and injury, so far as the woman is concerned, for it would be more grievous, if the adulterer oppressed her by violence. But this does not remove the injury as affecting her husband, since "the wife hath not power of her own body; but the husband" (1 Cor. 7:4). The same applies to similar cases. Of adultery, however, as it is opposed not only to justice but also to chastity, we shall speak in the treatise on Temperance (Q. 154, A. 8).

# QUESTION 66

OF THEFT AND ROBBERY (In Nine Articles)

We must now consider the sins opposed to justice, whereby a man injures his neighbor in his belongings; namely theft and robbery.

Under this head there are nine points of inquiry:

(1) Whether it is natural to man to possess external things?

(2) Whether it is lawful for a man to possess something as his own?

(3) Whether theft is the secret taking of another's property?

(4) Whether robbery is a species of sin distinct from theft?

(5) Whether every theft is a sin?

(6) Whether theft is a mortal sin?

(7) Whether it is lawful to thieve in a case of necessity?

(8) Whether every robbery is a mortal sin?

(9) Whether robbery is a more grievous sin than theft?

FIRST ARTICLE [II-II, Q. 66, Art. 1]

Whether It Is Natural for Man to Possess External Things?

Objection 1: It would seem that it is not natural for man to possess external things. For no man should ascribe to himself that which is God's. Now the dominion over all creatures is proper to God, according to Ps. 23:1, "The earth is the Lord's," etc. Therefore it is not natural for man to possess external things.

Obj. 2: Further, Basil in expounding the words of the rich man (Luke 12:18), "I will gather all things that are grown to me, and my goods," says [*Hom. in Luc. xii, 18]: "Tell me: which are thine? where did you take them from and bring them into being?" Now whatever man possesses naturally, he can fittingly call his own. Therefore man does not naturally possess external things.

Obj. 3: Further, according to Ambrose (De Trin. i [*De Fide, ad Gratianum, i, 1]) "dominion denotes power." But man has no power over external things, since he can work no change in their nature. Therefore the possession of external things is not natural to man.

*On the contrary,* It is written (Ps. 8:8): "Thou hast subjected all things under his feet."

*I answer that,* External things can be considered in two ways. First, as regards their nature, and this is not subject to the power of man, but only to the power of God Whose mere will all things obey. Secondly, as regards their use, and in this way, man has a natural dominion over external things, because, by his reason and will, he is able to use them for his own profit, as they were made on his account: for the imperfect is always for the sake of the perfect, as stated above (Q. 64, A. 1). It is by this argument that the Philosopher proves (Polit. i, 3) that the possession of external things is natural to man. Moreover, this natural dominion of man over other creatures, which is competent to man in respect of his reason wherein God's image resides, is shown forth in man's creation (Gen. 1:26) by the words: "Let us make man to our image and likeness: and let him have dominion over the fishes of the sea," etc.

Reply Obj. 1: God has sovereign dominion over all things: and He, according to His providence, directed certain things to the sustenance of man's body. For this reason man has a natural dominion over things, as regards the power to make use of them.

Reply Obj. 2: The rich man is reproved for deeming external things to belong to him principally, as though he had not received them from another, namely from God.

Reply Obj. 3: This argument considers the dominion over external things as regards their nature. Such a dominion belongs to God alone, as stated above.

SECOND ARTICLE [II-II, Q. 66, Art. 2]

Whether It Is Lawful for a Man to Possess a Thing As His Own?

Objection 1: It would seem unlawful for a man to possess a thing as his own. For whatever is contrary to the natural law is unlawful. Now according to the natural law all things are common property: and the possession of property is contrary to this community of goods. Therefore it is unlawful for any man to appropriate any external thing to himself.

Obj. 2: Further, Basil in expounding the words of the rich man quoted above (A. 1, Obj. 2), says: "The rich who deem as their own property the common goods they have seized upon, are like to those who by going beforehand to the play prevent others from coming, and appropriate to themselves what is intended for common use." Now it would be unlawful to prevent others from obtaining possession of common goods. Therefore it is unlawful to appropriate to oneself what belongs to the community.

Obj. 3: Further, Ambrose says [*Serm. lxiv, de temp.], and his words are quoted in the Decretals [*Dist. xlvii., Can. Sicut hi.]: "Let no man call his own that which is common property": and by "common" he means external things, as is clear from the context. Therefore it seems unlawful for a man to appropriate an external thing to himself.

*On the contrary,* Augustine says (De Haeres., haer. 40): "The 'Apostolici' are those who with extreme arrogance have given themselves that name, because they do not admit into their communion persons who are married or possess anything of their own, such as both monks and clerics who in considerable number are to be found in the Catholic Church." Now the reason why these people are heretics was because severing themselves from the Church, they think that those who enjoy the use of the above things, which they themselves lack, have no hope of salvation. Therefore it is erroneous to maintain that it is unlawful for a man to possess property.

*I answer that,* Two things are competent to man in respect of exterior things. One is the power to procure and dispense them, and in this regard it is lawful for man to possess property. Moreover this is necessary to human life for three reasons. First because every man is more careful to procure what is for himself alone than that which is common to many or to all: since each one would shirk the labor and leave to another that which concerns the community, as happens where there is a great number of servants. Secondly, because human affairs are conducted in more orderly fashion if each man is charged with taking care of some particular thing himself, whereas there would be confusion if everyone had to look after any one thing indeterminately. Thirdly, because a more peaceful state is ensured to man if each one is contented with his own. Hence it is to be observed that quarrels arise more frequently where there is no division of the things possessed.

The second thing that is competent to man with regard to external things is their use. In this respect man ought to possess external things, not as his own, but as common, so that, to wit, he is ready to communicate them to others in their need. Hence the Apostle says (1 Tim. 6:17, 18): "Charge the rich of this world ... to give easily, to communicate to others," etc.

Reply Obj. 1: Community of goods is ascribed to the natural law, not that the natural law dictates that all things should be possessed in common and that nothing should be possessed as one's own: but because the division of possessions is not according to the natural law, but rather arose from human agreement which belongs to positive law, as stated above (Q. 57, AA. 2, 3). Hence the ownership of possessions is not contrary to the natural law, but an addition thereto devised by human reason.

Reply Obj. 2: A man would not act unlawfully if by going beforehand to the play he prepared the way for others: but he acts unlawfully if by so doing he hinders others from going. In like manner a rich man does not act unlawfully if he anticipates someone in taking possession of something which at first was common property, and gives others a share: but he sins if he excludes others indiscriminately from using it. Hence Basil says (Hom. in Luc. xii, 18): "Why are you rich while another is poor, unless it be that you may have the merit of a good stewardship, and he the reward of patience?"

Reply Obj. 3: When Ambrose says: "Let no man call his own that which is common," he is speaking of ownership as regards use, wherefore he adds: "He who spends too much is a robber."

THIRD ARTICLE [II-II, Q. 66, Art. 3]

Whether the Essence of Theft Consists in Taking Another's Thing Secretly?

Objection 1: It would seem that it is not essential to theft to take another's thing secretly. For that which diminishes a sin, does not, apparently, belong to the essence of a sin. Now to sin secretly tends to diminish a sin, just as, *on the contrary,* it is written as indicating an aggravating circumstance of the sin of some (Isa. 3:9): "They have proclaimed abroad their sin as Sodom, and they have not hid it." Therefore it is not essential to theft that it should consist in taking another's thing secretly.

Obj. 2: Further, Ambrose says [*Serm. lxiv, de temp., A. 2, Obj. 3, Can. Sicut hi.]: and his words are embodied in the Decretals [*Dist. xlvii]: "It is no less a crime to take from him that has, than to refuse to succor the needy when you can and are well off." Therefore just as theft consists in taking another's thing, so does it consist in keeping it back.

Obj. 3: Further, a man may take by stealth from another, even that which is his own, for instance a thing that he has deposited with another, or that has been taken away from him unjustly. Therefore it is not essential to theft that it should consist in taking another's thing secretly.

*On the contrary,* Isidore says (Etym. x): " Fur (thief) is derived from furvus and so from fuscus (dark), because he takes advantage of the night."

*I answer that,* Three things combine together to constitute theft. The first belongs to theft as being contrary to justice, which gives to each one that which is his, so that it belongs to theft to take possession of what is another's. The second thing belongs to theft as distinct from those sins which are committed against the person, such as murder and adultery, and in this respect it belongs to theft to be about a thing possessed: for if a man takes what is another's not as a possession but as a part (for instance, if he amputates a limb), or as a person connected with him (for instance, if he carry off his daughter or his wife), it is not strictly speaking a case of theft. The third difference is that which completes the nature of theft, and consists in a thing being taken secretly: and in this respect it belongs properly to theft that it consists in "taking another's thing secretly."

Reply Obj. 1: Secrecy is sometimes a cause of sin, as when a man employs secrecy in order to commit a sin, for instance in fraud and guile. In this way it does not diminish sin, but constitutes a species of sin: and thus it is in theft. In another way secrecy is merely a circumstance of sin, and thus it diminishes sin, both because it is a sign of shame, and because it removes scandal.

Reply Obj. 2: To keep back what is due to another, inflicts the same kind of injury as taking a thing unjustly: wherefore an unjust detention is included in an unjust taking.

Reply Obj. 3: Nothing prevents that which belongs to one person simply, from belonging to another in some respect: thus a deposit belongs simply to the depositor, but with regard to its custody it is the depositary's, and the thing stolen is the thief's, not simply, but as regards its custody.

FOURTH ARTICLE [II-II, Q. 66, Art. 4]

Whether Theft and Robbery Are Sins of Different Species?

Objection 1: It would seem that theft and robbery are not sins of different species. For theft and robbery differ as "secret" and "manifest": because theft is taking something secretly, while robbery is to take something violently and openly. Now in the other kinds of sins, the secret and the manifest do not differ specifically. Therefore theft and robbery are not different species of sin.

Obj. 2: Further, moral actions take their species from the end, as stated above (I-II, Q. 1, A. 3; Q. 18, A. 6). Now theft and robbery are directed to the same end, viz. the possession of another's property. Therefore they do not differ specifically.

Obj. 3: Further, just as a thing is taken by force for the sake of possession, so is a woman taken by force for pleasure: wherefore Isidore says (Etym. x) that "he who commits a rape is called a corrupter, and the victim of the rape is said to be corrupted." Now it is a case of rape whether the woman be carried off publicly or secretly. Therefore the thing appropriated is said to be taken by force, whether it be done secretly or publicly. Therefore theft and robbery do not differ.

*On the contrary,* The Philosopher (Ethic. v, 2) distinguishes theft from robbery, and states that theft is done in secret, but that robbery is done openly.

*I answer that,* Theft and robbery are vices contrary to justice, in as much as one man does another an injustice. Now "no man suffers an injustice willingly," as stated in *Ethic.* v, 9. Wherefore theft and robbery derive their sinful nature, through the taking being involuntary on the part of the person from whom something is taken. Now the involuntary is twofold, namely, through violence and through ignorance, as stated in *Ethic.* iii, 1. Therefore the sinful aspect of robbery differs from that of theft: and consequently they differ specifically.

Reply Obj. 1: In the other kinds of sin the sinful nature is not derived from something involuntary, as in the sins opposed to justice: and so where there is a different kind of involuntary, there is a different species of sin.

Reply Obj. 2: The remote end of robbery and theft is the same. But this is not enough for identity of species, because there is a difference of proximate ends, since the robber wishes to take a thing by his own power, but the thief, by cunning.

Reply Obj. 3: The robbery of a woman cannot be secret on the part of the woman who is taken: wherefore even if it be secret as regards the others from whom she is taken, the nature of robbery remains on the part of the woman to whom violence is done.

FIFTH ARTICLE [II-II, Q. 66, Art. 5]

Whether Theft Is Always a Sin?

Objection 1: It would seem that theft is not always a sin. For no sin is commanded by God, since it is written (Ecclus. 15:21): "He hath commanded no man to do wickedly." Yet we find that God commanded theft, for it is written (Ex. 12:35, 36): "And the children of Israel did as the Lord had commanded Moses [Vulg.: 'as Moses had commanded']... and they stripped the Egyptians." Therefore theft is not always a sin.

Obj. 2: Further, if a man finds a thing that is not his and takes it, he seems to commit a theft, for he takes another's property. Yet this seems lawful according to natural equity, as the jurists hold. [*See loc. cit. in Reply.] Therefore it seems that theft is not always a sin.

Obj. 3: Further, he that takes what is his own does not seem to sin, because he does not act against justice, since he does not destroy its equality. Yet a man commits a theft even if he secretly take his own property that is detained by or in the safe-keeping of another. Therefore it seems that theft is not always a sin.

*On the contrary,* It is written (Ex. 20:15): "Thou shalt not steal."

*I answer that,* If anyone consider what is meant by theft, he will find that it is sinful on two counts. First, because of its opposition to justice, which gives to each one what is his, so that for this reason theft is contrary to justice, through being a taking of what belongs to another. Secondly, because of the guile or fraud committed by the thief, by laying hands on another's property secretly and cunningly. Wherefore it is evident that every theft is a sin.

Reply Obj. 1: It is no theft for a man to take another's property either secretly or openly by order of a judge who has commanded him to do so, because it becomes his due by the very fact that it is adjudicated to him by the sentence of the court. Hence still less was it a theft for the Israelites to take away the spoils of the Egyptians at the command of the Lord, Who ordered this to be done on account of the ill-treatment accorded to them by the Egyptians without any cause: wherefore it is written significantly (Wis. 10:19): "The just took the spoils of the wicked."

Reply Obj. 2: With regard to treasure-trove a distinction must be made. For some there are that were never in anyone's possession, for instance precious stones and jewels, found on the seashore, and such the finder is allowed to keep [*Dig. I, viii, De divis. rerum: Inst. II, i, De rerum divis.]. The same applies to treasure hidden underground long since and belonging to no man, except that according to civil law the finder is bound to give half to the owner of the land, if the treasure trove be in the land of another person [*Inst. II, i, 39: Cod. X, xv, De Thesauris]. Hence in the parable of the Gospel (Matt. 13:44) it is said of the finder of the treasure hidden in a field that he bought the field, as though he purposed thus to acquire the right of possessing the whole treasure. On the other Land the treasure-trove may be nearly in someone's possession: and then if anyone take it with the intention, not of keeping it but of returning it to the owner who does not look upon such things as unappropriated, he is not guilty of theft. In like manner if the thing found appears to be unappropriated, and if the finder believes it to be so, although he keep it, he does not commit a theft [*Inst. II, i, 47]. In any other case the sin of theft is committed [*Dig. XLI, i, De acquirend. rerum dominio, 9: Inst. II, i, 48]: wherefore Augustine says in a homily (Serm. clxxviii; De Verb. Apost.): "If thou hast found a thing and not returned it, thou hast stolen it" (Dig. xiv, 5, can. Si quid invenisti).

Reply Obj. 3: He who by stealth takes his own property which is deposited with another man burdens the depositary, who is bound either to restitution, or to prove himself innocent. Hence he is clearly guilty of sin, and is bound to ease the depositary of his burden. On the other hand he who, by stealth, takes his own property, if this be unjustly detained by another, he sins indeed; yet not because he burdens the retainer, and so he is not bound to restitution or compensation: but he sins against general justice by disregarding the order of justice and usurping judgment concerning his own property. Hence he must make satisfaction to God and endeavor to allay whatever scandal he may have given his neighbor by acting this way.

SIXTH ARTICLE [II-II, Q. 66, Art. 6]

Whether Theft Is a Mortal Sin?

Objection 1: It would seem that theft is not a mortal sin. For it is written (Prov. 6:30): "The fault is not so great when a man hath stolen." But every mortal sin is a great fault. Therefore theft is not a mortal sin.

Obj. 2: Further, mortal sin deserves to be punished with death. But in the Law theft is punished not by death but by indemnity, according to Ex. 22:1, "If any man steal an ox or a sheep ... he shall restore have oxen for one ox, and four sheep for one sheep." Therefore theft is not a mortal sin.

Obj. 3: Further, theft can be committed in small even as in great things. But it seems unreasonable for a man to be punished with eternal death for the theft of a small thing such as a needle or a quill. Therefore theft is not a mortal sin.

*On the contrary,* No man is condemned by the Divine judgment save for a mortal sin. Yet a man is condemned for theft, according to Zech. 5:3, "This is the curse that goeth forth over the face of the earth; for every thief shall be judged as is there written." Therefore theft is a mortal sin.

*I answer that,* As stated above (Q. 59, A. 4; I-II, Q. 72, A. 5), a mortal sin is one that is contrary to charity as the spiritual life of the soul. Now charity consists principally in the love of God, and secondarily in the love of our neighbor, which is shown in our wishing and doing him well. But theft is a means of doing harm to our neighbor in his belongings; and if men were to rob one another habitually, human society would be undone. Therefore theft, as being opposed to charity, is a mortal sin.

Reply Obj. 1: The statement that theft is not a great fault is in view of two cases. First, when a person is led to thieve through necessity. This necessity diminishes or entirely removes sin, as we shall show further on (A. 7). Hence the text continues: "For he stealeth to fill his hungry soul." Secondly, theft is stated not to be a great fault in comparison with the guilt of adultery, which is punished with death. Hence the text goes on to say of the thief that "if he be taken, he shall restore sevenfold ... but he that is an adulterer ... shall destroy his own soul."

Reply Obj. 2: The punishments of this life are medicinal rather than retributive. For retribution is reserved to the Divine judgment which is pronounced against sinners "according to truth" (Rom. 2:2). Wherefore, according to the judgment of the present life the death punishment is inflicted, not for every mortal sin, but only for such as inflict an irreparable harm, or again for such as contain some horrible deformity. Hence according to the present judgment the pain of death is not inflicted for theft which does not inflict an irreparable harm, except when it is aggravated by some grave circumstance, as in the case of sacrilege which is the theft of a sacred thing, of peculation, which is theft of common property, as Augustine states (Tract. 1, Super Joan.), and of kidnaping which is stealing a man, for which the pain of death is inflicted (Ex. 21:16).

Reply Obj. 3: Reason accounts as nothing that which is little: so that a man does not consider himself injured in very little matters: and the person who takes such things can presume that this is not against the will of the owner. And if a person take such like very little things, he may be proportionately excused from mortal sin. Yet if his intention is to rob and injure his neighbor, there may be a mortal sin even in these very little things, even as there may be through consent in a mere thought.

SEVENTH ARTICLE [II-II, Q. 66, Art. 7]

Whether It Is Lawful to Steal Through Stress of Need?

Objection 1: It would seem unlawful to steal through stress of need. For penance is not imposed except on one who has sinned. Now it is stated (Extra, De furtis, Cap. Si quis): "If anyone, through stress of hunger or nakedness, steal food, clothing or beast, he shall do penance for three weeks." Therefore it is not lawful to steal through stress of need.

Obj. 2: Further, the Philosopher says (Ethic. ii, 6) that "there are some actions whose very name implies wickedness," and among these he reckons theft. Now that which is wicked in itself may not be done for a good end. Therefore a man cannot lawfully steal in order to remedy a need.

Obj. 3: Further, a man should love his neighbor as himself. Now, according to Augustine (Contra Mendac. vii), it is unlawful to steal in order to succor one's neighbor by giving him an alms. Therefore neither is it lawful to steal in order to remedy one's own needs.

*On the contrary,* In cases of need all things are common property, so that there would seem to be no sin in taking another's property, for need has made it common.

*I answer that,* Things which are of human right cannot derogate from natural right or Divine right. Now according to the natural order established by

Divine Providence, inferior things are ordained for the purpose of succoring man's needs by their means. Wherefore the division and appropriation of things which are based on human law, do not preclude the fact that man's needs have to be remedied by means of these very things. Hence whatever certain people have in superabundance is due, by natural law, to the purpose of succoring the poor. For this reason Ambrose [*Loc. cit., A. 2, Obj. 3] says, and his words are embodied in the Decretals (Dist. xlvii, can. Sicut ii): "It is the hungry man's bread that you withhold, the naked man's cloak that you store away, the money that you bury in the earth is the price of the poor man's ransom and freedom."

Since, however, there are many who are in need, while it is impossible for all to be succored by means of the same thing, each one is entrusted with the stewardship of his own things, so that out of them he may come to the aid of those who are in need. Nevertheless, if the need be so manifest and urgent, that it is evident that the present need must be remedied by whatever means be at hand (for instance when a person is in some imminent danger, and there is no other possible remedy), then it is lawful for a man to succor his own need by means of another's property, by taking it either openly or secretly: nor is this properly speaking theft or robbery.

Reply Obj. 1: This decretal considers cases where there is no urgent need.

Reply Obj. 2: It is not theft, properly speaking, to take secretly and use another's property in a case of extreme need: because that which he takes for the support of his life becomes his own property by reason of that need.

Reply Obj. 3: In a case of a like need a man may also take secretly another's property in order to succor his neighbor in need.

EIGHTH ARTICLE [II-II, Q. 66, Art. 8]

Whether Robbery May Be Committed Without Sin?

Objection 1: It would seem that robbery may be committed without sin. For spoils are taken by violence, and this seems to belong to the essence of robbery, according to what has been said (A. 4). Now it is lawful to take spoils from the enemy; for Ambrose says (De Patriarch. 4 [*De Abraham i, 3]): "When the conqueror has taken possession of the spoils, military discipline demands that all should be reserved for the sovereign," in order, to wit, that he may distribute them. Therefore in certain cases robbery is lawful.

Obj. 2: Further, it is lawful to take from a man what is not his. Now the things which unbelievers have are not theirs, for Augustine says (Ep. ad Vincent. Donat. xciii.): "You falsely call things your own, for you do not possess them justly, and according to the laws of earthly kings you are commanded to forfeit them." Therefore it seems that one may lawfully rob unbelievers.

Obj. 3: Further, earthly princes violently extort many things from their subjects: and this seems to savor of robbery. Now it would seem a grievous matter to say that they sin in acting thus, for in that case nearly every prince would be damned. Therefore in some cases robbery is lawful.

*On the contrary,* Whatever is taken lawfully may be offered to God in sacrifice and oblation. Now this cannot be done with the proceeds of robbery, according to Isa. 61:8, "I am the Lord that love judgment, and hate robbery in a holocaust." Therefore it is not lawful to take anything by robbery.

*I answer that,* Robbery implies a certain violence and coercion employed in taking unjustly from a man that which is his. Now in human society no man can exercise coercion except through public authority: and, consequently, if a private individual not having public authority takes another's property by violence, he acts unlawfully and commits a robbery, as burglars do. As regards princes, the public power is entrusted to them that they may be the guardians of justice: hence it is unlawful for them to use violence or coercion, save within the bounds of justice—either by fighting against the enemy, or against the citizens, by punishing evil-doers: and whatever is taken by violence of this kind is not the spoils of robbery, since it is not contrary to justice. On the other hand to take other people's property violently and against justice, in the exercise of public authority, is to act unlawfully and to be guilty of robbery; and whoever does so is bound to restitution.

Reply Obj. 1: A distinction must be made in the matter of spoils. For if they who take spoils from the enemy, are waging a just war, such things as they seize in the war become their own property. This is no robbery, so that they are not bound to restitution. Nevertheless even they who are engaged in a just war may sin in taking spoils through cupidity arising from an evil intention, if, to wit, they fight chiefly not for justice but for spoil. For Augustine says (De Verb. Dom. xix; Serm. lxxxii) that "it is a sin to fight for booty." If, however, those who take the spoil, are waging an unjust war, they are guilty of robbery, and are bound to restitution.

Reply Obj. 2: Unbelievers possess their goods unjustly in so far as they are ordered by the laws of earthly princes to forfeit those goods. Hence these may be taken violently from them, not by private but by public authority.

Reply Obj. 3: It is no robbery if princes exact from their subjects that which is due to them for the safe-guarding of the common good, even if they use violence in so doing: but if they extort something unduly by means of violence, it is robbery even as burglary is. Hence Augustine says (De Civ. Dei iv, 4): "If justice be disregarded, what is a king but a mighty robber? since what is a robber but a little king?" And it is written (Ezech. 22:27): "Her princes in the midst of her, are like wolves ravening the prey." Wherefore they are bound to restitution, just as robbers are, and by so much do they sin more grievously than robbers, as their actions are fraught with greater and more universal danger to public justice whose wardens they are.

NINTH ARTICLE [II-II, Q. 66, Art. 9]

Whether Theft Is a More Grievous Sin Than Robbery?

Objection 1: It would seem that theft is a more grievous sin than robbery. For theft adds fraud and guile to the taking of another's property: and these things are not found in robbery. Now fraud and guile are sinful in themselves, as stated above (Q. 55, AA. 4, 5). Therefore theft is a more grievous sin than robbery.

Obj. 2: Further, shame is fear about a wicked deed, as stated in *Ethic.* iv, 9. Now men are more ashamed of theft than of robbery. Therefore theft is more wicked than robbery.

Obj. 3: Further, the more persons a sin injures the more grievous it would seem to be. Now the great and the lowly may be injured by theft: whereas only the weak can be injured by robbery, since it is possible to use violence towards them. Therefore the sin of theft seems to be more grievous than the sin of robbery.

*On the contrary,* According to the laws robbery is more severely punished than theft.

*I answer that,* Robbery and theft are sinful, as stated above (AA. 4, 6), on account of the involuntariness on the part of the person from whom something is taken: yet so that in theft the involuntariness is due to ignorance, whereas in robbery it is due to violence. Now a thing is more involuntary through violence than through ignorance, because violence is more directly opposed to the will than ignorance. Therefore robbery is a more grievous sin than theft. There is also another reason, since robbery not only inflicts a loss on a person in his things, but also conduces to the ignominy and injury of his person, and this is of graver import than fraud or guile which belong to theft. Hence the Reply to the First Objection is evident.

Reply Obj. 2: Men who adhere to sensible things think more of external strength which is evidenced in robbery, than of internal virtue which is forfeit through sin: wherefore they are less ashamed of robbery than of theft.

Reply Obj. 3: Although more persons may be injured by theft than by robbery, yet more grievous injuries may be inflicted by robbery than by theft: for which reason also robbery is more odious.

# QUESTION 67

OF THE INJUSTICE OF A JUDGE, IN JUDGING (In Four Articles)

We must now consider those vices opposed to commutative justice, that consist in words injurious to our neighbors. We shall consider (1) those which are connected with judicial proceedings, and (2) injurious words uttered extra-judicially.

Under the first head five points occur for our consideration: (1) The injustice of a judge in judging; (2) The injustice of the prosecutor in accusing; (3) The injustice of the defendant in defending himself; (4) The injustice of the witnesses in giving evidence; (5) The injustice of the advocate in defending.

Under the first head there are four points of inquiry:

(1) Whether a man can justly judge one who is not his subject?

(2) Whether it is lawful for a judge, on account of the evidence, to deliver judgment in opposition to the truth which is known to him?

(3) Whether a judge can justly sentence a man who is not accused?

(4) Whether he can justly remit the punishment?

FIRST ARTICLE [II-II, Q. 67, Art. 1]

Whether a Man Can Justly Judge One Who Is Not Subject to His Jurisdiction?

Objection 1: It would seem that a man can justly judge one who is not subject to his jurisdiction. For it is stated (Dan. 13) that Daniel sentenced the ancients who were convicted of bearing false witness. But these ancients were not subject to Daniel; indeed they were judges of the people. Therefore a man may lawfully judge one that is not subject to his jurisdiction.

Obj. 2: Further, Christ was no man's subject, indeed He was "King of kings and Lord of lords" (Apoc. 19:16). Yet He submitted to the judgment of a man. Therefore it seems that a man may lawfully judge one that is not subject to his jurisdiction.

Obj. 3: Further, according to the law [*Cap. Licet ratione, de Foro Comp.] a man is tried in this or that court according to his kind of offense. Now sometimes the defendant is not the subject of the man whose business it is to judge in that particular place, for instance when the defendant belongs to another diocese or is exempt. Therefore it seems that a man may judge one that is not his subject.

*On the contrary,* Gregory [*Regist. xi, epist. 64] in commenting on Deut. 23:25, "If thou go into thy friend's corn," etc. says: "Thou mayest not put the sickle of judgment to the corn that is entrusted to another."

*I answer that,* A judge's sentence is like a particular law regarding some particular fact. Wherefore just as a general law should have coercive power, as the Philosopher states (Ethic. x, 9), so too the sentence of a judge should have coercive power, whereby either party is compelled to comply with the judge's sentence; else the judgment would be of no effect. Now coercive power is not exercised in human affairs, save by those who hold public authority: and those who have this authority are accounted the superiors of those over whom they preside whether by ordinary or by delegated authority. Hence it is evident that no man can judge others than his subjects and this in virtue either of delegated or of ordinary authority.

Reply Obj. 1: In judging those ancients Daniel exercised an authority delegated to him by Divine instinct. This is indicated where it is said (Dan. 13:45) that "the Lord raised up the ... spirit of a young boy."

Reply Obj. 2: In human affairs a man may submit of his own accord to the judgment of others although these be not his superiors, an example of which is when parties agree to a settlement by arbitrators. Wherefore it is necessary that the arbitrator should be upheld by a penalty, since the arbitrators through not exercising authority in the case, have not of themselves full power of coercion. Accordingly in this way did Christ of his own accord submit to human judgment: and thus too did Pope Leo [*Leo IV] submit to the judgment of the emperor [*Can. Nos si incompetenter, caus. ii, qu. 7].

Reply Obj. 3: The bishop of the defendant's diocese becomes the latter's superior as regards the fault committed, even though he be exempt: unless perchance the defendant offend in a matter exempt from the bishop's authority, for instance in administering the property of an exempt monastery. But if an exempt person commits a theft, or a murder or the like, he may be justly condemned by the ordinary.

SECOND ARTICLE [II-II, Q. 67, Art. 2]

Whether It Is Lawful for a Judge to Pronounce Judgment Against the Truth That He Knows, on Account of Evidence to the Contrary?

Objection 1: It would seem unlawful for a judge to pronounce judgment against the truth that he knows, on account of evidence to the contrary. For it is written (Deut. 17:9): "Thou shalt come to the priests of the Levitical race, and to the judge that shall be at that time; and thou shalt ask of them, and they shall show thee the truth of the judgment." Now sometimes certain things are alleged against the truth, as when something is proved by means of false witnesses. Therefore it is unlawful for a judge to pronounce judgment according to what is alleged and proved in opposition to the truth which he knows.

Obj. 2: Further, in pronouncing judgment a man should conform to the Divine judgment, since "it is the judgment of God" (Deut. 1:17). Now "the judgment of God is according to the truth" (Rom. 2:2), and it was foretold of Christ (Isa. 11:3, 4): "He shall not judge according to the sight of the eyes, nor reprove according to the hearing of the ears. But He shall judge the poor with justice, and shall reprove with equity for the meek of the earth." Therefore the judge ought not to pronounce judgment according to the evidence before him if it be contrary to what he knows himself.

Obj. 3: Further, the reason why evidence is required in a court of law, is that the judge may have a faithful record of the truth of the matter, wherefore in matters of common knowledge there is no need of judicial procedure, according to 1 Tim. 5:24, "Some men's sins are manifest, going before to judgment." Consequently, if the judge by his personal knowledge is aware of the truth, he should pay no heed to the evidence, but should pronounce sentence according to the truth which he knows.

Obj. 4: Further, the word "conscience" denotes application of knowledge to a matter of action as stated in the First Part (Q. 79, A. 13). Now it is a sin to act contrary to one's knowledge. Therefore a judge sins if he pronounces sentence according to the evidence but against his conscience of the truth.

*On the contrary,* Augustine [*Ambrose, Super Ps. 118, serm. 20] says in his commentary on the Psalter: "A good judge does nothing according to his private opinion but pronounces sentence according to the law and the right." Now this is to pronounce judgment according to what is alleged and proved in court. Therefore a judge ought to pronounce judgment in accordance with these things, and not according to his private opinion.

*I answer that,* As stated above (A. 1; Q. 60, AA. 2, 6) it is the duty of a judge to pronounce judgment in as much as he exercises public authority, wherefore his judgment should be based on information acquired by him, not from his knowledge as a private individual, but from what he knows as a public person. Now the latter knowledge comes to him both in general and in particular—in general through the public laws, whether Divine or human, and he should admit no evidence that conflicts therewith—in some particular matter, through documents and witnesses, and other legal means of information, which in pronouncing his sentence, he ought to follow rather than the information he has acquired as a private individual. And yet this same information may be of use to him, so that he can more rigorously sift the evidence brought forward, and discover its weak points. If, however, he is unable to reject that evidence juridically, he must, as stated above, follow it in pronouncing sentence.

Reply Obj. 1: The reason why, in the passage quoted, it is stated that the judges should first of all be asked their reasons, is to make it clear that the judges ought to judge the truth in accordance with the evidence.

Reply Obj. 2: To judge belongs to God in virtue of His own power: wherefore His judgment is based on the truth which He Himself knows, and not on knowledge imparted by others: the same is to be said of Christ, Who is true God and true man: whereas other judges do not judge in virtue of their own power, so that there is no comparison.

Reply Obj. 3: The Apostle refers to the case where something is well known not to the judge alone, but both to him and to others, so that the guilty party can by no means deny his guilt (as in the case of notorious criminals), and is convicted at once from the evidence of the fact. If, on the other hand, it be well known to the judge, but not to others, or to others, but not to the judge, then it is necessary for the judge to sift the evidence.

Reply Obj. 4: In matters touching his own person, a man must form his conscience from his own knowledge, but in matters concerning the public authority, he must form his conscience in accordance with the knowledge attainable in the public judicial procedure.

THIRD ARTICLE [II-II, Q. 67, Art. 3]

Whether a Judge May Condemn a Man Who Is Not Accused?

Objection 1: It would seem that a judge may pass sentence on a man who is not accused. For human justice is derived from Divine justice. Now God judges the sinner even though there be no accuser. Therefore it seems that a man may pass sentence of condemnation on a man even though there be no accuser.

Obj. 2: Further, an accuser is required in judicial procedure in order that he may relate the crime to the judge. Now sometimes the crime may come to the judge's knowledge otherwise than by accusation; for instance, by denunciation, or by evil report, or through the judge himself being an eye-witness. Therefore a judge may condemn a man without there being an accuser.

Obj. 3: Further, the deeds of holy persons are related in Holy Writ, as models of human conduct. Now Daniel was at the same time the accuser and the judge of the wicked ancients (Dan. 13). Therefore it is not contrary to justice for a man to condemn anyone as judge while being at the same time his accuser.

*On the contrary,* Ambrose in his commentary on 1 Cor. 5:2, expounding the Apostle's sentence on the fornicator, says that "a judge should not condemn without an accuser, since our Lord did not banish Judas, who was a thief, yet was not accused."

*I answer that,* A judge is an interpreter of justice. Wherefore, as the Philosopher says (Ethic. v, 4), "men have recourse to a judge as to one who is the personification of justice." Now, as stated above (Q. 58, A. 2), justice is not between a man and himself but between one man and another. Hence a judge must needs judge between two parties, which is the case when one is the prosecutor, and the other the defendant. Therefore in criminal cases the judge cannot sentence a man unless the latter has an accuser, according to Acts 25:16: "It is not the custom of the Romans to condemn any man, before that he who is accused have his accusers present, and have liberty to make his answer, to clear himself of the crimes" of which he is accused.

Reply Obj. 1: God, in judging man, takes the sinner's conscience as his accuser, according to Rom. 2:15, "Their thoughts between themselves accusing, or also defending one another"; or again, He takes the evidence of the fact as regards the deed itself, according to Gen. 4:10, "The voice of thy brother's blood crieth to Me from the earth."

Reply Obj. 2: Public disgrace takes the place of an accuser. Hence a gloss on Gen. 4:10, "The voice of thy brother's blood," etc. says: "There is no need of an accuser when the crime committed is notorious." In a case of denunciation, as stated above (Q. 33, A. 7), the amendment, not the punishment, of the sinner is intended: wherefore when a man is denounced for a sin, nothing is done against him, but for him, so that no accuser is required. The punishment that is inflicted is on account of his rebellion against the Church, and since this rebellion is manifest, it stands instead of an accuser. The fact that the judge himself was an eye-witness, does not authorize him to proceed to pass sentence, except according to the order of judicial procedure.

Reply Obj. 3: God, in judging man, proceeds from His own knowledge of the truth, whereas man does not, as stated above (A. 2). Hence a man cannot be accuser, witness and judge at the same time, as God is. Daniel was at once accuser and judge, because he was the executor of the sentence of God, by whose instinct he was moved, as stated above (A. 1, ad 1).

FOURTH ARTICLE [II-II, Q. 67, Art. 4]

Whether the Judge Can Lawfully Remit the Punishment?

Objection 1: It would seem that the judge can lawfully remit the punishment. For it is written (James 2:13): "Judgment without mercy" shall be done "to him that hath not done mercy." Now no man is punished for not doing what he cannot do lawfully. Therefore any judge can lawfully do mercy by remitting the punishment.

Obj. 2: Further, human judgment should imitate the Divine judgment. Now God remits the punishment to sinners, because He desires not the death of the sinner, according to Ezech. 18:23. Therefore a human judge also may lawfully remit the punishment to one who repents.

Obj. 3: Further, it is lawful for anyone to do what is profitable to some one and harmful to none. Now the remission of his punishment profits the guilty man and harms nobody. Therefore the judge can lawfully loose a guilty man from his punishment.

*On the contrary,* It is written (Deut. 13:8, 9) concerning anyone who would persuade a man to serve strange gods: "Neither let thy eye spare him to pity and conceal him, but thou shalt presently put him to death": and of the murderer it is written (Deut. 19:12, 13): "He shall die. Thou shalt not pity him."

*I answer that,* As may be gathered from what has been said (AA. 2, 3), with regard to the question in point, two things may be observed in connection with a judge. One is that he has to judge between accuser and defendant, while the other is that he pronounces the judicial sentence, in virtue of his power, not as a private individual but as a public person. Accordingly on two counts a judge is hindered from loosing a guilty person from his punishment. First on the part of the accuser, whose right it sometimes is that the guilty party should be punished—for instance on account of some injury committed against the accuser—because it is not in the power of a judge to remit such punishment, since every judge is bound to give each man his right. Secondly, he finds a hindrance on the part of the commonwealth, whose power he exercises, and to whose good it belongs that evil-doers should be punished.

Nevertheless in this respect there is a difference between judges of lower degree and the supreme judge, i.e. the sovereign, to whom the entire public authority is entrusted. For the inferior judge has no power to exempt a guilty man from punishment against the laws imposed on him by his superior. Wherefore Augustine in commenting on John 19:11, "Thou shouldst not have any power against Me," says (Tract. cxvi in Joan.): "The power which God gave Pilate was such that he was under the power of Caesar, so that he was by no means free to acquit the person accused." On the other hand the sovereign who has full authority in the commonwealth, can lawfully remit the punishment to a guilty person, provided the injured party consent to the remission, and that this do not seem detrimental to the public good.

Reply Obj. 1: There is a place for the judge's mercy in matters that are left to the judge's discretion, because in like matters a good man is slow to punish as the Philosopher states (Ethic. v, 10). But in matters that are determined in accordance with Divine or human laws, it is not left to him to show mercy.

Reply Obj. 2: God has supreme power of judging, and it concerns Him whatever is done sinfully against anyone. Therefore He is free to remit the punishment, especially since punishment is due to sin chiefly because it is done against Him. He does not, however, remit the punishment, except in so far as it becomes His goodness, which is the source of all laws.

Reply Obj. 3: If the judge were to remit punishment inordinately, he would inflict an injury on the community, for whose good it behooves ill-deeds to be punished, in order that men may avoid sin. Hence the text, after appointing the punishment of the seducer, adds (Deut. 13:11): "That all Israel hearing may fear, and may do no more anything like this." He would also inflict harm on the injured person; who is compensated by having his honor restored in the punishment of the man who has injured him.

# QUESTION 68

OF MATTERS CONCERNING UNJUST ACCUSATION (In Four Articles)

We must now consider matters pertaining to unjust accusation. Under this head there are four points of inquiry:

(1) Whether a man is bound to accuse?

(2) Whether the accusation should be made in writing?

(3) How is an accusation vitiated?

(4) How should those be punished who have accused a man wrongfully?

FIRST ARTICLE [II-II, Q. 68, Art. 1]

Whether a Man Is Bound to Accuse?

Objection 1: It would seem that a man is not bound to accuse. For no man is excused on account of sin from fulfilling a Divine precept, since he would thus profit by his sin. Yet on account of sin some are disqualified from accusing, such as those who are excommunicate or of evil fame, or who are accused of grievous crimes and are not yet proved to be innocent [*1 Tim. 1:5]. Therefore a man is not bound by a Divine precept to accuse.

Obj. 2: Further, every duty depends on charity which is "the end of the precept" [*Can. Definimus, caus. iv, qu. 1; caus. vi, qu. 1]: wherefore it is written (Rom. 13:8): "Owe no man anything, but to love one another." Now that which belongs to charity is a duty that man owes to all both of high and of low degree, both superiors and inferiors. Since therefore subjects should not accuse their superiors, nor persons of lower degree, those of a higher degree, as shown in several chapters (Decret. II, qu. vii), it seems that it is no man's duty to accuse.

Obj. 3: Further, no man is bound to act against the fidelity which he owes his friend; because he ought not to do to another what he would not have others do to him. Now to accuse anyone is sometimes contrary to the fidelity that one owes a friend; for it is written (Prov. 11:13): "He that walketh deceitfully, revealeth secrets; but he that is faithful, concealeth the thing committed to him by his friend." Therefore a man is not bound to accuse.

*On the contrary,* It is written (Lev. 5:1): "If any one sin, and hear the voice of one swearing, and is a witness either because he himself hath seen, or is privy to it: if he do not utter it, he shall bear his iniquity."

*I answer that,* As stated above (Q. 33, AA. 6, 7; Q. 67, A. 3, ad 2), the difference between denunciation and accusation is that in denunciation we aim at a brother's amendment, whereas in accusation we intend the punishment of his crime. Now the punishments of this life are sought, not for their own sake, because this is not the final time of retribution, but in their character of medicine, conducing either to the amendment of the sinner, or to the good of the commonwealth whose calm is ensured by the punishment of evil-doers. The former of these is intended in denunciation, as stated, whereas the second regards properly accusation. Hence in the case of a crime that conduces to the injury of the commonwealth, a man is bound to accusation, provided he can offer sufficient proof, since it is the accuser's duty to prove: as, for example, when anyone's sin conduces to the bodily or spiritual corruption of the community. If, however, the sin be not such as to affect the community, or if he cannot offer sufficient proof, a man is not bound to attempt to accuse, since no man is bound to do what he cannot duly accomplish.

Reply Obj. 1: Nothing prevents a man being debarred by sin from doing what men are under an obligation to do: for instance from meriting eternal life, and from receiving the sacraments of the Church. Nor does a man profit by this: indeed it is a most grievous fault to fail to do what one is bound to do, since virtuous acts are perfections of man.

Reply Obj. 2: Subjects are debarred from accusing their superiors, "if it is not the affection of charity but their own wickedness that leads them to defame and disparage the conduct of their superiors" [*Append. Grat. ad can. Sunt nonnulli, caus. ii, qu. 7]—or again if the subject who wishes to accuse his superior is himself guilty of crime [*Decret. II, qu. vii, can. Praesumunt.]. Otherwise, provided they be in other respects qualified to accuse, it is lawful for subjects to accuse their superiors out of charity.

Reply Obj. 3: It is contrary to fidelity to make known secrets to the injury of a person; but not if they be revealed for the good of the community, which should always be preferred to a private good. Hence it is unlawful to receive any secret in detriment to the common good: and yet a thing is scarcely a secret when there are sufficient witnesses to prove it.

SECOND ARTICLE [II-II, Q. 68, Art. 2]

Whether It Is Necessary for the Accusation to Be Made in Writing?

Objection 1: It would seem unnecessary for the accusation to be made in writing. For writing was devised as an aid to the human memory of the past. But an accusation is made in the present. Therefore the accusation needs not to be made in writing.

Obj. 2: Further, it is laid down (Decret. II, qu. viii, can. Per scripta) that "no man may accuse or be accused in his absence." Now writing seems to be useful in the fact that it is a means of notifying something to one who is absent, as Augustine declares (De Trin. x, 1). Therefore the accusation need not be in writing: and all the more that the canon declares that "no accusation in writing should be accepted."

Obj. 3: Further, a man's crime is made known by denunciation, even as by accusation. Now writing is unnecessary in denunciation. Therefore it is seemingly unnecessary in accusation.

*On the contrary,* It is laid down (Decret. II, qu. viii, can. Accusatorum) that "the role of accuser must never be sanctioned without the accusation be in writing."

*I answer that,* As stated above (Q. 67, A. 3), when the process in a criminal case goes by way of accusation, the accuser is in the position of a party, so that the judge stands between the accuser and the accused for the purpose of the trial of justice, wherein it behooves one to proceed on certainties, as far as possible. Since however verbal utterances are apt to escape one's memory, the judge would be unable to know for certain what had been said and with what qualifications, when he comes to pronounce sentence, unless it were drawn up in writing. Hence it has with reason been established that the accusation, as well as other parts of the judicial procedure, should be put into writing.

Reply Obj. 1: Words are so many and so various that it is difficult to remember each one. A proof of this is the fact that if a number of people who have heard the same words be asked what was said, they will not agree in repeating them, even after a short time. And since a slight difference of words changes the sense, even though the judge's sentence may have to be pronounced soon afterwards, the certainty of judgment requires that the accusation be drawn up in writing.

Reply Obj. 2: Writing is needed not only on account of the absence of the person who has something to notify, or of the person to whom something is notified, but also on account of the delay of time as stated above (ad 1). Hence when the canon says, "Let no accusation be accepted in writing" it refers to the sending of an accusation by one who is absent: but it does not exclude the necessity of writing when the accuser is present.

Reply Obj. 3: The denouncer does not bind himself to give proofs: wherefore he is not punished if he is unable to prove. For this reason writing is unnecessary in a denunciation: and it suffices that the denunciation be made verbally to the Church, who will proceed, in virtue of her office, to the correction of the brother.

THIRD ARTICLE [II-II, Q. 68, Art. 3]

Whether an Accusation Is Rendered Unjust by Calumny, Collusion or Evasion?

Objection 1: It would seem that an accusation is not rendered unjust by calumny, collusion or evasion. For according to Decret. II, qu. iii [*Append. Grat. ad can. Si quem poenituerit.], "calumny consists in falsely charging a person with a crime." Now sometimes one man falsely accuses another of a crime through ignorance of fact which excuses him. Therefore it seems that an accusation is not always rendered unjust through being slanderous.

Obj. 2: Further, it is stated by the same authority that "collusion consists in hiding the truth about a crime." But seemingly this is not unlawful, because one is not bound to disclose every crime, as stated above (A. 1; Q. 33, A. 7). Therefore it seems that an accusation is not rendered unjust by collusion.

Obj. 3: Further, it is stated by the same authority that "evasion consists in withdrawing altogether from an accusation." But this can be done without injustice: for it is stated there also: "If a man repent of having made a wicked accusation and inscription* in a matter which he cannot prove, and come to an understanding with the innocent party whom he has accused, let them acquit one another." [*The accuser was bound by Roman Law to endorse (se inscribere) the writ of accusation. The effect of this endorsement or inscription was that the accuser bound himself, if he failed to prove the accusation, to suffer the same punishment as the accused would have to suffer if proved guilty.] Therefore evasion does not render an accusation unjust.

*On the contrary,* It is stated by the same authority: "The rashness of accusers shows itself in three ways. For they are guilty either of calumny, or of collusion, or of evasion."

*I answer that,* As stated above (A. 1), accusation is ordered for the common good which it aims at procuring by means of knowledge of the crime. Now no man ought to injure a person unjustly, in order to promote the common good. Wherefore a man may sin in two ways when making an accusation: first through acting unjustly against the accused, by charging him falsely with the commission of a crime, i.e. by calumniating him; secondly, on the part of the commonwealth, whose good is intended chiefly in an accusation, when anyone with wicked intent hinders a sin being punished. This again happens in two ways: first by having recourse to fraud in making the accusation. This belongs to collusion ( *prevaricatio* ) for "he that is guilty of collusion is like one who rides astraddle ( *varicator* ), because he helps the other party, and betrays his own side" [*Append. Grat. ad can. Si quem poenituerit.]. Secondly by withdrawing altogether from the accusation. This is evasion ( *tergiversatio* ) for by desisting from what he had begun he seems to turn his back ( *tergum vertere* ).

Reply Obj. 1: A man ought not to proceed to accuse except of what he is quite certain about, wherein ignorance of fact has no place. Yet he who falsely charges another with a crime is not a calumniator unless he gives utterance to false accusations out of malice. For it happens sometimes that a man through levity of mind proceeds to accuse someone, because he believes too readily what he hears, and this pertains to rashness; while, on the other hand sometimes a man is led to make an accusation on account of an error for which he is not to blame. All these things must be weighed according to the judge's prudence, lest he should declare a man to have been guilty of calumny, who through levity of mind or an error for which he is not to be blamed has uttered a false accusation.

Reply Obj. 2: Not everyone who hides the truth about a crime is guilty of collusion, but only he who deceitfully hides the matter about which he makes the accusation, by collusion with the defendant, dissembling his proofs, and admitting false excuses.

Reply Obj. 3: Evasion consists in withdrawing altogether from the accusation, by renouncing the intention of accusing, not anyhow, but inordinately. There are two ways, however, in which a man may rightly desist from accusing without committing a sin—in one way, in the very process of accusation, if it come to his knowledge that the matter of his accusation is false, and then by mutual consent the accuser and the defendant acquit one another—in another way, if the accusation be quashed by the sovereign to whom belongs the care of the common good, which it is intended to procure by the accusation.

FOURTH ARTICLE [II-II, Q. 68, Art. 4]

Whether an Accuser Who Fails to Prove His Indictment Is Bound to the Punishment of Retaliation?

Objection 1: It would seem that the accuser who fails to prove his indictment is not bound to the punishment of retaliation. For sometimes a man is led by a just error to make an accusation, in which case the judge acquit the accuser, as stated in Decret. II, qu. iii. [*Append. Grat., ad can. Si quem poenituerit.] Therefore the accuser who fails to prove his indictment is not bound to the punishment of retaliation.

Obj. 2: Further, if the punishment of retaliation ought to be inflicted on one who has accused unjustly, this will be on account of the injury he has done to someone—but not on account of any injury done to the person of the accused, for in that case the sovereign could not remit this punishment, nor on account of an injury to the commonwealth, because then the accused could not acquit him. Therefore the punishment of retaliation is not due to one who has failed to prove his accusation.

Obj. 3: Further, the one same sin does not deserve a twofold punishment, according to Nahum 1:9 [*Septuagint version]: "God shall not judge the same thing a second time." But he who fails to prove his accusation, incurs the punishment due to defamation [*Can. Infames, caus. vi, qu. 1], which punishment even the Pope seemingly cannot remit, according to a statement of Pope Gelasius [*Callist. I, Epist. ad omn. Gall. episc.]: "Although we are able to save souls by Penance, we are unable to remove the defamation." Therefore he is not bound to suffer the punishment of retaliation.

*On the contrary,* Pope Hadrian I says (Cap. lii): "He that fails to prove his accusation, must himself suffer the punishment which his accusation inferred."

*I answer that,* As stated above (A. 2), in a case, where the procedure is by way of accusation, the accuser holds the position of a party aiming at the punishment of the accused. Now the duty of the judge is to establish the equality of justice between them: and the equality of justice requires that a man should himself suffer whatever harm he has intended to be inflicted on another, according to Ex. 21:24, "Eye for eye, tooth for tooth." Consequently it is just that he who by accusing a man has put him in danger of being punished severely, should himself suffer a like punishment.

Reply Obj. 1: As the Philosopher says (Ethic. v, 5) justice does not always require counterpassion, because it matters considerably whether a man injures another voluntarily or not. Voluntary injury deserves punishment, involuntary deserves forgiveness. Hence when the judge becomes aware that a man has made a false accusation, not with a mind to do harm, but involuntarily through ignorance or a just error, he does not impose the punishment of retaliation.

Reply Obj. 2: He who accuses wrongfully sins both against the person of the accused and against the commonwealth; wherefore he is punished on both counts. This is the meaning of what is written (Deut. 19:18-20): "And when after most diligent inquisition, they shall find that the false witness hath told a lie against his brother: they shall render to him as he meant to do to his brother," and this refers to the injury done to the person: and afterwards, referring to the injury done to the commonwealth, the text continues: "And thou shalt take away the evil out of the midst of thee, that others hearing may fear, and may not dare to do such things." Specially, however, does he injure the person of the accused, if he accuse him falsely. Wherefore the accused, if innocent, may condone the injury done to himself, particularly if the accusation were made not calumniously but out of levity of mind. But if the accuser desist from accusing an innocent man, through collusion with the latter's adversary, he inflicts an injury on the commonwealth: and this cannot be condoned by the accused, although it can be remitted by the sovereign, who has charge of the commonwealth.

Reply Obj. 3: The accuser deserves the punishment of retaliation in compensation for the harm he attempts to inflict on his neighbor: but the punishment of disgrace is due to him for his wickedness in accusing another man calumniously. Sometimes the sovereign remits the punishment, and not the disgrace, and sometimes he removes the disgrace also: wherefore the Pope also can remove this disgrace. When Pope Gelasius says: "We cannot remove the disgrace," he may mean either the disgrace attaching to the deed ( *infamia facti* ), or that sometimes it is not expedient to remove it, or again he may be referring to the disgrace inflicted by the civil judge, as Gratian states (Callist. I, Epist. ad omn. Gall. episc.).

# QUESTION 69

OF SINS COMMITTED AGAINST JUSTICE ON THE PART OF THE DEFENDANT (In Four Articles)

We must now consider those sins which are committed against justice on the part of the defendant. Under this head there are four points of inquiry:

(1) Whether it is a mortal sin to deny the truth which would lead to one's condemnation?

(2) Whether it is lawful to defend oneself with calumnies?

(3) Whether it is lawful to escape condemnation by appealing?

(4) Whether it is lawful for one who has been condemned to defend himself by violence if he be able to do so?

FIRST ARTICLE [II-II, Q. 69, Art. 1]

Whether One Can, Without a Mortal Sin, Deny the Truth Which Would Lead to One's Condemnation?

Objection 1: It would seem one can, without a mortal sin, deny the truth which would lead to one's condemnation. For Chrysostom says (Hom. xxxi super Ep. ad Heb.): "I do not say that you should lay bare your guilt publicly, nor accuse yourself before others." Now if the accused were to confess the truth in court, he would lay bare his guilt and be his own accuser. Therefore he is not bound to tell the truth: and so he does not sin mortally if he tell a lie in court.

Obj. 2: Further, just as it is an officious lie when one tells a lie in order to rescue another man from death, so is it an officious lie when one tells a lie in order to free oneself from death, since one is more bound towards oneself than towards another. Now an officious lie is considered not a mortal but a venial sin. Therefore if the accused denies the truth in court, in order to escape death, he does not sin mortally.

Obj. 3: Further, every mortal sin is contrary to charity, as stated above (Q. 24, A. 12). But that the accused lie by denying himself to be guilty of the crime laid to his charge is not contrary to charity, neither as regards the love we owe God, nor as to the love due to our neighbor. Therefore such a lie is not a mortal sin.

*On the contrary,* Whatever is opposed to the glory of God is a mortal sin, because we are bound by precept to "do all to the glory of God" (1 Cor. 10:31). Now it is to the glory of God that the accused confess that which is alleged against him, as appears from the words of Josue to Achan, "My son, give glory to the Lord God of Israel, and confess and tell me what thou hast done, hide it not" (Joshua 7:19). Therefore it is a mortal sin to lie in order to cover one's guilt.

*I answer that,* Whoever acts against the due order of justice, sins mortally, as stated above (Q. 59, A. 4). Now it belongs to the order of justice that a man should obey his superior in those matters to which the rights of his authority extend. Again, the judge, as stated above (Q. 67, A. 1), is the superior in relation to the person whom he judges. Therefore the accused is in duty bound to tell the judge the truth which the latter exacts from him according to the form of law. Hence if he refuse to tell the truth which he is under obligation to tell, or if he mendaciously deny it, he sins mortally. If, on the other hand, the judge asks of him that which he cannot ask in accordance with the order of justice, the accused is not bound to satisfy him, and he may lawfully escape by appealing or otherwise: but it is not lawful for him to lie.

Reply Obj. 1: When a man is examined by the judge according to the order of justice, he does not lay bare his own guilt, but his guilt is unmasked by another, since the obligation of answering is imposed on him by one whom he is bound to obey.

Reply Obj. 2: To lie, with injury to another person, in order to rescue a man from death is not a purely officious lie, for it has an admixture of the pernicious lie: and when a man lies in court in order to exculpate himself, he does an injury to one whom he is bound to obey, since he refuses him his due, namely an avowal of the truth.

Reply Obj. 3: He who lies in court by denying his guilt, acts both against the love of God to whom judgment belongs, and against the love of his neighbor, and this not only as regards the judge, to whom he refuses his due, but also as regards his accuser, who is punished if he fail to prove his accusation. Hence it is written (Ps. 140:4): "Incline not my heart to evil words, to make excuses in sins": on which words a gloss says: "Shameless men are wont by lying to deny their guilt when they have been found out." And Gregory in expounding Job 31:33, "If as a man I have hid my sin," says (Moral. xxii, 15): "It is a common vice of mankind to sin in secret, by lying to hide the sin that has been committed, and when convicted to aggravate the sin by defending oneself."

SECOND ARTICLE [II-II, Q. 69, Art. 2]

Whether It Is Lawful for the Accused to Defend Himself with Calumnies?

Objection 1: It would seem lawful for the accused to defend himself with calumnies. Because, according to civil law (Cod. II, iv, De transact. 18), when a man is on trial for his life it is lawful for him to bribe his adversary. Now this is done chiefly by defending oneself with calumnies. Therefore the accused who is on trial for his life does not sin if he defend himself with calumnies.

Obj. 2: Further, an accuser who is guilty of collusion with the accused, is punishable by law (Decret. II, qu. iii, can. Si quem poenit.). Yet no punishment is imposed on the accused for collusion with the accuser. Therefore it would seem lawful for the accused to defend himself with calumnies.

Obj. 3: Further, it is written (Prov. 14:16): "A wise man feareth and declineth from evil, the fool leapeth over and is confident." Now what is done wisely is no sin. Therefore no matter how a man declines from evil, he does not sin.

*On the contrary,* In criminal cases an oath has to be taken against calumnious allegations (Extra, De juramento calumniae, cap. Inhaerentes): and this would not be the case if it were lawful to defend oneself with calumnies. Therefore it is not lawful for the accused to defend himself with calumnies.

*I answer that,* It is one thing to withhold the truth, and another to utter a falsehood. The former is lawful sometimes, for a man is not bound to divulge all truth, but only such as the judge can and must require of him according to the order of justice; as, for instance, when the accused is already disgraced through the commission of some crime, or certain indications of his guilt have already been discovered, or again when his guilt is already more or less proven. On the other hand it is never lawful to make a false declaration.

As regards what he may do lawfully, a man can employ either lawful means, and such as are adapted to the end in view, which belongs to prudence; or he can use unlawful means, unsuitable to the proposed end, and this belongs to craftiness, which is exercised by fraud and guile, as shown above (Q. 55, AA. 3, seqq.). His conduct in the former case is praiseworthy, in the latter sinful. Accordingly it is lawful for the accused to defend himself by withholding the truth that he is not bound to avow, by suitable means, for instance by not answering such questions as he is not bound to answer. This is not to defend himself with calumnies, but to escape prudently. But it is unlawful for him, either to utter a falsehood, or to withhold a truth that he is bound to avow, or to employ guile or fraud, because fraud and guile have the force of a lie, and so to use them would be to defend oneself with calumnies.

Reply Obj. 1: Human laws leave many things unpunished, which according to the Divine judgment are sins, as, for example, simple fornication; because human law does not exact perfect virtue from man, for such virtue belongs to few and cannot be found in so great a number of people as human law has to direct. That a man is sometimes unwilling to commit a sin in order to escape from the death of the body, the danger of which threatens the accused who is on trial for his life, is an act of perfect virtue, since "death is the most fearful of all temporal things" (Ethic. iii, 6). Wherefore if the accused, who is on trial for his life, bribes his adversary, he sins indeed by inducing him to do what is unlawful, yet the civil law does not punish this sin, and in this sense it is said to be lawful.

Reply Obj. 2: If the accuser is guilty of collusion with the accused and the latter is guilty, he incurs punishment, and so it is evident that he sins. Wherefore, since it is a sin to induce a man to sin, or to take part in a sin in any way—for the Apostle says (Rom. 1:32), that "they ... are worthy of death ... that consent" to those who sin—it is evident that the accused also sins if he is guilty of collusion with his adversary. Nevertheless according to human laws no punishment is inflicted on him, for the reason given above.

Reply Obj. 3: The wise man hides himself not by slandering others but by exercising prudence.

THIRD ARTICLE [II-II, Q. 69, Art. 3]

Whether It Is Lawful for the Accused to Escape Judgment by Appealing?

Objection 1: It would seem unlawful for the accused to escape judgment by appealing. The Apostle says (Rom. 13:1): "Let every soul be subject to the higher powers." Now the accused by appealing refuses to be subject to a higher power, viz. the judge. Therefore he commits a sin.

Obj. 2: Further, ordinary authority is more binding than that which we choose for ourselves. Now according to the Decretals (II, qu. vi, cap. A judicibus) it is unlawful to appeal from the judges chosen by common consent. Much less therefore is it lawful to appeal from ordinary judges.

Obj. 3: Further, whatever is lawful once is always lawful. But it is not lawful to appeal after the tenth day [*Can. Anteriorum, caus. ii, qu. 6], nor a third time on the same point [*Can. Si autem, caus. ii, qu. 6]. Therefore it would seem that an appeal is unlawful in itself.

*On the contrary,* Paul appealed to Caesar (Acts 25).

*I answer that,* There are two motives for which a man appeals. First through confidence in the justice of his cause, seeing that he is unjustly oppressed by the judge, and then it is lawful for him to appeal, because this is a prudent means of escape. Hence it is laid down (Decret. II, qu. vi, can. Omnis oppressus): "All those who are oppressed are free, if they so wish, to appeal to the judgment of the priests, and no man may stand in their way." Secondly, a man appeals in order to cause a delay, lest a just sentence be pronounced against him. This is to defend oneself calumniously, and is unlawful as stated above (A. 2). For he inflicts an injury both on the judge, whom he hinders in the exercise of his office, and on his adversary, whose justice he disturbs as far as he is able. Hence it is laid down (II, qu. vi, can. Omnino puniendus): "Without doubt a man should be punished if his appeal be declared unjust."

Reply Obj. 1: A man should submit to the lower authority in so far as the latter observes the order of the higher authority. If the lower authority departs from the order of the higher, we ought not to submit to it, for instance "if the proconsul order one thing and the emperor another," according to a gloss on Rom. 13:2. Now when a judge oppresses anyone unjustly, in this respect he departs from the order of the higher authority, whereby he is obliged to judge justly. Hence it is lawful for a man who is oppressed unjustly, to have recourse to the authority of the higher power, by appealing either before or after sentence has been pronounced. And since it is to be presumed that there is no rectitude where true faith is lacking, it is unlawful for a Catholic to appeal to an unbelieving judge, according to Decret. II, qu. vi, can. *Catholicus:* "The Catholic who appeals to the decision of a judge of another faith shall be excommunicated, whether his case be just or unjust." Hence the Apostle also rebuked those who went to law before unbelievers (1 Cor. 6:6).

Reply Obj. 2: It is due to a man's own fault or neglect that, of his own accord, he submits to the judgment of one in whose justice he has no confidence. Moreover it would seem to point to levity of mind for a man not to abide by what he has once approved of. Hence it is with reason that the law refuses us the faculty of appealing from the decision of judges of our own choice, who have no power save by virtue of the consent of the litigants. On the other hand the authority of an ordinary judge depends, not on the consent of those who are subject to his judgment, but on the authority of the king or prince who appointed him. Hence, as a remedy against his unjust oppression, the law allows one to have recourse to appeal, so that even if the judge be at the same time ordinary and chosen by the litigants, it is lawful to appeal from his decision, since seemingly his ordinary authority occasioned his being chosen as arbitrator. Nor is it to be imputed as a fault to the man who consented to his being arbitrator, without adverting to the fact that he was appointed ordinary judge by the prince.

Reply Obj. 3: The equity of the law so guards the interests of the one party that the other is not oppressed. Thus it allows ten days for appeal to be made, this being considered sufficient time for deliberating on the expediency of an appeal. If on the other hand there were no fixed time limit for appealing, the certainty of judgment would ever be in suspense, so that the other party would suffer an injury. The reason why it is not allowed to appeal a third time on the same point, is that it is not probable that the judges would fail to judge justly so many times.

FOURTH ARTICLE [II-II, Q. 69, Art. 4]

Whether a Man Who Is Condemned to Death May Lawfully Defend Himself If He Can?

Objection 1: It would seem that a man who is condemned to death may lawfully defend himself if he can. For it is always lawful to do that to which nature inclines us, as being of natural right, so to speak. Now, to resist corruption is an inclination of nature not only in men and animals but also in things devoid of sense. Therefore if he can do so, the accused, after condemnation, may lawfully resist being put to death.

Obj. 2: Further, just as a man, by resistance, escapes the death to which he has been condemned, so does he by flight. Now it is lawful seemingly to escape death by flight, according to Ecclus. 9:18, "Keep thee far from the man that hath power to kill [and not to quicken]" [*The words in the brackets are not in the Vulgate]. Therefore it is also lawful for the accused to resist.

Obj. 3: Further, it is written (Prov. 24:11): "Deliver them that are led to death: and those that are drawn to death forbear not to deliver." Now a man is under greater obligation to himself than to another. Therefore it is lawful for a condemned man to defend himself from being put to death.

*On the contrary,* The Apostle says (Rom. 13:2): "He that resisteth the power, resisteth the ordinance of God: and they that resist, purchase to themselves damnation." Now a condemned man, by defending himself, resists the power in the point of its being ordained by God "for the punishment of evil-doers, and for the praise of the good" [*1 Pet. 2:14]. Therefore he sins in defending himself.

*I answer that,* A man may be condemned to death in two ways. First justly, and then it is not lawful for the condemned to defend himself, because it is lawful for the judge to combat his resistance by force, so that on his part the fight is unjust, and consequently without any doubt he sins.

Secondly a man is condemned unjustly: and such a sentence is like the violence of robbers, according to Ezech. 22:21, "Her princes in the midst of her are like wolves ravening the prey to shed blood." Wherefore even as it is lawful to resist robbers, so is it lawful, in a like case, to resist wicked princes; except perhaps in order to avoid scandal, whence some grave disturbance might be feared to arise.

Reply Obj. 1: Reason was given to man that he might ensue those things to which his nature inclines, not in all cases, but in accordance with the order of reason. Hence not all self-defense is lawful, but only such as is accomplished with due moderation.

Reply Obj. 2: When a man is condemned to death, he has not to kill himself, but to suffer death: wherefore he is not bound to do anything from which death would result, such as to stay in the place whence he would be led to execution. But he may not resist those who lead him to death, in order that he may not suffer what is just for him to suffer. Even so, if a man were condemned to die of hunger, he does not sin if he partakes of food brought to him secretly, because to refrain from taking it would be to kill himself.

Reply Obj. 3: This saying of the wise man does not direct that one should deliver a man from death in opposition to the order of justice: wherefore neither should a man deliver himself from death by resisting against justice.

## QUESTION 70

OF INJUSTICE WITH REGARD TO THE PERSON OF THE WITNESS (In Four Articles)

We must now consider injustice with regard to the person of the witness. Under this head there are four points of inquiry:

(1) Whether a man is bound to give evidence?

(2) Whether the evidence of two or three witnesses suffices?

(3) Whether a man's evidence may be rejected without any fault on his part?

(4) Whether it is a mortal sin to bear false witness?

FIRST ARTICLE [II-II, Q. 70, Art. 1]

Whether a Man Is Bound to Give Evidence?

Objection 1: It would seem that a man is not bound to give evidence. Augustine says (QQ. Gen. 1:26) [*Cf. Contra Faust. xxii, 33, 34], that when Abraham said of his wife (Gen. 20:2), "She is my sister," he wished the truth to be concealed and not a lie be told. Now, by hiding the truth a man abstains from giving evidence. Therefore a man is not bound to give evidence.

Obj. 2: Further, no man is bound to act deceitfully. Now it is written (Prov. 11:13): "He that walketh deceitfully revealeth secrets, but he that is faithful concealeth the thing committed to him by his friend." Therefore a man is not always bound to give evidence, especially on matters committed to him as a secret by a friend.

Obj. 3: Further, clerics and priests, more than others, are bound to those things that are necessary for salvation. Yet clerics and priests are forbidden to give evidence when a man is on trial for his life. Therefore it is not necessary for salvation to give evidence.

*On the contrary,* Augustine [*Can. Quisquis, caus. xi, qu. 3, cap. Falsidicus; cf. Isidore, Sentent. iii, 55] says: "Both he who conceals the truth and he who tells a lie are guilty, the former because he is unwilling to do good, the latter because he desires to hurt."

*I answer that,* We must make a distinction in the matter of giving evidence: because sometimes a certain man's evidence is necessary, and sometimes not. If the necessary evidence is that of a man subject to a superior whom, in matters pertaining to justice, he is bound to obey, without doubt he is bound to give evidence on those points which are required of him in accordance with the order of justice, for instance on manifest things or when ill-report has preceded. If however he is required to give evidence on other points, for instance secret matters, and those of which no ill-report has preceded, he is not bound to give evidence. On the other hand, if his evidence be required by authority of a superior whom he is bound to obey, we must make a distinction: because if his evidence is required in order to deliver a man from an unjust death or any other penalty, or from false defamation, or some loss, in such cases he is bound to give evidence. Even if his evidence is not demanded, he is bound to do what he can to declare the truth to someone who may profit thereby. For it is written (Ps. 81:4): "Rescue the poor, and deliver the needy from the hand of the sinner"; and (Prov. 24:11): "Deliver them that are led to death"; and (Rom. 1:32): "They are worthy of death, not only they that do them, but they also that consent to them that do them," on which words a gloss says: "To be silent when one can disprove is to consent." In matters pertaining to a man's condemnation, one is not bound to give evidence, except when one is constrained by a superior in accordance with the order of justice; since if the truth of such a matter be concealed, no particular injury is inflicted on anyone. Or, if some danger threatens the accuser, it matters not since he risked the danger of his own accord: whereas it is different with the accused, who incurs the danger against his will.

Reply Obj. 1: Augustine is speaking of concealment of the truth in a case when a man is not compelled by his superior's authority to declare the truth, and when such concealment is not specially injurious to any person.

Reply Obj. 2: A man should by no means give evidence on matters secretly committed to him in confession, because he knows such things, not as man but as God's minister: and the sacrament is more binding than any human precept. But as regards matters committed to man in some other way under secrecy, we must make a distinction. Sometimes they are of such a nature that one is bound to make them known as soon as they come to our knowledge, for instance if they conduce to the spiritual or corporal corruption of the community, or to some grave personal injury, in short any like matter that a man is bound to make known either by giving evidence or by denouncing it. Against such a duty a man cannot be obliged to act on the plea that the matter is committed to him under secrecy, for he would break the faith he owes to another. On the other hand sometimes they are such as one is not bound to make known, so that one may be under obligation not to do so on account of their being committed to one under secrecy. In such a case one is by no means bound to make them known, even if the superior should command; because to keep faith is of natural right, and a man cannot be commanded to do what is contrary to natural right.

Reply Obj. 3: It is unbecoming for ministers of the altar to slay a man or to cooperate in his slaying, as stated above (Q. 64, A. 4); hence according to the order of justice they cannot be compelled to give evidence when a man is on trial for his life.

SECOND ARTICLE [II-II, Q. 70, Art. 2]

Whether the Evidence of Two or Three Persons Suffices?

Objection 1: It would seem that the evidence of two or three persons is not sufficient. For judgment requires certitude. Now certitude of the truth is not obtained by the assertions of two or three witnesses, for we read that Naboth was unjustly condemned on the evidence of two witnesses (3 Kings 21). Therefore the evidence of two or three witnesses does not suffice.

Obj. 2: Further, in order for evidence to be credible it must agree. But frequently the evidence of two or three disagrees in some point. Therefore it is of no use for proving the truth in court.

Obj. 3: Further, it is laid down (Decret. II, qu. iv, can. Praesul.): "A bishop shall not be condemned save on the evidence of seventy-two witnesses; nor a cardinal priest of the Roman Church, unless there be sixty-four witnesses. Nor a cardinal deacon of the Roman Church, unless there be twenty-seven witnesses; nor a subdeacon, an acolyte, an exorcist, a reader or a doorkeeper without seven witnesses." Now the sin of one who is of higher dignity is more grievous, and consequently should be treated more severely. Therefore neither is the evidence of two or three witnesses sufficient for the condemnation of other persons.

*On the contrary,* It is written (Deut. 17:6): "By the mouth of two or three witnesses shall he die that is to be slain," and further on (Deut. 19:15): "In the mouth of two or three witnesses every word shall stand."

*I answer that,* According to the Philosopher (Ethic. i, 3), "we must not expect to find certitude equally in every matter." For in human acts, on which judgments are passed and evidence required, it is impossible to have demonstrative certitude, because they are about things contingent and variable. Hence the certitude of probability suffices, such as may reach the truth in the greater number of cases, although it fail in the minority. Now it is probable that the assertion of several witnesses contains the truth rather than the assertion of one: and since the accused is the only one who denies, while several witness affirm the same as the prosecutor, it is reasonably established both by Divine and by human law, that the assertion of several witnesses should be upheld. Now all multitude is comprised of three elements, the beginning, the middle and the end. Wherefore, according to the Philosopher (De Coelo i, 1), "we reckon 'all' and 'whole' to consist of three parts." Now we have a triple voucher when two agree with the prosecutor: hence two witnesses are required; or for the sake of greater certitude three, which is the perfect number. Wherefore it is written (Eccles. 4:12): "A threefold cord is not easily broken": and Augustine, commenting on John 8:17, "The testimony of two men is true," says (Tract. xxxvi) that "there is here a mystery by which we are given to understand that Trinity wherein is perpetual stability of truth."

Reply Obj. 1: No matter how great a number of

witnesses may be determined, the evidence might sometimes be unjust, since is written (Ex. 23:2): "Thou shalt not follow the multitude to do evil." And yet the fact that in so many it is not possible to have certitude without fear of error, is no reason why we should reject the certitude which can probably be had through two or three witnesses, as stated above.

Reply Obj. 2: If the witnesses disagree in certain principal circumstances which change the substance of the fact, for instance in time, place, or persons, which are chiefly in question, their evidence is of no weight, because if they disagree in such things, each one would seem to be giving distinct evidence and to be speaking of different facts. For instance, one say that a certain thing happened at such and such a time or place, while another says it happened at another time or place, they seem not to be speaking of the same event. The evidence is not weakened if one witness says that he does not remember, while the other attests to a determinate time or place. And if on such points as these the witness for prosecution and defense disagree altogether, and if they be equal in number on either side, and of equal standing, the accused should have the benefit of the doubt, because the judge ought to be more inclined to acquit than to condemn, except perhaps in favorable suits, such as a pleading for liberty and the like. If, however, the witnesses for the same side disagree, the judge ought to use his own discretion in discerning which side to favor, by considering either the number of witnesses, or their standing, or the favorableness of the suit, or the nature of the business and of the evidence.

Much more ought the evidence of one witness to be rejected if he contradict himself when questioned about what he has seen and about what he knows; not, however, if he contradict himself when questioned about matters of opinion and report, since he may be moved to answer differently according to the different things he has seen and heard.

On the other hand if there be discrepancy of evidence in circumstances not touching the substance of the fact, for instance, whether the weather were cloudy or fine, whether the house were painted or not, or such like matters, such discrepancy does not weaken the evidence, because men are not wont to take much notice of such things, wherefore they easily forget them. Indeed, a discrepancy of this kind renders the evidence more credible, as Chrysostom states (Hom. i in Matth.), because if the witnesses agreed in every point, even in the minutest of details, they would seem to have conspired together to say the same thing: but this must be left to the prudent discernment of the judge.

Reply Obj. 3: This passage refers specially to the bishops, priests, deacons and clerics of the Roman Church, on account of its dignity: and this for three reasons. First because in that Church those men ought to be promoted whose sanctity makes their evidence of more weight than that of many witnesses. Secondly, because those who have to judge other men, often have many opponents on account of their justice, wherefore those who give evidence against them should not be believed indiscriminately, unless they be very numerous. Thirdly, because the condemnation of any one of them would detract in public opinion from the dignity and authority of that Church, a result which would be more fraught with danger than if one were to tolerate a sinner in that same Church, unless he were very notorious and manifest, so that a grave scandal would arise if he were tolerated.

THIRD ARTICLE [II-II, Q. 70, Art. 3]

Whether a Man's Evidence Can Be Rejected Without Any Fault of His?

Objection 1: It would seem that a man's evidence ought not to be rejected except on account of some fault. For it is inflicted as a penalty on some that their evidence is inadmissible, as in the case of those who are branded with infamy. Now a penalty must not be inflicted save for a fault. Therefore it would seem that no man's evidence ought to be rejected save on account of a fault.

Obj. 2: Further, "Good is to be presumed of every one, unless the contrary appear" [*Cap. Dudum, de Praesumpt.]. Now it pertains to a man's goodness that he should give true evidence. Since therefore there can be no proof of the contrary, unless there be some fault of his, it would seem that no man's evidence should be rejected save for some fault.

Obj. 3: Further, no man is rendered unfit for things necessary for salvation except by some sin. But it is necessary for salvation to give true evidence, as stated above (A. 1). Therefore no man should be excluded from giving evidence save for some fault.

*On the contrary,* Gregory says (Regist. xiii, 44): "As to the bishop who is said to have been accused by his servants, you are to know that they should by no means have been heard": which words are embodied in the Decretals (II, qu. 1, can. Imprimis).

*I answer that,* As stated above (A. 2), the authority of evidence is not infallible but probable; and consequently the evidence for one side is weakened by whatever strengthens the probability of the other. Now the reliability of a person's evidence is weakened, sometimes indeed on account of some fault of his, as in the case of unbelievers and persons of evil repute, as well as those who are guilty of a public crime and who are not allowed even to accuse; sometimes, without any fault on his part, and this owing either to a defect in the reason, as in the case of children, imbeciles and women, or to personal feeling, as in the case of enemies, or persons united by family or household ties, or again owing to some external condition, as in the case of poor people, slaves, and those who are under authority, concerning whom it is to be presumed that they might easily be induced to give evidence against the truth.

Thus it is manifest that a person's evidence may be rejected either with or without some fault of his.

Reply Obj. 1: If a person is disqualified from giving evidence this is done as a precaution against false evidence rather than as a punishment. Hence the argument does not prove.

Reply Obj. 2: Good is to be presumed of everyone unless the contrary appear, provided this does not threaten injury to another: because, in that case, one ought to be careful not to believe everyone readily, according to 1 John 4:1: "Believe not every spirit."

Reply Obj. 3: To give evidence is necessary for salvation, provided the witness be competent, and the order of justice observed. Hence nothing hinders certain persons being excused from giving evidence, if they be considered unfit according to law.

FOURTH ARTICLE [II-II, Q. 70, Art. 4]

Whether It Is Always a Mortal Sin to Give False Evidence?

Objection 1: It would seem that it is not always a mortal sin to give false evidence. For a person may happen to give false evidence, through ignorance of fact. Now such ignorance excuses from mortal sin. Therefore the giving of false evidence is not always a mortal sin.

Obj. 2: Further, a lie that benefits someone and hurts no man is officious, and this is not a mortal sin. Now sometimes a lie of this kind occurs in false evidence, as when a person gives false evidence in order to save a man from death, or from an unjust sentence which threatens him through other false witnesses or a perverse judge. Therefore in such cases it is not a mortal sin to give false evidence.

Obj. 3: Further, a witness is required to take an oath in order that he may fear to commit a mortal sin of perjury. But this would not be necessary, if it were already a mortal sin to give false evidence. Therefore the giving of false evidence is not always mortal sin.

*On the contrary,* It is written (Prov. 19:5): "A false witness shall not be unpunished."

*I answer that,* False evidence has a threefold deformity. The first is owing to perjury, since witnesses are admitted only on oath and on this count it is always a mortal sin. Secondly, owing to the violation of justice, and on this account it is a mortal sin generically, even as any kind of injustice. Hence the prohibition of false evidence by the precept of the decalogue is expressed in this form when it is said (Ex. 20:16), "Thou shalt not bear false witness against thy neighbor." For one does nothing against a man by preventing him from doing someone an injury, but only by taking away his justice. Thirdly, owing to the falsehood itself, by reason of which every lie is a sin: on this account, the giving of false evidence is not always a mortal sin.

Reply Obj. 1: In giving evidence a man ought not to affirm as certain, as though he knew it, that about which he is not certain; and he should confess his doubt in doubtful terms, and that which he is certain about, in terms of certainty. Owing however to the frailty of the human memory, a man sometimes thinks he is certain about something that is not true; and then if after thinking over the matter with due care he deems himself certain about that false thing, he does not sin mortally if he asserts it, because the evidence which he gives is not directly and intentionally, but accidentally contrary to what he intends.

Reply Obj. 2: An unjust judgment is not a judgment, wherefore the false evidence given in an unjust judgment, in order to prevent injustice is not a mortal sin by virtue of the judgment, but only by reason of the oath violated.

Reply Obj. 3: Men abhor chiefly those sins that are against God, as being most grievous; and among them is perjury: whereas they do not abhor so much sins against their neighbor. Consequently, for the greater certitude of evidence, the witness is required to take a oath.

# QUESTION 71

OF INJUSTICE IN JUDGMENT ON THE PART OF COUNSEL (In Four Articles)

We must now consider the injustice which takes place in judgment on the part of counsel, and under this head there are four points of inquiry:

(1) Whether an advocate is bound to defend the suits of the poor?

(2) Whether certain persons should be prohibited from exercising the office of advocate?

(3) Whether an advocate sins by defending an unjust cause?

(4) Whether he sins if he accept a fee for defending a suit?

FIRST ARTICLE [II-II, Q. 71, Art. 1]

Whether an Advocate Is Bound to Defend the Suits of the Poor?

Objection 1: It would seem that an advocate is bound to defend the suits of the poor. For it is written (Ex. 23:5): "If thou see the ass of him that hateth thee lie underneath his burden, thou shalt not pass by, but shall lift him up with him." Now no less a danger threatens the poor man whose suit is being unjustly prejudiced, than if his ass were to lie underneath its burden. Therefore an advocate is bound to defend the suits of the poor.

Obj. 2: Further, Gregory says in a homily (ix in Evang.): "Let him that hath understanding beware lest he withhold his knowledge; let him that hath abundance of wealth watch lest he slacken his merciful bounty; let him who is a servant to art share his skill with his neighbor; let him who has an opportunity of speaking with the wealthy plead the cause of the poor: for the slightest gift you have received will be reputed a talent." Now every man is bound, not to hide but faithfully to dispense the talent committed to him; as evidenced by the punishment inflicted on the servant who hid his talent (Matt. 25:30). Therefore an advocate is bound to plead for the poor.

Obj. 3: Further, the precept about performing works of mercy, being affirmative, is binding according to time and place, and this is chiefly in cases of need. Now it seems to be a case of need when the suit of a poor man is being prejudiced. Therefore it seems that in such a case an advocate is bound to defend the poor man's suit.

*On the contrary,* He that lacks food is no less in need than he that lacks an advocate. Yet he that is able to give food is not always bound to feed the needy. Therefore neither is an advocate always bound to defend the suits of the poor.

*I answer that,* Since defense of the poor man's suit belongs to the works of mercy, the answer to this inquiry is the same as the one given above with regard to the other works of mercy (Q. 32, AA. 5, 9). Now no man is sufficient to bestow a work of mercy on all those who need it. Wherefore, as Augustine says (De Doctr. Christ. i, 28), "since one cannot do good to all, we ought to consider those chiefly who by reason of place, time, or any other circumstance, by a kind of chance are more closely united to us." He says "by reason of place," because one is not bound to search throughout the world for the needy that one may succor them; and it suffices to do works of mercy to those one meets with. Hence it is written (Ex. 23:4): "If thou meet thy enemy's ass going astray, bring it back to him." He says also "by reason of time," because one is not bound to provide for the future needs of others, and it suffices to succor present needs. Hence it is written (1 John 3:17): "He that ... shall see his brother in need, and shall put up his bowels from him, how doth the charity of God abide in him?" Lastly he says, "or any other circumstance," because one ought to show kindness to those especially who are by any tie whatever united to us, according to 1 Tim. 5:8, "If any man have not care of his own, and especially of those of his house, he hath denied the faith and is worse than an infidel."

It may happen however that these circumstances concur, and then we have to consider whether this particular man stands in such a need that it is not easy to see how he can be succored otherwise, and then one is bound to bestow the work of mercy on him. If, however, it is easy to see how he can be otherwise succored, either by himself, or by some other person still more closely united to him, or in a better position to help him, one is not bound so strictly to help the one in need that it would be a sin not to do so: although it would be praiseworthy to do so where one is not bound to. Therefore an advocate is not always bound to defend the suits of the poor, but only when the aforesaid circumstances concur, else he would have to put aside all other business, and occupy himself entirely in defending the suits of poor people. The same applies to a physician with regard to attendance on the sick.

Reply Obj. 1: So long as the ass lies under the burden, there is no means of help in this case, unless those who are passing along come to the man's aid, and therefore they are bound to help. But they would not be so bound if help were possible from another quarter.

Reply Obj. 2: A man is bound to make good use of the talent bestowed on him, according to the opportunities afforded by time, place, and other circumstances, as stated above.

Reply Obj. 3: Not every need is such that it is one's duty to remedy it, but only such as we have stated above.

SECOND ARTICLE [II-II, Q. 71, Art. 2]

Whether It Is Fitting That the Law Should Debar Certain Persons from the Office of Advocate?

Objection 1: It would seem unfitting for the law to debar certain persons from the office of advocate. For no man should be debarred from doing works of mercy. Now it belongs to the works of mercy to defend a man's suit, as stated above (A. 1). Therefore no man should be debarred from this office.

Obj. 2: Further, contrary causes have not, seemingly, the same effect. Now to be busy with Divine things and to be busy about sin are contrary to one another. Therefore it is unfitting that some should be debarred from the office of advocate, on account of religion, as monks and clerics, while others are debarred on account of sin, as persons of ill-repute and heretics.

Obj. 3: Further, a man should love his neighbor as himself. Now it is a duty of love for an advocate to plead a person's cause. Therefore it is unfitting that certain persons should be debarred from pleading the cause of others, while they are allowed to advocate their own cause.

*On the contrary,* According to Decret. III, qu. vii, can. Infames, many persons are debarred from the office of advocate.

*I answer that,* In two ways a person is debarred from performing a certain act: first because it is impossible to him, secondly because it is unbecoming to him: but, whereas the man to whom a certain act is impossible, is absolutely debarred from performing it, he to whom an act is unbecoming is not debarred altogether, since necessity may do away with its unbecomingness. Accordingly some are debarred from the office of advocate because it is impossible to them through lack of sense—either interior, as in the case of madmen and minors—or exterior, as in the case of the deaf and dumb. For an advocate needs to have both interior skill so that he may be able to prove the justice of the cause he defends, and also speech and hearing, that he may speak and hear what is said to him. Consequently those who are defective in these points, are altogether debarred from being advocates either in their own or in another's cause. The becomingness of exercising this office is removed in two ways. First, through a man being engaged in higher things. Wherefore it is unfitting that monks or priests should be advocates in any cause whatever, or that clerics should plead in a secular court, because such persons are engaged in Divine things. Secondly, on account of some personal defect, either of body (for instance a blind man whose attendance in a court of justice would be unbecoming) or of soul, for it ill becomes one who has disdained to be just himself, to plead for the justice of another. Wherefore it is unbecoming that persons of ill repute, unbelievers, and those who have been convicted of grievous crimes should be advocates. Nevertheless this unbecomingness is outweighed by necessity: and for this reason such persons can plead either their own cause or that of persons closely connected with them. Moreover, clerics can be advocates in the cause of their own church, and monks in the cause of their own monastery, if the abbot direct them to do so.

Reply Obj. 1: Certain persons are sometimes debarred by unbecomingness, and others by inability from performing works of mercy: for not all the works of mercy are becoming to all persons: thus it ill becomes a fool to give counsel, or the ignorant to teach.

Reply Obj. 2: Just as virtue is destroyed by "too much" and "too little," so does a person become incompetent by "more" and "less." For this reason some, like religious and clerics, are debarred from pleading in causes, because they are above such an office; and others because they are less than competent to exercise it, such as persons of ill-repute and unbelievers.

Reply Obj. 3: The necessity of pleading the causes of others is not so pressing as the necessity of pleading one's own cause, because others are able to help themselves otherwise: hence the comparison fails.

THIRD ARTICLE [II-II, Q. 71, Art. 3]

Whether an Advocate Sins by Defending an Unjust Cause?

Objection 1: It would seem that an advocate does not sin by defending an unjust cause. For just as a physician proves his skill by healing a desperate disease, so does an advocate prove his skill, if he can defend an unjust cause. Now a physician is praised if he heals a desperate malady. Therefore an advocate also commits no sin, but ought to be praised, if he defends an unjust cause.

Obj. 2: Further, it is always lawful to desist from committing a sin. Yet an advocate is punished if he throws up his brief (Decret. II, qu. iii, can. Si quem poenit.). Therefore an advocate does not sin by defending an unjust cause, when once he has undertaken its defense.

Obj. 3: Further, it would seem to be a greater sin for an advocate to use unjust means in defense of a just cause (e.g. by producing false witnesses, or alleging false laws), than to defend an unjust cause, since the former is a sin against the form, the latter against the matter of justice. Yet it is seemingly lawful for an advocate to make use of such underhand means, even as it is lawful for a soldier to lay ambushes in a battle. Therefore it would seem that an advocate does not sin by defending an unjust cause.

*On the contrary,* It is said (2 Paralip. 19:2): "Thou helpest the ungodly ... and therefore thou didst deserve ... the wrath of the Lord." Now an advocate by defending an unjust cause, helps the ungodly. Therefore he sins and deserves the wrath of the Lord.

*I answer that,* It is unlawful to cooperate in an evil deed, by counseling, helping, or in any way consenting, because to counsel or assist an action is, in a way, to do it, and the Apostle says (Rom. 1:32) that "they ... are worthy of death, not only they that do" a sin, "but they also that consent to them that do" it. Hence it was stated above (Q. 62, A. 7), that all such are bound to restitution. Now it is evident that an advocate provides both assistance and counsel to the party for whom he pleads. Wherefore, if knowingly he defends an unjust cause, without doubt he sins grievously, and is bound to restitution of the loss unjustly incurred by the other party by reason of the assistance he has provided. If, however, he defends an unjust cause unknowingly, thinking it just, he is to be excused according to the measure in which ignorance is excusable.

Reply Obj. 1: The physician injures no man by undertaking to heal a desperate malady, whereas the advocate who accepts service in an unjust cause, unjustly injures the party against whom he pleads unjustly. Hence the comparison fails. For though he may seem to deserve praise for showing skill in his art, nevertheless he sins by reason of injustice in his will, since he abuses his art for an evil end.

Reply Obj. 2: If an advocate believes from the outset that the cause is just, and discovers afterwards while the case is proceeding that it is unjust, he ought not to throw up his brief in such a way as to help the other side, or so as to reveal the secrets of his client to the other party. But he can and must give up the case, or induce his client to give way, or make some compromise without prejudice to the opposing party.

Reply Obj. 3: As stated above (Q. 40, A. 3), it is lawful for a soldier, or a general to lay ambushes in a just war, by prudently concealing what he has a mind to do, but not by means of fraudulent falsehoods, since we should keep faith even with a foe, as Tully says (De offic. iii, 29). Hence it is lawful for an advocate, in defending his case, prudently to conceal whatever might hinder its happy issue, but it is unlawful for him to employ any kind of falsehood.

FOURTH ARTICLE [II-II, Q. 71, Art. 4]

Whether It Is Lawful for an Advocate to Take a Fee for Pleading?

Objection 1: It would seem unlawful for an advocate to take a fee for pleading. Works of mercy should not be done with a view to human remuneration, according to Luke 14:12, "When thou makest a dinner or a supper, call not thy friends ... nor thy neighbors who are rich: lest perhaps they also invite thee again, and a recompense be made to thee." Now it is a work of mercy to plead another's cause, as stated above (A. 1). Therefore it is not lawful for an advocate to take payment in money for pleading.

Obj. 2: Further, spiritual things are not to be bartered with temporal things. But pleading a person's cause seems to be a spiritual good since it consists in using one's knowledge of law. Therefore it is not lawful for an advocate to take a fee for pleading.

Obj. 3: Further, just as the person of the advocate concurs towards the pronouncement of the verdict, so do the persons of the judge and of the witness. Now, according to Augustine (Ep. cliii ad Macedon.), "the judge should not sell a just sentence, nor the witness true evidence." Therefore neither can an advocate sell a just pleading.

*On the contrary,* Augustine says (Ep. cliii ad Macedon.) that "an advocate may lawfully sell his pleading, and a lawyer his advice."

*I answer that,* A man may justly receive payment for granting what he is not bound to grant. Now it is evident that an advocate is not always bound to consent to plead, or to give advice in other people's causes. Wherefore, if he sell his pleading or advice, he does not act against justice. The same applies to the physician who attends on a sick person to heal him, and to all like persons; provided, however, they take a moderate fee, with due consideration for persons, for the matter in hand, for the labor entailed, and for the custom of the country. If, however, they wickedly extort an immoderate fee, they sin against justice. Hence Augustine says (Ep. cliii ad Macedon.) that "it is customary to demand from them restitution of what they have extorted by a wicked excess, but not what has been given to them in accordance with a commendable custom."

Reply Obj. 1: Man is not bound to do gratuitously whatever he can do from motives of mercy: else no man could lawfully sell anything, since anything may be given from motives of mercy. But when a man does give a thing out of mercy, he should seek, not a human, but a Divine reward. In like manner an advocate, when he mercifully pleads the cause of a poor man, should have in view not a human but a Divine meed; and yet he is not always bound to give his services gratuitously.

Reply Obj. 2: Though knowledge of law is something spiritual, the use of that knowledge is accomplished by the work of the body: hence it is lawful to take money in payment of that use, else no craftsman would be allowed to make profit by his art.

Reply Obj. 3: The judge and witnesses are common to either party, since the judge is bound to pronounce a just verdict, and the witness to give true evidence. Now justice and truth do not incline to one side rather than to the other: and consequently judges receive out of the public funds a fixed pay for their labor; and witnesses receive their expenses (not as payment for giving evidence, but as a fee for their labor) either from both parties or from the party by whom they are adduced, because no man "serveth as a soldier at any time at his own charge [*Vulg.: 'Who serveth as a soldier,']" (1 Cor. 9:7). On the other hand an advocate defends one party only, and so he may lawfully accept fee from the party he assists.

# QUESTION 72

OF REVILING (In Four Articles)

We must now consider injuries inflicted by words uttered extrajudicially. We shall consider (1) reviling, (2) backbiting, (3) tale bearing, (4) derision, (5) cursing.

Under the first head there are four points of inquiry:

(1) What is reviling?

(2) Whether every reviling is a mortal sin?

(3) Whether one ought to check revilers?

(4) Of the origin of reviling.

FIRST ARTICLE [II-II, Q. 72, Art. 1]

Whether Reviling Consists in Words?

Objection 1: It would seem that reviling does not consist in words. Reviling implies some injury inflicted on one's neighbor, since it is a kind of injustice. But words seem to inflict no injury on one's neighbor, either in his person, or in his belongings. Therefore reviling does not consist in words.

Obj. 2: Further, reviling seems to imply dishonor. But a man can be dishonored or slighted by deeds more than by words. Therefore it seems that reviling consists, not in words but in deeds.

Obj. 3: Further, a dishonor inflicted by words is called a railing or a taunt. But reviling seems to differ from railing or taunt. Therefore reviling does not consist in words.

*On the contrary,* Nothing, save words, is perceived by the hearing. Now reviling is perceived by the hearing according to Jer. 20:10, "I heard reviling [Douay: 'contumelies'] on every side." Therefore reviling consists in words.

*I answer that,* Reviling denotes the dishonoring of a person, and this happens in two ways: for since honor results from excellence, one person dishonors another, first, by depriving him of the excellence for which he is honored. This is done by sins of deed, whereof we have spoken above (Q. 64, seqq.). Secondly, when a man publishes something against another's honor, thus bringing it to the knowledge of the latter and of other men. This reviling properly so called, and is done by some kind of signs. Now, according to Augustine (De Doctr. Christ. ii, 3), "compared with words all other signs are very few, for words have obtained the chief place among men for the purpose of expressing whatever the mind conceives." Hence reviling, properly speaking, consists in words: wherefore, Isidore says (Etym. x) that a reviler ( *contumeliosus* ) "is hasty and bursts out ( *tumet* ) in injurious words." Since, however, things are also signified by deeds, which on this account have the same significance as words, it follows that reviling in a wider sense extends also to deeds. Wherefore a gloss on Rom. 1:30, "contumelious, proud," says: "The contumelious are those who by word or deed revile and shame others."

Reply Obj. 1: Our words, if we consider them in their essence, i.e. as audible sounds, injure no man, except perhaps by jarring of the ear, as when a person speaks too loud. But, considered as signs conveying something to the knowledge of others, they may do many kinds of harm. Such is the harm done to a man to the detriment of his honor, or of the respect due to him from others. Hence the reviling is greater if one man reproach another in the presence of many: and yet there may still be reviling if he reproach him by himself, in so far as the speaker acts unjustly against the respect due to the hearer.

Reply Obj. 2: One man slights another by deeds in so far as such deeds cause or signify that which is against that other man's honor. In the former case it is not a matter of reviling but of some other kind of injustice, of which we have spoken above (QQ. 64, 65, 66): where as in the latter case there is reviling, in so far as deeds have the significant force of words.

Reply Obj. 3: Railing and taunts consist in words, even as reviling, because by all of them a man's faults are exposed to the detriment of his honor. Such faults are of three kinds. First, there is the fault of guilt, which is exposed by *reviling* words. Secondly, there is the fault of both guilt and punishment, which is exposed by *taunts* ( *convicium* ), because vice is commonly spoken of in connection with not only the soul but also the body. Hence if one man says spitefully to another that he is blind, he taunts but does not revile him: whereas if one man calls another a thief, he not only taunts but also reviles him. Thirdly, a man reproaches another for his inferiority or indigence, so as to lessen the honor due to him for any kind of excellence. This is done by *upbraiding* words, and properly speaking, occurs when one spitefully reminds a man that one has succored him when he was in need. Hence it is written (Ecclus. 20:15): "He will give a few things and upbraid much." Nevertheless these terms are sometimes employed one for the other.

SECOND ARTICLE [II-II, Q. 72, Art. 2]

Whether Reviling or Railing Is a Mortal Sin?

Objection 1: It would seem that reviling or railing is not a mortal sin. For no mortal sin is an act of virtue. Now railing is the act of a virtue, viz. of wittiness ( *eutrapelia* ) [*Cf. I-II, Q. 60, A. 5] to which it pertains to rail well, according to the Philosopher (Ethic. iv, 8). Therefore railing or reviling is not a mortal sin.

Obj. 2: Further, mortal sin is not to be found in perfect men; and yet these sometimes give utterance to railing or reviling. Thus the Apostle says (Gal. 3:1): "O senseless Galatians!," and our Lord said (Luke 24:25): "O foolish and slow of heart to believe!" Therefore railing or reviling is not a mortal sin.

Obj. 3: Further, although that which is a venial sin by reason of its genus may become mortal, that which is mortal by reason of its genus cannot become venial, as stated above (I-II, Q. 88, AA. 4, 6). Hence if by reason of its genus it were a mortal sin to give utterance to railing or reviling, it would follow that it is always a mortal sin. But this is apparently untrue, as may be seen in the case of one who utters a reviling word indeliberately or through slight anger. Therefore reviling or railing is not a mortal sin, by reason of its genus.

*On the contrary,* Nothing but mortal sin deserves the eternal punishment of hell. Now railing or reviling deserves the punishment of hell, according to Matt. 5:22, "Whosoever shall say to his brother ... Thou fool, shall be in danger of hell fire." Therefore railing or reviling is a mortal sin.

*I answer that,* As stated above (A. 1), words are injurious to other persons, not as sounds, but as signs, and this signification depends on the speaker's inward intention. Hence, in sins of word, it seems that we ought to consider with what intention the words are uttered. Since then railing or reviling essentially denotes a dishonoring, if the intention of the utterer is to dishonor the other man, this is properly and essentially to give utterance to railing or reviling: and this is a mortal sin no less than theft or robbery, since a man loves his honor no less than his possessions. If, on the other hand, a man says to another a railing or reviling word, yet with the intention, not of dishonoring him, but rather perhaps of correcting him or with some like purpose, he utters a railing or reviling not formally and essentially, but accidentally and materially, in so far to wit as he says that which might be a railing or reviling. Hence this may be sometimes a venial sin, and sometimes without any sin at all. Nevertheless there is need of discretion in such matters, and one should use such words with moderation, because the railing might be so grave that being uttered inconsiderately it might dishonor the person against whom it is uttered. In such a case a man might commit a mortal sin, even though he did not intend to dishonor the other man: just as were a man incautiously to injure grievously another by striking him in fun, he would not be without blame.

Reply Obj. 1: It belongs to wittiness to utter some slight mockery, not with intent to dishonor or pain the person who is the object of the mockery, but rather with intent to please and amuse: and this may be without sin, if the due circumstances be observed. On the other hand if a man does not shrink from inflicting pain on the object of his witty mockery, so long as he makes others laugh, this is sinful, as stated in the passage quoted.

Reply Obj. 2: Just as it is lawful to strike a person, or damnify him in his belongings for the purpose of correction, so too, for the purpose of correction, may one say a mocking word to a person whom one has to correct. It is thus that our Lord called the disciples "foolish," and the Apostle called the Galatians "senseless." Yet, as Augustine says (De Serm. Dom. in Monte ii, 19), "seldom and only when it is very necessary should we have recourse to invectives, and then so as to urge God's service, not our own."

Reply Obj. 3: Since the sin of railing or reviling depends on the intention of the utterer, it may happen to be a venial sin, if it be a slight railing that does not inflict much dishonor on a man, and be uttered through lightness of heart or some slight anger, without the fixed purpose of dishonoring him, for instance when one intends by such a word to give but little pain.

THIRD ARTICLE [II-II, Q. 72, Art. 3]

Whether One Ought to Suffer Oneself to Be Reviled?

Objection 1: It would seem that one ought not to suffer oneself to be reviled. For he that suffers himself to be reviled, encourages the reviler. But one ought not to do this. Therefore one ought not to suffer oneself to be reviled, but rather reply to the reviler.

Obj. 2: Further, one ought to love oneself more than another. Now one ought not to suffer another to be reviled, wherefore it is written (Prov. 26:10): "He that putteth a fool to silence appeaseth anger." Therefore neither should one suffer oneself to be reviled.

Obj. 3: Further, a man is not allowed to revenge himself, for it is said: "Vengeance belongeth to Me, I will repay" [*Heb. 10:30]. Now by submitting to be reviled a man revenges himself, according to Chrysostom (Hom. xxii, in Ep. ad Rom.): "If thou wilt be revenged, be silent; thou hast dealt him a fatal blow." Therefore one ought not by silence to submit to reviling words, but rather answer back.

*On the contrary,* It is written (Ps. 37:13): "They that sought evils to me spoke vain things," and afterwards (Ps. 37:14) he says: "But I as a deaf man, heard not; and as a dumb man not opening his mouth."

*I answer that,* Just as we need patience in things done against us, so do we need it in those said against us. Now the precepts of patience in those things done against us refer to the preparedness of the mind, according to Augustine's (De Serm. Dom. in Monte i, 19) exposition on our Lord's precept, "If one strike thee on thy right cheek, turn to him also the other" [*The words as quoted by St. Thomas are a blending of Matt. 5:39 and Luke 6:29]: that is to say, a man ought to be prepared to do so if necessary. But he is not always bound to do this actually: since not even did our Lord do so, for when He received a blow, He said: "Why strikest thou Me?" (John 18:23). Consequently the same applies to the reviling words that are said against us. For we are bound to hold our minds prepared to submit to be reviled, if it should be expedient. Nevertheless it sometimes behooves us to withstand against being reviled, and this chiefly for two reasons. First, for the good of the reviler; namely, that his daring may be checked, and that he may not repeat the attempt, according to Prov. 26:5, "Answer a fool according to his folly, lest he imagine himself to be wise." Secondly, for the good of many who would be prevented from progressing in virtue on account of our being reviled. Hence Gregory says (Hom. ix, Super Ezech.): "Those who are so placed that their life should be an example to others, ought, if possible, to silence their detractors, lest their preaching be not heard by those who could have heard it, and they continue their evil conduct through contempt of a good life."

Reply Obj. 1: The daring of the railing reviler should be checked with moderation, i.e. as a duty of charity, and not through lust for one's own honor. Hence it is written (Prov. 26:4): "Answer not a fool according to his folly, lest thou be like him."

Reply Obj. 2: When one man prevents another from being reviled there is not the danger of lust for one's own honor as there is when a man defends himself from being reviled: indeed rather would it seem to proceed from a sense of charity.

Reply Obj. 3: It would be an act of revenge to keep silence with the intention of provoking the reviler to anger, but it would be praiseworthy to be silent, in order to give place to anger. Hence it is written (Ecclus. 8:4): "Strive not with a man that is full of tongue, and heap not wood upon his fire."

FOURTH ARTICLE [II-II, Q. 72, Art. 4]

Whether Reviling Arises from Anger?

Objection 1: It would seem that reviling does not arise from anger. For it is written (Prov. 11:2): "Where pride is, there shall also be reviling [Douay: 'reproach']." But anger is a vice distinct from pride. Therefore reviling does not arise from anger.

Obj. 2: Further, it is written (Prov. 20:3): "All fools are meddling with revilings [Douay: 'reproaches']." Now folly is a vice opposed to wisdom, as stated above (Q. 46, A. 1); whereas anger is opposed to meekness. Therefore reviling does not arise from anger.

Obj. 3: Further, no sin is diminished by its cause. But the sin of reviling is diminished if one gives vent to it through anger: for it is a more grievous sin to revile out of hatred than out of anger. Therefore reviling does not arise from anger.

*On the contrary,* Gregory says (Moral. xxxi, 45) that "anger gives rise to revilings."

*I answer that,* While one sin may arise from various causes, it is nevertheless said to have its source chiefly in that one from which it is wont to arise most frequently, through being closely connected with its end. Now reviling is closely connected with anger's end, which is revenge: since the easiest way for the angry man to take revenge on another is to revile him. Therefore reviling arises chiefly from anger.

Reply Obj. 1: Reviling is not directed to the end of pride which is excellency. Hence reviling does not arise directly from pride. Nevertheless pride disposes a man to revile, in so far as those who think themselves to excel, are more prone to despise others and inflict injuries on them, because they are more easily angered, through deeming it an affront to themselves whenever anything is done against their will.

Reply Obj. 2: According to the Philosopher (Ethic. vii, 6) "anger listens imperfectly to reason": wherefore an angry man suffers a defect of reason, and in this he is like the foolish man. Hence reviling arises from folly on account of the latter's kinship with anger.

Reply Obj. 3: According to the Philosopher (Rhet. ii, 4) "an angry man seeks an open offense, but he who hates does not worry about this." Hence reviling which denotes a manifest injury belongs to anger rather than to hatred.

## QUESTION 73

OF BACKBITING [*Or detraction] (In Four Articles)

We must now consider backbiting, under which head there are four points of inquiry:

(1) What is backbiting?

(2) Whether it is a mortal sin?

(3) Of its comparison with other sins;

(4) Whether it is a sin to listen to backbiting?

FIRST ARTICLE [II-II, Q. 73, Art. 1]

Whether Backbiting Is Suitably Defined As the Blackening of Another's Character by Secret Words?

Objection 1: It would seem that backbiting is not as defined by some [*Albert the Great, Sum. Theol. II, cxvii.], "the blackening of another's good name by words uttered in secret." For "secretly" and "openly" are circumstances that do not constitute the species of a sin, because it is accidental to a sin that it be known by many or by few. Now that which does not constitute the species of a sin, does not belong to its essence, and should not be included in its definition. Therefore it does not belong to the essence of backbiting that it should be done by secret words.

Obj. 2: Further, the notion of a good name implies something known to the public. If, therefore, a person's good name is blackened by backbiting, this cannot be done by secret words, but by words uttered openly.

Obj. 3: Further, to detract is to subtract, or to diminish something already existing. But sometimes a man's good name is blackened, even without subtracting from the truth: for instance, when one reveals the crimes which a man has in truth committed. Therefore not every blackening of a good name is backbiting.

*On the contrary,* It is written (Eccles. 10:11): "If a serpent bite in silence, he is nothing better that backbiteth."

*I answer that,* Just as one man injures another by deed in two ways—openly, as by robbery or by doing him any kind of violence—and secretly, as by theft, or by a crafty blow, so again one man injures another by words in two ways—in one way, openly, and this is done by reviling him, as stated above (Q. 72, A. 1)—and in another way secretly, and this is done by backbiting. Now from the fact that one man openly utters words against another man, he would appear to think little of him, so that for this reason he dishonors him, so that reviling is detrimental to the honor of the person reviled. On the other hand, he that speaks against another secretly, seems to respect rather than slight him, so that he injures directly, not his honor but his good name, in so far as by uttering such words secretly, he, for his own part, causes his hearers to have a bad opinion of the person against whom he speaks. For the backbiter apparently intends and aims at being believed. It is therefore evident that backbiting differs from reviling in two points: first, in the way in which the words are uttered, the reviler speaking openly against someone, and the backbiter secretly; secondly, as to the end in view, i.e. as regards the injury inflicted, the reviler injuring a man's honor, the backbiter injuring his good name.

Reply Obj. 1: In involuntary commutations, to which are reduced all injuries inflicted on our neighbor, whether by word or by deed, the kind of sin is differentiated by the circumstances "secretly" and "openly," because involuntariness itself is diversified by violence and by ignorance, as stated above (Q. 65, A. 4; I-II, Q. 6, AA. 5, 8).

Reply Obj. 2: The words of a backbiter are said to be secret, not altogether, but in relation to the person of whom they are said, because they are uttered in his absence and without his knowledge. On the other hand, the reviler speaks against a man to his face. Wherefore if a man speaks ill of another in the presence of several, it is a case of backbiting if he be absent, but of reviling if he alone be present: although if a man speak ill of an absent person to one man alone, he destroys his good name not altogether but partly.

Reply Obj. 3: A man is said to backbite ( *detrahere* ) another, not because he detracts from the truth, but because he lessens his good name. This is done sometimes directly, sometimes indirectly. Directly, in four ways: first, by saying that which is false about him; secondly, by stating his sin to be greater than it is; thirdly, by revealing something unknown about him; fourthly, by ascribing his good deeds to a bad intention. Indirectly, this is done either by gainsaying his good, or by maliciously concealing it, or by diminishing it.

SECOND ARTICLE [II-II, Q. 73, Art. 2]

Whether Backbiting Is a Mortal Sin?

Objection 1: It would seem that backbiting is not a mortal sin. For no act of virtue is a mortal sin. Now, to reveal an unknown sin, which pertains to backbiting, as stated above (A. 1, ad 3), is an act of the virtue of charity, whereby a man denounces his brother's sin in order that he may amend: or else it is an act of justice, whereby a man accuses his brother. Therefore backbiting is not a mortal sin.

Obj. 2: Further, a gloss on Prov. 24:21, "Have nothing to do with detractors," says: "The whole human race is in peril from this vice." But no mortal sin is to be found in the whole of mankind, since many refrain from mortal sin: whereas they are venial sins that are found in all. Therefore backbiting is a venial sin.

Obj. 3: Further, Augustine in a homily *on the Fire of Purgatory* [*Serm. civ in the appendix to St. Augustine's work] reckons it a slight sin "to speak ill without hesitation or forethought." But this pertains to backbiting. Therefore backbiting is a venial sin.

*On the contrary,* It is written (Rom. 1:30): "Backbiters, hateful to God," which epithet, according to a gloss, is inserted, "lest it be deemed a slight sin because it consists in words."

*I answer that,* As stated above (Q. 72, A. 2), sins of word should be judged chiefly from the intention of the speaker. Now backbiting by its very nature aims at blackening a man's good name. Wherefore, properly speaking, to backbite is to speak ill of an absent person in order to blacken his good name. Now it is a very grave matter to blacken a man's good name, because of all temporal things a man's good name seems the most precious, since for lack of it he is hindered from doing many things well. For this reason it is written (Ecclus. 41:15): "Take care of a good name, for this shall continue with thee, more than a thousand treasures precious and great." Therefore backbiting, properly speaking, is a mortal sin. Nevertheless it happens sometimes that a man utters words, whereby someone's good name is tarnished, and yet he does not intend this, but something else. This is not backbiting strictly and formally speaking, but only materially and accidentally as it were. And if such defamatory words be uttered for the sake of some necessary good, and with attention to the due circumstances, it is not a sin and cannot be called backbiting. But if they be uttered out of lightness of heart or for some unnecessary motive, it is not a mortal sin, unless perchance the spoken word be of such a grave nature, as to cause a notable injury to a man's good name, especially in matters pertaining to his moral character, because from the very nature of the words this would be a mortal sin. And one is bound to restore a man his good name, no less than any other thing one has taken from him, in the manner stated above (Q. 62, A. 2) when we were treating of restitution.

Reply Obj. 1: As stated above, it is not backbiting to reveal a man's hidden sin in order that he may mend, whether one denounce it, or accuse him for the good of public justice.

Reply Obj. 2: This gloss does not assert that backbiting is to be found throughout the whole of mankind, but "almost," both because "the number of fools is infinite," [*Eccles. 1:15] and few are they that walk in the way of salvation, [*Cf. Matt. 7:14] and because there are few or none at all who do not at times speak from lightness of heart, so as to injure someone's good name at least slightly, for it is written (James 3:2): "If any man offend not in word, the same is a perfect man."

Reply Obj. 3: Augustine is referring to the case when a man utters a slight evil about someone, not intending to injure him, but through lightness of heart or a slip of the tongue.

THIRD ARTICLE [II-II, Q. 73, Art. 3]

Whether Backbiting Is the Gravest of All Sins Committed Against One's Neighbor?

Objection 1: It would seem that backbiting is the gravest of all sins committed against one's neighbor. Because a gloss on Ps. 108:4, "Instead of making me a return of love they detracted me," a gloss says: "Those who detract Christ in His members and slay the souls of future believers are more guilty than those who killed the flesh that was soon to rise again." From this it seems to follow that backbiting is by so much a graver sin than murder, as it is a graver matter to kill the soul than to kill the body. Now murder is the gravest of the other sins that are committed against one's neighbor. Therefore backbiting is absolutely the gravest of all.

Obj. 2: Further, backbiting is apparently a graver sin than reviling, because a man can withstand reviling, but not a secret backbiting. Now backbiting is seemingly a graver sin than adultery, because adultery unites two persons in one flesh, whereas reviling severs utterly those who were united. Therefore backbiting is more grievous than adultery: and yet of all other sins a man commits against his neighbor, adultery is most grave.

Obj. 3: Further, reviling arises from anger, while backbiting arises from envy, according to Gregory (Moral. xxxi, 45). But envy is a graver sin than anger. Therefore backbiting is a graver sin than reviling; and so the same conclusion follows as before.

Obj. 4: Further, the gravity of a sin is measured by the gravity of the defect that it causes. Now backbiting causes a most grievous defect, viz. blindness of mind. For Gregory says (Regist. xi, Ep. 2): "What else do backbiters but blow on the dust and stir up the dirt into their eyes, so that the more they breathe of detraction, the less they see of the truth?" Therefore backbiting is the most grievous sin committed against one's neighbor.

*On the contrary,* It is more grievous to sin by deed than by word. But backbiting is a sin of word, while adultery, murder, and theft are sins of deed. Therefore backbiting is not graver than the other sins committed against one's neighbor.

*I answer that,* The essential gravity of sins committed against one's neighbor must be weighed by the injury they inflict on him, since it is thence that they derive their sinful nature. Now the greater the good taken away, the greater the injury. And while man's good is threefold, namely the good of his soul, the good of his body, and the good of external things; the good of the soul, which is the greatest of all, cannot be taken from him by another save as an occasional cause, for instance by an evil persuasion, which does not induce necessity. On the other hand the two latter goods, viz. of the body and of external things, can be taken away by violence. Since, however, the goods of the body excel the goods of external things, those sins which injure a man's body are more grievous than those which injure his external things. Consequently, among other sins committed against one's neighbor, murder is the most grievous, since it deprives man of the life which he already possesses: after this comes adultery, which is contrary to the right order of human generation, whereby man enters upon life. In the last place come external goods, among which a man's good name takes precedence of wealth because it is more akin to spiritual goods, wherefore it is written (Prov. 22:1): "A good name is better than great riches." Therefore backbiting according to its genus is a more grievous sin than theft, but is less grievous than murder or adultery. Nevertheless the order may differ by reason of aggravating or extenuating circumstances.

The accidental gravity of a sin is to be considered in relation to the sinner, who sins more grievously, if he sins deliberately than if he sins through weakness or carelessness. In this respect sins of word have a certain levity, in so far as they are apt to occur through a slip of the tongue, and without much forethought.

Reply Obj. 1: Those who detract Christ by hindering the faith of His members, disparage His Godhead, which is the foundation of our faith. Wherefore this is not simple backbiting but blasphemy.

Reply Obj. 2: Reviling is a more grievous sin than backbiting, in as much as it implies greater contempt of one's neighbor: even as robbery is a graver sin than theft, as stated above (Q. 66, A. 9). Yet reviling is not a more grievous sin than adultery. For the gravity of adultery is measured, not from its being a union of bodies, but from being a disorder in human generation. Moreover the reviler is not the sufficient cause of unfriendliness in another man, but is only the occasional cause of division among those who were united, in so far, to wit, as by declaring the evils of another, he for his own part severs that man from the friendship of other men, though they are not forced by his words to do so. Accordingly a backbiter is a murderer *occasionally,* since by his words he gives another man an occasion for hating or despising his neighbor. For this reason it is stated in the Epistle of Clement [*Ad Jacob. Ep. i] that "backbiters are murderers," i.e. occasionally; because "he that hateth his brother is a murderer" (1 John 3:15).

Reply Obj. 3: Anger seeks openly to be avenged, as the Philosopher states (Rhet. ii, 2): wherefore backbiting which takes place in secret, is not the daughter of anger, as reviling is, but rather of envy, which strives by any means to lessen one's neighbor's glory. Nor does it follow from this that backbiting is more grievous than reviling: since a lesser vice can give rise to a greater sin, just as anger gives birth to murder and blasphemy. For the origin of a sin depends on its inclination to an end, i.e. on the thing to which the sin turns, whereas the gravity of a sin depends on what it turns away from.

Reply Obj. 4: Since "a man rejoiceth in the sentence of his mouth" (Prov. 15:23), it follows that a backbiter more and more loves and believes what he says, and consequently more and more hates his neighbor, and thus his knowledge of the truth becomes less and less. This effect however may also result from other sins pertaining to hate of one's neighbor.

FOURTH ARTICLE [II-II, Q. 73, Art. 4]

Whether It Is a Grave Sin for the Listener to Suffer the Backbiter?

Objection 1: It would seem that the listener who suffers a backbiter does not sin grievously. For a man is not under greater obligations to others than to himself. But it is praiseworthy for a man to suffer his own backbiters: for Gregory says (Hom. ix, super Ezech): "Just as we ought not to incite the tongue of backbiters, lest they perish, so ought we to suffer them with equanimity when they have been incited by their own wickedness, in order that our merit may be the greater." Therefore a man does not sin if he does not withstand those who backbite others.

Obj. 2: Further, it is written (Ecclus. 4:30): "In

no wise speak against the truth." Now sometimes a person tells the truth while backbiting, as stated above (A. 1, ad 3). Therefore it seems that one is not always bound to withstand a backbiter.

Obj. 3: Further, no man should hinder what is profitable to others. Now backbiting is often profitable to those who are backbitten: for Pope Pius [*St. Pius I] says [*Append. Grat. ad can. Oves, caus. vi, qu. 1]: "Not unfrequently backbiting is directed against good persons, with the result that those who have been unduly exalted through the flattery of their kindred, or the favor of others, are humbled by backbiting." Therefore one ought not to withstand backbiters.

*On the contrary,* Jerome says (Ep. ad Nepot. lii): "Take care not to have an itching tongue, nor tingling ears, that is, neither detract others nor listen to backbiters."

*I answer that,* According to the Apostle (Rom. 1:32), they "are worthy of death ... not only they that" commit sins, "but they also that consent to them that do them." Now this happens in two ways. First, directly, when, to wit, one man induces another to sin, or when the sin is pleasing to him: secondly, indirectly, that is, if he does not withstand him when he might do so, and this happens sometimes, not because the sin is pleasing to him, but on account of some human fear.

Accordingly we must say that if a man listens to backbiting without resisting it, he seems to consent to the backbiter, so that he becomes a participator in his sin. And if he induces him to backbite, or at least if the detraction be pleasing to him on account of his hatred of the person detracted, he sins no less than the detractor, and sometimes more. Wherefore Bernard says (De Consid. ii, 13): "It is difficult to say which is the more to be condemned[:] the backbiter or he that listens to backbiting." If however the sin is not pleasing to him, and he fails to withstand the backbiter, through fear, negligence, or even shame, he sins indeed, but much less than the backbiter, and, as a rule venially. Sometimes too this may be a mortal sin, either because it is his official duty to correct the backbiter, or by reason of some consequent danger; or on account of the radical reason for which human fear may sometimes be a mortal sin, as stated above (Q. 19, A. 3).

Reply Obj. 1: No man hears himself backbitten, because when a man is spoken evil of in his hearing, it is not backbiting, properly speaking, but reviling, as stated above (A. 1, ad 2). Yet it is possible for the detractions uttered against a person to come to his knowledge through others telling him, and then it is left to his discretion whether he will suffer their detriment to his good name, unless this endanger the good of others, as stated above (Q. 72, A. 3). Wherefore his patience may deserve commendation for as much as he suffers patiently being detracted himself. But it is not left to his discretion to permit an injury to be done to another's good name, hence he is accounted guilty if he fails to resist when he can, for the same reason whereby a man is bound to raise another man's ass lying "underneath his burden," as commanded in Deut. 21:4 [*Ex. 23:5].

Reply Obj. 2: One ought not always to withstand a backbiter by endeavoring to convince him of falsehood, especially if one knows that he is speaking the truth: rather ought one to reprove him with words, for that he sins in backbiting his brother, or at least by our pained demeanor show him that we are displeased with his backbiting, because according to Prov. 25:23, "the north wind driveth away rain, as doth a sad countenance a backbiting tongue."

Reply Obj. 3: The profit one derives from being backbitten is due, not to the intention of the backbiter, but to the ordinance of God Who produces good out of every evil. Hence we should none the less withstand backbiters, just as those who rob or oppress others, even though the oppressed and the robbed may gain merit by patience.

# QUESTION 74

OF TALE-BEARING [* *Susurratio,* i.e. whispering] (In Two Articles)

We must now consider tale-bearing: under which head there are two points of inquiry:

(1) Whether tale-bearing is a sin distinct from backbiting?

(2) Which of the two is the more grievous?

FIRST ARTICLE [II-II, Q. 74, Art. 1]

Whether Tale-bearing Is a Sin Distinct from Backbiting?

Objection 1: It would seem that tale-bearing is not a distinct sin from backbiting. Isidore says (Etym. x): "The *susurro* (tale-bearer) takes his name from the sound of his speech, for he speaks disparagingly not to the face but into the ear." But to speak of another disparagingly belongs to backbiting. Therefore tale-bearing is not a distinct sin from backbiting.

Obj. 2: Further, it is written (Lev. 19:16): "Thou shalt not be an informer [Douay: 'a detractor'] nor a tale-bearer [Douay: 'whisperer'] among the people." But an informer is apparently the same as a backbiter. Therefore neither does tale-bearing differ from backbiting.

Obj. 3: Further, it is written (Ecclus. 28:15): "The tale-bearer [Douay: 'whisperer'] and the double-tongued is accursed." But a double-tongued man is apparently the same as a backbiter, because a backbiter speaks with a double tongue, with one in your absence, with another in your presence. Therefore a tale-bearer is the same as a backbiter.

*On the contrary,* A gloss on Rom. 1:29, 30, "Tale-bearers, backbiters [Douay: 'whisperers, detractors']" says: "Tale-bearers sow discord among friends; backbiters deny or disparage others' good points."

*I answer that,* The tale-bearer and the backbiter agree in matter, and also in form or mode of speaking, since they both speak evil secretly of their neighbor: and for this reason these terms are sometimes used one for the other. Hence a gloss on Ecclus. 5:16, "Be not called a tale-bearer [Douay: 'whisperer']" says: "i.e. a backbiter." They differ however in end, because the backbiter intends to blacken his neighbor's good name, wherefore he brings forward those evils especially about his neighbor which are likely to defame him, or at least to depreciate his good name: whereas a tale-bearer intends to sever friendship, as appears from the gloss quoted above and from the saying of Prov. 26:20, "Where the tale-bearer is taken away, contentions shall cease." Hence it is that a tale-bearer speaks such ill about his neighbors as may stir his hearer's mind against them, according to Ecclus. 28:11, "A sinful man will trouble his friends, and bring in debate in the midst of them that are at peace."

Reply Obj. 1: A tale-bearer is called a backbiter in so far as he speaks ill of another; yet he differs from a backbiter since he intends not to speak ill as such, but to say anything that may stir one man against another, though it be good simply, and yet has a semblance of evil through being unpleasant to the hearer.

Reply Obj. 2: An informer differs from a tale-bearer and a backbiter, for an informer is one who charges others publicly with crimes, either by accusing or by railing them, which does not apply to a backbiter or tale-bearer.

Reply Obj. 3: A double-tongued person is properly speaking a tale-bearer. For since friendship is between two, the tale-bearer strives to sever friendship on both sides. Hence he employs a double tongue towards two persons, by speaking ill of one to the other: wherefore it is written (Ecclus. 28:15): "The tale-bearer [Douay: 'whisperer'] and the double-tongued is accursed," and then it is added, "for he hath troubled many that were peace."

SECOND ARTICLE [II-II, Q. 74, Art. 2]

Whether Backbiting Is a Graver Sin Than Tale-bearing?

Objection 1: It would seem that backbiting is a graver sin than tale-bearing. For sins of word consist in speaking evil. Now a backbiter speaks of his neighbor things that are evil simply, for such things lead to the loss or depreciation of his good name: whereas a tale-bearer is only intent on saying what is apparently evil, because to wit they are unpleasant to the hearer. Therefore backbiting is a graver sin than tale-bearing.

Obj. 2: Further, he that deprives a man of his good name, deprives him not merely of one friend, but of many, because everyone is minded to scorn the friendship of a person with a bad name. Hence it is reproached against a certain individual [*King Josaphat] (2 Paralip. 19:2): "Thou art joined in friendship with them that hate the Lord." But tale-bearing deprives one of only one friend. Therefore backbiting is a graver sin than tale-bearing.

Obj. 3: Further, it is written (James 4:11): "He that backbiteth [Douay: 'detracteth'] his brother ... detracteth the law," and consequently God the giver of the law. Wherefore the sin of backbiting seems to be a sin against God, which is most grievous, as stated above (Q. 20, A. 3; I-II, Q. 73, A. 3). On the other hand the sin of tale-bearing is against one's neighbor. Therefore the sin of backbiting is graver than the sin of tale-bearing.

*On the contrary,* It is written (Ecclus. 5:17): "An evil mark of disgrace is upon the double-tongued; but to the tale-bearer [Douay: 'whisperer'] hatred, and enmity, and reproach."

*I answer that,* As stated above (Q. 73, A. 3; I-II, Q. 73, A. 8), sins against one's neighbor are the more grievous, according as they inflict a greater injury on him: and an injury is so much the greater, according to the greatness of the good which it takes away. Now of all one's external goods a friend takes the first place, since "no man can live without friends," as the Philosopher declares (Ethic. viii, 1). Hence it is written (Ecclus. 6:15): "Nothing can be compared to a faithful friend." Again, a man's good name whereof backbiting deprives him, is most necessary to him that he may be fitted for friendship. Therefore tale-bearing is a greater sin than backbiting or even reviling, because a friend is better than honor, and to be loved is better than to be honored, according to the Philosopher (Ethic. viii).

Reply Obj. 1: The species and gravity of a sin depend on the end rather than on the material object, wherefore, by reason of its end, tale-bearing is worse than backbiting, although sometimes the backbiter says worse things.

Reply Obj. 2: A good name is a disposition for friendship, and a bad name is a disposition for enmity. But a disposition falls short of the thing for which it disposes. Hence to do anything that leads to a disposition for enmity is a less grievous sin than to do what conduces directly to enmity.

Reply Obj. 3: He that backbites his brother, seems to detract the law, in so far as he despises the precept of love for one's neighbor: while he that strives to sever friendship seems to act more directly against this precept. Hence the latter sin is more specially against God, because "God is charity" (1 John 4:16), and for this reason it is written (Prov. 6:16): "Six things there are, which the Lord hateth, and the seventh His soul detesteth," and the seventh is "he (Prov. 6:19) that soweth discord among brethren."

# QUESTION 75

OF DERISION [*Or mockery] (In Two Articles)

We must now speak of derision, under which head there are two points of inquiry:

(1) Whether derision is a special sin distinct from the other sins whereby one's neighbor is injured by words?

(2) Whether derision is a mortal sin?

FIRST ARTICLE [II-II, Q. 75, Art. 1]

Whether Derision Is a Special Sin Distinct from Those Already Mentioned?

Objection 1: It would seem that derision is not a special sin distinct from those mentioned above. For laughing to scorn is apparently the same as derision. But laughing to scorn pertains to reviling. Therefore derision would seem not to differ from reviling.

Obj. 2: Further, no man is derided except for something reprehensible which puts him to shame. Now such are sins; and if they be imputed to a person publicly, it is a case of reviling, if privately, it amounts to backbiting or tale-bearing. Therefore derision is not distinct from the foregoing vices.

Obj. 3: Further, sins of this kind are distinguished by the injury they inflict on one's neighbor. Now the injury inflicted on a man by derision affects either his honor, or his good name, or is detrimental to his friendship. Therefore derision is not a sin distinct from the foregoing.

*On the contrary,* Derision is done in jest, wherefore it is described as "making fun." Now all the foregoing are done seriously and not in jest. Therefore derision differs from all of them.

*I answer that,* As stated above (Q. 72, A. 2), sins of word should be weighed chiefly by the intention of the speaker, wherefore these sins are differentiated according to the various intentions of those who speak against another. Now just as the railer intends to injure the honor of the person he rails, the backbiter to depreciate a good name, and the tale-bearer to destroy friendship, so too the derider intends to shame the person he derides. And since this end is distinct from the others, it follows that the sin of derision is distinct from the foregoing sins.

Reply Obj. 1: Laughing to scorn and derision agree as to the end but differ in mode, because derision is done with the "mouth," i.e. by words and laughter, while laughing to scorn is done by wrinkling the nose, as a gloss says on Ps. 2:4, "He that dwelleth in heaven shall laugh at them": and such a distinction does not differentiate the species. Yet they both differ from reviling, as being shamed differs from being dishonored: for to be ashamed is "to fear dishonor," as Damascene states (De Fide Orth. ii, 15).

Reply Obj. 2: For doing a virtuous deed a man deserves both respect and a good name in the eyes of others, and in his own eyes the glory of a good conscience, according to 2 Cor. 1:12, "Our glory is this, the testimony of our conscience." Hence, on the other hand, for doing a reprehensible, i.e. a vicious action, a man forfeits his honor and good name in the eyes of others—and for this purpose the reviler and the backbiter speak of another person—while in his own eyes, he loses the glory of his conscience through being confused and ashamed at reprehensible deeds being imputed to him—and for this purpose the derider speaks ill of him. It is accordingly evident that derision agrees with the foregoing vices as to the matter but differs as to the end.

Reply Obj. 3: A secure and calm conscience is a great good, according to Prov. 15:15, "A secure mind is like a continual feast." Wherefore he that disturbs another's conscience by confounding him inflicts a special injury on him: hence derision is a special kind of sin.

SECOND ARTICLE [II-II, Q. 75, Art. 2]

Whether Derision Can Be a Mortal Sin?

Objection 1: It would seem that derision cannot be a mortal sin. Every mortal sin is contrary to charity. But derision does not seem contrary to charity, for sometimes it takes place in jest among friends, wherefore it is known as "making fun." Therefore derision cannot be a mortal sin.

Obj. 2: Further, the greatest derision would appear to be that which is done as an injury to God. But derision is not always a mortal sin when it tends to the injury of God: else it would be a mortal sin to relapse into a venial sin of which one has repented. For Isidore says (De Sum. Bon. ii, 16) that "he who continues to do what he has repented of, is a derider and not a penitent." It would likewise follow that all hypocrisy is a mortal sin, because, according to Gregory (Moral. xxxi, 15) "the ostrich signifies the hypocrite, who derides the horse, i.e. the just man, and his rider, i.e. God." Therefore derision is not a mortal sin.

Obj. 3: Further, reviling and backbiting seem to be graver sins than derision, because it is more to do a thing seriously than in jest. But not all backbiting or reviling is a mortal sin. Much less therefore is derision a mortal sin.

*On the contrary,* It is written (Prov. 3:34): "He derideth [Vulg.: 'shall scorn'] the scorners." But God's derision is eternal punishment for mortal sin, as appears from the words of Ps. 2:4, "He that dwelleth in heaven shall laugh at them." Therefore derision is a mortal sin.

*I answer that,* The object of derision is always some evil or defect. Now when an evil is great, it is taken, not in jest, but seriously: consequently if it is taken in jest or turned to ridicule (whence the terms 'derision' and 'jesting'), this is because it is considered to be slight. Now an evil may be considered to be slight in two ways: first, in itself, secondly, in relation to the person. When anyone makes game or fun of another's evil or defect, because it is a slight evil in itself, this is a venial sin by reason of its genus. On the other hand this defect may be considered as a slight evil in relation to the person, just as we are wont to think little of the defects of children and imbeciles: and then to make game or fun of a person, is to scorn him altogether, and to think him so despicable that his misfortune troubles us not one whit, but is held as an object of derision. In this way derision is a mortal sin, and more grievous than reviling, which is also done openly: because the reviler would seem to take another's evil seriously; whereas the derider does so in fun, and so would seem the more to despise and dishonor the other man. Wherefore, in this sense, derision is a grievous sin, and all the more grievous according as a greater respect is due to the person derided.

Consequently it is an exceedingly grievous sin to deride God and the things of God, according to Isa. 37:23, "Whom hast thou reproached, and whom hast thou blasphemed, and against whom hast thou exalted thy voice?" and he replies: "Against the Holy One of Israel." In the second place comes derision of one's parents, wherefore it is written (Prov. 30:17): "The eye that mocketh at his father, and that despiseth the labor of his mother in bearing him, let the ravens of the brooks pick it out, and the young eagles eat it." Further, the derision of good persons is grievous, because honor is the reward of virtue, and against this it is written (Job 12:4): "The simplicity of the just man is laughed to scorn." Such like derision does very much harm: because it turns men away from good deeds, according to Gregory (Moral. xx, 14), "Who when they perceive any good points appearing in the acts of others, directly pluck them up with the hand of a mischievous reviling."

Reply Obj. 1: Jesting implies nothing contrary to charity in relation to the person with whom one jests, but it may imply something against charity in relation to the person who is the object of the jest, on account of contempt, as stated above.

Reply Obj. 2: Neither he that relapses into a sin of which he has repented, nor a hypocrite, derides God explicitly, but implicitly, in so far as either's behavior is like a derider's. Nor is it true that to commit a venial sin is to relapse or dissimulate altogether, but only dispositively and imperfectly.

Reply Obj. 3: Derision considered in itself is less grievous than backbiting or reviling, because it does not imply contempt, but jest. Sometimes however it includes greater contempt than reviling does, as stated above, and then it is a grave sin.

# QUESTION 76

OF CURSING (In Four Articles)

We must now consider cursing. Under this head there are four points of inquiry:

(1) Whether one may lawfully curse another?

(2) Whether one may lawfully curse an irrational creature?

(3) Whether cursing is a mortal sin?

(4) Of its comparison with other sins.

FIRST ARTICLE [II-II, Q. 76, Art. 1]

Whether It Is Lawful to Curse Anyone?

Objection 1: It would seem unlawful to curse anyone. For it is unlawful to disregard the command of the Apostle in whom Christ spoke, according to 2 Cor. 13:3. Now he commanded (Rom. 12:14), "Bless and curse not." Therefore it is not lawful to curse anyone.

Obj. 2: Further, all are bound to bless God, according to Dan. 3:82, "O ye sons of men, bless the Lord." Now the same mouth cannot both bless God and curse man, as proved in the third chapter of James. Therefore no man may lawfully curse another man.

Obj. 3: Further, he that curses another would seem to wish him some evil either of fault or of punishment, since a curse appears to be a kind of imprecation. But it is not lawful to wish ill to anyone, indeed we are bound to pray that all may be delivered from evil. Therefore it is unlawful for any man to curse.

Obj. 4: Further, the devil exceeds all in malice on account of his obstinacy. But it is not lawful to curse the devil, as neither is it lawful to curse oneself; for it is written (Ecclus. 21:30): "While the ungodly curseth the devil, he curseth his own soul." Much less therefore is it lawful to curse a man.

Obj. 5: Further, a gloss on Num. 23:8, "How shall I curse whom God hath not cursed?" says: "There cannot be a just cause for cursing a sinner if one be ignorant of his sentiments." Now one man cannot know another man's sentiments, nor whether he is cursed by God. Therefore no man may lawfully curse another.

*On the contrary,* It is written (Deut. 27:26): "Cursed be he that abideth not in the words of this law." Moreover Eliseus cursed the little boys who mocked him (4 Kings 2:24).

*I answer that,* To curse ( maledicere ) is the same as to speak ill ( *malum dicere* ). Now "speaking" has a threefold relation to the thing spoken. First, by way of assertion, as when a thing is expressed in the indicative mood: in this way *maledicere* signifies simply to tell someone of another's evil, and this pertains to backbiting, wherefore tellers of evil ( *maledici* ) are sometimes called backbiters. Secondly, speaking is related to the thing spoken, by way of cause, and this belongs to God first and foremost, since He made all things by His word, according to Ps. 32:9, "He spoke and they were made"; while secondarily it belongs to man, who, by his word, commands others and thus moves them to do something: it is for this purpose that we employ verbs in the imperative mood. Thirdly, "speaking" is related to the thing spoken by expressing the sentiments of one who desires that which is expressed in words; and for this purpose we employ the verb in the optative mood.

Accordingly we may omit the first kind of evil speaking which is by way of simple assertion of evil, and consider the other two kinds. And here we must observe that to do something and to will it are consequent on one another in the matter of goodness and wickedness, as shown above (I-II, Q. 20, A. 3). Hence in these two ways of evil speaking, by way of command and by way of desire, there is the same aspect of lawfulness and unlawfulness, for if a man commands or desires another's evil, as evil, being intent on the evil itself, then evil speaking will be unlawful in both ways, and this is what is meant by cursing. On the other hand if a man commands or desires another's evil under the aspect of good, it is lawful; and it may be called cursing, not strictly speaking, but accidentally, because the chief intention of the speaker is directed not to evil but to good.

Now evil may be spoken, by commanding or desiring it, under the aspect of a twofold good. Sometimes under the aspect of just, and thus a judge lawfully curses a man whom he condemns to a just penalty: thus too the Church curses by pronouncing anathema. In the same way the prophets in the Scriptures sometimes call down evils on sinners, as though conforming their will to Divine justice, although such like imprecation may be taken by way of foretelling. Sometimes evil is spoken under the aspect of useful, as when one wishes a sinner to suffer sickness or hindrance of some kind, either that he may himself reform, or at least that he may cease from harming others.

Reply Obj. 1: The Apostle forbids cursing strictly so called with an evil intent: and the same answer applies to the Second Objection.

Reply Obj. 3: To wish another man evil under the aspect of good, is not opposed to the sentiment whereby one wishes him good simply, in fact rather is it in conformity therewith.

Reply Obj. 4: In the devil both nature and guilt must be considered. His nature indeed is good and is from God nor is it lawful to curse it. On the other hand his guilt is deserving of being cursed, according to Job 3:8, "Let them curse it who curse the day." Yet when a sinner curses the devil on account of his guilt, for the same reason he judges himself worthy of being cursed; and in this sense he is said to curse his own soul.

Reply Obj. 5: Although the sinner's sentiments cannot be perceived in themselves, they can be perceived through some manifest sin, which has to be punished. Likewise although it is not possible to know whom God curses in respect of final reprobation, it is possible to know who is accursed of God in respect of being guilty of present sin.

SECOND ARTICLE [II-II, Q. 76, Art. 2]

Whether It Is Lawful to Curse an Irrational Creature?

Objection 1: It would seem that it is unlawful to curse an irrational creature. Cursing would seem to be lawful chiefly in its relation to punishment. Now irrational creatures are not competent subjects either of guilt or of punishment. Therefore it is unlawful to curse them.

Obj. 2: Further, in an irrational creature there is nothing but the nature which God made. But it is unlawful to curse this even in the devil, as stated above (A. 1). Therefore it is nowise lawful to curse an irrational creature.

Obj. 3: Further, irrational creatures are either stable, as bodies, or transient, as the seasons. Now, according to Gregory (Moral. iv, 2), "it is useless to curse what does not exist, and wicked to curse what exists." Therefore it is nowise lawful to curse an irrational creature.

*On the contrary,* our Lord cursed the fig tree, as related in Matt. 21:19; and Job cursed his day, according to Job 3:1.

*I answer that,* Benediction and malediction, properly speaking, regard things to which good or evil may happen, viz. rational creatures: while good and evil are said to happen to irrational creatures in relation to the rational creature for whose sake they are. Now they are related to the rational creature in several ways. First by way of ministration, in so far as irrational creatures minister to the needs of man. In this sense the Lord said to man (Gen. 3:17): "Cursed is the earth in thy work," so that its barrenness would be a punishment to man. Thus also David cursed the mountains of Gelboe, according to Gregory's expounding (Moral. iv, 3). Again the irrational creature is related to the rational creature by way of signification: and thus our Lord cursed the fig tree in signification of Judea. Thirdly, the irrational creature is related to rational creatures as something containing them, namely by way of time or place: and thus Job cursed the day of his birth, on account of the original sin which he contracted in birth, and on account of the consequent penalties. In this sense also we may understand David to have cursed the mountains of Gelboe, as we read in 2 Kings 1:21, namely on account of the people slaughtered there.

But to curse irrational beings, considered as creatures of God, is a sin of blasphemy; while to curse them considered in themselves is idle and vain and consequently unlawful.

From this the Replies to the objections may easily be gathered.

THIRD ARTICLE [II-II, Q. 76, Art. 3]

Whether Cursing Is a Mortal Sin?

Objection 1: It would seem that cursing is not a mortal sin. For Augustine in a homily *on the Fire of Purgatory* [*Serm. civ in the appendix of St. Augustine's works] reckons cursing among slight sins. But such sins are venial. Therefore cursing is not a mortal but a venial Sin.

Obj. 2: Further, that which proceeds from a slight movement of the mind does not seem to be generically a mortal sin. But cursing sometimes arises from a slight movement. Therefore cursing is not a mortal sin.

Obj. 3: Further, evil deeds are worse than evil words. But evil deeds are not always mortal sins. Much less therefore is cursing a mortal sin.

*On the contrary,* Nothing save mortal sin excludes one from the kingdom of God. But cursing excludes from the kingdom of God, according to 1 Cor. 6:10, "Nor cursers [Douay: 'railers'], nor extortioners shall possess the kingdom of God." Therefore cursing is a mortal sin.

*I answer that,* The evil words of which we are speaking now are those whereby evil is uttered against someone by way of command or desire. Now to wish evil to another man, or to conduce to that evil by commanding it, is, of its very nature, contrary to charity whereby we love our neighbor by desiring his good. Consequently it is a mortal sin, according to its genus, and so much the graver, as the person whom we curse has a greater claim on our love and respect. Hence it is written (Lev. 20:9): "He that curseth his father, or mother, dying let him die."

It may happen however that the word uttered in cursing is a venial sin either through the slightness of the evil invoked on another in cursing him, or on account of the sentiments of the person who utters the curse; because he may say such words through some slight movement, or in jest, or without deliberation, and sins of word should be weighed chiefly with regard to the speaker's intention, as stated above (Q. 72, A. 2).

From this the Replies to the Objections may be easily gathered.

FOURTH ARTICLE [II-II, Q. 76, Art. 4]

Whether Cursing Is a Graver Sin Than Backbiting?

Objection 1: It would seem that cursing is a graver sin than backbiting. Cursing would seem to be a kind of blasphemy, as implied in the canonical epistle of Jude (verse 9) where it is said that "when Michael the archangel, disputing with the devil, contended about the body of Moses, he durst not bring against him the judgment of blasphemy [Douay: 'railing speech']," where blasphemy stands for cursing, according to a gloss. Now blasphemy is a graver sin than backbiting. Therefore cursing is a graver sin than backbiting.

Obj. 2: Further, murder is more grievous than backbiting, as stated above (Q. 73, A. 3). But cursing is on a par with the sin of murder; for Chrysostom says (Hom. xix, super Matth.): "When thou sayest: 'Curse him down with his house, away with everything,' you are no better than a murderer." Therefore cursing is graver than backbiting.

Obj. 3: Further, to cause a thing is more than to signify it. But the curser causes evil by commanding it, whereas the backbiter merely signifies an evil already existing. Therefore the curser sins more grievously than the backbiter.

*On the contrary,* It is impossible to do well in backbiting, whereas cursing may be either a good or an evil deed, as appears from what has been said (A. 1). Therefore backbiting is graver than cursing.

*I answer that,* As stated in the First Part (Q. 48, A. 5), evil is twofold, evil of fault, and evil of punishment; and of the two, evil of fault is the worse (I, Q. 48, A. 6). Hence to speak evil of fault is worse than to speak evil of punishment, provided the mode of speaking be the same. Accordingly it belongs to the reviler, the tale-bearer, the backbiter and the derider to speak evil of fault, whereas it belongs to the evil-speaker, as we understand it here, to speak evil of punishment, and not evil of fault except under the aspect of punishment. But the mode of speaking is not the same, for in the case of the four vices mentioned above, evil of fault is spoken by way of assertion, whereas in the case of cursing evil of punishment is spoken, either by causing it in the form of a command, or by wishing it. Now the utterance itself of a person's fault is a sin, in as much as it inflicts an injury on one's neighbor, and it is more grievous to inflict an injury, than to wish to inflict it, other things being equal.

Hence backbiting considered in its generic aspect is a graver sin than the cursing which expresses a mere desire; while the cursing which is expressed by way of command, since it has the aspect of a cause, will be more or less grievous than backbiting, according as it inflicts an injury more or less grave than the blackening of a man's good name. Moreover this must be taken as applying to these vices considered in their essential aspects: for other accidental points might be taken into consideration, which would aggravate or extenuate the aforesaid vices.

Reply Obj. 1: To curse a creature, as such, reflects on God, and thus accidentally it has the character of blasphemy; not so if one curse a creature on account of its fault: and the same applies to backbiting.

Reply Obj. 2: As stated above (A. 3), cursing, in one way, includes the desire for evil, where if the curser desire the evil of another's violent death, he does not differ, in desire, from a murderer, but he differs from him in so far as the external act adds something to the act of the will.

Reply Obj. 3: This argument considers cursing by way of command.

## QUESTION 77

OF CHEATING, WHICH IS COMMITTED IN BUYING AND SELLING (In Four Articles)

We must now consider those sins which relate to voluntary commutations. First, we shall consider cheating, which is committed in buying and selling: secondly, we shall consider usury, which occurs in loans. In connection with the other voluntary commutations no special kind of sin is to be found distinct from rapine and theft.

Under the first head there are four points of inquiry:

(1) Of unjust sales as regards the price; namely, whether it is lawful to sell a thing for more than its worth?

(2) Of unjust sales on the part of the thing sold;

(3) Whether the seller is bound to reveal a fault in the thing sold?

(4) Whether it is lawful in trading to sell a thing at a higher price than was paid for it?

FIRST ARTICLE [II-II, Q. 77, Art. 1]

Whether It Is Lawful to Sell a Thing for More Than Its Worth?

Objection 1: It would seem that it is lawful to sell a thing for more than its worth. In the commutations of human life, civil laws determine that which is just. Now according to these laws it is just for buyer and seller to deceive one another (Cod. IV, xliv, De Rescind. Vend. 8, 15): and this occurs by the seller selling a thing for more than its worth, and the buyer buying a thing for less than its worth. Therefore it is lawful to sell a thing for more than its worth.

Obj. 2: Further, that which is common to all would seem to be natural and not sinful. Now Augustine relates that the saying of a certain jester was accepted by all, "You wish to buy for a song and to sell at a premium," which agrees with the saying of Prov. 20:14, "It is naught, it is naught, saith every buyer: and when he is gone away, then he will boast." Therefore it is lawful to sell a thing for more than its worth.

Obj. 3: Further, it does not seem unlawful if that which honesty demands be done by mutual agreement. Now, according to the Philosopher (Ethic. viii, 13), in the friendship which is based on utility, the amount of the recompense for a favor received should depend on the utility accruing to the receiver: and this utility sometimes is worth more than the thing given, for instance if the receiver be in great need of that thing, whether for the purpose of avoiding a danger, or of deriving some particular benefit. Therefore, in contracts of buying and selling, it is lawful to give a thing in return for more than its worth.

*On the contrary,* It is written (Matt. 7:12): "All things ... whatsoever you would that men should do to you, do you also to them." But no man wishes to buy a thing for more than its worth. Therefore no man should sell a thing to another man for more than its worth.

*I answer that,* It is altogether sinful to have recourse to deceit in order to sell a thing for more than its just price, because this is to deceive one's neighbor so as to injure him. Hence Tully says (De Offic. iii, 15): "Contracts should be entirely free from double-dealing: the seller must not impose upon the bidder, nor the buyer upon one that bids against him."

But, apart from fraud, we may speak of buying and selling in two ways. First, as considered in themselves, and from this point of view, buying and selling seem to be established for the common advantage of both parties, one of whom requires that which belongs to the other, and vice versa, as the Philosopher states (Polit. i, 3). Now whatever is established for the common advantage, should not be more of a burden to one party than to another, and consequently all contracts between them should observe equality of thing and thing. Again, the quality of a thing that comes into human use is measured by the price given for it, for which purpose money was invented, as stated in *Ethic.* v, 5. Therefore if either the price exceed the quantity of the thing's worth, or, conversely, the thing exceed the price, there is no longer the equality of justice: and consequently, to sell a thing for more than its worth, or to buy it for less than its worth, is in itself unjust and unlawful.

Secondly we may speak of buying and selling, considered as accidentally tending to the advantage of one party, and to the disadvantage of the other: for instance, when a man has great need of a certain thing, while another man will suffer if he be without it. In such a case the just price will depend not only on the thing sold, but on the loss which the sale brings on the seller. And thus it will be lawful to sell a thing for more than it is worth in itself, though the price paid be not more than it is worth to the owner. Yet if the one man derive a great advantage by becoming possessed of the other man's property, and the seller be not at a loss through being without that thing, the latter ought not to raise the price, because the advantage accruing to the buyer, is not due to the seller, but to a circumstance affecting the buyer. Now no man should sell what is not his, though he may charge for the loss he suffers.

On the other hand if a man find that he derives great advantage from something he has bought, he may, of his own accord, pay the seller something over and above: and this pertains to his honesty.

Reply Obj. 1: As stated above (I-II, Q. 96, A. 2) human law is given to the people among whom there are many lacking virtue, and it is not given to the virtuous alone. Hence human law was unable to forbid all that is contrary to virtue; and it suffices for it to prohibit whatever is destructive of human intercourse, while it treats other matters as though they were lawful, not by approving of them, but by not punishing them. Accordingly, if without employing deceit the seller disposes of his goods for more than their worth, or the buyer obtain them for less than their worth, the law looks upon this as licit, and provides no punishment for so doing, unless the excess be too great, because then even human law demands restitution to be made, for instance if a man be deceived in regard to more than half the amount of the just price of a thing [*Cod. IV, xliv, De Rescind. Vend. 2, 8].

On the other hand the Divine law leaves nothing unpunished that is contrary to virtue. Hence, according to the Divine law, it is reckoned unlawful if the equality of justice be not observed in buying and selling: and he who has received more than he ought must make compensation to him that has suffered loss, if the loss be considerable. I add this condition, because the just price of things is not fixed with mathematical precision, but depends on a kind of estimate, so that a slight addition or subtraction would not seem to destroy the equality of justice.

Reply Obj. 2: As Augustine says "this jester, either by looking into himself or by his experience of others, thought that all men are inclined to wish to buy for a song and sell at a premium. But since in reality this is wicked, it is in every man's power to acquire that justice whereby he may resist and overcome this inclination." And then he gives the example of a man who gave the just price for a book to a man who through ignorance asked a low price for it. Hence it is evident that this common desire is not from nature but from vice, wherefore it is common to many who walk along the broad road of sin.

Reply Obj. 3: In commutative justice we consider chiefly real equality. On the other hand, in friendship based on utility we consider equality of usefulness, so that the recompense should depend on the usefulness accruing, whereas in buying it should be equal to the thing bought.

SECOND ARTICLE [II-II, Q. 77, Art. 2]

Whether a Sale Is Rendered Unlawful Through a Fault in the Thing Sold?

Objection 1: It would seem that a sale is not rendered unjust and unlawful through a fault in the thing sold. For less account should be taken of the other parts of a thing than of what belongs to its substance. Yet the sale of a thing does not seem to be rendered unlawful through a fault in its substance: for instance, if a man sell instead of the real metal, silver or gold produced by some chemical process, which is adapted to all the human uses for which silver and gold are necessary, for instance in the making of vessels and the like. Much less therefore will it be an unlawful sale if the thing be defective in other ways.

Obj. 2: Further, any fault in the thing, affecting the quantity, would seem chiefly to be opposed to justice which consists in equality. Now quantity is known by being measured: and the measures of things that come into human use are not fixed, but in some places are greater, in others less, as the Philosopher states (Ethic. v, 7). Therefore just as it is impossible to avoid defects on the part of the thing sold, it seems that a sale is not rendered unlawful through the thing sold being defective.

Obj. 3: Further, the thing sold is rendered defective by lacking a fitting quality. But in order to know the quality of a thing, much knowledge is required that is lacking in most buyers. Therefore a sale is not rendered unlawful by a fault (in the thing sold).

*On the contrary,* Ambrose says (De Offic. iii, 11): "It is manifestly a rule of justice that a good man should not depart from the truth, nor inflict an unjust injury on anyone, nor have any connection with fraud."

*I answer that,* A threefold fault may be found pertaining to the thing which is sold. One, in respect of the thing's substance: and if the seller be aware of a fault in the thing he is selling, he is guilty of a fraudulent sale, so that the sale is rendered unlawful. Hence we find it written against certain people (Isa. 1:22), "Thy silver is turned into dross, thy wine is mingled with water": because that which is mixed is defective in its substance.

Another defect is in respect of quantity which is known by being measured: wherefore if anyone knowingly make use of a faulty measure in selling, he is guilty of fraud, and the sale is illicit. Hence it is written (Deut. 25:13, 14): "Thou shalt not have divers weights in thy bag, a greater and a less: neither shall there be in thy house a greater bushel and a less," and further on (Deut. 25:16): "For the Lord ... abhorreth him that doth these things, and He hateth all injustice."

A third defect is on the part of the quality, for instance, if a man sell an unhealthy animal as being a healthy one: and if anyone do this knowingly he is guilty of a fraudulent sale, and the sale, in consequence, is illicit.

In all these cases not only is the man guilty of a fraudulent sale, but he is also bound to restitution. But if any of the foregoing defects be in the thing sold, and he knows nothing about this, the seller does not sin, because he does that which is unjust materially, nor is his deed unjust, as shown above (Q. 59, A. 2). Nevertheless he is bound to compensate the buyer, when the defect comes to his knowledge. Moreover what has been said of the seller applies equally to the buyer. For sometimes it happens that the seller thinks his goods to be specifically of lower value, as when a man sells gold instead of copper, and then if the buyer be aware of this, he buys it unjustly and is bound to restitution: and the same applies to a defect in quantity as to a defect in quality.

Reply Obj. 1: Gold and silver are costly not only on account of the usefulness of the vessels and other like things made from them, but also on account of the excellence and purity of their substance. Hence if the gold or silver produced by alchemists has not the true specific nature of gold and silver, the sale thereof is fraudulent and unjust, especially as real gold and silver can produce certain results by their natural action, which the counterfeit gold and silver of alchemists cannot produce. Thus the true metal has the property of making people joyful, and is helpful medicinally against certain maladies. Moreover real gold can be employed more frequently, and lasts longer in its condition of purity than counterfeit gold. If however real gold were to be produced by alchemy, it would not be unlawful to sell it for the genuine article, for nothing prevents art from employing certain natural causes for the production of natural and true effects, as Augustine says (De Trin. iii, 8) of things produced by the art of the demons.

Reply Obj. 2: The measures of salable commodities must needs be different in different places, on account of the difference of supply: because where there is greater abundance, the measures are wont to be larger. However in each place those who govern the state must determine the just measures of things salable, with due consideration for the conditions of place and time. Hence it is not lawful to disregard such measures as are established by public authority or custom.

Reply Obj. 3: As Augustine says (De Civ. Dei xi, 16) the price of things salable does not depend on their degree of nature, since at times a horse fetches a higher price than a slave; but it depends on their usefulness to man. Hence it is not necessary for the seller or buyer to be cognizant of the hidden qualities of the thing sold, but only of such as render the thing adapted to man's use, for instance, that the horse be strong, run well and so forth. Such qualities the seller and buyer can easily discover.

THIRD ARTICLE [II-II, Q. 77, Art. 3]

Whether the Seller Is Bound to State the Defects of the Thing Sold?

Objection 1: It would seem that the seller is not bound to state the defects of the thing sold. Since the seller does not bind the buyer to buy, he would seem to leave it to him to judge of the goods offered for sale. Now judgment about a thing and knowledge of that thing belong to the same person. Therefore it does not seem imputable to the seller if the buyer be deceived in his judgment, and be hurried into buying a thing without carefully inquiring into its condition.

Obj. 2: Further, it seems foolish for anyone to do what prevents him carrying out his work. But if a man states the defects of the goods he has for sale, he prevents their sale: wherefore Tully (De Offic. iii, 13) pictures a man as saying: "Could anything be more absurd than for a public crier, instructed by the owner, to cry: 'I offer this unhealthy horse for sale?'" Therefore the seller is not bound to state the defects of the thing sold.

Obj. 3: Further, man needs more to know the road of virtue than to know the faults of things offered for sale. Now one is not bound to offer advice to all or to tell them the truth about matters pertaining to virtue, though one should not tell anyone what is false. Much less therefore is a seller bound to tell the faults of what he offers for sale, as though he were counseling the buyer.

Obj. 4: Further, if one were bound to tell the faults of what one offers for sale, this would only be in order to lower the price. Now sometimes the price would be lowered for some other reason, without any defect in the thing sold: for instance, if the seller carry wheat to a place where wheat fetches a high price, knowing that many will come after him carrying wheat; because if the buyers knew this they would give a lower price. But apparently the seller need not give the buyer this information. Therefore, in like manner, neither need he tell him the faults of the goods he is selling.

*On the contrary,* Ambrose says (De Offic. iii, 10): "In all contracts the defects of the salable commodity must be stated; and unless the seller make them known, although the buyer has already acquired a right to them, the contract is voided on account of the fraudulent action."

*I answer that,* It is always unlawful to give anyone an occasion of danger or loss, although a man need not always give another the help or counsel which would be for his advantage in any way; but only in certain fixed cases, for instance when someone is subject to him, or when he is the only one who can assist him. Now the seller who offers goods for sale, gives the buyer an occasion of loss or danger, by the very fact that he offers him defective goods, if such defect may occasion loss or danger to the buyer—loss, if, by reason of this defect, the goods are of less value, and he takes nothing off the price on that account—danger, if this defect either hinder the use of the goods or render it hurtful, for instance, if a man sells a lame for a fleet horse, a tottering house for a safe one, rotten or poisonous food for wholesome. Wherefore if such like defects be hidden, and the seller does not make them known, the sale will be illicit and fraudulent, and the seller will be bound to compensation for the loss incurred.

On the other hand, if the defect be manifest, for instance if a horse have but one eye, or if the goods though useless to the buyer, be useful to someone else, provided the seller take as much as he ought from the price, he is not bound to state the defect of the goods, since perhaps on account of that defect the buyer might want him to allow a greater rebate than he need. Wherefore the seller may look to his own indemnity, by withholding the defect of the goods.

Reply Obj. 1: Judgment cannot be pronounced save on what is manifest: for "a man judges of what he knows" (Ethic. i, 3). Hence if the defects of the goods offered for sale be hidden, judgment of them is not sufficiently left with the buyer unless such defects be made known to him. The case would be different if the defects were manifest.

Reply Obj. 2: There is no need to publish beforehand by the public crier the defects of the goods one is offering for sale, because if he were to begin by announcing its defects, the bidders would be frightened to buy, through ignorance of other qualities that might render the thing good and serviceable. Such defect ought to be stated to each individual that offers to buy: and then he will be able to compare the various points one with the other, the good with the bad: for nothing prevents that which is defective in one respect being useful in many others.

Reply Obj. 3: Although a man is not bound strictly speaking to tell everyone the truth about matters pertaining to virtue, yet he is so bound in a case when, unless he tells the truth, his conduct would endanger another man in detriment to virtue: and so it is in this case.

Reply Obj. 4: The defect in a thing makes it of less value now than it seems to be: but in the case cited, the goods are expected to be of less value at a future time, on account of the arrival of other merchants, which was not foreseen by the buyers. Wherefore the seller, since he sells his goods at the price actually offered him, does not seem to act contrary to justice through not stating what is going to happen. If however he were to do so, or if he lowered his price, it would be exceedingly virtuous on his part: although he does not seem to be bound to do this as a debt of justice.

FOURTH ARTICLE [II-II, Q. 77, Art. 4]

Whether, in Trading, It Is Lawful to Sell a Thing at a Higher Price Than What Was Paid for It?

Objection 1: It would seem that it is not lawful, in trading, to sell a thing for a higher price than we paid for it. For Chrysostom [*Hom. xxxviii in the Opus Imperfectum, falsely ascribed to St. John Chrysostom] says on Matt. 21:12: "He that buys a thing in order that he may sell it, entire and unchanged, at a profit, is the trader who is cast out of God's temple." Cassiodorus speaks in the same sense in his commentary on Ps. 70:15, "Because I have not known learning, or trading" according to another version [*The Septuagint]: "What is trade," says he, "but buying at a cheap price with the purpose of retailing at a higher price?" and he adds: "Such were the tradesmen whom Our Lord cast out of the temple." Now no man is cast out of the temple except for a sin. Therefore such like trading is sinful.

Obj. 2: Further, it is contrary to justice to sell goods at a higher price than their worth, or to buy them for less than their value, as shown above (A. 1). Now if you sell a thing for a higher price than you paid for it, you must either have bought it for less than its value, or sell it for more than its value. Therefore this cannot be done without sin.

Obj. 3: Further, Jerome says (Ep. ad Nepot. lii): "Shun, as you would the plague, a cleric who from being poor has become wealthy, or who, from being a nobody has become a celebrity." Now trading would net seem to be forbidden to clerics except on account of its sinfulness. Therefore it is a sin in trading, to buy at a low price and to sell at a higher price.

*On the contrary,* Augustine commenting on Ps. 70:15, "Because I have not known learning," [*Cf. Obj. 1] says: "The greedy tradesman blasphemes over his losses; he lies and perjures himself over the price of his wares. But these are vices of the man, not of the craft, which can be exercised without these vices." Therefore trading is not in itself unlawful.

*I answer that,* A tradesman is one whose business consists in the exchange of things. According to the Philosopher (Polit. i, 3), exchange of things is twofold; one, natural as it were, and necessary, whereby one commodity is exchanged for another, or money taken in exchange for a commodity, in order to satisfy the needs of life. Such like trading, properly speaking, does not belong to tradesmen, but rather to housekeepers or civil servants who have to provide the household or the state with the necessaries of life. The other kind of exchange is either that of money for money, or of any commodity for money, not on account of the necessities of life, but for profit, and this kind of exchange, properly speaking, regards tradesmen, according to the Philosopher (Polit. i, 3). The former kind of exchange is commendable because it supplies a natural need: but the latter is justly deserving of blame, because, considered in itself, it satisfies the greed for gain, which knows no limit and tends to infinity. Hence trading, considered in itself, has a certain debasement attaching thereto, in so far as, by its very nature, it does not imply a virtuous or necessary end. Nevertheless gain which is the end of trading, though not implying, by its nature, anything virtuous or necessary, does not, in itself, connote anything sinful or contrary to virtue: wherefore nothing prevents gain from being directed to some necessary or even virtuous end, and thus trading becomes lawful. Thus, for instance, a man may intend the moderate gain which he seeks to acquire by trading for the upkeep of his household, or for the assistance of the needy: or again, a man may take to trade for some public advantage, for instance, lest his country lack the necessaries of life, and seek gain, not as an end, but as payment for his labor.

Reply Obj. 1: The saying of Chrysostom refers to the trading which seeks gain as a last end. This is especially the case where a man sells something at a higher price without its undergoing any change. For if he sells at a higher price something that has changed for the better, he would seem to receive the reward of his labor. Nevertheless the gain itself may be lawfully intended, not as a last end, but for the sake of some other end which is necessary or virtuous, as stated above.

Reply Obj. 2: Not everyone that sells at a higher price than he bought is a tradesman, but only he who buys that he may sell at a profit. If, *on the contrary,* he buys not for sale but for possession, and afterwards, for some reason wishes to sell, it is not a trade transaction even if he sell at a profit. For he may lawfully do this, either because he has bettered the thing, or because the value of the thing has changed with the change of place or time, or on account of the danger he incurs in transferring the thing from one place to another, or again in having it carried by another. In this sense neither buying nor selling is unjust.

Reply Obj. 3: Clerics should abstain not only from things that are evil in themselves, but even from those that have an appearance of evil. This happens in trading, both because it is directed to worldly gain, which clerics should despise, and because trading is open to so many vices, since "a merchant is hardly free from sins of the lips" [*'A merchant is hardly free from negligence, and a huckster shall not be justified from the sins of the lips'] (Ecclus. 26:28). There is also another reason, because trading engages the mind too much with worldly cares, and consequently withdraws it from spiritual cares; wherefore the Apostle says (2 Tim. 2:4): "No man being a soldier to God entangleth himself with secular businesses." Nevertheless it is lawful for clerics to engage in the first mentioned kind of exchange, which is directed to supply the necessaries of life, either by buying or by selling.

# QUESTION 78

OF THE SIN OF USURY (In Four Articles)

We must now consider the sin of usury, which is committed in loans: and under this head there are four points of inquiry:

(1) Whether it is a sin to take money as a price for money lent, which is to receive usury?

(2) Whether it is lawful to lend money for any other kind of consideration, by way of payment for the loan?

(3) Whether a man is bound to restore just gains derived from money taken in usury?

(4) Whether it is lawful to borrow money under a condition of usury?

FIRST ARTICLE [II-II, Q. 78, Art. 1]

Whether It Is a Sin to Take Usury for Money Lent?

Objection 1: It would seem that it is not a sin to take usury for money lent. For no man sins through following the example of Christ. But Our Lord said of Himself (Luke 19:23): "At My coming I might have exacted it," i.e. the money lent, "with usury." Therefore it is not a sin to take usury for lending money.

Obj. 2: Further, according to Ps. 18:8, "The law of the Lord is unspotted," because, to wit, it forbids sin. Now usury of a kind is allowed in the Divine law, according to Deut. 23:19, 20: "Thou shalt not fenerate to thy brother money, nor corn, nor any other thing, but to the stranger": nay more, it is even promised as a reward for the observance of the Law, according to Deut. 28:12: "Thou shalt fenerate* to many nations, and shalt not borrow of any one." [* *Faeneraberis* —'Thou shalt lend upon usury.' The Douay version has simply 'lend.' The objection lays stress on the word *faeneraberis:* hence the necessity of rendering it by 'fenerate.'] Therefore it is not a sin to take usury.

Obj. 3: Further, in human affairs justice is determined by civil laws. Now civil law allows usury to be taken. Therefore it seems to be lawful.

Obj. 4: Further, the counsels are not binding under sin. But, among other counsels we find (Luke 6:35): "Lend, hoping for nothing thereby." Therefore it is not a sin to take usury.

Obj. 5: Further, it does not seem to be in itself sinful to accept a price for doing what one is not bound to do. But one who has money is not bound in every case to lend it to his neighbor. Therefore it is lawful for him sometimes to accept a price for lending it.

Obj. 6: Further, silver made into coins does not differ specifically from silver made into a vessel. But it is lawful to accept a price for the loan of a silver vessel. Therefore it is also lawful to accept a price for the loan of a silver coin. Therefore usury is not in itself a sin.

Obj. 7: Further, anyone may lawfully accept a thing which its owner freely gives him. Now he who accepts the loan, freely gives the usury. Therefore he who lends may lawfully take the usury.

*On the contrary,* It is written (Ex. 22:25): "If thou lend money to any of thy people that is poor, that dwelleth with thee, thou shalt not be hard upon them as an extortioner, nor oppress them with usuries."

*I answer that,* To take usury for money lent is unjust in itself, because this is to sell what does not exist, and this evidently leads to inequality which is contrary to justice. In order to make this evident, we must observe that there are certain things the use of which consists in their consumption: thus we consume wine when we use it for drink and we consume wheat when we use it for food. Wherefore in such like things the use of the thing must not be reckoned apart from the thing itself, and whoever is granted the use of the thing, is granted the thing itself and for this reason, to lend things of this kind is to transfer the ownership. Accordingly if a man wanted to sell wine separately from the use of the wine, he would be selling the same thing twice, or he would be selling what does not exist, wherefore he would evidently commit a sin of injustice. In like manner he commits an injustice who lends wine or wheat, and asks for double payment, viz. one, the return of the thing in equal measure, the other, the price of the use, which is called usury.

On the other hand, there are things the use of which does not consist in their consumption: thus to use a house is to dwell in it, not to destroy it. Wherefore in such things both may be granted: for instance, one man may hand over to another the ownership of his house while reserving to himself the use of it for a time, or vice versa, he may grant the use of the house, while retaining the ownership. For this reason a man may lawfully make a charge for the use of his house, and, besides this, revendicate the house from the person to whom he has granted its use, as happens in renting and letting a house.

Now money, according to the Philosopher (Ethic. v, 5; Polit. i, 3) was invented chiefly for the purpose of exchange: and consequently the proper and principal use of money is its consumption or alienation whereby it is sunk in exchange. Hence it is by its very nature unlawful to take payment for the use of money lent, which payment is known as usury: and just as a man is bound to restore other ill-gotten goods, so is he bound to restore the money which he has taken in usury.

Reply Obj. 1: In this passage usury must be taken figuratively for the increase of spiritual goods which God exacts from us, for He wishes us ever to advance in the goods which we receive from Him: and this is for our own profit not for His.

Reply Obj. 2: The Jews were forbidden to take usury from their brethren, i.e. from other Jews. By this we are given to understand that to take usury from any man is evil simply, because we ought to treat every man as our neighbor and brother, especially in the state of the Gospel, whereto all are called. Hence it is said without any distinction in Ps. 14:5: "He that hath not put out his money to usury," and (Ezech. 18:8): "Who hath not taken usury [*Vulg.: 'If a man … hath not lent upon money, nor taken any increase … he is just.']." They were permitted, however, to take usury from foreigners, not as though it were lawful, but in order to avoid a greater evil, lest, to wit, through avarice to which they were prone according to Isa. 56:11, they should take usury from the Jews who were worshippers of God.

Where we find it promised to them as a reward, "Thou shalt fenerate to many nations," etc., fenerating is to be taken in a broad sense for lending, as in Ecclus. 29:10, where we read: "Many have refused to fenerate, not out of wickedness," i.e. they would not lend. Accordingly the Jews are promised in reward an abundance of wealth, so that they would be able to lend to others.

Reply Obj. 3: Human laws leave certain things unpunished, on account of the condition of those who are imperfect, and who would be deprived of many advantages, if all sins were strictly forbidden and punishments appointed for them. Wherefore human law has permitted usury, not that it looks upon usury as harmonizing with justice, but lest the advantage of many should be hindered. Hence it is that in civil law [*Inst. II, iv, de Usufructu] it is stated that "those things according to natural reason and civil law which are consumed by being used, do not admit of usufruct," and that "the senate did not (nor could it) appoint a usufruct to such things, but established a quasi-usufruct," namely by permitting usury. Moreover the Philosopher, led by natural reason, says (Polit. i, 3) that "to make money by usury is exceedingly unnatural."

Reply Obj. 4: A man is not always bound to lend, and for this reason it is placed among the counsels. Yet it is a matter of precept not to seek profit by lending: although it may be called a matter of counsel in comparison with the maxims of the Pharisees, who deemed some kinds of usury to be lawful, just as love of one's enemies is a matter of counsel. Or again, He speaks here not of the hope of usurious gain, but of the hope which is put in man. For we ought not to lend or do any good deed through hope in man, but only through hope in God.

Reply Obj. 5: He that is not bound to lend, may accept repayment for what he has done, but he must not exact more. Now he is repaid according to equality of justice if he is repaid as much as he lent. Wherefore if he exacts more for the usufruct of a thing which has no other use but the consumption of its substance, he exacts a price of something non-existent: and so his exaction is unjust.

Reply Obj. 6: The principal use of a silver vessel is not its consumption, and so one may lawfully sell its use while retaining one's ownership of it. On the other hand the principal use of silver money is sinking it in exchange, so that it is not lawful to sell its use and at the same time expect the restitution of the amount lent. It must be observed, however, that the secondary use of silver vessels may be an exchange, and such use may not be lawfully sold. In like manner there may be some secondary use of silver money; for instance, a man might lend coins for show, or to be used as security.

Reply Obj. 7: He who gives usury does not give it voluntarily simply, but under a certain necessity, in so far as he needs to borrow money which the owner is unwilling to lend without usury.

SECOND ARTICLE [II-II, Q. 78, Art. 2]

Whether It Is Lawful to Ask for Any Other Kind of Consideration for Money Lent?

Objection 1: It would seem that one may ask for some other kind of consideration for money lent. For everyone may lawfully seek to indemnify himself. Now sometimes a man suffers loss through lending money. Therefore he may lawfully ask for or even exact something else besides the money lent.

Obj. 2: Further, as stated in *Ethic.* v, 5, one is in duty bound by a point of honor, to repay anyone who has done us a favor. Now to lend money to one who is in straits is to do him a favor for which he should be grateful. Therefore the recipient of a loan, is bound by a natural debt to repay something. Now it does not seem unlawful to bind oneself to an obligation of the natural law. Therefore it is not unlawful, in lending money to anyone, to demand some sort of compensation as condition of the loan.

Obj. 3: Further, just as there is real remuneration, so is there verbal remuneration, and remuneration by service, as a gloss says on Isa. 33:15, "Blessed is he that shaketh his hands from all bribes [*Vulg.: 'Which of you shall dwell with everlasting burnings? ... He that shaketh his hands from all bribes.']." Now it is lawful to accept service or praise from one to whom one has lent money. Therefore in like manner it is lawful to accept any other kind of remuneration.

Obj. 4: Further, seemingly the relation of gift to gift is the same as of loan to loan. But it is lawful to accept money for money given. Therefore it is lawful to accept repayment by loan in return for a loan granted.

Obj. 5: Further, the lender, by transferring his ownership of a sum of money removes the money further from himself than he who entrusts it to a merchant or craftsman. Now it is lawful to receive interest for money entrusted to a merchant or craftsman. Therefore it is also lawful to receive interest for money lent.

Obj. 6: Further, a man may accept a pledge for money lent, the use of which pledge he might sell for a price: as when a man mortgages his land or the house wherein he dwells. Therefore it is lawful to receive interest for money lent.

Obj. 7: Further, it sometimes happens that a man raises the price of his goods under guise of loan, or buys another's goods at a low figure; or raises his price through delay in being paid, and lowers his price that he may be paid the sooner. Now in all these cases there seems to be payment for a loan of money: nor does it appear to be manifestly illicit. Therefore it seems to be lawful to expect or exact some consideration for money lent.

*On the contrary,* Among other conditions requisite in a just man it is stated (Ezech. 18:17) that he "hath not taken usury and increase."

*I answer that,* According to the Philosopher (Ethic. iv, 1), a thing is reckoned as money "if its value can be measured by money." Consequently, just as it is a sin against justice, to take money, by tacit or express agreement, in return for lending money or anything else that is consumed by being used, so also is it a like sin, by tacit or express agreement to receive anything whose price can be measured by money. Yet there would be no sin in receiving something of the kind, not as exacting it, nor yet as though it were due on account of some agreement tacit or expressed, but as a gratuity: since, even before lending the money, one could accept a gratuity, nor is one in a worse condition through lending.

On the other hand it is lawful to exact compensation for a loan, in respect of such things as are not appreciated by a measure of money, for instance, benevolence, and love for the lender, and so forth.

Reply Obj. 1: A lender may without sin enter an agreement with the borrower for compensation for the loss he incurs of something he ought to have, for this is not to sell the use of money but to avoid a loss. It may also happen that the borrower avoids a greater loss than the lender incurs, wherefore the borrower may repay the lender with what he has gained. But the lender cannot enter an agreement for compensation, through the fact that he makes no profit out of his money: because he must not sell that which he has not yet and may be prevented in many ways from having.

Reply Obj. 2: Repayment for a favor may be made in two ways. In one way, as a debt of justice; and to such a debt a man may be bound by a fixed contract; and its amount is measured according to the favor received. Wherefore the borrower of money or any such thing the use of which is its consumption is not bound to repay more than he received in loan: and consequently it is against justice if he be obliged to pay back more. In another way a man's obligation to repayment for favor received is based on a debt of friendship, and the nature of this debt depends more on the feeling with which the favor was conferred than on the greatness of the favor itself. This debt does not carry with it a civil obligation, involving a kind of necessity that would exclude the spontaneous nature of such a repayment.

Reply Obj. 3: If a man were, in return for money lent, as though there had been an agreement tacit or expressed, to expect or exact repayment in the shape of some remuneration of service or words, it would be the same as if he expected or exacted some real remuneration, because both can be priced at a money value, as may be seen in the case of those who offer for hire the labor which they exercise by work or by tongue. If on the other hand the remuneration by service or words be given not as an obligation, but as a favor, which is not to be appreciated at a money value, it is lawful to take, exact, and expect it.

Reply Obj. 4: Money cannot be sold for a greater sum than the amount lent, which has to be paid back: nor should the loan be made with a demand or expectation of aught else but of a feeling of benevolence which cannot be priced at a pecuniary value, and which can be the basis of a spontaneous loan. Now the obligation to lend in return at some future time is repugnant to such a feeling, because again an obligation of this kind has its pecuniary value. Consequently it is lawful for the lender to borrow something else at the same time, but it is unlawful for him to bind the borrower to grant him a loan at some future time.

Reply Obj. 5: He who lends money transfers the ownership of the money to the borrower. Hence the borrower holds the money at his own risk and is bound to pay it all back: wherefore the lender must not exact more. On the other hand he that entrusts his money to a merchant or craftsman so as to form a kind of society, does not transfer the ownership of his money to them, for it remains his, so that at his risk the merchant speculates with it, or the craftsman uses it for his craft, and consequently he may lawfully demand as something belonging to him, part of the profits derived from his money.

Reply Obj. 6: If a man in return for money lent to him pledges something that can be valued at a price, the lender must allow for the use of that thing towards the repayment of the loan. Else if he wishes the gratuitous use of that thing in addition to repayment, it is the same as if he took money for lending, and that is usury, unless perhaps it were such a thing as friends are wont to lend to one another gratis, as in the case of the loan of a book.

Reply Obj. 7: If a man wish to sell his goods at a higher price than that which is just, so that he may wait for the buyer to pay, it is manifestly a case of usury: because this waiting for the payment of the price has the character of a loan, so that whatever he demands beyond the just price in consideration of this delay, is like a price for a loan, which pertains to usury. In like manner if a buyer wishes to buy goods at a lower price than what is just, for the reason that he pays for the goods before they can be delivered, it is a sin of usury; because again this anticipated payment of money has the character of a loan, the price of which is the rebate on the just price of the goods sold. On the other hand if a man wishes to allow a rebate on the just price in order that he may have his money sooner, he is not guilty of the sin of usury.

THIRD ARTICLE [II-II, Q. 78, Art. 3]

Whether a Man Is Bound to Restore Whatever Profits He Has Made Out of Money Gotten by Usury?

Objection 1: It would seem that a man is bound to restore whatever profits he has made out of money gotten by usury. For the Apostle says (Rom. 11:16): "If the root be holy, so are the branches." Therefore likewise if the root be rotten so are the branches. But the root was infected with usury. Therefore whatever profit is made therefrom is infected with usury. Therefore he is bound to restore it.

Obj. 2: Further, it is laid down (Extra, De Usuris, in the Decretal: 'Cum tu sicut asseris'): "Property accruing from usury must be sold, and the price repaid to the persons from whom the usury was extorted." Therefore, likewise, whatever else is acquired from usurious money must be restored.

Obj. 3: Further, that which a man buys with the proceeds of usury is due to him by reason of the money he paid for it. Therefore he has no more right to the thing purchased than to the money he paid. But he was bound to restore the money gained through usury. Therefore he is also bound to restore what he acquired with it.

*On the contrary,* A man may lawfully hold what he has lawfully acquired. Now that which is acquired by the proceeds of usury is sometimes lawfully acquired. Therefore it may be lawfully retained.

*I answer that,* As stated above (A. 1), there are certain things whose use is their consumption, and which do not admit of usufruct, according to law (ibid., ad 3). Wherefore if such like things be extorted by means of usury, for instance money, wheat, wine and so forth, the lender is not bound to restore more than he received (since what is acquired by such things is the fruit not of the thing but of human industry), unless indeed the other party by losing some of his own goods be injured through the lender retaining them: for then he is bound to make good the loss.

On the other hand, there are certain things whose use is not their consumption: such things admit of usufruct, for instance house or land property and so forth. Wherefore if a man has by usury extorted from another his house or land, he is bound to restore not only the house or land but also the fruits accruing to him therefrom, since they are the fruits of things owned by another man and consequently are due to him.

Reply Obj. 1: The root has not only the character of matter, as money made by usury has; but has also somewhat the character of an active cause, in so far as it administers nourishment. Hence the comparison fails.

Reply Obj. 2: Further, Property acquired from usury does not belong to the person who paid usury, but to the person who bought it. Yet he that paid usury has a certain claim on that property just as he has on the other goods of the usurer. Hence it is not prescribed that such property should be assigned to the persons who paid usury, since the property is perhaps worth more than what they paid in usury, but it is commanded that the property be sold, and the price be restored, of course according to the amount taken in usury.

Reply Obj. 3: The proceeds of money taken in usury are due to the person who acquired them not by reason of the usurious money as instrumental cause, but on account of his own industry as principal cause. Wherefore he has more right to the goods acquired with usurious money than to the usurious money itself.

FOURTH ARTICLE [II-II, Q. 78, Art. 4]

Whether It Is Lawful to Borrow Money Under a Condition of Usury?

Objection 1: It would seem that it is not lawful to borrow money under a condition of usury. For the Apostle says (Rom. 1:32) that they "are worthy of death ... not only they that do" these sins, "but they also that consent to them that do them." Now he that borrows money under a condition of usury consents in the sin of the usurer, and gives him an occasion of sin. Therefore he sins also.

Obj. 2: Further, for no temporal advantage ought one to give another an occasion of committing a sin: for this pertains to active scandal, which is always sinful, as stated above (Q. 43, A. 2). Now he that seeks to borrow from a usurer gives him an occasion of sin. Therefore he is not to be excused on account of any temporal advantage.

Obj. 3: Further, it seems no less necessary sometimes to deposit one's money with a usurer than to borrow from him. Now it seems altogether unlawful to deposit one's money with a usurer, even as it would be unlawful to deposit one's sword with a madman, a maiden with a libertine, or food with a glutton. Neither therefore is it lawful to borrow from a usurer.

*On the contrary,* He that suffers injury does not sin, according to the Philosopher (Ethic. v, 11), wherefore justice is not a mean between two vices, as stated in the same book (ch. 5). Now a usurer sins by doing an injury to the person who borrows from him under a condition of usury. Therefore he that accepts a loan under a condition of usury does not sin.

*I answer that,* It is by no means lawful to induce a man to sin, yet it is lawful to make use of another's sin for a good end, since even God uses all sin for some good, since He draws some good from every evil as stated in the Enchiridion (xi). Hence when Publicola asked whether it were lawful to make use of an oath taken by a man swearing by false gods (which is a manifest sin, for he gives Divine honor to them) Augustine (Ep. xlvii) answered that he who uses, not for a bad but for a good purpose, the oath of a man that swears by false gods, is a party, not to his sin of swearing by demons, but to his good compact whereby he kept his word. If however he were to induce him to swear by false gods, he would sin.

Accordingly we must also answer to the question in point that it is by no means lawful to induce a man to lend under a condition of usury: yet it is lawful to borrow for usury from a man who is ready to do so and is a usurer by profession; provided the borrower have a good end in view, such as the relief of his own or another's need. Thus too it is lawful for a man who has fallen among thieves to point out his property to them (which they sin in taking) in order to save his life, after the example of the ten men who said to Ismahel (Jer. 41:8): "Kill us not: for we have stores in the field."

Reply Obj. 1: He who borrows for usury does not consent to the usurer's sin but makes use of it. Nor is it the usurer's acceptance of usury that pleases him, but his lending, which is good.

Reply Obj. 2: He who borrows for usury gives the usurer an occasion, not for taking usury, but for lending; it is the usurer who finds an occasion of sin in the malice of his heart. Hence there is passive scandal on his part, while there is no active scandal on the part of the person who seeks to borrow. Nor is this passive scandal a reason why the other person should desist from borrowing if he is in need, since this passive scandal arises not from weakness or ignorance but from malice.

Reply Obj. 3: If one were to entrust one's money to a usurer lacking other means of practising usury; or with the intention of making a greater profit from his money by reason of the usury, one would be giving a sinner matter for sin, so that one would be a participator in his guilt. If, on the other hand, the usurer to whom one entrusts one's money has other means of practising usury, there is no sin in entrusting it to him that it may be in safer keeping, since this is to use a sinner for a good purpose.

## QUESTION 79

OF THE QUASI-INTEGRAL PARTS OF JUSTICE (In Four Articles)

We must now consider the quasi-integral parts of justice, which are *to do good,* and to decline from evil, and the opposite vices. Under this head there are four points of inquiry:

(1) Whether these two are parts of justice?
(2) Whether transgression is a special sin?
(3) Whether omission is a special sin?
(4) Of the comparison between omission and transgression.

FIRST ARTICLE [II-II, Q. 79, Art. 1]

Whether to Decline from Evil and to Do Good Are Parts of Justice?

Objection 1: It would seem that to decline from evil and to do good are not parts of justice. For it belongs to every virtue to perform a good deed and to avoid an evil one. But parts do not exceed the whole. Therefore to decline from evil and to do good should not be reckoned parts of justice, which is a special kind of virtue.

Obj. 2: Further, a gloss on Ps. 33:15, "Turn away from evil and do good," says: "The former," i.e. to turn away from evil, "avoids sin, the latter," i.e. to do good, "deserves the life and the palm." But any part of a virtue deserves the life and the palm. Therefore to decline from evil is not a part of justice.

Obj. 3: Further, things that are so related that one implies the other, are not mutually distinct as parts of a whole. Now declining from evil is implied in doing good: since no one does evil and good at the same time. Therefore declining from evil and doing good are not parts of justice.

*On the contrary,* Augustine (De Correp. et Grat. i) declares that "declining from evil and doing good" belong to the justice of the law.

*I answer that,* If we speak of good and evil in general, it belongs to every virtue to do good and to avoid evil: and in this sense they cannot be reckoned parts of justice, except justice be taken in the sense of "all virtue" [*Cf. Q. 58, A. 5]. And yet even if justice be taken in this sense it regards a certain special aspect of good; namely, the good as due in respect of Divine or human law.

On the other hand justice considered as a special virtue regards good as due to one's neighbor. And in this sense it belongs to special justice to do good considered as due to one's neighbor, and to avoid the opposite evil, that, namely, which is hurtful to one's neighbor; while it belongs to general justice to do good in relation to the community or in relation to God, and to avoid the opposite evil.

Now these two are said to be quasi-integral parts of general or of special justice, because each is required for the perfect act of justice. For it belongs to justice to establish equality in our relations with others, as shown above (Q. 58, A. 2): and it pertains to the same cause to establish and to preserve that which it has established. Now a person establishes the equality of justice by doing good, i.e. by rendering to another his due: and he preserves the already established equality of justice by declining from evil, that is by inflicting no injury on his neighbor.

Reply Obj. 1: Good and evil are here considered under a special aspect, by which they are appropriated to justice. The reason why these two are reckoned parts of justice under a special aspect of good and evil, while they are not reckoned parts of any other moral virtue, is that the other moral virtues are concerned with the passions wherein to do good is to observe the mean, which is the same as to avoid the extremes as evils: so that doing good and avoiding evil come to the same, with regard to the other virtues. On the other hand justice is concerned with operations and external things, wherein to establish equality is one thing, and not to disturb the equality established is another.

Reply Obj. 2: To decline from evil, considered as a part of justice, does not denote a pure negation, viz. "not to do evil"; for this does not deserve the palm, but only avoids the punishment. But it implies a movement of the will in repudiating evil, as the very term "decline" shows. This is meritorious; especially when a person resists against an instigation to do evil.

Reply Obj. 3: Doing good is the completive act of justice, and the principal part, so to speak, thereof. Declining from evil is a more imperfect act, and a secondary part of that virtue. Hence it is a material part, so to speak, thereof, and a necessary condition of the formal and completive part.

SECOND ARTICLE [II-II, Q. 79, Art. 2]

Whether Transgression Is a Special Sin?

Objection 1: It would seem that transgression is not a special sin. For no species is included in the definition of its genus. Now transgression is included in the definition of sin; because Ambrose says (De Parad. viii) that sin is "a transgression of the Divine law." Therefore transgression is not a species of sin.

Obj. 2: Further, no species is more comprehensive than its genus. But transgression is more comprehensive than sin, because sin is a "word, deed or desire against the law of God," according to Augustine (Contra Faust. xxii, 27), while transgression is also against nature, or custom. Therefore transgression is not a species of sin.

Obj. 3: Further, no species contains all the parts into which its genus is divided. Now the sin of transgression extends to all the capital vices, as well as to sins of thought, word and deed. Therefore transgression is not a special sin.

*On the contrary,* It is opposed to a special virtue, namely justice.

*I answer that,* The term transgression is derived from bodily movement and applied to moral actions. Now a person is said to transgress in bodily movement, when he steps (*graditur*) beyond (*trans*) a fixed boundary—and it is a negative precept that fixes the boundary that man must not exceed in his moral actions. Wherefore to transgress, properly speaking, is to act against a negative precept.

Now materially considered this may be common to all the species of sin, because man transgresses a Divine precept by any species of mortal sin. But if we consider it formally, namely under its special aspect of an act against a negative precept, it is a special sin in two ways. First, in so far as it is opposed to those kinds of sin that are opposed to the other virtues: for just as it belongs properly to legal justice to consider a precept as binding, so it belongs properly to a transgression to consider a precept as an object of contempt. Secondly, in so far as it is distinct from omission which is opposed to an affirmative precept.

Reply Obj. 1: Even as legal justice is "all virtue" (Q. 58, A. 5) as regards its subject and matter, so legal injustice is materially "all sin." It is in this way that Ambrose defined sin, considering it from the point of view of legal injustice.

Reply Obj. 2: The natural inclination concerns the precepts of the natural law. Again, a laudable custom has the force of a precept; since as Augustine says in an epistle *on the Fast of the Sabbath* (Ep. xxxvi), "a custom of God's people should be looked upon as law." Hence both sin and transgression may be against a laudable custom and against a natural inclination.

Reply Obj. 3: All these species of sin may include transgression, if we consider them not under their proper aspects, but under a special aspect, as stated above. The sin of omission, however, is altogether distinct from the sin of transgression.

THIRD ARTICLE [II-II, Q. 79, Art. 3]

Whether Omission Is a Special Sin?

Objection 1: It would seem that omission is not a special sin. For every sin is either original or actual. Now omission is not original sin, for it is not contracted through origin; nor is it actual sin, for it may be altogether without act, as stated above (I-II, Q. 71, A. 5) when we were treating of sins in general. Therefore omission is not a special sin.

Obj. 2: Further, every sin is voluntary. Now

omission sometimes is not voluntary but necessary, as when a woman is violated after taking a vow of virginity, or when one lose that which one is under an obligation to restore, or when a priest is bound to say Mass, and is prevented from doing so. Therefore omission is not always a sin.

Obj. 3: Further, it is possible to fix the time when any special sin begins. But this is not possible in the case of omission, since one is not altered by not doing a thing, no matter when the omission occurs, and yet the omission is not always sinful. Therefore omission is not a special sin.

Obj. 4: Further, every special sin is opposed to a special virtue. But it is not possible to assign any special virtue to which omission is opposed, both because the good of any virtue can be omitted, and because justice to which it would seem more particularly opposed, always requires an act, even in declining from evil, as stated above (A. 1, ad 2), while omission may be altogether without act. Therefore omission is not a special sin.

*On the contrary,* It is written (James 4:17): "To him ... who knoweth to do good and doth it not, to him it is sin."

*I answer that,* omission signifies the non-fulfilment of a good, not indeed of any good, but of a good that is due. Now good under the aspect of due belongs properly to justice; to legal justice, if the thing due depends on Divine or human law; to special justice, if the due is something in relation to one's neighbor. Wherefore, in the same way as justice is a special virtue, as stated above (Q. 58, AA. 6, 7), omission is a special sin distinct from the sins which are opposed to the other virtues; and just as doing good, which is the opposite of omitting it, is a special part of justice, distinct from avoiding evil, to which transgression is opposed, so too is omission distinct from transgression.

Reply Obj. 2: Omission is not original but actual sin, not as though it had some act essential to it, but for as much as the negation of an act is reduced to the genus of act, and in this sense non-action is a kind of action, as stated above (I-II, Q. 71, A. 6, ad 1).

Reply Obj. 2: Omission, as stated above, is only of such good as is due and to which one is bound. Now no man is bound to the impossible: wherefore no man sins by omission, if he does not do what he cannot. Accordingly she who is violated after vowing virginity, is guilty of an omission, not through not having virginity, but through not repenting of her past sin, or through not doing what she can to fulfil her vow by observing continence. Again a priest is not bound to say Mass, except he have a suitable opportunity, and if this be lacking, there is no omission. And in like manner, a person is bound to restitution, supposing he has the wherewithal; if he has not and cannot have it, he is not guilty of an omission, provided he does what he can. The same applies to other similar cases.

Reply Obj. 3: Just as the sin of transgression is opposed to negative precepts which regard the avoidance of evil, so the sin of omission is opposed to affirmative precepts, which regard the doing of good. Now affirmative precepts bind not for always, but for a fixed time, and at that time the sin of omission begins. But it may happen that then one is unable to do what one ought, and if this inability is without any fault on his part, he does not omit his duty, as stated above (ad 2; I-II, Q. 71, A. 5). On the other hand if this inability is due to some previous fault of his (for instance, if a man gets drunk at night, and cannot get up for matins, as he ought to), some say that the sin of omission begins when he engages in an action that is illicit and incompatible with the act to which he is bound. But this does not seem to be true, for supposing one were to rouse him by violence and that he went to matins, he would not omit to go, so that, evidently, the previous drunkenness was not an omission, but the cause of an omission. Consequently, we must say that the omission begins to be imputed to him as a sin, when the time comes for the action; and yet this is on account of a preceding cause by reason of which the subsequent omission becomes voluntary.

Reply Obj. 4: Omission is directly opposed to justice, as stated above; because it is a non-fulfilment of a good of virtue, but only under the aspect of due, which pertains to justice. Now more is required for an act to be virtuous and meritorious than for it to be sinful and demeritorious, because "good results from an entire cause, whereas evil arises from each single defect" [*Dionysius, De Div. Nom. iv]. Wherefore the merit of justice requires an act, whereas an omission does not.

FOURTH ARTICLE [II-II, Q. 79, Art. 4]

Whether a Sin of Omission Is More Grievous Than a Sin of Transgression?

Objection 1: It would seem that a sin of omission is more grievous than a sin of transgression. For *delictum* would seem to signify the same as *derelictum* [*Augustine, QQ. in Levit., qu. xx], and therefore is seemingly the same as an omission. But *delictum* denotes a more grievous offence than transgression, because it deserves more expiation as appears from Lev. 5. Therefore the sin of omission is more grievous than the sin of transgression.

Obj. 2: Further, the greater evil is opposed to the greater good, as the Philosopher declares (Ethic. viii, 10). Now to do good is a more excellent part of justice, than to decline from evil, to which transgression is opposed, as stated above (A. 1, ad 3). Therefore omission is a graver sin than transgression.

Obj. 3: Further, sins of transgression may be either venial or mortal. But sins of omission seem to be always mortal, since they are opposed to an affirmative precept. Therefore omission would seem to be a graver sin than transgression.

Obj. 4: Further, the pain of loss which consists in being deprived of seeing God and is inflicted for the sin of omission, is a greater punishment than the pain of sense, which is inflicted for the sin of transgression, as Chrysostom states (Hom. xxiii super Matth.). Now punishment is proportionate to fault. Therefore the sin of omission is graver than the sin of transgression.

*On the contrary,* It is easier to refrain from evil deeds than to accomplish good deeds. Therefore it is a graver sin not to refrain from an evil deed, i.e. to transgress, than not to accomplish a good deed, which is to omit.

*I answer that,* The gravity of a sin depends on its remoteness from virtue. Now contrariety is the greatest remoteness, according to *Metaph.* x [*Didot. ed. ix, 4]. Wherefore a thing is further removed from its contrary than from its simple negation; thus black is further removed from white than not-white is, since every black is not-white, but not conversely. Now it is evident that transgression is contrary to an act of virtue, while omission denotes the negation thereof: for instance it is a sin of omission, if one fail to give one's parents due reverence, while it is a sin of transgression to revile them or injure them in any way. Hence it is evident that, simply and absolutely speaking, transgression is a graver sin than omission, although a particular omission may be graver than a particular transgression.

Reply Obj. 1: *Delictum* in its widest sense denotes any kind of omission; but sometimes it is taken strictly for the omission of something concerning God, or for a man's intentional and as it were contemptuous dereliction of duty: and then it has a certain gravity, for which reason it demands a greater expiation.

Reply Obj. 2: The opposite of *doing good* is both not doing good, which is an omission, and doing evil, which is a transgression: but the first is opposed by contradiction, the second by contrariety, which implies greater remoteness: wherefore transgression is the more grievous sin.

Reply Obj. 3: Just as omission is opposed to affirmative precepts, so is transgression opposed to negative precepts: wherefore both, strictly speaking, have the character of mortal sin. Transgression and omission, however, may be taken broadly for any infringement of an affirmative or negative precept, disposing to the opposite of such precept: and so taking both in a broad sense they may be venial sins.

Reply Obj. 4: To the sin of transgression there correspond both the pain of loss on account of the aversion from God, and the pain of sense, on account of the inordinate conversion to a mutable good. In like manner omission deserves not only the pain of loss, but also the pain of sense, according to Matt. 7:19, "Every tree that bringeth not forth good fruit shall be cut down, and shall be cast into the fire"; and this on account of the root from which it grows, although it does not necessarily imply conversion to any mutable good.

## QUESTION 80

OF THE POTENTIAL PARTS OF JUSTICE (In One Article)

We must now consider the potential parts of justice, namely the virtues annexed thereto; under which head there are two points of consideration:

(1) What virtues are annexed to justice?

(2) The individual virtues annexed to justice.

ARTICLE [II-II, Q. 80, Art.]

Whether the Virtues Annexed to Justice Are Suitably Enumerated?

Objection 1: It would seem that the virtues annexed to justice are unsuitably enumerated. Tully [*De Invent. ii, 53] reckons six, viz. "religion, piety, gratitude, revenge, observance, truth." Now revenge is seemingly a species of commutative justice whereby revenge is taken for injuries inflicted, as stated above (Q. 61, A. 4). Therefore it should not be reckoned among the virtues annexed to justice.

Obj. 2: Further, Macrobius (Super Somn. Scip. i, 8) reckons seven, viz. "innocence, friendship, concord, piety, religion, affection, humanity," several of which are omitted by Tully. Therefore the virtues annexed to justice would seem to be insufficiently enumerated.

Obj. 3: Further, others reckon five parts of justice, viz. "obedience" in respect of one's superiors, "discipline" with regard to inferiors, "equity" as regards equals, "fidelity" and "truthfulness" towards all; and of these "truthfulness" alone is mentioned by Tully. Therefore he would seem to have enumerated insufficiently the virtues annexed to justice.

Obj. 4: Further, the peripatetic Andronicus [*De Affectibus] reckons nine parts annexed to justice viz. "liberality, kindliness, revenge, commonsense, [* *eugnomosyne* ] piety, gratitude, holiness, just exchange" and "just lawgiving"; and of all these it is evident that Tully mentions none but "revenge." Therefore he would appear to have made an incomplete enumeration.

Obj. 5: Further, Aristotle (Ethic. v, 10) mentions *epieikeia* as being annexed to justice: and yet seemingly it is not included in any of the foregoing enumerations. Therefore the virtues annexed to justice are insufficiently enumerated.

*I answer that,* Two points must be observed about the virtues annexed to a principal virtue. The first is that these virtues have something in common with the principal virtue; and the second is that in some respect they fall short of the perfection of that virtue. Accordingly since justice is of one man to another as stated above (Q. 58, A. 2), all the virtues that are directed to another person may by reason of this common aspect be annexed to justice. Now the essential character of justice consists in rendering to another his due according to equality, as stated above (Q. 58, A. 11). Wherefore in two ways may a virtue directed to another person fall short of the perfection of justice: first, by falling short of the aspect of equality; secondly, by falling short of the aspect of due. For certain virtues there are which render another his due, but are unable to render the equal due. In the first place, whatever man renders to God is due, yet it cannot be equal, as though man rendered to God as much as he owes Him, according to Ps. 115:12, "What shall I render to the Lord for all the things that He hath rendered to me?" In this respect *religion* is annexed to justice since, according to Tully (De invent. ii, 53), it consists in offering service and ceremonial rites or worship to "some superior nature that men call divine." Secondly, it is not possible to make to one's parents an equal return of what one owes to them, as the Philosopher declares (Ethic. viii, 14); and thus *piety* is annexed to justice, for thereby, as Tully says (De invent. ii, 53), a man "renders service and constant deference to his kindred and the well-wishers of his country." Thirdly, according to the Philosopher (Ethic. iv, 3), man is unable to offer an equal meed for virtue, and thus *observance* is annexed to justice, consisting according to Tully (De invent. ii, 53) in the "deference and honor rendered to those who excel in worth."

A falling short of the just due may be considered in respect of a twofold due, moral or legal: wherefore the Philosopher (Ethic. viii, 13) assigns a corresponding twofold just. The legal due is that which one is bound to render by reason of a legal obligation; and this due is chiefly the concern of justice, which is the principal virtue. On the other hand, the moral due is that to which one is bound in respect of the rectitude of virtue: and since a due implies necessity, this kind of due has two degrees. For one due is so necessary that without it moral rectitude cannot be ensured: and this has more of the character of due. Moreover this due may be considered from the point of view of the debtor, and in this way it pertains to this kind of due that a man represent himself to others just as he is, both in word and deed. Wherefore to justice is annexed *truth,* whereby, as Tully says (De invent. ii, 53), present, past and future things are told without perversion. It may also be considered from the point of view of the person to whom it is due, by comparing the reward he receives with what he has done—sometimes in good things; and then annexed to justice we have *gratitude* which "consists in recollecting the friendship and kindliness shown by others, and in desiring to pay them back," as Tully states (De invent. ii, 53)—and sometimes in evil things, and then to justice is annexed *revenge,* whereby, as Tully states (De invent. ii, 53), "we resist force, injury or anything obscure* by taking vengeance or by self-defense." [*St. Thomas read *obscurum,* and explains it as meaning *derogatory,* infra Q. 108, A. 2. Cicero, however, wrote obfuturum, i.e. *hurtful.* ]

There is another due that is necessary in the sense that it conduces to greater rectitude, although without it rectitude may be ensured. This due is the concern of *liberality,* affability or friendship, or the like, all of which Tully omits in the aforesaid enumeration because there is little of the nature of anything due in them.

Reply Obj. 1: The revenge taken by authority of a public power, in accordance with a judge's sentence, belongs to commutative justice: whereas the revenge which a man takes on his own initiative, though not against the law, or which a man seeks to obtain from a judge, belongs to the virtue annexed to justice.

Reply Obj. 2: Macrobius appears to have considered the two integral parts of justice, namely, *declining from evil,* to which innocence belongs, and *doing good,* to which the six others belong. Of these, two would seem to regard relations between equals, namely, *friendship* in the external conduct and concord internally; two regard our relations toward superiors, namely, *piety* to parents, and *religion* to God; while two regard our relations towards inferiors, namely, *condescension,* in so far as their good pleases us, and *humanity,* whereby we help them in their needs. For Isidore says (Etym. x) that a man is said to be "humane, through having a feeling of love and pity towards men: this gives its name to humanity whereby we uphold one another." In this sense *friendship* is understood as directing our external conduct towards others, from which point of view the Philosopher treats of it in *Ethic.* iv, 6. *Friendship* may also be taken as regarding properly the affections, and as the Philosopher describes it in *Ethic.* viii and ix. In this sense three things pertain to friendship, namely, *benevolence* which is here called *affection* ; concord, and beneficence which is here called *humanity.* These three, however, are omitted by Tully, because, as stated above, they have little of the nature of a due.

Reply Obj. 3: *Obedience* is included in observance, which Tully mentions, because both reverential honor and obedience are due to persons who excel. "Faithfulness whereby a man's acts agree with his words" [*Cicero, De Repub. iv, De Offic. i, 7], is contained in *truthfulness* as to the observance of one's promises: yet *truthfulness* covers a wider ground, as we shall state further on (Q. 109, AA. 1, 3). *Discipline* is not due as a necessary duty, because one is under no obligation to an inferior as such, although a superior may be under an obligation to watch over his inferiors, according to Matt. 24:45, "A faithful and wise servant, whom his lord hath appointed over his family": and for this reason it is omitted by Tully. It may, however, be included in humanity mentioned by Macrobius; and equity under *epieikeia* or under friendship.

Reply Obj. 4: This enumeration contains some belonging to true justice. To particular justice belongs *justice of exchange,* which he describes as "the habit of observing equality in commutations." To legal justice, as regards things to be observed by all, he ascribes *legislative justice,* which he describes as "the science of political commutations relating to the community." As regards things which have to be done in particular cases beside the general laws, he mentions *common sense* or good judgment, * which is our guide in such like matters, as stated above (Q. 51, A. 4) in the treatise on prudence: wherefore he says that it is a "voluntary justification," because by his own free will man observes what is just according to his judgment and not according to the written law. [*St. Thomas indicates the Greek derivation: *eugnomosyne* quasi 'bona gnome .'] These two are ascribed to prudence as their director, and to justice as their executor. *Eusebeia* (piety) means good worship and consequently is the same as religion, wherefore he says that it is the science of "the service of God" (he speaks after the manner of Socrates who said that 'all the virtues are sciences') [*Aristotle, *Ethic.* vi, 13]: and holiness comes to the same, as we shall state further on (Q. 81, A. 8). *Eucharistia* (gratitude) means "good thanksgiving," and is mentioned by Macrobius: wherefore Isidore says (Etym. x) that "a kind man is one who is ready of his own accord to do good, and is of gentle speech": and Andronicus too says that "kindliness is a habit of voluntary beneficence." *Liberality* would seem to pertain to *humanity.*

Reply Obj. 5: *Epieikeia* is annexed, not to particular but to legal justice, and apparently is the same as that which goes by the name of eugnomosyne (common sense).

# QUESTION 81

OF RELIGION (In Eight Articles)

We must now consider each of the foregoing virtues, in so far as our present scope demands. We shall consider (1) religion, (2) piety, (3) observance, (4) gratitude, (5) revenge, (6) truth, (7) friendship, (8) liberality, (9) *epieikeia* . Of the other virtues that have been mentioned we have spoken partly in the treatise on charity, viz. of concord and the like, and partly in this treatise on justice, for instance, of right commutations and of innocence. Of legislative justice we spoke in the treatise on prudence.

Religion offers a threefold consideration: (1) Religion considered in itself; (2) its acts; (3) the opposite vices.

Under the first head there are eight points of inquiry:

(1) Whether religion regards only our relation to God?

(2) Whether religion is a virtue?

(3) Whether religion is one virtue?

(4) Whether religion is a special virtue?

(5) Whether religion is a theological virtue?

(6) Whether religion should be preferred to the other moral virtues?

(7) Whether religion has any external actions?

(8) Whether religion is the same as holiness?

FIRST ARTICLE [II-II, Q. 81, Art. 1]

Whether Religion Directs Man to God Alone?

Objection 1: It would seem that religion does not direct man to God alone. It is written (James 1:27): "Religion clean and undefiled before God and the Father is this, to visit the fatherless and widows in their tribulation, and to keep oneself unspotted from this world." Now "to visit the fatherless and widows" indicates an order between oneself and one's neighbor, and "to keep oneself unspotted from this world" belongs to the order of a man within himself. Therefore religion does not imply order to God alone.

Obj. 2: Further, Augustine says (De Civ. Dei x, 1) that "since in speaking Latin not only unlettered but even most cultured persons ere wont to speak of religion as being exhibited, to our human kindred and relations as also to those who are linked with us by any kind of tie, that term does not escape ambiguity when it is a question of Divine worship, so that we be able to say without hesitation that religion is nothing else but the worship of God." Therefore religion signifies a relation not only to God but also to our kindred.

Obj. 3: Further, seemingly *latria* pertains to religion. Now " *latria* signifies servitude," as Augustine states (De Civ. Dei x, 1). And we are bound to serve not only God, but also our neighbor, according to Gal. 5:13, "By charity of the spirit serve one another." Therefore religion includes a relation to one's neighbor also.

Obj. 4: Further, worship belongs to religion. Now man is said to worship not only God, but also his neighbor, according to the saying of Cato [*Dionysius Cato, Breves Sententiae], "Worship thy parents." Therefore religion directs us also to our neighbor, and not only to God.

Obj. 5: Further, all those who are in the state of grace are subject to God. Yet not all who are in a state of grace are called religious, but only those who bind themselves by certain vows and observances, and to obedience to certain men. Therefore religion seemingly does not denote a relation of subjection of man to God.

*On the contrary,* Tully says (Rhet. ii, 53) that "religion consists in offering service and ceremonial rites to a superior nature that men call divine."

*I answer that,* as Isidore says (Etym. x), "according to Cicero, a man is said to be religious from *religio,* because he often ponders over, and, as it were, reads again ( *relegit* ), the things which pertain to the worship of God," so that religion would seem to take its name from reading over those things which belong to Divine worship because we ought frequently to ponder over such things in our hearts, according to Prov. 3:6, "In all thy ways think on Him." According to Augustine (De Civ. Dei x, 3) it may also take its name from the fact that "we ought to seek God again, whom we had lost by our neglect" [*St. Augustine plays on the words *reeligere,* i.e. to choose over again, and *negligere,* to neglect or despise.]. Or again, religion may be derived from *religare* (to bind together), wherefore Augustine says (De Vera Relig. 55): "May religion bind us to the one Almighty God." However, whether religion take its name from frequent reading, or from a repeated choice of what has been lost through negligence, or from being a bond, it denotes properly a relation to God. For it is He to Whom we ought to be bound as to our unfailing principle; to Whom also our choice should be resolutely directed as to our last end; and Whom we lose when we neglect Him by sin, and should recover by believing in Him and confessing our faith.

Reply Obj. 1: Religion has two kinds of acts. Some are its proper and immediate acts, which it elicits, and by which man is directed to God alone, for instance, sacrifice, adoration and the like. But it has other acts, which it produces through the medium of the virtues which it commands, directing them to the honor of God, because the virtue which is concerned with the end, commands the virtues which are concerned with the means. Accordingly "to visit the fatherless and widows in their tribulation" is an act of religion as commanding, and an act of mercy as eliciting; and "to keep oneself unspotted from this world" is an act of religion as commanding, but of temperance or of some similar virtue as eliciting.

Reply Obj. 2: Religion is referred to those things one exhibits to one's human kindred, if we take the term religion in a broad sense, but not if we take it in its proper sense. Hence, shortly before the passage quoted, Augustine says: "In a stricter sense religion seems to denote, not any kind of worship, but the worship of God."

Reply Obj. 3: Since servant implies relation to a lord, wherever there is a special kind of lordship there must needs be a special kind of service. Now it is evident that lordship belongs to God in a special and singular way, because He made all things, and has supreme dominion over all. Consequently a special kind of service is due to Him, which is known as *latria* in Greek; and therefore it belongs to religion.

Reply Obj. 4: We are said to worship those whom we honor, and to cultivate [*In the Latin the same word *colere* stands for "worship" and "cultivate"] a man's memory or presence: we even speak of cultivating things that are beneath us, thus a farmer ( *agricola* ) is one who cultivates the land, and an inhabitant ( *incola* ) is one who cultivates the place where he dwells. Since, however, special honor is due to God as the first principle of all things, to Him also is due a special kind of worship, which in Greek is *Eusebeia* or *Theosebeia* , as Augustine states (De Civ. Dei x, 1).

Reply Obj. 5: Although the name "religious" may be given to all in general who worship God, yet in a special way religious are those who consecrate their whole life to the Divine worship, by withdrawing from human affairs. Thus also the term "contemplative" is applied, not to those who contemplate, but to those who give up their whole lives to contemplation. Such men subject themselves to man, not for man's sake but for God's sake, according to the word of the Apostle (Gal. 4:14), "You ... received me as an angel of God, even as Christ Jesus."

SECOND ARTICLE [II-II, Q. 81, Art. 2]

Whether Religion Is a Virtue?

Objection 1: It would seem that religion is not a virtue. Seemingly it belongs to religion to pay reverence to God. But reverence is an act of fear which is a gift, as stated above (Q. 19, A. 9). Therefore religion is not a virtue but a gift.

Obj. 2: Further, every virtue is a free exercise of the will, wherefore it is described as an "elective" or voluntary "habit" [*Ethic. ii, 6]. Now, as stated above (A. 1, ad 3) *latria* belongs to religion, and *latria* denotes a kind of servitude. Therefore religion is not a virtue.

Obj. 3: Further, according to *Ethic.* ii, 1, aptitude for virtue is in us by nature, wherefore things pertaining to virtue belong to the dictate of natural reason. Now, it belongs to religion "to offer ceremonial worship to the Godhead" [*Cf. A. 1], and ceremonial matters, as stated above (I-II, Q. 99, A. 3, ad 2; Q. 101), do not belong to the dictate of natural reason. Therefore religion is not a virtue.

*On the contrary,* It is enumerated with the other virtues, as appears from what has been said above (Q. 80).

*I answer that,* As stated above (Q. 58, A. 3; I-II, Q. 55, AA. 3, 4) "a virtue is that which makes its possessor good, and his act good likewise," wherefore we must needs say that every good act belongs to a virtue. Now it is evident that to render anyone his due has the aspect of good, since by rendering a person his due, one becomes suitably proportioned to him, through being ordered to him in a becoming manner. But order comes under the aspect of good, just as mode and species, according to Augustine (De Nat. Boni iii). Since then it belongs to religion to pay due honor to someone, namely, to God, it is evident that religion is a virtue.

Reply Obj. 1: To pay reverence to God is an act of the gift of fear. Now it belongs to religion to do certain things through reverence for God. Hence it follows, not that religion is the same as the gift of fear, but that it is referred thereto as to something more excellent; for the gifts are more excellent than the moral virtues, as stated above (Q. 9, A. 1, ad 3; I-II, Q. 68, A. 8).

Reply Obj. 2: Even a slave can voluntarily do his duty by his master, and so "he makes a virtue of necessity" [*Jerome, Ep. liv, ad Furiam.], by doing his duty voluntarily. In like manner, to render due service to God may be an act of virtue, in so far as man does so voluntarily.

Reply Obj. 3: It belongs to the dictate of natural reason that man should do something through reverence for God. But that he should do this or that determinate thing does not belong to the dictate of natural reason, but is established by Divine or human law.

THIRD ARTICLE [II-II, Q. 81, Art. 3]

Whether Religion Is One Virtue?

Objection 1: It would seem that religion is not one virtue. Religion directs us to God, as stated above (A. 1). Now in God there are three Persons; and also many attributes, which differ at least logically from one another. Now a logical difference in the object suffices for a difference of virtue, as stated above (Q. 50, A. 2, ad 2). Therefore religion is not one virtue.

Obj. 2: Further, of one virtue there is seemingly one act, since habits are distinguished by their acts. Now there are many acts of religion, for instance to worship, to serve, to vow, to pray, to sacrifice and many such like. Therefore religion is not one virtue.

Obj. 3: Further, adoration belongs to religion. Now adoration is paid to images under one aspect, and under another aspect to God Himself. Since, then, a difference of aspect distinguishes virtues, it would seem that religion is not one virtue.

*On the contrary,* It is written (Eph. 4:5): "One God [Vulg.: 'Lord'], one faith." Now true religion professes faith in one God. Therefore religion is one virtue.

*I answer that,* As stated above (I-II, Q. 54, A. 2, ad 1), habits are differentiated according to a different aspect of the object. Now it belongs to religion to show reverence to one God under one aspect, namely, as the first principle of the creation and government of things. Wherefore He Himself says (Malach. 1:6): "If ... I be a father, where is My honor?" For it belongs to a father to beget and to govern. Therefore it is evident that religion is one virtue.

Reply Obj. 1: The three Divine Persons are the one principle of the creation and government of things, wherefore they are served by one religion. The different aspects of the attributes concur under the aspect of first principle, because God produces all things, and governs them by the wisdom, will and power of His goodness. Wherefore religion is one virtue.

Reply Obj. 2: By the one same act man both serves and worships God, for worship regards the excellence of God, to Whom reverence is due: while service regards the subjection of man who, by his condition, is under an obligation of showing reverence to God. To these two belong all acts ascribed to religion, because, by them all, man bears witness to the Divine excellence and to his own subjection to God, either by offering something to God, or by assuming something Divine.

Reply Obj. 3: The worship of religion is paid to images, not as considered in themselves, nor as things, but as images leading us to God incarnate. Now movement to an image as image does not stop at the image, but goes on to the thing it represents. Hence neither *latria* nor the virtue of religion is differentiated by the fact that religious worship is paid to the images of Christ.

FOURTH ARTICLE [II-II, Q. 81, Art. 4]

Whether Religion Is a Special Virtue, Distinct from the Others?

Objection 1: It would seem that religion is not a special virtue distinct from the others. Augustine says (De Civ. Dei x, 6): "Any action whereby we are united to God in holy fellowship, is a true sacrifice." But sacrifice belongs to religion. Therefore every virtuous deed belongs to religion; and consequently religion is not a special virtue.

Obj. 2: Further, the Apostle says (1 Cor. 10:31): "Do all to the glory of God." Now it belongs to religion to do anything in reverence of God, as stated above (A. 1, ad 2; A. 2). Therefore religion is not a special virtue.

Obj. 3: Further, the charity whereby we love God is not distinct from the charity whereby we love our neighbor. But according to *Ethic.* viii, 8 "to be honored is almost to be loved." Therefore the religion whereby we honor God is not a special virtue distinct from observance, or dulia, or piety whereby we honor our neighbor. Therefore religion is not a special virtue.

*On the contrary,* It is reckoned a part of justice, distinct from the other parts.

*I answer that,* Since virtue is directed to the good, wherever there is a special aspect of good, there must be a special virtue. Now the good to which religion is directed, is to give due honor to God. Again, honor is due to someone under the aspect of excellence: and to God a singular excellence is competent, since He infinitely surpasses all things and exceeds them in every way. Wherefore to Him is special honor due: even as in human affairs we see that different honor is due to different personal excellences, one kind of honor to a father, another to the king, and so on. Hence it is evident that religion is a special virtue.

Reply Obj. 1: Every virtuous deed is said to be a sacrifice, in so far as it is done out of reverence of God. Hence this does not prove that religion is a general virtue, but that it commands all other virtues, as stated above (A. 1, ad 1).

Reply Obj. 2: Every deed, in so far as it is done in God's honor, belongs to religion, not as eliciting but as commanding: those belong to religion as eliciting which pertain to the reverence of God by reason of their specific character.

Reply Obj. 3: The object of love is the good, but the object of honor and reverence is something excellent. Now God's goodness is communicated to the creature, but the excellence of His goodness is not. Hence the charity whereby God is loved is not distinct from the charity whereby our neighbor is loved; whereas the religion whereby God is honored, is distinct from the virtues whereby we honor our neighbor.

FIFTH ARTICLE [II-II, Q. 81, Art. 5]

Whether Religion Is a Theological Virtue?

Objection 1: It would seem that religion is a theological virtue. Augustine says (Enchiridion iii) that "God is worshiped by faith, hope and charity," which are theological virtues. Now it belongs to religion to pay worship to God. Therefore religion is a theological virtue.

Obj. 2: Further, a theological virtue is one that has God for its object. Now religion has God for its object, since it directs us to God alone, as stated above (A. 1). Therefore religion is a theological virtue.

Obj. 3: Further, every virtue is either theological, or intellectual, or moral, as is clear from what has been said (I-II, QQ. 57, 58, 62). Now it is evident that religion is not an intellectual virtue, because its perfection does not depend on the consideration of truth: nor is it a moral virtue, which consists properly in observing the mean between too much and too little, for one cannot worship God too much, according to Ecclus. 43:33, "Blessing the Lord, exalt Him as much as you can; for He is above all praise." Therefore it remains that it is a theological virtue.

*On the contrary,* It is reckoned a part of justice which is a moral virtue.

*I answer that,* As stated above (A. 4) religion pays due worship to God. Hence two things are to be considered in religion: first that which it offers to God, viz. worship, and this is by way of matter and object in religion; secondly, that to which something is offered, viz. God, to Whom worship is paid. And yet the acts whereby God is worshiped do not reach out to God himself, as when we believe God we reach out to Him by believing; for which reason it was stated (Q. 1, AA. 1, 2, 4) that God is the object of faith, not only because we believe in a God, but because we believe God.

Now due worship is paid to God, in so far as certain acts whereby God is worshiped, such as the offering of sacrifices and so forth, are done out of reverence for God. Hence it is evident that God is related to religion not as matter or object, but as end: and consequently religion is not a theological virtue whose object is the last end, but a moral virtue which is properly about things referred to the end.

Reply Obj. 1: The power or virtue whose action deals with an end, moves by its command the power or virtue whose action deals with matters directed to that end. Now the theological virtues, faith, hope and charity have an act in reference to God as their proper object: wherefore, by their command, they cause the act of religion, which performs certain deeds directed to God: and so Augustine says that God is worshiped by faith, hope and charity.

Reply Obj. 2: Religion directs man to God not as its object but as its end.

Reply Obj. 3: Religion is neither a theological nor an intellectual, but a moral virtue, since it is a part of justice, and observes a mean, not in the passions, but in actions directed to God, by establishing a kind of equality in them. And when I say "equality," I do not mean absolute equality, because it is not possible to pay God as much as we owe Him, but equality in consideration of man's ability and God's acceptance.

And it is possible to have too much in matters pertaining to the Divine worship, not as regards the circumstance of quantity, but as regards other circumstances, as when Divine worship is paid to whom it is not due, or when it is not due, or unduly in respect of some other circumstance.

SIXTH ARTICLE [II-II, Q. 81, Art. 6]

Whether Religion Should Be Preferred to the Other Moral Virtues?

Objection 1: It would seem that religion should not be preferred to the other moral virtues. The perfection of a moral virtue consists in its observing the mean, as stated in *Ethic.* ii, 6. But religion fails to observe the mean of justice, since it does not render an absolute equal to God. Therefore religion is not more excellent than the other moral virtues.

Obj. 2: Further, what is offered by one man to another is the more praiseworthy, according as the person it is offered to is in greater need: wherefore it is written (Isa. 57:7): "Deal thy bread to the hungry." But God needs nothing that we can offer Him, according to Ps. 15:2, "I have said: Thou art my God, for Thou hast no need of my goods." Therefore religion would seem less praiseworthy than the other virtues whereby man's needs are relieved.

Obj. 3: Further, the greater the obligation to do a thing, the less praise does it deserve, according to 1 Cor. 9:16, "If I preach the Gospel, it is no glory to me: a necessity lieth upon me." Now the more a thing is due, the greater the obligation of paying it. Since, then, what is paid to God by man is in the highest degree due to Him, it would seem that religion is less praiseworthy than the other human virtues.

*On the contrary,* The precepts pertaining to religion are given precedence (Ex. 20) as being of greatest importance. Now the order of precepts is proportionate to the order of virtues, since the precepts of the Law prescribe acts of virtue. Therefore religion is the chief of the moral virtues.

*I answer that,* Whatever is directed to an end takes its goodness from being ordered to that end; so that the nearer it is to the end the better it is. Now moral virtues, as stated above (A. 5; Q. 4, A. 7), are about matters that are ordered to God as their end. And religion approaches nearer to God than the other moral virtues, in so far as its actions are directly and immediately ordered to the honor of God. Hence religion excels among the moral virtues.

Reply Obj. 1: Virtue is praised because of the will, not because of the ability: and therefore if a man fall short of equality which is the mean of justice, through lack of ability, his virtue deserves no less praise, provided there be no failing on the part of his will.

Reply Obj. 2: In offering a thing to a man on account of its usefulness to him, the more needy the man the more praiseworthy the offering, because it is more useful: whereas we offer a thing to God not on account of its usefulness to Him, but for the sake of His glory, and on account of its usefulness to us.

Reply Obj. 3: Where there is an obligation to do a thing it loses the luster of supererogation, but not the merit of virtue, provided it be done voluntarily. Hence the argument proves nothing.

SEVENTH ARTICLE [II-II, Q. 81, Art. 7]

Whether Religion Has an External Act?

Objection 1: It would seem that religion has not an external act. It is written (John 4:24): "God is a spirit, and they that adore Him, must adore Him in spirit and in truth." Now external acts pertain, not to the spirit but to the body. Therefore religion, to which adoration belongs, has acts that are not external but internal.

Obj. 2: Further, the end of religion is to pay God reverence and honor. Now it would savor of irreverence towards a superior, if one were to offer him that which properly belongs to his inferior. Since then whatever man offers by bodily actions, seems to be directed properly to the relief of human needs, or to the reverence of inferior creatures, it would seem unbecoming to employ them in showing reverence to God.

Obj. 3: Further, Augustine (De Civ. Dei vi, 10) commends Seneca for finding fault with those who offered to idols those things that are wont to be offered to men, because, to wit, that which befits mortals is unbecoming to immortals. But such things are much less becoming to the true God, Who is "exalted above all gods" [*Ps. 94:3]. Therefore it would seem wrong to worship God with bodily actions. Therefore religion has no bodily actions.

*On the contrary,* It is written (Ps. 83:3): "My heart and my flesh have rejoiced in the living God." Now just as internal actions belong to the heart, so do external actions belong to the members of the flesh. Therefore it seems that God ought to be worshiped not only by internal but also by external actions.

*I answer that,* We pay God honor and reverence, not for His sake (because He is of Himself full of glory to which no creature can add anything), but for our own sake, because by the very fact that we revere and honor God, our mind is subjected to Him; wherein its perfection consists, since a thing is perfected by being subjected to its superior, for instance the body is perfected by being quickened by the soul, and the air by being enlightened by the sun. Now the human mind, in order to be united to God, needs to be guided by the sensible world, since "invisible things ... are clearly seen, being understood by the things that are made," as the Apostle says (Rom. 1:20). Wherefore in the Divine worship it is necessary to make use of corporeal things, that man's mind may be aroused thereby, as by signs, to the spiritual acts by means of which he is united to God. Therefore the internal acts of religion take precedence of the others and belong to religion essentially, while its external acts are secondary, and subordinate to the internal acts.

Reply Obj. 1: Our Lord is speaking of that which is most important and directly intended in the worship of God.

Reply Obj. 2: These external things are offered to God, not as though He stood in need of them, according to Ps. 49:13, "Shall I eat the flesh of bullocks? or shall I drink the blood of goats?" but as signs of the internal and spiritual works, which are of themselves acceptable to God. Hence Augustine says (De Civ. Dei x, 5): "The visible sacrifice is the sacrament or sacred sign of the invisible sacrifice."

Reply Obj. 3: Idolaters are ridiculed for offering to idols things pertaining to men, not as signs arousing them to certain spiritual things, but as though they were of themselves acceptable to the idols; and still more because they were foolish and wicked.

EIGHTH ARTICLE [II-II, Q. 81, Art. 8]

Whether Religion Is the Same As Sanctity?

Objection 1: It would seem that religion is not the same as sanctity. Religion is a special virtue, as stated above (A. 4): whereas sanctity is a general virtue, because it makes us faithful, and fulfil our just obligations to God, according to Andronicus [*De Affectibus]. Therefore sanctity is not the same as religion.

Obj. 2: Further, sanctity seems to denote a kind of purity. For Dionysius says (Div. Nom. xii) that "sanctity is free from all uncleanness, and is perfect and altogether unspotted purity." Now purity would seem above all to pertain to temperance which repels bodily uncleanness. Since then religion belongs to justice, it would seem that sanctity is not the same as religion.

Obj. 3: Further, things that are opposite members of a division are not identified with one another. But in an enumeration given above (Q. 80, ad 4) of the parts of justice, sanctity is reckoned as distinct from religion. Therefore sanctity is not the same as religion.

*On the contrary,* It is written (Luke 1:74, 75):

"That ... we may serve Him ... in holiness and justice." Now, "to serve God" belongs to religion, as stated above (A. 1, ad 3; A. 3, ad 2). Therefore religion is the same as sanctity.

*I answer that,* The word "sanctity" seems to have two significations. In one way it denotes purity; and this signification fits in with the Greek, for *hagios* means "unsoiled." In another way it denotes firmness, wherefore in olden times the term "sancta" was applied to such things as were upheld by law and were not to be violated. Hence a thing is said to be sacred ( *sancitum* ) when it is ratified by law. Again, in Latin, this word *sanctus* may be connected with purity, if it be resolved into *sanguine tinctus,* "since, in olden times, those who wished to be purified were sprinkled with the victim's blood," according to Isidore (Etym. x). In either case the signification requires sanctity to be ascribed to those things that are applied to the Divine worship; so that not only men, but also the temple, vessels and such like things are said to be sanctified through being applied to the worship of God. For purity is necessary in order that the mind be applied to God, since the human mind is soiled by contact with inferior things, even as all things depreciate by admixture with baser things, for instance, silver by being mixed with lead. Now in order for the mind to be united to the Supreme Being it must be withdrawn from inferior things: and hence it is that without purity the mind cannot be applied to God. Wherefore it is written (Heb. 12:14): "Follow peace with all men, and holiness, without which no man shall see God." Again, firmness is required for the mind to be applied to God, for it is applied to Him as its last end and first beginning, and such things must needs be most immovable. Hence the Apostle said (Rom. 8:38, 39): "I am sure that neither death, nor life ... shall separate me [*Vulg.: 'shall be able to separate us'] from the love of God."

Accordingly, it is by sanctity that the human mind applies itself and its acts to God: so that it differs from religion not essentially but only logically. For it takes the name of religion according as it gives God due service in matters pertaining specially to the Divine worship, such as sacrifices, oblations, and so forth; while it is called sanctity, according as man refers to God not only these but also the works of the other virtues, or according as man by means of certain good works disposes himself to the worship of God.

Reply Obj. 1: Sanctity is a special virtue according to its essence; and in this respect it is in a way identified with religion. But it has a certain generality, in so far as by its command it directs the acts of all the virtues to the Divine good, even as legal justice is said to be a general virtue, in so far as it directs the acts of all the virtues to the common good.

Reply Obj. 2: Temperance practices purity, yet not so as to have the character of sanctity unless it be referred to God. Hence of virginity itself Augustine says (De Virgin. viii) that "it is honored not for what it is, but for being consecrated to God."

Reply Obj. 3: Sanctity differs from religion as explained above, not really but logically.

## QUESTION 82

OF DEVOTION (In Four Articles)

We must now consider the acts of religion. First, we shall consider the interior acts, which, as stated above, are its principal acts; secondly, we shall consider its exterior acts, which are secondary. The interior acts of religion are seemingly devotion and prayer. Accordingly we shall treat first of devotion, and afterwards of prayer.

Under the first head there are four points of inquiry:

(1) Whether devotion is a special act?

(2) Whether it is an act of religion?

(3) Of the cause of devotion?

(4) Of its effect?

FIRST ARTICLE [II-II, Q. 82, Art. 1]

Whether Devotion Is a Special Act?

Objection 1: It would seem that devotion is not a special act. That which qualifies other acts is seemingly not a special act. Now devotion seems to qualify other acts, for it is written (2 Paralip. 29:31): "All the multitude offered victims, and praises, and holocausts with a devout mind." Therefore devotion is not a special act.

Obj. 2: Further, no special kind of act is common to various genera of acts. But devotion is common to various genera of acts, namely, corporal and spiritual acts: for a person is said to meditate devoutly and to genuflect devoutly. Therefore devotion is not a special act.

Obj. 3: Further, every special act belongs either to an appetitive or to a cognitive virtue or power. But devotion belongs to neither, as may be seen by going through the various species of acts of either faculty, as enumerated above (I, QQ. 78, seqq.; I-II, Q. 23, A. 4). Therefore devotion is not a special act.

*On the contrary,* Merits are acquired by acts as stated above (I-II, Q. 21, AA. 34). But devotion has a special reason for merit. Therefore devotion is a special act.

*I answer that,* Devotion is derived from "devote" [*The Latin *devovere* means "to vow"]; wherefore those persons are said to be "devout" who, in a way, devote themselves to God, so as to subject themselves wholly to Him. Hence in olden times among the heathens a devotee was one who vowed to his idols to suffer death for the safety of his army, as Livy relates of the two Decii (Decad. I, viii, 9; x, 28). Hence devotion is apparently nothing else but the will to give oneself readily to things concerning the service of God. Wherefore it is written (Ex. 35:20, 21) that "the multitude of the children of Israel ... offered first-fruits to the Lord with a most ready and devout mind." Now it is evident that the will to do readily what concerns the service of God is a special kind of act. Therefore devotion is a special act of the will.

Reply Obj. 1: The mover prescribes the mode of the movement of the thing moved. Now the will moves the other powers of the soul to their acts, and the will, in so far as it regards the end, moves both itself and whatever is directed to the end, as stated above (I-II, Q. 9, A. 3). Wherefore, since devotion is an act of the will whereby a man offers himself for the service of God Who is the last end, it follows that devotion prescribes the mode to human acts, whether they be acts of the will itself about things directed to the end, or acts of the other powers that are moved by the will.

Reply Obj. 2: Devotion is to be found in various genera of acts, not as a species of those genera, but as the motion of the mover is found virtually in the movements of the things moved.

Reply Obj. 3: Devotion is an act of the appetitive part of the soul, and is a movement of the will, as stated above.

SECOND ARTICLE [II-II, Q. 82, Art. 2]

Whether Devotion Is an Act of Religion?

Objection 1: It would seem that devotion is not an act of religion. Devotion, as stated above (A. 1), consists in giving oneself up to God. But this is done chiefly by charity, since according to Dionysius (Div. Nom. iv) "the Divine love produces ecstasy, for it takes the lover away from himself and gives him to the beloved." Therefore devotion is an act of charity rather than of religion.

Obj. 2: Further, charity precedes religion; and devotion seems to precede charity; since, in the Scriptures, charity is represented by fire, while devotion is signified by fatness which is the material of fire [*Cant. 8:6; Ps. 52:6]. Therefore devotion is not an act of religion.

Obj. 3: Further, by religion man is directed to God alone, as stated above (Q. 81, A. 1). But devotion is directed also to men; for we speak of people being devout to certain holy men, and subjects are said to be devoted to their masters; thus Pope Leo says [*Serm. viii, De Pass. Dom.] that the Jews "out of devotion to the Roman laws," said: "We have no king but Caesar." Therefore devotion is not an act of religion.

*On the contrary,* Devotion is derived from devovere, as stated (A. 1). But a vow is an act of religion. Therefore devotion is also an act of religion.

*I answer that,* It belongs to the same virtue, to will to do something, and to have the will ready to do it, because both acts have the same object. For this reason the Philosopher says (Ethic. v, 1): "It is justice whereby men both will end do just actions." Now it is evident that to do what pertains to the worship or service of God, belongs properly to religion, as stated above (Q. 81). Wherefore it belongs to that virtue to have the will ready to do such things, and this is to be devout. Hence it is evident that devotion is an act of religion.

Reply Obj. 1: It belongs immediately to charity that man should give himself to God, adhering to Him by a union of the spirit; but it belongs immediately to religion, and, through the medium of religion, to charity which is the principle of religion, that man should give himself to God for certain works of Divine worship.

Reply Obj. 2: Bodily fatness is produced by the natural heat in the process of digestion, and at the same time the natural heat thrives, as it were, on this fatness. In like manner charity both causes devotion (inasmuch as love makes one ready to serve one's friend) and feeds on devotion. Even so all friendship is safeguarded and increased by the practice and consideration of friendly deeds.

Reply Obj. 3: Devotion to God's holy ones, dead or living, does not terminate in them, but passes on to God, in so far as we honor God in His servants. But the devotion of subjects to their temporal masters is of another kind, just as service of a temporal master differs from the service of God.

THIRD ARTICLE [II-II, Q. 82, Art. 3]

Whether Contemplation or Meditation Is the Cause of Devotion?

Objection 1: It would seem that contemplation or meditation is not the cause of devotion. No cause hinders its effect. But subtle considerations about abstract matters are often a hindrance to devotion. Therefore contemplation or meditation is not the cause of devotion.

Obj. 2: Further, if contemplation were the proper and essential cause of devotion, the higher objects of contemplation would arouse greater devotion. But the contrary is the case: since frequently we are urged to greater devotion by considering Christ's Passion and other mysteries of His humanity than by considering the greatness of His Godhead. Therefore contemplation is not the proper cause of devotion.

Obj. 3: Further, if contemplation were the proper cause of devotion, it would follow that those who are most apt for contemplation, are also most apt for devotion. Yet the contrary is to be noticed, for devotion is frequently found in men of simplicity and members of the female sex, who are defective in contemplation. Therefore contemplation is not the proper cause of devotion.

*On the contrary,* It is written (Ps. 38:4): "In my meditation a fire shall flame out." But spiritual fire causes devotion. Therefore meditation is the cause of devotion.

*I answer that,* The extrinsic and chief cause of devotion is God, of Whom Ambrose, commenting on Luke 9:55, says that "God calls whom He deigns to call, and whom He wills He makes religious: the profane Samaritans, had He so willed, He would have made devout." But the intrinsic cause on our part must needs be meditation or contemplation. For it was stated above (A. 1) that devotion is an act of the will to the effect that man surrenders himself readily to the service of God. Now every act of the will proceeds from some consideration, since the object of the will is a good understood. Wherefore Augustine says (De Trin. ix, 12; xv, 23) that "the will arises from the intelligence." Consequently meditation must needs be the cause of devotion, in so far as through meditation man conceives the thought of surrendering himself to God's service. Indeed a twofold consideration leads him thereto. The one is the consideration of God's goodness and loving kindness, according to Ps. 72:28, "It is good for me to adhere to my God, to put my hope in the Lord God": and this consideration wakens love [* *Dilectio,* the interior act of charity; cf. Q. 27] which is the proximate cause of devotion. The other consideration is that of man's own shortcomings, on account of which he needs to lean on God, according to Ps. 120:1, 2, "I have lifted up my eyes to the mountains, from whence help shall come to me: my help is from the Lord, Who made heaven and earth"; and this consideration shuts out presumption whereby man is hindered from submitting to God, because he leans on His strength.

Reply Obj. 1: The consideration of such things as are of a nature to awaken our love [*Ibid.] of God, causes devotion; whereas the consideration of foreign matters that distract the mind from such things is a hindrance to devotion.

Reply Obj. 2: Matters concerning the Godhead are, in themselves, the strongest incentive to love [*Ibid.] and consequently to devotion, because God is supremely lovable. Yet such is the weakness of the human mind that it needs a guiding hand, not only to the knowledge, but also to the love of Divine things by means of certain sensible objects known to us. Chief among these is the humanity of Christ, according to the words of the Preface [*Preface for Christmastide], "that through knowing God visibly, we may be caught up to the love of things invisible." Wherefore matters relating to Christ's humanity are the chief incentive to devotion, leading us thither as a guiding hand, although devotion itself has for its object matters concerning the Godhead.

Reply Obj. 3: Science and anything else conducive to greatness, is to man an occasion of self-confidence, so that he does not wholly surrender himself to God. The result is that such like things sometimes occasion a hindrance to devotion; while in simple souls and women devotion abounds by repressing pride. If, however, a man perfectly submits to God his science or any other perfection, by this very fact his devotion is increased.

FOURTH ARTICLE [II-II, Q. 82, Art. 4]

Whether Joy Is an Effect of Devotion?

Objection 1: It would seem that joy is not an effect of devotion. As stated above (A. 3, ad 2), Christ's Passion is the chief incentive to devotion. But the consideration thereof causes an affliction of the soul, according to Lam. 3:19, "Remember my poverty ... the wormwood and the gall," which refers to the Passion, and afterwards (Lam. 3:20) it is said: "I will be mindful and remember, and my soul shall languish within me." Therefore delight or joy is not the effect of devotion.

Obj. 2: Further, devotion consists chiefly in an interior sacrifice of the spirit. But it is written (Ps. 50:19): "A sacrifice to God is an afflicted spirit." Therefore affliction is the effect of devotion rather than gladness or joy.

Obj. 3: Further, Gregory of Nyssa says (De Homine xii) [*Orat. funebr. de Placilla Imp.] that "just as laughter proceeds from joy, so tears and groans are signs of sorrow." But devotion makes some people shed tears. Therefore gladness or joy is not the effect of devotion.

*On the contrary,* We say in the Collect [*Thursday after fourth Sunday of Lent]: "That we who are punished by fasting may be comforted by a holy devotion."

*I answer that,* The direct and principal effect of devotion is the spiritual joy of the mind, though sorrow is its secondary and indirect effect. For it has been stated (A. 3) that devotion is caused by a twofold consideration: chiefly by the consideration of God's goodness, because this consideration belongs to the term, as it were, of the movement of the will in surrendering itself to God, and the direct result of this consideration is joy, according to Ps. 76:4, "I remembered God, and was delighted"; but accidentally this consideration causes a certain sorrow in those who do not yet enjoy God fully, according to Ps. 41:3, "My soul hath thirsted after the strong living God," and afterwards it is said (Ps. 41:4): "My tears have been my bread," etc. Secondarily devotion is caused as stated (A. 3), by the consideration of one's own failings; for this consideration regards the term from which man withdraws by the movement of his devout will, in that he trusts not in himself, but subjects himself to God. This consideration has an opposite tendency to the first: for it is of a nature to cause sorrow directly (when one thinks over one's own failings), and joy accidentally, namely, through hope of the Divine assistance. It is accordingly evident that the first and direct effect of devotion is joy, while the secondary and accidental effect is that "sorrow which is according to God" [*2 Cor. 7:10].

Reply Obj. 1: In the consideration of Christ's Passion there is something that causes sorrow, namely, the human defect, the removal of which made it necessary for Christ to suffer [*Luke 24:25]; and there is something that causes joy, namely, God's loving-kindness to us in giving us such a deliverance.

Reply Obj. 2: The spirit which on the one hand is afflicted on account of the defects of the present life, on the other hand is rejoiced, by the consideration of God's goodness, and by the hope of the Divine help.

Reply Obj. 3: Tears are caused not only through sorrow, but also through a certain tenderness of the affections, especially when one considers something that gives joy mixed with pain. Thus men are wont to shed tears through a sentiment of piety, when they recover their children or dear friends, whom they thought to have lost. In this way tears arise from devotion.

# QUESTION 83

OF PRAYER (In Seventeen Articles)

We must now consider prayer, under which head there are seventeen points of inquiry:

(1) Whether prayer is an act of the appetitive or of the cognitive power?

(2) Whether it is fitting to pray to God?

(3) Whether prayer is an act of religion?

(4) Whether we ought to pray to God alone?

(5) Whether we ought to ask for something definite when we pray?

(6) Whether we ought to ask for temporal things when we pray?

(7) Whether we ought to pray for others?

(8) Whether we ought to pray for our enemies?

(9) Of the seven petitions of the Lord's Prayer;

(10) Whether prayer is proper to the rational creature?

(11) Whether the saints in heaven pray for us?

(12) Whether prayer should be vocal?

(13) Whether attention is requisite in prayer?

(14) Whether prayer should last a long time?

(15) Whether prayer is meritorious? [*Art. 16]

(16) Whether sinners impetrate anything from God by praying? [*Art. 15]

(17) of the different kinds of prayer.

FIRST ARTICLE [II-II, Q. 83, Art. 1]

Whether Prayer Is an Act of the Appetitive Power?

Objection 1: It would seem that prayer is an act of the appetitive power. It belongs to prayer to be heard. Now it is the desire that is heard by God, according to Ps. 9:38, "The Lord hath heard the desire of the poor." Therefore prayer is desire. But desire is an act of the appetitive power: and therefore prayer is also.

Obj. 2: Further, Dionysius says (Div. Nom. iii): "It is useful to begin everything with prayer, because thereby we surrender ourselves to God and unite ourselves to Him." Now union with God is effected by love which belongs to the appetitive power. Therefore prayer belongs to the appetitive power.

Obj. 3: Further, the Philosopher states (De Anima iii, 6) that there are two operations of the intellective part. Of these the first is "the understanding of indivisibles," by which operation we apprehend what a thing is: while the second is "synthesis" and "analysis," whereby we apprehend that a thing is or is not. To these a third may be added, namely, "reasoning," whereby we proceed from the known to the unknown. Now prayer is not reducible to any of these operations. Therefore it is an operation, not of the intellective, but of the appetitive power.

*On the contrary,* Isidore says (Etym. x) that "to pray is to speak." Now speech belongs to the intellect. Therefore prayer is an act, not of the appetitive, but of the intellective power.

*I answer that,* According to Cassiodorus [*Comment. in Ps. 38:13] "prayer ( *oratio* ) is spoken reason ( oris ratio )." Now the speculative and practical reason differ in this, that the speculative merely apprehends its object, whereas the practical reason not only apprehends but causes. Now one thing is the cause of another in two ways: first perfectly, when it necessitates its effect, and this happens when the effect is wholly subject to the power of the cause; secondly imperfectly, by merely disposing to the effect, for the reason that the effect is not wholly subject to the power of the cause. Accordingly in this way the reason is cause of certain things in two ways: first, by imposing necessity; and in this way it belongs to reason, to command not only the lower powers and the members of the body, but also human subjects, which indeed is done by commanding; secondly, by leading up to the effect, and, in a way, disposing to it, and in this sense the reason asks for something to be done by things not subject to it, whether they be its equals or its superiors. Now both of these, namely, to command and to ask or beseech, imply a certain ordering, seeing that man proposes something to be effected by something else, wherefore they pertain to the reason to which it belongs to set in order. For this reason the Philosopher says (Ethic. i, 13) that the "reason exhorts us to do what is best."

Now in the present instance we are speaking of prayer [*This last paragraph refers to the Latin word *oratio* (prayer) which originally signified a speech, being derived in the first instance from *os, oris* (the mouth).] as signifying a beseeching or petition, in which sense Augustine [*Rabanus, De Univ. vi, 14]: says (De Verb. Dom.) that "prayer is a petition," and Damascene states (De Fide Orth. iii, 24) that "to pray is to ask becoming things of God." Accordingly it is evident that prayer, as we speak of it now, is an act of reason.

Reply Obj. 1: The Lord is said to hear the desire of the poor, either because desire is the cause of their petition, since a petition is like the interpreter of a desire, or in order to show how speedily they are heard, since no sooner do the poor desire something than God hears them before they put up a prayer, according to the saying of Isa. 65:24, "And it shall come to pass, that before they call, I will hear."

Reply Obj. 2: As stated above (I, Q. 82, A. 4; I-II, Q. 9, A. 1, ad 3), the will moves the reason to its end: wherefore nothing hinders the act of reason, under the motion of the will, from tending to an end such as charity which is union with God. Now prayer tends to God through being moved by the will of charity, as it were, and this in two ways. First, on the part of the object of our petition, because when we pray we ought principally to ask to be united to God, according to Ps. 26:4, "One thing I have asked of the Lord, this will I seek after, that I may dwell in the house of the Lord all the days of my life." Secondly, on the part of the petitioner, who ought to approach the person whom he petitions, either locally, as when he petitions a man, or mentally, as when he petitions God. Hence Dionysius says (Div. Nom. iii) that "when we call upon God in our prayers, we unveil our mind in His presence": and in the same sense Damascene says (De Fide Orth. iii, 24) that "prayer is the raising up of the mind to God."

Reply Obj. 3: These three acts belong to the speculative reason, but to the practical reason it belongs in addition to cause something by way of command or of petition, as stated above.

SECOND ARTICLE [II-II, Q. 83, Art. 2]

Whether It Is Becoming to Pray?

Objection 1: It would seem that it is unbecoming to pray. Prayer seems to be necessary in order that we may make our needs known to the person to whom we pray. But according to Matt. 6:32, "Your Father knoweth that you have need of all these things." Therefore it is not becoming to pray to God.

Obj. 2: Further, by prayer we bend the mind of the person to whom we pray, so that he may do what is asked of him. But God's mind is unchangeable and inflexible, according to 1 Kings 15:29, "But the Triumpher in Israel will not spare, and will not be moved to repentance." Therefore it is not fitting that we should pray to God.

Obj. 3: Further, it is more liberal to give to one that asks not, than to one who asks because, according to Seneca (De Benefic. ii, 1), "nothing is bought more dearly than what is bought with prayers." But God is supremely liberal. Therefore it would seem unbecoming to pray to God.

*On the contrary,* It is written (Luke 18:1): "We ought always to pray, and not to faint."

*I answer that,* Among the ancients there was a threefold error concerning prayer. Some held that human affairs are not ruled by Divine providence; whence it would follow that it is useless to pray and to worship God at all: of these it is written (Malach. 3:14): "You have said: He laboreth in vain that serveth God." Another opinion held that all things, even in human affairs, happen of necessity, whether by reason of the unchangeableness of Divine providence, or through the compelling influence of the stars, or on account of the connection of causes: and this opinion also excluded the utility of prayer. There was a third opinion of those who held that human affairs are indeed ruled by Divine providence, and that they do not happen of necessity; yet they deemed the disposition of Divine providence to be changeable, and that it is changed by prayers and other things pertaining to the worship of God. All these opinions were disproved in the First Part (Q. 19, AA. 7, 8; Q. 22, AA. 2, 4; Q. 115, A. 6; Q. 116). Wherefore it behooves us so to account for the utility of prayer as neither to impose necessity on human affairs subject to Divine providence, nor to imply changeableness on the part of the Divine disposition.

In order to throw light on this question we must consider that Divine providence disposes not only what effects shall take place, but also from what causes and in what order these effects shall proceed. Now among other causes human acts are the causes of certain effects. Wherefore it must be that men do certain actions, not that thereby they may change the Divine disposition, but that by those actions they may achieve certain effects according to the order of the Divine disposition: and the same is to be said of natural causes. And so is it with regard to prayer. For we pray not that we may change the Divine disposition, but that we may impetrate that which God has disposed to be fulfilled by our prayers, in other words "that by asking, men may deserve to receive what Almighty God from eternity has disposed to give," as Gregory says (Dial. i, 8).

Reply Obj. 1: We need to pray to God, not in order to make known to Him our needs or desires but that we ourselves may be reminded of the necessity of having recourse to God's help in these matters.

Reply Obj. 2: As stated above, our motive in praying is, not that we may change the Divine disposition, but that, by our prayers, we may obtain what God has appointed.

Reply Obj. 3: God bestows many things on us out of His liberality, even without our asking for them: but that He wishes to bestow certain things on us at our asking, is for the sake of our good, namely, that we may acquire confidence in having recourse to God, and that we may recognize in Him the Author of our goods. Hence Chrysostom says [*Implicitly (Hom. ii, de Orat.; Hom. xxx in Genes.; Cf. Caten. Aur. on Luke 18)]: "Think what happiness is granted thee, what honor bestowed on thee, when thou conversest with God in prayer, when thou talkest with Christ, when thou askest what thou wilt, whatever thou desirest."

THIRD ARTICLE [II-II, Q. 83, Art. 3]

Whether Prayer Is an Act of Religion?

Objection 1: It would seem that prayer is not an act of religion. Since religion is a part of justice, it resides in the will as in its subject. But prayer belongs to the intellective part, as stated above (A. 1). Therefore prayer seems to be an act, not of religion, but of the gift of understanding whereby the mind ascends to God.

Obj. 2: Further, the act of *latria* falls under a necessity of precept. But prayer does not seem to come under a necessity of precept, but to come from the mere will, since it is nothing else than a petition for what we will. Therefore prayer seemingly is not an act of religion.

Obj. 3: Further, it seems to belong to religion that one "offers worship and ceremonial rites to the Godhead" [*Cicero, Rhet. ii, 53]. But prayer seems not to offer anything to God, but to ask to obtain something from Him. Therefore prayer is not an act of religion.

*On the contrary,* It is written (Ps. 140:2): "Let my prayer be directed as incense in Thy sight": and a gloss on the passage says that "it was to signify this that under the Old Law incense was said to be offered for a sweet smell to the Lord." Now this belongs to religion. Therefore prayer is an act of religion.

*I answer that,* As stated above (Q. 81, AA. 2, 4), it belongs properly to religion to show honor to God, wherefore all those things through which reverence is shown to God, belong to religion. Now man shows reverence to God by means of prayer, in so far as he subjects himself to Him, and by praying confesses that he needs Him as the Author of his goods. Hence it is evident that prayer is properly an act of religion.

Reply Obj. 1: The will moves the other powers of the soul to its end, as stated above (Q. 82, A. 1, ad 1), and therefore religion, which is in the will, directs the acts of the other powers to the reverence of God. Now among the other powers of the soul the intellect is the highest, and the nearest to the will; and consequently after devotion which belongs to the will, prayer which belongs to the intellective part is the chief of the acts of religion, since by it religion directs man's intellect to God.

Reply Obj. 2: It is a matter of precept not only that we should ask for what we desire, but also that we should desire aright. But to desire comes under a precept of charity, whereas to ask comes under a precept of religion, which precept is expressed in Matt. 7:7, where it is said: "Ask and ye shall receive" [*Vulg.: 'Ask and it shall be given you.'].

Reply Obj. 3: By praying man surrenders his mind to God, since he subjects it to Him with reverence and, so to speak, presents it to Him, as appears from the words of Dionysius quoted above (A. 1, Obj. 2). Wherefore just as the human mind excels exterior things, whether bodily members, or those external things that are employed for God's service, so too, prayer surpasses other acts of religion.

FOURTH ARTICLE [II-II, Q. 83, Art. 4]

Whether We Ought to Pray to God Alone?

Objection 1: It would seem that we ought to pray to God alone. Prayer is an act of religion, as stated above (A. 3). But God alone is to be worshiped by religion. Therefore we should pray to God alone.

Obj. 2: Further, it is useless to pray to one who is ignorant of the prayer. But it belongs to God alone to know one's prayer, both because frequently prayer is uttered by an interior act which God alone knows, rather than by words, according to the saying of the Apostle (1 Cor. 14:15), "I will pray with the spirit, I will pray also with the understanding": and again because, as Augustine says (De Cura pro mortuis xiii) the "dead, even the saints, know not what the living, even their own children, are doing." Therefore we ought to pray to God alone.

Obj. 3: Further, if we pray to any of the saints, this is only because they are united to God. Now some yet living in this world, or even some who are in Purgatory, are closely united to God by grace, and yet we do not pray to them. Therefore neither should we pray to the saints who are in Paradise.

*On the contrary,* It is written (Job 5:1), "Call ... if there be any that will answer thee, and turn to some of the saints."

*I answer that,* Prayer is offered to a person in two ways: first, as to be fulfilled by him, secondly, as to be obtained through him. In the first way we offer prayer to God alone, since all our prayers ought to be directed to the acquisition of grace and glory, which God alone gives, according to Ps. 83:12, "The Lord will give grace and glory." But in the second way we pray to the saints, whether angels or men, not that God may through them know our petitions, but that our prayers may be effective through their prayers and merits. Hence it is written (Apoc. 8:4) that "the smoke of the incense," namely "the prayers of the saints ascended up before God." This is also clear from the very style employed by the Church in praying: since we beseech the Blessed Trinity "to have mercy on us," while we ask any of the saints "to pray for us."

Reply Obj. 1: To Him alone do we offer religious worship when praying, from Whom we seek to obtain what we pray for, because by so doing we confess that He is the Author of our goods: but not to those whom we call upon as our advocates in God's presence.

Reply Obj. 2: The dead, if we consider their natural condition, do not know what takes place in this world, especially the interior movements of the heart. Nevertheless, according to Gregory (Moral. xii, 21), whatever it is fitting the blessed should know about what happens to us, even as regards the interior movements of the heart, is made known to them in the Word: and it is most becoming to their exalted position that they should know the petitions we make to them by word or thought; and consequently the petitions which we raise to them are known to them through Divine manifestation.

Reply Obj. 3: Those who are in this world or in Purgatory, do not yet enjoy the vision of the Word, so as to be able to know what we think or say. Wherefore we do not seek their assistance by praying to them, but ask it of the living by speaking to them.

FIFTH ARTICLE [II-II, Q. 83, Art. 5]

Whether We Ought to Ask for Something Definite When We Pray?

Objection 1: It would seem that we ought not to ask for anything definite when we pray to God. According to Damascene (De Fide Orth. iii, 24), "to pray is to ask becoming things of God"; wherefore it is useless to pray for what is inexpedient, according to James 4:3, "You ask, and receive not: because you ask amiss." Now according to Rom. 8:26, "we know not what we should pray for as we ought." Therefore we ought not to ask for anything definite when we pray.

Obj. 2: Further, those who ask another person for something definite strive to incline his will to do what they wish themselves. But we ought not to endeavor to make God will what we will; *on the contrary,* we ought to strive to will what He wills, according to a gloss on Ps. 32:1, "Rejoice in the Lord, O ye just." Therefore we ought not to ask God for anything definite when we pray.

Obj. 3: Further, evil things are not to be sought from God; and as to good things, God Himself invites us to take them. Now it is useless to ask a person to give you what he invites you to take. Therefore we ought not to ask God for anything definite in our prayers.

*On the contrary,* our Lord (Matt. 6 and Luke 11) taught His disciples to ask definitely for those things which are contained in the petitions of the Lord's Prayer.

*I answer that,* According to Valerius Maximus [*Fact. et Dict. Memor. vii, 2], "Socrates deemed that we should ask the immortal gods for nothing else but that they should grant us good things, because they at any rate know what is good for each one whereas when we pray we frequently ask for what it had been better for us not to obtain." This opinion is true to a certain extent, as to those things which may have an evil result, and which man may use ill or well, such as "riches, by which," as stated by the same authority (Fact. et Dict. Memor. vii, 2), "many have come to an evil end; honors, which have ruined many; power, of which we frequently witness the unhappy results; splendid marriages, which sometimes bring about the total wreck of a family." Nevertheless there are certain goods which man cannot ill use, because they cannot have an evil result. Such are those which are the object of beatitude and whereby we merit it: and these the saints seek absolutely when they pray, as in Ps. 79:4, "Show us Thy face, and we shall be saved," and again in Ps. 118:35, "Lead me into the path of Thy commandments."

Reply Obj. 1: Although man cannot by himself know what he ought to pray for, "the Spirit," as stated in the same passage, "helpeth our infirmity," since by inspiring us with holy desires, He makes us ask for what is right. Hence our Lord said (John 4:24) that true adorers "must adore ... in spirit and in truth."

Reply Obj. 2: When in our prayers we ask for things concerning our salvation, we conform our will to God's, of Whom it is written (1 Tim. 2:4) that "He will have all men to be saved."

Reply Obj. 3: God so invites us to take good things, that we may approach to them not by the steps of the body, but by pious desires and devout prayers.

SIXTH ARTICLE [II-II, Q. 83, Art. 6]

Whether Man Ought to Ask God for Temporal Things When He Prays?

Objection 1: It would seem that man ought not to ask God for temporal things when he prays. We seek what we ask for in prayer. But we should not seek for temporal things, for it is written (Matt. 6:33): "Seek ye ... first the kingdom of God, and His justice: and all these things shall be added unto you," that is to say, temporal things, which, says He, we are not to seek, but they will be added to what we seek. Therefore temporal things are not to be asked of God in prayer.

Obj. 2: Further, no one asks save for that which he is solicitous about. Now we ought not to have solicitude for temporal things, according to the saying of Matt. 6:25, "Be not solicitous for your life, what you shall eat." Therefore we ought not to ask for temporal things when we pray.

Obj. 3: Further, by prayer our mind should be raised up to God. But by asking for temporal things, it descends to things beneath it, against the saying of the Apostle (2 Cor. 4:18), "While we look not at the things which are seen, but at the things which are not seen. For the things which are seen are temporal, but the things which are not seen are eternal." Therefore man ought not to ask God for temporal things when he prays.

Obj. 4: Further, man ought not to ask of God other than good and useful things. But sometimes temporal things, when we have them, are harmful, not only in a spiritual sense, but also in a material sense. Therefore we should not ask God for them in our prayers.

*On the contrary,* It is written (Prov. 30:8): "Give me only the necessaries of life."

*I answer that,* As Augustine says (ad Probam, de orando Deum, Ep. cxxx, 12): "It is lawful to pray for what it is lawful to desire." Now it is lawful to desire temporal things, not indeed principally, by placing our end therein, but as helps whereby we are assisted in tending towards beatitude, in so far, to wit, as they are the means of supporting the life of the body, and are of service to us as instruments in performing acts of virtue, as also the Philosopher states (Ethic. i, 8). Augustine too says the same to Proba (ad Probam, de orando Deum, Ep. cxxx, 6, 7) when he states that "it is not unbecoming for anyone to desire enough for a livelihood, and no more; for this sufficiency is desired, not for its own sake, but for the welfare of the body, or that we should desire to be clothed in a way befitting one's station, so as not to be out of keeping with those among whom we have to live. Accordingly we ought to pray that we may keep these things if we have them, and if we have them not, that we may gain possession of them."

Reply Obj. 1: We should seek temporal things not in the first but in the second place. Hence Augustine says (De Serm. Dom. in Monte ii, 16): "When He says that this" (i.e. the kingdom of God) "is to be sought first, He implies that the other" (i.e. temporal goods) "is to be sought afterwards, not in time but in importance, this as being our good, the other as our need."

Reply Obj. 2: Not all solicitude about temporal things is forbidden, but that which is superfluous and inordinate, as stated above (Q. 55, A. 6).

Reply Obj. 3: When our mind is intent on temporal things in order that it may rest in them, it remains immersed therein; but when it is intent on them in relation to the acquisition of beatitude, it is not lowered by them, but raises them to a higher level.

Reply Obj. 4: From the very fact that we ask for temporal things not as the principal object of our petition, but as subordinate to something else, we ask God for them in the sense that they may be granted to us in so far as they are expedient for salvation.

SEVENTH ARTICLE [II-II, Q. 83, Art. 7]

Whether We Ought to Pray for Others?

Objection 1: It would seem that we ought not to pray for others. In praying we ought to conform to the pattern given by our Lord. Now in the Lord's Prayer we make petitions for ourselves, not for others; thus we say: "Give us this day our daily bread," etc. Therefore we should not pray for others.

Obj. 2: Further, prayer is offered that it may be heard. Now one of the conditions required for prayer that it may be heard is that one pray for oneself, wherefore Augustine in commenting on John 16:23, "If you ask the Father anything in My name He will give it you," says (Tract. cii): "Everyone is heard when he prays for himself, not when he prays for all; wherefore He does not say simply 'He will give it,' but 'He will give it you.'" Therefore it would seem that we ought not to pray for others, but only for ourselves.

Obj. 3: Further, we are forbidden to pray for others, if they are wicked, according to Jer. 7:16, "Therefore do not then pray for this people ... and do not withstand Me, for I will not hear thee." On the other hand we are not bound to pray for the good, since they are heard when they pray for themselves. Therefore it would seem that we ought not to pray for others.

*On the contrary,* It is written (James 5:16): "Pray one for another, that you may be saved."

*I answer that,* As stated above (A. 6), when we pray we ought to ask for what we ought to desire. Now we ought to desire good things not only for ourselves, but also for others: for this is essential to the love which we owe to our neighbor, as stated above (Q. 25, AA. 1, 12; Q. 27, A. 2; Q. 31, A. 1). Therefore charity requires us to pray for others. Hence Chrysostom says (Hom. xiv in Matth.) [*Opus Imperfectum, falsely ascribed to St. John Chrysostom]: "Necessity binds us to pray for ourselves, fraternal charity urges us to pray for others: and the prayer that fraternal charity proffers is sweeter to God than that which is the outcome of necessity."

Reply Obj. 1: As Cyprian says (De orat. Dom.), "We say 'Our Father' and not 'My Father,' 'Give us' and not 'Give me,' because the Master of unity did not wish us to pray privately, that is for ourselves alone, for He wished each one to pray for all, even as He Himself bore all in one."

Reply Obj. 2: It is a condition of prayer that one pray for oneself: not as though it were necessary in order that prayer be meritorious, but as being necessary in order that prayer may not fail in its effect of impetration. For it sometimes happens that we pray for another with piety and perseverance, and ask for things relating to his salvation, and yet it is not granted on account of some obstacle on the part of the person we are praying for, according to Jer. 15:1, "If Moses and Samuel shall stand before Me, My soul is not towards this people." And yet the prayer will be meritorious for the person who prays thus out of charity, according to Ps. 34:13, "My prayer shall be turned into my bosom, i.e. though it profit them not, I am not deprived of my reward," as the gloss expounds it.

Reply Obj. 3: We ought to pray even for sinners, that they may be converted, and for the just that they may persevere and advance in holiness. Yet those who pray are heard not for all sinners but for some: since they are heard for the predestined, but not for those who are foreknown to death; even as the correction whereby we correct the brethren, has an effect in the predestined but not in the reprobate, according to Eccles. 7:14, "No man can correct whom God hath despised." Hence it is written (1 John 5:16): "He that knoweth his brother to sin a sin which is not to death, let him ask, and life shall be given to him, who sinneth not to death." Now just as the benefit of correction must not be refused to any man so long as he lives here below, because we cannot distinguish the predestined from the reprobate, as Augustine says (De Correp. et Grat. xv), so too no man should be denied the help of prayer.

We ought also to pray for the just for three reasons: First, because the prayers of a multitude are more easily heard, wherefore a gloss on Rom. 15:30, "Help me in your prayers," says: "The Apostle rightly tells the lesser brethren to pray for him, for many lesser ones, if they be united together in one mind, become great, and it is impossible for the prayers of a multitude not to obtain" that which is possible to be obtained by prayer. Secondly, that many may thank God for the graces conferred on the just, which graces conduce to the profit of many, according to the Apostle (2 Cor. 1:11). Thirdly, that the more perfect may not wax proud, seeing that they find that they need the prayers of the less perfect.

EIGHTH ARTICLE [II-II, Q. 83, Art. 8]

Whether We Ought to Pray for Our Enemies?

Objection 1: It would seem that we ought not to pray for our enemies. According to Rom. 15:4, "what things soever were written, were written for our learning." Now Holy Writ contains many imprecations against enemies; thus it is written (Ps. 6:11): "Let all my enemies be ashamed and be ... troubled, let them be ashamed and be troubled very speedily [*Vulg.: 'Let them be turned back and be ashamed.']." Therefore we too should pray against rather than for our enemies.

Obj. 2: Further, to be revenged on one's enemies is harmful to them. But holy men seek vengeance of their enemies according to Apoc. 6:10, "How long ... dost Thou not ... revenge our blood on them that dwell on earth?" Wherefore they rejoice in being revenged on their enemies, according to Ps. 57:11, "The just shall rejoice when he shall see the revenge." Therefore we should not pray for our enemies, but against them.

Obj. 3: Further, man's deed should not be contrary to his prayer. Now sometimes men lawfully attack their enemies, else all wars would be unlawful, which is opposed to what we have said above (Q. 40, A. 1). Therefore we should not pray for our enemies.

*On the contrary,* It is written (Matt. 5:44): "Pray for them that persecute and calumniate you."

*I answer that,* To pray for another is an act of charity, as stated above (A. 7). Wherefore we are bound to pray for our enemies in the same manner as we are bound to love them. Now it was explained above in the treatise on charity (Q. 25, AA. 8, 9), how we are bound to love our enemies, namely, that we must love in them their nature, not their sin, and that to love our enemies in general is a matter of precept, while to love them in the individual is not a matter of precept, except in the preparedness of the mind, so that a man must be prepared to love his enemy even in the individual and to help him in a case of necessity, or if his enemy should beg his forgiveness. But to love one's enemies absolutely in the individual, and to assist them, is an act of perfection.

In like manner it is a matter of obligation that we should not exclude our enemies from the general prayers which we offer up for others: but it is a matter of perfection, and not of obligation, to pray for them individually, except in certain special cases.

Reply Obj. 1: The imprecations contained in Holy Writ may be understood in four ways. First, according to the custom of the prophets "to foretell the future under the veil of an imprecation," as Augustine states [*De Serm. Dom. in Monte i, 21]. Secondly, in the sense that certain temporal evils are sometimes inflicted by God on the wicked for their correction. Thirdly, because they are understood to be pronounced, not against the men themselves, but against the kingdom of sin, with the purpose, to wit, of destroying sin by the correction of men. Fourthly, by way of conformity of our will to the Divine justice with regard to the damnation of those who are obstinate in sin.

Reply Obj. 2: As Augustine states in the same book (De Serm. Dom. in Monte i, 22), "the martyrs' vengeance is the overthrow of the kingdom of sin, because they suffered so much while it reigned": or as he says again (QQ. Vet. et Nov. Test. lxviii), "their prayer for vengeance is expressed not in words but in their minds, even as the blood of Abel cried from the earth." They rejoice in vengeance not for its own sake, but for the sake of Divine justice.

Reply Obj. 3: It is lawful to attack one's enemies, that they may be restrained from sin: and this is for their own good and for the good of others. Consequently it is even lawful in praying to ask that temporal evils be inflicted on our enemies in order that they may mend their ways. Thus prayer and deed will not be contrary to one another.

NINTH ARTICLE [II-II, Q. 83, Art. 9]

Whether the Seven Petitions of the Lord's Prayer Are Fittingly Assigned?

Objection 1: It would seem that the seven petitions of the Lord's Prayer are not fittingly assigned. It is useless to ask for that to be hallowed which is always holy. But the name of God is always holy, according to Luke 1:49, "Holy is His name." Again, His kingdom is everlasting, according to Ps. 144:13, "Thy kingdom is a kingdom of all ages." Again, God's will is always fulfilled, according to Isa 46:10, "All My will shall be done." Therefore it is useless to ask for "the name of God to be hallowed," for "His kingdom to come," and for "His will to be done."

Obj. 2: Further, one must withdraw from evil before attaining good. Therefore it seems unfitting for the petitions relating to the attainment of good to be set forth before those relating to the removal of evil.

Obj. 3: Further, one asks for a thing that it may be given to one. Now the chief gift of God is the Holy Ghost, and those gifts that we receive through Him. Therefore the petitions seem to be unfittingly assigned, since they do not correspond to the gifts of the Holy Ghost.

Obj. 4: Further, according to Luke, only five petitions are mentioned in the Lord's Prayer, as appears from the eleventh chapter. Therefore it was superfluous for Matthew to mention seven.

Obj. 5: Further, it seems useless to seek to win the benevolence of one who forestalls us by his benevolence. Now God forestalls us by His benevolence, since "He first hath loved us" ( 1 John 4:19). Therefore it is useless to preface the petitions with the words our "Father Who art in heaven," which seem to indicate a desire to win God's benevolence.

*On the contrary,* The authority of Christ, who composed this prayer, suffices.

*I answer that,* The Lord's Prayer is most perfect, because, as Augustine says (ad Probam Ep. cxxx, 12), "if we pray rightly and fittingly, we can say nothing else but what is contained in this prayer of our Lord." For since prayer interprets our desires, as it were, before God, then alone is it right to ask for something in our prayers when it is right that we should desire it. Now in the Lord's Prayer not only do we ask for all that we may rightly desire, but also in the order wherein we ought to desire them, so that this prayer not only teaches us to ask, but also directs all our affections. Thus it is evident that the first thing to be the object of our desire is the end, and afterwards whatever is directed to the end. Now our end is God towards Whom our affections tend in two ways: first, by our willing the glory of God, secondly, by willing to enjoy His glory. The first belongs to the love whereby we love God in Himself, while the second belongs to the love whereby we love ourselves in God. Wherefore the first petition is expressed thus: "Hallowed be Thy name," and the second thus: "Thy kingdom come," by which we ask to come to the glory of His kingdom.

To this same end a thing directs us in two ways: in one way, by its very nature, in another way, accidentally. Of its very nature the good which is useful for an end directs us to that end. Now a thing is useful in two ways to that end which is beatitude: in one way, directly and principally, according to the merit whereby we merit beatitude by obeying God, and in this respect we ask: "Thy will be done on earth as it is in heaven"; in another way instrumentally, and as it were helping us to merit, and in this respect we say: "Give us this day our daily bread," whether we understand this of the sacramental Bread, the daily use of which is profitable to man, and in which all the other sacraments are contained, or of the bread of the body, so that it denotes all sufficiency of food, as Augustine says (ad Probam, Ep. cxxx, 11), since the Eucharist is the chief sacrament, and bread is the chief food: thus in the Gospel of Matthew we read, "supersubstantial," i.e. "principal," as Jerome expounds it.

We are directed to beatitude accidentally by the removal of obstacles. Now there are three obstacles to our attainment of beatitude. First, there is sin, which directly excludes a man from the kingdom, according to 1 Cor. 6:9, 10, "Neither fornicators, nor idolaters, etc., shall possess the kingdom of God"; and to this refer the words, "Forgive us our trespasses." Secondly, there is temptation which hinders us from keeping God's will, and to this we refer when we say: "And lead us not into temptation," whereby we do not ask not to be tempted, but not to be conquered by temptation, which is to be led into temptation. Thirdly, there is the present penal state which is a kind of obstacle to a sufficiency of life, and to this we refer in the words, "Deliver us from evil."

Reply Obj. 1: As Augustine says (De Serm. Dom. in Monte ii, 5), when we say, "Hallowed be Thy name, we do not mean that God's name is not holy, but we ask that men may treat it as a holy thing," and this pertains to the diffusion of God's glory among men. When we say, "Thy kingdom come, we do not imply that God is not reigning now," but "we excite in ourselves the desire for that kingdom, that it may come to us, and that we may reign therein," as Augustine says (ad Probam, Ep. cxxx, 11). The words, "Thy will be done" rightly signify, "'May Thy commandments be obeyed' on earth as in heaven, i.e. by men as well as by angels" (De Serm. Dom. in Monte ii, 6). Hence these three petitions will be perfectly fulfilled in the life to come; while the other four, according to Augustine (Enchiridion cxv), belong to the needs of the present life.

Reply Obj. 2: Since prayer is the interpreter of desire, the order of the petitions corresponds with the order, not of execution, but of desire or intention, where the end precedes the things that are directed to the end, and attainment of good precedes removal of evil.

Reply Obj. 3: Augustine (De Serm. Dom. in Monte ii, 11) adapts the seven petitions to the gifts and beatitudes. He says: "If it is fear of God whereby blessed are the poor in spirit, let us ask that God's name be hallowed among men with a chaste fear. If it is piety whereby blessed are the meek, let us ask that His kingdom may come, so that we become meek and no longer resist Him. If it is knowledge whereby blessed are they that mourn, let us pray that His will be done, for thus we shall mourn no more. If it is fortitude whereby blessed ere they that hunger, let us pray that our daily bread be given to us. If it is counsel whereby blessed are the merciful, let us forgive the trespasses of others that our own may be forgiven. If it is understanding whereby blessed are the pure in heart, let us pray lest we have a double heart by seeking after worldly things which ere the occasion of our temptations. If it is wisdom whereby blessed are the peacemakers for they shall be called the children of God, let us pray to be delivered from evil: for if we be delivered we shall by that very fact become the free children of God."

Reply Obj. 4: According to Augustine (Enchiridion cxvi), "Luke included not seven but five petitions in the Lord's Prayer, for by omitting it, he shows that the third petition is a kind of repetition of the two that precede, and thus helps us to understand it"; because, to wit, the will of God tends chiefly to this—that we come to the knowledge of His holiness and to reign together with Him. Again the last petition mentioned by Matthew, "Deliver us from evil," is omitted by Luke, so that each one may know himself to be delivered from evil if he be not led into temptation.

Reply Obj. 5: Prayer is offered up to God, not that we may bend Him, but that we may excite in ourselves the confidence to ask: which confidence is excited in us chiefly by the consideration of His charity in our regard, whereby he wills our good—wherefore we say: "Our Father"; and of His excellence, whereby He is able to fulfil it—wherefore we say: "Who art in heaven."

TENTH ARTICLE [II-II, Q. 83, Art. 10]

Whether Prayer Is Proper to the Rational Creature?

Objection 1: It would seem that prayer is not proper to the rational creature. Asking and receiving apparently belong to the same subject. But receiving is becoming also to uncreated Persons, viz. the Son and Holy Ghost. Therefore it is competent to them to pray: for the Son said (John 14:16): "I will ask My [Vulg.: 'the'] Father," and the Apostle says of the Holy Ghost (Rom. 8:26): "The Spirit ... asketh for us."

Obj. 2: Angels are above rational creatures, since they are intellectual substances. Now prayer is becoming to the angels, wherefore we read in the Ps. 96:7: "Adore Him, all you His angels." Therefore prayer is not proper to the rational creature.

Obj. 3: Further, the same subject is fitted to pray as is fitted to call upon God, since this consists chiefly in prayer. But dumb animals are fitted to call upon God, according to Ps. 146:9, "Who giveth to beasts their food and to the young ravens that call upon Him." Therefore prayer is not proper to the rational creatures.

*On the contrary,* Prayer is an act of reason, as stated above (A. 1). But the rational creature is so called from his reason. Therefore prayer is proper to the rational creature.

*I answer that,* As stated above (A. 1) prayer is an act of reason, and consists in beseeching a superior; just as command is an act of reason, whereby an inferior is directed to something. Accordingly prayer is properly competent to one to whom it is competent to have reason, and a superior whom he may beseech. Now nothing is above the Divine Persons; and dumb animals are devoid of reason. Therefore prayer is unbecoming both the Divine Persons and dumb animals, and it is proper to the rational creature.

Reply Obj. 1: Receiving belongs to the Divine Persons in respect of their nature, whereas prayer belongs to one who receives through grace. The Son is said to ask or pray in respect of His assumed, i.e. His human, nature and not in respect of His Godhead: and the Holy Ghost is said to ask, because He makes us ask.

Reply Obj. 2: As stated in the First Part (Q. 79, A. 8), intellect and reason are not distinct powers in us: but they differ as the perfect from the imperfect. Hence intellectual creatures which are the angels are distinct from rational creatures, and sometimes are included under them. In this sense prayer is said to be proper to the rational creature.

Reply Obj. 3: The young ravens are said to call upon God, on account of the natural desire whereby all things, each in its own way, desire to attain the Divine goodness. Thus too dumb animals are said to obey God, on account of the natural instinct whereby they are moved by God.

ELEVENTH ARTICLE [II-II, Q. 83, Art. 11]

Whether the Saints in Heaven Pray for Us?

Objection 1: It would seem that the saints in heaven do not pray for us. A man's action is more meritorious for himself than for others. But the saints in heaven do not merit for themselves, neither do they pray for themselves, since they are already established in the term. Neither therefore do they pray for us.

Obj. 2: Further, the saints conform their will to God perfectly, so that they will only what God wills. Now what God wills is always fulfilled. Therefore it would be useless for the saints to pray for us.

Obj. 3: Further, just as the saints in heaven are above, so are those in Purgatory, for they can no longer sin. Now those in Purgatory do not pray for us, on the contrary we pray for them. Therefore neither do the saints in heaven pray for us.

Obj. 4: Further, if the saints in heaven pray for us, the prayers of the higher saints would be more efficacious; and so we ought not to implore the help of the lower saints' prayers but only of those of the higher saints.

Obj. 5: Further, the soul of Peter is not Peter. If therefore the souls of the saints pray for us, so long as they are separated from their bodies, we ought not to call upon Saint Peter, but on his soul, to pray for us: yet the Church does the contrary. The saints therefore do not pray for us, at least before the resurrection.

*On the contrary,* It is written (2 Macc. 15:14): "This is ... he that prayeth much for the people, and for all the holy city, Jeremias the prophet of God."

*I answer that,* As Jerome says (Cont. Vigilant. 6), the error of Vigilantius consisted in saying that "while we live, we can pray one for another; but that after we are dead, none of our prayers for others can be heard, seeing that not even the martyrs' prayers are granted when they pray for their blood to be avenged." But this is absolutely false, because, since prayers offered for others proceed from charity, as stated above (AA. 7, 8), the greater the charity of the saints in heaven, the more they pray for wayfarers, since the latter can be helped by prayers: and the more closely they are united to God, the more are their prayers efficacious: for the Divine order is such that lower beings receive an overflow of the excellence of the higher, even as the air receives the brightness of the sun. Wherefore it is said of Christ (Heb. 7:25): "Going to God by His own power ... to make intercession for us" [*Vulg.: 'He is able to save for ever them that come to God by Him, always living to make intercession for us.']. Hence Jerome says (Cont. Vigilant. 6): "If the apostles and martyrs while yet in the body and having to be solicitous for themselves, can pray for others, how much more now that they have the crown of victory and triumph."

Reply Obj. 1: The saints in heaven, since they are blessed, have no lack of bliss, save that of the body's glory, and for this they pray. But they pray for us who lack the ultimate perfection of bliss: and their prayers are efficacious in impetrating through their previous merits and through God's acceptance.

Reply Obj. 2: The saints impetrate what ever God wishes to take place through their prayers: and they pray for that which they deem will be granted through their prayers according to God's will.

Reply Obj. 3: Those who are in Purgatory though they are above us on account of their impeccability, yet they are below us as to the pains which they suffer: and in this respect they are not in a condition to pray, but rather in a condition that requires us to pray for them.

Reply Obj. 4: It is God's will that inferior beings should be helped by all those that are above them, wherefore we ought to pray not only to the higher but also to the lower saints; else we should have to implore the mercy of God alone. Nevertheless it happens sometime that prayers addressed to a saint of lower degree are more efficacious, either because he is implored with greater devotion, or because God wishes to make known his sanctity.

Reply Obj. 5: It is because the saints while living merited to pray for us, that we invoke them under the names by which they were known in this life, and by which they are better known to us: and also in order to indicate our belief in the resurrection, according to the saying of Ex. 3:6, "I am the God of Abraham," etc.

TWELFTH ARTICLE [II-II, Q. 83, Art. 12]

Whether Prayer Should Be Vocal?

Objection 1: It would seem that prayer ought not to be vocal. As stated above (A. 4), prayer is addressed chiefly to God. Now God knows the language of the heart. Therefore it is useless to employ vocal prayer.

Obj. 2: Further, prayer should lift man's mind to God, as stated above (A. 1, ad 2). But words, like other sensible objects, prevent man from ascending to God by contemplation. Therefore we should not use words in our prayers.

Obj. 3: Further, prayer should be offered to God in secret, according to Matt. 6:6, "But thou, when thou shalt pray, enter into thy chamber, and having shut the door, pray to thy Father in secret." But prayer loses its secrecy by being expressed vocally. Therefore prayer should not be vocal.

*On the contrary,* It is written (Ps. 141:2): "I cried to the Lord with my voice, with my voice I made supplication to the Lord."

*I answer that,* Prayer is twofold, common and individual. Common prayer is that which is offered to God by the ministers of the Church representing the body of the faithful: wherefore such like prayer should come to the knowledge of the whole people for whom it is offered: and this would not be possible unless it were vocal prayer. Therefore it is reasonably ordained that the ministers of the Church should say these prayers even in a loud voice, so that they may come to the knowledge of all.

On the other hand individual prayer is that which is offered by any single person, whether he pray for himself or for others; and it is not essential to such a prayer as this that it be vocal. And yet the voice is employed in such like prayers for three reasons. First, in order to excite interior devotion, whereby the mind of the person praying is raised to God, because by means of external signs, whether of words or of deeds, the human mind is moved as regards apprehension, and consequently also as regards the affections. Hence Augustine says (ad Probam. Ep. cxxx, 9) that "by means of words and other signs we arouse ourselves more effectively to an increase of holy desires." Hence then alone should we use words and such like signs when they help to excite the mind internally. But if they distract or in any way impede the mind we should abstain from them; and this happens chiefly to those whose mind is sufficiently prepared for devotion without having recourse to those signs. Wherefore the Psalmist (Ps. 26:8) said: "My heart hath said to Thee: 'My face hath sought Thee,'" and we read of Anna (1 Kings 1:13) that "she spoke in her heart." Secondly, the voice is used in praying as though to pay a debt, so that man may serve God with all that he has from God, that is to say, not only with his mind, but also with his body: and this applies to prayer considered especially as satisfactory. Hence it is written (Osee 14:3): "Take away all iniquity, and receive the good: and we will render the calves of our lips." Thirdly, we have recourse to vocal prayer, through a certain overflow from the soul into the body, through excess of feeling, according to Ps. 15:9, "My heart hath been glad, and my tongue hath rejoiced."

Reply Obj. 1: Vocal prayer is employed, not in order to tell God something He does not know, but in order to lift up the mind of the person praying or of other persons to God.

Reply Obj. 2: Words about other matters distract the mind and hinder the devotion of those who pray: but words signifying some object of devotion lift up the mind, especially one that is less devout.

Reply Obj. 3: As Chrysostom says [*Hom. xiii in the Opus Imperfectum falsely ascribed to St. John Chrysostom], "Our Lord forbids one to pray in presence of others in order that one may be seen by others. Hence when you pray, do nothing strange to draw men's attention, either by shouting so as to be heard by others, or by openly striking the heart, or extending the hands, so as to be seen by many. And yet, according to Augustine (De Serm. Dom. in Monte ii, 3), "it is not wrong to be seen by men, but to do this or that in order to be seen by men."

THIRTEENTH ARTICLE [II-II, Q. 83, Art. 13]

Whether Attention Is a Necessary Condition of Prayer?

Objection 1: It would seem that attention is a necessary condition of prayer. It is written (John 4:24): "God is a spirit, and they that adore Him must adore Him in spirit and in truth." But prayer is not in spirit unless it be attentive. Therefore attention is a necessary condition of prayer.

Obj. 2: Further, prayer is "the ascent of the mind to God" [*Damascene, De Fide Orth. iii, 24]. But the mind does not ascend to God if the prayer is inattentive. Therefore attention is a necessary condition of prayer.

Obj. 3: Further, it is a necessary condition of prayer that it should be altogether sinless. Now if a man allows his mind to wander while praying he is not free of sin, for he seems to make light of God; even as if he were to speak to another man without attending to what he was saying. Hence Basil says [*De Constit. Monach. i] that the "Divine assistance is to be implored, not lightly, nor with a mind wandering hither and thither: because he that prays thus not only will not obtain what he asks, nay rather will he provoke God to anger." Therefore it would seem a necessary condition of prayer that it should be attentive.

*On the contrary,* Even holy men sometimes suffer from a wandering of the mind when they pray, according to Ps. 39:13, "My heart hath forsaken me."

*I answer that,* This question applies chiefly to vocal prayer. Accordingly we must observe that a thing is necessary in two ways. First, a thing is necessary because thereby the end is better obtained: and thus attention is absolutely necessary for prayer. Secondly, a thing is said to be necessary when without it something cannot obtain its effect. Now the effect of prayer is threefold. The first is an effect which is common to all acts quickened by charity, and this is merit. In order to realize this effect, it is not necessary that prayer should be attentive throughout; because the force of the original intention with which one sets about praying renders the whole prayer meritorious, as is the case with other meritorious acts. The second effect of prayer is proper thereto, and consists in impetration: and again the original intention, to which God looks chiefly, suffices to obtain this effect. But if the original intention is lacking, prayer lacks both merit and impetration: because, as Gregory [*Hugh St. Victor, Expos. in Reg. S. Aug. iii] says, "God hears not the prayer of those who pay no attention to their prayer." The third effect of prayer is that which it produces at once; this is the spiritual refreshment of the mind, and for this effect attention is a necessary condition: wherefore it is written (1 Cor. 14:14): "If I pray in a tongue … my understanding is without fruit."

It must be observed, however, that there are three kinds of attention that can be brought to vocal prayer: one which attends to the words, lest we say them wrong, another which attends to the sense of the words, and a third, which attends to the end of prayer, namely, God, and to the thing we are praying for. That last kind of attention is most necessary, and even idiots are capable of it. Moreover this attention, whereby the mind is fixed on God, is sometimes so strong that the mind forgets all other things, as Hugh of St. Victor states [*De Modo Orandi ii].

Reply Obj. 1: To pray in spirit and in truth is to set about praying through the instigation of the Spirit, even though afterwards the mind wander through weakness.

Reply Obj. 2: The human mind is unable to remain aloft for long on account of the weakness of nature, because human weakness weighs down the soul to the level of inferior things: and hence it is that when, while praying, the mind ascends to God by contemplation, of a sudden it wanders off through weakness.

Reply Obj. 3: Purposely to allow one's mind to wander in prayer is sinful and hinders the prayer from having fruit. It is against this that Augustine says in his Rule (Ep. ccxi): "When you pray God with psalms and hymns, let your mind attend to that which your lips pronounce." But to wander in mind unintentionally does not deprive prayer of its fruit. Hence Basil says (De Constit. Monach. i): "If you are so truly weakened by sin that you are unable to pray attentively, strive as much as you can to curb yourself, and God will pardon you, seeing that you are unable to stand in His presence in a becoming manner, not through negligence but through frailty."

FOURTEENTH ARTICLE [II-II, Q. 83, Art. 14]

Whether Prayer Should Last a Long Time?

Objection 1: It would seem that prayer should not be continual. It is written (Matt. 6:7): "When you are praying, speak not much." Now one who prays a long time needs to speak much, especially if his be vocal prayer. Therefore prayer should not last a long time.

Obj. 2: Further, prayer expresses the desire. Now a desire is all the holier according as it is centered on one thing, according to Ps. 26:4, "One thing I have asked of the Lord, this will I seek after." Therefore the shorter prayer is, the more is it acceptable to God.

Obj. 3: Further, it seems to be wrong to transgress the limits fixed by God, especially in matters concerning Divine worship, according to Ex. 19:21: "Charge the people, lest they should have a mind to pass the limits to see the Lord, and a very great multitude of them should perish." But God has fixed for us the limits of prayer by instituting the Lord's Prayer (Matt. 6). Therefore it is not right to prolong our prayer beyond its limits.

Obj. 4: *On the contrary,* It would seem that we ought to pray continually. For our Lord said (Luke 18:1): "We ought always to pray, and not to faint": and it is written (1 Thess. 5:17): "Pray without ceasing."

*I answer that,* We may speak about prayer in two ways: first, by considering it in itself; secondly, by considering it in its cause. The cause of prayer is the desire of charity, from which prayer ought to arise: and this desire ought to be in us continually, either actually or virtually, for the virtue of this desire remains in whatever we do out of charity; and we ought to "do all things to the glory of God" (1 Cor. 10:31). From this point of view prayer ought to be continual: wherefore Augustine says (ad Probam, Ep. cxxx, 9): "Faith, hope and charity are by themselves a prayer of continual longing." But prayer, considered in itself, cannot be continual, because we have to be busy about other works, and, as Augustine says (ad Probam. Ep. cxxx, 9), "we pray to God with our lips at certain intervals and seasons, in order to admonish ourselves by means of such like signs, to take note of the amount of our progress in that desire, and to arouse ourselves more eagerly to an increase thereof." Now the quantity of a thing should be commensurate with its end, for instance the quantity of the dose should be commensurate with health. And so it is becoming that prayer should last long enough to arouse the fervor of the interior desire: and when it exceeds this measure, so that it cannot be continued any longer without causing weariness, it should be discontinued. Wherefore Augustine says (ad Probam. Ep. cxxx): "It is said that the brethren in Egypt make frequent but very short prayers, rapid ejaculations, as it were, lest that vigilant and erect attention which is so necessary in prayer slacken and languish, through the strain being prolonged. By so doing they make it sufficiently clear not only that this attention must not be forced if we are unable to keep it up, but also that if we are able to continue, it should not be broken off too soon." And just as we must judge of this in private prayers by considering the attention of the person praying, so too, in public prayers we must judge of it by considering the devotion of the people.

Reply Obj. 1: As Augustine says (ad Probam. Ep. cxxx), "to pray with many words is not the same as to pray long; to speak long is one thing, to be devout long is another. For it is written that our Lord passed the whole night in prayer, and that He 'prayed the longer' in order to set us an example." Further on he says: "When praying say little, yet pray much so long as your attention is fervent. For to say much in prayer is to discuss your need in too many words: whereas to pray much is to knock at the door of Him we pray, by the continuous and devout clamor of the heart. Indeed this business is frequently done with groans rather than with words, with tears rather than with speech."

Reply Obj. 2: Length of prayer consists, not in praying for many things, but in the affections persisting in the desire of one thing.

Reply Obj. 3: Our Lord instituted this prayer, not that we might use no other words when we pray, but that in our prayers we might have none but these things in view, no matter how we express them or think of them.

Reply Obj. 4: One may pray continually, either through having a continual desire, as stated above; or through praying at certain fixed times, though interruptedly; or by reason of the effect, whether in the person who prays—because he remains more devout even after praying, or in some other person—as when by his kindness a man incites another to pray for him, even after he himself has ceased praying.

FIFTEENTH ARTICLE [II-II, Q. 83, Art. 15]

Whether Prayer Is Meritorious?

Objection 1: It would seem that prayer is not meritorious. All merit proceeds from grace. But prayer precedes grace, since even grace is obtained by means of prayer according to Luke 11:13, "(How much more) will your Father from heaven give the good Spirit to them that ask Him!" Therefore prayer is not a meritorious act.

Obj. 2: Further, if prayer merits anything, this would seem to be chiefly that which is besought in prayer. Yet it does not always merit this, because even the saints' prayers are frequently not heard; thus Paul was not heard when he besought the sting of the flesh to be removed from him. Therefore prayer is not a meritorious act.

Obj. 3: Further, prayer is based chiefly on faith, according to James 1:6, "But let him ask in faith, nothing wavering." Now faith is not sufficient for merit, as instanced in those who have lifeless faith. Therefore prayer is not a meritorious act.

*On the contrary,* A gloss on the words of Ps. 34:13, "My prayer shall be turned into my bosom," explains them as meaning, "if my prayer does not profit them, yet shall not I be deprived of my reward." Now reward is not due save to merit. Therefore prayer is meritorious.

*I answer that,* As stated above (A. 13) prayer, besides causing spiritual consolation at the time of praying, has a twofold efficacy in respect of a future effect, namely, efficacy in meriting and efficacy in impetrating. Now prayer, like any other virtuous act, is efficacious in meriting, because it proceeds from charity as its root, the proper object of which is the eternal good that we merit to enjoy. Yet prayer proceeds from charity through the medium of religion, of which prayer is an act, as stated above (A. 3), and with the concurrence of other virtues requisite for the goodness of prayer, viz. humility and faith. For the offering of prayer itself to God belongs to religion, while the desire for the thing that we pray to be accomplished belongs to charity. Faith is necessary in reference to God to Whom we pray; that is, we need to believe that we can obtain from Him what we seek. Humility is necessary on the part of the person praying, because he recognizes his neediness. Devotion too is necessary: but this belongs to religion, for it is its first act and a necessary condition of all its secondary acts, as stated above (Q. 82, AA. 1, 2).

As to its efficacy in impetrating, prayer derives this from the grace of God to Whom we pray, and Who instigates us to pray. Wherefore Augustine says (De Verb. Dom., Serm. cv, 1): "He would not urge us to ask, unless He were willing to give"; and Chrysostom [*Cf. Catena Aurea of St. Thomas on Luke 18. The words as quoted are not to be found in the words of Chrysostom] says: "He never refuses to grant our prayers, since in His loving-kindness He urged us not to faint in praying."

Reply Obj. 1: Neither prayer nor any other virtuous act is meritorious without sanctifying grace. And yet even that prayer which impetrates sanctifying grace proceeds from some grace, as from a gratuitous gift, since the very act of praying is "a gift of God," as Augustine states (De Persever. xxiii).

Reply Obj. 2: Sometimes the merit of prayer regards chiefly something distinct from the object of one's petition. For the chief object of merit is beatitude, whereas the direct object of the petition of prayer extends sometimes to certain other things, as stated above (AA. 6, 7). Accordingly if this other thing that we ask for ourselves be not useful for our beatitude, we do not merit it; and sometimes by asking for and desiring such things we lose merit for instance if we ask of God the accomplishment of some sin, which would be an impious prayer. And sometimes it is not necessary for salvation, nor yet manifestly contrary thereto; and then although he who prays may merit eternal life by praying, yet he does not merit to obtain what he asks for. Hence Augustine says (Liber. Sentent. Prosperi sent. ccxii): "He who faithfully prays God for the necessaries of this life, is both mercifully heard, and mercifully not heard. For the physician knows better than the sick man what is good for the disease." For this reason, too, Paul was not heard when he prayed for the removal of the sting in his flesh, because this was not expedient. If, however, we pray for something that is useful for our beatitude, through being conducive to salvation, we merit it not only by praying, but also by doing other good deeds: therefore without any doubt we receive what we ask for, yet when we ought to receive it: "since certain things are not denied us, but are deferred that they may be granted at a suitable time," according to Augustine (Tract. cii in Joan.): and again this may be hindered if we persevere not in asking for it. Wherefore Basil says (De Constit. Monast. i): "The reason why sometimes thou hast asked and not received, is because thou hast asked amiss, either inconsistently, or lightly, or because thou hast asked for what was not good for thee, or because thou hast ceased asking." Since, however, a man cannot condignly merit eternal life for another, as stated above (I-II, Q. 114, A. 6), it follows that sometimes one cannot condignly merit for another things that pertain to eternal life. For this reason we are not always heard when we pray for others, as stated above (A. 7, ad 2, 3). Hence it is that four conditions are laid down; namely, to ask—"for ourselves—things necessary for salvation—piously—perseveringly"; when all these four concur, we always obtain what we ask for.

Reply Obj. 3: Prayer depends chiefly on faith, not for its efficacy in meriting, because thus it depends chiefly on charity, but for its efficacy in impetrating, because it is through faith that man comes to know of God's omnipotence and mercy, which are the source whence prayer impetrates what it asks for.

SIXTEENTH ARTICLE [II-II, Q. 83, Art. 16]

Whether Sinners Impetrate Anything from God by Their Prayers?

Objection 1: It would seem that sinners impetrate nothing from God by their prayers. It is written (John 9:31): "We know that God doth not hear sinners"; and this agrees with the saying of Prov. 28:9, "He that turneth away his ears from hearing the law, his prayer shall be an abomination." Now an abominable prayer impetrates nothing from God. Therefore sinners impetrate nothing from God.

Obj. 2: Further, the just impetrate from God what they merit, as stated above (A. 15, ad 2). But sinners cannot merit anything since they lack grace and charity which is the "power of godliness," according to a gloss on 2 Tim. 3:5, "Having an appearance indeed of godliness, but denying the power thereof." and so their prayer is impious, and yet piety is required in order that prayer may be impetrative, as stated above (A. 15, ad 2). Therefore sinners impetrate nothing by their prayers.

Obj. 3: Further, Chrysostom [*Hom. xiv in the Opus Imperfectum falsely ascribed to St. John Chrysostom] says: "The Father is unwilling to hear the prayer which the Son has not inspired." Now in the prayer inspired by Christ we say: "Forgive us our trespasses as we forgive them that trespass against us": and sinners do not fulfil this. Therefore either they lie in saying this, and so are unworthy to be heard, or, if they do not say it, they are not heard, because they do not observe the form of prayer instituted by Christ.

*On the contrary,* Augustine says (Tract. xliv, super Joan.): "If God were not to hear sinners, the publican would have vainly said: Lord, be merciful to me a sinner"; and Chrysostom [*Hom. xviii of the same Opus Imperfectum] says: "Everyone that asketh shall receive, that is to say whether he be righteous or sinful."

*I answer that,* In the sinner, two things are to be considered: his nature which God loves, and the sin which He hates. Accordingly when a sinner prays for something as sinner, i.e. in accordance with a sinful desire, God hears him not through mercy but sometimes through vengeance when He allows the sinner to fall yet deeper into sin. For "God refuses in mercy what He grants in anger," as Augustine declares (Tract. lxxiii in Joan.). On the other hand God hears the sinner's prayer if it proceed from a good natural desire, not out of justice, because the sinner does not merit to be heard, but out of pure mercy [*Cf. A. 15, ad 1], provided however he fulfil the four conditions given above, namely, that he beseech for himself things necessary for salvation, piously and perseveringly.

Reply Obj. 1: As Augustine states (Tract. xliv super Joan.), these words were spoken by the blind man before being anointed, i.e. perfectly enlightened, and consequently lack authority. And yet there is truth in the saying if it refers to a sinner as such, in which sense also the sinner's prayer is said to be an abomination.

Reply Obj. 2: There can be no godliness in the sinner's prayer as though his prayer were quickened by a habit of virtue: and yet his prayer may be godly in so far as he asks for something pertaining to godliness. Even so a man who has not the habit of justice is able to will something just, as stated above (Q. 59, A. 2). And though his prayer is not meritorious, it can be impetrative, because merit depends on justice, whereas impetration rests on grace.

Reply Obj. 3: As stated above (A. 7, ad 1) the Lord's Prayer is pronounced in the common person of the whole Church: and so if anyone say the Lord's Prayer while unwilling to forgive his neighbor's trespasses, he lies not, although his words do not apply to him personally: for they are true as referred to the person of the Church, from which he is excluded by merit, and consequently he is deprived of the fruit of his prayer. Sometimes, however, a sinner is prepared to forgive those who have trespassed against him, wherefore his prayers are heard, according to Ecclus. 28:2, "Forgive thy neighbor if he hath hurt thee, and then shall thy sins be forgiven to thee when thou prayest."

SEVENTEENTH ARTICLE [II-II, Q. 83, Art. 17]

Whether the Parts of Prayer Are Fittingly Described As Supplications, Prayers, Intercessions, and Thanksgivings?

Objection 1: It would seem that the parts of prayer are unfittingly described as supplications, prayers, intercessions, and thanksgivings. Supplication would seem to be a kind of adjuration. Yet, according to Origen (Super Matth. Tract. xxxv), "a man who wishes to live according to the gospel need not adjure another, for if it be unlawful to swear, it is also unlawful to adjure." Therefore supplication is unfittingly reckoned a part of prayer.

Obj. 2: Further, according to Damascene (De Fide Orth. iii, 24), "to pray is to ask becoming things of God." Therefore it is unfitting to distinguish "prayers" from "intercessions."

Obj. 3: Further, thanksgivings regard the past, while the others regard the future. But the past precedes the future. Therefore thanksgivings are unfittingly placed after the others.

*On the contrary,* suffices the authority of the Apostle (1 Tim. 2:1).

*I answer that,* Three conditions are requisite for prayer. First, that the person who prays should approach God Whom he prays: this is signified in the word "prayer," because prayer is "the raising up of one's mind to God." The second is that there should be a petition, and this is signified in the word "intercession." In this case sometimes one asks for something definite, and then some say it is "intercession" properly so called, or we may ask for some thing indefinitely, for instance to be helped by God, or we may simply indicate a fact, as in John 11:3, "Behold, he whom Thou lovest is sick," and then they call it "insinuation." The third condition is the reason for impetrating what we ask for: and this either on the part of God, or on the part of the person who asks. The reason of impetration on the part of God is His sanctity, on account of which we ask to be heard, according to Dan. 9:17, 18, "For Thy own sake, incline, O God, Thy ear"; and to this pertains "supplication" ( *obsecratio* ) which means a pleading through sacred things, as when we say, "Through Thy nativity, deliver us, O Lord." The reason for impetration on the part of the person who asks is "thanksgiving"; since "through giving thanks for benefits received we merit to receive yet greater benefits," as we say in the collect [*Ember Friday in September and Postcommunion of the common of a Confessor Bishop]. Hence a gloss on 1 Tim. 2:1 says that "in the Mass, the consecration is preceded by supplication," in which certain sacred things are called to mind; that "prayers are in the consecration itself," in which especially the mind should be raised up to God; and that "intercessions are in the petitions that follow, and thanksgivings at the end."

We may notice these four things in several of the Church's collects. Thus in the collect of Trinity Sunday the words, "Almighty eternal God" belong to the offering up of prayer to God; the words, "Who hast given to Thy servants," etc. belong to thanksgiving; the words, "grant, we beseech Thee," belong to intercession; and the words at the end, "Through Our Lord," etc. belong to supplication.

In the *Conferences of the Fathers* (ix, cap. 11, seqq.) we read: "Supplication is bewailing one's sins; prayer is vowing something to God; intercession is praying for others; thanksgiving is offered by the mind to God in ineffable ecstasy." The first explanation, however, is the better.

Reply Obj. 1: "Supplication" is an adjuration not for the purpose of compelling, for this is forbidden, but in order to implore mercy.

Reply Obj. 2: "Prayer" in the general sense includes all the things mentioned here; but when distinguished from the others it denotes properly the ascent to God.

Reply Obj. 3: Among things that are diverse the past precedes the future; but the one and same thing is future before it is past. Hence thanksgiving for other benefits precedes intercession: but one and the same benefit is first sought, and finally, when it has been received, we give thanks for it. Intercession is preceded by prayer whereby we approach Him of Whom we ask: and prayer is preceded by supplication, whereby through the consideration of God's goodness we dare approach Him.

## QUESTION 84

OF ADORATION (In Three Articles)

In due sequence we must consider the external acts of latria, and in the first place, adoration whereby one uses one's body to reverence God; secondly, those acts whereby some external thing is offered to God; thirdly, those acts whereby something belonging to God is assumed.

Under the first head there are three points of inquiry:

(1) Whether adoration is an act of latria?

(2) Whether adoration denotes an internal or an external act?

(3) Whether adoration requires a definite place?

FIRST ARTICLE [II-II, Q. 84, Art. 1]

Whether Adoration Is an Act of Latria or Religion?

Objection 1: It would seem that adoration is not an act of latria or religion. The worship of religion is due to God alone. But adoration is not due to God alone: since we read (Gen. 18:2) that Abraham adored the angels; and (3 Kings 1:23) that the prophet Nathan, when he was come in to king David, "worshiped him bowing down to the ground." Therefore adoration is not an act of religion.

Obj. 2: Further, the worship of religion is due to God as the object of beatitude, according to Augustine (De Civ. Dei x, 3): whereas adoration is due to Him by reason of His majesty, since a gloss on Ps. 28:2, "Adore ye the Lord in His holy court," says: "We pass from these courts into the court where we adore His majesty." Therefore adoration is not an act of latria.

Obj. 3: Further, the worship of one same religion is due to the three Persons. But we do not adore the three Persons with one adoration, for we genuflect at each separate invocation of Them [*At the adoration of the Cross, on Good Friday]. Therefore adoration is nol an act of latria.

*On the contrary,* are the words quoted Matt. 4:10: "The Lord thy God shalt thou adore and Him only shalt thou serve."

*I answer that,* Adoration is directed to the reverence of the person adored. Now it is evident from what we have said (Q. 81, AA. 2, 4) that it is proper to religion to show reverence to God. Hence the adoration whereby we adore God is an act of religion.

Reply Obj. 1: Reverence is due to God on account of His excellence, which is communicated to certain creatures not in equal measure, but according to a measure of proportion; and so the reverence which we pay to God, and which belongs to latria, differs from the reverence which we pay to certain excellent creatures; this belongs to dulia, and we shall speak of it further on (Q. 103). And since external actions are signs of internal reverence, certain external tokens significative of reverence are offered to creatures of excellence, and among these tokens the chief is adoration: yet there is one thing which is offered to God alone, and that is sacrifice. Hence Augustine says (De Civ. Dei x, 4): "Many tokens of Divine worship are employed in doing honor to men, either through excessive humility, or through pernicious flattery; yet so that those to whom these honors are given are recognized as being men to whom we owe esteem and reverence and even adoration if they be far above us. But who ever thought it his duty to sacrifice to any other than one whom he either knew or deemed or pretended to be a God?" Accordingly it was with the reverence due to an excellent creature that Nathan adored David; while it was the reverence due to God with which Mardochai refused to adore Aman fearing "lest he should transfer the honor of his God to a man" (Esther 13:14).

Again with the reverence due to an excellent creature Abraham adored the angels, as did also Josue (Jos. 5:15): though we may understand them to have adored, with the adoration of latria, God Who appeared and spoke to them in the guise of an angel. It was with the reverence due to God that John was forbidden to adore the angel (Apoc. 22:9), both to indicate the dignity which he had acquired through Christ, whereby man is made equal to an angel: wherefore the same text goes on: "I am thy fellow-servant and of thy brethren"; as also to exclude any occasion of idolatry, wherefore the text continues: "Adore God."

Reply Obj. 2: Every Divine excellency is included in His majesty: to which it pertains that we should be made happy in Him as in the sovereign good.

Reply Obj. 3: Since there is one excellence of the three Divine Persons, one honor and reverence is due to them and consequently one adoration. It is to represent this that where it is related (Gen. 18:2) that three men appeared to Abraham, we are told that he addressed one, saying: "Lord, if I have found favor in thy sight," etc. The triple genuflection represents the Trinity of Persons, not a difference of adoration.

SECOND ARTICLE [II-II, Q. 84, Art. 2]

Whether Adoration Denotes an Action of the Body?

Objection 1: It would seem that adoration does not denote an act of the body. It is written (John 4:23): "The true adorers shall adore the Father in spirit and in truth." Now what is done in spirit has nothing to do with an act of the body. Therefore adoration does not denote an act of the body.

Obj. 2: Further, the word adoration is taken from *oratio* (prayer). But prayer consists chiefly in an interior act, according to 1 Cor. 14:15, "I will pray with the spirit, I will pray also with the understanding." Therefore adoration denotes chiefly a spiritual act.

Obj. 3: Further, acts of the body pertain to sensible knowledge: whereas we approach God not by bodily but by spiritual sense. Therefore adoration does not denote an act of the body.

*On the contrary,* A gloss on Ex. 20:5, "Thou shalt not adore them, nor serve them," says: "Thou shalt neither worship them in mind, nor adore them outwardly."

*I answer that,* As Damascene says (De Fide Orth. iv, 12), since we are composed of a twofold nature, intellectual and sensible, we offer God a twofold adoration; namely, a spiritual adoration, consisting in the internal devotion of the mind; and a bodily adoration, which consists in an exterior humbling of the body. And since in all acts of latria that which is without is referred to that which is within as being of greater import, it follows that exterior adoration is offered on account of interior adoration, in other words we exhibit signs of humility in our bodies in order to incite our affections to submit to God, since it is connatural to us to proceed from the sensible to the intelligible.

Reply Obj. 1: Even bodily adoration is done in spirit, in so far as it proceeds from and is directed to spiritual devotion.

Reply Obj. 2: Just as prayer is primarily in the mind, and secondarily expressed in words, as stated above (Q. 83, A. 12), so too adoration consists chiefly in an interior reverence of God, but secondarily in certain bodily signs of humility; thus when we genuflect we signify our weakness in comparison with God, and when we prostrate ourselves we profess that we are nothing of ourselves.

Reply Obj. 3: Though we cannot reach God with the senses, our mind is urged by sensible signs to approach God.

THIRD ARTICLE [II-II, Q. 84, Art. 3]

Whether Adoration Requires a Definite Place?

Objection 1: It would seem that adoration does not require a definite place. It is written (John 4:21): "The hour cometh, when you shall neither on this mountain, nor in Jerusalem, adore the Father"; and the same reason seems to apply to other places. Therefore a definite place is not necessary for adoration.

Obj. 2: Further, exterior adoration is directed to interior adoration. But interior adoration is shown to God as existing everywhere. Therefore exterior adoration does not require a definite place.

Obj. 3: Further, the same God is adored in the New as in the Old Testament. Now in the Old Testament they adored towards the west, because the door of the Tabernacle looked to the east (Ex. 26:18 seqq.). Therefore for the same reason we ought now to adore towards the west, if any definite place be requisite for adoration.

*On the contrary,* It is written (Isa. 56:7): "My house shall be called the house of prayer," which words are also quoted (John 2:16).

*I answer that,* As stated above (A. 2), the chief part of adoration is the internal devotion of the mind, while the secondary part is something external pertaining to bodily signs. Now the mind internally apprehends God as not comprised in a place; while bodily signs must of necessity be in some definite place and position. Hence a definite place is required for adoration, not chiefly, as though it were essential thereto, but by reason of a certain fittingness, like other bodily signs.

Reply Obj. 1: By these words our Lord foretold the cessation of adoration, both according to the rite of the Jews who adored in Jerusalem, and according to the rite of the Samaritans who adored on Mount Garizim. For both these rites ceased with the advent of the spiritual truth of the Gospel, according to which "a sacrifice is offered to God in every place," as stated in Malach. 1:11.

Reply Obj. 2: A definite place is chosen for adoration, not on account of God Who is adored, as though He were enclosed in a place, but on account of the adorers; and this for three reasons. First, because the place is consecrated, so that those who pray there conceive a greater devotion and are more likely to be heard, as may be seen in the prayer of Solomon (3 Kings 8). Secondly, on account of the sacred mysteries and other signs of holiness contained therein. Thirdly, on account of the concourse of many adorers, by reason of which their prayer is more likely to be heard, according to Matt. 18:20, "Where there are two or three gathered together in My name, there am I in the midst of them."

Reply Obj. 3: There is a certain fittingness in adoring towards the east. First, because the Divine majesty is indicated in the movement of the heavens which is from the east. Secondly, because Paradise was situated in the east according to the Septuagint version of Gen. 2:8, and so we signify our desire to return to Paradise. Thirdly, on account of Christ Who is "the light of the world" [*John 8:12; 9:5], and is called "the Orient" (Zech. 6:12); "Who mounteth above the heaven of heavens to the east" (Ps. 67:34), and is expected to come from the east, according to Matt. 24:27, "As lightning cometh out of the east, and appeareth even into the west; so shall also the coming of the Son of Man be."

## QUESTION 85

OF SACRIFICE (In Four Articles)

In due sequence we must consider those acts whereby external things are offered to God. These give rise to a twofold consideration: (1) Of things given to God by the faithful; (2) Of vows, whereby something is promised to Him.

Under the first head we shall consider sacrifices, oblations, first-fruits, and tithes. About sacrifices there are four points of inquiry:

(1) Whether offering a sacrifice to God is of the law of nature?

(2) Whether sacrifice should be offered to God alone?

(3) Whether the offering of a sacrifice is a special act of virtue?

(4) Whether all are bound to offer sacrifice?

FIRST ARTICLE [II-II, Q. 85, Art. 1]

Whether Offering a Sacrifice to God Is of the Law of Nature?

Objection 1: It would seem that offering a sacrifice to God is not of the natural law. Things that are of the natural law are common among all men. Yet this is not the case with sacrifices: for we read of some, e.g. Melchisedech (Gen. 14:18), offering bread and wine in sacrifice, and of certain animals being offered by some, and others by others. Therefore the offering of sacrifices is not of the natural law.

Obj. 2: Further, things that are of the natural law were observed by all just men. Yet we do not read that Isaac offered sacrifice; nor that Adam did so, of whom nevertheless it is written (Wis. 10:2) that wisdom "brought him out of his sin." Therefore the offering of sacrifice is not of the natural law.

Obj. 3: Further, Augustine says (De Civ. Dei x, 5, 19) that sacrifices are offered in signification of something. Now words which are chief among signs, as he again says (De Doctr. Christ. ii, 3), "signify, not by nature but by convention," according to the Philosopher (Peri Herm. i, 2). Therefore sacrifices are not of the natural law.

*On the contrary,* At all times and among all nations there has always been the offering of sacrifices. Now that which is observed by all is seemingly natural. Therefore the offering of sacrifices is of the natural law.

*I answer that,* Natural reason tells man that he is subject to a higher being, on account of the defects which he perceives in himself, and in which he needs help and direction from someone above him: and whatever this superior being may be, it is known to all under the name of God. Now just as in natural things the lower are naturally subject to the higher, so too it is a dictate of natural reason in accordance with man's natural inclination that he should tender submission and honor, according to his mode, to that which is above man. Now the mode befitting to man is that he should employ sensible signs in order to signify anything, because he derives his knowledge from sensibles. Hence it is a dictate of natural reason that man should use certain sensibles, by offering them to God in sign of the subjection and honor due to Him, like those who make certain offerings to their lord in recognition of his authority. Now this is what we mean by a sacrifice, and consequently the offering of sacrifice is of the natural law.

Reply Obj. 1: As stated above (I-II, Q. 95, A. 2), certain things belong generically to the natural law, while their determination belongs to the positive law; thus the natural law requires that evildoers should be punished; but that this or that punishment should be inflicted on them is a matter determined by God or by man. In like manner the offering of sacrifice belongs generically to the natural law, and consequently all are agreed on this point, but the determination of sacrifices is established by God or by man, and this is the reason for their difference.

Reply Obj. 2: Adam, Isaac and other just men offered sacrifice to God in a manner befitting the times in which they lived, according to Gregory, who says (Moral. iv, 3) that in olden times original sin was remitted through the offering of sacrifices. Nor does Scripture mention all the sacrifices of the just, but only those that have something special connected with them. Perhaps the reason why we read of no sacrifice being offered by Adam may be that, as the origin of sin is ascribed to him, the origin of sanctification ought not to be represented as typified in him. Isaac was a type of Christ, being himself offered in sacrifice; and so there was no need that he should be represented as offering a sacrifice.

Reply Obj. 3: It is natural to man to express his ideas by signs, but the determination of those signs depends on man's pleasure.

SECOND ARTICLE [II-II, Q. 85, Art. 2]

Whether Sacrifice Should Be Offered to God Alone?

Objection 1: It would seem that sacrifice should not be offered to the most high God alone. Since sacrifice ought to be offered to God, it would seem that it ought to be offered to all such as are partakers of the Godhead. Now holy men are made "partakers of the Divine nature," according to 2 Pet. 1:4; wherefore of them is it written (Ps. 81:6): "I have said, You are gods": and angels too are called "sons of God," according to Job 1:6. Thus sacrifice should be offered to all these.

Obj. 2: Further, the greater a person is the greater the honor due to him from man. Now the angels and saints are far greater than any earthly princes: and yet the subjects of the latter pay them much greater honor, by prostrating before them, and offering them gifts, than is implied by offering an animal or any other thing in sacrifice. Much more therefore may one offer sacrifice to the angels and saints.

Obj. 3: Further, temples and altars are raised for the offering of sacrifices. Yet temples and altars are raised to angels and saints. Therefore sacrifices also may be offered to them.

*On the contrary,* It is written (Ex. 22:20): "He that sacrificeth to gods shall be put to death, save only to the Lord."

*I answer that,* As stated above (A. 1), a sacrifice is offered in order that something may be represented. Now the sacrifice that is offered outwardly represents the inward spiritual sacrifice, whereby the soul offers itself to God according to Ps. 50:19, "A sacrifice to God is an afflicted spirit," since, as stated above (Q. 81, A. 7; Q. 84, A. 2), the outward acts of religion are directed to the inward acts. Again the soul offers itself in sacrifice to God as its beginning by creation, and its end by beatification: and according to the true faith God alone is the creator of our souls, as stated in the First Part (QQ. 90, A. 3; 118, A. 2), while in Him alone the beatitude of our soul consists, as stated above (I-II, Q. 1, A. 8; Q. 2, A. 8; Q. 3, AA. 1, 7, 8). Wherefore just as to God alone ought we to offer spiritual sacrifice, so too ought we to offer outward sacrifices to Him alone: even so "in our prayers and praises we proffer significant words to Him to Whom in our hearts we offer the things which we designate thereby," as Augustine states (De Civ. Dei x, 19). Moreover we find that in every country the people are wont to show the sovereign ruler some special sign of honor, and that if this be shown to anyone else, it is a crime of high-treason. Therefore, in the Divine law, the death punishment is assigned to those who offer Divine honor to another than God.

Reply Obj. 1: The name of the Godhead is communicated to certain ones, not equally with God, but by participation; hence neither is equal honor due to them.

Reply Obj. 2: The offering of a sacrifice is measured not by the value of the animal killed, but by its signification, for it is done in honor of the sovereign Ruler of the whole universe. Wherefore, as Augustine says (De Civ. Dei x, 19), "the demons rejoice, not in the stench of corpses, but in receiving divine honors."

Reply Obj. 3: As Augustine says (De Civ. Dei viii, 19), "we do not raise temples and priesthoods to the martyrs, because not they but their God is our God. Wherefore the priest says not: I offer sacrifice to thee, Peter or Paul. But we give thanks to God for their triumphs, and urge ourselves to imitate them."

THIRD ARTICLE [II-II, Q. 85, Art. 3]

Whether the Offering of Sacrifice Is a Special Act of Virtue?

Objection 1: It would seem that the offering of sacrifice is not a special act of virtue. Augustine says (De Civ. Dei x, 6): "A true sacrifice is any work done that we may cleave to God in holy fellowship." But not every good work is a special act of some definite virtue. Therefore the offering of sacrifice is not a special act of a definite virtue.

Obj. 2: Further, the mortification of the body by fasting belongs to abstinence, by continence belongs to chastity, by martyrdom belongs to fortitude. Now all these things seem to be comprised in the offering of sacrifice, according to Rom. 12:1, "Present your bodies a living sacrifice." Again the Apostle says (Heb. 13:16): "Do not forget to do good and to impart, for by such sacrifices God's favor is obtained." Now it belongs to charity, mercy and liberality to do good and to impart. Therefore the offering of sacrifice is not a special act of a definite virtue.

Obj. 3: Further, a sacrifice is apparently anything offered to God. Now many things are offered to God, such as devotion, prayer, tithes, first-fruits, oblations, and holocausts. Therefore sacrifice does not appear to be a special act of a definite virtue.

*On the contrary,* The law contains special precepts about sacrifices, as appears from the beginning of Leviticus.

*I answer that,* As stated above (I-II, Q. 18, AA. 6, 7), where an act of one virtue is directed to the end of another virtue it partakes somewhat of its species; thus when a man thieves in order to commit fornication, his theft assumes, in a sense, the deformity of fornication, so that even though it were not a sin otherwise, it would be a sin from the very fact that it was directed to fornication. Accordingly, sacrifice is a special act deserving of praise in that it is done out of reverence for God; and for this reason it belongs to a definite virtue, viz. religion. But it happens that the acts of the other virtues are directed to the reverence of God, as when a man gives alms of his own things for God's sake, or when a man subjects his own body to some affliction out of reverence for God; and in this way the acts also of other virtues may be called sacrifices. On the other hand there are acts that are not deserving of praise save through being done out of reverence for God: such acts are properly called sacrifices, and belong to the virtue of religion.

Reply Obj. 1: The very fact that we wish to cling to God in a spiritual fellowship pertains to reverence for God: and consequently the act of any virtue assumes the character of a sacrifice through being done in order that we may cling to God in holy fellowship.

Reply Obj. 2: Man's good is threefold. There is first his soul's good which is offered to God in a certain inward sacrifice by devotion, prayer and other like interior acts: and this is the principal sacrifice. The second is his body's good, which is, so to speak, offered to God in martyrdom, and abstinence or continency. The third is the good which consists of external things: and of these we offer a sacrifice to God, directly when we offer our possession to God immediately, and indirectly when we share them with our neighbor for God's sake.

Reply Obj. 3: A "sacrifice," properly speaking, requires that something be done to the thing which is offered to God, for instance animals were slain and burnt, the bread is broken, eaten, blessed. The very word signifies this, since "sacrifice" is so called because a man does something sacred ( *facit sacrum* ). On the other hand an "oblation" is properly the offering of something to God even if nothing be done thereto, thus we speak of offering money or bread at the altar, and yet nothing is done to them. Hence every sacrifice is an oblation, but not conversely. "First-fruits" are oblations, because they were offered to God, according to Deut. 26, but they are not a sacrifice, because nothing sacred was done to them. "Tithes," however, are neither a sacrifice nor an oblation, properly speaking, because they are not offered immediately to God, but to the ministers of Divine worship.

FOURTH ARTICLE [II-II, Q. 85, Art. 4]

Whether All Are Bound to Offer Sacrifices?

Objection 1: It would seem that all are not bound to offer sacrifices. The Apostle says (Rom. 3:19): "What things soever the Law speaketh, it speaketh to them that are in the Law." Now the law of sacrifices was not given to all, but only to the Hebrew people. Therefore all are not bound to offer sacrifices.

Obj. 2: Further, sacrifices are offered to God in order to signify something. But not everyone is capable of understanding these significations. Therefore not all are bound to offer sacrifices.

Obj. 3: Further, priests [* *Sacerdotes:* Those who give or administer sacred things ( sacra dantes ): cf. 1 Cor. 4:1] are so called because they offer sacrifice to God. But all are not priests. Therefore not all are bound to offer sacrifices.

*On the contrary,* The offering of sacrifices of is of the natural law, as stated above (A. 1). Now all are bound to do that which is of the natural law. Therefore all are bound to offer sacrifice to God.

*I answer that,* Sacrifice is twofold, as stated above (A. 2). The first and principal is the inward sacrifice, which all are bound to offer, since all are obliged to offer to God a devout mind. The other is the outward sacrifice, and this again is twofold. There is a sacrifice which is deserving of praise merely through being offered to God in protestation of our subjection to God: and the obligation of offering this sacrifice was not the same for those under the New or the Old Law, as for those who were not under the Law. For those who are under the Law are bound to offer certain definite sacrifices according to the precepts of the Law, whereas those who were not under the Law were bound to perform certain outward actions in God's honor, as became those among whom they dwelt, but not definitely to this or that action. The other outward sacrifice is when the outward actions of the other virtues are performed out of reverence for God; some of which are a matter of precept; and to these all are bound, while others are works of supererogation, and to these all are not bound.

Reply Obj. 1: All were not bound to offer those particular sacrifices which were prescribed in the Law: but they were bound to some sacrifices inward or outward, as stated above.

Reply Obj. 2: Though all do not know explicitly the power of the sacrifices, they know it implicitly, even as they have implicit faith, as stated above (Q. 2, AA. 6, 7).

Reply Obj. 3: The priests offer those sacrifices which are specially directed to the Divine worship, not only for themselves but also for others. But there are other sacrifices, which anyone can offer to God for himself as explained above (AA. 2, 3).

# QUESTION 86

OF OBLATIONS AND FIRST-FRUITS (In Four Articles)

We must next consider oblations and first-fruits. Under this head there are four points of inquiry:

(1) Whether any oblations are necessary as a matter of precept?

(2) To whom are oblations due?

(3) of what things they should be made?

(4) In particular, as to first-fruits, whether men are bound to offer them?

FIRST ARTICLE [II-II, Q. 86, Art. 1]

Whether Men Are Under a Necessity of Precept to Make Oblations?

Objection 1: It would seem that men are not bound by precept to make oblations. Men are not bound, at the time of the Gospel, to observe the ceremonial precepts of the Old Law, as stated above (I-II, Q. 103, AA. 3, 4). Now the offering of oblations is one of the ceremonial precepts of the Old Law, since it is written (Ex. 23:14): "Three times every year you shall celebrate feasts with Me," and further on (Ex. 23:15): "Thou shalt not appear empty before Me." Therefore men are not now under a necessity of precept to make oblations.

Obj. 2: Further, before they are made, oblations depend on man's will, as appears from our Lord's saying (Matt. 5:23), "If ... thou offer thy gift at the altar," as though this were left to the choice of the offerer: and when once oblations have been made, there is no way of offering them again. Therefore in no way is a man under a necessity of precept to make oblations.

Obj. 3: Further, if anyone is bound to give a certain thing to the Church, and fails to give it, he can be compelled to do so by being deprived of the Church's sacraments. But it would seem unlawful to refuse the sacraments of the Church to those who refuse to make oblations according to a decree of the sixth council [*Can. Trullan, xxiii, quoted I, qu. i, can. Nullus]: "Let none who dispense Holy Communion exact anything of the recipient, and if they exact anything let them be deposed." Therefore it is not necessary that men should make oblations.

*On the contrary,* Gregory says [*Gregory VII; Concil. Roman. v, can. xii]: "Let every Christian take care that he offer something to God at the celebration of Mass."

*I answer that,* As stated above (Q. 85, A. 3, ad 3), the term "oblation" is common to all things offered for the Divine worship, so that if a thing be offered to be destroyed in worship of God, as though it were being made into something holy, it is both an oblation and a sacrifice. Wherefore it is written (Ex. 29:18): "Thou shalt offer the whole ram for a burnt-offering upon the altar; it is an oblation to the Lord, a most sweet savor of the victim of the Lord"; and (Lev. 2:1): "When anyone shall offer an oblation of sacrifice to the Lord, his offering shall be of fine flour." If, on the other hand, it be offered with a view to its remaining entire and being deputed to the worship of God or to the use of His ministers, it will be an oblation and not a sacrifice. Accordingly it is essential to oblations of this kind that they be offered voluntarily, according to Ex. 25:2, of "every man that offereth of his own accord you shall take them." Nevertheless it may happen in four ways that one is bound to make oblations. First, on account of a previous agreement: as when a person is granted a portion of Church land, that he may make certain oblations at fixed times, although this has the character of rent. Secondly, by reason of a previous assignment or promise; as when a man offers a gift among the living, or by will bequeaths to the Church something whether movable or immovable to be delivered at some future time. Thirdly, on account of the need of the Church, for instance if her ministers were without means of support. Fourthly, on account of custom; for the faithful are bound at certain solemn feasts to make certain customary oblations. In the last two cases, however, the oblation remains voluntary, as regards, to wit, the quantity or kind of the thing offered.

Reply Obj. 1: Under the New Law men are not bound to make oblations on account of legal solemnities, as stated in Exodus, but on account of certain other reasons, as stated above.

Reply Obj. 2: Some are bound to make oblations, both before making them, as in the first, third, and fourth cases, and after they have made them by assignment or promise: for they are bound to offer in reality that which has been already offered to the Church by way of assignment.

Reply Obj. 3: Those who do not make the oblations they are bound to make may be punished by being deprived of the sacraments, not by the priest himself to whom the oblations should be made, lest he seem to exact, something for bestowing the sacraments, but by someone superior to him.

SECOND ARTICLE [II-II, Q. 86, Art. 2]

Whether Oblations Are Due to Priests Alone?

Objection 1: It would seem that oblations are not due to priests alone. For chief among oblations would seem to be those that are deputed to the sacrifices of victims. Now whatever is given to the poor is called a "victim" in Scripture according to Heb. 13:16, "Do not forget to do good and to impart, for by such victims [Douay: 'sacrifices'] God's favor is obtained." Much more therefore are oblations due to the poor.

Obj. 2: Further, in many parishes monks have a share in the oblations. Now "the case of clerics is distinct from the case of monks," as Jerome states [*Ep. xiv, ad Heliod.]. Therefore oblations art not due to priests alone.

Obj. 3: Further, lay people with the consent of the Church buy oblations such as loaves and so forth, and they do so for no other reason than that they may make use thereof themselves. Therefore oblations may have reference to the laity.

*On the contrary,* A canon of Pope Damasus [*Damasus I] quoted X, qu. i [*Can. Hanc consuetudinem], says: "None but the priests whom day by day we see serving the Lord may eat and drink of the oblations which are offered within the precincts of the Holy Church: because in the Old Testament the Lord forbade the children of Israel to eat the sacred loaves, with the exception of Aaron and his sons" (Lev. 24:8, 9).

*I answer that,* The priest is appointed mediator and stands, so to speak, *between* the people and God, as we read of Moses (Deut. 5:5), wherefore it belongs to him to set forth the Divine teachings and sacraments before the people; and besides to offer to the Lord things appertaining to the people, their prayers, for instance, their sacrifices and oblations. Thus the Apostle says (Heb. 5:1): "Every high priest taken from among men is ordained for men in the things that appertain to God, that he may offer up gifts and sacrifices for sins." Hence the oblations which the people offer to God concern the priests, not only as regards their turning them to their own use, but also as regards the faithful dispensation thereof, by spending them partly on things appertaining to the Divine worship, partly on things touching their own livelihood (since they that serve the altar partake with the altar, according to 1 Cor. 9:13), and partly for the good of the poor, who, as far as possible, should be supported from the possessions of the Church: for our Lord had a purse for the use of the poor, as Jerome observes on Matt. 17:26, "That we may not scandalize them."

Reply Obj. 1: Whatever is given to the poor is not a sacrifice properly speaking; yet it is called a sacrifice in so far as it is given to them for God's sake. In like manner, and for the same reason, it can be called an oblation, though not properly speaking, since it is not given immediately to God. Oblations properly so called fall to the use of the poor, not by the dispensation of the offerers, but by the dispensation of the priests.

Reply Obj. 2: Monks or other religious may receive oblations under three counts. First, as poor, either by the dispensation of the priests, or by ordination of the Church; secondly, through being ministers of the altar, and then they can accept oblations that are freely offered; thirdly, if the parishes belong to them, and they can accept oblations, having a right to them as rectors of the Church.

Reply Obj. 3: Oblations when once they are consecrated, such as sacred vessels and vestments, cannot be granted to the use of the laity: and this is the meaning of the words of Pope Damasus. But those which are unconsecrated may be allowed to the use of layfolk by permission of the priests, whether by way of gift or by way of sale.

THIRD ARTICLE [II-II, Q. 86, Art. 3]

Whether a Man May Make Oblations of Whatever He Lawfully Possesses?

Objection 1: It would seem that a man may not make oblations of whatever he lawfully possesses. According to human law [*Dig. xii, v, de Condict. ob. turp. vel iniust. caus. 4] "the whore's is a shameful trade in what she does but not in what she takes," and consequently what she takes she possesses lawfully. Yet it is not lawful for her to make an oblation with her gains, according to Deut. 23:18, "Thou shalt not offer the hire of a strumpet ... in the house of the Lord thy God." Therefore it is not lawful to make an oblation of whatever one possesses lawfully.

Obj. 2: Further, in the same passage it is forbidden to offer "the price of a dog" in the house of God. But it is evident that a man possesses lawfully the price of a dog he has lawfully sold. Therefore it is not lawful to make an oblation of whatever we possess lawfully.

Obj. 3: Further, it is written (Malachi 1:8): "If you offer the lame and the sick, is it not evil?" Yet an animal though lame or sick is a lawful possession. Therefore it would seem that not of every lawful possession may one make an oblation.

*On the contrary,* It is written (Prov. 3:9): "Honor the Lord with thy substance." Now whatever a man possesses lawfully belongs to his substance. Therefore he may make oblations of whatever he possesses lawfully.

*I answer that,* As Augustine says (De Verb. Dom. Serm. cxiii), "shouldst thou plunder one weaker than thyself and give some of the spoil to the judge, if he should pronounce in thy favor, such is the force of justice that even thou wouldst not be pleased with him: and if this should not please thee, neither does it please thy God." Hence it is written (Ecclus. 34:21): "The offering of him that sacrificeth of a thing wrongfully gotten is stained." Therefore it is evident that an oblation must not be made of things unjustly acquired or possessed. In the Old Law, however, wherein the figure was predominant, certain things were reckoned unclean on account of their signification, and it was forbidden to offer them. But in the New Law all God's creatures are looked upon as clean, as stated in Titus 1:15: and consequently anything that is lawfully possessed, considered in itself, may be offered in oblation. But it may happen accidentally that one may not make an oblation of what one possesses lawfully; for instance if it be detrimental to another person, as in the case of a son who offers to God the means of supporting his father (which our Lord condemns, Matt. 15:5), or if it give rise to scandal or contempt, or the like.

Reply Obj. 1: In the Old Law it was forbidden to make an offering of the hire of a strumpet on account of its uncleanness, and in the New Law, on account of scandal, lest the Church seem to favor sin if she accept oblations from the profits of sin.

Reply Obj. 2: According to the Law, a dog was deemed an unclean animal. Yet other unclean animals were redeemed and their price could be offered, according to Lev. 27:27, "If it be an unclean animal, he that offereth it shall redeem it." But a dog was neither offered nor redeemed, both because idolaters used dogs in sacrifices to their idols, and because they signify robbery, the proceeds of which cannot be offered in oblation. However, this prohibition ceased under the New Law.

Reply Obj. 3: The oblation of a blind or lame animal was declared unlawful for three reasons. First, on account of the purpose for which it was offered, wherefore it is written (Malach. 1:8): "If you offer the blind in sacrifice, is it not evil?" and it behooved sacrifices to be without blemish. Secondly, on account of contempt, wherefore the same text goes on (Malach. 1:12): "You have profaned" My name, "in that you say: The table of the Lord is defiled and that which is laid thereupon is contemptible." Thirdly, on account of a previous vow, whereby a man has bound himself to offer without blemish whatever he has vowed: hence the same text says further on (Malach. 1:14): "Cursed is the deceitful man that hath in his flock a male, and making a vow offereth in sacrifice that which is feeble to the Lord." The same reasons avail still in the New Law, but when they do not apply the unlawfulness ceases.

FOURTH ARTICLE [II-II, Q. 86, Art. 4]

Whether Men Are Bound to Pay First-fruits?

Objection 1: It would seem that men are not bound to pay first-fruits. After giving the law of the first-born the text continues (Ex. 13:9): "It shall be as a sign in thy hand," so that, apparently, it is a ceremonial precept. But ceremonial precepts are not to be observed in the New Law. Neither therefore ought first-fruits to be paid.

Obj. 2: Further, first-fruits were offered to the Lord for a special favor conferred on that people, wherefore it is written (Deut. 26:2, 3): "Thou shalt take the first of all thy fruits ... and thou shalt go to the priest that shall be in those days, and say to him: I profess this day before the Lord thy God, that I am come into the land, for which He swore to our fathers, that He would give it us." Therefore other nations are not bound to pay first-fruits.

Obj. 3: That which one is bound to do should be something definite. But neither in the New Law nor in the Old do we find mention of a definite amount of first-fruits. Therefore one is not bound of necessity to pay them.

*On the contrary,* It is laid down (16, qu. vii, can. Decimas): "We confirm the right of priests to tithes and first-fruits, and everybody must pay them."

*I answer that,* First-fruits are a kind of oblation, because they are offered to God with a certain profession (Deut. 26); where the same passage continues: "The priest taking the basket containing the first-fruits from the hand of him that bringeth the first-fruits, shall set it before the altar of the Lord thy God," and further on (Deut. 26:10) he is commanded to say: "Therefore now I offer the first-fruits of the land, which the Lord hath given me." Now the first-fruits were offered for a special reason, namely, in recognition of the divine favor, as though man acknowledged that he had received the fruits of the earth from God, and that he ought to offer something to God in return, according to 1 Paral 29:14, "We have given Thee what we received of Thy hand." And since what we offer God ought to be something special, hence it is that man was commanded to offer God his first-fruits, as being a special part of the fruits of the earth: and since a priest is "ordained for the people in the things that appertain to God" (Heb. 5:1), the first-fruits offered by the people were granted to the priest's use. Wherefore it is written (Num. 18:8): "The Lord said to Aaron: Behold I have given thee the charge of My first-fruits." Now it is a point of natural law that man should make an offering in God's honor out of the things he has received from God, but that the offering should be made to any particular person, or out of his first-fruits, or in such or such a quantity, was indeed determined in the Old Law by divine command; but in the New Law it is fixed by the declaration of the Church, in virtue of which men are bound to pay first-fruits according to the custom of their country and the needs of the Church's ministers.

Reply Obj. 1: The ceremonial observances were properly speaking signs of the future, and consequently they ceased when the foreshadowed truth was actually present. But the offering of first-fruits was for a sign of a past favor, whence arises the duty of acknowledgment in accordance with the dictate of natural reason. Hence taken in a general sense this obligation remains.

Reply Obj. 2: First-fruits were offered in the Old Law, not only on account of the favor of the promised land given by God, but also on account of the favor of the fruits of the earth, which were given by God. Hence it is written (Deut. 26:10): "I offer the first-fruits of the land which the Lord hath given me," which second motive is common among all people. We may also reply that just as God granted the land of promise to the Jews by a special favor, so by a general favor He bestowed the lordship of the earth on the whole of mankind, according to Ps. 113:24, "The earth He has given to the children of men."

Reply Obj. 3: As Jerome says [*Comment. in Ezech. 45:13, 14; cf. Cap. Decimam, de Decim. Primit. et Oblat.]: "According to the tradition of the ancients the custom arose for those who had most to give the priests a fortieth part, and those who had least, one sixtieth, in lieu of first-fruits." Hence it would seem that first-fruits should vary between these limits according to the custom of one's country. And it was reasonable that the amount of first-fruits should not be fixed by law, since, as stated above, first-fruits are offered by way of oblation, a condition of which is that it should be voluntary.

# QUESTION 87

OF TITHES (In Four Articles)

Next we must consider tithes, under which head there are four points of inquiry:

(1) Whether men are bound by precept to pay tithes?

(2) Of what things ought tithes to be paid?

(3) To whom ought they to be paid?

(4) Who ought to pay tithes?

FIRST ARTICLE [II-II, Q. 87, Art. 1]

Whether Men Are Bound to Pay Tithes Under a Necessity of Precept?

Objection 1: It would seem that men are not bound by precept to pay tithes. The commandment to pay tithes is contained in the Old Law (Lev. 27:30), "All tithes of the land, whether of corn or of the fruits of trees, are the Lord's," and further on (Lev. 27:32): "Of all the tithes of oxen and sheep and goats, that pass under the shepherd's rod, every tenth that cometh shall be sanctified to the Lord." This cannot be reckoned among the moral precepts, because natural reason does not dictate that one ought to give a tenth part, rather than a ninth or eleventh. Therefore it is either a judicial or a ceremonial precept. Now, as stated above (I-II, Q. 103, A. 3; Q. 104, A. 3), during the time of grace men are hound neither to the ceremonial nor to the judicial precepts of the Old Law. Therefore men are not bound now to pay tithes.

Obj. 2: Further, during the time of grace men are bound only to those things which were commanded by Christ through the Apostles, according to Matt. 28:20, "Teaching them to observe all things whatsoever I have commanded you"; and Paul says

(Acts 20:27): "I have not spared to declare unto you all the counsel of God." Now neither in the teaching of Christ nor in that of the apostles is there any mention of the paying of tithes: for the saying of our Lord about tithes (Matt. 23:23), "These things you ought to have done" seems to refer to the past time of legal observance: thus Hilary says (Super Matth. can. xxiv): "The tithing of herbs, which was useful in foreshadowing the future, was not to be omitted." Therefore during the time of grace men are not bound to pay tithes.

Obj. 3: Further, during the time of grace, men are not more bound to the legal observances than before the Law. But before the Law tithes were given, by reason not of a precept but of a vow. For we read (Gen. 28:20, 22) that Jacob "made a vow" saying: "If God shall be with me, and shall keep me in the way by which I walk ... of all the things that Thou shalt give to me, I will offer tithes to Thee." Neither, therefore, during the time of grace are men bound to pay tithes.

Obj. 4: Further, in the Old Law men were bound to pay three kinds of tithe. For it is written (Num. 18:23, 24): "The sons of Levi ... shall ... be content with the oblation of tithes, which I have separated for their uses and necessities." Again, there were other tithes of which we read (Deut. 14:22, 23): "Every year thou shalt set aside the tithes of all thy fruits, that the earth bringeth forth year by year; and thou shalt eat before the Lord thy God in the place which He shall choose." And there were yet other tithes, of which it is written (Deut. 14:28): "The third year thou shalt separate another tithe of all things that grow to thee at that time, and shalt lay it up within thy gates. And the Levite that hath no other part nor possession with thee, and the stranger, and the fatherless, and the widow, that are within thy gates, shall ... eat and be filled." Now during the time of grace men are not bound to pay the second and third tithes. Neither therefore are they bound to pay the first.

Obj. 5: Further, a debt that is due without any time being fixed for its payment, must be paid at once under pain of sin. Accordingly if during the time of grace men are bound, under necessity of precept, to pay tithes in those countries where tithes are not paid, they would all be in a state of mortal sin, and so would also be the ministers of the Church for dissembling. But this seems unreasonable. Therefore during the time of grace men are not bound under necessity of precept to pay tithes.

*On the contrary,* Augustine [*Append. Serm. cclxxcii], whose words are quoted 16, qu. i [*Can. Decimae], says: "It is a duty to pay tithes, and whoever refuses to pay them takes what belongs to another."

*I answer that,* In the Old Law tithes were paid for the sustenance of the ministers of God. Hence it is written (Malach. 3:10): "Bring all the tithes into My [Vulg.: 'the'] store-house that there may be meat in My house." Hence the precept about the paying of tithes was partly moral and instilled in the natural reason; and partly judicial, deriving its force from its divine institution. Because natural reason dictates that the people should administer the necessaries of life to those who minister the divine worship for the welfare of the whole people even as it is the people's duty to provide a livelihood for their rulers and soldiers and so forth. Hence the Apostle proves this from human custom, saying (1 Cor. 9:7): "Who serveth as a soldier at any time at his own charge? Who planteth a vineyard and eateth not of the fruit thereof?" But the fixing of the proportion to be offered to the ministers of divine worship does not belong to the natural law, but was determined by divine institution, in accordance with the condition of that people to whom the law was being given. For they were divided into twelve tribes, and the twelfth tribe, namely that of Levi, was engaged exclusively in the divine ministry and had no possessions whence to derive a livelihood: and so it was becomingly ordained that the remaining eleven tribes should give one-tenth part of their revenues to the Levites [*Num. 18:21] that the latter might live respectably; and also because some, through negligence, would disregard this precept. Hence, so far as the tenth part was fixed, the precept was judicial, since all institutions established among this people for the special purpose of preserving equality among men, in accordance with this people's condition, are called "judicial precepts." Nevertheless by way of consequence these institutions foreshadowed something in the future, even as everything else connected with them, according to 1 Cor. 12, "All these things happened to them in figure." In this respect they had something in common with the *ceremonial precepts,* which were instituted chiefly that they might be signs of the future. Hence the precept about paying tithes foreshadowed something in the future. For ten is, in a way, the perfect number (being the first numerical limit, since the figures do not go beyond ten but begin over again from one), and therefore he that gave a tenth, which is the sign of perfection, reserving the nine other parts for himself, acknowledged by a sign that imperfection was his part, and that the perfection which was to come through Christ was to be hoped for from God. Yet this proves it to be, not a ceremonial but a judicial precept, as stated above.

There is this difference between the ceremonial and judicial precepts of the Law, as we stated above (I-II, Q. 104, A. 3), that it is unlawful to observe the ceremonial precepts at the time of the New Law, whereas there is no sin in keeping the judicial precepts during the time of grace although they are not binding. Indeed they are bound to be observed by some, if they be ordained by the authority of those who have power to make laws. Thus it was a judicial precept of the Old Law that he who stole a sheep should restore four sheep (Ex. 22:1), and if any king were to order this to be done his subjects would be bound to obey. In like manner during the time of the New Law the authority of the Church has established the payment of tithe; thus showing a certain kindliness, lest the people of the New Law should give less to the ministers of the New Testament than did the people of the Old Law to the ministers of the Old Testament; for the people of the New Law are under greater obligations, according to Matt. 5:20, "Unless your justice abound more than that of the Scribes and Pharisees, you shall not enter into the kingdom of heaven," and, moreover, the ministers of the New Testament are of greater dignity than the ministers of the Old Testament, as the Apostle shows (2 Cor. 3:7, 8).

Accordingly it is evident that man's obligation to pay tithes arises partly from natural law, partly from the institution of the Church; who, nevertheless, in consideration of the requirements of time and persons might ordain the payment of some other proportion.

This suffices for the Reply to the First Objection.

Reply Obj. 2: The precept about paying tithes, in so far as it was a moral precept, was given in the Gospel by our Lord when He said (Matt. 10:10) [*The words as quoted are from Luke 10:7: Matthew has 'meat' instead of 'hire']: "The workman is worthy of his hire," and the Apostle says the same (1 Cor. 9:4 seqq.). But the fixing of the particular proportion is left to the ordinance of the Church.

Reply Obj. 3: Before the time of the Old Law the ministry of the divine worship was not entrusted to any particular person; although it is stated that the first-born were priests, and that they received a double portion. For this very reason no particular portion was directed to be given to the ministers of the divine worship: but when they met with one, each man of his own accord gave him what he deemed right. Thus Abraham by a kind of prophetic instinct gave tithes to Melchisedech, the priest of the Most High God, according to Gen. 14:20, and again Jacob made a vow to give tithes [*Gen. 28:20], although he appears to have vowed to do so, not by paying them to ministers, but for the purpose of the divine worship, for instance for the fulfilling of sacrifices, hence he said significantly: "I will offer tithes to Thee."

Reply Obj. 4: The second kind of tithe, which was reserved for the offering of sacrifices, has no place in the New Law, since the legal victims had ceased. But the third kind of tithe which they had to eat with the poor, is increased in the New Law, for our Lord commanded us to give to the poor not merely the tenth part, but all our surplus, according to Luke 11:41: "That which remaineth, give alms." Moreover the tithes that are given to the ministers of the Church should be dispensed by them for the use of the poor.

Reply Obj. 5: The ministers of the Church ought to be more solicitous for the increase of spiritual goods in the people, than for the amassing of temporal goods: and hence the Apostle was unwilling to make use of the right given him by the Lord of receiving his livelihood from those to whom he preached the Gospel, lest he should occasion a hindrance to the Gospel of Christ [*1 Cor. 9:12]. Nor did they sin who did not contribute to his upkeep, else the Apostle would not have omitted to reprove them. In like manner the ministers of the Church rightly refrain from demanding the Church's tithes, when they could not demand them without scandal, on account of their having fallen into desuetude, or for some other reason. Nevertheless those who do not give tithes in places where the Church does not demand them are not in a state of damnation, unless they be obstinate, and unwilling to pay even if tithes were demanded of them.

SECOND ARTICLE [II-II, Q. 87, Art. 2]

Whether Men Are Bound to Pay Tithes of All Things?

Objection 1: It would seem that men are not bound to give tithes of all things. The paying of tithes seems to be an institution of the Old Law. Now the Old Law contains no precept about personal tithes, viz. those that are payable on property acquired by one's own act, for instance by commerce or soldiering. Therefore no man is bound to pay tithes on such things.

Obj. 2: Further, it is not right to make oblations of that which is ill-gotten, as stated above (Q. 86, A. 3). Now oblations, being offered to God immediately, seem to be more closely connected with the divine worship than tithes which are offered to the ministers. Therefore neither should tithes be paid on ill-gotten goods.

Obj. 3: Further, in the last chapter of Leviticus (30, 32) the precept of paying tithes refers only to "corn, fruits of trees" and animals "that pass under the shepherd's rod." But man derives a revenue from other smaller things, such as the herbs that grow in his garden and so forth. Therefore neither on these things is a man bound to pay tithes.

Obj. 4: Further, man cannot pay except what is in his power. Now a man does not always remain in possession of all his profit from land and stock, since sometimes he loses them by theft or robbery; sometimes they are transferred to another person by sale; sometimes they are due to some other person, thus taxes are due to princes, and wages due to workmen. Therefore one ought not to pay tithes on such like things.

*On the contrary,* It is written (Gen. 28:22): "Of all things that Thou shalt give to me, I will offer tithes to Thee."

*I answer that,* In judging about a thing we should look to its principle. Now the principle of the payment of tithes is the debt whereby carnal things are due to those who sow spiritual things, according to the saying of the Apostle (1 Cor. 9:11), "If we have sown unto you spiritual things, is it a great matter if we reap your carnal things?" [thus implying that on the contrary "it is no great matter if we reap your carnal things"] [*The phrase in the brackets is omitted in the Leonine edition]. For this debt is the principle on which is based the commandment of the Church about the payment of tithes. Now whatever man possesses comes under the designation of carnal things. Therefore tithes must be paid on whatever one possesses.

Reply Obj. 1: In accordance with the condition of that people there was a special reason why the Old Law did not include a precept about personal tithes; because, to wit, all the other tribes had certain possessions wherewith they were able to provide a sufficient livelihood for the Levites who had no possessions, but were not forbidden to make a profit out of other lawful occupations as the other Jews did. On the other hand the people of the New Law are spread abroad throughout the world, and many of them have no possessions, but live by trade, and these would contribute nothing to the support of God's ministers if they did not pay tithes on their trade profits. Moreover the ministers of the New Law are more strictly forbidden to occupy themselves in money-making trades, according to 2 Tim. 2:4, "No man being a soldier to God, entangleth himself with secular business." Wherefore in the New Law men are bound to pay personal tithes, according to the custom of their country and the needs of the ministers: hence Augustine, whose words are quoted 16, qu. 1, cap. Decimae, says [*Append. Serm. cclxxvii]: "Tithes must be paid on the profits of soldiering, trade or craft."

Reply Obj. 2: Things are ill-gotten in two ways. First, because the getting itself was unjust: such, for instance, are things gotten by robbery, theft or usury: and these a man is bound to restore, and not to pay tithes on them. If, however, a field be bought with the profits of usury, the usurer is bound to pay tithes on the produce, because the latter is not gotten usuriously but given by God. On the other hand certain things are said to be ill-gotten, because they are gotten of a shameful cause, for instance of whoredom or stage-playing, and the like. Such things a man is not bound to restore, and consequently he is bound to pay tithes on them in the same way as other personal tithes. Nevertheless the Church must not accept the tithe so long as those persons remain in sin, lest she appear to have a share in their sins: but when they have done penance, tithes may be accepted from them on these things.

Reply Obj. 3: Things directed to an end must be judged according to their fittingness to the end. Now the payment of tithes is due not for its own sake, but for the sake of the ministers, to whose dignity it is unbecoming that they should demand minute things with careful exactitude, for this is reckoned sinful according to the Philosopher (Ethic. iv, 2). Hence the Old Law did not order the payment of tithes on such like minute things, but left it to the judgment of those who are willing to pay, because minute things are counted as nothing. Wherefore the Pharisees who claimed for themselves the perfect justice of the Law, paid tithes even on these minute things: nor are they reproved by our Lord on that account, but only because they despised greater, i.e. spiritual, precepts; and rather did He show them to be deserving of praise in this particular, when He said (Matt. 23:23): "These things you ought to have done," i.e. during the time of the Law, according to Chrysostom's [*Hom. xliv in the Opus Imperfectum falsely ascribed to St. John Chrysostom] commentary. This also seems to denote fittingness rather than obligation. Therefore now too men are not bound to pay tithes on such minute things, except perhaps by reason of the custom of one's country.

Reply Obj. 4: A man is not bound to pay tithes on what he has lost by theft or robbery, before he recovers his property: unless he has incurred the loss through his own fault or neglect, because the Church ought not to be the loser on that account. If he sell wheat that has not been tithed, the Church can command the tithes due to her, both from the buyer who has a thing due to the Church, and from the seller, because so far as he is concerned he has defrauded the Church: yet if one pays, the other is not bound. Tithes are due on the fruits of the earth, in so far as these fruits are the gift of God. Wherefore tithes do not come under a tax, nor are they subject to workmen's wages. Hence it is not right to deduct one's taxes and the wages paid to workmen, before paying tithes: but tithes must be paid before anything else on one's entire produce.

THIRD ARTICLE [II-II, Q. 87, Art. 4]

Whether Tithes Should Be Paid to the Clergy?

Objection 1: It would seem that tithes should not be paid to the clergy. Tithes were paid to the Levites in the Old Testament, because they had no portion in the people's possessions, according to Num. 18:23, 24. But in the New Testament the clergy have possessions not only ecclesiastical, but sometimes also patrimonial: moreover they receive first-fruits, and oblations for the living and the dead. Therefore it is unnecessary to pay tithes to them.

Obj. 2: Further, it sometimes happens that a man dwells in one parish, and farms in another; or a shepherd may take his flock within the bounds of one parish during one part of the year, and within the bounds of another parish during the other part of the year; or he may have his sheepfold in one parish, and graze the sheep in another. Now in all these and similar cases it seems impossible to decide to which clergy the tithes ought to be paid. Therefore it would seem that no fixed tithe ought to be paid to the clergy.

Obj. 3: Further, it is the general custom in certain countries for the soldiers to hold the tithes from the Church in fee; and certain religious receive tithes. Therefore seemingly tithes are not due only to those of the clergy who have care of souls.

*On the contrary,* It is written (Num. 18:21): "I have given to the sons of Levi all the tithes of Israel for a possession, for the ministry wherewith they serve Me in the Tabernacle." Now the clergy are the successors of the sons of Levi in the New Testament. Therefore tithes are due to the clergy alone.

*I answer that,* Two things have to be considered with regard to tithes: namely, the right to receive tithes, and the things given in the name of tithes. The right to receive tithes is a spiritual thing, for it arises from the debt in virtue of which the ministers of the altar have a right to the expenses of their ministry, and temporal things are due to those who sow spiritual things. This debt concerns none but the clergy who have care of souls, and so they alone are competent to have this right.

On the other hand the things given in the name of tithes are material, wherefore they may come to be used by anyone, and thus it is that they fall into the hands of the laity.

Reply Obj. 1: In the Old Law, as stated above (A. 1, ad 4), special tithes were earmarked for the assistance of the poor. But in the New Law the tithes are given to the clergy, not only for their own support, but also that the clergy may use them in assisting the poor. Hence they are not unnecessary; indeed Church property, oblations and first-fruits as well as tithes are all necessary for this same purpose.

Reply Obj. 2: Personal tithes are due to the church in whose parish a man dwells, while predial tithes seem more reasonably to belong to the church within whose bounds the land is situated. The law, however, prescribes that in this matter a custom that has obtained for a long time must be observed [*Cap. Cum sint, and Cap. Ad apostolicae, de Decimis, etc.]. The shepherd who grazes his flock at different seasons in two parishes, should pay tithe proportionately to both churches. And since the fruit of the flock is derived from the pasture, the tithe of the flock is due to the church in whose lands the flock grazes, rather than to the church on whose land the fold is situated.

Reply Obj. 3: Just as the Church can hand over to a layman the things she receives under the title of tithe, so too can she allow him to receive tithes that are yet to be paid, the right of receiving being reserved to the ministers of the Church. The motive may be either the need of the Church, as when tithes are due to certain soldiers through being granted to them in fee by the Church, or it may be the succoring of the poor; thus certain tithes have been granted by way of alms to certain lay religious, or to those that have no care of souls. Some religious, however, are competent to receive tithes, because they have care of souls.

FOURTH ARTICLE [II-II, Q. 87, Art. 4]

Whether the Clergy Also Are Bound to Pay Tithes?

Objection 1: It would seem that clerics also are bound to pay tithes. By common law [*Cap. Cum homines, de Decimis, etc.] the parish church should receive the tithes on the lands which are in its territory. Now it happens sometimes that the clergy have certain lands of their own on the territory of some parish church, or that one church has ecclesiastical property on the territory of another. Therefore it would seem that the clergy are bound to pay predial tithes.

Obj. 2: Further, some religious are clerics; and yet they are bound to pay tithes to churches on account of the lands which they cultivate even with their own hands [*Cap. Ex parte, and Cap. Nuper.]. Therefore it would seem that the clergy are not immune from the payment of tithes.

Obj. 3: Further, in the eighteenth chapter of Numbers (26, 28), it is prescribed not only that the Levites should receive tithes from the people, but also that they should themselves pay tithes to the high-priest. Therefore the clergy are bound to pay tithes to the Sovereign Pontiff, no less than the laity are bound to pay tithes to the clergy.

Obj. 4: Further, tithes should serve not only for the support of the clergy, but also for the assistance of the poor. Therefore, if the clergy are exempt from paying tithes, so too are the poor. Yet the latter is not true. Therefore the former is false.

*On the contrary,* A decretal of Pope Paschal [*Paschal II] says: "It is a new form of exaction when the clergy demand tithes from the clergy" [*Cap. Novum genus, de Decimis, etc.].

*I answer that,* The cause of giving cannot be the cause of receiving, as neither can the cause of action be the cause of passion; yet it happens that one and the same person is giver and receiver, even as agent and patient, on account of different causes and from different points of view. Now tithes are due to the clergy as being ministers of the altar and sowers of spiritual things among the people. Wherefore those members of the clergy as such, i.e. as having ecclesiastical property, are not bound to pay tithes; whereas from some other cause through holding property in their own right, either by inheriting it from their kindred, or by purchase, or in any other similar manner, they are bound to the payment of tithes.

Hence the Reply to the First Objection is clear, because the clergy like anyone else are bound to pay tithes on their own lands to the parish church, even though they be the clergy of that same church, because to possess a thing as one's private property is not the same as possessing it in common. But church lands are not tithable, even though they be within the boundaries of another parish.

Reply Obj. 2: Religious who are clerics, if they have care of souls, and dispense spiritual things to the people, are not bound to pay tithes, but they may receive them. Another reason applies to other religious, who though clerics do not dispense spiritual things to the people; for according to the ordinary law they are bound to pay tithes, but they are somewhat exempt by reason of various concessions granted by the Apostolic See [*Cap. Ex multiplici, Ex parte, and Ad audientiam, de Decimis, etc.].

Reply Obj. 3: In the Old Law first-fruits were due to the priests, and tithes to the Levites; and since the Levites were below the priests, the Lord commanded that the former should pay the high-priest "the tenth part of the tenth" [*Num. 18:26] instead of first-fruits: wherefore for the same reason the clergy are bound now to pay tithes to the Sovereign Pontiff, if he demanded them. For natural reason dictates that he who has charge of the common estate of a multitude should be provided with all goods, so that he may be able to carry out whatever is necessary for the common welfare.

Reply Obj. 4: Tithes should be employed for the assistance of the poor, through the dispensation of the clergy. Hence the poor have no reason for accepting tithes, but they are bound to pay them.

## QUESTION 88

OF VOWS (In Twelve Articles)

We must now consider vows, whereby something is promised to God. Under this head there are twelve points of inquiry:

(1) What is a vow?

(2) What is the matter of a vow?

(3) Of the obligation of vows;

(4) Of the use of taking vows;

(5) Of what virtue is it an act?

(6) Whether it is more meritorious to do a thing from a vow, than without a vow?

(7) Of the solemnizing of a vow;

(8) Whether those who are under another's power can take vows?

(9) Whether children may be bound by vow to enter religion?

(10) Whether a vow is subject to dispensation or commutation?

(11) Whether a dispensation can be granted in a solemn vow of continence?

(12) Whether the authority of a superior is required in a dispensation from a vow?

FIRST ARTICLE [II-II, Q. 88, Art. 1]

Whether a Vow Consists in a Mere Purpose of the Will?

Objection 1: It would seem that a vow consists in nothing but a purpose of the will. According to some [*William of Auxerre, Sum. Aur. III, xxviii, qu. 1; Albertus Magnus, Sent. iv, D, 38], "a vow is a conception of a good purpose after a firm deliberation of the mind, whereby a man binds himself before God to do or not to do a certain thing." But the conception of a good purpose and so forth, may consist in a mere movement of the will. Therefore a vow consists in a mere purpose of the will.

Obj. 2: Further, the very word vow seems to be derived from *voluntas* (will), for one is said to do a thing proprio voto (by one's own vow) when one does it voluntarily. Now to purpose is an act of the will, while to promise is an act of the reason. Therefore a vow consists in a mere act of the will.

Obj. 3: Further, our Lord said (Luke 9:62): "No man putting his hand to the plough, and looking back, is fit for the kingdom of God." Now from the very fact that a man has a purpose of doing good, he puts his hand to the plough. Consequently, if he look back by desisting from his good purpose, he is not fit for the kingdom of God. Therefore by a mere good purpose a man is bound before God, even without making a promise; and consequently it would seem that a vow consists in a mere purpose of the will.

*On the contrary,* It is written (Eccles. 5:3): "If thou hast vowed anything to God, defer not to pay it, for an unfaithful and foolish promise displeaseth Him." Therefore to vow is to promise, and a vow is a promise.

*I answer that,* A vow denotes a binding to do or omit some particular thing. Now one man binds himself to another by means of a promise, which is an act of the reason to which faculty it belongs to direct. For just as a man by commanding or praying, directs, in a fashion, what others are to do for him, so by promising he directs what he himself is to do for another. Now a promise between man and man can only be expressed in words or any other outward signs; whereas a promise can be made to God by the mere inward thought, since according to 1 Kings 16:7, "Man seeth those things that appear, but the Lord beholdeth the heart." Yet we express words outwardly sometimes, either to arouse ourselves, as was stated above with regard to prayer (Q. 83, A. 12), or to call others to witness, so that one may refrain from breaking the vow, not only through fear of God, but also through respect of men. Now a promise is the outcome from a purpose of doing something: and a purpose presupposes deliberation, since it is the act of a deliberate will. Accordingly three things are essential to a vow: the first is deliberation; the second is a purpose of the will; and the third is a promise, wherein is completed the nature of a vow. Sometimes, however, two other things are added as a sort of confirmation of the vow, namely, pronouncement by word of mouth, according to Ps. 65:13, "I will pay Thee my vows which my lips have uttered"; and the witnessing of others. Hence the Master says (Sent. iv, D, 38) that a vow is "the witnessing of a spontaneous promise and ought to be made to God and about things relating to God": although the "witnessing" may strictly refer to the inward protestation.

Reply Obj. 1: The conceiving of a good purpose is not confirmed by the deliberation of the mind, unless the deliberation lead to a promise.

Reply Obj. 2: Man's will moves the reason to promise something relating to things subject to his will, and a vow takes its name from the will forasmuch as it proceeds from the will as first mover.

Reply Obj. 3: He that puts his hand to the plough does something already; while he that merely purposes to do something does nothing so far. When, however, he promises, he already sets about doing, although he does not yet fulfil his promise: even so, he that puts his hand to the plough does not plough yet, nevertheless he stretches out his hand for the purpose of ploughing.

SECOND ARTICLE [II-II, Q. 88, Art. 2]

Whether a Vow Should Always Be About a Better Good?

Objection 1: It would seem that a vow need not be always about a better good. A greater good is one that pertains to supererogation. But vows are not only about matters of supererogation, but also about matters of salvation: thus in Baptism men vow to renounce the devil and his pomps, and to keep the faith, as a gloss observes on Ps. 75:12, "Vow ye, and pay to the Lord your God"; and Jacob vowed (Gen. 28:21) that the Lord should be his God. Now this above all is necessary for salvation. Therefore vows are not only about a better good.

Obj. 2: Further, Jephte is included among the saints (Heb. 11:32). Yet he killed his innocent daughter on account of his vow (Judges 11). Since, then, the slaying of an innocent person is not a better good, but is in itself unlawful, it seems that a vow may be made not only about a better good, but also about something unlawful.

Obj. 3: Further, things that tend to be harmful to the person, or that are quite useless, do not come under the head of a better good. Yet sometimes vows are made about immoderate vigils or fasts which tend to injure the person: and sometimes vows are about indifferent matters and such as are useful to no purpose. Therefore a vow is not always about a better good.

*On the contrary,* It is written (Deut. 23:22): "If thou wilt not promise thou shalt be without sin."

*I answer that,* As stated above (A. 1), a vow is a promise made to God. Now a promise is about something that one does voluntarily for someone else: since it would be not a promise but a threat to say that one would do something against someone. In like manner it would be futile to promise anyone something unacceptable to him. Wherefore, as every sin is against God, and since no work is acceptable to God unless it be virtuous, it follows that nothing unlawful or indifferent, but only some act of virtue, should be the matter of a vow. But as a vow denotes a voluntary promise, while necessity excludes voluntariness, whatever is absolutely necessary, whether to be or not to be, can nowise be the matter of a vow. For it would be foolish to vow that one would die or that one would not fly.

On the other hand, if a thing be necessary, not absolutely but on the supposition of an end—for instance if salvation be unattainable without it—it may be the matter of a vow in so far as it is done voluntarily, but not in so far as there is a necessity for doing it. But that which is not necessary, neither absolutely, nor on the supposition of an end, is altogether voluntary, and therefore is most properly the matter of a vow. And this is said to be a greater good in comparison with that which is universally necessary for salvation. Therefore, properly speaking, a vow is said to be about a better good.

Reply Obj. 1: Renouncing the devil's pomps and keeping the faith of Christ are the matter of baptismal vows, in so far as these things are done voluntarily, although they are necessary for salvation. The same answer applies to Jacob's vow: although it may also be explained that Jacob vowed that he would have the Lord for his God, by giving Him a special form of worship to which he was not bound, for instance by offering tithes and so forth as mentioned further on in the same passage.

Reply Obj. 2: Certain things are good, whatever be their result; such are acts of virtue, and these can be, absolutely speaking, the matter of a vow: some are evil, whatever their result may be; as those things which are sins in themselves, and these can nowise be the matter of a vow: while some, considered in themselves, are good, and as such may be the matter of a vow, yet they may have an evil result, in which case the vow must not be kept. It was thus with the vow of Jephte, who as related in Judges 11:30, 31, "made a vow to the Lord, saying: If Thou wilt deliver the children of Ammon into my hands, whosoever shall first come forth out of the doors of my house, and shall meet me when I return in peace ... the same will I offer a holocaust to the Lord." For this could have an evil result if, as indeed happened, he were to be met by some animal which it would be unlawful to sacrifice, such as an ass or a human being. Hence Jerome says [*Implicitly 1 Contra Jovin.: Comment. in Micheam vi, viii: Comment. in Jerem. vii. The quotation is from Peter Comestor, Hist. Scholast.]: "In vowing he was foolish, through lack of discretion, and in keeping his vow he was wicked." Yet it is premised (Judges 11:29) that "the Spirit of the Lord came upon him," because his faith and devotion, which moved him to make that vow, were from the Holy Ghost; and for this reason he is reckoned among the saints, as also by reason of the victory which he obtained, and because it is probable that he repented of his sinful deed, which nevertheless foreshadowed something good.

Reply Obj. 3: The mortification of one's own body, for instance by vigils and fasting, is not acceptable to God except in so far as it is an act of virtue; and this depends on its being done with due discretion, namely, that concupiscence be curbed without overburdening nature. On this condition such things may be the matter of a vow. Hence the Apostle after saying (Rom. 12:1), "Present your bodies a living sacrifice, holy, pleasing to God," adds, "your reasonable service." Since, however, man is easily mistaken in judging of matters concerning himself, such vows as these are more fittingly kept or disregarded according to the judgment of a superior, yet so that, should a man find that without doubt he is seriously burdened by keeping such a vow, and should he be unable to appeal to his superior, he ought not to keep it. As to vows about vain and useless things they should be ridiculed rather than kept.

THIRD ARTICLE [II-II, Q. 88, Art. 3]

Whether All Vows Are Binding?

Objection 1: It would seem that vows are not all binding. For man needs things that are done by another, more than God does, since He has no need for our goods (Ps. 15:2). Now according to the prescription of human laws [*Dig. L. xii, de pollicitat., i] a simple promise made to a man is not binding; and this seems to be prescribed on account of the changeableness of the human will. Much less binding therefore is a simple promise made to God, which we call a vow.

Obj. 2: Further, no one is bound to do what is impossible. Now sometimes that which a man has vowed becomes impossible to him, either because it depends on another's decision, as when, for instance, a man vows to enter a monastery, the monks of which refuse to receive him: or on account of some defect arising, for instance when a woman vows virginity, and afterwards is deflowered; or when a man vows to give a sum of money, and afterwards loses it. Therefore a vow is not always binding.

Obj. 3: Further, if a man is bound to pay something, he must do so at once. But a man is not bound to pay his vow at once, especially if it be taken under a condition to be fulfilled in the future. Therefore a vow is not always binding.

*On the contrary,* It is written (Eccles. 5:3, 4): "Whatsoever thou hast vowed, pay it; and it is much better not to vow, than after a vow not to perform the things promised."

*I answer that,* For one to be accounted faithful one must keep one's promises. Wherefore, according to Augustine [*Ep. xxxii, 2: De Mendac. xx] faith takes its name "from a man's deed agreeing with his word" [* *Fides ... fiunt dicta.* Cicero gives the same etymology (De Offic. i, 7)]. Now man ought to be faithful to God above all, both on account of God's sovereignty, and on account of the favors he has received from God. Hence man is obliged before all to fulfill the vows he has made to God, since this is part of the fidelity he owes to God. On the other hand, the breaking of a vow is a kind of infidelity. Wherefore Solomon gives the reason why vows should be paid to God, because "an unfaithful ... promise displeaseth Him" [*Eccles. 5:3].

Reply Obj. 1: Honesty demands that a man should keep any promise he makes to another man, and this obligation is based on the natural law. But for a man to be under a civil obligation through a promise he has made, other conditions are requisite. And although God needs not our goods, we are under a very great obligation to Him: so that a vow made to Him is most binding.

Reply Obj. 2: If that which a man has vowed becomes impossible to him through any cause whatsoever, he must do what he can, so that he have at least a will ready to do what he can. Hence if a man has vowed to enter a monastery, he must endeavor to the best of his power to be received there. And if his intention was chiefly to bind himself to enter the religious life, so that, in consequence, he chose this particular form of religious life, or this place, as being most agreeable to him, he is bound, should he be unable to be received there, to enter the religious life elsewhere. But if his principal intention is to bind himself to this particular kind of religious life, or to this particular place, because the one or the other pleases him in some special way, he is not bound to enter another religious house, if they are unwilling to receive him into this particular one. On the other hand, if he be rendered incapable of fulfilling his vow through his own fault, he is bound over and above to do penance for his past fault: thus if a woman has vowed virginity and is afterwards violated, she is bound not only to observe what is in her power, namely, perpetual continency, but also to repent of what she has lost by sinning.

Reply Obj. 3: The obligation of a vow is caused by our own will and intention, wherefore it is written (Deut. 23:23): "That which is once gone out of thy lips, thou shalt observe, and shalt do as thou hast promised to the Lord thy God, and hast spoken with thy own will and with thy own mouth." Wherefore if in taking a vow, it is one's intention and will to bind oneself to fulfil it at once, one is bound to fulfil it immediately. But if one intend to fulfil it at a certain time, or under a certain condition, one is not bound to immediate fulfilment. And yet one ought not to delay longer than one intended to bind oneself, for it is written (Deut. 23:21): "When thou hast made a vow to the Lord thy God thou shalt not delay to pay it: because the Lord thy God will require it; and if thou delay, it shall be imputed to thee for a sin."

FOURTH ARTICLE [II-II, Q. 88, Art. 4]

Whether It Is Expedient to Take Vows?

Objection 1: It would seem that it is not expedient to take vows. It is not expedient to anyone to deprive himself of the good that God has given him. Now one of the greatest goods that God has given man is liberty whereof he seems to be deprived by the necessity implicated in a vow. Therefore it would seem inexpedient for man to take vows.

Obj. 2: Further, no one should expose himself to danger. But whoever takes a vow exposes himself to danger, since that which, before taking a vow, he could omit without danger, becomes a source of danger to him if he should not fulfil it after taking the vow. Hence Augustine says (Ep. cxxvii, ad Arment. et Paulin.): "Since thou hast vowed, thou hast bound thyself, thou canst not do otherwise. If thou dost not what thou hast vowed thou wilt not be as thou wouldst have been hadst thou not vowed. For then thou wouldst have been less great, not less good: whereas now if thou breakest faith with God (which God forbid) thou art the more unhappy, as thou wouldst have been happier, hadst thou kept thy vow." Therefore it is not expedient to take vows.

Obj. 3: Further, the Apostle says (1 Cor. 4:16): "Be ye followers of me, as I also am of Christ." But we do not read that either Christ or the Apostles took any vows. Therefore it would seem inexpedient to take vows.

*On the contrary,* It is written (Ps. 75:12): "Vow ye and pay to the Lord your God."

*I answer that,* As stated above (AA. 1, 2), a vow is a promise made to God. Now one makes a promise to a man under one aspect, and to God under another. Because we promise something to a man for his own profit; since it profits him that we should be of service to him, and that we should at first assure him of the future fulfilment of that service: whereas we make promises to God not for His but for our own profit. Hence Augustine says (Ep. cxxvii, ad Arment. et Paulin.): "He is a kind and not a needy exactor, for he does not grow rich on our payments, but makes those who pay Him grow rich in Him." And just as what we give God is useful not to Him but to us, since "what is given Him is added to the giver," as Augustine says (Ep. cxxvii, ad Arment. et Paulin.), so also a promise whereby we vow something to God, does not conduce to His profit, nor does He need to be assured by us, but it conduces to our profit, in so far as by vowing we fix our wills immovably on that which it is expedient to do. Hence it is expedient to take vows.

Reply Obj. 1: Even as one's liberty is not lessened by one being unable to sin, so, too, the necessity resulting from a will firmly fixed to good does not lessen the liberty, as instanced in God and the blessed. Such is the necessity implied by a vow, bearing a certain resemblance to the confirmation of the blessed. Hence, Augustine says (Ep. cxxvii, ad Arment. et Paulin.) that "happy is the necessity that compels us to do the better things."

Reply Obj. 2: When danger arises from the deed itself, this deed is not expedient, for instance that one cross a river by a tottering bridge: but if the danger arise through man's failure in the deed, the latter does not cease to be expedient: thus it is expedient to mount on horseback, though there be the danger of a fall from the horse: else it would behoove one to desist from all good things, that may become dangerous accidentally. Wherefore it is written (Eccles. 11:4): "He that observeth the wind shall not sow, and he that considereth the clouds shall never reap." Now a man incurs danger, not from the vow itself, but from his fault, when he changes his mind by breaking his vow. Hence, Augustine says (Ep. cxxvii, ad Arment. et Paulin.): "Repent not of thy vow: thou shouldst rather rejoice that thou canst no longer do what thou mightest lawfully have done to thy detriment."

Reply Obj. 3: It was incompetent for Christ, by His very nature, to take a vow, both because He was God, and because, as man, His will was firmly fixed on the good, since He was a *comprehensor.* By a kind of similitude, however, He is represented as saying (Ps. 21:26): "I will pay my vows in the sight of them that fear Him," when He is speaking of His body, which is the Church.

The apostles are understood to have vowed things pertaining to the state of perfection when "they left all things and followed Christ."

FIFTH ARTICLE [II-II, Q. 88, Art. 5]

Whether a Vow Is an Act of Latria or Religion?

Objection 1: It would seem that a vow is not an act of latria or religion. Every act of virtue is matter for a vow. Now it would seem to pertain to the same virtue to promise a thing and to do it. Therefore a vow pertains to any virtue and not to religion especially.

Obj. 2: Further, according to Tully (De Invent. ii, 53) it belongs to religion to offer God worship and ceremonial rites. But he who takes a vow does not yet offer something to God, but only promises it. Therefore, a vow is not an act of religion.

Obj. 3: Further, religious worship should be offered to none but God. But a vow is made not only to God, but also to the saints and to one's superiors, to whom religious vow obedience when they make their profession. Therefore, a vow is not an act of religion.

*On the contrary,* It is written (Isa. 19:21): "(The Egyptians) shall worship Him with sacrifices and offerings and they shall make vows to the Lord, and perform them." Now, the worship of God is properly the act of religion or latria. Therefore, a vow is an act of latria or religion.

*I answer that,* As stated above (Q. 81, A. 1, ad 1), every act of virtue belongs to religion or latria by way of command, in so far as it is directed to the reverence of God which is the proper end of latria. Now the direction of other actions to their end belongs to the commanding virtue, not to those which are commanded. Therefore the direction of the acts of any virtue to the service of God is the proper act of latria.

Now, it is evident from what has been said above (AA. 1, 2) that a vow is a promise made to God, and that a promise is nothing else than a directing of the thing promised to the person to whom the promise is made. Hence a vow is a directing of the thing vowed to the worship or service of God. And thus it is clear that to take a vow is properly an act of latria or religion.

Reply Obj. 1: The matter of a vow is sometimes the act of another virtue, as, for instance, keeping the fast or observing continency; while sometimes it is an act of religion, as offering a sacrifice or praying. But promising either of them to God belongs to religion, for the reason given above. Hence it is evident that some vows belong to religion by reason only of the promise made to God, which is the essence of a vow, while others belong thereto by reason also of the thing promised, which is the matter of the vow.

Reply Obj. 2: He who promises something gives it already in as far as he binds himself to give it: even as a thing is said to be made when its cause is made, because the effect is contained virtually in its cause. This is why we thank not only a giver, but also one who promises to give.

Reply Obj. 3: A vow is made to God alone, whereas a promise may be made to a man also: and this very promise of good, which is made to a man, may be the matter of a vow, and in so far as it is a virtuous act. This is how we are to understand vows whereby we vow something to the saints or to one's superiors: so that the promise made to the saints or to one's superiors is the matter of the vow, in so far as one vows to God to fulfil what one has promised to the saints or one's superiors.

SIXTH ARTICLE [II-II, Q. 88, Art. 6]

Whether It Is More Praiseworthy and Meritorious to Do Something in Fulfilment of a Vow, Than Without a Vow?

Objection 1: It would seem that it is more praiseworthy and meritorious to do a thing without a vow than in fulfilment of a vow. Prosper says (De Vita Contempl. ii): "We should abstain or fast without putting ourselves under the necessity of fasting, lest that which we are free to do be done without devotion and unwillingly." Now he who vows to fast puts himself under the necessity of fasting. Therefore it would be better for him to fast without taking the vow.

Obj. 2: Further, the Apostle says (2 Cor. 9:7): "Everyone as he hath determined in his heart, not with sadness, or of necessity: for God loveth a cheerful giver." Now some fulfil sorrowfully what they have vowed: and this seems to be due to the necessity arising from the vow, for necessity is a cause of sorrow according to *Metaph.* v [*Ed. Did. iv, 5]. Therefore, it is better to do something without a vow, than in fulfilment of a vow.

Obj. 3: Further, a vow is necessary for the purpose of fixing the will on that which is vowed, as stated above (A. 4). But the will cannot be more fixed on a thing than when it actually does that thing. Therefore it is no better to do a thing in fulfilment of a vow than without a vow.

*On the contrary,* A gloss on the words of Ps. 75:12, "Vow ye and pay," says: "Vows are counseled to the will." But a counsel is about none but a better good. Therefore it is better to do a deed in fulfilment of a vow than without a vow: since he that does it without a vow fulfils only one counsel, viz. the counsel to do it, whereas he that does it with a vow, fulfils two counsels, viz. the counsel to vow and the counsel to do it.

*I answer that,* For three reasons it is better and more meritorious to do one and the same deed with a vow than without. First, because to vow, as stated above (A. 5) is an act of religion which is the chief of the moral virtues. Now the more excellent the virtue the better and more meritorious the deed. Wherefore the act of an inferior virtue is the better and more meritorious for being commanded by a superior virtue, whose act it becomes through being commanded by it, just as the act of faith or hope is better if it be commanded by charity. Hence the works of the other moral virtues (for instance, fasting, which is an act of abstinence; and being continent, which is an act of chastity) are better and more meritorious, if they be done in fulfilment of a vow, since thus they belong to the divine worship, being like sacrifices to God. Wherefore Augustine says (De Virg. viii) that "not even is virginity honorable as such, but only when it is consecrated to God, and cherished by godly continence."

Secondly, because he that vows something and does it, subjects himself to God more than he that only does it; for he subjects himself to God not only as to the act, but also as to the power, since in future he cannot do something else. Even so he gives more who gives the tree with its fruit, than he that gives the fruit only, as Anselm [*Eadmer] observes (De Simil. viii). For this reason, we thank even those who promise, as stated above (A. 5, ad 2).

Thirdly, because a vow fixes the will on the good immovably and to do anything of a will that is fixed on the good belongs to the perfection of virtue, according to the Philosopher (Ethic. ii, 4), just as to sin with an obstinate mind aggravates the sin, and is called a sin against the Holy Ghost, as stated above (Q. 14, A. 2).

Reply Obj. 1: The passage quoted should be understood as referring to necessity of coercion which causes an act to be involuntary and excludes devotion. Hence he says pointedly: "Lest that which we are free to do be done without devotion and unwillingly." On the other hand the necessity resulting from a vow is caused by the immobility of the will, wherefore it strengthens the will and increases devotion. Hence the argument does not conclude.

Reply Obj. 2: According to the Philosopher, necessity of coercion, in so far as it is opposed to the will, causes sorrow. But the necessity resulting from a vow, in those who are well disposed, in so far as it strengthens the will, causes not sorrow but joy. Hence Augustine says (Ep. ad Arment. et Paulin. cxxcii): "Repent not of thy vow: thou shouldst rather rejoice that thou canst no longer do what thou mightest lawfully have done to thy detriment." If, however, the very deed, considered in itself, were to become disagreeable and involuntary after one has taken the vow, the will to fulfil it remaining withal, it is still more meritorious than if it were done without the vow, since the fulfilment of a vow is an act of religion which is a greater virtue than abstinence, of which fasting is an act.

Reply Obj. 3: He who does something without having vowed it has an immovable will as regards the individual deed which he does and at the time when he does it; but his will does not remain altogether fixed for the time to come, as does the will of one who makes a vow: for the latter has bound his will to do something, both before he did that particular deed, and perchance to do it many times.

SEVENTH ARTICLE [II-II, Q. 88, Art. 7]

Whether a Vow Is Solemnized by the Reception of Holy Orders, and by the Profession of a Certain Rule?

Objection 1: It would seem that a vow is not solemnized by the reception of holy orders and by the profession of a certain rule. As stated above (A. 1), a vow is a promise made to God. Now external actions pertaining to solemnity seem to be directed, not to God, but to men. Therefore they are related to vows accidentally: and consequently a solemnization of this kind is not a proper circumstance of a vow.

Obj. 2: Further, whatever belongs to the condition of a thing, would seem to be applicable to all in which that thing is found. Now many things may be the subject of a vow, which have no connection either with holy orders, or to any particular rule: as when a man vows a pilgrimage, or something of the kind. Therefore the solemnization that takes place in the reception of holy orders or in the profession of a certain rule does not belong to the condition of a vow.

Obj. 3: Further, a solemn vow seems to be the same as a public vow. Now many other vows may be made in public besides that which is pronounced in receiving holy orders or in professing a certain rule; which latter, moreover, may be made in private. Therefore not only these vows are solemn.

*On the contrary,* These vows alone are an impediment to the contract of marriage, and annul marriage if it be contracted, which is the effect of a solemn vow, as we shall state further on in the Third Part of this work [*Suppl., Q. 53, A. 2].

*I answer that,* The manner in which a thing is solemnized depends on its nature ( *conditio* ): thus when a man takes up arms he solemnizes the fact in one way, namely, with a certain display of horses and arms and a concourse of soldiers, while a marriage is solemnized in another way, namely, the array of the bridegroom and bride and the gathering of their kindred. Now a vow is a promise made to God: wherefore, the solemnization of a vow consists in something spiritual pertaining to God; i.e. in some spiritual blessing or consecration which, in accordance with the institution of the apostles, is given when a man makes profession of observing a certain rule, in the second degree after the reception of holy orders, as Dionysius states (Eccl. Hier. vi). The reason of this is that solemnization is not wont to be employed, save when a man gives himself up entirely to some particular thing. For the nuptial solemnization takes place only when the marriage is celebrated, and when the bride and bridegroom mutually deliver the power over their bodies to one another. In like manner a vow is solemnized when a man devotes himself to the divine ministry by receiving holy orders, or embraces the state of perfection by renouncing the world and his own will by the profession of a certain rule.

Reply Obj. 1: This kind of solemnization regards not only men but also God in so far as it is accompanied by a spiritual consecration or blessing, of which God is the author, though man is the minister, according to Num. 6:27, "They shall invoke My name upon the children of Israel, and I will bless them." Hence a solemn vow is more binding with God than a simple vow, and he who breaks a solemn vow sins more grievously. When it is said that a simple vow is no less binding than a solemn vow, this refers to the fact that the transgressor of either commits a mortal sin.

Reply Obj. 2: It is not customary to solemnize particular acts, but the embracing of a new state, as we have said above. Hence when a man vows particular deeds, such as a pilgrimage, or some special fast, such a vow is not competent to be solemnized, but only such as the vow whereby a man entirely devotes himself to the divine ministry or service: and yet many particular works are included under this vow as under a universal.

Reply Obj. 3: Through being pronounced in public vows may have a certain human solemnity, but not a spiritual and divine solemnity, as the aforesaid vows have, even when they are pronounced before a few persons. Hence the publicity of a vow differs from its solemnization.

EIGHTH ARTICLE [II-II, Q. 88, Art. 8]

Whether Those Who Are Subject to Another's Power Are Hindered from Taking Vows?

Objection 1: It would seem that those who are subject to another's power are not hindered from taking vows. The lesser bond is surpassed by the greater. Now the obligation of one man subject to another is a lesser bond than a vow whereby one is under an obligation to God. Therefore those who are subject to another's power are not hindered from taking vows.

Obj. 2: Further, children are under their parents' power. Yet children may make religious profession even without the consent of their parents. Therefore one is not hindered from taking vows, through being subject to another's power.

Obj. 3: Further, to do is more than to promise.

But religious who are under the power of their superiors can do certain things such as to say some psalms, or abstain from certain things. Much more therefore seemingly can they promise such things to God by means of vows.

Obj. 4: Further, whoever does what he cannot do lawfully sins. But subjects do not sin by taking vows, since nowhere do we find this forbidden. Therefore it would seem that they can lawfully take vows.

*On the contrary,* It is commanded (Num. 30:4-6) that "if a woman vow any thing ... being in her father's house, and yet but a girl in age," she is not bound by the vow, unless her father consent: and the same is said there (Num. 30:7-9) of the woman that has a husband. Therefore in like manner other persons that are subject to another's power cannot bind themselves by vow.

*I answer that,* As stated above (A. 1), a vow is a promise made to God. Now no man can firmly bind himself by a promise to do what is in another's power, but only to that which is entirely in his own power. Now whoever is subject to another, as to the matter wherein he is subject to him, it does not lie in his power to do as he will, but it depends on the will of the other. And therefore without the consent of his superior he cannot bind himself firmly by a vow in those matters wherein he is subject to another.

Reply Obj. 1: Nothing but what is virtuous can be the subject of a promise made to God, as stated above (A. 2). Now it is contrary to virtue for a man to offer to God that which belongs to another, as stated above (Q. 86, A. 3). Hence the conditions necessary for a vow are not altogether ensured, when a man who is under another's power vows that which is in that other's power, except under the condition that he whose power it concerns does not gainsay it.

Reply Obj. 2: As soon as a man comes of age, if he be a freeman he is in his own power in all matters concerning his person, for instance with regard to binding himself by vow to enter religion, or with regard to contracting marriage. But he is not in his own power as regards the arrangements of the household, so that in these matters he cannot vow anything that shall be valid without the consent of his father.

A slave, through being in his master's power, even as regards his personal deeds, cannot bind himself by vow to enter religion, since this would withdraw him from his master's service.

Reply Obj. 3: A religious is subject to his superior as to his actions connected with his profession of his rule. Wherefore even though one may be able to do something now and then, when one is not being occupied with other things by one's superior, yet since there is no time when his superior cannot occupy him with something, no vow of a religious stands without the consent of his superior, as neither does the vow of a girl while in (her father's) house without his consent; nor of a wife, without the consent of her husband.

Reply Obj. 4: Although the vow of one who is subject to another's power does not stand without the consent of the one to whom he is subject, he does not sin by vowing; because his vow is understood to contain the requisite condition, providing, namely, that his superior approve or do not gainsay it.

NINTH ARTICLE [II-II, Q. 88, Art. 9]

Whether Children Can Bind Themselves by Vow to Enter Religion?

Objection 1: It would seem that children cannot bind themselves by vow to enter religion. Since a vow requires deliberation of the mind, it is fitting that those alone should vow who have the use of reason. But this is lacking in children just as in imbeciles and madmen. Therefore just as imbeciles and madmen cannot bind themselves to anything by vow, so neither, seemingly, can children bind themselves by vow to enter religion.

Obj. 2: Further, that which can be validly done by one cannot be annulled by another. Now a vow to enter religion made by a boy or girl before the age of puberty can be revoked by the parents or guardian (20, qu. ii, cap. Puella). Therefore it seems that a boy or girl cannot validly make a vow before the age of fourteen.

Obj. 3: Further, according to the rule of Blessed Benedict [*Ch. 58] and a statute of Innocent IV, a year's probation is granted to those who enter religion, so that probation may precede the obligation of the vow. Therefore it seems unlawful, before the year of probation, for children to be bound by vow to enter religion.

*On the contrary,* That which is not done aright is invalid without being annulled by anyone. But the vow pronounced by a maiden, even before attaining the age of puberty, is valid, unless it be annulled by her parents within a year (20, qu. ii, cap. Puella). Therefore even before attaining to puberty children can lawfully and validly be bound by a vow to enter religion.

*I answer that,* As may be gathered from what has been said above (A. 7), vows are of two kinds, simple and solemn. And since, as stated in the same article, the solemnization of a vow consists in a spiritual blessing and consecration bestowed through the ministry of the Church, it follows that it comes under the Church's dispensation. Now a simple vow takes its efficacy from the deliberation of the mind, whereby one intends to put oneself under an obligation. That such an obligation be of no force may happen in two ways. First, through defect of reason, as in madmen and imbeciles, who cannot bind themselves by vow so long as they remain in a state of madness or imbecility. Secondly, through the maker of a vow being subject to another's power, as stated above (A. 8). Now these two circumstances concur in children before the age of puberty, because in most instances they are lacking in reason, and besides are naturally under the care of their parents, or guardians in place of their parents: wherefore in both events their vows are without force. It happens, however, through a natural disposition which is not subject to human laws, that the use of reason is accelerated in some, albeit few, who on this account are said to be capable of guile: and yet they are not, for this reason, exempt in any way from the care of their parents; for this care is subject to human law, which takes into account that which is of most frequent occurrence.

Accordingly we must say that boys or girls who have not reached the years of puberty and have not attained the use of reason can nowise bind themselves to anything by vow. If, however, they attain the use of reason, before reaching the years of puberty, they can for their own part, bind themselves by vow; but their vows can be annulled by their parents, under whose care they are still subject.

Yet no matter how much they be capable of guile before the years of puberty, they cannot be bound by a solemn religious vow, on account of the Church's decree [*Sext. Decret. cap. Is qui, de Reg. et transeunt. ad Relig.] which considers the majority of cases. But after the years of puberty have been reached, they can bind themselves by religious vows, simple or solemn, without the consent of their parents.

Reply Obj. 1: This argument avails in the case of children who have not yet reached the use of reason: for their vows then are invalid, as stated above.

Reply Obj. 2: The vows of persons subject to another's power contain an implied condition, namely, that they be not annulled by the superior. This condition renders them licit and valid if it be fulfilled, as stated above.

Reply Obj. 3: This argument avails in the case of solemn vows which are taken in profession.

TENTH ARTICLE [II-II, Q. 88, Art. 10]

Whether Vows Admit of Dispensation?

Objection 1: It would seem that vows are not subject to dispensation. It is less to have a vow commuted than to be dispensed from keeping it. But a vow cannot be commuted, according to Lev. 27:9, 10, "A beast that may be sacrificed to the Lord, if anyone shall vow, shall be holy, and cannot be changed, neither a better for a worse, nor a worse for a better." Much less, therefore, do vows admit of dispensation.

Obj. 2: Further, no man can grant a dispensation in matters concerning the natural law and in the Divine precepts, especially those of the First Table, since these aim directly at the love of God, which is the last end of the precepts. Now the fulfilment of a vow is a matter of the natural law, and is commanded by the Divine law, as shown above (A. 3), and belongs to the precepts of the First Table since it is an act of religion. Therefore vows do not admit of dispensation.

Obj. 3: Further, the obligation of a vow is based on the fidelity which a man owes to God, as stated above (A. 3). But no man can dispense in such a matter as this. Neither, therefore, can any one grant a dispensation from a vow.

*On the contrary,* That which proceeds from the common will of many has apparently greater stability than that which proceeds from the individual will of some one person. Now the law which derives its force from the common will admits of dispensation by a man. Therefore it seems that vows also admit of dispensation by a man.

*I answer that,* The dispensation from a vow is to be taken in the same sense as a dispensation given in the observance of a law because, as stated above (I-II, Q. 96, A. 6; Q. 97, A. 4), a law is made with an eye to that which is good in the majority of instances. But since in certain cases this is not good, there is need for someone to decide that in that particular case the law is not to be observed. This is properly speaking to dispense in the law: for a dispensation would seem to denote a commensurate distribution or application of some common thing to those that are contained under it, in the same way as a person is said to dispense food to a household.

In like manner a person who takes a vow makes a law for himself as it were, and binds himself to do something which in itself and in the majority of cases is a good. But it may happen that in some particular case this is simply evil, or useless, or a hindrance to a greater good: and this is essentially contrary to that which is the matter of a vow, as is clear from what has been said above (A. 2). Therefore it is necessary, in such a case, to decide that the vow is not to be observed. And if it be decided absolutely that a particular vow is not to be observed, this is called a "dispensation" from that vow; but if some other obligation be imposed in lieu of that which was to have been observed, the vow is said to be "commuted." Hence it is less to commute a vow than to dispense from a vow: both, however, are in the power of the Church.

Reply Obj. 1: An animal that could be lawfully sacrificed was deemed holy from the very moment that it was the subject of a vow, being, as it were, dedicated to the worship of God: and for this reason it could not be changed: even so neither may one now exchange for something better, or worse, that which one has vowed, if it be already consecrated, e.g. a chalice or a house. On the other hand, an animal that could not be sacrificed, through not being the lawful matter of a sacrifice, could and had to be bought back, as the law requires. Even so, vows can be commuted now, if no consecration has intervened.

Reply Obj. 2: Even as man is bound by natural law and Divine precept to fulfil his vow, so, too, is he bound under the same heads to obey the law or commands of his superiors. And yet when he is dispensed from keeping a human law, this does not involve disobedience to that human law, for this would be contrary to the natural law and the Divine command; but it amounts to this—that what was law is not law in this particular case. Even so, when a superior grants a dispensation, that which was contained under a vow is by his authority no longer so contained, in so far as he decides that in this case such and such a thing is not fitting matter for a vow. Consequently when an ecclesiastical superior dispenses someone from a vow, he does not dispense him from keeping a precept of the natural or of the Divine law, but he pronounces a decision on a matter to which a man had bound himself of his own accord, and of which he was unable to consider every circumstance.

Reply Obj. 3: The fidelity we owe to God does not require that we fulfil that which it would be wrong or useless to vow, or which would be an obstacle to the greater good whereunto the dispensation from that vow would conduce. Hence the dispensation from a vow is not contrary to the fidelity due to God.

ELEVENTH ARTICLE [II-II, Q. 88, Art. 11]

Whether It Is Possible to Be Dispensed from a Solemn Vow of Continency?

Objection 1: It would seem that it is possible to be dispensed from a solemn vow of continency. As stated above, one reason for granting a dispensation from a vow is if it be an obstacle to a greater good. But a vow of continency, even though it be solemn, may be an obstacle to a greater good, since the common good is more God-like than the good of an individual. Now one man's continency may be an obstacle to the good of the whole community, for instance, in the case where, if certain persons who have vowed continency were to marry, the peace of their country might be procured. Therefore it seems that it is possible to be dispensed even from a solemn vow of continency.

Obj. 2: Further, religion is a more excellent virtue than chastity. Now if a man vows an act of religion, e.g. to offer sacrifice to God he can be dispensed from that vow. Much more, therefore, can he be dispensed from the vow of continency which is about an act of chastity.

Obj. 3: Further, just as the observance of a vow of abstinence may be a source of danger to the person, so too may be the observance of a vow of continency. Now one who takes a vow of abstinence can be dispensed from that vow if it prove a source of danger to his body. Therefore for the same reason one may be dispensed from a vow of continency.

Obj. 4: Further, just as the vow of continency is part of the religious profession, whereby the vow is solemnized, so also are the vows of poverty and obedience. But it is possible to be dispensed from the vows of poverty and obedience, as in the case of those who are appointed bishops after making profession. Therefore it seems that it is possible to be dispensed from a solemn vow of continency.

*On the contrary,* It is written (Ecclus. 26:20): "No price is worthy of a continent soul."

Further, (Extra, De Statu Monach.) at the end of the Decretal, *Cum ad Monasterium,* it is stated that the "renouncing of property, like the keeping of chastity, is so bound up with the monastic rule, that not even the Sovereign Pontiff can disperse from its observance."

*I answer that,* Three things may be considered in a solemn vow of continency: first, the matter of the vow, namely, continency; secondly, the perpetuity of the vow, namely, when a person binds himself by vow to the perpetual observance of chastity: thirdly, the solemnity of the vow. Accordingly, some [*William of Auxerre, Sum. Aur. III. vii. 1, qu. 5] say that the solemn vow cannot be a matter of dispensation, on account of the continency itself for which no worthy price can be found, as is stated by the authority quoted above. The reason for this is assigned by some to the fact that by continency man overcomes a foe within himself, or to the fact that by continency man is perfectly conformed to Christ in respect of purity of both body and soul. But this reason does not seem to be cogent since the goods of the soul, such as contemplation and prayer, far surpass the goods of the body and still more conform us to God, and yet one may be dispensed from a vow of prayer or contemplation. Therefore, continency itself absolutely considered seems no reason why the solemn vow thereof cannot be a matter of dispensation; especially seeing that the Apostle (1 Cor. 7:34) exhorts us to be continent on account of contemplation, when he says that the unmarried woman ... "thinketh on the things of God [Vulg.: 'the Lord']," and since the end is of more account than the means.

Consequently others [*Albertus Magnus, Sent. iv, D, 38] find the reason for this in the perpetuity and universality of this vow. For they assert that the vow of continency cannot be canceled, save by something altogether contrary thereto, which is never lawful in any vow. But this is evidently false, because just as the practice of carnal intercourse is contrary to continency, so is eating flesh or drinking wine contrary to abstinence from such things, and yet these latter vows may be a matter for dispensation.

For this reason others [*Innocent IV, on the above decretal] maintain that one may be dispensed even from a solemn vow of continency, for the sake of some common good or common need, as in the case of the example given above (Obj. 1), of a country being restored to peace through a certain marriage to be contracted. Yet since the Decretal quoted says explicitly that "not even the Sovereign Pontiff can dispense a monk from keeping chastity," it follows seemingly, that we must maintain that, as stated above (A. 10, ad 1; cf. Lev. 27:9, 10, 28), whatsoever has once been sanctified to the Lord cannot be put to any other use. For no ecclesiastical prelate can make that which is sanctified to lose its consecration, not even though it be something inanimate, for instance a consecrated chalice to be not consecrated, so long as it remains entire. Much less, therefore, can a prelate make a man that is consecrated to God cease to be consecrated, so long as he lives. Now the solemnity of a vow consists in a kind of consecration or blessing of the person who takes the vow, as stated above (A. 7). Hence no prelate of the Church can make a man, who has pronounced a solemn vow, to be quit of that to which he was consecrated, e.g. one who is a priest, to be a priest no more, although a prelate may, for some particular reason, inhibit him from exercising his order. In like manner the Pope cannot make a man who has made his religious profession cease to be a religious, although certain jurists have ignorantly held the contrary.

We must therefore consider whether continency is essentially bound up with the purpose for which the vow is solemnized. Because if not, the solemnity of the consecration can remain without the obligation of continency, but not if continency is essentially bound up with that for which the vow is solemnized. Now the obligation of observing continency is connected with Holy Orders, not essentially but by the institution of the Church; wherefore it seems that the Church can grant a dispensation from the vow of continency solemnized by the reception of Holy Orders. On the other hand the obligation of observing continency is an essential condition of the religious state, whereby a man renounces the world and binds himself wholly to God's service, for this is incompatible with matrimony, in which state a man is under the obligation of taking to himself a wife, of begetting children, of looking after his household, and of procuring whatever is necessary for these purposes. Wherefore the Apostle says (1 Cor. 7:33) that "he that is with a wife, is solicitous for the things of the world, how he may please his wife; and he is divided." Hence the "monk" takes his name from "unity" [*The Greek *monos* ] in contrast with this division. For this reason the Church cannot dispense from a vow solemnized by the religious profession; and the reason assigned by the Decretal is because "chastity is bound up with the monastic rule."

Reply Obj. 1: Perils occasioned by human affairs should be obviated by human means, not by turning divine things to a human use. Now a professed religious is dead to the world and lives to God, and so he must not be called back to the human life on the pretext of any human contingency.

Reply Obj. 2: A vow of temporal continency can be a matter of dispensation, as also a vow of temporal prayer or of temporal abstinence. But the fact that no dispensation can be granted from a vow of continency solemnized by profession is due, not to its being an act of chastity, but because through the religious profession it is already an act of religion.

Reply Obj. 3: Food is directly ordered to the upkeep of the person, therefore abstinence from food may be a direct source of danger to the person: and so on this count a vow of abstinence is a matter of dispensation. On the other hand sexual intercourse is directly ordered to the upkeep not of the person but of the species, wherefore to abstain from such intercourse by continency does not endanger the person. And if indeed accidentally it prove a source of danger to the person, this danger may be obviated by some other means, for instance by abstinence, or other corporal remedies.

Reply Obj. 4: A religious who is made a bishop is no more absolved from his vow of poverty than from his vow of continency, since he must have nothing of his own and must hold himself as being the dispenser of the common goods of the Church. In like manner neither is he dispensed from his vow of obedience; it is an accident that he is not bound to obey if he have no superior; just as the abbot of a monastery, who nevertheless is not dispensed from his vow of obedience.

The passage of Ecclesiasticus, which is put forward in the contrary sense, should be taken as meaning that neither fruitfulness of the of the flesh nor any bodily good is to be compared with continency, which is reckoned one of the goods of the soul, as Augustine declares (De Sanct. Virg. viii). Wherefore it is said pointedly "of a continent soul," not "of a continent body."

TWELFTH ARTICLE [II-II, Q. 88, Art. 12]

Whether the Authority of a Prelate Is Required for the Commutation or the Dispensation of a Vow?

Objection 1: It would seem that the authority of a prelate is not required for the commutation or dispensation of a vow. A person may enter religion without the authority of a superior prelate. Now by entering religion one is absolved from the vows he made in the world, even from the vow of making a pilgrimage to the Holy Land [*Cap. Scripturae, de Voto et Voti redempt.]. Therefore the commutation or dispensation of a vow is possible without the authority of a superior prelate.

Obj. 2: Further, to dispense anyone from a vow seems to consist in deciding in what circumstances he need not keep that vow. But if the prelate is at fault in his decision, the person who took the vow does not seem to be absolved from his vow, since no prelate can grant a dispensation contrary to the divine precept about keeping one's vows, as stated above (A. 10, ad 2; A. 11). Likewise, when anyone rightly determines of his own authority that in his case a vow is not to be kept, he would seem not to be bound; since a vow need not be kept if it have an evil result (A. 2, ad 2). Therefore the Authority of a prelate is not required that one may be dispensed from a vow.

Obj. 3: Further, if it belongs to a prelate's power to grant dispensations from vows, on the same count it is competent to all prelates, but it does not belong to all to dispense from every vow. Therefore it does not belong to the power of a prelate to dispense from vows.

*On the contrary,* A vow binds one to do something, even as a law does. Now the superior's authority is requisite for a dispensation from a precept of the law, as stated above (I-II, Q. 96, A. 6; Q. 97, A. 4). Therefore it is likewise required in a dispensation from a vow.

*I answer that,* As stated above (AA. 1, 2), a vow is a promise made to God about something acceptable to Him. Now if you promise something to anyone it depends on his decision whether he accept what you promise. Again in the Church a prelate stands in God's place. Therefore a commutation or dispensation of vows requires the authority of a prelate who in God's stead declares what is acceptable to God, according to 2 Cor. 2:10: "For [I] ... have pardoned ... for your sakes ... in the person of Christ." And he says significantly "for your sakes," since whenever we ask a prelate for a dispensation we should do so to honor Christ in Whose person he dispenses, or to promote the interests of the Church which is His Body.

Reply Obj. 1: All other vows are about some particular works, whereas by the religious life a man consecrates his whole life to God's service. Now the particular is included in the universal, wherefore a Decretal [*Cap. Scripturae, de Voto et Voti redempt.] says that "a man is not deemed a vow-breaker if he exchange a temporal service for the perpetual service of religion." And yet a man who enters religion is not bound to fulfil the vows, whether of fasting or of praying or the like, which he made when in the world, because by entering religion he dies to his former life, and it is unsuitable to the religious life that each one should have his own observances, and because the burden of religion is onerous enough without requiring the addition of other burdens.

Reply Obj. 2: Some have held that prelates can dispense from vows at their will, for the reason that every vow supposes as a condition that the superior prelate be willing; thus it was stated above (A. 8) that the vow of a subject, e.g. of a slave or a son, supposes this condition, if "the father or master consent," or "does not dissent." And thus a subject might break his vow without any remorse of conscience, whenever his superior tells him to.

But this opinion is based on a false supposition: because a spiritual prelate being, not a master, but a dispenser, his power is given "unto edification, not for destruction" (2 Cor. 10:8), and consequently, just as he cannot command that which is in itself displeasing to God, namely, sin, so neither can he forbid what is in itself pleasing to God, namely, works of virtue. Therefore absolutely speaking man can vow them. But it does belong to a prelate to decide what is the more virtuous and the more acceptable to God. Consequently in matters presenting no difficulty, the prelate's dispensation would not excuse one from sin: for instance, if a prelate were to dispense a person from a vow to enter the religious life, without any apparent cause to prevent him from fulfilling his vow. But if some cause were to appear, giving rise, at least, to doubt, he could hold to the prelate's decision whether of commutation or of dispensation. He could not, however, follow his own judgment in the matter, because he does not stand in the place of God; except perhaps in the case when the thing he has vowed is clearly unlawful, and he is unable to have recourse to the prelate.

Reply Obj. 3: Since the Sovereign Pontiff holds the place of Christ throughout the whole Church, he exercises absolute power of dispensing from all vows that admit of dispensation. To other and inferior prelates is the power committed of dispensing from those vows that are commonly made and frequently require dispensation, in order that men may easily have recourse to someone; such are the vows of pilgrimage (Cap. de Peregin., de Voto et Voti redempt.), fasting and the like, and of pilgrimage to the Holy Land, are reserved to the Sovereign Pontiff [*Cap. Ex multa].

# QUESTION 89

OF OATHS (TEN ARTICLES)

We must now consider those external acts of religion, whereby something Divine is taken by man: and this is either a sacrament or the Name of God. The place for treating of the taking of a sacrament will be in the Third Part of this work: of the taking of God's Name we shall treat now. The Name of God is taken by man in three ways. First, by way oath in order to confirm one's own assertion: secondly, by way of adjuration as an inducement to others: thirdly, by way of invocation for the purpose of prayer or praise. Accordingly we must first treat of oaths: and under this head there are ten points of inquiry:

(1) What is an oath?

(2) Whether it is lawful?

(3) What are the accompanying conditions of an oath?

(4) Of what virtue is it an act?

(5) Whether oaths are desirable, and to be employed frequently as something useful and good?

(6) Whether it is lawful to swear by a creature?

(7) Whether an oath is binding?

(8) Which is more binding, an oath or a vow?

(9) Whether an oath is subject to dispensation?

(10) Who may lawfully swear, and when?

FIRST ARTICLE [II-II, Q. 89, Art. 1]

Whether to Swear Is to Call God to Witness?

Objection 1: It would seem that to swear is not to call God to witness. Whoever invokes the authority of Holy Writ calls God to witness, since it is His word that Holy Writ contains. Therefore, if to swear is to call God to witness, whoever invoked the authority of Holy Writ would swear. But this is false. Therefore the antecedent is false also.

Obj. 2: Further, one does not pay anything to a person by calling him to witness. But he who swears by God pays something to Him for it is written (Matt. 5:33): "Thou shall pay [Douay: 'perform'] thy oaths to the Lord"; and Augustine says [*Serm. clxxx] that to swear ( *jurare* ) is "to pay the right ( jus reddere ) of truth to God." Therefore to swear is not to call God to witness.

Obj. 3: Further, the duties of a judge differ from the duties of a witness, as shown above (QQ. 67, 70). Now sometimes a man, by swearing, implores the Divine judgment, according to Ps. 7:5, "If I have rendered to them that repaid me evils, let me deservedly fall empty before my enemies." Therefore to swear is not to call God to witness.

*On the contrary,* Augustine says in a sermon on perjury (Serm. clxxx): "When a man says: 'By God,' what else does he mean but that God is his witness?"

*I answer that,* As the Apostle says (Heb. 6:16), oaths are taken for the purpose of confirmation. Now speculative propositions receive confirmation from reason, which proceeds from principles known naturally and infallibly true. But particular contingent facts regarding man cannot be confirmed by a necessary reason, wherefore propositions regarding such things are wont to be confirmed by witnesses. Now a human witness does not suffice to confirm such matters for two reasons. First, on account of man's lack of truth, for many give way to lying, according to Ps. 16:10, "Their mouth hath spoken lies [Vulg.: 'proudly']." Secondly, on account of [his] lack of knowledge, since he can know neither the future, nor secret thoughts, nor distant things: and yet men speak about such things, and our everyday life requires that we should have some certitude about them. Hence the need to have recourse to a Divine witness, for neither can God lie, nor is anything hidden from Him. Now to call God to witness is named *jurare* (to swear) because it is established as though it were a principle of law ( *jure* ) that what a man asserts under the invocation of God as His witness should be accepted as true. Now sometimes God is called to witness when we assert present or past events, and this is termed a "declaratory oath"; while sometimes God is called to witness in confirmation of something future, and this is termed a "promissory oath." But oaths are not employed in order to substantiate necessary matters, and such as come under the investigation of reason; for it would seem absurd in a scientific discussion to wish to prove one's point by an oath.

Reply Obj. 1: It is one thing to employ a Divine witness already given, as when one adduces the authority of Holy Scripture; and another to implore God to bear witness, as in an oath.

Reply Obj. 2: A man is said to pay his oaths to God because he performs what he swears to do, or because, from the very fact that he calls upon God to witness, he recognizes Him as possessing universal knowledge and unerring truth.

Reply Obj. 3: A person is called to give witness, in order that he may make known the truth about what is alleged. Now there are two ways in which God makes known whether the alleged facts are true or not. In one way He reveals the truth simply, either by inward inspiration, or by unveiling the facts, namely, by making public what was hitherto secret: in another way by punishing the lying witness, and then He is at once judge and witness, since by punishing the liar He makes known his lie. Hence oaths are of two kinds: one is a simple contestation of God, as when a man says "God is my witness," or, "I speak before God," or, "By God," which has the same meaning, as Augustine states [*See argument On the contrary]; the other is by cursing, and consists in a man binding himself or something of his to punishment if what is alleged be not true.

SECOND ARTICLE [II-II, Q. 89, Art. 2]

Whether It Is Lawful to Swear?

Objection 1: It would seem that it is not lawful to swear. Nothing forbidden in the Divine Law is lawful. Now swearing is forbidden (Matt. 5:34), "But I say to you not to swear at all"; and (James 5:12), "Above all things, my brethren, swear not." Therefore swearing is unlawful.

Obj. 2: Further, whatever comes from an evil seems to be unlawful, because according to Matt. 7:18, "neither can an evil tree bring forth good fruit." Now swearing comes from an evil, for it is written (Matt. 5:37): "But let your speech be: Yea, yea: No, no. And that which is over and above these is of evil." Therefore swearing is apparently unlawful.

Obj. 3: Further, to seek a sign of Divine Providence is to tempt God, and this is altogether unlawful, according to Deut. 6:16, "Thou shalt not tempt the Lord thy God." Now he that swears seems to seek a sign of Divine Providence, since he asks God to bear witness, and this must be by some evident effect. Therefore it seems that swearing is altogether unlawful.

*On the contrary,* It is written (Deut. 6:13): "Thou shalt fear the Lord thy God ... and shalt swear by His name."

*I answer that,* Nothing prevents a thing being good in itself, and yet becoming a source of evil to one who makes use thereof unbecomingly: thus to receive the Eucharist is good, and yet he that receives it "unworthily, eateth and drinketh judgment to himself" (1 Cor. 11:29). Accordingly in answer to the question in point it must be stated that an oath is in itself lawful and commendable. This is proved from its origin and from its end. From its origin, because swearing owes its introduction to the faith whereby man believes that God possesses unerring truth and universal knowledge and foresight of all things: and from its end, since oaths are employed in order to justify men, and to put an end to controversy (Heb. 6:16).

Yet an oath becomes a source of evil to him that makes evil use of it, that is who employs it without necessity and due caution. For if a man calls God as witness, for some trifling reason, it would seemingly prove him to have but little reverence for God, since he would not treat even a good man in this manner. Moreover, he is in danger of committing perjury, because man easily offends in words, according to James 3:2, "If any man offend not in word, the same is a perfect man." Wherefore it is written (Ecclus. 23:9): "Let not thy mouth be accustomed to swearing, for in it there are many falls."

Reply Obj. 1: Jerome, commenting on Matt. 5:34, says: "Observe that our Saviour forbade us to swear, not by God, but by heaven and earth. For it is known that the Jews have this most evil custom of swearing by the elements." Yet this answer does not suffice, because James adds, "nor by any other oath." Wherefore we must reply that, as Augustine states (De Mendacio xv), "when the Apostle employs an oath in his epistles, he shows how we are to understand the saying, 'I say to you, not to swear at all'; lest, to wit, swearing lead us to swear easily and from swearing easily, we contract the habit, and, from swearing habitually, we fall into perjury. Hence we find that he swore only when writing, because thought brings caution and avoids hasty words."

Reply Obj. 2: According to Augustine (De Serm. Dom. in Monte i. 17): "If you have to swear, note that the necessity arises from the infirmity of those whom you convince, which infirmity is indeed an evil. Accordingly He did not say: 'That which is over and above is evil,' but 'is of evil.' For you do no evil; since you make good use of swearing, by persuading another to a useful purpose: yet it 'comes of the evil' of the person by whose infirmity you are forced to swear."

Reply Obj. 3: He who swears tempts not God, because it is not without usefulness and necessity that he implores the Divine assistance. Moreover, he does not expose himself to danger, if God be unwilling to bear witness there and then: for He certainly will bear witness at some future time, when He "will bring to light the hidden things of darkness, and will make manifest the counsels of hearts" (1 Cor. 4:5). And this witness will be lacking to none who swears, neither for nor against him.

THIRD ARTICLE [II-II, Q. 89, Art. 3]

Whether Three Accompanying Conditions of an Oath Are Suitably Assigned, Namely, Justice, Judgment, and Truth?

Objection 1: It would seem that justice, judgment and truth are unsuitably assigned as the conditions accompanying an oath. Things should not be enumerated as diverse, if one of them includes the other. Now of these three, one includes another, since truth is a part of justice, according to Tully (De Invent. Rhet. ii, 53): and judgment is an act of justice, as stated above (Q. 60, A. 1). Therefore the three accompanying conditions of an oath are unsuitably assigned.

Obj. 2: Further, many other things are required for an oath, namely, devotion, and faith whereby we believe that God knows all things and cannot lie. Therefore the accompanying conditions of an oath are insufficiently enumerated.

Obj. 3: Further, these three are requisite in man's every deed: since he ought to do nothing contrary to justice and truth, or without judgment, according to 1 Tim. 5:21, "Do nothing without prejudice," i.e. without previous judgment [*Vulg.: 'Observe these things without prejudice, doing nothing by declining to either side.']. Therefore these three should not be associated with an oath any more than with other human actions.

*On the contrary,* It is written (Jer. 4:2): "Thou shalt swear: As the Lord liveth, in truth, and in judgment, and in justice": which words Jerome expounds, saying: "Observe that an oath must be accompanied by these conditions, truth, judgment and justice."

*I answer that,* As stated above (A. 2), an oath is not good except for one who makes good use of it. Now two conditions are required for the good use of an oath. First, that one swear, not for frivolous, but for urgent reasons, and with discretion; and this requires judgment or discretion on the part of the person who swears. Secondly, as regards the point to be confirmed by oath, that it be neither false, nor unlawful, and this requires both truth, so that one employ an oath in order to confirm what is true, and justice, so that one confirm what is lawful. A rash oath lacks judgment, a false oath lacks truth, and a wicked or unlawful oath lacks justice.

Reply Obj. 1: Judgment does not signify here the execution of justice, but the judgment of discretion, as stated above. Nor is truth here to be taken for the part of justice, but for a condition of speech.

Reply Obj. 2: Devotion, faith and like conditions requisite for the right manner of swearing are implied by judgment: for the other two regard the things sworn to as stated above. We might also reply that justice regards the reason for swearing.

Reply Obj. 3: There is great danger in swearing, both on account of the greatness of God Who is called upon to bear witness, and on account of the frailty of the human tongue, the words of which are confirmed by oath. Hence these conditions are more requisite for an oath than for other human actions.

FOURTH ARTICLE [II-II, Q. 89, Art. 4]

Whether an Oath Is an Act of Religion, or Latria?

Objection 1: It would seem that an oath is not an act of religion, or latria. Acts of religion are about holy and divine things. But oaths are employed in connection with human disputes, as the Apostle declares (Heb. 6:16). Therefore swearing is not an act of religion or latria.

Obj. 2: Further, it belongs to religion to give worship to God, as Tully says (De Invent. Rhet. ii, 53). But he who swears offers nothing to God, but calls God to be his witness. Therefore swearing is not an act of religion or latria.

Obj. 3: Further, the end of religion or latria is to show reverence to God. But the end of an oath is not this, but rather the confirmation of some assertion. Therefore swearing is not an act of religion.

*On the contrary,* It is written (Deut. 6:13): "Thou shalt fear the Lord thy God, and shalt serve Him only, and thou shalt swear by His name." Now he speaks there of the servitude of religion. Therefore swearing is an act of religion.

*I answer that,* As appears from what has been said above (A. 1), he that swears calls God to witness in confirmation of what he says. Now nothing is confirmed save by what is more certain and more powerful. Therefore in the very fact that a man swears by God, he acknowledges God to be more powerful, by reason of His unfailing truth and His universal knowledge; and thus in a way he shows reverence to God. For this reason the Apostle says (Heb. 6:16) that "men swear by one greater than themselves," and Jerome commenting on Matt. 5:34, says that "he who swears either reveres or loves the person by whom he swears." The Philosopher, too, states (Metaph. i, 3) that "to swear is to give very great honor." Now to show reverence to God belongs to religion or latria. Wherefore it is evident that an oath is an act of religion or latria.

Reply Obj. 1: Two things may be observed in an oath. The witness adduced, and this is Divine: and the thing witnessed to, or that which makes it necessary to call the witness, and this is human. Accordingly an oath belongs to religion by reason of the former, and not of the latter.

Reply Obj. 2: In the very fact that a man takes God as witness by way of an oath, he acknowledges Him to be greater: and this pertains to the reverence and honor of God, so that he offers something to God, namely, reverence and honor.

Reply Obj. 3: Whatsoever we do, we should do it in honor of God: wherefore there is no hindrance, if by intending to assure a man, we show reverence to God. For we ought so to perform our actions in God's honor that they may conduce to our neighbor's good, since God also works for His own glory and for our good.

FIFTH ARTICLE [II-II, Q. 89, Art. 5]

Whether Oaths Are Desirable and to Be Used Frequently As Something Useful and Good?

Objection 1: It would seem that oaths are desirable and to be used frequently as something useful and good. Just as a vow is an act of religion, so is an oath. Now it is commendable and more meritorious to do a thing by vow, because a vow is an act of religion, as stated above (Q. 88, A. 5). Therefore for the same reason, to do or say a thing with an oath is more commendable, and consequently oaths are desirable as being good essentially.

Obj. 2: Further, Jerome, commenting on Matt. 5:34, says that "he who swears either reveres or loves the person by whom he swears." Now reverence and love of God are desirable as something good essentially. Therefore swearing is also.

Obj. 3: Further, swearing is directed to the purpose of confirming or assuring. But it is a good thing for a man to confirm his assertion. Therefore an oath is desirable as a good thing.

*On the contrary,* It is written (Ecclus. 23:12): "A man that sweareth much shall be filled with iniquity": and Augustine says (De Mendacio xv) that "the Lord forbade swearing, in order that for your own part you might not be fond of it, and take pleasure in seeking occasions of swearing, as though it were a good thing."

*I answer that,* Whatever is required merely as a remedy for an infirmity or a defect, is not reckoned among those things that are desirable for their own sake, but among those that are necessary: this is clear in the case of medicine which is required as a remedy for sickness. Now an oath is required as a remedy to a defect, namely, some man's lack of belief in another man. Wherefore an oath is not to be reckoned among those things that are desirable for their own sake, but among those that are necessary for this life; and such things are used unduly whenever they are used outside the bounds of necessity. For this reason Augustine says (De Serm. Dom. in Monte i, 17): "He who understands that swearing is not to be held as a good thing," i.e. desirable for its own sake, "restrains himself as far as he can from uttering oaths, unless there be urgent need."

Reply Obj. 1: There is no parity between a vow and an oath: because by a vow we direct something to the honor of God, so that for this very reason a vow is an act of religion. On the other hand, in an oath reverence for the name of God is taken in confirmation of a promise. Hence what is confirmed by oath does not, for this reason, become an act of religion, since moral acts take their species from the end.

Reply Obj. 2: He who swears does indeed make use of his reverence or love for the person by whom he swears: he does not, however, direct his oath to the reverence or love of that person, but to something else that is necessary for the present life.

Reply Obj. 3: Even as a medicine is useful for healing, and yet, the stronger it is, the greater harm it does if it be taken unduly, so too an oath is useful indeed as a means of confirmation, yet the greater the reverence it demands the more dangerous it is, unless it be employed aright; for, as it is written (Ecclus. 23:13), "if he make it void," i.e. if he deceive his brother, "his sin shall be upon him: and if he dissemble it," by swearing falsely, and with dissimulation, "he offendeth double," (because, to wit, "pretended equity is a twofold iniquity," as Augustine [*Enarr. in Ps. lxiii, 7] declares): "and if he swear in vain," i.e. without due cause and necessity, "he shall not be justified."

SIXTH ARTICLE [II-II, Q. 89, Art. 6]

Whether It Is Lawful to Swear by Creatures?

Objection 1: It would seem that it is not lawful to swear by creatures. It is written (Matt. 5:34-36): "I say to you not to swear at all, neither by heaven ... nor by the earth ... nor by Jerusalem ... nor by thy head": and Jerome, expounding these words, says: "Observe that the Saviour does not forbid swearing by God, but by heaven and earth," etc.

Obj. 2: Further, punishment is not due save for a fault. Now a punishment is appointed for one who swears by creatures: for it is written (22, qu. i, can. Clericum): "If a cleric swears by creatures he must be very severely rebuked: and if he shall persist in this vicious habit we wish that he be excommunicated." Therefore it is unlawful to swear by creatures.

Obj. 3: Further, an oath is an act of religion, as stated above (A. 4). But religious worship is not due to any creature, according to Rom. 1:23, 25. Therefore it is not lawful to swear by a creature.

*On the contrary,* Joseph swore "by the health of Pharaoh" (Gen. 42:16). Moreover it is customary to swear by the Gospel, by relics, and by the saints.

*I answer that,* As stated above (A. 1, ad 3), there are two kinds of oath. One is uttered as a simple contestation or calling God as witness: and this kind of oath, like faith, is based on God's truth. Now faith is essentially and chiefly about God Who is the very truth, and secondarily about creatures in which God's truth is reflected, as stated above (Q. 1, A. 1). In like manner an oath is chiefly referred to God Whose testimony is invoked; and secondarily an appeal by oath is made to certain creatures considered, not in themselves, but as reflecting the Divine truth. Thus we swear by the Gospel, i.e. by God Whose truth is made known in the Gospel; and by the saints who believed this truth and kept it.

The other way of swearing is by cursing and in this kind of oath a creature is adduced that the judgment of God may be wrought therein. Thus a man is wont to swear by his head, or by his son, or by some other thing that he loves, even as the Apostle swore (2 Cor. 1:23), saying: "I call God to witness upon my soul."

As to Joseph's oath by the health of Pharaoh this may be understood in both ways: either by way of a curse, as though he pledged Pharao's health to God; or by way of contestation, as though he appealed to the truth of God's justice which the princes of the earth are appointed to execute.

Reply Obj. 1: Our Lord forbade us to swear by creatures so as to give them the reverence due to God. Hence Jerome adds that "the Jews, through swearing by the angels and the like, worshipped creatures with a Divine honor."

In the same sense a cleric is punished, according to the canons (22, qu. i, can. Clericum, Obj. 2), for swearing by a creature, for this savors of the blasphemy of unbelief. Hence in the next chapter, it is said: "If any one swears by God's hair or head, or otherwise utter blasphemy against God, and he be in ecclesiastical orders, let him be degraded."

This suffices for the Reply to the Second Objection.

Reply Obj. 3: Religious worship is shown to one whose testimony is invoked by oath: hence the prohibition (Ex. 23:13): "By the name of strange gods you shall not swear." But religious worship is not given to creatures employed in an oath in the ways mentioned above.

SEVENTH ARTICLE [II-II, Q. 89, Art. 7]

Whether an Oath Has a Binding Force?

Objection 1: It would seem that an oath has no binding force. An oath is employed in order to confirm the truth of an assertion. But when a person makes an assertion about the future his assertion is true, though it may not be verified. Thus Paul lied not (2 Cor. 1:15, seqq.) though he went not to Corinth, as he had said he would (1 Cor. 16:5). Therefore it seems that an oath is not binding.

Obj. 2: Further, virtue is not contrary to virtue (Categ. viii, 22). Now an oath is an act of virtue, as stated above (A. 4). But it would sometimes be contrary to virtue, or an obstacle thereto, if one were to fulfil what one has sworn to do: for instance, if one were to swear to commit a sin, or to desist from some virtuous action. Therefore an oath is not always binding.

Obj. 3: Further, sometimes a man is compelled against his will to promise something under oath. Now, "such a person is loosed by the Roman Pontiffs from the bond of his oath" (Extra, De Jurejur., cap. Verum in ea quaest., etc.). Therefore an oath is not always binding.

Obj. 4: Further, no person can be under two opposite obligations. Yet sometimes the person who swears and the person to whom he swears have opposite intentions. Therefore an oath cannot always be binding.

*On the contrary,* It is written (Matt. 5:33): "Thou shalt perform thy oaths to the Lord."

*I answer that,* An obligation implies something to be done or omitted; so that apparently it regards neither the declaratory oath (which is about something present or past), nor such oaths as are about something to be effected by some other cause (as, for example, if one were to swear that it would rain tomorrow), but only such as are about things to be done by the person who swears.

Now just as a declaratory oath, which is about the future or the present, should contain the truth, so too ought the oath which is about something to be done by us in the future. Yet there is a difference: since, in the oath that is about the past or present, this obligation affects, not the thing that already has been or is, but the action of the swearer, in the point of his swearing to what is or was already true; whereas, *on the contrary,* in the oath that is made about something to be done by us, the obligation falls on the thing guaranteed by oath. For a man is bound to make true what he has sworn, else his oath lacks truth.

Now if this thing be such as not to be in his power, his oath is lacking in judgment of discretion: unless perchance what was possible when he swore become impossible to him through some mishap, as when a man swore to pay a sum of money, which is subsequently taken from him by force or theft. For then he would seem to be excused from fulfilling his oath, although he is bound to do what he can, as, in fact, we have already stated with regard to the obligation of a vow (Q. 88, A. 3, ad 2). If, on the other hand, it be something that he can do, but ought not to, either because it is essentially evil, or because it is a hindrance to a good, then his oath is lacking in justice: wherefore an oath must not be kept when it involves a sin or a hindrance to good. For in either case "its result is evil" [*Cf. Bede, Homil. xix, in Decoll. S. Joan. Bapt.]

Accordingly we must conclude that whoever swears to do something is bound to do what he can for the fulfilment of truth; provided always that the other two accompanying conditions be present, namely, judgment and justice.

Reply Obj. 1: It is not the same with a simple assertion, and with an oath wherein God is called to witness: because it suffices for the truth of an assertion, that a person say what he proposes to do, since it is already true in its cause, namely, the purpose of the doer. But an oath should not be employed, save in a matter about which one is firmly certain: and, consequently, if a man employ an oath, he is bound, as far as he can, to make true what he has sworn, through reverence of the Divine witness invoked, unless it leads to an evil result, as stated.

Reply Obj. 2: An oath may lead to an evil result in two ways. First, because from the very outset it has an evil result, either through being evil of its very nature (as, if a man were to swear to commit adultery), or through being a hindrance to a greater good, as if a man were to swear not to enter religion, or not to become a cleric, or that he would not accept a prelacy, supposing it would be expedient for him to accept, or in similar cases. For oaths of this kind are unlawful from the outset: yet with a difference: because if a man swear to commit a sin, he sinned in swearing, and sins in keeping his oath: whereas if a man swear not to perform a greater good, which he is not bound to do withal, he sins indeed in swearing (through placing an obstacle to the Holy Ghost, Who is the inspirer of good purposes), yet he does not sin in keeping his oath, though he does much better if he does not keep it.

Secondly, an oath leads to an evil result through some new and unforeseen emergency. An instance is the oath of Herod, who swore to the damsel, who danced before him, that he would give her what she would ask of him. For this oath could be lawful from the outset, supposing it to have the requisite conditions, namely, that the damsel asked what it was right to grant, but the fulfilment of the oath was unlawful. Hence Ambrose says (De Officiis i, 50): "Sometimes it is wrong to fulfil a promise, and to keep an oath; as Herod, who granted the slaying of John, rather than refuse what he had promised."

Reply Obj. 3: There is a twofold obligation in the oath which a man takes under compulsion: one, whereby he is beholden to the person to whom he promises something; and this obligation is cancelled by the compulsion, because he that used force deserves that the promise made to him should not be kept. The other is an obligation whereby a man is beholden to God, in virtue of which he is bound to fulfil what he has promised in His name. This obligation is not removed in the tribunal of conscience, because that man ought rather to suffer temporal loss, than violate his oath. He can, however, seek in a court of justice to recover what he has paid, or denounce the matter to his superior even if he has sworn to the contrary, because such an oath would lead to evil results since it would be contrary to public justice. The Roman Pontiffs, in absolving men from oaths of this kind, did not pronounce such oaths to be unbinding, but relaxed the obligation for some just cause.

Reply Obj. 4: When the intention of the swearer is not the same as the intention of the person to whom he swears, if this be due to the swearer's guile, he must keep his oath in accordance with the sound understanding of the person to whom the oath is made. Hence Isidore says (De Summo Bono ii, 31): "However artful a man may be in wording his oath, God Who witnesses his conscience accepts his oath as understood by the person to whom it is made." And that this refers to the deceitful oath is clear from what follows: "He is doubly guilty who both takes God's name in vain, and tricks his neighbor by guile." If, however, the swearer uses no guile, he is bound in accordance with his own intention. Wherefore Gregory says (Moral. xxvi, 7): "The human ear takes such like words in their natural outward sense, but the Divine judgment interprets them according to our inward intention."

EIGHTH ARTICLE [II-II, Q. 89, Art. 8]

Whether an Oath Is More Binding Than a Vow?

Objection 1: It would seem that an oath is more binding than a vow. A vow is a simple promise: whereas an oath includes, besides a promise, an appeal to God as witness. Therefore an oath is more binding than a vow.

Obj. 2: Further, the weaker is wont to be confirmed by the stronger. Now a vow is sometimes confirmed by an oath. Therefore an oath is stronger than a vow.

Obj. 3: Further, the obligation of a vow arises from the deliberation of the mind, a stated above (Q. 88, A. 1); while the obligation of an oath results from the truth of God Whose testimony is invoked. Since therefore God's truth is something greater than human deliberation, it seems that the obligation of an oath is greater than that of a vow.

*On the contrary,* A vow binds one to God while an oath sometimes binds one to man. Now one is more bound to God than to man. Therefore a vow is more binding than an oath.

*I answer that,* The obligation both of vow and of an oath arises from something Divine; but in different ways. For the obligation of a vow arises from the fidelity we owe God, which binds us to fulfil our promises to Him. On the other hand, the obligation of an oath arises from the reverence we owe Him which binds us to make true what we promise in His name. Now every act of infidelity includes an irreverence, but not conversely, because the infidelity of a subject to his lord would seem to be the greatest irreverence. Hence a vow by its very nature is more binding than an oath.

Reply Obj. 1: A vow is not any kind of promise, but a promise made to God; and to be unfaithful to God is most grievous.

Reply Obj. 2: An oath is added to a vow not because it is more stable, but because greater stability results from "two immutable things" [*Heb. 6:18].

Reply Obj. 3: Deliberation of the mind gives a vow its stability, on the part of the person who takes the vow: but it has a greater cause of stability on the part of God, to Whom the vow is offered.

NINTH ARTICLE [II-II, Q. 89, Art. 9]

Whether Anyone Can Dispense from an Oath?

Objection 1: It would seem that no one can dispense from an oath. Just as truth is required for a declaratory oath, which is about the past or the present, so too is it required for a promissory oath, which is about the future. Now no one can dispense a man from swearing to the truth about present or past things. Therefore neither can anyone dispense a man from making truth that which he has promised by oath to do in the future.

Obj. 2: Further, a promissory oath is used for the benefit of the person to whom the promise is made. But, apparently, he cannot release the other from his oath, since it would be contrary to the reverence of God. Much less therefore can a dispensation from this oath be granted by anyone.

Obj. 3: Further, any bishop can grant a dispensation from a vow, except certain vows reserved to the Pope alone, as stated above (Q. 88, A. 12, ad 3). Therefore in like manner, if an oath admits of dispensation, any bishop can dispense from an oath. And yet seemingly this is to be against the law [*Caus. XV, qu. 6, can. Auctoritatem, seqq.: Cap. Si vero, de Jurejurando]. Therefore it would seem that an oath does not admit of dispensation.

*On the contrary,* A vow is more binding than an oath, as stated above (A. 8). But a vow admits of dispensation and therefore an oath does also.

*I answer that,* As stated above (Q. 88, A. 10), the necessity of a dispensation both from the law and from a vow arises from the fact that something which is useful and morally good in itself and considered in general, may be morally evil and hurtful in respect of some particular emergency: and such a case comes under neither law nor vow. Now anything morally evil or hurtful is incompatible with the matter of an oath: for if it be morally evil it is opposed to justice, and if it be hurtful it is contrary to judgment. Therefore an oath likewise admits of dispensation.

Reply Obj. 1: A dispensation from an oath does not imply a permission to do anything against the oath: for this is impossible, since the keeping of an oath comes under a Divine precept, which does not admit of dispensation: but it implies that what hitherto came under an oath no longer comes under it, as not being due matter for an oath, just as we have said with regard to vows (Q. 88, A. 10, ad 2). Now the matter of a declaratory oath, which is about something past or present, has already acquired a certain necessity, and has become unchangeable, wherefore the dispensation will regard not the matter but the act itself of the oath: so that such a dispensation would be directly contrary to the Divine precept. On the other hand, the matter of a promissory oath is something future, which admits of change, so that, to wit, in certain emergencies, it may be unlawful or hurtful, and consequently undue matter for an oath. Therefore a promissory oath admits of dispensation, since such dispensation regards the matter of an oath, and is not contrary to the Divine precept about the keeping of oaths.

Reply Obj. 2: One man may promise something under oath to another in two ways. First, when he promises something for his benefit: for instance, if he promise to serve him, or to give him money: and from such a promise he can be released by the person to whom he made it: for he is understood to have already kept his promise to him when he acts towards him according to his will. Secondly, one man promises another something pertaining to God's honor or to the benefit of others: for instance, if a man promise another under oath that he will enter religion, or perform some act of kindness. In this case the person to whom the promise is made cannot release him that made the promise, because it was made principally not to him but to God: unless perchance it included some condition, for instance, "provided he give his consent" or some such like condition.

Reply Obj. 3: Sometimes that which is made the matter of a promissory oath is manifestly opposed to justice, either because it is a sin, as when a man swears to commit a murder, or because it is an obstacle to a greater good, as when a man swears not to enter religion: and such an oath requires no dispensation. But in the former case a man is bound not to keep such an oath, while in the latter it is lawful for him to keep or not to keep the oath, as stated above (A. 7, ad 2). Sometimes what is promised on oath is doubtfully right or wrong, useful or harmful, either in itself or under the circumstance. In this case any bishop can dispense. Sometimes, however, that which is promised under oath is manifestly lawful and beneficial. An oath of this kind seemingly admits not of dispensation but of commutation, when there occurs something better to be done for the common good, in which case the matter would seem to belong chiefly to the power of the Pope, who has charge over the whole Church; and even of absolute relaxation, for this too belongs in general to the Pope in all matters regarding the administration of things ecclesiastical. Thus it is competent to any man to cancel an oath made by one of his subjects in matters that come under his authority: for instance, a father may annul his daughter's oath, and a husband his wife's (Num. 30:6, seqq.), as stated above with regard to vows (Q. 88, AA. 8, 9).

TENTH ARTICLE [II-II, Q. 89, Art. 10]

Whether an Oath Is Voided by a Condition of Person or Time?

Objection 1: It would seem that an oath is not voided by a condition of person or time. An oath, according to the Apostle (Heb. 6:16), is employed for the purpose of confirmation. Now it is competent to anyone to confirm his assertion, and at any time. Therefore it would seem that an oath is not voided by a condition of person or time.

Obj. 2: Further, to swear by God is more than to swear by the Gospels: wherefore Chrysostom [*Hom. xliv in the Opus Imperfectum falsely ascribed to St. John Chrysostom] says: "If there is a reason for swearing, it seems a small thing to swear by God, but a great thing to swear by the Gospels. To those who think thus, it must be said: Nonsense! the Scriptures were made for God's sake, not God for the sake of the Scriptures." Now men of all conditions and at all times are wont to swear by God. Much more, therefore, is it lawful to swear by the Gospels.

Obj. 3: Further, the same effect does not proceed from contrary causes, since contrary causes produce contrary effects. Now some are debarred from swearing on account of some personal defect; children, for instance, before the age of fourteen, and persons who have already committed perjury. Therefore it would seem that a person ought not to be debarred from swearing either on account of his dignity, as clerics, or on account of the solemnity of the time.

Obj. 4: Further, in this world no living man is equal in dignity to an angel: for it is written (Matt. 11:11) that "he that is the lesser in the kingdom of heaven is greater than he," namely than John the Baptist, while yet living. Now an angel is competent to swear, for it is written (Apoc. 10:6) that the angel "swore by Him that liveth for ever and ever." Therefore no man ought to be excused from swearing, on account of his dignity.

*On the contrary,* It is stated (II, qu. v, can. Si quis presbyter): "Let a priest be examined 'by his sacred consecration,' instead of being put on his oath": and (22, qu. v, can. Nullus): "Let no one in ecclesiastical orders dare to swear on the Holy Gospels to a layman."

*I answer that,* Two things are to be considered in an oath. One is on the part of God, whose testimony is invoked, and in this respect we should hold an oath in the greatest reverence. For this reason children before the age of puberty are debarred from taking oaths [*Caus. XXII, qu. 5, can. Parvuli], and are not called upon to swear, because they have not yet attained the perfect use of reason, so as to be able to take a oath with due reverence. Perjurers also are debarred from taking an oath, because it is presumed from their antecedents that they will not treat an oath with the reverence due to it. For this same reason, in order that oaths might be treated with due reverence the law says (22, qu. v, can. Honestum): "It is becoming that he who ventures to swear on holy things should do so fasting, with all propriety and fear of God."

The other thing to be considered is on the part of the man, whose assertion is confirmed by oath. For a man's assertion needs no confirmation save because there is a doubt about it. Now it derogates from a person's dignity that one should doubt about the truth of what he says, wherefore "it becomes not persons of great dignity to swear." For this reason the law says (II, qu. v, can. Si quis presbyter) that "priests should not swear for trifling reasons." Nevertheless it is lawful for them to swear if there be need for it, or if great good may result therefrom. Especially is this the case in spiritual affairs, when moreover it is becoming that they should take oath on days of solemnity, since they ought then to devote themselves to spiritual matters. Nor should they on such occasions take oaths temporal matters, except perhaps in cases grave necessity.

Reply Obj. 1: Some are unable to confirm their own assertions on account of their own defect: and some there are whose words should be so certain that they need no confirmation.

Reply Obj. 2: The greater the thing sworn by, the holier and the more binding is the oath, considered in itself, as Augustine states (Ad Public., Ep. xlvii): and accordingly it is a graver matter to swear by God than the Gospels. Yet the contrary may be the case on account of the manner of swearing for instance, an oath by the Gospels might be taken with deliberation and solemnity, and an oath by God frivolously and without deliberation.

Reply Obj. 3: Nothing prevents the same thing from arising out of contrary causes, by way of superabundance and defect. It is in this way that some are debarred from swearing, through being of so great authority that it is unbecoming for them to swear; while others are of such little authority that their oaths have no standing.

Reply Obj. 4: The angel's oath is adduced not on account of any defect in the angel, as though one ought not to credit his mere word, but in order to show that the statement made issues from God's infallible disposition. Thus too God is sometimes spoken of by Scripture as swearing, in order to express the immutability of His word, as the Apostle declares (Heb. 6:17).

# QUESTION 90

OF THE TAKING OF GOD'S NAME BY WAY OF ADJURATION (In Three Articles)

We must now consider the taking of God's name by way of adjuration: under which head there are three points of inquiry:

(1) Whether it is lawful to adjure a man?

(2) Whether it is lawful to adjure the demons?

(3) Whether it is lawful to adjure irrational creatures?

FIRST ARTICLE [II-II, Q. 90, Art. 1]

Whether It Is Lawful to Adjure a Man?

Objection 1: It would seem that it is not lawful to adjure a man. Origen says (Tract. xxxv super Matth.): "I deem that a man who wishes to live according to the Gospel should not adjure another man. For if, according to the Gospel mandate of Christ, it be unlawful to swear, it is evident that neither is it lawful to adjure: and consequently it is manifest that the high-priest unlawfully adjured Jesus by the living God."

Obj. 2: Further, whoever adjures a man, compels him after a fashion. But it is unlawful to compel a man against his will. Therefore seemingly it is also unlawful to adjure a man.

Obj. 3: Further, to adjure is to induce a person to swear. Now it belongs to man's superior to induce him to swear, for the superior imposes an oath on his subject. Therefore subjects cannot adjure their superiors.

*On the contrary,* Even when we pray God we implore Him by certain holy things: and the Apostle too besought the faithful "by the mercy of God" (Rom. 12:1): and this seems to be a kind of adjuration. Therefore it is lawful to adjure.

*I answer that,* A man who utters a promissory oath, swearing by his reverence for the Divine name, which he invokes in confirmation of his promise, binds himself to do what he has undertaken, and so orders himself unchangeably to do a certain thing. Now just as a man can order himself to do a certain thing, so too can he order others, by beseeching his superiors, or by commanding his inferiors, as stated above (Q. 83, A. 1). Accordingly when either of these orderings is confirmed by something Divine it is an adjuration. Yet there is this difference between them, that man is master of his own actions but not of others; wherefore he can put himself under an obligation by invoking the Divine name, whereas he cannot put others under such an obligation unless they be his subjects, whom he can compel on the strength of the oath they have taken.

Therefore, if a man by invoking the name of God, or any holy thing, intends by this adjuration to put one who is not his subject under an obligation to do a certain thing, in the same way as he would bind himself by oath, such an adjuration is unlawful, because he usurps over another a power which he has not. But superiors may bind their inferiors by this kind of adjuration, if there be need for it.

If, however, he merely intend, through reverence of the Divine name or of some holy thing, to obtain something from the other man without putting him under any obligation, such an adjuration may be lawfully employed in respect of anyone.

Reply Obj. 1: Origen is speaking of an adjuration whereby a man intends to put another under an obligation, in the same way as he would bind himself by oath: for thus did the high-priest presume to adjure our Lord Jesus Christ [*Matt. 26:63].

Reply Obj. 2: This argument considers the adjuration which imposes an obligation.

Reply Obj. 3: To adjure is not to induce a man to swear, but to employ terms resembling an oath in order to provoke another to do a certain thing.

Moreover, we adjure God in one way and man in another; because when we adjure a man we intend to alter his will by appealing to his reverence for a holy thing: and we cannot have such an intention in respect of God Whose will is immutable. If we obtain something from God through His eternal will, it is due, not to our merits, but to His goodness.

SECOND ARTICLE [II-II, Q. 90, Art. 2]

Whether It Is Lawful to Adjure the Demons?

Objection 1: It would seem unlawful to adjure the demons. Origen says (Tract. xxxv, super Matth.): "To adjure the demons is not accordance with the power given by our Saviour: for this is a Jewish practice." Now rather than imitate the rites of the Jews, we should use the power given by Christ. Therefore it is not lawful to adjure the demons.

Obj. 2: Further, many make use of necromantic incantations when invoking the demons by something Divine: and this is an adjuration. Therefore, if it be lawful to adjure the demons, it is lawful to make use of necromantic incantations, which is evidently false. Therefore the antecedent is false also.

Obj. 3: Further, whoever adjures a person, by that very fact associates himself with him. Now it is not lawful to have fellowship with the demons, according to 1 Cor. 10:20, "I would not that you should be made partakers with devils." Therefore it is not lawful to adjure the demons.

*On the contrary,* It is written (Mk. 16:17): "In My name they shall cast out devils." Now to induce anyone to do a certain thing for the sake of God's name is to adjure. Therefore it is lawful to adjure the demons.

*I answer that,* As stated in the preceding article, there are two ways of adjuring: one by way of prayer or inducement through reverence of some holy thing: the other by way of compulsion. In the first way it is not lawful to adjure the demons because such a way seems to savor of benevolence or friendship, which it is unlawful to bear towards the demons. As to the second kind of adjuration, which is by compulsion, we may lawfully use it for some purposes, and not for others. For during the course of this life the demons are our adversaries: and their actions are not subject to our disposal but to that of God and the holy angels, because, as Augustine says (De Trin. iii, 4), "the rebel spirit is ruled by the just spirit." Accordingly we may repulse the demons, as being our enemies, by adjuring them through the power of God's name, lest they do us harm of soul or body, in accord with the Divine power given by Christ, as recorded by Luke 10:19: "Behold, I have given you power to tread upon serpents and scorpions, and upon all the power of the enemy: and nothing shall hurt you."

It is not, however, lawful to adjure them for the purpose of learning something from them, or of obtaining something through them, for this would amount to holding fellowship with them: except perhaps when certain holy men, by special instinct or Divine revelation, make use of the demons' actions in order to obtain certain results: thus we read of the Blessed James [*the Greater; cf. Apocrypha, N.T., Hist. Certam. Apost. vi, 19] that he caused Hermogenes to be brought to him, by the instrumentality of the demons.

Reply Obj. 1: Origen is speaking of adjuration made, not authoritatively by way of compulsion, but rather by way of a friendly appeal.

Reply Obj. 2: Necromancers adjure and invoke the demons in order to obtain or learn something from them: and this is unlawful, as stated above. Wherefore Chrysostom, commenting on our Lord's words to the unclean spirit (Mk. 1:25), "Speak no more, and go out of the man," says: "A salutary teaching is given us here, lest we believe the demons, however much they speak the truth."

Reply Obj. 3: This argument considers the adjuration whereby the demon's help is besought in doing or learning something: for this savors of fellowship with them. On the other hand, to repulse the demons by adjuring them, is to sever oneself from their fellowship.

THIRD ARTICLE [II-II, Q. 90, Art. 3]

Whether It Is Lawful to Adjure an Irrational Creature?

Objection 1: It would seem unlawful to adjure an irrational creature. An adjuration consists of spoken words. But it is useless to speak to one that understands not, such as an irrational creature. Therefore it is vain and unlawful to adjure an irrational creature.

Obj. 2: Further, seemingly wherever adjuration is admissible, swearing is also admissible. But swearing is not consistent with an irrational creature. Therefore it would seem unlawful to employ adjuration towards one.

Obj. 3: Further, there are two ways of adjuring, as explained above (AA. 1, 2). One is by way of appeal; and this cannot be employed towards irrational creatures, since they are not masters of their own actions. The other kind of adjuration is by way of compulsion: and, seemingly, neither is it lawful to use this towards them, because we have not the power to command irrational creatures, but only He of Whom it was said (Matt. 8:27): "For the winds and the sea obey Him." Therefore in no way, apparently, is it lawful to adjure irrational creatures.

*On the contrary,* Simon and Jude are related to have adjured dragons and to have commanded them to withdraw into the desert. [*From the apocryphal Historiae Certam. Apost. vi. 19.]

*I answer that,* Irrational creatures are directed to their own actions by some other agent. Now the action of what is directed and moved is also the action of the director and mover: thus the movement of the arrow is an operation of the archer. Wherefore the operation of the irrational creature is ascribed not only to it, but also and chiefly to God, Who disposes the movements of all things. It is also ascribed to the devil, who, by God's permission, makes use of irrational creatures in order to inflict harm on man.

Accordingly the adjuration of an irrational creature may be of two kinds. First, so that the adjuration is referred to the irrational creature in itself: and in this way it would be vain to adjure an irrational creature. Secondly, so that it be referred to the director and mover of the irrational creature, and in this sense a creature of this kind may be adjured in two ways. First, by way of appeal made to God, and this relates to those who work miracles by calling on God: secondly, by way of compulsion, which relates to the devil, who uses the irrational creature for our harm. This is the kind of adjuration used in the exorcisms of the Church, whereby the power of the demons is expelled from an irrational creature. But it is not lawful to adjure the demons by beseeching them to help us.

This suffices for the Replies to the Objections.

## QUESTION 91

OF TAKING THE DIVINE NAME FOR THE PURPOSE OF INVOKING IT BY MEANS OF PRAISE (In Two Articles)

We must now consider the taking of the Divine name for the purpose of invoking it by prayer or praise. Of prayer we have already spoken (Q. 83). Wherefore we must speak now of praise. Under this head there are two points of inquiry:

(1) Whether God should be praised with the lips?

(2) Whether God should be praised with song?

FIRST ARTICLE [II-II, Q. 91, Art. 1]

Whether God Should Be Praised with the Lips?

Objection 1: It would seem that God should not be praised with the lips. The Philosopher says (Ethic. 1, 12): "The best of men ere accorded not praise, but something greater." But God transcends the very best of all things. Therefore God ought to be given, not praise, but something greater than praise: wherefore He is said (Ecclus. 43:33) to be "above all praise."

Obj. 2: Further, divine praise is part of divine worship, for it is an act of religion. Now God is worshiped with the mind rather than with the lips: wherefore our Lord quoted against certain ones the words of Isa. 29:13, "This people ... honors [Vulg.: 'glorifies'] Me with their lips, but their heart is far from Me." Therefore the praise of God lies in the heart rather than on the lips.

Obj. 3: Further, men are praised with the lips that they may be encouraged to do better: since just as being praised makes the wicked proud, so does it incite the good to better things. Wherefore it is written (Prov. 27:21): "As silver is tried in the fining-pot ... so a man is tried by the mouth of him that praiseth." But God is not incited to better things by man's words, both because He is unchangeable, and because He is supremely good, and it is not possible for Him to grow better. Therefore God should not be praised with the lips.

*On the contrary,* It is written (Ps. 62:6): "My mouth shall praise Thee with joyful lips."

*I answer that,* We use words, in speaking to God, for one reason, and in speaking to man, for another reason. For when speaking to man we use words in order to tell him our thoughts which are unknown to him. Wherefore we praise a man with our lips, in order that he or others may learn that we have a good opinion of him: so that in consequence we may incite him to yet better things; and that we may induce others, who hear him praised, to think well of him, to reverence him, and to imitate him. On the other hand we employ words, in speaking to God, not indeed to make known our thoughts to Him Who is the searcher of hearts, but that we may bring ourselves and our hearers to reverence Him.

Consequently we need to praise God with our lips, not indeed for His sake, but for our own sake; since by praising Him our devotion is aroused towards Him, according to Ps. 49:23: "The sacrifice of praise shall glorify Me, and there is the way by which I will show him the salvation of God." And forasmuch as man, by praising God, ascends in his affections to God, by so much is he withdrawn from things opposed to God, according to Isa. 48:9, "For My praise I will bridle thee lest thou shouldst perish." The praise of the lips is also profitable to others by inciting their affections towards God, wherefore it is written (Ps. 33:2): "His praise shall always be in my mouth," and farther on: "Let the meek hear and rejoice. O magnify the Lord with me."

Reply Obj. 1: We may speak of God in two ways. First, with regard to His essence; and thus, since He is incomprehensible and ineffable, He is above all praise. In this respect we owe Him reverence and the honor of latria; wherefore Ps. 64:2 is rendered by Jerome in his Psalter [*Translated from the Hebrew]: "Praise to Thee is speechless, O God," as regards the first, and as to the second, "A vow shall be paid to Thee." Secondly, we may speak of God as to His effects which are ordained for our good. In this respect we owe Him praise; wherefore it is written (Isa. 63:7): "I will remember the tender mercies of the Lord, the praise of the Lord for all the things that the Lord hath bestowed upon us." Again, Dionysius says (Div. Nom. 1): "Thou wilt find that all the sacred hymns," i.e. divine praises "of the sacred writers, are directed respectively to the Blessed Processions of the Thearchy," i.e. of the Godhead, "showing forth and praising the names of God."

Reply Obj. 2: It profits one nothing to praise with the lips if one praise not with the heart. For the heart speaks God's praises when it fervently recalls "the glorious things of His works" [*Cf. Ecclus. 17:7, 8]. Yet the outward praise of the lips avails to arouse the inward fervor of those who praise, and to incite others to praise God, as stated above.

Reply Obj. 3: We praise God, not for His benefit, but for ours as stated.

SECOND ARTICLE [II-II, Q. 91, Art. 2]

Whether God Should Be Praised with Song?

Objection 1: It would seem that God should not be praised with song. For the Apostle says (Col. 3:16): "Teaching and admonishing one another in psalms, hymns and spiritual canticles." Now we should employ nothing in the divine worship, save what is delivered to us on the authority of Scripture. Therefore it would seem that, in praising God, we should employ, not corporal but spiritual canticles.

Obj. 2: Further, Jerome in his commentary on Eph. 5:19, "Singing and making melody in your hearts to the Lord," says: "Listen, young men whose duty it is to recite the office in church: God is to be sung not with the voice but with the heart. Nor should you, like play-actors, ease your throat and jaws with medicaments, and make the church resound with theatrical measures and airs." Therefore God should not be praised with song.

Obj. 3: Further, the praise of God is competent to little and great, according to Apoc. 14, "Give praise to our God, all ye His servants; and you that fear Him, little and great." But the great, who are in the church, ought not to sing: for Gregory says (Regist. iv, ep. 44): "I hereby ordain that in this See the ministers of the sacred altar must not sing" (Cf. Decret., dist. xcii., cap. In sancta Romana Ecclesia). Therefore singing is unsuitable to the divine praises.

Obj. 4: Further, in the Old Law God was praised with musical instruments and human song, according to Ps. 32:2, 3: "Give praise to the Lord on the harp, sing to Him with the psaltery, the instrument of ten strings. Sing to Him a new canticle." But the Church does not make use of musical instruments such as harps and psalteries, in the divine praises, for fear of seeming to imitate the Jews. Therefore in like manner neither should song be used in the divine praises.

Obj. 5: Further, the praise of the heart is more important than the praise of the lips. But the praise of the heart is hindered by singing, both because the attention of the singers is distracted from the consideration of what they are singing, so long as they give all their attention to the chant, and because others are less able to understand the things that are sung than if they were recited without chant. Therefore chants should not be employed in the divine praises.

*On the contrary,* Blessed Ambrose established singing in the Church of Milan, as Augustine relates (Confess. ix).

*I answer that,* As stated above (A. 1), the praise of the voice is necessary in order to arouse man's devotion towards God. Wherefore whatever is useful in conducing to this result is becomingly adopted in the divine praises. Now it is evident that the human soul is moved in various ways according to various melodies of sound, as the Philosopher state (Polit. viii, 5), and also Boethius (De Musica, prologue). Hence the use of music in the divine praises is a salutary institution, that the souls of the faint-hearted may be the more incited to devotion. Wherefore Augustine say (Confess. x, 33): "I am inclined to approve of the usage of singing in the church, that so by the delight of the ears the faint-hearted may rise to the feeling of devotion": and he says of himself (Confess. ix, 6): "I wept in Thy hymns and canticles, touched to the quick by the voices of Thy sweet-attuned Church."

Reply Obj. 1: The name of spiritual canticle may be given not only to those that are sung inwardly in spirit, but also to those that are sung outwardly with the lips, inasmuch as such like canticles arouse spiritual devotion.

Reply Obj. 2: Jerome does not absolutely condemn singing, but reproves those who sing theatrically in church not in order to arouse devotion, but in order to show off, or to provoke pleasure. Hence Augustine says (Confess. x, 33): "When it befalls me to be more moved by the voice than by the words sung, I confess to have sinned penally, and then had rather not hear the singer."

Reply Obj. 3: To arouse men to devotion by teaching and preaching is a more excellent way than by singing. Wherefore deacons and prelates, whom it becomes to incite men's minds towards God by means of preaching and teaching, ought not to be instant in singing, lest thereby they be withdrawn from greater things. Hence Gregory says (Regist. iv, ep. 44): "It is a most discreditable custom for those who have been raised to the diaconate to serve as choristers, for it behooves them to give their whole time to the duty of preaching and to taking charge of the alms."

Reply Obj. 4: As the Philosopher says (Polit. viii, 6), "Teaching should not be accompanied with a flute or any artificial instrument such as the harp or anything else of this kind: but only with such things as make good hearers." For such like musical instruments move the soul to pleasure rather than create a good disposition within it. In the Old Testament instruments of this description were employed, both because the people were more coarse and carnal—so that they needed to be aroused by such instruments as also by earthly promises—and because these material instruments were figures of something else.

Reply Obj. 5: The soul is distracted from that which is sung by a chant that is employed for the purpose of giving pleasure. But if the singer chant for the sake of devotion, he pays more attention to what he says, both because he lingers more thereon, and because, as Augustine remarks (Confess. x, 33), "each affection of our spirit, according to its variety, has its own appropriate measure in the voice, and singing, by some hidden correspondence wherewith it is stirred." The same applies to the hearers, for even if some of them understand not what is sung, yet they understand why it is sung, namely, for God's glory: and this is enough to arouse their devotion.

## QUESTION 92

OF SUPERSTITION (TWO ARTICLES)

In due sequence we must consider the vices that are opposed to religion. First we shall consider those which agree with religion in giving worship to God; secondly, we shall treat of those vices which are manifestly contrary to religion, through showing contempt of those things that pertain to the worship of God. The former come under the head of superstition, the latter under that of irreligion. Accordingly we must consider in the first place, superstition and its parts, and afterwards irreligion and its parts.

Under the first head there are two points of inquiry:

(1) Whether superstition is a vice opposed to religion?

(2) Whether it has several parts or species?

FIRST ARTICLE [II-II, Q. 92, Art. 1]

Whether Superstition Is a Vice Contrary to Religion?

Objection 1: It would seem that superstition is not a vice contrary to religion. One contrary is not included in the definition of the other. But religion is included in the definition of superstition: for the latter is defined as being "immoderate observance of religion," according to a gloss on Col. 2:23, "Which things have indeed a show of wisdom in superstition." Therefore superstition is not a vice contrary to religion.

Obj. 2: Further, Isidore says (Etym. x): "Cicero [*De Natura Deorum ii, 28] states that the superstitious were so called because they spent the day in praying and offering sacrifices that their children might survive ( *superstites* ) them." But this may be done even in accordance with true religious worship. Therefore superstition is not a vice opposed to religion.

Obj. 3: Further, superstition seems to denote an excess. But religion admits of no excess, since, as stated above (Q. 81, A. 5, ad 3), there is no possibility of rendering to God, by religion, the equal of what we owe Him. Therefore superstition is not a vice contrary to religion.

*On the contrary,* Augustine says (De Decem Chord. Serm. ix): "Thou strikest the first chord in the worship of one God, and the beast of superstition hath fallen." Now the worship of one God belongs to religion. Therefore superstition is contrary to religion.

*I answer that,* As stated above (Q. 81, A. 5), religion is a moral virtue. Now every moral virtue observes a mean, as stated above (I-II, Q. 64, A. 1). Therefore a twofold vice is opposed to a moral virtue; one by way of excess, the other by way of deficiency. Again, the mean of virtue may be exceeded, not only with regard to the circumstance called "how much," but also with regard to other circumstances: so that, in certain virtues such as magnanimity and magnificence; vice exceeds the mean of virtue, not through tending to something greater than the virtue, but possibly to something less, and yet it goes beyond the mean of virtue, through doing something to whom it ought not, or when it ought not, and in like manner as regards other circumstances, as the Philosopher shows (Ethic. iv, 1, 2, 3).

Accordingly superstition is a vice contrary to religion by excess, not that it offers more to the divine worship than true religion, but because it offers divine worship either to whom it ought not, or in a manner it ought not.

Reply Obj. 1: Just as we speak metaphorically of good among evil things—thus we speak of a good thief—so too sometimes the names of the virtues are employed by transposition in an evil sense. Thus prudence is sometimes used instead of cunning, according to Luke 16:8, "The children of this world are more prudent [Douay: 'wiser'] in their generation than the children of light." It is in this way that superstition is described as religion.

Reply Obj. 2: The etymology of a word differs from its meaning. For its etymology depends on what it is taken from for the purpose of signification: whereas its meaning depends on the thing to which it is applied for the purpose of signifying it. Now these things differ sometimes: for "lapis" (a stone) takes its name from hurting the foot ( *laedere pedem* ), but this is not its meaning, else iron, since it hurts the foot, would be a stone. In like manner it does not follow that "superstition" means that from which the word is derived.

Reply Obj. 3: Religion does not admit of excess, in respect of absolute quantity, but it does admit of excess in respect of proportionate quantity, in so far, to wit, as something may be done in divine worship that ought not to be done.

SECOND ARTICLE [II-II, Q. 92, Art. 2]

Whether There Are Various Species of Superstition?

Objection 1: It would seem that there are not various species of superstition. According to the Philosopher (Topic. i, 13), "if one contrary includes many kinds, so does the other." Now religion, to which superstition is contrary, does not include various species; but all its acts belong to the one species. Therefore neither has superstition various species.

Obj. 2: Further, opposites relate to one same thing. But religion, to which superstition is opposed, relates to those things whereby we are directed to God, as stated above (Q. 81, A. 1). Therefore superstition, which is opposed to religion, is not specified according to divinations of human occurrences, or by the observances of certain human actions.

Obj. 3: Further, a gloss on Col. 2:23, "Which things have ... a show of wisdom in superstition," adds: "that is to say in a hypocritical religion." Therefore hypocrisy should be reckoned a species of superstition.

*On the contrary,* Augustine assigns the various species of superstition (De Doctr. Christ. ii, 20).

*I answer that,* As stated above, sins against religion consist in going beyond the mean of virtue in respect of certain circumstances (A. 1). For as we have stated (I-II, Q. 72, A. 9), not every diversity of corrupt circumstances differentiates the species of a sin, but only that which is referred to diverse objects, for diverse ends: since it is in this respect that moral acts are diversified specifically, as stated above (I-II, Q. 1, A. 3; Q. 18, AA. 2, 6).

Accordingly the species of superstition are differentiated, first on the part of the mode, secondly on the part of the object. For the divine worship may be given either to whom it ought to be given, namely, to the true God, but *in an undue mode,* and this is the first species of superstition; or to whom it ought not to be given, namely, to any creature whatsoever, and this is another genus of superstition, divided into many species in respect of the various ends of divine worship. For the end of divine worship is in the first place to give reverence to God, and in this respect the first species of this genus is *idolatry,* which unduly gives divine honor to a creature. The second end of religion is that man may be taught by God Whom he worships; and to this must be referred *divinatory* superstition, which consults the demons through compacts made with them, whether tacit or explicit. Thirdly, the end of divine worship is a certain direction of human acts according to the precepts of God the object of that worship: and to this must be referred the superstition of certain *observances.*

Augustine alludes to these three (De Doctr. Christ. ii, 20), where he says that "anything invented by man for making and worshipping idols is superstitious," and this refers to the first species. Then he goes on to say, "or any agreement or covenant made with the demons for the purpose of consultation and of compact by tokens," which refers to the second species; and a little further on he adds: "To this kind belong all sorts of amulets and such like," and this refers to the third species.

Reply Obj. 1: As Dionysius says (Div. Nom. iv), "good results from a cause that is one and entire, whereas evil arises from each single defect." Wherefore several vices are opposed to one virtue, as stated above (A. 1; Q. 10, A. 5). The saying of the Philosopher is true of opposites wherein there is the same reason of multiplicity.

Reply Obj. 2: Divinations and certain observances come under the head of superstition, in so far as they depend on certain actions of the demons: and thus they pertain to compacts made with them.

Reply Obj. 3: Hypocritical religion is taken here for "religion as applied to human observances," as the gloss goes on to explain. Wherefore this hypocritical religion is nothing else than worship given to God in an undue mode: as, for instance, if a man were, in the time of grace, to wish to worship God according to the rite of the Old Law. It is of religion taken in this sense that the gloss speaks literally.

# QUESTION 93

OF SUPERSTITION CONSISTING IN UNDUE WORSHIP OF THE TRUE GOD (In Two Articles)

We must now consider the species of superstition. We shall treat (1) Of the superstition which consists in giving undue worship to the true God; (2) Of the superstition of idolatry; (3) of divinatory superstition; (4) of the superstition of observances.

Under the first head there are two points of inquiry:

(1) Whether there can be anything pernicious in the worship of the true God?

(2) Whether there can be anything superfluous therein?

FIRST ARTICLE [II-II, Q. 93, Art. 1]

Whether There Can Be Anything Pernicious in the Worship of the True God?

Objection 1: It would seem that there cannot be anything pernicious in the worship of the true God. It is written (Joel 2:32): "Everyone that shall call upon the name of the Lord shall be saved." Now whoever worships God calls upon His name. Therefore all worship of God is conducive to salvation, and consequently none is pernicious.

Obj. 2: Further, it is the same God that is worshiped by the just in any age of the world. Now before the giving of the Law the just worshiped God in whatever manner they pleased, without committing mortal sin: wherefore Jacob bound himself by his own vow to a special kind of worship, as related in Genesis 28. Therefore now also no worship of God is pernicious.

Obj. 3: Further, nothing pernicious is tolerated in the Church. Yet the Church tolerates various rites of divine worship: wherefore Gregory, replying to Augustine, bishop of the English (Regist. xi, ep. 64), who stated that there existed in the churches various customs in the celebration of Mass, wrote: "I wish you to choose carefully whatever you find likely to be most pleasing to God, whether in the Roman territory, or in the land of the Gauls, or in any part of the Church." Therefore no way of worshiping God is pernicious.

*On the contrary,* Augustine [*Jerome (Ep. lxxv, ad Aug.) See Opp. August. Ep. lxxxii] in a letter to Jerome (and the words are quoted in a gloss on Gal. 2:14) says that "after the Gospel truth had been preached the legal observances became deadly," and yet these observances belonged to the worship of God. Therefore there can be something deadly in the divine worship.

*I answer that,* As Augustine states (Cont. Mendac. xiv), "a most pernicious lie is that which is uttered in matters pertaining to Christian religion." Now it is a lie if one signify outwardly that which is contrary to the truth. But just as a thing is signified by word, so it is by deed: and it is in this signification by deed that the outward worship of religion consists, as shown above (Q. 81, A. 7). Consequently, if anything false is signified by outward worship, this worship will be pernicious.

Now this happens in two ways. In the first place, it happens on the part of the thing signified, through the worship signifying something discordant therefrom: and in this way, at the time of the New Law, the mysteries of Christ being already accomplished, it is pernicious to make use of the ceremonies of the Old Law whereby the mysteries of Christ were foreshadowed as things to come: just as it would be pernicious for anyone to declare that Christ has yet to suffer. In the second place, falsehood in outward worship occurs on the part of the worshiper, and especially in common worship which is offered by ministers impersonating the whole Church. For even as he would be guilty of falsehood who would, in the name of another person, proffer things that are not committed to him, so too does a man incur the guilt of falsehood who, on the part of the Church, gives worship to God contrary to the manner established by the Church or divine authority, and according to ecclesiastical custom. Hence Ambrose [*Comment. in 1 ad1 Cor. 11:27, quoted in the gloss of Peter Lombard] says: "He is unworthy who celebrates the mystery otherwise than Christ delivered it." For this reason, too, a gloss on Col. 2:23 says that superstition is "the use of human observances under the name of religion."

Reply Obj. 1: Since God is truth, to invoke God is to worship Him in spirit and truth, according to John 4:23. Hence a worship that contains falsehood, is inconsistent with a salutary calling upon God.

Reply Obj. 2: Before the time of the Law the just were instructed by an inward instinct as to the way of worshiping God, and others followed them. But afterwards men were instructed by outward precepts about this matter, and it is wicked to disobey them.

Reply Obj. 3: The various customs of the Church in the divine worship are in no way contrary to the truth: wherefore we must observe them, and to disregard them is unlawful.

SECOND ARTICLE [II-II, Q. 93, Art. 2]

Whether There Can Be Any Excess in the Worship of God?

Objection 1: It would seem that there cannot be excess in the worship of God. It is written (Ecclus. 43:32): "Glorify the Lord as much as ever you can, for He will yet far exceed." Now the divine worship is directed to the glorification of God. Therefore there can be no excess in it.

Obj. 2: Further, outward worship is a profession of inward worship, "whereby God is worshiped with faith, hope, and charity," as Augustine says (Enchiridion iii). Now there can be no excess in faith, hope, and charity. Neither, therefore, can there be in the worship of God.

Obj. 3: Further, to worship God consists in offering to Him what we have received from Him. But we have received all our goods from God. Therefore if we do all that we possibly can for God's honor, there will be no excess in the divine worship.

*On the contrary,* Augustine says (De Doctr. Christ. ii, 18) "that the good and true Christian rejects also superstitious fancies from Holy Writ." But Holy Writ teaches us to worship God. Therefore there can be superstition by reason of excess even in the worship of God.

*I answer that,* A thing is said to be in excess in two ways. First, with regard to absolute quantity, and in this way there cannot be excess in the worship of God, because whatever man does is less than he owes God. Secondly, a thing is in excess with regard to quantity of proportion, through not being proportionate to its end. Now the end of divine worship is that man may give glory to God, and submit to Him in mind and body. Consequently, whatever a man may do conducing to God's glory, and subjecting his mind to God, and his body, too, by a moderate curbing of the concupiscences, is not excessive in the divine worship, provided it be in accordance with the commandments of God and of the Church, and in keeping with the customs of those among whom he lives.

On the other hand if that which is done be, in itself, not conducive to God's glory, nor raise man's mind to God, nor curb inordinate concupiscence, or again if it be not in accordance with the commandments of God and of the Church, or if it be contrary to the general custom—which, according to Augustine [*Ad Casulan. Ep. xxxvi], "has the force of law"—all this must be reckoned excessive and superstitious, because consisting, as it does, of mere externals, it has no connection with the internal worship of God. Hence Augustine (De Vera Relig. iii) quotes the words of Luke 17:21, "The kingdom of God is within you," against the "superstitious," those, to wit, who pay more attention to externals.

Reply Obj. 1: The glorification of God implies that what is done is done for God's glory: and this excludes the excess denoted by superstition.

Reply Obj. 2: Faith, hope and charity subject the mind to God, so that there can be nothing excessive in them. It is different with external acts, which sometimes have no connection with these virtues.

Reply Obj. 3: This argument considers excess by way of absolute quantity.

# QUESTION 94

OF IDOLATRY (In Four Articles)

We must now consider idolatry: under which head there are four points of inquiry:

(1) Whether idolatry is a species of superstition?

(2) Whether it is a sin?

(3) Whether it is the gravest sin?

(4) Of the cause of this sin.

FIRST ARTICLE [II-II, Q. 94, Art. 1]

Whether Idolatry Is Rightly Reckoned a Species of Superstition?

Objection 1: It would seem that idolatry is not rightly reckoned a species of superstition. Just as heretics are unbelievers, so are idolaters. But heresy is a species of unbelief, as stated above (Q. 11, A. 1). Therefore idolatry is also a species of unbelief and not of superstition.

Obj. 2: Further, latria pertains to the virtue of religion to which superstition is opposed. But latria, apparently, is univocally applied to idolatry and to that which belongs to the true religion. For just as we speak univocally of the desire of false happiness, and of the desire of true happiness, so too, seemingly, we speak univocally of the worship of false gods, which is called idolatry, and of the worship of the true God, which is the latria of true religion. Therefore idolatry is not a species of superstition.

Obj. 3: Further, that which is nothing cannot be the species of any genus. But idolatry, apparently, is nothing: for the Apostle says (1 Cor. 8:4): "We know that an idol is nothing in the world," and fur ther on (1 Cor. 10:19): "What then? Do I say that what is offered in sacrifice to idols is anything? Or that the idol is anything?" implying an answer in the negative. Now offering things to idols belongs properly to idolatry. Therefore since idolatry is like to nothing, it cannot be a species of superstition.

Obj. 4: Further, it belongs to superstition to give divine honor to whom that honor is not due. Now divine honor is undue to idols, just as it is undue to other creatures, wherefore certain people are reproached (Rom. 1:25) for that they "worshipped and served the creature rather than the Creator." Therefore this species of superstition is unfittingly called idolatry, and should rather be named "worship of creatures."

*On the contrary,* It is related (Acts 17:16) that when Paul awaited Silas and Timothy at Athens, "his spirit was stirred within him seeing the whole city given to idolatry," and further on (Acts 17:22) he says: "Ye men of Athens, I perceive that in all things you are too superstitious." Therefore idolatry belongs to superstition.

*I answer that,* As stated above (Q. 92, A. 2), it belongs to superstition to exceed the due mode of divine worship, and this is done chiefly when divine worship is given to whom it should not be given. Now it should be given to the most high uncreated God alone, as stated above (Q. 81, A. 1) when we were treating of religion. Therefore it is superstition to give worship to any creature whatsoever.

Now just as this divine worship was given to sensible creatures by means of sensible signs, such as sacrifices, games, and the like, so too was it given to a creature represented by some sensible form or shape, which is called an "idol." Yet divine worship was given to idols in various ways. For some, by means of a nefarious art, constructed images which produced certain effects by the power of the demons: wherefore they deemed that the images themselves contained something God-like, and consequently that divine worship was due to them. This was the opinion of Hermes Trismegistus [*De Natura Deorum, ad Asclep.], as Augustine states (De Civ. Dei viii, 23): while others gave divine worship not to the images, but to the creatures represented thereby. The Apostle alludes to both of these (Rom. 1:23, 25). For, as regards the former, he says: "They changed the glory of the incorruptible God into the likeness of the image of a corruptible man, and of birds, and of four-footed beasts, and of creeping things," and of the latter he says: "Who worshipped and served the creature rather than the Creator."

These latter were of three ways of thinking. For some deemed certain men to have been gods, whom they worshipped in the images of those men: for instance, Jupiter, Mercury, and so forth. Others again deemed the whole world to be one god, not by reason of its material substance, but by reason of its soul, which they believed to be God, for they held God to be nothing else than a soul governing the world by movement and reason: even as a man is said to be wise in respect not of his body but of his soul. Hence they thought that divine worship ought to be given to the whole world and to all its parts, heaven, air, water, and to all such things: and to these they referred the names of their gods, as Varro asserted, and Augustine relates (De Civ. Dei vii, 5). Lastly, others, namely, the Platonists, said that there is one supreme god, the cause of all things. After him they placed certain spiritual substances created by the supreme god. These they called "gods," on account of their having a share of the godhead; but we call them "angels." After these they placed the souls of the heavenly bodies, and beneath these the demons which they stated to be certain animal denizens of the air, and beneath these again they placed human souls, which they believed to be taken up into the fellowship of the gods or of the demons by reason of the merit of their virtue. To all these they gave divine worship, as Augustine relates (De Civ . . Dei xviii, 14).

The last two opinions were held to belong to "natural theology" which the philosophers gathered from their study of the world and taught in the schools: while the other, relating to the worship of men, was said to belong to "mythical theology" which was wont to be represented on the stage according to the fancies of poets. The remaining opinion relating to images was held to belong to "civil theology," which was celebrated by the pontiffs in the temples [*De Civ. Dei vi, 5].

Now all these come under the head of the superstition of idolatry. Wherefore Augustine says (De Doctr. Christ. ii, 20): "Anything invented by man for making and worshipping idols, or for giving Divine worship to a creature or any part of a creature, is superstitious."

Reply Obj. 1: Just as religion is not faith, but a confession of faith by outward signs, so superstition is a confession of unbelief by external worship. Such a confession is signified by the term idolatry, but not by the term heresy, which only means a false opinion. Therefore heresy is a species of unbelief, but idolatry is a species of superstition.

Reply Obj. 2: The term latria may be taken in two senses. In one sense it may denote a human act pertaining to the worship of God: and then its signification remains the same, to whomsoever it be shown, because, in this sense, the thing to which it is shown is not included in its definition. Taken thus latria is applied univocally, whether to true religion or to idolatry, just as the payment of a tax is univocally the same, whether it is paid to the true or to a false king. In another sense latria denotes the same as religion, and then, since it is a virtue, it is essential thereto that divine worship be given to whom it ought to be given; and in this way latria is applied equivocally to the latria of true religion, and to idolatry: just as prudence is applied equivocally to the prudence that is a virtue, and to that which is carnal.

Reply Obj. 3: The saying of the Apostle that "an idol is nothing in the world" means that those images which were called idols, were not animated, or possessed of a divine power, as Hermes maintained, as though they were composed of spirit and body. In the same sense we must understand the saying that "what is offered in sacrifice to idols is not anything," because by being thus sacrificed the sacrificial flesh acquired neither sanctification, as the Gentiles thought, nor uncleanness, as the Jews held.

Reply Obj. 4: It was owing to the general custom among the Gentiles of worshipping any kind of creature under the form of images that the term "idolatry" was used to signify any worship of a creature, even without the use of images.

SECOND ARTICLE [II-II, Q. 94, Art. 2]

Whether Idolatry Is a Sin?

Objection 1: It would seem that idolatry is not a sin. Nothing is a sin that the true faith employs in worshipping God. Now the true faith employs images for the divine worship: since both in the Tabernacle were there images of the cherubim, as related in Ex. 25, and in the Church are images set up which the faithful worship. Therefore idolatry, whereby idols are worshipped, is not a sin.

Obj. 2: Further, reverence should be paid to every superior. But the angels and the souls of the blessed are our superiors. Therefore it will be no sin to pay them reverence by worship, of sacrifices or the like.

Obj. 3: Further, the most high God should be honored with an inward worship, according to John 4:24, "God ... they must adore ... in spirit and in truth": and Augustine says (Enchiridion iii), that "God is worshipped by faith, hope and charity." Now a man may happen to worship idols outwardly, and yet not wander from the true faith inwardly. Therefore it seems that we may worship idols outwardly without prejudice to the divine worship.

*On the contrary,* It is written (Ex. 20:5): "Thou shalt not adore them," i.e. outwardly, "nor serve them," i.e. inwardly, as a gloss explains it: and it is a question of graven things and images. Therefore it is a sin to worship idols whether outwardly or inwardly.

*I answer that,* There has been a twofold error in this matter. For some [*The School of Plato] have thought that to offer sacrifices and other things pertaining to latria, not only to God but also to the others aforesaid, is due and good in itself, since they held that divine honor should be paid to every superior nature, as being nearer to God. But this is unreasonable. For though we ought to revere all superiors, yet the same reverence is not due to them all: and something special is due to the most high God Who excels all in a singular manner: and this is the worship of latria.

Nor can it be said, as some have maintained, that "these visible sacrifices are fitting with regard to other gods, and that to the most high God, as being better than those others, better sacrifices, namely, the service of a pure mind, should be offered" [*Augustine, as quoted below]. The reason is that, as Augustine says (De Civ. Dei x, 19), "external sacrifices are signs of internal, just as audible words are signs of things. Wherefore, just as by prayer and praise we utter significant words to Him, and offer to Him in our hearts the things they signify, so too in our sacrifices we ought to realize that we should offer a visible sacrifice to no other than to Him Whose invisible sacrifice we ourselves should be in our hearts."

Others held that the outward worship of latria should be given to idols, not as though it were something good or fitting in itself, but as being in harmony with the general custom. Thus Augustine (De Civ. Dei vi, 10) quotes Seneca as saying: "We shall adore," says he, "in such a way as to remember that our worship is in accordance with custom rather than with the reality": and (De Vera Relig. v) Augustine says that "we must not seek religion from the philosophers, who accepted the same things for sacred, as did the people; and gave utterance in the schools to various and contrary opinions about the nature of their gods, and the sovereign good." This error was embraced also by certain heretics [*The Helcesaitae], who affirmed that it is not wrong for one who is seized in time of persecution to worship idols outwardly so long as he keeps the faith in his heart.

But this is evidently false. For since outward worship is a sign of the inward worship, just as it is a wicked lie to affirm the contrary of what one holds inwardly of the true faith so too is it a wicked falsehood to pay outward worship to anything counter to the sentiments of one's heart. Wherefore Augustine condemns Seneca (De Civ. Dei vi, 10) in that "his worship of idols was so much the more infamous forasmuch as the things he did dishonestly were so done by him that the people believed him to act honestly."

Reply Obj. 1: Neither in the Tabernacle or Temple of the Old Law, nor again now in the Church are images set up that the worship of latria may be paid to them, but for the purpose of signification, in order that belief in the excellence of angels and saints may be impressed and confirmed in the mind of man. It is different with the image of Christ, to which latria is due on account of His Divinity, as we shall state in the Third Part (Q. 25, A. 3).

The Replies to the Second and Third Objections are evident from what has been said above.

THIRD ARTICLE [II-II, Q. 94, Art. 3]

Whether Idolatry Is the Gravest of Sins?

Objection 1: It would seem that idolatry is not the gravest of sins. The worst is opposed to the best (Ethic. viii, 10). But interior worship, which consists of faith, hope and charity, is better than external worship. Therefore unbelief, despair and hatred of God, which are opposed to internal worship, are graver sins than idolatry, which is opposed to external worship.

Obj. 2: Further, the more a sin is against God the more grievous it is. Now, seemingly, a man acts more directly against God by blaspheming, or denying the faith, than by giving God's worship to another, which pertains to idolatry. Therefore blasphemy and denial of the faith are more grievous sins than idolatry.

Obj. 3: Further, it seems that lesser evils are punished with greater evils. But the sin of idolatry was punished with the sin against nature, as stated in Rom. 1:26. Therefore the sin against nature is a graver sin than idolatry.

Obj. 4: Further, Augustine says (Contra Faust. xx, 5): "Neither do we say that you," viz. the Manichees, "are pagans, or a sect of pagans, but that you bear a certain likeness to them since you worship many gods: and yet you are much worse than they are, for they worship things that exist, but should not be worshiped as gods, whereas you worship things that exist not at all." Therefore the vice of heretical depravity is more grievous than idolatry.

Obj. 5: Further, a gloss of Jerome on Gal. 4:9, "How turn you again to the weak and needy elements?" says: "The observance of the Law, to which they were then addicted, was a sin almost equal to the worship of idols, to which they had been given before their conversion." Therefore idolatry is not the most grievous sin.

*On the contrary,* A gloss on the saying of Lev. 15:25, about the uncleanness of a woman suffering from an issue of blood, says: "Every sin is an uncleanness of the soul, but especially idolatry."

*I answer that,* The gravity of a sin may be considered in two ways. First, on the part of the sin itself, and thus idolatry is the most grievous sin. For just as the most heinous crime in an earthly commonwealth would seem to be for a man to give royal honor to another than the true king, since, so far as he is concerned, he disturbs the whole order of the commonwealth, so, in sins that are committed against God, which indeed are the greater sins, the greatest of all seems to be for a man to give God's honor to a creature, since, so far as he is concerned, he sets up another God in the world, and lessens the divine sovereignty. Secondly, the gravity of a sin may be considered on the part of the sinner. Thus the sin of one that sins knowingly is said to be graver than the sin of one that sins through ignorance: and in this way nothing hinders heretics, if they knowingly corrupt the faith which they have received, from sinning more grievously than idolaters who sin through ignorance. Furthermore other sins may be more grievous on account of greater contempt on the part of the sinner.

Reply Obj. 1: Idolatry presupposes internal unbelief, and to this it adds undue worship. But in a case of external idolatry without internal unbelief, there is an additional sin of falsehood, as stated above (A. 2).

Reply Obj. 2: Idolatry includes a grievous blasphemy, inasmuch as it deprives God of the singleness of His dominion and denies the faith by deeds.

Reply Obj. 3: Since it is essential to punishment that it be against the will, a sin whereby another sin is punished needs to be more manifest, in order that it may make the man more hateful to himself and to others; but it need not be a more grievous sin: and in this way the sin against nature is less grievous than the sin of idolatry. But since it is more manifest, it is assigned as a fitting punishment of the sin of idolatry, in order that, as by idolatry man abuses the order of the divine honor, so by the sin against nature he may suffer confusion from the abuse of his own nature.

Reply Obj. 4: Even as to the genus of the sin, the Manichean heresy is more grievous than the sin of other idolaters, because it is more derogatory to the divine honor, since they set up two gods in opposition to one another, and hold many vain and fabulous fancies about God. It is different with other heretics, who confess their belief in one God and worship Him alone.

Reply Obj. 5: The observance of the Law during the time of grace is not quite equal to idolatry as to the genus of the sin, but almost equal, because both are species of pestiferous superstition.

FOURTH ARTICLE [II-II, Q. 94, Art. 4]

Whether the Cause of Idolatry Was on the Part of Man?

Objection 1: It would seem that the cause of idolatry was not on the part of man. In man there is nothing but either nature, virtue, or guilt. But the cause of idolatry could not be on the part of man's nature, since rather does man's natural reason dictate that there is one God, and that divine worship should not be paid to the dead or to inanimate beings. Likewise, neither could idolatry have its cause in man on the part of virtue, since "a good tree cannot bring forth evil fruit," according to Matt. 7:18: nor again could it be on the part of guilt, because, according to Wis. 14:27, "the worship of abominable idols is the cause and the beginning and end of all evil." Therefore idolatry has no cause on the part of man.

Obj. 2: Further, those things which have a cause in man are found among men at all times. Now idolatry was not always, but is stated [*Peter Comestor, Hist. Genes. xxxvii, xl] to have been originated either by Nimrod, who is related to have forced men to worship fire, or by Ninus, who caused the statue of his father Bel to be worshiped. Among the Greeks, as related by Isidore (Etym. viii, 11), Prometheus was the first to set up statues of men: and the Jews say that Ismael was the first to make idols of clay. Moreover, idolatry ceased to a great extent in the sixth age. Therefore idolatry had no cause on the part of man.

Obj. 3: Further, Augustine says (De Civ. Dei xxi, 6): "It was not possible to learn, for the first time, except from their" (i.e. the demons') "teaching, what each of them desired or disliked, and by what name to invite or compel him: so as to give birth to the magic arts and their professors": and the same observation seems to apply to idolatry. Therefore idolatry had no cause on the part of man.

*On the contrary,* It is written (Wis. 14:14): "By the vanity of men they," i.e. idols, "came into the world."

*I answer that,* Idolatry had a twofold cause. One was a dispositive cause; this was on the part of man, and in three ways. First, on account of his inordinate affections, forasmuch as he gave other men divine honor, through either loving or revering them too much. This cause is assigned (Wis. 14:15): "A father being afflicted with bitter grief, made to himself the image of his son, who was quickly taken away: and him who then had died as a man he began to worship as a god." The same passage goes on to say (Wis. 14:21) that "men serving either their affection, or their kings, gave the incommunicable name [Vulg.: 'names']," i.e. of the Godhead, "to stones and wood." Secondly, because man takes a natural pleasure in representations, as the Philosopher observes (Poet. iv), wherefore as soon as the uncultured man saw human images skillfully fashioned by the diligence of the craftsman, he gave them divine worship; hence it is written (Wis. 13:11-17): "If an artist, a carpenter, hath cut down a tree, proper for his use, in the wood ... and by the skill of his art fashioneth it, and maketh it like the image of a man ... and then maketh prayer to it, inquiring concerning his substance, and his children, or his marriage." Thirdly, on account of their ignorance of the true God, inasmuch as through failing to consider His excellence men gave divine worship to certain creatures, on account of their beauty or power, wherefore it is written (Wis. 13:1, 2): "All men ... neither by attending to the works have acknowledged who was the workman, but have imagined either the fire, or the wind, or the swift air, or the circle of the stars, or the great water, or the sun and the moon, to be the gods that rule the world."

The other cause of idolatry was completive, and this was on the part of the demons, who offered themselves to be worshipped by men, by giving answers in the idols, and doing things which to men seemed marvelous. Hence it is written (Ps. 95:5): "All the gods of the Gentiles are devils."

Reply Obj. 1: The dispositive cause of idolatry was, on the part of man, a defect of nature, either through ignorance in his intellect, or disorder in his affections, as stated above; and this pertains to guilt. Again, idolatry is stated to be the cause, beginning and end of all sin, because there is no kind of sin that idolatry does not produce at some time, either through leading expressly to that sin by causing it, or through being an occasion thereof, either as a beginning or as an end, in so far as certain sins were employed in the worship of idols; such as homicides, mutilations, and so forth. Nevertheless certain sins may precede idolatry and dispose man thereto.

Reply Obj. 2: There was no idolatry in the first age, owing to the recent remembrance of the creation of the world, so that man still retained in his mind the knowledge of one God. In the sixth age idolatry was banished by the doctrine and power of Christ, who triumphed over the devil.

Reply Obj. 3: This argument considers the consummative cause of idolatry.

# QUESTION 95

OF SUPERSTITION IN DIVINATIONS (In Eight Articles)

We must now consider superstition in divinations, under which head there are eight points of inquiry:

(1) Whether divination is a sin?

(2) Whether it is a species of superstition?

(3) Of the species of divination;

(4) Of divination by means of demons;

(5) Of divination by the stars;

(6) Of divination by dreams;

(7) Of divination by auguries and like observances;

(8) Of divination by lots.

FIRST ARTICLE [II-II, Q. 95, Art. 1]

Whether Divination Is a Sin?

Objection 1: It would seem that divination is not a sin. Divination is derived from something *divine:* and things that are divine pertain to holiness rather than to sin. Therefore it seems that divination is not a sin.

Obj. 2: Further, Augustine says (De Lib. Arb. i, 1): "Who dares to say that learning is an evil?" and again: "I could nowise admit that intelligence can be an evil." But some arts are divinatory, as the Philosopher states (De Memor. i): and divination itself would seem to pertain to a certain intelligence of the truth. Therefore it seems that divination is not a sin.

Obj. 3: Further, there is no natural inclination to evil; because nature inclines only to its like. But men by natural inclination seek to foreknow future events; and this belongs to divination. Therefore divination is not a sin.

*On the contrary,* It is written (Deut. 18:10, 11): "Neither let there be found among you ... any one that consulteth pythonic spirits, or fortune tellers": and it is stated in the Decretals (26, qu. v, can. Qui divinationes): "Those who seek for divinations shall be liable to a penance of five years' duration, according to the fixed grades of penance."

*I answer that,* Divination denotes a foretelling of the future. The future may be foreknown in two ways: first in its causes, secondly in itself. Now the causes of the future are threefold: for some produce their effects, of necessity and always; and such like future effects can be foreknown and foretold with certainty, from considering their causes, even as astrologers foretell a coming eclipse. Other causes produce their effects, not of necessity and always, but for the most part, yet they rarely fail: and from such like causes their future effects can be foreknown, not indeed with certainty, but by a kind of conjecture, even as astrologers by considering the stars can foreknow and foretell things concerning rains and droughts, and physicians, concerning health and death. Again, other causes, considered in themselves, are indifferent; and this is chiefly the case in the rational powers, which stand in relation to opposites, according to the Philosopher [*Metaph. viii, 2, 5, 8]. Such like effects, as also those which ensue from natural causes by chance and in the minority of instances, cannot be foreknown from a consideration of their causes, because these causes have no determinate inclination to produce these effects. Consequently such like effects cannot be foreknown unless they be considered in themselves. Now man cannot consider these effects in themselves except when they are present, as when he sees Socrates running or walking: the consideration of such things in themselves before they occur is proper to God, Who alone in His eternity sees the future as though it were present, as stated in the First Part (Q. 14, A. 13; Q. 57, A. 3; Q. 86, A. 4). Hence it is written (Isa. 41:23): "Show the things that are to come hereafter, and we shall know that ye are gods." Therefore if anyone presume to foreknow or foretell such like future things by any means whatever, except by divine revelation, he manifestly usurps what belongs to God. It is for this reason that certain men are called divines: wherefore Isidore says (Etym. viii, 9): "They are called divines, as though they were full of God. For they pretend to be filled with the Godhead, and by a deceitful fraud they forecast the future to men."

Accordingly it is not called divination, if a man foretells things that happen of necessity, or in the majority of instances, for the like can be foreknown by human reason: nor again if anyone knows other contingent future things, through divine revelation: for then he does not divine, i.e. cause something divine, but rather receives something divine. Then only is a man said to divine, when he usurps to himself, in an undue manner, the foretelling of future events: and this is manifestly a sin. Consequently divination is always a sin; and for this reason Jerome says in his commentary on Mic. 3:9, seqq. that "divination is always taken in an evil sense."

Reply Obj. 1: Divination takes its name not from a rightly ordered share of something divine, but from an undue usurpation thereof, as stated above.

Reply Obj. 2: There are certain arts for the foreknowledge of future events that occur of necessity or frequently, and these do not pertain to divination. But there are no true arts or sciences for the knowledge of other future events, but only vain inventions of the devil's deceit, as Augustine says (De Civ. Dei xxi, 8).

Reply Obj. 3: Man has a natural inclination to know the future by human means, but not by the undue means of divination.

SECOND ARTICLE [II-II, Q. 95, Art. 2]

Whether Divination Is a Species of Superstition?

Objection 1: It would seem that divination is not a species of superstition. The same thing cannot be a species of diverse genera. Now divination is apparently a species of curiosity, according to Augustine (De Vera Relig. xxxviii) [*Cf. De Doctr. Christ. ii, 23, 24; De Divin. Daem. 3]. Therefore it is not, seemingly, a species of superstition.

Obj. 2: Further, just as religion is due worship, so is superstition undue worship. But divination does not seem to pertain to undue worship. Therefore it does not pertain to superstition.

Obj. 3: Further, superstition is opposed to religion. But in true religion nothing is to be found corresponding as a contrary to divination. Therefore divination is not a species of superstition.

*On the contrary,* Origen says in his Peri Archon [*The quotation is from his sixteenth homily on the Book of Numbers]: "There is an operation of the demons in the administering of foreknowledge, comprised, seemingly, under the head of certain arts exercised by those who have enslaved themselves to the demons, by means of lots, omens, or the observance of shadows. I doubt not that all these things are done by the operation of the demons." Now, according to Augustine (De Doctr. Christ. ii, 20, 23), "whatever results from fellowship between demons and men is superstitious." Therefore divination is a species of superstition.

*I answer that,* As stated above (A. 1; QQ. 92, 94), superstition denotes undue divine worship. Now a thing pertains to the worship of God in two ways: in one way, it is something offered to God; as a sacrifice, an oblation, or something of the kind: in another way, it is something divine that is assumed, as stated above with regard to an oath (Q. 89, A. 4, ad 2). Wherefore superstition includes not only idolatrous sacrifices offered to demons, but also recourse to the help of the demons for the purpose of doing or knowing something. But all divination results from the demons' operation, either because the demons are expressly invoked that the future may be made known, or because the demons thrust themselves into futile searchings of the future, in order to entangle men's minds with vain conceits. Of this kind of vanity it is written (Ps. 39:5): "Who hath not regard to vanities and lying follies." Now it is vain to seek knowledge of the future, when one tries to get it from a source whence it cannot be foreknown. Therefore it is manifest that divination is a species of superstition.

Reply Obj. 1: Divination is a kind of curiosity with regard to the end in view, which is foreknowledge of the future; but it is a kind of superstition as regards the mode of operation.

Reply Obj. 2: This kind of divination pertains to the worship of the demons, inasmuch as one enters into a compact, tacit or express with the demons.

Reply Obj. 3: In the New Law man's mind is restrained from solicitude about temporal things: wherefore the New Law contains no institution for the foreknowledge of future events in temporal matters. On the other hand in the Old Law, which contained earthly promises, there were consultations about the future in connection with religious matters. Hence where it is written (Isa. 8:19): "And when they shall say to you: Seek of pythons and of diviners, who mutter in their enchantments," it is added by way of answer: "Should not the people seek of their God, a vision for the living and the dead? [*Vulg.: 'seek of their God, for the living of the dead?']"

In the New Testament, however, there were some possessed of the spirit of prophecy, who foretold many things about future events.

THIRD ARTICLE [II-II, Q. 95, Art. 3]

Whether We Ought to Distinguish Several Species of Divination?

Objection 1: It would seem that we should not distinguish several species of divination. Where the formality of sin is the same, there are not seemingly several species of sin. Now there is one formality of sin in all divinations, since they consist in entering into compact with the demons in order to know the future. Therefore there are not several species of divination.

Obj. 2: Further, a human act takes its species from its end, as stated above (I-II, Q. 1, A. 3; Q. 18, A. 6). But all divination is directed to one end, namely, the foretelling of the future. Therefore all divinations are of one species.

Obj. 3: Further, signs do not vary the species of a sin, for whether one detracts by word, writing or gestures, it is the same species of sin. Now divinations seem to differ merely according to the various signs whence the foreknowledge of the future is derived. Therefore there are not several species of divination.

*On the contrary,* Isidore enumerates various species of divination (Etym. viii, 9).

*I answer that,* As stated above (A. 2), all divinations seek to acquire foreknowledge of future events, by means of some counsel and help of a demon, who is either expressly called upon to give his help, or else thrusts himself in secretly, in order to foretell certain future things unknown to men, but known to him in such manners as have been explained in the First Part (Q. 57, A. 3). When demons are expressly invoked, they are wont to foretell the future in many ways. Sometimes they offer themselves to human sight and hearing by mock apparitions in order to foretell the future: and this species is called "prestigiation" because man's eyes are blindfolded ( *praestringuntur* ). Sometimes they make use of dreams, and this is called "divination by dreams": sometimes they employ apparitions or utterances of the dead, and this species is called "necromancy," for as Isidore observes (Etym. viii) in Greek, " *nekron* means dead, and *manteia* divination, because after certain incantations and the sprinkling of blood, the dead seem to come to life, to divine and to answer questions." Sometimes they foretell the future through living men, as in the case of those who are possessed: this is divination by "pythons," of whom Isidore says that "pythons are so called from Pythius Apollo, who was said to be the inventor of divination." Sometimes they foretell the future by means of shapes or signs which appear in inanimate beings. If these signs appear in some earthly body such as wood, iron or polished stone, it is called "geomancy," if in water "hydromancy," if in the air "aeromancy," if in fire "pyromancy," if in the entrails of animals sacrificed on the altars of demons, "aruspicy."

The divination which is practiced without express invocation of the demons is of two kinds. The first is when, with a view to obtain knowledge of the future, we take observations in the disposition of certain things. If one endeavor to know the future by observing the position and movements of the stars, this belongs to "astrologers," who are also called "genethliacs," because they take note of the days on which people are born. If one observe the movements and cries of birds or of any animals, or the sneezing of men, or the sudden movements of limbs, this belongs in general to "augury," which is so called from the chattering of birds ( *avium garritu* ), just as "auspice" is derived from watching birds ( *avium inspectione* ). These are chiefly wont to be observed in birds, the former by the ear, the latter by the eye. If, however, these observations have for their object men's words uttered unintentionally, which someone twist so as to apply to the future that he wishes to foreknow, then it is called an "omen": and as Valerius Maximus [*De Dict. Fact. Memor. i, 5] remarks, "the observing of omens has a touch of religion mingled with it, for it is believed to be founded not on a chance movement, but on divine providence. It was thus that when the Romans were deliberating whether they would change their position, a centurion happened to exclaim at the time: 'Standard-bearer, fix the banner, we had best stand here': and on hearing these words they took them as an omen, and abandoned their intention of advancing further." If, however, the observation regards the dispositions, that occur to the eye, of figures in certain bodies, there will be another species of divination: for the divination that is taken from observing the lines of the hand is called "chiromancy," i.e. divination of the hand (because *cheir* is the Greek for hand): while the divination which is taken from signs appearing in the shoulder-blades of an animal is called "spatulamancy."

To this second species of divination, which is without express invocation of the demons, belongs that which is practiced by observing certain things done seriously by men in the research of the occult, whether by drawing lots, which is called "geomancy"; or by observing the shapes resulting from molten lead poured into water; or by observing which of several sheets of paper, with or without writing upon them, a person may happen to draw; or by holding out several unequal sticks and noting who takes the greater or the lesser, or by throwing dice, and observing who throws the highest score; or by observing what catches the eye when one opens a book, all of which are named "sortilege."

Accordingly it is clear that there are three kinds of divination. The first is when the demons are invoked openly, this comes under the head of "necromancy"; the second is merely an observation of the disposition or movement of some other being, and this belongs to "augury"; while the third consists in doing something in order to discover the occult; and this belongs to "sortilege." Under each of these many others are contained, as explained above.

Reply Obj. 1: In all the aforesaid there is the same general, but not the same special, character of sin: for it is much more grievous to invoke the demons than to do things that deserve the demons' interference.

Reply Obj. 2: Knowledge of the future or of the occult is the ultimate end whence divination takes its general formality. But the various species are distinguished by their proper objects or matters, according as the knowledge of the occult is sought in various things.

Reply Obj. 3: The things observed by diviners are considered by them, not as signs expressing what they already know, as happens in detraction, but as principles of knowledge. Now it is evident that diversity of principles diversifies the species, even in demonstrative sciences.

FOURTH ARTICLE [II-II, Q. 95, Art. 4]

Whether Divination Practiced by Invoking the Demons Is Unlawful?

Objection 1: It would seem that divination practiced by invoking the demons is not unlawful. Christ did nothing unlawful, according to 1 Pet. 2:22, "Who did no sin." Yet our Lord asked the demon: "What is thy name?" and the latter replied: "My name is Legion, for we are many" (Mk. 5:9). Therefore it seems lawful to question the demons about the occult.

Obj. 2: Further, the souls of the saints do not encourage those who ask unlawfully. Yet Samuel appeared to Saul when the latter inquired of the woman that had a divining spirit, concerning the issue of the coming war (1 Kings 28:8, sqq.). Therefore the divination that consists in questioning demons is not unlawful.

Obj. 3: Further, it seems lawful to seek the truth from one who knows, if it be useful to know it. But it is sometimes useful to know what is hidden from us, and can be known through the demons, as in the discovery of thefts. Therefore divination by questioning demons is not unlawful.

*On the contrary,* It is written (Deut. 18:10, 11): "Neither let there there be found among you ... anyone that consulteth soothsayers ... nor ... that consulteth pythonic spirits."

*I answer that,* All divination by invoking demons is unlawful for two reasons. The first is gathered from the principle of divination, which is a compact made expressly with a demon by the very fact of invoking him. This is altogether unlawful; wherefore it is written against certain persons (Isa. 28:15): "You have said: We have entered into a league with death, and we have made a covenant with hell." And still more grievous would it be if sacrifice were offered or reverence paid to the demon invoked. The second reason is gathered from the result. For the demon who intends man's perdition endeavors, by his answers, even though he sometimes tells the truth, to accustom men to believe him, and so to lead him on to something prejudicial to the salvation of mankind. Hence Athanasius, commenting on the words of Luke 4:35, "He rebuked him, saying: Hold thy peace," says: "Although the demon confessed the truth, Christ put a stop to his speech, lest together with the truth he should publish his wickedness and accustom us to care little for such things, however much he may seem to speak the truth. For it is wicked, while we have the divine Scriptures, to seek knowledge from the demons."

Reply Obj. 1: According to Bede's commentary on Luke 8:30, "Our Lord inquired, not through ignorance, but in order that the disease, which he tolerated, being made public, the power of the Healer might shine forth more graciously." Now it is one thing to question a demon who comes to us of his own accord (and it is lawful to do so at times for the good of others, especially when he can be compelled, by the power of God, to tell the truth) and another to invoke a demon in order to gain from him knowledge of things hidden from us.

Reply Obj. 2: According to Augustine (Ad Simplic. ii, 3), "there is nothing absurd in believing that the spirit of the just man, being about to smite the king with the divine sentence, was permitted to appear to him, not by the sway of magic art or power, but by some occult dispensation of which neither the witch nor Saul was aware. Or else the spirit of Samuel was not in reality aroused from his rest, but some phantom or mock apparition formed by the machinations of the devil, and styled by Scripture under the name of Samuel, just as the images of things are wont to be called by the names of those things."

Reply Obj. 3: No temporal utility can compare with the harm to spiritual health that results from the research of the unknown by invoking the demon.

FIFTH ARTICLE [II-II, Q. 95, Art. 5]

Whether Divination by the Stars Is Unlawful?

Objection 1: It would seem that divination by the stars is not unlawful. It is lawful to foretell effects by observing their causes: thus a physician foretells death from the disposition of the disease. Now the heavenly bodies are the cause of what takes place in the world, according to Dionysius (Div. Nom. iv). Therefore divination by the stars is not unlawful.

Obj. 2: Further, human science originates from experiments, according to the Philosopher (Metaph. i, 1). Now it has been discovered through many experiments that the observation of the stars is a means whereby some future events may be known beforehand. Therefore it would seem not unlawful to make use of this kind of divination.

Obj. 3: Further, divination is declared to be unlawful in so far as it is based on a compact made with the demons. But divination by the stars contains nothing of the kind, but merely an observation of God's creatures. Therefore it would seem that this species of divination is not unlawful.

*On the contrary,* Augustine says (Confess. iv, 3): "Those astrologers whom they call mathematicians, I consulted without scruple; because they seemed to use no sacrifice, nor to pray to any spirit for their divinations which art, however, Christian and true piety rejects and condemns."

*I answer that,* As stated above (AA. 1, 2), the operation of the demon thrusts itself into those divinations which are based on false and vain opinions, in order that man's mind may become entangled in vanity and falsehood. Now one makes use of a vain and false opinion if, by observing the stars, one desires to foreknow the future that cannot be forecast by their means. Wherefore we must consider what things can be foreknown by observing the stars: and it is evident that those things which happen of necessity can be foreknown by this means: even so astrologers forecast a future eclipse.

However, with regard to the foreknowledge of future events acquired by observing the stars there have been various opinions. For some have stated that the stars signify rather than cause the things foretold by means of their observation. But this is an unreasonable statement: since every corporeal sign is either the effect of that for which it stands (thus smoke signifies fire whereby it is caused), or it proceeds from the same cause, so that by signifying the cause, in consequence it signifies the effect (thus a rainbow is sometimes a sign of fair weather, in so far as its cause is the cause of fair weather). Now it cannot be said that the dispositions and movements of the heavenly bodies are the effect of future events; nor again can they be ascribed to some common higher cause of a corporeal nature, although they are referable to a common higher cause, which is divine providence. On the contrary the appointment of the movements and positions of the heavenly bodies by divine providence is on a different principle from the appointment of the occurrence of future contingencies, because the former are appointed on a principle of necessity, so that they always occur in the same way, whereas the latter are appointed on a principle of contingency, so that the manner of their occurrence is variable. Consequently it is impossible to acquire foreknowledge of the future from an observation of the stars, except in so far as effects can be foreknown from their causes.

Now two kinds of effects escape the causality of heavenly bodies. In the first place all effects that occur accidentally, whether in human affairs or in the natural order, since, as it is proved in *Metaph.* vi [*Ed. Did. v, 3], an accidental being has no cause, least of all a natural cause, such as is the power of a heavenly body, because what occurs accidentally, neither is a *being* properly speaking, nor is *one* — for instance, that an earthquake occur when a stone falls, or that a treasure be discovered when a man digs a grave—for these and like occurrences are not one thing, but are simply several things. Whereas the operation of nature has always some one thing for its term, just as it proceeds from some one principle, which is the form of a natural thing.

In the second place, acts of the free-will, which is the faculty of will and reason, escape the causality of heavenly bodies. For the intellect or reason is not a body, nor the act of a bodily organ, and consequently neither is the will, since it is in the reason, as the Philosopher shows (De Anima iii, 4, 9). Now no body can make an impression on an incorporeal body. Wherefore it is impossible for heavenly bodies to make a direct impression on the intellect and will: for this would be to deny the difference between intellect and sense, with which position Aristotle reproaches (De Anima iii, 3) those who held that "such is the will of man, as is the day which the father of men and of gods," i.e. the sun or the heavens, "brings on" [*Odyssey xviii, 135].

Hence the heavenly bodies cannot be the direct cause of the free-will's operations. Nevertheless they can be a dispositive cause of an inclination to those operations, in so far as they make an impression on the human body, and consequently on the sensitive powers which are acts of bodily organs having an inclination for human acts. Since, however, the sensitive powers obey reason, as the Philosopher shows (De Anima iii, 11; *Ethic.* i, 13), this does not impose any necessity on the free-will, and man is able, by his reason, to act counter to the inclination of the heavenly bodies.

Accordingly if anyone take observation of the stars in order to foreknow casual or fortuitous future events, or to know with certitude future human actions, his conduct is based on a false and vain opinion; and so the operation of the demon introduces itself therein, wherefore it will be a superstitious and unlawful divination. On the other hand if one were to apply the observation of the stars in order to foreknow those future things that are caused by heavenly bodies, for instance, drought or rain and so forth, it will be neither an unlawful nor a superstitious divination.

Wherefore the Reply to the First Objection is evident.

Reply Obj. 2: That astrologers not unfrequently forecast the truth by observing the stars may be explained in two ways. First, because a great number of men follow their bodily passions, so that their actions are for the most part disposed in accordance with the inclination of the heavenly bodies: while there are few, namely, the wise alone, who moderate these inclinations by their reason. The result is that astrologers in many cases foretell the truth, especially in public occurrences which depend on the multitude. Secondly, because of the interference of the demons. Hence Augustine says (Gen. ad lit. ii, 17): "When astrologers tell the truth, it must be allowed that this is due to an instinct that, unknown to man, lies hidden in his mind. And since this happens through the action of unclean and lying spirits who desire to deceive man for they are permitted to know certain things about temporal affairs." Wherefore he concludes: "Thus a good Christian should beware of astrologers, and of all impious diviners, especially of those who tell the truth, lest his soul become the dupe of the demons and by making a compact of of partnership with them enmesh itself in their fellowship."

This suffices for the Reply to the Third Objection.

SIXTH ARTICLE [II-II, Q. 95, Art. 6]

Whether Divination by Dreams Is Unlawful?

Objection 1: It would seem that divination by dreams is not unlawful. It is not unlawful to make use of divine instruction. Now men are instructed by God in dreams, for it is written (Job 33:15, 16): "By a dream in a vision by night, when deep sleep falleth upon men, and they are sleeping in their beds, then He," God to wit, "openeth the ears of men, and teaching instructeth them in what they are to learn." Therefore it is not unlawful to make use of divination by dreams.

Obj. 2: Further, those who interpret dreams, properly speaking, make use of divination by dreams. Now we read of holy men interpreting dreams: thus Joseph interpreted the dreams of Pharaoh's butler and of his chief baker (Gen. 40), and Daniel interpreted the dream of the king of Babylon (Dan. 2, 4). Therefore divination by dreams is not unlawful.

Obj. 3: Further, it is unreasonable to deny the common experiences of men. Now it is the experience of all that dreams are significative of the future. Therefore it is useless to deny the efficacy of dreams for the purpose of divination, and it is lawful to listen to them.

*On the contrary,* It is written (Deut. 18:10): "Neither let there be found among you any one that ... observeth dreams."

*I answer that,* As stated above (AA. 2, 6), divination is superstitious and unlawful when it is based on a false opinion. Wherefore we must consider what is true in the matter of foreknowing the future from dreams. Now dreams are sometimes the cause of future occurrences; for instance, when a person's mind becomes anxious through what it has seen in a dream and is thereby led to do something or avoid something: while sometimes dreams are signs of future happenings, in so far as they are referable to some common cause of both dreams and future occurrences, and in this way the future is frequently known from dreams. We must, then, consider what is the cause of dreams, and whether it can be the cause of future occurrences, or be cognizant of them.

Accordingly it is to be observed that the cause of dreams is sometimes in us and sometimes outside us. The inward cause of dreams is twofold: one regards the soul, in so far as those things which have occupied a man's thoughts and affections while awake recur to his imagination while asleep. A such like cause of dreams is not a cause of future occurrences, so that dreams of this kind are related accidentally to future occurrences, and if at any time they concur it will be by chance. But sometimes the inward cause of dreams regards the body: because the inward disposition of the body leads to the formation of a movement in the imagination consistent with that disposition; thus a man in whom there is abundance of cold humors dreams that he is in the water or snow: and for this reason physicians say that we should take note of dreams in order to discover internal dispositions.

In like manner the outward cause of dreams is

twofold, corporal and spiritual. It is corporal in so far as the sleeper's imagination is affected either by the surrounding air, or through an impression of a heavenly body, so that certain images appear to the sleeper, in keeping with the disposition of the heavenly bodies. The spiritual cause is sometimes referable to God, Who reveals certain things to men in their dreams by the ministry of the angels, according Num. 12:6, "If there be among you a prophet of the Lord, I will appear to him in a vision, or I will speak to him in a dream." Sometimes, however, it is due to the action of the demons that certain images appear to persons in their sleep, and by this means they, at times, reveal certain future things to those who have entered into an unlawful compact with them.

Accordingly we must say that there is no unlawful divination in making use of dreams for the foreknowledge of the future, so long as those dreams are due to divine revelation, or to some natural cause inward or outward, and so far as the efficacy of that cause extends. But it will be an unlawful and superstitious divination if it be caused by a revelation of the demons, with whom a compact has been made, whether explicit, through their being invoked for the purpose, or implicit, through the divination extending beyond its possible limits.

This suffices for the Replies to the Objections.

SEVENTH ARTICLE [II-II, Q. 95, Art. 7]

Whether Divination by Auguries, Omens, and by Like Observations of External Things Is Unlawful?

Objection 1: It would seem that divination by auguries, omens, and by like observations of external things is not unlawful. If it were unlawful holy men would not make use thereof. Now we read of Joseph that he paid attention to auguries, for it is related (Gen. 44:5) that Joseph's steward said: "The cup which you have stolen is that in which my lord drinketh and in which he is wont to divine ( *augurari* )": and he himself afterwards said to his brethren (Gen. 44:15): "Know you not that there is no one like me in the science of divining?" Therefore it is not unlawful to make use of this kind of divination.

Obj. 2: Further, birds naturally know certain things regarding future occurrences of the seasons, according to Jer. 8:7, "The kite in the air hath known her time; the turtle, the swallow, and the stork have observed the time of their coming." Now natural knowledge is infallible and comes from God. Therefore it seems not unlawful to make use of the birds' knowledge in order to know the future, and this is divination by augury.

Obj. 3: Further, Gedeon is numbered among the saints (Heb. 11:32). Yet Gedeon made use of an omen, when he listened to the relation and interpreting of a dream (Judges 7:15): and Eliezer, Abraham's servant, acted in like manner (Gen. 24). Therefore it seems that this kind of divination is not unlawful.

*On the contrary,* It is written (Deut. 18:10): "Neither let there be found among you anyone ... that observeth omens."

*I answer that,* The movements or cries of birds, and whatever dispositions one may consider in such things, are manifestly not the cause of future events: wherefore the future cannot be known therefrom as from its cause. It follows therefore that if anything future can be known from them, it will be because the causes from which they proceed are also the causes of future occurrences or are cognizant of them. Now the cause of dumb animals' actions is a certain instinct whereby they are inclined by a natural movement, for they are not masters of their actions. This instinct may proceed from a twofold cause. In the first place it may be due to a bodily cause. For since dumb animals have naught but a sensitive soul, every power of which is the act of a bodily organ, their soul is subject to the disposition of surrounding bodies, and primarily to that of the heavenly bodies. Hence nothing prevents some of their actions from being signs of the future, in so far as they are conformed to the dispositions of the heavenly bodies and of the surrounding air, to which certain future events are due. Yet in this matter we must observe two things: first, that such observations must not be applied to the foreknowledge of future things other than those which can be foreknown from the movements of heavenly bodies, as stated above (AA. 5, 6): secondly, that they be not applied to other matters than those which in some way may have reference to these animals (since they acquire through the heavenly bodies a certain natural knowledge and instinct about things necessary for their life—such as changes resulting from rain and wind and so forth).

In the second place, this instinct is produced by a spiritual cause, namely, either by God, as may be seen in the dove that descended upon Christ, the raven that fed Elias, and the whale that swallowed and vomited Jonas, or by demons, who make use of these actions of dumb animals in order to entangle our minds with vain opinions. This seems to be true of all such like things; except omens, because human words which are taken for an omen are not subject to the disposition of the stars, yet are they ordered according to divine providence and sometimes according to the action of the demons.

Accordingly we must say that all such like divinations are superstitious and unlawful, if they be extended beyond the limits set according to the order of nature or of divine providence.

Reply Obj. 1: According to Augustine [*QQ. in Genes., qu. cxlv], when Joseph said that there was no one like him in the science of divining, he spoke in joke and not seriously, referring perhaps to the common opinion about him: in this sense also spoke his steward.

Reply Obj. 2: The passage quoted refers to the knowledge that birds have about things concerning them; and in order to know these things it is not unlawful to observe their cries and movements: thus from the frequent cawing of crows one might say that it will rain soon.

Reply Obj. 3: Gedeon listened to the recital and interpretation of a dream, seeing therein an omen, ordered by divine providence for his instruction. In like manner Eliezer listened to the damsel's words, having previously prayed to God.

EIGHTH ARTICLE [II-II, Q. 95, Art. 8]

Whether Divination by Drawing Lots Is Unlawful?

Objection 1: It would seem that divination by drawing lots is not unlawful, because a gloss of Augustine on Ps. 30:16, "My lots are in Thy hands," says: "It is not wrong to cast lots, for it is a means of ascertaining the divine will when a man is in doubt."

Obj. 2: There is, seemingly, nothing unlawful in the observances which the Scriptures relate as being practiced by holy men. Now both in the Old and in the New Testament we find holy men practicing the casting of lots. For it is related (Jos. 7:14, sqq.) that Josue, at the Lord's command, pronounced sentence by lot on Achan who had stolen of the anathema. Again Saul, by drawing lots, found that his son Jonathan had eaten honey (1 Kings 14:58, sqq.): Jonas, when fleeing from the face of the Lord, was discovered and thrown into the sea (Jonah 1:7, sqq.): Zacharias was chosen by lot to offer incense (Luke 1:9): and the apostles by drawing lots elected Matthias to the apostleship (Acts 1:26). Therefore it would seem that divination by lots is not unlawful.

Obj. 3: Further, fighting with the fists, or "monomachy," i.e. single combat as it is called, and trial by fire and water, which are called "popular" trials, seem to come under the head of sortilege, because something unknown is sought by their means. Yet these practices seem to be lawful, because David is related to have engaged in single combat with the Philistine (1 Kings 17:32, sqq.). Therefore it would seem that divination by lot is not unlawful.

*On the contrary,* It is written in the Decretals (XXVI, qu. v, can. Sortes): "We decree that the casting of lots, by which means you make up your mind in all your undertakings, and which the Fathers have condemned, is nothing but divination and witchcraft. For which reason we wish them to be condemned altogether, and henceforth not to be mentioned among Christians, and we forbid the practice thereof under pain of anathema."

*I answer that,* As stated above (A. 3), sortilege consists, properly speaking, in doing something, that by observing the result one may come to the knowledge of something unknown. If by casting lots one seeks to know what is to be given to whom, whether it be a possession, an honor, a dignity, a punishment, or some action or other, it is called "sortilege of allotment"; if one seeks to know what ought to be done, it is called "sortilege of consultation"; if one seeks to know what is going to happen, it is called "sortilege of divination." Now the actions of man that are required for sortilege and their results are not subject to the dispositions of the stars. Wherefore if anyone practicing sortilege is so minded as though the human acts requisite for sortilege depended for their result on the dispositions of the stars, his opinion is vain and false, and consequently is not free from the interference of the demons, so that a divination of this kind is superstitious and unlawful.

Apart from this cause, however, the result of sortilegious acts must needs be ascribed to chance, or to some directing spiritual cause. If we ascribe it to chance, and this can only take place in "sortilege of allotment," it does not seem to imply any vice other than vanity, as in the case of persons who, being unable to agree upon the division of something or other, are willing to draw lots for its division, thus leaving to chance what portion each is to receive.

If, on the other hand, the decision by lot be left to a spiritual cause, it is sometimes ascribed to demons. Thus we read (Ezech. 21:21) that "the king of Babylon stood in the highway, at the head of two ways, seeking divination, shuffling arrows; he inquired of the idols, and consulted entrails": sortilege of this kind is unlawful, and forbidden by the canons.

Sometimes, however, the decision is left to God, according to Prov. 16:33, "Lots are cast into the lap, but they are disposed of by the Lord": sortilege of this kind is not wrong in itself, as Augustine declares [*Enarr. ii in Ps. xxx, serm. 2; cf. Obj.[1]].

Yet this may happen to be sinful in four ways. First, if one have recourse to lots without any necessity: for this would seem to amount to tempting God. Hence Ambrose, commenting on the words of Luke 1:8, says: "He that is chosen by lot is not bound by the judgment of men." Secondly, if even in a case of necessity one were to have recourse to lots without reverence. Hence, on the Acts of the Apostles, Bede says (Super Act. Apost. i): "But if anyone, compelled by necessity, thinks that he ought, after the apostles' example, to consult God by casting lots, let him take note that the apostles themselves did not do so, except after calling together the assembly of the brethren and pouring forth prayer to God." Thirdly, if the Divine oracles be misapplied to earthly business. Hence Augustine says (ad inquisit. Januar. ii; Ep. lv): "Those who tell fortunes from the Gospel pages, though it is to be hoped that they do so rather than have recourse to consulting the demons, yet does this custom also displease me, that anyone should wish to apply the Divine oracles to worldly matters and to the vain things of this life." Fourthly, if anyone resort to the drawing of lots in ecclesiastical elections, which should be carried out by the inspiration of the Holy

Ghost. Wherefore, as Bede says (Super Act. Apost. i): "Before Pentecost the ordination of Matthias was decided by lot," because as yet the fulness of the Holy Ghost was not yet poured forth into the Church: "whereas the same deacons were ordained not by lot but by the choice of the disciples." It is different with earthly honors, which are directed to the disposal of earthly things: in elections of this kind men frequently have recourse to lots, even as in the distribution of earthly possessions.

If, however, there be urgent necessity it is lawful to seek the divine judgment by casting lots, provided due reverence be observed. Hence Augustine says (Ep. ad Honor. ccxxviii), "If, at a time of persecution, the ministers of God do not agree as to which of them is to remain at his post lest all should flee, and which of them is to flee, lest all die and the Church be forsaken, should there be no other means of coming to an agreement, so far as I can see, they must be chosen by lot." Again he says (De Doctr. Christ. xxviii): "If thou aboundest in that which it behooves thee to give to him who hath not, and which cannot be given to two; should two come to you, neither of whom surpasses the other either in need or in some claim on thee, thou couldst not act more justly than in choosing by lot to whom thou shalt give that which thou canst not give to both."

This suffices for the Reply to the First and Second Objections.

Reply Obj. 3: The trial by hot iron or boiling water is directed to the investigation of someone's hidden sin, by means of something done by a man, and in this it agrees with the drawing of lots. But in so far as a miraculous result is expected from God, it surpasses the common generality of sortilege. Hence this kind of trial is rendered unlawful, both because it is directed to the judgment of the occult, which is reserved to the divine judgment, and because such like trials are not sanctioned by divine authority. Hence we read in a decree of Pope Stephen V [*II, qu. v., can. Consuluist i]: "The sacred canons do not approve of extorting a confession from anyone by means of the trial by hot iron or boiling water, and no one must presume, by a superstitious innovation, to practice what is not sanctioned by the teaching of the holy fathers. For it is allowable that public crimes should be judged by our authority, after the culprit has made spontaneous confession, or when witnesses have been approved, with due regard to the fear of God; but hidden and unknown crimes must be left to Him Who alone knows the hearts of the children of men." The same would seem to apply to the law concerning duels, save that it approaches nearer to the common kind of sortilege, since no miraculous effect is expected thereupon, unless the combatants be very unequal in strength or skill.

# QUESTION 96

OF SUPERSTITION IN OBSERVANCES (In Four Articles)

We must now consider superstition in observances, under which head there are four points of inquiry:

(1) Of observances for acquiring knowledge, which are prescribed by the magic art;

(2) Of observances for causing alterations in certain bodies;

(3) Of observances practiced in fortune-telling;

(4) Of wearing sacred words at the neck.

FIRST ARTICLE [II-II, Q. 96, Art. 1]

Whether It Be Unlawful to Practice the Observances of the Magic Art?

Objection 1: It would seem that it is not unlawful to practice the observances of the magic art. A thing is said to be unlawful in two ways. First, by reason of the genus of the deed, as murder and theft: secondly, through being directed to an evil end, as when a person gives an alms for the sake of vainglory. Now the observances of the magic art are not evil as to the genus of the deed, for they consist in certain fasts and prayers to God; moreover, they are directed to a good end, namely, the acquisition of science. Therefore it is not unlawful to practice these observances.

Obj. 2: Further, it is written (Dan. 1:17) that "to the children" who abstained, "God gave knowledge, and understanding in every book, and wisdom." Now the observances of the magic art consist in certain fasts and abstinences. Therefore it seems that this art achieves its results through God: and consequently it is not unlawful to practice it.

Obj. 3: Further, seemingly, as stated above (A. 1), the reason why it is wrong to inquire of the demons concerning the future is because they have no knowledge of it, this knowledge being proper to God. Yet the demons know scientific truths: because sciences are about things necessary and invariable, and such things are subject to human knowledge, and much more to the knowledge of demons, who are of keener intellect, as Augustine says [*Gen. ad lit. ii, 17; De Divin. Daemon. 3, 4]. Therefore it seems to be no sin to practice the magic art, even though it achieve its result through the demons.

*On the contrary,* It is written (Deut. 18:10, 11): "Neither let there be found among you ... anyone ... that seeketh the truth from the dead": which search relies on the demons' help. Now through the observances of the magic art, knowledge of the truth is sought "by means of certain signs agreed upon by compact with the demons" [*Augustine, De Doctr. Christ. ii, 20; see above Q. 92, A. 2]. Therefore it is unlawful to practice the notary art.

*I answer that,* The magic art is both unlawful and futile. It is unlawful, because the means it employs for acquiring knowledge have not in themselves the power to cause science, consisting as they do in gazing certain shapes, and muttering certain strange words, and so forth. Wherefore this art does not make use of these things as causes, but as signs; not however as signs instituted by God, as are the sacramental signs. It follows, therefore, that they are empty signs, and consequently a kind of "agreement or covenant made with the demons for the purpose of consultation and of compact by tokens" [*Ibid.]. Wherefore the magic art is to be absolutely repudiated and avoided by Christians, even as other arts of vain and noxious superstition, as Augustine declares (De Doctr. Christ. ii, 23). This art is also useless for the acquisition of science. For since it is not intended by means of this art to acquire science in a manner connatural to man, namely, by discovery and instruction, the consequence is that this effect is expected either from God or from the demons. Now it is certain that some have received wisdom and science infused into them by God, as related of Solomon (3 Kings 3 and 2 Paralip. 1). Moreover, our Lord said to His disciples (Luke 21:15): "I will give you a mouth and wisdom, which all your adversaries shall not be able to resist and gainsay." However, this gift is not granted to all, or in connection with any particular observance, but according to the will of the Holy Ghost, as stated in 1 Cor. 12:8, "To one indeed by the Spirit is given the word of wisdom, to another the word of knowledge, according to the same Spirit," and afterwards it is said (1 Cor. 12:11): "All these things one and the same Spirit worketh, dividing to everyone according as He will." On the other hand it does not belong to the demons to enlighten the intellect, as stated in the First Part (Q. 109, A. 3). Now the acquisition of knowledge and wisdom is effected by the enlightening of the intellect, wherefore never did anyone acquire knowledge by means of the demons. Hence Augustine says (De Civ. Dei x, 9): "Porphyry confesses that the intellectual soul is in no way cleansed by theurgic inventions," i.e. the operations "of the demons, so as to be fitted to see its God, and discern what is true," such as are all scientific conclusions. The demons may, however, be able by speaking to men to express in words certain teachings of the sciences, but this is not what is sought by means of magic.

Reply Obj. 1: It is a good thing to acquire knowledge, but it is not good to acquire it by undue means, and it is to this end that the magic art tends.

Reply Obj. 2: The abstinence of these children was not in accordance with a vain observance of the notary art, but according to the authority of the divine law, for they refused to be defiled by the meat of Gentiles. Hence as a reward for their obedience they received knowledge from God, according to Ps. 118:100, "I have had understanding above the ancients, because I have sought Thy commandments."

Reply Obj. 3: To seek knowledge of the future from the demons is a sin not only because they are ignorant of the future, but also on account of the fellowship entered into with them, which also applies to the case in point.

SECOND ARTICLE [II-II, Q. 96, Art. 2]

Whether Observances Directed to the Alteration of Bodies, As for the Purpose of Acquiring Health or the Like, Are Unlawful?

Objection 1: It would seem that observances directed to the alteration of bodies, as for the purpose of acquiring health, or the like, are lawful. It is lawful to make use of the natural forces of bodies in order to produce their proper effects. Now in the physical order things have certain occult forces, the reason of which man is unable to assign; for instance that the magnet attracts iron, and many like instances, all of which Augustine enumerates (De Civ. Dei xxi, 5, 7). Therefore it would seem lawful to employ such like forces for the alteration of bodies.

Obj. 2: Further, artificial bodies are subject to the heavenly bodies, just as natural bodies are. Now natural bodies acquire certain occult forces resulting from their species through the influence of the heavenly bodies. Therefore artificial bodies, e.g. images, also acquire from the heavenly bodies a certain occult force for the production of certain effects. Therefore it is not unlawful to make use of them and of such like things.

Obj. 3: Further, the demons too are able to alter bodies in many ways, as Augustine states (De Trin. iii, 8, 9). But their power is from God. Therefore it is lawful to make use of their power for the purpose of producing these alterations.

*On the contrary,* Augustine says (De Doctr. Christ. ii, 20) that "to superstition belong the experiments of magic arts, amulets and nostrums condemned by the medical faculty, consisting either of incantations or of certain cyphers which they call characters, or of any kind of thing worn or fastened on."

*I answer that,* In things done for the purpose of producing some bodily effect we must consider whether they seem able to produce that effect naturally: for if so it will not be unlawful to do so, since it is lawful to employ natural causes in order to produce their proper effects. But, if they seem unable to produce those effects naturally, it follows that they are employed for the purpose of producing those effects, not as causes but only as signs, so that they come under the head of "compact by tokens entered into with the demons" [*Augustine, De Doctr. Christ.; see above Q. 92, A. 2]. Wherefore Augustine says (De Civ. Dei xxi, 6): "The demons are allured by means of creatures, which were made, not by them, but by God. They are enticed by various objects differing according to the various things in which they delight, not as animals by meat, but as spirits by signs, such as are to each one's liking, by means of various kinds of stones, herbs, trees, animals, songs and rites."

Reply Obj. 1: There is nothing superstitious or unlawful in employing natural things simply for the purpose of causing certain effects such as they are thought to have the natural power of producing. But if in addition there be employed certain characters, words, or any other vain observances which clearly have no efficacy by nature, it will be superstitious and unlawful.

Reply Obj. 2: The natural forces of natural bodies result from their substantial forms which they acquire through the influence of heavenly bodies; wherefore through this same influence they acquire certain active forces. On the other hand the forms of artificial bodies result from the conception of the craftsman; and since they are nothing else but composition, order and shape, as stated in *Phys.* i, 5, they cannot have a natural active force. Consequently, no force accrues to them from the influence of heavenly bodies, in so far as they are artificial, but only in respect of their natural matter. Hence it is false, what Porphyry held, according to Augustine (De Civ. Dei x, 11), that "by herbs, stones, animals, certain particular sounds, words, shapes and devices, or again by certain movements of the stars observed in the course of the heavens it is possible for men to fashion on earth forces capable of carrying into effect the various dispositions of the stars," as though the results of the magic arts were to be ascribed to the power of the heavenly bodies. In fact as Augustine adds (De Civ. Dei x, 11), "all these things are to be ascribed to the demons, who delude the souls that are subject to them."

Wherefore those images called astronomical also derive their efficacy from the actions of the demons: a sign of this is that it is requisite to inscribe certain characters on them which do not conduce to any effect naturally, since shape is not a principle of natural action. Yet astronomical images differ from necromantic images in this, that the latter include certain explicit invocations and trickery, wherefore they come under the head of explicit agreements made with the demons: whereas in the other images there are tacit agreements by means of tokens in certain shapes or characters.

Reply Obj. 3: It belongs to the domain of the divine majesty, to Whom the demons are subject, that God should employ them to whatever purpose He will. But man has not been entrusted with power over the demons, to employ them to whatsoever purpose he will; *on the contrary,* it is appointed that he should wage war against the demons. Hence in no way is it lawful for man to make use of the demons' help by compacts either tacit or express.

THIRD ARTICLE [II-II, Q. 96, Art. 3]

Whether Observances Directed to the Purpose of Fortune-telling Are Unlawful?

Objection 1: It would seem that observances directed to the purpose of fortune-telling are not unlawful. Sickness is one of the misfortunes that occur to man. Now sickness in man is preceded by certain symptoms, which the physician observes. Therefore it seems not unlawful to observe such like signs.

Obj. 2: Further, it is unreasonable to deny that which nearly everybody experiences. Now nearly everyone experiences that certain times, or places, hearing of certain words meetings of men or animals, uncanny or ungainly actions, are presages of good or evil to come. Therefore it seems not unlawful to observe these things.

Obj. 3: Further, human actions and occurrences are disposed by divine providence in a certain order: and this order seems to require that precedent events should be signs of subsequent occurrences: wherefore, according to the Apostle (1 Cor. 10:6), the things that happened to the fathers of old are signs of those that take place in our time. Now it is not unlawful to observe the order that proceeds from divine providence. Therefore it is seemingly not unlawful to observe these presages.

*On the contrary,* Augustine says (De Doctr. Christ. ii, 20) that "a thousand vain observances are comprised under the head of compacts entered into with the demons: for instance, the twitching of a limb; a stone, a dog, or a boy coming between friends walking together; kicking the door-post when anyone passes in front of one's house; to go back to bed if you happen to sneeze while putting on your shoes; to return home if you trip when going forth; when the rats have gnawed a hole in your clothes, to fear superstitiously a future evil rather than to regret the actual damage."

*I answer that,* Men attend to all these observances, not as causes but as signs of future events, good or evil. Nor do they observe them as signs given by God, since these signs are brought forward, not on divine authority, but rather by human vanity with the cooperation of the malice of the demons, who strive to entangle men's minds with such like trifles. Accordingly it is evident that all these observances are superstitious and unlawful: they are apparently remains of idolatry, which authorized the observance of auguries, of lucky and unlucky days which is allied to divination by the stars, in respect of which one day is differentiated from another: except that these observances are devoid of reason and art, wherefore they are yet more vain and superstitious.

Reply Obj. 1: The causes of sickness are seated in us, and they produce certain signs of sickness to come, which physicians lawfully observe. Wherefore it is not unlawful to consider a presage of future events as proceeding from its cause; as when a slave fears a flogging when he sees his master's anger. Possibly the same might be said if one were to fear for child lest it take harm from the evil eye, of which we have spoken in the First Part (Q. 117, A. 3, ad 2). But this does not apply to this kind of observances.

Reply Obj. 2: That men have at first experienced a certain degree of truth in these observances is due to chance. But afterwards when a man begins to entangle his mind with observances of this kind, many things occur in connection with them through the trickery of the demons, "so that men, through being entangled in these observances, become yet more curious, and more and more embroiled in the manifold snares of a pernicious error," as Augustine says (De Doctr. Christ. ii, 23).

Reply Obj. 3: Among the Jewish people of whom Christ was to be born, not only words but also deeds were prophetic, as Augustine states (Contra Faust. iv, 2; xxii, 24). Wherefore it is lawful to apply those deeds to our instruction, as signs given by God. Not all things, however, that occur through divine providence are ordered so as to be signs of the future. Hence the argument does not prove.

FOURTH ARTICLE [II-II, Q. 96, Art. 4]

Whether It Is Unlawful to Wear Divine Words at the Neck?

Objection 1: It would seem that it is not unlawful to wear divine words at the neck. Divine words are no less efficacious when written than when uttered. But it is lawful to utter sacred words for the purpose of producing certain effects; (for instance, in order to heal the sick), such as the "Our Father" or the "Hail Mary," or in any way whatever to call on the Lord's name, according to Mk. 16:17, 18, "In My name they shall cast out devils, they shall speak with new tongues, they shall take up serpents." Therefore it seems to be lawful to wear sacred words at one's neck, as a remedy for sickness or for any kind of distress.

Obj. 2: Further, sacred words are no less efficacious on the human body than on the bodies of serpents and other animals. Now certain incantations are efficacious in checking serpents, or in healing certain other animals: wherefore it is written (Ps. 57:5): "Their madness is according to the likeness of a serpent, like the deaf asp that stoppeth her ears, which will not hear the voice of the charmers, nor of the wizard that charmeth wisely." Therefore it is lawful to wear sacred words as a remedy for men.

Obj. 3: Further, God's word is no less holy than the relics of the saints; wherefore Augustine says (Lib. L. Hom. xxvi) that "God's word is of no less account than the Body of Christ." Now it is lawful for one to wear the relics of the saints at one's neck, or to carry them about one in any way for the purpose of self-protection. Therefore it is equally lawful to have recourse to the words of Holy Writ, whether uttered or written, for one's protection.

Obj. 4: On the other hand, Chrysostom says (Hom. xliii in Matth.) [*Cf. the Opus Imperfectum in Matthaeum, among St. Chrysostom's works, and falsely ascribed to him]: "Some wear round their necks a passage in writing from the Gospel. Yet is not the Gospel read in church and heard by all every day? How then, if it does a man no good to have the Gospels in his ears, will he find salvation by wearing them round his neck? Moreover, where is the power of the Gospel? In the shapes of the letters or in the understanding of the sense? If in the shapes, you do well to wear them round your neck; if in the understanding, you will then do better to bear them in your heart than to wear them round your neck."

*I answer that,* In every incantation or wearing of written words, two points seem to demand caution. The first is the thing said or written, because if it is connected with invocation of the demons it is clearly superstitious and unlawful. In like manner it seems that one should beware lest it contain strange words, for fear that they conceal something unlawful. Hence Chrysostom says [*Cf. the Opus Imperfectum in Matthaeum, among St. Chrysostom's works, falsely ascribed to him] that "many now after the example of the Pharisees who enlarged their fringes, invent and write Hebrew names of angels, and fasten them to their persons. Such things seem fearsome to those who do not understand them." Again, one should take care lest it contain anything false, because in that case also the effect could not be ascribed to God, Who does not bear witness to a falsehood.

In the second place, one should beware lest besides the sacred words it contain something vain, for instance certain written characters, except the sign of the Cross; or if hope be placed in the manner of writing or fastening, or in any like vanity, having no connection with reverence for God, because this would be pronounced superstitious: otherwise, however, it is lawful. Hence it is written in the Decretals (XXVI, qu. v, cap. Non liceat Christianis): "In blending together medicinal herbs, it is not lawful to make use of observances or incantations, other than the divine symbol, or the Lord's Prayer, so as to give honor to none but God the Creator of all."

Reply Obj. 1: It is indeed lawful to pronounce divine words, or to invoke the divine name, if one do so with a mind to honor God alone, from Whom the result is expected: but it is unlawful if it be done in connection with any vain observance.

Reply Obj. 2: Even in the case of incantations of serpents or any animals whatever, if the mind attend exclusively to the sacred words and to the divine power, it will not be unlawful. Such like incantations, however, often include unlawful observances, and rely on the demons for their result, especially in the case of serpents, because the serpent was the first instrument employed by the devil in order to deceive man. Hence a gloss on the passage quoted says: "Note that Scripture does not commend everything whence it draws its comparisons, as in the case of the unjust judge who scarcely heard the widow's request."

Reply Obj. 3: The same applies to the wearing of relics, for if they be worn out of confidence in God, and in the saints whose relics they are, it will not be unlawful. But if account were taken in this matter of some vain circumstance (for instance that the casket be three-cornered, or the like, having no bearing on the reverence due to God and the saints), it would be superstitious and unlawful.

Reply Obj. 4: Chrysostom is speaking of the case in which more attention is paid the written characters than to the understanding of the words.

## QUESTION 97

OF THE TEMPTATION OF GOD (In Four Articles)

We must now consider the vices that are opposed to religion, through lack of religion, and which are manifestly contrary thereto, so that they come under the head of irreligion. Such are the vices which pertain to contempt or irreverence for God and holy things. Accordingly we shall consider: (1) Vices pertaining directly to irreverence for God; (2) Vices pertaining to irreverence for holy things. With regard to the first we shall consider the temptation whereby God is tempted, and perjury, whereby God's name is taken with irreverence. Under the first head there are four points of inquiry:

(1) In what the temptation of God consists;

(2) Whether it is a sin?

(3) To what virtue it is opposed;

(4) Of its comparison with other vices.

FIRST ARTICLE [II-II, Q. 97, Art. 1]

Whether the Temptation of God Consists in Certain Deeds, Wherein the Expected Result Is Ascribed to the Power of God Alone?

Objection 1: It would seem that the temptation of God does not consist in certain deeds wherein the result is expected from the power of God alone. Just as God is tempted by man so is man tempted by God, man, and demons. But when man is tempted the result is not always expected from his power. Therefore neither is God tempted when the result is expected from His power alone.

Obj. 2: Further, all those who work miracles by invoking the divine name look for an effect due to God's power alone. Therefore, if the temptation of God consisted in such like deeds, all who work miracles would tempt God.

Obj. 3: Further, it seems to belong to man's perfection that he should put aside human aids and put his hope in God alone. Hence Ambrose, commenting on Luke 9:3, "Take nothing for your journey," etc. says: "The Gospel precept points out what is required of him that announces the kingdom of God, namely, that he should not depend on worldly assistance, and that, taking assurance from his faith, he should hold himself to be the more able to provide for himself, the less he seeks these things." And the Blessed Agatha said: "I have never treated my body with bodily medicine, I have my Lord Jesus Christ, Who restores all things by His mere word." [*Office of St. Agatha, eighth Responsory (Dominican Breviary).] But the temptation of God does not consist in anything pertaining to perfection. Therefore the temptation of God does not consist in such like deeds, wherein the help of God alone is expected.

*On the contrary,* Augustine says (Contra Faust. xxii, 36): "Christ who gave proof of God's power by teaching and reproving openly, yet not allowing the rage of His enemies to prevail against Him, nevertheless by fleeing and hiding, instructed human weakness, lest it should dare to tempt God when it has to strive to escape from that which it needs to avoid." From this it would seem that the temptation of God consists in omitting to do what one can in order to escape from danger, and relying on the assistance of God alone.

*I answer that,* Properly speaking, to tempt is to test the person tempted. Now we put a person to the test by words or by deeds. By words, that we may find out whether he knows what we ask, or whether he can and will grant it: by deeds, when, by what we do, we probe another's prudence, will or power. Either of these may happen in two ways. First, openly, as when one declares oneself a tempter: thus Samson (Judges 14:12) proposed a riddle to the Philistines in order to tempt them. In the second place it may be done with cunning and by stealth, as the Pharisees tempted Christ, as we read in Matt. 22:15, sqq. Again this is sometimes done explicitly, as when anyone intends, by word or deed, to put some person to the test; and sometimes implicitly, when, to wit, though he does not intend to test a person, yet that which he does or says can seemingly have no other purpose than putting him to a test.

Accordingly, man tempts God sometimes by words, sometimes by deeds. Now we speak with God in words when we pray. Hence a man tempts God explicitly in his prayers when he asks something of God with the intention of probing God's knowledge, power or will. He tempts God explicitly by deeds when he intends, by whatever he does, to experiment on God's power, good will or wisdom. But He will tempt God implicitly, if, though he does not intend to make an experiment on God, yet he asks for or does something which has no other use than to prove God's power, goodness or knowledge. Thus when a man wishes his horse to gallop in order to escape from the enemy, this is not giving the horse a trial: but if he make the horse gallop with out any useful purpose, it seems to be nothing else than a trial of the horse's speed; and the same applies to all other things. Accordingly when a man in his prayers or deeds entrusts himself to the divine assistance for some urgent or useful motive, this is not to tempt God: for it is written (2 Paralip 20:12): "As we know not what to do, we can only turn our eyes to Thee." But if this be done without any useful or urgent motive, this is to tempt God implicitly. Wherefore a gloss on Deut. 6:16, "Thou shalt not tempt the Lord thy God," says: "A man tempts God, if having the means at hand, without reason he chooses a dangerous course, trying whether he can be delivered by God."

Reply Obj. 1: Man also is sometimes tempted by means of deeds, to test his ability or knowledge or will to uphold or oppose those same deeds.

Reply Obj. 2: When saints work miracles by their prayers, they are moved by a motive of necessity or usefulness to ask for that which is an effect of the divine power.

Reply Obj. 3: The preachers of God's kingdom dispense with temporal aids, so as to be freer to give their time to the word of God: wherefore if they depend on God alone, it does not follow that they tempt God. But if they were to neglect human assistance without any useful or urgent motive, they would be tempting God. Hence Augustine (Contra Faust. xxii, 36) says that "Paul fled, not through ceasing to believe in God, but lest he should tempt God, were he not to flee when he had the means of flight." The Blessed Agatha had experience of God's kindness towards her, so that either she did not suffer such sickness as required bodily medicine, or else she felt herself suddenly cured by God.

SECOND ARTICLE [II-II, Q. 97, Art. 2]

Whether It Is a Sin to Tempt God?

Objection 1: It would seem that it is not a sin to tempt God. For God has not commanded sin. Yet He has commanded men to try, which is the same as to tempt, Him: for it is written (Malach. 3:10): "Bring all the tithes into the storehouse, that there may be meat in My house; and try Me in this, saith the Lord, if I open not unto you the flood-gates of heaven." Therefore it seems not to be a sin to tempt God.

Obj. 2: Further, a man is tempted not only in order to test his knowledge and his power, but also to try his goodness or his will. Now it is lawful to test the divine goodness or will, for it is written (Ps. 33:9): "O taste and see that the Lord is sweet," and (Rom. 12:2): "That you may prove what is the good, and the acceptable, and the perfect will of God." Therefore it is not a sin to tempt God.

Obj. 3: Further, Scripture never blames a man for ceasing from sin, but rather for committing a sin. Now Achaz is blamed because when the Lord said: "Ask thee a sign of the Lord thy God," he replied: "I will not ask, and I will not tempt the Lord," and then it was said to him: "Is it a small thing for you to be grievous to men, that you are grievous to my God also?" (Isa. 7:11-13). And we read of Abraham (Gen. 15:8) that he said to the Lord: "Whereby may I know that I shall possess it?" namely, the land which God had promised him. Again Gedeon asked God for a sign of the victory promised to him (Judges 6:36, sqq.). Yet they were not blamed for so doing. Therefore it is not a sin to tempt God.

*On the contrary,* It is forbidden in God's Law, for it is written (Deut. 6:10): "Thou shalt not tempt the Lord thy God."

*I answer that,* As stated above (A. 1), to tempt a person is to put him to a test. Now one never tests that of which one is certain. Wherefore all temptation proceeds from some ignorance or doubt, either in the tempter (as when one tests a thing in order to know its qualities), or in others (as when one tests a thing in order to prove it to others), and in this latter way God is said to tempt us. Now it is a sin to be ignorant of or to doubt that which pertains to God's perfection. Wherefore it is evident that it is a sin to tempt God in order that the tempter himself may know God's power.

On the other hand, if one were to test that which pertains to the divine perfection, not in order to know it oneself, but to prove it to others: this is not tempting God, provided there be just motive of urgency, or a pious motive of usefulness, and other requisite conditions. For thus did the apostles ask the Lord that signs might be wrought in the name of Jesus Christ, as related in Acts 4:30, in order, to wit, that Christ's power might be made manifest to unbelievers.

Reply Obj. 1: The paying of tithes was prescribed in the Law, as stated above (Q. 87, A. 1). Hence there was a motive of urgency to pay it, through the obligation of the Law, and also a motive of usefulness, as stated in the text quoted—"that there may be meat in God's house": wherefore they did not tempt God by paying tithes. The words that follow, "and try Me," are not to be understood causally, as though they had to pay tithes in order to try if "God would open the flood-gates of heaven," but consecutively, because, to wit, if they paid tithes, they would prove by experience the favors which God would shower upon them.

Reply Obj. 2: There is a twofold knowledge of God's goodness or will. One is speculative and as to this it is not lawful to doubt or to prove whether God's will be good, or whether God is sweet. The other knowledge of God's will or goodness is effective or experimental and thereby a man experiences in himself the taste of God's sweetness, and complacency in God's will, as Dionysius says of Hierotheos (Div. Nom. ii) that "he learnt divine things through experience of them." It is in this way that we are told to prove God's will, and to taste His sweetness.

Reply Obj. 3: God wished to give a sign to Achaz, not for him alone, but for the instruction of the whole people. Hence he was reproved because, by refusing to ask a sign, he was an obstacle to the common welfare. Nor would he have tempted God by asking, both because he would have asked through God commanding him to do so, and because it was a matter relating to the common good. Abraham asked for a sign through the divine instinct, and so he did not sin. Gedeon seems to have asked a sign through weakness of faith, wherefore he is not to be excused from sin, as a gloss observes: just as Zachary sinned in saying to the angel (Luke 1:18): "Whereby shall I know this?" so that he was punished for his unbelief.

It must be observed, however, that there are two ways of asking God for a sign: first in order to test God's power or the truth of His word, and this of its very nature pertains to the temptation of God. Secondly, in order to be instructed as to what is God's pleasure in some particular matter; and this nowise comes under the head of temptation of God.

THIRD ARTICLE [II-II, Q. 97, Art. 3]

Whether Temptation of God Is Opposed to the Virtue of Religion?

Objection 1: It would seem that the temptation of God is not opposed to the virtue of religion. The temptation of God is sinful, because a man doubts God, as stated above (A. 2). Now doubt about God comes under the head of unbelief, which is opposed to faith. Therefore temptation of God is opposed to faith rather than to religion.

Obj. 2: Further, it is written (Ecclus. 18:23): "Before prayer prepare thy soul, and be not as a man that tempteth God. Such a man," that is, who tempts God, says the interlinear gloss, "prays for what God taught him to pray for, yet does not what God has commanded him to do." Now this pertains to imprudence which is opposed to hope. Therefore it seems that temptation of God is a sin opposed to hope.

Obj. 3: Further, a gloss on Ps. 77:18, "And they tempted God in their hearts," says that "to tempt God is to pray to Him deceitfully, with simplicity in our words and wickedness in our hearts." Now deceit is opposed to the virtue of truth. Therefore temptation of God is opposed, not to religion, but to truth.

*On the contrary,* According to the gloss quoted above "to tempt God is to pray to Him inordinately." Now to pray to God becomingly is an act of religion as stated above (Q. 83, A. 15). Therefore to tempt God is a sin opposed to religion.

*I answer that,* As clearly shown above (Q. 81, A. 5), the end of religion is to pay reverence to God. Wherefore whatever pertains directly to irreverence for God is opposed to religion. Now it is evident that to tempt a person pertains to irreverence for him: since no one presumes to tempt one of whose excellence he is sure. Hence it is manifest that to tempt God is a sin opposed to religion.

Reply Obj. 1: As stated above (Q. 81, A. 7), it belongs to religion to declare one's faith by certain signs indicative of reverence towards God. Consequently it belongs to irreligion that, through doubtful faith, a man does things indicative of irreverence towards God. To tempt God is one of these; wherefore it is a species of irreligion.

Reply Obj. 2: He that prepares not his soul before prayer by forgiving those against whom he has anything, or in some other way disposing himself to devotion, does not do what he can to be heard by God, wherefore he tempts God implicitly as it were. And though this implicit temptation would seem to arise from presumption or indiscretion, yet the very fact that a man behaves presumptuously and without due care in matters relating to God implies irreverence towards Him. For it is written (1 Pet. 5:6): "Be you humbled ... under the mighty hand of God," and (2 Tim. 2:15): "Carefully study to present thyself approved unto God." Therefore also this kind of temptation is a species of irreligion.

Reply Obj. 3: A man is said to pray deceitfully, not in relation to God, Who knows the secrets of the heart, but in relation to man. Wherefore deceit is accidental to the temptation of God, and consequently it does not follow that to tempt God is directly opposed to the truth.

FOURTH ARTICLE [II-II, Q. 97, Art. 4]

Whether the Temptation of God Is a Graver Sin Than Superstition?

Objection 1: It would seem that the temptation of God is a graver sin than superstition. The greater sin receives the greater punishment. Now the sin of tempting God was more severely punished in the Jews than was the sin of idolatry; and yet the latter is the chief form of superstition: since for the sin of idolatry three thousand men of their number were slain, as related in Ex. 32:28 [*Septuagint version. The Vulgate has "twenty-three thousand."], whereas for the sin of temptation they all without exception perished in the desert, and entered not into the land of promise, according to Ps. 94:9, "Your fathers tempted Me," and further on, "so I swore in My wrath that they should not enter into My rest." Therefore to tempt God is a graver sin than superstition.

Obj. 2: Further, the more a sin is opposed to virtue the graver it would seem to be. Now irreligion, of which the temptation of God is a species, is more opposed to the virtue of religion, than superstition which bears some likeness to religion. Therefore to tempt God is a graver sin than superstition.

Obj. 3: Further, it seems to be a greater sin to behave disrespectfully to one's parents, than to pay others the respect we owe to our parents. Now God should be honored by us as the Father of all (Malach. 1:6). Therefore, temptation of God whereby we behave irreverently to God, seems to be a greater sin than idolatry, whereby we give to a creature the honor we owe to God.

*On the contrary,* A gloss on Deut. 17:2, "When there shall be found among you," etc. says: "The Law detests error and idolatry above all: for it is a very great sin to give to a creature the honor that belongs to the Creator."

*I answer that,* Among sins opposed to religion, the more grievous is that which is the more opposed to the reverence due to God. Now it is less opposed to this reverence that one should doubt the divine excellence than that one should hold the contrary for certain. For just as a man is more of an unbeliever if he be confirmed in his error, than if he doubt the truth of faith, so, too, a man acts more against the reverence due to God, if by his deeds he professes an error contrary to the divine excellence, than if he expresses a doubt. Now the superstitious man professes an error, as shown above (Q. 94, A. 1, ad 1), whereas he who tempts God by words or deeds expresses a doubt of the divine excellence, as stated above (A. 2). Therefore the sin of superstition is graver than the sin of tempting God.

Reply Obj. 1: The sin of idolatry was not punished in the above manner, as though it were a sufficient punishment; because a more severe punishment was reserved in the future for that sin, for it is written (Ex. 32:34): "And I, in the day of revenge, will visit this sin also of theirs."

Reply Obj. 2: Superstition bears a likeness to religion, as regards the material act which it pays just as religion does. But, as regards the end, it is more contrary to religion than the temptation of God, since it implies greater irreverence for God, as stated.

Reply Obj. 3: It belongs essentially to the divine excellence that it is singular and incommunicable. Consequently to give divine reverence to another is the same as to do a thing opposed to the divine excellence. There is no comparison with the honor due to our parents, which can without sin be given to others.

# QUESTION 98

OF PERJURY (In Four Articles)

We must now consider perjury: under which head there are four points of inquiry:

(1) Whether falsehood is necessary for perjury?

(2) Whether perjury is always a sin?

(3) Whether it is always a mortal sin?

(4) Whether it is a sin to enjoin an oath on a perjurer?

FIRST ARTICLE [II-II, Q. 98, Art. 1]

Whether It Is Necessary for Perjury That the Statement Confirmed on Oath Be False?

Objection 1: It would seem that it is not necessary for perjury that the statement confirmed on oath be false. As stated above (Q. 89, A. 3), an oath should be accompanied by judgment and justice no less than by truth. Since therefore perjury is incurred through lack of truth, it is incurred likewise through lack of judgment, as when one swears indiscreetly, and through lack of justice, as when one swears to something unjust.

Obj. 2: Further, that which confirms is more weighty than the thing confirmed thereby: thus in a syllogism the premises are more weighty than the conclusion. Now in an oath a man's statement is confirmed by calling on the name of God. Therefore perjury seems to consist in swearing by false gods rather than in a lack of truth in the human statement which is confirmed on oath.

Obj. 3: Further, Augustine says (De Verb. Apost. Jacobi; Serm. clxxx): "Men swear falsely both in deceiving others and when they are deceived themselves"; and he gives three examples. The first is: "Supposing a man to swear, thinking that what he swears to is true, whereas it is false"; the second is: "Take the instance of another who knows the statement to be false, and swears to it as though it were true"; and the third is: "Take another, who thinks his statement false, and swears to its being true, while perhaps it is true," of whom he says afterwards that he is a perjurer. Therefore one may be a perjurer while swearing to the truth. Therefore falsehood is not necessary for perjury.

*On the contrary,* Perjury is defined "a falsehood confirmed by oath" [*Hugh of St. Victor, Sum. Sent. iv, 5].

*I answer that,* As stated above (Q. 92, A. 2), moral acts take their species from their end. Now the end of an oath is the confirmation of a human assertion. To this confirmation falsehood is opposed: since an assertion is confirmed by being firmly shown to be true; and this cannot happen to that which is false. Hence falsehood directly annuls the end of an oath: and for this reason, that perversity in swearing, which is called perjury, takes its species chiefly from falsehood. Consequently falsehood is essential to perjury.

Reply Obj. 1: As Jerome says on Jer. 4:2, "whichever of these three be lacking, there is perjury," but in different order. For first and chiefly perjury consists in a lack of truth, for the reason stated in the Article. Secondly, there is perjury when justice is lacking, for in whatever way a man swears to that which is unlawful, for this very reason he is guilty of falsehood, since he is under an obligation to do the contrary. Thirdly, there is perjury when judgment is lacking, since by the very fact that a man swears indiscreetly, he incurs the danger of lapsing into falsehood.

Reply Obj. 2: In syllogisms the premises are of greater weight, since they are in the position of active principle, as stated in *Phys.* ii, 3: whereas in moral matters the end is of greater importance than the active principle. Hence though it is a perverse oath when a man swears to the truth by false gods, yet perjury takes its name from that kind of perversity in an oath, that deprives the oath of its end, by swearing what is false.

Reply Obj. 3: Moral acts proceed from the will, whose object is the apprehended good. Wherefore if the false be apprehended as true, it will be materially false, but formally true, as related to the will. If something false be apprehended as false, it will be false both materially and formally. If that which is true be apprehended as false, it will be materially true, and formally false. Hence in each of these cases the conditions required for perjury are to be found in some way, on account of some measure of falsehood. Since, however, that which is formal in anything is of greater importance than that which is material, he that swears to a falsehood thinking it true is not so much of a perjurer as he that swears to the truth thinking it false. For Augustine says (De Verb. Apost. Jacobi; Serm. clxxx): "It depends how the assertion proceeds from the mind, for the tongue is not guilty except the mind be guilty."

SECOND ARTICLE [II-II, Q. 98, Art. 2]

Whether All Perjury Is Sinful?

Objection 1: It would seem that not all perjury is sinful. Whoever does not fulfil what he has confirmed on oath is seemingly a perjurer. Yet sometimes a man swears he will do something unlawful (adultery, for instance, or murder): and if he does it, he commits a sin. If therefore he would commit a sin even if he did it not, it would follow that he is perplexed.

Obj. 2: Further, no man sins by doing what is best. Yet sometimes by committing a perjury one does what is best: as when a man swears not to enter religion, or not to do some kind of virtuous deed. Therefore not all perjury is sinful.

Obj. 3: Further, he that swears to do another's will would seem to be guilty of perjury unless he do it. Yet it may happen sometimes that he sins not, if he do not the man's will: for instance, if the latter order him to do something too hard and unbearable. Therefore seemingly not all perjury is sinful.

Obj. 4: Further, a promissory oath extends to future, just as a declaratory oath extends to past and present things. Now the obligation of an oath may be removed by some future occurrence: thus a state may swear to fulfil some obligation, and afterwards other citizens come on the scene who did not take the oath; or a canon may swear to keep the statutes of a certain church, and afterwards new statutes are made. Therefore seemingly he that breaks an oath does not sin.

*On the contrary,* Augustine says (De Verb. Apost. Jacobi; Serm. cxxx), in speaking of perjury: "See how you should detest this horrible beast and exterminate it from all human business."

*I answer that,* As stated above (Q. 89, A. 1), to swear is to call God as witness. Now it is an irreverence to God to call Him to witness to a falsehood, because by so doing one implies either that God ignores the truth or that He is willing to bear witness to a falsehood. Therefore perjury is manifestly a sin opposed to religion, to which it belongs to show reverence to God.

Reply Obj. 1: He that swears to do what is unlawful is thereby guilty of perjury through lack of justice: though, if he fails to keep his oath, he is not guilty of perjury in this respect, since that which he swore to do was not a fit matter of an oath.

Reply Obj. 2: A person who swears not to enter religion, or not to give an alms, or the like, is guilty of perjury through lack of judgment. Hence when he does that which is best it is not an act of perjury, but contrary thereto: for the contrary of that which he is doing could not be a matter of an oath.

Reply Obj. 3: When one man swears or promises to do another's will, there is to be understood this requisite condition—that the thing commanded be lawful and virtuous, and not unbearable or immoderate.

Reply Obj. 4: An oath is a personal act, and so when a man becomes a citizen of a state, he is not bound, as by oath, to fulfil whatever the state has sworn to do. Yet he is bound by a kind of fidelity, the nature of which obligation is that he should take his share of the state's burdens if he takes a share of its goods.

The canon who swears to keep the statutes that have force in some particular "college" is not bound by his oath to keep any that may be made in the future, unless he intends to bind himself to keep all, past and future. Nevertheless he is bound to keep them by virtue of the statutes themselves, since they are possessed of coercive force, as stated above (I-II, Q. 96, A. 4).

THIRD ARTICLE [II-II, Q. 98, Art. 3]

Whether All Perjury Is a Mortal Sin?

Objection 1: It would seem that not all perjury is a mortal sin. It is laid down (Extra, De Jurejur., cap. Verum): "Referring to the question whether an oath is binding on those who have taken one in order to safeguard their life and possessions, we have no other mind than that which our predecessors the Roman Pontiffs are known to have had, and who absolved such persons from the obligations of their oath. Henceforth, that discretion may be observed, and in order to avoid occasions of perjury, let them not be told expressly not to keep their oath: but if they should not keep it, they are not for this reason to be punished as for a mortal sin." Therefore not all perjury is a mortal sin.

Obj. 2. Further, as Chrysostom [*Hom. xliv in the Opus Imperfectum on St. Matthew, falsely ascribed to St. John Chrysostom] says, "it is a greater thing to swear by God than by the Gospels." Now it is not always a mortal sin to swear by God to something false; for instance, if we were to employ such an oath in fun or by a slip of the tongue in the course of an ordinary conversation. Therefore neither is it always a mortal sin to break an oath that has been taken solemnly on the Gospels.

Obj. 3: Further, according to the Law a man incurs infamy through committing perjury (VI, qu. i, cap. Infames). Now it would seem that infamy is not incurred through any kind of perjury, as it is prescribed in the case of a declaratory oath violated by perjury [*Cap. Cum dilectus, de Ord. Cognit.]. Therefore, seemingly, not all perjury is a mortal sin.

*On the contrary,* Every sin that is contrary to a divine precept is a mortal sin. Now perjury is contrary to a divine precept, for it is written (Lev. 19:12): "Thou shalt not swear falsely by My name." Therefore it is a mortal sin.

*I answer that,* According to the teaching of the Philosopher (Poster. i, 2), "that which causes a thing to be such is yet more so." Now we know that an action which is, by reason of its very nature, a venial sin, or even a good action, is a mortal sin if it be done out of contempt of God. Wherefore any action that of its nature, implies contempt of God is a mortal sin. Now perjury, of its very nature implies contempt of God, since, as stated above (A. 2), the reason why it is sinful is because it is an act of irreverence towards God. Therefore it is manifest that perjury, of its very nature, is a mortal sin.

Reply Obj. 1: As stated above (Q. 89, A. 7, ad 3), coercion does not deprive a promissory oath of its binding force, as regards that which can be done lawfully. Wherefore he who fails to fulfil an oath which he took under coercion is guilty of perjury and sins mortally. Nevertheless the Sovereign Pontiff can, by his authority, absolve a man from an obligation even of an oath, especially if the latter should have been coerced into taking the oath through such fear as may overcome a high-principled man.

When, however, it is said that these persons are not to be punished as for a mortal sin, this does not mean that they are not guilty of mortal sin, but that a lesser punishment is to be inflicted on them.

Reply Obj. 2: He that swears falsely in fun is nonetheless irreverent to God, indeed, in a way, he is more so, and consequently is not excused from mortal sin. He that swears falsely by a slip of tongue, if he adverts to the fact that he is swearing, and that he is swearing to something false, is not excused from mortal sin, as neither is he excused from contempt of God. If, however, he does not advert to this, he would seem to have no intention of swearing, and consequently is excused from the sin of perjury.

It is, however, a more grievous sin to swear solemnly by the Gospels, than to swear by God in ordinary conversation, both on account of scandal and on account of the greater deliberation. But if we consider them equally in comparison with one another, it is more grievous to commit perjury in swearing by God than in swearing by the Gospels.

Reply Obj. 3: Not every sin makes a man infamous in the eye of the law. Wherefore, if a man who has sworn falsely in a declaratory oath be not infamous in the eye of the law, but only when he has been so declared by sentence in a court of law, it does not follow that he has not sinned mortally. The reason why the law attaches infamy rather to one who breaks a promissory oath taken solemnly is that he still has it in his power after he has sworn to substantiate his oath, which is not the case in a declaratory oath.

FOURTH ARTICLE [II-II, Q. 98, Art. 4]

Whether He Sins Who Demands an Oath of a Perjurer?

Objection 1: It would seem that he who demands an oath of a perjurer commits a sin. Either he knows that he swears truly, or he knows that he swears falsely. If he knows him to swear truly, it is useless for him to demand an oath: and if he believes him to swear falsely, for his own part he leads him into sin. Therefore nowise seemingly should one enjoin an oath on another person.

Obj. 2: Further, to receive an oath from a person is less than to impose an oath on him. Now it would seem unlawful to receive an oath from a person, especially if he swear falsely, because he would then seem to consent in his sin. Much less therefore would it seem lawful to impose an oath on one who swears falsely.

Obj. 3: Further, it is written (Lev. 5:1): "If anyone sin, and hear the voice of one swearing falsely [*'Falsely' is not in the Vulgate], and is a witness either because he himself hath seen, or is privy to it: if he do not utter it, he shall bear his iniquity." Hence it would seem that when a man knows another to be swearing falsely, he is bound to denounce him. Therefore it is not lawful to demand an oath of such a man.

Obj. 4: On the other hand, Just as it is a sin to swear falsely so is it to swear by false gods. Yet it is lawful to take advantage of an oath of one who has sworn by false gods, as Augustine says (ad Public. Ep. xlvii). Therefore it is lawful to demand an oath from one who swears falsely.

*I answer that,* As regards a person who demands an oath from another, a distinction would seem to be necessary. For either he demands the oath on his own account and of his own accord, or he demands it on account of the exigencies of a duty imposed on him. If a man demands an oath on his own account as a private individual, we must make a distinction, as does Augustine (de Perjuriis. serm. clxxx): "For if he knows not that the man will swear falsely, and says to him accordingly: 'Swear to me' in order that he may be credited, there is no sin: yet it is a human temptation" (because, to wit, it proceeds from his weakness in doubting whether the man will speak the truth). "This is the evil whereof Our Lord says (Matt. 5:37): That which is over and above these, is of evil. But if he knows the man to have done so," i.e. the contrary of what he swears to, "and yet forces him to swear, he is a murderer: for the other destroys himself by his perjury, but it is he who urged the hand of the slayer."

If, on the other hand, a man demands an oath as a public person, in accordance with the requirements of the law, on the requisition of a third person: he does not seem to be at fault, if he demands an oath of a person, whether he knows that he will swear falsely or truly, because seemingly it is not he that exacts the oath but the person at whose instance he demands it.

Reply Obj. 1: This argument avails in the case of

one who demands an oath on his own account. Yet he does not always know that the other will swear truly or falsely, for at times he has doubts about the fact, and believes he will swear truly. In such a case he exacts an oath in order that he may be more certain.

Reply Obj. 2: As Augustine says (ad Public. serm. xlvii), "though we are forbidden to swear, I do not remember ever to have read in the Holy Scriptures that we must not accept oaths from others." Hence he that accepts an oath does not sin, except perchance when of his own accord he forces another to swear, knowing that he will swear falsely.

Reply Obj. 3: As Augustine says (QQ. Super Lev, qu. i), Moses in the passage quoted did not state to whom one man had to denounce another's perjury: wherefore it must be understood that the matter had to be denounced "to those who would do the perjurer good rather than harm." Again, neither did he state in what order the denunciation was to be made: wherefore seemingly the Gospel order should be followed, if the sin of perjury should be hidden, especially when it does not tend to another person's injury: because if it did, the Gospel order would not apply to the case, as stated above (Q. 33, A. 7; Q. 68, A. 1).

Reply Obj. 4: It is lawful to make use of an evil for the sake of good, as God does, but it is not lawful to lead anyone to do evil. Consequently it is lawful to accept the oath of one who is ready to swear by false gods, but it is not lawful to induce him to swear by false gods. Yet it seems to be different in the case of one who swears falsely by the true God, because an oath of this kind lacks the good of faith, which a man makes use of in the oath of one who swears truly by false gods, as Augustine says (ad Public. Ep. xlvii). Hence when a man swears falsely by the true God his oath seems to lack any good that one may use lawfully.

## QUESTION 99

OF SACRILEGE (In Four Articles)

We must now consider the vices which pertain to irreligion, whereby sacred things are treated with irreverence. We shall consider (1) Sacrilege; (2) Simony.

Under the first head there are four points of inquiry:

(1) What is sacrilege?

(2) Whether it is a special sin?

(3) Of the species of sacrilege;

(4) Of the punishment of sacrilege.

FIRST ARTICLE [II-II, Q. 99, Art. 1]

Whether Sacrilege Is the Violation of a Sacred Thing?

Objection 1: It would seem that sacrilege is not the violation of a sacred thing. It is stated (XVII, qu. iv [*Append. Gratian, on can. Si quis suadente]): "They are guilty of sacrilege who disagree about the sovereign's decision, and doubt whether the person chosen by the sovereign be worthy of honor." Now this seems to have no connection with anything sacred. Therefore sacrilege does not denote the violation of something sacred.

Obj. 2: Further, it is stated further on [*Append. Gratian, on can. Constituit.] that if any man shall allow the Jews to hold public offices, "he must be excommunicated as being guilty of sacrilege." Yet public offices have nothing to do with anything sacred. Therefore it seems that sacrilege does not denote the violation of a sacred thing.

Obj. 3: Further, God's power is greater than man's. Now sacred things receive their sacred character from God. Therefore they cannot be violated by man: and so a sacrilege would not seem to be the violation of a sacred thing.

*On the contrary,* Isidore says (Etym. x) that "a man is said to be sacrilegious because he selects," i.e. steals, "sacred things."

*I answer that,* As stated above (Q. 81, A. 5; I-II, Q. 101, A. 4), a thing is called "sacred" through being deputed to the divine worship. Now just as a thing acquires an aspect of good through being deputed to a good end, so does a thing assume a divine character through being deputed to the divine worship, and thus a certain reverence is due to it, which reverence is referred to God. Therefore whatever pertains to irreverence for sacred things is an injury to God, and comes under the head of sacrilege.

Reply Obj. 1: According to the Philosopher (Ethic. i, 2) the common good of the nation is a divine thing, wherefore in olden times the rulers of a commonwealth were called divines, as being the ministers of divine providence, according to Wis. 6:5, "Being ministers of His kingdom, you have not judged rightly." Hence by an extension of the term, whatever savors of irreverence for the sovereign, such as disputing his judgment, and questioning whether one ought to follow it, is called sacrilege by a kind of likeness.

Reply Obj. 2: Christians are sanctified by faith and the sacraments of Christ, according to 1 Cor. 6:11, "But you are washed, but you are sanctified." Wherefore it is written (1 Pet. 2:9): "You are a chosen generation, a kingly priesthood, a holy nation, a purchased people." Therefore any injury inflicted on the Christian people, for instance that unbelievers should be put in authority over it, is an irreverence for a sacred thing, and is reasonably called a sacrilege.

Reply Obj. 3: Violation here means any kind of irreverence or dishonor. Now as "honor is in the person who honors and not in the one who is honored" (Ethic. i, 5), so again irreverence is in the person who behaves irreverently even though he do no harm to the object of his irreverence. Hence, so far he is concerned, he violates the sacred thing, though the latter be not violated in itself.

SECOND ARTICLE [II-II, Q. 99, Art. 2]

Whether Sacrilege Is a Special Sin?

Objection 1: It would seem that sacrilege is not a special sin. It is stated (XVII, qu. iv) "They are guilty of sacrilege who through ignorance sin against the sanctity of the law, violate and defile it by their negligence." But this is done in every sin, because sin is "a word, deed or desire contrary to the law of God," according to Augustine (Contra Faust. xxi, 27). Therefore sacrilege is a general sin.

Obj. 2: Further, no special sin is comprised under different kinds of sin. Now sacrilege is comprised under different kinds of sin, for instance under murder, if one kill a priest under lust, as the violation of a consecrate virgin, or of any woman in a sacred place under theft, if one steal a sacred thing. Therefore sacrilege is not a special sin.

Obj. 3: Further, every special sin is to found apart from other sins as the Philosopher states, in speaking of special justice (Ethic. v, 11). But, seemingly, sacrilege is not to be found apart from other sins; for it is sometimes united to theft, sometimes to murder, as stated in the preceding objection. Therefore it is not a special sin.

*On the contrary,* That which is opposed to a special virtue is a special sin. But sacrilege is opposed to a special virtue, namely religion, to which it belongs to reverence God and divine things. Therefore sacrilege is a special sin.

*I answer that,* Wherever we find a special aspect of deformity, there must needs be a special sin; because the species of a thing is derived chiefly from its formal aspect, and not from its matter or subject. Now in sacrilege we find a special aspect of deformity, namely, the violation of a sacred thing by treating it irreverently. Hence it is a special sin.

Moreover, it is opposed to religion. For according to Damascene (De Fide Orth. iv, 3), "When the purple has been made into a royal robe, we pay it honor and homage, and if anyone dishonor it he is condemned to death," as acting against the king: and in the same way if a man violate a sacred thing, by so doing his behavior is contrary to the reverence due to God and consequently he is guilty of irreligion.

Reply Obj. 1: Those are said to sin against the sanctity of the divine law who assail God's law, as heretics and blasphemers do. These are guilty of unbelief, through not believing in God; and of sacrilege, through perverting the words of the divine law.

Reply Obj. 2: Nothing prevents one specific kind of sin being found in various generic kinds of sin, inasmuch as various sins are directed to the end of one sin, just as happens in the case of virtues commanded by one virtue. In this way, by whatever kind of sin a man acts counter to reverence due to sacred things, he commits a sacrilege formally; although his act contains various kinds of sin materially.

Reply Obj. 3: Sacrilege is sometimes found apart from other sins, through its act having no other deformity than the violation of a sacred thing: for instance, if a judge were to take a person from a sacred place, for he might lawfully have taken him from elsewhere.

THIRD ARTICLE [II-II, Q. 99, Art. 3]

Whether the Species of Sacrilege Are Distinguished According to the Sacred Things?

Objection 1: It would seem that the species of sacrilege are not distinguished according to the sacred things. Material diversity does not differentiate species, if the formal aspect remains the same. Now there would seem to be the same formal aspect of sin in all violations of sacred things, and that the only difference is one of matter. Therefore the species of sacrilege are not distinguished thereby.

Obj. 2: Further, it does not seem possible that things belonging to the same species should at the same time differ specifically. Now murder, theft, and unlawful intercourse, are different species of sin. Therefore they cannot belong to the one same species of sacrilege: and consequently it seems that the species of sacrilege are distinguished in accordance with the species of other sins, and not according to the various sacred things.

Obj. 3: Further, among sacred things sacred persons are reckoned. If, therefore, one species of sacrilege arises from the violation of a sacred person, it would follow that every sin committed by a sacred person is a sacrilege, since every sin violates the person of the sinner. Therefore the species of sacrilege are not reckoned according to the sacred things.

*On the contrary,* Acts and habits are distinguished by their objects. Now the sacred thing is the object of sacrilege, as stated above (A. 1). Therefore the species of sacrilege are distinguished according to the sacred things.

*I answer that,* As stated above (A. 1), the sin of sacrilege consists in the irreverent treatment of a sacred thing. Now reverence is due to a sacred thing by reason of its holiness: and consequently the species of sacrilege must needs be distinguished according to the different aspects of sanctity in the sacred things which are treated irreverently: for the greater the holiness ascribed to the sacred thing that is sinned against, the more grievous the sacrilege.

Now holiness is ascribed, not only to sacred persons, namely, those who are consecrated to the divine worship, but also to sacred places and to certain other sacred things. And the holiness of a place is directed to the holiness of man, who worships God in a holy place. For it is written (2 Macc. 5:19): "God did not choose the people for the place's sake, but the place for the people's sake." Hence sacrilege committed against a sacred person is a graver sin than that which is committed against a sacred place. Yet in either species there are various degrees of sacrilege, according to differences of sacred persons and places.

In like manner the third species of sacrilege, which is committed against other sacred things, has various degrees, according to the differences of sacred things. Among these the highest place belongs to the sacraments whereby man is sanctified: chief of which is the sacrament of the Eucharist, for it contains Christ Himself. Wherefore the sacrilege that is committed against this sacrament is the gravest of all. The second place, after the sacraments, belongs to the vessels consecrated for the administration of the sacraments; also sacred images, and the relics of the saints, wherein the very persons of the saints, so to speak, are reverenced and honored. After these come things connected with the apparel of the Church and its ministers; and those things, whether movable or immovable, that are deputed to the upkeep of the ministers. And whoever sins against any one of the aforesaid incurs the crime of sacrilege.

Reply Obj. 1: There is not the same aspect of holiness in all the aforesaid: wherefore the diversity of sacred things is not only a material, but also a formal difference.

Reply Obj. 2: Nothing hinders two things from belonging to one species in one respect, and to different species in another respect. Thus Socrates and Plato belong to the one species, "animal," but differ in the species "colored thing," if one be white and the other black. In like manner it is possible for two sins to differ specifically as to their material acts, and to belong to the same species as regards the one formal aspect of sacrilege: for instance, the violation of a nun by blows or by copulation.

Reply Obj. 3: Every sin committed by a sacred person is a sacrilege materially and accidentally as it were. Hence Jerome [*The quotation is from St. Bernard, De Consideration. ii, 13] says that "a trifle on a priest's lips is a sacrilege or a blasphemy." But formally and properly speaking a sin committed by a sacred person is a sacrilege only when it is committed against his holiness, for instance if a virgin consecrated to God be guilty of fornication: and the same is to be said of other instances.

FOURTH ARTICLE [II-II, Q. 99, Art. 4]

Whether the Punishment of Sacrilege Should Be Pecuniary?

Objection 1: It would seem that the punishment of sacrilege should not be pecuniary. A pecuniary punishment is not wont to be inflicted for a criminal fault. But sacrilege is a criminal fault, wherefore it is punished by capital sentence according to civil law [*Dig. xlviii, 13; Cod. i, 3, de Episc. et Cleric.]. Therefore sacrilege should not be awarded a pecuniary punishment.

Obj. 2: Further, the same sin should not receive a double punishment, according to Nahum 1:9, "There shall not rise a double affliction." But sacrilege is punished with excommunication; major excommunication, for violating a sacred person, and for burning or destroying a church, and minor excommunication for other sacrileges. Therefore sacrilege should not be awarded a pecuniary punishment.

Obj. 3: Further, the Apostle says (1 Thess. 2:5): "Neither have we taken an occasion of covetousness." But it seems to involve an occasion of covetousness that a pecuniary punishment should be exacted for the violation of a sacred thing. Therefore this does not seem to be a fitting punishment of sacrilege.

*On the contrary,* It is written [*XVII, qu. iv, can. Si quis contumax]: "If anyone contumaciously or arrogantly take away by force an escaped slave from the confines of a church he shall pay nine hundred soldi": and again further on (XVII, qu. iv, can. Quisquis inventus, can. 21): "Whoever is found guilty of sacrilege shall pay thirty pounds of tried purest silver."

*I answer that,* In the award of punishments two points must be considered. First equality, in order that the punishment may be just, and that "by what things a man sinneth by the same ... he may be tormented" (Wis. 11:17). In this respect the fitting punishment of one guilty of sacrilege, since he has done an injury to a sacred thing, is excommunication [*Append. Gratian. on can. Si quis contumax, quoted above] whereby sacred things are withheld from him. The second point to be considered is utility. For punishments are inflicted as medicines, that men being deterred thereby may desist from sin. Now it would seem that the sacrilegious man, who reverences not sacred things, is not sufficiently deterred from sinning by sacred things being withheld from him, since he has no care for them. Wherefore according to human laws he is sentenced to capital punishment, and according to the statutes of the Church, which does not inflict the death of the body, a pecuniary punishment is inflicted, in order that men may be deterred from sacrilege, at least by temporal punishments.

Reply Obj. 1: The Church inflicts not the death of the body, but excommunication in its stead.

Reply Obj. 2: When one punishment is not sufficient to deter a man from sin, a double punishment must be inflicted. Wherefore it was necessary to inflict some kind of temporal punishment in addition to the punishment of excommunication, in order to coerce those who despise spiritual things.

Reply Obj. 3: If money were exacted without a reasonable cause, this would seem to involve an occasion of covetousness. But when it is exacted for the purpose of man's correction, it has a manifest utility, and consequently involves no occasion of avarice.

## QUESTION 100

ON SIMONY (In Six Articles)

We must now consider simony, under which head there are six points of inquiry:

(1) What is simony?

(2) Whether it is lawful to accept money for the sacraments?

(3) Whether it is lawful to accept money for spiritual actions?

(4) Whether it is lawful to sell things connected with spirituals?

(5) Whether real remuneration alone makes a man guilty of simony, or also oral remuneration or remuneration by service?

(6) Of the punishment of simony.

FIRST ARTICLE [II-II, Q. 100, Art. 1]

Whether Simony Is an Intentional Will to Buy or Sell Something Spiritual or Connected with a Spiritual Thing?

Objection 1: It would seem that simony is not "an express will to buy or sell something spiritual or connected with a spiritual thing." Simony is heresy, since it is written (I, qu. i [*Can. Eos qui per pecunias]): "The impious heresy of Macedonius and of those who with him impugned the Holy Ghost, is more endurable than that of those who are guilty of simony: since the former in their ravings maintained that the Holy Spirit of Father and Son is a creature and the slave of God, whereas the latter make the same Holy Spirit to be their own slave. For every master sells what he has just as he wills, whether it be his slave or any other of his possessions." But unbelief, like faith, is an act not of the will but of the intellect, as shown above (Q. 10, A. 2). Therefore simony should not be defined as an act of the will.

Obj. 2: Further, to sin intentionally is to sin through malice, and this is to sin against the Holy Ghost. Therefore, if simony is an intentional will to sin, it would seem that it is always a sin against the Holy Ghost.

Obj. 3: Further, nothing is more spiritual than the kingdom of heaven. But it is lawful to buy the kingdom of heaven: for Gregory says in a homily (v, in Ev.): "The kingdom of heaven is worth as much as you possess." Therefore simony does not consist in a will to buy something spiritual.

Obj. 4: Further, simony takes its name from Simon the magician, of whom we read (Acts 8:18, 19) that "he offered the apostles money" that he might buy a spiritual power, in order, to wit, "that on whomsoever he imposed his hand they might receive the Holy Ghost." But we do not read that he wished to sell anything. Therefore simony is not the will to sell a spiritual thing.

Obj. 5: Further, there are many other voluntary commutations besides buying and selling, such as exchange and transaction [*A kind of legal compromise—Oxford Dictionary]. Therefore it would seem that simony is defined insufficiently.

Obj. 6: Further, anything connected with spiritual things is itself spiritual. Therefore it is superfluous to add "or connected with spiritual things."

Obj. 7: Further, according to some, the Pope cannot commit simony: yet he can buy or sell something spiritual. Therefore simony is not the will to buy or sell something spiritual or connected with a spiritual thing.

*On the contrary,* Gregory VII says (Regist. [*Caus. I, qu. i, can. Presbyter, qu. iii, can. Altare]): "None of the faithful is ignorant that buying or selling altars, tithes, or the Holy Ghost is the heresy of simony."

*I answer that,* As stated above (I-II, Q. 18, A. 2) an act is evil generically when it bears on undue matter. Now a spiritual thing is undue matter for buying and selling for three reasons. First, because a spiritual thing cannot be appraised at any earthly price, even as it is said concerning wisdom (Prov. 3:15), "she is more precious than all riches, and all things that are desired, are not to be compared with her": and for this reason Peter, in condemning the wickedness of Simon in its very source, said (Acts 8:20): "Keep thy money to thyself to perish with thee, because thou hast thought that the gift of God may be purchased with money."

Secondly, because a thing cannot be due matter for sale if the vendor is not the owner thereof, as appears from the authority quoted (Obj. 1). Now ecclesiastical superiors are not owners, but dispensers of spiritual things, according to 1 Cor. 4:1, "Let a man so account of us as of the ministers of Christ, and the dispensers of the ministers of God."

Thirdly, because sale is opposed to the source of spiritual things, since they flow from the gratuitous will of God. Wherefore Our Lord said (Matt. 10:8): "Freely have you received, freely give."

Therefore by buying or selling a spiritual thing, a man treats God and divine things with irreverence, and consequently commits a sin of irreligion.

Reply Obj. 1: Just as religion consists in a kind of protestation of faith, without, sometimes, faith being in one's heart, so too the vices opposed to religion include a certain protestation of unbelief without, sometimes, unbelief being in the mind. Accordingly simony is said to be a "heresy," as regards the outward protestation, since by selling a gift of the Holy Ghost a man declares, in a way, that he is the owner of a spiritual gift; and this is heretical. It must, however, be observed that Simon Magus, besides wishing the apostles to sell him a grace of the Holy Ghost for money, said that the world was not created by God, but by some heavenly power, as Isidore states (Etym. viii, 5): and so for this reason simoniacs are reckoned with other heretics, as appears from Augustine's book on heretics.

Reply Obj. 2: As stated above (Q. 58, A. 4), justice, with all its parts, and consequently all the opposite vices, is in the will as its subject. Hence simony is fittingly defined from its relation to the will. This act is furthermore described as "express," in order to signify that it proceeds from choice, which takes the principal part in virtue and vice. Nor does everyone sin against the Holy Ghost that sins from choice, but only he who chooses sin through contempt of those things whereby man is wont to be withdrawn from sin, as stated above (Q. 14, A. 1).

Reply Obj. 3: The kingdom of heaven is said to be bought when a man gives what he has for God's sake. But this is to employ the term "buying" in a wide sense, and as synonymous with merit: nor does it reach to the perfect signification of buying, both because neither "the sufferings of this time," nor any gift or deed of ours, "are worthy to be compared with the glory to come, that shall be revealed in us" (Rom. 8:18), and because merit consists chiefly, not in an outward gift, action or passion, but in an inward affection.

Reply Obj. 4: Simon the magician wished to buy a spiritual power in order that afterwards he might sell it. For it is written (I, qu. iii [*Can. Salvator]), that "Simon the magician wished to buy the gift of the Holy Ghost, in order that he might make money by selling the signs to be wrought by him." Hence those who sell spiritual things are likened in intention to Simon the magician: while those who wish to buy them are likened to him in act. Those who sell them imitate, in act, Giezi the disciple of Eliseus, of whom we read (4 Kings 5:20-24) that he received money from the leper who was healed: wherefore the sellers of spiritual things may be called not only "simoniacs" but also "giezites."

Reply Obj. 5: The terms "buying" and "selling" cover all kinds of non-gratuitous contracts. Wherefore it is impossible for the exchange or agency of prebends or ecclesiastical benefices to be made by authority of the parties concerned without danger of committing simony, as laid down by law [*Cap. Quaesitum, de rerum Permutat.; cap. Super, de Transact.]. Nevertheless the superior, in virtue of his office, can cause these exchanges to be made for useful or necessary reasons.

Reply Obj. 6: Even as the soul lives by itself, while the body lives through being united to the soul; so, too, certain things are spiritual by themselves, such as the sacraments and the like, while others are called spiritual, through adhering to those others. Hence (I, qu. iii, cap. Siquis objecerit) it is stated that "spiritual things do not progress without corporal things, even as the soul has no bodily life without the body."

Reply Obj. 7: The Pope can be guilty of the vice of simony, like any other man, since the higher a man's position the more grievous is his sin. For although the possessions of the Church belong to him as dispenser in chief, they are not his as master and owner. Therefore, were he to accept money from the income of any church in exchange for a spiritual thing, he would not escape being guilty of the vice of simony. In like manner he might commit simony by accepting from a layman moneys not belonging to the goods of the Church.

SECOND ARTICLE [II-II, Q. 100, Art. 2]

Whether It Is Always Unlawful to Give Money for the Sacraments?

Objection 1: It would seem that it is not always unlawful to give money for the sacraments. Baptism is the door of the sacraments, as we shall state in the Third Part (Q. 68, A. 6; Q. 73, A. 3). But seemingly it is lawful in certain cases to give money for Baptism, for instance if a priest were unwilling to baptize a dying child without being paid. Therefore it is not always unlawful to buy or sell the sacraments.

Obj. 2: Further, the greatest of the sacraments is the Eucharist, which is consecrated in the Mass. But some priests receive a prebend or money for singing masses. Much more therefore is it lawful to buy or sell the other sacraments.

Obj. 3: Further, the sacrament of Penance is a necessary sacrament consisting chiefly in the absolution. But some persons demand money when absolving from excommunication. Therefore it is not always unlawful to buy or sell a sacrament.

Obj. 4: Further, custom makes that which otherwise were sinful to be not sinful; thus Augustine says (Contra Faust. xxii, 47) that "it was no crime to have several wives, so long as it was the custom." Now it is the custom in some places to give something in the consecration of bishops, blessings of abbots, ordinations of the clergy, in exchange for the chrism, holy oil, and so forth. Therefore it would seem that it is not unlawful.

Obj. 5: Further, it happens sometimes that someone maliciously hinders a person from obtaining a bishopric or some like dignity. But it is lawful for a man to make good his grievance. Therefore it is lawful, seemingly, in such a case to give money for a bishopric or a like ecclesiastical dignity.

Obj. 6: Further, marriage is a sacrament. But sometimes money is given for marriage. Therefore it is lawful to sell a sacrament.

*On the contrary,* It is written (I, qu. i [*Can. Qui per pecunias]): "Whosoever shall consecrate anyone for money, let him be cut off from the priesthood."

*I answer that,* The sacraments of the New Law are of all things most spiritual, inasmuch as they are the cause of spiritual grace, on which no price can be set, and which is essentially incompatible with a non-gratuitous giving. Now the sacraments are dispensed through the ministers of the Church, whom the people are bound to support, according to the words of the Apostle (1 Cor. 9:13), "Know you not, that they who work in the holy place, eat the things that are of the holy place; and they that serve the altar, partake with the altar?"

Accordingly we must answer that to receive money for the spiritual grace of the sacraments, is the sin of simony, which cannot be excused by any custom whatever, since "custom does not prevail over natural or divine law" [*Cap. Cum tanto, de Consuetud.; cf. I-II, Q. 97, A. 3]. Now by money we are to understand anything that has a pecuniary value, as the Philosopher states (Ethic. iv, 1). On the other hand, to receive anything for the support of those who administer the sacraments, in accordance with the statutes of the Church and approved customs, is not simony, nor is it a sin. For it is received not as a price of goods, but as a payment for their need. Hence a gloss of Augustine on 1 Tim. 5:17, "Let the priests that rule well," says: "They should look to the people for a supply to their need, but to the Lord for the reward of their ministry."

Reply Obj. 1: In a case of necessity anyone may baptize. And since nowise ought one to sin, if the priest be unwilling to baptize without being paid, one must act as though there were no priest available for the baptism. Hence the person who is in charge of the child can, in such a case, lawfully baptize it, or cause it to be baptized by anyone else. He could, however, lawfully buy the water from the priest, because it is merely a bodily element. But if it were an adult in danger of death that wished to be baptized, and the priest were unwilling to baptize him without being paid, he ought, if possible, to be baptized by someone else. And if he is unable to have recourse to another, he must by no means pay a price for Baptism, and should rather die without being baptized, because for him the baptism of desire would supply the lack of the sacrament.

Reply Obj. 2: The priest receives money, not as the price for consecrating the Eucharist, or for singing the Mass (for this would be simoniacal), but as payment for his livelihood, as stated above.

Reply Obj. 3: The money exacted of the person absolved is not the price of his absolution (for this would be simoniacal), but a punishment of a past crime for which he was excommunicated.

Reply Obj. 4: As stated above, "custom does not prevail over natural or divine law" whereby simony is forbidden. Wherefore the custom, if such there be, of demanding anything as the price of a spiritual thing, with the intention of buying or selling it, is manifestly simoniacal, especially when the demand is made of a person unwilling to pay. But if the demand be made in payment of a stipend recognized by custom it is not simoniacal, provided there be no intention of buying or selling, but only of doing what is customary, and especially if the demand be acceded to voluntarily. In all these cases, however, one must beware of anything having an appearance of simony or avarice, according to the saying of the Apostle (1 Thess. 5:22), "From all appearance of evil restrain yourselves."

Reply Obj. 5: It would be simoniacal to buy off the opposition of one's rivals, before acquiring the right to a bishopric or any dignity or prebend, by election, appointment or presentation, since this would be to use money as a means of obtaining a spiritual thing. But it is lawful to use money as a means of removing unjust opposition, after one has already acquired that right.

Reply Obj. 6: Some [*Innocent IV on Cap. Cum in Ecclesia, de Simonia] say that it is lawful to give money for Matrimony because no grace is conferred thereby. But this is not altogether true, as we shall state in the Third Part of the work [* Supp., Q. 42, A. 3]. Wherefore we must reply that Matrimony is not only a sacrament of the Church, but also an office of nature. Consequently it is lawful to give money for Matrimony considered as an office of nature, but unlawful if it be considered as a sacrament of the Church. Hence, according to the law [*Cap. Cum in Ecclesia, de Simonia], it is forbidden to demand anything for the Nuptial Blessing.

THIRD ARTICLE [II-II, Q. 100, Art. 3]

Whether It Is Lawful to Give and Receive Money for Spiritual Actions?

Objection 1: It seems that it is lawful to give and receive money for spiritual actions. The use of prophecy is a spiritual action. But something used to be given of old for the use of prophecy, as appears from 1 Kings 9:7, 8, and 3 Kings 14:3. Therefore it would seem that it is lawful to give and receive money for a spiritual action.

Obj. 2: Further, prayer, preaching, divine praise, are most spiritual actions. Now money is given to holy persons in order to obtain the assistance of their prayers, according to Luke 16:9, "Make unto you friends of the mammon of iniquity." To preachers also, who sow spiritual things, temporal things are due according to the Apostle (1 Cor. 9:14). Moreover, something is given to those who celebrate the divine praises in the ecclesiastical office, and make processions: and sometimes an annual income is assigned to them. Therefore it is lawful to receive something for spiritual actions.

Obj. 3: Further, science is no less spiritual than power. Now it is lawful to receive money for the use of science: thus a lawyer may sell his just advocacy, a physician his advice for health, and a master the exercise of his teaching. Therefore in like manner it would seem lawful for a prelate to receive something for the use of his spiritual power, for instance, for correction, dispensation, and so forth.

Obj. 4: Further, religion is the state of spiritual perfection. Now in certain monasteries something is demanded from those who are received there. Therefore it is lawful to demand something for spiritual things.

*On the contrary,* It is stated (I, qu. i [*Can. Quidquid invisibilis]): "It is absolutely forbidden to make a charge for what is acquired by the consolation of invisible grace, whether by demanding a price or by seeking any kind of return whatever." Now all these spiritual things are acquired through an invisible grace. Therefore it is not lawful to charge a price or return for them.

*I answer that,* Just as the sacraments are called spiritual, because they confer a spiritual grace, so, too, certain other things are called spiritual, because they flow from spiritual grace and dispose thereto. And yet these things are obtainable through the ministry of men, according to 1 Cor. 9:7, "Who serveth as a soldier at any time at his own charges? Who feedeth the flock, and eateth not of the milk of the flock?" Hence it is simoniacal to sell or buy that which is spiritual in such like actions; but to receive or give something for the support of those who minister spiritual things in accordance with the statutes of the Church and approved customs is lawful, yet in such wise that there be no intention of buying or selling, and that no pressure be brought to bear on those who are unwilling to give, by withholding spiritual things that ought to be administered, for then there would be an appearance of simony. But after the spiritual things have been freely bestowed, then the statutory and customary offerings and other dues may be exacted from those who are unwilling but able to pay, if the superior authorize this to be done.

Reply Obj. 1: As Jerome says in his commentary on Mic. 3:9, certain gifts were freely offered to the good prophets, for their livelihood, but not as a price for the exercise of their gift of prophecy. Wicked prophets, however, abused this exercise by demanding payment for it.

Reply Obj. 2: Those who give alms to the poor in order to obtain from them the assistance of their prayers do not give with the intent of buying their prayers; but by their gratuitous beneficence inspire the poor with the mind to pray for them freely and out of charity. Temporal things are due to the preacher as means for his support, not as a price of the words he preaches. Hence a gloss on 1 Tim. 5:11, "Let the priests that rule well," says: "Their need allows them to receive the wherewithal to live, charity demands that this should be given to them: yet the Gospel is not for sale, nor is a livelihood the object of preaching: for if they sell it for this purpose, they sell a great thing for a contemptible price." In like manner temporal things are given to those who praise God by celebrating the divine office whether for the living or for the dead, not as a price but as a means of livelihood; and the same purpose is fulfilled when alms are received for making processions in funerals. Yet it is simoniacal to do such things by contract, or with the intention of buying or selling. Hence it would be an unlawful ordinance if it were decreed in any church that no procession would take place at a funeral unless a certain sum of money were paid, because such an ordinance would preclude the free granting of pious offices to any person. The ordinance would be more in keeping with the law, if it were decreed that this honor would be accorded to all who gave a certain alms, because this would not preclude its being granted to others. Moreover, the former ordinance has the appearance of an exaction, whereas the latter bears a likeness to a gratuitous remuneration.

Reply Obj. 3: A person to whom a spiritual power is entrusted is bound by virtue of his office to exercise the power entrusted to him in dispensing spiritual things. Moreover, he receives a statutory payment from the funds of the Church as a means of livelihood. Therefore, if he were to accept anything for the exercise of his spiritual power, this would imply, not a hiring of his labor (which he is bound to give, as a duty arising out of the office he has accepted), but a sale of the very use of a spiritual grace. For this reason it is unlawful for him to receive anything for any dispensing whatever, or for allowing someone else to take his duty, or for correcting his subjects, or for omitting to correct them. On the other hand it is lawful for him to receive "procurations," when he visits his subjects, not as a price for correcting them, but as a means of livelihood. He that is possessed of science, without having taken upon himself the obligation of using it for the benefit of others can lawfully receive a price for his learning or advice, since this is not a sale of truth or science, but a hiring of labor. If, on the other hand, he be so bound by virtue of his office, this would amount to a sale of the truth, and consequently he would sin grievously. For instance, those who in certain churches are appointed to instruct the clerics of that church and other poor persons, and are in receipt of an ecclesiastical benefice for so doing, are not allowed to receive anything in return, either for teaching, or for celebrating or omitting any feasts.

Reply Obj. 4: It is unlawful to exact or receive anything as price for entering a monastery: but, in the case of small monasteries, that are unable to support so many persons, it is lawful, while entrance to the monastery is free, to accept something for the support of those who are about to be received into the monastery, if its revenues are insufficient. In like manner it is lawful to be easier in admitting to a monastery a person who has proved his regard for that monastery by the generosity of his alms: just as, on the other hand, it is lawful to incite a person's regard for a monastery by means of temporal benefits, in order that he may thereby be induced to enter the monastery; although it is unlawful to agree to give or receive something for entrance into a monastery (I, qu. ii, cap. Quam pio).

FOURTH ARTICLE [II-II, Q. 100, Art. 4]

Whether It Is Lawful to Receive Money for Things Annexed to Spiritual Things?

Objection 1: It would seem lawful to receive money for things annexed to spiritual things. Seemingly all temporal things are annexed to spiritual things, since temporal things ought to be sought for the sake of spiritual things. If, therefore, it is unlawful to sell what is annexed to spiritual things, it will be unlawful to sell anything temporal, and this is clearly false.

Obj. 2: Further, nothing would seem to be more annexed to spiritual things than consecrated vessels. Yet it is lawful to sell a chalice for the ransom of prisoners, according to Ambrose (De Offic. ii, 28). Therefore it is lawful to sell things annexed to spiritual things.

Obj. 3: Further, things annexed to spiritual things include right of burial, right of patronage, and, according to ancient writers, right of the first-born (because before the Lord the first-born exercised the priestly office), and the right to receive tithes. Now Abraham bought from Ephron a double cave for a burying-place (Gen. 23:8, sqq.), and Jacob bought from Esau the right of the first-born (Gen. 25:31, sqq.). Again the right of patronage is transferred with the property sold, and is granted "in fee." Tithes are granted to certain soldiers, and can be redeemed. Prelates also at times retain for themselves the revenues of prebends of which they have the presentation, although a prebend is something annexed to a spiritual thing. Therefore it is lawful to sell things annexed to spiritual things.

*On the contrary,* Pope Paschal [*Paschal II] says (cf. I, qu. iii, cap. Si quis objecerit): "Whoever sells one of two such things, that the one is unproductive without the other, leaves neither unsold. Wherefore let no person sell a church, or a prebend, or anything ecclesiastical."

*I answer that,* A thing may be annexed to spiritual things in two ways. First, as being dependent on spiritual things. Thus to have ecclesiastical benefices is said to be annexed to spiritual things, because it is not competent save to those who hold a clerical office. Hence such things can by no means exist apart from spiritual things. Consequently it is altogether unlawful to sell such things, because the sale thereof implies the sale of things spiritual. Other things are annexed to spiritual things through being directed thereto, for instance the right of patronage, which is directed to the presentation of clerics to ecclesiastical benefices; and sacred vessels, which are directed to the use of the sacraments. Wherefore such things as these do not presuppose spiritual things, but precede them in the order of time. Hence in a way they can be sold, but not as annexed to spiritual things.

Reply Obj. 1: All things temporal are annexed to spiritual things, as to their end, wherefore it is lawful to sell temporal things, but their relation to spiritual things cannot be the matter of a lawful sale.

Reply Obj. 2: Sacred vessels also are annexed to spiritual things as to their end, wherefore their consecration cannot be sold. Yet their material can be sold for the needs of the Church or of the poor provided they first be broken, after prayer has been said over them, since when once broken, they are considered to be no longer sacred vessels but mere metal: so that if like vessels were to be made out of the same material they would have to be consecrated again.

Reply Obj. 3: We have no authority for supposing that the double cave which Abraham bought for a burial place was consecrated for that purpose: wherefore Abraham could lawfully buy that site to be used for burial, in order to turn it into a sepulchre: even so it would be lawful now to buy an ordinary field as a site for a cemetery or even a church. Nevertheless because even among the Gentiles burial places are looked upon as religious, if Ephron intended to accept the price as payment for a burial place, he sinned in selling, though Abraham did not sin in buying, because he intended merely to buy an ordinary plot of ground. Even now, it is lawful in a case of necessity to sell or buy land on which there has previously been a church, as we have also said with regard to sacred vessels (Reply Obj. 2). Or again, Abraham is to be excused because he thus freed himself of a grievance. For although Ephron offered him the burial place for nothing, Abraham deemed that he could not accept it gratis without prejudice to himself.

The right of the first-born was due to Jacob by reason of God's choice, according to Malach. 1:2, 3, "I have loved Jacob, but have hated Esau." Wherefore Esau sinned by selling his birthright, yet Jacob sinned not in buying, because he is understood to have freed himself of his grievance.

The right of patronage cannot be the matter of a direct sale, nor can it be granted "in fee," but is transferred with the property sold or granted.

The spiritual right of receiving tithes is not granted to layfolk, but merely the temporal commodities which are granted in the name of tithe, as stated above (Q. 87, A. 3).

With regard to the granting of benefices it must, however, be observed, that it is not unlawful for a bishop, before presenting a person to a benefice, to decide, for some reason, to retain part of the revenues of the benefice in question, and to spend it on some pious object. But, on the other hand, if he were to require part of the revenues of that benefice to be given to him by the beneficiary, it would be the same as though he demanded payment from him, and he would not escape the guilt of simony.

FIFTH ARTICLE [II-II, Q. 100, Art. 5]

Whether It Is Lawful to Grant Spiritual Things in Return for an Equivalent of Service, or for an Oral Remuneration?

Objection 1: It would seem that it is lawful to grant spiritual things in return for an equivalent of service, or an oral remuneration. Gregory says (Regist. iii, ep. 18): "It is right that those who serve the interests of the Church should be rewarded." Now an equivalent of service denotes serving the interests of the Church. Therefore it seems lawful to confer ecclesiastical benefices for services received.

Obj. 2: Further, to confer an ecclesiastical benefice for service received seems to indicate a carnal intention, no less than to do so on account of kinship. Yet the latter seemingly is not simoniacal since it implies no buying or selling. Therefore neither is the former simoniacal.

Obj. 3: Further, that which is done only at another's request would seem to be done gratis: so that apparently it does not involve simony, which consists in buying or selling. Now oral remuneration denotes the conferring of an ecclesiastical benefice at some person's request. Therefore this is not simoniacal.

Obj. 4: Further, hypocrites perform spiritual deeds in order that they may receive human praise, which seems to imply oral remuneration: and yet hypocrites are not said to be guilty of simony. Therefore oral remuneration does not entail simony.

*On the contrary,* Pope Urban [*Urban II, Ep. xvii ad Lucium] says: "Whoever grants or acquires ecclesiastical things, not for the purpose for which they were instituted but for his own profit, in consideration of an oral remuneration or of an equivalent in service rendered or money received, is guilty of simony."

*I answer that,* As stated above (A. 2), the term "money" denotes "anything that can have a pecuniary value." Now it is evident that a man's service is directed to some kind of usefulness, which has a pecuniary value, wherefore servants are hired for a money wage. Therefore to grant a spiritual thing for a service rendered or to be rendered is the same as to grant it for the money, received or promised, at which that service could be valued. Likewise, to grant a person's request for the bestowal of a temporary favor is directed to some kind of usefulness which has a pecuniary value. Wherefore just as a man contracts the guilt of simony by accepting money or any external thing which comes under the head of "real remuneration," so too does he contract it, by receiving "oral remuneration" or an "equivalent in service rendered."

Reply Obj. 1: If a cleric renders a prelate a lawful service, directed to spiritual things (e.g. to the good of the Church, or benefit of her ministers), he becomes worthy of an ecclesiastical benefice by reason of the devotion that led him to render the service, as he would by reason of any other good deed. Hence this is not a case of remuneration for service rendered, such as Gregory has in mind. But if the service be unlawful, or directed to carnal things (e.g. a service rendered to the prelate for the profit of his kindred, or the increase of his patrimony, or the like), it will be a case of remuneration for service rendered, and this will be simony.

Reply Obj. 2: The bestowal of a spiritual thing gratis on a person by reason of kinship or of any carnal affection is unlawful and carnal, but not simoniacal: since nothing is received in return, wherefore it does not imply a contract of buying and selling, on which simony is based. But to present a person to an ecclesiastical benefice with the understanding or intention that he provide for one's kindred from the revenue is manifest simony.

Reply Obj. 3: Oral remuneration denotes either praise that pertains to human favor, which has its price, or a request whereby man's favor is obtained or the contrary avoided. Hence if one intend this chiefly one commits simony. Now to grant a request made for an unworthy person implies, seemingly, that this is one's chief intention wherefore the deed itself is simoniacal. But if the request be made for a worthy person, the deed itself is not simoniacal, because it is based on a worthy cause, on account of which a spiritual thing is granted to the person for whom the request is made. Nevertheless there may be simony in the intention, if one look, not to the worthiness of the person, but to human favor. If, however, a person asks for himself, that he may obtain the cure of souls, his very presumption renders him unworthy, and so his request is made for an unworthy person. But, if one be in need, one may lawfully seek for oneself an ecclesiastical benefice without the cure of souls.

Reply Obj. 4: A hypocrite does not give a spiritual thing for the sake of praise, he only makes a show of it, and under false pretenses stealthily purloins rather than buys human praise: so that seemingly the hypocrite is not guilty of simony.

SIXTH ARTICLE [II-II, Q. 100, Art. 6]

Whether Those Who Are Guilty of Simony Are Fittingly Punished by Being Deprived of What They Have Acquired by Simony?

Objection 1: It would seem that those who are guilty of simony are not fittingly punished by being deprived of what they have acquired by simony. Simony is committed by acquiring spiritual things in return for a remuneration. Now certain spiritual things cannot be lost when once acquired, such as all characters that are imprinted by a consecration. Therefore it is not a fitting punishment for a person to be deprived of what he has acquired simoniacally.

Obj. 2: Further, it sometimes happens that one who has obtained the episcopate by simony commands a subject of his to receive orders from him: and apparently the subject should obey, so long as the Church tolerates him. Yet no one ought to receive from him that has not the power to give. Therefore a bishop does not lose his episcopal power, if he has acquired it by simony.

Obj. 3: Further, no one should be punished for what was done without his knowledge and consent, since punishment is due for sin which is voluntary, as was shown above (I-II, Q. 74, AA. 1, 2; Q. 77, A. 7). Now it happens sometimes that a person acquires something spiritual, which others have procured for him without his knowledge and consent. Therefore he should not be punished by being deprived of what has been bestowed on him.

Obj. 4: Further, no one should profit by his own sin. Yet, if a person who has acquired an ecclesiastical benefice by simony, were to restore what he has received, this would sometimes turn to the profit of those who had a share in his simony; for instance, when a prelate and his entire chapter have consented to the simony. Therefore that which has been acquired by simony ought not always to be restored.

Obj. 5: Further, sometimes a person obtains admission to a monastery by simony, and there takes the solemn vow of profession. But no one should be freed from the obligation of a vow on account of a fault he has committed. Therefore he should not be expelled from the monastic state which he has acquired by simony.

Obj. 6: Further, in this world external punishment is not inflicted for the internal movements of the heart, whereof God alone is the judge. Now simony is committed in the mere intention or will, wherefore it is defined in reference to the will, as stated above (A. 1, ad 2). Therefore a person should not always be deprived of what he has acquired by simony.

Obj. 7: Further, to be promoted to greater dignity is much less than to retain that which one has already received. Now sometimes those who are guilty of simony are, by dispensation, promoted to greater dignity. Therefore they should not always be deprived of what they have received.

*On the contrary,* It is written (I, qu. i, cap. Si quis Episcopus): "He that has been ordained shall profit nothing from his ordination or promotion that he has acquired by the bargain, but shall forfeit the dignity or cure that he has acquired with his money."

*I answer that,* No one can lawfully retain that which he has acquired against the owner's will. For instance, if a steward were to give some of his lord's property to a person, against his lord's will and orders, the recipient could not lawfully retain what he received. Now Our Lord, Whose stewards and ministers are the prelates of churches, ordered spiritual things to be given gratis, according to Matt. 10:8, "Freely have you received, freely give." Wherefore whosoever acquires spiritual things in return for a remuneration cannot lawfully retain them. Moreover, those who are guilty of simony, by either selling or buying spiritual things, as well as those who act as go-between, are sentenced to other punishments, namely, infamy and deposition, if they be clerics, and excommunication if they be laymen, as stated qu. i, cap. Si quis Episcopus [*Qu. iii, can. Si quis praebendas].

Reply Obj. 1: He that has received a sacred Order simoniacally, receives the character of the Order on account of the efficacy of the sacrament: but he does not receive the grace nor the exercise of the Order, because he has received the character by stealth as it were, and against the will of the Supreme Lord. Wherefore he is suspended, by virtue of the law, both as regards himself, namely, that he should not busy himself about exercising his Order, and as regards others, namely, that no one may communicate with him in the exercise of his Order, whether his sin be public or secret. Nor may he reclaim the money which he basely gave, although the other party unjustly retains it.

Again, a man who is guilty of simony, through having conferred Orders simoniacally, or through having simoniacally granted or received a benefice, or through having been a go-between in a simoniacal transaction, if he has done so publicly, is suspended by virtue of the law, as regards both himself and others; but if he has acted in secret he is suspended by virtue of the law, as regards himself alone, and not as regards others.

Reply Obj. 2: One ought not to receive Orders from a bishop one knows to have been promoted simoniacally, either on account of his command or for fear of his excommunication: and such as receive Orders from him do not receive the exercise of their Orders, even though they are ignorant of his being guilty of simony; and they need to receive a dispensation. Some, however, maintain that one ought to receive Orders in obedience to his command unless one can prove him to be guilty of simony, but that one ought not to exercise the Order without a dispensation. But this is an unreasonable statement, because no one should obey a man to the extent of communicating with him in an unlawful action. Now he that is, by virtue of the law, suspended as regards both himself and others, confers Orders unlawfully: wherefore no one should communicate with him, by receiving Orders from him for any cause whatever. If, however, one be not certain on the point, one ought not to give credence to another's sin, and so one ought with a good conscience to receive Orders from him. And if the bishop has been guilty of simony otherwise than by a simoniacal promotion, and the fact be a secret, one can receive Orders from him because he is not suspended as regards others, but only as regards himself, as stated above (ad 1).

Reply Obj. 3: To be deprived of what one has received is not only the punishment of a sin, but is also sometimes the effect of acquiring unjustly, as when one buys a thing of a person who cannot sell it. Wherefore if a man, knowingly and spontaneously, receives Orders or an ecclesiastical benefice simoniacally, not only is he deprived of what he has received, by forfeiting the exercise of his order, and resigning the benefice and the fruits acquired therefrom, but also in addition to this he is punished by being marked with infamy. Moreover, he is bound to restore not only the fruit actually acquired, but also such as could have been acquired by a careful possessor (which, however, is to be understood of the net fruits, allowance being made for expenses incurred on account of the fruits), excepting those fruits that have been expended for the good of the Church.

On the other hand, if a man's promotion be procured simoniacally by others, without his knowledge and consent, he forfeits the exercise of his Order, and is bound to resign the benefice obtained together with fruits still extant; but he is not bound to restore the fruits which he has consumed, since he possessed them in good faith. Exception must be made in the case when his promotion has been deceitfully procured by an enemy of his; or when he expressly opposes the transaction, for then he is not bound to resign, unless subsequently he agree to the transaction, by paying what was promised.

Reply Obj. 4: Money, property, or fruits simoniacally received, must be restored to the Church that has incurred loss by their transfer, notwithstanding the fact that the prelate or a member of the chapter of that church was at fault, since others ought not to be the losers by his sin: in suchwise, however, that, as far as possible, the guilty parties be not the gainers. But if the prelate and the entire chapter be at fault, restitution must be made, with the consent of superior authority, either to the poor or to some other church.

Reply Obj. 5: If there are any persons who have been simoniacally admitted into a monastery, they must quit: and if the simony was committed with their knowledge since the holding of the General Council [*Fourth Lateran Council, A.D. 1215, held by Innocent III], they must be expelled from their monastery without hope of return, and do perpetual penance under a stricter rule, or in some house of the same order, if a stricter one be not found. If, however, this took place before the Council, they must be placed in other houses of the same order. If this cannot be done, they must be received into monasteries of the same order, by way of compensation, lest they wander about the world, but they must not be admitted to their former rank, and must be assigned a lower place.

On the other hand, if they were received simoniacally, without their knowledge, whether before or after the Council, then after quitting they may be received again, their rank being changed as stated.

Reply Obj. 6: In God's sight the mere will makes a man guilty of simony; but as regards the external ecclesiastical punishment he is not punished as a simoniac, by being obliged to resign, but is bound to repent of his evil intention.

Reply Obj. 7: The Pope alone can grant a dispensation to one who has knowingly received a benefice (simoniacally). In other cases the bishop also can dispense, provided the beneficiary first of all renounce what he has received simoniacally, so that he will receive either the lesser dispensation allowing him to communicate with the laity, or a greater dispensation, allowing him after doing penance to retain his order in some other Church; or again a greater dispensation, allowing him to remain in the same Church, but in minor orders; or a full dispensation allowing him to exercise even the major orders in the same Church, but not to accept a prelacy.

## QUESTION 101

OF PIETY (In Four Articles)

After religion we must consider piety, the consideration of which will render the opposite vices manifest. Accordingly four points of inquiry arise with regard to piety:

(1) To whom does piety extend?

(2) What does piety make one offer a person?

(3) Whether piety is a special virtue?

(4) Whether the duties of piety should be omitted for the sake of religion?

FIRST ARTICLE [II-II, Q. 101, Art. 1]

Whether Piety Extends to Particular Human Individuals?

Objection 1: It seems that piety does not extend to particular human individuals. For Augustine says (De Civ. Dei x) that piety denotes, properly speaking, the worship of God, which the Greeks designate by the term *eusebeia* . But the worship of God does not denote relation to man, but only to God. Therefore piety does not extend definitely to certain human individuals.

Obj. 2: Further, Gregory says (Moral. i): "Piety, on her day, provides a banquet, because she fills the inmost recesses of the heart with works of mercy." Now the works of mercy are to be done to all, according to Augustine (De Doctr. Christ. i). Therefore piety does not extend definitely to certain special persons.

Obj. 3: Further, in human affairs there are many other mutual relations besides those of kindred and citizenship, as the Philosopher states (Ethic. viii, 11, 12), and on each of them is founded a kind of friendship, which would seem to be the virtue of piety, according to a gloss on 2 Tim. 3:5, "Having an appearance indeed of piety [Douay: 'godliness']." Therefore piety extends not only to one's kindred and fellow-citizens.

*On the contrary,* Tully says (De Invent. Rhet. ii) that "it is by piety that we do our duty towards our kindred and well-wishers of our country and render them faithful service."

*I answer that,* Man becomes a debtor to other men in various ways, according to their various excellence and the various benefits received from them. On both counts God holds first place, for He is supremely excellent, and is for us the first principle of being and government. In the second place, the principles of our being and government are our parents and our country, that have given us birth and nourishment. Consequently man is debtor chiefly to his parents and his country, after God. Wherefore just as it belongs to religion to give worship to God, so does it belong to piety, in the second place, to give worship to one's parents and one's country.

The worship due to our parents includes the worship given to all our kindred, since our kinsfolk are those who descend from the same parents, according to the Philosopher (Ethic. viii, 12). The worship given to our country includes homage to all our fellow-citizens and to all the friends of our country. Therefore piety extends chiefly to these.

Reply Obj. 1: The greater includes the lesser: wherefore the worship due to God includes the worship due to our parents as a particular. Hence it is written (Malach. 1:6): "If I be a father, where is My honor?" Consequently the term piety extends also to the divine worship.

Reply Obj. 2: As Augustine says (De Civ. Dei x), "the term piety is often used in connection with works of mercy, in the language of the common people; the reason for which I consider to be the fact that God Himself has declared that these works are more pleasing to Him than sacrifices. This custom has led to the application of the word 'pious' to God Himself."

Reply Obj. 3: The relations of a man with his kindred and fellow-citizens are more referable to the principles of his being than other relations: wherefore the term piety is more applicable to them.

SECOND ARTICLE [II-II, Q. 101, Art. 2]

Whether Piety Provides Support for Our Parents?

Objection 1: It seems that piety does not provide support for our parents. For, seemingly, the precept of the decalogue, "Honor thy father and mother," belongs to piety. But this prescribes only the giving of honor. Therefore it does not belong to piety to provide support for one's parents.

Obj. 2: Further, a man is bound to lay up for those whom he is bound to support. Now according to the Apostle (2 Cor. 12:14), "neither ought the children to lay up for the parents." Therefore piety does not oblige them to support their parents.

Obj. 3: Further, piety extends not only to one's parents, but also to other kinsmen and to one's fellow-citizens, as stated above (A. 1). But one is not bound to support all one's kindred and fellow-citizens. Therefore neither is one bound to support one's parents.

*On the contrary,* our Lord (Matt. 15:3-6) reproved the Pharisees for hindering children from supporting their parents.

*I answer that,* We owe something to our parents in two ways: that is to say, both essentially, and accidentally. We owe them essentially that which is due to a father as such: and since he is his son's superior through being the principle of his being, the latter owes him reverence and service. Accidentally, that is due to a father, which it befits him to receive in respect of something accidental to him, for instance, if he be ill, it is fitting that his children should visit him and see to his cure; if he be poor, it is fitting that they should support him; and so on in like instance, all of which come under the head of service due. Hence Tully says (De Invent. Rhet. ii) that "piety gives both duty and homage": "duty" referring to service, and "homage" to reverence or honor, because, as Augustine says (De Civ. Dei x), "we are said to give homage to those whose memory or presence we honor."

Reply Obj. 1: According to our Lord's interpretation (Matt. 15:3-6) the honor due to our parents includes whatever support we owe them; and the reason for this is that support is given to one's father because it is due to him as to one greater.

Reply Obj. 2: Since a father stands in the relation of principle, and his son in the relation of that which is from a principle, it is essentially fitting for a father to support his son: and consequently he is bound to support him not only for a time, but for all his life, and this is to lay by. On the other hand, for the son to bestow something on his father is accidental, arising from some momentary necessity, wherein he is bound to support him, but not to lay by as for a long time beforehand, because naturally parents are not the successors of their children, but children of their parents.

Reply Obj. 3: As Tully says (De Invent. Rhet. ii), "we offer homage and duty to all our kindred and to the well-wishers of our country"; not, however, equally to all, but chiefly to our parents, and to others according to our means and their personal claims.

THIRD ARTICLE [II-II, Q. 101, Art. 3]

Whether Piety Is a Special Virtue Distinct from Other Virtues?

Objection 1: It seems that piety is not a special virtue distinct from other virtues. For the giving of service and homage to anyone proceeds from love. But it belongs to piety. Therefore piety is not a distinct virtue from charity.

Obj. 2: Further, it is proper to religion to give worship to God. But piety also gives worship to God, according to Augustine (De Civ. Dei x). Therefore piety is not distinct from religion.

Obj. 3: Further, piety, whereby we give our country worship and duty, seems to be the same as legal justice, which looks to the common good. But legal justice is a general virtue, according to the Philosopher (Ethic. v, 1, 2). Therefore piety is not a special virtue.

*On the contrary,* It is accounted by Tully (De Invent. Rhet. ii) as a part of justice.

*I answer that,* A special virtue is one that regards an object under a special aspect. Since, then, the nature of justice consists in rendering another person his due, wherever there is a special aspect of something due to a person, there is a special virtue. Now a thing is indebted in a special way to that which is its connatural principle of being and government. And piety regards this principle, inasmuch as it pays duty and homage to our parents and country, and to those who are related thereto. Therefore piety is a special virtue.

Reply Obj. 1: Just as religion is a protestation of faith, hope and charity, whereby man is primarily directed to God, so again piety is a protestation of the charity we bear towards our parents and country.

Reply Obj. 2: God is the principle of our being and government in a far more excellent manner than one's father or country. Hence religion, which gives worship to God, is a distinct virtue from piety, which pays homage to our parents and country. But things relating to creatures are transferred to God as the summit of excellence and causality, as Dionysius says (Div. Nom. i): wherefore, by way of excellence, piety designates the worship of God, even as God, by way of excellence, is called "Our Father."

Reply Obj. 3: Piety extends to our country in so far as the latter is for us a principle of being: but legal justice regards the good of our country, considered as the common good: wherefore legal justice has more of the character of a general virtue than piety has.

FOURTH ARTICLE [II-II, Q. 101, Art. 4]

Whether the Duties of Piety Towards One's Parents Should Be Omitted for the Sake of Religion?

Objection 1: It seems that the duties of piety towards one's parents should be omitted for the sake of religion. For Our Lord said (Luke 14:26): "If any man come to Me, and hate not his father, and mother, and wife, and children, and brethren, and sisters, yea and his own life also, he cannot be My disciple." Hence it is said in praise of James and John (Matt. 4:22) that they left "their nets and father, and followed" Christ. Again it is said in praise of the Levites (Deut. 33:9): "Who hath said to his father, and to his mother: I do not know you; and to his brethren: I know you not; and their own children they have not known. These have kept Thy word." Now a man who knows not his parents and other kinsmen, or who even hates them, must needs omit the duties of piety. Therefore the duties of piety should be omitted for the sake of religion.

Obj. 2: Further, it is written (Luke 9:59, 60) that in answer to him who said: "Suffer me first to go and bury my father," Our Lord replied: "Let the dead bury their dead: but go thou, and preach the kingdom of God." Now the latter pertains to religion, while it is a duty of piety to bury one's father. Therefore a duty of piety should be omitted for the sake of religion.

Obj. 3: Further, God is called "Our Father" by excellence. Now just as we worship our parents by paying them the duties of piety so do we worship God by religion. Therefore the duties of piety should be omitted for the sake of the worship of religion.

Obj. 4: Further, religious are bound by a vow which they may not break to fulfil the observances of religion. Now in accordance with those observances they are hindered from supporting their parents, both on the score of poverty, since they have nothing of their own, and on the score of obedience, since they may not leave the cloister without the permission of their superior. Therefore the duties of piety towards one's parents should be omitted for the sake of religion.

*On the contrary,* Our Lord reproved the Pharisees (Matt. 15:3-6) who taught that for the sake of religion one ought to refrain from paying one's parents the honor we owe them.

*I answer that,* Religion and piety are two virtues. Now no virtue is opposed to another virtue, since according to the Philosopher, in his book on the Categories (Cap. De oppos.), "good is not opposed to good." Therefore it is impossible that religion and piety mutually hinder one another, so that the act of one be excluded by the act of the other. Now, as stated above (I-II, Q. 7, A. 2; Q. 18, A. 3), the act of every virtue is limited by the circumstances due thereto, and if it overstep them it will be an act no longer of virtue but of vice. Hence it belongs to piety to pay duty and homage to one's parents according to the due mode. But it is not the due mode that man should tend to worship his father rather than God, but, as Ambrose says on Luke 12:52, "the piety of divine religion takes precedence of the claims of kindred."

Accordingly, if the worship of one's parents take one away from the worship of God it would no longer be an act of piety to pay worship to one's parents to the prejudice of God. Hence Jerome says (Ep. ad Heliod.): "Though thou trample upon thy father, though thou spurn thy mother, turn not aside, but with dry eyes hasten to the standard of the cross; it is the highest degree of piety to be cruel in this matter." Therefore in such a case the duties of piety towards one's parents should be omitted for the sake of the worship religion gives to God. If, however, by paying the services due to our parents, we are not withdrawn from the service of God, then will it be an act of piety, and there will be no need to set piety aside for the sake of religion.

Reply Obj. 1: Gregory expounding this saying of our Lord says (Hom. xxxvii in Ev.) that "when we find our parents to be a hindrance in our way to God, we must ignore them by hating and fleeing from them." For if our parents incite us to sin, and withdraw us from the service of God, we must, as regards this point, abandon and hate them. It is in this sense that the Levites are said to have not known their kindred, because they obeyed the Lord's command, and spared not the idolaters (Ex. 32). James and John are praised for leaving their parents and following our Lord, not that their father incited them to evil, but because they deemed it possible for him to find another means of livelihood, if they followed Christ.

Reply Obj. 2: Our Lord forbade the disciple to bury his father because, according to Chrysostom (Hom. xxviii in Matth.), "Our Lord by so doing saved him from many evils, such as the sorrows and worries and other things that one anticipates under these circumstances. For after the burial the will had to be read, the estate had to be divided, and so forth: but chiefly, because there were others who could see to the funeral." Or, according to Cyril's commentary on Luke 9, "this disciple's request was, not that he might bury a dead father, but that he might support a yet living father in the latter's old age, until at length he should bury him. This is what Our Lord did not grant, because there were others, bound by the duties of kindred, to take care of him."

Reply Obj. 3: Whatever we give our parents out of piety is referred by us to God; just as other works of mercy which we perform with regard to any of our neighbors are offered to God, according to Matt. 25:40: "As long as you did it to one of ... My least ... you did it to Me." Accordingly, if our carnal parents stand in need of our assistance, so that they have no other means of support, provided they incite us to nothing against God, we must not abandon them for the sake of religion. But if we cannot devote ourselves to their service without sin, or if they can be supported without our assistance, it is lawful to forego their service, so as to give more time to religion.

Reply Obj. 4: We must speak differently of one who is yet in the world, and of one who has made his profession in religion. For he that is in the world, if he has parents unable to find support without him, he must not leave them and enter religion, because he would be breaking the commandment prescribing the honoring of parents. Some say, however, that even then he might abandon them, and leave them in God's care. But this, considered aright, would be to tempt God: since, while having human means at hand, he would be exposing his parents to danger, in the hope of God's assistance. On the other hand, if the parents can find means of livelihood without him, it is lawful for him to abandon them and enter religion, because children are not bound to support their parents except in cases of necessity, as stated above. He that has already made his profession in religion is deemed to be already dead to the world: wherefore he ought not, under pretext of supporting his parents, to leave the cloister where he is buried with Christ, and busy himself once more with worldly affairs. Nevertheless he is bound, saving his obedience to his superiors, and his religious state withal, to make points efforts for his parents' support.

## QUESTION 102

OF OBSERVANCE, CONSIDERED IN ITSELF, AND OF ITS PARTS (In Three Articles)

We must now consider observance and its parts, the considerations of which will manifest the contrary vices.

Under the head of observance there are three points of inquiry:

(1) Whether observance is a special virtue, distinct from other virtues?

(2) What does observance offer?

(3) Of its comparison with piety.

FIRST ARTICLE [II-II, Q. 102, Art. 1]

Whether Observance Is a Special Virtue, Distinct from Other Virtues?

Objection 1: It seems that observance is not a special virtue, distinct from other virtues. For virtues are distinguished by their objects. But the object of observance is not distinct from the object of piety: for Tully says (De Invent. Rhet. ii) that "it is by observance that we pay worship and honor to those who excel in some kind of dignity." But worship and honor are paid also by piety to our parents, who excel in dignity. Therefore observance is not a distinct virtue from piety.

Obj. 2: Further, just as honor and worship are due to those that are in a position of dignity, so also are they due to those who excel in science and virtue. But there is no special virtue whereby we pay honor and worship to those who excel in science and virtue. Therefore observance, whereby we pay worship and honor to those who excel in dignity, is not a special virtue distinct from other virtues.

Obj. 3: Further, we have many duties towards those who are in a position of dignity, the fulfilment of which is required by law, according to Rom. 13:7, "Render ... to all men their dues: tribute to whom tribute is due," etc. Now the fulfilment of the requirements of the law belongs to legal justice, or even to special justice. Therefore observance is not by itself a special virtue distinct from other virtues.

*On the contrary,* Tully (De Invent. Rhet. ii) reckons observance along with the other parts of justice, which are special virtues.

*I answer that,* As explained above (Q. 101, AA. 1, 3; Q. 80), according to the various excellences of those persons to whom something is due, there must needs be a corresponding distinction of virtues in a descending order. Now just as a carnal father partakes of the character of principle in a particular way, which character is found in God in a universal way, so too a person who, in some way, exercises providence in one respect, partakes of the character of father in a particular way, since a father is the principle of generation, of education, of learning and of whatever pertains to the perfection of human life: while a person who is in a position of dignity is as a principle of government with regard to certain things: for instance, the governor of a state in civil matters, the commander of an army in matters of warfare, a professor in matters of learning, and so forth. Hence it is that all such persons are designated as "fathers," on account of their being charged with like cares: thus the servants of

Naaman said to him (4 Kings 5:13): "Father, if the prophet had bid thee do some great thing," etc.

Therefore, just as, in a manner, beneath religion, whereby worship is given to God, we find piety, whereby we worship our parents; so under piety we find observance, whereby worship and honor are paid to persons in positions of dignity.

Reply Obj. 1: As stated above (Q. 101, A. 3, ad 2), religion goes by the name of piety by way of supereminence, although piety properly so called is distinct from religion; and in the same way piety can be called observance by way of excellence, although observance properly speaking is distinct from piety.

Reply Obj. 2: By the very fact of being in a position of dignity a man not only excels as regards his position, but also has a certain power of governing subjects, wherefore it is fitting that he should be considered as a principle inasmuch as he is the governor of others. On the other hand, the fact that a man has perfection of science and virtue does not give him the character of a principle in relation to others, but merely a certain excellence in himself. Wherefore a special virtue is appointed for the payment of worship and honor to persons in positions of dignity. Yet, forasmuch as science, virtue and all like things render a man fit for positions of dignity, the respect which is paid to anyone on account of any excellence whatever belongs to the same virtue.

Reply Obj. 3: It belongs to special justice, properly speaking, to pay the equivalent to those to whom we owe anything. Now this cannot be done to the virtuous, and to those who make good use of their position of dignity, as neither can it be done to God, nor to our parents. Consequently these matters belong to an annexed virtue, and not to special justice, which is a principal virtue.

Legal justice extends to the acts of all the virtues, as stated above (Q. 58, A. 6).

SECOND ARTICLE [II-II, Q. 102, Art. 2]

Whether It Belongs to Observance to Pay Worship and Honor to Those Who Are in Positions of Dignity?

Objection 1: It seems that it does not belong to observance to pay worship and honor to persons in positions of dignity. For according to Augustine (De Civ. Dei x), we are said to worship those persons whom we hold in honor, so that worship and honor would seem to be the same. Therefore it is unfitting to define observance as paying worship and honor to persons in positions of dignity.

Obj. 2: Further, it belongs to justice that we pay what we owe: wherefore this belongs to observance also, since it is a part of justice. Now we do not owe worship and honor to all persons in positions of dignity, but only to those who are placed over us. Therefore observance is unfittingly defined as giving worship and honor to all.

Obj. 3: Further, not only do we owe honor to persons of dignity who are placed over us; we owe them also fear and a certain payment of remuneration, according to Rom. 13:7, "Render ... to all men their dues; tribute to whom tribute is due; custom to whom custom; fear to whom fear; honor to whom honor." Moreover, we owe them reverence and subjection, according to Heb. 13:17, "Obey your prelates, and be subject to them." Therefore observance is not fittingly defined as paying worship and honor.

*On the contrary,* Tully says (De Invent. Rhet. ii) that "it is by observance that we pay worship and honor to those who excel in some kind of dignity."

*I answer that,* It belongs to persons in positions of dignity to govern subjects. Now to govern is to move certain ones to their due end: thus a sailor governs his ship by steering it to port. But every mover has a certain excellence and power over that which is moved. Wherefore, a person in a position of dignity is an object of twofold consideration: first, in so far as he obtains excellence of position, together with a certain power over subjects: secondly, as regards the exercise of his government. In respect of his excellence there is due to him honor, which is the recognition of some kind of excellence; and in respect of the exercise of his government, there is due to him worship, consisting in rendering him service, by obeying his commands, and by repaying him, according to one's faculty, for the benefits we received from him.

Reply Obj. 1: Worship includes not only honor, but also whatever other suitable actions are connected with the relations between man and man.

Reply Obj. 2: As stated above (Q. 80), debt is twofold. One is legal debt, to pay which man is compelled by law; and thus man owes honor and worship to those persons in positions of dignity who are placed over him. The other is moral debt, which is due by reason of a certain honesty: it is in this way that we owe worship and honor to persons in positions of dignity even though we be not their subjects.

Reply Obj. 3: Honor is due to the excellence of persons in positions of dignity, on account of their higher rank: while fear is due to them on account of their power to use compulsion: and to the exercise of their government there is due both obedience, whereby subjects are moved at the command of their superiors, and tributes, which are a repayment of their labor.

THIRD ARTICLE [II-II, Q. 102, Art. 3]

Whether Observance Is a Greater Virtue Than Piety?

Objection 1: It seems that observance is a greater virtue than piety. For the prince to whom worship is paid by observance is compared to a father who is worshiped by piety, as a universal to a particular governor; because the household which a father governs is part of the state which is governed by the prince. Now a universal power is greater, and inferiors are more subject thereto. Therefore observance is a greater virtue than piety.

Obj. 2: Further, persons in positions of dignity take care of the common good. Now our kindred pertain to the private good, which we ought to set aside for the common good: wherefore it is praiseworthy to expose oneself to the danger of death for the sake of the common good. Therefore observance, whereby worship is paid to persons in positions of dignity, is a greater virtue than piety, which pays worship to one's kindred.

Obj. 3: Further honor and reverence are due to the virtuous in the first place after God. Now honor and reverence are paid to the virtuous by the virtue of observance, as stated above (A. 1, ad 3). Therefore observance takes the first place after religion.

*On the contrary,* The precepts of the Law prescribe acts of virtue. Now, immediately after the precepts of religion, which belong to the first table, follows the precept of honoring our parents which refers to piety. Therefore piety follows immediately after religion in the order of excellence.

*I answer that,* Something may be paid to persons in positions of dignity in two ways. First, in relation to the common good, as when one serves them in the administration of the affairs of the state. This no longer belongs to observance, but to piety, which pays worship not only to one's father but also to one's fatherland. Secondly, that which is paid to persons in positions of dignity refers specially to their personal usefulness or renown, and this belongs properly to observance, as distinct from piety. Therefore in comparing observance with piety we must needs take into consideration the different relations in which other persons stand to ourselves, which relations both virtues regard. Now it is evident that the persons of our parents and of our kindred are more substantially akin to us than persons in positions of dignity, since birth and education, which originate in the father, belong more to one's substance than external government, the principle of which is seated in those who are in positions of dignity. For this reason piety takes precedence of observance, inasmuch as it pays worship to persons more akin to us, and to whom we are more strictly bound.

Reply Obj. 1: The prince is compared to the father as a universal to a particular power, as regards external government, but not as regards the father being a principle of generation: for in this way the father should be compared with the divine power from which all things derive their being.

Reply Obj. 2: In so far as persons in positions of dignity are related to the common good, their worship does not pertain to observance, but to piety, as stated above.

Reply Obj. 3: The rendering of honor or worship should be proportionate to the person to whom it is paid not only as considered in himself, but also as compared to those who pay them. Wherefore, though virtuous persons, considered in themselves, are more worthy of honor than the persons of one's parents, yet children are under a greater obligation, on account of the benefits they have received from their parents and their natural kinship with them, to pay worship and honor to their parents than to virtuous persons who are not of their kindred.

## QUESTION 103

OF DULIA (In Four Articles)

We must now consider the parts of observance. We shall consider (1) dulia, whereby we pay honor and other things pertaining thereto to those who are in a higher position; (2) obedience, whereby we obey their commands.

Under the first head there are four points of inquiry:

(1) Whether honor is a spiritual or a corporal thing?

(2) Whether honor is due to those only who are in a higher position?

(3) Whether dulia, which pays honor and worship to those who are above us, is a special virtue, distinct from latria?

(4) Whether it contains several species?

FIRST ARTICLE [II-II, Q. 103, Art. 1]

Whether Honor Denotes Something Corporal?

Objection 1: It seems that honor does not denote something corporal. For honor is showing reverence in acknowledgment of virtue, as may be gathered from the Philosopher (Ethic. i, 5). Now showing reverence is something spiritual, since to revere is an act of fear, as stated above (Q. 81, A. 2, ad 1). Therefore honor is something spiritual.

Obj. 2: Further, according to the Philosopher (Ethic. iv, 3), "honor is the reward of virtue." Now, since virtue consists chiefly of spiritual things, its reward is not something corporal, for the reward is more excellent than the merit. Therefore honor does not consist of corporal things.

Obj. 3: Further, honor is distinct from praise, as also from glory. Now praise and glory consist of external things. Therefore honor consists of things internal and spiritual.

*On the contrary,* Jerome in his exposition of 1 Tim. 5:3, "Honor widows that are widows indeed," and (1 Tim. 5:17), "let the priests that rule well be esteemed worthy of double honor" etc. says (Ep. ad Ageruch.): "Honor here stands either for almsgiving or for remuneration." Now both of these pertain to [corporal] things. Therefore honor consists of corporal things.

*I answer that,* Honor denotes a witnessing to a person's excellence. Therefore men who wish to be honored seek a witnessing to their excellence, according to the Philosopher (Ethic. i, 5; viii, 8). Now witness is borne either before God or before man. Before God, Who is the searcher of hearts, the witness of one's conscience suffices. wherefore honor, so far as God is concerned, may consist of the mere internal movement of the heart, for instance when a man acknowledges either God's excellence or another man's excellence before God. But, as regards men, one cannot bear witness, save by means of signs, either by words, as when one proclaims another's excellence by word of mouth, or by deeds, for instance by bowing, saluting, and so forth, or by external things, as by offering gifts, erecting statues, and the like. Accordingly honor consists of signs, external and corporal.

Reply Obj. 1: Reverence is not the same as honor: but on the one hand it is the primary motive for showing honor, in so far as one man honors another out of the reverence he has for him; and on the other hand, it is the end of honor, in so far as a person is honored in order that he may be held in reverence by others.

Reply Obj. 2: According to the Philosopher (Ethic. iv, 3), honor is not a sufficient reward of virtue: yet nothing in human and corporal things can be greater than honor, since these corporal things themselves are employed as signs in acknowledgment of excelling virtue. It is, however, due to the good and the beautiful, that they may be made known, according to Matt. 5:15, "Neither do men light a candle, and put it under a bushel, but upon a candlestick, that it may shine to all that are in the house." In this sense honor is said to be the reward of virtue.

Reply Obj. 3: Praise is distinguished from honor in two ways. First, because praise consists only of verbal signs, whereas honor consists of any external signs, so that praise is included in honor. Secondly, because by paying honor to a person we bear witness to a person's excelling goodness absolutely, whereas by praising him we bear witness to his goodness in reference to an end: thus we praise one that works well for an end. On the other hand, honor is given even to the best, which is not referred to an end, but has already arrived at the end, according to the Philosopher (Ethic. i, 5).

Glory is the effect of honor and praise, since the result of our bearing witness to a person's goodness is that his goodness becomes clear to the knowledge of many. The word "glory" signifies this, for "glory" is the same as *kleria* , wherefore a gloss of Augustine on Rom. 16:27 observes that glory is "clear knowledge together with praise."

SECOND ARTICLE [II-II, Q. 103, Art. 2]

Whether Honor Is Properly Due to Those Who Are Above Us?

Objection 1: It seems that honor is not properly due to those who are above us. For an angel is above any human wayfarer, according to Matt. 11:11, "He that is lesser in the kingdom of heaven is greater than John the Baptist." Yet an angel forbade John when the latter wished to honor him (Apoc. 22:10). Therefore honor is not due to those who are above us.

Obj. 2: Further, honor is due to a person in acknowledgment of his virtue, as stated above (A. 1; Q. 63, A. 3). But sometimes those who are above us are not virtuous. Therefore honor is not due to them, as neither is it due to the demons, who nevertheless are above us in the order of nature.

Obj. 3: Further, the Apostle says (Rom. 12:10): "With honor preventing one another," and we read (1 Pet. 2:17): "Honor all men." But this would not be so if honor were due to those alone who are above us. Therefore honor is not due properly to those who are above us.

Obj. 4: Further, it is written (Tob. 1:16) that Tobias "had ten talents of silver of that which he had been honored by the king": and we read (Esther 6:11) that Assuerus honored Mardochaeus, and ordered it to be proclaimed in his presence: "This honor is he worthy of whom the king hath a mind to honor." Therefore honor is paid to those also who are beneath us, and it seems, in consequence, that honor is not due properly to those who are above us.

*On the contrary,* The Philosopher says (Ethic. i, 12) that "honor is due to the best."

*I answer that,* As stated above (A. 1), honor is nothing but an acknowledgment of a person's excelling goodness. Now a person's excellence may be considered, not only in relation to those who honor him, in the point of his being more excellent than they, but also in itself, or in relation to other persons, and in this way honor is always due to a person, on account of some excellence or superiority.

For the person honored has no need to be more excellent than those who honor him; it may suffice for him to be more excellent than some others, or again he may be more excellent than those who honor him in some respect and not simply.

Reply Obj. 1: The angel forbade John to pay him, not any kind of honor, but the honor of adoration and latria, which is due to God. Or again, he forbade him to pay the honor of dulia, in order to indicate the dignity of John himself, for which Christ equaled him to the angels "according to the hope of glory of the children of God": wherefore he refused to be honored by him as though he were superior to him.

Reply Obj. 2: A wicked superior is honored for the excellence, not of his virtue but of his dignity, as being God's minister, and because the honor paid to him is paid to the whole community over which he presides. As for the demons, they are wicked beyond recall, and should be looked upon as enemies, rather than treated with honor.

Reply Obj. 3: In every man is to be found something that makes it possible to deem him better than ourselves, according to Phil. 2:3, "In humility, let each esteem others better than themselves," and thus, too, we should all be on the alert to do honor to one another.

Reply Obj. 4: Private individuals are sometimes honored by kings, not that they are above them in the order of dignity but on account of some excellence of their virtue: and in this way Tobias and Mardochaeus were honored by kings.

THIRD ARTICLE [II-II, Q. 103, Art. 3]

Whether Dulia Is a Special Virtue Distinct from Latria?

Objection 1. It seems that dulia is not a special virtue distinct from latria. For a gloss on Ps. 7:1, "O Lord my God, in Thee have I put my trust," says: "Lord of all by His power, to Whom dulia is due; God by creation, to Whom we owe latria." Now the virtue directed to God as Lord is not distinct from that which is directed to Him as God. Therefore dulia is not a distinct virtue from latria.

Obj. 2: Further, according to the Philosopher (Ethic. viii, 8), "to be loved is like being honored." Now the charity with which we love God is the same as that whereby we love our neighbor. Therefore dulia whereby we honor our neighbor is not a distinct virtue from latria with which we honor God.

Obj. 3: Further, the movement whereby one is moved towards an image is the same as the movement whereby one is moved towards the thing represented by the image. Now by dulia we honor a man as being made to the image of God. For it is written of the wicked (Wis. 2:22, 23) that "they esteemed not the honor of holy souls, for God created man incorruptible, and to the image of His own likeness He made him." Therefore dulia is not a distinct virtue from latria whereby God is honored.

*On the contrary,* Augustine says (De Civ. Dei x), that "the homage due to man, of which the Apostle spoke when he commanded servants to obey their masters and which in Greek is called dulia, is distinct from latria which denotes the homage that consists in the worship of God."

*I answer that,* According to what has been stated above (Q. 101, A. 3), where there are different aspects of that which is due, there must needs be different virtues to render those dues. Now servitude is due to God and to man under different aspects: even as lordship is competent to God and to man under different aspects. For God has absolute and paramount lordship over the creature wholly and singly, which is entirely subject to His power: whereas man partakes of a certain likeness to the divine lordship, forasmuch as he exercises a particular power over some man or creature. Wherefore dulia, which pays due service to a human lord, is a distinct virtue from latria, which pays due service to the lordship of God. It is, moreover, a species of observance, because by observance we honor all those who excel in dignity, while dulia properly speaking is the reverence of servants for their master, dulia being the Greek for servitude.

Reply Obj. 1: Just as religion is called piety by way of excellence, inasmuch as God is our Father by way of excellence, so again latria is called dulia by way of excellence, inasmuch as God is our Lord by way of excellence. Now the creature does not partake of the power to create by reason of which latria is due to God: and so this gloss drew a distinction, by ascribing latria to God in respect of creation, which is not communicated to a creature, but dulia in respect of lordship, which is communicated to a creature.

Reply Obj. 2: The reason why we love our neighbor is God, since that which we love in our neighbor through charity is God alone. Wherefore the charity with which we love God is the same as that with which we love our neighbor. Yet there are other friendships distinct from charity, in respect of the other reasons for which a man is loved. In like manner, since there is one reason for serving God and another for serving man, and for honoring the one or the other, latria and dulia are not the same virtue.

Reply Obj. 3: Movement towards an image as such is referred to the thing represented by the image: yet not every movement towards an image is referred to the image as such, and consequently sometimes the movement to the image differs specifically from the movement to the thing. Accordingly we must reply that the honor or subjection of dulia regards some dignity of a man absolutely. For though, in respect of that dignity, man is made to the image or likeness of God, yet in showing reverence to a person, one does not always refer this to God actually.

Or we may reply that the movement towards an image is, after a fashion, towards the thing, yet the movement towards the thing need not be towards its image. Wherefore reverence paid to a person as the image of God redounds somewhat to God: and yet this differs from the reverence that is paid to God Himself, for this in no way refers to His image.

FOURTH ARTICLE [II-II, Q. 103, Art. 4]

Whether Dulia Has Various Species?

Objection 1: It seems that dulia has various species. For by dulia we show honor to our neighbor. Now different neighbors are honored under different aspects, for instance king, father and master, as the Philosopher states (Ethic. ix, 2). Since this difference of aspect in the object differentiates the species of virtue, it seems that dulia is divided into specifically different virtues.

Obj. 2: Further, the mean differs specifically from the extremes, as pale differs from white and black. Now hyperdulia is apparently a mean between latria and dulia: for it is shown towards creatures having a special affinity to God, for instance to the Blessed Virgin as being the mother of God. Therefore it seems that there are different species of dulia, one being simply dulia, the other hyperdulia.

Obj. 3: Further, just as in the rational creature we find the image of God, for which reason it is honored, so too in the irrational creature we find the trace of God. Now the aspect of likeness denoted by an image differs from the aspect conveyed by a trace. Therefore we must distinguish a corresponding difference of dulia: and all the more since honor is shown to certain irrational creatures, as, for instance, to the wood of the Holy Cross.

*On the contrary,* Dulia is condivided with latria. But latria is not divided into different species. Neither therefore is dulia.

*I answer that,* Dulia may be taken in two ways. In one way it may be taken in a wide sense as denoting reverence paid to anyone on account of any kind of excellence, and thus it comprises piety and observance, and any similar virtue whereby reverence is shown towards a man. Taken in this sense it will have parts differing specifically from one another. In another way it may be taken in a strict sense as denoting the reverence of a servant for his lord, for dulia signifies servitude, as stated above (A. 3). Taken in this sense it is not divided into different species, but is one of the species of observance, mentioned by Tully (De Invent. Rhet. ii), for the reason that a servant reveres his lord under one aspect, a soldier his commanding officer under another, the disciple his master under another, and so on in similar cases.

Reply Obj. 1: This argument takes dulia in a wide sense.

Reply Obj. 2: Hyperdulia is the highest species of dulia taken in a wide sense, since the greatest reverence is that which is due to a man by reason of his having an affinity to God.

Reply Obj. 3: Man owes neither subjection nor honor to an irrational creature considered in itself, indeed all such creatures are naturally subject to man. As to the Cross of Christ, the honor we pay to it is the same as that which we pay to Christ, just as the king's robe receives the same honor as the king himself, according to Damascene (De Fide Orth. iv).

## QUESTION 104

OF OBEDIENCE (In Six Articles)

We must now consider obedience, under which head there are six points of inquiry:

(1) Whether one man is bound to obey another?

(2) Whether obedience is a special virtue?

(3) Of its comparison with other virtues;

(4) Whether God must be obeyed in all things?

(5) Whether subjects are bound to obey their superiors in all things?

(6) Whether the faithful are bound to obey the secular power?

FIRST ARTICLE [II-II, Q. 104, Art. 1]

Whether One Man Is Bound to Obey Another?

Objection 1: It seems that one man is not bound to obey another. For nothing should be done contrary to the divine ordinance. Now God has so ordered that man is ruled by his own counsel, according to Ecclus. 15:14, "God made man from the beginning, and left him in the hand of his own counsel." Therefore one man is not bound to obey another.

Obj. 2: Further, if one man were bound to obey another, he would have to look upon the will of the person commanding him, as being his rule of conduct. Now God's will alone, which is always right, is a rule of human conduct. Therefore man is bound to obey none but God.

Obj. 3: Further, the more gratuitous the service the more is it acceptable. Now what a man does out of duty is not gratuitous. Therefore if a man were bound in duty to obey others in doing good deeds, for this very reason his good deeds would be rendered less acceptable through being done out of obedience. Therefore one man is not bound to obey another.

*On the contrary,* It is prescribed (Heb. 13:17): "Obey your prelates and be subject to them."

*I answer that,* Just as the actions of natural things proceed from natural powers, so do human actions proceed from the human will. In natural things it behooved the higher to move the lower to their actions by the excellence of the natural power bestowed on them by God: and so in human affairs also the higher must move the lower by their will in virtue of a divinely established authority. Now to move by reason and will is to command. Wherefore just as in virtue of the divinely established natural order the lower natural things need to be subject to the movement of the higher, so too in human affairs, in virtue of the order of natural and divine law, inferiors are bound to obey their superiors.

Reply Obj. 1: God left man in the hand of his own counsel, not as though it were lawful to him to do whatever he will, but because, unlike irrational creatures, he is not compelled by natural necessity to do what he ought to do, but is left the free choice proceeding from his own counsel. And just as he has to proceed on his own counsel in doing other things, so too has he in the point of obeying his superiors. For Gregory says (Moral. xxxv), "When we humbly give way to another's voice, we overcome ourselves in our own hearts."

Reply Obj. 2: The will of God is the first rule whereby all rational wills are regulated: and to this rule one will approaches more than another, according to a divinely appointed order. Hence the will of the one man who issues a command may be as a second rule to the will of this other man who obeys him.

Reply Obj. 3: A thing may be deemed gratuitous in two ways. In one way on the part of the deed itself, because, to wit, one is not bound to do it; in another way, on the part of the doer, because he does it of his own free will. Now a deed is rendered virtuous, praiseworthy and meritorious, chiefly according as it proceeds from the will. Wherefore although obedience be a duty, if one obey with a prompt will, one's merit is not for that reason diminished, especially before God, Who sees not only the outward deed, but also the inward will.

SECOND ARTICLE [II-II, Q, 104, Art. 2]

Whether Obedience Is a Special Virtue?

Objection 1: It seems that obedience is not a special virtue. For disobedience is contrary to obedience. But disobedience is a general sin, because Ambrose says (De Parad. viii) that "sin is to disobey the divine law." Therefore obedience is not a special virtue.

Obj. 2: Further, every special virtue is either theological or moral. But obedience is not a theological virtue, since it is not comprised under faith, hope or charity. Nor is it a moral virtue, since it does not hold the mean between excess and deficiency, for the more obedient one is the more is one praised. Therefore obedience is not a special virtue.

Obj. 3: Further, Gregory says (Moral. xxxv) that "obedience is the more meritorious and praiseworthy, the less it holds its own." But every special virtue is the more to be praised the more it holds its own, since virtue requires a man to exercise his will and choice, as stated in *Ethic.* ii, 4. Therefore obedience is not a special virtue.

Obj. 4: Further, virtues differ in species according to their objects. Now the object of obedience would seem to be the command of a superior, of which, apparently, there are as many kinds as there are degrees of superiority. Therefore obedience is a general virtue, comprising many special virtues.

*On the contrary,* obedience is reckoned by some to be a part of justice, as stated above (Q. 80).

*I answer that,* A special virtue is assigned to all good deeds that have a special reason of praise: for it belongs properly to virtue to render a deed good. Now obedience to a superior is due in accordance with the divinely established order of things, as shown above (A. 1), and therefore it is a good, since good consists in mode, species and order, as Augustine states (De Natura Boni iii) [*Cf. First Part, Q. 5, A. 5]. Again, this act has a special aspect of praiseworthiness by reason of its object. For while subjects have many obligations towards their superiors, this one, that they are bound to obey their commands, stands out as special among the rest. Wherefore obedience is a special virtue, and its specific object is a command tacit or express, because the superior's will, however it become known, is a tacit precept, and a man's obedience seems to be all the more prompt, forasmuch as by obeying he forestalls the express command as soon as he understands his superior's will.

Reply Obj. 1: Nothing prevents the one same material object from admitting two special aspects to which two special virtues correspond: thus a soldier, by defending his king's fortress, fulfils both an act of fortitude, by facing the danger of death for a good end, and an act of justice, by rendering due service to his lord. Accordingly the aspect of precept, which obedience considers, occurs in acts of all virtues, but not in all acts of virtue, since not all acts of virtue are a matter of precept, as stated above (I-II, Q. 96, A. 3). Moreover, certain things are sometimes a matter of precept, and pertain to no other virtue, such things for instance as are not evil except because they are forbidden. Wherefore, if obedience be taken in its proper sense, as considering formally and intentionally the aspect of precept, it will be a special virtue, and disobedience a special sin: because in this way it is requisite for obedience that one perform an act of justice or of some other virtue with the intention of fulfilling a precept; and for disobedience that one treat the precept with actual contempt. On the other hand, if obedience be taken in a wide sense for the performance of any action that may be a matter of precept, and disobedience for the omission of that action through any intention whatever, then obedience will be a general virtue, and disobedience a general sin.

Reply Obj. 2: Obedience is not a theological virtue, for its direct object is not God, but the precept of any superior, whether expressed or inferred, namely, a simple word of the superior, indicating his will, and which the obedient subject obeys promptly, according to Titus 3:1, "Admonish them to be subject to princes, and to obey at a word," etc.

It is, however, a moral virtue, since it is a part of justice, and it observes the mean between excess and deficiency. Excess thereof is measured in respect, not of quantity, but of other circumstances, in so far as a man obeys either whom he ought not, or in matters wherein he ought not to obey, as we have stated above regarding religion (Q. 92, A. 2). We may also reply that as in justice, excess is in the person who retains another's property, and deficiency in the person who does not receive his due, according to the Philosopher (Ethic. v, 4), so too obedience observes the mean between excess on the part of him who fails to pay due obedience to his superior, since he exceeds in fulfilling his own will, and deficiency on the part of the superior, who does not receive obedience. Wherefore in this way obedience will be a mean between two forms of wickedness, as was stated above concerning justice (Q. 58, A. 10).

Reply Obj. 3: Obedience, like every virtue, requires the will to be prompt towards its proper object, but not towards that which is repugnant to it. Now the proper object of obedience is a precept, and this proceeds from another's will. Wherefore obedience makes a man's will prompt in fulfilling the will of another, the maker, namely, of the precept. If that which is prescribed to him is willed by him for its own sake apart from its being prescribed, as happens in agreeable matters, he tends towards it at once by his own will and seems to comply, not on account of the precept, but on account of his own will. But if that which is prescribed is nowise willed for its own sake, but, considered in itself, repugnant to his own will, as happens in disagreeable matters, then it is quite evident that it is not fulfilled except on account of the precept. Hence Gregory says (Moral. xxxv) that "obedience perishes or diminishes when it holds its own in agreeable matters," because, to wit, one's own will seems to tend principally, not to the accomplishment of the precept, but to the fulfilment of one's own desire; but that "it increases in disagreeable or difficult matters," because there one's own will tends to nothing beside the precept. Yet this must be understood as regards outward appearances: for, on the other hand, according to the judgment of God, Who searches the heart, it may happen that even in agreeable matters obedience, while holding its own, is nonetheless praiseworthy, provided the will of him that obeys tend no less devotedly [*Cf. Q. 82, A. 2] to the fulfilment of the precept.

Reply Obj. 4: Reverence regards directly the person that excels: wherefore it admits a various species according to the various aspects of excellence. Obedience, on the other hand, regards the precept of the person that excels, and therefore admits of only one aspect. And since obedience is due to a person's precept on account of reverence to him, it follows that obedience to a man is of one species, though the causes from which it proceeds differ specifically.

THIRD ARTICLE [II-II, Q. 104, Art. 3]

Whether Obedience Is the Greatest of the Virtues?

Objection 1: It seems that obedience is the greatest of the virtues. For it is written (1 Kings 15:22): "Obedience is better than sacrifices." Now the offering of sacrifices belongs to religion, which is the greatest of all moral virtues, as shown above (Q. 81, A. 6). Therefore obedience is the greatest of all virtues.

Obj. 2: Further, Gregory says (Moral. xxxv) that "obedience is the only virtue that ingrafts virtues in the soul and protects them when ingrafted." Now the cause is greater than the effect. Therefore obedience is greater than all the virtues.

Obj. 3: Further, Gregory says (Moral. xxxv) that "evil should never be done out of obedience: yet sometimes for the sake of obedience we should lay aside the good we are doing." Now one does not lay aside a thing except for something better. Therefore obedience, for whose sake the good of other virtues is set aside, is better than other virtues.

*On the contrary,* obedience deserves praise because it proceeds from charity: for Gregory says (Moral. xxxv) that "obedience should be practiced, not out of servile fear, but from a sense of charity, not through fear of punishment, but through love of justice." Therefore charity is a greater virtue than obedience.

*I answer that,* Just as sin consists in man contemning God and adhering to mutable things, so the merit of a virtuous act consists in man contemning created goods and adhering to God as his end. Now the end is greater than that which is directed to the end. Therefore if a man contemns created goods in order that he may adhere to God, his virtue derives greater praise from his adhering to God than from his contemning earthly things. And so those, namely the theological, virtues whereby he adheres to God in Himself, are greater than the moral virtues, whereby he holds in contempt some earthly thing in order to adhere to God.

Among the moral virtues, the greater the thing which a man contemns that he may adhere to God, the greater the virtue. Now there are three kinds of human goods that man may contemn for God's sake. The lowest of these are external goods, the goods of the body take the middle place, and the highest are the goods of the soul; and among these the chief, in a way, is the will, in so far as, by his will, man makes use of all other goods. Therefore, properly speaking, the virtue of obedience, whereby we contemn our own will for God's sake, is more praiseworthy than the other moral virtues, which contemn other goods for the sake of God.

Hence Gregory says (Moral. xxxv) that "obedience is rightly preferred to sacrifices, because by sacrifices another's body is slain whereas by obedience we slay our own will." Wherefore even any other acts of virtue are meritorious before God through being performed out of obedience to God's will. For were one to suffer even martyrdom, or to give all one's goods to the poor, unless one directed these things to the fulfilment of the divine will, which pertains directly to obedience, they could not be meritorious: as neither would they be if they were done without charity, which cannot exist apart from obedience. For it is written (1 John 2:4, 5): "He who saith that he knoweth God, and keepeth not His commandments, is a liar ... but he that keepeth His word, in him in very deed the charity of God is perfected": and this because friends have the same likes and dislikes.

Reply Obj. 1: Obedience proceeds from reverence, which pays worship and honor to a superior, and in this respect it is contained under different virtues, although considered in itself, as regarding the aspect of precept, it is one special virtue. Accordingly, in so far as it proceeds from reverence for a superior, it is contained, in a way, under observance; while in so far as it proceeds from reverence for one's parents, it is contained under piety; and in so far as it proceeds from reverence for God, it comes under religion, and pertains to devotion, which is the principal act of religion. Wherefore from this point of view it is more praiseworthy to obey God than to offer sacrifice, as well as because, "in a sacrifice we slay another's body, whereas by obedience we slay our own will," as Gregory says (Moral. xxxv). As to the special case in which Samuel spoke, it would have been better for Saul to obey God than to offer in sacrifice the fat animals of the Amalekites against the commandment of God.

Reply Obj. 2: All acts of virtue, in so far as they come under a precept, belong to obedience. Wherefore according as acts of virtue act causally or dispositively towards their generation and preservation, obedience is said to ingraft and protect all virtues. And yet it does not follow that obedience takes precedence of all virtues absolutely, for two reasons. First, because though an act of virtue come under a precept, one may nevertheless perform that act of virtue without considering the aspect of precept. Consequently, if there be any virtue, whose object is naturally prior to the precept, that virtue is said to be naturally prior to obedience. Such a virtue is faith, whereby we come to know the sublime nature of divine authority, by reason of which the power to command is competent to God. Secondly, because infusion of grace and virtues may precede, even in point of time, all virtuous acts: and in this way obedience is not prior to all virtues, neither in point of time nor by nature.

Reply Obj. 3: There are two kinds of good. There is that to which we are bound of necessity, for instance to love God, and so forth: and by no means may such a good be set aside on account of obedience. But there is another good to which man is not bound of necessity, and this good we ought sometimes to set aside for the sake of obedience to which we are bound of necessity, since we ought not to do good by falling into sin. Yet as Gregory remarks (Moral. xxxv), "he who forbids his subjects any single good, must needs allow them many others, lest the souls of those who obey perish utterly from starvation, through being deprived of every good." Thus the loss of one good may be compensated by obedience and other goods.

FOURTH ARTICLE [II-II, Q. 104, Art. 4]

Whether God Ought to Be Obeyed in All Things?

Objection 1: It seems that God need not be obeyed in all things. For it is written (Matt. 9:30, 31) that our Lord after healing the two blind men commanded them, saying: "See that no man know this. But they going out spread His fame abroad in all that country." Yet they are not blamed for so doing. Therefore it seems that we are not bound to obey God in all things.

Obj. 2: Further, no one is bound to do anything contrary to virtue. Now we find that God commanded certain things contrary to virtue: thus He commanded Abraham to slay his innocent son (Gen. 22); and the Jews to steal the property of the Egyptians (Ex. 11), which things are contrary to justice; and Osee to take to himself a woman who was an adulteress (Osee 3), and this is contrary to chastity. Therefore God is not to be obeyed in all things.

Obj. 3: Further, whoever obeys God conforms his will to the divine will even as to the thing willed. But we are not bound in all things to conform our will to the divine will as to the thing willed, as stated above (I-II, Q. 19, A. 10). Therefore man is not bound to obey God in all things.

*On the contrary,* It is written (Ex. 24:7): "All things that the Lord hath spoken we will do, and we will be obedient."

*I answer that,* As stated above (A. 1), he who obeys is moved by the command of the person he obeys, just as natural things are moved by their motive causes. Now just a God is the first mover of all things that are moved naturally, so too is He the first mover of all wills, as shown above (I-II, Q. 9, A. 6). Therefore just as all natural things are subject to the divine motion by a natural necessity so too all wills, by a kind of necessity of justice, are bound to obey the divine command.

Reply Obj. 1: Our Lord in telling the blind men to conceal the miracle had no intention of binding them with the force of a divine precept, but, as Gregory says (Moral. xix), "gave an example to His servants who follow Him that they might wish to hide their virtue and yet that it should be proclaimed against their will, in order that others might profit by their example."

Reply Obj. 2: Even as God does nothing contrary to nature (since "the nature of a thing is what God does therein," according to a gloss on Rom. 11), and yet does certain things contrary to the wonted course of nature; so to God can command nothing contrary to virtue since virtue and rectitude of human will consist chiefly in conformity with God's will and obedience to His command, although it be contrary to the wonted mode of virtue. Accordingly, then, the command given to Abraham to slay his innocent son was not contrary to justice, since God is the author of life and death. Nor again was it contrary to justice that He commanded the Jews to take things belonging to the Egyptians, because all things are His, and He gives them to whom He will. Nor was it contrary to chastity that Osee was commanded to take an adulteress, because God Himself is the ordainer of human generation, and the right manner of intercourse with woman is that which He appoints. Hence it is evident that the persons aforesaid did not sin, either by obeying God or by willing to obey Him.

Reply Obj. 3: Though man is not always bound to will what God wills, yet he is always bound to will what God wills him to will. This comes to man's knowledge chiefly through God's command, wherefore man is bound to obey God's commands in all things.

FIFTH ARTICLE [II-II, Q. 104, Art. 5]

Whether Subjects Are Bound to Obey Their Superiors in All Things?

Objection 1: It seems that subjects are bound to obey their superiors in all things. For the Apostle says (Col. 3:20): "Children, obey your parents in all things," and farther on (Col. 3:22): "Servants, obey in all things your masters according to the flesh." Therefore in like manner other subjects are bound to obey their superiors in all things.

Obj. 2: Further, superiors stand between God and their subjects, according to Deut. 5:5, "I was the mediator and stood between the Lord and you at that time, to show you His words." Now there is no going from extreme to extreme, except through that which stands between. Therefore the commands of a superior must be esteemed the commands of God, wherefore the Apostle says (Gal. 4:14): "You ... received me as an angel of God, even as Christ Jesus" and (1 Thess. 2:13): "When you had received of us the word of the hearing of God, you received it, not as the word of men, but, as it is indeed, the word of God." Therefore as man is bound to obey God in all things, so is he bound to obey his superiors.

Obj. 3: Further, just as religious in making their profession take vows of chastity and poverty, so do they also vow obedience. Now a religious is bound to observe chastity and poverty in all things. Therefore he is also bound to obey in all things.

*On the contrary,* It is written (Acts 5:29): "We ought to obey God rather than men." Now sometimes the things commanded by a superior are against God. Therefore superiors are not to be obeyed in all things.

*I answer that,* As stated above (AA. 1, 4), he who obeys is moved at the bidding of the person who commands him, by a certain necessity of justice, even as a natural thing is moved through the power of its mover by a natural necessity. That a natural thing be not moved by its mover, may happen in two ways. First, on account of a hindrance arising from the stronger power of some other mover; thus wood is not burnt by fire if a stronger force of water intervene. Secondly, through lack of order in the movable with regard to its mover, since, though it is subject to the latter's action in one respect, yet it is not subject thereto in every respect. Thus, a humor is sometimes subject to the action of heat, as regards being heated, but not as regards being dried up or consumed. In like manner there are two reasons, for which a subject may not be bound to obey his superior in all things. First on account of the command of a higher power. For as a gloss says on Rom. 13:2, "They that resist [Vulg.: 'He that resisteth'] the power, resist the ordinance of God" (cf. St. Augustine, De Verb. Dom. viii). "If a commissioner issue an order, are you to comply, if it is contrary to the bidding of the proconsul? Again if the proconsul command one thing, and the emperor another, will you hesitate to disregard the former and serve the latter? Therefore if the emperor commands one thing and God another, you must disregard the former and obey God." Secondly, a subject is not bound to obey his superior if the latter command him to do something wherein he is not subject to him. For Seneca says (De Beneficiis iii): "It is wrong to suppose that slavery falls upon the whole man: for the better part of him is excepted." His body is subjected and assigned to his master but his soul is his own. Consequently in matters touching the internal movement of the will man is not bound to obey his fellow-man, but God alone.

Nevertheless man is bound to obey his fellow-man in things that have to be done externally by means of the body: and yet, since by nature all men are equal, he is not bound to obey another man in matters touching the nature of the body, for instance in those relating to the support of his body or the begetting of his children. Wherefore servants are not bound to obey their masters, nor children their parents, in the question of contracting marriage or of remaining in the state of virginity or the like. But in matters concerning the disposal of actions and human affairs, a subject is bound to obey his superior within the sphere of his authority; for instance a soldier must obey his general in matters relating to war, a servant his master in matters touching the execution of the duties of his service, a son his father in matters relating to the conduct of his life and the care of the household; and so forth.

Reply Obj. 1: When the Apostle says "in all things," he refers to matters within the sphere of a father's or master's authority.

Reply Obj. 2: Man is subject to God simply as regards all things, both internal and external, wherefore he is bound to obey Him in all things. On the other hand, inferiors are not subject to their superiors in all things, but only in certain things and in a particular way, in respect of which the superior stands between God and his subjects, whereas in respect of other matters the subject is immediately under God, by Whom he is taught either by the natural or by the written law.

Reply Obj. 3: Religious profess obedience as to the regular mode of life, in respect of which they are subject to their superiors: wherefore they are bound to obey in those matters only which may belong to the regular mode of life, and this obedience suffices for salvation. If they be willing to obey even in other matters, this will belong to the superabundance of perfection; provided, however, such things be not contrary to God or to the rule they profess, for obedience in this case would be unlawful.

Accordingly we may distinguish a threefold obedience; one, sufficient for salvation, and consisting in obeying when one is bound to obey: secondly, perfect obedience, which obeys in all things lawful: thirdly, indiscreet obedience, which obeys even in matters unlawful.

SIXTH ARTICLE [II-II, Q. 104, Art. 6]

Whether Christians Are Bound to Obey the Secular Powers?

Objection 1: It seems that Christians are not bound to obey the secular power. For a gloss on Matt. 17:25, "Then the children are free," says: "If in every kingdom the children of the king who holds sway over that kingdom are free, then the children of that King, under Whose sway are all kingdoms, should be free in every kingdom." Now Christians, by their faith in Christ, are made children of God, according to John 1:12: "He gave them power to be made the sons of God, to them that believe in His name." Therefore they are not bound to obey the secular power.

Obj. 2: Further, it is written (Rom. 7:4): "You ... are become dead to the law by the body of Christ," and the law mentioned here is the divine law of the Old Testament. Now human law whereby men are subject to the secular power is of less account than the divine law of the Old Testament. Much more, therefore, since they have become members of Christ's body, are men freed from the law of subjection, whereby they were under the power of secular princes.

Obj. 3: Further, men are not bound to obey robbers, who oppress them with violence. Now, Augustine says (De Civ. Dei iv): "Without justice, what else is a kingdom but a huge robbery?" Since therefore the authority of secular princes is frequently exercised with injustice, or owes its origin to some unjust usurpation, it seems that Christians ought not to obey secular princes.

*On the contrary,* It is written (Titus 3:1): "Admonish them to be subject to princes and powers," and (1 Pet. 2:13, 14): "Be ye subject ... to every human creature for God's sake: whether it be to the king as excelling, or to governors as sent by him."

*I answer that,* Faith in Christ is the origin and cause of justice, according to Rom. 3:22, "The justice of God by faith of Jesus Christ:" wherefore faith in Christ does not void the order of justice, but strengthens it. Now the order of justice requires that subjects obey their superiors, else the stability of human affairs would cease. Hence faith in Christ does not excuse the faithful from the obligation of obeying secular princes.

Reply Obj. 1: As stated above (A. 5), subjection whereby one man is bound to another regards the body; not the soul, which retains its liberty. Now, in this state of life we are freed by the grace of Christ from defects of the soul, but not from defects of the body, as the Apostle declares by saying of himself (Rom. 7:23) that in his mind he served the law of God, but in his flesh the law of sin. Wherefore those that are made children of God by grace are free from the spiritual bondage of sin, but not from the bodily bondage, whereby they are held bound to earthly masters, as a gloss observes on 1 Tim. 6:1, "Whosoever are servants under the yoke," etc.

Reply Obj. 2: The Old Law was a figure of the New Testament, and therefore it had to cease on the advent of truth. And the comparison with human law does not stand because thereby one man is subject to another. Yet man is bound by divine law to obey his fellow-man.

Reply Obj. 3: Man is bound to obey secular princes in so far as this is required by order of justice. Wherefore if the prince's authority is not just but usurped, or if he commands what is unjust, his subjects are not bound to obey him, except perhaps accidentally, in order to avoid scandal or danger.

## QUESTION 105

OF DISOBEDIENCE (In Two Articles)

We must now consider disobedience, under which head there are two points of inquiry:

(1) Whether it is a mortal sin?

(2) Whether it is the most grievous of sins?

FIRST ARTICLE [II-II, Q. 105, Art. 2]

Whether Disobedience Is a Mortal Sin?

Objection 1: It seems that disobedience is not a mortal sin. For every sin is a disobedience, as appears from Ambrose's definition given above (Q. 104, A. 2, Obj. 1). Therefore if disobedience were a mortal sin, every sin would be mortal.

Obj. 2: Further, Gregory says (Moral. xxxi) that disobedience is born of vainglory. But vainglory is not a mortal sin. Neither therefore is disobedience.

Obj. 3: Further, a person is said to be disobedient when he does not fulfil a superior's command. But superiors often issue so many commands that it is seldom, if ever, possible to fulfil them. Therefore if disobedience were a mortal sin, it would follow that man cannot avoid mortal sin, which is absurd. Wherefore disobedience is not a mortal sin.

*On the contrary,* The sin of disobedience to parents is reckoned (Rom. 1:30; 2 Tim. 3:2) among other mortal sins.

*I answer that,* As stated above (Q. 24, A. 12; I-II, Q. 72, A. 5; I-II, Q. 88, A. 1), a mortal sin is one that is contrary to charity which is the cause of spiritual life. Now by charity we love God and our neighbor. The charity of God requires that we obey His commandments, as stated above (Q. 24, A. 12). Therefore to be disobedient to the commandments of God is a mortal sin, because it is contrary to the love of God.

Again, the commandments of God contain the precept of obedience to superiors. Wherefore also disobedience to the commands of a superior is a mortal sin, as being contrary to the love of God, according to Rom. 13:2, "He that resisteth the power, resisteth the ordinance of God." It is also contrary to the love of our neighbor, as it withdraws from the superior who is our neighbor the obedience that is his due.

Reply Obj. 1: The definition given by Ambrose refers to mortal sin, which has the character of perfect sin. Venial sin is not disobedience, because it is not contrary to a precept, but beside it. Nor again is every mortal sin disobedience, properly and essentially, but only when one contemns a precept, since moral acts take their species from the end. And when a thing is done contrary to a precept, not in contempt of the precept, but with some other purpose, it is not a sin of disobedience except materially, and belongs formally to another species of sin.

Reply Obj. 2: Vainglory desires display of excellence. And since it seems to point to a certain excellence that one be not subject to another's command, it follows that disobedience arises from vainglory. But there is nothing to hinder mortal sin from arising out of venial sin, since venial sin is a disposition to mortal.

Reply Obj. 3: No one is bound to do the impossible: wherefore if a superior makes a heap of precepts and lays them upon his subjects, so that they are unable to fulfil them, they are excused from sin. Wherefore superiors should refrain from making a multitude of precepts.

SECOND ARTICLE [II-II, Q. 105, Art. 2]

Whether Disobedience Is the Most Grievous of Sins?

Objection 1: It seems that disobedience is the most grievous of sins. For it is written (1 Kings 15:23): "It is like the sin of witchcraft to rebel, and like the crime of idolatry to refuse to obey." But idolatry is the most grievous of sins, as stated above (Q. 94, A. 3). Therefore disobedience is the most grievous of sins.

Obj. 2: Further, the sin against the Holy Ghost is one that removes the obstacles of sin, as stated above (Q. 14, A. 2). Now disobedience makes a man contemn a precept which, more than anything, prevents a man from sinning. Therefore disobedience is a sin against the Holy Ghost, and consequently is the most grievous of sins.

Obj. 3: Further, the Apostle says (Rom. 5:19) that "by the disobedience of one man, many were made sinners." Now the cause is seemingly greater than its effect. Therefore disobedience seems to be a more grievous sin than the others that are caused thereby.

*On the contrary,* Contempt of the commander is a more grievous sin than contempt of his command. Now some sins are against the very person of the commander, such as blasphemy and murder. Therefore disobedience is not the most grievous of sins.

*I answer that,* Not every disobedience is equally a sin: for one disobedience may be greater than another, in two ways. First, on the part of the superior commanding, since, although a man should take every care to obey each superior, yet it is a greater duty to obey a higher than a lower authority, in sign of which the command of a lower authority is set aside if it be contrary to the command of a higher authority. Consequently the higher the person who commands, the more grievous is it to disobey him: so that it is more grievous to disobey God than man. Secondly, on the part of the things commanded. For the person commanding does not equally desire the fulfilment of all his commands: since every such person desires above all the end, and that which is nearest to the end. Wherefore disobedience is the more grievous, according as the unfulfilled commandment is more in the intention of the person commanding. As to the commandments of God, it is evident that the greater the good commanded, the more grievous the disobedience of that commandment, because since God's will is essentially directed to the good, the greater the good the more does God wish it to be fulfilled. Consequently he that disobeys the commandment of the love of God sins more grievously than one who disobeys the commandment of the love of our neighbor. On the other hand, man's will is not always directed to the greater good: hence, when we are bound by a mere precept of man, a sin is more grievous, not through setting aside a greater good, but through setting aside that which is more in the intention of the person commanding.

Accordingly the various degrees of disobedience must correspond with the various degrees of precepts: because the disobedience in which there is contempt of God's precept, from the very nature of disobedience is more grievous than a sin committed against a man, apart from the latter being a disobedience to God. And I say this because whoever sins against his neighbor acts also against God's commandment. And if the divine precept be contemned in a yet graver matter, the sin is still more grievous. The disobedience that contains contempt of a man's precept is less grievous than the sin which contemns the man who made the precept, because reverence for the person commanding should give rise to reverence for his command. In like manner a sin that directly involves contempt of God, such as blasphemy, or the like, is more grievous (even if we mentally separate the disobedience from the sin) than would be a sin involving contempt of God's commandment alone.

Reply Obj. 1: This comparison of Samuel is one, not of equality but of likeness, because disobedience redounds to the contempt of God just as idolatry does, though the latter does so more.

Reply Obj. 2: Not every disobedience is sin against the Holy Ghost, but only that which obstinacy is added: for it is not the contempt of any obstacle to sin that constitutes sin against the Holy Ghost, else the contempt of any good would be a sin against the Holy Ghost, since any good may hinder a man from committing sin. The sin against the Holy Ghost consists in the contempt of those goods which lead directly to repentance and the remission of sins.

Reply Obj. 3: The first sin of our first parent, from which sin was transmitted to all men, was not disobedience considered as a special sin, but pride, from which then man proceeded to disobey. Hence the Apostle in these words seems to take disobedience in its relation to every sin.

## QUESTION 106

OF THANKFULNESS OR GRATITUDE (In Six Articles)

We must now consider thankfulness or gratitude, and ingratitude. Concerning thankfulness there are six points of inquiry:

(1) Whether thankfulness is a special virtue distinct from other virtues?

(2) Who owes more thanks to God, the innocent or the penitent?

(3) Whether man is always bound to give thanks for human favors?

(4) Whether thanksgiving should be deferred?

(5) Whether thanksgiving should be measured according to the favor received or the disposition of the giver?

(6) Whether one ought to pay back more than one has received?

FIRST ARTICLE [II-II, Q. 106, Art. 1]

Whether Thankfulness Is a Special Virtue, Distinct from Other Virtues?

Objection 1: It seems that thankfulness is not a special virtue, distinct from other virtues. For we have received the greatest benefits from God, and from our parents. Now the honor which we pay to God in return belongs to the virtue of religion, and the honor with which we repay our parents belongs to the virtue of piety. Therefore thankfulness or gratitude is not distinct from the other virtues.

Obj. 2: Further, proportionate repayment belongs to commutative justice, according to the Philosopher (Ethic. v, 4). Now the purpose of giving thanks is repayment (Ethic. 5, 4). Therefore thanksgiving, which belongs to gratitude, is an act of justice. Therefore gratitude is not a special virtue, distinct from other virtues.

Obj. 3: Further, acknowledgment of favor received is requisite for the preservation of friendship, according to the Philosopher (Ethic. viii, 13; ix, 1). Now friendship is associated with all the virtues, since they are the reason for which man is loved. Therefore thankfulness or gratitude, to which it belongs to repay favors received, is not a special virtue.

*On the contrary,* Tully reckons thankfulness a special part of justice (De Invent. Rhet. ii).

*I answer that,* As stated above (I-II, Q. 60, A. 3), the nature of the debt to be paid must needs vary according to various causes giving rise to the debt, yet so that the greater always includes the lesser. Now the cause of debt is found primarily and chiefly in God, in that He is the first principle of all our goods: secondarily it is found in our father, because he is the proximate principle of our begetting and upbringing: thirdly it is found in the person that excels in dignity, from whom general favors proceed; fourthly it is found in a benefactor, from whom we have received particular and private favors, on account of which we are under particular obligation to him.

Accordingly, since what we owe God, or our father, or a person excelling in dignity, is not the same as what we owe a benefactor from whom we have received some particular favor, it follows that after religion, whereby we pay God due worship, and piety, whereby we worship our parents, and observance, whereby we worship persons excelling in dignity, there is thankfulness or gratitude, whereby we give thanks to our benefactors. And it is distinct from the foregoing virtues, just as each of these is distinct from the one that precedes, as falling short thereof.

Reply Obj. 1: Just as religion is superexcelling piety, so is it excelling thankfulness or gratitude: wherefore giving thanks to God was reckoned above (Q. 83, A. 17) among things pertaining to religion.

Reply Obj. 2: Proportionate repayment belongs to commutative justice, when it answers to the legal due; for instance when it is contracted that so much be paid for so much. But the repayment that belongs to the virtue of thankfulness or gratitude answers to the moral debt, and is paid spontaneously. Hence thanksgiving is less thankful when compelled, as Seneca observes (De Beneficiis iii).

Reply Obj. 3: Since true friendship is based on virtue, whatever there is contrary to virtue in a friend is an obstacle to friendship, and whatever in him is virtuous is an incentive to friendship. In this way friendship is preserved by repayment of favors, although repayment of favors belongs specially to the virtue of gratitude.

SECOND ARTICLE [II-II, Q. 106, Art. 2]

Whether the Innocent Is More Bound to Give Thanks to God Than the Penitent?

Objection 1: It seems that the innocent is more bound to give thanks to God than the penitent. For the greater the gift one has received from God, the more one is bound to give Him thanks. Now the gift of innocence is greater than that of justice restored. Therefore it seems that the innocent is more bound to give thanks to God than the penitent.

Obj. 2: Further, a man owes love to his benefactor just as he owes him gratitude. Now Augustine says (Confess. ii): "What man, weighing his own infirmity, would dare to ascribe his purity and innocence to his own strength; that so he should love Thee the less, as if he had less needed Thy mercy, whereby Thou remittest sins to those that turn to Thee?" And farther on he says: "And for this let him love Thee as much, yea and more, since by Whom he sees me to have been recovered from such deep torpor of sin, by Him he sees himself to have been from the like torpor of sin preserved." Therefore the innocent is also more bound to give thanks than the penitent.

Obj. 3: Further, the more a gratuitous favor is continuous, the greater the thanksgiving due for it. Now the favor of divine grace is more continuous in the innocent than in the penitent. For Augustine says (Confess. iii): "To Thy grace I ascribe it, and to Thy mercy, that Thou hast melted away my sins as it were ice. To Thy grace I ascribe also whatsoever I have not done of evil; for what might I not have done? ... Yea, all I confess to have been forgiven me, both what evils I committed by my own wilfulness, and what by Thy guidance committed not." Therefore the innocent is more bound to give thanks than the penitent.

*On the contrary,* It is written (Luke 7:43): "To whom more is forgiven, he loveth more [*Vulg.: 'To whom less is forgiven, he loveth less' Luke 7:47]." Therefore for the same reason he is bound to greater thanksgiving.

*I answer that,* Thanksgiving ( gratiarum actio ) in the recipient corresponds to the favor ( *gratia* ) of the giver: so that when there is greater favor on the part of the giver, greater thanks are due on the part of the recipient. Now a favor is something bestowed *gratis:* wherefore on the part of the giver the favor may be greater on two counts. First, owing to the quantity of the thing given: and in this way the innocent owes greater thanksgiving, because he receives a greater gift from God, also, absolutely speaking, a more continuous gift, other things being equal. Secondly, a favor may be said to be greater, because it is given more gratuitously; and in this sense the penitent is more bound to give thanks than the innocent, because what he receives from God is more gratuitously given: since, whereas he was deserving of punishment, he has received grace. Wherefore, although the gift bestowed on the innocent is, considered absolutely, greater, yet the gift bestowed on the penitent is greater in relation to him: even as a small gift bestowed on a poor man is greater to him than a great gift is to a rich man. And since actions are about singulars, in matters of action, we have to take note of what is such here and now, rather than of what is such absolutely, as the Philosopher observes (Ethic. iii) in treating of the voluntary and the involuntary.

This suffices for the Replies to the Objections.

THIRD ARTICLE [II-II, Q. 106, Art. 3]

Whether a Man Is Bound to Give Thanks to Every Benefactor?

Objection 1: It seems that a man is not bound to give thanks to every benefactor. For a man may benefit himself just as he may harm himself, according to Ecclus. 14:5, "He that is evil to himself, to whom will he be good?" But a man cannot thank himself, since thanksgiving seems to pass from one person to another. Therefore thanksgiving is not due to every benefactor.

Obj. 2: Further, gratitude is a repayment of an act of grace. But some favors are granted without grace, and are rudely, slowly and grudgingly given. Therefore gratitude is not always due to a benefactor.

Obj. 3: Further, no thanks are due to one who works for his own profit. But sometimes people bestow favors for their own profit. Therefore thanks are not due to them.

Obj. 4: Further, no thanks are due to a slave, for all that he is belongs to his master. Yet sometimes a slave does a good turn to his master. Therefore gratitude is not due to every benefactor.

Obj. 5: Further, no one is bound to do what he cannot do equitably and advantageously. Now it happens at times that the benefactor is very well off, and it would be of no advantage to him to be repaid for a favor he has bestowed. Again it happens sometimes that the benefactor from being virtuous has become wicked, so that it would not seem equitable to repay him. Also the recipient of a favor may be a poor man, and is quite unable to repay. Therefore seemingly a man is not always bound to repayment for favors received.

Obj. 6: Further, no one is bound to do for another what is inexpedient and hurtful to him. Now sometimes it happens that repayment of a favor would be hurtful or useless to the person repaid. Therefore favors are not always to be repaid by gratitude.

*On the contrary,* It is written (1 Thess. 5:18): "In all things give thanks."

*I answer that,* Every effect turns naturally to its cause; wherefore Dionysius says (Div. Nom. i) that "God turns all things to Himself because He is the cause of all": for the effect must needs always be directed to the end of the agent. Now it is evident that a benefactor, as such, is cause of the beneficiary. Hence the natural order requires that he who has received a favor should, by repaying the favor, turn to his benefactor according to the mode of each. And, as stated above with regard to a father (Q. 31, A. 3; Q. 101, A. 2), a man owes his benefactor, as such, honor and reverence, since the latter stands to him in the relation of principle; but accidentally he owes him assistance or support, if he need it.

Reply Obj. 1: In the words of Seneca (1 Benef. v), "just as a man is liberal who gives not to himself but to others, and gracious who forgives not himself but others, and merciful who is moved, not by his own misfortunes but by another's, so too, no man confers a favor on himself, he is but following the bent of his nature, which moves him to resist what hurts him, and to seek what is profitable." Wherefore in things that one does for oneself, there is no place for gratitude or ingratitude, since a man cannot deny himself a thing except by keeping it. Nevertheless things which are properly spoken of in relation to others are spoken of metaphorically in relation to oneself, as the Philosopher states regarding justice (Ethic. v, 11), in so far, to wit, as the various parts of man are considered as though they were various persons.

Reply Obj. 2: It is the mark of a happy disposition to see good rather than evil. Wherefore if someone has conferred a favor, not as he ought to have conferred it, the recipient should not for that reason withhold his thanks. Yet he owes less thanks, than if the favor had been conferred duly, since in fact the favor is less, for, as Seneca remarks (De Benef. ii.) "promptness enhances, delay discounts a favor."

Reply Obj. 3: As Seneca observes (De Benef. vi), "it matters much whether a person does a kindness to us for his own sake, or for ours, or for both his and ours. He that considers himself only, and benefits because cannot otherwise benefit himself, seems to me like a man who seeks fodder for his cattle." And farther on: "If he has done it for me in common with himself, having both of us in his mind, I am ungrateful and not merely unjust, unless I rejoice that what was profitable to him is profitable to me also. It is the height of malevolence to refuse to recognize a kindness, unless the giver has been the loser thereby."

Reply Obj. 4: As Seneca observes (De Benef. iii), "when a slave does what is wont to be demanded of a slave, it is part of his service: when he does more than a slave is bound to do, it is a favor: for as soon as he does anything from a motive of friendship, if indeed that be his motive, it is no longer called service." Wherefore gratitude is due even to a slave, when he does more than his duty.

Reply Obj. 5: A poor man is certainly not ungrateful if he does what he can. For since kindness depends on the heart rather than on the deed, so too gratitude depends chiefly the heart. Hence Seneca says (De Benef. ii): "Who receives a favor gratefully, has already begun to pay it back: and that we are grateful for favors received should be shown by the outpourings of the heart, not only in his hearing but everywhere." From this it is evident that however well off a man may be, it is possible to thank him for his kindness by showing him reverence and honor. Wherefore the Philosopher says (Ethic. viii, 14): "He that abounds should be repaid with honor, he that is in want should be repaid with money": and Seneca writes (De Benef. vi): "There are many ways of repaying those who are well off, whatever we happen to owe them; such as good advice, frequent fellowship, affable and pleasant conversation without flattery." Therefore there is no need for a man to desire neediness or distress in his benefactor before repaying his kindness, because, as Seneca says (De Benef. vi), "it were inhuman to desire this in one from whom you have received no favor; how much more so to desire it in one whose kindness has made you his debtor!"

If, however, the benefactor has lapsed from virtue, nevertheless he should be repaid according to his state, that he may return to virtue if possible. But if he be so wicked as to be incurable, then his heart has changed, and consequently no repayment is due for his kindness, as heretofore. And yet, as far as it possible without sin, the kindness he has shown should be held in memory, as the Philosopher says (Ethic. ix, 3).

Reply Obj. 6: As stated in the preceding reply, repayment of a favor depends chiefly on the affection of the heart: wherefore repayment should be made in such a way as to prove most beneficial. If, however, through the benefactor's carelessness it prove detrimental to him, this is not imputed to the person who repays him, as Seneca observes (De Benef. vii): "It is my duty to repay, and not to keep back and safeguard my repayment."

FOURTH ARTICLE [II-II, Q. 106, Art. 4]

Whether a Man Is Bound to Repay a Favor at Once?

Objection 1: It seems that a man is bound to repay a favor at once. For we are bound to restore at once what we owe, unless the term be fixed. Now there is no term prescribed for the repayment of favors, and yet this repayment is a duty, as stated above (A. 3). Therefore a man is bound to repay a favor at once.

Obj. 2: Further, a good action would seem to be all the more praiseworthy according as it is done with greater earnestness. Now earnestness seems to make a man do his duty without any delay. Therefore it is apparently more praiseworthy to repay a favor at once.

Obj. 3: Further, Seneca says (De Benef. ii) that "it is proper to a benefactor to act freely and quickly." Now repayment ought to equal the favor received. Therefore it should be done at once.

*On the contrary,* Seneca says (De Benef. iv): "He that hastens to repay, is animated with a sense, not of gratitude but of indebtedness."

*I answer that,* Just as in conferring a favor two things are to be considered, namely, the affection of the heart and the gift, so also must these things be considered in repaying the favor. As regards the affection of the heart, repayment should be made at once, wherefore Seneca says (De Benef. ii): "Do you wish to repay a favor? Receive it graciously." As regards the gift, one ought to wait until such a time as will be convenient to the benefactor. In fact, if instead of choosing a convenient time, one wished to repay at once, favor for favor, it would not seem to be a virtuous, but a constrained repayment. For, as Seneca observes (De Benef. iv), "he that wishes to repay too soon, is an unwilling debtor, and an unwilling debtor is ungrateful."

Reply Obj. 1: A legal debt must be paid at once, else the equality of justice would not be preserved, if one kept another's property without his consent. But a moral debt depends on the equity of the debtor: and therefore it should be repaid in due time according as the rectitude of virtue demands.

Reply Obj. 2: Earnestness of the will is not virtuous unless it be regulated by reason; wherefore it is not praiseworthy to forestall the proper time through earnestness.

Reply Obj. 3: Favors also should be conferred at a convenient time and one should no longer delay when the convenient time comes; and the same is to be observed in repaying favors.

FIFTH ARTICLE [II-II, Q. 106, Art. 5]

Whether in Giving Thanks We Should Look at the Benefactor's Disposition or at the Deed?

Objection 1: It seems that in repaying favors we should not look at the benefactor's disposition but at the deed. For repayment is due to beneficence, and beneficence consists in deeds, as the word itself denotes. Therefore in repaying favors we should look at the deed.

Obj. 2: Further, thanksgiving, whereby we repay favors, is a part of justice. But justice considers equality between giving and taking. Therefore also in repaying favors we should consider the deed rather than the disposition of the benefactor.

Obj. 3: Further, no one can consider what he does not know. Now God alone knows the interior disposition. Therefore it is impossible to repay a favor according to the benefactor's disposition.

*On the contrary,* Seneca says (De Benef. i): "We are sometimes under a greater obligation to one who has given little with a large heart, and has bestowed a small favor, yet willingly."

*I answer that,* The repayment of a favor may belong to three virtues, namely, justice, gratitude and friendship. It belongs to justice when the repayment has the character of a legal debt, as in a loan and the like: and in such cases repayment must be made according to the quantity received.

On the other hand, repayment of a favor belongs, though in different ways, to friendship and likewise to the virtue of gratitude when it has the character of a moral debt. For in the repayment of friendship we have to consider the cause of friendship; so that in the friendship that is based on the useful, repayment should be made according to the usefulness accruing from the favor conferred, and in the friendship based on virtue repayment should be made with regard for the choice or disposition of the giver, since this is the chief requisite of virtue, as stated in *Ethic.* viii, 13. And likewise, since gratitude regards the favor inasmuch as it is bestowed gratis, and this regards the disposition of the giver, it follows again that repayment of a favor depends more on the disposition of the giver than on the effect.

Reply Obj. 1: Every moral act depends on the will. Hence a kindly action, in so far as it is praiseworthy and is deserving of gratitude, consists materially in the thing done, but formally and chiefly in the will. Hence Seneca says (De Benef. i): "A kindly action consists not in deed or gift, but in the disposition of the giver or doer."

Reply Obj. 2: Gratitude is a part of justice, not indeed as a species is part of a genus, but by a kind of reduction to the genus of justice, as stated above (Q. 80). Hence it does not follow that we shall find the same kind of debt in both virtues.

Reply Obj. 3: God alone sees man's disposition in itself: but in so far as it is shown by certain signs, man also can know it. It is thus that a benefactor's disposition is known by the way in which he does the kindly action, for instance through his doing it joyfully and readily.

SIXTH ARTICLE [II-II, Q. 106, Art. 6]

Whether the Repayment of Gratitude Should Surpass the Favor Received?

Objection 1: It seems that there is no need for the repayment of gratitude to surpass the favor received. For it is not possible to make even equal repayment to some, for instance, one's parents, as the Philosopher states (Ethic. viii, 14). Now virtue does not attempt the impossible. Therefore gratitude for a favor does not tend to something yet greater.

Obj. 2: Further, if one person repays another more than he has received by his favor, by that very fact he gives him something his turn, as it were. But the latter owes him repayment for the favor which in his turn the former has conferred on him. Therefore he that first conferred a favor will be bound to a yet greater repayment, and so on indefinitely. Now virtue does not strive at the indefinite, since "the indefinite removes the nature of good" (Metaph. ii, text. 8). Therefore repayment of gratitude should not surpass the favor received.

Obj. 3: Further, justice consists in equality. But "more" is excess of equality. Since therefore excess is sinful in every virtue, it seems that to repay more than the favor received is sinful and opposed to justice.

*On the contrary,* The Philosopher says (Ethic. v, 5): "We should repay those who are gracious to us, by being gracious to them return," and this is done by repaying more than we have received. Therefore gratitude should incline to do something greater.

*I answer that,* As stated above (A. 5), gratitude regards the favor received according the intention of the benefactor; who seems be deserving of praise, chiefly for having conferred the favor gratis without being bound to do so. Wherefore the beneficiary is under a moral obligation to bestow something gratis in return. Now he does not seem to bestow something gratis, unless he exceeds the quantity of the favor received: because so long as he repays less or an equivalent, he would seem to do nothing gratis, but only to return what he has received. Therefore gratitude always inclines, as far as possible, to pay back something more.

Reply Obj. 1: As stated above (A. 3, ad 5; A. 5), in repaying favors we must consider the disposition rather than the deed. Accordingly, if we consider the effect of beneficence, which a son receives from his parents namely, to be and to live, the son cannot make an equal repayment, as the Philosopher states (Ethic. viii, 14). But if we consider the will of the giver and of the repayer, then it is possible for the son to pay back something greater to his father, as Seneca declares (De Benef. iii). If, however, he were unable to do so, the will to pay back would be sufficient for gratitude.

Reply Obj. 2: The debt of gratitude flows from charity, which the more it is paid the more it is due, according to Rom. 13:8, "Owe no man anything, but to love one another." Wherefore it is not unreasonable if the obligation of gratitude has no limit.

Reply Obj. 3: As in injustice, which is a cardinal virtue, we consider equality of things, so in gratitude we consider equality of wills. For while on the one hand the benefactor of his own free-will gave something he was not bound to give, so on the other hand the beneficiary repays something over and above what he has received.

# QUESTION 107

OF INGRATITUDE (In Four Articles)

We must now consider ingratitude, under which head there are four points of inquiry:

(1) Whether ingratitude is always a sin?

(2) Whether ingratitude is a special sin?

(3) Whether every act of ingratitude is a mortal sin?

(4) Whether favors should be withdrawn from the ungrateful?

FIRST ARTICLE [II-II, Q. 107, Art. 1]

Whether Ingratitude Is Always a Sin?

Objection 1: It seems that ingratitude is not always a sin. For Seneca says (De Benef. iii) that "he who does not repay a favor is ungrateful." But sometimes it is impossible to repay a favor without sinning, for instance if one man has helped another to commit a sin. Therefore, since it is not a sin to refrain from sinning, it seems that ingratitude is not always a sin.

Obj. 2: Further, every sin is in the power of the person who commits it: because, according to Augustine (De Lib. Arb. iii; Retract. i), "no man sins in what he cannot avoid." Now sometimes it is not in the power of the sinner to avoid ingratitude, for instance when he has not the means of repaying. Again forgetfulness is not in our power, and yet Seneca declares (De Benef. iii) that "to forget a kindness is the height of ingratitude." Therefore ingratitude is not always a sin.

Obj. 3: Further, there would seem to be no repayment in being unwilling to owe anything, according to the Apostle (Rom. 13:8), "Owe no man anything." Yet "an unwilling debtor is ungrateful," as Seneca declares (De Benef. iv). Therefore ingratitude is not always a sin.

*On the contrary,* Ingratitude is reckoned among other sins (2 Tim. 3:2), where it is written: "Disobedient to parents, ungrateful, wicked." etc.

*I answer that,* As stated above (Q. 106, A. 4, ad 1, A. 6) a debt of gratitude is a moral debt required by virtue. Now a thing is a sin from the fact of its being contrary to virtue. Wherefore it is evident that every ingratitude is a sin.

Reply Obj. 1: Gratitude regards a favor received: and he that helps another to commit a sin does him not a favor but an injury: and so no thanks are due to him, except perhaps on account of his good will, supposing him to have been deceived, and to have thought to help him in doing good, whereas he helped him to sin. In such a case the repayment due to him is not that he should be helped to commit a sin, because this would be repaying not good but evil, and this is contrary to gratitude.

Reply Obj. 2: No man is excused from ingratitude through inability to repay, for the very reason that the mere will suffices for the repayment of the debt of gratitude, as stated above (Q. 106, A. 6, ad 1).

Forgetfulness of a favor received amounts to ingratitude, not indeed the forgetfulness that arises from a natural defect, that is not subject to the will, but that which arises from negligence. For, as Seneca observes (De Benef. iii), "when forgetfulness of favors lays hold of a man, he has apparently given little thought to their repayment."

Reply Obj. 3: The debt of gratitude flows from the debt of love, and from the latter no man should wish to be free. Hence that anyone should owe this debt unwillingly seems to arise from lack of love for his benefactor.

SECOND ARTICLE [II-II, Q. 107, Art. 2]

Whether Ingratitude Is a Special Sin?

Objection 1: It seems that ingratitude is not a special sin. For whoever sins acts against God his sovereign benefactor. But this pertains to ingratitude. Therefore ingratitude is not a special sin.

Obj. 2: Further, no special sin is contained under different kinds of sin. But one can be ungrateful by committing different kinds of sin, for instance by calumny, theft, or something similar committed against a benefactor. Therefore ingratitude is not a special sin.

Obj. 3: Further, Seneca writes (De Benef. iii): "It is ungrateful to take no notice of a kindness, it is ungrateful not to repay one, but it is the height of ingratitude to forget it." Now these do not seem to belong to the same species of sin. Therefore ingratitude is not a special sin.

*On the contrary,* Ingratitude is opposed to gratitude or thankfulness, which is a special virtue. Therefore it is a special sin.

*I answer that,* Every vice is denominated from a deficiency of virtue, because deficiency is more opposed to virtue: thus illiberality is more opposed to liberality than prodigality is. Now a vice may be opposed to the virtue of gratitude by way of excess, for instance if one were to show gratitude for things for which gratitude is not due, or sooner than it is due, as stated above (Q. 106, A. 4). But still more opposed to gratitude is the vice denoting deficiency of gratitude, because the virtue of gratitude, as stated above (Q. 106, A. 6), inclines to return something more. Wherefore ingratitude is properly denominated from being a deficiency of gratitude. Now every deficiency or privation takes its species from the opposite habit: for blindness and deafness differ according to the difference of sight and hearing. Therefore just as gratitude or thankfulness is one special virtue, so also is ingratitude one special sin.

It has, however, various degrees corresponding in their order to the things required for gratitude. The first of these is to recognize the favor received, the second to express one's appreciation and thanks, and the third to repay the favor at a suitable place and time according to one's means. And since what is last in the order of generation is first in the order of destruction, it follows that the first degree of ingratitude is when a man fails to repay a favor, the second when he declines to notice or indicate that he has received a favor, while the third and supreme degree is when a man fails to recognize the reception of a favor, whether by forgetting it or in any other way. Moreover, since opposite affirmation includes negation, it follows that it belongs to the first degree of ingratitude to return evil for good, to the second to find fault with a favor received, and to the third to esteem kindness as though it were unkindness.

Reply Obj. 1: In every sin there is material ingratitude to God, inasmuch as a man does something that may pertain to ingratitude. But formal ingratitude is when a favor is actually contemned, and this is a special sin.

Reply Obj. 2: Nothing hinders the formal aspect of some special sin from being found materially in several kinds of sin, and in this way the aspect of ingratitude is to be found in many kinds of sin.

Reply Obj. 3: These three are not different species but different degrees of one special sin.

THIRD ARTICLE [II-II, Q. 107, Art. 3]

Whether Ingratitude Is Always a Mortal Sin?

Objection 1: It seems that ingratitude is always a mortal sin. For one ought to be grateful to God above all. But one is not ungrateful to God by committing a venial sin: else every man would be guilty of ingratitude. Therefore no ingratitude is a venial sin.

Obj. 2: Further, a sin is mortal through being contrary to charity, as stated above (Q. 24, A. 12). But ingratitude is contrary to charity, since the debt of gratitude proceeds from that virtue, as stated above (Q. 106, A. 1, ad 3; A. 6, ad 2). Therefore ingratitude is always a mortal sin.

Obj. 3: Further, Seneca says (De Benef. ii): "Between the giver and the receiver of a favor there is this law, that the former should forthwith forget having given, and the latter should never forget having received." Now, seemingly, the reason why the giver should forget is that he may be unaware of the sin of the recipient, should the latter prove ungrateful; and there would be no necessity for that if ingratitude were a slight sin. Therefore ingratitude is always a mortal sin.

Obj. 4: *On the contrary,* No one should be put in the way of committing a mortal sin. Yet, according to Seneca (De Benef. ii), "sometimes it is necessary to deceive the person who receives assistance, in order that he may receive without knowing from whom he has received." But this would seem to put the recipient in the way of ingratitude. Therefore ingratitude is not always a mortal sin.

*I answer that,* As appears from what we have said above (A. 2), a man may be ungrateful in two ways: first, by mere omission, for instance by failing to recognize the favor received, or to express his appreciation of it or to pay something in return, and this is not always a mortal sin, because, as stated above (Q. 106, A. 6), the debt of gratitude requires a man to make a liberal return, which, however, he is not bound to do; wherefore if he fail to do so, he does not sin mortally. It is nevertheless a venial sin, because it arises either from some kind of negligence or from some disinclination to virtue in him. And yet ingratitude of this kind may happen to be a mortal sin, by reason either of inward contempt, or of the kind of thing withheld, this being needful to the benefactor, either simply, or in some case of necessity.

Secondly, a man may be ungrateful, because he not only omits to pay the debt of gratitude, but does the contrary. This again is sometimes a mortal and sometimes a venial sin, according to the kind of thing that is done.

It must be observed, however, that when ingratitude arises from a mortal sin, it has the perfect character of ingratitude, and when it arises from venial sin, it has the imperfect character.

Reply Obj. 1: By committing a venial sin one is not ungrateful to God to the extent of incurring the guilt of perfect ingratitude: but there is something of ingratitude in a venial sin, in so far as it removes a virtuous act of obedience to God.

Reply Obj. 2: When ingratitude is a venial sin it is not contrary to, but beside charity: since it does not destroy the habit of charity, but excludes some act thereof.

Reply Obj. 3: Seneca also says (De Benef. vii): "When we say that a man after conferring a favor should forget about it, it is a mistake to suppose that we mean him to shake off the recollection of a thing so very praiseworthy. When we say: He must not remember it, we mean that he must not publish it abroad and boast about it."

Reply Obj. 4: He that is unaware of a favor conferred on him is not ungrateful, if he fails to repay it, provided he be prepared to do so if he knew. It is nevertheless commendable at times that the object of a favor should remain in ignorance of it, both in order to avoid vainglory, as when Blessed Nicolas threw gold into a house secretly, wishing to avoid popularity: and because the kindness is all the greater through the benefactor wishing not to shame the person on whom he is conferring the favor.

FOURTH ARTICLE [II-II, Q. 107, Art. 4]

Whether Favors Should Be Withheld from the Ungrateful?

Objection 1: It seems that favors should withheld from the ungrateful. For it is written (Wis. 16:29): "The hope of the unthankful shall melt away as the winter's ice." But this hope would not melt away unless favors were withheld from him. Therefore favors should be withheld from the ungrateful.

Obj. 2: Further, no one should afford another an occasion of committing sin. But the ungrateful in receiving a favor is given an occasion of ingratitude. Therefore favors should not be bestowed on the ungrateful.

Obj. 3: Further, "By what things a man sinneth, by the same also he is tormented" (Wis. 11:17). Now he that is ungrateful when he receives a favor sins against the favor. Therefore he should be deprived of the favor.

*On the contrary,* It is written (Luke 6:35) that "the Highest ... is kind to the unthankful, and to the evil." Now we should prove ourselves His children by imitating Him (Luke 6:36). Therefore we should not withhold favors from the ungrateful.

*I answer that,* There are two points to be considered with regard to an ungrateful person. The first is what he deserves to suffer and thus it is certain that he deserves to be deprived of our favor. The second is, what ought his benefactor to do? For in the first place he should not easily judge him to be ungrateful, since, as Seneca remarks (De Benef. iii), "a man is often grateful although he repays not," because perhaps he has not the means or the opportunity of repaying. Secondly, he should be inclined to turn his ungratefulness into gratitude, and if he does not achieve this by being kind to him once, he may by being so a second time. If, however, the more he repeats his favors, the more ungrateful and evil the other becomes, he should cease from bestowing his favors upon him.

Reply Obj. 1: The passage quoted speaks of what the ungrateful man deserves to suffer.

Reply Obj. 2: He that bestows a favor on an ungrateful person affords him an occasion not of sin but of gratitude and love. And if the recipient takes therefrom an occasion of ingratitude, this is not to be imputed to the bestower.

Reply Obj. 3: He that bestows a favor must not at once act the part of a punisher of ingratitude, but rather that of a kindly physician, by healing the ingratitude with repeated favors.

# QUESTION 108

OF VENGEANCE (In Four Articles)

We must now consider vengeance, under which head there are four points of inquiry:

(1) Whether vengeance is lawful?

(2) Whether it is a special virtue?

(3) Of the manner of taking vengeance;

(4) On whom should vengeance be taken?

FIRST ARTICLE [II-II, Q. 108, Art. 1]

Whether Vengeance Is Lawful?

Objection 1: It seems that vengeance is not lawful. For whoever usurps what is God's sins. But vengeance belongs to God, for it is written (Deut. 32:35, Rom. 12:19): "Revenge to Me, and I will repay." Therefore all vengeance is unlawful.

Obj. 2: Further, he that takes vengeance on a man does not bear with him. But we ought to bear with the wicked, for a gloss on Cant. 2:2, "As the lily among the thorns," says: "He is not a good man that cannot bear with a wicked one." Therefore we should not take vengeance on the wicked.

Obj. 3: Further, vengeance is taken by inflicting punishment, which is the cause of servile fear. But the New Law is not a law of fear, but of love, as Augustine states (Contra Adamant. xvii). Therefore at least in the New Testament all vengeance is unlawful.

Obj. 4: Further, a man is said to avenge himself when he takes revenge for wrongs inflicted on himself. But, seemingly, it is unlawful even for a judge to punish those who have wronged him: for Chrysostom [*Cf. Opus Imperfectum, Hom. v in Matth., falsely ascribed to St. Chrysostom] says: "Let us learn after Christ's example to bear our own wrongs with magnanimity, yet not to suffer God's wrongs, not even by listening to them." Therefore vengeance seems to be unlawful.

Obj. 5: Further, the sin of a multitude is more harmful than the sin of only one: for it is written (Ecclus. 26:5-7): "Of three things my heart hath been afraid ... the accusation of a city, and the gathering together of the people, and a false calumny." But vengeance should not be taken on the sin of a multitude, for a gloss on Matt. 13:29, 30, "Lest perhaps ... you root up the wheat ... suffer both to grow," says that "a multitude should not be excommunicated, nor should the sovereign." Neither therefore is any other vengeance lawful.

*On the contrary,* We should look to God for nothing save what is good and lawful. But we are to look to God for vengeance on His enemies: for it is written (Luke 18:7): "Will not God revenge His elect who cry to Him day and night?" as if to say: "He will indeed." Therefore vengeance is not essentially evil and unlawful.

*I answer that,* Vengeance consists in the infliction of a penal evil on one who has sinned. Accordingly, in the matter of vengeance, we must consider the mind of the avenger. For if his intention is directed chiefly to the evil of the person on whom he takes vengeance and rests there, then his vengeance is altogether unlawful: because to take pleasure in another's evil belongs to hatred, which is contrary to the charity whereby we are bound to love all men. Nor is it an excuse that he intends the evil of one who has unjustly inflicted evil on him, as neither is a man excused for hating one that hates him: for a man may not sin against another just because the latter has already sinned against him, since this is to be overcome by evil, which was forbidden by the Apostle, who says (Rom. 12:21): "Be not overcome by evil, but overcome evil by good."

If, however, the avenger's intention be directed chiefly to some good, to be obtained by means of the punishment of the person who has sinned (for instance that the sinner may amend, or at least that he may be restrained and others be not disturbed, that justice may be upheld, and God honored), then vengeance may be lawful, provided other due circumstances be observed.

Reply Obj. 1: He who takes vengeance on the wicked in keeping with his rank and position does not usurp what belongs to God but makes use of the power granted him by God. For it is written (Rom. 13:4) of the earthly prince that "he is God's minister, an avenger to execute wrath upon him that doeth evil." If, however, a man takes vengeance outside the order of divine appointment, he usurps what is God's and therefore sins.

Reply Obj. 2: The good bear with the wicked by enduring patiently, and in due manner, the wrongs they themselves receive from them: but they do not bear with them as to endure the wrongs they inflict on God and their neighbor. For Chrysostom [*Cf. Opus Imperfectum, Hom. v in Matth., falsely ascribed to St. Chrysostom] says: "It is praiseworthy to be patient under our own wrongs, but to overlook God's wrongs is most wicked."

Reply Obj. 3: The law of the Gospel is the law of love, and therefore those who do good out of love, and who alone properly belong to the Gospel, ought not to be terrorized by means of punishment, but only those who are not moved by love to do good, and who, though they belong to the Church outwardly, do not belong to it in merit.

Reply Obj. 4: Sometimes a wrong done to a person reflects on God and the Church: and then it is the duty of that person to avenge the wrong. For example, Elias made fire descend on those who were come to seize him (4 Kings 1); likewise Eliseus cursed the boys that mocked him (4 Kings 2); and Pope Sylverius excommunicated those who sent him into exile (XXIII, Q. iv, Cap. Guilisarius). But in so far as the wrong inflicted on a man affects his person, he should bear it patiently if this be expedient. For these precepts of patience are to be understood as referring to preparedness of the mind, as Augustine states (De Serm. Dom. in Monte i).

Reply Obj. 5: When the whole multitude sins, vengeance must be taken on them, either in respect of the whole multitude—thus the Egyptians were drowned in the Red Sea while they were pursuing the children of Israel (Ex. 14), and the people of Sodom were entirely destroyed (Gen. 19)—or as regards part of the multitude, as may be seen in the punishment of those who worshipped the calf.

Sometimes, however, if there is hope of many making amends, the severity of vengeance should be brought to bear on a few of the principals, whose punishment fills the rest with fear; thus the Lord (Num. 25) commanded the princes of the people to be hanged for the sin of the multitude.

On the other hand, if it is not the whole but only a part of the multitude that has sinned, then if the guilty can be separated from the innocent, vengeance should be wrought on them: provided, however, that this can be done without scandal to others; else the multitude should be spared and severity foregone. The same applies to the sovereign, whom the multitude follow. For his sin should be borne with, if it cannot be punished without scandal to the multitude: unless indeed his sin were such, that it would do more harm to the multitude, either spiritually or temporally, than would the scandal that was feared to arise from his punishment.

SECOND ARTICLE [II-II, Q. 108, Art. 2]

Whether Vengeance Is a Special Virtue?

Objection 1: It seems that vengeance is not a special and distinct virtue. For just as the good are rewarded for their good deeds, so are the wicked punished for their evil deeds. Now the rewarding of the good does not belong to a special virtue, but is an act of commutative justice. Therefore in the same way vengeance should not be accounted a special virtue.

Obj. 2: Further, there is no need to appoint a special virtue for an act to which a man is sufficiently disposed by the other virtues. Now man is sufficiently disposed by the virtues of fortitude or zeal to avenge evil. Therefore vengeance should not be reckoned a special virtue.

Obj. 3: Further, there is a special vice opposed to every special virtue. But seemingly no special vice is opposed to vengeance. Therefore it is not a special virtue.

*On the contrary,* Tully (De Invent. Rhet. ii) reckons it a part of justice.

*I answer that,* As the Philosopher states (Ethic. ii, 1), aptitude to virtue is in us by nature, but the complement of virtue is in us through habituation or some other cause. Hence it is evident that virtues perfect us so that we follow in due manner our natural inclinations, which belong to the natural right. Wherefore to every definite natural inclination there corresponds a special virtue. Now there is a special inclination of nature to remove harm, for which reason animals have the irascible power distinct from the concupiscible. Man resists harm by defending himself against wrongs, lest they be inflicted on him, or he avenges those which have already been inflicted on him, with the intention, not of harming, but of removing the harm done. And this belongs to vengeance, for Tully says (De Invent. Rhet. ii) that by "vengeance we resist force, or wrong, and in general whatever is obscure" [* *Obscurum.* Cicero wrote *obfuturum* but the sense is the same as St. Thomas gives in the parenthesis] "(i.e. derogatory), either by self-defense or by avenging it." Therefore vengeance is a special virtue.

Reply Obj. 1: Just as repayment of a legal debt belongs to commutative justice, and as repayment of a moral debt, arising from the bestowal of a particular favor, belongs to the virtue of gratitude, so too the punishment of sins, so far as it is the concern of public justice, is an act of commutative justice; while so far as it is concerned in defending the rights of the individual by whom a wrong is resisted, it belongs to the virtue of revenge.

Reply Obj. 2: Fortitude disposes to vengeance by removing an obstacle thereto, namely, fear of an imminent danger. Zeal, as denoting the fervor of love, signifies the primary root of vengeance, in so far as a man avenges the wrong done to God and his neighbor, because charity makes him regard them as his own. Now every act of virtue proceeds from charity as its root, since, according to Gregory (Hom. xxvii in Ev.), "there are no green leaves on the bough of good works, unless charity be the root."

Reply Obj. 3: Two vices are opposed to vengeance: one by way of excess, namely, the sin of cruelty or brutality, which exceeds the measure in punishing: while the other is a vice by way of deficiency and consists in being remiss in punishing, wherefore it is written (Prov. 13:24): "He that spareth the rod hateth his son." But the virtue of vengeance consists in observing the due measure of vengeance with regard to all the circumstances.

THIRD ARTICLE [II-II, Q. 108, Art. 3]

Whether Vengeance Should Be Wrought by Means of Punishments Customary Among Men?

Objection 1: It seems that vengeance should not be wrought by means of punishments customary among men. For to put a man to death is to uproot him. But our Lord forbade (Matt. 13:29) the uprooting of the cockle, whereby the children of the wicked one are signified. Therefore sinners should not be put to death.

Obj. 2: Further, all who sin mortally seem to be deserving of the same punishment. Therefore if some who sin mortally are punished with death, it seems that all such persons should be punished with death: and this is evidently false.

Obj. 3: Further, to punish a man publicly for his sin seems to publish his sin: and this would seem to have a harmful effect on the multitude, since the example of sin is taken by them as an occasion for sin. Therefore it seems that the punishment of death should not be inflicted for a sin.

*On the contrary,* These punishments are fixed by the divine law as appears from what we have said above (I-II, Q. 105, A. 2).

*I answer that,* Vengeance is lawful and virtuous so far as it tends to the prevention of evil. Now some who are not influenced by motive of virtue are prevented from committing sin, through fear of losing those things which they love more than those they obtain by sinning, else fear would be no restraint to sin. Consequently vengeance for sin should be taken by depriving a man of what he loves most. Now the things which man loves most are life, bodily safety, his own freedom, and external goods such as riches, his country and his good name. Wherefore, according to Augustine's reckoning (De Civ. Dei xxi), "Tully writes that the laws recognize eight kinds of punishment": namely, "death," whereby man is deprived of life; "stripes," "retaliation," or the loss of eye for eye, whereby man forfeits his bodily safety; "slavery," and "imprisonment," whereby he is deprived of freedom; "exile" whereby he is banished from his country; "fines," whereby he is mulcted in his riches; "ignominy," whereby he loses his good name.

Reply Obj. 1: Our Lord forbids the uprooting of the cockle, when there is fear lest the wheat be uprooted together with it. But sometimes the wicked can be uprooted by death, not only without danger, but even with great profit, to the good. Wherefore in such a case the punishment of death may be inflicted on sinners.

Reply Obj. 2: All who sin mortally are deserving of eternal death, as regards future retribution, which is in accordance with the truth of the divine judgment. But the punishments of this life are more of a medicinal character; wherefore the punishment of death is inflicted on those sins alone which conduce to the grave undoing of others.

Reply Obj. 3: The very fact that the punishment, whether of death or of any kind that is fearsome to man, is made known at the same time as the sin, makes man's will avers to sin: because the fear of punishment is greater than the enticement of the example of sin.

FOURTH ARTICLE [II-II, Q. 108, Art. 4]

Whether Vengeance Should Be Taken on Those Who Have Sinned Involuntarily?

Objection 1: It seems that vengeance should be taken on those who have sinned involuntarily. For the will of one man does not follow from the will of another. Yet one man is punished for another, according to Ex. 20:5, "I am … God … jealous, visiting the iniquity of the fathers upon the children, unto the third and fourth generation." Thus for the sin of Cham, his son Chanaan was cursed (Gen. 9:25) and for the sin of Giezi, his descendants were struck with leprosy (4 Kings 5). Again the blood of Christ lays the descendants of the Jews under the ban of punishment, for they said (Matt. 27:25): "His blood be upon us and upon our children." Moreover we read (Josue 7) that the people of Israel were delivered into the hands of their enemies for the sin of Achan, and that the same people were overthrown by the Philistines on account of the sin of the sons of Heli (1 Kings 4). Therefore a person is to be punished without having deserved it voluntarily.

Obj. 2: Further, nothing is voluntary except what is in a man's power. But sometimes a man is punished for what is not in his power; thus a man is removed from the administration of the Church on account of being infected with leprosy; and a Church ceases to be an episcopal see on account of the depravity or evil of the people. Therefore vengeance is taken not only for voluntary sins.

Obj. 3: Further, ignorance makes an act involuntary. Now vengeance is sometimes taken on the ignorant. Thus the children of the people of Sodom, though they were in invincible ignorance, perished with their parents (Gen. 19). Again, for the sin of Dathan and Abiron their children were swallowed up together with them (Num 16). Moreover, dumb animals, which are devoid of reason, were commanded to be slain on account of the sin of the Amalekites (1 Kings 15). Therefore vengeance is sometimes taken on those who have deserved it involuntarily.

Obj. 4: Further, compulsion is most opposed to voluntariness. But a man does not escape the debt of punishment through being compelled by fear to commit a sin. Therefore vengeance is sometimes taken on those who have deserved it involuntarily.

Obj. 5: Further Ambrose says on Luke 5 that "the ship in which Judas was, was in distress"; wherefore "Peter, who was calm in the security of his own merits, was in distress about those of others." But Peter did not will the sin of Judas. Therefore a person is sometimes punished without having voluntarily deserved it.

*On the contrary,* Punishment is due to sin. But every sin is voluntary according to Augustine (De Lib. Arb. iii; Retract. i). Therefore vengeance should be taken only on those who have deserved it voluntarily.

*I answer that,* Punishment may be considered in two ways. First, under the aspect of punishment, and in this way punishment is not due save for sin, because by means of punishment the equality of justice is restored, in so far as he who by sinning has exceeded in following his own will suffers something that is contrary to this will. Wherefore, since every sin is voluntary, not excluding original sin, as stated above (I-II, Q. 81, A. 1), it follows that no one is punished in this way, except for something done voluntarily. Secondly, punishment may be considered as a medicine, not only healing the past sin, but also preserving from future sin, or conducing to some good, and in this way a person is sometimes punished without any fault of his own, yet not without cause.

It must, however, be observed that a medicine never removes a greater good in order to promote a lesser; thus the medicine of the body never blinds the eye, in order to repair the heel: yet sometimes it is harmful in lesser things that it may be helpful in things of greater consequence. And since spiritual goods are of the greatest consequence, while temporal goods are least important, sometimes a person is punished in his temporal goods without any fault of his own. Such are many of the punishments inflicted by God in this present life for our humiliation or probation. But no one is punished in spiritual goods without any fault on his part, neither in this nor in the future life, because in the latter punishment is not medicinal, but a result of spiritual condemnation.

Reply Obj. 1: A man is never condemned to a spiritual punishment for another man's sin, because spiritual punishment affects the soul, in respect of which each man is master of himself. But sometimes a man is condemned to punishment in temporal matters for the sin of another, and this for three reasons. First, because one man may be the temporal goods of another, and so he may be punished in punishment of the latter: thus children, as to the body, are a belonging of their father, and slaves are a possession of their master. Secondly, when one person's sin is transmitted to another, either by *imitation,* as children copy the sins of their parents, and slaves the sins of their masters, so as to sin with greater daring; or by way of *merit,* as the sinful subjects merit a sinful superior, according to Job 34:30, "Who maketh a man that is a hypocrite to reign for the sins of the people?" Hence the people of Israel were punished for David's sin in numbering the people (2 Kings 24). This may also happen through some kind of *consent* or *connivance:* thus sometimes even the good are punished in temporal matters together with the wicked, for not having condemned their sins, as Augustine says (De Civ. Dei i, 9). Thirdly, in order to mark the unity of human fellowship, whereby one man is bound to be solicitous for another, lest he sin; and in order to inculcate horror of sin, seeing that the punishment of one affects all, as though all were one body, as Augustine says in speaking of the sin of Achan (QQ. sup. Josue viii). The saying of the Lord, "Visiting the iniquity of the fathers upon the children unto the third and fourth generation," seems to belong to mercy rather than to severity, since He does not take vengeance forthwith, but waits for some future time, in order that the descendants at least may mend their ways; yet should the wickedness of the descendants increase, it becomes almost necessary to take vengeance on them.

Reply Obj. 2: As Augustine states (QQ. sup. Josue viii), human judgment should conform to the divine judgment, when this is manifest, and God condemns men spiritually for their own sins. But human judgment cannot be conformed to God's hidden judgments, whereby He punishes certain persons in temporal matters without any fault of theirs, since man is unable to grasp the reasons of these judgments so as to know what is expedient for each individual. Wherefore according to human judgment a man should never be condemned without fault of his own to an inflictive punishment, such as death, mutilation or flogging. But a man may be condemned, even according to human judgment, to a punishment of forfeiture, even without any fault on his part, but not without cause: and this in three ways.

First, through a person becoming, without any fault of his, disqualified for having or acquiring a certain good: thus for being infected with leprosy a man is removed from the administration of the Church: and for bigamy, or through pronouncing a death sentence a man is hindered from receiving sacred orders.

Secondly, because the particular good that he forfeits is not his own but common property: thus that an episcopal see be attached to a certain church belongs to the good of the whole city, and not only to the good of the clerics.

Thirdly, because the good of one person may depend on the good of another: thus in the crime of high treason a son loses his inheritance through the sin of his parent.

Reply Obj. 3: By the judgment of God children are punished in temporal matters together with their parents, both because they are a possession of their parents, so that their parents are punished also in their person, and because this is for their good lest, should they be spared, they might imitate the sins of their parents, and thus deserve to be punished still more severely. Vengeance is wrought on dumb animals and any other irrational creatures, because in this way their owners are punished; and also in horror of sin.

Reply Obj. 4: An act done through compulsion of fear is not involuntary simply, but has an admixture of voluntariness, as stated above (I-II, Q. 6, AA. 5, 6).

Reply Obj. 5: The other apostles were distressed about the sin of Judas, in the same way as the multitude is punished for the sin of one, in commendation of unity, as state above (Reply Obj. 1, 2).

# QUESTION 109

OF TRUTH (In Four Articles)

We must now consider truth and the vices opposed thereto. Concerning truth there are four points of inquiry:

(1) Whether truth is a virtue?

(2) Whether it is a special virtue?

(3) Whether it is a part of justice?

(4) Whether it inclines to that which is less?

FIRST ARTICLE [II-II, Q. 109, Art. 1]

Whether Truth Is a Virtue?

Objection 1: It seems that truth is not a virtue. For the first of virtues is faith, whose object is truth. Since then the object precedes the habit and the act, it seems that truth is not a virtue, but something prior to virtue.

Obj. 2: Further, according to the Philosopher (Ethic. iv, 7), it belongs to truth that a man should state things concerning himself to be neither more nor less than they are. But this is not always praiseworthy—neither in good things, since according to Prov. 27:2, "Let another praise thee, and not thy own mouth"—nor even in evil things, because it is written in condemnation of certain people (Isa. 3:9): "They have proclaimed abroad their sin as Sodom, and they have not hid it." Therefore truth is not a virtue.

Obj. 3: Further, every virtue is either theological, or intellectual, or moral. Now truth is not a theological virtue, because its object is not God but temporal things. For Tully says (De Invent. Rhet. ii) that by "truth we faithfully represent things as they are, were, or will be." Likewise it is not one of the intellectual virtues, but their end. Nor again is it a moral virtue, since it is not a mean between excess and deficiency, for the more one tells the truth, the better it is. Therefore truth is not a virtue.

*On the contrary,* The Philosopher both in the Second and in the Fourth Book of Ethics places truth among the other virtues.

*I answer that,* Truth can be taken in two ways. First, for that by reason of which a thing is said to be true, and thus truth is not a virtue, but the object or end of a virtue: because, taken in this way, truth is not a habit, which is the genus containing virtue, but a certain equality between the understanding or sign and the thing understood or signified, or again between a thing and its rule, as stated in the First Part (Q. 16, A. 1; Q. 21, A. 2). Secondly, truth may stand for that by which a person says what is true, in which sense one is said to be truthful. This truth or truthfulness must needs be a virtue, because to say what is true is a good act: and virtue is "that which makes its possessor good, and renders his action good."

Reply Obj. 1: This argument takes truth in the first sense.

Reply Obj. 2: To state that which concerns oneself, in so far as it is a statement of what is true, is good generically. Yet this does not suffice for it to be an act of virtue, since it is requisite for that purpose that it should also be clothed with the due circumstances, and if these be not observed, the act will be sinful. Accordingly it is sinful to praise oneself without due cause even for that which is true: and it is also sinful to publish one's sin, by praising oneself on that account, or in any way proclaiming it uselessly.

Reply Obj. 3: A person who says what is true, utters certain signs which are in conformity with things; and such signs are either words, or external actions, or any external thing. Now such kinds of things are the subject-matter of the moral virtues alone, for the latter are concerned with the use of the external members, in so far as this use is put into effect at the command of the will. Wherefore truth is neither a theological, nor an intellectual, but a moral virtue. And it is a mean between excess and deficiency in two ways. First, on the part of the object, secondly, on the part of the act. On the part of the object, because the true essentially denotes a kind of equality, and equal is a mean between more and less. Hence for the very reason that a man says what is true about himself, he observes the mean between one that says more than the truth about himself, and one that says less than the truth. On the part of the act, to observe the mean is to tell the truth, when one ought, and as one ought. Excess consists in making known one's own affairs out of season, and deficiency in hiding them when one ought to make them known.

SECOND ARTICLE [II-II, Q. 109, Art. 2]

Whether Truth Is a Special Virtue?

Objection 1: It seems that truth is not a special virtue. For the true and the good are convertible. Now goodness is not a special virtue, in fact every virtue is goodness, because "it makes its possessor good." Therefore truth is not a special virtue.

Obj. 2: Further, to make known what belongs to oneself is an act of truth as we understand it here. But this belongs to every virtue, since every virtuous habit is made known by its own act. Therefore truth is not a special virtue.

Obj. 3: Further, the truth of life is the truth whereby one lives aright, and of which it is written (Isa. 38:3): "I beseech Thee ... remember how I have walked before Thee in truth, and with a perfect heart." Now one lives aright by any virtue, as follows from the definition of virtue given above (I-II, Q. 55, A. 4). Therefore truth is not a special virtue.

Obj. 4: Further, truth seems to be the same as simplicity, since hypocrisy is opposed to both. But simplicity is not a special virtue, since it rectifies the intention, and that is required in every virtue. Therefore neither is truth a special virtue.

*On the contrary,* It is numbered together with other virtues (Ethic. ii, 7).

*I answer that,* The nature of human virtue consists in making a man's deed good. Consequently whenever we find a special aspect of goodness in human acts, it is necessary that man be disposed thereto by a special virtue. And since according to Augustine (De Nat. Boni iii) good consists in order, it follows that a special aspect of good will be found where there is a special order. Now there is a special order whereby our externals, whether words or deeds, are duly ordered in relation to some thing, as sign to thing signified: and thereto man is perfected by the virtue of truth. Wherefore it is evident that truth is a special virtue.

Reply Obj. 1: The true and the good are convertible as to subject, since every true thing is good, and every good thing is true. But considered logically, they exceed one another, even as the intellect and will exceed one another. For the intellect understands the will and many things besides, and the will desires things pertaining to the intellect, and many others. Wherefore the *true* considered in its proper aspect as a perfection of the intellect is a particular good, since it is something appetible: and in like manner the *good* considered in its proper aspect as the end of the appetite is something true, since it is something intelligible. Therefore since virtue includes the aspect of goodness, it is possible for truth to be a special virtue, just as the *true* is a special good; yet it is not possible for goodness to be a special virtue, since rather, considered logically, it is the genus of virtue.

Reply Obj. 2: The habits of virtue and vice take their species from what is directly intended, and not from that which is accidental and beside the intention. Now that a man states that which concerns himself, belongs to the virtue of truth, as something directly intended: although it may belong to other virtues consequently and beside his principal intention. For the brave man intends to act bravely: and that he shows his fortitude by acting bravely is a consequence beside his principal intention.

Reply Obj. 3: The truth of life is the truth whereby a thing is true, not whereby a person says what is true. Life like anything else is said to be true, from the fact that it attains its rule and measure, namely, the divine law; since rectitude of life depends on conformity to that law. This truth or rectitude is common to every virtue.

Reply Obj. 4: Simplicity is so called from its opposition to duplicity, whereby, to wit, a man shows one thing outwardly while having another in his heart: so that simplicity pertains to this virtue. And it rectifies the intention, not indeed directly (since this belongs to every virtue), but by excluding duplicity, whereby a man pretends one thing and intends another.

THIRD ARTICLE [II-II, Q. 109, Art. 3]

Whether Truth Is a Part of Justice?

Objection 1: It seems that truth is not a part of justice. For it seems proper to justice to give another man his due. But, by telling the truth, one does not seem to give another man his due, as is the case in all the foregoing parts of justice. Therefore truth is not a part of justice.

Obj. 2: Further, truth pertains to the intellect: whereas justice is in the will, as stated above (Q. 58, A. 4). Therefore truth is not a part of justice.

Obj. 3: Further, according to Jerome truth is threefold, namely, "truth of life," "truth of justice," and "truth of doctrine." But none of these is a part of justice. For truth of life comprises all virtues, as stated above (A. 2, ad 3): truth of justice is the same as justice, so that it is not one of its parts; and truth of doctrine belongs rather to the intellectual virtues. Therefore truth is nowise a part of justice.

*On the contrary,* Tully (De Invent. Rhet. ii) reckons truth among the parts of justice.

*I answer that,* As stated above (Q. 80), a virtue is annexed to justice, as secondary to a principal virtue, through having something in common with justice, while falling short from the perfect virtue thereof. Now the virtue of truth has two things in common with justice. In the first place it is directed to another, since the manifestation, which we have stated to be an act of truth, is directed to another, inasmuch as one person manifests to another the things that concern himself. In the second place, justice sets up a certain equality between things, and this the virtue of truth does also, for it equals signs to the things which concern man himself. Nevertheless it falls short of the proper aspect of justice, as to the notion of debt: for this virtue does not regard legal debt, which justice considers, but rather the moral debt, in so far as, out of equity, one man owes another a manifestation of the truth. Therefore truth is a part of justice, being annexed thereto as a secondary virtue to its principal.

Reply Obj. 1: Since man is a social animal, one man naturally owes another whatever is necessary for the preservation of human society. Now it would be impossible for men to live together, unless they believed one another, as declaring the truth one to another. Hence the virtue of truth does, in a manner, regard something as being due.

Reply Obj. 2: Truth, as known, belongs to the intellect. But man, by his own will, whereby he uses both habits and members, utters external signs in order to manifest the truth, and in this way the manifestation of the truth is an act of the will.

Reply Obj. 3: The truth of which we are speaking now differs from the truth of life, as stated in the preceding A. 2, ad 3.

We speak of the truth of justice in two ways. In one way we refer to the fact that justice itself is a certain rectitude regulated according to the rule of the divine law; and in this way the truth of justice differs from the truth of life, because by the truth of life a man lives aright in himself, whereas by the truth of justice a man observes the rectitude of the law in those judgments which refer to another man: and in this sense the truth of justice has nothing to do with the truth of which we speak now, as neither has the truth of life. In another way the truth of justice may be understood as referring to the fact that, out of justice, a man manifests the truth, as for instance when a man confesses the truth, or gives true evidence in a court of justice. This truth is a particular act of justice, and does not pertain directly to this truth of which we are now speaking, because, to wit, in this manifestation of the truth a man's chief intention is to give another man his due. Hence the Philosopher says (Ethic. iv, 7) in describing this virtue: "We are not speaking of one who is truthful in his agreements, nor does this apply to matters in which justice or injustice is questioned."

The truth of doctrine consists in a certain manifestation of truths relating to science wherefore neither does this truth directly pertain to this virtue, but only that truth whereby a man, both in life and in speech, shows himself to be such as he is, and the things that concern him, not other, and neither greater nor less, than they are. Nevertheless since truths of science, as known by us, are something concerning us, and pertain to this virtue, in this sense the truth of doctrine may pertain to this virtue, as well as any other kind of truth whereby a man manifests, by word or deed, what he knows.

FOURTH ARTICLE [II-II, Q. 109, Art. 4]

Whether the Virtue of Truth Inclines Rather to That Which Is Less?

Objection 1: It seems that the virtue of truth does not incline to that which is less. For as one incurs falsehood by saying more, so does one by saying less: thus it is no more false that four are five, than that four are three. But "every falsehood is in itself evil, and to be avoided," as the Philosopher declares (Ethic. iv, 7). Therefore the virtue of truth does not incline to that which is less rather than to that which is greater.

Obj. 2: Further, that a virtue inclines to the one extreme rather than to the other, is owing to the fact that the virtue's mean is nearer to the one extreme than to the other: thus fortitude is nearer to daring than to timidity. But the mean of truth is not nearer to one extreme than to the other; because truth, since it is a kind of equality, holds to the exact mean. Therefore truth does not more incline to that which is less.

Obj. 3: Further, to forsake the truth for that which is less seems to amount to a denial of the truth, since this is to subtract therefrom; and to forsake the truth for that which is greater seems to amount to an addition thereto. Now to deny the truth is more repugnant to truth than to add something to it, because truth is incompatible with the denial of truth, whereas it is compatible with addition. Therefore it seems that truth should incline to that which is greater rather than to that which is less.

*On the contrary,* The Philosopher says (Ethic. iv, 7) that "by this virtue a man declines rather from the truth towards that which is less."

*I answer that,* There are two ways of declining from the truth to that which is less. First, by affirming, as when a man does not show the whole good that is in him, for instance science, holiness and so forth. This is done without prejudice to truth, since the lesser is contained in the greater: and in this way this virtue inclines to what is less. For, as the Philosopher says (Ethic. iv, 7), "this seems to be more prudent because exaggerations give annoyance." For those who represent themselves as being greater than they are, are a source of annoyance to others, since they seem to wish to surpass others: whereas those who make less account of themselves are a source of pleasure, since they seem to defer to others by their moderation. Hence the Apostle says (2 Cor. 12:6): "Though I should have a mind to glory, I shall not be foolish: for I will say the truth. But I forbear, lest any man should think of me above that which he seeth in me or anything he heareth from me."

Secondly, one may incline to what is less by denying, so as to say that what is in us is not. In this way it does not belong to this virtue to incline to what is less, because this would imply falsehood. And yet this would be less repugnant to the truth, not indeed as regards the proper aspect of truth, but as regards the aspect of prudence, which should be safeguarded in all the virtues. For since it is fraught with greater danger and is more annoying to others, it is more repugnant to prudence to think or boast that one has what one has not, than to think or say that one has not what one has.

This suffices for the Replies to the Objections.

## QUESTION 110

OF THE VICES OPPOSED TO TRUTH, AND FIRST OF LYING (In Four Articles)

We must now consider the vices opposed to truth, and (1) lying: (2) dissimulation or hypocrisy: (3) boasting and the opposite vice. Concerning lying there are four points of inquiry:

(1) Whether lying, as containing falsehood, is always opposed to truth?

(2) Of the species of lying;

(3) Whether lying is always a sin?

(4) Whether it is always a mortal sin?

FIRST ARTICLE [II-II, Q. 110, Art. 1]

Whether Lying Is Always Opposed to Truth?

Objection 1: It seems that lying is not always opposed to truth. For opposites are incompatible with one another. But lying is compatible with truth, since he that speaks the truth, thinking it to be false, lies, according to Augustine (Lib. De Mendac. iii). Therefore lying is not opposed to truth.

Obj. 2: Further, the virtue of truth applies not only to words but also to deeds, since according to the Philosopher (Ethic. iv, 7) by this virtue one tells the truth both in one's speech and in one's life. But lying applies only to words, for Augustine says (Contra Mend. xii) that "a lie is a false signification by words." Accordingly, it seems that lying is not directly opposed to the virtue of truth.

Obj. 3: Further, Augustine says (Lib. De Mendac. iii) that the "liar's sin is the desire to deceive." But this is not opposed to truth, but rather to benevolence or justice. Therefore lying is not opposed to truth.

*On the contrary,* Augustine says (Contra Mend. x): "Let no one doubt that it is a lie to tell a falsehood in order to deceive. Wherefore a false statement uttered with intent to deceive is a manifest lie." But this is opposed to truth. Therefore lying is opposed to truth.

*I answer that,* A moral act takes its species from two things, its object, and its end: for the end is the object of the will, which is the first mover in moral acts. And the power moved by the will has its own object, which is the proximate object of the voluntary act, and stands in relation to the will's act towards the end, as material to formal, as stated above (I-II, Q. 18, AA. 6, 7).

Now it has been said above (Q. 109, A. 1, ad 3) that the virtue of truth—and consequently the opposite vices—regards a manifestation made by certain signs: and this manifestation or statement is an act of reason comparing sign with the thing signified; because every representation consists in comparison, which is the proper act of the reason. Wherefore though dumb animals manifest something, yet they do not intend to manifest anything: but they do something by natural instinct, and a manifestation is the result. But when this manifestation or statement is a moral act, it must needs be voluntary, and dependent on the intention of the will. Now the proper object of a manifestation or statement is the true or the false. And the intention of a bad will may bear on two things: one of which is that a falsehood may be told; while the other is the proper effect of a false statement, namely, that someone may be deceived.

Accordingly if these three things concur, namely, falsehood of what is said, the will to tell a falsehood, and finally the intention to deceive, then there is falsehood—materially, since what is said is false, formally, on account of the will to tell an untruth, and effectively, on account of the will to impart a falsehood.

However, the essential notion of a lie is taken from formal falsehood, from the fact namely, that a person intends to say what is false; wherefore also the word *mendacium* (lie) is derived from its being in opposition to the *mind.* Consequently if one says what is false, thinking it to be true, it is false materially, but not formally, because the falseness is beside the intention of the speaker so that it is not a perfect lie, since what is beside the speaker's intention is accidental for which reason it cannot be a specific difference. If, on the other hand, one utters falsehood formally, through having the will to deceive, even if what one says be true, yet inasmuch as this is a voluntary and moral act, it contains falseness essentially and truth accidentally, and attains the specific nature of a lie.

That a person intends to cause another to have a false opinion, by deceiving him, does not belong to the species of lying, but to perfection thereof, even as in the physical order, a thing acquires its species if it has its form, even though the form's effect be lacking; for instance a heavy body which is held up aloft by force, lest it come down in accordance with the exigency of its form. Therefore it is evident that lying is directly an formally opposed to the virtue of truth.

Reply Obj. 1: We judge of a thing according to what is in it formally and essentially rather than according to what is in it materially and accidentally. Hence it is more in opposition to truth, considered as a moral virtue, to tell the truth with the intention of telling a falsehood than to tell a falsehood with the intention of telling the truth.

Reply Obj. 2: As Augustine says (De Doctr. Christ. ii), words hold the chief place among other signs. And so when it is said that "a lie is a false signification by words," the term "words" denotes every kind of sign. Wherefore if a person intended to signify something false by means of signs, he would not be excused from lying.

Reply Obj. 3: The desire to deceive belongs to the perfection of lying, but not to its species, as neither does any effect belong to the species of its cause.

SECOND ARTICLE [II-II, Q. 110, Art. 2]

Whether Lies Are Sufficiently Divided into Officious, Jocose, and Mischievous Lies?

Objection 1: It seems that lies are not sufficiently divided into "officious," "jocose" and "mischievous" lies. For a division should be made according to that which pertains to a thing by reason of its nature, as the Philosopher states (Metaph. vii, text. 43; De Part. Animal i, 3). But seemingly the intention of the effect resulting from a moral act is something beside and accidental to the species of that act, so that an indefinite number of effects can result from one act. Now this division is made according to the intention of the effect: for a "jocose" lie is told in order to make fun, an "officious" lie for some useful purpose, and a "mischievous" lie in order to injure someone. Therefore lies are unfittingly divided in this way.

Obj. 2: Further, Augustine (Contra Mendac. xiv) gives eight kinds of lies. The first is "in religious doctrine"; the second is "a lie that profits no one and injures someone"; the third "profits one party so as to injure another"; the fourth is "told out of mere lust of lying and deceiving"; the fifth is "told out of the desire to please"; the sixth "injures no one, and profits someone in saving his money"; the seventh "injures no one and profits someone in saving him from death"; the eighth "injures no one, and profits someone in saving him from defilement of the body." Therefore it seems that the first division of lies is insufficient.

Obj. 3: Further, the Philosopher (Ethic. iv, 7) divides lying into "boasting," which exceeds the truth in speech, and "irony," which falls short of the truth by saying something less: and these two are not contained under any one of the kinds mentioned above. Therefore it seems that the aforesaid division of lies is inadequate.

*On the contrary,* A gloss on Ps. 5:7, "Thou wilt destroy all that speak a lie," says "that there are three kinds of lies; for some are told for the wellbeing and convenience of someone; and there is another kind of lie that is told in fun; but the third kind of lie is told out of malice." The first of these is called an officious lie, the second a jocose lie, the third a mischievous lie. Therefore lies are divided into these three kinds.

*I answer that,* Lies may be divided in three ways. First, with respect to their nature as lies: and this is the proper and essential division of lying. In this way, according to the Philosopher (Ethic. iv, 7), lies are of two kinds, namely, the lie which goes beyond the truth, and this belongs to "boasting," and the lie which stops short of the truth, and this belongs to "irony." This division is an essential division of lying itself, because lying as such is opposed to truth, as stated in the preceding Article: and truth is a kind of equality, to which more and less are in essential opposition.

Secondly, lies may be divided with respect to their nature as sins, and with regard to those things that aggravate or diminish the sin of lying, on the part of the end intended. Now the sin of lying is aggravated, if by lying a person intends to injure another, and this is called a "mischievous" lie, while the sin of lying is diminished if it be directed to some good—either of pleasure and then it is a "jocose" lie, or of usefulness, and then we have the "officious" lie, whereby it is intended to help another person, or to save him from being injured. In this way lies are divided into the three kinds aforesaid.

Thirdly, lies are divided in a more general way, with respect to their relation to some end, whether or not this increase or diminish their gravity: and in this way the division comprises eight kinds, as stated in the Second Objection. Here the first three kinds are contained under "mischievous" lies, which are either against God, and then we have the lie "in religious doctrine," or against man, and this either with the sole intention of injuring him, and then it is the second kind of lie, which "profits no one, and injures someone"; or with the intention of injuring one and at the same time profiting another, and this is the third kind of lie, "which profits one, and injures another." Of these the first is the most grievous, because sins against God are always more grievous, as stated above (I-II, Q. 73, A. 3): and the second is more grievous than the third, since the latter's gravity is diminished by the intention of profiting another.

After these three, which aggravate the sin of lying, we have a fourth, which has its own measure of gravity without addition or diminution; and this is the lie which is told "out of mere lust of lying and deceiving." This proceeds from a habit, wherefore the Philosopher says (Ethic. iv, 7) that "the liar, when he lies from habit, delights in lying."

The four kinds that follow lessen the gravity of the sin of lying. For the fifth kind is the jocose lie, which is told "with a desire to please": and the remaining three are comprised under the officious lie, wherein something useful to another person is intended. This usefulness regards either external things, and then we have the sixth kind of lie, which "profits someone in saving his money"; or his body, and this is the seventh kind, which "saves a man from death"; or the morality of his virtue, and this is the eighth kind, which "saves him from unlawful defilement of his body."

Now it is evident that the greater the good intended, the more is the sin of lying diminished in gravity. Wherefore a careful consideration of the matter will show that these various kinds of lies are enumerated in their order of gravity: since the useful good is better than the pleasurable good, and life of the body than money, and virtue than the life of the body.

This suffices for the Replies to the Objections.

THIRD ARTICLE [II-II, Q. 110, Art. 3]

Whether Every Lie Is a Sin?

Objection 1: It seems that not every lie is a sin. For it is evident that the evangelists did not sin in the writing of the Gospel. Yet they seem to have told something false: since their accounts of the words of Christ and of others often differ from one another: wherefore seemingly one of them must have given an untrue account. Therefore not every lie is a sin.

Obj. 2: Further, no one is rewarded by God for sin. But the midwives of Egypt were rewarded by God for a lie, for it is stated that "God built them houses" (Ex. 1:21). Therefore a lie is not a sin.

Obj. 3: Further, the deeds of holy men are related in Sacred Writ that they may be a model of human life. But we read of certain very holy men that they lied. Thus (Gen. 12 and 20) we are told that Abraham said of his wife that she was his sister. Jacob also lied when he said that he was Esau, and yet he received a blessing (Gen. 27:27-29). Again, Judith is commended (Judith 15:10, 11) although she lied to Holofernes. Therefore not every lie is a sin.

Obj. 4: Further, one ought to choose the lesser evil in order to avoid the greater: even so a physician cuts off a limb, lest the whole body perish. Yet less harm is done by raising a false opinion in a person's mind, than by someone slaying or being slain. Therefore a man may lawfully lie, to save another from committing murder, or another from being killed.

Obj. 5: Further, it is a lie not to fulfill what one has promised. Yet one is not bound to keep all one's promises: for Isidore says (Synonym. ii): "Break your faith when you have promised ill." Therefore not every lie is a sin.

Obj. 6: Further, apparently a lie is a sin because thereby we deceive our neighbor: wherefore Augustine says (Lib. De Mend. xxi): "Whoever thinks that there is any kind of lie that is not a sin deceives himself shamefully, since he deems himself an honest man when he deceives others." Yet not every lie is a cause of deception, since no one is deceived by a jocose lie; seeing that lies of this kind are told, not with the intention of being believed, but merely for the sake of giving pleasure. Hence again we find hyperbolical expressions in Holy Writ. Therefore not every lie is a sin.

*On the contrary,* It is written (Ecclus. 7:14): "Be not willing to make any manner of lie."

*I answer that,* An action that is naturally evil in respect of its genus can by no means be good and lawful, since in order for an action to be good it must be right in every respect: because good results from a complete cause, while evil results from any single defect, as Dionysius asserts (Div. Nom. iv). Now a lie is evil in respect of its genus, since it is an action bearing on undue matter. For as words are naturally signs of intellectual acts, it is unnatural and undue for anyone to signify by words something that is not in his mind. Hence the Philosopher says (Ethic. iv, 7) that "lying is in itself evil and to be shunned, while truthfulness is good and worthy of praise." Therefore every lie is a sin, as also Augustine declares (Contra Mend. i).

Reply Obj. 1: It is unlawful to hold that any false assertion is contained either in the Gospel or in any canonical Scripture, or that the writers thereof have told untruths, because faith would be deprived of its certitude which is based on the authority of Holy Writ. That the words of certain people are variously reported in the Gospel and other sacred writings does not constitute a lie. Hence Augustine says (De Consens. Evang. ii): "He that has the wit to understand that in order to know the truth it is necessary to get at the sense, will conclude that he must not be the least troubled, no matter by what words that sense is expressed." Hence it is evident, as he adds (De Consens. Evang. ii), that "we must not judge that someone is lying, if several persons fail to describe in the same way and in the same words a thing which they remember to have seen or heard."

Reply Obj. 2: The midwives were rewarded, not for their lie, but for their fear of God, and for their good-will, which latter led them to tell a lie. Hence it is expressly stated (Ex. 2:21): "And because the midwives feared God, He built them houses." But the subsequent lie was not meritorious.

Reply Obj. 3: In Holy Writ, as Augustine observes (Lib. De Mend. v), the deeds of certain persons are related as examples of perfect virtue: and we must not believe that such persons were liars. If, however, any of their statements appear to be untruthful, we must understand such statements to have been figurative and prophetic. Hence Augustine says (Lib. De Mend. v): "We must believe that whatever is related of those who, in prophetical times, are mentioned as being worthy of credit, was done and said by them prophetically." As to Abraham "when he said that Sara was his sister, he wished to hide the truth, not to tell a lie, for she is called his sister since she was the daughter of his father," Augustine says (QQ. Super. Gen. xxvi; Contra Mend. x; Contra Faust. xxii). Wherefore Abraham himself said (Gen. 20:12): "She is truly my sister, the daughter of my father, and not the daughter of my mother," being related to him on his father's side. Jacob's assertion that he was Esau, Isaac's first-born, was spoken in a mystical sense, because, to wit, the latter's birthright was due to him by right: and he made use of this mode of speech being moved by the spirit of prophecy, in order to signify a mystery, namely, that the younger people, i.e. the Gentiles, should supplant the first-born, i.e. the Jews.

Some, however, are commended in the Scriptures, not on account of perfect virtue, but for a certain virtuous disposition, seeing that it was owing to some praiseworthy sentiment that they were moved to do certain undue things. It is thus that Judith is praised, not for lying to Holofernes, but for her desire to save the people, to which end she exposed herself to danger. And yet one might also say that her words contain truth in some mystical sense.

Reply Obj. 4: A lie is sinful not only because it injures one's neighbor, but also on account of its inordinateness, as stated above in this Article. Now it is not allowed to make use of anything inordinate in order to ward off injury or defects from another: as neither is it lawful to steal in order to give an alms, except perhaps in a case of necessity when all things are common. Therefore it is not lawful to tell a lie in order to deliver another from any danger whatever. Nevertheless it is lawful to hide the truth prudently, by keeping it back, as Augustine says (Contra Mend. x).

Reply Obj. 5: A man does not lie, so long as he has a mind to do what he promises, because he does not speak contrary to what he has in mind: but if he does not keep his promise, he seems to act without faith in changing his mind. He may, however, be excused for two reasons. First, if he has promised something evidently unlawful, because he sinned in promise, and did well to change his mind. Secondly, if circumstances have changed with regard to persons and the business in hand. For, as Seneca states (De Benef. iv), for a man to be bound to keep a promise, it is necessary for everything to remain unchanged: otherwise neither did he lie in promising—since he promised what he had in his mind, due circumstances being taken for granted—nor was he faithless in not keeping his promise, because circumstances are no longer the same. Hence the Apostle, though he did not go to Corinth, whither he had promised to go (2 Cor. 1), did not lie, because obstacles had arisen which prevented him.

Reply Obj. 6: An action may be considered in two ways. First, in itself, secondly, with regard to the agent. Accordingly a jocose lie, from the very genus of the action, is of a nature to deceive; although in the intention of the speaker it is not told to deceive, nor does it deceive by the way it is told. Nor is there any similarity in the hyperbolical or any kind of figurative expressions, with which we meet in Holy Writ: because, as Augustine says (Lib. De Mend. v), "it is not a lie to do or say a thing figuratively: because every statement must be referred to the thing stated: and when a thing is done or said figuratively, it states what those to whom it is tendered understand it to signify."

FOURTH ARTICLE [II-II, Q. 110, Art. 4]

Whether Every Lie Is a Mortal Sin?

Objection 1: It seems that every lie is a mortal sin. For it is written (Ps. 6:7): "Thou wilt destroy all that speak a lie," and (Wis. 1:11): "The mouth that belieth killeth the soul." Now mortal sin alone causes destruction and death of the soul. Therefore every lie is a mortal sin.

Obj. 2: Further, whatever is against a precept of the decalogue is a mortal sin. Now lying is against this precept of the decalogue: "Thou shalt not bear false witness." Therefore every lie is a mortal sin.

Obj. 3: Further, Augustine says (De Doctr. Christ. i, 36): "Every liar breaks his faith in lying, since forsooth he wishes the person to whom he lies to have faith in him, and yet he does not keep faith with him, when he lies to him: and whoever breaks his faith is guilty of iniquity." Now no one is said to break his faith or "to be guilty of iniquity," for a venial sin. Therefore no lie is a venial sin.

Obj. 4: Further, the eternal reward is not lost save for a mortal sin. Now, for a lie the eternal reward was lost, being exchanged for a temporal meed. For Gregory says (Moral. xviii) that "we learn from the reward of the midwives what the sin of lying deserves: since the reward which they deserved for their kindness, and which they might have received in eternal life, dwindled into a temporal meed on account of the lie of which they were guilty." Therefore even an officious lie, such as was that of the midwives, which seemingly is the least of lies, is a mortal sin.

Obj. 5: Further, Augustine says (Lib. De Mend. xvii) that "it is a precept of perfection, not only not to lie at all, but not even to wish to lie." Now it is a mortal sin to act against a precept. Therefore every lie of the perfect is a mortal sin: and consequently so also is a lie told by anyone else, otherwise the perfect would be worse off than others.

*On the contrary,* Augustine says on Ps. 5:7, "Thou wilt destroy," etc.: "There are two kinds of lie, that are not grievously sinful yet are not devoid of sin, when we lie either in joking, or for the sake of our neighbor's good." But every mortal sin is grievous. Therefore jocose and officious lies are not mortal sins.

*I answer that,* A mortal sin is, properly speaking, one that is contrary to charity whereby the soul lives in union with God, as stated above (Q. 24, A. 12; Q. 35, A. 3). Now a lie may be contrary to charity in three ways: first, in itself; secondly, in respect of the evil intended; thirdly, accidentally.

A lie may be in itself contrary to charity by reason of its false signification. For if this be about divine things, it is contrary to the charity of God, whose truth one hides or corrupts by such a lie; so that a lie of this kind is opposed not only to the virtue of charity, but also to the virtues of faith and religion: wherefore it is a most grievous and a mortal sin. If, however, the false signification be about something the knowledge of which affects a man's good, for instance if it pertain to the perfection of science or to moral conduct, a lie of this description inflicts an injury on one's neighbor, since it causes him to have a false opinion, wherefore it is contrary to charity, as regards the love of our neighbor, and consequently is a mortal sin. On the other hand, if the false opinion engendered by the lie be about some matter the knowledge of which is of no consequence, then the lie in question does no harm to one's neighbor; for instance, if a person be deceived as to some contingent particulars that do not concern him. Wherefore a lie of this kind, considered in itself, is not a mortal sin.

As regards the end in view, a lie may be contrary to charity, through being told with the purpose of injuring God, and this is always a mortal sin, for it is opposed to religion; or in order to injure one's neighbor, in his person, his possessions or his good name, and this also is a mortal sin, since it is a mortal sin to injure one's neighbor, and one sins mortally if one has merely the intention of committing a mortal sin. But if the end intended be not contrary to charity, neither will the lie, considered under this aspect, be a mortal sin, as in the case of a jocose lie, where some little pleasure is intended, or in an officious lie, where the good also of one's neighbor is intended. Accidentally a lie may be contrary to charity by reason of scandal or any other injury resulting therefrom: and thus again it will be a mortal sin, for instance if a man were not deterred through scandal from lying publicly.

Reply Obj. 1: The passages quoted refer to the mischievous lie, as a gloss explains the words of Ps. 5:7, "Thou wilt destroy all that speak a lie."

Reply Obj. 2: Since all the precepts of the decalogue are directed to the love of God and our neighbor, as stated above (Q. 44, A. 1, ad 3; I-II, Q. 100, A. 5, ad 1), a lie is contrary to a precept of the decalogue, in so far as it is contrary to the love of God and our neighbor. Hence it is expressly forbidden to bear false witness against our neighbor.

Reply Obj. 3: Even a venial sin can be called "iniquity" in a broad sense, in so far as it is beside the equity of justice; wherefore it is written (1 John 3:4): "Every sin is iniquity [*Vulg.: 'And sin is iniquity.']." It is in this sense that Augustine is speaking.

Reply Obj. 4: The lie of the midwives may be considered in two ways. First as regards their feeling of kindliness towards the Jews, and their reverence and fear of God, for which their virtuous disposition is commended. For this an eternal reward is due. Wherefore Jerome (in his exposition of Isa. 65:21, 'And they shall build houses') explains that God "built them spiritual houses." Secondly, it may be considered with regard to the external act of lying. For thereby they could merit, not indeed eternal reward, but perhaps some temporal meed, the deserving of which was not inconsistent with the deformity of their lie, though this was inconsistent with their meriting an eternal reward. It is in this sense that we must understand the words of Gregory, and not that they merited by that lie to lose the eternal reward as though they had already merited it by their preceding kindliness, as the objection understands the words to mean.

Reply Obj. 5: Some say that for the perfect every lie is a mortal sin. But this assertion is unreasonable. For no circumstance causes a sin to be infinitely more grievous unless it transfers it to another species. Now a circumstance of person does not transfer a sin to another species, except perhaps by reason of something annexed to that person, for instance if it be against his vow: and this cannot apply to an officious or jocose lie. Wherefore an officious or a jocose lie is not a mortal sin in perfect men, except perhaps accidentally on account of scandal. We may take in this sense the saying of Augustine that "it is a precept of perfection not only not to lie at all, but not even to wish to lie": although Augustine says this not positively but dubiously, for he begins by saying: "Unless perhaps it is a precept," etc. Nor does it matter that they are placed in a position to safeguard the truth: because they are bound to safeguard the truth by virtue of their office in judging or teaching, and if they lie in these matters their lie will be a mortal sin: but it does not follow that they sin mortally when they lie in other matters.

# QUESTION 111

OF DISSIMULATION AND HYPOCRISY (In Four Articles)

In due sequence we must consider dissimulation and hypocrisy. Under this head there are four points of inquiry:

(1) Whether all dissimulation is a sin?
(2) Whether hypocrisy is dissimulation?
(3) Whether it is opposed to truth?
(4) Whether it is a mortal sin?

FIRST ARTICLE [II-II, Q. 111, Art. 1]

Whether All Dissimulation Is a Sin?

Objection 1: It seems that not all dissimulation is a sin. For it is written (Luke 24:28) that our Lord "pretended [Douay: 'made as though'] he would go farther"; and Ambrose in his book on the Patriarchs (De Abraham i) says of Abraham that he "spoke craftily to his servants, when he said" (Gen. 22:5): "I and the boy will go with speed as far as yonder, and after we have worshipped, will return to you." Now to pretend and to speak craftily savor of dissimulation: and yet it is not to be said that there was sin in Christ or Abraham. Therefore not all dissimulation is a sin.

Obj. 2: Further, no sin is profitable. But according to Jerome, in his commentary on Gal. 2:11, "When Peter [Vulg.: 'Cephas'] was come to Antioch:—The example of Jehu, king of Israel, who slew the priest of Baal, pretending that he desired to worship idols, should teach us that dissimulation is useful and sometimes to be employed"; and David "changed his countenance before" Achis, king of Geth (1 Kings 21:13). Therefore not all dissimulation is a sin.

Obj. 3: Further, good is contrary to evil. Therefore if it is evil to simulate good, it is good to simulate evil.

Obj. 4: Further, it is written in condemnation of certain people (Isa. 3:9): "They have proclaimed abroad their sin as Sodom, and they have not hid it." Now it pertains to dissimulation to hide one's sin. Therefore it is reprehensible sometimes not to simulate. But it is never reprehensible to avoid sin. Therefore dissimulation is not a sin.

*On the contrary,* A gloss on Isa. 16:14, "In three years," etc., says: "Of the two evils it is less to sin openly than to simulate holiness." But to sin openly is always a sin. Therefore dissimulation is always a sin.

*I answer that,* As stated above (Q. 109, A. 3; Q. 110, A. 1), it belongs to the virtue of truth to show oneself outwardly by outward signs to be such as one is. Now outward signs are not only words, but also deeds. Accordingly just as it is contrary to truth to signify by words something different from that which is in one's mind, so also is it contrary to truth to employ signs of deeds or things to signify the contrary of what is in oneself, and this is what is properly denoted by dissimulation. Consequently dissimulation is properly a lie told by the signs of outward deeds. Now it matters not whether one lie in word or in any other way, as stated above (Q. 110, A. 1, Obj. 2). Wherefore, since every lie is a sin, as stated above (Q. 110, A. 3), it follows that also all dissimulation is a sin.

Reply Obj. 1: As Augustine says (De QQ. Evang. ii), "To pretend is not always a lie: but only when the pretense has no signification, then it is a lie. When, however, our pretense refers to some signification, there is no lie, but a representation of the truth." And he cites figures of speech as an example, where a thing is "pretended," for we do not mean it to be taken literally but as a figure of something else that we wish to say. In this way our Lord "pretended He would go farther," because He acted as if wishing to go farther; in order to signify something figuratively either because He was far from their faith, according to Gregory (Hom. xxiii in Ev.); or, as Augustine says (De QQ. Evang. ii), because, "as He was about to go farther away from them by ascending into heaven, He was, so to speak, held back on earth by their hospitality."

Abraham also spoke figuratively. Wherefore Ambrose (De Abraham i) says that Abraham "foretold what he knew not": for he intended to return alone after sacrificing his son: but by his mouth the Lord expressed what He was about to do. It is evident therefore that neither dissembled.

Reply Obj. 2: Jerome employs the term "simulation" in a broad sense for any kind of pretense. David's change of countenance was a figurative pretense, as a gloss observes in commenting on the title of Ps. 33, "I will bless the Lord at all times." There is no need to excuse Jehu's dissimulation from sin or lie, because he was a wicked man, since he departed not from the idolatry of Jeroboam (4 Kings 10:29, 31). And yet he is praised withal and received an earthly reward from God, not for his dissimulation, but for his zeal in destroying the worship of Baal.

Reply Obj. 3: Some say that no one may pretend to be wicked, because no one pretends to be wicked by doing good deeds, and if he do evil deeds, he is evil. But this argument proves nothing. Because a man might pretend to be evil, by doing what is not evil in itself but has some appearance of evil: and nevertheless this dissimulation is evil, both because it is a lie, and because it gives scandal; and although he is wicked on this account, yet his wickedness is not the wickedness he simulates. And because dissimulation is evil in itself, its sinfulness is not derived from the thing simulated, whether this be good or evil.

Reply Obj. 4: Just as a man lies when he signifies by word that which he is not, yet lies not when he refrains from saying what he is, for this is sometimes lawful; so also does a man dissemble, when by outward signs of deeds or things he signifies that which he is not, yet he dissembles not if he omits to signify what he is. Hence one may hide one's sin without being guilty of dissimulation. It is thus that we must understand the saying of Jerome on the words of Isa. 3:9, that the "second remedy after shipwreck is to hide one's sin," lest, to wit, others be scandalized thereby.

SECOND ARTICLE [II-II, Q. 111, Art. 2]

Whether Hypocrisy Is the Same As Dissimulation?

Objection 1: It seems that hypocrisy is not the same as dissimulation. For dissimulation consists in lying by deeds. But there may be hypocrisy in showing outwardly what one does inwardly, according to Matt. 6:2, "When thou dost an almsdeed sound not a trumpet before thee, as the hypocrites do." Therefore hypocrisy is not the same as dissimulation.

Obj. 2: Further, Gregory says (Moral. xxxi, 7): "Some there are who wear the habit of holiness, yet are unable to attain the merit of perfection. We must by no means deem these to have joined the ranks of the hypocrites, since it is one thing to sin from weakness, and another to sin from malice." Now those who wear the habit of holiness, without attaining the merit of perfection, are dissemblers, since the outward habit signifies works of perfection. Therefore dissimulation is not the same as hypocrisy.

Obj. 3: Further, hypocrisy consists in the mere intention. For our Lord says of hypocrites (Matt. 23:5) that "all their works they do for to be seen of men": and Gregory says (Moral. xxxi, 7) that "they never consider what it is that they do, but how by their every action they may please men." But dissimulation consists, not in the mere intention, but in the outward action: wherefore a gloss on Job 36:13, "Dissemblers and crafty men prove the wrath of God," says that "the dissembler simulates one thing and does another: he pretends chastity, and delights in lewdness, he makes a show of poverty and fills his purse." Therefore hypocrisy is not the same as dissimulation.

*On the contrary,* Isidore says (Etym. x): "'Hypocrite' is a Greek word corresponding to the Latin 'simulator,' for whereas he is evil within," he "shows himself outwardly as being good; hypo denoting falsehood, and krisis , judgment."

*I answer that,* As Isidore says (Etym. x), "the word hypocrite is derived from the appearance of those who come on to the stage with a disguised face, by changing the color of their complexion, so as to imitate the complexion of the person they simulate, at one time under the guise of a man, at another under the guise of a woman, so as to deceive the people in their acting." Hence Augustine says (De Serm. Dom. ii) that "just as hypocrites by simulating other persons act the parts of those they are not (since he that acts the part of Agamemnon is not that man himself but pretends to be), so too in the Church and in every department of human life, whoever wishes to seem what he is not is a hypocrite: for he pretends to be just without being so in reality."

We must conclude, therefore, that hypocrisy is dissimulation, not, however, any form of dissimulation, but only when one person simulates another, as when a sinner simulates the person of a just man.

Reply Obj. 1: The outward deed is a natural sign of the intention. Accordingly when a man does good works pertaining by their genus to the service of God, and seeks by their means to please, not God but man, he simulates a right intention which he has not. Wherefore Gregory says (Moral.) that "hypocrites make God's interests subservient to worldly purposes, since by making a show of saintly conduct they seek, not to turn men to God, but to draw to themselves the applause of their approval:" and so they make a lying pretense of having a good intention, which they have not, although they do not pretend to do a good deed without doing it.

Reply Obj. 2: The habit of holiness, for instance the religious or the clerical habit, signifies a state whereby one is bound to perform works of perfection. And so when a man puts on the habit of holiness, with the intention of entering the state of perfection, if he fail through weakness, he is not a dissembler or a hypocrite, because he is not bound to disclose his sin by laying aside the habit of holiness. If, however, he were to put on the habit of holiness in order to make a show of righteousness, he would be a hypocrite and a dissembler.

Reply Obj. 3: In dissimulation, as in a lie, there are two things: one by way of sign, the other by way of thing signified. Accordingly the evil intention in hypocrisy is considered as a thing signified, which does not tally with the sign: and the outward words, or deeds, or any sensible objects are considered in every dissimulation and lie as a sign.

THIRD ARTICLE [II-II, Q. 111, Art. 3]

Whether Hypocrisy Is Contrary to the Virtue of Truth?

Objection 1: It seems that hypocrisy is not contrary to the virtue of truth. For in dissimulation or hypocrisy there is a sign and a thing signified. Now with regard to neither of these does it seem to be opposed to any special virtue: for a hypocrite simulates any virtue, and by means of any virtuous deeds, such as fasting, prayer and alms deeds, as stated in Matt. 6:1-18. Therefore hypocrisy is not specially opposed to the virtue of truth.

Obj. 2: Further, all dissimulation seems to proceed from guile, wherefore it is opposed to simplicity. Now guile is opposed to prudence as above stated (Q. 55, A. 4). Therefore, hypocrisy which is dissimulation is not opposed to truth, but rather to prudence or simplicity.

Obj. 3: Further, the species of moral acts is taken from their end. Now the end of hypocrisy is the acquisition of gain or vainglory: wherefore a gloss on Job 27:8, "What is the hope of the hypocrite, if through covetousness he take by violence," says: "A hypocrite or, as the Latin has it, a dissimulator, is a covetous thief: for through desire of being honored for holiness, though guilty of wickedness, he steals praise for a life which is not his." [*The quotation is from St. Gregory's *Moralia*, Bk XVIII.] Therefore since covetousness or vainglory is not directly opposed to truth, it seems that neither is hypocrisy or dissimulation.

*On the contrary,* All dissimulation is a lie, as stated above (A. 1). Now a lie is directly opposed to truth. Therefore dissimulation or hypocrisy is also.

*I answer that,* According to the Philosopher (Metaph. text. 13, 24, x), "contrariety is opposition as regards form," i.e. the specific form. Accordingly we must reply that dissimulation or hypocrisy may be opposed to a virtue in two ways, in one way directly, in another way indirectly. Its direct opposition or contrariety is to be considered with regard to the very species of the act, and this species depends on that act's proper object. Wherefore since hypocrisy is a kind of dissimulation, whereby a man simulates a character which is not his, as stated in the preceding article, it follows that it is directly opposed to truth whereby a man shows himself in life and speech to be what he is, as stated in *Ethic.* iv, 7.

The indirect opposition or contrariety of hypocrisy may be considered in relation to any accident, for instance a remote end, or an instrument of action, or anything else of that kind.

Reply Obj. 1: The hypocrite in simulating a virtue regards it as his end, not in respect of its existence, as though he wished to have it, but in respect of appearance, since he wishes to seem to have it. Hence his hypocrisy is not opposed to that virtue, but to truth, inasmuch as he wishes to deceive men with regard to that virtue. And he performs acts of that virtue, not as intending them for their own sake, but instrumentally, as signs of that virtue, wherefore his hypocrisy has not, on that account, a direct opposition to that virtue.

Reply Obj. 2: As stated above (Q. 55, AA. 3, 4, 5), the vice directly opposed to prudence is cunning, to which it belongs to discover ways of achieving a purpose, that are apparent and not real: while it accomplishes that purpose, by guile in words, and by fraud in deeds: and it stands in relation to prudence, as guile and fraud to simplicity. Now guile and fraud are directed chiefly to deception, and sometimes secondarily to injury. Wherefore it belongs directly to simplicity to guard oneself from deception, and in this way the virtue of simplicity is the same as the virtue of truth as stated above (Q. 109, A. 2, ad 4). There is, however, a mere logical difference between them, because by truth we mean the concordance between sign and thing signified, while simplicity indicates that one does not tend to different things, by intending one thing inwardly, and pretending another outwardly.

Reply Obj. 3: Gain or glory is the remote end of the dissembler as also of the liar. Hence it does not take its species from this end, but from the proximate end, which is to show oneself other than one is. Wherefore it sometimes happens to a man to pretend great things of himself, for no further purpose than the mere lust of hypocrisy, as the Philosopher says (Ethic. iv, 7), and as also we have said above with regard to lying (Q. 110, A. 2).

FOURTH ARTICLE [II-II, Q. 111, Art. 4]

Whether Hypocrisy Is Always a Mortal Sin?

Objection 1: It seems that hypocrisy is always a mortal sin. For Jerome says on Isa. 16:14: "Of the two evils it is less to sin openly than to simulate holiness": and a gloss on Job 1:21 [*St. Augustine, on Ps. 63:7], "As it hath pleased the Lord," etc., says that "pretended justice is no justice, but a twofold sin": and again a gloss on Lam. 4:6, "The iniquity ... of my people is made greater than the sin of Sodom," says: "He deplores the sins of the soul that falls into hypocrisy, which is a greater iniquity than the sin of Sodom." Now the sins of Sodom are mortal sin. Therefore hypocrisy is always a mortal sin.

Obj. 2: Further, Gregory says (Moral. xxxi, 8) that hypocrites sin out of malice. But this is most grievous, for it pertains to the sin against the Holy Ghost. Therefore a hypocrite always sins mortally.

Obj. 3: Further, no one deserves the anger of God and exclusion from seeing God, save on account of mortal sin. Now the anger of God is deserved through hypocrisy according to Job 36:13, "Dissemblers and crafty men prove the wrath of God": and the hypocrite is excluded from seeing God, according to Job 13:16, "No hypocrite shall come before His presence." Therefore hypocrisy is always a mortal sin.

*On the contrary,* Hypocrisy is lying by deed since it is a kind of dissimulation. But it is not always a mortal sin to lie by deed. Neither therefore is all hypocrisy a mortal sin.

Further, the intention of a hypocrite is to appear to be good. But this is not contrary to charity. Therefore hypocrisy is not of itself a mortal sin.

Further, hypocrisy is born of vainglory, as Gregory says (Moral. xxxi, 17). But vainglory is not always a mortal sin. Neither therefore is hypocrisy.

*I answer that,* There are two things in hypocrisy, lack of holiness, and simulation thereof. Accordingly if by a hypocrite we mean a person whose intention is directed to both the above, one, namely, who cares not to be holy but only to appear so, in which sense Sacred Scripture is wont to use the term, it is evident that hypocrisy is a mortal sin: for no one is entirely deprived of holiness save through mortal sin. But if by a hypocrite we mean one who intends to simulate holiness, which he lacks through mortal sin, then, although he is in mortal sin, whereby he is deprived of holiness, yet, in his case, the dissimulation itself is not always a mortal sin, but sometimes a venial sin. This will depend on the end in view; for if this be contrary to the love of God or of his neighbor, it will be a mortal sin: for instance if he were to simulate holiness in order to disseminate false doctrine, or that he may obtain ecclesiastical preferment, though unworthy, or that he may obtain any temporal good in which he fixes his end. If, however, the end intended be not contrary to charity, it will be a venial sin, as for instance when a man takes pleasure in the pretense itself: of such a man it is said in *Ethic.* iv, 7 that "he would seem to be vain rather than evil"; for the same applies to simulation as to a lie.

It happens also sometimes that a man simulates the perfection of holiness which is not necessary for spiritual welfare. Simulation of this kind is neither a mortal sin always, nor is it always associated with mortal sin.

This suffices for the Replies to the Objections.

## QUESTION 112

OF BOASTING (In Two Articles)

We must now consider boasting and irony, which are parts of lying according to the Philosopher (Ethic. iv, 7). Under the first head, namely, boasting, there are two points of inquiry:

(1) To which virtue is it opposed?

(2) Whether it is a mortal sin?

FIRST ARTICLE [II-II, Q. 112, Art. 1]

Whether Boasting Is Opposed to the Virtue of Truth?

Objection 1: It seems that boasting is not opposed to the virtue of truth. For lying is opposed to truth. But it is possible to boast even without lying, as when a man makes a show of his own excellence. Thus it is written (Esther 1:3, 4) that Assuerus "made a great feast ... that he might show the riches of the glory" and "of his kingdom, and the greatness and boasting of his power." Therefore boasting is not opposed to the virtue of truth.

Obj. 2: Further, boasting is reckoned by Gregory (Moral. xxiii, 4) to be one of the four species of pride, "when," to wit, "a man boasts of having what he has not." Hence it is written (Jer. 48:29, 30): "We have heard the pride of Moab, he is exceeding proud: his haughtiness, and his arrogancy, and his pride, and the loftiness of his heart. I know, saith the Lord, his boasting, and that the strength thereof is not according to it." Moreover, Gregory says (Moral. xxxi, 7) that boasting arises from vainglory. Now pride and vainglory are opposed to the virtue of humility. Therefore boasting is opposed, not to truth, but to humility.

Obj. 3: Further, boasting seems to be occasioned by riches; wherefore it is written (Wis. 5:8): "What hath pride profited us? or what advantage hath the boasting of riches brought us?" Now excess of riches seems to belong to the sin of covetousness, which is opposed to justice or liberality. Therefore boasting is not opposed to truth.

*On the contrary,* The Philosopher says (Ethic. ii, 7; iv, 7), that boasting is opposed to truth.

*I answer that,* Jactantia (boasting) seems properly to denote the uplifting of self by words: since if a man wishes to throw ( *jactare* ) a thing far away, he lifts it up high. And to uplift oneself, properly speaking, is to talk of oneself above oneself [*Or 'tall-talking' as we should say in English]. This happens in two ways. For sometimes a man speaks of himself, not above what he is in himself, but above that which he is esteemed by men to be: and this the Apostle declines to do when he says (2 Cor. 12:6): "I forbear lest any man should think of me above that which he seeth in me, or anything he heareth of me." In another way a man uplifts himself in words, by speaking of himself above that which he is in reality. And since we should judge of things as they are in themselves, rather than as others deem them to be, it follows that boasting denotes more properly the uplifting of self above what one is in oneself, than the uplifting of self above what others think of one: although in either case it may be called boasting. Hence boasting properly so called is opposed to truth by way of excess.

Reply Obj. 1: This argument takes boasting as exceeding men's opinion.

Reply Obj. 2: The sin of boasting may be considered in two ways. First, with regard to the species of the act, and thus it is opposed to truth; as stated (in the body of the article and Q. 110, A. 2). Secondly, with regard to its cause, from which more frequently though not always it arises: and thus it proceeds from pride as its inwardly moving and impelling cause. For when a man is uplifted inwardly by arrogance, it often results that outwardly he boasts of great things about himself; though sometimes a man takes to boasting, not from arrogance, but from some kind of vanity, and delights therein, because he is a boaster by habit. Hence arrogance, which is an uplifting of self above oneself, is a kind of pride; yet it is not the same as boasting, but is very often its cause. For this reason Gregory reckons boasting among the species of pride. Moreover, the boaster frequently aims at obtaining glory through his boasting, and so, according to Gregory, it arises from vainglory considered as its end.

Reply Obj. 3: Wealth also causes boasting, in two ways. First, as an occasional cause, inasmuch as a man prides himself on his riches. Hence (Prov. 8:18) "riches" are significantly described as "proud" [Douay: 'glorious']. Secondly, as being the end of boasting, since according to *Ethic.* iv, 7, some boast, not only for the sake of glory, but also for the sake of gain. Such people invent stories about themselves, so as to make profit thereby; for instance, they pretend to be skilled in medicine, wisdom, or divination.

SECOND ARTICLE [II-II, Q. 112, Art. 2]

Whether Boasting Is a Mortal Sin?

Objection 1: It seems that boasting is a mortal sin. For it is written (Prov. 28:25): "He that boasteth, and puffeth himself, stirreth up quarrels." Now it is a mortal sin to stir up quarrels, since God hates those that sow discord, according to Prov. 6:19. Therefore boasting is a mortal sin.

Obj. 2: Further, whatever is forbidden in God's law is a mortal sin. Now a gloss on Ecclus. 6:2, "Extol not thyself in the thoughts of thy soul," says: "This is a prohibition of boasting and pride." Therefore boasting is a mortal sin.

Obj. 3: Further, boasting is a kind of lie. But it is neither an officious nor a jocose lie. This is evident from the end of lying; for according to the Philosopher (Ethic. iv, 7), "the boaster pretends to something greater than he is, sometimes for no further purpose, sometimes for the sake of glory or honor, sometimes for the sake of money." Thus it is evident that it is neither an officious nor a jocose lie, and consequently it must be a mischievous lie. Therefore seemingly it is always a mortal sin.

*On the contrary,* Boasting arises from vainglory, according to Gregory (Moral. xxxi, 17). Now vainglory is not always a mortal sin, but is sometimes a venial sin which only the very perfect avoid. For Gregory says (Moral. viii, 30) that "it belongs to the very perfect, by outward deeds so to seek the glory of their author, that they are not inwardly uplifted by the praise awarded them." Therefore boasting is not always a mortal sin.

*I answer that,* As stated above (Q. 110, A. 4), a mortal sin is one that is contrary to charity. Accordingly boasting may be considered in two ways. First, in itself, as a lie, and thus it is sometimes a mortal, and sometimes a venial sin. It will be a mortal sin when a man boasts of that which is contrary to God's glory—thus it is said in the person of the king of Tyre (Ezech. 28:2): "Thy heart is lifted up, and thou hast said: I am God"—or contrary to the love of our neighbor, as when a man while boasting of himself breaks out into invectives against others, as told of the Pharisee who said (Luke 18:11): "I am not as the rest of men, extortioners, unjust, adulterers, as also is this publican." Sometimes it is a venial sin, when, to wit, a man boasts of things that are against neither God nor his neighbor. Secondly, it may be considered with regard to its cause, namely, pride, or the desire of gain or of vainglory: and then if it proceeds from pride or from such vainglory as is a mortal sin, then the boasting will also be a mortal sin: otherwise it will be a venial sin. Sometimes, however, a man breaks out into boasting through desire of gain, and for this very reason he would seem to be aiming at the deception and injury of his neighbor: wherefore boasting of this kind is more likely to be a mortal sin. Hence the Philosopher says (Ethic. iv, 7) that "a man who boasts for the sake of gain, is viler than one who boasts for the sake of glory or honor." Yet it is not always a mortal sin because the gain may be such as not to injure another man.

Reply Obj. 1: To boast in order to stir quarrels is a mortal sin. But it happens sometimes that boasts are the cause of quarrels, not intentionally but accidentally: and consequently boasting will not be a mortal sin on that account.

Reply Obj. 2: This gloss speaks of boasting as arising from pride that is a mortal sin.

Reply Obj. 3: Boasting does not always involve a mischievous lie, but only where it is contrary to the love of God or our neighbor, either in itself or in its cause. That a man boast, through mere pleasure in boasting, is an inane thing to do, as the Philosopher remarks (Ethic. iv, 7): wherefore it amounts to a jocose lie. Unless perchance he were to prefer this to the love of God, so as to contemn God's commandments for the sake of boasting: for then it would be against the charity of God, in Whom alone ought our mind to rest as in its last end.

To boast for the sake of glory or gain seems to involve an officious lie: provided it be done without injury to others, for then it would at once become a mischievous lie.

## QUESTION 113

IRONY* (In Two Articles) [*Irony here must be given the signification of the Greek *eironia* , whence it is derived: dissimulation of one's own good points.]

We must now consider irony, under which head there are two points of inquiry:

(1) Whether irony is a sin?

(2) Of its comparison with boasting.

FIRST ARTICLE [II-II, Q. 113, Art. 1]

Whether Irony Is a Sin?

Objection 1: It seems that irony, which consists in belittling oneself, is not a sin. For no sin arises from one's being strengthened by God: and yet this leads one to belittle oneself, according to Prov. 30:1, 2: "The vision which the man spoke, with whom is God, and who being strengthened by God, abiding with him, said, I am the most foolish of men." Also it is written (Amos 7:14): "Amos answered ... I am not a prophet." Therefore irony, whereby a man belittles himself in words, is not a sin.

Obj. 2: Further, Gregory says in a letter to Augustine, bishop of the English (Regist. xii): "It is the mark of a well-disposed mind to acknowledge one's fault when one is not guilty." But all sin is inconsistent with a well-disposed mind. Therefore irony is not a sin.

Obj. 3: Further, it is not a sin to shun pride. But "some belittle themselves in words, so as to avoid pride," according to the Philosopher (Ethic. iv, 7). Therefore irony is not a sin.

*On the contrary,* Augustine says (De Verb. Apost., Serm. xxix): "If thou liest on account of humility, if thou wert not a sinner before lying, thou hast become one by lying."

*I answer that,* To speak so as to belittle oneself may occur in two ways. First so as to safeguard truth, as when a man conceals the greater things in himself, but discovers and asserts lesser things of himself the presence of which in himself he perceives. To belittle oneself in this way does not belong to irony, nor is it a sin in respect of its genus, except through corruption of one of its circumstances. Secondly, a person belittles himself by forsaking the truth, for instance by ascribing to himself something mean the existence of which in himself he does not perceive, or by denying something great of himself, which nevertheless he perceives himself to possess: this pertains to irony, and is always a sin.

Reply Obj. 1: There is a twofold wisdom and a twofold folly. For there is a wisdom according to God, which has human or worldly folly annexed to it, according to 1 Cor. 3:18, "If any man among you seem to be wise in this world, let him become a fool that he may be wise." But there is another wisdom that is worldly, which as the same text goes on to say, "is foolishness with God." Accordingly, he that is strengthened by God acknowledges himself to be most foolish in the estimation of men, because, to wit, he despises human things, which human wisdom seeks. Hence the text quoted continues, "and the wisdom of men is not with me," and farther on, "and I have known the science of the saints" [*Vulg.: 'and I have not known the science of the saints'].

It may also be replied that "the wisdom of men" is that which is acquired by human reason, while the "wisdom of the saints" is that which is received by divine inspiration.

Amos denied that he was a prophet by birth, since, to wit, he was not of the race of prophets: hence the text goes on, "nor am I the son of a prophet."

Reply Obj. 2: It belongs to a well-disposed mind that a man tend to perfect righteousness, and consequently deem himself guilty, not only if he fall short of common righteousness, which is truly a sin, but also if he fall short of perfect righteousness, which sometimes is not a sin. But he does not call sinful that which he does not acknowledge to be sinful: which would be a lie of irony.

Reply Obj. 3: A man should not commit one sin in order to avoid another: and so he ought not to lie in any way at all in order to avoid pride. Hence Augustine says (Tract. xliii in Joan.): "Shun not arrogance so as to forsake truth": and Gregory says (Moral. xxvi, 3) that "it is a reckless humility that entangles itself with lies."

SECOND ARTICLE [II-II, Q. 113, Art. 2]

Whether Irony Is a Less Grievous Sin Than Boasting?

Objection 1: It seems that irony is not a less grievous sin than boasting. For each of them is a sin through forsaking truth, which is a kind of equality. But one does not forsake truth by exceeding it any more than by diminishing it. Therefore irony is not a less grievous sin than boasting.

Obj. 2: Further, according to the Philosopher (Ethic. iv, 7), irony sometimes is boasting. But boasting is not irony. Therefore irony is not a less grievous sin than boasting.

Obj. 3: Further, it is written (Prov. 26:25): "When he shall speak low, trust him not: because there are seven mischiefs in his heart." Now it belongs to irony to speak low. Therefore it contains a manifold wickedness.

*On the contrary,* The Philosopher says (Ethic. iv, 7): "Those who speak with irony and belittle themselves are more gracious, seemingly, in their manners."

*I answer that,* As stated above (Q. 110, AA. 2, 4), one lie is more grievous than another, sometimes on account of the matter which it is about—thus a lie about a matter of religious doctrine is most grievous—and sometimes on account of the motive for sinning; thus a mischievous lie is more grievous than an officious or jocose lie. Now irony and boasting lie about the same matter, either by words, or by any other outward signs, namely, about matters affecting the person: so that in this respect they are equal.

But for the most part boasting proceeds from a viler motive, namely, the desire of gain or honor: whereas irony arises from a man's averseness, albeit inordinate, to be disagreeable to others by uplifting himself: and in this respect the Philosopher says (Ethic. iv, 7) that "boasting is a more grievous sin than irony."

Sometimes, however, it happens that a man belittles himself for some other motive, for instance that he may deceive cunningly: and then irony is more grievous.

Reply Obj. 1: This argument applies to irony and boasting, according as a lie is considered to be grievous in itself or on account of its matter: for it has been said that in this way they are equal.

Reply Obj. 2: Excellence is twofold: one is in temporal, the other in spiritual things. Now it happens at times that a person, by outward words or signs, pretends to be lacking in external things, for instance by wearing shabby clothes, or by doing something of the kind, and that he intends by so doing to make a show of some spiritual excellence. Thus our Lord said of certain men (Matt. 6:16) that "they disfigure their faces that they may appear unto men to fast." Wherefore such persons are guilty of both vices, irony and boasting, although in different respects, and for this reason they sin more grievously. Hence the Philosopher says (Ethic. iv, 7) that it is "the practice of boasters both to make overmuch of themselves, and to make very little of themselves": and for the same reason it is related of Augustine that he was unwilling to possess clothes that were either too costly or too shabby, because by both do men seek glory.

Reply Obj. 3: According to the words of Ecclus. 19:23, "There is one that humbleth himself wickedly, and his interior is full of deceit," and it is in this sense that Solomon speaks of the man who, through deceitful humility, "speaks low" wickedly.

## QUESTION 114

OF THE FRIENDLINESS WHICH IS CALLED AFFABILITY (In Two Articles)

We must now consider the friendliness which is called affability, and the opposite vices which are flattery and quarreling. Concerning friendliness or affability, there are two points of inquiry:

(1) Whether it is a special virtue?

(2) Whether it is a part of justice?

FIRST ARTICLE [II-II, Q. 114, Art. 1]

Whether Friendliness Is a Special Virtue?

Objection 1: It seems that friendliness is not a special virtue. For the Philosopher says (Ethic. viii, 3) that "the perfect friendship is that which is on account of virtue." Now any virtue is the cause of friendship: "since the good is lovable to all," as Dionysius states (Div. Nom. iv). Therefore friendliness is not a special virtue, but a consequence of every virtue.

Obj. 2: Further, the Philosopher says (Ethic. iv, 6) of this kind of friend that he "takes everything in a right manner both from those he loves and from those who are not his friends." Now it seems to pertain to simulation that a person should show signs of friendship to those whom he loves not, and this is incompatible with virtue. Therefore this kind of friendliness is not a virtue.

Obj. 3: Further, virtue "observes the mean according as a wise man decides" (Ethic. ii, 6). Now it is written (Eccles. 7:5): "The heart of the wise is where there is mourning, and the heart of fools where there is mirth": wherefore "it belongs to a virtuous man to be most wary of pleasure" (Ethic. ii, 9). Now this kind of friendship, according to the Philosopher (Ethic. iv, 6), "is essentially desirous of sharing pleasures, but fears to give pain." Therefore this kind of friendliness is not a virtue.

*On the contrary,* The precepts of the law are about acts of virtue. Now it is written (Ecclus. 4:7): "Make thyself affable to the congregation of the poor." Therefore affability, which is what we mean by friendship, is a special virtue.

*I answer that,* As stated above (Q. 109, A. 2; I-II, Q. 55, A. 3), since virtue is directed to good, wherever there is a special kind of good, there must needs be a special kind of virtue. Now good consists in order, as stated above (Q. 109, A. 2). And it behooves man to be maintained in a becoming order towards other men as regards their mutual relations with one another, in point of both deeds and words, so that they behave towards one another in a becoming manner. Hence the need of a special virtue that maintains the becomingness of this order: and this virtue is called friendliness.

Reply Obj. 1: The Philosopher speaks of a twofold friendship in his *Ethics*. One consists chiefly in the affection whereby one man loves another and may result from any virtue. We have stated above, in treating of charity (Q. 23, A. 1, A. 3, ad 1; QQ. 25, 26), what things belong to this kind of friendship. But he mentions another friendliness, which consists merely in outward words or deeds; this has not the perfect nature of friendship, but bears a certain likeness thereto, in so far as a man behaves in a becoming manner towards those with whom he is in contact.

Reply Obj. 2: Every man is naturally every man's friend by a certain general love; even so it is written (Ecclus. 13:19) that "every beast loveth its like." This love is signified by signs of friendship, which we show outwardly by words or deeds, even to those who are strangers or unknown to us. Hence there is no dissimulation in this: because we do not show them signs of perfect friendship, for we do not treat strangers with the same intimacy as those who are united to us by special friendship.

Reply Obj. 3: When it is said that "the heart of the wise is where there is mourning" it is not that he may bring sorrow to his neighbor, for the Apostle says (Rom. 14:15): "If, because of thy meat, thy brother be grieved, thou walkest not now according to charity": but that he may bring consolation to the sorrowful, according to Ecclus. 7:38, "Be not wanting in comforting them that weep, and walk with them that mourn." Again, "the heart of fools is where there is mirth," not that they may gladden others, but that they may enjoy others' gladness. Accordingly, it belongs to the wise man to share his pleasures with those among whom he dwells, not lustful pleasures, which virtue shuns, but honest pleasures, according to Ps. 132:1, "Behold how good and how pleasant it is for brethren to dwell together in unity."

Nevertheless, as the Philosopher says (Ethic. iv, 6), for the sake of some good that will result, or in order to avoid some evil, the virtuous man will sometimes not shrink from bringing sorrow to those among whom he lives. Hence the Apostle says (2 Cor. 7:8): "Although I made you sorrowful by my epistle, I do not repent," and further on (2 Cor. 7:9), "I am glad; not because you were made sorrowful, but because you were made sorrowful unto repentance." For this reason we should not show a cheerful face to those who are given to sin, in order that we may please them, lest we seem to consent to their sin, and in a way encourage them to sin further. Hence it is written (Ecclus. 7:26): "Hast thou daughters? Have a care of their body, and show not thy countenance gay towards them."

SECOND ARTICLE [II-II, Q. 114, Art. 2]

Whether This Kind of Friendship Is a Part of Justice?

Objection 1: It seems that this kind of friendship is not a part of justice. For justice consists in giving another man his due. But this virtue does not consist in doing that, but in behaving agreeably towards those among whom we live. Therefore this virtue is not a part of justice.

Obj. 2: Further, according to the Philosopher (Ethic. iv, 6), this virtue is concerned about the joys and sorrows of those who dwell in fellowship. Now it belongs to temperance to moderate the greatest pleasures, as stated above (I-II, Q. 60, A. 5; Q. 61, A. 3). Therefore this virtue is a part of temperance rather than of justice.

Obj. 3: Further, to give equal things to those who are unequal is contrary to justice, as stated above (Q. 59, AA. 1, 2). Now, according to the Philosopher (Ethic. iv, 6), this virtue "treats in like manner known and unknown, companions and strangers." Therefore this virtue rather than being a part of justice is opposed thereto.

*On the contrary,* Macrobius (De Somno Scip. i) accounts friendship a part of justice.

*I answer that,* This virtue is a part of justice, being annexed to it as to a principal virtue. Because in common with justice it is directed to another person, even as justice is: yet it falls short of the notion of justice, because it lacks the full aspect of debt, whereby one man is bound to another, either by legal debt, which the law binds him to pay, or by some debt arising out of a favor received. For it regards merely a certain debt of equity, namely, that we behave pleasantly to those among whom we dwell, unless at times, for some reason, it be necessary to displease them for some good purpose.

Reply Obj. 1: As we have said above (Q. 109, A. 3, ad 1), because man is a social animal he owes his fellow-man, in equity, the manifestation of truth without which human society could not last. Now as man could not live in society without truth, so likewise, not without joy, because, as the Philosopher says (Ethic. viii), no one could abide a day with the sad nor with the joyless. Therefore, a certain natural equity obliges a man to live agreeably with his fellow-men; unless some reason should oblige him to sadden them for their good.

Reply Obj. 2: It belongs to temperance to curb pleasures of the senses. But this virtue regards the pleasures of fellowship, which have their origin in the reason, in so far as one man behaves becomingly towards another. Such pleasures need not to be curbed as though they were noisome.

Reply Obj. 3: This saying of the Philosopher does not mean that one ought to converse and behave in the same way with acquaintances and strangers, since, as he says (Ethic. iv, 6), "it is not fitting to please and displease intimate friends and strangers in the same way." This likeness consists in this, that we ought to behave towards all in a fitting manner.

## QUESTION 115

OF FLATTERY (In Two Articles)

We must now consider the vices opposed to the aforesaid virtue: (1) Flattery, and (2) Quarreling. Concerning flattery there are two points of inquiry:

(1) Whether flattery is a sin?

(2) Whether it is a mortal sin?

FIRST ARTICLE [II-II, Q. 115, Art. 1]

Whether Flattery Is a Sin?

Objection 1: It seems that flattery is not a sin. For flattery consists in words of praise offered to another in order to please him. But it is not a sin to praise a person, according to Prov. 31:28, "Her children rose up and called her blessed: her husband, and he praised her." Moreover, there is no evil in wishing to please others, according to 1 Cor. 10:33, "I ... in all things please all men." Therefore flattery is not a sin.

Obj. 2: Further, evil is contrary to good, and blame to praise. But it is not a sin to blame evil. Neither, then, is it a sin to praise good, which seems to belong to flattery. Therefore flattery is not a sin.

Obj. 3: Further, detraction is contrary to flattery. Wherefore Gregory says (Moral. xxii, 5) that detraction is a remedy against flattery. "It must be observed," says he, "that by the wonderful moderation of our Ruler, we are often allowed to be rent by detractions but are uplifted by immoderate praise, so that whom the voice of the flatterer upraises, the tongue of the detractor may humble." But detraction is an evil, as stated above (Q. 73, AA. 2, 3). Therefore flattery is a good.

*On the contrary,* A gloss on Ezech. 13:18, "Woe to them that sew cushions under every elbow," says, "that is to say, sweet flattery." Therefore flattery is a sin.

*I answer that,* As stated above (Q. 114, A. 1, ad 3), although the friendship of which we have been speaking, or affability, intends chiefly the pleasure of those among whom one lives, yet it does not fear to displease when it is a question of obtaining a certain good, or of avoiding a certain evil. Accordingly, if a man were to wish always to speak pleasantly to others, he would exceed the mode of pleasing, and would therefore sin by excess. If he do this with the mere intention of pleasing he is said to be "complaisant," according to the Philosopher (Ethic. iv, 6): whereas if he do it with the intention of making some gain out of it, he is called a "flatterer" or "adulator." As a rule, however, the term "flattery" is wont to be applied to all who wish to exceed the mode of virtue in pleasing others by words or deeds in their ordinary behavior towards their fellows.

Reply Obj. 1: One may praise a person both well and ill, according as one observes or omits the due circumstances. For if while observing other due circumstances one were to wish to please a person by praising him, in order thereby to console him, or that he may strive to make progress in good, this will belong to the aforesaid virtue of friendship. But it would belong to flattery, if one wished to praise a person for things in which he ought not to be praised; since perhaps they are evil, according to Ps. 9:24, "The sinner is praised in the desires of his soul"; or they may be uncertain, according to Ecclus. 27:8, "Praise not a man before he speaketh," and again (Ecclus. 11:2), "Praise not a man for his beauty"; or because there may be fear lest human praise should incite him to vainglory, wherefore it is written, (Ecclus. 11:30), "Praise not any man before death." Again, in like manner it is right to wish to please a man in order to foster charity, so that he may make spiritual progress therein. But it would be sinful to wish to please men for the sake of vainglory or gain, or to please them in something evil, according to Ps. 52:6, "God hath scattered the bones of them that please men," and according to the words of the Apostle (Gal. 1:10), "If I yet pleased men, I should not be the servant of Christ."

Reply Obj. 2: Even to blame evil is sinful, if due circumstances be not observed; and so too is it to praise good.

Reply Obj. 3: Nothing hinders two vices being contrary to one another. Wherefore even as detraction is evil, so is flattery, which is contrary thereto as regards what is said, but not directly as regards the end. Because flattery seeks to please the person flattered, whereas the detractor seeks not the displeasure of the person defamed, since at times he defames him in secret, but seeks rather his defamation.

SECOND ARTICLE [II-II, Q. 115, Art. 2]

Whether Flattery Is a Mortal Sin?

Objection 1: It seems that flattery is a mortal sin. For, according to Augustine (Enchiridion xii), "a thing is evil because it is harmful." But flattery is most harmful, according to Ps. 9:24, "For the sinner is praised in the desires of his soul, and the unjust man is blessed. The sinner hath provoked the Lord." Wherefore Jerome says (Ep. ad Celant): "Nothing so easily corrupts the human mind as flattery": and a gloss on Ps. 69:4, "Let them be presently turned away blushing for shame that say to me: 'Tis well, 'Tis well," says: "The tongue of the flatterer harms more than the sword of the persecutor." Therefore flattery is a most grievous sin.

Obj. 2: Further, whoever does harm by words, harms himself no less than others: wherefore it is written (Ps. 36:15): "Let their sword enter into their own hearts." Now he that flatters another induces him to sin mortally: hence a gloss on Ps. 140:5, "Let not the oil of the sinner fatten my head," says: "The false praise of the flatterer softens the mind by depriving it of the rigidity of truth and renders it susceptive of vice." Much more, therefore, does the flatterer sin in himself.

Obj. 3: Further, it is written in the Decretals (D. XLVI, Cap. 3): "The cleric who shall be found to spend his time in flattery and treachery shall be degraded from his office." Now such a punishment as this is not inflicted save for mortal sin. Therefore flattery is a mortal sin.

*On the contrary,* Augustine in a sermon on Purgatory (xli, de Sanctis) reckons among slight sins, "if one desire to flatter any person of higher standing, whether of one's own choice, or out of necessity."

*I answer that,* As stated above (Q. 112, A. 2), a mortal sin is one that is contrary to charity. Now flattery is sometimes contrary to charity and sometimes not. It is contrary to charity in three ways. First, by reason of the very matter, as when one man praises another's sin: for this is contrary to the love of God, against Whose justice he speaks, and contrary to the love of his neighbor, whom he encourages to sin. Wherefore this is a mortal sin, according to Isa. 5:20. "Woe to you that call evil good." Secondly, by reason of the intention, as when one man flatters another, so that by deceiving him he may injure him in body or in soul; this is also a mortal sin, and of this it is written (Prov. 27:6): "Better are the wounds of a friend than the deceitful kisses of an enemy." Thirdly, by way of occasion, as when the praise of a flatterer, even without his intending it, becomes to another an occasion of sin. In this case it is necessary to consider, whether the occasion were given or taken, and how grievous the consequent downfall, as may be understood from what has been said above concerning scandal (Q. 43, AA. 3, 4). If, however, one man flatters another from the mere craving to please others, or again in order to avoid some evil, or to acquire something in a case of necessity, this is not contrary to charity. Consequently it is not a mortal but a venial sin.

Reply Obj. 1: The passages quoted speak of the flatterer who praises another's sin. Flattery of this kind is said to harm more than the sword of the persecutor, since it does harm to goods that are of greater consequence, namely, spiritual goods. Yet it does not harm so efficaciously, since the sword of the persecutor slays effectively, being a sufficient cause of death; whereas no one by flattering can be a sufficient cause of another's sinning, as was shown above (Q. 43, A. 1, ad 3; I-II, Q. 73, A. 8, ad 3; I-II, Q. 80, A. 1).

Reply Obj. 2: This argument applies to one that flatters with the intention of doing harm: for such a man harms himself more than others, since he harms himself, as the sufficient cause of sinning, whereas he is only the occasional cause of the harm he does to others.

Reply Obj. 3: The passage quoted refers to the man who flatters another treacherously, in order to deceive him.

## QUESTION 116

OF QUARRELING (In Two Articles)

We must now consider quarreling; concerning which there are two points of inquiry:

(1) Whether it is opposed to the virtue of friendship?

(2) Of its comparison with flattery?

FIRST ARTICLE [II-II, Q. 116, Art. 1]

Whether Quarreling Is Opposed to the Virtue of Friendship or Affability?

Objection 1: It seems that quarreling is not opposed to the virtue of friendship or affability. For quarreling seems to pertain to discord, just as contention does. But discord is opposed to charity, as stated above (Q. 37, A. 1). Therefore quarreling is also.

Obj. 2: Further, it is written (Prov. 26:21): "An angry man stirreth up strife." Now anger is opposed to meekness. Therefore strife or quarreling is also.

Obj. 3: Further, it is written (James 4:1): "From whence are wars and quarrels [Douay: 'contentions'] among you? Are they not hence, from your concupiscences which war in your members?" Now it would seem contrary to temperance to follow one's concupiscences. Therefore it seems that quarreling is opposed not to friendship but to temperance.

*On the contrary,* The Philosopher opposes quarreling to friendship (Ethic. iv, 6).

*I answer that,* Quarreling consists properly in words, when, namely, one person contradicts another's words. Now two things may be observed in this contradiction. For sometimes contradiction arises on account of the person who speaks, the contradictor refusing to consent with him from lack of that love which unites minds together, and this seems to pertain to discord, which is contrary to charity. Whereas at times contradiction arises by reason of the speaker being a person to whom someone does not fear to be disagreeable: whence arises quarreling, which is opposed to the aforesaid friendship or affability, to which it belongs to behave agreeably towards those among whom we dwell. Hence the Philosopher says (Ethic. iv, 6) that "those who are opposed to everything with the intent of being disagreeable, and care for nobody, are said to be peevish and quarrelsome."

Reply Obj. 1: Contention pertains rather to the contradiction of discord, while quarreling belongs to the contradiction which has the intention of displeasing.

Reply Obj. 2: The direct opposition of virtues to vices depends, not on their causes, since one vice may arise from many causes, but on the species of their acts. And although quarreling arises at times from anger, it may arise from many other causes, hence it does not follow that it is directly opposed to meekness.

Reply Obj. 3: James speaks there of concupiscence considered as a general evil whence all vices arise. Thus, a gloss on Rom. 7:7 says: "The law is good, since by forbidding concupiscence, it forbids all evil."

SECOND ARTICLE [II-II, Q. 116, Art. 2]

Whether Quarreling Is a More Grievous Sin Than Flattery?

Objection 1: It seems that quarreling is a less grievous sin than the contrary vice, viz. adulation or flattery. For the more harm a sin does the more grievous it seems to be. Now flattery does more harm than quarreling, for it is written (Isa. 3:12): "O My people, they that call thee blessed, the same deceive thee, and destroy the way of thy steps." Therefore flattery is a more grievous sin than quarreling.

Obj. 2: Further, there appears to be a certain amount of deceit in flattery, since the flatterer says one thing, and thinks another: whereas the quarrelsome man is without deceit, for he contradicts openly. Now he that sins deceitfully is a viler man, according to the Philosopher (Ethic. vii, 6). Therefore flattery is a more grievous sin than quarreling.

Obj. 3: Further, shame is fear of what is vile, according to the Philosopher (Ethic. iv, 9). But a man is more ashamed to be a flatterer than a quarreler. Therefore quarreling is a less grievous sin than flattery.

*On the contrary,* The more a sin is inconsistent with the spiritual state, the more it appears to be grievous. Now quarreling seems to be more inconsistent with the spiritual state: for it is written (1 Tim. 3:2, 3) that it "behooveth a bishop to be ... not quarrelsome"; and (2 Tim. 3:24): "The servant of the Lord must not wrangle." Therefore quarreling seems to be a more grievous sin than flattery.

*I answer that,* We can speak of each of these sins in two ways. In one way we may consider the species of either sin, and thus the more a vice is at variance with the opposite virtue the more grievous it is. Now the virtue of friendship has a greater tendency to please than to displease: and so the quarrelsome man, who exceeds in giving displeasure sins more grievously than the adulator or flatterer, who exceeds in giving pleasure. In another way we may consider them as regards certain external motives, and thus flattery is sometimes more grievous, for instance when one intends by deception to acquire undue honor or gain: while sometimes quarreling is more grievous; for instance, when one intends either to deny the truth, or to hold up the speaker to contempt.

Reply Obj. 1: Just as the flatterer may do harm by deceiving secretly, so the quarreler may do harm sometimes by assailing openly. Now, other things being equal, it is more grievous to harm a person openly, by violence as it were, than secretly. Wherefore robbery is a more grievous sin than theft, as stated above (Q. 66, A. 9).

Reply Obj. 2: In human acts, the more grievous is not always the more vile. For the comeliness of a man has its source in his reason: wherefore the sins of the flesh, whereby the flesh enslaves the reason, are viler, although spiritual sins are more grievous, since they proceed from greater contempt. In like manner, sins that are committed through deceit are viler, in so far as they seem to arise from a certain weakness, and from a certain falseness of the reason, although sins that are committed openly proceed sometimes from a greater contempt. Hence flattery, through being accompanied by deceit, seems to be a viler sin; while quarreling, through proceeding from greater contempt, is apparently more grievous.

Reply Obj. 3: As stated in the objection, shame regards the vileness of a sin; wherefore a man is not always more ashamed of a more grievous sin, but of a viler sin. Hence it is that a man is more ashamed of flattery than of quarreling, although quarreling is more grievous.

## QUESTION 117

OF LIBERALITY (In Six Articles)

We must now consider liberality and the opposite vices, namely, covetousness and prodigality.

Concerning liberality there are six points of inquiry:

(1) Whether liberality is a virtue?

(2) What is its matter?

(3) Of its act;

(4) Whether it pertains thereto to give rather than to take?

(5) Whether liberality is a part of justice?

(6) Of its comparison with other virtues.

FIRST ARTICLE [II-II, Q. 117, Art. 1]

Whether Liberality Is a Virtue?

Objection 1: It seems that liberality is not a virtue. For no virtue is contrary to a natural inclination. Now it is a natural inclination for one to provide for oneself more than for others: and yet it pertains to the liberal man to do the contrary, since, according to the Philosopher (Ethic. iv, 1), "it is the mark of a liberal man not to look to himself, so that he leaves for himself the lesser things." Therefore liberality is not a virtue.

Obj. 2: Further, man sustains life by means of riches, and wealth contributes to happiness instrumentally, as stated in *Ethic.* i, 8. Since, then, every virtue is directed to happiness, it seems that the liberal man is not virtuous, for the Philosopher says of him (Ethic. iv, 1) that "he is inclined neither to receive nor to keep money, but to give it away."

Obj. 3: Further, the virtues are connected with one another. But liberality does not seem to be connected with the other virtues: since many are virtuous who cannot be liberal, for they have nothing to give; and many give or spend liberally who are not virtuous otherwise. Therefore liberality is not a virtue.

*On the contrary,* Ambrose says (De Offic. i) that "the Gospel contains many instances in which a just liberality is inculcated." Now in the Gospel nothing is taught that does not pertain to virtue. Therefore liberality is a virtue.

*I answer that,* As Augustine says (De Lib. Arb. ii, 19), "it belongs to virtue to use well the things that we can use ill." Now we may use both well and ill, not only the things that are within us, such as the powers and the passions of the soul, but also those that are without, such as the things of this world that are granted us for our livelihood. Wherefore since it belongs to liberality to use these things well, it follows that liberality is a virtue.

Reply Obj. 1: According to Ambrose (Serm. lxiv de Temp.) and Basil (Hom. in Luc. xii, 18) excess of riches is granted by God to some, in order that they may obtain the merit of a good stewardship. But it suffices for one man to have few things. Wherefore the liberal man commendably spends more on others than on himself. Nevertheless we are bound to be more provident for ourselves in spiritual goods, in which each one is able to look after himself in the first place. And yet it does not belong to the liberal man even in temporal things to attend so much to others as to lose sight of himself and those belonging to him. Wherefore Ambrose says (De Offic. i): "It is a commendable liberality not to neglect your relatives if you know them to be in want."

Reply Obj. 2: It does not belong to a liberal man so to give away his riches that nothing is left for his own support, nor the wherewithal to perform those acts of virtue whereby happiness is acquired. Hence the Philosopher says (Ethic. iv, 1) that "the liberal man does not neglect his own, wishing thus to be of help to certain people"; and Ambrose says (De Offic. i) that "Our Lord does not wish a man to pour out his riches all at once, but to dispense them: unless he do as Eliseus did, who slew his oxen and fed the poor, that he might not be bound by any household cares." For this belongs to the state of perfection, of which we shall speak farther on (Q. 184; Q. 186, A. 3).

It must be observed, however, that the very act of giving away one's possessions liberally, in so far as it is an act of virtue, is directed to happiness.

Reply Obj. 3: As the Philosopher says (Ethic. iv, 1), "those who spend much on intemperance are not liberal but prodigal"; and likewise whoever spends what he has for the sake of other sins. Hence Ambrose says (De Offic. i): "If you assist to rob others of their possessions, your honesty is not to be commended, nor is your liberality genuine if you give for the sake of boasting rather than of pity." Wherefore those who lack other virtues, though they spend much on certain evil works, are not liberal.

Again, nothing hinders certain people from spending much on good uses, without having the habit of liberality: even as men perform works of other virtues, before having the habit of virtue, though not in the same way as virtuous people, as stated above (I-II, Q. 65, A. 1). In like manner nothing prevents a virtuous man from being liberal, although he be poor. Hence the Philosopher says (Ethic. iv, 1): "Liberality is proportionate to a man's substance," i.e. his means, "for it consists, not in the quantity given, but in the habit of the giver": and Ambrose says (De Offic. i) that "it is the heart that makes a gift rich or poor, and gives things their value."

SECOND ARTICLE [II-II, Q. 117, Art. 2]

Whether Liberality Is About Money?

Objection 1: It seems that liberality is not about money. For every moral virtue is about operations and passions. Now it is proper to justice to be about operations, as stated in *Ethic.* v, 1. Therefore, since liberality is a moral virtue, it seems that it is about passions and not about money.

Obj. 2: Further, it belongs to a liberal man to make use of any kind of wealth. Now natural riches are more real than artificial riches, according to the Philosopher (Polit. i, 5, 6). Therefore liberality is not chiefly about money.

Obj. 3: Further, different virtues have different matter, since habits are distinguished by their objects. But external things are the matter of distributive and commutative justice. Therefore they are not the matter of liberality.

*On the contrary,* The Philosopher says (Ethic. iv, 1) that "liberality seems to be a mean in the matter of money."

*I answer that,* According to the Philosopher (Ethic. iv, 1) it belongs to the liberal man to part with things. Hence liberality is also called open-handedness ( *largitas* ), because that which is open does not withhold things but parts with them. The term "liberality" seems also to allude to this, since when a man quits hold of a thing he frees it ( *liberat* ), so to speak, from his keeping and ownership, and shows his mind to be free of attachment thereto. Now those things which are the subject of a man's free-handedness towards others are the goods he possesses, which are denoted by the term "money." Therefore the proper matter of liberality is money.

Reply Obj. 1: As stated above (A. 1, ad 3), liberality depends not on the quantity given, but on the heart of the giver. Now the heart of the giver is disposed according to the passions of love and desire, and consequently those of pleasure and sorrow, towards the things given. Hence the interior passions are the immediate matter of liberality, while exterior money is the object of those same passions.

Reply Obj. 2: As Augustine says in his book *De Disciplina Christi* (Tract. de divers, i), everything whatsoever man has on earth, and whatsoever he owns, goes by the name of pecunia (money), because in olden times men's possessions consisted entirely of pecora (flocks). And the Philosopher says (Ethic. iv, 1): "We give the name of money to anything that can be valued in currency."

Reply Obj. 3: Justice establishes equality in external things, but has nothing to do, properly speaking, with the regulation of internal passions: wherefore money is in one way the matter of liberality, and in another way of justice.

THIRD ARTICLE [II-II, Q. 117, Art. 3]

Whether Using Money Is the Act of Liberality?

Objection 1: It seems that using money is not the act of liberality. For different virtues have different acts. But using money is becoming to other virtues, such as justice and magnificence. Therefore it is not the proper act of liberality.

Obj. 2: Further, it belongs to a liberal man, not only to give but also to receive and keep. But receiving and keeping do not seem to be connected with the use of money. Therefore using money seems to be unsuitably assigned as the proper act of liberality.

Obj. 3: Further, the use of money consists not only in giving it but also in spending it. But the spending of money refers to the spender, and consequently is not an act of liberality: for Seneca says (De Benef. v): "A man is not liberal by giving to himself." Therefore not every use of money belongs to liberality.

*On the contrary,* The Philosopher says (Ethic. iv, 1): "In whatever matter a man is virtuous, he will make the best use of that matter: Therefore he that has the virtue with regard to money will make the best use of riches." Now such is the liberal man. Therefore the good use of money is the act of liberality.

*I answer that,* The species of an act is taken from its object, as stated above (I-II, Q. 18, A. 2). Now the object or matter of liberality is money and whatever has a money value, as stated in the foregoing Article (ad 2). And since every virtue is consistent with its object, it follows that, since liberality is a virtue, its act is consistent with money. Now money comes under the head of useful goods, since all external goods are directed to man's use. Hence the proper act of liberality is making use of money or riches.

Reply Obj. 1: It belongs to liberality to make good use of riches as such, because riches are the proper matter of liberality. On the other hand it belongs to justice to make use of riches under another aspect, namely, that of debt, in so far as an external thing is due to another. And it belongs to magnificence to make use of riches under a special aspect, in so far, to wit, as they are employed for the fulfilment of some great deed. Hence magnificence stands in relation to liberality as something in addition thereto, as we shall explain farther on (Q. 134).

Reply Obj. 2: It belongs to a virtuous man not only to make good use of his matter or instrument, but also to provide opportunities for that good use. Thus it belongs to a soldier's fortitude not only to wield his sword against the foe, but also to sharpen his sword and keep it in its sheath. Thus, too, it belongs to liberality not only to use money, but also to keep it in preparation and safety in order to make fitting use of it.

Reply Obj. 3: As stated (A. 2, ad 1), the internal passions whereby man is affected towards money are the proximate matter of liberality. Hence it belongs to liberality before all that a man should not be prevented from making any due use of money through an inordinate affection for it. Now there is a twofold use of money: one consists in applying it to one's own use, and would seem to come under the designation of costs or expenditure; while the other consists in devoting it to the use of others, and comes under the head of gifts. Hence it belongs to liberality that one be not hindered by an immoderate love of money, either from spending it becomingly, or from making suitable gifts. Therefore liberality is concerned with giving and spending, according to the Philosopher (Ethic. iv, 1). The saying of Seneca refers to liberality as regards giving: for a man is not said to be liberal for the reason that he gives something to himself.

FOURTH ARTICLE [II-II, Q. 117, Art. 4]

Whether It Belongs to a Liberal Man Chiefly to Give?

Objection 1: It seems that it does not belong to a liberal man chiefly to give. For liberality, like all other moral virtues, is regulated by prudence. Now it seems to belong very much to prudence that a man should keep his riches. Wherefore the Philosopher says (Ethic. iv, 1) that "those who have not earned money, but have received the money earned by others, spend it more liberally, because they have not experienced the want of it." Therefore it seems that giving does not chiefly belong to the liberal man.

Obj. 2: Further, no man is sorry for what he intends chiefly to do, nor does he cease from doing it. But a liberal man is sometimes sorry for what he has given, nor does he give to all, as stated in *Ethic.* iv, 1. Therefore it does not belong chiefly to a liberal man to give.

Obj. 3: Further, in order to accomplish what he intends chiefly, a man employs all the ways he can. Now a liberal man is not a beggar, as the Philosopher observes (Ethic. iv, 1); and yet by begging he might provide himself with the means of giving to others. Therefore it seems that he does not chiefly aim at giving.

Obj. 4: Further, man is bound to look after himself rather than others. But by spending he looks after himself, whereas by giving he looks after others. Therefore it belongs to a liberal man to spend rather than to give.

*On the contrary,* The Philosopher says (Ethic. iv, 1) that "it belongs to a liberal man to surpass in giving."

*I answer that,* It is proper to a liberal man to use money. Now the use of money consists in parting with it. For the acquisition of money is like generation rather than use: while the keeping of money, in so far as it is directed to facilitate the use of money, is like a habit. Now in parting with a thing—for instance, when we throw something—the farther we put it away the greater the force ( *virtus* ) employed. Hence parting with money by giving it to others proceeds from a greater virtue than when we spend it on ourselves. But it is proper to a virtue as such to tend to what is more perfect, since "virtue is a kind of perfection" (Phys. vii, text. 17, 18). Therefore a liberal man is praised chiefly for giving.

Reply Obj. 1: It belongs to prudence to keep money, lest it be stolen or spent uselessly. But to spend it usefully is not less but more prudent than to keep it usefully: since more things have to be considered in money's use, which is likened to movement, than in its keeping, which is likened to rest. As to those who, having received money that others have earned, spend it more liberally, through not having experienced the want of it, if their inexperience is the sole cause of their liberal expenditure they have not the virtue of liberality. Sometimes, however, this inexperience merely removes the impediment to liberality, so that it makes them all the more ready to act liberally, because, not unfrequently, the fear of want that results from the experience of want hinders those who have acquired money from using it up by acting with liberality; as does likewise the love they have for it as being their own effect, according to the Philosopher (Ethic. iv, 1).

Reply Obj. 2: As stated in this and the preceding Article, it belongs to liberality to make fitting use of money, and consequently to give it in a fitting manner, since this is a use of money. Again, every virtue is grieved by whatever is contrary to its act, and avoids whatever hinders that act. Now two things are opposed to suitable giving; namely, not giving what ought suitably to be given, and giving something unsuitably. Wherefore the liberal man is grieved at both: but especially at the former, since it is more opposed to his proper act. For this reason, too, he does not give to all: since his act would be hindered were he to give to everyone: for he would not have the means of giving to those to whom it were fitting for him to give.

Reply Obj. 3: Giving and receiving are related to one another as action and passion. Now the same thing is not the principle of both action and passion. Hence, since liberality is a principle of giving, it does not belong to the liberal man to be ready to receive, and still less to beg. Hence the verse:

In this world he that wishes to be pleasing to many Should give often, take seldom, ask never.

But he makes provision in order to give certain things according as liberality requires; such are the fruits of his own possessions, for he is careful about realizing them that he may make a liberal use thereof.

Reply Obj. 4: To spend on oneself is an inclination of nature; hence to spend money on others belongs properly to a virtue.

FIFTH ARTICLE [II-II, Q. 117, Art. 5]

Whether Liberality Is a Part of Justice?

Objection 1: It seems that liberality is not a part of justice. For justice regards that which is due. Now the more a thing is due the less liberally is it given. Therefore liberality is not a part of justice, but is incompatible with it.

Obj. 2: Further, justice is about operation as stated above (Q. 58, A. 9; I-II, Q. 60, AA. 2, 3): whereas liberality is chiefly about the love and desire of money, which are passions. Therefore liberality seems to belong to temperance rather than to justice.

Obj. 3: Further, it belongs chiefly to liberality to give becomingly, as stated (A. 4). But giving becomingly belongs to beneficence and mercy, which pertain to charity, as state above (QQ. 30, 31). Therefore liberality is a part of charity rather than of justice.

*On the contrary,* Ambrose says (De Offic. i): "Justice has to do with the fellowship of mankind. For the notion of fellowship is divided into two parts, justice and beneficence, also called liberality or kind-heartedness." Therefore liberality pertains to justice.

*I answer that,* Liberality is not a species of justice, since justice pays another what is his whereas liberality gives another what is one's own. There are, however, two points in which it agrees with justice: first, that it is directed chiefly to another, as justice is; secondly, that it is concerned with external things, and so is justice, albeit under a different aspect, a stated in this Article and above (A. 2, ad 3). Hence it is that liberality is reckoned by some to be a part of justice, being annexed thereto as to a principal virtue.

Reply Obj. 1: Although liberality does not consider the legal due that justice considers, it considers a certain moral due. This due is based on a certain fittingness and not on an obligation: so that it answers to the idea of due in the lowest degree.

Reply Obj. 2: Temperance is about concupiscence in pleasures of the body. But the concupiscence and delight in money is not referable to the body but rather to the soul. Hence liberality does not properly pertain to temperance.

Reply Obj. 3: The giving of beneficence and mercy proceeds from the fact that a man has a certain affection towards the person to whom he gives: wherefore this giving belongs to charity or friendship. But the giving of liberality arises from a person being affected in a certain way towards money, in that he desires it not nor loves it: so that when it is fitting he gives it not only to his friends but also to those whom he knows not. Hence it belong not to charity, but to justice, which is about external things.

SIXTH ARTICLE [II-II, Q. 117, Art. 6]

Whether Liberality Is the Greatest of the Virtues?

Objection 1: It seems that liberality is the greatest of the virtues. For every virtue of man is a likeness to the divine goodness. Now man is likened chiefly by liberality to God, "Who giveth to all men abundantly, and upbraideth not" (James 1:5). Therefore liberality is the greatest of the virtues.

Obj. 2: Further, according to Augustine (De Trin. vi, 8), "in things that are great, but not in bulk, to be greatest is to be best." Now the nature of goodness seems to pertain mostly to liberality, since "the good is self-communicative," according to Dionysius (Div. Nom. iv). Hence Ambrose says (De Offic. i) that "justice reclines to severity, liberality to goodness." Therefore liberality is the greatest of virtues.

Obj. 3: Further, men are honored and loved on account of virtue. Now Boethius says (De Consol. ii) that "bounty above all makes a man famous": and the Philosopher says (Ethic. iv, 1) that "among the virtuous the liberal are the most beloved." Therefore liberality is the greatest of virtues.

*On the contrary,* Ambrose says (De Offic. i) that "justice seems to be more excellent than liberality, although liberality is more pleasing." The Philosopher also says (Rhet. i, 9) that "brave and just men are honored chiefly and, after them, those who are liberal."

*I answer that,* Every virtue tends towards a good; wherefore the greater virtue is that which tends towards the greater good. Now liberality tends towards a good in two ways: in one way, primarily and of its own nature; in another way, consequently. Primarily and of its very nature it tends to set in order one's own affection towards the possession and use of money. In this way temperance, which moderates desires and pleasures relating to one's own body, takes precedence of liberality: and so do fortitude and justice, which, in a manner, are directed to the common good, one in time of peace, the other in time of war: while all these are preceded by those virtues which are directed to the Divine good. For the Divine good surpasses all manner of human good; and among human goods the public good surpasses the good of the individual; and of the last named the good of the body surpasses those goods that consist of external things. Again, liberality is ordained to a good consequently, and in this way it is directed to all the aforesaid goods. For by reason of his not being a lover of money, it follows that a man readily makes use of it, whether for himself, or for the good of others, or for God's glory. Thus it derives a certain excellence from being useful in many ways. Since, however, we should judge of things according to that which is competent to them primarily and in respect of their nature, rather than according to that which pertains to them. Consequently, it remains to be said that liberality is not the greatest of virtues.

Reply Obj. 1: God's giving proceeds from His love for those to whom He gives, not from His affection towards the things He gives, wherefore it seems to pertain to charity, the greatest of virtues, rather than to liberality.

Reply Obj. 2: Every virtue shares the nature of goodness by giving forth its own act: and the acts of certain other virtues are better than money which liberality gives forth.

Reply Obj. 3: The friendship whereby a liberal man is beloved is not that which is based on virtue, as though he were better than others, but that which is based on utility, because he is more useful in external goods, which as a rule men desire above all others. For the same reason he becomes famous.

# QUESTION 118

OF THE VICES OPPOSED TO LIBERALITY, AND IN THE FIRST PLACE, OF COVETOUSNESS (In Eight Articles)

We must now consider the vices opposed to liberality: and (1) covetousness; (2) prodigality.

Under the first head there are eight points of inquiry:

(1) Whether covetousness is a sin?
(2) Whether it is a special sin?
(3) To which virtue it is opposed;
(4) Whether it is a mortal sin?
(5) Whether it is the most grievous of sins?
(6) Whether it is a sin of the flesh or a spiritual sin?
(7) Whether it is a capital vice?
(8) Of its daughters.

FIRST ARTICLE [II-II, Q. 118, Art. 1]

Whether Covetousness Is a Sin?

Objection 1: It seems that covetousness is not a sin. For covetousness ( *avaritia* ) denotes a certain greed for gold ( aeris aviditas ),* because, to wit, it consists in a desire for money, under which all external goods may be comprised. [*The Latin for covetousness *avaritia* is derived from aveo to desire; but the Greek *philargyria* signifies literally "love of money": and it is to this that St. Thomas is alluding (cf. A. 2, Obj. 2)]. Now it is not a sin to desire external goods: since man desires them naturally, both because they are naturally subject to man, and because by their means man's life is sustained (for which reason they are spoken of as his substance). Therefore covetousness is not a sin.

Obj. 2: Further, every sin is against either God, or one's neighbor, or oneself, as stated above (I-II, Q. 72, A. 4). But covetousness is not, properly speaking, a sin against God: since it is opposed neither to religion nor to the theological virtues, by which man is directed to God. Nor again is it a sin against oneself, for this pertains properly to gluttony and lust, of which the Apostle says (1 Cor. 6:18): "He that committeth fornication sinneth against his own body." In like manner neither is it apparently a sin against one's neighbor, since a man harms no one by keeping what is his own. Therefore covetousness is not a sin.

Obj. 3: Further, things that occur naturally are not sins. Now covetousness comes naturally to old age and every kind of defect, according to the Philosopher (Ethic. iv, 1). Therefore covetousness is not a sin.

*On the contrary,* It is written (Heb. 13:5): "Let your manners be without covetousness, contented with such things as you have."

*I answer that,* In whatever things good consists in a due measure, evil must of necessity ensue through excess or deficiency of that measure. Now in all things that are for an end, the good consists in a certain measure: since whatever is directed to an end must needs be commensurate with the end, as, for instance, medicine is commensurate with health, as the Philosopher observes (Polit. i, 6). External goods come under the head of things useful for an end, as stated above (Q. 117, A. 3; I-II, Q. 2, A. 1). Hence it must needs be that man's good in their respect consists in a certain measure, in other words, that man seeks, according to a certain measure, to have external riches, in so far as they are necessary for him to live in keeping with his condition of life. Wherefore it will be a sin for him to exceed this measure, by wishing to acquire or keep them immoderately. This is what is meant by covetousness, which is defined as "immoderate love of possessing." It is therefore evident that covetousness is a sin.

Reply Obj. 1: It is natural to man to desire external things as means to an end: wherefore this desire is devoid of sin, in so far as it is held in check by the rule taken from the nature of the end. But covetousness exceeds this rule, and therefore is a sin.

Reply Obj. 2: Covetousness may signify immoderation about external things in two ways. First, so as to regard immediately the acquisition and keeping of such things, when, to wit, a man acquires or keeps them more than is due. In this way it is a sin directly against one's neighbor, since one man cannot over-abound in external riches, without another man lacking them, for temporal goods cannot be possessed by many at the same time. Secondly, it may signify immoderation in the internal affection which a man has for riches when, for instance, a man loves them, desires them, or delights in them, immoderately. In this way by covetousness a man sins against himself, because it causes disorder in his affections, though not in his body as do the sins of the flesh.

As a consequence, however, it is a sin against God, just as all mortal sins, inasmuch as man contemns things eternal for the sake of temporal things.

Reply Obj. 3: Natural inclinations should be regulated according to reason, which is the governing power in human nature. Hence though old people seek more greedily the aid of external things, just as everyone that is in need seeks to have his need supplied, they are not excused from sin if they exceed this due measure of reason with regard to riches.

SECOND ARTICLE [II-II, Q. 118, Art. 2]

Whether Covetousness Is a Special Sin?

Objection 1: It seems that covetousness is not a special sin. For Augustine says (De Lib. Arb. iii):

"Covetousness, which in Greek is called *philargyria* , applies not only to silver or money, but also to anything that is desired immoderately." Now in every sin there is immoderate desire of something, because sin consists in turning away from the immutable good, and adhering to mutable goods, as stated above (I-II, Q. 71, A. 6, Obj. 3). Therefore covetousness is a general sin.

Obj. 2: Further, according to Isidore (Etym. x), "the covetous ( *avarus* ) man" is so called because he is "greedy for brass ( avidus aeris )," i.e. money: wherefore in Greek covetousness is called *philargyria* , i.e. "love of silver." Now silver, which stands for money, signifies all external goods the value of which can be measured by money, as stated above (Q. 117, A. 2, ad 2). Therefore covetousness is a desire for any external thing: and consequently seems to be a general sin.

Obj. 3: Further, a gloss on Rom. 7:7, "For I had not known concupiscence," says: "The law is good, since by forbidding concupiscence, it forbids all evil." Now the law seems to forbid especially the concupiscence of covetousness: hence it is written (Ex. 20:17): "Thou shalt not covet thy neighbor's goods." Therefore the concupiscence of covetousness is all evil, and so covetousness is a general sin.

*On the contrary,* Covetousness is numbered together with other special sins (Rom. 1:29), where it is written: "Being filled with all iniquity, malice, fornication, covetousness" [Douay: 'avarice'], etc.

*I answer that,* Sins take their species from their objects, as stated above (I-II, Q. 72, A. 1). Now the object of a sin is the good towards which an inordinate appetite tends. Hence where there is a special aspect of good inordinately desired, there is a special kind of sin. Now the useful good differs in aspect from the delightful good. And riches, as such, come under the head of useful good, since they are desired under the aspect of being useful to man. Consequently covetousness is a special sin, forasmuch as it is an immoderate love of having possessions, which are comprised under the name of money, whence covetousness ( *avaritia* ) is denominated.

Since, however, the verb "to have," which seems to have been originally employed in connection with possessions whereof we are absolute masters, is applied to many other things (thus a man is said to have health, a wife, clothes, and so forth, as stated in De Praedicamentis ), consequently the term "covetousness" has been amplified to denote all immoderate desire for having anything whatever. Thus Gregory says in a homily (xvi in Ev.) that "covetousness is a desire not only for money, but also for knowledge and high places, when prominence is immoderately sought after." In this way covetousness is not a special sin: and in this sense Augustine speaks of covetousness in the passage quoted in the First Objection. Wherefore this suffices for the Reply to the First Objection.

Reply Obj. 2: All those external things that are subject to the uses of human life are comprised under the term "money," inasmuch as they have the aspect of useful good. But there are certain external goods that can be obtained by money, such as pleasures, honors, and so forth, which are desirable under another aspect. Wherefore the desire for such things is not properly called covetousness, in so far as it is a special vice.

Reply Obj. 3: This gloss speaks of the inordinate concupiscence for anything whatever. For it is easy to understand that if it is forbidden to covet another's possessions it is also forbidden to covet those things that can be obtained by means of those possessions.

THIRD ARTICLE [II-II, Q. 118, Art. 3]

Whether Covetousness Is Opposed to Liberality?

Objection 1: It seems that covetousness is not opposed to liberality. For Chrysostom, commenting on Matt. 5:6, "Blessed are they that hunger and thirst after justice," says, (Hom. xv in Matth.) that there are two kinds of justice, one general, and the other special, to which covetousness is opposed: and the Philosopher says the same (Ethic. v, 2). Therefore covetousness is not opposed to liberality.

Obj. 2: Further, the sin of covetousness consists in a man's exceeding the measure in the things he possesses. But this measure is appointed by justice. Therefore covetousness is directly opposed to justice and not to liberality.

Obj. 3: Further, liberality is a virtue that observes the mean between two contrary vices, as the Philosopher states (Ethic. i, 7; iv, 1). But covetousness has no contrary and opposite sin, according to the Philosopher (Ethic. v, 1, 2). Therefore covetousness is not opposed to liberality.

*On the contrary,* It is written (Eccles. 5:9): "A covetous man shall not be satisfied with money, and he that loveth riches shall have no fruits from them." Now not to be satisfied with money and to love it inordinately are opposed to liberality, which observes the mean in the desire of riches. Therefore covetousness is opposed to liberality.

*I answer that,* Covetousness denotes immoderation with regard to riches in two ways. First, immediately in respect of the acquisition and keeping of riches. In this way a man obtains money beyond his due, by stealing or retaining another's property. This is opposed to justice, and in this sense covetousness is mentioned (Ezech. 22:27): "Her princes in the midst of her are like wolves ravening the prey to shed blood ... and to run after gains through covetousness." Secondly, it denotes immoderation in the interior affections for riches; for instance, when a man loves or desires riches too much, or takes too much pleasure in them, even if he be unwilling to steal. In this way covetousness is opposed to liberality, which moderates these affections, as stated above (Q. 117, A. 2, ad 3; A. 3, ad 3; A. 6). In this sense covetousness is spoken of (2 Cor. 9:5): "That they would ... prepare this blessing before promised, to be ready, so as a blessing, not as covetousness," where a gloss observes: "Lest they should regret what they had given, and give but little."

Reply Obj. 1: Chrysostom and the Philosopher are speaking of covetousness in the first sense: covetousness in the second sense is called illiberality [* *aneleutheria* ] by the Philosopher.

Reply Obj. 2: It belongs properly to justice to appoint the measure in the acquisition and keeping of riches from the point of view of legal due, so that a man should neither take nor retain another's property. But liberality appoints the measure of reason, principally in the interior affections, and consequently in the exterior taking and keeping of money, and in the spending of the same, in so far as these proceed from the interior affection, looking at the matter from the point of view not of the legal but of the moral debt, which latter depends on the rule of reason.

Reply Obj. 3: Covetousness as opposed to justice has no opposite vice: since it consists in having more than one ought according to justice, the contrary of which is to have less than one ought, and this is not a sin but a punishment. But covetousness as opposed to liberality has the vice of prodigality opposed to it.

FOURTH ARTICLE [II-II, Q. 118, Art. 4]

Whether Covetousness Is Always a Mortal Sin?

Objection 1: It seems that covetousness is always a mortal sin. For no one is worthy of death save for a mortal sin. But men are worthy of death on account of covetousness. For the Apostle after saying (Rom. 1:29): "Being filled with all iniquity ... fornication, covetousness [Douay: 'avarice']," etc. adds (Rom. 1:32): "They who do such things are worthy of death." Therefore covetousness is a mortal sin.

Obj. 2: Further, the least degree of covetousness is to hold to one's own inordinately. But this seemingly is a mortal sin: for Basil says (Serm. super. Luc. xii, 18): "It is the hungry man's bread that thou keepest back, the naked man's cloak that thou hoardest, the needy man's money that thou possessest, hence thou despoilest as many as thou mightest succor."

Now it is a mortal sin to do an injustice to another, since it is contrary to the love of our neighbor. Much more therefore is all covetousness a mortal sin.

Obj. 3: Further, no one is struck with spiritual blindness save through a mortal sin, for this deprives a man of the light of grace. But, according to Chrysostom [*Hom. xv in the Opus Imperfectum, falsely ascribed to St. Chrysostom], "Lust for money brings darkness on the soul." Therefore covetousness, which is lust for money, is a mortal sin.

*On the contrary,* A gloss on 1 Cor. 3:12, "If any man build upon this foundation," says (cf. St. Augustine, De Fide et Oper. xvi) that "he builds wood, hay, stubble, who thinks in the things of the world, how he may please the world," which pertains to the sin of covetousness. Now he that builds wood, hay, stubble, sins not mortally but venially, for it is said of him that "he shall be saved, yet so as by fire." Therefore covetousness is some times a venial sin.

*I answer that,* As stated above (A. 3) covetousness is twofold. In one way it is opposed to justice, and thus it is a mortal sin in respect of its genus. For in this sense covetousness consists in the unjust taking or retaining of another's property, and this belongs to theft or robbery, which are mortal sins, as stated above (Q. 66, AA. 6, 8). Yet venial sin may occur in this kind of covetousness by reason of imperfection of the act, as stated above (Q. 66, A. 6, ad 3), when we were treating of theft.

In another way covetousness may be taken as opposed to liberality: in which sense it denotes inordinate love of riches. Accordingly if the love of riches becomes so great as to be preferred to charity, in such wise that a man, through love of riches, fear not to act counter to the love of God and his neighbor, covetousness will then be a mortal sin. If, on the other hand, the inordinate nature of his love stops short of this, so that although he love riches too much, yet he does not prefer the love of them to the love of God, and is unwilling for the sake of riches to do anything in opposition to God or his neighbor, then covetousness is a venial sin.

Reply Obj. 1: Covetousness is numbered together with mortal sins, by reason of the aspect under which it is a mortal sin.

Reply Obj. 2: Basil is speaking of a case wherein a man is bound by a legal debt to give of his goods to the poor, either through fear of their want or on account of his having too much.

Reply Obj. 3: Lust for riches, properly speaking, brings darkness on the soul, when it puts out the light of charity, by preferring the love of riches to the love of God.

FIFTH ARTICLE [II-II, Q. 118, Art. 5]

Whether Covetousness Is the Greatest of Sins?

Objection 1: It seems that covetousness is the greatest of sins. For it is written (Ecclus. 10:9): "Nothing is more wicked than a covetous man," and the text continues: "There is not a more wicked thing than to love money: for such a one setteth even his own soul to sale." Tully also says (De Offic. i, under the heading, 'True magnanimity is based chiefly on two things'): "Nothing is so narrow or little minded as to love money." But this pertains to covetousness. Therefore covetousness is the most grievous of sins.

Obj. 2: Further, the more a sin is opposed to charity, the more grievous it is. Now covetousness is most opposed to charity: for Augustine says (QQ. 83, qu. 36) that "greed is the bane of charity." Therefore covetousness is the greatest of sins.

Obj. 3: Further, the gravity of a sin is indicated by its being incurable: wherefore the sin against the

Holy Ghost is said to be most grievous, because it is irremissible. But covetousness is an incurable sin: hence the Philosopher says (Ethic. iv, 1) that "old age and helplessness of any kind make men illiberal." Therefore covetousness is the most grievous of sins.

Obj. 4: Further, the Apostle says (Eph. 5:5) that covetousness is "a serving of idols." Now idolatry is reckoned among the most grievous sins. Therefore covetousness is also.

*On the contrary,* Adultery is a more grievous sin than theft, according to Prov. 6:30. But theft pertains to covetousness. Therefore covetousness is not the most grievous of sins.

*I answer that,* Every sin, from the very fact that it is an evil, consists in the corruption or privation of some good: while, in so far as it is voluntary, it consists in the desire of some good. Consequently the order of sins may be considered in two ways. First, on the part of the good that is despised or corrupted by sin, and then the greater the good the graver the sin. From this point of view a sin that is against God is most grievous; after this comes a sin that is committed against a man's person, and after this comes a sin against external things, which are deputed to man's use, and this seems to belong to covetousness. Secondly, the degrees of sin may be considered on the part of the good to which the human appetite is inordinately subjected; and then the lesser the good, the more deformed is the sin: for it is more shameful to be subject to a lower than to a higher good. Now the good of external things is the lowest of human goods: since it is less than the good of the body, and this is less than the good of the soul, which is less than the Divine good. From this point of view the sin of covetousness, whereby the human appetite is subjected even to external things, has in a way a greater deformity. Since, however, corruption or privation of good is the formal element in sin, while conversion to a mutable good is the material element, the gravity of the sin is to be judged from the point of view of the good corrupted, rather than from that of the good to which the appetite is subjected. Hence we must assert that covetousness is not simply the most grievous of sins.

Reply Obj. 1: These authorities speak of covetousness on the part of the good to which the appetite is subjected. Hence (Ecclus. 10:10) it is given as a reason that the covetous man "setteth his own soul to sale"; because, to wit, he exposes his soul—that is, his life—to danger for the sake of money. Hence the text continues: "Because while he liveth he hath cast away"—that is, despised—"his bowels," in order to make money. Tully also adds that it is the mark of a "narrow mind," namely, that one be willing to be subject to money.

Reply Obj. 2: Augustine is taking greed generally, in reference to any temporal good, not in its special acceptation for covetousness: because greed for any temporal good is the bane of charity, inasmuch as a man turns away from the Divine good through cleaving to a temporal good.

Reply Obj. 3: The sin against the Holy Ghost is incurable in one way, covetousness in another. For the sin against the Holy Ghost is incurable by reason of contempt: for instance, because a man contemns God's mercy, or His justice, or some one of those things whereby man's sins are healed: wherefore incurability of this kind points to the greater gravity of the sin. on the other hand, covetousness is incurable on the part of a human defect; a thing which human nature ever seeks to remedy, since the more deficient one is the more one seeks relief from external things, and consequently the more one gives way to covetousness. Hence incurability of this kind is an indication not of the sin being more grievous, but of its being somewhat more dangerous.

Reply Obj. 4: Covetousness is compared to idolatry on account of a certain likeness that it bears to it: because the covetous man, like the idolater, subjects himself to an external creature, though not in the same way. For the idolater subjects himself to an external creature by paying it Divine honor, whereas the covetous man subjects himself to an external creature by desiring it immoderately for use, not for worship. Hence it does not follow that covetousness is as grievous a sin as idolatry.

SIXTH ARTICLE [II-II, Q. 118, Art. 6]

Whether Covetousness Is a Spiritual Sin?

Objection 1: It seems that covetousness is not a spiritual sin. For spiritual sins seem to regard spiritual goods. But the matter of covetousness is bodily goods, namely, external riches. Therefore covetousness is not a spiritual sin.

Obj. 2: Further, spiritual sin is condivided with sin of the flesh. Now covetousness is seemingly a sin of the flesh, for it results from the corruption of the flesh, as instanced in old people who, through corruption of carnal nature, fall into covetousness. Therefore covetousness is not a spiritual sin.

Obj. 3: Further, a sin of the flesh is one by which man's body is disordered, according to the saying of the Apostle (1 Cor. 6:18), "He that committeth fornication sinneth against his own body." Now covetousness disturbs man even in his body; wherefore Chrysostom (Hom. xxix in Matth.) compares the covetous man to the man who was possessed by the devil (Mk. 5) and was troubled in body. Therefore covetousness seems not to be a spiritual sin.

*On the contrary,* Gregory (Moral. xxxi) numbers covetousness among spiritual vices.

*I answer that,* Sins are seated chiefly in the affections: and all the affections or passions of the soul have their term in pleasure and sorrow, according to the Philosopher (Ethic. ii, 5). Now some pleasures are carnal and some spiritual. Carnal pleasures are those which are consummated in the carnal senses—for instance, the pleasures of the table and sexual pleasures: while spiritual pleasures are those which are consummated in the mere apprehension of the soul. Accordingly, sins of the flesh are those which are consummated in carnal pleasures, while spiritual sins are consummated in pleasures of the spirit without pleasure of the flesh. Such is covetousness: for the covetous man takes pleasure in the consideration of himself as a possessor of riches. Therefore covetousness is a spiritual sin.

Reply Obj. 1: Covetousness with regard to a bodily object seeks the pleasure, not of the body but only of the soul, forasmuch as a man takes pleasure in the fact that he possesses riches: wherefore it is not a sin of the flesh. Nevertheless by reason of its object it is a mean between purely spiritual sins, which seek spiritual pleasure in respect of spiritual objects (thus pride is about excellence), and purely carnal sins, which seek a purely bodily pleasure in respect of a bodily object.

Reply Obj. 2: Movement takes its species from the term *whereto* and not from the term wherefrom. Hence a vice of the flesh is so called from its tending to a pleasure of the flesh, and not from its originating in some defect of the flesh.

Reply Obj. 3: Chrysostom compares a covetous man to the man who was possessed by the devil, not that the former is troubled in the flesh in the same way as the latter, but by way of contrast, since while the possessed man, of whom we read in Mk. 5, stripped himself, the covetous man loads himself with an excess of riches.

SEVENTH ARTICLE [II-II, Q. 118, Art. 7]

Whether Covetousness Is a Capital Vice?

Objection 1: It seems that covetousness is not a capital vice. For covetousness is opposed to liberality as the mean, and to prodigality as extreme. But neither is liberality a principal virtue, nor prodigality a capital vice. Therefore covetousness also should not be reckoned a capital vice.

Obj. 2: Further, as stated above (I-II, Q. 84, AA. 3, 4), those vices are called capital which have principal ends, to which the ends of other vices are directed. But this does not apply to covetousness: since riches have the aspect, not of an end, but rather of something directed to an end, as stated in *Ethic.* i, 5. Therefore covetousness is not a capital vice.

Obj. 3: Further, Gregory says (Moral. xv), that "covetousness arises sometimes from pride, sometimes from fear. For there are those who, when they think that they lack the needful for their expenses, allow the mind to give way to covetousness. And there are others who, wishing to be thought more of, are incited to greed for other people's property." Therefore covetousness arises from other vices instead of being a capital vice in respect of other vices.

*On the contrary,* Gregory (Moral. xxxi) reckons covetousness among the capital vices.

*I answer that,* As stated in the Second Objection, a capital vice is one which under the aspect of end gives rise to other vices: because when an end is very desirable, the result is that through desire thereof man sets about doing many things either good or evil. Now the most desirable end is happiness or felicity, which is the last end of human life, as stated above (I-II, Q. 1, AA. 4, 7, 8): wherefore the more a thing is furnished with the conditions of happiness, the more desirable it is. Also one of the conditions of happiness is that it be self-sufficing, else it would not set man's appetite at rest, as the last end does. Now riches give great promise of self-sufficiency, as Boethius says (De Consol. iii): the reason of which, according to the Philosopher (Ethic. v, 5), is that we "use money in token of taking possession of something," and again it is written (Eccles. 10:19): "All things obey money." Therefore covetousness, which is desire for money, is a capital vice.

Reply Obj. 1: Virtue is perfected in accordance with reason, but vice is perfected in accordance with the inclination of the sensitive appetite. Now reason and sensitive appetite do not belong chiefly to the same genus, and consequently it does not follow that principal vice is opposed to principal virtue. Wherefore, although liberality is not a principal virtue, since it does not regard the principal good of the reason, yet covetousness is a principal vice, because it regards money, which occupies a principal place among sensible goods, for the reason given in the Article.

On the other hand, prodigality is not directed to an end that is desirable principally, indeed it seems rather to result from a lack of reason. Hence the Philosopher says (Ethic. iv, 1) that "a prodigal man is a fool rather than a knave."

Reply Obj. 2: It is true that money is directed to something else as its end: yet in so far as it is useful for obtaining all sensible things, it contains, in a way, all things virtually. Hence it has a certain likeness to happiness, as stated in the Article.

Reply Obj. 3: Nothing prevents a capital vice from arising sometimes out of other vices, as stated above (Q. 36, A. 4, ad 1; I-II, Q. 84, A. 4), provided that itself be frequently the source of others.

EIGHTH ARTICLE [II-II, Q. 118, Art. 8]

Whether Treachery, Fraud, Falsehood, Perjury, Restlessness, Violence, and Insensibility to Mercy Are Daughters of Covetousness?

Objection 1: It seems that the daughters of covetousness are not as commonly stated, namely, "treachery, fraud, falsehood, perjury, restlessness, violence, and insensibility to mercy." For covetousness is opposed to liberality, as stated above (A. 3). Now treachery, fraud, and falsehood are opposed to prudence, perjury to religion, restlessness to hope, or to charity which rests in the beloved object, violence to justice, insensibility to mercy. Therefore these vices have no connection with covetousness.

Obj. 2: Further, treachery, fraud and falsehood seem to pertain to the same thing, namely, the deceiving of one's neighbor. Therefore they should not be reckoned as different daughters of covetousness.

Obj. 3: Further, Isidore (Comment. in Deut.) enumerates nine daughters of covetousness; which are "lying, fraud, theft, perjury, greed of filthy lucre, false witnessing, violence, inhumanity, rapacity." Therefore the former reckoning of daughters is insufficient.

Obj. 4: Further, the Philosopher (Ethic. iv, 1) mentions many kinds of vices as belonging to covetousness which he calls illiberality, for he speaks of those who are "sparing, tight-fisted, skinflints [* *kyminopristes* ], misers [* kimbikes ], who do illiberal deeds," and of those who "batten on whoredom, usurers, gamblers, despoilers of the dead, and robbers." Therefore it seems that the aforesaid enumeration is insufficient.

Obj. 5: Further, tyrants use much violence against their subjects. But the Philosopher says (Ethic. iv, 1) that "tyrants who destroy cities and despoil sacred places are not to be called illiberal," i.e. covetous. Therefore violence should not be reckoned a daughter of covetousness.

*On the contrary,* Gregory (Moral. xxxi) assigns to covetousness the daughters mentioned above.

*I answer that,* The daughters of covetousness are the vices which arise therefrom, especially in respect of the desire of an end. Now since covetousness is excessive love of possessing riches, it exceeds in two things. For in the first place it exceeds in retaining, and in this respect covetousness gives rise to *insensibility to mercy,* because, to wit, a man's heart is not softened by mercy to assist the needy with his riches [*See Q. 30, A. 1]. In the second place it belongs to covetousness to exceed in receiving, and in this respect covetousness may be considered in two ways. First as in the thought ( *affectu* ). In this way it gives rise to restlessness, by hindering man with excessive anxiety and care, for "a covetous man shall not be satisfied with money" (Eccles. 5:9). Secondly, it may be considered in the execution ( *effectu* ). In this way the covetous man, in acquiring other people's goods, sometimes employs force, which pertains to *violence,* sometimes deceit, and then if he has recourse to words, it is *falsehood,* if it be mere words, perjury if he confirm his statement by oath; if he has recourse to deeds, and the deceit affects things, we have *fraud* ; if persons, then we have *treachery,* as in the case of Judas, who betrayed Christ through covetousness.

Reply Obj. 1: There is no need for the daughters of a capital sin to belong to that same kind of vice: because a sin of one kind allows of sins even of a different kind being directed to its end; seeing that it is one thing for a sin to have daughters, and another for it to have species.

Reply Obj. 2: These three are distinguished as stated in the Article.

Reply Obj. 3: These nine are reducible to the seven aforesaid. For lying and false witnessing are comprised under falsehood, since false witnessing is a special kind of lie, just as theft is a special kind of fraud, wherefore it is comprised under fraud; and greed of filthy lucre belongs to restlessness; rapacity is comprised under violence, since it is a species thereof; and inhumanity is the same as insensibility to mercy.

Reply Obj. 4: The vices mentioned by Aristotle are species rather than daughters of illiberality or covetousness. For a man may be said to be illiberal or covetous through a defect in giving. If he gives but little he is said to be "sparing"; if nothing, he is "tightfisted": if he gives with great reluctance, he is said to be *kyminopristes* ("skinflint"), a cumin-seller, as it were, because he makes a great fuss about things of little value. Sometimes a man is said to be illiberal or covetous, through an excess in receiving, and this in two ways. In one way, through making money by disgraceful means, whether in performing shameful and servile works by means of illiberal practices, or by acquiring more through sinful deeds, such as whoredom or the like, or by making a profit where one ought to have given gratis, as in the case of usury, or by laboring much to make little profit. In another way, in making money by unjust means, whether by using violence on the living, as robbers do, or by despoiling the dead, or by preying on one's friends, as gamblers do.

Reply Obj. 5: Just as liberality is about moderate sums of money, so is illiberality. Wherefore tyrants who take great things by violence, are said to be, not illiberal, but unjust.

## QUESTION 119

OF PRODIGALITY (In Three Articles)

We must now consider prodigality, under which head there are three points of inquiry:

(1) Whether prodigality is opposite to covetousness?

(2) Whether prodigality is a sin?

(3) Whether it is a graver sin that covetousness?

FIRST ARTICLE [II-II, Q. 119, Art. 1]

Whether Prodigality Is Opposite to Covetousness?

Objection 1: It seems that prodigality is not opposite to covetousness. For opposites cannot be together in the same subject. But some are at the same time prodigal and covetous. Therefore prodigality is not opposite to covetousness.

Obj. 2: Further, opposites relate to one same thing. But covetousness, as opposed to liberality, relates to certain passions whereby man is affected towards money: whereas prodigality does not seem to relate to any passions of the soul, since it is not affected towards money, or to anything else of the kind. Therefore prodigality is not opposite to covetousness.

Obj. 3: Further, sin takes its species chiefly from its end, as stated above (I-II, Q. 62, A. 3). Now prodigality seems always to be directed to some unlawful end, for the sake of which the prodigal squanders his goods. Especially is it directed to pleasures, wherefore it is stated (Luke 15:13) of the prodigal son that he "wasted his substance living riotously." Therefore it seems that prodigality is opposed to temperance and insensibility rather than to covetousness and liberality.

*On the contrary,* The Philosopher says (Ethic. ii, 7; iv, 1) that prodigality is opposed to liberality, and illiberality, to which we give here the name of covetousness.

*I answer that,* In morals vices are opposed to one another and to virtue in respect of excess and deficiency. Now covetousness and prodigality differ variously in respect of excess and deficiency. Thus, as regards affection for riches, the covetous man exceeds by loving them more than he ought, while the prodigal is deficient, by being less careful of them than he ought: and as regards external action, prodigality implies excess in giving, but deficiency in retaining and acquiring, while covetousness, *on the contrary,* denotes deficiency in giving, but excess in acquiring and retaining. Hence it is evident that prodigality is opposed to covetousness.

Reply Obj. 1: Nothing prevents opposites from being in the same subject in different respects. For a thing is denominated more from what is in it principally. Now just as in liberality, which observes the mean, the principal thing is giving, to which receiving and retaining are subordinate, so, too, covetousness and prodigality regard principally giving. Wherefore he who exceeds in giving is said to be "prodigal," while he who is deficient in giving is said to be "covetous." Now it happens sometimes that a man is deficient in giving, without exceeding in receiving, as the Philosopher observes (Ethic. iv, 1). And in like manner it happens sometimes that a man exceeds in giving, and therefore is prodigal, and yet at the same time exceeds in receiving. This may be due either to some kind of necessity, since while exceeding in giving he is lacking in goods of his own, so that he is driven to acquire unduly, and this pertains to covetousness; or it may be due to inordinateness of the mind, for he gives not for a good purpose, but, as though despising virtue, cares not whence or how he receives. Wherefore he is prodigal and covetous in different respects.

Reply Obj. 2: Prodigality regards passions in respect of money, not as exceeding, but as deficient in them.

Reply Obj. 3: The prodigal does not always exceed in giving for the sake of pleasures which are the matter of temperance, but sometimes through being so disposed as not to care about riches, and sometimes on account of something else. More frequently, however, he inclines to intemperance, both because through spending too much on other things he becomes fearless of spending on objects of pleasure, to which the concupiscence of the flesh is more prone; and because through taking no pleasure in virtuous goods, he seeks for himself pleasures of the body. Hence the Philosopher says (Ethic. iv, 1) "that many a prodigal ends in becoming intemperate."

SECOND ARTICLE [II-II, Q. 119, Art. 2]

Whether Prodigality Is a Sin?

Objection 1: It seems that prodigality is not a sin. For the Apostle says (1 Tim. 6:10): "Covetousness [Douay: 'desire of money'] is the root of all evils." But it is not the root of prodigality, since this is opposed to it. Therefore prodigality is not a sin.

Obj. 2: Further, the Apostle says (1 Tim. 6:17, 18): "Charge the rich of this world ... to give easily, to communicate to others." Now this is especially what prodigal persons do. Therefore prodigality is not a sin.

Obj. 3: Further, it belongs to prodigality to exceed in giving and to be deficient in solicitude about riches. But this is most becoming to the perfect, who fulfil the words of Our Lord (Matt. 6:34), "Be not ... solicitous for tomorrow," and (Matt. 19:21), "Sell all [Vulg.: 'what'] thou hast, and give to the poor." Therefore prodigality is not a sin.

*On the contrary,* The prodigal son is held to blame for his prodigality.

*I answer that,* As stated above (A. 1), the opposition between prodigality and covetousness is one of excess and deficiency; either of which destroys the mean of virtue. Now a thing is vicious and sinful through corrupting the good of virtue. Hence it follows that prodigality is a sin.

Reply Obj. 1: Some expound this saying of the Apostle as referring, not to actual covetousness, but to a kind of habitual covetousness, which is the concupiscence of the *fomes* [*Cf. I-II, Q. 81, A. 3, ad 2], whence all sins arise. Others say that he is speaking of a general covetousness with regard to any kind of good: and in this sense also it is evident that prodigality arises from covetousness; since the prodigal seeks to acquire some temporal good inordinately, namely, to give pleasure to others, or at least to satisfy his own will in giving. But to one that reviews the passage correctly, it is evident that the Apostle is speaking literally of the desire of riches, for he had said previously (1 Tim. 6:9): "They that will become rich," etc. In this sense covetousness is said to be "the root of all evils," not that all evils always arise from covetousness, but because there is no evil that does not at some time arise from covetousness. Wherefore prodigality sometimes is born of covetousness, as when a man is prodigal in going to great expense in order to curry favor with certain persons from whom he may receive riches.

Reply Obj. 2: The Apostle bids the rich to be ready to give and communicate their riches, according as they ought. The prodigal does not do this: since, as the Philosopher remarks (Ethic. iv,

1), "his giving is neither good, nor for a good end, nor according as it ought to be. For sometimes they give much to those who ought to be poor, namely, to buffoons and flatterers, whereas to the good they give nothing."

Reply Obj. 3: The excess in prodigality consists chiefly, not in the total amount given, but in the amount over and above what ought to be given. Hence sometimes the liberal man gives more than the prodigal man, if it be necessary. Accordingly we must reply that those who give all their possessions with the intention of following Christ, and banish from their minds all solicitude for temporal things, are not prodigal but perfectly liberal.

THIRD ARTICLE [II-II, Q. 119, Art. 3]

Whether Prodigality Is a More Grievous Sin Than Covetousness?

Objection 1: It seems that prodigality is a more grievous sin than covetousness. For by covetousness a man injures his neighbor by not communicating his goods to him, whereas by prodigality a man injures himself, because the Philosopher says (Ethic. iv, 1) that "the wasting of riches, which are the means whereby a man lives, is an undoing of his very being." Now he that injures himself sins more grievously, according to Ecclus. 14:5, "He that is evil to himself, to whom will he be good?" Therefore prodigality is a more grievous sin than covetousness.

Obj. 2: Further, a disorder that is accompanied by a laudable circumstance is less sinful. Now the disorder of covetousness is sometimes accompanied by a laudable circumstance, as in the case of those who are unwilling to spend their own, lest they be driven to accept from others: whereas the disorder of prodigality is accompanied by a circumstance that calls for blame, inasmuch as we ascribe prodigality to those who are intemperate, as the Philosopher observes (Ethic. iv, 1). Therefore prodigality is a more grievous sin than covetousness.

Obj. 3: Further, prudence is chief among the moral virtues, as stated above (Q. 56, A. 1, ad 1; I-II, Q. 61, A. 2, ad 1). Now prodigality is more opposed to prudence than covetousness is: for it is written (Prov. 21:20): "There is a treasure to be desired, and oil in the dwelling of the just; and the foolish man shall spend it": and the Philosopher says (Ethic. iv, 6) that "it is the mark of a fool to give too much and receive nothing." Therefore prodigality is a more grievous sin than covetousness.

*On the contrary,* The Philosopher says (Ethic. iv, 6) that "the prodigal seems to be much better than the illiberal man."

*I answer that,* Prodigality considered in itself is a less grievous sin than covetousness, and this for three reasons. First, because covetousness differs more from the opposite virtue: since giving, wherein the prodigal exceeds, belongs to liberality more than receiving or retaining, wherein the covetous man exceeds. Secondly, because the prodigal man is of use to the many to whom he gives, while the covetous man is of use to no one, not even to himself, as stated in *Ethic.* iv, 6. Thirdly, because prodigality is easily cured. For not only is the prodigal on the way to old age, which is opposed to prodigality, but he is easily reduced to a state of want, since much useless spending impoverishes him and makes him unable to exceed in giving. Moreover, prodigality is easily turned into virtue on account of its likeness thereto. On the other hand, the covetous man is not easily cured, for the reason given above (Q. 118, A. 5, ad 3).

Reply Obj. 1: The difference between the prodigal and the covetous man is not that the former sins against himself and the latter against another. For the prodigal sins against himself by spending that which is his, and his means of support, and against others by spending the wherewithal to help others. This applies chiefly to the clergy, who are the dispensers of the Church's goods, that belong to the poor whom they defraud by their prodigal expenditure. In like manner the covetous man sins against others, by being deficient in giving; and he sins against himself, through deficiency in spending: wherefore it is written (Eccles. 6:2): "A man to whom God hath given riches ... yet doth not give him the power to eat thereof." Nevertheless the prodigal man exceeds in this, that he injures both himself and others yet so as to profit some; whereas the covetous man profits neither others nor himself, since he does not even use his own goods for his own profit.

Reply Obj. 2: In speaking of vices in general, we judge of them according to their respective natures: thus, with regard to prodigality we note that it consumes riches to excess, and with regard to covetousness that it retains them to excess. That one spend too much for the sake of intemperance points already to several additional sins, wherefore the prodigal of this kind is worse, as stated in *Ethic.* iv, 1. That an illiberal or covetous man refrain from taking what belongs to others, although this appears in itself to call for praise, yet on account of the motive for which he does so it calls for blame, since he is unwilling to accept from others lest he be forced to give to others.

Reply Obj. 3: All vices are opposed to prudence, even as all virtues are directed by prudence: wherefore if a vice be opposed to prudence alone, for this very reason it is deemed less grievous.

# QUESTION 120

OF "EPIKEIA" OR EQUITY (In Two Articles)

We must now consider "epikeia," under which head there are two points of inquiry:

(1) Whether "epikeia" is a virtue?

(2) Whether it is a part of justice?

FIRST ARTICLE [II-II, Q. 120, Art. 1]

Whether "Epikeia" [* *Epieikeia* ] Is a Virtue?

Objection 1: It seems that *epikeia* is not a virtue. For no virtue does away with another virtue. Yet *epikeia* does away with another virtue, since it sets aside that which is just according to law, and seemingly is opposed to severity. Therefore *epikeia* is not a virtue.

Obj. 2: Further, Augustine says (De Vera Relig. xxxi): "With regard to these earthly laws, although men pass judgment on them when they make them, yet, when once they are made and established, the judge must pronounce judgment not on them but according to them." But seemingly *epikeia* pronounces judgment on the law, when it deems that the law should not be observed in some particular case. Therefore *epikeia* is a vice rather than a virtue.

Obj. 3: Further, apparently it belongs to *epikeia* to consider the intention of the lawgiver, as the Philosopher states (Ethic. v, 10). But it belongs to the sovereign alone to interpret the intention of the lawgiver, wherefore the Emperor says in the Codex of Laws and Constitutions,*under*Law i: "It is fitting and lawful that We alone should interpret between equity and law." Therefore the act of *epikeia* is unlawful: and consequently *epikeia* is not a virtue.

*On the contrary,* The Philosopher (Ethic. v, 10) states it to be a virtue.

*I answer that,* As stated above (I-II, Q. 96, A. 6), when we were treating of laws, since human actions, with which laws are concerned, are composed of contingent singulars and are innumerable in their diversity, it was not possible to lay down rules of law that would apply to every single case. Legislators in framing laws attend to what commonly happens: although if the law be applied to certain cases it will frustrate the equality of justice and be injurious to the common good, which the law has in view. Thus the law requires deposits to be restored, because in the majority of cases this is just. Yet it happens sometimes to be injurious—for instance, if a madman were to put his sword in deposit, and demand its delivery while in a state of madness, or if a man were to seek the return of his deposit in order to fight against his country. In these and like cases it is bad to follow the law, and it is good to set aside the letter of the law and to follow the dictates of justice and the common good. This is the object of *epikeia* which we call equity. Therefore it is evident that *epikeia* is a virtue.

Reply Obj. 1: *Epikeia* does not set aside that which is just in itself but that which is just as by law established. Nor is it opposed to severity, which follows the letter of the law when it ought to be followed. To follow the letter of the law when it ought not to be followed is sinful. Hence it is written in the Codex of Laws and Constitutions*under*Law v: "Without doubt he transgresses the law who by adhering to the letter of the law strives to defeat the intention of the lawgiver."

Reply Obj. 2: It would be passing judgment on a law to say that it was not well made; but to say that the letter of the law is not to be observed in some particular case is passing judgment not on the law, but on some particular contingency.

Reply Obj. 3: Interpretation is admissible in doubtful cases where it is not allowed to set aside the letter of the law without the interpretation of the sovereign. But when the case is manifest there is need, not of interpretation, but of execution.

SECOND ARTICLE [II-II, Q. 120, Art. 2]

Whether *Epikeia* Is a Part of Justice?

Objection 1: It seems that *epikeia* is not a part of justice. For, as stated above (Q. 58, A. 7), justice is twofold, particular and legal. Now *epikeia* is not a part of particular justice, since it extends to all virtues, even as legal justice does. In like manner, neither is it a part of legal justice, since its operation is beside that which is established by law. Therefore it seems that *epikeia* is not a part of justice.

Obj. 2: Further, a more principal virtue is not assigned as the part of a less principal virtue: for it is to the cardinal virtue, as being principal, that secondary virtues are assigned as parts. Now *epikeia* seems to be a more principal virtue than justice, as implied by its name: for it is derived from epi , i.e. "above," and dikaion , i.e. "just." Therefore *epikeia* is not a part of justice.

Obj. 3: Further, it seems that *epikeia* is the same as modesty. For where the Apostle says (Phil. 4:5), "Let your modesty be known to all men," the Greek has epieikeia [* to epieikes ]. Now, according to Tully (De Invent. Rhet. ii), modesty is a part of temperance. Therefore *epikeia* is not a part of justice.

*On the contrary,* The Philosopher says (Ethic. v, 10) that " epikeia is a kind of justice."

*I answer that,* As stated above (Q. 48), a virtue has three kinds of parts, subjective, integral, and potential. A subjective part is one of which the whole is predicated essentially, and it is less than the whole. This may happen in two ways. For sometimes one thing is predicated of many in one common ratio, as animal of horse and ox: and sometimes one thing is predicated of many according to priority and posteriority, as *being* of substance and accident.

Accordingly, *epikeia* is a part of justice taken in a general sense, for it is a kind of justice, as the Philosopher states (Ethic. v, 10). Wherefore it is evident that *epikeia* is a subjective part of justice; and justice is predicated of it with priority to being predicated of legal justice, since legal justice is subject to the direction of *epikeia.* Hence epikeia is by way of being a higher rule of human actions.

Reply Obj. 1: *Epikeia* corresponds properly to legal justice, and in one way is contained under it, and in another way exceeds it. For if legal justice denotes that which complies with the law, whether as regards the letter of the law, or as regards the intention of the lawgiver, which is of more account, then *epikeia* is the more important part of legal justice. But if legal justice denote merely that which complies with the law with regard to the letter, then *epikeia* is a part not of legal justice but of justice in its general acceptation, and is condivided with legal justice, as exceeding it.

Reply Obj. 2: As the Philosopher states (Ethic. v, 10), " *epikeia* is better than a certain," namely, legal, "justice," which observes the letter of the law: yet since it is itself a kind of justice, it is not better than all justice.

Reply Obj. 3: It belongs to *epikeia* to moderate something, namely, the observance of the letter of the law. But modesty, which is reckoned a part of temperance, moderates man's outward life—for instance, in his deportment, dress or the like. Possibly also the term *epieikeia* is applied in Greek by a similitude to all kinds of moderation.

# QUESTION 121

OF PIETY (In Two Articles)

We must now consider the gift that corresponds to justice; namely, piety. Under this head there are two points of inquiry:

(1) Whether it is a gift of the Holy Ghost?

(2) Which of the beatitudes and fruits corresponds to it?

FIRST ARTICLE [II-II, Q. 121, Art. 1]

Whether Piety Is a Gift?

Objection 1: It seems that piety is not a gift. For the gifts differ from the virtues, as stated above (I-II, Q. 68, A. 1). But piety is a virtue, as stated above (Q. 101, A. 3). Therefore piety is not a gift.

Obj. 2: Further, the gifts are more excellent than the virtues, above all the moral virtues, as above (I-II, Q. 68, A. 8). Now among the parts of justice religion is greater than piety. Therefore if any part of justice is to be accounted a gift, it seems that religion should be a gift rather than piety.

Obj. 3: Further, the gifts and their acts remain in heaven, as stated above (I-II, Q. 68, A. 6). But the act of piety cannot remain in heaven: for Gregory says (Moral. i) that "piety fills the inmost recesses of the heart with works of mercy": and so there will be no piety in heaven since there will be no unhappiness [*Cf. Q. 30, A. 1]. Therefore piety is not a gift.

*On the contrary,* It is reckoned among the gifts in the eleventh chapter of Isaias (verse 2) [Douay: "godliness"] [* Pietas, whence our English word "pity," which is the same as mercy.]

*I answer that,* As stated above (I-II, Q. 68, A. 1; Q. 69, AA. 1, 3), the gifts of the Holy Ghost are habitual dispositions of the soul, rendering it amenable to the motion of the Holy Ghost. Now the Holy Ghost moves us to this effect among others, of having a filial affection towards God, according to Rom. 8:15, "You have received the spirit of adoption of sons, whereby we cry: Abba (Father)." And since it belongs properly to piety to pay duty and worship to one's father, it follows that piety, whereby, at the Holy Ghost's instigation, we pay worship and duty to God as our Father, is a gift of the Holy Ghost.

Reply Obj. 1: The piety that pays duty and worship to a father in the flesh is a virtue: but the piety that is a gift pays this to God as Father.

Reply Obj. 2: To pay worship to God as Creator, as religion does, is more excellent than to pay worship to one's father in the flesh, as the piety that is a virtue does. But to pay worship to God as Father is yet more excellent than to pay worship to God as Creator and Lord. Wherefore religion is greater than the virtue of piety: while the gift of piety is greater than religion.

Reply Obj. 3: As by the virtue of piety man pays duty and worship not only to his father in the flesh, but also to all his kindred on account of their being related to his father, so by the gift of piety he pays worship and duty not only to God, but also to all men on account of their relationship to God. Hence it belongs to piety to honor the saints, and not to contradict the Scriptures whether one understands them or not, as Augustine says (De Doctr. Christ. ii). Consequently it also assists those who are in a state of unhappiness. And although this act has no place in heaven, especially after the Day of Judgment, yet piety will exercise its principal act, which is to revere God with filial affection: for it is then above all that this act will be fulfilled, according to Wis. 5:5, "Behold how they are numbered among the children of God." The saints will also mutually honor one another. Now, however, before the Judgment Day, the saints have pity on those also who are living in this unhappy state.

SECOND ARTICLE [II-II, Q. 121, Art. 2]

Whether the Second Beatitude, "Blessed Are the Meek," Corresponds to the Gift of Piety?

Objection 1: It seems that the second beatitude, "Blessed are the meek," does not correspond to the gift of piety. For piety is the gift corresponding to justice, to which rather belongs the fourth beatitude, "Blessed are they that hunger and thirst after justice," or the fifth beatitude, "Blessed are the merciful," since as stated above (A. 1, Obj. 3), the works of mercy belong to piety. Therefore the second beatitude does not pertain to the gift of piety.

Obj. 2: Further, the gift of piety is directed by the gift of knowledge, which is united to it in the enumeration of the gifts (Isa. 11). Now direction and execution extend to the same matter. Since, then, the third beatitude, "Blessed are they that mourn," corresponds to the gift of knowledge, it seems that the second beatitude corresponds to piety.

Obj. 3: Further, the fruits correspond to the beatitudes and gifts, as stated above (I-II, Q. 70, A. 2). Now among the fruits, goodness and benignity seem to agree with piety rather than mildness, which pertains to meekness. Therefore the second beatitude does not correspond to the gift of piety.

*On the contrary,* Augustine says (De Serm. Dom. in Monte i): "Piety is becoming to the meek."

*I answer that,* In adapting the beatitudes to the gifts a twofold congruity may be observed. One is according to the order in which they are given, and Augustine seems to have followed this: wherefore he assigns the first beatitude to the lowest gift, namely, fear, and the second beatitude, "Blessed are the meek," to piety, and so on. Another congruity may be observed in keeping with the special nature of each gift and beatitude. In this way one must adapt the beatitudes to the gifts according to their objects and acts: and thus the fourth and fifth beatitudes would correspond to piety, rather than the second. Yet the second beatitude has a certain congruity with piety, inasmuch as meekness removes the obstacles to acts of piety.

This suffices for the Reply to the First Objection.

Reply Obj. 2: Taking the beatitudes and gifts according to their proper natures, the same beatitude must needs correspond to knowledge and piety: but taking them according to their order, different beatitudes correspond to them, although a certain congruity may be observed, as stated above.

Reply Obj. 3: In the fruits goodness and benignity may be directly ascribed to piety; and mildness indirectly in so far as it removes obstacles to acts of piety, as stated above.

# QUESTION 122

OF THE PRECEPTS OF JUSTICE (In Six Articles)

We must now consider the precepts of justice, under which head there are six points of inquiry:

(1) Whether the precepts of the decalogue are precepts of justice?

(2) Of the first precept of the decalogue;

(3) Of the second;

(4) Of the third;

(5) Of the fourth;

(6) Of the other six.

FIRST ARTICLE [II-II, Q. 122, Art. 1]

Whether the Precepts of the Decalogue Are Precepts of Justice?

Objection 1: It seems that the precepts of the decalogue are not precepts of justice. For the intention of a lawgiver is "to make the citizens virtuous in respect of every virtue," as stated in *Ethic.* ii, 1. Wherefore, according to *Ethic.* v, 1, "the law prescribes about all acts of all virtues." Now the precepts of the decalogue are the first principles of the whole Divine Law. Therefore the precepts of the decalogue do not pertain to justice alone.

Obj. 2: Further, it would seem that to justice belong especially the judicial precepts, which are condivided with the moral precepts, as stated above (I-II, Q. 99, A. 4). But the precepts of the decalogue are moral precepts, as stated above (I-II, Q. 100, A. 3). Therefore the precepts of the decalogue are not precepts of justice.

Obj. 3: Further, the Law contains chiefly precepts about acts of justice regarding the common good, for instance about public officers and the like. But there is no mention of these in the precepts of the decalogue. Therefore it seems that the precepts of the decalogue do not properly belong to justice.

Obj. 4: Further, the precepts of the decalogue are divided into two tables, corresponding to the love of God and the love of our neighbor, both of which regard the virtue of charity. Therefore the precepts of the decalogue belong to charity rather than to justice.

*On the contrary,* Seemingly justice is the sole virtue whereby we are directed to another. Now we are directed to another by all the precepts of the decalogue, as is evident if one consider each of them. Therefore all the precepts of the decalogue pertain to justice.

*I answer that,* The precepts of the decalogue are the first principles of the Law: and the natural reason assents to them at once, as to principles that are most evident. Now it is altogether evident that the notion of duty, which is essential to a precept, appears in justice, which is of one towards another. Because in those matters that relate to himself it would seem at a glance that man is master of himself, and that he may do as he likes: whereas in matters that refer to another it appears manifestly that a man is under obligation to render to another that which is his due. Hence the precepts of the decalogue must needs pertain to justice. Wherefore the first three precepts are about acts of religion, which is the chief part of justice; the fourth precept is about acts of piety, which is the second part of justice; and the six remaining are about justice commonly so called, which is observed among equals.

Reply Obj. 1: The intention of the law is to make all men virtuous, but in a certain order, namely, by first of all giving them precepts about those things where the notion of duty is most manifest, as stated above.

Reply Obj. 2: The judicial precepts are determinations of the moral precepts, in so far as these are directed to one's neighbor, just as the ceremonial precepts are determinations of the moral precepts in so far as these are directed to God. Hence neither precepts are contained in the decalogue: and yet they are determinations of the precepts of the decalogue, and therefore pertain to justice.

Reply Obj. 3: Things that concern the common good must needs be administered in different ways according to the difference of men. Hence they were to be given a place not among the precepts of the decalogue, but among the judicial precepts.

Reply Obj. 4: The precepts of the decalogue pertain to charity as their end, according to 1 Tim. 1:5,

"The end of the commandment is charity": but they belong to justice, inasmuch as they refer immediately to acts of justice.

SECOND ARTICLE [II-II, Q. 122, Art. 2]

Whether the First Precept of the Decalogue Is Fittingly Expressed?

Objection 1: It seems that the first precept of the decalogue is unfittingly expressed. For man is more bound to God than to his father in the flesh, according to Heb. 12:9, "How much more shall we [Vulg.: 'shall we not much more'] obey the Father of spirits and live?" Now the precept of piety, whereby man honors his father, is expressed affirmatively in these words: "Honor thy father and thy mother." Much more, therefore, should the first precept of religion, whereby all honor God, be expressed affirmatively, especially as affirmation is naturally prior to negation.

Obj. 2: Further, the first precept of the decalogue pertains to religion, as stated above (A. 1). Now religion, since it is one virtue, has one act. Yet in the first precept three acts are forbidden: since we read first: "Thou shalt not have strange gods before Me"; secondly, "Thou shalt not make to thyself any graven thing"; and thirdly, "Thou shalt not adore them nor serve them." Therefore the first precept is unfittingly expressed.

Obj. 3: Further, Augustine says (De decem chord. ix) that "the first precept forbids the sin of superstition." But there are many wicked superstitions besides idolatry, as stated above (Q. 92, A. 2). Therefore it was insufficient to forbid idolatry alone.

*On the contrary,* stands the authority of Scripture.

*I answer that,* It pertains to law to make men good, wherefore it behooved the precepts of the Law to be set in order according to the order of generation, the order, to wit, of man's becoming good. Now two things must be observed in the order of generation. The first is that the first part is the first thing to be established; thus in the generation of an animal the first thing to be formed is the heart, and in building a home the first thing to be set up is the foundation: and in the goodness of the soul the first part is goodness of the will, the result of which is that a man makes good use of every other goodness. Now the goodness of the will depends on its object, which is its end. Wherefore since man was to be directed to virtue by means of the Law, the first thing necessary was, as it were, to lay the foundation of religion, whereby man is duly directed to God, Who is the last end of man's will.

The second thing to be observed in the order of generation is that in the first place contraries and obstacles have to be removed. Thus the farmer first purifies the soil, and afterwards sows his seed, according to Jer. 4:3, "Break up anew your fallow ground, and sow not upon thorns." Hence it behooved man, first of all to be instructed in religion, so as to remove the obstacles to true religion. Now the chief obstacle to religion is for man to adhere to a false god, according to Matt. 6:24, "You cannot serve God and mammon." Therefore in the first precept of the Law the worship of false gods is excluded.

Reply Obj. 1: In point of fact there is one affirmative precept about religion, namely: "Remember that thou keep holy the Sabbath Day." Still the negative precepts had to be given first, so that by their means the obstacles to religion might be removed. For though affirmation naturally precedes negation, yet in the process of generation, negation, whereby obstacles are removed, comes first, as stated in the Article. Especially is this true in matters concerning God, where negation is preferable to affirmation, on account of our insufficiency, as Dionysius observes (Coel. Hier. ii).

Reply Obj. 2: People worshiped strange gods in two ways. For some served certain creatures as gods without having recourse to images. Hence Varro says that for a long time the ancient Romans worshiped gods without using images: and this worship is first forbidden by the words, "Thou shalt not have strange gods." Among others the worship of false gods was observed by using certain images: and so the very making of images was fittingly forbidden by the words, "Thou shalt not make to thyself any graven thing," as also the worship of those same images, by the words, "Thou shalt not adore them," etc.

Reply Obj. 3: All other kinds of superstition proceed from some compact, tacit or explicit, with the demons; hence all are understood to be forbidden by the words, "Thou shalt not have strange gods."

THIRD ARTICLE [II-II, Q. 122, Art. 3]

Whether the Second Precept of the Decalogue Is Fittingly Expressed?

Objection 1: It seems that the second precept of the decalogue is unfittingly expressed. For this precept, "Thou shalt not take the name of thy God in vain" is thus explained by a gloss on Ex. 20:7: "Thou shalt not deem the Son of God to be a creature," so that it forbids an error against faith. Again, a gloss on the words of Deut. 5:11, "Thou shalt not take the name of ... thy God in vain," adds, i.e. "by giving the name of God to wood or stone," as though they forbade a false confession of faith, which, like error, is an act of unbelief. Now unbelief precedes superstition, as faith precedes religion. Therefore this precept should have preceded the first, whereby superstition is forbidden.

Obj. 2: Further, the name of God is taken for many purposes—for instance, those of praise, of working miracles, and generally speaking in conjunction with all we say or do, according to Col. 3:17, "All whatsoever you do in word or in work ... do ye in the name of the Lord." Therefore the precept forbidding the taking of God's name in vain seems to be more universal than the precept forbidding superstition, and thus should have preceded it.

Obj. 3: Further, a gloss on Ex. 20:7 expounds the precept, "Thou shalt not take the name of ... thy God in vain," namely, by swearing to nothing. Hence this precept would seem to forbid useless swearing, that is to say, swearing without judgment. But false swearing, which is without truth, and unjust swearing, which is without justice, are much more grievous. Therefore this precept should rather have forbidden them.

Obj. 4: Further, blasphemy or any word or deed that is an insult to God is much more grievous than perjury. Therefore blasphemy and other like sins should rather have been forbidden by this precept.

Obj. 5: Further, God's names are many. Therefore it should not have been said indefinitely: "Thou shalt not take the name of ... thy God in vain."

*On the contrary,* stands the authority of Scripture.

*I answer that,* In one who is being instructed in virtue it is necessary to remove obstacles to true religion before establishing him in true religion. Now a thing is opposed to true religion in two ways. First, by excess, when, to wit, that which belongs to religion is given to others than to whom it is due, and this pertains to superstition. Secondly, by lack, as it were, of reverence, when, to wit, God is contemned, and this pertains to the vice of irreligion, as stated above (Q. 97, in the preamble, and in the Article that follows). Now superstition hinders religion by preventing man from acknowledging God so as to worship Him: and when a man's mind is engrossed in some undue worship, he cannot at the same time give due worship to God, according to Isa. 28:20, "The bed is straitened, so that one must fall out," i.e. either the true God or a false god must fall out from man's heart, "and a short covering cannot cover both." On the other hand, irreligion hinders religion by preventing man from honoring God after he has acknowledged Him. Now one must first of all acknowledge God with a view to worship, before honoring Him we have acknowledged.

For this reason the precept forbidding superstition is placed before the second precept, which forbids perjury that pertains to irreligion.

Reply Obj. 1: These expositions are mystical. The literal explanation is that which is given Deut. 5:11: "Thou shalt not take the name of ... thy God in vain," namely, "by swearing on that which is not [*Vulg.: 'for he shall not be unpunished that taketh His name upon a vain thing']."

Reply Obj. 2: This precept does not forbid all taking of the name of God, but properly the taking of God's name in confirmation of a man's word by way of an oath, because men are wont to take God's name more frequently in this way. Nevertheless we may understand that in consequence all inordinate taking of the Divine name is forbidden by this precept: and it is in this sense that we are to take the explanation quoted in the First Objection.

Reply Obj. 3: To swear to nothing means to swear to that which is not. This pertains to false swearing, which is chiefly called perjury, as stated above (Q. 98, A. 1, ad 3). For when a man swears to that which is false, his swearing is vain in itself, since it is not supported by the truth. On the other hand, when a man swears without judgment, through levity, if he swear to the truth, there is no vanity on the part of the oath itself, but only on the part of the swearer.

Reply Obj. 4: Just as when we instruct a man in some science, we begin by putting before him certain general maxims, even so the Law, which forms man to virtue by instructing him in the precepts of the decalogue, which are the first of all precepts, gave expression, by prohibition or by command, to those things which are of most common occurrence in the course of human life. Hence the precepts of the decalogue include the prohibition of perjury, which is of more frequent occurrence than blasphemy, since man does not fall so often into the latter sin.

Reply Obj. 5: Reverence is due to the Divine names on the part of the thing signified, which is one, and not on the part of the signifying words, which are many. Hence it is expressed in the singular: "Thou shalt not take the name of ... thy God in vain": since it matters not in which of God's names perjury is committed.

FOURTH ARTICLE [II-II, Q. 122, Art. 4]

Whether the Third Precept of the Decalogue, Concerning the Hallowing of the Sabbath, Is Fittingly Expressed?

Objection 1: It seems that the third precept of the decalogue, concerning the hallowing of the Sabbath, is unfittingly expressed. For this, understood spiritually, is a general precept: since Bede in commenting on Luke 13:14, "The ruler of the synagogue being angry that He had healed on the Sabbath," says (Comment. iv): "The Law forbids, not to heal man on the Sabbath, but to do servile works," i.e. "to burden oneself with sin." Taken literally it is a ceremonial precept, for it is written (Ex. 31:13): "See that you keep My Sabbath: because it is a sign between Me and you in your generations." Now the precepts of the decalogue are both spiritual and moral. Therefore it is unfittingly placed among the precepts of the decalogue.

Obj. 2: Further, the ceremonial precepts of the Law contain "sacred things, sacrifices, sacraments and observances," as stated above (I-II, Q. 101, A. 4). Now sacred things comprised not only sacred days, but also sacred places and sacred vessels, and so on. Moreover, there were many sacred days other than the Sabbath. Therefore it was unfitting to omit all other ceremonial observances and to mention only that of the Sabbath.

Obj. 3: Further, whoever breaks a precept of

the decalogue, sins. But in the Old Law some who broke the observances of the Sabbath did not sin—for instance, those who circumcised their sons on the eighth day, and the priests who worked in the temple on the Sabbath. Also Elias (3 Kings 19), who journeyed for forty days unto the mount of God, Horeb, must have traveled on a Sabbath: the priests also who carried the ark of the Lord for seven days, as related in Josue 7, must be understood to have carried it on a Sabbath. Again it is written (Luke 13:15): "Doth not every one of you on the Sabbath day loose his ox or his ass ... and lead them to water?" Therefore it is unfittingly placed among the precepts of the decalogue.

Obj. 4: Further, the precepts of the decalogue have to be observed also under the New Law. Yet in the New Law this precept is not observed, neither in the point of the Sabbath day, nor as to the Lord's day, on which men cook their food, travel, fish, and do many like things. Therefore the precept of the observance of the Sabbath is unfittingly expressed.

*On the contrary,* stands the authority of Scripture.

*I answer that,* The obstacles to true religion being removed by the first and second precepts of the decalogue, as stated above (AA. 2, 3), it remained for the third precept to be given whereby man is established in true religion. Now it belongs to religion to give worship to God: and just as the Divine scriptures teach the interior worship under the guise of certain corporal similitudes, so is external worship given to God under the guise of sensible signs. And since for the most part man is induced to pay interior worship, consisting in prayer and devotion, by the interior prompting of the Holy Ghost, a precept of the Law as necessary respecting the exterior worship that consists in sensible signs. Now the precepts of the decalogue are, so to speak, first and common principles of the Law, and consequently the third precept of the decalogue describes the exterior worship of God as the sign of a universal boon that concerns all. This universal boon was the work of the Creation of the world, from which work God is stated to have rested on the seventh day: and sign of this we are commanded to keep holy seventh day—that is, to set it aside as a day to be given to God. Hence after the precept about the hallowing of the Sabbath the reason for it is given: "For in six days the Lord made heaven and earth ... and rested on the seventh day."

Reply Obj. 1: The precept about hallowing the Sabbath, understood literally, is partly moral and partly ceremonial. It is a moral precept in the point of commanding man to aside a certain time to be given to Divine things. For there is in man a natural inclination to set aside a certain time for each necessary thing, such as refreshment of the body, sleep, and so forth. Hence according to the dictate of reason, man sets aside a certain time for spiritual refreshment, by which man's mind is refreshed in God. And thus to have a certain time set aside for occupying oneself with Divine things is the matter of a moral precept. But, in so far as this precept specializes the time as a sign representing the Creation of the world, it is a ceremonial precept. Again, it is a ceremonial precept in its allegorical signification, as representative of Christ's rest in the tomb on the seventh day: also in its moral signification, as representing cessation from all sinful acts, and the mind's rest in God, in which sense, too, it is a general precept. Again, it is a ceremonial precept in its analogical signification, as foreshadowing the enjoyment of God in heaven. Hence the precept about hallowing the Sabbath is placed among the precepts of the decalogue, as a moral, but not as a ceremonial precept.

Reply Obj. 2: The other ceremonies of the Law are signs of certain particular Divine works: but the observance of the Sabbath is representative of a general boon, namely, the production of all creatures. Hence it was fitting that it should be placed among the general precepts of the decalogue, rather than any other ceremonial precept of the Law.

Reply Obj. 3: Two things are to be observed in the hallowing of the Sabbath. One of these is the end: and this is that man occupy himself with Divine things, and is signified in the words: "Remember that thou keep holy the Sabbath day." For in the Law those things are said to be holy which are applied to the Divine worship. The other thing is cessation from work, and is signified in the words (Ex. 20:11), "On the seventh day ... thou shalt do no work." The kind of work meant appears from Lev. 23:3, "You shall do no servile work on that day [*Vulg.: 'You shall do no work on that day']." Now servile work is so called from servitude: and servitude is threefold. One, whereby man is the servant of sin, according to John 8:34, "Whosoever committeth sin is the servant of sin," and in this sense all sinful acts are servile. Another servitude is whereby one man serves another. Now one man serves another not with his mind but with his body, as stated above (Q. 104, AA. 5, 6, ad 1). Wherefore in this respect those works are called servile whereby one man serves another. The third is the servitude of God; and in this way the work of worship, which pertains to the service of God, may be called a servile work. In this sense servile work is not forbidden on the Sabbath day, because that would be contrary to the end of the Sabbath observance: since man abstains from other works on the Sabbath day in order that he may occupy himself with works connected with God's service. For this reason, according to John 7:23, "a man [*Vulg.: 'If a man,' etc.] receives circumcision on the Sabbath day, that the law of Moses may not be broken": and for this reason too we read (Matt. 12:5), that "on the Sabbath days the priests in the temple break the Sabbath," i.e. do corporal works on the Sabbath, "and are without blame." Accordingly, the priests in carrying the ark on the Sabbath did not break the precept of the Sabbath observance. In like manner it is not contrary to the observance of the Sabbath to exercise any spiritual act, such as teaching by word or writing. Wherefore a gloss on Num 28 says that "smiths and like craftsmen rest on the Sabbath day, but the reader or teacher of the Divine law does not cease from his work. Yet he profanes not the Sabbath, even as the priests in the temple break the Sabbath, and are without blame." On the other hand, those works that are called servile in the first or second way are contrary to the observance of the Sabbath, in so far as they hinder man from applying himself to Divine things. And since man is hindered from applying himself to Divine things rather by sinful than by lawful albeit corporal works, it follows that to sin on a feast day is more against this precept than to do some other but lawful bodily work. Hence Augustine says (De decem chord. iii): "It would be better if the Jew did some useful work on his farm than spent his time seditiously in the theatre: and their womenfolk would do better to be making linen on the Sabbath than to be dancing lewdly all day in their feasts of the new moon." It is not, however, against this precept to sin venially on the Sabbath, because venial sin does not destroy holiness.

Again, corporal works, not pertaining to the spiritual worship of God, are said to be servile in so far as they belong properly to servants; while they are not said to be servile, in so far as they are common to those who serve and those who are free. Moreover, everyone, be he servant or free, is bound to provide necessaries both for himself and for his neighbor, chiefly in respect of things pertaining to the well-being of the body, according to Prov. 24:11, "Deliver them that are led to death": secondarily as regards avoiding damage to one's property, according to Deut. 22:1, "Thou shalt not pass by if thou seest thy brother's ox or his sheep go astray, but thou shalt bring them back to thy brother." Hence a corporal work pertaining to the preservation of one's own bodily well-being does not profane the Sabbath: for it is not against the observance of the Sabbath to eat and do such things as preserve the health of the body. For this reason the Machabees did not profane the Sabbath when they fought in self-defense on the Sabbath day (1 Macc. 2), nor Elias when he fled from the face of Jezabel on the Sabbath. For this same reason our Lord (Matt. 12:3) excused His disciples for plucking the ears of corn on account of the need which they suffered. In like manner a bodily work that is directed to the bodily well-being of another is not contrary to the observance of the Sabbath: wherefore it is written (John 7:23): "Are you angry at Me because I have healed the whole man on the Sabbath day?" And again, a bodily work that is done to avoid an imminent damage to some external thing does not profane the Sabbath, wherefore our Lord says (Matt. 12:11): "What man shall there be among you, that hath one sheep, and if the same fall into a pit on the Sabbath day, will he not take hold on it and lift it up?"

Reply Obj. 4: In the New Law the observance of the Lord's day took the place of the observance of the Sabbath, not by virtue of the precept but by the institution of the Church and the custom of Christian people. For this observance is not figurative, as was the observance of the Sabbath in the Old Law. Hence the prohibition to work on the Lord's day is not so strict as on the Sabbath: and certain works are permitted on the Lord's day which were forbidden on the Sabbath, such as the cooking of food and so forth. And again in the New Law, dispensation is more easily granted than in the Old, in the matter of certain forbidden works, on account of their necessity, because the figure pertains to the protestation of truth, which it is unlawful to omit even in small things; while works, considered in themselves, are changeable in point of place and time.

FIFTH ARTICLE [II-II, Q. 122, Art. 5]

Whether the Fourth Precept, About Honoring One's Parents, Is Fittingly Expressed?

Objection 1: It seems that the fourth precept, about honoring one's parents, is unfittingly expressed. For this is the precept pertaining to piety. Now, just as piety is a part of justice, so are observance, gratitude, and others of which we have spoken (QQ. 101, 102, seq.). Therefore it seems that there should not have been given a special precept of piety, as none is given regarding the others.

Obj. 2: Further, piety pays worship not only to one's parents, but also to one's country, and also to other blood kindred, and to the well-wishers of our country, as stated above (Q. 101, AA. 1, 2). Therefore it was unfitting for this precept to mention only the honoring of one's father and mother.

Obj. 3: Further, we owe our parents not merely honor but also support. Therefore the mere honoring of one's parents is unfittingly prescribed.

Obj. 4: Further, sometimes those who honor their parents die young, and on the contrary those who honor them not live a long time. Therefore it was unfitting to supplement this precept with the promise, "That thou mayest be long-lived upon earth."

*On the contrary,* stands the authority of Scripture.

*I answer that,* The precepts of the decalogue are directed to the love of God and of our neighbor. Now to our parents, of all our neighbors, we are under the greatest obligation. Hence, immediately after the precepts directing us to God, a place is given to the precept directing us to our parents, who are the particular principle of our being, just as God is the universal principle: so that this precept has a certain affinity to the precepts of the First Table.

Reply Obj. 1: As stated above (Q. 101, A. 2), piety

directs us to pay the debt due to our parents, a debt which is common to all. Hence, since the precepts of the decalogue are general precepts, they ought to contain some reference to piety rather than to the other parts of justice, which regard some special debt.

Reply Obj. 2: The debt to one's parents precedes the debt to one's kindred and country since it is because we are born of our parents that our kindred and country belong to us. Hence, since the precepts of the decalogue are the first precepts of the Law, they direct man to his parents rather than to his country and other kindred. Nevertheless this precept of honoring our parents is understood to command whatever concerns the payment of debt to any person, as secondary matter included in the principal matter.

Reply Obj. 3: Reverential honor is due to one's parents as such, whereas support and so forth are due to them accidentally, for instance, because they are in want, in slavery, or the like, as stated above (Q. 101, A. 2). And since that which belongs to a thing by nature precedes that which is accidental, it follows that among the first precepts of the Law, which are the precepts of the decalogue, there is a special precept of honoring our parents: and this honor, as a kind of principle, is understood to comprise support and whatever else is due to our parents.

Reply Obj. 4: A long life is promised to those who honor their parents not only as to the life to come, but also as to the present life, according to the saying of the Apostle (1 Tim. 4:8): "Piety [Douay: 'godliness'] is profitable to all things, having promise of the life that now is and of that which is to come." And with reason. Because the man who is grateful for a favor deserves, with a certain congruity, that the favor should be continued to him, and he who is ungrateful for a favor deserves to lose it. Now we owe the favor of bodily life to our parents after God: wherefore he that honors his parents deserves the prolongation of his life, because he is grateful for that favor: while he that honors not his parents deserves to be deprived of life because he is ungrateful for the favor. However, present goods or evils are not the subject of merit or demerit except in so far as they are directed to a future reward, as stated above (I-II, Q. 114, A. 12). Wherefore sometimes in accordance with the hidden design of the Divine judgments, which regard chiefly the future reward, some, who are dutiful to their parents, are sooner deprived of life, while others, who are undutiful to their parents, live longer.

SIXTH ARTICLE [II-II, Q. 122, Art. 6]

Whether the Other Six Precepts of the Decalogue Are Fittingly Expressed?

Objection 1: It seems that the other six precepts of the decalogue are unfittingly expressed. For it is not sufficient for salvation that one refrain from injuring one's neighbor; but it is required that one pay one's debts, according to Rom. 13:7, "Render ... to all men their dues." Now the last six precepts merely forbid one to injure one's neighbor. Therefore these precepts are unfittingly expressed.

Obj. 2: Further, these precepts forbid murder, adultery, stealing and bearing false witness. But many other injuries can be inflicted on one's neighbor, as appears from those which have been specified above (QQ. 72, seq.). Therefore it seems that the aforesaid precepts are unfittingly expressed.

Obj. 3: Further, concupiscence may be taken in two ways. First as denoting an act of the will, as in Wis. 6:21, "The desire ( *concupiscentia* ) of wisdom bringeth to the everlasting kingdom": secondly, as denoting an act of the sensuality, as in James 4:1, "From whence are wars and contentions among you? Are they not ... from your concupiscences which war in your members?" Now the concupiscence of the sensuality is not forbidden by a precept of the decalogue, otherwise first movements would be mortal sins, as they would be against a precept of the decalogue. Nor is the concupiscence of the will forbidden, since it is included in every sin. Therefore it is unfitting for the precepts of the decalogue to include some that forbid concupiscence.

Obj. 4: Further, murder is a more grievous sin than adultery or theft. But there is no precept forbidding the desire of murder. Therefore neither was it fitting to have precepts forbidding the desire of theft and of adultery.

*On the contrary,* stands the authority of Scripture.

*I answer that,* Just as by the parts of justice a man pays that which is due to certain definite persons, to whom he is bound for some special reason, so too by justice properly so called he pays that which is due to all in general. Hence, after the three precepts pertaining to religion, whereby man pays what is due God, and after the fourth precept pertaining to piety, whereby he pays what is due to his parents—which duty includes the paying of all that is due for any special reason—it was necessary in due sequence to give certain precepts pertaining to justice properly so called, which pays to all indifferently what is due to them.

Reply Obj. 1: Man is bound towards all persons in general to inflict injury on no one: hence the negative precepts, which forbid the doing of those injuries that can be inflicted on one's neighbor, had to be given a place, as general precepts, among the precepts of the decalogue. On the other hand, the duties we owe to our neighbor are paid in different ways to different people: hence it did not behoove to include affirmative precepts about those duties among the precepts of the decalogue.

Reply Obj. 2: All other injuries that are inflicted on our neighbor are reducible to those that are forbidden by these precepts, as taking precedence of others in point of generality and importance. For all injuries that are inflicted on the person of our neighbor are understood to be forbidden under the head of murder as being the principal of all. Those that are inflicted on a person connected with one's neighbor, especially by way of lust, are understood to be forbidden together with adultery: those that come under the head of damage done to property are understood to be forbidden together with theft: and those that are comprised under speech, such as detractions, insults, and so forth, are understood to be forbidden together with the bearing of false witness, which is more directly opposed to justice.

Reply Obj. 3: The precepts forbidding concupiscence do not include the prohibition of first movements of concupiscence, that do not go farther than the bounds of sensuality. The direct object of their prohibition is the consent of the will, which is directed to deed or pleasure.

Reply Obj. 4: Murder in itself is an object not of concupiscence but of horror, since it has not in itself the aspect of good. On the other hand, adultery has the aspect of a certain kind of good, i.e. of something pleasurable, and theft has an aspect of good, i.e. of something useful: and good of its very nature has the aspect of something concupiscible. Hence the concupiscence of theft and adultery had to be forbidden by special precepts, but not the concupiscence of murder.

TREATISE ON FORTITUDE AND TEMPERANCE (QQ. 123-170)

# QUESTION 123

OF FORTITUDE (In Twelve Articles)

After considering justice we must in due sequence consider fortitude. We must (1) consider the virtue itself of fortitude; (2) its parts; (3) the gift corresponding thereto; (4) the precepts that pertain to it.

Concerning fortitude three things have to be considered: (1) Fortitude itself; (2) its principal act, viz. martyrdom; (3) the vices opposed to fortitude.

Under the first head there are twelve points of inquiry:

(1) Whether fortitude is a virtue?

(2) Whether it is a special virtue?

(3) Whether fortitude is only about fear and daring?

(4) Whether it is only about fear of death?

(5) Whether it is only in warlike matters?

(6) Whether endurance is its chief act?

(7) Whether its action is directed to its own good?

(8) Whether it takes pleasure in its own action?

(9) Whether fortitude deals chiefly with sudden occurrences?

(10) Whether it makes use of anger in its action?

(11) Whether it is a cardinal virtue?

(12) Of its comparison with the other cardinal virtues.

FIRST ARTICLE [II-II, Q. 123, Art. 1]

Whether Fortitude Is a Virtue?

Objection 1: It seems that fortitude is not a virtue. For the Apostle says (2 Cor. 12:9): "Virtue is perfected in infirmity." But fortitude is contrary to infirmity. Therefore fortitude is not a virtue.

Obj. 2: Further, if it is a virtue, it is either theological, intellectual, or moral. Now fortitude is not contained among the theological virtues, nor among the intellectual virtues, as may be gathered from what we have said above (I-II, Q. 57, A. 2; Q. 62, A. 3). Neither, apparently, is it contained among the moral virtues, since according to the Philosopher (Ethic. iii, 7, 8): "Some seem to be brave through ignorance; or through experience, as soldiers," both of which cases seem to pertain to act rather than to moral virtue, "and some are called brave on account of certain passions"; for instance, on account of fear of threats, or of dishonor, or again on account of sorrow, anger, or hope. But moral virtue does not act from passion but from choice, as stated above (I-II, Q. 55, A. 4). Therefore fortitude is not a virtue.

Obj. 3: Further, human virtue resides chiefly in the soul, since it is a "good quality of the mind," as stated above (Ethic. iii, 7, 8). But fortitude, seemingly, resides in the body, or at least results from the temperament of the body. Therefore it seems that fortitude is not a virtue.

*On the contrary,* Augustine (De Morib. Eccl. xv, xxi, xxii) numbers fortitude among the virtues.

*I answer that,* According to the Philosopher (Ethic. ii, 6) "virtue is that which makes its possessor good, and renders his work good." Hence human virtue, of which we are speaking now, is that which makes a man good, and renders his work good. Now man's good is to be in accordance with reason, according to Dionysius (Div. Nom. iv, 22). Wherefore it belongs to human virtue to make man good, to make his work accord with reason. This happens in three ways: first, by rectifying reason itself, and this is done by the intellectual virtues; secondly, by establishing the rectitude of reason in human affairs, and this belongs to justice; thirdly, by removing the obstacles to the establishment of this rectitude in human affairs. Now the human will is hindered in two ways from following the rectitude of reason. First, through being drawn by some object of pleasure to something other than what the rectitude of reason requires; and this obstacle is removed by the virtue of temperance. Secondly, through the will being disinclined to follow that which is in accordance with reason, on account of some difficulty that presents itself. In order to remove this obstacle fortitude of the mind is requisite, whereby to resist the aforesaid difficulty even as a man, by fortitude of body, overcomes and removes bodily obstacles.

Hence it is evident that fortitude is a virtue, in so far as it conforms man to reason.

Reply Obj. 1: The virtue of the soul is perfected, not in the infirmity of the soul, but in the infirmity of the body, of which the Apostle was speaking. Now it belongs to fortitude of the mind to bear bravely with infirmities of the flesh, and this belongs to the virtue of patience or fortitude, as also to acknowledge one's own infirmity, and this belongs to the perfection that is called humility.

Reply Obj. 2: Sometimes a person performs the exterior act of a virtue without having the virtue, and from some other cause than virtue. Hence the Philosopher (Ethic. iii, 8) mentions five ways in which people are said to be brave by way of resemblance, through performing acts of fortitude without having the virtue. This may be done in three ways. First, because they tend to that which is difficult as though it were not difficult: and this again happens in three ways, for sometimes this is owing to ignorance, through not perceiving the greatness of the danger; sometimes it is owing to the fact that one is hopeful of overcoming dangers—when, for instance, one has often experienced escape from danger; and sometimes this is owing to a certain science and art, as in the case of soldiers who, through skill and practice in the use of arms, think little of the dangers of battle, as they reckon themselves capable of defending themselves against them; thus Vegetius says (De Re Milit. i), "No man fears to do what he is confident of having learned to do well." Secondly, a man performs an act of fortitude without having the virtue, through the impulse of a passion, whether of sorrow that he wishes to cast off, or again of anger. Thirdly, through choice, not indeed of a due end, but of some temporal advantage to be obtained, such as honor, pleasure, or gain, or of some disadvantage to be avoided, such as blame, pain, or loss.

Reply Obj. 3: The fortitude of the soul which is reckoned a virtue, as explained in the Reply to the First Objection, is so called from its likeness to fortitude of the body. Nor is it inconsistent with the notion of virtue, that a man should have a natural inclination to virtue by reason of his natural temperament, as stated above (I-II, Q. 63, A. 1).

SECOND ARTICLE [II-II, Q. 123, Art. 2]

Whether Fortitude Is a Special Virtue?

Objection 1: It seems that fortitude is not a special virtue. For it is written (Wis. 7:7): "She teacheth temperance, and prudence, and justice, and fortitude," where the text has "virtue" for "fortitude." Since then the term "virtue" is common to all virtues, it seems that fortitude is a general virtue.

Obj. 2: Further, Ambrose says (De Offic. i): "Fortitude is not lacking in courage, for alone she defends the honor of the virtues and guards their behests. She it is that wages an inexorable war on all vice, undeterred by toil, brave in face of dangers, steeled against pleasures, unyielding to lusts, avoiding covetousness as a deformity that weakens virtue"; and he says the same further on in connection with other vices. Now this cannot apply to any special virtue. Therefore fortitude is not a special virtue.

Obj. 3: Further, fortitude would seem to derive its name from firmness. But it belongs to every virtue to stand firm, as stated in *Ethic.* ii. Therefore fortitude is a general virtue.

*On the contrary,* Gregory (Moral. xxii) numbers it among the other virtues.

*I answer that,* As stated above (I-II, Q. 61, AA. 3, 4), the term "fortitude" can be taken in two ways. First, as simply denoting a certain firmness of mind, and in this sense it is a general virtue, or rather a condition of every virtue, since as the Philosopher states (Ethic. ii), it is requisite for every virtue to act firmly and immovably. Secondly, fortitude may be taken to denote firmness only in bearing and withstanding those things wherein it is most difficult to be firm, namely in certain grave dangers. Therefore Tully says (Rhet. ii), that "fortitude is deliberate facing of dangers and bearing of toils." In this sense fortitude is reckoned a special virtue, because it has a special matter.

Reply Obj. 1: According to the Philosopher (De Coelo i, 116) the word virtue refers to the extreme limit of a power. Now a natural power is, in one sense, the power of resisting corruptions, and in another sense is a principle of action, as stated in *Metaph.* v, 17. And since this latter meaning is the more common, the term "virtue," as denoting the extreme limit of such a power, is a common term, for virtue taken in a general sense is nothing else than a habit whereby one acts well. But as denoting the extreme limit of power in the first sense, which sense is more specific, it is applied to a special virtue, namely fortitude, to which it belongs to stand firm against all kinds of assaults.

Reply Obj. 2: Ambrose takes fortitude in a broad sense, as denoting firmness of mind in face of assaults of all kinds. Nevertheless even as a special virtue with a determinate matter, it helps to resist the assaults of all vices. For he that can stand firm in things that are most difficult to bear, is prepared, in consequence, to resist those which are less difficult.

Reply Obj. 3: This objection takes fortitude in the first sense.

THIRD ARTICLE [II-II, Q. 123, Art. 3]

Whether Fortitude Is About Fear and Daring?

Objection 1: It seems that fortitude is not about fear and daring. For Gregory says (Moral. vii): "The fortitude of the just man is to overcome the flesh, to withstand self-indulgence, to quench the lusts of the present life." Therefore fortitude seems to be about pleasures rather than about fear and daring.

Obj. 2: Further, Tully says (De Invent. Rhet. ii), that it belongs to fortitude to face dangers and to bear toil. But this seemingly has nothing to do with the passions of fear and daring, but rather with a man's toilsome deeds and external dangers. Therefore fortitude is not about fear and daring.

Obj. 3: Further, not only daring, but also hope, is opposed to fear, as stated above (I-II, Q. 45, A. 1, ad 2) in the treatise on passions. Therefore fortitude should not be about daring any more than about hope.

*On the contrary,* The Philosopher says (Ethic. ii, 7; iii, 9) that fortitude is about fear and daring.

*I answer that,* As stated above (A. 1), it belongs to the virtue of fortitude to remove any obstacle that withdraws the will from following the reason. Now to be withdrawn from something difficult belongs to the notion of fear, which denotes withdrawal from an evil that entails difficulty, as stated above (I-II, Q. 42, AA. 3, 5) in the treatise on passions. Hence fortitude is chiefly about fear of difficult things, which can withdraw the will from following the reason. And it behooves one not only firmly to bear the assault of these difficulties by restraining fear, but also moderately to withstand them, when, to wit, it is necessary to dispel them altogether in order to free oneself therefrom for the future, which seems to come under the notion of daring. Therefore fortitude is about fear and daring, as curbing fear and moderating daring.

Reply Obj. 1: Gregory is speaking then of the fortitude of the just man, as to its common relation to all virtues. Hence he first of all mentions matters pertaining to temperance, as in the words quoted, and then adds that which pertains properly to fortitude as a special virtue, by saying: "To love the trials of this life for the sake of an eternal reward."

Reply Obj. 2: Dangers and toils do not withdraw the will from the course of reason, except in so far as they are an object of fear. Hence fortitude needs to be immediately about fear and daring, but mediately about dangers and toils, these being the objects of those passions.

Reply Obj. 3: Hope is opposed to fear on the part of the object, for hope is of good, fear of evil: whereas daring is about the same object, and is opposed to fear by way of approach and withdrawal, as stated above (I-II, Q. 45, A. 1). And since fortitude properly regards those temporal evils that withdraw one from virtue, as appears from Tully's definition quoted in the Second Objection, it follows that fortitude properly is about fear and daring and not about hope, except in so far as it is connected with daring, as stated above (I-II, Q. 45, A. 2).

FOURTH ARTICLE [II-II, Q. 123, Art. 4]

Whether Fortitude Is Only About Dangers of Death?

Objection 1: It seems that fortitude is not only about dangers of death. For Augustine says (De Morib. Eccl. xv) that "fortitude is love bearing all things readily for the sake of the object beloved": and (Music. vi) he says that fortitude is "the love which dreads no hardship, not even death." Therefore fortitude is not only about danger of death, but also about other afflictions.

Obj. 2: Further, all the passions of the soul need to be reduced to a mean by some virtue. Now there is no other virtue reducing fears to a mean. Therefore fortitude is not only about fear of death, but also about other fears.

Obj. 3: Further, no virtue is about extremes. But fear of death is about an extreme, since it is the greatest of fears, as stated in *Ethic.* iii. Therefore the virtue of fortitude is not about fear of death.

*On the contrary,* Andronicus says that "fortitude is a virtue of the irascible faculty that is not easily deterred by the fear of death."

*I answer that,* As stated above (A. 3), it belongs to the virtue of fortitude to guard the will against being withdrawn from the good of reason through fear of bodily evil. Now it behooves one to hold firmly the good of reason against every evil whatsoever, since no bodily good is equivalent to the good of the reason. Hence fortitude of soul must be that which binds the will firmly to the good of reason in face of the greatest evils: because he that stands firm against great things, will in consequence stand firm against less things, but not conversely. Moreover it belongs to the notion of virtue that it should regard something extreme: and the most fearful of all bodily evils is death, since it does away all bodily goods. Wherefore Augustine says (De Morib. Eccl. xxii) that "the soul is shaken by its fellow body, with fear of toil and pain, lest the body be stricken and harassed with fear of death lest it be done away and destroyed." Therefore the virtue of fortitude is about the fear of dangers of death.

Reply Obj. 1: Fortitude behaves well in bearing all manner of adversity: yet a man is not reckoned brave simply through bearing any kind of adversity, but only through bearing well even the greatest evils; while through bearing others he is said to be brave in a restricted sense.

Reply Obj. 2: Since fear is born of love, any virtue that moderates the love of certain goods must in consequence moderate the fear of contrary evils: thus liberality, which moderates the love of money, as a consequence, moderates the fear of losing it, and the same is the case with temperance and other virtues. But to love one's own life is natural: and hence the necessity of a special virtue modifying the fear of death.

Reply Obj. 3: In virtues the extreme consists in exceeding right reason: wherefore to undergo the greatest dangers in accordance with reason is not contrary to virtue.

FIFTH ARTICLE [II-II, Q. 123, Art. 5]

Whether Fortitude Is Properly About Dangers of Death in Battle?

Objection 1: It seems that fortitude is not properly about dangers of death in battle. For martyrs above all are commended for their fortitude. But martyrs are not commended in connection with battle. Therefore fortitude is not properly about dangers of death in battle.

Obj. 2: Further, Ambrose says (De Offic. i) that "fortitude is applicable both to warlike and to civil matters": and Tully (De Offic. i), under the heading, "That it pertains to fortitude to excel in battle rather than in civil life," says: "Although not a few think that the business of war is of greater importance than the affairs of civil life, this opinion must be qualified: and if we wish to judge the matter truly, there are many things in civil life that are more important and more glorious than those connected with war." Now greater fortitude is about greater things. Therefore fortitude is not properly concerned with death in battle.

Obj. 3: Further, war is directed to the preservation of a country's temporal peace: for Augustine says (De Civ. Dei xix) that "wars are waged in order to insure peace." Now it does not seem that one ought to expose oneself to the danger of death for the temporal peace of one's country, since this same peace is the occasion of much license in morals. Therefore it seems that the virtue of fortitude is not about the danger of death in battle.

*On the contrary,* The Philosopher says (Ethic. iii) that fortitude is chiefly about death in battle.

*I answer that,* As stated above (A. 4), fortitude strengthens a man's mind against the greatest danger, which is that of death. Now fortitude is a virtue; and it is essential to virtue ever to tend to good; wherefore it is in order to pursue some good that man does not fly from the danger of death. But the dangers of death arising out of sickness, storms at sea, attacks from robbers, and the like, do not seem to come on a man through his pursuing some good. On the other hand, the dangers of death which occur in battle come to man directly on account of some good, because, to wit, he is defending the common good by a just fight. Now a just fight is of two kinds. First, there is the general combat, for instance, of those who fight in battle; secondly, there is the private combat, as when a judge or even private individual does not refrain from giving a just judgment through fear of the impending sword, or any other danger though it threaten death. Hence it belongs to fortitude to strengthen the mind against dangers of death, not only such as arise in a general battle, but also such as occur in singular combat, which may be called by the general name of battle. Accordingly it must be granted that fortitude is properly about dangers of death occurring in battle.

Moreover, a brave man behaves well in face of danger of any other kind of death; especially since man may be in danger of any kind of death on account of virtue: thus may a man not fail to attend on a sick friend through fear of deadly infection, or not refuse to undertake a journey with some godly object in view through fear of shipwreck or robbers.

Reply Obj. 1: Martyrs face the fight that is waged against their own person, and this for the sake of the sovereign good which is God; wherefore their fortitude is praised above all. Nor is it outside the genus of fortitude that regards warlike actions, for which reason they are said to have been valiant in battle. [*Office of Martyrs, ex. Heb. xi. 34.]

Reply Obj. 2: Personal and civil business is differentiated from the business of war that regards general wars. However, personal and civil affairs admit of dangers of death arising out of certain conflicts which are private wars, and so with regard to these also there may be fortitude properly so called.

Reply Obj. 3: The peace of the state is good in itself, nor does it become evil because certain persons make evil use of it. For there are many others who make good use of it; and many evils prevented by it, such as murders and sacrileges, are much greater than those which are occasioned by it, and which belong chiefly to the sins of the flesh.

SIXTH ARTICLE [II-II, Q. 123, Art. 6]

Whether Endurance Is the Chief Act of Fortitude?

Objection 1: It seems that endurance is not the chief act of fortitude. For virtue "is about the difficult and the good" (Ethic. ii, 3). Now it is more difficult to attack than to endure. Therefore endurance is not the chief act of fortitude.

Obj. 2: Further, to be able to act on another seems to argue greater power than not to be changed by another. Now to attack is to act on another, and to endure is to persevere unchangeably. Since then fortitude denotes perfection of power, it seems that it belongs to fortitude to attack rather than to endure.

Obj. 3: Further, one contrary is more distant from the other than its mere negation. Now to endure is merely not to fear, whereas to attack denotes a movement contrary to that of fear, since it implies pursuit. Since then fortitude above all withdraws the mind from fear, it seems that it regards attack rather than endurance.

*On the contrary,* The Philosopher says (Ethic. iii, 9) that "certain persons are" said to be brave chiefly because they endure affliction.

*I answer that,* As stated above (A. 3), and according to the Philosopher (Ethic. iii, 9), "fortitude is more concerned to allay fear, than to moderate daring." For it is more difficult to allay fear than to moderate daring, since the danger which is the object of daring and fear, tends by its very nature to check daring, but to increase fear. Now to attack belongs to fortitude in so far as the latter moderates daring, whereas to endure follows the repression of fear. Therefore the principal act of fortitude is endurance, that is to stand immovable in the midst of dangers rather than to attack them.

Reply Obj. 1: Endurance is more difficult than aggression, for three reasons. First, because endurance seemingly implies that one is being attacked by a stronger person, whereas aggression denotes that one is attacking as though one were the stronger party; and it is more difficult to contend with a stronger than with a weaker. Secondly, because he that endures already feels the presence of danger, whereas the aggressor looks upon danger as something to come; and it is more difficult to be unmoved by the present than by the future. Thirdly, because endurance implies length of time, whereas aggression is consistent with sudden movements; and it is more difficult to remain unmoved for a long time, than to be moved suddenly to something arduous. Hence the Philosopher says (Ethic. iii, 8) that "some hurry to meet danger, yet fly when the danger is present; this is not the behavior of a brave man."

Reply Obj. 2: Endurance denotes indeed a passion of the body, but an action of the soul cleaving most resolutely ( *fortissime* ) to good, the result being that it does not yield to the threatening passion of the body. Now virtue concerns the soul rather than the body.

Reply Obj. 3: He that endures fears not, though he is confronted with the cause of fear, whereas this cause is not present to the aggressor.

SEVENTH ARTICLE [II-II, Q. 123, Art. 7]

Whether the Brave Man Acts for the Sake of the Good of His Habit?

Objection 1: It seems that the brave man does not act for the sake of the good of his habit. For in matters of action the end, though first in intention, is last in execution. Now the act of fortitude, in the order of execution, follows the habit of fortitude. Therefore it is impossible for the brave man to act for the sake of the good of his habit.

Obj. 2: Further, Augustine says (De Trin. xiii): "We love virtues for the sake of happiness, and yet some make bold to counsel us to be virtuous," namely by saying that we should desire virtue for its own sake, "without loving happiness. If they succeed in their endeavor, we shall surely cease to love virtue itself, since we shall no longer love that for the sake of which alone we love virtue." But fortitude is a virtue. Therefore the act of fortitude is directed not to fortitude but to happiness.

Obj. 3: Further, Augustine says (De Morib. Eccl. xv) that "fortitude is love ready to bear all things for God's sake." Now God is not the habit of fortitude, but something better, since the end must needs be better than what is directed to the end. Therefore the brave man does not act for the sake of the good of his habit.

*On the contrary,* The Philosopher says (Ethic. iii, 7) that "to the brave man fortitude itself is a good": and such is his end.

*I answer that,* An end is twofold: proximate and ultimate. Now the proximate end of every agent is to introduce a likeness of that agent's form into something else: thus the end of fire in heating is to introduce the likeness of its heat into some passive matter, and the end of the builder is to introduce into matter the likeness of his art. Whatever good ensues from this, if it be intended, may be called the remote end of the agent. Now just as in things made, external matter is fashioned by art, so in things done, human deeds are fashioned by prudence. Accordingly we must conclude that the brave man intends as his proximate end to reproduce in action a likeness of his habit, for he intends to act in accordance with his habit: but his remote end is happiness or God.

This suffices for the Replies to the Objections: for the First Objection proceeds as though the very essence of a habit were its end, instead of the likeness of the habit in act, as stated. The other two objections consider the ultimate end.

EIGHTH ARTICLE [II-II, Q. 123, Art. 8]

Whether the Brave Man Delights in His Act?

Objection 1: It seems that the brave man delights in his act. For "delight is the unhindered action of a connatural habit" (Ethic. x, 4, 6, 8). Now the brave deed proceeds from a habit which acts after the manner of nature. Therefore the brave man takes pleasure in his act.

Obj. 2: Further, Ambrose, commenting on Gal. 5:22, "But the fruit of the Spirit is charity, joy, peace," says that deeds of virtue are called "fruits because they refresh man's mind with a holy and pure delight." Now the brave man performs acts of virtue. Therefore he takes pleasure in his act.

Obj. 3: Further, the weaker is overcome by the stronger. Now the brave man has a stronger love for the good of virtue than for his own body, which he exposes to the danger of death. Therefore the delight in the good of virtue banishes the pain of the body; and consequently the brave man does all things with pleasure.

*On the contrary,* The Philosopher says (Ethic. iii, 9) that "the brave man seems to have no delight in his act."

*I answer that,* As stated above (I-II, Q. 31, AA. 3, 4, 5) where we were treating of the passions, pleasure is twofold; one is bodily, resulting from bodily contact, the other is spiritual, resulting from an apprehension of the soul. It is the latter which properly results from deeds of virtue, since in them we consider the good of reason. Now the principal act of fortitude is to endure, not only certain things that are unpleasant as apprehended by the soul—for instance, the loss of bodily life, which the virtuous man loves not only as a natural good, but also as being necessary for acts of virtue, and things connected with them—but also to endure things unpleasant in respect of bodily contact, such as wounds and blows. Hence the brave man, on one side, has something that affords him delight, namely as regards spiritual pleasure, in the act itself of virtue and the end thereof: while, on the other hand, he has cause for both spiritual sorrow, in the thought of losing his life, and for bodily pain. Hence we read (2 Macc. 6:30) that Eleazar said: "I suffer grievous pains in body: but in soul am well content to suffer these things because I fear Thee."

Now the sensible pain of the body makes one insensible to the spiritual delight of virtue, without the copious assistance of God's grace, which has more strength to raise the soul to the Divine things in which it delights, than bodily pains have to afflict it. Thus the Blessed Tiburtius, while walking barefoot on the burning coal, said that he felt as though he were walking on roses.

Yet the virtue of fortitude prevents the reason from being entirely overcome by bodily pain. And the delight of virtue overcomes spiritual sorrow, inasmuch as a man prefers the good of virtue to the life of the body and to whatever appertains thereto. Hence the Philosopher says (Ethic. ii, 3; iii, 9) that "it is not necessary for a brave man to delight so as to perceive his delight, but it suffices for him not to be sad."

Reply Obj. 1: The vehemence of the action or passion of one power hinders the action of another power: wherefore the pain in his senses hinders the mind of the brave man from feeling delight in its proper operation.

Reply Obj. 2: Deeds of virtue are delightful chiefly on account of their end; yet they can be painful by their nature, and this is principally the case with fortitude. Hence the Philosopher says (Ethic. iii, 9) that "to perform deeds with pleasure does not happen in all virtues, except in so far as one attains the end."

Reply Obj. 3: In the brave man spiritual sorrow is overcome by the delight of virtue. Yet since bodily pain is more sensible, and the sensitive apprehension is more in evidence to man, it follows that spiritual pleasure in the end of virtue fades away, so to speak, in the presence of great bodily pain.

NINTH ARTICLE [II-II, Q. 123, Art. 9]

Whether Fortitude Deals Chiefly with Sudden Occurrences?

Objection 1: It seems that fortitude does not deal chiefly with sudden occurrences. For it would seem that things occur suddenly when they are unforeseen. But Tully says (De Invent. Rhet. ii) that "fortitude is the deliberate facing of danger, and bearing of toil." Therefore fortitude does not deal chiefly with sudden happenings.

Obj. 2: Further, Ambrose says (De Offic. i): "The brave man is not unmindful of what may be likely to happen; he takes measures beforehand, and looks out as from the conning-tower of his mind, so as to encounter the future by his forethought, lest he should say afterwards: This befell me because I did not think it could possibly happen." But it is not possible to be prepared for the future in the case of sudden occurrences. Therefore the operation of fortitude is not concerned with sudden happenings.

Obj. 3: Further, the Philosopher says (Ethic. iii, 8) that the "brave man is of good hope." But hope looks forward to the future, which is inconsistent with sudden occurrences. Therefore the operation of fortitude is not concerned with sudden happenings.

*On the contrary,* The Philosopher says (Ethic. iii, 8) that "fortitude is chiefly about sudden dangers of death."

*I answer that,* Two things must be considered in the operation of fortitude. One is in regard to its choice: and thus fortitude is not about sudden occurrences: because the brave man chooses to think beforehand of the dangers that may arise, in order to be able to withstand them, or to bear them more easily: since according to Gregory (Hom. xxv in Evang.), "the blow that is foreseen strikes with less force, and we are able more easily to bear earthly wrongs, if we are forearmed with the shield of foreknowledge." The other thing to be considered in the operation of fortitude regards the display of the virtuous habit: and in this way fortitude is chiefly about sudden occurrences, because according to the Philosopher (Ethic. iii, 8) the habit of fortitude is displayed chiefly in sudden dangers: since a habit works by way of nature. Wherefore if a person without forethought does that which pertains to virtue, when necessity urges on account of some sudden danger, this is a very strong proof that habitual fortitude is firmly seated in his mind.

Yet is it possible for a person even without the habit of fortitude, to prepare his mind against danger by long forethought: in the same way as a brave man prepares himself when necessary. This suffices for the Replies to the Objections.

TENTH ARTICLE [II-II, Q. 123, Art. 10]

Whether the Brave Man Makes Use of Anger in His Action?

Objection 1: It seems that the brave man does not use anger in his action. For no one should employ as an instrument of his action that which he cannot use at will. Now man cannot use anger at will, so as to take it up and lay it aside when he will. For, as the Philosopher says (De Memoria ii), when a bodily passion is in movement, it does not rest at once just as one wishes. Therefore a brave man should not employ anger for his action.

Obj. 2: Further, if a man is competent to do a thing by himself, he should not seek the assistance of something weaker and more imperfect. Now the reason is competent to achieve by itself deeds of fortitude, wherein anger is impotent: wherefore Seneca says (De Ira i): "Reason by itself suffices not only to make us prepared for action but also to accomplish it. In fact is there greater folly than for reason to seek help from anger? the steadfast from the unstaid, the trusty from the untrustworthy, the healthy from the sick?" Therefore a brave man should not make use of anger.

Obj. 3: Further, just as people are more earnest in doing deeds of fortitude on account of anger, so are they on account of sorrow or desire; wherefore the Philosopher says (Ethic. iii, 8) that wild beasts are incited to face danger through sorrow or pain, and adulterous persons dare many things for the sake of desire. Now fortitude employs neither sorrow nor desire for its action. Therefore in like manner it should not employ anger.

*On the contrary,* The Philosopher says (Ethic. iii, 8) that "anger helps the brave."

*I answer that,* As stated above (I-II, Q. 24, A. 2), concerning anger and the other passions there was a difference of opinion between the Peripatetics and the Stoics. For the Stoics excluded anger and all other passions of the soul from the mind of a wise or good man: whereas the Peripatetics, of whom Aristotle was the chief, ascribed to virtuous men both anger and the other passions of the soul albeit modified by reason. And possibly they differed not in reality but in their way of speaking. For the Peripatetics, as stated above (I-II, Q. 24, A. 2), gave the name of passions to all the movements of the sensitive appetite, however they may comport themselves. And since the sensitive appetite is moved by the command of reason, so that it may cooperate by rendering action more prompt, they held that virtuous persons should employ both anger and the other passions of the soul, modified according to the dictate of reason. On the other hand, the Stoics gave the name of passions to certain immoderate emotions of the sensitive appetite, wherefore they called them sicknesses or diseases, and for this reason severed them altogether from virtue.

Accordingly the brave man employs moderate anger for his action, but not immoderate anger.

Reply Obj. 1: Anger that is moderated in accordance with reason is subject to the command of reason: so that man uses it at his will, which would not be the case were it immoderate.

Reply Obj. 2: Reason employs anger for its action, not as seeking its assistance, but because it uses the sensitive appetite as an instrument, just as it uses the members of the body. Nor is it unbecoming for the instrument to be more imperfect than the principal agent, even as the hammer is more imperfect than the smith. Moreover, Seneca was a follower of the Stoics, and the above words were aimed by him directly at Aristotle.

Reply Obj. 3: Whereas fortitude, as stated above (A. 6), has two acts, namely endurance and aggression, it employs anger, not for the act of endurance, because the reason by itself performs this act, but for the act of aggression, for which it employs anger rather than the other passions, since it belongs to anger to strike at the cause of sorrow, so that it directly cooperates with fortitude in attacking. On the other hand, sorrow by its very nature gives way to the thing that hurts; though accidentally it helps in aggression, either as being the cause of anger, as stated above (I-II, Q. 47, A. 3), or as making a person expose himself to danger in order to escape from sorrow. In like manner desire, by its very nature, tends to a pleasurable good, to which it is directly contrary to withstand danger: yet accidentally sometimes it helps one to attack, in so far as one prefers to risk dangers rather than lack pleasure. Hence the Philosopher says (Ethic. iii, 5): "Of all the cases in which fortitude arises from a passion, the most natural is when a man is brave through anger, making his choice and acting for a purpose," i.e. for a due end; "this is true fortitude."

ELEVENTH ARTICLE [II-II, Q. 123, Art. 11]

Whether Fortitude Is a Cardinal Virtue?

Objection 1: It seems that fortitude is not a cardinal virtue. For, as stated above (A. 10), anger is closely allied with fortitude. Now anger is not accounted a principal passion; nor is daring which belongs to fortitude. Therefore neither should fortitude be reckoned a cardinal virtue.

Obj. 2: Further, the object of virtue is good. But the direct object of fortitude is not good, but evil, for it is endurance of evil and toil, as Tully says (De Invent. Rhet. ii). Therefore fortitude is not a cardinal virtue.

Obj. 3: Further, the cardinal virtues are about those things upon which human life is chiefly occupied, just as a door turns upon a hinge ( *cardine* ). But fortitude is about dangers of death which are of rare occurrence in human life. Therefore fortitude should not be reckoned a cardinal or principal virtue.

*On the contrary,* Gregory (Moral. xxii), Ambrose in his commentary on Luke 6:20, and Augustine (De Moribus Eccl. xv), number fortitude among the four cardinal or principal virtues.

*I answer that,* As stated above (I-II, Q. 61, AA. 3, 4), those virtues are said to be cardinal or principal which have a foremost claim to that which belongs to the virtues in common. And among other conditions of virtue in general one is that it is stated to "act steadfastly," according to *Ethic.* ii, 4. Now fortitude above all lays claim to praise for steadfastness. Because he that stands firm is so much the more praised, as he is more strongly impelled to fall or recede. Now man is impelled to recede from that which is in accordance with reason, both by the pleasing good and the displeasing evil. But bodily pain impels him more strongly than pleasure. For Augustine says (QQ. 83, qu. 36): "There is none that does not shun pain more than he desires pleasure. For we perceive that even the most untamed beasts are deterred from the greatest pleasures by the fear of pain." And among the pains of the mind and dangers those are mostly feared which lead to death, and it is against them that the brave man stands firm. Therefore fortitude is a cardinal virtue.

Reply Obj. 1: Daring and anger do not cooperate with fortitude in its act of endurance, wherein its steadfastness is chiefly commended: for it is by that act that the brave man curbs fear, which is a principal passion, as stated above (I-II, Q. 25, A. 4).

Reply Obj. 2: Virtue is directed to the good of

reason which it behooves to safeguard against the onslaught of evils. And fortitude is directed to evils of the body, as contraries which it withstands, and to the good of reason, as the end, which it intends to safeguard.

Reply Obj. 3: Though dangers of death are of rare occurrence, yet the occasions of those dangers occur frequently, since on account of justice which he pursues, and also on account of other good deeds, man encounters mortal adversaries.

TWELFTH ARTICLE [II-II, Q. 123, Art. 12]

Whether Fortitude Excels Among All Other Virtues?

Objection 1: It seems that fortitude excels among all other virtues. For Ambrose says (De Offic. i): "Fortitude is higher, so to speak, than the rest."

Obj. 2: Further, virtue is about that which is difficult and good. But fortitude is about most difficult things. Therefore it is the greatest of the virtues.

Obj. 3: Further, the person of a man is more excellent than his possessions. But fortitude is about a man's person, for it is this that a man exposes to the danger of death for the good of virtue: whereas justice and the other moral virtues are about other and external things. Therefore fortitude is the chief of the moral virtues.

Obj. 4: *On the contrary,* Tully says (De Offic. i): "Justice is the most resplendent of the virtues and gives its name to a good man."

Obj. 5: Further, the Philosopher says (Rhet. i, 19): "Those virtues must needs be greatest which are most profitable to others." Now liberality seems to be more useful than fortitude. Therefore it is a greater virtue.

*I answer that,* As Augustine says (De Trin. vi), "In things that are great, but not in bulk, to be great is to be good": wherefore the better a virtue the greater it is. Now reason's good is man's good, according to Dionysius (Div. Nom. iv) prudence, since it is a perfection of reason, has the good essentially: while justice effects this good, since it belongs to justice to establish the order of reason in all human affairs: whereas the other virtues safeguard this good, inasmuch as they moderate the passions, lest they lead man away from reason's good. As to the order of the latter, fortitude holds the first place, because fear of dangers of death has the greatest power to make man recede from the good of reason: and after fortitude comes temperance, since also pleasures of touch excel all others in hindering the good of reason. Now to be a thing essentially ranks before effecting it, and the latter ranks before safeguarding it by removing obstacles thereto. Wherefore among the cardinal virtues, prudence ranks first, justice second, fortitude third, temperance fourth, and after these the other virtues.

Reply Obj. 1: Ambrose places fortitude before the other virtues, in respect of a certain general utility, inasmuch as it is useful both in warfare, and in matters relating to civil or home life. Hence he begins by saying (De Offic. i): "Now we come to treat of fortitude, which being higher so to speak than the others, is applicable both to warlike and to civil matters."

Reply Obj. 2: Virtue essentially regards the good rather than the difficult. Hence the greatness of a virtue is measured according to its goodness rather than its difficulty.

Reply Obj. 3: A man does not expose his person to dangers of death except in order to safeguard justice: wherefore the praise awarded to fortitude depends somewhat on justice. Hence Ambrose says (De Offic. i) that "fortitude without justice is an occasion of injustice; since the stronger a man is the more ready is he to oppress the weaker."

The Fourth argument is granted.

Reply Obj. 5: Liberality is useful in conferring certain particular favors: whereas a certain general utility attaches to fortitude, since it safeguards the whole order of justice. Hence the Philosopher says (Rhet. i, 9) that "just and brave men are most beloved, because they are most useful in war and peace."

# QUESTION 124

OF MARTYRDOM (In Five Articles)

We must now consider martyrdom, under which head there are five points of inquiry:

(1) Whether martyrdom is an act of virtue?
(2) Of what virtue is it the act?
(3) Concerning the perfection of this act;
(4) The pain of martyrdom;
(5) Its cause.

FIRST ARTICLE [II-II, Q. 124, Art. 1]

Whether Martyrdom Is an Act of Virtue?

Objection 1: It seems that martyrdom is not an act of virtue. For all acts of virtue are voluntary. But martyrdom is sometimes not voluntary, as in the case of the Innocents who were slain for Christ's sake, and of whom Hilary says (Super Matth. i) that "they attained the ripe age of eternity through the glory of martyrdom." Therefore martyrdom is not an act of virtue.

Obj. 2: Further, nothing unlawful is an act of virtue. Now it is unlawful to kill oneself, as stated above (Q. 64, A. 5), and yet martyrdom is achieved by so doing: for Augustine says (De Civ. Dei i) that "during persecution certain holy women, in order to escape from those who threatened their chastity, threw themselves into a river, and so ended their lives, and their martyrdom is honored in the Catholic Church with most solemn veneration." Therefore martyrdom is not an act of virtue.

Obj. 3: Further, it is praiseworthy to offer oneself to do an act of virtue. But it is not praiseworthy to court martyrdom, rather would it seem to be presumptuous and rash. Therefore martyrdom is not an act of virtue.

*On the contrary,* The reward of beatitude is not due save to acts of virtue. Now it is due to martyrdom, since it is written (Matt. 5:10): "Blessed are they that suffer persecution for justice' sake, for theirs is the kingdom of heaven." Therefore martyrdom is an act of virtue.

*I answer that,* As stated above (Q. 123, AA. 1, 3), it belongs to virtue to safeguard man in the good of reason. Now the good of reason consists in the truth as its proper object, and in justice as its proper effect, as shown above (Q. 109, AA. 1, 2; Q. 123, A. 12). And martyrdom consists essentially in standing firmly to truth and justice against the assaults of persecution. Hence it is evident that martyrdom is an act of virtue.

Reply Obj. 1: Some have said that in the case of the Innocents the use of their free will was miraculously accelerated, so that they suffered martyrdom even voluntarily. Since, however, Scripture contains no proof of this, it is better to say that these babes in being slain obtained by God's grace the glory of martyrdom which others acquire by their own will. For the shedding of one's blood for Christ's sake takes the place of Baptism. Wherefore just as in the case of baptized children the merit of Christ is conducive to the acquisition of glory through the baptismal grace, so in those who were slain for Christ's sake the merit of Christ's martyrdom is conducive to the acquisition of the martyr's palm. Hence Augustine says in a sermon on the Epiphany (De Diversis lxvi), as though he were addressing them: "A man that does not believe that children are benefited by the baptism of Christ will doubt of your being crowned in suffering for Christ. You were not old enough to believe in Christ's future sufferings, but you had a body wherein you could endure suffering of Christ Who was to suffer."

Reply Obj. 2: Augustine says (De Civ. Dei i) that "possibly the Church was induced by certain credible witnesses of Divine authority thus to honor the memory of those holy women [*Cf. Q. 64, A. 1, ad 2]."

Reply Obj. 3: The precepts of the Law are about acts of virtue. Now it has been stated (I-II, Q. 108, A. 1, ad 4) that some of the precepts of the Divine Law are to be understood in reference to the preparation of the mind, in the sense that man ought to be prepared to do such and such a thing, whenever expedient. In the same way certain things belong to an act of virtue as regards the preparation of the mind, so that in such and such a case a man should act according to reason. And this observation would seem very much to the point in the case of martyrdom, which consists in the right endurance of sufferings unjustly inflicted. Nor ought a man to give another an occasion of acting unjustly: yet if anyone act unjustly, one ought to endure it in moderation.

SECOND ARTICLE [II-II, Q. 124, Art. 2]

Whether Martyrdom Is an Act of Fortitude?

Objection 1: It seems that martyrdom is not an act of fortitude. For the Greek *martyr* signifies a witness. Now witness is borne to the faith of Christ. according to Acts 1:8, "You shall be witnesses unto Me," etc. and Maximus says in a sermon: "The mother of martyrs is the Catholic faith which those glorious warriors have sealed with their blood." Therefore martyrdom is an act of faith rather than of fortitude.

Obj. 2: Further, a praiseworthy act belongs chiefly to the virtue which inclines thereto, is manifested thereby, and without which the act avails nothing. Now charity is the chief incentive to martyrdom: Thus Maximus says in a sermon: "The charity of Christ is victorious in His martyrs." Again the greatest proof of charity lies in the act of martyrdom, according to John 15:13, "Greater love than this no man hath, that a man lay down his life for his friends." Moreover without charity martyrdom avails nothing, according to 1 Cor. 13:3, "If I should deliver my body to be burned, and have not charity, it profiteth me nothing." Therefore martyrdom is an act of charity rather than of fortitude.

Obj. 3: Further, Augustine says in a sermon on St. Cyprian: "It is easy to honor a martyr by singing his praises, but it is a great thing to imitate his faith and patience." Now that which calls chiefly for praise in a virtuous act, is the virtue of which it is the act. Therefore martyrdom is an act of patience rather than of fortitude.

*On the contrary,* Cyprian says (Ep. ad Mart. et Conf. ii): "Blessed martyrs, with what praise shall I extol you? Most valiant warriors, how shall I find words to proclaim the strength of your courage?" Now a person is praised on account of the virtue whose act he performs. Therefore martyrdom is an act of fortitude.

*I answer that,* As stated above (Q. 123, A. 1, seqq.), it belongs to fortitude to strengthen man in the good of virtue, especially against dangers, and chiefly against dangers of death, and most of all against those that occur in battle. Now it is evident that in martyrdom man is firmly strengthened in the good of virtue, since he cleaves to faith and justice notwithstanding the threatening danger of death, the imminence of which is moreover due to a kind of particular contest with his persecutors. Hence Cyprian says in a sermon (Ep. ad Mart. et Conf. ii): "The crowd of onlookers wondered to see an unearthly battle, and Christ's servants fighting erect, undaunted in speech, with souls unmoved, and strength divine." Wherefore it is evident that martyrdom is an act of fortitude; for which reason the Church reads in the office of Martyrs: They "became valiant in battle" [*Heb. 11:34].

Reply Obj. 1: Two things must be considered in the act of fortitude. One is the good wherein the brave man is strengthened, and this is the end of fortitude; the other is the firmness itself, whereby a man does not yield to the contraries that hinder him from achieving that good, and in this consists the essence of fortitude. Now just as civic fortitude strengthens a man's mind in human justice, for the safeguarding of which he braves the danger of death, so gratuitous fortitude strengthens man's soul in the good of Divine justice, which is "through faith in Christ Jesus," according to Rom. 3:22. Thus martyrdom is related to faith as the end in which one is strengthened, but to fortitude as the eliciting habit.

Reply Obj. 2: Charity inclines one to the act of martyrdom, as its first and chief motive cause, being the virtue commanding it, whereas fortitude inclines thereto as being its proper motive cause, being the virtue that elicits it. Hence martyrdom is an act of charity as commanding, and of fortitude as eliciting. For this reason also it manifests both virtues. It is due to charity that it is meritorious, like any other act of virtue: and for this reason it avails not without charity.

Reply Obj. 3: As stated above (Q. 123, A. 6), the chief act of fortitude is endurance: to this and not to its secondary act, which is aggression, martyrdom belongs. And since patience serves fortitude on the part of its chief act, viz. endurance, hence it is that martyrs are also praised for their patience.

THIRD ARTICLE [II-II, Q. 124, Art. 3]

Whether Martyrdom Is an Act of the Greatest Perfection?

Objection 1: It seems that martyrdom is not an act of the greatest perfection. For seemingly that which is a matter of counsel and not of precept pertains to perfection, because, to wit, it is not necessary for salvation. But it would seem that martyrdom is necessary for salvation, since the Apostle says (Rom. 10:10), "With the heart we believe unto justice, but with the mouth confession is made unto salvation," and it is written (1 John 3:16), that "we ought to lay down our lives for the brethren." Therefore martyrdom does not pertain to perfection.

Obj. 2: Further, it seems to point to greater perfection that a man give his soul to God, which is done by obedience, than that he give God his body, which is done by martyrdom: wherefore Gregory says (Moral. xxxv) that "obedience is preferable to all sacrifices." Therefore martyrdom is not an act of the greatest perfection.

Obj. 3: Further, it would seem better to do good to others than to maintain oneself in good, since the "good of the nation is better than the good of the individual," according to the Philosopher (Ethic. i, 2). Now he that suffers martyrdom profits himself alone, whereas he that teaches does good to many. Therefore the act of teaching and guiding subjects is more perfect than the act of martyrdom.

*On the contrary,* Augustine (De Sanct. Virgin. xlvi) prefers martyrdom to virginity which pertains to perfection. Therefore martyrdom seems to belong to perfection in the highest degree.

*I answer that,* We may speak of an act of virtue in two ways. First, with regard to the species of that act, as compared to the virtue proximately eliciting it. In this way martyrdom, which consists in the due endurance of death, cannot be the most perfect of virtuous acts, because endurance of death is not praiseworthy in itself, but only in so far as it is directed to some good consisting in an act of virtue, such as faith or the love of God, so that this act of virtue being the end is better.

A virtuous act may be considered in another way, in comparison with its first motive cause, which is the love of charity, and it is in this respect that an act comes to belong to the perfection of life, since, as the Apostle says (Col. 3:14), that "charity ... is the bond of perfection." Now, of all virtuous acts martyrdom is the greatest proof of the perfection of charity: since a man's love for a thing is proved to be so much the greater, according as that which he despises for its sake is more dear to him, or that which he chooses to suffer for its sake is more odious. But it is evident that of all the goods of the present life man loves life itself most, and on the other hand he hates death more than anything, especially when it is accompanied by the pains of bodily torment, "from fear of which even dumb animals refrain from the greatest pleasures," as Augustine observes (QQ. 83, qu. 36). And from this point of view it is clear that martyrdom is the most perfect of human acts in respect of its genus, as being the sign of the greatest charity, according to John 15:13: "Greater love than this no man hath, that a man lay down his life for his friends."

Reply Obj. 1: There is no act of perfection, which is a matter of counsel, but what in certain cases is a matter of precept, as being necessary for salvation. Thus Augustine declares (De Adult. Conjug. xiii) that a man is under the obligation of observing continency, through the absence or sickness of his wife. Hence it is not contrary to the perfection of martyrdom if in certain cases it be necessary for salvation, since there are cases when it is not necessary for salvation to suffer martyrdom; thus we read of many holy martyrs who through zeal for the faith or brotherly love gave themselves up to martyrdom of their own accord. As to these precepts, they are to be understood as referring to the preparation of the mind.

Reply Obj. 2: Martyrdom embraces the highest possible degree of obedience, namely obedience unto death; thus we read of Christ (Phil. 2:8) that He became "obedient unto death." Hence it is evident that martyrdom is of itself more perfect than obedience considered absolutely.

Reply Obj. 3: This argument considers martyrdom according to the proper species of its act, whence it derives no excellence over all other virtuous acts; thus neither is fortitude more excellent than all virtues.

FOURTH ARTICLE [II-II, Q. 124, Art. 4]

Whether Death Is Essential to Martyrdom?

Objection 1: It seems that death is not essential to martyrdom. For Jerome says in a sermon on the Assumption (Epist. ad Paul. et Eustoch.): "I should say rightly that the Mother of God was both virgin and martyr, although she ended her days in peace": and Gregory says (Hom. iii in Evang.): "Although persecution has ceased to offer the opportunity, yet the peace we enjoy is not without its martyrdom, since even if we no longer yield the life of the body to the sword, yet do we slay fleshly desires in the soul with the sword of the spirit." Therefore there can be martyrdom without suffering death.

Obj. 2: Further, we read of certain women as commended for despising life for the sake of safeguarding the integrity of the flesh: wherefore seemingly the integrity of chastity is preferable to the life of the body. Now sometimes the integrity of the flesh has been forfeited or has been threatened in confession of the Christian faith, as in the case of Agnes and Lucy. Therefore it seems that the name of martyr should be accorded to a woman who forfeits the integrity of the flesh for the sake of Christ's faith, rather than if she were to forfeit even the life of the body: wherefore also Lucy said: "If thou causest me to be violated against my will, my chastity will gain me a twofold crown."

Obj. 3: Further, martyrdom is an act of fortitude. But it belongs to fortitude to brave not only death but also other hardships, as Augustine declares (Music. vi). Now there are many other hardships besides death, which one may suffer for Christ's faith, namely imprisonment, exile, being stripped of one's goods, as mentioned in Heb. 10:34, for which reason we celebrate the martyrdom of Pope Saint Marcellus, notwithstanding that he died in prison. Therefore it is not essential to martyrdom that one suffer the pain of death.

Obj. 4: Further, martyrdom is a meritorious act, as stated above (A. 2, ad 1; A. 3). Now it cannot be a meritorious act after death. Therefore it is before death; and consequently death is not essential to martyrdom.

*On the contrary,* Maximus says in a sermon on the martyrs that "in dying for the faith he conquers who would have been vanquished in living without faith."

*I answer that,* As stated above (A. 2), a martyr is so called as being a witness to the Christian faith, which teaches us to despise things visible for the sake of things invisible, as stated in Heb. 11. Accordingly it belongs to martyrdom that a man bear witness to the faith in showing by deed that he despises all things present, in order to obtain invisible goods to come. Now so long as a man retains the life of the body he does not show by deed that he despises all things relating to the body. For men are wont to despise both their kindred and all they possess, and even to suffer bodily pain, rather than lose life. Hence Satan testified against Job (Job 2:4): "Skin for skin, and all that a man hath he will give for his soul" [Douay: 'life'] i.e. for the life of his body. Therefore the perfect notion of martyrdom requires that a man suffer death for Christ's sake.

Reply Obj. 1: The authorities quoted, and the like that one may meet with, speak of martyrdom by way of similitude.

Reply Obj. 2: When a woman forfeits the integrity of the flesh, or is condemned to forfeit it under pretext of the Christian faith, it is not evident to men whether she suffers this for love of the Christian faith, or rather through contempt of chastity. Wherefore in the sight of men her testimony is not held to be sufficient, and consequently this is not martyrdom properly speaking. In the sight of God, however, Who searcheth the heart, this may be deemed worthy of a reward, as Lucy said.

Reply Obj. 3: As stated above (Q. 123, AA. 4, 5), fortitude regards danger of death chiefly, and other dangers consequently; wherefore a person is not called a martyr merely for suffering imprisonment, or exile, or forfeiture of his wealth, except in so far as these result in death.

Reply Obj. 4: The merit of martyrdom is not after death, but in the voluntary endurance of death, namely in the fact that a person willingly suffers being put to death. It happens sometimes, however, that a man lives for some time after being mortally wounded for Christ's sake, or after suffering for the faith of Christ any other kind of hardship inflicted by persecution and continued until death ensues. The act of martyrdom is meritorious while a man is in this state, and at the very time that he is suffering these hardships.

FIFTH ARTICLE [II-II, Q. 124, Art. 5]

Whether Faith Alone Is the Cause of Martyrdom?

Objection 1: It seems that faith alone is the cause of martyrdom. For it is written (1 Pet. 4:15, 16): "Let none of you suffer as a murderer, or a thief, or a railer, or a coveter of other men's things. But if as a Christian, let him not be ashamed, but let him glorify God in this name." Now a man is said to be a Christian because he holds the faith of Christ. Therefore only faith in Christ gives the glory of martyrdom to those who suffer.

Obj. 2: Further, a martyr is a kind of witness. But witness is borne to the truth alone. Now one is not called a martyr for bearing witness to any truth, but only for witnessing to the Divine truth, otherwise a man would be a martyr if he were to die for confessing a truth of geometry or some other speculative science, which seems ridiculous. Therefore faith alone is the cause of martyrdom.

Obj. 3: Further, those virtuous deeds would seem to be of most account which are directed to the common good, since "the good of the nation is better than the good of the individual," according to the Philosopher (Ethic. i, 2). If, then, some other good were the cause of martyrdom, it would seem that before all those would be martyrs who die for the defense of their country. Yet this is not consistent with Church observance, for we do not celebrate the martyrdom of those who die in a just war. Therefore faith alone is the cause of martyrdom.

*On the contrary,* It is written (Matt. 5:10): "Blessed are they that suffer persecution for justice' sake," which pertains to martyrdom, according to a gloss, as well as Jerome's commentary on this passage. Now not only faith but also the other virtues pertain to justice. Therefore other virtues can be the cause of martyrdom.

*I answer that,* As stated above (A. 4), martyrs are so called as being witnesses, because by suffering in body unto death they bear witness to the truth; not indeed to any truth, but to the truth which is in accordance with godliness, and was made known to us by Christ: wherefore Christ's martyrs are His witnesses. Now this truth is the truth of faith. Wherefore the cause of all martyrdom is the truth of faith.

But the truth of faith includes not only inward belief, but also outward profession, which is expressed not only by words, whereby one confesses the faith, but also by deeds, whereby a person shows that he has faith, according to James 2:18, "I will show thee, by works, my faith." Hence it is written of certain people (Titus 1:16): "They profess that they know God but in their works they deny Him." Thus all virtuous deeds, inasmuch as they are referred to God, are professions of the faith whereby we come to know that God requires these works of us, and rewards us for them: and in this way they can be the cause of martyrdom. For this reason the Church celebrates the martyrdom of Blessed John the Baptist, who suffered death, not for refusing to deny the faith, but for reproving adultery.

Reply Obj. 1: A Christian is one who is Christ's. Now a person is said to be Christ's, not only through having faith in Christ, but also because he is actuated to virtuous deeds by the Spirit of Christ, according to Rom. 8:9, "If any man have not the Spirit of Christ, he is none of His"; and again because in imitation of Christ he is dead to sins, according to Gal. 5:24, "They that are Christ's have crucified their flesh with the vices and concupiscences." Hence to suffer as a Christian is not only to suffer in confession of the faith, which is done by words, but also to suffer for doing any good work, or for avoiding any sin, for Christ's sake, because this all comes under the head of witnessing to the faith.

Reply Obj. 2: The truth of other sciences has no connection with the worship of the Godhead: hence it is not called truth according to godliness, and consequently the confession thereof cannot be said to be the direct cause of martyrdom. Yet, since every lie is a sin, as stated above (Q. 110, AA. 3, 4), avoidance of a lie, to whatever truth it may be contrary, may be the cause of martyrdom inasmuch as a lie is a sin against the Divine Law.

Reply Obj. 3: The good of one's country is paramount among human goods: yet the Divine good, which is the proper cause of martyrdom, is of more account than human good. Nevertheless, since human good may become Divine, for instance when it is referred to God, it follows that any human good in so far as it is referred to God, may be the cause of martyrdom.

# QUESTION 125

OF FEAR* (In Four Articles) [* St. Thomas calls this vice indifferently 'fear' or 'timidity.' The translation requires one to adhere to these terms on account of the connection with the passion of fear. Otherwise 'cowardice' would be a better rendering.]

We must now consider the vices opposed to fortitude: (1) Fear; (2) Fearlessness; (3) Daring.

Under the first head there are four points of inquiry:

(1) Whether fear is a sin?
(2) Whether it is opposed to fortitude?
(3) Whether it is a mortal sin?
(4) Whether it excuses from sin, or diminishes it?

FIRST ARTICLE [II-II, Q. 125, Art. 1]

Whether Fear Is a Sin?

Objection 1: It seems that fear is not a sin. For fear is a passion, as stated above (I-II, Q. 23, A. 4; Q. 42). Now we are neither praised nor blamed for passions, as stated in *Ethic.* ii. Since then every sin is blameworthy, it seems that fear is not a sin.

Obj. 2: Further, nothing that is commanded in the Divine Law is a sin: since the "law of the Lord is unspotted" (Ps. 18:8). Yet fear is commanded in God's law, for it is written (Eph. 6:5): "Servants, be obedient to them that are your lords according to the flesh, with fear and trembling." Therefore fear is not a sin.

Obj. 3: Further, nothing that is naturally in man is a sin, for sin is contrary to nature according to Damascene (De Fide Orth. iii). Now fear is natural to man: wherefore the Philosopher says (Ethic. iii, 7) that "a man would be insane or insensible to pain, if nothing, not even earthquakes nor deluges, inspired him with fear." Therefore fear is not a sin.

*On the contrary,* our Lord said (Matt. 10:28): "Fear ye not them that kill the body," and it is written (Ezech. 2:6): "Fear not, neither be thou afraid of their words."

*I answer that,* A human act is said to be a sin on account of its being inordinate, because the good of a human act consists in order, as stated above (Q. 109, A. 2; Q. 114, A. 1). Now this due order requires that the appetite be subject to the ruling of reason. And reason dictates that certain things should be shunned and some sought after. Among things to be shunned, it dictates that some are to be shunned more than others; and among things to be sought after, that some are to be sought after more than others. Moreover, the more a good is to be sought after, the more is the opposite evil to be shunned. The result is that reason dictates that certain goods are to be sought after more than certain evils are to be avoided. Accordingly when the appetite shuns what the reason dictates that we should endure rather than forfeit others that we should rather seek for, fear is inordinate and sinful. On the other hand, when the appetite fears so as to shun what reason requires to be shunned, the appetite is neither inordinate nor sinful.

Reply Obj. 1: Fear in its generic acceptation denotes avoidance in general. Hence in this way it does not include the notion of good or evil: and the same applies to every other passion. Wherefore the Philosopher says that passions call for neither praise nor blame, because, to wit, we neither praise nor blame those who are angry or afraid, but only those who behave thus in an ordinate or inordinate manner.

Reply Obj. 2: The fear which the Apostle inculcates is in accordance with reason, namely that servants should fear lest they be lacking in the service they owe their masters.

Reply Obj. 3: Reason dictates that we should shun the evils that we cannot withstand, and the endurance of which profits us nothing. Hence there is no sin in fearing them.

SECOND ARTICLE [II-II, Q. 125, Art. 2]

Whether the Sin of Fear Is Contrary to Fortitude?

Objection 1: It seems that the sin of fear is not contrary to fortitude: because fortitude is about dangers of death, as stated above (Q. 123, AA. 4, 5). But the sin of fear is not always connected with dangers of death, for a gloss on Ps. 127:1, "Blessed are all they that fear the Lord," says that "it is human fear whereby we dread to suffer carnal dangers, or to lose worldly goods." Again a gloss on Matt. 27:44, "He prayed the third time, saying the selfsame word," says that "evil fear is threefold, fear of death, fear of pain, and fear of contempt." Therefore the sin of fear is not contrary to fortitude.

Obj. 2: Further, the chief reason why a man is commended for fortitude is that he exposes himself to the danger of death. Now sometimes a man exposes himself to death through fear of slavery or shame. Thus Augustine relates (De Civ. Dei i) that Cato, in order not to be Caesar's slave, gave himself up to death. Therefore the sin of fear bears a certain likeness to fortitude instead of being opposed thereto.

Obj. 3: Further, all despair arises from fear. But despair is opposed not to fortitude but to hope, as stated above (Q. 20, A. 1; I-II, Q. 40, A. 4). Neither therefore is the sin of fear opposed to fortitude.

*On the contrary,* The Philosopher (Ethic. ii, 7; iii, 7) states that timidity is opposed to fortitude.

*I answer that,* As stated above (Q. 19, A. 3; I-II, Q. 43, A. 1), all fear arises from love; since no one fears save what is contrary to something he loves. Now love is not confined to any particular kind of virtue or vice: but ordinate love is included in every virtue, since every virtuous man loves the good proper to his virtue; while inordinate love is included in every sin, because inordinate love gives use to inordinate desire. Hence in like manner inordinate fear is included in every sin; thus the covetous man fears the loss of money, the intemperate man the loss of pleasure, and so on. But the greatest fear of all is that which has the danger of death for its object, as we find proved in *Ethic.* iii, 6. Wherefore the inordinateness of this fear is opposed to fortitude which regards dangers of death. For this reason timidity is said to be antonomastically* opposed to fortitude. [*Antonomasia is the figure of speech whereby we substitute the general for the individual term; e.g. The Philosopher for Aristotle: and so timidity, which is inordinate fear of any evil, is employed to denote inordinate fear of the danger of death.]

Reply Obj. 1: The passages quoted refer to inordinate fear in its generic acceptation, which can be opposed to various virtues.

Reply Obj. 2: Human acts are estimated chiefly with reference to the end, as stated above (I-II, Q. 1, A. 3; Q. 18, A. 6): and it belongs to a brave man to expose himself to danger of death for the sake of a good. But a man who exposes himself to danger of death in order to escape from slavery or hardships is overcome by fear, which is contrary to fortitude. Hence the Philosopher says (Ethic. iii, 7), that "to die in order to escape poverty, lust, or something disagreeable is an act not of fortitude but of cowardice: for to shun hardships is a mark of effeminacy."

Reply Obj. 3: As stated above (I-II, Q. 45, A. 2), fear is the beginning of despair even as hope is the beginning of daring. Wherefore, just as fortitude which employs daring in moderation presupposes hope, so on the other hand despair proceeds from some kind of fear. It does not follow, however, that any kind of despair results from any kind of fear, but that only from fear of the same kind. Now the despair that is opposed to hope is referred to another kind, namely to Divine things; whereas the fear that is opposed to fortitude regards dangers of death. Hence the argument does not prove.

THIRD ARTICLE [II-II, Q. 125, Art. 3]

Whether Fear Is a Mortal Sin?

Objection 1: It seems that fear is not a mortal sin. For, as stated above (I-II, Q. 23, A. 1), fear is in the irascible faculty which is a part of the sensuality. Now there is none but venial sin in the sensuality, as stated above (I-II, Q. 74, A. 4). Therefore fear is not a mortal sin.

Obj. 2: Further, every mortal sin turns the heart wholly from God. But fear does not this, for a gloss on Judges 7:3, "Whosoever is fearful," etc., says that "a man is fearful when he trembles at the very thought of conflict; yet he is not so wholly terrified at heart, but that he can rally and take courage." Therefore fear is not a mortal sin.

Obj. 3: Further, mortal sin is a lapse not only from perfection but also from a precept. But fear does not make one lapse from a precept, but only from perfection; for a gloss on Deut. 20:8, "What man is there that is fearful and fainthearted?" says: "We learn from this that no man can take up the profession of contemplation or spiritual warfare, if he still fears to be despoiled of earthly riches." Therefore fear is not a mortal sin.

*On the contrary,* For mortal sin alone is the pain of hell due: and yet this is due to the fearful, according to Apoc. 21:8, "But the fearful and unbelieving and the abominable," etc., "shall have their portion in the pool burning with fire and brimstone which is the second death." Therefore fear is a mortal sin.

*I answer that,* As stated above (A. 1), fear is a sin through being inordinate, that is to say, through shunning what ought not to be shunned according to reason. Now sometimes this inordinateness of fear is confined to the sensitive appetites, without the accession of the rational appetite's consent: and then it cannot be a mortal, but only a venial sin. But sometimes this inordinateness of fear reaches to the rational appetite which is called the will, which deliberately shuns something against the dictate of reason: and this inordinateness of fear is sometimes a mortal, sometimes a venial sin. For if a man through fear of the danger of death or of any other temporal evil is so disposed as to do what is forbidden, or to omit what is commanded by the Divine law, such fear is a mortal sin: otherwise it is a venial sin.

Reply Obj. 1: This argument considers fear as confined to the sensuality.

Reply Obj. 2: This gloss also can be understood as referring to the fear that is confined within the sensuality. Or better still we may reply that a man is terrified with his whole heart when fear banishes his courage beyond remedy. Now even when fear is a mortal sin, it may happen nevertheless that one is not so wilfully terrified that one cannot be persuaded to put fear aside: thus sometimes a man sins mortally by consenting to concupiscence, and is turned aside from accomplishing what he purposed doing.

Reply Obj. 3: This gloss speaks of the fear that turns man aside from a good that is necessary, not for the fulfilment of a precept, but for the perfection of a counsel. Such like fear is not a mortal sin, but is sometimes venial: and sometimes it is not a sin, for instance when one has a reasonable cause for fear.

FOURTH ARTICLE [II-II, Q. 125, Art. 4]

Whether Fear Excuses from Sin?

Objection 1: It seems that fear does not excuse from sin. For fear is a sin, as stated above (A. 1). But sin does not excuse from sin, rather does it aggravate it. Therefore fear does not excuse from sin.

Obj. 2: Further, if any fear excuses from sin, most of all would this be true of the fear of death, to which, as the saying is, a courageous man is subject. Yet this fear, seemingly, is no excuse, because, since death comes, of necessity, to all, it does not seem to be an object of fear. Therefore fear does not excuse from sin.

Obj. 3: Further, all fear is of evil, either temporal or spiritual. Now fear of spiritual evil cannot excuse sin, because instead of inducing one to sin, it withdraws one from sin: and fear of temporal evil does not excuse from sin, because according to the Philosopher (Ethic. iii, 6), "one should not fear poverty, nor sickness, nor anything that is not a result of one's own wickedness." Therefore it seems that in no sense does fear excuse from sin.

*On the contrary,* It is stated in the Decretals (I, Q. 1, Cap. Constat.): "A man who has been forcibly and unwillingly ordained by heretics, has an ostensible excuse."

*I answer that,* As stated above (A. 3), fear is sinful in so far as it runs counter to the order of reason. Now reason judges certain evils to be shunned rather than others. Wherefore it is no sin not to shun what is less to be shunned in order to avoid what reason judges to be more avoided: thus death of the body is more to be avoided than the loss of temporal goods. Hence a man would be excused from sin if through fear of death he were to promise or give something to a robber, and yet he would be guilty of sin were he to give to sinners, rather than to the good to whom he should give in preference. On the other hand, if through fear a man were to avoid evils which according to reason are less to be avoided, and so incur evils which according to reason are more to be avoided, he could not be wholly excused from sin, because such like fear would be inordinate. Now the evils of the soul are more to be feared than the evils of the body, and evils of the body more than evils of external things. Wherefore if one were to incur evils of the soul, namely sins, in order to avoid evils of the body, such as blows or death, or evils of external things, such as loss of money; or if one were to endure evils of the body in order to avoid loss of money, one would not be wholly excused from sin. Yet one's sin would be extenuated somewhat, for what is done through fear is less voluntary, because when fear lays hold of a man he is under a certain necessity of doing a certain thing. Hence the Philosopher (Ethic. iii, 1) says that these things that are done through fear are not simply voluntary, but a mixture of voluntary and involuntary.

Reply Obj. 1: Fear excuses, not in the point of its sinfulness, but in the point of its involuntariness.

Reply Obj. 2: Although death comes, of necessity, to all, yet the shortening of temporal life is an evil and consequently an object of fear.

Reply Obj. 3: According to the opinion of Stoics, who held temporal goods not to be man's goods, it follows in consequence that temporal evils are not man's evils, and that therefore they are nowise to be feared. But according to Augustine (De Lib. Arb. ii) these temporal things are goods of the least account, and this was also the opinion of the Peripatetics. Hence their contraries are indeed to be feared; but not so much that one ought for their sake to renounce that which is good according to virtue.

## QUESTION 126

OF FEARLESSNESS (In Two Articles)

We must now consider the vice of fearlessness: under which head there are two points of inquiry:

(1) Whether it is a sin to be fearless?

(2) Whether it is opposed to fortitude?

FIRST ARTICLE [II-II, Q. 126, Art. 1]

Whether Fearlessness Is a Sin?

Objection 1: It seems that fearlessness is not a sin. For that which is reckoned to the praise of a just man is not a sin. Now it is written in praise of the just man (Prov. 28:1): "The just, bold as a lion, shall be without dread." Therefore it is not a sin to be without fear.

Obj. 2: Further, nothing is so fearful as death, according to the Philosopher (Ethic. iii, 6). Yet one ought not to fear even death, according to Matt. 10:28, "Fear ye not them that kill the body," etc., nor anything that can be inflicted by man, according to Isa. 51:12, "Who art thou, that thou shouldst be afraid of a mortal man?" Therefore it is not a sin to be fearless.

Obj. 3: Further, fear is born of love, as stated above (Q. 125, A. 2). Now it belongs to the perfection of virtue to love nothing earthly, since according to Augustine (De Civ. Dei xiv), "the love of God to the abasement of self makes us citizens of the heavenly city." Therefore it is seemingly not a sin to fear nothing earthly.

*On the contrary,* It is said of the unjust judge (Luke 18:2) that "he feared not God nor regarded man."

*I answer that,* Since fear is born of love, we must seemingly judge alike of love and fear. Now it is here a question of that fear whereby one dreads temporal evils, and which results from the love of temporal goods. And every man has it instilled in him by nature to love his own life and whatever is directed thereto; and to do so in due measure, that is, to love these things not as placing his end therein, but as things to be used for the sake of his last end. Hence it is contrary to the natural inclination, and therefore a sin, to fall short of loving them in due measure. Nevertheless, one never lapses entirely from this love: since what is natural cannot be wholly lost: for which reason the Apostle says (Eph. 5:29): "No man ever hated his own flesh." Wherefore even those that slay themselves do so from love of their own flesh, which they desire to free from present stress. Hence it may happen that a man fears death and other temporal evils less than he ought, for the reason that he loves them* less than he ought. [*Viz. the contrary goods. One would expect 'se' instead of 'ea.' We should then read: For the reason that he loves himself less than he ought.] But that he fear none of these things cannot result from an entire lack of love, but only from the fact that he thinks it impossible for him to be afflicted by the evils contrary to the goods he loves. This is sometimes the result of pride of soul presuming on self and despising others, according to the saying of Job 41:24, 25: "He [Vulg.: 'who'] was made to fear no one, he beholdeth every high thing": and sometimes it happens through a defect in the reason; thus the Philosopher says (Ethic. iii, 7) that the "Celts, through lack of intelligence, fear nothing." [*"A man would deserve to be called insane and senseless if there were nothing that he feared, not even an earthquake nor a storm at sea, as is said to be the case with the Celts."] It is therefore evident that fearlessness is a vice, whether it result from lack of love, pride of soul, or dullness of understanding: yet the latter is excused from sin if it be invincible.

Reply Obj. 1: The just man is praised for being without fear that withdraws him from good; not that he is altogether fearless, for it is written (Ecclus. 1:28): "He that is without fear cannot be justified."

Reply Obj. 2: Death and whatever else can be inflicted by mortal man are not to be feared so that they make us forsake justice: but they are to be feared as hindering man in acts of virtue, either as regards himself, or as regards the progress he may cause in others. Hence it is written (Prov. 14:16): "A wise man feareth and declineth from evil."

Reply Obj. 3: Temporal goods are to be despised as hindering us from loving and serving God, and on the same score they are not to be feared; wherefore it is written (Ecclus. 34:16): "He that feareth the Lord shall tremble at nothing." But temporal goods are not to be despised, in so far as they are helping us instrumentally to attain those things that pertain to Divine fear and love.

SECOND ARTICLE [II-II, Q. 126, Art. 2]

Whether Fearlessness Is Opposed to Fortitude?

Objection 1: It seems that fearlessness is not opposed to fortitude. For we judge of habits by their acts. Now no act of fortitude is hindered by a man being fearless: since if fear be removed, one is both brave to endure, and daring to attack. Therefore fearlessness is not opposed to fortitude.

Obj. 2: Further, fearlessness is a vice, either through lack of due love, or on account of pride, or by reason of folly. Now lack of due love is opposed to charity, pride is contrary to humility, and folly to prudence or wisdom. Therefore the vice of fearlessness is not opposed to fortitude.

Obj. 3: Further, vices are opposed to virtue and extremes to the mean. But one mean has only one extreme on the one side. Since then fortitude has fear opposed to it on the one side and daring on the other, it seems that fearlessness is not opposed thereto.

*On the contrary,* The Philosopher (Ethic. iii) reckons fearlessness to be opposed to fortitude.

*I answer that,* As stated above (Q. 123, A. 3), fortitude is concerned about fear and daring. Now every moral virtue observes the rational mean in the matter about which it is concerned. Hence it belongs to fortitude that man should moderate his fear according to reason, namely that he should fear what he ought, and when he ought, and so forth. Now this mode of reason may be corrupted either by excess or by deficiency. Wherefore just as timidity is opposed to fortitude by excess of fear, in so far as a man fears what he ought not, and as he ought not, so too fearlessness is opposed thereto by deficiency of fear, in so far as a man fears not what he ought to fear.

Reply Obj. 1: The act of fortitude is to endure death without fear, and to be aggressive, not anyhow, but according to reason: this the fearless man does not do.

Reply Obj. 2: Fearlessness by its specific nature corrupts the mean of fortitude, wherefore it is opposed to fortitude directly. But in respect of its causes nothing hinders it from being opposed to other virtues.

Reply Obj. 3: The vice of daring is opposed to fortitude by excess of daring, and fearlessness by deficiency of fear. Fortitude imposes the mean on each passion. Hence there is nothing unreasonable in its having different extremes in different respects.

# QUESTION 127

OF DARING* [*Excessive daring or foolhardiness] (In Two Articles)

We must now consider daring; and under this head there are two points of inquiry:

(1) Whether daring is a sin?

(2) Whether it is opposed to fortitude?

FIRST ARTICLE [II-II, Q. 127, Art. 1]

Whether Daring Is a Sin?

Objection 1: It seems that daring is not a sin. For it is written (Job 39:21) concerning the horse, by which according to Gregory (Moral. xxxi) the godly preacher is denoted, that "he goeth forth boldly to meet armed men [*Vulg.: 'he pranceth boldly, he goeth forth to meet armed men']." But no vice redounds to a man's praise. Therefore it is not a sin to be daring.

Obj. 2: Further, according to the Philosopher (Ethic. vi, 9), "one should take counsel in thought, and do quickly what has been counseled." But daring helps this quickness in doing. Therefore daring is not sinful but praiseworthy.

Obj. 3: Further, daring is a passion caused by hope, as stated above (I-II, Q. 45, A. 2) when we were treating of the passions. But hope is accounted not a sin but a virtue. Neither therefore should daring be accounted a sin.

*On the contrary,* It is written (Ecclus. 8:18): "Go not on the way with a bold man, lest he burden thee with his evils." Now no man's fellowship is to be avoided save on account of sin. Therefore daring is a sin.

*I answer that,* Daring, as stated above (I-II, Q. 23, A. 1; Q. 55), is a passion. Now a passion is sometimes moderated according to reason, and sometimes it lacks moderation, either by excess or by deficiency, and on this account the passion is sinful. Again, the names of the passions are sometimes employed in the sense of excess, thus we speak of anger meaning not any but excessive anger, in which case it is sinful, and in the same way daring as implying excess is accounted a sin.

Reply Obj. 1: The daring spoken of there is that which is moderated by reason, for in that sense it belongs to the virtue of fortitude.

Reply Obj. 2: It is praiseworthy to act quickly after taking counsel, which is an act of reason. But to wish to act quickly before taking counsel is not praiseworthy but sinful; for this would be to act rashly, which is a vice contrary to prudence, as stated above (Q. 58, A. 3). Wherefore daring which leads one to act quickly is so far praiseworthy as it is directed by reason.

Reply Obj. 3: Some vices are unnamed, and so also are some virtues, as the Philosopher remarks (Ethic. ii, 7; iv, 4, 5, 6). Hence the names of certain passions have to be applied to certain vices and virtues: and in order to designate vices we employ especially the names of those passions the object of which is an evil, as in the case of hatred, fear, anger and daring. But hope and love have a good for this object, and so we use them rather to designate virtues.

SECOND ARTICLE [II-II, Q. 127, Art. 2]

Whether Daring Is Opposed to Fortitude?

Objection 1: It seems that daring is not opposed to fortitude. For excess of daring seems to result from presumption of mind. But presumption pertains to pride which is opposed to humility. Therefore daring is opposed to humility rather than to fortitude.

Obj. 2: Further, daring does not seem to call for blame, except in so far as it results in harm either to the daring person who puts himself in danger inordinately, or to others whom he attacks with daring, or exposes to danger. But this seemingly pertains to injustice. Therefore daring, as designating a sin, is opposed, not to fortitude but to justice.

Obj. 3: Further, fortitude is concerned about fear and daring, as stated above (Q. 123, A. 3). Now since timidity is opposed to fortitude in respect of an excess of fear, there is another vice opposed to timidity in respect of a lack of fear. If then, daring is opposed to fortitude, in the point of excessive daring, there will likewise be a vice opposed to it in the point of deficient daring. But there is no such vice. Therefore neither should daring be accounted a vice in opposition to fortitude.

*On the contrary,* The Philosopher in both the Second and Third Books of Ethics accounts daring to be opposed to fortitude.

*I answer that,* As stated above (Q. 126, A. 2), it belongs to a moral virtue to observe the rational mean in the matter about which it is concerned. Wherefore every vice that denotes lack of moderation in the matter of a moral virtue is opposed to that virtue, as immoderate to moderate. Now daring, in so far as it denotes a vice, implies excess of passion, and this excess goes by the name of daring. Wherefore it is evident that it is opposed to the virtue of fortitude which is concerned about fear and daring, as stated above (Q. 122, A. 3).

Reply Obj. 1: Opposition between vice and virtue does not depend chiefly on the cause of the vice but on the vice's very species. Wherefore it is not necessary that daring be opposed to the same virtue as presumption which is its cause.

Reply Obj. 2: Just as the direct opposition of a vice does not depend on its cause, so neither does it depend on its effect. Now the harm done by daring is its effect. Wherefore neither does the opposition of daring depend on this.

Reply Obj. 3: The movement of daring consists in a man taking the offensive against that which is in opposition to him: and nature inclines him to do this except in so far as such inclination is hindered by the fear of receiving harm from that source. Hence the vice which exceeds in daring has no contrary deficiency, save only timidity. Yet daring does not always accompany so great a lack of timidity, for as the Philosopher says (Ethic. iii, 7), "the daring are precipitate and eager to meet danger, yet fail when the danger is present," namely through fear.

# QUESTION 128

OF THE PARTS OF FORTITUDE

We must now consider the parts of fortitude; first we shall consider what are the parts of fortitude; and secondly we shall treat of each part.

ARTICLE [II-II, Q. 128, Art.]

Whether the Parts of Fortitude Are Suitably Assigned?

Objection 1: It seems that the parts of fortitude are unsuitably assigned. For Tully (De Invent. Rhet. ii) assigns four parts to fortitude, namely *magnificence, confidence, patience,* and *perseverance.* Now magnificence seems to pertain to liberality; since both are concerned about money, and "a magnificent man must needs be liberal," as the Philosopher observes (Ethic. iv, 2). But liberality is a part of justice, as stated above (Q. 117, A. 5). Therefore magnificence should not be reckoned a part of fortitude.

Obj. 2: Further, confidence is apparently the same as hope. But hope does not seem to pertain to fortitude, but is rather a virtue by itself. Therefore confidence should not be reckoned a part of fortitude.

Obj. 3: Further, fortitude makes a man behave aright in face of danger. But magnificence and confidence do not essentially imply any relation to danger. Therefore they are not suitably reckoned as parts of fortitude.

Obj. 4: Further, according to Tully (De Invent. Rhet. ii) patience denotes endurance of hardships, and he ascribes the same to fortitude. Therefore patience is the same as fortitude and not a part thereof.

Obj. 5: Further, that which is a requisite to every virtue should not be reckoned a part of a special virtue. But perseverance is required in every virtue: for it is written (Matt. 24:13): "He that shall persevere to the end he shall be saved." Therefore perseverance should not be accounted a part of fortitude.

Obj. 6: Further, Macrobius (De Somn. Scip. i) reckons seven parts of fortitude, namely "magnanimity, confidence, security, magnificence, constancy, forbearance, stability." Andronicus also reckons seven virtues annexed to fortitude, and these are, "courage, strength of will, magnanimity, manliness, perseverance, magnificence." Therefore it seems that Tully's reckoning of the parts of fortitude is incomplete.

Obj. 7: Further, Aristotle (Ethic. iii) reckons five parts of fortitude. The first is *civic* fortitude, which produces brave deeds through fear of dishonor or punishment; the second is *military* fortitude, which produces brave deeds as a result of warlike art or experience; the third is the fortitude which produces brave deeds resulting from passion, especially anger; the fourth is the fortitude which makes a man act bravely through being accustomed to overcome; the fifth is the fortitude which makes a man act bravely through being unaccustomed to danger. Now these kinds of fortitude are not comprised under any of the above enumerations. Therefore these enumerations of the parts of fortitude are unfitting.

*I answer that,* As stated above (Q. 48), a virtue can have three kinds of parts, subjective, integral, and potential. But fortitude, taken as a special virtue, cannot have subjective parts, since it is not divided into several specifically distinct virtues, for it is about a very special matter.

However, there are quasi-integral and potential parts assigned to it: integral parts, with regard to those things the concurrence of which is requisite for an act of fortitude; and potential parts, because what fortitude practices in face of the greatest hardships, namely dangers of death, certain other virtues practice in the matter of certain minor hardships and these virtues are annexed to fortitude as secondary virtues to the principal virtue. As stated above (Q. 123, AA. 3, 6), the act of fortitude is twofold, aggression and endurance. Now two things are required for the act of aggression. The first regards preparation of the mind, and consists in one's having a mind ready for aggression. In this respect Tully mentions *confidence,* of which he says (De Invent. Rhet. ii) that "with this the mind is much assured and firmly hopeful in great and honorable undertakings." The second regards the accomplishment of the deed, and consists in not failing to accomplish what one has confidently begun. In this respect Tully mentions *magnificence,* which he describes as being "the discussion and administration," i.e. accomplishment "of great and lofty undertakings, with a certain broad and noble purpose of mind," so as to combine execution with greatness of purpose. Accordingly if these two be confined to the proper matter of fortitude, namely to dangers of death, they will be quasi-integral parts thereof, because without them there can be no fortitude; whereas if they be referred to other matters involving less hardship, they will be virtues specifically distinct from fortitude, but annexed thereto as secondary virtues to principal: thus *magnificence* is referred by the Philosopher (Ethic. iv) to great expenses, and *magnanimity,* which seems to be the same as confidence, to great honors. Again, two things are requisite for the other act of fortitude, viz. endurance. The first is that the mind be not broken by sorrow, and fall away from its greatness, by reason of the stress of threatening evil. In this respect he mentions *patience,* which he describes as "the voluntary and prolonged endurance of arduous and difficult things for the sake of virtue or profit." The other is that by the prolonged suffering of hardships man be not wearied so as to lose courage, according to Heb. 12:3, "That you be not wearied, fainting in your minds." In this respect he mentions *perseverance,* which accordingly he describes as "the fixed and continued persistence in a well considered purpose." If these two be confined to the proper matter of fortitude, they will be quasi-integral parts thereof; but if they be referred to any kind of hardship they will be virtues distinct from fortitude, yet annexed thereto as secondary to principal.

Reply Obj. 1: Magnificence in the matter of liberality adds a certain greatness: this is connected with the notion of difficulty which is the object of the irascible faculty, that is perfected chiefly by fortitude: and to this virtue, in this respect, it belongs.

Reply Obj. 2: Hope whereby one confides in God is accounted a theological virtue, as stated above (Q. 17, A. 5; I-II, Q. 62, A. 3). But by confidence which here is accounted a part of fortitude, man hopes in himself, yet under God withal.

Reply Obj. 3: To venture on anything great seems to involve danger, since to fail in such things is very disastrous. Wherefore although magnificence and confidence are referred to the accomplishment of or venturing on any other great things, they have a certain connection with fortitude by reason of the imminent danger.

Reply Obj. 4: Patience endures not only dangers of death, with which fortitude is concerned, without excessive sorrow, but also any other hardships or dangers. In this respect it is accounted a virtue annexed to fortitude: but as referred to dangers of death, it is an integral part thereof.

Reply Obj. 5: Perseverance as denoting persistence in a good deed unto the end, may be a circumstance of every virtue, but it is reckoned a part of fortitude in the sense stated in the body of the Article.

Reply Obj. 6: Macrobius reckons the four aforesaid mentioned by Tully, namely *confidence, magnificence, forbearance,* which he puts in the place of patience, and *firmness,* which he substitutes for perseverance. And he adds three, two of which, namely *magnanimity* and *security,* are comprised by Tully under the head of confidence. But Macrobius is more specific in his enumeration. Because confidence denotes a man's hope for great things: and hope for anything presupposes an appetite stretching forth to great things by desire, and this belongs to magnanimity. For it has been stated above (I-II, Q. 40, A. 2) that hope presupposes love and desire of the thing hoped for.

A still better reply is that confidence pertains to the certitude of hope; while magnanimity refers to the magnitude of the thing hoped for. Now hope has no firmness unless its contrary be removed, for sometimes one, for one's own part, would hope for something, but hope is avoided on account of the obstacle of fear, since fear is somewhat contrary to hope, as stated above, (I-II, Q. 40, A. 4, ad 1). Hence Macrobius adds security, which banishes fear. He adds a third, namely constancy, which may be comprised under magnificence. For in performing deeds of magnificence one needs to have a constant mind. For this reason Tully says that magnificence consists not only in accomplishing great things, but also in discussing them generously in the mind. Constancy may also pertain to perseverance, so that one may be called persevering through not desisting on account of delays, and constant through not desisting on account of any other obstacles.

Those that are mentioned by Andronicus seem to amount to the same as the above. For with Tully and Macrobius he mentions *perseverance* and *magnificence,* and with Macrobius, magnanimity. Strength of will is the same as patience or forbearance, for he says that "strength of will is a habit that makes one ready to attempt what ought to be attempted, and to endure what reason says should be endured"—i.e. good courage seems to be the same as assurance, for he defines it as "strength of soul in the accomplishment of its purpose." Manliness is apparently the same as confidence, for he says that "manliness is a habit of self-sufficiency in matters of virtue." Besides magnificence he mentions *andragathia* , i.e. manly goodness which we may render "strenuousness." For magnificence consists not only in being constant in the accomplishment of great deeds, which belongs to constancy, but also in bringing a certain manly prudence and solicitude to that accomplishment, and this belongs to *andragathia* , strenuousness: wherefore he says that *andragathia* is the virtue of a man, whereby he thinks out profitable works.

Accordingly it is evident that all these parts may be reduced to the four principal parts mentioned by Tully.

Reply Obj. 7: The five mentioned by Aristotle fall short of the true notion of virtue, for though they concur in the act of fortitude, they differ as to motive, as stated above (Q. 123, A. 1, ad 2); wherefore they are not reckoned parts but modes of fortitude.

## QUESTION 129

OF MAGNANIMITY* [*Not in the ordinary restricted sense but as explained by the author] (In Eight Articles)

We must now consider each of the parts of fortitude, including, however, the other parts under those mentioned by Tully, with the exception of confidence, for which we shall substitute magnanimity, of which Aristotle treats. Accordingly we shall consider (1) Magnanimity; (2) Magnificence; (3) Patience; (4) Perseverance. As regards the first we shall treat (1) of magnanimity; (2) of its contrary vices. Under the first head there are eight points of inquiry:

(1) Whether magnanimity is about honors?

(2) Whether magnanimity is only about great honors?

(3) Whether it is a virtue?

(4) Whether it is a special virtue?

(5) Whether it is a part of fortitude?

(6) Of its relation to confidence;

(7) Of its relation to assurance;

(8) Of its relation to goods of fortune.

FIRST ARTICLE [II-II, Q. 129, Art. 1]

Whether Magnanimity Is About Honors?

Objection 1: It seems that magnanimity is not about honors. For magnanimity is in the irascible faculty, as its very name shows, since "magnanimity" signifies greatness of mind, and "mind" denotes the irascible part, as appears from *De Anima* iii, 42, where the Philosopher says that "in the sensitive appetite are desire and mind," i.e. the concupiscible and irascible parts. But honor is a concupiscible good since it is the reward of virtue. Therefore it seems that magnanimity is not about honors.

Obj. 2: Further, since magnanimity is a moral virtue, it must needs be about either passions or operations. Now it is not about operations, for then it would be a part of justice: whence it follows that it is about passions. But honor is not a passion. Therefore magnanimity is not about honors.

Obj. 3: Further, the nature of magnanimity seems to regard pursuit rather than avoidance, for a man is said to be magnanimous because he tends to great things. But the virtuous are praised not for desiring honors, but for shunning them. Therefore magnanimity is not about honors.

*On the contrary,* The Philosopher says (Ethic. iv, 3) that "magnanimity is about honor and dishonor."

*I answer that,* Magnanimity by its very name denotes stretching forth of the mind to great things. Now virtue bears a relationship to two things, first to the matter about which is the field of its activity, secondly to its proper act, which consists in the right use of such matter. And since a virtuous habit is denominated chiefly from its act, a man is said to be magnanimous chiefly because he is minded to do some great act. Now an act may be called great in two ways: in one way proportionately, in another absolutely. An act may be called great proportionately, even if it consist in the use of some small or ordinary thing, if, for instance, one make a very good use of it: but an act is simply and absolutely great when it consists in the best use of the greatest thing.

The things which come into man's use are external things, and among these honor is the greatest simply, both because it is the most akin to virtue, since it is an attestation to a person's virtue, as stated above (Q. 103, AA. 1, 2); and because it is offered to God and to the best; and again because, in order to obtain honor even as to avoid shame, men set aside all other things. Now a man is said to be magnanimous in respect of things that are great absolutely and simply, just as a man is said to be brave in respect of things that are difficult simply. It follows therefore that magnanimity is about honors.

Reply Obj. 1: Good and evil absolutely considered regard the concupiscible faculty, but in so far as the aspect of difficult is added, they belong to the irascible. Thus it is that magnanimity regards honor, inasmuch, to wit, as honor has the aspect of something great or difficult.

Reply Obj. 2: Although honor is neither a passion nor an operation, yet it is the object of a passion, namely hope, which tends to a difficult good. Wherefore magnanimity is immediately about the passions of hope, and mediately about honor as the object of hope: even so, we have stated (Q. 123, AA. 4, 5) with regard to fortitude that it is about dangers of death in so far as they are the object of fear and daring.

Reply Obj. 3: Those are worthy of praise who despise riches in such a way as to do nothing unbecoming in order to obtain them, nor have too great a desire for them. If, however, one were to despise honors so as not to care to do what is worthy of honor, this would be deserving of blame. Accordingly magnanimity is about honors in the sense that a man strives to do what is deserving of honor, yet not so as to think much of the honor accorded by man.

SECOND ARTICLE [II-II, Q. 129, Art. 2]

Whether Magnanimity Is Essentially About Great Honors?

Objection 1: It seems that magnanimity is not essentially about great honors. For the proper matter of magnanimity is honor, as stated above (A. 1). But great and little are accidental to honor. Therefore it is not essential to magnanimity to be about great honors.

Obj. 2: Further, just as magnanimity is about honor, so is meekness about anger. But it is not essential to meekness to be about either great or little anger. Therefore neither is it essential to magnanimity to be about great honor.

Obj. 3: Further, small honor is less aloof from great honor than is dishonor. But magnanimity is well ordered in relation to dishonor, and consequently in relation to small honors also. Therefore it is not only about great honors.

*On the contrary,* The Philosopher says (Ethic. ii, 7) that magnanimity is about great honors.

*I answer that,* According to the Philosopher (Phys. vii, 17, 18), virtue is a perfection, and by this we are to understand the perfection of a power, and that it regards the extreme limit of that power, as stated in *De Coelo* i, 116. Now the perfection of a power is not perceived in every operation of that power, but in such operations as are great or difficult: for every power, however imperfect, can extend to ordinary and trifling operations. Hence it is essential to a virtue to be about the difficult and the good, as stated in *Ethic.* ii, 3.

Now the difficult and the good (which amount to the same) in an act of virtue may be considered from two points of view. First, from the point of view of reason, in so far as it is difficult to find and establish the rational means in some particular matter: and this difficulty is found only in the act of intellectual virtues, and also of justice. The other difficulty is on the part of the matter, which may involve a certain opposition to the moderation of reason, which moderation has to be applied thereto: and this difficulty regards chiefly the other moral virtues, which are about the passions, because the passions resist reason as Dionysius states (Div. Nom. iv, 4).

Now as regards the passions it is to be observed that the greatness of this power of resistance to reason arises chiefly in some cases from the passions themselves, and in others from the things that are the objects of the passions. The passions themselves have no great power of resistance, unless they be violent, because the sensitive appetite, which is the seat of the passions, is naturally subject to reason. Hence the resisting virtues that are about these passions regard only that which is great in such passions: thus fortitude is about very great fear and daring; temperance about the concupiscence of the greatest pleasures, and likewise meekness about the greatest anger. On the other hand, some passions have great power of resistance to reason arising from the external things themselves that are the objects of those passions: such are the love or desire of money or of honor. And for these it is necessary to have a virtue not only regarding that which is greatest in those passions, but also about that which is ordinary or little: because things external, though they be little, are very desirable, as being necessary for human life. Hence with regard to the desire of money there are two virtues, one about ordinary or little sums of money, namely liberality, and another about large sums of money, namely "magnificence."

In like manner there are two virtues about honors, one about ordinary honors. This virtue has no name, but is denominated by its extremes, which are *philotimia* , i.e. love of honor, and aphilotimia , i.e. without love of honor: for sometimes a man is commended for loving honor, and sometimes for not caring about it, in so far, to wit, as both these things may be done in moderation. But with regard to great honors there is *magnanimity.* Wherefore we must conclude that the proper matter of magnanimity is great honor, and that a magnanimous man tends to such things as are deserving of honor.

Reply Obj. 1: Great and little are accidental to honor considered in itself: but they make a great difference in their relation to reason, the mode of which has to be observed in the use of honor, for it is much more difficult to observe it in great than in little honors.

Reply Obj. 2: In anger and other matters only that which is greatest presents any notable difficulty, and about this alone is there any need of a virtue. It is different with riches and honors which are things existing outside the soul.

Reply Obj. 3: He that makes good use of great things is much more able to make good use of little things. Accordingly the magnanimous man looks upon great honors as a thing of which he is worthy, or even little honors as something he deserves, because, to wit, man cannot sufficiently honor virtue which deserves to be honored by God. Hence he is not uplifted by great honors, because he does not deem them above him; rather does he despise them, and much more such as are ordinary or little. In like manner he is not cast down by dishonor, but despises it, since he recognizes that he does not deserve it.

THIRD ARTICLE [II-II, Q. 129, Art. 3]

Whether Magnanimity Is a Virtue?

Objection 1: It seems that magnanimity is not a virtue. For every moral virtue observes the mean. But magnanimity observes not the mean but the greater extreme: because the "magnanimous man deems himself worthy of the greatest things" (Ethic. iv, 3). Therefore magnanimity is not a virtue.

Obj. 2: Further, he that has one virtue has them all, as stated above (I-II, Q. 65, A. 1). But one may have a virtue without having magnanimity: since the Philosopher says (Ethic. iv, 3) that "whosoever is worthy of little things and deems himself worthy of them, is temperate, but he is not magnanimous." Therefore magnanimity is not a virtue.

Obj. 3: Further, "Virtue is a good quality of the mind," as stated above (I-II, Q. 55, A. 4). But magnanimity implies certain dispositions of the body: for the Philosopher says (Ethic. iv, 3) of "a magnanimous man that his gait is slow, his voice deep, and his utterance calm." Therefore magnanimity is not a virtue.

Obj. 4: Further, no virtue is opposed to another virtue. But magnanimity is opposed to humility, since "the magnanimous deems himself worthy of great things, and despises others," according to *Ethic.* iv, 3. Therefore magnanimity is not a virtue.

Obj. 5: Further, the properties of every virtue are praiseworthy. But magnanimity has certain properties that call for blame. For, in the first place, the magnanimous is unmindful of favors; secondly, he is remiss and slow of action; thirdly, he employs irony [*Cf. Q. 113] towards many; fourthly, he is unable to associate with others; fifthly, because he holds to the barren things rather than to those that are fruitful. Therefore magnanimity is not a virtue.

*On the contrary,* It is written in praise of certain men (2 Macc. 15:18): "Nicanor hearing of the valor of Judas' companions, and the greatness of courage ( animi magnitudinem ) with which they fought for their country, was afraid to try the matter by the sword." Now, only deeds of virtue are worthy of praise. Therefore magnanimity which consists in greatness of courage is a virtue.

*I answer that,* The essence of human virtue consists in safeguarding the good of reason in human affairs, for this is man's proper good. Now among external human things honors take precedence of all others, as stated above (A. 1; I-II, Q. 11, A. 2, Obj. 3). Therefore magnanimity, which observes the mode of reason in great honors, is a virtue.

Reply Obj. 1: As the Philosopher again says (Ethic. iv, 3), "the magnanimous in point of quantity goes to extremes," in so far as he tends to what is greatest, "but in the matter of becomingness, he follows the mean," because he tends to the greatest things according to reason, for "he deems himself worthy in accordance with his worth" (Ethic. iv, 3), since his aims do not surpass his deserts.

Reply Obj. 2: The mutual connection of the virtues does not apply to their acts, as though every one were competent to practice the acts of all the virtues. Wherefore the act of magnanimity is not becoming to every virtuous man, but only to great men. On the other hand, as regards the principles of virtue, namely prudence and grace, all virtues are connected together, since their habits reside together in the soul, either in act or by way of a proximate disposition thereto. Thus it is possible for one to whom the act of magnanimity is not competent, to have the habit of magnanimity, whereby he is disposed to practice that act if it were competent to him according to his state.

Reply Obj. 3: The movements of the body are differentiated according to the different apprehensions and emotions of the soul. And so it happens that to magnanimity there accrue certain fixed accidents by way of bodily movements. For quickness of movement results from a man being intent on many things which he is in a hurry to accomplish, whereas the magnanimous is intent only on great things; these are few and require great attention, wherefore they call for slow movement. Likewise shrill and rapid speaking is chiefly competent to those who are quick to quarrel about anything, and this becomes not the magnanimous who are busy only about great things. And just as these dispositions of bodily movements are competent to the magnanimous man according to the mode of his emotions, so too in those who are naturally disposed to magnanimity these conditions are found naturally.

Reply Obj. 4: There is in man something great which he possesses through the gift of God; and something defective which accrues to him through the weakness of nature. Accordingly magnanimity makes a man deem himself worthy of great things in consideration of the gifts he holds from God: thus if his soul is endowed with great virtue, magnanimity makes him tend to perfect works of virtue; and the same is to be said of the use of any other good, such as science or external fortune. On the other hand, humility makes a man think little of himself in consideration of his own deficiency, and magnanimity makes him despise others in so far as they fall away from God's gifts: since he does not think so much of others as to do anything wrong for their sake. Yet humility makes us honor others and esteem them better than ourselves, in so far as we see some of God's gifts in them. Hence it is written of the just man (Ps. 14:4): "In his sight a vile person is contemned [*Douay: 'The malignant is brought to nothing, but he glorifieth,' etc.]," which indicates the contempt of magnanimity, "but he honoreth them that fear the Lord," which points to the reverential bearing of humility. It is therefore evident that magnanimity and humility are not contrary to one another, although they seem to tend in contrary directions, because they proceed according to different considerations.

Reply Obj. 5: These properties in so far as they belong to a magnanimous man call not for blame, but for very great praise. For in the first place, when it is said that the magnanimous is not mindful of those from whom he has received favors, this points to the fact that he takes no pleasure in accepting favors from others unless he repay them with yet greater favor; this belongs to the perfection of gratitude, in the act of which he wishes to excel, even as in the acts of other virtues. Again, in the second place, it is said that he is remiss and slow of action, not that he is lacking in doing what becomes him, but because he does not busy himself with all kinds of works, but only with great works, such as are becoming to him. He is also said, in the third place, to employ irony, not as opposed to truth, and so as either to say of himself vile things that are not true, or deny of himself great things that are true, but because he does not disclose all his greatness, especially to the large number of those who are beneath him, since, as also the Philosopher says (Ethic. iv, 3), "it belongs to a magnanimous man to be great towards persons of dignity and affluence, and unassuming towards the middle class." In the fourth place, it is said that he cannot associate with others: this means that he is not at home with others than his friends: because he altogether shuns flattery and hypocrisy, which belong to littleness of mind. But he associates with all, both great and little, according as he ought, as stated above (ad 1). It is also said, fifthly, that he prefers to have barren things, not indeed any, but good, i.e. virtuous; for in all things he prefers the virtuous to the useful, as being greater: since the useful is sought in order to supply a defect which is inconsistent with magnanimity.

FOURTH ARTICLE [II-II, Q. 129, Art. 4]

Whether Magnanimity Is a Special Virtue?

Objection 1: It seems that magnanimity is not a special virtue. For no special virtue is operative in every virtue. But the Philosopher states (Ethic. iv, 3) that "whatever is great in each virtue belongs to the magnanimous." Therefore magnanimity is not a special virtue.

Obj. 2: Further, the acts of different virtues are not ascribed to any special virtue. But the acts of different virtues are ascribed to the magnanimous man. For it is stated in *Ethic.* iv, 3 that "it belongs to the magnanimous not to avoid reproof" (which is an act of prudence), "nor to act unjustly" (which is an act of justice), "that he is ready to do favors" (which is an act of charity), "that he gives his services readily" (which is an act of liberality), that "he is truthful" (which is an act of truthfulness), and that "he is not given to complaining" (which is an act of patience). Therefore magnanimity is not a special virtue.

Obj. 3: Further, every virtue is a special ornament of the soul, according to the saying of Isa. 61:10, "He hath clothed me with the garments of salvation," and afterwards he adds, "and as a bride adorned with her jewels." But magnanimity is the ornament of all the virtues, as stated in *Ethic.* iv. Therefore magnanimity is a general virtue.

*On the contrary,* The Philosopher (Ethic. ii, 7) distinguishes it from the other virtues.

*I answer that,* As stated above (Q. 123, A. 2), it belongs to a special virtue to establish the mode of reason in a determinate matter. Now magnanimity establishes the mode of reason in a determinate matter, namely honors, as stated above (AA. 1, 2): and honor, considered in itself, is a special good, and accordingly magnanimity considered in itself is a special virtue.

Since, however, honor is the reward of every virtue, as stated above (Q. 103, A. 1, ad 2), it follows that by reason of its matter it regards all the virtues.

Reply Obj. 1: Magnanimity is not about any kind of honor, but great honor. Now, as honor is due to virtue, so great honor is due to a great deed of virtue. Hence it is that the magnanimous is intent on doing great deeds in every virtue, in so far, to wit, as he tends to what is worthy of great honors.

Reply Obj. 2: Since the magnanimous tends to great things, it follows that he tends chiefly to things that involve a certain excellence, and shuns those that imply defect. Now it savors of excellence that a man is beneficent, generous and grateful. Wherefore he shows himself ready to perform actions of this kind, but not as acts of the other virtues. On the other hand, it is a proof of defect, that a man thinks so much of certain external goods or evils, that for their sake he abandons and gives up justice or any virtue whatever. Again, all concealment of the truth indicates a defect, since it seems to be the outcome of fear. Also that a man be given to complaining denotes a defect, because by so doing the mind seems to give way to external evils. Wherefore these and like things the magnanimous man avoids under a special aspect, inasmuch as they are contrary to his excellence or greatness.

Reply Obj. 3: Every virtue derives from its species a certain luster or adornment which is proper to each virtue: but further adornment results from the very greatness of a virtuous deed, through magnanimity which makes all virtues greater as stated in *Ethic.* iv, 3.

FIFTH ARTICLE [II-II, Q. 129, Art. 5]

Whether Magnanimity Is a Part of Fortitude?

Objection 1: It seems that magnanimity is not a part of fortitude. For a thing is not a part of itself. But magnanimity appears to be the same as fortitude. For Seneca says (De Quat. Virtut.): "If magnanimity, which is also called fortitude, be in thy soul, thou shalt live in great assurance": and Tully says (De Offic. i): "If a man is brave we expect him to be magnanimous, truth-loving, and far removed from deception." Therefore magnanimity is not a part of fortitude.

Obj. 2: Further, the Philosopher (Ethic. iv, 3) says that a magnanimous man is not *philokindynos* , that is, a lover of danger. But it belongs to a brave man to expose himself to danger. Therefore magnanimity has nothing in common with fortitude so as to be called a part thereof.

Obj. 3: Further, magnanimity regards the great in things to be hoped for, whereas fortitude regards the great in things to be feared or dared. But good is of more import than evil. Therefore magnanimity is a more important virtue than fortitude. Therefore it is not a part thereof.

*On the contrary,* Macrobius (De Somn. Scip. i) and Andronicus reckon magnanimity as a part of fortitude.

*I answer that,* As stated above (I-II, Q. 61, A. 3), a principal virtue is one to which it belongs to establish a general mode of virtue in a principal matter. Now one of the general modes of virtue is firmness of mind, because "a firm standing is necessary in every virtue," according to *Ethic.* ii. And this is chiefly commended in those virtues that tend to something difficult, in which it is most difficult to preserve firmness. Wherefore the more difficult it is to stand firm in some matter of difficulty, the more principal is the virtue which makes the mind firm in that matter.

Now it is more difficult to stand firm in dangers of death, wherein fortitude confirms the mind, than in hoping for or obtaining the greatest goods, wherein the mind is confirmed by magnanimity, for, as man loves his life above all things, so does he fly from dangers of death more than any others. Accordingly it is clear that magnanimity agrees with fortitude in confirming the mind about some difficult matter; but it falls short thereof, in that it confirms the mind about a matter wherein it is easier to stand firm. Hence magnanimity is reckoned a part of fortitude, because it is annexed thereto as secondary to principal.

Reply Obj. 1: As the Philosopher says (Ethic. v, 1, 3), "to lack evil is looked upon as a good," wherefore not to be overcome by a grievous evil, such as the danger of death, is looked upon as though it were the obtaining of a great good, the former belonging to fortitude, and the latter to magnanimity: in this sense fortitude and magnanimity may be considered as identical. Since, however, there is a difference as regards the difficulty on the part of either of the aforesaid, it follows that properly speaking magnanimity, according to the Philosopher (Ethic. ii, 7), is a distinct virtue from fortitude.

Reply Obj. 2: A man is said to love danger when he exposes himself to all kinds of dangers, which seems to be the mark of one who thinks "many" the same as "great." This is contrary to the nature of a magnanimous man, for no one seemingly exposes himself to danger for the sake of a thing that he does not deem great. But for things that are truly great, a magnanimous man is most ready to expose himself to danger, since he does something great in the act of fortitude, even as in the acts of the other virtues. Hence the Philosopher says (Ethic. ii, 7) that the magnanimous man is not *mikrokindynos* , i.e. endangering himself for small things, but *megalokindynos* , i.e. endangering himself for great things. And Seneca says (De Quat. Virtut.): "Thou wilt be magnanimous if thou neither seekest dangers like a rash man, nor fearest them like a coward. For nothing makes the soul a coward save the consciousness of a wicked life."

Reply Obj. 3: Evil as such is to be avoided: and that one has to withstand it is accidental; in so far, to wit, as one has to suffer an evil in order to safeguard a good. But good as such is to be desired, and that one avoids it is only accidental, in so far, to wit, as it is deemed to surpass the ability of the one who desires it. Now that which is so essentially is always of more account than that which is so accidentally. Wherefore the difficult in evil things is always more opposed to firmness of mind than the difficult in good things. Hence the virtue of fortitude takes precedence of the virtue of magnanimity. For though good is simply of more import than evil, evil is of more import in this particular respect.

SIXTH ARTICLE [II-II, Q. 129, Art. 6]

Whether Confidence Belongs to Magnanimity?

Objection 1: It seems that confidence does not belong to magnanimity. For a man may have assurance not only in himself, but also in another, according to 2 Cor. 3:4, 5, "Such confidence we have, through Christ towards God, not that we are sufficient to think anything of ourselves, as of ourselves." But this seems inconsistent with the idea of magnanimity. Therefore confidence does not belong to magnanimity.

Obj. 2: Further, confidence seems to be opposed to fear, according to Isa. 12:2, "I will deal confidently and will not fear." But to be without fear seems more akin to fortitude. Therefore confidence also belongs to fortitude rather than to magnanimity.

Obj. 3: Further, reward is not due except to virtue. But a reward is due to confidence, according to Heb. 3:6, where it is said that we are the house of Christ, "if we hold fast the confidence and glory of hope unto the end." Therefore confidence is a virtue distinct from magnanimity: and this is confirmed by the fact that Macrobius enumerates it with magnanimity (In Somn. Scip. i).

*On the contrary,* Tully (De Suv. Rhet. ii) seems to substitute confidence for magnanimity, as stated above in the preceding Question (ad 6) and in the prologue to this.

*I answer that,* Confidence takes its name from "fides" (faith): and it belongs to faith to believe something and in somebody. But confidence belongs to hope, according to Job 11:18, "Thou shalt have confidence, hope being set before thee."

Wherefore confidence apparently denotes chiefly that a man derives hope through believing the word of one who promises to help him. Since, however, faith signifies also a strong opinion, and since one may come to have a strong opinion about something, not only on account of another's statement, but also on account of something we observe in another, it follows that confidence may denote the hope of having something, which hope we conceive through observing something either in oneself—for instance, through observing that he is healthy, a man is confident that he will live long. Or in another, for instance, through observing that another is friendly to him and powerful, a man is confident that he will receive help from him.

Now it has been stated above (A. 1, ad 2) that magnanimity is chiefly about the hope of something difficult. Wherefore, since confidence denotes a certain strength of hope arising from some observation which gives one a strong opinion that one will obtain a certain good, it follows that confidence belongs to magnanimity.

Reply Obj. 1: As the Philosopher says (Ethic. iv, 3), it belongs to the "magnanimous to need nothing," for need is a mark of the deficient. But this is to be understood according to the mode of a man, hence he adds "or scarcely anything." For it surpasses man to need nothing at all. For every man needs, first, the Divine assistance, secondly, even human assistance, since man is naturally a social animal, for he is [not] sufficient by himself to provide for his own life. Accordingly, in so far as he needs others, it belongs to a magnanimous man to have confidence in others, for it is also a point of excellence in a man that he should have at hand those who are able to be of service to him. And in so far as his own ability goes, it belongs to a magnanimous man to be confident in himself.

Reply Obj. 2: As stated above (I-II, Q. 23, A. 2; Q. 40, A. 4), when we were treating of the passions, hope is directly opposed to despair, because the latter is about the same object, namely good. But as regards contrariety of objects it is opposed to fear, because the latter's object is evil. Now confidence denotes a certain strength of hope, wherefore it is opposed to fear even as hope is. Since, however, fortitude properly strengthens a man in respect of evil, and magnanimity in respect of the obtaining of good, it follows that confidence belongs more properly to magnanimity than to fortitude. Yet because hope causes daring, which belongs to fortitude, it follows in consequence that confidence pertains to fortitude.

Reply Obj. 3: Confidence, as stated above, denotes a certain mode of hope: for confidence is hope strengthened by a strong opinion. Now the mode applied to an affection may call for commendation of the act, so that it become meritorious, yet it is not this that draws it to a species of virtue, but its matter. Hence, properly speaking, confidence cannot denote a virtue, though it may denote the conditions of a virtue. For this reason it is reckoned among the parts of fortitude, not as an annexed virtue, except as identified with magnanimity by Tully (De Suv. Rhet. ii), but as an integral part, as stated in the preceding Question.

SEVENTH ARTICLE [II-II, Q. 129, Art. 7]

Whether Security Belongs to Magnanimity?

Objection 1: It seems that security does not belong to magnanimity. For security, as stated above (Q. 128, ad 6), denotes freedom from the disturbance of fear. But fortitude does this most effectively. Wherefore security is seemingly the same as fortitude. But fortitude does not belong to magnanimity; rather the reverse is the case. Neither therefore does security belong to magnanimity.

Obj. 2: Further, Isidore says (Etym. x) that a man "is said to be secure because he is without care." But this seems to be contrary to virtue, which has a care for honorable things, according to 2 Tim. 2:15, "Carefully study to present thyself approved unto God." Therefore security does not belong to magnanimity, which does great things in all the virtues.

Obj. 3: Further, virtue is not its own reward. But security is accounted the reward of virtue, according to Job 11:14, 18, "If thou wilt put away from thee the iniquity that is in thy hand ... being buried thou shalt sleep secure." Therefore security does not belong to magnanimity or to any other virtue, as a part thereof.

*On the contrary,* Tully says (De Offic. i) under the heading: "Magnanimity consists of two things," that "it belongs to magnanimity to give way neither to a troubled mind, nor to man, nor to fortune." But a man's security consists in this. Therefore security belongs to magnanimity.

*I answer that,* As the Philosopher says (Rhet. ii, 5), "fear makes a man take counsel," because, to wit he takes care to avoid what he fears. Now security takes its name from the removal of this care, of which fear is the cause: wherefore security denotes perfect freedom of the mind from fear, just as confidence denotes strength of hope. Now, as hope directly belongs to magnanimity, so fear directly regards fortitude. Wherefore as confidence belongs immediately to magnanimity, so security belongs immediately to fortitude.

It must be observed, however, that as hope is the cause of daring, so is fear the cause of despair, as stated above when we were treating of the passion (I-II, Q. 45, A. 2). Wherefore as confidence belongs indirectly to fortitude, in so far as it makes use of daring, so security belongs indirectly to magnanimity, in so far as it banishes despair.

Reply Obj. 1: Fortitude is chiefly commended, not because it banishes fear, which belongs to security, but because it denotes a firmness of mind in the matter of the passion. Wherefore security is not the same as fortitude, but is a condition thereof.

Reply Obj. 2: Not all security is worthy of praise but only when one puts care aside, as one ought, and in things when one should not fear: in this way it is a condition of fortitude and of magnanimity.

Reply Obj. 3: There is in the virtues a certain likeness to, and participation of, future happiness, as stated above (I-II, Q. 5, AA. 3, 7). Hence nothing hinders a certain security from being a condition of a virtue, although perfect security belongs to virtue's reward.

EIGHTH ARTICLE [II-II, Q. 129, Art. 8]

Whether Goods of Fortune Conduce to Magnanimity?

Objection 1: It seems that goods of fortune do not conduce to magnanimity. For according to Seneca (De Ira i: De vita beata xvi): "virtue suffices for itself." Now magnanimity takes every virtue great, as stated above (A. 4, ad 3). Therefore goods of fortune do not conduce to magnanimity.

Obj. 2: Further, no virtuous man despises what is helpful to him. But the magnanimous man despises whatever pertains to goods of fortune: for Tully says (De Offic. i) under the heading: "Magnanimity consists of two things," that "a great soul is commended for despising external things." Therefore a magnanimous man is not helped by goods of fortune.

Obj. 3: Further, Tully adds (De Offic. i) that "it belongs to a great soul so to bear what seems troublesome, as nowise to depart from his natural estate, or from the dignity of a wise man." And Aristotle says (Ethic. iv, 3) that "a magnanimous man does not grieve at misfortune." Now troubles and misfortunes are opposed to goods of fortune, for every one grieves at the loss of what is helpful to him. Therefore external goods of fortune do not conduce to magnanimity.

*On the contrary,* The Philosopher says (Ethic. iv, 3) that "good fortune seems to conduce to magnanimity."

*I answer that,* As stated above (A. 1), magnanimity regards two things: honor as its matter, and the accomplishment of something great as its end. Now goods of fortune conduce to both these things. For since honor is conferred on the virtuous, not only by the wise, but also by the multitude who hold these goods of fortune in the highest esteem, the result is that they show greater honor to those who possess goods of fortune. Likewise goods of fortune are useful organs or instruments of virtuous deeds: since we can easily accomplish things by means of riches, power and friends. Hence it is evident that goods of fortune conduce to magnanimity.

Reply Obj. 1: Virtue is said to be sufficient for itself, because it can be without even these external goods; yet it needs them in order to act more expeditiously.

Reply Obj. 2: The magnanimous man despises external goods, inasmuch as he does not think them so great as to be bound to do anything unbecoming for their sake. Yet he does not despise them, but that he esteems them useful for the accomplishment of virtuous deeds.

Reply Obj. 3: If a man does not think much of a thing, he is neither very joyful at obtaining it, nor very grieved at losing it. Wherefore, since the magnanimous man does not think much of external goods, that is goods of fortune, he is neither much uplifted by them if he has them, nor much cast down by their loss.

# QUESTION 130

OF PRESUMPTION (In Two Articles)

We must now consider the vices opposed to magnanimity; and in the first place, those that are opposed thereto by excess. These are three, namely, presumption, ambition, and vainglory. Secondly, we shall consider pusillanimity which is opposed to it by way of deficiency. Under the first head there are two points of inquiry:

(1) Whether presumption is a sin?

(2) Whether it is opposed to magnanimity by excess?

FIRST ARTICLE [II-II, Q. 130, Art. 1]

Whether Presumption Is a Sin?

Objection 1: It seems that presumption is not a sin. For the Apostle says: "Forgetting the things that are behind, I stretch forth [Vulg.: 'and stretching forth'] myself to those that are before." But it seems to savor of presumption that one should tend to what is above oneself. Therefore presumption is not a sin.

Obj. 2: Further, the Philosopher says (Ethic. i, 7) "we should not listen to those who would persuade us to relish human things because we are men, or mortal things because we are mortal, but we should relish those that make us immortal": and (Metaph. i) "that man should pursue divine things as far as possible." Now divine and immortal things are seemingly far above man. Since then presumption consists essentially in tending to what is above oneself, it seems that presumption is something praiseworthy, rather than a sin.

Obj. 3: Further, the Apostle says (2 Cor. 3:5): "Not that we are sufficient to think anything of ourselves, as of ourselves." If then presumption, by which one strives at that for which one is not sufficient, be a sin, it seems that man cannot lawfully even think of anything good: which is absurd. Therefore presumption is not a sin.

*On the contrary,* It is written (Ecclus. 37:3): "O wicked presumption, whence camest thou?" and a gloss answers: "From a creature's evil will." Now all that comes of the root of an evil will is a sin. Therefore presumption is a sin.

*I answer that,* Since whatever is according to nature, is ordered by the Divine Reason, which human reason ought to imitate, whatever is done in accordance with human reason in opposition to the order established in general throughout natural things is vicious and sinful. Now it is established throughout all natural things, that every action is commensurate with the power of the agent, nor does any natural agent strive to do what exceeds its ability. Hence it is vicious and sinful, as being contrary to the natural order, that any one should assume to do what is above his power: and this is what is meant by presumption, as its very name shows. Wherefore it is evident that presumption is a sin.

Reply Obj. 1: [A thing may be] above the active power of a natural thing, and yet not above the passive power of that same thing: thus the air is possessed of a passive power by reason of which it can be so changed as to obtain the action and movement of fire, which surpass the active power of air. Thus too it would be sinful and presumptuous for a man while in a state of imperfect virtue to attempt the immediate accomplishment of what belongs to perfect virtue. But it is not presumptuous or sinful for a man to endeavor to advance towards perfect virtue. In this way the Apostle stretched himself forth to the things that were before him, namely continually advancing forward.

Reply Obj. 2: Divine and immortal things surpass man according to the order of nature. Yet man is possessed of a natural power, namely the intellect, whereby he can be united to immortal and Divine things. In this respect the Philosopher says that "man ought to pursue immortal and divine things," not that he should do what it becomes God to do, but that he should be united to Him in intellect and will.

Reply Obj. 3: As the Philosopher says (Ethic. iii, 3), "what we can do by the help of others we can do by ourselves in a sense." Hence since we can think and do good by the help of God, this is not altogether above our ability. Hence it is not presumptuous for a man to attempt the accomplishment of a virtuous deed: but it would be presumptuous if one were to make the attempt without confidence in God's assistance.

SECOND ARTICLE [II-II, Q. 130, Art. 2]

Whether Presumption Is Opposed to Magnanimity by Excess?

Objection 1: It seems that presumption is not opposed to magnanimity by excess. For presumption is accounted a species of the sin against the Holy Ghost, as stated above (Q. 14, A. 2; Q. 21, A. 1). But the sin against the Holy Ghost is not opposed to magnanimity, but to charity. Neither therefore is presumption opposed to magnanimity.

Obj. 2: Further, it belongs to magnanimity that one should deem oneself worthy of great things. But a man is said to be presumptuous even if he deem himself worthy of small things, if they surpass his ability. Therefore presumption is not directly opposed to magnanimity.

Obj. 3: Further, the magnanimous man looks upon external goods as little things. Now according to the Philosopher (Ethic. iv, 3), "on account of external fortune the presumptuous disdain and wrong others, because they deem external goods as something great." Therefore presumption is opposed to magnanimity, not by excess, but only by deficiency.

*On the contrary,* The Philosopher says (Ethic. ii, 7; iv, 3) that the "vain man," i.e. a vaporer or a windbag, which with us denotes a presumptuous man, "is opposed to the magnanimous man by excess."

*I answer that,* As stated above (Q. 129, A. 3, ad 1), magnanimity observes the means, not as regards the quantity of that to which it tends, but in proportion to our own ability: for it does not tend to anything greater than is becoming to us.

Now the presumptuous man, as regards that to which he tends, does not exceed the magnanimous, but sometimes falls far short of him: but he does exceed in proportion to his own ability, whereas the magnanimous man does not exceed his. It is in this way that presumption is opposed to magnanimity by excess.

Reply Obj. 1: It is not every presumption that is accounted a sin against the Holy Ghost, but that by which one contemns the Divine justice through inordinate confidence in the Divine mercy. The latter kind of presumption, by reason of its matter, inasmuch, to wit, as it implies contempt of something Divine, is opposed to charity, or rather to the gift of fear, whereby we revere God. Nevertheless, in so far as this contempt exceeds the proportion to one's own ability, it can be opposed to magnanimity.

Reply Obj. 2: Presumption, like magnanimity, seems to tend to something great. For we are not, as a rule, wont to call a man presumptuous for going beyond his powers in something small. If, however, such a man be called presumptuous, this kind of presumption is not opposed to magnanimity, but to that virtue which is about ordinary honor, as stated above (Q. 129, A. 2).

Reply Obj. 3: No one attempts what is above his ability, except in so far as he deems his ability greater than it is. In this one may err in two ways. First only as regards quantity, as when a man thinks he has greater virtue, or knowledge, or the like, than he has. Secondly, as regards the kind of thing, as when he thinks himself great, and worthy of great things, by reason of something that does not make him so, for instance by reason of riches or goods of fortune. For, as the Philosopher says (Ethic. iv, 3), "those who have these things without virtue, neither justly deem themselves worthy of great things, nor are rightly called magnanimous."

Again, the thing to which a man sometimes tends in excess of his ability, is sometimes in very truth something great, simply as in the case of Peter, whose intent was to suffer for Christ, which has exceeded his power; while sometimes it is something great, not simply, but only in the opinion of fools, such as wearing costly clothes, despising and wronging others. This savors of an excess of magnanimity, not in any truth, but in people's opinion. Hence Seneca says (De Quat. Virtut.) that "when magnanimity exceeds its measure, it makes a man high-handed, proud, haughty restless, and bent on excelling in all things, whether in words or in deeds, without any considerations of virtue." Thus it is evident that the presumptuous man sometimes falls short of the magnanimous in reality, although in appearance he surpasses him.

## QUESTION 131

OF AMBITION (In Two Articles)

We must now consider ambition: and under this head there are two points of inquiry:

(1) Whether it is a sin?

(2) Whether it is opposed to magnanimity by excess?

FIRST ARTICLE [II-II, Q. 131, Art. 1]

Whether Ambition Is a Sin?

Objection 1: It seems that ambition is not a sin. For ambition denotes the desire of honor. Now honor is in itself a good thing, and the greatest of external goods: wherefore those who care not for honor are reproved. Therefore ambition is not a sin; rather is it something deserving of praise, in so far as a good is laudably desired.

Obj. 2: Further, anyone may, without sin, desire what is due to him as a reward. Now honor is the reward of virtue, as the Philosopher states (Ethic. i, 12; iv, 3; viii, 14). Therefore ambition of honor is not a sin.

Obj. 3: Further, that which heartens a man to do good and disheartens him from doing evil, is not a sin. Now honor heartens men to do good and to avoid evil; thus the Philosopher says (Ethic. iii, 8) that "with the bravest men, cowards are held in dishonor, and the brave in honor": and Tully says (De Tusc. Quaest. i) that "honor fosters the arts." Therefore ambition is not a sin.

*On the contrary,* It is written (1 Cor. 13:5) that "charity is not ambitious, seeketh not her own." Now nothing is contrary to charity, except sin. Therefore ambition is a sin.

*I answer that,* As stated above (Q. 103, AA. 1, 2), honor denotes reverence shown to a person in witness of his excellence. Now two things have to be considered with regard to man's honor. The first is that a man has not from himself the thing in which he excels, for this is, as it were, something Divine in him, wherefore on this count honor is due principally, not to him but to God. The second point that calls for observation is that the thing in which man excels is given to him by God, that he may profit others thereby: wherefore a man ought so far to be pleased that others bear witness to his excellence, as this enables him to profit others.

Now the desire of honor may be inordinate in three ways. First, when a man desires recognition of an excellence which he has not: this is to desire more than his share of honor. Secondly, when a man desires honor for himself without referring it to God. Thirdly, when a man's appetite rests in honor itself, without referring it to the profit of others. Since then ambition denotes inordinate desire of honor, it is evident that it is always a sin.

Reply Obj. 1: The desire for good should be regulated according to reason, and if it exceed this rule it will be sinful. In this way it is sinful to desire honor in disaccord with the order of reason. Now those are reproved who care not for honor in accordance with reason's dictate that they should avoid what is contrary to honor.

Reply Obj. 2: Honor is not the reward of virtue, as regards the virtuous man, in this sense that he should seek for it as his reward: since the reward he seeks is happiness, which is the end of virtue. But it is said to be the reward of virtue as regards others, who have nothing greater than honor whereby to reward the virtuous; which honor derives greatness from the very fact that it bears witness to virtue. Hence it is evident that it is not an adequate reward, as stated in *Ethic.* iv, 3.

Reply Obj. 3: Just as some are heartened to do good and disheartened from doing evil, by the desire of honor, if this be desired in due measure; so, if it be desired inordinately, it may become to man an occasion of doing many evil things, as when a man cares not by what means he obtains honor. Wherefore Sallust says (Catilin.) that "the good as well as the wicked covet honors for themselves, but the one," i.e. the good, "go about it in the right way," whereas "the other," i.e. the wicked, "through lack of the good arts, make use of deceit and falsehood." Yet they who, merely for the sake of honor, either do good or avoid evil, are not virtuous, according to the Philosopher (Ethic. iii, 8), where he says that they who do brave things for the sake of honor are not truly brave.

SECOND ARTICLE [II-II, Q. 131, Art. 2]

Whether Ambition Is Opposed to Magnanimity by Excess?

Objection 1: It seems that ambition is not opposed to magnanimity by excess. For one mean has only one extreme opposed to it on the one side. Now presumption is opposed to magnanimity by excess as stated above (Q. 130, A. 2). Therefore ambition is not opposed to it by excess.

Obj. 2: Further, magnanimity is about honors; whereas ambition seems to regard positions of dignity: for it is written (2 Macc. 4:7) that "Jason ambitiously sought the high priesthood." Therefore ambition is not opposed to magnanimity.

Obj. 3: Further, ambition seems to regard outward show: for it is written (Acts 25:27) that "Agrippa and Berenice ... with great pomp ( *ambitione* ) ... had entered into the hall of audience" [*'Praetorium.' The Vulgate has 'auditorium,' but the meaning is the same], and (2 Para. 16:14) that when Asa died they "burned spices and ... ointments over his body" with very great pomp ( *ambitione* ). But magnanimity is not about outward show. Therefore ambition is not opposed to magnanimity.

*On the contrary,* Tully says (De Offic. i) that "the more a man exceeds in magnanimity, the more he desires himself alone to dominate others." But this pertains to ambition. Therefore ambition denotes an excess of magnanimity.

*I answer that,* As stated above (A. 1), ambition signifies inordinate love of honor. Now magnanimity is about honors and makes use of them in a becoming manner. Wherefore it is evident that ambition is opposed to magnanimity as the inordinate to that which is well ordered.

Reply Obj. 1: Magnanimity regards two things. It regards one as its end, in so far as it is some great deed that the magnanimous man attempts in proportion to his ability. In this way presumption is opposed to magnanimity by excess: because the presumptuous man attempts great deeds beyond his ability. The other thing that magnanimity regards is its matter, viz. honor, of which it makes right use: and in this way ambition is opposed to magnanimity by excess. Nor is it impossible for one mean to be exceeded in various respects.

Reply Obj. 2: Honor is due to those who are in a position of dignity, on account of a certain excellence of their estate: and accordingly inordinate desire for positions of dignity pertains to ambition. For if a man were to have an inordinate desire for a position of dignity, not for the sake of honor, but for the sake of a right use of a dignity exceeding his ability, he would not be ambitious but presumptuous.

Reply Obj. 3: The very solemnity of outward worship is a kind of honor, wherefore in such cases honor is wont to be shown. This is signified by the words of James 2:2, 3: "If there shall come into your assembly a man having a golden ring, in fine apparel ... and you ... shall say to him: Sit thou here well," etc. Wherefore ambition does not regard outward worship, except in so far as this is a kind of honor.

# QUESTION 132

OF VAINGLORY (In Five Articles)

We must now consider vainglory: under which head there are five points of inquiry:

(1) Whether desire of glory is a sin?

(2) Whether it is opposed to magnanimity?

(3) Whether it is a mortal sin?

(4) Whether it is a capital vice?

(5) Of its daughters.

FIRST ARTICLE [II-II, Q. 132, Art. 1]

Whether the Desire of Glory Is a Sin?

Objection 1: It seems that the desire of glory is not a sin. For no one sins in being likened to God: in fact we are commanded (Eph. 5:1): "Be ye ... followers of God, as most dear children." Now by seeking glory man seems to imitate God, Who seeks glory from men: wherefore it is written (Isa. 43:6, 7): "Bring My sons from afar, and My daughters from the ends of the earth. And every one that calleth on My name, I have created him for My glory." Therefore the desire for glory is not a sin.

Obj. 2: Further, that which incites a man to do good is apparently not a sin. Now the desire of glory incites men to do good. For Tully says (De Tusc. Quaest. i) that "glory inflames every man to strive his utmost": and in Holy Writ glory is promised for good works, according to Rom. 2:7: "To them, indeed, who according to patience in good work ... glory and honor" [*Vulg.: 'Who will render to every man according to his works, to them indeed who ... seek glory and honor and incorruption, eternal life.']. Therefore the desire for glory is not a sin.

Obj. 3: Further, Tully says (De Invent. Rhet. ii) that glory is "consistent good report about a person, together with praise": and this comes to the same as what Augustine says (Contra Maximin. iii), viz. that glory is, "as it were, clear knowledge with praise." Now it is no sin to desire praiseworthy renown: indeed, it seems itself to call for praise, according to Ecclus. 41:15, "Take care of a good name," and Rom. 12:17, "Providing good things not only in the sight of God, but also in the sight of all men." Therefore the desire of vainglory is not a sin.

*On the contrary,* Augustine says (De Civ. Dei v): "He is better advised who acknowledges that even the love of praise is sinful."

*I answer that,* Glory signifies a certain clarity, wherefore Augustine says (Tract. lxxxii, c, cxiv in Joan.) that to be "glorified is the same as to be clarified." Now clarity and comeliness imply a certain display: wherefore the word glory properly denotes the display of something as regards its seeming comely in the sight of men, whether it be a bodily or a spiritual good. Since, however, that which is clear simply can be seen by many, and by those who are far away, it follows that the word glory properly denotes that somebody's good is known and approved by many, according to the saying of Sallust (Catilin.) [*The quotation is from Livy: Hist., Lib. XXII C, 39]: "I must not boast while I am addressing one man."

But if we take the word glory in a broader sense, it not only consists in the knowledge of many, but also in the knowledge of few, or of one, or of oneself alone, as when one considers one's own good as being worthy of praise. Now it is not a sin to know and approve one's own good: for it is written (1 Cor. 2:12): "Now we have received not the spirit of this world, but the Spirit that is of God that we may know the things that are given us from God." Likewise it is not a sin to be willing to approve one's own good works: for it is written (Matt. 5:16): "Let your light shine before men." Hence the desire for glory does not, of itself, denote a sin: but the desire for empty or vain glory denotes a sin: for it is sinful to desire anything vain, according to Ps. 4:3, "Why do you love vanity, and seek after lying?"

Now glory may be called vain in three ways. First, on the part of the thing for which one seeks glory: as when a man seeks glory for that which is unworthy of glory, for instance when he seeks it for something frail and perishable: secondly, on the part of him from whom he seeks glory, for instance a man whose judgment is uncertain: thirdly, on the part of the man himself who seeks glory, for that he does not refer the desire of his own glory to a due end, such as God's honor, or the spiritual welfare of his neighbor.

Reply Obj. 1: As Augustine says on John 13:13, "You call Me Master and Lord; and you say well" (Tract. lviii in Joan.): "Self-complacency is fraught with danger of one who has to beware of pride. But He Who is above all, however much He may praise Himself, does not uplift Himself. For knowledge of God is our need, not His: nor does any man know Him unless he be taught of Him Who knows." It is therefore evident that God seeks glory, not for His own sake, but for ours. In like manner a man may rightly seek his own glory for the good of others, according to Matt. 5:16, "That they may see your good works, and glorify your Father Who is in heaven."

Reply Obj. 2: That which we receive from God is not vain but true glory: it is this glory that is promised as a reward for good works, and of which it is written (2 Cor. 10:17, 18): "He that glorieth let him glory in the Lord, for not he who commendeth himself is approved, but he whom God commendeth." It is true that some are heartened to do works of virtue, through desire for human glory, as also through the desire for other earthly goods. Yet he is not truly virtuous who does virtuous deeds for the sake of human glory, as Augustine proves (De Civ. Dei v).

Reply Obj. 3: It is requisite for man's perfection that he should know himself; but not that he should be known by others, wherefore it is not to be desired in itself. It may, however, be desired as being useful for something, either in order that God may be glorified by men, or that men may become better by reason of the good they know to be in another man, or in order that man, knowing by the testimony of others' praise the good which is in him, may himself strive to persevere therein and to become better. In this sense it is praiseworthy that a man should "take care of his good name," and that he should "provide good things in the sight of God and men": but not that he should take an empty pleasure in human praise.

SECOND ARTICLE [II-II, Q. 132, Art. 2]

Whether Vainglory Is Opposed to Magnanimity?

Objection 1: It seems that vainglory is not opposed to magnanimity. For, as stated above (A. 1), vainglory consists in glorying in things that are not, which pertains to falsehood; or in earthly and perishable things, which pertains to covetousness; or in the testimony of men, whose judgment is uncertain, which pertains to imprudence. Now these vices are not contrary to magnanimity. Therefore vainglory is not opposed to magnanimity.

Obj. 2: Further, vainglory is not, like pusillanimity, opposed to magnanimity by way of deficiency, for this seems inconsistent with vainglory. Nor is it opposed to it by way of excess, for in this way presumption and ambition are opposed to magnanimity, as stated above (Q. 130, A. 2; Q. 131, A. 2): and these differ from vainglory. Therefore vainglory is not opposed to magnanimity.

Obj. 3: Further, a gloss on Phil. 2:3, "Let nothing be done through contention, neither by vainglory," says: "Some among them were given to dissension and restlessness, contending with one another for the sake of vainglory." But contention [*Cf. Q. 38] is not opposed to magnanimity. Neither therefore is vainglory.

*On the contrary,* Tully says (De Offic. i) under the heading, "Magnanimity consists in two things": "We should beware of the desire for glory, since it enslaves the mind, which a magnanimous man should ever strive to keep untrammeled." Therefore it is opposed to magnanimity.

*I answer that,* As stated above (Q. 103, A. 1, ad 3), glory is an effect of honor and praise: because from the fact that a man is praised, or shown any kind of reverence, he acquires charity in the knowledge of others. And since magnanimity is about honor, as stated above (Q. 129, AA. 1, 2), it follows that it also is about glory: seeing that as a man uses honor moderately, so too does he use glory in moderation. Wherefore inordinate desire of glory is directly opposed to magnanimity.

Reply Obj. 1: To think so much of little things as to glory in them is itself opposed to magnanimity. Wherefore it is said of the magnanimous man (Ethic. iv) that honor is of little account to him. In like manner he thinks little of other things that are sought for honor's sake, such as power and wealth. Likewise it is inconsistent with magnanimity to glory in things that are not; wherefore it is said of the magnanimous man (Ethic. iv) that he cares more for truth than for opinion. Again it is incompatible with magnanimity for a man to glory in the testimony of human praise, as though he deemed this something great; wherefore it is said of the magnanimous man (Ethic. iv), that he cares not to be praised. And so, when a man looks upon little things as though they were great, nothing hinders this from being contrary to magnanimity, as well as to other virtues.

Reply Obj. 2: He that is desirous of vainglory does in truth fall short of being magnanimous, because he glories in what the magnanimous man thinks little of, as stated in the preceding Reply. But if we consider his estimate, he is opposed to the magnanimous man by way of excess, because the glory which he seeks is something great in his estimation, and he tends thereto in excess of his deserts.

Reply Obj. 3: As stated above (Q. 127, A. 2, ad 2), the opposition of vices does not depend on their effects. Nevertheless contention, if done intentionally, is opposed to magnanimity: since no one contends save for what he deems great. Wherefore the Philosopher says (Ethic. iv, 3) that the magnanimous man is not contentious, because nothing is great in his estimation.

THIRD ARTICLE [II-II, Q. 132, Art. 3]

Whether Vainglory Is a Mortal Sin?

Objection 1: It seems that vainglory is a mortal sin. For nothing precludes the eternal reward except a mortal sin. Now vainglory precludes the eternal reward: for it is written (Matt. 6:1): "Take heed, that you do not give justice before men, to be seen by them: otherwise you shall not have a reward of your Father Who is in heaven." Therefore vainglory is a mortal sin.

Obj. 2: Further, whoever appropriates to himself that which is proper to God, sins mortally. Now by desiring vainglory, a man appropriates to himself that which is proper to God. For it is written (Isa. 42:8): "I will not give My glory to another," and (1 Tim. 1:17): "To ... the only God be honor and glory." Therefore vainglory is a mortal sin.

Obj. 3: Further, apparently a sin is mortal if it be most dangerous and harmful. Now vainglory is a sin of this kind, because a gloss of Augustine on 1 Thess. 2:4, "God, Who proveth our hearts," says: "Unless a man war against the love of human glory he does not perceive its baneful power, for though it be easy for anyone not to desire praise as long as one does not get it, it is difficult not to take pleasure in it, when it is given." Chrysostom also says (Hom. xix in Matth.) that "vainglory enters secretly, and robs us insensibly of all our inward possessions." Therefore vainglory is a mortal sin.

*On the contrary,* Chrysostom says [*Hom. xiii in the Opus Imperfectum falsely ascribed to St. John Chrysostom] that "while other vices find their abode in the servants of the devil, vainglory finds a place even in the servants of Christ." Yet in the latter there is no mortal sin. Therefore vainglory is not a mortal sin.

*I answer that,* As stated above (Q. 24, A. 12; Q. 110, A. 4; Q. 112, A. 2), a sin is mortal through being contrary to charity. Now the sin of vainglory, considered in itself, does not seem to be contrary to charity as regards the love of one's neighbor: yet as regards the love of God it may be contrary to charity in two ways. In one way, by reason of the matter about which one glories: for instance when one glories in something false that is opposed to the reverence we owe God, according to Ezech. 28:2, "Thy heart is lifted up, and Thou hast said: I am God," and 1 Cor. 4:7, "What hast thou that thou hast not received? And if thou hast received, why dost thou glory, as if thou hadst not received it?" Or again when a man prefers to God the temporal good in which he glories: for this is forbidden (Jer. 9:23, 24): "Let not the wise man glory in his wisdom, and let not the strong man glory in his strength, and let not the rich man glory in his riches. But let him that glorieth glory in this, that he understandeth and knoweth Me." Or again when a man prefers the testimony of man to God's; thus it is written in reproval of certain people (John 12:43): "For they loved the glory of men more than the glory of God."

In another way vainglory may be contrary to charity, on the part of the one who glories, in that he refers his intention to glory as his last end: so that he directs even virtuous deeds thereto, and, in order to obtain it, forbears not from doing even that which is against God. In this way it is a mortal sin. Wherefore Augustine says (De Civ. Dei v, 14) that "this vice," namely the love of human praise, "is so hostile to a godly faith, if the heart desires glory more than it fears or loves God, that our Lord said (John 5:44): How can you believe, who receive glory one from another, and the glory which is from God alone, you do not seek?"

If, however, the love of human glory, though it be vain, be not inconsistent with charity, neither as regards the matter gloried in, nor as to the intention of him that seeks glory, it is not a mortal but a venial sin.

Reply Obj. 1: No man, by sinning, merits eternal life: wherefore a virtuous deed loses its power to merit eternal life, if it be done for the sake of vainglory, even though that vainglory be not a mortal sin. On the other hand when a man loses the eternal reward simply through vainglory, and not merely in respect of one act, vainglory is a mortal sin.

Reply Obj. 2: Not every man that is desirous of vainglory, desires the excellence which belongs to God alone. For the glory due to God alone differs from the glory due to a virtuous or rich man.

Reply Obj. 3: Vainglory is stated to be a dangerous sin, not only on account of its gravity, but also because it is a disposition to grave sins, in so far as it renders man presumptuous and too self-confident: and so it gradually disposes a man to lose his inward goods.

FOURTH ARTICLE [II-II, Q. 132, Art. 4]

Whether Vainglory Is a Capital Vice?

Objection 1: It seems that vainglory is not a capital vice. For a vice that always arises from another vice is seemingly not capital. But vainglory always arises from pride. Therefore vainglory is not a capital vice.

Obj. 2: Further, honor would seem to take precedence of glory, for this is its effect. Now ambition which is inordinate desire of honor is not a capital vice. Neither therefore is the desire of vainglory.

Obj. 3: Further, a capital vice has a certain prominence. But vainglory seems to have no prominence, neither as a sin, because it is not always a mortal sin, nor considered as an appetible good, since human glory is apparently a frail thing, and is something outside man himself. Therefore vainglory is not a capital vice.

*On the contrary,* Gregory (Moral. xxxi) numbers vainglory among the seven capital vices.

*I answer that,* The capital vices are enumerated in two ways. For some reckon pride as one of their number: and these do not place vainglory among the capital vices. Gregory, however (Moral. xxxi), reckons pride to be the queen of all the vices, and vainglory, which is the immediate offspring of pride, he reckons to be a capital vice: and not without reason. For pride, as we shall state farther on (Q. 152, AA. 1, 2), denotes inordinate desire of excellence. But whatever good one may desire, one desires a certain perfection and excellence therefrom: wherefore the end of every vice is directed to the end of pride, so that this vice seems to exercise a kind of causality over the other vices, and ought not to be reckoned among the special sources of vice, known as the capital vices. Now among the goods that are the means whereby man acquires honor, glory seems to be the most conducive to that effect, inasmuch as it denotes the manifestation of a man's goodness: since good is naturally loved and honored by all. Wherefore, just as by the glory which is in God's sight man acquires honor in Divine things, so too by the glory which is in the sight of man he acquires excellence in human things. Hence on account of its close connection with excellence, which men desire above all, it follows that it is most desirable. And since many vices arise from the inordinate desire thereof, it follows that vainglory is a capital vice.

Reply Obj. 1: It is not impossible for a capital vice to arise from pride, since as stated above (in the body of the Article and I-II, Q. 84, A. 2) pride is the queen and mother of all the vices.

Reply Obj. 2: Praise and honor, as stated above (A. 2), stand in relation to glory as the causes from which it proceeds, so that glory is compared to them as their end. For the reason why a man loves to be honored and praised is that he thinks thereby to acquire a certain renown in the knowledge of others.

Reply Obj. 3: Vainglory stands prominent under the aspect of desirability, for the reason given above, and this suffices for it to be reckoned a capital vice. Nor is it always necessary for a capital vice to be a mortal sin; for mortal sin can arise from venial sin, inasmuch as venial sin can dispose man thereto.

FIFTH ARTICLE [II-II, Q. 132, Art. 5]

Whether the Daughters of Vainglory Are Suitably Reckoned to Be Disobedience, Boastfulness, Hypocrisy, Contention, Obstinacy, Discord, and Love of Novelties?

Objection 1: It seems that the daughters of vainglory are unsuitably reckoned to be "disobedience, boastfulness, hypocrisy, contention, obstinacy, discord, and eccentricity [* *Praesumptio novitatum,* literally 'presumption of novelties']." For according to Gregory (Moral. xxiii) boastfulness is numbered among the species of pride. Now pride does not arise from vainglory, rather is it the other way about, as Gregory says (Moral. xxxi). Therefore boastfulness should not be reckoned among the daughters of vainglory.

Obj. 2: Further, contention and discord seem to be the outcome chiefly of anger. But anger is a capital vice condivided with vainglory. Therefore it seems that they are not the daughters of vainglory.

Obj. 3: Further, Chrysostom says (Hom. xix in Matth.) that vainglory is always evil, but especially in philanthropy, i.e. mercy. And yet this is nothing new, for it is an established custom among men. Therefore eccentricity should not be specially reckoned as a daughter of vainglory.

*On the contrary,* stands the authority of Gregory (Moral. xxxi), who there assigns the above daughters to vainglory.

*I answer that,* As stated above (Q. 34, A. 5; Q. 35, A. 4; I-II, Q. 84, AA. 3, 4), the vices which by their very nature are such as to be directed to the end of a certain capital vice, are called its daughters. Now the end of vainglory is the manifestation of one's own excellence, as stated above (AA. 1, 4): and to this end a man may tend in two ways. In one way directly, either by words, and this is boasting, or by deeds, and then if they be true and call for astonishment, it is love of novelties which men are wont to wonder at most; but if they be false, it is hypocrisy. In another way a man strives to make known his excellence by showing that he is not inferior to another, and this in four ways. First, as regards the intellect, and thus we have *obstinacy,* by which a man is too much attached to his own opinion, being unwilling to believe one that is better. Secondly, as regards the will, and then we have *discord,* whereby a man is unwilling to give up his own will, and agree with others. Thirdly, as regards *speech,* and then we have contention, whereby a man quarrels noisily with another. Fourthly as regards deeds, and this is *disobedience,* whereby a man refuses to carry out the command of his superiors.

Reply Obj. 1: As stated above (Q. 112, A. 1, ad 2), boasting is reckoned a kind of pride, as regards its interior cause, which is arrogance: but outward boasting, according to *Ethic.* iv, is directed sometimes to gain, but more often to glory and honor, and thus it is the result of vainglory.

Reply Obj. 2: Anger is not the cause of discord and contention, except in conjunction with vainglory, in that a man thinks it a glorious thing for him not to yield to the will and words of others.

Reply Obj. 3: Vainglory is reproved in connection with almsdeeds on account of the lack of charity apparent in one who prefers vainglory to the good of his neighbor, seeing that he does the latter for the sake of the former. But a man is not reproved for presuming to give alms as though this were something novel.

# QUESTION 133

OF PUSILLANIMITY (In Two Articles)

We must now consider pusillanimity. Under this head there are two points of inquiry:

(1) Whether pusillanimity is a sin?

(2) To what virtue is it opposed?

FIRST ARTICLE [II-II, Q. 133, Art. 1]

Whether Pusillanimity Is a Sin?

Objection 1: It seems that pusillanimity is not a sin. For every sin makes a man evil, just as every virtue makes a man good. But a fainthearted man is not evil, as the Philosopher says (Ethic. iv, 3). Therefore pusillanimity is not a sin.

Obj. 2: Further, the Philosopher says (Ethic. iv, 3) that "a fainthearted man is especially one who is worthy of great goods, yet does not deem himself worthy of them." Now no one is worthy of great goods except the virtuous, since as the Philosopher again says (Ethic. iv, 3), "none but the virtuous are truly worthy of honor." Therefore the fainthearted are virtuous: and consequently pusillanimity is not a sin.

Obj. 3: Further, "Pride is the beginning of all sin" (Ecclus. 10:15). But pusillanimity does not proceed from pride, since the proud man sets himself above what he is, while the fainthearted man withdraws from the things he is worthy of. Therefore pusillanimity is not a sin.

Obj. 4: Further, the Philosopher says (Ethic. iv, 3) that "he who deems himself less worthy than he is, is said to be fainthearted." Now sometimes holy men deem themselves less worthy than they are; for instance, Moses and Jeremias, who were worthy of the office God chose them for, which they both humbly declined (Ex. 3:11; Jer. 1:6). Therefore pusillanimity is not a sin.

*On the contrary,* Nothing in human conduct is to be avoided save sin. Now pusillanimity is to be avoided: for it is written (Col. 3:21): "Fathers, provoke not your children to indignation, lest they be discouraged." Therefore pusillanimity is a sin.

*I answer that,* Whatever is contrary to a natural inclination is a sin, because it is contrary to a law of nature. Now everything has a natural inclination to accomplish an action that is commensurate with its power: as is evident in all natural things, whether animate or inanimate. Now just as presumption makes a man exceed what is proportionate to his power, by striving to do more than he can, so pusillanimity makes a man fall short of what is proportionate to his power, by refusing to tend to that which is commensurate thereto. Wherefore as presumption is a sin, so is pusillanimity. Hence it is that the servant who buried in the earth the money he had received from his master, and did not trade with it through fainthearted fear, was punished by his master (Matt. 25; Luke 19).

Reply Obj. 1: The Philosopher calls those evil who injure their neighbor: and accordingly the fainthearted is said not to be evil, because he injures no one, save accidentally, by omitting to do what might be profitable to others. For Gregory says (Pastoral. i) that if "they who demur to do good to their neighbor in preaching be judged strictly, without doubt their guilt is proportionate to the good they might have done had they been less retiring."

Reply Obj. 2: Nothing hinders a person who has a virtuous habit from sinning venially and without losing the habit, or mortally and with loss of the habit of gratuitous virtue. Hence it is possible for a man, by reason of the virtue which he has, to be worthy of doing certain great things that are worthy of great honor, and yet through not trying to make use of his virtue, he sins sometimes venially, sometimes mortally.

Again it may be replied that the fainthearted is worthy of great things in proportion to his ability for virtue, ability which he derives either from a good natural disposition, or from science, or from external fortune, and if he fails to use those things for virtue, he becomes guilty of pusillanimity.

Reply Obj. 3: Even pusillanimity may in some way be the result of pride: when, to wit, a man clings too much to his own opinion, whereby he thinks himself incompetent for those things for which he is competent. Hence it is written (Prov. 26:16): "The sluggard is wiser in his own conceit than seven men that speak sentences." For nothing hinders him from depreciating himself in some things, and having a high opinion of himself in others. Wherefore Gregory says (Pastoral. i) of Moses that "perchance he would have been proud, had he undertaken the leadership of a numerous people without misgiving: and again he would have been proud, had he refused to obey the command of his Creator."

Reply Obj. 4: Moses and Jeremias were worthy of the office to which they were appointed by God, but their worthiness was of Divine grace: yet they, considering the insufficiency of their own weakness, demurred; though not obstinately lest they should fall into pride.

SECOND ARTICLE [II-II, Q. 133, Art. 2]

Whether Pusillanimity Is Opposed to Magnanimity?

Objection 1: It seems that pusillanimity is not opposed to magnanimity. For the Philosopher says (Ethic., 3) that "the fainthearted man knows not himself: for he would desire the good things, of which he is worthy, if he knew himself." Now ignorance of self seems opposed to prudence. Therefore pusillanimity is opposed to prudence.

Obj. 2: Further our Lord calls the servant wicked and slothful who through pusillanimity refused to make use of the money. Moreover the Philosopher says (Ethic. iv, 3) that the fainthearted seem to be slothful. Now sloth is opposed to solicitude, which is an act of prudence, as stated above (Q. 47, A. 9). Therefore pusillanimity is not opposed to magnanimity.

Obj. 3: Further, pusillanimity seems to proceed from inordinate fear: hence it is written (Isa. 35:4): "Say to the fainthearted: Take courage and fear not." It also seems to proceed from inordinate anger, according to Col. 3:21, "Fathers, provoke not your children to indignation, lest they be discouraged." Now inordinate fear is opposed to fortitude, and inordinate anger to meekness. Therefore pusillanimity is not opposed to magnanimity.

Obj. 4: Further, the vice that is in opposition to a particular virtue is the more grievous according as it is more unlike that virtue. Now pusillanimity is more unlike magnanimity than presumption is. Therefore if pusillanimity is opposed to magnanimity, it follows that it is a more grievous sin than presumption: yet this is contrary to the saying of Ecclus. 37:3, "O wicked presumption, whence camest thou?" Therefore pusillanimity is not opposed to magnanimity.

*On the contrary,* Pusillanimity and magnanimity differ as greatness and littleness of soul, as their very names denote. Now great and little are opposites. Therefore pusillanimity is opposed to magnanimity.

*I answer that,* Pusillanimity may be considered in three ways. First, in itself; and thus it is evident that by its very nature it is opposed to magnanimity, from which it differs as great and little differ in connection with the same subject. For just as the magnanimous man tends to great things out of greatness of soul, so the pusillanimous man shrinks from great things out of littleness of soul. Secondly, it may be considered in reference to its cause, which on the part of the intellect is ignorance of one's own qualification, and on the part of the appetite is the fear of failure in what one falsely deems to exceed one's ability. Thirdly, it may be considered in reference to its effect, which is to shrink from the great things of which one is worthy. But, as stated above (Q. 132, A. 2, ad 3), opposition between vice and virtue depends rather on their respective species than on their cause or effect. Hence pusillanimity is directly opposed to magnanimity.

Reply Obj. 1: This argument considers pusillanimity as proceeding from a cause in the intellect. Yet it cannot be said properly that it is opposed to prudence, even in respect of its cause: because ignorance of this kind does not proceed from indiscretion but from laziness in considering one's own ability, according to *Ethic.* iv, 3, or in accomplishing what is within one's power.

Reply Obj. 2: This argument considers pusillanimity from the point of view of its effect.

Reply Obj. 3: This argument considers the point of view of cause. Nor is the fear that causes pusillanimity always a fear of the dangers of death: wherefore it does not follow from this standpoint that pusillanimity is opposed to fortitude. As regards anger, if we consider it under the aspect of its proper movement, whereby a man is roused to take vengeance, it does not cause pusillanimity, which disheartens the soul; *on the contrary,* it takes it away. If, however, we consider the causes of anger, which are injuries inflicted whereby the soul of the man who suffers them is disheartened, it conduces to pusillanimity.

Reply Obj. 4: According to its proper species pusillanimity is a graver sin than presumption, since thereby a man withdraws from good things, which is a very great evil according to *Ethic.* iv. Presumption, however, is stated to be "wicked" on account of pride whence it proceeds.

# QUESTION 134

OF MAGNIFICENCE (In Four Articles)

We must now consider magnificence and the vices opposed to it. With regard to magnificence there are four points of inquiry:

(1) Whether magnificence is a virtue?

(2) Whether it is a special virtue?

(3) What is its matter?

(4) Whether it is a part of fortitude?

FIRST ARTICLE [II-II, Q. 134, Art. 1]

Whether Magnificence Is a Virtue?

Objection 1: It seems that magnificence is not a virtue. For whoever has one virtue has all the virtues, as stated above (I-II, Q. 65, A. 1). But one may have the other virtues without having magnificence: because the Philosopher says (Ethic. iv, 2) that "not every liberal man is magnificent." Therefore magnificence is not a virtue.

Obj. 2: Further, moral virtue observes the mean, according to *Ethic.* ii, 6. But magnificence does not seemingly observe the mean, for it exceeds liberality in greatness. Now "great" and "little" are opposed to one another as extremes, the mean of which is "equal," as stated in Metaph. x. Hence magnificence observes not the mean, but the extreme. Therefore it is not a virtue.

Obj. 3: Further, no virtue is opposed to a natural inclination, but on the contrary perfects it, as stated above (Q. 108, A. 2; Q. 117, A. 1, Obj. 1). Now according to the Philosopher (Ethic. iv, 2) the "magnificent man is not lavish towards himself": and this is opposed to the natural inclination one has to look after oneself. Therefore magnificence is not a virtue.

Obj. 4: Further, according to the Philosopher (Ethic. vi, 4) "act is right reason about things to be made." Now magnificence is about things to be made, as its very name denotes [*Magnificence = *magna facere* —i.e. to make great things]. Therefore it is an act rather than a virtue.

*On the contrary,* Human virtue is a participation of Divine power. But magnificence ( virtutis ) belongs to Divine power, according to Ps. 47:35: "His magnificence and His power is in the clouds." Therefore magnificence is a virtue.

*I answer that,* According to De Coelo i, 16, "we speak of virtue in relation to the extreme limit of a thing's power," not as regards the limit of deficiency, but as regards the limit of excess, the very nature of which denotes something great. Wherefore to do something great, whence magnificence takes its name, belongs properly to the very notion of virtue. Hence magnificence denotes a virtue.

Reply Obj. 1: Not every liberal man is magnificent as regards his actions, because he lacks the wherewithal to perform magnificent deeds. Nevertheless every liberal man has the habit of magnificence, either actually or in respect of a proximate disposition thereto, as explained above (Q. 129, A. 3, ad 2), as also (I-II, Q. 65, A. 1) when we were treating of the connection of virtues.

Reply Obj. 2: It is true that magnificence observes the extreme, if we consider the quantity of the thing done: yet it observes the mean, if we consider the rule of reason, which it neither falls short of nor exceeds, as we have also said of magnanimity (Q. 129, A. 3, ad 1).

Reply Obj. 3: It belongs to magnificence to do something great. But that which regards a man's person is little in comparison with that which regards Divine things, or even the affairs of the community at large. Wherefore the magnificent man does not intend principally to be lavish towards himself, not that he does not seek his own good, but because to do so is not something great. Yet if anything regarding himself admits of greatness, the magnificent man accomplishes it magnificently: for instance, things that are done once, such as a wedding, or the like; or things that are of a lasting nature; thus it belongs to a magnificent man to provide himself with a suitable dwelling, as stated in *Ethic.* iv.

Reply Obj. 4: As the Philosopher says (Ethic. vi, 5) "there must needs be a virtue of act," i.e. a moral virtue, whereby the appetite is inclined to make good use of the rule of act: and this is what magnificence does. Hence it is not an act but a virtue.

SECOND ARTICLE [II-II, Q. 134, Art. 2]

Whether Magnificence Is a Special Virtue?

Objection 1: It seems that magnificence is not a special virtue. For magnificence would seem to consist in doing something great. But it may belong to any virtue to do something great, if the virtue be great: as in the case of one who has a great virtue of temperance, for he does a great work of temperance. Therefore, magnificence is not a special virtue, but denotes a perfect degree of any virtue.

Obj. 2: Further, seemingly that which tends to a thing is the same as that which does it. But it belongs to magnanimity to tend to something great, as stated above (Q. 129, AA. 1, 2). Therefore it belongs to magnanimity likewise to do something great. Therefore magnificence is not a special virtue distinct from magnanimity.

Obj. 3: Further, magnificence seems to belong to holiness, for it is written (Ex. 15:11): "Magnificent [Douay: 'glorious'] in holiness," and (Ps. 95:6): "Holiness and magnificence [Douay: 'Majesty'] in His sanctuary." Now holiness is the same as religion, as stated above (Q. 81, A. 8). Therefore magnificence is apparently the same as religion. Therefore it is not a special virtue, distinct from the others.

*On the contrary,* The Philosopher reckons it with other special virtues (Ethic. ii, 7; iv 2).

*I answer that,* It belongs to magnificence to do ( facere ) something great, as its name implies [* magnificence = magna facere —*i.e. to make great things]. Now*facere may be taken in two ways, in a strict sense, and in a broad sense. Strictly *facere* means to work something in external matter, for instance to make a house, or something of the kind; in a broad sense *facere* is employed to denote any action, whether it passes into external matter, as to burn or cut, or remain in the agent, as to understand or will.

Accordingly if magnificence be taken to denote the doing of something great, the doing ( *factio* ) being understood in the strict sense, it is then a special virtue. For the work done is produced by act: in the use of which it is possible to consider a special aspect of goodness, namely that the work produced ( *factum* ) by the act is something great, namely in quantity, value, or dignity, and this is what magnificence does. In this way magnificence is a special virtue.

If, on the other hand, magnificence take its name from doing something great, the doing ( *facere* ) being understood in a broad sense, it is not a special virtue.

Reply Obj. 1: It belongs to every perfect virtue to do something great in the genus of that virtue, if "doing" ( *facere* ) be taken in the broad sense, but not if it be taken strictly, for this is proper to magnificence.

Reply Obj. 2: It belongs to magnanimity not only to tend to something great, but also to do great works in all the virtues, either by making ( *faciendo* ), or by any kind of action, as stated in Ethic. iv, 3: yet so that magnanimity, in this respect, regards the sole aspect of great, while the other virtues which, if they be perfect, do something great, direct their principal intention, not to something great, but to that which is proper to each virtue: and the greatness of the thing done is sometimes consequent upon the greatness of the virtue.

On the other hand, it belongs to magnificence not only to do something great, "doing" ( *facere* ) being taken in the strict sense, but also to tend with the mind to the doing of great things. Hence Tully says (De Invent. Rhet. ii) that "magnificence is the discussing and administering of great and lofty undertakings, with a certain broad and noble purpose of mind," "discussion" referring to the inward intention, and "administration" to the outward accomplishment. Wherefore just as magnanimity intends something great in every matter, it follows that magnificence does the same in every work that can be produced in external matter ( *factibili* ).

Reply Obj. 3: The intention of magnificence is the production of a great work. Now works done by men are directed to an end: and no end of human works is so great as the honor of God: wherefore magnificence does a great work especially in reference to the Divine honor. Wherefore the Philosopher says (Ethic. iv, 2) that "the most commendable expenditure is that which is directed to Divine sacrifices": and this is the chief object of magnificence. For this reason magnificence is connected with holiness, since its chief effect is directed to religion or holiness.

THIRD ARTICLE [II-II, Q. 134, Art. 3]

Whether the Matter of Magnificence Is Great Expenditure?

Objection 1: It seems that the matter of magnificence is not great expenditure. For there are not two virtues about the same matter. But liberality is about expenditure, as stated above (Q. 117, A. 2). Therefore magnificence is not about expenditure.

Obj. 2: Further, "every magnificent man is liberal" (Ethic. iv, 2). But liberality is about gifts rather than about expenditure. Therefore magnificence also is not chiefly about expenditure, but about gifts.

Obj. 3: Further, it belongs to magnificence to produce an external work. But not even great expenditure is always the means of producing an external work, for instance when one spends much in sending presents. Therefore expenditure is not the proper matter of magnificence.

Obj. 4: Further, only the rich are capable of great expenditure. But the poor are able to possess all the virtues, since "the virtues do not necessarily require external fortune, but are sufficient for themselves," as Seneca says (De Ira i: De vita beata xvi). Therefore magnificence is not about great expenditure.

*On the contrary,* The Philosopher says (Ethic. iv, 2) that "magnificence does not extend, like liberality, to all transactions in money, but only to expensive ones, wherein it exceeds liberality in scale." Therefore it is only about great expenditure.

*I answer that,* As stated above (A. 2), it belongs to magnificence to intend doing some great work. Now for the doing of a great work, proportionate expenditure is necessary, for great works cannot be produced without great expenditure. Hence it belongs to magnificence to spend much in order that some great work may be accomplished in becoming manner. Wherefore the Philosopher says (Ethic. iv, 2) that "a magnificent man will produce a more magnificent work with equal," i.e. proportionate, "expenditure." Now expenditure is the outlay of a sum of money; and a man may be hindered from making that outlay if he love money too much. Hence the matter of magnificence may be said to be both this expenditure itself, which the magnificent man uses to produce a great work, and also the very money which he employs in going to great expense, and as well as the love of money, which love the magnificent man moderates, lest he be hindered from spending much.

Reply Obj. 1: As stated above (Q. 129, A. 2), those virtues that are about external things experience a certain difficulty arising from the genus itself of the thing about which the virtue is concerned, and another difficulty besides arising from the greatness of that same thing. Hence the need for two virtues, concerned about money and its use; namely, liberality, which regards the use of money in general, and magnificence, which regards that which is great in the use of money.

Reply Obj. 2: The use of money regards the liberal man in one way and the magnificent man in another. For it regards the liberal man, inasmuch as it proceeds from an ordinate affection in respect of money; wherefore all due use of money (such as gifts and expenditure), the obstacles to which are removed by a moderate love of money, belongs to liberality. But the use of money regards the magnificent man in relation to some great work which has to be produced, and this use is impossible without expenditure or outlay.

Reply Obj. 3: The magnificent man also makes gifts of presents, as stated in *Ethic.* iv, 2, but not under the aspect of gift, but rather under the aspect of expenditure directed to the production of some work, for instance in order to honor someone, or in order to do something which will reflect honor on the whole state: as when he brings to effect what the whole state is striving for.

Reply Obj. 4: The chief act of virtue is the inward choice, and a virtue may have this without outward fortune: so that even a poor man may be magnificent. But goods of fortune are requisite as instruments to the external acts of virtue: and in this way a poor man cannot accomplish the outward act of magnificence in things that are great simply. Perhaps, however, he may be able to do so in things that are great by comparison to some particular work; which, though little in itself, can nevertheless be done magnificently in proportion to its genus: for little and great are relative terms, as the Philosopher says (De Praedic. Cap. Ad aliquid.).

FOURTH ARTICLE [II-II, Q. 134, Art. 4]

Whether Magnificence Is a Part of Fortitude?

Objection 1: It seems that magnificence is not a part of fortitude. For magnificence agrees in matter with liberality, as stated above (A. 3). But liberality is a part, not of fortitude, but of justice. Therefore magnificence is not a part of fortitude.

Obj. 2: Further, fortitude is about fear and darings. But magnificence seems to have nothing to do with fear, but only with expenditure, which is a kind of action. Therefore magnificence seems to pertain to justice, which is about actions, rather than to fortitude.

Obj. 3: Further, the Philosopher says (Ethic. iv, 2) that "the magnificent man is like the man of science." Now science has more in common with prudence than with fortitude. Therefore magnificence should not be reckoned a part of fortitude.

*On the contrary,* Tully (De Invent. Rhet. ii) and Macrobius (De Somn. Scip. i) and Andronicus reckon magnificence to be a part of fortitude.

*I answer that,* Magnificence, in so far as it is a special virtue, cannot be reckoned a subjective part of fortitude, since it does not agree with this virtue in the point of matter: but it is reckoned a part thereof, as being annexed to it as secondary to principal virtue.

In order for a virtue to be annexed to a principal virtue, two things are necessary, as stated above (Q. 80). The one is that the secondary virtue agree with the principal, and the other is that in some respect it be exceeded thereby. Now magnificence agrees with fortitude in the point that as fortitude tends to something arduous and difficult, so also does magnificence: wherefore seemingly it is seated, like fortitude, in the irascible. Yet magnificence falls short of fortitude, in that the arduous thing to which fortitude tends derives its difficulty from a danger that threatens the person, whereas the arduous thing to which magnificence tends, derives its difficulty from the dispossession of one's property, which is of much less account than danger to one's person. Wherefore magnificence is accounted a part of fortitude.

Reply Obj. 1: Justice regards operations in themselves, as viewed under the aspect of something due: but liberality and magnificence regard sumptuary operations as related to the passions of the soul, albeit in different ways. For liberality regards expenditure in reference to the love and desire of money, which are passions of the concupiscible faculty, and do not hinder the liberal man from giving and spending: so that this virtue is in the concupiscible. On the other hand, magnificence regards expenditure in reference to hope, by attaining to the difficulty, not simply, as magnanimity does, but in a determinate matter, namely expenditure: wherefore magnificence, like magnanimity, is apparently in the irascible part.

Reply Obj. 2: Although magnificence does not agree with fortitude in matter, it agrees with it as the condition of its matter: since it tends to something difficult in the matter of expenditure, even as fortitude tends to something difficult in the matter of fear.

Reply Obj. 3: Magnificence directs the use of art to something great, as stated above and in the preceding Article. Now art is in the reason. Wherefore it belongs to the magnificent man to use his reason by observing proportion of expenditure to the work he has in hand. This is especially necessary on account of the greatness of both those things, since if he did not take careful thought, he would incur the risk of a great loss.

# QUESTION 135

OF MEANNESS* (In Two Articles) [*"Parvificentia," or doing mean things, just as "magnificentia" is doing great things.]

We must now consider the vices opposed to magnificence: under which head there are two points of inquiry:

(1) Whether meanness is a vice?

(2) Of the vice opposed to it.

FIRST ARTICLE [II-II, Q. 135, Art. 1]

Whether Meanness Is a Vice?

Objection 1: It seems that meanness is not a vice. For just as vice moderates great things, so does it moderate little things: wherefore both the liberal and the magnificent do little things. But magnificence is a virtue. Therefore likewise meanness is a virtue rather than a vice.

Obj. 2: Further, the Philosopher says (Ethic. iv, 2) that "careful reckoning is mean." But careful reckoning is apparently praiseworthy, since man's good is to be in accordance with reason, as Dionysius states (Div. Nom. iv, 4). Therefore meanness is not a vice.

Obj. 3: Further, the Philosopher says (Ethic. iv, 2) that "a mean man is loth to spend money." But this belongs to covetousness or illiberality. Therefore meanness is not a distinct vice from the others.

*On the contrary,* The Philosopher (Ethic. ii) accounts meanness a special vice opposed to magnificence.

*I answer that,* As stated above (I-II, Q. 1, A. 3; Q. 18, A. 6), moral acts take their species from their end, wherefore in many cases they are denominated from that end. Accordingly a man is said to be mean ( *parvificus* ) because he intends to do something little ( *parvum* ). Now according to the Philosopher (De Praedic. Cap. Ad aliquid.) great and little are relative terms: and when we say that a mean man intends to do something little, this must be understood in relation to the kind of work he does. This may be little or great in two ways: in one way as regards the work itself to be done, in another as regards the expense. Accordingly the magnificent man intends principally the greatness of his work, and secondarily he intends the greatness of the expense, which he does not shirk, so that he may produce a great work. Wherefore the Philosopher says (Ethic. iv, 4) that "the magnificent man with equal expenditure will produce a more magnificent result." On the other hand, the mean man intends principally to spend little, wherefore the Philosopher says (Ethic. iv, 2) that "he seeks how he may spend least." As a result of this he intends to produce a little work, that is, he does not shrink from producing a little work, so long as he spends little. Wherefore the Philosopher says that "the mean man after going to great expense forfeits the good" of the magnificent work, "for the trifle" that he is unwilling to spend. Therefore it is evident that the mean man fails to observe the proportion that reason demands between expenditure and work. Now the essence of vice is that it consists in failing to do what is in accordance with reason. Hence it is manifest that meanness is a vice.

Reply Obj. 1: Virtue moderates little things, according to the rule of reason: from which rule the mean man declines, as stated in the Article. For he is called mean, not for moderating little things, but for declining from the rule of reason in moderating great or little things: hence meanness is a vice.

Reply Obj. 2: As the Philosopher says (Rhet. ii, 5), "fear makes us take counsel": wherefore a mean man is careful in his reckonings, because he has an inordinate fear of spending his goods, even in things of the least account. Hence this is not praiseworthy, but sinful and reprehensible, because then a man does not regulate his affections according to reason, but, *on the contrary,* makes use of his reason in pursuance of his inordinate affections.

Reply Obj. 3: Just as the magnificent man has this in common with the liberal man, that he spends his money readily and with pleasure, so too the mean man in common with the illiberal or covetous man is loth and slow to spend. Yet they differ in this, that illiberality regards ordinary expenditure, while meanness regards great expenditure, which is a more difficult accomplishment: wherefore meanness is less sinful than illiberality. Hence the Philosopher says (Ethic. iv, 2) that "although meanness and its contrary vice are sinful, they do not bring shame on a man, since neither do they harm one's neighbor, nor are they very disgraceful."

SECOND ARTICLE [II-II, Q. 135, Art. 2]

Whether There Is a Vice Opposed to Meanness?

Objection 1: It seems that there is no vice opposed to meanness. For great is opposed to little. Now, magnificence is not a vice, but a virtue. Therefore no vice is opposed to meanness.

Obj. 2: Further, since meanness is a vice by deficiency, as stated above (A. 1), it seems that if any vice is opposed to meanness, it would merely consist in excessive spending. But those who spend much, where they ought to spend little, spend little where they ought to spend much, according to *Ethic.* iv, 2, and thus they have something of meanness. Therefore there is not a vice opposed to meanness.

Obj. 3: Further, moral acts take their species from their end, as stated above (A. 1). Now those who spend excessively, do so in order to make a show of their wealth, as stated in *Ethic.* iv, 2. But this belongs to vainglory, which is opposed to magnanimity, as stated above (Q. 131, A. 2). Therefore no vice is opposed to meanness.

*On the contrary,* stands the authority of the Philosopher who (Ethic. ii, 8; iv, 2) places magnificence as a mean between two opposite vices.

*I answer that,* Great is opposed to little. Also little and great are relative terms, as stated above (A. 1). Now just as expenditure may be little in comparison with the work, so may it be great in comparison with the work in that it exceeds the proportion which reason requires to exist between expenditure and work. Hence it is manifest that the vice of meanness, whereby a man intends to spend less than his work is worth, and thus fails to observe due proportion between his expenditure and his work, has a vice opposed to it, whereby a man exceeds this same proportion, by spending more than is proportionate to his work. This vice is called in Greek *banausia* , so called from the Greek *baunos* , because, like the fire in the furnace, it consumes everything. It is also called *apyrokalia* , i.e. lacking good fire, since like fire it consumes all, but not for a good purpose. Hence in Latin it may be called *consumptio* (waste).

Reply Obj. 1: Magnificence is so called from the great work done, but not from the expenditure being in excess of the work: for this belongs to the vice which is opposed to meanness.

Reply Obj. 2: To the one same vice there is opposed the virtue which observes the mean, and a contrary vice. Accordingly, then, the vice of waste is opposed to meanness in that it exceeds in expenditure the value of the work, by spending much where it behooved to spend little. But it is opposed to magnificence on the part of the great work, which the magnificent man intends principally, in so far as when it behooves to spend much, it spends little or nothing.

Reply Obj. 3: Wastefulness is opposed to meanness by the very species of its act, since it exceeds the rule of reason, whereas meanness falls short of it. Yet nothing hinders this from being directed to the end of another vice, such as vainglory or any other.

## QUESTION 136

OF PATIENCE (In Five Articles)

We must now consider patience. Under this head there are five points of inquiry:

(1) Whether patience is a virtue?

(2) Whether it is the greatest of the virtues?

(3) Whether it can be had without grace?

(4) Whether it is a part of fortitude?

(5) Whether it is the same as longanimity?

FIRST ARTICLE [II-II, Q. 136, Art. 1]

Whether Patience Is a Virtue?

Objection 1: It seems that patience is not a virtue. For the virtues are most perfect in heaven, as Augustine says (De Trin. xiv). Yet patience is not there, since no evils have to be borne there, according to Isa. 49:10 and Apoc. 7:16, "They shall not hunger nor thirst, neither shall the heat nor the sun strike them." Therefore patience is not a virtue.

Obj. 2: Further, no virtue can be found in the wicked, since virtue it is "that makes its possessor good." Yet patience is sometimes found in wicked men; for instance, in the covetous, who bear many evils patiently that they may amass money, according to Eccles. 5:16, "All the days of his life he eateth in darkness, and in many cares, and in misery and in sorrow." Therefore patience is not a virtue.

Obj. 3: Further, the fruits differ from the virtues, as stated above (I-II, Q. 70, A. 1, ad 3). But patience is reckoned among the fruits (Gal. 5:22). Therefore patience is not a virtue.

*On the contrary,* Augustine says (De Patientia i): "The virtue of the soul that is called patience, is so great a gift of God, that we even preach the patience of Him who bestows it upon us."

*I answer that,* As stated above (Q. 123, A. 1), the moral virtues are directed to the good, inasmuch as they safeguard the good of reason against the impulse of the passions. Now among the passions sorrow is strong to hinder the good of reason, according to 2 Cor. 7:10, "The sorrow of the world worketh death," and Ecclus. 30:25, "Sadness hath killed many, and there is no profit in it." Hence the necessity for a virtue to safeguard the good of reason against sorrow, lest reason give way to sorrow: and this patience does. Wherefore Augustine says (De Patientia ii): "A man's patience it is whereby he bears evil with an equal mind," i.e. without being disturbed by sorrow, "lest he abandon with an unequal mind the goods whereby he may advance to better things." It is therefore evident that patience is a virtue.

Reply Obj. 1: The moral virtues do not remain in heaven as regards the same act that they have on the way, in relation, namely, to the goods of the present life, which will not remain in heaven: but they will remain in their relation to the end, which will be in heaven. Thus justice will not be in heaven in relation to buying and selling and other matters pertaining to the present life, but it will remain in the point of being subject to God. In like manner the act of patience, in heaven, will not consist in bearing things, but in enjoying the goods to which we had aspired by suffering. Hence Augustine says (De Civ. Dei xiv) that "patience itself will not be in heaven, since there is no need for it except where evils have to be borne: yet that which we shall obtain by patience will be eternal."

Reply Obj. 2: As Augustine says (De Patientia ii; v) "properly speaking those are patient who would rather bear evils without inflicting them, than inflict them without bearing them. As for those who bear evils that they may inflict evil, their patience is neither marvelous nor praiseworthy, for it is no patience at all: we may marvel at their hardness of heart, but we must refuse to call them patient."

Reply Obj. 3: As stated above (I-II, Q. 11, A. 1), the very notion of fruit denotes pleasure. And works of virtue afford pleasure in themselves, as stated in *Ethic.* i, 8. Now the names of the virtues are wont to be applied to their acts. Wherefore patience as a habit is a virtue, but as to the pleasure which its act affords, it is reckoned a fruit, especially in this, that patience safeguards the mind from being overcome by sorrow.

SECOND ARTICLE [II-II, Q. 136, Art. 2]

Whether Patience Is the Greatest of the Virtues?

Objection 1: It seems that patience is the greatest of the virtues. For in every genus that which is perfect is the greatest. Now "patience hath a perfect work" (James 1:4). Therefore patience is the greatest of the virtues.

Obj. 2: Further, all the virtues are directed to the good of the soul. Now this seems to belong chiefly to patience; for it is written (Luke 21:19): "In your patience you shall possess your souls." Therefore patience is the greatest of the virtues.

Obj. 3: Further, seemingly that which is the safeguard and cause of other things is greater than they are. But according to Gregory (Hom. xxxv in Evang.) "patience is the root and safeguard of all the virtues." Therefore patience is the greatest of the virtues.

*On the contrary,* It is not reckoned among the four virtues which Gregory (Moral. xxii) and Augustine (De Morib. Eccl. xv) call principal.

*I answer that,* Virtues by their very nature are directed to good. For it is virtue that "makes its possessor good, and renders the latter's work good" (Ethic. ii, 6). Hence it follows that a virtue's superiority and preponderance over other virtues is the greater according as it inclines man to good more effectively and directly. Now those virtues which are effective of good, incline a man more directly to good than those which are a check on the things which lead man away from good: and just as among those that are effective of good, the greater is that which establishes man in a greater good (thus faith, hope, and charity are greater than prudence and justice); so too among those that are a check on things that withdraw man from good, the greater virtue is the one which is a check on a greater obstacle to good. But dangers of death, about which is fortitude, and pleasures of touch, with which temperance is concerned, withdraw man from good more than any kind of hardship, which is the object of patience. Therefore patience is not the greatest of the virtues, but falls short, not only of the theological virtues, and of prudence and justice which directly establish man in good, but also of fortitude and temperance which withdraw him from greater obstacles to good.

Reply Obj. 1: Patience is said to have a perfect work in bearing hardships: for these give rise first to sorrow, which is moderated by patience; secondly, to anger, which is moderated by meekness; thirdly, to hatred, which charity removes; fourthly, to unjust injury, which justice forbids. Now that which removes the principle is the most perfect.

Yet it does not follow, if patience be more perfect in this respect, that it is more perfect simply.

Reply Obj. 2: Possession denotes undisturbed ownership; wherefore man is said to possess his soul by patience, in so far as it removes by the root the passions that are evoked by hardships and disturb the soul.

Reply Obj. 3: Patience is said to be the root and safeguard of all the virtues, not as though it caused and preserved them directly, but merely because it removes their obstacles.

THIRD ARTICLE [II-II, Q. 136, Art. 3]

Whether It Is Possible to Have Patience Without Grace?

Objection 1: It seems that it is possible to have patience without grace. For the more his reason inclines to a thing, the more is it possible for the rational creature to accomplish it. Now it is more reasonable to suffer evil for the sake of good than for the sake of evil. Yet some suffer evil for evil's sake, by their own virtue and without the help of grace; for Augustine says (De Patientia iii) that "men endure many toils and sorrows for the sake of the things they love sinfully." Much more, therefore, is it possible for man, without the help of grace, to bear evil for the sake of good, and this is to be truly patient.

Obj. 2: Further, some who are not in a state of grace have more abhorrence for sinful evils than for bodily evils: hence some heathens are related to have endured many hardships rather than betray their country or commit some other misdeed. Now this is to be truly patient. Therefore it seems that it is possible to have patience without the help of grace.

Obj. 3: Further, it is quite evident that some go through much trouble and pain in order to regain health of the body. Now the health of the soul is not less desirable than bodily health. Therefore in like manner one may, without the help of grace, endure many evils for the health of the soul, and this is to be truly patient.

*On the contrary,* It is written (Ps. 61:6): "From Him," i.e. from God, "is my patience."

*I answer that,* As Augustine says (De Patientia iv), "the strength of desire helps a man to bear toil and pain: and no one willingly undertakes to bear what is painful, save for the sake of that which gives pleasure." The reason of this is because sorrow and pain are of themselves displeasing to the soul, wherefore it would never choose to suffer them for their own sake, but only for the sake of an end. Hence it follows that the good for the sake of which one is willing to endure evils, is more desired and loved than the good the privation of which causes the sorrow that we bear patiently. Now the fact that a man prefers the good of grace to all natural goods, the loss of which may cause sorrow, is to be referred to charity, which loves God above all things. Hence it is evident that patience, as a virtue, is caused by charity, according to 1 Cor. 13:4, "Charity is patient."

But it is manifest that it is impossible to have charity save through grace, according to Rom. 5:5, "The charity of God is poured forth in our hearts by the Holy Ghost Who is given to us." Therefore it is clearly impossible to have patience without the help of grace.

Reply Obj. 1: The inclination of reason would prevail in human nature in the state of integrity. But in corrupt nature the inclination of concupiscence prevails, because it is dominant in man. Hence man is more prone to bear evils for the sake of goods in which the concupiscence delights here and now, than to endure evils for the sake of goods to come, which are desired in accordance with reason: and yet it is this that pertains to true patience.

Reply Obj. 2: The good of a social virtue [*Cf. I-II, Q. 61, A. 5] is commensurate with human nature; and consequently the human will can tend thereto without the help of sanctifying grace, yet not without the help of God's grace [*Cf. I-II, Q. 109, A. 2]. On the other hand, the good of grace is supernatural, wherefore man cannot tend thereto by a natural virtue. Hence the comparison fails.

Reply Obj. 3: Even the endurance of those evils which a man bears for the sake of his body's health, proceeds from the love a man naturally has for his own flesh. Hence there is no comparison between this endurance and patience which proceeds from a supernatural love.

FOURTH ARTICLE [II-II, Q. 136, Art. 4]

Whether Patience Is a Part of Fortitude?

Objection 1: It seems that patience is not a part of fortitude. For a thing is not part of itself. Now patience is apparently the same as fortitude: because, as stated above (Q. 123, A. 6), the proper act of fortitude is to endure; and this belongs also to patience. For it is stated in the Liber Sententiarum Prosperi [*The quotation is from St. Gregory, Hom.

xxxv in Evang.] that "patience consists in enduring evils inflicted by others." Therefore patience is not a part of fortitude.

Obj. 2: Further, fortitude is about fear and daring, as stated above (Q. 123, A. 3), and thus it is in the irascible. But patience seems to be about sorrow, and consequently would seem to be in the concupiscible. Therefore patience is not a part of fortitude but of temperance.

Obj. 3: Further, the whole cannot be without its part. Therefore if patience is a part of fortitude, there can be no fortitude without patience. Yet sometimes a brave man does not endure evils patiently, but even attacks the person who inflicts the evil. Therefore patience is not a part of fortitude.

*On the contrary,* Tully (De Invent. Rhet. ii) reckons it a part of fortitude.

*I answer that,* Patience is a quasi-potential part of fortitude, because it is annexed thereto as secondary to principal virtue. For it belongs to patience "to suffer with an equal mind the evils inflicted by others," as Gregory says in a homily (xxxv in Evang.). Now of those evils that are inflicted by others, foremost and most difficult to endure are those that are connected with the danger of death, and about these evils fortitude is concerned. Hence it is clear that in this matter fortitude has the principal place, and that it lays claim to that which is principal in this matter. Wherefore patience is annexed to fortitude as secondary to principal virtue, for which reason Prosper calls patience brave (Sent. 811).

Reply Obj. 1: It belongs to fortitude to endure, not anything indeed, but that which is most difficult to endure, namely dangers of death: whereas it may pertain to patience to endure any kind of evil.

Reply Obj. 2: The act of fortitude consists not only in holding fast to good against the fear of future dangers, but also in not failing through sorrow or pain occasioned by things present; and it is in the latter respect that patience is akin to fortitude. Yet fortitude is chiefly about fear, which of itself evokes flight which fortitude avoids; while patience is chiefly about sorrow, for a man is said to be patient, not because he does not fly, but because he behaves in a praiseworthy manner by suffering ( *patiendo* ) things which hurt him here and now, in such a way as not to be inordinately saddened by them. Hence fortitude is properly in the irascible, while patience is in the concupiscible faculty.

Nor does this hinder patience from being a part of fortitude, because the annexing of virtue to virtue does not regard the subject, but the matter or the form. Nevertheless patience is not to be reckoned a part of temperance, although both are in the concupiscible, because temperance is only about those sorrows that are opposed to pleasures of touch, such as arise through abstinence from pleasures of food and sex: whereas patience is chiefly about sorrows inflicted by other persons. Moreover it belongs to temperance to control these sorrows besides their contrary pleasures: whereas it belongs to patience that a man forsake not the good of virtue on account of such like sorrows, however great they be.

Reply Obj. 3: It may be granted that patience in a certain respect is an integral part of justice, if we consider the fact that a man may patiently endure evils pertaining to dangers of death; and it is from this point of view that the objection argues. Nor is it inconsistent with patience that a man should, when necessary, rise up against the man who inflicts evils on him; for Chrysostom [*Homily v. in the Opus Imperfectum, falsely ascribed to St. John Chrysostom] says on Matt. 4:10, "Begone Satan," that "it is praiseworthy to be patient under our own wrongs, but to endure God's wrongs patiently is most wicked": and Augustine says in a letter to Marcellinus (Ep. cxxxviii) that "the precepts of patience are not opposed to the good of the commonwealth, since in order to ensure that good we fight against our enemies." But in so far as patience regards all kinds of evils, it is annexed to fortitude as secondary to principal virtue.

FIFTH ARTICLE [II-II, Q. 136, Art. 5]

Whether Patience Is the Same As Longanimity?* [*Longsuffering. It is necessary to preserve the Latin word, on account of the comparison with magnanimity.]

Objection 1: It seems that patience is the same as longanimity. For Augustine says (De Patientia i) that "we speak of patience in God, not as though any evil made Him suffer, but because He awaits the wicked, that they may be converted." Wherefore it is written (Ecclus. 5:4): "The Most High is a patient rewarder." Therefore it seems that patience is the same as longanimity.

Obj. 2: Further, the same thing is not contrary to two things. But impatience is contrary to longanimity, whereby one awaits a delay: for one is said to be impatient of delay, as of other evils. Therefore it seems that patience is the same as longanimity.

Obj. 3: Further, just as time is a circumstance of wrongs endured, so is place. But no virtue is distinct from patience on the score of place. Therefore in like manner longanimity which takes count of time, in so far as a person waits for a long time, is not distinct from patience.

Obj. 4: *On the contrary,* a gloss [*Origen, Comment. in Ep. ad Rom. ii] on Rom. 2:4, "Or despisest thou the riches of His goodness, and patience, and longsuffering?" says: "It seems that longanimity differs from patience, because those who offend from weakness rather than of set purpose are said to be borne with longanimity: while those who take a deliberate delight in their crimes are said to be borne patiently."

*I answer that,* Just as by magnanimity a man has a mind to tend to great things, so by longanimity a man has a mind to tend to something a long way off. Wherefore as magnanimity regards hope, which tends to good, rather than daring, fear, or sorrow, which have evil as their object, so also does longanimity. Hence longanimity has more in common with magnanimity than with patience.

Nevertheless it may have something in common with patience, for two reasons. First, because patience, like fortitude, endures certain evils for the sake of good, and if this good is awaited shortly, endurance is easier: whereas if it be delayed a long time, it is more difficult. Secondly, because the very delay of the good we hope for, is of a nature to cause sorrow, according to Prov. 13:12, "Hope that is deferred afflicteth the soul." Hence there may be patience in bearing this trial, as in enduring any other sorrows. Accordingly longanimity and constancy are both comprised under patience, in so far as both the delay of the hoped for good (which regards longanimity) and the toil which man endures in persistently accomplishing a good work (which regards constancy) may be considered under the one aspect of grievous evil.

For this reason Tully (De Invent. Rhet. ii) in defining patience, says that "patience is the voluntary and prolonged endurance of arduous and difficult things for the sake of virtue or profit." By saying "arduous" he refers to constancy in good; when he says "difficult" he refers to the grievousness of evil, which is the proper object of patience; and by adding "continued" or "long lasting," he refers to longanimity, in so far as it has something in common with patience.

This suffices for the Replies to the First and Second Objections.

Reply Obj. 3: That which is a long way off as to place, though distant from us, is not simply distant from things in nature, as that which is a long way off in point of time: hence the comparison fails. Moreover, what is remote as to place offers no difficulty save in the point of time, since what is placed a long way from us is a long time coming to us.

We grant the fourth argument. We must observe, however, that the reason for the difference assigned by this gloss is that it is hard to bear with those who sin through weakness, merely because they persist a long time in evil, wherefore it is said that they are borne with longanimity: whereas the very fact of sinning through pride seems to be unendurable; for which reason those who sin through pride are stated to be borne with patience.

# QUESTION 137

OF PERSEVERANCE (In Four Articles)

We must now consider perseverance and the vices opposed to it. Under the head of perseverance there are four points of inquiry:

(1) Whether perseverance is a virtue?

(2) Whether it is a part of fortitude?

(3) Of its relation to constancy;

(4) Whether it needs the help of grace?

FIRST ARTICLE [II-II, Q. 137, Art. 1]

Whether Perseverance Is a Virtue?

Objection 1: It seems that perseverance is not a virtue. For, according to the Philosopher (Ethic. vii, 7), continency is greater than perseverance. But continency is not a virtue, as stated in *Ethic.* iv, 9. Therefore perseverance is not a virtue.

Obj. 2: Further, "by virtue man lives aright," according to Augustine (De Lib. Arb. ii, 19). Now according to the same authority (De Persever. i), no one can be said to have perseverance while living, unless he persevere until death. Therefore perseverance is not a virtue.

Obj. 3: Further, it is requisite of every virtue that one should persist unchangeably in the work of that virtue, as stated in *Ethic.* ii, 4. But this is what we understand by perseverance: for Tully says (De Invent. Rhet. ii) that "perseverance is the fixed and continued persistence in a well-considered purpose." Therefore perseverance is not a special virtue, but a condition of every virtue.

*On the contrary,* Andronicus [*Chrysippus: in De Affect.] says that "perseverance is a habit regarding things to which we ought to stand, and those to which we ought not to stand, as well as those that are indifferent." Now a habit that directs us to do something well, or to omit something, is a virtue. Therefore perseverance is a virtue.

*I answer that,* According to the Philosopher (Ethic. ii, 3), "virtue is about the difficult and the good"; and so where there is a special kind of difficulty or goodness, there is a special virtue. Now a virtuous deed may involve goodness or difficulty on two counts. First, from the act's very species, which is considered in respect of the proper object of that act: secondly, from the length of time, since to persist long in something difficult involves a special difficulty. Hence to persist long in something good until it is accomplished belongs to a special virtue.

Accordingly just as temperance and fortitude are special virtues, for the reason that the one moderates pleasures of touch (which is of itself a difficult thing), while the other moderates fear and daring in connection with dangers of death (which also is something difficult in itself), so perseverance is a special virtue, since it consists in enduring delays in the above or other virtuous deeds, so far as necessity requires.

Reply Obj. 1: The Philosopher is taking perseverance there, as it is found in one who bears those things which are most difficult to endure long. Now it is difficult to endure, not good, but evil. And evils that involve danger of death, for the most part are not endured for a long time, because often they soon pass away: wherefore it is not on this account that perseverance has its chief title to praise. Among other evils foremost are those which are opposed to pleasures of touch, because evils of this kind affect the necessaries of life: such are the lack of food and the like, which at times call for long endurance. Now it is not difficult to endure these things for a long time for one who grieves not much at them, nor delights much in the contrary goods; as in the case of the temperate man, in whom these passions are not violent. But they are most difficult to bear for one who is strongly affected by such things, through lacking the perfect virtue that moderates these passions. Wherefore if perseverance be taken in this sense it is not a perfect virtue, but something imperfect in the genus of virtue. On the other hand, if we take perseverance as denoting long persistence in any kind of difficult good, it is consistent in one who has even perfect virtue: for even if it is less difficult for him to persist, yet he persists in the more perfect good. Wherefore such like perseverance may be a virtue, because virtue derives perfection from the aspect of good rather than from the aspect of difficulty.

Reply Obj. 2: Sometimes a virtue and its act go by the same name: thus Augustine says (Tract. in Joan. lxxix): "Faith is to believe without seeing." Yet it is possible to have a habit of virtue without performing the act: thus a poor man has the habit of magnificence without exercising the act. Sometimes, however, a person who has the habit, begins to perform the act, yet does not accomplish it, for instance a builder begins to build a house, but does not complete it. Accordingly we must reply that the term "perseverance" is sometimes used to denote the habit whereby one chooses to persevere, sometimes for the act of persevering: and sometimes one who has the habit of perseverance chooses to persevere and begins to carry out his choice by persisting for a time, yet completes not the act, through not persisting to the end. Now the end is twofold: one is the end of the work, the other is the end of human life. Properly speaking it belongs to perseverance to persevere to the end of the virtuous work, for instance that a soldier persevere to the end of the fight, and the magnificent man until his work be accomplished. There are, however, some virtues whose acts must endure throughout the whole of life, such as faith, hope, and charity, since they regard the last end of the entire life of man. Wherefore as regards these which are the principal virtues, the act of perseverance is not accomplished until the end of life. It is in this sense that Augustine speaks of perseverance as denoting the consummate act of perseverance.

Reply Obj. 3: Unchangeable persistence may belong to a virtue in two ways. First, on account of the intended end that is proper to that virtue; and thus to persist in good for a long time until the end, belongs to a special virtue called perseverance, which intends this as its special end. Secondly, by reason of the relation of the habit to its subject: and thus unchangeable persistence is consequent upon every virtue, inasmuch as virtue is a "quality difficult to change."

SECOND ARTICLE [II-II, Q. 137, Art. 2]

Whether Perseverance Is a Part of Fortitude?

Objection 1: It seems that perseverance is not a part of fortitude. For, according to the Philosopher (Ethic. viii, 7), "perseverance is about pains of touch." But these belong to temperance. Therefore perseverance is a part of temperance rather than of fortitude.

Obj. 2: Further, every part of a moral virtue is about certain passions which that virtue moderates. Now perseverance does not imply moderation of the passions: since the more violent the passions, the more praiseworthy is it to persevere in accordance with reason. Therefore it seems that perseverance is a part not of a moral virtue, but rather of prudence which perfects the reason.

Obj. 3: Further, Augustine says (De Persev. i) that no one can lose perseverance; whereas one can lose the other virtues. Therefore perseverance is greater than all the other virtues. Now a principal virtue is greater than its part. Therefore perseverance is not a part of a virtue, but is itself a principal virtue.

*On the contrary,* Tully (De Invent. Rhet. ii) reckons perseverance as a part of fortitude.

*I answer that,* As stated above (Q. 123, A. 2; I-II, Q. 61, AA. 3, 4), a principal virtue is one to which is principally ascribed something that lays claim to the praise of virtue, inasmuch as it practices it in connection with its own matter, wherein it is most difficult of accomplishment. In accordance with this it has been stated (Q. 123, A. 2) that fortitude is a principal virtue, because it observes firmness in matters wherein it is most difficult to stand firm, namely in dangers of death. Wherefore it follows of necessity that every virtue which has a title to praise for the firm endurance of something difficult must be annexed to fortitude as secondary to principal virtue. Now the endurance of difficulty arising from delay in accomplishing a good work gives perseverance its claim to praise: nor is this so difficult as to endure dangers of death. Therefore perseverance is annexed to fortitude, as secondary to principal virtue.

Reply Obj. 1: The annexing of secondary to principal virtues depends not only on the matter [*Cf. Q. 136, A. 4, ad 2], but also on the mode, because in everything form is of more account than matter. Wherefore although, as to matter, perseverance seems to have more in common with temperance than with fortitude, yet, in mode, it has more in common with fortitude, in the point of standing firm against the difficulty arising from length of time.

Reply Obj. 2: The perseverance of which the Philosopher speaks (Ethic. vii, 4, 7) does not moderate any passions, but consists merely in a certain firmness of reason and will. But perseverance, considered as a virtue, moderates certain passions, namely fear of weariness or failure on account of the delay. Hence this virtue, like fortitude, is in the irascible.

Reply Obj. 3: Augustine speaks there of perseverance, as denoting, not a virtuous habit, but a virtuous act sustained to the end, according to Matt. 24:13, "He that shall persevere to the end, he shall be saved." Hence it is incompatible with such like perseverance for it to be lost, since it would no longer endure to the end.

THIRD ARTICLE [II-II, Q. 137. Art. 3]

Whether Constancy Pertains to Perseverance?

Objection 1: It seems that constancy does not pertain to perseverance. For constancy pertains to patience, as stated above (Q. 137, A. 5): and patience differs from perseverance. Therefore constancy does not pertain to perseverance.

Obj. 2: Further, "virtue is about the difficult and the good." Now it does not seem difficult to be constant in little works, but only in great deeds, which pertain to magnificence. Therefore constancy pertains to magnificence rather than to perseverance.

Obj. 3: Further, if constancy pertained to perseverance, it would seem nowise to differ from it, since both denote a kind of unchangeableness. Yet they differ: for Macrobius (In Somn. Scip. i) condivides constancy with firmness by which he indicates perseverance, as stated above (Q. 128, A. 6). Therefore constancy does not pertain to perseverance.

*On the contrary,* One is said to be constant because one stands to a thing. Now it belongs to perseverance to stand to certain things, as appears from the definition given by Andronicus. Therefore constancy belongs to perseverance.

*I answer that,* Perseverance and constancy agree as to end, since it belongs to both to persist firmly in some good: but they differ as to those things which make it difficult to persist in good. Because the virtue of perseverance properly makes man persist firmly in good, against the difficulty that arises from the very continuance of the act: whereas constancy makes him persist firmly in good against difficulties arising from any other external hindrances. Hence perseverance takes precedence of constancy as a part of fortitude, because the difficulty arising from continuance of action is more intrinsic to the act of virtue than that which arises from external obstacles.

Reply Obj. 1: External obstacles to persistence in good are especially those which cause sorrow. Now patience is about sorrow, as stated above (Q. 136, A. 1). Hence constancy agrees with perseverance as to end: while it agrees with patience as to those things which occasion difficulty. Now the end is of most account: wherefore constancy pertains to perseverance rather than to patience.

Reply Obj. 2: It is more difficult to persist in great deeds: yet in little or ordinary deeds, it is difficult to persist for any length of time, if not on account of the greatness of the deed which magnificence considers, yet from its very continuance which perseverance regards. Hence constancy may pertain to both.

Reply Obj. 3: Constancy pertains to perseverance in so far as it has something in common with it: but it is not the same thing in the point of their difference, as stated in the Article.

FOURTH ARTICLE [II-II, Q. 137, Art. 4]

Whether Perseverance Needs the Help of Grace? [*Cf. I-II, Q. 109, A. 10]

Objection 1: It seems that perseverance does not need the help of grace. For perseverance is a virtue, as stated above (A. 1). Now according to Tully (De Invent. Rhet. ii) virtue acts after the manner of nature. Therefore the sole inclination of virtue suffices for perseverance. Therefore this does not need the help of grace.

Obj. 2: Further, the gift of Christ's grace is greater than the harm brought upon us by Adam, as appears from Rom. 5:15, seqq. Now "before sin man was so framed that he could persevere by means of what he had received," as Augustine says (De Correp. et Grat. xi). Much more therefore can man, after being repaired by the grace of Christ, persevere without the help of a further grace.

Obj. 3: Further, sinful deeds are sometimes more difficult than deeds of virtue: hence it is said in the person of the wicked (Wis. 5:7): "We ... have walked through hard ways." Now some persevere in sinful deeds without the help of another. Therefore man can also persevere in deeds of virtue without the help of grace.

*On the contrary,* Augustine says (De Persev. i): "We hold that perseverance is a gift of God, whereby we persevere unto the end, in Christ."

*I answer that,* As stated above (A. 1, ad 2; A. 2, ad 3), perseverance has a twofold signification. First, it denotes the habit of perseverance, considered as a virtue. In this way it needs the gift of habitual grace, even as the other infused virtues. Secondly, it may be taken to denote the act of perseverance enduring until death: and in this sense it needs not only habitual grace, but also the gratuitous help of God sustaining man in good until the end of life, as stated above (I-II, Q. 109, A. 10), when we were treating of grace. Because, since the free-will is changeable by its very nature, which changeableness is not taken away from it by the habitual grace bestowed in the present life, it is not in the power of the free-will, albeit repaired by grace, to abide unchangeably in good, though it is in its power to choose this: for it is often in our power to choose yet not to accomplish.

Reply Obj. 1: The virtue of perseverance, so far as it is concerned, inclines one to persevere: yet since it is a habit, and a habit is a thing one uses at will, it does not follow that a person who has the habit of virtue uses it unchangeably until death.

Reply Obj. 2: As Augustine says (De Correp. et

Grat. xi), "it was given to the first man, not to persevere, but to be able to persevere of his free-will: because then no corruption was in human nature to make perseverance difficult. Now, however, by the grace of Christ, the predestined receive not only the possibility of persevering, but perseverance itself. Wherefore the first man whom no man threatened, of his own free-will rebelling against a threatening God, forfeited so great a happiness and so great a facility of avoiding sin: whereas these, although the world rage against their constancy, have persevered in faith."

Reply Obj. 3: Man is able by himself to fall into sin, but he cannot by himself arise from sin without the help of grace. Hence by falling into sin, so far as he is concerned man makes himself to be persevering in sin, unless he be delivered by God's grace. On the other hand, by doing good he does not make himself to be persevering in good, because he is able, by himself, to sin: wherefore he needs the help of grace for that end.

# QUESTION 138

OF THE VICES OPPOSED TO PERSEVERANCE (In Two Articles)

We must now consider the vices opposed to perseverance; under which head there are two points of inquiry:

(1) Of effeminacy;

(2) Of pertinacity.

FIRST ARTICLE [II-II, Q. 138, Art. 1]

Whether Effeminacy* Is Opposed to Perseverance? [* *Mollities,* literally "softness"]

Objection 1: It seems that effeminacy is not opposed to perseverance. For a gloss on 1 Cor. 6:9, 10, "Nor adulterers, nor the effeminate, nor liers with mankind," expounds the text thus: "Effeminate—i.e. obscene, given to unnatural vice." But this is opposed to chastity. Therefore effeminacy is not a vice opposed to perseverance.

Obj. 2: Further, the Philosopher says (Ethic. vii, 7) that "delicacy is a kind of effeminacy." But to be delicate seems akin to intemperance. Therefore effeminacy is not opposed to perseverance but to temperance.

Obj. 3: Further, the Philosopher says (Ethic. vii, 7) that "the man who is fond of amusement is effeminate." Now immoderate fondness of amusement is opposed to *eutrapelia* , which is the virtue about pleasures of play, as stated in Ethic. iv, 8. Therefore effeminacy is not opposed to perseverance.

*On the contrary,* The Philosopher says (Ethic. vii, 7) that "the persevering man is opposed to the effeminate."

*I answer that,* As stated above (Q. 137, AA. 1, 2), perseverance is deserving of praise because thereby a man does not forsake a good on account of long endurance of difficulties and toils: and it is directly opposed to this, seemingly, for a man to be ready to forsake a good on account of difficulties which he cannot endure. This is what we understand by effeminacy, because a thing is said to be "soft" if it readily yields to the touch. Now a thing is not declared to be soft through yielding to a heavy blow, for walls yield to the battering-ram. Wherefore a man is not said to be effeminate if he yields to heavy blows. Hence the Philosopher says (Ethic. vii, 7) that "it is no wonder, if a person is overcome by strong and overwhelming pleasures or sorrows; but he is to be pardoned if he struggles against them." Now it is evident that fear of danger is more impelling than the desire of pleasure: wherefore Tully says (De Offic. i) under the heading "True magnanimity consists of two things": "It is inconsistent for one who is not cast down by fear, to be defeated by lust, or who has proved himself unbeaten by toil, to yield to pleasure." Moreover, pleasure itself is a stronger motive of attraction than sorrow, for the lack of pleasure is a motive of withdrawal, since lack of pleasure is a pure privation. Wherefore, according to the Philosopher (Ethic. vii, 7), properly speaking an effeminate man is one who withdraws from good on account of sorrow caused by lack of pleasure, yielding as it were to a weak motion.

Reply Obj. 1: This effeminacy is caused in two ways. In one way, by custom: for where a man is accustomed to enjoy pleasures, it is more difficult for him to endure the lack of them. In another way, by natural disposition, because, to wit, his mind is less persevering through the frailty of his temperament. This is how women are compared to men, as the Philosopher says (Ethic. vii, 7): wherefore those who are passively sodomitical are said to be effeminate, being womanish themselves, as it were.

Reply Obj. 2: Toil is opposed to bodily pleasure: wherefore it is only toilsome things that are a hindrance to pleasures. Now the delicate are those who cannot endure toils, nor anything that diminishes pleasure. Hence it is written (Deut. 28:56): "The tender and delicate woman, that could not go upon the ground, nor set down her foot for ... softness [Douay: 'niceness']." Thus delicacy is a kind of effeminacy. But properly speaking effeminacy regards lack of pleasures, while delicacy regards the cause that hinders pleasure, for instance toil or the like.

Reply Obj. 3: In play two things may be considered. In the first place there is the pleasure, and thus inordinate fondness of play is opposed to *eutrapelia* . Secondly, we may consider the relaxation or rest which is opposed to toil. Accordingly just as it belongs to effeminacy to be unable to endure toilsome things, so too it belongs thereto to desire play or any other relaxation inordinately.

SECOND ARTICLE [II-II, Q. 138, Art. 2]

Whether Pertinacity Is Opposed to Perseverance?

Objection 1: It seems that pertinacity is not opposed to perseverance. For Gregory says (Moral. xxxi) that pertinacity arises from vainglory. But vainglory is not opposed to perseverance but to magnanimity, as stated above (Q. 132, A. 2). Therefore pertinacity is not opposed to perseverance.

Obj. 2: Further, if it is opposed to perseverance, this is so either by excess or by deficiency. Now it is not opposed by excess: because the pertinacious also yield to certain pleasure and sorrow, since according to the Philosopher (Ethic. vii, 9) "they rejoice when they prevail, and grieve when their opinions are rejected." And if it be opposed by deficiency, it will be the same as effeminacy, which is clearly false. Therefore pertinacity is nowise opposed to perseverance.

Obj. 3: Further, just as the persevering man persists in good against sorrow, so too do the continent and the temperate against pleasures, the brave against fear, and the meek against anger. But pertinacity is over-persistence in something. Therefore pertinacity is not opposed to perseverance more than to other virtues.

*On the contrary,* Tully says (De Invent. Rhet. ii) that pertinacity is to perseverance as superstition is to religion. But superstition is opposed to religion, as stated above (Q. 92, A. 1). Therefore pertinacity is opposed to perseverance.

*I answer that,* As Isidore says (Etym. x) "a person is said to be pertinacious who holds on impudently, as being utterly tenacious." "Pervicacious" has the same meaning, for it signifies that a man "perseveres in his purpose until he is victorious: for the ancients called 'vicia' what we call victory." These the Philosopher (Ethic. vii, 9) calls *ischyrognomones* , that is "head-strong," or *idiognomones* , that is "self-opinionated," because they abide by their opinions more than they should; whereas the effeminate man does so less than he ought, and the persevering man, as he ought. Hence it is clear that perseverance is commended for observing the mean, while pertinacity is reproved for exceeding the mean, and effeminacy for falling short of it.

Reply Obj. 1: The reason why a man is too persistent in his own opinion, is that he wishes by this means to make a show of his own excellence: wherefore this is the result of vainglory as its cause. Now it has been stated above (Q. 127, A. 2, ad 1; Q. 133, A. 2), that opposition of vices to virtues depends, not on their cause, but on their species.

Reply Obj. 2: The pertinacious man exceeds by persisting inordinately in something against many difficulties: yet he takes a certain pleasure in the end, just as the brave and the persevering man. Since, however, this pleasure is sinful, seeing that he desires it too much, and shuns the contrary pain, he is like the incontinent or effeminate man.

Reply Obj. 3: Although the other virtues persist against the onslaught of the passions, they are not commended for persisting in the same way as perseverance is. As to continence, its claim to praise seems to lie rather in overcoming pleasures. Hence pertinacity is directly opposed to perseverance.

# QUESTION 139

OF THE GIFT OF FORTITUDE (In Two Articles)

We must next consider the gift corresponding to fortitude, and this is the gift of fortitude. Under this head there are two points of inquiry:

(1) Whether fortitude is a gift?

(2) Which among the beatitudes and fruits correspond to it?

FIRST ARTICLE [II-II, Q. 139, Art. 1]

Whether Fortitude Is a Gift?

Objection 1: It seems that fortitude is not a gift. For the virtues differ from the gifts: and fortitude is a virtue. Therefore it should not be reckoned a gift.

Obj. 2: Further, the acts of the gifts remain in heaven, as stated above (I-II, Q. 68, A. 6). But the act of fortitude does not remain in heaven: for Gregory says (Moral. i) that "fortitude encourages the fainthearted against hardships, which will be altogether absent from heaven." Therefore fortitude is not a gift.

Obj. 3: Further, Augustine says (De Doctr. Christ. ii) that "it is a sign of fortitude to cut oneself adrift from all the deadly pleasures of the passing show." Now noisome pleasures and delights are the concern of temperance rather than of fortitude. Therefore it seems that fortitude is not the gift corresponding to the virtue of fortitude.

*On the contrary,* Fortitude is reckoned among the other gifts of the Holy Ghost (Isa. 11:2).

*I answer that,* Fortitude denotes a certain firmness of mind, as stated above (Q. 123, A. 2; I-II, Q. 61, A. 3): and this firmness of mind is required both in doing good and in enduring evil, especially with regard to goods or evils that are difficult. Now man, according to his proper and connatural mode, is able to have this firmness in both these respects, so as not to forsake the good on account of difficulties, whether in accomplishing an arduous work, or in enduring grievous evil. In this sense fortitude denotes a special or general virtue, as stated above (Q. 123, A. 2).

Yet furthermore man's mind is moved by the Holy Ghost, in order that he may attain the end of each work begun, and avoid whatever perils may threaten. This surpasses human nature: for sometimes it is not in a man's power to attain the end of his work, or to avoid evils or dangers, since these may happen to overwhelm him in death. But the Holy Ghost works this in man, by bringing him to everlasting life, which is the end of all good deeds, and the release from all perils. A certain confidence of this is infused into the mind by the Holy Ghost Who expels any fear of the contrary. It is in this sense that fortitude is reckoned a gift of the Holy Ghost. For it has been stated above (I-II, Q. 68, AA. 1, 2) that the gifts regard the motion of the mind by the Holy Ghost.

Reply Obj. 1: Fortitude, as a virtue, perfects the mind in the endurance of all perils whatever; but it does not go so far as to give confidence of overcoming all dangers: this belongs to the fortitude that is a gift of the Holy Ghost.

Reply Obj. 2: The gifts have not the same acts in heaven as on the way: for they exercise acts in connection with the enjoyment of the end. Hence the act of fortitude there is to enjoy full security from toil and evil.

Reply Obj. 3: The gift of fortitude regards the virtue of fortitude not only because it consists in enduring dangers, but also inasmuch as it consists in accomplishing any difficult work. Wherefore the gift of fortitude is directed by the gift of counsel, which seems to be concerned chiefly with the greater goods.

SECOND ARTICLE [II-II, Q. 139, Art. 2]

Whether the Fourth Beatitude: "Blessed Are They That Hunger and Thirst After Justice," Corresponds to the Gift of Fortitude?

Objection 1: It seems that the fourth beatitude, "Blessed are they that hunger and thirst after justice," does not correspond to the gift of fortitude. For the gift of piety and not the gift of fortitude corresponds to the virtue of justice. Now hungering and thirsting after justice pertain to the act of justice. Therefore this beatitude corresponds to the gift of piety rather than to the gift of fortitude.

Obj. 2: Further, hunger and thirst after justice imply a desire for good. Now this belongs properly to charity, to which the gift of wisdom, and not the gift of fortitude, corresponds, as stated above (Q. 45). Therefore this beatitude corresponds, not to the gift of fortitude, but to the gift of wisdom.

Obj. 3: Further, the fruits are consequent upon the beatitudes, since delight is essential to beatitude, according to *Ethic.* i, 8. Now the fruits, apparently, include none pertaining to fortitude. Therefore neither does any beatitude correspond to it.

*On the contrary,* Augustine says (De Serm. Dom. in Monte i): "Fortitude becomes the hungry and thirsty: since those who desire to enjoy true goods, and wish to avoid loving earthly and material things, must toil."

*I answer that,* As stated above (Q. 121, A. 2), Augustine makes the beatitudes correspond to the gifts according to the order in which they are set forth, observing at the same time a certain fittingness between them. Wherefore he ascribes the fourth beatitude, concerning the hunger and thirst for justice, to the fourth gift, namely fortitude.

Yet there is a certain congruity between them, because, as stated (A. 1), fortitude is about difficult things. Now it is very difficult, not merely to do virtuous deeds, which receive the common designation of works of justice, but furthermore to do them with an unsatiable desire, which may be signified by hunger and thirst for justice.

Reply Obj. 1: As Chrysostom says (Hom. xv in Matth.), we may understand here not only particular, but also universal justice, which is related to all virtuous deeds according to *Ethic.* v, 1, wherein whatever is hard is the object of that fortitude which is a gift.

Reply Obj. 2: Charity is the root of all the virtues and gifts, as stated above (Q. 23, A. 8, ad 3; I-II, Q. 68, A. 4, ad 3). Hence whatever pertains to fortitude may also be referred to charity.

Reply Obj. 3: There are two of the fruits which correspond sufficiently to the gift of fortitude: namely, patience, which regards the enduring of evils: and longanimity, which may regard the long delay and accomplishment of goods.

# QUESTION 140

OF THE PRECEPTS OF FORTITUDE (In Two Articles)

We must next consider the precepts of fortitude:

(1) The precepts of fortitude itself;

(2) The precepts of its parts.

FIRST ARTICLE [II-II, Q. 140, Art. 1]

Whether the Precepts of Fortitude Are Suitably Given in the Divine Law?

Objection 1: It seems that the precepts of fortitude are not suitably given in the Divine Law. For the New Law is more perfect than the Old Law. Yet the Old Law contains precepts of fortitude (Deut. 20). Therefore precepts of fortitude should have been given in the New Law also.

Obj. 2: Further, affirmative precepts are of greater import than negative precepts, since the affirmative include the negative, but not vice versa. Therefore it is unsuitable for the Divine Law to contain none but negative precepts in prohibition of fear.

Obj. 3: Further, fortitude is one of the principal virtues, as stated above (Q. 123, A. 2; I-II, Q. 61, A. 2). Now the precepts are directed to the virtues as to their end: wherefore they should be proportionate to them. Therefore the precepts of fortitude should have been placed among the precepts of the decalogue, which are the chief precepts of the Law.

*On the contrary,* stands Holy Writ which contains these precepts.

*I answer that,* Precepts of law are directed to the end intended by the lawgiver. Wherefore precepts of law must needs be framed in various ways according to the various ends intended by lawgivers, so that even in human affairs there are laws of democracies, others of kingdoms, and others again of tyrannical governments. Now the end of the Divine Law is that man may adhere to God: wherefore the Divine Law contains precepts both of fortitude and of the other virtues, with a view to directing the mind to God. For this reason it is written (Deut. 20:3, 4): "Fear ye them not: because the Lord your God is in the midst of you, and will fight for you against your enemies."

As to human laws, they are directed to certain earthly goods, and among them we find precepts of fortitude according to the requirements of those goods.

Reply Obj. 1: The Old Testament contained temporal promises, while the promises of the New Testament are spiritual and eternal, according to Augustine (Contra Faust. iv). Hence in the Old Law there was need for the people to be taught how to fight, even in a bodily contest, in order to obtain an earthly possession. But in the New Testament men were to be taught how to come to the possession of eternal life by fighting spiritually, according to Matt. 11:12, "The kingdom of heaven suffereth violence, and the violent bear it away." Hence Peter commands (1 Pet. 5:8, 9): "Your adversary the devil, as a roaring lion, goeth about, seeking whom he may devour: whom resist ye, strong in faith," as also James 4:7: "Resist the devil, and he will fly from you." Since, however, men while tending to spiritual goods may be withdrawn from them by corporal dangers, precepts of fortitude had to be given even in the New Law, that they might bravely endure temporal evils, according to Matt. 10:28, "Fear ye not them that kill the body."

Reply Obj. 2: The law gives general directions in its precepts. But the things that have to be done in cases of danger are not, like the things to be avoided, reducible to some common thing. Hence the precepts of fortitude are negative rather than affirmative.

Reply Obj. 3: As stated above (Q. 122, A. 1), the precepts of the decalogue are placed in the Law, as first principles, which need to be known to all from the outset. Wherefore the precepts of the decalogue had to be chiefly about those acts of justice in which the notion of duty is manifest, and not about acts of fortitude, because it is not so evident that it is a duty for a person not to fear dangers of death.

SECOND ARTICLE [II-II, Q. 140, Art. 2]

Whether the Precepts of the Parts of Fortitude Are Suitably Given in the Divine Law?

Objection 1: It seems that the precept of the parts of fortitude are unsuitably given in the Divine Law. For just as patience and perseverance are parts of fortitude, so also are magnificence, magnanimity, and confidence, as stated above (Q. 128). Now we find precepts of patience in the Divine Law, as also of perseverance. Therefore there should also have been precepts of magnificence and magnanimity.

Obj. 2: Further, patience is a very necessary virtue, since it is the guardian of the other virtues, as Gregory says (Hom. in Evang. xxxv). Now the other virtues are commanded absolutely. Therefore patience should not have been commanded merely, as Augustine says (De Serm. Dom. in Monte i), as to the preparedness of the mind.

Obj. 3: Further, patience and perseverance are parts of fortitude, as stated above (Q. 128; Q. 136, A. 4; Q. 137, A. 2). Now the precepts of fortitude are not affirmative but only negative, as stated above (A. 1, ad 2). Therefore the precepts of patience and perseverance should have been negative and not affirmative.

The contrary, however, follows from the way in which they are given by Holy Writ.

*I answer that,* The Divine Law instructs man perfectly about such things as are necessary for right living. Now in order to live aright man needs not only the principal virtues, but also the secondary and annexed virtues. Wherefore the Divine Law contains precepts not only about the acts of the principal virtues, but also about the acts of the secondary and annexed virtues.

Reply Obj. 1: Magnificence and magnanimity do not belong to the genus of fortitude, except by reason of a certain excellence of greatness which they regard in their respective matters. Now things pertaining to excellence come under the counsels of perfection rather than under precepts of obligation. Wherefore, there was need of counsels, rather than of precepts about magnificence and magnanimity. On the other hand, the hardships and toils of the present life pertain to patience and perseverance, not by reason of any greatness observable in them, but on account of the very nature of those virtues. Hence the need of precepts of patience and perseverance.

Reply Obj. 2: As stated above (Q. 3, A. 2), although affirmative precepts are always binding, they are not binding for always, but according to place and time. Wherefore just as the affirmative precepts about the other virtues are to be understood as to the preparedness of the mind, in the sense that man be prepared to fulfil them when necessary, so too are the precepts of patience to be understood in the same way.

Reply Obj. 3: Fortitude, as distinct from patience and perseverance, is about the greatest dangers wherein one must proceed with caution; nor is it necessary to determine what is to be done in particular. On the other hand, patience and perseverance are about minor hardships and toils, wherefore there is less danger in determining, especially in general, what is to be done in such cases.

# QUESTION 141

OF TEMPERANCE (In Eight Articles)

In the next place we must consider temperance: (1) Temperance itself; (2) its parts; (3) its precepts. With regard to temperance we must consider (1) temperance itself; (2) the contrary vices.

Under the first head there are eight points of inquiry:

(1) Whether temperance is a virtue?

(2) Whether it is a special virtue?

(3) Whether it is only about desires and pleasures?

(4) Whether it is only about pleasures of touch?

(5) Whether it is about pleasures of taste, as such, or only as a kind of touch?

(6) What is the rule of temperance?

(7) Whether it is a cardinal, or principal, virtue?

(8) Whether it is the greatest of virtues?

FIRST ARTICLE [II-II, Q. 141, Art. 1]

Whether Temperance Is a Virtue?

Objection 1: It seems that temperance is not a virtue. For no virtue goes against the inclination of nature, since "there is in us a natural aptitude for virtue," as stated in *Ethic.* ii, 1. Now temperance withdraws us from pleasures to which nature inclines, according to *Ethic.* ii, 3, 8. Therefore temperance is not a virtue.

Obj. 2: Further, virtues are connected with one another, as stated above (I-II, Q. 65, A. 1). But some people have temperance without having the other virtues: for we find many who are temperate, and yet covetous or timid. Therefore temperance is not a virtue.

Obj. 3: Further, to every virtue there is a corresponding gift, as appears from what we have said above (I-II, Q. 68, A. 4). But seemingly no gift corresponds to temperance, since all the gifts have been already ascribed to the other virtues (QQ. 8, 9, 19, 45, 52, 71, 139). Therefore temperance is not a virtue.

*On the contrary,* Augustine says (Music. vi, 15): "Temperance is the name of a virtue."

*I answer that,* As stated above (I-II, Q. 55, A. 3), it is essential to virtue to incline man to good. Now the good of man is to be in accordance with reason, as Dionysius states (Div. Nom. iv). Hence human virtue is that which inclines man to something in accordance with reason. Now temperance evidently inclines man to this, since its very name implies moderation or temperateness, which reason causes. Therefore temperance is a virtue.

Reply Obj. 1: Nature inclines everything to whatever is becoming to it. Wherefore man naturally desires pleasures that are becoming to him. Since, however, man as such is a rational being, it follows that those pleasures are becoming to man which are in accordance with reason. From such pleasures temperance does not withdraw him, but from those which are contrary to reason. Wherefore it is clear that temperance is not contrary to the inclination of human nature, but is in accord with it. It is, however, contrary to the inclination of the animal nature that is not subject to reason.

Reply Obj. 2: The temperance which fulfils the conditions of perfect virtue is not without prudence, while this is lacking to all who are in sin. Hence those who lack other virtues, through being subject to the opposite vices, have not the temperance which is a virtue, though they do acts of temperance from a certain natural disposition, in so far as certain imperfect virtues are either natural to man, as stated above (I-II, Q. 63, A. 1), or acquired by habituation, which virtues, through lack of prudence, are not perfected by reason, as stated above (I-II, Q. 65, A. 1).

Reply Obj. 3: Temperance also has a corresponding gift, namely, fear, whereby man is withheld from the pleasures of the flesh, according to Ps. 118:120: "Pierce Thou my flesh with Thy fear." The gift of fear has for its principal object God, Whom it avoids offending, and in this respect it corresponds to the virtue of hope, as stated above (Q. 19, A. 9, ad 1). But it may have for its secondary object whatever a man shuns in order to avoid offending God. Now man stands in the greatest need of the fear of God in order to shun those things which are most seductive, and these are the matter of temperance: wherefore the gift of fear corresponds to temperance also.

SECOND ARTICLE [II-II, Q. 141, Art. 2]

Whether Temperance Is a Special Virtue?

Objection 1: It would seem that temperance is not a special virtue. For Augustine says (De Morib. Eccl. xv) that "it belongs to temperance to preserve one's integrity and freedom from corruption for God's sake." But this is common to every virtue. Therefore temperance is not a special virtue.

Obj. 2: Further, Ambrose says (De Offic. i, 42) that "what we observe and seek most in temperance is tranquillity of soul." But this is common to every virtue. Therefore temperance is not a special virtue.

Obj. 3: Further, Tully says (De Offic. i, 27) that "we cannot separate the beautiful from the virtuous," and that "whatever is just is beautiful." Now the beautiful is considered as proper to temperance, according to the same authority (Tully, De Offic. i, 27). Therefore temperance is not a special virtue.

*On the contrary,* The Philosopher (Ethic. ii, 7; iii, 10) reckons it a special virtue.

*I answer that,* It is customary in human speech to employ a common term in a restricted sense in order to designate the principal things to which that common term is applicable: thus the word "city" is used antonomastically* to designate Rome. [*Antonomasia is the figure of speech whereby we substitute the general for the individual term; e.g. The Philosopher for Aristotle]. Accordingly the word "temperance" has a twofold acceptation. First, in accordance with its common signification: and thus temperance is not a special but a general virtue, because the word "temperance" signifies a certain temperateness or moderation, which reason appoints to human operations and passions: and this is common to every moral virtue. Yet there is a logical difference between temperance and fortitude, even if we take them both as general virtues: since temperance withdraws man from things which seduce the appetite from obeying reason, while fortitude incites him to endure or withstand those things on account of which he forsakes the good of reason.

On the other hand, if we take temperance antonomastically, as withholding the appetite from those things which are most seductive to man, it is a special virtue, for thus it has, like fortitude, a special matter.

Reply Obj. 1: Man's appetite is corrupted chiefly by those things which seduce him into forsaking the rule of reason and Divine law. Wherefore integrity, which Augustine ascribes to temperance, can, like the latter, be taken in two ways: first, in a general sense, and secondly in a sense of excellence.

Reply Obj. 2: The things about which temperance is concerned have a most disturbing effect on the soul, for the reason that they are natural to man, as we shall state further on (AA. 4, 5). Hence tranquillity of soul is ascribed to temperance by way of excellence, although it is a common property of all the virtues.

Reply Obj. 3: Although beauty is becoming to every virtue, it is ascribed to temperance, by way of excellence, for two reasons. First, in respect of the generic notion of temperance, which consists in a certain moderate and fitting proportion, and this is what we understand by beauty, as attested by Dionysius (Div. Nom. iv). Secondly, because the things from which temperance withholds us, hold the lowest place in man, and are becoming to him by reason of his animal nature, as we shall state further on (AA. 4, 5; Q. 142, A. 4), wherefore it is natural that such things should defile him. In consequence beauty is a foremost attribute of temperance which above all hinders man from being defiled. In like manner honesty [*Honesty must be taken here in its broad sense as synonymous with moral goodness, from the point of view of decorum] is a special attribute of temperance: for Isidore says (Etym. x): "An honest man is one who has no defilement, for honesty means an honorable state." This is most applicable to temperance, which withstands the vices that bring most dishonor on man, as we shall state further on (Q. 142, A. 4).

THIRD ARTICLE [II-II, Q. 141, Art. 3]

Whether Temperance Is Only About Desires and Pleasures?

Objection 1: It would seem that temperance is not only about desires and pleasures. For Tully says (De Invent. Rhet. ii, 54) that "temperance is reason's firm and moderate mastery of lust and other wanton emotions of the mind." Now all the passions of the soul are called emotions of the mind. Therefore it seems that temperance is not only about desires and pleasures.

Obj. 2: Further, "Virtue is about the difficult and the good" [*Ethic. ii, 3]. Now it seems more difficult to temper fear, especially with regard to dangers of death, than to moderate desires and pleasures, which are despised on account of deadly pains and dangers, according to Augustine (QQ. 83, qu. 36). Therefore it seems that the virtue of temperance is not chiefly about desires and pleasures.

Obj. 3: Further, according to Ambrose (De Offic. i, 43) "the grace of moderation belongs to temperance": and Tully says (De Offic. ii, 27) that "it is the concern of temperance to calm all disturbances of the mind and to enforce moderation." Now moderation is needed, not only in desires and pleasures, but also in external acts and whatever pertains to the exterior. Therefore temperance is not only about desires and pleasures.

*On the contrary,* Isidore says (Etym.) [*The words quoted do not occur in the work referred to; Cf. his De Summo Bono xxxvii, xlii, and De Different. ii, 39]: that "it is temperance whereby lust and desire are kept under control."

*I answer that,* As stated above (Q. 123, A. 12; Q. 136, A. 1), it belongs to moral virtue to safeguard the good of reason against the passions that rebel against reason. Now the movement of the soul's passions is twofold, as stated above (I-II, Q. 23, A. 2), when we were treating of the passions: the one, whereby the sensitive appetite pursues sensible and bodily goods, the other whereby it flies from sensible and bodily evils.

The first of these movements of the sensitive appetite rebels against reason chiefly by lack of moderation. Because sensible and bodily goods, considered in their species, are not in opposition to reason, but are subject to it as instruments which reason employs in order to attain its proper end: and that they are opposed to reason is owing to the fact that the sensitive appetite fails to tend towards them in accord with the mode of reason. Hence it belongs properly to moral virtue to moderate those passions which denote a pursuit of the good.

On the other hand, the movement of the sensitive appetite in flying from sensible evil is mostly in opposition to reason, not through being immoderate, but chiefly in respect of its flight: because, when a man flies from sensible and bodily evils, which sometimes accompany the good of reason, the result is that he flies from the good of reason. Hence it belongs to moral virtue to make man while flying from evil to remain firm in the good of reason.

Accordingly, just as the virtue of fortitude, which by its very nature bestows firmness, is chiefly concerned with the passion, viz. fear, which regards flight from bodily evils, and consequently with daring, which attacks the objects of fear in the hope of attaining some good, so, too, temperance, which denotes a kind of moderation, is chiefly concerned with those passions that tend towards sensible goods, viz. desire and pleasure, and consequently with the sorrows that arise from the absence of those pleasures. For just as daring presupposes objects of fear, so too such like sorrow arises from the absence of the aforesaid pleasures.

Reply Obj. 1: As stated above (I-II, Q. 23, AA. 1, 2; I-II, Q. 25, A. 1), when we were treating of the passions, those passions which pertain to avoidance of evil, presuppose the passions pertaining to the pursuit of good; and the passions of the irascible presuppose the passions of the concupiscible. Hence, while temperance directly moderates the passions of the concupiscible which tend towards good, as a consequence, it moderates all the other passions, inasmuch as moderation of the passions that precede results in moderation of the passions that follow: since he that is not immoderate in desire is moderate in hope, and grieves moderately for the absence of the things he desires.

Reply Obj. 2: Desire denotes an impulse of the appetite towards the object of pleasure and this impulse needs control, which belongs to temperance. On the other hand fear denotes a withdrawal of the mind from certain evils, against which man needs firmness of mind, which fortitude bestows. Hence temperance is properly about desires, and fortitude about fears.

Reply Obj. 3: External acts proceed from the internal passions of the soul: wherefore their moderation depends on the moderation of the internal passions.

FOURTH ARTICLE [II-II, Q. 141, Art. 4]

Whether Temperance Is Only About Desires and Pleasures of Touch?

Objection 1: It would seem that temperance is not only about desires and pleasures of touch. For Augustine says (De Morib. Eccl. xix) that "the function of temperance is to control and quell the desires which draw us to the things which withdraw us from the laws of God and from the fruit of His goodness"; and a little further on he adds that "it is the duty of temperance to spurn all bodily allurements and popular praise." Now we are withdrawn from God's laws not only by the desire for pleasures of touch, but also by the desire for pleasures of the other senses, for these, too, belong to the bodily allurements, and again by the desire for riches or for worldly glory: wherefore it is written (1 Tim. 6:10). "Desire [* *Cupiditas,* which the Douay version following the Greek *philargyria* renders 'desire of money'] is the root of all evils." Therefore temperance is not only about desires of pleasures of touch.

Obj. 2: Further, the Philosopher says (Ethic. iv, 3) that "one who is worthy of small things and deems himself worthy of them is temperate, but he is not magnificent." Now honors, whether small or great, of which he is speaking there, are an object of pleasure, not of touch, but in the soul's apprehension. Therefore temperance is not only about desires for pleasures of touch.

Obj. 3: Further, things that are of the same genus would seem to pertain to the matter of a particular virtue under one same aspect. Now all pleasures of sense are apparently of the same genus. Therefore they all equally belong to the matter of temperance.

Obj. 4: Further, spiritual pleasures are greater than the pleasures of the body, as stated above (I-II, Q. 31, A. 5) in the treatise on the passions. Now sometimes men forsake God's laws and the state of virtue through desire for spiritual pleasures, for instance, through curiosity in matters of knowledge: wherefore the devil promised man knowledge, saying (Gen. 3:5): "Ye shall be as Gods, knowing good and evil." Therefore temperance is not only about pleasures of touch.

Obj. 5: Further, if pleasures of touch were the proper matter of temperance, it would follow that temperance is about all pleasures of touch. But it is not about all, for instance, about those which occur in games. Therefore pleasures of touch are not the proper matter of temperance.

*On the contrary,* The Philosopher says (Ethic. iii, 10) that "temperance is properly about desires of pleasures of touch."

*I answer that,* As stated above (A. 3), temperance is about desires and pleasures in the same way as fortitude is about fear and daring. Now fortitude is about fear and daring with respect to the greatest evils whereby nature itself is dissolved; and such are dangers of death. Wherefore in like manner temperance must needs be about desires for the greatest pleasures. And since pleasure results from a natural operation, it is so much the greater according as it results from a more natural operation. Now to animals the most natural operations are those which preserve the nature of the individual by means of meat and drink, and the nature of the species by the union of the sexes. Hence temperance is properly about pleasures of meat and drink and sexual pleasures. Now these pleasures result from the sense of touch. Wherefore it follows that temperance is about pleasures of touch.

Reply Obj. 1: In the passage quoted Augustine apparently takes temperance, not as a special virtue having a determinate matter, but as concerned with the moderation of reason, in any matter whatever: and this is a general condition of every virtue. However, we may also reply that if a man can control the greatest pleasures, much more can he control lesser ones. Wherefore it belongs chiefly and properly to temperance to moderate desires and pleasures of touch, and secondarily other pleasures.

Reply Obj. 2: The Philosopher takes temperance as denoting moderation in external things, when, to wit, a man tends to that which is proportionate to him, but not as denoting moderation in the soul's emotions, which pertains to the virtue of temperance.

Reply Obj. 3: The pleasures of the other senses play a different part in man and in other animals. For in other animals pleasures do not result from the other senses save in relation to sensibles of touch: thus the lion is pleased to see the stag, or to hear its voice, in relation to his food. On the other hand man derives pleasure from the other senses, not only for this reason, but also on account of the becomingness of the sensible object. Wherefore temperance is about the pleasures of the other senses, in relation to pleasures of touch, not principally but consequently: while in so far as the sensible objects of the other senses are pleasant on account of their becomingness, as when a man is pleased at a well-harmonized sound, this pleasure has nothing to do with the preservation of nature. Hence these passions are not of such importance that temperance can be referred to them antonomastically.

Reply Obj. 4: Although spiritual pleasures are by their nature greater than bodily pleasures, they are not so perceptible to the senses, and consequently they do not so strongly affect the sensitive appetite, against whose impulse the good of reason is safeguarded by moral virtue. We may also reply that spiritual pleasures, strictly speaking, are in accordance with reason, wherefore they need no control, save accidentally, in so far as one spiritual pleasure is a hindrance to another greater and more binding.

Reply Obj. 5: Not all pleasures of touch regard the preservation of nature, and consequently it does not follow that temperance is about all pleasures of touch.

FIFTH ARTICLE [II-II, Q. 141, Art. 5]

Whether Temperance Is About the Pleasures Proper to the Taste?

Objection 1: It would seem that temperance is about pleasures proper to the taste. For pleasures of the taste result from food and drink, which are more necessary to man's life than sexual pleasures, which regard the touch. But according to what has been said (A. 4), temperance is about pleasures in things that are necessary to human life. Therefore temperance is about pleasures proper to the taste rather than about those proper to the touch.

Obj. 2: Further, temperance is about the passions rather than about things themselves. Now, according to *De Anima* ii, 3, "the touch is the sense of food," as regards the very substance of the food, whereas "savor" which is the proper object of the taste, is "the pleasing quality of the food." Therefore temperance is about the taste rather than about the touch.

Obj. 3: Further, according to *Ethic.* vii, 4, 7: "temperance and intemperance are about the same things, and so are continence and incontinence, perseverance, and effeminacy," to which delicacy pertains. Now delicacy seems to regard the delight taken in savors which are the object of the taste. Therefore temperance is about pleasures proper to the taste.

*On the contrary,* The Philosopher says (Ethic. iii, 10) that "seemingly temperance and intemperance have little if anything to do with the taste."

*I answer that,* As stated above (A. 4), temperance is about the greatest pleasures, which chiefly regard the preservation of human life either in the species or in the individual. In these matters certain things are to be considered as principal and others as secondary. The principal thing is the use itself of the necessary means, of the woman who is necessary for the preservation of the species, or of food and drink which are necessary for the preservation of the individual: while the very use of these necessary things has a certain essential pleasure annexed thereto.

In regard to either use we consider as secondary whatever makes the use more pleasurable, such as beauty and adornment in woman, and a pleasing savor and likewise odor in food. Hence temperance is chiefly about the pleasure of touch, that results essentially from the use of these necessary things, which use is in all cases attained by the touch. Secondarily, however, temperance and intemperance are about pleasures of the taste, smell, or sight, inasmuch as the sensible objects of these senses conduce to the pleasurable use of the necessary things that have relation to the touch. But since the taste is more akin to the touch than the other senses are, it follows that temperance is more about the taste than about the other senses.

Reply Obj. 1: The use of food and the pleasure that essentially results therefrom pertain to the touch. Hence the Philosopher says (De Anima ii, 3) that "touch is the sense of food, for food is hot or cold, wet or dry." To the taste belongs the discernment of savors, which make the food pleasant to eat, in so far as they are signs of its being suitable for nourishment.

Reply Obj. 2: The pleasure resulting from savor is additional, so to speak, whereas the pleasure of touch results essentially from the use of food and drink.

Reply Obj. 3: Delicacy regards principally the substance of the food, but secondarily it regards its delicious savor and the way in which it is served.

SIXTH ARTICLE [II-II, Q. 141, Art. 6]

Whether the Rule of Temperance Depends on the Need of the Present Life?

Objection 1: It would seem that the rule of temperance does not depend on the needs of the present life. For higher things are not regulated according to lower. Now, as temperance is a virtue of the soul, it is above the needs of the body. Therefore the rule of temperance does not depend on the needs of the body.

Obj. 2: Further, whoever exceeds a rule sins. Therefore if the needs of the body were the rule of temperance, it would be a sin against temperance to indulge in any other pleasure than those required by nature, which is content with very little. But this would seem unreasonable.

Obj. 3: Further, no one sins in observing a rule.

Therefore if the need of the body were the rule of temperance, there would be no sin in using any pleasure for the needs of the body, for instance, for the sake of health. But this is apparently false. Therefore the need of the body is not the rule of temperance.

*On the contrary,* Augustine says (De Morib. Eccl. xxi): "In both Testaments the temperate man finds confirmation of the rule forbidding him to love the things of this life, or to deem any of them desirable for its own sake, and commanding him to avail himself of those things with the moderation of a user not the attachment of a lover, in so far as they are requisite for the needs of this life and of his station."

*I answer that,* As stated above (A. 1; Q. 109, A. 2; Q. 123, A. 12), the good of moral virtue consists chiefly in the order of reason: because "man's good is to be in accord with reason," as Dionysius asserts (Div. Nom. iv). Now the principal order of reason is that by which it directs certain things towards their end, and the good of reason consists chiefly in this order; since good has the aspect of end, and the end is the rule of whatever is directed to the end. Now all the pleasurable objects that are at man's disposal, are directed to some necessity of this life as to their end. Wherefore temperance takes the need of this life, as the rule of the pleasurable objects of which it makes use, and uses them only for as much as the need of this life requires.

Reply Obj. 1: As stated above, the need of this life is regarded as a rule in so far as it is an end. Now it must be observed that sometimes the end of the worker differs from the end of the work, thus it is clear that the end of building is a house, whereas sometimes the end of the builder is profit. Accordingly the end and rule of temperance itself is happiness; while the end and rule of the thing it makes use of is the need of human life, to which whatever is useful for life is subordinate.

Reply Obj. 2: The need of human life may be taken in two ways. First, it may be taken in the sense in which we apply the term "necessary" to that without which a thing cannot be at all; thus food is necessary to an animal. Secondly, it may be taken for something without which a thing cannot be becomingly. Now temperance regards not only the former of these needs, but also the latter. Wherefore the Philosopher says (Ethic. iii, 11) that "the temperate man desires pleasant things for the sake of health, or for the sake of a sound condition of body." Other things that are not necessary for this purpose may be divided into two classes. For some are a hindrance to health and a sound condition of body; and these temperance makes not use of whatever, for this would be a sin against temperance. But others are not a hindrance to those things, and these temperance uses moderately, according to the demands of place and time, and in keeping with those among whom one dwells. Hence the Philosopher (Ethic. iii, 11) says that the "temperate man also desires other pleasant things," those namely that are not necessary for health or a sound condition of body, "so long as they are not prejudicial to these things."

Reply Obj. 3: As stated (ad 2), temperance regards need according to the requirements of life, and this depends not only on the requirements of the body, but also on the requirements of external things, such as riches and station, and more still on the requirements of good conduct. Hence the Philosopher adds (Ethic. iii, 11) that "the temperate man makes use of pleasant things provided that not only they be not prejudicial to health and a sound bodily condition, but also that they be not inconsistent with good," i.e. good conduct, nor "beyond his substance," i.e. his means. And Augustine says (De Morib. Eccl. xxi) that the "temperate man considers the need" not only "of this life" but also "of his station."

SEVENTH ARTICLE [II-II, Q. 141, Art. 7]

Whether Temperance Is a Cardinal Virtue?

Objection 1: It would seem that temperance is not a cardinal virtue. For the good of moral virtue depends on reason. But temperance is about those things that are furthest removed from reason, namely about pleasures common to us and the lower animals, as stated in *Ethic.* iii, 10. Therefore temperance, seemingly, is not a principal virtue.

Obj. 2: Further, the greater the impetus the more difficult is it to control. Now anger, which is controlled by meekness, seems to be more impetuous than desire, which is controlled by temperance. For it is written (Prov. 27:4): "Anger hath no mercy, nor fury when it breaketh forth; and who can bear the violence ( *impetum* ) of one provoked?" Therefore meekness is a principal virtue rather than temperance.

Obj. 3: Further, hope as a movement of the soul takes precedence of desire and concupiscence, as stated above (I-II, Q. 25, A. 4). But humility controls the presumption of immoderate hope. Therefore, seemingly, humility is a principal virtue rather than temperance which controls concupiscence.

*On the contrary,* Gregory reckons temperance among the principal virtues (Moral. ii, 49).

*I answer that,* As stated above (Q. 123, A. 11; Q. 61, A. 3), a principal or cardinal virtue is so called because it has a foremost claim to praise on account of one of those things that are requisite for the notion of virtue in general. Now moderation, which is requisite in every virtue, deserves praise principally in pleasures of touch, with which temperance is concerned, both because these pleasures are most natural to us, so that it is more difficult to abstain from them, and to control the desire for them, and because their objects are more necessary to the present life, as stated above (A. 4). For this reason temperance is reckoned a principal or cardinal virtue.

Reply Obj. 1: The longer the range of its operation, the greater is the agent's power ( *virtus* ) shown to be: wherefore the very fact that the reason is able to moderate desires and pleasures that are furthest removed from it, proves the greatness of reason's power. This is how temperance comes to be a principal virtue.

Reply Obj. 2: The impetuousness of anger is caused by an accident, for instance, a painful hurt; wherefore it soon passes, although its impetus be great. On the other hand, the impetuousness of the desire for pleasures of touch proceeds from a natural cause, wherefore it is more lasting and more general, and consequently its control regards a more principal virtue.

Reply Obj. 3: The object of hope is higher than the object of desire, wherefore hope is accounted the principal passion in the irascible. But the objects of desires and pleasures of touch move the appetite with greater force, since they are more natural. Therefore temperance, which appoints the mean in such things, is a principal virtue.

EIGHTH ARTICLE [II-II, Q. 141, Art. 8]

Whether Temperance Is the Greatest of the Virtues?

Objection 1: It would seem that temperance is the greatest of the virtues. For Ambrose says (De Offic. i, 43) that "what we observe and seek most in temperance is the safeguarding of what is honorable, and the regard for what is beautiful." Now virtue deserves praise for being honorable and beautiful. Therefore temperance is the greatest of the virtues.

Obj. 2: Further, the more difficult the deed the greater the virtue. Now it is more difficult to control desires and pleasures of touch than to regulate external actions, the former pertaining to temperance and the latter to justice. Therefore temperance is a greater virtue than justice.

Obj. 3: Further, seemingly the more general a thing is, the more necessary and the better it is. Now fortitude is about dangers of death which occur less frequently than pleasures of touch, for these occur every day; so that temperance is in more general use than fortitude. Therefore temperance is a more excellent virtue than fortitude.

*On the contrary,* The Philosopher says (Rhet. i, 9) that the "greatest virtues are those which are most profitable to others, for which reason we give the greatest honor to the brave and the just."

*I answer that,* As the Philosopher declares (Ethic. i, 2) "the good of the many is more of the godlike than the good of the individual," wherefore the more a virtue regards the good of the many, the better it is. Now justice and fortitude regard the good of the many more than temperance does, since justice regards the relations between one man and another, while fortitude regards dangers of battle which are endured for the common weal: whereas temperance moderates only the desires and pleasures which affect man himself. Hence it is evident that justice and fortitude are more excellent virtues than temperance: while prudence and the theological virtues are more excellent still.

Reply Obj. 1: Honor and beauty are especially ascribed to temperance, not on account of the excellence of the good proper to temperance, but on account of the disgrace of the contrary evil from which it withdraws us, by moderating the pleasures common to us and the lower animals.

Reply Obj. 2: Since virtue is about the difficult and the good, the excellence of a virtue is considered more under the aspect of good, wherein justice excels, than under the aspect of difficult, wherein temperance excels.

Reply Obj. 3: That which is general because it regards the many conduces more to the excellence of goodness than that which is general because it occurs frequently: fortitude excels in the former way, temperance in the latter. Hence fortitude is greater simply, although in some respects temperance may be described as greater not only than fortitude but also than justice.

# QUESTION 142

OF THE VICES OPPOSED TO TEMPERANCE (In Four Articles)

We must now consider the vices opposed to temperance. Under this head there are four points of inquiry:

(1) Whether insensibility is a sin?

(2) Whether intemperance is a childish sin?

(3) Of the comparison between intemperance and timidity;

(4) Whether intemperance is the most disgraceful of vices?

FIRST ARTICLE [II-II, Q. 142, Art. 1]

Whether Insensibility Is a Vice?

Objection 1: It would seem that insensibility is not a vice. For those are called insensible who are deficient with regard to pleasures of touch. Now seemingly it is praiseworthy and virtuous to be altogether deficient in such matters: for it is written (Dan. 10:2, 3): "In those days Daniel mourned the days of three weeks, I ate no desirable bread, and neither flesh nor wine entered my mouth, neither was I anointed with ointment." Therefore insensibility is not a sin.

Obj. 2: Further, "man's good is to be in accord with reason," according to Dionysius (Div. Nom. iv). Now abstinence from all pleasures of touch is most conducive to man's progress in the good of reason: for it is written (Dan. 1:17) that "to the children" who took pulse for their food (Dan. 1:12), "God gave knowledge, and understanding in every book and wisdom." Therefore insensibility, which rejects these pleasures altogether, is not sinful.

Obj. 3: Further, that which is a very effective means of avoiding sin would seem not to be sinful. Now the most effective remedy in avoiding sin is to shun pleasures, and this pertains to insensibility. For the Philosopher says (Ethic. ii, 9) that "if we deny ourselves pleasures we are less liable to sin." Therefore there is nothing vicious in insensibility.

*On the contrary,* Nothing save vice is opposed to virtue. Now insensibility is opposed to the virtue of temperance according to the Philosopher (Ethic. ii, 7; iii, 11). Therefore insensibility is a vice.

*I answer that,* Whatever is contrary to the natural order is vicious. Now nature has introduced pleasure into the operations that are necessary for man's life. Wherefore the natural order requires that man should make use of these pleasures, in so far as they are necessary for man's well-being, as regards the preservation either of the individual or of the species. Accordingly, if anyone were to reject pleasure to the extent of omitting things that are necessary for nature's preservation, he would sin, as acting counter to the order of nature. And this pertains to the vice of insensibility.

It must, however, be observed that it is sometimes praiseworthy, and even necessary for the sake of an end, to abstain from such pleasures as result from these operations. Thus, for the sake of the body's health, certain persons refrain from pleasures of meat, drink, and sex; as also for the fulfilment of certain engagements: thus athletes and soldiers have to deny themselves many pleasures, in order to fulfil their respective duties. In like manner penitents, in order to recover health of soul, have recourse to abstinence from pleasures, as a kind of diet, and those who are desirous of giving themselves up to contemplation and Divine things need much to refrain from carnal things. Nor do any of these things pertain to the vice of insensibility, because they are in accord with right reason.

Reply Obj. 1: Daniel abstained thus from pleasures, not through any horror of pleasure as though it were evil in itself, but for some praiseworthy end, in order, namely, to adapt himself to the heights of contemplation by abstaining from pleasures of the body. Hence the text goes on to tell of the revelation that he received immediately afterwards.

Reply Obj. 2: Since man cannot use his reason without his sensitive powers, which need a bodily organ, as stated in the First Part (Q. 84, AA. 7, 8), man needs to sustain his body in order that he may use his reason. Now the body is sustained by means of operations that afford pleasure: wherefore the good of reason cannot be in a man if he abstain from all pleasures. Yet this need for using pleasures of the body will be greater or less, according as man needs more or less the powers of his body in accomplishing the act of reason. Wherefore it is commendable for those who undertake the duty of giving themselves to contemplation, and of imparting to others a spiritual good, by a kind of spiritual procreation, as it were, to abstain from many pleasures, but not for those who are in duty bound to bodily occupations and carnal procreation.

Reply Obj. 3: In order to avoid sin, pleasure must be shunned, not altogether, but so that it is not sought more than necessity requires.

SECOND ARTICLE [II-II, Q. 142, Art. 2]

Whether Intemperance Is a Childish Sin?

Objection 1: It would seem that intemperance is not a childish sin. For Jerome in commenting on Matt. 18:3, "Unless you be converted, and become as little children," says that "a child persists not in anger, is unmindful of injuries, takes no pleasure in seeing a beautiful woman," all of which is contrary to intemperance. Therefore intemperance is not a childish sin.

Obj. 2: Further, children have none but natural desires. Now "in respect of natural desires few sin by intemperance," according to the Philosopher (Ethic. iii, 11). Therefore intemperance is not a childish sin.

Obj. 3: Further, children should be fostered and nourished: whereas concupiscence and pleasure, about which intemperance is concerned, are always to be thwarted and uprooted, according to Col. 3:5, "Mortify ... your members upon the earth, which are ... concupiscence" [*Vulg.: 'your members which are upon the earth, fornication . . concupiscence'], etc. Therefore intemperance is not a childish sin.

*On the contrary,* The Philosopher says (Ethic. iii, 12) that "we apply the term intemperance* to childish faults." [* Akolasia which Aristotle refers to kolazo to punish, so that its original sense would be 'impunity' or 'unrestraint.']

*I answer that,* A thing is said to be childish for two reasons. First, because it is becoming to children, and the Philosopher does not mean that the sin of intemperance is childish in this sense. Secondly. by way of likeness, and it is in this sense that sins of intemperance are said to be childish. For the sin of intemperance is one of unchecked concupiscence, which is likened to a child in three ways. First, as regards that which they both desire, for like a child concupiscence desires something disgraceful. This is because in human affairs a thing is beautiful according as it harmonizes with reason. Wherefore Tully says (De Offic. i, 27) under the heading "Comeliness is twofold," that "the beautiful is that which is in keeping with man's excellence in so far as his nature differs from other animals." Now a child does not attend to the order of reason; and in like manner "concupiscence does not listen to reason," according to *Ethic.* vii, 6. Secondly, they are alike as to the result. For a child, if left to his own will, becomes more self-willed: hence it is written (Ecclus. 30:8): "A horse not broken becometh stubborn, and a child left to himself will become headstrong." So, too, concupiscence, if indulged, gathers strength: wherefore Augustine says (Confess. viii, 5): "Lust served became a custom, and custom not resisted became necessity." Thirdly, as to the remedy which is applied to both. For a child is corrected by being restrained; hence it is written (Prov. 23:13, 14): "Withhold not correction from a child ... Thou shalt beat him with a rod, and deliver his soul from Hell." In like manner by resisting concupiscence we moderate it according to the demands of virtue. Augustine indicates this when he says (Music. vi, 11) that if the mind be lifted up to spiritual things, and remain fixed "thereon, the impulse of custom," i.e. carnal concupiscence, "is broken, and being suppressed is gradually weakened: for it was stronger when we followed it, and though not wholly destroyed, it is certainly less strong when we curb it." Hence the Philosopher says (Ethic. iii, 12) that "as a child ought to live according to the direction of his tutor, so ought the concupiscible to accord with reason."

Reply Obj. 1: This argument takes the term "childish" as denoting what is observed in children. It is not in this sense that the sin of intemperance is said to be childish, but by way of likeness, as stated above.

Reply Obj. 2: A desire may be said to be natural in two ways. First, with regard to its genus, and thus temperance and intemperance are about natural desires, since they are about desires of food and sex, which are directed to the preservation of nature. Secondly, a desire may be called natural with regard to the species of the thing that nature requires for its own preservation; and in this way it does not happen often that one sins in the matter of natural desires, for nature requires only that which supplies its need, and there is no sin in desiring this, save only where it is desired in excess as to quantity. This is the only way in which sin can occur with regard to natural desires, according to the Philosopher (Ethic. iii, 11).

There are other things in respect of which sins frequently occur, and these are certain incentives to desire devised by human curiosity [*Cf. Q. 167], such as the nice ( *curiosa* ) preparation of food, or the adornment of women. And though children do not affect these things much, yet intemperance is called a childish sin for the reason given above.

Reply Obj. 3: That which regards nature should be nourished and fostered in children, but that which pertains to the lack of reason in them should not be fostered, but corrected, as stated above.

THIRD ARTICLE [II-II, Q. 142, Art. 3]

Whether Cowardice* Is a Greater Vice Than Intemperance? [*Cf. Q. 125]

Objection 1: It would seem that cowardice is a greater vice than intemperance. For a vice deserves reproach through being opposed to the good of virtue. Now cowardice is opposed to fortitude, which is a more excellent virtue than temperance, as stated above (A. 2; Q. 141, A. 8). Therefore cowardice is a greater vice than intemperance.

Obj. 2: Further, the greater the difficulty to be surmounted, the less is a man to be reproached for failure, wherefore the Philosopher says (Ethic. vii, 7) that "it is no wonder, in fact it is pardonable, if a man is mastered by strong and overwhelming pleasures or pains." Now seemingly it is more difficult to control pleasures than other passions; hence it is stated in *Ethic.* ii, 3, that "it is more difficult to contend against pleasure than against anger, which would seem to be stronger than fear." Therefore intemperance, which is overcome by pleasure, is a less grievous sin than cowardice, which is overcome by fear.

Obj. 3: Further, it is essential to sin that it be voluntary. Now cowardice is more voluntary than intemperance, since no man desires to be intemperate, whereas some desire to avoid dangers of death, which pertains to cowardice. Therefore cowardice is a more grievous sin than intemperance.

*On the contrary,* The Philosopher says (Ethic. iii, 12) that "intemperance seems more akin to voluntary action than cowardice." Therefore it is more sinful.

*I answer that,* one may be compared with another in two ways. First, with regard to the matter or object; secondly, on the part of the man who sins: and in both ways intemperance is a more grievous sin than cowardice.

First, as regards the matter. For cowardice shuns dangers of death, to avoid which the principal motive is the necessity of preserving life. On the other hand, intemperance is about pleasures, the desire of which is not so necessary for the preservation of life, because, as stated above (A. 2, ad 2), intemperance is more about certain annexed pleasures or desires than about natural desires or pleasures. Now the more necessary the motive of sin the less grievous the sin. Wherefore intemperance is a more grievous vice than cowardice, on the part of the object or motive matter.

In like manner again, on the part of the man who sins, and this for three reasons. First, because the more sound-minded a man is, the more grievous his sin, wherefore sins are not imputed to those who are demented. Now grave fear and sorrow, especially in dangers of death, stun the human mind, but not so pleasure which is the motive of intemperance. Secondly, because the more voluntary a sin the graver it is. Now intemperance has more of the voluntary in it than cowardice has, and this for two reasons. The first is because actions done through fear have their origin in the compulsion of an external agent, so that they are not simply voluntary but mixed, as stated in *Ethic.* iii, 1, whereas actions done for the sake of pleasure are simply voluntary. The second reason is because the actions of an intemperate man are more voluntary individually and less voluntary generically. For no one would wish to be intemperate, yet man is enticed by individual pleasures which make of him an intemperate man. Hence the most effective remedy against intemperance is not to dwell on the consideration of singulars. It is the other way about in matters relating to cowardice: because the particular action that imposes itself on a man is less voluntary, for instance to cast aside his shield, and the like, whereas the general purpose is more voluntary, for instance to save himself by flight. Now that which is more voluntary in the particular circumstances in which the act takes place, is simply more voluntary. Wherefore intemperance, being simply more voluntary than cowardice, is a greater vice. Thirdly, because it is easier to find a remedy for intemperance than for cowardice, since pleasures of food and sex, which are the matter of intemperance, are of everyday occurrence, and it is possible for man without danger by frequent practice in their regard to become temperate; whereas dangers of death are of rare occurrence, and it is more dangerous for man to encounter them frequently in order to cease being a coward.

Reply Obj. 1: The excellence of fortitude in comparison with temperance may be considered from two standpoints. First, with regard to the end, which has the aspect of good: because fortitude is directed to the common good more than temperance is. And from this point of view cowardice has a certain precedence over intemperance, since by cowardice some people forsake the defense of the common good. Secondly, with regard to the difficulty, because it is more difficult to endure dangers of death than to refrain from any pleasures whatever: and from this point of view there is no need for cowardice to take precedence of intemperance. For just as it is a greater strength that does not succumb to a stronger force, so on the other hand to be overcome by a stronger force is proof of a lesser vice, and to succumb to a weaker force, is the proof of a greater vice.

Reply Obj. 2: Love of self-preservation, for the sake of which one shuns perils of death, is much more connatural than any pleasures whatever of food and sex which are directed to the preservation of life. Hence it is more difficult to overcome the fear of dangers of death, than the desire of pleasure in matters of food and sex: although the latter is more difficult to resist than anger, sorrow, and fear, occasioned by certain other evils.

Reply Obj. 3: The voluntary, in cowardice, depends rather on a general than on a particular consideration: wherefore in such cases we have the voluntary not simply but in a restricted sense.

FOURTH ARTICLE [II-II, Q. 142, Art. 4]

Whether Intemperance Is the Most Disgraceful of Sins?

Objection 1: It would seem that intemperance is not the most disgraceful of sins. As honor is due to virtue so is disgrace due to sin. Now some sins are more grievous than intemperance: for instance murder, blasphemy, and the like. Therefore intemperance is not the most disgraceful of sins.

Obj. 2: Further, those sins which are the more common are seemingly less disgraceful, since men are less ashamed of them. Now sins of intemperance are most common, because they are about things connected with the common use of human life, and in which many happen to sin. Therefore sins of intemperance do not seem to be most disgraceful.

Obj. 3: Further, the Philosopher says (Ethic. vii, 6) temperance and intemperance are about human desires and pleasures. Now certain desires and pleasures are more shameful than human desires and pleasures; such are brutal pleasures and those caused by disease as the Philosopher states (Ethic. vii, 5). Therefore intemperance is not the most disgraceful of sins.

*On the contrary,* The Philosopher says (Ethic. iii, 10) that "intemperance is justly more deserving of reproach than other vices."

*I answer that,* Disgrace is seemingly opposed to honor and glory. Now honor is due to excellence, as stated above (Q. 103, A. 1), and glory denotes clarity (Q. 103, A. 1, ad 3). Accordingly intemperance is most disgraceful for two reasons. First, because it is most repugnant to human excellence, since it is about pleasures common to us and the lower animals, as stated above (Q. 141, AA. 2, 3). Wherefore it is written (Ps. 48:21): "Man, when he was in honor, did not understand: he hath been compared to senseless beasts, and made like to them." Secondly, because it is most repugnant to man's clarity or beauty; inasmuch as the pleasures which are the matter of intemperance dim the light of reason from which all the clarity and beauty of virtue arises: wherefore these pleasures are described as being most slavish.

Reply Obj. 1: As Gregory says [*Moral. xxxiii. 12] "the sins of the flesh," which are comprised under the head of intemperance, although less culpable, are more disgraceful. The reason is that culpability is measured by inordinateness in respect of the end, while disgrace regards shamefulness, which depends chiefly on the unbecomingness of the sin in respect of the sinner.

Reply Obj. 2: The commonness of a sin diminishes the shamefulness and disgrace of a sin in the opinion of men, but not as regards the nature of the vices themselves.

Reply Obj. 3: When we say that intemperance is most disgraceful, we mean in comparison with human vices, those, namely, that are connected with human passions which to a certain extent are in conformity with human nature. But those vices which exceed the mode of human nature are still more disgraceful. Nevertheless such vices are apparently reducible to the genus of intemperance, by way of excess: for instance, if a man delight in eating human flesh, or in committing the unnatural vice.

## QUESTION 143

OF THE PARTS OF TEMPERANCE, IN GENERAL

We must now consider the parts of temperance: we shall consider these same parts (1) in general; (2) each of them in particular.

ARTICLE [II-II, Q. 143, Art.]

Whether the Parts of Temperance Are Rightly Assigned?

Objection 1: It would seem that Tully (De Invent. Rhet. ii, 54) unbecomingly assigns the parts of temperance, when he asserts them to be "continence, mildness, and modesty." For continence is reckoned to be distinct from virtue (Ethic. vii, 1): whereas temperance is comprised under virtue. Therefore continence is not a part of temperance.

Obj. 2: Further, mildness seemingly softens hatred or anger. But temperance is not about these things, but about pleasures of touch, as stated above (Q. 141, A. 4). Therefore mildness is not a part of temperance.

Obj. 3: Further, modesty concerns external action, wherefore the Apostle says (Phil. 4:5): "Let your modesty be known to all men." Now external actions are the matter of justice, as stated above (Q. 58, A. 8). Therefore modesty is a part of justice rather than of temperance.

Obj. 4: Further, Macrobius (In Somn. Scip. i, 8) reckons many more parts of temperance: for he says that "temperance results in modesty, shamefacedness, abstinence, chastity, honesty, moderation, lowliness, sobriety, purity." Andronicus also says [*De Affectibus] that "the companions of temperance are gravity, continence, humility, simplicity, refinement, method, contentment." [* *Per-se-sufficientiam* which could be rendered "self-sufficiency," but for the fact that this is taken in a bad sense. See Q. 169, A. 1.] Therefore it seems that Tully insufficiently reckoned the parts of temperance.

*I answer that,* As stated above (QQ. 48, 128), a cardinal virtue may have three kinds of parts, namely integral, subjective, and potential. The integral parts of a virtue are the conditions the concurrence of which are necessary for virtue: and in this respect there are two integral parts of temperance, *shamefacedness,* whereby one recoils from the disgrace that is contrary to temperance, and *honesty,* whereby one loves the beauty of temperance. For, as stated above (Q. 141, A. 2, ad 3), temperance more than any other virtue lays claim to a certain comeliness, and the vices of intemperance excel others in disgrace.

The subjective parts of a virtue are its species: and the species of a virtue have to be differentiated according to the difference of matter or object. Now temperance is about pleasures of touch, which are of two kinds. For some are directed to nourishment: and in these as regards meat, there is *abstinence,* and as regards drink properly there is *sobriety.* Other pleasures are directed to the power of procreation, and in these as regards the principal pleasure of the act itself of procreation, there is *chastity,* and as to the pleasures incidental to the act, resulting, for instance, from kissing, touching, or fondling, we have *purity.*

The potential parts of a principal virtue are called secondary virtues: for while the principal virtue observes the mode in some principal matter, these observe the mode in some other matter wherein moderation is not so difficult. Now it belongs to temperance to moderate pleasures of touch, which are most difficult to moderate. Wherefore any virtue that is effective of moderation in some matter or other, and restrains the appetite in its impulse towards something, may be reckoned a part of temperance, as a virtue annexed thereto.

This happens in three ways: first, in the inward movements of the soul; secondly, in the outward movements and actions of the body; thirdly, in outward things. Now besides the movement of concupiscence, which temperance moderates and restrains, we find in the soul three movements towards a particular object. In the first place there is the movement of the will when stirred by the impulse of passion: and this movement is restrained by *continence,* the effect of which is that, although a man suffer immoderate concupiscences, his will does not succumb to them. Another inward movement towards something is the movement of hope, and of the resultant daring, and this is moderated or restrained by *humility.* The third movement is that of anger, which tends towards revenge, and this is restrained by *meekness* or mildness.

With regard to bodily movements and actions, moderation and restraint is the effect of *modesty,* which, according to Andronicus, has three parts. The first of these enables one to discern what to do and what not to do, and to observe the right order, and to persevere in what we do: this he assigns to *method.* The second is that a man observe decorum in what he does, and this he ascribes to *refinement.* The third has to do with the conversation or any other intercourse between a man and his friends, and this is called *gravity.*

With regard to external things, a twofold moderation has to be observed. First, we must not desire too many, and to this Macrobius assigns *lowliness,* and Andronicus contentment ; secondly, we must not be too nice in our requirements, and to this Macrobius ascribes moderation, Andronicus simplicity.

Reply Obj. 1: It is true that continence differs from virtue, just as imperfect differs from perfect, as we shall state further on (Q. 165, A. 1); and in this sense it is condivided with virtue. Yet it has something in common with temperance both as to matter, since it is about pleasures of touch, and as to mode, since it is a kind of restraint. Hence it is suitably assigned as a part of temperance.

Reply Obj. 2: Mildness or meekness is reckoned a part of temperance not because of a likeness of matter, but because they agree as to the mode of restraint and moderation as stated above.

Reply Obj. 3: In the matter of external action justice considers what is due to another. Modesty does not consider this, but only a certain moderation. Hence it is reckoned a part not of justice but of temperance.

Reply Obj. 4: Under modesty Tully includes whatever pertains to the moderation of bodily movements and external things, as well as the moderation of hope which we reckoned as pertaining to humility.

# QUESTION 144

OF SHAMEFACEDNESS (In Four Articles)

We must now consider the parts of temperance in particular: and in the first place the integral parts, which are shamefacedness and honesty. With regard to shamefacedness there are four points of inquiry:

(1) Whether shamefacedness is a virtue?

(2) What is its object?

(3) Who are the cause of a man being ashamed?

(4) What kind of people are ashamed?

FIRST ARTICLE [II-II, Q. 144, Art. 1]

Whether Shamefacedness Is a Virtue?

Objection 1: It seems that shamefacedness is a virtue. For it is proper to a virtue "to observe the mean as fixed by reason": this is clear from the definition of virtue given in *Ethic.* ii, 6. Now shamefacedness observes the mean in this way, as the Philosopher observes (Ethic. ii, 7). Therefore shamefacedness is a virtue.

Obj. 2: Further, whatever is praiseworthy is either a virtue or something connected with virtue. Now shamefacedness is praiseworthy. But it is not part of a virtue. For it is not a part of prudence, since it is not in the reason but in the appetite; nor is it a part of justice. Since shamefacedness implies a certain passion, whereas justice is not about the passions; nor again is it a part of fortitude, because it belongs to fortitude to be persistent and aggressive, while it belongs to shamefacedness to recoil from something; nor lastly is it a part of temperance, since the latter is about desires, whereas shamefacedness is a kind of fear according as the Philosopher states (Ethic. iv, 9) and Damascene (De Fide Orth. ii, 15). Hence it follows that shamefacedness is a virtue.

Obj. 3: Further, the honest and the virtuous are convertible according to Tully (De Offic. i, 27). Now shamefacedness is a part of honesty: for Ambrose says (De Offic. i, 43) that "shamefacedness is the companion and familiar of the restful mind, averse to wantonness, a stranger to any kind of excess, the friend of sobriety and the support of what is honest, a seeker after the beautiful." Therefore shamefacedness is a virtue.

Obj. 4: Further, every vice is opposed to a virtue. Now certain vices are opposed to shamefacedness, namely shamelessness and inordinate prudery. Therefore shamefacedness is a virtue.

Obj. 5: Further, "like acts beget like habits," according to *Ethic.* ii, 1. Now shamefacedness implies a praiseworthy act; wherefore from many such acts a habit results. But a habit of praiseworthy deeds is a virtue, according to the Philosopher (Ethic. i, 12). Therefore shamefacedness is a virtue.

*On the contrary,* The Philosopher says (Ethic. ii, 7; iv, 9) that shamefacedness is not a virtue.

*I answer that,* Virtue is taken in two ways, in a strict sense and in a broad sense. Taken strictly virtue is a perfection, as stated in *Phys.* vii, 17, 18. Wherefore anything that is inconsistent with perfection, though it be good, falls short of the notion of virtue. Now shamefacedness is inconsistent with perfection, because it is the fear of something base, namely of that which is disgraceful. Hence Damascene says (De Fide Orth. ii, 15) that "shamefacedness is fear of a base action." Now just as hope is about a possible and difficult good, so is fear about a possible and arduous evil, as stated above (I-II, Q. 40, A. 1; Q. 41, A. 2; Q. 42, A. 3), when we were treating of the passions. But one who is perfect as to a virtuous habit, does not apprehend that which would be disgraceful and base to do, as being possible and arduous, that is to say difficult for him to avoid; nor does he actually do anything base, so as to be in fear of disgrace. Therefore shamefacedness, properly speaking, is not a virtue, since it falls short of the perfection of virtue.

Taken, however, in a broad sense virtue denotes whatever is good and praiseworthy in human acts or passions; and in this way shamefacedness is sometimes called a virtue, since it is a praiseworthy passion.

Reply Obj. 1: Observing the mean is not sufficient for the notion of virtue, although it is one of the conditions included in virtue's definition: but it is requisite, in addition to this, that it be "an elective habit," that is to say, operating from choice. Now shamefacedness denotes, not a habit but a passion, nor does its movement result from choice, but from an impulse of passion. Hence it falls short of the notion of virtue.

Reply Obj. 2: As stated above, shamefacedness is fear of baseness and disgrace. Now it has been stated (Q. 142, A. 4) that the vice of intemperance is most base and disgraceful. Wherefore shamefacedness pertains more to temperance than to any other virtue, by reason of its motive cause, which is a base action though not according to the species of the passion, namely fear. Nevertheless in so far as the vices opposed to other virtues are base and disgraceful, shamefacedness may also pertain to other virtues.

Reply Obj. 3: Shamefacedness fosters honesty, by removing that which is contrary thereto, but not so as to attain to the perfection of honesty.

Reply Obj. 4: Every defect causes a vice, but not every good is sufficient for the notion of virtue. Consequently it does not follow that whatever is directly opposed to vice is a virtue, although every vice is opposed to a virtue, as regards its origin. Hence shamelessness, in so far as it results from excessive love of disgraceful things, is opposed to temperance.

Reply Obj. 5: Being frequently ashamed causes the habit of an acquired virtue whereby one avoids disgraceful things which are the object of shamefacedness, without continuing to be ashamed in their regard: although as a consequence of this acquired virtue, a man would be more ashamed, if confronted with the matter of shamefacedness.

SECOND ARTICLE [II-II, Q. 144, Art. 2]

Whether Shamefacedness Is About a Disgraceful Action?

Objection 1: It would seem that shamefacedness is not about a disgraceful action. For the Philosopher says (Ethic. iv, 9) that "shamefacedness is fear of disgrace." Now sometimes those who do nothing wrong suffer ignominy, according to Ps. 67:8, "For thy sake I have borne reproach, shame hath covered my face." Therefore shamefacedness is not properly about a disgraceful action.

Obj. 2: Further, nothing apparently is disgraceful but what is sinful. Yet man is ashamed of things that are not sins, for instance when he performs a menial occupation. Therefore it seems that shamefacedness is not properly about a disgraceful action.

Obj. 3: Further, virtuous deeds are not disgraceful but most beautiful according to *Ethic.* i, 8. Yet sometimes people are ashamed to do virtuous deeds, according to Luke 9:26, "He that shall be ashamed of Me and My words, of him the Son of man shall be ashamed," etc. Therefore shamefacedness is not about a disgraceful action.

Obj. 4: Further, if shamefacedness were properly about a disgraceful action, it would follow that the more disgraceful the action the more ashamed would one be. Yet sometimes a man is more ashamed of lesser sins, while he glories in those which are most grievous, according to Ps. 51:3, "Why dost thou glory in malice?" Therefore shamefacedness is not properly about a disgraceful action.

*On the contrary,* Damascene (De Fide Orth. ii, 15) and Gregory of Nyssa [*Nemesius, (De Nat. Hom. xx)] say that "shamefacedness is fear of doing a disgraceful deed or of a disgraceful deed done."

*I answer that,* As stated above (I-II, Q. 41, A. 2; Q. 42, A. 3), when we were treating of the passions, fear is properly about an arduous evil, one, namely, that is difficult to avoid. Now disgrace is twofold. There is the disgrace inherent to vice, which consists in the deformity of a voluntary act: and this, properly speaking, has not the character of an arduous evil. For that which depends on the will alone does not appear to be arduous and above man's ability: wherefore it is not apprehended as fearful, and for this reason the Philosopher says (Rhet. ii, 5) that such evils are not a matter of fear.

The other kind of disgrace is penal so to speak, and it consists in the reproach that attaches to a person, just as the clarity of glory consists in a person being honored. And since this reproach has the character of an arduous evil, just as honor has the character of an arduous good, shamefacedness, which is fear of disgrace, regards first and foremost reproach or ignominy. And since reproach is properly due to vice, as honor is due to virtue, it follows that shamefacedness regards also the disgrace inherent to vice. Hence the Philosopher says (Rhet. ii, 5) that "a man is less ashamed of those defects which are not the result of any fault of his own."

Now shamefacedness regards fault in two ways. In one way a man refrains from vicious acts through fear of reproach: in another way a man while doing a disgraceful deed avoids the public eye through fear of reproach. In the former case, according to Gregory of Nyssa (Nemesius, De Nat. Hom. xx), we speak of a person "blushing," in the latter we say that he is "ashamed." Hence he says that "the man who is ashamed acts in secret, but he who blushes fears to be disgraced."

Reply Obj. 1: Shamefacedness properly regards disgrace as due to sin which is a voluntary defect. Hence the Philosopher says (Rhet. ii, 6) that "a man is more ashamed of those things of which he is the cause." Now the virtuous man despises the disgrace to which he is subject on account of virtue, because he does not deserve it; as the Philosopher says of the magnanimous (Ethic. iv, 3). Thus we find it said of the apostles (Acts 5:41) that "they (the apostles) went from the presence of the council, rejoicing that they were accounted worthy to suffer reproach for the name of Jesus." It is owing to imperfection of virtue that a man is sometimes ashamed of the reproaches which he suffers on account of virtue, since the more virtuous a man is, the more he despises external things, whether good or evil. Wherefore it is written (Isa. 51:7): "Fear ye not the reproach of men."

Reply Obj. 2: As stated above (Q. 63, A. 3), though honor is not really due save to virtue alone, yet it regards a certain excellence: and the same applies to reproach, for though it is properly due to sin alone, yet, at least in man's opinion, it regards any kind of defect. Hence a man is ashamed of poverty, disrepute, servitude, and the like.

Reply Obj. 3: Shamefacedness does not regard virtuous deeds as such. Yet it happens accidentally that a man is ashamed of them either because he looks upon them as vicious according to human opinion, or because he is afraid of being marked as presumptuous or hypocritical for doing virtuous deeds.

Reply Obj. 4: Sometimes more grievous sins are less shameful, either because they are less disgraceful, as spiritual sins in comparison with sins of the flesh, or because they connote a certain abundance of some temporal good; thus a man is more ashamed of cowardice than of daring, of theft than of robbery, on account of a semblance of power. The same applies to other sins.

THIRD ARTICLE [II-II, Q. 144, Art. 3]

Whether Man Is More Shamefaced of Those Who Are More Closely Connected with Him?

Objection 1: It would seem that man is not more shamefaced of those who are more closely connected with him. For it is stated in *Rhet.* ii, 6 that "men are more shamefaced of those from whom they desire approbation." Now men desire this especially from people of the better sort who are sometimes not connected with them. Therefore man is not more shamefaced of those who are more closely connected with him.

Obj. 2: Further, seemingly those are more closely connected who perform like deeds. Now man is not made ashamed of his sin by those whom he knows to be guilty of the same sin, because according to *Rhet.* ii, 6, "a man does not forbid his neighbor what he does himself." Therefore he is not more shamefaced of those who are most closely connected with him.

Obj. 3: Further, the Philosopher says (Rhet. ii, 6) that "men take more shame from those who retail their information to many, such as jokers and fable-tellers." But those who are more closely connected with a man do not retail his vices. Therefore one should not take shame chiefly from them.

Obj. 4: Further, the Philosopher says (Rhet. ii, 6) that "men are most liable to be made ashamed by those among whom they have done nothing amiss; by those of whom they ask something for the first time; by those whose friends they wish to become." Now these are less closely connected with us. Therefore man is not made most ashamed by those who are more closely united to him.

*On the contrary,* It is stated in Rhet. ii, 6 that "man is made most ashamed by those who are to be continually with him."

*I answer that,* Since reproach is opposed to honor, just as honor denotes attestation to someone's excellence, especially the excellence which is according to virtue, so too reproach, the fear of which is shamefacedness, denotes attestation to a person's defect, especially that which results from sin. Hence the more weighty a person's attestation is considered to be, the more does he make another person ashamed. Now a person's attestation may be considered as being more weighty, either because he is certain of the truth or because of its effect. Certitude of the truth attaches to a person's attestations for two reasons. First on account of the rectitude of his judgement, as in the case of wise and virtuous men, by whom man is more desirous of being honored and by whom he is brought to a greater sense of shame. Hence children and the lower animals inspire no one with shame, by reason of their lack of judgment. Secondly, on account of his knowledge of the matter attested, because "everyone judges well of what is known to him" [*Ethic. i, 3]. In this way we are more liable to be made ashamed by persons connected with us, since they are better acquainted with our deeds: whereas strangers and persons entirely unknown to us, who are ignorant of what we do, inspire us with no shame at all.

An attestation receives weight from its effect by reason of some advantage or harm resulting therefrom; wherefore men are more desirous of being honored by those who can be of use to them, and are more liable to be made ashamed by those who are able to do them some harm. And for this reason again, in a certain respect, persons connected with us make us more ashamed, since we are to be continually in their society, as though this entailed a continual harm to us: whereas the harm that comes from strangers and passersby ceases almost at once.

Reply Obj. 1: People of the better sort make us ashamed for the same reason as those who are more closely connected with us; because just as the attestation of the better men carries more weight since they have a more universal knowledge of things, and in their judgments hold fast to the truth: so, too, the attestation of those among whom we live is more cogent since they know more about our concerns in detail.

Reply Obj. 2: We fear not the attestation of those who are connected with us in the likeness of sin, because we do not think that they look upon our defect as disgraceful.

Reply Obj. 3: Tale-bearers make us ashamed on account of the harm they do by making many think ill of us.

Reply Obj. 4: Even those among whom we have done no wrong, make us more ashamed, on account of the harm that would follow, because, to wit, we should forfeit the good opinion they had of us: and again because when contraries are put in juxtaposition their opposition seems greater, so that when a man notices something disgraceful in one whom he esteemed good, he apprehends it as being the more disgraceful. The reason why we are made more ashamed by those of whom we ask something for the first time, or whose friends we wish to be, is that we fear to suffer some injury, by being disappointed in our request, or by failing to become their friends.

FOURTH ARTICLE [II-II, Q. 144, Art. 4]

Whether Even Virtuous Men Can Be Ashamed?

Objection 1: It would seem that even virtuous men can be ashamed. For contraries have contrary effects. Now those who excel in wickedness are not ashamed, according to Jer. 3:3, "Thou hadst a harlot's forehead, thou wouldst not blush." Therefore those who are virtuous are more inclined to be ashamed.

Obj. 2: Further, the Philosopher says (Rhet. ii, 6) that "men are ashamed not only of vice, but also of the signs of evil": and this happens also in the virtuous. Therefore virtuous men can be ashamed.

Obj. 3: Further, shamefacedness is "fear of disgrace" [*Ethic. iv, 9]. Now virtuous people may happen to be ignominious, for instance if they are slandered, or if they suffer reproach undeservedly. Therefore a virtuous man can be ashamed.

Obj. 4: Further, shamefacedness is a part of temperance, as stated above (Q. 143). Now a part is not separated from its whole. Since then temperance is in a virtuous man, it means that shamefacedness is also.

*On the contrary,* The Philosopher says (Ethic. iv, 9) that a "virtuous man is not shamefaced."

*I answer that,* As stated above (AA. 1, 2) shamefacedness is fear of some disgrace. Now it may happen in two ways that an evil is not feared: first, because it is not reckoned an evil; secondly because one reckons it impossible with regard to oneself, or as not difficult to avoid.

Accordingly shame may be lacking in a person in two ways. First, because the things that should make him ashamed are not deemed by him to be disgraceful; and in this way those who are steeped in sin are without shame, for instead of disapproving of their sins, they boast of them. Secondly, because they apprehend disgrace as impossible to themselves, or as easy to avoid. In this way the old and the virtuous are not shamefaced. Yet they are so disposed, that if there were anything disgraceful in them they would be ashamed of it. Wherefore the Philosopher says (Ethic. iv, 9) that "shame is in the virtuous hypothetically."

Reply Obj. 1: Lack of shame occurs in the best and in the worst men through different causes, as stated in the Article. In the average men it is found, in so far as they have a certain love of good, and yet are not altogether free from evil.

Reply Obj. 2: It belongs to the virtuous man to avoid not only vice, but also whatever has the semblance of vice, according to 1 Thess. 5:22, "From all appearance of evil refrain yourselves." The Philosopher, too, says (Ethic. iv, 9) that the virtuous man should avoid "not only what is really evil, but also those things that are regarded as evil."

Reply Obj. 3: As stated above (A. 1, ad 1) the virtuous man despises ignominy and reproach, as being things he does not deserve, wherefore he is not much ashamed of them. Nevertheless, to a certain extent, shame, like the other passions, may forestall reason.

Reply Obj. 4: Shamefacedness is a part of temperance, not as though it entered into its essence, but as a disposition to it: wherefore Ambrose says (De Offic. i, 43) that "shamefacedness lays the first foundation of temperance," by inspiring man with the horror of whatever is disgraceful.

## QUESTION 145

OF HONESTY* (In Four Articles) [*Honesty must be taken here in its broad sense as synonymous with moral goodness, from the point of view of decorum.]

We must now consider honesty, under which head there are four points of inquiry:

(1) The relation between the honest and the virtuous;

(2) Its relation with the beautiful [*As honesty here denotes moral goodness, so beauty stands for moral beauty];

(3) Its relation with the useful and the pleasant;

(4) Whether honesty is a part of temperance?

FIRST ARTICLE [II-II, Q. 145, Art. 1]

Whether Honesty Is the Same As Virtue?

Objection 1: It would seem that honesty is not the same as virtue. For Tully says (De Invent. Rhet. ii, 53) that "the honest is what is desired for its own sake." Now virtue is desired, not for its own sake, but for the sake of happiness, for the Philosopher says (Ethic. i, 9) that "happiness is the reward and the end of virtue." Therefore honesty is not the same as virtue.

Obj. 2: Further, according to Isidore (Etym. x) "honesty means an honorable state." Now honor is due to many things besides virtue, since "it is praise that is the proper due of virtue" (Ethic. i, 12). Therefore honesty is not the same as virtue.

Obj. 3: Further, the "principal part of virtue is the interior choice," as the Philosopher says (Ethic. viii, 13). But honesty seems to pertain rather to exterior conduct, according to 1 Cor. 14:40, "Let all things be done decently ( *honeste* ) and according to order" among you. Therefore honesty is not the same as virtue.

Obj. 4: Further, honesty apparently consists in external wealth. According to Ecclus. 11:14, "good things and evil, life and death [poverty and riches] are from God" [*The words in brackets are omitted in the Leonine edition. For riches the Vulgate has *honestas* ]. But virtue does not consist in external wealth. Therefore honesty is not the same as virtue.

*On the contrary,* Tully (De Offic. i, 5; Rhet. ii, 53) divides honesty into the four principal virtues, into which virtue is also divided. Therefore honesty is the same as virtue.

*I answer that,* As Isidore says (Etym. x) "honesty means an honorable state," wherefore a thing may be said to be honest through being worthy of honor. Now honor, as stated above (Q. 144, A. 2, ad 2), is due to excellence: and the excellence of a man is gauged chiefly according to his virtue, as stated in *Phys.* vii, 17. Therefore, properly speaking, honesty refers to the same thing as virtue.

Reply Obj. 1: According to the Philosopher (Ethic. i, 7), of those things that are desired for their own sake, some are desired for their own sake alone, and never for the sake of something else, such as happiness which is the last end; while some are desired, not only for their own sake, inasmuch as they have an aspect of goodness in themselves, even if no further good accrued to us through them, but also for the sake of something else, inasmuch as they are conducive to some more perfect good. It is thus that the virtues are desirable for their own sake: wherefore Tully says (De Invent. Rhet. ii, 52) that "some things allure us by their own force, and attract us by their own worth, such as virtue, truth, knowledge." And this suffices to give a thing the character of honest.

Reply Obj. 2: Some of the things which are honored besides virtue are more excellent than virtue, namely God and happiness, and such like things are not so well known to us by experience as virtue which we practice day by day. Hence virtue has a greater claim to the name of honesty. Other things which are beneath virtue are honored, in so far as they are a help to the practice of virtue, such as rank, power, and riches [*Ethic. i, 8]. For as the Philosopher says (Ethic. iv, 3) that these things "are honored by some people, but in truth it is only the good man who is worthy of honor." Now a man is good in respect of virtue. Wherefore praise is due to virtue in so far as the latter is desirable for the sake of something else, while honor is due to virtue for its own sake: and it is thus that virtue has the character of honesty.

Reply Obj. 3: As we have stated honest denotes that to which honor is due. Now honor is an attestation to someone's excellence, as stated above (Q. 103, AA. 1, 2). But one attests only to what one knows; and the internal choice is not made known save by external actions. Wherefore external conduct has the character of honesty, in so far as it reflects internal rectitude. For this reason honesty consists radically in the internal choice, but its expression lies in the external conduct.

Reply Obj. 4: It is because the excellence of wealth is commonly regarded as making a man deserving of honor, that sometimes the name of honesty is given to external prosperity.

SECOND ARTICLE [II-II, Q. 145, Art. 2]

Whether the Honest Is the Same As the Beautiful?

Objection 1: It would seem that the honest is not the same as the beautiful. For the aspect of honest is derived from the appetite, since the honest is "what is desirable for its own sake" [*Cicero, De Invent. Rhet. ii, 53]. But the beautiful regards rather the faculty of vision to which it is pleasing. Therefore the beautiful is not the same as the honest.

Obj. 2: Further, beauty requires a certain clarity, which is characteristic of glory: whereas the honest regards honor. Since then honor and glory differ, as stated above (Q. 103, A. 1, ad 3), it seems also that the honest and the beautiful differ.

Obj. 3: Further, honesty is the same as virtue, as stated above (A. 1). But a certain beauty is contrary to virtue, wherefore it is written (Ezech. 16:15): "Trusting in thy beauty thou playest the harlot because of thy renown." Therefore the honest is not the same as the beautiful.

*On the contrary,* The Apostle says (1 Cor. 12:23, 24): "Those that are our uncomely ( inhonesta ) parts, have more abundant comeliness ( honestatem ), but our comely ( honesta ) parts have no need." Now by uncomely parts he means the baser members, and by comely parts the beautiful members. Therefore the honest and the beautiful are apparently the same.

*I answer that,* As may be gathered from the words of Dionysius (Div. Nom. iv), beauty or comeliness results from the concurrence of clarity and due proportion. For he states that God is said to be beautiful, as being "the cause of the harmony and clarity of the universe." Hence the beauty of the body consists in a man having his bodily limbs well proportioned, together with a certain clarity of color. In like manner spiritual beauty consists in a man's conduct or actions being well proportioned in respect of the spiritual clarity of reason. Now this is what is meant by honesty, which we have stated (A. 1) to be the same as virtue; and it is virtue that moderates according to reason all that is connected with man. Wherefore "honesty is the same as spiritual beauty." Hence Augustine says (QQ. 83, qu. 30): "By honesty I mean intelligible beauty, which we properly designate as spiritual," and further on he adds that "many things are beautiful to the eye, which it would be hardly proper to call honest."

Reply Obj. 1: The object that moves the appetite is an apprehended good. Now if a thing is perceived to be beautiful as soon as it is apprehended, it is taken to be something becoming and good. Hence Dionysius says (Div. Nom. iv) that "the beautiful and the good are beloved by all." Wherefore the honest, inasmuch as it implies spiritual beauty, is an object of desire, and for this reason Tully says (De Offic. i, 5): "Thou perceivest the form and the features, so to speak, of honesty; and were it to be seen with the eye, would, as Plato declares, arouse a wondrous love of wisdom."

Reply Obj. 2: As stated above (Q. 103, A. 1, ad 3), glory is the effect of honor: because through being honored or praised, a person acquires clarity in the eyes of others. Wherefore, just as the same thing makes a man honorable and glorious, so is the same thing honest and beautiful.

Reply Obj. 3: This argument applies to the beauty of the body: although it might be replied that to be proud of one's honesty is to play the harlot because of one's spiritual beauty, according to Ezech. 28:17, "Thy heart was lifted up with thy beauty, thou hast lost thy wisdom in thy beauty."

THIRD ARTICLE [II-II, Q. 145, Art. 3]

Whether the Honest Differs from the Useful and the Pleasant?

Objection 1: It would seem that the honest does not differ from the useful and the pleasant. For the honest is "what is desirable for its own sake" [*Cicero, De Invent. Rhet. ii, 53]. Now pleasure is desired for its own sake, for "it seems ridiculous to ask a man why he wishes to be pleased," as the Philosopher remarks (Ethic. x, 2). Therefore the honest does not differ from the pleasant.

Obj. 2: Further, riches are comprised under the head of useful good: for Tully says (De Invent. Rhet. ii, 52): "There is a thing that attracts the desire not by any force of its own, nor by its very nature, but on account of its fruitfulness and utility": and "that is money." Now riches come under the head of honesty, for it is written (Ecclus. 11:14): "Poverty and riches ( honestas ) are from God," and (Ecclus. 13:2): "He shall take a burden upon him that hath fellowship with one more honorable," i.e. richer, "than himself." Therefore the honest differs not from the useful.

Obj. 3: Further, Tully proves (De Offic. ii, 3) that nothing can be useful unless it be honest: and Ambrose makes the same statement (De Offic. ii, 6). Therefore the useful differs not from the honest.

*On the contrary,* Augustine says (Q. 83, qu. 30): "The honest is that which is desirable for its own sake: the useful implies reference to something else."

*I answer that,* The honest concurs in the same subject with the useful and the pleasant, but it differs from them in aspect. For, as stated above (A. 2), a thing is said to be honest, in so far as it has a certain beauty through being regulated by reason. Now whatever is regulated in accordance with reason is naturally becoming to man. Again, it is natural for a thing to take pleasure in that which is becoming to it. Wherefore an honest thing is naturally pleasing to man: and the Philosopher proves this with regard to acts of virtue (Ethic. i, 8). Yet not all that is pleasing is honest, since a thing may be becoming according to the senses, but not according to reason. A pleasing thing of this kind is beside man's reason which perfects his nature. Even virtue itself, which is essentially honest, is referred to something else as its end namely happiness. Accordingly the honest the useful, and the pleasant concur in the one subject.

Nevertheless they differ in aspect. For a thing is said to be honest as having a certain excellence deserving of honor on account of its spiritual beauty: while it is said to be pleasing, as bringing rest to desire, and useful, as referred to something else. The pleasant, however, extends to more things than the useful and the honest: since whatever is useful and honest is pleasing in some respect, whereas the converse does not hold (Ethic. ii, 3).

Reply Obj. 1: A thing is said to be honest, if it is desired for its own sake by the rational appetite, which tends to that which is in accordance with reason: while a thing is said to be pleasant if it is desired for its own sake by the sensitive appetite.

Reply Obj. 2: Riches are denominated honesty according of the opinion of the many who honor wealth: or because they are intended to be the instruments of virtuous deeds, as stated above (A. 1, ad 2).

Reply Obj. 3: Tully and Ambrose mean to say that nothing incompatible with honesty can be simply and truly useful, since it follows that it is contrary to man's last end, which is a good in accordance with reason; although it may perhaps be useful in some respect, with regard to a particular end. But they do not mean to say that every useful thing as such may be classed among those that are honest.

FOURTH ARTICLE [II-II, Q. 145, Art. 4]

Whether Honesty Should Be Reckoned a Part of Temperance?

Objection 1: It would seem that honesty should not be reckoned a part of temperance. For it is not possible for a thing to be part and whole in respect of one same thing. Now "temperance is a part of honesty," according to Tully (De Invent. Rhet. ii, 53). Therefore honesty is not a part of temperance.

Obj. 2: Further, it is stated (3 Esdra 3:21) that "wine ... makes all thoughts honest." But the use of wine, especially in excess, in which sense the passage quoted should seemingly be taken, pertains to intemperance rather than to temperance. Therefore honesty is not a part of temperance.

Obj. 3: Further, the honest is that which is deserving of honor. Now "it is the just and the brave who receive most honor," according to the Philosopher (Rhet. i, 9). Therefore honesty pertains, not to temperance, but rather to justice and fortitude: wherefore Eleazar said as related in 2 Macc. 6:28: "I suffer an honorable ( *honesta* ) death, for the most venerable and most holy laws."

*On the contrary,* Macrobius [*In Somn. Scip. i] reckons honesty a part of temperance, and Ambrose (De Offic. i, 43) ascribes honesty as pertaining especially to temperance.

*I answer that,* As stated above (A. 2), honesty is a kind of spiritual beauty. Now the disgraceful is opposed to the beautiful: and opposites are most manifest of one another. Wherefore seemingly honesty belongs especially to temperance, since the latter repels that which is most disgraceful and unbecoming to man, namely animal lusts. Hence by its very name temperance is most significative of the good of reason to which it belongs to moderate and temper evil desires. Accordingly honesty, as being ascribed for a special reason to temperance, is reckoned as a part thereof, not as a subjective part, nor as an annexed virtue, but as an integral part or condition attaching thereto.

Reply Obj. 1: Temperance is accounted a subjective part of honesty taken in a wide sense: it is not thus that the latter is reckoned a part of temperance.

Reply Obj. 2: When a man is intoxicated, "the wine makes his thoughts honest" according to his own reckoning because he deems himself great and deserving of honor [*Cf. Q. 148, A. 6].

Reply Obj. 3: Greater honor is due to justice and fortitude than to temperance, because they excel in the point of a greater good: yet greater honor is due to temperance, because the vices which it holds in check are the most deserving of reproach, as stated above. Thus honesty is more to be ascribed to temperance according to the rule given by the Apostle (1 Cor. 12:23) when he says that "our uncomely parts have more abundant comeliness," which, namely, destroys whatever is uncomely.

# QUESTION 146

OF ABSTINENCE (In Two Articles)

We must now consider the subjective parts of temperance: first, those which are about pleasures of food; secondly, those which are about pleasures of sex. The first consideration will include abstinence, which is about meat and drink, and sobriety, which is specifically about drink.

With regard to abstinence three points have to be considered: (1) Abstinence itself; (2) its act which is fasting; (3) its opposite vice which is gluttony. Under the first head there are two points of inquiry:

(1) Whether abstinence is a virtue?

(2) Whether it is a special virtue?

FIRST ARTICLE [II-II, Q. 146, Art. 1]

Whether Abstinence Is a Virtue?

Objection 1: It seems that abstinence is not a virtue. For the Apostle says (1 Cor. 4:20): "The kingdom of God is not in speech but in power ( *virtute* )." Now the kingdom of God does not consist in abstinence, for the Apostle says (Rom. 14:17): "The kingdom of God is not meat and drink," where a gloss [*Cf. St. Augustine, QQ. Evang. ii, qu. 11] observes that "justice consists neither in abstaining nor in eating." Therefore abstinence is not a virtue.

Obj. 2: Further, Augustine says (Confess. x, 11) addressing himself to God: "This hast Thou taught me, that I should set myself to take food as physic." Now it belongs not to virtue, but to the medical art to regulate medicine. Therefore, in like manner, to regulate one's food, which belongs to abstinence, is an act not of virtue but of art.

Obj. 3: Further, every virtue "observes the mean," as stated in *Ethic.* ii, 6, 7. But abstinence seemingly inclines not to the mean but to deficiency, since it denotes retrenchment. Therefore abstinence is not a virtue.

Obj. 4: Further, no virtue excludes another virtue. But abstinence excludes patience: for Gregory says (Pastor. iii, 19) that "impatience not unfrequently dislodges the abstainer's mind from its peaceful seclusion." Likewise he says (Pastor. iii, 19) that "sometimes the sin of pride pierces the thoughts of the abstainer," so that abstinence excludes humility. Therefore abstinence is not a virtue.

*On the contrary,* It is written (2 Pet. 1:5, 6): "Join with your faith virtue, and with virtue knowledge, and with knowledge abstinence"; where abstinence is numbered among other virtues. Therefore abstinence is a virtue.

*I answer that,* Abstinence by its very name denotes retrenchment of food. Hence the term abstinence may be taken in two ways. First, as denoting retrenchment of food absolutely, and in this way it signifies neither a virtue nor a virtuous act, but something indifferent. Secondly, it may be taken as regulated by reason, and then it signifies either a virtuous habit or a virtuous act. This is the meaning of Peter's words quoted above, where he says that we ought "to join abstinence with knowledge," namely that in abstaining from food a man should act with due regard for those among whom he lives, for his own person, and for the requirements of health.

Reply Obj. 1: The use of and abstinence from food, considered in themselves, do not pertain to the kingdom of God, since the Apostle says (1 Cor. 8:8): "Meat doth not commend us to God. For neither, if we eat not [*Vulg.: 'Neither if we eat ... nor if we eat not'], shall we have the less, nor if we eat, shall we have the more," i.e. spiritually. Nevertheless they both belong to the kingdom of God, in so far as they are done reasonably through faith and love of God.

Reply Obj. 2: The regulation of food, in the point of quantity and quality, belongs to the art of medicine as regards the health of the body: but in the point of internal affections with regard to the good of reason, it belongs to abstinence. Hence Augustine says (QQ. Evang. ii, qu. 11): "It makes no difference whatever to virtue what or how much food a man takes, so long as he does it with due regard for the people among whom he lives, for his own person, and for the requirements of his health: but it matters how readily and uncomplainingly he does without food when bound by duty or necessity to abstain."

Reply Obj. 3: It belongs to temperance to bridle the pleasures which are too alluring to the soul, just as it belongs to fortitude to strengthen the soul against fears that deter it from the good of reason. Wherefore, just as fortitude is commended on account of a certain excess, from which all the parts of fortitude take their name, so temperance is commended for a kind of deficiency, from which all its parts are denominated. Hence abstinence, since it is a part of temperance, is named from deficiency, and yet it observes the mean, in so far as it is in accord with right reason.

Reply Obj. 4: Those vices result from abstinence in so far as it is not in accord with right reason. For right reason makes one abstain as one ought, i.e. with gladness of heart, and for the due end, i.e. for God's glory and not one's own.

SECOND ARTICLE [II-II, Q. 146, Art. 1]

Whether Abstinence Is a Special Virtue?

Objection 1: It would seem that abstinence is not a special virtue. For every virtue is praiseworthy by itself. But abstinence is not praiseworthy by itself; for Gregory says (Pastor. iii, 19) that "the virtue of abstinence is praised only on account of the other virtues." Therefore abstinence is not a special virtue.

Obj. 2: Further, Augustine [*Fulgentius] says (De Fide ad Pet. xlii) that "the saints abstain from meat and drink, not that any creature of God is evil, but merely in order to chastise the body." Now this belongs to chastity, as its very name denotes. Therefore abstinence is not a special virtue distinct from chastity.

Obj. 3: Further, as man should be content with moderate meat, so should he be satisfied with moderate clothes, according to 1 Tim. 6:8, "Having food, and wherewith to be covered, with these we should be [Vulg.: 'are'] content." Now there is no special virtue in being content with moderate clothes. Neither, therefore, is there in abstinence which moderates food.

*On the contrary,* Macrobius [*In Somn. Scip. i, 8] reckons abstinence as a special part of temperance.

*I answer that,* As stated above (Q. 136, A. 1; Q. 141, A. 3) moral virtue maintains the good of reason against the onslaught of the passions: hence whenever we find a special motive why a passion departs from the good of reason, there is need of a special virtue. Now pleasures of the table are of a nature to withdraw man from the good of reason, both because they are so great, and because food is necessary to man who needs it for the maintenance of life, which he desires above all other things. Therefore abstinence is a special virtue.

Reply Obj. 1: Virtues are of necessity connected together, as stated above (I-II, Q. 65, A. 1). Wherefore one virtue receives help and commendation from another, as justice from fortitude. Accordingly in this way the virtue of abstinence receives commendation on account of the other virtues.

Reply Obj. 2: The body is chastised by means of abstinence, not only against the allurements of lust, but also against those of gluttony: since by abstaining a man gains strength for overcoming the onslaughts of gluttony, which increase in force the more he yields to them. Yet abstinence is not prevented from being a special virtue through being a help to chastity, since one virtue helps another.

Reply Obj. 3: The use of clothing was devised by art, whereas the use of food is from nature. Hence it is more necessary to have a special virtue for the moderation of food than for the moderation of clothing.

# QUESTION 147

OF FASTING (In Eight Articles)

We must now consider fasting: under which head there are eight points of inquiry:

(1) Whether fasting is an act of virtue?

(2) Of what virtue is it the act?

(3) Whether it is a matter of precept?

(4) Whether anyone is excused from fulfilling this precept?

(5) The time of fasting;

(6) Whether it is requisite for fasting to eat but once?

(7) The hour of eating for those who fast;

(8) The meats from which it is necessary to abstain.

FIRST ARTICLE [II-II, Q. 147, Art. 1]

Whether Fasting Is an Act of Virtue?

Objection 1: It would seem that fasting is not an act of virtue. For every act of virtue is acceptable to God. But fasting is not always acceptable to God, according to Isa. 58:3, "Why have we fasted and Thou hast not regarded?" Therefore fasting is not an act of virtue.

Obj. 2: Further, no act of virtue forsakes the mean of virtue. Now fasting forsakes the mean of virtue, which in the virtue of abstinence takes account of the necessity of supplying the needs of nature, whereas by fasting something is retrenched therefrom: else those who do not fast would not have the virtue of abstinence. Therefore fasting is not an act of virtue.

Obj. 3: Further, that which is competent to all, both good and evil, is not an act of virtue. Now such is fasting, since every one is fasting before eating. Therefore fasting is not an act of virtue.

*On the contrary,* It is reckoned together with other virtuous acts (2 Cor. 6:5, 6) where the Apostle says: "In fasting, in knowledge, in chastity, etc. [Vulg.: 'in chastity, in knowledge']."

*I answer that,* An act is virtuous through being directed by reason to some virtuous ( *honestum* ) [*Cf. Q. 145, A. 1] good. Now this is consistent with fasting, because fasting is practiced for a threefold purpose. First, in order to bridle the lusts of the flesh, wherefore the Apostle says (2 Cor. 6:5, 6): "In fasting, in chastity," since fasting is the guardian of chastity. For, according to Jerome [*Contra Jov. ii.] "Venus is cold when Ceres and Bacchus are not there," that is to say, lust is cooled by abstinence in meat and drink. Secondly, we have recourse to fasting in order that the mind may arise more freely to the contemplation of heavenly things: hence it is related (Dan. 10) of Daniel that he received a revelation from God after fasting for three weeks. Thirdly, in order to satisfy for sins: wherefore it is written (Joel 2:12): "Be converted to Me with all your heart, in fasting and in weeping and in mourning." The same is declared by Augustine in a sermon (De orat. et Jejun. [*Serm. lxxii] (ccxxx, de Tempore)): "Fasting cleanses the soul, raises the mind, subjects one's flesh to the spirit, renders the heart contrite and humble, scatters the clouds of concupiscence, quenches the fire of lust, kindles the true light of chastity."

Reply Obj. 1: An act that is virtuous generically may be rendered vicious by its connection with certain circumstances. Hence the text goes on to say: "Behold in the day of your fast your own will is founded," and a little further on (Isa. 58:4): "You fast for debates and strife and strike with the fist wickedly." These words are expounded by Gregory (Pastor. iii, 19) as follows: "The will indicates joy and the fist anger. In vain then is the flesh restrained if the mind allowed to drift to inordinate movements be wrecked by vice." And Augustine says (in the same sermon) that "fasting loves not many words, deems wealth superfluous, scorns pride, commends humility, helps man to perceive what is frail and paltry."

Reply Obj. 2: The mean of virtue is measured not according to quantity but according to right reason, as stated in *Ethic.* ii, 6. Now reason judges it expedient, on account of some special motive, for a man to take less food than would be becoming to him under ordinary circumstances, for instance in order to avoid sickness, or in order to perform certain bodily works with greater ease: and much more does reason direct this to the avoidance of spiritual evils and the pursuit of spiritual goods. Yet reason does not retrench so much from one's food as to refuse nature its necessary support: thus Jerome says:* "It matters not whether thou art a long or a short time in destroying thyself, since to afflict the body immoderately, whether by excessive lack of nourishment, or by eating or sleeping too little, is to offer a sacrifice of stolen goods." [*The quotation is from the Corpus of Canon Law (Cap. Non mediocriter, De Consecrationibus, dist. 5). Gratian there ascribes the quotation to St. Jerome, but it is not to be found in the saint's works.] In like manner right reason does not retrench so much from a man's food as to render him incapable of fulfilling his duty. Hence Jerome says (in the same reference) "Rational man forfeits his dignity, if he sets fasting before chastity, or night-watchings before the well-being of his senses."

Reply Obj. 3: The fasting of nature, in respect of which a man is said to be fasting until he partakes of food, consists in a pure negation, wherefore it cannot be reckoned a virtuous act. Such is only the fasting of one who abstains in some measure from food for a reasonable purpose. Hence the former is called natural fasting ( *jejunium jejunii* ) [*Literally the 'fast of fasting']: while the latter is called the faster's fast, because he fasts for a purpose.

SECOND ARTICLE [II-II, Q. 147, Art. 2]

Whether Fasting Is an Act of Abstinence?

Objection 1: It would seem that fasting is not an act of abstinence. For Jerome [*The quotation is from the Ordinary Gloss, where the reference is lacking] commenting on Matt. 17:20, "This kind of devil" says: "To fast is to abstain not only from food but also from all manner of lusts." Now this belongs to every virtue. Therefore fasting is not exclusively an act of abstinence.

Obj. 2: Further, Gregory says in a Lenten Homily (xvi in Evang.) that "the Lenten fast is a tithe of the whole year." Now paying tithes is an act of religion, as stated above (Q. 87, A. 1). Therefore fasting is an act of religion and not of abstinence.

Obj. 3: Further, abstinence is a part of temperance, as stated above (QQ. 143, 146, A. 1, ad 3). Now temperance is condivided with fortitude, to which it belongs to endure hardships, and this seems very applicable to fasting. Therefore fasting is not an act of abstinence.

*On the contrary,* Isidore says (Etym. vi, 19) that "fasting is frugality of fare and abstinence from food."

*I answer that,* Habit and act have the same matter. Wherefore every virtuous act about some particular matter belongs to the virtue that appoints the mean in that matter. Now fasting is concerned with food, wherein the mean is appointed by abstinence. Wherefore it is evident that fasting is an act of abstinence.

Reply Obj. 1: Properly speaking fasting consists in abstaining from food, but speaking metaphorically it denotes abstinence from anything harmful, and such especially is sin.

We may also reply that even properly speaking fasting is abstinence from all manner of lust, since, as stated above (A. 1, ad 1), an act ceases to be virtuous by the conjunction of any vice.

Reply Obj. 2: Nothing prevents the act of one virtue belonging to another virtue, in so far as it is directed to the end of that virtue, as explained above (Q. 32, A. 1, ad 2; Q. 85, A. 3). Accordingly there is no reason why fasting should not be an act of religion, or of chastity, or of any other virtue.

Reply Obj. 3: It belongs to fortitude as a special virtue, to endure, not any kind of hardship, but only those connected with the danger of death. To endure hardships resulting from privation of pleasure of touch, belongs to temperance and its parts: and such are the hardships of fasting.

THIRD ARTICLE [II-II, Q. 147, Art. 3]

Whether Fasting Is a Matter of Precept?

Objection 1: It would seem that fasting is not a matter of precept. For precepts are not given about works of supererogation which are a matter of counsel. Now fasting is a work of supererogation: else it would have to be equally observed at all places and times. Therefore fasting is not a matter of precept.

Obj. 2: Further, whoever infringes a precept commits a mortal sin. Therefore if fasting were a matter of precept, all who do not fast would sin mortally, and a widespreading snare would be laid for men.

Obj. 3: Further, Augustine says (De Vera Relig. 17) that "the Wisdom of God having taken human nature, and called us to a state of freedom, instituted a few most salutary sacraments whereby the community of the Christian people, that is, of the free multitude, should be bound together in subjection to one God." Now the liberty of the Christian people seems to be hindered by a great number of observances no less than by a great number of sacraments. For Augustine says (Ad inquis. Januar., Ep. lv) that "whereas God in His mercy wished our religion to be distinguished by its freedom and the evidence and small number of its solemn sacraments, some people render it oppressive with slavish burdens." Therefore it seems that the Church should not have made fasting a matter of precept.

*On the contrary,* Jerome (Ad Lucin., Ep. lxxi) speaking of fasting says: "Let each province keep to its own practice, and look upon the commands of the elders as though they were laws of the apostles." Therefore fasting is a matter of precept.

*I answer that,* Just as it belongs to the secular authority to make legal precepts which apply the natural law to matters of common weal in temporal affairs, so it belongs to ecclesiastical superiors to prescribe by statute those things that concern the common weal of the faithful in spiritual goods.

Now it has been stated above (A. 1) that fasting is useful as atoning for and preventing sin, and as raising the mind to spiritual things. And everyone is bound by the natural dictate of reason to practice fasting as far as it is necessary for these purposes. Wherefore fasting in general is a matter of precept of the natural law, while the fixing of the time and manner of fasting as becoming and profitable to the Christian people, is a matter of precept of positive law established by ecclesiastical authority: the latter is the Church fast, the former is the fast prescribed by nature.

Reply Obj. 1: Fasting considered in itself denotes something not eligible but penal: yet it becomes eligible in so far as it is useful to some end. Wherefore considered absolutely it is not binding under precept, but it is binding under precept to each one that stands in need of such a remedy. And since men, for the most part, need this remedy, both because "in many things we all offend" (James 3:2), and because "the flesh lusteth against the spirit" (Gal. 5:17), it was fitting that the Church should appoint certain fasts to be kept by all in common. In doing this the Church does not make a precept of a matter of supererogation, but particularizes in detail that which is of general obligation.

Reply Obj. 2: Those commandments which are given under the form of a general precept, do not bind all persons in the same way, but subject to the requirements of the end intended by the lawgiver. It will be a mortal sin to disobey a commandment through contempt of the lawgiver's authority, or to disobey it in such a way as to frustrate the end intended by him: but it is not a mortal sin if one fails to keep a commandment, when there is a reasonable motive, and especially if the lawgiver would not insist on its observance if he were present. Hence it is that not all, who do not keep the fasts of the Church, sin mortally.

Reply Obj. 3: Augustine is speaking there of those things "that are neither contained in the authorities of Holy Scripture, nor found among the ordinances of bishops in council, nor sanctioned by the custom of the universal Church." On the other hand, the fasts that are of obligation are appointed by the councils of bishops and are sanctioned by the custom of the universal Church. Nor are they opposed to the freedom of the faithful, rather are they of use in hindering the slavery of sin, which is opposed to spiritual freedom, of which it is written (Gal. 5:13): "You, brethren, have been called unto liberty; only make not liberty an occasion to the flesh."

FOURTH ARTICLE [II-II, Q. 147, Art. 4]

Whether All Are Bound to Keep the Fasts of the Church?

Objection 1: It would seem that all are bound to keep the fasts of the Church. For the commandments of the Church are binding even as the commandments of God, according to Luke 10:16, "He that heareth you heareth Me." Now all are bound to keep the commandments of God. Therefore in like manner all are bound to keep the fasts appointed by the Church.

Obj. 2: Further, children especially are seemingly not exempt from fasting, on account of their age: for it is written (Joel 2:15): "Sanctify a fast," and further on (Joel 2:16): "Gather together the little ones, and them that suck the breasts." Much more therefore are all others bound to keep the fasts.

Obj. 3: Further, spiritual things should be preferred to temporal, and necessary things to those that are not necessary. Now bodily works are directed to temporal gain; and pilgrimages, though directed to spiritual things, are not a matter of necessity. Therefore, since fasting is directed to a spiritual gain, and is made a necessary thing by the commandment of the Church, it seems that the fasts of the Church ought not to be omitted on account of a pilgrimage, or bodily works.

Obj. 4: Further, it is better to do a thing willingly than through necessity, as stated in 2 Cor. 9:7. Now the poor are wont to fast through necessity, owing to lack of food. Much more therefore ought they to fast willingly.

*On the contrary,* It seems that no righteous man is bound to fast. For the commandments of the Church are not binding in opposition to Christ's teaching. But our Lord said (Luke 5:34) that "the children of the bridegroom cannot fast whilst the bridegroom is with them [*Vulg.: 'Can you make the children of the bridegroom fast, whilst the bridegroom is with them?']." Now He is with all the righteous by dwelling in them in a special manner [*Cf. I, Q. 8, A. 3], wherefore our Lord said (Matt. 28:20): "Behold I am with you ... even to the consummation of the world." Therefore the righteous are not bound by the commandment of the Church to fast.

*I answer that,* As stated above (I-II, Q. 90, A. 2; Q. 98, AA. 2, 6), general precepts are framed according to the requirements of the many. Wherefore in making such precepts the lawgiver considers what happens generally and for the most part, and he does not intend the precept to be binding on a person in whom for some special reason there is something incompatible with observance of the precept. Yet discretion must be brought to bear on the point. For if the reason be evident, it is lawful for a man to use his own judgment in omitting to fulfil the precept, especially if custom be in his favor, or if it be difficult for him to have recourse to superior authority. On the other hand, if the reason be doubtful, one should have recourse to the superior who has power to grant a dispensation in such cases. And this must be done in the fasts appointed by the Church, to which all are bound in general, unless there be some special obstacle to this observance.

Reply Obj. 1: The commandments of God are precepts of the natural law, which are, of themselves, necessary for salvation. But the commandments of the Church are about matters which are necessary for salvation, not of themselves, but only through the ordinance of the Church. Hence there may be certain obstacles on account of which certain persons are not bound to keep the fasts in question.

Reply Obj. 2: In children there is a most evident reason for not fasting, both on account of their natural weakness, owing to which they need to take food frequently, and not much at a time, and because they need much nourishment owing to the demands of growth, which results from the residuum of nourishment. Wherefore as long as the stage of growth lasts, which as a rule lasts until they have completed the third period of seven years, they are not bound to keep the Church fasts: and yet it is fitting that even during that time they should exercise themselves in fasting, more or less, in accordance with their age. Nevertheless when some great calamity threatens, even children are commanded to fast, in sign of more severe penance, according to Jonah 3:7, "Let neither men nor beasts ... taste anything ... nor drink water."

Reply Obj. 3: Apparently a distinction should be made with regard to pilgrims and working people. For if the pilgrimage or laborious work can be conveniently deferred or lessened without detriment to the bodily health and such external conditions as are necessary for the upkeep of bodily or spiritual life, there is no reason for omitting the fasts of the Church. But if one be under the necessity of starting on the pilgrimage at once, and of making long stages, or of doing much work, either for one's bodily livelihood, or for some need of the spiritual life, and it be impossible at the same time to keep the fasts of the Church, one is not bound to fast: because in ordering fasts the Church would not seem to have intended to prevent other pious and more necessary undertakings. Nevertheless, in such cases one ought seemingly, to seek the superior's dispensation; except perhaps when the above course is recognized by custom, since when superiors are silent they would seem to consent.

Reply Obj. 4: Those poor who can provide themselves with sufficient for one meal are not excused, on account of poverty, from keeping the fasts of the Church. On the other hand, those would seem to be exempt who beg their food piecemeal, since they are unable at any one time to have a sufficiency of food.

Reply Obj. 5: This saying of our Lord may be expounded in three ways. First, according to Chrysostom (Hom. xxx in Matth.), who says that "the disciples, who are called children of the bridegroom, were as yet of a weakly disposition, wherefore they are compared to an old garment." Hence while Christ was with them in body they were to be fostered with kindness rather than drilled with the harshness of fasting. According to this interpretation, it is fitting that dispensations should be granted to the imperfect and to beginners, rather than to the elders and the perfect, according to a gloss on Ps. 130:2, "As a child that is weaned is towards his mother." Secondly, we may say with Jerome [*Bede, Comment. in Luc. v] that our Lord is speaking here of the fasts of the observances of the Old Law. Wherefore our Lord means to say that the apostles were not to be held back by the old observances, since they were to be filled with the newness of grace. Thirdly, according to Augustine (De Consensu Evang. ii, 27), who states that fasting is of two kinds. One pertains to those who are humbled by disquietude, and this is not befitting perfect men, for they are called "children of the bridegroom"; hence when we read in Luke: "The children of the bridegroom cannot fast [*Hom. xiii, in Matth.]," we read in Matt. 9:15: "The children of the bridegroom cannot mourn [*Vulg.: 'Can the children of the bridegroom mourn?']." The other pertains to the mind that rejoices in adhering to spiritual things: and this fasting is befitting the perfect.

FIFTH ARTICLE [II-II, Q. 147, Art. 5]

Whether the Times for the Church Fast Are Fittingly Ascribed?

Objection 1: It would seem that the times for the Church fast are unfittingly appointed. For we read (Matt. 4) that Christ began to fast immediately after being baptized. Now we ought to imitate Christ, according to 1 Cor. 4:16, "Be ye followers of me, as I also am of Christ." Therefore we ought to fast immediately after the Epiphany when Christ's baptism is celebrated.

Obj. 2: Further, it is unlawful in the New Law to observe the ceremonies of the Old Law. Now it belongs to the solemnities of the Old Law to fast in certain particular months: for it is written (Zech. 8:19): "The fast of the fourth month and the fast of the fifth, and the fast of the seventh, and the fast of the tenth shall be to the house of Judah, joy and gladness and great solemnities." Therefore the fast of certain months, which are called Ember days, are unfittingly kept in the Church.

Obj. 3: Further, according to Augustine (De Consensu Evang. ii, 27), just as there is a fast "of sorrow," so is there a fast "of joy." Now it is most becoming that the faithful should rejoice spiritually in Christ's Resurrection. Therefore during the five weeks which the Church solemnizes on account of Christ's Resurrection, and on Sundays which commemorate the Resurrection, fasts ought to be appointed.

*On the contrary,* stands the general custom of the Church.

*I answer that,* As stated above (AA. 1, 3), fasting is directed to two things, the deletion of sin, and the raising of the mind to heavenly things. Wherefore fasting ought to be appointed specially for those times, when it behooves man to be cleansed from sin, and the minds of the faithful to be raised to God by devotion: and these things are particularly requisite before the feast of Easter, when sins are loosed by baptism, which is solemnly conferred on Easter-eve, on which day our Lord's burial is commemorated, because "we are buried together with Christ by baptism unto death" (Rom. 6:4). Moreover at the Easter festival the mind of man ought to be devoutly raised to the glory of eternity, which Christ restored by rising from the dead, and so the Church ordered a fast to be observed immediately before the Paschal feast; and for the same reason, on the eve of the chief festivals, because it is then that one ought to make ready to keep the coming feast devoutly. Again it is the custom in the Church for Holy Orders to be conferred every quarter of the year (in sign whereof our Lord fed four thousand men with seven loaves, which signify the New Testament year as Jerome says [*Comment. in Marc. viii]): and then both the ordainer, and the candidates for ordination, and even the whole people, for whose good they are ordained, need to fast in order to make themselves ready for the ordination. Hence it is related (Luke 6:12) that before choosing His disciples our Lord "went out into a mountain to pray": and Ambrose [*Exposit. in Luc.] commenting on these words says: "What shouldst thou do, when thou desirest to undertake some pious work, since Christ prayed before sending His apostles?"

With regard to the forty day's fast, according to Gregory (Hom. xvi in Evang.) there are three reasons for the number. First, "because the power of the Decalogue is accomplished in the four books of the Holy Gospels: since forty is the product of ten multiplied by four." Or "because we are composed of four elements in this mortal body through whose lusts we transgress the Lord's commandments which are delivered to us in the Decalogue. Wherefore it is fitting we should punish that same body forty times. Or, because, just as under the Law it was commanded that tithes should be paid of things, so we strive to pay God a tithe of days, for since a year is composed of three hundred and sixty-six days, by punishing ourselves for thirty-six days" (namely, the fasting days during the six weeks of Lent) "we pay God a tithe of our year." According to Augustine (De Doctr. Christ. ii, 16) a fourth reason may be added. For the Creator is the *Trinity,* Father, Son, and Holy Ghost: while the number three refers to the invisible creature, since we are commanded to love God, with our whole heart, with our whole soul, and with our whole mind: and the number *four* refers to the visible creature, by reason of heat, cold, wet and dry. Thus the number *ten* [*Ten is the sum of three, three, and four] signifies all things, and if this be multiplied by four which refers to the body whereby we make use of things, we have the number forty.

Each fast of the Ember days is composed of three days, on account of the number of months in each season: or on account of the number of Holy orders which are conferred at these times.

Reply Obj. 1: Christ needed not baptism for His own sake, but in order to commend baptism to us. Wherefore it was competent for Him to fast, not before, but after His baptism, in order to invite us to fast before our baptism.

Reply Obj. 2: The Church keeps the Ember fasts, neither at the very same time as the Jews, nor for the same reasons. For they fasted in July, which is the fourth month from April (which they count as the first), because it was then that Moses coming down from Mount Sinai broke the tables of the Law (Ex. 32), and that, according to Jer. 39:2, "the walls of the city were first broken through." In the fifth month, which we call August, they fasted because they were commanded not to go up on to the mountain, when the people had rebelled on account of the spies (Num. 14): also in this month the temple of Jerusalem was burnt down by Nabuchodonosor (Jer. 52) and afterwards by Titus. In the seventh month which we call October, Godolias was slain, and the remnants of the people were dispersed (Jer. 51). In the tenth month, which we call January, the people who were with Ezechiel in captivity heard of the destruction of the temple (Ezech. 4).

Reply Obj. 3: The "fasting of joy" proceeds from the instigation of the Holy Ghost Who is the Spirit of liberty, wherefore this fasting should not be a matter of precept. Accordingly the fasts appointed by the commandment of the Church are rather "fasts of sorrow" which are inconsistent with days of joy. For this reason fasting is not ordered by the Church during the whole of the Paschal season, nor on Sundays: and if anyone were to fast at these times in contradiction to the custom of Christian people, which as Augustine declares (Ep. xxxvi) "is to be considered as law," or even through some erroneous opinion (thus the Manichees fast, because they deem such fasting to be of obligation)—he would not be free from sin. Nevertheless fasting considered in itself is commendable at all times; thus Jerome wrote (Ad Lucin., Ep. lxxi): "Would that we might fast always."

SIXTH ARTICLE [II-II, Q. 147, Art. 6]

Whether It Is Requisite for Fasting That One Eat but Once?

Objection 1: It would seem that it is not requisite for fasting that one eat but once. For, as stated above (A. 2), fasting is an act of the virtue of abstinence, which observes due quantity of food not less than the number of meals. Now the quantity of food is not limited for those who fast. Therefore neither should the number of meals be limited.

Obj. 2: Further, Just as man is nourished by meat, so is he by drink: wherefore drink breaks the fast, and for this reason we cannot receive the Eucharist after drinking. Now we are not forbidden to drink at various hours of the day. Therefore those who fast should not be forbidden to eat several times.

Obj. 3: Further, digestives are a kind of food: and yet many take them on fasting days after eating. Therefore it is not essential to fasting to take only one meal.

*On the contrary,* stands the common custom of the Christian people.

*I answer that,* Fasting is instituted by the Church in order to bridle concupiscence, yet so as to safeguard nature. Now only one meal is seemingly sufficient for this purpose, since thereby man is able to satisfy nature; and yet he withdraws something from concupiscence by minimizing the number of meals. Therefore it is appointed by the Church, in her moderation, that those who fast should take one meal in the day.

Reply Obj. 1: It was not possible to fix the same quantity of food for all, on account of the various bodily temperaments, the result being that one person needs more, and another less food: whereas, for the most part, all are able to satisfy nature by only one meal.

Reply Obj. 2: Fasting is of two kinds [*Cf. A. 1, ad 3]. One is the natural fast, which is requisite for receiving the Eucharist. This is broken by any kind of drink, even of water, after which it is not lawful to receive the Eucharist. The fast of the Church is another kind and is called the "fasting of the faster," and this is not broken save by such things as the Church intended to forbid in instituting the fast. Now the Church does not intend to command abstinence from drink, for this is taken more for bodily refreshment, and digestion of the food consumed, although it nourishes somewhat. It is, however, possible to sin and lose the merit of fasting, by partaking of too much drink: as also by eating immoderately at one meal.

Reply Obj. 3: Although digestives nourish somewhat they are not taken chiefly for nourishment, but for digestion. Hence one does not break one's fast by taking them or any other medicines, unless one were to take digestives, with a fraudulent intention, in great quantity and by way of food.

SEVENTH ARTICLE [II-II, Q. 147, Art. 7]

Whether the Ninth Hour Is Suitably Fixed for the Faster's Meal?

Objection 1: It would seem that the ninth hour is not suitably fixed for the faster's meal. For the state of the New Law is more perfect than the state of the Old Law. Now in the Old Testament they fasted until evening, for it is written (Lev. 23:32): "It is a sabbath ... you shall afflict your souls," and then the text continues: "From evening until evening you shall celebrate your sabbaths." Much more therefore under the New Testament should the fast be ordered until the evening.

Obj. 2: Further, the fast ordered by the Church is binding on all. But all are not able to know exactly the ninth hour. Therefore it seems that the fixing of the ninth hour should not form part of the commandment to fast.

Obj. 3: Further, fasting is an act of the virtue of abstinence, as stated above (A. 2). Now the mean of moral virtue does not apply in the same way to all, since what is much for one is little for another, as stated in *Ethic.* ii, 6. Therefore the ninth hour should not be fixed for those who fast.

*On the contrary,* The Council of Chalons [*The quotation is from the Capitularies (Cap. 39) of Theodulf, bishop of Orleans (760-821) and is said to be found in the Corpus Juris, Cap. Solent, dist. 1, De Consecratione] says: "During Lent those are by no means to be credited with fasting who eat before the celebration of the office of Vespers," which in the Lenten season is said after the ninth hour. Therefore we ought to fast until the ninth hour.

*I answer that,* As stated above (AA. 1, 3, 5), fasting is directed to the deletion and prevention of sin. Hence it ought to add something to the common custom, yet so as not to be a heavy burden to nature. Now the right and common custom is for men to eat about the sixth hour: both because digestion is seemingly finished (the natural heat being withdrawn inwardly at night-time on account of the surrounding cold of the night), and the humor spread about through the limbs (to which result the heat of the day conduces until the sun has reached its zenith), and again because it is then chiefly that the nature of the human body needs assistance against the external heat that is in the air, lest the humors be parched within. Hence, in order that those who fast may feel some pain in satisfaction for their sins, the ninth hour is suitably fixed for their meal.

Moreover, this hour agrees with the mystery of Christ's Passion, which was brought to a close at the ninth hour, when "bowing His head, He gave up the ghost" (John 19:30): because those who fast by punishing their flesh, are conformed to the Passion of Christ, according to Gal. 5:24, "They that are Christ's, have crucified their flesh with the vices and concupiscences."

Reply Obj. 1: The state of the Old Testament is compared to the night, while the state of the New Testament is compared to the day, according to Rom. 13:12, "The night is passed and the day is at hand." Therefore in the Old Testament they fasted until night, but not in the New Testament.

Reply Obj. 2: Fasting requires a fixed hour based, not on a strict calculation, but on a rough estimate: for it suffices that it be about the ninth hour, and this is easy for anyone to ascertain.

Reply Obj. 3: A little more or a little less cannot do much harm. Now it is not a long space of time from the sixth hour at which men for the most part are wont to eat, until the ninth hour, which is fixed for those who fast. Wherefore the fixing of such a time cannot do much harm to anyone, whatever his circumstances may be. If however this were to prove a heavy burden to a man on account of sickness, age, or some similar reason, he should be dispensed from fasting, or be allowed to forestall the hour by a little.

EIGHTH ARTICLE [II-II, Q. 147, Art. 8]

Whether It Is Fitting That Those Who Fast Should Be Bidden to Abstain from Flesh Meat, Eggs, and Milk Foods?

Objection 1: It would seem unfitting that those who fast should be bidden to abstain from flesh meat, eggs, and milk foods. For it has been stated above (A. 6) that fasting was instituted as a curb on the concupiscence of the flesh. Now concupiscence is kindled by drinking wine more than by eating flesh; according to Prov. 20:1, "Wine is a luxurious thing," and Eph. 5:18, "Be not drunk with wine, wherein is luxury." Since then those who fast are not forbidden to drink wine, it seems that they should not be forbidden to eat flesh meat.

Obj. 2: Further, some fish are as delectable to eat as the flesh of certain animals. Now "concupiscence is desire of the delectable," as stated above (I-II, Q. 30, A. 1). Therefore since fasting which was instituted in order to bridle concupiscence does not exclude the eating of fish, neither should it exclude the eating of flesh meat.

Obj. 3: Further, on certain fasting days people make use of eggs and cheese. Therefore one can likewise make use of them during the Lenten fast.

*On the contrary,* stands the common custom of the faithful.

*I answer that,* As stated above (A. 6), fasting was instituted by the Church in order to bridle the concupiscences of the flesh, which regard pleasures of touch in connection with food and sex. Wherefore the Church forbade those who fast to partake of those foods which both afford most pleasure to the palate, and besides are a very great incentive to lust. Such are the flesh of animals that take their rest on the earth, and of those that breathe the air and their products, such as milk from those that walk on the earth, and eggs from birds. For, since such like animals are more like man in body, they afford greater pleasure as food, and greater nourishment to the human body, so that from their consumption there results a greater surplus available for seminal matter, which when abundant becomes a great incentive to lust. Hence the Church has bidden those who fast to abstain especially from these foods.

Reply Obj. 1: Three things concur in the act of procreation, namely, heat, spirit [*Cf. P. I., Q. 118, A. 1, ad 3], and humor. Wine and other things that heat the body conduce especially to heat: flatulent foods seemingly cooperate in the production of the vital spirit: but it is chiefly the use of flesh meat which is most productive of nourishment, that conduces to the production of humor. Now the alteration occasioned by heat, and the increase in vital spirits are of short duration, whereas the substance of the humor remains a long time. Hence those who fast are forbidden the use of flesh meat rather than of wine or vegetables which are flatulent foods.

Reply Obj. 2: In the institution of fasting, the Church takes account of the more common occurrences. Now, generally speaking, eating flesh meat affords more pleasure than eating fish, although this is not always the case. Hence the Church forbade those who fast to eat flesh meat, rather than to eat fish.

Reply Obj. 3: Eggs and milk foods are forbidden to those who fast, for as much as they originate from animals that provide us with flesh: wherefore the prohibition of flesh meat takes precedence of the prohibition of eggs and milk foods. Again the Lenten fast is the most solemn of all, both because it is kept in imitation of Christ, and because it disposes us to celebrate devoutly the mysteries of our redemption. For this reason the eating of flesh meat is forbidden in every fast, while the Lenten fast lays a general prohibition even on eggs and milk foods. As to the use of the latter things in other fasts the custom varies among different people, and each person is bound to conform to that custom which is in vogue with those among whom he is dwelling. Hence Jerome says [*Augustine, De Lib. Arb. iii, 18; cf. De Nat. et Grat. lxvii]: "Let each province keep to its own practice, and look upon the commands of the elders as though they were the laws of the apostles."

# QUESTION 148

OF GLUTTONY (In Six Articles)

We must now consider gluttony. Under this head there are six points of inquiry:

(1) Whether gluttony is a sin?
(2) Whether it is a mortal sin?
(3) Whether it is the greatest of sins?
(4) Its species;
(5) Whether it is a capital sin?
(6) Its daughters.

FIRST ARTICLE [II-II, Q. 148, Art. 1]

Whether Gluttony Is a Sin?

Objection 1: It would seem that gluttony is not a sin. For our Lord said (Matt. 15:11): "Not that which goeth into the mouth defileth a man." Now gluttony regards food which goes into a man. Therefore, since every sin defiles a man, it seems that gluttony is not a sin.

Obj. 2: Further, "No man sins in what he cannot avoid" [*Ep. lxxi, ad Lucin.]. Now gluttony is immoderation in food; and man cannot avoid this, for Gregory says (Moral. xxx, 18): "Since in eating pleasure and necessity go together, we fail to discern between the call of necessity and the seduction of pleasure," and Augustine says (Confess. x, 31): "Who is it, Lord, that does not eat a little more than necessary?" Therefore gluttony is not a sin.

Obj. 3: Further, in every kind of sin the first movement is a sin. But the first movement in taking food is not a sin, else hunger and thirst would be sinful. Therefore gluttony is not a sin.

*On the contrary,* Gregory says (Moral. xxx, 18) that "unless we first tame the enemy dwelling within us, namely our gluttonous appetite, we have not even stood up to engage in the spiritual combat." But man's inward enemy is sin. Therefore gluttony is a sin.

*I answer that,* Gluttony denotes, not any desire of eating and drinking, but an inordinate desire. Now desire is said to be inordinate through leaving the order of reason, wherein the good of moral virtue consists: and a thing is said to be a sin through being contrary to virtue. Wherefore it is evident that gluttony is a sin.

Reply Obj. 1: That which goes into man by way of food, by reason of its substance and nature, does not defile a man spiritually. But the Jews, against whom our Lord is speaking, and the Manichees deemed certain foods to make a man unclean, not on account of their signification, but by reason of their nature [*Cf. I-II, Q. 102, A. 6, ad 1]. It is the inordinate desire of food that defiles a man spiritually.

Reply Obj. 2: As stated above, the vice of gluttony does not regard the substance of food, but in the desire thereof not being regulated by reason. Wherefore if a man exceed in quantity of food, not from desire of food, but through deeming it necessary to him, this pertains, not to gluttony, but to some kind of inexperience. It is a case of gluttony only when a man knowingly exceeds the measure in eating, from a desire for the pleasures of the palate.

Reply Obj. 3: The appetite is twofold. There is the natural appetite, which belongs to the powers of the vegetal soul. In these powers virtue and vice are impossible, since they cannot be subject to reason; wherefore the appetitive power is differentiated from the powers of secretion, digestion, and excretion, and to it hunger and thirst are to be referred. Besides this there is another, the sensitive appetite, and it is in the concupiscence of this appetite that the vice of gluttony consists. Hence the first movement of gluttony denotes inordinateness in the sensitive appetite, and this is not without sin.

SECOND ARTICLE [II-II, Q. 148, Art. 2]

Whether Gluttony Is a Mortal Sin?

Objection 1: It would seem that gluttony is not a mortal sin. For every mortal sin is contrary to a precept of the Decalogue: and this, apparently, does not apply to gluttony. Therefore gluttony is not a mortal sin.

Obj. 2: Further, every mortal sin is contrary to charity, as stated above (Q. 132, A. 3). But gluttony is not opposed to charity, neither as regards the love of God, nor as regards the love of one's neighbor. Therefore gluttony is never a mortal sin.

Obj. 3: Further, Augustine says in a sermon on Purgatory [*Cf. Append. to St. Augustine's works: Serm. civ (xli, de sanctis)]: "Whenever a man takes more meat and drink than is necessary, he should know that this is one of the lesser sins." But this pertains to gluttony. Therefore gluttony is accounted among the lesser, that is to say venial, sins.

Obj. 4: *On the contrary,* Gregory says (Moral. xxx, 18): "As long as the vice of gluttony has a hold on a man, all that he has done valiantly is forfeited by him: and as long as the belly is unrestrained, all virtue comes to naught." But virtue is not done away save by mortal sin. Therefore gluttony is a mortal sin.

*I answer that,* As stated above (A. 1), the vice of gluttony properly consists in inordinate concupiscence. Now the order of reason in regulating the concupiscence may be considered from two points of view. First, with regard to things directed to the end, inasmuch as they may be incommensurate and consequently improportionate to the end; secondly, with regard to the end itself, inasmuch as concupiscence turns man away from his due end. Accordingly, if the inordinate concupiscence in gluttony be found to turn man away from the last end, gluttony will be a mortal sin. This is the case when he adheres to the pleasure of gluttony as his end, for the sake of which he contemns God, being ready to disobey God's commandments, in order to obtain those pleasures. On the other hand, if the inordinate concupiscence in the vice of gluttony be found to affect only such things as are directed to the end, for instance when a man has too great a desire for the pleasures of the palate, yet would not for their sake do anything contrary to God's law, it is a venial sin.

Reply Obj. 1: The vice of gluttony becomes a mortal sin by turning man away from his last end: and accordingly, by a kind of reduction, it is opposed to the precept of hallowing the sabbath, which commands us to rest in our last end. For mortal sins are not all directly opposed to the precepts of the Decalogue, but only those which contain injustice: because the precepts of the Decalogue pertain specially to justice and its parts, as stated above (Q. 122, A. 1).

Reply Obj. 2: In so far as it turns man away from his last end, gluttony is opposed to the love of God, who is to be loved, as our last end, above all things: and only in this respect is gluttony a mortal sin.

Reply Obj. 3: This saying of Augustine refers to gluttony as denoting inordinate concupiscence merely in regard of things directed to the end.

Reply Obj. 4: Gluttony is said to bring virtue to naught, not so much on its own account, as on account of the vices which arise from it. For Gregory says (Pastor. iii, 19): "When the belly is distended by gluttony, the virtues of the soul are destroyed by lust."

THIRD ARTICLE [II-II, Q. 148, Art. 3]

Whether Gluttony Is the Greatest of Sins?

Objection 1: It would seem that gluttony is the greatest of sins. For the grievousness of a sin is measured by the grievousness of the punishment. Now the sin of gluttony is most grievously punished, for Chrysostom says [*Hom. xiii in Matth.]: "Gluttony turned Adam out of Paradise, gluttony it was that drew down the deluge at the time of Noah." According to Ezech. 16:49, "This was the iniquity of Sodom, thy sister ... fulness of bread," etc. Therefore the sin of gluttony is the greatest of all.

Obj. 2: Further, in every genus the cause is the most powerful. Now gluttony is apparently the cause of other sins, for a gloss on Ps. 135:10, "Who smote Egypt with their first-born," says: "Lust, concupiscence, pride are the first-born of gluttony." Therefore gluttony is the greatest of sins.

Obj. 3: Further, man should love himself in the first place after God, as stated above (Q. 25, A. 4). Now man, by the vice of gluttony, inflicts an injury on himself: for it is written (Ecclus. 37:34): "By surfeiting many have perished." Therefore gluttony is the greatest of sins, at least excepting those that are against God.

*On the contrary,* The sins of the flesh, among which gluttony is reckoned, are less culpable according to Gregory (Moral. xxxiii).

*I answer that,* The gravity of a sin may be measured in three ways. First and foremost it depends on the matter in which the sin is committed: and in this way sins committed in connection with Divine things are the greatest. From this point of view gluttony is not the greatest sin, for it is about matters connected with the nourishment of the body. Secondly, the gravity of a sin depends on the person who sins, and from this point of view the sin of gluttony is diminished rather than aggravated, both on account of the necessity of taking food, and on account of the difficulty of proper discretion and moderation in such matters. Thirdly, from the point of view of the result that follows, and in this way gluttony has a certain gravity, inasmuch as certain sins are occasioned thereby.

Reply Obj. 1: These punishments are to be referred to the vices that resulted from gluttony, or to the root from which gluttony sprang, rather than to gluttony itself. For the first man was expelled from Paradise on account of pride, from which he went on to an act of gluttony: while the deluge and the punishment of the people of Sodom were inflicted for sins occasioned by gluttony.

Reply Obj. 2: This objection argues from the standpoint of the sins that result from gluttony. Nor is a cause necessarily more powerful, unless it be a direct cause: and gluttony is not the direct cause but the accidental cause, as it were, and the occasion of other vices.

Reply Obj. 3: The glutton intends, not the harm to his body, but the pleasure of eating: and if injury results to his body, this is accidental. Hence this does not directly affect the gravity of gluttony, the guilt of which is nevertheless aggravated, if a man incur some bodily injury through taking too much food.

FOURTH ARTICLE [II-II, Q. 148, Art. 4]

Whether the Species of Gluttony Are Fittingly Distinguished?

Objection 1: It seems that the species of gluttony are unfittingly distinguished by Gregory who says (Moral. xxx, 18): "The vice of gluttony tempts us in five ways. Sometimes it forestalls the hour of need; sometimes it seeks costly meats; sometimes it requires the food to be daintily cooked; sometimes it exceeds the measure of refreshment by taking too much; sometimes we sin by the very heat of an immoderate appetite"—which are contained in the following verse: "Hastily, sumptuously, too much, greedily, daintily."

For the above are distinguished according to diversity of circumstance. Now circumstances, being the accidents of an act, do not differentiate its species. Therefore the species of gluttony are not distinguished according to the aforesaid.

Obj. 2: Further, as time is a circumstance, so is place. If then gluttony admits of one species in respect of time, it seems that there should likewise be others in respect of place and other circumstances.

Obj. 3: Further, just as temperance observes due circumstances, so do the other moral virtues. Now the species of the vices opposed to the other moral virtues are not distinguished according to various circumstances. Neither, therefore, are the species of gluttony distinguished thus.

*On the contrary,* stands the authority of Gregory quoted above.

*I answer that,* As stated above (A. 1), gluttony denotes inordinate concupiscence in eating. Now two things are to be considered in eating, namely the food we eat, and the eating thereof. Accordingly, the inordinate concupiscence may be considered in two ways. First, with regard to the food consumed: and thus, as regards the substance or species of food a man seeks "sumptuous"—i.e. costly food; as regards its quality, he seeks food prepared too nicely—i.e. "daintily"; and as regards quantity, he exceeds by eating "too much."

Secondly, the inordinate concupiscence is considered as to the consumption of food: either because one forestalls the proper time for eating, which is to eat "hastily," or one fails to observe the due manner of eating, by eating "greedily."

Isidore [*De Summo Bon. ii, 42] comprises the first and second under one heading, when he says that the glutton exceeds in "what" he eats, or in "how much," "how" or "when he eats."

Reply Obj. 1: The corruption of various circumstances causes the various species of gluttony, on account of the various motives, by reason of which the species of moral things are differentiated. For in him that seeks sumptuous food, concupiscence is aroused by the very species of the food; in him that forestalls the time concupiscence is disordered through impatience of delay, and so forth.

Reply Obj. 2: Place and other circumstances include no special motive connected with eating, that can cause a different species of gluttony.

Reply Obj. 3: In all other vices, whenever different circumstances correspond to different motives, the difference of circumstances argues a specific difference of vice: but this does not apply to all circumstances, as stated above (I-II, Q. 72, A. 9).

FIFTH ARTICLE [II-II, Q. 148, Art. 5]

Whether Gluttony Is a Capital Vice?

Objection 1: It would seem that gluttony is not a capital vice. For capital vices denote those whence, under the aspect of final cause, other vices originate. Now food, which is the matter of gluttony, has not the aspect of end, since it is sought, not for its own sake, but for the body's nourishment. Therefore gluttony is not a capital vice.

Obj. 2: Further, a capital vice would seem to have a certain pre-eminence in sinfulness. But this does not apply to gluttony, which, in respect of its genus, is apparently the least of sins, seeing that it is most akin to what is [according to nature]. Therefore gluttony is not a capital vice.

Obj. 3: Further, sin results from a man forsaking the [good] of virtue on account of something useful to the present life, or pleasing to the senses. Now as regards goods having the aspect of utility, there is but one capital vice, namely covetousness. Therefore, seemingly, there would be but one capital vice in respect of pleasures: and this is lust, which is a greater vice than gluttony, and is about greater pleasures. Therefore gluttony is not a capital vice.

*On the contrary,* Gregory (Moral. xxxi, 45) reckons gluttony among the capital vices.

*I answer that,* As stated above (I-II, Q. 84, A. 3), a capital vice denotes one from which, considered as final cause, i.e. as having a most desirable end, other vices originate: wherefore through desiring that end men are incited to sin in many ways. Now an end is rendered most desirable through having one of the conditions of happiness which is desirable by its very nature: and pleasure is essential to happiness, according to *Ethic.* i, 8; x, 3, 7, 8. Therefore the vice of gluttony, being about pleasures of touch which stand foremost among other pleasures, is fittingly reckoned among the capital vices.

Reply Obj. 1: It is true that food itself is directed to something as its end: but since that end, namely the sustaining of life, is most desirable and whereas life cannot be sustained without food, it follows that food too is most desirable: indeed, nearly all the toil of man's life is directed thereto, according to Eccles. 6:7, "All the labor of man is for his mouth." Yet gluttony seems to be about pleasures of food rather than about food itself; wherefore, as Augustine says (De Vera Relig. liii), "with such food as is good for the worthless body, men desire to be fed," wherein namely the pleasure consists, "rather than to be filled: since the whole end of that desire is this—not to thirst and not to hunger."

Reply Obj. 2: In sin the end is ascertained with respect to the conversion, while the gravity of sin is determined with regard to the aversion. Wherefore it does not follow that the capital sin which has the most desirable end surpasses the others in gravity.

Reply Obj. 3: That which gives pleasure is desirable in itself: and consequently corresponding to its diversity there are two capital vices, namely gluttony and lust. On the other hand, that which is useful is desirable, not in itself, but as directed to something else: wherefore seemingly in all useful things there is one aspect of desirability. Hence there is but one capital vice, in respect of such things.

SIXTH ARTICLE [II-II, Q. 148, Art. 6]

Whether [Five] Daughters Are Fittingly Assigned to Gluttony?

Objection 1: It would seem that [five] daughters are unfittingly assigned to gluttony, to wit, "unseemly joy, scurrility, uncleanness, loquaciousness, and dullness of mind as regards the understanding." For unseemly joy results from every sin, according to Prov. 2:14, "Who are glad when they have done evil, and rejoice in most wicked things." Likewise dullness of mind is associated with every sin, according to Prov. 14:22, "They err that work evil." Therefore they are unfittingly reckoned to be daughters of gluttony.

Obj. 2: Further, the uncleanness which is particularly the result of gluttony would seem to be connected with vomiting, according to Isa. 28:8, "All tables were full of vomit and filth." But this seems to be not a sin but a punishment; or even a useful thing that is a matter of counsel, according to Ecclus. 31:25, "If thou hast been forced to eat much, arise, go out, and vomit; and it shall refresh thee." Therefore it should not be reckoned among the daughters of gluttony.

Obj. 3: Further, Isidore (QQ. in Deut. xvi) reckons scurrility as a daughter of lust. Therefore it should not be reckoned among the daughters of gluttony.

*On the contrary,* Gregory (Moral. xxxi, 45) assigns these daughters to gluttony.

*I answer that,* As stated above (AA. 1, 2, 3), gluttony consists properly in an immoderate pleasure in eating and drinking. Wherefore those vices are reckoned among the daughters of gluttony, which are the results of eating and drinking immoderately. These may be accounted for either on the part of the soul or on the part of the body. On the part of the soul these results are of four kinds. First, as regards the reason, whose keenness is dulled by immoderate meat and drink, and in this respect we reckon as a daughter of gluttony, "dullness of sense in the understanding," on account of the fumes of food disturbing the brain. Even so, on the other hand, abstinence conduces to the penetrating power of wisdom, according to Eccles. 2:3, "I thought in my heart to withdraw my flesh from wine, that I might turn my mind in wisdom." Secondly, as regards the appetite, which is disordered in many ways by immoderation in eating and drinking, as though reason were fast asleep at the helm, and in this respect "unseemly joy" is reckoned, because all the other inordinate passions are directed to joy or sorrow, as stated in *Ethic.* ii, 5. To this we must refer the saying of 3 Esdr. 3:20, that "wine ... gives every one a confident and joyful mind." Thirdly, as regards inordinate words, and thus we have "loquaciousness," because as Gregory says (Pastor. iii, 19), "unless gluttons were carried away by immoderate speech, that rich man who is stated to have feasted sumptuously every day would not have been so tortured in his tongue." Fourthly, as regards inordinate action, and in this way we have "scurrility," i.e. a kind of levity resulting from lack of reason, which is unable not only to bridle the speech, but also to restrain outward behavior. Hence a gloss on Eph. 5:4, "Or foolish talking or scurrility," says that "fools call this geniality—i.e. jocularity, because it is wont to raise a laugh." Both of these, however, may be referred to the words which may happen to be sinful, either by reason of excess which belongs to "loquaciousness," or by reason of unbecomingness, which belongs to "scurrility."

On the part of the body, mention is made of "uncleanness," which may refer either to the inordinate emission of any kind of superfluities, or especially to the emission of the semen. Hence a gloss on Eph. 5:3, "But fornication and all uncleanness," says: "That is, any kind of incontinence that has reference to lust."

Reply Obj. 1: Joy in the act or end of sin results from every sin, especially the sin that proceeds from habit, but the random riotous joy which is described as "unseemly" arises chiefly from immoderate partaking of meat or drink. In like manner, we reply that dullness of sense as regards matters of choice is common to all sin, whereas dullness of sense in speculative matters arises chiefly from gluttony, for the reason given above.

Reply Obj. 2: Although it does one good to vomit after eating too much, yet it is sinful to expose oneself to its necessity by immoderate meat or drink. However, it is no sin to procure vomiting as a remedy for sickness if the physician prescribes it.

Reply Obj. 3: Scurrility proceeds from the act of gluttony, and not from the lustful act, but from the lustful will: wherefore it may be referred to either vice.

# QUESTION 149

OF SOBRIETY (In Four Articles)

We must now consider sobriety and the contrary vice, namely drunkenness. As regards sobriety there are four points of inquiry:

(1) What is the matter of sobriety?

(2) Whether it is a special virtue?

(3) Whether the use of wine is lawful?

(4) To whom especially is sobriety becoming?

FIRST ARTICLE [II-II, Q. 149, Art. 1]

Whether Drink Is the Matter of Sobriety?

Objection 1: It would seem that drink is not the matter proper to sobriety. For it is written (Rom. 12:3): "Not to be more wise than it behooveth to be wise, but to be wise unto sobriety." Therefore sobriety is also about wisdom, and not only about drink.

Obj. 2: Further, concerning the wisdom of God, it is written (Wis. 8:7) that "she teacheth sobriety [Douay: 'temperance'], and prudence, and justice, and fortitude," where sobriety stands for temperance. Now temperance is not only about drink, but also about meat and sexual matters. Therefore sobriety is not only about drink.

Obj. 3: Further, sobriety would seem to take its name from "measure" [* *Bria*, a measure, a cup; Cf. Facciolati and Forcellini's *Lexicon* ]. Now we ought to be guided by the measure in all things appertaining to us: for it is written (Titus 2:12): "We should live soberly and justly and godly," where a gloss remarks: "Soberly, in ourselves"; and (1 Tim. 2:9): "Women ... in decent apparel, adorning themselves with modesty and sobriety." Consequently it would seem that sobriety regards not only the interior man, but also things appertaining to external apparel. Therefore drink is not the matter proper to sobriety.

*On the contrary,* It is written (Ecclus. 31:32): "Wine taken with sobriety is equal life to men; if thou drink it moderately, thou shalt be sober."

*I answer that,* When a virtue is denominated from some condition common to the virtues, the matter specially belonging to it is that in which it is most difficult and most commendable to satisfy that condition of virtue: thus fortitude is about dangers of death, and temperance about pleasures of touch. Now sobriety takes its name from "measure," for a man is said to be sober because he observes the *bria,* i.e. the measure. Wherefore sobriety lays a special claim to that matter wherein the observance of the measure is most deserving of praise. Such matter is the drinking of intoxicants, because the measured use thereof is most profitable, while immoderate excess therein is most harmful, since it hinders the use of reason even more than excessive eating. Hence it is written (Ecclus. 31:37, 38): "Sober drinking is health to soul and body; wine drunken with excess raiseth quarrels, and wrath and many ruins." For this reason sobriety is especially concerned with drink, not any kind of drink, but that which by reason of its volatility is liable to disturb the brain, such as wine and all intoxicants. Nevertheless, sobriety may be employed in a general sense so as to apply to any matter, as stated above (Q. 123, A. 2; Q. 141, A. 2) with regard to fortitude and temperance.

Reply Obj. 1: Just as the material wine intoxicates a man as to his body, so too, speaking figuratively, the consideration of wisdom is said to be an inebriating draught, because it allures the mind by its delight, according to Ps. 22:5, "My chalice which inebriateth me, how goodly is it!" Hence sobriety is applied by a kind of metaphor in speaking of the contemplation of wisdom.

Reply Obj. 2: All the things that belong properly to temperance are necessary to the present life, and their excess is harmful. Wherefore it behooves one to apply a measure in all such things. This is the business of sobriety: and for this reason sobriety is used to designate temperance. Yet slight excess is more harmful in drink than in other things, wherefore sobriety is especially concerned with drink.

Reply Obj. 3: Although a measure is needful in all things, sobriety is not properly employed in connection with all things, but only in those wherein there is most need for a measure.

SECOND ARTICLE [II-II, Q. 149, Art. 2]

Whether Sobriety Is by Itself a Special Virtue?

Objection 1: It would seem that sobriety is not by itself a special virtue. For abstinence is concerned with both meat and drink. Now there is no special virtue about meat. Therefore neither is sobriety, which is about drink, a special virtue.

Obj. 2: Further, abstinence and gluttony are about pleasures of touch as sensitive to food. Now meat and drink combine together to make food, since an animal needs a combination of wet and dry nourishment. Therefore sobriety, which is about drink, is not a. special virtue.

Obj. 3: Further, just as in things pertaining to nourishment, drink is distinguished from meat, so are there various kinds of meats and of drinks. Therefore if sobriety is by itself a special virtue, seemingly there will be a special virtue corresponding to each different kind of meat or drink, which is unreasonable. Therefore it would seem that sobriety is not a special virtue.

*On the contrary,* Macrobius [*In Somno Scip. i, 8] reckons sobriety to be a special part of temperance.

*I answer that,* As stated above (Q. 146, A. 2), it belongs to moral virtue to safeguard the good of reason against those things which may hinder it. Hence wherever we find a special hindrance to reason, there must needs be a special virtue to remove it. Now intoxicating drink is a special kind of hindrance to the use of reason, inasmuch as it disturbs the brain by its fumes. Wherefore in order to remove this hindrance to reason a special virtue, which is sobriety, is requisite.

Reply Obj. 1: Meat and drink are alike capable of hindering the good of reason, by embroiling the reason with immoderate pleasure: and in this respect abstinence is about both meat and drink alike. But intoxicating drink is a special kind of hindrance, as stated above, wherefore it requires a special virtue.

Reply Obj. 2: The virtue of abstinence is about meat and drink, considered, not as food but as a hindrance to reason. Hence it does not follow that special kinds of virtue correspond to different kinds of food.

Reply Obj. 3: In all intoxicating drinks there is one kind of hindrance to the use of reason: so that the difference of drinks bears an accidental relation to virtue. Hence this difference does not call for a difference of virtue. The same applies to the difference of meats.

THIRD ARTICLE [II-II, Q. 149, Art. 3]

Whether the Use of Wine Is Altogether Unlawful?

Objection 1: It would seem that the use of wine is altogether unlawful. For without wisdom, a man cannot be in the state of salvation: since it is written (Wis. 7:28): "God loveth none but him that dwelleth with wisdom," and further on (Wis. 9:19): "By wisdom they were healed, whosoever have pleased Thee, O Lord, from the beginning." Now the use of wine is a hindrance to wisdom, for it is written (Eccles. 2:3): "I thought in my heart to withdraw my flesh from wine, that I might turn my mind to wisdom." Therefore wine-drinking is altogether unlawful.

Obj. 2: Further, the Apostle says (Rom. 14:21): "It is good not to eat flesh, and not to drink wine, nor anything whereby thy brother is offended or scandalized, or made weak." Now it is sinful to forsake the good of virtue, as likewise to scandalize one's brethren. Therefore it is unlawful to make use of wine.

Obj. 3: Further, Jerome says [*Contra Jovin. i] that "after the deluge wine and flesh were sanctioned: but Christ came in the last of the ages and brought back the end into line with the beginning." Therefore it seems unlawful to use wine under the Christian law.

*On the contrary,* The Apostle says (1 Tim. 5:23): "Do not still drink water, but use a little wine for thy stomach's sake, and thy frequent infirmities"; and it is written (Ecclus. 31:36): "Wine drunken with moderation is the joy of the soul and the heart."

*I answer that,* No meat or drink, considered in itself, is unlawful, according to Matt. 15:11, "Not that which goeth into the mouth defileth a man." Wherefore it is not unlawful to drink wine as such. Yet it may become unlawful accidentally. This is sometimes owing to a circumstance on the part of the drinker, either because he is easily the worse for taking wine, or because he is bound by a vow not to drink wine: sometimes it results from the mode of drinking, because to wit he exceeds the measure in drinking: and sometimes it is on account of others who would be scandalized thereby.

Reply Obj. 1: A man may have wisdom in two ways. First, in a general way, according as it is sufficient for salvation: and in this way it is required, in order to have wisdom, not that a man abstain altogether from wine, but that he abstain from its immoderate use. Secondly, a man may have wisdom in some degree of perfection: and in this way, in order to receive wisdom perfectly, it is requisite for certain persons that they abstain altogether from wine, and this depends on circumstances of certain persons and places.

Reply Obj. 2: The Apostle does not declare simply that it is good to abstain from wine, but that it is good in the case where this would give scandal to certain people.

Reply Obj. 3: Christ withdraws us from some things as being altogether unlawful, and from others as being obstacles to perfection. It is in the latter way that he withdraws some from the use of wine, that they may aim at perfection, even as from riches and the like.

FOURTH ARTICLE [II-II, Q. 149, Art. 4]

Whether Sobriety Is More Requisite in Persons of Greater Standing?

Objection 1: It would seem that sobriety is more requisite in persons of greater standing. For old age gives a man a certain standing; wherefore honor and reverence are due to the old, according to Lev. 19:32, "Rise up before the hoary head, and honor the person of the aged man." Now the Apostle declares that old men especially should be exhorted to sobriety, according to Titus 2:2, "That the aged man be sober." Therefore sobriety is most requisite in persons of standing.

Obj. 2: Further, a bishop has the highest degree in the Church: and the Apostle commands him to be sober, according to 1 Tim. 3:2, "It behooveth ... a bishop to be blameless, the husband of one wife, sober, prudent," etc. Therefore sobriety is chiefly required in persons of high standing.

Obj. 3: Further, sobriety denotes abstinence from wine. Now wine is forbidden to kings, who hold the highest place in human affairs: while it is allowed to those who are in a state of affliction, according to Prov. 31:4, "Give not wine to kings," and further on (Prov. 31:6), "Give strong drink to them that are sad, and wine to them that are grieved in mind." Therefore sobriety is more requisite in persons of standing.

*On the contrary,* The Apostle says (1 Tim. 3:11): "The women in like manner, chaste ... sober," etc., and (Titus 2:6) "Young men in like manner exhort that they be sober."

*I answer that,* Virtue includes relationship to two things, to the contrary vices which it removes, and to the end to which it leads. Accordingly a particular virtue is more requisite in certain persons for two reasons. First, because they are more prone to the concupiscences which need to be restrained by virtue, and to the vices which are removed by virtue. In this respect, sobriety is most requisite in the young and in women, because concupiscence of pleasure thrives in the young on account of the heat of youth, while in women there is not sufficient strength of mind to resist concupiscence. Hence, according to Valerius Maximus [*Dict. Fact. Memor. ii, 1] among the ancient Romans women drank no wine. Secondly, sobriety is more requisite in certain persons, as being more necessary for the operations proper to them. Now immoderate use of wine is a notable obstacle to the use of reason: wherefore sobriety is specially prescribed to the old, in whom reason should be vigorous in instructing others: to bishops and all ministers of the Church, who should fulfil their spiritual duties with a devout mind; and to kings, who should rule their subjects with wisdom.

This suffices for the Replies to the Objections.

# QUESTION 150

OF DRUNKENNESS (In Four Articles)

We must now consider drunkenness. Under this head there are four points of inquiry:

(1) Whether drunkenness is a sin?

(2) Whether it is a mortal sin?

(3) Whether it is the most grievous sin?

(4) Whether it excuses from sin?

FIRST ARTICLE [II-II, Q. 150, Art. 1]

Whether Drunkenness Is a Sin?

Objection 1: It would seem that drunkenness is not a sin. For every sin has a corresponding contrary sin, thus timidity is opposed to daring, and presumption to pusillanimity. But no sin is opposed to drunkenness. Therefore drunkenness is not a sin.

Obj. 2: Further, every sin is voluntary [*Augustine, De Vera Relig. xiv]. But no man wishes to be drunk, since no man wishes to be deprived of the use of reason. Therefore drunkenness is not a sin.

Obj. 3: Further, whoever causes another to sin, sins himself. Therefore, if drunkenness were a sin, it would follow that it is a sin to ask a man to drink that which makes him drunk, which would seem very hard.

Obj. 4: Further, every sin calls for correction. But correction is not applied to drunkards: for Gregory [*Cf. Canon Denique, dist. 4 where Gratian refers to a letter of St. Gregory to St. Augustine of Canterbury] says that "we must forbear with their ways, lest they become worse if they be compelled to give up the habit." Therefore drunkenness is not a sin.

*On the contrary,* The Apostle says (Rom. 13:13): "Not in rioting and drunkenness."

*I answer that,* Drunkenness may be understood in two ways. First, it may signify the defect itself of a man resulting from his drinking much wine, the consequence being that he loses the use of reason. In this sense drunkenness denotes not a sin, but a penal defect resulting from a fault. Secondly, drunkenness may denote the act by which a man incurs this defect. This act may cause drunkenness in two ways. In one way, through the wine being too strong, without the drinker being cognizant of this: and in this way too, drunkenness may occur without sin, especially if it is not through his negligence, and thus we believe that Noah was made drunk as related in Gen. 9. In another way drunkenness may result from inordinate concupiscence and use of wine: in this way it is accounted a sin, and is comprised under gluttony as a species under its genus. For gluttony is divided into "surfeiting [Douay: 'rioting'] and drunkenness," which are forbidden by the Apostle (Rom. 13:13).

Reply Obj. 1: As the Philosopher says (Ethic. iii, 11), insensibility which is opposed to temperance "is not very common," so that like its species which are opposed to the species of intemperance it has no name. Hence the vice opposed to drunkenness is unnamed; and yet if a man were knowingly to abstain from wine to the extent of molesting nature grievously, he would not be free from sin.

Reply Obj. 2: This objection regards the resulting defect which is involuntary: whereas immoderate use of wine is voluntary, and it is in this that the sin consists.

Reply Obj. 3: Even as he that is drunk is excused if he knows not the strength of the wine, so too is he that invites another to drink excused from sin, if he be unaware that the drinker is the kind of person to be made drunk by the drink offered. But if ignorance be lacking neither is excused from sin.

Reply Obj. 4: Sometimes the correction of a sinner is to be foregone, as stated above (Q. 33, A. 6). Hence Augustine says in a letter (Ad Aurel. Episc. Ep. xxii), "Meseems, such things are cured not by bitterness, severity, harshness, but by teaching rather than commanding, by advice rather than threats. Such is the course to be followed with the majority of sinners: few are they whose sins should be treated with severity."

SECOND ARTICLE [II-II, Q. 150, Art. 2]

Whether Drunkenness Is a Mortal Sin?

Objection 1: It would seem that drunkenness is not a mortal sin. For Augustine says in a sermon on Purgatory [*Serm. civ in the Appendix to St. Augustine's works] that "drunkenness if indulged in assiduously, is a mortal sin." Now assiduity denotes a circumstance which does not change the species of a sin; so that it cannot aggravate a sin infinitely, and make a mortal sin of a venial sin, as shown above (I-II, Q. 88, A. 5). Therefore if drunkenness is not a mortal sin for some other reason, neither is it for this.

Obj. 2: Further, Augustine says [*Serm. civ in the Appendix to St. Augustine's works]: "Whenever a man takes more meat and drink than is necessary, he should know that this is one of the lesser sins." Now the lesser sins are called venial. Therefore drunkenness, which is caused by immoderate drink, is a venial sin.

Obj. 3: Further, no mortal sin should be committed on the score of medicine. Now some drink too much at the advice of the physician, that they may be purged by vomiting; and from this excessive drink drunkenness ensues. Therefore drunkenness is not a mortal sin.

*On the contrary,* We read in the Canons of the apostles (Can. xli, xlii): "A bishop, priest or deacon who is given to drunkenness or gambling, or incites others thereto, must either cease or be deposed; a subdeacon, reader or precentor who does these things must either give them up or be excommunicated; the same applies to the laity." Now such punishments are not inflicted save for mortal sins. Therefore drunkenness is a mortal sin.

*I answer that,* The sin of drunkenness, as stated in the foregoing Article, consists in the immoderate use and concupiscence of wine. Now this may happen to a man in three ways. First, so that he knows not the drink to be immoderate and intoxicating: and then drunkenness may be without sin, as stated above (A. 1). Secondly, so that he perceives the drink to be immoderate, but without knowing it to be intoxicating, and then drunkenness may involve a venial sin. Thirdly, it may happen that a man is well aware that the drink is immoderate and intoxicating, and yet he would rather be drunk than abstain from drink. Such a man is a drunkard properly speaking, because morals take their species not from things that occur accidentally and beside the intention, but from that which is directly intended. In this way drunkenness is a mortal sin, because then a man willingly and knowingly deprives himself of the use of reason, whereby he performs virtuous deeds and avoids sin, and thus he sins mortally by running the risk of falling into sin. For Ambrose says (De Patriarch. [*De Abraham i.]): "We learn that we should shun drunkenness, which prevents us from avoiding grievous sins. For the things we avoid when sober, we unknowingly commit through drunkenness." Therefore drunkenness, properly speaking, is a mortal sin.

Reply Obj. 1: Assiduity makes drunkenness a mortal sin, not on account of the mere repetition of the act, but because it is impossible for a man to become drunk assiduously, without exposing himself to drunkenness knowingly and willingly, since he has many times experienced the strength of wine and his own liability to drunkenness.

Reply Obj. 2: To take more meat or drink than is necessary belongs to the vice of gluttony, which is not always a mortal sin: but knowingly to take too much drink to the point of being drunk, is a mortal sin. Hence Augustine says (Confess. x, 31): "Drunkenness is far from me: Thou wilt have mercy, that it come not near me. But full feeding sometimes hath crept upon Thy servant."

Reply Obj. 3: As stated above (Q. 141, A. 6), meat and drink should be moderate in accordance with the demands of the body's health. Wherefore, just as it happens sometimes that the meat and drink which are moderate for a healthy man are immoderate for a sick man, so too it may happen conversely, that what is excessive for a healthy man is moderate for one that is ailing. In this way when a man eats or drinks much at the physician's advice in order to provoke vomiting, he is not to be deemed to have taken excessive meat or drink. There is, however, no need for intoxicating drink in order to procure vomiting, since this is caused by drinking lukewarm water: wherefore this is no sufficient cause for excusing a man from drunkenness.

THIRD ARTICLE [II-II, Q. 150, Art. 3]

Whether drunkenness is the gravest of sins?

Objection 1: It would seem that drunkenness is the gravest of sins. For Chrysostom says (Hom. lviii in Matth.) that "nothing gains the devil's favor so much as drunkenness and lust, the mother of all the vices." And it is written in the Decretals (Dist. xxxv, can. Ante omnia): "Drunkenness, more than anything else, is to be avoided by the clergy, for it foments and fosters all the vices."

Obj. 2: Further, from the very fact that a thing excludes the good of reason, it is a sin. Now this is especially the effect of drunkenness. Therefore drunkenness is the greatest of sins.

Obj. 3: Further, the gravity of a sin is shown by the gravity of its punishment. Now seemingly drunkenness is punished most severely; for Ambrose says [*De Elia et de Jejunio v] that "there would be no slavery, were there no drunkards." Therefore drunkenness is the greatest of sins.

*On the contrary,* According to Gregory (Moral. xxxiii, 12), spiritual vices are greater than carnal vices. Now drunkenness is one of the carnal vices. Therefore it is not the greatest of sins.

*I answer that,* A thing is said to be evil because it removes a good. Wherefore the greater the good removed by an evil, the graver the evil. Now it is evident that a Divine good is greater than a human good. Wherefore the sins that are directly against God are graver than the sin of drunkenness, which is directly opposed to the good of human reason.

Reply Obj. 1: Man is most prone to sins of intemperance, because such like concupiscences and pleasures are connatural to us, and for this reason these sins are said to find greatest favor with the devil, not for being graver than other sins, but because they occur more frequently among men.

Reply Obj. 2: The good of reason is hindered in two ways: in one way by that which is contrary to reason, in another by that which takes away the use of reason. Now that which is contrary to reason has more the character of an evil, than that which takes away the use of reason for a time, since the use of reason, which is taken away by drunkenness, may be either good or evil, whereas the goods of virtue, which are taken away by things that are contrary to reason, are always good.

Reply Obj. 3: Drunkenness was the occasional cause of slavery, in so far as Cham brought the curse of slavery on to his descendants, for having laughed at his father when the latter was made drunk. But slavery was not the direct punishment of drunkenness.

FOURTH ARTICLE [II-II, Q. 150, Art. 4]

Whether Drunkenness Excuses from Sin?

Objection 1: It would seem that drunkenness does not excuse from sin. For the Philosopher says (Ethic. iii, 5) that "the drunkard deserves double punishment." Therefore drunkenness aggravates a sin instead of excusing from it.

Obj. 2: Further, one sin does not excuse another, but increases it. Now drunkenness is a sin. Therefore it is not an excuse for sin.

Obj. 3: Further, the Philosopher says (Ethic. vii, 3) that just as man's reason is tied by drunkenness, so is it by concupiscence. But concupiscence is not an excuse for sin: neither therefore is drunkenness.

*On the contrary,* According to Augustine (Contra Faust. xxii, 43), Lot was to be excused from incest on account of drunkenness.

*I answer that,* Two things are to be observed in drunkenness, as stated above (A. 1), namely the resulting defect and the preceding act. On the part of the resulting defect whereby the use of reason is fettered, drunkenness may be an excuse for sin, in so far as it causes an act to be involuntary through ignorance. But on the part of the preceding act, a distinction would seem necessary; because, if the drunkenness that results from that act be without sin, the subsequent sin is entirely excused from fault, as perhaps in the case of Lot. If, however, the preceding act was sinful, the person is not altogether excused from the subsequent sin, because the latter is rendered voluntary through the voluntariness of the preceding act, inasmuch as it was through doing something unlawful that he fell into the subsequent sin. Nevertheless, the resulting sin is diminished, even as the character of voluntariness is diminished. Wherefore Augustine says (Contra Faust. xxii, 44) that "Lot's guilt is to be measured, not by the incest, but by his drunkenness."

Reply Obj. 1: The Philosopher does not say that the drunkard deserves more severe punishment, but that he deserves double punishment for his twofold sin. Or we may reply that he is speaking in view of the law of a certain Pittacus, who, as stated in Polit. ii, 9, ordered "those guilty of assault while drunk to be more severely punished than if they had been sober, because they do wrong in more ways than one." In this, as Aristotle observes (Polit. ii, 9), "he seems to have considered the advantage," namely of the prevention of wrong, "rather than the leniency which one should have for drunkards," seeing that they are not in possession of their faculties.

Reply Obj. 2: Drunkenness may be an excuse for sin, not in the point of its being itself a sin, but in the point of the defect that results from it, as stated above.

Reply Obj. 3: Concupiscence does not altogether fetter the reason, as drunkenness does, unless perchance it be so vehement as to make a man insane. Yet the passion of concupiscence diminishes sin, because it is less grievous to sin through weakness than through malice.

## QUESTION 151

OF CHASTITY (In Four Articles)

We must next consider chastity: (1) The virtue itself of chastity: (2) virginity, which is a part of chastity: (3) lust, which is the contrary vice. Under the first head there are four points of inquiry:

(1) Whether chastity is a virtue?

(2) Whether it is a general virtue?

(3) Whether it is a virtue distinct from abstinence?

(4) Of its relation to purity.

FIRST ARTICLE [II-II, Q. 151, Art. 1]

Whether Chastity Is a Virtue?

Objection 1: It would seem that chastity is not a virtue. For here we are treating of virtues of the soul. But chastity, seemingly, belongs to the body: for a person is said to be chaste because he behaves in a certain way as regards the use of certain parts of the body. Therefore chastity is not a virtue.

Obj. 2: Further, virtue is "a voluntary habit," as stated in *Ethic.* ii, 6. But chastity, apparently, is not voluntary, since it can be taken away by force from a woman to whom violence is done. Therefore it seems that chastity is not a virtue.

Obj. 3: Further, there is no virtue in unbelievers. Yet some unbelievers are chaste. Therefore chastity is not a virtue.

Obj. 4: Further, the fruits are distinct from the virtues. But chastity is reckoned among the fruits (Gal. 5:23). Therefore chastity is not a virtue.

*On the contrary,* Augustine says (De Decem Chord. [*Serm. ix de Tempore]): "Whereas thou shouldst excel thy wife in virtue, since chastity is a virtue, thou yieldest to the first onslaught of lust, while thou wishest thy wife to be victorious."

*I answer that,* Chastity takes its name from the fact that reason "chastises" concupiscence, which, like a child, needs curbing, as the Philosopher states (Ethic. iii, 12). Now the essence of human virtue consists in being something moderated by reason, as shown above (I-II, Q. 64, A. 1). Therefore it is evident that chastity is a virtue.

Reply Obj. 1: Chastity does indeed reside in the soul as its subject, though its matter is in the body. For it belongs to chastity that a man make moderate use of bodily members in accordance with the judgment of his reason and the choice of his will.

Reply Obj. 2: As Augustine says (De Civ. Dei i, 18), "so long as her mind holds to its purpose, whereby she has merited to be holy even in body, not even the violence of another's lust can deprive her body of its holiness, which is safeguarded by her persevering continency." He also says (De Civ. Dei i, 18) that "in the mind there is a virtue which is the companion of fortitude, whereby it is resolved to suffer any evil whatsoever rather than consent to evil."

Reply Obj. 3: As Augustine says (Contra Julian. iv, 3), "it is impossible to have any true virtue unless one be truly just; nor is it possible to be just unless one live by faith." Whence he argues that in unbelievers there is neither true chastity, nor any other virtue, because, to wit, they are not referred to the due end, and as he adds (Contra Julian. iv, 3) "virtues are distinguished from vices not by their functions," i.e. their acts, "but by their ends."

Reply Obj. 4: Chastity is a virtue in so far as it works in accordance with reason, but in so far as it delights in its act, it is reckoned among the fruits.

SECOND ARTICLE [II-II, Q. 151, Art. 2]

Whether Chastity Is a General Virtue?

Objection 1: It would seem that chastity is a general virtue. For Augustine says (De Mendacio xx) that "chastity of the mind is the well-ordered movement of the mind that does not prefer the lesser to the greater things." But this belongs to every virtue. Therefore chastity is a general virtue.

Obj. 2: Further, "Chastity" takes its name from "chastisement" [*Cf. A. 1]. Now every movement of the appetitive part should be chastised by reason. Since, then, every moral virtue curbs some movement of the appetite, it seems that every moral virtue is chastity.

Obj. 3: Further, chastity is opposed to fornication. But fornication seems to belong to every kind of sin: for it is written (Ps. 72:27): "Thou shalt destroy [Vulg.: 'hast destroyed'] all them that go awhoring from [Douay: 'are disloyal to'] Thee." Therefore chastity is a general virtue.

*On the contrary,* Macrobius [*In Somn. Scip. i, 8] reckons it to be a part of temperance.

*I answer that,* The word "chastity" is employed in two ways. First, properly; and thus it is a special virtue having a special matter, namely the concupiscences relating to venereal pleasures. Secondly, the word "chastity" is employed metaphorically: for just as a mingling of bodies conduces to venereal pleasure which is the proper matter of chastity and of lust its contrary vice, so too the spiritual union of the mind with certain things conduces to a pleasure which is the matter of a spiritual chastity metaphorically speaking, as well as of a spiritual fornication likewise metaphorically so called. For if the human mind delight in the spiritual union with that to which it behooves it to be united, namely God, and refrains from delighting in union with other things against the requirements of the order established by God, this may be called a spiritual chastity, according to 2 Cor. 11:2, "I have espoused you to one husband, that I may present you as a chaste virgin to Christ." If, on the other hand, the mind be united to any other things whatsoever, against the prescription of the Divine order, it will be called spiritual fornication, according to Jer. 3:1, "But thou hast prostituted thyself to many lovers." Taking chastity in this sense, it is a general virtue, because every virtue withdraws the human mind from delighting in a union with unlawful things. Nevertheless, the essence of this chastity consists principally in charity and the other theological virtues, whereby the human mind is united to God.

Reply Obj. 1: This argument takes chastity in the metaphorical sense.

Reply Obj. 2: As stated above (A. 1; Q. 142, A. 2), the concupiscence of that which gives pleasure is especially likened to a child, because the desire of pleasure is connatural to us, especially of pleasures of touch which are directed to the maintenance of nature. Hence it is that if the concupiscence of such pleasures be fostered by consenting to it, it will wax very strong, as in the case of a child left to his own will. Wherefore the concupiscence of these pleasures stands in very great need of being chastised: and consequently chastity is applied antonomastically to such like concupiscences, even as fortitude is about those matters wherein we stand in the greatest need of strength of mind.

Reply Obj. 3: This argument considers spiritual fornication metaphorically so called, which is opposed to spiritual chastity, as stated.

THIRD ARTICLE [II-II, Q. 151, Art. 3]

Whether Chastity Is a Distinct Virtue from Abstinence?

Objection 1: It would seem that chastity is not a distinct virtue from abstinence. Because where the matter is generically the same, one virtue suffices. Now it would seem that things pertaining to the same sense are of one genus. Therefore, since pleasures of the palate which are the matter of abstinence, and venereal pleasures which are the matter of chastity, pertain to the touch, it seems that chastity is not a distinct virtue from abstinence.

Obj. 2: Further, the Philosopher (Ethic. iii, 12) likens all vices of intemperance to childish sins, which need chastising. Now "chastity" takes its name from "chastisement" of the contrary vices. Since then certain vices are bridled by abstinence, it seems that abstinence is chastity.

Obj. 3: Further, the pleasures of the other senses are the concern of temperance in so far as they refer to pleasures of touch; which are the matter of temperance. Now pleasures of the palate, which are the matter of abstinence, are directed to venereal pleasures, which are the matter of chastity: wherefore Jerome says [*Ep. cxlvii ad Amand. Cf. Gratian, Dist. xliv.], commenting on Titus 1:7, "Not given to wine, no striker," etc.: "The belly and the organs of generation are neighbors, that the neighborhood of the organs may indicate their complicity in vice." Therefore abstinence and chastity are not distinct virtues.

*On the contrary,* The Apostle (2 Cor. 6:5, 6) reckons "chastity" together with "fastings" which pertain to abstinence.

*I answer that,* As stated above (Q. 141, A. 4), temperance is properly about the concupiscences of the pleasures of touch: so that where there are different kinds of pleasure, there are different virtues comprised under temperance. Now pleasures are proportionate to the actions whose perfections they are, as stated in *Ethic.* ix, 4, 5: and it is evident that actions connected with the use of food whereby the nature of the individual is maintained differ generically from actions connected with the use of matters venereal, whereby the nature of the species is preserved. Therefore chastity, which is about venereal pleasures, is a distinct virtue from abstinence, which is about pleasures of the palate.

Reply Obj. 1: Temperance is chiefly about pleasures of touch, not as regards the sense's judgment concerning the objects of touch, which judgment is of uniform character concerning all such objects, but as regards the use itself of those objects, as stated in *Ethic.* iii, 10. Now the uses of meats, drinks, and venereal matters differ in character. Wherefore there must needs be different virtues, though they regard the one sense.

Reply Obj. 2: Venereal pleasures are more impetuous, and are more oppressive on the reason than the pleasures of the palate: and therefore they are in greater need of chastisement and restraint, since if one consent to them this increases the force of concupiscence and weakens the strength of the mind. Hence Augustine says (Soliloq. i, 10): "I consider that nothing so casts down the manly mind from its heights as the fondling of women, and those bodily contacts which belong to the married state."

Reply Obj. 3: The pleasures of the other senses do not pertain to the maintenance of man's nature, except in so far as they are directed to pleasures of touch. Wherefore in the matter of such pleasures there is no other virtue comprised under temperance. But the pleasures of the palate, though directed somewhat to venereal pleasures, are essentially directed to the preservation of man's life: wherefore by their very nature they have a special virtue, although this virtue which is called abstinence directs its act to chastity as its end.

FOURTH ARTICLE [II-II, Q. 151, Art. 4]

Whether Purity Belongs Especially to Chastity?

Objection 1: It would seem that purity does not belong especially to chastity. For Augustine says (De Civ. Dei i, 18) that "purity is a virtue of the soul." Therefore it is not something belonging to chastity, but is of itself a virtue distinct from chastity.

Obj. 2: Further, *pudicitia* (purity) is derived from pudor, which is equivalent to shame. Now shame, according to Damascene [*De Fide Orth. ii, 15], is about a disgraceful act, and this is common to all sinful acts. Therefore purity belongs no more to chastity than to the other virtues.

Obj. 3: Further, the Philosopher says (Ethic. iii, 12) that "every kind of intemperance is most deserving of reproach." Now it would seem to belong to purity to avoid all that is deserving of reproach. Therefore purity belongs to all the parts of temperance, and not especially to chastity.

*On the contrary,* Augustine says (De Perseverantia xx): "We must give praise to purity, that he who has ears to hear, may put to none but a lawful use the organs intended for procreation." Now the use of these organs is the proper matter of chastity. Therefore purity belongs properly to chastity.

*I answer that,* As stated above (Obj. 2), pudicitia (purity) takes its name from *pudor,* which signifies shame. Hence purity must needs be properly about the things of which man is most ashamed. Now men are most ashamed of venereal acts, as Augustine remarks (De Civ. Dei xiv, 18), so much so that even the conjugal act, which is adorned by the honesty [*Cf. Q. 145] of marriage, is not devoid of shame: and this because the movement of the organs of generation is not subject to the command of reason, as are the movements of the other external members. Now man is ashamed not only of this sexual union but also of all the signs thereof, as the Philosopher observes (Rhet. ii, 6). Consequently purity regards venereal matters properly, and especially the signs thereof, such as impure looks, kisses, and touches. And since the latter are more wont to be observed, purity regards rather these external signs, while chastity regards rather sexual union. Therefore purity is directed to chastity, not as a virtue distinct therefrom, but as expressing a circumstance of chastity. Nevertheless the one is sometimes used to designate the other.

Reply Obj. 1: Augustine is here speaking of purity as designating chastity.

Reply Obj. 2: Although every vice has a certain disgrace, the vices of intemperance are especially disgraceful, as stated above (Q. 142, A. 4).

Reply Obj. 3: Among the vices of intemperance, venereal sins are most deserving of reproach, both on account of the insubordination of the genital organs, and because by these sins especially, the reason is absorbed.

## QUESTION 152

OF VIRGINITY (In Five Articles)

We must now consider virginity: and under this head there are five points of inquiry:

(1) In what does virginity consist?

(2) Whether it is lawful?

(3) Whether it is a virtue?

(4) Of its excellence in comparison with marriage;

(5) Of its excellence in comparison with the other virtues.

FIRST ARTICLE [II-II, Q. 152, Art. 1]

Whether Virginity Consists in Integrity of the Flesh?

Objection 1: It would seem that virginity does not consist in integrity of the flesh. For Augustine says (De Nup. et Concup.) [*The quotation is from De Sancta Virgin. xiii] that "virginity is the continual meditation on incorruption in a corruptible flesh." But meditation does not concern the flesh. Therefore virginity is not situated in the flesh.

Obj. 2: Further, virginity denotes a kind of purity. Now Augustine says (De Civ. Dei i, 18) that "purity dwells in the soul." Therefore virginity is not incorruption of the flesh.

Obj. 3: Further, the integrity of the flesh would seem to consist in the seal of virginal purity. Yet sometimes the seal is broken without loss of virginity. For Augustine says (De Civ. Dei i, 18) that "those organs may be injured through being wounded by mischance. Physicians, too, sometimes do for the sake of health that which makes one shudder to see: and a midwife has been known to destroy by touch the proof of virginity that she sought." And he adds: "Nobody, I think, would be so foolish as to deem this maiden to have forfeited even bodily sanctity, though she lost the integrity of that organ." Therefore virginity does not consist in incorruption of the flesh.

Obj. 4: Further, corruption of the flesh consists chiefly in resolution of the semen: and this may take place without copulation, whether one be asleep or awake. Yet seemingly virginity is not lost without copulation: for Augustine says (De Virgin. xiii) that "virginal integrity and holy continency that refrains from all sexual intercourse is the portion of angels." Therefore virginity does not consist in incorruption of the flesh.

*On the contrary,* Augustine says (De Virgin. viii) that "virginity is continence whereby integrity of the flesh is vowed, consecrated and observed in honor of the Creator of both soul and flesh."

*I answer that,* Virginity takes its name apparently from viror (freshness), and just as a thing is described as fresh and retaining its freshness, so long as it is not parched by excessive heat, so too, virginity denotes that the person possessed thereof is unseared by the heat of concupiscence which is experienced in achieving the greatest bodily pleasure which is that of sexual intercourse. Hence, Ambrose says (De Virgin. i, 5) that "virginal chastity is integrity free of pollution."

Now venereal pleasures offer three points for consideration. The first is on the part of the body, viz. the violation of the seal of virginity. The second is the link between that which concerns the soul and that which concerns the body, and this is the resolution of the semen, causing sensible pleasure. The third is entirely on the part of the soul, namely the purpose of attaining this pleasure. Of these three the first is accidental to the moral act, which as such must be considered in reference to the soul. The second stands in the relation of matter to the moral act, since the sensible passions are the matters of moral acts. But the third stands in the position of form and complement, because the essence of morality is perfected in that which concerns the reason. Since then virginity consists in freedom from the aforesaid corruption, it follows that the integrity of the bodily organ is accidental to virginity; while freedom from pleasure in resolution of the semen is related thereto materially; and the purpose of perpetually abstaining from this pleasure is the formal and completive element in virginity.

Reply Obj. 1: This definition of Augustine's expresses directly that which is formal in virginity. For "meditation" denotes reason's purpose; and the addition "perpetual" does not imply that a virgin must always retain this meditation actually, but that she should bear in mind the purpose of always persevering therein. The material element is expressed indirectly by the words "on incorruption in a corruptible body." This is added to show the difficulty of virginity: for if the flesh were incorruptible, it would not be difficult to maintain a perpetual meditation on incorruption.

Reply Obj. 2: It is true that purity, as to its essence, is in the soul; but as to its matter, it is in the body: and it is the same with virginity. Wherefore Augustine says (De Virgin. viii) that "although virginity resides in the flesh," and for this reason is a bodily quality, "yet it is a spiritual thing, which a holy continency fosters and preserves."

Reply Obj. 3: As stated above, the integrity of a bodily organ is accidental to virginity, in so far as a person, through purposely abstaining from venereal pleasure, retains the integrity of a bodily organ. Hence if the organ lose its integrity by chance in some other way, this is no more prejudicial to virginity than being deprived of a hand or foot.

Reply Obj. 4: Pleasure resulting from resolution of semen may arise in two ways. If this be the result of the mind's purpose, it destroys virginity, whether copulation takes place or not. Augustine, however, mentions copulation, because such like resolution is the ordinary and natural result thereof. In another way this may happen beside the purpose of the mind, either during sleep, or through violence and without the mind's consent, although the flesh derives pleasure from it, or again through weakness of nature, as in the case of those who are subject to a flow of semen. In such cases virginity is not forfeit, because such like pollution is not the result of impurity which excludes virginity.

SECOND ARTICLE [II-II, Q. 152, Art. 2]

Whether Virginity Is Unlawful?

Objection 1: It would seem that virginity is unlawful. For whatever is contrary to a precept of the natural law is unlawful. Now just as the words of Gen. 2:16, "Of every tree" that is in "paradise, thou shalt eat," indicate a precept of the natural law, in reference to the preservation of the individual, so also the words of Gen. 1:28, "Increase and multiply, and fill the earth," express a precept of the natural law, in reference to the preservation of the species. Therefore just as it would be a sin to abstain from all food, as this would be to act counter to the good of the individual, so too it is a sin to abstain altogether from the act of procreation, for this is to act against the good of the species.

Obj. 2: Further, whatever declines from the mean of virtue is apparently sinful. Now virginity declines from the mean of virtue, since it abstains from all venereal pleasures: for the Philosopher says (Ethic. ii, 2), that "he who revels in every pleasure, and abstains from not even one, is intemperate: but he who refrains from all is loutish and insensible." Therefore virginity is something sinful.

Obj. 3: Further, punishment is not due save for a vice. Now in olden times those were punished who led a celibate life, as Valerius Maximus asserts [*Dict. Fact. Mem. ii, 9]. Hence according to Augustine (De Vera Relig. iii) Plato "is said to have sacrificed to nature, in order that he might atone for his perpetual continency as though it were a sin." Therefore virginity is a sin.

*On the contrary,* No sin is a matter of direct counsel. But virginity is a matter of direct counsel: for it is written (1 Cor. 7:25): "Concerning virgins I have no commandment of the Lord: but I give counsel." Therefore virginity is not an unlawful thing.

*I answer that,* In human acts, those are sinful which are against right reason. Now right reason requires that things directed to an end should be used in a measure proportionate to that end. Again, man's good is threefold as stated in *Ethic.* i, 8; one consisting in external things, for instance riches; another, consisting in bodily goods; the third, consisting in the goods of the soul among which the goods of the contemplative life take precedence of the goods of the active life, as the Philosopher shows (Ethic. x, 7), and as our Lord declared (Luke 10:42), "Mary hath chosen the better part." Of these goods those that are external are directed to those which belong to the body, and those which belong to the body are directed to those which belong to the soul; and furthermore those which belong to the active life are directed to those which belong to the life of contemplation. Accordingly, right reason dictates that one use external goods in a measure proportionate to the body, and in like manner as regards the rest. Wherefore if a man refrain from possessing certain things (which otherwise it were good for him to possess), for the sake of his body's good, or of the contemplation of truth, this is not sinful, but in accord with right reason. In like manner if a man abstain from bodily pleasures, in order more freely to give himself to the contemplation of truth, this is in accordance with the rectitude of reason. Now holy virginity refrains from all venereal pleasure in order more freely to have leisure for Divine contemplation: for the Apostle says (1 Cor. 7:34): "The unmarried woman and the virgin thinketh on the things of the Lord: that she may be holy in both body and in spirit. But she that is married thinketh on the things of the world, how she may please her husband." Therefore it follows that virginity instead of being sinful is worthy of praise.

Reply Obj. 1: A precept implies a duty, as stated above (Q. 122, A. 1). Now there are two kinds of duty. There is the duty that has to be fulfilled by one person; and a duty of this kind cannot be set aside without sin. The other duty has to be fulfilled by the multitude, and the fulfilment of this kind of duty is not binding on each one of the multitude. For the multitude has many obligations which cannot be discharged by the individual; but are fulfilled by one person doing this, and another doing that. Accordingly the precept of natural law which binds man to eat must needs be fulfilled by each individual, otherwise the individual cannot be sustained. On the other hand, the precept of procreation regards the whole multitude of men, which needs not only to multiply in body, but also to advance spiritually. Wherefore sufficient provision is made for the human multitude, if some betake themselves to carnal procreation, while others abstaining from this betake themselves to the contemplation of Divine things, for the beauty and welfare of the whole human race. Thus too in an army, some take sentry duty, others are standard-bearers, and others fight with the sword: yet all these things are necessary for the multitude, although they cannot be done by one person.

Reply Obj. 2: The person who, beside the dictate of right reason, abstains from all pleasures through aversion, as it were, for pleasure as such, is insensible as a country lout. But a virgin does not refrain from every pleasure, but only from that which is venereal: and abstains therefrom according to right reason, as stated above. Now the mean of virtue is fixed with reference, not to quantity but to right reason, as stated in *Ethic.* ii, 6: wherefore it is said of the magnanimous (Ethic. iv, 3) that "in point of quantity he goes to the extreme, but in point of becomingness he follows the mean."

Reply Obj. 3: Laws are framed according to what occurs more frequently. Now it seldom happened in olden times that anyone refrained from all venereal pleasure through love of the contemplation of truth: as Plato alone is related to have done. Hence it was not through thinking this a sin, that he offered sacrifice, but "because he yielded to the false opinion of his fellow countrymen," as Augustine remarks (De Vera Relig. iii).

THIRD ARTICLE [II-II, Q. 152, Art. 3]

Whether Virginity Is a Virtue?

Objection 1: It would seem that virginity is not a virtue. For "no virtue is in us by nature," as the Philosopher says (Ethic. ii, 1). Now virginity is in us by nature, since all are virgins when born. Therefore virginity is not a virtue.

Obj. 2: Further, whoever has one virtue has all virtues, as stated above (I-II, Q. 65, A. 1). Yet some have other virtues without having virginity: else, since none can go to the heavenly kingdom without virtue, no one could go there without virginity, which would involve the condemnation of marriage. Therefore virginity is not a virtue.

Obj. 3: Further, every virtue is recovered by penance. But virginity is not recovered by penance: wherefore Jerome says [*Ep. xxii ad Eustoch.]: "Other things God can do, but He cannot restore the virgin after her downfall." Therefore seemingly virginity is not a virtue.

Obj. 4: Further, no virtue is lost without sin. Yet virginity is lost without sin, namely by marriage. Therefore virginity is not a virtue.

Obj. 5: Further, virginity is condivided with widowhood and conjugal purity. But neither of these is a virtue. Therefore virginity is not a virtue.

*On the contrary,* Ambrose says (De Virgin. i, 3): "Love of virginity moves us to say something about virginity, lest by passing it over we should seem to cast a slight on what is a virtue of high degree."

*I answer that,* As stated above (A. 1), the formal and completive element in virginity is the purpose of abstaining from venereal pleasure, which purpose is rendered praiseworthy by its end, in so far, to wit, as this is done in order to have leisure for Divine things: while the material element in virginity is integrity of the flesh free of all experience of venereal pleasure. Now it is manifest that where a good action has a special matter through having a special excellence, there is a special kind of virtue: for example, magnificence which is about great expenditure is for this reason a special virtue distinct from liberality, which is about all uses of money in general. Now to keep oneself free from the experience of venereal pleasure has an excellence of its own deserving of greater praise than keeping oneself free from inordinate venereal pleasure. Wherefore virginity is a special virtue being related to chastity as magnificence to liberality.

Reply Obj. 1: Men have from their birth that which is material in virginity, namely integrity of the flesh and freedom from venereal experience. But they have not that which is formal in virginity, namely the purpose of safeguarding this integrity for God's sake, which purpose gives virginity its character of virtue. Hence Augustine says (De Virgin. xi): "Nor do we praise virgins for being virgins, but, because their virginity is consecrated to God by holy continency."

Reply Obj. 2: Virtues are connected together by reason of that which is formal in them, namely charity, or by reason of prudence, as stated above (Q. 129, A. 3, ad 2), but not by reason of that which is material in them. For nothing hinders a virtuous man from providing the matter of one virtue, and not the matter of another virtue: thus a poor man has the matter of temperance, but not that of magnificence. It is in this way that one who has the other virtues lacks the matter of virginity, namely the aforesaid integrity of the flesh: nevertheless he can have that which is formal in virginity, his mind being so prepared that he has the purpose of safeguarding this same integrity of the flesh, should it be fitting for him to do so: even as a poor man may be so prepared in mind as to have the purpose of being magnificent in his expenditure, were he in a position to do so: or again as a prosperous man is so prepared in mind as to purpose bearing misfortune with equanimity: without which preparedness of the mind no man can be virtuous.

Reply Obj. 3: Virtue can be recovered by penance as regards that which is formal in virtue, but not as to that which is material therein. For if a magnificent man has squandered all his wealth he does not recover his riches by repenting of his sin. In like manner a person who has lost virginity by sin, recovers by repenting, not the matter of virginity but the purpose of virginity.

As regards the matter of virginity there is that which can be miraculously restored by God, namely the integrity of the organ, which we hold to be accidental to virginity: while there is something else which cannot be restored even by miracle, to wit, that one who has experienced venereal lust should cease to have had that experience. For God cannot make that which is done not to have been done, as stated in the First Part (Q. 25, A. 4).

Reply Obj. 4: Virginity as a virtue denotes the purpose, confirmed by vow, of observing perpetual integrity. For Augustine says (De Virgin. viii) that "by virginity, integrity of the flesh is vowed, consecrated and observed in honor of the Creator of both soul and flesh." Hence virginity, as a virtue, is never lost without sin.

Reply Obj. 5: Conjugal chastity is deserving of praise merely because it abstains from unlawful pleasures: hence no excellence attaches to it above that of chastity in general. Widowhood, however, adds something to chastity in general; but it does not attain to that which is perfect in this matter, namely to entire freedom from venereal pleasure; virginity alone achieves this. Wherefore virginity alone is accounted a virtue above chastity, even as magnificence is reckoned above liberality.

FOURTH ARTICLE [II-II, Q. 152, Art. 4]

Whether Virginity Is More Excellent Than Marriage?

Objection 1: It would seem that virginity is not more excellent than marriage. For Augustine says (De Bono Conjug. xxi): "Continence was equally meritorious in John who remained unmarried and Abraham who begot children." Now a greater virtue has greater merit. Therefore virginity is not a greater virtue than conjugal chastity.

Obj. 2: Further, the praise accorded a virtuous man depends on his virtue. If, then, virginity were preferable to conjugal continence, it would seem to follow that every virgin is to be praised more than any married woman. But this is untrue. Therefore virginity is not preferable to marriage.

Obj. 3: Further, the common good takes precedence of the private good, according to the Philosopher (Ethic. i, 2). Now marriage is directed to the common good: for Augustine says (De Bono Conjug. xvi): "What food is to a man's wellbeing, such is sexual intercourse to the welfare of the human race." On the other hand, virginity is ordered to the individual good, namely in order to avoid what the Apostle calls the "tribulation of the flesh," to which married people are subject (1 Cor. 7:28). Therefore virginity is not greater than conjugal continence.

*On the contrary,* Augustine says (De Virgin. xix): "Both solid reason and the authority of Holy Writ show that neither is marriage sinful, nor is it to be equaled to the good of virginal continence or even to that of widowhood."

*I answer that,* According to Jerome (Contra Jovin. i) the error of Jovinian consisted in holding virginity not to be preferable to marriage. This error is refuted above all by the example of Christ Who both chose a virgin for His mother, and remained Himself a virgin, and by the teaching of the Apostle who (1 Cor. 7) counsels virginity as the greater good. It is also refuted by reason, both because a Divine good takes precedence of a human good, and because the good of the soul is preferable to the good of the body, and again because the good of the contemplative life is better than that of the active life. Now virginity is directed to the good of the soul in respect of the contemplative life, which consists in thinking "on the things of God" [Vulg.: 'the Lord'], whereas marriage is directed to the good of the body, namely the bodily increase of the human race, and belongs to the active life, since the man and woman who embrace the married life have to think "on the things of the world," as the Apostle says (1 Cor. 7:34). Without doubt therefore virginity is preferable to conjugal continence.

Reply Obj. 1: Merit is measured not only by the kind of action, but still more by the mind of the agent. Now Abraham had a mind so disposed, that he was prepared to observe virginity, if it were in keeping with the times for him to do so. Wherefore in him conjugal continence was equally meritorious with the virginal continence of John, as regards the essential reward, but not as regards the accidental reward. Hence Augustine says (De Bono Conjug. xxi) that both "the celibacy of John and the marriage of Abraham fought Christ's battle in keeping with the difference of the times: but John was continent even in deed, whereas Abraham was continent only in habit."

Reply Obj. 2: Though virginity is better than conjugal continence, a married person may be better than a virgin for two reasons. First, on the part of chastity itself; if to wit, the married person is more prepared in mind to observe virginity, if it should be expedient, than the one who is actually a virgin. Hence Augustine (De Bono Conjug. xxii) charges the virgin to say: "I am no better than Abraham, although the chastity of celibacy is better than the chastity of marriage." Further on he gives the reason for this: "For what I do now, he would have done better, if it were fitting for him to do it then; and what they did I would even do now if it behooved me now to do it." Secondly, because perhaps the person who is not a virgin has some more excellent virtue. Wherefore Augustine says (De Virgin. xliv): "Whence does a virgin know the things that belong to the Lord, however solicitous she be about them, if perchance on account of some mental fault she be not yet ripe for martyrdom, whereas this woman to whom she delighted in preferring herself is already able to drink the chalice of the Lord?"

Reply Obj. 3: The common good takes precedence of the private good, if it be of the same genus: but it may be that the private good is better generically. It is thus that the virginity that is consecrated to God is preferable to carnal fruitfulness. Hence Augustine says (De Virgin. ix): "It must be confessed that the fruitfulness of the flesh, even of those women who in these times seek naught else from marriage but children in order to make them servants of Christ, cannot compensate for lost virginity."

FIFTH ARTICLE [II-II, Q. 152, Art. 5]

Whether Virginity Is the Greatest of Virtues?

Objection 1: It would seem that virginity is the greatest of virtues. For Cyprian says (De Virgin. [*De Habitu Virg.]): "We address ourselves now to the virgins. Sublime is their glory, but no less exalted is their vocation. They are a flower of the Church's sowing, the pride and ornament of spiritual grace, the most honored portion of Christ's flock."

Obj. 2: Further, a greater reward is due to the greater virtue. Now the greatest reward is due to virginity, namely the hundredfold fruit, according to a gloss on Matt. 13:23. Therefore virginity is the greatest of the virtues.

Obj. 3: Further, the more a virtue conforms us to Christ, the greater it is. Now virginity above all conforms us to Christ; for it is declared in the Apocalypse (14:4) that virgins "follow the Lamb whithersoever He goeth," and (Apoc. 14:3) that they sing "a new canticle," which "no" other "man" could say. Therefore virginity is the greatest of the virtues.

*On the contrary,* Augustine says (De Virgin. xlvi): "No one, methinks, would dare prefer virginity to martyrdom," and (De Virgin. xlv): "The authority of the Church informs the faithful in no uncertain manner, so that they know in what place the martyrs and the holy virgins who have departed this life are commemorated in the Sacrament of the Altar." By this we are given to understand that martyrdom, and also the monastic state, are preferable to virginity.

*I answer that,* A thing may excel all others in two ways. First, in some particular genus: and thus virginity is most excellent, namely in the genus of chastity, since it surpasses the chastity both of widowhood and of marriage. And because comeliness is ascribed to chastity antonomastically, it follows that surpassing beauty is ascribed to chastity. Wherefore Ambrose says (De Virgin. i, 7): "Can anyone esteem any beauty greater than a virgin's, since she is beloved of her King, approved by her Judge, dedicated to her Lord, consecrated to her God?" Secondly, a thing may be most excellent simply, and in this way virginity is not the most excellent of the virtues. Because the end always excels that which is directed to the end; and the more effectively a thing is directed to the end, the better it is. Now the end which renders virginity praiseworthy is that one may have leisure for Divine things, as stated above (A. 4). Wherefore the theological virtues as well as the virtue of religion, the acts of which consist in being occupied about Divine things, are preferable to virginity. Moreover, martyrs work more mightily in order to cleave to God—since for this end they hold their own life in contempt; and those who dwell in monasteries—since for this end they give up their own will and all that they may possess—than virgins who renounce venereal pleasure for that same purpose. Therefore virginity is not simply the greatest of virtues.

Reply Obj. 1: Virgins are "the more honored portion of Christ's flock," and "their glory more sublime" in comparison with widows and married women.

Reply Obj. 2: The hundredfold fruit is ascribed to virginity, according to Jerome [*Ep. cxxiii ad Ageruch.], on account of its superiority to widowhood, to which the sixtyfold fruit is ascribed, and to marriage, to which is ascribed the thirtyfold fruit. But according to Augustine (De QQ. Evang. i, 9), "the hundredfold fruit is given to martyrs, the sixtyfold to virgins, and the thirtyfold to married persons." Wherefore it does not follow that virginity is simply the greatest of virtues, but only in comparison with other degrees of chastity.

Reply Obj. 3: Virgins "follow the Lamb whithersoever He goeth," because they imitate Christ, by integrity not only of the mind but also of the flesh, as Augustine says (De Virgin. xxvii). Wherefore they follow the Lamb in more ways, but this does not imply that they follow more closely, because other virtues make us cleave to God more closely by imitation of the mind. The "new hymn" which virgins alone sing, is their joy at having preserved integrity of the flesh.

# QUESTION 153

OF LUST (In Five Articles)

We must next consider the vice of lust which is opposed to chastity: (1) Lust in general; (2) its species. Under the first head there are five points of inquiry:

(1) What is the matter of lust?

(2) Whether all copulation is unlawful?

(3) Whether lust is a mortal sin?

(4) Whether lust is a capital vice?

(5) Concerning its daughters.

FIRST ARTICLE [II-II, Q. 153, Art. 1]

Whether the Matter of Lust Is Only Venereal Desires and Pleasures?

Objection 1: It would seem that the matter of lust is not only venereal desires and pleasures. For Augustine says (Confess. ii, 6) that "lust affects to be called surfeit and abundance." But surfeit regards meat and drink, while abundance refers to riches. Therefore lust is not properly about venereal desires and pleasures.

Obj. 2: Further, it is written (Prov. 20:1): "Wine is a lustful [Douay: 'luxurious'] thing." Now wine is connected with pleasure of meat and drink. Therefore these would seem to be the matter of lust.

Obj. 3: Further, lust is defined "as the desire of wanton pleasure" [*Alexander of Hales, Summ. Theol. ii, cxvli]. But wanton pleasure regards not only venereal matters but also many others. Therefore lust is not only about venereal desires and pleasures.

*On the contrary,* To the lustful it is said (De Vera Relig. iii [*Written by St. Augustine]): "He that soweth in the flesh, of the flesh shall reap corruption." Now the sowing of the flesh refers to venereal pleasures. Therefore these belong to lust.

*I answer that,* As Isidore says (Etym. x), "a lustful man is one who is debauched with pleasures." Now venereal pleasures above all debauch a man's mind. Therefore lust is especially concerned with such like pleasures.

Reply Obj. 1: Even as temperance chiefly and properly applies to pleasures of touch, yet consequently and by a kind of likeness is referred to other matters, so too, lust applies chiefly to venereal pleasures, which more than anything else work the greatest havoc in a man's mind, yet secondarily it applies to any other matters pertaining to excess. Hence a gloss on Gal. 5:19 says "lust is any kind of surfeit."

Reply Obj. 2: Wine is said to be a lustful thing, either in the sense in which surfeit in any matter is ascribed to lust, or because the use of too much wine affords an incentive to venereal pleasure.

Reply Obj. 3: Although wanton pleasure applies to other matters, the name of lust has a special application to venereal pleasures, to which also wantonness is specially applicable, as Augustine remarks (De Civ. xiv, 15, 16).

SECOND ARTICLE [II-II, Q. 153, Art. 2]

Whether No Venereal Act Can Be Without Sin?

Objection 1: It would seem that no venereal act can be without sin. For nothing but sin would seem to hinder virtue. Now every venereal act is a great hindrance to virtue. For Augustine says (Soliloq. i, 10): "I consider that nothing so casts down the manly mind from its height as the fondling of a woman, and those bodily contacts." Therefore, seemingly, no venereal act is without sin.

Obj. 2: Further, any excess that makes one forsake the good of reason is sinful, because virtue is corrupted by "excess" and "deficiency" as stated in *Ethic.* ii, 2. Now in every venereal act there is excess of pleasure, since it so absorbs the mind, that "it is incompatible with the act of understanding," as the Philosopher observes (Ethic. vii, 11); and as Jerome [*Origen, Hom. vi in Num.; Cf. Jerome, Ep. cxxiii ad Ageruch.] states, rendered the hearts of the prophets, for the moment, insensible to the spirit of prophecy. Therefore no venereal act can be without sin.

Obj. 3: Further, the cause is more powerful than its effect. Now original sin is transmitted to children by concupiscence, without which no venereal act is possible, as Augustine declares (De Nup. et Concup. i, 24). Therefore no venereal act can be without sin.

*On the contrary,* Augustine says (De Bono Conjug. xxv): "This is a sufficient answer to heretics, if only they will understand that no sin is committed in that which is against neither nature, nor morals, nor a commandment": and he refers to the act of sexual intercourse between the patriarchs of old and their several wives. Therefore not every venereal act is a sin.

*I answer that,* A sin, in human acts, is that which is against the order of reason. Now the order of reason consists in its ordering everything to its end in a fitting manner. Wherefore it is no sin if one, by the dictate of reason, makes use of certain things in a fitting manner and order for the end to which they are adapted, provided this end be something truly good. Now just as the preservation of the bodily nature of one individual is a true good, so, too, is the preservation of the nature of the human species a very great good. And just as the use of food is directed to the preservation of life in the individual, so is the use of venereal acts directed to the preservation of the whole human race. Hence Augustine says (De Bono Conjug. xvi): "What food is to a man's well being, such is sexual intercourse to the welfare of the whole human race." Wherefore just as the use of food can be without sin, if it be taken in due manner and order, as required for the welfare of the body, so also the use of venereal acts can be without sin, provided they be performed in due manner and order, in keeping with the end of human procreation.

Reply Obj. 1: A thing may be a hindrance to virtue in two ways. First, as regards the ordinary degree of virtue, and as to this nothing but sin is an obstacle to virtue. Secondly, as regards the perfect degree of virtue, and as to this virtue may be hindered by that which is not a sin, but a lesser good. In this way sexual intercourse casts down the mind not from virtue, but from the height, i.e. the perfection of virtue. Hence Augustine says (De Bono Conjug. viii): "Just as that was good which Martha did when busy about serving holy men, yet better still that which Mary did in hearing the word of God: so, too, we praise the good of Susanna's conjugal chastity, yet we prefer the good of the widow Anna, and much more that of the Virgin Mary."

Reply Obj. 2: As stated above (Q. 152, A. 2, ad 2; I-II, Q. 64, A. 2), the mean of virtue depends not on quantity but on conformity with right reason: and consequently the exceeding pleasure attaching to a venereal act directed according to reason, is not opposed to the mean of virtue. Moreover, virtue is not concerned with the amount of pleasure experienced by the external sense, as this depends on the disposition of the body; what matters is how much the interior appetite is affected by that pleasure. Nor does it follow that the act in question is contrary to virtue, from the fact that the free act of reason in considering spiritual things is incompatible with the aforesaid pleasure. For it is not contrary to virtue, if the act of reason be sometimes interrupted for something that is done in accordance with reason, else it would be against virtue for a person to set himself to sleep. That venereal concupiscence and pleasure are not subject to the command and moderation of reason, is due to the punishment of the first sin, inasmuch as the reason, for rebelling against God, deserved that its body should rebel against it, as Augustine says (De Civ. Dei xiii, 13).

Reply Obj. 3: As Augustine says (De Civ. Dei xiii, 13), "the child, shackled with original sin, is born of fleshly concupiscence (which is not imputed as sin to the regenerate) as of a daughter of sin." Hence it does not follow that the act in question is a sin, but that it contains something penal resulting from the first sin.

THIRD ARTICLE [II-II, Q. 153, Art. 3]

Whether the Lust That Is About Venereal Acts Can Be a Sin?

Objection 1: It would seem that lust about venereal acts cannot be a sin. For the venereal act consists in the emission of semen which is the surplus from food, according to the Philosopher (De Gener. Anim. i, 18). But there is no sin attaching to the emission of other superfluities. Therefore neither can there be any sin in venereal acts.

Obj. 2: Further, everyone can lawfully make what use he pleases of what is his. But in the venereal act a man uses only what is his own, except perhaps in adultery or rape. Therefore there can be no sin in venereal acts, and consequently lust is no sin.

Obj. 3: Further, every sin has an opposite vice. But, seemingly, no vice is opposed to lust. Therefore lust is not a sin.

*On the contrary,* The cause is more powerful than its effect. Now wine is forbidden on account of lust, according to the saying of the Apostle (Eph. 5:18), "Be not drunk with wine wherein is lust [Douay: 'luxury']." Therefore lust is forbidden.

Further, it is numbered among the works of the flesh: Gal. 5:19 [Douay: 'luxury'].

*I answer that,* The more necessary a thing is, the more it behooves one to observe the order of reason in its regard; wherefore the more sinful it becomes if the order of reason be forsaken. Now the use of venereal acts, as stated in the foregoing Article, is most necessary for the common good, namely the preservation of the human race. Wherefore there is the greatest necessity for observing the order of reason in this matter: so that if anything be done in this connection against the dictate of reason's ordering, it will be a sin. Now lust consists essentially in exceeding the order and mode of reason in the matter of venereal acts. Wherefore without any doubt lust is a sin.

Reply Obj. 1: As the Philosopher says in the same book (De Gener. Anim. i, 18), "the semen is a surplus that is needed." For it is said to be superfluous, because it is the residue from the action of the nutritive power, yet it is needed for the work of the generative power. But the other superfluities of the human body are such as not to be needed, so that it matters not how they are emitted, provided one observe the decencies of social life. It is different with the emission of semen, which should be accomplished in a manner befitting the end for which it is needed.

Reply Obj. 2: As the Apostle says (1 Cor. 6:20) in speaking against lust, "You are bought with a great price: glorify and bear God in your body." Wherefore by inordinately using the body through lust a man wrongs God Who is the Supreme Lord of our body. Hence Augustine says (De Decem. Chord. 10 [*Serm. ix (xcvi de Temp.)]): "God Who thus governs His servants for their good, not for His, made this order and commandment, lest unlawful pleasures should destroy His temple which thou hast begun to be."

Reply Obj. 3: The opposite of lust is not found in many, since men are more inclined to pleasure. Yet the contrary vice is comprised under insensibility, and occurs in one who has such a dislike for sexual intercourse as not to pay the marriage debt.

FOURTH ARTICLE [II-II, Q. 153, Art. 4]

Whether Lust Is a Capital Vice?

Objection 1: It seems that lust is not a capital vice. For lust is apparently the same as "uncleanness," according to a gloss on Eph. 5:3 (Cf. 2 Cor. 12:21). But uncleanness is a daughter of gluttony, according to Gregory (Moral. xxxi, 45). Therefore lust is not a capital vice.

Obj. 2: Further, Isidore says (De Summo Bono ii, 39) that "as pride of mind leads to the depravity of lust, so does humility of mind safeguard the chastity of the flesh." Now it is seemingly contrary to the nature of a capital vice to arise from another vice. Therefore lust is not a capital vice.

Obj. 3: Further, lust is caused by despair, according to Eph. 4:19, "Who despairing, have given themselves up to lasciviousness." But despair is not a capital vice; indeed, it is accounted a daughter of sloth, as stated above (Q. 35, A. 4, ad 2). Much less, therefore, is lust a capital vice.

*On the contrary,* Gregory (Moral. xxxi, 45) places lust among the capital vices.

*I answer that,* As stated above (Q. 148, A. 5; I-II, Q. 84, AA. 3, 4), a capital vice is one that has a very desirable end, so that through desire for that end, a man proceeds to commit many sins, all of which are said to arise from that vice as from a principal vice. Now the end of lust is venereal pleasure, which is very great. Wherefore this pleasure is very desirable as regards the sensitive appetite, both on account of the intensity of the pleasure, and because such like concupiscence is connatural to man. Therefore it is evident that lust is a capital vice.

Reply Obj. 1: As stated above (Q. 148, A. 6), according to some, the uncleanness which is reckoned a daughter of gluttony is a certain uncleanness of the body, and thus the objection is not to the point. If, however, it denote the uncleanness of lust, we must reply that it is caused by gluttony materially—in so far as gluttony provides the bodily matter of lust—and not under the aspect of final cause, in which respect chiefly the capital vices are said to be the cause of others.

Reply Obj. 2: As stated above (Q. 132, A. 4, ad 1), when we were treating of vainglory, pride is accounted the common mother of all sins, so that even the capital vices originate therefrom.

Reply Obj. 3: Certain persons refrain from lustful pleasures chiefly through hope of the glory to come, which hope is removed by despair, so that the latter is a cause of lust, as removing an obstacle thereto, not as its direct cause; whereas this is seemingly necessary for a capital vice.

FIFTH ARTICLE [II-II, Q. 153, Art. 5]

Whether the Daughters of Lust Are Fittingly Described?

Objection 1: It would seem that the daughters of lust are unfittingly reckoned to be "blindness of mind, thoughtlessness, inconstancy, rashness, self-love, hatred of God, love of this world and abhorrence or despair of a future world." For mental blindness, thoughtlessness and rashness pertain to imprudence, which is to be found in every sin, even as prudence is in every virtue. Therefore they should not be reckoned especially as daughters of lust.

Obj. 2: Further, constancy is reckoned a part of fortitude, as stated above (Q. 128, ad 6; Q. 137, A. 3). But lust is contrary, not to fortitude but to temperance. Therefore inconstancy is not a daughter of lust.

Obj. 3: Further, "Self-love extending to the contempt of God" is the origin of every sin, as Augustine says (De Civ. Dei xiv, 28). Therefore it should not be accounted a daughter of lust.

Obj. 4: Further, Isidore [*QQ. in Deut., qu. xvi] mentions four, namely, "obscene," "scurrilous," "wanton" and "foolish talking." There the aforesaid enumeration would seem to be superfluous.

*On the contrary,* stands the authority of Gregory (Moral. xxxi, 45).

*I answer that,* When the lower powers are strongly moved towards their objects, the result is that the higher powers are hindered and disordered in their acts. Now the effect of the vice of lust is that the lower appetite, namely the concupiscible, is most vehemently intent on its object, to wit, the object of pleasure, on account of the vehemence of the pleasure. Consequently the higher powers, namely the reason and the will, are most grievously disordered by lust.

Now the reason has four acts in matters of action. First there is simple understanding, which apprehends some end as good, and this act is hindered by lust, according to Dan. 13:56, "Beauty hath deceived thee, and lust hath perverted thy heart." In this respect we have "blindness of mind." The second act is counsel about what is to be done for the sake of the end: and this is also hindered by the concupiscence of lust. Hence Terence says (Eunuch., act 1, sc. 1), speaking of lecherous love: "This thing admits of neither counsel nor moderation, thou canst not control it by counseling." In this respect there is "rashness," which denotes absence of counsel, as stated above (Q. 53, A. 3). The third act is judgment about the things to be done, and this again is hindered by lust. For it is said of the lustful old men (Dan. 13:9): "They perverted their own mind ... that they might not ... remember just judgments." In this respect there is "thoughtlessness." The fourth act is the reason's command about the thing to be done, and this also is impeded by lust, in so far as through being carried away by concupiscence, a man is hindered from doing what his reason ordered to be done. [To this "inconstancy" must be referred.] [*The sentence in brackets is omitted in the Leonine edition.] Hence Terence says (Eunuch., act 1, sc. 1) of a man who declared that he would leave his mistress: "One little false tear will undo those words."

On the part of the will there results a twofold inordinate act. One is the desire for the end, to which we refer "self-love," which regards the pleasure which a man desires inordinately, while on the other hand there is "hatred of God," by reason of His forbidding the desired pleasure. The other act is the desire for the things directed to the end. With regard to this there is "love of this world," whose pleasures a man desires to enjoy, while on the other hand there is "despair of a future world," because through being held back by carnal pleasures he cares not to obtain spiritual pleasures, since they are distasteful to him.

Reply Obj. 1: According to the Philosopher (Ethic. vi, 5), intemperance is the chief corruptive of prudence: wherefore the vices opposed to prudence arise chiefly from lust, which is the principal species of intemperance.

Reply Obj. 2: The constancy which is a part of fortitude regards hardships and objects of fear; but constancy in refraining from pleasures pertains to continence which is a part of temperance, as stated above (Q. 143). Hence the inconstancy which is opposed thereto is to be reckoned a daughter of lust. Nevertheless even the first named inconstancy arises from lust, inasmuch as the latter enfeebles a man's heart and renders it effeminate, according to Osee 4:11, "Fornication and wine and drunkenness take away the heart [Douay: 'understanding']." Vegetius, too, says (De Re Milit. iii) that "the less a man knows of the pleasures of life, the less he fears death." Nor is there any need, as we have repeatedly stated, for the daughters of a capital vice to agree with it in matter (cf. Q. 35, A. 4, ad 2; Q. 118, A. 8, ad 1; Q. 148, A. 6).

Reply Obj. 3: Self-love in respect of any goods that a man desires for himself is the common origin of all sins; but in the special point of desiring carnal pleasures for oneself, it is reckoned a daughter of lust.

Reply Obj. 4: The sins mentioned by Isidore are inordinate external acts, pertaining in the main to speech; wherein there is a fourfold inordinateness. First, on account of the matter, and to this we refer "obscene words": for since "out of the abundance of the heart the mouth speaketh" (Matt. 12:34), the lustful man, whose heart is full of lewd concupiscences, readily breaks out into lewd words. Secondly, on account of the cause: for, since lust causes thoughtlessness and rashness, the result is that it makes a man speak without weighing or giving a thought to his words, which are described as "scurrilous." Thirdly, on account of the end: for since the lustful man seeks pleasure, he directs his speech thereto, and so gives utterance to "wanton words." Fourthly, on account of the sentiments expressed by his words, for through causing blindness of mind, lust perverts a man's sentiments, and so he gives way "to foolish talking," for instance, by expressing a preference for the pleasures he desires to anything else.

# QUESTION 154

OF THE PARTS OF LUST (In Twelve Articles)

We must now consider the parts of lust, under which head there are twelve points of inquiry:

(1) Into what parts is lust divided?

(2) Whether simple fornication is a mortal sin?

(3) Whether it is the greatest of sins?

(4) Whether there is mortal sin in touches, kisses and such like seduction?

(5) Whether nocturnal pollution is a mortal sin?

(6) Of seduction;

(7) Of rape;

(8) Of adultery;

(9) Of incest;

(10) Of sacrilege;

(11) Of the sin against nature;

(12) Of the order of gravity in the aforesaid sins.

FIRST ARTICLE [II-II, Q. 154, Art. 1]

Whether Six Species Are Fittingly Assigned to Lust?

Objection 1: It would seem that six species are unfittingly assigned to lust, namely, "simple fornication, adultery, incest, seduction, rape, and the unnatural vice." For diversity of matter does not diversify the species. Now the aforesaid division is made with regard to diversity of matter, according as the woman with whom a man has intercourse is married or a virgin, or of some other condition. Therefore it seems that the species of lust are diversified in this way.

Obj. 2: Further, seemingly the species of one vice are not differentiated by things that belong to another vice. Now adultery does not differ from simple fornication, save in the point of a man having intercourse with one who is another's, so that he commits an injustice. Therefore it seems that adultery should not be reckoned a species of lust.

Obj. 3: Further, just as a man may happen to have intercourse with a woman who is bound to another man by marriage, so may it happen that a man has intercourse with a woman who is bound to God by vow. Therefore sacrilege should be reckoned a species of lust, even as adultery is.

Obj. 4: Further, a married man sins not only if he be with another woman, but also if he use his own wife inordinately. But the latter sin is comprised under lust. Therefore it should be reckoned among the species thereof.

Obj. 5: Further, the Apostle says (2 Cor. 12:21): "Lest again, when I come, God humble me among you, and I mourn many of them that sinned before, and have not done penance for the uncleanness and fornication and lasciviousness that they have committed." Therefore it seems that also uncleanness and lasciviousness should be reckoned species of lust, as well as fornication.

Obj. 6: Further, the thing divided is not to be reckoned among its parts. But lust is reckoned together with the aforesaid: for it is written (Gal. 5:19): "The works of the flesh are manifest, which are fornication, uncleanness, immodesty, lust [Douay: 'luxury']." Therefore it seems that fornication is unfittingly reckoned a species of lust.

*On the contrary,* The aforesaid division is given in the Decretals 36, qu. i [*Append. Grat. ad can. Lex illa].

*I answer that,* As stated above (Q. 153, A. 3), the sin of lust consists in seeking venereal pleasure not in accordance with right reason. This may happen in two ways. First, in respect of the matter wherein this pleasure is sought; secondly, when, whereas there is due matter, other due circumstances are not observed. And since a circumstance, as such, does not specify a moral act, whose species is derived from its object which is also its matter, it follows that the species of lust must be assigned with respect to its matter or object.

Now this same matter may be discordant with right reason in two ways. First, because it is inconsistent with the end of the venereal act. In this way, as hindering the begetting of children, there is the *vice against nature,* which attaches to every venereal act from which generation cannot follow; and, as hindering the due upbringing and advancement of the child when born, there is simple fornication, which is the union of an unmarried man with an unmarried woman. Secondly, the matter wherein the venereal act is consummated may be discordant with right reason in relation to other persons; and this in two ways. First, with regard to the woman, with whom a man has connection, by reason of due honor not being paid to her; and thus there is *incest,* which consists in the misuse of a woman who is related by consanguinity or affinity. Secondly, with regard to the person under whose authority the woman is placed: and if she be under the authority of a husband, it is *adultery,* if under the authority of her father, it is *seduction,* in the absence of violence, and *rape* if violence be employed.

These species are differentiated on the part of the woman rather than of the man, because in the venereal act the woman is passive and is by way of matter, whereas the man is by way of agent; and it has been stated above (Obj. 1) that the aforesaid species are assigned with regard to a difference of matter.

Reply Obj. 1: The aforesaid diversity of matter is connected with a formal difference of object, which difference results from different modes of opposition to right reason, as stated above.

Reply Obj. 2: As stated above (I-II, Q. 18, A. 7), nothing hinders the deformities of different vices concurring in the one act, and in this way adultery is comprised under lust and injustice. Nor is this deformity of injustice altogether accidental to lust: since the lust that obeys concupiscence so far as to lead to injustice, is thereby shown to be more grievous.

Reply Obj. 3: Since a woman, by vowing continence, contracts a spiritual marriage with God, the sacrilege that is committed in the violation of such a woman is a spiritual adultery. In like manner, the other kinds of sacrilege pertaining to lustful matter are reduced to other species of lust.

Reply Obj. 4: The sin of a husband with his wife is not connected with undue matter, but with other circumstances, which do not constitute the species of a moral act, as stated above (I-II, Q. 18, A. 2).

Reply Obj. 5: As a gloss says on this passage, "uncleanness" stands for lust against nature, while "lasciviousness" is a man's abuse of boys, wherefore it would appear to pertain to seduction. We may also reply that "lasciviousness" relates to certain acts circumstantial to the venereal act, for instance kisses, touches, and so forth.

Reply Obj. 6: According to a gloss on this passage "lust" there signifies any kind of excess.

SECOND ARTICLE [II-II, Q. 154, Art. 2]

Whether Simple Fornication Is a Mortal Sin?

Objection 1: It would seem that simple fornication is not a mortal sin. For things that come under the same head would seem to be on a par with one another. Now fornication comes under the same head as things that are not mortal sins: for it is written (Acts 15:29): "That you abstain from things sacrificed to idols, and from blood, and from things strangled, and from fornication." But there is not mortal sin in these observances, according to 1 Tim. 4:4, "Nothing is rejected that is received with thanksgiving." Therefore fornication is not a mortal sin.

Obj. 2: Further, no mortal sin is the matter of a Divine precept. But the Lord commanded (Osee 1:2): "Go take thee a wife of fornications, and have of her children of fornications." Therefore fornication is not a mortal sin.

Obj. 3: Further, no mortal sin is mentioned in Holy Writ without disapprobation. Yet simple fornication is mentioned without disapprobation by Holy Writ in connection with the patriarchs. Thus we read (Gen. 16:4) that Abraham went in to his handmaid Agar; and further on (Gen. 30:5, 9) that Jacob went in to Bala and Zelpha the handmaids of his wives; and again (Gen. 38:18) that Juda was with Thamar whom he thought to be a harlot. Therefore simple fornication is not a mortal sin.

Obj. 4: Further, every mortal sin is contrary to charity. But simple fornication is not contrary to charity, neither as regards the love of God, since it is not a sin directly against God, nor as regards the love of our neighbor, since thereby no one is injured. Therefore simple fornication is not a mortal sin.

Obj. 5: Further, every mortal sin leads to eternal perdition. But simple fornication has not this result: because a gloss of Ambrose [*The quotation is from the Gloss of Peter Lombard, who refers it to St. Ambrose: whereas it is from Hilary the deacon] on 1 Tim. 4:8, "Godliness is profitable to all things," says: "The whole of Christian teaching is summed up in mercy and godliness: if a man conforms to this, even though he gives way to the inconstancy of the flesh, doubtless he will be punished, but he will not perish." Therefore simple fornication is not a mortal sin.

Obj. 6: Further, Augustine says (De Bono Conjug. xvi) that "what food is to the well-being of the body, such is sexual intercourse to the welfare of the human race." But inordinate use of food is not always a mortal sin. Therefore neither is all inordinate sexual intercourse; and this would seem to apply especially to simple fornication, which is the least grievous of the aforesaid species.

*On the contrary,* It is written (Tob. 4:13): "Take heed to keep thyself ... from all fornication, and beside thy wife never endure to know a crime." Now crime denotes a mortal sin. Therefore fornication and all intercourse with other than one's wife is a mortal sin.

Further, nothing but mortal sin debars a man from God's kingdom. But fornication debars him, as shown by the words of the Apostle (Gal. 5:21), who after mentioning fornication and certain other vices, adds: "They who do such things shall not obtain the kingdom of God." Therefore simple fornication is a mortal sin.

Further, it is written in the Decretals (XXII, qu. i, can. Praedicandum): "They should know that the same penance is to be enjoined for perjury as for adultery, fornication, and wilful murder and other criminal offenses." Therefore simple fornication is a criminal or mortal sin.

*I answer that,* Without any doubt we must hold simple fornication to be a mortal sin, notwithstanding that a gloss [*St. Augustine, QQ. in Deut., qu. 37] on Deut. 23:17, says: "This is a prohibition against going with whores, whose vileness is venial." For instead of "venial" it should be "venal," since such is the wanton's trade. In order to make this evident, we must take note that every sin committed directly against human life is a mortal sin. Now simple fornication implies an inordinateness that tends to injure the life of the offspring to be born of this union. For we find in all animals where the upbringing of the offspring needs care of both male and female, that these come together not indeterminately, but the male with a certain female, whether one or several; such is the case with all birds: while, on the other hand, among those animals, where the female alone suffices for the offspring's upbringing, the union is indeterminate, as in the case of dogs and like animals. Now it is evident that the upbringing of a human child requires not only the mother's care for his nourishment, but much more the care of his father as guide and guardian, and under whom he progresses in goods both internal and external. Hence human nature rebels against an indeterminate union of the sexes and demands that a man should be united to a determinate woman and should abide with her a long time or even for a whole lifetime. Hence it is that in the human race the male has a natural solicitude for the certainty of offspring, because on him devolves the upbringing of the child: and this certainly would cease if the union of sexes were indeterminate.

This union with a certain definite woman is called matrimony; which for the above reason is said to belong to the natural law. Since, however, the union of the sexes is directed to the common good of the whole human race, and common goods depend on the law for their determination, as stated above (I-II, Q. 90, A. 2), it follows that this union of man and woman, which is called matrimony, is determined by some law. What this determination is for us will be stated in the Third Part of this work (Suppl., Q. 50, seqq.), where we shall treat of the sacrament of matrimony. Wherefore, since fornication is an indeterminate union of the sexes, as something incompatible with matrimony, it is opposed to the good of the child's upbringing, and consequently it is a mortal sin.

Nor does it matter if a man having knowledge of a woman by fornication, make sufficient provision for the upbringing of the child: because a matter that comes under the determination of the law is judged according to what happens in general, and not according to what may happen in a particular case.

Reply Obj. 1: Fornication is reckoned in conjunction with these things, not as being on a par with them in sinfulness, but because the matters mentioned there were equally liable to cause dispute between Jews and Gentiles, and thus prevent them from agreeing unanimously. For among the Gentiles, fornication was not deemed unlawful, on account of the corruption of natural reason: whereas the Jews, taught by the Divine law, considered it to be unlawful. The other things mentioned were loathsome to the Jews through custom introduced by the law into their daily life. Hence the Apostles forbade these things to the Gentiles, not as though they were unlawful in themselves, but because they were loathsome to the Jews, as stated above (I-II, Q. 103, A. 4, ad 3).

Reply Obj. 2: Fornication is said to be a sin, because it is contrary to right reason. Now man's reason is right, in so far as it is ruled by the Divine Will, the first and supreme rule. Wherefore that which a man does by God's will and in obedience to His command, is not contrary to right reason, though it may seem contrary to the general order of reason: even so, that which is done miraculously by the Divine power is not contrary to nature, though it be contrary to the usual course of nature. Therefore just as Abraham did not sin in being willing to slay his innocent son, because he obeyed God, although considered in itself it was contrary to right human reason in general, so, too, Osee sinned not in committing fornication by God's command. Nor should such a copulation be strictly called fornication, though it be so called in reference to the general course of things. Hence Augustine says (Confess. iii, 8): "When God commands a thing to be done against the customs or agreement of any people, though it were never done by them heretofore, it is to be done"; and afterwards he adds: "For as among the powers of human society, the greater authority is obeyed in preference to the lesser, so must God in preference to all."

Reply Obj. 3: Abraham and Jacob went in to their handmaidens with no purpose of fornication, as we shall show further on when we treat of matrimony (Suppl., Q. 65, A. 5, ad 2). As to Juda there is no need to excuse him, for he also caused Joseph to be sold.

Reply Obj. 4: Simple fornication is contrary to the love of our neighbor, because it is opposed to the good of the child to be born, as we have shown, since it is an act of generation accomplished in a manner disadvantageous to the future child.

Reply Obj. 5: A person, who, while given to works of piety, yields to the inconstancy of the flesh, is freed from eternal loss, in so far as these works dispose him to receive the grace to repent, and because by such works he makes satisfaction for his past inconstancy; but not so as to be freed by pious works, if he persist in carnal inconstancy impenitent until death.

Reply Obj. 6: One copulation may result in the begetting of a man, wherefore inordinate copulation, which hinders the good of the future child, is a mortal sin as to the very genus of the act, and not only as to the inordinateness of concupiscence. On the other hand, one meal does not hinder the good of a man's whole life, wherefore the act of gluttony is not a mortal sin by reason of its genus. It would, however, be a mortal sin, if a man were knowingly to partake of a food which would alter the whole condition of his life, as was the case with Adam.

Nor is it true that fornication is the least of the sins comprised under lust, for the marriage act that is done out of sensuous pleasure is a lesser sin.

THIRD ARTICLE [II-II, Q. 154, Art. 3]

Whether Fornication Is the Most Grievous of Sins?

Objection 1: It would seem that fornication is the most grievous of sins. For seemingly a sin is the more grievous according as it proceeds from a greater sensuous pleasure. Now the greatest sensuous pleasure is in fornication, for a gloss on 1 Cor. 7:9 says that the "flame of sensuous pleasure is most fierce in lust." Therefore it seems that fornication is the gravest of sins.

Obj. 2: Further, a sin is the more grievous that is committed against a person more closely united to the sinner: thus he sins more grievously who strikes his father than one who strikes a stranger. Now according to 1 Cor. 6:18, "He that committeth fornication sinneth against his own body," which is most intimately connected with a man. Therefore it seems that fornication is the most grievous of sins.

Obj. 3: Further, the greater a good is, the graver would seem to be the sin committed against it. Now the sin of fornication is seemingly opposed to the good of the whole human race, as appears from what was said in the foregoing Article. It is also against Christ, according to 1 Cor. 6:15, "Shall I ... take the members of Christ, and make them the members of a harlot?" Therefore fornication is the most grievous of sins.

*On the contrary,* Gregory says (Moral. xxxiii, 12) that the sins of the flesh are less grievous than spiritual sins.

*I answer that,* The gravity of a sin may be measured in two ways, first with regard to the sin in itself, secondly with regard to some accident. The gravity of a sin is measured with regard to the sin itself, by reason of its species, which is determined according to the good to which that sin is opposed. Now fornication is contrary to the good of the child to be born. Wherefore it is a graver sin, as to its species, than those sins which are contrary to external goods, such as theft and the like; while it is less grievous than those which are directly against God, and sins that are injurious to the life of one already born, such as murder.

Reply Obj. 1: The sensual pleasure that aggravates a sin is that which is in the inclination of the will. But the sensual pleasure that is in the sensitive appetite, lessens sin, because a sin is the less grievous according as it is committed under the impulse of a greater passion. It is in this way that the greatest sensual pleasure is in fornication. Hence Augustine says (De Agone Christiano [*Serm. ccxciii; ccl de Temp.; see Appendix to St. Augustine's works]) that of all a Christian's conflicts, the most difficult combats are those of chastity; wherein the fight is a daily one, but victory rare: and Isidore declares (De Summo Bono ii, 39) that "mankind is subjected to the devil by carnal lust more than by anything else," because, to wit, the vehemence of this passion is more difficult to overcome.

Reply Obj. 2: The fornicator is said to sin against his own body, not merely because the pleasure of fornication is consummated in the flesh, which is also the case in gluttony, but also because he acts against the good of his own body by an undue resolution and defilement thereof, and an undue association with another. Nor does it follow from this that fornication is the most grievous sin, because in man reason is of greater value than the body, wherefore if there be a sin more opposed to reason, it will be more grievous.

Reply Obj. 3: The sin of fornication is contrary to the good of the human race, in so far as it is prejudicial to the individual begetting of the one man that may be born. Now one who is already an actual member of the human species attains to the perfection of the species more than one who is a man potentially, and from this point of view murder is a more grievous sin than fornication and every kind of lust, through being more opposed to the good of the human species. Again, a Divine good is greater than the good of the human race: and therefore those sins also that are against God are more grievous. Moreover, fornication is a sin against God, not directly as though the fornicator intended to offend God, but consequently, in the same way as all mortal sins. And just as the members of our body are Christ's members, so too, our spirit is one with Christ, according to 1 Cor. 6:17, "He who is joined to the Lord is one spirit." Wherefore also spiritual sins are more against Christ than fornication is.

FOURTH ARTICLE [II-II, Q. 154, Art. 4]

Whether There Can Be Mortal Sin in Touches and Kisses?

Objection 1: It would seem that there is no mortal sin in touches and kisses. For the Apostle says (Eph. 5:3): "Fornication and all uncleanness, or covetousness, let it not so much as be named among you, as becometh saints," then he adds: "Or obscenity" (which a gloss refers to "kissing and fondling"), "or foolish talking" (as "soft speeches"), "or scurrility" (which "fools call geniality—i.e. jocularity"), and afterwards he continues (Eph. 5:5): "For know ye this and understand that no fornicator, or unclean, or covetous person (which is the serving of idols), hath inheritance in the kingdom of Christ and of God," thus making no further mention of obscenity, as neither of foolish talking or scurrility. Therefore these are not mortal sins.

Obj. 2: Further, fornication is stated to be a mortal sin as being prejudicial to the good of the future child's begetting and upbringing. But these are not affected by kisses and touches or blandishments. Therefore there is no mortal sin in these.

Obj. 3: Further, things that are mortal sins in themselves can never be good actions. Yet kisses, touches, and the like can be done sometimes without sin. Therefore they are not mortal sins in themselves.

*On the contrary,* A lustful look is less than a touch, a caress or a kiss. But according to Matt. 5:28, "Whosoever shall look on a woman to lust after her hath already committed adultery with her in his heart." Much more therefore are lustful kisses and other like things mortal sins.

Further, Cyprian says (Ad Pompon, de Virgin., Ep. lxii), "By their very intercourse, their blandishments, their converse, their embraces, those who are associated in a sleep that knows neither honor nor shame, acknowledge their disgrace and crime." Therefore by doing these things a man is guilty of a crime, that is, of mortal sin.

*I answer that,* A thing is said to be a mortal sin in two ways. First, by reason of its species, and in this way a kiss, caress, or touch does not, of its very nature, imply a mortal sin, for it is possible to do such things without lustful pleasure, either as being the custom of one's country, or on account of some obligation or reasonable cause. Secondly, a thing is said to be a mortal sin by reason of its cause: thus he who gives an alms, in order to lead someone into heresy, sins mortally on account of his corrupt intention. Now it has been stated above (I-II, Q. 74, A. 8), that it is a mortal sin not only to consent to the act, but also to the delectation of a mortal sin. Wherefore since fornication is a mortal sin, and much more so the other kinds of lust, it follows that in such like sins not only consent to the act but also consent to the pleasure is a mortal sin. Consequently, when these kisses and caresses are done for this delectation, it follows that they are mortal sins, and only in this way are they said to be lustful. Therefore in so far as they are lustful, they are mortal sins.

Reply Obj. 1: The Apostle makes no further mention of these three because they are not sinful except as directed to those that he had mentioned before.

Reply Obj. 2: Although kisses and touches do not by their very nature hinder the good of the human offspring, they proceed from lust, which is the source of this hindrance: and on this account they are mortally sinful.

Reply Obj. 3: This argument proves that such things are not mortal sins in their species.

FIFTH ARTICLE [II-II, Q. 154, Art. 5]

Whether Nocturnal Pollution Is a Mortal Sin?

Objection 1: It would seem that nocturnal pollution is a sin. For the same things are the matter of merit and demerit. Now a man may merit while he sleeps, as was the case with Solomon, who while asleep obtained the gift of wisdom from the Lord (3 Kings 3:2, Par. 1). Therefore a man may demerit while asleep; and thus nocturnal pollution would seem to be a sin.

Obj. 2: Further, whoever has the use of reason can sin. Now a man has the use of reason while asleep, since in our sleep we frequently discuss matters, choose this rather than that, consenting to one thing, or dissenting to another. Therefore one may sin while asleep, so that nocturnal pollution is not prevented by sleep from being a sin, seeing that it is a sin according to its genus.

Obj. 3: Further, it is useless to reprove and instruct one who cannot act according to or against reason. Now man, while asleep, is instructed and reproved by God, according to Job 33:15, 16, "By a dream in a vision by night, when deep sleep is wont to lay hold of men [*Vulg.: 'When deep sleep falleth upon men.' St. Thomas is apparently quoting from memory, as the passage is given correctly above, Q. 95, A. 6, Obj. 1.] ... Then He openeth the ears of men, and teaching instructeth them in what they are to learn." Therefore a man, while asleep, can act according to or against his reason, and this is to do good or sinful actions, and thus it seems that nocturnal pollution is a sin.

*On the contrary,* Augustine says (Gen. ad lit. xii, 15): "When the same image that comes into the mind of a speaker presents itself to the mind of the sleeper, so that the latter is unable to distinguish the imaginary from the real union of bodies, the flesh is at once moved, with the result that usually follows such motions; and yet there is as little sin in this as there is in speaking and therefore thinking about such things while one is awake."

*I answer that,* Nocturnal pollution may be considered in two ways. First, in itself; and thus it has not the character of a sin. For every sin depends on the judgment of reason, since even the first movement of the sensuality has nothing sinful in it, except in so far as it can be suppressed by reason; wherefore in the absence of reason's judgment, there is no sin in it. Now during sleep reason has not a free judgment. For there is no one who while sleeping does not regard some of the images formed by his imagination as though they were real, as stated above in the First Part (Q. 84, A. 8, ad 2). Wherefore what a man does while he sleeps and is deprived of reason's judgment, is not imputed to him as a sin, as neither are the actions of a maniac or an imbecile.

Secondly, nocturnal pollution may be considered with reference to its cause. This may be threefold. One is a bodily cause. For when there is excess of seminal humor in the body, or when the humor is disintegrated either through overheating of the body or some other disturbance, the sleeper dreams things that are connected with the discharge of this excessive or disintegrated humor: the same thing happens when nature is cumbered with other superfluities, so that phantasms relating to the discharge of those superfluities are formed in the imagination. Accordingly if this excess of humor be due to a sinful cause (for instance excessive eating or drinking), nocturnal pollution has the character of sin from its cause: whereas if the excess or disintegration of these superfluities be not due to a sinful cause, nocturnal pollution is not sinful, neither in itself nor in its cause.

A second cause of nocturnal pollution is on the part of the soul and the inner man: for instance when it happens to the sleeper on account of some previous thought. For the thought which preceded while he was awake, is sometimes purely speculative, for instance when one thinks about the sins of the flesh for the purpose of discussion; while sometimes it is accompanied by a certain emotion either of concupiscence or of abhorrence. Now nocturnal pollution is more apt to arise from thinking about carnal sins with concupiscence for such pleasures, because this leaves its trace and inclination in the soul, so that the sleeper is more easily led in his imagination to consent to acts productive of pollution. In this sense the Philosopher says (Ethic. i, 13) that "in so far as certain movements in some degree pass" from the waking state to the state of sleep, "the dreams of good men are better than those of any other people": and Augustine says (Gen. ad lit. xii, 15) that "even during sleep, the soul may have conspicuous merit on account of its good disposition." Thus it is evident that nocturnal pollution may be sinful on the part of its cause. On the other hand, it may happen that nocturnal pollution ensues after thoughts about carnal acts, though they were speculative, or accompanied by abhorrence, and then it is not sinful, neither in itself nor in its cause.

The third cause is spiritual and external; for instance when by the work of a devil the sleeper's phantasms are disturbed so as to induce the aforesaid result. Sometimes this is associated with a previous sin, namely the neglect to guard against the wiles of the devil. Hence the words of the hymn at even: "Our enemy repress, that so our bodies no uncleanness know" [*Translation W. K. Blount].

On the other hand, this may occur without any fault on man's part, and through the wickedness of the devil alone. Thus we read in the *Collationes Patrum* (Coll. xxii, 6) of a man who was ever wont to suffer from nocturnal pollution on festivals, and that the devil brought this about in order to prevent him from receiving Holy Communion. Hence it is manifest that nocturnal pollution is never a sin, but is sometimes the result of a previous sin.

Reply Obj. 1: Solomon did not merit to receive wisdom from God while he was asleep. He received it in token of his previous desire. It is for this reason that his petition is stated to have been pleasing to God (3 Kings 3:10), as Augustine observes (Gen. ad lit. xii, 15).

Reply Obj. 2: The use of reason is more or less hindered in sleep, according as the inner sensitive powers are more or less overcome by sleep, on account of the violence or attenuation of the evaporations. Nevertheless it is always hindered somewhat, so as to be unable to elicit a judgment altogether free, as stated in the First Part (Q. 84, A. 8, ad 2). Therefore what it does then is not imputed to it as a sin.

Reply Obj. 3: Reason's apprehension is not hindered during sleep to the same extent as its judgment, for this is accomplished by reason turning to sensible objects, which are the first principles of human thought. Hence nothing hinders man's reason during sleep from apprehending anew something arising out of the traces left by his previous thoughts and phantasms presented to him, or again through Divine revelation, or the interference of a good or bad angel.

SIXTH ARTICLE [II-II, Q. 154, Art. 6]

Whether Seduction Should Be Reckoned a Species of Lust?

Objection 1: It would seem that seduction should not be reckoned a species of lust. For seduction denotes the unlawful violation of a virgin, according to the Decretals (XXXVI, qu. 1) [*Append. Grat. ad can. Lex illa]. But this may occur between an unmarried man and an unmarried woman, which pertains to fornication. Therefore seduction should not be reckoned a species of lust, distinct from fornication.

Obj. 2: Further, Ambrose says (De Patriarch. [*De Abraham i, 4]): "Let no man be deluded by human laws: all seduction is adultery." Now a species is not contained under another that is differentiated in opposition to it. Therefore since adultery is a species of lust, it seems that seduction should not be reckoned a species of lust.

Obj. 3: Further, to do a person an injury would seem to pertain to injustice rather than to lust. Now the seducer does an injury to another, namely the violated maiden's father, who "can take the injury as personal to himself" [*Gratian, ad can. Lex illa], and sue the seducer for damages. Therefore seduction should not be reckoned a species of lust.

*On the contrary,* Seduction consists properly in the venereal act whereby a virgin is violated. Therefore, since lust is properly about venereal actions, it would seem that seduction is a species of lust.

*I answer that,* When the matter of a vice has a special deformity, we must reckon it to be a determinate species of that vice. Now lust is a sin concerned with venereal matter, as stated above (Q. 153, A. 1). And a special deformity attaches to the violation of a virgin who is under her father's care: both on the part of the maid, who through being violated without any previous compact of marriage is both hindered from contracting a lawful marriage and is put on the road to a wanton life from which she was withheld lest she should lose the seal of virginity: and on the part of the father, who is her guardian, according to Ecclus. 42:11, "Keep a sure watch over a shameless daughter, lest at any time she make thee become a laughing-stock to thy enemies." Therefore it is evident that seduction which denotes the unlawful violation of a virgin, while still under the guardianship of her parents, is a determinate species of lust.

Reply Obj. 1: Although a virgin is free from the bond of marriage, she is not free from her father's power. Moreover, the seal of virginity is a special obstacle to the intercourse of fornication, in that it should be removed by marriage only. Hence seduction is not simple fornication, since the latter is intercourse with harlots, women, namely, who are no longer virgins, as a gloss observes on 2 Cor. 12: "And have not done penance for the uncleanness and fornication," etc.

Reply Obj. 2: Ambrose here takes seduction in another sense, as applicable in a general way to any sin of lust. Wherefore seduction, in the words quoted, signifies the intercourse between a married man and any woman other than his wife. This is clear from his adding: "Nor is it lawful for the husband to do what the wife may not." In this sense, too, we are to understand the words of Num. 5:13: "If [Vulg.: 'But'] the adultery is secret, and cannot be provided by witnesses, because she was not found in adultery ( *stupro* )."

Reply Obj. 3: Nothing prevents a sin from having a greater deformity through being united to another sin. Now the sin of lust obtains a greater deformity from the sin of injustice, because the concupiscence would seem to be more inordinate, seeing that it refrains not from the pleasurable object so that it may avoid an injustice. In fact a twofold injustice attaches to it. One is on the part of the virgin, who, though not violated by force, is nevertheless seduced, and thus the seducer is bound to compensation. Hence it is written (Ex. 22:16, 17): "If a man seduce a virgin not yet espoused, and lie with her, he shall endow her and have her to wife. If the maid's father will not give her to him, he shall give money according to the dowry, which virgins are wont to receive." The other injury is done to the maid's father: wherefore the seducer is bound by the Law to a penalty in his regard. For it is written (Deut. 22:28, 29): "If a man find a damsel that is a virgin, who is not espoused, and taking her, lie with her, and the matter come to judgment: he that lay with her shall give to the father of the maid fifty sicles of silver, and shall have her to wife, and because he hath humbled her, he may not put her away all the days of his life": and this, lest he should prove to have married her in mockery, as Augustine observes. [*QQ. in Deut., qu. xxxiv.]

SEVENTH ARTICLE [II-II, Q. 154, Art. 7]

Whether Rape Is a Species of Lust, Distinct from Seduction?

Objection 1: It would seem that rape is not a species of lust, distinct from seduction. For Isidore says (Etym. v, 26) that "seduction ( *stuprum* ), or rape, properly speaking, is unlawful intercourse, and takes its name from its causing corruption: wherefore he that is guilty of rape is a seducer." Therefore it seems that rape should not be reckoned a species of lust distinct from seduction.

Obj. 2: Further, rape, apparently, implies violence. For it is stated in the Decretals (XXXVI, qu. 1 [*Append. Grat. ad can. Lex illa]) that "rape is committed when a maid is taken away by force from her father's house that after being violated she may be taken to wife." But the employment of force is accidental to lust, for this essentially regards the pleasure of intercourse. Therefore it seems that rape should not be reckoned a determinate species of lust.

Obj. 3: Further, the sin of lust is curbed by marriage: for it is written (1 Cor. 7:2): "For fear of fornication, let every man have his own wife." Now rape is an obstacle to subsequent marriage, for it was enacted in the council of Meaux: "We decree that those who are guilty of rape, or of abducting or seducing women, should not have those women in marriage, although they should have subsequently married them with the consent of their parents." Therefore rape is not a determinate species of lust distinct from seduction.

Obj. 4: Further, a man may have knowledge of his newly married wife without committing a sin of lust. Yet he may commit rape if he take her away by force from her parents' house, and have carnal knowledge of her. Therefore rape should not be reckoned a determinate species of lust.

*On the contrary,* Rape is unlawful sexual intercourse, as Isidore states (Etym. v, 26). But this pertains to the sin of lust. Therefore rape is a species of lust.

*I answer that,* Rape, in the sense in which we speak of it now, is a species of lust: and sometimes it coincides with seduction; sometimes there is rape without seduction, and sometimes seduction without rape.

They coincide when a man employs force in order unlawfully to violate a virgin. This force is employed sometimes both towards the virgin and towards her father; and sometimes towards the father and not to the virgin, for instance if she allows herself to be taken away by force from her father's house. Again, the force employed in rape differs in another way, because sometimes a maid is taken away by force from her parents' house, and is forcibly violated: while sometimes, though taken away by force, she is not forcibly violated, but of her own consent, whether by act of fornication or by the act of marriage: for the conditions of rape remain no matter how force is employed. There is rape without seduction if a man abduct a widow or one who is not a virgin. Hence Pope Symmachus says [*Ep. v ad Caesarium; Cf. can. Raptores xxxvi, qu. 2], "We abhor abductors whether of widows or of virgins on account of the heinousness of their crime."

There is seduction without rape when a man, without employing force, violates a virgin unlawfully.

Reply Obj. 1: Since rape frequently coincides with seduction, the one is sometimes used to signify the other.

Reply Obj. 2: The employment of force would seem to arise from the greatness of concupiscence, the result being that a man does not fear to endanger himself by offering violence.

Reply Obj. 3: The rape of a maiden who is promised in marriage is to be judged differently from that of one who is not so promised. For one who is promised in marriage must be restored to her betrothed, who has a right to her in virtue of their betrothal: whereas one that is not promised to another must first of all be restored to her father's care, and then the abductor may lawfully marry her with her parents' consent. Otherwise the marriage is unlawful, since whosoever steals a thing he is bound to restore it. Nevertheless rape does not dissolve a marriage already contracted, although it is an impediment to its being contracted. As to the decree of the council in question, it was made in abhorrence of this crime, and has been abrogated. Wherefore Jerome [*The quotation is from Can. Tria. xxxvi, qu. 2] declares the contrary: "Three kinds of lawful marriage," says he, "are mentioned in Holy Writ. The first is that of a chaste maiden given away lawfully in her maidenhood to a man. The second is when a man finds a maiden in the city, and by force has carnal knowledge of her. If the father be willing, the man shall endow her according to the father's estimate, and shall pay the price of her purity [*Cf. Deut. 22:23-29]. The third is, when the maiden is taken away from such a man, and is given to another at the father's will."

We may also take this decree to refer to those who are promised to others in marriage, especially if the betrothal be expressed by words in the present tense.

Reply Obj. 4: The man who is just married has, in virtue of the betrothal, a certain right in her: wherefore, although he sins by using violence, he is not guilty of the crime of rape. Hence Pope Gelasius says [*Can. Lex illa, xxvii, qu. 2; xxxvi, qu. 1]: "This law of bygone rulers stated that rape was committed when a maiden, with regard to whose marriage nothing had so far been decided, was taken away by force."

EIGHTH ARTICLE [II-II, Q. 154, Art. 8]

Whether Adultery Is Determinate Species of Lust, Distinct from the Other Species?

Objection 1: It would seem that adultery is not a determinate species of lust, distinct from the other species. For adultery takes its name from a man having intercourse "with a woman who is not his own [ad alteram]," according to a gloss [*St. Augustine: Serm. li, 13 de Divers. lxiii] on Ex. 20:14. Now a woman who is not one's own may be of various conditions, namely either a virgin, or under her father's care, or a harlot, or of any other description. Therefore it seems that adultery is not a species of lust distinct from the others.

Obj. 2: Further, Jerome says [*Contra Jovin. i]: "It matters not for what reason a man behaves as one demented. Hence Sixtus the Pythagorean says in his Maxims: He that is insatiable of his wife is an adulterer," and in like manner one who is over enamored of any woman. Now every kind of lust includes a too ardent love. Therefore adultery is in every kind of lust: and consequently it should not be reckoned a species of lust.

Obj. 3: Further, where there is the same kind of deformity, there would seem to be the same species of sin. Now, apparently, there is the same kind of deformity in seduction and adultery: since in either case a woman is violated who is under another person's authority. Therefore adultery is not a determinate species of lust, distinct from the others.

*On the contrary,* Pope Leo [*St. Augustine, De Bono Conjug. iv; Cf. Append. Grat. ad can. Ille autem. xxxii, qu. 5] says that "adultery is sexual intercourse with another man or woman in contravention of the marriage compact, whether through the impulse of one's own lust, or with the consent of the other party." Now this implies a special deformity of lust. Therefore adultery is a determinate species of lust.

*I answer that,* Adultery, as its name implies, "is access to another's marriage-bed ( *ad alienum torum* )" [*Cf. Append. Gratian, ad can. Ille autem. xxxii, qu. 1]. By so doing a man is guilty of a twofold offense against chastity and the good of human procreation. First, by accession to a woman who is not joined to him in marriage, which is contrary to the good of the upbringing of his own children. Secondly, by accession to a woman who is united to another in marriage, and thus he hinders the good of another's children. The same applies to the married woman who is corrupted by adultery. Wherefore it is written (Ecclus. 23:32, 33): "Every woman ... that leaveth her husband ... shall be guilty of sin. For first she hath been unfaithful to the law of the Most High" (since there it is commanded: "Thou shalt not commit adultery"); "and secondly, she hath offended against her husband," by making it uncertain that the children are his: "thirdly, she hath fornicated in adultery, and hath gotten children of another man," which is contrary to the good of her offspring. The first of these, however, is common to all mortal sins, while the two others belong especially to the deformity of adultery. Hence it is manifest that adultery is a determinate species of lust, through having a special deformity in venereal acts.

Reply Obj. 1: If a married man has intercourse with another woman, his sin may be denominated either with regard to him, and thus it is always adultery, since his action is contrary to the fidelity of marriage, or with regard to the woman with whom he has intercourse; and thus sometimes it is adultery, as when a married man has intercourse with another's wife; and sometimes it has the character of seduction, or of some other sin, according to various conditions affecting the woman with whom he has intercourse: and it has been stated above (A. 1) that the species of lust correspond to the various conditions of women.

Reply Obj. 2: Matrimony is specially ordained for the good of human offspring, as stated above (A. 2). But adultery is specially opposed to matrimony, in the point of breaking the marriage faith which is due between husband and wife. And since the man who is too ardent a lover of his wife acts counter to the good of marriage if he use her indecently, although he be not unfaithful, he may in a sense be called an adulterer; and even more so than he that is too ardent a lover of another woman.

Reply Obj. 3: The wife is under her husband's authority, as united to him in marriage: whereas the maid is under her father's authority, as one who is to be married by that authority. Hence the sin of adultery is contrary to the good of marriage in one way, and the sin of seduction in another; wherefore they are reckoned to differ specifically. Of other matters concerning adultery we shall speak in the Third Part [* Cf. Suppl., Q. 59, A. 3; QQ. 60, 62], when we treat of matrimony.

NINTH ARTICLE [II-II, Q. 154, Art. 9]

Whether Incest Is a Determinate Species of Lust?

Objection 1: It would seem that incest is not a determinate species of lust. For incest [* *Incestus* is equivalent to in-castus = "unchaste"] takes its name from being a privation of chastity. But all kinds of lust are opposed to chastity. Therefore it seems that incest is not a species of lust, but is lust itself in general.

Obj. 2: Further, it is stated in the Decretals (XXXVI, qu. 1 [*Cf. Append. Grat. ad can. Lex illa]) that "incest is intercourse between a man and a woman related by consanguinity or affinity." Now affinity differs from consanguinity. Therefore it is not one but several species of lust.

Obj. 3: Further, that which does not, of itself, imply a deformity, does not constitute a determinate species of vice. But intercourse between those who are related by consanguinity or affinity does not, of itself, contain any deformity, else it would never have been lawful. Therefore incest is not a determinate species of lust.

*On the contrary,* The species of lust are distinguished according to the various conditions of women with whom a man has unlawful intercourse. Now incest implies a special condition on the part of the woman, because it is unlawful intercourse with a woman related by consanguinity or affinity as stated (Obj. 2). Therefore incest is a determinate species of lust.

*I answer that,* As stated above (AA. 1, 6) wherever we find something incompatible with the right use of venereal actions, there must needs be a determinate species of lust. Now sexual intercourse with women related by consanguinity or affinity is unbecoming to venereal union on three counts. First, because man naturally owes a certain respect to his parents and therefore to his other blood relations, who are descended in near degree from the same parents: so much so indeed that among the ancients, as Valerius Maximus relates [*Dict. Fact. Memor. ii, 1], it was not deemed right for a son to bathe with his father, lest they should see one another naked. Now from what has been said (Q. 142, A. 4; Q. 151, A. 4), it is evident that in venereal acts there is a certain shamefulness inconsistent with respect, wherefore men are ashamed of them. Wherefore it is unseemly that such persons should be united in venereal intercourse. This reason seems to be indicated (Lev. 18:7) where we read: "She is thy mother, thou shalt not uncover her nakedness," and the same is expressed further on with regard to others.

The second reason is because blood relations must needs live in close touch with one another. Wherefore if they were not debarred from venereal union, opportunities of venereal intercourse would be very frequent and thus men's minds would be enervated by lust. Hence in the Old Law [*Lev. 18] the prohibition was apparently directed specially to those persons who must needs live together.

The third reason is, because this would hinder a man from having many friends: since through a man taking a stranger to wife, all his wife's relations are united to him by a special kind of friendship, as though they were of the same blood as himself. Wherefore Augustine says (De Civ. Dei xv, 16): "The demands of charity are most perfectly satisfied by men uniting together in the bonds that the various ties of friendship require, so that they may live together in a useful and becoming amity; nor should one man have many relationships in one, but each should have one."

Aristotle adds another reason (2 Polit. ii): for since it is natural that a man should have a liking for a woman of his kindred, if to this be added the love that has its origin in venereal intercourse, his love would be too ardent and would become a very great incentive to lust: and this is contrary to chastity. Hence it is evident that incest is a determinate species of lust.

Reply Obj. 1: Unlawful intercourse between persons related to one another would be most prejudicial to chastity, both on account of the opportunities it affords, and because of the excessive ardor of love, as stated in the Article. Wherefore the unlawful intercourse between such persons is called "incest" antonomastically.

Reply Obj. 2: Persons are related by affinity through one who is related by consanguinity: and therefore since the one depends on the other, consanguinity and affinity entail the same kind of unbecomingness.

Reply Obj. 3: There is something essentially unbecoming and contrary to natural reason in sexual intercourse between persons related by blood, for instance between parents and children who are directly and immediately related to one another, since children naturally owe their parents honor. Hence the Philosopher instances a horse (De Animal. ix, 47) which covered its own mother by mistake and threw itself over a precipice as though horrified at what it had done, because some animals even have a natural respect for those that have begotten them. There is not the same essential unbecomingness attaching to other persons who are related to one another not directly but through their parents: and, as to this, becomingness or unbecomingness varies according to custom, and human or Divine law: because, as stated above (A. 2), sexual intercourse, being directed to the common good, is subject to law. Wherefore, as Augustine says (De Civ. Dei xv, 16), whereas the union of brothers and sisters goes back to olden times, it became all the more worthy of condemnation when religion forbade it.

TENTH ARTICLE [II-II, Q. 154, Art. 1]

Whether Sacrilege Can Be a Species of Lust?

Objection 1: It would seem that sacrilege cannot be a species of lust. For the same species is not contained under different genera that are not subalternated to one another. Now sacrilege is a species of irreligion, as stated above (Q. 99, A. 2). Therefore sacrilege cannot be reckoned a species of lust.

Obj. 2: Further, the Decretals (XXXVI, qu. 1 [*Append. Grat. ad can. Lex illa]), do not place sacrilege among other sins which are reckoned species of lust. Therefore it would seem not to be a species of lust.

Obj. 3: Further, something derogatory to a sacred thing may be done by the other kinds of vice, as well as by lust. But sacrilege is not reckoned a species of gluttony, or of any other similar vice. Therefore neither should it be reckoned a species of lust.

*On the contrary,* Augustine says (De Civ. Dei xv, 16) that "if it is wicked, through covetousness, to go beyond one's earthly bounds, how much more wicked is it through venereal lust to transgress the bounds of morals!" Now to go beyond one's earthly bounds in sacred matters is a sin of sacrilege. Therefore it is likewise a sin of sacrilege to overthrow the bounds of morals through venereal desire in sacred matters. But venereal desire pertains to lust. Therefore sacrilege is a species of lust.

*I answer that,* As stated above (I-II, Q. 18, AA. 6, 7), the act of a virtue or vice, that is directed to the end of another virtue or vice, assumes the latter's species: thus, theft committed for the sake of adultery, passes into the species of adultery. Now it is evident that as Augustine states (De Virgin. 8), the observance of chastity, by being directed to the worship of God, becomes an act of religion, as in the case of those who vow and keep chastity. Wherefore it is manifest that lust also, by violating something pertaining to the worship of God, belongs to the species of sacrilege: and in this way sacrilege may be accounted a species of lust.

Reply Obj. 1: Lust, by being directed to another vice as its end, becomes a species of that vice: and so a species of lust may be also a species of irreligion, as of a higher genus.

Reply Obj. 2: The enumeration referred to, includes those sins which are species of lust by their very nature: whereas sacrilege is a species of lust in so far as it is directed to another vice as its end, and may coincide with the various species of lust. For unlawful intercourse between persons mutually united by spiritual relationship, is a sacrilege after the manner of incest. Intercourse with a virgin consecrated to God, inasmuch as she is the spouse of Christ, is sacrilege resembling adultery. If the maiden be under her father's authority, it will be spiritual seduction; and if force be employed it will be spiritual rape, which kind of rape even the civil law punishes more severely than others. Thus the Emperor Justinian says [*Cod. i, iii de Episc. et Cler. 5]: "If any man dare, I will not say to rape, but even to tempt a consecrated virgin with a view to marriage, he shall be liable to capital punishment."

Reply Obj. 3: Sacrilege is committed on a consecrated thing. Now a consecrated thing is either a consecrated person, who is desired for sexual intercourse, and thus it is a kind of lust, or it is desired for possession, and thus it is a kind of injustice. Sacrilege may also come under the head of anger, for instance, if through anger an injury be done to a consecrated person. Again, one may commit a sacrilege by partaking gluttonously of sacred food. Nevertheless, sacrilege is ascribed more specially to lust which is opposed to chastity for the observance of which certain persons are specially consecrated.

ELEVENTH ARTICLE [II-II, Q. 154, Art. 11]

Whether the Unnatural Vice Is a Species of Lust?

Objection 1: It would seem that the unnatural vice is not a species of lust. For no mention of the vice against nature is made in the enumeration given above (A. 1, Obj. 1). Therefore it is not a species of lust.

Obj. 2: Further, lust is contrary to virtue; and so it is comprised under vice. But the unnatural vice is comprised not under vice, but under bestiality, according to the Philosopher (Ethic. vii, 5). Therefore the unnatural vice is not a species of lust.

Obj. 3: Further, lust regards acts directed to human generation, as stated above (Q. 153, A. 2): Whereas the unnatural vice concerns acts from which generation cannot follow. Therefore the unnatural vice is not a species of lust.

*On the contrary,* It is reckoned together with the other species of lust (2 Cor. 12:21) where we read: "And have not done penance for the uncleanness, and fornication, and lasciviousness," where a gloss says: "Lasciviousness, i.e., unnatural lust."

*I answer that,* As stated above (AA. 6, 9) wherever there occurs a special kind of deformity whereby the venereal act is rendered unbecoming, there is a determinate species of lust. This may occur in two ways: First, through being contrary to right reason, and this is common to all lustful vices; secondly, because, in addition, it is contrary to the natural order of the venereal act as becoming to the human race: and this is called "the unnatural vice." This may happen in several ways. First, by procuring pollution, without any copulation, for the sake of venereal pleasure: this pertains to the sin of "uncleanness" which some call "effeminacy." Secondly, by copulation with a thing of undue species, and this is called "bestiality." Thirdly, by copulation with an undue sex, male with male, or female with female, as the Apostle states (Rom. 1:27): and this is called the "vice of sodomy." Fourthly, by not observing the natural manner of copulation, either as to undue means, or as to other monstrous and bestial manners of copulation.

Reply Obj. 1: There we enumerated the species of lust that are not contrary to human nature: wherefore the unnatural vice was omitted.

Reply Obj. 2: Bestiality differs from vice, for the latter is opposed to human virtue by a certain excess in the same matter as the virtue, and therefore is reducible to the same genus.

Reply Obj. 3: The lustful man intends not human generation but venereal pleasures. It is possible to have this without those acts from which human generation follows: and it is that which is sought in the unnatural vice.

TWELFTH ARTICLE [II-II, Q. 154, Art. 12]

Whether the Unnatural Vice Is the Greatest Sin Among the Species of Lust?

Objection 1: It would seem that the unnatural vice is not the greatest sin among the species of lust. For the more a sin is contrary to charity the graver it is. Now adultery, seduction and rape which are injurious to our neighbor are seemingly more contrary to the love of our neighbor, than unnatural sins, by which no other person is injured. Therefore the unnatural sin is not the greatest among the species of lust.

Obj. 2: Further, sins committed against God would seem to be the most grievous. Now sacrilege is committed directly against God, since it is injurious to the Divine worship. Therefore sacrilege is a graver sin than the unnatural vice.

Obj. 3: Further, seemingly, a sin is all the more grievous according as we owe a greater love to the person against whom that sin is committed. Now the order of charity requires that a man love more those persons who are united to him—and such are those whom he defiles by incest—than persons who are not connected with him, and whom in certain cases he defiles by the unnatural vice. Therefore incest is a graver sin than the unnatural vice.

Obj. 4: Further, if the unnatural vice is most grievous, the more it is against nature the graver it would seem to be. Now the sin of uncleanness or effeminacy would seem to be most contrary to nature, since it would seem especially in accord with nature that agent and patient should be distinct from one another. Hence it would follow that uncleanness is the gravest of unnatural vices. But this is not true. Therefore unnatural vices are not the most grievous among sins of lust.

*On the contrary,* Augustine says (De adult. conjug. [*The quotation is from Cap. Adulterii xxxii, qu. 7. Cf. Augustine, De Bono Conjugali, viii.]) that "of all these," namely the sins belonging to lust, "that which is against nature is the worst."

*I answer that,* In every genus, worst of all is the corruption of the principle on which the rest depend. Now the principles of reason are those things that are according to nature, because reason presupposes things as determined by nature, before disposing of other things according as it is fitting. This may be observed both in speculative and in practical matters. Wherefore just as in speculative matters the most grievous and shameful error is that which is about things the knowledge of which is naturally bestowed on man, so in matters of action it is most grave and shameful to act against things as determined by nature. Therefore, since by the unnatural vices man transgresses that which has been determined by nature with regard to the use of venereal actions, it follows that in this matter this sin is gravest of all. After it comes incest, which, as stated above (A. 9), is contrary to the natural respect which we owe persons related to us.

With regard to the other species of lust they imply a transgression merely of that which is determined by right reason, on the presupposition, however, of natural principles. Now it is more against reason to make use of the venereal act not only with prejudice to the future offspring, but also so as to injure another person besides. Wherefore simple fornication, which is committed without injustice to another person, is the least grave among the species of lust. Then, it is a greater injustice to have intercourse with a woman who is subject to another's authority as regards the act of generation, than as regards merely her guardianship. Wherefore adultery is more grievous than seduction. And both of these are aggravated by the use of violence. Hence rape of a virgin is graver than seduction, and rape of a wife than adultery. And all these are aggravated by coming under the head of sacrilege, as stated above (A. 10, ad 2).

Reply Obj. 1: Just as the ordering of right reason proceeds from man, so the order of nature is from God Himself: wherefore in sins contrary to nature, whereby the very order of nature is violated, an injury is done to God, the Author of nature. Hence Augustine says (Confess. iii, 8): "Those foul offenses that are against nature should be everywhere and at all times detested and punished, such as were those of the people of Sodom, which should all nations commit, they should all stand guilty of the same crime, by the law of God which hath not so made men that they should so abuse one another. For even that very intercourse which should be between God and us is violated, when that same nature, of which He is the Author, is polluted by the perversity of lust."

Reply Obj. 2: Vices against nature are also against God, as stated above (ad 1), and are so much more grievous than the depravity of sacrilege, as the order impressed on human nature is prior to and more firm than any subsequently established order.

Reply Obj. 3: The nature of the species is more intimately united to each individual, than any other individual is. Wherefore sins against the specific nature are more grievous.

Reply Obj. 4: Gravity of a sin depends more on the abuse of a thing than on the omission of the right use. Wherefore among sins against nature, the lowest place belongs to the sin of uncleanness, which consists in the mere omission of copulation with another. While the most grievous is the sin of bestiality, because use of the due species is not observed. Hence a gloss on Gen. 37:2, "He accused his brethren of a most wicked crime," says that "they copulated with cattle." After this comes the sin of sodomy, because use of the right sex is not observed. Lastly comes the sin of not observing the right manner of copulation, which is more grievous if the abuse regards the "vas" than if it affects the manner of copulation in respect of other circumstances.

# QUESTION 155

OF CONTINENCE (In Four Articles)

We must next consider the potential parts of temperance: (1) continence; (2) clemency; (3) modesty. Under the first head we must consider continence and incontinence. With regard to continence there are four points of inquiry:

(1) Whether continence is a virtue?

(2) What is its matter?
(3) What is its subject?
(4) Of its comparison with temperance.

FIRST ARTICLE [II-II, Q. 155, Art. 1]

Whether Continence Is a Virtue?

Objection 1: It would seem that continence is not a virtue. For species and genus are not co-ordinate members of the same division. But continence is co-ordinated with virtue, according to the Philosopher (Ethic. vii, 1, 9). Therefore continence is not a virtue.

Obj. 2: Further, no one sins by using a virtue, since, according to Augustine (De Lib. Arb. ii, 18, 19), "a virtue is a thing that no one makes ill use of." Yet one may sin by containing oneself: for instance, if one desire to do a good, and contain oneself from doing it. Therefore continence is not a virtue.

Obj. 3: Further, no virtue withdraws man from that which is lawful, but only from unlawful things: for a gloss on Gal. 5:23, "Faith, modesty," etc., says that by continence a man refrains even from things that are lawful. Therefore continence is not a virtue.

*On the contrary,* Every praiseworthy habit would seem to be a virtue. Now such is continence, for Andronicus says [*De Affectibus] that "continence is a habit unconquered by pleasure." Therefore continence is a virtue.

*I answer that,* The word "continence" is taken by various people in two ways. For some understand continence to denote abstention from all venereal pleasure: thus the Apostle joins continence to chastity (Gal. 5:23). In this sense perfect continence is virginity in the first place, and widowhood in the second. Wherefore the same applies to continence understood thus, as to virginity which we have stated above (Q. 152, A. 3) to be a virtue. Others, however, understand continence as signifying that whereby a man resists evil desires, which in him are vehement. In this sense the Philosopher takes continence (Ethic. vii, 7), and thus also it is used in the Conferences of the Fathers (Collat. xii, 10, 11). In this way continence has something of the nature of a virtue, in so far, to wit, as the reason stands firm in opposition to the passions, lest it be led astray by them: yet it does not attain to the perfect nature of a moral virtue, by which even the sensitive appetite is subject to reason so that vehement passions contrary to reason do not arise in the sensitive appetite. Hence the Philosopher says (Ethic. iv, 9) that "continence is not a virtue but a mixture," inasmuch as it has something of virtue, and somewhat falls short of virtue.

If, however, we take virtue in a broad sense, for any principle of commendable actions, we may say that continence is a virtue.

Reply Obj. 1: The Philosopher includes continence in the same division with virtue in so far as the former falls short of virtue.

Reply Obj. 2: Properly speaking, man is that which is according to reason. Wherefore from the very fact that a man holds ( *tenet se* ) to that which is in accord with reason, he is said to contain himself. Now whatever pertains to perversion of reason is not according to reason. Hence he alone is truly said to be continent who stands to that which is in accord with right reason, and not to that which is in accord with perverse reason. Now evil desires are opposed to right reason, even as good desires are opposed to perverse reason. Wherefore he is properly and truly continent who holds to right reason, by abstaining from evil desires, and not he who holds to perverse reason, by abstaining from good desires: indeed, the latter should rather be said to be obstinate in evil.

Reply Obj. 3: The gloss quoted takes continence in the first sense, as denoting a perfect virtue, which refrains not merely from unlawful goods, but also from certain lawful things that are lesser goods, in order to give its whole attention to the more perfect goods.

SECOND ARTICLE [II-II, Q. 155, Art. 2]

Whether Desires for Pleasures of Touch Are the Matter of Continence?

Objection 1: It would seem that desires for pleasures of touch are not the matter of continence. For Ambrose says (De Offic. i, 46): "General decorum by its consistent form and the perfection of what is virtuous is restrained* in its every action." [*"Continentem" according to St. Thomas' reading; St. Ambrose wrote "concinentem = harmonious"].

Obj. 2: Further, continence takes its name from a man standing for the good of right reason, as stated above (A. 1, ad 2). Now other passions lead men astray from right reason with greater vehemence than the desire for pleasures of touch: for instance, the fear of mortal dangers, which stupefies a man, and anger which makes him behave like a madman, as Seneca remarks [*De Ira i, 1]. Therefore continence does not properly regard the desires for pleasures of touch.

Obj. 3: Further, Tully says (De Invent. Rhet. ii, 54): "It is continence that restrains cupidity with the guiding hand of counsel." Now cupidity is generally used to denote the desire for riches rather than the desire for pleasures of touch, according to 1 Tim. 6:10, "Cupidity [Douay: 'The desire of money'] ( *philargyria* ), is the root of all evils." Therefore continence is not properly about the desires for pleasures of touch.

Obj. 4: Further, there are pleasures of touch not only in venereal matters but also in eating. But continence is wont to be applied only to the use of venereal matters. Therefore the desire for pleasures of touch is not its proper matter.

Obj. 5: Further, among pleasures of touch some are not human but bestial, both as regards food—for instance, the pleasure of eating human flesh; and as regards venereal matters—for instance the abuse of animals or boys. But continence is not about such like things, as stated in *Ethic.* vii, 5. Therefore desires for pleasures of touch are not the proper matter of continence.

*On the contrary,* The Philosopher says (Ethic. vii, 4) that "continence and incontinence are about the same things as temperance and intemperance." Now temperance and intemperance are about the desires for pleasures of touch, as stated above (Q. 141, A. 4). Therefore continence and incontinence are also about that same matter.

*I answer that,* Continence denotes, by its very name, a certain curbing, in so far as a man contains himself from following his passions. Hence continence is properly said in reference to those passions which urge a man towards the pursuit of something, wherein it is praiseworthy that reason should withhold man from pursuing: whereas it is not properly about those passions, such as fear and the like, which denote some kind of withdrawal: since in these it is praiseworthy to remain firm in pursuing what reason dictates, as stated above (Q. 123, AA. 3, 4). Now it is to be observed that natural inclinations are the principles of all supervening inclinations, as stated above (I, Q. 60, A. 2). Wherefore the more they follow the inclination of nature, the more strongly do the passions urge to the pursuance of an object. Now nature inclines chiefly to those things that are necessary to it, whether for the maintenance of the individual, such as food, or for the maintenance of the species, such as venereal acts, the pleasures of which pertain to the touch. Therefore continence and incontinence refer properly to desires for pleasures of touch.

Reply Obj. 1: Just as temperance may be used in a general sense in connection with any matter; but is properly applied to that matter wherein it is best for man to be curbed: so, too, continence properly speaking regards that matter wherein it is best and most difficult to contain oneself, namely desires for pleasures of touch, and yet in a general sense and relatively may be applied to any other matter: and in this sense Ambrose speaks of continence.

Reply Obj. 2: Properly speaking we do not speak of continence in relation to fear, but rather of firmness of mind which fortitude implies. As to anger, it is true that it begets an impulse to the pursuit of something, but this impulse follows an apprehension of the soul—in so far as a man apprehends that someone has injured him—rather than an inclination of nature. Wherefore a man may be said to be continent of anger, relatively but not simply.

Reply Obj. 3: External goods, such as honors, riches and the like, as the Philosopher says (Ethic. vii, 4), seem to be objects of choice in themselves indeed, but not as being necessary for the maintenance of nature. Wherefore in reference to such things we speak of a person as being continent or incontinent, not simply, but relatively, by adding that they are continent or incontinent in regard to wealth, or honor and so forth. Hence Tully either understood continence in a general sense, as including relative continence, or understood cupidity in a restricted sense as denoting desire for pleasures of touch.

Reply Obj. 4: Venereal pleasures are more vehement than pleasures of the palate: wherefore we are wont to speak of continence and incontinence in reference to venereal matters rather than in reference to food; although according to the Philosopher they are applicable to both.

Reply Obj. 5: Continence is a good of the human reason: wherefore it regards those passions which can be connatural to man. Hence the Philosopher says (Ethic. vii, 5) that "if a man were to lay hold of a child with desire of eating him or of satisfying an unnatural passion whether he follow up his desire or not, he is said to be continent [*See A. 4], not absolutely, but relatively."

THIRD ARTICLE [II-II, Q. 155, Art. 3]

Whether the Subject of Continence Is the Concupiscible Power?

Objection 1: It would seem that the subject of continence is the concupiscible power. For the subject of a virtue should be proportionate to the virtue's matter. Now the matter of continence, as stated (A. 2), is desires for the pleasures of touch, which pertain to the concupiscible power. Therefore continence is in the concupiscible power.

Obj. 2: Further, "Opposites are referred to one same thing" [*Categ. viii]. But incontinence is in the concupiscible, whose passions overcome reason, for Andronicus says [*De Affectibus] that "incontinence is the evil inclination of the concupiscible, by following which it chooses wicked pleasures in disobedience to reason." Therefore continence is likewise in the concupiscible.

Obj. 3: Further, the subject of a human virtue is either the reason, or the appetitive power, which is divided into the will, the concupiscible and the irascible. Now continence is not in the reason, for then it would be an intellectual virtue; nor is it in the will, since continence is about the passions which are not in the will; nor again is it in the irascible, because it is not properly about the passions of the irascible, as stated above (A. 2, ad 2). Therefore it follows that it is in the concupiscible.

*On the contrary,* Every virtue residing in a certain power removes the evil act of that power. But continence does not remove the evil act of the concupiscible: since "the continent man has evil desires," according to the Philosopher (Ethic. vii, 9). Therefore continence is not in the concupiscible power.

*I answer that,* Every virtue while residing in a subject, makes that subject have a different disposition from that which it has while subjected to the opposite vice. Now the concupiscible has the same disposition in one who is continent and in one who is incontinent, since in both of them it breaks out into vehement evil desires. Wherefore it is manifest that continence is not in the concupiscible as its subject. Again the reason has the same disposition in both, since both the continent and the incontinent have right reason, and each of them, while undisturbed by passion, purposes not to follow his unlawful desires. Now the primary difference between them is to be found in their choice: since the continent man, though subject to vehement desires, chooses not to follow them, because of his reason; whereas the incontinent man chooses to follow them, although his reason forbids. Hence continence must needs reside in that power of the soul, whose act it is to choose; and that is the will, as stated above (I-II, Q. 13, A. 1).

Reply Obj. 1: Continence has for its matter the desires for pleasures of touch, not as moderating them (this belongs to temperance which is in the concupiscible), but its business with them is to resist them. For this reason it must be in another power, since resistance is of one thing against another.

Reply Obj. 2: The will stands between reason and the concupiscible, and may be moved by either. In the continent man it is moved by the reason, in the incontinent man it is moved by the concupiscible. Hence continence may be ascribed to the reason as to its first mover, and incontinence to the concupiscible power: though both belong immediately to the will as their proper subject.

Reply Obj. 3: Although the passions are not in the will as their subject, yet it is in the power of the will to resist them: thus it is that the will of the continent man resists desires.

FOURTH ARTICLE [II-II, Q. 155, Art. 4]

Whether Continence Is Better Than Temperance?

Objection 1: It would seem that continence is better than temperance. For it is written (Ecclus. 26:20): "No price is worthy of a continent soul." Therefore no virtue can be equalled to continence.

Obj. 2: Further, the greater the reward a virtue merits, the greater the virtue. Now continence apparently merits the greater reward; for it is written (2 Tim. 2:5): "He ... is not crowned, except he strive lawfully," and the continent man, since he is subject to vehement evil desires, strives more than the temperate man, in whom these things are not vehement. Therefore continence is a greater virtue than temperance.

Obj. 3: Further, the will is a more excellent power than the concupiscible. But continence is in the will, whereas temperance is in the concupiscible, as stated above (A. 3). Therefore continence is a greater virtue than temperance.

*On the contrary,* Tully (De Invent. Rhet. ii, 54) and Andronicus [*De Affectibus] reckon continence to be annexed to temperance, as to a principal virtue.

*I answer that,* As stated above (A. 1), continence has a twofold signification. In one way it denotes cessation from all venereal pleasures; and if continence be taken in this sense, it is greater than temperance considered absolutely, as may be gathered from what we said above (Q. 152, A. 5) concerning the preeminence of virginity over chastity considered absolutely. In another way continence may be taken as denoting the resistance of the reason to evil desires when they are vehement in a man: and in this sense temperance is far greater than continence, because the good of a virtue derives its praise from that which is in accord with reason. Now the good of reason flourishes more in the temperate man than in the continent man, because in the former even the sensitive appetite is obedient to reason, being tamed by reason so to speak, whereas in the continent man the sensitive appetite strongly resists reason by its evil desires. Hence continence is compared to temperance, as the imperfect to the perfect.

Reply Obj. 1: The passage quoted may be understood in two ways. First in reference to the sense in which continence denotes abstinence from all things venereal: and thus it means that "no price is worthy of a continent soul," in the genus of chastity; since not even the fruitfulness of the flesh which is the purpose of marriage is equalled to the continence of virginity or of widowhood, as stated above (Q. 152, AA. 4, 5). Secondly it may be understood in reference to the general sense in which continence denotes any abstinence from things unlawful: and thus it means that "no price is worthy of a continent soul," because its value is not measured with gold or silver, which are appreciable according to weight.

Reply Obj. 2: The strength or weakness of concupiscence may proceed from two causes. For sometimes it is owing to a bodily cause: because some people by their natural temperament are more prone to concupiscence than others; and again opportunities for pleasure which inflame the concupiscence are nearer to hand for some people than for others. Such like weakness of concupiscence diminishes merit, whereas strength of concupiscence increases it. On the other hand, weakness or strength of concupiscence arises from a praiseworthy spiritual cause, for instance the vehemence of charity, or the strength of reason, as in the case of a temperate man. In this way weakness of concupiscence, by reason of its cause, increases merit, whereas strength of concupiscence diminishes it.

Reply Obj. 3: The will is more akin to the reason than the concupiscible power is. Wherefore the good of reason—on account of which virtue is praised by the very fact that it reaches not only to the will but also to the concupiscible power, as happens in the temperate man—is shown to be greater than if it reach only to the will, as in the case of one who is continent.

## QUESTION 156

OF INCONTINENCE (In Four Articles)

We must now consider incontinence: and under this head there are four points of inquiry:

(1) Whether incontinence pertains to the soul or to the body?

(2) Whether incontinence is a sin?

(3) The comparison between incontinence and intemperance;

(4) Which is the worse, incontinence in anger, or incontinence in desire?

FIRST ARTICLE [II-II, Q. 156, Art. 1]

Whether Incontinence Pertains to the Soul or to the Body?

Objection 1: It would seem that incontinence pertains not to the soul but to the body. For sexual diversity comes not from the soul but from the body. Now sexual diversity causes diversity of incontinence: for the Philosopher says (Ethic. vii, 5) that women are not described either as continent or as incontinent. Therefore incontinence pertains not to the soul but to the body.

Obj. 2: Further, that which pertains to the soul does not result from the temperament of the body. But incontinence results from the bodily temperament: for the Philosopher says (Ethic. vii, 7) that "it is especially people of a quick or choleric and atrabilious temper whose incontinence is one of unbridled desire." Therefore incontinence regards the body.

Obj. 3: Further, victory concerns the victor rather than the vanquished. Now a man is said to be incontinent, because "the flesh lusteth against the spirit," and overcomes it. Therefore incontinence pertains to the flesh rather than to the soul.

*On the contrary,* Man differs from beast chiefly as regards the soul. Now they differ in respect of continence and incontinence, for we ascribe neither continence nor incontinence to the beasts, as the Philosopher states (Ethic. vii, 3). Therefore incontinence is chiefly on the part of the soul.

*I answer that,* Things are ascribed to their direct causes rather than to those which merely occasion them. Now that which is on the part of the body is merely an occasional cause of incontinence; since it is owing to a bodily disposition that vehement passions can arise in the sensitive appetite which is a power of the organic body. Yet these passions, however vehement they be, are not the sufficient cause of incontinence, but are merely the occasion thereof, since, so long as the use of reason remains, man is always able to resist his passions. If, however, the passions gain such strength as to take away the use of reason altogether—as in the case of those who become insane through the vehemence of their passions—the essential conditions of continence or incontinence cease, because such people do not retain the judgment of reason, which the continent man follows and the incontinent forsakes. From this it follows that the direct cause of incontinence is on the part of the soul, which fails to resist a passion by the reason. This happens in two ways, according to the Philosopher (Ethic. vii, 7): first, when the soul yields to the passions, before the reason has given its counsel; and this is called "unbridled incontinence" or "impetuosity": secondly, when a man does not stand to what has been counselled, through holding weakly to reason's judgment; wherefore this kind of incontinence is called "weakness." Hence it is manifest that incontinence pertains chiefly to the soul.

Reply Obj. 1: The human soul is the form of the body, and has certain powers which make use of bodily organs. The operations of these organs conduce somewhat to those operations of the soul which are accomplished without bodily instruments, namely to the acts of the intellect and of the will, in so far as the intellect receives from the senses, and the will is urged by passions of the sensitive appetite. Accordingly, since woman, as regards the body, has a weak temperament, the result is that for the most part, whatever she holds to, she holds to it weakly; although in rare cases the opposite occurs, according to Prov. 31:10, "Who shall find a valiant woman?" And since small and weak things "are accounted as though they were not" [*Aristotle, *Phys.* ii, 5] the Philosopher speaks of women as though they had not the firm judgment of reason, although the contrary happens in some women. Hence he states that "we do not describe women as being continent, because they are vacillating" through being unstable of reason, and "are easily led" so that they follow their passions readily.

Reply Obj. 2: It is owing to the impulse of passion that a man at once follows his passion before his reason counsels him. Now the impulse of passion may arise either from its quickness, as in bilious persons [*Cf. I-II, Q. 46, A. 5], or from its vehemence, as in the melancholic, who on account of their earthy temperament are most vehemently aroused. Even so, on the other hand, a man fails to stand to that which is counselled, because he holds to it in weakly fashion by reason of the softness of his temperament, as we have stated with regard to woman (ad 1). This is also the case with phlegmatic temperaments, for the same reason as in women. And these results are due to the fact that the bodily temperament is an occasional but not a sufficient cause of incontinence, as stated above.

Reply Obj. 3: In the incontinent man concupiscence of the flesh overcomes the spirit, not necessarily, but through a certain negligence of the spirit in not resisting strongly.

SECOND ARTICLE [II-II, Q. 156, Art. 2]

Whether Incontinence Is a Sin?

Objection 1: It would seem that incontinence is not a sin. For as Augustine says (De Lib. Arb. iii, 18): "No man sins in what he cannot avoid." Now no man can by himself avoid incontinence, according to Wis. 8:21, "I know [Vulg.: 'knew'] that I could not ... be continent, except God gave it." Therefore incontinence is not a sin.

Obj. 2: Further, apparently every sin originates in the reason. But the judgment of reason is overcome in the incontinent man. Therefore incontinence is not a sin.

Obj. 3: Further, no one sins in loving God vehemently. Now a man becomes incontinent through the vehemence of divine love: for Dionysius says (Div. Nom. iv) that "Paul, through incontinence of divine love, exclaimed: I live, now not I" (Gal. 2:20). Therefore incontinence is not a sin.

*On the contrary,* It is numbered together with other sins (2 Tim. 3:3) where it is written: "Slanderers, incontinent, unmerciful," etc. Therefore incontinence is a sin.

*I answer that,* Incontinence about a matter may be considered in two ways. First it may be considered properly and simply: and thus incontinence is about concupiscences of pleasures of touch, even as intemperance is, as we have said in reference to continence (Q. 155, A. 2). In this way incontinence is a sin for two reasons: first, because the incontinent man goes astray from that which is in accord with reason; secondly, because he plunges into shameful pleasures. Hence the Philosopher says (Ethic. vii, 4) that "incontinence is censurable not only because it is wrong"—that is, by straying from reason—"but also because it is wicked"—that is, by following evil desires. Secondly, incontinence about a matter is considered, properly—inasmuch as it is a straying from reason—but not simply; for instance when a man does not observe the mode of reason in his desire for honor, riches, and so forth, which seem to be good in themselves. About such things there is incontinence, not simply but relatively, even as we have said above in reference to continence (Q. 155, A. 2, ad 3). In this way incontinence is a sin, not from the fact that one gives way to wicked desires, but because one fails to observe the mode of reason even in the desire for things that are of themselves desirable.

Thirdly, incontinence is said to be about a matter, not properly, but metaphorically, for instance about the desires for things of which one cannot make an evil use, such as the desire for virtue. A man may be said to be incontinent in these matters metaphorically, because just as the incontinent man is entirely led by his evil desire, even so is a man entirely led by his good desire which is in accord with reason. Such like incontinence is no sin, but pertains to the perfection of virtue.

Reply Obj. 1: Man can avoid sin and do good, yet not without God's help, according to John 15:5: "Without Me you can do nothing." Wherefore the fact that man needs God's help in order to be continent, does not show incontinence to be no sin, for, as stated in *Ethic.* iii, 3, "what we can do by means of a friend we do, in a way, ourselves."

Reply Obj. 2: The judgment of reason is overcome in the incontinent man, not necessarily, for then he would commit no sin, but through a certain negligence on account of his not standing firm in resisting the passion by holding to the judgment formed by his reason.

Reply Obj. 3: This argument takes incontinence metaphorically and not properly.

THIRD ARTICLE [II-II, Q. 156, Art. 3]

Whether the Incontinent Man Sins More Gravely Than the Intemperate?

Objection 1: It would seem that the incontinent man sins more gravely than the intemperate. For, seemingly, the more a man acts against his conscience, the more gravely he sins, according to Luke 12:47, "That servant who knew the will of his lord ... and did not ... shall be beaten with many stripes." Now the incontinent man would seem to act against his conscience more than the intemperate because, according to *Ethic.* vii, 3, the incontinent man, though knowing how wicked are the things he desires, nevertheless acts through passion, whereas the intemperate man judges what he desires to be good. Therefore the incontinent man sins more gravely than the intemperate.

Obj. 2: Further, apparently, the graver a sin is, the more incurable it is: wherefore the sins against the Holy Ghost, being most grave, are declared to be unpardonable. Now the sin of incontinence would appear to be more incurable than the sin of intemperance. For a person's sin is cured by admonishment and correction, which seemingly are no good to the incontinent man, since he knows he is doing wrong, and does wrong notwithstanding: whereas it seems to the intemperate man that he is doing well, so that it were good for him to be admonished. Therefore it would appear that the incontinent man sins more gravely than the intemperate.

Obj. 3: Further, the more eagerly man sins, the more grievous his sin. Now the incontinent sins more eagerly than the intemperate, since the incontinent man has vehement passions and desires, which the intemperate man does not always have. Therefore the incontinent man sins more gravely than the intemperate.

*On the contrary,* Impenitence aggravates every sin: wherefore Augustine says (De Verb. Dom. serm. xi, 12, 13) that "impenitence is a sin against the Holy Ghost." Now according to the Philosopher (Ethic. vii, 8) "the intemperate man is not inclined to be penitent, for he holds on to his choice: but every incontinent man is inclined to repentance." Therefore the intemperate man sins more gravely than the incontinent.

*I answer that,* According to Augustine [*De Duab. Anim. x, xi] sin is chiefly an act of the will, because "by the will we sin and live aright" [*Retract. i, 9]. Consequently where there is a greater inclination of the will to sin, there is a graver sin. Now in the intemperate man, the will is inclined to sin in virtue of its own choice, which proceeds from a habit acquired through custom: whereas in the incontinent man, the will is inclined to sin through a passion. And since passion soon passes, whereas a habit is "a disposition difficult to remove," the result is that the incontinent man repents at once, as soon as the passion has passed; but not so the intemperate man; in fact he rejoices in having sinned, because the sinful act has become connatural to him by reason of his habit. Wherefore in reference to such persons it is written (Prov. 2:14) that "they are glad when they have done evil, and rejoice in most wicked things." Hence it follows that "the intemperate man is much worse than the incontinent," as also the Philosopher declares (Ethic. vii, 7).

Reply Obj. 1: Ignorance in the intellect sometimes precedes the inclination of the appetite and causes it, and then the greater the ignorance, the more does it diminish or entirely excuse the sin, in so far as it renders it involuntary. On the other hand, ignorance in the reason sometimes follows the inclination of the appetite, and then such like ignorance, the greater it is, the graver the sin, because the inclination of the appetite is shown thereby to be greater. Now in both the incontinent and the intemperate man, ignorance arises from the appetite being inclined to something, either by passion, as in the incontinent, or by habit, as in the intemperate. Nevertheless greater ignorance results thus in the intemperate than in the incontinent. In one respect as regards duration, since in the incontinent man this ignorance lasts only while the passion endures, just as an attack of intermittent fever lasts as long as the humor is disturbed: whereas the ignorance of the intemperate man endures without ceasing, on account of the endurance of the habit, wherefore it is likened to phthisis or any chronic disease, as the Philosopher says (Ethic. vii, 8). In another respect the ignorance of the intemperate man is greater as regards the thing ignored. For the ignorance of the incontinent man regards some particular detail of choice (in so far as he deems that he must choose this particular thing now): whereas the intemperate man's ignorance is about the end itself, inasmuch as he judges this thing good, in order that he may follow his desires without being curbed. Hence the Philosopher says (Ethic. vii, 7, 8) that "the incontinent man is better than the intemperate, because he retains the best principle [* *To beltiston, e arche*, 'the best thing, i.e. the principle'']," to wit, the right estimate of the end.

Reply Obj. 2: Mere knowledge does not suffice to cure the incontinent man, for he needs the inward assistance of grace which quenches concupiscence, besides the application of the external remedy of admonishment and correction, which induce him to begin to resist his desires, so that concupiscence is weakened, as stated above (Q. 142, A. 2). By these same means the intemperate man can be cured. But his curing is more difficult, for two reasons. The first is on the part of reason, which is corrupt as regards the estimate of the last end, which holds the same position as the principle in demonstrations. Now it is more difficult to bring back to the truth one who errs as to the principle; and it is the same in practical matters with one who errs in regard to the end. The other reason is on the part of the inclination of the appetite: for in the intemperate man this proceeds from a habit, which is difficult to remove, whereas the inclination of the incontinent man proceeds from a passion, which is more easily suppressed.

Reply Obj. 3: The eagerness of the will, which increases a sin, is greater in the intemperate man than in the incontinent, as explained above. But the eagerness of concupiscence in the sensitive appetite is sometimes greater in the incontinent man, because he does not sin except through vehement concupiscence, whereas the intemperate man sins even through slight concupiscence and sometimes forestalls it. Hence the Philosopher says (Ethic. vii, 7) that we blame more the intemperate man, "because he pursues pleasure without desiring it or with calm," i.e. slight desire. "For what would he have done if he had desired it with passion?"

FOURTH ARTICLE [II-II, Q. 156, Art. 4]

Whether the Incontinent in Anger Is Worse Than the Incontinent in Desire?

Objection 1: It would seem that the incontinent in anger is worse than the incontinent in desire. For the more difficult it is to resist the passion, the less grievous, apparently is incontinence: wherefore the Philosopher says (Ethic. vii, 7): "It is not wonderful, indeed it is pardonable if a person is overcome by strong and overwhelming pleasures or pains." Now, "as Heraclitus says, it is more difficult to resist desire than anger" [*Ethic. ii. 3]. Therefore incontinence of desire is less grievous than incontinence of anger.

Obj. 2: Further, one is altogether excused from sin if the passion be so vehement as to deprive one of the judgment of reason, as in the case of one who becomes demented through passion. Now he that is incontinent in anger retains more of the judgment of reason, than one who is incontinent in desire: since "anger listens to reason somewhat, but desire does not" as the Philosopher states (Ethic. vii, 6). Therefore the incontinent in anger is worse than the incontinent in desire.

Obj. 3: Further, the more dangerous a sin the more grievous it is. Now incontinence of anger would seem to be more dangerous, since it leads a man to a greater sin, namely murder, for this is a more grievous sin than adultery, to which incontinence of desire leads. Therefore incontinence of anger is graver than incontinence of desire.

*On the contrary,* The Philosopher says (Ethic. vii, 6) that "incontinence of anger is less disgraceful than incontinence of desire."

*I answer that,* The sin of incontinence may be considered in two ways. First, on the part of the passion which occasions the downfall of reason.

In this way incontinence of desire is worse than incontinence of anger, because the movement of desire is more inordinate than the movement of anger. There are four reasons for this, and the Philosopher indicates them, *Ethic.* vii, 6: First, because the movement of anger partakes somewhat of reason, since the angry man tends to avenge the injury done to him, and reason dictates this in a certain degree. Yet he does not tend thereto perfectly, because he does not intend the due mode of vengeance. On the other hand, the movement of desire is altogether in accord with sense and nowise in accord with reason. Secondly, because the movement of anger results more from the bodily temperament owing to the quickness of the movement of the bile which tends to anger. Hence one who by bodily temperament is disposed to anger is more readily angry than one who is disposed to concupiscence is liable to be concupiscent: wherefore also it happens more often that the children of those who are disposed to anger are themselves disposed to anger, than that the children of those who are disposed to concupiscence are also disposed to concupiscence. Now that which results from the natural disposition of the body is deemed more deserving of pardon. Thirdly, because anger seeks to work openly, whereas concupiscence is fain to disguise itself and creeps in by stealth. Fourthly, because he who is subject to concupiscence works with pleasure, whereas the angry man works as though forced by a certain previous displeasure.

Secondly, the sin of incontinence may be considered with regard to the evil into which one falls through forsaking reason; and thus incontinence of anger is, for the most part, more grievous, because it leads to things that are harmful to one's neighbor.

Reply Obj. 1: It is more difficult to resist pleasure perseveringly than anger, because concupiscence is enduring. But for the moment it is more difficult to resist anger, on account of its impetuousness.

Reply Obj. 2: Concupiscence is stated to be without reason, not as though it destroyed altogether the judgment of reason, but because nowise does it follow the judgment of reason: and for this reason it is more disgraceful.

Reply Obj. 3: This argument considers incontinence with regard to its result.

## QUESTION 157

OF CLEMENCY AND MEEKNESS (In Four Articles)

We must next consider clemency and meekness, and the contrary vices. Concerning the virtues themselves there are four points of inquiry:

(1) Whether clemency and meekness are altogether identical?

(2) Whether each of them is a virtue?

(3) Whether each is a part of temperance?

(4) Of their comparison with the other virtues.

FIRST ARTICLE [II-II, Q. 157, Art. 1]

Whether Clemency and Meekness Are Absolutely the Same?

Objection 1: It would seem that clemency and meekness are absolutely the same. For meekness moderates anger, according to the Philosopher (Ethic. iv, 5). Now anger is "desire of vengeance" [*Aristotle, Rhet. ii, 2]. Since, then, clemency "is leniency of a superior in inflicting punishment on an inferior," as Seneca states (De Clementia ii, 3), and vengeance is taken by means of punishment, it would seem that clemency and meekness are the same.

Obj. 2: Further, Tully says (De Invent. Rhet. ii, 54) that "clemency is a virtue whereby the mind is restrained by kindness when unreasonably provoked to hatred of a person," so that apparently clemency moderates hatred. Now, according to Augustine [*Ep. ccxi], hatred is caused by anger; and this is the matter of meekness and clemency. Therefore seemingly clemency and meekness are absolutely the same.

Obj. 3: Further, the same vice is not opposed to different virtues. But the same vice, namely cruelty, is opposed to meekness and clemency. Therefore it seems that meekness and clemency are absolutely the same.

*On the contrary,* According to the aforesaid definition of Seneca (Obj. 1) "clemency is leniency of a superior towards an inferior": whereas meekness is not merely of superior to inferior, but of each to everyone. Therefore meekness and clemency are not absolutely the same.

*I answer that,* As stated in Ethic. ii, 3, a moral virtue is "about passions and actions." Now internal passions are principles of external actions, and are likewise obstacles thereto. Wherefore virtues that moderate passions, to a certain extent, concur towards the same effect as virtues that moderate actions, although they differ specifically. Thus it belongs properly to justice to restrain man from theft, whereunto he is inclined by immoderate love or desire of money, which is restrained by liberality; so that liberality concurs with justice towards the effect, which is abstention from theft. This applies to the case in point; because through the passion of anger a man is provoked to inflict a too severe punishment, while it belongs directly to clemency to mitigate punishment, and this might be prevented by excessive anger.

Consequently meekness, in so far as it restrains the onslaught of anger, concurs with clemency towards the same effect; yet they differ from one another, inasmuch as clemency moderates external punishment, while meekness properly mitigates the passion of anger.

Reply Obj. 1: Meekness regards properly the desire itself of vengeance; whereas clemency regards the punishment itself which is applied externally for the purpose of vengeance.

Reply Obj. 2: Man's affections incline to the moderation of things that are unpleasant to him in themselves. Now it results from one man loving another that he takes no pleasure in the latter's punishment in itself, but only as directed to something else, for instance justice, or the correction of the person punished. Hence love makes one quick to mitigate punishment—and this pertains to clemency—while hatred is an obstacle to such mitigation. For this reason Tully says that "the mind provoked to hatred" that is to punish too severely, "is restrained by clemency," from inflicting too severe a punishment, so that clemency directly moderates not hatred but punishment.

Reply Obj. 3: The vice of anger, which denotes excess in the passion of anger, is properly opposed to meekness, which is directly concerned with the passion of anger; while cruelty denotes excess in punishing. Wherefore Seneca says (De Clementia ii, 4) that "those are called cruel who have reason for punishing, but lack moderation in punishing." Those who delight in a man's punishment for its own sake may be called savage or brutal, as though lacking the human feeling that leads one man to love another.

SECOND ARTICLE [II-II, Q. 157, Art. 2]

Whether Both Clemency and Meekness Are Virtues?

Objection 1: It would seem that neither clemency nor meekness is a virtue. For no virtue is opposed to another virtue. Yet both of these are apparently opposed to severity, which is a virtue. Therefore neither clemency nor meekness is a virtue.

Obj. 2: Further, "Virtue is destroyed by excess and defect" [*Ethic. ii, 2]. But both clemency and meekness consist in a certain decrease; for clemency decreases punishment, and meekness decreases anger. Therefore neither clemency nor meekness is a virtue.

Obj. 3: Further, meekness or mildness is included (Matt. 5:4) among the beatitudes, and (Gal. 5:23) among the fruits. Now the virtues differ from the beatitudes and fruits. Therefore they are not comprised under virtue.

*On the contrary,* Seneca says (De Clementia ii, 5): "Every good man is conspicuous for his clemency and meekness." Now it is virtue properly that belongs to a good man, since "virtue it is that makes its possessor good, and renders his works good also" (Ethic. ii, 6). Therefore clemency and meekness are virtues.

*I answer that,* The nature of moral virtue consists in the subjection of appetite to reason, as the Philosopher declares (Ethic. i, 13). Now this is verified both in clemency and in meekness. For clemency, in mitigating punishment, "is guided by reason," according to Seneca (De Clementia ii, 5), and meekness, likewise, moderates anger according to right reason, as stated in *Ethic.* iv, 5. Wherefore it is manifest that both clemency and meekness are virtues.

Reply Obj. 1: Meekness is not directly opposed to severity; for meekness is about anger. On the other hand, severity regards the external infliction of punishment, so that accordingly it would seem rather to be opposed to clemency, which also regards external punishing, as stated above (A. 1). Yet they are not really opposed to one another, since they are both according to right reason. For severity is inflexible in the infliction of punishment when right reason requires it; while clemency mitigates punishment also according to right reason, when and where this is requisite. Wherefore they are not opposed to one another as they are not about the same thing.

Reply Obj. 2: According to the Philosopher (Ethic. iv, 5), "the habit that observes the mean in anger is unnamed; so that the virtue is denominated from the diminution of anger, and is designated by the name of meekness." For the virtue is more akin to diminution than to excess, because it is more natural to man to desire vengeance for injuries done to him, than to be lacking in that desire, since "scarcely anyone belittles an injury done to himself," as Sallust observes [*Cf. Q. 120]. As to clemency, it mitigates punishment, not in respect of that which is according to right reason, but as regards that which is according to common law, which is the object of legal justice: yet on account of some particular consideration, it mitigates the punishment, deciding, as it were, that a man is not to be punished any further. Hence Seneca says (De Clementia ii, 1): "Clemency grants this, in the first place, that those whom she sets free are declared immune from all further punishment; and remission of punishment due amounts to a pardon." Wherefore it is clear that clemency is related to severity as equity [the Greek *epieikeia* [*Cf. Q. 120]] to legal justice, whereof severity is a part, as regards the infliction of punishment in accordance with the law. Yet clemency differs from equity, as we shall state further on (A. 3, ad 1).

Reply Obj. 3: The beatitudes are acts of virtue: while the fruits are delights in virtuous acts. Wherefore nothing hinders meekness being reckoned both virtue, and beatitude and fruit.

THIRD ARTICLE [II-II, Q. 157, Art. 3]

Whether the Aforesaid Virtues Are Parts of Temperance?

Objection 1: It would seem that the aforesaid virtues are not parts of temperance. For clemency mitigates punishment, as stated above (A. 2). But the Philosopher (Ethic. v, 10) ascribes this to equity, which pertains to justice, as stated above (Q. 120, A. 2). Therefore seemingly clemency is not a part of temperance.

Obj. 2: Further, temperance is concerned with concupiscences; whereas meekness and clemency regard, not concupiscences, but anger and vengeance. Therefore they should not be reckoned parts of temperance.

Obj. 3: Further, Seneca says (De Clementia ii, 4): "A man may be said to be of unsound mind when he takes pleasure in cruelty." Now this is opposed to clemency and meekness. Since then an unsound mind is opposed to prudence, it seems that clemency and meekness are parts of prudence rather than of temperance.

*On the contrary,* Seneca says (De Clementia ii, 3) that "clemency is temperance of the soul in exercising the power of taking revenge." Tully also (De Invent. Rhet. ii, 54) reckons clemency a part of temperance.

*I answer that,* Parts are assigned to the principal virtues, in so far as they imitate them in some secondary matter as to the mode whence the virtue derives its praise and likewise its name. Thus the mode and name of justice consist in a certain *equality,* those of fortitude in a certain *strength of mind,* those of temperance in a certain *restraint,* inasmuch as it restrains the most vehement concupiscences of the pleasures of touch. Now clemency and meekness likewise consist in a certain restraint, since clemency mitigates punishment, while meekness represses anger, as stated above (AA. 1, 2). Therefore both clemency and meekness are annexed to temperance as principal virtue, and accordingly are reckoned to be parts thereof.

Reply Obj. 1: Two points must be considered in the mitigation of punishment. One is that punishment should be mitigated in accordance with the lawgiver's intention, although not according to the letter of the law; and in this respect it pertains to equity. The other point is a certain moderation of a man's inward disposition, so that he does not exercise his power of inflicting punishment. This belongs properly to clemency, wherefore Seneca says (De Clementia ii, 3) that "it is temperance of the soul in exercising the power of taking revenge." This moderation of soul comes from a certain sweetness of disposition, whereby a man recoils from anything that may be painful to another. Wherefore Seneca says (De Clementia ii, 3) that "clemency is a certain smoothness of the soul"; for, on the other hand, there would seem to be a certain roughness of soul in one who fears not to pain others.

Reply Obj. 2: The annexation of secondary to principal virtues depends on the mode of virtue, which is, so to speak, a kind of form of the virtue, rather than on the matter. Now meekness and clemency agree with temperance in mode, as stated above, though they agree not in matter.

Reply Obj. 3: *Unsoundness* is corruption of soundness. Now just as soundness of body is corrupted by the body lapsing from the condition due to the human species, so unsoundness of mind is due to the mind lapsing from the disposition due to the human species. This occurs both in respect of the reason, as when a man loses the use of reason, and in respect of the appetitive power, as when a man loses that humane feeling whereby "every man is naturally friendly towards all other men" (Ethic. viii, 1). The unsoundness of mind that excludes the use of reason is opposed to prudence. But that a man who takes pleasure in the punishment of others is said to be of unsound mind, is because he seems on this account to be devoid of the humane feeling which gives rise to clemency.

FOURTH ARTICLE [II-II, Q. 157, Art. 4]

Whether Clemency and Meekness Are the Greatest Virtues?

Objection 1: It would seem that clemency and meekness are the greatest virtues. For virtue is deserving of praise chiefly because it directs man to happiness that consists in the knowledge of God. Now meekness above all directs man to the knowledge of God: for it is written (James 1:21): "With meekness receive the ingrafted word," and (Ecclus. 5:13): "Be meek to hear the word" of God. Again, Dionysius says (Ep. viii ad Demophil.) that "Moses was deemed worthy of the Divine apparition on account of his great meekness." Therefore meekness is the greatest of virtues.

Obj. 2: Further, seemingly a virtue is all the greater according as it is more acceptable to God and men. Now meekness would appear to be most acceptable to God. For it is written (Ecclus. 1:34, 35): "That which is agreeable" to God is "faith and meekness"; wherefore Christ expressly invites us to be meek like unto Himself (Matt. 11:29), where He says: "Learn of Me, because I am meek and humble of heart"; and Hilary declares [*Comment. in Matth. iv, 3] that "Christ dwells in us by our meekness of soul." Again, it is most acceptable to men; wherefore it is written (Ecclus. 3:19): "My son, do thy works in meekness, and thou shalt be beloved above the glory of men": for which reason it is also declared (Prov. 20:28) that the King's "throne is strengthened by clemency." Therefore meekness and clemency are the greatest of virtues.

Obj. 3: Further, Augustine says (De Serm. Dom. in Monte i, 2) that "the meek are they who yield to reproaches, and resist not evil, but overcome evil by good." Now this seems to pertain to mercy or piety which would seem to be the greatest of virtues: because a gloss of Ambrose [*Hilary the deacon] on 1 Tim. 4:8, "Piety [Douay: 'Godliness'] is profitable to all things," observes that "piety is the sum total of the Christian religion." Therefore meekness and clemency are the greatest virtues.

*On the contrary,* They are not reckoned as principal virtues, but are annexed to another, as to a principal, virtue.

*I answer that,* Nothing prevents certain virtues from being greatest, not indeed simply, nor in every respect, but in a particular genus. It is impossible for clemency or meekness to be absolutely the greatest virtues, since they owe their praise to the fact that they withdraw a man from evil, by mitigating anger or punishment. Now it is more perfect to obtain good than to lack evil. Wherefore those virtues like faith, hope, charity, and likewise prudence and justice, which direct one to good simply, are absolutely greater virtues than clemency and meekness.

Yet nothing prevents clemency and meekness from having a certain restricted excellence among the virtues which resist evil inclinations. For anger, which is mitigated by meekness, is, on account of its impetuousness, a very great obstacle to man's free judgment of truth: wherefore meekness above all makes a man self-possessed. Hence it is written (Ecclus. 10:31): "My son, keep thy soul in meekness." Yet the concupiscences of the pleasures of touch are more shameful, and harass more incessantly, for which reason temperance is more rightly reckoned as a principal virtue. as stated above (Q. 141, A. 7, ad 2). As to clemency, inasmuch as it mitigates punishment, it would seem to approach nearest to charity, the greatest of the virtues, since thereby we do good towards our neighbor, and hinder his evil.

Reply Obj. 1: Meekness disposes man to the knowledge of God, by removing an obstacle; and this in two ways. First, because it makes man self-possessed by mitigating his anger, as stated above; secondly, because it pertains to meekness that a man does not contradict the words of truth, which many do through being disturbed by anger. Wherefore Augustine says (De Doctr. Christ. ii, 7): "To be meek is not to contradict Holy Writ, whether we understand it, if it condemn our evil ways, or understand it not, as though we might know better and have a clearer insight of the truth."

Reply Obj. 2: Meekness and clemency make us acceptable to God and men, in so far as they concur with charity, the greatest of the virtues, towards the same effect, namely the mitigation of our neighbor's evils.

Reply Obj. 3: Mercy and piety agree indeed with meekness and clemency by concurring towards the same effect, namely the mitigation of our neighbor's evils. Nevertheless they differ as to motive. For piety relieves a neighbor's evil through reverence for a superior, for instance God or one's parents: mercy relieves a neighbor's evil, because this evil is displeasing to one, in so far as one looks upon it as affecting oneself, as stated above (Q. 30, A. 2): and this results from friendship which makes friends rejoice and grieve for the same things: meekness does this, by removing anger that urges to vengeance, and clemency does this through leniency of soul, in so far as it judges equitable that a person be no further punished.

## QUESTION 158

OF ANGER (In Eight Articles)

We must next consider the contrary vices: (1) Anger that is opposed to meekness; (2) Cruelty that is opposed to clemency. Concerning anger there are eight points of inquiry:

(1) Whether it is lawful to be angry?
(2) Whether anger is a sin?
(3) Whether it is a mortal sin?
(4) Whether it is the most grievous of sins?
(5) Of its species;
(6) Whether anger is a capital vice?
(7) Of its daughters;
(8) Whether it has a contrary vice?

FIRST ARTICLE [II-II, Q. 158, Art. 1]

Whether It Is Lawful to Be Angry?

Objection 1: It would seem that it cannot be lawful to be angry. For Jerome in his exposition on Matt. 5:22, "Whosoever is angry with his brother," etc. says: "Some codices add 'without cause.' However, in the genuine codices the sentence is unqualified, and anger is forbidden altogether." Therefore it is nowise lawful to be angry.

Obj. 2: Further, according to Dionysius (Div. Nom. iv) "The soul's evil is to be without reason." Now anger is always without reason: for the Philosopher says (Ethic. vii, 6) that "anger does not listen perfectly to reason"; and Gregory says (Moral. v, 45) that "when anger sunders the tranquil surface of the soul, it mangles and rends it by its riot"; and Cassian says (De Inst. Caenob. viii, 6): "From whatever cause it arises, the angry passion boils over and blinds the eye of the mind." Therefore it is always evil to be angry.

Obj. 3: Further, anger is "desire for vengeance" [*Aristotle, Rhet. ii, 2] according to a gloss on Lev. 19:17, "Thou shalt not hate thy brother in thy heart." Now it would seem unlawful to desire vengeance, since this should be left to God, according to Deut. 32:35, "Revenge is Mine." Therefore it would seem that to be angry is always an evil.

Obj. 4: Further, all that makes us depart from likeness to God is evil. Now anger always makes us depart from likeness to God, since God judges with tranquillity according to Wis. 12:18. Therefore to be angry is always an evil.

*On the contrary,* Chrysostom [*Hom. xi in the Opus Imperfectum, falsely ascribed to St. John Chrysostom] says: "He that is angry without cause, shall be in danger; but he that is angry with cause, shall not be in danger: for without anger, teaching will be useless, judgments unstable, crimes unchecked." Therefore to be angry is not always an evil.

*I answer that,* Properly speaking anger is a passion of the sensitive appetite, and gives its name to the irascible power, as stated above (I-II, Q. 46, A. 1) when we were treating of the passions. Now with regard to the passions of the soul, it is to be observed that evil may be found in them in two ways. First by reason of the passion's very species, which is derived from the passion's object. Thus envy, in respect of its species, denotes an evil, since it is displeasure at another's good, and such displeasure is in itself contrary to reason: wherefore, as the Philosopher remarks (Ethic. ii, 6), "the very mention of envy denotes something evil." Now this does not apply to anger, which is the desire for revenge, since revenge may be desired both well and ill. Secondly, evil is found in a passion in respect of the passion's quantity, that is in respect of its excess or deficiency; and thus evil may be found in anger, when, to wit, one is angry, more or less than right reason demands. But if one is angry in accordance with right reason, one's anger is deserving of praise.

Reply Obj. 1: The Stoics designated anger and all the other passions as emotions opposed to the order of reason; and accordingly they deemed anger and all other passions to be evil, as stated above (I-II, Q. 24, A. 2) when we were treating of the passions. It is in this sense that Jerome considers anger; for he speaks of the anger whereby one is angry with one's neighbor, with the intent of doing him a wrong.—But, according to the Peripatetics, to whose opinion Augustine inclines (De Civ. Dei ix, 4), anger and the other passions of the soul are movements of the sensitive appetite, whether they be moderated or not, according to reason: and in this sense anger is not always evil.

Reply Obj. 2: Anger may stand in a twofold relation to reason. First, antecedently; in this way it withdraws reason from its rectitude, and has therefore the character of evil. Secondly, consequently, inasmuch as the movement of the sensitive appetite is directed against vice and in accordance with reason, this anger is good, and is called "zealous anger." Wherefore Gregory says (Moral. v, 45): "We must beware lest, when we use anger as an instrument of virtue, it overrule the mind, and go before it as its mistress, instead of following in reason's train, ever ready, as its handmaid, to obey." This latter anger, although it hinder somewhat the judgment of reason in the execution of the act, does not destroy the rectitude of reason. Hence Gregory says (Moral. v, 45) that "zealous anger troubles the eye of reason, whereas sinful anger blinds it." Nor is it incompatible with virtue that the deliberation of reason be interrupted in the execution of what reason has deliberated: since art also would be hindered in its act, if it were to deliberate about what has to be done, while having to act.

Reply Obj. 3: It is unlawful to desire vengeance considered as evil to the man who is to be punished, but it is praiseworthy to desire vengeance as a corrective of vice and for the good of justice; and to this the sensitive appetite can tend, in so far as it is moved thereto by the reason: and when revenge is taken in accordance with the order of judgment, it is God's work, since he who has power to punish "is God's minister," as stated in Rom. 13:4.

Reply Obj. 4: We can and ought to be like to God in the desire for good; but we cannot be altogether likened to Him in the mode of our desire, since in God there is no sensitive appetite, as in us, the movement of which has to obey reason. Wherefore Gregory says (Moral. v, 45) that "anger is more firmly erect in withstanding vice, when it bows to the command of reason."

SECOND ARTICLE [II-II, Q. 158, Art. 2]

Whether Anger Is a Sin?

Objection 1: It would seem that anger is not a sin. For we demerit by sinning. But "we do not demerit by the passions, even as neither do we incur blame thereby," as stated in *Ethic.* ii, 5. Consequently no passion is a sin. Now anger is a passion as stated above (I-II, Q. 46, A. 1) in the treatise on the passions. Therefore anger is not a sin.

Obj. 2: Further, in every sin there is conversion to some mutable good. But in anger there is conversion not to a mutable good, but to a person's evil. Therefore anger is not a sin.

Obj. 3: Further, "No man sins in what he cannot avoid," as Augustine asserts [*De Lib. Arb. iii, 18]. But man cannot avoid anger, for a gloss on Ps. 4:5, "Be ye angry and sin not," says: "The movement of anger is not in our power." Again, the Philosopher asserts (Ethic. vii, 6) that "the angry man acts with displeasure." Now displeasure is contrary to the will. Therefore anger is not a sin.

Obj. 4: Further, sin is contrary to nature, according to Damascene [*De Fide Orth. ii, 4, 30]. But it is not contrary to man's nature to be angry, and it is the natural act of a power, namely the irascible; wherefore Jerome says in a letter [*Ep. xii ad Anton. Monach.] that "to be angry is the property of man." Therefore it is not a sin to be angry.

*On the contrary,* The Apostle says (Eph. 4:31): "Let all indignation and anger [*Vulg.: 'Anger and indignation'] ... be put away from you."

*I answer that,* Anger, as stated above (A. 1), is properly the name of a passion. A passion of the sensitive appetite is good in so far as it is regulated by reason, whereas it is evil if it set the order of reason aside. Now the order of reason, in regard to anger, may be considered in relation to two things. First, in relation to the appetible object to which anger tends, and that is revenge. Wherefore if one desire revenge to be taken in accordance with the order of reason, the desire of anger is praiseworthy, and is called "zealous anger" [*Cf. Greg., Moral. v, 45]. On the other hand, if one desire the taking of vengeance in any way whatever contrary to the order of reason, for instance if he desire the punishment of one who has not deserved it, or beyond his deserts, or again contrary to the order prescribed by law, or not for the due end, namely the maintaining of justice and the correction of defaults, then the desire of anger will be sinful, and this is called sinful anger.

Secondly, the order of reason in regard to anger may be considered in relation to the mode of being angry, namely that the movement of anger should not be immoderately fierce, neither internally nor externally; and if this condition be disregarded, anger will not lack sin, even though just vengeance be desired.

Reply Obj. 1: Since passion may be either regulated or not regulated by reason, it follows that a passion considered absolutely does not include the notion of merit or demerit, of praise or blame. But as regulated by reason, it may be something meritorious and deserving of praise; while on the other hand, as not regulated by reason, it may be demeritorious and blameworthy. Wherefore the Philosopher says (Ethic. ii, 5) that "it is he who is angry in a certain way, that is praised or blamed."

Reply Obj. 2: The angry man desires the evil of another, not for its own sake but for the sake of revenge, towards which his appetite turns as to a mutable good.

Reply Obj. 3: Man is master of his actions through the judgment of his reason, wherefore as to the movements that forestall that judgment, it is not in man's power to prevent them as a whole, i.e. so that none of them arise, although his reason is able to check each one, if it arise. Accordingly it is stated that the movement of anger is not in man's power, to the extent namely that no such movement arise. Yet since this movement is somewhat in his power, it is not entirely sinless if it be inordinate. The statement of the Philosopher that "the angry man acts with displeasure," means that he is displeased, not with his being angry, but with the injury which he deems done to himself: and through this displeasure he is moved to seek vengeance.

Reply Obj. 4: The irascible power in man is naturally subject to his reason, wherefore its act is natural to man, in so far as it is in accord with reason, and in so far as it is against reason, it is contrary to man's nature.

THIRD ARTICLE [II-II, Q. 158, Art. 3]

Whether All Anger Is a Mortal Sin?

Objection 1: It would seem that all anger is a mortal sin. For it is written (Job 5:2): "Anger killeth the foolish man [*Vulg.: 'Anger indeed killeth the foolish'];" and he speaks of the spiritual killing, whence mortal sin takes its name. Therefore all anger is a mortal sin.

Obj. 2: Further, nothing save mortal sin is deserving of eternal condemnation. Now anger deserves eternal condemnation; for our Lord said (Matt. 5:22): "Whosoever is angry with his brother shall be in danger of the judgment": and a gloss on this passage says that "the three things mentioned there, namely judgment, council, and hell-fire, signify in a pointed manner different abodes in the state of eternal damnation corresponding to various sins." Therefore anger is a mortal sin.

Obj. 3: Further, whatsoever is contrary to charity is a mortal sin. Now anger is of itself contrary to charity, as Jerome declares in his commentary on Matt. 5:22, "Whosoever is angry with his brother," etc. where he says that this is contrary to the love of your neighbor. Therefore anger is a mortal sin.

*On the contrary,* A gloss on Ps. 4:5, "Be ye angry and sin not," says: "Anger is venial if it does not proceed to action."

*I answer that,* The movement of anger may be inordinate and sinful in two ways, as stated above (A. 2). First, on the part of the appetible object, as when one desires unjust revenge; and thus anger is a mortal sin in the point of its genus, because it is contrary to charity and justice. Nevertheless such like anger may happen to be a venial sin by reason of the imperfection of the act. This imperfection is considered either in relation to the subject desirous of vengeance, as when the movement of anger forestalls the judgment of his reason; or in relation to the desired object, as when one desires to be avenged in a trifling matter, which should be deemed of no account, so that even if one proceeded to action, it would not be a mortal sin, for instance by pulling a child slightly by the hair, or by some other like action. Secondly, the movement of anger may be inordinate in the mode of being angry, for instance, if one be too fiercely angry inwardly, or if one exceed in the outward signs of anger. In this way anger is not a mortal sin in the point of its genus; yet it may happen to be a mortal sin, for instance if through the fierceness of his anger a man fall away from the love of God and his neighbor.

Reply Obj. 1: It does not follow from the passage quoted that all anger is a mortal sin, but that the foolish are killed spiritually by anger, because, through not checking the movement of anger by their reason, they fall into mortal sins, for instance by blaspheming God or by doing injury to their neighbor.

Reply Obj. 2: Our Lord said this of anger, by way of addition to the words of the Law: "Whosoever shall kill shall be in danger of the judgment" (Matt. 5:21). Consequently our Lord is speaking here of the movement of anger wherein a man desires the killing or any grave injury of his neighbor: and should the consent of reason be given to this desire, without doubt it will be a mortal sin.

Reply Obj. 3: In the case where anger is contrary to charity, it is a mortal sin, but it is not always so, as appears from what we have said.

FOURTH ARTICLE [II-II, Q. 158, Art. 4]

Whether Anger Is the Most Grievous Sin?

Objection 1: It would seem that anger is the most grievous sin. For Chrysostom says [*Hom. xlviii in Joan.] that "nothing is more repulsive than the look of an angry man, and nothing uglier than a ruthless* face, and most of all than a cruel soul." [* *Severo* . The correct text is *Si vero.* The translation would then run thus ... "and nothing uglier." And if his "face is ugly, how much uglier is his soul!"]. Therefore anger is the most grievous sin.

Obj. 2: Further, the more hurtful a sin is, the worse it would seem to be; since, according to Augustine (Enchiridion xii), "a thing is said to be evil because it hurts." Now anger is most hurtful, because it deprives man of his reason, whereby he is master of himself; for Chrysostom says (Hom. xlviii in Joan.) that "anger differs in no way from madness; it is a demon while it lasts, indeed more troublesome than one harassed by a demon." Therefore anger is the most grievous sin.

Obj. 3: Further, inward movements are judged according to their outward effects. Now the effect of anger is murder, which is a most grievous sin. Therefore anger is a most grievous sin.

*On the contrary,* Anger is compared to hatred as the mote to the beam; for Augustine says in his Rule (Ep. ccxi): "Lest anger grow into hatred and a mote become a beam." Therefore anger is not the most grievous sin.

*I answer that,* As stated above (AA. 1, 2), the inordinateness of anger is considered in a twofold respect, namely with regard to an undue object, and with regard to an undue mode of being angry. As to the appetible object which it desires, anger would seem to be the least of sins, for anger desires the evil of punishment for some person, under the aspect of a good that is vengeance. Hence on the part of the evil which it desires the sin of anger agrees with those sins which desire the evil of our neighbor, such as envy and hatred; but while hatred desires absolutely another's evil as such, and the envious man desires another's evil through desire of his own glory, the angry man desires another's evil under the aspect of just revenge. Wherefore it is evident that hatred is more grievous than envy, and envy than anger: since it is worse to desire evil as an evil, than as a good; and to desire evil as an external good such as honor or glory, than under the aspect of the rectitude of justice. On the part of the good, under the aspect of which the angry man desires an evil, anger concurs with the sin of concupiscence that tends to a good. In this respect again, absolutely speaking, the sin of anger is apparently less grievous than that of concupiscence, according as the good of justice, which the angry man desires, is better than the pleasurable or useful good which is desired by the subject of concupiscence. Wherefore the Philosopher says (Ethic. vii, 4) that "the incontinent in desire is more disgraceful than the incontinent in anger."

On the other hand, as to the inordinateness which regards the mode of being angry, anger would seem to have a certain pre-eminence on account of the strength and quickness of its movement, according to Prov. 27:4, "Anger hath no mercy, nor fury when it breaketh forth: and who can bear the violence of one provoked?" Hence Gregory says (Moral. v, 45): "The heart goaded by the pricks of anger is convulsed, the body trembles, the tongue entangles itself, the face is inflamed, the eyes are enraged and fail utterly to recognize those whom we know: the tongue makes sounds indeed, but there is no sense in its utterance."

Reply Obj. 1: Chrysostom is alluding to the repulsiveness of the outward gestures which result from the impetuousness of anger.

Reply Obj. 2: This argument considers the inordinate movement of anger, that results from its impetuousness, as stated above.

Reply Obj. 3: Murder results from hatred and envy no less than from anger: yet anger is less grievous, inasmuch as it considers the aspect of justice, as stated above.

FIFTH ARTICLE [II-II, Q. 158, Art. 5]

Whether the Philosopher Suitably Assigns the Species of Anger?

Objection 1: It would seem that the species of anger are unsuitably assigned by the Philosopher (Ethic. iv, 5) where he says that some angry persons are "choleric," some "sullen," and some "ill-tempered" or "stern." According to him, a person is said to be "sullen" whose anger "is appeased with difficulty and endures a long time." But this apparently pertains to the circumstance of time. Therefore it seems that anger can be differentiated specifically in respect also of the other circumstances.

Obj. 2: Further, he says (Ethic. iv, 5) that "ill-tempered" or "stern" persons "are those whose anger is not appeased without revenge, or punishment." Now this also pertains to the unquenchableness of anger. Therefore seemingly the ill-tempered is the same as bitterness.

Obj. 3: Further, our Lord mentions three degrees of anger, when He says (Matt. 5:22): "Whosoever is angry with his brother, shall be in danger of the judgment: and whosoever shall say to his brother, Raca, shall be in danger of the council, and whosoever shall say" to his brother, "Thou fool." But these degrees are not referable to the aforesaid species. Therefore it seems that the above division of anger is not fitting.

*On the contrary,* Gregory of Nyssa [*Nemesius, De Nat. Hom. xxi] says "there are three species of irascibility," namely, "the anger which is called wrath [* *Fellea*, i.e. like gall. But in I-II, Q. 46, A. 8, St. Thomas quoting the same authority has *Cholos* which we render 'wrath']," and "ill-will" which is a disease of the mind, and "rancour." Now these three seem to coincide with the three aforesaid. For "wrath" he describes as "having beginning and movement," and the Philosopher (Ethic. iv, 5) ascribes this to "choleric" persons: "ill-will" he describes as "an anger that endures and grows old," and this the Philosopher ascribes to "sullenness"; while he describes "rancour" as "reckoning the time for vengeance," which tallies with the Philosopher's description of the "ill-tempered." The same division is given by Damascene (De Fide Orth. ii, 16). Therefore the aforesaid division assigned by the Philosopher is not unfitting.

*I answer that,* The aforesaid distinction may be referred either to the passion, or to the sin itself of anger. We have already stated when treating of the passions (I-II, Q. 46, A. 8) how it is to be applied to the passion of anger. And it would seem that this is chiefly what Gregory of Nyssa and Damascene had in view. Here, however, we have to take the distinction of these species in its application to the sin of anger, and as set down by the Philosopher.

For the inordinateness of anger may be considered in relation to two things. First, in relation to the origin of anger, and this regards "choleric" persons, who are angry too quickly and for any slight cause. Secondly, in relation to the duration of anger, for that anger endures too long; and this may happen in two ways. In one way, because the cause of anger, to wit, the inflicted injury, remains too long in a man's memory, the result being that it gives rise to a lasting displeasure, wherefore he is "grievous" and "sullen" to himself. In another way, it happens on the part of vengeance, which a man seeks with a stubborn desire: this applies to "ill-tempered" or "stern" people, who do not put aside their anger until they have inflicted punishment.

Reply Obj. 1: It is not time, but a man's propensity to anger, or his pertinacity in anger, that is the chief point of consideration in the aforesaid species.

Reply Obj. 2: Both "sullen" and "ill-tempered" people have a long-lasting anger, but for different reasons. For a "sullen" person has an abiding anger on account of an abiding displeasure, which he holds locked in his breast; and as he does not break forth into the outward signs of anger, others cannot reason him out of it, nor does he of his own accord lay aside his anger, except his displeasure wear away with time and thus his anger cease. On the other hand, the anger of "ill-tempered" persons is long-lasting on account of their intense desire for revenge, so that it does not wear out with time, and can be quelled only by revenge.

Reply Obj. 3: The degrees of anger mentioned by our Lord do not refer to the different species of anger, but correspond to the course of the human act [*Cf. I-II, Q. 46, A. 8, Obj. 3]. For the first degree is an inward conception, and in reference to this He says: "Whosoever is angry with his brother." The second degree is when the anger is manifested by outward signs, even before it breaks out into effect; and in reference to this He says: "Whosoever shall say to his brother, Raca!" which is an angry exclamation. The third degree is when the sin conceived inwardly breaks out into effect. Now the effect of anger is another's hurt under the aspect of revenge; and the least of hurts is that which is done by a mere word; wherefore in reference to this He says: "Whosoever shall say to his brother Thou fool!" Consequently it is clear that the second adds to the first, and the third to both the others; so that, if the first is a mortal sin, in the case referred to by our Lord, as stated above (A. 3, ad 2), much more so are the others. Wherefore some kind of condemnation is assigned as corresponding to each one of them. In the first case "judgment" is assigned, and this is the least severe, for as Augustine says [*Serm. Dom. in Monte i, 9], "where judgment is to be delivered, there is an opportunity for defense": in the second case "council" is assigned, "whereby the judges deliberate together on the punishment to be inflicted": to the third case is assigned "hell-fire," i.e. "decisive condemnation."

SIXTH ARTICLE [II-II, Q. 158, Art. 6]

Whether Anger Should Be Reckoned Among the Capital Vices?

Objection 1: It would seem that anger should not be reckoned among the capital sins. For anger is born of sorrow which is a capital vice known by the name of sloth. Therefore anger should not be reckoned a capital vice.

Obj. 2: Further, hatred is a graver sin than anger. Therefore it should be reckoned a capital vice rather than anger.

Obj. 3: Further, a gloss on Prov. 29:22, "An angry [Douay: 'passionate'] man provoketh quarrels," says: "Anger is the door to all vices: if it be closed, peace is ensured within to all the virtues; if it be opened, the soul is armed for every crime." Now no capital vice is the origin of all sins, but only of certain definite ones. Therefore anger should not be reckoned among the capital vices.

*On the contrary,* Gregory (Moral. xxxi, 45) places anger among the capital vices.

*I answer that,* As stated above (I-II, Q. 84, A. 3, 4), a capital vice is defined as one from which many vices arise. Now there are two reasons for which many vices can arise from anger. The first is on the part of its object which has much of the aspect of desirability, in so far as revenge is desired under the aspect of just or honest*, which is attractive by its excellence, as stated above (A. 4). [*Honesty must be taken here in its broad sense as synonymous with moral goodness, from the point of view of decorum; Cf. Q. 145, A. 1.] The second is on the part of its impetuosity, whereby it precipitates the mind into all kinds of inordinate action. Therefore it is evident that anger is a capital vice.

Reply Obj. 1: The sorrow whence anger arises is not, for the most part, the vice of sloth, but the passion of sorrow, which results from an injury inflicted.

Reply Obj. 2: As stated above (Q. 118, A. 7; Q. 148, A. 5; Q. 153, A. 4; I-II, Q. 84, A. 4), it belongs to the notion of a capital vice to have a most desirable end, so that many sins are committed through the desire thereof. Now anger, which desires evil under the aspect of good, has a more desirable end than hatred has, since the latter desires evil under the aspect of evil: wherefore anger is more a capital vice than hatred is.

Reply Obj. 3: Anger is stated to be the door to the vices accidentally, that is by removing obstacles, to wit by hindering the judgment of reason, whereby man is withdrawn from evil. It is, however, directly the cause of certain special sins, which are called its daughters.

SEVENTH ARTICLE [II-II, Q. 158, Art. 7]

Whether Six Daughters Are Fittingly Assigned to Anger?

Objection 1: It would seem that six daughters are unfittingly assigned to anger, namely "quarreling, swelling of the mind, contumely, clamor, indignation and blasphemy." For blasphemy is reckoned by Isidore [*QQ. in Deut., qu. xvi] to be a daughter of pride. Therefore it should not be accounted a daughter of anger.

Obj. 2: Further, hatred is born of anger, as Augustine says in his rule (Ep. ccxi). Therefore it should be placed among the daughters of anger.

Obj. 3: Further, "a swollen mind" would seem to be the same as pride. Now pride is not the daughter of a vice, but "the mother of all vices," as Gregory states (Moral. xxxi, 45). Therefore swelling of the mind should not be reckoned among the daughters of anger.

*On the contrary,* Gregory (Moral. xxxi, 45) assigns these daughters to anger.

*I answer that,* Anger may be considered in three ways. First, as consisting in thought, and thus two vices arise from anger. One is on the part of the person with whom a man is angry, and whom he deems unworthy ( *indignum* ) of acting thus towards him, and this is called "indignation." The other vice is on the part of the man himself, in so far as he devises various means of vengeance, and with such like thoughts fills his mind, according to Job 15:2, "Will a wise man ... fill his stomach with burning heat?" And thus we have "swelling of the mind."

Secondly, anger may be considered, as expressed in words: and thus a twofold disorder arises from anger. One is when a man manifests his anger in his manner of speech, as stated above (A. 5, ad 3) of the man who says to his brother, "Raca": and this refers to "clamor," which denotes disorderly and confused speech. The other disorder is when a man breaks out into injurious words, and if these be against God, it is "blasphemy," if against one's neighbor, it is "contumely."

Thirdly, anger may be considered as proceeding to deeds; and thus anger gives rise to "quarrels," by which we are to understand all manner of injuries inflicted on one's neighbor through anger.

Reply Obj. 1: The blasphemy into which a man breaks out deliberately proceeds from pride, whereby a man lifts himself up against God: since, according to Ecclus. 10:14, "the beginning of the pride of man is to fall off from God," i.e. to fall away from reverence for Him is the first part of pride [*Cf. Q. 162, A. 7, ad 2]; and this gives rise to blasphemy. But the blasphemy into which a man breaks out through a disturbance of the mind, proceeds from anger.

Reply Obj. 2: Although hatred sometimes arises from anger, it has a previous cause, from which it arises more directly, namely displeasure, even as, on the other hand, love is born of pleasure. Now through displeasure, a man is moved sometimes to anger, sometimes to hatred. Wherefore it was fitting to reckon that hatred arises from sloth rather than from anger.

Reply Obj. 3: Swelling of the mind is not taken here as identical with pride, but for a certain effort or daring attempt to take vengeance; and daring is a vice opposed to fortitude.

EIGHTH ARTICLE [II-II, Q. 158, Art. 8]

Whether There Is a Vice Opposed to Anger Resulting from Lack of Anger?

Objection 1: It would seem that there is not a vice opposed to anger, resulting from lack of anger. For no vice makes us like to God. Now by being entirely without anger, a man becomes like to God, Who judges "with tranquillity" (Wis. 12:18). Therefore seemingly it is not a vice to be altogether without anger.

Obj. 2: Further, it is not a vice to lack what is altogether useless. But the movement of anger is useful for no purpose, as Seneca proves in the book he wrote on anger (De Ira i, 9, seqq.). Therefore it seems that lack of anger is not a vice.

Obj. 3: Further, according to Dionysius (Div. Nom. iv), "man's evil is to be without reason." Now the judgment of reason remains unimpaired, if all movement of anger be done away. Therefore no lack of anger amounts to a vice.

*On the contrary,* Chrysostom [*Hom. xi in Matth. in the Opus Imperfectum, falsely ascribed to St. John Chrysostom] says: "He who is not angry, whereas he has cause to be, sins. For unreasonable patience is the hotbed of many vices, it fosters negligence, and incites not only the wicked but even the good to do wrong."

*I answer that,* Anger may be understood in two ways. In one way, as a simple movement of the will, whereby one inflicts punishment, not through passion, but in virtue of a judgment of the reason: and thus without doubt lack of anger is a sin. This is the sense in which anger is taken in the saying of Chrysostom, for he says (Hom. xi in Matth., in the Opus Imperfectum, falsely ascribed to St. John Chrysostom): "Anger, when it has a cause, is not anger but judgment. For anger, properly speaking, denotes a movement of passion": and when a man is angry with reason, his anger is no longer from passion: wherefore he is said to judge, not to be angry. In another way anger is taken for a movement of the sensitive appetite, which is with passion resulting from a bodily transmutation. This movement is a necessary sequel, in man, to the movement of his will, since the lower appetite necessarily follows the movement of the higher appetite, unless there be an obstacle. Hence the movement of anger in the sensitive appetite cannot be lacking altogether, unless the movement of the will be altogether lacking or weak. Consequently lack of the passion of anger is also a vice, even as the lack of movement in the will directed to punishment by the judgment of reason.

Reply Obj. 1: He that is entirely without anger when he ought to be angry, imitates God as to lack of passion, but not as to God's punishing by judgment.

Reply Obj. 2: The passion of anger, like all other movements of the sensitive appetite, is useful, as being conducive to the more prompt execution [*Cf. I-II, Q. 24, A. 3] of reason's dictate: else, the sensitive appetite in man would be to no purpose, whereas "nature does nothing without purpose" [*Aristotle, De Coelo i, 4].

Reply Obj. 3: When a man acts inordinately, the judgment of his reason is cause not only of the simple movement of the will but also of the passion in the sensitive appetite, as stated above. Wherefore just as the removal of the effect is a sign that the cause is removed, so the lack of anger is a sign that the judgment of reason is lacking.

# QUESTION 159

OF CRUELTY (In Two Articles)

We must now consider cruelty, under which head there are two points of inquiry:

(1) Whether cruelty is opposed to clemency?

(2) Of its comparison with savagery or brutality.

FIRST ARTICLE [II-II, Q. 159, Art. 1]

Whether Cruelty Is Opposed to Clemency?

Objection 1: It would seem that cruelty is not opposed to clemency. For Seneca says (De Clementia ii, 4) that "those are said to be cruel who exceed in punishing," which is contrary to justice. Now clemency is reckoned a part, not of justice but of temperance. Therefore apparently cruelty is not opposed to clemency.

Obj. 2: Further, it is written (Jer. 6:23): "They are cruel, and will have no mercy"; so that cruelty would seem opposed to mercy. Now mercy is not the same as clemency, as stated above (Q. 157, A. 4, ad 3). Therefore cruelty is not opposed to clemency.

Obj. 3: Further, clemency is concerned with the infliction of punishment, as stated above (Q. 157, A. 1): whereas cruelty applies to the withdrawal of beneficence, according to Prov. 11:17, "But he that is cruel casteth off even his own kindred." Therefore cruelty is not opposed to clemency.

*On the contrary,* Seneca says (De Clementia ii, 4) that "the opposite of clemency is cruelty, which is nothing else but hardness of heart in exacting punishment."

*I answer that,* Cruelty apparently takes its name from cruditas (rawness). Now just as things when cooked and prepared are wont to have an agreeable and sweet savor, so when raw they have a disagreeable and bitter taste. Now it has been stated above (Q. 157, A. 3, ad 1; A. 4, ad 3) that clemency denotes a certain smoothness or sweetness of soul, whereby one is inclined to mitigate punishment. Hence cruelty is directly opposed to clemency.

Reply Obj. 1: Just as it belongs to equity to mitigate punishment according to reason, while the sweetness of soul which inclines one to this belongs to clemency: so too, excess in punishing, as regards the external action, belongs to injustice; but as regards the hardness of heart, which makes one ready to increase punishment, belongs to cruelty.

Reply Obj. 2: Mercy and clemency concur in this, that both shun and recoil from another's unhappiness, but in different ways. For it belongs to mercy [*Cf. Q. 30, A. 1] to relieve another's unhappiness by a beneficent action, while it belongs to clemency to mitigate another's unhappiness by the cessation of punishment. And since cruelty denotes excess in exacting punishment, it is more directly opposed to clemency than to mercy; yet on account of the mutual likeness of these virtues, cruelty is sometimes taken for mercilessness.

Reply Obj. 3: Cruelty is there taken for mercilessness, which is lack of beneficence. We may also reply that withdrawal of beneficence is in itself a punishment.

SECOND ARTICLE [II-II, Q. 159, Art. 2]

Whether Cruelty Differs from Savagery or Brutality?

Objection 1: It would seem that cruelty differs not from savagery or brutality. For seemingly one vice is opposed in one way to one virtue. Now both savagery and cruelty are opposed to clemency by way of excess. Therefore it would seem that savagery and cruelty are the same.

Obj. 2: Further, Isidore says (Etym. x) that "severity is as it were savagery with verity, because it holds to justice without attending to piety": so that savagery would seem to exclude that mitigation of punishment in delivering judgment which is demanded by piety. Now this has been stated to belong to cruelty (A. 1, ad 1). Therefore cruelty is the same as savagery.

Obj. 3: Further, just as there is a vice opposed to a virtue by way of excess, so is there a vice opposed to it by way of deficiency, which latter is opposed both to the virtue which is the mean, and to the vice which is in excess. Now the same vice pertaining to deficiency is opposed to both cruelty and savagery, namely remission or laxity. For Gregory says (Moral. xx, 5): "Let there be love, but not that which enervates, let there be severity, but without fury, let there be zeal without unseemly savagery, let there be piety without undue clemency." Therefore savagery is the same as cruelty.

*On the contrary,* Seneca says (De Clementia ii, 4) that "a man who is angry without being hurt, or with one who has not offended him, is not said to be cruel, but to be brutal or savage."

*I answer that,* "Savagery" and "brutality" take their names from a likeness to wild beasts which are also described as savage. For animals of this kind attack man that they may feed on his body, and not for some motive of justice the consideration of which belongs to reason alone. Wherefore, properly speaking, brutality or savagery applies to those who in inflicting punishment have not in view a default of the person punished, but merely the pleasure they derive from a man's torture. Consequently it is evident that it is comprised under bestiality: for such like pleasure is not human but bestial, and resulting as it does either from evil custom, or from a corrupt nature, as do other bestial emotions. On the other hand, cruelty not only regards the default of the person punished, but exceeds in the mode of punishing: wherefore cruelty differs from savagery or brutality, as human wickedness differs from bestiality, as stated in *Ethic.* vii, 5.

Reply Obj. 1: Clemency is a human virtue; wherefore directly opposed to it is cruelty which is a form of human wickedness. But savagery or brutality is comprised under bestiality, wherefore it is directly opposed not to clemency, but to a more excellent virtue, which the Philosopher (Ethic. vii, 5) calls "heroic" or "god-like," which according to us, would seem to pertain to the gifts of the Holy Ghost. Consequently we may say that savagery is directly opposed to the gift of piety.

Reply Obj. 2: A severe man is not said to be simply savage, because this implies a vice; but he is said to be "savage as regards the truth," on account of some likeness to savagery which is not inclined to mitigate punishment.

Reply Obj. 3: Remission of punishment is not a vice, except it disregard the order of justice, which requires a man to be punished on account of his offense, and which cruelty exceeds. On the other hand, cruelty disregards this order altogether. Wherefore remission of punishment is opposed to cruelty, but not to savagery.

## QUESTION 160

OF MODESTY (In Two Articles)

We must now consider modesty: and (1) Modesty in general; (2) Each of its species. Under the first head there are two points of inquiry:

(1) Whether modesty is a part of temperance?

(2) What is the matter of modesty?

FIRST ARTICLE [II-II, Q. 160, Art. 1]

Whether Modesty Is a Part of Temperance?

Objection 1: It would seem that modesty is not a part of temperance. For modesty is denominated from mode. Now mode is requisite in every virtue: since virtue is directed to good; and "good," according to Augustine (De Nat. Boni 3), "consists in mode, species, and order." Therefore modesty is a general virtue, and consequently should not be reckoned a part of temperance.

Obj. 2: Further, temperance would seem to be deserving of praise chiefly on account of its moderation. Now this gives modesty its name. Therefore modesty is the same as temperance, and not one of its parts.

Obj. 3: Further, modesty would seem to regard the correction of our neighbor, according to 2 Tim. 2:24, 25, "The servant of the Lord must not wrangle, but be mild towards all men ... with modesty admonishing them that resist the truth." Now admonishing wrong-doers is an act of justice or of charity, as stated above (Q. 33, A. 1). Therefore seemingly modesty is a part of justice rather than of temperance.

*On the contrary,* Tully (De Invent. Rhet. ii, 54) reckons modesty as a part of temperance.

*I answer that,* As stated above (Q. 141, A. 4; Q. 157, A. 3), temperance brings moderation into those things wherein it is most difficult to be moderate, namely the concupiscences of pleasures of touch. Now whenever there is a special virtue about some matter of very great moment, there must needs be another virtue about matters of lesser import: because the life of man requires to be regulated by the virtues with regard to everything: thus it was stated above (Q. 134, A. 3, ad 1), that while magnificence is about great expenditure, there is need in addition for liberality, which is concerned with ordinary expenditure. Hence there is need for a virtue to moderate other lesser matters where moderation is not so difficult. This virtue is called modesty, and is annexed to temperance as its principal.

Reply Obj. 1: When a name is common to many it is sometimes appropriated to those of the lowest rank; thus the common name of angel is appropriated to the lowest order of angels. In the same way, mode which is observed by all virtues in common, is specially appropriated to the virtue which prescribes the mode in the slightest things.

Reply Obj. 2: Some things need tempering on account of their strength, thus we temper strong wine. But moderation is necessary in all things: wherefore temperance is more concerned with strong passions, and modesty about weaker passions.

Reply Obj. 3: Modesty is to be taken there for the general moderation which is necessary in all virtues.

SECOND ARTICLE [II-II, Q. 160, Art. 2]

Whether Modesty Is Only About Outward Actions?

Objection 1: It would seem that modesty is only about outward actions. For the inward movements of the passions cannot be known to other persons. Yet the Apostle enjoins (Phil. 4:5): "Let your modesty be known to all men." Therefore modesty is only about outward actions.

Obj. 2: Further, the virtues that are about the passions are distinguished from justice which is about operations. Now modesty is seemingly one virtue. Therefore, if it be about outward works, it will not be concerned with inward passions.

Obj. 3: Further, no one same virtue is both about things pertaining to the appetite—which is proper to the moral virtues—and about things pertaining to knowledge—which is proper to the intellectual virtues—and again about things pertaining to the irascible and concupiscible faculties. Therefore, if modesty be one virtue, it cannot be about all these things.

*On the contrary,* In all these things it is necessary to observe the "mode" whence modesty takes its name. Therefore modesty is about all of them.

*I answer that,* As stated above (A. 1), modesty differs from temperance, in that temperance moderates those matters where restraint is most difficult, while modesty moderates those that present less difficulty. Authorities seem to have had various opinions about modesty. For wherever they found a special kind of good or a special difficulty of moderation, they withdrew it from the province of modesty, which they confined to lesser matters. Now it is clear to all that the restraint of pleasures of touch presents a special difficulty: wherefore all distinguished temperance from modesty.

In addition to this, moreover, Tully (De Invent. Rhet. ii, 54) considered that there was a special kind of good in the moderation of punishment; wherefore he severed clemency also from modesty, and held modesty to be about the remaining ordinary matters that require moderation. These seemingly are of four kinds. One is the movement of the mind towards some excellence, and this is moderated by *humility.* The second is the desire of things pertaining to knowledge, and this is moderated by *studiousness* which is opposed to curiosity. The third regards bodily movements and actions, which require to be done becomingly and honestly [*Cf. Q. 145, A. 1], whether we act seriously or in play. The fourth regards outward show, for instance in dress and the like.

To some of these matters, however, other authorities appointed certain special virtues: thus Andronicus [*De Affectibus] mentions "meekness, simplicity, humility," and other kindred virtues, of which we have spoken above (Q. 143); while Aristotle (Ethic. ii, 7) assigned *eutrapelia* to pleasures in games, as stated above (I-II, Q. 60, A. 5). All these are comprised under modesty as understood by Tully; and in this way modesty regards not only outward but also inward actions.

Reply Obj. 1: The Apostle speaks of modesty as regarding externals. Nevertheless the moderation of the inner man may be shown by certain outward signs.

Reply Obj. 2: Various virtues assigned by various authorities are comprised under modesty. Wherefore nothing prevents modesty from regarding matters which require different virtues. Yet there is not so great a difference between the various parts of modesty, as there is between justice, which is about operations, and temperance, which is about passions, because in actions and passions that present no great difficulty on the part of the matter, but only on the part of moderation, there is but one virtue, one namely for each kind of moderation.

Wherefore the Reply to the Third Objection also is clear.

## QUESTION 161

OF HUMILITY (In Six Articles)

We must consider next the species of modesty: (1) Humility, and pride which is opposed to it; (2) Studiousness, and its opposite, Curiosity; (3) Modesty as affecting words or deeds; (4) Modesty as affecting outward attire.

Concerning humility there are six points of inquiry:

(1) Whether humility is a virtue?

(2) Whether it resides in the appetite, or in the judgment of reason?

(3) Whether by humility one ought to subject oneself to all men?

(4) Whether it is a part of modesty or temperance?

(5) Of its comparison with the other virtues;

(6) Of the degrees of humility.

FIRST ARTICLE [II-II, Q. 161, Art. 1]

Whether Humility Is a Virtue?

Objection 1: It would seem that humility is not a virtue. For virtue conveys the notion of a good. But humility conveys the notion of a penal evil, according to Ps. 104:18, "They humbled his feet in fetters." Therefore humility is not a virtue.

Obj. 2: Further, virtue and vice are mutually opposed. Now humility seemingly denotes a vice, for it is written (Ecclus. 19:23): "There is one that humbleth himself wickedly." Therefore humility is not a virtue.

Obj. 3: Further, no virtue is opposed to another virtue. But humility is apparently opposed to the virtue of magnanimity, which aims at great things, whereas humility shuns them. Therefore it would seem that humility is not a virtue.

Obj. 4: Further, virtue is "the disposition of that which is perfect" (Phys. vii, text. 17). But humility seemingly belongs to the imperfect: wherefore it becomes not God to be humble, since He can be subject to none. Therefore it seems that humility is not a virtue.

Obj. 5: Further, every moral virtue is about actions and passions, according to *Ethic.* ii, 3. But humility is not reckoned by the Philosopher among the virtues that are about passions, nor is it comprised under justice which is about actions. Therefore it would seem not to be a virtue.

*On the contrary,* Origen commenting on Luke 1:48, "He hath regarded the humility of His handmaid," says (Hom. viii in Luc.): "One of the virtues, humility, is particularly commended in Holy Writ; for our Saviour said: 'Learn of Me, because I am meek, and humble of heart.'"

*I answer that,* As stated above (I-II, Q. 23, A. 2) when we were treating of the passions, the difficult good has something attractive to the appetite, namely the aspect of good, and likewise something repulsive to the appetite, namely the difficulty of obtaining it. In respect of the former there arises the movement of hope, and in respect of the latter, the movement of despair. Now it has been stated above (I-II, Q. 61, A. 2) that for those appetitive movements which are a kind of impulse towards an object, there is need of a moderating and restraining moral virtue, while for those which are a kind of recoil, there is need, on the part of the appetite, of a moral virtue to strengthen it and urge it on. Wherefore a twofold virtue is necessary with regard to the difficult good: one, to temper and restrain the mind, lest it tend to high things immoderately; and this belongs to the virtue of humility: and another to strengthen the mind against despair, and urge it on to the pursuit of great things according to right reason; and this is magnanimity. Therefore it is evident that humility is a virtue.

Reply Obj. 1: As Isidore observes (Etym. x), "a humble man is so called because he is, as it were, *humo acclinis*" [*Literally, "bent to the ground"], i.e. inclined to the lowest place. This may happen in two ways. First, through an extrinsic principle, for instance when one is cast down by another, and thus humility is a punishment. Secondly, through an intrinsic principle: and this may be done sometimes well, for instance when a man, considering his own failings, assumes the lowest place according to his mode: thus Abraham said to the Lord (Gen. 18:27), "I will speak to my Lord, whereas I am dust and ashes." In this way humility is a virtue. Sometimes, however, this may be ill-done, for instance when man, "not understanding his honor, compares himself to senseless beasts, and becomes like to them" (Ps. 48:13).

Reply Obj. 2: As stated (ad 1), humility, in so far as it is a virtue, conveys the notion of a praiseworthy self-abasement to the lowest place. Now this is sometimes done merely as to outward signs and pretense: wherefore this is "false humility," of which Augustine says in a letter (Ep. cxlix) that it is "grievous pride," since to wit, it would seem to aim at excellence of glory. Sometimes, however, this is done by an inward movement of the soul, and in this way, properly speaking, humility is reckoned a virtue, because virtue does not consist in externals, but chiefly in the inward choice of the mind, as the Philosopher states (Ethic. ii, 5).

Reply Obj. 3: Humility restrains the appetite from aiming at great things against right reason: while magnanimity urges the mind to great things in accord with right reason. Hence it is clear that magnanimity is not opposed to humility: indeed they concur in this, that each is according to right reason.

Reply Obj. 4: A thing is said to be perfect in two ways. First absolutely; such a thing contains no defect, neither in its nature nor in respect of anything else, and thus God alone is perfect. To Him humility is fitting, not as regards His Divine nature, but only as regards His assumed nature. Secondly, a thing may be said to be perfect in a restricted sense, for instance in respect of its nature or state or time. Thus a virtuous man is perfect: although in comparison with God his perfection is found wanting, according to the word of Isa. 40:17, "All nations are before Him as if they had no being at all." In this way humility may be competent to every man.

Reply Obj. 5: The Philosopher intended to treat of virtues as directed to civic life, wherein the subjection of one man to another is defined according to the ordinance of the law, and consequently is a matter of legal justice. But humility, considered as a special virtue, regards chiefly the subjection of man to God, for Whose sake he humbles himself by subjecting himself to others.

SECOND ARTICLE [II-II, Q. 161, Art. 2]

Whether Humility Has to Do with the Appetite?

Objection 1: It would seem that humility concerns, not the appetite but the judgment of reason. Because humility is opposed to pride. Now pride concerns things pertaining to knowledge: for Gregory says (Moral. xxxiv, 22) that "pride, when it extends outwardly to the body, is first of all shown in the eyes": wherefore it is written (Ps. 130:1), "Lord, my heart is not exalted, nor are my eyes lofty." Now eyes are the chief aids to knowledge. Therefore it would seem that humility is chiefly concerned with knowledge, whereby one thinks little of oneself.

Obj. 2: Further, Augustine says (De Virginit. xxxi) that "almost the whole of Christian teaching is humility." Consequently nothing contained in Christian teaching is incompatible with humility. Now Christian teaching admonishes us to seek the better things, according to 1 Cor. 12:31, "Be zealous for the better gifts." Therefore it belongs to humility to restrain not the desire of difficult things but the estimate thereof.

Obj. 3: Further, it belongs to the same virtue both to restrain excessive movement, and to strengthen the soul against excessive withdrawal: thus fortitude both curbs daring and fortifies the soul against fear. Now it is magnanimity that strengthens the soul against the difficulties that occur in the pursuit of great things. Therefore if humility were to curb the desire of great things, it would follow that humility is not a distinct virtue from magnanimity, which is evidently false. Therefore humility is concerned, not with the desire but with the estimate of great things.

Obj. 4: Further, Andronicus [*De Affectibus] assigns humility to outward show; for he says that humility is "the habit of avoiding excessive expenditure and parade." Therefore it is not concerned with the movement of the appetite.

*On the contrary,* Augustine says (De Poenit. [*Serm. cccli]) that "the humble man is one who chooses to be an abject in the house of the Lord, rather than to dwell in the tents of sinners." But choice concerns the appetite. Therefore humility has to do with the appetite rather than with the estimative power.

*I answer that,* As stated above (A. 1), it belongs properly to humility, that a man restrain himself from being borne towards that which is above him. For this purpose he must know his disproportion to that which surpasses his capacity. Hence knowledge of one's own deficiency belongs to humility, as a rule guiding the appetite. Nevertheless humility is essentially in the appetite itself; and consequently it must be said that humility, properly speaking, moderates the movement of the appetite.

Reply Obj. 1: Lofty eyes are a sign of pride, inasmuch as it excludes respect and fear: for fearing and respectful persons are especially wont to lower the eyes, as though not daring to compare themselves with others. But it does not follow from this that humility is essentially concerned with knowledge.

Reply Obj. 2: It is contrary to humility to aim at greater things through confiding in one's own powers: but to aim at greater things through confidence in God's help, is not contrary to humility; especially since the more one subjects oneself to God, the more is one exalted in God's sight. Hence Augustine says (De Virginit. xxxi): "It is one thing to raise oneself to God, and another to raise oneself up against God. He that abases himself before Him, him He raiseth up; he that raises himself up against Him, him He casteth down."

Reply Obj. 3: In fortitude there is the same reason for restraining daring and for strengthening the soul against fear: since the reason in both cases is that man should set the good of reason before dangers of death. But the reason for restraining presumptuous hope which pertains to humility is not the same as the reason for strengthening the soul against despair. Because the reason for strengthening the soul against despair is the acquisition of one's proper good lest man, by despair, render himself unworthy of a good which was competent to him; while the chief reason for suppressing presumptuous hope is based on divine reverence, which shows that man ought not to ascribe to himself more than is competent to him according to the position in which God has placed him. Wherefore humility would seem to denote in the first place man's subjection to God; and for this reason Augustine (De Serm. Dom. in Monte i, 4) ascribes humility, which he understands by poverty of spirit, to the gift of fear whereby man reveres God. Hence it follows that the relation of fortitude to daring differs from that of humility to hope. Because fortitude uses daring more than it suppresses it: so that excess of daring is more like fortitude than lack of daring is. On the other hand, humility suppresses hope or confidence in self more than it uses it; wherefore excessive self-confidence is more opposed to humility than lack of confidence is.

Reply Obj. 4: Excess in outward expenditure and parade is wont to be done with a view of boasting, which is suppressed by humility. Accordingly humility has to do, in a secondary way, with externals, as signs of the inward movement of the appetite.

THIRD ARTICLE [II-II, Q. 161, Art. 3]

Whether One Ought, by Humility, to Subject Oneself to All Men?

Objection 1: It would seem that one ought not, by humility, to subject oneself to all men. For, as stated above (A. 2, ad 3), humility consists chiefly in man's subjection to God. Now one ought not to offer to a man that which is due to God, as is the case with all acts of religious worship. Therefore, by humility, one ought not to subject oneself to man.

Obj. 2: Further, Augustine says (De Nat. et Gratia xxxiv): "Humility should take the part of truth, not of falsehood." Now some men are of the highest rank, who cannot, without falsehood, subject themselves to their inferiors. Therefore one ought not, by humility, to subject oneself to all men.

Obj. 3: Further no one ought to do that which conduces to the detriment of another's spiritual welfare. But if a man subject himself to another by humility, this is detrimental to the person to whom he subjects himself; for the latter might wax proud, or despise the other. Hence Augustine says in his Rule (Ep. ccxi): "Lest through excessive humility the superior lose his authority." Therefore a man ought not, by humility, to subject himself to all.

*On the contrary,* It is written (Phil. 2:3): "In humility, let each esteem others better than themselves."

*I answer that,* We may consider two things in man, namely that which is God's, and that which is man's. Whatever pertains to defect is man's: but whatever pertains to man's welfare and perfection is God's, according to the saying of Osee 13:9, "Destruction is thy own, O Israel; thy help is only in Me." Now humility, as stated above (A. 1, ad 5; A. 2, ad 3), properly regards the reverence whereby man is subject to God. Wherefore every man, in respect of that which is his own, ought to subject himself to every neighbor, in respect of that which the latter has of God's: but humility does not require a man to subject what he has of God's to that which may seem to be God's in another. For those who have a share of God's gifts know that they have them, according to 1 Cor. 2:12: "That we may know the things that are given us from God." Wherefore without prejudice to humility they may set the gifts they have received from God above those that others appear to have received from Him; thus the Apostle says (Eph. 3:5): "(The mystery of Christ) was not known to the sons of men as it is now revealed to His holy apostles." In like manner, humility does not require a man to subject that which he has of his own to that which his neighbor has of man's: otherwise each one would have to esteem himself a greater sinner than anyone else: whereas the Apostle says without prejudice to humility (Gal. 2:15): "We by nature are Jews, and not of the Gentiles, sinners." Nevertheless a man may esteem his neighbor to have some good which he lacks himself, or himself to have some evil which another has not: by reason of which, he may subject himself to him with humility.

Reply Obj. 1: We must not only revere God in Himself, but also that which is His in each one, although not with the same measure of reverence as we revere God. Wherefore we should subject ourselves with humility to all our neighbors for God's sake, according to 1 Pet. 2:13, "Be ye subject ... to every human creature for God's sake"; but to God alone do we owe the worship of latria.

Reply Obj. 2: If we set what our neighbor has of God's above that which we have of our own, we cannot incur falsehood. Wherefore a gloss [*St. Augustine, QQ. lxxxiii, qu. 71] on Phil. 2:3, "Esteem others better than themselves," says: "We must not esteem by pretending to esteem; but we should in truth think it possible for another person to have something that is hidden to us and whereby he is better than we are, although our own good whereby we are apparently better than he, be not hidden."

Reply Obj. 3: Humility, like other virtues, resides chiefly inwardly in the soul. Consequently a man, by an inward act of the soul, may subject himself to another, without giving the other man an occasion of detriment to his spiritual welfare. This is what Augustine means in his Rule (Ep. ccxi): "With fear, the superior should prostrate himself at your feet in the sight of God." On the other hand, due moderation must be observed in the outward acts of humility even as of other virtues, lest they conduce to the detriment of others. If, however, a man does as he ought, and others take therefrom an occasion of sin, this is not imputed to the man who acts with humility; since he does not give scandal, although others take it.

FOURTH ARTICLE [II-II, Q. 161, Art. 4]

Whether Humility Is a Part of Modesty or Temperance?

Objection 1: It would seem that humility is not a part of modesty or temperance. For humility regards chiefly the reverence whereby one is subject to God, as stated above (A. 3). Now it belongs to a theological virtue to have God for its object. Therefore humility should be reckoned a theological virtue rather than a part of temperance or modesty.

Obj. 2: Further, temperance is in the concupiscible, whereas humility would seem to be in the irascible, just as pride which is opposed to it, and whose object is something difficult. Therefore apparently humility is not a part of temperance or modesty.

Obj. 3: Further, humility and magnanimity are about the same object, as stated above (A. 1, ad 3). But magnanimity is reckoned a part, not of temperance but of fortitude, as stated above (Q. 129, A. 5). Therefore it would seem that humility is not a part of temperance or modesty.

*On the contrary,* Origen says (Hom. viii super Luc.): "If thou wilt hear the name of this virtue, and what it was called by the philosophers, know that humility which God regards is the same as what they called metriotes , i.e. measure or moderation." Now this evidently pertains to modesty or temperance. Therefore humility is a part of modesty or temperance.

*I answer that,* As stated above (Q. 137, A. 2, ad 1; Q. 157, A. 3, ad 2), in assigning parts to a virtue we consider chiefly the likeness that results from the mode of the virtue. Now the mode of temperance, whence it chiefly derives its praise, is the restraint or suppression of the impetuosity of a passion. Hence whatever virtues restrain or suppress, and the actions which moderate the impetuosity of the emotions, are reckoned parts of temperance. Now just as meekness suppresses the movement of anger, so does humility suppress the movement of hope, which is the movement of a spirit aiming at great things. Wherefore, like meekness, humility is accounted a part of temperance. For this reason the Philosopher (Ethic. iv, 3) says that a man who aims at small things in proportion to his mode is not magnanimous but "temperate," and such a man we may call humble. Moreover, for the reason given above (Q. 160, A. 2), among the various parts of temperance, the one under which humility is comprised is modesty as understood by Tully (De Invent. Rhet. ii, 54), inasmuch as humility is nothing else than a moderation of spirit: wherefore it is written (1 Pet. 3:4): "In the incorruptibility of a quiet and meek spirit."

Reply Obj. 1: The theological virtues, whose object is our last end, which is the first principle in matters of appetite, are the causes of all the other virtues. Hence the fact that humility is caused by reverence for God does not prevent it from being a part of modesty or temperance.

Reply Obj. 2: Parts are assigned to a principal virtue by reason of a sameness, not of subject or matter, but of formal mode, as stated above (Q. 137, A. 2, ad 1; Q. 157, A. 3, ad 2). Consequently, although humility is in the irascible as its subject, it is assigned as a part of modesty or temperance by reason of its mode.

Reply Obj. 3: Although humility and magnanimity agree as to matter, they differ as to mode, by reason of which magnanimity is reckoned a part of fortitude, and humility a part of temperance.

FIFTH ARTICLE [II-II, Q. 161, Art. 5]

Whether Humility Is the Greatest of the Virtues?

Objection 1: It would seem that humility is the greatest of the virtues. For Chrysostom, expounding the story of the Pharisee and the publican (Luke 18), says [*Eclog. hom. vii de Humil. Animi.] that "if humility is such a fleet runner even when hampered by sin that it overtakes the justice that is the companion of pride, whither will it not reach if you couple it with justice? It will stand among the angels by the judgment seat of God." Hence it is clear that humility is set above justice. Now justice is either the most exalted of all the virtues, or includes all virtues, according to the Philosopher (Ethic. v, 1). Therefore humility is the greatest of the virtues.

Obj. 2: Further, Augustine says (De Verb. Dom., Serm. [*S. 10, C. 1]): "Are you thinking of raising the great fabric of spirituality? Attend first of all to the foundation of humility." Now this would seem to imply that humility is the foundation of all virtue. Therefore apparently it is greater than the other virtues.

Obj. 3: Further, the greater virtue deserves the greater reward. Now the greatest reward is due to humility, since "he that humbleth himself shall be exalted" (Luke 14:11). Therefore humility is the greatest of virtues.

Obj. 4: Further, according to Augustine (De Vera Relig. 16), "Christ's whole life on earth was a lesson in moral conduct through the human nature which He assumed." Now He especially proposed His humility for our example, saying (Matt. 11:29): "Learn of Me, because I am meek and humble of heart." Moreover, Gregory says (Pastor. iii, 1) that the "lesson proposed to us in the mystery of our redemption is the humility of God." Therefore humility would seem to be the greatest of virtues.

*On the contrary,* Charity is set above all the virtues, according to Col. 3:14, "Above all ... things have charity." Therefore humility is not the greatest of virtues.

*I answer that,* The good of human virtue pertains to the order of reason: which order is considered chiefly in reference to the end: wherefore the theological virtues are the greatest because they have the last end for their object. Secondarily, however, it is considered in reference to the ordering of the means to the end. This ordinance, as to its essence, is in the reason itself from which it issues, but by participation it is in the appetite ordered by the reason; and this ordinance is the effect of justice, especially of legal justice. Now humility makes a man a good subject to ordinance of all kinds and in all matters; while every other virtue has this effect in some special matter. Therefore after the theological virtues, after the intellectual virtues which regard the reason itself, and after justice, especially legal justice, humility stands before all others.

Reply Obj. 1: Humility is not set before justice, but before that justice which is coupled with pride, and is no longer a virtue; even so, on the other hand, sin is pardoned through humility: for it is said of the publican (Luke 18:14) that through the merit of his humility "he went down into his house justified." Hence Chrysostom says [*De incompr. Nat. Dei, Hom. v]: "Bring me a pair of two-horse chariots: in the one harness pride with justice, in the other sin with humility: and you will see that sin outrunning justice wins not by its own strength, but by that of humility: while you will see the other pair beaten, not by the weakness of justice, but by the weight and size of pride."

Reply Obj. 2: Just as the orderly assembly of virtues is, by reason of a certain likeness, compared to a building, so again that which is the first step in the acquisition of virtue is likened to the foundation, which is first laid before the rest of the building. Now the virtues are in truth infused by God. Wherefore the first step in the acquisition of virtue may be understood in two ways. First by way of removing obstacles: and thus humility holds the first place, inasmuch as it expels pride, which "God resisteth," and makes man submissive and ever open to receive the influx of Divine grace. Hence it is written (James 4:6): "God resisteth the proud, and giveth grace to the humble." In this sense humility is said to be the foundation of the spiritual edifice. Secondly, a thing is first among virtues directly, because it is the first step towards God. Now the first step towards God is by faith, according to Heb. 11:6, "He that cometh to God must believe." In this sense faith is the foundation in a more excellent way than humility.

Reply Obj. 3: To him that despises earthly things, heavenly things are promised: thus heavenly treasures are promised to those who despise earthly riches, according to Matt. 6:19, 20, "Lay not up to yourselves treasures on earth ... but lay up to yourselves treasures in heaven." Likewise heavenly consolations are promised to those who despise worldly joys, according to Matt. 4:5, "Blessed are they that mourn, for they shall be comforted." In the same way spiritual uplifting is promised to humility, not that humility alone merits it, but because it is proper to it to despise earthly uplifting. Wherefore Augustine says (De Poenit. [*Serm. cccli]): "Think not that he who humbles himself remains for ever abased, for it is written: 'He shall be exalted.' And do not imagine that his exaltation in men's eyes is effected by bodily uplifting."

Reply Obj. 4: The reason why Christ chiefly proposed humility to us, was because it especially removes the obstacle to man's spiritual welfare consisting in man's aiming at heavenly and spiritual things, in which he is hindered by striving to become great in earthly things. Hence our Lord, in order to remove an obstacle to our spiritual welfare, showed by giving an example of humility, that outward exaltation is to be despised. Thus humility is, as it were, a disposition to man's untrammeled access to spiritual and divine goods. Accordingly as perfection is greater than disposition, so charity, and other virtues whereby man approaches God directly, are greater than humility.

SIXTH ARTICLE [II-II, Q. 161, Art. 6]

Whether Twelve Degrees of Humility Are Fittingly Distinguished in the Rule of the Blessed Benedict?

Objection 1: It would seem that the twelve degrees of humility that are set down in the Rule of the Blessed Benedict [*St. Thomas gives these degrees in the reverse order to that followed by St. Benedict] are unfittingly distinguished. The first is to be "humble not only in heart, but also to show it in one's very person, one's eyes fixed on the ground"; the second is "to speak few and sensible words, and not to be loud of voice"; the third is "not to be easily moved, and disposed to laughter"; the fourth is "to maintain silence until one is asked"; the fifth is "to do nothing but to what one is exhorted by the common rule of the monastery"; the sixth is "to believe and acknowledge oneself viler than all"; the seventh is "to think oneself worthless and unprofitable for all purposes"; the eighth is "to confess one's sin"; the ninth is "to embrace patience by obeying under difficult and contrary circumstances"; the tenth is "to subject oneself to a superior"; the eleventh is "not to delight in fulfilling one's own desires"; the twelfth is "to fear God and to be always mindful of everything that God has commanded." For among these there are some things pertaining to the other virtues, such as obedience and patience. Again there are some that seem to involve a false opinion—and this is inconsistent with any virtue—namely to declare oneself more despicable than all men, and to confess and believe oneself to be in all ways worthless and unprofitable. Therefore these are unfittingly placed among the degrees of humility.

Obj. 2: Further, humility proceeds from within to externals, as do other virtues. Therefore in the aforesaid degrees, those which concern outward actions are unfittingly placed before those which pertain to inward actions.

Obj. 3: Further, Anselm (De Simil. ci, seqq.) gives seven degrees of humility, the first of which is "to acknowledge oneself contemptible"; the second, "to grieve for this"; the third, "to confess it"; the fourth, "to convince others of this, that is to wish them to believe it"; the fifth, "to bear patiently that this be said of us"; the sixth, "to suffer oneself to be treated with contempt"; the seventh, "to love being thus treated." Therefore the aforesaid degrees would seem to be too numerous.

Obj. 4: Further, a gloss on Matt. 3:15 says: "Perfect humility has three degrees. The first is to subject ourselves to those who are above us, and not to set ourselves above our equals: this is sufficient. The second is to submit to our equals, and not to set ourselves before our inferiors; this is called abundant humility. The third degree is to subject ourselves to inferiors, and in this is perfect righteousness." Therefore the aforesaid degrees would seem to be too numerous.

Obj. 5: Further, Augustine says (De Virginit. xxxi): "The measure of humility is apportioned to each one according to his rank. It is imperiled by pride, for the greater a man is the more liable is he to be entrapped." Now the measure of a man's greatness cannot be fixed according to a definite number of degrees. Therefore it would seem that it is not possible to assign the aforesaid degrees to humility.

*I answer that,* As stated above (A. 2) humility has essentially to do with the appetite, in so far as a man restrains the impetuosity of his soul, from tending inordinately to great things: yet its rule is in the cognitive faculty, in that we should not deem ourselves to be above what we are. Also, the principle and origin of both these things is the reverence we bear to God. Now the inward disposition of humility leads to certain outward signs in words, deeds, and gestures, which manifest that which is hidden within, as happens also with the other virtues. For "a man is known by his look, and a wise man, when thou meetest him, by his countenance" (Ecclus. 19:26). Wherefore the aforesaid degrees of humility include something regarding the root of humility, namely the twelfth degree, "that a man fear God and bear all His commandments in mind."

Again, they include certain things with regard to the appetite, lest one aim inordinately at one's own excellence. This is done in three ways. First, by not following one's own will, and this pertains to the eleventh degree; secondly, by regulating it according to one's superior judgment, and this applies to the tenth degree; thirdly, by not being deterred from this on account of the difficulties and hardships that come in our way, and this belongs to the ninth degree.

Certain things also are included referring to the estimate a man forms in acknowledging his own deficiency, and this in three ways. First by acknowledging and avowing his own shortcomings; this belongs to the eighth degree: secondly, by deeming oneself incapable of great things, and this pertains to the seventh degree: thirdly, that in this respect one should put others before oneself, and this belongs to the sixth degree.

Again, some things are included that refer to outward signs. One of these regards deeds, namely that in one's work one should not depart from the ordinary way; this applies to the fifth degree. Two others have reference to words, namely that one should not be in a hurry to speak, which pertains to the fourth degree, and that one be not immoderate in speech, which refers to the second. The others have to do with outward gestures, for instance in restraining haughty looks, which regards the first, and in outwardly checking laughter and other signs of senseless mirth, and this belongs to the third degree.

Reply Obj. 1: It is possible, without falsehood, to deem and avow oneself the most despicable of men, as regards the hidden faults which we acknowledge in ourselves, and the hidden gifts of God which others have. Hence Augustine says (De Virginit. lii): "Bethink you that some persons are in some hidden way better than you, although outwardly you are better than they." Again, without falsehood one may avow and believe oneself in all ways unprofitable and useless in respect of one's own capability, so as to refer all one's sufficiency to God, according to 2 Cor. 3:5, "Not that we are sufficient to think anything of ourselves as of ourselves: but our sufficiency is from God." And there is nothing unbecoming in ascribing to humility those things that pertain to other virtues, since, just as one vice arises from another, so, by a natural sequence, the act of one virtue proceeds from the act of another.

Reply Obj. 2: Man arrives at humility in two ways. First and chiefly by a gift of grace, and in this way the inner man precedes the outward man. The other way is by human effort, whereby he first of all restrains the outward man, and afterwards succeeds in plucking out the inward root. It is according to this order that the degrees of humility are here enumerated.

Reply Obj. 3: All the degrees mentioned by Anselm are reducible to knowledge, avowal, and desire of one's own abasement. For the first degree belongs to the knowledge of one's own deficiency; but since it would be wrong for one to love one's own failings, this is excluded by the second degree. The third and fourth degrees regard the avowal of one's own deficiency; namely that not merely one simply assert one's failing, but that one convince another of it. The other three degrees have to do with the appetite, which seeks, not outward excellence, but outward abasement, or bears it with equanimity, whether it consist of words or deeds. For as Gregory says (Regist. ii, 10, Ep. 36), "there is nothing great in being humble towards those who treat us with regard, for even worldly people do this: but we should especially be humble towards those who make us suffer," and this belongs to the fifth and sixth degrees: or the appetite may even go so far as lovingly to embrace external abasement, and this pertains to the seventh degree; so that all these degrees are comprised under the sixth and seventh mentioned above.

Reply Obj. 4: These degrees refer, not to the thing itself, namely the nature of humility, but to the degrees among men, who are either of higher or lower or of equal degree.

Reply Obj. 5: This argument also considers the degrees of humility not according to the nature of the thing, in respect of which the aforesaid degrees are assigned, but according to the various conditions of men.

## QUESTION 162

OF PRIDE (In Eight Articles)

We must next consider pride, and (1) pride in general; (2) the first man's sin, which we hold to have been pride. Under the first head there are eight points of inquiry:

(1) Whether pride is a sin?
(2) Whether it is a special vice?
(3) Wherein does it reside as in its subject?
(4) Of its species;
(5) Whether it is a mortal sin?
(6) Whether it is the most grievous of all sins?
(7) Of its relation to other sins;
(8) Whether it should be reckoned a capital vice?

FIRST ARTICLE [II-II, Q. 162, Art. 1]

Whether Pride Is a Sin?

Objection 1: It would seem that pride is not a sin. For no sin is the object of God's promise. For God's promises refer to what He will do; and He is not the author of sin. Now pride is numbered among the Divine promises: for it is written (Isa. 60:15): "I will make thee to be an everlasting pride [Douay: 'glory'], a joy unto generation and generation." Therefore pride is not a sin.

Obj. 2: Further, it is not a sin to wish to be like unto God: for every creature has a natural desire for this; and especially does this become the rational creature which is made to God's image and likeness. Now it is said in Prosper's Lib. Sent. 294, that "pride is love of one's own excellence, whereby one is likened to God who is supremely excellent." Hence Augustine says (Confess. ii, 6): "Pride imitates exaltedness; whereas Thou alone art God exalted over all." Therefore pride is not a sin.

Obj. 3: Further, a sin is opposed not only to a virtue but also to a contrary vice, as the Philosopher states (Ethic. ii, 8). But no vice is found to be opposed to pride. Therefore pride is not a sin.

*On the contrary,* It is written (Tob. 4:14): "Never suffer pride to reign in thy mind or in thy words."

*I answer that,* Pride ( superbia ) is so called because a man thereby aims higher ( *supra* ) than he is; wherefore Isidore says (Etym. x): "A man is said to be proud, because he wishes to appear above (super) what he really is"; for he who wishes to overstep beyond what he is, is proud. Now right reason requires that every man's will should tend to that which is proportionate to him. Therefore it is evident that pride denotes something opposed to right reason, and this shows it to have the character of sin, because according to Dionysius (Div. Nom.

iv, 4), "the soul's evil is to be opposed to reason." Therefore it is evident that pride is a sin.

Reply Obj. 1: Pride ( *superbia* ) may be understood in two ways. First, as overpassing ( *supergreditur* ) the rule of reason, and in this sense we say that it is a sin. Secondly, it may simply denominate "super-abundance"; in which sense any super-abundant thing may be called pride: and it is thus that God promises pride as significant of super-abundant good. Hence a gloss of Jerome on the same passage (Isa. 61:6) says that "there is a good and an evil pride"; or "a sinful pride which God resists, and a pride that denotes the glory which He bestows."

It may also be replied that pride there signifies abundance of those things in which men may take pride.

Reply Obj. 2: Reason has the direction of those things for which man has a natural appetite; so that if the appetite wander from the rule of reason, whether by excess or by default, it will be sinful, as is the case with the appetite for food which man desires naturally. Now pride is the appetite for excellence in excess of right reason. Wherefore Augustine says (De Civ. Dei xiv, 13) that pride is the "desire for inordinate exaltation": and hence it is that, as he asserts (De Civ. Dei xiv, 13; xix, 12), "pride imitates God inordinately: for it hath equality of fellowship under Him, and wishes to usurp His dominion over our fellow-creatures."

Reply Obj. 3: Pride is directly opposed to the virtue of humility, which, in a way, is concerned about the same matter as magnanimity, as stated above (Q. 161, A. 1, ad 3). Hence the vice opposed to pride by default is akin to the vice of pusillanimity, which is opposed by default to magnanimity. For just as it belongs to magnanimity to urge the mind to great things against despair, so it belongs to humility to withdraw the mind from the inordinate desire of great things against presumption. Now pusillanimity, if we take it for a deficiency in pursuing great things, is properly opposed to magnanimity by default; but if we take it for the mind's attachment to things beneath what is becoming to a man, it is opposed to humility by default; since each proceeds from a smallness of mind. In the same way, on the other hand, pride may be opposed by excess, both to magnanimity and humility, from different points of view: to humility, inasmuch as it scorns subjection, to magnanimity, inasmuch as it tends to great things inordinately. Since, however, pride implies a certain elation, it is more directly opposed to humility, even as pusillanimity, which denotes littleness of soul in tending towards great things, is more directly opposed to magnanimity.

SECOND ARTICLE [II-II, Q. 162, Art. 2]

Whether Pride Is a Special Sin?

Objection 1: It would seem that pride is not a special sin. For Augustine says (De Nat. et Grat. xxix) that "you will find no sin that is not labelled pride"; and Prosper says (De Vita Contempl. iii, 2) that "without pride no sin is, or was, or ever will be possible." Therefore pride is a general sin.

Obj. 2: Further, a gloss on Job 33:17, "That He may withdraw man from wickedness [*Vulg.: 'From the things that he is doing, and may deliver him from pride'']," says that "a man prides himself when he transgresses His commandments by sin." Now according to Ambrose [*De Parad. viii], "every sin is a transgression of the Divine law, and a disobedience of the heavenly commandments." Therefore every sin is pride.

Obj. 3: Further, every special sin is opposed to a special virtue. But pride is opposed to all the virtues, for Gregory says (Moral. xxxiv, 23): "Pride is by no means content with the destruction of one virtue; it raises itself up against all the powers of the soul, and like an all-pervading and poisonous disease corrupts the whole body"; and Isidore says (Etym. [*De Summo Bono ii, 38]) that it is "the downfall of all virtues." Therefore pride is not a special sin.

Obj. 4: Further, every special sin has a special matter. Now pride has a general matter, for Gregory says (Moral. xxxiv, 23) that "one man is proud of his gold, another of his eloquence: one is elated by mean and earthly things, another by sublime and heavenly virtues." Therefore pride is not a special but a general sin.

*On the contrary,* Augustine says (De Nat. et Grat. xxix): "If he look into the question carefully, he will find that, according to God's law, pride is a very different sin from other vices." Now the genus is not different from its species. Therefore pride is not a general but a special sin.

*I answer that,* The sin of pride may be considered in two ways. First with regard to its proper species, which it has under the aspect of its proper object. In this way pride is a special sin, because it has a special object: for it is inordinate desire of one's own excellence, as stated (A. 1, ad 2). Secondly, it may be considered as having a certain influence towards other sins. In this way it has somewhat of a generic character, inasmuch as all sins may arise from pride, in two ways. First directly, through other sins being directed to the end of pride which is one's own excellence, to which may be directed anything that is inordinately desired. Secondly, indirectly and accidentally as it were, that is by removing an obstacle, since pride makes a man despise the Divine law which hinders him from sinning, according to Jer. 2:20, "Thou hast broken My yoke, thou hast burst My bands, and thou saidst: I will not serve."

It must, however, be observed that this generic character of pride admits of the possibility of all vices arising from pride sometimes, but it does not imply that all vices originate from pride always. For though one may break the commandments of the Law by any kind of sin, through contempt which pertains to pride, yet one does not always break the Divine commandments through contempt, but sometimes through ignorance, and sometimes through weakness: and for this reason Augustine says (De Nat. et Grat. xxix) that "many things are done amiss which are not done through pride."

Reply Obj. 1: These words are introduced by Augustine into his book *De Nat. et Grat.*, not as being his own, but as those of someone with whom he is arguing. Hence he subsequently disproves the assertion, and shows that not all sins are committed through pride. We might, however, reply that these authorities must be understood as referring to the outward effect of pride, namely the breaking of the commandments, which applies to every sin, and not to the inward act of pride, namely contempt of the commandment. For sin is committed, not always through contempt, but sometimes through ignorance, sometimes through weakness, as stated above.

Reply Obj. 2: A man may sometimes commit a sin effectively, but not affectively; thus he who, in ignorance, slays his father, is a parricide effectively, but not affectively, since he did not intend it. Accordingly he who breaks God's commandment is said to pride himself against God, effectively always, but not always affectively.

Reply Obj. 3: A sin may destroy a virtue in two ways. In one way by direct contrariety to a virtue, and thus pride does not corrupt every virtue, but only humility; even as every special sin destroys the special virtue opposed to it, by acting counter thereto. In another way a sin destroys a virtue, by making ill use of that virtue: and thus pride destroys every virtue, in so far as it finds an occasion of pride in every virtue, just as in everything else pertaining to excellence. Hence it does not follow that it is a general sin.

Reply Obj. 4: Pride regards a special aspect in its object, which aspect may be found in various matters: for it is inordinate love of one's excellence, and excellence may be found in various things.

THIRD ARTICLE [II-II, Q. 162, Art. 3]

Whether the Subject of Pride Is the Irascible Faculty?

Objection 1: It would seem that the subject of pride is not the irascible faculty. For Gregory says (Moral. xxiii, 17): "A swollen mind is an obstacle to truth, for the swelling shuts out the light." Now the knowledge of truth pertains, not to the irascible but to the rational faculty. Therefore pride is not in the irascible.

Obj. 2: Further, Gregory says (Moral. xxiv, 8) that "the proud observe other people's conduct not so as to set themselves beneath them with humility, but so as to set themselves above them with pride": wherefore it would seem that pride originates in undue observation. Now observation pertains not to the irascible but to the rational faculty.

Obj. 3: Further, pride seeks pre-eminence not only in sensible things, but also in spiritual and intelligible things: while it consists essentially in the contempt of God, according to Ecclus. 10:14, "The beginning of the pride of man is to fall off from God." Now the irascible, since it is a part of the sensitive appetite, cannot extend to God and things intelligible. Therefore pride cannot be in the irascible.

Obj. 4: Further, as stated in Prosper's *Liber Sententiarum,* sent. 294, "Pride is love of one's own excellence." But love is not in the irascible, but in the concupiscible. Therefore pride is not in the irascible.

*On the contrary,* Gregory (Moral. ii, 49) opposes pride to the gift of fear. Now fear belongs to the irascible. Therefore pride is in the irascible.

*I answer that,* The subject of any virtue or vice is to be ascertained from its proper object: for the object of a habit or act cannot be other than the object of the power, which is the subject of both. Now the proper object of pride is something difficult, for pride is the desire of one's own excellence, as stated above (AA. 1, 2). Wherefore pride must needs pertain in some way to the irascible faculty. Now the irascible may be taken in two ways. First in a strict sense, and thus it is a part of the sensitive appetite, even as anger, strictly speaking, is a passion of the sensitive appetite. Secondly, the irascible may be taken in a broader sense, so as to belong also to the intellective appetite, to which also anger is sometimes ascribed. It is thus that we attribute anger to God and the angels, not as a passion, but as denoting the sentence of justice pronouncing judgment. Nevertheless the irascible understood in this broad sense is not distinct from the concupiscible power, as stated above in the First Part (Q. 59, A. 4; I-II, Q. 82, A. 5, ad 1 and 2).

Consequently if the difficult thing which is the object of pride, were merely some sensible object, whereto the sensitive appetite might tend, pride would have to be in the irascible which is part of the sensitive appetite. But since the difficult thing which pride has in view is common both to sensible and to spiritual things, we must needs say that the subject of pride is the irascible not only strictly so called, as a part of the sensitive appetite, but also in its wider acceptation, as applicable to the intellective appetite. Wherefore pride is ascribed also to the demons.

Reply Obj. 1: Knowledge of truth is twofold. One is purely speculative, and pride hinders this indirectly by removing its cause. For the proud man subjects not his intellect to God, that he may receive the knowledge of truth from Him, according to Matt. 11:25, "Thou hast hid these things from the wise and the prudent," i.e. from the proud, who are wise and prudent in their own eyes, "and hast revealed them to little ones," i.e. to the humble.

Nor does he deign to learn anything from man, whereas it is written (Ecclus. 6:34): "If thou wilt incline thy ear, thou shalt receive instruction."

The other knowledge of truth is affective, and this is directly hindered by pride, because the proud, through delighting in their own excellence, disdain the excellence of truth; thus Gregory says (Moral. xxiii, 17) that "the proud, although certain hidden truths be conveyed to their understanding, cannot realize their sweetness: and if they know of them they cannot relish them." Hence it is written (Prov. 11:2): "Where humility is there also is wisdom."

Reply Obj. 2: As stated above (Q. 161, AA. 2, 6), humility observes the rule of right reason whereby a man has true self-esteem. Now pride does not observe this rule of right reason, for he esteems himself greater than he is: and this is the outcome of an inordinate desire for his own excellence, since a man is ready to believe what he desires very much, the result being that his appetite is borne towards things higher than what become him. Consequently whatsoever things lead a man to inordinate self-esteem lead him to pride: and one of those is the observing of other people's failings, just as, on the other hand, in the words of Gregory (Moral. xxiii, 17), "holy men, by a like observation of other people's virtues, set others above themselves." Accordingly the conclusion is not that pride is in the rational faculty, but that one of its causes is in the reason.

Reply Obj. 3: Pride is in the irascible, not only as a part of the sensitive appetite, but also as having a more general signification, as stated above.

Reply Obj. 4: According to Augustine (De Civ. Dei xiv, 7, 9), "love precedes all other emotions of the soul, and is their cause," wherefore it may be employed to denote any of the other emotions. It is in this sense that pride is said to be "love of one's own excellence," inasmuch as love makes a man presume inordinately on his superiority over others, and this belongs properly to pride.

FOURTH ARTICLE [II-II, Q. 162, Art. 4]

Whether the Four Species of Pride Are Fittingly Assigned by Gregory?

Objection 1: It seems that the four species of pride are unfittingly assigned by Gregory, who says (Moral. xxiii, 6): "There are four marks by which every kind of pride of the arrogant betrays itself; either when they think that their good is from themselves, or if they believe it to be from above, yet they think that it is due to their own merits; or when they boast of having what they have not, or despise others and wish to appear the exclusive possessors of what they have." For pride is a vice distinct from unbelief, just as humility is a distinct virtue from faith. Now it pertains to unbelief, if a man deem that he has not received his good from God, or that he has the good of grace through his own merits. Therefore this should not be reckoned a species of pride.

Obj. 2: Further, the same thing should not be reckoned a species of different genera. Now boasting is reckoned a species of lying, as stated above (Q. 110, A. 2; Q. 112). Therefore it should not be accounted a species of pride.

Obj. 3: Further, some other things apparently pertain to pride, which are not mentioned here. For Jerome [*Reference unknown] says that "nothing is so indicative of pride as to show oneself ungrateful": and Augustine says (De Civ. Dei xiv, 14) that "it belongs to pride to excuse oneself of a sin one has committed." Again, presumption whereby one aims at having what is above one, would seem to have much to do with pride. Therefore the aforesaid division does not sufficiently account for the different species of pride.

Obj. 4: Further, we find other divisions of pride. For Anselm [*Eadmer, De Similit. xxii, seqq.] divides the uplifting of pride, saying that there is "pride of will, pride of speech, end pride of deed." Bernard [*De Grad. Humil. et Superb. x, seqq.] also reckons twelve degrees of pride, namely "curiosity, frivolity of mind, senseless mirth, boasting, singularity, arrogance, presumption, defense of one's sins, deceitful confession, rebelliousness, license, sinful habit." Now these apparently are not comprised under the species mentioned by Gregory. Therefore the latter would seem to be assigned unfittingly.

*On the contrary,* The authority of Gregory suffices.

*I answer that,* As stated above (AA. 1, 2, 3), pride denotes immoderate desire of one's own excellence, a desire, to wit, that is not in accord with right reason. Now it must be observed that all excellence results from a good possessed. Such a good may be considered in three ways. First, in itself. For it is evident that the greater the good that one has, the greater the excellence that one derives from it. Hence when a man ascribes to himself a good greater than what he has, it follows that his appetite tends to his own excellence in a measure exceeding his competency: and thus we have the third species of pride, namely "boasting of having what one has not."

Secondly, it may be considered with regard to its cause, in so far as to have a thing of oneself is more excellent than to have it of another. Hence when a man esteems the good he has received of another as though he had it of himself, the result is that his appetite is borne towards his own excellence immoderately. Now one is cause of one's own good in two ways, efficiently and meritoriously: and thus we have the first two species of pride, namely "when a man thinks he has from himself that which he has from God," or "when he believes that which he has received from above to be due to his own merits."

Thirdly, it may be considered with regard to the manner of having it, in so far as a man obtains greater excellence through possessing some good more excellently than other men; the result again being that his appetite is borne inordinately towards his own excellence: and thus we have the fourth species of pride, which is "when a man despises others and wishes to be singularly conspicuous."

Reply Obj. 1: A true judgment may be destroyed in two ways. First, universally: and thus in matters of faith, a true judgment is destroyed by unbelief. Secondly, in some particular matter of choice, and unbelief does not do this. Thus a man who commits fornication, judges that for the time being it is good for him to commit fornication; yet he is not an unbeliever, as he would be, were he to say that universally fornication is good. It is thus in the question in point: for it pertains to unbelief to assert universally that there is a good which is not from God, or that grace is given to men for their merits, whereas, properly speaking, it belongs to pride and not to unbelief, through inordinate desire of one's own excellence, to boast of one's goods as though one had them of oneself, or of one's own merits.

Reply Obj. 2: Boasting is reckoned a species of lying, as regards the outward act whereby a man falsely ascribes to himself what he has not: but as regards the inward arrogance of the heart it is reckoned by Gregory to be a species of pride.

Reply Obj. 3: The ungrateful man ascribes to himself what he has from another: wherefore the first two species of pride pertain to ingratitude. To excuse oneself of a sin one has committed, belongs to the third species, since by so doing a man ascribes to himself the good of innocence which he has not. To aim presumptuously at what is above one, would seem to belong chiefly to the fourth species, which consists in wishing to be preferred to others.

Reply Obj. 4: The three mentioned by Anselm correspond to the progress of any particular sin: for it begins by being conceived in thought, then is uttered in word, and thirdly is accomplished in deed.

The twelve degrees mentioned by Bernard are reckoned by way of opposition to the twelve degrees of humility, of which we have spoken above (Q. 161, A. 6). For the first degree of humility is to "be humble in heart, and to show it in one's very person, one's eyes fixed on the ground": and to this is opposed "curiosity," which consists in looking around in all directions curiously and inordinately. The second degree of humility is "to speak few and sensible words, and not to be loud of voice": to this is opposed "frivolity of mind," by which a man is proud of speech. The third degree of humility is "not to be easily moved and disposed to laughter," to which is opposed "senseless mirth." The fourth degree of humility is "to maintain silence until one is asked," to which is opposed "boasting". The fifth degree of humility is "to do nothing but to what one is exhorted by the common rule of the monastery," to which is opposed "singularity," whereby a man wishes to seem more holy than others. The sixth degree of humility is "to believe and acknowledge oneself viler than all," to which is opposed "arrogance," whereby a man sets himself above others. The seventh degree of humility is "to think oneself worthless and unprofitable for all purposes," to which is opposed "presumption," whereby a man thinks himself capable of things that are above him. The eighth degree of humility is "to confess one's sins," to which is opposed "defense of one's sins." The ninth degree is "to embrace patience by obeying under difficult and contrary circumstances," to which is opposed "deceitful confession," whereby a man being unwilling to be punished for his sins confesses them deceitfully. The tenth degree of humility is "obedience," to which is opposed "rebelliousness." The eleventh degree of humility is "not to delight in fulfilling one's own desires"; to this is opposed "license," whereby a man delights in doing freely whatever he will. The last degree of humility is "fear of God": to this is opposed "the habit of sinning," which implies contempt of God.

In these twelve degrees not only are the species of pride indicated, but also certain things that precede and follow them, as we have stated above with regard to humility (Q. 161, A. 6).

FIFTH ARTICLE [II-II, Q. 162, Art. 5]

Whether Pride Is a Mortal Sin?

Objection 1: It would seem that pride is not a mortal sin. For a gloss on Ps. 7:4, "O Lord my God, if I have done this thing," says: "Namely, the universal sin which is pride." Therefore if pride were a mortal sin, so would every sin be.

Obj. 2: Further, every mortal sin is contrary to charity. But pride is apparently not contrary to charity, neither as to the love of God, nor as to the love of one's neighbor, because the excellence which, by pride, one desires inordinately, is not always opposed to God's honor, or our neighbor's good. Therefore pride is not a mortal sin.

Obj. 3: Further, every mortal sin is opposed to virtue. But pride is not opposed to virtue; *on the contrary,* it arises therefrom, for as Gregory says (Moral. xxxiv, 23), "sometimes a man is elated by sublime and heavenly virtues." Therefore pride is not a mortal sin.

*On the contrary,* Gregory says (Moral. xxxiv, 23) that "pride is a most evident sign of the reprobate, and contrariwise, humility of the elect." But men do not become reprobate on account of venial sins. Therefore pride is not a venial but a mortal sin.

*I answer that,* Pride is opposed to humility. Now humility properly regards the subjection of man to God, as stated above (Q. 161, A. 1, ad 5). Hence pride properly regards lack of this subjection, in so far as a man raises himself above that which is appointed to him according to the Divine rule or measure, against the saying of the Apostle (2 Cor. 10:13), "But we will not glory beyond our measure; but according to the measure of the rule which God hath measured to us." Wherefore it is written (Ecclus. 10:14): "The beginning of the pride of man is to fall off from God" because, to wit, the root of pride is found to consist in man not being, in some way, subject to God and His rule. Now it is evident that not to be subject to God is of its very nature a mortal sin, for this consists in turning away from God: and consequently pride is, of its genus, a mortal sin. Nevertheless just as in other sins which are mortal by their genus (for instance fornication and adultery) there are certain motions that are venial by reason of their imperfection (through forestalling the judgment of reason, and being without its consent), so too in the matter of pride it happens that certain motions of pride are venial sins, when reason does not consent to them.

Reply Obj. 1: As stated above (A. 2) pride is a general sin, not by its essence but by a kind of influence, in so far as all sins may have their origin in pride. Hence it does not follow that all sins are mortal, but only such as arise from perfect pride, which we have stated to be a mortal sin.

Reply Obj. 2: Pride is always contrary to the love of God, inasmuch as the proud man does not subject himself to the Divine rule as he ought. Sometimes it is also contrary to the love of our neighbor; when, namely, a man sets himself inordinately above his neighbor: and this again is a transgression of the Divine rule, which has established order among men, so that one ought to be subject to another.

Reply Obj. 3: Pride arises from virtue, not as from its direct cause, but as from an accidental cause, in so far as a man makes a virtue an occasion for pride. And nothing prevents one contrary from being the accidental cause of another, as stated in *Phys.* viii, 1. Hence some are even proud of their humility.

SIXTH ARTICLE [II-II, Q. 162, Art. 6]

Whether Pride Is the Most Grievous of Sins?

Objection 1: It would seem that pride is not the most grievous of sins. For the more difficult a sin is to avoid, the less grievous it would seem to be. Now pride is most difficult to avoid; for Augustine says in his Rule (Ep. ccxi), "Other sins find their vent in the accomplishment of evil deeds, whereas pride lies in wait for good deeds to destroy them." Therefore pride is not the most grievous of sins.

Obj. 2: Further, "The greater evil is opposed to the greater good," as the Philosopher asserts (Ethic. viii, 10). Now humility to which pride is opposed is not the greatest of virtues, as stated above (Q. 61, A. 5). Therefore the vices that are opposed to greater virtues, such as unbelief, despair, hatred of God, murder, and so forth, are more grievous sins than pride.

Obj. 3: Further, the greater evil is not punished by a lesser evil. But pride is sometimes punished by other sins according to Rom. 1:28, where it is stated that on account of their pride of heart, men of science were delivered "to a reprobate sense, to do those things which are not convenient." Therefore pride is not the most grievous of sins.

*On the contrary,* A gloss on Ps. 118:51, "The proud did iniquitously," says: "The greatest sin in man is pride."

*I answer that,* Two things are to be observed in sin, conversion to a mutable good, and this is the material part of sin; and aversion from the immutable good, and this gives sin its formal aspect and complement. Now on the part of the conversion, there is no reason for pride being the greatest of sins, because uplifting which pride covets inordinately, is not essentially most incompatible with the good of virtue. But on the part of the aversion, pride has extreme gravity, because in other sins man turns away from God, either through ignorance or through weakness, or through desire for any other good whatever; whereas pride denotes aversion from God simply through being unwilling to be subject to God and His rule. Hence Boethius [*Cf. Cassian, de Caenob. Inst. xii, 7] says that "while all vices flee from God, pride alone withstands God"; for which reason it is specially stated (James 4:6) that "God resisteth the proud." Wherefore aversion from God and His commandments, which is a consequence as it were in other sins, belongs to pride by its very nature, for its act is the contempt of God. And since that which belongs to a thing by its nature is always of greater weight than that which belongs to it through something else, it follows that pride is the most grievous of sins by its genus, because it exceeds in aversion which is the formal complement of sin.

Reply Obj. 1: A sin is difficult to avoid in two ways. First, on account of the violence of its onslaught; thus anger is violent in its onslaught on account of its impetuosity; and "still more difficult is it to resist concupiscence, on account of its connaturality," as stated in *Ethic.* ii, 3, 9. A difficulty of this kind in avoiding sin diminishes the gravity of the sin; because a man sins the more grievously, according as he yields to a less impetuous temptation, as Augustine says (De Civ. Dei xiv, 12, 15).

Secondly, it is difficult to avoid a sin, on account of its being hidden. In this way it is difficult to avoid pride, since it takes occasion even from good deeds, as stated (A. 5, ad 3). Hence Augustine says pointedly that it "lies in wait for good deeds"; and it is written (Ps. 141:4): "In the way wherein I walked, the proud [*Cf. Ps. 139:6, 'The proud have hidden a net for me.'] [Vulg.: 'they'] have hidden a snare for me." Hence no very great gravity attaches to the movement of pride while creeping in secretly, and before it is discovered by the judgment of reason: but once discovered by reason, it is easily avoided, both by considering one's own infirmity, according to Ecclus. 10:9, "Why is earth and ashes proud?" and by considering God's greatness, according to Job 15:13, "Why doth thy spirit swell against God?" as well as by considering the imperfection of the goods on which man prides himself, according to Isa. 40:6, "All flesh is grass, and all the glory thereof as the flower of the field"; and farther on (Isa. 64:6), "all our justices" are become "like the rag of a menstruous woman."

Reply Obj. 2: Opposition between a vice and a virtue is inferred from the object, which is considered on the part of conversion. In this way pride has no claim to be the greatest of sins, as neither has humility to be the greatest of virtues. But it is the greatest on the part of aversion, since it brings greatness upon other sins. For unbelief, by the very fact of its arising out of proud contempt, is rendered more grievous than if it be the outcome of ignorance or weakness. The same applies to despair and the like.

Reply Obj. 3: Just as in syllogisms that lead to an impossible conclusion one is sometimes convinced by being faced with a more evident absurdity, so too, in order to overcome their pride, God punishes certain men by allowing them to fall into sins of the flesh, which though they be less grievous are more evidently shameful. Hence Isidore says (De Summo Bono ii, 38) that "pride is the worst of all vices; whether because it is appropriate to those who are of highest and foremost rank, or because it originates from just and virtuous deeds, so that its guilt is less perceptible. On the other hand, carnal lust is apparent to all, because from the outset it is of a shameful nature: and yet, under God's dispensation, it is less grievous than pride. For he who is in the clutches of pride and feels it not, falls into the lusts of the flesh, that being thus humbled he may rise from his abasement."

From this indeed the gravity of pride is made manifest. For just as a wise physician, in order to cure a worse disease, allows the patient to contract one that is less dangerous, so the sin of pride is shown to be more grievous by the very fact that, as a remedy, God allows men to fall into other sins.

SEVENTH ARTICLE [II-II, Q. 162, Art. 7]

Whether Pride Is the First Sin of All?

Objection 1: It would seem that pride is not the first sin of all. For the first is maintained in all that follows. Now pride does not accompany all sins, nor is it the origin of all: for Augustine says (De Nat. et Grat. xx) that many things are done "amiss which are not done with pride." Therefore pride is not the first sin of all.

Obj. 2: Further, it is written (Ecclus. 10:14) that the "beginning of ... pride is to fall off from God." Therefore falling away from God precedes pride.

Obj. 3: Further, the order of sins would seem to be according to the order of virtues. Now, not humility but faith is the first of all virtues. Therefore pride is not the first sin of all.

Obj. 4: Further, it is written (2 Tim. 3:13): "Evil men and seducers shall grow worse and worse"; so that apparently man's beginning of wickedness is not the greatest of sins. But pride is the greatest of sins as stated in the foregoing Article. Therefore pride is not the first sin.

Obj. 5: Further, resemblance and pretense come after the reality. Now the Philosopher says (Ethic. iii, 7) that "pride apes fortitude and daring." Therefore the vice of daring precedes the vice of pride.

*On the contrary,* It is written (Ecclus. 10:15): "Pride is the beginning of all sin."

*I answer that,* The first thing in every genus is that which is essential. Now it has been stated above (A. 6) that aversion from God, which is the formal complement of sin, belongs to pride essentially, and to other sins, consequently. Hence it is that pride fulfils the conditions of a first thing, and is "the beginning of all sins," as stated above (I-II, Q. 84, A. 2), when we were treating of the causes of sin on the part of the aversion which is the chief part of sin.

Reply Obj. 1: Pride is said to be "the beginning of all sin," not as though every sin originated from pride, but because any kind of sin is naturally liable to arise from pride.

Reply Obj. 2: To fall off from God is said to be the beginning of pride, not as though it were a distinct sin from pride, but as being the first part of pride. For it has been said above (A. 5) that pride regards chiefly subjection to God which it scorns, and in consequence it scorns to be subject to a creature for God's sake.

Reply Obj. 3: There is no need for the order of virtues to be the same as that of vices. For vice is corruptive of virtue. Now that which is first to be generated is the last to be corrupted. Wherefore as faith is the first of virtues, so unbelief is the last of sins, to which sometimes man is led by other sins. Hence a gloss on Ps. 136:7, "Rase it, rase it, even to the foundation thereof," says that "by heaping vice upon vice a man will lapse into unbelief," and the Apostle says (1 Tim. 1:19) that "some rejecting a good conscience have made shipwreck concerning the faith."

Reply Obj. 4: Pride is said to be the most grievous of sins because that which gives sin its gravity is essential to pride. Hence pride is the cause of gravity in other sins. Accordingly previous to pride there may be certain less grievous sins that are committed through ignorance or weakness. But among the grievous sins the first is pride, as the cause whereby other sins are rendered more grievous. And as that which is the first in causing sins is the last in the withdrawal from sin, a gloss on Ps. 18:13, "I shall be cleansed from the greatest sin," says: "Namely from the sin of pride, which is the last in those who return to God, and the first in those who withdraw from God."

Reply Obj. 5: The Philosopher associates pride with feigned fortitude, not that it consists precisely in this, but because man thinks he is more likely to be uplifted before men, if he seem to be daring or brave.

EIGHTH ARTICLE [II-II, Q. 162, Art. 8]

Whether Pride Should Be Reckoned a Capital Vice?

Objection 1: It would seem that pride should be reckoned a capital vice, since Isidore [*Comment. in Deut. xvi] and Cassian [*De Inst. Caenob. v, 1: Collat. v, 2] number pride among the capital vices.

Obj. 2: Further, pride is apparently the same as vainglory, since both covet excellence. Now vainglory is reckoned a capital vice. Therefore pride also should be reckoned a capital vice.

Obj. 3: Further, Augustine says (De Virginit. xxxi) that "pride begets envy, nor is it ever without this companion." Now envy is reckoned a capital vice, as stated above (Q. 36, A. 4). Much more therefore is pride a capital vice.

*On the contrary,* Gregory (Moral. xxxi, 45) does not include pride among the capital vices.

*I answer that,* As stated above (AA. 2, 5, ad 1) pride may be considered in two ways; first in itself, as being a special sin; secondly, as having a general influence towards all sins. Now the capital vices are said to be certain special sins from which many kinds of sin arise. Wherefore some, considering pride in the light of a special sin, numbered it together with the other capital vices. But Gregory, taking into consideration its general influence towards all vices, as explained above (A. 2, Obj. 3), did not place it among the capital vices, but held it to be the "queen and mother of all the vices." Hence he says (Moral. xxxi, 45): "Pride, the queen of vices, when it has vanquished and captured the heart, forthwith delivers it into the hands of its lieutenants the seven principal vices, that they may despoil it and produce vices of all kinds."

This suffices for the Reply to the First Objection.

Reply Obj. 2: Pride is not the same as vainglory, but is the cause thereof: for pride covets excellence inordinately: while vainglory covets the outward show of excellence.

Reply Obj. 3: The fact that envy, which is a capital vice, arises from pride, does not prove that pride is a capital vice, but that it is still more principal than the capital vices themselves.

## QUESTION 163

OF THE FIRST MAN'S SIN (In Four Articles)

We must now consider the first man's sin which was pride: and (1) his sin; (2) its punishment; (3) the temptation whereby he was led to sin.

Under the first head there are four points of inquiry:

(1) Whether pride was the first man's first sin?

(2) What the first man coveted by sinning?

(3) Whether his sin was more grievous than all other sins?

(4) Which sinned more grievously, the man or the woman?

FIRST ARTICLE [II-II, Q. 163, Art. 1]

Whether Pride Was the First Man's First Sin?

Objection 1: It would seem that pride was not the first man's first sin. For the Apostle says (Rom. 5:19) that "by the disobedience of one man many were made sinners." Now the first man's first sin is the one by which all men were made sinners in the point of original sin. Therefore disobedience, and not pride, was the first man's first sin.

Obj. 2: Further, Ambrose says, commenting on Luke 4:3, "And the devil said to Him," that the devil in tempting Christ observed the same order as in overcoming the first man. Now Christ was first tempted to gluttony, as appears from Matt. 4:3, where it was said to Him: "If thou be the Son of God, command that these stones be made bread." Therefore the first man's first sin was not pride but gluttony.

Obj. 3: Further, man sinned at the devil's suggestion. Now the devil in tempting man promised him knowledge (Gen. 3:5). Therefore inordinateness in man was through the desire of knowledge, which pertains to curiosity. Therefore curiosity, and not pride, was the first sin.

Obj. 4: Further, a gloss [*St. Augustine, Gen. ad lit. xi] on 1 Tim. 2:14, "The woman being seduced was in the transgression," says: "The Apostle rightly calls this seduction, for they were persuaded to accept a falsehood as being true; namely that God had forbidden them to touch that tree, because He knew that if they touched it, they would be like gods, as though He who made them men, begrudged them the godhead ..." Now it pertains to unbelief to believe such a thing. Therefore man's first sin was unbelief and not pride.

*On the contrary,* It is written (Ecclus. 10:15): "Pride is the beginning of all sin." Now man's first sin is the beginning of all sin, according to Rom. 5:12, "By one man sin entered into this world." Therefore man's first sin was pride.

*I answer that,* Many movements may concur towards one sin, and the character of sin attaches to that one in which inordinateness is first found. And it is evident that inordinateness is in the inward movement of the soul before being in the outward act of the body; since, as Augustine says (De Civ. Dei i, 18), the sanctity of the body is not forfeited so long as the sanctity of the soul remains. Also, among the inward movements, the appetite is moved towards the end before being moved towards that which is desired for the sake of the end; and consequently man's first sin was where it was possible for his appetite to be directed to an inordinate end. Now man was so appointed in the state of innocence, that there was no rebellion of the flesh against the spirit. Wherefore it was not possible for the first inordinateness in the human appetite to result from his coveting a sensible good, to which the concupiscence of the flesh tends against the order of reason. It remains therefore that the first inordinateness of the human appetite resulted from his coveting inordinately some spiritual good. Now he would not have coveted it inordinately, by desiring it according to his measure as established by the Divine rule. Hence it follows that man's first sin consisted in his coveting some spiritual good above his measure: and this pertains to pride. Therefore it is evident that man's first sin was pride.

Reply Obj. 1: Man's disobedience to the Divine command was not willed by man for his own sake, for this could not happen unless one presuppose inordinateness in his will. It remains therefore that he willed it for the sake of something else. Now the first thing he coveted inordinately was his own excellence; and consequently his disobedience was the result of his pride. This agrees with the statement of Augustine, who says (Ad Oros [*Dial. QQ. lxv, qu. 4]) that "man puffed up with pride obeyed the serpent's prompting, and scorned God's commands."

Reply Obj. 2: Gluttony also had a place in the sin of our first parents. For it is written (Gen. 3:6): "The woman saw that the tree was good to eat, and fair to the eyes, and delightful to behold, and she took of the fruit thereof, and did eat." Yet the very goodness and beauty of the fruit was not their first motive for sinning, but the persuasive words of the serpent, who said (Gen. 3:5): "Your eyes shall be opened and you shall be as Gods": and it was by coveting this that the woman fell into pride. Hence the sin of gluttony resulted from the sin of pride.

Reply Obj. 3: The desire for knowledge resulted in our first parents from their inordinate desire for excellence. Hence the serpent began by saying: "You shall be as Gods," and added: "Knowing good and evil."

Reply Obj. 4: According to Augustine (Gen. ad lit. xi, 30), "the woman had not believed the serpent's statement that they were debarred by God from a good and useful thing, were her mind not already filled with the love of her own power, and a certain proud self-presumption." This does not mean that pride preceded the promptings of the serpent, but that as soon as the serpent had spoken his words of persuasion, her mind was puffed up, the result being that she believed the demon to have spoken truly.

SECOND ARTICLE [II-II, Q. 163, Art. 2]

Whether the First Man's Pride Consisted in His Coveting God's Likeness?

Objection 1: It would seem that the first man's pride did not consist in his coveting the Divine likeness. For no one sins by coveting that which is competent to him according to his nature. Now God's likeness is competent to man according to his nature: for it is written (Gen. 1:26): "Let us make man to our image and likeness." Therefore he did not sin by coveting God's likeness.

Obj. 2: Further, it would seem that man coveted God's likeness in order that he might obtain knowledge of good and evil: for this was the serpent's suggestion: "You shall be as Gods knowing good and evil." Now the desire of knowledge is natural to man, according to the saying of the Philosopher at the beginning of his Metaphysics i, 1: "All men naturally desire knowledge." Therefore he did not sin by coveting God's likeness.

Obj. 3: Further, no wise man chooses the impossible. Now the first man was endowed with wisdom, according to Ecclus. 17:5, "He filled them with the knowledge of understanding." Since then every sin consists in a deliberate act of the appetite, namely choice, it would seem that the first man did not sin by coveting something impossible. But it is impossible for man to be like God, according to the saying of Ex. 15:11, "Who is like to Thee among the strong, O Lord?" Therefore the first man did not sin by coveting God's likeness.

*On the contrary,* Augustine commenting on Ps. 68:5 [*Enarr. in Ps. 68], "Then did I restore [Douay: 'pay'] that which I took not away," says: "Adam and Eve wished to rob the Godhead and they lost happiness."

*I answer that,* likeness is twofold. One is a likeness of absolute equality [*Cf. I, Q. 93, A. 1]: and such a likeness to God our first parents did not covet, since such a likeness to God is not conceivable to the mind, especially of a wise man.

The other is a likeness of imitation, such as is possible for a creature in reference to God, in so far as the creature participates somewhat of God's likeness according to its measure. For Dionysius says (Div. Nom. ix): "The same things are like and unlike to God; like, according as they imitate Him, as far as He can be imitated; unlike, according as an effect falls short of its cause." Now every good existing in a creature is a participated likeness of the first good.

Wherefore from the very fact that man coveted a spiritual good above his measure, as stated in the foregoing Article, it follows that he coveted God's likeness inordinately.

It must, however, be observed that the proper object of the appetite is a thing not possessed. Now spiritual good, in so far as the rational creature participates in the Divine likeness, may be considered in reference to three things. First, as to natural being: and this likeness was imprinted from the very outset of their creation, both on man—of whom it is written (Gen. 1:26) that God made man "to His image and likeness"—and on the angel, of whom it is written (Ezech. 28:12): "Thou wast the seal of resemblance." Secondly, as to knowledge: and this likeness was bestowed on the angel at his creation, wherefore immediately after the words just quoted, "Thou wast the seal of resemblance," we read: "Full of wisdom." But the first man, at his creation, had not yet received this likeness actually but only in potentiality. Thirdly, as to the power of operation: and neither angel nor man received this likeness actually at the very outset of his creation, because to each there remained something to be done whereby to obtain happiness.

Accordingly, while both (namely the devil and the first man) coveted God's likeness inordinately, neither of them sinned by coveting a likeness of nature. But the first man sinned chiefly by coveting God's likeness as regards "knowledge of good and evil," according to the serpent's instigation, namely that by his own natural power he might decide what was good, and what was evil for him to do; or again that he should of himself foreknow what good and what evil would befall him. Secondarily he sinned by coveting God's likeness as regards his own power of operation, namely that by his own natural power he might act so as to obtain happiness. Hence Augustine says (Gen. ad lit. xi, 30) that "the woman's mind was filled with love of her own power." On the other hand, the devil sinned by coveting God's likeness, as regards power. Wherefore Augustine says (De Vera Relig. 13) that "he wished to enjoy his own power rather than God's." Nevertheless both coveted somewhat to be equal to God, in so far as each wished to rely on himself in contempt of the order of the Divine rule.

Reply Obj. 1: This argument considers the likeness of nature: and man did not sin by coveting this, as stated.

Reply Obj. 2: It is not a sin to covet God's likeness as to knowledge, absolutely; but to covet this likeness inordinately, that is, above one's measure, this is a sin. Hence Augustine commenting on Ps. 70:18, "O God, who is like Thee?" says: "He who desires to be of himself, even as God is of no one, wishes wickedly to be like God. Thus did the devil, who was unwilling to be subject to Him, and man who refused to be, as a servant, bound by His command."

Reply Obj. 3: This argument considers the likeness of equality.

THIRD ARTICLE [II-II, Q. 163, Art. 7]

Whether the Sin of Our First Parents Was More Grievous Than Other Sins?

Objection 1: It would seem that the sin of our first parents was more grievous than other sins. For Augustine says (De Civ. Dei xiv, 15): "Great was the wickedness in sinning, when it was so easy to avoid sin." Now it was very easy for our first parents to avoid sin, because they had nothing within them urging them to sin. Therefore the sin of our first parents was more grievous than other sins.

Obj. 2: Further, punishment is proportionate to guilt. Now the sin of our first parents was most severely punished, since by it "death entered into this world," as the Apostle says (Rom. 5:12). Therefore that sin was more grievous than other sins.

Obj. 3: Further, the first in every genus is seemingly the greatest (Metaph. ii, 4 [*Ed. Diel. i, 1]). Now the sin of our first parents was the first among sins of men. Therefore it was the greatest.

*On the contrary,* Origen says [*Peri Archon i, 3]: "I think that a man who stands on the highest step of perfection cannot fail or fall suddenly: this can happen only by degrees and little by little." Now our first parents were established on the highest and perfect grade. Therefore their first sin was not the greatest of all sins.

*I answer that,* There is a twofold gravity to be observed in sin. one results from the very species of the sin: thus we say that adultery is a graver sin than simple fornication. The other gravity of sin results from some circumstance of place, person, or time. The former gravity is more essential to sin and is of greater moment: hence a sin is said to be grave in respect of this gravity rather than of the other. Accordingly we must say that the first man's sin was not graver than all other sins of men, as regards the species of the sin. For though pride, of its genus, has a certain pre-eminence over other sins, yet the pride whereby one denies or blasphemes God is greater than the pride whereby one covets God's likeness inordinately, such as the pride of our first parents, as stated (A. 2).

But if we consider the circumstances of the persons who sinned, that sin was most grave on account of the perfection of their state. We must accordingly conclude that this sin was most grievous relatively but not simply.

Reply Obj. 1: This argument considers the gravity of sin as resulting from the person of the sinner.

Reply Obj. 2: The severity of the punishment awarded to that first sin corresponds to the magnitude of the sin, not as regards its species but as regards its being the first sin: because it destroyed the innocence of our original state, and by robbing it of innocence brought disorder upon the whole human nature.

Reply Obj. 3: Where things are directly subordinate, the first must needs be the greatest. Such is not the order among sins, for one follows from another accidentally. And thus it does not follow that the first sin is the greatest.

FOURTH ARTICLE [II-II, Q. 163, Art. 4]

Whether Adam's Sin Was More Grievous Than Eve's?

Objection 1: It would seem that Adam's sin was more grievous than Eve's. For it is written (1 Tim. 2:14): "Adam was not seduced, but the woman being seduced was in the transgression": and so it would seem that the woman sinned through ignorance, but the man through assured knowledge. Now the latter is the graver sin, according to Luke 12:47, 48, "That servant who knew the will of his lord ... and did not according to his will, shall be beaten with many stripes: but he that knew not, and did things worthy of stripes, shall be beaten with few stripes." Therefore Adam's sin was more grievous than Eve's.

Obj. 2: Further, Augustine says (De Decem Chordis 3 [*Serm. ix; xcvi de Temp.]): "If the man is the head, he should live better, and give an example of good deeds to his wife, that she may imitate him." Now he who ought to do better, sins more grievously, if he commit a sin. Therefore Adam sinned more grievously than Eve.

Obj. 3: Further, the sin against the Holy Ghost would seem to be the most grievous. Now Adam, apparently, sinned against the Holy Ghost, because while sinning he relied on God's mercy [*Cf. Q. 21, A. 2, Obj. 3. St. Thomas is evidently alluding to the words of Peter Lombard quoted there], and this pertains to the sin of presumption. Therefore it seems that Adam sinned more grievously than Eve.

*On the contrary,* Punishment corresponds to guilt. Now the woman was more grievously punished than the man, as appears from Gen. 3. Therefore she sinned more grievously than the man.

*I answer that,* As stated (A. 3), the gravity of a sin depends on the species rather than on a circumstance of that sin. Accordingly we must assert that, if we consider the condition attaching to these persons, the man's sin is the more grievous, because he was more perfect than the woman.

As regards the genus itself of the sin, the sin of each is considered to be equal, for each sinned by pride. Hence Augustine says (Gen. ad lit. xi, 35): "Eve in excusing herself betrays disparity of sex, though parity of pride."

But as regards the species of pride, the woman sinned more grievously, for three reasons. First, because she was more puffed up than the man. For the woman believed in the serpent's persuasive words, namely that God had forbidden them to eat of the tree, lest they should become like to Him; so that in wishing to attain to God's likeness by eating of the forbidden fruit, her pride rose to the height of desiring to obtain something against God's will. On the other hand, the man did not believe this to be true; wherefore he did not wish to attain to God's likeness against God's will: but his pride consisted in wishing to attain thereto by his own power. Secondly, the woman not only herself sinned, but suggested sin to the man; wherefore she sinned against both God and her neighbor. Thirdly, the man's sin was diminished by the fact that, as Augustine says (Gen. ad lit. xi, 42), "he consented to the sin out of a certain friendly good-will, on account of which a man sometimes will offend God rather than make an enemy of his friend. That he ought not to have done so is shown by the just issue of the Divine sentence."

It is therefore evident that the woman's sin was more grievous than the man's.

Reply Obj. 1: The woman was deceived because she was first of all puffed up with pride. Wherefore her ignorance did not excuse, but aggravated her sin, in so far as it was the cause of her being puffed up with still greater pride.

Reply Obj. 2: This argument considers the circumstance of personal condition, on account of which the man's sin was more grievous than the woman's.

Reply Obj. 3: The man's reliance on God's mercy did not reach to contempt of God's justice, wherein consists the sin against the Holy Ghost, but as Augustine says (Gen. ad lit. xi [*De Civ. Dei xiv, 11]), it was due to the fact that, "having had no experience of God's severity, he thought the sin to be venial," i.e. easily forgiven [*Cf. I-II, Q. 89, A. 3, ad 1].

# QUESTION 164

OF THE PUNISHMENTS OF THE FIRST MAN'S SIN (In Two Articles)

We must now consider the punishments of the first sin; and under this head there are two points of inquiry: (1) Death, which is the common punishment; (2) the other particular punishments mentioned in Genesis.

FIRST ARTICLE [II-II, Q. 164, Art. 1]

Whether Death Is the Punishment of Our First Parents' Sin?

Objection 1: It would seem that death is not the punishment of our first parents' sin. For that which is natural to man cannot be called a punishment of sin, because sin does not perfect nature but vitiates it. Now death is natural to man: and this is evident both from the fact that his body is composed of contraries, and because "mortal" is included in the definition of man. Therefore death is not a punishment of our first parents' sin.

Obj. 2: Further, death and other bodily defects are similarly found in man as well as in other animals, according to Eccles. 3:19, "The death of man and of beasts is one, and the condition of them both equal." But in dumb animals death is not a punishment of sin. Therefore neither is it so in men.

Obj. 3: Further, the sin of our first parents was the sin of particular individuals: whereas death affects the entire human nature. Therefore it would seem that it is not a punishment of our first parents' sin.

Obj. 4: Further, all are equally descended from our first parents. Therefore if death were the punishment of our first parents' sin, it would follow that all men would suffer death in equal measure. But this is clearly untrue, since some die sooner, and some more painfully, than others. Therefore death is not the punishment of the first sin.

Obj. 5: Further, the evil of punishment is from God, as stated above (I, Q. 48, A. 6; Q. 49, A. 2). But death, apparently, is not from God: for it is written (Wis. 1:13): "God made not death." Therefore death is not the punishment of the first sin.

Obj. 6: Further, seemingly, punishments are not meritorious, since merit is comprised under good, and punishment under evil. Now death is sometimes meritorious, as in the case of a martyr's death. Therefore it would seem that death is not a punishment.

Obj. 7: Further, punishment would seem to be

painful. But death apparently cannot be painful, since man does not feel it when he is dead, and he cannot feel it when he is not dying. Therefore death is not a punishment of sin.

Obj. 8: Further, if death were a punishment of sin, it would have followed sin immediately. But this is not true, for our first parents lived a long time after their sin (Gen. 5:5). Therefore, seemingly, death is not a punishment of sin.

*On the contrary,* The Apostle says (Rom. 5:12): "By one man sin entered into this world, and by sin death."

*I answer that,* If any one, on account of his fault, be deprived of a favor bestowed on him the privation of that favor is a punishment of that fault. Now as we stated in the First Part (Q. 95, A. 1; Q. 97, A. 1), God bestowed this favor on man, in his primitive state, that as long as his mind was subject to God, the lower powers of his soul would be subject to his rational mind, and his body to his soul. But inasmuch as through sin man's mind withdrew from subjection to God, the result was that neither were his lower powers wholly subject to his reason, whence there followed so great a rebellion of the carnal appetite against the reason: nor was the body wholly subject to the soul; whence arose death and other bodily defects. For life and soundness of body depend on the body being subject to the soul, as the perfectible is subject to its perfection. Consequently, on the other hand, death, sickness, and all defects of the body are due to the lack of the body's subjection to the soul.

It is therefore evident that as the rebellion of the carnal appetite against the spirit is a punishment of our first parents' sin, so also are death and all defects of the body.

Reply Obj. 1: A thing is said to be natural if it proceeds from the principles of nature. Now the essential principles of nature are form and matter. The form of man is his rational soul, which is, of itself, immortal: wherefore death is not natural to man on the part of his form. The matter of man is a body such as is composed of contraries, of which corruptibility is a necessary consequence, and in this respect death is natural to man. Now this condition attached to the nature of the human body results from a natural necessity, since it was necessary for the human body to be the organ of touch, and consequently a mean between objects of touch: and this was impossible, were it not composed of contraries, as the Philosopher states (De Anima ii, 11). On the other hand, this condition is not attached to the adaptability of matter to form because, if it were possible, since the form is incorruptible, its matter should rather be incorruptible. In the same way a saw needs to be of iron, this being suitable to its form and action, so that its hardness may make it fit for cutting. But that it be liable to rust is a necessary result of such a matter and is not according to the agent's choice; for, if the craftsman were able, of the iron he would make a saw that would not rust. Now God Who is the author of man is all-powerful, wherefore when He first made man, He conferred on him the favor of being exempt from the necessity resulting from such a matter: which favor, however, was withdrawn through the sin of our first parents. Accordingly death is both natural on account of a condition attaching to matter, and penal on account of the loss of the Divine favor preserving man from death [*Cf. I-II, Q. 85, A. 6].

Reply Obj. 2: This likeness of man to other animals regards a condition attaching to matter, namely the body being composed of contraries. But it does not regard the form, for man's soul is immortal, whereas the souls of dumb animals are mortal.

Reply Obj. 3: Our first parents were made by God not only as particular individuals, but also as principles of the whole human nature to be transmitted by them to their posterity, together with the Divine favor preserving them from death. Hence through their sin the entire human nature, being deprived of that favor in their posterity, incurred death.

Reply Obj. 4: A twofold defect arises from sin. One is by way of a punishment appointed by a judge: and such a defect should be equal in those to whom the sin pertains equally. The other defect is that which results accidentally from this punishment; for instance, that one who has been deprived of his sight for a sin he has committed, should fall down in the road. Such a defect is not proportionate to the sin, nor does a human judge take it into account, since he cannot foresee chance happenings. Accordingly, the punishment appointed for the first sin and proportionately corresponding thereto, was the withdrawal of the Divine favor whereby the rectitude and integrity of human nature was maintained. But the defects resulting from this withdrawal are death and other penalties of the present life. Wherefore these punishments need not be equal in those to whom the first sin equally appertains. Nevertheless, since God foreknows all future events, Divine providence has so disposed that these penalties are apportioned in different ways to various people. This is not on account of any merits or demerits previous to this life, as Origen held [*Peri Archon ii, 9]: for this is contrary to the words of Rom. 9:11, "When they ... had not done any good or evil"; and also contrary to statements made in the First Part (Q. 90, A. 4; Q. 118, A. 3), namely that the soul is not created before the body: but either in punishment of their parents' sins, inasmuch as the child is something belonging to the father, wherefore parents are often punished in their children; or again it is for a remedy intended for the spiritual welfare of the person who suffers these penalties, to wit that he may thus be turned away from his sins, or lest he take pride in his virtues, and that he may be crowned for his patience.

Reply Obj. 5: Death may be considered in two ways. First, as an evil of human nature, and thus it is not of God, but is a defect befalling man through his fault. Secondly, as having an aspect of good, namely as being a just punishment, and thus it is from God. Wherefore Augustine says (Retract. i, 21) that God is not the author of death, except in so far as it is a punishment.

Reply Obj. 6: As Augustine says (De Civ. Dei xiii, 5), "just as the wicked abuse not only evil but also good things, so do the righteous make good use not only of good but also of evil things. Hence it is that both evil men make evil use of the law, though the law is good, while good men die well, although death is an evil." Wherefore inasmuch as holy men make good use of death, their death is to them meritorious.

Reply Obj. 7: Death may be considered in two ways. First, as the privation of life, and thus death cannot be felt, since it is the privation of sense and life. In this way it involves not pain of sense but pain of loss. Secondly, it may be considered as denoting the corruption which ends in the aforesaid privation. Now we may speak of corruption even as of generation in two ways: in one way as being the term of alteration, and thus in the first instant in which life departs, death is said to be present. In this way also death has no pain of sense. In another way corruption may be taken as including the previous alteration: thus a person is said to die, when he is in motion towards death; just as a thing is said to be engendered, while in motion towards the state of having been engendered: and thus death may be painful.

Reply Obj. 8: According to Augustine (Gen. ad lit. [*De Pecc. Mer. et Rem. i, 16. Cf. Gen. ad lit. ii. 32]), "although our first parents lived thereafter many years, they began to die on the day when they heard the death-decree, condemning them to decline to old age."

SECOND ARTICLE [II-II, Q. 164, Art. 2]

Whether the Particular Punishments of Our First Parents Are Suitably Appointed in Scripture?

Objection 1: It would seem that the particular punishments of our first parents are unsuitably appointed in Scripture. For that which would have occurred even without sin should not be described as a punishment for sin. Now seemingly there would have been "pain in child-bearing," even had there been no sin: for the disposition of the female sex is such that offspring cannot be born without pain to the bearer. Likewise the "subjection of woman to man" results from the perfection of the male, and the imperfection of the female sex. Again it belongs to the nature of the earth "to bring forth thorns and thistles," and this would have occurred even had there been no sin. Therefore these are unsuitable punishments of the first sin.

Obj. 2: Further, that which pertains to a person's dignity does not, seemingly, pertain to his punishment. But the "multiplying of conceptions" pertains to a woman's dignity. Therefore it should not be described as the woman's punishment.

Obj. 3: Further, the punishment of our first parents' sin is transmitted to all, as we have stated with regard to death (A. 1). But all "women's conceptions" are not "multiplied," nor does "every man eat bread in the sweat of his face." Therefore these are not suitable punishments of the first sin.

Obj. 4: Further, the place of paradise was made for man. Now nothing in the order of things should be without purpose. Therefore it would seem that the exclusion of man from paradise was not a suitable punishment of man.

Obj. 5: Further, this place of the earthly paradise is said to be naturally inaccessible. Therefore it was useless to put other obstacles in the way lest man should return thither, to wit the cherubim, and the "flaming sword turning every way."

Obj. 6: Further, immediately after his sin man was subject to the necessity of dying, so that he could not be restored to immortality by the beneficial tree of life. Therefore it was useless to forbid him to eat of the tree of life, as instanced by the words of Gen. 3:22: "See, lest perhaps he ... take ... of the tree of life ... and live for ever."

Obj. 7: Further, to mock the unhappy seems inconsistent with mercy and clemency, which are most of all ascribed to God in Scripture, according to Ps. 144:9, "His tender mercies are over all His works." Therefore God is unbecomingly described as mocking our first parents, already reduced through sin to unhappy straits, in the words of Gen. 3:22, "Behold Adam is become as one of Us, knowing good and evil."

Obj. 8: Further, clothes are necessary to man, like food, according to 1 Tim. 6:8, "Having food, and wherewith to be covered, with these we are content." Therefore just as food was appointed to our first parents before their sin, so also should clothing have been ascribed to them. Therefore after their sin it was unsuitable to say that God made for them garments of skin.

Objection 9: Further, the punishment inflicted for a sin should outweigh in evil the gain realized through the sin: else the punishment would not deter one from sinning. Now through sin our first parents gained in this, that their eyes were opened, according to Gen. 3:7. But this outweighs in good all the penal evils which are stated to have resulted from sin. Therefore the punishments resulting from our first parents' sin are unsuitably described.

*On the contrary,* These punishments were appointed by God, Who does all things, "in number, weight, and measure [*Vulg.: 'Thou hast ordered all things in measure, and number, and weight.']" (Wis. 11:21).

*I answer that,* As stated in the foregoing Article, on account of their sin, our first parents were deprived of the Divine favor, whereby the integrity of human nature was maintained in them, and by the withdrawal of this favor human nature incurred penal defects. Hence they were punished in two ways. In the first place by being deprived of that which was befitting the state of integrity, namely the place of the earthly paradise: and this is indicated (Gen. 3:23) where it is stated that "God sent him out of the paradise of pleasure." And since he was unable, of himself, to return to that state of original innocence, it was fitting that obstacles should be placed against his recovering those things that were befitting his original state, namely food (lest he should take of the tree of life) and place; for "God placed before ... paradise ... Cherubim, and a flaming sword." Secondly, they were punished by having appointed to them things befitting a nature bereft of the aforesaid favor: and this as regards both the body and the soul. With regard to the body, to which pertains the distinction of sex, one punishment was appointed to the woman and another to the man. To the woman punishment was appointed in respect of two things on account of which she is united to the man; and these are the begetting of children, and community of works pertaining to family life. As regards the begetting of children, she was punished in two ways: first in the weariness to which she is subject while carrying the child after conception, and this is indicated in the words (Gen. 3:16), "I will multiply thy sorrows, and thy conceptions"; secondly, in the pain which she suffers in giving birth, and this is indicated by the words (Gen. 3:16), "In sorrow shalt thou bring forth." As regards family life she was punished by being subjected to her husband's authority, and this is conveyed in the words (Gen. 3:16), "Thou shalt be under thy husband's power."

Now, just as it belongs to the woman to be subject to her husband in matters relating to the family life, so it belongs to the husband to provide the necessaries of that life. In this respect he was punished in three ways. First, by the barrenness of the earth, in the words (Gen. 3:17), "Cursed is the earth in thy work." Secondly, by the cares of his toil, without which he does not win the fruits of the earth; hence the words (Gen. 3:17), "With labor and toil shalt thou eat thereof all the days of thy life." Thirdly, by the obstacles encountered by the tillers of the soil, wherefore it is written (Gen. 3:18), "Thorns and thistles shall it bring forth to thee."

Likewise a triple punishment is ascribed to them on the part of the soul. First, by reason of the confusion they experienced at the rebellion of the flesh against the spirit; hence it is written (Gen. 3:7): "The eyes of them both were opened; and ... they perceived themselves to be naked." Secondly, by the reproach for their sin, indicated by the words (Gen. 3:22), "Behold Adam is become as one of Us." Thirdly, by the reminder of their coming death, when it was said to him (Gen. 3:19): "Dust thou art and into dust thou shalt return." To this also pertains that God made them garments of skin, as a sign of their mortality.

Reply Obj. 1: In the state of innocence child-bearing would have been painless: for Augustine says (De Civ. Dei xiv, 26): "Just as, in giving birth, the mother would then be relieved not by groans of pain, but by the instigations of maturity, so in bearing and conceiving the union of both sexes would be one not of lustful desire but of deliberate action" [*Cf. I, Q. 98, A. 2].

The subjection of the woman to her husband is to be understood as inflicted in punishment of the woman, not as to his headship (since even before sin the man was the "head" and governor "of the woman"), but as to her having now to obey her husband's will even against her own.

If man had not sinned, the earth would have brought forth thorns and thistles to be the food of animals, but not to punish man, because their growth would bring no labor or punishment for the tiller of the soil, as Augustine says (Gen. ad lit. iii, 18). Alcuin [*Interrog. et Resp. in Gen. lxxix], however, holds that, before sin, the earth brought forth no thorns and thistles, whatever: but the former opinion is the better.

Reply Obj. 2: The multiplying of her conceptions was appointed as a punishment to the woman, not on account of the begetting of children, for this would have been the same even before sin, but on account of the numerous sufferings to which the woman is subject, through carrying her offspring after conception. Hence it is expressly stated: "I will multiply thy sorrows, and thy conceptions."

Reply Obj. 3: These punishments affect all somewhat. For any woman who conceives must needs suffer sorrows and bring forth her child with pain: except the Blessed Virgin, who "conceived without corruption, and bore without pain" [*St. Bernard, Serm. in Dom. inf. oct. Assum. B. V. M.], because her conceiving was not according to the law of nature, transmitted from our first parents. And if a woman neither conceives nor bears, she suffers from the defect of barrenness, which outweighs the aforesaid punishments. Likewise whoever tills the soil must needs eat his bread in the sweat of his brow: while those who do not themselves work on the land, are busied with other labors, for "man is born to labor" (Job 5:7): and thus they eat the bread for which others have labored in the sweat of their brow.

Reply Obj. 4: Although the place of the earthly paradise avails not man for his use, it avails him for a lesson; because he knows himself deprived of that place on account of sin, and because by the things that have a bodily existence in that paradise, he is instructed in things pertaining to the heavenly paradise, the way to which is prepared for man by Christ.

Reply Obj. 5: Apart from the mysteries of the spiritual interpretation, this place would seem to be inaccessible, chiefly on account of the extreme heat in the middle zone by reason of the nighness of the sun. This is denoted by the "flaming sword," which is described as "turning every way," as being appropriate to the circular movement that causes this heat. And since the movements of corporal creatures are set in order through the ministry of the angels, according to Augustine (De Trin. iii, 4), it was fitting that, besides the sword turning every way, there should be cherubim "to keep the way of the tree of life." Hence Augustine says (Gen. ad lit. xi, 40): "It is to be believed that even in the visible paradise this was done by heavenly powers indeed, so that there was a fiery guard set there by the ministry of angels."

Reply Obj. 6: After sin, if man had [eaten] of the tree of life, he would not thereby have recovered immortality, but by means of that beneficial food he might have prolonged his life. Hence in the words "And live for ever," "for ever" signifies "for a long time." For it was not expedient for man to remain longer in the unhappiness of this life.

Reply Obj. 7: According to Augustine (Gen. ad lit. xi, 39), "these words of God are not so much a mockery of our first parents as a deterrent to others, for whose benefit these things are written, lest they be proud likewise, because Adam not only failed to become that which he coveted to be, but did not keep that to which he was made."

Reply Obj. 8: Clothing is necessary to man in his present state of unhappiness for two reasons. First, to supply a deficiency in respect of external harm caused by, for instance, extreme heat or cold. Secondly, to hide his ignominy and to cover the shame of those members wherein the rebellion of the flesh against the spirit is most manifest. Now these two motives do not apply to the primitive state. because then man's body could not be hurt by any outward thing, as stated in the First Part (Q. 97, A. 2), nor was there in man's body anything shameful that would bring confusion on him. Hence it is written (Gen. 2:23): "And they were both naked, to wit Adam and his wife, and were not ashamed." The same cannot be said of food, which is necessary to entertain the natural heat, and to sustain the body.

Reply Obj. 9: As Augustine says (Gen. ad lit. xi, 31), "We must not imagine that our first parents were created with their eyes closed, especially since it is stated that the woman saw that the tree was fair, and good to eat. Accordingly the eyes of both were opened so that they saw and thought on things which had not occurred to their minds before, this was a mutual concupiscence such as they had not hitherto."

# QUESTION 165

OF OUR FIRST PARENTS' TEMPTATION (In Two Articles)

We must now consider our first parents' temptation, concerning which there are two points of inquiry:

(1) Whether it was fitting for man to be tempted by the devil?

(2) Of the manner and order of that temptation.

FIRST ARTICLE [II-II, Q. 165, Art. 1]

Whether It Was Fitting for Man to Be Tempted by the Devil?

Objection 1: It would seem that it was not fitting for man to be tempted by the devil. For the same final punishment is appointed to the angels' sin and to man's, according to Matt. 25:41, "Go [Vulg.: 'Depart from Me'] you cursed into everlasting fire, which was prepared for the devil and his angels." Now the angels' first sin did not follow a temptation from without. Therefore neither should man's first sin have resulted from an outward temptation.

Obj. 2: Further, God, Who foreknows the future, knew that through the demon's temptation man would fall into sin, and thus He knew full well that it was not expedient for man to be tempted. Therefore it would seem unfitting for God to allow him to be tempted.

Obj. 3: Further, it seems to savor of punishment that anyone should have an assailant, just as on the other hand the cessation of an assault is akin to a reward. Now punishment should not precede fault. Therefore it was unfitting for man to be tempted before he sinned.

*On the contrary,* It is written (Ecclus. 34:11): "He that hath not been tempted [Douay: 'tried'], what manner of things doth he know?"

*I answer that,* God's wisdom "orders all things sweetly" (Wis. 8:1), inasmuch as His providence appoints to each one that which is befitting it according to its nature. For as Dionysius says (Div. Nom. iv), "it belongs to providence not to destroy, but to maintain, nature." Now it is a condition attaching to human nature that one creature can be helped or impeded by another. Wherefore it was fitting that God should both allow man in the state of innocence to be tempted by evil angels, and should cause him to be helped by good angels. And by a special favor of grace, it was granted him that no creature outside himself could harm him against his own will, whereby he was able even to resist the temptation of the demon.

Reply Obj. 1: Above the human nature there is another that admits of the possibility of the evil of fault: but there is not above the angelic nature. Now only one that is already become evil through sin can tempt by leading another into evil. Hence it was fitting that by an evil angel man should be tempted to sin, even as according to the order of nature he is moved forward to perfection by means of a good angel. An angel could be perfected in good by something above him, namely by God, but he could not thus be led into sin, because according to James 1:13, "God is not a tempter of evils."

Reply Obj. 2: Just as God knew that man, through being tempted, would fall into sin, so too He knew that man was able, by his free will, to resist the tempter. Now the condition attaching to man's nature required that he should be left to his own will, according to Ecclus. 15:14, "God left" man "in the hand of his own counsel." Hence Augustine says (Gen. ad lit. xi, 4): "It seems to me that man would have had no prospect of any special praise, if he were able to lead a good life simply because there was none to persuade him to lead an evil life; since both by nature he had the power, and in his power he had the will, not to consent to the persuader."

Reply Obj. 3: An assault is penal if it be difficult to resist it: but, in the state of innocence, man was able, without any difficulty, to resist temptation. Consequently the tempter's assault was not a punishment to man.

SECOND ARTICLE [II-II, Q. 165, Art. 2]

Whether the Manner and Order of the First Temptation Was Fitting?

Objection 1: It would seem that the manner and order of the first temptation was not fitting. For just as in the order of nature the angel was above man, so was the man above the woman. Now sin came upon man through an angel: therefore in like manner it should have come upon the woman through the man; in other words the woman should have been tempted by the man, and not the other way about.

Obj. 2: Further, the temptation of our first parents was by suggestion. Now the devil is able to make suggestions to man without making use of an outward sensible creature. Since then our first parents were endowed with a spiritual mind, and adhered less to sensible than to intelligible things, it would have been more fitting for man to be tempted with a merely spiritual, instead of an outward, temptation.

Obj. 3: Further, one cannot fittingly suggest an evil except through some apparent good. But many other animals have a greater appearance of good than the serpent has. Therefore man was unfittingly tempted by the devil through a serpent.

Obj. 4: Further, the serpent is an irrational animal. Now wisdom, speech, and punishment are not befitting an irrational animal. Therefore the serpent is unfittingly described (Gen. 3:1) as "more subtle than any of the beasts of the earth," or as "the most prudent of all beasts" according to another version [*The Septuagint]: and likewise is unfittingly stated to have spoken to the woman, and to have been punished by God.

*On the contrary,* That which is first in any genus should be proportionate to all that follow it in that genus. Now in every kind of sin we find the same order as in the first temptation. For, according to Augustine (De Trin. xii, 12), it begins with the concupiscence of sin in the sensuality, signified by the serpent; extends to the lower reason, by pleasure, signified by the woman; and reaches to the higher reason by consent in the sin, signified by the man. Therefore the order of the first temptation was fitting.

*I answer that,* Man is composed of a twofold nature, intellective and sensitive. Hence the devil, in tempting man, made use of a twofold incentive to sin: one on the part of the intellect, by promising the Divine likeness through the acquisition of knowledge which man naturally desires to have; the other on the part of sense. This he did by having recourse to those sensible things, which are most akin to man, partly by tempting the man through the woman who was akin to him in the same species; partly by tempting the woman through the serpent, who was akin to them in the same genus; partly by suggesting to them to eat of the forbidden fruit, which was akin to them in the proximate genus.

Reply Obj. 1: In the act of tempting the devil was by way of principal agent; whereas the woman was employed as an instrument of temptation in bringing about the downfall of the man, both because the woman was weaker than the man, and consequently more liable to be deceived, and because, on account of her union with man, the devil was able to deceive the man especially through her. Now there is no parity between principal agent and instrument, because the principal agent must exceed in power, which is not requisite in the instrumental agent.

Reply Obj. 2: A suggestion whereby the devil suggests something to man spiritually, shows the devil to have more power against man than outward suggestion has, since by an inward suggestion, at least, man's imagination is changed by the devil [*Cf. First Part, Q. 91, A. 3]; whereas by an outward suggestion, a change is wrought merely on an outward creature. Now the devil had a minimum of power against man before sin, wherefore he was unable to tempt him by inward suggestion, but only by outward suggestion.

Reply Obj. 3: According to Augustine (Gen. ad lit. xi, 3), "we are not to suppose that the devil chose the serpent as his means of temptation; but as he was possessed of the lust of deceit, he could only do so by the animal he was allowed to use for that purpose."

Reply Obj. 4: According to Augustine (Gen. ad lit. xi, 29), "the serpent is described as most prudent or subtle, on account of the cunning of the devil, who wrought his wiles in it: thus, we speak of a prudent or cunning tongue, because it is the instrument of a prudent or cunning man in advising something prudently or cunningly. Nor indeed (Gen. ad lit. xi, 28) did the serpent understand the sounds which were conveyed through it to the woman; nor again are we to believe that its soul was changed into a rational nature, since not even men, who are rational by nature, know what they say when a demon speaks in them. Accordingly (Gen. ad lit. xi, 29) the serpent spoke to man, even as the ass on which Balaam sat spoke to him, except that the former was the work of a devil, whereas the latter was the work of an angel. Hence (Gen. ad lit. xi, 36) the serpent was not asked why it had done this, because it had not done this in its own nature, but the devil in it, who was already condemned to everlasting fire on account of his sin: and the words addressed to the serpent were directed to him who wrought through the serpent."

Moreover, as again Augustine says (Super Gen. contra Manich. ii, 17, 18), "his, that is, the devil's, punishment mentioned here is that for which we must be on our guard against him, not that which is reserved till the last judgment. For when it was said to him: 'Thou art cursed among all cattle and beasts of the earth,' the cattle are set above him, not in power, but in the preservation of their nature, since the cattle lost no heavenly bliss, seeing that they never had it, but they continue to live in the nature which they received." It is also said to him: "'Upon thy breast and belly shalt thou creep,'" according to another version [*The Septuagint] "Here the breast signifies pride, because it is there that the impulse of the soul dominates, while the belly denotes carnal desire, because this part of the body is softest to the touch: and on these he creeps to those whom he wishes to deceive." The words, "'Earth shalt thou eat all the days of thy life' may be understood in two ways. Either 'Those shall belong to thee, whom thou shalt deceive by earthly lust,' namely sinners who are signified under the name of earth, or a third kind of temptation, namely curiosity, is signified by these words: for to eat earth is to look into things deep and dark." The putting of enmities between him and the woman "means that we cannot be tempted by the devil, except through that part of the soul which bears or reflects the likeness of a woman. The seed of the devil is the temptation to evil, the seed of the woman is the fruit of good works, whereby the temptation to evil is resisted. Wherefore the serpent lies in wait for the woman's heel, that if at any time she fall away towards what is unlawful, pleasure may seize hold of her: and she watches his head that she may shut him out at the very outset of the evil temptation."

## QUESTION 166

OF STUDIOUSNESS (In Two Articles)

We must next consider studiousness and its opposite, curiosity. Concerning studiousness there are two points of inquiry:

(1) What is the matter of studiousness?

(2) Whether it is a part of temperance?

FIRST ARTICLE [II-II, Q. 166, Art. 1]

Whether the Proper Matter of Studiousness Is Knowledge?

Objection 1: It would seem that knowledge is not the proper matter of studiousness. For a person is said to be studious because he applies study to certain things. Now a man ought to apply study to every matter, in order to do aright what has to be done. Therefore seemingly knowledge is not the special matter of studiousness.

Obj. 2: Further, studiousness is opposed to curiosity. Now curiosity, which is derived from *cura* (care), may also refer to elegance of apparel and other such things, which regard the body; wherefore the Apostle says (Rom. 13:14): "Make not provision ( curam ) for the flesh in its concupiscences."

Obj. 3: Further it is written (Jer. 6:13): "From the least of them even to the greatest, all study [Douay: 'are given to'] covetousness." Now covetousness is not properly about knowledge, but rather about the possession of wealth, as stated above (Q. 118, A. 2). Therefore studiousness, which is derived from "study," is not properly about knowledge.

*On the contrary,* It is written (Prov. 27:11): "Study wisdom, my son, and make my heart joyful, that thou mayest give an answer to him that reproacheth." Now study, which is commended as a virtue, is the same as that to which the Law urges. Therefore studiousness is properly about knowledge.

*I answer that,* Properly speaking, study denotes keen application of the mind to something. Now the mind is not applied to a thing except by knowing that thing. Wherefore the mind's application to knowledge precedes its application to those things to which man is directed by his knowledge. Hence study regards knowledge in the first place, and as a result it regards any other things the working of which requires to be directed by knowledge. Now the virtues lay claim to that matter about which they are first and foremost; thus fortitude is concerned about dangers of death, and temperance about pleasures of touch. Therefore studiousness is properly ascribed to knowledge.

Reply Obj. 1: Nothing can be done aright as regards other matters, except in so far as is previously directed by the knowing reason. Hence studiousness, to whatever matter it be applied, has a prior regard for knowledge.

Reply Obj. 2: Man's mind is drawn, on account of his affections, towards the things for which he has an affection, according to Matt. 6:21, "Where thy treasure is, there is thy heart also." And since man has special affection for those things which foster the flesh, it follows that man's thoughts are concerned about things that foster his flesh, so that man seeks to know how he may best sustain his body. Accordingly curiosity is accounted to be about things pertaining to the body by reason of things pertaining to knowledge.

Reply Obj. 3: Covetousness craves the acquisition of gain, and for this it is very necessary to be skilled in earthly things. Accordingly studiousness is ascribed to things pertaining to covetousness.

SECOND ARTICLE [II-II, Q. 166, Art. 2]

Whether Studiousness Is a Part of Temperance?

Objection 1: It would seem that studiousness is not a part of temperance. For a man is said to be studious by reason of his studiousness. Now all virtuous persons without exception are called studious according to the Philosopher, who frequently employs the term "studious" ( *spoudaios* ) in this sense (Ethic. ix, 4, 8, 9). [*In the same sense Aristotle says in *Ethic.* iii, 2, that "every vicious person is ignorant of what he ought to do."] Therefore studiousness is a general virtue, and not a part of temperance.

Obj. 2: Further, studiousness, as stated (A. 1), pertains to knowledge. But knowledge has no connection with the moral virtues which are in the appetitive part of the soul, and pertains rather to the intellectual virtues which are in the cognitive part: wherefore solicitude is an act of prudence as stated above (Q. 47, A. 9). Therefore studiousness is not a part of temperance.

Obj. 3: Further, a virtue that is ascribed as part of a principal virtue resembles the latter as to mode. Now studiousness does not resemble temperance as to mode, because temperance takes its name from being a kind of restraint, wherefore it is more opposed to the vice that is in excess: whereas studiousness is denominated from being the application of the mind to something, so that it would seem to be opposed to the vice that is in default, namely, neglect of study, rather than to the vice which is in excess, namely curiosity. wherefore, on account of its resemblance to the latter, Isidore says (Etym. x) that "a studious man is one who is curious to study." Therefore studiousness is not a part of temperance.

*On the contrary,* Augustine says (De Morib. Eccl. 21): "We are forbidden to be curious: and this is a great gift that temperance bestows." Now curiosity is prevented by moderate studiousness. Therefore studiousness is a part of temperance.

*I answer that,* As stated above (Q. 141, AA. 3, 4, 5), it belongs to temperance to moderate the movement of the appetite, lest it tend excessively to that which is desired naturally. Now just as in respect of his corporeal nature man naturally desires the pleasures of food and sex, so, in respect of his soul, he naturally desires to know something; thus the Philosopher observes at the beginning of his *Metaphysics* (i, 1): "All men have a natural desire for knowledge."

The moderation of this desire pertains to the virtue of studiousness; wherefore it follows that studiousness is a potential part of temperance, as a subordinate virtue annexed to a principal virtue. Moreover, it is comprised under modesty for the reason given above (Q. 160, A. 2).

Reply Obj. 1: Prudence is the complement of all the moral virtues, as stated in *Ethic.* vi, 13. Consequently, in so far as the knowledge of prudence pertains to all the virtues, the term "studiousness," which properly regards knowledge, is applied to all the virtues.

Reply Obj. 2: The act of a cognitive power is commanded by the appetitive power, which moves all the powers, as stated above (I-II, Q. 9, A. 1). Wherefore knowledge regards a twofold good. One is connected with the act of knowledge itself; and this good pertains to the intellectual virtues, and consists in man having a true estimate about each thing. The other good pertains to the act of the appetitive power, and consists in man's appetite being directed aright in applying the cognitive power in this or that way to this or that thing. And this belongs to the virtue of seriousness. Wherefore it is reckoned among the moral virtues.

Reply Obj. 3: As the Philosopher says (Ethic. ii, 93) in order to be virtuous we must avoid those things to which we are most naturally inclined. Hence it is that, since nature inclines us chiefly to fear dangers of death, and to seek pleasures of the flesh, fortitude is chiefly commended for a certain steadfast perseverance against such dangers, and temperance for a certain restraint from pleasures of the flesh. But as regards knowledge, man has contrary inclinations. For on the part of the soul, he is inclined to desire knowledge of things; and so it behooves him to exercise a praiseworthy restraint on this desire, lest he seek knowledge immoderately: whereas on the part of his bodily nature, man is inclined to avoid the trouble of seeking knowledge. Accordingly, as regards the first inclination studiousness is a kind of restraint, and it is in this sense that it is reckoned a part of temperance. But as to the second inclination, this virtue derives its praise from a certain keenness of interest in seeking knowledge of things; and from this it takes its name. The former is more essential to this virtue than the latter: since the desire to know directly regards knowledge, to which studiousness is directed, whereas the trouble of learning is an obstacle to knowledge, wherefore it is regarded by this virtue indirectly, as by that which removes an obstacle.

## QUESTION 167

OF CURIOSITY (In Two Articles)

We must next consider curiosity, under which head there are two points of inquiry:

(1) Whether the vice of curiosity can regard intellective knowledge?

(2) Whether it is about sensitive knowledge?

FIRST ARTICLE [II-II, Q. 167, Art. 1]

Whether Curiosity Can Be About Intellective Knowledge?

Objection 1: It would seem that curiosity cannot be about intellective knowledge. Because, according to the Philosopher (Ethic. ii, 6), there can be no mean and extremes in things which are essentially good. Now intellective knowledge is essentially good: because man's perfection would seem to consist in his intellect being reduced from potentiality to act, and this is done by the knowledge of truth. For Dionysius says (Div. Nom. iv) that "the good of the human soul is to be in accordance with reason," whose perfection consists in knowing the truth. Therefore the vice of curiosity cannot be about intellective knowledge.

Obj. 2: Further, that which makes man like to God, and which he receives from God, cannot be an evil. Now all abundance of knowledge is from God, according to Ecclus. 1:1, "All wisdom is from the Lord God," and Wis. 7:17, "He hath given me the true knowledge of things that are, to know the disposition of the whole world, and the virtues of the elements," etc. Again, by knowing the truth man is likened to God, since "all things are naked and open to His eyes" (Heb. 4:13), and "the Lord is a God of all knowledge" (1 Kings 2:3). Therefore however abundant knowledge of truth may be, it is not evil but good. Now the desire of good is not sinful. Therefore the vice of curiosity cannot be about the intellective knowledge of truth.

Obj. 3: Further, if the vice of curiosity can be about any kind of intellective knowledge, it would be chiefly about the philosophical sciences. But, seemingly, there is no sin in being intent on them: for Jerome says (Super Daniel 1:8): "Those who refused to partake of the king's meat and wine, lest they should be defiled, if they had considered the wisdom and teaching of the Babylonians to be sinful, would never have consented to learn that which was unlawful": and Augustine says (De Doctr. Christ. ii, 40) that "if the philosophers made any true statements, we must claim them for our own use, as from unjust possessors." Therefore curiosity about intellective knowledge cannot be sinful.

*On the contrary,* Jerome [*Comment. in Ep. ad Ephes. iv, 17] says: "Is it not evident that a man who day and night wrestles with the dialectic art, the student of natural science whose gaze pierces the heavens, walks in vanity of understanding and darkness of mind?" Now vanity of understanding and darkness of mind are sinful. Therefore curiosity about intellective sciences may be sinful.

*I answer that,* As stated above (Q. 166, A. 2, ad 2) studiousness is directly, not about knowledge itself, but about the desire and study in the pursuit of knowledge. Now we must judge differently of the knowledge itself of truth, and of the desire and study in the pursuit of the knowledge of truth. For the knowledge of truth, strictly speaking, is good, but it may be evil accidentally, by reason of some result, either because one takes pride in knowing the truth, according to 1 Cor. 8:1, "Knowledge puffeth up," or because one uses the knowledge of truth in order to sin.

On the other hand, the desire or study in pursuing the knowledge of truth may be right or wrong. First, when one tends by his study to the knowledge of truth as having evil accidentally annexed to it, for instance those who study to know the truth that they may take pride in their knowledge. Hence Augustine says (De Morib. Eccl. 21): "Some there are who forsaking virtue, and ignorant of what God is, and of the majesty of that nature which ever remains the same, imagine they are doing something great, if with surpassing curiosity and keenness they explore the whole mass of this body which we call the world. So great a pride is thus begotten, that one would think they dwelt in the very heavens about which they argue." In like manner, those who study to learn something in order to sin are engaged in a sinful study, according to the saying of Jer. 9:5, "They have taught their tongue to speak lies, they have labored to commit iniquity."

Secondly, there may be sin by reason of the appetite or study directed to the learning of truth being itself inordinate; and this in four ways. First, when a man is withdrawn by a less profitable study from a study that is an obligation incumbent on him; hence Jerome says [*Epist. xxi ad Damas]: "We see priests forsaking the gospels and the prophets, reading stage-plays, and singing the love songs of pastoral idylls." Secondly, when a man studies to learn of one, by whom it is unlawful to be taught, as in the case of those who seek to know the future through the demons. This is superstitious curiosity, of which Augustine says (De Vera Relig. 4): "Maybe, the philosophers were debarred from the faith by their sinful curiosity in seeking knowledge from the demons."

Thirdly, when a man desires to know the truth about creatures, without referring his knowledge to its due end, namely, the knowledge of God. Hence Augustine says (De Vera Relig. 29) that "in studying creatures, we must not be moved by empty and perishable curiosity; but we should ever mount towards immortal and abiding things."

Fourthly, when a man studies to know the truth above the capacity of his own intelligence, since by so doing men easily fall into error: wherefore it is written (Ecclus. 3:22): "Seek not the things that are too high for thee, and search not into things above thy ability ... and in many of His works be not curious," and further on (Ecclus. 3:26), "For ... the suspicion of them hath deceived many, and hath detained their minds in vanity."

Reply Obj. 1: Man's good consists in the knowledge of truth; yet man's sovereign good consists, not in the knowledge of any truth, but in the perfect knowledge of the sovereign truth, as the Philosopher states (Ethic. x, 7, 8). Hence there may be sin in the knowledge of certain truths, in so far as the desire of such knowledge is not directed in due manner to the knowledge of the sovereign truth, wherein supreme happiness consists.

Reply Obj. 2: Although this argument shows that the knowledge of truth is good in itself, this does not prevent a man from misusing the knowledge of truth for an evil purpose, or from desiring the knowledge of truth inordinately, since even the desire for good should be regulated in due manner.

Reply Obj. 3: The study of philosophy is in itself lawful and commendable, on account of the truth which the philosophers acquired through God revealing it to them, as stated in Rom. 1:19. Since, however, certain philosophers misuse the truth in order to assail the faith, the Apostle says (Col. 2:8): "Beware lest any man cheat you by philosophy and vain deceit, according to the tradition of men ... and not according to Christ": and Dionysius says (Ep. vii ad Polycarp.) of certain philosophers that "they make an unholy use of divine things against that which is divine, and by divine wisdom strive to destroy the worship of God."

SECOND ARTICLE [II-II, Q. 167, Art. 2]

Whether the Vice of Curiosity Is About Sensitive Knowledge?

Objection 1: It would seem that the vice of curiosity is not about sensitive knowledge. For just as some things are known by the sense of sight, so too are some things known by the senses of touch and taste. Now the vice concerned about objects of touch and taste is not curiosity but lust or gluttony. Therefore seemingly neither is the vice of curiosity about things known by the sight.

Obj. 2: Further, curiosity would seem to refer to watching games; wherefore Augustine says (Confess. vi, 8) that when "a fall occurred in the fight, a mighty cry of the whole people struck him strongly, and overcome by curiosity Alypius opened his eyes." But it does not seem to be sinful to watch games, because it gives pleasure on account of the representation, wherein man takes a natural delight, as the Philosopher states (Poet. vi). Therefore the vice of curiosity is not about the knowledge of sensible objects.

Obj. 3: Further, it would seem to pertain to curiosity to inquire into our neighbor's actions, as Bede observes [*Comment. in 1 John 2:16]. Now, seemingly, it is not a sin to inquire into the actions of others, because according to Ecclus. 17:12, God "gave to every one of them commandment concerning his neighbor." Therefore the vice of curiosity does not regard the knowledge of such like particular sensible objects.

*On the contrary,* Augustine says (De Vera Relig. 38) that "concupiscence of the eyes makes men curious." Now according to Bede (Comment. in 1 John 2:16) "concupiscence of the eyes refers not only to the learning of magic arts, but also to sight-seeing, and to the discovery and dispraise of our neighbor's faults," and all these are particular objects of sense. Therefore since concupiscence of the eves is a sin, even as concupiscence of the flesh and pride of life, which are members of the same division (1 John 2:16), it seems that the vice of curiosity is about the knowledge of sensible things.

*I answer that,* The knowledge of sensible things is directed to two things. For in the first place, both in man and in other animals, it is directed to the upkeep of the body, because by knowledge of this kind, man and other animals avoid what is harmful to them, and seek those things that are necessary for the body's sustenance. In the second place, it is directed in a manner special to man, to intellective knowledge, whether speculative or practical. Accordingly to employ study for the purpose of knowing sensible things may be sinful in two ways. First, when the sensitive knowledge is not directed to something useful, but turns man away from some useful consideration. Hence Augustine says (Confess. x, 35), "I go no more to see a dog coursing a hare in the circus; but in the open country, if I happen to be passing, that coursing haply will distract me from some weighty thought, and draw me after it ... and unless Thou, having made me see my weakness, didst speedily admonish me, I become foolishly dull." Secondly, when the knowledge of sensible things is directed to something harmful, as looking on a woman is directed to lust: even so the busy inquiry into other people's actions is directed to detraction. On the other hand, if one be ordinately intent on the knowledge of sensible things by reason of the necessity of sustaining nature, or for the sake of the study of intelligible truth, this studiousness about the knowledge of sensible things is virtuous.

Reply Obj. 1: Lust and gluttony are about pleasures arising from the use of objects of touch, whereas curiosity is about pleasures arising from the knowledge acquired through all the senses. According to Augustine (Confess. x, 35) "it is called concupiscence of the eyes" because "the sight is the sense chiefly used for obtaining knowledge, so that all sensible things are said to be seen," and as he says further on: "By this it may more evidently be discerned wherein pleasure and wherein curiosity is the object of the senses; for pleasure seeketh objects beautiful, melodious, fragrant, savory, soft; but curiosity, for trial's sake, seeketh even the contraries of these, not for the sake of suffering annoyance, but out of the lust of experiment and knowledge."

Reply Obj. 2: Sight-seeing becomes sinful, when it renders a man prone to the vices of lust and cruelty on account of things he sees represented. Hence Chrysostom says [*Hom. vi in Matth.] that such sights make men adulterers and shameless.

Reply Obj. 3: One may watch other people's actions or inquire into them, with a good intent, either for one's own good—that is in order to be encouraged to better deeds by the deeds of our neighbor—or for our neighbor's good—that is in order to correct him, if he do anything wrong, according to the rule of charity and the duty of one's position. This is praiseworthy, according to Heb. 10:24, "Consider one another to provoke unto charity and to good works." But to observe our neighbor's faults with the intention of looking down upon them, or of detracting them, or even with no further purpose than that of disturbing them, is sinful: hence it is written (Prov. 24:15), "Lie not in wait, nor seek after wickedness in the house of the just, nor spoil his rest."

# QUESTION 168

OF MODESTY AS CONSISTING IN THE OUTWARD MOVEMENTS OF THE BODY (In Four Articles)

We must next consider modesty as consisting in the outward movements of the body, and under this head there are four points of inquiry:

(1) Whether there can be virtue and vice in the outward movements of the body that are done seriously?

(2) Whether there can be a virtue about playful actions?

(3) Of the sin consisting in excess of play;

(4) Of the sin consisting in lack of play.

FIRST ARTICLE [II-II, Q. 168, Art. 1]

Whether Any Virtue Regards the Outward Movements of the Body?

Objection 1: It would seem that no virtue regards the outward movements of the body. For every virtue pertains to the spiritual beauty of the soul, according to Ps. 44:14, "All the glory of the king's daughter is within," and a gloss adds, "namely, in the conscience." Now the movements of the body are not within, but without. Therefore there can be no virtue about them.

Obj. 2: Further, "Virtues are not in us by nature," as the Philosopher states (Ethic. ii, 1). But outward bodily movements are in man by nature, since it is by nature that some are quick, and some slow of movement, and the same applies to other differences of outward movements. Therefore there is no virtue about movements of this kind.

Obj. 3: Further, every moral virtue is either about actions directed to another person, as justice, or about passions, as temperance and fortitude. Now outward bodily movements are not directed to another person, nor are they passions. Therefore no virtue is connected with them.

Obj. 4: Further, study should be applied to all works of virtue, as stated above (Q. 166, A. 1, Obj. 1; A. 2, ad 1). Now it is censurable to apply study to the ordering of one's outward movements: for Ambrose says (De Offic. i, 18): "A becoming gait is one that reflects the carriage of authority, has the tread of gravity, and the foot-print of tranquillity: yet so that there be neither study nor affectation, but natural and artless movement." Therefore seemingly there is no virtue about the style of outward movements.

*On the contrary,* The beauty of honesty [*Cf. Q. 145, A. 1] pertains to virtue. Now the style of outward movements pertains to the beauty of honesty. For Ambrose says (De Offic. i, 18): "The sound of the voice and the gesture of the body are distasteful to me, whether they be unduly soft and nerveless, or coarse and boorish. Let nature be our model; her reflection is gracefulness of conduct and beauty of honesty." Therefore there is a virtue about the style of outward movement.

*I answer that,* Moral virtue consists in the things pertaining to man being directed by his reason. Now it is manifest that the outward movements of man are dirigible by reason, since the outward members are set in motion at the command of reason. Hence it is evident that there is a moral virtue concerned with the direction of these movements.

Now the direction of these movements may be considered from a twofold standpoint. First, in respect of fittingness to the person; secondly, in respect of fittingness to externals, whether persons, business, or place. Hence Ambrose says (De Offic. i, 18): "Beauty of conduct consists in becoming behavior towards others, according to their sex and person," and this regards the first. As to the second, he adds: "This is the best way to order our behavior, this is the polish becoming to every action."

Hence Andronicus [*De Affectibus] ascribes two things to these outward movements: namely "taste" ( *ornatus* ) which regards what is becoming to the person, wherefore he says that it is the knowledge of what is becoming in movement and behavior; and "methodicalness" ( *bona ordinatio* ) which regards what is becoming to the business in hand, and to one's surroundings, wherefore he calls it "the practical knowledge of separation," i.e. of the distinction of "acts."

Reply Obj. 1: Outward movements are signs of the inward disposition, according to Ecclus. 19:27, "The attire of the body, and the laughter of the teeth, and the gait of the man, show what he is"; and Ambrose says (De Offic. i, 18) that "the habit of mind is seen in the gesture of the body," and that "the body's movement is an index of the soul."

Reply Obj. 2: Although it is from natural disposition that a man is inclined to this or that style of outward movement, nevertheless what is lacking to nature can be supplied by the efforts of reason. Hence Ambrose says (De Offic. i, 18): "Let nature guide the movement: and if nature fail in any respect, surely effort will supply the defect."

Reply Obj. 3: As stated (ad 1) outward movements are indications of the inward disposition, and this regards chiefly the passions of the soul. Wherefore Ambrose says (De Offic. i, 18) that "from these things," i.e. the outward movements, "the man that lies hidden in our hearts is esteemed to be either frivolous, or boastful, or impure, or on the other hand sedate, steady, pure, and free from blemish." It is moreover from our outward movements that other men form their judgment about us, according to Ecclus. 19:26, "A man is known by his look, and a wise man, when thou meetest him, is known by his countenance." Hence moderation of outward movements is directed somewhat to other persons, according to the saying of Augustine in his Rule (Ep. ccxi), "In all your movements, let nothing be done to offend the eye of another, but only that which is becoming to the holiness of your state." Wherefore the moderation of outward movements may be reduced to two virtues, which the Philosopher mentions in *Ethic.* iv, 6, 7. For, in so far as by outward movements we are directed to other persons, the moderation of our outward movements belongs to "friendliness or affability" [*Cf. Q. 114, A. 1]. This regards pleasure or pain which may arise from words or deeds in reference to others with whom a man comes in contact. And, in so far as outward movements are signs of our inward disposition, their moderation belongs to the virtue of truthfulness [*Cf. Q. 9], whereby a man, by word and deed, shows himself to be such as he is inwardly.

Reply Obj. 4: It is censurable to study the style of one's outward movements, by having recourse to pretense in them, so that they do not agree with one's inward disposition. Nevertheless it behooves one to study them, so that if they be in any way inordinate, this may be corrected. Hence Ambrose says (De Offic. i, 18): "Let them be without artifice, but not without correction."

SECOND ARTICLE [II-II, Q. 168, Art. 2]

Whether There Can Be a Virtue About Games?

Objection 1: It would seem that there cannot be a virtue about games. For Ambrose says (De Offic. i, 23): "Our Lord said: 'Woe to you who laugh, for you shall weep.' Wherefore I consider that all, and not only excessive, games should be avoided." Now that which can be done virtuously is not to be avoided altogether. Therefore there cannot be a virtue about games.

Obj. 2: Further, "Virtue is that which God forms in us, without us," as stated above (I-II, Q. 55, A. 4). Now Chrysostom says [*Hom. vi in Matth.]: "It is not God, but the devil, that is the author of fun. Listen to what happened to those who played: 'The people sat down to eat and drink, and they rose up to play.'" Therefore there can be no virtue about games.

Obj. 3: Further, the Philosopher says (Ethic. x, 6) that "playful actions are not directed to something else." But it is a requisite of virtue that the agent in choosing should "direct his action to something else," as the Philosopher states (Ethic. ii, 4). Therefore there can be no virtue about games.

*On the contrary,* Augustine says (Music. ii, 15): "I pray thee, spare thyself at times: for it becomes a wise man sometimes to relax the high pressure of his attention to work." Now this relaxation of the mind from work consists in playful words or deeds. Therefore it becomes a wise and virtuous man to have recourse to such things at times. Moreover the Philosopher [*Ethic. ii, 7; iv, 8] assigns to games the virtue of *eutrapelia* , which we may call "pleasantness."

*I answer that,* Just as man needs bodily rest for the body's refreshment, because he cannot always be at work, since his power is finite and equal to a certain fixed amount of labor, so too is it with his soul, whose power is also finite and equal to a fixed amount of work. Consequently when he goes beyond his measure in a certain work, he is oppressed and becomes weary, and all the more since when the soul works, the body is at work likewise, in so far as the intellective soul employs forces that operate through bodily organs. Now sensible goods are connatural to man, and therefore, when the soul arises above sensibles, through being intent on the operations of reason, there results in consequence a certain weariness of soul, whether the operations with which it is occupied be those of the practical or of the speculative reason. Yet this weariness is greater if the soul be occupied with the work of contemplation, since thereby it is raised higher above sensible things; although perhaps certain outward works of the practical reason entail a greater bodily labor. In either case, however, one man is more soul-wearied than another, according as he is more intensely occupied with works of reason. Now just as weariness of the body is dispelled by resting the body, so weariness of the soul must needs be remedied by resting the soul: and the soul's rest is pleasure, as stated above (I-II, Q. 25, A. 2; I-II, Q. 31, A. 1, ad 2). Consequently, the remedy for weariness of soul must needs consist in the application of some pleasure, by slackening the tension of the reason's study. Thus in the *Conferences of the Fathers* (xxiv, 21), it is related of Blessed John the Evangelist, that when some people were scandalized on finding him playing together with his disciples, he is said to have told one of them who carried a bow to shoot an arrow. And when the latter had done this several times, he asked him whether he could do it indefinitely, and the man answered that if he continued doing it, the bow would break. Whence the Blessed John drew the inference that in like manner man's mind would break if its tension were never relaxed.

Now such like words or deeds wherein nothing further is sought than the soul's delight, are called playful or humorous. Hence it is necessary at times to make use of them, in order to give rest, as it were, to the soul. This is in agreement with the statement of the Philosopher (Ethic. iv, 8) that "in the intercourse of this life there is a kind of rest that is associated with games": and consequently it is sometimes necessary to make use of such things.

Nevertheless it would seem that in this matter there are three points which require especial caution. The first and chief is that the pleasure in question should not be sought in indecent or injurious deeds or words. Wherefore Tully says (De Offic. i, 29) that "one kind of joke is discourteous, insolent, scandalous, obscene." Another thing to be observed is that one lose not the balance of one's mind altogether. Hence Ambrose says (De Offic. i, 20): "We should beware lest, when we seek relaxation of mind, we destroy all that harmony which is the concord of good works": and Tully says (De Offic. i, 29), that, "just as we do not allow children to enjoy absolute freedom in their games, but only that which is consistent with good behavior, so our very fun should reflect something of an upright mind." Thirdly, we must be careful, as in all other human actions, to conform ourselves to persons, time, and place, and take due account of other circumstances, so that our fun "befit the hour and the man," as Tully says (De Offic. i, 29).

Now these things are directed according to the rule of reason: and a habit that operates according to reason is virtue. Therefore there can be a virtue about games. The Philosopher gives it the name of wittiness ( *eutrapelia* ), and a man is said to be pleasant through having a happy turn* of mind, whereby he gives his words and deeds a cheerful turn: and inasmuch as this virtue restrains a man from immoderate fun, it is comprised under modesty. [* *Eutrapelia* is derived from *trepein* = "to turn"].

Reply Obj. 1: As stated above, fun should fit with business and persons; wherefore Tully says (De Invent. Rhet. i, 17) that "when the audience is weary, it will be useful for the speaker to try something novel or amusing, provided that joking be not incompatible with the gravity of the subject." Now the sacred doctrine is concerned with things of the greatest moment, according to Prov. 8:6, "Hear, for I will speak of great things." Wherefore Ambrose does not altogether exclude fun from human speech, but from the sacred doctrine; hence he begins by saying: "Although jokes are at times fitting and pleasant, nevertheless they are incompatible with the ecclesiastical rule; since how can we have recourse to things which are not to be found in Holy Writ?"

Reply Obj. 2: This saying of Chrysostom refers to the inordinate use of fun, especially by those who make the pleasure of games their end; of whom it is written (Wis. 15:12): "They have accounted our life a pastime." Against these Tully says (De Offic. i, 29): "We are so begotten by nature that we appear to be made not for play and fun, but rather for hardships, and for occupations of greater gravity and moment."

Reply Obj. 3: Playful actions themselves considered in their species are not directed to an end: but the pleasure derived from such actions is directed to the recreation and rest of the soul, and accordingly if this be done with moderation, it is lawful to make use of fun. Hence Tully says (De Offic. i, 29): "It is indeed lawful to make use of play and fun, but in the same way as we have recourse to sleep and other kinds of rest, then only when we have done our duty by grave and serious matters."

THIRD ARTICLE [II-II, Q. 168, Art. 3]

Whether There Can Be Sin in the Excess of Play?

Objection 1: It would seem that there cannot be sin in the excess of play. For that which is an excuse for sin is not held to be sinful. Now play is sometimes an excuse for sin, for many things would be grave sins if they were done seriously, whereas if they be done in fun, are either no sin or but slightly sinful. Therefore it seems that there is no sin in excessive play.

Obj. 2: Further, all other vices are reducible to the seven capital vices, as Gregory states (Moral. xxxi, 17). But excess of play does not seem reducible to any of the capital vices. Therefore it would seem not to be a sin.

Obj. 3: Further, comedians especially would seem to exceed in play, since they direct their whole life to playing. Therefore if excess of play were a sin, all actors would be in a state of sin; moreover all those who employ them, as well as those who make them any payment, would sin as accomplices of their sin. But this would seem untrue; for it is related in the Lives of the Fathers (ii. 16; viii. 63) that is was revealed to the Blessed Paphnutius that a certain jester would be with him in the life to come.

*On the contrary,* A gloss on Prov. 14:13, "Laughter shall be mingled with sorrow and mourning taketh hold of the end of joy," remarks: "A mourning that will last for ever." Now there is inordinate laughter and inordinate joy in excessive play. Therefore there is mortal sin therein, since mortal sin alone is deserving of everlasting mourning.

*I answer that,* In all things dirigible according to reason, the excessive is that which goes beyond, and the deficient is that which falls short of the rule of reason. Now it has been stated (A. 2) that playful or jesting words or deeds are dirigible according to reason. Wherefore excessive play is that which goes beyond the rule of reason: and this happens in two ways. First, on account of the very species of the acts employed for the purpose of fun, and this kind of jesting, according to Tully (De Offic. i, 29), is stated to be "discourteous, insolent, scandalous, and obscene," when to wit a man, for the purpose of jesting, employs indecent words or deeds, or such as are injurious to his neighbor, these being of themselves mortal sins. And thus it is evident that excessive play is a mortal sin.

Secondly, there may be excess in play, through lack of due circumstances: for instance when people make use of fun at undue times or places, or out of keeping with the matter in hand, or persons. This may be sometimes a mortal sin on account of the strong attachment to play, when a man prefers the pleasure he derives therefrom to the love of God, so as to be willing to disobey a commandment of

God or of the Church rather than forego, such like amusements. Sometimes, however, it is a venial sin, for instance where a man is not so attached to amusement as to be willing for its sake to do anything in disobedience to God.

Reply Obj. 1: Certain things are sinful on account of the intention alone, because they are done in order to injure someone. Such an intention is excluded by their being done in fun, the intention of which is to please, not to injure: in these cases fun excuses from sin, or diminishes it. Other things, however, are sins according to their species, such as murder, fornication, and the like: and fun is no excuse for these; in fact they make fun scandalous and obscene.

Reply Obj. 2: Excessive play pertains to senseless mirth, which Gregory (Moral. xxxi, 17) calls a daughter of gluttony. Wherefore it is written (Ex. 32:6): "The people sat down to eat and drink, and they rose up to play."

Reply Obj. 3: As stated (A. 2), play is necessary for the intercourse of human life. Now whatever is useful to human intercourse may have a lawful employment ascribed to it. Wherefore the occupation of play-actors, the object of which is to cheer the heart of man, is not unlawful in itself; nor are they in a state of sin provided that their playing be moderated, namely that they use no unlawful words or deeds in order to amuse, and that they do not introduce play into undue matters and seasons. And although in human affairs, they have no other occupation in reference to other men, nevertheless in reference to themselves, and to God, they perform other actions both serious and virtuous, such as prayer and the moderation of their own passions and operations, while sometimes they give alms to the poor. Wherefore those who maintain them in moderation do not sin but act justly, by rewarding them for their services. On the other hand, if a man spends too much on such persons, or maintains those comedians who practice unlawful mirth, he sins as encouraging them in their sin. Hence Augustine says (Tract. c. in Joan.) that "to give one's property to comedians is a great sin, not a virtue"; unless by chance some play-actor were in extreme need, in which case one would have to assist him, for Ambrose says (De Offic. [*Quoted in Canon Pasce, dist. 86]): "Feed him that dies of hunger; for whenever thou canst save a man by feeding him, if thou hast not fed him, thou hast slain him."

FOURTH ARTICLE [II-II, Q. 168, Art. 4]

Whether There Is a Sin in Lack of Mirth?

Objection 1: It would seem that there is no sin in lack of mirth. For no sin is prescribed to a penitent. But Augustine speaking of a penitent says (De Vera et Falsa Poenit. 15) [*Spurious]: "Let him refrain from games and the sights of the world, if he wishes to obtain the grace of a full pardon." Therefore there is no sin in lack of mirth.

Obj. 2: Further, no sin is included in the praise given to holy men. But some persons are praised for having refrained from mirth; for it is written (Jer. 15:17): "I sat not in the assembly of jesters," and (Tobias 3:17): "Never have I joined myself with them that play; neither have I made myself partaker with them that walk in lightness." Therefore there can be no sin in the lack of mirth.

Obj. 3: Further, Andronicus counts austerity to be one of the virtues, and he describes it as a habit whereby a man neither gives nor receives the pleasures of conversation. Now this pertains to the lack of mirth. Therefore the lack of mirth is virtuous rather than sinful.

*On the contrary,* The Philosopher (Ethic. ii, 7; iv, 8) reckons the lack of mirth to be a vice.

*I answer that,* In human affairs whatever is against reason is a sin. Now it is against reason for a man to be burdensome to others, by offering no pleasure to others, and by hindering their enjoyment. Wherefore Seneca [*Martin of Braga, Formula Vitae Honestae: cap. De Continentia] says (De Quat. Virt., cap. De Continentia): "Let your conduct be guided by wisdom so that no one will think you rude, or despise you as a cad." Now a man who is without mirth, not only is lacking in playful speech, but is also burdensome to others, since he is deaf to the moderate mirth of others. Consequently they are vicious, and are said to be boorish or rude, as the Philosopher states (Ethic. iv, 8).

Since, however, mirth is useful for the sake of the rest and pleasures it affords; and since, in human life, pleasure and rest are not in quest for their own sake, but for the sake of operation, as stated in *Ethic.* x, 6, it follows that "lack of mirth is less sinful than excess thereof." Hence the Philosopher says (Ethic. ix, 10): "We should make few friends for the sake of pleasure, since but little sweetness suffices to season life, just as little salt suffices for our meat."

Reply Obj. 1: Mirth is forbidden the penitent because he is called upon to mourn for his sins. Nor does this imply a vice in default, because this very diminishment of mirth in them is in accordance with reason.

Reply Obj. 2: Jeremias speaks there in accordance with the times, the state of which required that man should mourn; wherefore he adds: "I sat alone, because Thou hast filled me with threats." The words of Tobias 3 refer to excessive mirth; and this is evident from his adding: "Neither have I made myself partaker with them that walk in lightness."

Reply Obj. 3: Austerity, as a virtue, does not exclude all pleasures, but only such as are excessive and inordinate; wherefore it would seem to pertain to affability, which the Philosopher (Ethic. iv, 6) calls "friendliness," or *eutrapelia* , otherwise wittiness. Nevertheless he names and defines it thus in respect of its agreement with temperance, to which it belongs to restrain pleasure.

# QUESTION 169

OF MODESTY IN THE OUTWARD APPAREL (In Two Articles)

We must now consider modesty as connected with the outward apparel, and under this head there are two points of inquiry:

(1) Whether there can be virtue and vice in connection with outward apparel?

(2) Whether women sin mortally by excessive adornment?

FIRST ARTICLE [II-II, Q. 169, Art. 1]

Whether There Can Be Virtue and Vice in Connection with Outward Apparel?

Objection 1: It would seem that there cannot be virtue and vice in connection with outward apparel. For outward adornment does not belong to us by nature, wherefore it varies according to different times and places. Hence Augustine says (De Doctr. Christ. iii, 12) that "among the ancient Romans it was scandalous for one to wear a cloak with sleeves and reaching to the ankles, whereas now it is scandalous for anyone hailing from a reputable place to be without them." Now according to the Philosopher (Ethic. ii, 1) there is in us a natural aptitude for the virtues. Therefore there is no virtue or vice about such things.

Obj. 2: Further, if there were virtue and vice in connection with outward attire, excess in this matter would be sinful. Now excess in outward attire is not apparently sinful, since even the ministers of the altar use most precious vestments in the sacred ministry. Likewise it would seem not to be sinful to be lacking in this, for it is said in praise of certain people (Heb. 11:37): "They wandered about in sheepskins and in goatskins." Therefore it seems that there cannot be virtue and vice in this matter.

Obj. 3: Further, every virtue is either theological, or moral, or intellectual. Now an intellectual virtue is not conversant with matter of this kind, since it is a perfection regarding the knowledge of truth. Nor is there a theological virtue connected therewith, since that has God for its object; nor are any of the moral virtues enumerated by the Philosopher (Ethic. ii, 7), connected with it. Therefore it seems that there cannot be virtue and vice in connection with this kind of attire.

*On the contrary,* Honesty [*Cf. Q. 145] pertains to virtue. Now a certain honesty is observed in the outward apparel; for Ambrose says (De Offic. i, 19): "The body should be bedecked naturally and without affectation, with simplicity, with negligence rather than nicety, not with costly and dazzling apparel, but with ordinary clothes, so that nothing be lacking to honesty and necessity, yet nothing be added to increase its beauty." Therefore there can be virtue and vice in the outward attire.

*I answer that,* It is not in the outward things themselves which man uses, that there is vice, but on the part of man who uses them immoderately. This lack of moderation occurs in two ways. First, in comparison with the customs of those among whom one lives; wherefore Augustine says (Confess. iii, 8): "Those offenses which are contrary to the customs of men, are to be avoided according to the customs generally prevailing, so that a thing agreed upon and confirmed by custom or law of any city or nation may not be violated at the lawless pleasure of any, whether citizen or foreigner. For any part, which harmonizeth not with its whole, is offensive." Secondly, the lack of moderation in the use of these things may arise from the inordinate attachment of the user, the result being that a man sometimes takes too much pleasure in using them, either in accordance with the custom of those among whom he dwells or contrary to such custom. Hence Augustine says (De Doctr. Christ. iii, 12): "We must avoid excessive pleasure in the use of things, for it leads not only wickedly to abuse the customs of those among whom we dwell, but frequently to exceed their bounds, so that, whereas it lay hidden, while under the restraint of established morality, it displays its deformity in a most lawless outbreak."

In point of excess, this inordinate attachment occurs in three ways. First when a man seeks glory from excessive attention to dress; in so far as dress and such like things are a kind of ornament. Hence Gregory says (Hom. xl in Ev.): "There are some who think that attention to finery and costly dress is no sin. Surely, if this were no fault, the word of God would not say so expressly that the rich man who was tortured in hell had been clothed in purple and fine linen. No one, forsooth, seeks costly apparel" (such, namely, as exceeds his estate) "save for vainglory." Secondly, when a man seeks sensuous pleasure from excessive attention to dress, in so far as dress is directed to the body's comfort. Thirdly, when a man is too solicitous [*Cf. Q. 55, A. 6] in his attention to outward apparel.

Accordingly Andronicus [*De Affectibus] reckons three virtues in connection with outward attire; namely "humility," which excludes the seeking of glory, wherefore he says that humility is "the habit of avoiding excessive expenditure and parade"; "contentment" [*Cf. Q. 143, Obj. 4], which excludes the seeking of sensuous pleasure, wherefore he says that "contentedness is the habit that makes a man satisfied with what is suitable, and enables him to determine what is becoming in his manner of life" (according to the saying of the Apostle, 1 Tim. 6:8): "Having food and wherewith to be covered, with these let us be content;"—and "simplicity," which excludes excessive solicitude about such things, wherefore he says that "simplicity is a habit that makes a man contented with what he has."

In the point of deficiency there may be inordinate attachment in two ways. First, through a man's neglect to give the requisite study or trouble to the use of outward apparel. Wherefore the Philosopher says (Ethic. vii, 7) that "it is a mark of effeminacy to let one's cloak trail on the ground to avoid the trouble of lifting it up." Secondly, by seeking glory from the very lack of attention to outward attire. Hence Augustine says (De Serm. Dom. in Monte ii, 12) that "not only the glare and pomp of outward things, but even dirt and the weeds of mourning may be a subject of ostentation, all the more dangerous as being a decoy under the guise of God's service"; and the Philosopher says (Ethic. iv, 7) that "both excess and inordinate defect are a subject of ostentation."

Reply Obj. 1: Although outward attire does not come from nature, it belongs to natural reason to moderate it; so that we are naturally inclined to be the recipients of the virtue that moderates outward raiment.

Reply Obj. 2: Those who are placed in a position of dignity, or again the ministers of the altar, are attired in more costly apparel than others, not for the sake of their own glory, but to indicate the excellence of their office or of the Divine worship: wherefore this is not sinful in them. Hence Augustine says (De Doctr. Christ. iii, 12): "Whoever uses outward things in such a way as to exceed the bounds observed by the good people among whom he dwells, either signifies something by so doing, or is guilty of sin, inasmuch as he uses these things for sensual pleasure or ostentation."

Likewise there may be sin on the part of deficiency: although it is not always a sin to wear coarser clothes than other people. For, if this be done through ostentation or pride, in order to set oneself above others, it is a sin of superstition; whereas, if this be done to tame the flesh, or to humble the spirit, it belongs to the virtue of temperance. Hence Augustine says (De Doctr. Christ. iii, 12): "Whoever uses transitory things with greater restraint than is customary with those among whom he dwells, is either temperate or superstitious." Especially, however, is the use of coarse raiment befitting to those who by word and example urge others to repentance, as did the prophets of whom the Apostle is speaking in the passage quoted. Wherefore a gloss on Matt. 3:4, says: "He who preaches penance, wears the garb of penance."

Reply Obj. 3: This outward apparel is an indication of man's estate; wherefore excess, deficiency, and mean therein, are referable to the virtue of truthfulness, which the Philosopher (Ethic. ii, 7) assigns to deeds and words, which are indications of something connected with man's estate.

SECOND ARTICLE [II-II, Q. 169, Art. 2]

Whether the Adornment of Women Is Devoid of Mortal Sin?

Objection 1: It would seem that the adornment of women is not devoid of mortal sin. For whatever is contrary to a precept of the Divine law is a mortal sin. Now the adornment of women is contrary to a precept of the Divine law; for it is written (1 Pet. 3:3): "Whose," namely women's, "adorning, let it not be the outward plaiting of the hair, or the wearing of gold, or the putting on of apparel." Wherefore a gloss of Cyprian says: "Those who are clothed in silk and purple cannot sincerely put on Christ: those who are bedecked with gold and pearls and trinkets have forfeited the adornments of mind and body." Now this is not done without a mortal sin. Therefore the adornment of women cannot be devoid of mortal sin.

Obj. 2: Further, Cyprian says (De Habit. Virg.): "I hold that not only virgins and widows, but also wives and all women without exception, should be admonished that nowise should they deface God's work and fabric, the clay that He has fashioned, with the aid of yellow pigments, black powders or rouge, or by applying any dye that alters the natural features." And afterwards he adds: "They lay hands on God, when they strive to reform what He has formed. This is an assault on the Divine handiwork, a distortion of the truth. Thou shalt not be able to see God, having no longer the eyes that God made, but those the devil has unmade; with him shalt thou burn on whose account thou art bedecked." But this is not due except to mortal sin. Therefore the adornment of women is not devoid of mortal sin.

Obj. 3: Further, just as it is unbecoming for a woman to wear man's clothes, so is it unbecoming for her to adorn herself inordinately. Now the former is a sin, for it is written (Deut. 22:5): "A woman shall not be clothed with man's apparel, neither shall a man use woman's apparel." Therefore it seems that also the excessive adornment of women is a mortal sin.

Obj. 4: *On the contrary,* If this were true it would seem that the makers of these means of adornment sin mortally.

*I answer that,* As regards the adornment of women, we must bear in mind the general statements made above (A. 1) concerning outward apparel, and also something special, namely that a woman's apparel may incite men to lust, according to Prov. 7:10, "Behold a woman meeteth him in harlot's attire, prepared to deceive souls."

Nevertheless a woman may use means to please her husband, lest through despising her he fall into adultery. Hence it is written (1 Cor. 7:34) that the woman "that is married thinketh on the things of the world, how she may please her husband." Wherefore if a married woman adorn herself in order to please her husband she can do this without sin.

But those women who have no husband nor wish to have one, or who are in a state of life inconsistent with marriage, cannot without sin desire to give lustful pleasure to those men who see them, because this is to incite them to sin. And if indeed they adorn themselves with this intention of provoking others to lust, they sin mortally; whereas if they do so from frivolity, or from vanity for the sake of ostentation, it is not always mortal, but sometimes venial. And the same applies to men in this respect. Hence Augustine says (Ep. ccxlv ad Possid.): "I do not wish you to be hasty in forbidding the wearing of gold or costly attire except in the case of those who being neither married nor wishful to marry, should think how they may please God: whereas the others think on the things of the world, either husbands how they may please their wives, or wives how they may please their husbands, except that it is unbecoming for women though married to uncover their hair, since the Apostle commands them to cover the head." Yet in this case some might be excused from sin, when they do this not through vanity but on account of some contrary custom: although such a custom is not to be commended.

Reply Obj. 1: As a gloss says on this passage, "The wives of those who were in distress despised their husbands, and decked themselves that they might please other men": and the Apostle forbids this. Cyprian is speaking in the same sense; yet he does not forbid married women to adorn themselves in order to please their husbands, lest the latter be afforded an occasion of sin with other women. Hence the Apostle says (1 Tim. 2:9): "Women ... in ornate [Douay: 'decent'] apparel, adorning themselves with modesty and sobriety, not with plaited hair, or gold, or pearls, or costly attire": whence we are given to understand that women are not forbidden to adorn themselves soberly and moderately but to do so excessively, shamelessly, and immodestly.

Reply Obj. 2: Cyprian is speaking of women painting themselves: this is a kind of falsification, which cannot be devoid of sin. Wherefore Augustine says (Ep. ccxlv ad Possid.): "To dye oneself with paints in order to have a rosier or a paler complexion is a lying counterfeit. I doubt whether even their husbands are willing to be deceived by it, by whom alone" (i.e. the husbands) "are they to be permitted, but not ordered, to adorn themselves." However, such painting does not always involve a mortal sin, but only when it is done for the sake of sensuous pleasure or in contempt of God, and it is to like cases that Cyprian refers.

It must, however, be observed that it is one thing to counterfeit a beauty one has not, and another to hide a disfigurement arising from some cause such as sickness or the like. For this is lawful, since according to the Apostle (1 Cor. 12:23), "such as we think to be the less honorable members of the body, about these we put more abundant honor."

Reply Obj. 3: As stated in the foregoing Article, outward apparel should be consistent with the estate of the person, according to the general custom. Hence it is in itself sinful for a woman to wear man's clothes, or vice versa; especially since this may be a cause of sensuous pleasure; and it is expressly forbidden in the Law (Deut. 22) because the Gentiles used to practice this change of attire for the purpose of idolatrous superstition. Nevertheless this may be done sometimes without sin on account of some necessity, either in order to hide oneself from enemies, or through lack of other clothes, or for some similar motive.

Reply Obj. 4: In the case of an art directed to the production of goods which men cannot use without sin, it follows that the workmen sin in making such things, as directly affording others an occasion of sin; for instance, if a man were to make idols or anything pertaining to idolatrous worship. But in the case of an art the products of which may be employed by man either for a good or for an evil use, such as swords, arrows, and the like, the practice of such an art is not sinful. These alone should be called arts; wherefore Chrysostom says [*Hom. xlix super Matth.]: "The name of art should be applied to those only which contribute towards and produce necessaries and mainstays of life." In the case of an art that produces things which for the most part some people put to an evil use, although such arts are not unlawful in themselves, nevertheless, according to the teaching of Plato, they should be extirpated from the State by the governing authority. Accordingly, since women may lawfully adorn themselves, whether to maintain the fitness of their estate, or even by adding something thereto, in order to please their husbands, it follows that those who make such means of adornment do not sin in the practice of their art, except perhaps by inventing means that are superfluous and fantastic. Hence Chrysostom says (Super Matth.) that "even the shoemakers' and clothiers' arts stand in need of restraint, for they have lent their art to lust, by abusing its needs, and debasing art by art."

## QUESTION 170

OF THE PRECEPTS OF TEMPERANCE (In Two Articles)

We must next consider the precepts of temperance:

(1) The precepts of temperance itself;

(2) The precepts of its parts.

FIRST ARTICLE [II-II, Q. 170, Art. 1]

Whether the Precepts of Temperance Are Suitably Given in the Divine Law?

Objection 1: It would seem that the precepts of temperance are unsuitably given in the Divine law. Because fortitude is a greater virtue than temperance, as stated above (Q. 123, A. 12; Q. 141, A. 8; I-II, Q. 66, A. 4). Now there is no precept of fortitude among the precepts of the decalogue, which are the most important among the precepts of the

Law. Therefore it was unfitting to include among the precepts of the decalogue the prohibition of adultery, which is contrary to temperance, as stated above (Q. 154, AA. 1, 8).

Obj. 2: Further, temperance is not only about venereal matters, but also about pleasures of meat and drink. Now the precepts of the decalogue include no prohibition of a vice pertaining to pleasures of meat and drink, or to any other species of lust. Neither, therefore, should they include a precept prohibiting adultery, which pertains to venereal pleasure.

Obj. 3: Further, in the lawgiver's intention inducement to virtue precedes the prohibition of vice, since vices are forbidden in order that obstacles to virtue may be removed. Now the precepts of the decalogue are the most important in the Divine law. Therefore the precepts of the decalogue should have included an affirmative precept directly prescribing the virtue of temperance, rather than a negative precept forbidding adultery which is directly opposed thereto.

*On the contrary,* stands the authority of Scripture in the decalogue (Ex. 20:14, 17).

*I answer that,* As the Apostle says (1 Tim. 1:5), "the end of the commandment is charity," which is enjoined upon us in the two precepts concerning the love of God and of our neighbor. Wherefore the decalogue contains those precepts which tend more directly to the love of God and of our neighbor. Now among the vices opposed to temperance, adultery would seem most of all opposed to the love of our neighbor, since thereby a man lays hold of another's property for his own use, by abusing his neighbor's wife. Wherefore the precepts of the decalogue include a special prohibition of adultery, not only as committed in deed, but also as desired in thought.

Reply Obj. 1: Among the species of vices opposed to fortitude there is not one that is so directly opposed to the love of our neighbor as adultery, which is a species of lust that is opposed to temperance. And yet the vice of daring, which is opposed to fortitude, is wont to be sometimes the cause of murder, which is forbidden by one of the precepts of the decalogue: for it is written (Eccus. 8:18): "Go not on the way with a bold man lest he burden thee with his evils."

Reply Obj. 2: Gluttony is not directly opposed to the love of our neighbor, as adultery is. Nor indeed is any other species of lust, for a father is not so wronged by the seduction of the virgin over whom he has no connubial right, as is the husband by the adultery of his wife, for he, not the wife herself, has power over her body [*1 Cor. 7:4].

Reply Obj. 3: As stated above (Q. 122, AA. 1, 4) the precepts of the decalogue are universal principles of the Divine law; hence they need to be common precepts. Now it was not possible to give any common affirmative precepts of temperance, because the practice of temperance varies according to different times, as Augustine remarks (De Bono Conjug. xv, 7), and according to different human laws and customs.

SECOND ARTICLE [II-II, Q. 170, Art. 2]

Whether the Precepts of the Virtues Annexed to Temperance Are Suitably Given in the Divine Law?

Objection 1: It would seem that the precepts of the virtues annexed to temperance are unsuitably given in the Divine law. For the precepts of the Decalogue, as stated above (A. 1, ad 3), are certain universal principles of the whole Divine law. Now "pride is the beginning of all sin," according to Ecclus. 10:15. Therefore among the precepts of the Decalogue there should have been one forbidding pride.

Obj. 2: Further, a place before all should have been given in the decalogue to those precepts by which men are especially induced to fulfil the Law, because these would seem to be the most important. Now since humility subjects man to God, it would seem most of all to dispose man to the fulfilment of the Divine law; wherefore obedience is accounted one of the degrees of humility, as stated above (Q. 161, A. 6); and the same apparently applies to meekness, the effect of which is that a man does not contradict the Divine Scriptures, as Augustine observes (De Doctr. Christ. ii, 7). Therefore it seems that the Decalogue should have contained precepts of humility and meekness.

Obj. 3: Further, it was stated in the foregoing Article that adultery is forbidden in the decalogue, because it is contrary to the love of our neighbor. But inordinateness of outward movements, which is contrary to modesty, is opposed to neighborly love: wherefore Augustine says in his Rule (Ep. ccxii): "In all your movements let nothing be done to offend the eye of any person whatever." Therefore it seems that this kind of inordinateness should also have been forbidden by a precept of the Decalogue.

*On the contrary,* suffices the authority of Scripture.

*I answer that,* The virtues annexed to temperance may be considered in two ways: first, in themselves; secondly, in their effects. Considered in themselves they have no direct connection with the love of God or of our neighbor; rather do they regard a certain moderation of things pertaining to man himself. But considered in their effects, they may regard the love of God or of our neighbor: and in this respect the decalogue contains precepts that relate to the prohibition of the effects of the vices opposed to the parts of temperance. Thus the effect of anger, which is opposed to meekness, is sometimes that a man goes on to commit murder (and this is forbidden in the Decalogue), and sometimes that he refuses due honor to his parents, which may also be the result of pride, which leads many to transgress the precepts of the first table.

Reply Obj. 1: Pride is the beginning of sin, but it lies hidden in the heart; and its inordinateness is not perceived by all in common. Hence there was no place for its prohibition among the precepts of the Decalogue, which are like first self-evident principles.

Reply Obj. 2: Those precepts which are essentially an inducement to the observance of the Law presuppose the Law to be already given, wherefore they cannot be first precepts of the Law so as to have a place in the Decalogue.

Reply Obj. 3: Inordinate outward movement is not injurious to one's neighbor, if we consider the species of the act, as are murder, adultery, and theft, which are forbidden in the decalogue; but only as being signs of an inward inordinateness, as stated above (Q. 168, A. 1, ad 1, 3).

TREATISE ON GRATUITOUS GRACES (QQ. 171-182)

# QUESTION 171

OF PROPHECY (In Six Articles)

After treating individually of all the virtues and vices that pertain to men of all conditions and estates, we must now consider those things which pertain especially to certain men. Now there is a triple difference between men as regards things connected with the soul's habits and acts. First, in reference to the various gratuitous graces, according to 1 Cor. 12:4, 7: "There are diversities of graces ... and to one ... by the Spirit is given the word of wisdom, to another the word of knowledge," etc. Another difference arises from the diversities of life, namely the active and the contemplative life, which correspond to diverse purposes of operation, wherefore it is stated (1 Cor. 12:4, 7) that "there are diversities of operations." For the purpose of operation in Martha, who "was busy about much serving," which pertains to the active life, differed from the purpose of operation in Mary, "who sitting ... at the Lord's feet, heard His word" (Luke 10:39, 40), which pertains to the contemplative life. A third difference corresponds to the various duties and states of life, as expressed in Eph. 4:11, "And He gave some apostles; and some prophets; and other some evangelists; and other some pastors and doctors": and this pertains to diversity of ministries, of which it is written (1 Cor. 12:5): "There are diversities of ministries."

With regard to gratuitous graces, which are the first object to be considered, it must be observed that some of them pertain to knowledge, some to speech, and some to operation. Now all things pertaining to knowledge may be comprised under *prophecy,* since prophetic revelation extends not only to future events relating to man, but also to things relating to God, both as to those which are to be believed by all and are matters of *faith,* and as to yet higher mysteries, which concern the perfect and belong to *wisdom.* Again, prophetic revelation is about things pertaining to spiritual substances, by whom we are urged to good or evil; this pertains to the *discernment of spirits.* Moreover it extends to the direction of human acts, and this pertains to *knowledge,* as we shall explain further on (Q. 177). Accordingly we must first of all consider prophecy, and rapture which is a degree of prophecy.

Prophecy admits of four heads of consideration: (1) its essence; (2) its cause; (3) the mode of prophetic knowledge; (4) the division of prophecy.

Under the first head there are six points of inquiry:

(1) Whether prophecy pertains to knowledge?

(2) Whether it is a habit?

(3) Whether it is only about future contingencies?

(4) Whether a prophet knows all possible matters of prophecy?

(5) Whether a prophet distinguishes that which he perceives by the gift of God, from that which he perceives by his own spirit?

(6) Whether anything false can be the matter of prophecy?

FIRST ARTICLE [II-II, Q. 171, Art. 1]

Whether Prophecy Pertains to Knowledge?

Objection 1: It would seem that prophecy does not pertain to knowledge. For it is written (Ecclus. 48:14) that after death the body of Eliseus prophesied, and further on (Ecclus. 49:18) it is said of Joseph that "his bones were visited, and after death they prophesied." Now no knowledge remains in the body or in the bones after death. Therefore prophecy does not pertain to knowledge.

Obj. 2: Further, it is written (1 Cor. 14:3): "He that prophesieth, speaketh to men unto edification." Now speech is not knowledge itself, but its effect. Therefore it would seem that prophecy does not pertain to knowledge.

Obj. 3: Further, every cognitive perfection excludes folly and madness. Yet both of these are consistent with prophecy; for it is written (Osee 9:7): "Know ye, O Israel, that the prophet was foolish and mad [*Vulg.: 'the spiritual man was mad']." Therefore prophecy is not a cognitive perfection.

Obj. 4: Further, just as revelation regards the intellect, so inspiration regards, apparently, the affections, since it denotes a kind of motion. Now prophecy is described as "inspiration" or "revelation," according to Cassiodorus [*Prolog. super Psalt. i]. Therefore it would seem that prophecy does not pertain to the intellect more than to the affections.

*On the contrary,* It is written (1 Kings 9:9): "For he that is now called a prophet, in time past was called a seer." Now sight pertains to knowledge. Therefore prophecy pertains to knowledge.

*I answer that,* Prophecy first and chiefly consists in knowledge, because, to wit, prophets know things that are far ( *procul* ) removed from man's knowledge. Wherefore they may be said to take their name from *phanos* , "apparition," because things appear to them from afar. Wherefore, as Isidore states (Etym. vii, 8), "in the Old Testament, they were called Seers, because they saw what others saw not, and surveyed things hidden in mystery." Hence among heathen nations they were known as *vates,* "on account of their power of mind ( vi mentis )," [*The Latinvates is from the Greek phates , and may be rendered "soothsayer"] (ibid. viii, 7).

Since, however, it is written (1 Cor. 12:7): "The manifestation of the Spirit is given to every man unto profit," and further on (1 Cor. 14:12): "Seek to abound unto the edification of the Church," it follows that prophecy consists secondarily in speech, in so far as the prophets declare for the instruction of others, the things they know through being taught of God, according to the saying of Isa. 21:10, "That which I have heard of the Lord of hosts, the God of Israel, I have declared unto you." Accordingly, as Isidore says (Etym. viii, 7), "prophets" may be described as *praefatores* (foretellers), "because they tell from afar ( *porro fantur* )," that is, speak from a distance, "and foretell the truth about things to come."

Now those things above human ken which are revealed by God cannot be confirmed by human reason, which they surpass as regards the operation of the Divine power, according to Mk. 16:20, "They ... preached everywhere, the Lord working withal and confirming the word with signs that followed." Hence, thirdly, prophecy is concerned with the working of miracles, as a kind of confirmation of the prophetic utterances. Wherefore it is written (Deut. 34:10, 11): "There arose no more a prophet in Israel like unto Moses, whom the Lord knew face to face, in all the signs and wonders."

Reply Obj. 1: These passages speak of prophecy in reference to the third point just mentioned, which regards the proof of prophecy.

Reply Obj. 2: The Apostle is speaking there of the prophetic utterances.

Reply Obj. 3: Those prophets who are described as foolish and mad are not true but false prophets, of whom it is said (Jer. 3:16): "Hearken not to the words of the prophets that prophesy to you, and deceive you; they speak a vision of their own heart, and not out of the mouth of the Lord," and (Ezech. 13:3): "Woe to the foolish prophets, that follow their own spirit, and see nothing."

Reply Obj. 4: It is requisite to prophecy that the intention of the mind be raised to the perception of Divine things: wherefore it is written (Ezech. 2:1): "Son of man, stand upon thy feet, and I will speak to thee." This raising of the intention is brought about by the motion of the Holy Ghost, wherefore the text goes on to say: "And the Spirit entered into me ... and He set me upon my feet." After the mind's intention has been raised to heavenly things, it perceives the things of God; hence the text continues: "And I heard Him speaking to me." Accordingly inspiration is requisite for prophecy, as regards the raising of the mind, according to Job 32:8, "The inspiration of the Almighty giveth understanding": while revelation is necessary, as regards the very perception of Divine things, whereby prophecy is completed; by its means the veil of darkness and ignorance is removed, according to Job 12:22, "He discovereth great things out of darkness."

SECOND ARTICLE [II-II, Q. 171, Art. 2]

Whether Prophecy Is a Habit?

Objection 1: It would seem that prophecy is a habit. For according to *Ethic.* ii, 5, "there are three things in the soul, power, passion, and habit." Now prophecy is not a power, for then it would be in all men, since the powers of the soul are common to them. Again it is not a passion, since the passions belong to the appetitive faculty, as stated above (I-II, Q. 22, A. 2); whereas prophecy pertains principally to knowledge, as stated in the foregoing Article. Therefore prophecy is a habit.

Obj. 2: Further, every perfection of the soul, which is not always in act, is a habit. Now prophecy is a perfection of the soul; and it is not always in act, else a prophet could not be described as asleep. Therefore seemingly prophecy is a habit.

Obj. 3: Further, prophecy is reckoned among the gratuitous graces. Now grace is something in the soul, after the manner of a habit, as stated above (I-II, Q. 110, A. 2). Therefore prophecy is a habit.

*On the contrary,* A habit is something "whereby we act when we will," as the Commentator [*Averroes or Ibn Roshd, 1120-1198] says (De Anima iii). But a man cannot make use of prophecy when he will, as appears in the case of Eliseus (4 Kings 3:15), "who on Josaphat inquiring of him concerning the future, and the spirit of prophecy failing him, caused a minstrel to be brought to him, that the spirit of prophecy might come down upon him through the praise of psalmody, and fill his mind with things to come," as Gregory observes (Hom. i super Ezech.). Therefore prophecy is not a habit.

*I answer that,* As the Apostle says (Eph. 5:13), "all that is made manifest is light," because, to wit, just as the manifestation of the material sight takes place through material light, so too the manifestation of intellectual sight takes place through intellectual light. Accordingly manifestation must be proportionate to the light by means of which it takes place, even as an effect is proportionate to its cause. Since then prophecy pertains to a knowledge that surpasses natural reason, as stated above (A. 1), it follows that prophecy requires an intellectual light surpassing the light of natural reason. Hence the saying of Micah 7:8: "When I sit in darkness, the Lord is my light." Now light may be in a subject in two ways: first, by way of an abiding form, as material light is in the sun, and in fire; secondly, by way of a passion, or passing impression, as light is in the air. Now the prophetic light is not in the prophet's intellect by way of an abiding form, else a prophet would always be able to prophesy, which is clearly false. For Gregory says (Hom. i super Ezech.): "Sometimes the spirit of prophecy is lacking to the prophet, nor is it always within the call of his mind, yet so that in its absence he knows that its presence is due to a gift." Hence Eliseus said of the Sunamite woman (4 Kings 4:27): "Her soul is in anguish, and the Lord hath hid it from me, and hath not told me." The reason for this is that the intellectual light that is in a subject by way of an abiding and complete form, perfects the intellect chiefly to the effect of knowing the principle of the things manifested by that light; thus by the light of the active intellect the intellect knows chiefly the first principles of all things known naturally. Now the principle of things pertaining to supernatural knowledge, which are manifested by prophecy, is God Himself, Whom the prophets do not see in His essence, although He is seen by the blessed in heaven, in whom this light is by way of an abiding and complete form, according to Ps. 35:10, "In Thy light we shall see light."

It follows therefore that the prophetic light is in the prophet's soul by way of a passion or transitory impression. This is indicated Ex. 33:22: "When my glory shall pass, I will set thee in a hole of the rock," etc., and 3 Kings 19:11: "Go forth and stand upon the mount before the Lord; and behold the Lord passeth," etc. Hence it is that even as the air is ever in need of a fresh enlightening, so too the prophet's mind is always in need of a fresh revelation; thus a disciple who has not yet acquired the principles of an art needs to have every detail explained to him. Wherefore it is written (Isa. 1:4): "In the morning He wakeneth my ear, so that I may hear Him as a master." This is also indicated by the very manner in which prophecies are uttered: thus it is stated that "the Lord spake to such and such a prophet," or that "the word of the Lord," or "the hand of the Lord was made upon him."

But a habit is an abiding form. Wherefore it is evident that, properly speaking, prophecy is not a habit.

Reply Obj. 1: This division of the Philosopher's does not comprise absolutely all that is in the soul, but only such as can be principles of moral actions, which are done sometimes from passion, sometimes from habit, sometimes from mere power, as in the case of those who perform an action from the judgment of their reason before having the habit of that action.

However, prophecy may be reduced to a passion, provided we understand passion to denote any kind of receiving, in which sense the Philosopher says (De Anima iii, 4) that "to understand is, in a way, to be passive." For just as, in natural knowledge, the possible intellect is passive to the light of the active intellect, so too in prophetic knowledge the human intellect is passive to the enlightening of the Divine light.

Reply Obj. 2: Just as in corporeal things, when a passion ceases, there remains a certain aptitude to a repetition of the passion—thus wood once ignited is more easily ignited again, so too in the prophet's intellect, after the actual enlightenment has ceased, there remains an aptitude to be enlightened anew—thus when the mind has once been aroused to devotion, it is more easily recalled to its former devotion. Hence Augustine says (De orando Deum. Ep. cxxx, 9) that our prayers need to be frequent, "lest devotion be extinguished as soon as it is kindled."

We might, however, reply that a person is called a prophet, even while his prophetic enlightenment ceases to be actual, on account of his being deputed by God, according to Jer. 1:5, "And I made thee a prophet unto the nations."

Reply Obj. 3: Every gift of grace raises man to something above human nature, and this may happen in two ways. First, as to the substance of the act—for instance, the working of miracles, and the knowledge of the uncertain and hidden things of Divine wisdom—and for such acts man is not granted a habitual gift of grace. Secondly, a thing is above human nature as to the mode but not the substance of the act—for instance to love God and to know Him in the mirror of His creatures—and for this a habitual gift of grace is bestowed.

THIRD ARTICLE [II-II, Q. 171, Art. 3]

Whether Prophecy Is Only About Future Contingencies?

Objection 1: It would seem that prophecy is only about future contingencies. For Cassiodorus says [*Prol. super Psalt. i] that "prophecy is a Divine inspiration or revelation, announcing the issue of things with unchangeable truth." Now issues pertain to future contingencies. Therefore the prophetic revelation is about future contingencies alone.

Obj. 2: Further, according to 1 Cor. 12, the grace of prophecy is differentiated from wisdom and faith, which are about Divine things; and from the discernment of spirits, which is about created spirits; and from knowledge, which is about human things. Now habits and acts are differentiated by their objects, as stated above (I-II, Q. 54, A. 2). Therefore it seems that the object of prophecy is not connected with any of the above. Therefore it follows that it is about future contingencies alone.

Obj. 3: Further, difference of object causes difference of species, as stated above (I-II, Q. 54, A. 2). Therefore, if one prophecy is about future contingencies, and another about other things, it would seem to follow that these are different species of prophecy.

*On the contrary,* Gregory says (Hom. i super Ezech.) that some prophecies are "about the future, for instance (Isa. 7:14), 'Behold a virgin shall conceive, and bear a son'"; some are "about the past, as (Gen. 1:1), 'In the beginning God created heaven and earth'"; some are "about the present," as (1 Cor. 14:24, 25), "If all prophesy, and there come in one that believeth not ... the secrets of his heart are made manifest." Therefore prophecy is not about future contingencies alone.

*I answer that,* A manifestation made by means of a certain light can extend to all those things that are subject to that light: thus the body's sight extends to all colors, and the soul's natural knowledge extends to whatever is subject to the light of the active intellect. Now prophetic knowledge comes through a Divine light, whereby it is possible to know all things both Divine and human, both spiritual and corporeal; and consequently the prophetic revelation extends to them all. Thus by the ministry of spirits a prophetic revelation concerning the perfections of God and the angels was made to Isa. 6:1, where it is written, "I saw the Lord sitting upon a throne high and elevated." Moreover his prophecy contains matters referring to natural bodies, according to the words of Isa. 40:12, "Who hath measured the waters in the hollow of His hand," etc. It also contains matters relating to human conduct, according to Isa. 58:1, "Deal thy bread to the hungry," etc.; and besides this it contains things pertaining to future events, according to Isa. 47:9, "Two things shall come upon thee suddenly in one day, barrenness and widowhood."

Since, however, prophecy is about things remote from our knowledge, it must be observed that the more remote things are from our knowledge the more pertinent they are to prophecy. Of such things there are three degrees. One degree comprises things remote from the knowledge, either sensitive or intellective, of some particular man, but not from the knowledge of all men; thus a particular man knows by sense things present to him locally, which another man does not know by human sense, since they are removed from him. Thus Eliseus knew prophetically what his disciple Giezi had done in his absence (4 Kings 5:26), and in like manner the secret thoughts of one man are manifested prophetically to another, according to 1 Cor. 14:25; and again in this way what one man knows by demonstration may be revealed to another prophetically.

The second degree comprises those things which surpass the knowledge of all men without exception, not that they are in themselves unknowable, but on account of a defect in human knowledge; such as the mystery of the Trinity, which was revealed by the Seraphim saying: "Holy, Holy, Holy," etc. (Isa. 6:3).

The last degree comprises things remote from the knowledge of all men, through being in themselves unknowable; such are future contingencies, the truth of which is indeterminate. And since that which is predicated universally and by its very nature, takes precedence of that which is predicated in a limited and relative sense, it follows that revelation of future events belongs most properly to prophecy, and from this prophecy apparently takes its name. Hence Gregory says (Hom. i super Ezech.): "And since a prophet is so called because he foretells the future, his name loses its significance when he speaks of the past or present."

Reply Obj. 1: Prophecy is there defined according to its proper signification; and it is in this sense that it is differentiated from the other gratuitous graces.

Reply Obj. 2: This is evident from what has just been said. We might also reply that all those things that are the matter of prophecy have the common aspect of being unknowable to man except by Divine revelation; whereas those that are the matter of *wisdom, knowledge,* and the *interpretation of speeches,* can be known by man through natural reason, but are manifested in a higher way through the enlightening of the Divine light. As to *faith,* although it is about things invisible to man, it is not concerned with the knowledge of the things believed, but with a man's certitude of assent to things known by others.

Reply Obj. 3: The formal element in prophetic knowledge is the Divine light, which being one, gives unity of species to prophecy, although the things prophetically manifested by the Divine light are diverse.

FOURTH ARTICLE [II-II, Q. 171, Art. 4]

Whether by the Divine Revelation a Prophet Knows All That Can Be Known Prophetically?

Objection 1: It would seem that by the Divine revelation a prophet knows all that can be known prophetically. For it is written (Amos 3:7): "The Lord God doth nothing without revealing His secret to His servants the prophets." Now whatever is revealed prophetically is something done by God. Therefore there is not one of them but what is revealed to the prophet.

Obj. 2: Further, "God's works are perfect" (Deut. 32:4). Now prophecy is a "Divine revelation," as stated above (A. 3). Therefore it is perfect; and this would not be so unless all possible matters of prophecy were revealed prophetically, since "the perfect is that which lacks nothing" (Phys. iii, 6). Therefore all possible matters of prophecy are revealed to the prophet.

Obj. 3: Further, the Divine light which causes prophecy is more powerful than the right of natural reason which is the cause of human science. Now a man who has acquired a science knows whatever pertains to that science; thus a grammarian knows all matters of grammar. Therefore it would seem that a prophet knows all matters of prophecy.

*On the contrary,* Gregory says (Hom. i super Ezech.) that "sometimes the spirit of prophecy indicates the present to the prophet's mind and nowise the future; and sometimes it points not to the present but to the future." Therefore the prophet does not know all matters of prophecy.

*I answer that,* Things which differ from one another need not exist simultaneously, save by reason of some one thing in which they are connected and on which they depend: thus it has been stated above (I-II, Q. 65, AA. 1, 2) that all the virtues must needs exist simultaneously on account of prudence and charity. Now all the things that are known through some principle are connected in that principle and depend thereon. Hence he who knows a principle perfectly, as regards all to which its virtue extends, knows at the same time all that can be known through that principle; whereas if the common principle is unknown, or known only in a general way, it does not follow that one knows all those things at the same time, but each of them has to be manifested by itself, so that consequently some of them may be known, and some not.

Now the principle of those things that are prophetically manifested by the Divine light is the first truth, which the prophets do not see in itself. Wherefore there is no need for their knowing all possible matters of prophecy; but each one knows some of them according to the special revelation of this or that matter.

Reply Obj. 1: The Lord reveals to the prophets all things that are necessary for the instruction of the faithful; yet not all to every one, but some to one, and some to another.

Reply Obj. 2: Prophecy is by way of being something imperfect in the genus of Divine revelation: hence it is written (1 Cor. 13:8) that "prophecies shall be made void," and that "we prophesy in part," i.e. imperfectly. The Divine revelation will be brought to its perfection in heaven; wherefore the same text continues (1 Cor. 113:10): "When that which is perfect is come, that which is in part shall be done away." Consequently it does not follow that nothing is lacking to prophetic revelation, but that it lacks none of those things to which prophecy is directed.

Reply Obj. 3: He who has a science knows the principles of that science, whence whatever is pertinent to that science depends; wherefore to have the habit of a science perfectly, is to know whatever is pertinent to that science. But God Who is the principle of prophetic knowledge is not known in Himself through prophecy; wherefore the comparison fails.

FIFTH ARTICLE [II-II, Q. 171, Art. 5]

Whether the Prophet Always Distinguishes What He Says by His Own Spirit from What He Says by the Prophetic Spirit?

Objection 1: It would seem that the prophet always distinguishes what he says by his own spirit from what he says by the prophetic spirit. For Augustine states (Confess. vi, 13) that his mother said "she could, through a certain feeling, which in words she could not express, discern betwixt Divine revelations, and the dreams of her own soul." Now prophecy is a Divine revelation, as stated above (A. 3). Therefore the prophet always distinguishes what he says by the spirit of prophecy, from what he says by his own spirit.

Obj. 2: Further, God commands nothing impossible, as Jerome [*Pelagius. Ep. xvi, among the supposititious works of St. Jerome] says. Now the prophets were commanded (Jer. 23:28): "The prophet that hath a dream, let him tell a dream; and he that hath My word, let him speak My word with truth." Therefore the prophet can distinguish what he has through the spirit of prophecy from what he sees otherwise.

Obj. 3: Further, the certitude resulting from a Divine light is greater than that which results from the light of natural reason. Now he that has science, by the light of natural reason knows for certain that he has it. Therefore he that has prophecy by a Divine light is much more certain that he has it.

*On the contrary,* Gregory says (Hom. i super Ezech.): "It must be observed that sometimes the holy prophets, when consulted, utter certain things by their own spirit, through being much accustomed to prophesying, and think they are speaking by the prophetic spirit."

*I answer that,* The prophet's mind is instructed by God in two ways: in one way by an express revelation, in another way by a most mysterious instinct to "which the human mind is subjected without knowing it," as Augustine says (Gen. ad lit. ii, 17). Accordingly the prophet has the greatest certitude about those things which he knows by an express revelation, and he has it for certain that they are revealed to him by God; wherefore it is written (Jer. 26:15): "In truth the Lord sent me to you, to speak all these words in your hearing." Else, were he not certain about this, the faith which relies on the utterances of the prophet would not be certain. A sign of the prophet's certitude may be gathered from the fact that Abraham being admonished in a prophetic vision, prepared to sacrifice his only-begotten son, which he nowise would have done had he not been most certain of the Divine revelation.

On the other hand, his position with regard to the things he knows by instinct is sometimes such that he is unable to distinguish fully whether his thoughts are conceived of Divine instinct or of his own spirit. And those things which we know by Divine instinct are not all manifested with prophetic certitude, for this instinct is something imperfect in the genus of prophecy. It is thus that we are to understand the saying of Gregory. Lest, however, this should lead to error, "they are very soon set aright by the Holy Ghost [*For instance, cf. 2 Kings 7:3 seqq.], and from Him they hear the truth, so that they reproach themselves for having said what was untrue," as Gregory adds (Hom. i super Ezech.).

The arguments set down in the first place consider the revelation that is made by the prophetic spirit; wherefore the answer to all the objections is clear.

SIXTH ARTICLE [II-II, Q. 171, Art. 6]

Whether Things Known or Declared Prophetically Can Be False?

Objection 1: It would seem that things known or declared prophetically can be false. For prophecy is about future contingencies, as stated above (A. 3). Now future contingencies may possibly not happen; else they would happen of necessity. Therefore the matter of prophecy can be false.

Obj. 2: Further, Isaias prophesied to Ezechias saying (Isa. 38:1): "Take order with thy house, for thou shalt surely die, and shalt not live," and yet fifteen years were added to his life (4 Kings 20:6). Again the Lord said (Jer. 18:7, 8): "I will suddenly speak against a nation and against a kingdom, to root out and to pull down and to destroy it. If that nation against which I have spoken shall repent of their evil, I also will repent of the evil that I have thought to do them." This is instanced in the example of the Ninevites, according to John 3:10: "The Lord [Vulg.: 'God'] had mercy with regard to the evil which He had said that He would do to them, and He did it not." Therefore the matter of prophecy can be false.

Obj. 3: Further, in a conditional proposition, whenever the antecedent is absolutely necessary, the consequent is absolutely necessary, because the consequent of a conditional proposition stands in the same relation to the antecedent, as the conclusion to the premises in a syllogism, and a syllogism whose premises are necessary always leads to a necessary conclusion, as we find proved in I Poster. 6. But if the matter of a prophecy cannot be false, the following conditional proposition must needs be true: "If a thing has been prophesied, it will be." Now the antecedent of this conditional proposition is absolutely necessary, since it is about the past. Therefore the consequent is also necessary absolutely; yet this is unfitting, for then prophecy would not be about contingencies. Therefore it is untrue that the matter of prophecy cannot be false.

*On the contrary,* Cassiodorus says [*Prol. in Psalt. i] that "prophecy is a Divine inspiration or revelation, announcing the issue of things with invariable truth." Now the truth of prophecy would not be invariable, if its matter could be false. Therefore nothing false can come under prophecy.

*I answer that,* As may be gathered from what has been said (AA. 1, 3, 5), prophecy is a kind of knowledge impressed under the form of teaching on the prophet's intellect, by Divine revelation. Now the truth of knowledge is the same in disciple and teacher since the knowledge of the disciple is a likeness of the knowledge of the teacher, even as in natural things the form of the thing generated is a likeness of the form of the generator. Jerome speaks in this sense when he says [*Comment. in Daniel ii, 10] that "prophecy is the seal of the Divine foreknowledge." Consequently the same truth must needs be in prophetic knowledge and utterances, as in the Divine knowledge, under which nothing false can possibly come, as stated in the First Part (Q. 16, A. 8). Therefore nothing false can come under prophecy.

Reply Obj. 1: As stated in the First Part (Q. 14, A. 13) the certitude of the Divine foreknowledge does not exclude the contingency of future singular events, because that knowledge regards the future as present and already determinate to one thing. Wherefore prophecy also, which is an "impressed likeness" or "seal of the Divine foreknowledge," does not by its unchangeable truth exclude the contingency of future things.

Reply Obj. 2: The Divine foreknowledge regards future things in two ways. First, as they are in themselves, in so far, to wit, as it sees them in their presentiality: secondly, as in their causes, inasmuch as it sees the order of causes in relation to their effects. And though future contingencies, considered as in themselves, are determinate to one thing, yet, considered as in their causes, they are not so determined but that they can happen otherwise. Again, though this twofold knowledge is always united in the Divine intellect, it is not always united in the prophetic revelation, because an imprint made by an active cause is not always on a par with the virtue of that cause. Hence sometimes the prophetic revelation is an imprinted likeness of the Divine foreknowledge, in so far as the latter regards future contingencies in themselves: and such things happen in the same way as foretold, for example this saying of Isa. 7:14: "Behold a virgin shall conceive." Sometimes, however, the prophetic revelation is an imprinted likeness of the Divine foreknowledge as knowing the order of causes to effects; and then at times the event is otherwise than foretold. Yet the prophecy does not cover a falsehood, for the meaning of the prophecy is that inferior causes, whether they be natural causes or human acts, are so disposed as to lead to such a result. In this way we are to understand the saying of Isa. 38:1: "Thou shalt die, and not live"; in other words, "The disposition of thy body has a tendency to death": and the saying of Jonah 3:4, "Yet forty days, and Nineveh shall be destroyed," that is to say, "Its merits demand that it should be destroyed." God is said "to repent," metaphorically, inasmuch as He bears Himself after the manner of one who repents, by "changing His sentence, although He changes not His counsel" [*Cf. I, Q. 19, A. 7, ad 2].

Reply Obj. 3: Since the same truth of prophecy is the same as the truth of Divine foreknowledge, as stated above, the conditional proposition: "If this was prophesied, it will be," is true in the same way as the proposition: "If this was foreknown, it will be": for in both cases it is impossible for the antecedent not to be. Hence the consequent is necessary, considered, not as something future in our regard, but as being present to the Divine foreknowledge, as stated in the First Part (Q. 14, A. 13, ad 2).

## QUESTION 172

OF THE CAUSE OF PROPHECY (In Six Articles)

We must now consider the cause of prophecy. Under this head there are six points of inquiry:

(1) Whether prophecy is natural?

(2) Whether it is from God by means of the angels?

(3) Whether a natural disposition is requisite for prophecy?

(4) Whether a good life is requisite?

(5) Whether any prophecy is from the demons?

(6) Whether prophets of the demons ever tell what is true?

FIRST ARTICLE [II-II, Q. 172, Art. 1]

Whether Prophecy Can Be Natural?

Objection 1: It would seem that prophecy can be natural. For Gregory says (Dial. iv, 26) that "sometimes the mere strength of the soul is sufficiently cunning to foresee certain things": and Augustine says (Gen. ad lit. xii, 13) that the human soul, according as it is withdrawn from the sense of the body, is able to foresee the future [*Cf. I, Q. 86, A. 4, ad 2]. Now this pertains to prophecy. Therefore the soul can acquire prophecy naturally.

Obj. 2: Further, the human soul's knowledge is more alert while one wakes than while one sleeps. Now some, during sleep, naturally foresee the future, as the Philosopher asserts (De Somn. et Vigil. [*De Divinat. per Somn. ii, which is annexed to the work quoted]). Much more therefore can a man naturally foreknow the future.

Obj. 3: Further, man, by his nature, is more perfect than dumb animals. Yet some dumb animals have foreknowledge of future things that concern them. Thus ants foreknow the coming rains, which is evident from their gathering grain into their nest before the rain commences; and in like manner fish foreknow a coming storm, as may be gathered from their movements in avoiding places exposed to storm. Much more therefore can men foreknow the future that concerns themselves, and of such things is prophecy. Therefore prophecy comes from nature.

Obj. 4: Further, it is written (Prov. 29:18): "When prophecy shall fail, the people shall be scattered abroad"; wherefore it is evident that prophecy is necessary for the stability of the human race. Now "nature does not fail in necessaries" [*Aristotle, *De Anima* iii, 9]. Therefore it seems that prophecy is from nature.

*On the contrary,* It is written (2 Pet. 1:21): "For prophecy came not by the will of man at any time, but the holy men of God spoke, inspired by the Holy Ghost." Therefore prophecy comes not from nature, but through the gift of the Holy Ghost.

*I answer that,* As stated above (Q. 171, A. 6, ad 2) prophetic foreknowledge may regard future things in two ways: in one way, as they are in themselves; in another way, as they are in their causes. Now, to foreknow future things, as they are in themselves, is proper to the Divine intellect, to Whose eternity all things are present, as stated in the First Part (Q. 14, A. 13). Wherefore such like foreknowledge of the future cannot come from nature, but from Divine revelation alone. On the other hand, future things can be foreknown in their causes with a natural knowledge even by man: thus a physician foreknows future health or death in certain causes, through previous experimental knowledge of the order of those causes to such effects. Such like knowledge of the future may be understood to be in a man by nature in two ways. In one way that the soul, from that which it holds, is able to foreknow the future, and thus Augustine says (Gen. ad lit. xii, 13): "Some have deemed the human soul to contain a certain power of divination." This seems to be in accord with the opinion of Plato [*Phaed. xxvii; Civit. vi], who held that our souls have knowledge of all things by participating in the ideas; but that this knowledge is obscured in them by union with the body; yet in some more, in others less, according to a difference in bodily purity. According to this it might be said that men, whose souls are not much obscured through union with the body, are able to foreknow such like future things by their own knowledge. Against this opinion Augustine says (Gen. ad lit. xii, 13): "How is it that the soul cannot always have this power of divination, since it always wishes to have it?"

Since, however, it seems truer, according to the opinion of Aristotle, that the soul acquires knowledge from sensibles, as stated in the First Part (Q. 84, A. 6), it is better to have recourse to another explanation, and to hold that men have no such foreknowledge of the future, but that they can acquire it by means of experience, wherein they are helped by their natural disposition, which depends on the perfection of a man's imaginative power, and the clarity of his understanding.

Nevertheless this latter foreknowledge of the future differs in two ways from the former, which comes through Divine revelation. First, because the former can be about any events whatever, and this infallibly; whereas the latter foreknowledge, which can be had naturally, is about certain effects, to which human experience may extend. Secondly, because the former prophecy is "according to the unchangeable truth" [*Q. 171, A. 3, Obj. 1], while the latter is not, and can cover a falsehood. Now the former foreknowledge, and not the latter, properly belongs to prophecy, because, as stated above (Q. 171, A. 3), prophetic knowledge is of things which naturally surpass human knowledge. Consequently we must say that prophecy strictly so called cannot be from nature, but only from Divine revelation.

Reply Obj. 1: When the soul is withdrawn from corporeal things, it becomes more adapted to receive the influence of spiritual substances [*Cf. I, Q. 88, A. 4, ad 2], and also is more inclined to receive the subtle motions which take place in the human imagination through the impression of natural causes, whereas it is hindered from receiving them while occupied with sensible things. Hence Gregory says (Dial. iv, 26) that "the soul, at the approach of death, foresees certain future things, by reason of the subtlety of its nature," inasmuch as it is receptive even of slight impressions. Or again, it knows future things by a revelation of the angels; but not by its own power, because according to Augustine (Gen. ad lit. xii, 13), "if this were so, it would be able to foreknow the future whenever it willed," which is clearly false.

Obj. 2: Knowledge of the future by means of dreams, comes either from the revelation of spiritual substances, or from a corporeal cause, as stated above (Q. 95, A. 6), when we were treating of divination. Now both these causes are more applicable to a person while asleep than while awake, because, while awake, the soul is occupied with external sensibles, so that it is less receptive of the subtle impressions either of spiritual substances, or even of natural causes; although as regards the perfection of judgment, the reason is more alert in waking than in sleeping.

Reply Obj. 3: Even dumb animals have no foreknowledge of future events, except as these are foreknown in their causes, whereby their imagination is moved more than man's, because man's imagination, especially in waking, is more disposed according to reason than according to the impression of natural causes. Yet reason effects much more amply in man, that which the impression of natural causes effects in dumb animals; and Divine grace by inspiring the prophecy assists man still more.

Reply Obj. 4: The prophetic light extends even to the direction of human acts; and in this way prophecy is requisite for the government of a people, especially in relation to Divine worship; since for this nature is not sufficient, and grace is necessary.

SECOND ARTICLE [II-II, Q. 172, Art. 2]

Whether Prophetic Revelation Comes Through the Angels?

Objection 1: It would seem that prophetic revelation does not come through the angels. For it is written (Wis. 7:27) that Divine wisdom "conveyeth herself into holy souls," and "maketh the friends of God, and the prophets." Now wisdom makes the friends of God immediately. Therefore it also makes the prophets immediately, and not through the medium of the angels.

Obj. 2: Further, prophecy is reckoned among the gratuitous graces. But the gratuitous graces are from the Holy Ghost, according to 1 Cor. 12:4, "There are diversities of graces, but the same Spirit." Therefore the prophetic revelation is not made by means of an angel.

Obj. 3: Further, Cassiodorus [*Prol. in Psalt. i] says that prophecy is a "Divine revelation": whereas if it were conveyed by the angels, it would be called an angelic revelation. Therefore prophecy is not bestowed by means of the angels.

*On the contrary,* Dionysius says (Coel. Hier. iv): "Our glorious fathers received Divine visions by means of the heavenly powers"; and he is speaking there of prophetic visions. Therefore prophetic revelation is conveyed by means of the angels.

*I answer that,* As the Apostle says (Rom. 13:1), "Things that are of God are well ordered [*Vulg.: 'Those that are, are ordained of God.']." Now the Divine ordering, according to Dionysius [*Coel. Hier. iv; Eccl. Hier. v], is such that the lowest things are directed by middle things. Now the angels hold a middle position between God and men, in that they have a greater share in the perfection of the Divine goodness than men have. Wherefore the Divine enlightenments and revelations are conveyed from God to men by the angels. Now prophetic knowledge is bestowed by Divine enlightenment and revelation. Therefore it is evident that it is conveyed by the angels.

Reply Obj. 1: Charity which makes man a friend of God, is a perfection of the will, in which God alone can form an impression; whereas prophecy is a perfection of the intellect, in which an angel also can form an impression, as stated in the First Part (Q. 111, A. 1), wherefore the comparison fails between the two.

Reply Obj. 2: The gratuitous graces are ascribed to the Holy Ghost as their first principle: yet He works grace of this kind in men by means of the angels.

Reply Obj. 3: The work of the instrument is ascribed to the principal agent by whose power the instrument acts. And since a minister is like an instrument, prophetic revelation, which is conveyed by the ministry of the angels, is said to be Divine.

THIRD ARTICLE [II-II, Q. 172, Art. 3]

Whether a Natural Disposition Is Requisite for Prophecy?

Objection 1: It would seem that a natural disposition is requisite for prophecy. For prophecy is received by the prophet according to the disposition of the recipient, since a gloss of Jerome on Amos 1:2, "The Lord will roar from Sion," says: "Anyone who wishes to make a comparison naturally turns to those things of which he has experience, and among which his life is spent. For example, sailors compare their enemies to the winds, and their losses to a shipwreck. In like manner Amos, who was a shepherd, likens the fear of God to that which is inspired by the lion's roar." Now that which is received by a thing according to the mode of the recipient requires a natural disposition. Therefore prophecy requires a natural disposition.

Obj. 2: Further, the considerations of prophecy are more lofty than those of acquired science. Now natural indisposition hinders the considerations of acquired science, since many are prevented by natural indisposition from succeeding to grasp the speculations of science. Much more therefore is a natural disposition requisite for the contemplation of prophecy.

Obj. 3: Further, natural indisposition is a much greater obstacle than an accidental impediment. Now the considerations of prophecy are hindered by an accidental occurrence. For Jerome says in his commentary on Matthew [*The quotation is from Origen, Hom. vi in Num.] that "at the time of the marriage act, the presence of the Holy Ghost will not be vouchsafed, even though it be a prophet that fulfils the duty of procreation." Much more therefore does a natural indisposition hinder prophecy; and thus it would seem that a good natural disposition is requisite for prophecy.

*On the contrary,* Gregory says in a homily for Pentecost (xxx in Ev.): "He," namely the Holy Ghost, "fills the boy harpist and makes him a Psalmist; He fills the herdsman plucking wild figs, and makes him a prophet." Therefore prophecy requires no previous disposition, but depends on the will alone of the Holy Ghost, of Whom it is written (1 Cor. 12:2): "All these things, one and the same Spirit worketh, dividing to every one according as He will."

*I answer that,* As stated above (A. 1), prophecy in its true and exact sense comes from Divine inspiration; while that which comes from a natural cause is not called prophecy except in a relative sense. Now we must observe that as God Who is the universal efficient cause requires neither previous matter nor previous disposition of matter in His corporeal effects, for He is able at the same instant to bring into being matter and disposition and form, so neither does He require a previous disposition in His spiritual effects, but is able to produce both the spiritual effect and at the same time the fitting disposition as requisite according to the order of nature. More than this, He is able at the same time, by creation, to produce the subject, so as to dispose a soul for prophecy and give it the prophetic grace, at the very instant of its creation.

Reply Obj. 1: It matters not to prophecy by what comparisons the thing prophesied is expressed; and so the Divine operation makes no change in a prophet in this respect. Yet if there be anything in him incompatible with prophecy, it is removed by the Divine power.

Reply Obj. 2: The considerations of science proceed from a natural cause, and nature cannot work without a previous disposition in matter. This cannot be said of God Who is the cause of prophecy.

Reply Obj. 3: A natural indisposition, if not removed, might be an obstacle to prophetic revelation, for instance if a man were altogether deprived of the natural senses. In the same way a man might be hindered from the act of prophesying by some very strong passion, whether of anger, or of concupiscence as in coition, or by any other passion. But such a natural indisposition as this is removed by the Divine power, which is the cause of prophecy.

FOURTH ARTICLE [II-II, Q. 172, Art. 4]

Whether a Good Life Is Requisite for Prophecy?

Objection 1: It would seem that a good life is requisite for prophecy. For it is written (Wis. 7:27) that the wisdom of God "through nations conveyeth herself into holy souls," and "maketh the friends of God, and prophets." Now there can be no holiness without a good life and sanctifying grace. Therefore prophecy cannot be without a good life and sanctifying grace.

Obj. 2: Further, secrets are not revealed save to a friend, according to John 15:15, "But I have called you friends, because all things whatsoever I have heard of My Father, I have made known to you." Now God reveals His secrets to the prophets (Amos 3:7). Therefore it would seem that the prophets are the friends of God; which is impossible without charity. Therefore seemingly prophecy cannot be without charity; and charity is impossible without sanctifying grace.

Obj. 3: Further, it is written (Matt. 7:15): "Beware of false prophets, who come to you in the clothing of sheep, but inwardly they are ravening wolves." Now all who are without grace are likened inwardly to a ravening wolf, and consequently all such are false prophets. Therefore no man is a true prophet except he be good by grace.

Obj. 4: Further, the Philosopher says (De Somn. et Vigil. [*Cf. De Divinat. per Somn. i, which is annexed to the work quoted]) that "if interpretation of dreams is from God, it is unfitting for it to be bestowed on any but the best." Now it is evident that the gift of prophecy is from God. Therefore the gift of prophecy is vouchsafed only to the best men.

*On the contrary,* To those who had said, "Lord, have we not prophesied in Thy name?" this reply is made: "I never knew you" (Matt. 7:22, 23). Now "the Lord knoweth who are His" (2 Tim. 2:19). Therefore prophecy can be in those who are not God's by grace.

*I answer that,* A good life may be considered from two points of view. First, with regard to its inward root, which is sanctifying grace. Secondly, with regard to the inward passions of the soul and the outward actions. Now sanctifying grace is given chiefly in order that man's soul may be united to God by charity. Wherefore Augustine says (De Trin. xv, 18): "A man is not transferred from the left side to the right, unless he receive the Holy Ghost, by Whom he is made a lover of God and of his neighbor." Hence whatever can be without charity can be without sanctifying grace, and consequently without goodness of life. Now prophecy can be without charity; and this is clear on two counts. First, on account of their respective acts: for prophecy pertains to the intellect, whose act precedes the act of the will, which power is perfected by charity. For this reason the Apostle (1 Cor. 13) reckons prophecy with other things pertinent to the intellect, that can be had without charity. Secondly, on account of their respective ends. For prophecy like other gratuitous graces is given for the good of the Church, according to 1 Cor. 12:7, "The manifestation of the Spirit is given to every man unto profit"; and is not directly intended to unite man's affections to God, which is the purpose of charity. Therefore prophecy can be without a good life, as regards the first root of this goodness.

If, however, we consider a good life, with regard to the passions of the soul, and external actions, from this point of view an evil life is an obstacle to prophecy. For prophecy requires the mind to be raised very high in order to contemplate spiritual things, and this is hindered by strong passions, and the inordinate pursuit of external things. Hence we read of the sons of the prophets (4 Kings 4:38) that they "dwelt together with [Vulg.: 'before']" Eliseus, leading a solitary life, as it were, lest worldly employment should be a hindrance to the gift of prophecy.

Reply Obj. 1: Sometimes the gift of prophecy is given to a man both for the good of others, and in order to enlighten his own mind; and such are those whom Divine wisdom, "conveying itself" by sanctifying grace to their minds, "maketh the friends of God, and prophets." Others, however, receive the gift of prophecy merely for the good of others. Hence Jerome commenting on Matt. 7:22, says: "Sometimes prophesying, the working of miracles, and the casting out of demons are accorded not to the merit of those who do these things, but either to the invoking the name of Christ, or to the condemnation of those who invoke, and for the good of those who see and hear."

Reply Obj. 2: Gregory [*Hom. xxvii in Ev.] expounding this passage [*John 15:15] says: "Since we love the lofty things of heaven as soon as we hear them, we know them as soon as we love them, for to love is to know. Accordingly He had made all things known to them, because having renounced earthly desires they were kindled by the torches of perfect love." In this way the Divine secrets are not always revealed to prophets.

Reply Obj. 3: Not all wicked men are ravening wolves, but only those whose purpose is to injure others. For Chrysostom says [*Opus Imperf. in Matth., Hom. xix, among the works of St. John Chrysostom, and falsely ascribed to him] that "Catholic teachers, though they be sinners, are called slaves of the flesh, but never ravening wolves, because they do not purpose the destruction of Christians." And since prophecy is directed to the good of others, it is manifest that such are false prophets, because they are not sent for this purpose by God.

Reply Obj. 4: God's gifts are not always bestowed on those who are simply the best, but sometimes are vouchsafed to those who are best as regards the receiving of this or that gift. Accordingly God grants the gift of prophecy to those whom He judges best to give it to.

FIFTH ARTICLE [II-II, Q. 172, Art. 5]

Whether Any Prophecy Comes from the Demons?

Objection 1: It would seem that no prophecy comes from the demons. For prophecy is "a Divine revelation," according to Cassiodorus [*Prol. in Psalt. i]. But that which is done by a demon is not Divine. Therefore no prophecy can be from a demon.

Obj. 2: Further, some kind of enlightenment is requisite for prophetic knowledge, as stated above (Q. 171, AA. 2, 3). Now the demons do not enlighten the human intellect, as stated above in the First Part (Q. 119, A. 3). Therefore no prophecy can come from the demons.

Obj. 3: Further, a sign is worthless if it betokens contraries. Now prophecy is a sign in confirmation of faith; wherefore a gloss on Rom. 12:6, "Either prophecy to be used according to the rule of faith," says: "Observe that in reckoning the graces, he begins with prophecy, which is the first proof of the reasonableness of our faith; since believers, after receiving the Spirit, prophesied." Therefore prophecy cannot be bestowed by the demons.

*On the contrary,* It is written (3 Kings 18:19): "Gather unto me all Israel unto mount Carmel, and the prophets of Baal four hundred and fifty, and the prophets of the grove four hundred, who eat at Jezebel's table." Now these were worshippers of demons. Therefore it would seem that there is also a prophecy from the demons.

*I answer that,* As stated above (Q. 171, A. 1), prophecy denotes knowledge far removed from human knowledge. Now it is evident that an intellect of a higher order can know some things that are far removed from the knowledge of an inferior intellect. Again, above the human intellect there is not only the Divine intellect, but also the intellects of good and bad angels according to the order of nature. Hence the demons, even by their natural knowledge, know certain things remote from men's knowledge, which they can reveal to men: although those things which God alone knows are remote simply and most of all.

Accordingly prophecy, properly and simply, is conveyed by Divine revelations alone; yet the revelation which is made by the demons may be called prophecy in a restricted sense. Wherefore those men to whom something is revealed by the demons are styled in the Scriptures as prophets, not simply, but with an addition, for instance as "false prophets," or "prophets of idols." Hence Augustine says (Gen. ad lit. xii, 19): "When the evil spirit lays hold of a man for such purposes as these," namely visions, "he makes him either devilish, or possessed, or a false prophet."

Reply Obj. 1: Cassiodorus is here defining prophecy in its proper and simple acceptation.

Reply Obj. 2: The demons reveal what they know to men, not by enlightening the intellect, but by an imaginary vision, or even by audible speech; and in this way this prophecy differs from true prophecy.

Reply Obj. 3: The prophecy of the demons can be distinguished from Divine prophecy by certain, and even outward, signs. Hence Chrysostom says [*Opus Imperf. in Matth., Hom. xix, falsely ascribed to St. John Chrysostom] that "some prophesy by the spirit of the devil, such as diviners, but they may be discerned by the fact that the devil sometimes utters what is false, the Holy Ghost never." Wherefore it is written (Deut. 18:21, 22): "If in silent thought thou answer: How shall I know the word that the Lord hath spoken? Thou shalt have this sign: Whatsoever that same prophet foretelleth in the name of the Lord, and it come not to pass, that thing the Lord hath not spoken."

SIXTH ARTICLE [II-II, Q. 172, Art. 6]

Whether the Prophets of the Demons Ever Foretell the Truth?

Objection 1: It would seem that the prophets of the demons never foretell the truth. For Ambrose [*Hilary the Deacon (Ambrosiaster) on 1 Cor. 12:3] says that "Every truth, by whomsoever spoken, is from the Holy Ghost." Now the prophets of the demons do not speak from the Holy Ghost, because "there is no concord between Christ and Belial [*'What concord hath Christ with Belial?']" (2 Cor. 6:15). Therefore it would seem that they never foretell the truth.

Obj. 2: Further, just as true prophets are inspired by the Spirit of truth, so the prophets of the demons are inspired by the spirit of untruth, according to 3 Kings 22:22, "I will go forth, and be a lying spirit in the mouth of all his prophets." Now the prophets inspired by the Holy Ghost never speak false, as stated above (Q. 111, A. 6). Therefore the prophets of the demons never speak truth.

Obj. 3: Further, it is said of the devil (John 8:44) that "when he speaketh a lie, he speaketh of his own, for the devil is a liar, and the father thereof," i.e. of lying. Now by inspiring his prophets, the devil speaks only of his own, for he is not appointed God's minister to declare the truth, since "light hath no fellowship with darkness [*Vulg.: 'What fellowship hath light with darkness?']" (2 Cor. 6:14). Therefore the prophets of the demons never foretell the truth.

*On the contrary,* A gloss on Num. 22:14, says that "Balaam was a diviner, for he sometimes foreknew the future by help of the demons and the magic art." Now he foretold many true things, for instance that which is to be found in Num. 24:17: "A star shall rise out of Jacob, and a scepter shall spring up from Israel." Therefore even the prophets of the demons foretell the truth.

*I answer that,* As the good is in relation to things, so is the true in relation to knowledge. Now in things it is impossible to find one that is wholly devoid of good. Wherefore it is also impossible for any knowledge to be wholly false, without some mixture of truth. Hence Bede says [*Comment. in Luc. xvii, 12; Cf. Augustine, QQ. Evang. ii, 40] that "no teaching is so false that it never mingles truth with falsehood." Hence the teaching of the demons, with which they instruct their prophets, contains some truths whereby it is rendered acceptable. For the intellect is led astray to falsehood by the semblance of truth, even as the will is seduced to evil by the semblance of goodness. Wherefore Chrysostom says [*Opus Imperf. in Matth., Hom. xix, falsely ascribed to St. John Chrysostom]: "The devil is allowed sometimes to speak true things, in order that his unwonted truthfulness may gain credit for his lie."

Reply Obj. 1: The prophets of the demons do not always speak from the demons' revelation, but sometimes by Divine inspiration. This was evidently the case with Balaam, of whom we read that the Lord spoke to him (Num. 22:12), though he was a prophet of the demons, because God makes use even of the wicked for the profit of the good. Hence He foretells certain truths even by the demons' prophets, both that the truth may be rendered more credible, since even its foes bear witness to it, and also in order that men, by believing such men, may be more easily led on to truth. Wherefore also the Sibyls foretold many true things about Christ.

Yet even when the demons' prophets are instructed by the demons, they foretell the truth, sometimes by virtue of their own nature, the author of which is the Holy Ghost, and sometimes by revelation of the good spirits, as Augustine declares (Gen. ad lit. xii, 19): so that even then this truth which the demons proclaim is from the Holy Ghost.

Reply Obj. 2: A true prophet is always inspired by the Spirit of truth, in Whom there is no falsehood, wherefore He never says what is not true; whereas a false prophet is not always instructed by the spirit of untruth, but sometimes even by the Spirit of truth. Even the very spirit of untruth sometimes declares true things, sometimes false, as stated above.

Reply Obj. 3: Those things are called the demons' own, which they have of themselves, namely lies and sins; while they have, not of themselves but of God, those things which belong to them by nature: and it is by virtue of their own nature that they sometimes foretell the truth, as stated above (ad 1). Moreover God makes use of them to make known the truth which is to be accomplished through them, by revealing Divine mysteries to them through the angels, as already stated (Gen. ad lit. xii, 19; I, Q. 109, A. 4, ad 1).

## QUESTION 173

OF THE MANNER IN WHICH PROPHETIC KNOWLEDGE IS CONVEYED (In Four Articles)

We must now consider the manner in which prophetic knowledge is conveyed, and under this head there are four points of inquiry:

(1) Whether the prophets see God's very essence?

(2) Whether the prophetic revelation is effected by the infusion of certain species, or by the infusion of Divine light alone?

(3) Whether prophetic revelation is always accompanied by abstraction from the sense?

(4) Whether prophecy is always accompanied by knowledge of the things prophesied?

FIRST ARTICLE [II-II, Q. 173, Art. 1]

Whether the Prophets See the Very Essence of God?

Objection 1: It would seem that the prophets see the very essence of God, for a gloss on Isa. 38:1, "Take order with thy house, for thou shalt die and not live," says: "Prophets can read in the book of God's foreknowledge in which all things are written." Now God's foreknowledge is His very essence. Therefore prophets see God's very essence.

Obj. 2: Further, Augustine says (De Trin. ix, 7) that "in that eternal truth from which all temporal things are made, we see with the mind's eye the type both of our being and of our actions." Now, of all men, prophets have the highest knowledge of Divine things. Therefore they, especially, see the Divine essence.

Obj. 3: Further, future contingencies are foreknown by the prophets "with unchangeable truth." Now future contingencies exist thus in God alone. Therefore the prophets see God Himself.

*On the contrary,* The vision of the Divine essence is not made void in heaven; whereas "prophecy is made void" (1 Cor. 13:8). Therefore prophecy is not conveyed by a vision of the Divine essence.

*I answer that,* Prophecy denotes Divine knowledge as existing afar off. Wherefore it is said of the prophets (Heb. 11:13) that "they were beholding ... afar off." But those who are in heaven and in the state of bliss see, not as from afar off, but rather, as it were, from near at hand, according to Ps. 139:14, "The upright shall dwell with Thy countenance." Hence it is evident that prophetic knowledge differs from the perfect knowledge, which we shall have in heaven, so that it is distinguished therefrom as the imperfect from the perfect, and when the latter comes the former is made void, as appears from the words of the Apostle (1 Cor. 13:10).

Some, however, wishing to discriminate between prophetic knowledge and the knowledge of the blessed, have maintained that the prophets see the very essence of God (which they call the "mirror of eternity") [*Cf. De Veritate, xii, 6; Sent. II, D, XI, part 2, art. 2, ad 4], not, however, in the way in which it is the object of the blessed, but as containing the types [*Cf. I, Q. 15] of future events. But this is altogether impossible. For God is the object of bliss in His very essence, according to the saying of Augustine (Confess. v, 4): "Happy whoso knoweth Thee, though he know not these," i.e. creatures. Now it is not possible to see the types of creatures in the very essence of God without seeing It, both because the Divine essence is Itself the type of all things that are made—the ideal type adding nothing to the Divine essence save only a relationship to the creature—and because knowledge of a thing in itself—and such is the knowledge of God as the object of heavenly bliss—precedes knowledge of that thing in its relation to something else—and such is the knowledge of God as containing the types of things. Consequently it is impossible for prophets to see God as containing the types of creatures, and yet not as the object of bliss. Therefore we must conclude that the prophetic vision is not the vision of the very essence of God, and that the prophets do not see in the Divine essence Itself the things they do see, but that they see them in certain images, according as they are enlightened by the Divine light.

Wherefore Dionysius (Coel. Hier. iv), in speaking of prophetic visions, says that "the wise theologian calls that vision divine which is effected by images of things lacking a bodily form through the seer being rapt in divine things." And these images illumined by the Divine light have more of the nature of a mirror than the Divine essence: since in a mirror images are formed from other things, and this cannot be said of God. Yet the prophet's mind thus enlightened may be called a mirror, in so far as a likeness of the truth of the Divine foreknowledge is formed therein, for which reason it is called the "mirror of eternity," as representing God's foreknowledge, for God in His eternity sees all things as present before Him, as stated above (Q. 172, A. 1).

Reply Obj. 1: The prophets are said to read the book of God's foreknowledge, inasmuch as the truth is reflected from God's foreknowledge on the prophet's mind.

Reply Obj. 2: Man is said to see in the First Truth the type of his existence, in so far as the image of the First Truth shines forth on man's mind, so that he is able to know himself.

Reply Obj. 3: From the very fact that future contingencies are in God according to unalterable truth, it follows that God can impress a like knowledge on the prophet's mind without the prophet seeing God in His essence.

SECOND ARTICLE [II-II, Q. 173, Art. 2]

Whether, in Prophetic Revelation, New Species of Things Are Impressed on the Prophet's Mind, or Merely a New Light?

Objection 1: It would seem that in prophetic revelation no new species of things are impressed on the prophet's mind, but only a new light. For a gloss of Jerome on Amos 1:2 says that "prophets draw comparisons from things with which they are conversant." But if prophetic vision were effected by means of species newly impressed, the prophet's previous experience of things would be inoperative. Therefore no new species are impressed on the prophet's soul, but only the prophetic light.

Obj. 2: Further, according to Augustine (Gen. ad lit. xii, 9), "it is not imaginative but intellective vision that makes the prophet"; wherefore it is declared (Dan. 10:1) that "there is need of understanding in a vision." Now intellective vision, as stated in the same book (Gen. ad lit. xii, 6) is not effected by means of images, but by the very truth of things. Therefore it would seem that prophetic revelation is not effected by impressing species on the soul.

Obj. 3: Further, by the gift of prophecy the Holy Ghost endows man with something that surpasses the faculty of nature. Now man can by his natural faculties form all kinds of species of things. Therefore it would seem that in prophetic revelation no new species of things are impressed, but merely an intellectual light.

*On the contrary,* It is written (Osee 12:10): "I have multiplied" their "visions, and I have used similitudes, by the ministry of the prophets." Now multiplicity of visions results, not from a diversity of intellectual light, which is common to every prophetic vision, but from a diversity of species, whence similitudes also result. Therefore it seems that in prophetic revelation new species of things are impressed, and not merely an intellectual light.

*I answer that,* As Augustine says (Gen. ad lit. xii, 9), "prophetic knowledge pertains most of all to the intellect." Now two things have to be considered in connection with the knowledge possessed by the human mind, namely the acceptance or representation of things, and the judgment of the things represented. Now things are represented to the human mind under the form of species: and according to the order of nature, they must be represented first to the senses, secondly to the imagination, thirdly to the passive intellect, and these are changed by the species derived from the phantasms, which change results from the enlightening action of the active intellect. Now in the imagination there are the forms of sensible things not only as received from the senses, but also transformed in various ways, either on account of some bodily transformation (as in the case of people who are asleep or out of their senses), or through the coordination of the phantasms, at the command of reason, for the purpose of understanding something. For just as the various arrangements of the letters of the alphabet convey various ideas to the understanding, so the various coordinations of the phantasms produce various intelligible species of the intellect.

As to the judgment formed by the human mind, it depends on the power of the intellectual light.

Now the gift of prophecy confers on the human mind something which surpasses the natural faculty in both these respects, namely as to the judgment which depends on the inflow of intellectual light, and as to the acceptance or representation of things, which is effected by means of certain species. Human teaching may be likened to prophetic revelation in the second of these respects, but not in the first. For a man represents certain things to his disciple by signs of speech, but he cannot enlighten him inwardly as God does.

But it is the first of these two that holds the chief place in prophecy, since judgment is the complement of knowledge. Wherefore if certain things are divinely represented to any man by means of imaginary likenesses, as happened to Pharaoh (Gen. 41:1-7) and to Nabuchodonosor (Dan. 4:1-2), or even by bodily likenesses, as happened to Balthasar (Dan. 5:5), such a man is not to be considered a prophet, unless his mind be enlightened for the purpose of judgment; and such an apparition is something imperfect in the genus of prophecy. Wherefore some [*Rabbi Moyses, Doct. Perplex. II, xxxvi] have called this "prophetic ecstasy," and such is divination by dreams. And yet a man will be a prophet, if his intellect be enlightened merely for the purpose of judging of things seen in imagination by others, as in the case of Joseph who interpreted Pharaoh's dream. But, as Augustine says (Gen. ad lit. xii, 9), "especially is he a prophet who excels in both respects, so," to wit, "as to see in spirit likenesses significant of things corporeal, and understand them by the quickness of his intellect."

Now sensible forms are divinely presented to the prophet's mind, sometimes externally by means of the senses—thus Daniel saw the writing on the wall (Dan. 5:25)—sometimes by means of imaginary forms, either of exclusively Divine origin and not received through the senses (for instance, if images of colors were imprinted on the imagination of one blind from birth), or divinely coordinated from those derived from the senses—thus Jeremiah saw the "boiling caldron ... from the face of the north" (Jer. 1:13)—or by the direct impression of intelligible species on the mind, as in the case of those who receive infused scientific knowledge or wisdom, such as Solomon or the apostles.

But intellectual light is divinely imprinted on the human mind—sometimes for the purpose of judging of things seen by others, as in the case of Joseph, quoted above, and of the apostles whose understanding our Lord opened "that they might understand the scriptures" (Luke 24:45); and to this pertains the "interpretation of speeches"—sometimes for the purpose of judging according to Divine truth, of the things which a man apprehends in the ordinary course of nature—sometimes for the purpose of discerning truthfully and efficaciously what is to be done, according to Isa. 63:14, "The Spirit of the Lord was their leader."

Hence it is evident that prophetic revelation is conveyed sometimes by the mere infusion of light, sometimes by imprinting species anew, or by a new coordination of species.

Reply Obj. 1: As stated above, sometimes in prophetic revelation imaginary species previously derived from the senses are divinely coordinated so as to accord with the truth to be revealed, and then previous experience is operative in the production of the images, but not when they are impressed on the mind wholly from without.

Reply Obj. 2: Intellectual vision is not effected by means of bodily and individual images, but by an intelligible image. Hence Augustine says (De Trin. ix, 11) that "the soul possesses a certain likeness of the species known to it." Sometimes this intelligible image is, in prophetic revelation, imprinted immediately by God, sometimes it results from pictures in the imagination, by the aid of the prophetic light, since a deeper truth is gathered from these pictures in the imagination by means of the enlightenment of the higher light.

Reply Obj. 3: It is true that man is able by his natural powers to form all kinds of pictures in the imagination, by simply considering these pictures, but not so that they be directed to the representation of intelligible truths that surpass his intellect, since for this purpose he needs the assistance of a supernatural light.

THIRD ARTICLE [II-II, Q. 173, Art. 3]

Whether the Prophetic Vision Is Always Accompanied by Abstraction from the Senses?

Objection 1: It would seem that the prophetic vision is always accompanied by abstraction from the senses. For it is written (Num. 12:6): "If there be among you a prophet of the Lord, I will appear to him in a vision, or I will speak to him in a dream." Now a gloss says at the beginning of the Psalter, "a vision that takes place by dreams and apparitions consists of things which seem to be said or done." But when things seem to be said or done, which are neither said nor done, there is abstraction from the senses. Therefore prophecy is always accompanied by abstraction from the senses.

Obj. 2: Further, when one power is very intent on its own operation, other powers are drawn away from theirs; thus men who are very intent on hearing something fail to see what takes place before them. Now in the prophetic vision the intellect is very much uplifted, and intent on its act. Therefore it seems that the prophetic vision is always accompanied by abstraction from the senses.

Obj. 3: Further, the same thing cannot, at the same time, tend in opposite directions. Now in the prophetic vision the mind tends to the acceptance of things from above, and consequently it cannot at the same time tend to sensible objects. Therefore it would seem necessary for prophetic revelation to be always accompanied by abstraction from the senses.

Obj. 4: *On the contrary,* It is written (1 Cor. 14:32): "The spirits of the prophets are subject to the prophets." Now this were impossible if the prophet were not in possession of his faculties, but abstracted from his senses. Therefore it would seem that prophetic vision is not accompanied by abstraction from the senses.

*I answer that,* As stated in the foregoing Article, the prophetic revelation takes place in four ways: namely, by the infusion of an intelligible light, by the infusion of intelligible species, by impression or coordination of pictures in the imagination, and by the outward presentation of sensible images. Now it is evident that there is no abstraction from the senses, when something is presented to the prophet's mind by means of sensible species—whether these be divinely formed for this special purpose, as the bush shown to Moses (Ex. 3:2), and the writing shown to Daniel (Dan. 5:)—or whether they be produced by other causes; yet so that they are ordained by Divine providence to be prophetically significant of something, as, for instance, the Church was signified by the ark of Noah.

Again, abstraction from the external senses is not rendered necessary when the prophet's mind is enlightened by an intellectual light, or impressed with intelligible species, since in us the perfect judgment of the intellect is effected by its turning to sensible objects, which are the first principles of our knowledge, as stated in the First Part (Q. 84, A. 6).

When, however, prophetic revelation is conveyed by images in the imagination, abstraction from the senses is necessary lest the things thus seen in imagination be taken for objects of external sensation. Yet this abstraction from the senses is sometimes complete, so that a man perceives nothing with his senses; and sometimes it is incomplete, so that he perceives something with his senses, yet does not fully discern the things he perceives outwardly from those he sees in imagination. Hence Augustine says (Gen. ad lit. xii, 12): "Those images of bodies which are formed in the soul are seen just as bodily things themselves are seen by the body, so that we see with our eyes one who is present, and at the same time we see with the soul one who is absent, as though we saw him with our eyes."

Yet this abstraction from the senses takes place in the prophets without subverting the order of nature, as is the case with those who are possessed or out of their senses; but is due to some well-ordered cause. This cause may be natural—for instance, sleep—or spiritual—for instance, the intenseness of the prophets' contemplation; thus we read of Peter (Acts 10:9) that while he was praying in the supper-room [*Vulg.: 'the house-top' or 'upper-chamber'] "he fell into an ecstasy"—or he may be carried away by the Divine power, according to the saying of Ezechiel 1:3: "The hand of the Lord was upon him."

Reply Obj. 1: The passage quoted refers to prophets in whom imaginary pictures were formed or coordinated, either while asleep, which is denoted by the word "dream," or while awake, which is signified by the word "vision."

Reply Obj. 2: When the mind is intent, in its act, upon distant things which are far removed from the senses, the intensity of its application leads to abstraction from the senses; but when it is intent, in its act, upon the coordination of or judgment concerning objects of sense, there is no need for abstraction from the senses.

Reply Obj. 3: The movement of the prophetic mind results not from its own power, but from a power acting on it from above. Hence there is no abstraction from the senses when the prophet's mind is led to judge or coordinate matters relating to objects of sense, but only when the mind is raised to the contemplation of certain more lofty things.

Reply Obj. 4: The spirit of the prophets is said to be subject to the prophets as regards the prophetic utterances to which the Apostle refers in the words quoted; because, to wit, the prophets in declaring what they have seen speak their own mind, and are not thrown off their mental balance, like persons who are possessed, as Priscilla and Montanus maintained. But as regards the prophetic revelation itself, it would be more correct to say that the prophets are subject to the spirit of prophecy, i.e. to the prophetic gift.

FOURTH ARTICLE [II-II, Q. 173, Art. 4]

Whether Prophets Always Know the Things Which They Prophesy?

Objection 1: It would seem that the prophets always know the things which they prophesy. For, as Augustine says (Gen. ad lit. xii, 9), "those to whom signs were shown in spirit by means of the likenesses of bodily things, had not the gift of prophecy, unless the mind was brought into action, so that those signs were also understood by them." Now what is understood cannot be unknown. Therefore the prophet is not ignorant of what he prophesies.

Obj. 2: Further, the light of prophecy surpasses the light of natural reason. Now one who possesses a science by his natural light, is not ignorant of his scientific acquirements. Therefore he who utters things by the prophetic light cannot ignore them.

Obj. 3: Further, prophecy is directed for man's enlightenment; wherefore it is written (2 Pet. 1:19): "We have the more firm prophetical word, whereunto you do well to attend, as to a light that shineth in a dark place." Now nothing can enlighten others unless it be lightsome in itself. Therefore it would seem that the prophet is first enlightened so as to know what he declares to others.

*On the contrary,* It is written (John 11:51): "And this he" (Caiphas) "spoke, not of himself, but being the High Priest of that year, he prophesied that Jesus should die for the nation," etc. Now Caiphas knew this not. Therefore not every prophet knows what he prophesies.

*I answer that,* In prophetic revelation the prophet's mind is moved by the Holy Ghost, as an instrument that is deficient in regard to the principal agent. Now the prophet's mind is moved not only to apprehend something, but also to speak or to do something; sometimes indeed to all these three together, sometimes to two, sometimes to one only, and in each case there may be a defect in the prophet's knowledge. For when the prophet's mind is moved to think or apprehend a thing, sometimes he is led merely to apprehend that thing, and sometimes he is further led to know that it is divinely revealed to him.

Again, sometimes the prophet's mind is moved to speak something, so that he understands what the Holy Ghost means by the words he utters; like David who said (2 Kings 23:2): "The Spirit of the Lord hath spoken by me"; while, on the other hand, sometimes the person whose mind is moved to utter certain words knows not what the Holy Ghost means by them, as was the case with Caiphas (John 11:51).

Again, when the Holy Ghost moves a man's mind to do something, sometimes the latter understands the meaning of it, like Jeremias who hid his loin-cloth in the Euphrates (Jer. 13:1-11); while sometimes he does not understand it—thus the soldiers, who divided Christ's garments, understood not the meaning of what they did.

Accordingly, when a man knows that he is being moved by the Holy Ghost to think something, or signify something by word or deed, this belongs properly to prophecy; whereas when he is moved, without his knowing it, this is not perfect prophecy, but a prophetic instinct. Nevertheless it must be observed that since the prophet's mind is a defective instrument, as stated above, even true prophets know not all that the Holy Ghost means by the things they see, or speak, or even do.

And this suffices for the Replies to the Objections, since the arguments given at the beginning refer to true prophets whose minds are perfectly enlightened from above.

## QUESTION 174

OF THE DIVISION OF PROPHECY (SIX ARTICLES)

We must now consider the division of prophecy, and under this head there are six points of inquiry:

(1) The division of prophecy into its species;

(2) Whether the more excellent prophecy is that which is without imaginative vision?

(3) The various degrees of prophecy;

(4) Whether Moses was the greatest of the prophets?

(5) Whether a comprehensor can be a prophet?

(6) Whether prophecy advanced in perfection as time went on?

FIRST ARTICLE [II-II, Q. 174, Art. 1]

Whether Prophecy Is Fittingly Divided into the Prophecy of Divine Predestination, of Foreknowledge, and of Denunciation?

Objection 1: It would seem that prophecy is unfittingly divided according to a gloss on Matt. 1:23, "Behold a virgin shall be with child," where it is stated that "one kind of prophecy proceeds from the Divine predestination, and must in all respects be accomplished so that its fulfillment is independent of our will, for instance the one in question. Another prophecy proceeds from God's foreknowledge: and into this our will enters. And another prophecy is called denunciation, which is significative of God's disapproval." For that which results from every prophecy should not be reckoned a part of prophecy. Now all prophecy is according to the Divine foreknowledge, since the prophets "read in the book of foreknowledge," as a gloss says on Isa. 38:1. Therefore it would seem that prophecy according to foreknowledge should not be reckoned a species of prophecy.

Obj. 2: Further, just as something is foretold in denunciation, so is something foretold in promise, and both of these are subject to alteration. For it is written (Jer. 18:7, 8): "I will suddenly speak against a nation and against a kingdom, to root out, and to pull down, and to destroy it. If that nation against which I have spoken shall repent of their evil, I also will repent"—and this pertains to the prophecy of denunciation, and afterwards the text continues in reference to the prophecy of promise (Jer. 18:9, 10): "I will suddenly speak of a nation and of a kingdom, to build up and plant it. If it shall do evil in My sight ... I will repent of the good that I have spoken to do unto it." Therefore as there is reckoned to be a prophecy of denunciation, so should there be a prophecy of promise.

Obj. 3: Further, Isidore says (Etym. vii, 8): "There are seven kinds of prophecy. The first is an ecstasy, which is the transport of the mind: thus Peter saw a vessel descending from heaven with all manner of beasts therein. The second kind is a vision, as we read in Isaias, who says (Isa. 6:1): 'I saw the Lord sitting,' etc. The third kind is a dream: thus Jacob in a dream, saw a ladder. The fourth kind is from the midst of a cloud: thus God spake to Moses. The fifth kind is a voice from heaven, as that which called to Abraham saying (Gen. 22:11): 'Lay not thy hand upon the boy.' The sixth kind is taking up a parable, as in the example of Balaam (Num. 23:7; 24:15). The seventh kind is the fullness of the Holy Ghost, as in the case of nearly all the prophets." Further, he mentions three kinds of vision; "one by the eyes of the body, another by the soul's imagination, a third by the eyes of the mind." Now these are not included in the aforesaid division. Therefore it is insufficient.

*On the contrary,* stands the authority of Jerome to whom the gloss above quoted is ascribed.

*I answer that,* The species of moral habits and acts are distinguished according to their objects. Now the object of prophecy is something known by God and surpassing the faculty of man. Wherefore, according to the difference of such things, prophecy is divided into various species, as assigned above. Now it has been stated above (Q. 71, A. 6, ad 2) that the future is contained in the Divine knowledge in two ways. First, as in its cause: and thus we have the prophecy of *denunciation,* which is not always fulfilled. but it foretells the relation of cause to effect, which is sometimes hindered by some other occurrence supervening. Secondly, God foreknows certain things in themselves—either as to be accomplished by Himself, and of such things is the prophecy of *predestination,* since, according to Damascene (De Fide Orth. ii, 30), "God predestines things which are not in our power"—or as to be accomplished through man's free-will, and of such is the prophecy of *foreknowledge.* This may regard either good or evil, which does not apply to the prophecy of predestination, since the latter regards good alone. And since predestination is comprised under foreknowledge, the gloss in the beginning of the Psalter assigns only two species to prophecy, namely of *foreknowledge,* and of *denunciation.*

Reply Obj. 1: Foreknowledge, properly speaking, denotes precognition of future events in themselves, and in this sense it is reckoned a species of prophecy. But in so far as it is used in connection with future events, whether as in themselves, or as in their causes, it is common to every species of prophecy.

Reply Obj. 2: The prophecy of promise is included in the prophecy of denunciation, because the aspect of truth is the same in both. But it is denominated in preference from denunciation, because God is more inclined to remit punishment than to withdraw promised blessings.

Reply Obj. 3: Isidore divides prophecy according to the manner of prophesying. Now we may distinguish the manner of prophesying—either according to man's cognitive powers, which are sense, imagination, and intellect, and then we have the three kinds of vision mentioned both by him and by Augustine (Gen. ad lit. xii, 6, 7)—or according to the different ways in which the prophetic current is received. Thus as regards the enlightening of the intellect there is the "fullness of the Holy Ghost" which he mentions in the seventh place. As to the imprinting of pictures on the imagination he mentions three, namely "dreams," to which he gives the third place; "vision," which occurs to the prophet while awake and regards any kind of ordinary object, and this he puts in the second place; and "ecstasy," which results from the mind being uplifted to certain lofty things, and to this he assigns the first place. As regards sensible signs he reckons three kinds of prophecy, because a sensible sign is—either a corporeal thing offered externally to the sight, such as "a cloud," which he mentions in the fourth place—or a "voice" sounding from without and conveyed to man's hearing—this he puts in the fifth place—or a voice proceeding from a man, conveying something under a similitude, and this pertains to the "parable" to which he assigns the sixth place.

SECOND ARTICLE [II-II, Q. 174, Art. 2]

Whether the Prophecy Which Is Accompanied by Intellective and Imaginative Vision Is More Excellent Than That Which Is Accompanied by Intellective Vision Alone?

Objection 1: It would seem that the prophecy which has intellective and imaginative vision is more excellent than that which is accompanied by intellective vision alone. For Augustine says (Gen. ad lit. xii, 9): "He is less a prophet, who sees in spirit nothing but the signs representative of things, by means of the images of things corporeal: he is more a prophet, who is merely endowed with the understanding of these signs; but most of all is he a prophet, who excels in both ways," and this refers to the prophet who has intellective together with imaginative vision. Therefore this kind of prophecy is more excellent.

Obj. 2: Further, the greater a thing's power is, the greater the distance to which it extends. Now the prophetic light pertains chiefly to the mind, as stated above (Q. 173, A. 2). Therefore apparently the prophecy that extends to the imagination is greater than that which is confined to the intellect.

Obj. 3: Further, Jerome (Prol. in Lib. Reg.) distinguishes the "prophets" from the "sacred writers." Now all those whom he calls prophets (such as Isaias, Jeremias, and the like) had intellective together with imaginative vision: but not those whom he calls sacred writers, as writing by the inspiration of the Holy Ghost (such as Job, David, Solomon, and the like). Therefore it would seem more proper to call prophets those who had intellective together with imaginative vision, than those who had intellective vision alone.

Obj. 4: Further, Dionysius says (Coel. Hier. i) that "it is impossible for the Divine ray to shine on us, except as screened round about by the many-colored sacred veils." Now the prophetic revelation is conveyed by the infusion of the divine ray. Therefore it seems that it cannot be without the veils of phantasms.

*On the contrary,* A gloss says at the beginning of the Psalter that "the most excellent manner of prophecy is when a man prophesies by the mere inspiration of the Holy Ghost, apart from any outward assistance of deed, word, vision, or dream."

*I answer that,* The excellence of the means is measured chiefly by the end. Now the end of prophecy is the manifestation of a truth that surpasses the faculty of man. Wherefore the more effective this manifestation is, the more excellent the prophecy. But it is evident that the manifestation of divine truth by means of the bare contemplation of the truth itself, is more effective than that which is conveyed under the similitude of corporeal things, for it approaches nearer to the heavenly vision whereby the truth is seen in God's essence. Hence it follows that the prophecy whereby a supernatural truth is seen by intellectual vision, is more excellent than that in which a supernatural truth is manifested by means of the similitudes of corporeal things in the vision of the imagination.

Moreover the prophet's mind is shown thereby to be more lofty: even as in human teaching the hearer, who is able to grasp the bare intelligible truth the master propounds, is shown to have a better understanding than one who needs to be taken by the hand and helped by means of examples taken from objects of sense. Hence it is said in commendation of David's prophecy (2 Kings 23:3): "The strong one of Israel spoke to me," and further on (2 Kings 23:4): "As the light of the morning, when the sun riseth, shineth in the morning without clouds."

Reply Obj. 1: When a particular supernatural truth has to be revealed by means of corporeal images, he that has both, namely the intellectual light and the imaginary vision, is more a prophet than he that has only one, because his prophecy is more perfect; and it is in this sense that Augustine speaks as quoted above. Nevertheless the prophecy in which the bare intelligible truth is revealed is greater than all.

Reply Obj. 2: The same judgment does not apply to things that are sought for their own sake, as to things sought for the sake of something else. For in things sought for their own sake, the agent's power is the more effective according as it extends to more numerous and more remote objects; even so a physician is thought more of, if he is able to heal more people, and those who are further removed from health. On the other hand, in things sought only for the sake of something else, that agent would seem to have greater power, who is able to achieve his purpose with fewer means and those nearest to hand: thus more praise is awarded the physician who is able to heal a sick person by means of fewer and more gentle remedies. Now, in the prophetic knowledge, imaginary vision is required, not for its own sake, but on account of the manifestation of the intelligible truth. Wherefore prophecy is all the more excellent according as it needs it less.

Reply Obj. 3: The fact that a particular predicate

is applicable to one thing and less properly to another, does not prevent this latter from being simply better than the former: thus the knowledge of the blessed is more excellent than the knowledge of the wayfarer, although faith is more properly predicated of the latter knowledge, because faith implies an imperfection of knowledge. In like manner prophecy implies a certain obscurity, and remoteness from the intelligible truth; wherefore the name of prophet is more properly applied to those who see by imaginary vision. And yet the more excellent prophecy is that which is conveyed by intellectual vision, provided the same truth be revealed in either case. If, however, the intellectual light be divinely infused in a person, not that he may know some supernatural things, but that he may be able to judge, with the certitude of divine truth, of things that can be known by human reason, such intellectual prophecy is beneath that which is conveyed by an imaginary vision leading to a supernatural truth. It was this kind of prophecy that all those had who are included in the ranks of the prophets, who moreover were called prophets for the special reason that they exercised the prophetic calling officially. Hence they spoke as God's representatives, saying to the people: "Thus saith the Lord": but not so the authors of the *sacred writings,* several of whom treated more frequently of things that can be known by human reason, not in God's name, but in their own, yet with the assistance of the Divine light withal.

Reply Obj. 4: In the present life the enlightenment by the divine ray is not altogether without any veil of phantasms, because according to his present state of life it is unnatural to man not to understand without a phantasm. Sometimes, however, it is sufficient to have phantasms abstracted in the usual way from the senses without any imaginary vision divinely vouchsafed, and thus prophetic vision is said to be without imaginary vision.

THIRD ARTICLE [II-II, Q. 174, Art. 3]

Whether the Degrees of Prophecy Can Be Distinguished According to the Imaginary Vision?

Objection 1: It would seem that the degrees of prophecy cannot be distinguished according to the imaginary vision. For the degrees of a thing bear relation to something that is on its own account, not on account of something else. Now, in prophecy, intellectual vision is sought on its own account, and imaginary vision on account of something else, as stated above (A. 2, ad 2). Therefore it would seem that the degrees of prophecy are distinguished not according to imaginary, but only according to intellectual, vision.

Obj. 2: Further, seemingly for one prophet there is one degree of prophecy. Now one prophet receives revelation through various imaginary visions. Therefore a difference of imaginary visions does not entail a difference of prophecy.

Obj. 3: Further, according to a gloss [*Cassiodorus, super Prolog. Hieron. in Psalt.], prophecy consists of words, deeds, dreams, and visions. Therefore the degrees of prophecy should not be distinguished according to imaginary vision, to which vision and dreams pertain, rather than according to words and deeds.

*On the contrary,* The medium differentiates the degrees of knowledge: thus science based on direct [* *Propter quid* ] proofs is more excellent than science based on indirect [* *Quia* ] premises or than opinion, because it comes through a more excellent medium. Now imaginary vision is a kind of medium in prophetic knowledge. Therefore the degrees of prophecy should be distinguished according to imaginary vision.

*I answer that,* As stated above (Q. 173, A. 2), the prophecy wherein, by the intelligible light, a supernatural truth is revealed through an imaginary vision, holds the mean between the prophecy wherein a supernatural truth is revealed without imaginary vision, and that wherein through the intelligible light and without an imaginary vision, man is directed to know or do things pertaining to human conduct. Now knowledge is more proper to prophecy than is action; wherefore the lowest degree of prophecy is when a man, by an inward instinct, is moved to perform some outward action. Thus it is related of Samson (Judges 15:14) that "the Spirit of the Lord came strongly upon him, and as the flax [* *Lina.* St. Thomas apparently read *ligna* ('wood')] is wont to be consumed at the approach of fire, so the bands with which he was bound were broken and loosed." The second degree of prophecy is when a man is enlightened by an inward light so as to know certain things, which, however, do not go beyond the bounds of natural knowledge: thus it is related of Solomon (3 Kings 4:32, 33) that "he spoke ... parables ... and he treated about trees from the cedar that is in Libanus unto the hyssop that cometh out of the wall, and he discoursed of beasts and of fowls, and of creeping things and of fishes": and all of this came from divine inspiration, for it was stated previously (3 Kings 4:29): "God gave to Solomon wisdom and understanding exceeding much."

Nevertheless these two degrees are beneath prophecy properly so called, because they do not attain to supernatural truth. The prophecy wherein supernatural truth is manifested through imaginary vision is differentiated first according to the difference between dreams which occur during sleep, and vision which occurs while one is awake. The latter belongs to a higher degree of prophecy, since the prophetic light that draws the soul away to supernatural things while it is awake and occupied with sensible things would seem to be stronger than that which finds a man's soul asleep and withdrawn from objects of sense. Secondly the degrees of this prophecy are differentiated according to the expressiveness of the imaginary signs whereby the intelligible truth is conveyed. And since words are the most expressive signs of intelligible truth, it would seem to be a higher degree of prophecy when the prophet, whether awake or asleep, hears words expressive of an intelligible truth, than when he sees things significative of truth, for instance "the seven full ears of corn" signified "seven years of plenty" (Gen. 41:22, 26). In such like signs prophecy would seem to be the more excellent, according as the signs are more expressive, for instance when Jeremias saw the burning of the city under the figure of a boiling cauldron (Jer. 1:13). Thirdly, it is evidently a still higher degree of prophecy when a prophet not only sees signs of words or deeds, but also, either awake or asleep, sees someone speaking or showing something to him, since this proves the prophet's mind to have approached nearer to the cause of the revelation. Fourthly, the height of a degree of prophecy may be measured according to the appearance of the person seen: for it is a higher degree of prophecy, if he who speaks or shows something to the waking or sleeping prophet be seen by him under the form of an angel, than if he be seen by him under the form of man: and higher still is it, if he be seen by the prophet whether asleep or awake, under the appearance of God, according to Isa. 6:1, "I saw the Lord sitting."

But above all these degrees there is a third kind of prophecy, wherein an intelligible and supernatural truth is shown without any imaginary vision. However, this goes beyond the bounds of prophecy properly so called, as stated above (A. 2, ad 3); and consequently the degrees of prophecy are properly distinguished according to imaginary vision.

Reply Obj. 1: We are unable to know how to distinguish the intellectual light, except by means of imaginary or sensible signs. Hence the difference in the intellectual light is gathered from the difference in the things presented to the imagination.

Reply Obj. 2: As stated above (Q. 171, A. 2), prophecy is by way, not of an abiding habit, but of a transitory passion; wherefore there is nothing inconsistent if one and the same prophet, at different times, receive various degrees of prophetic revelation.

Reply Obj. 3: The words and deeds mentioned there do not pertain to the prophetic revelation, but to the announcement, which is made according to the disposition of those to whom that which is revealed to the prophet is announced; and this is done sometimes by words, sometimes by deeds. Now this announcement, and the working of miracles, are something consequent upon prophecy, as stated above (Q. 171, A. 1).

FOURTH ARTICLE [II-II, Q. 174, Art. 4]

Whether Moses Was the Greatest of the Prophets?

Objection 1: It would seem that Moses was not the greatest of the prophets. For a gloss at the beginning of the Psalter says that "David is called the prophet by way of excellence." Therefore Moses was not the greatest of all.

Obj. 2: Further, greater miracles were wrought by Josue, who made the sun and moon to stand still (Josh. 10:12-14), and by Isaias, who made the sun to turn back (Isa. 38:8), than by Moses, who divided the Red Sea (Ex. 14:21). In like manner greater miracles were wrought by Elias, of whom it is written (Ecclus. 48:4, 5): "Who can glory like to thee? Who raisedst up a dead man from below." Therefore Moses was not the greatest of the prophets.

Obj. 3: Further, it is written (Matt. 11:11) that "there hath not risen, among them that are born of women, a greater than John the Baptist." Therefore Moses was not greater than all the prophets.

*On the contrary,* It is written (Deut. 34:10): "There arose no more a prophet in Israel like unto Moses."

*I answer that,* Although in some respect one or other of the prophets was greater than Moses, yet Moses was simply the greatest of all. For, as stated above (A. 3; Q. 171, A. 1), in prophecy we may consider not only the knowledge, whether by intellectual or by imaginary vision, but also the announcement and the confirmation by miracles. Accordingly Moses was greater than the other prophets. First, as regards the intellectual vision, since he saw God's very essence, even as Paul in his rapture did, according to Augustine (Gen. ad lit. xii, 27). Hence it is written (Num. 12:8) that he saw God "plainly and not by riddles." Secondly, as regards the imaginary vision, which he had at his call, as it were, for not only did he hear words, but also saw one speaking to him under the form of God, and this not only while asleep, but even when he was awake. Hence it is written (Ex. 33:11) that "the Lord spoke to Moses face to face, as a man is wont to speak to his friend." Thirdly, as regards the working of miracles which he wrought on a whole nation of unbelievers. Wherefore it is written (Deut. 34:10, 11): "There arose no more a prophet in Israel like unto Moses, whom the Lord knew face to face: in all the signs and wonders, which He sent by him, to do in the land of Egypt to Pharaoh, and to all his servants, and to his whole land."

Reply Obj. 1: The prophecy of David approaches near to the vision of Moses, as regards the intellectual vision, because both received a revelation of intelligible and supernatural truth, without any imaginary vision. Yet the vision of Moses was more excellent as regards the knowledge of the Godhead; while David more fully knew and expressed the mysteries of Christ's incarnation.

Reply Obj. 2: These signs of the prophets mentioned were greater as to the substance of the thing done; yet the miracles of Moses were greater as regards the way in which they were done, since they were wrought on a whole people.

Reply Obj. 3: John belongs to the New Testament, whose ministers take precedence even of

Moses, since they are spectators of a fuller revelation, as stated in 2 Cor. 3.

FIFTH ARTICLE [II-II, Q. 174, Art. 6]

Whether There Is a Degree of Prophecy in the Blessed?

Objection 1: It would seem that there is a degree of prophecy in the blessed. For, as stated above (A. 4), Moses saw the Divine essence, and yet he is called a prophet. Therefore in like manner the blessed can be called prophets.

Obj. 2: Further, prophecy is a "divine revelation." Now divine revelations are made even to the blessed angels. Therefore even blessed angels can be prophets.

Obj. 3: Further, Christ was a comprehensor from the moment of His conception; and yet He calls Himself a prophet (Matt. 13:57), when He says: "A prophet is not without honor, save in his own country." Therefore even comprehensors and the blessed can be called prophets.

Obj. 4: Further, it is written of Samuel (Ecclus. 46:23): "He lifted up his voice from the earth in prophecy to blot out the wickedness of the nation." Therefore other saints can likewise be called prophets after they have died.

*On the contrary,* The prophetic word is compared (2 Pet. 1:19) to a "light that shineth in a dark place." Now there is no darkness in the blessed. Therefore they cannot be called prophets.

*I answer that,* Prophecy denotes vision of some supernatural truth as being far remote from us. This happens in two ways. First, on the part of the knowledge itself, because, to wit, the supernatural truth is not known in itself, but in some of its effects; and this truth will be more remote if it be known by means of images of corporeal things, than if it be known in its intelligible effects; and such most of all is the prophetic vision, which is conveyed by images and likenesses of corporeal things. Secondly, vision is remote on the part of the seer, because, to wit, he has not yet attained completely to his ultimate perfection, according to 2 Cor. 5:6, "While we are in the body, we are absent from the Lord."

Now in neither of these ways are the blessed remote; wherefore they cannot be called prophets.

Reply Obj. 1: This vision of Moses was interrupted after the manner of a passion, and was not permanent like the beatific vision, wherefore he was as yet a seer from afar. For this reason his vision did not entirely lose the character of prophecy.

Reply Obj. 2: The divine revelation is made to the angels, not as being far distant, but as already wholly united to God; wherefore their revelation has not the character of prophecy.

Reply Obj. 3: Christ was at the same time comprehensor and wayfarer [*Cf. III, QQ. 9, seqq.]. Consequently the notion of prophecy is not applicable to Him as a comprehensor, but only as a wayfarer.

Reply Obj. 4: Samuel had not yet attained to the state of blessedness. Wherefore although by God's will the soul itself of Samuel foretold to Saul the issue of the war as revealed to him by God, this pertains to the nature of prophecy. It is not the same with the saints who are now in heaven. Nor does it make any difference that this is stated to have been brought about by the demons' art, because although the demons are unable to evoke the soul of a saint, or to force it to do any particular thing, this can be done by the power of God, so that when the demon is consulted, God Himself declares the truth by His messenger: even as He gave a true answer by Elias to the King's messengers who were sent to consult the god of Accaron (4 Kings 1).

It might also be replied [*The Book of Ecclesiasticus was not as yet declared by the Church to be Canonical Scripture; Cf. I, Q. 89, A. 8, ad 2] that it was not the soul of Samuel, but a demon impersonating him; and that the wise man calls him Samuel, and describes his prediction as prophetic, in accordance with the thoughts of Saul and the bystanders who were of this opinion.

SIXTH ARTICLE [II-II, Q. 174, Art. 6]

Whether the Degrees of Prophecy Change As Time Goes On?

Objection 1: It would seem that the degrees of prophecy change as time goes on. For prophecy is directed to the knowledge of Divine things, as stated above (A. 2). Now according to Gregory (Hom. in Ezech.), "knowledge of God went on increasing as time went on." Therefore degrees of prophecy should be distinguished according to the process of time.

Obj. 2: Further, prophetic revelation is conveyed by God speaking to man; while the prophets declared both in words and in writing the things revealed to them. Now it is written (1 Kings 3:1) that before the time of Samuel "the word of the Lord was precious," i.e. rare; and yet afterwards it was delivered to many. In like manner the books of the prophets do not appear to have been written before the time of Isaias, to whom it was said (Isa. 8:1): "Take thee a great book and write in it with a man's pen," after which many prophets wrote their prophecies. Therefore it would seem that in course of time the degree of prophecy made progress.

Obj. 3: Further, our Lord said (Matt. 11:13): "The prophets and the law prophesied until John"; and afterwards the gift of prophecy was in Christ's disciples in a much more excellent manner than in the prophets of old, according to Eph. 3:5, "In other generations" the mystery of Christ "was not known to the sons of men, as it is now revealed to His holy apostles and prophets in the Spirit." Therefore it would seem that in course of time the degree of prophecy advanced.

*On the contrary,* As stated above (A. 4), Moses was the greatest of the prophets, and yet he preceded the other prophets. Therefore prophecy did not advance in degree as time went on.

*I answer that,* As stated above (A. 2), prophecy is directed to the knowledge of Divine truth, by the contemplation of which we are not only instructed in faith, but also guided in our actions, according to Ps. 42:3, "Send forth Thy light and Thy truth: they have conducted me." Now our faith consists chiefly in two things: first, in the true knowledge of God, according to Heb. 11:6, "He that cometh to God must believe that He is"; secondly, in the mystery of Christ's incarnation, according to John 14:1, "You believe in God, believe also in Me." Accordingly, if we speak of prophecy as directed to the Godhead as its end, it progressed according to three divisions of time, namely before the law, under the law, and under grace. For before the law, Abraham and the other patriarchs were prophetically taught things pertinent to faith in the Godhead. Hence they are called prophets, according to Ps. 104:15, "Do no evil to My prophets," which words are said especially on behalf of Abraham and Isaac. Under the Law prophetic revelation of things pertinent to faith in the Godhead was made in a yet more excellent way than hitherto, because then not only certain special persons or families but the whole people had to be instructed in these matters. Hence the Lord said to Moses (Ex. 6:2, 3): "I am the Lord that appeared to Abraham, to Isaac, and to Jacob, by the name of God almighty, and My name Adonai I did not show to them"; because previously the patriarchs had been taught to believe in a general way in God, one and Almighty, while Moses was more fully instructed in the simplicity of the Divine essence, when it was said to him (Ex. 3:14): "I am Who am"; and this name is signified by Jews in the word "Adonai" on account of their veneration for that unspeakable name. Afterwards in the time of grace the mystery of the Trinity was revealed by the Son of God Himself, according to Matt. 28:19: "Going ... teach ye all nations, baptizing them in the name of the Father, and of the Son, and of the Holy Ghost."

In each state, however, the most excellent revelation was that which was given first. Now the first revelation, before the Law, was given to Abraham, for it was at that time that men began to stray from faith in one God by turning aside to idolatry, whereas hitherto no such revelation was necessary while all persevered in the worship of one God. A less excellent revelation was made to Isaac, being founded on that which was made to Abraham. Wherefore it was said to him (Gen. 26:24): "I am the God of Abraham thy father," and in like manner to Jacob (Gen. 28:13): "I am the God of Abraham thy father, and the God of Isaac." Again in the state of the Law the first revelation which was given to Moses was more excellent, and on this revelation all the other revelations to the prophets were founded. And so, too, in the time of grace the entire faith of the Church is founded on the revelation vouchsafed to the apostles, concerning the faith in one God and three Persons, according to Matt. 16:18, "On this rock," i.e. of thy confession, "I will build My Church."

As to the faith in Christ's incarnation, it is evident that the nearer men were to Christ, whether before or after Him, the more fully, for the most part, were they instructed on this point, and after Him more fully than before, as the Apostle declares (Eph. 3:5).

As regards the guidance of human acts, the prophetic revelation varied not according to the course of time, but according as circumstances required, because as it is written (Prov. 29:18), "When prophecy shall fail, the people shall be scattered abroad." Wherefore at all times men were divinely instructed about what they were to do, according as it was expedient for the spiritual welfare of the elect.

Reply Obj. 1: The saying of Gregory is to be referred to the time before Christ's incarnation, as regards the knowledge of this mystery.

Reply Obj. 2: As Augustine says (De Civ. Dei xviii, 27), "just as in the early days of the Assyrian kingdom promises were made most explicitly to Abraham, so at the outset of the western Babylon," which is Rome, "and under its sway Christ was to come, in Whom were to be fulfilled the promises made through the prophetic oracles testifying in word and writing to that great event to come," the promises, namely, which were made to Abraham. "For while prophets were scarcely ever lacking to the people of Israel from the time that they began to have kings, it was exclusively for their benefit, not for that of the nations. But when those prophetic writings were being set up with greater publicity, which at some future time were to benefit the nations, it was fitting to begin when this city," Rome to wit, "was being built, which was to govern the nations."

The reason why it behooved that nation to have a number of prophets especially at the time of the kings, was that then it was not over-ridden by other nations, but had its own king; wherefore it behooved the people, as enjoying liberty, to have prophets to teach them what to do.

Reply Obj. 3: The prophets who foretold the coming of Christ could not continue further than John, who with his finger pointed to Christ actually present. Nevertheless as Jerome says on this passage, "This does not mean that there were no more prophets after John. For we read in the Acts of the apostles that Agabus and the four maidens, daughters of Philip, prophesied." John, too, wrote a prophetic book about the end of the Church; and at all times there have not been lacking persons having the spirit of prophecy, not indeed for the declaration of any new doctrine of faith, but for the direction of human acts. Thus Augustine says (De Civ. Dei v, 26) that "the emperor Theodosius sent to John who dwelt in the Egyptian desert, and whom he knew by his ever-increasing fame to be endowed with the prophetic spirit: and from him he received a message assuring him of victory."

## QUESTION 175

OF RAPTURE (In Six Articles)

We must now consider rapture. Under this head there are six points of inquiry:

(1) Whether the soul of man is carried away to things divine?

(2) Whether rapture pertains to the cognitive or to the appetitive power?

(3) Whether Paul when in rapture saw the essence of God?

(4) Whether he was withdrawn from his senses?

(5) Whether, when in that state, his soul was wholly separated from his body?

(6) What did he know, and what did he not know about this matter?

FIRST ARTICLE [II-II, Q. 175, Art. 1]

Whether the Soul of Man Is Carried Away to Things Divine?

Objection 1: It would seem that the soul of man is not carried away to things divine. For some define rapture as "an uplifting by the power of a higher nature, from that which is according to nature to that which is above nature" [*Reference unknown; Cf. De Veritate xiii, 1]. Now it is in accordance with man's nature that he be uplifted to things divine; for Augustine says at the beginning of his Confessions: "Thou madest us, Lord, for Thyself, and our heart is restless, till it rest in Thee." Therefore man's soul is not carried away to things divine.

Obj. 2: Further, Dionysius says (Div. Nom. viii) that "God's justice is seen in this that He treats all things according to their mode and dignity." But it is not in accordance with man's mode and worth that he be raised above what he is according to nature. Therefore it would seem that man's soul is not carried away to things divine.

Obj. 3: Further, rapture denotes violence of some kind. But God rules us not by violence or force, as Damascene says [*De Fide Orth. ii, 30]. Therefore man's soul is not carried away to things divine.

*On the contrary,* The Apostle says (2 Cor. 12:2): "I know a man in Christ ... rapt even to the third heaven." On which words a gloss says: "Rapt, that is to say, uplifted contrary to nature."

*I answer that,* Rapture denotes violence of a kind as stated above (Obj. 3); and "the violent is that which has its principle without, and in which he that suffers violence concurs not at all" (Ethic. iii, 1). Now everything concurs in that to which it tends in accordance with its proper inclination, whether voluntary or natural. Wherefore he who is carried away by some external agent, must be carried to something different from that to which his inclination tends. This difference arises in two ways: in one way from the end of the inclination—for instance a stone, which is naturally inclined to be borne downwards, may be thrown upwards; in another way from the manner of tending—for instance a stone may be thrown downwards with greater velocity than consistent with its natural movement.

Accordingly man's soul also is said to be carried away, in a twofold manner, to that which is contrary to its nature: in one way, as regards the term of transport—as when it is carried away to punishment, according to Ps. 49:22, "Lest He snatch you away, and there be none to deliver you"; in another way, as regards the manner connatural to man, which is that he should understand the truth through sensible things. Hence when he is withdrawn from the apprehension of sensibles, he is said to be carried away, even though he be uplifted to things whereunto he is directed naturally: provided this be not done intentionally, as when a man betakes himself to sleep which is in accordance with nature, wherefore sleep cannot be called rapture, properly speaking.

This withdrawal, whatever its term may be, may arise from a threefold cause. First, from a bodily cause, as happens to those who suffer abstraction from the senses through weakness: secondly, by the power of the demons, as in those who are possessed: thirdly, by the power of God. In this last sense we are now speaking of rapture, whereby a man is uplifted by the spirit of God to things supernatural, and withdrawn from his senses, according to Ezech. 8:3, "The spirit lifted me up between the earth and the heaven, and brought me in the vision of God into Jerusalem."

It must be observed, however, that sometimes a person is said to be carried away, not only through being withdrawn from his senses, but also through being withdrawn from the things to which he was attending, as when a person's mind wanders contrary to his purpose. But this is to use the expression in a less proper signification.

Reply Obj. 1: It is natural to man to tend to divine things through the apprehension of things sensible, according to Rom. 1:20, "The invisible things of God ... are clearly seen, being understood by the things that are made." But the mode, whereby a man is uplifted to divine things and withdrawn from his senses, is not natural to man.

Reply Obj. 2: It belongs to man's mode and dignity that he be uplifted to divine things, from the very fact that he is made to God's image. And since a divine good infinitely surpasses the faculty of man in order to attain that good, he needs the divine assistance which is bestowed on him in every gift of grace. Hence it is not contrary to nature, but above the faculty of nature that man's mind be thus uplifted in rapture by God.

Reply Obj. 3: The saying of Damascene refers to those things which a man does by himself. But as to those things which are beyond the scope of the free-will, man needs to be uplifted by a stronger operation, which in a certain respect may be called force if we consider the mode of operation, but not if we consider its term to which man is directed both by nature and by his intention.

SECOND ARTICLE [II-II, Q. 175, Art. 2]

Whether Rapture Pertains to the Cognitive Rather Than to the Appetitive Power?

Objection 1: It would seem that rapture pertains to the appetitive rather than to the cognitive power. For Dionysius says (Div. Nom. iv): "The Divine love causes ecstasy." Now love pertains to the appetitive power. Therefore so does ecstasy or rapture.

Obj. 2: Further, Gregory says (Dial. ii, 3) that "he who fed the swine debased himself by a dissipated mind and an unclean life; whereas Peter, when the angel delivered him and carried him into ecstasy, was not beside himself, but above himself." Now the prodigal son sank into the depths by his appetite. Therefore in those also who are carried up into the heights it is the appetite that is affected.

Obj. 3: Further, a gloss on Ps. 30:1, "In Thee, O Lord, have I hoped, let me never be confounded," says in explaining the title [*Unto the end, a psalm for David, in an ecstasy]: " *Ekstasis* in Greek signifies in Latin *excessus mentis,* an aberration of the mind. This happens in two ways, either through dread of earthly things or through the mind being rapt in heavenly things and forgetful of this lower world." Now dread of earthly things pertains to the appetite. Therefore rapture of the mind in heavenly things, being placed in opposition to this dread, also pertains to the appetite.

*On the contrary,* A gloss on Ps. 115:2, "I said in my excess: Every man is a liar," says: "We speak of ecstasy, not when the mind wanders through fear, but when it is carried aloft on the wings of revelation." Now revelation pertains to the intellective power. Therefore ecstasy or rapture does also.

*I answer that,* We can speak of rapture in two ways. First, with regard to the term of rapture, and thus, properly speaking, rapture cannot pertain to the appetitive, but only to the cognitive power. For it was stated (A. 1) that rapture is outside the inclination of the person who is rapt; whereas the movement of the appetitive power is an inclination to an appetible good. Wherefore, properly speaking, in desiring something, a man is not rapt, but is moved by himself.

Secondly, rapture may be considered with regard to its cause, and thus it may have a cause on the part of the appetitive power. For from the very fact that the appetite is strongly affected towards something, it may happen, owing to the violence of his affection, that a man is carried away from everything else. Moreover, it has an effect on the appetitive power, when for instance a man delights in the things to which he is rapt. Hence the Apostle said that he was rapt, not only "to the third heaven"—which pertains to the contemplation of the intellect—but also into "paradise," which pertains to the appetite.

Reply Obj. 1: Rapture adds something to ecstasy. For ecstasy means simply a going out of oneself by being placed outside one's proper order [*Cf. I-II, Q. 28, A. 3]; while rapture denotes a certain violence in addition. Accordingly ecstasy may pertain to the appetitive power, as when a man's appetite tends to something outside him, and in this sense Dionysius says that "the Divine love causes ecstasy," inasmuch as it makes man's appetite tend to the object loved. Hence he says afterwards that "even God Himself, the cause of all things, through the overflow of His loving goodness, goes outside Himself in His providence for all beings." But even if this were said expressly of rapture, it would merely signify that love is the cause of rapture.

Reply Obj. 2: There is a twofold appetite in man; to wit, the intellective appetite which is called the will, and the sensitive appetite known as the sensuality. Now it is proper to man that his lower appetite be subject to the higher appetite, and that the higher move the lower. Hence man may become outside himself as regards the appetite, in two ways. In one way, when a man's intellective appetite tends wholly to divine things, and takes no account of those things whereto the sensitive appetite inclines him; thus Dionysius says (Div. Nom. iv) that "Paul being in ecstasy through the vehemence of Divine love" exclaimed: "I live, now not I, but Christ liveth in me."

In another way, when a man tends wholly to things pertaining to the lower appetite, and takes no account of his higher appetite. It is thus that "he who fed the swine debased himself"; and this latter kind of going out of oneself, or being beside oneself, is more akin than the former to the nature of rapture because the higher appetite is more proper to man. Hence when through the violence of his lower appetite a man is withdrawn from the movement of his higher appetite, it is more a case of being withdrawn from that which is proper to him. Yet, because there is no violence therein, since the will is able to resist the passion, it falls short of the true nature of rapture, unless perchance the passion be so strong that it takes away entirely the use of reason, as happens to those who are mad with anger or love.

It must be observed, however, that both these excesses affecting the appetite may cause an excess in the cognitive power, either because the mind is carried away to certain intelligible objects, through being drawn away from objects of sense, or because it is caught up into some imaginary vision or fanciful apparition.

Reply Obj. 3: Just as love is a movement of the appetite with regard to good, so fear is a movement of the appetite with regard to evil. Wherefore either of them may equally cause an aberration of mind;

and all the more since fear arises from love, as Augustine says (De Civ. Dei xiv, 7, 9).

THIRD ARTICLE [II-II, Q. 175, Art. 3]

Whether Paul, When in Rapture, Saw the Essence of God?

Objection 1: It would seem that Paul, when in rapture, did not see the essence of God. For just as we read of Paul that he was rapt to the third heaven, so we read of Peter (Acts 10:10) that "there came upon him an ecstasy of mind." Now Peter, in his ecstasy, saw not God's essence but an imaginary vision. Therefore it would seem that neither did Paul see the essence of God.

Obj. 2: Further, the vision of God is beatific. But Paul, in his rapture, was not beatified; else he would never have returned to the unhappiness of this life, but his body would have been glorified by the overflow from his soul, as will happen to the saints after the resurrection, and this clearly was not the case. Therefore Paul when in rapture saw not the essence of God.

Obj. 3: Further, according to 1 Cor. 13:10-12, faith and hope are incompatible with the vision of the Divine essence. But Paul when in this state had faith and hope. Therefore he saw not the essence of God.

Obj. 4: Further, as Augustine states (Gen. ad lit. xii, 6, 7), "pictures of bodies are seen in the imaginary vision." Now Paul is stated (2 Cor. 12:2, 4) to have seen certain pictures in his rapture, for instance of the "third heaven" and of "paradise." Therefore he would seem to have been rapt to an imaginary vision rather than to the vision of the Divine essence.

*On the contrary,* Augustine (Ep. CXLVII, 13; ad Paulin., de videndo Deum) concludes that "possibly God's very substance was seen by some while yet in this life: for instance by Moses, and by Paul who in rapture heard unspeakable words, which it is not granted unto man to utter."

*I answer that,* Some have said that Paul, when in rapture, saw "not the very essence of God, but a certain reflection of His clarity." But Augustine clearly comes to an opposite decision, not only in his book (De videndo Deum), but also in Gen. ad lit. xii, 28 (quoted in a gloss on 2 Cor. 12:2). Indeed the words themselves of the Apostle indicate this. For he says that "he heard secret words, which it is not granted unto man to utter": and such would seem to be words pertaining to the vision of the blessed, which transcends the state of the wayfarer, according to Isa. 64:4, "Eye hath not seen, O God, besides Thee, what things Thou hast prepared for them that love [Vulg.: 'wait for'] Thee" [*1 Cor. 2:9]. Therefore it is more becoming to hold that he saw God in His essence.

Reply Obj. 1: Man's mind is rapt by God to the contemplation of divine truth in three ways. First, so that he contemplates it through certain imaginary pictures, and such was the ecstasy that came upon Peter. Secondly, so that he contemplates the divine truth through its intelligible effects; such was the ecstasy of David, who said (Ps. 115:11): "I said in my excess: Every man is a liar." Thirdly, so that he contemplates it in its essence. Such was the rapture of Paul, as also of Moses [*Cf. Q. 174, A. 4]; and not without reason, since as Moses was the first Teacher of the Jews, so was Paul the first "Teacher of the gentiles" [*Cf. I, Q. 68, A. 4].

Reply Obj. 2: The Divine essence cannot be seen by a created intellect save through the light of glory, of which it is written (Ps. 35:10): "In Thy light we shall see light." But this light can be shared in two ways. First by way of an abiding form, and thus it beatifies the saints in heaven. Secondly, by way of a transitory passion, as stated above (Q. 171, A. 2) of the light of prophecy; and in this way that light was in Paul when he was in rapture. Hence this vision did not beatify him simply, so as to overflow into his body, but only in a restricted sense. Consequently this rapture pertains somewhat to prophecy.

Reply Obj. 3: Since, in his rapture, Paul was beatified not as to the habit, but only as to the act of the blessed, it follows that he had not the act of faith at the same time, although he had the habit.

Reply Obj. 4: In one way by the third heaven we may understand something corporeal, and thus the third heaven denotes the empyrean [*1 Tim. 2:7; Cf. I, Q. 12, A. 11, ad 2], which is described as the "third," in relation to the aerial and starry heavens, or better still, in relation to the aqueous and crystalline heavens. Moreover Paul is stated to be rapt to the "third heaven," not as though his rapture consisted in the vision of something corporeal, but because this place is appointed for the contemplation of the blessed. Hence the gloss on 2 Cor. 12 says that the "third heaven is a spiritual heaven, where the angels and the holy souls enjoy the contemplation of God: and when Paul says that he was rapt to this heaven he means that God showed him the life wherein He is to be seen forevermore."

In another way the third heaven may signify a supra-mundane vision. Such a vision may be called the third heaven in three ways. First, according to the order of the cognitive powers. In this way the first heaven would indicate a supramundane bodily vision, conveyed through the senses; thus was seen the hand of one writing on the wall (Dan. 5:5); the second heaven would be an imaginary vision such as Isaias saw, and John in the Apocalypse; and the third heaven would denote an intellectual vision according to Augustine's explanation (Gen. ad lit. xii, 26, 28, 34). Secondly, the third heaven may be taken according to the order of things knowable, the first heaven being "the knowledge of heavenly bodies, the second the knowledge of heavenly spirits, the third the knowledge of God Himself." Thirdly, the third heaven may denote the contemplation of God according to the degrees of knowledge whereby God is seen. The first of these degrees belongs to the angels of the lowest hierarchy [*Cf. I, Q. 108, A. 1], the second to the angels of the middle hierarchy, the third to the angels of the highest hierarchy, according to the gloss on 2 Cor. 12.

And since the vision of God cannot be without delight, he says that he was not only "rapt to the third heaven" by reason of his contemplation, but also into "Paradise" by reason of the consequent delight.

FOURTH ARTICLE [II-II, Q. 175, Art. 4]

Whether Paul, When in Rapture, Was Withdrawn from His Senses?

Objection 1: It would seem that Paul, when in rapture, was not withdrawn from his senses. For Augustine says (Gen. ad lit. xii, 28): "Why should we not believe that when so great an apostle, the teacher of the gentiles, was rapt to this most sublime vision, God was willing to vouchsafe him a glimpse of that eternal life which is to take the place of the present life?" Now in that future life after the resurrection the saints will see the Divine essence without being withdrawn from the senses of the body. Therefore neither did such a withdrawal take place in Paul.

Obj. 2: Further, Christ was truly a wayfarer, and also enjoyed an uninterrupted vision of the Divine essence, without, however, being withdrawn from His senses. Therefore there was no need for Paul to be withdrawn from his senses in order for him to see the essence of God.

Obj. 3: Further, after seeing God in His essence, Paul remembered what he had seen in that vision; hence he said (2 Cor. 12:4): "He heard secret words, which it is not granted to man to utter." Now the memory belongs to the sensitive faculty according to the Philosopher (De Mem. et Remin. i). Therefore it seems that Paul, while seeing the essence of God, was not withdrawn from his senses.

*On the contrary,* Augustine says (Gen. ad lit. xii, 27): "Unless a man in some way depart this life, whether by going altogether out of his body or by turning away and withdrawing from his carnal senses, so that he truly knows not as the Apostle said, whether he be in the body or out of the body, he is not rapt and caught up into that vision.*" [*The text of St. Augustine reads: "when he is rapt," etc.]

*I answer that,* The Divine essence cannot be seen by man through any cognitive power other than the intellect. Now the human intellect does not turn to intelligible objects except by means of the phantasms [*Cf. I, Q. 84, A. 7] which it takes from the senses through the intelligible species; and it is in considering these phantasms that the intellect judges of and coordinates sensible objects. Hence in any operation that requires abstraction of the intellect from phantasms, there must be also withdrawal of the intellect from the senses. Now in the state of the wayfarer it is necessary for man's intellect, if it see God's essence, to be withdrawn from phantasms. For God's essence cannot be seen by means of a phantasm, nor indeed by any created intelligible species [*Cf. I, Q. 12, A. 2], since God's essence infinitely transcends not only all bodies, which are represented by phantasms, but also all intelligible creatures. Now when man's intellect is uplifted to the sublime vision of God's essence, it is necessary that his mind's whole attention should be summoned to that purpose in such a way that he understand naught else by phantasms, and be absorbed entirely in God. Therefore it is impossible for man while a wayfarer to see God in His essence without being withdrawn from his senses.

Reply Obj. 1: As stated above (A. 3, Obj. 2), after the resurrection, in the blessed who see God in His essence, there will be an overflow from the intellect to the lower powers and even to the body. Hence it is in keeping with the rule itself of the divine vision that the soul will turn towards phantasms and sensible objects. But there is no such overflow in those who are raptured, as stated (A. 3, Obj. 2, ad 2), and consequently the comparison fails.

Reply Obj. 2: The intellect of Christ's soul was glorified by the habit of the light of glory, whereby He saw the Divine essence much more fully than an angel or a man. He was, however, a wayfarer on account of the passibility of His body, in respect of which He was "made a little lower than the angels" (Heb. 2:9), by dispensation, and not on account of any defect on the part of His intellect. Hence there is no comparison between Him and other wayfarers.

Reply Obj. 3: Paul, after seeing God in His essence, remembered what he had known in that vision, by means of certain intelligible species that remained in his intellect by way of habit; even as in the absence of the sensible object, certain impressions remain in the soul which it recollects when it turns to the phantasms. And so this was the knowledge that he was unable wholly to think over or express in words.

FIFTH ARTICLE [II-II, Q. 175, Art. 5]

Whether, While in This State, Paul's Soul Was Wholly Separated from His Body?

Objection 1: It would seem that, while in this state, Paul's soul was wholly separated from his body. For the Apostle says (2 Cor. 5:6, 7): "While we are in the body we are absent from the Lord. For we walk by faith, and not by sight" [* *Per speciem,* i.e. by an intelligible species]. Now, while in that state, Paul was not absent from the Lord, for he saw Him by a species, as stated above (A. 3). Therefore he was not in the body.

Obj. 2: Further, a power of the soul cannot be uplifted above the soul's essence wherein it is rooted. Now in this rapture the intellect, which is a power of the soul, was withdrawn from its bodily surroundings through being uplifted to divine contemplation. Much more therefore was the essence of the soul separated from the body.

Obj. 3: Further, the forces of the vegetative soul

are more material than those of the sensitive soul. Now in order for him to be rapt to the vision of God, it was necessary for him to be withdrawn from the forces of the sensitive soul, as stated above (A. 4). Much more, therefore, was it necessary for him to be withdrawn from the forces of the vegetative soul. Now when these forces cease to operate, the soul is no longer in any way united to the body. Therefore it would seem that in Paul's rapture it was necessary for the soul to be wholly separated from the body.

*On the contrary,* Augustine says (Ep. CXLVII, 13, ad Paulin.; de videndo Deum): "It is not incredible that this sublime revelation" (namely, that they should see God in His essence) "was vouchsafed certain saints, without their departing this life so completely as to leave nothing but a corpse for burial." Therefore it was not necessary for Paul's soul, when in rapture, to be wholly separated from his body.

*I answer that,* As stated above (A. 1, Obj. 1), in the rapture of which we are speaking now, man is uplifted by God's power, "from that which is according to nature to that which is above nature." Wherefore two things have to be considered: first, what pertains to man according to nature; secondly, what has to be done by God in man above his nature. Now, since the soul is united to the body as its natural form, it belongs to the soul to have a natural disposition to understand by turning to phantasms; and this is not withdrawn by the divine power from the soul in rapture, since its state undergoes no change, as stated above (A. 3, ad 2, 3). Yet, this state remaining, actual conversion to phantasms and sensible objects is withdrawn from the soul, lest it be hindered from being uplifted to that which transcends all phantasms, as stated above (A. 4). Therefore it was not necessary that his soul in rapture should be so separated from the body as to cease to be united thereto as its form; and yet it was necessary for his intellect to be withdrawn from phantasms and the perception of sensible objects.

Reply Obj. 1: In this rapture Paul was absent from the Lord as regards his state, since he was still in the state of a wayfarer, but not as regards the act by which he saw God by a species, as stated above (A. 3, ad 2, 3).

Reply Obj. 2: A faculty of the soul is not uplifted by the natural power above the mode becoming the essence of the soul; but it can be uplifted by the divine power to something higher, even as a body by the violence of a stronger power is lifted up above the place befitting it according to its specific nature.

Reply Obj. 3: The forces of the vegetative soul do not operate through the soul being intent thereon, as do the sensitive forces, but by way of nature. Hence in the case of rapture there is no need for withdrawal from them, as from the sensitive powers, whose operations would lessen the intentness of the soul on intellective knowledge.

SIXTH ARTICLE [II-II, Q. 175, Art. 6]

Did Paul Know Whether His Soul Were Separated from His Body?

Objection 1: It would seem that Paul was not ignorant whether his soul were separated from his body. For he says (2 Cor. 12:2): "I know a man in Christ rapt even to the third heaven." Now man denotes something composed of soul and body; and rapture differs from death. Seemingly therefore he knew that his soul was not separated from his body by death, which is the more probable seeing that this is the common opinion of the Doctors.

Obj. 2: Further, it appears from the same words of the Apostle that he knew whither he was rapt, since it was "to the third heaven." Now this shows that he knew whether he was in the body or not, for if he knew the third heaven to be something corporeal, he must have known that his soul was not separated from his body, since a corporeal thing cannot be an object of sight save through the body. Therefore it would seem that he was not ignorant whether his soul were separated from his body.

Obj. 3: Further, Augustine says (Gen. ad lit. xii, 28) that "when in rapture, he saw God with the same vision as the saints see Him in heaven." Now from the very fact that the saints see God, they know whether their soul is separated from their body. Therefore Paul too knew this.

*On the contrary,* It is written (2 Cor. 12:3): "Whether in the body, or out of the body, I know not, God knoweth."

*I answer that,* The true answer to this question must be gathered from the Apostle's very words, whereby he says he knew something, namely that he was "rapt even to the third heaven," and that something he knew not, namely "whether" he were "in the body or out of the body." This may be understood in two ways. First, the words "whether in the body or out of the body" may refer not to the very being of the man who was rapt (as though he knew not whether his soul were in his body or not), but to the mode of rapture, so that he ignored whether his body besides his soul, or, on the other hand, his soul alone, were rapt to the third heaven. Thus Ezechiel is stated (Ezech. 8:3) to have been "brought in the vision of God into Jerusalem." This was the explanation of a certain Jew according to Jerome (Prolog. super Daniel.), where he says that "lastly our Apostle" (thus said the Jew) "durst not assert that he was rapt in his body, but said: 'Whether in the body or out of the body, I know not.'"

Augustine, however, disapproves of this explanation (Gen. ad lit. xii, 3 seqq.) for this reason that the Apostle states that he knew he was rapt even to the third heaven. Wherefore he knew it to be really the third heaven to which he was rapt, and not an imaginary likeness of the third heaven: otherwise if he gave the name of third heaven to an imaginary third heaven, in the same way he might state that he was rapt in the body, meaning, by body, an image of his body, such as appears in one's dreams. Now if he knew it to be really the third heaven, it follows that either he knew it to be something spiritual and incorporeal, and then his body could not be rapt thither; or he knew it to be something corporeal, and then his soul could not be rapt thither without his body, unless it were separated from his body. Consequently we must explain the matter otherwise, by saying that the Apostle knew himself to be rapt both in soul and body, but that he ignored how his soul stood in relation to his body, to wit, whether it were accompanied by his body or not.

Here we find a diversity of opinions. For some say that the Apostle knew his soul to be united to his body as its form, but ignored whether it were abstracted from its senses, or again whether it were abstracted from the operations of the vegetative soul. But he could not but know that it was abstracted from the senses, seeing that he knew himself to be rapt; and as to his being abstracted from the operation of the vegetative soul, this was not of such importance as to require him to be so careful in mentioning it. It follows, then, that the Apostle ignored whether his soul were united to his body as its form, or separated from it by death. Some, however, granting this say that the Apostle did not consider the matter while he was in rapture, because he was wholly intent upon God, but that afterwards he questioned the point, when taking cognizance of what he had seen. But this also is contrary to the Apostle's words, for he there distinguishes between the past and what happened subsequently, since he states that at the present time he knows that he was rapt "fourteen years ago," and that at the present time he knows not "whether he was in the body or out of the body."

Consequently we must assert that both before and after he ignored whether his soul were separated from his body. Wherefore Augustine (Gen. ad lit. xii, 5), after discussing the question at length, concludes: "Perhaps then we must infer that he ignored whether, when he was rapt to the third heaven, his soul was in his body (in the same way as the soul is in the body, when we speak of a living body either of a waking or of a sleeping man, or of one that is withdrawn from his bodily senses during ecstasy), or whether his soul went out of his body altogether, so that his body lay dead."

Reply Obj. 1: Sometimes by the figure of synecdoche a part of man, especially the soul which is the principal part, denotes a man. Or again we might take this to mean that he whom he states to have been rapt was a man not at the time of his rapture, but fourteen years afterwards: for he says "I know a man," not "I know a rapt man." Again nothing hinders death brought about by God being called rapture; and thus Augustine says (Gen. ad lit. xii, 3): "If the Apostle doubted the matter, who of us will dare to be certain about it?" Wherefore those who have something to say on this subject speak with more conjecture than certainty.

Reply Obj. 2: The Apostle knew that either the heaven in question was something incorporeal, or that he saw something incorporeal in that heaven; yet this could be done by his intellect, even without his soul being separated from his body.

Reply Obj. 3: Paul's vision, while he was in rapture, was like the vision of the blessed in one respect, namely as to the thing seen; and, unlike, in another respect, namely as to the mode of seeing, because he saw not so perfectly as do the saints in heaven. Hence Augustine says (Gen. ad lit. xii, 36): "Although, when the Apostle was rapt from his carnal senses to the third heaven, he lacked that full and perfect knowledge of things which is in the angels, in that he knew not whether he was in the body, or out of the body, this will surely not be lacking after reunion with the body in the resurrection of the dead, when this corruptible will put on incorruption."

## QUESTION 176

OF THE GRACE OF TONGUES (In Two Articles)

We must now consider those gratuitous graces that pertain to speech, and (1) the grace of tongues; (2) the grace of the word of wisdom and knowledge. Under the first head there are two points of inquiry:

(1) Whether by the grace of tongues a man acquires the knowledge of all languages?

(2) Of the comparison between this gift and the grace of prophecy.

FIRST ARTICLE [II-II, Q. 176, Art. 1]

Whether Those Who Received the Gift of Tongues Spoke in Every Language?

Objection 1: It seems that those who received the gift of tongues did not speak in every language. For that which is granted to certain persons by the divine power is the best of its kind: thus our Lord turned the water into good wine, as stated in John 2:10. Now those who had the gift of tongues spoke better in their own language; since a gloss on Heb. 1, says that "it is not surprising that the epistle to the Hebrews is more graceful in style than the other epistles, since it is natural for a man to have more command over his own than over a strange language. For the Apostle wrote the other epistles in a foreign, namely the Greek, idiom; whereas he wrote this in the Hebrew tongue." Therefore the apostles did not receive the knowledge of all languages by a gratuitous grace.

Obj. 2: Further, nature does not employ many means where one is sufficient; and much less does God Whose work is more orderly than nature's. Now God could make His disciples to be understood by all, while speaking one tongue: hence a gloss on Acts 2:6, "Every man heard them speak in his own tongue," says that "they spoke in every tongue, or speaking in their own, namely the Hebrew language, were understood by all, as though they spoke the language proper to each." Therefore it would seem that they had not the knowledge to speak in all languages.

Obj. 3: Further, all graces flow from Christ to His body, which is the Church, according to John 1:16, "Of His fullness we all have received." Now we do not read that Christ spoke more than one language, nor does each one of the faithful now speak save in one tongue. Therefore it would seem that Christ's disciples did not receive the grace to the extent of speaking in all languages.

*On the contrary,* It is written (Acts 2:4) that "they were all filled with the Holy Ghost, and they began to speak with divers tongues, according as the Holy Ghost gave them to speak"; on which passage a gloss of Gregory [*Hom. xxx in Ev.] says that "the Holy Ghost appeared over the disciples under the form of fiery tongues, and gave them the knowledge of all tongues."

*I answer that,* Christ's first disciples were chosen by Him in order that they might disperse throughout the whole world, and preach His faith everywhere, according to Matt. 28:19, "Going ... teach ye all nations." Now it was not fitting that they who were being sent to teach others should need to be taught by others, either as to how they should speak to other people, or as to how they were to understand those who spoke to them; and all the more seeing that those who were being sent were of one nation, that of Judea, according to Isa. 27:6, "When they shall rush out from Jacob [*Vulg.: 'When they shall rush in unto Jacob,' etc.] ... they shall fill the face of the world with seed." Moreover those who were being sent were poor and powerless; nor at the outset could they have easily found someone to interpret their words faithfully to others, or to explain what others said to them, especially as they were sent to unbelievers. Consequently it was necessary, in this respect, that God should provide them with the gift of tongues; in order that, as the diversity of tongues was brought upon the nations when they fell away to idolatry, according to Gen. 11, so when the nations were to be recalled to the worship of one God a remedy to this diversity might be applied by the gift of tongues.

Reply Obj. 1: As it is written (1 Cor. 12:7), "the manifestation of the Spirit is given to every man unto profit"; and consequently both Paul and the other apostles were divinely instructed in the languages of all nations sufficiently for the requirements of the teaching of the faith. But as regards the grace and elegance of style which human art adds to a language, the Apostle was instructed in his own, but not in a foreign tongue. Even so they were sufficiently instructed in wisdom and scientific knowledge, as required for teaching the faith, but not as to all things known by acquired science, for instance the conclusions of arithmetic and geometry.

Reply Obj. 2: Although either was possible, namely that, while speaking in one tongue they should be understood by all, or that they should speak in all tongues, it was more fitting that they should speak in all tongues, because this pertained to the perfection of their knowledge, whereby they were able not only to speak, but also to understand what was said by others. Whereas if their one language were intelligible to all, this would either have been due to the knowledge of those who understood their speech, or it would have amounted to an illusion, since a man's words would have had a different sound in another's ears, from that with which they were uttered. Hence a gloss says on Acts 2:6 that "it was a greater miracle that they should speak all kinds of tongues"; and Paul says (1 Cor. 14:18): "I thank my God I speak with all your tongues."

Reply Obj. 3: Christ in His own person purposed preaching to only one nation, namely the Jews. Consequently, although without any doubt He possessed most perfectly the knowledge of all languages, there was no need for Him to speak in every tongue. And therefore, as Augustine says (Tract. xxxii in Joan.), "whereas even now the Holy Ghost is received, yet no one speaks in the tongues of all nations, because the Church herself already speaks the languages of all nations: since whoever is not in the Church, receives not the Holy Ghost."

SECOND ARTICLE [II-II, Q. 176, Art. 2]

Whether the Gift of Tongues Is More Excellent Than the Grace of Prophecy?

Objection 1: It would seem that the gift of tongues is more excellent than the grace of prophecy. For, seemingly, better things are proper to better persons, according to the Philosopher (Topic. iii, 1). Now the gift of tongues is proper to the New Testament, hence we sing in the sequence of Pentecost [*The sequence: Sancti Spiritus adsit nobis gratia ascribed to King Robert of France, the reputed author of the *Veni Sancte Spiritus.* Cf. Migne, Patr. Lat. tom. CXLI]: "On this day Thou gavest Christ's apostles an unwonted gift, a marvel to all time": whereas prophecy is more pertinent to the Old Testament, according to Heb. 1:1, "God Who at sundry times and in divers manners spoke in times past to the fathers by the prophets." Therefore it would seem that the gift of tongues is more excellent than the gift of prophecy.

Obj. 2: Further, that whereby we are directed to God is seemingly more excellent than that whereby we are directed to men. Now, by the gift of tongues, man is directed to God, whereas by prophecy he is directed to man; for it is written (1 Cor. 14:2, 3): "He that speaketh in a tongue, speaketh not unto men, but unto God ... but he that prophesieth, speaketh unto men unto edification." Therefore it would seem that the gift of tongues is more excellent than the gift of prophecy.

Obj. 3: Further, the gift of tongues abides like a habit in the person who has it, and "he can use it when he will"; wherefore it is written (1 Cor. 14:18): "I thank my God I speak with all your tongues." But it is not so with the gift of prophecy, as stated above (Q. 171, A. 2). Therefore the gift of tongues would seem to be more excellent than the gift of prophecy.

Obj. 4: Further, the "interpretation of speeches" would seem to be contained under prophecy, because the Scriptures are expounded by the same Spirit from Whom they originated. Now the interpretation of speeches is placed after "divers kinds of tongues" (1 Cor. 12:10). Therefore it seems that the gift of tongues is more excellent than the gift of prophecy, particularly as regards a part of the latter.

*On the contrary,* The Apostle says (1 Cor. 14:5): "Greater is he that prophesieth than he that speaketh with tongues."

*I answer that,* The gift of prophecy surpasses the gift of tongues, in three ways. First, because the gift of tongues regards the utterance of certain words, which signify an intelligible truth, and this again is signified by the phantasms which appear in an imaginary vision; wherefore Augustine compares (Gen. ad lit. xii, 8) the gift of tongues to an imaginary vision. On the other hand, it has been stated above (Q. 173, A. 2) that the gift of prophecy consists in the mind itself being enlightened so as to know an intelligible truth. Wherefore, as the prophetic enlightenment is more excellent than the imaginary vision, as stated above (Q. 174, A. 2), so also is prophecy more excellent than the gift of tongues considered in itself. Secondly, because the gift of prophecy regards the knowledge of things, which is more excellent than the knowledge of words, to which the gift of tongues pertains.

Thirdly, because the gift of prophecy is more profitable. The Apostle proves this in three ways (1 Cor. 14); first, because prophecy is more profitable to the edification of the Church, for which purpose he that speaketh in tongues profiteth nothing, unless interpretation follow (1 Cor. 14:4, 5). Secondly, as regards the speaker himself, for if he be enabled to speak in divers tongues without understanding them, which pertains to the gift of prophecy, his own mind would not be edified (1 Cor. 14:7-14). Thirdly, as to unbelievers for whose especial benefit the gift of tongues seems to have been given; since perchance they might think those who speak in tongues to be mad (1 Cor. 14:23), for instance the Jews deemed the apostles drunk when the latter spoke in various tongues (Acts 2:13): whereas by prophecies the unbeliever is convinced, because the secrets of his heart are made manifest (Acts 2:25).

Reply Obj. 1: As stated above (Q. 174, A. 3, ad 1), it belongs to the excellence of prophecy that a man is not only enlightened by an intelligible light, but also that he should perceive an imaginary vision: and so again it belongs to the perfection of the Holy Ghost's operation, not only to fill the mind with the prophetic light, and the imagination with the imaginary vision, as happened in the Old Testament, but also to endow the tongue with external erudition, in the utterance of various signs of speech. All this is done in the New Testament, according to 1 Cor. 14:26, "Every one of you hath a psalm, hath a doctrine, hath a tongue, hath a revelation," i.e. a prophetic revelation.

Reply Obj. 2: By the gift of prophecy man is directed to God in his mind, which is more excellent than being directed to Him in his tongue. "He that speaketh in a tongue" is said to speak "not unto men," i.e. to men's understanding or profit, but unto God's understanding and praise. On the other hand, by prophecy a man is directed both to God and to man; wherefore it is the more perfect gift.

Reply Obj. 3: Prophetic revelation extends to the knowledge of all things supernatural; wherefore from its very perfection it results that in this imperfect state of life it cannot be had perfectly by way of habit, but only imperfectly by way of passion. On the other hand, the gift of tongues is confined to a certain particular knowledge, namely of human words; wherefore it is not inconsistent with the imperfection of this life, that it should be had perfectly and by way of habit.

Reply Obj. 4: The interpretation of speeches is reducible to the gift of prophecy, inasmuch as the mind is enlightened so as to understand and explain any obscurities of speech arising either from a difficulty in the things signified, or from the words uttered being unknown, or from the figures of speech employed, according to Dan. 5:16, "I have heard of thee, that thou canst interpret obscure things, and resolve difficult things." Hence the interpretation of speeches is more excellent than the gift of tongues, as appears from the saying of the Apostle (1 Cor. 14:5), "Greater is he that prophesieth than he that speaketh with tongues; unless perhaps he interpret." Yet the interpretation of speeches is placed after the gift of tongues, because the interpretation of speeches extends even to the interpretation of divers kinds of tongues.

## QUESTION 177

OF THE GRATUITOUS GRACE CONSISTING IN WORDS (In Two Articles)

We must now consider the gratuitous grace that attaches to words; of which the Apostle says (1 Cor. 12:8): "To one ... by the Spirit is given the word of wisdom, and to another the word of knowledge." Under this head there are two points of inquiry:

(1) Whether any gratuitous grace attaches to words?

(2) To whom is the grace becoming?

FIRST ARTICLE [II-II, Q. 177, Art. 1]

Whether Any Gratuitous Grace Attaches to Words?

Objection 1: It would seem that a gratuitous grace does not attach to words. For grace is given for that which surpasses the faculty of nature. But natural reason has devised the art of rhetoric whereby a man is able to speak so as to teach, please, and persuade, as Augustine says (De Doctr. Christ. iv, 12). Now this belongs to the grace of words. Therefore it would seem that the grace of words is not a gratuitous grace.

Obj. 2: Further, all grace pertains to the kingdom of God. But the Apostle says (1 Cor. 4:20): "The kingdom of God is not in speech, but in power." Therefore there is no gratuitous grace connected with words.

Obj. 3: Further, no grace is given through merit, since "if by grace, it is not now of works" (Rom. 11:6). But the word is sometimes given to a man on his merits. For Gregory says (Moral. xi, 15) in explanation of Ps. 118:43, "Take not Thou the word of truth utterly out of my mouth" that "the word of truth is that which Almighty God gives to them that do it, and takes away from them that do it not." Therefore it would seem that the gift of the word is not a gratuitous grace.

Obj. 4: Further, it behooves man to declare in words things pertaining to the virtue of faith, no less than those pertaining to the gift of wisdom or of knowledge. Therefore if the word of wisdom and the word of knowledge are reckoned gratuitous graces, the word of faith should likewise be placed among the gratuitous graces.

*On the contrary,* It is written (Ecclus. 6:5): "A gracious tongue in a good man shall abound [Vulg.: 'aboundeth']." Now man's goodness is by grace. Therefore graciousness in words is also by grace.

*I answer that,* The gratuitous graces are given for the profit of others, as stated above (I-II, Q. 111, AA. 1, 4). Now the knowledge a man receives from God cannot be turned to another's profit, except by means of speech. And since the Holy Ghost does not fail in anything that pertains to the profit of the Church, He provides also the members of the Church with speech; to the effect that a man not only speaks so as to be understood by different people, which pertains to the gift of tongues, but also speaks with effect, and this pertains to the grace *of the word.*

This happens in three ways. First, in order to instruct the intellect, and this is the case when a man speaks so as *to teach.* Secondly, in order to move the affections, so that a man willingly hearkens to the word of God. This is the case when a man speaks so as *to please* his hearers, not indeed with a view to his own favor, but in order to draw them to listen to God's word. Thirdly, in order that men may love that which is signified by the word, and desire to fulfill it, and this is the case when a man so speaks as *to sway* his hearers. In order to effect this the Holy Ghost makes use of the human tongue as of an instrument; but He it is Who perfects the work within. Hence Gregory says in a homily for Pentecost (Hom. xxx in Ev.): "Unless the Holy Ghost fill the hearts of the hearers, in vain does the voice of the teacher resound in the ears of the body."

Reply Obj. 1: Even as by a miracle God sometimes works in a more excellent way those things which nature also can work, so too the Holy Ghost effects more excellently by the grace of words that which art can effect in a less efficient manner.

Reply Obj. 2: The Apostle is speaking there of the word that relies on human eloquence without the power of the Holy Ghost. Wherefore he says just before (1 Cor. 4:19): "I ... will know, not the speech of them that are puffed up, but the power": and of himself he had already said (1 Cor. 2:4): "My speech and my preaching was not in the persuasive words of human wisdom, but in the showing of the spirit and power."

Reply Obj. 3: As stated above, the grace of the word is given to a man for the profit of others. Hence it is withdrawn sometimes through the fault of the hearer, and sometimes through the fault of the speaker. The good works of either of them do not merit this grace directly, but only remove the obstacles thereto. For sanctifying grace also is withdrawn on account of a person's fault, and yet he does not merit it by his good works, which, however, remove the obstacles to grace.

Reply Obj. 4: As stated above, the grace of the word is directed to the profit of others. Now if a man communicates his faith to others this is by the word of knowledge or of wisdom. Hence Augustine says (De Trin. xiv, 1) that "to know how faith may profit the godly and be defended against the ungodly, is apparently what the Apostle means by knowledge." Hence it was not necessary for him to mention the word of faith, but it was sufficient for him to mention the word of knowledge and of wisdom.

SECOND ARTICLE [II-II, Q. 177, Art. 2]

Whether the Grace of the Word of Wisdom and Knowledge Is Becoming to Women?

Objection 1: It would seem that the grace of the word of wisdom and knowledge is becoming even to women. For teaching is pertinent to this grace, as stated in the foregoing Article. Now it is becoming to a woman to teach; for it is written (Prov. 4:3, 4): "I was an only son in the sight of my mother, and she taught me [*Vulg.: 'I was my father's son, tender, and as an only son in the sight of my mother. And he taught me.']." Therefore this grace is becoming to women.

Obj. 2: Further, the grace of prophecy is greater than the grace of the word, even as the contemplation of truth is greater than its utterance. But prophecy is granted to women, as we read of Deborah (Judges 4:4), and of Holda the prophetess, the wife of Sellum (4 Kings 22:14), and of the four daughters of Philip (Acts 21:9). Moreover the Apostle says (1 Cor. 11:5): "Every woman praying or prophesying," etc. Much more therefore would it seem that the grace of the word is becoming to a woman.

Obj. 3: Further, it is written (1 Pet. 4:10): "As every man hath received grace ministering the same one to another." Now some women receive the grace of wisdom and knowledge, which they cannot minister to others except by the grace of the word. Therefore the grace of the word is becoming to women.

*On the contrary,* The Apostle says (1 Cor. 14:34): "Let women keep silence in the churches," and (1 Tim. 2:12): "I suffer not a woman to teach." Now this pertains especially to the grace of the word. Therefore the grace of the word is not becoming to women.

*I answer that,* Speech may be employed in two ways: in one way privately, to one or a few, in familiar conversation, and in this respect the grace of the word may be becoming to women; in another way, publicly, addressing oneself to the whole church, and this is not permitted to women. First and chiefly, on account of the condition attaching to the female sex, whereby woman should be subject to man, as appears from Gen. 3:16. Now teaching and persuading publicly in the church belong not to subjects but to the prelates (although men who are subjects may do these things if they be so commissioned, because their subjection is not a result of their natural sex, as it is with women, but of some thing supervening by accident). Secondly, lest men's minds be enticed to lust, for it is written (Ecclus. 9:11): "Her conversation burneth as fire." Thirdly, because as a rule women are not perfected in wisdom, so as to be fit to be intrusted with public teaching.

Reply Obj. 1: The passage quoted speaks of private teaching whereby a father instructs his son.

Reply Obj. 2: The grace of prophecy consists in God enlightening the mind, on the part of which there is no difference of sex among men, according to Col. 3:10, 11, "Putting on the new" man, "him who is renewed unto knowledge, according to the image of Him that created him, where there is neither male nor female [*Vulg.: 'Neither Gentile nor Jew, circumcision nor uncircumcision, Barbarian nor Scythian, bond nor free.' Cf. I, Q. 93, A. 6, ad 2 footnote]." Now the grace of the word pertains to the instruction of men among whom the difference of sex is found. Hence the comparison fails.

Reply Obj. 3: The recipients of a divinely conferred grace administer it in different ways according to their various conditions. Hence women, if they have the grace of wisdom or of knowledge, can administer it by teaching privately but not publicly.

## QUESTION 178

OF THE GRACE OF MIRACLES (In Two Articles)

We must next consider the grace of miracles, under which head there are two points of inquiry:

(1) Whether there is a gratuitous grace of working miracles?

(2) To whom is it becoming?

FIRST ARTICLE [II-II, Q. 178, Art. 1]

Whether There Is a Gratuitous Grace of Working Miracles?

Objection 1: It would seem that no gratuitous grace is directed to the working of miracles. For every grace puts something in the one to whom it is given (Cf. I-II, Q. 90, A. 1). Now the working of miracles puts nothing in the soul of the man who receives it since miracles are wrought at the touch even of a dead body. Thus we read (4 Kings 13:21) that "some ... cast the body into the sepulchre of Eliseus. And when it had touched the bones of Eliseus, the man came to life, and stood upon his feet." Therefore the working of miracles does not belong to a gratuitous grace.

Obj. 2: Further, the gratuitous graces are from the Holy Ghost, according to 1 Cor. 12:4, "There are diversities of graces, but the same Spirit." Now the working of miracles is effected even by the unclean spirit, according to Matt. 24:24, "There shall arise false Christs and false prophets, and shall show great signs and wonders." Therefore it would seem that the working of miracles does not belong to a gratuitous grace.

Obj. 3: Further, miracles are divided into "signs," "wonders" or "portents," and "virtues." [*Cf. 2 Thess. 2:9, where the Douay version renders *virtus* by "power." The use of the word "virtue" in the sense of a miracle is now obsolete, and the generic term "miracle" is elsewhere used in its stead: Cf. 1 Cor. 12:10, 28; Heb. 2:4; Acts 2:22]. Therefore it is unreasonable to reckon the "working of miracles" a gratuitous grace, any more than the "working of signs" and "wonders."

Obj. 4: Further, the miraculous restoring to health is done by the power of God. Therefore the grace of healing should not be distinguished from the working of miracles.

Obj. 5: Further, the working of miracles results from faith—either of the worker, according to 1 Cor. 13:2, "If I should have all faith, so that I could remove mountains," or of other persons for whose sake miracles are wrought, according to Matt. 13:58, "And He wrought not many miracles there, because of their unbelief." Therefore, if faith be reckoned a gratuitous grace, it is superfluous to reckon in addition the working of signs as another gratuitous grace.

*On the contrary,* The Apostle (1 Cor. 12:9, 10)

says that among other gratuitous graces, "to another" is given "the grace of healing ... to another, the working of miracles."

*I answer that,* As stated above (Q. 177, A. 1), the Holy Ghost provides sufficiently for the Church in matters profitable unto salvation, to which purpose the gratuitous graces are directed. Now just as the knowledge which a man receives from God needs to be brought to the knowledge of others through the gift of tongues and the grace of the word, so too the word uttered needs to be confirmed in order that it be rendered credible. This is done by the working of miracles, according to Mk. 16:20, "And confirming the word with signs that followed": and reasonably so. For it is natural to man to arrive at the intelligible truth through its sensible effects. Wherefore just as man led by his natural reason is able to arrive at some knowledge of God through His natural effects, so is he brought to a certain degree of supernatural knowledge of the objects of faith by certain supernatural effects which are called miracles. Therefore the working of miracles belongs to a gratuitous grace.

Reply Obj. 1: Just as prophecy extends to whatever can be known supernaturally, so the working of miracles extends to all things that can be done supernaturally; the cause whereof is the divine omnipotence which cannot be communicated to any creature. Hence it is impossible for the principle of working miracles to be a quality abiding as a habit in the soul. On the other hand, just as the prophet's mind is moved by divine inspiration to know something supernaturally, so too is it possible for the mind of the miracle worker to be moved to do something resulting in the miraculous effect which God causes by His power. Sometimes this takes place after prayer, as when Peter raised to life the dead Tabitha (Acts 9:40): sometimes without any previous prayer being expressed, as when Peter by upbraiding the lying Ananias and Saphira delivered them to death (Acts 5:4, 9). Hence Gregory says (Dial. ii, 30) that "the saints work miracles, sometimes by authority, sometimes by prayer." In either case, however, God is the principal worker, for He uses instrumentally either man's inward movement, or his speech, or some outward action, or again the bodily contact of even a dead body. Thus when Josue had said as though authoritatively (Josh. 10:12): "Move not, O sun, toward Gabaon," it is said afterwards (Josh. 10:14): "There was not before or after so long a day, the Lord obeying the voice of a man."

Reply Obj. 2: Our Lord is speaking there of the miracles to be wrought at the time of Antichrist, of which the Apostle says (2 Thess. 2:9) that the coming of Antichrist will be "according to the working of Satan, in all power, and signs, and lying wonders." To quote the words of Augustine (De Civ. Dei xx, 19), "it is a matter of debate whether they are called signs and lying wonders, because he will deceive the senses of mortals by imaginary visions, in that he will seem to do what he does not, or because, though they be real wonders, they will seduce into falsehood them that believe." They are said to be real, because the things themselves will be real, just as Pharaoh's magicians made real frogs and real serpents; but they will not be real miracles, because they will be done by the power of natural causes, as stated in the First Part (Q. 114, A. 4); whereas the working of miracles which is ascribed to a gratuitous grace, is done by God's power for man's profit.

Reply Obj. 3: Two things may be considered in miracles. One is that which is done: this is something surpassing the faculty of nature, and in this respect miracles are called "virtues." The other thing is the purpose for which miracles are wrought, namely the manifestation of something supernatural, and in this respect they are commonly called "signs": but on account of some excellence they receive the name of "wonder" or "prodigy," as showing something from afar ( *procul* ).

Reply Obj. 4: The "grace of healing" is mentioned separately, because by its means a benefit, namely bodily health, is conferred on man in addition to the common benefit bestowed in all miracles, namely the bringing of men to the knowledge of God.

Reply Obj. 5: The working of miracles is ascribed to faith for two reasons. First, because it is directed to the confirmation of faith, secondly, because it proceeds from God's omnipotence on which faith relies. Nevertheless, just as besides the grace of faith, the grace of the word is necessary that people may be instructed in the faith, so too is the grace of miracles necessary that people may be confirmed in their faith.

SECOND ARTICLE [II-II, Q. 178, Art. 2]

Whether the Wicked Can Work Miracles?

Objection 1: It would seem that the wicked cannot work miracles. For miracles are wrought through prayer, as stated above (A. 1, ad 1). Now the prayer of a sinner is not granted, according to John 9:31, "We know that God doth not hear sinners," and Prov. 28:9, "He that turneth away his ear from hearing the law, his prayer shall be an abomination." Therefore it would seem that the wicked cannot work miracles.

Obj. 2: Further, miracles are ascribed to faith, according to Matt. 17:19, "If you have faith as a grain of mustard seed you shall say to this mountain: Remove from hence hither, and it shall remove." Now "faith without works is dead," according to James 2:20, so that, seemingly, it is devoid of its proper operation. Therefore it would seem that the wicked, since they do not good works, cannot work miracles.

Obj. 3: Further, miracles are divine attestations, according to Heb. 2:4, "God also bearing them witness by signs and wonders and divers miracles": wherefore in the Church the canonization of certain persons is based on the attestation of miracles. Now God cannot bear witness to a falsehood. Therefore it would seem that wicked men cannot work miracles.

Obj. 4: Further, the good are more closely united to God than the wicked. But the good do not all work miracles. Much less therefore do the wicked.

*On the contrary,* The Apostle says (1 Cor. 13:2): "If I should have all faith, so that I could remove mountains, and have not charity, I am nothing." Now whosoever has not charity is wicked, because "this gift alone of the Holy Ghost distinguishes the children of the kingdom from the children of perdition," as Augustine says (De Trin. xv, 18). Therefore it would seem that even the wicked can work miracles.

*I answer that,* Some miracles are not true but imaginary deeds, because they delude man by the appearance of that which is not; while others are true deeds, yet they have not the character of a true miracle, because they are done by the power of some natural cause. Both of these can be done by the demons, as stated above (A. 1, ad 2).

True miracles cannot be wrought save by the power of God, because God works them for man's benefit, and this in two ways: in one way for the confirmation of truth declared, in another way in proof of a person's holiness, which God desires to propose as an example of virtue. In the first way miracles can be wrought by any one who preaches the true faith and calls upon Christ's name, as even the wicked do sometimes. In this way even the wicked can work miracles. Hence Jerome commenting on Matt. 7:22, "Have not we prophesied in Thy name?" says: "Sometimes prophesying, the working of miracles, and the casting out of demons are accorded not to the merit of those who do these things, but to the invoking of Christ's name, that men may honor God, by invoking Whom such great miracles are wrought."

In the second way miracles are not wrought except by the saints, since it is in proof of their holiness that miracles are wrought during their lifetime or after death, either by themselves or by others. For we read (Acts 19:11, 12) that "God wrought by the hand of Paul ... miracles" and "even there were brought from his body to the sick, handkerchiefs ... and the diseases departed from them." In this way indeed there is nothing to prevent a sinner from working miracles by invoking a saint; but the miracle is ascribed not to him, but to the one in proof of whose holiness such things are done.

Reply Obj. 1: As stated above (Q. 83, A. 16) when we were treating of prayer, the prayer of impetration relies not on merit but on God's mercy, which extends even to the wicked, wherefore the prayers even of sinners are sometimes granted by God. Hence Augustine says (Tract. xliv in Joan.) that "the blind man spoke these words before he was anointed," that is, before he was perfectly enlightened; "since God does hear sinners." When it is said that the prayer of one who hears not the law is an abomination, this must be understood so far as the sinner's merit is concerned; yet it is sometimes granted, either for the spiritual welfare of the one who prays—as the publican was heard (Luke 18:14)—or for the good of others and for God's glory.

Reply Obj. 2: Faith without works is said to be dead, as regards the believer, who lives not, by faith, with the life of grace. But nothing hinders a living thing from working through a dead instrument, as a man through a stick. It is thus that God works while employing instrumentally the faith of a sinner.

Reply Obj. 3: Miracles are always true witnesses to the purpose for which they are wrought. Hence wicked men who teach a false doctrine never work true miracles in confirmation of their teaching, although sometimes they may do so in praise of Christ's name which they invoke, and by the power of the sacraments which they administer. If they teach a true doctrine, sometimes they work true miracles as confirming their teaching, but not as an attestation of holiness. Hence Augustine says (QQ. lxxxiii, qu. 79): "Magicians work miracles in one way, good Christians in another, wicked Christians in another. Magicians by private compact with the demons, good Christians by their manifest righteousness, evil Christians by the outward signs of righteousness."

Reply Obj. 4: As Augustine says (QQ. lxxxiii, qu. 79), "the reason why these are not granted to all holy men is lest by a most baneful error the weak be deceived into thinking such deeds to imply greater gifts than the deeds of righteousness whereby eternal life is obtained."

## QUESTION 179

OF THE DIVISION OF LIFE INTO ACTIVE AND CONTEMPLATIVE (In Two Articles)

We must next consider active and contemplative life. This consideration will be fourfold: (1) Of the division of life into active and contemplative; (2) Of the contemplative life; (3) Of the active life; (4) Of the comparison between the active and the contemplative life.

Under the first head there are two points of inquiry:

(1) Whether life is fittingly divided into active and contemplative?

(2) Whether this is an adequate division?

FIRST ARTICLE [II-II, Q. 179, Art. 1]

Whether Life Is Fittingly Divided into Active and Contemplative?

Objection 1: It would seem that life is not fittingly divided into active and contemplative. For the soul is the principle of life by its essence: since the

Philosopher says (De Anima ii, 4) that "in living things to live is to be." Now the soul is the principle of action and contemplation by its powers. Therefore it would seem that life is not fittingly divided into active and contemplative.

Obj. 2: Further, the division of that which comes afterwards is unfittingly applied to that which comes first. Now active and contemplative, or "speculative" and "practical," are differences of the intellect (De Anima iii, 10); while "to live" comes before "to understand," since "to live" comes first to living things through the vegetative soul, as the Philosopher states (De Anima ii, 4). Therefore life is unfittingly divided into active and contemplative.

Obj. 3: Further, the word "life" implies movement, according to Dionysius (Div. Nom. vi): whereas contemplation consists rather in rest, according to Wis. 8:16: "When I enter into my house, I shall repose myself with her." Therefore it would seem that life is unfittingly divided into active and contemplative.

*On the contrary,* Gregory says (Hom. xiv super Ezech.): "There is a twofold life wherein Almighty God instructs us by His holy word, the active life and the contemplative."

*I answer that,* Properly speaking, those things are said to live whose movement or operation is from within themselves. Now that which is proper to a thing and to which it is most inclined is that which is most becoming to it from itself; wherefore every living thing gives proof of its life by that operation which is most proper to it, and to which it is most inclined. Thus the life of plants is said to consist in nourishment and generation; the life of animals in sensation and movement; and the life of men in their understanding and acting according to reason. Wherefore also in men the life of every man would seem to be that wherein he delights most, and on which he is most intent; thus especially does he wish "to associate with his friends" (Ethic. ix, 12).

Accordingly since certain men are especially intent on the contemplation of truth, while others are especially intent on external actions, it follows that man's life is fittingly divided into active and contemplative.

Reply Obj. 1: Each thing's proper form that makes it actually *to be* is properly that thing's principle of operation. Hence to live is, in living things, to be, because living things through having being from their form, act in such and such a way.

Reply Obj. 2: Life in general is not divided into active and contemplative, but the life of man, who derives his species from having an intellect, wherefore the same division applies to intellect and human life.

Reply Obj. 3: It is true that contemplation enjoys rest from external movements. Nevertheless to contemplate is itself a movement of the intellect, in so far as every operation is described as a movement; in which sense the Philosopher says (De Anima iii, 7) that sensation and understanding are movements of a kind, in so far as movement is defined "the act of a perfect thing." In this way Dionysius (Div. Nom. iv) ascribes three movements to the soul in contemplation, namely, "straight," "circular," and "oblique" [*Cf. Q. 180, A. 6].

SECOND ARTICLE [II-II, Q. 179, Art. 2]

Whether Life Is Adequately Divided into Active and Contemplative?

Objection 1: It would seem that life is not adequately divided into active and contemplative. For the Philosopher says (Ethic. i, 5) that there are three most prominent kinds of life, the life of "pleasure," the "civil" which would seem to be the same as the active, and the "contemplative" life. Therefore the division of life into active and contemplative would seem to be inadequate.

Obj. 2: Further, Augustine (De Civ. Dei xix, 1, 2, 3, 19) mentions three kinds of life, namely the life of "leisure" which pertains to the contemplative, the "busy" life which pertains to the active, and a third "composed of both." Therefore it would seem that life is inadequately divided into active and contemplative.

Obj. 3: Further, man's life is diversified according to the divers actions in which men are occupied. Now there are more than two occupations of human actions. Therefore it would seem that life should be divided into more kinds than the active and the contemplative.

*On the contrary,* These two lives are signified by the two wives of Jacob; the active by Lia, and the contemplative by Rachel: and by the two hostesses of our Lord; the contemplative life by Mary, and the active life by Martha, as Gregory declares (Moral. vi, 37 [*Hom. xiv in Ezech.]). Now this signification would not be fitting if there were more than two lives. Therefore life is adequately divided into active and contemplative.

*I answer that,* As stated above (A. 1, ad 2), this division applies to the human life as derived from the intellect. Now the intellect is divided into active and contemplative, since the end of intellective knowledge is either the knowledge itself of truth, which pertains to the contemplative intellect, or some external action, which pertains to the practical or active intellect. Therefore life too is adequately divided into active and contemplative.

Reply Obj. 1: The life of pleasure places its end in pleasures of the body, which are common to us and dumb animals; wherefore as the Philosopher says (Ethic. *Ethic.* i, 5), it is the life "of a beast." Hence it is not included in this division of the life of a man into active and contemplative.

Reply Obj. 2: A mean is a combination of extremes, wherefore it is virtually contained in them, as tepid in hot and cold, and pale in white and black. In like manner active and contemplative comprise that which is composed of both. Nevertheless as in every mixture one of the simples predominates, so too in the mean state of life sometimes the contemplative, sometimes the active element, abounds.

Reply Obj. 3: All the occupations of human actions, if directed to the requirements of the present life in accord with right reason, belong to the active life which provides for the necessities of the present life by means of well-ordered activity. If, on the other hand, they minister to any concupiscence whatever, they belong to the life of pleasure, which is not comprised under the active life. Those human occupations that are directed to the consideration of truth belong to the contemplative life.

## QUESTION 180

OF THE CONTEMPLATIVE LIFE (In Eight Articles)

We must now consider the contemplative life, under which head there are eight points of inquiry:

(1) Whether the contemplative life pertains to the intellect only, or also to the affections?

(2) Whether the moral virtues pertain to the contemplative life?

(3) Whether the contemplative life consists in one action or in several?

(4) Whether the consideration of any truth whatever pertains to the contemplative life?

(5) Whether the contemplative life of man in this state can arise to the vision of God?

(6) Of the movements of contemplation assigned by Dionysius (Div. Nom. iv);

(7) Of the pleasure of contemplation;

(8) Of the duration of contemplation.

FIRST ARTICLE [II-II, Q. 180, Art. 1]

Whether the Contemplative Life Has Nothing to Do with the Affections, and Pertains Wholly to the Intellect?

Objection 1: It would seem that the contemplative life has nothing to do with the affections and pertains wholly to the intellect. For the Philosopher says (Metaph. ii, text. 3 [*Ed Did. ia, 1]) that "the end of contemplation is truth." Now truth pertains wholly to the intellect. Therefore it would seem that the contemplative life wholly regards the intellect.

Obj. 2: Further, Gregory says (Moral. vi, 37; Hom. xix in Ezech.) that "Rachel, which is interpreted 'vision of the principle' [*Or rather, 'One seeing the principle,' if derived from *rah* and irzn ; Cf. Jerome, De Nom. Hebr.], signifies the contemplative life." Now the vision of a principle belongs properly to the intellect. Therefore the contemplative life belongs properly to the intellect.

Obj. 3: Further, Gregory says (Hom. xiv in Ezech.) that it belongs to the contemplative life, "to rest from external action." Now the affective or appetitive power inclines to external actions. Therefore it would seem that the contemplative life has nothing to do with the appetitive power.

*On the contrary,* Gregory says (Hom. xiv in Ezech.) that "the contemplative life is to cling with our whole mind to the love of God and our neighbor, and to desire nothing beside our Creator." Now desire and love pertain to the affective or appetitive power, as stated above (I-II, Q. 25, A. 2; Q. 26, A. 2). Therefore the contemplative life has also something to do with the affective or appetitive power.

*I answer that,* As stated above (Q. 179, A. 1) theirs is said to be the contemplative who are chiefly intent on the contemplation of truth. Now intention is an act of the will, as stated above (I-II, Q. 12, A. 1), because intention is of the end which is the object of the will. Consequently the contemplative life, as regards the essence of the action, pertains to the intellect, but as regards the motive cause of the exercise of that action it belongs to the will, which moves all the other powers, even the intellect, to their actions, as stated above (I, Q. 82, A. 4; I-II, Q. 9, A. 1).

Now the appetitive power moves one to observe things either with the senses or with the intellect, sometimes for love of the thing seen because, as it is written (Matt. 6:21), "where thy treasure is, there is thy heart also," sometimes for love of the very knowledge that one acquires by observation. Wherefore Gregory makes the contemplative life to consist in the "love of God," inasmuch as through loving God we are aflame to gaze on His beauty. And since everyone delights when he obtains what he loves, it follows that the contemplative life terminates in delight, which is seated in the affective power, the result being that love also becomes more intense.

Reply Obj. 1: From the very fact that truth is the end of contemplation, it has the aspect of an appetible good, both lovable and delightful, and in this respect it pertains to the appetitive power.

Reply Obj. 2: We are urged to the vision of the first principle, namely God, by the love thereof; wherefore Gregory says (Hom. xiv in Ezech.) that "the contemplative life tramples on all cares and longs to see the face of its Creator."

Reply Obj. 3: The appetitive power moves not only the bodily members to perform external actions, but also the intellect to practice the act of contemplation, as stated above.

SECOND ARTICLE [II-II, Q. 180, Art. 2]

Whether the Moral Virtues Pertain to the Contemplative Life?

Objection 1: It would seem that the moral virtues pertain to the contemplative life. For Gregory says (Hom. xiv in Ezech.) that "the contemplative life is to cling to the love of God and our neighbor with the whole mind." Now all the moral virtues, since their acts are prescribed by the precepts of the Law, are reducible to the love of God and of our neighbor, for "love ... is the fulfilling of the Law" (Rom. 13:10). Therefore it would seem that the moral virtues belong to the contemplative life.

Obj. 2: Further, the contemplative life is chiefly directed to the contemplation of God; for Gregory says (Hom. xiv in Ezech.) that "the mind tramples on all cares and longs to gaze on the face of its Creator." Now no one can accomplish this without cleanness of heart, which is a result of moral virtue [*Cf. Q. 8, A. 7]. For it is written (Matt. 5:8): "Blessed are the clean of heart, for they shall see God": and (Heb. 12:14): "Follow peace with all men, and holiness, without which no man shall see God." Therefore it would seem that the moral virtues pertain to the contemplative life.

Obj. 3: Further, Gregory says (Hom. xiv in Ezech.) that "the contemplative life gives beauty to the soul," wherefore it is signified by Rachel, of whom it is said (Gen. 29:17) that she was "of a beautiful countenance." Now the beauty of the soul consists in the moral virtues, especially temperance, as Ambrose says (De Offic. i, 43, 45, 46). Therefore it seems that the moral virtues pertain to the contemplative life.

*On the contrary,* The moral virtues are directed to external actions. Now Gregory says (Moral. vi [*Hom. xiv in Ezech.; Cf. A. 1, Obj. 3]) that it belongs to the contemplative life "to rest from external action." Therefore the moral virtues do not pertain to the contemplative life.

*I answer that,* A thing may belong to the contemplative life in two ways, essentially or dispositively. The moral virtues do not belong to the contemplative life essentially, because the end of the contemplative life is the consideration of truth: and as the Philosopher states (Ethic. ii, 4), "knowledge," which pertains to the consideration of truth, "has little influence on the moral virtues": wherefore he declares (Ethic. x, 8) that the moral virtues pertain to active but not to contemplative happiness.

On the other hand, the moral virtues belong to the contemplative life dispositively. For the act of contemplation, wherein the contemplative life essentially consists, is hindered both by the impetuosity of the passions which withdraw the soul's intention from intelligible to sensible things, and by outward disturbances. Now the moral virtues curb the impetuosity of the passions, and quell the disturbance of outward occupations. Hence moral virtues belong dispositively to the contemplative life.

Reply Obj. 1: As stated above (A. 1), the contemplative life has its motive cause on the part of the affections, and in this respect the love of God and our neighbor is requisite to the contemplative life. Now motive causes do not enter into the essence of a thing, but dispose and perfect it. Wherefore it does not follow that the moral virtues belong essentially to the contemplative life.

Reply Obj. 2: Holiness or cleanness of heart is caused by the virtues that are concerned with the passions which hinder the purity of the reason; and peace is caused by justice which is about operations, according to Isa. 32:17, "The work of justice shall be peace": since he who refrains from wronging others lessens the occasions of quarrels and disturbances. Hence the moral virtues dispose one to the contemplative life by causing peace and cleanness of heart.

Reply Obj. 3: Beauty, as stated above (Q. 145, A. 2), consists in a certain clarity and due proportion. Now each of these is found radically in the reason; because both the light that makes beauty seen, and the establishing of due proportion among things belong to reason. Hence since the contemplative life consists in an act of the reason, there is beauty in it by its very nature and essence; wherefore it is written (Wis. 8:2) of the contemplation of wisdom: "I became a lover of her beauty."

On the other hand, beauty is in the moral virtues by participation, in so far as they participate in the order of reason; and especially is it in temperance, which restrains the concupiscences which especially darken the light of reason. Hence it is that the virtue of chastity most of all makes man apt for contemplation, since venereal pleasures most of all weigh the mind down to sensible objects, as Augustine says (Soliloq. i, 10).

THIRD ARTICLE [II-II, Q. 180, Art. 3]

Whether There Are Various Actions Pertaining to the Contemplative Life?

Objection 1: It would seem that there are various actions pertaining to the contemplative life. For Richard of St. Victor [*De Grat. Contempl. i, 3, 4] distinguishes between "contemplation," "meditation," and "cogitation." Yet all these apparently pertain to contemplation. Therefore it would seem that there are various actions pertaining to the contemplative life.

Obj. 2: Further, the Apostle says (2 Cor. 3:18): "But we ... beholding ( *speculantes* ) the glory of the Lord with open face, are transformed into the same clarity [*Vulg.: 'into the same image from glory to glory.']." Now this belongs to the contemplative life. Therefore in addition to the three aforesaid, vision ( speculatio ) belongs to the contemplative life.

Obj. 3: Further, Bernard says (De Consid. v, 14) that "the first and greatest contemplation is admiration of the Majesty." Now according to Damascene (De Fide Orth. ii, 15) admiration is a kind of fear. Therefore it would seem that several acts are requisite for the contemplative life.

Obj. 4: Further, "Prayer," "reading," and "meditation" [*Hugh of St. Victor, Alleg. in N.T. iii, 4] are said to belong to the contemplative life. Again, "hearing" belongs to the contemplative life: since it is stated that Mary (by whom the contemplative life is signified) "sitting ... at the Lord's feet, heard His word" (Luke 10:39). Therefore it would seem that several acts are requisite for the contemplative life.

*On the contrary,* Life signifies here the operation on which a man is chiefly intent. Wherefore if there are several operations of the contemplative life, there will be, not one, but several contemplative lives.

*I answer that,* We are now speaking of the contemplative life as applicable to man. Now according to Dionysius (Div. Nom. vii) between man and angel there is this difference, that an angel perceives the truth by simple apprehension, whereas man arrives at the perception of a simple truth by a process from several premises. Accordingly, then, the contemplative life has one act wherein it is finally completed, namely the contemplation of truth, and from this act it derives its unity. Yet it has many acts whereby it arrives at this final act. Some of these pertain to the reception of principles, from which it proceeds to the contemplation of truth; others are concerned with deducing from the principles, the truth, the knowledge of which is sought; and the last and crowning act is the contemplation itself of the truth.

Reply Obj. 1: According to Richard of St. Victor "cogitation" would seem to regard the consideration of the many things from which a person intends to gather one simple truth. Hence cogitation may comprise not only the perceptions of the senses in taking cognizance of certain effects, but also the imaginations. And again the reason's discussion of the various signs or of anything that conduces to the truth in view: although, according to Augustine (De Trin. xiv, 7), cogitation may signify any actual operation of the intellect. "Meditation" would seem to be the process of reason from certain principles that lead to the contemplation of some truth: and "consideration" has the same meaning, according to Bernard (De Consid. ii, 2), although, according to the Philosopher (De Anima ii, 1), every operation of the intellect may be called "consideration." But "contemplation" regards the simple act of gazing on the truth; wherefore Richard says again (De Grat. Contempl. i, 4) that "contemplation is the soul's clear and free dwelling upon the object of its gaze; meditation is the survey of the mind while occupied in searching for the truth: and cogitation is the mind's glance which is prone to wander."

Reply Obj. 2: According to a gloss [*Cf. De Trin. xv, 8] of Augustine on this passage, "beholding" ( *speculatio* ) denotes "seeing in a mirror ( speculo ), not from a watch-tower ( specula )." Now to see a thing in a mirror is to see a cause in its effect wherein its likeness is reflected. Hence "beholding" would seem to be reducible to meditation.

Reply Obj. 3: Admiration is a kind of fear resulting from the apprehension of a thing that surpasses our faculties: hence it results from the contemplation of the sublime truth. For it was stated above (A. 1) that contemplation terminates in the affections.

Reply Obj. 4: Man reaches the knowledge of truth in two ways. First, by means of things received from another. In this way, as regards the things he receives from God, he needs *prayer,* according to Wis. 7:7, "I called upon" God, "and the spirit of wisdom came upon me": while as regards the things he receives from man, he needs *hearing,* in so far as he receives from the spoken word, and *reading,* in so far as he receives from the tradition of Holy Writ. Secondly, he needs to apply himself by his personal study, and thus he requires *meditation.*

FOURTH ARTICLE [II-II, Q. 180, Art. 4]

Whether the Contemplative Life Consists in the Mere Contemplation of God, or Also in the Consideration of Any Truth Whatever?

Objection 1: It would seem that the contemplative life consists not only in the contemplation of God, but also in the consideration of any truth. For it is written (Ps. 138:14): "Wonderful are Thy works, and my soul knoweth right well." Now the knowledge of God's works is effected by any contemplation of the truth. Therefore it would seem that it pertains to the contemplative life to contemplate not only the divine truth, but also any other.

Obj. 2: Further, Bernard says (De Consid. v, 14) that "contemplation consists in admiration first of God's majesty, secondly of His judgments, thirdly of His benefits, fourthly of His promises." Now of these four the first alone regards the divine truth, and the other three pertain to His effects. Therefore the contemplative life consists not only in the contemplation of the divine truth, but also in the consideration of truth regarding the divine effects.

Obj. 3: Further, Richard of St. Victor [*De Grat. Contempl. i, 6] distinguishes six species of contemplation. The first belongs to "the imagination alone," and consists in thinking of corporeal things. The second is in "the imagination guided by reason," and consists in considering the order and disposition of sensible objects. The third is in "the reason based on the imagination"; when, to wit, from the consideration of the visible we rise to the invisible. The fourth is in "the reason and conducted by the reason," when the mind is intent on things invisible of which the imagination has no cognizance. The fifth is "above the reason," but not contrary to reason, when by divine revelation we become cognizant of things that cannot be comprehended by the human reason. The sixth is "above reason and contrary to reason"; when, to wit, by the divine enlightening we know things that seem contrary to human reason, such as the doctrine of the mystery of the Trinity. Now only the last of these would seem to pertain to the divine truth. Therefore the contemplation of truth regards not only the divine truth, but also that which is considered in creatures.

Obj. 4: Further, in the contemplative life the contemplation of truth is sought as being the perfection of man. Now any truth is a perfection of the human intellect. Therefore the contemplative life consists in the contemplation of any truth.

*On the contrary,* Gregory says (Moral. vi, 37) that "in contemplation we seek the principle which is God."

*I answer that,* As stated above (A. 2), a thing may belong to the contemplative life in two ways: principally, and secondarily, or dispositively. That which belongs principally to the contemplative life is the contemplation of the divine truth, because this contemplation is the end of the whole human life. Hence Augustine says (De Trin. i, 8) that "the contemplation of God is promised us as being the goal of all our actions and the everlasting perfection of our joys." This contemplation will be perfect in the life to come, when we shall see God face to face, wherefore it will make us perfectly happy: whereas now the contemplation of the divine truth is competent to us imperfectly, namely "through a glass" and "in a dark manner" (1 Cor. 13:12). Hence it bestows on us a certain inchoate beatitude, which begins now and will be continued in the life to come; wherefore the Philosopher (Ethic. x, 7) places man's ultimate happiness in the contemplation of the supreme intelligible good.

Since, however, God's effects show us the way to the contemplation of God Himself, according to Rom. 1:20, "The invisible things of God … are clearly seen, being understood by the things that are made," it follows that the contemplation of the divine effects also belongs to the contemplative life, inasmuch as man is guided thereby to the knowledge of God. Hence Augustine says (De Vera Relig. xxix) that "in the study of creatures we must not exercise an empty and futile curiosity, but should make them the stepping-stone to things unperishable and everlasting."

Accordingly it is clear from what has been said (AA. 1, 2, 3) that four things pertain, in a certain order, to the contemplative life; first, the moral virtues; secondly, other acts exclusive of contemplation; thirdly, contemplation of the divine effects; fourthly, the complement of all which is the contemplation of the divine truth itself.

Reply Obj. 1: David sought the knowledge of God's works, so that he might be led by them to God; wherefore he says elsewhere (Ps. 142:5, 6): "I meditated on all Thy works: I meditated upon the works of Thy hands: I stretched forth my hands to Thee."

Reply Obj. 2: By considering the divine judgments man is guided to the consideration of the divine justice; and by considering the divine benefits and promises, man is led to the knowledge of God's mercy or goodness, as by effects already manifested or yet to be vouchsafed.

Reply Obj. 3: These six denote the steps whereby we ascend by means of creatures to the contemplation of God. For the first step consists in the mere consideration of sensible objects; the second step consists in going forward from sensible to intelligible objects; the third step is to judge of sensible objects according to intelligible things; the fourth is the absolute consideration of the intelligible objects to which one has attained by means of sensibles; the fifth is the contemplation of those intelligible objects that are unattainable by means of sensibles, but which the reason is able to grasp; the sixth step is the consideration of such intelligible things as the reason can neither discover nor grasp, which pertain to the sublime contemplation of divine truth, wherein contemplation is ultimately perfected.

Reply Obj. 4: The ultimate perfection of the human intellect is the divine truth: and other truths perfect the intellect in relation to the divine truth.

FIFTH ARTICLE [II-II, Q. 180, Art. 5]

Whether in the Present State of Life the Contemplative Life Can Reach to the Vision of the Divine Essence?

Objection 1: It would seem that in the present state of life the contemplative life can reach to the vision of the Divine essence. For, as stated in Gen. 32:30, Jacob said: "I have seen God face to face, and my soul has been saved." Now the vision of God's face is the vision of the Divine essence. Therefore it would seem that in the present life one may come, by means of contemplation, to see God in His essence.

Obj. 2: Further, Gregory says (Moral. vi, 37) that "contemplative men withdraw within themselves in order to explore spiritual things, nor do they ever carry with them the shadows of things corporeal, or if these follow them they prudently drive them away: but being desirous of seeing the incomprehensible light, they suppress all the images of their limited comprehension, and through longing to reach what is above them, they overcome that which they are." Now man is not hindered from seeing the Divine essence, which is the incomprehensible light, save by the necessity of turning to corporeal phantasms. Therefore it would seem that the contemplation of the present life can extend to the vision of the incomprehensible light in its essence.

Obj. 3: Further, Gregory says (Dial. ii, 35): "All creatures are small to the soul that sees its Creator: wherefore when the man of God," the blessed Benedict, to wit, "saw a fiery globe in the tower and angels returning to heaven, without doubt he could only see such things by the light of God." Now the blessed Benedict was still in this life. Therefore the contemplation of the present life can extend to the vision of the essence of God.

*On the contrary,* Gregory says (Hom. xiv in Ezech.): "As long as we live in this mortal flesh, no one reaches such a height of contemplation as to fix the eyes of his mind on the ray itself of incomprehensible light."

*I answer that,* As Augustine says (Gen. ad lit. xii, 27), "no one seeing God lives this mortal life wherein the bodily senses have their play: and unless in some way he depart this life, whether by going altogether out of his body, or by withdrawing from his carnal senses, he is not caught up into that vision." This has been carefully discussed above (Q. 175, AA. 4, 5), where we spoke of rapture, and in the First Part (Q. 12, A. 2), where we treated of the vision of God.

Accordingly we must state that one may be in this life in two ways. First, with regard to act, that is to say by actually making use of the bodily senses, and thus contemplation in the present life can nowise attain to the vision of God's essence. Secondly, one may be in this life potentially and not with regard to act, that is to say, when the soul is united to the mortal body as its form, yet so as to make use neither of the bodily senses, nor even of the imagination, as happens in rapture; and in this way the contemplation of the present life can attain to the vision of the Divine essence. Consequently the highest degree of contemplation in the present life is that which Paul had in rapture, whereby he was in a middle state between the present life and the life to come.

Reply Obj. 1: As Dionysius says (Ep. i ad Caium. Monach.), "if anyone seeing God, understood what he saw, he saw not God Himself, but something belonging to God." And Gregory says (Hom. xiv in Ezech.): "By no means is God seen now in His glory; but the soul sees something of lower degree, and is thereby refreshed so that afterwards it may attain to the glory of vision." Accordingly the words of Jacob, "I saw God face to face" do not imply that he saw God's essence, but that he saw some shape [*Cf. I, Q. 12, A. 11, ad 1], imaginary of course, wherein God spoke to him. Or, "since we know a man by his face, by the face of God he signified his knowledge of Him," according to a gloss of Gregory on the same passage.

Reply Obj. 2: In the present state of life human contemplation is impossible without phantasms, because it is connatural to man to see the intelligible species in the phantasms, as the Philosopher states (De Anima iii, 7). Yet intellectual knowledge does not consist in the phantasms themselves, but in our contemplating in them the purity of the intelligible truth: and this not only in natural knowledge, but also in that which we obtain by revelation. For Dionysius says (Coel. Hier. i) that "the Divine glory shows us the angelic hierarchies under certain symbolic figures, and by its power we are brought back to the single ray of light," i.e. to the simple knowledge of the intelligible truth. It is in this sense that we must understand the statement of Gregory that "contemplatives do not carry along with them the shadows of things corporeal," since their contemplation is not fixed on them, but on the consideration of the intelligible truth.

Reply Obj. 3: By these words Gregory does not imply that the blessed Benedict, in that vision, saw God in His essence, but he wishes to show that because "all creatures are small to him that sees God," it follows that all things can easily be seen through the enlightenment of the Divine light. Wherefore he adds: "For however little he may see of the Creator's light, all created things become petty to him."

SIXTH ARTICLE [II-II, Q. 180, Art. 6]

Whether the Operation of Contemplation Is Fittingly Divided into a Threefold Movement, Circular, Straight and Oblique?

Objection 1: It would seem that the operation of contemplation is unfittingly divided into a threefold movement, "circular," "straight," and "oblique" (Div. Nom. iv). For contemplation pertains exclusively to rest, according to Wis. 8:16, "When I go into my house, I shall repose myself with her." Now movement is opposed to rest. Therefore the operations of the contemplative life should not be described as movements.

Obj. 2: Further, the action of the contemplative life pertains to the intellect, whereby man is like the angels. Now Dionysius describes these movements as being different in the angels from what they are in the soul. For he says (Div. Nom. iv) that the "circular" movement in the angel is "according to his enlightenment by the beautiful and the good." On the other hand, he assigns the circular movement of the soul to several things: the first of which is the "withdrawal of the soul into itself from externals"; the second is "a certain concentration of its powers, whereby it is rendered free of error and of outward occupation"; and the third is "union with those things that are above it." Again, he describes differently their respective straight movements. For he says that the straight movement of the angel is that by which he proceeds to the care of those things that are beneath him. On the other hand, he describes the straight movement of the soul as being twofold: first, "its progress towards things that are near it"; secondly, "its uplifting from external things to simple contemplation." Further, he assigns a different oblique movement to each. For he assigns the oblique movement of the angels to the fact that "while providing for those who have less they remain unchanged in relation to God": whereas he assigns the oblique movement of the soul to the fact that "the soul is enlightened in Divine knowledge by reasoning and discoursing." Therefore it would seem that the operations of contemplation are unfittingly assigned according to the ways mentioned above.

Obj. 3: Further, Richard of St. Victor (De Contempl. i, 5) mentions many other different movements in likeness to the birds of the air. "For some of these rise at one time to a great height, at another swoop down to earth, and they do so repeatedly; others fly now to the right, now to the left again and again; others go forwards or lag behind many times; others fly in a circle now more now less extended; and others remain suspended almost immovably in one place." Therefore it would seem that there are only three movements of contemplation.

*On the contrary,* stands the authority of Dionysius (Div. Nom. iv).

*I answer that,* As stated above (Q. 119, A. 1, ad

3), the operation of the intellect, wherein contemplation essentially consists, is called a movement, in so far as movement is the act of a perfect thing, according to the Philosopher (De Anima iii, 1). Since, however, it is through sensible objects that we come to the knowledge of intelligible things, and since sensible operations do not take place without movement, the result is that even intelligible operations are described as movements, and are differentiated in likeness to various movements. Now of bodily movements, local movements are the most perfect and come first, as proved in *Phys.* viii, 7; wherefore the foremost among intelligible operations are described by being likened to them. These movements are of three kinds; for there is the "circular" movement, by which a thing moves uniformly round one point as center, another is the "straight" movement, by which a thing goes from one point to another; the third is "oblique," being composed as it were of both the others. Consequently, in intelligible operations, that which is simply uniform is compared to circular movement; the intelligible operation by which one proceeds from one point to another is compared to the straight movement; while the intelligible operation which unites something of uniformity with progress to various points is compared to the oblique movement.

Reply Obj. 1: External bodily movements are opposed to the quiet of contemplation, which consists in rest from outward occupations: but the movements of intellectual operations belong to the quiet of contemplation.

Reply Obj. 2: Man is like the angels in intellect generically, but the intellective power is much higher in the angel than in man. Consequently these movements must be ascribed to souls and angels in different ways, according as they are differently related to uniformity. For the angelic intellect has uniform knowledge in two respects. First, because it does not acquire intelligible truth from the variety of composite objects; secondly, because it understands the truth of intelligible objects not discursively, but by simple intuition. On the other hand, the intellect of the soul acquires intelligible truth from sensible objects, and understands it by a certain discoursing of the reason.

Wherefore Dionysius assigns the "circular" movement of the angels to the fact that their intuition of God is uniform and unceasing, having neither beginning nor end: even as a circular movement having neither beginning nor end is uniformly around the one same center. But on the part of the soul, ere it arrive at this uniformity, its twofold lack of uniformity needs to be removed. First, that which arises from the variety of external things: this is removed by the soul withdrawing from externals, and so the first thing he mentions regarding the circular movement of the soul is "the soul's withdrawal into itself from external objects." Secondly, another lack of uniformity requires to be removed from the soul, and this is owing to the discoursing of reason. This is done by directing all the soul's operations to the simple contemplation of the intelligible truth, and this is indicated by his saying in the second place that "the soul's intellectual powers must be uniformly concentrated," in other words that discoursing must be laid aside and the soul's gaze fixed on the contemplation of the one simple truth. In this operation of the soul there is no error, even as there is clearly no error in the understanding of first principles which we know by simple intuition. Afterwards these two things being done, he mentions thirdly the uniformity which is like that of the angels, for then all things being laid aside, the soul continues in the contemplation of God alone. This he expresses by saying: "Then being thus made uniform unitedly," i.e. conformably, "by the union of its powers, it is conducted to the good and the beautiful." The "straight" movement of the angel cannot apply to his proceeding from one thing to another by considering them, but only to the order of his providence, namely to the fact that the higher angel enlightens the lower angels through the angels that are intermediate. He indicates this when he says: "The angel's movement takes a straight line when he proceeds to the care of things subject to him, taking in his course whatever things are direct," i.e. in keeping with the dispositions of the direct order. Whereas he ascribes the "straight" movement in the soul to the soul's proceeding from exterior sensibles to the knowledge of intelligible objects. The "oblique" movement in the angels he describes as being composed of the straight and circular movements, inasmuch as their care for those beneath them is in accordance with their contemplation of God: while the "oblique" movement in the soul he also declares to be partly straight and partly circular, in so far as in reasoning it makes use of the light received from God.

Reply Obj. 3: These varieties of movement that are taken from the distinction between above and below, right and left, forwards and backwards, and from varying circles, are all comprised under either straight [or] oblique movement, because they all denote discursions of reason. For if the reason pass from the genus to the species, or from the part to the whole, it will be, as he explains, from above to below: if from one opposite to another, it will be from right to left; if from the cause to the effect, it will be backwards and forwards; if it be about accidents that surround a thing near at hand or far remote, the movement will be circular. The discoursing of reason from sensible to intelligible objects, if it be according to the order of natural reason, belongs to the straight movement; but if it be according to the Divine enlightenment, it will belong to the oblique movement as explained above (ad 2). That alone which he describes as immobility belongs to the circular movement.

Wherefore it is evident that Dionysius describes the movement of contemplation with much greater fulness and depth.

SEVENTH ARTICLE [II-II, Q. 180, Art. 7]

Whether There Is Delight in Contemplation?

Objection 1: It would seem that there is no delight in contemplation. For delight belongs to the appetitive power; whereas contemplation resides chiefly in the intellect. Therefore it would seem that there is no delight in contemplation.

Obj. 2: Further, all strife and struggle is a hindrance to delight. Now there is strife and struggle in contemplation. For Gregory says (Hom. xiv in Ezech.) that "when the soul strives to contemplate God, it is in a state of struggle; at one time it almost overcomes, because by understanding and feeling it tastes something of the incomprehensible light, and at another time it almost succumbs, because even while tasting, it fails." Therefore there is no delight in contemplation.

Obj. 3: Further, delight is the result of a perfect operation, as stated in *Ethic.* x, 4. Now the contemplation of wayfarers is imperfect, according to 1 Cor. 13:12, "We see now through a glass in a dark manner." Therefore seemingly there is no delight in the contemplative life.

Obj. 4: Further, a lesion of the body is an obstacle to delight. Now contemplation causes a lesion of the body; wherefore it is stated (Gen. 32) that after Jacob had said (Gen. 32:30), "'I have seen God face to face' ... he halted on his foot (Gen. 32:31) ... because he touched the sinew of his thigh and it shrank" (Gen. 32:32). Therefore seemingly there is no delight in contemplation.

*On the contrary,* It is written of the contemplation of wisdom (Wis. 8:16): "Her conversation hath no bitterness, nor her company any tediousness, but joy and gladness": and Gregory says (Hom. xiv in Ezech.) that "the contemplative life is sweetness exceedingly lovable."

*I answer that,* There may be delight in any particular contemplation in two ways. First by reason of the operation itself [*Cf. I-II, Q. 3, A. 5], because each individual delights in the operation which befits him according to his own nature or habit. Now contemplation of the truth befits a man according to his nature as a rational animal: the result being that "all men naturally desire to know," so that consequently they delight in the knowledge of truth. And more delightful still does this become to one who has the habit of wisdom and knowledge, the result of which is that he contemplates without difficulty. Secondly, contemplation may be delightful on the part of its object, in so far as one contemplates that which one loves; even as bodily vision gives pleasure, not only because to see is pleasurable in itself, but because one sees a person whom one loves. Since, then, the contemplative life consists chiefly in the contemplation of God, of which charity is the motive, as stated above (AA. 1, 2, ad 1), it follows that there is delight in the contemplative life, not only by reason of the contemplation itself, but also by reason of the Divine love.

In both respects the delight thereof surpasses all human delight, both because spiritual delight is greater than carnal pleasure, as stated above (I-II, Q. 31, A. 5), when we were treating of the passions, and because the love whereby God is loved out of charity surpasses all love. Hence it is written (Ps. 33:9): "O taste and see that the Lord is sweet."

Reply Obj. 1: Although the contemplative life consists chiefly in an act of the intellect, it has its beginning in the appetite, since it is through charity that one is urged to the contemplation of God. And since the end corresponds to the beginning, it follows that the term also and the end of the contemplative life has its being in the appetite, since one delights in seeing the object loved, and the very delight in the object seen arouses a yet greater love. Wherefore Gregory says (Hom. xiv in Ezech.) that "when we see one whom we love, we are so aflame as to love him more." And this is the ultimate perfection of the contemplative life, namely that the Divine truth be not only seen but also loved.

Reply Obj. 2: Strife or struggle arising from the opposition of an external thing, hinders delight in that thing. For a man delights not in a thing against which he strives: but in that for which he strives; when he has obtained it, other things being equal, he delights yet more: wherefore Augustine says (Confess. viii, 3) that "the more peril there was in the battle, the greater the joy in the triumph." But there is no strife or struggle in contemplation on the part of the truth which we contemplate, though there is on the part of our defective understanding and our corruptible body which drags us down to lower things, according to Wis. 9:15, "The corruptible body is a load upon the soul, and the earthly habitation presseth down the mind that museth upon many things." Hence it is that when man attains to the contemplation of truth, he loves it yet more, while he hates the more his own deficiency and the weight of his corruptible body, so as to say with the Apostle (Rom. 7:24): "Unhappy man that I am, who shall deliver me from the body of this death?" Wherefore Gregory say (Hom. xiv in Ezech.): "When God is once known by desire and understanding, He withers all carnal pleasure in us."

Reply Obj. 3: The contemplation of God in this life is imperfect in comparison with the contemplation in heaven; and in like manner the delight of the wayfarer's contemplation is imperfect as compared with the delight of contemplation in heaven, of which it is written (Ps. 35:9): "Thou shalt make them drink of the torrent of Thy pleasure." Yet, though the contemplation of Divine things which is to be had by wayfarers is imperfect, it is more delightful than all other contemplation however perfect, on account of the excellence of that which is contemplated. Hence the Philosopher says (De Part. Animal. i, 5): "We may happen to have our own little theories about those sublime beings and godlike substances, and though we grasp them but feebly, nevertheless so elevating is the knowledge that they give us more delight than any of those things that are round about us": and Gregory says in the same sense (Hom. xiv in Ezech.): "The contemplative life is sweetness exceedingly lovable; for it carries the soul away above itself, it opens heaven and discovers the spiritual world to the eyes of the mind."

Reply Obj. 4: After contemplation Jacob halted with one foot, "because we need to grow weak in the love of the world ere we wax strong in the love of God," as Gregory says (Hom. xiv in Ezech.). "Thus when we have known the sweetness of God, we have one foot sound while the other halts; since every one who halts on one foot leans only on that foot which is sound."

EIGHTH ARTICLE [II-II, Q. 180, Art. 8]

Whether the Contemplative Life Is Continuous?

Objection 1: It would seem that the contemplative life is not continuous. For the contemplative life consists essentially in things pertaining to the intellect. Now all the intellectual perfections of this life will be made void, according to 1 Cor. 13:8, "Whether prophecies shall be made void, or tongues shall cease, or knowledge shall be destroyed." Therefore the contemplative life is made void.

Obj. 2: Further, a man tastes the sweetness of contemplation by snatches and for a short time only: wherefore Augustine says (Confess. x, 40), "Thou admittest me to a most unwonted affection in my inmost soul, to a strange sweetness ... yet through my grievous weight I sink down again." Again, Gregory commenting on the words of Job 4:15, "When a spirit passed before me," says (Moral. v, 33): "The mind does not remain long at rest in the sweetness of inward contemplation, for it is recalled to itself and beaten back by the very immensity of the light." Therefore the contemplative life is not continuous.

Obj. 3: Further, that which is not connatural to man cannot be continuous. Now the contemplative life, according to the Philosopher (Ethic. x, 7), "is better than the life which is according to man." Therefore seemingly the contemplative life is not continuous.

*On the contrary,* our Lord said (Luke 10:42): "Mary hath chosen the best part, which shall not be taken away from her," since as Gregory says (Hom. xiv in Ezech.), "the contemplative life begins here so that it may be perfected in our heavenly home."

*I answer that,* A thing may be described as continuous in two ways: first, in regard to its nature; secondly, in regard to us. It is evident that in regard to itself contemplative life is continuous for two reasons: first, because it is about incorruptible and unchangeable things; secondly, because it has no contrary, for there is nothing contrary to the pleasure of contemplation, as stated in *Topic.* i, 13. But even in our regard contemplative life is continuous—both because it is competent to us in respect of the incorruptible part of the soul, namely the intellect, wherefore it can endure after this life—and because in the works of the contemplative life we work not with our bodies, so that we are the more able to persevere in the works thereof, as the Philosopher observes (Ethic. x, 7).

Reply Obj. 1: The manner of contemplation is not the same here as in heaven: yet the contemplative life is said to remain by reason of charity, wherein it has both its beginning and its end. Gregory speaks in this sense (Hom. xiv in Ezech.): "The contemplative life begins here, so as to be perfected in our heavenly home, because the fire of love which begins to burn here is aflame with a yet greater love when we see Him Whom we love."

Reply Obj. 2: No action can last long at its highest pitch. Now the highest point of contemplation is to reach the uniformity of Divine contemplation, according to Dionysius [*Cf. Coel. Hier. iii], and as we have stated above (A. 6, ad 2). Hence although contemplation cannot last long in this respect, it can be of long duration as regards the other contemplative acts.

Reply Obj. 3: The Philosopher declares the contemplative life to be above man, because it befits us "so far as there is in us something divine" (Ethic. x, 7), namely the intellect, which is incorruptible and impassible in itself, wherefore its act can endure longer.

## QUESTION 181

OF THE ACTIVE LIFE (In Four Articles)

We must now consider the active life, under which head there are four points of inquiry:

(1) Whether all the works of the moral virtues pertain to the active life?

(2) Whether prudence pertains to the active life?

(3) Whether teaching pertains to the active life?

(4) Of the duration of the active life.

FIRST ARTICLE [II-II, Q. 181, Art. 1]

Whether All the Actions of the Moral Virtues Pertain to the Active Life?

Objection 1: It would seem that the acts of the moral virtues do not all pertain to the active life. For seemingly the active life regards only our relations with other persons: hence Gregory says (Hom. xiv in Ezech.) that "the active life is to give bread to the hungry," and after mentioning many things that regard our relations with other people he adds finally, "and to give to each and every one whatever he needs." Now we are directed in our relations to others, not by all the acts of moral virtues, but only by those of justice and its parts, as stated above (Q. 58, AA. 2, 8; I-II, Q. 60, AA. 2, 3). Therefore the acts of the moral virtues do not all pertain to the active life.

Obj. 2: Further, Gregory says (Hom. xiv in Ezech.) that Lia who was blear-eyed but fruitful signifies the active life: which "being occupied with work, sees less, and yet since it urges one's neighbor both by word and example to its imitation it begets a numerous offspring of good deeds." Now this would seem to belong to charity, whereby we love our neighbor, rather than to the moral virtues. Therefore seemingly the acts of moral virtue do not pertain to the active life.

Obj. 3: Further, as stated above (Q. 180, A. 2), the moral virtues dispose one to the contemplative life. Now disposition and perfection belong to the same thing. Therefore it would seem that the moral virtues do not pertain to the active life.

*On the contrary,* Isidore says (De Summo Bono iii, 15): "In the active life all vices must first of all be extirpated by the practice of good works, in order that in the contemplative life the mind's eye being purified one may advance to the contemplation of the Divine light." Now all vices are not extirpated save by acts of the moral virtues. Therefore the acts of the moral virtues pertain to the active life.

*I answer that,* As stated above (Q. 179, A. 1) the active and the contemplative life differ according to the different occupations of men intent on different ends: one of which occupations is the consideration of the truth; and this is the end of the contemplative life, while the other is external work to which the active life is directed.

Now it is evident that the moral virtues are directed chiefly, not to the contemplation of truth but to operation. Wherefore the Philosopher says (Ethic. ii, 4) that "for virtue knowledge is of little or no avail." Hence it is clear that the moral virtues belong essentially to the active life; for which reason the Philosopher (Ethic. x, 8) subordinates the moral virtues to active happiness.

Reply Obj. 1: The chief of the moral virtues is justice by which one man is directed in his relations towards another, as the Philosopher proves (Ethic. v, 1). Hence the active life is described with reference to our relations with other people, because it consists in these things, not exclusively, but principally.

Reply Obj. 2: It is possible, by the acts of all the moral virtues, for one to direct one's neighbor to good by example: and this is what Gregory here ascribes to the active life.

Reply Obj. 3: Even as the virtue that is directed to the end of another virtue passes, as it were, into the species of the latter virtue, so again when a man makes use of things pertaining to the active life, merely as dispositions to contemplation, such things are comprised under the contemplative life. On the other hand, when we practice the works of the moral virtues, as being good in themselves, and not as dispositions to the contemplative life, the moral virtues belong to the active life.

It may also be replied, however, that the active life is a disposition to the contemplative life.

SECOND ARTICLE [II-II, Q. 181, Art. 2]

Whether Prudence Pertains to the Active Life?

Objection 1: It would seem that prudence does not pertain to the active life. For just as the contemplative life belongs to the cognitive power, so the active life belongs to the appetitive power. Now prudence belongs not to the appetitive but to the cognitive power. Therefore prudence does not belong to the active life.

Obj. 2: Further, Gregory says (Hom. xiv in Ezech.) that the "active life being occupied with work, sees less," wherefore it is signified by Lia who was blear-eyed. But prudence requires clear eyes, so that one may judge aright of what has to be done. Therefore it seems that prudence does not pertain to the active life.

Obj. 3: Further, prudence stands between the moral and the intellectual virtues. Now just as the moral virtues belong to the active life, as stated above (A. 1), so do the intellectual virtues pertain to the contemplative life. Therefore it would seem that prudence pertains neither to the active nor to the contemplative life, but to an intermediate kind of life, of which Augustine makes mention (De Civ. Dei xix, 2, 3, 19).

*On the contrary,* The Philosopher says (Ethic. x, 8) that prudence pertains to active happiness, to which the moral virtues belong.

*I answer that,* As stated above (A. 1, ad 3; I-II, Q. 18, A. 6), if one thing be directed to another as its end, it is drawn, especially in moral matters, to the species of the thing to which it is directed: for instance "he who commits adultery that he may steal, is a thief rather than an adulterer," according to the Philosopher (Ethic. v, 2). Now it is evident that the knowledge of prudence is directed to the works of the moral virtues as its end, since it is "right reason applied to action" (Ethic. vi, 5); so that the ends of the moral virtues are the principles of prudence, as the Philosopher says in the same book. Accordingly, as it was stated above (A. 1, ad 3) that the moral virtues in one who directs them to the quiet of contemplation belong to the contemplative life, so the knowledge of prudence, which is of itself directed to the works of the moral virtues, belongs directly to the active life, provided we take prudence in its proper sense as the Philosopher speaks of it.

If, however, we take it in a more general sense, as comprising any kind of human knowledge, then prudence, as regards a certain part thereof, belongs to the contemplative life. In this sense Tully (De Offic. i, 5) says that "the man who is able most clearly and quickly to grasp the truth and to unfold his reasons, is wont to be considered most prudent and wise."

Reply Obj. 1: Moral works take their species from their end, as stated above (I-II, Q. 18, AA. 4, 6), wherefore the knowledge pertaining to the contemplative life is that which has its end in the very knowledge of truth; whereas the knowledge of prudence, through having its end in an act of the appetitive power, belongs to the active life.

Reply Obj. 2: External occupation makes a man see less in intelligible things, which are separated from sensible objects with which the works of the active life are concerned. Nevertheless the external occupation of the active life enables a man to see more clearly in judging of what is to be done, which belongs to prudence, both on account of experience, and on account of the mind's attention, since "brains avail when the mind is attentive" as Sallust observes [*Bell. Catilin., LI].

Reply Obj. 3: Prudence is said to be intermediate between the intellectual and the moral virtues because it resides in the same subject as the intellectual virtues, and has absolutely the same matter as the moral virtues. But this third kind of life is intermediate between the active and the contemplative life as regards the things about which it is occupied, because it is occupied sometimes with the contemplation of the truth, sometimes with eternal things.

THIRD ARTICLE [II-II, Q. 811, Art. 3]

Whether Teaching Is a Work of the Active or of the Contemplative Life?

Objection 1: It would seem that teaching is a work not of the active but of the contemplative life. For Gregory says (Hom. v in Ezech.) that "the perfect who have been able to contemplate heavenly goods, at least through a glass, proclaim them to their brethren, whose minds they inflame with love for their hidden beauty." But this pertains to teaching. Therefore teaching is a work of the contemplative life.

Obj. 2: Further, act and habit would seem to be referable to the same kind of life. Now teaching is an act of wisdom: for the Philosopher says (Metaph. i, 1) that "to be able to teach is an indication of knowledge." Therefore since wisdom or knowledge pertain to the contemplative life, it would seem that teaching also belongs to the contemplative life.

Obj. 3: Further, prayer, no less than contemplation, is an act of the contemplative life. Now prayer, even when one prays for another, belongs to the contemplative life. Therefore it would seem that it belongs also to the contemplative life to acquaint another, by teaching him, of the truth we have meditated.

*On the contrary,* Gregory says (Hom. xiv in Ezech.): "The active life is to give bread to the hungry, to teach the ignorant the words of wisdom."

*I answer that,* The act of teaching has a twofold object. For teaching is conveyed by speech, and speech is the audible sign of the interior concept. Accordingly one object of teaching is the matter or object of the interior concept; and as to this object teaching belongs sometimes to the active, sometimes to the contemplative life. It belongs to the active life, when a man conceives a truth inwardly, so as to be directed thereby in his outward action; but it belongs to the contemplative life when a man conceives an intelligible truth, in the consideration and love whereof he delights. Hence Augustine says (De Verb. Dom. Serm. civ, 1): "Let them choose for themselves the better part," namely the contemplative life, "let them be busy with the word, long for the sweetness of teaching, occupy themselves with salutary knowledge," thus stating clearly that teaching belongs to the contemplative life.

The other object of teaching is on the part of the speech heard, and thus the object of teaching is the hearer. As to this object all doctrine belongs to the active life to which external actions pertain.

Reply Obj. 1: The authority quoted speaks expressly of doctrine as to its matter, in so far as it is concerned with the consideration and love of truth.

Reply Obj. 2: Habit and act have a common object. Hence this argument clearly considers the matter of the interior concept. For it pertains to the man having wisdom and knowledge to be able to teach, in so far as he is able to express his interior concept in words, so as to bring another man to understand the truth.

Reply Obj. 3: He who prays for another does nothing towards the man for whom he prays, but only towards God Who is the intelligible truth; whereas he who teaches another does something in his regard by external action. Hence the comparison fails.

FOURTH ARTICLE [II-II, Q. 181, Art. 4]

Whether the Active Life Remains After This Life?

Objection 1: It would seem that the active life remains after this life. For the acts of the moral virtues belong to the active life, as stated above (A. 1). But the moral virtues endure after this life according to Augustine (De Trin. xiv, 9). Therefore the active life remains after this life.

Obj. 2: Further, teaching others belongs to the active life, as stated above (A. 3). But in the life to come when "we shall be like the angels," teaching will be possible: even as apparently it is in the angels of whom one "enlightens, cleanses, and perfects" [*Coel. Hier. iii, viii] another, which refers to the "receiving of knowledge," according to Dionysius (Coel. Hier. vii). Therefore it would seem that the active life remains after this life.

Obj. 3: Further, the more lasting a thing is in itself, the more is it able to endure after this life. But the active life is seemingly more lasting in itself: for Gregory says (Hom. v in Ezech.) that "we can remain fixed in the active life, whereas we are nowise able to maintain an attentive mind in the contemplative life." Therefore the active life is much more able than the contemplative to endure after this life.

*On the contrary,* Gregory says (Hom. xiv in Ezech.): "The active life ends with this world, but the contemplative life begins here, to be perfected in our heavenly home."

*I answer that,* As stated above (A. 1), the active life has its end in external actions: and if these be referred to the quiet of contemplation, for that very reason they belong to the contemplative life. But in the future life of the blessed the occupation of external actions will cease, and if there be any external actions at all, these will be referred to contemplation as their end. For, as Augustine says at the end of *De Civitate Dei* xxii, 30, "there we shall rest and we shall see, we shall see and love, we shall love and praise." And he had said before (De Civ. Dei xxii, 30) that "there God will be seen without end, loved without wearying, praised without tiring: such will be the occupation of all, the common love, the universal activity."

Reply Obj. 1: As stated above (Q. 136, A. 1, ad 1), the moral virtues will remain not as to those actions which are about the means, but as to the actions which are about the end. Such acts are those that conduce to the quiet of contemplation, which in the words quoted above Augustine denotes by "rest," and this rest excludes not only outward disturbances but also the inward disturbance of the passions.

Reply Obj. 2: The contemplative life, as stated above (Q. 180, A. 4), consists chiefly in the contemplation of God, and as to this, one angel does not teach another, since according to Matt. 18:10, "the little ones' angels," who belong to the lower order, "always see the face of the Father"; and so, in the life to come, no man will teach another of God, but "we shall" all "see Him as He is" (1 John 3:2). This is in keeping with the saying of Jeremiah 31:34: "They shall teach no more every man his neighbor ... saying: Know the Lord: for all shall know me, from the least of them even to the greatest."

But as regards things pertaining to the "dispensation of the mysteries of God," one angel teaches another by cleansing, enlightening, and perfecting him: and thus they have something of the active life so long as the world lasts, from the fact that they are occupied in administering to the creatures below them. This is signified by the fact that Jacob saw angels "ascending" the ladder—which refers to contemplation—and "descending"—which refers to action. Nevertheless, as Gregory remarks (Moral. ii, 3), "they do not wander abroad from the Divine vision, so as to be deprived of the joys of inward contemplation." Hence in them the active life does not differ from the contemplative life as it does in us for whom the works of the active life are a hindrance to contemplation.

Nor is the likeness to the angels promised to us as regards the administering to lower creatures, for this is competent to us not by reason of our natural order, as it is to the angels, but by reason of our seeing God.

Reply Obj. 3: That the durability of the active life in the present state surpasses the durability of the contemplative life arises not from any property of either life considered in itself, but from our own deficiency, since we are withheld from the heights of contemplation by the weight of the body. Hence Gregory adds (Moral. ii, 3) that "the mind through its very weakness being repelled from that immense height recoils on itself."

## QUESTION 182

OF THE ACTIVE LIFE IN COMPARISON WITH THE CONTEMPLATIVE LIFE (In Four Articles)

We must now consider the active life in comparison with the contemplative life, under which head there are four points of inquiry:

(1) Which of them is of greater import or excellence?

(2) Which of them has the greater merit?

(3) Whether the contemplative life is hindered by the active life?

(4) Of their order.

FIRST ARTICLE [II-II, Q. 182, Art. 1]

Whether the Active Life Is More Excellent Than the Contemplative?

Objection 1: It would seem that the active life is more excellent than the contemplative. For "that which belongs to better men would seem to be worthier and better," as the Philosopher says (Top. iii, 1). Now the active life belongs to persons of higher rank, namely prelates, who are placed in a position of honor and power; wherefore Augustine says (De Civ. Dei xix, 19) that "in our actions we must not love honor or power in this life." Therefore it would seem that the active life is more excellent than the contemplative.

Obj. 2: Further, in all habits and acts, direction belongs to the more important; thus the military art, being the more important, directs the art of the bridle-maker [*Ethic. i, 1]. Now it belongs to the active life to direct and command the contemplative, as appears from the words addressed to Moses (Ex. 19:21), "Go down and charge the people, lest they should have a mind to pass the" fixed "limits to see the Lord." Therefore the active life is more excellent than the contemplative.

Obj. 3: Further, no man should be taken away from a greater thing in order to be occupied with lesser things: for the Apostle says (1 Cor. 12:31): "Be zealous for the better gifts." Now some are taken away from the state of the contemplative life to the occupations of the active life, as in the case of those who are transferred to the state of prelacy. Therefore it would seem that the active life is more excellent than the contemplative.

*On the contrary,* Our Lord said (Luke 10:42):

"Mary hath chosen the best part, which shall not be taken away from her." Now Mary figures the contemplative life. Therefore the contemplative life is more excellent than the active.

*I answer that,* Nothing prevents certain things being more excellent in themselves, whereas they are surpassed by another in some respect. Accordingly we must reply that the contemplative life is simply more excellent than the active: and the Philosopher proves this by eight reasons (Ethic. x, 7, 8). The first is, because the contemplative life becomes man according to that which is best in him, namely the intellect, and according to its proper objects, namely things intelligible; whereas the active life is occupied with externals. Hence Rachael, by whom the contemplative life is signified, is interpreted "the vision of the principle," [*Or rather, 'One seeing the principle,' if derived from *rah* and irzn ; Cf. Jerome, De Nom. Hebr.] whereas as Gregory says (Moral. vi, 37) the active life is signified by Lia who was blear-eyed. The second reason is because the contemplative life can be more continuous, although not as regards the highest degree of contemplation, as stated above (Q. 180, A. 8, ad 2; Q. 181, A. 4, ad 3), wherefore Mary, by whom the contemplative life is signified, is described as "sitting" all the time "at the Lord's feet." Thirdly, because the contemplative life is more delightful than the active; wherefore Augustine says (De Verb. Dom. Serm. ciii) that "Martha was troubled, but Mary feasted." Fourthly, because in the contemplative life man is more self-sufficient, since he needs fewer things for that purpose; wherefore it was said (Luke 10:41): "Martha, Martha, thou art careful and art troubled about many things." Fifthly, because the contemplative life is loved more for its own sake, while the active life is directed to something else. Hence it is written (Ps. 36:4): "One thing I have asked of the Lord, this will I seek after, that I may dwell in the house of the Lord all the days of my life, that I may see the delight of the Lord." Sixthly, because the contemplative life consists in leisure and rest, according to Ps. 45:11, "Be still and see that I am God." Seventhly, because the contemplative life is according to Divine things, whereas active life is according to human things; wherefore Augustine says (De Verb. Dom. Serm. civ): "'In the beginning was the Word': to Him was Mary hearkening: 'The Word was made flesh': Him was Martha serving." Eighthly, because the contemplative life is according to that which is most proper to man, namely his intellect; whereas in the works of the active life the lower powers also, which are common to us and brutes, have their part; wherefore (Ps. 35:7) after the words, "Men and beasts Thou wilt preserve, O Lord," that which is special to man is added (Ps. 35:10): "In Thy light we shall see light."

Our Lord adds a ninth reason (Luke 10:42) when He says: "Mary hath chosen the best part, which shall not be taken away from her," which words Augustine (De Verb. Dom. Serm. ciii) expounds thus: "Not—Thou hast chosen badly but—She has chosen better. Why better? Listen—because it shall not be taken away from her. But the burden of necessity shall at length be taken from thee: whereas the sweetness of truth is eternal."

Yet in a restricted sense and in a particular case one should prefer the active life on account of the needs of the present life. Thus too the Philosopher says (Topic. iii, 2): "It is better to be wise than to be rich, yet for one who is in need, it is better to be rich ..."

Reply Obj. 1: Not only the active life concerns prelates, they should also excel in the contemplative life; hence Gregory says (Pastor. ii, 1): "A prelate should be foremost in action, more uplifted than others in contemplation."

Reply Obj. 2: The contemplative life consists in a certain liberty of mind. For Gregory says (Hom. iii in Ezech.) that "the contemplative life obtains a certain freedom of mind, for it thinks not of temporal but of eternal things." And Boethius says (De Consol. v, 2): "The soul of man must needs be more free while it continues to gaze on the Divine mind, and less so when it stoops to bodily things." Wherefore it is evident that the active life does not directly command the contemplative life, but prescribes certain works of the active life as dispositions to the contemplative life; which it accordingly serves rather than commands. Gregory refers to this when he says (Hom. iii in Ezech.) that "the active life is bondage, whereas the contemplative life is freedom."

Reply Obj. 3: Sometimes a man is called away from the contemplative life to the works of the active life, on account of some necessity of the present life, yet not so as to be compelled to forsake contemplation altogether. Hence Augustine says (De Civ. Dei xix, 19): "The love of truth seeks a holy leisure, the demands of charity undertake an honest toil," the work namely of the active life. "If no one imposes this burden upon us we must devote ourselves to the research and contemplation of truth, but if it be imposed on us, we must bear it because charity demands it of us. Yet even then we must not altogether forsake the delights of truth, lest we deprive ourselves of its sweetness, and this burden overwhelm us." Hence it is clear that when a person is called from the contemplative life to the active life, this is done by way not of subtraction but of addition.

SECOND ARTICLE [II-II, Q. 182, Art. 2]

Whether the Active Life Is of Greater Merit Than the Contemplative?

Objection 1: It would seem that the active life is of greater merit than the contemplative. For merit implies relation to meed; and meed is due to labor, according to 1 Cor. 3:8, "Every man shall receive his own reward according to his own labor." Now labor is ascribed to the active life, and rest to the contemplative life; for Gregory says (Hom. xiv in Ezech.): "Whosoever is converted to God must first of all sweat from labor, i.e. he must take Lia, that afterwards he may rest in the embraces of Rachel so as to see the principle." Therefore the active life is of greater merit than the contemplative.

Obj. 2: Further, the contemplative life is a beginning of the happiness to come; wherefore Augustine commenting on John 21:22, "So I will have him to remain till I come," says (Tract. cxxiv in Joan.): "This may be expressed more clearly: Let perfect works follow Me conformed to the example of My passion, and let contemplation begun here remain until I come, that it may be perfected when I shall come." And Gregory says (Hom. xiv in Ezech.) that "contemplation begins here, so as to be perfected in our heavenly home." Now the life to come will be a state not of meriting but of receiving the reward of our merits. Therefore the contemplative life would seem to have less of the character of merit than the active, but more of the character of reward.

Obj. 3: Further, Gregory says (Hom. xii in Ezech.) that "no sacrifice is more acceptable to God than zeal for souls." Now by the zeal for souls a man turns to the occupations of the active life. Therefore it would seem that the contemplative life is not of greater merit than the active.

*On the contrary,* Gregory says (Moral. vi, 37): "Great are the merits of the active life, but greater still those of the contemplative."

*I answer that,* As stated above (I-II, Q. 114, A. 4), the root of merit is charity; and, while, as stated above (Q. 25, A. 1), charity consists in the love of God and our neighbor, the love of God is by itself more meritorious than the love of our neighbor, as stated above (Q. 27, A. 8). Wherefore that which pertains more directly to the love of God is generically more meritorious than that which pertains directly to the love of our neighbor for God's sake. Now the contemplative life pertains directly and immediately to the love of God; for Augustine says (De Civ. Dei xix, 19) that "the love of" the Divine "truth seeks a holy leisure," namely of the contemplative life, for it is that truth above all which the contemplative life seeks, as stated above (Q. 181, A. 4, ad 2). On the other hand, the active life is more directly concerned with the love of our neighbor, because it is "busy about much serving" (Luke 10:40). Wherefore the contemplative life is generically of greater merit than the active life. This is moreover asserted by Gregory (Hom. iii in Ezech.): "The contemplative life surpasses in merit the active life, because the latter labors under the stress of present work," by reason of the necessity of assisting our neighbor, "while the former with heartfelt relish has a foretaste of the coming rest," i.e. the contemplation of God.

Nevertheless it may happen that one man merits more by the works of the active life than another by the works of the contemplative life. For instance through excess of Divine love a man may now and then suffer separation from the sweetness of Divine contemplation for the time being, that God's will may be done and for His glory's sake. Thus the Apostle says (Rom. 9:3): "I wished myself to be an anathema from Christ, for my brethren"; which words Chrysostom expounds as follows (De Compunct. i, 7 [*Ad Demetr. de Compunct. Cordis.]): "His mind was so steeped in the love of Christ that, although he desired above all to be with Christ, he despised even this, because thus he pleased Christ."

Reply Obj. 1: External labor conduces to the increase of the accidental reward; but the increase of merit with regard to the essential reward consists chiefly in charity, whereof external labor borne for Christ's sake is a sign. Yet a much more expressive sign thereof is shown when a man, renouncing whatsoever pertains to this life, delights to occupy himself entirely with Divine contemplation.

Reply Obj. 2: In the state of future happiness man has arrived at perfection, wherefore there is no room for advancement by merit; and if there were, the merit would be more efficacious by reason of the greater charity. But in the present life contemplation is not without some imperfection, and can always become more perfect; wherefore it does not remove the idea of merit, but causes a yet greater merit on account of the practice of greater Divine charity.

Reply Obj. 3: A sacrifice is rendered to God spiritually when something is offered to Him; and of all man's goods, God specially accepts that of the human soul when it is offered to Him in sacrifice. Now a man ought to offer to God, in the first place, his soul, according to Ecclus. 30:24, "Have pity on thy own soul, pleasing God"; in the second place, the souls of others, according to Apoc. 22:17, "He that heareth, let him say: Come." And the more closely a man unites his own or another's soul to God, the more acceptable is his sacrifice to God; wherefore it is more acceptable to God that one apply one's own soul and the souls of others to contemplation than to action. Consequently the statement that "no sacrifice is more acceptable to God than zeal for souls," does not mean that the merit of the active life is preferable to the merit of the contemplative life, but that it is more meritorious to offer to God one's own soul and the souls of others, than any other external gifts.

THIRD ARTICLE [II-II, Q. 182, Art. 3]

Whether the Contemplative Life Is Hindered by the Active Life?

Objection 1: It would seem that the contemplative life is hindered by the active life. For the contemplative life requires a certain stillness of mind, according to Ps. 45:11, "Be still, and see that I am God"; whereas the active life involves restlessness, according to Luke 10:41, "Martha, Martha, thou art careful and troubled about many things." Therefore the active life hinders the contemplative.

Obj. 2: Further, clearness of vision is a requisite for the contemplative life. Now active life is a hindrance to clear vision; for Gregory says (Hom. xiv in Ezech.) that it "is blear-eyed and fruitful, because the active life, being occupied with work, sees less." Therefore the active life hinders the contemplative.

Obj. 3: Further, one contrary hinders the other. Now the active and the contemplative life are apparently contrary to one another, since the active life is busy about many things, while the contemplative life attends to the contemplation of one; wherefore they differ in opposition to one another. Therefore it would seem that the contemplative life is hindered by the active.

*On the contrary,* Gregory says (Moral. vi, 37): "Those who wish to hold the fortress of contemplation, must first of all train in the camp of action."

*I answer that,* The active life may be considered from two points of view. First, as regards the attention to and practice of external works: and thus it is evident that the active life hinders the contemplative, in so far as it is impossible for one to be busy with external action, and at the same time give oneself to Divine contemplation. Secondly, active life may be considered as quieting and directing the internal passions of the soul; and from this point of view the active life is a help to the contemplative, since the latter is hindered by the inordinateness of the internal passions. Hence Gregory says (Moral. vi, 37): "Those who wish to hold the fortress of contemplation must first of all train in the camp of action. Thus after careful study they will learn whether they no longer wrong their neighbor, whether they bear with equanimity the wrongs their neighbors do to them, whether their soul is neither overcome with joy in the presence of temporal goods, nor cast down with too great a sorrow when those goods are withdrawn. In this way they will know when they withdraw within themselves, in order to explore spiritual things, whether they no longer carry with them the shadows of the things corporeal, or, if these follow them, whether they prudently drive them away." Hence the work of the active life conduces to the contemplative, by quelling the interior passions which give rise to the phantasms whereby contemplation is hindered.

This suffices for the Replies to the Objections; for these arguments consider the occupation itself of external actions, and not the effect which is the quelling of the passions.

FOURTH ARTICLE [II-II, Q. 182, Art. 4]

Whether the Active Life Precedes the Contemplative?

Objection 1: It would seem that the active life does not precede the contemplative. For the contemplative life pertains directly to the love of God; while the active life pertains to the love of our neighbor. Now the love of God precedes the love of our neighbor, since we love our neighbor for God's sake. Seemingly therefore the contemplative life also precedes the active life.

Obj. 2: Further, Gregory says (Hom. xiv in Ezech.): "It should be observed that while a well-ordered life proceeds from action to contemplation, sometimes it is useful for the soul to turn from the contemplative to the active life." Therefore the active is not simply prior to the contemplative.

Obj. 3: Further, it would seem that there is not necessarily any order between things that are suitable to different subjects. Now the active and the contemplative life are suitable to different subjects; for Gregory says (Moral. vi, 37): "Often those who were able to contemplate God so long as they were undisturbed have fallen when pressed with occupation; and frequently they who might live advantageously occupied with the service of their fellow-creatures are killed by the sword of their inaction."

*I answer that,* A thing is said to precede in two ways. First, with regard to its nature; and in this way the contemplative life precedes the active, inasmuch as it applies itself to things which precede and are better than others, wherefore it moves and directs the active life. For the higher reason which is assigned to contemplation is compared to the lower reason which is assigned to action, and the husband is compared to his wife, who should be ruled by her husband, as Augustine says (De Trin. xii, 3, 7, 12).

Secondly, a thing precedes with regard to us, because it comes first in the order of generation. In this way the active precedes the contemplative life, because it disposes one to it, as stated above (A. 1; Q. 181, A. 1, ad 3); and, in the order of generation, disposition precedes form, although the latter precedes simply and according to its nature.

Reply Obj. 1: The contemplative life is directed to the love of God, not of any degree, but to that which is perfect; whereas the active life is necessary for any degree of the love of our neighbor. Hence Gregory says (Hom. iii in Ezech.): "Without the contemplative life it is possible to enter the heavenly kingdom, provided one omit not the good actions we are able to do; but we cannot enter therein without the active life, if we neglect to do the good we can do."

From this it is also evident that the active precedes the contemplative life, as that which is common to all precedes, in the order of generation, that which is proper to the perfect.

Reply Obj. 2: Progress from the active to the contemplative life is according to the order of generation; whereas the return from the contemplative life to the active is according to the order of direction, in so far as the active life is directed by the contemplative. Even thus habit is acquired by acts, and by the acquired habit one acts yet more perfectly, as stated in *Ethic.* ii, 7.

Reply Obj. 3: He that is prone to yield to his passions on account of his impulse to action is simply more apt for the active life by reason of his restless spirit. Hence Gregory says (Moral. vi, 37) that "there be some so restless that when they are free from labor they labor all the more, because the more leisure they have for thought, the worse interior turmoil they have to bear." Others, *on the contrary,* have the mind naturally pure and restful, so that they are apt for contemplation, and if they were to apply themselves wholly to action, this would be detrimental to them. Wherefore Gregory says (Moral. vi, 37) that "some are so slothful of mind that if they chance to have any hard work to do they give way at the very outset." Yet, as he adds further on, "often ... love stimulates slothful souls to work, and fear restrains souls that are disturbed in contemplation." Consequently those who are more adapted to the active life can prepare themselves for the contemplative by the practice of the active life; while none the less, those who are more adapted to the contemplative life can take upon themselves the works of the active life, so as to become yet more apt for contemplation.

TREATISE ON THE STATES OF LIFE (QQ. 183-189)

OF MAN'S VARIOUS DUTIES AND STATES IN GENERAL (In Four Articles)

We must next consider man's various states and duties. We shall consider (1) man's duties and states in general; (2) the state of the perfect in particular.

Under the first head there are four points of inquiry:

(1) What constitutes a state among men?

(2) Whether among men there should be various states and duties?

(3) Of the diversity of duties;

(4) Of the diversity of states.

FIRST ARTICLE [II-II, Q. 183, Art. 1]

Whether the Notion of a State Denotes a Condition of Freedom or Servitude?

Objection 1: It would seem that the notion of a state does not denote a condition of freedom or servitude. For "state" takes its name from "standing." Now a person is said to stand on account of his being upright; and Gregory says (Moral. vii, 17): "To fall by speaking harmful words is to forfeit entirely the state of righteousness." But a man acquires spiritual uprightness by submitting his will to God; wherefore a gloss on Ps. 32:1, "Praise becometh the upright," says: "The upright are those who direct their heart according to God's will." Therefore it would seem that obedience to the Divine commandments suffices alone for the notion of a state.

Obj. 2: Further, the word "state" seems to denote immobility according to 1 Cor. 15:48, "Be ye steadfast ( *stabiles* ) and immovable"; wherefore Gregory says (Hom. xxi in Ezech.): "The stone is foursquare, and is stable on all sides, if no disturbance will make it fall." Now it is virtue that enables us "to act with immobility," according to *Ethic.* ii, 4. Therefore it would seem that a state is acquired by every virtuous action.

Obj. 3: Further, the word "state" seems to indicate height of a kind; because to stand is to be raised upwards. Now one man is made higher than another by various duties; and in like manner men are raised upwards in various ways by various grades and orders. Therefore the mere difference of grades, orders, or duties suffices for a difference of states.

*On the contrary,* It is thus laid down in the Decretals (II, qu. vi, can. Si Quando): "Whenever anyone intervene in a cause where life or state is at stake he must do so, not by a proxy, but in his own person"; and "state" here has reference to freedom or servitude. Therefore it would seem that nothing differentiates a man's state, except that which refers to freedom or servitude.

*I answer that,* "State," properly speaking, denotes a kind of position, whereby a thing is disposed with a certain immobility in a manner according with its nature. For it is natural to man that his head should be directed upwards, his feet set firmly on the ground, and his other intermediate members disposed in becoming order; and this is not the case if he lie down, sit, or recline, but only when he stands upright: nor again is he said to stand, if he move, but only when he is still. Hence it is again that even in human acts, a matter is said to have stability ( *statum* ) in reference to its own disposition in the point of a certain immobility or restfulness. Consequently matters which easily change and are extrinsic to them do not constitute a state among men, for instance that a man be rich or poor, of high or low rank, and so forth. Wherefore in the civil law [*Dig. I, IX, De Senatoribus] (Lib. Cassius ff. De Senatoribus) it is said that if a man be removed from the senate, he is deprived of his dignity rather than of his state. But that alone seemingly pertains to a man's state, which regards an obligation binding his person, in so far, to wit, as a man is his own master or subject to another, not indeed from any slight or unstable cause, but from one that is firmly established; and this is something pertaining to the nature of freedom or servitude. Therefore state properly regards freedom or servitude whether in spiritual or in civil matters.

Reply Obj. 1: Uprightness as such does not pertain to the notion of state, except in so far as it is connatural to man with the addition of a certain restfulness. Hence other animals are said to stand without its being required that they should be upright; nor again are men said to stand, however upright their position be, unless they be still.

Reply Obj. 2: Immobility does not suffice for the notion of state; since even one who sits or lies down is still, and yet he is not said to stand.

Reply Obj. 3: Duty implies relation to act; while grades denote an order of superiority and inferiority. But state requires immobility in that which regards a condition of the person himself.

SECOND ARTICLE [II-II, Q. 183, Art. 2]

Whether There Should Be Different Duties or States in the Church?

Objection 1: It would seem that there should not be different duties or states in the Church. For distinction is opposed to unity. Now the faithful of Christ are called to unity according to John 17:21, 22: "That they ... may be one in Us ... as We also are one." Therefore there should not be a distinction of duties and states in the Church.

Obj. 2: Further, nature does not employ many means where one suffices. But the working of grace is much more orderly than the working of nature. Therefore it were more fitting for things pertaining to the operations of grace to be administered by the same persons, so that there would not be a distinction of duties and states in the Church.

Obj. 3: Further, the good of the Church seemingly consists chiefly in peace, according to Ps. 147:3, "Who hath placed peace in thy borders," and 2 Cor. 13:11, "Have peace, and the God of peace ... shall be with you." Now distinction is a hindrance to peace, for peace would seem to result from likeness, according to Ecclus. 13:19, "Every beast loveth its like," while the Philosopher says (Polit. vii, 5) that "a little difference causes dissension in a state." Therefore it would seem that there ought not to be a distinction of states and duties in the Church.

*On the contrary,* It is written in praise of the Church (Ps. 44:10) that she is "surrounded with variety": and a gloss on these words says that "the Queen," namely the Church, "is bedecked with the teaching of the apostles, the confession of martyrs, the purity of virgins, the sorrowings of penitents."

*I answer that,* The difference of states and duties in the Church regards three things. In the first place it regards the perfection of the Church. For even as in the order of natural things, perfection, which in God is simple and uniform, is not to be found in the created universe except in a multiform and manifold manner, so too, the fulness of grace, which is centered in Christ as head, flows forth to His members in various ways, for the perfecting of the body of the Church. This is the meaning of the Apostle's words (Eph. 4:11, 12): "He gave some apostles, and some prophets, and other some evangelists, and other some pastors and doctors for the perfecting of the saints." Secondly, it regards the need of those actions which are necessary in the Church. For a diversity of actions requires a diversity of men appointed to them, in order that all things may be accomplished without delay or confusion; and this is indicated by the Apostle (Rom. 12:4, 5), "As in one body we have many members, but all the members have not the same office, so we being many are one body in Christ." Thirdly, this belongs to the dignity and beauty of the Church, which consist in a certain order; wherefore it is written (3 Kings 10:4, 5) that "when the queen of Saba saw all the wisdom of Solomon ... and the apartments of his servants, and the order of his ministers ... she had no longer any spirit in her." Hence the Apostle says (2 Tim. 2:20) that "in a great house there are not only vessels of gold and silver, but also of wood and of earth."

Reply Obj. 1: The distinction of states and duties is not an obstacle to the unity of the Church, for this results from the unity of faith, charity, and mutual service, according to the saying of the Apostle (Eph. 4:16): "From whom the whole body being compacted," namely by faith, "and fitly joined together," namely by charity, "by what every joint supplieth," namely by one man serving another.

Reply Obj. 2: Just as nature does not employ many means where one suffices, so neither does it confine itself to one where many are required, according to the saying of the Apostle (1 Cor. 12:17), "If the whole body were the eye, where would be the hearing?" Hence there was need in the Church, which is Christ's body, for the members to be differentiated by various duties, states, and grades.

Reply Obj. 3: Just as in the natural body the various members are held together in unity by the power of the quickening spirit, and are dissociated from one another as soon as that spirit departs, so too in the Church's body the peace of the various members is preserved by the power of the Holy Spirit, Who quickens the body of the Church, as stated in John 6:64. Hence the Apostle says (Eph. 4:3): "Careful to keep the unity of the Spirit in the bond of peace." Now a man departs from this unity of spirit when he seeks his own; just as in an earthly kingdom peace ceases when the citizens seek each man his own. Besides, the peace both of mind and of an earthly commonwealth is the better preserved by a distinction of duties and states, since thereby the greater number have a share in public actions. Wherefore the Apostle says (1 Cor. 12:24, 25) that "God hath tempered ( *the body* ) together that there might be no schism in the body, but the members might be mutually careful one for another."

THIRD ARTICLE [II-II, Q. 183, Art. 3]

Whether Duties Differ According to Their Actions?

Objection 1: It would seem that duties do not differ according to their actions. For there are infinite varieties of human acts both in spirituals and in temporals. Now there can be no certain distinction among things that are infinite in number. Therefore human duties cannot be differentiated according to a difference of acts.

Obj. 2: Further, the active and the contemplative life differ according to their acts, as stated above (Q. 179, A. 1). But the distinction of duties seems to be other than the distinction of lives. Therefore duties do not differ according to their acts.

Obj. 3: Further, even ecclesiastical orders, states, and grades seemingly differ according to their acts. If, then, duties differ according to their acts it would seem that duties, grades, and states differ in the same way. Yet this is not true, since they are divided into their respective parts in different ways. Therefore duties do not differ according to their acts.

*On the contrary,* Isidore says (Etym. vi, 19) that " officium (duty) takes its name from efficere (to effect), as though it were instead of efficium, by the change of one letter for the sake of the sound." But effecting pertains to action. Therefore duties differ according to their acts.

*I answer that,* As stated above (A. 2), difference among the members of the Church is directed to three things: perfection, action, and beauty; and according to these three we may distinguish a threefold distinction among the faithful. One, with regard to perfection, and thus we have the difference of states, in reference to which some persons are more perfect than others. Another distinction regards action and this is the distinction of duties: for persons are said to have various duties when they are appointed to various actions. A third distinction regards the order of ecclesiastical beauty: and thus we distinguish various grades according as in the same state or duty one person is above another. Hence according to a variant text [*The Septuagint] it is written (Ps. 47:4): "In her grades shall God be known."

Reply Obj. 1: The material diversity of human acts is infinite. It is not thus that duties differ, but by their formal diversity which results from diverse species of acts, and in this way human acts are not infinite.

Reply Obj. 2: Life is predicated of a thing absolutely: wherefore diversity of lives results from a diversity of acts which are becoming to man considered in himself. But efficiency, whence we have the word "office" (as stated above), denotes action tending to something else according to *Metaph.* ix, text. 16 [*Ed. Did. viii, 8]. Hence offices differ properly in respect of acts that are referred to other persons; thus a teacher is said to have an office, and so is a judge, and so forth. Wherefore Isidore says (Etym. vi, 19) that "to have an office is to be officious," i.e. harmful "to no one, but to be useful to all."

Reply Obj. 3: Differences of state, offices and grades are taken from different things, as stated above (A. 1, ad 3). Yet these three things may concur in the same subject: thus when a person is appointed to a higher action, he attains thereby both office and grade, and sometimes, besides this, a state of perfection, on account of the sublimity of the act, as in the case of a bishop. The ecclesiastical orders are particularly distinct according to divine offices. For Isidore says (Etym. vi): "There are various kinds of offices; but the foremost is that which relates to sacred and Divine things."

FOURTH ARTICLE [II-II, Q. 183, Art. 4]

Whether the Difference of States Applies to Those Who Are Beginning, Progressing, or Perfect?

Objection 1: It would seem that the difference of states does not apply to those who are beginning, progressing, or perfect. For "diverse genera have diverse species and differences" [*Aristotle, Categ. ii]. Now this difference of beginning, progress, and perfection is applied to the degrees of charity, as stated above (Q. 24, A. 9), where we were treating of charity. Therefore it would seem that the differences of states should not be assigned in this manner.

Obj. 2: Further, as stated above (A. 1), state regards a condition of servitude or freedom, which apparently has no connection with the aforesaid difference of beginning, progress, and perfection. Therefore it is unfitting to divide state in this way.

Obj. 3: Further, the distinction of beginning, progress, and perfection seems to refer to *more* and less, and this seemingly implies the notion of grades. But the distinction of grades differs from that of states, as we have said above (AA. 2, 3). Therefore state is unfittingly divided according to beginning, progress, and perfection.

*On the contrary,* Gregory says (Moral. xxiv, 11): "There are three states of the converted, the beginning, the middle, and the perfection"; and (Hom. xv in Ezech.): "Other is the beginning of virtue, other its progress, and other still its perfection."

*I answer that,* As stated above (A. 1) state regards freedom or servitude. Now in spiritual things there is a twofold servitude and a twofold freedom: for there is the servitude of sin and the servitude of justice; and there is likewise a twofold freedom, from sin, and from justice, as appears from the words of the Apostle (Rom. 6:20, 22), "When you were the servants of sin, you were free men to justice ... but now being made free from sin," you are ... "become servants to God."

Now the servitude of sin or justice consists in being inclined to evil by a habit of sin, or inclined to good by a habit of justice: and in like manner freedom from sin is not to be overcome by the inclination to sin, and freedom from justice is not to be held back from evil for the love of justice. Nevertheless, since man, by his natural reason, is inclined to justice, while sin is contrary to natural reason, it follows that freedom from sin is true freedom which is united to the servitude of justice, since they both incline man to that which is becoming to him. In like manner true servitude is the servitude of sin, which is connected with freedom from justice, because man is thereby hindered from attaining that which is proper to him. That a man become the servant of justice or sin results from his efforts, as the Apostle declares (Rom. 6:16): "To whom you yield yourselves servants to obey, his servants you are whom you obey, whether it be of sin unto death, or of obedience unto justice." Now in every human effort we can distinguish a beginning, a middle, and a term; and consequently the state of spiritual servitude and freedom is differentiated according to these things, namely, the beginning—to which pertains the state of beginners—the middle, to which pertains the state of the proficient—and the term, to which belongs the state of the perfect.

Reply Obj. 1: Freedom from sin results from charity which "is poured forth in our hearts by the Holy Ghost, Who is given to us" (Rom. 5:5). Hence it is written (2 Cor. 3:17): "Where the Spirit of the Lord is, there is liberty." Wherefore the same division applies to charity as to the state of those who enjoy spiritual freedom.

Reply Obj. 2: Men are said to be beginners, proficient, and perfect (so far as these terms indicate different states), not in relation to any occupation whatever, but in relation to such occupations as pertain to spiritual freedom or servitude, as stated above (A. 1).

Reply Obj. 3: As already observed (A. 3, ad 3), nothing hinders grade and state from concurring in the same subject. For even in earthly affairs those who are free, not only belong to a different state from those who are in service, but are also of a different grade.

# QUESTION 184

OF THE STATE OF PERFECTION IN GENERAL (In Eight Articles)

We must now consider those things that pertain to the state of perfection whereto the other states are directed. For the consideration of offices in relation to other acts belongs to the legislator; and in relation to the sacred ministry it comes under the consideration of orders of which we shall treat in the Third Part [*Suppl., Q. 34].

Concerning the state of the perfect, a three-fold consideration presents itself: (1) The state of perfection in general; (2) Things relating to the perfection of bishops; (3) Things relating to the perfection of religious.

Under the first head there are eight points of inquiry:

(1) Whether perfection bears any relation to charity?

(2) Whether one can be perfect in this life?

(3) Whether the perfection of this life consists chiefly in observing the counsels or the commandments?

(4) Whether whoever is perfect is in the state of perfection?

(5) Whether especially prelates and religious are in the state of perfection?

(6) Whether all prelates are in the state of perfection?

(7) Which is the more perfect, the episcopal or the religious state?

(8) The comparison between religious and parish priests and archdeacons.

FIRST ARTICLE [II-II, Q. 184, Art. 1]

Whether the Perfection of the Christian Life Consists Chiefly in Charity?

Objection 1: It would seem that the perfection of the Christian life does not consist chiefly in charity. For the Apostle says (1 Cor. 14:20): "In malice be children, but in sense be perfect." But charity regards not the senses but the affections. Therefore it would seem that the perfection of the Christian life does not chiefly consist in charity.

Obj. 2: Further, it is written (Eph. 6:13): "Take unto you the armor of God, that you may be able to resist in the evil day, and to stand in all things perfect"; and the text continues (Eph. 6:14, 16), speaking of the armor of God: "Stand therefore having your loins girt about with truth, and having on the breast-plate of justice ... in all things taking the shield of faith." Therefore the perfection of the Christian life consists not only in charity, but also in other virtues.

Obj. 3: Further, virtues like other habits, are specified by their acts. Now it is written (James 1:4) that "patience hath a perfect work." Therefore seemingly the state of perfection consists more specially in patience.

*On the contrary,* It is written (Col. 3:14): "Above all things have charity, which is the bond of perfection," because it binds, as it were, all the other virtues together in perfect unity.

*I answer that,* A thing is said to be perfect in so far as it attains its proper end, which is the ultimate perfection thereof. Now it is charity that unites us to God, Who is the last end of the human mind, since "he that abideth in charity abideth in God, and God in him" (1 John 4:16). Therefore the perfection of the Christian life consists radically in charity.

Reply Obj. 1: The perfection of the human senses would seem to consist chiefly in their concurring together in the unity of truth, according to 1 Cor. 1:10, "That you be perfect in the same mind ( *sensu* ), and in the same judgment." Now this is effected by charity which operates consent in us men. Wherefore even the perfection of the senses consists radically in the perfection of charity.

Reply Obj. 2: A man may be said to be perfect in two ways. First, simply: and this perfection regards that which belongs to a thing's nature, for instance an animal may be said to be perfect when it lacks nothing in the disposition of its members and in such things as are necessary for an animal's life. Secondly, a thing is said to be perfect relatively: and this perfection regards something connected with the thing externally, such as whiteness or blackness or something of the kind. Now the Christian life consists chiefly in charity whereby the soul is united to God; wherefore it is written (1 John 3:14): "He that loveth not abideth in death." Hence the perfection of the Christian life consists simply in charity, but in the other virtues relatively. And since that which is simply, is paramount and greatest in comparison with other things, it follows that the perfection of charity is paramount in relation to the perfection that regards the other virtues.

Reply Obj. 3: Patience is stated to have a perfect work in relation to charity, in so far as it is an effect of the abundance of charity that a man bears hardships patiently, according to Rom. 8:35, "Who ... shall separate us from the love of Christ? Shall tribulation? Or distress?" etc.

SECOND ARTICLE [II-II, Q. 184, Art. 2]

Whether Any One Can Be Perfect in This Life?

Objection 1: It would seem that none can be perfect in this life. For the Apostle says (1 Cor. 13:10): "When that which is perfect is come, that which is in part shall be done away." Now in this life that which is in part is not done away; for in this life faith and hope, which are in part, remain. Therefore none can be perfect in this life.

Obj. 2: Further, "The perfect is that which lacks nothing" (Phys. iii, 6). Now there is no one in this life who lacks nothing; for it is written (James 3:2): "In many things we all offend"; and (Ps. 138:16): "Thy eyes did see my imperfect being." Therefore none is perfect in this life.

Obj. 3: Further, the perfection of the Christian life, as stated (A. 1), relates to charity, which comprises the love of God and of our neighbor. Now, neither as to the love of God can one have perfect charity in this life, since according to Gregory (Hom. xiv in Ezech.) "the furnace of love which begins to burn here, will burn more fiercely when we see Him Whom we love"; nor as to the love of our neighbor, since in this life we cannot love all our neighbors actually, even though we love them habitually; and habitual love is imperfect. Therefore it seems that no one can be perfect in this life.

*On the contrary,* The Divine law does not prescribe the impossible. Yet it prescribes perfection according to Matt. 5:48, "Be you ... perfect, as also your heavenly Father is perfect." Therefore seemingly one can be perfect in this life.

*I answer that,* As stated above (A. 1), the perfection of the Christian life consists in charity. Now perfection implies a certain universality because according to *Phys.* iii, 6, "the perfect is that which lacks nothing." Hence we may consider a threefold perfection. One is absolute, and answers to a totality not only on the part of the lover, but also on the part of the object loved, so that God be loved as much as He is lovable. Such perfection as this is not possible to any creature, but is competent to God alone, in Whom good is wholly and essentially.

Another perfection answers to an absolute totality on the part of the lover, so that the affective faculty always actually tends to God as much as it possibly can; and such perfection as this is not possible so long as we are on the way, but we shall have it in heaven.

The third perfection answers to a totality neither on the part of the object served, nor on the part of the lover as regards his always actually tending to God, but on the part of the lover as regards the removal of obstacles to the movement of love towards God, in which sense Augustine says (QQ. LXXXIII, qu. 36) that "carnal desire is the bane of charity; to have no carnal desires is the perfection of charity." Such perfection as this can be had in this life, and in two ways. First, by the removal from man's affections of all that is contrary to charity, such as mortal sin; and there can be no charity apart from this perfection, wherefore it is necessary for salvation. Secondly, by the removal from man's affections not only of whatever is contrary to charity, but also of whatever hinders the mind's affections from tending wholly to God. Charity is possible apart from this perfection, for instance in those who are beginners and in those who are proficient.

Reply Obj. 1: The Apostle is speaking there of heavenly perfection which is not possible to those who are on the way.

Reply Obj. 2: Those who are perfect in this life are said to "offend in many things" with regard to venial sins, which result from the weakness of the present life: and in this respect they have an "imperfect being" in comparison with the perfection of heaven.

Reply Obj. 3: As the conditions of the present life do not allow of a man always tending actually to God, so neither does it allow of his tending actually to each individual neighbor; but it suffices for him to tend to all in common and collectively, and to each individual habitually and according to the preparedness of his mind. Now in the love of our neighbor, as in the love of God we may observe a twofold perfection: one without which charity is impossible, and consisting in one's having in one's affections nothing that is contrary to the love of one's neighbor; and another without which it is possible to have charity. The latter perfection may be considered in three ways. First, as to the extent of love, through a man loving not only his friends and acquaintances but also strangers and even his enemies, for as Augustine says (Enchiridion lxxiii) this is a mark of the perfect children of God. Secondly, as to the intensity of love, which is shown by the things which man despises for his neighbor's sake, through his despising not only external goods for the sake of his neighbor, but also bodily hardships and even death, according to John 15:13, "Greater love than this no man hath, that a man lay down his life for his friends." Thirdly, as to the effect of love, so that a man will surrender not only temporal but also spiritual goods and even himself, for his neighbor's sake, according to the words of the Apostle (2 Cor. 12:15), "But I most gladly will spend and be spent myself for your souls."

THIRD ARTICLE [II-II, Q. 184, Art. 3]

Whether, in This Life, Perfection Consists in the Observance of the Commandments or of the Counsels?

Objection 1: It would seem that, in this life,

perfection consists in the observance not of the commandments but of the counsels. For our Lord said (Matt. 19:21): "If thou wilt be perfect, go sell all [Vulg.: 'what'] thou hast, and give to the poor ... and come, follow Me." Now this is a counsel. Therefore perfection regards the counsels and not the precepts.

Obj. 2: Further, all are bound to the observance of the commandments, since this is necessary for salvation. Therefore, if the perfection of the Christian life consists in observing the commandments, it follows that perfection is necessary for salvation, and that all are bound thereto; and this is evidently false.

Obj. 3: Further, the perfection of the Christian life is gauged according to charity, as stated above (A. 1). Now the perfection of charity, seemingly, does not consist in the observance of the commandments, since the perfection of charity is preceded both by its increase and by its beginning, as Augustine says (Super Canonic. Joan. Tract. ix). But the beginning of charity cannot precede the observance of the commandments, since according to John 14:23, "If any one love Me, he will keep My word." Therefore the perfection of life regards not the commandments but the counsels.

*On the contrary,* It is written (Deut. 6:5): "Thou shalt love the Lord thy God with thy whole heart," and (Lev. 19:18): "Thou shalt love thy neighbor [Vulg.: 'friend'] as thyself"; and these are the commandments of which our Lord said (Matt. 22:40): "On these two commandments dependeth the whole law and the prophets." Now the perfection of charity, in respect of which the Christian life is said to be perfect, consists in our loving God with our whole heart, and our neighbor as ourselves. Therefore it would seem that perfection consists in the observance of the precepts.

*I answer that,* Perfection is said to consist in a thing in two ways: in one way, primarily and essentially; in another, secondarily and accidentally. Primarily and essentially the perfection of the Christian life consists in charity, principally as to the love of God, secondarily as to the love of our neighbor, both of which are the matter of the chief commandments of the Divine law, as stated above. Now the love of God and of our neighbor is not commanded according to a measure, so that what is in excess of the measure be a matter of counsel. This is evident from the very form of the commandment, pointing, as it does, to perfection—for instance in the words, "Thou shalt love the Lord thy God with thy whole heart": since "the whole" is the same as "the perfect," according to the Philosopher (Phys. iii, 6), and in the words, "Thou shalt love thy neighbor as thyself," since every one loves himself most. The reason of this is that "the end of the commandment is charity," according to the Apostle (1 Tim. 1:5); and the end is not subject to a measure, but only such things as are directed to the end, as the Philosopher observes (Polit. i, 3); thus a physician does not measure the amount of his healing, but how much medicine or diet he shall employ for the purpose of healing. Consequently it is evident that perfection consists essentially in the observance of the commandments; wherefore Augustine says (De Perf. Justit. viii): "Why then should not this perfection be prescribed to man, although no man has it in this life?"

Secondarily and instrumentally, however, perfection consists in the observance of the counsels, all of which, like the commandments, are directed to charity; yet not in the same way. For the commandments, other than the precepts of charity, are directed to the removal of things contrary to charity, with which, namely, charity is incompatible, whereas the counsels are directed to the removal of things that hinder the act of charity, and yet are not contrary to charity, such as marriage, the occupation of worldly business, and so forth. Hence Augustine says (Enchiridion cxxi): "Whatever things God commands, for instance, 'Thou shalt not commit adultery,' and whatever are not commanded, yet suggested by a special counsel, for instance, 'It is good for a man not to touch a woman,' are then done aright when they are referred to the love of God, and of our neighbor for God's sake, both in this world and in the world to come." Hence it is that in the Conferences of the Fathers (Coll. i, cap. vii) the abbot Moses says: "Fastings, watchings, meditating on the Scriptures, penury and loss of all one's wealth, these are not perfection but means to perfection, since not in them does the school of perfection find its end, but through them it achieves its end," and he had already said that "we endeavor to ascend by these steps to the perfection of charity."

Reply Obj. 1: In this saying of our Lord something is indicated as being the way to perfection by the words, "Go, sell all thou hast, and give to the poor"; and something else is added wherein perfection consists, when He said, "And follow Me." Hence Jerome in his commentary on Matt. 19:27, says that "since it is not enough merely to leave, Peter added that which is perfect: 'And have followed Thee'"; and Ambrose, commenting on Luke 5:27, "Follow Me," says: "He commands him to follow, not with steps of the body, but with devotion of the soul, which is the effect of charity." Wherefore it is evident from the very way of speaking that the counsels are means of attaining to perfection, since it is thus expressed: "If thou wilt be perfect, go, sell," etc., as though He said: "By so doing thou shalt accomplish this end."

Reply Obj. 2: As Augustine says (De Perf. Justit. viii) "the perfection of charity is prescribed to man in this life, because one runs not right unless one knows whither to run. And how shall we know this if no commandment declares it to us?" And since that which is a matter of precept can be fulfilled variously, one does not break a commandment through not fulfilling it in the best way, but it is enough to fulfil it in any way whatever. Now the perfection of Divine love is a matter of precept for all without exception, so that even the perfection of heaven is not excepted from this precept, as Augustine says (De Perf. Justit. viii [*Cf. De Spir. et Lit. XXXVI]), and one escapes transgressing the precept, in whatever measure one attains to the perfection of Divine love. The lowest degree of Divine love is to love nothing more than God, or contrary to God, or equally with God, and whoever fails from this degree of perfection nowise fulfils the precept. There is another degree of the Divine love, which cannot be fulfilled so long as we are on the way, as stated above (A. 2), and it is evident that to fail from this is not to be a transgressor of the precept; and in like manner one does not transgress the precept, if one does not attain to the intermediate degrees of perfection, provided one attain to the lowest.

Reply Obj. 3: Just as man has a certain perfection of his nature as soon as he is born, which perfection belongs to the very essence of his species, while there is another perfection which he acquires by growth, so again there is a perfection of charity which belongs to the very essence of charity, namely that man love God above all things, and love nothing contrary to God, while there is another perfection of charity even in this life, whereto a man attains by a kind of spiritual growth, for instance when a man refrains even from lawful things, in order more freely to give himself to the service of God.

FOURTH ARTICLE [II-II, Q. 184, Art. 4]

Whether Whoever Is Perfect Is in the State of Perfection?

Objection 1: It would seem that whoever is perfect is in the state of perfection. For, as stated above (A. 3, ad 3), just as bodily perfection is reached by bodily growth, so spiritual perfection is acquired by spiritual growth. Now after bodily growth one is said to have reached the state of perfect age. Therefore seemingly also after spiritual growth, when one has already reached spiritual perfection, one is in the state of perfection.

Obj. 2: Further, according to *Phys.* v, 2, movement "from one contrary to another" has the same aspect as "movement from less to more." Now when a man is changed from sin to grace, he is said to change his state, in so far as the state of sin differs from the state of grace. Therefore it would seem that in the same manner, when one progresses from a lesser to a greater grace, so as to reach the perfect degree, one is in the state of perfection.

Obj. 3: Further, a man acquires a state by being freed from servitude. But one is freed from the servitude of sin by charity, because "charity covereth all sins" (Prov. 10:12). Now one is said to be perfect on account of charity, as stated above (A. 1). Therefore, seemingly, whoever has perfection, for this very reason has the state of perfection.

*On the contrary,* Some are in the state of perfection, who are wholly lacking in charity and grace, for instance wicked bishops or religious. Therefore it would seem that on the other hand some have the perfection of life, who nevertheless have not the state of perfection.

*I answer that,* As stated above (Q. 183, A. 1), state properly regards a condition of freedom or servitude. Now spiritual freedom or servitude may be considered in man in two ways: first, with respect to his internal actions; secondly, with respect to his external actions. And since according to 1 Kings 16:7, "man seeth those things that appear, but the Lord beholdeth the heart," it follows that with regard to man's internal disposition we consider his spiritual state in relation to the Divine judgment, while with regard to his external actions we consider man's spiritual state in relation to the Church. It is in this latter sense that we are now speaking of states, namely in so far as the Church derives a certain beauty from the variety of states [*Cf. Q. 183, A. 2].

Now it must be observed, that so far as men are concerned, in order that any one attain to a state of freedom or servitude there is required first of all an obligation or a release. For the mere fact of serving someone does not make a man a slave, since even the free serve, according to Gal. 5:13, "By charity of the spirit serve one another": nor again does the mere fact of ceasing to serve make a man free, as in the case of a runaway slave; but properly speaking a man is a slave if he be bound to serve, and a man is free if he be released from service. Secondly, it is required that the aforesaid obligation be imposed with a certain solemnity; even as a certain solemnity is observed in other matters which among men obtain a settlement in perpetuity.

Accordingly, properly speaking, one is said to be in the state of perfection, not through having the act of perfect love, but through binding himself in perpetuity and with a certain solemnity to those things that pertain to perfection. Moreover it happens that some persons bind themselves to that which they do not keep, and some fulfil that to which they have not bound themselves, as in the case of the two sons (Matt. 21:28, 30), one of whom when his father said: "Work in my vineyard," answered: "I will not," and "afterwards ... he went," while the other "answering said: I go ... and he went not." Wherefore nothing hinders some from being perfect without being in the state of perfection, and some in the state of perfection without being perfect.

Reply Obj. 1: By bodily growth a man progresses in things pertaining to nature, wherefore he attains to the state of nature; especially since "what is according to nature is," in a way, "unchangeable" [*Ethic. v, 7], inasmuch as nature is determinate to one thing. In like manner by inward spiritual growth a man reaches the state of perfection in relation to the Divine judgment. But as regards the distinctions of ecclesiastical states, a man does not reach the state of perfection except by growth in respect of external actions.

Reply Obj. 2: This argument also regards the interior state. Yet when a man passes from sin to grace, he passes from servitude to freedom; and this does not result from a mere progress in grace, except when a man binds himself to things pertaining to grace.

Reply Obj. 3: Again this argument considers the interior state. Nevertheless, although charity causes the change of condition from spiritual servitude to spiritual freedom, an increase of charity has not the same effect.

FIFTH ARTICLE [II-II, Q. 184, Art. 5]

Whether Religious and Prelates Are in the State of Perfection?

Objection 1: It would seem that prelates and religious are not in the state of perfection. For the state of perfection differs from the state of the beginners and the proficient. Now no class of men is specially assigned to the state of the proficient or of the beginners. Therefore it would seem that neither should any class of men be assigned to the state of perfection.

Obj. 2: Further, the outward state should answer to the inward, else one is guilty of lying, "which consists not only in false words, but also in deceitful deeds," according to Ambrose in one of his sermons (xxx de Tempore). Now there are many prelates and religious who have not the inward perfection of charity. Therefore, if all religious and prelates are in the state of perfection, it would follow that all of them that are not perfect are in mortal sin, as deceivers and liars.

Obj. 3: Further, as stated above (A. 1), perfection is measured according to charity. Now the most perfect charity would seem to be in the martyrs, according to John 15:13, "Greater love than this no man hath, that a man lay down his life for his friends": and a gloss on Heb. 12:4, "For you have not yet resisted unto blood," says: "In this life no love is more perfect than that to which the holy martyrs attained, who strove against sin even unto blood." Therefore it would seem that the state of perfection should be ascribed to the martyrs rather than to religious and bishops.

*On the contrary,* Dionysius (Eccl. Hier. v) ascribes perfection to bishops as being perfecters, and (Eccl. Hier. vi) to religious (whom he calls monks or therapeutai , i.e. servants of God) as being perfected.

*I answer that,* As stated above (A. 4), there is required for the state of perfection a perpetual obligation to things pertaining to perfection, together with a certain solemnity. Now both these conditions are competent to religious and bishops. For religious bind themselves by vow to refrain from worldly affairs, which they might lawfully use, in order more freely to give themselves to God, wherein consists the perfection of the present life. Hence Dionysius says (Eccl. Hier. vi), speaking of religious: "Some call them *therapeutai* ," i.e. servants, "on account of their rendering pure service and homage to God; others call them *monachoi* " [*i.e. solitaries; whence the English word 'monk'], "on account of the indivisible and single-minded life which by their being wrapped in," i.e. contemplating, "indivisible things, unites them in a God-like union and a perfection beloved of God" [*Cf. Q. 180, A. 6]. Moreover, the obligation in both cases is undertaken with a certain solemnity of profession and consecration; wherefore Dionysius adds (Eccl. Hier. vi): "Hence the holy legislation in bestowing perfect grace on them accords them a hallowing invocation."

In like manner bishops bind themselves to things pertaining to perfection when they take up the pastoral duty, to which it belongs that a shepherd "lay down his life for his sheep," according to John 10:15. Wherefore the Apostle says (1 Tim. 6:12): "Thou ... hast confessed a good confession before many witnesses," that is to say, "when he was ordained," as a gloss says on this passage. Again, a certain solemnity of consecration is employed together with the aforesaid profession, according to 2 Tim. 1:6: "Stir up the grace of God which is in thee by the imposition of my hands," which the gloss ascribes to the grace of the episcopate. And Dionysius says (Eccl. Hier. v) that "when the high priest," i.e. the bishop, "is ordained, he receives on his head the most holy imposition of the sacred oracles, whereby it is signified that he is a participator in the whole and entire hierarchical power, and that not only is he the enlightener in all things pertaining to his holy discourses and actions, but that he also confers this on others."

Reply Obj. 1: Beginning and increase are sought not for their own sake, but for the sake of perfection; hence it is only to the state of perfection that some are admitted under certain obligations and with solemnity.

Reply Obj. 2: Those who enter the state of perfection do not profess to be perfect, but to tend to perfection. Hence the Apostle says (Phil. 3:12): "Not as though I had already attained, or were already perfect; but I follow after, if I may by any means apprehend": and afterwards (Phil. 3:15): "Let us therefore as many as are perfect, be thus minded." Hence a man who takes up the state of perfection is not guilty of lying or deceit through not being perfect, but through withdrawing his mind from the intention of reaching perfection.

Reply Obj. 3: Martyrdom is the most perfect act of charity. But an act of perfection does not suffice to make the state of perfection, as stated above (A. 4).

SIXTH ARTICLE [II-II, Q. 184, Art. 6]

Whether All Ecclesiastical Prelates Are in the State of Perfection?

Objection 1: It would seem that all ecclesiastical prelates are in a state of perfection. For Jerome commenting on Titus 1:5, "Ordain ... in every city," etc. says: "Formerly priest was the same as bishop," and afterwards he adds: "Just as priests know that by the custom of the Church they are subject to the one who is placed over them, so too, bishops should recognize that, by custom rather than by the very ordinance of our Lord, they are above the priests, and are together the rightful governors of the Church." Now bishops are in the state of perfection. Therefore those priests also are who have the cure of souls.

Obj. 2: Further, just as bishops together with their consecration receive the cure of souls, so also do parish priests and archdeacons, of whom a gloss on Acts 6:3, "Brethren, look ye out ... seven men of good reputation," says: "The apostles decided here to appoint throughout the Church seven deacons, who were to be of a higher degree, and as it were the supports of that which is nearest to the altar." Therefore it would seem that these also are in the state of perfection.

Obj. 3: Further, just as bishops are bound to "lay down their life for their sheep," so too are parish priests and archdeacons. But this belongs to the perfection of charity, as stated above (A. 2, ad 3). Therefore it would seem that parish priests and archdeacons also are in the state of perfection.

*On the contrary,* Dionysius says (Eccl. Hier. v): "The order of pontiffs is consummative and perfecting, that of the priests is illuminative and light-giving, that of the ministers is cleansing and discretive." Hence it is evident that perfection is ascribed to bishops only.

*I answer that,* In priests and deacons having cure of souls two things may be considered, namely their order and their cure. Their order is directed to some act in the Divine offices. Wherefore it has been stated above (Q. 183, A. 3, ad 3) that the distinction of orders is comprised under the distinction of offices. Hence by receiving a certain order a man receives the power of exercising certain sacred acts, but he is not bound on this account to things pertaining to perfection, except in so far as in the Western Church the receiving of a sacred order includes the taking of a vow of continence, which is one of the things pertaining to perfection, as we shall state further on (Q. 186, A. 4). Therefore it is clear that from the fact that a man receives a sacred order a man is not placed simply in the state of perfection, although inward perfection is required in order that one exercise such acts worthily.

In like manner, neither are they placed in the state of perfection on the part of the cure which they take upon themselves. For they are not bound by this very fact under the obligation of a perpetual vow to retain the cure of souls; but they can surrender it—either by entering religion, even without their bishop's permission (cf. Decret. xix, qu. 2, can. Duae sunt)—or again an archdeacon may with his bishop's permission resign his arch-deaconry or parish, and accept a simple prebend without cure, which would be nowise lawful, if he were in the state of perfection; for "no man putting his hand to the plough and looking back is fit for the kingdom of God" (Luke 9:62). On the other hand bishops, since they are in the state of perfection, cannot abandon the episcopal cure, save by the authority of the Sovereign Pontiff (to whom alone it belongs also to dispense from perpetual vows), and this for certain causes, as we shall state further on (Q. 185, A. 4). Wherefore it is manifest that not all prelates are in the state of perfection, but only bishops.

Reply Obj. 1: We may speak of priest and bishop in two ways. First, with regard to the name: and thus formerly bishops and priests were not distinct. For bishops are so called "because they watch over others," as Augustine observes (De Civ. Dei xix, 19); while the priests according to the Greek are "elders." [*Referring to the Greek *episkopos* and presbyteros from which the English 'bishop' and 'priest' are derived.] Hence the Apostle employs the term "priests" in reference to both, when he says (1 Tim. 5:17): "Let the priests that rule well be esteemed worthy of double honor"; and again he uses the term "bishops" in the same way, wherefore addressing the priests of the Church of Ephesus he says (Acts 20:28): "Take heed to yourselves" and "to the whole flock, wherein the Holy Ghost hath placed you bishops, to rule the church of God."

But as regards the thing signified by these terms, there was always a difference between them, even at the time of the apostles. This is clear on the authority of Dionysius (Eccl. Hier. v), and of a gloss on Luke 10:1, "After these things the Lord appointed," etc. which says: "Just as the apostles were made bishops, so the seventy-two disciples were made priests of the second order." Subsequently, however, in order to avoid schism, it became necessary to distinguish even the terms, by calling the higher ones bishops and the lower ones priests. But to assert that priests nowise differ from bishops is reckoned by Augustine among heretical doctrines (De Heres. liii), where he says that the Arians maintained that "no distinction existed between a priest and a bishop."

Reply Obj. 2: Bishops have the chief cure of the sheep of their diocese, while parish priests and archdeacons exercise an inferior ministry under the bishops. Hence a gloss on 1 Cor. 12:28, "to one, helps, to another, governments [*Vulg.: 'God hath set some in the church ... helps, governments,' etc.]," says: "Helps, namely assistants to those who are in authority," as Titus was to the Apostle, or as archdeacons to the bishop; "governments, namely persons of lesser authority, such as priests who have to instruct the people": and Dionysius says (Eccl. Hier. v) that "just as we see the whole hierarchy culminating in Jesus, so each office culminates in its respective godlike hierarch or bishop." Also it is said (XVI, qu. i, can. Cunctis): "Priests and deacons must all take care not to do anything without their bishop's permission." Wherefore it is evident that they stand in relation to their bishop as wardens or mayors to the king; and for this reason, just as in earthly governments the king alone receives a solemn blessing, while others are appointed by simple commission, so too in the Church the episcopal cure is conferred with the solemnity of consecration, while the archdeacon or parish priest receives his cure by simple appointment; although they are consecrated by receiving orders before having a cure.

Reply Obj. 3: As parish priests and archdeacons have not the chief cure, but a certain ministry as committed to them by the bishop, so the pastoral office does not belong to them in chief, nor are they bound to lay down their life for the sheep, except in so far as they have a share in their cure. Hence we should say that they have an office pertaining to perfection rather than that they attain the state of perfection.

SEVENTH ARTICLE [II-II, Q. 184, Art. 7]

Whether the Religious State Is More Perfect Than That of Prelates?

Objection 1: It would seem that the religious state is more perfect than that of prelates. For our Lord said (Matt. 19:21): "If thou wilt be perfect, go" and "sell" all [Vulg.: 'what'] "thou hast, and give to the poor"; and religious do this. But bishops are not bound to do so; for it is said (XII, qu. i, can. Episcopi de rebus): "Bishops, if they wish, may bequeath to their heirs their personal or acquired property, and whatever belongs to them personally." Therefore religious are in a more perfect state than bishops.

Obj. 2: Further, perfection consists more especially in the love of God than in the love of our neighbor. Now the religious state is directly ordered to the love of God, wherefore it takes its name from "service and homage to God," as Dionysius says (Eccl. Hier. vi); [*Quoted above A. 5] whereas the bishop's state would seem to be ordered to the love of our neighbor, of whose cure he is the "warden," and from this he takes his name, as Augustine observes (De Civ. Dei. xix, 19). Therefore it would seem that the religious state is more perfect than that of bishops.

Obj. 3: Further, the religious state is directed to the contemplative life, which is more excellent than the active life to which the episcopal state is directed. For Gregory says (Pastor. i, 7) that "Isaias wishing to be of profit to his neighbor by means of the active life desired the office of preaching, whereas Jeremias, who was fain to hold fast to the love of his Creator, exclaimed against being sent to preach." Therefore it would seem that the religious state is more perfect than the episcopal state.

*On the contrary,* It is not lawful for anyone to pass from a more excellent to a less excellent state; for this would be to look back [*Cf. Luke 9:62]. Yet a man may pass from the religious to the episcopal state, for it is said (XVIII, qu. i, can. Statutum) that "the holy ordination makes a monk to be a bishop." Therefore the episcopal state is more perfect than the religious.

*I answer that,* As Augustine says (Gen. ad lit. xii, 16), "the agent is ever more excellent than the patient." Now in the genus of perfection according to Dionysius (Eccl. Hier. v, vi), bishops are in the position of "perfecters," whereas religious are in the position of being "perfected"; the former of which pertains to action, and the latter to passion. Whence it is evident that the state of perfection is more excellent in bishops than in religious.

Reply Obj. 1: Renunciation of one's possessions may be considered in two ways. First, as being actual: and thus it is not essential, but a means, to perfection, as stated above (A. 3). Hence nothing hinders the state of perfection from being without renunciation of one's possessions, and the same applies to other outward practices. Secondly, it may be considered in relation to one's preparedness, in the sense of being prepared to renounce or give away all: and this belongs directly to perfection. Hence Augustine says (De QQ. Evang. ii, qu. 11): "Our Lord shows that the children of wisdom understand righteousness to consist neither in eating nor in abstaining, but in bearing want patiently." Wherefore the Apostle says (Phil. 4:12): "I know ... both to abound and to suffer need." Now bishops especially are bound to despise all things for the honor of God and the spiritual welfare of their flock, when it is necessary for them to do so, either by giving to the poor of their flock, or by suffering "with joy the being stripped of" their "own goods" [*Heb. 10:34].

Reply Obj. 2: That bishops are busy about things pertaining to the love of their neighbor, arises out of the abundance of their love of God. Hence our Lord asked Peter first of all whether he loved Him, and afterwards committed the care of His flock to him. And Gregory says (Pastor. i, 5): "If the pastoral care is a proof of love, he who refuses to feed God's flock, though having the means to do so, is convicted of not loving the supreme Pastor." And it is a sign of greater love if a man devotes himself to others for his friend's sake, than if he be willing only to serve his friend.

Reply Obj. 3: As Gregory says (Pastor. ii, 1), "a prelate should be foremost in action, and more uplifted than others in contemplation," because it is incumbent on him to contemplate, not only for his own sake, but also for the purpose of instructing others. Hence Gregory applies (Hom. v in Ezech.) the words of Ps. 144:7, "They shall publish the memory ... of Thy sweetness," to perfect men returning after their contemplation.

EIGHTH ARTICLE [II-II, Q. 184, Art. 8]

Whether Parish Priests and Archdeacons Are More Perfect Than Religious?

Objection 1: It would seem that also parish priests and archdeacons are more perfect than religious. For Chrysostom says in his Dialogue (De Sacerdot. vi): "Take for example a monk, such as Elias, if I may exaggerate somewhat, he is not to be compared with one who, cast among the people and compelled to carry the sins of many, remains firm and strong." A little further on he says: "If I were given the choice, where would I prefer to please, in the priestly office, or in the monastic solitude, without hesitation I should choose the former." Again in the same book (ch. 5) he says: "If you compare the toils of this project, namely of the monastic life, with a well-employed priesthood, you will find them as far distant from one another as a common citizen is from a king." Therefore it would seem that priests who have the cure of souls are more perfect than religious.

Obj. 2: Further, Augustine says (ad Valerium, Ep. xxi): "Let thy religious prudence observe that in this life, and especially at these times, there is nothing so difficult, so onerous, so perilous as the office of bishop, priest, or deacon; while in God's sight there is no greater blessing, if one engage in the fight as ordered by our Commander-in-chief." Therefore religious are not more perfect than priests or deacons.

Obj. 3: Further, Augustine says (Ep. lx, ad Aurel.): "It would be most regrettable, were we to exalt monks to such a disastrous degree of pride, and deem the clergy deserving of such a grievous insult," as to assert that "'a bad monk is a good clerk,' since sometimes even a good monk makes a bad clerk." And a little before this he says that "God's servants," i.e. monks, "must not be allowed to think that they may easily be chosen for something better," namely the clerical state, "if they should become worse thereby," namely by leaving the monastic state. Therefore it would seem that those who are in the clerical state are more perfect than religious.

Obj. 4: Further, it is not lawful to pass from a more perfect to a less perfect state. Yet it is lawful to pass from the monastic state to a priestly office with a cure attached, as appears (XVI, qu. i, can. Si quis monachus) from a decree of Pope Gelasius, who says: "If there be a monk, who by the merit of his exemplary life is worthy of the priesthood, and the abbot under whose authority he fights for Christ his King, ask that he be made a priest, the bishop shall take him and ordain him in such place as he shall choose fitting." And Jerome says (Ad Rustic. Monach., Ep. cxxv): "In the monastery so live as to deserve to be a clerk." Therefore parish priests and archdeacons are more perfect than religious.

Obj. 5: Further, bishops are in a more perfect state than religious, as shown above (A. 7). But parish priests and archdeacons, through having cure of souls, are more like bishops than religious are. Therefore they are more perfect.

Obj. 6: Further, virtue "is concerned with the difficult and the good" (Ethic. ii, 3). Now it is more difficult to lead a good life in the office of parish priest or archdeacon than in the religious state. Therefore parish priests and archdeacons have more perfect virtue than religious.

*On the contrary,* It is stated (XIX, qu. ii, cap. Duce): "If a man while governing the people in his church under the bishop and leading a secular life is inspired by the Holy Ghost to desire to work out his salvation in a monastery or under some canonical rule, since he is led by a private law, there is no reason why he should be constrained by a public law." Now a man is not led by the law of the Holy Ghost, which is here called a "private law," except to something more perfect. Therefore it would seem that religious are more perfect than archdeacons or parish priests.

*I answer that,* When we compare things in the point of super-eminence, we look not at that in which they agree, but at that wherein they differ. Now in parish priests and archdeacons three things may be considered, their state, their order, and their office. It belongs to their state that they are seculars, to their order that they are priests or deacons, to their office that they have the cure of souls committed to them.

Accordingly, if we compare these with one who is a religious by state, a deacon or priest by order, having the cure of souls by office, as many monks and canons regular have, this one will excel in the first point, and in the other points he will be equal. But if the latter differ from the former in state and office, but agree in order, such as religious priests and deacons not having the cure of souls, it is evident that the latter will be more excellent than the former in state, less excellent in office, and equal in order.

We must therefore consider which is the greater, preeminence of state or of office; and here, seemingly, we should take note of two things, goodness and difficulty. Accordingly, if we make the comparison with a view to goodness, the religious state surpasses the office of parish priest or archdeacon, because a religious pledges his whole life to the quest of perfection, whereas the parish priest or archdeacon does not pledge his whole life to the cure of souls, as a bishop does, nor is it competent to him, as it is to a bishop, to exercise the cure of souls in chief, but only in certain particulars regarding the cure of souls committed to his charge, as stated above (A. 6, ad 2). Wherefore the comparison of their religious state with their office is like the comparisons of the universal with the particular, and of a holocaust with a sacrifice which is less than a holocaust according to Gregory (Hom. xx in Ezech.). Hence it is said (XIX, qu. i, can. Clerici qui monachorum.): "Clerics who wish to take the monastic vows through being desirous of a better life must be allowed by their bishops the free entrance into the monastery."

This comparison, however, must be considered as regarding the genus of the deed; for as regards the charity of the doer it happens sometimes that a deed which is of less account in its genus is of greater merit if it be done out of greater charity.

On the other hand, if we consider the difficulty of leading a good life in religion, and in the office of one having the cure of souls, in this way it is more difficult to lead a good life together with the exercise of the cure of souls, on account of outward dangers: although the religious life is more difficult as regards the genus of the deed, by reason of the strictness of religious observance. If, however, the religious is also without orders, as in the case of religious lay brethren, then it is evident that the pre-eminence of order excels in the point of dignity, since by holy orders a man is appointed to the most august ministry of serving Christ Himself in the sacrament of the altar. For this requires a greater inward holiness than that which is requisite for the religious state, since as Dionysius says (Eccl. Hier. vi) the monastic order must follow the priestly orders, and ascend to Divine things in imitation of them. Hence, other things being equal, a cleric who is in holy orders, sins more grievously if he do something contrary to holiness than a religious who is not in holy orders: although a religious who is not in orders is bound to regular observance to which persons in holy orders are not bound.

Reply Obj. 1: We might answer briefly these quotations from Chrysostom by saying that he speaks not of a priest of lesser order who has the cure of souls, but of a bishop, who is called a high-priest; and this agrees with the purpose of that book wherein he consoles himself and Basil in that they were chosen to be bishops. We may, however, pass this over and reply that he speaks in view of the difficulty. For he had already said: "When the pilot is surrounded by the stormy sea and is able to bring the ship safely out of the tempest, then he deserves to be acknowledged by all as a perfect pilot"; and afterwards he concludes, as quoted, with regard to the monk, "who is not to be compared with one who, cast among the people ... remains firm"; and he gives the reason why, because "both in the calm and in the storm he piloted himself to safety." This proves nothing more than that the state of one who has the cure of souls is fraught with more danger than the monastic state; and to keep oneself innocent in face of a greater peril is proof of greater virtue. on the other hand, it also indicates greatness of virtue if a man avoid dangers by entering religion; hence he does not say that "he would prefer the priestly office to the monastic solitude," but that "he would rather please" in the former than in the latter, since this is a proof of greater virtue.

Reply Obj. 2: This passage quoted from Augustine also clearly refers to the question of difficulty which proves the greatness of virtue in those who lead a good life, as stated above (ad 1).

Reply Obj. 3: Augustine there compares monks with clerics as regards the pre-eminence of order, not as regards the distinction between religious and secular life.

Reply Obj. 4: Those who are taken from the religious state to receive the cure of souls, being already in sacred orders, attain to something they had not hitherto, namely the office of the cure, yet they do not put aside what they had already. For it is said in the Decretals (XVI, qu. i, can. De Monachis): "With regard to those monks who after long residence in a monastery attain to the order of clerics, we bid them not to lay aside their former purpose."

On the other hand, parish priests and archdeacons, when they enter religion, resign their cure, in order to enter the state of perfection. This very fact shows the excellence of the religious life. When religious who are not in orders are admitted to the clerical state and to the sacred orders, they are clearly promoted to something better, as stated: this is indicated by the very way in which Jerome expresses himself: "So live in the monastery as to deserve to be a clerk."

Reply Obj. 5: Parish priests and archdeacons are more like bishops than religious are, in a certain respect, namely as regards the cure of souls which they have subordinately; but as regards the obligation in perpetuity, religious are more like a bishop, as appears from what we have said above (AA. 5, 6).

Reply Obj. 6: The difficulty that arises from the arduousness of the deed adds to the perfection of virtue; but the difficulty that results from outward obstacles sometimes lessens the perfection of virtue—for instance, when a man loves not virtue so much as to wish to avoid the obstacles to virtue, according to the saying of the Apostle (1 Cor. 9:25), "Everyone that striveth for the mastery refraineth himself from all things": and sometimes it is a sign of perfect virtue—for instance, when a man forsakes not virtue, although he is hindered in the practice of virtue unawares or by some unavoidable cause. In the religious state there is greater difficulty arising from the arduousness of deeds; whereas for those who in any way at all live in the world, there is greater difficulty resulting from obstacles to virtue, which obstacles the religious has had the foresight to avoid.

# QUESTION 185

OF THINGS PERTAINING TO THE EPISCOPAL STATE (In Eight Articles)

We must now consider things pertaining to the episcopal state. Under this head there are eight points of inquiry:

(1) Whether it is lawful to desire the office of a bishop?

(2) Whether it is lawful to refuse the office of bishop definitively?

(3) Whether the better man should be chosen for the episcopal office?

(4) Whether a bishop may pass over to the religious state?

(5) Whether he may lawfully abandon his subjects in a bodily manner?

(6) Whether he can have anything of his own?

(7) Whether he sins mortally by not distributing ecclesiastical goods to the poor?

(8) Whether religious who are appointed to the episcopal office are bound to religious observances?

FIRST ARTICLE [II-II, Q. 185, Art. 1]

Whether It Is Lawful to Desire the Office of a Bishop?

Objection 1: It would seem that it is lawful to desire the office of a bishop. For the Apostle says (1 Tim. 3:1): "He that desires [Vulg.: 'If a man desire'] the office of a bishop, he desireth a good work." Now it is lawful and praiseworthy to desire a good work. Therefore it is even praiseworthy to desire the office of a bishop.

Obj. 2: Further, the episcopal state is more perfect than the religious, as we have said above (Q. 184, A. 7). But it is praiseworthy to desire to enter the religious state. Therefore it is also praiseworthy to desire promotion to the episcopal state.

Obj. 3: Further, it is written (Prov. 11:26): "He that hideth up corn shall be cursed among the people; but a blessing upon the head of them that sell." Now a man who is apt, both in manner of life and by knowledge, for the episcopal office, would seem to hide up the spiritual corn, if he shun the episcopal state, whereas by accepting the episcopal office he enters the state of a dispenser of spiritual corn. Therefore it would seem praiseworthy to desire the office of a bishop, and blameworthy to refuse it.

Obj. 4: Further, the deeds of the saints related in Holy Writ are set before us as an example, according to Rom. 15:4, "What things soever were written, were written for our learning." Now we read (Isa. 6:8) that Isaias offered himself for the office of preacher, which belongs chiefly to bishops. Therefore it would seem praiseworthy to desire the office of a bishop.

*On the contrary,* Augustine says (De Civ. Dei xix, 19): "The higher place, without which the people cannot be ruled, though it be filled becomingly, is unbecomingly desired."

*I answer that,* Three things may be considered in the episcopal office. One is principal and final, namely the bishop's work, whereby the good of our neighbor is intended, according to John 21:17, "Feed My sheep." Another thing is the height of degree, for a bishop is placed above others, according to Matt. 24:45, "A faithful and a wise servant, whom his lord hath appointed over his family." The third is something resulting from these, namely reverence, honor, and a sufficiency of temporalities, according to 1 Tim. 5:17, "Let the priests that rule well be esteemed worthy of double honor." Accordingly, to desire the episcopal office on account of these incidental goods is manifestly unlawful, and pertains to covetousness or ambition. Wherefore our Lord said against the Pharisees (Matt. 23:6, 7): "They love the first places at feasts, and the first chairs in the synagogues, and salutations in the market-place, and to be called by men, Rabbi." As regards the second, namely the height of degree, it is presumptuous to desire the episcopal office. Hence our Lord reproved His disciples for seeking precedence, by saying to them (Matt. 20:25): "You know that the princes of the gentiles lord it over them." Here Chrysostom says (Hom. lxv in Matth.) that in these words "He points out that it is heathenish to seek precedence; and thus by comparing them to the gentiles He converted their impetuous soul."

On the other hand, to desire to do good to one's neighbor is in itself praiseworthy, and virtuous. Nevertheless, since considered as an episcopal act it has the height of degree attached to it, it would seem that, unless there be manifest and urgent reason for it, it would be presumptuous for any man to desire to be set over others in order to do them good. Thus Gregory says (Pastor. i, 8) that "it was praiseworthy to seek the office of a bishop when it was certain to bring one into graver dangers." Wherefore it was not easy to find a person to accept this burden, especially seeing that it is through the zeal of charity that one divinely instigated to do so, according to Gregory, who says (Pastor. i, 7) that "Isaias being desirous of profiting his neighbor, commendably desired the office of preacher."

Nevertheless, anyone may, without presumption, desire to do such like works if he should happen to be in that office, or to be worthy of doing them; so that the object of his desire is the good work and not the precedence in dignity. Hence Chrysostom* says: "It is indeed good to desire a good work, but to desire the primacy of honor is vanity. For primacy seeks one that shuns it, and abhors one that desires it." [*The quotation is from the Opus Imperfectum in Matth. (Hom. xxxv), falsely ascribed to St. John Chrysostom.]

Reply Obj. 1: As Gregory says (Pastor. i, 8), "when the Apostle said this he who was set over the people was the first to be dragged to the torments of martyrdom," so that there was nothing to be desired in the episcopal office, save the good work. Wherefore Augustine says (De Civ. Dei xix, 19) that when the Apostle said, "'Whoever desireth the office of bishop, desireth a good work,' he wished to explain what the episcopacy is: for it denotes work and not honor: since *skopos* signifies 'watching.' Wherefore if we like we may render *episkopein* by the Latin superintendere (to watch over): thus a man may know himself to be no bishop if he loves to precede rather than to profit others." For, as he observed shortly before, "in our actions we should seek, not honor nor power in this life, since all things beneath the sun are vanity, but the work itself which that honor or power enables us to do." Nevertheless, as Gregory says (Pastor. i, 8), "while praising the desire" (namely of the good work) "he forthwith turns this object of praise into one of fear, when he adds: It behooveth ... a bishop to be blameless," as though to say: "I praise what you seek, but learn first what it is you seek."

Reply Obj. 2: There is no parity between the religious and the episcopal state, for two reasons. First, because perfection of life is a prerequisite of the episcopal state, as appears from our Lord asking Peter if he loved Him more than the others, before committing the pastoral office to him, whereas perfection is not a prerequisite of the religious state, since the latter is the way to perfection. Hence our Lord did not say (Matt. 19:21): "If thou art perfect, go, sell all [Vulg.: 'what'] thou hast," but "If thou wilt be perfect." The reason for this difference is because, according to Dionysius (Eccl. Hier. vi), perfection pertains actively to the bishop, as the "perfecter," but to the monk passively as one who is "perfected": and one needs to be perfect in order to bring others to perfection, but not in order to be brought to perfection. Now it is presumptuous to think oneself perfect, but it is not presumptuous to tend to perfection. Secondly, because he who enters the religious state subjects himself to others for the sake of a spiritual profit, and anyone may lawfully do this. Wherefore Augustine says (De Civ. Dei xix, 19): "No man is debarred from striving for the knowledge of truth, since this pertains to a praiseworthy ease." On the other hand, he who enters the episcopal state is raised up in order to watch over others, and no man should seek to be raised thus, according to Heb. 5:4, "Neither doth any man take the honor to himself, but he that is called by God": and Chrysostom says: "To desire supremacy in the Church is neither just nor useful. For what wise man seeks of his own accord to submit to such servitude and peril, as to have to render an account of the whole Church? None save him who fears not God's judgment, and makes a secular abuse of his ecclesiastical authority, by turning it to secular uses."

Reply Obj. 3: The dispensing of spiritual corn is not to be carried on in an arbitrary fashion, but chiefly according to the appointment and disposition of God, and in the second place according to the appointment of the higher prelates, in whose person it is said (1 Cor. 4:1): "Let a man so account of us as of the ministers of Christ, and the dispensers of the mysteries of God." Wherefore a man is not deemed to hide spiritual corn if he avoids governing or correcting others, and is not competent to do so, neither in virtue of his office nor of his superior's command; thus alone is he deemed to hide it, when he neglects to dispense it while under obligation to do so in virtue of his office, or obstinately refuses to accept the office when it is imposed on him. Hence Augustine says (De Civ. Dei xix, 19): "The love of truth seeks a holy leisure, the demands of charity undertake an honest labor. If no one imposes this burden upon us, we must devote ourselves to the research and contemplation of truth, but if it be imposed on us, we must bear it because charity demands it of us. *On the contrary,* our Lord commanded the apostles, whose successors bishops are (Matt. 10:23): "When they shall persecute you in this city, flee into another."

*I answer that,* In any obligation the chief thing to be considered is the end of the obligation. Now bishops bind themselves to fulfil the pastoral office for the sake of the salvation of their subjects. Consequently when the salvation of his subjects demands the personal presence of the pastor, the pastor should not withdraw his personal presence from his flock, neither for the sake of some temporal advantage, nor even on account of some impending danger to his person, since the good shepherd is bound to lay down his life for his sheep.

On the other hand, if the salvation of his subjects can be sufficiently provided for by another person in the absence of the pastor, it is lawful for the pastor to withdraw his bodily presence from his flock, either for the sake of some advantage to the Church, or on account of some danger to his person. Hence Augustine says (Ep. ccxxviii ad Honorat.): "Christ's servants may flee from one city to another, when one of them is specially sought out by persecutors: in order that the Church be not abandoned by others who are not so sought for. When, however, the same danger threatens all, those who stand in need of others must not be abandoned by those whom they need." For "if it is dangerous for the helmsman to leave the ship when the sea is calm, how much more so when it is stormy," as Pope Nicholas I says (cf. VII, qu. i, can. Sciscitaris).

Reply Obj. 1: To flee as a hireling is to prefer temporal advantage or one's bodily welfare to the spiritual welfare of one's neighbor. Hence Gregory says (Hom. xiv in Ev.): "A man cannot endanger himself for the sake of his sheep, if he uses his authority over them not through love of them but for the sake of earthly gain: wherefore he fears to stand in the way of danger lest he lose what he loves." But he who, in order to avoid danger, leaves the flock without endangering the flock, does not flee as a hireling.

Reply Obj. 2: If he who is surety for another be unable to fulfil his engagement, it suffices that he fulfil it through another. Hence if a superior is hindered from attending personally to the care of his subjects, he fulfils his obligation if he do so through another.

Reply Obj. 3: When a man is appointed to a bishopric, he embraces the state of perfection as regards one kind of perfection; and if he be hindered from the practice thereof, he is not bound to another kind of perfection, so as to be obliged to enter the religious state. Yet he is under the obligation of retaining the intention of devoting himself to his neighbor's salvation, should an opportunity offer, and necessity require it of him.

SIXTH ARTICLE [II-II, Q. 185, Art. 6]

Whether It Is Lawful for a Bishop to Have Property of His Own?

Objection 1: It would seem that it is not lawful for a bishop to have property of his own. For our Lord said (Matt. 19:21): "If thou wilt be perfect, go sell all [Vulg.: 'what'] thou hast, and give to the poor . . . and come, follow Me"; whence it would seem to follow that voluntary poverty is requisite for perfection. Now bishops are in the state of perfection. Therefore it would seem unlawful for them to possess anything as their own.

Obj. 2: Further, bishops take the place of the apostles in the Church, according to a gloss on Luke 10:1. Now our Lord commanded the apostles to possess nothing of their own, according to Matt. 10:9, "Do not possess gold, nor silver, nor money in your purses"; wherefore Peter said for himself and the other apostles (Matt. 19:27): "Behold we have left all things and have followed Thee." Therefore it would seem that bishops are bound to keep this command, and to possess nothing of their own.

Obj. 3: Further, Jerome says (Ep. lii ad Nepotian.): "The Greek kleros denotes the Latin sors. Hence clerics are so called either because they are of the Lord's estate, or because the Lord Himself is the estate, i.e. portion of clerics. Now he that possesses the Lord, can have nothing besides God; and if he have gold and silver, possessions, and chattels of all kinds, with such a portion the Lord does not vouchsafe to be his portion also." Therefore it would seem that not only bishops but even clerics should have nothing of their own.

*On the contrary,* It is stated (XII, qu. i, can. Episcopi de rebus): "Bishops, if they wish, may bequeath to their heirs their personal or acquired property, and whatever belongs to them personally."

*I answer that,* No one is bound to works of supererogation, unless he binds himself specially thereto by vow. Hence Augustine says (Ep. cxxvii ad Paulin. et Arment.): "Since you have taken the vow, you have already bound yourself, you can no longer do otherwise. Before you were bound by the vow, you were free to submit." Now it is evident that to live without possessing anything is a work of supererogation, for it is a matter not of precept but of counsel. Wherefore our Lord after saying to the young man: "If thou wilt enter into life, keep the commandments," said afterwards by way of addition: "If thou wilt be perfect go sell" all "that thou hast, and give to the poor" (Matt. 19:17, 21). Bishops, however, do not bind themselves at their ordination to live without possessions of their own; nor indeed does the pastoral office, to which they bind themselves, make it necessary for them to live without anything of their own. Therefore bishops are not bound to live without possessions of their own.

Reply Obj. 1: As stated above (Q. 184, A. 3, ad 1) the perfection of the Christian life does not essentially consist in voluntary poverty, but voluntary poverty conduces instrumentally to the perfection of life. Hence it does not follow that where there is greater poverty there is greater perfection; indeed the highest perfection is compatible with great wealth, since Abraham, to whom it was said (Gen. 17:1): "Walk before Me and be perfect," is stated to have been rich (Gen. 13:2).

Reply Obj. 2: This saying of our Lord can be understood in three ways. First, mystically, that we should possess neither gold nor silver means that the preacher should not rely chiefly on temporal wisdom and eloquence; thus Jerome expounds the passage.

Secondly, according to Augustine's explanation (De Consens. Ev. ii, 30), we are to understand that our Lord said this not in command but in permission. For he permitted them to go preaching without gold or silver or other means, since they were to receive the means of livelihood from those to whom they preached; wherefore He added: "For the workman is worthy of his meat." And yet if anyone were to use his own means in preaching the Gospel, this would be a work of supererogation, as Paul says in reference to himself (1 Cor. 9:12, 15).

Thirdly, according to the exposition of Chrysostom [*Hom. ii in Rom. xvi, 3, we are to understand that our Lord laid these commands on His disciples in reference to the mission on which they were sent to preach to the Jews, so that they might be encouraged to trust in His power, seeing that He provided for their wants without their having means of their own. But it does not follow from this that they, or their successors, were obliged to preach the Gospel without having means of their own: since we read of Paul (2 Cor. 11:8) that he "received wages" of other churches for preaching to the Corinthians, wherefore it is clear that he possessed something sent to him by others. And it seems foolish to say that so many holy bishops as Athanasius, Ambrose, and Augustine would have disobeyed these commandments if they believed themselves bound to observe them.

Reply Obj. 3: Every part is less than the whole. Accordingly a man has other portions together with God, if he becomes less intent on things pertaining to God by occupying himself with things of the world. Now neither bishops nor clerics ought thus to possess means of their own, that while busy with their own they neglect those that concern the worship of God.

SEVENTH ARTICLE [II-II, Q. 185, Art. 7]

Whether Bishops Sin Mortally If They Distribute Not to the Poor the Ecclesiastical Goods Which Accrue to Them?

Objection 1: It would seem that bishops sin mortally if they distribute not to the poor the ecclesiastical goods which they acquire. For Ambrose [*Basil, Serm. lxiv, de Temp., among the supposititious works of St. Jerome] expounding Luke 12:16, "The land of a certain . . . man brought forth plenty of fruits," says: "Let no man claim as his own that which he has taken and obtained by violence from the common property in excess of his requirements"; and afterwards he adds: "It is not less criminal to take from him who has, than, when you are able and have plenty to refuse him who has not." Now it is a mortal sin to take another's property by violence. Therefore bishops sin mortally if they give not to the poor that which they have in excess.

Obj. 2: Further, a gloss of Jerome on Isa. 3:14, "The spoil of the poor is in your house," says that "ecclesiastical goods belong to the poor." Now whoever keeps for himself or gives to others that which belongs to another, sins mortally and is bound to restitution. Therefore if bishops keep for themselves, or give to their relations or friends, their surplus of ecclesiastical goods, it would seem that they are bound to restitution.

Obj. 3: Further, much more may one take what is necessary for oneself from the goods of the Church, than accumulate a surplus therefrom. Yet Jerome says in a letter to Pope Damasus [*Cf. Can. Clericos, cause. i, qu. 2; Can. Quoniam; cause. xvi, qu. 1; Regul. Monach. iv, among the supposititious works of St. Jerome]: "It is right that those clerics who receive no goods from their parents and relations should be supported from the funds of the Church. But those who have sufficient income from their parents and their own possessions, if they take what belongs to the poor, they commit and incur the guilt of sacrilege." Wherefore the Apostle says (1 Tim. 5:16): "If any of the faithful have widows, let him minister to them, and let not the Church be charged, that there may be sufficient for them that are widows indeed." Much more therefore do bishops sin mortally if they give not to the poor the surplus of their ecclesiastical goods.

*On the contrary,* Many bishops do not give their surplus to the poor, but would seem commendably to lay it out so as to increase the revenue of the Church.

*I answer that,* The same is not to be said of their own goods which bishops may possess, and of ecclesiastical goods. For they have real dominion over their own goods; wherefore from the very nature of the case they are not bound to give these things to others, and may either keep them for themselves or bestow them on others at will. Nevertheless they may sin in this disposal by inordinate affection, which leads them either to accumulate more than they should, or not to assist others, in accordance with the demands of charity; yet they are not bound to restitution, because such things are entrusted to their ownership.

On the other hand, they hold ecclesiastical goods as dispensers or trustees. For Augustine says (Ep. clxxxv ad Bonif.): "If we possess privately what is enough for us, other things belong not to us but to the poor, and we have the dispensing of them; but we can claim ownership of them only by wicked theft." Now dispensing requires good faith, according to 1 Cor. 4:2, "Here now it is required among the dispensers that a man be found faithful." Moreover ecclesiastical goods are to be applied not only to the good of the poor, but also to the divine worship and the needs of its ministers. Hence it is said (XII, qu. ii, can. de reditibus): "Of the Church's revenues or the offerings of the faithful only one part is to be assigned to the bishop, two parts are to be used by the priest, under pain of suspension, for the ecclesiastical fabric, and for the benefit of the poor; the remaining part is to be divided among the clergy according to their respective merits." Accordingly if the goods which are assigned to the use of the bishop are distinct from those which are appointed for the use of the poor, or the ministers, or for the ecclesiastical worship, and if the bishop keeps back for himself part of that which should be given to the poor, or to the ministers for their use, or expended on the divine worship, without doubt he is an unfaithful dispenser, sins mortally, and is bound to restitution.

But as regards those goods which are deputed to his private use, the same apparently applies as to his own property, namely that he sins through immoderate attachment thereto or use thereof, if he exceeds moderation in what he keeps for himself, and fails to assist others according to the demands of charity.

On the other hand, if no distinction is made in the aforesaid goods, their distribution is entrusted to his good faith; and if he fail or exceed in a slight degree, this may happen without prejudice to his good faith, because in such matters a man cannot possibly decide precisely what ought to be done. On the other hand, if the excess be very great he cannot be ignorant of the fact; consequently he would seem to be lacking in good faith, and is guilty of mortal sin. For it is written (Matt. 24:48-51) that "if that evil servant shall say in his heart: My lord is long a-coming," which shows contempt of God's judgment, "and shall begin to strike his fellow-servants," which is a sign of pride, "and shall eat and drink with drunkards," which proceeds from lust, "the lord of that servant shall come in a day that he hopeth not . . . and shall separate him," namely from the fellowship of good men, "and appoint his portion with hypocrites," namely in hell.

Reply Obj. 1: This saying of Ambrose refers to the administration not only of ecclesiastical things but also of any goods whatever from which a man is bound, as a duty of charity, to provide for those who are in need. But it is not possible to state definitely when this need is such as to impose an obligation under pain of mortal sin, as is the case in other points of detail that have to be considered in human acts: for the decision in such matters is left to human prudence.

Reply Obj. 2: As stated above the goods of the Church have to be employed not only for the use of the poor, but also for other purposes. Hence if a bishop or cleric wish to deprive himself of that which is assigned to his own use, and give it to his relations or others, he sins not so long as he observes moderation, so, to wit, that they cease to be in want without becoming the richer thereby. Hence Ambrose says (De Offic. i, 30): "It is a commendable liberality if you overlook not your kindred when you know them to be in want; yet not so as to wish to make them rich with what you can give to the poor."

Reply Obj. 3: The goods of churches should not all be given to the poor, except in a case of necessity: for then, as Ambrose says (De Offic. ii, 28), even the vessels consecrated to the divine worship are to be sold for the ransom of prisoners, and other needs of the poor. In such a case of necessity a cleric would sin if he chose to maintain himself on the goods of the Church, always supposing him to have a patrimony of his own on which to support himself.

Reply Obj. 4: The goods of the churches should be employed for the good of the poor. Consequently a man is to be commended if, there being no present necessity for helping the poor, he spends the surplus from the Church revenue, in buying property, or lays it by for some future use connected with the Church or the needs of the poor. But if there be a pressing need for helping the poor, to lay by for the future is a superfluous and inordinate saving, and is forbidden by our Lord Who said (Matt. 6:34): "Be . . . not solicitous for the morrow."

EIGHTH ARTICLE [II-II, Q. 185, Art. 8]

Whether Religious Who Are Raised to the Episcopate Are Bound to Religious Observances?

Objection 1: It would seem that religious who are raised to the episcopate are not bound to religious observances. For it is said (XVIII, qu. i, can. Statutum) that a "canonical election loosens a monk from the yoke imposed by the rule of the monastic profession, and the holy ordination makes of a monk a bishop." Now the regular observances pertain to the yoke of the rule. Therefore religious who are appointed bishops are not bound to religious observances.

Obj. 2: Further, he who ascends from a lower to a higher degree is seemingly not bound to those things which pertain to the lower degree: thus it was stated above (Q. 88, A. 12, ad 1) that a religious is not bound to keep the vows he made in the world. But a religious who is appointed to the episcopate ascends to something greater, as stated above (Q. 84, A. 7). Therefore it would seem that a bishop is not bound to those things whereto he was bound in the state of religion.

Obj. 3: Further, religious would seem to be bound above all to obedience, and to live without property of their own. But religious who are appointed bishops, are not bound to obey the superiors of their order, since they are above them; nor apparently are they bound to poverty, since according to the decree quoted above (Obj. 1) "when the holy ordination has made of a monk a bishop he enjoys the right, as the lawful heir, of claiming his paternal inheritance." Moreover they are sometimes allowed to make a will. Much less therefore are they bound to other regular observances.

*On the contrary,* It is said in the Decretals (XVI, qu. i, can. De Monachis): "With regard to those who after long residence in a monastery attain to the order of clerics, we bid them not to lay aside their former purpose."

*I answer that,* As stated above (A. 1, ad 2) the religious state pertains to perfection, as a way of tending to perfection, while the episcopal state pertains to perfection, as a professorship of perfection. Hence the religious state is compared to the episcopal state, as the school to the professorial chair, and as disposition to perfection. Now the disposition is not voided at the advent of perfection, except as regards what perchance is incompatible with perfection, whereas as to that wherein it is in accord with perfection, it is confirmed the more. Thus when the scholar has become a professor it no longer becomes him to be a listener, but it becomes him to read and meditate even more than before. Accordingly we must assert that if there be among religious observances any that instead of being an obstacle to the episcopal office, are a safeguard of perfection, such as continence, poverty, and so forth, a religious, even after he has been made a bishop, remains bound to observe these, and consequently to wear the habit of his order, which is a sign of this obligation.

On the other hand, a man is not bound to keep such religious observances as may be incompatible with the episcopal office, for instance solitude, silence, and certain severe abstinences or watchings and such as would render him bodily unable to exercise the episcopal office. For the rest he may dispense himself from them, according to the needs of his person or office, and the manner of life of those among whom he dwells, in the same way as religious superiors dispense themselves in such matters.

Reply Obj. 1: He who from being a monk becomes a bishop is loosened from the yoke of the monastic profession, not in everything, but in those that are incompatible with the episcopal office, as stated above.

Reply Obj. 2: The vows of those who are living in the world are compared to the vows of religion as the particular to the universal, as stated above (Q. 88, A. 12, ad 1). But the vows of religion are compared to the episcopal dignity as disposition to perfection. Now the particular is superfluous when one has the universal, whereas the disposition is still necessary when perfection has been attained.

Reply Obj. 3: It is accidental that religious who are bishops are not bound to obey the superiors of their order, because, to wit, they have ceased to be their subjects; even as those same religious superiors. Nevertheless the obligation of the vow remains virtually, so that if any person be lawfully set above them, they would be bound to obey them, inasmuch as they are bound to obey both the statutes of their rule in the way mentioned above, and their superiors if they have any.

As to property they can nowise have it. For they claim their paternal inheritance not as their own, but as due to the Church. Hence it is added (XVIII, qu. i, can. Statutum) that after he has been ordained bishop at the altar to which he is consecrated and appointed according to the holy canons, he must restore whatever he may acquire.

Nor can he make any testament at all, because he is entrusted with the sole administration of things ecclesiastical, and this ends with his death, after which a testament comes into force according to the Apostle (Heb. 9:17). If, however, by the Pope's permission he make a will, he is not to be understood to bequeath property of his own, but we are to understand that by apostolic authority the power of his administration has been prolonged so as to remain in force after his death.

# QUESTION 186

OF THOSE THINGS IN WHICH THE RELIGIOUS STATE PROPERLY CONSISTS (In Ten Articles)

We must now consider things pertaining to the religious state: which consideration will be fourfold. In the first place we shall consider those things in which the religious state consists chiefly; secondly, those things which are lawfully befitting to religious; thirdly, the different kinds of religious orders; fourthly, the entrance into the religious state.

Under the first head there are ten points of inquiry:

(1) Whether the religious state is perfect?

(2) Whether religious are bound to all the counsels?

(3) Whether voluntary poverty is required for the religious state?

(4) Whether continency is necessary?

(5) Whether obedience is necessary?

(6) Whether it is necessary that these should be the matter of a vow?

(7) Of the sufficiency of these vows;

(8) Of their comparison one with another;

(9) Whether a religious sins mortally whenever he transgresses a statute of his rule?

(10) Whether, other things being equal, a religious sins more grievously by the same kind of sin than a secular person?

FIRST ARTICLE [II-II, Q. 186, Art. 1]

Whether Religion Implies a State of Perfection?

Objection 1: It would seem that religion does not imply a state of perfection. For that which is necessary for salvation does not seemingly pertain to perfection. But religion is necessary for salvation, whether because "thereby we are bound ( religamur ) to the one almighty God," as Augustine says (De Vera Relig. 55), or because it takes its name from "our returning ( religimus ) to God Whom we had lost by neglecting Him" [*Cf. Q. 81, A. 1], according to Augustine (De Civ. Dei x, 3). Therefore it would seem that religion does not denote the state of perfection.

Obj. 2: Further, religion according to Tully (De Invent. Rhet. ii, 53) is that "which offers worship and ceremony to the Divine nature." Now the offering of worship and ceremony to God would seem to pertain to the ministry of holy orders rather than to the diversity of states, as stated above (Q. 40, A. 2; Q. 183, A. 3). Therefore it would seem that religion does not denote the state of perfection.

Obj. 3: Further, the state of perfection is distinct from the state of beginners and that of the proficient. But in religion also some are beginners, and some are proficient. Therefore religion does not denote the state of perfection.

Obj. 4: Further, religion would seem a place of repentance; for it is said in the Decrees (VII, qu. i, can. Hoc nequaquam): "The holy synod orders that any man who has been degraded from the episcopal dignity to the monastic life and a place of repentance, should by no means rise again to the episcopate." Now a place of repentance is opposed to the state of perfection; hence Dionysius (Eccl. Hier. vi) places penitents in the lowest place, namely among those who are to be cleansed. Therefore it would seem that religion is not the state of perfection.

*On the contrary,* In the Conferences of the Fathers (Collat. i, 7) abbot Moses speaking of religious says: "We must recognize that we have to undertake the hunger of fasting, watchings, bodily toil, privation, reading, and other acts of virtue, in order by these degrees to mount to the perfection of charity." Now things pertaining to human acts are specified and denominated from the intention of the end. Therefore religious belong to the state of perfection.

Moreover Dionysius says (Eccl. Hier. vi) that those who are called servants of God, by reason of their rendering pure service and subjection to God, are united to the perfection beloved of Him.

*I answer that,* As stated above (Q. 141, A. 2) that which is applicable to many things in common is ascribed antonomastically to that to which it is applicable by way of excellence. Thus the name of "fortitude" is claimed by the virtue which preserves the firmness of the mind in regard to most difficult things, and the name of "temperance," by that virtue which tempers the greatest pleasures. Now religion as stated above (Q. 81, A. 2; A. 3, ad 2) is a virtue whereby a man offers something to the service and worship of God. Wherefore those are called religious antonomastically, who give themselves up entirely to the divine service, as offering a holocaust to God. Hence Gregory says (Hom. xx in Ezech.): "Some there are who keep nothing for themselves, but sacrifice to almighty God their tongue, their senses, their life, and the property they possess." Now the perfection of man consists in adhering wholly to God, as stated above (Q. 184, A. 2), and in this sense religion denotes the state of perfection.

Reply Obj. 1: To offer something to the worship of God is necessary for salvation, but to offer oneself wholly, and one's possessions to the worship of God belongs to perfection.

Reply Obj. 2: As stated above (Q. 81, A. 1, ad 1; A. 4, ad 1, 2; Q. 85, A. 3) when we were treating of the virtue of religion, religion has reference not only to the offering of sacrifices and other like things that are proper to religion, but also to the acts of all the virtues which in so far as these are referred to God's service and honor become acts of religion. Accordingly if a man devotes his whole life to the divine service, his whole life belongs to religion, and thus by reason of the religious life that they lead, those who are in the state of perfection are called religious.

Reply Obj. 3: As stated above (Q. 184, AA. 4, 6) religion denotes the state of perfection by reason of the end intended. Hence it does not follow that whoever is in the state of perfection is already perfect, but that he tends to perfection. Hence Origen commenting on Matt. 19:21, "If thou wilt be perfect," etc., says (Tract. viii in Matth.) that "he who has exchanged riches for poverty in order to become perfect does not become perfect at the very moment of giving his goods to the poor; but from that day the contemplation of God will begin to lead him to all the virtues." Thus all are not perfect in religion, but some are beginners, some proficient.

Reply Obj. 4: The religious state was instituted chiefly that we might obtain perfection by means of certain exercises, whereby the obstacles to perfect charity are removed. By the removal of the obstacles of perfect charity, much more are the occasions of sin cut off, for sin destroys charity altogether. Wherefore since it belongs to penance to cut out the causes of sin, it follows that the religious state is a most fitting place for penance. Hence (XXXIII, qu. ii, cap. Admonere) a man who had killed his wife is counseled to enter a monastery which is described as "better and lighter," rather than to do public penance while remaining in the world.

SECOND ARTICLE [II-II, Q. 186, Art. 2]

Whether Every Religious Is Bound to Keep All the Counsels?

Objection 1: It would seem that every religious is bound to keep all the counsels. For whoever professes a certain state of life is bound to observe whatever belongs to that state. Now each religious professes the state of perfection. Therefore every religious is bound to keep all the counsels that pertain to the state of perfection.

Obj. 2: Further, Gregory says (Hom. xx in Ezech.) that "he who renounces this world, and does all the good he can, is like one who has gone out of Egypt and offers sacrifice in the wilderness." Now it belongs specially to religious to renounce the world. Therefore it belongs to them also to do all the good they can. and so it would seem that each of them is bound to fulfil all the counsels.

Obj. 3: Further, if it is not requisite for the state of perfection to fulfil all the counsels, it would seem enough to fulfil some of them. But this is false, since some who lead a secular life fulfil some of the counsels, for instance those who observe continence. Therefore it would seem that every religious who is in the state of perfection is bound to fulfil whatever pertains to perfection: and such are the counsels.

*On the contrary,* one is not bound, unless one bind oneself, to do works of supererogation. But every religious does not bind himself to keep all the counsels, but to certain definite ones, some to some, others to others. Therefore all are not bound to keep all of them.

*I answer that,* A thing pertains to perfection in three ways. First, essentially, and thus, as stated above (Q. 184, A. 3) the perfect observance of the precepts of charity belongs to perfection. Secondly, a thing belongs to perfection consequently: such are those things that result from the perfection of charity, for instance to bless them that curse you (Luke 6:27), and to keep counsels of a like kind, which though they be binding as regards the preparedness of the mind, so that one has to fulfil them when necessity requires; yet are sometimes fulfilled, without there being any necessity, through superabundance of charity. Thirdly, a thing belongs to perfection instrumentally and dispositively, as poverty, continence, abstinence, and the like.

Now it has been stated (A. 1) that the perfection of charity is the end of the religious state. And the religious state is a school or exercise for the attainment of perfection, which men strive to reach by various practices, just as a physician may use various remedies in order to heal. But it is evident that for him who works for an end it is not necessary that he should already have attained the end, but it is requisite that he should by some means tend thereto. Hence he who enters the religious state is not bound to have perfect charity, but he is bound to tend to this, and use his endeavors to have perfect charity.

For the same reason he is not bound to fulfil those things that result from the perfection of charity, although he is bound to intend to fulfil them: against which intention he acts if he contemns them, wherefore he sins not by omitting them but by contempt of them.

In like manner he is not bound to observe all the practices whereby perfection may be attained, but only those which are definitely prescribed to him by the rule which he has professed.

Reply Obj. 1: He who enters religion does not make profession to be perfect, but he professes to endeavor to attain perfection; even as he who enters the schools does not profess to have knowledge, but to study in order to acquire knowledge. Wherefore as Augustine says (De Civ. Dei viii, 2), Pythagoras was unwilling to profess to be a wise man, but acknowledged himself, "a lover of wisdom." Hence a religious does not violate his profession if he be not perfect, but only if he despises to tend to perfection.

Reply Obj. 2: Just as, though all are bound to love God with their whole heart, yet there is a certain wholeness of perfection which cannot be omitted without sin, and another wholeness which can be omitted without sin (Q. 184, A. 2, ad 3), provided there be no contempt, as stated above (ad 1), so too, all, both religious and seculars, are bound, in a certain measure, to do whatever good they can, for to all without exception it is said (Eccles. 9:10): "Whatsoever thy hand is able to do, do it earnestly." Yet there is a way of fulfilling this precept, so as to avoid sin, namely if one do what one can as required by the conditions of one's state of life: provided there be no contempt of doing better things, which contempt sets the mind against spiritual progress.

Reply Obj. 3: There are some counsels such that if they be omitted, man's whole life would be taken up with secular business; for instance if he have property of his own, or enter the married state, or do something of the kind that regards the essential vows of religion themselves; wherefore religious are bound to keep all such like counsels. Other counsels there are, however, about certain particular better actions, which can be omitted without one's life being taken up with secular actions; wherefore there is no need for religious to be bound to fulfil all of them.

THIRD ARTICLE [II-II, Q. 186, Art. 3]

Whether Poverty Is Required for Religious Perfection?

Objection 1: It would seem that poverty is not required for religious perfection. For that which it is unlawful to do does not apparently belong to the state of perfection. But it would seem to be unlawful for a man to give up all he possesses; since the Apostle (2 Cor. 8:12) lays down the way in which the faithful are to give alms saying: "If the will be forward, it is accepted according to that which a man hath," i.e. "you should keep back what you need," and afterwards he adds (2 Cor. 8:13): "For I mean not that others should be eased, and you burthened," i.e. "with poverty," according to a gloss. Moreover a gloss on 1 Tim. 6:8, "Having food, and wherewith to be covered," says: "Though we brought nothing, and will carry nothing away, we must not give up these temporal things altogether." Therefore it seems that voluntary poverty is not requisite for religious perfection.

Obj. 2: Further, whosoever exposes himself to danger sins. But he who renounces all he has and embraces voluntary poverty exposes himself to danger--not only spiritual, according to Prov. 30:9, "Lest perhaps . . . being compelled by poverty, I should steal and forswear the name of my God," and Ecclus. 27:1, "Through poverty many have sinned"--but also corporal, for it is written (Eccles. 7:13): "As wisdom is a defense, so money is a defense," and the Philosopher says (Ethic. iv, 1) that "the waste of property appears to be a sort of ruining of one's self, since thereby man lives." Therefore it would seem that voluntary poverty is not requisite for the perfection of religious life.

Obj. 3: Further, "Virtue observes the mean," as stated in Ethic. ii, 6. But he who renounces all by voluntary poverty seems to go to the extreme rather than to observe the mean. Therefore he does not act virtuously: and so this does not pertain to the perfection of life.

Obj. 4: Further, the ultimate perfection of man consists in happiness. Now riches conduce to happiness; for it is written (Ecclus. 31:8): "Blessed is the rich man that is found without blemish," and the Philosopher says (Ethic. i, 8) that "riches contribute instrumentally to happiness." Therefore voluntary poverty is not requisite for religious perfection.

Obj. 5: Further, the episcopal state is more perfect than the religious state. But bishops may have property, as stated above (Q. 185, A. 6). Therefore religious may also.

Obj. 6: Further, almsgiving is a work most acceptable to God, and as Chrysostom says (Hom. ix in Ep. ad Hebr.) "is a most effective remedy in repentance." Now poverty excludes almsgiving. Therefore it would seem that poverty does not pertain to religious perfection.

*On the contrary,* Gregory says (Moral. viii, 26): "There are some of the righteous who bracing themselves up to lay hold of the very height of perfection, while they aim at higher objects within, abandon all things without." Now, as stated above, (AA. 1, 2), it belongs properly to religious to brace themselves up in order to lay hold of the very height of perfection. Therefore it belongs to them to abandon all outward things by voluntary poverty.

*I answer that,* As stated above (A. 2), the religious state is an exercise and a school for attaining to the perfection of charity. For this it is necessary that a man wholly withdraw his affections from worldly things; since Augustine says (Confess. x, 29), speaking to God: "Too little doth he love Thee, who loves anything with Thee, which he loveth not for Thee." Wherefore he says (QQ. lxxxiii, qu. 36) that "greater charity means less cupidity, perfect charity means no cupidity." Now the possession of worldly things draws a man's mind to the love of them: hence Augustine says (Ep. xxxi ad Paulin. et Theras.) that "we are more firmly attached to earthly things when we have them than when we desire them: since why did that young man go away sad, save because he had great wealth? For it is one thing not to wish to lay hold of what one has not, and another to renounce what one already has; the former are rejected as foreign to us, the latter are cut off as a limb." And Chrysostom says (Hom. lxiii in Matth.) that "the possession of wealth kindles a greater flame and the desire for it becomes stronger."

Hence it is that in the attainment of the perfection of charity the first foundation is voluntary poverty, whereby a man lives without property of his own, according to the saying of our Lord (Matt. 19:21), "If thou wilt be perfect, go, sell all [Vulg.: 'what'] thou hast, and give to the poor . . . and come, follow Me."

Reply Obj. 1: As the gloss adds, "when the Apostle said this (namely 'not that you should be burthened,' i.e. with poverty)," he did not mean that "it were better not to give: but he feared for the weak, whom he admonished so to give as not to suffer privation." Hence in like manner the other gloss means not that it is unlawful to renounce all one's temporal goods, but that this is not required of necessity. Wherefore Ambrose says (De Offic. i, 30): "Our Lord does not wish," namely does not command us "to pour out our wealth all at once, but to dispense it; or perhaps to do as did Eliseus who slew his oxen, and fed the poor with that which was his own so that no household care might hold him back."

Reply Obj. 2: He who renounces all his possessions for Christ's sake exposes himself to no danger, neither spiritual nor corporal. For spiritual danger ensues from poverty when the latter is not voluntary; because those who are unwillingly poor, through the desire of money-getting, fall into many sins, according to 1 Tim. 6:9, "They that will become rich, fall into temptation and into the snare of the devil." This attachment is put away by those who embrace voluntary poverty, but it gathers strength in those who have wealth, as stated above. Again bodily danger does not threaten those who, intent on following Christ, renounce all their possessions and entrust themselves to divine providence. Hence Augustine says (De Serm. Dom. in Monte ii, 17): "Those who seek first the kingdom of God and His justice are not weighed down by anxiety lest they lack what is necessary."

Reply Obj. 3: According to the Philosopher (Ethic. ii, 6), the mean of virtue is taken according to right reason, not according to the quantity of a thing. Consequently whatever may be done in accordance with right reason is not rendered sinful by the greatness of the quantity, but all the more virtuous. It would, however, be against right reason to throw away all one's possessions through intemperance, or without any useful purpose; whereas it is in accordance with right reason to renounce wealth in order to devote oneself to the contemplation of wisdom. Even certain philosophers are said to have done this; for Jerome says (Ep. xlviii ad Paulin.): "The famous Theban, Crates, once a very wealthy man, when he was going to Athens to study philosophy, cast away a large amount of gold; for he considered that he could not possess both gold and virtue at the same time." Much more therefore is it according to right reason for a man to renounce all he has, in order perfectly to follow Christ. Wherefore Jerome says (Ep. cxxv ad Rust. Monach.): "Poor thyself, follow Christ poor."

Reply Obj. 4: Happiness or felicity is twofold. One is perfect, to which we look forward in the life to come; the other is imperfect, in respect of which some are said to be happy in this life. The happiness of this life is twofold, one is according to the active life, the other according to the contemplative life, as the Philosopher asserts (Ethic. x, 7, 8). Now wealth conduces instrumentally to the happiness of the active life which consists in external actions, because as the Philosopher says (Ethic. i, 8) "we do many things by friends, by riches, by political influence, as it were by instruments." On the other hand, it does not conduce to the happiness of the contemplative life, rather is it an obstacle thereto, inasmuch as the anxiety it involves disturbs the quiet of the soul, which is most necessary to one who contemplates. Hence it is that the Philosopher asserts (Ethic. x, 8) that "for actions many things are needed, but the contemplative man needs no such things," namely external goods, "for his operation; in fact they are obstacles to his contemplation."

Man is directed to future happiness by charity; and since voluntary poverty is an efficient exercise for the attaining of perfect charity, it follows that it is of great avail in acquiring the happiness of heaven. Wherefore our Lord said (Matt. 19:21): "Go, sell all [Vulg.: 'what'] thou hast, and give to the poor, and thou shalt have treasure in heaven." Now riches once they are possessed are in themselves of a nature to hinder the perfection of charity, especially by enticing and distracting the mind. Hence it is written (Matt. 13:22) that "the care of this world and the deceitfulness of riches choketh up the word" of God, for as Gregory says (Hom. xv in Ev.) by "preventing the good desire from entering into the heart, they destroy life at its very outset." Consequently it is difficult to safeguard charity amidst riches: wherefore our Lord said (Matt. 19:23) that "a rich man shall hardly enter into the kingdom of heaven," which we must understand as referring to one who actually has wealth, since He says that this is impossible for him who places his affection in riches, according to the explanation of Chrysostom (Hom. lxiii in Matth.), for He adds (Matt. 19:24): "It is easier for a camel to pass through the eye of a needle, than for a rich man to enter into the kingdom of heaven." Hence it is not said simply that the "rich man" is blessed, but "the rich man that is found without blemish, and that hath not gone after gold," and this because he has done a difficult thing, wherefore the text continues (Matt. 19:9): "Who is he? and we will praise him; for he hath done wonderful things in his life," namely by not loving riches though placed in the midst of them.

Reply Obj. 5: The episcopal state is not directed to the attainment of perfection, but rather to the effect that, in virtue of the perfection which he already has, a man may govern others, by administering not only spiritual but also temporal things. This belongs to the active life, wherein many things occur that may be done by means of wealth as an instrument, as stated (ad 4). Wherefore it is not required of bishops, who make profession of governing Christ's flock, that they have nothing of their own, whereas it is required of religious who make profession of learning to obtain perfection.

Reply Obj. 6: The renouncement of one's own wealth is compared to almsgiving as the universal to the particular, and as the holocaust to the sacrifice. Hence Gregory says (Hom. xx in Ezech.) that those who assist "the needy with the things they possess, by their good deeds offer sacrifice, since they offer up something to God and keep back something for themselves; whereas those who keep nothing for themselves offer a holocaust which is greater than a sacrifice." Wherefore Jerome also says (Contra Vigilant.): "When you declare that those do better who retain the use of their possessions, and dole out the fruits of their possessions to the poor, it is not I but the Lord Who answers you; If thou wilt be perfect," etc., and afterwards he goes on to say: "This man whom you praise belongs to the second and third degree, and we too commend him: provided we acknowledge the first as to be preferred to the second and third." For this reason in order to exclude the error of Vigilantius it is said (De Eccl. Dogm. xxxviii): "It is a good thing to give away one's goods by dispensing them to the poor: it is better to give them away once for all with the intention of following the Lord, and, free of solicitude, to be poor with Christ."

FOURTH ARTICLE [II-II, Q. 186, Art. 4]

Whether Perpetual Continence Is Required for Religious Perfection?

Objection 1: It would seem that perpetual continence is not required for religious perfection. For all perfection of the Christian life began with Christ's apostles. Now the apostles do not appear to have observed continence, as evidenced by Peter, of whose mother-in-law we read Matt. 8:14. Therefore it would seem that perpetual continence is not requisite for religious perfection.

Obj. 2: Further, the first example of perfection is shown to us in the person of Abraham, to whom the Lord said (Gen. 17:1): "Walk before Me, and be perfect." Now the copy should not surpass the example. Therefore perpetual continence is not requisite for religious perfection.

Obj. 3: Further, that which is required for religious perfection is to be found in every religious order. Now there are some religious who lead a married life. Therefore religious perfection does not require perpetual continence.

*On the contrary,* The Apostle says (2 Cor. 7:1): "Let us cleanse ourselves from all defilement of the flesh and of the spirit, perfecting sanctification in the fear of God." Now cleanness of flesh and spirit is safeguarded by continence, for it is said (1 Cor. 7:34): "The unmarried woman and the virgin thinketh on the things of the Lord that she may be holy both in spirit and in body [Vulg.: 'both in body and in spirit']." Therefore religious perfection requires continence.

*I answer that,* The religious state requires the removal of whatever hinders man from devoting himself entirely to God's service. Now the use of sexual union hinders the mind from giving itself wholly to the service of God, and this for two reasons. First, on account of its vehement delectation, which by frequent repetition increases concupiscence, as also the Philosopher observes (Ethic. iii, 12): and hence it is that the use of venery withdraws the mind from that perfect intentness on tending to God. Augustine expresses this when he says (Solil. i, 10): "I consider that nothing so casts down the manly mind from its height as the fondling of women, and those bodily contacts which belong to the married state." Secondly, because it involves man in solicitude for the control of his wife, his children, and his temporalities which serve for their upkeep. Hence the Apostle says (1 Cor. 7:32, 33): "He that is without a wife is solicitous for the things that belong to the Lord, how he may please God: but he that is with a wife is solicitous for the things of the world, how he may please his wife."

Therefore perpetual continence, as well as voluntary poverty, is requisite for religious perfection. Wherefore just as Vigilantius was condemned for equaling riches to poverty, so was Jovinian condemned for equaling marriage to virginity.

Reply Obj. 1: The perfection not only of poverty but also of continence was introduced by Christ Who said (Matt. 19:12): "There are eunuchs who have made themselves eunuchs, for the kingdom of heaven," and then added: "He that can take, let him take it." And lest anyone should be deprived of the hope of attaining perfection, he admitted to the state of perfection those even who were married. Now the husbands could not without committing an injustice forsake their wives, whereas men could without injustice renounce riches. Wherefore Peter whom He found married, He severed not from his wife, while "He withheld from marriage John who wished to marry" [*Prolog. in Joan. among the supposititious works of St. Jerome].

Reply Obj. 2: As Augustine says (De Bono Conjug. xxii), "the chastity of celibacy is better than the chastity of marriage, one of which Abraham had in use, both of them in habit. For he lived chastely, and he might have been chaste without marrying, but it was not requisite then." Nevertheless if the patriarchs of old had perfection of mind together with wealth and marriage, which is a mark of the greatness of their virtue, this is no reason why any weaker person should presume to have such great virtue that he can attain to perfection though rich and married; as neither does a man unarmed presume to attack his enemy, because Samson slew many foes with the jaw-bone of an ass. For those fathers, had it been seasonable to observe continence and poverty, would have been most careful to observe them.

Reply Obj. 3: Such ways of living as admit of the use of marriage are not the religious life simply and absolutely speaking, but in a restricted sense, in so far as they have a certain share in those things that belong to the religious state.

FIFTH ARTICLE [II-II, Q. 186, Art. 5]

Whether Obedience Belongs to Religious Perfection?

Objection 1: It would seem that obedience does not belong to religious perfection. For those things seemingly belong to religious perfection, which are works of supererogation and are not binding upon all. But all are bound to obey their superiors, according to the saying of the Apostle (Heb. 13:17), "Obey your prelates, and be subject to them." Therefore it would seem that obedience does not belong to religious perfection.

Obj. 2: Further, obedience would seem to belong properly to those who have to be guided by the sense of others, and such persons are lacking in discernment. Now the Apostle says (Heb. 5:14) that "strong meat is for the perfect, for them who by custom have their senses exercised to the discerning of good and evil." Therefore it would seem that obedience does not belong to the state of the perfect.

Obj. 3: Further, if obedience were requisite for religious perfection, it would follow that it is befitting to all religious. But it is not becoming to all; since some religious lead a solitary life, and have no superior whom they obey. Again religious superiors apparently are not bound to obedience. Therefore obedience would seem not to pertain to religious perfection.

Obj. 4: Further, if the vow of obedience were requisite for religion, it would follow that religious are bound to obey their superiors in all things, just as they are bound to abstain from all venery by their vow of continence. But they are not bound to obey them in all things, as stated above (Q. 104, A. 5), when we were treating of the virtue of obedience. Therefore the vow of obedience is not requisite for religion.

Obj. 5: Further, those services are most acceptable to God which are done freely and not of necessity, according to 2 Cor. 9:7, "Not with sadness or of necessity." Now that which is done out of obedience is done of necessity of precept. Therefore those good works are more deserving of praise which are done of one's own accord. Therefore the vow of obedience is unbecoming to religion whereby men seek to attain to that which is better.

*On the contrary,* Religious perfection consists chiefly in the imitation of Christ, according to Matt. 19:21, "If thou wilt be perfect, go sell all [Vulg.: 'what'] thou hast, and give to the poor, and follow Me." Now in Christ obedience is commended above all according to Phil. 2:8, "He became [Vulg.: 'becoming'] obedient unto death." Therefore seemingly obedience belongs to religious perfection.

*I answer that,* As stated above (AA. 2, 3) the religious state is a school and exercise for tending to perfection. Now those who are being instructed or exercised in order to attain a certain end must needs follow the direction of someone under whose control they are instructed or exercised so as to attain that end as disciples under a master. Hence religious need to be placed under the instruction and command of someone as regards things pertaining to the religious life; wherefore it is said (VII, qu. i, can. Hoc nequaquam): "The monastic life denotes subjection and discipleship." Now one man is subjected to another's command and instruction by obedience: and consequently obedience is requisite for religious perfection.

Reply Obj. 1: To obey one's superiors in matters that are essential to virtue is not a work of supererogation, but is common to all: whereas to obey in matters pertaining to the practice of perfection belongs properly to religious. This latter obedience is compared to the former as the universal to the particular. For those who live in the world, keep something for themselves, and offer something to God; and in the latter respect they are under obedience to their superiors: whereas those who live in religion give themselves wholly and their possessions to God, as stated above (AA. 1, 3). Hence their obedience is universal.

Reply Obj. 2: As the Philosopher says (Ethic. ii,

1, 2), by performing actions we contract certain habits, and when we have acquired the habit we are best able to perform the actions. Accordingly those who have not attained to perfection, acquire perfection by obeying, while those who have already acquired perfection are most ready to obey, not as though they need to be directed to the acquisition of perfection, but as maintaining themselves by this means in that which belongs to perfection.

Reply Obj. 3: The subjection of religious is chiefly in reference to bishops, who are compared to them as perfecters to perfected, as Dionysius states (Eccl. Hier. vi), where he also says that the "monastic order is subjected to the perfecting virtues of the bishops, and is taught by their godlike enlightenment." Hence neither hermits nor religious superiors are exempt from obedience to bishops; and if they be wholly or partly exempt from obedience to the bishop of the diocese, they are nevertheless bound to obey the Sovereign Pontiff, not only in matters affecting all in common, but also in those which pertain specially to religious discipline.

Reply Obj. 4: The vow of obedience taken by religious, extends to the disposition of a man's whole life, and in this way it has a certain universality, although it does not extend to all individual acts. For some of these do not belong to religion, through not being of those things that concern the love of God and of our neighbor, such as rubbing one's beard, lifting a stick from the ground and so forth, which do not come under a vow nor under obedience; and some are contrary to religion. Nor is there any comparison with continence whereby acts are excluded which are altogether contrary to religion.

Reply Obj. 5: The necessity of coercion makes an act involuntary and consequently deprives it of the character of praise or merit; whereas the necessity which is consequent upon obedience is a necessity not of coercion but of a free will, inasmuch as a man is willing to obey, although perhaps he would not be willing to do the thing commanded considered in itself. Wherefore since by the vow of obedience a man lays himself under the necessity of doing for God's sake certain things that are not pleasing in themselves, for this very reason that which he does is the more acceptable to God, though it be of less account, because man can give nothing greater to God, than by subjecting his will to another man's for God's sake. Hence in the Conferences of the Fathers (Coll. xviii, 7) it is stated that "the Sarabaitae are the worst class of monks, because through providing for their own needs without being subject to superiors, they are free to do as they will; and yet day and night they are more busily occupied in work than those who live in monasteries."

SIXTH ARTICLE [II-II, Q. 186, Art. 6]

Whether It Is Requisite for Religious Perfection That Poverty, Continence, and Obedience Should Come Under a Vow?

Objection 1: It would seem that it is not requisite for religious perfection that the three aforesaid, namely poverty, continence, and obedience, should come under a vow. For the school of perfection is founded on the principles laid down by our Lord. Now our Lord in formulating perfection (Matt. 19:21) said: "If thou wilt be perfect, go, sell all [Vulg.: 'what'] thou hast, and give to the poor," without any mention of a vow. Therefore it would seem that a vow is not necessary for the school of religion.

Obj. 2: Further, a vow is a promise made to God, wherefore (Eccles. 5:3) the wise man after saying: "If thou hast vowed anything to God, defer not to pay it," adds at once, "for an unfaithful and foolish promise displeaseth Him." But when a thing is being actually given there is no need for a promise. Therefore it suffices for religious perfection that one keep poverty, continence, and obedience without. vowing them.

Obj. 3: Further, Augustine says (Ad Pollent., de Adult. Conjug. i, 14): "The services we render are more pleasing when we might lawfully not render them, yet do so out of love." Now it is lawful not to render a service which we have not vowed, whereas it is unlawful if we have vowed to render it. Therefore seemingly it is more pleasing to God to keep poverty, continence, and obedience without a vow. Therefore a vow is not requisite for religious perfection.

*On the contrary,* In the Old Law the Nazareans were consecrated by vow according to Num. 6:2, "When a man or woman shall make a vow to be sanctified and will consecrate themselves to the Lord," etc. Now these were a figure of those "who attain the summit of perfection," as a gloss [*Cf. Moral. ii] of Gregory states. Therefore a vow is requisite for religious perfection.

*I answer that,* It belongs to religious to be in the state of perfection, as shown above (Q. 174, A. 5). Now the state of perfection requires an obligation to whatever belongs to perfection: and this obligation consists in binding oneself to God by means of a vow. But it is evident from what has been said (AA. 3, 4, 5) that poverty, continence, and obedience belong to the perfection of the Christian life. Consequently the religious state requires that one be bound to these three by vow. Hence Gregory says (Hom. xx in Ezech.): "When a man vows to God all his possessions, all his life, all his knowledge, it is a holocaust"; and afterwards he says that this refers to those who renounce the present world.

Reply Obj. 1: Our Lord declared that it belongs to the perfection of life that a man follow Him, not anyhow, but in such a way as not to turn back. Wherefore He says again (Luke 9:62): "No man putting his hand to the plough, and looking back, is fit for the kingdom of God." And though some of His disciples went back, yet when our Lord asked (John 6:68, 69), "Will you also go away?" Peter answered for the others: "Lord, to whom shall we go?" Hence Augustine says (De Consensu Ev. ii, 17) that "as Matthew and Mark relate, Peter and Andrew followed Him after drawing their boats on to the beach, not as though they purposed to return, but as following Him at His command." Now this unwavering following of Christ is made fast by a vow: wherefore a vow is requisite for religious perfection.

Reply Obj. 2: As Gregory says (Moral. ii) religious perfection requires that a man give "his whole life" to God. But a man cannot actually give God his whole life, because that life taken as a whole is not simultaneous but successive. Hence a man cannot give his whole life to God otherwise than by the obligation of a vow.

Reply Obj. 3: Among other services that we can lawfully give, is our liberty, which is dearer to man than aught else. Consequently when a man of his own accord deprives himself by vow of the liberty of abstaining from things pertaining to God's service, this is most acceptable to God. Hence Augustine says (Ep. cxxvii ad Paulin. et Arment.): "Repent not of thy vow; rejoice rather that thou canst no longer do lawfully, what thou mightest have done lawfully but to thy own cost. Happy the obligation that compels to better things."

SEVENTH ARTICLE [II-II, Q. 186, Art. 7]

Whether It Is Right to Say That Religious Perfection Consists in These Three Vows?

Objection 1: It would seem that it is not right to say that religious perfection consists in these three vows. For the perfection of life consists of inward rather than of outward acts, according to Rom. 14:17, "The Kingdom of God is not meat and drink, but justice and peace and joy in the Holy Ghost." Now the religious vow binds a man to things belonging to perfection. Therefore vows of inward actions, such as contemplation, love of God and our neighbor, and so forth, should pertain to the religious state, rather than the vows of poverty, continence, and obedience which refer to outward actions.

Obj. 2: Further, the three aforesaid come under the religious vow, in so far as they belong to the practice of tending to perfection. But there are many other things that religious practice, such as abstinence, watchings, and the like. Therefore it would seem that these three vows are incorrectly described as pertaining to the state of perfection.

Obj. 3: Further, by the vow of obedience a man is bound to do according to his superior's command whatever pertains to the practice of perfection. Therefore the vow of obedience suffices without the two other vows.

Obj. 4: Further, external goods comprise not only riches but also honors. Therefore, if religious, by the vow of poverty, renounce earthly riches, there should be another vow whereby they may despise worldly honors.

*On the contrary,* It is stated (Extra, de Statu Monach., cap. Cum ad monasterium) that "the keeping of chastity and the renouncing of property are affixed to the monastic rule."

*I answer that,* The religious state may be considered in three ways. First, as being a practice of tending to the perfection of charity: secondly, as quieting the human mind from outward solicitude, according to 1 Cor. 7:32: "I would have you to be without solicitude": thirdly, as a holocaust whereby a man offers himself and his possessions wholly to God; and in corresponding manner the religious state is constituted by these three vows.

First, as regards the practice of perfection a man is required to remove from himself whatever may hinder his affections from tending wholly to God, for it is in this that the perfection of charity consists. Such hindrances are of three kinds. First, the attachment to external goods, which is removed by the vow of poverty; secondly, the concupiscence of sensible pleasures, chief among which are venereal pleasures, and these are removed by the vow of continence; thirdly, the inordinateness of the human will, and this is removed by the vow of obedience. In like manner the disquiet of worldly solicitude is aroused in man in reference especially to three things. First, as regards the dispensing of external things, and this solicitude is removed from man by the vow of poverty; secondly, as regards the control of wife and children, which is cut away by the vow of continence; thirdly, as regards the disposal of one's own actions, which is eliminated by the vow of obedience, whereby a man commits himself to the disposal of another.

Again, "a holocaust is the offering to God of all that one has," according to Gregory (Hom. xx in Ezech.). Now man has a threefold good, according to the Philosopher (Ethic. i, 8). First, the good of external things, which he wholly offers to God by the vow of voluntary poverty: secondly, the good of his own body, and this good he offers to God especially by the vow of continence, whereby he renounces the greatest bodily pleasures. The third is the good of the soul, which man wholly offers to God by the vow of obedience, whereby he offers God his own will by which he makes use of all the powers and habits of the soul. Therefore the religious state is fittingly constituted by the three vows.

Reply Obj. 1: As stated above (A. 1), the end whereunto the religious vow is directed is the perfection of charity, since all the interior acts of virtue belong to charity as to their mother, according to 1 Cor. 13:4, "Charity is patient, is kind," etc. Hence the interior acts of virtue, for instance humility, patience, and so forth, do not come under the religious vow, but this is directed to them as its end.

Reply Obj. 2: All other religious observances are directed to the three aforesaid principal vows; for if any of them are ordained for the purpose of procuring a livelihood, such as labor, questing, and so on, they are to be referred to poverty; for the safeguarding of which religious seek a livelihood by these means. Other observances whereby the body is chastised, such as watching, fasting, and the like, are directly ordained for the observance of the vow of continence. And such religious observances as regard human actions whereby a man is directed to the end of religion, namely the love of God and his neighbor (such as reading, prayer, visiting the sick, and the like), are comprised under the vow of obedience that applies to the will, which directs its actions to the end according to the ordering of another person. The distinction of habit belongs to all three vows, as a sign of being bound by them: wherefore the religious habit is given or blessed at the time of profession.

Reply Obj. 3: By obedience a man offers to God his will, to which though all human affairs are subject, yet some are subject to it alone in a special manner, namely human actions, since passions belong also to the sensitive appetite. Wherefore in order to restrain the passions of carnal pleasures and of external objects of appetite, which hinder the perfection of life, there was need for the vows of continence and poverty; but for the ordering of one's own actions accordingly as the state of perfection requires, there was need for the vow of obedience.

Reply Obj. 4: As the Philosopher says (Ethic. iv, 3), strictly and truly speaking honor is not due save to virtue. Since, however, external goods serve instrumentally for certain acts of virtue, the consequence is that a certain honor is given to their excellence especially by the common people who acknowledge none but outward excellence. Therefore since religious tend to the perfection of virtue it becomes them not to renounce the honor which God and all holy men accord to virtue, according to Ps. 138:17, "But to me Thy friends, O God, are made exceedingly honorable." On the other hand, they renounce the honor that is given to outward excellence, by the very fact that they withdraw from a worldly life: hence no special vow is needed for this.

EIGHTH ARTICLE [II-II, Q. 186, Art. 8]

Whether the Vow of Obedience Is the Chief of the Three Religious Vows?

Objection 1: It would seem that the vow of obedience is not the chief of the three religious vows. For the perfection of the religious life was inaugurated by Christ. Now Christ gave a special counsel of poverty; whereas He is not stated to have given a special counsel of obedience. Therefore the vow of poverty is greater than the vow of obedience.

Obj. 2: Further, it is written (Ecclus. 26:20) that "no price is worthy of a continent soul." Now the vow of that which is more worthy is itself more excellent. Therefore the vow of continence is more excellent than the vow of obedience.

Obj. 3: Further, the greater a vow the more indispensable it would seem to be. Now the vows of poverty and continence "are so inseparable from the monastic rule, that not even the Sovereign Pontiff can allow them to be broken," according to a Decretal (De Statu Monach., cap. Cum ad monasterium): yet he can dispense a religious from obeying his superior. Therefore it would seem that the vow of obedience is less than the vow of poverty and continence.

*On the contrary,* Gregory says (Moral. xxxv, 14): "Obedience is rightly placed before victims, since by victims another's flesh, but by obedience one's own will, is sacrificed." Now the religious vows are holocausts, as stated above (AA. 1, 3, ad 6). Therefore the vow of obedience is the chief of all religious vows.

*I answer that,* The vow of obedience is the chief of the three religious vows, and this for three reasons.

First, because by the vow of obedience man offers God something greater, namely his own will; for this is of more account than his own body, which he offers God by continence, and than external things, which he offers God by the vow of poverty. Wherefore that which is done out of obedience is more acceptable to God than that which is done of one's own will, according to the saying of Jerome (Ep. cxxv ad Rustic Monach.): "My words are intended to teach you not to rely on your own judgment": and a little further on he says: "You may not do what you will; you must eat what you are bidden to eat, you may possess as much as you receive, clothe yourself with what is given to you." Hence fasting is not acceptable to God if it is done of one's own will, according to Isa. 58:3, "Behold in the day of your fast your own will is found."

Secondly, because the vow of obedience includes the other vows, but not vice versa: for a religious, though bound by vow to observe continence and poverty, yet these also come under obedience, as well as many other things besides the keeping of continence and poverty.

Thirdly, because the vow of obedience extends properly to those acts that are closely connected with the end of religion; and the more closely a thing is connected with the end, the better it is.

It follows from this that the vow of obedience is more essential to the religious life. For if a man without taking a vow of obedience were to observe, even by vow, voluntary poverty and continence, he would not therefore belong to the religious state, which is to be preferred to virginity observed even by vow; for Augustine says (De Virgin. xlvi): "No one, methinks, would prefer virginity to the monastic life." [*St. Augustine wrote not monasterio but martyrio --to "martyrdom"; and St. Thomas quotes the passage correctly above, Q. 124, A. 3, and Q. 152, A. 5].

Reply Obj. 1: The counsel of obedience was included in the very following of Christ, since to obey is to follow another's will. Consequently it is more pertinent to perfection than the vow of poverty, because as Jerome, commenting on Matt. 19:27, "Behold we have left all things," observes, "Peter added that which is perfect when he said: And have followed Thee."

Reply Obj. 2: The words quoted mean that continence is to be preferred, not to all other acts of virtue, but to conjugal chastity, or to external riches of gold and silver which are measured by weight [* Pondere, referring to the Latin ponderatio in the Vulgate, which the Douay version renders "price."]. Or again continence is taken in a general sense for abstinence from all evil, as stated above (Q. 155, A. 4, ad 1).

Reply Obj. 3: The Pope cannot dispense a religious from his vow of obedience so as to release him from obedience to every superior in matters relating to the perfection of life, for he cannot exempt him from obedience to himself. He can, however, exempt him from subjection to a lower superior, but this is not to dispense him from his vow of obedience.

NINTH ARTICLE [II-II, Q. 186, Art. 9]

Whether a Religious Sins Mortally Whenever He Transgresses the Things Contained in His Rule?

Objection 1: It would seem that a religious sins mortally whenever he transgresses the things contained in his rule. For to break a vow is a sin worthy of condemnation, as appears from 1 Tim. 5:11, 12, where the Apostle says that widows who "will marry have [Vulg.: 'having'] damnation, because they have made void their first faith." But religious are bound to a rule by the vows of their profession. Therefore they sin mortally by transgressing the things contained in their rule.

Obj. 2: Further, the rule is enjoined upon a religious in the same way as a law. Now he who transgresses a precept of law sins mortally. Therefore it would seem that a monk sins mortally if he transgresses the things contained in his rule.

Obj. 3: Further, contempt involves a mortal sin. Now whoever repeatedly does what he ought not to do seems to sin from contempt. Therefore it would seem that a religious sins mortally by frequently transgressing the things contained in his rule.

*On the contrary,* The religious state is safer than the secular state; wherefore Gregory at the beginning of his Morals [*Epist. Missoria, ad Leand. Episc. i] compares the secular life to the stormy sea, and the religious life to the calm port. But if every transgression of the things contained in his rule were to involve a religious in mortal sin, the religious life would be fraught with danger of account of its multitude of observances. Therefore not every transgression of the things contained in the rule is a mortal sin.

*I answer that,* As stated above (A. 1, ad 1, 2), a thing is contained in the rule in two ways. First, as the end of the rule, for instance things that pertain to the acts of the virtues; and the transgression of these, as regards those which come under a common precept, involves a mortal sin; but as regards those which are not included in the common obligation of a precept, the transgression thereof does not involve a mortal sin, except by reason of contempt, because, as stated above (A. 2), a religious is not bound to be perfect, but to tend to perfection, to which the contempt of perfection is opposed.

Secondly, a thing is contained in the rule through pertaining to the outward practice, such as all external observances, to some of which a religious is bound by the vow of his profession. Now the vow of profession regards chiefly the three things aforesaid, namely poverty, continence, and obedience, while all others are directed to these. Consequently the transgression of these three involves a mortal sin, while the transgression of the others does not involve a mortal sin, except either by reason of contempt of the rule (since this is directly contrary to the profession whereby a man vows to live according to the rule), or by reason of a precept, whether given orally by a superior, or expressed in the rule, since this would be to act contrary to the vow of obedience.

Reply Obj. 1: He who professes a rule does not vow to observe all the things contained in the rule, but he vows the regular life which consists essentially in the three aforesaid things. Hence in certain religious orders precaution is taken to profess, not the rule, but to live according to the rule, i.e. to tend to form one's conduct in accordance with the rule as a kind of model; and this is set aside by contempt. Yet greater precaution is observed in some religious orders by professing obedience according to the rule, so that only that which is contrary to a precept of the rule is contrary to the profession, while the transgression or omission of other things binds only under pain of venial sin, because, as stated above (A. 7, ad 2), such things are dispositions to the chief vows. And venial sin is a disposition to mortal, as stated above (I-II, Q. 88, A. 3), inasmuch as it hinders those things whereby a man is disposed to keep the chief precepts of Christ's law, namely the precepts of charity.

There is also a religious order, that of the Friars Preachers, where such like transgressions or omissions do not, by their very nature, involve sin, either mortal or venial; but they bind one to suffer the punishment affixed thereto, because it is in this way that they are bound to observe such things. Nevertheless they may sin venially or mortally through neglect, concupiscence, or contempt.

Reply Obj. 2: Not all the contents of the law are set forth by way of precept; for some are expressed under the form of ordinance or statute binding under pain of a fixed punishment. Accordingly, just as in the civil law the transgression of a legal statute does not always render a man deserving of bodily death, so neither in the law of the Church does every ordinance or statute bind under mortal sin; and the same applies to the statutes of the rule.

Reply Obj. 3: An action or transgression proceeds from contempt when a man's will refuses to submit to the ordinance of the law or rule, and from this he proceeds to act against the law or rule. On the other hand, he does not sin from contempt, but from some other cause, when he is led to do something against the ordinance of the law or rule through some particular cause such as concupiscence or anger, even though he often repeat the same kind of sin through the same or some other cause. Thus Augustine says (De Nat. et Grat. xxix) that "not all sins are committed through proud contempt." Nevertheless the frequent repetition of a sin leads dispositively to contempt, according to the words of Prov. 18:3, "The wicked man, when he is come into the depth of sins, contemneth."

TENTH ARTICLE [II-II, Q. 186, Art. 10]

Whether a Religious Sins More Grievously Than a Secular by the Same Kind of Sin?

Objection 1: It would seem that a religious does not sin more grievously than a secular by the same kind of sin. For it is written (2 Paralip. 30:18, 19): "The Lord Who is good will show mercy to all them who with their whole heart seek the Lord the God of their fathers, and will not impute it to them that they are not sanctified." Now religious apparently follow the Lord the God of their fathers with their whole heart rather than seculars, who partly give themselves and their possessions to God and reserve part for themselves, as Gregory says (Hom. xx in Ezech.). Therefore it would seem that it is less imputed to them if they fall short somewhat of their sanctification.

Obj. 2: Further, God is less angered at a man's sins if he does some good deeds, according to 2 Paralip. 19:2, 3, "Thou helpest the ungodly, and thou art joined in friendship with them that hate the Lord, and therefore thou didst deserve indeed the wrath of the Lord: but good works are found in thee." Now religious do more good works than seculars. Therefore if they commit any sins, God is less angry with them.

Obj. 3: Further, this present life is not carried through without sin, according to James 3:2, "In many things we all offend." Therefore if the sins of religious were more grievous than those of seculars it would follow that religious are worse off than seculars: and consequently it would not be a wholesome counsel to enter religion.

*On the contrary,* The greater the evil the more it would seem to be deplored. But seemingly the sins of those who are in the state of holiness and perfection are the most deplorable, for it is written (Jer. 23:9): "My heart is broken within me," and afterwards (Jer. 23:11): "For the prophet and the priest are defiled; and in My house I have found their wickedness." Therefore religious and others who are in the state of perfection, other things being equal, sin more grievously.

*I answer that,* A sin committed by a religious may be in three ways more grievous than a like sin committed by a secular. First, if it be against his religious vow; for instance if he be guilty of fornication or theft, because by fornication he acts against the vow of continence, and by theft against the vow of poverty; and not merely against a precept of the divine law. Secondly, if he sin out of contempt, because thereby he would seem to be the more ungrateful for the divine favors which have raised him to the state of perfection. Thus the Apostle says (Heb. 10:29) that the believer "deserveth worse punishments" who through contempt tramples under foot the Son of God. Hence the Lord complains (Jer. 11:15): "What is the meaning that My beloved hath wrought much wickedness in My house?" Thirdly, the sin of a religious may be greater on account of scandal, because many take note of his manner of life: wherefore it is written (Jer. 23:14): "I have seen the likeness of adulterers, and the way of lying in the Prophets of Jerusalem; and they strengthened the hands of the wicked, that no man should return from his evil doings."

On the other hand, if a religious, not out of contempt, but out of weakness or ignorance, commit a sin that is not against the vow of his profession, without giving scandal (for instance if he commit it in secret) he sins less grievously in the same kind of sin than a secular, because his sin if slight is absorbed as it were by his many good works, and if it be mortal, he more easily recovers from it. First, because he has a right intention towards God, and though it be intercepted for the moment, it is easily restored to its former object. Hence Origen commenting on Ps. 36:24, "When he shall fall he shall not be bruised," says (Hom. iv in Ps. 36): "The wicked man, if he sin, repents not, and fails to make amends for his sin. But the just man knows how to make amends and recover himself; even as he who had said: 'I know not the man,' shortly afterwards when the Lord had looked on him, knew to shed most bitter tears, and he who from the roof had seen a woman and desired her knew to say: 'I have sinned and done evil before Thee.'" Secondly, he is assisted by his fellow-religious to rise again, according to Eccles. 4:10, "If one fall he shall be supported by the other: woe to him that is alone, for when he falleth he hath none to lift him up."

Reply Obj. 1: The words quoted refer to things done through weakness or ignorance, but not to those that are done out of contempt.

Reply Obj. 2: Josaphat also, to whom these words were addressed, sinned not out of contempt, but out of a certain weakness of human affection.

Reply Obj. 3: The just sin not easily out of contempt; but sometimes they fall into a sin through ignorance or weakness from which they easily arise. If, however, they go so far as to sin out of contempt, they become most wicked and incorrigible, according to the word of Jer. 2:20: "Thou hast broken My yoke, thou hast burst My bands, and thou hast said: 'I will not serve.' For on every high hill and under every green tree thou didst prostitute thyself." Hence Augustine says (Ep. lxxviii ad Pleb. Hippon.): "From the time I began to serve God, even as I scarcely found better men than those who made progress in monasteries, so have I not found worse than those who in the monastery have fallen."

## QUESTION 187

OF THOSE THINGS THAT ARE COMPETENT TO RELIGIOUS (In Six Articles)

We must now consider the things that are competent to religious; and under this head there are six points of inquiry:

(1) Whether it is lawful for them to teach, preach, and do like things?

(2) Whether it is lawful for them to meddle in secular business?

(3) Whether they are bound to manual labor?

(4) Whether it is lawful for them to live on alms?

(5) Whether it is lawful for them to quest?

(6) Whether it is lawful for them to wear coarser clothes than other persons?

FIRST ARTICLE [II-II, Q. 187, Art. 1]

Whether It Is Lawful for Religious to Teach, Preach, and the Like?

Objection 1: It would seem unlawful for religious to teach, preach, and the like. For it is said (VII, qu. i, can. Hoc nequaquam) in an ordinance of a synod of Constantinople [*Pseudosynod held by Photius in the year 879]: "The monastic life is one of subjection and discipleship, not of teaching, authority, or pastoral care." And Jerome says (ad Ripar. et Desider. [*Contra Vigilant. xvi]): "A monk's duty is not to teach but to lament." Again Pope Leo [*Leo I, Ep. cxx ad Theodoret., 6, cf. XVI, qu. i, can. Adjicimus]: says "Let none dare to preach save the priests of the Lord, be he monk or layman, and no matter what knowledge he may boast of having." Now it is not lawful to exceed the bounds of one's office or transgress the ordinance of the Church. Therefore seemingly it is unlawful for religious to teach, preach, and the like.

Obj. 2: Further, in an ordinance of the Council of Nicea (cf. XVI, qu. i, can. Placuit) it is laid down as follows: "It is our absolute and peremptory command addressed to all that monks shall not hear confessions except of one another, as is right, that they shall not bury the dead except those dwelling with them in the monastery, or if by chance a brother happen to die while on a visit." But just as the above belong to the duty of clerics, so also do preaching and teaching. Therefore since "the business of a monk differs from that of a cleric," as Jerome says (Ep. xiv ad Heliod.), it would seem unlawful for religious to preach, teach, and the like.

Obj. 3: Further, Gregory says (Regist. v, Ep. 1): "No man can fulfil ecclesiastical duties, and keep consistently to the monastic rule": and this is quoted XVI, qu. i, can. Nemo potest. Now monks are bound to keep consistently to the monastic rule. Therefore it would seem that they cannot fulfil ecclesiastical duties, whereof teaching and preaching are a part. Therefore seemingly it is unlawful for them to preach, teach, and do similar things.

*On the contrary,* Gregory is quoted (XVI, qu. i, can. Ex auctoritate) as saying: "By authority of this decree framed in virtue of our apostolic power and the duty of our office, be it lawful to monk priests who are configured to the apostles, to preach, baptize, give communion, pray for sinners, impose penance, and absolve from sin."

*I answer that,* A thing is declared to be unlawful to a person in two ways. First, because there is something in him contrary to that which is declared unlawful to him: thus to no man is it lawful to sin, because each man has in himself reason and an obligation to God's law, to which things sin is contrary. And in this way it is said to be unlawful for a person to preach, teach, or do like things, because there is in him something incompatible with these things, either by reason of a precept--thus those who are irregular by ordinance of the Church may not be raised to the sacred orders--or by reason of sin, according to Ps. 49:16, "But to the sinner God hath said: Why dost thou declare My justice?"

In this way it is not unlawful for religious to preach, teach, and do like things, both because they are bound neither by vow nor by precept of their rule to abstain from these things, and because they are not rendered less apt for these things by any sin committed, but on the contrary they are the more apt through having taken upon themselves the practice of holiness. For it is foolish to say that a man is rendered less fit for spiritual duties through advancing himself in holiness; and consequently it is foolish to declare that the religious state is an obstacle to the fulfilment of such like duties. This error is rejected by Pope Boniface [*Boniface IV] for the reasons given above. His words which are quoted (XVI, qu. i, can. Sunt. nonnulli) are these: "There are some who without any dogmatic proof, and with extreme daring, inspired with a zeal rather of bitterness than of love, assert that monks though they be dead to the world and live to God, are unworthy of the power of the priestly office, and that they cannot confer penance, nor christen, nor absolve in virtue of the power divinely bestowed on them in the priestly office. But they are altogether wrong." He proves this first because it is not contrary to the rule; thus he continues: "For neither did the Blessed Benedict the saintly teacher of monks forbid this in any way," nor is it forbidden in other rules. Secondly, he refutes the above error from the usefulness of the monks, when he adds at the end of the same chapter: "The more perfect a man is, the more effective is he in these, namely in spiritual works."

Secondly, a thing is said to be unlawful for a man, not on account of there being in him something contrary thereto, but because he lacks that which enables him to do it: thus it is unlawful for a deacon to say mass, because he is not in priestly orders; and it is unlawful for a priest to deliver judgment because he lacks the episcopal authority. Here, however, a distinction must be made. Because those things which are a matter of an order, cannot be deputed to one who has not the order, whereas matters of jurisdiction can be deputed to those who have not ordinary jurisdiction: thus the delivery of a judgment is deputed by the bishop to a simple priest. In this sense it is said to be unlawful for monks and other religious to preach, teach, and so forth, because the religious state does not give them the power to do these things. They can, however, do them if they receive orders, or ordinary jurisdiction, or if matters of jurisdiction be delegated to them.

Reply Obj. 1: It results from the words quoted that the fact of their being monks does not give monks the power to do these things, yet it does not involve in them anything contrary to the performance of these acts.

Reply Obj. 2: Again, this ordinance of the Council of Nicea forbids monks to claim the power of exercising those acts on the ground of their being monks, but it does not forbid those acts being delegated to them.

Reply Obj. 3: These two things are incompatible, namely, the ordinary cure of ecclesiastical duties, and the observance of the monastic rule in a monastery. But this does not prevent monks and other religious from being sometimes occupied with ecclesiastical duties through being deputed thereto by superiors having ordinary cure; especially members of religious orders that are especially instituted for that purpose, as we shall say further on (Q. 188, A. 4).

SECOND ARTICLE [II-II, Q. 187, Art. 2]

Whether It Is Lawful for Religious to Occupy Themselves with Secular Business?

Objection 1: It would seem unlawful for religious to occupy themselves with secular business. For in the decree quoted above (A. 1) of Pope Boniface it is said that the "Blessed Benedict bade them to be altogether free from secular business; and this is most explicitly prescribed by the apostolic doctrine and the teaching of all the Fathers, not only to religious, but also to all the canonical clergy," according to 2 Tim. 2:4, "No man being a soldier to God, entangleth himself with secular business." Now it is the duty of all religious to be soldiers of God. Therefore it is unlawful for them to occupy themselves with secular business.

Obj. 2: Further, the Apostle says (1 Thess. 4:11): "That you use your endeavor to be quiet, and that you do your own business," which a gloss explains thus--"by refraining from other people's affairs, so as to be the better able to attend to the amendment of your own life." Now religious devote themselves in a special way to the amendment of their life. Therefore they should not occupy themselves with secular business.

Obj. 3: Further, Jerome, commenting on Matt. 11:8, "Behold they that are clothed in soft garments are in the houses of kings," says: "Hence we gather that an austere life and severe preaching should avoid the palaces of kings and the mansions of the voluptuous." But the needs of secular business induce men to frequent the palaces of kings. Therefore it is unlawful for religious to occupy themselves with secular business.

*On the contrary,* The Apostle says (Rom. 16:1): "I commend to you Phoebe our Sister," and further on (Rom. 16:2), "that you assist her in whatsoever business she shall have need of you."

*I answer that,* As stated above (Q. 186, AA. 1, 7, ad 1), the religious state is directed to the attainment of the perfection of charity, consisting principally in the love of God and secondarily in the love of our neighbor. Consequently that which religious intend chiefly and for its own sake is to give themselves to God. Yet if their neighbor be in need, they should attend to his affairs out of charity, according to Gal. 6:2, "Bear ye one another's burthens: and so you shall fulfil the law of Christ," since through serving their neighbor for God's sake, they are obedient to the divine love. Hence it is written (James 1:27): "Religion clean and undefiled before God and the Father, is this: to visit the fatherless and widows in their tribulation," which means, according to a gloss, to assist the helpless in their time of need.

We must conclude therefore that it is unlawful for either monks or clerics to carry on secular business from motives of avarice; but from motives of charity, and with their superior's permission, they may occupy themselves with due moderation in the administration and direction of secular business. Wherefore it is said in the Decretals (Dist. xxxviii, can. Decrevit): "The holy synod decrees that henceforth no cleric shall buy property or occupy himself with secular business, save with a view to the care of the fatherless, orphans, or widows, or when the bishop of the city commands him to take charge of the business connected with the Church." And the same applies to religious as to clerics, because they are both debarred from secular business on the same grounds, as stated above.

Reply Obj. 1: Monks are forbidden to occupy themselves with secular business from motives of avarice, but not from motives of charity.

Reply Obj. 2: To occupy oneself with secular business on account of another's need is not officiousness but charity.

Reply Obj. 3: To haunt the palaces of kings from motives of pleasure, glory, or avarice is not becoming to religious, but there is nothing unseemly in their visiting them from motives of piety. Hence it is written (4 Kings 4:13): "Hast thou any business, and wilt thou that I speak to the king or to the general of the army?" Likewise it becomes religious to go to the palaces of kings to rebuke and guide them, even as John the Baptist rebuked Herod, as related in Matt. 14:4.

THIRD ARTICLE [II-II, Q. 187, Art. 3]

Whether Religious Are Bound to Manual Labor?

Objection 1: It would seem that religious are bound to manual labor. For religious are not exempt from the observance of precepts. Now manual labor is a matter of precept according to 1 Thess. 4:11, "Work with your own hands as we commanded you"; wherefore Augustine says (De oper. Monach. xxx): "But who can allow these insolent men," namely religious that do no work, of whom he is speaking there, "who disregard the most salutary admonishment of the Apostle, not merely to be borne with as being weaker than others, but even to preach as though they were holier than others." Therefore it would seem that religious are bound to manual labor.

Obj. 2: Further, a gloss [*St. Augustine, (De oper. Monach. xxi)] on 2 Thess. 3:10, "If any man will not work, neither let him eat," says: "Some say that this command of the Apostle refers to spiritual works, and not to the bodily labor of the farmer or craftsman"; and further on: "But it is useless for them to try to hide from themselves and from others the fact that they are unwilling not only to fulfil, but even to understand the useful admonishments of charity"; and again: "He wishes God's servants to make a living by working with their bodies." Now religious especially are called servants of God, because they give themselves entirely to the service of God, as Dionysius asserts (Eccl. Hier. vi). Therefore it would seem that they are bound to manual labor.

Obj. 3: Further, Augustine says (De oper. Monach. xvii): "I would fain know how they would occupy themselves, who are unwilling to work with their body. We occupy our time, say they, with prayers, psalms, reading, and the word of God." Yet these things are no excuse, and he proves this, as regards each in particular. For in the first place, as to prayer, he says: "One prayer of the obedient man is sooner granted than ten thousand prayers of the contemptuous": meaning that those are contemptuous and unworthy to be heard who work not with their hands. Secondly, as to the divine praises he adds: "Even while working with their hands they can easily sing hymns to God." Thirdly, with regard to reading, he goes on to say: "Those who say they are occupied in reading, do they not find there what the Apostle commanded? What sort of perverseness is this, to wish to read but not to obey what one reads?" Fourthly, he adds in reference to preaching [*Cap. xviii]: "If one has to speak, and is so busy that he cannot spare time for manual work, can all in the monastery do this? And since all cannot do this, why should all make this a pretext for being exempt? And even if all were able, they should do so by turns, not only so that the others may be occupied in other works, but also because it suffices that one speak while many listen." Therefore it would seem that religious should not desist from manual labor on account of such like spiritual works to which they devote themselves.

Obj. 4: Further, a gloss on Luke 12:33, "Sell what you possess," says: "Not only give your clothes to the poor, but sell what you possess, that having once for all renounced all your possessions for the Lord's sake, you may henceforth work with the labor of your hands, so as to have wherewith to live or to give alms." Now it belongs properly to religious to renounce all they have. Therefore it would seem likewise to belong to them to live and give alms through the labor of their hands.

Obj. 5: Further, religious especially would seem to be bound to imitate the life of the apostles, since they profess the state of perfection. Now the apostles worked with their own hands, according to 1 Cor. 4:12: "We labor, working with our own hands." Therefore it would seem that religious are bound to manual labor.

*On the contrary,* Those precepts that are commonly enjoined upon all are equally binding on religious and seculars. But the precept of manual labor is enjoined upon all in common, as appears from 2 Thess. 3:6, "Withdraw yourselves from every brother walking disorderly," etc. (for by brother he signifies every Christian, according to 1 Cor. 7:12, "If any brother have a wife that believeth not"). Now it is written in the same passage (2 Thess. 3:10): "If any man will not work, neither let him eat." Therefore religious are not bound to manual labor any more than seculars are.

*I answer that,* Manual labor is directed to four things. First and principally to obtain food; wherefore it was said to the first man (Gen. 3:19): "In the sweat of thy face shalt thou eat bread," and it is written (Ps. 127:2): "For thou shalt eat the labors of thy hands." Secondly, it is directed to the removal of idleness whence arise many evils; hence it is written (Ecclus. 33:28, 29): "Send" thy slave "to work, that he be not idle, for idleness hath taught much evil." Thirdly, it is directed to the curbing of concupiscence, inasmuch as it is a means of afflicting the body; hence it is written (2 Cor. 6:5, 6): "In labors, in watchings, in fastings, in chastity." Fourthly, it is directed to almsgiving, wherefore it is written (Eph. 4:28): "He that stole, let him now steal no more; but rather let him labor, working with his hands the thing which is good, that he may have something to give to him that suffereth need." Accordingly, in so far as manual labor is directed to obtaining food, it comes under a necessity of precept in so far as it is necessary for that end: since that which is directed to an end derives its necessity from that end, being, in effect, so far necessary as the end cannot be obtained without it. Consequently he who has no other means of livelihood is bound to work with his hands, whatever his condition may be. This is signified by the words of the Apostle: "If any man will not work, neither let him eat," as though to say: "The necessity of manual labor is the necessity of meat." So that if one could live without eating, one would not be bound to work with one's hands. The same applies to those who have no other lawful means of livelihood: since a man is understood to be unable to do what he cannot do lawfully. Wherefore we find that the Apostle prescribed manual labor merely as a remedy for the sin of those who gained their livelihood by unlawful means. For the Apostle ordered manual labor first of all in order to avoid theft, as appears from Eph. 4:28, "He that stole, let him now steal no more; but rather let him labor, working with his hands." Secondly, to avoid the coveting of others' property, wherefore it is written (1 Thess. 4:11): "Work with your own hands, as we commanded you, and that you walk honestly towards them that are without." Thirdly, to avoid the discreditable pursuits whereby some seek a livelihood. Hence he says (2 Thess. 3:10-12): "When we were with you, this we declared to you: that if any man will not work, neither let him eat. For we have heard that there are some among you who walk disorderly, working not at all, but curiously meddling" (namely, as a gloss explains it, "who make a living by meddling in unlawful things). Now we charge them that are such, and beseech them . . . that working with silence, they would eat their own bread." Hence Jerome states (Super epist. ad Galat. [*Preface to Bk. ii of Commentary]) that the Apostle said this "not so much in his capacity of teacher as on account of the faults of the people."

It must, however, be observed that under manual labor are comprised all those human occupations whereby man can lawfully gain a livelihood, whether by using his hands, his feet, or his tongue. For watchmen, couriers, and such like who live by their labor, are understood to live by their handiwork: because, since the hand is "the organ of organs" [*De Anima iii, 8], handiwork denotes all kinds of work, whereby a man may lawfully gain a livelihood.

In so far as manual labor is directed to the removal of idleness, or the affliction of the body, it does not come under a necessity of precept if we consider it in itself, since there are many other means besides manual labor of afflicting the body or of removing idleness: for the flesh is afflicted by fastings and watchings, and idleness is removed by meditation on the Holy Scriptures and by the divine praises. Hence a gloss on Ps. 118:82, "My eyes have failed for Thy word," says: "He is not idle who meditates only on God's word; nor is he who works abroad any better than he who devotes himself to the study of knowing the truth." Consequently for these reasons religious are not bound to manual labor, as neither are seculars, except when they are so bound by the statutes of their order. Thus Jerome says (Ep. cxxv ad Rustic Monach.): "The Egyptian monasteries are wont to admit none unless they work or labor, not so much for the necessities of life, as for the welfare of the soul, lest it be led astray by wicked thoughts." But in so far as manual labor is directed to almsgiving, it does not come under the necessity of precept, save perchance in some particular case, when a man is under an obligation to give alms, and has no other means of having the wherewithal to assist the poor: for in such a case religious would be bound as well as seculars to do manual labor.

Reply Obj. 1: This command of the Apostle is of natural law: wherefore a gloss on 2 Thess. 3:6, "That you withdraw yourselves from every brother walking disorderly," says, "otherwise than the natural order requires," and he is speaking of those who abstained from manual labor. Hence nature has provided man with hands instead of arms and clothes, with which she has provided other animals, in order that with his hands he may obtain these and all other necessaries. Hence it is clear that this precept, even as all the precepts of the natural law, is binding on both religious and seculars alike. Yet not everyone sins that works not with his hands, because those precepts of the natural law which regard the good of the many are not binding on each individual, but it suffices that one person apply himself to this business and another to that; for instance, that some be craftsmen, others husbandmen, others judges, and others teachers, and so forth, according to the words of the Apostle (1 Cor. 12:17), "If the whole body were the eye, where would be the hearing? If the whole were the hearing, where would be the smelling?"

Reply Obj. 2: This gloss is taken from Augustine's De operibus Monachorum, cap. 21, where he speaks against certain monks who declared it to be unlawful for the servants of God to work with their hands, on account of our Lord's saying (Matt. 6:25): "Be not solicitous for your life, what you shall eat." Nevertheless his words do not imply that religious are bound to work with their hands, if they have other means of livelihood. This is clear from his adding: "He wishes the servants of God to make a living by working with their bodies." Now this does not apply to religious any more than to seculars, which is evident for two reasons. First, on account of the way in which the Apostle expresses himself, by saying: "That you withdraw yourselves from every brother walking disorderly." For he calls all Christians brothers, since at that time religious orders were not as yet founded. Secondly, because religious have no other obligations than what seculars have, except as required by the rule they profess: wherefore if their rule contain nothing about manual labor, religious are not otherwise bound to manual labor than seculars are.

Reply Obj. 3: A man may devote himself in two ways to all the spiritual works mentioned by Augustine in the passage quoted: in one way with a view to the common good, in another with a view to his private advantage. Accordingly those who devote themselves publicly to the aforesaid spiritual works are thereby exempt from manual labor for two reasons: first, because it behooves them to be occupied exclusively with such like works; secondly, because those who devote themselves to such works have a claim to be supported by those for whose advantage they work.

On the other hand, those who devote themselves to such works not publicly but privately as it were, ought not on that account to be exempt from manual labor, nor have they a claim to be supported by the offerings of the faithful, and it is of these that Augustine is speaking. For when he says: "They can sing hymns to God even while working with their hands; like the craftsmen who give tongue to fable telling without withdrawing their hands from their work," it is clear that he cannot refer to those who sing the canonical hours in the church, but to those who tell psalms or hymns as private prayers. Likewise what he says of reading and prayer is to be referred to the private prayer and reading which even lay people do at times, and not to those who perform public prayers in the church, or give public lectures in the schools. Hence he does not say: "Those who say they are occupied in teaching and instructing," but: "Those who say they are occupied in reading." Again he speaks of that preaching which is addressed, not publicly to the people, but to one or a few in particular by way of private admonishment. Hence he says expressly: "If one has to speak." For according to a gloss on 1 Cor. 2:4, "Speech is addressed privately, preaching to many."

Reply Obj. 4: Those who despise all for God's sake are bound to work with their hands, when they have no other means of livelihood, or of almsgiving (should the case occur where almsgiving were a matter of precept), but not otherwise, as stated in the Article. It is in this sense that the gloss quoted is to be understood.

Reply Obj. 5: That the apostles worked with their hands was sometimes a matter of necessity, sometimes a work of supererogation. It was of necessity when they failed to receive a livelihood from others. Hence a gloss on 1 Cor. 4:12, "We labor, working with our own hands," adds, "because no man giveth to us." It was supererogation, as appears from 1 Cor. 9:12, where the Apostle says that he did not use the power he had of living by the Gospel. The Apostle had recourse to this supererogation for three motives. First, in order to deprive the false apostles of the pretext for preaching, for they preached merely for a temporal advantage; hence he says (2 Cor. 11:12): "But what I do, that I will do that I may cut off the occasion from them," etc. Secondly, in order to avoid burdening those to whom he preached; hence he says (2 Cor. 12:13): "What is there that you have had less than the other churches, but that I myself was not burthensome to you?" Thirdly, in order to give an example of work to the idle; hence he says (2 Thess. 3:8, 9): "We worked night and day . . . that we might give ourselves a pattern unto you, to imitate us." However, the Apostle did not do this in places like Athens where he had facilities for preaching daily, as Augustine observes (De oper. Monach. xviii). Yet religious are not for this reason bound to imitate the Apostle in this matter, since they are not bound to all works of supererogation: wherefore neither did the other apostles work with their hands.

FOURTH ARTICLE [II-II, Q. 187, Art. 4]

Whether It Is Lawful for Religious to Live on Alms?

Objection 1: It would seem unlawful for religious to live on alms. For the Apostle (1 Tim. 5:16) forbids those widows who have other means of livelihood to live on the alms of the Church, so that the Church may have "sufficient for them that are widows indeed." And Jerome says to Pope Damasus [*Cf. Cf. Can. Clericos, cause. i, qu. 2; Can. Quoniam, cause xvi, qu. 1; Regul. Monach. iv among the supposititious works of St. Jerome] that "those who have sufficient income from their parents and their own possessions, if they take what belongs to the poor they commit and incur the guilt of sacrilege, and by the abuse of such things they eat and drink judgment to themselves." Now religious if they be able-bodied can support themselves by the work of their hands. Therefore it would seem that they sin if they consume the alms belonging to the poor.

Obj. 2: Further, to live at the expense of the faithful is the stipend appointed to those who preach the Gospel in payment of their labor or work, according to Matt. 10:10: "The workman is worthy of his meat." Now it belongs not to religious to preach the Gospel, but chiefly to prelates who are pastors and teachers. Therefore religious cannot lawfully live on the alms of the faithful.

Obj. 3: Further, religious are in the state of perfection. But it is more perfect to give than to receive alms; for it is written (Acts 20:35): "It is a more blessed thing to give, rather than to receive." Therefore they should not live on alms, but rather should they give alms of their handiwork.

Obj. 4: Further, it belongs to religious to avoid obstacles to virtue and occasions of sin. Now the receiving of alms offers an occasion of sin, and hinders an act of virtue; hence a gloss on 2 Thess. 3:9, "That we might give ourselves a pattern unto you," says: "He who through idleness eats often at another's table, must needs flatter the one who feeds him." It is also written (Ex. 23:8): "Neither shalt thou take bribes which . . . blind the wise, and pervert the words of the just," and (Prov. 22:7): "The borrower is servant to him that lendeth." This is contrary to religion, wherefore a gloss on 2 Thess. 3:9, "That we might give ourselves a pattern," etc., says, "our religion calls men to liberty." Therefore it would seem that religious should not live on alms.

Obj. 5: Further, religious especially are bound to imitate the perfection of the apostles; wherefore the Apostle says (Phil. 3:15): "Let us . . . as many as are perfect, be thus minded." But the Apostle was unwilling to live at the expense of the faithful, either in order to cut off the occasion from the false apostles as he himself says (2 Cor. 11:12), or to avoid giving scandal to the weak, as appears from 1 Cor. 9:12. It would seem therefore that religious ought for the same reasons to refrain from living on alms. Hence Augustine says (De oper. Monach. 28): "Cut off the occasion of disgraceful marketing whereby you lower yourselves in the esteem of others, and give scandal to the weak: and show men that you seek not an easy livelihood in idleness, but the kingdom of God by the narrow and strait way."

*On the contrary,* Gregory says (Dial. ii, 1): The Blessed Benedict after leaving his home and parents dwelt for three years in a cave, and while there lived on the food brought to him by a monk from Rome. Nevertheless, although he was able-bodied, we do not read that he sought to live by the labor of his hands. Therefore religious may lawfully live on alms.

*I answer that,* A man may lawfully live on what is his or due to him. Now that which is given out of liberality becomes the property of the person to whom it is given. Wherefore religious and clerics whose monasteries or churches have received from the munificence of princes or of any of the faithful any endowment whatsoever for their support, can lawfully live on such endowment without working with their hands, and yet without doubt they live on alms. Wherefore in like manner if religious receive movable goods from the faithful they can lawfully live on them. For it is absurd to say that a person may accept an alms of some great property but not bread or some small sum of money. Nevertheless since these gifts would seem to be bestowed on religious in order that they may have more leisure for religious works, in which the donors of temporal goods wish to have a share, the use of such gifts would become unlawful for them if they abstained from religious works, because in that case, so far as they are concerned, they would be thwarting the intention of those who bestowed those gifts.

A thing is due to a person in two ways. First, on account of necessity, which makes all things common, as Ambrose [*Basil, Serm. de Temp. lxiv, among the supposititious works of St. Ambrose] asserts. Consequently if religious be in need they can lawfully live on alms. Such necessity may occur in three ways. First, through weakness of body, the result being that they are unable to make a living by working with their hands. Secondly, because that which they gain by their handiwork is insufficient for their livelihood: wherefore Augustine says (De oper. Monach. xvii) that "the good works of the faithful should not leave God's servants who work with their hands without a supply of necessaries, that when the hour comes for them to nourish their souls, so as to make it impossible for them to do these corporal works, they be not oppressed by want." Thirdly, because of the former mode of life of those who were unwont to work with their hands: wherefore Augustine says (De oper. Monach. xxi) that "if they had in the world the wherewithal easily to support this life without working, and gave it to the needy when they were converted to God, we must credit their weakness and bear with it." For those who have thus been delicately brought up are wont to be unable to bear the toil of bodily labor.

In another way a thing becomes due to a person through his affording others something whether temporal or spiritual, according to 1 Cor. 9:11, "If we have sown unto you spiritual things, is it a great matter if we reap your carnal things?" And in this sense religious may live on alms as being due to them in four ways. First, if they preach by the authority of the prelates. Secondly, if they be ministers of the altar, according to 1 Cor. 9:13, 14, "They that serve the altar partake with the altar. So also the lord ordained that they who preach the Gospel should live by the Gospel." Hence Augustine says (De oper. Monach. xxi): "If they be gospelers, I allow, they have" (a claim to live at the charge of the faithful): "if they be ministers of the altar and dispensers of the sacraments, they need not insist on it, but it is theirs by perfect right." The reason for this is because the sacrament of the altar wherever it be offered is common to all the faithful. Thirdly, if they devote themselves to the study of Holy Writ to the common profit of the whole Church. Wherefore Jerome says (Contra Vigil. xiii): "It is still the custom in Judea, not only among us but also among the Hebrews, for those who meditate on the law of the Lord day and night, and have no other share on earth but God alone, to be supported by the subscriptions of the synagogues and of the whole world." Fourthly, if they have endowed the monastery with the goods they possessed, they may live on the alms given to the monastery. Hence Augustine says (De oper. Monach. xxv) that "those who renouncing or distributing their means, whether ample or of any amount whatever, have desired with pious and salutary humility to be numbered among the poor of Christ, have a claim on the community and on brotherly love to receive a livelihood in return. They are to be commended indeed if they work with their hands, but if they be unwilling, who will dare to force them? Nor does it matter, as he goes on to say, to which monasteries, or in what place any one of them has bestowed his goods on his needy brethren; for all Christians belong to one commonwealth."

On the other hand, in the default of any necessity, or of their affording any profit to others, it is unlawful for religious to wish to live in idleness on the alms given to the poor. Hence Augustine says (De oper. Monach. xxii): "Sometimes those who enter the profession of God's service come from a servile condition of life, from tilling the soil or working at some trade or lowly occupation. In their case it is not so clear whether they came with the purpose of serving God, or of evading a life of want and toil with a view to being fed and clothed in idleness, and furthermore to being honored by those by whom they were wont to be despised and downtrodden. Such persons surely cannot excuse themselves from work on the score of bodily weakness, for their former mode of life is evidence against them." And he adds further on (De oper. Monach. xxv): "If they be unwilling to work, neither let them eat. For if the rich humble themselves to piety, it is not that the poor may be exalted to pride; since it is altogether unseemly that in a life wherein senators become laborers, laborers should become idle, and that where the lords of the manor have come after renouncing their ease, the serfs should live in comfort."

Reply Obj. 1: These authorities must be understood as referring to cases of necessity, that is to say, when there is no other means of succoring the poor: for then they would be bound not only to refrain from accepting alms, but also to give what they have for the support of the needy.

Reply Obj. 2: Prelates are competent to preach in virtue of their office, but religious may be competent to do so in virtue of delegation; and thus when they work in the field of the Lord, they may make their living thereby, according to 2 Tim. 2:6, "The husbandman that laboreth must first partake of the fruits," which a gloss explains thus, "that is to say, the preacher, who in the field of the Church tills the hearts of his hearers with the plough of God's word." Those also who minister to the preachers may live on alms. Hence a gloss on Rom. 15:27, "If the Gentiles have been made partakers of their spiritual things, they ought also in carnal things to minister to them," says, "namely, to the Jews who sent preachers from Jerusalem." There are moreover other reasons for which a person has a claim to live at the charge of the faithful, as stated above.

Reply Obj. 3: Other things being equal, it is more perfect to give than to receive. Nevertheless to give or to give up all one's possessions for Christ's sake, and to receive a little for one's livelihood is better than to give to the poor part by part, as stated above (Q. 186, A. 3, ad 6).

Reply Obj. 4: To receive gifts so as to increase one's wealth, or to accept a livelihood from another without having a claim to it, and without profit to others or being in need oneself, affords an occasion of sin. But this does not apply to religious, as stated above.

Reply Obj. 5: Whenever there is evident necessity for religious living on alms without doing any manual work, as well as an evident profit to be derived by others, it is not the weak who are scandalized, but those who are full of malice like the Pharisees, whose scandal our Lord teaches us to despise (Matt. 15:12-14). If, however, these motives of necessity and profit be lacking, the weak might possibly be scandalized thereby; and this should be avoided. Yet the same scandal might be occasioned through those who live in idleness on the common revenues.

FIFTH ARTICLE [II-II, Q. 187, Art. 5]

Whether It Is Lawful for Religious to Beg?

Objection 1: It would seem unlawful for religious to beg. For Augustine says (De oper. Monach. xxviii): "The most cunning foe has scattered on all sides a great number of hypocrites wearing the monastic habit, who go wandering about the country," and afterwards he adds: "They all ask, they all demand to be supported in their profitable penury, or to be paid for a pretended holiness." Therefore it would seem that the life of mendicant religious is to be condemned.

Obj. 2: Further, it is written (1 Thess. 4:11): "That you . . . work with your own hands as we commanded you, and that you walk honestly towards them that are without: and that you want nothing of any man's": and a gloss on this passage says: "You must work and not be idle, because work is both honorable and a light to the unbeliever: and you must not covet that which belongs to another and much less beg or take anything." Again a gloss [*St. Augustine, (De oper. Monach. iii)] on 2 Thess. 3:10, "If any man will not work," etc. says: "He wishes the servants of God to work with the body, so as to gain a livelihood, and not be compelled by want to ask for necessaries." Now this is to beg. Therefore it would seem unlawful to beg while omitting to work with one's hands.

Obj. 3: Further, that which is forbidden by law and contrary to justice, is unbecoming to religious. Now begging is forbidden in the divine law; for it is written (Deut. 15:4): "There shall be no poor nor beggar among you," and (Ps. 36:25): "I have not seen the just forsaken, nor his seed seeking bread." Moreover an able-bodied mendicant is punished by civil law, according to the law (XI, xxvi, de Valid. Mendicant.). Therefore it is unfitting for religious to beg.

Obj. 4: Further, "Shame is about that which is disgraceful," as Damascene says (De Fide Orth. ii, 15). Now Ambrose says (De Offic. i, 30) that "to be ashamed to beg is a sign of good birth." Therefore it is disgraceful to beg: and consequently this is unbecoming to religious.

Obj. 5: Further, according to our Lord's command it is especially becoming to preachers of the Gospel to live on alms, as stated above (A. 4). Yet it is not becoming that they should beg, since a gloss on 2 Tim. 2:6, "The husbandman, that laboreth," etc. says: "The Apostle wishes the gospeler to understand that to accept necessaries from those among whom he labors is not mendicancy but a right." Therefore it would seem unbecoming for religious to beg.

*On the contrary,* It becomes religious to live in imitation of Christ. Now Christ was a mendicant, according to Ps. 39:18, "But I am a beggar and poor"; where a gloss says: "Christ said this of Himself as bearing the 'form of a servant,'" and further on: "A beggar is one who entreats another, and a poor man is one who has not enough for himself." Again it is written (Ps. 69:6): "I am needy and poor"; where a gloss says: "'Needy,' that is a suppliant; 'and poor,' that is, not having enough for myself, because I have no worldly wealth." And Jerome says in a letter [*Reference unknown]: "Beware lest whereas thy Lord," i.e. Christ, "begged, thou amass other people's wealth." Therefore it becomes religious to beg.

*I answer that,* Two things may be considered in reference to mendicancy. The first is on the part of the act itself of begging, which has a certain abasement attaching to it; since of all men those would seem most abased who are not only poor, but are so needy that they have to receive their meat from others. In this way some deserve praise for begging out of humility, just as they abase themselves in other ways, as being the most efficacious remedy against pride which they desire to quench either in themselves or in others by their example. For just as a disease that arises from excessive heat is most efficaciously healed by things that excel in cold, so proneness to pride is most efficaciously healed by those things which savor most of abasement. Hence it is said in the Decretals (II, cap. Si quis semel, de Paenitentia): "To condescend to the humblest duties, and to devote oneself to the lowliest service is an exercise of humility; for thus one is able to heal the disease of pride and human glory." Hence Jerome praises Fabiola (Ep. lxxvii ad ocean.) for that she desired "to receive alms, having poured forth all her wealth for Christ's sake." The Blessed Alexis acted in like manner, for, having renounced all his possessions for Christ's sake he rejoiced in receiving alms even from his own servants. It is also related of the Blessed Arsenius in the Lives of the Fathers (v, 6) that he gave thanks because he was forced by necessity to ask for alms. Hence it is enjoined to some people as a penance for grievous sins to go on a pilgrimage begging. Since, however, humility like the other virtues should not be without discretion, it behooves one to be discreet in becoming a mendicant for the purpose of humiliation, lest a man thereby incur the mark of covetousness or of anything else unbecoming. Secondly, mendicancy may be considered on the part of that which one gets by begging: and thus a man may be led to beg by a twofold motive. First, by the desire to have wealth or meat without working for it, and such like mendicancy is unlawful; secondly, by a motive of necessity or usefulness. The motive is one of necessity if a man has no other means of livelihood save begging; and it is a motive of usefulness if he wishes to accomplish something useful, and is unable to do so without the alms of the faithful. Thus alms are besought for the building of a bridge, or church, or for any other work whatever that is conducive to the common good: thus scholars may seek alms that they may devote themselves to the study of wisdom. In this way mendicancy is lawful to religious no less than to seculars.

Reply Obj. 1: Augustine is speaking there explicitly of those who beg from motives of covetousness.

Reply Obj. 2: The first gloss speaks of begging from motives of covetousness, as appears from the words of the Apostle; while the second gloss speaks of those who without effecting any useful purpose, beg their livelihood in order to live in idleness. On the other hand, he lives not idly who in any way lives usefully.

Reply Obj. 3: This precept of the divine law does not forbid anyone to beg, but it forbids the rich to be so stingy that some are compelled by necessity to beg. The civil law imposes a penalty on able-bodied mendicants who beg from motives neither of utility nor of necessity.

Reply Obj. 4: Disgrace is twofold; one arises from lack of honesty [*Cf. Q. 145, A. 1], the other from an external defect, thus it is disgraceful for a man to be sick or poor. Such like uncomeliness of mendicancy does not pertain to sin, but it may pertain to humility, as stated above.

Reply Obj. 5: Preachers have the right to be fed by those to whom they preach: yet if they wish to seek this by begging so as to receive it as a free gift and not as a right this will be a mark of greater humility.

SIXTH ARTICLE [II-II, Q. 187, Art. 6]

Whether It Is Lawful for Religious to Wear Coarser Clothes Than Others?

Objection 1: It would seem unlawful for religious to wear coarser clothes than others. For according to the Apostle (1 Thess. 5:22) we ought to "refrain from all appearance of evil." Now coarseness of clothes has an appearance of evil; for our Lord said (Matt. 7:15): "Beware of false prophets who come to you in the clothing of sheep": and a gloss on Apoc. 6:8, "Behold a pale horse," says: "The devil finding that he cannot succeed, neither by outward afflictions nor by manifest heresies, sends in advance false brethren, who under the guise of religion assume the characteristics of the black and red horses by corrupting the faith." Therefore it would seem that religious should not wear coarse clothes.

Obj. 2: Further, Jerome says (Ep. lii ad Nepotian.): "Avoid somber," i.e. black, "equally with glittering apparel. Fine and coarse clothes are equally to be shunned, for the one exhales pleasure, the other vainglory." Therefore, since vainglory is a graver sin than the use of pleasure, it would seem that religious who should aim at what is more perfect ought to avoid coarse rather than fine clothes.

Obj. 3: Further, religious should aim especially at doing works of penance. Now in works of penance we should use, not outward signs of sorrow, but rather signs of joy; for our Lord said (Matt. 6:16): "When you fast, be not, as the hypocrites, sad," and afterwards He added: "But thou, when thou fastest, anoint thy head and wash thy face." Augustine commenting on these words (De Serm. Dom. in Monte ii, 12): "In this chapter we must observe that not only the glare and pomp of outward things, but even the weeds of mourning may be a subject of ostentation, all the more dangerous as being a decoy under the guise of God's service." Therefore seemingly religious ought not to wear coarse clothes.

*On the contrary,* The Apostle says (Heb. 11:37): "They wandered about in sheep-skins, in goatskins," and a gloss adds--"as Elias and others." Moreover it is said in the Decretal XXI, qu. iv, can. Omnis jactantia: "If any persons be found to deride those who wear coarse and religious apparel they must be reproved. For in the early times all those who were consecrated to God went about in common and coarse apparel."

*I answer that,* As Augustine says (De Doctr. Christ. iii, 12), "in all external things, it is not the use but the intention of the user that is at fault." In order to judge of this it is necessary to observe that coarse and homely apparel may be considered in two ways. First, as being a sign of a man's disposition or condition, because according to Ecclus. 19:27, "the attire . . . of the man" shows "what he is." In this way coarseness of attire is sometimes a sign of sorrow: wherefore those who are beset with sorrow are wont to wear coarser clothes, just as on the other hand in times of festivity and joy they wear finer clothes. Hence penitents make use of coarse apparel, for example, the king (Jonah 3:6) who "was clothed with sack-cloth," and Achab (3 Kings 21:27) who "put hair-cloth upon his flesh." Sometimes, however, it is a sign of the contempt of riches and worldly ostentation. Wherefore Jerome says (Ep. cxxv ad Rustico Monach.): "Let your somber attire indicate your purity of mind, your coarse robe prove your contempt of the world, yet so that your mind be not inflated withal, lest your speech belie your habit." In both these ways it is becoming for religious to wear coarse attire, since religion is a state of penance and of contempt of worldly glory.

But that a person wish to signify this to others arises from three motives. First, in order to humble himself: for just as a man's mind is uplifted by fine clothes, so is it humbled by lowly apparel. Hence speaking of Achab who "put hair-cloth on his flesh," the Lord said to Elias: "Hast thou not seen Achab humbled before Me?" (3 Kings 21:29). Secondly, in order to set an example to others; wherefore a gloss on Matt. 3:4, "(John) had his garments of camel's hair," says: "He who preaches penance is clothed in the habit of penance." Thirdly, on account of vainglory; thus Augustine says (cf. Obj. 3) that "even the weeds of mourning may be a subject of ostentation."

Accordingly in the first two ways it is praiseworthy to wear humble apparel, but in the third way it is sinful.

Secondly, coarse and homely attire may be considered as the result of covetousness or negligence, and thus also it is sinful.

Reply Obj. 1: Coarseness of attire has not of itself the appearance of evil, indeed it has more the appearance of good, namely of the contempt of worldly glory. Hence it is that wicked persons hide their wickedness under coarse clothing. Hence Augustine says (De Serm. Dom. in Monte ii, 24) that "the sheep should not dislike their clothing for the reason that the wolves sometimes hide themselves under it."

Reply Obj. 2: Jerome is speaking there of the coarse attire that is worn on account of human glory.

Reply Obj. 3: According to our Lord's teaching men should do no deeds of holiness for the sake of show: and this is especially the case when one does something strange. Hence Chrysostom [*Hom. xiii in Matth. in the Opus Imperfectum, falsely ascribed to St. John Chrysostom] says: "While praying a man should do nothing strange, so as to draw the gaze of others, either by shouting or striking his breast, or casting up his hands," because the very strangeness draws people's attention to him. Yet blame does not attach to all strange behavior that draws people's attention, for it may be done well or ill. Hence Augustine says (De Serm. Dom. in Monte ii, 12) that "in the practice of the Christian religion when a man draws attention to himself by unwonted squalor and shabbiness, since he acts thus voluntarily and not of necessity, we can gather from his other deeds whether his behavior is motivated by contempt of excessive dress or by affectation." Religious, however, would especially seem not to act thus from affectation, since they wear a coarse habit as a sign of their profession whereby they profess contempt of the world.

# QUESTION 188

OF THE DIFFERENT KINDS OF RELIGIOUS LIFE (In Eight Articles)

We must now consider the different kinds of religious life, and under this head there are eight points of inquiry:

(1) Whether there are different kinds of religious life or only one?

(2) Whether a religious order can be established for the works of the active life?

(3) Whether a religious order can be directed to soldiering?

(4) Whether a religious order can be established for preaching and the exercise of like works?

(5) Whether a religious order can be established for the study of science?

(6) Whether a religious order that is directed to the contemplative life is more excellent than one that is directed to the active life?

(7) Whether religious perfection is diminished by possessing something in common?

(8) Whether the religious life of solitaries is to be preferred to the religious life of those who live in community?

FIRST ARTICLE [II-II, Q. 188, Art. 1]

Whether There Is Only One Religious Order?

Objection 1: It would seem that there is but one religious order. For there can be no diversity in that which is possessed wholly and perfectly; wherefore there can be only one sovereign good, as stated in the First Part (Q. 6, AA. 2, 3, 4). Now as Gregory says (Hom. xx in Ezech.), "when a man vows to Almighty God all that he has, all his life, all his knowledge, it is a holocaust," without which there is no religious life. Therefore it would seem that there are not many religious orders but only one.

Obj. 2: Further, things which agree in essentials differ only accidentally. Now there is no religious order without the three essential vows of religion, as stated above (Q. 186, AA. 6, 7). Therefore it would seem that religious orders differ not specifically, but only accidentally.

Obj. 3: Further, the state of perfection is competent both to religious and to bishops, as stated above (Q. 185, AA. 5, 7). Now the episcopate is not diversified specifically, but is one wherever it may be; wherefore Jerome says (Ep. cxlvi ad Evan.): "Wherever a bishop is, whether at Rome, or Gubbio, or Constantinople, or Reggio, he has the same excellence, the same priesthood." Therefore in like manner there is but one religious order.

Obj. 4: Further, anything that may lead to confusion should be removed from the Church. Now it would seem that a diversity of religious orders might confuse the Christian people, as stated in the Decretal de Statu Monach. et Canon. Reg. [*Cap. Ne Nimia, de Relig. Dom.]. Therefore seemingly there ought not to be different religious orders.

*On the contrary,* It is written (Ps. 44:10) that it pertains to the adornment of the queen that she is "surrounded with variety."

*I answer that,* As stated above (Q. 186, A, 7; Q. 187, A. 2), the religious state is a training school wherein one aims by practice at the perfection of charity. Now there are various works of charity to which a man may devote himself; and there are also various kinds of exercise. Wherefore religious orders may be differentiated in two ways. First, according to the different things to which they may be directed: thus one may be directed to the lodging of pilgrims, another to visiting or ransoming captives. Secondly, there may be various religious orders according to the diversity of practices; thus in one religious order the body is chastised by abstinence in food, in another by the practice of manual labor, scantiness of clothes, or the like.

Since, however, the end imports most in every matter, [*Arist., Topic. vi 8] religious orders differ more especially according to their various ends than according to their various practices.

Reply Obj. 1: The obligation to devote oneself wholly to God's service is common to every religious order; hence religious do not differ in this respect, as though in one religious order a person retained some one thing of his own, and in another order some other thing. But the difference is in respect of the different things wherein one may serve God, and whereby a man may dispose himself to the service of God.

Reply Obj. 2: The three essential vows of religion pertain to the practice of religion as principles to which all other matters are reduced, as stated above (Q. 186, A. 7). But there are various ways of disposing oneself to the observance of each of them. For instance one disposes oneself to observe the vow of continence, by solitude of place, by abstinence, by mutual fellowship, and by many like means. Accordingly it is evident that the community of the essential vows is compatible with diversity of religious life, both on account of the different dispositions and on account of the different ends, as explained above.

Reply Obj. 3: In matters relating to perfection, the bishop stands in the position of agent, and the religious as passive, as stated above (Q. 184, A. 7). Now the agent, even in natural things, the higher it is, is so much the more one, whereas the things that are passive are various. Hence with reason the episcopal state is one, while religious orders are many.

Reply Obj. 4: Confusion is opposed to distinction and order. Accordingly the multitude of religious orders would lead to confusion, if different religious orders were directed to the same end and in the same way, without necessity or utility. Wherefore to prevent this happening it has been wholesomely forbidden to establish a new religious order without the authority of the Sovereign Pontiff.

SECOND ARTICLE [II-II, Q. 188, Art. 2]

Whether a Religious Order Should Be Established for the Works of the Active Life?

Objection 1: It would seem that no religious order should be established for the works of the active life. For every religious order belongs to the state of perfection, as stated above (Q. 184, A. 5; Q. 186, A. 1). Now the perfection of the religious state consists in the contemplation of divine things. For Dionysius says (Eccl. Hier. vi) that they are "called servants of God by reason of their rendering pure service and subjection to God, and on account of the indivisible and singular life which unites them by holy reflections," i.e. contemplations, "on invisible things, to the Godlike unity and the perfection beloved of God." Therefore seemingly no religious order should be established for the works of the active life.

Obj. 2: Further, seemingly the same judgment applies to canons regular as to monks, according to Extra, De Postul., cap. Ex parte; and De Statu Monach., cap. Quod Dei timorem: for it is stated that "they are not considered to be separated from the fellowship of monks": and the same would seem to apply to all other religious. Now the monastic rule was established for the purpose of the contemplative life; wherefore Jerome says (Ep. lviii ad Paulin.): "If you wish to be what you are called, a monk," i.e. a solitary, "what business have you in a city?" The same is found stated in Extra, De Renuntiatione, cap. Nisi cum pridem; and De Regular., cap. Licet quibusdam. Therefore it would seem that every religious order is directed to the contemplative life, and none to the active life.

Obj. 3: Further, the active life is concerned with the present world. Now all religious are said to renounce the world; wherefore Gregory says (Hom. xx in Ezech.): "He who renounces this world, and does all the good he can, is like one who has gone out of Egypt and offers sacrifice in the wilderness." Therefore it would seem that no religious order can be directed to the active life.

*On the contrary,* It is written (James 1:27): "Religion clean and undefiled before God and the Father, is this: to visit the fatherless and widows in their tribulation." Now this belongs to the active life. Therefore religious life can be fittingly directed to the active life.

*I answer that,* As stated above (A. 1), the religious state is directed to the perfection of charity, which extends to the love of God and of our neighbor. Now the contemplative life which seeks to devote itself to God alone belongs directly to the love of God, while the active life, which ministers to our neighbor's needs, belongs directly to the love of one's neighbor. And just as out of charity we love our neighbor for God's sake, so the services we render our neighbor redound to God, according to Matt. 25:40, "What you have done [Vulg.: 'As long as you did it'] to one of these My least brethren, you did it to Me." Consequently those services which we render our neighbor, in so far as we refer them to God, are described as sacrifices, according to Heb. 13:16, "Do not forget to do good and to impart, for by such sacrifices God's favor is obtained." And since it belongs properly to religion to offer sacrifice to God, as stated above (Q. 81, A. 1, ad 1; A. 4, ad 1), it follows that certain religious orders are fittingly directed to the works of the active life. Wherefore in the Conferences of the Fathers (Coll. xiv, 4) the Abbot Nesteros in distinguishing the various aims of religious orders says: "Some direct their intention exclusively to the hidden life of the desert and purity of heart; some are occupied with the instruction of the brethren and the care of the monasteries; while others delight in the service of the guesthouse," i.e. in hospitality.

Reply Obj. 1: Service and subjection rendered to God are not precluded by the works of the active life, whereby a man serves his neighbor for God's sake, as stated in the Article. Nor do these works preclude singularity of life; not that they involve man's living apart from his fellow-men, but in the sense that each man individually devotes himself to things pertaining to the service of God; and since religious occupy themselves with the works of the active life for God's sake, it follows that their action results from their contemplation of divine things. Hence they are not entirely deprived of the fruit of the contemplative life.

Reply Obj. 2: The same judgment applies to monks and to all other religious, as regards things common to all religious orders: for instance as regards their devoting themselves wholly to the divine service, their observance of the essential vows of religion, and their refraining from worldly business. But it does not follow that this likeness extends to other things that are proper to the monastic profession, and are directed especially to the contemplative life. Hence in the aforesaid Decretal, De Postulando, it is not simply stated that "the same judgment applies to canons regular" as "to monks," but that it applies "in matters already mentioned," namely that "they are not to act as advocates in lawsuits." Again the Decretal quoted, De Statu Monach., after the statement that "canons regular are not considered to be separated from the fellowship of monks," goes on to say: "Nevertheless they obey an easier rule." Hence it is evident that they are not bound to all that monks are bound.

Reply Obj. 3: A man may be in the world in two ways: in one way by his bodily presence, in another way by the bent of his mind. Hence our Lord said to His disciples (John 15:19): "I have chosen you out of the world," and yet speaking of them to His Father He said (John 17:11): "These are in the world, and I come to Thee." Although, then, religious who are occupied with the works of the active life are in the world as to the presence of the body, they are not in the world as regards their bent of mind, because they are occupied with external things, not as seeking anything of the world, but merely for the sake of serving God: for "they . . . use this world, as if they used it not," to quote 1 Cor. 7:31. Hence (James 1:27) after it is stated that "religion clean and undefiled . . . is . . . to visit the fatherless and widows in their tribulation," it is added, "and to keep one's self unspotted from this world," namely to avoid being attached to worldly things.

THIRD ARTICLE [II-II, Q. 188, Art. 3]

Whether a Religious Order Can Be Directed to Soldiering?

Objection 1: It would seem that no religious order can be directed to soldiering. For all religious orders belong to the state of perfection. Now our Lord said with reference to the perfection of Christian life (Matt. 5:39): "I say to you not to resist evil; but if one strike thee on the right cheek, turn to him also the other," which is inconsistent with the duties of a soldier. Therefore no religious order can be established for soldiering.

Obj. 2: Further, the bodily encounter of the battlefield is more grievous than the encounter in words that takes place between counsel at law. Yet religious are forbidden to plead at law, as appears from the Decretal De Postulando quoted above (A. 2, Obj. 2). Therefore it is much less seemly for a religious order to be established for soldiering.

Obj. 3: Further, the religious state is a state of penance, as we have said above (Q. 187, A. 6). Now according to the code of laws soldiering is forbidden to penitents. For it is said in the Decretal De Poenit., Dist. v, cap. 3: "It is altogether opposed to the rules of the Church, to return to worldly soldiering after doing penance." Therefore it is unfitting for any religious order to be established for soldiering.

Obj. 4: Further, no religious order may be established for an unjust object. But as Isidore says (Etym. xviii, 1), "A just war is one that is waged by order of the emperor." Since then religious are private individuals, it would seem unlawful for them to wage war; and consequently no religious order may be established for this purpose.

*On the contrary,* Augustine says (Ep. clxxxix; ad Bonifac.), "Beware of thinking that none of those can please God who handle war-like weapons. Of such was holy David to whom the Lord gave great testimony." Now religious orders are established in order that men may please God. Therefore nothing hinders the establishing of a religious order for the purpose of soldiering.

*I answer that,* As stated above (A. 2), a religious order may be established not only for the works of the contemplative life, but also for the works of the active life, in so far as they are concerned in helping our neighbor and in the service of God, but not in so far as they are directed to a worldly object. Now the occupation of soldiering may be directed to the assistance of our neighbor, not only as regards private individuals, but also as regards the defense of the whole commonwealth. Hence it is said of Judas Machabeus (1 Macc. 3:2, 3) that "he [Vulg.: 'they'] fought with cheerfulness the battle of Israel, and he got his people great honor." It can also be directed to the upkeep of divine worship, wherefore (1 Macc. 3:21) Judas is stated to have said: "We will fight for our lives and our laws," and further on (1 Macc. 13:3) Simon said: "You know what great battles I and my brethren, and the house of my father, have fought for the laws and the sanctuary."

Hence a religious order may be fittingly established for soldiering, not indeed for any worldly purpose, but for the defense of divine worship and public safety, or also of the poor and oppressed, according to Ps. 81:4: "Rescue the poor, and deliver the needy out of the hand of the sinner."

Reply Obj. 1: Not to resist evil may be understood in two ways. First, in the sense of forgiving the wrong done to oneself, and thus it may pertain to perfection, when it is expedient to act thus for the spiritual welfare of others. Secondly, in the sense of tolerating patiently the wrongs done to others: and this pertains to imperfection, or even to vice, if one be able to resist the wrongdoer in a becoming manner. Hence Ambrose says (De Offic. i, 27): "The courage whereby a man in battle defends his country against barbarians, or protects the weak at home, or his friends against robbers is full of justice": even so our Lord says in the passage quoted [*Luke 6:30: "Of him that taketh away thy goods, ask them not again"; Cf. Matt. 5:40," . . . thy goods, ask them not again."] If, however, a man were not to demand the return of that which belongs to another, he would sin if it were his business to do so: for it is praiseworthy to give away one's own, but not another's property. And much less should the things of God be neglected, for as Chrysostom [*Hom. v in Matth. in the Opus Imperfectum, falsely ascribed to St. John Chrysostom] says, "it is most wicked to overlook the wrongs done to God."

Reply Obj. 2: It is inconsistent with any religious order to act as counsel at law for a worldly object, but it is not inconsistent to do so at the orders of one's superior and in favor of one's monastery, as stated in the same Decretal, or for the defense of the poor and widows. Wherefore it is said in the Decretals (Dist. lxxxviii, cap. 1): "The holy synod has decreed that henceforth no cleric is to buy property or occupy himself with secular business, save with a view to the care of the fatherless . . . and widows." Likewise to be a soldier for the sake of some worldly object is contrary to all religious life, but this does not apply to those who are soldiers for the sake of God's service.

Reply Obj. 3: Worldly soldiering is forbidden to penitents, but the soldiering which is directed to the service of God is imposed as a penance on some people, as in the case of those upon whom it is enjoined to take arms in defense of the Holy Land.

Reply Obj. 4: The establishment of a religious order for the purpose of soldiering does not imply that the religious can wage war on their own authority; but they can do so only on the authority of the sovereign or of the Church.

FOURTH ARTICLE [II-II, Q. 188, Art. 4]

Whether a Religious Order Can Be Established for Preaching or Hearing Confessions?

Objection 1: It would seem that no religious order may be established for preaching, or hearing confessions. For it is said (VII, qu. i [*Cap. Hoc nequaquam; Cf. Q. 187, A. 1, Obj. 1]): "The monastic life is one of subjection and discipleship, not of teaching, authority, or pastoral care," and the same apparently applies to religious. Now preaching and hearing confessions are the actions of a pastor and teacher. Therefore a religious order should not be established for this purpose.

Obj. 2: Further, the purpose for which a religious order is established would seem to be something most proper to the religious life, as stated above (A. 1). Now the aforesaid actions are not proper to religious but to bishops. Therefore a religious order should not be established for the purpose of such actions.

Obj. 3: Further, it seems unfitting that the authority to preach and hear confessions should be committed to an unlimited number of men; and there is no fixed number of those who are received into a religious order. Therefore it is unfitting for a religious order to be established for the purpose of the aforesaid actions.

Obj. 4: Further, preachers have a right to receive their livelihood from the faithful of Christ, according to 1 Cor. 9. If then the office of preaching be committed to a religious order established for that purpose, it follows that the faithful of Christ are bound to support an unlimited number of persons, which would be a heavy burden on them. Therefore a religious order should not be established for the exercise of these actions.

Obj. 5: Further, the organization of the Church should be in accordance with Christ's institution. Now Christ sent first the twelve apostles to preach, as related in Luke 9, and afterwards He sent the seventy-two disciples, as stated in Luke 10. Moreover, according to the gloss of Bede on "And after these things" (Luke 10:1), "the apostles are represented by the bishops, the seventy-two disciples by the lesser priests," i.e. the parish priests. Therefore in addition to bishops and parish priests, no religious order should be established for the purpose of preaching and hearing confessions.

*On the contrary,* In the Conferences of the Fathers (Coll. xiv, 4), Abbot Nesteros, speaking of the various kinds of religious orders, says: "Some choosing the care of the sick, others devoting themselves to the relief of the afflicted and oppressed, or applying themselves to teaching, or giving alms to the poor, have been most highly esteemed on account of their devotion and piety." Therefore just as a religious order may be established for the care of the sick, so also may one be established for teaching the people by preaching and like works.

*I answer that,* As stated above (A. 2), it is fitting for a religious order to be established for the works of the active life, in so far as they are directed to the good of our neighbor, the service of God, and the upkeep of divine worship. Now the good of our neighbor is advanced by things pertaining to the spiritual welfare of the soul rather than by things pertaining to the supplying of bodily needs, in proportion to the excellence of spiritual over corporal things. Hence it was stated above (Q. 32, A. 3) that spiritual works of mercy surpass corporal works of mercy. Moreover this is more pertinent to the service of God, to Whom no sacrifice is more acceptable than zeal for souls, as Gregory says (Hom. xii in Ezech.). Furthermore, it is a greater thing to employ spiritual arms in defending the faithful against the errors of heretics and the temptations of the devil, than to protect the faithful by means of bodily weapons. Therefore it is most fitting for a religious order to be established for preaching and similar works pertaining to the salvation of souls.

Reply Obj. 1: He who works by virtue of another, acts as an instrument. And a minister is like an "animated instrument," as the Philosopher says (Polit. i, 2 [*Cf. Ethic. viii, 11]). Hence if a man preach or do something similar by the authority of his superiors, he does not rise above the degree of "discipleship" or "subjection," which is competent to religious.

Reply Obj. 2: Some religious orders are established for soldiering, to wage war, not indeed on their own authority, but on that of the sovereign or of the Church who are competent to wage war by virtue of their office, as stated above (A. 3, ad 4). In the same way certain religious orders are established for preaching and hearing confessions, not indeed by their own authority, but by the authority of the higher and lower superiors, to whom these things belong by virtue of their office. Consequently to assist one's superiors in such a ministry is proper to a religious order of this kind.

Reply Obj. 3: Bishops do not allow these religious severally and indiscriminately to preach or hear confessions, but according to the discretion of the religious superiors, or according to their own appointment.

Reply Obj. 4: The faithful are not bound by law to contribute to the support of other than their ordinary prelates, who receive the tithes and offerings of the faithful for that purpose, as well as other ecclesiastical revenues. But if some men are willing to minister to the faithful by exercising the aforesaid acts gratuitously, and without demanding payment as of right, the faithful are not burdened thereby because their temporal contributions can be liberally repaid by those men, nor are they bound by law to contribute, but by charity, and yet not so that they be burdened thereby and others eased, as stated in 2 Cor. 8:13. If, however, none be found to devote themselves gratuitously to services of this kind, the ordinary prelate is bound, if he cannot suffice by himself, to seek other suitable persons and support them himself.

Reply Obj. 5: The seventy-two disciples are represented not only by the parish priests, but by all those of lower order who in any way assist the bishops in their office. For we do not read that our

Lord appointed the seventy-two disciples to certain fixed parishes, but that "He sent them two and two before His face into every city and place whither He Himself was to come." It was fitting, however, that in addition to the ordinary prelates others should be chosen for these duties on account of the multitude of the faithful, and the difficulty of finding a sufficient number of persons to be appointed to each locality, just as it was necessary to establish religious orders for military service, on account of the secular princes being unable to cope with unbelievers in certain countries.

FIFTH ARTICLE [II-II, Q. 188, Art. 5]

Whether a Religious Order Should Be Established for the Purpose of Study?

Objection 1: It would seem that a religious order should not be established for the purpose of study. For it is written (Ps. 70:15, 16): "Because I have not known letters [Douay: 'learning'], I will enter into the powers of the Lord," i.e. "Christian virtue," according to a gloss. Now the perfection of Christian virtue, seemingly, pertains especially to religious. Therefore it is not for them to apply themselves to the study of letters.

Obj. 2: Further, that which is a source of dissent is unbecoming to religious, who are gathered together in the unity of peace. Now study leads to dissent: wherefore different schools of thought arose among the philosophers. Hence Jerome (Super Epist. ad Tit. 1:5) says: "Before a diabolical instinct brought study into religion, and people said: I am of Paul, I of Apollo, I of Cephas," etc. Therefore it would seem that no religious order should be established for the purpose of study.

Obj. 3: Further, those who profess the Christian religion should profess nothing in common with the Gentiles. Now among the Gentiles were some who professed philosophy, and even now some secular persons are known as professors of certain sciences. Therefore the study of letters does not become religious.

*On the contrary,* Jerome (Ep. liii ad Paulin.) urges him to acquire learning in the monastic state, saying: "Let us learn on earth those things the knowledge of which will remain in heaven," and further on: "Whatever you seek to know, I will endeavor to know with you."

I answer that As stated above (A. 2), religion may be ordained to the active and to the contemplative life. Now chief among the works of the active life are those which are directly ordained to the salvation of souls, such as preaching and the like. Accordingly the study of letters is becoming to the religious life in three ways. First, as regards that which is proper to the contemplative life, to which the study of letters helps in a twofold manner. In one way by helping directly to contemplate, namely by enlightening the intellect. For the contemplative life of which we are now speaking is directed chiefly to the consideration of divine things, as stated above (Q. 180, A. 4), to which consideration man is directed by study; for which reason it is said in praise of the righteous (Ps. 1:2) that "he shall meditate day and night" on the law of the Lord, and (Ecclus. 39:1): "The wise man will seek out the wisdom of all the ancients, and will be occupied in the prophets." In another way the study of letters is a help to the contemplative life indirectly, by removing the obstacles to contemplation, namely the errors which in the contemplation of divine things frequently beset those who are ignorant of the scriptures. Thus we read in the Conferences of the Fathers (Coll. x, 3) that the Abbot Serapion through simplicity fell into the error of the Anthropomorphites, who thought that God had a human shape. Hence Gregory says (Moral. vi) that "some through seeking in contemplation more than they are able to grasp, fall away into perverse doctrines, and by failing to be the humble disciples of truth become the masters of error." Hence it is written (Eccles. 2:3): "I thought in my heart to withdraw my flesh from wine, that I might turn my mind to wisdom and might avoid folly."

Secondly, the study of letters is necessary in those religious orders that are founded for preaching and other like works; wherefore the Apostle (Titus 1:9), speaking of bishops to whose office these acts belong, says: "Embracing that faithful word which is according to doctrine, that he may be able to exhort in sound doctrine and to convince the gainsayers." Nor does it matter that the apostles were sent to preach without having studied letters, because, as Jerome says (Ep. liii ad Paulin.), "whatever others acquire by exercise and daily meditation in God's law, was taught them by the Holy Ghost."

Thirdly, the study of letters is becoming to religious as regards that which is common to all religious orders. For it helps us to avoid the lusts of the flesh; wherefore Jerome says (Ep. cxxv ad Rust. Monach.): "Love the science of the Scriptures and thou shalt have no love for carnal vice." For it turns the mind away from lustful thoughts, and tames the flesh on account of the toil that study entails according to Ecclus. 31:1, "Watching for riches* consumeth the flesh." [* Vigilia honestatis. St. Thomas would seem to have taken honestas in the sense of virtue]. It also helps to remove the desire of riches, wherefore it is written (Wis. 7:8): "I . . . esteemed riches nothing in comparison with her," and (1 Macc. 12:9): "We needed none of these things," namely assistance from without, "having for our comfort the holy books that are in our hands." It also helps to teach obedience, wherefore Augustine says (De oper. Monach. xvii): "What sort of perverseness is this, to wish to read, but not to obey what one reads?" Hence it is clearly fitting that a religious order be established for the study of letters.

Reply Obj. 1: This commentary of the gloss is an exposition of the Old Law of which the Apostle says (2 Cor. 3:6): "The letter killeth." Hence not to know letters is to disapprove of the circumcision of the "letter" and other carnal observances.

Reply Obj. 2: Study is directed to knowledge which, without charity, "puffeth up," and consequently leads to dissent, according to Prov. 13:10, "Among the proud there are always dissensions": whereas, with charity, it "edifieth and begets concord." Hence the Apostle after saying (1 Cor. 1:5): "You are made rich . . . in all utterance and in all knowledge," adds (1 Cor. 1:10): "That you all speak the same thing, and that there be no schisms among you." But Jerome is not speaking here of the study of letters, but of the study of dissensions which heretics and schismatics have brought into the Christian religion.

Reply Obj. 3: The philosophers professed the study of letters in the matter of secular learning: whereas it becomes religious to devote themselves chiefly to the study of letters in reference to the doctrine that is "according to godliness" (Titus 1:1). It becomes not religious, whose whole life is devoted to the service of God, to seek for other learning, save in so far as it is referred to the sacred doctrine. Hence Augustine says at the end of De Musica vi, 17: "Whilst we think that we should not overlook those whom heretics delude by the deceitful assurance of reason and knowledge, we are slow to advance in the consideration of their methods. Yet we should not be praised for doing this, were it not that many holy sons of their most loving mother the Catholic Church had done the same under the necessity of confounding heretics."

SIXTH ARTICLE [II-II, Q. 188, Art. 6]

Whether a Religious Order That Is Devoted to the Contemplative Life Is More Excellent Than on That Is Given to the Active Life?

Objection 1: It would seem that a religious order which is devoted to the contemplative life is not more excellent than one which is given to the active life. For it is said (Extra, de Regular. et Transeunt. ad Relig., cap. Licet), quoting the words of Innocent III: "Even as a greater good is preferred to a lesser, so the common profit takes precedence of private profit: and in this case teaching is rightly preferred to silence, responsibility to contemplation, work to rest." Now the religious order which is directed to the greater good is better. Therefore it would seem that those religious orders that are directed to the active life are more excellent than those which are directed to the contemplative life.

Obj. 2: Further, every religious order is directed to the perfection of charity, as stated above (AA. 1, 2). Now a gloss on Heb. 12:4, "For you have not yet resisted unto blood," says: "In this life there is no more perfect love than that to which the holy martyrs attained, who fought against sin unto blood." Now to fight unto blood is becoming those religious who are directed to military service, and yet this pertains to the active life. Therefore it would seem that religious orders of this kind are the most excellent.

Obj. 3: Further, seemingly the stricter a religious order is, the more excellent it is. But there is no reason why certain religious orders directed to the active life should not be of stricter observance than those directed to the contemplative life. Therefore they are more excellent.

*On the contrary,* our Lord said (Luke 10:42) that the "best part" was Mary's, by whom the contemplative life is signified.

*I answer that,* As stated above (A. 1), the difference between one religious order and another depends chiefly on the end, and secondarily on the exercise. And since one thing cannot be said to be more excellent than another save in respect of that in which it differs therefrom, it follows that the excellence of one religious order over another depends chiefly on their ends, and secondarily on their respective exercises. Nevertheless each of these comparisons is considered in a different way. For the comparison with respect to the end is absolute, since the end is sought for its own sake; whereas the comparison with respect to exercise is relative, since exercise is sought not for its own sake, but for the sake of the end. Hence a religious order is preferable to another, if it be directed to an end that is absolutely more excellent either because it is a greater good or because it is directed to more goods. If, however, the end be the same, the excellence of one religious order over another depends secondarily, not on the amount of exercise, but on the proportion of the exercise to the end in view. Wherefore in the Conferences of the Fathers (Coll. ii, 2) Blessed Antony is quoted, as preferring discretion whereby a man moderates all his actions, to fastings, watchings, and all such observances.

Accordingly we must say that the work of the active life is twofold. one proceeds from the fulness of contemplation, such as teaching and preaching. Wherefore Gregory says (Hom. v in Ezech.) that the words of Ps. 144:7, "They shall publish the memory of . . . Thy sweetness," refer "to perfect men returning from their contemplation." And this work is more excellent than simple contemplation. For even as it is better to enlighten than merely to shine, so is it better to give to others the fruits of one's contemplation than merely to contemplate. The other work of the active life consists entirely in outward occupation, for instance almsgiving, receiving guests, and the like, which are less excellent than the works of contemplation, except in cases of necessity, as stated above (Q. 182, A. 1). Accordingly the highest place in religious orders is held by those which are directed to teaching and preaching, which, moreover, are nearest to the episcopal perfection, even as in other things "the end of that which is first is in conjunction with the beginning of that which is second," as Dionysius states (Div. Nom. vii). The second place belongs to those which are directed to contemplation, and the third to those which are occupied with external actions.

Moreover, in each of these degrees it may be noted that one religious order excels another through being directed to higher action in the same genus; thus among the works of the active life it is better to ransom captives than to receive guests, and among the works of the contemplative life prayer is better than study. Again one will excel another if it be directed to more of these actions than another, or if it have statutes more adapted to the attainment of the end in view.

Reply Obj. 1: This Decretal refers to the active life as directed to the salvation of souls.

Reply Obj. 2: Those religious orders that are established for the purpose of military service aim more directly at shedding the enemy's blood than at the shedding of their own, which latter is more properly competent to martyrs. Yet there is no reason why religious of this description should not acquire the merit of martyrdom in certain cases, and in this respect stand higher than other religious; even as in some cases the works of the active life take precedence of contemplation.

Reply Obj. 3: Strictness of observances, as the Blessed Antony remarks (Conferences of the Fathers; Coll. ii, 2), is not the chief object of commendation in a religious order; and it is written (Isa. 58:5): "Is this such a fast as I have chosen, for a man to afflict his soul for a day?" Nevertheless it is adopted in religious life as being necessary for taming the flesh, "which if done without discretion, is liable to make us fail altogether," as the Blessed Antony observes. Wherefore a religious order is not more excellent through having stricter observances, but because its observances are directed by greater discretion to the end of religion. Thus the taming of the flesh is more efficaciously directed to continence by means of abstinence in meat and drink, which pertain to hunger and thirst, than by the privation of clothing, which pertains to cold and nakedness, or by bodily labor.

SEVENTH ARTICLE [II-II, Q. 188, Art. 7]

Whether Religious Perfection Is Diminished by Possessing Something in Common?

Objection 1: It would seem that religious perfection is diminished by possessing something in common. For our Lord said (Matt. 19:21): "If thou wilt be perfect, go sell all [Vulg.: 'what'] thou hast and give to the poor." Hence it is clear that to lack worldly wealth belongs to the perfection of Christian life. Now those who possess something in common do not lack worldly wealth. Therefore it would seem that they do not quite reach to the perfection of Christian life.

Obj. 2: Further, the perfection of the counsels requires that one should be without worldly solicitude; wherefore the Apostle in giving the counsel of virginity said (1 Cor. 7:32): "I would have you to be without solicitude." Now it belongs to the solicitude of the present life that certain people keep something to themselves for the morrow; and this solicitude was forbidden His disciples by our Lord (Matt. 6:34) saying: "Be not . . . solicitous for tomorrow." Therefore it would seem that the perfection of Christian life is diminished by having something in common.

Obj. 3: Further, possessions held in common belong in some way to each member of the community; wherefore Jerome (Ep. lx ad Heliod. Episc.) says in reference to certain people: "They are richer in the monastery than they had been in the world; though serving the poor Christ they have wealth which they had not while serving the rich devil; the Church rejects them now that they are rich, who in the world were beggars." But it is derogatory to religious perfection that one should possess wealth of one's own. Therefore it is also derogatory to religious perfection to possess anything in common.

Obj. 4: Further, Gregory (Dial. iii, 14) relates of a very holy man named Isaac, that "when his disciples humbly signified that he should accept the possessions offered to him for the use of the monastery, he being solicitous for the safeguarding of his poverty, held firmly to his opinion, saying: A monk who seeks earthly possessions is no monk at all": and this refers to possessions held in common, and which were offered him for the common use of the monastery. Therefore it would seem destructive of religious perfection to possess anything in common.

Obj. 5: Further, our Lord in prescribing religious perfection to His disciples, said (Matt. 10:9, 10): "Do not possess gold, nor silver, nor money in your purses, nor script for your journey." By these words, as Jerome says in his commentary, "He reproves those philosophers who are commonly called Bactroperatae [*i.e. staff and scrip bearers], who as despising the world and valuing all things at naught carried their pantry about with them." Therefore it would seem derogatory to religious perfection that one should keep something whether for oneself or for the common use.

*On the contrary,* Prosper [*Julianus Pomerius, among the works of Prosper] says (De Vita Contempl. ix) and his words are quoted (XII, qu. 1, can. Expedit): "It is sufficiently clear both that for the sake of perfection one should renounce having anything of one's own, and that the possession of revenues, which are of course common property, is no hindrance to the perfection of the Church."

*I answer that,* As stated above (Q. 184, A. 3, ad 1; Q. 185, A. 6, ad 1), perfection consists, essentially, not in poverty, but in following Christ, according to the saying of Jerome (Super Matth. xix, 27): "Since it is not enough to leave all, Peter adds that which is perfect, namely, 'We have followed Thee,'" while poverty is like an instrument or exercise for the attainment of perfection. Hence in the Conferences of the Fathers (Coll. i, 7) the abbot Moses says: "Fastings, watchings, meditating on the Scriptures, poverty, and privation of all one's possessions are not perfection, but means of perfection."

Now the privation of one's possessions, or poverty, is a means of perfection, inasmuch as by doing away with riches we remove certain obstacles to charity; and these are chiefly three. The first is the cares which riches bring with them; wherefore our Lord said (Matt. 13:22): "That which was sown [Vulg.: 'He that received the seed'] among thorns, is he that heareth the word, and the care of this world, and the deceitfulness of riches, choketh up the word." The second is the love of riches, which increases with the possession of wealth; wherefore Jerome says (Super Matth. xix, 23) that "since it is difficult to despise riches when we have them, our Lord did not say: 'It is impossible for a rich man to enter the kingdom of heaven,' but: 'It is difficult.'" The third is vainglory or elation which results from riches, according to Ps. 48:7, "They that trust in their own strength, and glory in the multitude of their riches."

Accordingly the first of these three cannot be altogether separated from riches whether great or small. For man must needs take a certain amount of care in acquiring or keeping external things. But so long as external things are sought or possessed only in a small quantity, and as much as is required for a mere livelihood, such like care does not hinder one much; and consequently is not inconsistent with the perfection of Christian life. For our Lord did not forbid all care, but only such as is excessive and hurtful; wherefore Augustine, commenting on Matt. 6:25, "Be not solicitous for your life, what you shall eat," says (De Serm. in Monte [*The words quoted are from De Operibus Monach. xxvi]): "In saying this He does not forbid them to procure these things in so far as they needed them, but to be intent on them, and for their sake to do whatever they are bidden to do in preaching the Gospel." Yet the possession of much wealth increases the weight of care, which is a great distraction to man's mind and hinders him from giving himself wholly to God's service. The other two, however, namely the love of riches and taking pride or glorying in riches, result only from an abundance of wealth.

Nevertheless it makes a difference in this matter if riches, whether abundant or moderate, be possessed in private or in common. For the care that one takes of one's own wealth, pertains to love of self, whereby a man loves himself in temporal matters; whereas the care that is given to things held in common pertains to the love of charity which "seeketh not her own," but looks to the common good. And since religion is directed to the perfection of charity, and charity is perfected in "the love of God extending to contempt of self" [*Augustine, De Civ. Dei xiv, 28,] it is contrary to religious perfection to possess anything in private. But the care that is given to common goods may pertain to charity, although it may prove an obstacle to some higher act of charity, such as divine contemplation or the instructing of one's neighbor. Hence it is evident that to have excessive riches in common, whether in movable or in immovable property, is an obstacle to perfection, though not absolutely incompatible with it; while it is not an obstacle to religious perfection to have enough external things, whether movables or immovables, as suffice for a livelihood, if we consider poverty in relation to the common end of religious orders, which is to devote oneself to the service of God. But if we consider poverty in relation to the special end of any religious order, then this end being presupposed, a greater or lesser degree of poverty is adapted to that religious order; and each religious order will be the more perfect in respect of poverty, according as it professes a poverty more adapted to its end. For it is evident that for the purpose of the outward and bodily works of the active life a man needs the assistance of outward things, whereas few are required for contemplation. Hence the Philosopher says (Ethic. x, 8) that "many things are needed for action, and the more so, the greater and nobler the actions are. But the contemplative man requires no such things for the exercise of his act: he needs only the necessaries; other things are an obstacle to his contemplation." Accordingly it is clear that a religious order directed to the bodily actions of the active life, such as soldiering or the lodging of guests, would be imperfect if it lacked common riches; whereas those religious orders which are directed to the contemplative life are the more perfect, according as the poverty they profess burdens them with less care for temporal things. And the care of temporal things is so much a greater obstacle to religious life as the religious life requires a greater care of spiritual things.

Now it is manifest that a religious order established for the purpose of contemplating and of giving to others the fruits of one's contemplation by teaching and preaching, requires greater care of spiritual things than one that is established for contemplation only. Wherefore it becomes a religious order of this kind to embrace a poverty that burdens one with the least amount of care. Again it is clear that to keep what one has acquired at a fitting time for one's necessary use involves the least burden of care. Wherefore a threefold degree of poverty corresponds to the three aforesaid degrees of religious life. For it is fitting that a religious order which is directed to the bodily actions of the active life should have an abundance of riches in common; that the common possession of a religious order directed to contemplation should be more moderate, unless the said religious be bound, either themselves or through others, to give hospitality or to assist the poor; and that those who aim at giving the fruits of their contemplation to others should have their life most exempt from external cares; this being accomplished by their laying up the necessaries of life procured at a fitting time.

This, our Lord, the Founder of poverty, taught by His example. For He had a purse which He entrusted to Judas, and in which were kept the things that were offered to Him, as related in John 12:6.

Nor should it be argued that Jerome (Super Matth. xvii, 26) says: "If anyone object that Judas carried money in the purse, we answer that He deemed it unlawful to spend the property of the poor on His own uses," namely by paying the tax--because among those poor His disciples held a foremost place, and the money in Christ's purse was spent chiefly on their needs. For it is stated (John 4:8) that "His disciples were gone into the city to buy meats," and (John 13:29) that the disciples "thought, because Judas had the purse, that Jesus had said to him: But those things which we have need of for the festival day, or that he should give something to the poor." From this it is evident that to keep money by, or any other common property for the support of religious of the same order, or of any other poor, is in accordance with the perfection which Christ taught by His example. Moreover, after the resurrection, the disciples from whom all religious orders took their origin kept the price of the lands, and distributed it according as each one had need (Acts 4:34, 35).

Reply Obj. 1: As stated above (Q. 184, A. 3, ad 1), this saying of our Lord does not mean that poverty itself is perfection, but that it is the means of perfection. Indeed, as shown above (Q. 186, A. 8), it is the least of the three chief means of perfection; since the vow of continence excels the vow of poverty, and the vow of obedience excels them both. Since, however, the means are sought not for their own sake, but for the sake of the end, a thing is better, not for being a greater instrument, but for being more adapted to the end. Thus a physician does not heal the more the more medicine he gives, but the more the medicine is adapted to the disease. Accordingly it does not follow that a religious order is the more perfect, according as the poverty it professes is more perfect, but according as its poverty is more adapted to the end both common and special. Granted even that the religious order which exceeds others in poverty be more perfect in so far as it is poorer, this would not make it more perfect simply. For possibly some other religious order might surpass it in matters relating to continence, or obedience, and thus be more perfect simply, since to excel in better things is to be better simply.

Reply Obj. 2: Our Lord's words (Matt. 6:34), "Be not solicitous for tomorrow," do not mean that we are to keep nothing for the morrow; for the Blessed Antony shows the danger of so doing, in the Conferences of the Fathers (Coll. ii, 2), where he says: "It has been our experience that those who have attempted to practice the privation of all means of livelihood, so as not to have the wherewithal to procure themselves food for one day, have been deceived so unawares that they were unable to finish properly the work they had undertaken." And, as Augustine says (De oper. Monach. xxiii), "if this saying of our Lord, 'Be not solicitous for tomorrow,' means that we are to lay nothing by for the morrow, those who shut themselves up for many days from the sight of men, and apply their whole mind to a life of prayer, will be unable to provide themselves with these things." Again he adds afterwards: "Are we to suppose that the more holy they are, the less do they resemble the birds?" And further on (De oper. Monach. xxiv): "For if it be argued from the Gospel that they should lay nothing by, they answer rightly: Why then did our Lord have a purse, wherein He kept the money that was collected? Why, in days long gone by, when famine was imminent, was grain sent to the holy fathers? Why did the apostles thus provide for the needs of the saints?"

Accordingly the saying: "Be not solicitous for tomorrow," according to Jerome (Super Matth.) is to be rendered thus: "It is enough that we think of the present; the future being uncertain, let us leave it to God": according to Chrysostom [*Hom. xvi in the Opus Imperfectum, falsely ascribed to St. John Chrysostom], "It is enough to endure the toil for necessary things, labor not in excess for unnecessary things": according to Augustine (De Serm. Dom. in Monte ii, 17): "When we do any good action, we should bear in mind not temporal things which are denoted by the morrow, but eternal things."

Reply Obj. 3: The saying of Jerome applies where there are excessive riches, possessed in private as it were, or by the abuse of which even the individual members of a community wax proud and wanton. But they do not apply to moderate wealth, set by for the common use, merely as a means of livelihood of which each one stands in need. For it amounts to the same that each one makes use of things pertaining to the necessaries of life, and that these things be set by for the common use.

Reply Obj. 4: Isaac refused to accept the offer of possessions, because he feared lest this should lead him to have excessive wealth, the abuse of which would be an obstacle to religious perfection. Hence Gregory adds (Dial. iii, 14): "He was as afraid of forfeiting the security of his poverty, as the rich miser is careful of his perishable wealth." It is not, however, related that he refused to accept such things as are commonly necessary for the upkeep of life.

Reply Obj. 5: The Philosopher says (Polit. i, 5, 6) that bread, wine, and the like are natural riches, while money is artificial riches. Hence it is that certain philosophers declined to make use of money, and employed other things, living according to nature. Wherefore Jerome shows by the words of our Lord, Who equally forbade both, that it comes to the same to have money and to possess other things necessary for life. And though our Lord commanded those who were sent to preach not to carry these things on the way, He did not forbid them to be possessed in common. How these words of our Lord should be understood has been shown above (Q. 185, A. 6 ad 2; I-II, Q. 108, A. 2, ad 3).

EIGHTH ARTICLE [II-II, Q. 188, Art. 8]

Whether the Religious Life of Those Who Live in Community Is More Perfect Than That of Those Who Lead a Solitary Life?

Objection 1: It would seem that the religious life of those who live in community is more perfect than that of those who lead a solitary life. For it is written (Eccles. 4:9): "It is better . . . that two should be together, than one; for they have the advantage of their society." Therefore the religious life of those who live in community would seem to be more perfect.

Obj. 2: Further, it is written (Matt. 18:20): "Where there are two or three gathered together in My name, there am I in the midst of them." But nothing can be better than the fellowship of Christ. Therefore it would seem better to live in community than in solitude.

Obj. 3: Further, the vow of obedience is more excellent than the other religious vows; and humility is most acceptable to God. Now obedience and humility are better observed in company than in solitude; for Jerome says (Ep. cxxv ad Rustic. Monach.): "In solitude pride quickly takes man unawares, he sleeps as much as he will, he does what he likes"; whereas when instructing one who lives in community, he says: "You may not do what you will, you must eat what you are bidden to eat, you may possess so much as you receive, you must obey one you prefer not to obey, you must be a servant to your brethren, you must fear the superior of the monastery as God, love him as a father." Therefore it would seem that the religious life of those who live in community is more perfect than that of those who lead a solitary life.

Obj. 4: Further, our Lord said (Luke 11:33): "No man lighteth a candle and putteth it in a hidden place, nor under a bushel." Now those who lead a solitary life are seemingly in a hidden place, and to be doing no good to any man. Therefore it would seem that their religious life is not more perfect.

Obj. 5: Further, that which is in accord with man's nature is apparently more pertinent to the perfection of virtue. But man is naturally a social animal, as the Philosopher says (Polit. i, 1). Therefore it would seem that to lead a solitary life is not more perfect than to lead a community life.

*On the contrary,* Augustine says (De oper. Monach. xxiii) that "those are holier who keep themselves aloof from the approach of all, and give their whole mind to a life of prayer."

*I answer that,* Solitude, like poverty, is not the essence of perfection, but a means thereto. Hence in the Conferences of the Fathers (Coll. i, 7) the Abbot Moses says that "solitude," even as fasting and other like things, is "a sure means of acquiring purity of heart." Now it is evident that solitude is a means adapted not to action but to contemplation, according to Osee 2:14, "I . . . will lead her into solitude [Douay: 'the wilderness']; and I will speak to her heart." Wherefore it is not suitable to those religious orders that are directed to the works whether corporal or spiritual of the active life; except perhaps for a time, after the example of Christ, Who as Luke relates (6:12), "went out into a mountain to pray; and He passed the whole night in the prayer of God." On the other hand, it is suitable to those religious orders that are directed to contemplation.

It must, however, be observed that what is solitary should be self-sufficing by itself. Now such a thing is one "that lacks nothing," and this belongs to the idea of a perfect thing [*Aristotle, Phys. iii, 6]. Wherefore solitude befits the contemplative who has already attained to perfection. This happens in two ways: in one way by the gift only of God, as in the case of John the Baptist, who was "filled with the Holy Ghost even from his mother's womb" (Luke 1:11), so that he was in the desert even as a boy; in another way by the practice of virtuous action, according to Heb. 5:14: "Strong meat is for the perfect; for them who by custom have their senses exercised to the discerning of good and evil."

Now man is assisted in this practice by the fellowship of others in two ways. First, as regards his intellect, to the effect of his being instructed in that which he has to contemplate; wherefore Jerome says (ad Rustic. Monach., Ep. cxxv): "It pleases me that you have the fellowship of holy men, and teach not yourself." Secondly, as regards the affections, seeing that man's noisome affections are restrained by the example and reproof which he receives from others; for as Gregory says (Moral. xxx, 23), commenting on the words, "To whom I have given a house in the wilderness" (Job 39:6), "What profits solitude of the body, if solitude of the heart be lacking?" Hence a social life is necessary for the practice of perfection. Now solitude befits those who are already perfect; wherefore Jerome says (ad Rustic. Monach., Ep. cxxv): "Far from condemning the solitary life, we have often commended it. But we wish the soldiers who pass from the monastic school to be such as not to be deterred by the hard noviciate of the desert, and such as have given proof of their conduct for a considerable time."

Accordingly, just as that which is already perfect surpasses that which is being schooled in perfection, so the life of the solitaries, if duly practiced, surpasses the community life. But if it be undertaken without the aforesaid practice, it is fraught with very great danger, unless the grace of God supply that which others acquire by practice, as in the case of the Blessed Antony and the Blessed Benedict.

Reply Obj. 1: Solomon shows that two are better than one, on account of the help which one affords the other either by "lifting him" up, or by "warming him," i.e. giving him spiritual heat (Eccles. 4:10,

11). But those who have already attained to perfection do not require this help.

Reply Obj. 2: According to 1 John 4:16, "He that abideth in charity abideth in God and God in him." Wherefore just as Christ is in the midst of those who are united together in the fellowship of brotherly love, so does He dwell in the heart of the man who devotes himself to divine contemplation through love of God.

Reply Obj. 3: Actual obedience is required of those who need to be schooled according to the direction of others in the attainment of perfection; but those who are already perfect are sufficiently "led by the spirit of God" so that they need not to obey others actually. Nevertheless they have obedience in the preparedness of the mind.

Reply Obj. 4: As Augustine says (De Civ. Dei xix, 19), "no one is forbidden to seek the knowledge of truth, for this pertains to a praiseworthy leisure." That a man be placed "on a candlestick," does not concern him but his superiors, and "if this burden is not placed on us," as Augustine goes on to say (De Civ. Dei xix, 19), "we must devote ourselves to the contemplation of truth," for which purpose solitude is most helpful. Nevertheless, those who lead a solitary life are most useful to mankind. Hence, referring to them, Augustine says (De Morib. Eccl. xxxi): "They dwell in the most lonely places, content to live on water and the bread that is brought to them from time to time, enjoying colloquy with God to whom they have adhered with a pure mind. To some they seem to have renounced human intercourse more than is right: but these understand not how much such men profit us by the spirit of their prayers, what an example to us is the life of those whom we are forbidden to see in the body."

Reply Obj. 5: A man may lead a solitary life for two motives. One is because he is unable, as it were, to bear with human fellowship on account of his uncouthness of mind; and this is beast-like. The other is with a view to adhering wholly to divine things; and this is superhuman. Hence the Philosopher says (Polit. i, 1) that "he who associates not with others is either a beast or a god," i.e. a godly man.

## QUESTION 189

OF THE ENTRANCE INTO RELIGIOUS LIFE (In Ten Articles)

We must now consider the entrance into religious life. Under this head there are ten points of inquiry:

(1) Whether those who are not practiced in the observance of the commandments should enter religion?

(2) Whether it is lawful for a person to be bound by vow to enter religion?

(3) Whether those who are bound by vow to enter religion are bound to fulfil their vow?

(4) Whether those who vow to enter religion are bound to remain there in perpetuity?

(5) Whether children should be received into religion?

(6) Whether one should be withheld from entering religion through deference to one's parents?

(7) Whether parish priests or archdeacons may enter religion?

(8) Whether one may pass from one religious order to another?

(9) Whether one ought to induce others to enter religion?

(10) Whether serious deliberation with one's relations and friends is requisite for entrance into religion?

FIRST ARTICLE [II-II, Q. 189, Art. 1]

Whether Those Who Are Not Practiced in Keeping the Commandments Should Enter Religion?

Objection 1: It would seem that none should enter religion but those who are practiced in the observance of the commandments. For our Lord gave the counsel of perfection to the young man who said that he had kept the commandments "from his youth." Now all religious orders originate from Christ. Therefore it would seem that none should be allowed to enter religion but those who are practiced in the observance of the commandments.

Obj. 2: Further, Gregory says (Hom. xv in Ezech., and Moral. xxii): "No one comes suddenly to the summit; but he must make a beginning of a good life in the smallest matters, so as to accomplish great things." Now the great things are the counsels which pertain to the perfection of life, while the lesser things are the commandments which belong to common righteousness. Therefore it would seem that one ought not to enter religion for the purpose of keeping the counsels, unless one be already practiced in the observance of the precepts.

Obj. 3: Further, the religious state, like the holy orders, has a place of eminence in the Church. Now, as Gregory writes to the bishop Siagrius [*Regist. ix, Ep. 106], "order should be observed in ascending to orders. For he seeks a fall who aspires to mount to the summit by overpassing the steps." [*The rest of the quotation is from Regist. v, Ep. 53, ad Virgil. Episc.]. "For we are well aware that walls when built receive not the weight of the beams until the new fabric is rid of its moisture, lest if they should be burdened with weight before they are seasoned they bring down the whole building" (Dist. xlviii, can. Sicut neophytus). Therefore it would seem that one should not enter religion unless one be practiced in the observance of the precepts.

Obj. 4: Further, a gloss on Ps. 130:2, "As a child that is weaned is towards his mother," says: "First we are conceived in the womb of Mother Church, by being taught the rudiments of faith. Then we are nourished as it were in her womb, by progressing in those same elements. Afterwards we are brought forth to the light by being regenerated in baptism. Then the Church bears us as it were in her hands and feeds us with milk, when after baptism we are instructed in good works and are nourished with the milk of simple doctrine while we progress; until having grown out of infancy we leave our mother's milk for a father's control, that is to say, we pass from simple doctrine, by which we are taught the Word made flesh, to the Word that was in the beginning with God." Afterwards it goes on to say: "For those who are just baptized on Holy Saturday are borne in the hands of the Church as it were and fed with milk until Pentecost, during which time nothing arduous is prescribed, no fasts, no rising at midnight. Afterwards they are confirmed by the Paraclete Spirit, and being weaned so to speak, begin to fast and keep other difficult observances. Many, like the heretics and schismatics, have perverted this order by being weaned before the time. Hence they have come to naught." Now this order is apparently perverted by those who enter religion, or induce others to enter religion, before they are practiced in the easier observance of the commandments. Therefore they would seem to be heretics or schismatics.

Obj. 5: Further, one should proceed from that which precedes to that which follows after. Now the commandments precede the counsels, because they are more universal, for "the implication of the one by the other is not convertible" [*Categor. ix], since whoever keeps the counsels keeps the commandments, but the converse does not hold. Seeing then that the right order requires one to pass from that which comes first to that which comes after, it follows that one ought not to pass to the observance of the counsels in religion, without being first of all practiced in the observance of the commandments.

*On the contrary,* Matthew the publican who was not practiced in the observance of the commandments was called by our Lord to the observance of the counsels. For it is stated (Luke 5:28) that "leaving all things he . . . followed Him." Therefore it is not necessary for a person to be practiced in the observance of the commandments before passing to the perfection of the counsels.

*I answer that,* As shown above (Q. 188, A. 1), the religious state is a spiritual schooling for the attainment of the perfection of charity. This is accomplished through the removal of the obstacles to perfect charity by religious observances; and these obstacles are those things which attach man's affections to earthly things. Now the attachment of man's affections to earthly things is not only an obstacle to the perfection of charity, but sometimes leads to the loss of charity, when through turning inordinately to temporal goods man turns away from the immutable good by sinning mortally. Hence it is evident that the observances of the religious state, while removing the obstacles to perfect charity, remove also the occasions of sin: for instance, it is clear that fasting, watching, obedience, and the like withdraw man from sins of gluttony and lust and all other manner of sins.

Consequently it is right that not only those who are practiced in the observance of the commandments should enter religion in order to attain to yet greater perfection, but also those who are not practiced, in order the more easily to avoid sin and attain to perfection.

Reply Obj. 1: Jerome (Super Matth. xix, 20) says: "The young man lies when he says: 'All these have I kept from my youth.' For if he had fulfilled this commandment, 'Thou shalt love thy neighbor as thyself,' why did he go away sad when he heard: Go, sell all thou hast and give to the poor?" But this means that he lied as to the perfect observance of this commandment. Hence Origen says (Tract. viii super Matth.) that "it is written in the Gospel according to the Hebrews that when our Lord had said to him: 'Go, sell all thou hast,' the rich man began to scratch his head; and that our Lord said to him: How sayest thou: I have fulfilled the law and the prophets, seeing that it is written in the law: Thou shalt love thy neighbor as thyself? Behold many of thy brethren, children of Abraham, are clothed in filth, and die of hunger, whilst thy house is full of all manner of good things, and nothing whatever hath passed thence to them. And thus our Lord reproves him saying: If thou wilt be perfect, go, etc. For it is impossible to fulfil the commandment which says, Thou shalt love thy neighbor as thyself, and to be rich, especially to have such great wealth." This also refers to the perfect fulfilment of this precept. On the other hand, it is true that he kept the commandments imperfectly and in a general way. For perfection consists chiefly in the observance of the precepts of charity, as stated above (Q. 184, A. 3). Wherefore in order to show that the perfection of the counsels is useful both to the innocent and to sinners, our Lord called not only the innocent youth but also the sinner Matthew. Yet Matthew obeyed His call, and the youth obeyed not, because sinners are converted to the religious life more easily than those who presume on their innocency. It is to the former that our Lord says (Matt. 21:31): "The publicans and the harlots shall go into the kingdom of God before you."

Reply Obj. 2: The highest and the lowest place can be taken in three ways. First, in reference to the same state and the same man; and thus it is evident that no one comes to the summit suddenly, since every man that lives aright, progresses during the whole course of his life, so as to arrive at the summit. Secondly, in comparison with various states; and thus he who desires to reach to a higher state need not begin from a lower state: for instance, if a man wish to be a cleric he need not first of all be practiced in the life of a layman. Thirdly, in comparison with different persons; and in this way it is clear that one man begins straightway not only from a higher state, but even from a higher degree of holiness, than the highest degree to which another man attains throughout his whole life. Hence Gregory says (Dial. ii, 1): "All are agreed that the boy Benedict began at a high degree of grace and perfection in his daily life."

Reply Obj. 3: As stated above (Q. 184, A. 6) the holy orders prerequire holiness, whereas the religious state is a school for the attainment of holiness. Hence the burden of orders should be laid on the walls when these are already seasoned with holiness, whereas the burden of religion seasons the walls, i.e. men, by drawing out the damp of vice.

Reply Obj. 4: It is manifest from the words of this gloss that it is chiefly a question of the order of doctrine, in so far as one has to pass from easy matter to that which is more difficult. Hence it is clear from what follows that the statement that certain "heretics" and "schismatics have perverted this order" refers to the order of doctrine. For it continues thus: "But he says that he has kept these things, namely the aforesaid order, binding himself by an oath [*Referring to the last words of the verse, and taking retributio, which Douay renders reward, as meaning 'punishment']. Thus I was humble not only in other things but also in knowledge, for 'I was humbly minded'; because I was first of all fed with milk, which is the Word made flesh, so that I grew up to partake of the bread of angels, namely the Word that is in the beginning with God." The example which is given in proof, of the newly baptized not being commanded to fast until Pentecost, shows that no difficult things are to be laid on them as an obligation before the Holy Ghost inspires them inwardly to take upon themselves difficult things of their own choice. Hence after Pentecost and the receiving of the Holy Ghost the Church observes a fast. Now the Holy Ghost, according to Ambrose (Super Luc. 1:15), "is not confined to any particular age; He ceases not when men die, He is not excluded from the maternal womb." Gregory also in a homily for Pentecost (xxx in Ev.) says: "He fills the boy harpist and makes him a psalmist: He fills the boy abstainer and makes him a wise judge [*Dan. 1:8-17]," and afterwards he adds: "No time is needed to learn whatsoever He will, for He teaches the mind by the merest touch." Again it is written (Eccles. 8:8), "It is not in man's power to stop the Spirit," and the Apostle admonishes us (1 Thess. 5:19): "Extinguish not the Spirit," and (Acts 7:51) it is said against certain persons: "You always resist the Holy Ghost."

Reply Obj. 5: There are certain chief precepts which are the ends, so to say, of the commandments and counsels. These are the precepts of charity, and the counsels are directed to them, not that these precepts cannot be observed without keeping the counsels, but that the keeping of the counsels conduces to the better observance of the precepts. The other precepts are secondary and are directed to the precepts of charity; in such a way that unless one observe them it is altogether impossible to keep the precepts of charity. Accordingly in the intention the perfect observance of the precepts of charity precedes the counsels, and yet sometimes it follows them in point of time. For such is the order of the end in relation to things directed to the end. But the observance in a general way of the precepts of charity together with the other precepts, is compared to the counsels as the common to the proper, because one can observe the precepts without observing the counsels, but not vice versa. Hence the common observance of the precepts precedes the counsels in the order of nature; but it does not follow that it precedes them in point of time, for a thing is not in the genus before being in one of the species. But the observance of the precepts apart from the counsels is directed to the observance of the precepts together with the counsels; as an imperfect to a perfect species, even as the irrational to the rational animal. Now the perfect is naturally prior to the imperfect, since "nature," as Boethius says (De Consol. iii, 10), "begins with perfect things." And yet it is not necessary for the precepts first of all to be observed without the counsels, and afterwards with the counsels, just as it is not necessary for one to be an ass before being a man, or married before being a virgin. In like manner it is not necessary for a person first of all to keep the commandments in the world before entering religion; especially as the worldly life does not dispose one to religious perfection, but is more an obstacle thereto.

SECOND ARTICLE [II-II, Q. 189, Art. 2]

Whether One Ought to Be Bound by Vow to Enter Religion?

Objection 1: It would seem that one ought not to be bound by vow to enter religion. For in making his profession a man is bound by the religious vow. Now before profession a year of probation is allowed, according to the rule of the Blessed Benedict (lviii) and according to the decree of Innocent IV [*Sext. Decret., cap. Non solum., de Regular. et Transeunt, ad Relig.] who moreover forbade anyone to be bound to the religious life by profession before completing the year of probation. Therefore it would seem that much less ought anyone while yet in the world to be bound by vow to enter religion.

Obj. 2: Further, Gregory says (Regist. xi, Ep. 15): Jews "should be persuaded to be converted, not by compulsion but of their own free will" (Dist. xlv, can. De Judaeis). Now one is compelled to fulfil what one has vowed. Therefore no one should be bound by vow to enter religion.

Obj. 3: Further, no one should give another an occasion of falling; wherefore it is written (Ex. 21:33, 34): "If a man open a pit . . . and an ox or an ass fall into it, the owner of the pit shall pay the price of the beasts." Now through being bound by vow to enter religion it often happens that people fall into despair and various sins. Therefore it would seem that one ought not to be bound by vow to enter religion.

*On the contrary,* It is written, (Ps. 75:12): "Vow ye, and pay to the Lord your God"; and a gloss of Augustine says that "some vows concern the individual, such as vows of chastity, virginity, and the like." Consequently Holy Scripture invites us to vow these things. But Holy Scripture invites us only to that which is better. Therefore it is better to bind oneself by vow to enter religion.

*I answer that,* As stated above (Q. 88, A. 6), when we were treating of vows, one and the same work done in fulfilment of a vow is more praiseworthy than if it be done apart from a vow, both because to vow is an act of religion, which has a certain pre-eminence among the virtues, and because a vow strengthens a man's will to do good; and just as a sin is more grievous through proceeding from a will obstinate in evil, so a good work is the more praiseworthy through proceeding from a will confirmed in good by means of a vow. Therefore it is in itself praiseworthy to bind oneself by vow to enter religion.

Reply Obj. 1: The religious vow is twofold. One is the solemn vow which makes a man a monk or a brother in some other religious order. This is called the profession, and such a vow should be preceded by a year's probation, as the objection proves. The other is the simple vow which does not make a man a monk or a religious, but only binds him to enter religion, and such a vow need not be preceded by a year's probation.

Reply Obj. 2: The words quoted from Gregory must be understood as referring to absolute violence. But the compulsion arising from the obligation of a vow is not absolute necessity, but a necessity of end, because after such a vow one cannot attain to the end of salvation unless one fulfil that vow. Such a necessity is not to be avoided; indeed, as Augustine says (Ep. cxxvii ad Armentar. et Paulin.), "happy is the necessity that compels us to better things."

Reply Obj. 3: The vow to enter religion is a strengthening of the will for better things, and consequently, considered in itself, instead of giving a man an occasion of falling, withdraws him from it. But if one who breaks a vow falls more grievously, this does not derogate from the goodness of the vow, as neither does it derogate from the goodness of Baptism that some sin more grievously after being baptized.

THIRD ARTICLE [II-II, Q. 189, Art. 3]

Whether One Who Is Bound by a Vow to Enter Religion Is Under an Obligation of Entering Religion?

Objection 1: It would seem that one who is bound by the vow to enter religion is not under an obligation of entering religion. For it is said in the Decretals (XVII, qu. ii, can. Consaldus): "Consaldus, a priest under pressure of sickness and emotional fervour, promised to become a monk. He did not, however, bind himself to a monastery or abbot; nor did he commit his promise to writing, but he renounced his benefice in the hands of a notary; and when he was restored to health he refused to become a monk." And afterwards it is added: "We adjudge and by apostolic authority we command that the aforesaid priest be admitted to his benefice and sacred duties, and that he be allowed to retain them in peace." Now this would not be if he were bound to enter religion. Therefore it would seem that one is not bound to keep one's vow of entering religion.

Obj. 2: Further, no one is bound to do what is not in his power. Now it is not in a person's power to enter religion, since this depends on the consent of those whom he wishes to join. Therefore it would seem that a man is not obliged to fulfil the vow by which he bound himself to enter religion.

Obj. 3: Further, a less useful vow cannot remit a more useful one. Now the fulfilment of a vow to enter religion might hinder the fulfilment of a vow to take up the cross in defense of the Holy Land; and the latter apparently is the more useful vow, since thereby a man obtains the forgiveness of his sins. Therefore it would seem that the vow by which a man has bound himself to enter religion is not necessarily to be fulfilled.

*On the contrary,* It is written (Eccles. 5:3): "If thou hast vowed anything to God, defer not to pay it, for an unfaithful and foolish promise displeaseth him"; and a gloss on Ps. 75:12, "Vow ye, and pay to the Lord your God," says: "To vow depends on the will: but after the vow has been taken the fulfilment is of obligation."

*I answer that,* As stated above (Q. 88, A. 1), when we were treating of vows, a vow is a promise made to God in matters concerning God. Now, as Gregory says in a letter to Boniface [*Innoc. I, Epist. ii, Victricio Epo. Rotomag., cap. 14; Cf. can. Viduas: cause. xxvii, qu. 1]: "If among men of good faith contracts are wont to be absolutely irrevocable, how much more shall the breaking of this promise given to God be deserving of punishment!" Therefore a man is under an obligation to fulfil what he has vowed, provided this be something pertaining to God.

Now it is evident that entrance into religion pertains very much to God, since thereby man devotes himself entirely to the divine service, as stated above (Q. 186, A. 1). Hence it follows that he who binds himself to enter religion is under an obligation to enter religion according as he intends to bind himself by his vow: so that if he intend to bind himself absolutely, he is obliged to enter as soon as he can, through the cessation of a lawful impediment; whereas if he intend to bind himself to a certain fixed time, or under a certain fixed condition, he is bound to enter religion when the time comes or the condition is fulfilled.

Reply Obj. 1: This priest had made, not a solemn, but a simple vow. Hence he was not a monk in effect, so as to be bound by law to dwell in a monastery and renounce his cure. However, in the court of conscience one ought to advise him to renounce all and enter religion. Hence (Extra, De Voto et Voti Redemptione, cap. Per tuas) the Bishop of Grenoble, who had accepted the episcopate after vowing to enter religion, without having fulfilled his vow, is counseled that if "he wish to heal his conscience he should renounce the government of his see and pay his vows to the Most High."

Reply Obj. 2: As stated above (Q. 88, A. 3, ad 2), when we were treating of vows, he who has bound himself by vow to enter a certain religious order is bound to do what is in his power in order to be received in that order; and if he intend to bind himself simply to enter the religious life, if he be not admitted to one, he is bound to go to another; whereas if he intend to bind himself only to one particular order, he is bound only according to the measure of the obligation to which he has engaged himself.

Reply Obj. 3: The vow to enter religion being perpetual is greater than the vow of pilgrimage to the Holy Land, which is a temporal vow; and as Alexander III says (Extra, De Voto et Voti Redemptione, cap. Scripturae), "he who exchanges a temporary service for the perpetual service of religion is in no way guilty of breaking his vow."

Moreover it may be reasonably stated that also by entrance into religion a man obtains remission of all his sins. For if by giving alms a man may forthwith satisfy for his sins, according to Dan. 4:24, "Redeem thou thy sins with alms," much more does it suffice to satisfy for all his sins that a man devote himself wholly to the divine service by entering religion, for this surpasses all manner of satisfaction, even that of public penance, according to the Decretals (XXXIII, qu. i, cap. Admonere) just as a holocaust exceeds a sacrifice, as Gregory declares (Hom. xx in Ezech.). Hence we read in the Lives of the Fathers (vi, 1) that by entering religion one receives the same grace as by being baptized. And yet even if one were not thereby absolved from all debt of punishment, nevertheless the entrance into religion is more profitable than a pilgrimage to the Holy Land, as regards the advancement in good, which is preferable to absolution from punishment.

FOURTH ARTICLE [II-II, Q. 189, Art. 4]

Whether He Who Has Vowed to Enter Religion Is Bound to Remain in Religion in Perpetuity?

Objection 1: It would seem that he who has vowed to enter religion, is bound in perpetuity to remain in religion. For it is better not to enter religion than to leave after entering, according to 2 Pet. 2:21, "It had been better for them not to have known the way of justice, than after they have known it to turn back," and Luke 9:62, "No man putting his hand to the plough, and looking back, is fit for the kingdom of God." But he who bound himself by the vow to enter religion, is under the obligation to enter, as stated above (A. 3). Therefore he is also bound to remain for always.

Obj. 2: Further, everyone is bound to avoid that which gives rise to scandal, and is a bad example to others. Now by leaving after entering religion a man gives a bad example and is an occasion of scandal to others, who are thereby withdrawn from entering or incited to leave. Therefore it seems that he who enters religion in order to fulfil a vow which he had previously taken, is bound to remain evermore.

Obj. 3: Further, the vow to enter religion is accounted a perpetual vow: wherefore it is preferred to temporal vows, as stated above (A. 3, ad 3; Q. 88, A. 12, ad 1). But this would not be so if a person after vowing to enter religion were to enter with the intention of leaving. It seems, therefore, that he who vows to enter religion is bound also to remain in perpetuity.

*On the contrary,* The vow of religious profession, for the reason that it binds a man to remain in religion for evermore, has to be preceded by a year of probation; whereas this is not required before the simple vow whereby a man binds himself to enter religion. Therefore it seems that he who vows to enter religion is not for that reason bound to remain there in perpetuity.

*I answer that,* The obligation of a vow proceeds from the will: because "to vow is an act of the will" according to Augustine [*Gloss of Peter Lombard on Ps. 75:12]. Consequently the obligation of a vow extends as far as the will and intention of the person who takes the vow. Accordingly if in vowing he intend to bind himself not only to enter religion, but also to remain there evermore, he is bound to remain in perpetuity. If, on the other hand, he intend to bind himself to enter religion for the purpose of trial, while retaining the freedom to remain or not remain, it is clear that he is not bound to remain. If, however, in vowing he thought merely of entering religion, without thinking of being free to leave, or of remaining in perpetuity, it would seem that he is bound to enter religion according to the form prescribed by common law, which is that those who enter should be given a year's probation. Wherefore he is not bound to remain for ever.

Reply Obj. 1: It is better to enter religion with the purpose of making a trial than not to enter at all, because by so doing one disposes oneself to remain always. Nor is a person accounted to turn or to look back, save when he omits to do that which he engaged to do: else whoever does a good work for a time, would be unfit for the kingdom of God, unless he did it always, which is evidently false.

Reply Obj. 2: A man who has entered religion gives neither scandal nor bad example by leaving, especially if he do so for a reasonable motive; and if others are scandalized, it will be passive scandal on their part, and not active scandal on the part of the person leaving, since in doing so, he has done what was lawful, and expedient on account of some reasonable motive, such as sickness, weakness, and the like.

Reply Obj. 3: He who enters with the purpose of leaving forthwith, does not seem to fulfil his vow, since this was not his intention in vowing. Hence he must change that purpose, at least so as to wish to try whether it is good for him to remain in religion, but he is not bound to remain for evermore.

FIFTH ARTICLE [II-II, Q. 189, Art. 5]

Whether Children Should Be Received in Religion?

Objection 1: It would seem that children ought not to be received in religion. Because it is said (Extra, De Regular. et Transeunt. ad Relig., cap. Nullus): "No one should be tonsured unless he be of legal age and willing." But children, seemingly, are not of legal age; nor have they a will of their own, not having perfect use of reason. Therefore it seems that they ought not to be received in religion.

Obj. 2: Further, the state of religion would seem to be a state of repentance; wherefore religion is derived [*Cf. Q. 81, A. 1] from religare (to bind) or from re-eligere (to choose again), as Augustine says (De Civ. Dei x, 3 [*Cf. De Vera Relig. lv]). But repentance does not become children. Therefore it seems that they should not enter religion.

Obj. 3: Further, the obligation of a vow is like that of an oath. But children under the age of fourteen ought not to be bound by oath (Decret. XXII, qu. v, cap. Pueri and cap. Honestum.). Therefore it would seem that neither should they be bound by vow.

Obj. 4: Further, it is seemingly unlawful to bind a person to an obligation that can be justly canceled. Now if any persons of unripe age bind themselves to religion, they can be withdrawn by their parents or guardians. For it is written in the Decretals (XX, qu. ii, can. Puella) that "if a maid under twelve years of age shall take the sacred veil of her own accord, her parents or guardians, if they choose, can at once declare the deed null and void." It is therefore unlawful for children, especially of unripe age, to be admitted or bound to religion.

*On the contrary,* our Lord said (Matt. 19:14): "Suffer the little children, and forbid them not to come to Me." Expounding these words Origen says (Tract. vii in Matth.) that "the disciples of Jesus before they have been taught the conditions of righteousness [*Cf. Matt. 19:16-30], rebuke those who offer children and babes to Christ: but our Lord urges His disciples to stoop to the service of children. We must therefore take note of this, lest deeming ourselves to excel in wisdom we despise the Church's little ones, as though we were great, and forbid the children to come to Jesus."

*I answer that,* As stated above (A. 2, ad 1), the religious vow is twofold. One is the simple vow consisting in a mere promise made to God, and proceeding from the interior deliberation of the mind. Such a vow derives its efficacy from the divine law. Nevertheless it may encounter a twofold obstacle. First, through lack of deliberation, as in the case of the insane, whose vows are not binding [*Extra, De Regular. et Transeunt. ad Relig., cap. Sicut tenor]. The same applies to children who have not reached the required use of reason, so as to be capable of guile, which use boys attain, as a rule, at about the age of fourteen, and girls at the age of twelve, this being what is called "the age of puberty," although in some it comes earlier and in others it is delayed, according to the various dispositions of nature. Secondly, the efficacy of a simple vow encounters an obstacle, if the person who makes a vow to God is not his own master; for instance, if a slave, though having the use of reason, vows to enter religion, or even is ordained, without the knowledge of his master: for his master can annul this, as stated in the Decretals (Dist. LIV, cap. Si servus). And since boys and girls under the age of puberty are naturally in their father's power as regards the disposal of their manner of life, their father may either cancel or approve their vow, if it please him to do so, as it is expressly said with regard to a woman (Num. 30:4).

Accordingly if before reaching the age of puberty a child makes a simple vow, not yet having full use of reason, he is not bound in virtue of the vow; but if he has the use of reason before reaching the age of puberty, he is bound, so far as he is concerned, by his vow; yet this obligation may be removed by his father's authority, under whose control he still remains, because the ordinance of the law whereby one man is subject to another considers what happens in the majority of cases. If, however, the child has passed the age of puberty, his vow cannot be annulled by the authority of his parents; though if he has not the full use of reason, he would not be bound in the sight of God.

The other is the solemn vow which makes a man a monk or a religious. Such a vow is subject to the ordinance of the Church, on account of the solemnity attached to it. And since the Church considers what happens in the majority of cases, a profession made before the age of puberty, however much the person who makes profession may have the use of reason, or be capable of guile, does not take effect so as to make him a religious (Extra, De Regular., etc. cap. Significatum est.).

Nevertheless, although they cannot be professed before the age of puberty, they can, with the consent of their parents, be received into religion to be educated there: thus it is related of John the Baptist (Luke 1:80) that "the child grew and was strengthened in spirit, and was in the deserts." Hence, as

Gregory states (Dial. ii, 3), "the Roman nobles began to give their sons to the blessed Benedict to be nurtured for Almighty God"; and this is most fitting, according to Lam. 3:27, "It is good for a man when he has borne the yoke from his youth." It is for this reason that by common custom children are made to apply themselves to those duties or arts with which they are to pass their lives.

Reply Obj. 1: The legal age for receiving the tonsure and taking the solemn vow of religion is the age of puberty, when a man is able to make use of his own will; but before the age of puberty it is possible to have reached the lawful age to receive the tonsure and be educated in a religious house.

Reply Obj. 2: The religious state is chiefly directed to the atta[in]ment of perfection, as stated above (Q. 186, A. 1, ad 4); and accordingly it is becoming to children, who are easily drawn to it. But as a consequence it is called a state of repentance, inasmuch as occasions of sin are removed by religious observances, as stated above (Q. 186, A. 1, ad 4).

Reply Obj. 3: Even as children are not bound to take oaths (as the canon states), so are they not bound to take vows. If, however, they bind themselves by vow or oath to do something, they are bound in God's sight, if they have the use of reason, but they are not bound in the sight of the Church before reaching the age of fourteen.

Reply Obj. 4: A woman who has not reached the age of puberty is not rebuked (Num. 30:4) for taking a vow without her parents' consent: but the vow can be made void by her parents. Hence it is evident that she does not sin in vowing. But we are given to understand that she binds herself by vow, so far as she may, without prejudice to her parents' authority.

SIXTH ARTICLE [II-II, Q. 189, Art. 6]

Whether One Ought to Be Withdrawn from Entering Religion Through Deference to One's Parents?

Objection 1: It would seem that one ought to be withdrawn from entering religion through deference to one's parents. For it is not lawful to omit that which is of obligation in order to do that which is optional. Now deference to one's parents comes under an obligation of the precept concerning the honoring of our parents (Ex. 20:12); wherefore the Apostle says (1 Tim. 5:4): "If any widow have children or grandchildren, let her learn first to govern her own house, and to make a return of duty to her parents." But the entrance to religion is optional. Therefore it would seem that one ought not to omit deference to one's parents for the sake of entering religion.

Obj. 2: Further, seemingly the subjection of a son to his father is greater than that of a slave to his master, since sonship is natural, while slavery results from the curse of sin, as appears from Gen. 9:25. Now a slave cannot set aside the service of his master in order to enter religion or take holy orders, as stated in the Decretals (Dist. LIV, cap. Si servus). Much less therefore can a son set aside the deference due to his father in order to enter religion.

Obj. 3: Further, a man is more indebted to his parents than to those to whom he owes money. Now persons who owe money to anyone cannot enter religion. For Gregory says (Regist. viii, Ep. 5) that "those who are engaged in trade must by no means be admitted into a monastery, when they seek admittance, unless first of all they withdraw from public business" (Dist. liii, can. Legem.). Therefore seemingly much less may children enter religion in despite of their duty to their parents.

*On the contrary,* It is related (Matt. 4:22) that James and John "left their nets and father, and followed our Lord." By this, says Hilary (Can. iii in Matth.), "we learn that we who intend to follow Christ are not bound by the cares of the secular life, and by the ties of home."

*I answer that,* As stated above (Q. 101, A. 2, ad 2) when we were treating of piety, parents as such have the character of a principle, wherefore it is competent to them as such to have the care of their children. Hence it is unlawful for a person having children to enter religion so as altogether to set aside the care for their children, namely without providing for their education. For it is written (1 Tim. 5:8) that "if any man have not care of his own . . . he hath denied the faith, and is worse than an infidel."

Nevertheless it is accidentally competent to parents to be assisted by their children, in so far, to wit, as they are placed in a condition of necessity. Consequently we must say that when their parents are in such need that they cannot fittingly be supported otherwise than by the help of their children, these latter may not lawfully enter religion in despite of their duty to their parents. If, however, the parents' necessity be not such as to stand in great need of their children's assistance, the latter may, in despite of the duty they owe their parents, enter religion even against their parents' command, because after the age of puberty every freeman enjoys freedom in things concerning the ordering of his state of life, especially in such as belong to the service of God, and "we should more obey the Father of spirits that we may live [*'Shall we not much more obey the Father of Spirits, and live?'']," as says the Apostle (Heb. 12:9), than obey our parents. Hence as we read (Matt. 8:22; Luke 9:62) our Lord rebuked the disciple who was unwilling to follow him forthwith on account of his father's burial: for there were others who could see to this, as Chrysostom remarks [*Hom. xxvii in Matth.].

Reply Obj. 1: The commandment of honoring our parents extends not only to bodily but also to spiritual service, and to the paying of deference. Hence even those who are in religion can fulfil the commandment of honoring their parents, by praying for them and by revering and assisting them, as becomes religious, since even those who live in the world honor their parents in different ways as befits their condition.

Reply Obj. 2: Since slavery was imposed in punishment of sin, it follows that by slavery man forfeits something which otherwise he would be competent to have, namely the free disposal of his person, for "a slave belongs wholly to his master" [*Aristotle, Polit. i, 2]. On the other hand, the son, through being subject to his father, is not hindered from freely disposing of his person by transferring himself to the service of God; which is most conducive to man's good.

Reply Obj. 3: He who is under a certain fixed obligation cannot lawfully set it aside so long as he is able to fulfil it. Wherefore if a person is under an obligation to give an account to someone or to pay a certain fixed debt, he cannot lawfully evade this obligation in order to enter religion. If, however, he owes a sum of money, and has not wherewithal to pay the debt, he must do what he can, namely by surrendering his goods to his creditor. According to civil law [*Cod. IV, x, de Oblig. et Action, 12] money lays an obligation not on the person of a freeman, but on his property, because the person of a freeman "is above all pecuniary consideration" [*Dig. L, xvii, de div. reg. Jur. ant. 106, 176]. Hence, after surrendering his property, he may lawfully enter religion, nor is he bound to remain in the world in order to earn the means of paying the debt.

On the other hand, he does not owe his father a special debt, except as may arise in a case of necessity, as stated above.

SEVENTH ARTICLE [II-II, Q. 189, Art. 7]

Whether Parish Priests May Lawfully Enter Religion?

Objection 1: It would seem that parish priests cannot lawfully enter religion. For Gregory says (Past. iii, 4) that "he who undertakes the cure of souls, receives an awful warning in the words: 'My son, if thou be surety for thy friend, thou hast engaged fast thy hand to a stranger'" (Prov. 6:1); and he goes on to say, "because to be surety for a friend is to take charge of the soul of another on the surety of one's own behavior." Now he who is under an obligation to a man for a debt, cannot enter religion, unless he pay what he owes, if he can. Since then a priest is able to fulfil the cure of souls, to which obligation he has pledged his soul, it would seem unlawful for him to lay aside the cure of souls in order to enter religion.

Obj. 2: Further, what is lawful to one is likewise lawful to all. But if all priests having cure of souls were to enter religion, the people would be left without a pastor's care, which would be unfitting. Therefore it seems that parish priests cannot lawfully enter religion.

Obj. 3: Further, chief among the acts to which religious orders are directed are those whereby a man gives to others the fruit of his contemplation. Now such acts are competent to parish priests and archdeacons, whom it becomes by virtue of their office to preach and hear confessions. Therefore it would seem unlawful for a parish priest or archdeacon to pass over to religion.

*On the contrary,* It is said in the Decretals (XIX, qu. ii, cap. Duce sunt leges.): "If a man, while governing the people in his church under the bishop and leading a secular life, is inspired by the Holy Ghost to desire to work out his salvation in a monastery or under some canonical rule, even though his bishop withstand him, we authorize him to go freely."

*I answer that,* As stated above (A. 3, ad 3; Q. 88, A. 12, ad 1), the obligation of a perpetual vow stands before every other obligation. Now it belongs properly to bishops and religious to be bound by perpetual vow to devote themselves to the divine service [*Cf. Q. 184, A. 5], while parish priests and archdeacons are not, as bishops are, bound by a perpetual and solemn vow to retain the cure of souls. Wherefore bishops "cannot lay aside their bishopric for any pretext whatever, without the authority of the Roman Pontiff" (Extra, De Regular. et Transeunt. ad Relig., cap. Licet.): whereas archdeacons and parish priests are free to renounce in the hands of the bishop the cure entrusted to them, without the Pope's special permission, who alone can dispense from perpetual vows. Therefore it is evident that archdeacons and parish priests may lawfully enter religion.

Reply Obj. 1: Parish priests and archdeacons have bound themselves to the care of their subjects, as long as they retain their archdeaconry or parish, but they did not bind themselves to retain their archdeaconry or parish for ever.

Reply Obj. 2: As Jerome says (Contra Vigil.): "Although they," namely religious, "are sorely smitten by thy poisonous tongue, about whom you argue, saying; 'If all shut themselves up and live in solitude, who will go to church? who will convert worldlings? who will be able to urge sinners to virtue?' If this holds true, if all are fools with thee, who can be wise? Nor will virginity be commendable, for if all be virgins, and none marry, the human race will perish. Virtue is rare, and is not desired by many." It is therefore evident that this is a foolish alarm; thus might a man fear to draw water lest the river run dry. [*St. Thomas gives no reply to the third objection, which is sufficiently solved in the body of the article.]

EIGHTH ARTICLE [II-II, Q. 189, Art. 8]

Whether It Is Lawful to Pass from One Religious Order to Another?

Objection 1: It seems unlawful to pass from one religious order to another, even a stricter one. For the Apostle says (Heb. 10:25): "Not forsaking our assembly, as some are accustomed"; and a gloss observes: "Those namely who yield through fear of persecution, or who presuming on themselves withdraw from the company of sinners or of the imperfect, that they may appear to be righteous." Now those who pass from one religious order to another more perfect one would seem to do this. Therefore this is seemingly unlawful.

Obj. 2: Further, the profession of monks is stricter than that of canons regular (Extra, De Statu Monach. et Canonic. Reg., cap. Quod Dei timorem). But it is unlawful for anyone to pass from the state of canon regular to the monastic state. For it is said in the Decretals (XIX, qu. iii, can. Mandamus): "We ordain and without any exception forbid any professed canon regular to become a monk, unless (which God forbid) he have fallen into public sin." Therefore it would seem unlawful for anyone to pass from one religious order to another of higher rank.

Obj. 3: Further, a person is bound to fulfil what he has vowed, as long as he is able lawfully to do so; thus if a man has vowed to observe continence, he is bound, even after contracting marriage by words in the present tense, to fulfil his vow so long as the marriage is not consummated, because he can fulfil the vow by entering religion. Therefore if a person may lawfully pass from one religious order to another, he will be bound to do so if he vowed it previously while in the world. But this would seem objectionable, since in many cases it might give rise to scandal. Therefore a religious may not pass from one religious order to another stricter one.

*On the contrary,* It is said in the Decretals (XX, qu. iv, can. Virgines): "If sacred virgins design for the good of their soul to pass to another monastery on account of a stricter life, and decide to remain there, the holy synod allows them to do so": and the same would seem to apply to any religious. Therefore one may lawfully pass from one religious order to another.

*I answer that,* It is not commendable to pass from one religious order to another: both because this frequently gives scandal to those who remain; and because, other things being equal, it is easier to make progress in a religious order to which one is accustomed than in one to which one is not habituated. Hence in the Conferences of the Fathers (Coll. xiv, 5) Abbot Nesteros says: "It is best for each one that he should, according to the resolve he has made, hasten with the greatest zeal and care to reach the perfection of the work he has undertaken, and nowise forsake the profession he has chosen." And further on he adds (cap. 6) by way of reason: "For it is impossible that one and the same man should excel in all the virtues at once, since if he endeavor to practice them equally, he will of necessity, while trying to attain them all, end in acquiring none of them perfectly": because the various religious orders excel in respect of various works of virtue.

Nevertheless one may commendably pass from one religious order to another for three reasons. First, through zeal for a more perfect religious life, which excellence depends, as stated above (Q. 188, A. 6), not merely on severity, but chiefly on the end to which a religious order is directed, and secondarily on the discretion whereby the observances are proportionate to the due end. Secondly, on account of a religious order falling away from the perfection it ought to have: for instance, if in a more severe religious order, the religious begin to live less strictly, it is commendable for one to pass even to a less severe religious order if the observance is better. Hence in the Conferences of the Fathers (Coll. xix, 3, 5, 6) Abbot John says of himself that he had passed from the solitary life, in which he was professed, to a less severe life, namely of those who lived in community, because the hermetical life had fallen into decline and laxity. Thirdly, on account of sickness or weakness, the result of which sometimes is that one is unable to keep the ordinances of a more severe religious order, though able to observe those of a less strict religion.

There is, however, a difference in these three cases. For in the first case one ought, on account of humility, to seek permission: yet this cannot be denied, provided it be certain that this other religion is more severe. "And if there be a probable doubt about this, one should ask one's superior to decide" (Extra, De Regular. et Transeunt. ad Relig., cap. Licet.). In like manner the superior's decision should be sought in the second case. In the third case it is also necessary to have a dispensation.

Reply Obj. 1: Those who pass to a stricter religious order, do so not out of presumption that they may appear righteous, but out of devotion, that they may become more righteous.

Reply Obj. 2: Religious orders whether of monks or of canons regular are destined to the works of the contemplative life. Chief among these are those which are performed in the divine mysteries, and these are the direct object of the orders of canons regular, the members of which are essentially religious clerics. On the other hand, monastic religious are not essentially clerics, according to the Decretals (XVI, qu. i, cap. Alia causa). Hence although monastic orders are more severe, it would be lawful, supposing the members to be lay monks, to pass from the monastic order to an order of canons regular, according to the statement of Jerome (Ep. cxxv, ad Rustic. Monach.): "So live in the monastery as to deserve to become a cleric"; but not conversely, as expressed in the Decretal quoted (XIX, qu. iii). If, however, the monks be clerics devoting themselves to the sacred ministry, they have this in common with canons regular coupled with greater severity, and consequently it will be lawful to pass from an order of canons regular to a monastic order, provided withal that one seek the superior's permission (XIX, qu. iii; cap. Statuimus).

Reply Obj. 3: The solemn vow whereby a person is bound to a less strict order, is more binding than the simple vow whereby a person is bound to a stricter order. For if after taking a simple vow a person were to be married, his marriage would not be invalid, as it would be after his taking a solemn vow. Consequently a person who is professed in a less severe order is not bound to fulfil a simple vow he has taken on entering a more severe order.

NINTH ARTICLE [II-II, Q. 189, Art. 9]

Whether One Ought to Induce Others to Enter Religion?

Objection 1: It would seem that no one ought to induce others to enter religion. For the blessed Benedict prescribes in his Rule (lviii) that "those who seek to enter religion must not easily be admitted, but spirits must be tested whether they be of God"; and Cassian has the same instruction (De Inst. Caenob. iv, 3). Much less therefore is it lawful to induce anyone to enter religion.

Obj. 2: Further, our Lord said (Matt. 23:15): "Woe to you . . . because you go round about the sea and the land to make one proselyte, and when he is made you make him the child of hell twofold more than yourselves." Now thus would seem to do those who induce persons to enter religion. Therefore this would seem blameworthy.

Obj. 3: Further, no one should induce another to do what is to his prejudice. But those who are induced to enter religion, sometimes take harm therefrom, for sometimes they are under obligation to enter a stricter religion. Therefore it would not seem praiseworthy to induce others to enter religion.

*On the contrary,* It is written (Ex. 26:3, seqq. [*St. Thomas quotes the sense, not the words]): "Let one curtain draw the other." Therefore one man should draw another to God's service.

*I answer that,* Those who induce others to enter religion not only do not sin, but merit a great reward. For it is written (James 5:20): "He who causeth a sinner to be converted from the error of his way, shall save his soul from death, and shall cover a multitude of sins"; and (Dan. 12:3): "They that instruct many to justice shall be as stars for all eternity."

Nevertheless such inducement may be affected by a threefold inordinateness. First, if one person force another by violence to enter religion: and this is forbidden in the Decretals (XX, qu. iii, cap. Praesens). Secondly, if one person persuade another simoniacally to enter religion, by giving him presents: and this is forbidden in the Decretal (I, qu. ii, cap. Quam pio). But this does not apply to the case where one provides a poor person with necessaries by educating him in the world for the religious life; or when without any compact one gives a person little presents for the sake of good fellowship. Thirdly, if one person entices another by lies: for it is to be feared that the person thus enticed may turn back on finding himself deceived, and thus "the last state of that man" may become "worse than the first" (Luke 11:26).

Reply Obj. 1: Those who are induced to enter religion have still a time of probation wherein they make a trial of the hardships of religion, so that they are not easily admitted to the religious life.

Reply Obj. 2: According to Hilary (Can. xxiv in Matth.) this saying of our Lord was a forecast of the wicked endeavors of the Jews, after the preaching of Christ, to draw Gentiles or even Christians to observe the Jewish ritual, thereby making them doubly children of hell, because, to wit, they were not forgiven the former sins which they committed while adherents of Judaism, and furthermore they incurred the guilt of Jewish perfidy; and thus interpreted these words have nothing to do with the case in point.

According to Jerome, however, in his commentary on this passage of Matthew, the reference is to the Jews even at the time when it was yet lawful to keep the legal observances, in so far as he whom they converted to Judaism "from paganism, was merely misled; but when he saw the wickedness of his teachers, he returned to his vomit, and becoming a pagan deserved greater punishment for his treachery." Hence it is manifest that it is not blameworthy to draw others to the service of God or to the religious life, but only when one gives a bad example to the person converted, whence he becomes worse.

Reply Obj. 3: The lesser is included in the greater. Wherefore a person who is bound by vow or oath to enter a lesser order, may be lawfully induced to enter a greater one, unless there be some special obstacle, such as ill-health, or the hope of making greater progress in the lesser order. On the other hand, one who is bound by vow or oath to enter a greater order, cannot be lawfully induced to enter a lesser order, except for some special and evident motive, and then with the superior's dispensation.

TENTH ARTICLE [II-II, Q. 189, Art. 10]

Whether It Is Praiseworthy to Enter Religion Without Taking Counsel of Many, and Previously Deliberating for a Long Time?

Objection 1: It would not seem praiseworthy to enter religion without taking counsel of many, and previously deliberating for a long time. For it is written (1 John 4:1): "Believe not every spirit, but try the spirits if they be of God." Now sometimes a man's purpose of entering religion is not of God, since it often comes to naught through his leaving the religious life; for it is written (Acts 5:38, 39): "If this counsel or this work be of God, you cannot overthrow it." Therefore it would seem that one ought to make a searching inquiry before entering religion.

Obj. 2: Further, it is written (Prov. 25:9): "Treat thy cause with thy friend." Now a man's cause would seem to be especially one that concerns a change in his state of life. Therefore seemingly one ought not to enter religion without discussing the matter with one's friends.

Obj. 3: Further, our Lord (Luke 14:28) in making a comparison with a man who has a mind to build a tower, says that he doth "first sit down and reckon the charges that are necessary, whether he have wherewithal to finish it," lest he become an object of mockery, for that "this man began to build and was not able to finish." Now the wherewithal to build the tower, as Augustine says (Ep. ad Laetum ccxliii), is nothing less than that "each one should renounce all his possessions." Yet it happens sometimes that many cannot do this, nor keep other religious observances; and in signification of this it is stated (1 Kings 17:39) that David could not walk in Saul's armor, for he was not used to it. Therefore it would seem that one ought not to enter religion without long deliberation beforehand and taking counsel of many.

*On the contrary,* It is stated (Matt. 4:20) that upon our Lord's calling them, Peter and Andrew "immediately leaving their nets, followed Him." Here Chrysostom says (Hom. xiv in Matth.): "Such obedience as this does Christ require of us, that we delay not even for a moment."

*I answer that,* Long deliberation and the advice of many are required in great matters of doubt, as the Philosopher says (Ethic. iii, 3); while advice is unnecessary in matters that are certain and fixed. Now with regard to entering religion three points may be considered. First, the entrance itself into religion, considered by itself; and thus it is certain that entrance into religion is a greater good, and to doubt about this is to disparage Christ Who gave this counsel. Hence Augustine says (De Verb. Dom., Serm. c, 2): "The East," that is Christ, "calleth thee, and thou turnest to the West," namely mortal and fallible man. Secondly, the entrance into religion may be considered in relation to the strength of the person who intends to enter. And here again there is no room for doubt about the entrance to religion, since those who enter religion trust not to be able to stay by their own power, but by the assistance of the divine power, according to Isa. 40:31, "They that hope in the Lord shall renew their strength, they shall take wings as eagles, they shall run and not be weary, they shall walk and not faint." Yet if there be some special obstacle (such as bodily weakness, a burden of debts, or the like) in such cases a man must deliberate and take counsel with such as are likely to help and not hinder him. Hence it is written (Ecclus. 37:12): "Treat with a man without religion concerning holiness [*The Douay version supplies the negative: 'Treat not . . . nor with . . .'], with an unjust man concerning justice," meaning that one should not do so, wherefore the text goes on (Ecclus. 37:14, 15), "Give no heed to these in any matter of counsel, but be continually with a holy man." In these matters, however, one should not take long deliberation. Wherefore Jerome says (Ep. and Paulin. liii): "Hasten, I pray thee, cut off rather than loosen the rope that holds the boat to the shore." Thirdly, we may consider the way of entering religion, and which order one ought to enter, and about such matters also one may take counsel of those who will not stand in one's way.

Reply Obj. 1: The saying: "Try the spirits, if they be of God," applies to matters admitting of doubt whether the spirits be of God; thus those who are already in religion may doubt whether he who offers himself to religion be led by the spirit of God, or be moved by hypocrisy. Wherefore they must try the postulant whether he be moved by the divine spirit. But for him who seeks to enter religion there can be no doubt but that the purpose of entering religion to which his heart has given birth is from the spirit of God, for it is His spirit "that leads" man "into the land of uprightness" (Ps. 142:10).

Nor does this prove that it is not of God that some turn back; since not all that is of God is incorruptible: else corruptible creatures would not be of God, as the Manicheans hold, nor could some who have grace from God lose it, which is also heretical. But God's "counsel" whereby He makes even things corruptible and changeable, is imperishable according to Isa. 46:10, "My counsel shall stand and all My will shall be done." Hence the purpose of entering religion needs not to be tried whether it be of God, because "it requires no further demonstration," as a gloss says on 1 Thess. 5:21, "Prove all things."

Reply Obj. 2: Even as "the flesh lusteth against the spirit" (Gal. 5:17), so too carnal friends often thwart our spiritual progress, according to Mic. 7:6, "A man's enemies are they of his own household." Wherefore Cyril expounding Luke 9:61, "Let me first take my leave of them that are at my house," says [*Cf. St. Thomas's Catena Aurea]: "By asking first to take his leave of them that were at his house, he shows he was somewhat of two minds. For to communicate with his neighbors, and consult those who are unwilling to relish righteousness, is an indication of weakness and turning back. Hence he hears our Lord say: 'No man putting his hand to the plough, and looking back, is fit for the kingdom of God,' because he looks back who seeks delay in order to go home and confer with his kinsfolk."

Reply Obj. 3: The building of the tower signifies the perfection of Christian life; and the renunciation of one's possessions is the wherewithal to build this tower. Now no one doubts or deliberates about wishing to have the wherewithal, or whether he is able to build the tower if he have the wherewithal, but what does come under deliberation is whether one has the wherewithal. Again it need not be a matter of deliberation whether one ought to renounce all that one has, or whether by so doing one may be able to attain to perfection; whereas it is a matter of deliberation whether that which one is doing amounts to the renunciation of all that he has, since unless he does renounce (which is to have the wherewithal) he cannot, as the text goes on to state, be Christ's disciple, and this is to build the tower.

The misgiving of those who hesitate as to whether they may be able to attain to perfection by entering religion is shown by many examples to be unreasonable. Hence Augustine says (Confess. viii, 11): "On that side whither I had set my face, and whither I trembled to go, there appeared to me the chaste dignity of continency . . . honestly alluring me to come and doubt not, and stretching forth to receive and embrace me, her holy hands full of multitudes of good examples. There were so many young men and maidens here, a multitude of youth and every age, grave widows and aged virgins . . . And she smiled at me with a persuasive mockery as though to say: Canst not thou what these youths and these maidens can? Or can they either in themselves, and not rather in the Lord their God? . . . Why standest thou in thyself, and so standest not? Cast thyself upon Him; fear not, He will not withdraw Himself that thou shouldst fall. Cast thyself fearlessly upon Him: He will receive and will heal thee."

The example quoted of David is not to the point, because "the arms of Saul," as a gloss on the passage observes, "are the sacraments of the Law, as being burdensome": whereas religion is the sweet yoke of Christ, for as Gregory says (Moral. iv, 33), "what burden does He lay on the shoulders of the mind, Who commands us to shun all troublesome desires, Who warns us to turn aside from the rough paths of this world?"

To those indeed who take this sweet yoke upon themselves He promises the refreshment of the divine fruition and the eternal rest of their souls.

To which may He Who made this promise bring us, Jesus Christ our Lord, "Who is over all things God blessed for ever. Amen."

---

The End

# SUMMA THEOLOGICA PART III ("Tertia Pars")

## PROLOGUE

Forasmuch as our Saviour the Lord Jesus Christ, in order to "save His people from their sins" (Matt. 1:21), as the angel announced, showed unto us in His own Person the way of truth, whereby we may attain to the bliss of eternal life by rising again, it is necessary, in order to complete the work of theology, that after considering the last end of human life, and the virtues and vices, there should follow the consideration of the Saviour of all, and of the benefits bestowed by Him on the human race.

Concerning this we must consider (1) the Saviour Himself; (2) the sacraments by which we attain to our salvation; (3) the end of immortal life to which we attain by the resurrection.

Concerning the first, a double consideration occurs: the first, about the mystery of the Incarnation itself, whereby God was made man for our salvation; the second, about such things as were done and suffered by our Saviour--i.e. God incarnate.

TREATISE ON THE INCARNATION (QQ. 1-59)

## QUESTION 1

OF THE FITNESS OF THE INCARNATION (In Six Articles)

Concerning the first, three things occur to be considered: first, the fitness of the Incarnation; secondly, the mode of union of the Word Incarnate; thirdly, what follows this union.

Under the first head there are six points of inquiry:

(1) Whether it was fitting for God to become incarnate?

(2) Whether it was necessary for the restoration of the human race?

(3) Whether if there had been no sin God would have become incarnate?

(4) Whether He became incarnate to take away original sin rather than actual?

(5) Whether it was fitting for God to become incarnate from the beginning of the world?

(6) Whether His Incarnation ought to have been deferred to the end of the world?

FIRST ARTICLE [III, Q. 1, Art. 1]

Whether It Was Fitting That God Should Become Incarnate?

Objection 1: It would seem that it was not fitting for God to become incarnate. Since God from all eternity is the very essence of goodness, it was best for Him to be as He had been from all eternity. But from all eternity He had been without flesh. Therefore it was most fitting for Him not to be united to flesh. Therefore it was not fitting for God to become incarnate.

Obj. 2: Further, it is not fitting to unite things that are infinitely apart, even as it would not be a fitting union if one were "to paint a figure in which the neck of a horse was joined to the head of a man" [*Horace, Ars. Poet., line 1]. But God and flesh are infinitely apart; since God is most simple, and flesh is most composite--especially human flesh. Therefore it was not fitting that God should be united to human flesh.

Obj. 3: Further, a body is as distant from the highest spirit as evil is from the highest good. But it was wholly unfitting that God, Who is the highest good, should assume evil. Therefore it was not fitting that the highest uncreated spirit should assume a body.

Obj. 4: Further, it is not becoming that He Who surpassed the greatest things should be contained in the least, and He upon Whom rests the care of great things should leave them for lesser things. But God--Who takes care of the whole world--the whole universe of things cannot contain. Therefore it would seem unfitting that "He should be hid under the frail body of a babe in swathing bands, in comparison with Whom the whole universe is accounted as little; and that this Prince should quit His throne for so long, and transfer the government of the whole world to so frail a body," as Volusianus writes to Augustine (Ep. cxxxv).

*On the contrary,* It would seem most fitting that by visible things the invisible things of God should be made known; for to this end was the whole world made, as is clear from the word of the Apostle (Rom. 1:20): "For the invisible things of God . . . are clearly seen, being understood by the things that are made." But, as Damascene says (De Fide Orth. iii, 1), by the mystery of the Incarnation are made known at once the goodness, the wisdom, the justice, and the power or might of God--"His goodness, for He did not despise the weakness of His own handiwork; His justice, since, on man's defeat, He caused the tyrant to be overcome by none other than man, and yet He did not snatch men forcibly from death; His wisdom, for He found a suitable discharge for a most heavy debt; His power, or infinite might, for there is nothing greater than for God to become incarnate . . ."

*I answer that,* To each thing, that is befitting which belongs to it by reason of its very nature; thus, to reason befits man, since this belongs to him because he is of a rational nature. But the very nature of God is goodness, as is clear from Dionysius (Div. Nom. i). Hence, what belongs to the essence of goodness befits God. But it belongs to the essence of goodness to communicate itself to others, as is plain from Dionysius (Div. Nom. iv). Hence it belongs to the essence of the highest good to communicate itself in the highest manner to the creature, and this is brought about chiefly by "His so joining created nature to Himself that one Person is made up of these three--the Word, a soul and flesh," as Augustine says (De Trin. xiii). Hence it is manifest that it was fitting that God should become incarnate.

Reply Obj. 1: The mystery of the Incarnation was not completed through God being changed in any way from the state in which He had been from eternity, but through His having united Himself to the creature in a new way, or rather through having united it to Himself. But it is fitting that a creature which by nature is mutable, should not always be in one way. And therefore, as the creature began to be, although it had not been before, so likewise, not having been previously united to God in Person, it was afterwards united to Him.

Reply Obj. 2: To be united to God in unity of person was not fitting to human flesh, according to its natural endowments, since it was above its dignity; nevertheless, it was fitting that God, by reason of His infinite goodness, should unite it to Himself for man's salvation.

Reply Obj. 3: Every mode of being wherein any creature whatsoever differs from the Creator has been established by God's wisdom, and is ordained to God's goodness. For God, Who is uncreated, immutable, and incorporeal, produced mutable and corporeal creatures for His own goodness. And so also the evil of punishment was established by God's justice for God's glory. But evil of fault is committed by withdrawing from the art of the Divine wisdom and from the order of the Divine goodness. And therefore it could be fitting to God to assume a nature created, mutable, corporeal, and subject to penalty, but it did not become Him to assume the evil of fault.

Reply Obj. 4: As Augustine replies (Ep. ad Volusian. cxxxvii): "The Christian doctrine nowhere holds that God was so joined to human flesh as either to desert or lose, or to transfer and as it were, contract within this frail body, the care of governing the universe. This is the thought of men unable to see anything but corporeal things . . . God is great not in mass, but in might. Hence the greatness of His might feels no straits in narrow surroundings. Nor, if the passing word of a man is heard at once by many, and wholly by each, is it incredible that the abiding Word of God should be everywhere at once?" Hence nothing unfitting arises from God becoming incarnate.

SECOND ARTICLE [III, Q. 1, Art. 2]

Whether It Was Necessary for the Restoration of the Human Race That the Word of God Should Become Incarnate?

Objection 1: It would seem that it was not necessary for the reparation of the human race that the Word of God should become incarnate. For since the Word of God is perfect God, as has been said (I, Q. 4, AA. 1, 2), no power was added to Him by the assumption of flesh. Therefore, if the incarnate Word of God restored human nature. He could also have restored it without assuming flesh.

Obj. 2: Further, for the restoration of human nature, which had fallen through sin, nothing more is required than that man should satisfy for sin. Now man can satisfy, as it would seem, for sin; for God cannot require from man more than man can do, and since He is more inclined to be merciful than to punish, as He lays the act of sin to man's charge, so He ought to credit him with the contrary act. Therefore it was not necessary for the restoration of human nature that the Word of God should become incarnate.

Obj. 3: Further, to revere God pertains especially to man's salvation; hence it is written (Mal. 1:6): "If, then, I be a father, where is my honor? and if I be a master, where is my fear?" But men revere God the more by considering Him as elevated above all, and far beyond man's senses, hence (Ps. 112:4) it is written: "The Lord is high above all nations, and His glory above the heavens"; and farther on: "Who is as the Lord our God?" which pertains to reverence. Therefore it would seem unfitting to man's salvation that God should be made like unto us by assuming flesh.

*On the contrary,* What frees the human race from perdition is necessary for the salvation of man. But the mystery of the Incarnation is such; according to John 3:16: "God so loved the world as to give His only-begotten Son, that whosoever believeth in Him may not perish, but may have life everlasting." Therefore it was necessary for man's salvation that God should become incarnate.

*I answer that,* A thing is said to be necessary for a certain end in two ways. First, when the end cannot be without it; as food is necessary for the preservation of human life. Secondly, when the end is attained better and more conveniently, as a horse is necessary for a journey. In the first way it was not necessary that God should become incarnate for the restoration of human nature. For God with His omnipotent power could have restored human nature in many other ways. But in the second way it was necessary that God should become incarnate for the restoration of human nature. Hence Augustine says (De Trin. xii, 10): "We shall also show that other ways were not wanting to God, to Whose power all things are equally subject; but that there was not a more fitting way of healing our misery."

Now this may be viewed with respect to our "furtherance in good." First, with regard to faith, which is made more certain by believing God Himself Who speaks; hence Augustine says (De Civ. Dei xi, 2): "In order that man might journey more trustfully toward the truth, the Truth itself, the Son of God, having assumed human nature, established and founded faith." Secondly, with regard to hope, which is thereby greatly strengthened; hence Augustine says (De Trin. xiii): "Nothing was so necessary for raising our hope as to show us how deeply God loved us. And what could afford us a stronger proof of this than that the Son of God should become a partner with us of human nature?" Thirdly, with regard to charity, which is greatly enkindled by this; hence Augustine says (De Catech. Rudib. iv): "What greater cause is there of the Lord's coming than to show God's love for us?" And he afterwards adds: "If we have been slow to love, at least let us hasten to love in return." Fourthly, with regard to well-doing, in which He set us an example; hence Augustine says in a sermon (xxii de Temp.): "Man who might be seen was not to be followed; but God was to be followed, Who could not be seen. And therefore God was made man, that He Who might be seen by man, and Whom man might follow, might be shown to man." Fifthly, with regard to the full participation of the Divinity, which is the true bliss of man and end of human life; and this is bestowed upon us by Christ's humanity; for Augustine says in a sermon (xiii de Temp.): "God was made man, that man might be made God."

So also was this useful for our withdrawal from evil. First, because man is taught by it not to prefer the devil to himself, nor to honor him who is the author of sin; hence Augustine says (De Trin. xiii, 17): "Since human nature is so united to God as to become one person, let not these proud spirits dare to prefer themselves to man, because they have no bodies." Secondly, because we are thereby taught how great is man's dignity, lest we should sully it with sin; hence Augustine says (De Vera Relig. xvi): "God has proved to us how high a place human nature holds amongst creatures, inasmuch as He appeared to men as a true man." And Pope Leo says in a sermon on the Nativity (xxi): "Learn, O Christian, thy worth; and being made a partner of the Divine nature, refuse to return by evil deeds to your former worthlessness." Thirdly, because, "in order to do away with man's presumption, the grace of God is commended in Jesus Christ, though no merits of ours went before," as Augustine says (De Trin. xiii, 17). Fourthly, because "man's pride, which is the greatest stumbling-block to our clinging to God, can be convinced and cured by humility so great," as Augustine says in the same place. Fifthly, in order to free man from the thraldom of sin, which, as Augustine says (De Trin. xiii, 13), "ought to be done in such a way that the devil should be overcome by the justice of the man Jesus Christ," and this was done by Christ satisfying for us. Now a mere man could not have satisfied for the whole human race, and God was not bound to satisfy; hence it behooved Jesus Christ to be both God and man. Hence Pope Leo says in the same sermon: "Weakness is assumed by strength, lowliness by majesty, mortality by eternity, in order that one and the same Mediator of God and men might die in one and rise in the other--for this was our fitting remedy. Unless He was God, He would not have brought a remedy; and unless He was man, He would not have set an example."

And there are very many other advantages which accrued, above man's apprehension.

Reply Obj. 1: This reason has to do with the first kind of necessity, without which we cannot attain to the end.

Reply Obj. 2: Satisfaction may be said to be sufficient in two ways--first, perfectly, inasmuch as it is condign, being adequate to make good the fault committed, and in this way the satisfaction of a mere man cannot be sufficient for sin, both because the whole of human nature has been corrupted by sin, whereas the goodness of any person or persons could not be made up adequately for the harm done to the whole of the nature; and also because a sin committed against God has a kind of infinity from the infinity of the Divine majesty, because the greater the person we offend, the more grievous the offense. Hence for condign satisfaction it was necessary that the act of the one satisfying should have an infinite efficiency, as being of God and man. Secondly, man's satisfaction may be termed sufficient, imperfectly--i.e. in the acceptation of him who is content with it, even though it is not condign, and in this way the satisfaction of a mere man is sufficient. And forasmuch as every imperfect presupposes some perfect thing, by which it is sustained, hence it is that satisfaction of every mere man has its efficiency from the satisfaction of Christ.

Reply Obj. 3: By taking flesh, God did not lessen His majesty; and in consequence did not lessen the reason for reverencing Him, which is increased by the increase of knowledge of Him. But, *on the contrary,* inasmuch as He wished to draw nigh to us by taking flesh, He greatly drew us to know Him.

THIRD ARTICLE [III, Q. 1, Art. 3]

Whether, If Man Had Not Sinned, God Would Have Become Incarnate?

Objection 1: It would seem that if man had not sinned, God would still have become incarnate. For the cause remaining, the effect also remains. But as Augustine says (De Trin. xiii, 17): "Many other things are to be considered in the Incarnation of Christ besides absolution from sin"; and these were discussed above (A. 2). Therefore if man had not sinned, God would have become incarnate.

Obj. 2: Further, it belongs to the omnipotence of the Divine power to perfect His works, and to manifest Himself by some infinite effect. But no mere creature can be called an infinite effect, since it is finite of its very essence. Now, seemingly, in the work of the Incarnation alone is an infinite effect of the Divine power manifested in a special manner by which power things infinitely distant are united, inasmuch as it has been brought about that man is God. And in this work especially the universe would seem to be perfected, inasmuch as the last creature--viz. man--is united to the first principle--viz. God. Therefore, even if man had not sinned, God would have become incarnate.

Obj. 3: Further, human nature has not been made more capable of grace by sin. But after sin it is capable of the grace of union, which is the greatest grace. Therefore, if man had not sinned, human nature would have been capable of this grace; nor would God have withheld from human nature any good it was capable of. Therefore, if man had not sinned, God would have become incarnate.

Obj. 4: Further, God's predestination is eternal. But it is said of Christ (Rom. 1:4): "Who was predestined the Son of God in power." Therefore, even before sin, it was necessary that the Son of God should become incarnate, in order to fulfil God's predestination.

Obj. 5: Further, the mystery of the Incarnation was revealed to the first man, as is plain from Gen. 2:23. "This now is bone of my bones," etc. which the Apostle says is "a great sacrament . . . in Christ and in the Church," as is plain from Eph. 5:32. But man could not be fore-conscious of his fall, for the same reason that the angels could not, as Augustine proves (Gen. ad lit. xi, 18). Therefore, even if man had not sinned, God would have become incarnate.

*On the contrary,* Augustine says (De Verb. Apost. viii, 2), expounding what is set down in Luke 19:10, "For the Son of Man is come to seek and to save that which was lost"; "Therefore, if man had not sinned, the Son of Man would not have come." And on 1 Tim. 1:15, "Christ Jesus came into this world to save sinners," a gloss says, "There was no cause of Christ's coming into the world, except to save sinners. Take away diseases, take away wounds, and there is no need of medicine."

*I answer that,* There are different opinions about this question. For some say that even if man had not sinned, the Son of Man would have become incarnate. Others assert the contrary, and seemingly our assent ought rather to be given to this opinion.

For such things as spring from God's will, and beyond the creature's due, can be made known to us only through being revealed in the Sacred Scripture, in which the Divine Will is made known to us. Hence, since everywhere in the Sacred Scripture the sin of the first man is assigned as the reason of the Incarnation, it is more in accordance with this to say that the work of the Incarnation was ordained by God as a remedy for sin; so that, had sin not existed, the Incarnation would not have been. And yet the power of God is not limited to this; even had sin not existed, God could have become incarnate.

Reply Obj. 1: All the other causes which are assigned in the preceding article have to do with a remedy for sin. For if man had not sinned, he would have been endowed with the light of Divine wisdom, and would have been perfected by God with the righteousness of justice in order to know and carry out everything needful. But because man, on deserting God, had stooped to corporeal things, it was necessary that God should take flesh, and by corporeal things should afford him the remedy of salvation. Hence, on John 1:14, "And the Word was made flesh," St. Augustine says (Tract. ii): "Flesh had blinded thee, flesh heals thee; for Christ came and overthrew the vices of the flesh."

Reply Obj. 2: The infinity of Divine power is shown in the mode of production of things from nothing. Again, it suffices for the perfection of the universe that the creature be ordained in a natural manner to God as to an end. But that a creature should be united to God in person exceeds the limits of the perfection of nature.

Reply Obj. 3: A double capability may be remarked in human nature: one, in respect of the order of natural power, and this is always fulfilled by God, Who apportions to each according to its natural capability; the other in respect to the order of the Divine power, which all creatures implicitly obey; and the capability we speak of pertains to this. But God does not fulfil all such capabilities, otherwise God could do only what He has done in creatures, and this is false, as stated above (I, Q. 105, A. 6). But there is no reason why human nature should not have been raised to something greater after sin. For God allows evils to happen in order to bring a greater good therefrom; hence it is written (Rom. 5:20): "Where sin abounded, grace did more abound." Hence, too, in the blessing of the Paschal candle, we say: "O happy fault, that merited such and so great a Redeemer!"

Reply Obj. 4: Predestination presupposes the foreknowledge of future things; and hence, as God predestines the salvation of anyone to be brought about by the prayers of others, so also He predestined the work of the Incarnation to be the remedy of human sin.

Reply Obj. 5: Nothing prevents an effect from being revealed to one to whom the cause is not revealed. Hence, the mystery of the Incarnation could be revealed to the first man without his being fore-conscious of his fall. For not everyone who knows the effect knows the cause.

FOURTH ARTICLE [III, Q. 1, Art. 4]

Whether God Became Incarnate in Order to Take Away Actual Sin, Rather Than to Take Away Original Sin?

Objection 1: It would seem that God became incarnate as a remedy for actual sins rather than for original sin. For the more grievous the sin, the more it runs counter to man's salvation, for which God became incarnate. But actual sin is more grievous than original sin; for the lightest punishment is due to original sin, as Augustine says (Contra Julian. v, 11). Therefore the Incarnation of Christ is chiefly directed to taking away actual sins.

Obj. 2: Further, pain of sense is not due to original

sin, but merely pain of loss, as has been shown (I-II, Q. 87, A. 5). But Christ came to suffer the pain of sense on the Cross in satisfaction for sins--and not the pain of loss, for He had no defect of either the beatific vision or fruition. Therefore He came in order to take away actual sin rather than original sin.

Obj. 3: Further, as Chrysostom says (De Compunctione Cordis ii, 3): "This must be the mind of the faithful servant, to account the benefits of his Lord, which have been bestowed on all alike, as though they were bestowed on himself alone. For as if speaking of himself alone, Paul writes to the Galatians 2:20: 'Christ . . . loved me and delivered Himself for me.'" But our individual sins are actual sins; for original sin is the common sin. Therefore we ought to have this conviction, so as to believe that He has come chiefly for actual sins.

*On the contrary,* It is written (John 1:29): "Behold the Lamb of God, behold Him Who taketh away the sins [Vulg.: 'sin'] of the world."

*I answer that,* It is certain that Christ came into this world not only to take away that sin which is handed on originally to posterity, but also in order to take away all sins subsequently added to it; not that all are taken away (and this is from men's fault, inasmuch as they do not adhere to Christ, according to John 3:19: "The light is come into the world, and men loved darkness rather than the light"), but because He offered what was sufficient for blotting out all sins. Hence it is written (Rom. 5:15-16): "But not as the offense, so also the gift . . . For judgment indeed was by one unto condemnation, but grace is of many offenses unto justification."

Moreover, the more grievous the sin, the more particularly did Christ come to blot it out. But "greater" is said in two ways: in one way "intensively," as a more intense whiteness is said to be greater, and in this way actual sin is greater than original sin; for it has more of the nature of voluntary, as has been shown (I-II, Q. 81, A. 1). In another way a thing is said to be greater "extensively," as whiteness on a greater superficies is said to be greater; and in this way original sin, whereby the whole human race is infected, is greater than any actual sin, which is proper to one person. And in this respect Christ came principally to take away original sin, inasmuch as "the good of the race is a more Divine thing than the good of an individual," as is said Ethic. i, 2.

Reply Obj. 1: This reason looks to the intensive greatness of sin.

Reply Obj. 2: In the future award the pain of sense will not be meted out to original sin. Yet the penalties, such as hunger, thirst, death, and the like, which we suffer sensibly in this life flow from original sin. And hence Christ, in order to satisfy fully for original sin, wished to suffer sensible pain, that He might consume death and the like in Himself.

Reply Obj. 3: Chrysostom says (De Compunctione Cordis ii, 6): "The Apostle used these words, not as if wishing to diminish Christ's gifts, ample as they are, and spreading throughout the whole world, but that he might account himself alone the occasion of them. For what does it matter that they are given to others, if what are given to you are as complete and perfect as if none of them were given to another than yourself?" And hence, although a man ought to account Christ's gifts as given to himself, yet he ought not to consider them not to be given to others. And thus we do not exclude that He came to wipe away the sin of the whole nature rather than the sin of one person. But the sin of the nature is as perfectly healed in each one as if it were healed in him alone. Hence, on account of the union of charity, what is vouchsafed to all ought to be accounted his own by each one.

FIFTH ARTICLE [III, Q. 1, Art. 5]

Whether It Was Fitting That God Should Become Incarnate in the Beginning of the Human Race?

Objection 1: It would seem that it was fitting that God should become incarnate in the beginning of the human race. For the work of the Incarnation sprang from the immensity of Divine charity, according to Eph. 2:4, 5: "But God (Who is rich in mercy), for His exceeding charity wherewith He loved us . . . even when we were dead in sins, hath quickened us together in Christ." But charity does not tarry in bringing assistance to a friend who is suffering need, according to Prov. 3:28: "Say not to thy friend: Go, and come again, and tomorrow I will give to thee, when thou canst give at present." Therefore God ought not to have put off the work of the Incarnation, but ought thereby to have brought relief to the human race from the beginning.

Obj. 2: Further, it is written (1 Tim. 1:15): "Christ Jesus came into this world to save sinners." But more would have been saved had God become incarnate at the beginning of the human race; for in the various centuries very many, through not knowing God, perished in their sin. Therefore it was fitting that God should become incarnate at the beginning of the human race.

Obj. 3: Further, the work of grace is not less orderly than the work of nature. But nature takes its rise with the more perfect, as Boethius says (De Consol. iii). Therefore the work of Christ ought to have been perfect from the beginning. But in the work of the Incarnation we see the perfection of grace, according to John 1:14: "The Word was made flesh"; and afterwards it is added: "Full of grace and truth." Therefore Christ ought to have become incarnate at the beginning of the human race.

*On the contrary,* It is written (Gal. 4:4): "But when the fulness of the time was come, God sent His Son, made of a woman, made under the law": upon which a gloss says that "the fulness of the time is when it was decreed by God the Father to send His Son." But God decreed everything by His wisdom. Therefore God became incarnate at the most fitting time; and it was not fitting that God should become incarnate at the beginning of the human race.

*I answer that,* Since the work of the Incarnation is principally ordained to the restoration of the human race by blotting out sin, it is manifest that it was not fitting for God to become incarnate at the beginning of the human race before sin. For medicine is given only to the sick. Hence our Lord Himself says (Matt. 9:12, 13): "They that are in health need not a physician, but they that are ill . . . For I am not come to call the just, but sinners."

Nor was it fitting that God should become incarnate immediately after sin. First, on account of the manner of man's sin, which had come of pride; hence man was to be liberated in such a manner that he might be humbled, and see how he stood in need of a deliverer. Hence on the words in Gal. 3:19, "Being ordained by angels in the hand of a mediator," a gloss says: "With great wisdom was it so ordered that the Son of Man should not be sent immediately after man's fall. For first of all God left man under the natural law, with the freedom of his will, in order that he might know his natural strength; and when he failed in it, he received the law; whereupon, by the fault, not of the law, but of his nature, the disease gained strength; so that having recognized his infirmity he might cry out for a physician, and beseech the aid of grace."

Secondly, on account of the order of furtherance in good, whereby we proceed from imperfection to perfection. Hence the Apostle says (1 Cor. 15:46, 47): "Yet that was not first which is spiritual, but that which is natural; afterwards that which is spiritual . . . The first man was of the earth, earthy; the second man from heaven, heavenly."

Thirdly, on account of the dignity of the incarnate Word, for on the words (Gal. 4:4), "But when the fulness of the time was come," a gloss says: "The greater the judge who was coming, the more numerous was the band of heralds who ought to have preceded him."

Fourthly, lest the fervor of faith should cool by the length of time, for the charity of many will grow cold at the end of the world. Hence (Luke 18:8) it is written: "But yet the Son of Man, when He cometh, shall He find think you, faith on earth?"

Reply Obj. 1: Charity does not put off bringing assistance to a friend: always bearing in mind the circumstances as well as the state of the persons. For if the physician were to give the medicine at the very outset of the ailment, it would do less good, and would hurt rather than benefit. And hence the Lord did not bestow upon the human race the remedy of the Incarnation in the beginning, lest they should despise it through pride, if they did not already recognize their disease.

Reply Obj. 2: Augustine replies to this (De Sex Quest. Pagan., Ep. cii), saying (Q. 2) that "Christ wished to appear to man and to have His doctrine preached to them when and where He knew those were who would believe in Him. But in such times and places as His Gospel was not preached He foresaw that not all, indeed, but many would so bear themselves towards His preaching as not to believe in His corporeal presence, even were He to raise the dead." But the same Augustine, taking exception to this reply in his book (De Perseverantia ix), says: "How can we say the inhabitants of Tyre and Sidon would not believe when such great wonders were wrought in their midst, or would not have believed had they been wrought, when God Himself bears witness that they would have done penance with great humility if these signs of Divine power had been wrought in their midst?" And he adds in answer (De Perseverantia xi): "Hence, as the Apostle says (Rom. 9:16), 'it is not of him that willeth nor of him that runneth, but of God that showeth mercy'; Who (succors whom He will of) those who, as He foresaw, would believe in His miracles if wrought amongst them, (while others) He succors not, having judged them in His predestination secretly yet justly. Therefore let us unshrinkingly believe His mercy to be with those who are set free, and His truth with those who are condemned." [*The words in brackets are not in the text of St. Augustine].

Reply Obj. 3: Perfection is prior to imperfection, both in time and nature, in things that are different (for what brings others to perfection must itself be perfect); but in one and the same, imperfection is prior in time though posterior in nature. And thus the eternal perfection of God precedes in duration the imperfection of human nature; but the latter's ultimate perfection in union with God follows.

SIXTH ARTICLE [III, Q. 1, Art. 6]

Whether the Incarnation Ought to Have Been Put Off Till the End of the World?

Objection 1: It would seem that the work of the Incarnation ought to have been put off till the end of the world. For it is written (Ps. 91:11): "My old age in plentiful mercy"--i.e. "in the last days," as a gloss says. But the time of the Incarnation is especially the time of mercy, according to Ps. 101:14: "For it is time to have mercy on it." Therefore the Incarnation ought to have been put off till the end of the world.

Obj. 2: Further, as has been said (A. 5, ad 3), in the same subject, perfection is subsequent in time to imperfection. Therefore, what is most perfect ought to be the very last in time. But the highest perfection of human nature is in the union with the Word, because "in Christ it hath pleased the Father that all the fulness of the Godhead should dwell," as the Apostle says (Col. 1:19, and 2:9). Therefore the Incarnation ought to have been put off till the end of the world.

Obj. 3: Further, what can be done by one ought not to be done by two. But the one coming of Christ at the end of the world was sufficient for the salvation of human nature. Therefore it was not necessary for Him to come beforehand in His Incarnation; and hence the Incarnation ought to have been put off till the end of the world.

*On the contrary,* It is written (Hab. 3:2): "In the midst of the years Thou shalt make it known." Therefore the mystery of the Incarnation which was made known to the world ought not to have been put off till the end of the world.

*I answer that,* As it was not fitting that God should become incarnate at the beginning of the world, so also it was not fitting that the Incarnation should be put off till the end of the world. And this is shown first from the union of the Divine and human nature. For, as it has been said (A. 5, ad 3), perfection precedes imperfection in time in one way, and contrariwise in another way imperfection precedes perfection. For in that which is made perfect from being imperfect, imperfection precedes perfection in time, whereas in that which is the efficient cause of perfection, perfection precedes imperfection in time. Now in the work of the Incarnation both concur; for by the Incarnation human nature is raised to its highest perfection; and in this way it was not becoming that the Incarnation should take place at the beginning of the human race. And the Word incarnate is the efficient cause of the perfection of human nature, according to John 1:16: "Of His fulness we have all received"; and hence the work of the Incarnation ought not to have been put off till the end of the world. But the perfection of glory to which human nature is to be finally raised by the Word Incarnate will be at the end of the world.

Secondly, from the effect of man's salvation; for, as is said Qq. Vet. et Nov. Test., qu. 83, "it is in the power of the Giver to have pity when, or as much as, He wills. Hence He came when He knew it was fitting to succor, and when His boons would be welcome. For when by the feebleness of the human race men's knowledge of God began to grow dim and their morals lax, He was pleased to choose Abraham as a standard of the restored knowledge of God and of holy living; and later on when reverence grew weaker, He gave the law to Moses in writing; and because the gentiles despised it and would not take it upon themselves, and they who received it would not keep it, being touched with pity, God sent His Son, to grant to all remission of their sin and to offer them, justified, to God the Father." But if this remedy had been put off till the end of the world, all knowledge and reverence of God and all uprightness of morals would have been swept away from the earth.

Thirdly, this appears fitting to the manifestation of the Divine power, which has saved men in several ways--not only by faith in some future thing, but also by faith in something present and past.

Reply Obj. 1: This gloss has in view the mercy of God, which leads us to glory. Nevertheless, if it is referred to the mercy shown the human race by the Incarnation of Christ, we must reflect that, as Augustine says (Retract. i), the time of the Incarnation may be compared to the youth of the human race, "on account of the strength and fervor of faith, which works by charity"; and to old age--i.e. the sixth age--on account of the number of centuries, for Christ came in the sixth age. And although youth and old age cannot be together in a body, yet they can be together in a soul, the former on account of quickness, the latter on account of gravity. And hence Augustine says elsewhere (Qq. lxxxiii, qu. 44) that "it was not becoming that the Master by Whose imitation the human race was to be formed to the highest virtue should come from heaven, save in the time of youth." But in another work (De Gen. cont. Manich. i, 23) he says: that Christ came in the sixth age--i.e. in the old age--of the human race.

Reply Obj. 2: The work of the Incarnation is to be viewed not as merely the terminus of a movement from imperfection to perfection, but also as a principle of perfection to human nature, as has been said.

Reply Obj. 3: As Chrysostom says on John 3:11, "For God sent not His Son into the world to judge the world" (Hom. xxviii): "There are two comings of Christ: the first, for the remission of sins; the second, to judge the world. For if He had not done so, all would have perished together, since all have sinned and need the glory of God." Hence it is plain that He ought not to have put off the coming in mercy till the end of the world.

## QUESTION 2

OF THE MODE OF UNION OF THE WORD INCARNATE (In Twelve Articles)

Now we must consider the mode of union of the Incarnate Word; and, first, the union itself; secondly, the Person assuming; thirdly, the nature assumed.

Under the first head there are twelve points of inquiry:

(1) Whether the union of the Word Incarnate took place in the nature?

(2) Whether it took place in the Person?

(3) Whether it took place in the suppositum or hypostasis?

(4) Whether the Person or hypostasis of Christ is composite after the Incarnation?

(5) Whether any union of body and soul took place in Christ?

(6) Whether the human nature was united to the Word accidentally?

(7) Whether the union itself is something created?

(8) Whether it is the same as assumption?

(9) Whether the union of the two natures is the greatest union?

(10) Whether the union of the two natures in Christ was brought about by grace?

(11) Whether any merits preceded it?

(12) Whether the grace of union was natural to the man Christ?

FIRST ARTICLE [III, Q. 2, Art. 1]

Whether the Union of the Incarnate Word Took Place in the Nature?

Objection 1: It would seem that the Union of the Word Incarnate took place in the nature. For Cyril says (he is quoted in the acts of the Council of Chalcedon, part ii, act. 1): "We must understand not two natures, but one incarnate nature of the Word of God"; and this could not be unless the union took place in the nature. Therefore the union of the Word Incarnate took place in the nature.

Obj. 2: Further, Athanasius says that, as the rational soul and the flesh together form the human nature, so God and man together form a certain one nature; therefore the union took place in the nature.

Obj. 3: Further, of two natures one is not denominated by the other unless they are to some extent mutually transmuted. But the Divine and human natures in Christ are denominated one by the other; for Cyril says (quoted in the acts of the Council of Chalcedon, part ii, act. 1) that the Divine nature "is incarnate"; and Gregory Nazianzen says (Ep. i ad Cledon.) that the human nature is "deified," as appears from Damascene (De Fide Orth. iii, 6, 11). Therefore from two natures one seems to have resulted.

*On the contrary,* It is said in the declaration of the Council of Chalcedon: "We confess that in these latter times the only-begotten Son of God appeared in two natures, without confusion, without change, without division, without separation--the distinction of natures not having been taken away by the union." Therefore the union did not take place in the nature.

*I answer that,* To make this question clear we must consider what is "nature." Now it is to be observed that the word "nature" comes from nativity. Hence this word was used first of all to signify the begetting of living beings, which is called "birth" or "sprouting forth," the word "natura" meaning, as it were, "nascitura." Afterwards this word "nature" was taken to signify the principle of this begetting; and because in living things the principle of generation is an intrinsic principle, this word "nature" was further employed to signify any intrinsic principle of motion: thus the Philosopher says (Phys. ii) that "nature is the principle of motion in that in which it is essentially and not accidentally." Now this principle is either form or matter. Hence sometimes form is called nature, and sometimes matter. And because the end of natural generation, in that which is generated, is the essence of the species, which the definition signifies, this essence of the species is called the "nature." And thus Boethius defines nature (De Duab. Nat.): "Nature is what informs a thing with its specific difference, "--i.e. which perfects the specific definition. But we are now speaking of nature as it signifies the essence, or the "what-it-is," or the quiddity of the species.

Now, if we take nature in this way, it is impossible that the union of the Incarnate Word took place in the nature. For one thing is made of two or more in three ways. First, from two complete things which remain in their perfection. This can only happen to those whose form is composition, order, or figure, as a heap is made up of many stones brought together without any order, but solely with juxtaposition; and a house is made of stones and beams arranged in order, and fashioned to a figure. And in this way some said the union was by manner of confusion (which is without order) or by manner of commensuration (which is with order). But this cannot be. First, because neither composition nor order nor figure is a substantial form, but accidental; and hence it would follow that the union of the Incarnation was not essential, but accidental, which will be disproved later on (A. 6). Secondly, because thereby we should not have an absolute unity, but relative only, for there remain several things actually. Thirdly, because the form of such is not a nature, but an art, as the form of a house; and thus one nature would not be constituted in Christ, as they wish.

Secondly, one thing is made up of several things, perfect but changed, as a mixture is made up of its elements; and in this way some have said that the union of the Incarnation was brought about by manner of combination. But this cannot be. First, because the Divine Nature is altogether immutable, as has been said (I, Q. 9, AA. 1, 2), hence neither can it be changed into something else, since it is incorruptible; nor can anything else be changed into it, for it cannot be generated. Secondly, because what is mixed is of the same species with none of the elements; for flesh differs in species from any of its elements. And thus Christ would be of the same nature neither with His Father nor with His Mother. Thirdly, because there can be no mingling of things widely apart; for the species of one of them is absorbed, e.g. if we were to put a drop of water in a flagon of wine. And hence, since the Divine Nature infinitely exceeds the human nature, there could be no mixture, but the Divine Nature alone would remain.

Thirdly, a thing is made up of things not mixed nor changed, but imperfect; as man is made up of soul and body, and likewise of divers members. But this cannot be said of the mystery of the Incarnation. First, because each nature, i.e. the Divine and the human, has its specific perfection. Secondly, because the Divine and human natures cannot constitute anything after the manner of quantitative parts, as the members make up the body; for the Divine Nature is incorporeal; nor after the manner of form and matter, for the Divine Nature cannot be the form of anything, especially of anything corporeal, since it would follow that the species resulting therefrom would be communicable to several, and thus there would be several Christs. Thirdly, because Christ would exist neither in human nature nor in the Divine Nature: since any difference varies the species, as unity varies number, as is said (Metaph. viii, text. 10).

Reply Obj. 1: This authority of Cyril is expounded in the Fifth Synod (i.e. Constantinople II, coll. viii, can. 8) thus: "If anyone proclaiming one nature of the Word of God to be incarnate does not receive it as the Fathers taught, viz. that from the Divine and human natures (a union in subsistence having taken place) one Christ results, but endeavors from these words to introduce one nature or substance of the Divinity and flesh of Christ, let such a one be anathema." Hence the sense is not that from two natures one results; but that the Nature of the Word of God united flesh to Itself in Person.

Reply Obj. 2: From the soul and body a double unity, viz. of nature and person--results in each individual--of nature inasmuch as the soul is united to the body, and formally perfects it, so that one nature springs from the two as from act and potentiality or from matter and form. But the comparison is not in this sense, for the Divine Nature cannot be the form of a body, as was proved (I, Q. 3, A. 8). Unity of person results from them, however, inasmuch as there is an individual subsisting in flesh and soul; and herein lies the likeness, for the one Christ subsists in the Divine and human natures.

Reply Obj. 3: As Damascene says (De Fide Orth. iii, 6, 11), the Divine Nature is said to be incarnate because It is united to flesh personally, and not that It is changed into flesh. So likewise the flesh is said to be deified, as he also says (De Fide Orth. 15, 17), not by change, but by union with the Word, its natural properties still remaining, and hence it may be considered as deified, inasmuch as it becomes the flesh of the Word of God, but not that it becomes God.

SECOND ARTICLE [III, Q. 2, Art. 2]

Whether the Union of the Incarnate Word Took Place in the Person?

Objection 1: It would seem that the union of the Incarnate Word did not take place in the person. For the Person of God is not distinct from His Nature, as we said (I, Q. 39, A. 1). If, therefore, the union did not take place in the nature, it follows that it did not take place in the person.

Obj. 2: Further, Christ's human nature has no less dignity than ours. But personality belongs to dignity, as was stated above (I, Q. 29, A. 3, ad 2). Hence, since our human nature has its proper personality, much more reason was there that Christ's should have its proper personality.

Obj. 3: Further, as Boethius says (De Duab. Nat.), a person is an individual substance of rational nature. But the Word of God assumed an individual human nature, for "universal human nature does not exist of itself, but is the object of pure thought," as Damascene says (De Fide Orth. iii, 11). Therefore the human nature of Christ has its personality. Hence it does not seem that the union took place in the person.

*On the contrary,* We read in the Synod of Chalcedon (Part ii, act. 5): "We confess that our Lord Jesus Christ is not parted or divided into two persons, but is one and the same only-Begotten Son and Word of God." Therefore the union took place in the person.

*I answer that,* Person has a different meaning from "nature." For nature, as has been said (A. 1), designates the specific essence which is signified by the definition. And if nothing was found to be added to what belongs to the notion of the species, there would be no need to distinguish the nature from the suppositum of the nature (which is the individual subsisting in this nature), because every individual subsisting in a nature would be altogether one with its nature. Now in certain subsisting things we happen to find what does not belong to the notion of the species, viz. accidents and individuating principles, which appears chiefly in such as are composed of matter and form. Hence in such as these the nature and the suppositum really differ; not indeed as if they were wholly separate, but because the suppositum includes the nature, and in addition certain other things outside the notion of the species. Hence the suppositum is taken to be a whole which has the nature as its formal part to perfect it; and consequently in such as are composed of matter and form the nature is not predicated of the suppositum, for we do not say that this man is his manhood. But if there is a thing in which there is nothing outside the species or its nature (as in God), the suppositum and the nature are not really distinct in it, but only in our way of thinking, inasmuch it is called "nature" as it is an essence, and a suppositum as it is subsisting. And what is said of a suppositum is to be applied to a person in rational or intellectual creatures; for a person is nothing else than "an individual substance of rational nature," according to Boethius. Therefore, whatever adheres to a person is united to it in person, whether it belongs to its nature or not. Hence, if the human nature is not united to God the Word in person, it is nowise united to Him; and thus belief in the Incarnation is altogether done away with, and Christian faith wholly overturned. Therefore, inasmuch as the Word has a human nature united to Him, which does not belong to His Divine Nature, it follows that the union took place in the Person of the Word, and not in the nature.

Reply Obj. 1: Although in God Nature and Person are not really distinct, yet they have distinct meanings, as was said above, inasmuch as person signifies after the manner of something subsisting. And because human nature is united to the Word, so that the Word subsists in it, and not so that His Nature receives therefrom any addition or change, it follows that the union of human nature to the Word of God took place in the person, and not in the nature.

Reply Obj. 2: Personality pertains of necessity to the dignity of a thing, and to its perfection so far as it pertains to the dignity and perfection of that thing to exist by itself (which is understood by the word "person"). Now it is a greater dignity to exist in something nobler than oneself than to exist by oneself. Hence the human nature of Christ has a greater dignity than ours, from this very fact that in us, being existent by itself, it has its own personality, but in Christ it exists in the Person of the Word. Thus to perfect the species belongs to the dignity of a form, yet the sensitive part in man, on account of its union with the nobler form which perfects the species, is more noble than in brutes, where it is itself the form which perfects.

Reply Obj. 3: The Word of God "did not assume human nature in general, but in atomo "--that is, in an individual--as Damascene says (De Fide Orth. iii, 11) otherwise every man would be the Word of God, even as Christ was. Yet we must bear in mind that not every individual in the genus of substance, even in rational nature, is a person, but that alone which exists by itself, and not that which exists in some more perfect thing. Hence the hand of Socrates, although it is a kind of individual, is not a person, because it does not exist by itself, but in something more perfect, viz. in the whole. And hence, too, this is signified by a "person" being defined as "an individual substance," for the hand is not a complete substance, but part of a substance. Therefore, although this human nature is a kind of individual in the genus of substance, it has not its own personality, because it does not exist separately, but in something more perfect, viz. in the Person of the Word. Therefore the union took place in the person.

THIRD ARTICLE [III, Q. 2, Art. 3]

Whether the Union of the Word Incarnate Took Place in the Suppositum or Hypostasis?

Objection 1: It would seem that the union of the Word Incarnate did not take place in the suppositum or hypostasis. For Augustine says (Enchiridion xxxv, xxxviii): "Both the Divine and human substance are one Son of God, but they are one thing ( aliud ) by reason of the Word and another thing ( aliud ) by reason of the man." And Pope Leo says in his letter to Flavian (Ep. xxviii): "One of these is glorious with miracles, the other succumbs under injuries." But "one" ( aliud ) and "the other" ( aliud ) differ in suppositum. Therefore the union of the Word Incarnate did not take place in the suppositum.

Obj. 2: Further, hypostasis is nothing more than a "particular substance," as Boethius says (De Duab. Nat.). But it is plain that in Christ there is another particular substance beyond the hypostasis of the Word, viz. the body and the soul and the resultant of these. Therefore there is another hypostasis in Him besides the hypostasis of the Word.

Obj. 3: Further, the hypostasis of the Word is not included in any genus or species, as is plain from the First Part (Q. 3, A. 5). But Christ, inasmuch as He is made man, is contained under the species of man; for Dionysius says (Div. Nom. 1): "Within the limits of our nature He came, Who far surpasses the whole order of nature supersubstantially." Now nothing is contained under the human species unless it be a hypostasis of the human species. Therefore in Christ there is another hypostasis besides the hypostasis of the Word of God; and hence the same conclusion follows as above.

*On the contrary,* Damascene says (De Fide Orth. iii, 3, 4, 5): "In our Lord Jesus Christ we acknowledge two natures and one hypostasis."

*I answer that,* Some who did not know the relation of hypostasis to person, although granting that there is but one person in Christ, held, nevertheless, that there is one hypostasis of God and another of man, and hence that the union took place in the person and not in the hypostasis. Now this, for three reasons, is clearly erroneous. First, because person only adds to hypostasis a determinate nature, viz. rational, according to what Boethius says (De Duab. Nat.), "a person is an individual substance of rational nature"; and hence it is the same to attribute to the human nature in Christ a proper hypostasis and a proper person. And the holy Fathers, seeing this, condemned both in the Fifth Council held at Constantinople, saying: "If anyone seeks to introduce into the mystery of the Incarnation two subsistences or two persons, let him be anathema. For by the incarnation of one of the Holy Trinity, God the Word, the Holy Trinity received no augment of person or subsistence." Now "subsistence" is the same as the subsisting thing, which is proper to hypostasis, as is plain from Boethius (De Duab. Nat.). Secondly, because if it is granted that person adds to hypostasis something in which the union can take place, this something is nothing else than a property pertaining to dignity; according as it is said by some that a person is a "hypostasis distinguished by a property pertaining to dignity." If, therefore, the union took place in the person and not in the hypostasis, it follows that the union only took place in regard to some dignity. And this is what Cyril, with the approval of the Council of Ephesus (part iii, can. 3), condemned in these terms: "If anyone after the uniting divides the subsistences in the one Christ, only joining them in a union of dignity or authority or power, and not rather in a concourse of natural union, let him be anathema." Thirdly, because to the hypostasis alone are attributed the operations and the natural properties, and whatever belongs to the nature in the concrete; for we say that this man reasons, and is risible, and is a rational animal. So likewise this man is said to be a suppositum, because he underlies ( supponitur ) whatever belongs to man and receives its predication. Therefore, if there is any hypostasis in Christ besides the hypostasis of the Word, it follows that whatever pertains to man is verified of some other than the Word, e.g. that He was born of a Virgin, suffered, was crucified, was buried. And this, too, was condemned with the approval of the Council of Ephesus (part iii, can. 4) in these words: "If anyone ascribes to two persons or subsistences such words as are in the evangelical and apostolic Scriptures, or have been said of Christ by the saints, or by Himself of Himself, and, moreover, applies some of them to the man, taken as distinct from the Word of God, and some of them (as if they could be used of God alone) only to the Word of God the Father, let him be anathema." Therefore it is plainly a heresy condemned long since by the Church to say that in Christ there are two hypostases, or two supposita, or that the union did not take place in the hypostasis or suppositum. Hence in the same Synod (can. 2) it is said: "If anyone does not confess that the Word was united to flesh in subsistence, and that Christ with His flesh is both--to wit, God and man--let him be anathema."

Reply Obj. 1: As accidental difference makes a thing "other" ( alterum ), so essential difference makes "another thing" ( aliud ). Now it is plain that the "otherness" which springs from accidental difference may pertain to the same hypostasis or suppositum in created things, since the same thing numerically can underlie different accidents. But it does not happen in created things that the same numerically can subsist in divers essences or natures. Hence just as when we speak of "otherness" in regard to creatures we do not signify diversity of suppositum, but only diversity of accidental forms, so likewise when Christ is said to be one thing or another thing, we do not imply diversity of suppositum or hypostasis, but diversity of nature. Hence Gregory Nazianzen says in a letter to Chelidonius (Ep. ci): "In the Saviour we may find one thing and another, yet He is not one person and another. And I say 'one thing and another'; whereas, *on the contrary,* in the Trinity we say one Person and another (so as not to confuse the subsistences), but not one thing and another."

Reply Obj. 2: Hypostasis signifies a particular substance, not in every way, but as it is in its complement. Yet as it is in union with something more complete, it is not said to be a hypostasis, as a hand or a foot. So likewise the human nature in Christ, although it is a particular substance, nevertheless cannot be called a hypostasis or suppositum, seeing that it is in union with a completed thing, viz. the whole Christ, as He is God and man. But the complete being with which it concurs is said to be a hypostasis or suppositum.

Reply Obj. 3: In created things a singular thing is placed in a genus or species, not on account of what belongs to its individuation, but on account of its nature, which springs from its form, and in composite things individuation is taken more from matter. Hence we say that Christ is in the human species by reason of the nature assumed, and not by reason of the hypostasis.

FOURTH ARTICLE [III, Q. 2, Art. 4]

Whether After the Incarnation the Person or Hypostasis of Christ Is Composite?

Objection 1: It would seem that the Person of Christ is not composite. For the Person of Christ is naught else than the Person or hypostasis of the Word, as appears from what has been said (A. 2). But in the Word, Person and Nature do not differ, as appears from First Part (Q. 39, A. 1). Therefore since the Nature of the Word is simple, as was shown above (I, Q. 3, A. 7), it is impossible that the Person of Christ be composite.

Obj. 2: Further, all composition requires parts. But the Divine Nature is incompatible with the notion of a part, for every part implicates the notion of imperfection. Therefore it is impossible that the Person of Christ be composed of two natures.

Obj. 3: Further, what is composed of others would seem to be homogeneous with them, as from bodies only a body can be composed. Therefore if there is anything in Christ composed of the two natures, it follows that this will not be a person but a nature; and hence the union in Christ will take place in the nature, which is contrary to A. 2.

*On the contrary,* Damascene says (De Fide Orth. iii, 3, 4, 5), "In the Lord Jesus Christ we acknowledge two natures, but one hypostasis composed from both."

*I answer that,* The Person or hypostasis of Christ may be viewed in two ways. First as it is in itself, and thus it is altogether simple, even as the Nature of the Word. Secondly, in the aspect of person or hypostasis to which it belongs to subsist in a nature; and thus the Person of Christ subsists in two natures. Hence though there is one subsisting being in Him, yet there are different aspects of subsistence, and hence He is said to be a composite person, insomuch as one being subsists in two.

And thereby the solution to the first is clear.

Reply Obj. 2: This composition of a person from natures is not so called on account of parts, but by reason of number, even as that in which two things concur may be said to be composed of them.

Reply Obj. 3: It is not verified in every composition, that the thing composed is homogeneous with its component parts, but only in the parts of a continuous thing; for the continuous is composed solely of continuous [parts]. But an animal is composed of soul and body, and neither of these is an animal.

FIFTH ARTICLE [III, Q. 2, Art. 5]

Whether in Christ There Is Any Union of Soul and Body?

Objection 1: It would seem that in Christ there was no union of soul and body. For from the union of soul and body in us a person or a human hypostasis is caused. Hence if the soul and body were united in Christ, it follows that a hypostasis resulted from their union. But this was not the hypostasis of God the Word, for It is eternal. Therefore in Christ there would be a person or hypostasis besides the hypostasis of the Word, which is contrary to AA. 2, 3.

Obj. 2: Further, from the union of soul and body results the nature of the human species. But Damascene says (De Fide Orth. iii, 3), that "we must not conceive a common species in the Lord Jesus Christ." Therefore there was no union of soul and body in Him.

Obj. 3: Further, the soul is united to the body for the sole purpose of quickening it. But the body of Christ could be quickened by the Word of God Himself, seeing He is the fount and principle of life. Therefore in Christ there was no union of soul and body.

*On the contrary,* The body is not said to be animated save from its union with the soul. Now the body of Christ is said to be animated, as the Church chants: "Taking an animate body, He deigned to be born of a Virgin" [*Feast of the Circumcision, Ant. ii, Lauds]. Therefore in Christ there was a union of soul and body.

*I answer that,* Christ is called a man univocally with other men, as being of the same species, according to the Apostle (Phil. 2:7), "being made in the likeness of a man." Now it belongs essentially to the human species that the soul be united to the body, for the form does not constitute the species, except inasmuch as it becomes the act of matter, and this is the terminus of generation through which nature intends the species. Hence it must be said that in Christ the soul was united to the body; and the contrary is heretical, since it destroys the truth of Christ's humanity.

Reply Obj. 1: This would seem to be the reason which was of weight with such as denied the union of the soul and body in Christ, viz. lest they should thereby be forced to admit a second person or hypostasis in Christ, since they saw that the union of soul and body in mere men resulted in a person. But this happens in mere men because the soul and body are so united in them as to exist by themselves. But in Christ they are united together, so as to be united to something higher, which subsists in the nature composed of them. And hence from the union of the soul and body in Christ a new hypostasis or person does not result, but what is composed of them is united to the already existing hypostasis or Person. Nor does it therefore follow that the union of the soul and body in Christ is of less effect than in us, for its union with something nobler does not lessen but increases its virtue and worth; just as the sensitive soul in animals constitutes the species, as being considered the ultimate form, yet it does not do so in man, although it is of greater effect and dignity, and this because of its union with a further and nobler perfection, viz. the rational soul, as has been said above (A. 2, ad 2).

Reply Obj. 2: This saying of Damascene may be taken in two ways: First, as referring to human nature, which, as it is in one individual alone, has not the nature of a common species, but only inasmuch as either it is abstracted from every individual, and considered in itself by the mind, or according as it is in all individuals. Now the Son of God did not assume human nature as it exists in the pure thought of the intellect, since in this way He would not have assumed human nature in reality, unless it be said that human nature is a separate idea, just as the Platonists conceived of man without matter. But in this way the Son of God would not have assumed flesh, contrary to what is written (Luke 24:39), "A spirit hath not flesh and bones as you see Me to have." Neither can it be said that the Son of God assumed human nature as it is in all the individuals of the same species, otherwise He would have assumed all men. Therefore it remains, as Damascene says further on (De Fide Orth. iii, 11) that He assumed human nature in atomo, i.e. in an individual; not, indeed, in another individual which is a suppositum or a person of that nature, but in the Person of the Son of God.

Secondly, this saying of Damascene may be taken not as referring to human nature, as if from the union of soul and body one common nature (viz. human) did not result, but as referring to the union of the two natures Divine and human: which do not combine so as to form a third something that becomes a common nature, for in this way it would become predicable of many, and this is what he is aiming at, since he adds: "For there was not generated, neither will there ever be generated, another Christ, Who from the Godhead and manhood, and in the Godhead and manhood, is perfect God and perfect man."

Reply Obj. 3: There are two principles of corporeal life: one the effective principle, and in this way the Word of God is the principle of all life; the other, the formal principle of life, for since "in living things to be is to live," as the Philosopher says (De Anima ii, 37), just as everything is formally by its form, so likewise the body lives by the soul: in this way a body could not live by the Word, Which cannot be the form of a body.

SIXTH ARTICLE [III, Q. 2, Art. 6]

Whether the Human Nature Was United to the Word of God Accidentally?

Objection 1: It would seem that the human nature was united to the Word of God accidentally. For the Apostle says (Phil. 2:7) of the Son of God, that He was "in habit found as a man." But habit is accidentally associated with that to which it pertains, whether habit be taken for one of the ten predicaments or as a species of quality. Therefore human nature is accidentally united to the Son of God.

Obj. 2: Further, whatever comes to a thing that is complete in being comes to it accidentally, for an accident is said to be what can come or go without the subject being corrupted. But human nature came to Christ in time, Who had perfect being from eternity. Therefore it came to Him accidentally.

Obj. 3: Further, whatever does not pertain to the nature or the essence of a thing is its accident, for whatever is, is either a substance or an accident. But human nature does not pertain to the Divine Essence or Nature of the Son of God, for the union did not take place in the nature, as was said above (A. 1). Hence the human nature must have accrued accidentally to the Son of God.

Obj. 4: Further, an instrument accrues accidentally. But the human nature was the instrument of the Godhead in Christ, for Damascene says (De Fide Orth. iii, 15), that "the flesh of Christ is the instrument of the Godhead." Therefore it seems that the human nature was united to the Son of God accidentally.

*On the contrary,* Whatever is predicated accidentally, predicates, not substance, but quantity, or quality, or some other mode of being. If therefore the human nature accrues accidentally, when we say Christ is man, we do not predicate substance, but quality or quantity, or some other mode of being, which is contrary to the Decretal of Pope Alexander III, who says (Conc. Later. iii): "Since Christ is perfect God and perfect man, what foolhardiness have some to dare to affirm that Christ as man is not a substance?"

*I answer that,* In evidence of this question we must know that two heresies have arisen with regard to the mystery of the union of the two natures in Christ. The first confused the natures, as Eutyches and Dioscorus, who held that from the two natures one nature resulted, so that they confessed Christ to be "from" two natures (which were distinct before the union), but not "in" two natures (the distinction of nature coming to an end after the union). The second was the heresy of Nestorius and Theodore of Mopsuestia, who separated the persons. For they held the Person of the Son of God to be distinct from the Person of the Son of man, and said these were mutually united: first, "by indwelling," inasmuch as the Word of God dwelt in the man, as in a temple; secondly, "by unity of intention," inasmuch as the will of the man was always in agreement with the will of the Word of God; thirdly, "by operation," inasmuch as they said the man was the instrument of the Word of God; fourthly, "by greatness of honor," inasmuch as all honor shown to the Son of God was equally shown to the Son of man, on account of His union with the Son of God; fifthly, "by equivocation," i.e. communication of names, inasmuch as we say that this man is God and the Son of God. Now it is plain that these modes imply an accidental union.

But some more recent masters, thinking to avoid these heresies, through ignorance fell into them. For some conceded one person in Christ, but maintained two hypostases, or two supposita, saying that a man, composed of body and soul, was from the beginning of his conception assumed by the Word of God. And this is the first opinion set down by the Master (Sent. iii, D, 6). But others desirous of keeping the unity of person, held that the soul of Christ was not united to the body, but that these two were mutually separate, and were united to the Word accidentally, so that the number of persons might not be increased. And this is the third opinion which the Master sets down (Sent. iii, D, 6).

But both of these opinions fall into the heresy of Nestorius; the first, indeed, because to maintain two hypostases or supposita in Christ is the same as to maintain two persons, as was shown above (A. 3). And if stress is laid on the word "person," we must have in mind that even Nestorius spoke of unity of person on account of the unity of dignity and honor. Hence the fifth Council (Constantinople II, coll. viii, can. 5) directs an anathema against such a one as holds "one person in dignity, honor and adoration, as Theodore and Nestorius foolishly wrote." But the other opinion falls into the error of Nestorius by maintaining an accidental union. For there is no difference in saying that the Word of God is united to the Man Christ by indwelling, as in His temple (as Nestorius said), or by putting on man, as a garment, which is the third opinion; rather it says something worse than Nestorius--to wit, that the soul and body are not united.

Now the Catholic faith, holding the mean between the aforesaid positions, does not affirm that the union of God and man took place in the essence or nature, nor yet in something accidental, but midway, in a subsistence or hypostasis. Hence in the fifth Council (Constantinople II, coll. viii, can. 5) we read: "Since the unity may be understood in many ways, those who follow the impiety of Apollinaris and Eutyches, professing the destruction of what came together" (i.e. destroying both natures), "confess a union by mingling; but the followers of Theodore and Nestorius, maintaining division, introduce a union of purpose. But the Holy Church of God, rejecting the impiety of both these treasons, confesses a union of the Word of God with flesh, by composition, which is in subsistence." Therefore it is plain that the second of the three opinions, mentioned by the Master (Sent. iii, D, 6), which holds one hypostasis of God and man, is not to be called an opinion, but an article of Catholic faith. So likewise the first opinion which holds two hypostases, and the third which holds an accidental union, are not to be styled opinions, but heresies condemned by the Church in Councils.

Reply Obj. 1: As Damascene says (De Fide Orth. iii, 26): "Examples need not be wholly and at all points similar, for what is wholly similar is the same, and not an example, and especially in Divine things, for it is impossible to find a wholly similar example in the Theology," i.e. in the Godhead of Persons, "and in the Dispensation," i.e. the mystery of the Incarnation. Hence the human nature in Christ is likened to a habit, i.e. a garment, not indeed in regard to accidental union, but inasmuch as the Word is seen by the human nature, as a man by his garment, and also inasmuch as the garment is changed, for it is shaped according to the figure of him who puts it on, and yet he is not changed from his form on account of the garment. So likewise the human nature assumed by the Word of God is ennobled, but the Word of God is not changed, as Augustine says (Qq. 83, qu. 73).

Reply Obj. 2: Whatever accrues after the completion of the being comes accidentally, unless it be taken into communion with the complete being, just as in the resurrection the body comes to the soul which pre-exists, yet not accidentally, because it is assumed unto the same being, so that the body has vital being through the soul; but it is not so with whiteness, for the being of whiteness is other than the being of man to which whiteness comes. But the Word of God from all eternity had complete being in hypostasis or person; while in time the human nature accrued to it, not as if it were assumed unto one being inasmuch as this is of the nature (even as the body is assumed to the being of the soul), but to one being inasmuch as this is of the hypostasis or person. Hence the human nature is not accidentally united to the Son of God.

Reply Obj. 3: Accident is divided against substance. Now substance, as is plain from Metaph. v, 25, is taken in two ways: first, for essence or nature; secondly, for suppositum or hypostasis--hence the union having taken place in the hypostasis, is enough to show that it is not an accidental union, although the union did not take place in the nature.

Reply Obj. 4: Not everything that is assumed as an instrument pertains to the hypostasis of the one who assumes, as is plain in the case of a saw or a sword; yet nothing prevents what is assumed into the unity of the hypostasis from being as an instrument, even as the body of man or his members. Hence Nestorius held that the human nature was assumed by the Word merely as an instrument, and not into the unity of the hypostasis. And therefore he did not concede that the man was really the Son of God, but His instrument. Hence Cyril says (Epist. ad Monach. Aegyptii): "The Scripture does not affirm that this Emmanuel," i.e. Christ, "was assumed for the office of an instrument, but as God truly humanized," i.e. made man. But Damascene held that the human nature in Christ is an instrument belonging to the unity of the hypostasis.

SEVENTH ARTICLE [III, Q. 2, Art. 7]

Whether the Union of the Divine Nature and the Human Is Anything Created?

Objection 1: It would seem that the union of the Divine and human natures is not anything created. For there can be nothing created in God, because whatever is in God is God. But the union is in God, for God Himself is united to human nature. Therefore it seems that the union is not anything created.

Obj. 2: Further, the end holds first place in everything. But the end of the union is the Divine hypostasis or Person in which the union is terminated. Therefore it seems that this union ought chiefly to be judged with reference to the dignity of the Divine hypostasis, which is not anything created. Therefore the union is nothing created.

Obj. 3: Further, "That which is the cause of a thing being such is still more so" (Poster. i). But man is said to be the Creator on account of the union. Therefore much more is the union itself nothing created, but the Creator.

*On the contrary,* Whatever has a beginning in time is created. Now this union was not from eternity, but began in time. Therefore the union is something created.

*I answer that,* The union of which we are speaking is a relation which we consider between the Divine and the human nature, inasmuch as they come together in one Person of the Son of God. Now, as was said above (I, Q. 13, A. 7), every relation which we consider between God and the creature is really in the creature, by whose change the relation is brought into being; whereas it is not really in God, but only in our way of thinking, since it does not arise from any change in God. And hence we must say that the union of which we are speaking is not really in God, except only in our way of thinking; but in the human nature, which is a creature, it is really. Therefore we must say it is something created.

Reply Obj. 1: This union is not really in God, but only in our way of thinking, for God is said to be united to a creature inasmuch as the creature is really united to God without any change in Him.

Reply Obj. 2: The specific nature of a relation, as of motion, depends on the subject. And since this union has its being nowhere save in a created nature, as was said above, it follows that it has a created being.

Reply Obj. 3: A man is called Creator and is God because of the union, inasmuch as it is terminated in the Divine hypostasis; yet it does not follow that the union itself is the Creator or God, because that a thing is said to be created regards its being rather than its relation.

EIGHTH ARTICLE [III, Q. 2, Art. 8]

Whether Union Is the Same As Assumption?

Objection 1: It would seem that union is the same as assumption. For relations, as motions, are specified by their termini. Now the term of assumption and union is one and the same, viz. the Divine hypostasis. Therefore it seems that union and assumption are not different.

Obj. 2: Further, in the mystery of the Incarnation the same thing seems to be what unites and what assumes, and what is united and what is assumed. But union and assumption seem to follow the action and passion of the thing uniting and the united, of the thing assuming and the assumed. Therefore union seems to be the same as assumption.

Obj. 3: Further, Damascene says (De Fide Orth. iii, 11): "Union is one thing, incarnation is another; for union demands mere copulation, and leaves unsaid the end of the copulation; but incarnation and humanation determine the end of copulation." But likewise assumption does not determine the end of copulation. Therefore it seems that union is the same as assumption.

*On the contrary,* The Divine Nature is said to be united, not assumed.

*I answer that,* As was stated above (A. 7), union implies a certain relation of the Divine Nature and the human, according as they come together in one Person. Now all relations which begin in time are brought about by some change; and change consists in action and passion. Hence the first and principal difference between assumption and union must be said to be that union implies the relation: whereas assumption implies the action, whereby someone is said to assume, or the passion, whereby something is said to be assumed. Now from this difference another second difference arises, for assumption implies becoming, whereas union implies having become, and therefore the thing uniting is said to be united, but the thing assuming is not said to be assumed. For the human nature is taken to be in the terminus of assumption unto the Divine hypostasis when man is spoken of; and hence we can truly say that the Son of God, Who assumes human nature unto Himself, is man. But human nature, considered in itself, i.e. in the abstract, is viewed as assumed; and we do not say the Son of God is human nature. From this same follows a third difference, which is that a relation, especially one of equiparance, is no more to one extreme than to the other, whereas action and passion bear themselves differently to the agent and the patient, and to different termini. And hence assumption determines the term whence and the term whither; for assumption means a taking to oneself from another. But union determines none of these things. Hence it may be said indifferently that the human nature is united with the Divine, or conversely. But the Divine Nature is not said to be assumed by the human, but conversely, because the human nature is joined to the Divine personality, so that the Divine Person subsists in human nature.

Reply Obj. 1: Union and assumption have not the same relation to the term, but a different relation, as was said above.

Reply Obj. 2: What unites and what assumes are not the same. For whatsoever Person assumes unites, and not conversely. For the Person of the Father united the human nature to the Son, but not to Himself; and hence He is said to unite and not to assume. So likewise the united and the assumed are not identical, for the Divine Nature is said to be united, but not assumed.

Reply Obj. 3: Assumption determines with whom the union is made on the part of the one assuming, inasmuch as assumption means taking unto oneself ( ad se sumere ), whereas incarnation and humanation (determine with whom the union is made) on the part of the thing assumed, which is flesh or human nature. And thus assumption differs logically both from union and from incarnation or humanation.

NINTH ARTICLE [III, Q. 2, Art. 9]

Whether the Union of the Two Natures in Christ Is the Greatest of All Unions?

Objection 1: It would seem that the union of the two natures in Christ is not the greatest of all unions. For what is united falls short of the unity of what is one, since what is united is by participation, but one is by essence. Now in created things there are some that are simply one, as is shown especially in unity itself, which is the principle of number. Therefore the union of which we are speaking does not imply the greatest of all unions.

Obj. 2: Further, the greater the distance between things united, the less the union. Now, the things united by this union are most distant--namely, the Divine and human natures; for they are infinitely apart. Therefore their union is the least of all.

Obj. 3: Further, from union there results one. But from the union of soul and body in us there arises what is one in person and nature; whereas from the union of the Divine and human nature there results what is one in person only. Therefore the union of soul and body is greater than that of the Divine and human natures; and hence the union of which we speak does not imply the greatest unity.

*On the contrary,* Augustine says (De Trin. i, 10) that "man is in the Son of God, more than the Son in the Father." But the Son is in the Father by unity of essence, and man is in the Son by the union of the Incarnation. Therefore the union of the Incarnation is greater than the unity of the Divine Essence, which nevertheless is the greatest union; and thus the union of the Incarnation implies the greatest unity.

*I answer that,* Union implies the joining of several in some one thing. Therefore the union of the Incarnation may be taken in two ways: first, in regard to the things united; secondly, in regard to that in which they are united. And in this regard this union has a pre-eminence over other unions; for the unity of the Divine Person, in which the two natures are united, is the greatest. But it has no pre-eminence in regard to the things united.

Reply Obj. 1: The unity of the Divine Person is greater than numerical unity, which is the principle of number. For the unity of a Divine Person is an uncreated and self-subsisting unity, not received into another by participation. Also, it is complete in itself, having in itself whatever pertains to the nature of unity; and therefore it is not compatible with the nature of a part, as in numerical unity, which is a part of number, and which is shared in by the things numbered. And hence in this respect the union of the Incarnation is higher than numerical unity by reason of the unity of the Divine Person, and not by reason of the human nature, which is not the unity of the Divine Person, but is united to it.

Reply Obj. 2: This reason regards the things united, and not the Person in Whom the union takes place.

Reply Obj. 3: The unity of the Divine Person is greater than the unity of person and nature in us; and hence the union of the Incarnation is greater than the union of soul and body in us.

And because what is urged in the argument "on the contrary" rests upon what is untrue--namely, that the union of the Incarnation is greater than the unity of the Divine Persons in Essence--we must say to the authority of Augustine that the human nature is not more in the Son of God than the Son of God in the Father, but much less. But the man in some respects is more in the Son than the Son in the Father--namely, inasmuch as the same suppositum is signified when I say "man," meaning Christ, and when I say "Son of God"; whereas it is not the same suppositum of Father and Son.

TENTH ARTICLE [III, Q. 2, Art. 10]

Whether the Union of the Incarnation Took Place by Grace?

Objection 1: It would seem that the union of the Incarnation did not take place by grace. For grace is an accident, as was shown above (I-II, Q. 110, A. 2). But the union of the human nature to the Divine did not take place accidentally, as was shown above (A. 6). Therefore it seems that the union of the Incarnation did not take place by grace.

Obj. 2: Further, the subject of grace is the soul. But it is written (Col. 2:9): "In Christ [Vulg.: 'Him'] dwelleth all the fulness of the Godhead corporeally." Therefore it seems that this union did not take place by grace.

Obj. 3: Further, every saint is united to God by grace. If, therefore, the union of the Incarnation was by grace, it would seem that Christ is said to be God no more than other holy men.

*On the contrary,* Augustine says (De Praed. Sanct. xv): "By the same grace every man is made a Christian, from the beginning of his faith, as this man from His beginning was made Christ." But this man became Christ by union with the Divine Nature. Therefore this union was by grace.

*I answer that,* As was said above (I-II, Q. 110, A. 1), grace is taken in two ways:--first, as the will of God gratuitously bestowing something; secondly, as the free gift of God. Now human nature stands in need of the gratuitous will of God in order to be lifted up to God, since this is above its natural capability. Moreover, human nature is lifted up to God in two ways: first, by operation, as the saints know and love God; secondly, by personal being, and this mode belongs exclusively to Christ, in Whom human nature is assumed so as to be in the Person of the Son of God. But it is plain that for the perfection of operation the power needs to be perfected by a habit, whereas that a nature has being in its own suppositum does not take place by means of a habit.

And hence we must say that if grace be understood as the will of God gratuitously doing something or reputing anything as well-pleasing or acceptable to Him, the union of the Incarnation took place by grace, even as the union of the saints with God by knowledge and love. But if grace be taken as the free gift of God, then the fact that the human nature is united to the Divine Person may be called a grace, inasmuch as it took place without being preceded by any merits--but not as though there were an habitual grace, by means of which the union took place.

Reply Obj. 1: The grace which is an accident is a certain likeness of the Divinity participated by man. But by the Incarnation human nature is not said to have participated a likeness of the Divine nature, but is said to be united to the Divine Nature itself in the Person of the Son. Now the thing itself is greater than a participated likeness of it.

Reply Obj. 2: Habitual grace is only in the soul; but the grace, i.e. the free gift of God, of being united to the Divine Person belongs to the whole human nature, which is composed of soul and body. And hence it is said that the fulness of the Godhead dwelt corporeally in Christ because the Divine Nature is united not merely to the soul, but to the body also. Although it may also be said that it dwelt in Christ corporeally, i.e. not as in a shadow, as it dwelt in the sacraments of the old law, of which it is said in the same place (Col. 2:17) that they are the "shadow of things to come but the body is Christ" [Vulg.: 'Christ's'], inasmuch as the body is opposed to the shadow. And some say that the Godhead is said to have dwelt in Christ corporeally, i.e. in three ways, just as a body has three dimensions: first, by essence, presence, and power, as in other creatures; secondly, by sanctifying grace, as in the saints; thirdly, by personal union, which is proper to Christ.

Hence the reply to the third is manifest, viz. because the union of the Incarnation did not take place by habitual grace alone, but in subsistence or person.

ELEVENTH ARTICLE [III, Q. 2, Art. 11]

Whether Any Merits Preceded the Union of the Incarnation?

Objection 1: It would seem that the union of the Incarnation followed upon certain merits, because upon Ps. 32:22, "Let Thy mercy, o Lord, be upon us, as," etc. a gloss says: "Here the prophet's desire for the Incarnation and its merited fulfilment are hinted at." Therefore the Incarnation falls under merit.

Obj. 2: Further, whoever merits anything merits that without which it cannot be. But the ancient Fathers merited eternal life, to which they were able to attain only by the Incarnation; for Gregory says (Moral. xiii): "Those who came into this world before Christ's coming, whatsoever eminency of righteousness they may have had, could not, on being divested of the body, at once be admitted into the bosom of the heavenly country, seeing that He had not as yet come Who, by His own descending, should place the souls of the righteous in their everlasting seat." Therefore it would seem that they merited the Incarnation.

Obj. 3: Further, of the Blessed Virgin it is sung that "she merited to bear the Lord of all" [*Little Office of B. V. M., Dominican Rite, Ant. at Benedictus], and this took place through the Incarnation. Therefore the Incarnation falls under merit.

*On the contrary,* Augustine says (De Praed. Sanct. xv): "Whoever can find merits preceding the singular generation of our Head, may also find merits preceding the repeated regeneration of us His members." But no merits preceded our regeneration, according to Titus 3:5: "Not by the works of justice which we have done, but according to His mercy He saved us, by the laver of regeneration." Therefore no merits preceded the generation of Christ.

*I answer that,* With regard to Christ Himself, it is clear from the above (A. 10) that no merits of His could have preceded the union. For we do not hold that He was first of all a mere man, and that afterwards by the merits of a good life it was granted Him to become the Son of God, as Photinus held; but we hold that from the beginning of His conception this man was truly the Son of God, seeing that He had no other hypostasis but that of the Son of God, according to Luke 1:35: "The Holy which shall be born of thee shall be called the Son of God." And hence every operation of this man followed the union. Therefore no operation of His could have been meritorious of the union.

Neither could the needs of any other man whatsoever have merited this union condignly: first, because the meritorious works of man are properly ordained to beatitude, which is the reward of virtue, and consists in the full enjoyment of God. Whereas the union of the Incarnation, inasmuch as it is in the personal being, transcends the union of the beatified mind with God, which is by the act of the soul in fruition; and therefore it cannot fall under merit. Secondly, because grace cannot fall under merit, for the principle of merit does not fall under merit; and therefore neither does grace, for it is the principle of merit. Hence, still less does the Incarnation fall under merit, since it is the principle of grace, according to John 1:17: "Grace and truth came by Jesus Christ." Thirdly, because the Incarnation is for the reformation of the entire human nature, and therefore it does not fall under the merit of any individual man, since the goodness of a mere man cannot be the cause of the good of the entire nature. Yet the holy Fathers merited the Incarnation congruously by desiring and beseeching; for it was becoming that God should harken to those who obeyed Him.

And thereby the reply to the First Objection is manifest.

Reply Obj. 2: It is false that under merit falls everything without which there can be no reward. For there is something pre-required not merely for reward, but also for merit, as the Divine goodness and grace and the very nature of man. And again, the mystery of the Incarnation is the principle of merit, because "of His fulness we all have received" (John 1:16).

Reply Obj. 3: The Blessed Virgin is said to have merited to bear the Lord of all; not that she merited His Incarnation, but because by the grace bestowed upon her she merited that grade of purity and holiness, which fitted her to be the Mother of God.

TWELFTH ARTICLE [III, Q. 2, Art. 12]

Whether the Grace of Union Was Natural to the Man Christ?

Objection 1: It would seem that the grace of union was not natural to the man Christ. For the union of the Incarnation did not take place in the nature, but in the Person, as was said above (A. 2). Now a thing is denominated from its terminus. Therefore this grace ought rather to be called personal than natural.

Obj. 2: Further, grace is divided against nature, even as gratuitous things, which are from God, are distinguished from natural things, which are from an intrinsic principle. But if things are divided in opposition to one another, one is not denominated by the other. Therefore the grace of Christ was not natural to Him.

Obj. 3: Further, natural is that which is according to nature. But the grace of union is not natural to Christ in regard to the Divine Nature, otherwise it would belong to the other Persons; nor is it natural to Him according to the human nature, otherwise it would belong to all men, since they are of the same nature as He. Therefore it would seem that the grace of union is nowise natural to Christ.

*On the contrary,* Augustine says (Enchiridion xl): "In the assumption of human nature, grace itself became somewhat natural to that man, so as to leave no room for sin in Him."

*I answer that,* According to the Philosopher (Metaph. v, 5), nature designates, in one way, nativity; in another, the essence of a thing. Hence natural may be taken in two ways: first, for what is only from the essential principles of a thing, as it is natural to fire to mount; secondly, we call natural to man what he has had from his birth, according to Eph. 2:3: "We were by nature children of wrath"; and Wis. 12:10: "They were a wicked generation, and their malice natural." Therefore the grace of Christ, whether of union or habitual, cannot be called natural as if caused by the principles of the human nature of Christ, although it may be called natural, as if coming to the human nature of Christ by the causality of His Divine Nature. But these two kinds of grace are said to be natural to Christ, inasmuch as He had them from His nativity, since from the beginning of His conception the human nature was united to the Divine Person, and His soul was filled with the gift of grace.

Reply Obj. 1: Although the union did not take place in the nature, yet it was caused by the power of the Divine Nature, which is truly the nature of Christ, and it, moreover, belonged to Christ from the beginning of His nativity.

Reply Obj. 2: The union is not said to be grace and natural in the same respect; for it is called grace inasmuch as it is not from merit; and it is said to be natural inasmuch as by the power of the Divine Nature it was in the humanity of Christ from His nativity.

Reply Obj. 3: The grace of union is not natural to Christ according to His human nature, as if it were caused by the principles of the human nature, and hence it need not belong to all men. Nevertheless, it is natural to Him in regard to the human nature on account of the property of His birth, seeing that He was conceived by the Holy Ghost, so that He might be the natural Son of God and of man. But it is natural to Him in regard to the Divine Nature, inasmuch as the Divine Nature is the active principle of this grace; and this belongs to the whole Trinity--to wit, to be the active principle of this grace.

## QUESTION 3

OF THE MODE OF UNION ON THE PART OF THE PERSON ASSUMING (In Eight Articles)

We must now consider the union on the part of the Person assuming, and under this head there are eight points of inquiry:

(1) Whether to assume is befitting to a Divine Person?

(2) Whether it is befitting to the Divine Nature?

(3) Whether the Nature abstracted from the Personality can assume?

(4) Whether one Person can assume without another?

(5) Whether each Person can assume?

(6) Whether several Persons can assume one individual nature?

(7) Whether one Person can assume two individual natures?

(8) Whether it was more fitting for the Person of the Son of God to assume human nature than for another Divine Person?

FIRST ARTICLE [III, Q. 3, Art. 1]

Whether It Is Befitting for a Divine Person to Assume?

Objection 1: It would seem that it is not befitting to a Divine Person to assume a created nature. For a Divine Person signifies something most perfect. Now no addition can be made to what is perfect. Therefore, since to assume is to take to oneself, and consequently what is assumed is added to the one who assumes, it does not seem to be befitting to a Divine Person to assume a created nature.

Obj. 2: Further, that to which anything is assumed is communicated in some degree to what is assumed to it, just as dignity is communicated to whosoever is assumed to a dignity. But it is of the nature of a person to be incommunicable, as was said above (I, Q. 29, A. 1). Therefore it is not befitting to a Divine Person to assume, i.e. to take to Himself.

Obj. 3: Further, person is constituted by nature. But it is repugnant that the thing constituted should assume the constituent, since the effect does not act on its cause. Hence it is not befitting to a Person to assume a nature.

*On the contrary,* Augustine [*Fulgentius] says (De Fide ad Petrum ii): "This God, i.e. the only-Begotten one, took the form," i.e. the nature, "of a servant to His own Person." But the only-Begotten God is a Person. Therefore it is befitting to a Person to take, i.e. to assume a nature.

*I answer that,* In the word "assumption" are implied two things, viz. the principle and the term of the act, for to assume is to take something to oneself. Now of this assumption a Person is both the principle and the term. The principle--because it properly belongs to a person to act, and this assuming of flesh took place by the Divine action. Likewise a Person is the term of this assumption, because, as was said above (Q. 2, AA. 1, 2), the union took place in the Person, and not in the nature. Hence it is plain that to assume a nature is most properly befitting to a Person.

Reply Obj. 1: Since the Divine Person is infinite, no addition can be made to it: Hence Cyril says [*Council of Ephesus, Part I, ch. 26]: "We do not conceive the mode of conjunction to be according to addition"; just as in the union of man with God, nothing is added to God by the grace of adoption, but what is Divine is united to man; hence, not God but man is perfected.

Reply Obj. 2: A Divine Person is said to be incommunicable inasmuch as It cannot be predicated of several supposita, but nothing prevents several things being predicated of the Person. Hence it is not contrary to the nature of person to be communicated so as to subsist in several natures, for even in a created person several natures may concur accidentally, as in the person of one man we find quantity and quality. But this is proper to a Divine Person, on account of its infinity, that there should be a concourse of natures in it, not accidentally, but in subsistence.

Reply Obj. 3: As was said above (Q. 2, A. 1), the human nature constitutes a Divine Person, not simply, but forasmuch as the Person is denominated from such a nature. For human nature does not make the Son of Man to be simply, since He was from eternity, but only to be man. It is by the Divine Nature that a Divine Person is constituted simply. Hence the Divine Person is not said to assume the Divine Nature, but to assume the human nature.

SECOND ARTICLE [III, Q. 3, Art. 2]

Whether It Is Befitting to the Divine Nature to Assume?

Objection 1: It would seem that it is not befitting to the Divine Nature to assume. Because, as was said above (A. 1), to assume is to take to oneself. But the Divine Nature did not take to Itself human nature, for the union did not take place in the nature, as was said above (Q. 2, AA. 1, 3). Hence it is not befitting to the Divine Nature to assume human nature.

Obj. 2: Further, the Divine Nature is common to the three Persons. If, therefore, it is befitting to the Divine Nature to assume, it consequently is befitting to the three Persons; and thus the Father assumed human nature even as the Son, which is erroneous.

Obj. 3: Further, to assume is to act. But to act befits a person, not a nature, which is rather taken to be the principle by which the agent acts. Therefore to assume is not befitting to the nature.

*On the contrary,* Augustine (Fulgentius) says (De Fide ad Petrum ii): "That nature which remains eternally begotten of the Father" (i.e. which is received from the Father by eternal generation) "took our nature free of sin from His Mother."

*I answer that,* As was said above (A. 1), in the word assumption two things are signified--to wit, the principle and the term of the action. Now to be the principle of the assumption belongs to the Divine Nature in itself, because the assumption took place by Its power; but to be the term of the assumption does not belong to the Divine Nature in itself, but by reason of the Person in Whom It is considered to be. Hence a Person is primarily and more properly said to assume, but it may be said secondarily that the Nature assumed a nature to Its Person. And after the same manner the Nature is also said to be incarnate, not that it is changed to flesh, but that it assumed the nature of flesh. Hence Damascene says (De Fide Orth. iii, 6): "Following the blessed Athanasius and Cyril we say that the Nature of God is incarnate."

Reply Obj. 1: "Oneself" is reciprocal, and points to the same suppositum. But the Divine Nature is not a distinct suppositum from the Person of the Word. Hence, inasmuch as the Divine Nature took human nature to the Person of the Word, It is said to take it to Itself. But although the Father takes human nature to the Person of the Word, He did not thereby take it to Himself, for the suppositum of the Father and the Son is not one, and hence it cannot properly be said that the Father assumes human nature.

Reply Obj. 2: What is befitting to the Divine Nature in Itself is befitting to the three Persons, as goodness, wisdom, and the like. But to assume belongs to It by reason of the Person of the Word, as was said above, and hence it is befitting to that Person alone.

Reply Obj. 3: As in God what is and whereby it is are the same, so likewise in Him what acts and whereby it acts are the same, since everything acts, inasmuch as it is a being. Hence the Divine Nature is both that whereby God acts, and the very God Who acts.

THIRD ARTICLE [III, Q. 3, Art. 3]

Whether the Nature Abstracted from the Personality Can Assume?

Objection 1: It would seem that if we abstract the Personality by our mind, the Nature cannot assume. For it was said above (A. 1) that it belongs to the Nature to assume by reason of the Person. But what belongs to one by reason of another cannot belong to it if the other is removed; as a body, which is visible by reason of color, without color cannot be seen. Hence if the Personality be mentally abstracted, the Nature cannot assume.

Obj. 2: Further, assumption implies the term of union, as was said above (A. 1). But the union cannot take place in the nature, but only in the Person. Therefore, if the Personality be abstracted, the Divine Nature cannot assume.

Obj. 3: Further, it has been said above (I, Q. 40, A. 3) that in the Godhead if the Personality is abstracted, nothing remains. But the one who assumes is something. Therefore, if the Personality is abstracted, the Divine Nature cannot assume.

*On the contrary,* In the Godhead Personality signifies a personal property; and this is threefold, viz. Paternity, Filiation and Procession, as was said above (I, Q. 30, A. 2). Now if we mentally abstract these, there still remains the omnipotence of God, by which the Incarnation was wrought, as the angel says (Luke 1:37): "No word shall be impossible with God." Therefore it seems that if the Personality be removed, the Divine Nature can still assume.

*I answer that,* The intellect stands in two ways towards God. First, to know God as He is, and in this manner it is impossible for the intellect to circumscribe something in God and leave the rest, for all that is in God is one, except the distinction of Persons; and as regards these, if one is removed the other is taken away, since they are distinguished by relations only which must be together at the same time. Secondly, the intellect stands towards God, not indeed as knowing God as He is, but in its own way, i.e. understanding manifoldly and separately what in God is one: and in this way our intellect can understand the Divine goodness and wisdom, and the like, which are called essential attributes, without understanding Paternity or Filiation, which are called Personalities. And hence if we abstract Personality by our intellect, we may still understand the Nature assuming.

Reply Obj. 1: Because in God what is, and whereby it is, are one, if any one of the things which are attributed to God in the abstract is considered in itself, abstracted from all else, it will still be something subsisting, and consequently a Person, since it is an intellectual nature. Hence just as we now say three Persons, on account of holding three personal properties, so likewise if we mentally exclude the personal properties there will still remain in our thought the Divine Nature as subsisting and as a Person. And in this way It may be understood to assume human nature by reason of Its subsistence or Personality.

Reply Obj. 2: Even if the personal properties of the three Persons are abstracted by our mind, nevertheless there will remain in our thoughts the one Personality of God, as the Jews consider. And the assumption can be terminated in It, as we now say it is terminated in the Person of the Word.

Reply Obj. 3: If we mentally abstract the Personality, it is said that nothing remains by way of resolution, i.e. as if the subject of the relation and the relation itself were distinct because all we can think of in God is considered as a subsisting suppositum. However, some of the things predicated of God can be understood without others, not by way of resolution, but by the way mentioned above.

FOURTH ARTICLE [III, Q. 3, Art. 4]

Whether One Person Without Another Can Assume a Created Nature?

Objection 1: It would seem that one Person cannot assume a created nature without another assuming it. For "the works of the Trinity are inseparable," as Augustine says (Enchiridion xxxviii). But as the three Persons have one essence, so likewise They have one operation. Now to assume is an operation. Therefore it cannot belong to one without belonging to another.

Obj. 2: Further, as we say the Person of the Son became incarnate, so also did the Nature; for "the whole Divine Nature became incarnate in one of Its hypostases," as Damascene says (De Fide Orth. iii, 6). But the Nature is common to the three Persons. Therefore the assumption is.

Obj. 3: Further, as the human nature in Christ is assumed by God, so likewise are men assumed by Him through grace, according to Rom. 14:3: "God hath taken him to Him." But this assumption pertains to all the Persons; therefore the first also.

*On the contrary,* Dionysius says (Div. Nom. ii) that the mystery of the Incarnation pertains to "discrete theology," i.e. according to which something "distinct" is said of the Divine Persons.

*I answer that,* As was said above (A. 1), assumption implies two things, viz. the act of assuming and the term of assumption. Now the act of assumption proceeds from the Divine power, which is common to the three Persons, but the term of the assumption is a Person, as stated above (A. 2). Hence what has to do with action in the assumption is common to the three Persons; but what pertains to the nature of term belongs to one Person in such a manner as not to belong to another; for the three Persons caused the human nature to be united to the one Person of the Son.

Reply Obj. 1: This reason regards the operation, and the conclusion would follow if it implied this operation only, without the term, which is a Person.

Reply Obj. 2: The Nature is said to be incarnate, and to assume by reason of the Person in Whom the union is terminated, as stated above (AA. 1, 2), and not as it is common to the three Persons. Now "the whole Divine Nature is" said to be "incarnate"; not that It is incarnate in all the Persons, but inasmuch as nothing is wanting to the perfection of the Divine Nature of the Person incarnate, as Damascene explains there.

Reply Obj. 3: The assumption which takes place by the grace of adoption is terminated in a certain participation of the Divine Nature, by an assimilation to Its goodness, according to 2 Pet. 1:4: "That you may be made partakers of the Divine Nature"; and hence this assumption is common to the three Persons, in regard to the principle and the term. But the assumption which is by the grace of union is common on the part of the principle, but not on the part of the term, as was said above.

FIFTH ARTICLE [III, Q. 3, Art. 5]

Whether Each of the Divine Persons Could Have Assumed Human Nature?

Objection 1: It would seem that no other Divine Person could have assumed human nature except the Person of the Son. For by this assumption it has been brought about that God is the Son of Man. But it was not becoming that either the Father or the Holy Ghost should be said to be a Son; for this would tend to the confusion of the Divine Persons. Therefore the Father and Holy Ghost could not have assumed flesh.

Obj. 2: Further, by the Divine Incarnation men have come into possession of the adoption of sons, according to Rom. 8:15: "For you have not received the spirit of bondage again in fear, but the spirit of adoption of sons." But sonship by adoption is a participated likeness of natural sonship which does not belong to the Father nor the Holy Ghost; hence it is said (Rom. 8:29): "For whom He foreknew He also predestinated to be made conformable to the image of His Son." Therefore it seems that no other Person except the Person of the Son could have become incarnate.

Obj. 3: Further, the Son is said to be sent and to be begotten by the temporal nativity, inasmuch as He became incarnate. But it does not belong to the Father to be sent, for He is innascible, as was said above (I, Q. 32, A. 3; First Part, Q. 43, A. 4). Therefore at least the Person of the Father cannot become incarnate.

*On the contrary,* Whatever the Son can do, so can the Father and the Holy Ghost, otherwise the power of the three Persons would not be one. But the Son was able to become incarnate. Therefore the Father and the Holy Ghost were able to become incarnate.

*I answer that,* As was said above (AA. 1, 2, 4), assumption implies two things, viz. the act of the one assuming and the term of the assumption. Now the principle of the act is the Divine power, and the term is a Person. But the Divine power is indifferently and commonly in all the Persons. Moreover, the nature of Personality is common to all the Persons, although the personal properties are different. Now whenever a power regards several things indifferently, it can terminate its action in any of them indifferently, as is plain in rational powers, which regard opposites, and can do either of them. Therefore the Divine power could have united human nature to the Person of the Father or of the Holy Ghost, as It united it to the Person of the Son. And hence we must say that the Father or the Holy Ghost could have assumed flesh even as the Son.

Reply Obj. 1: The temporal sonship, whereby Christ is said to be the Son of Man, does not constitute His Person, as does the eternal Sonship; but is something following upon the temporal nativity. Hence, if the name of son were transferred to the Father or the Holy Ghost in this manner, there would be no confusion of the Divine Persons.

Reply Obj. 2: Adoptive sonship is a certain participation of natural sonship; but it takes place in us, by appropriation, by the Father, Who is the principle of natural sonship, and by the gift of the Holy Ghost, Who is the love of the Father and Son, according to Gal. 4:6: "God hath sent the Spirit of His Son into your hearts crying, Abba, Father." And therefore, even as by the Incarnation of the Son we receive adoptive sonship in the likeness of His natural sonship, so likewise, had the Father become incarnate, we should have received adoptive sonship from Him, as from the principle of the natural sonship, and from the Holy Ghost as from the common bond of Father and Son.

Reply Obj. 3: It belongs to the Father to be innascible as to eternal birth, and the temporal birth would not destroy this. But the Son of God is said to be sent in regard to the Incarnation, inasmuch as He is from another, without which the Incarnation would not suffice for the nature of mission.

SIXTH ARTICLE [III, Q. 3, Art. 6]

Whether Several Divine Persons Can Assume One and the Same Individual Nature?

Objection 1: It would seem that two Divine Persons cannot assume one and the same individual nature. For, this being granted, there would either be several men or one. But not several, for just as one Divine Nature in several Persons does not make several gods, so one human nature in several persons does not make several men. Nor would there be only one man, for one man is "this man," which signifies one person; and hence the distinction of three Divine Persons would be destroyed, which cannot be allowed. Therefore neither two nor three Persons can take one human nature.

Obj. 2: Further, the assumption is terminated in the unity of Person, as has been said above (A. 2). But the Father, Son, and Holy Ghost are not one Person. Therefore the three Persons cannot assume one human nature.

Obj. 3: Further, Damascene says (De Fide Orth. iii, 3, 4), and Augustine (De Trin. i, 11, 12, 13), that from the Incarnation of God the Son it follows that whatever is said of the Son of God is said of the Son of Man, and conversely. Hence, if three Persons were to assume one human nature, it would follow that whatever is said of each of the three Persons would be said of the man; and conversely, what was said of the man could be said of each of the three Persons. Therefore what is proper to the Father, viz. to beget the Son, would be said of the man, and consequently would be said of the Son of God; and this could not be. Therefore it is impossible that the three Persons should assume one human nature.

*On the contrary,* The Incarnate Person subsists in two natures. But the three Persons can subsist in one Divine Nature. Therefore they can also subsist in one human nature in such a way that the human nature be assumed by the three Persons.

*I answer that,* As was said above (Q. 2, A. 5, ad 1), by the union of the soul and body in Christ neither a new person is made nor a new hypostasis, but one human nature is assumed to the Divine Person or hypostasis, which, indeed, does not take place by the power of the human nature, but by the power of the Divine Person. Now such is the characteristic of the Divine Persons that one does not exclude another from communicating in the same nature, but only in the same Person. Hence, since in the mystery of the Incarnation "the whole reason of the deed is the power of the doer," as Augustine says (Ep. ad Volusianum cxxxvii), we must judge of it in regard to the quality of the Divine Person assuming, and not according to the quality of the human nature assumed. Therefore it is not impossible that two or three Divine Persons should assume one human nature, but it would be impossible for them to assume one human hypostasis or person; thus Anselm says in the book De Concep. Virg. (Cur Deus Homo ii, 9), that "several Persons cannot assume one and the same man to unity of Person."

Reply Obj. 1: In the hypothesis that three Persons assume one human nature, it would be true to say that the three Persons were one man, because of the one human nature. For just as it is now true to say the three Persons are one God on account of the one Divine Nature, so it would be true to say they are one man on account of the one human nature. Nor would "one" imply unity of person, but unity in human nature; for it could not be argued that because the three Persons were one man they were one simply. For nothing hinders our saying that men, who are many simply, are in some respect one, e.g. one people, and as Augustine says (De Trin. vi, 3): "The Spirit of God and the spirit of man are by nature different, but by inherence one spirit results," according to 1 Cor. 6:17: "He who is joined to the Lord is one spirit."

Reply Obj. 2: In this supposition the human nature would be assumed to the unity, not indeed of one Person, but to the unity of each Person, so that even as the Divine Nature has a natural unity with each Person, so also the human nature would have a unity with each Person by assumption.

Reply Obj. 3: In the mystery of the Incarnation, there results a communication of the properties belonging to the nature, because whatever belongs to the nature can be predicated of the Person subsisting in that nature, no matter to which of the natures it may apply. Hence in this hypothesis, of the Person of the Father may be predicated what belongs to the human nature and what belongs to the Divine; and likewise of the Person of the Son and of the Holy Ghost. But what belongs to the Person of the Father by reason of His own Person could not be attributed to the Person of the Son or Holy Ghost on account of the distinction of Persons which would still remain. Therefore it might be said that as the Father was unbegotten, so the man was unbegotten, inasmuch as "man" stood for the Person of the Father. But if one were to go on to say, "The man is unbegotten; the Son is man; therefore the Son is unbegotten," it would be the fallacy of figure of speech or of accident; even as we now say God is unbegotten, because the Father is unbegotten, yet we cannot conclude that the Son is unbegotten, although He is God.

SEVENTH ARTICLE [III, Q. 3, Art. 7]

Whether One Divine Person Can Assume Two Human Natures?

Objection 1: It would seem that one Divine Person cannot assume two human natures. For the nature assumed in the mystery of the Incarnation has no other suppositum than the suppositum of the Divine Person, as is plain from what has been stated above (Q. 2, AA. 3, 6). Therefore, if we suppose one Person to assume two human natures, there would be one suppositum of two natures of the same species; which would seem to imply a contradiction, for the nature of one species is only multiplied by distinct supposita.

Obj. 2: Further, in this hypothesis it could not be said that the Divine Person incarnate was one man, seeing that He would not have one human nature; neither could it be said that there were several, for several men have distinct supposita, whereas in this case there would be only one suppositum. Therefore the aforesaid hypothesis is impossible.

Obj. 3: Further, in the mystery of the Incarnation the whole Divine Nature is united to the whole nature assumed, i.e. to every part of it, for Christ is "perfect God and perfect man, complete God and complete man," as Damascene says (De Fide Orth. iii, 7). But two human natures cannot be wholly united together, inasmuch as the soul of one would be united to the body of the other; and, again, two bodies would be together, which would give rise to confusion of natures. Therefore it is not possibly for one Divine Person to assume two human natures.

*On the contrary,* Whatever the Father can do, that also can the Son do. But after the Incarnation the Father can still assume a human nature distinct from that which the Son has assumed; for in nothing is the power of the Father or the Son lessened by the Incarnation of the Son. Therefore it seems that after the Incarnation the Son can assume another human nature distinct from the one He has assumed.

*I answer that,* What has power for one thing, and no more, has a power limited to one. Now the power of a Divine Person is infinite, nor can it be limited by any created thing. Hence it may not be said that a Divine Person so assumed one human nature as to be unable to assume another. For it would seem to follow from this that the Personality of the Divine Nature was so comprehended by one human nature as to be unable to assume another to its Personality; and this is impossible, for the Uncreated cannot be comprehended by any creature. Hence it is plain that, whether we consider the Divine Person in regard to His power, which is the principle of the union, or in regard to His Personality, which is the term of the union, it has to be said that the Divine Person, over and beyond the human nature which He has assumed, can assume another distinct human nature.

Reply Obj. 1: A created nature is completed in its essentials by its form, which is multiplied according to the division of matter. And hence, if the composition of matter and form constitutes a new suppositum, the consequence is that the nature is multiplied by the multiplication of supposita. But in the mystery of the Incarnation the union of form and matter, i.e. of soul and body, does not constitute a new suppositum, as was said above (A. 6). Hence there can be a numerical multitude on the part of the nature, on account of the division of matter, without distinction of supposita.

Reply Obj. 2: It might seem possible to reply that in such a hypothesis it would follow that there were two men by reason of the two natures, just as, *on the contrary,* the three Persons would be called one man, on account of the one nature assumed, as was said above (A. 6, ad 1). But this does not seem to be true; because we must use words according to the purpose of their signification, which is in relation to our surroundings. Consequently, in order to judge of a word's signification or co-signification, we must consider the things which are around us, in which a word derived from some form is never used in the plural unless there are several supposita. For a man who has on two garments is not said to be "two persons clothed," but "one clothed with two garments"; and whoever has two qualities is designated in the singular as "such by reason of the two qualities." Now the assumed nature is, as it were, a garment, although this similitude does not fit at all points, as has been said above (Q. 2, A. 6, ad 1). And hence, if the Divine Person were to assume two human natures, He would be called, on account of the unity of suppositum, one man having two human natures. Now many men are said to be one people, inasmuch as they have some one thing in common, and not on account of the unity of suppositum. So likewise, if two Divine Persons were to assume one singular human nature, they would be said to be one man, as stated (A. 6, ad 1), not from the unity of suppositum, but because they have some one thing in common.

Reply Obj. 3: The Divine and human natures do not bear the same relation to the one Divine Person, but the Divine Nature is related first of all thereto, inasmuch as It is one with It from eternity; and afterwards the human nature is related to the Divine Person, inasmuch as it is assumed by the Divine Person in time, not indeed that the nature is the Person, but that the Person of God subsists in human nature. For the Son of God is His Godhead, but is not His manhood. And hence, in order that the human nature may be assumed by the Divine Person, the Divine Nature must be united by a personal union with the whole nature assumed, i.e. in all its parts. Now in the two natures assumed there would be a uniform relation to the Divine Person, nor would one assume the other. Hence it would not be necessary for one of them to be altogether united to the other, i.e. all the parts of one with all the parts of the other.

EIGHTH ARTICLE [III, Q. 3, Art. 8]

Whether it was more fitting that the Person of the Son rather than any other Divine Person should assume human nature?

Objection 1: It would seem that it was not more fitting that the Son of God should become incarnate than the Father or the Holy Ghost. For by the mystery of the Incarnation men are led to the true knowledge of God, according to John 18:37: "For this was I born, and for this came I into the world, to give testimony to the truth." But by the Person of the Son of God becoming incarnate many have been kept back from the true knowledge of God, since they referred to the very Person of the Son what was said of the Son in His human nature, as Arius, who held an inequality of Persons, according to what is said (John 14:28): "The Father is greater than I." Now this error would not have arisen if the Person of the Father had become incarnate, for no one would have taken the Father to be less than the Son. Hence it seems fitting that the Person of the Father, rather than the Person of the Son, should have become incarnate.

Obj. 2: Further, the effect of the Incarnation would seem to be, as it were, a second creation of human nature, according to Gal. 6:15: "For in Christ Jesus neither circumcision availeth anything, nor uncircumcision, but a new creature." But the power of creation is appropriated to the Father. Therefore it would have been more becoming to the Father than to the Son to become incarnate.

Obj. 3: Further, the Incarnation is ordained to the remission of sins, according to Matt. 1:21: "Thou shalt call His name Jesus. For He shall save His people from their sins." Now the remission of sins is attributed to the Holy Ghost according to John 20:22, 23: "Receive ye the Holy Ghost. Whose sins you shall forgive, they are forgiven them." Therefore it became the Person of the Holy Ghost rather than the Person of the Son to become incarnate.

*On the contrary,* Damascene says (De Fide Orth. iii, 1): "In the mystery of the Incarnation the wisdom and power of God are made known: the wisdom, for He found a most suitable discharge for a most heavy debt; the power, for He made the conquered conquer." But power and wisdom are appropriated to the Son, according to 1 Cor. 1:24: "Christ, the power of God and the wisdom of God." Therefore it was fitting that the Person of the Son should become incarnate.

*I answer that,* It was most fitting that the Person of the Son should become incarnate. First, on the part of the union; for such as are similar are fittingly united. Now the Person of the Son, Who is the Word of God, has a certain common agreement with all creatures, because the word of the craftsman, i.e. his concept, is an exemplar likeness of whatever is made by him. Hence the Word of God, Who is His eternal concept, is the exemplar likeness of all creatures. And therefore as creatures are established in their proper species, though movably, by the participation of this likeness, so by the non-participated and personal union of the Word with a creature, it was fitting that the creature should be restored in order to its eternal and unchangeable perfection; for the craftsman by the intelligible form of his art, whereby he fashioned his handiwork, restores it when it has fallen into ruin. Moreover, He has a particular agreement with human nature, since the Word is a concept of the eternal Wisdom, from Whom all man's wisdom is derived. And hence man is perfected in wisdom (which is his proper perfection, as he is rational) by participating the Word of God, as the disciple is instructed by receiving the word of his master. Hence it is said (Ecclus. 1:5): "The Word of God on high is the fountain of wisdom." And hence for the consummate perfection of man it was fitting that the very Word of God should be personally united to human nature.

Secondly, the reason of this fitness may be taken from the end of the union, which is the fulfilling of predestination, i.e. of such as are preordained to the heavenly inheritance, which is bestowed only on sons, according to Rom. 8:17: "If sons, heirs also." Hence it was fitting that by Him Who is the natural Son, men should share this likeness of sonship by adoption, as the Apostle says in the same chapter (Rom. 8:29): "For whom He foreknew, He also predestinated to be made conformable to the image of His Son."

Thirdly, the reason for this fitness may be taken from the sin of our first parent, for which the Incarnation supplied the remedy. For the first man sinned by seeking knowledge, as is plain from the words of the serpent, promising to man the knowledge of good and evil. Hence it was fitting that by the Word of true knowledge man might be led back to God, having wandered from God through an inordinate thirst for knowledge.

Reply Obj. 1: There is nothing which human malice cannot abuse, since it even abuses God's goodness, according to Rom. 2:4: "Or despisest thou the riches of His goodness?" Hence, even if the Person of the Father had become incarnate, men would have been capable of finding an occasion of error, as though the Son were not able to restore human nature.

Reply Obj. 2: The first creation of things was made by the power of God the Father through the Word; hence the second creation ought to have been brought about through the Word, by the power of God the Father, in order that restoration should correspond to creation according to 2 Cor. 5:19: "For God indeed was in Christ reconciling the world to Himself."

Reply Obj. 3: To be the gift of the Father and the Son is proper to the Holy Ghost. But the remission of sins is caused by the Holy Ghost, as by the gift of God. And hence it was more fitting to man's justification that the Son should become incarnate, Whose gift the Holy Ghost is.

# QUESTION 4

OF THE MODE OF UNION ON THE PART OF THE HUMAN NATURE (In Six Articles)

We must now consider the union on the part of what was assumed. About which we must consider first what things were assumed by the Word of God; secondly, what were co-assumed, whether perfections or defects.

Now the Son of God assumed human nature and its parts. Hence a threefold consideration arises. First, with regard to the nature; secondly, with regard to its parts; thirdly, with regard to the order of the assumption.

Under the first head there are six points of inquiry:

(1) Whether human nature was more capable of being assumed than any other nature?

(2) Whether He assumed a person?

(3) Whether He assumed a man?

(4) Whether it was becoming that He should assume human nature abstracted from all individuals?

(5) Whether it was becoming that He should assume human nature in all its individuals?

(6) Whether it was becoming that He should assume human nature in any man begotten of the stock of Adam?

FIRST ARTICLE [III, Q. 4, Art. 1]

Whether Human Nature Was More Assumable by the Son of God Than Any Other Nature?

Objection 1: It would seem that human nature is not more capable of being assumed by the Son of God than any other nature. For Augustine says (Ep. ad Volusianum cxxxvii): "In deeds wrought miraculously the whole reason of the deed is the power of the doer." Now the power of God Who wrought the Incarnation, which is a most miraculous work, is not limited to one nature, since the power of God is infinite. Therefore human nature is not more capable of being assumed than any other creature.

Obj. 2: Further, likeness is the foundation of the fittingness of the Incarnation of the Divine Person, as above stated (Q. 3, A. 8). But as in rational creatures we find the likeness of image, so in irrational creatures we find the image of trace. Therefore the irrational creature was as capable of assumption as human nature.

Obj. 3: Further, in the angelic nature we find a more perfect likeness than in human nature, as Gregory says: (Hom. de Cent. Ovib.; xxxiv in Ev.), where he introduces Ezech. 28:12: "Thou wast the seal of resemblance." And sin is found in angels, even as in man, according to Job 4:18: "And in His angels He found wickedness." Therefore the angelic nature was as capable of assumption as the nature of man.

Obj. 4: Further, since the highest perfection belongs to God, the more like to God a thing is, the more perfect it is. But the whole universe is more perfect than its parts, amongst which is human nature. Therefore the whole universe is more capable of being assumed than human nature.

*On the contrary,* It is said (Prov. 8:31) by the mouth of Begotten Wisdom: "My delights were to be with the children of men"; and hence there would seem some fitness in the union of the Son of God with human nature.

*I answer that,* A thing is said to be assumable as

being capable of being assumed by a Divine Person, and this capability cannot be taken with reference to the natural passive power, which does not extend to what transcends the natural order, as the personal union of a creature with God transcends it. Hence it follows that a thing is said to be assumable according to some fitness for such a union. Now this fitness in human nature may be taken from two things, viz. according to its dignity, and according to its need. According to its dignity, because human nature, as being rational and intellectual, was made for attaining to the Word to some extent by its operation, viz. by knowing and loving Him. According to its need--because it stood in need of restoration, having fallen under original sin. Now these two things belong to human nature alone. For in the irrational creature the fitness of dignity is wanting, and in the angelic nature the aforesaid fitness of need is wanting. Hence it follows that only human nature was assumable.

Reply Obj. 1: Creatures are said to be "such" with reference to their proper causes, not with reference to what belongs to them from their first and universal causes; thus we call a disease incurable, not that it cannot be cured by God, but that it cannot be cured by the proper principles of the subject. Therefore a creature is said to be not assumable, not as if we withdrew anything from the power of God, but in order to show the condition of the creature, which has no capability for this.

Reply Obj. 2: The likeness of image is found in human nature, forasmuch as it is capable of God, viz. by attaining to Him through its own operation of knowledge and love. But the likeness of trace regards only a representation by Divine impression, existing in the creature, and does not imply that the irrational creature, in which such a likeness is, can attain to God by its own operation alone. For what does not come up to the less, has no fitness for the greater; as a body which is not fitted to be perfected by a sensitive soul is much less fitted for an intellectual soul. Now much greater and more perfect is the union with God in personal being than the union by operation. And hence the irrational creature which falls short of the union with God by operation has no fitness to be united with Him in personal being.

Reply Obj. 3: Some say that angels are not assumable, since they are perfect in their personality from the beginning of their creation, inasmuch as they are not subject to generation and corruption; hence they cannot be assumed to the unity of a Divine Person, unless their personality be destroyed, and this does not befit the incorruptibility of their nature nor the goodness of the one assuming, to Whom it does not belong to corrupt any perfection in the creature assumed. But this would not seem totally to disprove the fitness of the angelic nature for being assumed. For God by producing a new angelic nature could join it to Himself in unity of Person, and in this way nothing pre-existing would be corrupted in it. But as was said above, there is wanting the fitness of need, because, although the angelic nature in some is the subject of sin, their sin is irremediable, as stated above (I, Q. 64, A. 2).

Reply Obj. 4: The perfection of the universe is not the perfection of one person or suppositum, but of something which is one by position or order, whereof very many parts are not capable of assumption, as was said above. Hence it follows that only human nature is capable of being assumed.

SECOND ARTICLE [III, Q. 4, Art. 2]

Whether the Son of God Assumed a Person?

Objection 1: It would seem that the Son of God assumed a person. For Damascene says (De Fide Orth. iii, 11) that the Son of God "assumed human nature in atomo," i.e. in an individual. But an individual in rational nature is a person, as is plain from Boethius (De Duab. Nat.). Therefore the Son of God assumed a person.

Obj. 2: Further, Damascene says (De Fide Orth. iii, 6) that the Son of God "assumed what He had sown in our nature." But He sowed our personality there. Therefore the Son of God assumed a person.

Obj. 3: Further, nothing is absorbed unless it exist. But Innocent III [*Paschas. Diac., De Spiritu Sanct. ii] says in a Decretal that "the Person of God absorbed the person of man." Therefore it would seem that the person of man existed previous to its being assumed.

*On the contrary,* Augustine [*Fulgentius] says (De Fide ad Petrum ii) that "God assumed the nature, not the person, of man."

*I answer that,* A thing is said to be assumed inasmuch as it is taken into another. Hence, what is assumed must be presupposed to the assumption, as what is moved locally is presupposed to the motion. Now a person in human nature is not presupposed to assumption; rather, it is the term of the assumption, as was said (Q. 3, AA. 1, 2). For if it were presupposed, it must either have been corrupted--in which case it was useless; or it remains after the union--and thus there would be two persons, one assuming and the other assumed, which is false, as was shown above (Q. 2, A. 6). Hence it follows that the Son of God nowise assumed a human person.

Reply Obj. 1: The Son of God assumed human nature in atomo, i.e. in an individual, which is no other than the uncreated suppositum, the Person of the Son of God. Hence it does not follow that a person was assumed.

Reply Obj. 2: Its proper personality is not wanting to the nature assumed through the loss of anything pertaining to the perfection of the human nature but through the addition of something which is above human nature, viz. the union with a Divine Person.

Reply Obj. 3: Absorption does not here imply the destruction of anything pre-existing, but the hindering what might otherwise have been. For if the human nature had not been assumed by a Divine Person, the human nature would have had its own personality; and in this way is it said, although improperly, that the Person "absorbed the person," inasmuch as the Divine Person by His union hindered the human nature from having its personality.

THIRD ARTICLE [III, Q. 4, Art. 3]

Whether the Divine Person Assumed a Man?

Objection 1: It would seem that the Divine Person assumed a man. For it is written (Ps. 64:5): "Blessed is he whom Thou hast chosen and taken to Thee," which a gloss expounds of Christ; and Augustine says (De Agone Christ. xi): "The Son of God assumed a man, and in him bore things human."

Obj. 2: Further, the word "man" signifies a human nature. But the Son of God assumed a human nature. Therefore He assumed a man.

Obj. 3: Further, the Son of God is a man. But He is not one of the men He did not assume, for with equal reason He would be Peter or any other man. Therefore He is the man whom He assumed.

*On the contrary,* Is the authority of Felix, Pope and Martyr, which is quoted by the Council of Ephesus: "We believe in our Lord Jesus Christ, born of the Virgin Mary, because He is the Eternal Son and Word of God, and not a man assumed by God, in such sort that there is another besides Him. For the Son of God did not assume a man, so that there be another besides Him."

*I answer that,* As has been said above (A. 2), what is assumed is not the term of the assumption, but is presupposed to the assumption. Now it was said (Q. 3, AA. 1, 2) that the individual to Whom the human nature is assumed is none other than the Divine Person, Who is the term of the assumption. Now this word "man" signifies human nature, as it is in a suppositum, because, as Damascene says (De Fide Orth. iii, 4, 11), this word God signifies Him Who has human nature. And hence it cannot properly be said that the Son assumed a man, granted (as it must be, in fact) that in Christ there is but one suppositum and one hypostasis. But according to such as hold that there are two hypostases or two supposita in Christ, it may fittingly and properly be said that the Son of God assumed a man. Hence the first opinion quoted in Sent. iii, D. 6, grants that a man was assumed. But this opinion is erroneous, as was said above (Q. 2, A. 6).

Reply Obj. 1: These phrases are not to be taken too literally, but are to be loyally explained, wherever they are used by holy doctors; so as to say that a man was assumed, inasmuch as his nature was assumed; and because the assumption terminated in this--that the Son of God is man.

Reply Obj. 2: The word "man" signifies human nature in the concrete, inasmuch as it is in a suppositum; and hence, since we cannot say a suppositum was assumed, so we cannot say a man was assumed.

Reply Obj. 3: The Son of God is not the man whom He assumed, but the man whose nature He assumed.

FOURTH ARTICLE [III, Q. 4, Art. 4]

Whether the Son of God Ought to Have Assumed Human Nature Abstracted from All Individuals?

Objection 1: It would seem that the Son of God ought to have assumed human nature abstracted from all individuals. For the assumption of human nature took place for the common salvation of all men; hence it is said of Christ (1 Tim. 4:10) that He is "the Saviour of all men, especially of the faithful." But nature as it is in individuals withdraws from its universality. Therefore the Son of God ought to have assumed human nature as it is abstracted from all individuals.

Obj. 2: Further, what is noblest in all things ought to be attributed to God. But in every genus what is of itself is best. Therefore the Son of God ought to have assumed self-existing ( per se ) man, which, according to Platonists, is human nature abstracted from its individuals. Therefore the Son of God ought to have assumed this.

Obj. 3: Further, human nature was not assumed by the Son of God in the concrete as is signified by the word "man," as was said above (A. 3). Now in this way it signifies human nature as it is in individuals, as is plain from what has been said (A. 3). Therefore the Son of God assumed human nature as it is separated from individuals.

*On the contrary,* Damascene says (De Fide Orth. iii, 11): "God the Word Incarnate did not assume a nature which exists in pure thought; for this would have been no Incarnation, but a false and fictitious Incarnation." But human nature as it is separated or abstracted from individuals is "taken to be a pure conception, since it does not exist in itself," as Damascene says (De Fide Orth. iii, 11). Therefore the Son of God did not assume human nature, as it is separated from individuals.

*I answer that,* The nature of man or of any other sensible thing, beyond the being which it has in individuals, may be taken in two ways: first, as if it had being of itself, away from matter, as the Platonists held; secondly, as existing in an intellect either human or Divine. Now it cannot subsist of itself, as the Philosopher proves (Metaph. vii, 26, 27, 29, 51), because sensible matter belongs to the specific nature of sensible things, and is placed in its definition, as flesh and bones in the definition of man. Hence human nature cannot be without sensible matter. Nevertheless, if human nature were subsistent in this way, it would not be fitting that it should be assumed by the Word of God. First, because this assumption is terminated in a Person, and it is contrary to the nature of a common form to be thus individualized in a person. Secondly, because to a common nature can only be attributed common and universal operations, according to which man neither merits nor demerits, whereas, *on the contrary*, the assumption took place in order that the Son of God, having assumed our nature, might merit for us. Thirdly, because a nature so existing would not be sensible, but intelligible. But the Son of God assumed human nature in order to show Himself in men's sight, according to Baruch 3:38: "Afterwards He was seen upon earth, and conversed with men."

Likewise, neither could human nature have been assumed by the Son of God, as it is in the Divine intellect, since it would be none other than the Divine Nature; and, according to this, human nature would be in the Son of God from eternity. Neither can we say that the Son of God assumed human nature as it is in a human intellect, for this would mean nothing else but that He is understood to assume a human nature; and thus if He did not assume it in reality, this would be a false understanding; nor would this assumption of the human nature be anything but a fictitious Incarnation, as Damascene says (De Fide Orth. iii, 11).

Reply Obj. 1: The incarnate Son of God is the common Saviour of all, not by a generic or specific community, such as is attributed to the nature separated from the individuals, but by a community of cause, whereby the incarnate Son of God is the universal cause of human salvation.

Reply Obj. 2: Self-existing ( per se ) man is not to be found in nature in such a way as to be outside the singular, as the Platonists held, although some say Plato believed that the separate man was only in the Divine intellect. And hence it was not necessary for it to be assumed by the Word, since it had been with Him from eternity.

Reply Obj. 3: Although human nature was not assumed in the concrete, as if the suppositum were presupposed to the assumption, nevertheless it is assumed in an individual, since it is assumed so as to be in an individual.

FIFTH ARTICLE [III, Q. 4, Art. 5]

Whether the Son of God Ought to Have Assumed Human Nature in All Individuals?

Objection 1: It would seem that the Son of God ought to have assumed human nature in all individuals. For what is assumed first and by itself is human nature. But what belongs essentially to a nature belongs to all who exist in the nature. Therefore it was fitting that human nature should be assumed by the Word of God in all its supposita.

Obj. 2: Further, the Divine Incarnation proceeded from Divine Love; hence it is written (John 3:16): "God so loved the world as to give His only-begotten Son." But love makes us give ourselves to our friends as much as we can, and it was possible for the Son of God to assume several human natures, as was said above (Q. 3, A. 7), and with equal reason all. Hence it was fitting for the Son of God to assume human nature in all its supposita.

Obj. 3: Further, a skilful workman completes his work in the shortest manner possible. But it would have been a shorter way if all men had been assumed to the natural sonship than for one natural Son to lead many to the adoption of sons, as is written Gal. 4:5 (cf. Heb. 2:10). Therefore human nature ought to have been assumed by God in all its supposita.

*On the contrary,* Damascene says (De Fide Orth. iii, 11) that the Son of God "did not assume human nature as a species, nor did He assume all its hypostases."

*I answer that,* It was unfitting for human nature to be assumed by the Word in all its supposita. First, because the multitude of supposita of human nature, which are natural to it, would have been taken away. For since we must not see any other suppositum in the assumed nature, except the Person assuming, as was said above (A. 3), if there was no human nature except what was assumed, it would follow that there was but one suppositum of human nature, which is the Person assuming. Secondly, because this would have been derogatory to the dignity of the incarnate Son of God, as He is the First-born of many brethren, according to the human nature, even as He is the First-born of all creatures according to the Divine, for then all men would be of equal dignity. Thirdly, because it is fitting that as one Divine suppositum is incarnate, so He should assume one human nature, so that on both sides unity might be found.

Reply Obj. 1: To be assumed belongs to the human nature of itself, because it does not belong to it by reason of a person, as it belongs to the Divine Nature to assume by reason of the Person; not, however, that it belongs to it of itself as if belonging to its essential principles, or as its natural property in which manner it would belong to all its supposita.

Reply Obj. 2: The love of God to men is shown not merely in the assumption of human nature, but especially in what He suffered in human nature for other men, according to Rom. 5:8: "But God commendeth His charity towards us; because when as yet we were sinners . . . Christ died for us," which would not have taken place had He assumed human nature in all its supposita.

Reply Obj. 3: In order to shorten the way, which every skilful workman does, what can be done by one must not be done by many. Hence it was most fitting that by one man all the rest should be saved.

SIXTH ARTICLE [III, Q. 4, Art. 6]

Whether It Was Fitting for the Son of God to Assume Human Nature of the Stock of Adam?

Objection 1: It would seem that it was not fitting for the Son of God to assume human nature of the stock of Adam, for the Apostle says (Heb. 7:26): "For it was fitting that we should have such a high priest . . . separated from sinners." But He would have been still further separated from sinners had He not assumed human nature of the stock of Adam, a sinner. Hence it seems that He ought not to have assumed human nature of the stock of Adam.

Obj. 2: Further, in every genus the principle is nobler than what is from the principle. Hence, if He wished to assume human nature, He ought to have assumed it in Adam himself.

Obj. 3: Further, the Gentiles were greater sinners than the Jews, as a gloss says on Gal. 2:15: "For we by nature are Jews, and not of the Gentiles, sinners." Hence, if He wished to assume human nature from sinners, He ought rather to have assumed it from the Gentiles than from the stock of Abraham, who was just.

*On the contrary,* (Luke 3), the genealogy of our Lord is traced back to Adam.

*I answer that,* As Augustine says (De Trin. xiii, 18): "God was able to assume human nature elsewhere than from the stock of Adam, who by his sin had fettered the whole human race; yet God judged it better to assume human nature from the vanquished race, and thus to vanquish the enemy of the human race." And this for three reasons: First, because it would seem to belong to justice that he who sinned should make amends; and hence that from the nature which he had corrupted should be assumed that whereby satisfaction was to be made for the whole nature. Secondly, it pertains to man's greater dignity that the conqueror of the devil should spring from the stock conquered by the devil. Thirdly, because God's power is thereby made more manifest, since, from a corrupt and weakened nature, He assumed that which was raised to such might and glory.

Reply Obj. 1: Christ ought to be separated from sinners as regards sin, which He came to overthrow, and not as regards nature which He came to save, and in which "it behooved Him in all things to be made like to His brethren," as the Apostle says (Heb. 2:17). And in this is His innocence the more wonderful, seeing that though assumed from a mass tainted by sin, His nature was endowed with such purity.

Reply Obj. 2: As was said above (ad 1) it behooved Him Who came to take away sins to be separated from sinners as regards sin, to which Adam was subject, whom Christ "brought out of his sin," as is written (Wis. 10:2). For it behooved Him Who came to cleanse all, not to need cleansing Himself; just as in every genus of motion the first mover is immovable as regards that motion, and the first to alter is itself unalterable. Hence it was not fitting that He should assume human nature in Adam himself.

Reply Obj. 3: Since Christ ought especially to be separated from sinners as regards sin, and to possess the highest innocence, it was fitting that between the first sinner and Christ some just men should stand midway, in whom certain forecasts of (His) future holiness should shine forth. And hence, even in the people from whom Christ was to be born, God appointed signs of holiness, which began in Abraham, who was the first to receive the promise of Christ, and circumcision, as a sign that the covenant should be kept, as is written (Gen. 17:11).

## QUESTION 5

OF THE PARTS OF HUMAN NATURE WHICH WERE ASSUMED (In Four Articles)

We must now consider the assumption of the parts of human nature; and under this head there are four points of inquiry:

(1) Whether the Son of God ought to have assumed a true body?

(2) Whether He ought to have assumed an earthly body, i.e. one of flesh and blood?

(3) Whether He ought to have assumed a soul?

(4) Whether He ought to have assumed an intellect?

FIRST ARTICLE [III, Q. 5, Art. 1]

Whether the Son of God Ought to Have Assumed a True Body?

Objection 1: It would seem that the Son of God did not assume a true body. For it is written (Phil. 2:7), that He was "made in the likeness of men." But what is something in truth is not said to be in the likeness thereof. Therefore the Son of God did not assume a true body.

Obj. 2: Further, the assumption of a body in no way diminishes the dignity of the Godhead; for Pope Leo says (Serm. de Nativ.) that "the glorification did not absorb the lesser nature, nor did the assumption lessen the higher." But it pertains to the dignity of God to be altogether separated from bodies. Therefore it seems that by the assumption God was not united to a body.

Obj. 3: Further, signs ought to correspond to the realities. But the apparitions of the Old Testament which were signs of the manifestation of Christ were not in a real body, but by visions in the imagination, as is plain from Isa. 60:1: "I saw the Lord sitting," etc. Hence it would seem that the apparition of the Son of God in the world was not in a real body, but only in imagination.

*On the contrary,* Augustine says (Qq. lxxxiii, qu. 13): "If the body of Christ was a phantom, Christ deceived us, and if He deceived us, He is not the Truth. But Christ is the Truth. Therefore His body was not a phantom." Hence it is plain that He assumed a true body.

*I answer that,* As is said (De Eccles. Dogm. ii). The Son of God was not born in appearance only, as if He had an imaginary body; but His body was real. The proof of this is threefold. First, from the essence of human nature to which it pertains to have a true body. Therefore granted, as already proved (Q. 4, A. 1), that it was fitting for the Son of God to assume human nature, He must consequently have assumed a real body. The second reason is taken from what was done in the mystery of the Incarnation. For if His body was not real but imaginary, He neither underwent a real death, nor of those things which the Evangelists recount of Him, did He do any in very truth, but only in appearance; and hence it would also follow that the real salvation of man has not taken place; since the effect must be proportionate to the cause. The third reason is taken from the dignity of the Person assuming, Whom it did not become to have anything fictitious in His work, since He is the Truth. Hence our Lord Himself deigned to refute this error (Luke 24:37, 39), when the disciples, "troubled and frighted, supposed that they saw a spirit," and not a true body; wherefore He offered Himself to their touch, saying: "Handle, and see; for a spirit hath not flesh and bones, as you see Me to have."

Reply Obj. 1: This likeness indicates the truth of the human nature in Christ--just as all that truly exist in human nature are said to be like in species--and not a mere imaginary likeness. In proof of this the Apostle subjoins (Phil. 2:8) that He became "obedient unto death, even to the death of the cross"; which would have been impossible, had it been only an imaginary likeness.

Reply Obj. 2: By assuming a true body the dignity of the Son of God is nowise lessened. Hence Augustine [*Fulgentius] says (De Fide ad Petrum ii): "He emptied Himself, taking the form of a servant, that He might become a servant; yet did He not lose the fulness of the form of God." For the Son of God assumed a true body, not so as to become the form of a body, which is repugnant to the Divine simplicity and purity--for this would be to assume a body to the unity of the nature, which is impossible, as is plain from what has been stated above (Q. 2, A. 1): but, the natures remaining distinct, He assumed a body to the unity of Person.

Reply Obj. 3: The figure ought to correspond to the reality as regards the likeness and not as regards the truth of the thing. For if they were alike in all points, it would no longer be a likeness but the reality itself, as Damascene says (De Fide Orth. iii, 26). Hence it was more fitting that the apparitions of the old Testament should be in appearance only, being figures; and that the apparition of the Son of God in the world should be in a real body, being the thing prefigured by these figures. Hence the Apostle says (Col. 2:17): "Which are a shadow of things to come, but the body is Christ's."

SECOND ARTICLE [III, Q. 5, Art. 2]

Whether the Son of God Ought to Have Assumed a Carnal or Earthly Body?

Objection 1: It would seem that Christ had not a carnal or earthly, but a heavenly body. For the Apostle says (1 Cor. 15:41): "The first man was of the earth, earthy; the second man from heaven, heavenly." But the first man, i.e. Adam, was of the earth as regards his body, as is plain from Gen. 1. Therefore the second man, i.e. Christ, was of heaven as regards the body.

Obj. 2: Further, it is said (1 Cor. 15:50): "Flesh and blood shall not [Vulg.: 'cannot'] possess the kingdom of God." But the kingdom of God is in Christ chiefly. Therefore there is no flesh or blood in Him, but rather a heavenly body.

Obj. 3: Further, whatever is best is to be attributed to God. But of all bodies a heavenly body is the best. Therefore it behooved Christ to assume such a body.

*On the contrary,* our Lord says (Luke 24:39): "A spirit hath not flesh and bones, as you see Me to have." Now flesh and bones are not of the matter of heavenly bodies, but are composed of the inferior elements. Therefore the body of Christ was not a heavenly, but a carnal and earthly body.

*I answer that,* By the reasons which proved that the body of Christ was not an imaginary one, it may also be shown that it was not a heavenly body. First, because even as the truth of the human nature of Christ would not have been maintained had His body been an imaginary one, such as Manes supposed, so likewise it would not have been maintained if we supposed, as did Valentine, that it was a heavenly body. For since the form of man is a natural thing, it requires determinate matter, to wit, flesh and bones, which must be placed in the definition of man, as is plain from the Philosopher (Metaph. vii, 39). Secondly, because this would lessen the truth of such things as Christ did in the body. For since a heavenly body is impassible and incorruptible, as is proved De Coel. i, 20, if the Son of God had assumed a heavenly body, He would not have truly hungered or thirsted, nor would he have undergone His passion and death. Thirdly, this would have detracted from God's truthfulness. For since the Son of God showed Himself to men, as if He had a carnal and earthly body, the manifestation would have been false, had He had a heavenly body. Hence (De Eccles. Dogm. ii) it is said: "The Son of God was born, taking flesh of the Virgin's body, and not bringing it with Him from heaven."

Reply Obj. 1: Christ is said in two ways to have come down from heaven. First, as regards His Divine Nature; not indeed that the Divine Nature ceased to be in heaven, but inasmuch as He began to be here below in a new way, viz. by His assumed nature, according to John 3:13: "No man hath ascended into heaven, but He that descended from heaven, the Son of Man, Who is in heaven."

Secondly, as regards His body, not indeed that the very substance of the body of Christ descended from heaven, but that His body was formed by a heavenly power, i.e. by the Holy Ghost. Hence Augustine, explaining the passage quoted, says (Ad Orosium [*Dial. Qq. lxv, qu. 4, work of an unknown author]): "I call Christ a heavenly man because He was not conceived of human seed." And Hilary expounds it in the same way (De Trin. x).

Reply Obj. 2: Flesh and blood are not taken here for the substance of flesh and blood, but for the corruption of flesh, which was not in Christ as far as it was sinful; but as far as it was a punishment; thus, for a time, it was in Christ, that He might carry through the work of our redemption.

Reply Obj. 3: It pertains to the greatest glory of God to have raised a weak and earthly body to such sublimity. Hence in the General Council of Ephesus (P. II, Act. I) we read the saying of St. Theophilus: "Just as the best workmen are esteemed not merely for displaying their skill in precious materials, but very often because by making use of the poorest clay and commonest earth, they show the power of their craft; so the best of all workmen, the Word of God, did not come down to us by taking a heavenly body of some most precious matter, but shewed the greatness of His skill in clay."

THIRD ARTICLE [III, Q. 5, Art. 3]

Whether the Son of God Assumed a Soul?

Objection 1: It would seem that the Son of God did not assume a soul. For John has said, teaching the mystery of the Incarnation (John 1:14): "The Word was made flesh"--no mention being made of a soul. Now it is not said that "the Word was made flesh" as if changed to flesh, but because He assumed flesh. Therefore He seems not to have assumed a soul.

Obj. 2: Further, a soul is necessary to the body, in order to quicken it. But this was not necessary for the body of Christ, as it would seem, for of the Word of God it is written (Ps. 35:10): Lord, "with Thee is the fountain of life." Therefore it would seem altogether superfluous for the soul to be there, when the Word was present. But "God and nature do nothing uselessly," as the Philosopher says (De Coel. i, 32; ii, 56). Therefore the Word would seem not to have assumed a soul.

Obj. 3: Further, by the union of soul and body is constituted the common nature, which is the human species. But "in the Lord Jesus Christ we are not to look for a common species," as Damascene says (De Fide Orth. iii, 3). Therefore He did not assume a soul.

*On the contrary,* Augustine says (De Agone Christ. xxi): "Let us not hearken to such as say that only a human body was assumed by the Word of God; and take 'the Word was made flesh' to mean that the man had no soul nor any other part of a man, save flesh."

*I answer that,* As Augustine says (De Haeres. 69, 55), it was first of all the opinion of Arius and then of Apollinaris that the Son of God assumed only flesh, without a soul, holding that the Word took the place of a soul to the body. And consequently it followed that there were not two natures in Christ, but only one; for from a soul and body one human nature is constituted. But this opinion cannot hold, for three reasons. First, because it is counter to the authority of Scripture, in which our Lord makes mention of His soul, Matt. 26:38: "My soul is sorrowful even unto death"; and John 10:18: "I have power to lay down My soul [ animam meam: Douay: 'My life']." But to this Apollinaris replied that in these words soul is taken metaphorically, in which way mention is made in the Old Testament of the soul of God (Isa. 1:14): "My soul hateth your new moons and your solemnities." But, as Augustine says (Qq. lxxxiii, qu. 80), the Evangelists relate how Jesus wondered, was angered, sad, and hungry. Now these show that He had a true soul, just as that He ate, slept and was weary shows that He had a true human body: otherwise, if these things are a metaphor, because the like are said of God in the Old Testament, the trustworthiness of the Gospel story is undermined. For it is one thing that things were foretold in a figure, and another that historical events were related in very truth by the Evangelists. Secondly, this error lessens the utility of the Incarnation, which is man's liberation. For Augustine [*Vigilius Tapsensis] argues thus (Contra Felician. xiii): "If the Son of God in taking flesh passed over the soul, either He knew its sinlessness, and trusted it did not need a remedy; or He considered it unsuitable to Him, and did not bestow on it the boon of redemption; or He reckoned it altogether incurable, and was unable to heal it; or He cast it off as worthless and seemingly unfit for any use. Now two of these reasons imply a blasphemy against God. For how shall we call Him omnipotent, if He is unable to heal what is beyond hope? Or God of all, if He has not made our soul. And as regards the other two reasons, in one the cause of the soul is ignored, and in the other no place is given to merit. Is He to be considered to understand the cause of the soul, Who seeks to separate it from the sin of wilful transgression, enabled as it is to receive the law by the endowment of the habit of reason? Or how can His generosity be known to any one who says it was despised on account of its ignoble sinfulness? If you look at its origin, the substance of the soul is more precious than the body: but if at the sin of transgression, on account of its intelligence it is worse than the body. Now I know and declare that Christ is perfect wisdom, nor have I any doubt that He is most loving; and because of the first of these He did not despise what was better and more capable of prudence; and because of the second He protected what was most wounded." Thirdly, this position is against the truth of the Incarnation. For flesh and the other parts of man receive their species through the soul. Hence, if the soul is absent, there are no bones nor flesh, except equivocally, as is plain from the Philosopher (De Anima ii, 9; Metaph. vii, 34).

Reply Obj. 1: When we say, "The Word was made

flesh," "flesh" is taken for the whole man, as if we were to say, "The Word was made man," as Isa. 40:5: "All flesh together shall see that the mouth of the Lord hath spoken." And the whole man is signified by flesh, because, as is said in the authority quoted, the Son of God became visible by flesh; hence it is subjoined: "And we saw His glory." Or because, as Augustine says (Qq. lxxxiii, qu. 80), "in all that union the Word is the highest, and flesh the last and lowest. Hence, wishing to commend the love of God's humility to us, the Evangelist mentioned the Word and flesh, leaving the soul on one side, since it is less than the Word and nobler than flesh." Again, it was reasonable to mention flesh, which, as being farther away from the Word, was less assumable, as it would seem.

Reply Obj. 2: The Word is the fountain of life, as the first effective cause of life; but the soul is the principle of the life of the body, as its form. Now the form is the effect of the agent. Hence from the presence of the Word it might rather have been concluded that the body was animated, just as from the presence of fire it may be concluded that the body, in which fire adheres, is warm.

Reply Obj. 3: It is not unfitting, indeed it is necessary to say that in Christ there was a nature which was constituted by the soul coming to the body. But Damascene denied that in Jesus Christ there was a common species, i.e. a third something resulting from the Godhead and the humanity.

FOURTH ARTICLE [II-II, Q. 5, Art. 4]

Whether the Son of God Assumed a Human Mind or Intellect?

Objection 1: It would seem that the Son of God did not assume a human mind or intellect. For where a thing is present, its image is not required. But man is made to God's image, as regards his mind, as Augustine says (De Trin. xiv, 3, 6). Hence, since in Christ there was the presence of the Divine Word itself, there was no need of a human mind.

Obj. 2: Further, the greater light dims the lesser. But the Word of God, Who is "the light, which enlighteneth every man that cometh into this world," as is written John 1:9, is compared to the mind as the greater light to the lesser; since our mind is a light, being as it were a lamp enkindled by the First Light (Prov. 20:27): "The spirit of a man is the lamp of the Lord." Therefore in Christ Who is the Word of God, there is no need of a human mind.

Obj. 3: Further, the assumption of human nature by the Word of God is called His Incarnation. But the intellect or human mind is nothing carnal, either in its substance or in its act, for it is not the act of a body, as is proved De Anima iii, 6. Hence it would seem that the Son of God did not assume a human mind.

*On the contrary,* Augustine [*Fulgentius] says (De Fide ad Petrum xiv): "Firmly hold and nowise doubt that Christ the Son of God has true flesh and a rational soul of the same kind as ours, since of His flesh He says (Luke 24:39): 'Handle, and see; for a spirit hath not flesh and bones, as you see Me to have.' And He proves that He has a soul, saying (John 17): 'I lay down My soul [Douay: 'life'] that I may take it again.' And He proves that He has an intellect, saying (Matt. 11:29): 'Learn of Me, because I am meek and humble of heart.' And God says of Him by the prophet (Isa. 52:13): 'Behold my servant shall understand.'"

*I answer that,* As Augustine says (De Haeres. 49, 50), "the Apollinarists thought differently from the Catholic Church concerning the soul of Christ, saying with the Arians, that Christ took flesh alone, without a soul; and on being overcome on this point by the Gospel witness, they went on to say that the mind was wanting to Christ's soul, but that the Word supplied its place." But this position is refuted by the same arguments as the preceding. First, because it runs counter to the Gospel story, which relates how He marveled (as is plain from Matt. 8:10). Now marveling cannot be without reason, since it implies the collation of effect and cause, i.e. inasmuch as when we see an effect and are ignorant of its cause, we seek to know it, as is said Metaph. i, 2. Secondly, it is inconsistent with the purpose of the Incarnation, which is the justification of man from sin. For the human soul is not capable of sin nor of justifying grace except through the mind. Hence it was especially necessary for the mind to be assumed. Hence Damascene says (De Fide Orth. iii, 6) that "the Word of God assumed a body and an intellectual and rational soul," and adds afterwards: "The whole was united to the whole, that He might bestow salvation on me wholly; for what was not assumed is not curable." Thirdly, it is against the truth of the Incarnation. For since the body is proportioned to the soul as matter to its proper form, it is not truly human flesh if it is not perfected by human, i.e. a rational soul. And hence if Christ had had a soul without a mind, He would not have had true human flesh, but irrational flesh, since our soul differs from an animal soul by the mind alone. Hence Augustine says (Qq. lxxxiii, qu. 80) that from this error it would have followed that the Son of God "took an animal with the form of a human body," which, again, is against the Divine truth, which cannot suffer any fictitious untruth.

Reply Obj. 1: Where a thing is by its presence, its image is not required to supply the place of the thing, as where the emperor is the soldiers do not pay homage to his image. Yet the image of a thing is required together with its presence, that it may be perfected by the presence of the thing, just as the image in the wax is perfected by the impression of the seal, and as the image of man is reflected in the mirror by his presence. Hence in order to perfect the human mind it was necessary that the Word should unite it to Himself.

Reply Obj. 2: The greater light dims the lesser light of another luminous body; but it does not dim, rather it perfects the light of the body illuminated--at the presence of the sun the light of the stars is put out, but the light of the air is perfected. Now the intellect or mind of man is, as it were, a light lit up by the light of the Divine Word; and hence by the presence of the Word the mind of man is perfected rather than overshadowed.

Reply Obj. 3: Although the intellective power is not the act of a body, nevertheless the essence of the human soul, which is the form of the body, requires that it should be more noble, in order that it may have the power of understanding; and hence it is necessary that a better disposed body should correspond to it.

# QUESTION 6

OF THE ORDER OF ASSUMPTION (In Six Articles)

We must now consider the order of the foregoing assumption, and under this head there are six points of inquiry:

(1) Whether the Son of God assumed flesh through the medium of the soul?

(2) Whether He assumed the soul through the medium of the spirit or mind?

(3) Whether the soul was assumed previous to the flesh?

(4) Whether the flesh of Christ was assumed by the Word previous to being united to the soul?

(5) Whether the whole human nature was assumed through the medium of the parts?

(6) Whether it was assumed through the medium of grace?

FIRST ARTICLE [III, Q. 6, Art. 1]

Whether the Son of God Assumed Flesh Through the Medium of the Soul?

Objection 1: It would seem that the Son of God did not assume flesh through the medium of the soul. For the mode in which the Son of God is united to human nature and its parts, is more perfect than the mode whereby He is in all creatures. But He is in all creatures immediately by essence, power and presence. Much more, therefore, is the Son of God united to flesh without the medium of the soul.

Obj. 2: Further, the soul and flesh are united to the Word of God in unity of hypostasis or person. But the body pertains immediately to the human hypostasis or person, even as the soul. Indeed, the human body, since it is matter, would rather seem to be nearer the hypostasis than the soul, which is a form, since the principle of individuation, which is implied in the word "hypostasis," would seem to be matter. Hence the Son of God did not assume flesh through the medium of the soul.

Obj. 3: Further, take away the medium and you separate what were joined by the medium; for example, if the superficies be removed color would leave the body, since it adheres to the body through the medium of the superficies. But though the soul was separated from the body by death, yet there still remained the union of the Word to the flesh, as will be shown (Q. 50, AA. 2, 3). Hence the Word was not joined to flesh through the medium of the soul.

*On the contrary,* Augustine says (Ep. ad Volusianum cxxxvi): "The greatness of the Divine power fitted to itself a rational soul, and through it a human body, so as to raise the whole man to something higher."

*I answer that,* A medium is in reference to a beginning and an end. Hence as beginning and end imply order, so also does a medium. Now there is a twofold order: one, of time; the other, of nature. But in the mystery of the Incarnation nothing is said to be a medium in the order of time, for the Word of God united the whole human nature to Himself at the same time, as will appear (Q. 30, A. 3). An order of nature between things may be taken in two ways: first, as regards rank of dignity, as we say the angels are midway between man and God; secondly, as regards the idea of causality, as we say a cause is midway between the first cause and the last effect. And this second order follows the first to some extent; for as Dionysius says (Coel. Hier. xiii), God acts upon the more remote substances through the less remote. Hence if we consider the rank of dignity, the soul is found to be midway between God and flesh; and in this way it may be said that the Son of God united flesh to Himself, through the medium of the soul. But even as regards the second order of causality the soul is to some extent the cause of flesh being united to the Son of God. For the flesh would not have been assumable, except by its relation to the rational soul, through which it becomes human flesh. For it was said above (Q. 4, A. 1) that human nature was assumable before all others.

Reply Obj. 1: We may consider a twofold order between creatures and God: the first is by reason of creatures being caused by God and depending on Him as on the principle of their being; and thus on account of the infinitude of His power God touches each thing immediately, by causing and preserving it, and so it is that God is in all things by essence, presence and power. But the second order is by reason of things being directed to God as to their end; and it is here that there is a medium between the creature and God, since lower creatures are directed to God by higher, as Dionysius says (Eccl. Hier. v); and to this order pertains the assumption of human nature by the Word of God, Who is the term of the assumption; and hence it is united to flesh through the soul.

Reply Obj. 2: If the hypostasis of the Word of God were constituted simply by human nature, it would follow that the body was nearest to it, since it is matter which is the principle of individuation;

even as the soul, being the specific form, would be nearer the human nature. But because the hypostasis of the Word is prior to and more exalted than the human nature, the more exalted any part of the human nature is, the nearer it is to the hypostasis of the Word. And hence the soul is nearer the Word of God than the body is.

Reply Obj. 3: Nothing prevents one thing being the cause of the aptitude and congruity of another, and yet if it be taken away the other remains; because although a thing's becoming may depend on another, yet when it is in being it no longer depends on it, just as a friendship brought about by some other may endure when the latter has gone; or as a woman is taken in marriage on account of her beauty, which makes a woman's fittingness for the marriage tie, yet when her beauty passes away, the marriage tie still remains. So likewise, when the soul was separated, the union of the Word with flesh still endured.

SECOND ARTICLE [III, Q. 6, Art. 2]

Whether the Son of God Assumed a Soul Through the Medium of the Spirit or Mind?

Objection 1: It would seem that the Son of God did not assume a soul through the medium of the spirit or mind. For nothing is a medium between itself and another. But the spirit is nothing else in essence but the soul itself, as was said above (I, Q. 77, A. 1, ad 1). Therefore the Son of God did not assume a soul through the medium of the spirit or mind.

Obj. 2: Further, what is the medium of the assumption is itself more assumable. But the spirit or mind is not more assumable than the soul; which is plain from the fact that angelic spirits are not assumable, as was said above (Q. 4, A. 1). Hence it seems that the Son of God did not assume a soul through the medium of the spirit.

Obj. 3: Further, that which comes later is assumed by the first through the medium of what comes before. But the soul implies the very essence, which naturally comes before its power--the mind. Therefore it would seem that the Son of God did not assume a soul through the medium of the spirit or mind.

*On the contrary,* Augustine says (De Agone Christ. xviii): "The invisible and unchangeable Truth took a soul by means of the spirit, and a body by means of the soul."

*I answer that,* As stated above (A. 1), the Son of God is said to have assumed flesh through the medium of the soul, on account of the order of dignity, and the congruity of the assumption. Now both these may be applied to the intellect, which is called the spirit, if we compare it with the other parts of the soul. For the soul is assumed congruously only inasmuch as it has a capacity for God, being in His likeness: which is in respect of the mind that is called the spirit, according to Eph. 4:23: "Be renewed in the spirit of your mind." So, too, the intellect is the highest and noblest of the parts of the soul, and the most like to God, and hence Damascene says (De Fide Orth. iii, 6) that "the Word of God is united to flesh through the medium of the intellect; for the intellect is the purest part of the soul, God Himself being an intellect."

Reply Obj. 1: Although the intellect is not distinct from the soul in essence, it is distinct from the other parts of the soul as a power; and it is in this way that it has the nature of a medium.

Reply Obj. 2: Fitness for assumption is wanting to the angelic spirits, not from any lack of dignity, but because of the irremediableness of their fall, which cannot be said of the human spirit, as is clear from what has been said above (I, Q. 62, A. 8; First Part, Q. 64, A. 2).

Reply Obj. 3: The soul, between which and the Word of God the intellect is said to be a medium, does not stand for the essence of the soul, which is common to all the powers, but for the lower powers, which are common to every soul.

THIRD ARTICLE [III, Q. 6, Art. 3]

Whether the Soul Was Assumed Before the Flesh by the Son of God?

Objection 1: It would seem that the soul of Christ was assumed before the flesh by the Word. For the Son of God assumed flesh through the medium of the soul, as was said above (A. 1). Now the medium is reached before the end. Therefore the Son of God assumed the soul before the body.

Obj. 2: Further, the soul of Christ is nobler than the angels, according to Ps. 96:8: "Adore Him, all you His angels." But the angels were created in the beginning, as was said above (I, Q. 46, A. 3). Therefore the soul of Christ also (was created in the beginning). But it was not created before it was assumed, for Damascene says (De Fide Orth. iii, 2, 3, 9), that "neither the soul nor the body of Christ ever had any hypostasis save the hypostasis of the Word." Therefore it would seem that the soul was assumed before the flesh, which was conceived in the womb of the Virgin.

Obj. 3: Further, it is written (John 1:14): "We saw Him [Vulg.: 'His glory'] full of grace and truth," and it is added afterwards that "of His fulness we have all received" (John 1:16), i.e. all the faithful of all time, as Chrysostom expounds it (Hom. xiii in Joan.). Now this could not have been unless the soul of Christ had all fulness of grace and truth before all the saints, who were from the beginning of the world, for the cause is not subsequent to the effect. Hence since the fulness of grace and truth was in the soul of Christ from union with the Word, according to what is written in the same place: "We saw His glory, the glory as it were of the Only-begotten of the Father, full of grace and truth," it would seem in consequence that from the beginning of the world the soul of Christ was assumed by the Word of God.

*On the contrary,* Damascene says (De Fide Orth. iv, 6): "The intellect was not, as some untruthfully say, united to the true God, and henceforth called Christ, before the Incarnation which was of the Virgin."

*I answer that,* Origen (Peri Archon i, 7, 8; ii, 8) maintained that all souls, amongst which he placed Christ's soul, were created in the beginning. But this is not fitting, if we suppose that it was first of all created, but not at once joined to the Word, since it would follow that this soul once had its proper subsistence without the Word; and thus, since it was assumed by the Word, either the union did not take place in the subsistence, or the pre-existing subsistence of the soul was corrupted. So likewise it is not fitting to suppose that this soul was united to the Word from the beginning, and that it afterwards became incarnate in the womb of the Virgin; for thus His soul would not seem to be of the same nature as ours, which are created at the same time that they are infused into bodies. Hence Pope Leo says (Ep. ad Julian. xxxv) that "Christ's flesh was not of a different nature to ours, nor was a different soul infused into it in the beginning than into other men."

Reply Obj. 1: As was said above (A. 1), the soul of Christ is said to be the medium in the union of the flesh with the Word, in the order of nature; but it does not follow from this that it was the medium in the order of time.

Reply Obj. 2: As Pope Leo says in the same Epistle, Christ's soul excels our soul "not by diversity of genus, but by sublimity of power"; for it is of the same genus as our souls, yet excels even the angels in "fulness of grace and truth." But the mode of creation is in harmony with the generic property of the soul; and since it is the form of the body, it is consequently created at the same time that it is infused into and united with the body; which does not happen to angels, since they are substances entirely free from matter.

Reply Obj. 3: Of the fulness of Christ all men receive according to the faith they have in Him; for it is written (Rom. 3:22) that "the justice of God is by faith of Jesus Christ unto all and upon all them that believe in Him." Now just as we believe in Him as already born; so the ancients believed in Him as about to be born, since "having the same spirit of faith . . . we also believe," as it is written (2 Cor. 4:13). But the faith which is in Christ has the power of justifying by reason of the purpose of the grace of God, according to Rom. 4:5: "But to him that worketh not, yet believeth in Him that justifieth the ungodly, his faith is reputed to justice according to the purpose of the grace of God." Hence because this purpose is eternal, there is nothing to hinder some from being justified by the faith of Jesus Christ, even before His soul was full of grace and truth.

FOURTH ARTICLE [III, Q. 6, Art. 4]

Whether the Flesh of Christ Was Assumed by the Word Before Being United to the Soul?

Objection 1: It would seem that the flesh of Christ was assumed by the Word before being united to the soul. For Augustine [*Fulgentius] says (De Fide ad Petrum xviii): "Most firmly hold, and nowise doubt that the flesh of Christ was not conceived in the womb of the Virgin without the Godhead before it was assumed by the Word." But the flesh of Christ would seem to have been conceived before being united to the rational soul, because matter or disposition is prior to the completive form in order of generation. Therefore the flesh of Christ was assumed before being united to the soul.

Obj. 2: Further, as the soul is a part of human nature, so is the body. But the human soul in Christ had no other principle of being than in other men, as is clear from the authority of Pope Leo, quoted above (A. 3). Therefore it would seem that the body of Christ had no other principle of being than we have. But in us the body is begotten before the rational soul comes to it. Therefore it was the same in Christ; and thus the flesh was assumed by the Word before being united to the soul.

Obj. 3: Further, as is said (De Causis), the first cause excels the second in bringing about the effect, and precedes it in its union with the effect. But the soul of Christ is compared to the Word as a second cause to a first. Hence the Word was united to the flesh before it was to the soul.

*On the contrary,* Damascene says (De Fide Orth. iii, 2): "At the same time the Word of God was made flesh, and flesh was united to a rational and intellectual soul." Therefore the union of the Word with the flesh did not precede the union with the soul.

*I answer that,* The human flesh is assumable by the Word on account of the order which it has to the rational soul as to its proper form. Now it has not this order before the rational soul comes to it, because when any matter becomes proper to any form, at the same time it receives that form; hence the alteration is terminated at the same instant in which the substantial form is introduced. And hence it is that the flesh ought not to have been assumed before it was human flesh; and this happened when the rational soul came to it. Therefore since the soul was not assumed before the flesh, inasmuch as it is against the nature of the soul to be before it is united to the body, so likewise the flesh ought not to have been assumed before the soul, since it is not human flesh before it has a rational soul.

Reply Obj. 1: Human flesh depends upon the soul for its being; and hence, before the coming of the soul, there is no human flesh, but there may be a disposition towards human flesh. Yet in the conception of Christ, the Holy Ghost, Who is an agent of infinite might, disposed the matter and brought it to its perfection at the same time.

Reply Obj. 2: The form actually gives the species; but the matter in itself is in potentiality to the species. And hence it would be against the nature of a form to exist before the specific nature. And therefore the dissimilarity between our origin and Christ's origin, inasmuch as we are conceived before being animated, and Christ's flesh is not, is by reason of what precedes the perfection of the nature, viz. that we are conceived from the seed of man, and Christ is not. But a difference which would be with reference to the origin of the soul, would bespeak a diversity of nature.

Reply Obj. 3: The Word of God is understood to be united to the flesh before the soul by the common mode whereby He is in the rest of creatures by essence, power, and presence. Yet I say "before," not in time, but in nature; for the flesh is understood as a being, which it has from the Word, before it is understood as animated, which it has from the soul. But by the personal union we understand the flesh as united to the soul before it is united to the Word, for it is from its union with the soul that it is capable of being united to the Word in Person; especially since a person is found only in the rational nature.

FIFTH ARTICLE [III, Q. 6, Art. 5]

Whether the Whole Human Nature Was Assumed Through the Medium of the Parts?

Objection 1: It would seem that the Son of God assumed the whole human nature through the medium of its parts. For Augustine says (De Agone Christ. xviii) that "the invisible and unchangeable Truth assumed the soul through the medium of the spirit, and the body through the medium of the soul, and in this way the whole man." But the spirit, soul, and body are parts of the whole man. Therefore He assumed all, through the medium of the parts.

Obj. 2: Further, the Son of God assumed flesh through the medium of the soul because the soul is more like to God than the body. But the parts of human nature, since they are simpler than the body, would seem to be more like to God, Who is most simple, than the whole. Therefore He assumed the whole through the medium of the parts.

Obj. 3: Further, the whole results from the union of parts. But the union is taken to be the term of the assumption, and the parts are presupposed to the assumption. Therefore He assumed the whole by the parts.

*On the contrary,* Damascene says (De Fide Orth. iii, 16): "In our Lord Jesus Christ we do not behold parts of parts, but such as are immediately joined, i.e. the Godhead and the manhood." Now the humanity is a whole, which is composed of soul and body, as parts. Therefore the Son of God assumed the parts through the medium of the whole.

*I answer that,* When anything is said to be a medium in the assumption of the Incarnation, we do not signify order of time, because the assumption of the whole and the parts was simultaneous. For it has been shown (AA. 3, 4) that the soul and body were mutually united at the same time in order to constitute the human nature of the Word. But it is order of nature that is signified. Hence by what is prior in nature, that is assumed which is posterior in nature. Now a thing is prior in nature in two ways: First on the part of the agent, secondly on the part of the matter; for these two causes precede the thing. On the part of the agent--that is simply first, which is first included in his intention; but that is relatively first, with which his operation begins--and this because the intention is prior to the operation. On the part of the matter--that is first which exists first in the transmutation of the matter. Now in the Incarnation the order depending on the agent must be particularly considered, because, as Augustine says (Ep. ad Volusianum cxxxvii), "in such things the whole reason of the deed is the power of the doer." But it is manifest that, according to the intention of the doer, what is complete is prior to what is incomplete, and, consequently, the whole to the parts. Hence it must be said that the Word of God assumed the parts of human nature, through the medium of the whole; for even as He assumed the body on account of its relation to the rational soul, so likewise He assumed a body and soul on account of their relation to human nature.

Reply Obj. 1: From these words nothing may be gathered, except that the Word, by assuming the parts of human nature, assumed the whole human nature. And thus the assumption of parts is prior in the order of the intellect, if we consider the operation, but not in order of time; whereas the assumption of the nature is prior if we consider the intention: and this is to be simply first, as was said above.

Reply Obj. 2: God is so simple that He is also most perfect; and hence the whole is more like to God than the parts, inasmuch as it is more perfect.

Reply Obj. 3: It is a personal union wherein the assumption is terminated, not a union of nature, which springs from a conjunction of parts.

SIXTH ARTICLE [III, Q. 6, Art. 6]

Whether the Human Nature Was Assumed Through the Medium of Grace?

Objection 1: It would seem that the Son of God assumed human nature through the medium of grace. For by grace we are united to God. But the human nature in Christ was most closely united to God. Therefore the union took place by grace.

Obj. 2: Further, as the body lives by the soul, which is its perfection, so does the soul by grace. But the human nature was fitted for the assumption by the soul. Therefore the Son of God assumed the soul through the medium of grace.

Obj. 3: Further, Augustine says (De Trin. xv, 11) that the incarnate Word is like our spoken word. But our word is united to our speech by means of breathing ( spiritus ). Therefore the Word of God is united to flesh by means of the Holy Spirit, and hence by means of grace, which is attributed to the Holy Spirit, according to 1 Cor. 12:4: "Now there are diversities of graces, but the same Spirit."

*On the contrary,* Grace is an accident in the soul, as was shown above (I-II, Q. 110, A. 2). Now the union of the Word with human nature took place in the subsistence, and not accidentally, as was shown above (Q. 2, A. 6). Therefore the human nature was not assumed by means of grace.

*I answer that,* In Christ there was the grace of union and habitual grace. Therefore grace cannot be taken to be the medium of the assumption of the human nature, whether we speak of the grace of union or of habitual grace. For the grace of union is the personal being that is given gratis from above to the human nature in the Person of the Word, and is the term of the assumption. Whereas the habitual grace pertaining to the spiritual holiness of the man is an effect following the union, according to John 1:14: "We saw His glory . . . as it were of the Only-begotten of the Father, full of grace and truth"--by which we are given to understand that because this Man (as a result of the union) is the Only-begotten of the Father, He is full of grace and truth. But if by grace we understand the will of God doing or bestowing something gratis, the union took place by grace, not as a means, but as the efficient cause.

Reply Obj. 1: Our union with God is by operation, inasmuch as we know and love Him; and hence this union is by habitual grace, inasmuch as a perfect operation proceeds from a habit. Now the union of the human nature with the Word of God is in personal being, which depends not on any habit, but on the nature itself.

Reply Obj. 2: The soul is the substantial perfection of the body; grace is but an accidental perfection of the soul. Hence grace cannot ordain the soul to personal union, which is not accidental, as the soul ordains the body.

Reply Obj. 3: Our word is united to our speech, by means of breathing ( spiritus ), not as a formal medium, but as a moving medium. For from the word conceived within, the breathing proceeds, from which the speech is formed. And similarly from the eternal Word proceeds the Holy Spirit, Who formed the body of Christ, as will be shown (Q. 32, A. 1). But it does not follow from this that the grace of the Holy Spirit is the formal medium in the aforesaid union.

## QUESTION 7

OF THE GRACE OF CHRIST AS AN INDIVIDUAL MAN (In Thirteen Articles)

We must now consider such things as were co-assumed by the Son of God in human nature; and first what belongs to perfection; secondly, what belongs to defect.

Concerning the first, there are three points of consideration: (1) The grace of Christ; (2) His knowledge; (3) His power.

With regard to His grace we must consider two things: (1) His grace as He is an individual man; (2) His grace as He is the Head of the Church. Of the grace of union we have already spoken (Q. 2).

Under the first head there are thirteen points of inquiry:

(1) Whether in the soul of Christ there was any habitual grace?

(2) Whether in Christ there were virtues?

(3) Whether He had faith?

(4) Whether He had hope?

(5) Whether in Christ there were the gifts?

(6) Whether in Christ there was the gift of fear?

(7) Whether in Christ there were any gratuitous graces?

(8) Whether in Christ there was prophecy?

(9) Whether there was the fulness of grace in Him?

(10) Whether such fulness was proper to Christ?

(11) Whether the grace of Christ was infinite?

(12) Whether it could have been increased?

(13) How this grace stood towards the union?

FIRST ARTICLE [III, Q. 7, Art. 1]

Whether in the Soul of Christ There Was Any Habitual Grace?

Objection 1: It would seem there was no habitual grace in the soul assumed by the Word. For grace is a certain partaking of the Godhead by the rational creature, according to 2 Pet. 1:4: "By Whom He hath given us most great and precious promises, that by these you may be made partakers of the Divine Nature." Now Christ is God not by participation, but in truth. Therefore there was no habitual grace in Him.

Obj. 2: Further, grace is necessary to man, that he may operate well, according to 1 Cor. 15:10: "I have labored more abundantly than all they; yet not I, but the grace of God with me"; and in order that he may reach eternal life, according to Rom. 6:23: "The grace of God (is) life everlasting." Now the inheritance of everlasting life was due to Christ by the mere fact of His being the natural Son of God; and by the fact of His being the Word, by Whom all things were made, He had the power of doing all things well. Therefore His human nature needed no further grace beyond union with the Word.

Obj. 3: Further, what operates as an instrument does not need a habit for its own operations, since habits are rooted in the principal agent. Now the human nature in Christ was "as the instrument of the Godhead," as Damascene says (De Fide Orth. iii, 15). Therefore there was no need of habitual grace in Christ.

*On the contrary,* It is written (Isa. 11:2): "The Spirit of the Lord shall rest upon Him"--which (Spirit), indeed, is said to be in man by habitual grace, as was said above (I, Q. 8, A. 3; Q. 43, AA. 3, 6). Therefore there was habitual grace in Christ.

*I answer that,* It is necessary to suppose habitual grace in Christ for three reasons. First, on account of the union of His soul with the Word of God. For the nearer any recipient is to an inflowing cause, the more does it partake of its influence. Now the influx of grace is from God, according to Ps. 83:12: "The Lord will give grace and glory." And hence it was most fitting that His soul should receive the influx of Divine grace. Secondly, on account of the dignity of this soul, whose operations were to attain so closely to God by knowledge and love, to which it is necessary for human nature to be raised by grace. Thirdly, on account of the relation of Christ to the human race. For Christ, as man, is the "Mediator of God and men," as is written, 1 Tim. 2:5; and hence it behooved Him to have grace which would overflow upon others, according to John 1:16: "And of His fulness we have all received, and grace for grace."

Reply Obj. 1: Christ is the true God in Divine Person and Nature. Yet because together with unity of person there remains distinction of natures, as stated above (Q. 2, AA. 1, 2), the soul of Christ is not essentially Divine. Hence it behooves it to be Divine by participation, which is by grace.

Reply Obj. 2: To Christ, inasmuch as He is the natural Son of God, is due an eternal inheritance, which is the uncreated beatitude through the uncreated act of knowledge and love of God, i.e. the same whereby the Father knows and loves Himself. Now the soul was not capable of this act, on account of the difference of natures. Hence it behooved it to attain to God by a created act of fruition which could not be without grace. Likewise, inasmuch as He was the Word of God, He had the power of doing all things well by the Divine operation. And because it is necessary to admit a human operation, distinct from the Divine operation, as will be shown (Q. 19, A. 1), it was necessary for Him to have habitual grace, whereby this operation might be perfect in Him.

Reply Obj. 3: The humanity of Christ is the instrument of the Godhead--not, indeed, an inanimate instrument, which nowise acts, but is merely acted upon; but an instrument animated by a rational soul, which is so acted upon as to act. And hence the nature of the action demanded that he should have habitual grace.

SECOND ARTICLE [III, Q. 7, Art. 2]

Whether in Christ There Were Virtues?

Objection 1: It would seem that in Christ there were no virtues. For Christ had the plenitude of grace. Now grace is sufficient for every good act, according to 2 Cor. 12:9: "My grace is sufficient for thee." Therefore there were no virtues in Christ.

Obj. 2: Further, according to the Philosopher (Ethic. vii, 1), virtue is contrasted with a "certain heroic or godlike habit" which is attributed to godlike men. But this belongs chiefly to Christ. Therefore Christ had not virtues, but something higher than virtue.

Obj. 3: Further, as was said above (I-II, Q. 65, AA. 1, 2), all the virtues are bound together. But it was not becoming for Christ to have all the virtues, as is clear in the case of liberality and magnificence, for these have to do with riches, which Christ spurned, according to Matt. 8:20: "The Son of man hath not where to lay His head." Temperance and continence also regard wicked desires, from which Christ was free. Therefore Christ had not the virtues.

*On the contrary,* on Ps. 1:2, "But His will is in the law of the Lord," a gloss says: "This refers to Christ, Who is full of all good." But a good quality of the mind is a virtue. Therefore Christ was full of all virtue.

*I answer that,* As was said above (I-II, Q. 110, AA. 3, 4), as grace regards the essence of the soul, so does virtue regard its power. Hence it is necessary that as the powers of the soul flow from its essence, so do the virtues flow from grace. Now the more perfect a principle is, the more it impresses its effects. Hence, since the grace of Christ was most perfect, there flowed from it, in consequence, the virtues which perfect the several powers of the soul for all the soul's acts; and thus Christ had all the virtues.

Reply Obj. 1: Grace suffices a man for all whereby he is ordained to beatitude; nevertheless, it effects some of these by itself--as to make him pleasing to God, and the like; and some others through the medium of the virtues which proceed from grace.

Reply Obj. 2: A heroic or godlike habit only differs from virtue commonly so called by a more perfect mode, inasmuch as one is disposed to good in a higher way than is common to all. Hence it is not hereby proved that Christ had not the virtues, but that He had them most perfectly beyond the common mode. In this sense Plotinus gave to a certain sublime degree of virtue the name of "virtue of the purified soul" (cf. I-II, Q. 61, A. 5).

Reply Obj. 3: Liberality and magnificence are praiseworthy in regard to riches, inasmuch as anyone does not esteem wealth to the extent of wishing to retain it, so as to forego what ought to be done. But he esteems them least who wholly despises them, and casts them aside for love of perfection. And hence by altogether contemning all riches, Christ showed the highest kind of liberality and magnificence; although He also performed the act of liberality, as far as it became Him, by causing to be distributed to the poor what was given to Himself. Hence, when our Lord said to Judas (John 13:21), "That which thou dost do quickly," the disciples understood our Lord to have ordered him to give something to the poor. But Christ had no evil desires whatever, as will be shown (Q. 15, AA. 1, 2); yet He was not thereby prevented from having temperance, which is the more perfect in man, as he is without evil desires. Hence, according to the Philosopher (Ethic. vii, 9), the temperate man differs from the continent in this--that the temperate has not the evil desires which the continent suffers. Hence, taking continence in this sense, as the Philosopher takes it, Christ, from the very fact that He had all virtue, had not continence, since it is not a virtue, but something less than virtue.

THIRD ARTICLE [III, Q. 7, Art. 3]

Whether in Christ There Was Faith?

Objection 1: It would seem that there was faith in Christ. For faith is a nobler virtue than the moral virtues, e.g. temperance and liberality. Now these were in Christ, as stated above (A. 2). Much more, therefore, was there faith in Him.

Obj. 2: Further, Christ did not teach virtues which He had not Himself, according to Acts 1:1: "Jesus began to do and to teach." But of Christ it is said (Heb. 12:2) that He is "the author and finisher of our faith." Therefore there was faith in Him before all others.

Obj. 3: Further, everything imperfect is excluded from the blessed. But in the blessed there is faith; for on Rom. 1:17, "the justice of God is revealed therein from faith to faith," a gloss says: "From the faith of words and hope to the faith of things and sight." Therefore it would seem that in Christ also there was faith, since it implies nothing imperfect.

*On the contrary,* It is written (Heb. 11:1): "Faith is the evidence of things that appear not." But there was nothing that did not appear to Christ, according to what Peter said to Him (John 21:17): "Thou knowest all things." Therefore there was no faith in Christ.

*I answer that,* As was said above (II-II, Q. 1, A. 4), the object of faith is a Divine thing not seen. Now the habit of virtue, as every other habit, takes its species from the object. Hence, if we deny that the Divine thing was not seen, we exclude the very essence of faith. Now from the first moment of His conception Christ saw God's Essence fully, as will be made clear (Q. 34, A. 1). Hence there could be no faith in Him.

Reply Obj. 1: Faith is a nobler virtue than the moral virtues, seeing that it has to do with nobler matter; nevertheless, it implies a certain defect with regard to that matter; and this defect was not in Christ. And hence there could be no faith in Him, although the moral virtues were in Him, since in their nature they imply no defect with regard to their matter.

Reply Obj. 2: The merit of faith consists in this--that man through obedience assents to what things he does not see, according to Rom. 1:5: "For obedience to the faith in all nations for His name." Now Christ had most perfect obedience to God, according to Phil. 2:8: "Becoming obedient unto death." And hence He taught nothing pertaining to merit which He did not fulfil more perfectly Himself.

Reply Obj. 3: As a gloss says in the same place, faith is that "whereby such things as are not seen are believed." But faith in things seen is improperly so called, and only after a certain similitude with regard to the certainty and firmness of the assent.

FOURTH ARTICLE [III, Q. 7, Art. 4]

Whether in Christ There Was Hope?

Objection 1: It would seem that there was hope in Christ. For it is said in the Person of Christ (Ps. 30:1): "In Thee, O Lord, have I hoped." But the virtue of hope is that whereby a man hopes in God. Therefore the virtue of hope was in Christ.

Obj. 2: Further, hope is the expectation of the bliss to come, as was shown above (II-II, Q. 17, A. 5, ad 3). But Christ awaited something pertaining to bliss, viz. the glorifying of His body. Therefore it seems there was hope in Him.

Obj. 3: Further, everyone may hope for what pertains to his perfection, if it has yet to come. But there was something still to come pertaining to Christ's perfection, according to Eph. 4:12: "For the perfecting of the saints, for the work of the ministry, for the building up [Douay: 'edifying'] of the body of Christ." Hence it seems that it befitted Christ to have hope.

*On the contrary,* It is written (Rom. 8:24): "What a man seeth, why doth he hope for?" Thus it is clear that as faith is of the unseen, so also is hope. But there was no faith in Christ, as was said above (A. 1): neither, consequently, was there hope.

*I answer that,* As it is of the nature of faith that one assents to what one sees not, so is it of the nature of hope that one expects what as yet one has not; and as faith, forasmuch as it is a theological virtue, does not regard everything unseen, but only God; so likewise hope, as a theological virtue, has God Himself for its object, the fruition of Whom man chiefly expects by the virtue of hope; yet, in consequence, whoever has the virtue of hope may expect the Divine aid in other things, even as he who has the virtue of faith believes God not only in Divine things, but even in whatsoever is divinely revealed. Now from the beginning of His conception Christ had the Divine fruition fully, as will be shown (Q. 34, A. 4), and hence he had not the virtue of hope. Nevertheless He had hope as regards such things as He did not yet possess, although He had not faith with regard to anything; because, although He knew all things fully, wherefore faith was altogether wanting to Him, nevertheless He did not as yet fully possess all that pertained to His perfection, viz. immortality and glory of the body, which He could hope for.

Reply Obj. 1: This is said of Christ with reference to hope, not as a theological virtue, but inasmuch as He hoped for some other things not yet possessed, as was said above.

Reply Obj. 2: The glory of the body does not pertain to beatitude as being that in which beatitude principally consists, but by a certain outpouring from the soul's glory, as was said above (I-II, Q. 4, A. 6). Hence hope, as a theological virtue, does not regard the bliss of the body but the soul's bliss, which consists in the Divine fruition.

Reply Obj. 3: The building up of the church by

the conversion of the faithful does not pertain to the perfection of Christ, whereby He is perfect in Himself, but inasmuch as it leads others to a share of His perfection. And because hope properly regards what is expected by him who hopes, the virtue of hope cannot properly be said to be in Christ, because of the aforesaid reason.

FIFTH ARTICLE [III, Q. 7, Art. 5]

Whether in Christ There Were the Gifts?

Objection 1: It would seem that the gifts were not in Christ. For, as is commonly said, the gifts are given to help the virtues. But what is perfect in itself does not need an exterior help. Therefore, since the virtues of Christ were perfect, it seems there were no gifts in Him.

Obj. 2: Further, to give and to receive gifts would not seem to belong to the same; since to give pertains to one who has, and to receive pertains to one who has not. But it belongs to Christ to give gifts according to Ps. 67:19. "Thou hast given gifts to men [Vulg.: 'Thou hast received gifts in men']." Therefore it was not becoming that Christ should receive gifts of the Holy Ghost.

Obj. 3: Further, four gifts would seem to pertain to the contemplation of earth, viz. wisdom, knowledge, understanding, and counsel which pertains to prudence; hence the Philosopher (Ethic. vi, 3) enumerates these with the intellectual virtues. But Christ had the contemplation of heaven. Therefore He had not these gifts.

*On the contrary,* It is written (Isa. 4:1): "Seven women shall take hold of one man": on which a gloss says: "That is, the seven gifts of the Holy Ghost shall take hold of Christ."

*I answer that,* As was said above (I-II, Q. 68, A. 1), the gifts, properly, are certain perfections of the soul's powers, inasmuch as these have a natural aptitude to be moved by the Holy Ghost, according to Luke 4:1: "And Jesus, being full of the Holy Ghost, returned from the Jordan, and was led by the Spirit into the desert." Hence it is manifest that in Christ the gifts were in a pre-eminent degree.

Reply Obj. 1: What is perfect in the order of its nature needs to be helped by something of a higher nature; as man, however perfect, needs to be helped by God. And in this way the virtues, which perfect the powers of the soul, as they are controlled by reason, no matter how perfect they are, need to be helped by the gifts, which perfect the soul's powers, inasmuch as these are moved by the Holy Ghost.

Reply Obj. 2: Christ is not a recipient and a giver of the gifts of the Holy Ghost, in the same respect; for He gives them as God and receives them as man. Hence Gregory says (Moral. ii) that "the Holy Ghost never quitted the human nature of Christ, from Whose Divine nature He proceedeth."

Reply Obj. 3: In Christ there was not only heavenly knowledge, but also earthly knowledge, as will be said (Q. 15, A. 10). And yet even in heaven the gifts of the Holy Ghost will still exist, in a certain manner, as was said above (I-II, Q. 68, A. 6).

SIXTH ARTICLE [III, Q. 7, Art. 6]

Whether in Christ There Was the Gift of Fear?

Objection 1: It would seem that in Christ there was not the gift of fear. For hope would seem to be stronger than fear; since the object of hope is goodness, and of fear, evil, as was said above (I-II, Q. 40, A. 1; I-II, Q. 42, A. 1). But in Christ there was not the virtue of hope, as was said above (A. 4). Hence, likewise, there was not the gift of fear in Him.

Obj. 2: Further, by the gift of fear we fear either to be separated from God, which pertains to chaste fear--or to be punished by Him, which pertains to servile fear, as Augustine says (In Joan. Tract. ix). But Christ did not fear being separated from God by sin, nor being punished by Him on account of a fault, since it was impossible for Him to sin, as will be said (Q. 15, AA. 1, 2). Now fear is not of the impossible. Therefore in Christ there was not the gift of fear.

Obj. 3: Further, it is written (1 John 4:18) that "perfect charity casteth out fear." But in Christ there was most perfect charity, according to Eph. 3:19: "The charity of Christ which surpasseth all knowledge." Therefore in Christ there was not the gift of fear.

*On the contrary,* It is written (Isa. 11:3): "And He shall be filled with the spirit of the fear of the Lord."

*I answer that,* As was said above (I-II, Q. 42, A. 1), fear regards two objects, one of which is an evil causing terror; the other is that by whose power an evil can be inflicted, as we fear the king inasmuch as he has the power of putting to death. Now whoever can hurt would not be feared unless he had a certain greatness of might, to which resistance could not easily be offered; for what we easily repel we do not fear. And hence it is plain that no one is feared except for some pre-eminence. And in this way it is said that in Christ there was the fear of God, not indeed as it regards the evil of separation from God by fault, nor as it regards the evil of punishment for fault; but inasmuch as it regards the Divine pre-eminence, on account of which the soul of Christ, led by the Holy Spirit, was borne towards God in an act of reverence. Hence it is said (Heb. 5:7) that in all things "he was heard for his reverence." For Christ as man had this act of reverence towards God in a fuller sense and beyond all others. And hence Scripture attributes to Him the fulness of the fear of the Lord.

Reply Obj. 1: The habits of virtues and gifts regard goodness properly and of themselves; but evil, consequently; since it pertains to the nature of virtue to render acts good, as is said Ethic. ii, 6. And hence the nature of the gift of fear regards not that evil which fear is concerned with, but the pre-eminence of that goodness, viz. of God, by Whose power evil may be inflicted. On the other hand, hope, as a virtue, regards not only the author of good, but even the good itself, as far as it is not yet possessed. And hence to Christ, Who already possessed the perfect good of beatitude, we do not attribute the virtue of hope, but we do attribute the gift of fear.

Reply Obj. 2: This reason is based on fear in so far as it regards the evil object.

Reply Obj. 3: Perfect charity casts out servile fear, which principally regards punishment. But this kind of fear was not in Christ.

SEVENTH ARTICLE [III, Q. 7, Art. 7]

Whether the Gratuitous Graces Were in Christ?

Objection 1: It would seem that the gratuitous graces were not in Christ. For whoever has anything in its fulness, to him it does not pertain to have it by participation. Now Christ has grace in its fulness, according to John 1:14: "Full of grace and truth." But the gratuitous graces would seem to be certain participations, bestowed distributively and particularly upon divers subjects, according to 1 Cor. 12:4: "Now there are diversities of graces." Therefore it would seem that there were no gratuitous graces in Christ.

Obj. 2: Further, what is due to anyone would not seem to be gratuitously bestowed on him. But it was due to the man Christ that He should abound in the word of wisdom and knowledge, and to be mighty in doing wonderful works and the like, all of which pertain to gratuitous graces: since He is "the power of God and the wisdom of God," as is written 1 Cor. 1:24. Therefore it was not fitting for Christ to have the gratuitous graces.

Obj. 3: Further, gratuitous graces are ordained to the benefit of the faithful. But it does not seem that a habit which a man does not use is for the benefit of others, according to Ecclus. 20:32: "Wisdom that is hid and treasure that is not seen: what profit is there in them both?" Now we do not read that Christ made use of these gratuitously given graces, especially as regards the gift of tongues. Therefore not all the gratuitous graces were in Christ.

*On the contrary,* Augustine says (Ep. ad Dardan. cclxxxvii) that "as in the head are all the senses, so in Christ were all the graces."

*I answer that,* As was said above (I-II, Q. 3, AA. 1, 4), the gratuitous graces are ordained for the manifestation of faith and spiritual doctrine. For it behooves him who teaches to have the means of making his doctrine clear; otherwise his doctrine would be useless. Now Christ is the first and chief teacher of spiritual doctrine and faith, according to Heb. 2:3, 4: "Which having begun to be declared by the Lord was confirmed unto us by them that heard Him, God also bearing them witness by signs and wonders." Hence it is clear that all the gratuitous graces were most excellently in Christ, as in the first and chief teacher of the faith.

Reply Obj. 1: As sanctifying grace is ordained to meritorious acts both interior and exterior, so likewise gratuitous grace is ordained to certain exterior acts manifestive of the faith, as the working of miracles, and the like. Now of both these graces Christ had the fulness, since inasmuch as His soul was united to the Godhead, He had the perfect power of effecting all these acts. But other saints who are moved by God as separated and not united instruments, receive power in a particular manner in order to bring about this or that act. And hence in other saints these graces are divided, but not in Christ.

Reply Obj. 2: Christ is said to be the power of God and the wisdom of God, inasmuch as He is the Eternal Son of God. But in this respect it does not pertain to Him to have grace, but rather to be the bestower of grace; but it pertains to Him in His human nature to have grace.

Reply Obj. 3: The gift of tongues was bestowed on the apostles, because they were sent to teach all nations; but Christ wished to preach personally only in the one nation of the Jews, as He Himself says (Matt. 15:24): "I was not sent but to the sheep that are lost of the house of Israel"; and the Apostle says (Rom. 15:8): "I say that Christ Jesus was minister of the circumcision." And hence it was not necessary for Him to speak several languages. Yet was a knowledge of all languages not wanting to Him, since even the secrets of hearts, of which all words are signs, were not hidden from Him, as will be shown (Q. 10, A. 2). Nor was this knowledge uselessly possessed, just as it is not useless to have a habit, which we do not use when there is no occasion.

EIGHTH ARTICLE [III, Q. 7, Art. 8]

Whether in Christ There Was the Gift of Prophecy?

Objection 1: It would seem that in Christ there was not the gift of prophecy. For prophecy implies a certain obscure and imperfect knowledge, according to Num. 12:6: "If there be among you a prophet of the Lord, I will appear to him in a vision, or I will speak to him in a dream." But Christ had full and unveiled knowledge, much more than Moses, of whom it is subjoined that "plainly and not by riddles and figures doth he see God" (Num. 6:8). Therefore we ought not to admit prophecy in Christ.

Obj. 2: Further, as faith has to do with what is not seen, and hope with what is not possessed, so prophecy has to do with what is not present, but distant; for a prophet means, as it were, a teller of far-off things. But in Christ there could be neither faith nor hope, as was said above (AA. 3, 4). Hence prophecy also ought not to be admitted in Christ.

Obj. 3: Further, a prophet is in an inferior order to an angel; hence Moses, who was the greatest of the prophets, as was said above (II-II, Q. 174, A. 4) is said (Acts 7:38) to have spoken with an angel in the desert. But Christ was "made lower than the angels," not as to the knowledge of His soul, but only as regards the sufferings of His body, as is shown Heb. 2:9. Therefore it seems that Christ was not a prophet.

*On the contrary,* It is written of Him (Deut. 18:15): "Thy God will raise up to thee a prophet of thy nation and of thy brethren," and He says of Himself (Matt. 13:57; John 4:44): "A prophet is not without honor, save in his own country."

*I answer that,* A prophet means, as it were, a teller or seer of far-off things, inasmuch as he knows and announces what things are far from men's senses, as Augustine says (Contra Faust. xvi, 18). Now we must bear in mind that no one can be called a prophet for knowing and announcing what is distant from others, with whom he is not. And this is clear in regard to place and time. For if anyone living in France were to know and announce to others living in France what things were transpiring in Syria, it would be prophetical, as Eliseus told Giezi (4 Kings 5:26) how the man had leaped down from his chariot to meet him. But if anyone living in Syria were to announce what things were there, it would not be prophetical. And the same appears in regard to time. For it was prophetical of Isaias to announce that Cyrus, King of the Persians, would rebuild the temple of God, as is clear from Isa. 44:28. But it was not prophetical of Esdras to write it, in whose time it took place. Hence if God or angels, or even the blessed, know and announce what is beyond our knowing, this does not pertain to prophecy, since they nowise touch our state. Now Christ before His passion touched our state, inasmuch as He was not merely a "comprehensor," but a "wayfarer." Hence it was prophetical in Him to know and announce what was beyond the knowledge of other "wayfarers": and for this reason He is called a prophet.

Reply Obj. 1: These words do not prove that enigmatical knowledge, viz. by dream and vision, belongs to the nature of prophecy; but the comparison is drawn between other prophets, who saw Divine things in dreams and visions, and Moses, who saw God plainly and not by riddles, and who yet is called a prophet, according to Deut. 24:10: "And there arose no more a prophet in Israel like unto Moses." Nevertheless it may be said that although Christ had full and unveiled knowledge as regards the intellective part, yet in the imaginative part He had certain similitudes, in which Divine things could be viewed, inasmuch as He was not only a "comprehensor," but a "wayfarer."

Reply Obj. 2: Faith regards such things as are unseen by him who believes; and hope, too, is of such things as are not possessed by the one who hopes; but prophecy is of such things as are beyond the sense of men, with whom the prophet dwells and converses in this state of life. And hence faith and hope are repugnant to the perfection of Christ's beatitude; but prophecy is not.

Reply Obj. 3: Angels, being "comprehensors," are above prophets, who are merely "wayfarers"; but not above Christ, Who was both a "comprehensor" and a "wayfarer."

NINTH ARTICLE [III, Q. 7, Art. 9]

Whether in Christ There Was the Fulness of Grace?

Objection 1: It would seem that in Christ there was not the fulness of grace. For the virtues flow from grace, as was said above (I-II, Q. 110, A. 4). But in Christ there were not all the virtues; for there was neither faith nor hope in Him, as was shown above (AA. 3, 4). Therefore in Christ there was not the fulness of grace.

Obj. 2: Further, as is plain from what was said above (I-II, Q. 111, A. 2), grace is divided into operating and cooperating. Now operating grace signifies that whereby the ungodly is justified, which has no place in Christ, Who never lay under any sin. Therefore in Christ there was not the fulness of grace.

Obj. 3: Further, it is written (James 1:17): "Every best gift and every perfect gift is from above, coming down from the Father of lights." But what comes thus is possessed partially, and not fully. Therefore no creature, not even the soul of Christ, can have the fulness of the gifts of grace.

*On the contrary,* It is written (John 1:14): "We saw Him [Vulg.: 'His glory'] full of grace and truth."

*I answer that,* To have fully is to have wholly and perfectly. Now totality and perfection can be taken in two ways: First as regards theirintensive quantity; for instance, I may say that some man has whiteness fully, because he has as much of it as can naturally be in him; secondly,as regards power ; for instance, if anyone be said to have life fully, inasmuch as he has it in all the effects or works of life; and thus man has life fully, but senseless animals or plants have not. Now in both these ways Christ has the fulness of grace. First, since He has grace in its highest degree, in the most perfect way it can be had. And this appears, first, from the nearness of Christ's soul to the cause of grace. For it was said above (A. 1) that the nearer a recipient is to the inflowing cause, the more it receives. And hence the soul of Christ, which is more closely united to God than all other rational creatures, receives the greatest outpouring of His grace. Secondly, in His relation to the effect. For the soul of Christ so received grace, that, in a manner, it is poured out from it upon others. And hence it behooved Him to have the greatest grace; as fire which is the cause of heat in other hot things, is of all things the hottest.

Likewise, as regards the virtue of grace, He had grace fully, since He had it for all the operations and effects of grace; and this, because grace was bestowed on Him, as upon a universal principle in the genus of such as have grace. Now the virtue of the first principle of a genus universally extends itself to all the effects of that genus; thus the force of the sun, which is the universal cause of generation, as Dionysius says (Div. Nom. i), extends to all things that come under generation. Hence the second fulness of grace is seen in Christ inasmuch as His grace extends to all the effects of grace, which are the virtues, gifts, and the like.

Reply Obj. 1: Faith and hope signify effects of grace with certain defects on the part of the recipient of grace, inasmuch as faith is of the unseen, and hope of what is not yet possessed. Hence it was not necessary that in Christ, Who is the author of grace, there should be any defects such as faith and hope imply; but whatever perfection is in faith and hope was in Christ most perfectly; as in fire there are not all the modes of heat which are defective by the subject's defect, but whatever belongs to the perfection of heat.

Reply Obj. 2: It pertains essentially to operating grace to justify; but that it makes the ungodly to be just is accidental to it on the part of the subject, in which sin is found. Therefore the soul of Christ was justified by operating grace, inasmuch as it was rendered just and holy by it from the beginning of His conception; not that it was until then sinful, or even not just.

Reply Obj. 3: The fulness of grace is attributed to the soul of Christ according to the capacity of the creature and not by comparison with the infinite fulness of the Divine goodness.

TENTH ARTICLE [III, Q. 7, Art. 10]

Whether the Fulness of Grace Is Proper to Christ?

Objection 1: It would seem that the fulness of grace is not proper to Christ. For what is proper to anyone belongs to him alone. But to be full of grace is attributed to some others; for it was said to the Blessed Virgin (Luke 1:28): "Hail, full of grace"; and again it is written (Acts 6:8): "Stephen, full of grace and fortitude." Therefore the fulness of grace is not proper to Christ.

Obj. 2: Further, what can be communicated to others through Christ does not seem to be proper to Christ. But the fulness of grace can be communicated to others through Christ, since the Apostle says (Eph. 3:19): "That you may be filled unto all the fulness of God." Therefore the fulness of grace is not proper to Christ.

Obj. 3: Further, the state of the wayfarer seems to be proportioned to the state of the comprehensor. But in the state of the comprehensor there will be a certain fulness, since "in our heavenly country with its fulness of all good, although some things are bestowed in a pre-eminent way, yet nothing is possessed singularly," as is clear from Gregory (Hom. De Cent. Ovib.; xxxiv in Ev.). Therefore in the state of the comprehensor the fulness of grace is possessed by everyone, and hence the fulness of grace is not proper to Christ. *On the contrary,* The fulness of grace is attributed to Christ inasmuch as He is the only-begotten of the Father, according to John 1:14: "We saw Him [Vulg.: 'His glory'] as it were . . . the Only-begotten of the Father, full of grace and truth." But to be the Only-begotten of the Father is proper to Christ. Therefore it is proper to Him to be full of grace and truth.

*I answer that,* The fulness of grace may be taken in two ways: First, on the part of grace itself, or secondly on the part of the one who has grace. Now on the part of grace itself there is said to be the fulness of grace when the limit of grace is attained, as to essence and power, inasmuch as grace is possessed in its highest possible excellence and in its greatest possible extension to all its effects. And this fulness of grace is proper to Christ. But on the part of the subject there is said to be the fulness of grace when anyone fully possesses grace according to his condition--whether as regards intensity, by reason of grace being intense in him, to the limit assigned by God, according to Eph. 4:1: "But to every one of us is given grace according to the measure of the giving of Christ"--or "as regards power," by reason of a man having the help of grace for all that belongs to his office or state, as the Apostle says (Eph. 3:8): "To me, the least of all the saints, is given this grace . . . to enlighten all men." And this fulness of grace is not proper to Christ, but is communicated to others by Christ.

Reply Obj. 1: The Blessed Virgin is said to be full of grace, not on the part of grace itself--since she had not grace in its greatest possible excellence--nor for all the effects of grace; but she is said to be full of grace in reference to herself, i.e. inasmuch as she had sufficient grace for the state to which God had chosen her, i.e. to be the mother of His Only-begotten. So, too, Stephen is said to be full of grace, since he had sufficient grace to be a fit minister and witness of God, to which office he had been called. And the same must be said of others. Of these fulnesses one is greater than another, according as one is divinely pre-ordained to a higher or lower state.

Reply Obj. 2: The Apostle is there speaking of that fulness which has reference to the subject, in comparison with what man is divinely pre-ordained to; and this is either something in common, to which all the saints are pre-ordained, or something special, which pertains to the pre-eminence of some. And in this manner a certain fulness of grace is common to all the saints, viz. to have grace enough to merit eternal life, which consists in the enjoyment of God. And this is the fulness of grace which the Apostle desires for the faithful to whom he writes.

Reply Obj. 3: These gifts which are in common in heaven, viz.: vision, possession and fruition, and the like, have certain gifts corresponding to them in this life which are also common to all the saints. Yet there are certain prerogatives of saints, both in heaven and on earth, which are not possessed by all.

ELEVENTH ARTICLE [III, Q. 7, Art. 11]

Whether the Grace of Christ Is Infinite?

Objection 1: It would seem that Christ's grace is infinite. For everything immeasurable is infinite.

But the grace of Christ is immeasurable; since it is written (John 3:34): "For God doth not give the Spirit by measure to His Son [*'To His Son' is lacking in the Vulgate], namely Christ." Therefore the grace of Christ is infinite.

Obj. 2: Further, an infinite effect betokens an infinite power which can only spring from an infinite essence. But the effect of Christ's grace is infinite, since it extends to the salvation of the whole human race; for He is the propitiation for our sins . . . and for those of the whole world, as is said (1 John 2:2). Therefore the grace of Christ is infinite.

Obj. 3: Further, every finite thing by addition can attain to the quantity of any other finite thing. Therefore if the grace of Christ is finite the grace of any other man could increase to such an extent as to reach to an equality with Christ's grace, against what is written (Job 28:17): "Gold nor crystal cannot equal it," as Gregory expounds it (Moral. xviii). Therefore the grace of Christ is infinite.

*On the contrary,* Grace is something created in the soul. But every created thing is finite, according to Wis. 11:21: "Thou hast ordered all things in measure and number and weight." Therefore the grace of Christ is not infinite.

*I answer that,* As was made clear above (Q. 2, A. 10), a twofold grace may be considered in Christ; the first being the grace of union, which, as was said (Q. 6, A. 6), is for Him to be personally united to the Son of God, which union has been bestowed gratis on the human nature; and it is clear that this grace is infinite, as the Person of God is infinite. The second is habitual grace; which may be taken in two ways: first as a being, and in this way it must be a finite being, since it is in the soul of Christ, as in a subject, and Christ's soul is a creature having a finite capacity; hence the being of grace cannot be infinite, since it cannot exceed its subject. Secondly it may be viewed in its specific nature of grace; and thus the grace of Christ can be termed infinite, since it is not limited, i.e. it has whatsoever can pertain to the nature of grace, and what pertains to the nature of grace is not bestowed on Him in a fixed measure; seeing that "according to the purpose" of God to Whom it pertains to measure grace, it is bestowed on Christ's soul as on a universal principle for bestowing grace on human nature, according to Eph. 1:5, 6, "He hath graced us in His beloved Son"; thus we might say that the light of the sun is infinite, not indeed in being, but in the nature of light, as having whatever can pertain to the nature of light.

Reply Obj. 1: When it is said that the Father "doth not give the Spirit by measure," it may be expounded of the gift which God the Father from all eternity gave the Son, viz. the Divine Nature, which is an infinite gift. Hence the comment of a certain gloss: "So that the Son may be as great as the Father is." Or again, it may be referred to the gift which is given the human nature, to be united to the Divine Person, and this also is an infinite gift. Hence a gloss says on this text: "As the Father begot a full and perfect Word, it is united thus full and perfect to human nature." Thirdly, it may be referred to habitual grace, inasmuch as the grace of Christ extends to whatever belongs to grace. Hence Augustine expounding this (Tract. xiv in Joan.) says: "The division of the gifts is a measurement. For to one indeed by the Spirit is given the word of wisdom, to another the word of knowledge." But Christ the giver does not receive by measure.

Reply Obj. 2: The grace of Christ has an infinite effect, both because of the aforesaid infinity of grace, and because of the unity [*Perhaps we should read 'infinity'--Ed.] of the Divine Person, to Whom Christ's soul is united.

Reply Obj. 3: The lesser can attain by augment to the quantity of the greater, when both have the same kind of quantity. But the grace of any man is compared to the grace of Christ as a particular to a universal power; hence as the force of fire, no matter how much it increases, can never equal the sun's strength, so the grace of a man, no matter how much it increases, can never equal the grace of Christ.

TWELFTH ARTICLE [III, Q. 7, Art. 12]

Whether the Grace of Christ Could Increase?

Objection 1: It would seem that the grace of Christ could increase. For to every finite thing addition can be made. But the grace of Christ was finite. Therefore it could increase.

Obj. 2: Further, it is by Divine power that grace is increased, according to 2 Cor. 9:8: "And God is able to make all grace abound in you." But the Divine power, being infinite, is confined by no limits. Therefore it seems that the grace of Christ could have been greater.

Obj. 3: Further, it is written (Luke 2:52) that the child "Jesus advanced in wisdom and age and grace with God and men." Therefore the grace of Christ could increase.

*On the contrary,* It is written (John 1:14): "We saw Him [Vulg.: 'His glory'] as it were . . . the Only-begotten of the Father, full of grace and truth." But nothing can be or can be thought greater than that anyone should be the Only-begotten of the Father. Therefore no greater grace can be or can be thought than that of which Christ was full.

*I answer that,* For a form to be incapable of increase happens in two ways: First on the part of the subject; secondly, on the part of the form itself. On the part of the subject, indeed, when the subject reaches the utmost limit wherein it partakes of this form, after its own manner, e.g. if we say that air cannot increase in heat, when it has reached the utmost limit of heat which can exist in the nature of air, although there may be greater heat in actual existence, viz. the heat of fire. But on the part of the form, the possibility of increase is excluded when a subject reaches the utmost perfection which this form can have by nature, e.g. if we say the heat of fire cannot be increased because there cannot be a more perfect grade of heat than that to which fire attains. Now the proper measure of grace, like that of other forms, is determined by the Divine wisdom, according to Wis. 11:21: "Thou hast ordered all things in number, weight and measure." And it is with reference to its end that a measure is set to every form, as there is no greater gravity than that of the earth, because there is no lower place than that of the earth. Now the end of grace is the union of the rational creature with God. But there can neither be nor be thought a greater union of the rational creature with God than that which is in the Person. And hence the grace of Christ reached the highest measure of grace. Hence it is clear that the grace of Christ cannot be increased on the part of grace. But neither can it be increased on the part of the subject, since Christ as man was a true and full comprehensor from the first instant of His conception. Hence there could have been no increase of grace in Him, as there could be none in the rest of the blessed, whose grace could not increase, seeing that they have reached their last end. But as regards men who are wholly wayfarers, their grace can be increased not merely on the part of the form, since they have not attained the highest degree of grace, but also on the part of the subject, since they have not yet attained their end.

Reply Obj. 1: If we speak of mathematical quantity, addition can be made to any finite quantity, since there is nothing on the part of finite quantity which is repugnant to addition. But if we speak of natural quantity, there may be repugnance on the part of the form to which a determined quantity is due, even as other accidents are determined. Hence the Philosopher says (De Anima ii, 41) that "there is naturally a term of all things, and a fixed limit of magnitude and increase." And hence to the quantity of the whole there can be no addition. And still more must we suppose a term in the forms themselves, beyond which they may not go. Hence it is not necessary that addition should be capable of being made to Christ's grace, although it is finite in its essence.

Reply Obj. 2: Although the Divine power can make something greater and better than the habitual grace of Christ, yet it could not make it to be ordained to anything greater than the personal union with the Only-begotten Son of the Father; and to this union, by the purpose of the Divine wisdom, the measure of grace is sufficient.

Reply Obj. 3: Anyone may increase in wisdom and grace in two ways. First inasmuch as the very habits of wisdom and grace are increased; and in this way Christ did not increase. Secondly, as regards the effects, i.e. inasmuch as they do wiser and greater works; and in this way Christ increased in wisdom and grace even as in age, since in the course of time He did more perfect works, to prove Himself true man, both in the things of God, and in the things of man.

THIRTEENTH ARTICLE [III, Q. 7, Art. 13]

Whether the Habitual Grace of Christ Followed After the Union?

Objection 1: It would seem that the habitual grace did not follow after the union. For nothing follows itself. But this habitual grace seems to be the same as the grace of union; for Augustine says (De Praedest. Sanct. xv): "Every man becomes a Christian from the beginning of his belief, by the same grace whereby this Man from His beginning became Christ"; and of these two the first pertains to habitual grace and the second to the grace of union. Therefore it would seem that habitual grace did not follow upon the union.

Obj. 2: Further, disposition precedes perfection, if not in time, at least in thought. But the habitual grace seems to be a disposition in human nature for the personal union. Therefore it seems that the habitual grace did not follow but rather preceded the union.

Obj. 3: Further, the common precedes the proper. But habitual grace is common to Christ and other men; and the grace of union is proper to Christ. Therefore habitual grace is prior in thought to the union. Therefore it does not follow it.

*On the contrary,* It is written (Isa. 42:1): "Behold my servant, I will uphold Him . . . "and farther on: "I have given My Spirit upon Him"; and this pertains to the gift of habitual grace. Hence it remains that the assumption of human nature to the unity of the Person preceded the habitual grace of Christ.

*I answer that,* The union of the human nature with the Divine Person, which, as we have said above (Q. 2, A. 10; Q. 6, A. 6), is the grace of union, precedes the habitual grace of Christ, not in order of time, but by nature and in thought; and this for a triple reason: First, with reference to the order of the principles of both. For the principle of the union is the Person of the Son assuming human nature, Who is said to be sent into the world, inasmuch as He assumed human nature; but the principle of habitual grace, which is given with charity, is the Holy Ghost, Who is said to be sent inasmuch as He dwells in the mind by charity. Now the mission of the Son is prior, in the order of nature, to the mission of the Holy Ghost, even as in the order of nature the Holy Ghost proceeds from the Son, and love from wisdom. Hence the personal union, according to which the mission of the Son took place, is prior in the order of nature to habitual grace, according to which the mission of the Holy Ghost takes place. Secondly, the reason of this order may be taken from the relation of grace to its cause. For grace is caused in man by the presence of the Godhead, as light in the air by the presence of the sun. Hence it is written (Ezech. 43:2): "The glory of the God of Israel came in by the way of the east . . . and the earth shone with His majesty."

But the presence of God in Christ is by the union of human nature with the Divine Person. Hence the habitual grace of Christ is understood to follow this union, as light follows the sun. Thirdly, the reason of this union can be taken from the end of grace, since it is ordained to acting rightly, and action belongs to the suppositum and the individual. Hence action and, in consequence, grace ordaining thereto, presuppose the hypostasis which operates. Now the hypostasis did not exist in the human nature before the union, as is clear from Q. 4, A. 2. Therefore the grace of union precedes, in thought, habitual grace.

Reply Obj. 1: Augustine here means by grace the gratuitous will of God, bestowing benefits gratis; and hence every man is said to be made a Christian by the same grace whereby a Man became Christ, since both take place by the gratuitous will of God without merits.

Reply Obj. 2: As disposition in the order of generation precedes the perfection to which it disposes, in such things as are gradually perfected; so it naturally follows the perfection which one has already obtained; as heat, which was a disposition to the form of fire, is an effect flowing from the form of already existing fire. Now the human nature in Christ is united to the Person of the Word from the beginning without succession. Hence habitual grace is not understood to have preceded the union, but to have followed it; as a natural property. Hence, as Augustine says (Enchiridion xl): "Grace is in a manner natural to the Man Christ."

Reply Obj. 3: The common precedes the proper, when both are of the same genus; but when they are of divers genera, there is nothing to prevent the proper being prior to the common. Now the grace of union is not in the same genus as habitual grace; but is above all genera even as the Divine Person Himself. Hence there is nothing to prevent this proper from being before the common since it does not result from something being added to the common, but is rather the principle and source of that which is common.

## QUESTION 8

OF THE GRACE OF CHRIST, AS HE IS THE HEAD OF THE CHURCH (In Eight Articles)

We must now consider the grace of Christ as the Head of the Church; and under this head there are eight points of inquiry:

(1) Whether Christ is the Head of the Church?

(2) Whether He is the Head of men as regards their bodies or only as regards their souls?

(3) Whether He is the Head of all men?

(4) Whether He is the Head of the angels?

(5) Whether the grace of Christ as Head of the Church is the same as His habitual grace as an individual man?

(6) Whether to be Head of the Church is proper to Christ?

(7) Whether the devil is the head of all the wicked?

(8) Whether Antichrist can be called the head of all the wicked?

FIRST ARTICLE [III, Q. 8, Art. 1]

Whether Christ Is the Head of the Church?

Objection 1: It would seem that it does not belong to Christ as man to be Head of the Church. For the head imparts sense and motion to the members. Now spiritual sense and motion which are by grace, are not imparted to us by the Man Christ, because, as Augustine says (De Trin. i, 12; xv, 24), "not even Christ, as man, but only as God, bestows the Holy Ghost." Therefore it does not belong to Him as man to be Head of the Church.

Obj. 2: Further, it is not fitting for the head to have a head. But God is the Head of Christ, as man, according to 1 Cor. 11:3, "The Head of Christ is God." Therefore Christ Himself is not a head.

Obj. 3: Furthermore, the head of a man is a particular member, receiving an influx from the heart. But Christ is the universal principle of the whole Church. Therefore He is not the Head of the Church.

*On the contrary,* It is written (Eph. 1:22): "And He . . . hath made Him head over all the Church."

*I answer that,* As the whole Church is termed one mystic body from its likeness to the natural body of a man, which in divers members has divers acts, as the Apostle teaches (Rom. 12; 1 Cor. 12), so likewise Christ is called the Head of the Church from a likeness with the human head, in which we may consider three things, viz. order, perfection, and power: "Order," indeed; for the head is the first part of man, beginning from the higher part; and hence it is that every principle is usually called a head according to Ezech. 16:25: "At every head of the way, thou hast set up a sign of thy prostitution"--"Perfection," inasmuch as in the head dwell all the senses, both interior and exterior, whereas in the other members there is only touch, and hence it is said (Isa. 9:15): "The aged and honorable, he is the head"--"Power," because the power and movement of the other members, together with the direction of them in their acts, is from the head, by reason of the sensitive and motive power there ruling; hence the ruler is called the head of a people, according to 1 Kings 15:17: "When thou wast a little one in thy own eyes, wast thou not made the head of the tribes of Israel?" Now these three things belong spiritually to Christ. First, on account of His nearness to God His grace is the highest and first, though not in time, since all have received grace on account of His grace, according to Rom. 8:29: "For whom He foreknew, He also predestinated to be made conformable to the image of His Son; that He might be the first-born amongst many brethren." Secondly, He had perfection as regards the fulness of all graces, according to John 1:14, "We saw Him [Vulg.: 'His glory'] . . . full of grace and truth," as was shown (Q. 7, A. 9). Thirdly, He has the power of bestowing grace on all the members of the Church, according to John 1:16: "Of His fulness we have all received." And thus it is plain that Christ is fittingly called the Head of the Church.

Reply Obj. 1: To give grace or the Holy Ghost belongs to Christ as He is God, authoritatively; but instrumentally it belongs also to Him as man, inasmuch as His manhood is the instrument of His Godhead. And hence by the power of the Godhead His actions were beneficial, i.e. by causing grace in us, both meritoriously and efficiently. But Augustine denies that Christ as man gives the Holy Ghost authoritatively. Even other saints are said to give the Holy Ghost instrumentally, or ministerially, according to Gal. 3:5: "He . . . who giveth to you the Spirit."

Reply Obj. 2: In metaphorical speech we must not expect a likeness in all respects; for thus there would be not likeness but identity. Accordingly a natural head has not another head because one human body is not part of another; but a metaphorical body, i.e. an ordered multitude, is part of another multitude as the domestic multitude is part of the civil multitude; and hence the father who is head of the domestic multitude has a head above him, i.e. the civil governor. And hence there is no reason why God should not be the Head of Christ, although Christ Himself is Head of the Church.

Reply Obj. 3: The head has a manifest pre-eminence over the other exterior members; but the heart has a certain hidden influence. And hence the Holy Ghost is likened to the heart, since He invisibly quickens and unifies the Church; but Christ is likened to the Head in His visible nature in which man is set over man.

SECOND ARTICLE [III, Q. 8, Art. 2]

Whether Christ Is the Head of Men As to Their Bodies or Only As to Their Souls?

Objection 1: It would seem that Christ is not the Head of men as to their bodies. For Christ is said to be the Head of the Church inasmuch as He bestows spiritual sense and the movement of grace on the Church. But a body is not capable of this spiritual sense and movement. Therefore Christ is not the Head of men as regards their bodies.

Obj. 2: Further, we share bodies with the brutes. If therefore Christ was the Head of men as to their bodies, it would follow that He was the Head of brute animals; and this is not fitting.

Obj. 3: Further, Christ took His body from other men, as is clear from Matt. 1 and Luke 3. But the head is the first of the members, as was said above (A. 1, ad 3). Therefore Christ is not the Head of the Church as regards bodies.

*On the contrary,* It is written (Phil. 3:21): "Who will reform the body of our lowness, made like to the body of His glory."

*I answer that,* The human body has a natural relation to the rational soul, which is its proper form and motor. Inasmuch as the soul is its form, it receives from the soul life and the other properties which belong specifically to man; but inasmuch as the soul is its motor, the body serves the soul instrumentally. Therefore we must hold that the manhood of Christ had the power of influence, inasmuch as it is united to the Word of God, to Whom His body is united through the soul, as stated above (Q. 6, A. 1). Hence the whole manhood of Christ, i.e. according to soul and body, influences all, both in soul and body; but principally the soul, and secondarily the body: First, inasmuch as the "members of the body are presented as instruments of justice" in the soul that lives through Christ, as the Apostle says (Rom. 6:13): secondly, inasmuch as the life of glory flows from the soul on to the body, according to Rom. 8:11: "He that raised up Jesus from the dead shall quicken also your mortal bodies, because of His Spirit that dwelleth in you."

Reply Obj. 1: The spiritual sense of grace does not reach to the body first and principally, but secondarily and instrumentally, as was said above.

Reply Obj. 2: The body of an animal has no relation to a rational soul, as the human body has. Hence there is no parity.

Reply Obj. 3: Although Christ drew the matter of His body from other men, yet all draw from Him the immortal life of their body, according to 1 Cor. 15:22: "And as in Adam all die, so also in Christ all shall be made alive."

THIRD ARTICLE [III, Q. 8, Art. 3]

Whether Christ Is the Head of All Men?

Objection 1: It would seem that Christ is not the Head of all men. For the head has no relation except to the members of its body. Now the unbaptized are nowise members of the Church which is the body of Christ, as it is written (Eph. 1:23). Therefore Christ is not the Head of all men.

Obj. 2: Further, the Apostle writes to the Ephesians (5:25, 27): "Christ delivered Himself up for" the Church "that He might present it to Himself a glorious Church, not having spot or wrinkle or any such thing." But there are many of the faithful in whom is found the spot or the wrinkle of sin. Therefore Christ is not the Head of all the faithful.

Obj. 3: Further, the sacraments of the Old Law are compared to Christ as the shadow to the body, as is written (Col. 2:17). But the fathers of the Old Testament in their day served unto these sacraments, according to Heb. 8:5: "Who serve unto the example and shadow of heavenly things." Hence they did not pertain to Christ's body, and therefore Christ is not the Head of all men.

*On the contrary,* It is written (1 Tim. 4:10): "Who is the Saviour of all men, especially of the faithful," and (1 John 2:2): "He is the propitiation for our sins, and not for ours only, but also for those of the whole world." Now to save men and to be a propitiation for their sins belongs to Christ as Head. Therefore Christ is the Head of all men.

*I answer that,* This is the difference between the natural body of man and the Church's mystical body, that the members of the natural body are all together, and the members of the mystical are not all together--neither as regards their natural being, since the body of the Church is made up of the men who have been from the beginning of the world until its end--nor as regards their supernatural being, since, of those who are at any one time, some there are who are without grace, yet will afterwards obtain it, and some have it already. We must therefore consider the members of the mystical body not only as they are in act, but as they are in potentiality. Nevertheless, some are in potentiality who will never be reduced to act, and some are reduced at some time to act; and this according to the triple class, of which the first is by faith, the second by the charity of this life, the third by the fruition of the life to come. Hence we must say that if we take the whole time of the world in general, Christ is the Head of all men, but diversely. For, first and principally, He is the Head of such as are united to Him by glory; secondly, of those who are actually united to Him by charity; thirdly, of those who are actually united to Him by faith; fourthly, of those who are united to Him merely in potentiality, which is not yet reduced to act, yet will be reduced to act according to Divine predestination; fifthly, of those who are united to Him in potentiality, which will never be reduced to act; such are those men existing in the world, who are not predestined, who, however, on their departure from this world, wholly cease to be members of Christ, as being no longer in potentiality to be united to Christ.

Reply Obj. 1: Those who are unbaptized, though not actually in the Church, are in the Church potentially. And this potentiality is rooted in two things--first and principally, in the power of Christ, which is sufficient for the salvation of the whole human race; secondly, in free-will.

Reply Obj. 2: To be "a glorious Church not having spot or wrinkle" is the ultimate end to which we are brought by the Passion of Christ. Hence this will be in heaven, and not on earth, in which "if we say we have no sin, we deceive ourselves," as is written (1 John 1:8). Nevertheless, there are some, viz. mortal, sins from which they are free who are members of Christ by the actual union of charity; but such as are tainted with these sins are not members of Christ actually, but potentially; except, perhaps, imperfectly, by formless faith, which unites to God, relatively but not simply, viz. so that man partake of the life of grace. For, as is written (James 2:20): "Faith without works is dead." Yet such as these receive from Christ a certain vital act, i.e. to believe, as if a lifeless limb were moved by a man to some extent.

Reply Obj. 3: The holy Fathers made use of the legal sacraments, not as realities, but as images and shadows of what was to come. Now it is the same motion to an image as image, and to the reality, as is clear from the Philosopher (De Memor. et Remin. ii). Hence the ancient Fathers, by observing the legal sacraments, were borne to Christ by the same faith and love whereby we also are borne to Him, and hence the ancient Fathers belong to the same Church as we.

FOURTH ARTICLE [III, Q. 8, Art. 4]

Whether Christ Is the Head of the Angels?

Objection 1: It would seem that Christ as man is not the head of the angels. For the head and members are of one nature. But Christ as man is not of the same nature with the angels, but only with men, since, as is written (Heb. 2:16): "For nowhere doth He take hold of the angels, but of the seed of Abraham He taketh hold." Therefore Christ as man is not the head of the angels.

Obj. 2: Further, Christ is the head of such as belong to the Church, which is His Body, as is written (Eph. 1:23). But the angels do not belong to the Church. For the Church is the congregation of the faithful: and in the angels there is no faith, for they do not "walk by faith" but "by sight," otherwise they would be "absent from the Lord," as the Apostle argues (2 Cor. 5:6, 7). Therefore Christ as man is not head of the angels.

Obj. 3: Further, Augustine says (Tract. xix; xxiii in Joan.), that as "the Word" which "was in the beginning with the Father" quickens souls, so the "Word made flesh" quickens bodies, which angels lack. But the Word made flesh is Christ as man. Therefore Christ as man does not give life to angels, and hence as man He is not the head of the angels.

*On the contrary,* The Apostle says (Col. 2:10), "Who is the head of all Principality and Power," and the same reason holds good with the other orders of angels. Therefore Christ is the Head of the angels.

*I answer that,* As was said above (A. 1, ad 2), where there is one body we must allow that there is one head. Now a multitude ordained to one end, with distinct acts and duties, may be metaphorically called one body. But it is manifest that both men and angels are ordained to one end, which is the glory of the Divine fruition. Hence the mystical body of the Church consists not only of men but of angels. Now of all this multitude Christ is the Head, since He is nearer God, and shares His gifts more fully, not only than man, but even than angels; and of His influence not only men but even angels partake, since it is written (Eph. 1:20-22): that God the Father set "Him," namely Christ, "on His right hand in the heavenly places, above all Principality and Power and Virtue and Dominion and every name that is named not only in this world, but also in that which is to come. And He hath subjected all things under His feet." Therefore Christ is not only the Head of men, but of angels. Hence we read (Matt. 4:11) that "angels came and ministered to Him."

Reply Obj. 1: Christ's influence over men is chiefly with regard to their souls; wherein men agree with angels in generic nature, though not in specific nature. By reason of this agreement Christ can be said to be the Head of the angels, although the agreement falls short as regards the body.

Reply Obj. 2: The Church, on earth, is the congregation of the faithful; but, in heaven, it is the congregation of comprehensors. Now Christ was not merely a wayfarer, but a comprehensor. And therefore He is the Head not merely of the faithful, but of comprehensors, as having grace and glory most fully.

Reply Obj. 3: Augustine here uses the similitude of cause and effect, i.e. inasmuch as corporeal things act on bodies, and spiritual things on spiritual things. Nevertheless, the humanity of Christ, by virtue of the spiritual nature, i.e. the Divine, can cause something not only in the spirits of men, but also in the spirits of angels, on account of its most close conjunction with God, i.e. by personal union.

FIFTH ARTICLE [III, Q. 8, Art. 5]

Whether the Grace of Christ, As Head of the Church, Is the Same As His Habitual Grace, Inasmuch As He Is Man?

Objection 1: It would seem that the grace whereby Christ is Head of the Church and the individual grace of the Man are not the same. For the Apostle says (Rom. 5:15): "If by the offense of one many died, much more the grace of God and the gift, by the grace of one man, Jesus Christ, hath abounded unto many." But the actual sin of Adam is distinct from original sin which he transmitted to his posterity. Hence the personal grace which is proper to Christ is distinct from His grace, inasmuch as He is the Head of the Church, which flows to others from Him.

Obj. 2: Further, habits are distinguished by acts. But the personal grace of Christ is ordained to one act, viz. the sanctification of His soul; and the capital grace is ordained to another, viz. to sanctifying others. Therefore the personal grace of Christ is distinct from His grace as He is the Head of the Church.

Obj. 3: Further, as was said above (Q. 6, A. 6), in Christ we distinguish a threefold grace, viz. the grace of union, capital grace, and the individual grace of the Man. Now the individual grace of Christ is distinct from the grace of union. Therefore it is also distinct from the capital grace.

*On the contrary,* It is written (John 1:16): "Of His fulness we all have received." Now He is our Head, inasmuch as we receive from Him. Therefore He is our Head, inasmuch as He has the fulness of grace. Now He had the fulness of grace, inasmuch as personal grace was in Him in its perfection, as was said above (Q. 7, A. 9). Hence His capital and personal grace are not distinct.

*I answer that,* Since everything acts inasmuch as it is a being in act, it must be the same act whereby it is in act and whereby it acts, as it is the same heat whereby fire is hot and whereby it heats. Yet not every act whereby anything is in act suffices for its being the principle of acting upon others. For since the agent is nobler than the patient, as Augustine says (Gen. ad lit. xii, 16) and the Philosopher (De Anima iii, 19), the agent must act on others by reason of a certain pre-eminence. Now it was said above (A. 1; Q. 7, A. 9) grace was received by the soul of Christ in the highest way; and therefore from this pre-eminence of grace which He received, it is from Him that this grace is bestowed on others--and this belongs to the nature of head. Hence the personal grace, whereby the soul of Christ is justified, is essentially the same as His grace, as He is the Head of the Church, and justifies others; but there is a distinction of reason between them.

Reply Obj. 1: Original sin in Adam, which is a sin of the nature, is derived from his actual sin, which is a personal sin, because in him the person corrupted the nature; and by means of this corruption the sin of the first man is transmitted to posterity, inasmuch as the corrupt nature corrupts the person. Now grace is not vouchsafed us by means of human nature, but solely by the personal action of Christ Himself. Hence we must not distinguish a twofold grace in Christ, one corresponding to the nature, the other to the person as in Adam we distinguish the sin of the nature and of the person.

Reply Obj. 2: Different acts, one of which is the reason and the cause of the other, do not diversify a habit. Now the act of the personal grace which is formally to sanctify its subject, is the reason of the justification of others, which pertains to capital grace. Hence it is that the essence of the habit is not diversified by this difference.

Reply Obj. 3: Personal and capital grace are ordained to an act; but the grace of union is not ordained to an act, but to the personal being. Hence the personal and the capital grace agree in the essence of the habit; but the grace of union does not, although the personal grace can be called in a manner the grace of union, inasmuch as it brings about a fitness for the union; and thus the grace of union, the capital, and the personal grace are one in essence, though there is a distinction of reason between them.

SIXTH ARTICLE [III, Q. 8, Art. 6]

Whether It Is Proper to Christ to Be Head of the Church?

Objection 1: It seems that it is not proper to Christ to be Head of the Church. For it is written (1 Kings 15:17): "When thou wast a little one in thy own eyes, wast thou not made the head of the tribes of Israel?" Now there is but one Church in the New and the Old Testament. Therefore it seems that with equal reason any other man than Christ might be head of the Church.

Obj. 2: Further, Christ is called Head of the Church from His bestowing grace on the Church's members. But it belongs to others also to grant grace to others, according to Eph. 4:29: "Let no evil speech proceed from your mouth; but that which is good to the edification of faith, that it may administer grace to the hearers." Therefore it seems to belong also to others than Christ to be head of the Church.

Obj. 3: Further, Christ by His ruling over the Church is not only called "Head," but also "Shepherd" and "Foundation." Now Christ did not retain for Himself alone the name of Shepherd, according to 1 Pet. 5:4, "And when the prince of pastors shall appear, you shall receive a never-fading crown of glory"; nor the name of Foundation, according to Apoc. 21:14: "And the wall of the city had twelve foundations." Therefore it seems that He did not retain the name of Head for Himself alone.

*On the contrary,* It is written (Col. 2:19): "The head" of the Church is that "from which the whole body, by joints and bands being supplied with nourishment and compacted groweth unto the increase of God." But this belongs only to Christ. Therefore Christ alone is Head of the Church.

*I answer that,* The head influences the other members in two ways. First, by a certain intrinsic influence, inasmuch as motive and sensitive force flow from the head to the other members; secondly, by a certain exterior guidance, inasmuch as by sight and the senses, which are rooted in the head, man is guided in his exterior acts. Now the interior influx of grace is from no one save Christ, Whose manhood, through its union with the Godhead, has the power of justifying; but the influence over the members of the Church, as regards their exterior guidance, can belong to others; and in this way others may be called heads of the Church, according to Amos 6:1, "Ye great men, heads of the people"; differently, however, from Christ. First, inasmuch as Christ is the Head of all who pertain to the Church in every place and time and state; but all other men are called heads with reference to certain special places, as bishops of their Churches. Or with reference to a determined time as the Pope is the head of the whole Church, viz. during the time of his Pontificate, and with reference to a determined state, inasmuch as they are in the state of wayfarers. Secondly, because Christ is the Head of the Church by His own power and authority; while others are called heads, as taking Christ's place, according to 2 Cor. 2:10, "For what I have pardoned, if I have pardoned anything, for your sakes I have done it in the person of Christ," and 2 Cor. 5:20, "For Christ therefore we are ambassadors, God, as it were, exhorting by us."

Reply Obj. 1: The word "head" is employed in that passage in regard to exterior government; as a king is said to be the head of his kingdom.

Reply Obj. 2: Man does not distribute grace by interior influx, but by exteriorly persuading to the effects of grace.

Reply Obj. 3: As Augustine says (Tract. xlvi in Joan.): "If the rulers of the Church are Shepherds, how is there one Shepherd, except that all these are members of one Shepherd?" So likewise others may be called foundations and heads, inasmuch as they are members of the one Head and Foundation. Nevertheless, as Augustine says (Tract. xlvii), "He gave to His members to be shepherds; yet none of us calleth himself the Door. He kept this for Himself alone." And this because by door is implied the principal authority, inasmuch as it is by the door that all enter the house; and it is Christ alone by "Whom also we have access . . . into this grace, wherein we stand" (Rom. 5:2); but by the other names above-mentioned there may be implied not merely the principal but also the secondary authority.

SEVENTH ARTICLE [III, Q. 8, Art. 7]

Whether the Devil Is the Head of All the Wicked?

Objection 1: It would seem that the devil is not the head of the wicked. For it belongs to the head to diffuse sense and movement into the members, as a gloss says, on Eph. 1:22, "And made Him head," etc. But the devil has no power of spreading the evil of sin, which proceeds from the will of the sinner. Therefore the devil cannot be called the head of the wicked.

Obj. 2: Further, by every sin a man is made evil. But not every sin is from the devil; and this is plain as regards the demons, who did not sin through the persuasion of another; so likewise not every sin of man proceeds from the devil, for it is said (De Eccles. Dogm. lxxxii): "Not all our wicked thoughts are always raised up by the suggestion of the devil; but sometimes they spring from the movement of our will." Therefore the devil is not the head of all the wicked.

Obj. 3: Further, one head is placed on one body. But the whole multitude of the wicked do not seem to have anything in which they are united, for evil is contrary to evil and springs from divers defects, as Dionysius says (Div. Nom. iv). Therefore the devil cannot be called the head of all the wicked.

*On the contrary,* A gloss [*St. Gregory, Moral. xiv] on Job 18:17, "Let the memory of him perish from the earth," says: "This is said of every evil one, yet so as to be referred to the head," i.e. the devil.

*I answer that,* As was said above (A. 6), the head not only influences the members interiorly, but also governs them exteriorly, directing their actions to an end. Hence it may be said that anyone is the head of a multitude, either as regards both, i.e. by interior influence and exterior governance, and thus Christ is the Head of the Church, as was stated (A. 6); or as regards exterior governance, and thus every prince or prelate is head of the multitude subject to him. And in this way the devil is head of all the wicked. For, as is written (Job 41:25): "He is king over all the children of pride." Now it belongs to a governor to lead those whom he governs to their end. But the end of the devil is the aversion of the rational creature from God; hence from the beginning he has endeavored to lead man from obeying the Divine precept. But aversion from God has the nature of an end, inasmuch as it is sought for under the appearance of liberty, according to Jer. 2:20: "Of old time thou hast broken my yoke, thou hast burst my bands, and thou saidst, 'I will not serve.'" Hence, inasmuch as some are brought to this end by sinning, they fall under the rule and government of the devil, and therefore he is called their head.

Reply Obj. 1: Although the devil does not influence the rational mind interiorly, yet he beguiles it to evil by persuasion.

Reply Obj. 2: A governor does not always suggest to his subjects to obey his will; but proposes to all the sign of his will, in consequence of which some are incited by inducement, and some of their own free-will, as is plain in the leader of an army, whose standard all the soldiers follow, though no one persuades them. Therefore in the same way, the first sin of the devil, who "sinneth from the beginning" (1 John 3:8), is held out to all to be followed, and some imitate at his suggestion, and some of their own will without any suggestion. And hence the devil is the head of all the wicked, inasmuch as they imitate Him, according to Wis. 2:24, 25: "By the envy of the devil, death came into the world. And they follow him that are of his side."

Reply Obj. 3: All sins agree in aversion from God, although they differ by conversion to different changeable goods.

EIGHTH ARTICLE [III, Q. 8, Art. 8]

Whether Antichrist May Be Called the Head of All the Wicked?

Objection 1: It would seem that Antichrist is not the head of the wicked. For there are not several heads of one body. But the devil is the head of the multitude of the wicked. Therefore Antichrist is not their head.

Obj. 2: Further, Antichrist is a member of the devil. Now the head is distinguished from the members. Therefore Antichrist is not the head of the wicked.

Obj. 3: Further, the head has an influence over the members. But Antichrist has no influence over the wicked who have preceded him. Therefore Antichrist is not the head of the wicked.

*On the contrary,* A gloss [*St. Gregory, Moral. xv] on Job 21:29, "Ask any of them that go by the way," says: "Whilst he was speaking of the body of all the wicked, suddenly he turned his speech to Antichrist the head of all evil-doers."

*I answer that,* As was said above (A. 1), in the head are found three things: order, perfection, and the power of influencing. But as regards the order of the body, Antichrist is not said to be the head of the wicked as if his sin had preceded, as the sin of the devil preceded. So likewise he is not called the head of the wicked from the power of influencing, although he will pervert some in his day by exterior persuasion; nevertheless those who were before him were not beguiled into wickedness by him nor have imitated his wickedness. Hence he cannot be called the head of all the wicked in this way, but of some. Therefore it remains to be said that he is the head of all the wicked by reason of the perfection of his wickedness. Hence, on 2 Thess. 2:4, "Showing himself as if he were God," a gloss says: "As in Christ dwelt the fulness of the Godhead, so in Antichrist the fulness of all wickedness." Not indeed as if his humanity were assumed by the devil into unity of person, as the humanity of Christ by the Son of God; but that the devil by suggestion infuses his wickedness more copiously into him than into all others. And in this way all the wicked who have gone before are signs of Antichrist, according to 2 Thess. 2:7, "For the mystery of iniquity already worketh."

Reply Obj. 1: The devil and Antichrist are not two heads, but one; since Antichrist is called the head, inasmuch as the wickedness of the devil is most fully impressed on him. Hence, on 2 Thess. 2:4, "Showing himself as if he were God," a gloss says: "The head of all the wicked, namely the devil, who is king over all the children of pride will be in him." Now he is said to be in him not by personal union, nor by indwelling, since "the Trinity alone dwells in the mind" (as is said De Eccles. Dogm. lxxxiii), but by the effect of wickedness.

Reply Obj. 2: As the head of Christ is God, and yet He is the Head of the Church, as was said above (A. 1, ad 2), so likewise Antichrist is a member of the devil and yet is head of the wicked.

Reply Obj. 3: Antichrist is said to be the head of all the wicked not by a likeness of influence, but by a likeness of perfection. For in him the devil, as it were, brings his wickedness to a head, in the same way that anyone is said to bring his purpose to a head when he executes it.

## QUESTION 9

OF CHRIST'S KNOWLEDGE IN GENERAL (In Four Articles)

We must now consider Christ's knowledge; concerning which the consideration will be twofold. First, of Christ's knowledge in general; secondly, of each particular kind of knowledge He had.

Under the first head there are four points of inquiry:

(1) Whether Christ had any knowledge besides the Divine?

(2) Whether He had the knowledge which the blessed or comprehensors have?

(3) Whether He had an imprinted or infused knowledge?

(4) Whether He had any acquired knowledge?

FIRST ARTICLE [III, Q. 9, Art. 1]

Whether Christ Had Any Knowledge Besides the Divine?

Objection 1: It would seem that in Christ there was no knowledge except the Divine. For knowledge is necessary that things may be known thereby. But by His Divine knowledge Christ knew all things. Therefore any other knowledge would have been superfluous in Him.

Obj. 2: Further, the lesser light is dimmed by the greater. But all created knowledge in comparison with the uncreated knowledge of God is as the lesser to the greater light. Therefore there shone in Christ no other knowledge except the Divine.

Obj. 3: Further, the union of the human nature with the Divine took place in the Person, as is clear from Q. 2, A. 2. Now, according to some there is in Christ a certain "knowledge of the union," whereby Christ knew what belongs to the mystery of the Incarnation more fully than anyone else. Hence, since the personal union contains two natures, it would seem that there are not two knowledges in Christ, but one only, pertaining to both natures.

*On the contrary,* Ambrose says (De Incarnat. vii): "God assumed the perfection of human nature in the flesh; He took upon Himself the sense of man, but not the swollen sense of the flesh." But created knowledge pertains to the sense of man. Therefore in Christ there was created knowledge.

*I answer that,* As said above (Q. 5), the Son of God assumed an entire human nature, i.e. not only a body, but also a soul, and not only a sensitive, but also a rational soul. And therefore it behooved Him to have created knowledge, for three reasons. First, on account of the soul's perfection. For the soul, considered in itself, is in potentiality to knowing intelligible things. since it is like "a tablet on which nothing is written," and yet it may be written upon through the possible intellect, whereby it may become all things, as is said De Anima iii, 18. Now what is in potentiality is imperfect unless reduced to act. But it was fitting that the Son of God should assume, not an imperfect, but a perfect human nature, since the whole human race was to be brought back to perfection by its means. Hence it behooved the soul of Christ to be perfected by a knowledge, which would be its proper perfection. And therefore it was necessary that there should be another knowledge in Christ besides the Divine knowledge, otherwise the soul of Christ would have been more imperfect than the souls of the rest of men. Secondly, because, since everything is on account of its operation, as stated De Coel. ii, 17, Christ would have had an intellective soul to no purpose if He had not understood by it; and this pertains to created knowledge. Thirdly, because some created knowledge pertains to the nature of the human soul, viz. that whereby we naturally know first principles; since we are here taking knowledge for any cognition of the human intellect. Now nothing natural was wanting to Christ, since He took the whole human nature, as stated above (Q. 5). And hence the Sixth Council [*Third Council of Constantinople, Act. 4] condemned the opinion of those who denied that in Christ there are two knowledges or wisdoms.

Reply Obj. 1: Christ knew all things with the Divine knowledge by an uncreated operation which is the very Essence of God; since God's understanding is His substance, as the Philosopher proves (Metaph. xii, text. 39). Hence this act could not belong to the human soul of Christ, seeing that it belongs to another nature. Therefore, if there had been no other knowledge in the soul of Christ, it would have known nothing; and thus it would have been assumed to no purpose, since everything is on account of its operation.

Reply Obj. 2: If the two lights are supposed to be in the same order, the lesser is dimmed by the greater, as the light of the sun dims the light of a candle, both being in the class of illuminants. But if we suppose two lights, one of which is in the class of illuminants and the other in the class of illuminated, the lesser light is not dimmed by the greater, but rather is strengthened, as the light of the air by the light of the sun. And in this manner the light of knowledge is not dimmed, but rather is heightened in the soul of Christ by the light of the Divine knowledge, which is "the true light which enlighteneth every man that cometh into this world," as is written John 1:9.

Reply Obj. 3: On the part of what are united we hold there is a knowledge in Christ, both as to His Divine and as to His human nature; so that, by reason of the union whereby there is one hypostasis of God and man, the things of God are attributed to man, and the things of man are attributed to God, as was said above (Q. 3, AA. 1, 6). But on the part of the union itself we cannot admit any knowledge in Christ. For this union is in personal being, and knowledge belongs to person only by reason of a nature.

SECOND ARTICLE [III, Q. 9, Art. 2]

Whether Christ Had the Knowledge Which the Blessed or Comprehensors Have?

Objection 1: It would seem that in Christ there was not the knowledge of the blessed or comprehensors. For the knowledge of the blessed is a participation of Divine light, according to Ps. 35:10: "In Thy light we shall see light." Now Christ had not a participated light, but He had the Godhead Itself substantially abiding in Him, according to Col. 2:9: "For in Him dwelleth all the fulness of the Godhead corporeally." Therefore in Christ there was not the knowledge of the blessed.

Obj. 2: Further, the knowledge of the blessed makes them blessed, according to John 17:3: "This is eternal life: that they may know Thee, the only true God, and Jesus Christ Whom Thou hast sent." But this Man was blessed through being united to God in person, according to Ps. 64:5: "Blessed is He Whom Thou hast chosen and taken to Thee." Therefore it is not necessary to suppose the knowledge of the blessed in Him.

Obj. 3: Further, to man belongs a double knowledge--one by nature, one above nature. Now the knowledge of the blessed, which consists in the vision of God, is not natural to man, but above his nature. But in Christ there was another and much higher supernatural knowledge, i.e. the Divine knowledge. Therefore there was no need of the knowledge of the blessed in Christ.

*On the contrary,* The knowledge of the blessed consists in the knowledge of God. But He knew God fully, even as He was man, according to John 8:55: "I do know Him, and do keep His word." Therefore in Christ there was the knowledge of the blessed.

*I answer that,* What is in potentiality is reduced to act by what is in act; for that whereby things are heated must itself be hot. Now man is in potentiality to the knowledge of the blessed, which consists in the vision of God; and is ordained to it as to an end; since the rational creature is capable of that blessed knowledge, inasmuch as he is made in the image of God. Now men are brought to this end of beatitude by the humanity of Christ, according to Heb. 2:10: "For it became Him, for Whom are all things, and by Whom are all things, Who had brought many children unto glory, to perfect the author of their salvation by His passion." And hence it was necessary that the beatific knowledge, which consists in the vision of God, should belong to Christ pre-eminently, since the cause ought always to be more efficacious than the effect.

Reply Obj. 1: The Godhead is united to the manhood of Christ in Person, not in essence or nature; yet with the unity of Person remains the distinction of natures. And therefore the soul of Christ, which is a part of human nature, through a light participated from the Divine Nature, is perfected with the beatific knowledge whereby it sees God in essence.

Reply Obj. 2: By the union this Man is blessed with the uncreated beatitude, even as by the union He is God; yet besides the uncreated beatitude it was necessary that there should be in the human nature of Christ a created beatitude, whereby His soul was established in the last end of human nature.

Reply Obj. 3: The beatific vision and knowledge are to some extent above the nature of the rational soul, inasmuch as it cannot reach it of its own strength; but in another way it is in accordance with its nature, inasmuch as it is capable of it by nature, having been made to the likeness of God, as stated above. But the uncreated knowledge is in every way above the nature of the human soul.

THIRD ARTICLE [III, Q. 9, Art. 3]

Whether Christ Had an Imprinted or Infused Knowledge?

Objection 1: It would seem that there was not in Christ another infused knowledge besides the beatific knowledge. For all other knowledge compared to the beatific knowledge is like imperfect to perfect. But imperfect knowledge is removed by the presence of perfect knowledge, as the clear "face-to-face" vision removes the enigmatical vision of faith, as is plain from 1 Cor. 13:10, 12. Since, therefore, in Christ there was the beatific knowledge, as stated above (A. 2), it would seem that there could not be any other imprinted knowledge.

Obj. 2: Further, an imperfect mode of cognition disposes towards a more perfect, as opinion, the result of dialectical syllogisms, disposes towards science, which results from demonstrative syllogisms. Now, when perfection is reached, there is no further need of the disposition, even as on reaching the end motion is no longer necessary. Hence, since every created cognition is compared to beatific cognition, as imperfect to perfect and as disposition to its term, it seems that since Christ had beatific knowledge, it was not necessary for Him to have any other knowledge.

Obj. 3: Further, as corporeal matter is in potentiality to sensible forms, so the possible intellect is in potentiality to intelligible forms. Now corporeal matter cannot receive two forms at once, one more perfect and the other less perfect. Therefore neither can the soul receive a double knowledge at once, one more perfect and the other less perfect; and hence the same conclusion as above.

*On the contrary,* It is written (Col. 2:3) that in Christ "are hid all the treasures of wisdom and knowledge."

*I answer that,* As stated above (A. 1), it was fitting that the human nature assumed by the Word of God should not be imperfect. Now everything in potentiality is imperfect unless it be reduced to act. But the passive intellect of man is in potentiality to all intelligible things, and it is reduced to act by intelligible species, which are its completive forms, as is plain from what is said De Anima iii, 32, 38. And hence we must admit in the soul of Christ an infused knowledge, inasmuch as the Word of God imprinted upon the soul of Christ, which is personally united to Him, intelligible species of all things to which the possible intellect is in potentiality; even as in the beginning of the creation of things, the Word of God imprinted intelligible species upon the angelic mind, as is clear from Augustine (Gen. ad lit. ii, 8). And therefore, even as in the angels, according to Augustine (Gen. ad lit. iv, 22, 24, 30), there is a double knowledge--one the morning knowledge, whereby they know things in the Word; the other the evening knowledge, whereby they know things in their proper natures by infused species; so likewise, besides the Divine and uncreated knowledge in Christ, there is in His soul a beatific knowledge, whereby He knows the Word, and things in the Word; and an infused or imprinted knowledge, whereby He knows things in their proper nature by intelligible species proportioned to the human mind.

Reply Obj. 1: The imperfect vision of faith is essentially opposed to manifest vision, seeing that it is of the essence of faith to have reference to the unseen, as was said above (II-II, Q. 1, A. 4). But cognition by infused species includes no opposition to beatific cognition. Therefore there is no parity.

Reply Obj. 2: Disposition is referred to perfection in two ways: first, as a way leading to perfection; secondly, as an effect proceeding from perfection; thus matter is disposed by heat to receive the form of fire, and, when this comes, the heat does not cease, but remains as an effect of this form. So, too, opinion caused by a dialectical syllogism is a way to knowledge, which is acquired by demonstration, yet, when this has been acquired, there may still remain the knowledge gained by the dialectical syllogism, following, so to say, the demonstrative knowledge, which is based on the cause, since he who knows the cause is thereby enabled the better to understand the probable signs from which dialectical syllogisms proceed. So likewise in Christ, together with the beatific knowledge, there still remains infused knowledge, not as a way to beatitude, but as strengthened by beatitude.

Reply Obj. 3: The beatific knowledge is not by a species, that is a similitude of the Divine Essence, or of whatever is known in the Divine Essence, as is plain from what has been said in the First Part (Q. 12, A. 2); but it is a knowledge of the Divine Essence immediately, inasmuch as the Divine Essence itself is united to the beatified mind as an intelligible to an intelligent being; and the Divine Essence is a form exceeding the capacity of any creature whatsoever. Hence, together with this super-exceeding form, there is nothing to hinder from being in the rational mind, intelligible species, proportioned to its nature.

FOURTH ARTICLE [III, Q. 9, Art. 4]

Whether Christ Had Any Acquired Knowledge?

Objection 1: It would seem that in Christ there was no empiric and acquired knowledge. For whatever befitted Christ, He had most perfectly. Now Christ did not possess acquired knowledge most perfectly, since He did not devote Himself to the study of letters, by which knowledge is acquired in its perfection; for it is said (John 7:15): "The Jews wondered, saying: How doth this Man know letters, having never learned?" Therefore it seems that in Christ there was no acquired knowledge.

Obj. 2: Further, nothing can be added to what is full. But the power of Christ's soul was filled with intelligible species divinely infused, as was said above (A. 3). Therefore no acquired species could accrue to His soul.

Obj. 3: Further, he who already has the habit of knowledge, acquires no new habit, through what he receives from the senses (otherwise two forms of the same species would be in the same thing together); but the habit which previously existed is strengthened and increased. Therefore, since Christ had the habit of infused knowledge, it does not seem that He acquired a new knowledge through what He perceived by the senses.

*On the contrary,* It is written (Heb. 5:8): "Whereas . . . He was the Son of God, He learned obedience by the things which He suffered," i.e. "experienced," says a gloss. Therefore there was in the soul of Christ an empiric knowledge, which is acquired knowledge.

*I answer that,* As is plain from A. 1, nothing that God planted in our nature was wanting to the human nature assumed by the Word of God. Now it is manifest that God planted in human nature not only a passive, but an active intellect. Hence it is necessary to say that in the soul of Christ there was not merely a passive, but also an active intellect. But if in other things God and nature make nothing in vain, as the Philosopher says (De Coel. i, 31; ii, 59), still less in the soul of Christ is there anything in vain. Now what has not its proper operation is useless, as is said inDe Coel. ii, 17. Now the proper operation of the active intellect is to make intelligible species in act, by abstracting them from phantasms; hence, it is said (De Anima iii, 18) that the active intellect is that "whereby everything is made actual." And thus it is necessary to say that in Christ there were intelligible species received in the passive intellect by the action of the active intellect--which means that there was acquired knowledge in Him, which some call empiric. And hence, although I wrote differently (Sent. iii, D, xiv, A. 3; D, xviii, A. 3), it must be said that in Christ there was acquired knowledge, which is properly knowledge in a human fashion, both as regards the subject receiving and as regards the active cause. For such knowledge springs from Christ's active intellect, which is natural to the human soul. But infused knowledge is attributed to the soul, on account of a light infused from on high, and this manner of knowing is proportioned to the angelic nature. But the beatific knowledge, whereby the very Essence of God is seen, is proper and natural to God alone, as was said in the First Part (Q. 12, A. 4).

Reply Obj. 1: Since there is a twofold way of acquiring knowledge--by discovery and by being taught--the way of discovery is the higher, and the way of being taught is secondary. Hence it is said (Ethic. i, 4): "He indeed is the best who knows everything by himself: yet he is good who obeys him that speaks aright." And hence it was more fitting for Christ to possess a knowledge acquired by discovery than by being taught, especially since He was given to be the Teacher of all, according to Joel 2:23: "Be joyful in the Lord your God, because He hath given you a Teacher of justice."

Reply Obj. 2: The human mind has two relations--one to higher things, and in this respect the soul of Christ was full of the infused knowledge. The other relation is to lower things, i.e. to phantasms, which naturally move the human mind by virtue of the active intellect. Now it was necessary that even in this respect the soul of Christ should be filled with knowledge, not that the first fulness was insufficient for the human mind in itself, but that it behooved it to be also perfected with regard to phantasms.

Reply Obj. 3: Acquired and infused habits are not to be classed together; for the habit of knowledge is acquired by the relation of the human mind to phantasms; hence, another habit of the same kind cannot be again acquired. But the habit of infused knowledge is of a different nature, as coming down to the soul from on high, and not from phantasms. And hence there is no parity between these habits.

## QUESTION 10

OF THE BEATIFIC KNOWLEDGE OF CHRIST'S SOUL (In Four Articles)

Now we must consider each of the aforesaid knowledges. Since, however, we have treated of the Divine knowledge in the First Part (Q. 14), it now remains to speak of the three others: (1) of the beatific knowledge; (2) of the infused knowledge; (3) of the acquired knowledge.

But again, because much has been said in the First Part (Q. 12) of the beatific knowledge, which consists in the vision of God, we shall speak here only of such things as belong properly to the soul of Christ. Under this head there are four points of inquiry:

(1) Whether the soul of Christ comprehended the Word or the Divine Essence?

(2) Whether it knew all things in the Word?

(3) Whether the soul of Christ knew the infinite in the Word?

(4) Whether it saw the Word or the Divine Essence clearer than did any other creature?

FIRST ARTICLE [III, Q. 10, Art. 1]

Whether the Soul of Christ Comprehended the Word or the Divine Essence?

Objection 1: It would seem that the soul of Christ comprehended and comprehends the Word or Divine Essence. For Isidore says (De Summo Bono i, 3) that "the Trinity is known only to Itself and to the Man assumed." Therefore the Man assumed communicates with the Holy Trinity in that knowledge of Itself which is proper to the Trinity. Now this is the knowledge of comprehension. Therefore the soul of Christ comprehends the Divine Essence.

Obj. 2: Further, to be united to God in personal being is greater than to be united by vision. But as Damascene says (De Fide Orth. iii, 6), "the whole Godhead in one Person is united to the human nature in Christ." Therefore much more is the whole Divine Nature seen by the soul of Christ; and hence it would seem that the soul of Christ comprehended the Divine Essence.

Obj. 3: Further, what belongs by nature to the Son of God belongs by grace to the Son of Man, as Augustine says (De Trin. i, 13). But to comprehend the Divine Essence belongs by nature to the Son of God. Therefore it belongs by grace to the Son of Man; and thus it seems that the soul of Christ comprehended the Divine Essence by grace.

*On the contrary,* Augustine says (Qq. lxxxiii, qu. 14): "Whatsoever comprehends itself is finite to itself." But the Divine Essence is not finite with respect to the soul of Christ, since It infinitely exceeds it. Therefore the soul of Christ does not comprehend the Word.

*I answer that,* As is plain from Q. 2, AA. 1, 6, the union of the two natures in the Person of Christ took place in such a way that the properties of both natures remained unconfused, i.e. "the uncreated remained uncreated, and the created remained within the limits of the creature," as Damascene says (De Fide Orth. iii, 3, 4). Now it is impossible for any creature to comprehend the Divine Essence, as was shown in the First Part (Q. 12, AA. 1, 4, 7), seeing that the infinite is not comprehended by the finite. And hence it must be said that the soul of Christ nowise comprehends the Divine Essence.

Reply Obj. 1: The Man assumed is reckoned with the Divine Trinity in the knowledge of Itself, not indeed as regards comprehension, but by reason of a certain most excellent knowledge above the rest of creatures.

Reply Obj. 2: Not even in the union by personal being does the human nature comprehend the Word of God or the Divine Nature, for although it was wholly united to the human nature in the one Person of the Son, yet the whole power of the Godhead was not circumscribed by the human nature. Hence Augustine says (Ep. ad Volusian. cxxxvii): "I would have you know that it is not the Christian doctrine that God was united to flesh in such a manner as to quit or lose the care of the world's government, neither did He narrow or reduce it when He transferred it to that little body." So likewise the soul of Christ sees the whole Essence of God, yet does not comprehend It; since it does not see It totally, i.e. not as perfectly as It is knowable, as was said in the First Part (Q. 12, A. 7).

Reply Obj. 3: This saying of Augustine is to be understood of the grace of union, by reason of which all that is said of the Son of God in His Divine Nature is also said of the Son of Man on account of the identity of suppositum. And in this way it may be said that the Son of Man is a comprehensor of the Divine Essence, not indeed by His soul, but in His Divine Nature; even as we may also say that the Son of Man is the Creator.

SECOND ARTICLE [III, Q. 10, Art. 2]

Whether the Son of God Knew All Things in the Word?

Obj. 1: It would seem that the soul of Christ does not know all things in the Word. For it is written (Mk. 13:32): "But of that day or hour no man knoweth, neither the angels in heaven nor the Son, but the Father." Therefore He does not know all things in the Word.

Obj. 2: Further, the more perfectly anyone knows a principle the more he knows in the principle. But God sees His Essence more perfectly than the soul of Christ does. Therefore He knows more than the soul of Christ knows in the Word. Therefore the soul of Christ does not know all things in the Word.

Obj. 3: Further, the extent of knowledge depends on the number of things known. If, therefore, the soul of Christ knew in the Word all that the Word knows, it would follow that the knowledge of the soul of Christ would equal the Divine knowledge, i.e. the created would equal the uncreated, which is impossible.

*On the contrary,* on Apoc. 5:12, "The Lamb that was slain is worthy to receive . . . divinity and wisdom," a gloss says, i.e. "the knowledge of all things."

*I answer that,* When it is inquired whether Christ knows all things in the Word, "all things" may be taken in two ways: First, properly, to stand for all that in any way whatsoever is, will be, or was done, said, or thought, by whomsoever and at any time. And in this way it must be said that the soul of Christ knows all things in the Word. For every created intellect knows in the Word, not all simply, but so many more things the more perfectly it sees the Word. Yet no beatified intellect fails to know in the Word whatever pertains to itself. Now to Christ and to His dignity all things to some extent belong, inasmuch as all things are subject to Him. Moreover, He has been appointed Judge of all by God, "because He is the Son of Man," as is said John 5:27; and therefore the soul of Christ knows in the Word all things existing in whatever time, and the thoughts of men, of which He is the Judge, so that what is said of Him (John 2:25), "For He knew what was in man," can be understood not merely of the Divine knowledge, but also of His soul's knowledge, which it had in the Word. Secondly, "all things" may be taken widely, as extending not merely to such things as are in act at some time, but even to such things as are in potentiality, and never have been nor ever will be reduced to act. Now some of these are in the Divine power alone, and not all of these does the soul of Christ know in the Word. For this would be to comprehend all that God could do, which would be to comprehend the Divine power, and, consequently, the Divine Essence. For every power is known from the knowledge of all it can do. Some, however, are not only in the power of God, but also in the power of the creature; and all of these the soul of Christ knows in the Word; for it comprehends in the Word the essence of every creature, and, consequently, its power and virtue, and all things that are in the power of the creature.

Reply Obj. 1: Arius and Eunomius understood this saying, not of the knowledge of the soul, which they did not hold to be in Christ, as was said above (Q. 9, A. 1), but of the Divine knowledge of the Son, Whom they held to be less than the Father as regards knowledge. But this will not stand, since all things were made by the Word of God, as is said John 1:3, and, amongst other things, all times were made by Him. Now He is not ignorant of anything that was made by Him.

He is said, therefore, not to know the day and the hour of the Judgment, for that He does not make it known, since, on being asked by the apostles (Acts 1:7), He was unwilling to reveal it; and, *on the contrary,* we read (Gen. 22:12): "Now I know that thou fearest God," i.e. "Now I have made thee know." But the Father is said to know, because He imparted this knowledge to the Son. Hence, by saying "but the Father," we are given to understand that the Son knows, not merely in the Divine Nature, but also in the human, because, as Chrysostom argues (Hom. lxxviii in Matth.), if it is given to Christ as man to know how to judge--which is greater--much more is it given to Him to know the less, viz. the time of Judgment. Origen, however (in Matth. Tract. xxx), expounds it of His body, which is the Church, which is ignorant of this time. Lastly, some say this is to be understood of the adoptive, and not of the natural Son of God.

Reply Obj. 2: God knows His Essence so much the more perfectly than the soul of Christ, as He comprehends it. And hence He knows all things, not merely whatever are in act at any time, which things He is said to know by knowledge of vision, but also what ever He Himself can do, which He is said to know by simple intelligence, as was shown in the First Part (Q. 14, A. 9). Therefore the soul of Christ knows all things that God knows in Himself by the knowledge of vision, but not all that God knows in Himself by knowledge of simple intelligence; and thus in Himself God knows many more things than the soul of Christ.

Reply Obj. 3: The extent of knowledge depends not merely on the number of knowable things, but also on the clearness of the knowledge. Therefore, although the knowledge of the soul of Christ which He has in the Word is equal to the knowledge of vision as regards the number of things known, nevertheless the knowledge of God infinitely exceeds the knowledge of the soul of Christ in clearness of cognition, since the uncreated light of the Divine intellect infinitely exceeds any created light received by the soul of Christ; although, absolutely speaking, the Divine knowledge exceeds the knowledge of the soul of Christ, not only as regards the mode of knowing, but also as regards the number of things known, as was stated above.

THIRD ARTICLE [III, Q. 10, Art. 3]

Whether the Soul of Christ Can Know the Infinite in the Word?

Objection 1: It would seem that the soul of Christ cannot know the infinite in the Word. For that the infinite should be known is repugnant to the definition of the infinite which (Phys. iii, 63) is said to be that "from which, however much we may take, there always remains something to be taken." But it is impossible for the definition to be separated from the thing defined, since this would mean that contradictories exist together. Therefore it is impossible that the soul of Christ knows the infinite.

Obj. 2: Further, the knowledge of the infinite is infinite. But the knowledge of the soul of Christ cannot be infinite, because its capacity is finite, since it is created. Therefore the soul of Christ cannot know the infinite.

Obj. 3: Further, there can be nothing greater than the infinite. But more is contained in the Divine knowledge, absolutely speaking, than in the knowledge of Christ's soul, as stated above (A. 2). Therefore the soul of Christ does not know the infinite.

*On the contrary,* The soul of Christ knows all its power and all it can do. Now it can cleanse infinite sins, according to 1 John 2:2: "He is the propitiation for our sins, and not for ours only, but also for those of the whole world." Therefore the soul of Christ knows the infinite.

*I answer that,* Knowledge regards only being, since being and truth are convertible. Now a thing is said to be a being in two ways: First, simply, i.e. whatever is a being in act; secondly, relatively, i.e. whatever is a being in potentiality. And because, as is said Metaph. ix, 20, everything is known as it is in act, and not as it is in potentiality, knowledge primarily and essentially regards being in act, and secondarily regards being in potentiality, which is not knowable of itself, but inasmuch as that in whose power it exists is known. Hence, with regard to the first mode of knowledge, the soul of Christ does not know the infinite. Because there is not an infinite number in act, even though we were to reckon all that are in act at any time whatsoever, since the state of generation and corruption will not last for ever: consequently there is a certain number not only of things lacking generation and corruption, but also of things capable of generation and corruption. But with regard to the other mode of knowing, the soul of Christ knows infinite things in the Word, for it knows, as stated above (A. 2), all that is in the power of the creature. Hence, since in the power of the creature there is an infinite number of things, it knows the infinite, as it were, by a certain knowledge of simple intelligence, and not by a knowledge of vision.

Reply Obj. 1: As we said in the First Part (Q. 8, A. 1), the infinite is taken in two ways. First, on the part of a form, and thus we have the negatively infinite, i.e. a form or act not limited by being received into matter or a subject; and this infinite of itself is most knowable on account of the perfection of the act, although it is not comprehensible by the finite power of the creature; for thus God is said to be infinite. And this infinite the soul of Christ knows, yet does not comprehend. Secondly, there is the infinite as regards matter, which is taken privatively, i.e. inasmuch as it has not the form it ought naturally to have, and in this way we have infinite in quantity. Now such an infinite of itself, is unknown: inasmuch as it is, as it were, matter with privation of form as is said Phys. iii, 65. But all knowledge is by form or act. Therefore if this infinite is to be known according to its mode of being, it cannot be known. For its mode is that part be taken after part, as is said Phys. iii, 62, 63. And in this way it is true that, if we take something from it, i.e. taking part after part, there always remains something to be taken. But as material things can be received by the intellect immaterially, and many things unitedly, so can infinite things be received by the intellect, not after the manner of infinite, but finitely; and thus what are in themselves infinite are, in the intellect of the knower, finite. And in this way the soul of Christ knows an infinite number of things, inasmuch as it knows them not by discoursing from one to another, but in a certain unity, i.e. in any creature in whose potentiality infinite things exist, and principally in the Word Himself.

Reply Obj. 2: There is nothing to hinder a thing from being infinite in one way and finite in another, as when in quantities we imagine a surface infinite in length and finite in breadth. Hence, if there were an infinite number of men, they would have a relative infinity, i.e. in multitude; but, as regards the essence, they would be finite, since the essence of all would be limited to one specific nature. But what is simply infinite in its essence is God, as was said in the First Part (Q. 7, A. 2). Now the proper object of the intellect is "what a thing is," as is said De Anima iii, 26, to which pertains the notion of the species. And thus the soul of Christ, since it has a finite capacity, attains to, but does not comprehend, what is simply infinite in essence, as stated above (A. 1). But the infinite in potentiality which is in creatures can be comprehended by the soul of Christ, since it is compared to that soul according to its essence, in which respect it is not infinite. For even our intellect understands a universal--for example, the nature of a genus or species, which in a manner has infinity, inasmuch as it can be predicated of an infinite number.

Reply Obj. 3: That which is infinite in every way can be but one. Hence the Philosopher says (De Coel. i, 2, 3) that, since bodies have dimensions in every part, there cannot be several infinite bodies. Yet if anything were infinite in one way only, nothing would hinder the existence of several such infinite things; as if we were to suppose several lines of infinite length drawn on a surface of finite breadth. Hence, because infinitude is not a substance, but is accidental to things that are said to be infinite, as the Philosopher says (Phys. iii, 37, 38); as the infinite is multiplied by different subjects, so, too, a property of the infinite must be multiplied, in such a way that it belongs to each of them according to that particular subject. Now it is a property of the infinite that nothing is greater than it. Hence, if we take one infinite line, there is nothing greater in it than the infinite; so, too, if we take any one of other infinite lines, it is plain that each has infinite parts. Therefore of necessity in this particular line there is nothing greater than all these infinite parts; yet in another or a third line there will be more infinite parts besides these. We observe this in numbers also, for the species of even numbers are infinite, and likewise the species of odd numbers are infinite; yet there are more even and odd numbers than even. And thus it must be said that nothing is greater than the simply and in every way infinite; but than the infinite which is limited in some respect, nothing is greater in that order; yet we may suppose something greater outside that order. In this way, therefore, there are infinite things in the potentiality of the creature, and yet there are more in the power of God than in the potentiality of the creature. So, too, the soul of Christ knows infinite things by the knowledge of simple intelligence; yet God knows more by this manner of knowledge or understanding.

FOURTH ARTICLE [III, Q. 10, Art. 4]

Whether the Soul of Christ Sees the Word or the Divine Essence More Clearly Than Does Any Other Creature?

Objection 1: It would seem that the soul of Christ does not see the Word more perfectly than does any other creature. For the perfection of knowledge depends upon the medium of knowing; as the knowledge we have by means of a demonstrative syllogism is more perfect than that which we have by means of a probable syllogism. But all the blessed see the Word immediately in the Divine Essence Itself, as was said in the First Part (Q. 12, A. 2). Therefore the soul of Christ does not see the Word more perfectly than any other creature.

Obj. 2: Further, the perfection of vision does not exceed the power of seeing. But the rational power of a soul such as is the soul of Christ is below the intellective power of an angel, as is plain from Dionysius (Coel. Hier. iv). Therefore the soul of Christ did not see the Word more perfectly than the angels.

Obj. 3: Further, God sees His Word infinitely more perfectly than does the soul of Christ. Hence there are infinite possible mediate degrees between the manner in which God sees His Word, and the manner in which the soul of Christ sees the Word. Therefore we cannot assert that the soul of Christ sees the Word or the Divine Essence more perfectly than does every other creature.

*On the contrary,* The Apostle says (Eph. 1:20, 21) that God set Christ "on His right hand in the heavenly places, above all principality and power and virtue and dominion and every name that is named not only in this world, but also in that which is to come." But in that heavenly glory the higher anyone is the more perfectly does he know God. Therefore the soul of Christ sees God more perfectly than does any other creature.

*I answer that,* The vision of the Divine Essence is granted to all the blessed by a partaking of the Divine light which is shed upon them from the fountain of the Word of God, according to Ecclus. 1:5: "The Word of God on high is the fountain of Wisdom." Now the soul of Christ, since it is united to the Word in person, is more closely joined to the Word of God than any other creature. Hence it more fully receives the light in which God is seen by the Word Himself than any other creature. And therefore more perfectly than the rest of creatures it sees the First Truth itself, which is the Essence of God; hence it is written (John 1:14): "And we saw His glory, the glory as it were of the Only-begotten of the Father," "full" not only of "grace" but also of "truth."

Reply Obj. 1: Perfection of knowledge, on the part of the thing known, depends on the medium; but as regards the knower, it depends on the power or habit. And hence it is that even amongst men one sees a conclusion in a medium more perfectly than another does. And in this way the soul of Christ, which is filled with a more abundant light, knows the Divine Essence more perfectly than do the other blessed, although all see the Divine Essence in itself.

Reply Obj. 2: The vision of the Divine Essence exceeds the natural power of any creature, as was said in the First Part (Q. 12, A. 4). And hence the degrees thereof depend rather on the order of grace in which Christ is supreme, than on the order of nature, in which the angelic nature is placed before the human.

Reply Obj. 3: As stated above (Q. 7, A. 12), there cannot be a greater grace than the grace of Christ with respect to the union with the Word; and the same is to be said of the perfection of the Divine vision; although, absolutely speaking, there could be a higher and more sublime degree by the infinity of the Divine power.

# QUESTION 11

OF THE KNOWLEDGE IMPRINTED OR INFUSED IN THE SOUL OF CHRIST (In Six Articles)

We must now consider the knowledge imprinted or infused in the soul of Christ, and under this head there are six points of inquiry:

(1) Whether Christ knows all things by this knowledge?

(2) Whether He could use this knowledge by turning to phantasms?

(3) Whether this knowledge was collative?

(4) Of the comparison of this knowledge with the angelic knowledge;

(5) Whether it was a habitual knowledge?

(6) Whether it was distinguished by various habits?

FIRST ARTICLE [III, Q. 11, Art. 1]

Whether by This Imprinted or Infused Knowledge Christ Knew All Things?

Objection 1: It would seem that by this knowledge Christ did not know all things. For this knowledge is imprinted upon Christ for the perfection of the passive intellect. Now the passive intellect of the human soul does not seem to be in potentiality to all things simply, but only to those things with regard to which it can be reduced to act by the active intellect, which is its proper motor; and these are knowable by natural reason. Therefore by this knowledge Christ did not know what exceeded the natural reason.

Obj. 2: Further, phantasms are to the human intellect as colors to sight, as is said De Anima iii, 18, 31, 39. But it does not pertain to the perfection of the power of seeing to know what is without color. Therefore it does not pertain to the perfection of human intellect to know things of which there are no phantasms, such as separate substances. Hence, since this knowledge was in Christ for the perfection of His intellective soul, it seems that by this knowledge He did not know separate substances.

Obj. 3: Further, it does not belong to the perfection of the intellect to know singulars. Hence it would seem that by this knowledge the soul of Christ did not know singulars.

*On the contrary,* It is written (Isa. 11:2) that "the Spirit of wisdom and understanding, of knowledge and counsel shall fill Him [*Vulg.: 'The Spirit of the Lord shall rest upon Him, the Spirit of wisdom and understanding, the Spirit of counsel . . . the Spirit of knowledge . . . '; cf. Ecclus. 15:5," under which are included all that may be known; for the knowledge of all Divine things belongs to wisdom, the knowledge of all immaterial things to understanding, the knowledge of all conclusions to knowledge ( scientia ), the knowledge of all practical things to counsel. Hence it would seem that by this knowledge Christ had the knowledge of all things.

*I answer that,* As was said above (Q. 9, A. 1), it was fitting that the soul of Christ should be wholly perfected by having each of its powers reduced to act. Now it must be borne in mind that in the human soul, as in every creature, there is a double passive power: one in comparison with a natural agent; the other in comparison with the first agent, which can reduce any creature to a higher act than a natural agent can reduce it, and this is usually called the obediential power of a creature. Now both powers of Christ's soul were reduced to act by this divinely imprinted knowledge. And hence, by it the soul of Christ knew: First, whatever can be known by force of a man's active intellect, e.g. whatever pertains to human sciences; secondly, by this knowledge Christ knew all things made known to man by Divine revelation, whether they belong to the gift of wisdom or the gift of prophecy, or any other gift of the Holy Ghost; since the soul of Christ knew these things more fully and completely than others. Yet He did not know the Essence of God by this knowledge, but by the first alone, of which we spoke above (Q. 10).

Reply Obj. 1: This reason refers to the natural power of an intellective soul in comparison with its natural agent, which is the active intellect.

Reply Obj. 2: The human soul in the state of this life, since it is somewhat fettered by the body, so as to be unable to understand without phantasms, cannot understand separate substances. But after the state of this life the separated soul will be able, in a measure, to know separate substances by itself, as was said in the First Part (Q. 89, AA. 1, 2), and this is especially clear as regards the souls of the blessed. Now before His Passion, Christ was not merely a wayfarer but also a comprehensor; hence His soul could know separate substances in the same way that a separated soul could.

Reply Obj. 3: The knowledge of singulars pertains to the perfection of the intellective soul, not in speculative knowledge, but in practical knowledge, which is imperfect without the knowledge of singulars, in which operations exist, as is said Ethic. vi, 7. Hence for prudence are required the remembrance of past things, knowledge of present things, and foresight of future things, as Tully says (De Invent. ii). Therefore, since Christ had the fulness of prudence by the gift of counsel, He consequently knew all singular things--present, past, and future.

SECOND ARTICLE [III, Q. 11, Art. 2]

Whether Christ Could Use This Knowledge by Turning to Phantasms?

Objection 1: It would seem that the soul of Christ could not understand by this knowledge except by turning to phantasms, because, as is stated De Anima iii, 18, 31, 39, phantasms are compared to man's intellective soul as colors to sight. But Christ's power of seeing could not become actual save by turning to colors. Therefore His intellective soul could understand nothing except by turning to phantasms.

Obj. 2: Further, Christ's soul is of the same nature as ours. otherwise He would not be of the same species as we, contrary to what the Apostle says (Phil. 2:7) " . . . being made in the likeness of men." But our soul cannot understand except by turning to phantasms. Hence, neither can Christ's soul otherwise understand.

Obj. 3: Further, senses are given to man to help his intellect. Hence, if the soul of Christ could understand without turning to phantasms, which arise in the senses, it would follow that in the soul of Christ the senses were useless, which is not fitting. Therefore it seems that the soul of Christ can only understand by turning to phantasms.

*On the contrary,* The soul of Christ knew certain things which could not be known by the senses, viz. separate substances. Therefore it could understand without turning to phantasms.

*I answer that,* In the state before His Passion Christ was at the same time a wayfarer and a comprehensor, as will be more clearly shown (Q. 15, A. 10). Especially had He the conditions of a wayfarer on the part of the body, which was passible; but the conditions of a comprehensor He had chiefly on the part of the soul. Now this is the condition of the soul of a comprehensor, viz. that it is nowise subject to its body, or dependent upon it, but wholly dominates it. Hence after the resurrection glory will flow from the soul to the body. But the soul of man on earth needs to turn to phantasms, because it is fettered by the body and in a measure subject to and dependent upon it. And hence the blessed both before and after the resurrection can understand without turning to phantasms. And this must be said of the soul of Christ, which had fully the capabilities of a comprehensor.

Reply Obj. 1: This likeness which the Philosopher asserts is not with regard to everything. For it is manifest that the end of the power of seeing is to know colors; but the end of the intellective power is not to know phantasms, but to know intelligible species, which it apprehends from and in phantasms, according to the state of the present life. Therefore there is a likeness in respect of what both powers regard, but not in respect of that in which the condition of both powers is terminated. Now nothing prevents a thing in different states from reaching its end by different ways: albeit there is never but one proper end of a thing. Hence, although the sight knows nothing without color; nevertheless in a certain state the intellect can know without phantasms, but not without intelligible species.

Reply Obj. 2: Although the soul of Christ was of the same nature as our souls, yet it had a state which our souls have not yet in fact, but only in hope, i.e. the state of comprehension.

Reply Obj. 3: Although the soul of Christ could understand without turning to phantasms, yet it could also understand by turning to phantasms. Hence the senses were not useless in it; especially as the senses are not afforded to man solely for intellectual knowledge, but for the need of animal life.

THIRD ARTICLE [III, Q. 11, Art. 3]

Whether This Knowledge Is Collative?

Objection 1: It would seem that the soul of Christ had not this knowledge by way of comparison. For Damascene says (De Fide Orth. iii, 14): "We do not uphold counsel or choice in Christ." Now these things are withheld from Christ only inasmuch as they imply comparison and discursion. Therefore it seems that there was no collative or discursive knowledge in Christ.

Obj. 2: Further, man needs comparison and discursion of reason in order to find out the unknown. But the soul of Christ knew everything, as was said above (Q. 10, A. 2). Hence there was no discursive or collative knowledge in Him.

Obj. 3: Further, the knowledge in Christ's soul was like that of comprehensors, who are likened to the angels, according to Matt. 22:30. Now there is no collative or discursive knowledge in the angels, as Dionysius shows (Div. Nom. vii). Therefore there was no discursive or collative knowledge in the soul of Christ.

*On the contrary,* Christ had a rational soul, as was shown (Q. 5, A. 4). Now the proper operation of a rational soul consists in comparison and discursion from one thing to another. Therefore there was collative and discursive knowledge in Christ.

*I answer that,* Knowledge may be discursive or collative in two ways. First, in the acquisition of the knowledge, as happens to us, who proceed from one thing to the knowledge of another, as from causes to effects, and conversely. And in this way the knowledge in Christ's soul was not discursive or collative, since this knowledge which we are now considering was divinely infused, and not acquired by a process of reasoning. Secondly, knowledge may be called discursive or collative in use; as at times those who know, reason from cause to effect, not in order to learn anew, but wishing to use the knowledge they have. And in this way the knowledge in Christ's soul could be collative or discursive; since it could conclude one thing from another, as it pleased, as in Matt. 17:24, 25, when our Lord asked Peter: "Of whom do the kings of the earth receive tribute, of their own children, or of strangers?" On Peter replying: "Of strangers," He concluded: "Then the children are free."

Reply Obj. 1: From Christ is excluded that counsel which is with doubt; and consequently choice, which essentially includes such counsel; but the practice of using counsel is not excluded from Christ.

Reply Obj. 2: This reason rests upon discursion and comparison, as used to acquire knowledge.

Reply Obj. 3: The blessed are likened to the angels in the gifts of graces; yet there still remains the difference of natures. And hence to use comparison and discursion is connatural to the souls of the blessed, but not to angels.

FOURTH ARTICLE [III, Q. 11, Art. 4]

Whether in Christ This Knowledge Was Greater Than the Knowledge of the Angels?

Objection 1: It would seem that this knowledge was not greater in Christ than in the angels. For perfection is proportioned to the thing perfected. But the human soul in the order of nature is below the angelic nature. Therefore since the knowledge we are now speaking of is imprinted upon Christ's soul for its perfection, it seems that this knowledge is less than the knowledge by which the angelic nature is perfected.

Obj. 2: Further, the knowledge of Christ's soul was in a measure comparative and discursive, which cannot be said of the angelic knowledge. Therefore the knowledge of Christ's soul was less than the knowledge of the angels.

Obj. 3: Further, the more immaterial knowledge is, the greater it is. But the knowledge of the angels is more immaterial than the knowledge of Christ's soul, since the soul of Christ is the act of a body, and turns to phantasms, which cannot be said of the angels. Therefore the knowledge of angels is greater than the knowledge of Christ's soul.

*On the contrary,* The Apostle says (Heb. 2:9): "For we see Jesus, Who was made a little lower than the angels, for the suffering of death, crowned with glory and honor"; from which it is plain that Christ is said to be lower than the angels only in regard to the suffering of death. And hence, not in knowledge.

*I answer that,* The knowledge imprinted on Christ's soul may be looked at in two ways: First, as regards what it has from the inflowing cause; secondly, as regards what it has from the subject receiving it. Now with regard to the first, the knowledge imprinted upon the soul of Christ was more excellent than the knowledge of the angels, both in the number of things known and in the certainty of the knowledge; since the spiritual light, which is imprinted on the soul of Christ, is much more excellent than the light which pertains to the angelic nature. But as regards the second, the knowledge imprinted on the soul of Christ is less than the angelic knowledge, in the manner of knowing that is natural to the human soul, i.e. by turning to phantasms, and by comparison and discursion.

And hereby the reply to the objections is made clear.

FIFTH ARTICLE [III, Q. 11, Art. 5]

Whether This Knowledge Was Habitual?

Objection 1: It would seem that in Christ there was no habitual knowledge. For it has been said (Q. 9, A. 1) that the highest perfection of knowledge befitted Christ's soul. But the perfection of an actually existing knowledge is greater than that of a potentially or habitually existing knowledge. Therefore it was fitting for Him to know all things actually. Therefore He had not habitual knowledge.

Obj. 2: Further, since habits are ordained to acts, a habitual knowledge which is never reduced to act would seem useless. Now, since Christ knew all things, as was said (Q. 10, A. 2), He could not have considered all things actually, thinking over one after another, since the infinite cannot be passed over by enumeration. Therefore the habitual knowledge of certain things would have been useless to Him--which is unfitting. Therefore He had an actual and not a habitual knowledge of what He knew.

Obj. 3: Further, habitual knowledge is a perfection of the knower. But perfection is more noble than the thing perfected. If, therefore, in the soul of Christ there was any created habit of knowledge, it would follow that this created thing was nobler than the soul of Christ. Therefore there was no habitual knowledge in Christ's soul.

*On the contrary,* The knowledge of Christ we are now speaking about was univocal with our knowledge, even as His soul was of the same species as ours. But our knowledge is in the genus of habit. Therefore the knowledge of Christ was habitual.

*I answer that,* As stated above (A. 4), the mode of the knowledge impressed on the soul of Christ befitted the subject receiving it. For the received is in the recipient after the mode of the recipient. Now the connatural mode of the human soul is that it should understand sometimes actually, and sometimes potentially. But the medium between a pure power and a completed act is a habit: and extremes and medium are of the same genus. Thus it is plain that it is the connatural mode of the human soul to receive knowledge as a habit. Hence it must be said that the knowledge imprinted on the soul of Christ was habitual, for He could use it when He pleased.

Reply Obj. 1: In Christ's soul there was a twofold knowledge--each most perfect of its kind: the first exceeding the mode of human nature, as by it He saw the Essence of God, and other things in It, and this was the most perfect, simply. Nor was this knowledge habitual, but actual with respect to everything He knew in this way. But the second knowledge was in Christ in a manner proportioned to human nature, i.e. inasmuch as He knew things by species divinely imprinted upon Him, and of this knowledge we are now speaking. Now this knowledge was not most perfect, simply, but merely in the genus of human knowledge; hence it did not behoove it to be always in act.

Reply Obj. 2: Habits are reduced to act by the command of the will, since a habit is that "with which we act when we wish." Now the will is indeterminate in regard to infinite things. Yet it is not useless, even when it does not actually tend to all; provided it actually tends to everything in fitting place and time. And hence neither is a habit useless, even if all that it extends to is not reduced to act; provided that that which befits the due end of the will be reduced to act according as the matter in hand and the time require.

Reply Obj. 3: Goodness and being are taken in two ways: First, simply; and thus a substance, which subsists in its being and goodness, is a good and a being; secondly, being and goodness are taken relatively, and in this way an accident is a being and a good, not that it has being and goodness, but that its subject is a being and a good. And hence habitual knowledge is not simply better or more excellent than the soul of Christ; but relatively, since the whole goodness of habitual knowledge is added to the goodness of the subject.

SIXTH ARTICLE [III, Q. 11, Art. 6]

Whether This Knowledge Was Distinguished by Divers Habits?

Objection 1: It would seem that in the soul of Christ there was only one habit of knowledge. For the more perfect knowledge is, the more united it is; hence the higher angels understand by the more universal forms, as was said in the First Part (Q. 55, A. 3). Now Christ's knowledge was most perfect. Therefore it was most one. Therefore it was not distinguished by several habits.

Obj. 2: Further, our faith is derived from Christ's knowledge; hence it is written (Heb. 12:2): "Looking on Jesus the author and finisher of faith." But there is only one habit of faith about all things believed, as was said in the Second Part (II-II, Q. 4, A. 6). Much more, therefore, was there only one habit of knowledge in Christ.

Obj. 3: Further, knowledge is distinguished by the divers formalities of knowable things. But the soul of Christ knew everything under one formality, i.e. by a divinely infused light. Therefore in Christ there was only one habit of knowledge.

*On the contrary,* It is written (Zech. 3:9) that on "one" stone, i.e. Christ, "there are seven eyes." Now by the eye is understood knowledge. Therefore it would seem that in Christ there were several habits of knowledge.

*I answer that,* As stated above (AA. 4, 5), the knowledge imprinted on Christ's soul has a mode connatural to a human soul. Now it is connatural to a human soul to receive species of a lesser universality than the angels receive; so that it knows different specific natures by different intelligible species. But it so happens that we have different habits of knowledge, because there are different classes of knowable things, inasmuch as what are in one genus are known by one habit; thus it is said (Poster. i, 42) that "one science is of one class of object." And hence the knowledge imprinted on Christ's soul was distinguished by different habits.

Reply Obj. 1: As was said (A. 4), the knowledge of Christ's soul is most perfect, and exceeds the knowledge of angels with regard to what is in it on the part of God's gift; but it is below the angelic knowledge as regards the mode of the recipient. And it pertains to this mode that this knowledge is distinguished by various habits, inasmuch as it regards more particular species.

Reply Obj. 2: Our faith rests upon the First Truth; and hence Christ is the author of our faith by the Divine knowledge, which is simply one.

Reply Obj. 3: The divinely infused light is the common formality for understanding what is divinely revealed, as the light of the active intellect is with regard to what is naturally known. Hence, in the soul of Christ there must be the proper species of singular things, in order to know each with proper knowledge; and in this way there must be divers habits of knowledge in Christ's soul, as stated above.

# QUESTION 12

OF THE ACQUIRED OR EMPIRIC KNOWLEDGE OF CHRIST'S SOUL (In Four Articles)

We must now consider the acquired or empiric knowledge of Christ's soul; and under this head there are four points of inquiry:

(1) Whether Christ knew all things by this knowledge?

(2) Whether He advanced in this knowledge?

(3) Whether He learned anything from man?

(4) Whether He received anything from angels?

FIRST ARTICLE [III, Q. 12, Art. 1]

Whether Christ Knew All Things by This Acquired or Empiric Knowledge?

Objection 1: It would seem that Christ did not know everything by this knowledge. For this knowledge is acquired by experience. But Christ did not experience everything. Therefore He did not know everything by this knowledge.

Obj. 2: Further, man acquires knowledge through the senses. But not all sensible things were subjected to Christ's bodily senses. Therefore Christ did not know everything by this knowledge.

Obj. 3: Further, the extent of knowledge depends on the things knowable. Therefore if Christ knew all things by this knowledge, His acquired knowledge would have been equal to His infused and beatific knowledge; which is not fitting. Therefore Christ did not know all things by this knowledge.

*On the contrary,* Nothing imperfect was in Christ's soul. Now this knowledge of His would have been imperfect if He had not known all things by it, since the imperfect is that to which addition may be made. Hence Christ knew all things by this knowledge.

*I answer that,* Acquired knowledge is held to be in Christ's soul, as we have said (Q. 9, A. 4), by reason of the active intellect, lest its action, which is to make things actually intelligible, should be wanting; even as imprinted or infused knowledge is held to be in Christ's soul for the perfection of the passive intellect. Now as the passive intellect is that by which "all things are in potentiality," so the active intellect is that by which "all are in act," as is said De Anima iii, 18. And hence, as the soul of Christ knew by infused knowledge all things to which the passive intellect is in any way in potentiality, so by acquired knowledge it knew whatever can be known by the action of the active intellect.

Reply Obj. 1: The knowledge of things may be acquired not merely by experiencing the things themselves, but by experiencing other things; since by virtue of the light of the active intellect man can go on to understand effects from causes, and causes from effects, like from like, contrary from contrary. Therefore Christ, though He did not experience all things, came to the knowledge of all things from what He did experience.

Reply Obj. 2: Although all sensible things were not subjected to Christ's bodily senses, yet other sensible things were subjected to His senses; and from this He could come to know other things by the most excellent force of His reason, in the manner described in the previous reply; just as in seeing heavenly bodies He could comprehend their powers and the effects they have upon things here below, which were not subjected to His senses; and for the same reason, from any other things whatsoever, He could come to the knowledge of yet other things.

Reply Obj. 3: By this knowledge the soul of Christ did not know all things simply, but all such as are knowable by the light of man's active intellect. Hence by this knowledge He did not know the essences of separate substances, nor past, present, or future singulars, which, nevertheless, He knew by infused knowledge, as was said above (Q. 11).

SECOND ARTICLE [III, Q. 12, Art. 2]

Whether Christ Advanced in Acquired or Empiric Knowledge?

Objection 1: It would seem that Christ did not advance in this knowledge. For even as Christ knew all things by His beatific and His infused knowledge, so also did He by this acquired knowledge, as is plain from what has been said (A. 1). But He did not advance in these knowledges. Therefore neither in this.

Obj. 2: Further, to advance belongs to the imperfect, since the perfect cannot be added to. Now we cannot suppose an imperfect knowledge in Christ. Therefore Christ did not advance in this knowledge.

Obj. 3: Further, Damascene says (De Fide Orth. iii, 22): "Whoever say that Christ advanced in wisdom and grace, as if receiving additional sensations, do not venerate the union which is in hypostasis." But it is impious not to venerate this union. Therefore it is impious to say that His knowledge received increase.

*On the contrary,* It is written (Luke 2:52): "Jesus advanced in wisdom and age and grace with God and men"; and Ambrose says (De Incar. Dom. vii) that "He advanced in human wisdom." Now human wisdom is that which is acquired in a human manner, i.e. by the light of the active intellect. Therefore Christ advanced in this knowledge.

*I answer that,* There is a twofold advancement in knowledge: one in essence, inasmuch as the habit of knowledge is increased; the other in effect--e.g. if someone were with one and the same habit of knowledge to prove to someone else some minor truths at first, and afterwards greater and more subtle conclusions. Now in this second way it is plain that Christ advanced in knowledge and grace, even as in age, since as His age increased He wrought greater deeds, and showed greater knowledge and grace.

But as regards the habit of knowledge, it is plain that His habit of infused knowledge did not increase, since from the beginning He had perfect infused knowledge of all things; and still less could His beatific knowledge increase; while in the First Part (Q. 14, A. 15), we have already said that His Divine knowledge could not increase. Therefore, if in the soul of Christ there was no habit of acquired knowledge, beyond the habit of infused knowledge, as appears to some [*Blessed Albert the Great, Alexander of Hales, St. Bonaventure], and sometime appeared to me (Sent. iii, D, xiv), no knowledge in Christ increased in essence, but merely by experience, i.e. by comparing the infused intelligible species with phantasms. And in this way they maintain that Christ's knowledge grew in experience, e.g. by comparing the infused intelligible species with what He received through the senses for the first time. But because it seems unfitting that any natural intelligible action should be wanting to Christ, and because to extract intelligible species from phantasms is a natural action of man's active intellect, it seems becoming to place even this action in Christ. And it follows from this that in the soul of Christ there was a habit of knowledge which could increase by this abstraction of species; inasmuch as the active intellect, after abstracting the first intelligible species from phantasms, could abstract others, and others again.

Reply Obj. 1: Both the infused knowledge and the beatific knowledge of Christ's soul were the effects of an agent of infinite power, which could produce the whole at once; and thus in neither knowledge did Christ advance; since from the beginning He had them perfectly. But the acquired knowledge of Christ is caused by the active intellect which does not produce the whole at once, but successively; and hence by this knowledge Christ did not know everything from the beginning, but step by step, and after a time, i.e. in His perfect age; and this is plain from what the Evangelist says, viz. that He increased in "knowledge and age" together.

Reply Obj. 2: Even this knowledge was always perfect for the time being, although it was not always perfect, simply and in comparison to the nature; hence it could increase.

Reply Obj. 3: This saying of Damascene regards those who say absolutely that addition was made to Christ's knowledge, i.e. as regards any knowledge of His, and especially as regards the infused knowledge which is caused in Christ's soul by union with the Word; but it does not regard the increase of knowledge caused by the natural agent.

THIRD ARTICLE [III, Q. 12, Art. 3]

Whether Christ Learned Anything from Man?

Objection 1: It would seem that Christ learned something from man. For it is written (Luke 2:46, 47) that, "They found Him in the temple in the midst of the doctors, hearing them, and asking them questions." But to ask questions and to reply pertains to a learner. Therefore Christ learned something from man.

Obj. 2: Further, to acquire knowledge from a man's teaching seems more noble than to acquire it from sensible things, since in the soul of the man who teaches the intelligible species are in act; but in sensible things the intelligible species are only in potentiality. Now Christ received empiric knowledge from sensible things, as stated above (A. 2). Much more, therefore, could He receive knowledge by learning from men.

Obj. 3: Further, by empiric knowledge Christ did not know everything from the beginning, but advanced in it, as was said above (A. 2). But anyone hearing words which mean something, may learn something he does not know. Therefore Christ could learn from men something He did not know by this knowledge.

*On the contrary,* It is written (Ps. 45:4): "Behold, I have given Him for a witness to the people, for a leader and a master to the Gentiles." Now a master is not taught, but teaches. Therefore Christ did not receive any knowledge by the teaching of any man.

*I answer that,* In every genus that which is the first mover is not moved according to the same species of movement; just as the first alterative is not itself altered. Now Christ is established by God the Head of the Church--yea, of all men, as was said above (Q. 8, A. 3), so that not only all might receive grace through Him, but that all might receive the doctrine of Truth from Him. Hence He Himself says (John 18:37): "For this was I born, and for this came I into the world; that I should give testimony to the truth." And thus it did not befit His dignity that He should be taught by any man.

Reply Obj. 1: As Origen says (Hom. xix in Luc.): "Our Lord asked questions not in order to learn anything, but in order to teach by questioning. For from the same well of knowledge came the question and the wise reply." Hence the Gospel goes on to say that "all that heard Him were astonished at His wisdom and His answers."

Reply Obj. 2: Whoever learns from man does not receive knowledge immediately from the intelligible species which are in his mind, but through sensible words, which are signs of intelligible concepts. Now as words formed by a man are signs of his intellectual knowledge; so are creatures, formed by God, signs of His wisdom. Hence it is written (Ecclus. 1:10) that God "poured" wisdom "out upon all His works." Hence, just as it is better to be taught by God than by man, so it is better to receive our knowledge from sensible creatures and not by man's teaching.

Reply Obj. 3: Jesus advanced in empiric knowledge, as in age, as stated above (A. 2). Now as a fitting age is required for a man to acquire knowledge by discovery, so also that he may acquire it by being taught. But our Lord did nothing unbecoming to His age; and hence He did not give ear to hearing the lessons of doctrine until such time as He was able to have reached that grade of knowledge by way of experience. Hence Gregory says (Sup. Ezech. Lib. i, Hom. ii): "In the twelfth year of His age He deigned to question men on earth, since in the course of reason, the word of doctrine is not vouchsafed before the age of perfection."

FOURTH ARTICLE [III, Q. 12, Art. 4]

Whether Christ Received Knowledge from the Angels?

Objection 1: It would seem that Christ received knowledge from the angels. For it is written (Luke 22:43) that "there appeared to Him an angel from heaven, strengthening Him." But we are strengthened by the comforting words of a teacher, according to Job 4:3, 4: "Behold thou hast taught many and hast strengthened the weary hand. Thy words have confirmed them that were staggering." Therefore Christ was taught sby angels.

Obj. 2: Further, Dionysius says (Coel. Hier. iv): "For I see that even Jesus--the super-substantial substance of supercelestial substances--when without change He took our substance upon Himself, was subject in obedience to the instructions of the Father and God by the angels." Hence it seems that even Christ wished to be subject to the ordinations of the Divine law, whereby men are taught by means of angels.

Obj. 3: Further, as in the natural order the human body is subject to the celestial bodies, so likewise is the human mind to angelic minds. Now Christ's body was subject to the impressions of the heavenly bodies, for He felt the heat in summer and the cold in winter, and other human passions. Therefore His human mind was subject to the illuminations of supercelestial spirits.

*On the contrary,* Dionysius says (Coel. Hier. vii) that "the highest angels question Jesus, and learn the knowledge of His Divine work, and of the flesh assumed for us; and Jesus teaches them directly." Now to teach and to be taught do not belong to the same. Therefore Christ did not receive knowledge from the angels.

*I answer that,* Since the human soul is midway between spiritual substances and corporeal things, it is perfected naturally in two ways. First by knowledge received from sensible things; secondly, by knowledge imprinted or infused by the illumination of spiritual substances. Now in both these ways the soul of Christ was perfected; first by empirical knowledge of sensible things, for which there is no need of angelic light, since the light of the active intellect suffices; secondly, by the higher impression of infused knowledge, which He received directly from God. For as His soul was united to the Word above the common mode, in unity of person, so above the common manner of men was it filled with knowledge and grace by the Word of God Himself; and not by the medium of angels, who in their beginning received the knowledge of things by the influence of the Word, as Augustine says (Gen. ad lit. ii, 8).

Reply Obj. 1: This strengthening by the angel was for the purpose not of instructing Him, but of proving the truth of His human nature. Hence Bede says (on Luke 22:43): "In testimony of both natures are the angels said to have ministered to Him and to have strengthened Him. For the Creator did not need help from His creature; but having become man, even as it was for our sake that He was sad, so was it for our sake that He was strengthened," i.e. in order that our faith in the Incarnation might be strengthened.

Reply Obj. 2: Dionysius says that Christ was subject to the angelic instructions, not by reason of Himself, but by reason of what happened at His Incarnation, and as regards the care of Him whilst He was a child. Hence in the same place he adds that "Jesus' withdrawal to Egypt decreed by the Father is announced to Joseph by angels, and again His return to Judaea from Egypt."

Reply Obj. 3: The Son of God assumed a passible body (as will be said hereafter (Q. 14, A. 1)) and a soul perfect in knowledge and grace (Q. 14, A. 1, ad 1; A. 4). Hence His body was rightly subject to the impression of heavenly bodies; but His soul was not subject to the impression of heavenly spirits.

## QUESTION 13

OF THE POWER OF CHRIST'S SOUL (In Four Articles)

We must now consider the power of Christ's soul; and under this head there are four points of inquiry:

(1) Whether He had omnipotence simply?

(2) Whether He had omnipotence with regard to corporeal creatures?

(3) Whether He had omnipotence with regard to His own body?

(4) Whether He had omnipotence as regards the execution of His own will?

FIRST ARTICLE [III, Q. 13, Art. 1]

Whether the Soul of Christ Had Omnipotence?

Objection 1: It would seem that the soul of Christ had omnipotence. For Ambrose [*Gloss, Ord.] says on Luke 1:32: "The power which the Son of God had naturally, the Man was about to receive in time." Now this would seem to regard the soul principally, since it is the chief part of man. Hence since the Son of God had omnipotence from all eternity, it would seem that the soul of Christ received omnipotence in time.

Obj. 2: Further, as the power of God is infinite, so is His knowledge. But the soul of Christ in a manner had the knowledge of all that God knows, as was said above (Q. 10, A. 2). Therefore He had all power; and thus He was omnipotent.

Obj. 3: Further, the soul of Christ has all knowledge. Now knowledge is either practical or speculative. Therefore He has a practical knowledge of what He knows, i.e. He knew how to do what He knows; and thus it seems that He can do all things.

*On the contrary,* What is proper to God cannot belong to any creature. But it is proper to God to be omnipotent, according to Ex. 15:2, 3: "He is my God and I will glorify Him," and further on, "Almighty is His name." Therefore the soul of Christ, as being a creature, has not omnipotence.

*I answer that,* As was said above (Q. 2, A. 1; Q. 10, A. 1) in the mystery of the Incarnation the union in person so took place that there still remained the distinction of natures, each nature still retaining what belonged to it. Now the active principle of a thing follows its form, which is the principle of action. But the form is either the very nature of the thing, as in simple things; or is the constituent of the nature of the thing; as in such as are composed of matter and form.

And it is in this way that omnipotence flows, so to say, from the Divine Nature. For since the Divine Nature is the very uncircumscribed Being of God, as is plain from Dionysius (Div. Nom. v), it has an active power over everything that can have the nature of being; and this is to have omnipotence; just as every other thing has an active power over such things as the perfection of its nature extends to; as what is hot gives heat. Therefore since the soul of Christ is a part of human nature, it cannot possibly have omnipotence.

Reply Obj. 1: By union with the Person, the Man receives omnipotence in time, which the Son of God had from eternity; the result of which union is that as the Man is said to be God, so is He said to be omnipotent; not that the omnipotence of the Man is distinct (as neither is His Godhead) from that of the Son of God, but because there is one Person of God and man.

Reply Obj. 2: According to some, knowledge and active power are not in the same ratio; for an active power flows from the very nature of the thing, inasmuch as action is considered to come forth from the agent; but knowledge is not always possessed by the very essence or form of the knower, since it may be had by assimilation of the knower to the thing known by the aid of received species. But this reason seems not to suffice, because even as we may understand by a likeness obtained from another, so also may we act by a form obtained from another, as water or iron heats, by heat borrowed from fire. Hence there would be no reason why the soul of Christ, as it can know all things by the similitudes of all things impressed upon it by God, cannot do these things by the same similitudes.

It has, therefore, to be further considered that what is received in the lower nature from the higher is possessed in an inferior manner; for heat is not received by water in the perfection and strength it had in fire. Therefore, since the soul of Christ is of an inferior nature to the Divine Nature, the similitudes of things are not received in the soul of Christ in the perfection and strength they had in the Divine Nature. And hence it is that the knowledge of Christ's soul is inferior to Divine knowledge as regards the manner of knowing, for God knows (things) more perfectly than the soul of Christ; and also as regards the number of things known, since the soul of Christ does not know all that God can do, and these God knows by the knowledge of simple intelligence; although it knows all things present, past, and future, which God knows by the knowledge of vision. So, too, the similitudes of things infused into Christ's soul do not equal the Divine power in acting, i.e. so as to do all that God can do, or to do in the same manner as God does, Who acts with an infinite might whereof the creature is not capable. Now there is no thing, to know which in some way an infinite power is needed, although a certain kind of knowledge belongs to an infinite power; yet there are things which can be done only by an infinite power, as creation and the like, as is plain from what has been said in the First Part (Q. 45). Hence Christ's soul which, being a creature, is finite in might, can know, indeed, all things, but not in every way; yet it cannot do all things, which pertains to the nature of omnipotence; and, amongst other things, it is clear it cannot create itself.

Reply Obj. 3: Christ's soul has practical and speculative knowledge; yet it is not necessary that it should have practical knowledge of those things of which it has speculative knowledge. Because for speculative knowledge a mere conformity or assimilation of the knower to the thing known suffices; whereas for practical knowledge it is required that the forms of the things in the intellect should be operative. Now to have a form and to impress this form upon something else is more than merely to have the form; as to be lightsome and to enlighten is more than merely to be lightsome. Hence the soul of Christ has a speculative knowledge of creation (for it knows the mode of God's creation), but it has no practical knowledge of this mode, since it has no knowledge operative of creation.

SECOND ARTICLE [III, Q. 13, Art. 2]

Whether the Soul of Christ Had Omnipotence with Regard to the Transmutation of Creatures?

Objection 1: It would seem that the soul of Christ had omnipotence with regard to the transmutation of creatures. For He Himself says (Matt. 28:18): "All power is given to Me in heaven and on earth." Now by the words "heaven and earth" are meant all creatures, as is plain from Gen. 1:1: "In the beginning God created heaven and earth." Therefore it seems that the soul of Christ had omnipotence with regard to the transmutation of creatures.

Obj. 2: Further, the soul of Christ is the most perfect of all creatures. But every creature can be moved by another creature; for Augustine says (De Trin. iii, 4) that "even as the denser and lower bodies are ruled in a fixed way by the subtler and stronger bodies; so are all bodies by the spirit of life, and the irrational spirit of life by the rational spirit of life, and the truant and sinful rational spirit of life by the rational, loyal, and righteous spirit of life." But the soul of Christ moves even the highest spirits, enlightening them, as Dionysius says (Coel. Hier. vii). Therefore it seems that the soul of Christ has omnipotence with regard to the transmutation of creatures.

Obj. 3: Further, Christ's soul had in its highest degree the "grace of miracles" or works of might. But every transmutation of the creature can belong to the grace of miracles; since even the heavenly bodies were miraculously changed from their course, as Dionysius proves (Ep. ad Polycarp). Therefore Christ's soul had omnipotence with regard to the transmutation of creatures.

*On the contrary,* To transmute creatures belongs to Him Who preserves them. Now this belongs to God alone, according to Heb. 1:3: "Upholding all things by the word of His power." Therefore God alone has omnipotence with regard to the transmutation of creatures. Therefore this does not belong to Christ's soul.

*I answer that,* Two distinctions are here needed. Of these the first is with respect to the transmutation of creatures, which is three-fold. The first is natural, being brought about by the proper agent naturally; the second is miraculous, being brought about by a supernatural agent above the wonted order and course of nature, as to raise the dead; the third is inasmuch as every creature may be brought to nothing.

The second distinction has to do with Christ's soul, which may be looked at in two ways: first in its proper nature and with its power of nature or of grace; secondly, as it is the instrument of the Word of God, personally united to Him. Therefore if we speak of the soul of Christ in its proper nature and with its power of nature or of grace, it had power to cause those effects proper to a soul (e.g. to rule the body and direct human acts, and also, by the fulness of grace and knowledge to enlighten all rational creatures falling short of its perfection), in a manner befitting a rational creature. But if we speak of the soul of Christ as it is the instrument of the Word united to Him, it had an instrumental power to effect all the miraculous transmutations ordainable to the end of the Incarnation, which is "to re-establish all things that are in heaven and on earth" [*Eph. 1:10]. But the transmutation of creatures, inasmuch as they may be brought to nothing, corresponds to their creation, whereby they were brought from nothing. And hence even as God alone can create, so, too, He alone can bring creatures to nothing, and He alone upholds them in being, lest they fall back to nothing. And thus it must be said that the soul of Christ had not omnipotence with regard to the transmutation of creatures.

Reply Obj. 1: As Jerome says (on the text quoted): "Power is given Him," i.e. to Christ as man, "Who a little while before was crucified, buried in the tomb, and afterwards rose again." But power is said to have been given Him, by reason of the union whereby it was brought about that a Man was omnipotent, as was said above (A. 1, ad 1). And although this was made known to the angels before the Resurrection, yet after the Resurrection it was made known to all men, as Remigius says (cf. Catena Aurea). Now, "things are said to happen when they are made known" [*Hugh of St. Victor: Qq. in Ep. ad Philip.]. Hence after the Resurrection our Lord says "that all power is given" to Him "in heaven and on earth."

Reply Obj. 2: Although every creature is transmutable by some other creature, except, indeed, the highest angel, and even it can be enlightened by Christ's soul; yet not every transmutation that can be made in a creature can be made by a creature; since some transmutations can be made by God alone. Yet all transmutations that can be made in creatures can be made by the soul of Christ, as the instrument of the Word, but not in its proper nature and power, since some of these transmutations pertain to the soul neither in the order of nature nor in the order of grace.

Reply Obj. 3: As was said in the Second Part (Q. 178, A. 1, ad 1), the grace of mighty works or miracles is given to the soul of a saint, so that these miracles are wrought not by his own, but by Divine power. Now this grace was bestowed on Christ's soul most excellently, i.e. not only that He might work miracles, but also that He might communicate this grace to others. Hence it is written (Matt. 10:1) that, "having called His twelve disciples together, He gave them power over unclean spirits, to cast them out, and to heal all manner of diseases, and all manner of infirmities."

THIRD ARTICLE [III, Q. 13, Art. 3]

Whether the Soul of Christ Had Omnipotence with Regard to His Own Body?

Objection 1: It would seem that Christ's soul had omnipotence with regard to His own body. For Damascene says (De Fide Orth. iii, 20, 23) that "all natural things were voluntary to Christ; He willed to hunger, He willed to thirst, He willed to fear, He willed to die." Now God is called omnipotent because "He hath done all things whatsoever He would" (Ps. 113:11). Therefore it seems that Christ's soul had omnipotence with regard to the natural operations of the body.

Obj. 2: Further, human nature was more perfect in Christ than in Adam, who had a body entirely subject to the soul, so that nothing could happen to the body against the will of the soul--and this on account of the original justice which it had in the state of innocence. Much more, therefore, had Christ's soul omnipotence with regard to His body.

Obj. 3: Further, the body is naturally changed by the imaginations of the soul; and so much more changed, the stronger the soul's imagination, as was said in the First Part (Q. 117, A. 3, ad 3). Now the soul of Christ had most perfect strength as regards both the imagination and the other powers. Therefore the soul of Christ was omnipotent with regard to His own body.

*On the contrary,* It is written (Heb. 2:17) that "it behooved Him in all things to be made like unto His brethren," and especially as regards what belongs to the condition of human nature. But it belongs to the condition of human nature that the health of the body and its nourishment and growth are not subject to the bidding of reason or will, since natural things are subject to God alone Who is the author of nature. Therefore they were not subject in Christ. Therefore Christ's soul was not omnipotent with regard to His own body.

*I answer that,* As stated above (A. 2), Christ's soul may be viewed in two ways. First, in its proper nature and power; and in this way, as it was incapable of making exterior bodies swerve from the course and order of nature, so, too, was it incapable of changing its own body from its natural disposition, since the soul, of its own nature, has a determinate relation to its body. Secondly, Christ's soul may be viewed as an instrument united in person to God's Word; and thus every disposition of His own body was wholly subject to His power. Nevertheless, since the power of an action is not properly attributed to the instrument, but to the principal agent, this omnipotence is attributed to the Word of God rather than to Christ's soul.

Reply Obj. 1: This saying of Damascene refers to the Divine will of Christ, since, as he says in the preceding chapter (De Fide Orth. xix, 14, 15), it was by the consent of the Divine will that the flesh was allowed to suffer and do what was proper to it.

Reply Obj. 2: It was no part of the original justice which Adam had in the state of innocence that a man's soul should have the power of changing his own body to any form, but that it should keep it from any hurt. Yet Christ could have assumed even this power if He had wished. But since man has three states--viz. innocence, sin, and glory, even as from the state of glory He assumed comprehension and from the state of innocence, freedom from sin-

-so also from the state of sin did He assume the necessity of being under the penalties of this life, as will be said (Q. 14, A. 2).

Reply Obj. 3: If the imagination be strong, the body obeys naturally in some things, e.g. as regards falling from a beam set on high, since the imagination was formed to be a principle of local motion, as is said De Anima iii, 9, 10. So, too, as regards alteration in heat and cold, and their consequences; for the passions of the soul, wherewith the heart is moved, naturally follow the imagination, and thus by commotion of the spirits the whole body is altered. But the other corporeal dispositions which have no natural relation to the imagination are not transmuted by the imagination, however strong it is, e.g. the shape of the hand, or foot, or such like.

FOURTH ARTICLE [III, Q. 13, Art. 4]

Whether the Soul of Christ Had Omnipotence As Regards the Execution of His Will?

Objection 1: It would seem that the soul of Christ had not omnipotence as regards the execution of His own will. For it is written (Mk. 7:24) that "entering into a house, He would that no man should know it, and He could not be hid." Therefore He could not carry out the purpose of His will in all things.

Obj. 2: Further, a command is a sign of will, as was said in the First Part (Q. 19, A. 12). But our Lord commanded certain things to be done, and the contrary came to pass, for it is written (Matt. 9:30, 31) that Jesus strictly charged them whose eyes had been opened, saying: "See that no man know this. But they going out spread His fame abroad in all that country." Therefore He could not carry out the purpose of His will in everything.

Obj. 3: Further, a man does not ask from another for what he can do himself. But our Lord besought the Father, praying for what He wished to be done, for it is written (Luke 6:12): "He went out into a mountain to pray, and He passed the whole night in the prayer of God." Therefore He could not carry out the purpose of His will in all things.

*On the contrary,* Augustine says (Qq. Nov. et Vet. Test., qu. 77): "It is impossible for the will of the Saviour not to be fulfilled: nor is it possible for Him to will what He knows ought not to come to pass."

*I answer that,* Christ's soul willed things in two ways. First, what was to be brought about by Himself; and it must be said that He was capable of whatever He willed thus, since it would not befit His wisdom if He willed to do anything of Himself that was not subject to His will. Secondly, He wished things to be brought about by the Divine power, as the resurrection of His own body and such like miraculous deeds, which He could not effect by His own power, except as the instrument of the Godhead, as was said above (A. 2).

Reply Obj. 1: As Augustine says (Qq. Nov. et Vet. Test., qu. 77): "What came to pass, this Christ must be said to have willed. For it must be remarked that this happened in the country of the Gentiles, to whom it was not yet time to preach. Yet it would have been invidious not to welcome such as came spontaneously for the faith. Hence He did not wish to be heralded by His own, and yet He wished to be sought; and so it came to pass." Or it may be said that this will of Christ was not with regard to what was to be carried out by it, but with regard to what was to be done by others, which did not come under His human will. Hence in the letter of Pope Agatho, which was approved in the Sixth Council [*Third Council of Constantinople, Act. iv], we read: "When He, the Creator and Redeemer of all, wished to be hid and could not, must not this be referred only to His human will which He deigned to assume in time?"

Reply Obj. 2: As Gregory says (Moral. xix), by the fact that "Our Lord charged His mighty works to be kept secret, He gave an example to His servants coming after Him that they should wish their miracles to be hidden; and yet, that others may profit by their example, they are made public against their will." And thus this command signified His will to fly from human glory, according to John 8:50, "I seek not My own glory." Yet He wished absolutely, and especially by His Divine will, that the miracle wrought should be published for the good of others.

Reply Obj. 3: Christ prayed both for things that were to be brought about by the Divine power, and for what He Himself was to do by His human will, since the power and operation of Christ's soul depended on God, "Who works in all [Vulg.: 'you'], both to will and to accomplish" (Phil. 2:13).

# QUESTION 14

OF THE DEFECTS OF BODY ASSUMED BY THE SON OF GOD (In Four Articles)

We must now consider the defects Christ assumed in the human nature; and first, of the defects of body; secondly, of the defects of soul.

Under the first head there are four points of inquiry:

(1) Whether the Son of God should have assumed in human nature defects of body?

(2) Whether He assumed the obligation of being subject to these defects?

(3) Whether He contracted these defects?

(4) Whether He assumed all these defects?

FIRST ARTICLE [III, Q. 14, Art. 1]

Whether the Son of God in Human Nature Ought to Have Assumed Defects of Body?

Objection 1: It would seem that the Son of God ought not to have assumed human nature with defects of body. For as His soul is personally united to the Word of God, so also is His body. But the soul of Christ had every perfection, both of grace and truth, as was said above (Q. 7, A. 9; Q. 9, seqq.). Hence, His body also ought to have been in every way perfect, not having any imperfection in it.

Obj. 2: Further, the soul of Christ saw the Word of God by the vision wherein the blessed see, as was said above (Q. 9, A. 2), and thus the soul of Christ was blessed. Now by the beatification of the soul the body is glorified; since, as Augustine says (Ep. ad Dios. cxviii), "God made the soul of a nature so strong that from the fulness of its blessedness there pours over even into the lower nature" (i.e. the body), "not indeed the bliss proper to the beatific fruition and vision, but the fulness of health" (i.e. the vigor of incorruptibility). Therefore the body of Christ was incorruptible and without any defect.

Obj. 3: Further, penalty is the consequence of fault. But there was no fault in Christ, according to 1 Pet. 2:22: "Who did no guile." Therefore defects of body, which are penalties, ought not to have been in Him.

Obj. 4: Further, no reasonable man assumes what keeps him from his proper end. But by such like bodily defects, the end of the Incarnation seems to be hindered in many ways. First, because by these infirmities men were kept back from knowing Him, according to Isa. 53:2, 3: "[There was no sightliness] that we should be desirous of Him. Despised and the most abject of men, a man of sorrows and acquainted with infirmity, and His look was, as it were, hidden and despised, whereupon we esteemed Him not." Secondly, because the desire of the Fathers would not seem to be fulfilled, in whose person it is written (Isa. 51:9): "Arise, arise, put on Thy strength, O Thou Arm of the Lord." Thirdly, because it would seem more fitting for the devil's power to be overcome and man's weakness healed, by strength than by weakness. Therefore it does not seem to have been fitting that the Son of God assumed human nature with infirmities or defects of body.

*On the contrary,* It is written (Heb. 2:18): "For in that, wherein He Himself hath suffered and been tempted, He is able to succor them also that are tempted." Now He came to succor us. Hence David said of Him (Ps. 120:1): "I have lifted up my eyes to the mountains, from whence help shall come to me." Therefore it was fitting for the Son of God to assume flesh subject to human infirmities, in order to suffer and be tempted in it and so bring succor to us.

*I answer that,* It was fitting for the body assumed by the Son of God to be subject to human infirmities and defects; and especially for three reasons. First, because it was in order to satisfy for the sin of the human race that the Son of God, having taken flesh, came into the world. Now one satisfies for another's sin by taking on himself the punishment due to the sin of the other. But these bodily defects, to wit, death, hunger, thirst, and the like, are the punishment of sin, which was brought into the world by Adam, according to Rom. 5:12: "By one man sin entered into this world, and by sin death." Hence it was useful for the end of the Incarnation that He should assume these penalties in our flesh and in our stead, according to Isa. 53:4, "Surely He hath borne our infirmities." Secondly, in order to cause belief in the Incarnation. For since human nature is known to men only as it is subject to these defects, if the Son of God had assumed human nature without these defects, He would not have seemed to be true man, nor to have true, but imaginary, flesh, as the Manicheans held. And so, as is said, Phil. 2:7: "He . . . emptied Himself, taking the form of a servant, being made in the likeness of men, and in habit found as a man." Hence, Thomas, by the sight of His wounds, was recalled to the faith, as related John 20:26. Thirdly, in order to show us an example of patience by valiantly bearing up against human passibility and defects. Hence it is said (Heb. 12:3) that He "endured such opposition from sinners against Himself, that you be not wearied, fainting in your minds."

Reply Obj. 1: The penalties one suffers for another's sin are the matter, as it were, of the satisfaction for that sin; but the principle is the habit of soul, whereby one is inclined to wish to satisfy for another, and from which the satisfaction has its efficacy, for satisfaction would not be efficacious unless it proceeded from charity, as will be explained (Supp., Q. 14, A. 2). Hence, it behooved the soul of Christ to be perfect as regards the habit of knowledge and virtue, in order to have the power of satisfying; but His body was subject to infirmities, that the matter of satisfaction should not be wanting.

Reply Obj. 2: From the natural relationship which is between the soul and the body, glory flows into the body from the soul's glory. Yet this natural relationship in Christ was subject to the will of His Godhead, and thereby it came to pass that the beatitude remained in the soul, and did not flow into the body; but the flesh suffered what belongs to a passible nature; thus Damascene says (De Fide Orth. iii, 15) that, "it was by the consent of the Divine will that the flesh was allowed to suffer and do what belonged to it."

Reply Obj. 3: Punishment always follows sin actual or original, sometimes of the one punished, sometimes of the one for whom he who suffers the punishment satisfies. And so it was with Christ, according to Isa. 53:5: "He was wounded for our iniquities, He was bruised for our sins."

Reply Obj. 4: The infirmity assumed by Christ did not impede, but greatly furthered the end of the Incarnation, as above stated. And although these infirmities concealed His Godhead, they made known His Manhood, which is the way of coming to the Godhead, according to Rom. 5:1, 2: "By Jesus Christ we have access to God." Moreover, the ancient Fathers did not desire bodily strength in Christ, but spiritual strength, wherewith He vanquished the devil and healed human weakness.

SECOND ARTICLE [III, Q. 14, Art. 2]

Whether Christ Was of Necessity Subject to These Defects?

Objection 1: It would seem that Christ was not of necessity subject to these defects. For it is written (Isa. 53:7): "He was offered because it was His own will"; and the prophet is speaking of the offering of the Passion. But will is opposed to necessity. Therefore Christ was not of necessity subject to bodily defects.

Obj. 2: Further, Damascene says (De Fide Orth. iii, 20): "Nothing obligatory is seen in Christ: all is voluntary." Now what is voluntary is not necessary. Therefore these defects were not of necessity in Christ.

Obj. 3: Further, necessity is induced by something more powerful. But no creature is more powerful than the soul of Christ, to which it pertained to preserve its own body. Therefore these defects were not of necessity in Christ.

*On the contrary,* The Apostle says (Rom. 8:3) that "God" sent "His own Son in the likeness of sinful flesh." Now it is a condition of sinful flesh to be under the necessity of dying, and suffering other like passions. Therefore the necessity of suffering these defects was in Christ's flesh.

*I answer that,* Necessity is twofold. One is a necessity of constraint, brought about by an external agent; and this necessity is contrary to both nature and will, since these flow from an internal principle. The other is natural necessity, resulting from the natural principles--either the form (as it is necessary for fire to heat), or the matter (as it is necessary for a body composed of contraries to be dissolved). Hence, with this necessity, which results from the matter, Christ's body was subject to the necessity of death and other like defects, since, as was said (A. 1, ad 2), "it was by the consent of the Divine will that the flesh was allowed to do and suffer what belonged to it." And this necessity results from the principles of human nature, as was said above in this article. But if we speak of necessity of constraint, as repugnant to the bodily nature, thus again was Christ's body in its own natural condition subject to necessity in regard to the nail that pierced and the scourge that struck. Yet inasmuch as such necessity is repugnant to the will, it is clear that in Christ these defects were not of necessity as regards either the Divine will, or the human will of Christ considered absolutely, as following the deliberation of reason; but only as regards the natural movement of the will, inasmuch as it naturally shrinks from death and bodily hurt.

Reply Obj. 1: Christ is said to be "offered because it was His own will," i.e. Divine will and deliberate human will; although death was contrary to the natural movement of His human will, as Damascene says (De Fide Orth. iii, 23, 24).

Reply Obj. 2: This is plain from what has been said.

Reply Obj. 3: Nothing was more powerful than Christ's soul, absolutely; yet there was nothing to hinder a thing being more powerful in regard to this or that effect, as a nail for piercing. And this I say, in so far as Christ's soul is considered in its own proper nature and power.

THIRD ARTICLE [III, Q. 14, Art. 3]

Whether Christ Contracted These Defects?

Objection 1: It would seem that Christ contracted bodily defects. For we are said to contract what we derive with our nature from birth. But Christ, together with human nature, derived His bodily defects and infirmities through His birth from His mother, whose flesh was subject to these defects. Therefore it seems that He contracted these defects.

Obj. 2: Further, what is caused by the principles of nature is derived together with nature, and hence is contracted. Now these penalties are caused by the principles of human nature. Therefore Christ contracted them.

Obj. 3: Further, Christ is likened to other men in these defects, as is written Heb. 2:17. But other men contract these defects. Therefore it seems that Christ contracted these defects.

*On the contrary,* These defects are contracted through sin, according to Rom. 5:12: "By one man sin entered into this world and by sin, death." Now sin had no place in Christ. Therefore Christ did not contract these defects.

*I answer that,* In the verb "to contract" is understood the relation of effect to cause, i.e. that is said to be contracted which is derived of necessity together with its cause. Now the cause of death and such like defects in human nature is sin, since "by sin death entered into this world," according to Rom. 5:12. And hence they who incur these defects, as due to sin, are properly said to contract them. Now Christ had not these defects, as due to sin, since, as Augustine [*Alcuin in the Gloss, Ord.], expounding John 3:31, "He that cometh from above, is above all," says: "Christ came from above, i.e. from the height of human nature, which it had before the fall of the first man." For He received human nature without sin, in the purity which it had in the state of innocence. In the same way He might have assumed human nature without defects. Thus it is clear that Christ did not contract these defects as if taking them upon Himself as due to sin, but by His own will.

Reply Obj. 1: The flesh of the Virgin was conceived in original sin, [*See introductory note to Q. 27] and therefore contracted these defects. But from the Virgin, Christ's flesh assumed the nature without sin, and He might likewise have assumed the nature without its penalties. But He wished to bear its penalties in order to carry out the work of our redemption, as stated above (A. 1). Therefore He had these defects--not that He contracted them, but that He assumed them.

Reply Obj. 2: The cause of death and other corporeal defects of human nature is twofold: the first is remote, and results from the material principles of the human body, inasmuch as it is made up of contraries. But this cause was held in check by original justice. Hence the proximate cause of death and other defects is sin, whereby original justice is withdrawn. And thus, because Christ was without sin, He is said not to have contracted these defects, but to have assumed them.

Reply Obj. 3: Christ was made like to other men in the quality and not in the cause of these defects; and hence, unlike others, He did not contract them.

FOURTH ARTICLE [III, Q. 14, Art. 4]

Whether Christ Ought to Have Assumed All the Bodily Defects of Men?

Objection 1: It would seem that Christ ought to have assumed all the bodily defects of men. For Damascene says (De Fide Orth. iii, 6, 18): "What is unassumable is incurable." But Christ came to cure all our defects. Therefore He ought to have assumed all our defects.

Obj. 2: Further it was said (A. 1), that in order to satisfy for us, Christ ought to have had perfective habits of soul and defects of body. Now as regards the soul, He assumed the fulness of all grace. Therefore as regards the body, He ought to have assumed all defects.

Obj. 3: Further, amongst all bodily defects death holds the chief place. Now Christ assumed death. Much more, therefore, ought He to have assumed other defects.

*On the contrary,* Contraries cannot take place simultaneously in the same. Now some infirmities are contrary to each other, being caused by contrary principles. Hence it could not be that Christ assumed all human infirmities.

*I answer that,* As stated above (AA. 1, 2), Christ assumed human defects in order to satisfy for the sin of human nature, and for this it was necessary for Him to have the fulness of knowledge and grace in His soul. Hence Christ ought to have assumed those defects which flow from the common sin of the whole nature, yet are not incompatible with the perfection of knowledge and grace. And thus it was not fitting for Him to assume all human defects or infirmities. For there are some defects that are incompatible with the perfection of knowledge and grace, as ignorance, a proneness towards evil, and a difficulty in well-doing. Some other defects do not flow from the whole of human nature in common on account of the sin of our first parent, but are caused in some men by certain particular causes, as leprosy, epilepsy, and the like; and these defects are sometimes brought about by the fault of the man, e.g. from inordinate eating; sometimes by a defect in the formative power. Now neither of these pertains to Christ, since His flesh was conceived of the Holy Ghost, Who has infinite wisdom and power, and cannot err or fail; and He Himself did nothing wrong in the order of His life. But there are some third defects, to be found amongst all men in common, by reason of the sin of our first parent, as death, hunger, thirst, and the like; and all these defects Christ assumed, which Damascene (De Fide Orth. i, 11; iii, 20) calls "natural and indetractible passions" --natural, as following all human nature in common; indetractible, as implying no defect of knowledge or grace.

Reply Obj. 1: All particular defects of men are caused by the corruptibility and passibility of the body, some particular causes being added; and hence, since Christ healed the passibility and corruptibility of our body by assuming it, He consequently healed all other defects.

Reply Obj. 2: The fulness of all grace and knowledge was due to Christ's soul of itself, from the fact of its being assumed by the Word of God; and hence Christ assumed all the fulness of knowledge and wisdom absolutely. But He assumed our defects economically, in order to satisfy for our sin, and not that they belonged to Him of Himself. Hence it was not necessary for Him to assume them all, but only such as sufficed to satisfy for the sin of the whole nature.

Reply Obj. 3: Death comes to all men from the sin of our first parent; but not other defects, although they are less than death. Hence there is no parity.

## QUESTION 15

OF THE DEFECTS OF SOUL ASSUMED BY CHRIST (In Ten Articles)

We must now consider the defects pertaining to the soul; and under this head there are ten points of inquiry:

(1) Whether there was sin in Christ?

(2) Whether there was the fomes of sin in Him?

(3) Whether there was ignorance?

(4) Whether His soul was passible?

(5) Whether in Him there was sensible pain?

(6) Whether there was sorrow?

(7) Whether there was fear?

(8) Whether there was wonder?

(9) Whether there was anger?

(10) Whether He was at once wayfarer and comprehensor?

FIRST ARTICLE [III, Q. 15, Art. 1]

Whether There Was Sin in Christ?

Objection 1: It would seem that there was sin in Christ. For it is written (Ps. 21:2): "O God, My God . . . why hast Thou forsaken Me? Far from My salvation are the words of My sins." Now these words are said in the person of Christ Himself, as appears from His having uttered them on the cross. Therefore it would seem that in Christ there were sins.

Obj. 2: Further, the Apostle says (Rom. 5:12) that "in Adam all have sinned"--namely, because all were in Adam by origin. Now Christ also was in Adam by origin. Therefore He sinned in him.

Obj. 3: Further, the Apostle says (Heb. 2:18) that "in that, wherein He Himself hath suffered and been tempted, He is able to succor them also that are tempted." Now above all do we require His help against sin. Therefore it seems that there was sin in Him.

Obj. 4: Further, it is written (2 Cor. 5:21) that "Him that knew no sin" (i.e. Christ), "for us" God "hath made sin." But that really is, which has been made by God. Therefore there was really sin in Christ.

Obj. 5: Further, as Augustine says (De Agone Christ. xi), "in the man Christ the Son of God gave Himself to us as a pattern of living." Now man needs a pattern not merely of right living, but also of repentance for sin. Therefore it seems that in Christ there ought to have been sin, that He might repent of His sin, and thus afford us a pattern of repentance.

*On the contrary,* He Himself says (John 8:46): "Which of you shall convince Me of sin?"

*I answer that,* As was said above (Q. 14, A. 1), Christ assumed our defects that He might satisfy for us, that He might prove the truth of His human nature, and that He might become an example of virtue to us. Now it is plain that by reason of these three things He ought not to have assumed the defect of sin. First, because sin nowise works our satisfaction; rather, it impedes the power of satisfying, since, as it is written (Ecclus. 34:23), "The Most High approveth not the gifts of the wicked." Secondly, the truth of His human nature is not proved by sin, since sin does not belong to human nature, whereof God is the cause; but rather has been sown in it against its nature by the devil, as Damascene says (De Fide Orth. iii, 20). Thirdly, because by sinning He could afford no example of virtue, since sin is opposed to virtue. Hence Christ nowise assumed the defect of sin--either original or actual--according to what is written (1 Pet. 2:22): "Who did no sin, neither was guile found in His mouth."

Reply Obj. 1: As Damascene says (De Fide Orth. iii, 25), things are said of Christ, first, with reference to His natural and hypostatic property, as when it is said that God became man, and that He suffered for us; secondly, with reference to His personal and relative property, when things are said of Him in our person which nowise belong to Him of Himself. Hence, in the seven rules of Tichonius which Augustine quotes in De Doctr. Christ. iii, 31, the first regards "Our Lord and His Body," since "Christ and His Church are taken as one person." And thus Christ, speaking in the person of His members, says (Ps. 21:2): "The words of My sins"--not that there were any sins in the Head.

Reply Obj. 2: As Augustine says (Gen. ad lit. x, 20), Christ was in Adam and the other fathers not altogether as we were. For we were in Adam as regards both seminal virtue and bodily substance, since, as he goes on to say: "As in the seed there is a visible bulk and an invisible virtue, both have come from Adam. Now Christ took the visible substance of His flesh from the Virgin's flesh; but the virtue of His conception did not spring from the seed of man, but far otherwise--from on high." Hence He was not in Adam according to seminal virtue, but only according to bodily substance. And therefore Christ did not receive human nature from Adam actively, but only materially--and from the Holy Ghost actively; even as Adam received his body materially from the slime of the earth--actively from God. And thus Christ did not sin in Adam, in whom He was only as regards His matter.

Reply Obj. 3: In His temptation and passion Christ has succored us by satisfying for us. Now sin does not further satisfaction, but hinders it, as has been said. Hence, it behooved Him not to have sin, but to be wholly free from sin; otherwise the punishment He bore would have been due to Him for His own sin.

Reply Obj. 4: God "made Christ sin"--not, indeed, in such sort that He had sin, but that He made Him a sacrifice for sin: even as it is written (Osee 4:8): "They shall eat the sins of My people"--they, i.e. the priests, who by the law ate the sacrifices offered for sin. And in that way it is written (Isa. 53:6) that "the Lord hath laid on Him the iniquity of us all" (i.e. He gave Him up to be a victim for the sins of all men); or "He made Him sin" (i.e. made Him to have "the likeness of sinful flesh"), as is written (Rom. 8:3), and this on account of the passible and mortal body He assumed.

Reply Obj. 5: A penitent can give a praiseworthy example, not by having sinned, but by freely bearing the punishment of sin. And hence Christ set the highest example to penitents, since He willingly bore the punishment, not of His own sin, but of the sins of others.

SECOND ARTICLE [III, Q. 15, Art. 2]

Whether There Was the Fomes of Sin in Christ?

Objection 1: It would seem that in Christ there was the fomes of sin. For the fomes of sin, and the passibility and mortality of the body spring from the same principle, to wit, from the withdrawal of original justice, whereby the inferior powers of the soul were subject to the reason, and the body to the soul. Now passibility and mortality of body were in Christ. Therefore there was also the fomes of sin.

Obj. 2: Further, as Damascene says (De Fide Orth. iii, 19), "it was by consent of the Divine will that the flesh of Christ was allowed to suffer and do what belonged to it." But it is proper to the flesh to lust after its pleasures. Now since the fomes of sin is nothing more than concupiscence, as the gloss says on Rom. 7:8, it seems that in Christ there was the fomes of sin.

Obj. 3: Further, it is by reason of the fomes of sin that "the flesh lusteth against the spirit," as is written (Gal. 5:17). But the spirit is shown to be so much the stronger and worthier to be crowned according as the more completely it overcomes its enemy--to wit, the concupiscence of the flesh, according to 2 Tim. 2:5, he "is not crowned except he strive lawfully." Now Christ had a most valiant and conquering spirit, and one most worthy of a crown, according to Apoc. 6:2: "There was a crown given Him, and He went forth conquering that He might conquer." Therefore it would especially seem that the fomes of sin ought to have been in Christ.

*On the contrary,* It is written (Matt. 1:20): "That which is conceived in her is of the Holy Ghost." Now the Holy Ghost drives out sin and the inclination to sin, which is implied in the word fomes. Therefore in Christ there ought not to have been the fomes of sin.

*I answer that,* As was said above (Q. 7, AA. 2, 9), Christ had grace and all the virtues most perfectly. Now moral virtues, which are in the irrational part of the soul, make it subject to reason, and so much the more as the virtue is more perfect; thus, temperance controls the concupiscible appetite, fortitude and meekness the irascible appetite, as was said in the Second Part (I-II, Q. 56, A. 4). But there belongs to the very nature of the fomes of sin an inclination of the sensual appetite to what is contrary to reason. And hence it is plain that the more perfect the virtues are in any man, the weaker the fomes of sin becomes in him. Hence, since in Christ the virtues were in their highest degree, the fomes of sin was nowise in Him; inasmuch, also, as this defect cannot be ordained to satisfaction, but rather inclined to what is contrary to satisfaction.

Reply Obj. 1: The inferior powers pertaining to the sensitive appetite have a natural capacity to be obedient to reason; but not the bodily powers, nor those of the bodily humors, nor those of the vegetative soul, as is made plain Ethic. i, 13. And hence perfection of virtue, which is in accordance with right reason, does not exclude passibility of body; yet it excludes the fomes of sin, the nature of which consists in the resistance of the sensitive appetite to reason.

Reply Obj. 2: The flesh naturally seeks what is pleasing to it by the concupiscence of the sensitive appetite; but the flesh of man, who is a rational animal, seeks this after the manner and order of reason. And thus with the concupiscence of the sensitive appetite Christ's flesh naturally sought food, drink, and sleep, and all else that is sought in right reason, as is plain from Damascene (De Fide Orth. iii, 14). Yet it does not therefore follow that in Christ there was the fomes of sin, for this implies the lust after pleasurable things against the order of reason.

Reply Obj. 3: The spirit gives evidence of fortitude to some extent by resisting that concupiscence of the flesh which is opposed to it; yet a greater fortitude of spirit is shown, if by its strength the flesh is thoroughly overcome, so as to be incapable of lusting against the spirit. And hence this belonged to Christ, whose spirit reached the highest degree of fortitude. And although He suffered no internal assault on the part of the fomes of sin, He sustained an external assault on the part of the world and the devil, and won the crown of victory by overcoming them.

THIRD ARTICLE [III, Q. 15, Art. 3]

Whether in Christ There Was Ignorance?

Objection 1: It would seem that there was ignorance in Christ. For that is truly in Christ which belongs to Him in His human nature, although it does not belong to Him in His Divine Nature, as suffering and death. But ignorance belongs to Christ in His human nature; for Damascene says (De Fide Orth. iii, 21) that "He assumed an ignorant and enslaved nature." Therefore ignorance was truly in Christ.

Obj. 2: Further, one is said to be ignorant through defect of knowledge. Now some kind of knowledge was wanting to Christ, for the Apostle says (2 Cor. 5:21) "Him that knew no sin, for us He hath made sin." Therefore there was ignorance in Christ.

Obj. 3: Further, it is written (Isa. 8:4): "For before the child know to call his Father and his mother, the strength of Damascus . . . shall be taken away." Therefore in Christ there was ignorance of certain things.

*On the contrary,* Ignorance is not taken away by ignorance. But Christ came to take away our ignorance; for "He came to enlighten them that sit in darkness and in the shadow of death" (Luke 1:79). Therefore there was no ignorance in Christ.

*I answer that,* As there was the fulness of grace and virtue in Christ, so too there was the fulness of all knowledge, as is plain from what has been said above (Q. 7, A. 9; Q. 9). Now as the fulness of grace and virtue in Christ excluded the fomes of sin, so the fulness of knowledge excluded ignorance, which is opposed to knowledge. Hence, even as the fomes of sin was not in Christ, neither was there ignorance in Him.

Reply Obj. 1: The nature assumed by Christ may be viewed in two ways. First, in its specific nature, and thus Damascene calls it "ignorant and enslaved"; hence he adds: "For man's nature is a slave of Him" (i.e. God) "Who made it; and it has no knowledge of future things." Secondly, it may be considered with regard to what it has from its union with the Divine hypostasis, from which it has the fulness of knowledge and grace, according to John 1:14: "We saw Him [Vulg.: 'His glory'] as it were the Only-begotten of the Father, full of grace and truth"; and in this way the human nature in Christ was not affected with ignorance.

Reply Obj. 2: Christ is said not to have known sin, because He did not know it by experience; but He knew it by simple cognition.

Reply Obj. 3: The prophet is speaking in this

passage of the human knowledge of Christ; thus he says: "Before the Child" (i.e. in His human nature) "know to call His father" (i.e. Joseph, who was His reputed father), "and His mother" (i.e. Mary), "the strength of Damascus . . . shall be taken away." Nor are we to understand this as if He had been some time a man without knowing it; but "before He know" (i.e. before He is a man having human knowledge)--literally, "the strength of Damascus and the spoils of Samaria shall be taken away by the King of the Assyrians"--or spiritually, "before His birth He will save His people solely by invocation," as a gloss expounds it. Augustine however (Serm. xxxii de Temp.) says that this was fulfilled in the adoration of the Magi. For he says: "Before He uttered human words in human flesh, He received the strength of Damascus, i.e. the riches which Damascus vaunted (for in riches the first place is given to gold). They themselves were the spoils of Samaria. Because Samaria is taken to signify idolatry; since this people, having turned away from the Lord, turned to the worship of idols. Hence these were the first spoils which the child took from the domination of idolatry." And in this way "before the child know" may be taken to mean "before he show himself to know."

FOURTH ARTICLE [III, Q. 15, Art. 4]

Whether Christ's Soul Was Passible?

Objection 1: It would seem that the soul of Christ was not passible. For nothing suffers except by reason of something stronger; since "the agent is greater than the patient," as is clear from Augustine (Gen. ad lit. xii, 16), and from the Philosopher (De Anima iii, 5). Now no creature was stronger than Christ's soul. Therefore Christ's soul could not suffer at the hands of any creature; and hence it was not passible; for its capability of suffering would have been to no purpose if it could not have suffered at the hands of anything.

Obj. 2: Further, Tully (De Tusc. Quaes. iii) says that the soul's passions are ailments [*Cf. I-II, Q. 24, A. 2]. But Christ's soul had no ailment; for the soul's ailment results from sin, as is plain from Ps. 40:5: "Heal my soul, for I have sinned against Thee." Therefore in Christ's soul there were no passions.

Obj. 3: Further, the soul's passions would seem to be the same as the fomes of sin, hence the Apostle (Rom. 7:5) calls them the "passions of sins." Now the fomes of sin was not in Christ, as was said (A. 2). Therefore it seems that there were no passions in His soul; and hence His soul was not passible.

*On the contrary,* It is written (Ps. 87:4) in the person of Christ: "My soul is filled with evils"--not sins, indeed, but human evils, i.e. "pains," as a gloss expounds it. Hence the soul of Christ was passible.

*I answer that,* A soul placed in a body may suffer in two ways: first with a bodily passion; secondly, with an animal passion. It suffers with a bodily passion through bodily hurt; for since the soul is the form of the body, soul and body have but one being; and hence, when the body is disturbed by any bodily passion, the soul, too, must be disturbed, i.e. in the being which it has in the body. Therefore, since Christ's body was passible and mortal, as was said above (Q. 14, A. 2), His soul also was of necessity passible in like manner. But the soul suffers with an animal passion, in its operations--either in such as are proper to the soul, or in such as are of the soul more than of the body. And although the soul is said to suffer in this way through sensation and intelligence, as was said in the Second Part (I-II, Q. 22, A. 3; I-II, Q. 41, A. 1); nevertheless the affections of the sensitive appetite are most properly called passions of the soul. Now these were in Christ, even as all else pertaining to man's nature. Hence Augustine says (De Civ. Dei xiv, 9): "Our Lord having deigned to live in the form of a servant, took these upon Himself whenever He judged they ought to be assumed; for there was no false human affection in Him Who had a true body and a true human soul."

Nevertheless we must know that the passions were in Christ otherwise than in us, in three ways. First, as regards the object, since in us these passions very often tend towards what is unlawful, but not so in Christ. Secondly, as regards the principle, since these passions in us frequently forestall the judgment of reason; but in Christ all movements of the sensitive appetite sprang from the disposition of the reason. Hence Augustine says (De Civ. Dei xiv, 9), that "Christ assumed these movements, in His human soul, by an unfailing dispensation, when He willed; even as He became man when He willed." Thirdly, as regards the effect, because in us these movements, at times, do not remain in the sensitive appetite, but deflect the reason; but not so in Christ, since by His disposition the movements that are naturally becoming to human flesh so remained in the sensitive appetite that the reason was nowise hindered in doing what was right. Hence Jerome says (on Matt. 26:37) that "Our Lord, in order to prove the reality of the assumed manhood, 'was sorrowful' in very deed; yet lest a passion should hold sway over His soul, it is by a propassion that He is said to have 'begun to grow sorrowful and to be sad'"; so that it is a perfect "passion" when it dominates the soul, i.e. the reason; and a "propassion" when it has its beginning in the sensitive appetite, but goes no further.

Reply Obj. 1: The soul of Christ could have prevented these passions from coming upon it, and especially by the Divine power; yet of His own will He subjected Himself to these corporeal and animal passions.

Reply Obj. 2: Tully is speaking there according to the opinions of the Stoics, who did not give the name of passions to all, but only to the disorderly movements of the sensitive appetite. Now, it is manifest that passions like these were not in Christ.

Reply Obj. 3: The "passions of sins" are movements of the sensitive appetite that tend to unlawful things; and these were not in Christ, as neither was the fomes of sin.

FIFTH ARTICLE [III, Q. 15, Art. 5]

Whether There Was Sensible Pain in Christ?

Objection 1: It would seem that there was no true sensible pain in Christ. For Hilary says (De Trin. x): "Since with Christ to die was life, what pain may He be supposed to have suffered in the mystery of His death, Who bestows life on such as die for Him?" And further on he says: "The Only-begotten assumed human nature, not ceasing to be God; and although blows struck Him and wounds were inflicted on Him, and scourges fell upon Him, and the cross lifted Him up, yet these wrought in deed the vehemence of the passion, but brought no pain; as a dart piercing the water." Hence there was no true pain in Christ.

Obj. 2: Further, it would seem to be proper to flesh conceived in original sin, to be subject to the necessity of pain. But the flesh of Christ was not conceived in sin, but of the Holy Ghost in the Virgin's womb. Therefore it lay under no necessity of suffering pain.

Obj. 3: Further, the delight of the contemplation of Divine things dulls the sense of pain; hence the martyrs in their passions bore up more bravely by thinking of the Divine love. But Christ's soul was in the perfect enjoyment of contemplating God, Whom He saw in essence, as was said above (Q. 9, A. 2). Therefore He could feel no pain.

*On the contrary,* It is written (Isa. 53:4): "Surely He hath borne our infirmities and carried our sorrows."

*I answer that,* As is plain from what has been said in the Second Part (I-II, Q. 35, A. 7), for true bodily pain are required bodily hurt and the sense of hurt. Now Christ's body was able to be hurt, since it was passible and mortal, as above stated (Q. 14, AA. 1, 2); neither was the sense of hurt wanting to it, since Christ's soul possessed perfectly all natural powers. Therefore no one should doubt but that in Christ there was true pain.

Reply Obj. 1: In all these and similar words, Hilary does not intend to exclude the reality of the pain, but the necessity of it. Hence after the foregoing he adds: "Nor, when He thirsted, or hungered, or wept, was the Lord seen to drink, or eat, or grieve. But in order to prove the reality of the body, the body's customs were assumed, so that the custom of our body was atoned for by the custom of our nature. Or when He took drink or food, He acceded, not to the body's necessity, but to its custom." And he uses the word "necessity" in reference to the first cause of these defects, which is sin, as above stated (Q. 14, AA. 1, 3), so that Christ's flesh is said not to have lain under the necessity of these defects, in the sense that there was no sin in it. Hence he adds: "For He" (i.e. Christ) "had a body--one proper to His origin, which did not exist through the unholiness of our conception, but subsisted in the form of our body by the strength of His power." But as regards the proximate cause of these defects, which is composition of contraries, the flesh of Christ lay under the necessity of these defects, as was said above (Q. 14, A. 2).

Reply Obj. 2: Flesh conceived in sin is subject to pain, not merely on account of the necessity of its natural principles, but from the necessity of the guilt of sin. Now this necessity was not in Christ; but only the necessity of natural principles.

Reply Obj. 3: As was said above (Q. 14, A. 1, ad 2), by the power of the Godhead of Christ the beatitude was economically kept in the soul, so as not to overflow into the body, lest His passibility and mortality should be taken away; and for the same reason the delight of contemplation was so kept in the mind as not to overflow into the sensitive powers, lest sensible pain should thereby be prevented.

SIXTH ARTICLE [III, Q. 15, Art. 6]

Whether There Was Sorrow in Christ?

Objection 1: It would seem that in Christ there was no sorrow. For it is written of Christ (Isa. 42:4): "He shall not be sad nor troublesome."

Obj. 2: Further, it is written (Prov. 12:21): "Whatever shall befall the just man, it shall not make him sad." And the reason of this the Stoics asserted to be that no one is saddened save by the loss of his goods. Now the just man esteems only justice and virtue as his goods, and these he cannot lose; otherwise the just man would be subject to fortune if he was saddened by the loss of the goods fortune has given him. But Christ was most just, according to Jer. 23:6: "This is the name that they shall call Him: The Lord, our just one." Therefore there was no sorrow in Him.

Obj. 3: Further, the Philosopher says (Ethic. vii, 13, 14) that all sorrow is "evil, and to be shunned." But in Christ there was no evil to be shunned. Therefore there was no sorrow in Christ.

Obj. 4: Furthermore, as Augustine says (De Civ. Dei xiv, 6): "Sorrow regards the things we suffer unwillingly." But Christ suffered nothing against His will, for it is written (Isa. 53:7): "He was offered because it was His own will." Hence there was no sorrow in Christ.

*On the contrary,* Our Lord said (Matt. 26:38): "My soul is sorrowful even unto death." And Ambrose says (De Trin. ii.) that "as a man He had sorrow; for He bore my sorrow. I call it sorrow, fearlessly, since I preach the cross."

*I answer that,* As was said above (A. 5, ad 3), by Divine dispensation the joy of contemplation remained in Christ's mind so as not to overflow into the sensitive powers, and thereby shut out sensible pain. Now even as sensible pain is in the sensitive appetite, so also is sorrow. But there is a difference of motive or object; for the object and motive of pain is hurt perceived by the sense of touch, as when anyone is wounded; but the object and motive of sorrow is anything hurtful or evil interiorly, apprehended by the reason or the imagination, as was said in the Second Part (I-II, Q. 35, AA. 2, 7), as when anyone grieves over the loss of grace or money. Now Christ's soul could apprehend things as hurtful either to Himself, as His passion and death--or to others, as the sin of His disciples, or of the Jews that killed Him. And hence, as there could be true pain in Christ, so too could there be true sorrow; otherwise, indeed, than in us, in the three ways above stated (A. 4), when we were speaking of the passions of Christ's soul in general.

Reply Obj. 1: Sorrow was not in Christ, as a perfect passion; yet it was inchoatively in Him as a "propassion." Hence it is written (Matt. 26:37): "He began to grow sorrowful and to be sad." For "it is one thing to be sorrowful and another to grow sorrowful," as Jerome says, on this text.

Reply Obj. 2: As Augustine says (De Civ. Dei xiv, 8), "for the three passions"--desire, joy, and fear--the Stoics held three eupatheias i.e. good passions, in the soul of the wise man, viz. for desire, will--for joy, delight--for fear, caution. But as regards sorrow, they denied it could be in the soul of the wise man, for sorrow regards evil already present, and they thought that no evil could befall a wise man; and for this reason, because they believed that only the virtuous is good, since it makes men good, and that nothing is evil, except what is sinful, whereby men become wicked. Now although what is virtuous is man's chief good, and what is sinful is man's chief evil, since these pertain to reason which is supreme in man, yet there are certain secondary goods of man, which pertain to the body, or to the exterior things that minister to the body. And hence in the soul of the wise man there may be sorrow in the sensitive appetite by his apprehending these evils; without this sorrow disturbing the reason. And in this way are we to understand that "whatsoever shall befall the just man, it shall not make him sad," because his reason is troubled by no misfortune. And thus Christ's sorrow was a propassion, and not a passion.

Reply Obj. 3: All sorrow is an evil of punishment; but it is not always an evil of fault, except only when it proceeds from an inordinate affection. Hence Augustine says (De Civ. Dei xiv, 9): "Whenever these affections follow reason, and are caused when and where needed, who will dare to call them diseases or vicious passions?"

Reply Obj. 4: There is no reason why a thing may not of itself be contrary to the will, and yet be willed by reason of the end, to which it is ordained, as bitter medicine is not of itself desired, but only as it is ordained to health. And thus Christ's death and passion were of themselves involuntary, and caused sorrow, although they were voluntary as ordained to the end, which is the redemption of the human race.

SEVENTH ARTICLE [III, Q. 15, Art. 7]

Whether There Was Fear in Christ?

Objection 1: It would seem that there was no fear in Christ. For it is written (Prov. 28:1): "The just, bold as a lion, shall be without dread." But Christ was most just. Therefore there was no fear in Christ.

Obj. 2: Further, Hilary says (De Trin. x): "I ask those who think thus, does it stand to reason that He should dread to die, Who by expelling all dread of death from the Apostles, encouraged them to the glory of martyrdom?" Therefore it is unreasonable that there should be fear in Christ.

Obj. 3: Further, fear seems only to regard what a man cannot avoid. Now Christ could have avoided both the evil of punishment which He endured, and the evil of fault which befell others. Therefore there was no fear in Christ.

*On the contrary,* It is written (Mk. 4:33): Jesus "began to fear and to be heavy."

*I answer that,* As sorrow is caused by the apprehension of a present evil, so also is fear caused by the apprehension of a future evil. Now the apprehension of a future evil, if the evil be quite certain, does not arouse fear. Hence the Philosopher says (Rhet. ii, 5) that we do not fear a thing unless there is some hope of avoiding it. For when there is no hope of avoiding it the evil is considered present, and thus it causes sorrow rather than fear. Hence fear may be considered in two ways. First, inasmuch as the sensitive appetite naturally shrinks from bodily hurt, by sorrow if it is present, and by fear if it is future; and thus fear was in Christ, even as sorrow. Secondly, fear may be considered in the uncertainty of the future event, as when at night we are frightened at a sound, not knowing what it is; and in this way there was no fear in Christ, as Damascene says (De Fide Orth. iii, 23).

Reply Obj. 1: The just man is said to be "without dread," in so far as dread implies a perfect passion drawing man from what reason dictates. And thus fear was not in Christ, but only as a propassion. Hence it is said (Mk. 14:33) that Jesus "began to fear and to be heavy," with a propassion, as Jerome expounds (Matt. 26:37).

Reply Obj. 2: Hilary excludes fear from Christ in the same way that he excludes sorrow, i.e. as regards the necessity of fearing. And yet to show the reality of His human nature, He voluntarily assumed fear, even as sorrow.

Reply Obj. 3: Although Christ could have avoided future evils by the power of His Godhead, yet they were unavoidable, or not easily avoidable by the weakness of the flesh.

EIGHTH ARTICLE [III, Q. 15, Art. 8]

Whether There Was Wonder in Christ?

Objection 1: It would seem that in Christ there was no wonder. For the Philosopher says (Metaph. i, 2) that wonder results when we see an effect without knowing its cause; and thus wonder belongs only to the ignorant. Now there was no ignorance in Christ, as was said (A. 3). Therefore there was no wonder in Christ.

Obj. 2: Further, Damascene says (De Fide Orth. ii, 15) that "wonder is fear springing from the imagination of something great"; and hence the Philosopher says (Ethic. iv, 3) that the "magnanimous man does not wonder." But Christ was most magnanimous. Therefore there was no wonder in Christ.

Obj. 3: Further, no man wonders at what he himself can do. Now Christ could do whatsoever was great. Therefore it seems that He wondered at nothing.

*On the contrary,* It is written (Matt. 8:10): "Jesus hearing this," i.e. the words of the centurion, "marveled."

*I answer that,* Wonder properly regards what is new and unwonted. Now there could be nothing new and unwonted as regards Christ's Divine knowledge, whereby He saw things in the Word; nor as regards the human knowledge, whereby He saw things by infused species. Yet things could be new and unwonted with regard to His empiric knowledge, in regard to which new things could occur to Him day by day. Hence, if we speak of Christ with respect to His Divine knowledge, and His beatific and even His infused knowledge, there was no wonder in Christ. But if we speak of Him with respect to empiric knowledge, wonder could be in Him; and He assumed this affection for our instruction, i.e. in order to teach us to wonder at what He Himself wondered at. Hence Augustine says (Super Gen. Cont. Manich. i, 8): "Our Lord wondered in order to show us that we, who still need to be so affected, must wonder. Hence all these emotions are not signs of a disturbed mind, but of a master teaching."

Reply Obj. 1: Although Christ was ignorant of nothing, yet new things might occur to His empiric knowledge, and thus wonder would be caused.

Reply Obj. 2: Christ did not marvel at the Centurion's faith as if it was great with respect to Himself, but because it was great with respect to others.

Reply Obj. 3: He could do all things by the Divine power, for with respect to this there was no wonder in Him, but only with respect to His human empiric knowledge, as was said above.

NINTH ARTICLE [III, Q. 15, Art. 9]

Whether There Was Anger in Christ?

Objection 1: It would seem that there was no anger in Christ. For it is written (James 1:20): "The anger of man worketh not the justice of God." Now whatever was in Christ pertained to the justice of God, since of Him it is written (1 Cor. 1:30): "For He [Vulg.: 'Who'] of God is made unto us . . . justice." Therefore it seems that there was no anger in Christ.

Obj. 2: Further, anger is opposed to meekness, as is plain from Ethic. iv, 5. But Christ was most meek. Therefore there was no anger in Him.

Obj. 3: Further, Gregory says (Moral. v, 45) that "anger that comes of evil blinds the eye of the mind, but anger that comes of zeal disturbs it." Now the mind's eye in Christ was neither blinded nor disturbed. Therefore in Christ there was neither sinful anger nor zealous anger.

*On the contrary,* It is written (John 2:17) that the words of Ps. 58:10, "the zeal of Thy house hath eaten me up," were fulfilled in Him.

*I answer that,* As was said in the Second Part (I-II, Q. 46, A. 3, ad 3, and II-II, Q. 158, A. 2, ad 3), anger is an effect of sorrow. For when sorrow is inflicted upon someone, there arises within him a desire of the sensitive appetite to repel this injury brought upon himself or others. Hence anger is a passion composed of sorrow and the desire of revenge. Now it was said (A. 6) that sorrow could be in Christ. As to the desire of revenge it is sometimes with sin, i.e. when anyone seeks revenge beyond the order of reason: and in this way anger could not be in Christ, for this kind of anger is sinful. Sometimes, however, this desire is without sin--nay, is praiseworthy, e.g. when anyone seeks revenge according to justice, and this is zealous anger. For Augustine says (on John 2:17) that "he is eaten up by zeal for the house of God, who seeks to better whatever He sees to be evil in it, and if he cannot right it, bears with it and sighs." Such was the anger that was in Christ.

Reply Obj. 1: As Gregory says (Moral. v), anger is in man in two ways--sometimes it forestalls reason, and causes it to operate, and in this way it is properly said to work, for operations are attributed to the principal agent. It is in this way that we must understand that "the anger of man worketh not the justice of God." Sometimes anger follows reason, and is, as it were, its instrument, and then the operation, which pertains to justice, is not attributed to anger but to reason.

Reply Obj. 2: It is the anger which outsteps the bounds of reason that is opposed to meekness, and not the anger which is controlled and brought within its proper bounds by reason, for meekness holds the mean in anger.

Reply Obj. 3: In us the natural order is that the soul's powers mutually impede each other, i.e. if the operation of one power is intense, the operation of the other is weakened. This is the reason why any movement whatsoever of anger, even if it be tempered by reason, dims the mind's eye of him who contemplates. But in Christ, by control of the Divine power, "every faculty was allowed to do what was proper to it," and one power was not impeded by another. Hence, as the joy of His mind in contemplation did not impede the sorrow or pain of the inferior part, so, conversely, the passions of the inferior part no-wise impeded the act of reason.

TENTH ARTICLE [III, Q. 15, Art. 10]

Whether Christ Was at Once a Wayfarer and a Comprehensor?

Objection 1: It would seem that Christ was not at once a wayfarer and a comprehensor. For it belongs to a wayfarer to be moving toward the end of beatitude, and to a comprehensor it belongs to be resting in the end. Now to be moving towards the end and to be resting in the end cannot belong to the same. Therefore Christ could not be at once wayfarer and comprehensor.

Obj. 2: Further, to tend to beatitude, or to obtain it, does not pertain to man's body, but to his soul; hence Augustine says (Ep. ad Dios. cxviii) that "upon the inferior nature, which is the body, there overflows, not indeed the beatitude which belongs to such as enjoy and understand, the fulness of health, i.e. the vigor of incorruption." Now although Christ had a passible body, He fully enjoyed God in His mind. Therefore Christ was not a wayfarer but a comprehensor.

Obj. 3: Further, the Saints, whose souls are in heaven and whose bodies are in the tomb, enjoy beatitude in their souls, although their bodies are subject to death, yet they are called not wayfarers, but only comprehensors. Hence, with equal reason, would it seem that Christ was a pure comprehensor and nowise a wayfarer, since His mind enjoyed God although His body was mortal.

*On the contrary,* It is written (Jer. 14:8): "Why wilt Thou be as a stranger in the land, and as a wayfaring man turning in to lodge?"

*I answer that,* A man is called a wayfarer from tending to beatitude, and a comprehensor from having already obtained beatitude, according to 1 Cor. 9:24: "So run that you may comprehend [Douay: 'obtain']"; and Phil. 3:12: "I follow after, if by any means I may comprehend [Douay: 'obtain']". Now man's perfect beatitude consists in both soul and body, as stated in the Second Part (I-II, Q. 4, A. 6). In the soul, as regards what is proper to it, inasmuch as the mind sees and enjoys God; in the body, inasmuch as the body "will rise spiritual in power and glory and incorruption," as is written 1 Cor. 15:42. Now before His passion Christ's mind saw God fully, and thus He had beatitude as far as it regards what is proper to the soul; but beatitude was wanting with regard to all else, since His soul was passible, and His body both passible and mortal, as is clear from the above (A. 4; Q. 14, AA. 1, 2). Hence He was at once comprehensor, inasmuch as He had the beatitude proper to the soul, and at the same time wayfarer, inasmuch as He was tending to beatitude, as regards what was wanting to His beatitude.

Reply Obj. 1: It is impossible to be moving towards the end and resting in the end, in the same respect; but there is nothing against this under a different respect--as when a man is at once acquainted with what he already knows, and yet is a learner with regard to what he does not know.

Reply Obj. 2: Beatitude principally and properly belongs to the soul with regard to the mind, yet secondarily and, so to say, instrumentally, bodily goods are required for beatitude; thus the Philosopher says (Ethic. i, 8), that exterior goods minister "organically" to beatitude.

Reply Obj. 3: There is no parity between the soul of a saint and of Christ, for two reasons: first, because the souls of saints are not passible, as Christ's soul was; secondly, because their bodies do nothing by which they tend to beatitude, as Christ by His bodily sufferings tended to beatitude as regards the glory of His body.

## QUESTION 16

OF THOSE THINGS WHICH ARE APPLICABLE TO CHRIST IN HIS BEING AND BECOMING (In Twelve Articles)

We must now consider the consequences of the union; and first as to what belongs to Christ in Himself; secondly, as to what belongs to Christ in relation with His Father; thirdly, as to what belongs to Christ in relation to us.

Concerning the first, there occurs a double consideration. The first is about such things as belong to Christ in being and becoming; the second regards such things as belong to Christ by reason of unity.

Under the first head there are twelve points of inquiry:

(1) Whether this is true: "God is man"?

(2) Whether this is true: "Man is God"?

(3) Whether Christ may be called a lordly man?

(4) Whether what belongs to the Son of Man may be predicated of the Son of God, and conversely?

(5) Whether what belongs to the Son of Man may be predicated of the Divine Nature, and what belongs to the Son of God of the human nature?

(6) Whether this is true: "The Son of God was made man"?

(7) Whether this is true: "Man became God"?

(8) Whether this is true: "Christ is a creature"?

(9) Whether this is true: "This man," pointing out Christ, "began to be"? or "always was"?

(10) Whether this is true: "Christ as man is a creature"?

(11) Whether this is true: "Christ as man is God"?

(12) Whether this is true: "Christ as man is a hypostasis or person"?

FIRST ARTICLE [III, Q. 16, Art. 1]

Whether This Is True: "God Is Man"?

Objection 1: It would seem that this is false: "God is man." For every affirmative proposition of remote matter is false. Now this proposition, "God is man," is on remote matter, since the forms signified by the subject and predicate are most widely apart. Therefore, since the aforesaid proposition is affirmative, it would seem to be false.

Obj. 2: Further, the three Divine Persons are in greater mutual agreement than the human nature and the Divine. But in the mystery of the Incarnation one Person is not predicated of another; for we do not say that the Father is the Son, or conversely. Therefore it seems that the human nature ought not to be predicated of God by saying that God is man.

Obj. 3: Further, Athanasius says (Symb. Fid.) that, "as the soul and the flesh are one man, so are God and man one Christ." But this is false: "The soul is the body." Therefore this also is false: "God is man."

Obj. 4: Further, it was said in the First Part (Q. 39, A. 4) that what is predicated of God not relatively but absolutely, belongs to the whole Trinity and to each of the Persons. But this word "man" is not relative, but absolute. Hence, if it is predicated of God, it would follow that the whole Trinity and each of the Persons is man; and this is clearly false.

*On the contrary,* It is written (Phil. 2:6, 7): "Who being in the form of God . . . emptied Himself, taking the form of a servant, being made in the likeness of man, and in habit found as a man"; and thus He Who is in the form of God is man. Now He Who is in the form of God is God. Therefore God is man.

*I answer that,* This proposition "God is man," is admitted by all Christians, yet not in the same way by all. For some admit the proposition, but not in the proper acceptation of the terms. Thus the Manicheans say the Word of God is man, not indeed true, but fictitious man, inasmuch as they say that the Son of God assumed an imaginary body, and thus God is called man as a bronze figure is called man if it has the figure of a man. So, too, those who held that Christ's body and soul were not united, could not say that God is true man, but that He is figuratively called man by reason of the parts. Now both these opinions were disproved above (Q. 2, A. 5; Q. 5, A. 1).

Some, *on the contrary,* hold the reality on the part of man, but deny the reality on the part of God. For they say that Christ, Who is God and man, is God not naturally, but by participation, i.e. by grace; even as all other holy men are called gods--Christ being more excellently so than the rest, on account of His more abundant grace. And thus, when it is said that "God is man," God does not stand for the true and natural God. And this is the heresy of Photinus, which was disproved above (Q. 2, AA. 10, 11). But some admit this proposition, together with the reality of both terms, holding that Christ is true God and true man; yet they do not preserve the truth of the predication. For they say that man is predicated of God by reason of a certain conjunction either of dignity, or of authority, or of affection or indwelling. It was thus that Nestorius held God to be man--nothing further being meant than that God is joined to man by such a conjunction that man is dwelt in by God, and united to Him in affection, and in a share of the Divine authority and honor. And into the same error fall those who suppose two supposita or hypostases in Christ, since it is impossible to understand how, of two things distinct in suppositum or hypostasis, one can be properly predicated of the other: unless merely by a figurative expression, inasmuch as they are united in something, as if we were to say that Peter is John because they are somehow mutually joined together. And these opinions also were disproved above (Q. 2, AA. 3, 6).

Hence, supposing the truth of the Catholic belief, that the true Divine Nature is united with true human nature not only in person, but also in suppositum or hypostasis; we say that this proposition is true and proper, "God is man"--not only by the truth of its terms, i.e. because Christ is true God and true man, but by the truth of the predication. For a word signifying the common nature in the concrete may stand for all contained in the common nature, as this word "man" may stand for any individual man. And thus this word "God," from its very mode of signification, may stand for the Person of the Son of God, as was said in the First Part (Q. 39, A. 4). Now of every suppositum of any nature we may truly and properly predicate a word signifying that nature in the concrete, as "man" may properly and truly be predicated of Socrates and Plato. Hence, since the Person of the Son of God for Whom this word "God" stands, is a suppositum of human nature this word man may be truly and properly predicated of this word "God," as it stands for the Person of the Son of God.

Reply Obj. 1: When different forms cannot come together in one suppositum, the proposition is necessarily in remote matter, the subject signifying one form and the predicate another. But when two forms can come together in one suppositum, the matter is not remote, but natural or contingent, as when I say: "Something white is musical." Now the Divine and human natures, although most widely apart, nevertheless come together by the mystery of the Incarnation in one suppositum, in which neither exists accidentally, but [both] essentially. Hence this proposition is neither in remote nor in contingent, but in natural matter; and man is not predicated of God accidentally, but essentially, as being predicated of its hypostasis--not, indeed, by reason of the form signified by this word "God," but by reason of the suppositum, which is a hypostasis of human nature.

Reply Obj. 2: The three Divine Persons agree in one Nature, and are distinguished in suppositum; and hence they are not predicated one of another. But in the mystery of the Incarnation the natures, being distinct, are not predicated one of the other, in the abstract. For the Divine Nature is not the human nature. But because they agree in suppositum, they are predicated of each other in the concrete.

Reply Obj. 3: "Soul" and "flesh" are taken in the abstract, even as Godhead and manhood; but in the concrete we say "animate" and "carnal" or "corporeal," as, on the other hand, "God" and "man." Hence in both cases the abstract is not predicated of the abstract, but only the concrete of the concrete.

Reply Obj. 4: This word "man" is predicated of God, because of the union in person, and this union implies a relation. Hence it does not follow the rule of those words which are absolutely predicated of God from eternity.

SECOND ARTICLE [III, Q. 16, Art. 2]

Whether This Is True: "Man Is God"?

Objection 1: It would seem that this is false: "Man is God." For God is an incommunicable name; hence (Wis. 13:10; 14:21) idolaters are rebuked for giving the name of God, which is incommunicable, to wood and stones. Hence with equal reason does it seem unbecoming that this word "God" should be predicated of man.

Obj. 2: Further, whatever is predicated of the predicate may be predicated of the subject. But this is true: "God is the Father," or "God is the Trinity." Therefore, if it is true that "Man is God," it seems that this also is true: "Man is the Father," or "Man is the Trinity." But these are false. Therefore the first is false.

Obj. 3: Further, it is written (Ps. 80:10): "There shall be no new God in thee." But man is something new; for Christ was not always man. Therefore this is false: "Man is God."

*On the contrary,* It is written (Rom. 9:5): "Of whom is Christ according to the flesh, Who is over all things, God blessed for ever." Now Christ, according to the flesh, is man. Therefore this is true: "Man is God."

*I answer that,* Granted the reality of both natures, i.e. Divine and human, and of the union in person and hypostasis, this is true and proper: "Man is God," even as this: "God is man." For this word "man" may stand for any hypostasis of human nature; and thus it may stand for the Person of the Son of God, Whom we say is a hypostasis of human nature. Now it is manifest that the word "God" is truly and properly predicated of the Person of the Son of God, as was said in the First Part (Q. 39, A. 4). Hence it remains that this is true and proper: "Man is God."

Reply Obj. 1: Idolaters attributed the name of the Deity to stones and wood, considered in their own nature, because they thought there was something divine in them. But we do not attribute the name of the Deity to the man in His human nature, but in the eternal suppositum, which by union is a suppositum of human nature, as stated above.

Reply Obj. 2: This word "Father" is predicated of this word "God," inasmuch as this word "God" stands for the Person of the Father. And in this way it is not predicated of the Person of the Son, because the Person of the Son is not the Person of the Father. And, consequently, it is not necessary that this word "Father" be predicated of this word "Man," of which the Word "God" is predicated, inasmuch as "Man" stands for the Person of the Son.

Reply Obj. 3: Although the human nature in Christ is something new, yet the suppositum of the human nature is not new, but eternal. And because this word "God" is predicated of man not on account of the human nature, but by reason of the suppositum, it does not follow that we assert a new God. But this would follow, if we held that "Man" stands for a created suppositum: even as must be said by those who assert that there are two supposita in Christ [*Cf. Q. 2, AA. 3, 6].

THIRD ARTICLE [III, Q. 16, Art. 3]

Whether Christ Can Be Called a Lordly Man?*

[*The question is hardly apposite in English. St. Thomas explains why we can say in Latin, e.g. oratio dominica (the Lord's Prayer) or passio dominica (Our Lord's Passion), but not speak of our Lord as homo dominicus (a lordly man)].

Objection 1: It would seem that Christ can be called a lordly man. For Augustine says (Qq. lxxxiii, qu. 36) that "we are to be counseled to hope for the goods that were in the Lordly Man"; and he is speaking of Christ. Therefore it seems that Christ was a lordly man.

Obj. 2: Further, as lordship belongs to Christ by reason of His Divine Nature, so does manhood belong to the human nature. Now God is said to be "humanized," as is plain from Damascene (De Fide Orth. iii, 11), where he says that "being humanized manifests the conjunction with man." Hence with like reason may it be said denominatively that this man is lordly.

Obj. 3: Further, as "lordly" is derived from "lord," so is "Divine" derived from "Deus" [God]. But Dionysius (Eccl. Hier. iv) calls Christ the "most Divine Jesus." Therefore with like reason may Christ be called a lordly man.

*On the contrary,* Augustine says (Retract. i, 19): "I do not see that we may rightly call Jesus Christ a lordly man, since He is the Lord Himself."

*I answer that,* As was said above (A. 2, ad 3), when we say "the Man Christ Jesus," we signify the eternal suppositum, which is the Person of the Son of God, because there is only one suppositum of both natures. Now "God" and "Lord" are predicated essentially of the Son of God; and hence they ought not to be predicated denominatively, since this is derogatory to the truth of the union. Hence, since we say "lordly" denominatively from lord, it cannot truly and properly be said that this Man is lordly, but rather that He is Lord. But if, when we say "the Man Christ Jesus," we mean a created suppositum, as those who assert two supposita in Christ, this man might be called lordly, inasmuch as he is assumed to a participation of Divine honor, as the Nestorians said. And, even in this way, the human nature is not called "divine" by essence, but "deified"--not, indeed, by its being converted into the Divine Nature, but by its conjunction with the Divine Nature in one hypostasis, as is plain from Damascene (De Fide Orth. iii, 11, 17).

Reply Obj. 1: Augustine retracts these and the like words (Retract. i, 19); hence, after the foregoing words (Retract. i, 19), he adds: "Wherever I have said this," viz. that Christ Jesus is a lordly man, "I wish it unsaid, having afterwards seen that it ought not to be said although it may be defended with some reason," i.e. because one might say that He was called a lordly man by reason of the human nature, which this word "man" signifies, and not by reason of the suppositum.

Reply Obj. 2: This one suppositum, which is of the human and Divine natures, was first of the Divine Nature, i.e. from eternity. Afterwards in time it was made a suppositum of human nature by the Incarnation. And for this reason it is said to be "humanized" not that it assumed a man, but that it assumed human nature. But the converse of this is not true, viz. that a suppositum of human nature assumed the Divine Nature; hence we may not say a "deified" or "lordly" man.

Reply Obj. 3: This word Divine is wont to be predicated even of things of which the word God is predicated essentially; thus we say that "the Divine Essence is God," by reason of identity; and that "the Essence belongs to God," or is "Divine," on account of the different way of signifying; and we speak of the "Divine Word," though the Word is God. So, too, we say "a Divine Person," just as we say "the person of Plato," on account of its different mode of signification. But "lordly" is not predicated of those of which "lord" is predicated; for we are not wont to call a man who is a lord, lordly; but whatsoever belongs to a lord is called lordly, as the "lordly will," or the "lordly hand," or the "lordly possession." And hence the man Christ, Who is our Lord, cannot be called lordly; yet His flesh can be called "lordly flesh" and His passion the "lordly passion."

FOURTH ARTICLE [III, Q. 16, Art. 4]

Whether What Belongs to the Human Nature Can Be Predicated of God?

Objection 1: It would seem that what belongs to the human nature cannot be said of God. For contrary things cannot be said of the same. Now, what belongs to human nature is contrary to what is proper to God, since God is uncreated, immutable, and eternal, and it belongs to the human nature to be created temporal and mutable. Therefore what belongs to the human nature cannot be said of God.

Obj. 2: Further, to attribute to God what is defective seems to be derogatory to the Divine honor, and to be a blasphemy. Now what pertains to the human nature contains a kind of defect, as to suffer, to die, and the like. Hence it seems that what pertains to the human nature can nowise be said of God.

Obj. 3: Further, to be assumed pertains to the human nature; yet it does not pertain to God. Therefore what belongs to the human nature cannot be said of God.

*On the contrary,* Damascene says (De Fide Orth. iii, 4) that "God assumed the idioms," i.e. the properties, "of flesh, since God is said to be passible, and the God of glory was crucified."

*I answer that,* On this question there was a difference of opinion between Nestorians and Catholics. The Nestorians wished to divide words predicated of Christ, in this way, viz. that such as pertained to human nature should not be predicated of God, and that such as pertained to the Divine Nature should not be predicated of the Man. Hence Nestorius said: "If anyone attempt to attribute sufferings to the Word, let him be anathema" [*Council of Ephesus, Part I, ch. 29]. But if there are any words applicable to both natures, of them they predicated what pertained to both natures, as "Christ" or "Lord." Hence they granted that Christ was born of a Virgin, and that He was from eternity; but they did not say that God was born of a virgin, or that the Man was from eternity. Catholics on the other hand maintained that words which are said of Christ either in His Divine or in His human nature may be said either of God or of man. Hence Cyril says [*Council of Ephesus, Part I, ch. 26]: "If anyone ascribes to two persons or substances," i.e. hypostases, "such words as are in the evangelical and apostolic Scriptures, or have been said of Christ by the Saints, or by Himself of Himself, and believes that some are to be applied to the Man, and apportions some to the Word alone--let him be anathema." And the reason of this is that, since there is one hypostasis of both natures, the same hypostasis is signified by the name of either nature. Thus whether we say "man" or "God," the hypostasis of Divine and human nature is signified. And hence, of the Man may be said what belongs to the Divine Nature, as of a hypostasis of the Divine Nature; and of God may be said what belongs to the human nature, as of a hypostasis of human nature.

Nevertheless, it must be borne in mind that in a proposition in which something is predicated of another, we must not merely consider what the predicate is predicated of, but also the reason of its being predicated. Thus, although we do not distinguish things predicated of Christ, yet we distinguish that by reason of which they are predicated, since those things that belong to the Divine Nature are predicated of Christ in His Divine Nature, and those that belong to the human nature are predicated of Christ in His human nature. Hence Augustine says (De Trin. i, 11): "We must distinguish what is said by Scripture in reference to the form of God, wherein He is equal to the Father, and what in reference to the form of a servant, wherein He is less than the Father": and further on he says (De Trin. i, 13): "The prudent, careful, and devout reader will discern the reason and point of view of what is said."

Reply Obj. 1: It is impossible for contraries to be predicated of the same in the same respects, but nothing prevents their being predicated of the same in different aspects. And thus contraries are predicated of Christ, not in the same, but in different natures.

Reply Obj. 2: If the things pertaining to defect were attributed to God in His Divine Nature, it would be a blasphemy, since it would be derogatory to His honor. But there is no kind of wrong done to God if they are attributed to Him in His assumed nature. Hence in a discourse of the Council of Ephesus [*Part III, ch. 10] it is said: "God accounts nothing a wrong which is the occasion of man's salvation. For no lowliness that He assumed for us injures that Nature which can be subject to no injury, yet makes lower things Its own, to save our nature. Therefore, since these lowly and worthless things do no harm to the Divine Nature, but bring about our salvation, how dost thou maintain that what was the cause of our salvation was the occasion of harm to God?"

Reply Obj. 3: To be assumed pertains to human nature, not in its suppositum, but in itself; and thus it does not belong to God.

FIFTH ARTICLE [III, Q. 16, Art. 5]

Whether What Belongs to the Human Nature Can Be Predicated of the Divine Nature?

Objection 1: It would seem that what belongs to the human nature can be said of the Divine Nature. For what belongs to the human nature is predicated of the Son of God, and of God. But God is His own Nature. Therefore, what belongs to the human nature may be predicated of the Divine Nature.

Obj. 2: Further, the flesh pertains to human nature. But as Damascene says (De Fide Orth. iii, 6), "we say, after the blessed Athanasius and Cyril, that the Nature of the Word was incarnate." Therefore it would seem with equal reason that what belongs to the human nature may be said of the Divine Nature.

Obj. 3: Further, what belongs to the Divine Nature belongs to Christ's human nature; such as to know future things and to possess saving power. Therefore it would seem with equal reason that what belongs to the human may be said of the Divine Nature.

*On the contrary,* Damascene says (De Fide Orth. iii, 4): "When we mention the Godhead we do not predicate of it the idioms," i.e. the properties, "of the humanity; for we do not say that the Godhead is passible or creatable." Now the Godhead is the Divine Nature. Therefore what is proper to the human nature cannot be said of the Divine Nature.

*I answer that,* What belongs to one cannot be said of another, unless they are both the same; thus "risible" can be predicated only of man. Now in the mystery of the Incarnation the Divine and human natures are not the same; but the hypostasis of the two natures is the same. And hence what belongs to one nature cannot be predicated of the other if they are taken in the abstract. Now concrete words stand for the hypostasis of the nature; and hence of concrete words we may predicate indifferently what belongs to either nature--whether the word of which they are predicated refers to one nature, as the word "Christ," by which is signified "both the Godhead anointing and the manhood anointed"; or to the Divine Nature alone, as this word "God" or "the Son of God"; or to the manhood alone, as this word "Man" or "Jesus." Hence Pope Leo says (Ep. ad Palaest. cxxiv): "It is of no consequence from what substance we name Christ; because since the unity of person remains inseparably, one and the same is altogether Son of Man by His flesh, and altogether Son of God by the Godhead which He has with the Father."

Reply Obj. 1: In God, Person and Nature are really the same; and by reason of this identity the Divine Nature is predicated of the Son of God. Nevertheless, its mode of predication is different; and hence certain things are said of the Son of God which are not said of the Divine Nature; thus we say that the Son of God is born, yet we do not say that the Divine Nature is born; as was said in the First Part (Q. 39, A. 5). So, too, in the mystery of the Incarnation we say that the Son of God suffered, yet we do not say that the Divine Nature suffered.

Reply Obj. 2: Incarnation implies union with flesh, rather than any property of flesh. Now in Christ each nature is united to the other in person; and by reason of this union the Divine Nature is said to be incarnate and the human nature deified, as stated above (Q. 2, A. 1, ad 3).

Reply Obj. 3: What belongs to the Divine Nature is predicated of the human nature--not, indeed, as it belongs essentially to the Divine Nature, but as it is participated by the human nature. Hence, whatever cannot be participated by the human nature (as to be uncreated and omnipotent), is nowise predicated of the human nature. But the Divine Nature received nothing by participation from the human nature; and hence what belongs to the human nature can nowise be predicated of the Divine Nature.

SIXTH ARTICLE [III, Q. 16, Art. 6]

Whether This Is True: "God Was Made Man"?

Objection 1: It would seem that this is false: "God was made man." For since man signifies a substance, to be made man is to be made simply. But this is false: "God was made simply." Therefore this is false: "God was made man."

Obj. 2: Further, to be made man is to be changed. But God cannot be the subject of change, according to Malachi 3:6: "I am the Lord, and I change not." Hence this is false: "God was made man."

Obj. 3: Further, man as predicated of Christ stands for the Person of the Son of God. But this is false: "God was made the Person of the Son of God." Therefore this is false: "God was made man."

*On the contrary,* It is written (John 1:14): "The Word was made flesh": and as Athanasius says (Ep. ad Epictetum), "when he said, 'The Word was made flesh,' it is as if it were said that God was made man."

*I answer that,* A thing is said to be made that which begins to be predicated of it for the first time. Now to be man is truly predicated of God, as stated above (A. 1), yet in such sort that it pertains to God to be man, not from eternity, but from the time of His assuming human nature. Hence, this is true, "God was made man"; though it is understood differently by some: even as this, "God is man," as we said above (A. 1).

Reply Obj. 1: To be made man is to be made simply, in all those in whom human nature begins to be in a newly created suppositum. But God is said to have been made man, inasmuch as the human nature began to be in an eternally pre-existing suppositum of the Divine Nature. And hence for God to be made man does not mean that God was made simply.

Reply Obj. 2: As stated above, to be made implies that something is newly predicated of another. Hence, whenever anything is predicated of another, and there is a change in that of which it is predicated, then to be made is to be changed; and this takes place in whatever is predicated absolutely, for whiteness or greatness cannot newly affect anything, unless it be newly changed to whiteness or greatness. But whatever is predicated relatively can be newly predicated of anything without its change, as a man may be made to be on the right side without being changed and merely by the change of him on whose left side he was. Hence in such cases, not all that is said to be made is changed, since it may happen by the change of something else. And it is thus we say of God: "Lord, Thou art made [Douay: 'hast been'] our refuge" (Ps. 89:1). Now to be man belongs to God by reason of the union, which is a relation. And hence to be man is newly predicated of God without any change in Him, by a change in the human nature, which is assumed to a Divine Person. And hence, when it is said, "God was made man," we understand no change on the part of God, but only on the part of the human nature.

Reply Obj. 3: Man stands not for the bare Person of the Son of God, but inasmuch as it subsists in human nature. Hence, although this is false, "God was made the Person of the Son of God," yet this is true: "God was made man" by being united to human nature.

SEVENTH ARTICLE [III, Q. 16, Art. 7]

Whether This Is True: "Man Was Made God"?

Objection 1: It would seem that this is true: "Man was made God." For it is written (Rom. 1:2, 3): "Which He had promised before by His prophets in the holy Scriptures, concerning His Son Who was made to Him of the seed of David according to the flesh." Now Christ, as man, is of the seed of David according to the flesh. Therefore man was made the Son of God.

Obj. 2: Further, Augustine says (De Trin. i, 13) that "such was this assumption, which made God man, and man God." But by reason of this assumption this is true: "God was made man." Therefore, in like manner, this is true: "Man was made God."

Obj. 3: Further, Gregory Nazianzen says (Ep. ad Chelid. ci): "God was humanized and man was deified, or whatever else one may like to call it." Now God is said to be humanized by being made man. Therefore with equal reason man is said to be deified by being made God; and thus it is true that "Man was made God."

Obj. 4: Further, when it is said that "God was made man," the subject of the making or uniting is not God, but human nature, which the word "man" signifies. Now that seems to be the subject of the making, to which the making is attributed. Hence "Man was made God" is truer than "God was made man."

*On the contrary,* Damascene says (De Fide Orth. iii, 2): "We do not say that man was deified, but that God was humanized." Now to be made God is the same as to be deified. Hence this is false: "Man was made God."

*I answer that,* This proposition, Man was made God, may be understood in three ways. First, so that the participle "made" absolutely determines either the subject or the predicate; and in this sense it is false, since neither the Man of Whom it is predicated was made, nor is God made, as will be said (AA. 8, 9). And in the same sense this is false: "God was made man." But it is not of this sense that we are now speaking. Secondly, it may be so understood that the word "made" determines the composition, with this meaning: "Man was made God, i.e. it was brought about that Man is God." And in this sense both are true, viz. that "Man was made God" and that "God was made Man." But this is not the proper sense of these phrases; unless, indeed, we are to understand that "man" has not a personal but a simple supposition. For although "this man" was not made God, because this suppositum, viz. the Person of the Son of God, was eternally God, yet man, speaking commonly, was not always God. Thirdly, properly understood, this participle "made" attaches making to man with relation to God, as the term of the making. And in this sense, granted that the Person or hypostasis in Christ are the same as the suppositum of God and Man, as was shown (Q. 2, AA. 2, 3), this proposition is false, because, when it is said, "Man was made God," "man" has a personal suppositum: because, to be God is not verified of the Man in His human nature, but in His suppositum. Now the suppositum of human nature, of Whom "to be God" is verified, is the same as the hypostasis or Person of the Son of God, Who was always God. Hence it cannot be said that this Man began to be God, or is made God, or that He was made God.

But if there were a different hypostasis of God and man, so that "to be God" was predicated of the man, and, conversely, by reason of a certain conjunction of supposita, or of personal dignity, or of affection or indwelling, as the Nestorians said, then with equal reason might it be said that Man was made God, i.e. joined to God, and that God was made Man, i.e. joined to man.

Reply Obj. 1: In these words of the Apostle the relative "Who" which refers to the Person of the Son of God ought not to be considered as affecting the predicate, as if someone already existing of the "seed of David according to the flesh" was made the Son of God--and it is in this sense that the objection takes it. But it ought to be taken as affecting the subject, with this meaning--that the "Son of God was made to Him ('namely to the honor of the Father,' as a gloss expounds it), being of the seed of David according to the flesh," as if to say "the Son of God having flesh of the seed of David to the honor of God."

Reply Obj. 2: This saying of Augustine is to be taken in the sense that by the assumption that took place in the Incarnation it was brought about that Man is God and God is Man; and in this sense both sayings are true as stated above.

The same is to be said in reply to the third, since to be deified is the same as to be made God.

Reply Obj. 4: A term placed in the subject is taken materially, i.e. for the suppositum; placed in the predicate it is taken formally, i.e. for the nature signified. Hence when it is said that "Man was made God," the being made is not attributed to the human nature but to the suppositum of the human nature, Which is God from eternity, and hence it does not befit Him to be made God. But when it is said that "God was made Man," the making is taken to be terminated in the human nature. Hence, properly speaking, this is true: "God was made Man," and this is false: "Man was made God"; even as if Socrates, who was already a man, were made white, and were pointed out, this would be true: "This man was made white today," and this would be false; "This white thing was made man today." Nevertheless, if on the part of the subject there is added some word signifying human nature in the abstract, it might be taken in this way for the subject of the making, e.g. if it were said that "human nature was made the Son of God's."

EIGHTH ARTICLE [III, Q. 16, Art. 8]

Whether This Is True: "Christ Is a Creature"?

Objection 1: It would seem that this is true: "Christ is a creature." For Pope Leo says [*Cf. Append. Opp. August., Serm. xii de Nativ.]: "A new and unheard of covenant: God Who is and was, is made a creature." Now we may predicate of Christ whatever the Son of God became by the Incarnation. Therefore this is true; Christ is a creature.

Obj. 2: Further, the properties of both natures may be predicated of the common hypostasis of both natures, no matter by what word they are signified, as stated above (A. 5). But it is the property of human nature to be created, as it is the property of the Divine Nature to be Creator. Hence both may be said of Christ, viz. that He is a creature and that he is uncreated and Creator.

Obj. 3: Further, the principal part of a man is the soul rather than the body. But Christ, by reason of the body which He took from the Virgin, is said simply to be born of the Virgin. Therefore by reason of the soul which is created by God, it ought simply to be said that He is a creature.

*On the contrary,* Ambrose says (De Trin. i): "Was Christ made by a word? Was Christ created by a command?" as if to say: "No!" Hence he adds: "How can there be a creature in God? For God has a simple not a composite Nature." Therefore it must not be granted that "Christ is a creature."

*I answer that,* As Jerome [*Gloss, Ord. in Osee 2:16] says, "words spoken amiss lead to heresy"; hence with us and heretics the very words ought not to be in common, lest we seem to countenance their error. Now the Arian heretics said that Christ was a creature and less than the Father, not only in His human nature, but even in His Divine Person. And hence we must not say absolutely that Christ is a "creature" or "less than the Father"; but with a qualification, viz. "in His human nature." But such things as could not be considered to belong to the Divine Person in Itself may be predicated simply of Christ by reason of His human nature; thus we say simply that Christ suffered, died and was buried: even as in corporeal and human beings, things of which we may doubt whether they belong to the whole or the part, if they are observed to exist in a part, are not predicated of the whole simply, i.e. without qualification, for we do not say that the Ethiopian is white but that he is white as regards his teeth; but we say without qualification that he is curly, since this can only belong to him as regards his hair.

Reply Obj. 1: Sometimes, for the sake of brevity, the holy doctors use the word "creature" of Christ, without any qualifying term; we should however take as understood the qualification, "as man."

Reply Obj. 2: All the properties of the human, just as of the Divine Nature, may be predicated equally of Christ. Hence Damascene says (De Fide Orth. iii, 4) that "Christ Who God and Man, is called created and uncreated, passible and impassible." Nevertheless things of which we may doubt to what nature they belong, are not to be predicated without a qualification. Hence he afterwards adds (De Fide Orth. iv, 5) that "the one hypostasis," i.e. of Christ, "is uncreated in its Godhead and created in its manhood": even so conversely, we may not say without qualification, "Christ is incorporeal" or "impassible"; in order to avoid the error of Manes, who held that Christ had not a true body, nor truly suffered, but we must say, with a qualification, that Christ was incorporeal and impassible "in His Godhead."

Reply Obj. 3: There can be no doubt how the birth from the Virgin applies to the Person of the Son of God, as there can be in the case of creation; and hence there is no parity.

NINTH ARTICLE [III, Q. 16, Art. 9]

Whether This Man, i.e. Christ, Began to Be?

Objection 1: It would seem that this Man, i.e. Christ, began to be. For Augustine says (Tract. cv in Joan.) that "before the world was, neither were we, nor the Mediator of God and men--the Man Jesus Christ." But what was not always, has begun to be. Therefore this Man, i.e. Christ, began to be.

Obj. 2: Further, Christ began to be Man. But to be man is to be simply. Therefore this man began to be, simply.

Obj. 3: Further, "man" implies a suppositum of human nature. But Christ was not always a suppositum of human nature. Therefore this Man began to be.

*On the contrary,* It is written (Heb. 13:8): "Jesus Christ yesterday and today: and the same for ever."

*I answer that,* We must not say that "this Man"--pointing to Christ--"began to be," unless we add something. And this for a twofold reason. First, for this proposition is simply false, in the judgment of the Catholic Faith, which affirms that in Christ there is one suppositum and one hypostasis, as also one Person. For according to this, when we say "this Man," pointing to Christ, the eternal suppositum is necessarily meant, with Whose eternity a beginning in time is incompatible. Hence this is false: "This Man began to be." Nor does it matter that to begin to be refers to the human nature, which is signified by this word "man"; because the term placed in the subject is not taken formally so as to signify the nature, but is taken materially so as to signify the suppositum, as was said (A. 1, ad 4). Secondly, because even if this proposition were true, it ought not to be made use of without qualification; in order to avoid the heresy of Arius, who, since he pretended that the Person of the Son of God is a creature, and less than the Father, so he maintained that He began to be, saying "there was a time when He was not."

Reply Obj. 1: The words quoted must be qualified, i.e. we must say that the Man Jesus Christ was not, before the world was, "in His humanity."

Reply Obj. 2: With this word "begin" we cannot argue from the lower species to the higher. For it does not follow if "this began to be white," that therefore "it began to be colored." And this because "to begin" implies being now and not heretofore: for it does not follow if "this was not white hitherto" that "therefore it was not colored hitherto." Now, to be simply is higher than to be man. Hence this does not follow: "Christ began to be Man--therefore He began to be."

Reply Obj. 3: This word "Man," as it is taken for Christ, although it signifies the human nature, which began to be, nevertheless signifies the eternal suppositum which did not begin to be. Hence, since it signifies the suppositum when placed in the subject, and refers to the nature when placed in the predicate, therefore this is false: "The Man Christ began to be": but this is true: "Christ began to be Man."

TENTH ARTICLE [III, Q. 16, Art. 10]

Whether This Is True: "Christ As Man Is a Creature"?

Objection 1: It would seem that this is false: "Christ as Man is a creature," or "began to be." For nothing in Christ is created except the human nature. But this is false: "Christ as Man is the human nature." Therefore this is also false; Christ as Man is a creature.

Obj. 2: Further, the predicate is predicated of the term placed in reduplication, rather than of the subject of the proposition; as when I say: "A body as colored is visible," it follows that the colored is visible. But as stated (AA. 8, 9) we must not absolutely grant that "the Man Christ is a creature"; nor consequently that "Christ as Man is a creature."

Obj. 3: Further, whatever is predicated of a man as man is predicated of him per se and simply, for per se is the same as "inasmuch as itself," as is said Metaph. v, text. 23. But this is false: "Christ as Man is per se and simply a creature." Hence this, too, is false; "Christ as Man is a creature."

*On the contrary,* Whatever is, is either Creator or creature. But this is false: "Christ as Man is Creator." Therefore this is true: "Christ as Man is a creature."

*I answer that,* When we say "Christ as Man" this word "man" may be added in the reduplication, either by reason of the suppositum or by reason of the nature. If it be added by reason of the suppositum, since the suppositum of the human nature in Christ is eternal and uncreated, this will be false: "Christ as Man is a creature." But if it be added by reason of the human nature, it is true, since by reason of the human nature or in the human nature, it belongs to Him to be a creature, as was said (A. 8).

It must however be borne in mind that the term covered by the reduplication signifies the nature rather than the suppositum, since it is added as a predicate, which is taken formally, for it is the same to say "Christ as Man" and to say "Christ as He is a Man." Hence this is to be granted rather than denied: "Christ as Man is a creature." But if something further be added whereby [the term covered by the reduplication] is attracted to the suppositum, this proposition is to be denied rather than granted, for instance were one to say: "Christ as 'this' Man is a creature."

Reply Obj. 1: Although Christ is not the human nature, He has human nature. Now the word "creature" is naturally predicated not only of abstract, but also of concrete things; since we say that "manhood is a creature" and that "man is a creature."

Reply Obj. 2: Man as placed in the subject refers to the suppositum--and as placed in the reduplication refers to the nature, as was stated above. And because the nature is created and the suppositum uncreated, therefore, although it is not granted that "this man is a creature," yet it is granted that "Christ as Man is a creature."

Reply Obj. 3: It belongs to every man who is a suppositum of human nature alone to have his being only in human nature. Hence of every such suppositum it follows that if it is a creature as man, it is a creature simply. But Christ is a suppositum not merely of human nature, but also of the Divine Nature, in which He has an uncreated being. Hence it does not follow that, if He is a creature as Man, He is a creature simply.

ELEVENTH ARTICLE [III, Q. 16, Art. 11]

Whether This Is True: "Christ As Man Is God"?

Objection 1: It would seem that Christ, as Man, is God. For Christ is God by the grace of union. But Christ, as Man, has the grace of union. Therefore Christ as Man is God.

Obj. 2: Further, to forgive sins is proper to God, according to Isa. 43:25: "I am He that blot out thy iniquities for My own sake." But Christ as Man forgives sin, according to Matt. 9:6: "But that you may know that the Son of Man hath power on earth to forgive sins," etc. Therefore Christ as Man is God.

Obj. 3: Further, Christ is not Man in common, but is this particular Man. Now Christ, as this Man, is God, since by "this Man" we signify the eternal suppositum which is God naturally. Therefore Christ as Man is God.

*On the contrary,* Whatever belongs to Christ as Man belongs to every man. Now, if Christ as Man is God, it follows that every man is God--which is clearly false.

*I answer that,* This term "man" when placed in the reduplication may be taken in two ways. First as referring to the nature; and in this way it is not true that Christ as Man is God, because the human nature is distinct from the Divine by a difference of nature. Secondly it may be taken as referring to the suppositum; and in this way, since the suppositum of the human nature in Christ is the Person of the Son of God, to Whom it essentially belongs to be God, it is true that Christ, as Man, is God. Nevertheless because the term placed in the reduplication signifies the nature rather than the suppositum, as stated above (A. 10), hence this is to be denied rather than granted: "Christ as Man is God."

Reply Obj. 1: It is not with regard to the same, that a thing moves towards, and that it is, something; for to move belongs to a thing because of its matter or subject--and to be in act belongs to it because of its form. So too it is not with regard to the same, that it belongs to Christ to be ordained to be God by the grace of union, and to be God. For the first belongs to Him in His human nature, and the second, in His Divine Nature. Hence this is true: "Christ as Man has the grace of union"; yet not this: "Christ as Man is God."

Reply Obj. 2: The Son of Man has on earth the power of forgiving sins, not by virtue of the human nature, but by virtue of the Divine Nature, in which Divine Nature resides the power of forgiving sins authoritatively; whereas in the human nature it resides instrumentally and ministerially. Hence Chrysostom expounding this passage says [*Implicitly. Hom. xxx in Matth; cf. St. Thomas, Catena Aurea on Mk. 2:10]: "He said pointedly 'on earth to forgive sins,' in order to show that by an indivisible union He united human nature to the power of the Godhead, since although He was made Man, yet He remained the Word of God."

Reply Obj. 3: When we say "this man," the demonstrative pronoun "this" attracts "man" to the suppositum; and hence "Christ as this Man, is God, is a truer proposition than Christ as Man is God."

TWELFTH ARTICLE [III, Q. 16, Art. 12]

Whether This Is True: "Christ As Man Is a Hypostasis or Person"?

Objection 1: It would seem that Christ as Man is a hypostasis or person. For what belongs to every man belongs to Christ as Man, since He is like other men according to Phil. 2:7: "Being made in the likeness of men." But every man is a person. Therefore Christ as Man is a person.

Obj. 2: Further, Christ as Man is a substance of rational nature. But He is not a universal substance: therefore He is an individual substance. Now a person is nothing else than an individual substance of rational nature; as Boethius says (De Duab. Nat.). Therefore Christ as Man is a person.

Obj. 3: Further, Christ as Man is a being of human nature, and a suppositum and a hypostasis of the same nature. But every hypostasis and suppositum and being of human nature is a person. Therefore Christ as Man is a person.

*On the contrary,* Christ as Man is not an eternal person. Therefore if Christ as Man is a person it would follow that in Christ there are two persons--one temporal and the other eternal, which is erroneous, as was said above (Q. 2, A. 6; Q. 4, A. 2).

*I answer that,* As was said (AA. 10, 11), the term "Man" placed in the reduplication may refer either to the suppositum or to the nature. Hence when it is said: "Christ as Man is a person," if it is taken as referring to the suppositum, it is clear that Christ as Man is a person, since the suppositum of human nature is nothing else than the Person of the Son of God. But if it be taken as referring to the nature, it may be understood in two ways. First, we may so understand it as if it belonged to human nature to be in a person, and in this way it is true, for whatever subsists in human nature is a person. Secondly it may be taken that in Christ a proper personality, caused by the principles of the human nature, is due to the human nature; and in this way Christ as Man is not a person, since the human nature does not exist of itself apart from the Divine Nature, and yet the notion of person requires this.

Reply Obj. 1: It belongs to every man to be a person, inasmuch as everything subsisting in human nature is a person. Now this is proper to the Man Christ that the Person subsisting in His human nature is not caused by the principles of the human nature, but is eternal. Hence in one way He is a person, as Man; and in another way He is not, as stated above.

Reply Obj. 2: The "individual substance," which is included in the definition of a person, implies a complete substance subsisting of itself and separate from all else; otherwise, a man's hand might be called a person, since it is an individual substance; nevertheless, because it is an individual substance existing in something else, it cannot be called a person; nor, for the same reason, can the human nature in Christ, although it may be called something individual and singular.

Reply Obj. 3: As a person signifies something complete and self-subsisting in rational nature, so a hypostasis, suppositum, and being of nature in the genus of substance, signify something that subsists of itself. Hence, as human nature is not of itself a person apart from the Person of the Son of God, so likewise it is not of itself a hypostasis or suppositum or a being of nature. Hence in the sense in which we deny that "Christ as Man is a person" we must deny all the other propositions.

# QUESTION 17

OF CHRIST'S UNITY OF BEING (In Two Articles)

We must now consider what pertains to Christ's unity in common. For, in their proper place, we must consider what pertains to unity and plurality in detail: thus we concluded (Q. 9) that there is not only one knowledge in Christ, and it will be concluded hereafter (Q. 35, A. 2) that there is not only one nativity in Christ.

Hence we must consider Christ's unity (1) of being; (2) of will; (3) of operation.

Under the first head there are two points of inquiry:

(1) Whether Christ is one or two?

(2) Whether there is only one being in Christ?

FIRST ARTICLE [III, Q. 17, Art. 1]

Whether Christ Is One or Two?

Objection 1: It would seem that Christ is not one, but two. For Augustine says (De Trin. i, 7): "Because the form of God took the form of a servant, both are God by reason of God Who assumed, yet both are Man by reason of the man assumed." Now "both" may only be said when there are two. Therefore Christ is two.

Obj. 2: Further, where there is one thing and another there are two. Now Christ is one thing and another; for Augustine says (Enchiridion xxxv): "Being in the form of God . . . He took the form of a servant . . . being both in one; but He was one of these as Word, and the other as man." Therefore Christ is two.

Obj. 3: Further, Christ is not only man; for, if He were a mere man, He would not be God. Therefore He is something else than man, and thus in Christ there is one thing and another. Therefore Christ is two.

Obj. 4: Further, Christ is something that the Father is, and something that the Father is not. Therefore Christ is one thing and another. Therefore Christ is two.

Obj. 5: Further, as in the mystery of the Trinity there are three Persons in one Nature, so in the mystery of the Incarnation there are two natures in one Person. But on account of the unity of the Nature, notwithstanding the distinction of Person, the Father and Son are one, according to John 10:30: "I and the Father are one." Therefore, notwithstanding the unity of Person, Christ is two on account of the duality of nature.

Obj. 6: Further, the Philosopher says (Phys. iii, text. 18) that "one" and "two" are predicated denominatively. Now Christ has a duality of nature. Therefore Christ is two.

Obj. 7: Further, as accidental form makes a thing otherwise ( alterum ) so does substantial form make another thing ( aliud ) as Porphyry says (Praedic.). Now in Christ there are two substantial natures, the human and the Divine. Therefore Christ is one thing and another. Therefore Christ is two.

*On the contrary,* Boethius says (De Duab. Nat.): "Whatever is, inasmuch as it is, is one." But we confess that Christ is. Therefore Christ is one.

*I answer that,* Nature, considered in itself, as it is used in the abstract, cannot truly be predicated of the suppositum or person, except in God, in Whom "what it is" and "whereby it is" do not differ, as stated in the First Part (Q. 29, A. 4, ad 1). But in Christ, since there are two natures, viz. the Divine and the human, one of them, viz. the Divine, may be predicated of Him both in the abstract and in the concrete, for we say that the Son of God, Who is signified by the word Christ, is the Divine Nature and is God. But the human nature cannot be predicated of Christ in the abstract, but only in the concrete, i.e. as it is signified by the suppositum. For we cannot truly say that "Christ is human nature," because human nature is not naturally predicated of its suppositum. But we say that Christ is a man, even as Christ is God. Now God signifies one having the Godhead, and man signifies one having manhood. Yet one having manhood is differently signified by the word "man" and by the word "Jesus" or "Peter." For this word "man" implies one having manhood indistinctly, even as the word "God" implies indistinctly one having the Godhead; but the word "Peter" or "Jesus" implies one having manhood distinctly, i.e. with its determinate individual properties, as "Son of God" implies one having the Godhead under a determinate personal property. Now the dual number is placed in Christ with regard to the natures. Hence, if both the natures were predicated in the abstract of Christ, it would follow that Christ is two. But because the two natures are not predicated of Christ, except as they are signified in the suppositum, it must be by reason of the suppositum that "one" or "two" be predicated of Christ.

Now some placed two supposita in Christ, and one Person, which, in their opinion, would seem to be the suppositum completed with its final completion. Hence, since they placed two supposita in Christ, they said that God is two, in the neuter. But because they asserted one Person, they said that Christ is one, in the masculine, for the neuter gender signifies something unformed and imperfect, whereas the masculine signifies something formed and perfect. On the other hand, the Nestorians, who asserted two Persons in Christ, said that Christ is two not only in the neuter, but also in the masculine. But since we maintain one person and one suppositum in Christ, as is clear from Q. 2, AA. 2, 3, it follows that we say that Christ is one not merely in the masculine, but also in the neuter.

Reply Obj. 1: This saying of Augustine is not to be taken as if "both" referred to the predicate, so as to mean that Christ is both; but it refers to the subject. And thus "both" does not stand for two supposita, but for two words signifying two natures in the concrete. For I can say that "both, viz. God and Man, are God" on account of God Who assumes; and "both, viz. God and Man," are Man on account of the man assumed.

Reply Obj. 2: When it is said that "Christ is one thing and another," this saying is to be explained in this sense--"having this nature and another." And it is in this way that Augustine explains it (Contra Felic. xi), where, after saying, "In the mediator of God and man, the Son of God is one thing, and the Son of Man another," he adds: "I say another thing by reason of the difference of substance, and not another thing by reason of the unity of person." Hence Gregory Nazianzen says (Ep. ad Chelid. ci): "If we must speak briefly, that of which the Saviour is, is one thing and another; thus the invisible is not the same as the visible; and what is without time is not the same as what is in time. Yet they are not one and another: far from it; for both these are one."

Reply Obj. 3: This is false, "Christ is only man"; because it does not exclude another suppositum, but another nature, since terms placed in the predicate are taken formally. But if anything is added whereby it is drawn to the suppositum, it would be a true proposition--for instance, "Christ is only that which is man." Nevertheless, it would not follow that He is "any other thing than man," because "another thing," inasmuch as it refers to a diversity of substance, properly refers to the suppositum, even as all relative things bearing a personal relation. But it does follow: "Therefore He has another nature."

Reply Obj. 4: When it is said, "Christ is something that the Father is"; "something" signifies the Divine Nature, which is predicated even in the abstract of the Father and Son. But when it is said: "Christ is something that is not the Father"; "something" signifies, not the human nature as it is in the abstract, but as it is in the concrete; not, indeed, in a distinct, but in an indistinct suppositum, i.e. inasmuch as it underlies the nature and not the individuating properties. Hence it does not follow that Christ is one thing and another, or that He is two, since the suppositum of the human nature in Christ, which is the Person of the Son of God, does not reckon numerically with the Divine Nature, which is predicated of the Father and Son.

Reply Obj. 5: In the mystery of the Divine Trinity the Divine Nature is predicated, even in the abstract of the three Persons; hence it may be said simply that the three Persons are one. But in the mystery of the Incarnation both natures are not predicated in the abstract of Christ; hence it cannot be said simply that Christ is two.

Reply Obj. 6: Two signifies what has duality, not in another, but in the same thing of which "two" is predicated. Now what is predicated is said of the suppositum, which is implied by the word "Christ." Hence, although Christ has duality of nature, yet, because He has not duality of suppositum, it cannot be said that Christ is two.

Reply Obj. 7: Otherwise implies diversity of accident. Hence diversity of accident suffices for anything to be called "otherwise" simply. But "another thing" implies diversity of substance. Now not merely the nature, but also the suppositum is said to be a substance, as is said Metaph.v, text. 15. Hence diversity of nature does not suffice for anything to be called "another thing" simply, unless there is diversity of suppositum. But diversity of nature makes "another thing" relatively, i.e. in nature, if there is no diversity of suppositum.

SECOND ARTICLE [III, Q. 17, Art. 2]

Whether There Is Only One Being in Christ?

Objection 1: It would seem that in Christ there is not merely one being, but two. For Damascene says (De Fide Orth. iii, 13) that whatever follows the nature is doubled in Christ. But being follows the nature, for being is from the form. Hence in Christ there are two beings.

Obj. 2: Further, the being of the Son of God is the Divine Nature itself, and is eternal: whereas the being of the Man Christ is not the Divine Nature, but is a temporal being. Therefore there is not only one being in Christ.

Obj. 3: Further, in the Trinity, although there are three Persons, yet on account of the unity of nature there is only one being. But in Christ there are two natures, though there is one Person. Therefore in Christ there is not only one being.

Obj. 4: Further, in Christ the soul gives some being to the body, since it is its form. But it does not give the Divine being, since this is uncreated. Therefore in Christ there is another being besides the Divine being; and thus in Christ there is not only one being.

*On the contrary,* Everything is said to be a being, inasmuch as it is one, for one and being are convertible. Therefore, if there were two beings in Christ, and not one only, Christ would be two, and not one.

*I answer that,* Because in Christ there are two natures and one hypostasis, it follows that things belonging to the nature in Christ must be two; and that those belonging to the hypostasis in Christ must be only one. Now being pertains both to the nature and to the hypostasis; to the hypostasis as to that which has being--and to the nature as to that whereby it has being. For nature is taken after the manner of a form, which is said to be a being because something is by it; as by whiteness a thing is white, and by manhood a thing is man. Now it must be borne in mind that if there is a form or nature which does not pertain to the personal being of the subsisting hypostasis, this being is not said to belong to the person simply, but relatively; as to be white is the being of Socrates, not as he is Socrates, but inasmuch as he is white. And there is no reason why this being should not be multiplied in one hypostasis or person; for the being whereby Socrates is white is distinct from the being whereby he is a musician. But the being which belongs to the very hypostasis or person in itself cannot possibly be multiplied in one hypostasis or person, since it is impossible that there should not be one being for one thing.

If, therefore, the human nature accrued to the Son of God, not hypostatically or personally, but accidentally, as some maintained, it would be necessary to assert two beings in Christ--one, inasmuch as He is God--the other, inasmuch as He is Man; even as in Socrates we place one being inasmuch as he is white, and another inasmuch as he is a man, since "being white" does not pertain to the personal being of Socrates. But being possessed of a head, being corporeal, being animated--all these pertain to the one person of Socrates, and hence there arises from these only the one being of Socrates. And if it so happened that after the person of Socrates was constituted there accrued to him hands or feet or eyes, as happened to him who was born blind, no new being would be thereby added to Socrates, but only a relation to these, i.e. inasmuch as he would be said to be, not only with reference to what he had previously, but also with reference to what accrued to him afterwards. And thus, since the human nature is united to the Son of God, hypostatically or personally as was said above (Q. 2, AA. 5, 6), and not accidentally, it follows that by the human nature there accrued to Him no new personal being, but only a new relation of the pre-existing personal being to the human nature, in such a way that the Person is said to subsist not merely in the Divine, but also in the human nature.

Reply Obj. 1: Being is consequent upon nature, not as upon that which has being, but as upon that whereby a thing is: whereas it is consequent upon person or hypostasis, as upon that which has being. Hence it has unity from the unity of hypostasis, rather than duality from the duality of the nature.

Reply Obj. 2: The eternal being of the Son of God, which is the Divine Nature, becomes the being of man, inasmuch as the human nature is assumed by the Son of God to unity of Person.

Reply Obj. 3: As was said in the First Part (Q. 50, A. 2, ad 3; Q. 75, A. 5, ad 4), since the Divine Person is the same as the Nature, there is no distinction in the Divine Persons between the being of the Person and the being of the Nature, and, consequently, the three Persons have only one being. But they would have a triple being if the being of the Person were distinct in them from the being of the Nature.

Reply Obj. 4: In Christ the soul gives being to the body, inasmuch as it makes it actually animated, which is to give it the complement of its nature and species. But if we consider the body perfected by the soul, without the hypostasis having both--this whole, composed of soul and body, as signified by the word "humanity," does not signify what is, but whereby it is. Hence being belongs to the subsisting person, inasmuch as it has a relation to such a nature, and of this relation the soul is the cause, inasmuch as it perfects human nature by informing the body.

## QUESTION 18

OF CHRIST'S UNITY OF WILL (In Six Articles)

We must now consider unity as regards the will; and under this head there are six points of inquiry:

(1) Whether the Divine will and the human are distinct in Christ?

(2) Whether in Christ's human nature the will of sensuality is distinct from the will of reason?

(3) Whether as regards the reason there were several wills in Christ?

(4) Whether there was free-will in Christ?

(5) Whether Christ's human will was always conformed to the Divine will in the thing willed?

(6) Whether there was any contrariety of wills in Christ?

FIRST ARTICLE [III, Q. 18, Art. 1]

Whether There Are Two Wills in Christ?

Objection 1: It would seem that in Christ there are not two wills, one Divine, the other human. For the will is the first mover and first commander in whoever wills. But in Christ the first mover and commander was the Divine will, since in Christ everything human was moved by the Divine will. Hence it seems that in Christ there was only one will, viz. the Divine.

Obj. 2: Further, an instrument is not moved by its own will but by the will of its mover. Now the human nature of Christ was the instrument of His Godhead. Hence the human nature of Christ was not moved by its own will, but by the Divine will.

Obj. 3: Further, that alone is multiplied in Christ which belongs to the nature. But the will does not seem to pertain to nature: for natural things are of necessity; whereas what is voluntary is not of necessity. Therefore there is but one will in Christ.

Obj. 4: Further, Damascene says (De Fide Orth. iii, 14) that "to will in this or that way belongs not to our nature but to our intellect," i.e. our personal intellect. But every will is this or that will, since there is nothing in a genus which is not at the same time in some one of its species. Therefore all will belongs to the person. But in Christ there was and is but one person. Therefore in Christ there is only one will.

*On the contrary,* our Lord says (Luke 22:42): "Father, if Thou wilt, remove this chalice from Me. But yet not My will but Thine be done." And Ambrose, quoting this to the Emperor Gratian (De Fide ii, 7) says: "As He assumed my will, He assumed my sorrow;" and on Luke 22:42 he says: "His will, He refers to the Man--the Father's, to the Godhead. For the will of man is temporal, and the will of the Godhead eternal."

*I answer that,* Some placed only one will in Christ; but they seem to have had different motives for holding this. For Apollinaris did not hold an intellectual soul in Christ, but maintained that the Word was in place of the soul, or even in place of the intellect. Hence since "the will is in the reason," as the Philosopher says (De Anima iii, 9), it followed that in Christ there was no human will; and thus there was only one will in Him. So, too, Eutyches and all who held one composite nature in Christ were forced to place one will in Him. Nestorius, too, who maintained that the union of God and man was one of affection and will, held only one will in Christ. But later on, Macarius, Patriarch of Antioch, Cyrus of Alexandria, and Sergius of Constantinople and some of their followers, held that there is one will in Christ, although they held that in Christ there are two natures united in a hypostasis; because they believed that Christ's human nature never moved with its own motion, but only inasmuch as it was moved by the Godhead, as is plain from the synodical letter of Pope Agatho [*Third Council of Constantinople, Act. 4].

And hence in the sixth Council held at Constantinople [*Act. 18] it was decreed that it must be said that there are two wills in Christ, in the following passage: "In accordance with what the Prophets of old taught us concerning Christ, and as He taught us Himself, and the Symbol of the Holy Fathers has handed down to us, we confess two natural wills in Him and two natural operations." And this much it was necessary to say. For it is manifest that the Son of God assumed a perfect human nature, as was shown above (Q. 5; Q. 9, A. 1). Now the will pertains to the perfection of human nature, being one of its natural powers, even as the intellect, as was stated in the First Part (QQ. 79, 80). Hence we must say that the Son of God assumed a human will, together with human nature. Now by the assumption of human nature the Son of God suffered no diminution of what pertains to His Divine Nature, to which it belongs to have a will, as was said in the First Part (Q. 19, A. 1). Hence it must be said that there are two wills in Christ, i.e. one human, the other Divine.

Reply Obj. 1: Whatever was in the human nature of Christ was moved at the bidding of the Divine will; yet it does not follow that in Christ there was no movement of the will proper to human nature, for the good wills of other saints are moved by God's will, "Who worketh" in them "both to will and to accomplish," as is written Phil. 2:13. For although the will cannot be inwardly moved by any creature, yet it can be moved inwardly by God, as was said in the First Part (Q. 105, A. 4). And thus, too, Christ by His human will followed the Divine will according to Ps. 39:9; "That I should do Thy will, O my God, I have desired it." Hence Augustine says (Contra Maxim. ii, 20): "Where the Son says to the Father, 'Not what I will, but what Thou willest,' what do you gain by adding your own words and saying 'He shows that His will was truly subject to His Father,' as if we denied that man's will ought to be subject to God's will?"

Reply Obj. 2: It is proper to an instrument to be moved by the principal agent, yet diversely, according to the property of its nature. For an inanimate instrument, as an axe or a saw, is moved by the craftsman with only a corporeal movement; but an instrument animated by a sensitive soul is moved by the sensitive appetite, as a horse by its rider; and an instrument animated with a rational soul is moved by its will, as by the command of his lord the servant is moved to act, the servant being like an animate instrument, as the Philosopher says (Polit. i, 2, 4; Ethic. viii, 11). And hence it was in this manner that the human nature of Christ was the instrument of the Godhead, and was moved by its own will.

Reply Obj. 3: The power of the will is natural, and necessarily follows upon the nature; but the movement or act of this power--which is also called will--is sometimes natural and necessary, e.g. with respect to beatitude; and sometimes springs from free-will and is neither necessary nor natural, as is plain from what has been stated in the Second Part (I-II, Q. 10, AA. 1, 2) [*Cf. I, Q. 82, A. 2]. And yet even reason itself, which is the principle of this movement, is natural. Hence besides the Divine will it is necessary to place in Christ a human will, not merely as a natural power, or a natural movement, but even as a rational movement.

Reply Obj. 4: When we say "to will in a certain way," we signify a determinate mode of willing. Now a determinate mode regards the thing of which it is the mode. Hence since the will pertains to the nature, "to will in a certain way" belongs to the nature, not indeed considered absolutely, but as it is in the hypostasis. Hence the human will of Christ had a determinate mode from the fact of being in a Divine hypostasis, i.e. it was always moved in accordance with the bidding of the Divine will.

SECOND ARTICLE [III, Q. 18, Art. 2]

Whether in Christ There Was a Will of Sensuality Besides the Will of Reason?

Objection 1: It would seem that in Christ there was no will of sensuality besides the will of reason. For the Philosopher says (De Anima iii, text. 42) that "the will is in the reason, and in the sensitive appetite are the irascible and concupiscible parts." Now sensuality signifies the sensitive appetite. Hence in Christ there was no will of sensuality.

Obj. 2: Further, according to Augustine (De Trin. xii, 12, 13) the sensuality is signified by the serpent. But there was nothing serpent-like in Christ; for He had the likeness of a venomous animal without the venom, as Augustine says (De Pecc. Merit. et Remiss. i, 32). Hence in Christ there was no will of sensuality.

Obj. 3: Further, will is consequent upon nature, as was said (A. 1). But in Christ there was only one nature besides the Divine. Hence in Christ there was only one human will.

*On the contrary,* Ambrose says (De Fide ii, 7): "Mine is the will which He calls His own; because as Man He assumed my sorrow." From this we are given to understand that sorrow pertains to the human will of Christ. Now sorrow pertains to the sensuality, as was said in the Second Part (I-II, Q. 23, A. 1; Q. 25, A. 1). Therefore, seemingly, in Christ there is a will of sensuality besides the will of reason.

*I answer that,* As was said (Q. 9, A. 1), the Son of God assumed human nature together with everything pertaining to the perfection of human nature. Now in human nature is included animal nature, as the genus in its species. Hence the Son of God must have assumed together with the human nature whatever belongs to animal nature; one of which things is the sensitive appetite, which is called the sensuality. Consequently it must be allowed that in Christ there was a sensual appetite, or sensuality. But it must be borne in mind that sensuality or the sensual appetite, inasmuch as it naturally obeys reason, is said to be "rational by participation," as is clear from the Philosopher (Ethic. i, 13). And because "the will is in the reason," as stated above, it may equally be said that the sensuality is "a will by participation."

Reply Obj. 1: This argument is based on the will, essentially so called, which is only in the intellectual part; but the will by participation can be in the sensitive part, inasmuch as it obeys reason.

Reply Obj. 2: The sensuality is signified by the serpent--not as regards the nature of the sensuality, which Christ assumed, but as regards the corruption of the fomes, which was not in Christ.

Reply Obj. 3: "Where there is one thing on account of another, there seems to be only one" (Aristotle, Topic. iii); thus a surface which is visible by color is one visible thing with the color. So, too, because the sensuality is called the will, only because it partakes of the rational will, there is said to be but one human will in Christ, even as there is but one human nature.

THIRD ARTICLE [III, Q. 18, Art. 3]

Whether in Christ There Were Two Wills As Regards the Reason?

Objection 1: It would seem that in Christ there were two wills as regards the reason. For Damascene says (De Fide Orth. ii, 22) that there is a double will in man, viz. the natural will which is called thelesis , and the rational will which is called boulesis . Now Christ in His human nature had whatever belongs to the perfection of human nature. Hence both the foregoing wills were in Christ.

Obj. 2: Further, the appetitive power is diversified in man by the difference of the apprehensive power, and hence according to the difference of sense and intellect is the difference of sensitive and intellective appetite in man. But in the same way as regards man's apprehension, we hold the difference of reason and intellect; both of which were in Christ. Therefore there was a double will in Him, one intellectual and the other rational.

Obj. 3: Further, some [*Hugh of St. Victor, De Quat. Volunt. Christ.] ascribe to Christ "a will of piety," which can only be on the part of reason. Therefore in Christ on the part of reason there are several wills.

*On the contrary,* In every order there is one first mover. But the will is the first mover in the genus of human acts. Therefore in one man there is only one will, properly speaking, which is the will of reason. But Christ is one man. Therefore in Christ there is only one human will.

*I answer that,* As stated above (A. 1, ad 3), the will is sometimes taken for the power, and sometimes for the act. Hence if the will is taken for the act, it is necessary to place two wills, i.e. two species of acts of the will in Christ on the part of the reason. For the will, as was said in the I-II, Q. 8, AA. 2, 3, regards both the end and the means; and is affected differently towards both. For towards the end it is borne simply and absolutely, as towards what is good in itself; but towards the means it is borne under a certain relation, as the goodness of the means depends on something else. Hence the act of the will, inasmuch as it is drawn to anything desired of itself, as health, which act is called by Damascene-thelesis --i.e. simple will, and by the masters "will as nature," is different from the act of the will as it is drawn to anything that is desired only in order to something else, as to take medicine; and this act of the will Damascene calls boulesis --i.e. counseling will, and the masters, "will as reason." But this diversity of acts does not diversify the power, since both acts regard the one common ratio of the object, which is goodness. Hence we must say that if we are speaking of the power of the will, in Christ there is but one human will, essentially so called and not by participation; but if we are speaking of the will as an act, we thus distinguish in Christ a will as nature, which is called thelesis , and a will as reason, which is called boulesis .

Reply Obj. 1: These two wills do not diversify the power but only the act, as we have said.

Reply Obj. 2: The intellect and the reason are not distinct powers, as was said in the First Part (Q. 79, A. 8).

Reply Obj. 3: The "will of piety" would not seem to be distinct from the will considered as nature, inasmuch as it shrinks from another's evil, absolutely considered.

FOURTH ARTICLE [III, Q. 18, Art. 4]

Whether There Was Free-will in Christ?

Objection 1: It would seem that in Christ there was no free-will. For Damascene says (De Fide Orth. iii, 14) that gnome , i.e. opinion, thinking or cogitation, and proairesis , i.e. choice, "cannot possibly be attributed to our Lord, if we wish to speak with propriety." But in the things of faith especially we must speak with propriety. Therefore there was no choice in Christ and consequently no free-will, of which choice is the act.

Obj. 2: Further, the Philosopher says (Ethic. iii, 2) that choice is "a desire of something after taking counsel." Now counsel does not appear to be in Christ, because we do not take counsel concerning such things as we are certain of. But Christ was certain of everything. Hence there was no counsel and consequently no free-will in Christ.

Obj. 3: Further, free-will is indifferent. But Christ's will was determined to good, since He could not sin; as stated above (Q. 15, AA. 1, 2). Hence there was no free-will in Christ.

*On the contrary,* It is written (Isa. 7:15): "He shall eat butter and honey, that He may know to refuse the evil and to choose the good," which is an act of the free-will. Therefore there was free-will in Christ.

*I answer that,* As was said above (A. 3), there was a twofold act of the will in Christ; one whereby He was drawn to anything willed in itself, which implies the nature of an end; the other whereby His will was drawn to anything willed on account of its being ordained to another--which pertains to the nature of means. Now, as the Philosopher says (Ethic. iii, 2) choice differs from will in this, that will of itself regards the end, while choice regards the means. And thus simple will is the same as the "will as nature"; but choice is the same as the "will as reason," and is the proper act of free-will, as was said in the First Part (Q. 83, A. 3). Hence, since "will as reason" is placed in Christ, we must also place choice, and consequently free-will, whose act is choice, as was said in the First Part (Q. 83, A. 3; I-II, Q. 13, A. 1).

Reply Obj. 1: Damascene excludes choice from Christ, in so far as he considers that doubt is implied in the word choice. Nevertheless doubt is not necessary to choice, since it belongs even to God Himself to choose, according to Eph. 1:4: "He chose us in Him before the foundation of the world," although in God there is no doubt. Yet doubt is accidental to choice when it is in an ignorant nature. We may also say the same of whatever else is mentioned in the passage quoted.

Reply Obj. 2: Choice presupposes counsel; yet it follows counsel only as determined by judgment. For what we judge to be done, we choose, after the inquiry of counsel, as is stated (Ethic. iii, 2, 3). Hence if anything is judged necessary to be done, without any preceding doubt or inquiry, this suffices for choice. Therefore it is plain that doubt or inquiry belong to choice not essentially, but only when it is in an ignorant nature.

Reply Obj. 3: The will of Christ, though determined to good, is not determined to this or that good. Hence it pertains to Christ, even as to the blessed, to choose with a free-will confirmed in good.

FIFTH ARTICLE [III, Q. 18, Art. 5]

Whether the Human Will of Christ Was Altogether Conformed to the Divine Will in the Thing Willed?

Objection 1: It would seem that the human will in Christ did not will anything except what God willed. For it is written (Ps. 39:9) in the person of Christ: "That I should do Thy will: O my God, I have desired it." Now he who desires to do another's will, wills what the other wills. Hence it seems that Christ's human will willed nothing but what was willed by His Divine will.

Obj. 2: Further, Christ's soul had most perfect charity, which, indeed, surpasses the comprehension of all our knowledge, according to Eph. 3:19, "the charity of Christ, which surpasseth all knowledge." Now charity makes men will what God wills; hence the Philosopher says (Ethic. ix, 4) that one mark of friendship is "to will and choose the same." Therefore the human will in Christ willed nothing else than was willed by His Divine will.

Obj. 3: Further, Christ was a true comprehensor. But the Saints who are comprehensors in heaven will only what God wills, otherwise they would not be happy, because they would not obtain whatever they will, for "blessed is he who has what he wills, and wills nothing amiss," as Augustine says (De Trin. xiii, 5). Hence in His human will Christ wills nothing else than does the Divine will.

*On the contrary,* Augustine says (Contra Maxim. ii, 20): "When Christ says 'Not what I will, but what Thou wilt' He shows Himself to have willed something else than did His Father; and this could only have been by His human heart, since He did not transfigure our weakness into His Divine but into His human will."

*I answer that,* As was said (AA. 2, 3), in Christ according to His human nature there is a twofold will, viz. the will of sensuality, which is called will by participation, and the rational will, whether considered after the manner of nature, or after the manner of reason. Now it was said above (Q. 13, A. 3, ad 1; Q. 14, A. 1, ad 2) that by a certain dispensation the Son of God before His Passion "allowed His flesh to do and suffer what belonged to it." And in like manner He allowed all the powers of His soul to do what belonged to them. Now it is clear that the will of sensuality naturally shrinks from sensible pains and bodily hurt. In like manner, the will as nature turns from what is against nature and what is evil in itself, as death and the like; yet the will as reason may at time choose these things in relation to an end, as in a mere man the sensuality and the will absolutely considered shrink from burning, which, nevertheless, the will as reason may choose for the sake of health. Now it was the will of God that Christ should undergo pain, suffering, and death, not that these of themselves were willed by God, but for the sake of man's salvation. Hence it is plain that in His will of sensuality and in His rational will considered as nature, Christ could will what God did not; but in His will as reason He always willed the same as God, which appears from what He says (Matt. 26:39): "Not as I will, but as Thou wilt." For He willed in His reason that the Divine will should be fulfilled although He said that He willed something else by another will.

Reply Obj. 1: By His rational will Christ willed the Divine will to be fulfilled; but not by His will of sensuality, the movement of which does not extend to the will of God--nor by His will considered as nature which regards things absolutely considered and not in relation to the Divine will.

Reply Obj. 2: The conformity of the human will to the Divine regards the will of reason: according to which the wills even of friends agree, inasmuch as reason considers something willed in its relation to the will of a friend.

Reply Obj. 3: Christ was at once comprehensor and wayfarer, inasmuch as He was enjoying God in His mind and had a passible body. Hence things repugnant to His natural will and to His sensitive appetite could happen to Him in His passible flesh.

SIXTH ARTICLE [III, Q. 18, Art. 6]

Whether There Was Contrariety of Wills in Christ?

Objection 1: It would seem that there was contrariety of wills in Christ. For contrariety of wills regards contrariety of objects, as contrariety of movements springs from contrariety of termini, as is plain from the Philosopher (Phys. v, text. 49, seq.). Now Christ in His different wills wished contrary things. For in His Divine will He wished for death, from which He shrank in His human will, hence Athanasius says [*De Incarnat. et Cont. Arianos, written against Apollinarius]: "When Christ says 'Father, if it be possible, let this chalice pass from Me; yet not My will, but Thine be done,' and again, 'The spirit indeed is willing, but the flesh weak,' He denotes two wills--the human, which through the weakness of the flesh shrank from the passion--and His Divine will eager for the passion." Hence there was contrariety of wills in Christ.

Obj. 2: Further, it is written (Gal. 5:17) that "the flesh lusteth against the spirit, and the spirit against the flesh." Now when the spirit desires one thing, and the flesh another, there is contrariety of wills. But this was in Christ; for by the will of charity which the Holy Spirit was causing in His mind, He willed the passion, according to Isa. 53:7: "He was offered because it was His own will," yet in His flesh He shrank from the passion. Therefore there was contrariety of wills in Him.

Obj. 3: Further, it is written (Luke 22:43) that "being in an agony, He prayed the longer." Now agony seems to imply a certain struggle [*Greek, agonia ] in a soul drawn to contrary things. Hence it seems that there was contrariety of will in Christ.

*On the contrary,* In the decisions of the Sixth Council [*Third Council of Constantinople, Act. 18] it is said: "We confess two natural wills, not in opposition, as evil-minded heretics assert, but following His human will, and neither withstanding nor striving against, but rather being subject to, His Divine and omnipotent will."

*I answer that,* Contrariety can exist only where there is opposition in the same and as regards the same. For if the diversity exists as regards diverse things, and in diverse subjects, this would not suffice for the nature of contrariety, nor even for the nature of contradiction, e.g. if a man were well formed or healthy as regards his hand, but not as regards his foot. Hence for there to be contrariety of wills in anyone it is necessary, first, that the diversity of wills should regard the same. For if the will of one regards the doing of something with reference to some universal reason, and the will of another regards the not doing the same with reference to some particular reason, there is not complete contrariety of will, e.g. when a judge wishes a brigand to be hanged for the good of the commonwealth, and one of the latter's kindred wishes him not to be hanged on account of a private love, there is no contrariety of wills; unless, indeed, the desire of the private good went so far as to wish to hinder the public good for the private good--in that case the opposition of wills would regard the same.

Secondly, for contrariety of wills it is necessary that it should be in the same will. For if a man wishes one thing with his rational appetite, and wishes another thing with his sensitive appetite, there is no contrariety, unless the sensitive appetite so far prevailed as to change or at least keep back the rational appetite; for in this case something of the contrary movement of the sensitive appetite would reach the rational will.

And hence it must be said that although the natural and the sensitive will in Christ wished what the Divine will did not wish, yet there was no contrariety of wills in Him. First, because neither the natural will nor the will of sensuality rejected the reason for which the Divine will and the will of the human reason in Christ wished the passion. For the absolute will of Christ wished the salvation of the human race, although it did not pertain to it to will this for the sake of something further; but the movement of sensuality could nowise extend so far. Secondly, because neither the Divine will nor the will of reason in Christ was impeded or retarded by the natural will or the appetite of sensuality. So, too, on the other hand, neither the Divine will nor the will of reason in Christ shrank from or retarded the movement of the natural human will and the movement of the sensuality in Christ. For it pleased Christ, in His Divine will, and in His will of reason, that His natural will and will of sensuality should be moved according to the order of their nature. Hence it is clear that in Christ there was no opposition or contrariety of wills.

Reply Obj. 1: The fact of any will in Christ willing something else than did the Divine will, proceeded from the Divine will, by whose permission the human nature in Christ was moved by its proper movements, as Damascene says (De Fide Orth. ii, 15, 18, 19).

Reply Obj. 2: In us the desires of the spirit are impeded or retarded by the desires of the flesh: this did not occur in Christ. Hence in Christ there was no contrariety of flesh and spirit, as in us.

Reply Obj. 3: The agony in Christ was not in the rational soul, in as far as it implies a struggle in the will arising from a diversity of motives, as when anyone, on his reason considering one, wishes one thing, and on its considering another, wishes the contrary. For this springs from the weakness of the reason, which is unable to judge which is the best simply. Now this did not occur in Christ, since by His reason He judged it best that the Divine will regarding the salvation of the human race should be fulfilled by His passion. Nevertheless, there was an agony in Christ as regards the sensitive part, inasmuch as it implied a dread of coming trial, as Damascene says (De Fide Orth. ii, 15; iii, 18, 23).

## QUESTION 19

OF THE UNITY OF CHRIST'S OPERATION (In Four Articles)

We must now consider the unity of Christ's operation; and under this head there are four points of inquiry:

(1) Whether in Christ there was one or several operations of the Godhead and Manhood?

(2) Whether in Christ there were several operations of the human nature?

(3) Whether Christ by His human operation merited anything for Himself?

(4) Whether He merited anything for us by it?

FIRST ARTICLE [III, Q. 19, Art. 1]

Whether in Christ There Is Only One Operation of the Godhead and Manhood?

Objection 1: It would seem that in Christ there is but one operation of the Godhead and the Manhood. For Dionysius says (Div. Nom. ii): "The most loving operation of God is made manifest to us by the supersubstantial Word having taken flesh integrally and truly, and having operated and suffered whatsoever befits His human and Divine operation." But he here mentions only one human and Divine operation, which is written in Greek theandrike , i.e. God-manlike. Hence it seems that there is but one composite operation in Christ.

Obj. 2: Further, there is but one operation of the principal and instrumental agent. Now the human nature in Christ was the instrument of the Divine, as was said above (Q. 7, A. 1, ad 3; Q. 8, A. 1, ad 1; Q. 18, A. 1, ad 2). Hence the operations of the Divine and human natures in Christ are the same.

Obj. 3: Further, since in Christ there are two natures in one hypostasis or person, whatever pertains to the hypostasis or person is one and the same. But operation pertains to the hypostasis or person, for it is only a subsisting suppositum that operates; hence, according to the Philosopher (Metaph. i, 1), acts belong to singulars. Hence in Christ there is only one operation of the Godhead and the Manhood.

Obj. 4: Further, as being belongs to a subsisting hypostasis, so also does operation. But on account of the unity of hypostasis there is only one operation of the Godhead and the (Q. 17, A. 2). Hence, on account of the same unity, there is one operation in Christ.

Obj. [5]: Further, [where there is one thing] operated there is one operation. But the same thing was operated by the Godhead and the Manhood, as the healing of the lepers or the raising of the dead. Hence it seems that in Christ there is but one operation of the Godhead and the Manhood.

*On the contrary,* Ambrose says (De Fide ii, 8): "How can the same operation spring from different powers? Cannot the lesser operate as the greater? And can there be one operation where there are different substances?"

*I answer that,* As was said above (Q. 18, A. 1), the aforesaid heretics who placed one will in Christ placed one operation in Christ. Now in order better to understand their erroneous opinion, we must bear in mind that wherever there are several mutually ordained agents, the inferior is moved by the superior, as in man the body is moved by the soul and the lower powers by the reason. And thus the actions and movements of the inferior principle are things operated rather than operations. Now what pertains to the highest principle is properly the operation; thus we say of man that to walk, which belongs to the feet, and to touch, which belongs to the hand, are things operated by the man--one of which is operated by the soul through the feet, the other through the hands. And because it is the same soul that operates in both cases, there is only one indifferent operation, on the part of the thing operating, which is the first moving principle; but difference is found on the part of what is operated. Now, as in a mere man the body is moved by the soul, and the sensitive by the rational appetite, so in the Lord Jesus Christ the human nature is moved and ruled by the Divine. Hence they said that there is one indifferent operation on the part of the Godhead operating, but divers things operated, inasmuch as the Godhead of Christ did one thing by Itself, as to uphold all things by the word of His power--and another thing by His human nature, as to walk in body. Hence the Sixth Council [*Third Council of Constantinople, Act. 10] quotes the words of Severus the heretic, who said: "What things were done and wrought by the one Christ, differ greatly; for some are becoming to God, and some are human, as to walk bodily on the earth is indeed human, but to give hale steps to sickly limbs, wholly unable to walk on the ground, is becoming to God. Yet one, i.e. the Incarnate Word, wrought one and the other--neither was this from one nature, and that from another; nor can we justly affirm that because there are distinct things operated there are therefore two operating natures and forms."

But herein they were deceived, for what is moved by another has a twofold action--one which it has from its own form--the other, which it has inasmuch as it is moved by another; thus the operation of an axe of itself is to cleave; but inasmuch as it is moved by the craftsman, its operation is to make benches. Hence the operation which belongs to a thing by its form is proper to it, nor does it belong to the mover, except in so far as he makes use of this kind of thing for his work: thus to heat is the proper operation of fire, but not of a smith, except in so far as he makes use of fire for heating iron. But the operation which belongs to the thing, as moved by another, is not distinct from the operation of the mover; thus to make a bench is not the work of the axe independently of the workman. Hence, wheresoever the mover and the moved have different forms or operative faculties, there must the operation of the mover and the proper operation of the moved be distinct; although the moved shares in the operation of the mover, and the mover makes use of the operation of the moved, and, consequently, each acts in communion with the other.

Therefore in Christ the human nature has its proper form and power whereby it acts; and so has the Divine. Hence the human nature has its proper operation distinct from the Divine, and conversely. Nevertheless, the Divine Nature makes use of the operation of the human nature, as of the operation of its instrument; and in the same way the human nature shares in the operation of the Divine Nature, as an instrument shares in the operation of the principal agent. And this is what Pope Leo says (Ep. ad Flavian. xxviii): "Both forms" (i.e. both the Divine and the human nature in Christ) "do what is proper to each in union with the other, i.e. the Word operates what belongs to the Word, and the flesh carries out what belongs to flesh."

But if there were only one operation of the Godhead and manhood in Christ, it would be necessary to say either that the human nature had not its proper form and power (for this could not possibly be said of the Divine), whence it would follow that in Christ there was only the Divine operation; or it would be necessary to say that from the Divine and human power there was made up one power. Now both of these are impossible. For by the first the human nature in Christ is supposed to be imperfect; and by the second a confusion of the natures is supposed. Hence it is with reason that the Sixth Council (Act. 18) condemned this opinion, and decreed as follows: "We confess two natural, indivisible, unconvertible, unconfused, and inseparable operations in the same Lord Jesus Christ our true God"; i.e. the Divine operation and the human operation.

Reply Obj. 1: Dionysius places in Christ a theandric, i.e. a God-manlike or Divino-human, operation not by any confusion of the operations or powers of both natures, but inasmuch as His Divine operation employs the human, and His human operation shares in the power of the Divine. Hence, as he says in a certain epistle (Ad Caium iv), "what is of man He works beyond man; and this is shown by the Virgin conceiving supernaturally and by the unstable waters bearing up the weight of bodily feet." Now it is clear that to be begotten belongs to human nature, and likewise to walk; yet both were in Christ supernaturally. So, too, He wrought Divine things humanly, as when He healed the leper with a touch. Hence in the same epistle he adds: "He performed Divine works not as God does, and human works not as man does, but, God having been made man, by a new operation of God and man."

Now, that he understood two operations in Christ, one of the Divine and the other of the human nature, is clear from what he says, Div. Nom. ii: "Whatever pertains to His human operation the Father and the Holy Ghost no-wise share in, except, as one might say, by their most gracious and merciful will," i.e. inasmuch as the Father and the Holy Ghost in their mercy wished Christ to do and to suffer human things. And he adds: "He is truly the unchangeable God, and God's Word by the sublime and unspeakable operation of God, which, being made man for us, He wrought." Hence it is clear that the human operation, in which the Father and the Holy Ghost do not share, except by Their merciful consent, is distinct from His operation, as the Word of God, wherein the Father and the Holy Ghost share.

Reply Obj. 2: The instrument is said to act through being moved by the principal agent; and yet, besides this, it can have its proper operation through its own form, as stated above of fire. And hence the action of the instrument as instrument is not distinct from the action of the principal agent; yet it may have another operation, inasmuch as it is a thing. Hence the operation of Christ's human nature, as the instrument of the Godhead, is not distinct from the operation of the Godhead; for the salvation wherewith the manhood of Christ saves us and that wherewith His Godhead saves us are not distinct; nevertheless, the human nature in Christ, inasmuch as it is a certain nature, has a proper operation distinct from the Divine, as stated above.

Reply Obj. 3: To operate belongs to a subsisting hypostasis; in accordance, however, with the form and nature from which the operation receives its species. Hence from the diversity of forms or natures spring the divers species of operations, but from the unity of hypostasis springs the numerical unity as regards the operation of the species: thus fire has two operations specifically different, namely, to illuminate and to heat, from the difference of light and heat, and yet the illumination of the fire that illuminates at one and the same time is numerically one. So, likewise, in Christ there are necessarily two specifically different operations by reason of His two natures; nevertheless, each of the operations at one and the same time is numerically one, as one walking and one healing.

Reply Obj. 4: Being and operation belong to the person by reason of the nature; yet in a different manner. For being belongs to the very constitution of the person, and in this respect it has the nature of a term; consequently, unity of person requires unity of the complete and personal being. But operation is an effect of the person by reason of a form or nature. Hence plurality of operations is not incompatible with personal unity.

Reply Obj. 5: The proper work of the Divine operation is different from the proper work of the human operation. Thus to heal a leper is a proper work of the Divine operation, but to touch him is the proper work of the human operation. Now both these operations concur in one work, inasmuch as one nature acts in union with the other.

SECOND ARTICLE [III, Q. 19, Art. 2]

Whether in Christ There Are Several Human Operations?

Objection 1: It would seem that in Christ there are several human operations. For Christ as man communicates with plants by His nutritive soul, with the brutes by His sensitive soul, and with the angels by His intellective soul, even as other men do. Now the operations of a plant as plant and of an animal as animal are different. Therefore Christ as man has several operations.

Obj. 2: Further, powers and habits are distinguished by their acts. Now in Christ's soul there were divers powers and habits; therefore also divers operations.

Obj. 3: Further, instruments ought to be proportioned to their operations. Now the human body has divers members of different form, and consequently fitted to divers operations. Therefore in Christ there are divers operations in the human nature.

*On the contrary,* As Damascene says (De Fide Orth. iii, 15), "operation is consequent upon the nature." But in Christ there is only one human nature. Therefore in Christ there is only one human operation.

*I answer that,* Since it is by his reason that man is what he is; that operation is called human simply, which proceeds from the reason through the will, which is the rational appetite. Now if there is any operation in man which does not proceed from the reason and the will, it is not simply a human operation, but belongs to man by reason of some part of human nature--sometimes by reason of the nature of elementary bodies, as to be borne downwards--sometimes by reason of the force of the vegetative soul, as to be nourished, and to grow--sometimes by reason of the sensitive part, as to see and hear, to imagine and remember, to desire and to be angry. Now between these operations there is a difference. For the operations of the sensitive soul are to some extent obedient to reason, and consequently they are somewhat rational and human inasmuch as they obey reason, as is clear from the Philosopher (Ethic. i, 13). But the operations that spring from the vegetative soul, or from the nature of elemental bodies, are not subject to reason; consequently they are nowise rational; nor simply human, but only as regards a part of human nature. Now it was said (A. 1) that when a subordinate agent acts by its own form, the operations of the inferior and of the superior agent are distinct; but when the inferior agent acts only as moved by the superior agent, then the operation of the superior and the inferior agent is one.

And hence in every mere man the operations of the elemental body and of the vegetative soul are distinct from the will's operation, which is properly human; so likewise the operations of the sensitive soul inasmuch as it is not moved by reason; but inasmuch as it is moved by reason, the operations of the sensitive and the rational part are the same. Now there is but one operation of the rational part if we consider the principle of the operation, which is the reason and the will; but the operations are many if we consider their relationship to various objects. And there were some who called this a diversity of things operated rather than of operations, judging the unity of the operation solely from the operative principle. And it is in this respect that we are now considering the unity and plurality of operations in Christ.

Hence in every mere man there is but one operation, which is properly called human; but besides this there are in a mere man certain other operations, which are not strictly human, as was said above. But in the Man Jesus Christ there was no motion of the sensitive part which was not ordered by reason. Even the natural and bodily operations pertained in some respects to His will, inasmuch as it was His will "that His flesh should do and suffer what belonged to it," as stated above (Q. 18, A. 5). Much more, therefore, is there one operation in Christ, than in any other man whatsoever.

Reply Obj. 1: The operations of the sensitive and nutritive parts are not strictly human, as stated above; yet in Christ these operations were more human than in others.

Reply Obj. 2: Powers and habits are diversified by comparison with their objects. Hence in this way the diversity of operations corresponds to the divers powers and habits, as likewise to the divers objects. Now we do not wish to exclude this diversity of operations from Christ's humanity, nor that which springs from a diversity of time, but only that which regards the first active principle, as was said above.

(St. Thomas gives no reply to Obj. 3; some codices add: Hence may be gathered the reply to the third objection.)

THIRD ARTICLE [III, Q. 19, Art. 3]

Whether the Human Action of Christ Could Be Meritorious to Him?

Objection 1: It would seem that the human action of Christ could not be meritorious to Him. For before His death Christ was a comprehensor even as He is now. But comprehensors do not merit: because the charity of the comprehensor belongs to the reward of beatitude, since fruition depends upon it. Hence it does not seem to be the principle of merit, since merit and reward are not the same. Therefore Christ before His passion did not merit, even as He does not merit now.

Obj. 2: Further, no one merits what is due to him. But because Christ is the Son of God by nature, the eternal inheritance is due to Him, which other men merit by their works. And hence Christ Who, from the beginning, was the Word of God, could not merit anything for Himself.

Obj. 3: Further, whoever has the principle does not properly merit what flows from its possession. But Christ has the glory of the soul, whence, in the natural course, flowed the glory of the body, as Augustine says (Ep. ad Dios cxviii); though by a dispensation it was brought about that in Christ the glory of the soul should not overflow to the body. Hence Christ did not merit the glory of the body.

Obj. 4: Further, the manifestation of Christ's excellence is a good, not of Christ Himself, but of those who know Him. Hence it is promised as a reward to such as love Christ that He will be manifested to them, according to John 14:21: "He that loveth Me, shall be loved of My Father, and I will love him and will manifest Myself to him." Therefore Christ did not merit the manifestation of His greatness.

*On the contrary,* The Apostle says (Phil. 2:8, 9): "Becoming obedient unto death . . . For which cause God also hath exalted Him." Therefore by obeying He merited His exaltation and thus He merited something for Himself.

*I answer that,* To have any good thing of oneself is more excellent than to have it from another, for "what is of itself a cause is always more excellent than what is a cause through another," as is said Phys. viii, 5. Now a thing is said to have, of itself, that of which it is to some extent the cause. But of whatever good we possess the first cause by authority is God; and in this way no creature has any good of itself, according to 1 Cor. 4:7: "What hast thou that thou hast not received?" Nevertheless, in a secondary manner anyone may be a cause, to himself, of having certain good things, inasmuch as he cooperates with God in the matter, and thus whoever has anything by his own merit has it, in a manner, of himself. Hence it is better to have a thing by merit than without merit.

Now since all perfection and greatness must be attributed to Christ, consequently He must have by merit what others have by merit; unless it be of such a nature that its want would detract from Christ's dignity and perfection more than would accrue to Him by merit. Hence He merited neither grace nor knowledge nor the beatitude of His soul, nor the Godhead, because, since merit regards only what is not yet possessed, it would be necessary that Christ should have been without these at some time; and to be without them would have diminished Christ's dignity more than His merit would have increased it. But the glory of the body, and the like, are less than the dignity of meriting, which pertains to the virtue of charity. Hence we must say that Christ had, by merit, the glory of His body and whatever pertained to His outward excellence, as His Ascension, veneration, and the rest. And thus it is clear that He could merit for Himself.

Reply Obj. 1: Fruition, which is an act of charity,

pertains to the glory of the soul, which Christ did not merit. Hence if He merited by charity, it does not follow that the merit and the reward are the same. Nor did He merit by charity inasmuch as it was the charity of a comprehensor, but inasmuch as it was that of a wayfarer. For He was at once a wayfarer and a comprehensor, as was said above (Q. 15, A. 10). And therefore, since He is no longer a wayfarer, He is not in the state of meriting.

Reply Obj. 2: Because by nature Christ is God and the Son of God, the Divine glory and the lordship of all things are due to Him, as to the first and supreme Lord. Nevertheless a glory is due to Him as a beatified man; and this He has partly without merit, and partly with merit, as is clear from what has been said.

Reply Obj. 3: It is by Divine appointment that there is an overflow of glory from the soul to the body, in keeping with human merit; so that as man merits by the act of the soul which he performs in the body, so he may be rewarded by the glory of the soul overflowing to the body. And hence not only the glory of the soul, but also the glory of the body falls under merit, according to Rom. 8:11: "He . . . shall quicken also our [Vulg.: 'your'] mortal bodies, because of His Spirit that dwelleth in us [Vulg.: 'you']." And thus it could fall under Christ's merit.

Reply Obj. 4: The manifestation of Christ's excellence is His good as regards the being which it has in the knowledge of others; although in regard to the being which they have in themselves it chiefly belongs to the good of those who know Him. Yet even this is referred to Christ inasmuch as they are His members.

FOURTH ARTICLE [III, Q. 19, Art. 4]

Whether Christ Could Merit for Others?

Objection 1: It would seem that Christ could not merit for others. For it is written (Ezech. 18:4): "The soul that sinneth, the same shall die." Hence, for a like reason, the soul that meriteth, the same shall be recompensed. Therefore it is not possible that Christ merited for others.

Obj. 2: Further, of the fulness of Christ's grace we all receive, as is written John 1:16. Now other men having Christ's grace cannot merit for others. For it is written (Ezech. 14:20) that if "Noe and Daniel and Job be in the city [Vulg.: 'the midst thereof'] . . . they shall deliver neither son nor daughter; but they shall only deliver their own souls by their justice." Hence Christ could not merit anything for us.

Obj. 3: Further, the "reward" that we merit is due "according to justice [Vulg.: 'debt'] and not according to grace," as is clear from Rom. 4:4. Therefore if Christ merited our salvation it follows that our salvation is not by God's grace but by justice, and that He acts unjustly with those whom He does not save, since Christ's merit extends to all.

*On the contrary,* It is written (Rom. 5:18): "As by the offense of one, unto all men to condemnation; so also by the justice of one, unto all men to justification of life." But Adam's demerits reached to the condemnation of others. Much more, therefore, does the merit of Christ reach others.

*I answer that,* As stated above (Q. 8, AA. 1, 5), grace was in Christ not merely as in an individual, but also as in the Head of the whole Church, to Whom all are united, as members to a head, who constitute one mystical person. And hence it is that Christ's merit extends to others inasmuch as they are His members; even as in a man the action of the head reaches in a manner to all his members, since it perceives not merely for itself alone, but for all the members.

Reply Obj. 1: The sin of an individual harms himself alone; but the sin of Adam, who was appointed by God to be the principle of the whole nature, is transmitted to others by carnal propagation. So, too, the merit of Christ, Who has been appointed by God to be the head of all men in regard to grace, extends to all His members.

Reply Obj. 2: Others receive of Christ's fulness not indeed the fount of grace, but some particular grace. And hence it need not be that men merit for others, as Christ did.

Reply Obj. 3: As the sin of Adam reaches others only by carnal generation, so, too, the merit of Christ reaches others only by spiritual regeneration, which takes place in baptism; wherein we are incorporated with Christ, according to Gal. 3:27, "As many of you as have been baptized in Christ, have put on Christ"; and it is by grace that it is granted to man to be incorporated with Christ. And thus man's salvation is from grace.

# QUESTION 20

OF CHRIST'S SUBJECTION TO THE FATHER (In Two Articles)

We must now consider such things as belong to Christ in relation to the Father. Some of these things are predicated of Him because of His relation to the Father, e.g. that He was subject to Him, that He prayed to Him, that He ministered, to Him by priesthood. And some are predicated, or may be predicated, of Him because of the Father's relation to Him, e.g. that the Father adopted Him and that He predestined Him.

Hence we must consider (1) Christ's subjection to the Father; (2) His prayer; (3) His priesthood; (4) Adoption--whether it is becoming to Him; (5) His predestination.

Under the first head there are two points of inquiry:

(1) Whether Christ is subject to the Father?

(2) Whether He is subject to Himself?

FIRST ARTICLE [III, Q. 20, Art. 1]

Whether We May Say That Christ Is Subject to the Father?

Objection 1: It would seem that we may not say that Christ was subject to the Father. For everything subject to the Father is a creature, since, as is said in De Eccles. Dogm. iv, "in the Trinity there is no dependence or subjection." But we cannot say simply that Christ is a creature, as was stated above (Q. 16, A. 8). Therefore we cannot say simply that Christ is subject to God the Father.

Obj. 2: Further, a thing is said to be subject to God when it is subservient to His dominion. But we cannot attribute subservience to the human nature of Christ; for Damascene says (De Fide Orth. iii, 21): "We must bear in mind that we may not call it" (i.e. Christ's human nature) "a servant; for the words 'subservience' and 'domination' are not names of the nature, but of relations, as the words 'paternity' and 'filiation.'" Hence Christ in His human nature is not subject to God the Father.

Obj. 3: Further, it is written (1 Cor. 15:28): "And when all things shall be subdued unto Him, then the Son also Himself shall be subject unto Him that put all things under Him." But, as is written (Heb. 2:8): "We see not as yet all things subject to Him." Hence He is not yet subject to the Father, Who has subjected all things to Him.

*On the contrary,* Our Lord says (John 14:28), "The Father is greater than I"; and Augustine says (De Trin. i, 7): "It is not without reason that the Scripture mentions both, that the Son is equal to the Father and the Father greater than the Son, for the first is said on account of the form of God, and the second on account of the form of a servant, without any confusion." Now the less is subject to the greater. Therefore in the form of a servant Christ is subject to the Father.

*I answer that,* Whoever has a nature is competent to have what is proper to that nature. Now human nature from its beginning has a threefold subjection to God. The first regards the degree of goodness, inasmuch as the Divine Nature is the very essence of goodness as is clear from Dionysius (Div. Nom. i) while a created nature has a participation of the Divine goodness, being subject, so to say, to the rays of this goodness. Secondly, human nature is subject to God, as regards God's power, inasmuch as human nature, even as every creature, is subject to the operation of the Divine ordinance. Thirdly, human nature is especially subject to God through its proper act, inasmuch as by its own will it obeys His command. This triple subjection to God Christ professes of Himself. The first (Matt. 19:17): "Why askest thou Me concerning good? One is good, God." And on this Jerome remarks: "He who had called Him a good master, and had not confessed Him to be God or the Son of God, learns that no man, however holy, is good in comparison with God." And hereby He gave us to understand that He Himself, in His human nature, did not attain to the height of Divine goodness. And because "in such things as are great, but not in bulk, to be great is the same as to be good," as Augustine says (De Trin. vi, 8), for this reason the Father is said to be greater than Christ in His human nature. The second subjection is attributed to Christ, inasmuch as all that befell Christ is believed to have happened by Divine appointment; hence Dionysius says (Coel. Hier. iv) that Christ "is subject to the ordinance of God the Father." And this is the subjection of subservience, whereby "every creature serves God" (Judith 16:17), being subject to His ordinance, according to Wis. 16:24: "The creature serving Thee the Creator." And in this way the Son of God (Phil. 2:7) is said to have taken "the form of a servant." The third subjection He attributes to Himself, saying (John 8:29): "I do always the things that please Him." And this is the subjection to the Father, of obedience unto death. Hence it is written (Phil. 2:8) that he became "obedient" to the Father "unto death."

Reply Obj. 1: As we are not to understand that Christ is a creature simply, but only in His human nature, whether this qualification be added or not, as stated above (Q. 16, A. 8), so also we are to understand that Christ is subject to the Father not simply but in His human nature, even if this qualification be not added; and yet it is better to add this qualification in order to avoid the error of Arius, who held the Son to be less than the Father.

Reply Obj. 2: The relation of subservience and dominion is based upon action and passion, inasmuch as it belongs to a servant to be moved by the will of his master. Now to act is not attributed to the nature as agent, but to the person, since "acts belong to supposita and to singulars," according to the Philosopher (Metaph. i, 1). Nevertheless action is attributed to the nature as to that whereby the person or hypostasis acts. Hence, although the nature is not properly said to rule or serve, yet every hypostasis or person may be properly said to be ruling or serving in this or that nature. And in this way nothing prevents Christ being subject or servant to the Father in human nature.

Reply Obj. 3: As Augustine says (De Trin. i, 8): "Christ will give the kingdom to God and the Father, when He has brought the faithful, over whom He now reigns by faith, to the vision," i.e. to see the essence common to the Father and the Son: and then He will be totally subject to the Father not only in Himself, but also in His members by the full participation of the Godhead. And then all things will be fully subject to Him by the final accomplishment of His will concerning them; although even now all things are subject to Him as regards His power, according to Matt. 28:18: "All power is given to Me in heaven and in earth."

SECOND ARTICLE [III, Q. 20, Art. 2]

Whether Christ Is Subject to Himself?

Objection 1: It would seem that Christ is not subject to Himself. For Cyril says in a synodal letter which the Council of Ephesus (Part I, ch. xxvi) received: "Christ is neither servant nor master of Himself. It is foolish, or rather impious, to think or say this." And Damascene says the same (De Fide Orth. iii, 21): "The one Being, Christ, cannot be the servant or master of Himself." Now Christ is said to be the servant of the Father inasmuch as He is subject to Him. Hence Christ is not subject to Himself.

Obj. 2: Further, servant has reference to master. Now nothing has a relation to itself, hence Hilary says (De Trin. vii) that nothing is like or equal to itself. Hence Christ cannot be said to be the servant of Himself, and consequently to be subject to Himself.

Obj. 3: Further, "as the rational soul and flesh are one man; so God and man are one Christ," as Athanasius says (Symb. Fid.). Now man is not said to be subject to himself or servant to himself or greater than himself because his body is subject to his soul. Therefore, Christ is not said to be subject to Himself because His Manhood is subject to His Godhead.

*On the contrary,* Augustine says (De Trin. i, 7): "Truth shows in this way" (i.e. whereby the Father is greater than Christ in human nature) "that the Son is less than Himself."

Further, as he argues (De Trin. i, 7), the form of a servant was so taken by the Son of God that the form of God was not lost. But because of the form of God, which is common to the Father and the Son, the Father is greater than the Son in human nature. Therefore the Son is greater than Himself in human nature.

Further, Christ in His human nature is the servant of God the Father, according to John 20:17: "I ascend to My Father and to your Father to My God and your God." Now whoever is the servant of the Father is the servant of the Son; otherwise not everything that belongs to the Father would belong to the Son. Therefore Christ is His own servant and is subject to Himself.

*I answer that,* As was said above (A. 1, ad 2), to be master or servant is attributed to a person or hypostasis according to a nature. Hence when it is said that Christ is the master or servant of Himself, or that the Word of God is the Master of the Man Christ, this may be understood in two ways. First, so that this is understood to be said by reason of another hypostasis or person, as if there was the person of the Word of God ruling and the person of the man serving; and this is the heresy of Nestorius. Hence in the condemnation of Nestorius it is said in the Council of Ephesus (Part III, ch. i, anath. 6): "If anyone say that the Word begotten of God the Father is the God or Lord of Christ, and does not rather confess the same to be at once God and man as the Word made flesh, according to the Scriptures, let him be anathema." And in this sense it is denied by Cyril and Damascene (Obj. 1); and in the same sense must it be denied that Christ is less than Himself or subject to Himself. Secondly, it may be understood of the diversity of natures in the one person or hypostasis. And thus we may say that in one of them, in which He agrees with the Father, He presides and rules together with the Father; and in the other nature, in which He agrees with us, He is subject and serves, and in this sense Augustine says that "the Son is less than Himself."

Yet it must be borne in mind that since this name "Christ" is the name of a Person, even as the name "Son," those things can be predicated essentially and absolutely of Christ which belong to Him by reason of the Person, Which is eternal; and especially those relations which seem more properly to pertain to the Person or the hypostasis. But whatever pertains to Him in His human nature is rather to be attributed to Him with a qualification; so that we say that Christ is simply greatest, Lord, Ruler, whereas to be subject or servant or less is to be attributed to Him with the qualification, in His human nature.

Reply Obj. 1: Cyril and Damascene deny that Christ is the head of Himself inasmuch as this implies a plurality of supposita, which is required in order that anyone may be the master of another.

Reply Obj. 2: Simply speaking it is necessary that the master and the servant should be distinct; yet a certain notion of mastership and subservience may be preserved inasmuch as the same one is master of Himself in different respects.

Reply Obj. 3: On account of the divers parts of man, one of which is superior and the other inferior, the Philosopher says (Ethic. v, 11) that there is justice between a man and himself inasmuch as the irascible and concupiscible powers obey reason. Hence this way a man may be said to be subject and subservient to Himself as regards His different parts.

To the other arguments, the reply is clear from what has been said. For Augustine asserts that the Son is less than, or subject to, Himself in His human nature, and not by a diversity of supposita.

## QUESTION 21

OF CHRIST'S PRAYER (In Four Articles)

We must now consider Christ's prayer; and under this head there are four points of inquiry:

(1) Whether it is becoming that Christ should pray?

(2) Whether it pertains to Him in respect of His sensuality?

(3) Whether it is becoming to Him to pray for Himself or only for others?

(4) Whether every prayer of His was heard?

FIRST ARTICLE [III, Q. 21, Art. 1]

Whether It Is Becoming of Christ to Pray?

Objection 1: It would seem unbecoming that Christ should pray. For, as Damascene says (De Fide Orth. iii, 24), "prayer is the asking for becoming things from God." But since Christ could do all things, it does not seem becoming to Him to ask anything from anyone. Therefore it does not seem fitting that Christ should pray.

Obj. 2: Further, we need not ask in prayer for what we know for certain will happen; thus, we do not pray that the sun may rise tomorrow. Nor is it fitting that anyone should ask in prayer for what he knows will not happen. But Christ in all things knew what would happen. Therefore it was not fitting that He should ask anything in prayer.

Obj. 3: Further, Damascene says (De Fide Orth. iii, 24) that "prayer is the raising up of the mind to God." Now Christ's mind needed no uplifting to God, since His mind was always united to God, not only by the union of the hypostasis, but by the fruition of beatitude. Therefore it was not fitting that Christ should pray.

*On the contrary,* It is written (Luke 6:12): "And it came to pass in those days, that He went out into a mountain, and He passed the whole night in the prayer of God."

*I answer that,* As was said in the Second Part (Q. 83, AA. 1, 2), prayer is the unfolding of our will to God, that He may fulfill it. If, therefore, there had been but one will in Christ, viz. the Divine, it would nowise belong to Him to pray, since the Divine will of itself is effective of whatever He wishes by it, according to Ps. 134:6: "Whatsoever the Lord pleased, He hath done." But because the Divine and the human wills are distinct in Christ, and the human will of itself is not efficacious enough to do what it wishes, except by Divine power, hence to pray belongs to Christ as man and as having a human will.

Reply Obj. 1: Christ as God and not as man was able to carry out all He wished, since as man He was not omnipotent, as stated above (Q. 13, A. 1). Nevertheless being both God and man, He wished to offer prayers to the Father, not as though He were incompetent, but for our instruction. First, that He might show Himself to be from the Father; hence He says (John 11:42): "Because of the people who stand about I have said it" (i.e. the words of the prayer) "that they may believe that Thou hast sent Me." Hence Hilary says (De Trin. x): "He did not need prayer. It was for us He prayed, lest the Son should be unknown." Secondly, to give us an example of prayer; hence Ambrose says (on Luke 6:12): "Be not deceived, nor think that the Son of God prays as a weakling, in order to beseech what He cannot effect. For the Author of power, the Master of obedience persuades us to the precepts of virtue by His example." Hence Augustine says (Tract. civ in Joan.): "Our Lord in the form of a servant could have prayed in silence, if need be, but He wished to show Himself a suppliant of the Father, in such sort as to bear in mind that He was our Teacher."

Reply Obj. 2: Amongst the other things which He knew would happen, He knew that some would be brought about by His prayer; and for these He not unbecomingly besought God.

Reply Obj. 3: To rise is nothing more than to move towards what is above. Now movement is taken in two ways, as is said De Anima iii, 7; first, strictly, according as it implies the passing from potentiality to act, inasmuch as it is the act of something imperfect, and thus to rise pertains to what is potentially and not actually above. Now in this sense, as Damascene says (De Fide Orth. iii, 24), "the human mind of Christ did not need to rise to God, since it was ever united to God both by personal being and by the blessed vision." Secondly, movement signifies the act of something perfect, i.e. something existing in act, as to understand and to feel are called movements; and in this sense the mind of Christ was always raised up to God, since He was always contemplating Him as existing above Himself.

SECOND ARTICLE [III, Q. 21, Art. 2]

Whether It Pertains to Christ to Pray According to His Sensuality?

Objection 1: It would seem that it pertains to Christ to pray according to His sensuality. For it is written (Ps. 83:3) in the person of Christ: "My heart and My flesh have rejoiced in the Living God." Now sensuality is called the appetite of the flesh. Hence Christ's sensuality could ascend to the Living God by rejoicing; and with equal reason by praying.

Obj. 2: Further, prayer would seem to pertain to that which desires what is besought. Now Christ besought something that His sensuality desired when He said (Matt. 26:39): "Let this chalice pass from Me." Therefore Christ's sensuality prayed.

Obj. 3: Further, it is a greater thing to be united to God in person than to mount to Him in prayer. But the sensuality was assumed by God to the unity of Person, even as every other part of human nature. Much more, therefore, could it mount to God by prayer.

*On the contrary,* It is written (Phil. 2:7) that the Son of God in the nature that He assumed was "made in the likeness of men." But the rest of men do not pray with their sensuality. Therefore, neither did Christ pray according to His sensuality.

*I answer that,* To pray according to sensuality may be understood in two ways. First as if prayer itself were an act of the sensuality; and in this sense Christ did not pray with His sensuality, since His sensuality was of the same nature and species in Christ as in us. Now in us the sensuality cannot pray for two reasons; first because the movement of the sensuality cannot transcend sensible things, and, consequently, it cannot mount to God, which is required for prayer; secondly, because prayer implies a certain ordering inasmuch as we desire something to be fulfilled by God; and this is the work of reason alone. Hence prayer is an act of the reason, as was said in the Second Part (II-II, Q. 83, A. 1).

Secondly, we may be said to pray according to the sensuality when our prayer lays before God what is in our appetite of sensuality; and in this sense Christ prayed with His sensuality inasmuch as His prayer expressed the desire of His sensuality, as if it were the advocate of the sensuality--and this, that He might teach us three things. First, to show that He had taken a true human nature, with all its natural affections: secondly, to show that a man may wish with his natural desire what God does not wish: thirdly, to show that man should subject his own will to the Divine will. Hence Augustine says in the Enchiridion (Serm. 1 in Ps. 32): "Christ acting as a man, shows the proper will of a man when He says 'Let this chalice pass from Me'; for this was the human will desiring something proper to itself and, so to say, private. But because He wishes man to be righteous and to be directed to God, He adds: 'Nevertheless not as I will but as Thou wilt,' as if to say, 'See thyself in Me, for thou canst desire something proper to thee, even though God wishes something else.'"

Reply Obj. 1: The flesh rejoices in the Living God, not by the act of the flesh mounting to God, but by the outpouring of the heart into the flesh, inasmuch as the sensitive appetite follows the movement of the rational appetite.

Reply Obj. 2: Although the sensuality wished what the reason besought, it did not belong to the sensuality to seek this by praying, but to the reason, as stated above.

Reply Obj. 3: The union in person is according to the personal being, which pertains to every part of the human nature; but the uplifting of prayer is by an act which pertains only to the reason, as stated above. Hence there is no parity.

THIRD ARTICLE [III, Q. 21, Art. 3]

Whether It Was Fitting That Christ Should Pray for Himself?

Objection 1: It would seem that it was not fitting that Christ should pray for Himself. For Hilary says (De Trin. x): "Although His word of beseeching did not benefit Himself, yet He spoke for the profit of our faith." Hence it seems that Christ prayed not for Himself but for us.

Obj. 2: Further, no one prays save for what He wishes, because, as was said (A. 1), prayer is an unfolding of our will to God that He may fulfil it. Now Christ wished to suffer what He suffered. For Augustine says (Contra Faust. xxvi): "A man, though unwilling, is often angry; though unwilling, is sad; though unwilling, sleeps; though unwilling, hungers and thirsts. But He" (i.e. Christ) "did all these things, because He wished." Therefore it was not fitting that He should pray for Himself.

Obj. 3: Further, Cyprian says (De Orat. Dom.): "The Doctor of Peace and Master of Unity did not wish prayers to be offered individually and privately, lest when we prayed we should pray for ourselves alone." Now Christ did what He taught, according to Acts 1:1: "Jesus began to do and to teach." Therefore Christ never prayed for Himself alone.

*On the contrary,* our Lord Himself said while praying (John 17:1): "Glorify Thy Son."

*I answer that,* Christ prayed for Himself in two ways. First, by expressing the desire of His sensuality, as stated above (A. 2); or also of His simple will, considered as a nature; as when He prayed that the chalice of His Passion might pass from Him (Matt. 26:39). Secondly, by expressing the desire of His deliberate will, which is considered as reason; as when He prayed for the glory of His Resurrection (John 17:1). And this is reasonable. For as we have said above (A. 1, ad 1) Christ wished to pray to His Father in order to give us an example of praying; and also to show that His Father is the author both of His eternal procession in the Divine Nature, and of all the good that He possesses in the human nature. Now just as in His human nature He had already received certain gifts from His Father. so there were other gifts which He had not yet received, but which He expected to receive. And therefore, as He gave thanks to the Father for gifts already received in His human nature, by acknowledging Him as the author thereof, as we read (Matt. 26:27; John 11:41): so also, in recognition of His Father, He besought Him in prayer for those gifts still due to Him in His human nature, such as the glory of His body, and the like. And in this He gave us an example, that we should give thanks for benefits received, and ask in prayer for those we have not as yet.

Reply Obj. 1: Hilary is speaking of vocal prayer, which was not necessary to Him for His own sake, but only for ours. Whence he says pointedly that "His word of beseeching did not benefit Himself." For if "the Lord hears the desire of the poor," as is said in the Ps. 9:38, much more the mere will of Christ has the force of a prayer with the Father: wherefore He said (John 11:42): "I know that Thou hearest Me always, but because of the people who stand about have I said it, that they may believe that Thou hast sent Me."

Reply Obj. 2: Christ wished indeed to suffer what He suffered, at that particular time: nevertheless He wished to obtain, after His passion, the glory of His body, which as yet He had not. This glory He expected to receive from His Father as the author thereof, and therefore it was fitting that He should pray to Him for it.

Reply Obj. 3: This very glory which Christ, while praying, besought for Himself, pertained to the salvation of others according to Rom. 4:25: "He rose again for our justification." Consequently the prayer which He offered for Himself was also in a manner offered for others. So also anyone that asks a boon of God that he may use it for the good of others, prays not only for himself, but also for others.

FOURTH ARTICLE [III, Q. 21, Art. 4]

Whether Christ's Prayer Was Always Heard?

Objection 1: It would seem that Christ's prayer was not always heard. For He besought that the chalice of His passion might be taken from Him, as we read (Matt. 26:39): and yet it was not taken from Him. Therefore it seems that not every prayer of His was heard.

Obj. 2: Further, He prayed that the sin of those who crucified Him might be forgiven, as is related (Luke 23:34). Yet not all were pardoned this sin, since the Jews were punished on account thereof. Therefore it seems that not every prayer of His was heard.

Obj. 3: Further, our Lord prayed for them "who would believe in Him through the word" of the apostles, that they "might all be one in Him," and that they might attain to being with Him (John 17:20, 21, 24). But not all attain to this. Therefore not every prayer of His was heard.

Obj. 4: Further, it is said (Ps. 21:3) in the person of Christ: "I shall cry by day, and Thou wilt not hear." Not every prayer of His, therefore, was heard.

*On the contrary,* The Apostle says (Heb. 5:7): "With a strong cry and tears offering up prayers . . . He was heard for His reverence."

*I answer that,* As stated above (A. 1), prayer is a certain manifestation of the human will. Wherefore, then is the request of one who prays granted, when his will is fulfilled. Now absolutely speaking the will of man is the will of reason; for we will absolutely that which we will in accordance with reason's deliberation. Whereas what we will in accordance with the movement of sensuality, or even of the simple will, which is considered as nature is willed not absolutely but conditionally ( secundum quid )--that is, provided no obstacle be discovered by reason's deliberation. Wherefore such a will should rather be called a "velleity" than an absolute will; because one would will ( vellet ) if there were no obstacle.

But according to the will of reason, Christ willed nothing but what He knew God to will. Wherefore every absolute will of Christ, even human, was fulfilled, because it was in conformity with God; and consequently His every prayer was fulfilled. For in this respect also is it that other men's prayers are fulfilled, in that their will is in conformity with God, according to Rom. 8:27: "And He that searcheth the hearts knoweth," that is, approves of, "what the Spirit desireth," that is, what the Spirit makes the saints to desire: "because He asketh for the saints according to God," that is, in conformity with the Divine will.

Reply Obj. 1: This prayer for the passing of the chalice is variously explained by the Saints. For Hilary (Super Matth. 31) says: "When He asks that this may pass from Him, He does not pray that it may pass by Him, but that others may share in that which passes on from Him to them; So that the sense is: As I am partaking of the chalice of the passion, so may others drink of it, with unfailing hope, with unflinching anguish, without fear of death."

Or according to Jerome (on Matt. 26:39): "He says pointedly, 'This chalice,' that is of the Jewish people, who cannot allege ignorance as an excuse for putting Me to death, since they have the Law and the Prophets, who foretold concerning Me."

Or, according to Dionysius of Alexandria (De Martyr. ad Origen 7): "When He says 'Remove this chalice from Me,' He does not mean, 'Let it not come to Me'; for if it come not, it cannot be removed. But, as that which passes is neither untouched nor yet permanent, so the Saviour beseeches, that a slightly pressing trial may be repulsed."

Lastly, Ambrose, Origen and Chrysostom say that He prayed thus "as man," being reluctant to die according to His natural will.

Thus, therefore, whether we understand, according to Hilary, that He thus prayed that other martyrs might be imitators of His Passion, or that He prayed that the fear of drinking His chalice might not trouble Him, or that death might not withhold Him, His prayer was entirely fulfilled. But if we understand that He prayed that He might not drink the chalice of His passion and death; or that He might not drink it at the hands of the Jews; what He besought was not indeed fulfilled, because His reason which formed the petition did not desire its fulfilment, but for our instruction, it was His will to make known to us His natural will, and the movement of His sensuality, which was His as man.

Reply Obj. 2: Our Lord did not pray for all those who crucified Him, as neither did He for all those who would believe in Him; but for those only who were predestinated to obtain eternal life through Him.

Wherefore the reply to the third objection is also manifest.

Reply Obj. 4: When He says: "I shall cry and Thou wilt not hear," we must take this as referring to the desire of sensuality, which shunned death. But He is heard as to the desire of His reason, as stated above.

## QUESTION 22

OF THE PRIESTHOOD OF CHRIST (In Six Articles)

We have now to consider the Priesthood of Christ; and under this head there are six points of inquiry:

(1) Whether it is fitting that Christ should be a priest?

(2) Of the victim offered by this priest;

(3) Of the effect of this priesthood;

(4) Whether the effect of His priesthood pertains to Himself, or only to others?

(5) Of the eternal duration of His priesthood;

(6) Whether He should be called "a priest according to the order of Melchisedech"?

FIRST ARTICLE [III, Q. 22, Art. 1]

Whether It Is Fitting That Christ Should Be a Priest?

Objection 1: It would seem unfitting that Christ should be a priest. For a priest is less than an angel; whence it is written (Zech. 3:1): "The Lord showed me the high-priest standing before the angel of the Lord." But Christ is greater than the angels, according to Heb. 1:4: "Being made so much better than the angels, as He hath inherited a more excellent name than they." Therefore it is unfitting that Christ should be a priest.

Obj. 2: Further, things which were in the Old Testament were figures of Christ, according to Col. 2:17: "Which are a shadow of things to come, but the body is Christ's." But Christ was not descended from the priests of the Old Law, for the Apostle says (Heb. 7:14): "It is evident that our Lord sprang out of Judah, in which tribe Moses spoke nothing concerning priests." Therefore it is not fitting that Christ should be a priest.

Obj. 3: Further, in the Old Law, which is a figure of Christ, the lawgivers and the priests were distinct: wherefore the Lord said to Moses the lawgiver (Ex. 28:1): "Take unto thee Aaron, thy brother . . . that he [Vulg.: 'they'] may minister to Me in the priest's office." But Christ is the giver of the New Law, according to Jer. 31:33: "I will give My law in their bowels." Therefore it is unfitting that Christ should be a priest.

*On the contrary,* It is written (Heb. 4:14): "We have [Vulg.: 'Having'] therefore a great high-priest that hath passed into the heavens, Jesus, the Son of God."

*I answer that,* The office proper to a priest is to be a mediator between God and the people: to wit, inasmuch as He bestows Divine things on the people, wherefore sacerdos (priest) means a giver of sacred things ( sacra dans ), according to Malachi 2:7: "They shall seek the law at his," i.e. the priest's, "mouth"; and again, forasmuch as he offers up the people's prayers to God, and, in a manner, makes satisfaction to God for their sins; wherefore the Apostle says (Heb. 5:1): "Every high-priest taken from among men is ordained for men in the things that appertain to God, that he may offer up gifts and sacrifices for sins." Now this is most befitting to Christ. For through Him are gifts bestowed on men, according to 2 Pet. 1:4: "By Whom" (i.e. Christ) "He hath given us most great and precious promises, that by these you may be made partakers of the Divine Nature." Moreover, He reconciled the human race to God, according to Col. 1:19, 20: "In Him" (i.e. Christ) "it hath well pleased (the Father) that all fulness should dwell, and through Him to reconcile all things unto Himself." Therefore it is most fitting that Christ should be a priest.

Reply Obj. 1: Hierarchical power appertains to the angels, inasmuch as they also are between God and man, as Dionysius explains (Coel. Hier. ix), so that the priest himself, as being between God and man, is called an angel, according to Malachi 2:7: "He is the angel of the Lord of hosts." Now Christ was greater than the angels, not only in His Godhead, but also in His humanity, as having the fulness of grace and glory. Wherefore also He had the hierarchical or priestly power in a higher degree than the angels, so that even the angels were ministers of His priesthood, according to Matt. 4:11: "Angels came and ministered unto Him." But, in regard to His passibility, He "was made a little lower than the angels," as the Apostle says (Heb. 2:9): and thus He was conformed to those wayfarers who are ordained to the priesthood.

Reply Obj. 2: As Damascene says (De Fide Orth. iii, 26): "What is like in every particular must be, of course, identical, and not a copy." Since, therefore, the priesthood of the Old Law was a figure of the priesthood of Christ, He did not wish to be born of the stock of the figurative priests, that it might be made clear that His priesthood is not quite the same as theirs, but differs therefrom as truth from figure.

Reply Obj. 3: As stated above (Q. 7, A. 7, ad 1), other men have certain graces distributed among them: but Christ, as being the Head of all, has the perfection of all graces. Wherefore, as to others, one is a lawgiver, another is a priest, another is a king; but all these concur in Christ, as the fount of all grace. Hence it is written (Isa. 33:22): "The Lord is our Judge, the Lord is our law-giver, the Lord is our King: He will" come and "save us."

SECOND ARTICLE [III, Q. 22, Art. 2]

Whether Christ Was Himself Both Priest and Victim?

Objection 1: It would seem that Christ Himself was not both priest and victim. For it is the duty of the priest to slay the victim. But Christ did not kill Himself. Therefore He was not both priest and victim.

Obj. 2: Further, the priesthood of Christ has a greater similarity to the Jewish priesthood, instituted by God, than to the priesthood of the Gentiles, by which the demons were worshiped. Now in the old Law man was never offered up in sacrifice: whereas this was very much to be reprehended in the sacrifices of the Gentiles, according to Ps. 105:38: "They shed innocent blood; the blood of their sons and of their daughters, which they sacrificed to the idols of Chanaan." Therefore in Christ's priesthood the Man Christ should not have been the victim.

Obj. 3: Further, every victim, through being offered to God, is consecrated to God. But the humanity of Christ was from the beginning consecrated and united to God. Therefore it cannot be said fittingly that Christ as man was a victim.

*On the contrary,* The Apostle says (Eph. 5:2): "Christ hath loved us, and hath delivered Himself for us, an oblation and a victim [Douay: 'sacrifice'] to God for an odor of sweetness."

*I answer that,* As Augustine says (De Civ. Dei x, 5): "Every visible sacrifice is a sacrament, that is a sacred sign, of the invisible sacrifice." Now the invisible sacrifice is that by which a man offers his spirit to God, according to Ps. 50:19: "A sacrifice to God is an afflicted spirit." Wherefore, whatever is offered to God in order to raise man's spirit to Him, may be called a sacrifice.

Now man is required to offer sacrifice for three reasons. First, for the remission of sin, by which he is turned away from God. Hence the Apostle says (Heb. 5:1) that it appertains to the priest "to offer gifts and sacrifices for sins." Secondly, that man may be preserved in a state of grace, by ever adhering to God, wherein his peace and salvation consist. Wherefore under the old Law the sacrifice of peace-offerings was offered up for the salvation of the offerers, as is prescribed in the third chapter of Leviticus. Thirdly, in order that the spirit of man be perfectly united to God: which will be most perfectly realized in glory. Hence, under the Old Law, the holocaust was offered, so called because the victim was wholly burnt, as we read in the first chapter of Leviticus.

Now these effects were conferred on us by the humanity of Christ. For, in the first place, our sins were blotted out, according to Rom. 4:25: "Who was delivered up for our sins." Secondly, through Him we received the grace of salvation, according to Heb. 5:9: "He became to all that obey Him the cause of eternal salvation." Thirdly, through Him we have acquired the perfection of glory, according to Heb. 10:19: "We have [Vulg.: 'Having'] a confidence in the entering into the Holies" (i.e. the heavenly glory) "through His Blood." Therefore Christ Himself, as man, was not only priest, but also a perfect victim, being at the same time victim for sin, victim for a peace-offering, and a holocaust.

Reply Obj. 1: Christ did not slay Himself, but of His own free-will He exposed Himself to death, according to Isa. 53:7: "He was offered because it was His own will." Thus He is said to have offered Himself.

Reply Obj. 2: The slaying of the Man Christ may be referred to a twofold will. First, to the will of those who slew Him: and in this respect He was not a victim: for the slayers of Christ are not accounted as offering a sacrifice to God, but as guilty of a great crime: a similitude of which was borne by the wicked sacrifices of the Gentiles, in which they offered up men to idols. Secondly, the slaying of Christ may be considered in reference to the will of the Sufferer, Who freely offered Himself to suffering. In this respect He is a victim, and in this He differs from the sacrifices of the Gentiles.

(The reply to the third objection is wanting in the original manuscripts, but it may be gathered from the above.--Ed.)

[*Some editions, however, give the following reply:

Reply Obj. 3: The fact that Christ's manhood was holy from its beginning does not prevent that same manhood, when it was offered to God in the Passion, being sanctified in a new way--namely, as a victim actually offered then. For it acquired then the actual holiness of a victim, from the charity which it had from the beginning, and from the grace of union sanctifying it absolutely.]

THIRD ARTICLE [III, Q. 22, Art. 3]

Whether the Effect of Christ's Priesthood Is the Expiation of Sins?

Objection 1: It would seem that the effect of Christ's priesthood is not the expiation of sins. For it belongs to God alone to blot out sins, according to Isa. 43:25: "I am He that blot out thy iniquities for My own sake." But Christ is priest, not as God, but as man. Therefore the priesthood of Christ does not expiate sins.

Obj. 2: Further, the Apostle says (Heb. 10:1-3) that the victims of the Old Testament could not "make" (the comers thereunto) "perfect: for then they would have ceased to be offered; because the worshipers once cleansed should have no conscience of sin any longer; but in them there is made a commemoration of sins every year." But in like manner under the priesthood of Christ a commemoration of sins is made in the words: "Forgive us our trespasses" (Matt. 6:12). Moreover, the Sacrifice is offered continuously in the Church; wherefore again we say: "Give us this day our daily bread." Therefore sins are not expiated by the priesthood of Christ.

Obj. 3: Further, in the sin-offerings of the Old Law, a he-goat was mostly offered for the sin of a prince, a she-goat for the sin of some private individual, a calf for the sin of a priest, as we gather from Lev. 4:3, 23, 28. But Christ is compared to none of these, but to the lamb, according to Jer. 11:19: "I was as a meek lamb, that is carried to be a victim." Therefore it seems that His priesthood does not expiate sins.

*On the contrary,* The Apostle says (Heb. 9:14): "The blood of Christ, Who by the Holy Ghost offered Himself unspotted unto God, shall cleanse our conscience from dead works, to serve the living God." But dead works denote sins. Therefore the priesthood of Christ has the power to cleanse from sins.

*I answer that,* Two things are required for the perfect cleansing from sins, corresponding to the two things comprised in sin--namely, the stain of sin and the debt of punishment. The stain of sin is, indeed, blotted out by grace, by which the sinner's heart is turned to God: whereas the debt of punishment is entirely removed by the satisfaction that man offers to God. Now the priesthood of Christ produces both these effects. For by its virtue grace is given to us, by which our hearts are turned to

God, according to Rom. 3:24, 25: "Being justified freely by His grace, through the redemption that is in Christ Jesus, Whom God hath proposed to be a propitiation, through faith in His blood." Moreover, He satisfied for us fully, inasmuch as "He hath borne our infirmities and carried our sorrows" (Isa. 53:4). Wherefore it is clear that the priesthood of Christ has full power to expiate sins.

Reply Obj. 1: Although Christ was a priest, not as God, but as man, yet one and the same was both priest and God. Wherefore in the Council of Ephesus [*Part III, ch. i, anath. 10] we read: "If anyone say that the very Word of God did not become our High-Priest and Apostle, when He became flesh and a man like us, but altogether another one, the man born of a woman, let him be anathema." Hence in so far as His human nature operated by virtue of the Divine, that sacrifice was most efficacious for the blotting out of sins. For this reason Augustine says (De Trin. iv, 14): "So that, since four things are to be observed in every sacrifice--to whom it is offered, by whom it is offered, what is offered, for whom it is offered; the same one true Mediator reconciling us to God by the sacrifice of peace, was one with Him to Whom it was offered, united in Himself those for whom He offered it, at the same time offered it Himself, and was Himself that which He offered."

Reply Obj. 2: Sins are commemorated in the New Law, not on account of the inefficacy of the priesthood of Christ, as though sins were not sufficiently expiated by Him: but in regard to those who either are not willing to be participators in His sacrifice, such as unbelievers, for whose sins we pray that they be converted; or who, after taking part in this sacrifice, fall away from it by whatsoever kind of sin. The Sacrifice which is offered every day in the Church is not distinct from that which Christ Himself offered, but is a commemoration thereof. Wherefore Augustine says (De Civ. De. x, 20): "Christ Himself both is the priest who offers it and the victim: the sacred token of which He wished to be the daily Sacrifice of the Church."

Reply Obj. 3: As Origen says (Sup. Joan. i, 29), though various animals were offered up under the Old Law, yet the daily sacrifice, which was offered up morning and evening, was a lamb, as appears from Num. 38:3, 4. By which it was signified that the offering up of the true lamb, i.e. Christ, was the culminating sacrifice of all. Hence (John 1:29) it is said: "Behold the Lamb of God, behold Him Who taketh away the sins [Vulg.: 'sin'] of the world."

FOURTH ARTICLE [III, Q. 22, Art. 4]

Whether the Effect of the Priesthood of Christ Pertained Not Only to Others, but Also to Himself?

Objection 1: It would seem that the effect of the priesthood of Christ pertained not only to others, but also to Himself. For it belongs to the priest's office to pray for the people, according to 2 Macc. 1:23: "The priests made prayer while the sacrifice was consuming." Now Christ prayed not only for others, but also for Himself, as we have said above (Q. 21, A. 3), and as expressly stated (Heb. 5:7): "In the days of His flesh, with a strong cry and tears He offered [Vulg.: 'offering'] up prayers and supplications to Him that was able to save Him from death." Therefore the priesthood of Christ had an effect not only in others, but also in Himself.

Obj. 2: Further, in His passion Christ offered Himself as a sacrifice. But by His passion He merited, not only for others, but also for Himself, as stated above (Q. 19, AA. 3, 4). Therefore the priesthood of Christ had an effect not only in others, but also in Himself.

Obj. 3: Further, the priesthood of the Old Law was a figure of the priesthood of Christ. But the priest of the Old Law offered sacrifice not only for others, but also for himself: for it is written (Lev. 16:17) that "the high-priest goeth into the sanctuary to pray for himself and his house, and for the whole congregation of Israel." Therefore the priesthood of Christ also had an effect not merely in others, but also in Himself.

*On the contrary,* We read in the acts of the Council of Ephesus [*Part III, ch. i, anath. 10]: "If anyone say that Christ offered sacrifice for Himself, and not rather for us alone (for He Who knew not sin needed no sacrifice), let him be anathema." But the priest's office consists principally in offering sacrifice. Therefore the priesthood of Christ had no effect in Himself.

*I answer that,* As stated above (A. 1), a priest is set between God and man. Now he needs someone between himself and God, who of himself cannot approach to God; and such a one is subject to the priesthood by sharing in the effect thereof. But this cannot be said of Christ; for the Apostle says (Heb. 7:25): "Coming of Himself to God, always living to make intercession for us [Vulg.: 'He is able to save for ever them that come to God by Him; always living,' etc.]." And therefore it is not fitting for Christ to be the recipient of the effect of His priesthood, but rather to communicate it to others. For the influence of the first agent in every genus is such that it receives nothing in that genus: thus the sun gives but does not receive light; fire gives but does not receive heat. Now Christ is the fountain-head of the entire priesthood: for the priest of the Old Law was a figure of Him; while the priest of the New Law works in His person, according to 2 Cor. 2:10: "For what I have pardoned, if I have pardoned anything, for your sakes have I done it in the person of Christ." Therefore it is not fitting that Christ should receive the effect of His priesthood.

Reply Obj. 1: Although prayer is befitting to priests, it is not their proper office, for it is befitting to everyone to pray both for himself and for others, according to James 5:16: "Pray for one another that you may be saved." And so we may say that the prayer by which Christ prayed for Himself was not an action of His priesthood. But this answer seems to be precluded by the Apostle, who, after saying (Heb. 5:6), "Thou art a priest for ever according to the order of Melchisedech," adds, "Who in the days of His flesh offering up payers," etc., as quoted above (Obj. 1): so that it seems that the prayer which Christ offered pertained to His priesthood. We must therefore say that other priests partake in the effect of their priesthood, not as priests, but as sinners, as we shall state farther on (ad 3). But Christ had, simply speaking, no sin; though He had the "likeness of sin in the flesh [Vulg.: 'sinful flesh']," as is written Rom. 8:3. And, consequently, we must not say simply that He partook of the effect of His priesthood but with this qualification--in regard to the passibility of the flesh. Wherefore he adds pointedly, "that was able to save Him from death."

Reply Obj. 2: Two things may be considered in the offering of a sacrifice by any priest--namely, the sacrifice itself which is offered, and the devotion of the offerer. Now the proper effect of priesthood is that which results from the sacrifice itself. But Christ obtained a result from His passion, not as by virtue of the sacrifice, which is offered by way of satisfaction, but by the very devotion with which out of charity He humbly endured the passion.

Reply Obj. 3: A figure cannot equal the reality, wherefore the figural priest of the Old Law could not attain to such perfection as not to need a sacrifice of satisfaction. But Christ did not stand in need of this. Consequently, there is no comparison between the two; and this is what the Apostle says (Heb. 7:28): "The Law maketh men priests, who have infirmity; but the word of the oath, which was since the Law, the Son Who is perfected for evermore."

FIFTH ARTICLE [III, Q. 22, Art. 5]

Whether the Priesthood of Christ Endures for Ever?

Objection 1: It would seem that the priesthood of Christ does not endure for ever. For as stated above (A. 4, ad 1, 3) those alone need the effect of the priesthood who have the weakness of sin, which can be expiated by the priest's sacrifice. But this will not be for ever. For in the Saints there will be no weakness, according to Isa. 60:21: "Thy people shall be all just": while no expiation will be possible for the weakness of sin, since "there is no redemption in hell" (Office of the Dead, Resp. vii). Therefore the priesthood of Christ endures not for ever.

Obj. 2: Further, the priesthood of Christ was made manifest most of all in His passion and death, when "by His own blood He entered into the Holies" (Heb. 9:12). But the passion and death of Christ will not endure for ever, as stated Rom. 6:9: "Christ rising again from the dead, dieth now no more." Therefore the priesthood of Christ will not endure for ever.

Obj. 3: Further, Christ is a priest, not as God, but as man. But at one time Christ was not man, namely during the three days He lay dead. Therefore the priesthood of Christ endures not for ever.

*On the contrary,* It is written (Ps. 109:4): "Thou art a priest for ever."

*I answer that,* In the priestly office, we may consider two things: first, the offering of the sacrifice; secondly, the consummation of the sacrifice, consisting in this, that those for whom the sacrifice is offered, obtain the end of the sacrifice. Now the end of the sacrifice which Christ offered consisted not in temporal but in eternal good, which we obtain through His death, according to Heb. 9:11: "Christ is [Vulg.: 'being come'] a high-priest of the good things to come"; for which reason the priesthood of Christ is said to be eternal. Now this consummation of Christ's sacrifice was foreshadowed in this, that the high-priest of the Old Law, once a year, entered into the Holy of Holies with the blood of a he-goat and a calf, as laid down, Lev. 16:11, and yet he offered up the he-goat and calf not within the Holy of Holies, but without. In like manner Christ entered into the Holy of Holies--that is, into heaven--and prepared the way for us, that we might enter by the virtue of His blood, which He shed for us on earth.

Reply Obj. 1: The Saints who will be in heaven will not need any further expiation by the priesthood of Christ, but having expiated, they will need consummation through Christ Himself, on Whom their glory depends, as is written (Apoc. 21:23): "The glory of God hath enlightened it"--that is, the city of the Saints--"and the Lamb is the lamp thereof."

Reply Obj. 2: Although Christ's passion and death are not to be repeated, yet the virtue of that Victim endures for ever, for, as it is written (Heb. 10:14), "by one oblation He hath perfected for ever them that are sanctified."

Wherefore the reply to the third objection is clear.

As to the unity of this sacrifice, it was foreshadowed in the Law in that, once a year, the high-priest of the Law entered into the Holies, with a solemn oblation of blood, as set down, Lev. 16:11. But the figure fell short of the reality in this, that the victim had not an everlasting virtue, for which reason those sacrifices were renewed every year.

SIXTH ARTICLE [III, Q. 22, Art. 6]

Whether the Priesthood of Christ Was According to the Order of Melchisedech?

Objection 1: It would seem that Christ's priesthood was not according to the order of Melchisedech. For Christ is the fountain-head of the entire priesthood, as being the principal priest. Now that which is principal is not secondary in regard to others, but others are secondary in its regard. Therefore Christ should not be called a priest according to the order of Melchisedech.

Obj. 2: Further, the priesthood of the Old Law

was more akin to Christ's priesthood than was the priesthood that existed before the Law. But the nearer the sacraments were to Christ, the more clearly they signified Him; as is clear from what we have said in the Second Part (II-II, Q. 2, A. 7). Therefore the priesthood of Christ should be denominated after the priesthood of the Law, rather than after the order of Melchisedech, which was before the Law.

Obj. 3: Further, it is written (Heb. 7:2, 3): "That is 'king of peace,' without father, without mother, without genealogy; having neither beginning of days nor ending of life": which can be referred only to the Son of God. Therefore Christ should not be called a priest according to the order of Melchisedech, as of some one else, but according to His own order.

*On the contrary,* It is written (Ps. 109:4): "Thou art a priest for ever according to the order of Melchisedech."

*I answer that,* As stated above (A. 4, ad 3) the priesthood of the Law was a figure of the priesthood of Christ, not as adequately representing the reality, but as falling far short thereof: both because the priesthood of the Law did not wash away sins, and because it was not eternal, as the priesthood of Christ. Now the excellence of Christ's over the Levitical priesthood was foreshadowed in the priesthood of Melchisedech, who received tithes from Abraham, in whose loins the priesthood of the Law was tithed. Consequently the priesthood of Christ is said to be "according to the order of Melchisedech," on account of the excellence of the true priesthood over the figural priesthood of the Law.

Reply Obj. 1: Christ is said to be according to the order of Melchisedech not as though the latter were a more excellent priest, but because he foreshadowed the excellence of Christ's over the Levitical priesthood.

Reply Obj. 2: Two things may be considered in Christ's priesthood: namely, the offering made by Christ, and (our) partaking thereof. As to the actual offering, the priesthood of Christ was more distinctly foreshadowed by the priesthood of the Law, by reason of the shedding of blood, than by the priesthood of Melchisedech in which there was no blood-shedding. But if we consider the participation of this sacrifice and the effect thereof, wherein the excellence of Christ's priesthood over the priesthood of the Law principally consists, then the former was more distinctly foreshadowed by the priesthood of Melchisedech, who offered bread and wine, signifying, as Augustine says (Tract. xxvi in Joan.) ecclesiastical unity, which is established by our taking part in the sacrifice of Christ [*Cf. Q. 79, A. 1]. Wherefore also in the New Law the true sacrifice of Christ is presented to the faithful under the form of bread and wine.

Reply Obj. 3: Melchisedech is described as "without father, without mother, without genealogy," and as "having neither beginning of days nor ending of life," not as though he had not these things, but because these details in his regard are not supplied by Holy Scripture. And this it is that, as the Apostle says in the same passage, he is "likened unto the Son of God," Who had no earthly father, no heavenly mother, and no genealogy, according to Isa. 53:8: "Who shall declare His generation?" and Who in His Godhead has neither beginning nor end of days.

## QUESTION 23

OF ADOPTION AS BEFITTING TO CHRIST (In Four Articles)

We must now come to consider whether adoption befits Christ: and under this head there are four points of inquiry:

(1) Whether it is fitting that God should adopt sons?

(2) Whether this is fitting to God the Father alone?

(3) Whether it is proper to man to be adopted to the sonship of God?

(4) Whether Christ can be called the adopted Son?

FIRST ARTICLE [III, Q. 23, Art. 1]

Whether It Is Fitting That God Should Adopt Sons?

Objection 1: It would seem that it is not fitting that God should adopt sons. For, as jurists say, no one adopts anyone but a stranger as his son. But no one is a stranger in relation to God, Who is the Creator of all. Therefore it seems unfitting that God should adopt.

Obj. 2: Further, adoption seems to have been introduced in default of natural sonship. But in God there is natural sonship, as set down in the First Part (Q. 27, A. 2). Therefore it is unfitting that God should adopt.

Obj. 3: Further, the purpose of adopting anyone is that he may succeed, as heir, the person who adopts him. But it does not seem possible for anyone to succeed God as heir, for He can never die. Therefore it is unfitting that God should adopt.

*On the contrary,* It is written (Eph. 1:5) that "He hath predestinated us unto the adoption of children of God." But the predestination of God is not ineffectual. Therefore God does adopt some as His sons.

*I answer that,* A man adopts someone as his son forasmuch as out of goodness he admits him as heir to his estate. Now God is infinitely good: for which reason He admits His creatures to a participation of good things; especially rational creatures, who forasmuch as they are made to the image of God, are capable of Divine beatitude. And this consists in the enjoyment of God, by which also God Himself is happy and rich in Himself--that is, in the enjoyment of Himself. Now a man's inheritance is that which makes him rich. Wherefore, inasmuch as God, of His goodness, admits men to the inheritance of beatitude, He is said to adopt them. Moreover Divine exceeds human adoption, forasmuch as God, by bestowing His grace, makes man whom He adopts worthy to receive the heavenly inheritance; whereas man does not make him worthy whom he adopts; but rather in adopting him he chooses one who is already worthy.

Reply Obj. 1: Considered in his nature man is not a stranger in respect to God, as to the natural gifts bestowed on him: but he is as to the gifts of grace and glory; in regard to which he is adopted.

Reply Obj. 2: Man works in order to supply his wants: not so God, Who works in order to communicate to others the abundance of His perfection. Wherefore, as by the work of creation the Divine goodness is communicated to all creatures in a certain likeness, so by the work of adoption the likeness of natural sonship is communicated to men, according to Rom. 8:29: "Whom He foreknew . . . to be made conformable to the image of His Son."

Reply Obj. 3: Spiritual goods can be possessed by many at the same time; not so material goods. Wherefore none can receive a material inheritance except the successor of a deceased person: whereas all receive the spiritual inheritance at the same time in its entirety without detriment to the ever-living Father.

Yet it might be said that God ceases to be, according as He is in us by faith, so as to begin to be in us by vision, as a gloss says on Rom. 8:17: "If sons, heirs also."

SECOND ARTICLE [III, Q. 23, Art. 2]

Whether It Is Fitting That the Whole Trinity Should Adopt?

Objection 1: It would seem unfitting that the whole Trinity should adopt. For adoption is said of God in likeness to human custom. But among men those only adopt who can beget: and in God this can be applied only to the Father. Therefore in God the Father alone can adopt.

Obj. 2: Further, by adoption men become the brethren of Christ, according to Rom. 8:29: "That He might be the first-born among many brethren." Now brethren are the sons of the same father; wherefore our Lord says (John 20:17): "I ascend to My Father and to your Father." Therefore Christ's Father alone has adopted sons.

Obj. 3: Further, it is written (Gal. 4:4, 5, 6): "God sent His Son . . . that we might receive the adoption of sons. And because you are sons of God, God hath sent the Spirit of His Son into your hearts, crying: 'Abba' (Father)." Therefore it belongs to Him to adopt, Who has the Son and the Holy Ghost. But this belongs to the Father alone. Therefore it befits the Father alone to adopt.

*On the contrary,* It belongs to Him to adopt us as sons, Whom we can call Father; whence it is written (Rom. 8:15): "You have received the spirit of adoption of sons, whereby we cry: 'Abba' (Father)." But when we say to God, "Our Father," we address the whole Trinity: as is the case with the other names which are said of God in respect of creatures, as stated in the First Part (Q. 33, A. 3, Obj. 1; cf. Q. 45, A. 6). Therefore to adopt is befitting to the whole Trinity.

*I answer that,* There is this difference between an adopted son of God and the natural Son of God, that the latter is "begotten not made"; whereas the former is made, according to John 1:12: "He gave them power to be made the sons of God." Yet sometimes the adopted son is said to be begotten, by reason of the spiritual regeneration which is by grace, not by nature; wherefore it is written (James 1:18): "Of His own will hath He begotten us by the word of truth." Now although, in God, to beget belongs to the Person of the Father, yet to produce any effect in creatures is common to the whole Trinity, by reason of the oneness of their Nature: since, where there is one nature, there must needs be one power and one operation: whence our Lord says (John 5:19): "What things soever the Father doth, these the Son also doth in like manner." Therefore it belongs to the whole Trinity to adopt men as sons of God.

Reply Obj. 1: All human individuals are not of one individual nature, so that there need be one operation and one effect of them all, as is the case in God. Consequently in this respect no comparison is possible.

Reply Obj. 2: By adoption we are made the brethren of Christ, as having with Him the same Father: Who, nevertheless, is His Father in one way, and ours in another. Whence pointedly our Lord says, separately, "My Father," and "Your Father" (John 20:17). For He is Christ's Father by natural generation; and this is proper to Him: whereas He is our Father by a voluntary operation, which is common to Him and to the Son and Holy Ghost: so that Christ is not the Son of the whole Trinity, as we are.

Reply Obj. 3: As stated above (A. 1, ad 2), adoptive sonship is a certain likeness of the eternal Sonship: just as all that takes place in time is a certain likeness of what has been from eternity. Now man is likened to the splendor of the Eternal Son by reason of the light of grace which is attributed to the Holy Ghost. Therefore adoption, though common to the whole Trinity, is appropriated to the Father as its author; to the Son, as its exemplar; to the Holy Ghost, as imprinting on us the likeness of this exemplar.

THIRD ARTICLE [III, Q. 23, Art. 3]

Whether It Is Proper to the Rational Nature to Be Adopted?

Objection 1: It would seem that it is not proper to the rational nature to be adopted. For God is not said to be the Father of the rational creature, save by adoption. But God is called the Father even of the irrational creature, according to Job 38:28: "Who is father of the rain? Or who begot the drops of dew?" Therefore it is not proper to the rational creature to be adopted.

Obj. 2: Further, by reason of adoption some are called sons of God. But to be sons of God seems to be properly attributed by the Scriptures to the angels; according to Job 1:6: "On a certain day when the sons of God came to stand before the Lord." Therefore it is not proper to the rational creature to be adopted.

Obj. 3: Further, whatever is proper to a nature, belongs to all that have that nature: just as risibility belongs to all men. But to be adopted does not belong to every rational nature. Therefore it is not proper to human nature.

*On the contrary,* Adopted sons are the "heirs of God," as is stated Rom. 8:17. But such an inheritance belongs to none but the rational nature. Therefore it is proper to the rational nature to be adopted.

*I answer that,* As stated above (A. 2, ad 3), the sonship of adoption is a certain likeness of natural sonship. Now the Son of God proceeds naturally from the Father as the Intellectual Word, in oneness of nature with the Father. To this Word, therefore, something may be likened in three ways. First, on the part of the form but not on the part of its intelligibility: thus the form of a house already built is like the mental word of the builder in its specific form, but not in intelligibility, because the material form of a house is not intelligible, as it was in the mind of the builder. In this way every creature is like the Eternal Word; since it was made through the Word. Secondly, the creature is likened to the Word, not only as to its form, but also as to its intelligibility: thus the knowledge which is begotten in the disciple's mind is likened to the word in the mind of the master. In this way the rational creature, even in its nature, is likened to the Word of God. Thirdly, a creature is likened to the Eternal Word, as to the oneness of the Word with the Father, which is by reason of grace and charity: wherefore our Lord prays (John 17:21, 22): "That they may be one in Us . . . as We also are one." And this likeness perfects the adoption: for to those who are thus like Him the eternal inheritance is due. It is therefore clear that to be adopted belongs to the rational creature alone: not indeed to all, but only to those who have charity; which is "poured forth in our hearts by the Holy Ghost" (Rom. 5:5); for which reason (Rom. 8:15) the Holy Ghost is called "the Spirit of adoption of sons."

Reply Obj. 1: God is called the Father of the irrational creature, not properly speaking, by reason of adoption, but by reason of creation; according to the first-mentioned participation of likeness.

Reply Obj. 2: Angels are called sons of God by adoptive sonship, not that it belongs to them first; but because they were the first to receive the adoption of sons.

Reply Obj. 3: Adoption is a property resulting not from nature, but from grace, of which the rational nature is capable. Therefore it need not belong to every rational nature: but every rational creature must needs be capable of adoption.

FOURTH ARTICLE [III, Q. 23, Art. 4]

Whether Christ As Man Is the Adopted Son of God?

Objection 1: It would seem that Christ as man is the adopted Son of God. For Hilary says (De Trin. ii) speaking of Christ: "The dignity of power is not forfeited when carnal humanity [*Some editions read 'humilitas'--'the humility or lowliness of the flesh'] is adopted." Therefore Christ as man is the adopted Son of God.

Obj. 2: Further, Augustine says (De Praedest. Sanct. xv) that "by the same grace that Man is Christ, as from the birth of faith every man is a Christian." But other men are Christians by the grace of adoption. Therefore this Man is Christ by adoption: and consequently He would seem to be an adopted son.

Obj. 3: Further, Christ, as man, is a servant. But it is of greater dignity to be an adopted son than to be a servant. Therefore much more is Christ, as man, an adopted Son.

*On the contrary,* Ambrose says (De Incarn. viii): "We do not call an adopted son a natural son: the natural son is a true son." But Christ is the true and natural Son of God, according to 1 John 5:20: "That we may . . . be in His true Son, Jesus Christ." Therefore Christ, as Man, is not an adopted Son.

*I answer that,* Sonship belongs properly to the hypostasis or person, not to the nature; whence in the First Part (Q. 32, A. 3) we have stated that Filiation is a personal property. Now in Christ there is no other than the uncreated person or hypostasis, to Whom it belongs by nature to be the Son. But it has been said above (A. 1, ad 2), that the sonship of adoption is a participated likeness of natural sonship: nor can a thing be said to participate in what it has essentially. Therefore Christ, Who is the natural Son of God, can nowise be called an adopted Son.

But according to those who suppose two persons or two hypostases or two supposita in Christ, no reason prevents Christ being called the adopted Son of God.

Reply Obj. 1: As sonship does not properly belong to the nature, so neither does adoption. Consequently, when it is said that "carnal humanity is adopted," the expression is metaphorical: and adoption is used to signify the union of human nature to the Person of the Son.

Reply Obj. 2: This comparison of Augustine is to be referred to the principle because, to wit, just as it is granted to any man without meriting it to be a Christian, so did it happen that this man without meriting it was Christ. But there is a difference on the part of the term: because by the grace of union Christ is the natural Son; whereas another man by habitual grace is an adopted son. Yet habitual grace in Christ does not make one who was not a son to be an adopted son, but is a certain effect of Filiation in the soul of Christ, according to John 1:14: "We saw His glory . . . as it were of the Only-begotten of the Father; full of grace and truth."

Reply Obj. 3: To be a creature, as also to be subservient or subject to God, regards not only the person, but also the nature: but this cannot be said of sonship. Wherefore the comparison does not hold.

## QUESTION 24

OF THE PREDESTINATION OF CHRIST (In Four Articles)

We shall now consider the predestination of Christ. Under this head there are four points of inquiry:

(1) Whether Christ was predestinated?

(2) Whether He was predestinated as man?

(3) Whether His predestination is the exemplar of ours?

(4) Whether it is the cause of our predestination?

FIRST ARTICLE [III, Q. 24, Art. 1]

Whether It Is Befitting That Christ Should Be Predestinated?

Objection 1: It would seem unfitting that Christ should be predestinated. For the term of anyone's predestination seems to be the adoption of sons, according to Eph. 1:5: "Who hath predestinated us unto the adoption of children." But it is not befitting to Christ to be an adopted Son, as stated above (Q. 23, A. 4). Therefore it is not fitting that Christ be predestinated.

Obj. 2: Further, we may consider two things in Christ: His human nature and His person. But it cannot be said that Christ is predestinated by reason of His human nature; for this proposition is false--"The human nature is Son of God." In like manner neither by reason of the person; for this person is the Son of God, not by grace, but by nature: whereas predestination regards what is of grace, as stated in the First Part, Q. 23, AA. 2, 5. Therefore Christ was not predestinated to be the Son of God.

Obj. 3: Further, just as that which has been made was not always, so also that which was predestinated; since predestination implies a certain antecedence. But, because Christ was always God and the Son of God, it cannot be said that that Man was "made the Son of God." Therefore, for a like reason, we ought not to say that Christ was "predestinated the Son of God."

*On the contrary,* The Apostle says, speaking of Christ (Rom. 1:4): "Who was predestinated the Son of God in power."

*I answer that,* As is clear from what has been said in the First Part (Q. 23, AA. 1, 2), predestination, in its proper sense, is a certain Divine preordination from eternity of those things which are to be done in time by the grace of God. Now, that man is God, and that God is man, is something done in time by God through the grace of union. Nor can it be said that God has not from eternity pre-ordained to do this in time: since it would follow that something would come anew into the Divine Mind. And we must needs admit that the union itself of natures in the Person of Christ falls under the eternal predestination of God. For this reason do we say that Christ was predestinated.

Reply Obj. 1: The Apostle there speaks of that predestination by which we are predestinated to be adopted sons. And just as Christ in a singular manner above all others is the natural Son of God, so in a singular manner is He predestinated.

Reply Obj. 2: As a gloss [*From St. Augustine, De Praed. Sanct. xv] says on Rom. 1:4, some understood that predestination to refer to the nature and not to the Person--that is to say, that on human nature was bestowed the grace of being united to the Son of God in unity of Person.

But in that case the phrase of the Apostle would be improper, for two reasons. First, for a general reason: for we do not speak of a person's nature, but of his person, as being predestinated: because to be predestinated is to be directed towards salvation, which belongs to a suppositum acting for the end of beatitude. Secondly, for a special reason. Because to be Son of God is not befitting to human nature; for this proposition is false: "The human nature is the Son of God": unless one were to force from it such an exposition as: "Who was predestinated the Son of God in power"--that is, "It was predestinated that the Human nature should be united to the Son of God in the Person."

Hence we must attribute predestination to the Person of Christ: not, indeed, in Himself or as subsisting in the Divine Nature, but as subsisting in the human nature. Wherefore the Apostle, after saying, "Who was made to Him of the seed of David according to the flesh," added, "Who was predestinated the Son of God in power": so as to give us to understand that in respect of His being of the seed of David according to the flesh, He was predestinated the Son of God in power. For although it is natural to that Person, considered in Himself, to be the Son of God in power, yet this is not natural to Him, considered in the human nature, in respect of which this befits Him according to the grace of union.

Reply Obj. 3: Origen commenting on Rom. 1:4 says that the true reading of this passage of the Apostle is: "Who was destined to be the Son of God in power"; so that no antecedence is implied. And so there would be no difficulty. Others refer the antecedence implied in the participle "predestinated," not to the fact of being the Son of God, but to the manifestation thereof, according to the customary way of speaking in Holy Scripture, by which things are said to take place when they are made known; so that the sense would be--"Christ was predestinated to be made known as the Son of God." But this is an improper signification of predestination. For a person is properly said to be predestinated by reason of his being directed to the end of beatitude: but the beatitude of Christ does not depend on our knowledge thereof.

It is therefore better to say that the antecedence implied in the participle "predestinated" is to be referred to the Person not in Himself, but by reason of the human nature: since, although that Person was the Son of God from eternity, it was not always true that one subsisting in human nature was the Son of God. Hence Augustine says (De Praedest. Sanct. xv): "Jesus was predestinated, so that He Who according to the flesh was to be the son of David, should be nevertheless Son of God in power."

Moreover, it must be observed that, although the participle "predestinated," just as this participle "made," implies antecedence, yet there is a difference. For "to be made" belongs to the thing in itself: whereas "to be predestinated" belongs to someone as being in the apprehension of one who pre-ordains. Now that which is the subject of a form or nature in reality, can be apprehended either as under that form or absolutely. And since it cannot be said absolutely of the Person of Christ that He began to be the Son of God, yet this is becoming to Him as understood or apprehended to exist in human nature, because at one time it began to be true that one existing in human nature was the Son of God; therefore this proposition--"Christ was predestinated the Son of God"--is truer than this--"Christ was made the Son of God."

SECOND ARTICLE [III, Q. 24, Art. 2]

Whether This Proposition Is False: "Christ As Man Was Predestinated to Be the Son of God"?

Objection 1: It would seem that this proposition is false: "Christ as man was predestinated to be the Son of God." For at some time a man is that which he was predestinated to be: since God's predestination does not fail. If, therefore, Christ as man was predestinated the Son of God, it seems to follow that as man He is the Son of God. But the latter is false. Therefore the former is false.

Obj. 2: Further, what is befitting to Christ as man is befitting to any man; since He belongs to the same species as other men. If, therefore, Christ, as man, was predestinated the Son of God, it will follow that this is befitting to any other man. But the latter is false. Therefore the former is false.

Obj. 3: Further, that is predestinated from eternity which is to take place at some time. But this proposition, "The Son of God was made man," is truer than this, "Man was made the Son of God." Therefore this proposition, "Christ, as the Son of God, was predestinated to be man," is truer than this, "Christ as Man was predestinated to be the Son of God."

*On the contrary,* Augustine (De Praedest. Sanct. xv) says: "Forasmuch as God the Son was made Man, we say that the Lord of Glory was predestinated."

*I answer that,* Two things may be considered in predestination. One on the part of eternal predestination itself: and in this respect it implies a certain antecedence in regard to that which comes under predestination. Secondly, predestination may be considered as regards its temporal effect, which is some gratuitous gift of God. Therefore from both points of view we must say that predestination is ascribed to Christ by reason of His human nature alone: for human nature was not always united to the Word; and by grace bestowed on it was it united in Person to the Son of God. Consequently, by reason of human nature alone can predestination be attributed to Christ. Wherefore Augustine says (De Praedest. Sanct. xv): "This human nature of ours was predestinated to be raised to so great, so lofty, so exalted a position, that it would be impossible to raise it higher." Now that is said to belong to anyone as man which belongs to him by reason of human nature. Consequently, we must say that "Christ, as Man, was predestinated the Son of God."

Reply Obj. 1: When we say, "Christ, as Man, was predestinated the Son of God," this qualification, "as Man," can be referred in two ways to the action signified by the participle. First, as regards what comes under predestination materially, and thus it is false. For the sense would be that it was predestinated that Christ, as Man, should be the Son of God. And in this sense the objection takes it.

Secondly, it may be referred to the very nature of the action itself: that is, forasmuch as predestination implies antecedence and gratuitous effect. And thus predestination belongs to Christ by reason of His human nature, as stated above. And in this sense He is said to be predestinated as Man.

Reply Obj. 2: Something may be befitting to a man by reason of human nature, in two ways. First, so that human nature be the cause thereof: thus risibility is befitting to Socrates by reason of human nature, being caused by its principles. In this manner predestination is not befitting either to Christ or to any other man, by reason of human nature. This is the sense of the objection. Secondly, a thing may be befitting to someone by reason of human nature, because human nature is susceptible of it. And in this sense we say that Christ was predestinated by reason of human nature; because predestination refers to the exaltation of human nature in Him, as stated above.

Reply Obj. 3: As Augustine says (Praedest. Sanct. xv): "The Word of God assumed Man to Himself in such a singular and ineffable manner that at the same time He may be truly and correctly called the Son of Man, because He assumed Man to Himself; and the Son of God, because it was the Only-begotten of God Who assumed human nature." Consequently, since this assumption comes under predestination by reason of its being gratuitous, we can say both that the Son of God was predestinated to be man, and that the Son of Man was predestinated to be the Son of God. But because grace was not bestowed on the Son of God that He might be man, but rather on human nature, that it might be united to the Son of God; it is more proper to say that "Christ, as Man, was predestinated to be the Son of God," than that, "Christ, as Son of God, was predestinated to be Man."

THIRD ARTICLE [III, Q. 24, Art. 3]

Whether Christ's Predestination Is the Exemplar of Ours?

Objection 1: It would seem that Christ's predestination is not the exemplar of ours. For the exemplar exists before the exemplate. But nothing exists before the eternal. Since, therefore, our predestination is eternal, it seems that Christ's predestination is not the exemplar of ours.

Obj. 2: Further, the exemplar leads us to knowledge of the exemplate. But there was no need for God to be led from something else to knowledge of our predestination; since it is written (Rom. 8:29): "Whom He foreknew, He also predestinated." Therefore Christ's predestination is not the exemplar of ours.

Obj. 3: Further, the exemplar is conformed to the exemplate. But Christ's predestination seems to be of a different nature from ours: because we are predestinated to the sonship of adoption, whereas Christ was predestinated "Son of God in power," as is written (Rom. 1:4). Therefore His predestination is not the exemplar of ours.

*On the contrary,* Augustine says (De Praedest. Sanct. xv): "The Saviour Himself, the Mediator of God and men, the Man Christ Jesus is the most splendid light of predestination and grace." Now He is called the light of predestination and grace, inasmuch as our predestination is made manifest by His predestination and grace; and this seems to pertain to the nature of an exemplar. Therefore Christ's predestination is the exemplar of ours.

*I answer that,* Predestination may be considered in two ways. First, on the part of the act of predestination: and thus Christ's predestination cannot be said to be the exemplar of ours: for in the same way and by the same eternal act God predestinated us and Christ.

Secondly, predestination may be considered on the part of that to which anyone is predestinated, and this is the term and effect of predestination. In this sense Christ's predestination is the exemplar of ours, and this in two ways. First, in respect of the good to which we are predestinated: for He was predestinated to be the natural Son of God, whereas we are predestinated to the adoption of sons, which is a participated likeness of natural sonship. Whence it is written (Rom. 8:29): "Whom He foreknew, He also predestinated to be made conformable to the image of His Son." Secondly, in respect of the manner of obtaining this good--that is, by grace. This is most manifest in Christ; because human nature in Him, without any antecedent merits, was united to the Son of God: and of the fulness of His grace we all have received, as it is written (John 1:16).

Reply Obj. 1: This argument considers the aforesaid act of the predestinator.

The same is to be said of the second objection.

Reply Obj. 3: The exemplate need not be conformed to the exemplar in all respects: it is sufficient that it imitate it in some.

FOURTH ARTICLE [III, Q. 24, Art. 4]

Whether Christ's Predestination Is the Cause of Ours?

Objection 1: It would seem that Christ's predestination is not the cause of ours. For that which is eternal has no cause. But our predestination is eternal. Therefore Christ's predestination is not the cause of ours.

Obj. 2: Further, that which depends on the simple will of God has no other cause but God's will. Now, our predestination depends on the simple will of God, for it is written (Eph. 1:11): "Being predestinated according to the purpose of Him, Who worketh all things according to the counsel of His will." Therefore Christ's predestination is not the cause of ours.

Obj. 3: Further, if the cause be taken away, the effect is also taken away. But if we take away Christ's predestination, ours is not taken away; since even if the Son of God were not incarnate, our salvation might yet have been achieved in a different manner, as Augustine says (De Trin. xiii, 10). Therefore Christ's predestination is not the cause of ours.

*On the contrary,* It is written (Eph. 1:5): "(Who) hath predestinated us unto the adoption of children through Jesus Christ."

*I answer that,* if we consider predestination on the part of the very act of predestinating, then Christ's predestination is not the cause of ours; because by one and the same act God predestinated both Christ and us. But if we consider predestination on the part of its term, thus Christ's predestination is the cause of ours: for God, by predestinating from eternity, so decreed our salvation, that it should be achieved through Jesus Christ. For eternal predestination covers not only that which is to be accomplished in time, but also the mode and order in which it is to be accomplished in time.

Replies Obj. 1 and 2: These arguments consider predestination on the part of the act of predestinating.

Reply Obj. 3: If Christ were not to have been incarnate, God would have decreed men's salvation by other means. But since He decreed the Incarnation of Christ, He decreed at the same time that He should be the cause of our salvation.

## QUESTION 25

OF THE ADORATION OF CHRIST (In Six Articles)

We have now to consider things pertaining to Christ in reference to us; and first, the adoration of Christ, by which we adore Him; secondly, we must consider how He is our Mediator with God.

Under the first head there are six points of inquiry:

(1) Whether Christ's Godhead and humanity are to be adored with one and the same adoration?

(2) Whether His flesh is to be adored with the adoration of latria?

(3) Whether the adoration of latria is to be given to the image of Christ?

(4) Whether latria is to be given to the Cross of Christ?

(5) Whether to His Mother?

(6) Concerning the adoration of the relics of Saints.

FIRST ARTICLE [III, Q. 25, Art. 1]

Whether Christ's Humanity and Godhead Are to Be Adored with the Same Adoration?

Objection 1: It would seem that Christ's humanity and Godhead are not to be adored with the same adoration. For Christ's Godhead is to be adored, as being common to Father and Son; wherefore it is written (John 5:23): "That all may honor the Son, as they honor the Father." But Christ's humanity is not common to Him and the Father. Therefore Christ's humanity and Godhead are not to be adored with the same adoration.

Obj. 2: Further, honor is properly "the reward of virtue," as the Philosopher says (Ethic. iv, 3). But virtue merits its reward by action. Since, therefore, in Christ the action of the Divine Nature is distinct from that of the human nature, as stated above (Q. 19, A. 1), it seems that Christ's humanity is to be adored with a different adoration from that which is given to His Godhead.

Obj. 3: Further, if the soul of Christ were not united to the Word, it would have been worthy of veneration on account of the excellence of its wisdom and grace. But by being united to the Word it lost nothing of its worthiness. Therefore His human nature should receive a certain veneration proper thereto, besides the veneration which is given to His Godhead.

*On the contrary,* We read in the chapters of the Fifth Council [*Second Council of Constantinople, coll. viii, can. 9]: "If anyone say that Christ is adored in two natures, so as to introduce two distinct adorations, and does not adore God the Word made flesh with the one and the same adoration as His flesh, as the Church has handed down from the beginning; let such a one be anathema."

*I answer that,* We may consider two things in a person to whom honor is given: the person himself, and the cause of his being honored. Now properly speaking honor is given to a subsistent thing in its entirety: for we do not speak of honoring a man's hand, but the man himself. And if at any time it happen that we speak of honoring a man's hand or foot, it is not by reason of these members being honored of themselves: but by reason of the whole being honored in them. In this way a man may be honored even in something external; for instance in his vesture, his image, or his messenger.

The cause of honor is that by reason of which the person honored has a certain excellence, for honor is reverence given to something on account of its excellence, as stated in the Second Part (II-II, Q. 103, A. 1). If therefore in one man there are several causes of honor, for instance, rank, knowledge, and virtue, the honor given to him will be one in respect of the person honored, but several in respect of the causes of honor: for it is the man that is honored, both on account of knowledge and by reason of his virtue.

Since, therefore, in Christ there is but one Person of the Divine and human natures, and one hypostasis, and one suppositum, He is given one adoration and one honor on the part of the Person adored: but on the part of the cause for which He is honored, we can say that there are several adorations, for instance that He receives one honor on account of His uncreated knowledge, and another on account of His created knowledge.

But if it be said that there are several persons or hypostases in Christ, it would follow that there would be, absolutely speaking, several adorations. And this is what is condemned in the Councils. For it is written in the chapters of Cyril [*Council of Ephesus, Part I, ch. 26]: "If anyone dare to say that the man assumed should be adored besides the Divine Word, as though these were distinct persons; and does not rather honor the Emmanuel with one single adoration, inasmuch as the Word was made flesh; let him be anathema."

Reply Obj. 1: In the Trinity there are three Who are honored, but only one cause of honor. In the mystery of the Incarnation it is the reverse: and therefore only one honor is given to the Trinity and only one to Christ, but in a different way.

Reply Obj. 2: Operation is not the object but the motive of honor. And therefore there being two operations in Christ proves, not two adorations, but two causes of adoration.

Reply Obj. 3: If the soul of Christ were not united to the Word of God, it would be the principal thing in that Man. Wherefore honor would be due to it principally, since man is that which is principal in him [*Cf. Ethic. ix, 8]. But since Christ's soul is united to a Person of greater dignity, to that Person is honor principally due to Whom Christ's soul is united. Nor is the dignity of Christ's soul hereby diminished, but rather increased, as stated above (Q. 2, A. 2, ad 2).

SECOND ARTICLE [III, Q. 25, Art. 2]

Whether Christ's Humanity Should Be Adored with the Adoration of Latria?

Objection 1: It would seem that Christ's soul should not be adored with the adoration of latria. For on the words of Ps. 98:5, "Adore His footstool for it is holy," a gloss says: "The flesh assumed by the Word of God is rightly adored by us: for no one partakes spiritually of His flesh unless he first adore it; but not indeed with the adoration called latria, which is due to the Creator alone." Now the flesh is part of the humanity. Therefore Christ's humanity is not to be adored with the adoration of latria.

Obj. 2: Further, the worship of latria is not to be given to any creature: since for this reason were the Gentiles reproved, that they "worshiped and served the creature," as it is written (Rom. 1:25). But Christ's humanity is a creature. Therefore it should not be adored with the adoration of latria.

Obj. 3: Further, the adoration of latria is due to God in recognition of His supreme dominion, according to Deut. 6:13: "Thou shalt adore [Vulg.: 'fear'; cf. Matt. 4:10] the Lord thy God, and shalt serve Him only." But Christ as man is less than the Father. Therefore His humanity is not to be adored with the adoration of latria.

*On the contrary,* Damascene says (De Fide Orth. iv, 3): "On account of the incarnation of the Divine Word, we adore the flesh of Christ not for its own sake, but because the Word of God is united thereto in person." And on Ps. 98:5, "Adore His foot-stool," a gloss says: "He who adores the body of Christ, regards not the earth, but rather Him whose footstool it is, in Whose honor he adores the footstool." But the incarnate Word is adored with the adoration of latria. Therefore also His body or His humanity.

*I answer that,* As stated above (A. 1) adoration is due to the subsisting hypostasis: yet the reason for honoring may be something non-subsistent, on account of which the person, in whom it is, is honored. And so the adoration of Christ's humanity may be understood in two ways. First, so that the humanity is the thing adored: and thus to adore the flesh of Christ is nothing else than to adore the incarnate Word of God: just as to adore a King's robe is nothing else than to adore a robed King. And in this sense the adoration of Christ's humanity is the adoration oflatria. Secondly, the adoration of Christ's humanity may be taken as given by reason of its being perfected with every gift of grace. And so in this sense the adoration of Christ's humanity is the adoration not of latria but of dulia. So that one and the same Person of Christ is adored with latriaon account of His Divinity, and with dulia on account of His perfect humanity.

Nor is this unfitting. For the honor of latria is due to God the Father Himself on account of His Godhead; and the honor of dulia on account of the dominion by which He rules over creatures. Wherefore on Ps. 7:1, "O Lord my God, in Thee have I hoped," a gloss says: "Lord of all by power, to Whom dulia is due: God of all by creation, to Whom latria is due."

Reply Obj. 1: That gloss is not to be understood as though the flesh of Christ were adored separately from its Godhead: for this could happen only, if there were one hypostasis of God, and another of man. But since, as Damascene says (De Fide Orth. iv, 3): "If by a subtle distinction you divide what is seen from what is understood, it cannot be adored because it is a creature"--that is, with adoration of latria. And then thus understood as distinct from the Word of God, it should be adored with the adoration of dulia ; not any kind of dulia, such as is given to other creatures, but with a certain higher adoration, which is called hyperdulia.

Hence appear the answers to the second and third objections. Because the adoration of latria is not given to Christ's humanity in respect of itself; but in respect of the Godhead to which it is united, by reason of which Christ is not less than the Father.

THIRD ARTICLE [III, Q. 25, Art. 3]

Whether the Image of Christ Should Be Adored with the Adoration of Latria ?

Objection 1: It would seem that Christ's image should not be adored with the adoration of latria. For it is written (Ex. 20:4): "Thou shalt not make to thyself a graven thing, nor the likeness of anything." But no adoration should be given against the commandment of God. Therefore Christ's image should not be adored with the adoration of latria.

Obj. 2: Further, we should have nothing in common with the works of the Gentiles, as the Apostle says (Eph. 5:11). But the Gentiles are reproached principally for that "they changed the glory of the incorruptible God into the likeness of the image of a corruptible man," as is written (Rom. 1:23). Therefore Christ's image is not to be adored with the adoration of latria.

Obj. 3: Further, to Christ the adoration of latria is due by reason of His Godhead, not of His humanity. But the adoration of latria is not due to the image of His Godhead, which is imprinted on the rational soul. Much less, therefore, is it due to the material image which represents the humanity of Christ Himself.

Obj. 4: Further, it seems that nothing should be done in the Divine worship that is not instituted by God; wherefore the Apostle (1 Cor. 11:23) when about to lay down the doctrine of the sacrifice of the Church, says: "I have received of the Lord that which also I delivered unto you." But Scripture does not lay down anything concerning the adoration of images. Therefore Christ's image is not to be adored with the adoration oflatria.

*On the contrary,* Damascene (De Fide Orth. iv, 16) quotes Basil as saying: "The honor given to an image reaches to the prototype," i.e. the exemplar. But the exemplar itself--namely, Christ--is to be adored with the adoration of latria ; therefore also His image.

*I answer that,* As the Philosopher says (De Memor. et Remin. i), there is a twofold movement of the mind towards an image: one indeed towards the image itself as a certain thing; another, towards the image in so far as it is the image of something else. And between these movements there is this difference; that the former, by which one is moved towards an image as a certain thing, is different from the movement towards the thing: whereas the latter movement, which is towards the image as an image, is one and the same as that which is towards the thing. Thus therefore we must say that no reverence is shown to Christ's image, as a thing--for instance, carved or painted wood: because reverence is not due save to a rational creature. It follow therefore that reverence should be shown to it, in so far only as it is an image. Consequently the same reverence should be shown to Christ's image as to Christ Himself. Since, therefore, Christ is adored with the adoration of latria, it follows that His image should be adored with the adoration of latria.

Reply Obj. 1: This commandment does not forbid the making of any graven thing or likeness, but the making thereof for the purpose of adoration, wherefore it is added: "Thou shalt not adore them nor serve them." And because, as stated above, the movement towards the image is the same as the movement towards the thing, adoration thereof is forbidden in the same way as adoration of the thing whose image it is. Wherefore in the passage quoted we are to understand the prohibition to adore those images which the Gentiles made for the purpose of venerating their own gods, i.e. the demons, and so it is premised: "Thou shalt not have strange gods before Me." But no corporeal image could be raised to the true God Himself, since He is incorporeal; because, as Damascene observes (De Fide Orth. iv, 16): "It is the highest absurdity and impiety to fashion a figure of what is Divine." But because in the New Testament God was made man, He can be adored in His corporeal image.

Reply Obj. 2: The Apostle forbids us to have anything in common with the "unfruitful works" of the Gentiles, but not with their useful works. Now the adoration of images must be numbered among the unfruitful works in two respects. First, because some of the Gentiles used to adore the images themselves, as things, believing that there was something Divine therein, on account of the answers which the demons used to give in them, and on account of other such like wonderful effects. Secondly on account of the things of which they were images; for they set up images to certain creatures, to whom in these images they gave the veneration of latria. Whereas we give the adoration of latria to the image of Christ, Who is true God, not for the sake of the image, but for the sake of the thing whose image it is, as stated above.

Reply Obj. 3: Reverence is due to the rational creature for its own sake. Consequently, if the adoration of latria were shown to the rational creature in which this image is, there might be an occasion of error--namely, lest the movement of adoration might stop short at the man, as a thing, and not be carried on to God, Whose image he is. This cannot happen in the case of a graven or painted image in insensible material.

Reply Obj. 4: The Apostles, led by the inward instinct of the Holy Ghost, handed down to the churches certain instructions which they did not put in writing, but which have been ordained, in accordance with the observance of the Church as practiced by the faithful as time went on. Wherefore the Apostle says (2 Thess. 2:14): "Stand fast; and hold the traditions which you have learned, whether by word"--that is by word of mouth--"or by our epistle"--that is by word put into writing. Among these traditions is the worship of Christ's image. Wherefore it is said that Blessed Luke painted the image of Christ, which is in Rome.

FOURTH ARTICLE [III, Q. 25, Art. 4]

Whether Christ's Cross Should Be Worshipped with the Adoration of Latria ?

Objection 1: It would seem that Christ's cross should not be worshiped with the adoration of latria. For no dutiful son honors that which dishonors his father, as the scourge with which he was scourged, or the gibbet on which he was hanged; rather does he abhor it. Now Christ underwent the most shameful death on the cross; according to Wis. 2:20: "Let us condemn Him to a most shameful death." Therefore we should not venerate the cross but rather we should abhor it.

Obj. 2: Further, Christ's humanity is worshiped with the adoration of latria, inasmuch as it is united to the Son of God in Person. But this cannot be said of the cross. Therefore Christ's cross should not be worshiped with the adoration of latria.

Obj. 3: Further, as Christ's cross was the instrument of His passion and death, so were also many other things, for instance, the nails, the crown, the lance; yet to these we do not show the worship of latria. It seems, therefore, that Christ's cross should not be worshiped with the adoration of latria.

*On the contrary,* We show the worship of latria to that in which we place our hope of salvation. But we place our hope in Christ's cross, for the Church sings:

"Dear Cross, best hope o'er all beside, That cheers the solemn passion-tide: Give to the just increase of grace, Give to each contrite sinner peace."

[*Hymn Vexilla Regis: translation of Father Aylward, O.P.]

Therefore Christ's cross should be worshiped with the adoration of latria.

*I answer that,* As stated above (A. 3), honor or reverence is due to a rational creature only; while to an insensible creature, no honor or reverence is due save by reason of a rational nature. And this in two ways. First, inasmuch as it represents a rational nature: secondly, inasmuch as it is united to it in any way whatsoever. In the first way men are wont to venerate the king's image; in the second way, his robe. And both are venerated by men with the same veneration as they show to the king.

If, therefore, we speak of the cross itself on which Christ was crucified, it is to be venerated by us in both ways--namely, in one way in so far as it represents to us the figure of Christ extended thereon; in the other way, from its contact with the limbs of Christ, and from its being saturated with His blood. Wherefore in each way it is worshiped with the same adoration as Christ, viz. the adoration of latria. And for this reason also we speak to the cross and pray to it, as to the Crucified Himself. But if we speak of the effigy of Christ's cross in any other material whatever--for instance, in stone or wood, silver or gold--thus we venerate the cross merely as Christ's image, which we worship with the adoration of latria, as stated above (A. 3).

Reply Obj. 1: If in Christ's cross we consider the point of view and intention of those who did not believe in Him, it will appear as His shame: but if we consider its effect, which is our salvation, it will appear as endowed with Divine power, by which it triumphed over the enemy, according to Col. 2:14, 15: "He hath taken the same out of the way, fastening it to the cross, and despoiling the principalities and powers, He hath exposed them confidently, in open show, triumphing over them in Himself." Wherefore the Apostle says (1 Cor. 1:18): "The Word of the cross to them indeed that perish is foolishness; but to them that are saved--that is, to us--it is the power of God."

Reply Obj. 2: Although Christ's cross was not united to the Word of God in Person, yet it was united to Him in some other way, viz. by representation and contact. And for this sole reason reverence is shown to it.

Reply Obj. 3: By reason of the contact of Christ's limbs we worship not only the cross, but all that belongs to Christ. Wherefore Damascene says (De Fide Orth. iv, 11): "The precious wood, as having been sanctified by the contact of His holy body and blood, should be meetly worshiped; as also His nails, His lance, and His sacred dwelling-places, such as the manger, the cave and so forth." Yet these very things do not represent Christ's image as the cross does, which is called "the Sign of the Son of Man" that "will appear in heaven," as it is written (Matt. 24:30). Wherefore the angel said to the women (Mk. 16:6): "You seek Jesus of Nazareth, Who was crucified": he said not "pierced," but "crucified." For this reason we worship the image of Christ's cross in any material, but not the image of the nails or of any such thing.

FIFTH ARTICLE [III, Q. 25, Art. 5]

Whether the Mother of God Should Be Worshipped with the Adoration of Latria ?

Objection 1: It would seem that the Mother of God is to be worshiped with the adoration of latria. For it seems that the same honor is due to the king's mother as to the king: whence it is written (3 Kings 2:19) that "a throne was set for the king's mother, and she sat on His right hand." Moreover, Augustine [*Sermon on the Assumption, work of an anonymous author] says: "It is right that the throne of God, the resting-place of the Lord of Heaven, the abode of Christ, should be there where He is Himself." But Christ is worshiped with the adoration of latria. Therefore His Mother also should be.

Obj. 2: Further, Damascene says (De Fide Orth. iv, 16): "The honor of the Mother reflects on the Son." But the Son is worshiped with the adoration of latria. Therefore the Mother also.

Obj. 3: Further, Christ's Mother is more akin to Him than the cross. But the cross is worshiped with the adoration of latria. Therefore also His Mother is to be worshiped with the same adoration.

*On the contrary,* The Mother of God is a mere creature. Therefore the worship of latria is not due to her.

*I answer that,* Since latria is due to God alone, it is not due to a creature so far as we venerate a creature for its own sake. For though insensible creatures are not capable of being venerated for their own sake, yet the rational creature is capable of being venerated for its own sake. Consequently the worship of latria is not due to any mere rational creature for its own sake. Since, therefore, the Blessed Virgin is a mere rational creature, the worship of latria is not due to her, but only that of dulia : but in a higher degree than to other creatures, inasmuch as she is the Mother of God. For this reason we say that not any kind of dulia is due to her, but hyperdulia.

Reply Obj. 1: The honor due to the king's mother is not equal to the honor which is due to the king: but is somewhat like it, by reason of a certain excellence on her part. This is what is meant by the authorities quoted.

Reply Obj. 2: The honor given to the Mother reflects on her Son, because the Mother is to be honored for her Son's sake. But not in the same way as honor given to an image reflects on its exemplar: because the image itself, considered as a thing, is not to be venerated in any way at all.

Reply Obj. 3: The cross, considered in itself, is not an object of veneration, as stated above (AA. 4,

5). But the Blessed Virgin is in herself an object of veneration. Hence there is no comparison.

SIXTH ARTICLE [III, Q. 25, Art. 6]

Whether Any Kind of Worship Is Due to the Relics of the Saints?

Objection 1: It would seem that the relics of the saints are not to be worshiped at all. For we should avoid doing what may be the occasion of error. But to worship the relics of the dead seems to savor of the error of the Gentiles, who gave honor to dead men. Therefore the relics of the saints are not to be honored.

Obj. 2: Further, it seems absurd to venerate what is insensible. But the relics of the saints are insensible. Therefore it is absurd to venerate them.

Obj. 3: Further, a dead body is not of the same species as a living body: consequently it does not seem to be identical with it. Therefore, after a saint's death, it seems that his body should not be worshiped.

*On the contrary,* It is written (De Eccles. Dogm. xl): "We believe that the bodies of the saints, above all the relics of the blessed martyrs, as being the members of Christ, should be worshiped in all sincerity": and further on: "If anyone holds a contrary opinion, he is not accounted a Christian, but a follower of Eunomius and Vigilantius."

*I answer that,* As Augustine says (De Civ. Dei i, 13): "If a father's coat or ring, or anything else of that kind, is so much more cherished by his children, as love for one's parents is greater, in no way are the bodies themselves to be despised, which are much more intimately and closely united to us than any garment; for they belong to man's very nature." It is clear from this that he who has a certain affection for anyone, venerates whatever of his is left after his death, not only his body and the parts thereof, but even external things, such as his clothes, and such like. Now it is manifest that we should show honor to the saints of God, as being members of Christ, the children and friends of God, and our intercessors. Wherefore in memory of them we ought to honor any relics of theirs in a fitting manner: principally their bodies, which were temples, and organs of the Holy Ghost dwelling and operating in them, and are destined to be likened to the body of Christ by the glory of the Resurrection. Hence God Himself fittingly honors such relics by working miracles at their presence.

Reply Obj. 1: This was the argument of Vigilantius, whose words are quoted by Jerome in the book he wrote against him (ch. ii) as follows: "We see something like a pagan rite introduced under pretext of religion; they worship with kisses I know not what tiny heap of dust in a mean vase surrounded with precious linen." To him Jerome replies (Ep. ad Ripar. cix): "We do not adore, I will not say the relics of the martyrs, but either the sun or the moon or even the angels"--that is to say, with the worship of latria. "But we honor the martyrs' relics, so that thereby we give honor to Him Whose martyrs [*The original meaning of the word 'martyr,' i.e. the Greek martys is 'a witness'] they are: we honor the servants, that the honor shown to them may reflect on their Master." Consequently, by honoring the martyrs' relics we do not fall into the error of the Gentiles, who gave the worship of latria to dead men.

Reply Obj. 2: We worship that insensible body, not for its own sake, but for the sake of the soul, which was once united thereto, and now enjoys God; and for God's sake, whose ministers the saints were.

Reply Obj. 3: The dead body of a saint is not identical with that which the saint had during life, on account of the difference of form, viz. the soul: but it is the same by identity of matter, which is destined to be reunited to its form.

## QUESTION 26

OF CHRIST AS CALLED THE MEDIATOR OF GOD AND MAN (In Two Articles)

We have now to consider how Christ is called the Mediator of God and man, and under this head there are two points of inquiry:

(1) Whether it is proper to Christ to be the Mediator of God and man?

(2) Whether this belongs to Him by reason of His human nature?

FIRST ARTICLE [III, Q. 26, Art. 1]

Whether It Is Proper to Christ to Be the Mediator of God and Man?

Objection 1: It would seem that it is not proper to Christ to be the Mediator of God and man. For a priest and a prophet seem to be mediators between God and man, according to Deut. 5:5: "I was the mediator and stood between God [Vulg.: 'the Lord'] and you at that time." But it is not proper to Christ to be a priest and a prophet. Neither, therefore, is it proper to Him to be Mediator.

Obj. 2: Further, that which is fitting to angels, both good and bad, cannot be said to be proper to Christ. But to be between God and man is fitting to the good angels, as Dionysius says (Div. Nom. iv). It is also fitting to the bad angels--that is, the demons: for they have something in common with God--namely, immortality; and something they have in common with men--namely, passibility of soul and consequently unhappiness; as appears from what Augustine says (De Civ. Dei ix, 13, 15). Therefore it is not proper to Christ to be a Mediator of God and man.

Obj. 3: Further, it belongs to the office of Mediator to beseech one of those, between whom he mediates, for the other. But the Holy Ghost, as it is written (Rom. 8:26), "asketh" God "for us with unspeakable groanings." Therefore the Holy Ghost is a Mediator between God and man. Therefore this is not proper to Christ.

*On the contrary,* It is written (1 Tim. 2:5): "There is . . . one Mediator of God and man, the man Christ Jesus."

*I answer that,* Properly speaking, the office of a mediator is to join together and unite those between whom he mediates: for extremes are united in the mean ( medio ). Now to unite men to God perfectively belongs to Christ, through Whom men are reconciled to God, according to 2 Cor. 5:19: "God was in Christ reconciling the world to Himself." And, consequently, Christ alone is the perfect Mediator of God and men, inasmuch as, by His death, He reconciled the human race to God. Hence the Apostle, after saying, "Mediator of God and man, the man Christ Jesus," added: "Who gave Himself a redemption for all."

However, nothing hinders certain others from being called mediators, in some respect, between God and man, forasmuch as they cooperate in uniting men to God, dispositively or ministerially.

Reply Obj. 1: The prophets and priests of the Old Law were called mediators between God and man, dispositively and ministerially: inasmuch as they foretold and foreshadowed the true and perfect Mediator of God and men. As to the priests of the New Law, they may be called mediators of God and men, inasmuch as they are the ministers of the true Mediator by administering, in His stead, the saving sacraments to men.

Reply Obj. 2: The good angels, as Augustine says (De Civ. Dei ix, 13), cannot rightly be called mediators between God and men. "For since, in common with God, they have both beatitude and immortality, and none of these things in common with unhappy and mortal man, how much rather are they not aloof from men and akin to God, than established between them?" Dionysius, however, says that they do occupy a middle place, because, in the order of nature, they are established below God and above man. Moreover, they fulfill the office of mediator, not indeed principally and perfectively, but ministerially and dispositively: whence (Matt. 4:11) it is said that "angels came and ministered unto Him"--namely, Christ. As to the demons, it is true that they have immortality in common with God, and unhappiness in common with men. "Hence for this purpose does the immortal and unhappy demon intervene, in order that he may hinder men from passing to a happy immortality," and may allure them to an unhappy immortality. Whence he is like "an evil mediator, who separates friends" [*Augustine, De Civ. Dei xv].

But Christ had beatitude in common with God, mortality in common with men. Hence "for this purpose did He intervene, that having fulfilled the span of His mortality, He might from dead men make immortal--which He showed in Himself by rising again; and that He might confer beatitude on those who were deprived of it--for which reason He never forsook us." Wherefore He is "the good Mediator, Who reconciles enemies" (De Civ. Dei xv).

Reply Obj. 3: Since the Holy Ghost is in everything equal to God, He cannot be said to be between, or a Mediator of, God and men: but Christ alone, Who, though equal to the Father in His Godhead, yet is less than the Father in His human nature, as stated above (Q. 20, A. 1). Hence on Gal. 3:20, "Christ is a Mediator [Vulg.: 'Now a mediator is not of one, but God is one']," the gloss says: "Not the Father nor the Holy Ghost." The Holy Ghost, however, is said "to ask for us," because He makes us ask.

SECOND ARTICLE [III, Q. 26, Art. 2]

Whether Christ, as Man, Is the Mediator of God and Men?

Objection 1: It would seem that Christ is not, as man, the Mediator of God and men. For Augustine says (Contra Felic. x): "One is the Person of Christ: lest there be not one Christ, not one substance; lest, the office of Mediator being denied, He be called the Son either of God alone, or merely the Son of a man." But He is the Son of God and man, not as man, but as at the same time God and man. Therefore neither should we say that, as man alone, He is Mediator of God and man.

Obj. 2: Further, just as Christ, as God, has a common nature with the Father and the Holy Ghost; so, as man, He has a common nature with men. But for the reason that, as God, He has the same nature as the Father and the Holy Ghost, He cannot be called Mediator, as God: for on 1 Tim. 2:5, "Mediator of God and man," a gloss says: "As the Word, He is not a Mediator, because He is equal to God, and God 'with God,' and at the same time one God." Therefore neither, as man, can He be called Mediator, on account of His having the same nature as men.

Obj. 3: Further, Christ is called Mediator, inasmuch as He reconciled us to God: and this He did by taking away sin, which separated us from God. But to take away sin belongs to Christ, not as man, but as God. Therefore Christ is our Mediator, not as man, but as God.

*On the contrary,* Augustine says (De Civ. Dei ix, 15): "Not because He is the Word, is Christ Mediator, since He Who is supremely immortal and supremely happy is far from us unhappy mortals; but He is Mediator, as man."

*I answer that,* We may consider two things in a mediator: first, that he is a mean; secondly, that he unites others. Now it is of the nature of a mean to be distant from each extreme: while it unites by communicating to one that which belongs to the other. Now neither of these can be applied to Christ as God, but only as man. For, as God, He does not differ from the Father and the Holy Ghost in nature and power of dominion: nor have the Father and the Holy Ghost anything that the Son has not, so that He be able to communicate to others something belonging to the Father or the Holy Ghost, as though it were belonging to others than Himself. But both can be applied to Him as man. Because, as man, He is distant both from God, by nature, and from man by dignity of both grace and glory. Again, it belongs to Him, as man, to unite men to God, by communicating to men both precepts and gifts, and by offering satisfaction and prayers to God for men. And therefore He is most truly called Mediator, as man.

Reply Obj. 1: If we take the Divine Nature from Christ, we consequently take from Him the singular fulness of grace, which belongs to Him as the Only-begotten of the Father, as it is written (John 1:14). From which fulness it resulted that He was established over all men, and approached nearer to God.

Reply Obj. 2: Christ, as God, is in all things equal to the Father. But even in the human nature He is above all men. Therefore, as man, He can be Mediator, but not as God.

Reply Obj. 3: Although it belongs to Christ as God to take away sin authoritatively, yet it belongs to Him, as man, to satisfy for the sin of the human race. And in this sense He is called the Mediator of God and men.

ST. THOMAS AND THE IMMACULATE CONCEPTION (EDITORIAL NOTE)

The privilege of the Virgin-Mother of God and the supreme prerogative of her Son may be seen from the following diagram:

THE LAW AND COURSE OF ORIGINAL SIN.

[The following content was presented in the form of a three-column table in the original.]

[COLUMN 1] UNDER THE LAW.

All descendants from Adam.

Spring from Adam materially and seminally.

The body lies (not under the guilt, but) under the effects of original sin.

The stricken body dispositively causes the soul to contract the guilt of original sin.

The soul at the moment of union with the body contracts the stain.

All contract both debt and stain.

All need a Redeemer to destroy the stain contracted.

[COLUMN 2] PARTIALLY EXEMPT FROM THE LAW; PRIVILEGE OF IMMACULATE CONCEPTION.

Spring from Adam materially and seminally.

The body lies (not under the guilt, but) under the effects of original sin.

The stricken body would have dispositively caused the soul to contract the guilt of original sin.

The soul at the moment of union with the body was prevented by the infusion of grace from contracting the stain.

Mary contracted the debt, but not the stain.

Mary needed a Redeemer to prevent her from contracting the stain.

[COLUMN 3] WHOLLY EXEMPT FROM THE LAW; MIRACULOUS CONCEPTION.

Springs from Adam materially, not seminally. (Q. 31, A. 1)

His body lay under neither guilt nor effects of original sin.

The body being entirely free, could not transmit the stain to His soul.

No preventive grace needed.

Jesus Christ contracted neither debt nor stain.

Jesus Christ is not redeemed, but the Redeemer.

It will thus be seen how accurately St. Thomas speaks of the "flesh" or body of our Blessed Lady. For it should be remembered that, according to St. Thomas, the human body is animated in succession by (1) a vegetative, (2) a sensitive, and (3) a rational soul. Hence his assertion that "the flesh of the Blessed Virgin was conceived in original sin" (Q. 14, A. 3, ad 1) means that the body of the Blessed Virgin, being descended from Adam both materially and seminally, contracted the bodily defects which are conveyed by seminal generation, and are the results of the privation of original justice (Q. 69, A. 4, ad 3). Before animation, therefore the body of the Blessed Virgin would not be infected with the guilt of original sin, because privation of grace can only be in that which is the subject of grace, viz. the rational soul. Nevertheless, before animation the body of the Blessed Virgin, being seminally descended from Adam, was such that it would have been the means of transmitting the taint of original sin to the rational soul at the very first instant of animation, unless the grace of the Redeemer intervened and sanctified her soul "in that self-same instant," thus redeeming her and preventing her from contracting the guilt of original sin.

Why, then, does St. Thomas say that because the Blessed Virgin was not sanctified before animation, therefore she could be sanctified only after animation?

Such a conclusion would hold if it were a question of the order of Nature: "a thing must be before it is such ( prius est esse quam esse tale )"; and therefore the soul must be, before it is sanctified. But if St. Thomas held for a posteriority of time, no matter how short, we ask how it was that he did not perceive the fallacy of the argument, since it might be neither before nor after, but in the very instant of, animation.

The question is answered thus: St. Thomas as a Doctor of the Church and in matters which were not then de fide, is a witness to the expression of the faith of his time. Hence his line of argument coincides with, because it follows, that of St. Bernard, Peter Lombard, Alexander of Hales, Albert the Great, St. Bonaventure. It was not likely that St. Thomas would differ from the great masters of his time, who failed to understand that the grace of redemption might at the same time be one of preservation and prevention. Nor is it likely that St. Thomas had any reliable information about the movement* in progress at that time towards a belief in the Immaculate Conception. [*Principally in England, where, owing to the influence of St. Anselm (1109), the doctrine was maintained by Eadmer (1137). Nicolas of St. Albans (1175), Osbert of Clare (1170), Robert Grosseteste, Bishop of Lincoln (1253), William of Ware (1300), who was the master of Duns Scotus (1308)]. No doubt he knew something of it, but the names of its promoters would have weighed little with him as against those of Bernard, Albert, Peter, Alexander, and Bonaventure. And it must not be forgotten that among those who upheld the doctrine of the Immaculate Conception, not a few ascribed the privilege as being absolute and not one of preservation and Redemption. Hence it is that St. Thomas insists on two things: (1) that the Mother of God was redeemed, and (2) that the grace of her sanctification was a grace of preservation. And, be it remarked in conclusion, these two points, so much insisted on by St. Thomas, are at the very basis of the Catholic doctrine of the Immaculate Conception.

## QUESTION 27

OF THE SANCTIFICATION OF THE BLESSED VIRGIN (In Six Articles)

After the foregoing treatise of the union of God and man and the consequences thereof, it remains for us to consider what things the Incarnate Son of God did or suffered in the human nature united to Him. This consideration will be fourfold. For we shall consider: (1) Those things that relate to His coming into the world; (2) Those things that relate to the course of His life in this world; (3) His departure from this world; (4) Those things that concern His exaltation after this life.

The first of these offers four points of consideration: (1) The Conception of Christ; (2) His Birth; (3) His Circumcision; (4) His Baptism. Concerning His Conception there are some points to be considered: (1) As to the Mother who conceived Him; (2) as to the mode of His Conception; (3) as to the perfection of the offspring conceived.

On the part of the Mother four points offer themselves to our consideration: (1) Her sanctification. (2) her virginity; (3) her espousals; (4) her annunciation, or preparation for conception.

Concerning the first there are six points of inquiry:

(1) Whether the Blessed Virgin, Mother of God, was sanctified before her birth from the womb?

(2) Whether she was sanctified before animation?

(3) Whether in virtue of this sanctification the fomes of sin was entirely taken away from her?

(4) Whether the result of this sanctification was that she never sinned?

(5) Whether in virtue of this sanctification she received the fulness of grace?

(6) Whether it was proper to her to be thus sanctified?

FIRST ARTICLE [III, Q. 27, Art. 1]

Whether the Blessed Virgin Was Sanctified Before Her Birth from the Womb?

Objection 1: It would seem that the Blessed Virgin was not sanctified before her birth from the womb. For the Apostle says (1 Cor. 15:46): "That was not first which is spiritual but that which is natural; afterwards that which is spiritual." But by sanctifying grace man is born spiritually into a son of God according to John 1:13: "(who) are born of God." But birth from the womb is a natural birth. Therefore the Blessed Virgin was not sanctified before her birth from the womb.

Obj. 2: Further, Augustine says (Ep. ad Dardan.): "The sanctification, by which we become temples of God, is only of those who are born again." But no one is born again, who was not born previously. Therefore the Blessed Virgin was not sanctified before her birth from the womb.

Obj. 3: Further, whoever is sanctified by grace is cleansed from sin, both original and actual. If, therefore, the Blessed Virgin was sanctified before her birth from the womb, it follows that she was then cleansed from original sin. Now nothing but original sin could hinder her from entering the heavenly kingdom. If therefore she had died then, it seems that she would have entered the gates of heaven. But this was not possible before the Passion of Christ, according to the Apostle (Heb. 10:19): "We have [Vulg.: 'having'] therefore a confidence in the entering into the Holies by His blood." It seems therefore that the Blessed Virgin was not sanctified before her birth from the womb.

Obj. 4: Further, original sin is contracted through the origin, just as actual sin is contracted through an act. But as long as one is in the act of sinning, one cannot be cleansed from actual sin. Therefore neither could the Blessed Virgin be cleansed from original sin as long as she was in the act of origin, by existence in her mother's womb.

*On the contrary,* The Church celebrates the feast of our Lady's Nativity. Now the Church does not celebrate feasts except of those who are holy. Therefore even in her birth the Blessed Virgin was holy. Therefore she was sanctified in the womb.

*I answer that,* Nothing is handed down in the canonical Scriptures concerning the sanctification of the Blessed Mary as to her being sanctified in the womb; indeed, they do not even mention her birth. But as Augustine, in his tractate on the Assumption of the Virgin, argues with reason, since her body was assumed into heaven, and yet Scripture does not relate this; so it may be reasonably argued that she was sanctified in the womb. For it is reasonable to believe that she, who brought forth "the Only-Begotten of the Father full of grace and truth," received greater privileges of grace than all others: hence we read (Luke 1:28) that the angel addressed her in the words: "Hail full of grace!"

Moreover, it is to be observed that it was granted, by way of privilege, to others, to be sanctified in the womb; for instance, to Jeremias, to whom it was said (Jer. 1:5): "Before thou camest forth out of the womb, I sanctified thee"; and again, to John the Baptist, of whom it is written (Luke 1:15): "He shall be filled with the Holy Ghost even from his mother's womb." It is therefore with reason that we believe the Blessed Virgin to have been sanctified before her birth from the womb.

Reply Obj. 1: Even in the Blessed Virgin, first was that which is natural, and afterwards that which is spiritual: for she was first conceived in the flesh, and afterwards sanctified in the spirit.

Reply Obj. 2: Augustine speaks according to the common law, by reason of which no one is regenerated by the sacraments, save those who are previously born. But God did not so limit His power to the law of the sacraments, but that He can bestow His grace, by special privilege, on some before they are born from the womb.

Reply Obj. 3: The Blessed Virgin was sanctified in the womb from original sin, as to the personal stain; but she was not freed from the guilt to which the whole nature is subject, so as to enter into Paradise otherwise than through the Sacrifice of Christ; the same also is to be said of the Holy Fathers who lived before Christ.

Reply Obj. 4: Original sin is transmitted through the origin, inasmuch as through the origin the human nature is transmitted, and original sin, properly speaking, affects the nature. And this takes place when the offspring conceived is animated. Wherefore nothing hinders the offspring conceived from being sanctified after animation: for after this it remains in the mother's womb not for the purpose of receiving human nature, but for a certain perfecting of that which it has already received.

SECOND ARTICLE [III, Q. 27, Art. 2]

Whether the Blessed Virgin Was Sanctified Before Animation?

Objection 1: It would seem that the Blessed Virgin was sanctified before animation. Because, as we have stated (A. 1), more grace was bestowed on the Virgin Mother of God than on any saint. Now it seems to have been granted to some, to be sanctified before animation. For it is written (Jer. 1:5): "Before I formed thee in the bowels of thy mother, I knew thee": and the soul is not infused before the formation of the body. Likewise Ambrose says of John the Baptist (Comment. in Luc. i, 15): "As yet the spirit of life was not in him and already he possessed the Spirit of grace." Much more therefore could the Blessed Virgin be sanctified before animation.

Obj. 2: Further, as Anselm says (De Concep. Virg. xviii), "it was fitting that this Virgin should shine with such a purity that under God none greater can be imagined": wherefore it is written (Canticles 4:7): "Thou art all fair, O my love, and there is not a spot in thee." But the purity of the Blessed Virgin would have been greater, if she had never been stained by the contagion of original sin. Therefore it was granted to her to be sanctified before her flesh was animated.

Obj. 3: Further, as it has been stated above, no feast is celebrated except of some saint. But some keep the feast of the Conception of the Blessed Virgin. Therefore it seems that in her very Conception she was holy; and hence that she was sanctified before animation.

Obj. 4: Further, the Apostle says (Rom. 11:16): "If the root be holy, so are the branches." Now the root of the children is their parents. Therefore the Blessed Virgin could be sanctified even in her parents, before animation.

*On the contrary,* The things of the Old Testament were figures of the New, according to 1 Cor. 10:11: "All things happened to them in figure." Now the sanctification of the tabernacle, of which it is written (Ps. 45:5): "The most High hath sanctified His own tabernacle," seems to signify the sanctification of the Mother of God, who is called "God's Tabernacle," according to Ps. 18:6: "He hath set His tabernacle in the sun." But of the tabernacle it is written (Ex. 40:31, 32): "After all things were perfected, the cloud covered the tabernacle of the testimony, and the glory of the Lord filled it." Therefore also the Blessed Virgin was not sanctified until after all in her was perfected, viz. her body and soul.

*I answer that,* The sanctification of the Blessed Virgin cannot be understood as having taken place before animation, for two reasons. First, because the sanctification of which we are speaking, is nothing but the cleansing from original sin: for sanctification is a "perfect cleansing," as Dionysius says (Div. Nom. xii). Now sin cannot be taken away except by grace, the subject of which is the rational creature alone. Therefore before the infusion of the rational soul, the Blessed Virgin was not sanctified.

Secondly, because, since the rational creature alone can be the subject of sin; before the infusion of the rational soul, the offspring conceived is not liable to sin. And thus, in whatever manner the Blessed Virgin would have been sanctified before animation, she could never have incurred the stain of original sin: and thus she would not have needed redemption and salvation which is by Christ, of whom it is written (Matt. 1:21): "He shall save His people from their sins." But this is unfitting, through implying that Christ is not the "Saviour of all men," as He is called (1 Tim. 4:10). It remains, therefore, that the Blessed Virgin was sanctified after animation.

Reply Obj. 1: The Lord says that He "knew" Jeremias before he was formed in the womb, by knowledge, that is to say, of predestination: but He says that He "sanctified" him, not before formation, but before he "came forth out of the womb," etc.

As to what Ambrose says, viz. that in John the Baptist there was not the spirit of life when there was already the Spirit of grace, by spirit of life we are not to understand the life-giving soul, but the air which we breathe out ( respiratus ). Or it may be said that in him as yet there was not the spirit of life, that is the soul, as to its manifest and complete operations.

Reply Obj. 2: If the soul of the Blessed Virgin had never incurred the stain of original sin, this would be derogatory to the dignity of Christ, by reason of His being the universal Saviour of all. Consequently after Christ, who, as the universal Saviour of all, needed not to be saved, the purity of the Blessed Virgin holds the highest place. For Christ did not contract original sin in any way whatever, but was holy in His very Conception, according to Luke 1:35: "The Holy which shall be born of thee, shall be called the Son of God." But the Blessed Virgin did indeed contract original sin, but was cleansed therefrom before her birth from the womb. This is what is signified (Job 3:9) where it is written of the night of original sin: "Let it expect light," i.e. Christ, "and not see it"--(because "no defiled thing cometh into her," as is written Wis. 7:25), "nor the rising of the dawning of the day," that is of the Blessed Virgin, who in her birth was immune from original sin.

Reply Obj. 3: Although the Church of Rome does not celebrate the Conception of the Blessed Virgin, yet it tolerates the custom of certain churches that do keep that feast, wherefore this is not to be entirely reprobated. Nevertheless the celebration of this feast does not give us to understand that she was holy in her conception. But since it is not known when she was sanctified, the feast of her Sanctification, rather than the feast of her Conception, is kept on the day of her conception.

Reply Obj. 4: Sanctification is twofold. One is that of the whole nature: inasmuch as the whole human nature is freed from all corruption of sin and punishment. This will take place at the resurrection. The other is personal sanctification. This is not transmitted to the children begotten of the flesh: because it does not regard the flesh but the mind. Consequently, though the parents of the Blessed Virgin were cleansed from original sin, nevertheless she contracted original sin, since she was conceived by way of fleshly concupiscence and the intercourse of man and woman: for Augustine says (De Nup. et Concup. i): "All flesh born of carnal intercourse is sinful."

THIRD ARTICLE [III, Q. 27, Art. 3]

Whether the Blessed Virgin Was Cleansed from the Infection of the Fomes?

Objection 1: It would seem that the Blessed Virgin was not cleansed from the infection of the fomes. For just as the fomes, consisting in the rebellion of the lower powers against the reason, is a punishment of original sin; so also are death and other corporeal penalties. Therefore the fomes was not entirely removed from her.

Obj. 2: Further, it is written (2 Cor. 12:9): "Power is made perfect in infirmity," which refers to the weakness of the fomes, by reason of which he (the Apostle) felt the "sting of the flesh." But it was not fitting that anything should be taken away from the Blessed Virgin, pertaining to the perfection of virtue. Therefore it was unfitting that the fomes should be entirely taken away from her.

Obj. 3: Further, Damascene says (De Fide Orth. iii) that "the Holy Ghost came upon" the Blessed Virgin, "purifying her," before she conceived the Son of God. But this can only be understood of purification from the fomes: for she committed no sin, as Augustine says (De Nat. et Grat. xxvi). Therefore by the sanctification in the womb she was not absolutely cleansed from the fomes.

*On the contrary,* It is written (Canticles 4:7): "Thou art all fair, O my love, and there is not a spot in thee!" But the fomes implies a blemish, at any rate in the flesh. Therefore the fomes was not in the Blessed Virgin.

*I answer that,* on this point there are various opinions. For some have held that the fomes was entirely taken away in that sanctification whereby the Blessed Virgin was sanctified in the womb. Others say that it remained as far as it causes a difficulty in doing good, but was taken away as far as it causes a proneness to evil. Others again, that it was taken away as to the personal corruption, by which it makes us quick to do evil and slow to do good: but that it remained as to the corruption of nature, inasmuch as it is the cause of transmitting original sin to the offspring. Lastly, others say that, in her first sanctification, the fomes remained essentially, but was fettered; and that, when she conceived the Son of God, it was entirely taken away. In order to understand the question at issue, it must be observed that the fomes is nothing but a certain inordinate, but habitual, concupiscence of the sensitive appetite, for actual concupiscence is a sinful motion. Now sensual concupiscence is said to be inordinate, in so far as it rebels against reason; and this it does by inclining to evil, or hindering from good. Consequently it is essential to the fomes to incline to evil, or hinder from good. Wherefore to say that the fomes was in the Blessed Virgin without an inclination to evil, is to combine two contradictory statements.

In like manner it seems to imply a contradiction to say that the fomes remained as to the corruption of nature, but not as to the personal corruption. For, according to Augustine (De Nup. et Concup. i.), it is lust that transmits original sin to the offspring. Now lust implies inordinate concupiscence, not entirely subject to reason: and therefore, if the fomes were entirely taken away as to personal corruption, it could not remain as to the corruption of nature.

It remains, therefore, for us to say, either that the fomes was entirely taken away from her by her first sanctification or that it was fettered. Now that the fomes was entirely taken away, might be understood in this way, that, by the abundance of grace bestowed on the Blessed Virgin, such a disposition of the soul's powers was granted to her, that the lower powers were never moved without the command of her reason: just as we have stated to have been the case with Christ (Q. 15, A. 2), who certainly did not have the fomes of sin; as also was the case with Adam, before he sinned, by reason of original justice: so that, in this respect, the grace of sanctification in the Virgin had the force of original justice. And although this appears to be part of the dignity of the Virgin Mother, yet it is somewhat derogatory to the dignity of Christ, without whose power no one had been freed from the first sentence of condemnation. And though, through faith in Christ, some were freed from that condemnation, according to the spirit, before Christ's Incarnation, yet it does not seem fitting that any one should be freed from that condemnation, according to the flesh, except after His Incarnation, for it was then that immunity from condemnation was first to appear. Consequently, just as before the immortality of the flesh of Christ rising again, none obtained immortality of the flesh, so it seems unfitting to say that before Christ appeared in sinless flesh, His Virgin Mother's or anyone else's flesh should be without the fomes, which is called "the law of the flesh" or "of the members" (Rom. 7:23, 25).

Therefore it seems better to say that by the sanctification in the womb, the Virgin was not freed from the fomes in its essence, but that it remained fettered: not indeed by an act of her reason, as in holy men, since she had not the use of reason from the very first moment of her existence in her mother's womb, for this was the singular privilege of Christ: but by reason of the abundant grace bestowed on her in her sanctification, and still more perfectly by Divine Providence preserving her sensitive soul, in a singular manner, from any inordinate movement. Afterwards, however, at the conception of Christ's flesh, in which for the first time immunity from sin was to be conspicuous, it is to be believed that entire freedom from the fomes redounded from the Child to the Mother. This indeed is signified (Ezech. 43:2): "Behold the glory of the God of Israel came in by the way of the east," i.e. by the Blessed Virgin, "and the earth," i.e. her flesh, "shone with His," i.e. Christ's, "majesty."

Reply Obj. 1: Death and such like penalties do not of themselves incline us to sin. Wherefore though Christ assumed them, He did not assume the fomes. Consequently in order that the Blessed Virgin might be conformed to her Son, from "whose fulness" her grace was derived, the fomes was at first fettered and afterwards taken away: while she was not freed from death and other such penalties.

Reply Obj. 2: The "infirmity" of the flesh, that pertains to the fomes, is indeed to holy men an occasional cause of perfect virtue: but not the "sine qua non" of perfection: and it is quite enough to ascribe to the Blessed Virgin perfect virtue and abundant grace: nor is there any need to attribute to her every occasional cause of perfection.

Reply Obj. 3: The Holy Ghost effected a twofold purification in the Blessed Virgin. The first was, as it were, preparatory to Christ's conception: which did not cleanse her from the stain of sin or fomes, but rather gave her mind a unity of purpose and disengaged it from a multiplicity of things (Cf. Dionysius, Div. Nom. iv), since even the angels are said to be purified, in whom there is no stain, as Dionysius says (Eccl. Hier. vi). The second purification effected in her by the Holy Ghost was by means of the conception of Christ which was the operation of the Holy Ghost. And in respect of this, it may be said that He purified her entirely from the fomes.

FOURTH ARTICLE [III, Q. 27, Art. 4]

Whether by Being Sanctified in the Womb the Blessed Virgin Was Preserved from All Actual Sin?

Objection 1: It would seem that by being sanctified in the womb the Blessed Virgin was not preserved from all actual sin. For, as we have already stated (A. 3), after her first sanctification the fomes remained in the Virgin. Now the motion of the fomes, even if it precede the act of the reason, is a venial sin, albeit extremely slight, as Augustine says in his work De Trinitate [*Cf. Sent. ii, D, 24]. Therefore there was some venial sin in the Blessed Virgin.

Obj. 2: Further, Augustine (Qq. Nov. et Vet. Test. lxxiii on Luke 2:35: "Thy own soul a sword shall pierce") says that the Blessed Virgin "was troubled with wondering doubt at the death of our Lord." But doubt in matters of faith is a sin. Therefore the Blessed Virgin was not preserved from all actual sin.

Obj. 3: Further, Chrysostom (Hom. xlv in Matth.) expounding the text: "Behold thy mother and thy brethren stand without, seeking thee," says: "It is clear that they did this from mere vain glory." Again, on John 2:3: "They have no wine," the same Chrysostom says that "she wished to do them a favor, and raise herself in their esteem, by means of her Son: and perchance she succumbed to human frailty, just as did His brethren when they said: 'Manifest Thyself to the world.'" And a little further on he says: "For as yet she did not believe in Him as she ought." Now it is quite clear that all this was sinful. Therefore the Blessed Virgin was not preserved from all sin.

*On the contrary,* Augustine says (De Nat. et Grat. xxxvi): "In the matter of sin, it is my wish to exclude absolutely all questions concerning the holy Virgin Mary, on account of the honor due to Christ. For since she conceived and brought forth Him who most certainly was guilty of no sin, we know that an abundance of grace was given her that she might be in every way the conqueror of sin."

*I answer that,* God so prepares and endows those, whom He chooses for some particular office, that they are rendered capable of fulfilling it, according to 2 Cor. 3:6: "(Who) hath made us fit ministers of the New Testament." Now the Blessed Virgin was chosen by God to be His Mother. Therefore there can be no doubt that God, by His grace, made her worthy of that office, according to the words spoken to her by the angel (Luke 1:30, 31): "Thou hast found grace with God: behold thou shalt conceive," etc. But she would not have been worthy to be the Mother of God, if she had ever sinned. First, because the honor of the parents reflects on the child, according to Prov. 17:6: "The glory of children are their fathers": and consequently, on the other hand, the Mother's shame would have reflected on her Son. Secondly, because of the singular affinity between her and Christ, who took flesh from her: and it is written ( 2 Cor. 6:15): "What concord hath Christ with Belial?" Thirdly, because of the singular manner in which the Son of God, who is the "Divine Wisdom" (1 Cor. 1:24) dwelt in her, not only in her soul but in her womb. And it is written (Wis. 1:4): "Wisdom will not enter into a malicious soul, nor dwell in a body subject to sins."

We must therefore confess simply that the Blessed Virgin committed no actual sin, neither mortal nor venial; so that what is written (Cant 4:7) is fulfilled: "Thou art all fair, O my love, and there is not a spot in thee," etc.

Reply Obj. 1: After her sanctification the fomes remained in the Blessed Virgin, but fettered; lest she should be surprised by some sudden inordinate act, antecedent to the act of reason. And although the grace of her sanctification contributed to this effect, yet it did not suffice; for otherwise the result of her sanctification would have been to render impossible in her any sensual movement not preceded by an act of reason, and thus she would not have had the fomes, which is contrary to what we have said above (A. 3). We must therefore say that the above mentioned fettering (of the fomes) was perfected by divine providence not permitting any inordinate motion to result from the fomes.

Reply Obj. 2: Origen (Hom. xvii in Luc.) and certain other doctors expound these words of Simeon as referring to the sorrow which she suffered at the time of our Lord's Passion. Ambrose (in Luc. 2:35) says that the sword signifies "Mary's prudence which took note of the heavenly mystery. For the word of God is living and effectual, and more piercing than any two-edged sword" (Heb. 4:12).

Others again take the sword to signify doubt. But this is to be understood of the doubt, not of unbelief, but of wonder and discussion. Thus Basil says (Ep. ad Optim.) that "the Blessed Virgin while standing by the cross, and observing every detail, after the message of Gabriel, and the ineffable knowledge of the Divine Conception, after that wondrous manifestation of miracles, was troubled in mind": that is to say, on the one side seeing Him suffer such humiliation, and on the other considering His marvelous works.

Reply Obj. 3: In those words Chrysostom goes too far. They may, however, be explained as meaning that our Lord corrected in her, not the inordinate motion of vain glory in regard to herself, but that which might be in the thoughts of others.

FIFTH ARTICLE [III, Q. 27, Art. 5]

Whether, by Her Sanctification in the Womb, the Blessed Virgin Received the Fulness of Grace?

Objection 1: It would seem that, by her sanctification in the womb, the Blessed Virgin did not receive the fulness or perfection of grace. For this seems to be Christ's privilege, according to John 1:14: "We saw Him [Vulg.: 'His glory'] as the Only-Begotten [Vulg.: 'as it were of the Only-Begotten'] full of grace and truth." But what is proper to Christ ought not to be ascribed to some one else. Therefore the Blessed Virgin did not receive the fulness of grace at the time of her sanctification.

Obj. 2: Further, nothing remains to be added to that which is full and perfect: for "the perfect is that which lacks nothing," as is said Phys. iii. But the Blessed Virgin received additional grace afterwards when she conceived Christ; for to her was it said (Luke 1:35): "The Holy Ghost shall come upon thee: and again, when she was assumed into glory." Therefore it seems that she did not receive the fulness of grace at the time of her first sanctification.

Obj. 3: Further, "God does nothing useless," as is said De Coelo et Mundo i. But it would have been useless for her to have certain graces, for she would never have put them to use: since we do not read that she taught which is the act of wisdom; or that she worked miracles, which is the act of one of the gratuitous graces. Therefore she had not the fulness of grace.

*On the contrary,* The angel said to her: "Hail, full of grace" (Luke 1:28); which words Jerome expounds as follows, in a sermon on the Assumption (cf. Ep. ad Paul. et Eustoch.): "Full indeed of grace: for to others it is given in portions; whereas on Mary the fulness of grace was showered all at once."

*I answer that,* In every genus, the nearer a thing is to the principle, the greater the part which it has in the effect of that principle, whence Dionysius says (Coel. Hier. iv) that angels, being nearer to God, have a greater share than men, in the effects of the Divine goodness. Now Christ is the principle of grace, authoritatively as to His Godhead, instrumentally as to His humanity: whence (John 1:17) it is written: "Grace and truth came by Jesus Christ." But the Blessed Virgin Mary was nearest to Christ in His humanity: because He received His human nature from her. Therefore it was due to her to receive a greater fulness of grace than others.

Reply Obj. 1: God gives to each one according to the purpose for which He has chosen him. And since Christ as man was predestinated and chosen to be "predestinated the Son of God in power . . . of sanctification" (Rom. 1:4), it was proper to Him to have such a fulness of grace that it overflowed from Him into all, according to John 1:16: "Of His fulness we have all received." Whereas the Blessed Virgin Mary received such a fulness of grace that she was nearest of all to the Author of grace; so that she received within her Him Who is full of all grace; and by bringing Him forth, she, in a manner, dispensed grace to all.

Reply Obj. 2: In natural things at first there is perfection of disposition, for instance when matter is perfectly disposed for the form. Secondly, there is the perfection of the form; and this is the more excellent, for the heat that proceeds from the form of fire is more perfect than that which disposed to the form of fire. Thirdly, there is the perfection of the end: for instance when fire has its qualities in the most perfect degree, having mounted to its own place.

In like manner there was a threefold perfection of grace in the Blessed Virgin. The first was a kind of disposition, by which she was made worthy to be the mother of Christ: and this was the perfection of her sanctification. The second perfection of grace in the Blessed Virgin was through the presence of the Son of God Incarnate in her womb. The third perfection of the end is that which she has in glory.

That the second perfection excels the first, and the third the second, appears (1) from the point of view of deliverance from evil. For at first in her sanctification she was delivered from original sin: afterwards, in the conception of the Son of God, she was entirely cleansed from the fomes: lastly, in her glorification she was also delivered from all affliction whatever. It appears (2) from the point of view of ordering to good. For at first in her sanctification she received grace inclining her to good: in the conception of the Son of God she received consummate grace confirming her in good; and in her glorification her grace was further consummated so as to perfect her in the enjoyment of all good.

Reply Obj. 3: There is no doubt that the Blessed Virgin received in a high degree both the gift of wisdom and the grace of miracles and even of prophecy, just as Christ had them. But she did not so receive them, as to put them and such like graces to every use, as did Christ: but accordingly as it befitted her condition of life. For she had the use of wisdom in contemplation, according to Luke 2:19: "But Mary kept all these words, pondering them in her heart." But she had not the use of wisdom as to teaching: since this befitted not the female sex, according to 1 Tim. 2:12: "But I suffer not a woman to teach." The use of miracles did not become her while she lived: because at that time the Teaching of Christ was to be confirmed by miracles, and therefore it was befitting that Christ alone, and His disciples who were the bearers of His doctrine, should work miracles. Hence of John the Baptist it is written (John 10:41) that he "did no sign"; that is, in order that all might fix their attention on Christ. As to the use of prophecy, it is clear that she had it, from the canticle spoken by her: "My soul doth magnify the Lord" (Luke 1:46, etc.).

SIXTH ARTICLE [III, Q. 27, Art. 6]

Whether After Christ, It Was Proper to the Blessed Virgin to Be Sanctified in the Womb?

Objection 1: It would seem that it was proper for the Blessed Virgin, after Christ, to be sanctified in the womb. For it has been said (A. 4) that the Blessed Virgin was sanctified in the womb, in order that she might be worthy to be the mother of God. But this is proper to her. Therefore she alone was sanctified in the womb.

Obj. 2: Further, some men seem to have been more closely connected with Christ than Jeremias and John the Baptist, who are said to have been sanctified in the womb. For Christ is specially called the Son of David and of Abraham, by reason of the promise specially made to them concerning Christ. Isaias also prophesied of Christ in the most express terms. And the apostles were in converse with Christ Himself. And yet these are not mentioned as having been sanctified in the womb. Therefore it was not befitting that either Jeremias or John the Baptist should be sanctified in the womb.

Obj. 3: Further, Job says of himself (Job 31:18): "From my infancy mercy grew up with me; and it came out with me from [my mother's] womb." Nevertheless we do not for this reason say that he was sanctified in the womb. Neither therefore are we bound to say that Jeremias and John the Baptist were sanctified in the womb.

*On the contrary,* It is written of Jeremias (Jer. 1:5): "Before thou camest forth out of the womb I sanctified thee." And of John the Baptist it is written (Luke 1:15): "He shall be filled with the Holy Ghost, even from his mother's womb."

*I answer that,* Augustine (Ep. ad Dardan.) seems to speak dubiously of their (Jeremias' and John the Baptist's) sanctification in the womb. For the leaping of John in the womb "might," as he says, "signify the great truth," viz. that the woman was the mother of God, "which was to be made known to his elders, though as yet unknown to the infant. Hence in the Gospel it is written, not that the infant in her womb believed, but that it 'leaped': and our eyes are witness that not only infants leap but also cattle. But this was unwonted because it was in the womb. And therefore, just as other miracles are wont to be done, this was done divinely, in the infant; not humanly by the infant. Perhaps also in this child the use of reason and will was so far accelerated that while yet in his mother's womb he was able to acknowledge, believe, and consent, whereas in other children we have to wait for these things till they grow older: this again I count as a miraculous result of the divine power."

But since it is expressly said (of John) in the Gospel that "he shall be filled with the Holy Ghost, even from his mother's womb"; and of Jeremias, "Before thou camest forth out of the womb, I sanctified thee"; it seems that we must needs assert that they were sanctified in the womb, although, while in the womb, they had not the use of reason (which is the point discussed by Augustine); just as neither do children enjoy the use of free will as soon as they are sanctified by baptism.

Nor are we to believe that any others, not mentioned by Scripture, were sanctified in the womb. For such privileges of grace, which are bestowed on some, outside the common law, are ordered for the salvation of others, according to 1 Cor. 12:7: "The manifestation of the Spirit is given to every man unto profit," which would not result from the sanctification of anyone unless it were made known to the Church.

And although it is not possible to assign a reason for God's judgments, for instance, why He bestows such a grace on one and not on another, yet there seems to be a certain fittingness in both of these being sanctified in the womb, by their foreshadowing the sanctification which was to be effected through Christ. First, as to His Passion, according to Heb. 13:12: "Jesus, that He might sanctify the people by His own blood, suffered without the gate": which Passion Jeremias foretold openly by words and by symbols, and most clearly foreshadowed by his own sufferings. Secondly, as to His Baptism (1 Cor. 6:11): "But you are washed, but you are sanctified"; to which Baptism John prepared men by his baptism.

Reply Obj. 1: The blessed Virgin, who was chosen by God to be His Mother, received a fuller grace of sanctification than John the Baptist and Jeremias, who were chosen to foreshadow in a special way the sanctification effected by Christ. A sign of this is that it was granted to the Blessed Virgin thenceforward never to sin either mortally or venially: whereas to the others who were thus sanctified it was granted thenceforward not to sin mortally, through the protection of God's grace.

Reply Obj. 2: In other respects these saints might be more closely united to Christ than Jeremias and John the Baptist. But the latter were most closely united to Him by clearly foreshadowing His sanctification, as explained above.

Reply Obj. 3: The mercy of which Job speaks is not the infused virtue; but a certain natural inclination to the act of that virtue.

# QUESTION 28

OF THE VIRGINITY OF THE MOTHER OF GOD (In Four Articles)

We now have to consider the virginity of the Mother of God; concerning which there are four points of inquiry:

(1) Whether she was a virgin in conceiving?

(2) Whether she was a virgin in His Birth?

(3) Whether she remained a virgin after His Birth?

(4) Whether she took a vow of virginity?

FIRST ARTICLE [III, Q. 28, Art. 1]

Whether the Mother of God Was a Virgin in Conceiving Christ?

Objection 1: It would seem that the Mother of God was not a virgin in conceiving Christ. For no child having father and mother is conceived by a virgin mother. But Christ is said to have had not only a mother, but also a father, according to Luke 2:33: "His father and mother were wondering at those things which were spoken concerning Him": and further on (Luke 2:48) in the same chapter she says: "Behold I and Thy father [Vulg.: 'Thy father and I'] have sought Thee sorrowing." Therefore Christ was not conceived of a virgin mother.

Obj. 2: Further (Matt. 1) it is proved that Christ was the Son of Abraham and David, through Joseph being descended from David. But this proof would have availed nothing if Joseph were not the father of Christ. Therefore it seems that Christ's Mother conceived Him of the seed of Joseph; and consequently that she was not a virgin in conceiving Him.

Obj. 3: Further, it is written (Gal. 4:4): "God sent His Son, made of a woman." But according to the customary mode of speaking, the term "woman" applies to one who is known of a man. Therefore Christ was not conceived by a virgin mother.

Obj. 4: Further, things of the same species have the same mode of generation: since generation is specified by its terminus just as are other motions. But Christ belonged to the same species as other men, according to Phil. 2:7: "Being made in the likeness of men, and in habit found as a man." Since therefore other men are begotten of the mingling of male and female, it seems that Christ was begotten in the same manner; and that consequently He was not conceived of a virgin mother.

Obj. 5: Further, every natural form has its determinate matter, outside which it cannot be. But the matter of human form appears to be the semen of male and female. If therefore Christ's body was not conceived of the semen of male and female, it would not have been truly a human body; which cannot be asserted. It seems therefore that He was not conceived of a virgin mother.

*On the contrary,* It is written (Isa. 7:14): "Behold a virgin shall conceive."

*I answer that,* We must confess simply that the Mother of Christ was a virgin in conceiving for to deny this belongs to the heresy of the Ebionites and Cerinthus, who held Christ to be a mere man, and maintained that He was born of both sexes.

It is fitting for four reasons that Christ should be born of a virgin. First, in order to maintain the dignity or the Father Who sent Him. For since Christ is the true and natural Son of God, it was not fitting that He should have another father than God: lest the dignity belonging to God be transferred to another.

Secondly, this was befitting to a property of the Son Himself, Who is sent. For He is the Word of God: and the word is conceived without any interior corruption: indeed, interior corruption is incompatible with perfect conception of the word. Since therefore flesh was so assumed by the Word of God, as to be the flesh of the Word of God, it was fitting that it also should be conceived without corruption of the mother.

Thirdly, this was befitting to the dignity of Christ's humanity in which there could be no sin, since by it the sin of the world was taken away, according to John 1:29: "Behold the Lamb of God" (i.e. the Lamb without stain) "who taketh away the sin of the world." Now it was not possible in a nature already corrupt, for flesh to be born from sexual intercourse without incurring the infection of original sin. Whence Augustine says (De Nup. et Concup. i): "In that union," viz. the marriage of Mary and Joseph, "the nuptial intercourse alone was lacking: because in sinful flesh this could not be without fleshly concupiscence which arises from sin, and without which He wished to be conceived, Who was to be without sin."

Fourthly, on account of the very end of the Incarnation of Christ, which was that men might be born again as sons of God, "not of the will of the flesh, nor of the will of man, but of God" (John 1:13), i.e. of the power of God, of which fact the very conception of Christ was to appear as an exemplar. Whence Augustine says (De Sanct. Virg.): "It behooved that our Head, by a notable miracle, should be born, after the flesh, of a virgin, that He might thereby signify that His members would be born, after the Spirit, of a virgin Church."

Reply Obj. 1: As Bede says on Luke 1:33: Joseph is called the father of the Saviour, not that he really was His father, as the Photinians pretended: but that he was considered by men to be so, for the safeguarding of Mary's good name. Wherefore Luke adds (Luke 3:23): "Being, as it was supposed, the son of Joseph."

Or, according to Augustine (De Cons. Evang. ii), Joseph is called the father of Christ just as "he is called the husband of Mary, without fleshly mingling, by the mere bond of marriage: being thereby united to Him much more closely than if he were adopted from another family. Consequently that Christ was not begotten of Joseph by fleshly union is no reason why Joseph should not be called His father; since he would be the father even of an adopted son not born of his wife."

Reply Obj. 2: As Jerome says on Matt. 1:18: "Though Joseph was not the father of our Lord and Saviour, the order of His genealogy is traced down to Joseph"--first, because "the Scriptures are not wont to trace the female line in genealogies": secondly, "Mary and Joseph were of the same tribe"; wherefore by law he was bound to take her as being of his kin. Likewise, as Augustine says (De Nup. et Concup. i), "it was befitting to trace the genealogy down to Joseph, lest in that marriage any slight should be offered to the male sex, which is indeed the stronger: for truth suffered nothing thereby, since both Joseph and Mary were of the family of David."

Reply Obj. 3: As the gloss says on this passage, the word " mulier is here used instead of femina, according to the custom of the Hebrew tongue: which applies the term signifying woman to those of the female sex who are virgins."

Reply Obj. 4: This argument is true of those things which come into existence by the way of nature: since nature, just as it is fixed to one particular effect, so it is determinate to one mode of producing that effect. But as the supernatural power of God extends to the infinite: just as it is not determinate to one effect, so neither is it determinate to one mode of producing any effect whatever. Consequently, just as it was possible for the first man to be produced, by the Divine power, "from the slime of the earth," so too was it possible for Christ's body to be made, by Divine power, from a virgin without the seed of the male.

Reply Obj. 5: According to the Philosopher (De Gener. Animal. i, ii, iv), in conception the seed of the male is not by way of matter, but by way of agent: and the female alone supplies the matter. Wherefore though the seed of the male was lacking in Christ's conception, it does not follow that due matter was lacking.

But if the seed of the male were the matter of the fetus in animal conception, it is nevertheless manifest that it is not a matter remaining under one form, but subject to transformation. And though the natural power cannot transmute other than determinate matter to a determinate form; nevertheless the Divine power, which is infinite, can transmute all matter to any form whatsoever. Consequently, just as it transmuted the slime of the earth into Adam's body, so could it transmute the matter supplied by His Mother into Christ's body, even though it were not the sufficient matter for a natural conception.

SECOND ARTICLE [III, Q. 28, Art. 2]

Whether Christ's Mother Was a Virgin in His Birth?

Objection 1: It would seem that Christ's Mother was not a virgin in His Birth. For Ambrose says on Luke 2:23: "He who sanctified a strange womb, for the birth of a prophet, He it is who opened His Mother's womb, that He might go forth unspotted." But opening of the womb excludes virginity. Therefore Christ's Mother was not a virgin in His Birth.

Obj. 2: Further, nothing should have taken place in the mystery of Christ, which would make His body to seem unreal. Now it seems to pertain not to a true but to an unreal body, to be able to go through a closed passage; since two bodies cannot be in one place at the same time. It was therefore unfitting that Christ's body should come forth from His Mother's closed womb: and consequently that she should remain a virgin in giving birth to Him.

Obj. 3: Further, as Gregory says in the Homily for the octave of Easter [*xxvi in Evang.], that by entering after His Resurrection where the disciples were gathered, the doors being shut, our Lord "showed that His body was the same in nature but differed in glory": so that it seems that to go through a closed passage pertains to a glorified body. But Christ's body was not glorified in its conception, but was passible, having "the likeness of sinful flesh," as the Apostle says (Rom. 8:3). Therefore He did not come forth through the closed womb of the Virgin.

*On the contrary,* In a sermon of the Council of Ephesus (P. III, Cap. ix) it is said: "After giving birth, nature knows not a virgin: but grace enhances her fruitfulness, and effects her motherhood, while in no way does it injure her virginity." Therefore Christ's Mother was a virgin also in giving birth to Him.

*I answer that,* Without any doubt whatever we must assert that the Mother of Christ was a virgin even in His Birth: for the prophet says not only: "Behold a virgin shall conceive," but adds: "and shall bear a son." This indeed was befitting for three reasons. First, because this was in keeping with a property of Him whose Birth is in question, for He is the Word of God. For the word is not only conceived in the mind without corruption, but also proceeds from the mind without corruption. Wherefore in order to show that body to be the body of the very Word of God, it was fitting that it should be born of a virgin incorrupt. Whence in the sermon of the Council of Ephesus (quoted above) we read: "Whosoever brings forth mere flesh, ceases to be a virgin. But since she gave birth to the Word made flesh, God safeguarded her virginity so as to manifest His Word, by which Word He thus manifested Himself: for neither does our word, when brought forth, corrupt the mind; nor does God, the substantial Word, deigning to be born, destroy virginity."

Secondly, this is fitting as regards the effect of Christ's Incarnation: since He came for this purpose, that He might take away our corruption. Wherefore it is unfitting that in His Birth He should corrupt His Mother's virginity. Thus Augustine says in a sermon on the Nativity of Our Lord: "It was not right that He who came to heal corruption, should by His advent violate integrity."

Thirdly, it was fitting that He Who commanded us to honor our father and mother should not in His Birth lessen the honor due to His Mother.

Reply Obj. 1: Ambrose says this in expounding the evangelist's quotation from the Law: "Every male opening the womb shall be called holy to the Lord." This, says Bede, "is said in regard to the wonted manner of birth; not that we are to believe that our Lord in coming forth violated the abode of her sacred womb, which His entrance therein had hallowed." Wherefore the opening here spoken of does not imply the unlocking of the enclosure of virginal purity; but the mere coming forth of the infant from the maternal womb.

Reply Obj. 2: Christ wished so to show the reality of His body, as to manifest His Godhead at the same time. For this reason He mingled wondrous with lowly things. Wherefore, to show that His body was real, He was born of a woman. But in order to manifest His Godhead, He was born of a virgin, for "such a Birth befits a God," as Ambrose says in the Christmas hymn.

Reply Obj. 3: Some have held that Christ, in His Birth, assumed the gift of "subtlety," when He came forth from the closed womb of a virgin; and that He assumed the gift of "agility" when with dry feet He walked on the sea. But this is not consistent with what has been decided above (Q. 14). For these gifts of a glorified body result from an overflow of the soul's glory on to the body, as we shall explain further on, in treating of glorified bodies (Suppl., Q. 82): and it has been said above (Q. 13, A. 3, ad 1; Q. 16, A. 1, ad 2) that before His Passion Christ "allowed His flesh to do and to suffer what was proper to it" (Damascene, De Fide Orth. iii): nor was there such an overflow of glory from His soul on to His body.

We must therefore say that all these things took place miraculously by Divine power. Whence Augustine says (Sup. Joan. Tract. 121): "To the substance of a body in which was the Godhead closed doors were no obstacle. For truly He had power to enter in by doors not open, in Whose Birth His Mother's virginity remained inviolate." And Dionysius says in an epistle (Ad Caium iv) that "Christ excelled man in doing that which is proper to man: this is shown in His supernatural conception, of a virgin, and in the unstable waters bearing the weight of earthly feet."

THIRD ARTICLE [III, Q. 28, Art. 3]

Whether Christ's Mother Remained a Virgin After His Birth?

Objection 1: It would seem that Christ's Mother did not remain a virgin after His Birth. For it is written (Matt. 1:18): "Before Joseph and Mary came together, she was found with child of the Holy Ghost." Now the Evangelist would not have said this--"before they came together"--unless he were certain of their subsequent coming together; for no one says of one who does not eventually dine "before he dines" (cf. Jerome, Contra Helvid.). It seems, therefore, that the Blessed Virgin subsequently had intercourse with Joseph; and consequently that she did not remain a virgin after (Christ's) Birth.

Obj. 2: Further, in the same passage (Matt. 1:20) are related the words of the angel to Joseph: "Fear not to take unto thee Mary thy wife." But marriage is consummated by carnal intercourse. Therefore it seems that this must have at some time taken place between Mary and Joseph: and that, consequently she did not remain a virgin after (Christ's) Birth.

Obj. 3: Further, again in the same passage a little further on (Matt. 1:24, 25) we read: "And" (Joseph) "took unto him his wife; and he knew her not till she brought forth her first-born Son." Now this conjunction "till" is wont to designate a fixed time, on the completion of which that takes place which previously had not taken place. And the verb "knew" refers here to knowledge by intercourse (cf. Jerome, Contra Helvid.); just as (Gen. 4:1) it is said that "Adam knew his wife." Therefore it seems that after (Christ's) Birth, the Blessed Virgin was known by Joseph; and, consequently, that she did not remain a virgin after the Birth (of Christ).

Obj. 4: Further, "first-born" can only be said of one who has brothers afterwards: wherefore (Rom. 8:29): "Whom He foreknew, He also predestinated to be made conformable to the image of His Son; that He might be the first-born among many brethren." But the evangelist calls Christ the first-born by His Mother. Therefore she had other children after Christ. And therefore it seems that Christ's Mother did not remain a virgin after His Birth.

Obj. 5: Further, it is written (John 2:12): "After this He went down to Capharnaum, He"--that is, Christ--"and His Mother and His brethren." But brethren are those who are begotten of the same parent. Therefore it seems that the Blessed Virgin had other sons after Christ.

Obj. 6: Further, it is written (Matt. 27:55, 56): "There were there"--that is, by the cross of Christ--"many women afar off, who had followed Jesus from Galilee, ministering unto Him; among whom was Mary Magdalen, and Mary the mother of James and Joseph, and the mother of the sons of Zebedee." Now this Mary who is called "the mother of James and Joseph" seems to have been also the Mother of Christ; for it is written (John 19:25) that "there stood by the cross of Jesus, Mary His Mother." Therefore it seems that Christ's Mother did not remain a virgin after His Birth.

*On the contrary,* It is written (Ezech. 44:2): "This gate shall be shut, it shall not be opened, and no man shall pass through it; because the Lord the God of Israel hath entered in by it." Expounding these words, Augustine says in a sermon (De Annunt. Dom. iii): "What means this closed gate in the House of the Lord, except that Mary is to be ever inviolate? What does it mean that 'no man shall pass through it,' save that Joseph shall not know her? And what is this--'The Lord alone enters in and goeth out by it'--except that the Holy Ghost shall impregnate her, and that the Lord of angels shall be born of her? And what means this--'it shall be shut for evermore'--but that Mary is a virgin before His Birth, a virgin in His Birth, and a virgin after His Birth?"

*I answer that,* Without any hesitation we must abhor the error of Helvidius, who dared to assert that Christ's Mother, after His Birth, was carnally known by Joseph, and bore other children. For, in the first place, this is derogatory to Christ's perfection: for as He is in His Godhead the Only-Begotten of the Father, being thus His Son in every respect perfect, so it was becoming that He should be the Only-begotten son of His Mother, as being her perfect offspring.

Secondly, this error is an insult to the Holy Ghost, whose "shrine" was the virginal womb [*"Sacrarium Spiritus Sancti" (Office of B. M. V., Ant. ad Benedictus, T. P.)], wherein He had formed the flesh of Christ: wherefore it was unbecoming that it should be desecrated by intercourse with man.

Thirdly, this is derogatory to the dignity and holiness of God's Mother: for thus she would seem to be most ungrateful, were she not content with such a Son; and were she, of her own accord, by carnal intercourse to forfeit that virginity which had been miraculously preserved in her.

Fourthly, it would be tantamount to an imputation of extreme presumption in Joseph, to assume that he attempted to violate her whom by the angel's revelation he knew to have conceived by the Holy Ghost.

We must therefore simply assert that the Mother of God, as she was a virgin in conceiving Him and a virgin in giving Him birth, did she remain a virgin ever afterwards.

Reply Obj. 1: As Jerome says (Contra Helvid. i): "Although this particle 'before' often indicates a subsequent event, yet we must observe that it not infrequently points merely to some thing previously in the mind: nor is there need that what was in the mind take place eventually, since something may occur to prevent its happening. Thus if a man say: 'Before I dined in the port, I set sail,' we do not understand him to have dined in port after he set sail: but that his mind was set on dining in port." In like manner the evangelist says: "Before they came together" Mary "was found with child, of the Holy Ghost," not that they came together afterwards: but that, when it seemed that they would come together, this was forestalled through her conceiving by the Holy Ghost, the result being that afterwards they did not come together.

Reply Obj. 2: As Augustine says (De Nup. et Concup. i): "The Mother of God is called (Joseph's) wife from the first promise of her espousals, whom he had not known nor ever was to know by carnal intercourse." For, as Ambrose says on Luke 1:27: "The fact of her marriage is declared, not to insinuate the loss of virginity, but to witness to the reality of the union."

Reply Obj. 3: Some have said that this is not to be understood of carnal knowledge, but of acquaintance. Thus Chrysostom says [*Opus Imperf. in Matth., Hom. 1: among the spurious works ascribed to Chrysostom] that "Joseph did not know her, until she gave birth, being unaware of her dignity: but after she had given birth, then did he know her. Because by reason of her child she surpassed the whole world in beauty and dignity: since she alone in the narrow abode of her womb received Him Whom the world cannot contain."

Others again refer this to knowledge by sight. For as, while Moses was speaking with God, his face was so bright "that the children of Israel could not steadfastly behold it"; so Mary, while being "overshadowed" by the brightness of the "power of the Most High," could not be gazed on by Joseph, until she gave birth. But afterwards she is acknowledged by Joseph, by looking on her face, not by lustful contact.

Jerome, however, grants that this is to be understood of knowledge by intercourse; but he observes that "before" or "until" has a twofold sense in Scripture. For sometimes it indicates a fixed time, as Gal. 3:19: The law "was set because of transgressions, until the seed should come, to whom He made the promise." On the other hand, it sometimes indicates an indefinite time, as in Ps. 122:2: "Our eyes are unto the Lord our God, until He have mercy on us"; from which it is not to be gathered that our eyes are turned from God as soon as His mercy has been obtained. In this sense those things are indicated "of which we might doubt if they had not been written down: while others are left out to be supplied by our understanding. Thus the evangelist says that the Mother of God was not known by her husband until she gave birth, that we may be given to understand that still less did he know her afterwards" (Adversus Helvid. v).

Reply Obj. 4: The Scriptures are wont to designate as the first-born, not only a child who is followed by others, but also the one that is born first. "Otherwise, if a child were not first-born unless followed by others, the first-fruits would not be due as long as there was no further produce" [*Jerome, Adversus Helvid. x]: which is clearly false, since according to the law the first-fruits had to be redeemed within a month (Num. 18:16).

Reply Obj. 5: Some, as Jerome says on Matt. 12:49, 50, "suppose that the brethren of the Lord were Joseph's sons by another wife. But we understand the brethren of the Lord to be not sons of Joseph, but cousins of the Saviour, the sons of Mary, His Mother's sister." For "Scripture speaks of brethren in four senses; namely, those who are united by being of the same parents, of the same nation, of the same family, by common affection." Wherefore the brethren of the Lord are so called, not by birth, as being born of the same mother; but by relationship, as being blood-relations of His. But Joseph, as Jerome says (Contra Helvid. ix), is rather to be believed to have remained a virgin, "since he is not said to have had another wife," and "a holy man does not live otherwise than chastely."

Reply Obj. 6: Mary who is called "the mother of James and Joseph" is not to be taken for the Mother of our Lord, who is not wont to be named in the Gospels save under this designation of her dignity--"the Mother of Jesus." This Mary is to be taken for the wife of Alphaeus, whose son was James the less, known as the "brother of the Lord" (Gal. 1:19).

FOURTH ARTICLE [III, Q. 28, Art. 4]

Whether the Mother of God Took a Vow of Virginity?

Objection 1: It would seem that the Mother of God did not take a vow of virginity. For it is written (Deut. 7:14): "No one shall be barren among you of either sex." But sterility is a consequence of virginity. Therefore the keeping of virginity was contrary to the commandment of the Old Law. But before Christ was born the old law was still in force. Therefore at that time the Blessed Virgin could not lawfully take a vow of virginity.

Obj. 2: Further, the Apostle says (1 Cor. 7:25): "Concerning virgins I have no commandment of the Lord; but I give counsel." But the perfection of the counsels was to take its beginning from Christ, who is the "end of the Law," as the Apostle says (Rom. 10:4). It was not therefore becoming that the Virgin should take a vow of virginity.

Obj. 3: Further, the gloss of Jerome says on 1 Tim. 5:12, that "for those who are vowed to virginity, it is reprehensible not only to marry, but also to desire to be married." But the Mother of Christ committed no sin for which she could be reprehended, as stated above (Q. 27, A. 4). Since therefore she was "espoused," as related by Luke 1:27 it seems that she did not take a vow of virginity.

*On the contrary,* Augustine says (De Sanct. Virg. iv): "Mary answered the announcing angel: 'How shall this be done, because I know not man?' She would not have said this unless she had already vowed her virginity to God."

*I answer that,* As we have stated in the Second Part (II-II, Q. 88, A. 6), works of perfection are more praiseworthy when performed in fulfilment of a vow. Now it is clear that for reasons already given (AA. 1, 2, 3) virginity had a special place in the Mother of God. It was therefore fitting that her virginity should be consecrated to God by vow. Nevertheless because, while the Law was in force both men and women were bound to attend to the duty of begetting, since the worship of God was spread according to carnal origin, until Christ was born of that people; the Mother of God is not believed to have taken an absolute vow of virginity, before being espoused to Joseph, although she desired to do so, yet yielding her own will to God's judgment. Afterwards, however, having taken a husband, according as the custom of the time required, together with him she took a vow of virginity.

Reply Obj. 1: Because it seemed to be forbidden by the law not to take the necessary steps for leaving a posterity on earth, therefore the Mother of God did not vow virginity absolutely, but under the condition that it were pleasing to God. When, however, she knew that it was acceptable to God, she made the vow absolute, before the angel's Annunciation.

Reply Obj. 2: Just as the fulness of grace was in Christ perfectly, yet some beginning of the fulness preceded in His Mother; so also the observance of the counsels, which is an effect of God's grace, began its perfection in Christ, but was begun after a fashion in His Virgin Mother.

Reply Obj. 3: These words of the Apostle are to be understood of those who vow chastity absolutely. Christ's Mother did not do this until she was espoused to Joseph. After her espousals, however, by their common consent she took a vow of virginity together with her spouse.

## QUESTION 29

OF THE ESPOUSALS OF THE MOTHER OF GOD (In Two Articles)

We now consider the espousals of God's Mother: concerning which two points arise for inquiry:

(1) Whether Christ should have been born of an espoused virgin?

(2) Whether there was true marriage between our Lord's Mother and Joseph?

FIRST ARTICLE [III, Q. 29, Art. 1]

Whether Christ Should Have Been Born of an Espoused Virgin?

Objection 1: It would seem that Christ should not have been born of an espoused virgin. For espousals are ordered to carnal intercourse. But our Lord's Mother never wished to have carnal intercourse with her husband; because this would be derogatory to the virginity of her mind. Therefore she should not have been espoused.

Obj. 2: Further, that Christ was born of a virgin was miraculous, whence Augustine says (Ep. ad Volus. cxxxvii): "This same power of God brought forth the infant's limbs out of the virginal womb of His inviolate Mother, by which in the vigor of manhood He passed through the closed doors. If we are told why this happened, it will cease to be wonderful; if another instance be alleged, it will no longer be unique." But miracles that are wrought in confirmation of the Faith should be manifest. Since, therefore, by her Espousals this miracle would be less evident, it seems that it was unfitting that Christ should be born of an espoused virgin.

Obj. 3: Further, the martyr Ignatius, as Jerome says on Matt. 1:18, gives as a reason of the espousals of the Mother of God, "that the manner of His Birth might be hidden from the devil, who would think Him to be begotten not of a virgin but of a wife." But this seems to be no reason at all. First, because by his natural cunning he knows whatever takes place in bodies. Secondly, because later on the demons, through many evident signs, knew Christ after a fashion: whence it is written (Mk. 1:23, 24): "A man with an unclean spirit . . . cried out, saying: What have we to do with Thee, Jesus of Nazareth? Art Thou come to destroy us? I know . . . Thou art the Holy one of God." Therefore it does not seem fitting that the Mother of God should have been espoused.

Obj. 4: Further, Jerome gives as another reason, "lest the Mother of God should be stoned by the Jews as an adulteress." But this reason seems to have no weight, for if she were not espoused, she could not be condemned for adultery. Therefore it does not seem reasonable that Christ should be born of an espoused virgin.

*On the contrary,* It is written (Matt. 1:18): "When as His Mother Mary was espoused to Joseph": and (Luke 1:26, 27): "The angel Gabriel was sent . . . to a virgin espoused to a man whose name was Joseph."

*I answer that,* It was fitting that Christ should be born of an espoused virgin; first, for His own sake; secondly, for His Mother's sake; thirdly, for our sake. For the sake of Christ Himself, for four reasons. First, lest He should be rejected by unbelievers as illegitimate: wherefore Ambrose says on Luke 1:26, 27: "How could we blame Herod or the Jews if they seem to persecute one who was born of adultery?"

Secondly, in order that in the customary way His genealogy might be traced through the male line. Thus Ambrose says on Luke 3:23: "He Who came into the world, according to the custom of the world had to be enrolled. Now for this purpose, it is the men that are required, because they represent the family in the senate and other courts. The custom of the Scriptures, too, shows that the ancestry of the men is always traced out."

Thirdly, for the safety of the new-born Child: lest the devil should plot serious hurt against Him. Hence Ignatius says that she was espoused "that the manner of His Birth might be hidden from the devil."

Fourthly, that He might be fostered by Joseph: who is therefore called His "father," as bread-winner.

It was also fitting for the sake of the Virgin. First, because thus she was rendered exempt from punishment; that is, "lest she should be stoned by the Jews as an adulteress," as Jerome says.

Secondly, that thus she might be safeguarded from ill fame. Whence Ambrose says on Luke 1:26, 27: "She was espoused lest she be wounded by the ill-fame of violated virginity, in whom the pregnant womb would betoken corruption."

Thirdly, that, as Jerome says, Joseph might administer to her wants.

This was fitting, again, for our sake. First, because Joseph is thus a witness to Christ's being born of a virgin. Wherefore Ambrose says: "Her husband is the more trustworthy witness of her purity, in that he would deplore the dishonor, and avenge the disgrace, were it not that he acknowledged the mystery."

Secondly, because thereby the very words of the Virgin are rendered more credible by which she asserted her virginity. Thus Ambrose says: "Belief in Mary's words is strengthened, the motive for a lie is removed. If she had not been espoused when pregnant, she would seem to have wished to hide her sin by a lie: being espoused, she had no motive for lying, since a woman's pregnancy is the reward of marriage and gives grace to the nuptial bond." These two reasons add strength to our faith.

Thirdly, that all excuse be removed from those virgins who, through want of caution, fall into dishonor. Hence Ambrose says: "It was not becoming that virgins should expose themselves to evil report, and cover themselves with the excuse that the Mother of the Lord had also been oppressed by ill-fame."

Fourthly, because by this the universal Church is typified, which is a virgin and yet is espoused to one Man, Christ, as Augustine says (De Sanct. Virg. xii).

A fifth reason may be added: since the Mother of the Lord being both espoused and a virgin, both virginity and wedlock are honored in her person, in contradiction to those heretics who disparaged one or the other.

Reply Obj. 1: We must believe that the Blessed Virgin, Mother of God, desired, from an intimate inspiration of the Holy Ghost, to be espoused, being confident that by the help of God she would never come to have carnal intercourse: yet she left this to God's discretion. Wherefore she suffered nothing in detriment to her virginity.

Reply Obj. 2: As Ambrose says on Luke 1:26: "Our Lord preferred that men should doubt of His origin rather than of His Mother's purity. For he knew the delicacy of virgin modesty, and how easily the fair name of chastity is disparaged: nor did He choose that our faith in His Birth should be strengthened in detriment to His Mother." We must observe, however, that some miracles wrought by God are the direct object of faith; such are the miracles of the virginal Birth, the Resurrection of our Lord, and the Sacrament of the Altar. Wherefore our Lord wished these to be more hidden, that belief in them might have greater merit. Whereas other miracles are for the strengthening of faith: and these it behooves to be manifest.

Reply Obj. 3: As Augustine says (De Trin. iii), the devil can do many things by his natural power which he is hindered by the Divine power from doing. Thus it may be that by his natural power the devil could know that the Mother of God knew not man, but was a virgin; yet was prevented by God from knowing the manner of the Divine Birth. That afterwards the devil after a fashion knew that He was the Son of God, makes no difficulty: because then the time had already come for Christ to make known His power against the devil, and to suffer persecution aroused by him. But during His infancy it behooved the malice of the devil to be withheld, lest he should persecute Him too severely: for Christ did not wish to suffer such things then, nor to make His power known, but to show Himself to be in all things like other infants. Hence Pope Leo (Serm. in Epiph. iv) says that "the Magi found the Child Jesus small in body, dependent on others, unable to speak, and in no way differing from the generality of human infants." Ambrose, however, expounding Luke 1:26, seems to understand this of the devil's members. For, after giving the above reason--namely, that the prince of the world might be deceived--he continues thus: "Yet still more did He deceive the princes of the world, since the evil disposition of the demons easily discovers even hidden things: but those who spend their lives in worldly vanities can have no acquaintance of Divine things."

Reply Obj. 4: The sentence of adulteresses according to the Law was that they should be stoned, not only if they were already espoused or married, but also if their maidenhood were still under the protection of the paternal roof, until the day when they enter the married state. Thus it is written (Deut. 22:20, 21): "If . . . virginity be not found in the damsel . . . the men of the city shall stone her to death, and she shall die; because she hath done a wicked thing in Israel, to play the whore in her father's house."

It may also be said, according to some writers, that the Blessed Virgin was of the family or kindred of Aaron, so that she was related to Elizabeth, as we are told (Luke 1:36). Now a virgin of the priestly tribe was condemned to death for whoredom; for we read (Lev. 21:9): "If the daughter of a priest be taken in whoredom, and dishonor the name of her father, she shall be burnt with fire."

Lastly, some understand the passage of Jerome to refer to the throwing of stones by ill-fame.

SECOND ARTICLE [III, Q. 29, Art. 2]

Whether there was a true marriage between Mary and Joseph?

Objection 1: It would seem that there was no true marriage between Mary and Joseph. For Jerome says against Helvidius that Joseph "was Mary's guardian rather than her husband." But if this was a true marriage, Joseph was truly her husband. Therefore there was no true marriage between Mary and Joseph.

Obj. 2: Further, on Matt. 1:16: "Jacob begot Joseph the husband of Mary," Jerome says: "When thou readest 'husband' suspect not a marriage; but remember that Scripture is wont to speak of those who are betrothed as husband and wife." But a true marriage is not effected by the betrothal, but by the wedding. Therefore, there was no true marriage between the Blessed Virgin and Joseph.

Obj. 3: Further, it is written (Matt. 1:19): "Joseph, her husband, being a just man, and not willing to take her away [*Douay: 'publicly to expose her'], i.e. to take her to his home in order to cohabit with her, was minded to put her away privately, i.e. to postpone the wedding," as Remigius [*Cf. Catena Aurea in Matth.] expounds. Therefore, it seems that, as the wedding was not yet solemnized, there was no true marriage: especially since, after the marriage contract, no one can lawfully put his wife away.

*On the contrary,* Augustine says (De Consensu Evang. ii): "It cannot be allowed that the evangelist thought that Joseph ought to sever his union with Mary" (since he said that Joseph was Mary's husband) "on the ground that in giving birth to Christ, she had not conceived of him, but remained a virgin. For by this example the faithful are taught that if after marriage they remain continent by mutual consent, their union is still and is rightly called marriage, even without intercourse of the sexes."

*I answer that,* Marriage or wedlock is said to be true by reason of its attaining its perfection. Now perfection of anything is twofold; first, and second. The first perfection of a thing consists in its very form, from which it receives its species; while the second perfection of a thing consists in its operation, by which in some way a thing attains its end. Now the form of matrimony consists in a certain inseparable union of souls, by which husband and wife are pledged by a bond of mutual affection that cannot be sundered. And the end of matrimony is the begetting and upbringing of children: the first of which is attained by conjugal intercourse; the second by the other duties of husband and wife, by which they help one another in rearing their offspring.

Thus we may say, as to the first perfection, that the marriage of the Virgin Mother of God and Joseph was absolutely true: because both consented to the nuptial bond, but not expressly to the bond of the flesh, save on the condition that it was pleasing to God. For this reason the angel calls Mary the wife of Joseph, saying to him (Matt. 1:20): "Fear not to take unto thee Mary thy wife": on which words Augustine says (De Nup. et Concup. i): "She is called his wife from the first promise of her espousals, whom he had not known nor ever was to know by carnal intercourse."

But as to the second perfection which is attained by the marriage act, if this be referred to carnal intercourse, by which children are begotten; thus this marriage was not consummated. Wherefore Ambrose says on Luke 1:26, 27: "Be not surprised that Scripture calls Mary a wife. The fact of her marriage is declared, not to insinuate the loss of virginity, but to witness to the reality of the union." Nevertheless, this marriage had the second perfection, as to upbringing of the child. Thus Augustine says (De Nup. et Concup. i): "All the nuptial blessings are fulfilled in the marriage of Christ's parents, offspring, faith and sacrament. The offspring we know to have been the Lord Jesus; faith, for there was no adultery: sacrament, since there was no divorce. Carnal intercourse alone there was none."

Reply Obj. 1: Jerome uses the term "husband" in reference to marriage consummated.

Reply Obj. 2: By marriage Jerome means the nuptial intercourse.

Reply Obj. 3: As Chrysostom says (Hom. i super Matth. [*Opus Imperfectum, among the supposititious works ascribed to St. Chrysostom]) the Blessed Virgin was so espoused to Joseph that she dwelt in his home: "for just as she who conceives in her husband's house is understood to have conceived of him, so she who conceives elsewhere is suspect." Consequently sufficient precaution would not have been taken to safeguard the fair fame of the Blessed Virgin, if she had not the entry of her husband's house. Wherefore the words, "not willing to take her away" are better rendered as meaning, "not willing publicly to expose her," than understood of taking her to his house. Hence the evangelist adds that "he was minded to put her away privately." But although she had the entry of Joseph's house by reason of her first promise of espousals, yet the time had not yet come for the solemnizing of the wedding; for which reason they had not yet consummated the marriage. Therefore, as Chrysostom says (Hom. iv in Matth.): "The evangelist does not say, 'before she was taken to the house of her husband,' because she was already in the house. For it was the custom among the ancients for espoused maidens to enter frequently the houses of them to whom they were betrothed." Therefore the angel also said to Joseph: "Fear not to take unto thee Mary thy wife"; that is: "Fear not to solemnize your marriage with her." Others, however, say that she was not yet admitted to his house, but only betrothed to him. But the first is more in keeping with the Gospel narrative.

# QUESTION 30

OF THE ANNUNCIATION OF THE BLESSED VIRGIN (In Four Articles)

We now have to consider the Blessed Virgin's Annunciation, concerning which there are four points of inquiry:

(1) Whether it was befitting that announcement should be made to her of that which was to be begotten of her?

(2) By whom should this announcement be made?

(3) In what manner should this announcement be made?

(4) Of the order observed in the Annunciation.

FIRST ARTICLE [III, Q. 30, Art. 1]

Whether It Was Necessary to Announce to the Blessed Virgin That Which Was to Be Done in Her?

Objection 1: It would seem that it was unnecessary to announce to the Blessed Virgin that which was to be done in her. For there seems to have been no need of the Annunciation except for the purpose of receiving the Virgin's consent. But her consent seems to have been unnecessary: because the Virginal Conception was foretold by a prophecy of "predestination," which is "fulfilled without our consent," as a gloss says on Matt. 1:22. There was no need, therefore, for this Annunciation.

Obj. 2: Further, the Blessed Virgin believed in the Incarnation, for to disbelieve therein excludes man from the way of salvation; because, as the Apostle says (Rom. 3:22): "The justice of God (is) by faith of Jesus Christ." But one needs no further instruction concerning what one believes without doubt. Therefore the Blessed Virgin had no need for the Incarnation of her Son to be announced to her.

Obj. 3: Further, just as the Blessed Virgin conceived Christ in her body, so every pious soul conceives Him spiritually. Thus the Apostle says (Gal. 4:19): "My little children, of whom I am in labor again, until Christ be formed in you." But to those who conceive Him spiritually no announcement is made of this conception. Therefore neither should it have been announced to the Blessed Virgin that she was to conceive the Son of God in her womb.

*On the contrary,* It is related (Luke 1:31) that the angel said to her: "Behold, thou shalt conceive in thy womb, and shalt bring forth a son."

*I answer that,* It was reasonable that it should be announced to the Blessed Virgin that she was to conceive Christ. First, in order to maintain a becoming order in the union of the Son of God with the Virgin--namely, that she should be informed in mind concerning Him, before conceiving Him in the flesh. Thus Augustine says (De Sancta Virgin. iii): "Mary is more blessed in receiving the faith of Christ, than in conceiving the flesh of Christ"; and further on he adds: "Her nearness as a Mother would have been of no profit to Mary, had she not borne Christ in her heart after a more blessed manner than in her flesh."

Secondly, that she might be a more certain witness of this mystery, being instructed therein by God.

Thirdly, that she might offer to God the free gift of her obedience: which she proved herself right ready to do, saying: "Behold the handmaid of the Lord."

Fourthly, in order to show that there is a certain spiritual wedlock between the Son of God and human nature. Wherefore in the Annunciation the Virgin's consent was besought in lieu of that of the entire human nature.

Reply Obj. 1: The prophecy of predestination is fulfilled without the causality of our will; not without its consent.

Reply Obj. 2: The Blessed Virgin did indeed believe explicitly in the future Incarnation; but, being humble, she did not think such high things of herself. Consequently she required instruction in this matter.

Reply Obj. 3: The spiritual conception of Christ through faith is preceded by the preaching of the faith, for as much as "faith is by hearing" (Rom. 10:17). Yet man does not know for certain thereby that he has grace; but he does know that the faith, which he has received, is true.

SECOND ARTICLE [III, Q. 30, Art. 2]

Whether the annunciation should have been made by an angel to the Blessed Virgin?

Objection 1: It would seem that the Annunciation should not have been made by an angel to our Blessed Lady. For revelations to the highest angels are made immediately by God, as Dionysius says (Coel. Hier. vii). But the Mother of God is exalted above all the angels. Therefore it seems that the mystery of the Incarnation should have been announced to her by God immediately, and not by an angel.

Obj. 2: Further, if in this matter it behooved the common order to be observed, by which Divine things are announced to men by angels; in like manner Divine things are announced to a woman by a man: wherefore the Apostle says (1 Cor. 14:34, 35): "Let women keep silence in the churches . . . but if they would learn anything, let them ask their husbands at home." Therefore it seems that the mystery of the Incarnation should have been announced to the Blessed Virgin by some man: especially seeing that Joseph, her husband, was instructed thereupon by an angel, as is related (Matt. 1:20, 21)

Obj. 3: Further, none can becomingly announce what he knows not. But the highest angels did not fully know the mystery of the Incarnation: wherefore Dionysius says (Coel. Hier. vii) that the question, "Who is this that cometh from Edom?" (Isa. 63:1) is to be understood as made by them. Therefore it seems that the announcement of the Incarnation could not be made becomingly by any angel.

Obj. 4: Further, greater things should be announced by messengers of greater dignity. But the mystery of the Incarnation is the greatest of all things announced by angels to men. It seems, therefore, if it behooved to be announced by an angel at all, that this should have been done by an angel of the highest order. But Gabriel is not of the highest order, but of the order of archangels, which is the last but one: wherefore the Church sings: "We know that the archangel Gabriel brought thee a message from God" [*Feast of Purification B.V.M. ix Resp. Brev. O.P.]. Therefore this announcement was not becomingly made by the archangel Gabriel.

*On the contrary,* It is written (Luke 1:26): "The angel Gabriel was sent by God," etc.

*I answer that,* It was fitting for the mystery of the Incarnation to be announced to the Mother of God by an angel, for three reasons. First, that in this also might be maintained the order established by God, by which Divine things are brought to men by means of the angels. Wherefore Dionysius says (Coel. Hier. iv) that "the angels were the first to be taught the Divine mystery of the loving kindness of Jesus: afterwards the grace of knowledge was imparted to us through them. Thus, then, the most god-like Gabriel made known to Zachary that a prophet son would be born to him; and, to Mary, how the Divine mystery of the ineffable conception of God would be realized in her."

Secondly, this was becoming to the restoration of human nature which was to be effected by Christ. Wherefore Bede says in a homily (in Annunt.): "It was an apt beginning of man's restoration that an angel should be sent by God to the Virgin who was to be hallowed by the Divine Birth: since the first cause of man's ruin was through the serpent being sent by the devil to cajole the woman by the spirit of pride."

Thirdly, because this was becoming to the virginity of the Mother of God. Wherefore Jerome says in a sermon on the Assumption [*Ascribed to St. Jerome but not his work]: "It is well that an angel be sent to the Virgin; because virginity is ever akin to the angelic nature. Surely to live in the flesh and not according to the flesh is not an earthly but a heavenly life."

Reply Obj. 1: The Mother of God was above the angels as regards the dignity to which she was chosen by God. But as regards the present state of life, she was beneath the angels. For even Christ Himself, by reason of His passible life, "was made a little lower than the angels," according to Heb. 2:9. But because Christ was both wayfarer and comprehensor, He did not need to be instructed by angels, as regards knowledge of Divine things. The Mother of God, however, was not yet in the state of comprehension: and therefore she had to be instructed by angels concerning the Divine Conception.

Reply Obj. 2: As Augustine says in a sermon on the Assumption (De Assump. B.V.M. [*Work of another author: among the works of St. Augustine]) a true estimation of the Blessed Virgin excludes her from certain general rules. For "neither did she 'multiply her conceptions' nor was she 'under man's, i.e. her husband's,' power (Gen. 3:16), who in her spotless womb conceived Christ of the Holy Ghost." Therefore it was fitting that she should be informed of the mystery of the Incarnation by means not of a man, but of an angel. For this reason it was made known to her before Joseph: since the message was brought to her before she conceived, but to Joseph after she had conceived.

Reply Obj. 3: As may be gathered from the passage quoted from Dionysius, the angels were acquainted with the mystery of the Incarnation: and yet they put this question, being desirous that Christ should give them more perfect knowledge of the details of this mystery, which are incomprehensible to any created intellect. Thus Maximus [*Maximus of Constantinople] says that "there can be no question that the angels knew that the Incarnation was to take place. But it was not given to them to trace the manner of our Lord's conception, nor how it was that He remained whole in the Father, whole throughout the universe, and was whole in the narrow abode of the Virgin."

Reply Obj. 4: Some say that Gabriel was of the highest order; because Gregory says (Hom. de Centum Ovibus [*34 in Evang.]): "It was right that one of the highest angels should come, since his message was most sublime." But this does nat imply that he was of the highest order of all, but in regard to the angels: since he was an archangel. Thus the Church calls him an archangel, and Gregory himself in a homily (De Centum Ovibus 34) says that "those are called archangels who announce sublime things." It is therefore sufficiently credible that he was the highest of the archangels. And, as Gregory says (De Centum Ovibus 34), this name agrees with his office: for "Gabriel means 'Power of God.' This message therefore was fittingly brought by the 'Power of God,' because the Lord of hosts and mighty in battle was coming to overcome the powers of the air."

THIRD ARTICLE [III, Q. 30, Art. 3]

Whether the Angel of Annunciation Should Have Appeared to the Virgin in a Bodily Vision?

Objection 1: It would seem that the angel of the Annunciation should not have appeared to the Virgin in a bodily vision. For "intellectual vision is more excellent than bodily vision," as Augustine says (Gen. ad lit. xii), and especially more becoming to an angel: since by intellectual vision an angel is seen in his substance; whereas in a bodily vision he is seen in the bodily shape which he assumes. Now since it behooved a sublime messenger to come to announce the Divine Conception, so, seemingly, he should have appeared in the most excellent kind of vision. Therefore it seems that the angel of the Annunciation appeared to the Virgin in an intellectual vision.

Obj. 2: Further, imaginary vision also seems to excel bodily vision: just as the imagination is a higher power than the senses. But "the angel . . . appeared to Joseph in his sleep" (Matt. 1:20), which was clearly an imaginary vision. Therefore it seems that he should have appeared to the Blessed Virgin also in an imaginary vision.

Obj. 3: Further, the bodily vision of a spiritual substance stupefies the beholder; thus we sing of the Virgin herself: "And the Virgin seeing the light was filled with fear" [*Feast of Annunciation, B.V.M. ii Resp. Brev. O.P.]. But it was better that her mind should be preserved from being thus troubled. Therefore it was not fitting that this announcement should be made in a bodily vision.

*On the contrary,* Augustine in a sermon (De Annunt. iii) pictures the Blessed Virgin as speaking thus: "To me came the archangel Gabriel with glowing countenance, gleaming robe, and wondrous step." But these cannot pertain to other than bodily vision. Therefore the angel of the Annunciation appeared in a bodily vision to the Blessed Virgin.

*I answer that,* The angel of the Annunciation appeared in a bodily vision to the Blessed Virgin. And this indeed was fitting, first in regard to that which was announced. For the angel came to announce the Incarnation of the invisible God. Wherefore it was becoming that, in order to make this known, an invisible creature should assume a form in which to appear visibly: forasmuch as all the apparitions of the Old Testament are ordered to that apparition in which the Son of God appeared in the flesh.

Secondly, it was fitting as regards the dignity of the Mother of God, who was to receive the Son of God not only in her mind, but in her bodily womb. Therefore it behooved not only her mind, but also her bodily senses to be refreshed by the angelic vision.

Thirdly, it is in keeping with the certainty of that which was announced. For we apprehend with greater certainty that which is before our eyes, than what is in our imagination. Thus Chrysostom says (Hom. iv in Matth.) that the angel "came to the Virgin not in her sleep, but visibly. For since she was receiving from the angel a message exceeding great, before such an event she needed a vision of great solemnity."

Reply Obj. 1: Intellectual vision excels merely imaginary and merely bodily vision. But Augustine himself says (De Annunt. iii) that prophecy is more excellent if accompanied by intellectual and imaginary vision, than if accompanied by only one of them. Now the Blessed Virgin perceived not only the bodily vision, but also the intellectual illumination. Wherefore this was a more excellent vision. Yet it would have been more excellent if she had perceived the angel himself in his substance by her intellectual vision. But it was incompatible with her state of wayfarer that she should see an angel in his essence.

Reply Obj. 2: The imagination is indeed a higher power than the exterior sense: but because the senses are the principle of human knowledge, the greatest certainty is in them, for the principles of knowledge must needs always be most certain. Consequently Joseph, to whom the angel appeared in his sleep, did not have so excellent a vision as the Blessed Virgin.

Reply Obj. 3: As Ambrose says on Luke 1:11: "We are disturbed, and lose our presence of mind, when we are confronted by the presence of a superior power." And this happens not only in bodily, but also in imaginary vision. Wherefore it is written (Gen. 15:12) that "when the sun was setting, a deep sleep fell upon Abram, and a great and darksome horror seized upon him." But by being thus disturbed man is not harmed to such an extent that therefore he ought to forego the vision of an angel. First because from the very fact that man is raised above himself, in which matter his dignity is concerned, his inferior powers are weakened; and from this results the aforesaid disturbance: thus, also, when the natural heat is drawn within a body, the exterior parts tremble. Secondly, because, as Origen says (Hom. iv in Luc.): "The angel who appeared, knowing hers was a human nature, first sought to remedy the disturbance of mind to which a man is subject." Wherefore both to Zachary and to Mary, as soon as they were disturbed, he said: "Fear not." For this reason, as we read in the life of Anthony, "it is difficult to discern good from evil spirits. For if joy succeed fear, we should know that the help is from the Lord: because security of soul is a sign of present majesty. But if the fear with which we are stricken persevere, it is an enemy that we see."

Moreover it was becoming to virginal modesty that the Virgin should be troubled. Because, as Ambrose says on Luke 1:20: "It is the part of a virgin to be timid, to fear the advances of men, and to shrink from men's addresses."

But others say that as the Blessed Virgin was accustomed to angelic visions, she was not troubled at seeing this angel, but with wonder at hearing what the angel said to her, for she did not think so highly of herself. Wherefore the evangelist does not say that she was troubled at seeing the angel, but "at his saying."

FOURTH ARTICLE [III, Q. 30, Art. 4]

Whether the Annunciation Took Place in Becoming Order?

Objection 1: It would seem that the Annunciation did not take place in becoming order. For the dignity of the Mother of God results from the child she conceived. But the cause should be made known before the effect. Therefore the angel should have announced to the Virgin the conception of her child before acknowledging her dignity in greeting her.

Obj. 2: Further, proof should be omitted in things which admit of no doubt; and premised where doubt is possible. But the angel seems first to have announced what the virgin might doubt, and which, because of her doubt, would make her ask: "How shall this be done?" and afterwards to have given the proof, alleging both the instance of Elizabeth and the omnipotence of God. Therefore the Annunciation was made by the angel in unbecoming order.

Obj. 3: Further, the greater cannot be adequately proved by the less. But it was a greater wonder for a virgin than for an old woman to be with child. Therefore the angel's proof was insufficient to demonstrate the conception of a virgin from that of an old woman.

*On the contrary,* it is written (Rom. 13:1): "Those that are of God, are well ordered [Vulg.: 'Those that are, are ordained of God']." Now the angel was "sent by God" to announce unto the Virgin, as is related Luke 1:26. Therefore the Annunciation was made by the angel in the most perfect order.

*I answer that,* The Annunciation was made by the angel in a becoming manner. For the angel had a threefold purpose in regard to the Virgin. First, to draw her attention to the consideration of a matter of such moment. This he did by greeting her by a new and unwonted salutation. Wherefore Origen says, commenting on Luke (Hom. vi), that if "she had known that similar words had been addressed to anyone else, she, who had knowledge of the Law, would never have been astonished at the seeming strangeness of the salutation." In which salutation he began by asserting her worthiness of the conception, by saying, "Full of grace"; then he announced the conception in the words, "The Lord is with thee"; and then foretold the honor which would result to her therefrom, by saying, "Blessed art thou among women."

Secondly, he purposed to instruct her about the mystery of the Incarnation, which was to be fulfilled in her. This he did by foretelling the conception and birth, saying: "Behold, thou shalt conceive in thy womb," etc.; and by declaring the dignity of the child conceived, saying: "He shall be great"; and further, by making known the mode of conception, when he said: "The Holy Ghost shall come upon thee."

Thirdly, he purposed to lead her mind to consent. This he did by the instance of Elizabeth, and by the argument from Divine omnipotence.

Reply Obj. 1: To a humble mind nothing is more astonishing than to hear its own excellence. Now, wonder is most effective in drawing the mind's attention. Therefore the angel, desirous of drawing the Virgin's attention to the hearing of so great a mystery, began by praising her.

Reply Obj. 2: Ambrose says explicitly on Luke 1:34, that the Blessed Virgin did not doubt the angel's words. For he says: "Mary's answer is more temperate than the words of the priest. She says: How shall this be? He replies: Whereby shall I know this? He denies that he believes, since he denies that he knows this. She does not doubt fulfilment when she asks how it shall be done."

Augustine, however, seems to assert that she doubted. For he says (De Qq. Vet. et Nov. Test. qu. li): "To Mary, in doubt about the conception, the angel declares the possibility thereof." But such a doubt is one of wonder rather than of unbelief. And so the angel adduces a proof, not as a cure for unbelief, but in order to remove her astonishment.

Reply Obj. 3: As Ambrose says (Hexaemeron v): "For this reason had many barren women borne children, that the virginal birth might be credible."

The conception of the sterile Elizabeth is therefore adduced, not as a sufficient argument, but as a kind of figurative example: consequently in support of this instance, the convincing argument is added taken from the Divine omnipotence.

## QUESTION 31

OF THE MATTER FROM WHICH THE SAVIOUR'S BODY WAS CONCEIVED (In Eight Articles)

We have now to consider the Saviour's conception. First, as to the matter from which His body was conceived; secondly, as to the author of His conception; thirdly, as to the manner and order of His conception.

Concerning the first there are eight points of inquiry:

(1) Whether the flesh of Christ was derived from Adam?

(2) Whether it was derived from David?

(3) Of the genealogy of Christ which is given in the Gospels;

(4) Whether it was fitting for Christ to be born of a woman?

(5) Whether His body was formed from the purest blood of the Virgin?

(6) Whether the flesh of Christ was in the patriarchs as to something signate?

(7) Whether the flesh of Christ in the patriarchs was subject to sin?

(8) Whether Christ paid tithes in the loins of Abraham?

FIRST ARTICLE [III, Q. 31, Art. 1]

Whether the Flesh of Christ Was Derived from Adam?

Objection 1: It would seem that Christ's flesh was not derived from Adam. For the Apostle says (1 Cor. 15:47): "The first man was of the earth, earthly: the second man, from heaven, heavenly." Now, the first man is Adam: and the second man is Christ. Therefore Christ is not derived from Adam, but has an origin distinct from him.

Obj. 2: Further, the conception of Christ should have been most miraculous. But it is a greater miracle to form man's body from the slime of the earth, than from human matter derived from Adam. It seems therefore unfitting that Christ should take flesh from Adam. Therefore the body of Christ should not have been formed from the mass of the human race derived from Adam, but of some other matter.

Obj. 3: Further, by "one man sin entered into this world," i.e. by Adam, because in him all nations sinned originally, as is clear from Rom. 5:12. But if Christ's body was derived from Adam, He would have been in Adam originally when he sinned: therefore he would have contracted original sin; which is unbecoming in His purity. Therefore the body of Christ was not formed of matter derived from Adam.

*On the contrary,* The Apostle says (Heb. 2:16): "Nowhere doth He"--that is, the Son of God--"take hold of the angels: but of the seed of Abraham He taketh hold." But the seed of Abraham was derived from Adam. Therefore Christ's body was formed of matter derived from Adam.

*I answer that,* Christ assumed human nature in order to cleanse it of corruption. But human nature did not need to be cleansed save in as far as it was soiled in its tainted origin whereby it was descended from Adam. Therefore it was becoming that He should assume flesh of matter derived from Adam, that the nature itself might be healed by the assumption.

Reply Obj. 1: The second man, i.e. Christ, is said to be of heaven, not indeed as to the matter from which His body was formed, but either as to the virtue whereby it was formed; or even as to His very Godhead. But as to matter, Christ's body was earthly, as Adam's body was.

Reply Obj. 2: As stated above (Q. 29, A. 1, ad 2) the mystery of Christ's Incarnation is miraculous, not as ordained to strengthen faith, but as an article of faith. And therefore in the mystery of the Incarnation we do not seek that which is most miraculous, as in those miracles that are wrought for the confirmation of faith, but what is most becoming to Divine wisdom, and most expedient to the salvation of man, since this is what we seek in all matters of faith.

It may also be said that in the mystery of the Incarnation the miracle is not only in reference to the matter of the conception, but rather in respect of the manner of the conception and birth; inasmuch as a virgin conceived and gave birth to God.

Reply Obj. 3: As stated above (Q. 15, A. 1, ad 2), Christ's body was in Adam in respect of a bodily substance--that is to say, that the corporeal matter of Christ's body was derived from Adam: but it was not there by reason of seminal virtue, because it was not conceived from the seed of man. Thus it did not contract original sin, as others who are descended from Adam by man's seed.

SECOND ARTICLE [III, Q. 31, Art. 2]

Whether Christ Took Flesh of the Seed of David?

Objection 1: It would seem that Christ did not take flesh of the seed of David. For Matthew, in tracing the genealogy of Christ, brings it down to Joseph. But Joseph was not Christ's father, as shown above (Q. 28, A. 1, ad 1, 2). Therefore it seems that Christ was not descended from David.

Obj. 2: Further, Aaron was of the tribe of Levi, as related Ex. 6. Now Mary the Mother of Christ is called the cousin of Elizabeth, who was a daughter of Aaron, as is clear from Luke 1:5, 36. Therefore, since David was of the tribe of Juda, as is shown Matt. 1, it seems that Christ was not descended from David.

Obj. 3: Further, it is written of Jechonias (Jer. 22:30): "Write this man barren . . . for there shall not be a man of his seed that shall sit upon the throne of David." Whereas of Christ it is written (Isa. 9:7): "He shall sit upon the throne of David." Therefore Christ was not of the seed of Jechonias: nor, consequently, of the family of David, since Matthew traces the genealogy from David through Jechonias.

*On the contrary,* It is written (Rom. 1:3): "Who was made to him of the seed of David according to the flesh."

*I answer that,* Christ is said to have been the son especially of two of the patriarchs, Abraham and David, as is clear from Matt. 1:1. There are many reasons for this. First to these especially was the promise made concerning Christ. For it was said to Abraham (Gen. 22:18): "In thy seed shall all the nations of the earth be blessed": which words the Apostle expounds of Christ (Gal. 3:16): "To Abraham were the promises made and to his seed. He saith not, 'And to his seeds' as of many; but as of one, 'And to thy seed,' which is Christ." And to David it was said (Ps. 131:11): "Of the fruit of thy womb I will set upon thy throne." Wherefore the Jewish people, receiving Him with kingly honor, said (Matt. 21:9): "Hosanna to the Son of David."

A second reason is because Christ was to be king, prophet, and priest. Now Abraham was a priest; which is clear from the Lord saying unto him (Gen. 15:9): "Take thee [Vulg.: 'Me'] a cow of three years old," etc. He was also a prophet, according to Gen. 20:7: "He is a prophet; and he shall pray for thee." Lastly David was both king and prophet.

A third reason is because circumcision had its beginning in Abraham: while in David God's election was most clearly made manifest, according to 1 Kings 13:14: "The Lord hath sought Him a man according to His own heart." And consequently Christ is called in a most special way the Son of both, in order to show that He came for the salvation both of the circumcised and of the elect among the Gentiles.

Reply Obj. 1: Faustus the Manichean argued thus, in the desire to prove that Christ is not the Son of David, because He was not conceived of Joseph, in whom Matthew's genealogy terminates. Augustine answered this argument thus (Contra Faust. xxii): "Since the same evangelist affirms that Joseph was Mary's husband and that Christ's mother was a virgin, and that Christ was of the seed of Abraham, what must we believe, but that Mary was not a stranger to the family of David: and that it is not without reason that she was called the wife of Joseph, by reason of the close alliance of their hearts, although not mingled in the flesh; and that the genealogy is traced down to Joseph rather than to her by reason of the dignity of the husband? So therefore we believe that Mary was also of the family of David: because we believe the Scriptures, which assert both that Christ was of the seed of David according to the flesh, and that Mary was His Mother, not by sexual intercourse but retaining her virginity." For as Jerome says on Matt. 1:18: "Joseph and Mary were of the same tribe: wherefore he was bound by law to marry her as she was his kinswoman. Hence it was that they were enrolled together at Bethlehem, as being descended from the same stock."

Reply Obj. 2: Gregory of Nazianzum answers this objection by saying that it happened by God's will, that the royal family was united to the priestly race, so that Christ, who is both king and priest, should be born of both according to the flesh. Wherefore Aaron, who was the first priest according to the Law, married a wife of the tribe of Juda, Elizabeth, daughter of Aminadab. It is therefore possible that Elizabeth's father married a wife of the family of David, through whom the Blessed Virgin Mary, who was of the family of David, would be a cousin of Elizabeth. Or conversely, and with greater likelihood, that the Blessed Mary's father, who was of the family of David, married a wife of the family of Aaron.

Again, it may be said with Augustine (Contra Faust. xxii) that if Joachim, Mary's father, was of the family of Aaron (as the heretic Faustus pretended to prove from certain apocryphal writings), then we must believe that Joachim's mother, or else his wife, was of the family of David, so long as we say that Mary was in some way descended from David.

Reply Obj. 3: As Ambrose says on Luke 3:25, this prophetical passage does not deny that a posterity will be born of the seed of Jechonias. And so Christ is of his seed. Neither is the fact that Christ reigned contrary to prophecy, for He did not reign with worldly honor; since He declared: "My kingdom is not of this world."

THIRD ARTICLE [III, Q. 31, Art. 3]

Whether Christ's Genealogy Is Suitably Traced by the Evangelists?

Objection 1: It would seem that Christ's genealogy is not suitably traced by the Evangelists. For it is written (Isa. 53:8): "Who shall declare His generation?" Therefore Christ's genealogy should not have been set down.

Obj. 2: Further, one man cannot possibly have two fathers. But Matthew says that "Jacob begot Joseph, the husband of Mary": whereas Luke says that Joseph was the son of Heli. Therefore they contradict one another.

Obj. 3: Further, there seem to be divergencies between them on several points. For Matthew, at the commencement of his book, beginning from Abraham and coming down to Joseph, enumerates forty-two generations. Whereas Luke sets down Christ's genealogy after His Baptism, and beginning from Christ traces the series of generations back to God, counting in all seventy-seven generations, the first and last included. It seems therefore that their accounts of Christ's genealogy do not agree.

Obj. 4: Further, we read (4 Kings 8:24) that Joram begot Ochozias, who was succeeded by his son Joas: who was succeeded by his son Amasius: after whom reigned his son Azarias, called Ozias; who was succeeded by his son Joathan. But Matthew says that Joram begot Ozias. Therefore it seems that his account of Christ's genealogy is unsuitable, since he omits three kings in the middle thereof.

Obj. 5: Further, all those who are mentioned in Christ's genealogy had both a father and a mother, and many of them had brothers also. Now in Christ's genealogy Matthew mentions only three mothers--namely, Thamar, Ruth, and the wife of Urias. He also mentions the brothers of Judas and Jechonias, and also Phares and Zara. But Luke mentions none of these. Therefore the evangelists seem to have described the genealogy of Christ in an unsuitable manner.

*On the contrary,* The authority of Scripture suffices.

*I answer that,* As is written (2 Tim. 3:16), "All Holy Scripture is inspired of God [Vulg.: 'All scripture inspired of God is profitable'], etc. Now what is done by God is done in perfect order, according to Rom. 13:1: "Those that are of God are ordained [Vulg.: 'Those that are, are ordained of God']." Therefore Christ's genealogy is set down by the evangelists in a suitable order.

Reply Obj. 1: As Jerome says on Matt. 1, Isaias speaks of the generation of Christ's Godhead. Whereas Matthew relates the generation of Christ in His humanity; not indeed by explaining the manner of the Incarnation, which is also unspeakable; but by enumerating Christ's forefathers from whom He was descended according to the flesh.

Reply Obj. 2: Various answers have been made by certain writers to this objection which was raised by Julian the Apostate; for some, as Gregory of Nazianzum, say that the people mentioned by the two evangelists are the same, but under different names, as though they each had two. But this will not stand: because Matthew mentions one of David's sons--namely, Solomon; whereas Luke mentions another--namely, Nathan, who according to the history of the kings (2 Kings 5:14) were clearly brothers.

Wherefore others said that Matthew gave the true genealogy of Christ: while Luke gave the supposititious genealogy; hence he began: "Being (as it was supposed) the son of Joseph." For among the Jews there were some who believed that, on account of the crimes of the kings of Juda, Christ would be born of the family of David, not through the kings, but through some other line of private individuals.

Others again have supposed that Matthew gave the forefathers according to the flesh: whereas Luke gave these according to the spirit, that is, righteous men, who are called (Christ's) forefathers by likeness of virtue.

But an answer is given in the Qq. Vet. et Nov. Test. [*Part i, qu. lvi; part 2, qu. vi] to the effect that we are not to understand that Joseph is said by Luke to be the son of Heli: but that at the time of Christ, Heli and Joseph were differently descended from David. Hence Christ is said to have been supposed to be the son of Joseph, and also to have been the son of Heli as though (the Evangelist) were to say that Christ, from the fact that He was the son of Joseph, could be called the son of Heli and of all those who were descended from David; as the Apostle says (Rom. 9:5): "Of whom" (viz. the Jews) "is Christ according to the flesh."

Augustine again gives three solutions (De Qq. Evang. ii), saying: "There are three motives by one or other of which the evangelist was guided. For either one evangelist mentions Joseph's father of whom he was begotten; whilst the other gives either his maternal grandfather or some other of his later forefathers; or one was Joseph's natural father: the other is father by adoption. Or, according to the Jewish custom, one of those having died without children, a near relation of his married his wife, the son born of the latter union being reckoned as the son of the former": which is a kind of legal adoption, as Augustine himself says (De Consensu Evang. ii, Cf. Retract. ii).

This last motive is the truest: Jerome also gives it commenting on Matt. 1:16; and Eusebius of Caesarea in his Church history (I, vii), says that it is given by Africanus the historian. For these writers say that Mathan and Melchi, at different times, each begot a son of one and the same wife, named Estha. For Mathan, who traced his descent through Solomon, had married her first, and died, leaving one son, whose name was Jacob: and after his death, as the law did not forbid his widow to remarry, Melchi, who traced his descent through Mathan, being of the same tribe though not of the same family as Mathan, married his widow, who bore him a son, called Heli; so that Jacob and Heli were uterine brothers born to different fathers. Now one of these, Jacob, on his brother Heli dying without issue, married the latter's widow, according to the prescription of the law, of whom he had a son, Joseph, who by nature was his own son, but by law was accounted the son of Heli. Wherefore Matthew says "Jacob begot Joseph": whereas Luke, who was giving the legal genealogy, speaks of no one as begetting.

And although Damascene (De Fide Orth. iv) says that the Blessed Virgin Mary was connected with Joseph in as far as Heli was accounted as his father, for he says that she was descended from Melchi: yet must we also believe that she was in some way descended from Solomon through those patriarchs enumerated by Matthew, who is said to have set down Christ's genealogy according to the flesh; and all the more since Ambrose states that Christ was of the seed of Jechonias.

Reply Obj. 3: According to Augustine (De Consensu Evang. ii) "Matthew purposed to delineate the royal personality of Christ; Luke the priestly personality: so that in Matthew's genealogy is signified the assumption of our sins by our Lord Jesus Christ": inasmuch as by his carnal origin "He assumed 'the likeness of sinful flesh.' But in Luke's genealogy the washing away of our sins is signified," which is effected by Christ's sacrifice. "For which reason Matthew traces the generations downwards, Luke upwards." For the same reason too "Matthew descends from David through Solomon, in whose mother David sinned; whereas Luke ascends to David through Nathan, through whose namesake, the prophet, God expiated his sin." And hence it is also that, because "Matthew wished to signify that Christ had condescended to our mortal nature, he set down the genealogy of Christ at the very outset of his Gospel, beginning with Abraham and descending to Joseph and the birth of Christ Himself. Luke, *on the contrary,* sets forth Christ's genealogy not at the outset, but after Christ's Baptism, and not in the descending but in the ascending order: as though giving prominence to the office of the priest in expiating our sins, to which John bore witness, saying: 'Behold Him who taketh away the sin of the world.' And in the ascending order, he passes Abraham and continues up to God, to whom we are reconciled by cleansing and expiating. With reason too he follows the origin of adoption; because by adoption we become children of God: whereas by carnal generation the Son of God became the Son of Man. Moreover he shows sufficiently that he does not say that Joseph was the son of Heli as though begotten by him, but because he was adopted by him, since he says that Adam was the son of God, inasmuch as he was created by God."

Again, the number forty pertains to the time of our present life: because of the four parts of the world in which we pass this mortal life under the rule of Christ. And forty is the product of four multiplied by ten: while ten is the sum of the numbers from one to four. The number ten may also refer to the decalogue; and the number four to the present life; or again to the four Gospels, according to which Christ reigns in us. And thus "Matthew, putting forward the royal personality of Christ, enumerates forty persons not counting Him" (cf. Augustine, De Consensu Evang. ii). But this is to be taken on the supposition that it be the same Jechonias at the end of the second, and at the commencement of the third series of fourteen, as Augustine understands it. According to him this was done in order to signify "that under Jechonias there was a certain defection to strange nations during the Babylonian captivity; which also foreshadowed the fact that Christ would pass from the Jews to the Gentiles."

On the other hand, Jerome (on Matt. 1:12-15) says that there were two Joachims--that is, Jechonias, father and son: both of whom are mentioned in Christ's genealogy, so as to make clear the distinction of the generations, which the evangelist divides into three series of fourteen; which amounts in all to forty-two persons. Which number may also be applied to the Holy Church: for it is the product of six, which signifies the labor of the present life, and seven, which signifies the rest of the life to come: for six times seven are forty-two. The number fourteen, which is the sum of ten and four, can also be given the same signification as that given to the number forty, which is the product of the same numbers by multiplication.

But the number used by Luke in Christ's genealogy signifies the generality of sins. "For the number ten is shown in the ten precepts of the Law to be the number of righteousness. Now, to sin is to go beyond the restriction of the Law. And eleven is the number beyond ten." And seven signifies universality: because "universal time is involved in seven days." Now seven times eleven are seventy-seven: so that this number signifies the generality of sins which are taken away by Christ.

Reply Obj. 4: As Jerome says on Matt. 1:8, 11: "Because Joram allied himself with the family of the most wicked Jezabel, therefore his memory is omitted down to the third generation, lest it should be inserted among the holy predecessors of the Nativity." Hence as Chrysostom [*Cf. Opus Imperf. in Matth. Hom. i, falsely ascribed to Chrysostom] says: "Just as great was the blessing conferred on Jehu, who wrought vengeance on the house of Achab and Jezabel, so also great was the curse on the house of Joram, through the wicked daughter of Achab and Jezabel, so that until the fourth generation his posterity is cut off from the number of kings, according to Ex. 20:5: I shall visit [Vulg.: 'Visiting'] the iniquity of the fathers upon the children unto the third and fourth generations."

It must also be observed that there were other kings who sinned and are mentioned in Christ's genealogy: but their impiety was not continuous. For, as it is stated in the book De Qq. Vet. et Nov. Test. qu. lxxxv: "Solomon through his father's merits is included in the series of kings; and Roboam . . . through the merits of Asa," who was son of his (Roboam's) son, Abiam. "But the impiety of those three [*i.e. Ochozias, Joas, and Amasias, of whom St. Augustine asks in this question lxxxv, why they were omitted by St. Matthew] was continuous."

Reply Obj. 5: As Jerome says on Matt. 1:3: "None of the holy women are mentioned in the Saviour's genealogy, but only those whom Scripture censures, so that He who came for the sake of sinners, by being born of sinners, might blot out all sin." Thus Thamar is mentioned, who is censured for her sin with her father-in-law; Rahab who was a whore; Ruth who was a foreigner; and Bethsabee, the wife of Urias, who was an adulteress. The last, however, is not mentioned by name, but is designated through her husband; both on account of his sin, for he was cognizant of the adultery and murder; and further in order that, by mentioning the husband by name, David's sin might be recalled. And because Luke purposes to delineate Christ as the expiator of our sins, he makes no mention of these women. But he does mention Juda's brethren, in order to show that they belong to God's people: whereas Ismael, the brother of Isaac, and Esau, Jacob's brother, were cut off from God's people, and for this reason are not mentioned in Christ's genealogy. Another motive was to show the emptiness of pride of birth: for many of Juda's brethren were born of hand-maidens, and yet all were patriarchs and heads of tribes. Phares and Zara are mentioned together, because, as Ambrose says on Luke 3:23, "they are the type of the twofold life of man: one, according to the Law," signified by Zara; "the other by Faith," of which Phares is the type. The brethren of Jechonias are included, because they all reigned at various times: which was not the case with other kings: or, again, because they were alike in wickedness and misfortune.

FOURTH ARTICLE [III, Q. 31, Art. 4]

Whether the Matter of Christ's Body Should Have Been Taken from a Woman?

Objection 1: It would seem that the matter of Christ's body should not have been taken from a woman. For the male sex is more noble than the female. But it was most suitable that Christ should assume that which is perfect in human nature. Therefore it seems that He should not have taken flesh from a woman but rather from man: just as Eve was formed from the rib of a man.

Obj. 2: Further, whoever is conceived of a woman is shut up in her womb. But it ill becomes God, Who fills heaven and earth, as is written Jer. 23:24, to be shut up within the narrow limits of the womb. Therefore it seems that He should not have been conceived of a woman.

Obj. 3: Further, those who are conceived of a woman contract a certain uncleanness: as it is written (Job 25:4): "Can man be justified compared with God? Or he that is born of a woman appear clean?" But it was unbecoming that any uncleanness should be in Christ: for He is the Wisdom of God, of whom it is written (Wis. 7:25) that "no defiled thing cometh into her." Therefore it does not seem right that He should have taken flesh from a woman.

*On the contrary,* It is written (Gal. 4:4): "God sent His Son, made of a woman."

*I answer that,* Although the Son of God could have taken flesh from whatever matter He willed, it was nevertheless most becoming that He should take flesh from a woman. First because in this way the entire human nature was ennobled. Hence Augustine says (QQ. lxxxiii, qu. 11): "It was suitable that man's liberation should be made manifest in both sexes. Consequently, since it behooved a man, being of the nobler sex, to assume, it was becoming that the liberation of the female sex should be manifested in that man being born of a woman."

Secondly, because thus the truth of the Incarnation is made evident. Wherefore Ambrose says (De Incarn. vi): "Thou shalt find in Christ many things both natural, and supernatural. In accordance with nature He was within the womb," viz. of a woman's body: "but it was above nature that a virgin should conceive and give birth: that thou mightest believe that He was God, who was renewing nature; and that He was man who, according to nature, was being born of a man." And Augustine says (Ep. ad Volus. cxxxvii): "If Almighty God had created a man formed otherwise than in a mother's womb, and had suddenly produced him to sight . . . would He not have strengthened an erroneous opinion, and made it impossible for us to believe that He had become a true man? And whilst He is doing all things wondrously, would He have taken away that which He accomplished in mercy? But now, He, the mediator between God and man, has so shown Himself, that, uniting both natures in the unity of one Person, He has given a dignity to ordinary by extraordinary things, and tempered the extraordinary by the ordinary."

Thirdly, because in this fashion the begetting of man is accomplished in every variety of manner. For the first man was made from the "slime of the earth," without the concurrence of man or woman: Eve was made of man but not of woman: and other men are made from both man and woman. So that this fourth manner remained as it were proper to Christ, that He should be made of a woman without the concurrence of a man.

Reply Obj. 1: The male sex is more noble than the female, and for this reason He took human nature in the male sex. But lest the female sex should be despised, it was fitting that He should take flesh of a woman. Hence Augustine says (De Agone Christ. xi): "Men, despise not yourselves: the Son of God became a man: despise not yourselves, women; the Son of God was born of a woman."

Reply Obj. 2: Augustine thus (Contra Faust. xxiii) replies to Faustus, who urged this objection; "By no means," says he, "does the Catholic Faith, which believes that Christ the Son of God was born of a virgin, according to the flesh, suppose that the same Son of God was so shut up in His Mother's womb, as to cease to be elsewhere, as though He no longer continued to govern heaven and earth, and as though He had withdrawn Himself from the Father. But you, Manicheans, being of a mind that admits of nought but material images, are utterly unable to grasp these things." For, as he again says (Ep. ad Volus. cxxxvii), "it belongs to the sense of man to form conceptions only through tangible bodies, none of which can be entire everywhere, because they must of necessity be diffused through their innumerable parts in various places . . . Far otherwise is the nature of the soul from that of the body: how much more the nature of God, the Creator of soul and body! . . . He is able to be entire everywhere, and to be contained in no place. He is able to come without moving from the place where He was; and to go without leaving the spot whence He came."

Reply Obj. 3: There is no uncleanness in the conception of man from a woman, as far as this is the work of God: wherefore it is written (Acts 10:15): "That which God hath cleansed do not thou call common," i.e. unclean. There is, however, a certain uncleanness therein, resulting from sin, as far as lustful desire accompanies conception by sexual union. But this was not the case with Christ, as shown above (Q. 28, A. 1). But if there were any uncleanness therein, the Word of God would not have been sullied thereby, for He is utterly unchangeable. Wherefore Augustine says (Contra Quinque Haereses v): "God saith, the Creator of man: What is it that troubles thee in My Birth? I was not conceived by lustful desire. I made Myself a mother of whom to be born. If the sun's rays can dry up the filth in the drain, and yet not be defiled: much more can the Splendor of eternal light cleanse whatever It shines upon, but Itself cannot be sullied."

FIFTH ARTICLE [III, Q. 31, Art. 5]

Whether the Flesh of Christ Was Conceived of the Virgin's Purest Blood?

Objection 1: It would seem that the flesh of Christ was not conceived of the Virgin's purest blood: For it is said in the collect (Feast of the Annunciation) that God "willed that His Word should take flesh from a Virgin." But flesh differs from blood. Therefore Christ's body was not taken from the Virgin's blood.

Obj. 2: Further, as the woman was miraculously formed from the man, so Christ's body was formed miraculously from the Virgin. But the woman is not said to have been formed from the man's blood, but rather from his flesh and bones, according to Gen. 2:23: "This now is bone of my bones, and flesh of my flesh." It seems therefore that neither should Christ's body have been formed from the Virgin's blood, but from her flesh and bones.

Obj. 3: Further, Christ's body was of the same species as other men's bodies. But other men's bodies are not formed from the purest blood but from the semen and the menstrual blood. Therefore it seems that neither was Christ's body conceived of the purest blood of the Virgin.

*On the contrary,* Damascene says (De Fide Orth. iii) that "the Son of God, from the Virgin's purest blood, formed Himself flesh, animated with a rational soul."

*I answer that,* As stated above (A. 4), in Christ's conception His being born of a woman was in accordance with the laws of nature, but that He was born of a virgin was above the laws of nature. Now, such is the law of nature that in the generation of an animal the female supplies the matter, while the male is the active principle of generation; as the Philosopher proves (De Gener. Animal. i). But a woman who conceives of a man is not a virgin. And consequently it belongs to the supernatural mode of Christ's generation, that the active principle of generation was the supernatural power of God: but it belongs to the natural mode of His generation, that the matter from which His body was conceived is similar to the matter which other women supply for the conception of their offspring. Now, this matter, according to the Philosopher (De Gener. Animal.), is the woman's blood, not any of her blood, but brought to a more perfect stage of secretion by the mother's generative power, so as to be apt for conception. And therefore of such matter was Christ's body conceived.

Reply Obj. 1: Since the Blessed Virgin was of the same nature as other women, it follows that she had flesh and bones of the same nature as theirs. Now, flesh and bones in other women are actual parts of the body, the integrity of which results therefrom: and consequently they cannot be taken from the body without its being corrupted or diminished. But as Christ came to heal what was corrupt, it was not fitting that He should bring corruption or diminution to the integrity of His Mother. Therefore it was becoming that Christ's body should be formed not from the flesh or bones of the Virgin, but from her blood, which as yet is not actually a part, but is potentially the whole, as stated in De Gener. Animal. i. Hence He is said to have taken flesh from the Virgin, not that the matter from which His body was formed was actual flesh, but blood, which is flesh potentially.

Reply Obj. 2: As stated in the First Part (Q. 92, A. 3, ad 2), Adam, through being established as a kind of principle of human nature, had in his body a certain proportion of flesh and bone, which belonged to him, not as an integral part of his personality, but in regard to his state as a principle of human nature. And from this was the woman formed, without detriment to the man. But in the Virgin's body there was nothing of this sort, from which Christ's body could be formed without detriment to His Mother's body.

Reply Obj. 3: Woman's semen is not apt for generation, but is something imperfect in the seminal order, which, on account of the imperfection of the female power, it has not been possible to bring to complete seminal perfection. Consequently this semen is not the necessary matter of conception; as the Philosopher says (De Gener. Animal. i): wherefore there was none such in Christ's conception: all the more since, though it is imperfect in the seminal order, a certain concupiscence accompanies its emission, as also that of the male semen: whereas in that virginal conception there could be no concupiscence. Wherefore Damascene says (De Fide Orth. iii) that Christ's body was not conceived "seminally." But the menstrual blood, the flow of which is subject to monthly periods, has a certain natural impurity of corruption: like other superfluities, which nature does not heed, and therefore expels. Of such menstrual blood infected with corruption and repudiated by nature, the conception is not formed; but from a certain secretion of the pure blood which by a process of elimination is prepared for conception, being, as it were, more pure and more perfect than the rest of the blood. Nevertheless, it is tainted with the impurity of lust in the conception of other men: inasmuch as by sexual intercourse this blood is drawn to a place apt for conception. This, however, did not take place in Christ's conception: because this blood was brought together in the Virgin's womb and fashioned into a child by the operation of the Holy Ghost. Therefore is Christ's body said to be "formed of the most chaste and purest blood of the Virgin."

SIXTH ARTICLE [III, Q. 31, Art. 6]

Whether Christ's Body Was in Adam and the Other Patriarchs, As to Something Signate?

Objection 1: It would seem that Christ's body was in Adam and the patriarchs as to something signate. For Augustine says (Gen. ad lit. x) that the flesh of Christ was in Adam and Abraham "by way of a bodily substance." But bodily substance is something signate. Therefore Christ's flesh was in Adam, Abraham, and the other patriarchs, according to something signate.

Obj. 2: Further, it is said (Rom. 1:3) that Christ "was made . . . of the seed of David according to the flesh." But the seed of David was something signate in him. Therefore Christ was in David, according to something signate, and for the same reason in the other patriarchs.

Obj. 3: Further, the human race is Christ's kindred, inasmuch as He took flesh therefrom. But if that flesh were not something signate in Adam, the human race, which is descended from Adam, would seem to have no kindred with Christ: but rather with those other things from which the matter of His flesh was taken. Therefore it seems that Christ's flesh was in Adam and the other patriarchs according to something signate.

*On the contrary,* Augustine says (Gen. ad lit. x) that in whatever way Christ was in Adam and Abraham, other men were there also; but not conversely. But other men were not in Adam and Abraham by way of some signate matter, but only according to origin, as stated in the First Part (Q. 119, A. 1, A. 2, ad 4). Therefore neither was Christ in Adam and Abraham according to something signate; and, for the same reason, neither was He in the other patriarchs.

*I answer that,* As stated above (A. 5, ad 1), the matter of Christ's body was not the flesh and bones of the Blessed Virgin, nor anything that was actually a part of her body, but her blood which was her flesh potentially. Now, whatever was in the Blessed Virgin, as received from her parents, was actually a part of her body. Consequently that which the Blessed Virgin received from her parents was not the matter of Christ's body. Therefore we must say that Christ's body was not in Adam and the other patriarchs according to something signate, in the sense that some part of Adam's or of anyone else's body could be singled out and designated as the very matter from which Christ's body was to be formed: but it was there according to origin, just as was the flesh of other men. For Christ's body is related to Adam and the other patriarchs through the medium of His Mother's body. Consequently Christ's body was in the patriarchs, in no other way than was His Mother's body, which was not in the patriarchs according to signate matter: as neither were the bodies of other men, as stated in the First Part (Q. 119, A. 1, A. 2, ad 4).

Reply Obj. 1: The expression "Christ was in Adam according to bodily substance," does not mean that Christ's body was a bodily substance in Adam: but that the bodily substance of Christ's body, i.e. the matter which He took from the Virgin, was in Adam as in its active principle, but not as in its material principle: in other words, by the generative power of Adam and his descendants down to the Blessed Virgin, this matter was prepared for Christ's conception. But this matter was not fashioned into Christ's body by the seminal power derived from Adam. Therefore Christ is said to have been in Adam by way of origin, according to bodily substance: but not according to seminal virtue.

Reply Obj. 2: Although Christ's body was not in Adam and the other patriarchs, according to seminal virtue, yet the Blessed Virgin's body was thus in them, through her being conceived from the seed of a man. For this reason, through the medium of the Blessed Virgin, Christ is said to be of the seed of David, according to the flesh, by way of origin.

Reply Obj. 3: Christ and the human race are kindred, through the likeness of species. Now, specific likeness results not from remote but from proximate matter, and from the active principle which begets its like in species. Thus, then, the kinship of Christ and the human race is sufficiently preserved by His body being formed from the Virgin's blood, derived in its origin from Adam and the other patriarchs. Nor is this kinship affected by the matter whence this blood is taken, as neither is it in the generation of other men, as stated in the First Part (Q. 119, A. 2, ad 3).

SEVENTH ARTICLE [III, Q. 31, Art. 7]

Whether Christ's Flesh in the Patriarchs Was Infected by Sin?

Objection 1: It would seem that Christ's flesh was not infected by sin in the patriarchs. For it is written (Wis. 7:25) that "no defiled thing cometh into" Divine Wisdom. But Christ is the Wisdom of God according to 1 Cor. 1:24. Therefore Christ's flesh was never defiled by sin.

Obj. 2: Further, Damascene says (De Fide Orth. iii) that Christ "assumed the first-fruits of our nature." But in the primitive state human flesh was not infected by sin. Therefore Christ's flesh was not infected either in Adam or in the other patriarchs.

Obj. 3: Further, Augustine says (Gen. ad lit. x) that "human nature ever had, together with the wound, the balm with which to heal it." But that which is infected cannot heal a wound; rather does it need to be healed itself. Therefore in human nature there was ever something preserved from infection, from which afterwards Christ's body was formed.

*On the contrary,* Christ's body is not related to Adam and the other patriarchs, save through the medium of the Blessed Virgin's body, of whom He took flesh. But the body of the Blessed Virgin was wholly conceived in original sin, as stated above (Q. 14, A. 3, ad 1), and thus, as far as it was in the patriarchs, it was subject to sin. Therefore the flesh of Christ, as far as it was in the patriarchs, was subject to sin.

*I answer that,* When we say that Christ or His flesh was in Adam and the other patriarchs, we compare Him, or His flesh, to Adam and the other patriarchs. Now, it is manifest that the condition of the patriarchs differed from that of Christ: for the patriarchs were subject to sin, whereas Christ was absolutely free from sin. Consequently a twofold error may occur on this point. First, by attributing to Christ, or to His flesh, that condition which was in the patriarchs; by saying, for instance, that Christ sinned in Adam, since after some fashion He was in him. But this is false; because Christ was not in Adam in such a way that Adam's sin belonged to Christ: forasmuch as He is not descended from him according to the law of concupiscence, or according to seminal virtue; as stated above (A. 1, ad 3, A. 6, ad 1; Q. 15, A. 1, ad 2).

Secondly, error may occur by attributing the condition of Christ or of His flesh to that which was actually in the patriarchs: by saying, for instance, that, because Christ's flesh, as existing in Christ, was not subject to sin, therefore in Adam also and in the patriarchs there was some part of his body that was not subject to sin, and from which afterwards Christ's body was formed; as some indeed held. For this is quite impossible. First, because Christ's flesh was not in Adam and in the other patriarchs, according to something signate, distinguishable from the rest of his flesh, as pure from impure; as already stated (A. 6). Secondly, because since human flesh is infected by sin, through being conceived in lust, just as the entire flesh of a man is conceived through lust, so also is it entirely defiled by sin. Consequently we must say that the entire flesh of the patriarchs was subjected to sin, nor was there anything in them that was free from sin, and from which afterwards Christ's body could be formed.

Reply Obj. 1: Christ did not assume the flesh of the human race subject to sin, but cleansed from all infection of sin. Thus it is that "no defiled thing cometh into the Wisdom of God."

Reply Obj. 2: Christ is said to have assumed the first-fruits of our nature, as to the likeness of condition; forasmuch as He assumed flesh not infected by sin, like unto the flesh of man before sin. But this is not to be understood to imply a continuation of that primitive purity, as though the flesh of innocent man was preserved in its freedom from sin until the formation of Christ's body.

Reply Obj. 3: Before Christ, there was actually in human nature a wound, i.e. the infection of original sin. But the balm to heal the wound was not there actually, but only by a certain virtue of origin, forasmuch as from those patriarchs the flesh of Christ was to be propagated.

EIGHTH ARTICLE [III, Q. 31, Art. 8]

Whether Christ Paid Tithes in Abraham's Loins?

Objection 1: It would seem that Christ "paid tithes" in Abraham's loins. For the Apostle says (Heb. 7:6-9) that Levi, the great-grandson of Abraham, "paid tithes in Abraham," because, when the latter paid tithes to Melchisedech, "he was yet in his loins." In like manner Christ was in Abraham's loins when the latter paid tithes. Therefore Christ Himself also paid tithes in Abraham.

Obj. 2: Further, Christ is of the seed of Abraham according to the flesh which He received from His Mother. But His Mother paid tithes in Abraham. Therefore for a like reason did Christ.

Obj. 3: Further, "in Abraham tithe was levied on that which needed healing," as Augustine says (Gen. ad lit. x). But all flesh subject to sin needed healing. Since therefore Christ's flesh was the subject of sin, as stated above (A. 7), it seems that Christ's flesh paid tithes in Abraham.

Obj. 4: Further, this does not seem to be at all derogatory to Christ's dignity. For the fact that the father of a bishop pays tithes to a priest does not hinder his son, the bishop, from being of higher rank than an ordinary priest. Consequently, although we may say that Christ paid tithes when Abraham paid them to Melchisedech, it does not follow that Christ was not greater than Melchisedech.

*On the contrary,* Augustine says (Gen. ad lit. x) that "Christ did not pay tithes there," i.e. in Abraham, "for His flesh derived from him, not the heat of the wound, but the matter of the antidote."

*I answer that,* It behooves us to say that the sense of the passage quoted from the Apostle is that Christ did not pay tithes in Abraham. For the Apostle proves that the priesthood according to the order of Melchisedech is greater than the Levitical priesthood, from the fact that Abraham paid tithes to Melchisedech, while Levi, from whom the legal priesthood was derived, was yet in his loins. Now, if Christ had also paid tithes in Abraham, His priesthood would not have been according to the order of Melchisedech, but of a lower order. Consequently we must say that Christ did not pay tithes in Abraham's loins, as Levi did.

For since he who pays a tithe keeps nine parts to himself, and surrenders the tenth to another, inasmuch as the number ten is the sign of perfection, as being, in a sort, the terminus of all numbers which mount from one to ten, it follows that he who pays a tithe bears witness to his own imperfection and to the perfection of another. Now, to sin is due the imperfection of the human race, which needs to be perfected by Him who cleanses from sin. But to heal from sin belongs to Christ alone, for He is the "Lamb that taketh away the sin of the world" (John 1:29), whose figure was Melchisedech, as the Apostle proves (Heb. 7). Therefore by giving tithes to Melchisedech, Abraham foreshadowed that he, as being conceived in sin, and all who were to be his descendants in contracting original sin, needed that healing which is through Christ. And Isaac, Jacob, and Levi, and all the others were in Abraham in such a way so as to be descended from him, not only as to bodily substance, but also as to seminal virtue, by which original sin is transmitted. Consequently, they all paid tithes in Abraham, i.e. foreshadowed as needing to be healed by Christ. And Christ alone was in Abraham in such a manner as to descend from him, not by seminal virtue, but according to bodily substance. Therefore He was not in Abraham so as to need to be healed, but rather "as the balm with which the wound was to be healed." Therefore He did not pay tithes in Abraham's loins.

Thus the answer to the first objection is made manifest.

Reply Obj. 2: Because the Blessed Virgin was conceived in original sin, she was in Abraham as needing to be healed. Therefore she paid tithes in him, as descending from him according to seminal virtue. But this is not true of Christ's body, as stated above.

Reply Obj. 3: Christ's flesh is said to have been subject to sin, according as it was in the patriarchs, by reason of the condition in which it was in His forefathers, who paid the tithes: but not by reason of its condition as actually in Christ, who did not pay the tithes.

Reply Obj. 4: The levitical priesthood was handed down through carnal origin: wherefore it was not less in Abraham than in Levi. Consequently, since Abraham paid tithes to Melchisedech as to one greater than he, it follows that the priesthood of Melchisedech, inasmuch as he was a figure of Christ, was greater than that of Levi. But the priesthood of Christ does not result from carnal origin, but from spiritual grace. Therefore it is possible that a father pay tithes to a priest, as the less to the greater, and yet his son, if he be a bishop, is greater than that priest, not through carnal origin, but through the spiritual grace which he has received from Christ.

## QUESTION 32

OF THE ACTIVE PRINCIPLE IN CHRIST'S CONCEPTION (In Four Articles)

We shall now consider the active principle in Christ's conception: concerning which there are four points of inquiry:

(1) Whether the Holy Ghost was the active principle of Christ's conception?

(2) Whether it can be said that Christ was conceived of the Holy Ghost?

(3) Whether it can be said that the Holy Ghost is Christ's father according to the flesh?

(4) Whether the Blessed Virgin cooperated actively in Christ's conception?

FIRST ARTICLE [III, Q. 32, Art. 1]

Whether the Accomplishment of Christ's Conception Should Be Attributed to the Holy Ghost?

Objection 1: It would seem that the accomplishment of Christ's conception should not be attributed to the Holy Ghost, because, as Augustine says (De Trin. i), "The works of the Trinity are indivisible, just as the Essence of the Trinity is indivisible." But the accomplishment of Christ's conception was the work of God. Therefore it seems that it should not be attributed to the Holy Ghost any more than to the Father or the Son.

Obj. 2: Further, the Apostle says (Gal. 4:4): "When the fulness of time was come, God sent His Son, made of a woman"; which words Augustine expounds by saying (De Trin. iv): "Sent, in so far as made of a woman." But the sending of the Son is especially attributed to the Father, as stated in the First Part (Q. 43, A. 8). Therefore His conception also, by reason of which He was "made of a woman," should be attributed principally to the Father.

Obj. 3: Further, it is written (Prov. 9:1): "Wisdom hath built herself a house." Now, Christ is Himself the Wisdom of God; according to 1 Cor. 1:24: "Christ the Power of God and the Wisdom of God." And the house of this Wisdom is Christ's body, which is also called His temple, according to John 2:21: "But He spoke of the temple of His body." Therefore it seems that the accomplishment of Christ's conception should be attributed principally to the Son, and not, therefore, to the Holy Ghost.

*On the contrary,* It is written (Luke 1:35): "The Holy Ghost shall come upon Thee."

*I answer that,* The whole Trinity effected the conception of Christ's body: nevertheless, this is attributed to the Holy Ghost, for three reasons. First, because this is befitting to the cause of the Incarnation, considered on the part of God. For the Holy Ghost is the love of Father and Son, as stated in the First Part (Q. 37, A. 1). Now, that the Son of God took to Himself flesh from the Virgin's womb was due to the exceeding love of God: wherefore it is said (John 3:16): "God so loved the world as to give His only-begotten Son."

Secondly, this is befitting to the cause of the Incarnation, on the part of the nature assumed. Because we are thus given to understand that human nature was assumed by the Son of God into the unity of Person, not by reason of its merits, but through grace alone; which is attributed to the Holy Ghost, according to 1 Cor. 12:4: "There are diversities of graces, but the same Spirit." Wherefore Augustine says (Enchiridion xl): "The manner in which Christ was born of the Holy Ghost . . . suggests to us the grace of God, whereby man, without any merits going before, in the very beginning of his nature when he began to exist was joined to God the Word, into so great unity of Person, that He Himself should be the Son of God."

Thirdly, because this is befitting the term of the Incarnation. For the term of the Incarnation was that that man, who was being conceived, should be the Holy one and the Son of God. Now, both of these are attributed to the Holy Ghost. For by Him men are made to be sons of God, according to Gal. 4:6: "Because you are sons, God hath sent the Spirit of His Son into your [Vulg.: 'our'] hearts, crying: Abba, Father." Again, He is the "Spirit of sanctification," according to Rom. 1:4. Therefore, just as other men are sanctified spiritually by the Holy Ghost; so as to be the adopted sons of God, so was Christ conceived in sanctity by the Holy Ghost, so as to be the natural Son of God. Hence, according to a gloss on Rom. 1:4, the words, "Who was predestinated the Son of God, in power," are explained by what immediately follows: "According to the Spirit of sanctification, i.e. through being conceived of the Holy Ghost." And the Angel of the Annunciation himself, after saying, "The Holy Ghost shall come upon thee," draws the conclusion: "Therefore also the Holy which shall be born of thee shall be called the Son of God."

Reply Obj. 1: The work of the conception is indeed common to the whole Trinity; yet in some way it is attributed to each of the Persons. For to the Father is attributed authority in regard to the Person of the Son, who by this conception took to Himself (human nature). The taking itself (of human nature) is attributed to the Son: but the formation of the body taken by the Son is attributed to the Holy Ghost. For the Holy Ghost is the Spirit of the Son, according to Gal. 4:6: "God sent the Spirit of His Son." For just as the power of the soul which is in the semen, through the spirit enclosed therein, fashions the body in the generation of other men, so the Power of God, which is the Son Himself, according to 1 Cor. 1:24: "Christ, the Power of God," through the Holy Ghost formed the body which He assumed. This is also shown by the words of the angel: "The Holy Ghost shall come upon thee," as it were, in order to prepare and fashion the matter of Christ's body; "and the Power of the Most High," i.e. Christ, "shall overshadow thee--that is to say, the incorporeal Light of the Godhead shall in thee take the corporeal substance of human nature: for a shadow is formed by light and body," as Gregory says (Moral. xviii). The "Most High" is the Father, whose Power is the Son.

Reply Obj. 2: The mission refers to the Person assuming, who is sent by the Father; but the conception refers to the body assumed, which is formed by the operation of the Holy Ghost. And therefore, though mission and conception are in the same subject; since they differ in our consideration of them, mission is attributed to the Father, but the accomplishment of the conception to the Holy Ghost; whereas the assumption of flesh is attributed to the Son.

Reply Obj. 3: As Augustine says (QQ. Vet. et Nov. Test., qu. 52): "This may be understood in two ways. For, first, Christ's house is the Church, which He built with His blood. Secondly, His body may be called His house, just as it is called His temple . . . and what is done by the Holy Ghost is done by the Son of God, because Theirs is one Nature and one Will."

SECOND ARTICLE [III, Q. 32, Art. 2]

Whether It Should Be Said That Christ Was Conceived of ( de ) the Holy Ghost?

Objection 1: It would seem that we should not say that Christ was conceived of ( de ) the Holy Ghost. Because on Rom. 11:36: "For of Him (ex ipso ) and by Him, and in Him, are all things," the gloss of Augustine says: "Notice that he does not say, 'of Him' ( de ipso ), but 'of Him' ( ex ipso ). For of Him ( ex ipso ), are heaven and earth, since He made them: but not of Him [de ipso, since they are not made of His substance." But the Holy Ghost did not form Christ's body of ( de ) His own substance. Therefore we should not say that Christ was conceived of ( de ) the Holy Ghost.

Obj. 2: Further, the active principle of ( de ) which something is conceived is as the seed in generation. But the Holy Ghost did not take the place of seed in Christ's conception. For Jerome says (Expos. Cathol. Fidei) [*Written by Pelagius]: "We do not say, as some wicked wretches hold, that the Holy Ghost took the place of seed: but we say that Christ's body was wrought," i.e. formed, "by the power and might of the Creator." Therefore we should not say that Christ's body was conceived of ( de ) the Holy Ghost.

Obj. 3: Further, no one thing is made of two, except they be in some way mingled. But Christ's body was formed of ( de ) the Virgin Mary. If therefore we say that Christ was conceived of ( de ) the Holy Ghost, it seems that a mingling took place of the Holy Ghost with the matter supplied by the Virgin: and this is clearly false. Therefore we should not say that Christ was conceived of ( de ) the Holy Ghost.

*On the contrary,* It is written (Matt. 1:18): "Before they came together, she was found with child, of ( de ) the Holy Ghost."

*I answer that,* Conception is not attributed to Christ's body alone, but also to Christ Himself by reason of His body. Now, in the Holy Ghost we may observe a twofold habitude to Christ. For to the Son of God Himself, who is said to have been conceived, He has a habitude of consubstantiality: while to His body He has the habitude of efficient cause. And this preposition of ( de ) signifies both habitudes: thus we say that a certain man is "of ( de ) his father." And therefore we can fittingly say that Christ was conceived of the Holy Ghost in such a way that the efficiency of the Holy Ghost be referred to the body assumed, and the consubstantiality to the Person assuming.

Reply Obj. 1: Christ's body, through not being consubstantial with the Holy Ghost, cannot properly be said to be conceived "of" ( de ) the Holy Ghost, but rather "from ( ex ) the Holy Ghost," as Ambrose says (De Spir. Sanct. ii.): "What is from someone is either from his substance or from his power: from his substance, as the Son who is from the Father; from his power, as all things are from God, just as Mary conceived from the Holy Ghost."

Reply Obj. 2: It seems that on this point there is a difference of opinion between Jerome and certain other Doctors, who assert that the Holy Ghost took the place of seed in this conception. For Chrysostom says (Hom. i in Matth. [*Opus Imperf., among the supposititious writings]): "When God's Only-Begotten was about to enter into the Virgin, the Holy Ghost preceded Him; that by the previous entrance of the Holy Ghost, Christ might be born unto sanctification according to His body, the Godhead entering instead of the seed." And Damascene says (De Fide Orth. iii): "God's wisdom and power overshadowed her, like unto a Divine seed."

But these expressions are easily explained. Because Chrysostom and Damascene compare the Holy Ghost, or also the Son, who is the Power of the Most High, to seed, by reason of the active power therein; while Jerome denies that the Holy Ghost took the place of seed, considered as a corporeal substance which is transformed in conception.

Reply Obj. 3: As Augustine says (Enchiridion xl), Christ is said to be conceived or born of the Holy Ghost in one sense; of the Virgin Mary in another--of the Virgin Mary materially; of the Holy Ghost efficiently. Therefore there was no mingling here.

THIRD ARTICLE [III, Q. 32, Art. 3]

Whether the Holy Ghost Should Be Called Christ's Father in Respect of His Humanity?

Objection 1: It would seem that the Holy Ghost should be called Christ's father in respect of His humanity. Because, according to the Philosopher (De Gener. Animal. i): "The Father is the active principle in generation, the Mother supplies the matter." But the Blessed Virgin is called Christ's Mother, by reason of the matter which she supplied in His conception. Therefore it seems that the Holy Ghost can be called His father, through being the active principle in His conception.

Obj. 2: Further, as the minds of other holy men are fashioned by the Holy Ghost, so also was Christ's body fashioned by the Holy Ghost. But other holy men, on account of the aforesaid fashioning, are called the children of the whole Trinity, and consequently of the Holy Ghost. Therefore it seems that Christ should be called the Son of the Holy Ghost, forasmuch as His body was fashioned by the Holy Ghost.

Obj. 3: Further, God is called our Father by reason of His having made us, according to Deut. 32:6: "Is not He thy Father, that hath possessed thee, and made thee and created thee?" But the Holy Ghost made Christ's body, as stated above (AA. 1, 2). Therefore the Holy Ghost should be called Christ's Father in respect of the body fashioned by Him.

*On the contrary,* Augustine says (Enchiridion xl): "Christ was born of the Holy Ghost not as a Son, and of the Virgin Mary as a Son."

*I answer that,* The words "fatherhood," "motherhood," and "sonship," result from generation; yet not from any generation, but from that of living things, especially animals. For we do not say that fire generated is the son of the fire generating it, except, perhaps, metaphorically; we speak thus only of animals in whom generation is more perfect. Nevertheless, the word "son" is not applied to everything generated in animals, but only to that which is generated into likeness of the generator. Wherefore, as Augustine says (Enchiridion xxxix), we do not say that a hair which is generated in a man is his son; nor do we say that a man who is born is the son of the seed; for neither is the hair like the man nor is the man born like the seed, but like the man who begot him. And if the likeness be perfect, the sonship is perfect, whether in God or in man. But if the likeness be imperfect, the sonship is imperfect. Thus in man there is a certain imperfect likeness to God, both as regards his being created to God's image and as regards His being created unto the likeness of grace. Therefore in both ways man can be called His son, both because he is created to His image and because he is likened to Him by grace. Now, it must be observed that what is said in its perfect sense of a thing should not be said thereof in its imperfect sense: thus, because Socrates is said to be naturally a man, in the proper sense of "man," never is he called man in the sense in which the portrait of a man is called a man, although, perhaps, he may resemble another man. Now, Christ is the Son of God in the perfect sense of sonship. Wherefore, although in His human nature He was created and justified, He ought not to be called the Son of God, either in respect of His being created or of His being justified, but only in respect of His eternal generation, by reason of which He is the Son of the Father alone. Therefore nowise should Christ be called the Son of the Holy Ghost, nor even of the whole Trinity.

Reply Obj. 1: Christ was conceived of the Virgin Mary, who supplied the matter of His conception unto likeness of species. For this reason He is called her Son. But as man He was conceived of the Holy Ghost as the active principle of His conception, but not unto likeness of species, as a man is born of his father. Therefore Christ is not called the Son of the Holy Ghost.

Reply Obj. 2: Men who are fashioned spiritually by the Holy Ghost cannot be called sons of God in the perfect sense of sonship. And therefore they are called sons of God in respect of imperfect sonship, which is by reason of the likeness of grace, which flows from the whole Trinity.

But with Christ it is different, as stated above.

The same reply avails for the Third Objection.

FOURTH ARTICLE [III, Q. 32, Art. 4]

Whether the Blessed Virgin Cooperated Actively in the Conception of Christ's Body?

Objection 1: It would seem that the Blessed Virgin cooperated actively in the conception of Christ's body. For Damascene says (De Fide Orth. iii) that "the Holy Ghost came upon the Virgin, purifying her, and bestowing on her the power to receive and to bring forth the Word of God." But she had from nature the passive power of generation, like any other woman. Therefore He bestowed on her an active power of generation. And thus she cooperated actively in Christ's conception.

Obj. 2: Further, all the powers of the vegetative soul are active, as the Commentator says (De Anima ii). But the generative power, in both man and woman, belongs to the vegetative soul. Therefore, both in man and woman, it cooperates actively in the conception of the child.

Obj. 3: Further, in the conception of a child the woman supplies the matter from which the child's body is naturally formed. But nature is an intrinsic principle of movement. Therefore it seems that in the very matter supplied by the Blessed Virgin there was an active principle.

*On the contrary,* The active principle in generation is called the "seminal virtue." But, as Augustine says (Gen. ad lit. x), Christ's body "was taken from the Virgin, only as to corporeal matter, by the Divine power of conception and formation, but not by any human seminal virtue." Therefore the Blessed Virgin did not cooperate actively in, the conception of Christ's body.

*I answer that,* Some say that the Blessed Virgin cooperated actively in Christ's conception, both by natural and by a supernatural power. By natural power, because they hold that in all natural matter there is an active principle; otherwise they believe that there would be no such thing as natural transformation. But in this they are deceived. Because a transformation is said to be natural by reason not only of an active but also of a passive intrinsic principle: for the Philosopher says expressly (Phys. viii) that in heavy and light things there is a passive, and not an active, principle of natural movement. Nor is it possible for matter to be active in its own formation, since it is not in act. Nor, again, is it possible for anything to put itself in motion except it be divided into two parts, one being the mover, the other being moved: which happens in animate things only, as is proved Phys. viii.

By a supernatural power, because they say that the mother requires not only to supply the matter, which is the menstrual blood, but also the semen, which, being mingled with that of the male, has an active power in generation. And since in the Blessed Virgin there was no resolution of semen, by reason of her inviolate virginity, they say that the Holy Ghost supernaturally bestowed on her an active power in the conception of Christ's body, which power other mothers have by reason of the semen resolved. But this cannot stand, because, since "each thing is on account of its operation" (De Coel. ii), nature would not, for the purpose of the act of generation, distinguish the male and female sexes, unless the action of the male were distinct from that of the female. Now, in generation there are two distinct operations--that of the agent and that of the patient. Wherefore it follows that the entire active operation is on the part of the male, and the passive on the part of the female. For this reason in plants, where both forces are mingled, there is no distinction of male and female.

Since, therefore, the Blessed Virgin was not Christ's Father, but His Mother, it follows that it was not given to her to exercise an active power in His conception: whether to cooperate actively so as to be His Father, or not to cooperate at all, as some say. Whence it would follow that this active power was bestowed on her to no purpose. We must therefore say that in Christ's conception itself she did not cooperate actively, but merely supplied the matter thereof. Nevertheless, before the conception she cooperated actively in the preparation of the matter so that it should be apt for the conception.

Reply Obj. 1: This conception had three privileges--namely, that it was without original sin; that it was not that of a man only, but of God and man; and that it was a virginal conception. And all three were effected by the Holy Ghost. Therefore Damascene says, as to the first, that the Holy Ghost "came upon the Virgin, purifying her"--that is, preserving her from conceiving with original sin. As to the second, he says: "And bestowing on her the power to receive," i.e. to conceive, "the Word of God." As to the third, he says: "And to give birth" to Him, i.e. that she might, while remaining a virgin, bring Him forth, not actively, but passively, just as other mothers achieve this through the action of the male seed.

Reply Obj. 2: The generative power of the female is imperfect compared to that of the male. And, therefore, just as in the arts the inferior art gives a disposition to the matter to which the higher art gives the form, as is stated Phys. ii, so also the generative power of the female prepares the matter, which is then fashioned by the active power of the male.

Reply Obj. 3: In order for a transformation to be natural, there is no need for an active principle in matter, but only for a passive principle, as stated above.

# QUESTION 33

OF THE MODE AND ORDER OF CHRIST'S CONCEPTION (In Four Articles)

We have now to consider the mode and order of Christ's conception, concerning which there are four points of inquiry:

(1) Whether Christ's body was formed in the first instant of its conception?

(2) Whether it was animated in the first instant of its conception?

(3) Whether it was assumed by the Word in the first instant of its conception?

(4) Whether this conception was natural or miraculous?

FIRST ARTICLE [III, Q. 33, Art. 1]

Whether Christ's Body Was Formed in the First Instant of Its Conception?

Objection 1: It would seem that Christ's body was not formed in the first instant of its conception. For it is written (John 2:20): "Six-and-forty years was this Temple in building"; on which words Augustine comments as follows (De Trin. iv): "This number applies manifestly to the perfection of our Lord's body." He says, further (QQ. lxxxiii, qu. 56): "It is not without reason that the Temple, which was a type of His body, is said to have been forty-six years in building: so that as many years as it took to build the Temple, in so many days was our Lord's body perfected." Therefore Christ's body was not perfectly formed in the first instant of its conception.

Obj. 2: Further, there was need of local movement for the formation of Christ's body in order that the purest blood of the Virgin's body might be brought where generation might aptly take place. Now, no body can be moved locally in an instant: since the time taken in movement is divided according to the division of the thing moved, as is proved Phys. vi. Therefore Christ's body was not formed in an instant.

Obj. 3: Further, Christ's body was formed of the purest blood of the Virgin, as stated above (Q. 31, A. 5). But that matter could not be in the same instant both blood and flesh, because thus matter would have been at the same time the subject of two forms. Therefore the last instant in which it was blood was distinct from the first instant in which it was flesh. But between any two instants there is an interval of time. Therefore Christ's body was not formed in an instant, but during a space of time.

Obj. 4: Further, as the augmentative power requires a fixed time for its act, so also does the generative power: for both are natural powers belonging to the vegetative soul. But Christ's body took a fixed time to grow, like the bodies of other men: for it is written (Luke 2:52) that He "advanced in wisdom and age." Therefore it seems for the same reason that the formation of His body, since that, too, belongs to the generative power, was not instantaneous, but took a fixed time, like the bodies of other men.

*On the contrary,* Gregory says (Moral. xviii): "As soon as the angel announced it, as soon as the Spirit came down, the Word was in the womb, within the womb the Word was made flesh."

*I answer that,* In the conception of Christ's body three points may be considered: first, the local movement of the blood to the place of generation; secondly, the formation of the body from that matter; thirdly, the development whereby it was brought to perfection of quantity. Of these, the second is the conception itself; the first is a preamble; the third, a result of the conception.

Now, the first could not be instantaneous: since this would be contrary to the very nature of the local movement of any body whatever, the parts of which come into a place successively. The third also requires a succession of time: both because there is no increase without local movement, and because increase is effected by the power of the soul already informing the body, the operation of which power is subject to time.

But the body's very formation, in which conception principally consists, was instantaneous, for two reasons. First, because of the infinite power of the agent, viz. the Holy Ghost, by whom Christ's body was formed, as stated above (Q. 32, A. 1). For the greater the power of an agent, the more quickly can it dispose matter; and, consequently, an agent of infinite power can dispose matter instantaneously to its due form. Secondly, on the part of the Person of the Son, whose body was being formed. For it was unbecoming that He should take to Himself a body as yet unformed. While, if the conception had been going on for any time before the perfect formation of the body, the whole conception could not be attributed to the Son of God, since it is not attributed to Him except by reason of the assumption of that body. Therefore in the first instant in which the various parts of the matter were united together in the place of generation, Christ's body was both perfectly formed and assumed. And thus is the Son of God said to have been conceived; nor could it be said otherwise.

Reply Obj. 1: Neither quotation from Augustine refers to formation alone of Christ's body, but to its formation, together with a fixed development up to the time of His birth. Wherefore in the aforesaid number are foreshadowed the number of months during which Christ was in the Virgin's womb.

Reply Obj. 2: This local movement is not comprised within the conception itself, but is a preamble thereto.

Reply Obj. 3: It is not possible to fix the last instant in which that matter was blood: but it is possible to fix the last period of time which continued without any interval up to the first instant in which Christ's body was formed. And this instant was the terminus of the time occupied by the local movement of the matter towards the place of generation.

Reply Obj. 4: Increase is caused by the augmentative power of that which is the subject of increase: but the formation of the body is caused by the generative power, not of that which is generated, but of the father generating from seed, in which the formative power derived from the father's soul has its operation. But Christ's body was not formed by the seed of man, as stated above (Q. 31, A. 5, ad 3), but by the operation of the Holy Ghost. Therefore the formation thereof should be such as to be worthy of the Holy Ghost. But the development of Christ's body was the effect of the augmentative power in Christ's soul: and since this was of the same species as ours, it behooved His body to develop in the same way as the bodies of other men, so as to prove the reality of His human nature.

SECOND ARTICLE [III, Q. 33, Art. 2]

Whether Christ's Body Was Animated in the First Instant of Its Conception?

Objection 1: It would seem that Christ's body was not animated in the first instant of its conception. For Pope Leo says (Ep. ad Julian.): "Christ's flesh was not of another nature than ours: nor was the beginning of His animation different from that of other men." But the soul is not infused into other men at the first instant of their conception. Therefore neither should Christ's soul have been infused into His body in the first instant of its conception.

Obj. 2: Further, the soul, like any natural form, requires determinate quantity in its matter. But in the first instant of its conception Christ's body was not of the same quantity as the bodies of other men when they are animated: otherwise, if afterwards its development had been continuous, either its birth would have occurred sooner, or at the time of birth He would have been a bigger child than others. The former alternative is contrary to what Augustine says (De Trin. iv), where he proves that Christ was in the Virgin's womb for the space of nine months: while the latter is contrary to what Pope Leo says (Serm. iv in Epiph.): "They found the child Jesus nowise differing from the generality of infants." Therefore Christ's body was not animated in the first instant of its conception.

Obj. 3: Further, whenever there is "before" and "after" there must be several instants. But according to the Philosopher (De Gener. Animal. ii) in the generation of a man there must needs be "before" and "after": for he is first of all a living thing, and afterwards, an animal, and after that, a man. Therefore the animation of Christ could not be effected in the first instant of His conception.

*On the contrary,* Damascene says (De Fide Orth. iii): "At the very instant that there was flesh, it was the flesh of the Word of God, it was flesh animated with a rational and intellectual soul."

*I answer that,* For the conception to be attributed to the very Son of God, as we confess in the Creed, when we say, "who was conceived by the Holy Ghost," we must needs say that the body itself, in being conceived, was assumed by the Word of God. Now it has been shown above (Q. 6, AA. 1, 2) that the Word of God assumed the body by means of the soul, and the soul by means of the spirit, i.e. the intellect. Wherefore in the first instant of its conception Christ's body must needs have been animated by the rational soul.

Reply Obj. 1: The beginning of the infusion of the soul may be considered in two ways. First, in regard to the disposition of the body. And thus, the beginning of the infusion of the soul into Christ's body was the same as in other men's bodies: for just as the soul is infused into another man's body as soon as it is formed, so was it with Christ. Secondly, this beginning may be considered merely in regard to time. And thus, because Christ's body was perfectly formed in a shorter space of time, so after a shorter space of time was it animated.

Reply Obj. 2: The soul requires due quantity in the matter into which it is infused: but this quantity allows of a certain latitude because it is not fixed to a certain amount. Now the quantity that a body has when the soul is first infused into it is in proportion to the perfect quantity to which it will attain by development: that is to say, men of greater stature have greater bodies at the time of first animation. But Christ at the perfect age was of becoming and middle stature: in proportion to which was the quantity of His body at the time when other men's bodies are animated; though it was less than theirs at the first instant of His conception. Nevertheless that quantity was not too small to safeguard the nature of an animated body; since it would have sufficed for the animation of a small man's body.

Reply Obj. 3: What the Philosopher says is true in the generation of other men, because the body is successively formed and disposed for the soul: whence, first, as being imperfectly disposed, it receives an imperfect soul; and afterwards, when it is perfectly disposed, it receives a perfect soul. But Christ's body, on account of the infinite power of the agent, was perfectly disposed instantaneously. Wherefore, at once and in the first instant it received a perfect form, that is, the rational soul.

THIRD ARTICLE [III, Q. 33, Art. 3]

Whether Christ's Flesh Was First of All Conceived and Afterwards Assumed?

Objection 1: It would seem that Christ's flesh was first of all conceived, and afterwards assumed. Because what is not cannot be assumed. But Christ's flesh began to exist when it was conceived. Therefore it seems that it was assumed by the Word of God after it was conceived.

Obj. 2: Further, Christ's flesh was assumed by the Word of God, by means of the rational soul. But it received the rational soul at the term of the conception. Therefore it was assumed at the term of the conception. But at the term of the conception it was already conceived. Therefore it was first of all conceived and afterwards assumed.

Obj. 3: Further, in everything generated, that which is imperfect precedes in time that which is perfect: which is made clear by the Philosopher (Metaph. ix). But Christ's body is something generated. Therefore it did not attain to its ultimate perfection, which consisted in the union with the Word of God, at the first instant of its conception; but, first of all, the flesh was conceived and afterwards assumed.

*On the contrary,* Augustine says (De Fide ad Petrum xviii [*Written by Fulgentius]): "Hold steadfastly, and doubt not for a moment that Christ's flesh was not conceived in the Virgin's womb, before being assumed by the Word."

*I answer that,* As stated above, we may say properly that "God was made man," but not that "man was made God": because God took to Himself that which belongs to man--and that which belongs to man did not pre-exist, as subsisting in itself, before being assumed by the Word. But if Christ's flesh had been conceived before being assumed by the Word, it would have had at some time an hypostasis other than that of the Word of God. And this is against the very nature of the Incarnation, which we hold to consist in this, that the Word of God was united to human nature and to all its parts in the unity of hypostasis: nor was it becoming that the Word of God should, by assuming human nature, destroy a pre-existing hypostasis of human nature or of any part thereof. It is consequently contrary to faith to assert that Christ's flesh was first of all conceived and afterwards assumed by the Word of God.

Reply Obj. 1: If Christ's flesh had been formed or conceived, not instantaneously, but successively, one of two things would follow: either that what was assumed was not yet flesh, or that the flesh was conceived before it was assumed. But since we hold that the conception was effected instantaneously, it follows that in that flesh the beginning and the completion of its conception were in the same instant. So that, as Augustine [*Fulgentius, De Fide ad Petrum xviii] says: "We say that the very Word of God was conceived in taking flesh, and that His very flesh was conceived by the Word taking flesh."

From the above the reply to the Second Objection is clear. For in the same moment that this flesh began to be conceived, its conception and animation were completed.

Reply Obj. 3: The mystery of the Incarnation is not to be looked upon as an ascent, as it were, of a man already existing and mounting up to the dignity of the Union: as the heretic Photinus maintained. Rather is it to be considered as a descent, by reason of the perfect Word of God taking unto Himself the imperfection of our nature; according to John 6:38: "I came down from heaven."

FOURTH ARTICLE [III, Q. 33, Art. 4]

Whether Christ's Conception Was Natural?

Objection 1: It would seem that Christ's conception was natural. For Christ is called the Son of Man by reason of His conception in the flesh. But He is a true and natural Son of Man: as also is He the true and natural Son of God. Therefore His conception was natural.

Obj. 2: Further, no creature can be the cause of a miraculous effect. But Christ's conception is attributed to the Blessed Virgin, who is a mere creature: for we say that the Virgin conceived Christ. Therefore it seems that His conception was not miraculous, but natural.

Obj. 3: Further, for a transformation to be natural, it is enough that the passive principle be natural, as stated above (Q. 32, A. 4). But in Christ's conception the passive principle on the part of His Mother was natural, as we have shown (Q. 32, A. 4). Therefore Christ's conception was natural.

*On the contrary,* Dionysius says (Ep. ad Caium Monach.): "Christ does in a superhuman way those things that pertain to man: this is shown in the miraculous virginal conception."

*I answer that,* As Ambrose says (De Incarn. vi): "In this mystery thou shalt find many things that are natural, and many that are supernatural." For if we consider in this conception anything connected with the matter thereof, which was supplied by the mother, it was in all such things natural. But if we consider it on the part of the active power, thus it was entirely miraculous. And since judgment of a thing should be pronounced in respect of its form rather than of its matter: and likewise in respect of its activity rather than of its passiveness: therefore is it that Christ's conception should be described simply as miraculous and supernatural, although in a certain respect it was natural.

Reply Obj. 1: Christ is said to be a natural Son of Man, by reason of His having a true human nature, through which He is a Son of Man, although He had it miraculously; thus, too, the blind man to whom sight has been restored sees naturally by sight miraculously received.

Reply Obj. 2: The conception is attributed to the Blessed Virgin, not as the active principle thereof, but because she supplied the matter, and because the conception took place in her womb.

Reply Obj. 3: A natural passive principle suffices for a transformation to be natural, when it is moved by its proper active principle in a natural and wonted way. But this is not so in the case in point. Therefore this conception cannot be called simply natural.

## QUESTION 34

OF THE PERFECTION OF THE CHILD CONCEIVED (In Four Articles)

We must now consider the perfection of the child conceived: and concerning this there are four points of inquiry:

(1) Whether Christ was sanctified by grace in the first instant of His conception?

(2) Whether in that same instant He had the use of free-will?

(3) Whether in that same instant He could merit?

(4) Whether in that same instant He was a perfect comprehensor?

FIRST ARTICLE [III, Q. 34, Art. 1]

Whether Christ Was Sanctified in the First Instant of His Conception?

Objection 1: It would seem that Christ was not sanctified in the first instant of His conception. For it is written (1 Cor. 15:46): "That was not first which is spiritual, but that which is natural: afterwards that which is spiritual." But sanctification by grace is something spiritual. Therefore Christ received the grace of sanctification, not at the very beginning of His conception, but after a space of time.

Obj. 2: Further, sanctification seems to be a cleansing from sin: according to 1 Cor. 6:1: "And such some of you were," namely, sinners, "but you are washed, but you are sanctified." But sin was never in Christ. Therefore it was not becoming that He should be sanctified by grace.

Obj. 3: Further, as by the Word of God "all things were made," so from the Word incarnate all men who are made holy receive holiness, according to Heb. 2:11: "Both he that sanctifieth and they who are sanctified are all of one." But "the Word of God, by whom all things were made, was not Himself made"; as Augustine says (De Trin. i). Therefore Christ, by whom all are made holy, was not Himself made holy.

*On the contrary,* It is written (Luke 1:35): "The Holy which shall be born of thee shall be called the Son of God"; and (John 10:36): "Whom the Father hath sanctified and sent into the world."

*I answer that,* As stated above (Q. 7, AA. 9, 10, 12), the abundance of grace sanctifying Christ's soul flows from the very union of the Word, according to John 1:14: "We saw His glory . . . as it were of the Only-Begotten of the Father, full of grace and truth." For it has been shown above (Q. 33, AA. 2, 3) that in the first instant of conception, Christ's body was both animated and assumed by the Word of God. Consequently, in the first instant of His conception, Christ had the fulness of grace sanctifying His body and His soul.

Reply Obj. 1: The order set down by the Apostle in this passage refers to those who by advancing attain to the spiritual state. But the mystery of the Incarnation is considered as a condescension of the fulness of the Godhead into human nature rather than as the promotion of human nature, already existing, as it were, to the Godhead. Therefore in the man Christ there was perfection of spiritual life from the very beginning.

Reply Obj. 2: To be sanctified is to be made holy. Now something is made not only from its contrary, but also from that which is opposite to it, either by negation or by privation: thus white is made either from black or from not-white. We indeed from being sinners are made holy: so that our sanctification is a cleansing from sin. Whereas Christ, as man, was made holy, because He was not always thus sanctified by grace: yet He was not made holy from being a sinner, because He never sinned; but He was made holy from not-holy as man, not indeed by privation, as though He were at some time a man and not holy; but by negation--that is, when He was not man He had not human sanctity. Therefore at the same time He was made man and a holy man. For this reason the angel said (Luke 1:35): "The Holy which shall be born of thee." Which words Gregory expounds as follows (Moral. xviii): "In order to show the distinction between His holiness and ours, it is declared that He shall be born holy. For we, though we are made holy, yet are not born holy, because by the mere condition of a corruptible nature we are tied . . . But He alone is truly born holy who . . . was not conceived by the combining of carnal union."

Reply Obj. 3: The Father creates things through the Son, and the whole Trinity sanctifies men through the Man Christ, but not in the same way. For the Word of God has the same power and operation as God the Father: hence the Father does not work through the Son as an instrument, which is both mover and moved. Whereas the humanity of Christ is as the instrument of the Godhead, as stated above (Q. 7, A. 1, ad 3; Q. 8, A. 1, ad 1). Therefore Christ's humanity is both sanctified and sanctifier.

SECOND ARTICLE [III, Q. 34, Art. 2]

Whether Christ As Man Had the Use of Free-will in the First Instant of His Conception?

Objection 1: It would seem that Christ as man had not the use of free-will in the first instant of His conception. For a thing is, before it acts or operates. Now the use of free-will is an operation. Since, therefore, Christ's soul began to exist in the first instant of His conception, as was made clear above (Q. 33, A. 2), it seems impossible that He should have the use of free-will in the first instant of His conception.

Obj. 2: Further, the use of free-will consists in choice. But choice presupposes the deliberation of counsel: for the Philosopher says (Ethic. iii) that choice is "the desire of what has been previously the object of deliberation." Therefore it seems impossible that Christ should have had the use of free-will in the first instant of His conception.

Obj. 3: Further, the free-will is "a faculty of the will and reason," as stated in the First Part (Q. 83, A. 2, Obj. 2): consequently the use of free-will is an act of the will and the reason or intellect. But the act of the intellect presupposes an act of the senses; and this cannot exist without proper disposition of the organs--a condition which would seem impossible in the first instant of Christ's conception. Therefore it seems that Christ could not have the use of free-will at the first instant of His conception.

*On the contrary,* Augustine says in his book on the Trinity (Gregory: Regist. ix, Ep. 61): "As soon as the Word entered the womb, while retaining the reality of His Nature, He was made flesh, and a perfect man." But a perfect man has the use of free-will. Therefore Christ had the use of free-will in the first instant of His conception.

*I answer that,* As stated above (A. 1), spiritual perfection was becoming to the human nature which Christ took, which perfection He attained not by making progress, but by receiving it from the very first. Now ultimate perfection does not consist in power or habit, but in operation; wherefore it is said (De Anima ii, text. 5) that operation is a "second act." We must, therefore, say that in the first instant of His conception Christ had that operation of the soul which can be had in an instant. And such is the operation of the will and intellect, in which the use of free-will consists. For the operation of the intellect and will is sudden and instantaneous, much more, indeed, than corporeal vision; inasmuch as to understand, to will, and to feel, are not movements that may be described as "acts of an imperfect being," which attains perfection successively, but are "the acts of an already perfect being," as is said, De Anima iii, text. 28. We must therefore say that Christ had the use of free-will in the first instant of His conception.

Reply Obj. 1: Existence precedes action by nature, but not in time; but at the same time the agent has perfect existence, and begins to act unless it is hindered. Thus fire, as soon as it is generated, begins to give heat and light. The action of heating, however, is not terminated in an instant, but continues for a time; whereas the action of giving light is perfected in an instant. And such an operation is the use of free-will, as stated above.

Reply Obj. 2: As soon as counsel or deliberation is ended, there may be choice. But those who need the deliberation of counsel, as soon as this comes to an end are certain of what ought to be chosen: and consequently they choose at once. From this it is clear that the deliberation of counsel does not of necessity precede choice save for the purpose of inquiring into what is uncertain. But Christ, in the first instant of His conception, had the fulness of sanctifying grace, and in like manner the fulness of known truth; according to John 1:14: "Full of grace and truth." Wherefore, as being possessed of certainty about all things, He could choose at once in an instant.

Reply Obj. 3: Christ's intellect, in regard to His infused knowledge, could understand without turning to phantasms, as stated above (Q. 11, A. 2). Consequently His intellect and will could act without any action of the senses.

Nevertheless it was possible for Him, in the first instant of His conception, to have an operation of the senses: especially as to the sense of touch, which the infant can exercise in the womb even before it has received the rational soul, as is said, De Gener. Animal. ii, 3, 4. Wherefore, since Christ had the rational soul in the first instant of His conception, through His body being already fashioned and endowed with sensible organs, much more was it possible for Him to exercise the sense of touch in that same instant.

THIRD ARTICLE [III, Q. 34, Art. 3]

Whether Christ Could Merit in the First Instant of His Conception?

Objection 1: It would seem that Christ could not merit in the first instant of His conception. For the free-will bears the same relation to merit as to demerit. But the devil could not sin in the first instant of his creation, as was shown in the First Part, Q. 63, A. 5. Therefore neither could Christ's soul merit in the first instant of its creation--that is, in the first instant of Christ's conception.

Obj. 2: Further, that which man has in the first instant of his conception seems to be natural to him: for it is in this that his natural generation is terminated. But we do not merit by what is natural to us, as is clear from what has been said in the Second Part (I-II, Q. 109, A. 5; Q. 114, A. 2). Therefore it seems that the use of free-will, which Christ as man had in the first instant of His conception, was not meritorious.

Obj. 3: Further, that which a man has once merited he makes, in a way, his own: consequently it seems that he cannot merit the same thing again: for no one merits what is already his. If, therefore, Christ merited in the first instant of His conception, it follows that afterwards He merited nothing. But this is evidently untrue. Therefore Christ did not merit in the first instant of His conception.

*On the contrary,* Augustine [*Paterius, Expos. Vet. et Nov. Test. super Ex. 40] says: "Increase of merit was absolutely impossible to the soul of Christ." But increase of merit would have been possible had He not merited in the first instant of His conception. Therefore Christ merited in the first instant of His conception.

*I answer that,* As stated above (A. 1), Christ was sanctified by grace in the first instant of His conception. Now, sanctification is twofold: that of adults who are sanctified in consideration of their own act; and that of infants who are sanctified in consideration of, not their own act of faith, but that of their parents or of the Church. The former sanctification is more perfect than the latter: just as act is more perfect than habit; and "that which is by itself, than that which is by another" [*Aristotle, Phys. viii]. Since, therefore, the sanctification of Christ was most perfect, because He was so sanctified that He might sanctify others; consequently He was sanctified by reason of His own movement of the free-will towards God. Which movement, indeed, of the free-will is meritorious. Consequently, Christ did merit in the first instant of His conception.

Reply Obj. 1: Free-will does not bear the same relation to good as to evil: for to good it is related of itself, and naturally; whereas to evil it is related as to a defect, and beside nature. Now, as the Philosopher says (De Coelo ii, text. 18): "That which is beside nature is subsequent to that which is according to nature; because that which is beside nature is an exception to nature." Therefore the free-will of a creature can be moved to good meritoriously in the first instant of its creation, but not to evil sinfully; provided, however, its nature be unimpaired.

Reply Obj. 2: That which man has at the first moment of his creation, in the ordinary course of nature, is natural to him; but nothing hinders a creature from receiving from God a gift of grace at the very beginning of its creation. In this way did Christ's soul in the first instant of its creation receive grace by which it could merit. And for this reason is that grace, by way of a certain likeness, said to be natural to this Man, as explained by Augustine (Enchiridion xl).

Reply Obj. 3: Nothing prevents the same thing belonging to someone from several causes. And thus it is that Christ was able by subsequent actions and sufferings to merit the glory of immortality, which He also merited in the first instant of His conception: not, indeed, so that it became thereby more due to Him than before, but so that it was due to Him from more causes than before.

FOURTH ARTICLE [III, Q. 34, Art. 4]

Whether Christ Was a Perfect Comprehensor in the First Instant of His Conception?

Objection 1: It would seem that Christ was not a perfect comprehensor in the first instant of His conception. For merit precedes reward, as fault precedes punishment. But Christ merited in the first instant of His conception, as stated above (A. 3). Since, therefore, the state of comprehension is the principal reward, it seems that Christ was not a comprehensor in the first instant of His conception.

Obj. 2: Further, our Lord said (Luke 24:26): "Ought not Christ to have suffered these things, and so to enter into His glory?" But glory belongs to the state of comprehension. Therefore Christ was not in the state of comprehension in the first instant of His conception, when as yet He had not suffered.

Obj. 3: Further, what befits neither man nor angel seems proper to God; and therefore is not becoming to Christ as man. But to be always in the state of beatitude befits neither man nor angel: for if they had been created in beatitude, they would not have sinned afterwards. Therefore Christ, as man, was not in the state of beatitude in the first instant of His conception.

*On the contrary,* It is written (Ps. 64:5): "Blessed is he whom Thou hast chosen, and taken to Thee"; which words, according to the gloss, refer to Christ's human nature, which "was taken by the Word of God unto the unity of Person." But human nature was taken by the Word of God in the first instant of His conception. Therefore, in the first instant of His conception, Christ, as man, was in the state of beatitude; which is to be a comprehensor.

*I answer that,* As appears from what was said above (A. 3), it was unbecoming that in His conception Christ should receive merely habitual grace without the act. Now, He received grace "not by measure" (John 3:34), as stated above (Q. 7, A. 11). But the grace of the "wayfarer," being short of that of the "comprehensor," is in less measure than that of the comprehensor. Wherefore it is manifest that in the first instant of His conception Christ received not only as much grace as comprehensors have, but also greater than that which they all have. And because that grace was not without its act, it follows that He was a comprehensor in act, seeing God in His Essence more clearly than other creatures.

Reply Obj. 1: As stated above (Q. 19, A. 3), Christ did not merit the glory of the soul, in respect of which He is said to have been a comprehensor, but the glory of the body, to which He came through His Passion.

Wherefore the reply to the Second Objection is clear.

Reply Obj. 3: Since Christ was both God and man, He had, even in His humanity, something more than other creatures--namely, that He was in the state of beatitude from the very beginning.

## QUESTION 35

OF CHRIST'S NATIVITY (In Eight Articles)

After considering Christ's conception, we must treat of His nativity. First, as to the nativity itself; secondly, as to His manifestation after birth.

Concerning the first there are eight points of inquiry:

(1) Whether nativity regards the nature or the person?

(2) Whether another, besides His eternal, birth should be attributed to Christ?

(3) Whether the Blessed Virgin is His Mother in respect of His temporal birth?

(4) Whether she ought to be called the Mother of God?

(5) Whether Christ is the Son of God the Father and of the Virgin Mother in respect of two filiations?

(6) Of the mode of the Nativity;

(7) Of its place;

(8) Of the time of the Nativity.

FIRST ARTICLE [III, Q. 35, Art. 1]

Whether Nativity Regards the Nature Rather Than the Person?

Objection 1: It would seem that nativity regards the nature rather than the person. For Augustine [*Fulgentius] says (De Fide ad Petrum): "The eternal Divine Nature could not be conceived and born of human nature, except in a true human nature." Consequently it becomes the Divine Nature to be conceived and born by reason of the human nature. Much more, therefore, does it regard human nature itself.

Obj. 2: Further, according to the Philosopher (Metaph. v), "nature" is so denominated from "nativity." But things are denominated from one another by reason of some likeness. Therefore it seems that nativity regards the nature rather than the person.

Obj. 3: Further, properly speaking, that is born which begins to exist by nativity. But Christ's Person did not begin to exist by His nativity, whereas His human nature did. Therefore it seems that the nativity properly regards the nature, and not the person.

*On the contrary,* Damascene says (De Fide Orth. iii): "Nativity regards the hypostasis, not the nature."

*I answer that,* Nativity can be attributed to someone in two ways: first, as to its subject; secondly, as to its terminus. To him that is born it is attributed as to its subject: and this, properly speaking, is the hypostasis, not the nature. For since to be born is to be generated; as a thing is generated in order for it to be, so is a thing born in order for it to be. Now, to be, properly speaking, belongs to that which subsists; since a form that does not subsist is said to be only inasmuch as by it something is: and whereas person or hypostasis designates something as subsisting, nature designates form, whereby something subsists. Consequently, nativity is attributed to the person or hypostasis as to the proper subject of being born, but not to the nature.

But to the nature nativity is attributed as to its terminus. For the terminus of generation and of every nativity is the form. Now, nature designates something as a form: wherefore nativity is said to be "the road to nature," as the Philosopher states (Phys. ii): for the purpose of nature is terminated in the form or nature of the species.

Reply Obj. 1: On account of the identity of nature and hypostasis in God, nature is sometimes put instead of person or hypostasis. And in this sense Augustine says that the Divine Nature was conceived and born, inasmuch as the Person of the Son was conceived and born in the human nature.

Reply Obj. 2: No movement or change is denominated from the subject moved, but from the terminus of the movement, whence the subject has its species. For this reason nativity is not denominated from the person born, but from nature, which is the terminus of nativity.

Reply Obj. 3: Nature, properly speaking, does not begin to exist: rather is it the person that begins to exist in some nature. Because, as stated above, nature designates that by which something is; whereas person designates something as having subsistent being.

SECOND ARTICLE [III, Q. 35, Art. 2]

Whether a Temporal Nativity Should Be Attributed to Christ?

Objection 1: It would seem that temporal nativity is not to be attributed to Christ. For "to be born is a certain movement of a thing that did not exist before it was born, which movement procures for it the benefit of existence" [*Cf. Augustine, De Unit. Trin. xii]. But Christ was from all eternity. Therefore He could not be born in time.

Obj. 2: Further, what is perfect in itself needs not to be born. But the Person of the Son of God was perfect from eternity. Therefore He needs not to be born in time. Therefore it seems that He had no temporal birth.

Obj. 3: Further, properly speaking, nativity regards the person. But in Christ there is only one person. Therefore in Christ there is but one nativity.

Obj. 4: Further, what is born by two nativities is born twice. But this proposition is false; "Christ was born twice": because the nativity whereby He was born of the Father suffers no interruption; since it is eternal. Whereas interruption is required to warrant the use of the adverb "twice": for a man is said to run twice whose running is interrupted. Therefore it seems that we should not admit a double nativity in Christ.

*On the contrary,* Damascene says (De Fide Orth. iii): "We confess two nativities in Christ: one of the Father--eternal; and one which occurred in these latter times for our sake."

*I answer that,* As stated above (A. 1), nature is compared to nativity, as the terminus to movement or change. Now, movement is diversified according to the diversity of its termini, as the Philosopher shows (Phys. v). But, in Christ there is a twofold nature: one which He received of the Father from eternity, the other which He received from His Mother in time. Therefore we must needs attribute to Christ a twofold nativity: one by which He was born of the Father from all eternity; one by which He was born of His Mother in time.

Reply Obj. 1: This was the argument of a certain heretic, Felician, and is solved thus by Augustine (Contra Felic. xii). "Let us suppose," says he, "as many maintain, that in the world there is a universal soul, which, by its ineffable movement, so gives life to all seed, that it is not compounded with things begotten, but bestows life that they may be begotten. Without doubt, when this soul reaches the womb, being intent on fashioning the passible matter to its own purpose, it unites itself to the personality thereof, though manifestly it is not of the same substance; and thus of the active soul and passive matter, one man is made out of two substances. And so we confess that the soul is born from out the womb; but not as though, before birth, it was nothing at all in itself. Thus, then, but in a way much more sublime, the Son of God was born as man, just as the soul is held to be born together with the body: not as though they both made one substance, but that from both, one person results. Yet we do not say that the Son of God began thus to exist: lest it be thought that His Divinity is temporal. Nor do we acknowledge the flesh of the Son of God to have been from eternity: lest it be thought that He took, not a true human body, but some resemblance thereof."

Reply Obj. 2: This was an argument of Nestorius, and it is thus solved by Cyril in an epistle [*Cf. Acta Concil. Ephes., p. 1, cap. viii]: "We do not say that the Son of God had need, for His own sake, of a second nativity, after that which is from the Father: for it is foolish and a mark of ignorance to say that He who is from all eternity, and co-eternal with the Father, needs to begin again to exist. But because for us and for our salvation, uniting the human nature to His Person, He became the child of a woman, for this reason do we say that He was born in the flesh."

Reply Obj. 3: Nativity regards the person as its subject, the nature as its terminus. Now, it is possible for several transformations to be in the same subject: yet must they be diversified in respect of their termini. But we do not say this as though the eternal nativity were a transformation or a movement, but because it is designated by way of a transformation or movement.

Reply Obj. 4: Christ can be said to have been born twice in respect of His two nativities. For just as he is said to run twice who runs at two different times, so can He be said to be born twice who is born once from eternity and once in time: because eternity and time differ much more than two different times, although each signifies a measure of duration.

THIRD ARTICLE [III, Q. 35, Art. 3]

Whether the Blessed Virgin Can Be Called Christ's Mother in Respect of His Temporal Nativity?

Objection 1: It would seem that the Blessed Virgin cannot be called Christ's Mother in respect of His temporal nativity. For, as stated above (Q. 32, A. 4), the Blessed Virgin Mary did not cooperate actively in begetting Christ, but merely supplied the matter. But this does not seem sufficient to make her His Mother: otherwise wood might be called the mother of the bed or bench. Therefore it seems that the Blessed Virgin cannot be called the Mother of Christ.

Obj. 2: Further, Christ was born miraculously of the Blessed Virgin. But a miraculous begetting does not suffice for motherhood or sonship: for we do not speak of Eve as being the daughter of Adam. Therefore neither should Christ be called the Son of the Blessed Virgin.

Obj. 3: Further, motherhood seems to imply partial separation of the semen. But, as Damascene says (De Fide Orth. iii), "Christ's body was formed, not by a seminal process, but by the operation of the Holy Ghost." Therefore it seems that the Blessed Virgin should not be called the Mother of Christ.

*On the contrary,* It is written (Matt. 1:18): "The generation of Christ was in this wise. When His Mother Mary was espoused to Joseph," etc.

*I answer that,* The Blessed Virgin Mary is in truth and by nature the Mother of Christ. For, as we have said above (Q. 5, A. 2; Q. 31, A. 5), Christ's body was not brought down from heaven, as the heretic Valentine maintained, but was taken from the Virgin Mother, and formed from her purest blood. And this is all that is required for motherhood, as has been made clear above (Q. 31, A. 5; Q. 32, A. 4). Therefore the Blessed Virgin is truly Christ's Mother.

Reply Obj. 1: As stated above (Q. 32, A. 3), not every generation implies fatherhood or motherhood and sonship, but only the generation of living things. Consequently when inanimate things are made from some matter, the relationship of motherhood and sonship does not follow from this, but only in the generation of living things, which is properly called nativity.

Reply Obj. 2: As Damascene says (De Fide Orth. iii): "The temporal nativity by which Christ was born for our salvation is, in a way, natural, since a Man was born of a woman, and after the due lapse of time from His conception: but it is also supernatural, because He was begotten, not of seed, but of the Holy Ghost and the Blessed Virgin, above the law of conception." Thus, then, on the part of the mother, this nativity was natural, but on the part of the operation of the Holy Ghost it was supernatural. Therefore the Blessed Virgin is the true and natural Mother of Christ.

Reply Obj. 3: As stated above (Q. 31, A. 5, ad 3; Q. 32, A. 4), the resolution of the woman's semen is not necessary for conception; neither, therefore, is it required for motherhood.

FOURTH ARTICLE [III, Q. 35, Art. 4]

Whether the Blessed Virgin should be called the Mother of God?

Objection 1: It would seem that the Blessed Virgin should not be called the Mother of God. For in the Divine mysteries we should not make any assertion that is not taken from Holy Scripture. But we read nowhere in Holy Scripture that she is the mother or parent of God, but that she is the "mother of Christ" or of "the Child," as may be seen from Matt. 1:18. Therefore we should not say that the Blessed Virgin is the Mother of God.

Obj. 2: Further, Christ is called God in respect of His Divine Nature. But the Divine Nature did not first originate from the Virgin. Therefore the Blessed Virgin should not be called the Mother of God.

Obj. 3: Further, the word "God" is predicated in common of Father, Son, and Holy Ghost. If, therefore, the Blessed Virgin is Mother of God it seems to follow that she was the Mother of Father, Son, and Holy Ghost, which cannot be allowed. Therefore the Blessed Virgin should not be called Mother of God.

*On the contrary,* In the chapters of Cyril, approved in the Council of Ephesus (P. 1, Cap. xxvi), we read: "If anyone confess not that the Emmanuel is truly God, and that for this reason the Holy Virgin is the Mother of God, since she begot of her flesh the Word of God made flesh, let him be anathema."

*I answer that,* As stated above (Q. 16, A. 1), every word that signifies a nature in the concrete can stand for any hypostasis of that nature. Now, since the union of the Incarnation took place in the hypostasis, as above stated (Q. 2, A. 3), it is manifest that this word "God" can stand for the hypostasis, having a human and a Divine nature. Therefore whatever belongs to the Divine and to the human nature can be attributed to that Person: both when a word is employed to stand for it, signifying the Divine Nature, and when a word is used signifying the human nature. Now, conception and birth are attributed to the person and hypostasis in respect of that nature in which it is conceived and born. Since, therefore, the human nature was taken by the Divine Person in the very beginning of the conception, as stated above (Q. 33, A. 3), it follows that it can be truly said that God was conceived and born of the Virgin. Now from this is a woman called a man's mother, that she conceived him and gave birth to him. Therefore the Blessed Virgin is truly called the Mother of God. For the only way in which it could be denied that the Blessed Virgin is the Mother of God would be either if the humanity were first subject to conception and birth, before this man were the Son of God, as Photinus said; or if the humanity were not assumed unto unity of the Person or hypostasis of the Word of God, as Nestorius maintained. But both of these are erroneous. Therefore it is heretical to deny that the Blessed Virgin is the Mother of God.

Reply Obj. 1: This was an argument of Nestorius, and it is solved by saying that, although we do not find it said expressly in Scripture that the Blessed Virgin is the Mother of God, yet we do find it expressly said in Scripture that "Jesus Christ is true God," as may be seen 1 John 5:20, and that the Blessed Virgin is the "Mother of Jesus Christ," which is clearly expressed Matt. 1:18. Therefore, from the words of Scripture it follows of necessity that she is the Mother of God.

Again, it is written (Rom. 9:5) that Christ is of the Jews "according to the flesh, who is over all things, God blessed for ever." But He is not of the Jews except through the Blessed Virgin. Therefore He who is "above all things, God blessed for ever," is truly born of the Blessed Virgin as of His Mother.

Reply Obj. 2: This was an argument of Nestorius. But Cyril, in a letter against Nestorius [*Cf. Acta Conc. Ephes., p. 1, cap. ii], answers it thus: "Just as when a man's soul is born with its body, they are considered as one being: and if anyone wish to say that the mother of the flesh is not the mother of the soul, he says too much. Something like this may be perceived in the generation of Christ. For the Word of God was born of the substance of God the Father: but because He took flesh, we must of necessity confess that in the flesh He was born of a woman." Consequently we must say that the Blessed Virgin is called the Mother of God, not as though she were the Mother of the Godhead, but because she is the mother, according to His human nature, of the Person who has both the divine and the human nature.

Reply Obj. 3: Although the name "God" is common to the three Persons, yet sometimes it stands for the Person of the Father alone, sometimes only for the Person of the Son or of the Holy Ghost, as stated above (Q. 16, A. 1; First Part, Q. 39, A. 4). So that when we say, "The Blessed Virgin is the Mother of God," this word "God" stands only for the incarnate Person of the Son.

FIFTH ARTICLE [III, Q. 35, Art. 5]

Whether There Are Two Filiations in Christ?

Objection 1: It would seem that there are two filiations in Christ. For nativity is the cause of filiation. But in Christ there are two nativities. Therefore in Christ there are also two filiations.

Obj. 2: Further, filiation, which is said of a man as being the son of someone, his father or his mother, depends, in a way, on him: because the very being of a relation consists in being referred to another; wherefore if one of two relatives be destroyed, the other is destroyed also. But the eternal filiation by which Christ is the Son of God the Father depends not on His Mother, because nothing eternal depends on what is temporal. Therefore Christ is not His Mother's Son by temporal filiation. Either, therefore, He is not her Son at all, which is in contradiction to what has been said above (AA. 3, 4), or He must needs be her Son by some other temporal filiation. Therefore in Christ there are two filiations.

Obj. 3: Further, one of two relatives enters the definition of the other; hence it is clear that of two relatives, one is specified from the other. But one and the same cannot be in diverse species. Therefore it seems impossible that one and the same relation be referred to extremes which are altogether diverse. But Christ is said to be the Son of the Eternal Father and a temporal mother, who are terms altogether diverse. Therefore it seems that Christ cannot, by the same relation, be called the Son of the Father and of His Mother Therefore in Christ there are two filiations.

*On the contrary,* As Damascene says (De Fide Orth. iii), things pertaining to the nature are multiple in Christ; but not those things that pertain to the Person. But filiation belongs especially to the Person, since it is a personal property, as appears from what was said in the First Part (Q. 32, A. 3; Q. 40, A. 2). Therefore there is but one filiation in Christ.

*I answer that,* opinions differ on this question. For some, considering only the cause of filiation, which is nativity, put two filiations in Christ, just as there are two nativities. *On the contrary,* others, considering only the subject of filiation, which is the person or hypostasis, put only one filiation in Christ, just as there is but one hypostasis or person. Because the unity or plurality of a relation is considered in respect, not of its terms, but of its cause or of its subject. For if it were considered in respect of its terms, every man would of necessity have in himself two filiations--one in reference to his father, and another in reference to his mother. But if we consider the question aright, we shall see that every man bears but one relation to both his father and his mother, on account of the unity of the cause thereof. For man is born by one birth of both father and mother: whence he bears but one relation to both. The same is said of one master who teaches many disciples the same doctrine, and of one lord who governs many subjects by the same power. But if there be various causes specifically diverse, it seems that in consequence the relations differ in species: wherefore nothing hinders several such relations being in the same subject. Thus if a man teach grammar to some and logic to others, his teaching is of a different kind in one case and in the other; and therefore one and the same man may have different relations as the master of different disciples, or of the same disciples in regard to diverse doctrines. Sometimes, however, it happens that a man bears a relation to several in respect of various causes, but of the same species: thus a father may have several sons by several acts of generation. Wherefore the paternity cannot differ specifically, since the acts of generation are specifically the same. And because several forms of the same species cannot at the same time be in the same subject, it is impossible for several paternities to be in a man who is the father of several sons by natural generation. But it would not be so were he the father of one son by natural generation and of another by adoption.

Now, it is manifest that Christ was not born by one and the same nativity, of the Father from eternity, and of His Mother in time: indeed, these two nativities differ specifically. Wherefore, as to this, we must say that there are various filiations, one temporal and the other eternal. Since, however, the subject of filiation is neither the nature nor part of the nature, but the person or hypostasis alone; and since in Christ there is no other hypostasis or person than the eternal, there can be no other filiation in Christ but that which is in the eternal hypostasis. Now, every relation which is predicated of God from time does not put something real in the eternal God, but only something according to our way of thinking, as we have said in the First Part (Q. 13, A. 7). Therefore the filiation by which Christ is referred to His Mother cannot be a real relation, but only a relation of reason.

Consequently each opinion is true to a certain extent. For if we consider the adequate causes of filiation, we must needs say that there are two filiations in respect of the twofold nativity. But if we consider the subject of filiation, which can only be the eternal suppositum, then no other than the eternal filiation in Christ is a real relation. Nevertheless, He has the relation of Son in regard to His Mother, because it is implied in the relation of motherhood to Christ. Thus God is called Lord by a relation which is implied in the real relation by which the creature is subject to God. And although lordship is not a real relation in God, yet is He really Lord through the real subjection of the creature to Him. In the same way Christ is really the Son of the Virgin Mother through the real relation of her motherhood to Christ.

Reply Obj. 1: Temporal nativity would cause a real temporal filiation in Christ if there were in Him a subject capable of such filiation. But this cannot be; since the eternal suppositum cannot be receptive of a temporal relation, as stated above. Nor can it be said that it is receptive of temporal filiation by reason of the human nature, just as it is receptive of the temporal nativity; because human nature would need in some way to be the subject of filiation, just as in a way it is the subject of nativity; for since an Ethiopian is said to be white by reason of his teeth, it must be that his teeth are the subject of whiteness. But human nature can nowise be the subject of filiation, because this relation regards directly the person.

Reply Obj. 2: Eternal filiation does not depend on a temporal mother, but together with this eternal filiation we understand a certain temporal relation dependent on the mother, in respect of which relation Christ is called the Son of His Mother.

Reply Obj. 3: One and being are mutually consequent, as is said Metaph. iv. Therefore, just as it happens that in one of the extremes of a relation there is something real, whereas in the other there is not something real, but merely a certain aspect, as the Philosopher observes of knowledge and the thing known; so also it happens that on the part of one extreme there is one relation, whereas on the part of the other there are many. Thus in man on the part of his parents there is a twofold relation, the one of paternity, the other of motherhood, which are specifically diverse, inasmuch as the father is the principle of generation in one way, and the mother in another (whereas if many be the principle of one action and in the same way--for instance, if many together draw a ship along--there would be one and the same relation in all of them); but on the part of the child there is but one filiation in reality, though there be two in aspect, corresponding to the two relations in the parents, as considered by the intellect. And thus in one way there is only one real filiation in Christ, which is in respect of the Eternal Father: yet there is another temporal relation in regard to His temporal mother.

SIXTH ARTICLE [III, Q. 35, Art. 6]

Whether Christ Was Born Without His Mother Suffering?

Objection 1: It would seem that Christ was not born without His Mother suffering. For just as man's death was a result of the sin of our first parents, according to Gen. 2:17: "In what day soever ye shall eat, ye shall [Vulg.: 'thou shalt eat of it, thou shalt] die"; so were the pains of childbirth, according to Gen. 3:16: "In sorrow shalt thou bring forth children." But Christ was willing to undergo death. Therefore for the same reason it seems that His birth should have been with pain.

Obj. 2: Further, the end is proportionate to the beginning. But Christ ended His life in pain, according to Isa. 53:4: "Surely . . . He hath carried our sorrows." Therefore it seems that His nativity was not without the pains of childbirth.

Obj. 3: Further, in the book on the birth of our Saviour [*Protevangelium Jacobi xix, xx] it is related that midwives were present at Christ's birth; and they would be wanted by reason of the mother's suffering pain. Therefore it seems that the Blessed Virgin suffered pain in giving birth to her Child.

*On the contrary,* Augustine says (Serm. de Nativ. [*Supposititious]), addressing himself to the Virgin-Mother: "In conceiving thou wast all pure, in giving birth thou wast without pain."

*I answer that,* The pains of childbirth are caused by the infant opening the passage from the womb. Now it has been said above (Q. 28, A. 2, Replies to objections), that Christ came forth from the closed womb of His Mother, and, consequently, without opening the passage. Consequently there was no pain in that birth, as neither was there any corruption; *on the contrary,* there was much joy therein for that God-Man "was born into the world," according to Isa. 35:1, 2: "Like the lily, it shall bud forth and blossom, and shall rejoice with joy and praise."

Reply Obj. 1: The pains of childbirth in the woman follow from the mingling of the sexes. Wherefore (Gen. 3:16) after the words, "in sorrow shalt thou bring forth children," the following are added: "and thou shalt be under thy husband's power." But, as Augustine says (Serm. de Assumpt. B. Virg., [*Supposititious]), from this sentence we must exclude the Virgin-Mother of God; who, "because she conceived Christ without the defilement of sin, and without the stain of sexual mingling, therefore did she bring Him forth without pain, without violation of her virginal integrity, without detriment to the purity of her maidenhood." Christ, indeed, suffered death, but through His own spontaneous desire, in order to atone for us, not as a necessary result of that sentence, for He was not a debtor unto death.

Reply Obj. 2: As "by His death" Christ "destroyed our death" [*Preface of the Mass in Paschal-time], so by His pains He freed us from our pains; and so He wished to die a painful death. But the mother's pains in childbirth did not concern Christ, who came to atone for our sins. And therefore there was no need for His Mother to suffer in giving birth.

Reply Obj. 3: We are told (Luke 2:7) that the Blessed Virgin herself "wrapped up in swaddling clothes" the Child whom she had brought forth, "and laid Him in a manger." Consequently the narrative of this book, which is apocryphal, is untrue. Wherefore Jerome says (Adv. Helvid. iv): "No midwife was there, no officious women interfered. She was both mother and midwife. 'With swaddling clothes,' says he, 'she wrapped up the child, and laid Him in a manger.'" These words prove the falseness of the apocryphal ravings.

SEVENTH ARTICLE [III, Q. 35, Art. 7]

Whether Christ Should Have Been Born in Bethlehem?

Objection 1: It would seem that Christ should not have been born in Bethlehem. For it is written (Isa. 2:3): "The law shall come forth from Sion, and the Word of the Lord from Jerusalem." But Christ is truly the Word of God. Therefore He should have come into the world at Jerusalem.

Obj. 2: Further, it is said (Matt. 2:23) that it is written of Christ that "He shall be called a Nazarene"; which is taken from Isa. 11:1: "A flower shall rise up out of his root"; for "Nazareth" is interpreted "a flower." But a man is named especially from the place of his birth. Therefore it seems that He should have been born in Nazareth, where also He was conceived and brought up.

Obj. 3: Further, for this was our Lord born into the world, that He might make known the true faith, according to John 18:37: "For this was I born, and for this came I into the world; that I should give testimony to the truth." But this would have been easier if He had been born in the city of Rome, which at that time ruled the world; whence Paul, writing to the Romans (1:8) says: "Your faith is spoken of in the whole world." Therefore it seems that He should not have been born in Bethlehem.

*On the contrary,* It is written (Mic. 5:2): "And thou, Bethlehem, Ephrata . . . out of thee shall He come forth unto Me, that is to be the ruler in Israel."

*I answer that,* Christ willed to be born in Bethlehem for two reasons. First, because "He was made . . . of the seed of David according to the flesh," as it is written (Rom. 1:3); to whom also was a special promise made concerning Christ; according to 2 Kings 23:1: "The man to whom it was appointed concerning the Christ of the God of Jacob . . . said." Therefore He willed to be born at Bethlehem, where David was born, in order that by the very birthplace the promise made to David might be shown to be fulfilled. The Evangelist points this out by saying: "Because He was of the house and of the family of David." Secondly, because, as Gregory says (Hom. viii in Evang.): "Bethlehem is interpreted 'the house of bread.' It is Christ Himself who said, 'I am the living Bread which came down from heaven.'"

Reply Obj. 1: As David was born in Bethlehem, so also did he choose Jerusalem to set up his throne there, and to build there the Temple of God, so that Jerusalem was at the same time a royal and a priestly city. Now, Christ's priesthood and kingdom were "consummated" principally in His Passion. Therefore it was becoming that He should choose Bethlehem for His Birthplace and Jerusalem for the scene of His Passion.

At the same time, too, He put to silence the vain boasting of men who take pride in being born in great cities, where also they desire especially to receive honor. Christ, *on the contrary,* willed to be born in a mean city, and to suffer reproach in a great city.

Reply Obj. 2: Christ wished "to flower" by His holy life, not in His carnal birth. Therefore He wished to be fostered and brought up at Nazareth. But He wished to be born at Bethlehem away from home; because, as Gregory says (Hom. viii in Evang.), through the human nature which He had taken, He was born, as it were, in a foreign place--foreign not to His power, but to His Nature. And, again, as Bede says on Luke 2:7: "In order that He who found no room at the inn might prepare many mansions for us in His Father's house."

Reply Obj. 3: According to a sermon in the

Council of Ephesus [*P. iii, cap. ix]: "If He had chosen the great city of Rome, the change in the world would be ascribed to the influence of her citizens. If He had been the son of the Emperor, His benefits would have been attributed to the latter's power. But that we might acknowledge the work of God in the transformation of the whole earth, He chose a poor mother and a birthplace poorer still."

"But the weak things of the world hath God chosen, that He may confound the strong" (1 Cor. 1:27). And therefore, in order the more to show His power, He set up the head of His Church in Rome itself, which was the head of the world, in sign of His complete victory, in order that from that city the faith might spread throughout the world; according to Isa. 26:5, 6: "The high city He shall lay low . . . the feet of the poor," i.e. of Christ, "shall tread it down; the steps of the needy," i.e. of the apostles Peter and Paul.

EIGHTH ARTICLE [III, Q. 35, Art. 8]

Whether Christ Was Born at a Fitting Time?

Objection 1: It would seem that Christ was not born at a fitting time. Because Christ came in order to restore liberty to His own. But He was born at a time of subjection--namely, when the whole world, as it were, tributary to Augustus, was being enrolled, at his command as Luke relates (2:1). Therefore it seems that Christ was not born at a fitting time.

Obj. 2: Further, the promises concerning the coming of Christ were not made to the Gentiles; according to Rom. 9:4: "To whom belong . . . the promises." But Christ was born during the reign of a foreigner, as appears from Matt. 2:1: "When Jesus was born in the days of King Herod." Therefore it seems that He was not born at a fitting time.

Obj. 3: Further, the time of Christ's presence on earth is compared to the day, because He is the "Light of the world"; wherefore He says Himself (John 9:4): "I must work the works of Him that sent Me, whilst it is day." But in summer the days are longer than in winter. Therefore, since He was born in the depth of winter, eight days before the Kalends of January, it seems that He was not born at a fitting time.

*On the contrary,* It is written (Gal. 4:4): "When the fulness of the time was come, God sent His Son, made of a woman, made under the law."

*I answer that,* There is this difference between Christ and other men, that, whereas they are born subject to the restrictions of time, Christ, as Lord and Maker of all time, chose a time in which to be born, just as He chose a mother and a birthplace. And since "what is of God is well ordered" and becomingly arranged, it follows that Christ was born at a most fitting time.

Reply Obj. 1: Christ came in order to bring us back from a state of bondage to a state of liberty. And therefore, as He took our mortal nature in order to restore us to life, so, as Bede says (Super Luc. ii, 4, 5), "He deigned to take flesh at such a time that, shortly after His birth, He would be enrolled in Caesar's census, and thus submit Himself to bondage for the sake of our liberty."

Moreover, at that time, when the whole world lived under one ruler, peace abounded on the earth. Therefore it was a fitting time for the birth of Christ, for "He is our peace, who hath made both one," as it is written (Eph. 2:14). Wherefore Jerome says on Isa. 2:4: "If we search the page of ancient history, we shall find that throughout the whole world there was discord until the twenty-eighth year of Augustus Caesar: but when our Lord was born, all war ceased"; according to Isa. 2:4: "Nation shall not lift up sword against nation."

Again, it was fitting that Christ should be born while the world was governed by one ruler, because "He came to gather His own [Vulg.: 'the children of God'] together in one" (John 11:52), that there might be "one fold and one shepherd" (John 10:16).

Reply Obj. 2: Christ wished to be born during the reign of a foreigner, that the prophecy of Jacob might be fulfilled (Gen. 49:10): "The sceptre shall not be taken away from Juda, nor a ruler from his thigh, till He come that is to be sent." Because, as Chrysostom says (Hom. ii in Matth. [*Opus Imperf., falsely ascribed to Chrysostom]), as long as the Jewish "people was governed by Jewish kings, however wicked, prophets were sent for their healing. But now that the Law of God is under the power of a wicked king, Christ is born; because a grave and hopeless disease demanded a more skilful physician."

Reply Obj. 3: As says the author of the book De Qq. Nov. et Vet. Test., "Christ wished to be born, when the light of day begins to increase in length," so as to show that He came in order that man might come nearer to the Divine Light, according to Luke 1:79: "To enlighten them that sit in darkness and in the shadow of death."

In like manner He chose to be born in the rough winter season, that He might begin from then to suffer in body for us.

## QUESTION 36

OF THE MANIFESTATION OF THE NEWLY BORN CHRIST (In Eight Articles)

We must now consider the manifestation of the newly born Christ: concerning which there are eight points of inquiry:

(1) Whether Christ's birth should have been made known to all?

(2) Whether it should have been made known to some?

(3) To whom should it have been made known?

(4) Whether He should have made Himself known, or should He rather have been manifested by others?

(5) By what other means should it have been made known?

(6) Of the order of these manifestations;

(7) Of the star by means of which His birth was made known;

(8) of the adoration of the Magi, who were informed of Christ's nativity by means of the star.

FIRST ARTICLE [III, Q. 36, Art. 1]

Whether Christ's Birth Should Have Been Made Known to All?

Objection 1: It would seem that Christ's birth should have been made known to all. Because fulfilment should correspond to promise. Now, the promise of Christ's coming is thus expressed (Ps. 49:3): "God shall come manifestly. But He came by His birth in the flesh." Therefore it seems that His birth should have been made known to the whole world.

Obj. 2: Further, it is written (1 Tim. 1:15): "Christ came into this world to save sinners." But this is not effected save in as far as the grace of Christ is made known to them; according to Titus 2:11, 12: "The grace of God our Saviour hath appeared to all men, instructing us, that denying ungodliness and worldly desires, we should live soberly, and justly, and godly in this world." Therefore it seems that Christ's birth should have been made known to all.

Obj. 3: Further, God is most especially inclined to mercy; according to Ps. 144:9: "His tender mercies are over all His works." But in His second coming, when He will "judge justices" (Ps. 70:3), He will come before the eyes of all; according to Matt. 24:27: "As lightning cometh out of the east, and appeareth even into the west, so shall also the coming of the Son of Man be." Much more, therefore, should His first coming, when He was born into the world according to the flesh, have been made known to all.

*On the contrary,* It is written (Isa. 45:15): "Thou art a hidden God, the Holy [Vulg.: 'the God] of Israel, the Saviour." And, again (Isa. 43:3): "His look was, as it were, hidden and despised."

*I answer that,* It was unfitting that Christ's birth should be made known to all men without distinction. First, because this would have been a hindrance to the redemption of man, which was accomplished by means of the Cross; for, as it is written (1 Cor. 2:8): "If they had known it, they would never have crucified the Lord of glory."

Secondly, because this would have lessened the merit of faith, which He came to offer men as the way to righteousness, according to Rom. 3:22: "The justice of God by faith of Jesus Christ." For if, when Christ was born, His birth had been made known to all by evident signs, the very nature of faith would have been destroyed, since it is "the evidence of things that appear not," as stated, Heb. 11:1.

Thirdly, because thus the reality of His human nature would have come into doubt. Whence Augustine says (Ep. ad Volusianum cxxxvii): "If He had not passed through the different stages of age from babyhood to youth, had neither eaten nor slept, would He not have strengthened an erroneous opinion, and made it impossible for us to believe that He had become true man? And while He is doing all things wondrously, would He have taken away that which He accomplished in mercy?"

Reply Obj. 1: According to the gloss, the words quoted must be understood of Christ's coming as judge.

Reply Obj. 2: All men were to be instructed unto salvation, concerning the grace of God our Saviour, not at the very time of His birth, but afterwards, in due time, after He had "wrought salvation in the midst of the earth" (Ps. 73:12). Wherefore after His Passion and Resurrection, He said to His disciples (Matt. 28:19): "Going . . . teach ye all nations."

Reply Obj. 3: For judgment to be passed, the authority of the judge needs to be known: and for this reason it behooves that the coming of Christ unto judgment should be manifest. But His first coming was unto the salvation of all, which is by faith that is of things not seen. And therefore it was fitting that His first coming should be hidden.

SECOND ARTICLE [III, Q. 36, Art. 2]

Whether Christ's Birth Should Have Been Made Known to Some?

Objection 1: It would seem that Christ's birth should not have been made known to anyone. For, as stated above (A. 1, ad 3), it befitted the salvation of mankind that Christ's first coming should be hidden. But Christ came to save all; according to 1 Tim. 4:10: "Who is the Saviour of all men, especially of the faithful." Therefore Christ's birth should not have been made known to anyone.

Obj. 2: Further, before Christ was born, His future birth was made known to the Blessed Virgin and Joseph. Therefore it was not necessary that it should be made known to others after His birth.

Obj. 3: Further, no wise man makes known that from which arise disturbance and harm to others. But, when Christ's birth was made known, disturbance arose: for it is written (Matt. 2:3) that "King Herod, hearing" of Christ's birth, "was troubled, and all Jerusalem with him." Moreover, this brought harm to others; because it was the occasion of Herod's killing "all the male children that were in Bethlehem . . . from two years old and under." Therefore it seems unfitting for Christ's birth to have been made known to anyone.

*On the contrary,* Christ's birth would have been profitable to none if it had been hidden from all. But it behooved Christ's birth to be profitable: else He were born in vain. Therefore it seems that Christ's birth should have been made known to some.

*I answer that,* As the Apostle says (Rom. 13:1) "what is of God is well ordered." Now it belongs to the order of Divine wisdom that God's gifts and the secrets of His wisdom are not bestowed on all equally, but to some immediately, through whom they are made known to others. Wherefore, with regard to the mystery of the Resurrection it is written (Acts 10:40, 41): "God . . . gave" Christ rising again "to be made manifest, not to all the people, but to witnesses pre-ordained by God." Consequently, that His birth might be consistent with this, it should have been made known, not to all, but to some, through whom it could be made known to others.

Reply Obj. 1: As it would have been prejudicial to the salvation of mankind if God's birth had been made known to all men, so also would it have been if none had been informed of it. Because in either case faith is destroyed, whether a thing be perfectly manifest, or whether it be entirely unknown, so that no one can hear it from another; for "faith cometh by hearing" (Rom. 10:17).

Reply Obj. 2: Mary and Joseph needed to be instructed concerning Christ's birth before He was born, because it devolved on them to show reverence to the child conceived in the womb, and to serve Him even before He was born. But their testimony, being of a domestic character, would have aroused suspicion in regard to Christ's greatness: and so it behooved it to be made known to others, whose testimony could not be suspect.

Reply Obj. 3: The very disturbance that arose when it was known that Christ was born was becoming to His birth. First, because thus the heavenly dignity of Christ is made manifest. Wherefore Gregory says (Hom. x in Evang.): "After the birth of the King of heaven, the earthly king is troubled: doubtless because earthly grandeur is covered with confusion when the heavenly majesty is revealed."

Secondly, thereby the judicial power of Christ was foreshadowed. Thus Augustine says in a sermon (30 de Temp.) on the Epiphany: "What will He be like in the judgment-seat; since from His cradle He struck terror into the heart of a proud king?"

Thirdly, because thus the overthrow of the devil's kingdom was foreshadowed. For, as Pope Leo says in a sermon on the Epiphany (Serm. v [*Opus Imperfectum in Matth., Hom. ii, falsely ascribed to St. John Chrysostom]): "Herod was not so much troubled in himself as the devil in Herod. For Herod thought Him to be a man, but the devil thought Him to be God. Each feared a successor to his kingdom: the devil, a heavenly successor; Herod, an earthly successor." But their fear was needless: since Christ had not come to set up an earthly kingdom, as Pope Leo says, addressing himself to Herod: "Thy palace cannot hold Christ: nor is the Lord of the world content with the paltry power of thy scepter." That the Jews were troubled, who, *on the contrary,* should have rejoiced, was either because, as Chrysostom says, "wicked men could not rejoice at the coming of the Holy one," or because they wished to court favor with Herod, whom they feared; for "the populace is inclined to favor too much those whose cruelty it endures."

And that the children were slain by Herod was not harmful to them, but profitable. For Augustine says in a sermon on the Epiphany (66 de Diversis): "It cannot be questioned that Christ, who came to set man free, rewarded those who were slain for Him; since, while hanging on the cross, He prayed for those who were putting Him to death."

THIRD ARTICLE [III, Q. 36, Art. 3]

Whether Those to Whom Christ's Birth Was Made Known Were Suitably Chosen?

Objection 1: It would seem that those to whom Christ's birth was made known were not suitably chosen. For our Lord (Matt. 10:5) commanded His disciples, "Go ye not into the way of the Gentiles," so that He might be made known to the Jews before the Gentiles. Therefore it seems that much less should Christ's birth have been at once revealed to the Gentiles who "came from the east," as stated Matt. 2:1.

Obj. 2: Further, the revelation of Divine truth should be made especially to the friends of God, according to Job 37 [Vulg.: Job 36:33]: "He sheweth His friend concerning it." But the Magi seem to be God's foes; for it is written (Lev. 19:31): "Go not aside after wizards ( magi ), neither ask anything of soothsayers." Therefore Christ's birth should not have been made known to the Magi.

Obj. 3: Further, Christ came in order to set free the whole world from the power of the devil; whence it is written (Malachi 1:11): "From the rising of the sun even to the going down, My name is great among the Gentiles." Therefore He should have been made known, not only to those who dwelt in the east, but also to some from all parts of the world.

Obj. 4: Further, all the sacraments of the Old Law were figures of Christ. But the sacraments of the Old Law were dispensed through the ministry of the legal priesthood. Therefore it seems that Christ's birth should have been made known rather to the priests in the Temple than to the shepherds in the fields.

Obj. 5: Further, Christ was born of a Virgin-Mother, and was as yet a little child. It was therefore more suitable that He should be made known to youths and virgins than to old and married people or to widows, such as Simeon and Anna.

*On the contrary,* It is written (John 13:18): "I know whom I have chosen." But what is done by God's wisdom is done becomingly. Therefore those to whom Christ's birth was made known were suitably chosen.

*I answer that,* Salvation, which was to be accomplished by Christ, concerns all sorts and conditions of men: because, as it is written (Col. 3:11), in Christ "there is neither male nor female, [*These words are in reality from Gal. 3:28] neither Gentile nor Jew . . . bond nor free," and so forth. And in order that this might be foreshadowed in Christ's birth, He was made known to men of all conditions. Because, as Augustine says in a sermon on the Epiphany (32 de Temp.), "the shepherds were Israelites, the Magi were Gentiles. The former were nigh to Him, the latter far from Him. Both hastened to Him together as to the cornerstone." There was also another point of contrast: for the Magi were wise and powerful; the shepherds simple and lowly. He was also made known to the righteous as Simeon and Anna; and to sinners, as the Magi. He was made known both to men, and to women--namely, to Anna--so as to show no condition of men to be excluded from Christ's redemption.

Reply Obj. 1: That manifestation of Christ's birth was a kind of foretaste of the full manifestation which was to come. And as in the later manifestation the first announcement of the grace of Christ was made by Him and His Apostles to the Jews and afterwards to the Gentiles, so the first to come to Christ were the shepherds, who were the first-fruits of the Jews, as being near to Him; and afterwards came the Magi from afar, who were "the first-fruits of the Gentiles," as Augustine says (Serm. 30 de Temp. cc.).

Reply Obj. 2: As Augustine says in a sermon on the Epiphany (Serm. 30 de Temp.): "As unskilfulness predominates in the rustic manners of the shepherd, so ungodliness abounds in the profane rites of the Magi. Yet did this Corner-Stone draw both to Itself; inasmuch as He came 'to choose the foolish things that He might confound the wise,' and 'not to call the just, but sinners,'" so that "the proud might not boast, nor the weak despair." Nevertheless, there are those who say that these Magi were not wizards, but wise astronomers, who are called Magi among the Persians or Chaldees.

Reply Obj. 3: As Chrysostom says [*Hom. ii in Matth. in the Opus Imperf., among the supposititious works of Chrysostom]: "The Magi came from the east, because the first beginning of faith came from the land where the day is born; since faith is the light of the soul." Or, "because all who come to Christ come from Him and through Him": whence it is written (Zech. 6:12): "Behold a Man, the Orient is His name." Now, they are said to come from the east literally, either because, as some say, they came from the farthest parts of the east, or because they came from the neighboring parts of Judea that lie to the east of the region inhabited by the Jews. Yet it is to be believed that certain signs of Christ's birth appeared also in other parts of the world: thus, at Rome the river flowed with oil [*Eusebius, Chronic. II, Olymp. 185]; and in Spain three suns were seen, which gradually merged into one [*Cf. Eusebius, Chronic. II, Olymp. 184].

Reply Obj. 4: As Chrysostom observes (Theophylact., Enarr. in Luc. ii, 8), the angel who announced Christ's birth did not go to Jerusalem, nor did he seek the Scribes and Pharisees, for they were corrupted, and full of ill-will. But the shepherds were single-minded, and were like the patriarchs and Moses in their mode of life.

Moreover, these shepherds were types of the Doctors of the Church, to whom are revealed the mysteries of Christ that were hidden from the Jews.

Reply Obj. 5: As Ambrose says (on Luke 2:25): "It was right that our Lord's birth should be attested not only by the shepherds, but also by people advanced in age and virtue": whose testimony is rendered the more credible by reason of their righteousness.

FOURTH ARTICLE [III, Q. 36, Art. 4]

Whether Christ Himself Should Have Made His Birth Known?

Objection 1: It would seem that Christ should have Himself made His birth known. For "a direct cause is always of greater power than an indirect cause," as is stated Phys. viii. But Christ made His birth known through others--for instance, to the shepherds through the angels, and to the Magi through the star. Much more, therefore, should He Himself have made His birth known.

Obj. 2: Further, it is written (Ecclus. 20:32): "Wisdom that is hid and treasure that is not seen; what profit is there in them both?" But Christ had, to perfection, the treasure of wisdom and grace from the beginning of His conception. Therefore, unless He had made the fulness of these gifts known by words and deeds, wisdom and grace would have been given Him to no purpose. But this is unreasonable: because "God and nature do nothing without a purpose" (De Coelo i).

Obj. 3: Further, we read in the book De Infantia Salvatoris that in His infancy Christ worked many miracles. It seems therefore that He did Himself make His birth known.

*On the contrary,* Pope Leo says (Serm. xxxiv) that the Magi found the "infant Jesus in no way different from the generality of human infants." But other infants do not make themselves known. Therefore it was not fitting that Christ should Himself make His birth known.

*I answer that,* Christ's birth was ordered unto man's salvation, which is by faith. But saving faith confesses Christ's Godhead and humanity. It behooved, therefore, Christ's birth to be made known in such a way that the proof of His Godhead should not be prejudicial to faith in His human nature. But this took place while Christ presented a likeness of human weakness, and yet, by means of God's creatures, He showed the power of the Godhead in Himself. Therefore Christ made His birth known, not by Himself, but by means of certain other creatures.

Reply Obj. 1: By the way of generation and movement we must of necessity come to the imperfect before the perfect. And therefore Christ was made known first through other creatures, and afterwards He Himself manifested Himself perfectly.

Reply Obj. 2: Although hidden wisdom is useless, yet there is no need for a wise man to make himself known at all times, but at a suitable time; for it is written (Ecclus. 20:6): "There is one that holdeth his peace because he knoweth not what to say: and there is another that holdeth his peace, knowing the proper time." Hence the wisdom given to Christ was not useless, because at a suitable time He manifested Himself. And the very fact that He was hidden at a suitable time is a sign of wisdom.

Reply Obj. 3: The book De Infantia Salvatoris is apocryphal. Moreover, Chrysostom (Hom. xxi super Joan.) says that Christ worked no miracles before changing the water into wine, according to John 2:11: "'This beginning of miracles did Jesus.' For if He had worked miracles at an early age, there would have been no need for anyone else to manifest Him to the Israelites; whereas John the Baptist says (John 1:31): 'That He may be made manifest in Israel; therefore am I come baptizing with water.' Moreover, it was fitting that He should not begin to work miracles at an early age. For people would have thought the Incarnation to be unreal, and, out of sheer spite, would have crucified Him before the proper time."

FIFTH ARTICLE [III, Q. 36, Art. 5]

Whether Christ's Birth Should Have Been Manifested by Means of the Angels and the Star?

Objection 1: It would seem that Christ's birth should not have been manifested by means of the angels. For angels are spiritual substances, according to Ps. 103:4: "Who maketh His [Vulg.: 'makest Thy'] angels, spirits." But Christ's birth was in the flesh, and not in His spiritual substance. Therefore it should not have been manifested by means of angels.

Obj. 2: Further, the righteous are more akin to the angels than to any other, according to Ps. 33:8: "The angel of the Lord shall encamp round about them that fear Him, and shall deliver them." But Christ's birth was not announced to the righteous, viz. Simeon and Anna, through the angels. Therefore neither should it have been announced to the shepherds by means of the angels.

Obj. 3: Further, it seems that neither ought it to have been announced to the Magi by means of the star. For this seems to favor the error of those who think that man's birth is influenced by the stars. But occasions of sin should be taken away from man. Therefore it was not fitting that Christ's birth should be announced by a star.

Obj. 4: Further, a sign should be certain, in order that something be made known thereby. But a star does not seem to be a certain sign of Christ's birth. Therefore Christ's birth was not suitably announced by a star.

*On the contrary,* It is written (Deut. 32:4): "The works of God are perfect." But this manifestation is the work of God. Therefore it was accomplished by means of suitable signs.

*I answer that,* As knowledge is imparted through a syllogism from something which we know better, so knowledge given by signs must be conveyed through things which are familiar to those to whom the knowledge is imparted. Now, it is clear that the righteous have, through the spirit of prophecy, a certain familiarity with the interior instinct of the Holy Ghost, and are wont to be taught thereby, without the guidance of sensible signs. Whereas others, occupied with material things, are led through the domain of the senses to that of the intellect. The Jews, however, were accustomed to receive Divine answers through the angels; through whom they also received the Law, according to Acts 7:53: "You [Vulg.: 'who'] . . . have received the Law by the disposition of angels." And the Gentiles, especially astrologers, were wont to observe the course of the stars. And therefore Christ's birth was made known to the righteous, viz. Simeon and Anna, by the interior instinct of the Holy Ghost, according to Luke 2:26: "He had received an answer from the Holy Ghost that he should not see death before he had seen the Christ of the Lord." But to the shepherds and Magi, as being occupied with material things, Christ's birth was made known by means of visible apparitions. And since this birth was not only earthly, but also, in a way, heavenly, to both (shepherds and Magi) it is revealed through heavenly signs: for, as Augustine says in a sermon on the Epiphany (cciv): "The angels inhabit, and the stars adorn, the heavens: by both, therefore, do the 'heavens show forth the glory of God.'" Moreover, it was not without reason that Christ's birth was made known, by means of angels, to the shepherds, who, being Jews, were accustomed to frequent apparitions of the angels: whereas it was revealed by means of a star to the Magi, who were wont to consider the heavenly bodies. Because, as Chrysostom says (Hom. vi in Matth.): "Our Lord deigned to call them through things to which they were accustomed." There is also another reason. For, as Gregory says (Hom. x in Evang.): "To the Jews, as rational beings, it was fitting that a rational animal [*Cf. I, Q. 51, A. 1, ad 2]," viz. an angel, "should preach. Whereas the Gentiles, who were unable to come to the knowledge of God through the reason, were led to God, not by words, but by signs. And as our Lord, when He was able to speak, was announced by heralds who spoke, so before He could speak He was manifested by speechless elements." Again, there is yet another reason. For, as Augustine [*Pope Leo] says in a sermon on the Epiphany: "To Abraham was promised an innumerable progeny, begotten, not of carnal propagation, but of the fruitfulness of faith. For this reason it is compared to the multitude of stars; that a heavenly progeny might be hoped for." Wherefore the Gentiles, "who are thus designated by the stars, are by the rising of a new star stimulated" to seek Christ, through whom they are made the seed of Abraham.

Reply Obj. 1: That which of itself is hidden needs to be manifested, but not that which in itself is manifest. Now, the flesh of Him who was born was manifest, whereas the Godhead was hidden. And therefore it was fitting that this birth should be made known by angels, who are the ministers of God. Wherefore also a certain "brightness" (Luke 2:9) accompanied the angelic apparition, to indicate that He who was just born was the "Brightness of" the Father's "glory."

Reply Obj. 2: The righteous did not need the visible apparition of the angel; on account of their perfection the interior instinct of the Holy Ghost was enough for them.

Reply Obj. 3: The star which manifested Christ's birth removed all occasion of error. For, as Augustine says (Contra Faust. ii): "No astrologer has ever so far connected the stars with man's fate at the time of his birth as to assert that one of the stars, at the birth of any man, left its orbit and made its way to him who was just born": as happened in the case of the star which made known the birth of Christ. Consequently this does not corroborate the error of those who "think there is a connection between man's birth and the course of the stars, for they do not hold that the course of the stars can be changed at a man's birth."

In the same sense Chrysostom says (Hom. vi in Matth.): "It is not an astronomer's business to know from the stars those who are born, but to tell the future from the hour of a man's birth: whereas the Magi did not know the time of the birth, so as to conclude therefrom some knowledge of the future; rather was it the other way about."

Reply Obj. 4: Chrysostom relates (Hom. ii in Matth.) that, according to some apocryphal books, a certain tribe in the far east near the ocean was in the possession of a document written by Seth, referring to this star and to the presents to be offered: which tribe watched attentively for the rising of this star, twelve men being appointed to take observations, who at stated times repaired to the summit of a mountain with faithful assiduity: whence they subsequently perceived the star containing the figure of a small child, and above it the form of a cross.

Or we may say, as may be read in the book De Qq. Vet. et Nov. Test., qu. lxiii, that "these Magi followed the tradition of Balaam," who said, "'A star shall rise out of Jacob.' Wherefore observing this star to be a stranger to the system of this world, they gathered that it was the one foretold by Balaam to indicate the King of the Jews."

Or again, it may be said with Augustine, in a sermon on the Epiphany (ccclxxiv), that "the Magi had received a revelation through the angels" that the star was a sign of the birth of Christ: and he thinks it probable that these were "good angels; since in adoring Christ they were seeking for salvation."

Or with Pope Leo, in a sermon on the Epiphany (xxxiv), that "besides the outward form which aroused the attention of their corporeal eyes, a more brilliant ray enlightened their minds with the light of faith."

SIXTH ARTICLE [III, Q. 36, Art. 6]

Whether Christ's Birth Was Made Known in a Becoming Order?

Objection 1: It would seem that Christ's birth was made known in an unbecoming order. For Christ's birth should have been made known to them first who were nearest to Christ, and who longed for Him most; according to Wis. 6:14: "She preventeth them that covet her, so that she first showeth herself unto them." But the righteous were nearest to Christ by faith, and longed most for His coming; whence it is written (Luke 2:25) of Simeon that "he was just and devout, waiting for the consolation of Israel." Therefore Christ's birth should have been made known to Simeon before the shepherds and Magi.

Obj. 2: Further, the Magi were the "first-fruits of the Gentiles," who were to believe in Christ. But first the "fulness of the Gentiles . . . come in" unto faith, and afterwards "all Israel" shall "be saved," as is written (Rom. 11:25). Therefore Christ's birth should have been made known to the Magi before the shepherds.

Obj. 3: Further, it is written (Matt. 2:16) that "Herod killed all the male children that were in Bethlehem, and in all the borders thereof, from two years old and under, according to the time which he had diligently inquired from the wise men": so that it seems that the Magi were two years in coming to Christ after His birth. It was therefore unbecoming that Christ should be made known to the Gentiles so long after His birth.

*On the contrary,* It is written (Dan. 2:21): "He changes time and ages." Consequently the time of the manifestation of Christ's birth seems to have been arranged in a suitable order.

*I answer that,* Christ's birth was first made known to the shepherds on the very day that He was born. For, as it is written (Luke 2:8, 15, 16): "There were in the same country shepherds watching, and keeping the night-watches over their flock . . . And it came to pass, after the angels departed from them into heaven they [Vulg.: 'the shepherds'] said one to another: Let us go over to Bethlehem . . . and they came with haste." Second in order were the Magi, who came to Christ on the thirteenth day after His birth, on which day is kept the feast of the Epiphany. For if they had come after a year, or even two years, they would not have found Him in Bethlehem, since it is written (Luke 2:39) that "after they had performed all things according to the law of the Lord"--that is to say, after they had offered up the Child Jesus in the Temple--"they returned into Galilee, to their city"--namely, "Nazareth." In the third place, it was made known in the Temple to the righteous on the fortieth day after His birth, as related by Luke (2:22).

The reason of this order is that the shepherds represent the apostles and other believers of the Jews, to whom the faith of Christ was made known first; among whom there were "not many mighty, not many noble," as we read 1 Cor. 1:26. Secondly, the faith of Christ came to the "fulness of the Gentiles"; and this is foreshadowed in the Magi. Thirdly it came to the fulness of the Jews, which is foreshadowed in the righteous. Wherefore also Christ was manifested to them in the Jewish Temple.

Reply Obj. 1: As the Apostle says (Rom. 9:30, 31): "Israel, by following after the law of justice, is not come unto the law of justice": but the Gentiles, "who followed not after justice," forestalled the generality of the Jews in the justice which is of faith. As a figure of this, Simeon, "who was waiting for the consolation of Israel," was the last to know Christ born: and he was preceded by the Magi and the shepherds, who did not await the coming of Christ with such longing.

Reply Obj. 2: Although the "fulness of the Gentiles came in" unto faith before the fulness of the Jews, yet the first-fruits of the Jews preceded the first-fruits of the Gentiles in faith. For this reason the birth of Christ was made known to the shepherds before the Magi.

Reply Obj. 3: There are two opinions about the apparition of the star seen by the Magi. For Chrysostom (Hom. ii in Matth. [*Opus Imperf. in Matth., falsely ascribed to Chrysostom]), and Augustine in a sermon on the Epiphany (cxxxi, cxxxii), say that the star was seen by the Magi during the two years that preceded the birth of Christ: and then, having first considered the matter and prepared themselves for the journey, they came from the farthest east to Christ, arriving on the thirteenth day after His birth. Wherefore Herod, immediately after the departure of the Magi, "perceiving that He was deluded by them," commanded the male children to be killed "from two years old and under," being doubtful lest Christ were already born when the star appeared, according as he had heard from the Magi.

But others say that the star first appeared when Christ was born, and that the Magi set off as soon as they saw the star, and accomplished a journey of very great length in thirteen days, owing partly to the Divine assistance, and partly to the fleetness of the dromedaries. And I say this on the supposition that they came from the far east. But others, again, say that they came from a neighboring country, whence also was Balaam, to whose teaching they were heirs; and they are said to have come from the east, because their country was to the east of the country of the Jews. In this case Herod killed the babes, not as soon as the Magi departed, but two years after: and that either because he is said to have gone to Rome in the meanwhile on account of an accusation brought against him, or because he was troubled at some imminent peril, and for the time being desisted from his anxiety to slay the child, or because he may have thought that the Magi, "being deceived by the illusory appearance of the star, and not finding the child, as they had expected to, were ashamed to return to him": as Augustine says (De Consensu Evang. ii). And the reason why he killed not only those who were two years old, but also the younger children, would be, as Augustine says in a sermon on the Innocents, because he feared lest a child whom the stars obey, might make himself appear older or younger.

SEVENTH ARTICLE [III, Q. 36, Art. 7]

Whether the Star Which Appeared to the Magi Belonged to the Heavenly System?

Objection 1: It would seem that the star which appeared to the Magi belonged to the heavenly system. For Augustine says in a sermon on the Epiphany (cxxii): "While God yet clings to the breast, and suffers Himself to be wrapped in humble swaddling clothes, suddenly a new star shines forth in the heavens." Therefore the star which appeared to the Magi belonged to the heavenly system.

Obj. 2: Further, Augustine says in a sermon on the Epiphany (cci): "Christ was made known to the shepherds by angels, to the Magi by a star. A heavenly tongue speaks to both, because the tongue of the prophets spoke no longer." But the angels who appeared to the shepherds were really angels from heaven. Therefore also the star which appeared to the Magi was really a star from the heavens.

Obj. 3: Further, stars which are not in the heavens but in the air are called comets, which do not appear at the birth of kings, but rather are signs of their approaching death. But this star was a sign of the King's birth: wherefore the Magi said (Matt. 2:2): "Where is He that is born King of the Jews? For we have seen His star in the east." Therefore it seems that it was a star from the heavens.

*On the contrary,* Augustine says (Contra Faust. ii): "It was not one of those stars which since the beginning of the creation observe the course appointed to them by the Creator; but this star was a stranger to the heavens, and made its appearance at the strange sight of a virgin in childbirth."

*I answer that,* As Chrysostom says (Hom. vi in Matth.), it is clear, for many reasons, that the star which appeared to the Magi did not belong to the heavenly system. First, because no other star approaches from the same quarter as this star, whose course was from north to south, these being the relative positions of Persia, whence the Magi came, and Judea. Secondly, from the time [at which it was seen]. For it appeared not only at night, but also at midday: and no star can do this, not even the moon. Thirdly, because it was visible at one time and hidden at another. For when they entered Jerusalem it hid itself: then, when they had left Herod, it showed itself again. Fourthly, because its movement was not continuous, but when the Magi had to continue their journey the star moved on; when they had to stop the star stood still; as happened to the pillar of a cloud in the desert. Fifthly, because it indicated the virginal Birth, not by remaining aloft, but by coming down below. For it is written (Matt. 2:9) that "the star which they had seen in the east went before them, until it came and stood over where the child was." Whence it is evident that the words of the Magi, "We have seen His star in the east," are to be taken as meaning, not that when they were in the east the star appeared over the country of Judea, but that when they saw the star it was in the east, and that it preceded them into Judea (although this is considered doubtful by some). But it could not have indicated the house distinctly, unless it were near the earth. And, as he [Chrysostom] observes, this does not seem fitting to a star, but "of some power endowed with reason." Consequently "it seems that this was some invisible force made visible under the form of a star."

Wherefore some say that, as the Holy Ghost, after our Lord's Baptism, came down on Him under the form of a dove, so did He appear to the Magi under the form of a star. While others say that the angel who, under a human form, appeared to the shepherds, under the form of a star, appeared to the Magi. But it seems more probable that it was a newly created star, not in the heavens, but in the air near the earth, and that its movement varied according to God's will. Wherefore Pope Leo says in a sermon on the Epiphany (xxxi): "A star of unusual brightness appeared to the three Magi in the east, which, through being more brilliant and more beautiful than the other stars, drew men's gaze and attention: so that they understood at once that such an unwonted event could not be devoid of purpose."

Reply Obj. 1: In Holy Scripture the air is sometimes called the heavens--for instance, "The birds of the heavens [Douay: 'air'] and the fishes of the sea."

Reply Obj. 2: The angels of heaven, by reason of their very office, come down to us, being "sent to minister." But the stars of heaven do not change their position. Wherefore there is no comparison.

Reply Obj. 3: As the star did not follow the course of the heavenly stars, so neither did it follow the course of the comets, which neither appear during the daytime nor vary their customary course. Nevertheless in its signification it has something in common with the comets. Because the heavenly kingdom of Christ "shall break in pieces, and shall consume all the kingdoms" of the earth, "and itself shall stand for ever" (Dan. 2:44).

EIGHTH ARTICLE [III, Q. 36, Art. 8]

Whether It Was Becoming That the Magi Should Come to Adore Christ and Pay Homage to Him?

Objection 1: It would seem that it was unbecoming that the Magi should come to adore Christ and pay homage to Him. For reverence is due to a king from his subjects. But the Magi did not belong to the kingdom of the Jews. Therefore, since they knew by seeing the star that He that was born was the "King of the Jews," it seems unbecoming that they should come to adore Him.

Obj. 2: Further, it seems absurd during the reign of one king to proclaim a stranger. But in Judea Herod was reigning. Therefore it was foolish of the Magi to proclaim the birth of a king.

Obj. 3: Further, a heavenly sign is more certain than a human sign. But the Magi had come to Judea from the east, under the guidance of a heavenly sign. Therefore it was foolish of them to seek human guidance besides that of the star, saying: "Where is He that is born King of the Jews?"

Obj. 4: Further, the offering of gifts and the homage of adoration are not due save to kings already reigning. But the Magi did not find Christ resplendent with kingly grandeur. Therefore it was unbecoming for them to offer Him gifts and homage.

*On the contrary,* It is written (Isa. 60:3): "[The Gentiles] shall walk in the light, and kings in the brightness of thy rising." But those who walk in the Divine light do not err. Therefore the Magi were right in offering homage to Christ.

*I answer that,* As stated above (A. 3, ad 1), the Magi are the "first-fruits of the Gentiles" that believed in Christ; because their faith was a presage of the faith and devotion of the nations who were to come to Christ from afar. And therefore, as the devotion and faith of the nations is without any error through the inspiration of the Holy Ghost, so also we must believe that the Magi, inspired by the Holy Ghost, did wisely in paying homage to Christ.

Reply Obj. 1: As Augustine says in a sermon on the Epiphany (cc.): "Though many kings of the Jews had been born and died, none of them did the Magi seek to adore. And so they who came from a distant foreign land to a kingdom that was entirely strange to them, had no idea of showing such great homage to such a king as the Jews were wont to have. But they had learnt that such a King was born that by adoring Him they might be sure of obtaining from Him the salvation which is of God."

Reply Obj. 2: By proclaiming [Christ King] the Magi foreshadowed the constancy of the Gentiles in confessing Christ even until death. Whence Chrysostom says (Hom. ii in Matth.) that, while they thought of the King who was to come, the Magi feared not the king who was actually present. They had not yet seen Christ, and they were already prepared to die for Him.

Reply Obj. 3: As Augustine says in a sermon on the Epiphany (cc.): "The star which led the Magi to the place where the Divine Infant was with His Virgin-Mother could bring them to the town of Bethlehem, in which Christ was born. Yet it hid itself until the Jews also bore testimony of the city in which Christ was to be born: so that, being encouraged by a twofold witness," as Pope Leo says (Serm. xxxiv), "they might seek with more ardent faith Him, whom both the brightness of the star and the authority of prophecy revealed." Thus they "proclaim" that Christ is born, and "inquire where; they believe and ask, as it were, betokening those who walk by faith and desire to see," as Augustine says in a sermon on the Epiphany (cxcix). But the Jews, by indicating to them the place of Christ's birth, "are like the carpenters who built the Ark of Noe, who provided others with the means of escape, and themselves perished in the flood. Those who asked, heard and went their way: the teachers spoke and stayed where they were; like the milestones that point out the way but walk not" (Augustine, Serm. cclxxiii). It was also by God's will that, when they no longer saw the star, the Magi, by human instinct, went to Jerusalem, to seek in the royal city the newborn King, in order that Christ's birth might be publicly proclaimed first in Jerusalem, according to Isa. 2:3: "The Law shall come forth from Sion, and the Word of the Lord from Jerusalem"; and also "in order that by the zeal of the Magi who came from afar, the indolence of the Jews who lived near at hand, might be proved worthy of condemnation" (Remig., Hom. in Matth. ii, 1).

Reply Obj. 4: As Chrysostom says (Hom. ii in Matth. [*From the supposititious Opus Imperfectum]): "If the Magi had come in search of an earthly King, they would have been disconcerted at finding that they had taken the trouble to come such a long way for nothing. Consequently they would have neither adored nor offered gifts. But since they sought a heavenly King, though they found in Him no signs of royal pre-eminence, yet, content with the testimony of the star alone, they adored: for they saw a man, and they acknowledged a God." Moreover, they offer gifts in keeping with Christ's greatness: "gold, as to the great King; they offer up incense as to God, because it is used in the Divine Sacrifice; and myrrh, which is used in embalming the bodies of the dead, is offered as to Him who is to die for the salvation of all" (Gregory, Hom. x in Evang.). And hereby, as Gregory says (Hom. x in Evang.), we are taught to offer gold, "which signifies wisdom, to the new-born King, by the luster of our wisdom in His sight." We offer God incense, "which signifies fervor in prayer, if our constant prayers mount up to God with an odor of sweetness"; and we offer myrrh, "which signifies mortification of the flesh, if we mortify the ill-deeds of the flesh by refraining from them."

## QUESTION 37

OF CHRIST'S CIRCUMCISION, AND OF THE OTHER LEGAL OBSERVANCES ACCOMPLISHED IN REGARD TO THE CHILD CHRIST (In Four Articles)

We must now consider Christ's circumcision. And since the circumcision is a kind of profession of observing the Law, according to Gal. 5:3: "I testify . . . to every man circumcising himself that he is a debtor to do the whole Law," we shall have at the same time to inquire about the other legal observances accomplished in regard to the Child Christ. Therefore there are four points of inquiry:

(1) His circumcision;

(2) The imposition of His name;

(3) His presentation;

(4) His Mother's purification.

FIRST ARTICLE [III, Q. 37, Art. 1]

Whether Christ Should Have Been Circumcised?

Objection 1: It would seem that Christ should not have been circumcised. For on the advent of the reality, the figure ceases. But circumcision was prescribed to Abraham as a sign of the covenant concerning his posterity, as may be seen from Gen. 17. Now this covenant was fulfilled in Christ's birth. Therefore circumcision should have ceased at once.

Obj. 2: Further, "every action of Christ is a lesson to us" [*Innoc. III, Serm. xxii de Temp.]; wherefore it is written (John 3:15): "I have given you an example, that as I have done to you, so you do also." But we ought not to be circumcised; according to Gal. 5:2: "If you be circumcised, Christ shall profit you nothing." Therefore it seems that neither should Christ have been circumcised.

Obj. 3: Further, circumcision was prescribed as a remedy of original sin. But Christ did not contract original sin, as stated above (Q. 14, A. 3; Q. 15, A. 1). Therefore Christ should not have been circumcised.

*On the contrary,* It is written (Luke 2:21): "After eight days were accomplished, that the child should be circumcised."

*I answer that,* For several reasons Christ ought to have been circumcised. First, in order to prove the reality of His human nature, in contradiction to the Manicheans, who said that He had an imaginary body: and in contradiction to Apollinarius, who said that Christ's body was consubstantial with His Godhead; and in contradiction to Valentine, who said that Christ brought His body from heaven. Secondly, in order to show His approval of circumcision, which God had instituted of old. Thirdly, in order to prove that He was descended from Abraham, who had received the commandment of circumcision as a sign of his faith in Him. Fourthly, in order to take away from the Jews an excuse for not receiving Him, if He were uncircumcised. Fifthly, "in order by His example to exhort us to be obedient" [*Bede, Hom. x in Evang.]. Wherefore He was circumcised on the eighth day according to the prescription of the Law (Lev. 12:3). Sixthly, "that He who had come in the likeness of sinful flesh might not reject the remedy whereby sinful flesh was wont to be healed." Seventhly, that by taking on Himself the burden of the Law, He might set others free therefrom, according to Gal. 4:4, 5: "God sent His Son . . . made under the Law, that He might redeem them who were under the Law."

Reply Obj. 1: Circumcision by the removal of the piece of skin in the member of generation, signified "the passing away of the old generation" [*Athanasius, De Sabb. et Circumcis.]: from the decrepitude of which we are freed by Christ's Passion. Consequently this figure was not completely fulfilled in Christ's birth, but in His Passion, until which time the circumcision retained its virtue and status. Therefore it behooved Christ to be circumcised as a son of Abraham before His Passion.

Reply Obj. 2: Christ submitted to circumcision while it was yet of obligation. And thus His action in this should be imitated by us, in fulfilling those things which are of obligation in our own time. Because "there is a time and opportunity for every business" (Eccl 8:6).

Moreover, according to Origen (Hom. xiv in Luc.), "as we died when He died, and rose again when Christ rose from the dead, so were we circumcised spiritually through Christ: wherefore we need no carnal circumcision." And this is what the Apostle says (Col. 2:11): "In whom," [i.e. Christ] "you are circumcised with circumcision not made by hand in despoiling of the body of the flesh, but in the circumcision of" our Lord Jesus "Christ."

Reply Obj. 3: As Christ voluntarily took upon Himself our death, which is the effect of sin, whereas He had no sin Himself, in order to deliver us from death, and to make us to die spiritually unto sin, so also He took upon Himself circumcision, which was a remedy against original sin, whereas He contracted no original sin, in order to deliver us from the yoke of the Law, and to accomplish a spiritual circumcision in us--in order, that is to say, that, by taking upon Himself the shadow, He might accomplish the reality.

SECOND ARTICLE [III, Q. 37, Art. 2]

Whether His Name Was Suitably Given to Christ?

Objection 1: It would seem that an unsuitable name was given to Christ. For the Gospel reality should correspond to the prophetic foretelling. But the prophets foretold another name for Christ: for it is written (Isa. 7:14): "Behold a virgin shall conceive and bear a son, and His name shall be called Emmanuel"; and (Isa. 8:3): "Call His name, Hasten to take away the spoils; Make haste to take away the prey"; and (Isa. 9:6): "His name shall be called Wonderful, Counselor God the Mighty, the Father of the world to come, the Prince of Peace"; and (Zech. 6:12): "Behold a Man, the Orient is His name." Thus it was unsuitable that His name should be called Jesus.

Obj. 2: Further, it is written (Isa. 62:2): "Thou shalt be called by a new name, which the mouth of the Lord hath named [Vulg.: 'shall name']." But the name Jesus is not a new name, but was given to several in the Old Testament: as may be seen in the genealogy of Christ (Luke 3:29), "Therefore it seems that it was unfitting for His name to be called Jesus."

Obj. 3: Further, the name Jesus signifies "salvation"; as is clear from Matt. 1:21: "She shall bring forth a son, and thou shalt call His name Jesus. For He shall save His people from their sins." But salvation through Christ was accomplished not only in the circumcision, but also in uncircumcision, as is declared by the Apostle (Rom. 4:11, 12). Therefore this name was not suitably given to Christ at His circumcision.

On the contrary is the authority of Scripture, in which it is written (Luke 2:21): "After eight days were accomplished, that the child should be circumcised, His name was called Jesus."

*I answer that,* A name should answer to the nature of a thing. This is clear in the names of genera and species, as stated Metaph. iv: "Since a name is but an expression of the definition" which designates a thing's proper nature.

Now, the names of individual men are always taken from some property of the men to whom they are given. Either in regard to time; thus men are named after the Saints on whose feasts they are born: or in respect of some blood relation; thus a son is named after his father or some other relation; and thus the kinsfolk of John the Baptist wished to call him "by his father's name Zachary," not by the name John, because "there" was "none of" his "kindred that" was "called by this name," as related Luke 1:59-61. Or, again, from some occurrence; thus Joseph "called the name of" the "first-born Manasses, saying: God hath made me to forget all my labors" (Gen. 41:51). Or, again, from some quality of the person who receives the name; thus it is written (Gen. 25:25) that "he that came forth first was red and hairy like a skin; and his name was called Esau," which is interpreted "red."

But names given to men by God always signify some gratuitous gift bestowed on them by Him; thus it was said to Abraham (Gen. 17:5): "Thou shalt be called Abraham; because I have made thee a father of many nations": and it was said to Peter (Matt. 16:18): "Thou art Peter, and upon this rock I will build My Church." Since, therefore, this prerogative of grace was bestowed on the Man Christ that through Him all men might be saved, therefore He was becomingly named Jesus, i.e. Saviour: the angel having foretold this name not only to His Mother, but also to Joseph, who was to be his foster-father.

Reply Obj. 1: All these names in some way mean the same as Jesus, which means "salvation." For the name "Emmanuel, which being interpreted is 'God with us,'" designates the cause of salvation, which is the union of the Divine and human natures in the Person of the Son of God, the result of which union was that "God is with us."

When it was said, "Call his name, Hasten to take away," etc., these words indicate from what He saved us, viz. from the devil, whose spoils He took away, according to Col. 2:15: "Despoiling the principalities and powers, He hath exposed them confidently."

When it was said, "His name shall be called Wonderful," etc., the way and term of our salvation are pointed out: inasmuch as "by the wonderful counsel and might of the Godhead we are brought to the inheritance of the life to come," in which the children of God will enjoy "perfect peace" under "God their Prince."

When it was said, "Behold a Man, the Orient is His name," reference is made to the same, as in the first, viz. to the mystery of the Incarnation, by reason of which "to the righteous a light is risen up in darkness" (Ps. 111:4).

Reply Obj. 2: The name Jesus could be suitable for some other reason to those who lived before Christ--for instance, because they were saviours in a particular and temporal sense. But in the sense of spiritual and universal salvation, this name is proper to Christ, and thus it is called a "new" name.

Reply Obj. 3: As is related Gen. 17, Abraham received from God and at the same time both his name and the commandment of circumcision. For this reason it was customary among the Jews to name children on the very day of circumcision, as though before being circumcised they had not as yet perfect existence: just as now also children receive their names in Baptism. Wherefore on Prov. 4:3, "I was my father's son, tender, and as an only son in the sight of my mother," the gloss says: "Why does Solomon call himself an only son in the sight of his mother, when Scripture testifies that he had an elder brother of the same mother, unless it be that the latter died unnamed soon after birth?" Therefore it was that Christ received His name at the time of His circumcision.

THIRD ARTICLE [III, Q. 37, Art. 3]

Whether Christ Was Becomingly Presented in the Temple?

Objection 1: It would seem that Christ was unbecomingly presented in the Temple. For it is written (Ex. 13:2): "Sanctify unto Me every first-born that openeth the womb among the children of Israel." But Christ came forth from the closed womb of the Virgin; and thus He did not open His Mother's womb. Therefore Christ was not bound by this law to be presented in the Temple.

Obj. 2: Further, that which is always in one's presence cannot be presented to one. But Christ's humanity was always in God's presence in the highest degree, as being always united to Him in unity of person. Therefore there was no need for Him to be presented to the Lord.

Obj. 3: Further, Christ is the principal victim, to whom all the victims of the old Law are referred, as the figure to the reality. But a victim should not be offered up for a victim. Therefore it was not fitting that another victim should be offered up for Christ.

Obj. 4: Further, among the legal victims the principal was the lamb, which was a "continual sacrifice" [Vulg.: 'holocaust'], as is stated Num. 28:6: for which reason Christ is also called "the Lamb--Behold the Lamb of God" (John 1: 29). It was therefore more fitting that a lamb should be offered for Christ than "a pair of turtle doves or two young pigeons."

On the contrary is the authority of Scripture which relates this as having taken place (Luke 2:22).

*I answer that,* As stated above (A. 1), Christ wished to be "made under the Law, that He might redeem them who were under the Law" (Gal. 4:4, 5), and that the "justification of the Law might be" spiritually "fulfilled" in His members. Now, the Law contained a twofold precept touching the children born. One was a general precept which affected all--namely, that "when the days of the mother's purification were expired," a sacrifice was to be offered either "for a son or for a daughter," as laid down Lev. 12:6. And this sacrifice was for the expiation of the sin in which the child was conceived and born; and also for a certain consecration of the child, because it was then presented in the Temple for the first time. Wherefore one offering was made as a holocaust and another for sin.

The other was a special precept in the law concerning the first-born of "both man and beast": for the Lord claimed for Himself all the first-born in Israel, because, in order to deliver the Israelites, He "slew every first-born in the land of Egypt, both men and cattle" (Ex. 12:12, 13, 29), the first-born of Israel being saved; which law is set down Ex. 13. Here also was Christ foreshadowed, who is "the First-born amongst many brethren" (Rom. 8:29).

Therefore, since Christ was born of a woman and was her first-born, and since He wished to be "made under the Law," the Evangelist Luke shows that both these precepts were fulfilled in His regard. First, as to that which concerns the first-born, when he says (Luke 2:22, 23): "They carried Him to Jerusalem to present Him to the Lord: as it is written in the law of the Lord, 'Every male opening the womb shall be called holy to the Lord.'" Secondly, as to the general precept which concerned all, when he says (Luke 2:24): "And to offer a sacrifice according as it is written in the law of the Lord, a pair of turtle doves or two young pigeons."

Reply Obj. 1: As Gregory of Nyssa says (De Occursu Dom.): "It seems that this precept of the Law was fulfilled in God incarnate alone in a special manner exclusively proper to Him. For He alone, whose conception was ineffable, and whose birth was incomprehensible, opened the virginal womb which had been closed to sexual union, in such a way that after birth the seal of chastity remained inviolate." Consequently the words "opening the womb" imply that nothing hitherto had entered or gone forth therefrom. Again, for a special reason is it written "'a male,' because He contracted nothing of the woman's sin": and in a singular way "is He called 'holy,' because He felt no contagion of earthly corruption, whose birth was wondrously immaculate" (Ambrose, on Luke 2:23).

Reply Obj. 2: As the Son of God "became man, and was circumcised in the flesh, not for His own sake, but that He might make us to be God's through grace, and that we might be circumcised in the spirit; so, again, for our sake He was presented to the Lord, that we may learn to offer ourselves to God" [*Athanasius, on Luke 2:23]. And this was done after His circumcision, in order to show that "no one who is not circumcised from vice is worthy of Divine regard" [*Bede, on Luke 2:23].

Reply Obj. 3: For this very reason He wished the legal victims to be offered for Him who was the true Victim, in order that the figure might be united to and confirmed by the reality, against those who denied that in the Gospel Christ preached the God of the Law. "For we must not think," says Origen (Hom. xiv in Luc.) "that the good God subjected His Son to the enemy's law, which He Himself had not given."

Reply Obj. 4: The law of Lev. 12:6, 8 "commanded those who could, to offer, for a son or a daughter, a lamb and also a turtle dove or a pigeon: but those who were unable to offer a lamb were commanded to offer two turtle doves or two young pigeons" [*Bede, Hom. xv in Purif.]. "And so the Lord, who, 'being rich, became poor for our [Vulg.: 'your'] sakes, that through His poverty we [you] might be rich,'' as is written 2 Cor. 8:9, "wished the poor man's victim to be offered for Him" just as in His birth He was "wrapped in swaddling clothes and laid in a manger" [*Bede on Luke 1]. Nevertheless, these birds have a figurative sense. For the turtle dove, being a loquacious bird, represents the preaching and confession of faith; and because it is a chaste animal, it signifies chastity; and being a solitary animal, it signifies contemplation. The pigeon is a gentle and simple animal, and therefore signifies gentleness and simplicity. It is also a gregarious animal; wherefore it signifies the active life. Consequently this sacrifice signified the perfection of Christ and His members. Again, "both these animals, by the plaintiveness of their song, represented the mourning of the saints in this life: but the turtle dove, being solitary, signifies the tears of prayer; whereas the pigeon, being gregarious, signifies the public prayers of the Church" [*Bede, Hom. xv in Purif.]. Lastly, two of each of these animals are offered, to show that holiness should be not only in the soul, but also in the body.

FOURTH ARTICLE [III, Q. 37, Art. 4]

Whether It Was Fitting That the Mother of God Should Go to the Temple to Be Purified?

Objection 1: It would seem that it was unfitting for the Mother of God to go to the Temple to be purified. For purification presupposes uncleanness. But there was no uncleanness in the Blessed Virgin, as stated above (QQ. 27, 28). Therefore she should not have gone to the Temple to be purified.

Obj. 2: Further, it is written (Lev. 12:2-4): "If a woman, having received seed, shall bear a man-child, she shall be unclean seven days"; and consequently she is forbidden "to enter into the sanctuary until the days of her purification be fulfilled." But the Blessed Virgin brought forth a male child without receiving the seed of man. Therefore she had no need to come to the Temple to be purified.

Obj. 3: Further, purification from uncleanness is accomplished by grace alone. But the sacraments of the Old Law did not confer grace; rather, indeed, did she have the very Author of grace with her. Therefore it was not fitting that the Blessed Virgin should come to the Temple to be purified.

On the contrary is the authority of Scripture, where it is stated (Luke 2:22) that "the days of" Mary's "purification were accomplished according to the law of Moses."

*I answer that,* As the fulness of grace flowed from Christ on to His Mother, so it was becoming that the mother should be like her Son in humility: for "God giveth grace to the humble," as is written James 4:6. And therefore, just as Christ, though not subject to the Law, wished, nevertheless, to submit to circumcision and the other burdens of the Law, in order to give an example of humility and obedience; and in order to show His approval of the Law; and, again, in order to take away from the Jews an excuse for calumniating Him: for the same reasons He wished His Mother also to fulfil the prescriptions of the Law, to which, nevertheless, she was not subject.

Reply Obj. 1: Although the Blessed Virgin had no uncleanness, yet she wished to fulfil the observance of purification, not because she needed it, but on account of the precept of the Law. Thus the Evangelist says pointedly that the days of her purification "according to the Law" were accomplished; for she needed no purification in herself.

Reply Obj. 2: Moses seems to have chosen his words in order to exclude uncleanness from the Mother of God, who was with child "without receiving seed." It is therefore clear that she was not bound to fulfil that precept, but fulfilled the observance of purification of her own accord, as stated above.

Reply Obj. 3: The sacraments of the Law did not cleanse from the uncleanness of sin which is accomplished by grace, but they foreshadowed this purification: for they cleansed by a kind of carnal purification, from the uncleanness of a certain irregularity, as stated in the Second Part (I-II, Q. 102, A. 5; Q. 103, A. 2). But the Blessed Virgin contracted neither uncleanness, and consequently did not need to be purified.

## QUESTION 38

OF THE BAPTISM OF JOHN (In Six Articles)

We now proceed to consider the baptism wherewith Christ was baptized. And since Christ was baptized with the baptism of John, we shall consider (1) the baptism of John in general; (2) the baptizing of Christ. In regard to the former there are six points of inquiry:

(1) Whether it was fitting that John should baptize?

(2) Whether that baptism was from God?

(3) Whether it conferred grace?

(4) Whether others besides Christ should have received that baptism?

(5) Whether that baptism should have ceased when Christ was baptized?

(6) Whether those who received John's baptism had afterwards to receive Christ's baptism?

FIRST ARTICLE [III, Q. 38, Art. 1]

Whether It Was Fitting That John Should Baptize?

Objection 1: It would seem that it was not fitting that John should baptize. For every sacramental rite belongs to some law. But John did not introduce a new law. Therefore it was not fitting that he should introduce the new rite of baptism.

Obj. 2: Further, John "was sent by God . . . for a witness" (John 1:6, 7) as a prophet; according to Luke 1:76: "Thou, child, shalt be called the prophet of the Highest." But the prophets who lived before Christ did not introduce any new rite, but persuaded men to observe the rites of the Law. as is clearly stated Malachi 4:4: "Remember the law of Moses My servant." Therefore neither should John have introduced a new rite of baptism.

Obj. 3: Further, when there is too much of anything, nothing should be added to it. But the Jews observed a superfluity of baptisms; for it is written (Mk. 7:3, 4) that "the Pharisees and all the Jews eat not without often washing their hands . . . and when they come from the market, unless they be washed, they eat not; and many other things there are that have been delivered to them to observe, the washings of cups and of pots, and of brazen vessels, and of beds." Therefore it was unfitting that John should baptize.

On the contrary is the authority of Scripture (Matt. 3:5, 6), which, after stating the holiness of John, adds many went out to him, "and were baptized in the Jordan."

*I answer that,* It was fitting for John to baptize, for four reasons: first, it was necessary for Christ to be baptized by John, in order that He might sanctify baptism; as Augustine observes, super Joan. (Tract. xiii in Joan.).

Secondly, that Christ might be manifested. Whence John himself says (John 1:31): "That He," i.e. Christ, "may be made manifest in Israel, therefore am I come baptizing with water." For he announced Christ to the crowds that gathered around him; which was thus done much more easily than if he had gone in search of each individual, as Chrysostom observes, commenting on St. John (Hom. x in Matth.).

Thirdly, that by his baptism he might accustom men to the baptism of Christ; wherefore Gregory says in a homily (Hom. vii in Evang.) that therefore did John baptize, "that, being consistent with his office of precursor, as he had preceded our Lord in birth, so he might also by baptizing precede Him who was about to baptize."

Fourthly, that by persuading men to do penance, he might prepare men to receive worthily the baptism of Christ. Wherefore Bede [*Cf. Scot. Erig. in Joan. iii, 24] says that "the baptism of John was as profitable before the baptism of Christ, as instruction in the faith profits the catechumens not yet baptized. For just as he preached penance, and foretold the baptism of Christ, and drew men to the knowledge of the Truth that hath appeared to the world, so do the ministers of the Church, after instructing men, chide them for their sins, and lastly promise them forgiveness in the baptism of Christ."

Reply Obj. 1: The baptism of John was not a sacrament properly so called ( per se ), but a kind of sacramental, preparatory to the baptism of Christ. Consequently, in a way, it belonged to the law of Christ, but not to the law of Moses.

Reply Obj. 2: John was not only a prophet, but "more than a prophet," as stated Matt. 11:9: for he was the term of the Law and the beginning of the Gospel. Therefore it was in his province to lead men, both by word and deed, to the law of Christ rather than to the observance of the Old Law.

Reply Obj. 3: Those baptisms of the Pharisees were vain, being ordered merely unto carnal cleanliness. But the baptism of John was ordered unto spiritual cleanliness, since it led men to do penance, as stated above.

SECOND ARTICLE [III, Q. 38, Art. 2]

Whether the Baptism of John Was from God?

Objection 1: It would seem that the baptism of John was not from God. For nothing sacramental that is from God is named after a mere man: thus the baptism of the New Law is not named after Peter or Paul, but after Christ. But that baptism is named after John, according to Matt. 21:25: "The baptism of John . . . was it from heaven or from men?" Therefore the baptism of John was not from God.

Obj. 2: Further, every doctrine that proceeds from God anew is confirmed by some signs: thus the Lord (Ex. 4) gave Moses the power of working signs; and it is written (Heb. 2:3, 4) that our faith "having begun to be declared by the Lord, was confirmed unto us by them that heard Him, God also bearing them witness by signs and wonders." But it is written of John the Baptist (John 10:41) that "John did no sign." Therefore it seems that the baptism wherewith he baptized was not from God.

Obj. 3: Further, those sacraments which are instituted by God are contained in certain precepts of Holy Scripture. But there is no precept of Holy Writ commanding the baptism of John. Therefore it seems that it was not from God.

*On the contrary,* It is written (John 1:33): "He who sent me to baptize with water said to me: 'He upon whom thou shalt see the Spirit,'" etc.

*I answer that,* Two things may be considered in the baptism of John--namely, the rite of baptism and the effect of baptism. The rite of baptism was not from men, but from God, who by an interior revelation of the Holy Ghost sent John to baptize. But the effect of that baptism was from man, because it effected nothing that man could not accomplish. Wherefore it was not from God alone, except in as far as God works in man.

Reply Obj. 1: By the baptism of the New Law men are baptized inwardly by the Holy Ghost, and this is accomplished by God alone. But by the baptism of John the body alone was cleansed by the water. Wherefore it is written (Matt. 3:11): "I baptize you in water; but . . . He shall baptize you in the Holy Ghost." For this reason the baptism of John was named after him, because it effected nothing that he did not accomplish. But the baptism of the New Law is not named after the minister thereof, because he does not accomplish its principal effect, which is the inward cleansing.

Reply Obj. 2: The whole teaching and work of John was ordered unto Christ, who, by many miracles confirmed both His own teaching and that of John. But if John had worked signs, men would have paid equal attention to John and to Christ. Wherefore, in order that men might pay greater attention to Christ, it was not given to John to work a sign. Yet when the Jews asked him why he baptized, he confirmed his office by the authority of Scripture, saying: "I am the voice of one crying in the wilderness," etc. as related, John 1:23 (cf. Isa. 40:3). Moreover, the very austerity of his life was a commendation of his office, because, as Chrysostom says, commenting on Matthew (Hom. x in Matth.), "it was wonderful to witness such endurance in a human body."

Reply Obj. 3: The baptism of John was intended by God to last only for a short time, for the reasons given above (A. 1). Therefore it was not the subject of a general commandment set down in Sacred Writ, but of a certain interior revelation of the Holy Ghost, as stated above.

THIRD ARTICLE [III, Q. 38, Art. 3]

Whether Grace Was Given in the Baptism of John?

Objection 1: It would seem that grace was given in the baptism of John. For it is written (Mk. 1:4): "John was in the desert baptizing and preaching the baptism of penance unto remission of sins." But penance and remission of sins are the effect of grace. Therefore the baptism of John conferred grace.

Obj. 2: Further, those who were about to be baptized by John "confessed their sins," as related Matt. 3:6 and Mk. 1:5. But the confession of sins is ordered to their remission, which is effected by grace. Therefore grace was conferred in the baptism of John.

Obj. 3: Further, the baptism of John was more akin than circumcision to the baptism of Christ. But original sin was remitted through circumcision: because, as Bede says (Hom. x in Circumcis.), "under the Law, circumcision brought the same saving aid to heal the wound of original sin as baptism is wont to bring now that grace is revealed." Much more, therefore, did the baptism of John effect the remission of sins, which cannot be accomplished without grace.

*On the contrary,* It is written (Matt. 3:11): "I indeed baptize you in water unto penance." Which words Gregory thus expounds in a certain homily (Hom. vii in Evang.): "John baptized, not in the Spirit, but in water: because he could not forgive sins." But grace is given by the Holy Ghost, and by means thereof sins are taken away. Therefore the baptism of John did not confer grace.

*I answer that,* As stated above (A. 2, ad 2), the whole teaching and work of John was in preparation for Christ: just as it is the duty of the servant and of the under-craftsman to prepare the matter for the form which is accomplished by the head-craftsman. Now grace was to be conferred on men through Christ, according to John 1:17: "Grace and truth came through Jesus Christ." Therefore the baptism of John did not confer grace, but only prepared the way for grace; and this in three ways: first, by John's teaching, which led men to faith in Christ; secondly, by accustoming men to the rite of Christ's baptism; thirdly, by penance, preparing men to receive the effect of Christ's baptism.

Reply Obj. 1: In these words, as Bede says (on Mk. 1:4), a twofold baptism of penance may be understood. One is that which John conferred by baptizing, which is called "a baptism of penance," etc., by reason of its inducing men to do penance, and of its being a kind of protestation by which men avowed their purpose of doing penance. The other is the baptism of Christ, by which sins are remitted, and which John could not give, but only preach, saying: "He will baptize you in the Holy Ghost."

Or it may be said that he preached the "baptism of penance," i.e. which induced men to do penance, which penance leads men on to "the remission of sins."

Or again, it may be said with Jerome [*Another author on Mk. 1 (inter op. Hier.)] that "by the baptism of Christ grace is given, by which sins are remitted gratis; and that what is accomplished by the bridegroom is begun by the bridesman," i.e. by John. Consequently it is said that "he baptized and preached the baptism of penance unto remission of sins," not as though he accomplished this himself, but because he began it by preparing the way for it.

Reply Obj. 2: That confession of sins was not made unto the remission of sins, to be realized immediately through the baptism of John, but to be obtained through subsequent penance and through the baptism of Christ, for which that penance was a preparation.

Reply Obj. 3: Circumcision was instituted as a remedy for original sin. Whereas the baptism of John was not instituted for this purpose, but was merely in preparation for the baptism of Christ, as stated above; whereas the sacraments attain their effect through the force of their institution.

FOURTH ARTICLE [III, Q. 38, Art. 4]

Whether Christ Alone Should Have Been Baptized with the Baptism of John?

Objection 1: It would seem that Christ alone should have been baptized with the baptism of John. For, as stated above (A. 1), "the reason why John baptized was that Christ might receive baptism," as Augustine says (Super Joan., Tract. xiii). But what is proper to Christ should not be applicable to others. Therefore no others should have received that baptism.

Obj. 2: Further, whoever is baptized either receives something from the baptism or confers something on the baptism. But no one could receive anything from the baptism of John, because thereby grace was not conferred, as stated above (A. 3). On the other hand, no one could confer anything on baptism save Christ, who "sanctified the waters by the touch of His most pure flesh" [*Mag. Sent. iv, 3]. Therefore it seems that Christ alone should have been baptized with the baptism of John.

Obj. 3: Further, if others were baptized with that baptism, this was only in order that they might be prepared for the baptism of Christ: and thus it would seem fitting that the baptism of John should be conferred on all, old and young, Gentile and Jew, just as the baptism of Christ. But we do not read that either children or Gentiles were baptized by the latter; for it is written (Mk. 1:5) that "there went out to him . . . all they of Jerusalem, and were baptized by him." Therefore it seems that Christ alone should have been baptized by John.

*On the contrary,* It is written (Luke 3:21): "It came to pass, when all the people were baptized, that Jesus also being baptized and praying, heaven was opened."

*I answer that,* For two reasons it behooved others besides Christ to be baptized with the baptism of John. First, as Augustine says (Super Joan., Tract. iv, v), "if Christ alone had been baptized with the baptism of John, some would have said that John's baptism, with which Christ was baptized, was more excellent than that of Christ, with which others are baptized."

Secondly, because, as above stated, it behooved others to be prepared by John's baptism for the baptism of Christ.

Reply Obj. 1: The baptism of John was instituted not only that Christ might be baptized, but also for other reasons, as stated above (A. 1). And yet, even if it were instituted merely in order that Christ might be baptized therewith, it was still necessary for others to receive this baptism, in order to avoid the objection mentioned above.

Reply Obj. 2: Others who approached to be baptized by John could not, indeed, confer anything on his baptism: yet neither did they receive anything therefrom, save only the sign of penance.

Reply Obj. 3: This was the baptism of "penance," for which children were not suited; wherefore they were not baptized therewith. But to bring the nations into the way of salvation was reserved to Christ alone, who is the "expectation of the nations," as we read Gen. 49:10. Indeed, Christ forbade the apostles to preach the Gospel to the Gentiles before His Passion and Resurrection. Much less fitting, therefore, was it for the Gentiles to be baptized by John.

FIFTH ARTICLE [III, Q. 38, Art. 5]

Whether John's Baptism Should Have Ceased After Christ Was Baptized?

Objection 1: It would seem that John's baptism should have ceased after Christ was baptized. For it is written (John 1:31): "That He may be made manifest in Israel, therefore am I come baptizing in water." But when Christ had been baptized, He was made sufficiently manifest, both by the testimony of John and by the dove coming down upon Him, and again by the voice of the Father bearing witness to Him. Therefore it seems that John's baptism should not have endured thereafter.

Obj. 2: Further, Augustine says (Super Joan., Tract. iv): "Christ was baptized, and John's baptism ceased to avail." Therefore it seems that, after Christ's baptism, John should not have continued to baptize.

Obj. 3: Further, John's baptism prepared the way for Christ's. But Christ's baptism began as soon as He had been baptized; because "by the touch of His most pure flesh He endowed the waters with a regenerating virtue," as Bede asserts (Mag. Sent. iv, 3). Therefore it seems that John's baptism ceased when Christ had been baptized.

*On the contrary,* It is written (John 3:22, 23): "Jesus . . . came into the land of Judea . . . and baptized: and John also was baptizing." But Christ did not baptize before being baptized. Therefore it seems that John continued to baptize after Christ had been baptized.

*I answer that,* It was not fitting for the baptism of John to cease when Christ had been baptized. First, because, as Chrysostom says (Hom. xxix in Joan.), "if John had ceased to baptize" when Christ had been baptized, "men would think that he was moved by jealousy or anger." Secondly, if he had ceased to baptize when Christ baptized, "he would have given His disciples a motive for yet greater envy." Thirdly, because, by continuing to baptize, "he sent his hearers to Christ" (Hom. xxix in Joan.). Fourthly, because, as Bede [*Scot. Erig. Comment. in Joan.] says, "there still remained a shadow of the Old Law: nor should the forerunner withdraw until the truth be made manifest."

Reply Obj. 1: When Christ was baptized, He was not as yet fully manifested: consequently there was still need for John to continue baptizing.

Reply Obj. 2: The baptism of John ceased after Christ had been baptized, not immediately, but when the former was cast into prison. Thus Chrysostom says (Hom. xxix in Joan.): "I consider that John's death was allowed to take place, and that Christ's preaching began in a great measure after John had died, so that the undivided allegiance of the multitude was transferred to Christ, and there was no further motive for the divergence of opinions concerning both of them."

Reply Obj. 3: John's baptism prepared the way not only for Christ to be baptized, but also for others to approach to Christ's baptism: and this did not take place as soon as Christ was baptized.

SIXTH ARTICLE [III, Q. 38, Art. 6]

Whether Those Who Had Been Baptized with John's Baptism Had to Be Baptized with the Baptism of Christ?

Objection 1: It would seem that those who had been baptized with John's baptism had not to be baptized with the baptism of Christ. For John was not less than the apostles, since of him is it written (Matt. 11:11): "There hath not risen among them that are born of women a greater than John the Baptist." But those who were baptized by the apostles were not baptized again, but only received the imposition of hands; for it is written (Acts 8:16, 17) that some were "only baptized" by Philip "in the name of the Lord Jesus": then the apostles--namely, Peter and John--"laid their hands upon them, and they received the Holy Ghost." Therefore it seems that those who had been baptized by John had not to be baptized with the baptism of Christ.

Obj. 2: Further, the apostles were baptized with John's baptism, since some of them were his disciples, as is clear from John 1:37. But the apostles do not seem to have been baptized with the baptism of Christ: for it is written (John 4:2) that "Jesus did not baptize, but His disciples." Therefore it seems that those who had been baptized with John's baptism had not to be baptized with the baptism of Christ.

Obj. 3: Further, he who is baptized is less than he who baptizes. But we are not told that John himself was baptized with the baptism of Christ. Therefore much less did those who had been baptized by John need to receive the baptism of Christ.

Obj. 4: Further, it is written (Acts 19:1-5) that "Paul . . . found certain disciples; and he said to them: Have you received the Holy Ghost since ye believed? But they said to him: We have not so much as heard whether there be a Holy Ghost. And he said: In what then were you baptized? Who said: In John's baptism." Wherefore "they were" again "baptized in the name of our [Vulg.: 'the'] Lord Jesus Christ." Hence it seems that they needed to be baptized again, because they did not know of the Holy Ghost: as Jerome says on Joel 2:28 and in an epistle (lxix De Viro unius uxoris), and likewise Ambrose (De Spiritu Sancto). But some were baptized with John's baptism who had full knowledge of the Trinity. Therefore these had no need to be baptized again with Christ's baptism.

Obj. 5: Further, on Rom. 10:8, "This is the word of faith, which we preach," the gloss of Augustine says: "Whence this virtue in the water, that it touches the body and cleanses the heart, save by the efficacy of the word, not because it is uttered, but because it is believed?" Whence it is clear that the virtue of baptism depends on faith. But the form of John's baptism signified the faith in which we are baptized; for Paul says (Acts 19:4): "John baptized the people with the baptism of penance, saying: That they should believe in Him who was to come after him--that is to say, in Jesus." Therefore it seems that those who had been baptized with John's baptism had no need to be baptized again with the baptism of Christ.

*On the contrary,* Augustine says (Super Joan., Tract. v): "Those who were baptized with John's baptism needed to be baptized with the baptism of our Lord."

*I answer that,* According to the opinion of the Master (Sent. iv, D, 2), "those who had been baptized by John without knowing of the existence of the Holy Ghost, and who based their hopes on his baptism, were afterwards baptized with the baptism of Christ: but those who did not base their hope on John's baptism, and who believed in the Father, Son, and Holy Ghost, were not baptized afterwards, but received the Holy Ghost by the imposition of hands made over them by the apostles."

And this, indeed, is true as to the first part, and is confirmed by many authorities. But as to the second part, the assertion is altogether unreasonable. First, because John's baptism neither conferred grace nor imprinted a character, but was merely "in water," as he says himself (Matt. 3:11). Wherefore the faith or hope which the person baptized had in Christ could not supply this defect. Secondly, because, when in a sacrament, that is omitted which belongs of necessity to the sacrament, not only must the omission be supplied, but the whole must be entirely renewed. Now, it belongs of necessity to Christ's baptism that it be given not only in water, but also in the Holy Ghost, according to John 3:5: "Unless a man be born of water and the Holy Ghost, he cannot enter into the kingdom of God." Wherefore in the case of those who had been baptized with John's baptism in water only, not merely had the omission to be supplied by giving them the Holy Ghost by the imposition of hands, but they had to be baptized wholly anew "in water and the Holy Ghost."

Reply Obj. 1: As Augustine says (Super Joan., Tract. v): "After John, baptism was administered, and the reason why was because he gave not Christ's baptism, but his own . . . That which Peter gave . . . and if any were given by Judas, that was Christ's. And therefore if Judas baptized anyone, yet were they not rebaptized . . . For the baptism corresponds with him by whose authority it is given, not with him by whose ministry it is given." For the same reason those who were baptized by the deacon Philip, who gave the baptism of Christ, were not baptized again, but received the imposition of hands by the apostles, just as those who are baptized by priests are confirmed by bishops.

Reply Obj. 2: As Augustine says to Seleucianus (Ep. cclxv), "we deem that Christ's disciples were baptized either with John's baptism, as some maintain, or with Christ's baptism, which is more probable. For He would not fail to administer baptism so as to have baptized servants through whom He baptized others, since He did not fail in His humble service to wash their feet."

Reply Obj. 3: As Chrysostom says (Hom. iv in Matth. [*From the supposititious Opus Imperfectum]): "Since, when John said, 'I ought to be baptized by Thee,' Christ answered, 'Suffer it to be so now': it follows that afterwards Christ did baptize John." Moreover, he asserts that "this is distinctly set down in some of the apocryphal books." At any rate, it is certain, as Jerome says on Matt. 3:13, that, "as Christ was baptized in water by John, so had John to be baptized in the Spirit by Christ."

Reply Obj. 4: The reason why these persons were baptized after being baptized by John was not only because they knew not of the Holy Ghost, but also because they had not received the baptism of Christ.

Reply Obj. 5: As Augustine says (Contra Faust. xix), our sacraments are signs of present grace, whereas the sacraments of the Old Law were signs of future grace. Wherefore the very fact that John baptized in the name of one who was to come, shows that he did not give the baptism of Christ, which is a sacrament of the New Law.

## QUESTION 39

OF THE BAPTIZING OF CHRIST (In Eight Articles)

We have now to consider the baptizing of Christ, concerning which there are eight points of inquiry:

(1) Whether Christ should have been baptized?

(2) Whether He should have been baptized with the baptism of John?

(3) Of the time when He was baptized;

(4) Of the place;

(5) Of the heavens being opened unto Him;

(6) Of the apparition of the Holy Ghost under the form of a dove;

(7) Whether that dove was a real animal?

(8) Of the voice of the Father witnessing unto Him.

FIRST ARTICLE [III, Q. 39, Art. 1]

Whether It Was Fitting That Christ Should Be Baptized?

Objection 1: It would seem that it was not fitting for Christ to be baptized. For to be baptized is to be washed. But it was not fitting for Christ to be washed, since there was no uncleanness in Him. Therefore it seems unfitting for Christ to be baptized.

Obj. 2: Further, Christ was circumcised in order to fulfil the law. But baptism was not prescribed by the law. Therefore He should not have been baptized.

Obj. 3: Further, the first mover in every genus is unmoved in regard to that movement; thus the heaven, which is the first cause of alteration, is unalterable. But Christ is the first principle of baptism, according to John 1:33: "He upon whom thou shalt see the Spirit descending and remaining upon Him, He it is that baptizeth." Therefore it was unfitting for Christ to be baptized.

*On the contrary,* It is written (Matt. 3:13) that "Jesus cometh from Galilee to the Jordan, unto John, to be baptized by him."

*I answer that,* It was fitting for Christ to be baptized. First, because, as Ambrose says on Luke 3:21: "Our Lord was baptized because He wished, not to be cleansed, but to cleanse the waters, that, being purified by the flesh of Christ that knew no sin, they might have the virtue of baptism"; and, as Chrysostom says (Hom. iv in Matth.), "that He might bequeath the sanctified waters to those who were to be baptized afterwards." Secondly, as Chrysostom says (Hom. iv in Matth.), "although Christ was not a sinner, yet did He take a sinful nature and 'the likeness of sinful flesh.' Wherefore, though He needed not baptism for His own sake, yet carnal nature in others had need thereof." And, as Gregory Nazianzen says (Orat. xxxix) "Christ was baptized that He might plunge the old Adam entirely in the water." Thirdly, He wished to be baptized, as Augustine says in a sermon on the Epiphany (cxxxvi), "because He wished to do what He had commanded all to do." And this is what He means by saying: "So it becometh us to fulfil all justice" (Matt. 3:15). For, as Ambrose says (on Luke 3:21), "this is justice, to do first thyself that which thou wishest another to do, and so encourage others by thy example."

Reply Obj. 1: Christ was baptized, not that He might be cleansed, but that He might cleanse, as stated above.

Reply Obj. 2: It was fitting that Christ should not only fulfil what was prescribed by the Old Law, but also begin what appertained to the New Law. Therefore He wished not only to be circumcised, but also to be baptized.

Reply Obj. 3: Christ is the first principle of baptism's spiritual effect. Unto this He was not baptized, but only in water.

SECOND ARTICLE [III, Q. 39, Art. 2]

Whether It Was Fitting for Christ to Be Baptized with John's Baptism?

Objection 1: It would seem that it was unfitting for Christ to be baptized with John's baptism. For John's baptism was the "baptism of penance." But penance is unbecoming to Christ, since He had no sin. Therefore it seems that He should not have been baptized with John's baptism.

Obj. 2: Further, John's baptism, as Chrysostom says (Hom. de Bapt. Christi), "was a mean between the baptism of the Jews and that of Christ." But "the mean savors of the nature of the extremes" (Aristotle, De Partib. Animal.). Since, therefore, Christ was not baptized with the Jewish baptism, nor yet with His own, on the same grounds He should not have been baptized with the baptism of John.

Obj. 3: Further, whatever is best in human things should be ascribed to Christ. But John's baptism does not hold the first place among baptisms. Therefore it was not fitting for Christ to be baptized with John's baptism.

*On the contrary,* It is written (Matt. 3:13) that "Jesus cometh to the Jordan, unto John, to be baptized by him."

*I answer that,* As Augustine says (Super Joan., Tract. xiii): "After being baptized, the Lord baptized, not with that baptism wherewith He was baptized." Wherefore, since He Himself baptized with His own baptism, it follows that He was not baptized with His own, but with John's baptism. And this was befitting: first, because John's baptism was peculiar in this, that he baptized, not in the Spirit, but only "in water"; while Christ did not need spiritual baptism, since He was filled with the grace of the Holy Ghost from the beginning of His conception, as we have made clear above (Q. 34, A. 1). And this is the reason given by Chrysostom (Hom. de Bapt. Christi). Secondly, as Bede says on Mk. 1:9, He was baptized with the baptism of John, that, "by being thus baptized, He might show His approval of John's baptism." Thirdly, as Gregory Nazianzen says (Orat. xxxix), "by going to John to be baptized by him, He sanctified baptism."

Reply Obj. 1: As stated above (A. 1), Christ wished to be baptized in order by His example to lead us to baptism. And so, in order that He might lead us thereto more efficaciously, He wished to be baptized with a baptism which He clearly needed not, that men who needed it might approach unto it. Wherefore Ambrose says on Luke 3:21: "Let none decline the laver of grace, since Christ did not refuse the laver of penance."

Reply Obj. 2: The Jewish baptism prescribed by the law was merely figurative, whereas John's baptism, in a measure, was real, inasmuch as it induced men to refrain from sin; but Christ's baptism is efficacious unto the remission of sin and the conferring of grace. Now Christ needed neither the remission of sin, which was not in Him, nor the bestowal of grace, with which He was filled. Moreover, since He is "the Truth," it was not fitting that He should receive that which was no more than a figure. Consequently it was more fitting that He should receive the intermediate baptism than one of the extremes.

Reply Obj. 3: Baptism is a spiritual remedy. Now, the more perfect a thing is, the less remedy does it need. Consequently, from the very fact that Christ is most perfect, it follows that it was fitting that He should not receive the most perfect baptism: just as one who is healthy does not need a strong medicine.

THIRD ARTICLE [III, Q. 39, Art. 3]

Whether Christ Was Baptized at a Fitting Time?

Objection 1: It would seem that Christ was baptized at an unfitting time. For Christ was baptized in order that He might lead others to baptism by His example. But it is commendable that the faithful of Christ should be baptized, not merely before their thirtieth year, but even in infancy. Therefore it seems that Christ should not have been baptized at the age of thirty.

Obj. 2: Further, we do not read that Christ taught or worked miracles before being baptized. But it would have been more profitable to the world if He had taught for a longer time, beginning at the age of twenty, or even before. Therefore it seems that Christ, who came for man's profit, should have been baptized before His thirtieth year.

Obj. 3: Further, the sign of wisdom infused by God should have been especially manifest in Christ. But in the case of Daniel this was manifested at the time of his boyhood; according to Dan. 13:45: "The Lord raised up the holy spirit of a young boy, whose name was Daniel." Much more, therefore, should Christ have been baptized or have taught in His boyhood.

Obj. 4: Further, John's baptism was ordered to that of Christ as to its end. But "the end is first in intention and last in execution." Therefore He should have been baptized by John either before all the others, or after them.

*On the contrary,* It is written (Luke 3:21): "It came to pass, when all the people were baptized, that Jesus also being baptized, and praying;" and further on (Luke 3:23): "And Jesus Himself was beginning about the age of thirty years."

*I answer that,* Christ was fittingly baptized in His thirtieth year. First, because Christ was baptized as though for the reason that He was about forthwith to begin to teach and preach: for which purpose perfect age is required, such as is the age of thirty. Thus we read (Gen. 41:46) that "Joseph was thirty" years old when he undertook the government of Egypt. In like manner we read (2 Kings 5:4) that "David was thirty years old when he began to reign." Again, Ezechiel began to prophesy in "his thirtieth year," as we read Ezech. 1:1.

Secondly, because, as Chrysostom says (Hom. x in Matth.), "the law was about to pass away after Christ's baptism: wherefore Christ came to be baptized at this age which admits of all sins; in order that by His observing the law, no one might say that because He Himself could not fulfil it, He did away with it."

Thirdly, because by Christ's being baptized at the perfect age, we are given to understand that baptism brings forth perfect men, according to Eph. 4:13: "Until we all meet into the unity of faith, and of the knowledge of the Son of God, unto a perfect man, unto the measure of the age of the fulness of Christ." Hence the very property of the number seems to point to this. For thirty is product of three and ten: and by the number three is implied faith in the Trinity, while ten signifies the fulfilment of the commandments of the Law: in which two things the perfection of Christian life consists.

Reply Obj. 1: As Gregory Nazianzen says (Orat. xl), Christ was baptized, not "as though He needed to be cleansed, or as though some peril threatened Him if He delayed to be baptized. But no small danger besets any other man who departs from this life without being clothed with the garment of incorruptibility"--namely, grace. And though it be a good thing to remain clean after baptism, "yet is it still better," as he says, "to be slightly sullied now and then than to be altogether deprived of grace."

Reply Obj. 2: The profit which accrues to men from Christ is chiefly through faith and humility: to both of which He conduced by beginning to teach not in His boyhood or youth, but at the perfect age. To faith, because in this manner His human nature is shown to be real, by its making bodily progress with the advance of time; and lest this progress should be deemed imaginary, He did not wish to show His wisdom and power before His body had reached the perfect age: to humility, lest anyone should presume to govern or teach others before attaining to perfect age.

Reply Obj. 3: Christ was set before men as an example to all. Wherefore it behooved that to be shown forth in Him, which is becoming to all according to the common law--namely, that He should teach after reaching the perfect age. But, as Gregory Nazianzen says (Orat. xxxix), that which seldom occurs is not the law of the Church; as "neither does one swallow make the spring." For by special dispensation, in accordance with the ruling of Divine wisdom, it has been granted to some, contrary to the common law, to exercise the functions of governing or teaching, such as Solomon, Daniel, and Jeremias.

Reply Obj. 4: It was not fitting that Christ should be baptized by John either before or after all others. Because, as Chrysostom says (Hom. iv in Matth. [*From the supposititious Opus Imperfectum]), for this was Christ baptized, "that He might confirm the preaching and the baptism of John, and that John might bear witness to Him." Now, men would not have had faith in John's testimony except after many had been baptized by him. Consequently it was not fitting that John should baptize Him before baptizing anyone else. In like manner, neither was it fitting that he should baptize Him last. For as he (Chrysostom) says in the same passage: "As the light of the sun does not wait for the setting of the morning star, but comes forth while the latter is still above the horizon, and by its brilliance dims its shining: so Christ did not wait till John had run his course, but appeared while he was yet teaching and baptizing."

FOURTH ARTICLE [III, Q. 39, Art. 4]

Whether Christ Should Have Been Baptized in the Jordan?

Objection 1: It would seem that Christ should not have been baptized in the Jordan. For the reality should correspond to the figure. But baptism was prefigured in the crossing of the Red Sea, where the Egyptians were drowned, just as our sins are blotted out in baptism. Therefore it seems that Christ should rather have been baptized in the sea than in the river Jordan.

Obj. 2: Further, "Jordan" is interpreted a "going down." But by baptism a man goes up rather than down: wherefore it is written (Matt. 3:16) that "Jesus being baptized, forthwith came up [Douay: 'out'] from the water." Therefore it seems unfitting that Christ should be baptized in the Jordan.

Obj. 3: Further, while the children of Israel were crossing, the waters of the Jordan "were turned back," as it is related Jos. 4, and as it is written Ps. 113:3, 5. But those who are baptized go forward, not back. Therefore it was not fitting that Christ should be baptized in the Jordan.

*On the contrary,* It is written (Mk. 1:9) that "Jesus was baptized by John in the Jordan."

*I answer that,* It was through the river Jordan that the children of Israel entered into the land of promise. Now, this is the prerogative of Christ's baptism over all other baptisms: that it is the entrance to the kingdom of God, which is signified by the land of promise; wherefore it is said (John 3:5): "Unless a man be born again of water and the Holy Ghost, he cannot enter into the kingdom of God." To this also is to be referred the dividing of the water of the Jordan by Elias, who was to be snatched up into heaven in a fiery chariot, as it is related 4 Kings 2: because, to wit, the approach to heaven is laid open by the fire of the Holy Ghost, to those who pass through the waters of baptism. Therefore it was fitting that Christ should be baptized in the Jordan.

Reply Obj. 1: The crossing of the Red Sea foreshadowed baptism in this--that baptism washes away sin: whereas the crossing of the Jordan foreshadows it in this--that it opens the gate to the heavenly kingdom: and this is the principal effect of baptism, and accomplished through Christ alone. And therefore it was fitting that Christ should be baptized in the Jordan rather than in the sea.

Reply Obj. 2: In baptism we "go up" by advancing in grace: for which we need to "go down" by humility, according to James 4:6: "He giveth grace to the humble." And to this "going down" must the name of the Jordan be referred.

Reply Obj. 3: As Augustine says in a sermon for the Epiphany (x): "As of yore the waters of the Jordan were held back, so now, when Christ was baptized, the torrent of sin was held back." Or else this may signify that against the downward flow of the waters the river of blessings flowed upwards.

FIFTH ARTICLE [III, Q. 39, Art. 5]

Whether the Heavens Should Have Been Opened Unto Christ at His Baptism?

Objection 1: It would seem that the heavens should not have been opened unto Christ at His baptism. For the heavens should be opened unto one who needs to enter heaven, by reason of his being out of heaven. But Christ was always in heaven, according to John 3:13: "The Son of Man who is in heaven." Therefore it seems that the heavens should not have been opened unto Him.

Obj. 2: Further, the opening of the heavens is understood either in a corporal or in a spiritual sense. But it cannot be understood in a corporal sense: because the heavenly bodies are impassible and indissoluble, according to Job 37:18: "Thou perhaps hast made the heavens with Him, which are most strong, as if they were of molten brass." In like manner neither can it be understood in a spiritual sense, because the heavens were not previously closed to the eyes of the Son of God. Therefore it seems unbecoming to say that when Christ was baptized "the heavens were opened."

Obj. 3: Further, heaven was opened to the faithful through Christ's Passion, according to Heb. 10:19: "We have [Vulg.: 'Having'] a confidence in the entering into the holies by the blood of Christ." Wherefore not even those who were baptized with Christ's baptism, and died before His Passion, could enter heaven. Therefore the heavens should have been opened when Christ was suffering rather than when He was baptized.

*On the contrary,* It is written (Luke 3:21): "Jesus being baptized and praying, heaven was opened."

*I answer that,* As stated above (A. 1; Q. 38, A. 1), Christ wished to be baptized in order to consecrate the baptism wherewith we were to be baptized. And therefore it behooved those things to be shown forth which belong to the efficacy of our baptism: concerning which efficacy three points are to be considered. First, the principal power from which it is derived; and this, indeed, is a heavenly power. For which reason, when Christ was baptized, heaven was opened, to show that in future the heavenly power would sanctify baptism.

Secondly, the faith of the Church and of the person baptized conduces to the efficacy of baptism: wherefore those who are baptized make a profession of faith, and baptism is called the "sacrament of faith." Now by faith we gaze on heavenly things, which surpass the senses and human reason. And in order to signify this, the heavens were opened when Christ was baptized.

Thirdly, because the entrance to the heavenly kingdom was opened to us by the baptism of Christ in a special manner, which entrance had been closed to the first man through sin. Hence, when Christ was baptized, the heavens were opened, to show that the way to heaven is open to the baptized.

Now after baptism man needs to pray continually, in order to enter heaven: for though sins are remitted through baptism, there still remain the fomes of sin assailing us from within, and the world and the devils assailing us from without. And therefore it is said pointedly (Luke 3:21) that "Jesus being baptized and praying, heaven was opened": because, to wit, the faithful after baptism stand in need of prayer. Or else, that we may be led to understand that the very fact that through baptism heaven is opened to believers is in virtue of the prayer of Christ. Hence it is said pointedly (Matt. 3:16) that "heaven was opened to Him"--that is, "to all for His sake." Thus, for example, the Emperor might say to one asking a favor for another: "Behold, I grant this favor, not to him, but to thee"--that is, "to him for thy sake," as Chrysostom says (Hom. iv in Matth. [*From the supposititious Opus Imperfectum]).

Reply Obj. 1: According to Chrysostom (Hom. iv in Matth.; from the supposititious Opus Imperfectum), as Christ was baptized for man's sake, though He needed no baptism for His own sake, so the heavens were opened unto Him as man, whereas in respect of His Divine Nature He was ever in heaven.

Reply Obj. 2: As Jerome says on Matt. 3:16, 17, the heavens were opened to Christ when He was baptized, not by an unfolding of the elements, but by a spiritual vision: thus does Ezechiel relate the opening of the heavens at the beginning of his book. And Chrysostom proves this (Hom. iv in Matth.; from the supposititious Opus Imperfectum) by saying that "if the creature"--namely, heaven--"had been sundered he would not have said, 'were opened to Him,' since what is opened in a corporeal sense is open to all." Hence it is said expressly (Mk. 1:10) that Jesus "forthwith coming up out of the water, saw the heavens opened"; as though the opening of the heavens were to be considered as seen by Christ. Some, indeed, refer this to the corporeal vision, and say that such a brilliant light shone round about Christ when He was baptized, that the heavens seemed to be opened. It can also be referred to the imaginary vision, in which manner Ezechiel saw the heavens opened: since such a vision was formed in Christ's imagination by the Divine power and by His rational will, so as to signify that the entrance to heaven is opened to men through baptism. Lastly, it can be referred to intellectual vision: forasmuch as Christ, when He had sanctified baptism, saw that heaven was opened to men: nevertheless He had seen before that this would be accomplished.

Reply Obj. 3: Christ's Passion is the common cause of the opening of heaven to men. But it behooves this cause to be applied to each one, in order that he enter heaven. And this is effected by baptism, according to Rom. 6:3: "All we who are baptized in Christ Jesus are baptized in His death." Wherefore mention is made of the opening of the heavens at His baptism rather than at His Passion.

Or, as Chrysostom says (Hom. iv in Matth.; from the supposititious Opus Imperfectum): "When Christ was baptized, the heavens were merely opened: but after He had vanquished the tyrant by the cross; since gates were no longer needed for a heaven which thenceforth would be never closed, the angels said, not 'open the gates,' but 'Take them away.'" Thus Chrysostom gives us to understand that the obstacles which had hitherto hindered the souls of the departed from entering into heaven were entirely removed by the Passion: but at Christ's baptism they were opened, as though the way had been shown by which men were to enter into heaven.

SIXTH ARTICLE [III, Q. 39, Art. 6]

Whether It Is Fitting to Say That When Christ Was Baptized the Holy Ghost Came Down on Him in the Form of a Dove?

Objection 1: It would seem that it is not fitting to say that when Christ was baptized the Holy Ghost came down on Him in the form of a dove. For the Holy Ghost dwells in man by grace. But the fulness of grace was in the Man-Christ from the beginning of His conception, because He was the "Only-begotten of the Father," as is clear from what has been said above (Q. 7, A. 12; Q. 34, A. 1). Therefore the Holy Ghost should not have been sent to Him at His baptism.

Obj. 2: Further, Christ is said to have "descended" into the world in the mystery of the Incarnation, when "He emptied Himself, taking the form of a servant" (Phil. 2:7). But the Holy Ghost did not become incarnate. Therefore it is unbecoming to say that the Holy Ghost "descended upon Him."

Obj. 3: Further, that which is accomplished in our baptism should have been shown in Christ's baptism, as in an exemplar. But in our baptism no visible mission of the Holy Ghost takes place. Therefore neither should a visible mission of the Holy Ghost have taken place in Christ's baptism.

Obj. 4: Further, the Holy Ghost is poured forth on others through Christ, according to John 1:16: "Of His fulness we all have received." But the Holy Ghost came down on the apostles in the form, not of a dove, but of fire. Therefore neither should He have come down on Christ in the form of a dove, but in the form of fire.

*On the contrary,* It is written (Luke 3:22): "The Holy Ghost descended in a bodily shape as a dove upon Him."

*I answer that,* What took place with respect to Christ in His baptism, as Chrysostom says (Hom. iv in Matth. [*From the supposititious Opus Imperfectum]), "is connected with the mystery accomplished in all who were to be baptized afterwards." Now, all those who are baptized with the baptism of Christ receive the Holy Ghost, unless they approach unworthily; according to Matt. 3:11: "He shall baptize you in the Holy Ghost." Therefore it was fitting that when our Lord was baptized the Holy Ghost should descend upon Him.

Reply Obj. 1: As Augustine says (De Trin. xv): "It is most absurd to say that Christ received the Holy Ghost, when He was already thirty years old: for when He came to be baptized, since He was without sin, therefore was He not without the Holy Ghost. For if it is written of John that 'he shall be filled with the Holy Ghost from his mother's womb,' what must we say of the Man-Christ, whose conception in the flesh was not carnal, but spiritual? Therefore now," i.e. at His baptism, "He deigned to foreshadow His body," i.e. the Church, "in which those who are baptized receive the Holy Ghost in a special manner."

Reply Obj. 2: As Augustine says (De Trin. ii), the Holy Ghost is said to have descended on Christ in a bodily shape, as a dove, not because the very substance of the Holy Ghost was seen, for He is invisible: nor as though that visible creature were assumed into the unity of the Divine Person; since it is not said that the Holy Ghost was the dove, as it is said that the Son of God is man by reason of the union. Nor, again, was the Holy Ghost seen under the form of a dove, after the manner in which John saw the slain Lamb in the Apocalypse (5:6): "For the latter vision took place in the spirit through spiritual images of bodies; whereas no one ever doubted that this dove was seen by the eyes of the body." Nor, again, did the Holy Ghost appear under the form of a dove in the sense in which it is said (1 Cor. 10:4): "'Now, the rock was Christ': for the latter had already a created existence, and through the manner of its action was called by the name of Christ, whom it signified: whereas this dove came suddenly into existence, to fulfil the purpose of its signification, and afterwards ceased to exist, like the flame which appeared in the bush to Moses."

Hence the Holy Ghost is said to have descended upon Christ, not by reason of His being united to the dove: but either because the dove itself signified the Holy Ghost, inasmuch as it "descended" when it came upon Him; or, again, by reason of the spiritual grace, which is poured out by God, so as to descend, as it were, on the creature, according to James 1:17: "Every best gift and every perfect gift is from above, coming down from the Father of lights."

Reply Obj. 3: As Chrysostom says (Hom. xii in Matth.): "At the beginning of all spiritual transactions sensible visions appear, for the sake of them who cannot conceive at all an incorporeal nature . . . so that, though afterwards no such thing occur, they may shape their faith according to that which has occurred once for all." And therefore the Holy Ghost descended visibly, under a bodily shape, on Christ at His baptism, in order that we may believe Him to descend invisibly on all those who are baptized.

Reply Obj. 4: The Holy Ghost appeared over Christ at His baptism, under the form of a dove, for four reasons. First, on account of the disposition required in the one baptized--namely, that he approach in good faith: since, as it is written (Wis. 1:5): "The holy spirit of discipline will flee from the deceitful." For the dove is an animal of a simple character, void of cunning and deceit: whence it is said (Matt. 10:16): "Be ye simple as doves."

Secondly, in order to designate the seven gifts of the Holy Ghost, which are signified by the properties of the dove. For the dove dwells beside the running stream, in order that, on perceiving the hawk, it may plunge in and escape. This refers to the gift of wisdom, whereby the saints dwell beside the running waters of Holy Scripture, in order to escape the assaults of the devil. Again, the dove prefers the more choice seeds. This refers to the gift of knowledge, whereby the saints make choice of sound doctrines, with which they nourish themselves. Further, the dove feeds the brood of other birds. This refers to the gift of counsel, with which the saints, by teaching and example, feed men who have been the brood, i.e. imitators, of the devil. Again, the dove tears not with its beak. This refers to the gift of understanding, wherewith the saints do not rend sound doctrines, as heretics do. Again, the dove has no gall. This refers to the gift of piety, by reason of which the saints are free from unreasonable anger. Again, the dove builds its nest in the cleft of a rock. This refers to the gift of fortitude, wherewith the saints build their nest, i.e. take refuge and hope, in the death wounds of Christ, who is the Rock of strength. Lastly, the dove has a plaintive song. This refers to the gift of fear, wherewith the saints delight in bewailing sins.

Thirdly, the Holy Ghost appeared under the form of a dove on account of the proper effect of baptism, which is the remission of sins and reconciliation with God: for the dove is a gentle creature. Wherefore, as Chrysostom says, (Hom. xii in Matth.), "at the Deluge this creature appeared bearing an olive branch, and publishing the tidings of the universal peace of the whole world: and now again the dove appears at the baptism, pointing to our Deliverer."

Fourthly, the Holy Ghost appeared over our Lord at His baptism in the form of a dove, in order to designate the common effect of baptism--namely, the building up of the unity of the Church. Hence it is written (Eph. 5:25-27): "Christ delivered Himself up . . . that He might present . . . to Himself a glorious Church, not having spot or wrinkle, or any such thing . . . cleansing it by the laver of water in the word of life." Therefore it was fitting that the Holy Ghost should appear at the baptism under the form of a dove, which is a creature both loving and gregarious. Wherefore also it is said of the Church (Cant 6:8): "One is my dove."

But on the apostles the Holy Ghost descended under the form of fire, for two reasons. First, to show with what fervor their hearts were to be moved, so as to preach Christ everywhere, though surrounded by opposition. And therefore He appeared as a fiery tongue. Hence Augustine says (Super Joan., Tract. vi): Our Lord "manifests" the Holy Ghost "visibly in two ways"--namely, "by the dove coming upon the Lord when He was baptized; by fire, coming upon the disciples when they were met together . . . In the former case simplicity is shown, in the latter fervor . . . We learn, then, from the dove, that those who are sanctified by the Spirit should be without guile: and from the fire, that their simplicity should not be left to wax cold. Nor let it disturb anyone that the tongues were cloven . . . in the dove recognize unity."

Secondly, because, as Chrysostom says (Gregory, Hom. xxx in Ev.): "Since sins had to be forgiven," which is effected in baptism, "meekness was required"; this is shown by the dove: "but when we have obtained grace we must look forward to be judged"; and this is signified by the fire.

SEVENTH ARTICLE [III, Q. 39, Art. 7]

Whether the Dove in Which the Holy Ghost Appeared Was Real?

Objection 1: It would seem that the dove in which the Holy Ghost appeared was not real. For that seems to be a mere apparition which appears in its semblance. But it is stated (Luke 3:22) that the "Holy Ghost descended in a bodily shape as a dove upon Him." Therefore it was not a real dove, but a semblance of a dove.

Obj. 2: Further, just as "Nature does nothing useless, so neither does God" (De Coelo i). Now since this dove came merely "in order to signify something and pass away," as Augustine says (De Trin. ii), a real dove would have been useless: because the semblance of a dove was sufficient for that purpose. Therefore it was not a real dove.

Obj. 3: Further, the properties of a thing lead us to a knowledge of that thing. If, therefore, this were a real dove, its properties would have signified the nature of the real animal, and not the effect of the Holy Ghost. Therefore it seems that it was not a real dove.

*On the contrary,* Augustine says (De Agone Christ. xxii): "Nor do we say this as though we asserted that our Lord Jesus Christ alone had a real body, and that the Holy Ghost appeared to men's eyes in a fallacious manner: but we say that both those bodies were real."

*I answer that,* As stated above (Q. 5, A. 1), it was unbecoming that the Son of God, who is the Truth of the Father, should make use of anything unreal; wherefore He took, not an imaginary, but a real body. And since the Holy Ghost is called the Spirit of Truth, as appears from John 16:13, therefore He too made a real dove in which to appear, though He did not assume it into unity of person. Wherefore, after the words quoted above, Augustine adds: "Just as it behooved the Son of God not to deceive men, so it behooved the Holy Ghost not to deceive. But it was easy for Almighty God, who created all creatures out of nothing, to frame the body of a real dove without the help of other doves, just as it was easy for Him to form a true body in Mary's womb without the seed of a man: since the corporeal creature obeys its Lord's command and will, both in the mother's womb in forming a man, and in the world itself in forming a dove."

Reply Obj. 1: The Holy Ghost is said to have descended in the shape or semblance of a dove, not in the sense that the dove was not real, but in order to show that He did not appear in the form of His substance.

Reply Obj. 2: It was not superfluous to form a real dove, in which the Holy Ghost might appear, because by the very reality of the dove the reality of the Holy Ghost and of His effects is signified.

Reply Obj. 3: The properties of the dove lead us to understand the dove's nature and the effects of the Holy Ghost in the same way. Because from the very fact that the dove has such properties, it results that it signifies the Holy Ghost.

EIGHTH ARTICLE [III, Q. 39, Art. 8]

Whether It Was Becoming, When Christ Was Baptized That the Father's Voice Should Be Heard, Bearing Witness to the Son?

Objection 1: It would seem that it was unbecoming when Christ was baptized for the Father's voice to be heard bearing witness to the Son. For the Son and the Holy Ghost, according as they have appeared visibly, are said to have been visibly sent. But it does not become the Father to be sent, as Augustine makes it clear (De Trin. ii). Neither, therefore, (does it become Him) to appear.

Obj. 2: Further, the voice gives expression to the word conceived in the heart. But the Father is not the Word. Therefore He is unfittingly manifested by a voice.

Obj. 3: Further, the Man-Christ did not begin to be Son of God at His baptism, as some heretics have stated: but He was the Son of God from the beginning of His conception. Therefore the Father's voice should have proclaimed Christ's Godhead at His nativity rather than at His baptism.

*On the contrary,* It is written (Matt. 3:17): "Behold a voice from heaven, saying: This is My beloved Son in whom I am well pleased."

*I answer that,* As stated above (A. 5), that which is accomplished in our baptism should be manifested in Christ's baptism, which was the exemplar of ours. Now the baptism which the faithful receive is hallowed by the invocation and the power of the Trinity; according to Matt. 28:19: "Go ye and teach all nations, baptizing them in the name of the Father, and of the Son, and of the Holy Ghost." Wherefore, as Jerome says on Matt. 3:16, 17: "The mystery of the Trinity is shown forth in Christ's baptism. Our Lord Himself is baptized in His human nature; the Holy Ghost descended in the shape of a dove: the Father's voice is heard bearing witness to the Son." Therefore it was becoming that in that baptism the Father should be manifested by a voice.

Reply Obj. 1: The visible mission adds something to the apparition, to wit, the authority of the sender. Therefore the Son and the Holy Ghost who are from another, are said not only to appear, but also to be sent visibly. But the Father, who is not from another, can appear indeed, but cannot be sent visibly.

Reply Obj. 2: The Father is manifested by the voice, only as producing the voice or speaking by it. And since it is proper to the Father to produce the Word--that is, to utter or to speak--therefore was it most becoming that the Father should be manifested by a voice, because the voice designates the word. Wherefore the very voice to which the Father gave utterance bore witness to the Sonship of the Word. And just as the form of the dove, in which the Holy Ghost was made manifest, is not the Nature of the Holy Ghost, nor is the form of man in which the Son Himself was manifested, the very Nature of the Son of God, so neither does the voice belong to the Nature of the Word or of the Father who spoke. Hence (John 5:37) our Lord says: "Neither have you heard His," i.e. the Father's, "voice at any time, nor seen His shape." By which words, as Chrysostom says (Hom. xl in Joan.), "He gradually leads them to the knowledge of the philosophical truth, and shows them that God has neither voice nor shape, but is above all such forms and utterances." And just as the whole Trinity made both the dove and the human nature assumed by Christ, so also they formed the voice: yet the Father alone as speaking is manifested by the voice, just as the Son alone assumed human nature, and the Holy Ghost alone is manifested in the dove, as Augustine [*Fulgentius, De Fide ad Petrum] makes evident.

Reply Obj. 3: It was becoming that Christ's Godhead should not be proclaimed to all in His nativity, but rather that It should be hidden while He was subject to the defects of infancy. But when He attained to the perfect age, when the time came for Him to teach, to work miracles, and to draw men to Himself then did it behoove His Godhead to be attested from on high by the Father's testimony, so that His teaching might become the more credible. Hence He says (John 5:37): "The Father Himself who sent Me, hath given testimony of Me." And specially at the time of baptism, by which men are born again into adopted sons of God; since God's sons by adoption are made to be like unto His natural Son, according to Rom. 8:29: "Whom He foreknew, He also predestinated to be made conformable to the image of His Son." Hence Hilary says (Super Matth. ii) that when Jesus was baptized, the Holy Ghost descended on Him, and the Father's voice was heard saying: "'This is My beloved Son,' that we might know, from what was accomplished in Christ, that after being washed in the waters of baptism the Holy Ghost comes down upon us from on high, and that the Father's voice declares us to have become the adopted sons of God."

## QUESTION 40

OF CHRIST'S MANNER OF LIFE (In Four Articles)

Having considered those things which relate to Christ's entrance into the world, or to His beginning, it remains for us to consider those that relate to the process of His life. And we must consider (1) His manner of life; (2) His temptation; (3) His doctrine; (4) His miracles.

Concerning the first there are four points of inquiry:

(1) Whether Christ should have led a solitary life, or have associated with men?

(2) Whether He should have led an austere life as regards food, drink, and clothing? Or should He have conformed Himself to others in these respects?

(3) Whether He should have adopted a lowly state of life, or one of wealth and honor?

(4) Whether He should have lived in conformity with the Law?

FIRST ARTICLE [III, Q. 40, Art. 1]

Whether Christ Should Have Associated with Men, or Led a Solitary Life?

Objection 1: It would seem that Christ should not have associated with men, but should have led a solitary life. For it behooved Christ to show by His manner of life not only that He was man, but also that He was God. But it is not becoming that God should associate with men, for it is written (Dan. 2:11): "Except the gods, whose conversation is not with men"; and the Philosopher says (Polit. i) that he who lives alone is "either a beast"--that is, if he do this from being wild--"or a god," if his motive be the contemplation of truth. Therefore it seems that it was not becoming for Christ to associate with men.

Obj. 2: Further, while He lived in mortal flesh, it behooved Christ to lead a most perfect life. But the most perfect is the contemplative life, as we have stated in the Second Part (II-II, Q. 182, AA. 1, 2). Now, solitude is most suitable to the contemplative life; according to Osee 2:14: "I will lead her into the wilderness, and I will speak to her heart." Therefore it seems that Christ should have led a solitary life.

Obj. 3: Further, Christ's manner of life should have been uniform: because it should always have given evidence of that which is best. But at times Christ avoided the crowd and sought lonely places: hence Remigius [*Cf. Catena Aurea, Matth. 5:1], commenting on Matthew, says: "We read that our Lord had three places of refuge: the ship, the mountain, the desert; to one or other of which He betook Himself whenever he was harassed by the crowd." Therefore He ought always to have led a solitary life.

*On the contrary,* It is written (Baruch 3:38): "Afterwards He was seen upon earth and conversed with men."

*I answer that,* Christ's manner of life had to be in keeping with the end of His Incarnation, by reason of which He came into the world. Now He came into the world, first, that He might publish the truth. Thus He says Himself (John 18:37): "For this was I born, and for this came I into the world, that I should give testimony to the truth." Hence it was fitting not that He should hide Himself by leading a solitary life, but that He should appear openly and preach in public. Wherefore (Luke 4:42, 43) He says to those who wished to stay Him: "To other cities also I must preach the kingdom of God: for therefore am I sent."

Secondly, He came in order to free men from sin; according to 1 Tim. 1:15: "Christ Jesus came into this world to save sinners." And hence, as Chrysostom says, "although Christ might, while staying in the same place, have drawn all men to Himself, to hear His preaching, yet He did not do so; thus giving us the example to go about and seek those who perish, like the shepherd in his search of the lost sheep, and the physician in his attendance on the sick."

Thirdly, He came that by Him "we might have access to God," as it is written (Rom. 5:2). And thus it was fitting that He should give men confidence in approaching Him by associating familiarly with them. Wherefore it is written (Matt. 9:10): "It came to pass as He was sitting . . . in the house, behold, many publicans and sinners came, and sat down with Jesus and His disciples." On which Jerome comments as follows: "They had seen the publican who had been converted from a sinful to a better life: and consequently they did not despair of their own salvation."

Reply Obj. 1: Christ wished to make His Godhead known through His human nature. And therefore, since it is proper to man to do so, He associated with men, at the same time manifesting His Godhead to all, by preaching and working miracles, and by leading among men a blameless and righteous life.

Reply Obj. 2: As stated in the Second Part (II-II, Q. 182, A. 1; Q. 188, A. 6), the contemplative life is, absolutely speaking, more perfect than the active life, because the latter is taken up with bodily actions: yet that form of active life in which a man, by preaching and teaching, delivers to others the fruits of his contemplation, is more perfect than the life that stops at contemplation, because such a life is built on an abundance of contemplation, and consequently such was the life chosen by Christ.

Reply Obj. 3: Christ's action is our instruction. And therefore, in order to teach preachers that they ought not to be for ever before the public, our Lord withdrew Himself sometimes from the crowd. We are told of three reasons for His doing this. First, for the rest of the body: hence (Mk. 6:31) it is stated that our Lord said to His disciples: "Come apart into a desert place, and rest a little. For there were many coming and going: and they had not so much as time to eat." But sometimes it was for the sake of prayer; thus it is written (Luke 6:12): "It came to pass in those days, that He went out into a mountain to pray; and He passed the whole night in the prayer of God." On this Ambrose remarks that "by His example He instructs us in the precepts of virtue." And sometimes He did so in order to teach us to avoid the favor of men. Wherefore Chrysostom, commenting on Matt. 5:1, Jesus, "seeing the multitude, went up into a mountain," says: "By sitting not in the city and in the market-place, but on a mountain and in a place of solitude, He taught us to do nothing for show, and to withdraw from the crowd, especially when we have to discourse of needful things."

SECOND ARTICLE [III, Q. 40, Art. 2]

Whether It Was Becoming That Christ Should Lead an Austere Life in This World?

Objection 1: It would seem that it was becoming that Christ should lead an austere life in this world. For Christ preached the perfection of life much more than John did. But John led an austere life in order that he might persuade men by his example to embrace a perfect life; for it is written (Matt. 3:4) that "the same John had his garment of camel's hair and a leathern girdle about his loins: and his meat was locusts and wild honey"; on which Chrysostom comments as follows (Hom. x): "It was a marvelous and strange thing to behold such austerity in a human frame: which thing also particularly attracted the Jews." Therefore it seems that an austere life was much more becoming to Christ.

Obj. 2: Further, abstinence is ordained to continency; for it is written (Osee 4:10): "They shall eat and shall not be filled; they have committed fornication, and have not ceased." But Christ both observed continency in Himself and proposed it to be observed by others when He said (Matt. 19:12): "There are eunuchs who have made themselves eunuchs for the kingdom of heaven: he that can take it let him take it." Therefore it seems that Christ should have observed an austere life both in Himself and in His disciples.

Obj. 3: Further, it seems absurd for a man to begin a stricter form of life and to return to an easier life: for one might quote to his discredit that which is written, Luke 14:30: "This man began to build, and was not able to finish." Now Christ began a very strict life after His baptism, remaining in the desert and fasting for "forty days and forty nights." Therefore it seems unbecoming that, after leading such a strict life, He should return to the common manner of living.

*On the contrary,* It is written (Matt. 11:19): "The Son of Man came eating and drinking."

*I answer that,* As stated above (A. 1), it was in keeping with the end of the Incarnation that Christ should not lead a solitary life, but should associate with men. Now it is most fitting that he who associates with others should conform to their manner of living; according to the words of the Apostle (1 Cor. 9:22): "I became all things to all men." And therefore it was most fitting that Christ should conform to others in the matter of eating and drinking. Hence Augustine says (Contra Faust. xvi) that "John is described as 'neither eating nor drinking,' because he did not take the same food as the Jews. Therefore, unless our Lord had taken it, it would not be said of Him, in contrast, 'eating and drinking.'"

Reply Obj. 1: In His manner of living our Lord gave an example of perfection as to all those things which of themselves relate to salvation. Now abstinence in eating and drinking does not of itself relate to salvation, according to Rom. 14:17: "The kingdom of God is not meat and drink." And Augustine (De Qq. Evang. ii, qu. 11) explains Matt. 11:19, "Wisdom is justified by her children," saying that this is because the holy apostles "understood that the kingdom of God does not consist in eating and drinking, but in suffering indigence with equanimity," for they are neither uplifted by affluence, nor distressed by want. Again (De Doctr. Christ. iii), he says that in all such things "it is not making use of them, but the wantonness of the user, that is sinful." Now both these lives are lawful and praiseworthy--namely, that a man withdraw from the society of other men and observe abstinence; and that he associate with other men and live like them. And therefore our Lord wished to give men an example of either kind of life.

As to John, according to Chrysostom (Hom. xxxvii super Matth.), "he exhibited no more than his life and righteous conduct . . . but Christ had the testimony also of miracles. Leaving, therefore, John to be illustrious by his fasting, He Himself came the opposite way, both coming unto publicans' tables and eating and drinking."

Reply Obj. 2: Just as by abstinence other men acquire the power of self-restraint, so also Christ, in Himself and in those that are His, subdued the flesh by the power of His Godhead. Wherefore, as we read Matt. 9:14, the Pharisees and the disciples of John fasted, but not the disciples of Christ. On which Bede comments, saying that "John drank neither wine nor strong drink: because abstinence is meritorious where the nature is weak. But why should our Lord, whose right by nature it is to forgive sins, avoid those whom He could make holier than such as abstain?"

Reply Obj. 3: As Chrysostom says (Hom. xiii super Matth.), "that thou mightest learn how great a good is fasting, and how it is a shield against the devil, and that after baptism thou shouldst give thyself up, not to luxury, but to fasting--for this cause did He fast, not as needing it Himself, but as teaching us . . . And for this did He proceed no further than Moses and Elias, lest His assumption of our flesh might seem incredible." The mystical meaning, as Gregory says (Hom. xvi in Evang.), is that by Christ's example the number "forty" is observed in His fast, because the power of the "decalogue is fulfilled throughout the four books of the Holy Gospel: since ten multiplied by four amounts to forty." Or, because "we live in this mortal body composed of the four elements, and by its lusts we transgress the commandments of the Lord, which are expressed in the decalogue." Or, according to Augustine (QQ. lxxxiii, qu. 81): "To know the Creator and the creature is the entire teaching of wisdom. The Creator is the Trinity, the Father, the Son, and the Holy Ghost. Now the creature is partly invisible, as the soul, to which the number three may be ascribed, for we are commanded to love God in three ways, 'with our whole heart, our whole soul, and our whole mind'; and partly visible, as the body, to which the number four is applicable on account of its being subject to heat, moisture, cold, and dryness. Hence if we multiply ten, which may be referred to the entire moral code, by four, which number may be applied to the body, because it is the body that executes the law, the product is the number forty: in which," consequently, "the time during which we sigh and grieve is shown forth." And yet there was no inconsistency in Christ's returning to the common manner of living, after fasting and (retiring into the) desert. For it is becoming to that kind of life, which we hold Christ to have embraced, wherein a man delivers to others the fruits of his contemplation, that he devote himself first of all to contemplation, and that he afterwards come down to the publicity of active life by associating with other men. Hence Bede says on Mk. 2:18: "Christ fasted, that thou mightest not disobey the commandment; He ate with sinners, that thou mightest discern His sanctity and acknowledge His power."

THIRD ARTICLE [III, Q. 40, Art. 3]

Whether Christ Should Have Led a Life of Poverty in This World?

Objection 1: It would seem that Christ should not have led a life of poverty in this world. Because Christ should have embraced the most eligible form of life. But the most eligible form of life is that which is a mean between riches and poverty; for it is written (Prov. 30:8): "Give me neither beggary nor riches; give me only the necessaries of life." Therefore Christ should have led a life, not of poverty, but of moderation.

Obj. 2: Further, external wealth is ordained to bodily use as to food and raiment. But Christ conformed His manner of life to those among whom He lived, in the matter of food and raiment. Therefore it seems that He should have observed the ordinary manner of life as to riches and poverty, and have avoided extreme poverty.

Obj. 3: Further, Christ specially invited men to imitate His example of humility, according to Matt. 11:29: "Learn of Me, because I am meek and humble of heart." But humility is most commendable in the rich; thus it is written (1 Tim. 6:11): "Charge the rich of this world not to be high-minded." Therefore it seems that Christ should not have chosen a life of poverty.

*On the contrary,* It is written (Matt. 8:20): "The Son of Man hath not where to lay His head": as though He were to say as Jerome observes: "Why desirest thou to follow Me for the sake of riches and worldly gain, since I am so poor that I have not even the smallest dwelling-place, and I am sheltered by a roof that is not Mine?" And on Matt. 17:26: "That we may not scandalize them, go to the sea," Jerome says: "This incident, taken literally, affords edification to those who hear it when they are told that our Lord was so poor that He had not the wherewithal to pay the tax for Himself and His apostles."

*I answer that,* It was fitting for Christ to lead a life of poverty in this world. First, because this was in keeping with the duty of preaching, for which purpose He says that He came (Mk. 1:38): "Let us go into the neighboring towns and cities, that I may preach there also: for to this purpose am I come." Now in order that the preachers of God's word may be able to give all their time to preaching, they must be wholly free from care of worldly matters: which is impossible for those who are possessed of wealth. Wherefore the Lord Himself, when sending the apostles to preach, said to them (Matt. 10:9): "Do not possess gold nor silver." And the apostles (Acts 6:2) say: "It is not reasonable that we should leave the word of God and serve tables."

Secondly, because just as He took upon Himself the death of the body in order to bestow spiritual life on us, so did He bear bodily poverty, in order to enrich us spiritually, according to 2 Cor. 8:9: "You know the grace of our Lord Jesus Christ: that . . . He became poor for our [Vulg.: 'your'] sakes that through His poverty we [Vulg.: 'you'] might be rich."

Thirdly, lest if He were rich His preaching might be ascribed to cupidity. Wherefore Jerome says on Matt. 10:9, that if the disciples had been possessed of wealth, "they had seemed to preach for gain, not for the salvation of mankind." And the same reason applies to Christ.

Fourthly, that the more lowly He seemed by reason of His poverty, the greater might the power of His Godhead be shown to be. Hence in a sermon of the Council of Ephesus (P. iii, c. ix) we read: "He chose all that was poor and despicable, all that was of small account and hidden from the majority, that we might recognize His Godhead to have transformed the terrestrial sphere. For this reason did He choose a poor maid for His Mother, a poorer birthplace; for this reason did He live in want. Learn this from the manger."

Reply Obj. 1: Those who wish to live virtuously need to avoid abundance of riches and beggary, in as far as these are occasions of sin: since abundance of riches is an occasion for being proud; and beggary is an occasion of thieving and lying, or even of perjury. But forasmuch as Christ was incapable of sin, He had not the same motive as Solomon for avoiding these things. Yet neither is every kind of beggary an occasion of theft and perjury, as Solomon seems to add (Prov. 30:8); but only that which is involuntary, in order to avoid which, a man is guilty of theft and perjury. But voluntary poverty is not open to this danger: and such was the poverty chosen by Christ.

Reply Obj. 2: A man may feed and clothe himself in conformity with others, not only by possessing riches, but also by receiving the necessaries of life from those who are rich. This is what happened in regard to Christ: for it is written (Luke 8:2, 3) that certain women followed Christ and "ministered unto Him of their substance." For, as Jerome says on Matt. 27:55, "It was a Jewish custom, nor was it thought wrong for women, following the ancient tradition of their nation, out of their private means to provide their instructors with food and clothing. But as this might give scandal to the heathens, Paul says that he gave it up": thus it was possible for them to be fed out of a common fund, but not to possess wealth, without their duty of preaching being hindered by anxiety.

Reply Obj. 3: Humility is not much to be praised in one who is poor of necessity. But in one who, like Christ, is poor willingly, poverty itself is a sign of very great humility.

FOURTH ARTICLE [III, Q. 40, Art. 4]

Whether Christ Conformed His Conduct to the Law?

Objection 1: It would seem that Christ did not conform His conduct to the Law. For the Law forbade any work whatsoever to be done on the Sabbath, since God "rested on the seventh day from all His work which He had done." But He healed a man on the Sabbath, and commanded him to take up his bed. Therefore it seems that He did not conform His conduct to the Law.

Obj. 2: Further, what Christ taught, that He also did, according to Acts 1:1: "Jesus began to do and to teach." But He taught (Matt. 15:11) that "not" all "that which goeth into the mouth defileth a man": and this is contrary to the precept of the Law, which declared that a man was made unclean by eating and touching certain animals, as stated Lev. 11. Therefore it seems that He did not conform His conduct to the Law.

Obj. 3: Further, he who consents to anything is of the same mind as he who does it, according to Rom. 1:32: "Not only they that do them, but they also that consent to them that do them." But Christ, by excusing His disciples, consented to their breaking the Law by plucking the ears of corn on the Sabbath; as is related Matt. 12:1-8. Therefore it seems that Christ did not conform His conduct to the Law.

*On the contrary,* It is written (Matt. 5:17): "Do not think that I am come to destroy the Law or the Prophets." Commenting on these words, Chrysostom says: "He fulfilled the Law . . . in one way, by transgressing none of the precepts of the Law; secondly, by justifying us through faith, which the Law, in the letter, was unable to do."

*I answer that,* Christ conformed His conduct in all things to the precepts of the Law. In token of this He wished even to be circumcised; for the circumcision is a kind of protestation of a man's purpose of keeping the Law, according to Gal. 5:3: "I testify to every man circumcising himself, that he is a debtor to do the whole Law."

And Christ, indeed, wished to conform His conduct to the Law, first, to show His approval of the Old Law. Secondly, that by obeying the Law He might perfect it and bring it to an end in His own self, so as to show that it was ordained to Him. Thirdly, to deprive the Jews of an excuse for slandering Him. Fourthly, in order to deliver men from subjection to the Law, according to Gal. 4:4, 5: "God sent His Son . . . made under the Law that He might redeem them who were under the Law."

Reply Obj. 1: Our Lord excuses Himself from any transgression of the Law in this matter, for three reasons. First, the precept of the hallowing of the Sabbath forbids not Divine work, but human work: for though God ceased on the seventh day from the creation of new creatures, yet He ever works by keeping and governing His creatures. Now that Christ wrought miracles was a Divine work: hence He says (John 5:17): "My Father worketh until now; and I work."

Secondly, He excuses Himself on the ground that this precept does not forbid works which are needful for bodily health. Wherefore He says (Luke 13:15): "Doth not every one of you on the Sabbath-day loose his ox or his ass from the manger, and lead them to water?" And farther on (Luke 14:5): "Which of you shall have an ass or an ox fall into a pit, and will not immediately draw him out on the Sabbath-day?" Now it is manifest that the miraculous works done by Christ related to health of body and soul.

Thirdly, because this precept does not forbid works pertaining to the worship of God. Wherefore He says (Matt. 12:5): "Have ye not read in the Law that on the Sabbath-days the priests in the Temple break the Sabbath, and are without blame?" And (John 7:23) it is written that a man receives circumcision on the Sabbath-day. Now when Christ commanded the paralytic to carry his bed on the Sabbath-day, this pertained to the worship of God, i.e. to the praise of God's power. And thus it is clear that He did not break the Sabbath: although the Jews threw this false accusation in His face, saying (John 9:16): "This man is not of God, who keepeth not the Sabbath."

Reply Obj. 2: By those words Christ wished to show that man is made unclean as to his soul, by the use of any sort of foods considered not in their nature, but only in some signification. And that certain foods are in the Law called "unclean" is due to some signification; whence Augustine says (Contra Faust. vi): "If a question be raised about swine and lambs, both are clean by nature, since 'all God's creatures are good'; but by a certain signification lambs are clean and swine unclean."

Reply Obj. 3: The disciples also, when, being hungry, they plucked the ears of corn on the Sabbath, are to be excused from transgressing the Law, since they were pressed by hunger: just as David did not transgress the Law when, through being compelled by hunger, he ate the loaves which it was not lawful for him to eat.

## QUESTION 41

OF CHRIST'S TEMPTATION (In Four Articles)

We have now to consider Christ's temptation, concerning which there are four points of inquiry:

(1) Whether it was becoming that Christ should be tempted?

(2) Of the place;

(3) Of the time;

(4) Of the mode and order of the temptation.

FIRST ARTICLE [III, Q. 41, Art. 1]

Whether It Was Becoming That Christ Should Be Tempted?

Objection 1: It would seem that it was not becoming for Christ to be tempted. For to tempt is to make an experiment, which is not done save in regard to something unknown. But the power of Christ was known even to the demons; for it is written (Luke 4:41) that "He suffered them not to speak, for they knew that He was Christ." Therefore it seems that it was unbecoming for Christ to be tempted.

Obj. 2: Further, Christ was come in order to destroy the works of the devil, according to 1 John 3:8: "For this purpose the Son of God appeared, that He might destroy the works of the devil." But it is not for the same to destroy the works of a certain one and to suffer them. Therefore it seems unbecoming that Christ should suffer Himself to be tempted by the devil.

Obj. 3: Further, temptation is from a threefold source--the flesh, the world, and the devil. But Christ was not tempted either by the flesh or by the world. Therefore neither should He have been tempted by the devil.

*On the contrary,* It is written (Matt. 4:1): "Jesus was led by the Spirit into the desert to be tempted by the devil."

*I answer that,* Christ wished to be tempted; first that He might strengthen us against temptations. Hence Gregory says in a homily (xvi in Evang.): "It was not unworthy of our Redeemer to wish to be tempted, who came also to be slain; in order that by His temptations He might conquer our temptations, just as by His death He overcame our death."

Secondly, that we might be warned, so that none, however holy, may think himself safe or free from temptation. Wherefore also He wished to be tempted after His baptism, because, as Hilary says (Super Matth., cap. iii.): "The temptations of the devil assail those principally who are sanctified, for he desires, above all, to overcome the holy. Hence also it is written (Ecclus. 2): Son, when thou comest to the service of God, stand in justice and in fear, and prepare thy soul for temptation."

Thirdly, in order to give us an example: to teach us, to wit, how to overcome the temptations of the devil. Hence Augustine says (De Trin. iv) that Christ "allowed Himself to be tempted" by the devil, "that He might be our Mediator in overcoming temptations, not only by helping us, but also by giving us an example."

Fourthly, in order to fill us with confidence in His mercy. Hence it is written (Heb. 4:15): "We have not a high-priest, who cannot have compassion on our infirmities, but one tempted in all things like as we are, without sin."

Reply Obj. 1: As Augustine says (De Civ. Dei ix): "Christ was known to the demons only so far as He willed; not as the Author of eternal life, but as the cause of certain temporal effects," from which they formed a certain conjecture that Christ was the Son of God. But since they also observed in Him certain signs of human frailty, they did not know for certain that He was the Son of God: wherefore (the devil) wished to tempt Him. This is implied by the words of Matt. 4:2, 3, saying that, after "He was hungry, the tempter" came "to Him," because, as Hilary says (Super Matth., cap. iii), "Had not Christ's weakness in hungering betrayed His human nature, the devil would not have dared to tempt Him." Moreover, this appears from the very manner of the temptation, when he said: "If Thou be the Son of God." Which words Ambrose explains as follows (In Luc. iv): "What means this way of addressing Him, save that, though he knew that the Son of God was to come, yet he did not think that He had come in the weakness of the flesh?"

Reply Obj. 2: Christ came to destroy the works of the devil, not by powerful deeds, but rather by suffering from him and his members, so as to conquer the devil by righteousness, not by power; thus Augustine says (De Trin. xiii) that "the devil was to be overcome, not by the power of God, but by righteousness." And therefore in regard to Christ's temptation we must consider what He did of His own will and what He suffered from the devil. For that He allowed Himself to be tempted was due to His own will. Wherefore it is written (Matt. 4:1): "Jesus was led by the Spirit into the desert, to be tempted by the devil"; and Gregory (Hom. xvi in Evang.) says this is to be understood of the Holy Ghost, to wit, that "thither did His Spirit lead Him, where the wicked spirit would find Him and tempt Him." But He suffered from the devil in being "taken up" on to "the pinnacle of the Temple" and again "into a very high mountain." Nor is it strange, as Gregory observes, "that He allowed Himself to be taken by him on to a mountain, who allowed Himself to be crucified by His members." And we understand Him to have been taken up by the devil, not, as it were, by force, but because, as Origen says (Hom. xxi super Luc.), "He followed Him in the course of His temptation like a wrestler advancing of his own accord."

Reply Obj. 3: As the Apostle says (Heb. 4:15), Christ wished to be "tempted in all things, without sin." Now temptation which comes from an enemy can be without sin: because it comes about by merely outward suggestion. But temptation which comes from the flesh cannot be without sin, because such a temptation is caused by pleasure and concupiscence; and, as Augustine says (De Civ. Dei xix), "it is not without sin that 'the flesh desireth against the spirit.'" And hence Christ wished to be tempted by an enemy, but not by the flesh.

SECOND ARTICLE [III, Q. 41, Art. 2]

Whether Christ Should Have Been Tempted in the Desert?

Objection 1: It would seem that Christ should not have been tempted in the desert. Because Christ wished to be tempted in order to give us an example, as stated above (A. 1). But an example should be set openly before those who are to follow it. Therefore He should not have been tempted in the desert.

Obj. 2: Further, Chrysostom says (Hom. xii in Matth.): "Then most especially does the devil assail by tempting us, when he sees us alone. Thus did he tempt the woman in the beginning when he found her apart from her husband." Hence it seems that, by going into the desert to be tempted, He exposed Himself to temptation. Since, therefore, His temptation is an example to us, it seems that others too should take such steps as will lead them into temptation. And yet this seems a dangerous thing to do, since rather should we avoid the occasion of being tempted.

Obj. 3: Further, Matt. 4:5, Christ's second temptation is set down, in which "the devil took" Christ up "into the Holy City, and set Him upon the pinnacle of the Temple": which is certainly not in the desert. Therefore He was not tempted in the desert only.

*On the contrary,* It is written (Mk. 1:13) that Jesus "was in the desert forty days and forty nights, and was tempted by Satan."

*I answer that,* As stated above (A. 1, ad 2), Christ of His own free-will exposed Himself to be tempted by the devil, just as by His own free-will He submitted to be killed by his members; else the devil would not have dared to approach Him. Now the devil prefers to assail a man who is alone, for, as it is written (Eccles. 4:12), "if a man prevail against one, two shall withstand him." And so it was that Christ went out into the desert, as to a field of battle, to be tempted there by the devil. Hence Ambrose says on Luke 4:1, that "Christ was led into the desert for the purpose of provoking the devil. For had he," i.e. the devil, "not fought, He," i.e. Christ, "would not have conquered." He adds other reasons, saying that "Christ in doing this set forth the mystery of Adam's delivery from exile," who had been expelled from paradise into the desert, and "set an example to us, by showing that the devil envies those who strive for better things."

Reply Obj. 1: Christ is set as an example to all through faith, according to Heb. 12:2: "Looking on Jesus, the author and finisher of faith." Now faith, as it is written (Rom. 10:17), "cometh by hearing," but not by seeing: nay, it is even said (John 20:29): "Blessed are they that have not seen and have believed." And therefore, in order that Christ's temptation might be an example to us, it behooved that men should not see it, and it was enough that they should hear it related.

Reply Obj. 2: The occasions of temptation are twofold. One is on the part of man--for instance, when a man causes himself to be near to sin by not avoiding the occasion of sinning. And such occasions of temptation should be avoided, as it is written of Lot (Gen. 19:17): "Neither stay thou in all the country about" Sodom.

Another occasion of temptation is on the part of the devil, who always "envies those who strive for better things," as Ambrose says (In Luc. iv, 1). And such occasions of temptation are not to be avoided. Hence Chrysostom says (Hom. v in Matth. [*From the supposititious Opus Imperfectum]): "Not only Christ was led into the desert by the Spirit, but all God's children that have the Holy Ghost. For it is not enough for them to sit idle; the Holy Ghost urges them to endeavor to do something great: which is for them to be in the desert from the devil's standpoint, for no unrighteousness, in which the devil delights, is there. Again, every good work, compared to the flesh and the world, is the desert; because it is not according to the will of the flesh and of the world." Now, there is no danger in giving the devil such an occasion of temptation; since the help of the Holy Ghost, who is the Author of the perfect deed, is more powerful* than the assault of the envious devil. [*All the codices read 'majus.' One of the earliest printed editions has 'magis,' which has much to commend it, since St. Thomas is commenting the text quoted from St. Chrysostom. The translation would run thus: 'since rather is it (the temptation) a help from the Holy Ghost, who,' etc.].

Reply Obj. 3: Some say that all the temptations took place in the desert. Of these some say that Christ was led into the Holy City, not really, but in an imaginary vision; while others say that the Holy City itself, i.e. Jerusalem, is called "a desert," because it was deserted by God. But there is no need for this explanation. For Mark says that He was tempted in the desert by the devil, but not that He was tempted in the desert only.

THIRD ARTICLE [III, Q. 41, Art. 3]

Whether Christ's Temptation Should Have Taken Place After His Fast?

Objection 1: It would seem that Christ's temptation should not have taken place after His fast. For it has been said above (Q. 40, A. 2) that an austere mode of life was not becoming to Christ. But it savors of extreme austerity that He should have eaten nothing for forty days and forty nights, for Gregory (Hom. xvi in Evang.) explains the fact that "He fasted forty days and forty nights," saying that "during that time He partook of no food whatever." It seems, therefore, that He should not thus have fasted before His temptation.

Obj. 2: Further, it is written (Mk. 1:13) that "He was in the desert forty days and forty nights; and was tempted by Satan." Now, He fasted forty days and forty nights. Therefore it seems that He was tempted by the devil, not after, but during, His fast.

Obj. 3: Further, we read that Christ fasted but once. But He was tempted by the devil, not only once, for it is written (Luke 4:13) "that all the temptation being ended, the devil departed from Him for a time." As, therefore, He did not fast before the second temptation, so neither should He have fasted before the first.

*On the contrary,* It is written (Matt. 4:2, 3): "When He had fasted forty days and forty nights, afterwards He was hungry": and then "the tempter came to Him."

*I answer that,* It was becoming that Christ should wish to fast before His temptation. First, in order to give us an example. For since we are all in urgent need of strengthening ourselves against temptation, as stated above (A. 1), by fasting before being tempted, He teaches us the need of fasting in order to equip ourselves against temptation. Hence the Apostle (2 Cor. 6:5, 7) reckons "fastings" together with the "armor of justice."

Secondly, in order to show that the devil assails with temptations even those who fast, as likewise those who are given to other good works. And so Christ's temptation took place after His fast, as also after His baptism. Hence since rather Chrysostom says (Hom. xiii super Matth.): "To instruct thee how great a good is fasting, and how it is a most powerful shield against the devil; and that after baptism thou shouldst give thyself up, not to luxury, but to fasting; for this cause Christ fasted, not as needing it Himself, but as teaching us."

Thirdly, because after the fast, hunger followed, which made the devil dare to approach Him, as already stated (A. 1, ad 1). Now, when "our Lord was hungry," says Hilary (Super Matth. iii), "it was not because He was overcome by want of food, but because He abandoned His manhood to its nature. For the devil was to be conquered, not by God, but by the flesh." Wherefore Chrysostom too says: "He proceeded no farther than Moses and Elias, lest His assumption of our flesh might seem incredible."

Reply Obj. 1: It was becoming for Christ not to adopt an extreme form of austere life in order to show Himself outwardly in conformity with those to whom He preached. Now, no one should take up the office of preacher unless he be already cleansed and perfect in virtue, according to what is said of Christ, that "Jesus began to do and to teach" (Acts 1:1). Consequently, immediately after His baptism Christ adopted an austere form of life, in order to teach us the need of taming the flesh before passing on to the office of preaching, according to the Apostle (1 Cor. 9:27): "I chastise my body, and bring it into subjection, lest perhaps when I have preached to others, I myself should become a castaway."

Reply Obj. 2: These words of Mark may be understood as meaning that "He was in the desert forty days and forty nights," and that He fasted during that time: and the words, "and He was tempted by Satan," may be taken as referring, not to the time during which He fasted, but to the time that followed: since Matthew says that "after He had fasted forty days and forty nights, afterwards He was hungry," thus affording the devil a pretext for approaching Him. And so the words that follow, and the angels ministered to Him, are to be taken in sequence, which is clear from the words of Matthew (4:11): "Then the devil left Him," i.e. after the temptation, "and behold angels came and ministered to Him." And as to the words inserted by Mark, "and He was with the beasts," according to Chrysostom (Hom. xiii in Matth.), they are set down in order to describe the desert as being impassable to man and full of beasts.

On the other hand, according to Bede's exposition of Mk. 1:12, 13, our Lord was tempted forty days and forty nights. But this is not to be understood of the visible temptations which are related by Matthew and Luke, and occurred after the fast, but of certain other assaults which perhaps Christ suffered from the devil during that time of His fast.

Reply Obj. 3: As Ambrose says on Luke 4:13, the devil departed from Christ "for a time, because, later on, he returned, not to tempt Him, but to assail Him openly"--namely, at the time of His Passion. Nevertheless, He seemed in this later assault to tempt Christ to dejection and hatred of His neighbor; just as in the desert he had tempted Him to gluttonous pleasure and idolatrous contempt of God.

FOURTH ARTICLE [III, Q. 41, Art. 4]

Whether the Mode and Order of the Temptation Were Becoming?

Objection 1: It would seem that the mode and order of the temptation were unbecoming. For the devil tempts in order to induce us to sin. But if Christ had assuaged His bodily hunger by changing the stones into bread, He would not have sinned; just as neither did He sin when He multiplied the loaves, which was no less a miracle, in order to succor the hungry crowd. Therefore it seems that this was nowise a temptation.

Obj. 2: Further, a counselor is inconsistent if he persuades the contrary to what he intends. But when the devil set Christ on a pinnacle of the Temple, he purposed to tempt Him to pride or vainglory. Therefore it was inconsistent to urge Him to cast Himself thence: for this would be contrary to pride or vainglory, which always seeks to rise.

Obj. 3: Further, one temptation should lead to one sin. But in the temptation on the mountain he counseled two sins--namely, covetousness and idolatry. Therefore the mode of the temptation was unfitting.

Obj. 4: Further, temptations are ordained to sin. But there are seven deadly sins, as we have stated in the Second Part (I-II, Q. 84, A. 4). But the tempter only deals with three, viz. gluttony, vainglory, and covetousness. Therefore the temptation seems to have been incomplete.

Obj. 5: Further, after overcoming all the vices, man is still tempted to pride or vainglory: since pride "worms itself in stealthily, and destroys even good works," as Augustine says (Ep. ccxi). Therefore Matthew unfittingly gives the last place to the temptation to covetousness on the mountain, and the second place to the temptation to vainglory in the Temple, especially since Luke puts them in the reverse order.

Obj. 6: Further, Jerome says on Matt. 4:4 that "Christ purposed to overcome the devil by humility, not by might." Therefore He should not have repulsed him with a haughty rebuke, saying: "Begone, Satan."

Obj. 7: Further, the gospel narrative seems to be false. For it seems impossible that Christ could have been set on a pinnacle of the Temple without being seen by others. Nor is there to be found a mountain so high that all the world can be seen from it, so that all the kingdoms of the earth could be shown to Christ from its summit. It seems, therefore, that Christ's temptation is unfittingly described.

On the contrary is the authority of Scripture.

*I answer that,* The temptation which comes from the enemy takes the form of a suggestion, as Gregory says (Hom. xvi in Evang.). Now a suggestion cannot be made to everybody in the same way; it must arise from those things towards which each one has an inclination. Consequently the devil does not straight away tempt the spiritual man to grave sins, but he begins with lighter sins, so as gradually to lead him to those of greater magnitude. Wherefore Gregory (Moral. xxxi), expounding Job 39:25, "He smelleth the battle afar off, the encouraging of the captains and the shouting of the army," says: "The captains are fittingly described as encouraging, and the army as shouting. Because vices begin by insinuating themselves into the mind under some specious pretext: then they come on the mind in such numbers as to drag it into all sorts of folly, deafening it with their bestial clamor."

Thus, too, did the devil set about the temptation of the first man. For at first he enticed his mind to consent to the eating of the forbidden fruit, saying (Gen. 3:1): "Why hath God commanded you that you should not eat of every tree of paradise?" Secondly [he tempted him] to vainglory by saying: "Your eyes shall be opened." Thirdly, he led the temptation to the extreme height of pride, saying: "You shall be as gods, knowing good and evil." This same order did he observe in tempting Christ. For at first he tempted Him to that which men desire, however spiritual they may be--namely, the support of the corporeal nature by food. Secondly, he advanced to that matter in which spiritual men are sometimes found wanting, inasmuch as they do certain things for show, which pertains to vainglory. Thirdly, he led the temptation on to that in which no spiritual men, but only carnal men, have a part--namely, to desire worldly riches and fame, to the extent of holding God in contempt. And so in the first two temptations he said: "If Thou be the Son of God"; but not in the third, which is inapplicable to spiritual men, who are sons of God by adoption, whereas it does apply to the two preceding temptations.

And Christ resisted these temptations by quoting the authority of the Law, not by enforcing His power, "so as to give more honor to His human nature and a greater punishment to His adversary, since the foe of the human race was vanquished, not as by God, but as by man"; as Pope Leo says (Serm. 1, De Quadrag. 3).

Reply Obj. 1: To make use of what is needful for self-support is not the sin of gluttony; but if a man do anything inordinate out of the desire for such support, it can pertain to the sin of gluttony. Now it is inordinate for a man who has human assistance at his command to seek to obtain food miraculously for mere bodily support. Hence the Lord miraculously provided the children of Israel with manna in the desert, where there was no means of obtaining food otherwise. And in like fashion Christ miraculously provided the crowds with food in the desert, when there was no other means of getting food. But in order to assuage His hunger, He could have done otherwise than work a miracle, as did John the Baptist, according to Matthew (3:4); or He could have hastened to the neighboring country. Consequently the devil esteemed that if Christ was a mere man, He would fall into sin by attempting to assuage His hunger by a miracle.

Reply Obj. 2: It often happens that a man seeks to derive glory from external humiliation, whereby he is exalted by reason of spiritual good. Hence Augustine says (De Serm. Dom. in Monte ii, 12): "It must be noted that it is possible to boast not only of the beauty and splendor of material things, but even of filthy squalor." And this is signified by the devil urging Christ to seek spiritual glory by casting His body down.

Reply Obj. 3: It is a sin to desire worldly riches and honors in an inordinate fashion. And the principal sign of this is when a man does something wrong in order to acquire such things. And so the devil was not satisfied with instigating to a desire for riches and honors, but he went so far as to tempt Christ, for the sake of gaining possession of these things, to fall down and adore him, which is a very great crime, and against God. Nor does he say merely, "if Thou wilt adore me," but he adds, "if, falling down"; because, as Ambrose says on Luke 4:5: "Ambition harbors yet another danger within itself: for, while seeking to rule, it will serve; it will bow in submission that it may be crowned with honor; and the higher it aims, the lower it abases itself."

In like manner [the devil] in the preceding temptations tried to lead [Christ] from the desire of one sin to the commission of another; thus from the desire of food he tried to lead Him to the vanity of the needless working of a miracle; and from the desire of glory to tempt God by casting Himself headlong.

Reply Obj. 4: As Ambrose says on Luke 4:13, Scripture would not have said that "'all the temptation being ended, the devil departed from Him,' unless the matter of all sins were included in the three temptations already related. For the causes of temptations are the causes of desires"--namely, "lust of the flesh, hope of glory, eagerness for power."

Reply Obj. 5: As Augustine says (De Consensu Evang. ii): "It is not certain which happened first; whether the kingdoms of the earth were first shown to Him, and afterwards He was set on the pinnacle of the Temple; or the latter first, and the former afterwards. However, it matters not, provided it be made clear that all these things did take place." It may be that the Evangelists set these things in different orders, because sometimes cupidity arises from vainglory, sometimes the reverse happens.

Reply Obj. 6: When Christ had suffered the wrong of being tempted by the devil saying, "If Thou be the Son of God cast Thyself down," He was not troubled, nor did He upbraid the devil. But when the devil usurped to himself the honor due to God, saying, "All these things will I give Thee, if, falling down, Thou wilt adore me," He was exasperated, and repulsed him, saying, "Begone, Satan": that we might learn from His example to bear bravely insults leveled at ourselves, but not to allow ourselves so much as to listen to those which are aimed at God.

Reply Obj. 7: As Chrysostom says (Hom. v in Matth.): "The devil set Him" (on a pinnacle of the Temple) "that He might be seen by all, whereas, unawares to the devil, He acted in such sort that He was seen by none."

In regard to the words, "'He showed Him all the kingdoms of the world, and the glory of them,' we are not to understand that He saw the very kingdoms, with the cities and inhabitants, their gold and silver: but that the devil pointed out the quarters in which each kingdom or city lay, and set forth to Him in words their glory and estate." Or, again, as Origen says (Hom. xxx in Luc.), "he showed Him how, by means of the various vices, he was the lord of the world."

## QUESTION 42

OF CHRIST'S DOCTRINE (In Four Articles)

We have now to consider Christ's doctrine, about which there are four points of inquiry:

(1) Whether Christ should have preached to the Jews only, or to the Gentiles also?

(2) Whether in preaching He should have avoided the opposition of the Jews?

(3) Whether He should have preached in an open or in a hidden manner?

(4) Whether He should have preached by word only, or also by writing?

Concerning the time when He began to teach, we have spoken above when treating of His baptism (Q. 29, A. 3).

FIRST ARTICLE [III, Q. 42, Art. 1]

Whether Christ Should Have Preached Not Only to the Jews, but Also to the Gentiles?

Objection 1: It would seem that Christ should have preached not only to the Jews, but also to the Gentiles. For it is written (Isa. 49:6): "It is a small thing that thou shouldst be My servant to raise up the tribes of Israel [Vulg.: 'Jacob'] and to convert the dregs of Jacob [Vulg.: 'Israel']: behold, I have given thee to be the light of the Gentiles, that thou mayest be my salvation even to the farthest part of the earth." But Christ gave light and salvation through His doctrine. Therefore it seems that it was "a small thing" that He preached to Jews alone, and not to the Gentiles.

Obj. 2: Further, as it is written (Matt. 7:29): "He was teaching them as one having power." Now the power of doctrine is made more manifest in the instruction of those who, like the Gentiles, have received no tidings whatever; hence the Apostle says (Rom. 15:20): "I have so preached the [Vulg.: 'this'] gospel, not where Christ was named, lest I should build upon another man's foundation." Therefore much rather should Christ have preached to the Gentiles than to the Jews.

Obj. 3: Further, it is more useful to instruct many than one. But Christ instructed some individual Gentiles, such as the Samaritan woman (John 4) and the Chananaean woman (Matt. 15). Much more reason, therefore, was there for Christ to preach to the Gentiles in general.

*On the contrary,* our Lord said (Matt. 15:24): "I was not sent but to the sheep that are lost of the house of Israel." And (Rom. 10:15) it is written: "How shall they preach unless they be sent?" Therefore Christ should not have preached to the Gentiles.

*I answer that,* It was fitting that Christ's preaching, whether through Himself or through His apostles, should be directed at first to the Jews alone. First, in order to show that by His coming the promises were fulfilled which had been made to the Jews of old, and not to the Gentiles. Thus the Apostle says (Rom. 15:8): "I say that Christ . . . was minister of the circumcision," i.e. the apostle and preacher of the Jews, "for the truth of God, to confirm the promises made unto the fathers."

Secondly, in order to show that His coming was of God; because, as is written Rom. 13:1: "Those things which are of God are well ordered [Vulg.: 'those that are, are ordained of God']." Now the right order demanded that the doctrine of Christ should be made known first to the Jews, who, by believing in and worshiping one God, were nearer to God, and that it should be transmitted through them to the Gentiles: just as in the heavenly hierarchy the Divine enlightenment comes to the lower angels through the higher. Hence on Matt. 15:24, "I was not sent but to the sheep that are lost in the house of Israel," Jerome says: "He does not mean by this that He was not sent to the Gentiles, but that He was sent to the Jews first." And so we read (Isa. 66:19): "I will send of them that shall be saved," i.e. of the Jews, "to the Gentiles . . . and they shall declare My glory unto the Gentiles."

Thirdly, in order to deprive the Jews of ground for quibbling. Hence on Matt. 10:5, "Go ye not into the way of the Gentiles." Jerome says: "It behooved Christ's coming to be announced to the Jews first, lest they should have a valid excuse, and say that they had rejected our Lord because He had sent His apostles to the Gentiles and Samaritans."

Fourthly, because it was through the triumph of the cross that Christ merited power and lordship over the Gentiles. Hence it is written (Apoc. 2:26, 28): "He that shall overcome . . . I will give him power over the nations . . . as I also have received of My Father"; and that because He became "obedient unto the death of the cross, God hath exalted Him . . . that in the name of Jesus every knee should bow . . ." and that "every tongue should confess Him" (Phil. 2:8-11). Consequently He did not wish His doctrine to be preached to the Gentiles before His Passion: it was after His Passion that He said to His disciples (Matt. 28:19): "Going, teach ye all nations." For this reason it was that when, shortly before His Passion, certain Gentiles wished to see Jesus, He said: "Unless the grain of wheat falling into the ground dieth, itself remaineth alone: but if it die it bringeth forth much fruit" (John 12:20-25); and as Augustine says, commenting on this passage: "He called Himself the grain of wheat that must be mortified by the unbelief of the Jews, multiplied by the faith of the nations."

Reply Obj. 1: Christ was given to be the light and salvation of the Gentiles through His disciples, whom He sent to preach to them.

Reply Obj. 2: It is a sign, not of lesser, but of greater power to do something by means of others rather than by oneself. And thus the Divine power of Christ was specially shown in this, that He bestowed on the teaching of His disciples such a power that they converted the Gentiles to Christ, although these had heard nothing of Him.

Now the power of Christ's teaching is to be considered in the miracles by which He confirmed His doctrine, in the efficacy of His persuasion, and in the authority of His words, for He spoke as being Himself above the Law when He said: "But I say to you" (Matt. 5:22, 28, 32, 34, 39, 44); and, again, in the force of His righteousness shown in His sinless manner of life.

Reply Obj. 3: Just as it was unfitting that Christ should at the outset make His doctrine known to the Gentiles equally with the Jews, in order that He might appear as being sent to the Jews, as to the first-born people; so neither was it fitting for Him to neglect the Gentiles altogether, lest they should be deprived of the hope of salvation. For this reason certain individual Gentiles were admitted, on account of the excellence of their faith and devotedness.

SECOND ARTICLE [III, Q. 42, Art. 2]

Whether Christ Should Have Preached to the Jews Without Offending Them?

Objection 1: It would seem that Christ should have preached to the Jews without offending them. For, as Augustine says (De Agone Christ. xi): "In the Man Jesus Christ, a model of life is given us by the Son of God." But we should avoid offending not only the faithful, but even unbelievers, according to 1 Cor. 10:32: "Be without offense to the Jews, and to the Gentiles, and to the Church of God." Therefore it seems that, in His teaching, Christ should also have avoided giving offense to the Jews.

Obj. 2: Further, no wise man should do anything that will hinder the result of his labor. Now through the disturbance which His teaching occasioned among the Jews, it was deprived of its results; for it is written (Luke 11:53, 54) that when our Lord reproved the Pharisees and Scribes, they "began vehemently to urge Him, end to oppress His mouth about many things; lying in wait for Him, and seeking to catch something from His mouth, that they might accuse Him." It seems therefore unfitting that He should have given them offense by His teaching.

Obj. 3: Further, the Apostle says (1 Tim. 5:1): "An ancient man rebuke not; but entreat him as a father." But the priests and princes of the Jews were the elders of that people. Therefore it seems that they should not have been rebuked with severity.

*On the contrary,* It was foretold (Isa. 8:14) that Christ would be "for a stone of stumbling and for a rock of offense to the two houses of Israel."

*I answer that,* The salvation of the multitude is to be preferred to the peace of any individuals whatsoever. Consequently, when certain ones, by their perverseness, hinder the salvation of the multitude, the preacher and the teacher should not fear to offend those men, in order that he may insure the salvation of the multitude. Now the Scribes and Pharisees and the princes of the Jews were by their malice a considerable hindrance to the salvation of the people, both because they opposed themselves to Christ's doctrine, which was the only way to salvation, and because their evil ways corrupted the morals of the people. For which reason our Lord, undeterred by their taking offense, publicly taught the truth which they hated, and condemned their vices. Hence we read (Matt. 15:12, 14) that when the disciples of our Lord said: "Dost Thou know that the Pharisees, when they heard this word, were scandalized?" He answered: "Let them alone: they are blind and leaders of the blind; and if the blind lead the blind, both fall into the pit."

Reply Obj. 1: A man ought so to avoid giving offense, as neither by wrong deed or word to be the occasion of anyone's downfall. "But if scandal arise from truth, the scandal should be borne rather than the truth be set aside," as Gregory says (Hom. vii in Ezech.).

Reply Obj. 2: By publicly reproving the Scribes and Pharisees, Christ promoted rather than hindered the effect of His teaching. Because when the people came to know the vices of those men, they were less inclined to be prejudiced against Christ by hearing what was said of Him by the Scribes and Pharisees, who were ever withstanding His doctrine.

Reply Obj. 3: This saying of the Apostle is to be understood of those elders whose years are reckoned not only in age and authority, but also in probity; according to Num. 11:16: "Gather unto Me seventy men of the ancients of Israel, whom thou knowest to be ancients . . . of the people." But if by sinning openly they turn the authority of their years into an instrument of wickedness, they should be rebuked openly and severely, as also Daniel says (Dan. 13:52): "O thou that art grown old in evil days," etc.

THIRD ARTICLE [III, Q. 42, Art. 3]

Whether Christ Should Have Taught All Things Openly?

Objection 1: It would seem that Christ should not have taught all things openly. For we read that He taught many things to His disciples apart: as is seen clearly in the sermon at the Supper. Wherefore He said: "That which you heard in the ear in the chambers shall be preached on the housetops" [*St. Thomas, probably quoting from memory, combines Matt. 10:27 with Luke 12:3]. Therefore He did not teach all things openly.

Obj. 2: Further, the depths of wisdom should not be expounded save to the perfect, according to 1 Cor. 2:6: "We speak wisdom among the perfect." Now Christ's doctrine contained the most profound wisdom. Therefore it should not have been made known to the imperfect crowd.

Obj. 3: Further, it comes to the same, to hide the truth, whether by saying nothing or by making use of a language that is difficult to understand. Now Christ, by speaking to the multitudes a language they would not understand, hid from them the truth that He preached; since "without parables He did not speak to them" (Matt. 13:34). In the same way, therefore, He could have hidden it from them by saying nothing at all.

*On the contrary,* He says Himself (John 18:20): "In secret I have spoken nothing."

*I answer that,* Anyone's doctrine may be hidden in three ways. First, on the part of the intention of the teacher, who does not wish to make his doctrine known to many, but rather to hide it. And this may happen in two ways--sometimes through envy on the part of the teacher, who desires to excel in his knowledge, wherefore he is unwilling to communicate it to others. But this was not the case with Christ, in whose person the following words are spoken (Wis. 7:13): "Which I have learned without guile, and communicate without envy, and her riches I hide not." But sometimes this happens through the vileness of the things taught; thus Augustine says on John 16:12: "There are some things so bad that no sort of human modesty can bear them." Wherefore of heretical doctrine it is written (Prov. 9:17): "Stolen waters are sweeter." Now, Christ's doctrine is "not of error nor of uncleanness" (1 Thess. 2:3). Wherefore our Lord says (Mk. 4:21): "Doth a candle," i.e. true and pure doctrine, "come in to be put under a bushel?"

Secondly, doctrine is hidden because it is put before few. And thus, again, did Christ teach nothing in secret: for He propounded His entire doctrine either to the whole crowd or to His disciples gathered together. Hence Augustine says on John 18:20: "How can it be said that He speaks in secret when He speaks before so many men? . . . especially if what He says to few He wishes through them to be made known to many?"

Thirdly, doctrine is hidden, as to the manner in which it is propounded. And thus Christ spoke certain things in secret to the crowds, by employing parables in teaching them spiritual mysteries which they were either unable or unworthy to grasp: and yet it was better for them to be instructed in the knowledge of spiritual things, albeit hidden under the garb of parables, than to be deprived of it altogether. Nevertheless our Lord expounded the open and unveiled truth of these parables to His disciples, so that they might hand it down to others worthy of it; according to 2 Tim. 2:2: "The things which thou hast heard of me by many witnesses, the same command to faithful men, who shall be fit to teach others." This is foreshadowed, Num. 4, where the sons of Aaron are commanded to wrap up the sacred vessels that were to be carried by the Levites.

Reply Obj. 1: As Hilary says, commenting on the passage quoted, "we do not read that our Lord was wont to preach at night, and expound His doctrine in the dark: but He says this because His speech is darkness to the carnal-minded, and His words are night to the unbeliever. His meaning, therefore, is that whatever He said we also should say in the midst of unbelievers, by openly believing and professing it."

Or, according to Jerome, He speaks comparatively--that is to say, because He was instructing them in Judea, which was a small place compared with the whole world, where Christ's doctrine was to be published by the preaching of the apostles.

Reply Obj. 2: By His doctrine our Lord did not make known all the depths of His wisdom, neither to the multitudes, nor, indeed, to His disciples, to whom He said (John 16:12): "I have yet many things to say to you, but you cannot bear them now." Yet whatever things out of His wisdom He judged it right to make known to others, He expounded, not in secret, but openly; although He was not understood by all. Hence Augustine says on John 18:20: "We must understand this, 'I have spoken openly to the world,' as though our Lord had said, 'Many have heard Me' . . . and, again, it was not 'openly,' because they did not understand."

Reply Obj. 3: As stated above, our Lord spoke to the multitudes in parables, because they were neither able nor worthy to receive the naked truth, which He revealed to His disciples.

And when it is said that "without parables He did not speak to them," according to Chrysostom (Hom. xlvii in Matth.), we are to understand this of that particular sermon, since on other occasions He said many things to the multitude without parables. Or, as Augustine says (De Qq. Evang., qu. xvii), this means, "not that He spoke nothing literally, but that He scarcely ever spoke without introducing a parable, although He also spoke some things in the literal sense."

FOURTH ARTICLE [III, Q. 42, Art. 4]

Whether Christ Should Have Committed His Doctrine to Writing?

Objection 1: It would seem that Christ should have committed His doctrine to writing. For the purpose of writing is to hand down doctrine to posterity. Now Christ's doctrine was destined to endure for ever, according to Luke 21:33: "Heaven and earth shall pass away, but My words shall not pass away." Therefore it seems that Christ should have committed His doctrine to writing.

Obj. 2: Further, the Old Law was a foreshadowing of Christ, according to Heb. 10:1: "The Law has [Vulg.: 'having'] a shadow of the good things to come." Now the Old Law was put into writing by God, according to Ex. 24:12: "I will give thee" two "tables of stone and the law, and the commandments which I have written." Therefore it seems that Christ also should have put His doctrine into writing.

Obj. 3: Further, to Christ, who came to enlighten them that sit in darkness (Luke 1:79), it belonged to remove occasions of error, and to open out the road to faith. Now He would have done this by putting His teaching into writing: for Augustine says (De Consensu Evang. i) that "some there are who wonder why our Lord wrote nothing, so that we have to believe what others have written about Him. Especially do those pagans ask this question who dare not blame or blaspheme Christ, and who ascribe to Him most excellent, but merely human, wisdom. These say that the disciples made out the Master to be more than He really was when they said that He was the Son of God and the Word of God, by whom all things were made." And farther on he adds: "It seems as though they were prepared to believe whatever He might have written of Himself, but not what others at their discretion published about Him." Therefore it seems that Christ should have Himself committed His doctrine to writing.

*On the contrary,* No books written by Him were to be found in the canon of Scripture.

*I answer that,* It was fitting that Christ should not commit His doctrine to writing. First, on account of His dignity: for the more excellent the teacher, the more excellent should be his manner of teaching. Consequently it was fitting that Christ, as the most excellent of teachers, should adopt that manner of teaching whereby His doctrine is imprinted on the hearts of His hearers; wherefore it is written (Matt. 7:29) that "He was teaching them as one having power." And so it was that among the Gentiles, Pythagoras and Socrates, who were teachers of great excellence, were unwilling to write anything. For writings are ordained, as to an end, unto the imprinting of doctrine in the hearts of the hearers.

Secondly, on account of the excellence of Christ's doctrine, which cannot be expressed in writing; according to John 21:25: "There are also many other things which Jesus did: which, if they were written everyone, the world itself, I think, would not be able to contain the books that should be written." Which Augustine explains by saying: "We are not to believe that in respect of space the world could not contain them . . . but that by the capacity of the readers they could not be comprehended." And if Christ had committed His doctrine to writing, men would have had no deeper thought of His doctrine than that which appears on the surface of the writing.

Thirdly, that His doctrine might reach all in an orderly manner: Himself teaching His disciples immediately, and they subsequently teaching others, by preaching and writing: whereas if He Himself had written, His doctrine would have reached all immediately.

Hence it is said of Wisdom (Prov. 9:3) that "she hath sent her maids to invite to the tower." It is to be observed, however, that, as Augustine says (De Consensu Evang. i), some of the Gentiles thought that Christ wrote certain books treating of the magic art whereby He worked miracles: which art is condemned by the Christian learning. "And yet they who claim to have read those books of Christ do none of those things which they marvel at His doing according to those same books. Moreover, it is by a Divine judgment that they err so far as to assert that these books were, as it were, entitled as letters to Peter and Paul, for that they found them in several places depicted in company with Christ. No wonder that the inventors were deceived by the painters: for as long as Christ lived in the mortal flesh with His disciples, Paul was no disciple of His."

Reply Obj. 1: As Augustine says in the same book: "Christ is the head of all His disciples who are members of His body. Consequently, when they put into writing what He showed forth and said to them, by no means must we say that He wrote nothing: since His members put forth that which they knew under His dictation. For at His command they, being His hands, as it were, wrote whatever He wished us to read concerning His deeds and words."

Reply Obj. 2: Since the old Law was given under the form of sensible signs, therefore also was it fittingly written with sensible signs. But Christ's doctrine, which is "the law of the spirit of life" (Rom. 8:2), had to be "written not with ink, but with the Spirit of the living God; not in tables of stone, but in the fleshly tables of the heart," as the Apostle says (2 Cor. 3:3).

Reply Obj. 3: Those who were unwilling to believe what the apostles wrote of Christ would have refused to believe the writings of Christ, whom they deemed to work miracles by the magic art.

## QUESTION 43

OF THE MIRACLES WORKED BY CHRIST, IN GENERAL (In Four Articles)

We must now consider the miracles worked by Christ: (1) In general; (2) Specifically, of each kind of miracle; (3) In particular, of His transfiguration.

Concerning the first, there are four points of inquiry:

(1) Whether Christ should have worked miracles?

(2) Whether He worked them by Divine power?

(3) When did He begin to work miracles?

(4) Whether His miracles are a sufficient proof of His Godhead?

FIRST ARTICLE [III, Q. 43, Art. 1]

Whether Christ Should Have Worked Miracles?

Objection 1: It would seem that Christ should not have worked miracles. For Christ's deeds should have been consistent with His words. But He Himself said (Matt. 16:4): "A wicked and adulterous generation seeketh after a sign; and a sign shall not be given it, but the sign of Jonas the prophet." Therefore He should not have worked miracles.

Obj. 2: Further, just as Christ, at His second coming, is to come with great power and majesty, as is written Matt. 24:30, so at His first coming He came in infirmity, according to Isa. 53:3: "A man of sorrows and acquainted with infirmity." But the working of miracles belongs to power rather than to infirmity. Therefore it was not fitting that He should work miracles in His first coming.

Obj. 3: Further, Christ came that He might save men by faith; according to Heb. 12:2: "Looking on Jesus, the author and finisher of faith." But miracles lessen the merit of faith; hence our Lord says (John 4:48): "Unless you see signs and wonders you believe not." Therefore it seems that Christ should not have worked miracles.

*On the contrary,* It was said in the person of His adversaries (John 11:47): "What do we; for this man doth many miracles?"

*I answer that,* God enables man to work miracles for two reasons. First and principally, in confirmation of the doctrine that a man teaches. For since those things which are of faith surpass human reason, they cannot be proved by human arguments, but need to be proved by the argument of Divine power: so that when a man does works that God alone can do, we may believe that what he says is from God: just as when a man is the bearer of letters sealed with the king's ring, it is to be believed that what they contain expresses the king's will.

Secondly, in order to make known God's presence in a man by the grace of the Holy Ghost: so that when a man does the works of God we may believe that God dwells in him by His grace. Wherefore it is written (Gal. 3:5): "He who giveth to you the Spirit, and worketh miracles among you."

Now both these things were to be made known to men concerning Christ--namely, that God dwelt in Him by grace, not of adoption, but of union: and that His supernatural doctrine was from God. And therefore it was most fitting that He should work miracles. Wherefore He Himself says (John 10:38): "Though you will not believe Me, believe the works"; and (John 5:36): "The works which the Father hath given Me to perfect . . . themselves . . . give testimony to Me."

Reply Obj. 1: These words, "a sign shall not be given it, but the sign of Jonas," mean, as Chrysostom says (Hom. xliii in Matth.), that "they did not receive a sign such as they sought, viz. from heaven": but not that He gave them no sign at all. Or that "He worked signs not for the sake of those whom He knew to be hardened, but to amend others." Therefore those signs were given, not to them, but to others.

Reply Obj. 2: Although Christ came "in the infirmity" of the flesh, which is manifested in the passions, yet He came "in the power of God" [*Cf. 2 Cor. 13:4], and this had to be made manifest by miracles.

Reply Obj. 3: Miracles lessen the merit of faith in so far as those are shown to be hard of heart who are unwilling to believe what is proved from the Scriptures unless (they are convinced) by miracles. Yet it is better for them to be converted to the faith even by miracles than that they should remain altogether in their unbelief. For it is written (1 Cor. 14:22) that signs are given "to unbelievers," viz. that they may be converted to the faith.

SECOND ARTICLE [III, Q. 43, Art. 2]

Whether Christ Worked Miracles by Divine Power?

Objection 1: It would seem that Christ did not work miracles by Divine power. For the Divine power is omnipotent. But it seems that Christ was not omnipotent in working miracles; for it is written (Mk. 6:5) that "He could not do any miracles there," i.e. in His own country. Therefore it seems that He did not work miracles by Divine power.

Obj. 2: Further, God does not pray. But Christ sometimes prayed when working miracles; as may be seen in the raising of Lazarus (John 11:41, 42), and in the multiplication of the loaves, as related Matt. 14:19. Therefore it seems that He did not work miracles by Divine power.

Obj. 3: Further, what is done by Divine power cannot be done by the power of any creature. But the things which Christ did could be done also by the power of a creature: wherefore the Pharisees said (Luke 11:15) that He cast out devils "by Beelzebub the prince of devils." Therefore it seems that Christ did not work miracles by Divine power.

*On the contrary,* our Lord said (John 14:10): "The Father who abideth in Me, He doth the works."

*I answer that,* as stated in the First Part (Q. 110, A. 4), true miracles cannot be wrought save by Divine power: because God alone can change the order of nature; and this is what is meant by a miracle. Wherefore Pope Leo says (Ep. ad Flav. xxviii) that, while there are two natures in Christ, there is "one," viz. the Divine, which shines forth in miracles; and "another," viz. the human, "which submits to insults"; yet "each communicates its actions to the other": in as far as the human nature is the instrument of the Divine action, and the human action receives power from the Divine Nature, as stated above (Q. 19, A. 1).

Reply Obj. 1: When it is said that "He could not do any miracles there," it is not to be understood that He could not do them absolutely, but that it was not fitting for Him to do them: for it was unfitting for Him to work miracles among unbelievers. Wherefore it is said farther on: "And He wondered because of their unbelief." In like manner it is said (Gen. 18:17): "Can I hide from Abraham what I am about to do?" and Gen. 19:22: "I cannot do anything till thou go in thither."

Reply Obj. 2: As Chrysostom says on Matt. 14:19, "He took the five loaves and the two fishes, and, looking up to heaven, He blessed and brake: It was to be believed of Him, both that He is of the Father and that He is equal to Him . . . Therefore that He might prove both, He works miracles now with authority, now with prayer . . . in the lesser things, indeed, He looks up to heaven"--for instance, in multiplying the loaves--"but in the greater, which belong to God alone, He acts with authority; for example, when He forgave sins and raised the dead."

When it is said that in raising Lazarus He lifted up His eyes (John 11:41), this was not because He needed to pray, but because He wished to teach us how to pray. Wherefore He said: "Because of the people who stand about have I said it: that they may believe that Thou hast sent Me."

Reply Obj. 3: Christ cast out demons otherwise than they are cast out by the power of demons. For demons are cast out from bodies by the power of higher demons in such a way that they retain their power over the soul: since the devil does not work against his own kingdom. On the other hand, Christ cast out demons, not only from the body, but still more from the soul. For this reason our Lord rebuked the blasphemy of the Jews, who said that He cast out demons by the power of the demons: first, by saying that Satan is not divided against himself; secondly, by quoting the instance of others who cast out demons by the Spirit of God; thirdly, because He could not have cast out a demon unless He had overcome Him by Divine power; fourthly, because there was nothing in common between His works and their effects and those of Satan; since Satan's purpose was to "scatter" those whom Christ "gathered" together [*Cf. Matt. 12:24-30; Mk. 3:22; Luke 11:15-32].

THIRD ARTICLE [III, Q. 43, Art. 3]

Whether Christ Began to Work Miracles When He Changed Water into Wine at the Marriage Feast?

Objection 1: It would seem that Christ did not begin to work miracles when He changed water into wine at the marriage feast. For we read in the book De Infantia Salvatoris that Christ worked many miracles in His childhood. But the miracle of changing water into wine at the marriage feast took place in the thirtieth or thirty-first year of His age. Therefore it seems that it was not then that He began to work miracles.

Obj. 2: Further, Christ worked miracles by Divine power. Now He was possessed of Divine power from the first moment of His conception; for from that instant He was both God and man. Therefore it seems that He worked miracles from the very first.

Obj. 3: Further, Christ began to gather His disciples after His baptism and temptation, as related Matt. 4:18 and John 1:35. But the disciples gathered around Him, principally on account of His miracles: thus it is written (Luke 5:4) that He called Peter when "he was astonished at" the miracle which He had worked in "the draught of fishes." Therefore it seems that He worked other miracles before that of the marriage feast.

*On the contrary,* It is written (John 2:11): "This beginning of miracles did Jesus in Cana of Galilee."

*I answer that,* Christ worked miracles in order to confirm His doctrine, and in order to show forth His Divine power. Therefore, as to the first, it was unbecoming for Him to work miracles before He began to teach. And it was unfitting that He should begin to teach until He reached the perfect age, as we stated above, in speaking of His baptism (Q. 39, A. 3). But as to the second, it was right that He should so manifest His Godhead by working miracles that men should believe in the reality of His manhood. And, consequently, as Chrysostom says (Hom. xxi in Joan.), "it was fitting that He should not begin to work wonders from His early years: for men would have deemed the Incarnation to be imaginary and would have crucified Him before the proper time."

Reply Obj. 1: As Chrysostom says (Hom. xvii in Joan.), in regard to the saying of John the Baptist, "'That He may be made manifest in Israel, therefore am I come baptizing with water,' it is clear that the wonders which some pretend to have been worked by Christ in His childhood are untrue and fictitious. For had Christ worked miracles from His early years, John would by no means have been unacquainted with Him, nor would the rest of the people have stood in need of a teacher to point Him out to them."

Reply Obj. 2: What the Divine power achieved in Christ was in proportion to the needs of the salvation of mankind, the achievement of which was the purpose of His taking flesh. Consequently He so worked miracles by the Divine power as not to prejudice our belief in the reality of His flesh.

Reply Obj. 3: The disciples were to be commended precisely because they followed Christ "without having seen Him work any miracles," as Gregory says in a homily (Hom. v in Evang.). And, as Chrysostom says (Hom. xxiii in Joan.), "the need for working miracles arose then, especially when the disciples were already gathered around and attached to Him, and attentive to what was going on around them. Hence it is added: 'And His disciples believed in Him,'" not because they then believed in Him for the first time, but because then "they believed with greater discernment and perfection." Or they are called "disciples" because "they were to be disciples later on," as Augustine observes (De Consensu Evang. ii).

FOURTH ARTICLE [III, Q. 43, Art. 4]

Whether the Miracles Which Christ Worked Were a Sufficient Proof of His Godhead?

Objection 1: It would seem that the miracles which Christ worked were not a sufficient proof of His Godhead. For it is proper to Christ to be both God and man. But the miracles which Christ worked have been done by others also. Therefore they were not a sufficient proof of His Godhead.

Obj. 2: Further, no power surpasses that of the Godhead. But some have worked greater miracles than Christ, for it is written (John 14:12): "He that believeth in Me, the works that I do, he also shall do, and greater than these shall he do." Therefore it seems that the miracles which Christ worked are not sufficient proof of His Godhead.

Obj. 3: Further, the particular is not a sufficient proof of the universal. But any one of Christ's miracles was one particular work. Therefore none of them was a sufficient proof of His Godhead, by reason of which He had universal power over all things.

*On the contrary,* our Lord said (John 5:36): "The works which the Father hath given Me to perfect . . . themselves . . . give testimony of Me."

*I answer that,* The miracles which Christ worked were a sufficient proof of His Godhead in three respects. First, as to the very nature of the works, which surpassed the entire capability of created power, and therefore could not be done save by Divine power. For this reason the blind man, after his sight had been restored, said (John 9:32, 33): "From the beginning of the world it has not been heard, that any man hath opened the eyes of one born blind. Unless this man were of God, he could not do anything."

Secondly, as to the way in which He worked miracles--namely, because He worked miracles as though of His own power, and not by praying, as others do. Wherefore it is written (Luke 6:19) that "virtue went out from Him and healed all." Whereby it is proved, as Cyril says (Comment. in Lucam) that "He did not receive power from another, but, being God by nature, He showed His own power over the sick. And this is how He worked countless miracles." Hence on Matt. 8:16: "He cast out spirits with His word, and all that were sick He healed," Chrysostom says: "Mark how great a multitude of persons healed, the Evangelists pass quickly over, not mentioning one by one . . . but in one word traversing an unspeakable sea of miracles." And thus it was shown that His power was co-equal with that of God the Father, according to John 5:19: "What things soever" the Father "doth, these the Son doth also in like manner"; and, again (John 5:21): "As the Father raiseth up the dead and giveth life, so the Son also giveth life to whom He will."

Thirdly, from the very fact that He taught that He was God; for unless this were true it would not be confirmed by miracles worked by Divine power. Hence it was said (Mk. 1:27): "What is this new doctrine? For with power He commandeth the unclean spirits, and they obey Him."

Reply Obj. 1: This was the argument of the Gentiles. Wherefore Augustine says (Ep. ad Volusian. cxxxvii): "No suitable wonders, say they, show forth the presence of so great majesty, for the ghostly cleansing" whereby He cast out demons, "the cure of the sick, the raising of the dead to life, if other miracles be taken into account, are small things before God." To this Augustine answers thus: "We own that the prophets did as much . . . But even Moses himself and the other prophets made Christ the Lord the object of their prophecy, and gave Him great glory . . . He, therefore, chose to do similar things to avoid the inconsistency of failing to do what He had done through others. Yet still He was bound to do something which no other had done: to be born of a virgin, to rise from the dead, and to ascend into heaven. If anyone deem this a slight thing for God to do, I know not what more he can expect. Having become man, ought He to have made another world, that we might believe Him to be Him by whom the world was made? But in this world neither a greater world could be made nor one equal to it: and if He had made a lesser world in comparison with this, that too would have been deemed a small thing."

As to the miracles worked by others, Christ did greater still. Hence on John 15:24: "If I had not done in [Douay: 'among'] them the works that no other men hath done," etc., Augustine says: "None of the works of Christ seem to be greater than the raising of the dead: which thing we know the ancient prophets also did . . . Yet Christ did some works 'which no other man hath done.' But we are told in answer that others did works which He did not, and which none other did . . . But to heal with so great a power so many defects and ailments and grievances of mortal men, this we read concerning none soever of the men of old. To say nothing of those, each of whom by His bidding, as they came in His way, He made whole . . . Mark saith (6:56): 'Whithersoever He entered, into towns or into villages or into cities, they laid the sick in the streets, and besought Him that they might touch but the hem of His garment: and as many as touched Him were made whole.' These things none other did in them; for when He saith 'In them,' it is not to be understood to mean 'Among them,' or 'In their presence,' but wholly 'In them,' because He healed them . . . Therefore whatever works He did in them are works that none ever did; since if ever any other man did any one of them, by His doing he did it; whereas these works He did, not by their doing, but by Himself."

Reply Obj. 2: Augustine explains this passage of John as follows (Tract. lxxi): "What are these 'greater works' which believers in Him would do? That, as they passed by, their very shadow healed the sick? For it is greater that a shadow should heal than the hem of a garment . . . When, however, He said these words, it was the deeds and works of His words that He spoke of: for when He said . . . 'The Father who abideth in Me, He doth the works,' what works did He mean, then, but the words He was speaking? . . . and the fruits of those same words was the faith of those (who believed): but when the disciples preached the Gospel, not some few like those, but the very nations believed . . . (Tract. lxxii). Did not that rich man go away from His presence sorrowful? . . . and yet afterwards, what one individual, having heard from Him, did not, that many did when He spake by the mouth of His disciples . . . Behold, He did greater works when spoken of by men believing than when speaking to men hearing. But there is yet this difficulty: that He did these 'greater works' by the apostles: whereas He saith as meaning not only them: . . . 'He that believeth in Me' . . . Listen! . . . 'He that believeth in Me, the works that I do, he also shall do': first, 'I do,' then 'he also shall do,' because I do that he may do. What works--but that from ungodly he should be made righteous? . . . Which thing Christ worketh in him, truly, but not without him. Yes, I may affirm this to be altogether greater than to create" [*The words 'to create' are not in the text of St. Augustine] "heaven and earth . . . for 'heaven and earth shall pass away'; but the salvation and justification of the predestinate shall remain . . . But also in the heavens . . . the angels are the works of Christ: and does that man do greater works than these, who co-operates with Christ in the work of his justification? . . . let him, who can, judge whether it be greater to create a righteous being than to justify an ungodly one. Certainly if both are works of equal power, the latter is a work of greater mercy."

"But there is no need for us to understand all the works of Christ, where He saith 'Greater than these shall he do.' For by 'these' He meant, perhaps, those which He was doing at that hour: now at that time He was speaking words of faith: . . . and certainly it is less to preach words of righteousness, which thing He did without us, than to justify the ungodly, which thing He so doth in us that we also do it ourselves."

Reply Obj. 3: When some particular work is proper to some agent, then that particular work is a sufficient proof of the whole power of that agent: thus, since the act of reasoning is proper to man, the mere fact that someone reasons about any particular proposition proves him to be a man. In like manner, since it is proper to God to work miracles by His own power, any single miracle worked by Christ by His own power is a sufficient proof that He is God.

## QUESTION 44

OF (CHRIST'S) MIRACLES CONSIDERED SPECIFICALLY (In Four Articles)

We have now to consider each kind of miracle:

(1) The miracles which He worked in spiritual substances;

(2) The miracles which He worked in heavenly bodies;

(3) The miracles which He worked in man;

(4) The miracles which He worked in irrational creatures.

FIRST ARTICLE [III, Q. 44, Art. 1]

Whether Those Miracles Were Fitting Which Christ Worked in Spiritual Substances?

Objection 1: It would seem that those miracles were unfitting which Christ worked in spiritual substances. For among spiritual substances the holy angels are above the demons; for, as Augustine says (De Trin. iii): "The treacherous and sinful rational spirit of life is ruled by the rational, pious, and just spirit of life." But we read of no miracles worked by Christ in the good angels. Therefore neither should He have worked miracles in the demons.

Obj. 2: Further, Christ's miracles were ordained to make known His Godhead. But Christ's Godhead was not to be made known to the demons: since this would have hindered the mystery of His Passion, according to 1 Cor. 2:8: "If they had known it, they would never have crucified the Lord of glory." Therefore He should not have worked miracles in the demons.

Obj. 3: Further, Christ's miracles were ordained to the glory of God: hence it is written (Matt. 9:8) that "the multitudes seeing" that the man sick of the palsy had been healed by Christ, "feared, and glorified God that gave such power to men." But the demons have no part in glorifying God; since "praise is not seemly in the mouth of a sinner" (Ecclus. 15:9). For which reason also "He suffered them not to speak" (Mk. 1:34; Luke 4:41) those things which reflected glory on Him. Therefore it seems that it was unfitting for Him to work miracles in the demons.

Obj. 4: Further, Christ's miracles are ordained to the salvation of mankind. But sometimes the casting out of demons from men was detrimental to man, in some cases to the body: thus it is related (Mk. 9:24, 25) that a demon at Christ's command, "crying out and greatly tearing" the man, "went out of him; and he became as dead, so that many said: He is dead"; sometimes also to things: as when He sent the demons, at their own request, into the swine, which they cast headlong into the sea; wherefore the inhabitants of those parts "besought Him that He would depart from their coasts" (Matt. 8:31-34). Therefore it seems unfitting that He should have worked such like miracles.

*On the contrary,* this was foretold (Zech. 13:2), where it is written: "I will take away . . . the unclean spirit out of the earth."

*I answer that,* The miracles worked by Christ were arguments for the faith which He taught. Now, by the power of His Godhead He was to rescue those who would believe in Him, from the power of the demons; according to John 12:31: "Now shall the prince of this world be cast out." Consequently it was fitting that, among other miracles, He should also deliver those who were obsessed by demons.

Reply Obj. 1: Just as men were to be delivered by Christ from the power of the demons, so by Him were they to be brought to the companionship of the angels, according to Col. 1:20: "Making peace through the blood of His cross, both as to the things on earth and the things that are in heaven." Therefore it was not fitting to show forth to men other miracles as regards the angels, except by angels appearing to men: as happened in His Nativity, His Resurrection, and His Ascension.

Reply Obj. 2: As Augustine says (De Civ. Dei ix): "Christ was known to the demons just as much as He willed; and He willed just as far as there was need. But He was known to them, not as to the holy angels, by that which is eternal life, but by certain temporal effects of His power." First, when they saw that Christ was hungry after fasting they deemed Him not to be the Son of God. Hence, on Luke 4:3,

"If Thou be the Son of God," etc., Ambrose says: "What means this way of addressing Him? save that, though He knew that the Son of God was to come, yet he did not think that He had come in the weakness of the flesh?" But afterwards, when he saw Him work miracles, he had a sort of conjectural suspicion that He was the Son of God. Hence on Mk. 1:24, "I know who Thou art, the Holy one of God," Chrysostom [*Victor of Antioch. Cf. Catena Aurea] says that "he had no certain or firm knowledge of God's coming." Yet he knew that He was "the Christ promised in the Law," wherefore it is said (Luke 4:41) that "they knew that He was Christ." But it was rather from suspicion than from certainty that they confessed Him to be the Son of God. Hence Bede says on Luke 4:41: "The demons confess the Son of God, and, as stated farther on, 'they knew that He was Christ.' For when the devil saw Him weakened by His fast, He knew Him to be a real man: but when He failed to overcome Him by temptation, He doubted lest He should be the Son of God. And now from the power of His miracles He either knew, or rather suspected that He was the Son of God. His reason therefore for persuading the Jews to crucify Him was not that he deemed Him not to be Christ or the Son of God, but because he did not foresee that he would be the loser by His death. For the Apostle says of this mystery" (1 Cor. 2:7, 8), "which is hidden from the beginning, that 'none of the princes of this world knew it,' for if they had known it they would never have crucified the Lord of glory."

Reply Obj. 3: The miracles which Christ worked in expelling demons were for the benefit, not of the demons, but of men, that they might glorify Him. Wherefore He forbade them to speak in His praise. First, to give us an example. For, as Athanasius says, "He restrained his speech, although he was confessing the truth; to teach us not to care about such things, although it may seem that what is said is true. For it is wrong to seek to learn from the devil when we have the Divine Scripture": Besides, it is dangerous, since the demons frequently mix falsehood with truth. Or, as Chrysostom [*Cyril of Alexandria, Comment. in Luc.] says: "It was not meet for them to usurp the prerogative of the apostolic office. Nor was it fitting that the mystery of Christ should be proclaimed by a corrupt tongue" because "praise is not seemly in the mouth of a sinner" [*Cf. Theophylact, Enarr. in Luc.]. Thirdly, because, as Bede says, "He did not wish the envy of the Jews to be aroused thereby" [*Bede, Expos. in Luc. iv, 41]. Hence "even the apostles are commanded to be silent about Him, lest, if His Divine majesty were proclaimed, the gift of His Passion should be deferred."

Reply Obj. 4: Christ came specially to teach and to work miracles for the good of man, and principally as to the salvation of his soul. Consequently, He allowed the demons, that He cast out, to do man some harm, either in his body or in his goods, for the salvation of man's soul--namely, for man's instruction. Hence Chrysostom says on Matt. 8:32 that Christ let the demons depart into the swine, "not as yielding to the demons, but first, to show . . . how harmful are the demons who attack men; secondly, that all might learn that the demons would not dare to hurt even the swine, except He allow them; thirdly, that they would have treated those men more grievously than they treated the swine, unless they had been protected by God's providence."

And for the same motives He allowed the man, who was being delivered from the demons, to suffer grievously for the moment; yet did He release him at once from that distress. By this, moreover, we are taught, as Bede says on Mk. 9:25, that "often, when after falling into sin we strive to return to God, we experience further and more grievous attacks from the old enemy. This he does, either that he may inspire us with a distaste for virtue, or that he may avenge the shame of having been cast out." For the man who was healed "became as dead," says Jerome, "because to those who are healed it is said, 'You are dead; and your life is hid with Christ in God'" (Col. 3:3)

SECOND ARTICLE [III, Q. 44, Art. 2]

Whether It Was Fitting That Christ Should Work Miracles in the Heavenly Bodies?

Objection 1: It would seem that it was unfitting that Christ should work miracles in the heavenly bodies. For, as Dionysius says (Div. Nom. iv), "it beseems Divine providence not to destroy, but to preserve, nature." Now, the heavenly bodies are by nature incorruptible and unchangeable, as is proved De Coelo i. Therefore it was unfitting that Christ should cause any change in the order of the heavenly bodies.

Obj. 2: Further, the course of time is marked out by the movement of the heavenly bodies, according to Gen. 1:14: "Let there be lights made in the firmament of heaven . . . and let them be for signs, and for seasons, and for days and years." Consequently if the movement of the heavenly bodies be changed, the distinction and order of the seasons is changed. But there is no report of this having been perceived by astronomers, "who gaze at the stars and observe the months," as it is written (Isa. 47:13). Therefore it seems that Christ did not work any change in the movements of the heavenly bodies.

Obj. 3: Further, it was more fitting that Christ should work miracles in life and when teaching, than in death: both because, as it is written (2 Cor. 13:4), "He was crucified through weakness, yet He liveth by the power of God," by which He worked miracles; and because His miracles were in confirmation of His doctrine. But there is no record of Christ having worked any miracles in the heavenly bodies during His lifetime: nay, more; when the Pharisees asked Him to give "a sign from heaven," He refused, as Matthew relates (12, 16). Therefore it seems that neither in His death should He have worked any miracles in the heavenly bodies.

*On the contrary,* It is written (Luke 23:44, 45): "There was darkness over all the earth until the ninth hour; and the sun was darkened."

*I answer that,* As stated above (Q. 43, A. 4) it behooved Christ's miracles to be a sufficient proof of His Godhead. Now this is not so sufficiently proved by changes wrought in the lower bodies, which changes can be brought about by other causes, as it is by changes wrought in the course of the heavenly bodies, which have been established by God alone in an unchangeable order. This is what Dionysius says in his epistle to Polycarp: "We must recognize that no alteration can take place in the order end movement of the heavens that is not caused by Him who made all and changes all by His word." Therefore it was fitting that Christ should work miracles even in the heavenly bodies.

Reply Obj. 1: Just as it is natural to the lower bodies to be moved by the heavenly bodies, which are higher in the order of nature, so is it natural to any creature whatsoever to be changed by God, according to His will. Hence Augustine says (Contra Faust. xxvi; quoted by the gloss on Rom. 11:24: "Contrary to nature thou wert grafted," etc.): "God, the Creator and Author of all natures, does nothing contrary to nature: for whatsoever He does in each thing, that is its nature." Consequently the nature of a heavenly body is not destroyed when God changes its course: but it would be if the change were due to any other cause.

Reply Obj. 2: The order of the seasons was not disturbed by the miracle worked by Christ. For, according to some, this gloom or darkening of the sun, which occurred at the time of Christ's passion, was caused by the sun withdrawing its rays, without any change in the movement of the heavenly bodies, which measures the duration of the seasons. Hence Jerome says on Matt. 27:45: "It seems as though the 'greater light' withdrew its rays, lest it should look on its Lord hanging on the Cross, or bestow its radiancy on the impious blasphemers." And this withdrawal of the rays is not to be understood as though it were in the sun's power to send forth or withdraw its rays: for it sheds its light, not from choice, but by nature, as Dionysius says (Div. Nom. iv). But the sun is said to withdraw its rays in so far as the Divine power caused the sun's rays not to reach the earth. On the other hand, Origen says this was caused by clouds coming between (the earth and the sun). Hence on Matt. 27:45 he says: "We must therefore suppose that many large and very dense clouds were massed together over Jerusalem and the land of Judea; so that it was exceedingly dark from the sixth to the ninth hour. Hence I am of opinion that, just as the other signs which occurred at the time of the Passion"--namely, "the rending of the veil, the quaking of the earth," etc.--"took place in Jerusalem only, so this also: . . . or if anyone prefer, it may be extended to the whole of Judea," since it is said that "'there was darkness over the whole earth,' which expression refers to the land of Judea, as may be gathered from 3 Kings 18:10, where Abdias says to Elias: 'As the Lord thy God liveth, there is no nation or kingdom whither my lord hath not sent to seek thee': which shows that they sought him among the nations in the neighborhood of Judea."

On this point, however, credence is to be given rather to Dionysius, who is an eyewitness as to this having occurred by the moon eclipsing the sun. For he says (Ep. ad Polycarp): "Without any doubt we saw the moon encroach on the sun," he being in Egypt at the time, as he says in the same letter. And in this he points out four miracles. The first is that the natural eclipse of the sun by interposition of the moon never takes place except when the sun and moon are in conjunction. But then the sun and moon were in opposition, it being the fifteenth day, since it was the Jewish Passover. Wherefore he says: "For it was not the time of conjunction."--The second miracle is that whereas at the sixth hour the moon was seen, together with the sun, in the middle of the heavens, in the evening it was seen to be in its place, i.e. in the east, opposite the sun. Wherefore he says: "Again we saw it," i.e. the moon, "return supernaturally into opposition with the sun," so as to be diametrically opposite, having withdrawn from the sun "at the ninth hour," when the darkness ceased, "until evening." From this it is clear that the wonted course of the seasons was not disturbed, because the Divine power caused the moon both to approach the sun supernaturally at an unwonted season, and to withdraw from the sun and return to its proper place according to the season. The third miracle was that the eclipse of the sun naturally always begins in that part of the sun which is to the west and spreads towards the east: and this is because the moon's proper movement from west to east is more rapid than that of the sun, and consequently the moon, coming up from the west, overtakes the sun and passes it on its eastward course. But in this case the moon had already passed the sun, and was distant from it by the length of half the heavenly circle, being opposite to it: consequently it had to return eastwards towards the sun, so as to come into apparent contact with it from the east, and continue in a westerly direction. This is what he refers to when he says: "Moreover, we saw the eclipse begin to the east and spread towards the western edge of the sun," for it was a total eclipse, "and afterwards pass away." The fourth miracle consisted in this, that in a natural eclipse that part of the sun which is first eclipsed is the first to reappear (because the moon, coming in front of the sun, by its natural movement passes on to the east, so as to come away first from the western portion of the sun, which was the first part to be eclipsed), whereas in this case the moon, while returning miraculously from the east to the west, did not pass the sun so as to be to the west of it: but having reached the western edge of the sun returned towards the east: so that the last portion of the sun to be eclipsed was the first to reappear. Consequently the eclipse began towards the east, whereas the sun began to reappear towards the west. And to this he refers by saying: "Again we observed that the occultation and emersion did not begin from the same point," i.e. on the same side of the sun, "but on opposite sides."

Chrysostom adds a fifth miracle (Hom. lxxxviii in Matth.), saying that "the darkness in this case lasted for three hours, whereas an eclipse of the sun lasts but a short time, for it is soon over, as those know who have seen one." Hence we are given to understand that the moon was stationary below the sun, except we prefer to say that the duration of the darkness was measured from the first moment of occultation of the sun to the moment when the sun had completely emerged from the eclipse.

But, as Origen says (on Matt. 27:45), "against this the children of this world object: How is it such a phenomenal occurrence is not related by any writer, whether Greek or barbarian?" And he says that someone of the name of Phlegon "relates in his chronicles that this took place during the reign of Tiberius Caesar, but he does not say that it occurred at the full moon." It may be, therefore, that because it was not the time for an eclipse, the various astronomers living then throughout the world were not on the look-out for one, and that they ascribed this darkness to some disturbance of the atmosphere. But in Egypt, where clouds are few on account of the tranquillity of the air, Dionysius and his companions were considerably astonished so as to make the aforesaid observations about this darkness.

Reply Obj. 3: Then, above all, was there need for miraculous proof of Christ's Godhead, when the weakness of human nature was most apparent in Him. Hence it was that at His birth a new star appeared in the heavens. Wherefore Maximus says (Serm. de Nativ. viii): "If thou disdain the manger, raise thine eyes a little and gaze on the new star in the heavens, proclaiming to the world the birth of our Lord." But in His Passion yet greater weakness appeared in His manhood. Therefore there was need for yet greater miracles in the greater lights of the world. And, as Chrysostom says (Hom. lxxxviii in Matth.): "This is the sign which He promised to them who sought for one saying: 'An evil and adulterous generation seeketh a sign; and a sign shall not be given it, but the sign of Jonas the prophet,' referring to His Cross . . . and Resurrection . . . For it was much more wonderful that this should happen when He was crucified than when He was walking on earth."

THIRD ARTICLE [III, Q. 44, Art. 3]

Whether Christ Worked Miracles Fittingly on Men?

Objection 1: It would seem that Christ worked miracles unfittingly on men. For in man the soul is of more import than the body. Now Christ worked many miracles on bodies, but we do not read of His working any miracles on souls: for neither did He convert any unbelievers to the faith mightily, but by persuading and convincing them with outward miracles, nor is it related of Him that He made wise men out of fools. Therefore it seems that He worked miracles on men in an unfitting manner.

Obj. 2: Further, as stated above (Q. 43, A. 2), Christ worked miracles by Divine power: to which it is proper to work suddenly, perfectly, and without any assistance. Now Christ did not always heal men suddenly as to their bodies: for it is written (Mk. 8:22-25) that, "taking the blind man by the hand, He led him out of the town; and, spitting upon his eyes, laying His hands on him, He asked him if he saw anything. And, looking up, he said: I see men as it were trees walking. After that again He laid His hands upon his eyes, and he began to see, and was restored, so that he saw all things clearly." It is clear from this that He did not heal him suddenly, but at first imperfectly, and by means of His spittle. Therefore it seems that He worked miracles on men unfittingly.

Obj. 3: Further, there is no need to remove at the same time things which do not follow from one another. Now bodily ailments are not always the result of sin, as appears from our Lord's words (John 9:3): "Neither hath this man sinned, nor his parents, that he should be born blind." It was unseemly, therefore, for Him to forgive the sins of those who sought the healing of the body, as He is related to have done in the case of the man sick of the palsy (Matt. 9:2): the more that the healing of the body, being of less account than the forgiveness of sins, does not seem a sufficient argument for the power of forgiving sins.

Obj. 4: Further, Christ's miracles were worked in order to confirm His doctrine, and witness to His Godhead, as stated above (Q. 43, A. 4). Now no man should hinder the purpose of his own work. Therefore it seems unfitting that Christ commanded those who had been healed miraculously to tell no one, as appears from Matt. 9:30 and Mk. 8:26: the more so, since He commanded others to proclaim the miracles worked on them; thus it is related (Mk. 5:19) that, after delivering a man from the demons, He said to him: "Go into thy house to thy friends, and tell them, how great things the Lord hath done for thee."

*On the contrary,* It is written (Mk. 7:37): "He hath done all things well: He hath made both the deaf to hear and the dumb to speak."

*I answer that,* The means should be proportionate to the end. Now Christ came into the world and taught in order to save man, according to John 3:17: "For God sent not His Son into the world to judge the world, but that the world may be saved by Him." Therefore it was fitting that Christ, by miraculously healing men in particular, should prove Himself to be the universal and spiritual Saviour of all.

Reply Obj. 1: The means are distinct from the end. Now the end for which Christ's miracles were worked was the health of the rational part, which is healed by the light of wisdom, and the gift of righteousness: the former of which presupposes the latter, since, as it is written (Wis. 1:4): "Wisdom will not enter into a malicious soul, nor dwell in a body subject to sins." Now it was unfitting that man should be made righteous unless he willed: for this would be both against the nature of righteousness, which implies rectitude of the will, and contrary to the very nature of man, which requires to be led to good by the free-will, not by force. Christ, therefore, justified man inwardly by the Divine power, but not against man's will. Nor did this pertain to His miracles, but to the end of His miracles. In like manner by the Divine power He infused wisdom into the simple minds of His disciples: hence He said to them (Luke 21:15): "I will give you a mouth and wisdom" which "all your adversaries will not be able to resist and gainsay." And this, in so far as the enlightenment was inward, is not to be reckoned as a miracle, but only as regards the outward action--namely, in so far as men saw that those who had been unlettered and simple spoke with such wisdom and constancy. Wherefore it is written (Acts 4:13) that the Jews, "seeing the constancy of Peter and of John, understanding that they were illiterate and ignorant men . . . wondered."--And though such like spiritual effects are different from visible miracles, yet do they testify to Christ's doctrine and power, according to Heb. 2:4: "God also bearing them witness by signs and wonders and divers miracles, and distributions of the Holy Ghost."

Nevertheless Christ did work some miracles on the soul of man, principally by changing its lower powers. Hence Jerome, commenting on Matt. 9:9, "He rose up and followed Him," says: "Such was the splendor and majesty of His hidden Godhead, which shone forth even in His human countenance, that those who gazed on it were drawn to Him at first sight." And on Matt. 21:12, "(Jesus) cast out all them that sold and bought," the same Jerome says: "Of all the signs worked by our Lord, this seems to me the most wondrous--that one man, at that time despised, could, with the blows of one scourge, cast out such a multitude. For a fiery and heavenly light flashed from His eyes, and the majesty of His Godhead shone in His countenance." And Origen says on John 2:15 that "this was a greater miracle than when He changed water into wine, for there He shows His power over inanimate matter, whereas here He tames the minds of thousands of men." Again, on John 18:6, "They went backward and fell to the ground," Augustine says: "Though that crowd was fierce in hate and terrible with arms, yet did that one word . . . without any weapon, smite them through, drive them back, lay them prostrate: for God lay hidden in that flesh." Moreover, to this must be referred what Luke says (4:30) --namely, that Jesus, "passing through the midst of them, went His way," on which Chrysostom observes (Hom. xlviii in Joan.): "That He stood in the midst of those who were lying in wait for Him, and was not seized by them, shows the power of His Godhead"; and, again, that which is written John 8:59, "Jesus hid Himself and went out of the Temple," on which Theophylact says: "He did not hide Himself in a corner of the Temple, as if afraid, or take shelter behind a wall or pillar; but by His heavenly power making Himself invisible to those who were threatening Him, He passed through the midst of them."

From all these instances it is clear that Christ, when He willed, changed the minds of men by His Divine power, not only by the bestowal of righteousness and the infusion of wisdom, which pertains to the end of miracles, but also by outwardly drawing men to Himself, or by terrifying or stupefying them, which pertains to the miraculous itself.

Reply Obj. 2: Christ came to save the world, not only by Divine power, but also through the mystery of His Incarnation. Consequently in healing the sick He frequently not only made use of His Divine power, healing by way of command, but also by applying something pertaining to His human nature. Hence on Luke 4:40, "He, laying His hands on every one of them, healed them," Cyril says: "Although, as God, He might, by one word, have driven out all diseases, yet He touched them, showing that His own flesh was endowed with a healing virtue." And on Mk. 8:23, "Spitting upon his eyes, laying His hands on him," etc., Chrysostom [*Victor of Antioch] says: "He spat and laid His hands upon the blind man, wishing to show that His Divine word, accompanied by His operation, works wonders: for the hand signifies operation; the spittle signifies the word which proceeds from the mouth." Again, on John 9:6, "He made clay of the spittle, and spread the clay upon the eyes of the blind man," Augustine says: "Of His spittle He made clay--because 'the Word was made flesh.'" Or, again, as Chrysostom says, to signify that it was He who made man of "the slime of the earth."

It is furthermore to be observed concerning Christ's miracles that generally what He did was most perfect. Hence on John 2:10, "Every man at first setteth forth good wine," Chrysostom says: "Christ's miracles are such as to far surpass the works of nature in splendor and usefulness." Likewise in an instant He conferred perfect health on the sick. Hence on Matt. 8:15, "She arose and ministered to them," Jerome says: "Health restored by our Lord returns wholly and instantly."

There was, however, special reason for the contrary happening in the case of the man born blind, and this was his want of faith, as Chrysostom [*Victor of Antioch] says. Or as Bede observes on Mk. 8:23: "Whom He might have healed wholly and instantly by a single word, He heals little by little, to show the extent of human blindness, which hardly, and that only by degrees, can come back to the light: and to point out that each step forward in the way of perfection is due to the help of His grace."

Reply Obj. 3: As stated above (Q. 43, A. 2), Christ worked miracles by Divine power. Now "the works of God are perfect" (Deut. 32:4). But nothing is perfect except it attain its end. Now the end of the outward healing worked by Christ is the healing of the soul. Consequently it was not fitting that Christ should heal a man's body without healing his soul. Wherefore on John 7:23, "I have healed the whole man on a Sabbath day," Augustine says: "Because he was cured, so as to be whole in body; he believed, so as to be whole in soul." To the man sick of the palsy it is said specially, "Thy sins are forgiven thee," because, as Jerome observes on Matt. 9:5, 6: "We are hereby given to understand that ailments of the body are frequently due to sin: for which reason, perhaps, first are his sins forgiven, that the cause of the ailment being removed, health may return." Wherefore, also (John 4:14), it is said: "Sin no more, lest some worse thing happen to thee." Whence, says Chrysostom, "we learn that his sickness was the result of sin."

Nevertheless, as Chrysostom says on Matt. 9:5: "By how much a soul is of more account than a body, by so much is the forgiving of sins a greater work than healing the body; but because the one is unseen He does the lesser and more manifest thing in order to prove the greater and more unseen."

Reply Obj. 4: On Matt. 9:30, "See that no man know this," Chrysostom says: "If in another place we find Him saying, 'Go and declare the glory of God' (cf. Mk. 5:19; Luke 8:39), that is not contrary to this. For He instructs us to forbid them that would praise us on our own account: but if the glory be referred to God, then we must not forbid, but command, that it be done."

FOURTH ARTICLE [III, Q. 44, Art. 4]

Whether Christ Worked Miracles Fittingly on Irrational Creatures?

Objection 1: It would seem that Christ worked miracles unfittingly on irrational creatures. For brute animals are more noble than plants. But Christ worked a miracle on plants as when the fig-tree withered away at His command (Matt. 21:19). Therefore Christ should have worked miracles also on brute animals.

Obj. 2: Further, punishment is not justly inflicted save for fault. But it was not the fault of the fig-tree that Christ found no fruit on it, when fruit was not in season (Mk. 11:13). Therefore it seems unfitting that He withered it up.

Obj. 3: Further, air and water are between heaven and earth. But Christ worked some miracles in the heavens, as stated above (A. 2), and likewise in the earth, when it quaked at the time of His Passion (Matt. 27:51). Therefore it seems that He should also have worked miracles in the air and water, such as to divide the sea, as did Moses (Ex. 14:21); or a river, as did Josue (Josh. 3:16) and Elias (4 Kings 2:8); and to cause thunder to be heard in the air, as occurred on Mount Sinai when the Law was given (Ex. 19:16), and like to what Elias did (3 Kings 18:45).

Obj. 4: Further, miraculous works pertain to the work of Divine providence in governing the world. But this work presupposes creation. It seems, therefore, unfitting that in His miracles Christ made use of creation: when, to wit, He multiplied the loaves. Therefore His miracles in regard to irrational creatures seem to have been unfitting.

*On the contrary,* Christ is "the wisdom of God" (1 Cor. 1:24), of whom it is said (Wis. 8:1) that "she ordereth all things sweetly."

*I answer that,* As stated above, Christ's miracles were ordained to the end that He should be recognized as having Divine power, unto the salvation of mankind. Now it belongs to the Divine power that every creature be subject thereto. Consequently it behooved Him to work miracles on every kind of creature, not only on man, but also on irrational creatures.

Reply Obj. 1: Brute animals are akin generically to man, wherefore they were created on the same day as man. And since He had worked many miracles on the bodies of men, there was no need for Him to work miracles on the bodies of brute animals. And so much the less that, as to their sensible and corporeal nature, the same reason applies to both men and animals, especially terrestrial. But fish, from living in water, are more alien from human nature; wherefore they were made on another day. On them Christ worked a miracle in the plentiful draught of fishes, related Luke 5 and John 21; and, again, in the fish caught by Peter, who found a stater in it (Matt. 17:26). As to the swine who were cast headlong into the sea, this was not the effect of a Divine miracle, but of the action of the demons, God permitting.

Reply Obj. 2: As Chrysostom says on Matt. 21:19: "When our Lord does any such like thing" on plants or brute animals, "ask not how it was just to wither up the fig-tree, since it was not the fruit season; to ask such a question is foolish in the extreme," because such things cannot commit a fault or be punished: "but look at the miracle, and wonder at the worker." Nor does the Creator "inflict" any hurt on the owner, if He choose to make use of His own creature for the salvation of others; rather, as Hilary says on Matt. 21:19, "we should see in this a proof of God's goodness, for when He wished to afford an example of salvation as being procured by Him, He exercised His mighty power on the human body: but when He wished to picture to them His severity towards those who wilfully disobey Him, He foreshadows their doom by His sentence on the tree." This is the more noteworthy in a fig-tree which, as Chrysostom observes (on Matt. 21:19), "being full of moisture, makes the miracle all the more remarkable."

Reply Obj. 3: Christ also worked miracles befitting to Himself in the air and water: when, to wit, as related Matt. 8:26, "He commanded the winds, and the sea, and there came a great calm." But it was not befitting that He who came to restore all things to a state of peace and calm should cause either a disturbance in the atmosphere or a division of waters. Hence the Apostle says (Heb. 12:18): "You are not come to a fire that may be touched and approached [Vulg.: 'a mountain that might be touched, and a burning fire'], and a whirlwind, and darkness, and storm."

At the time of His Passion, however, the "veil was rent," to signify the unfolding of the mysteries of the Law; "the graves were opened," to signify that His death gave life to the dead; "the earth quaked and the rocks were rent," to signify that man's stony heart would be softened, and the whole world changed for the better by the virtue of His Passion.

Reply Obj. 4: The multiplication of the loaves was not effected by way of creation, but by an addition of extraneous matter transformed into loaves; hence Augustine says on John 6:1-14: "Whence He multiplieth a few grains into harvests, thence in His hands He multiplied the five loaves": and it is clearly by a process of transformation that grains are multiplied into harvests.

# QUESTION 45

OF CHRIST'S TRANSFIGURATION (In Four Articles)

We now consider Christ's transfiguration; and here there are four points of inquiry:

(1) Whether it was fitting that Christ should be transfigured?

(2) Whether the clarity of the transfiguration was the clarity of glory?

(3) Of the witnesses of the transfiguration;

(4) Of the testimony of the Father's voice.

FIRST ARTICLE [III, Q. 45, Art. 1]

Whether It Was Fitting That Christ Should Be Transfigured?

Objection 1: It would seem that it was not fitting that Christ should be transfigured. For it is not fitting for a true body to be changed into various shapes ( figuras ), but only for an imaginary body. Now Christ's body was not imaginary, but real, as stated above (Q. 5, A. 1). Therefore it seems that it should not have been transfigured.

Obj. 2: Further, figure is in the fourth species of quality, whereas clarity is in the third, since it is a sensible quality. Therefore Christ's assuming clarity should not be called a transfiguration.

Obj. 3: Further, a glorified body has four gifts, as we shall state farther on (Suppl., Q. 82), viz. impassibility, agility, subtlety, and clarity. Therefore His transfiguration should not have consisted in an assumption of clarity rather than of the other gifts.

*On the contrary,* It is written (Matt. 17:2) that Jesus "was transfigured" in the presence of three of His disciples.

*I answer that,* Our Lord, after foretelling His Passion to His disciples, had exhorted them to follow the path of His sufferings (Matt. 16:21, 24). Now in order that anyone go straight along a road, he must have some knowledge of the end: thus an archer will not shoot the arrow straight unless he first see the target. Hence Thomas said (John 14:5): "Lord, we know not whither Thou goest; and how can we know the way?" Above all is this necessary when hard and rough is the road, heavy the going, but delightful the end. Now by His Passion Christ achieved glory, not only of His soul, not only of His soul, which He had from the first moment of His conception, but also of His body; according to Luke (24:26): "Christ ought [Vulg.: 'ought not Christ'] to have suffered these things, and so to enter into His glory (?)." To which glory He brings those who follow the footsteps of His Passion, according to Acts 14:21: "Through many tribulations we must enter into the kingdom of God." Therefore it was fitting that He should show His disciples the glory of His clarity (which is to be transfigured), to which He will configure those who are His; according to Phil. 3:21: "(Who) will reform the body of our lowness configured [Douay: 'made like'] to the body of His glory." Hence Bede says on Mk. 8:39: "By His loving foresight He allowed them to taste for a short time the contemplation of eternal joy, so that they might bear persecution bravely."

Reply Obj. 1: As Jerome says on Matt. 17:2: "Let no one suppose that Christ," through being said to be transfigured, "laid aside His natural shape and countenance, or substituted an imaginary or aerial body for His real body. The Evangelist describes the manner of His transfiguration when he says: 'His face did shine as the sun, and His garments became white as snow.' Brightness of face and whiteness of garments argue not a change of substance, but a putting on of glory."

Reply Obj. 2: Figure is seen in the outline of a body, for it is "that which is enclosed by one or more boundaries" [*Euclid, bk i, def. xiv]. Therefore whatever has to do with the outline of a body seems to pertain to the figure. Now the clarity, just as the color, of a non-transparent body is seen on its surface, and consequently the assumption of clarity is called transfiguration.

Reply Obj. 3: Of those four gifts, clarity alone is a quality of the very person in himself; whereas the other three are not perceptible, save in some action or movement, or in some passion. Christ, then, did show in Himself certain indications of those three gifts--of agility, for instance, when He walked on the waves of the sea; of subtlety, when He came forth from the closed womb of the Virgin; of impassibility, when He escaped unhurt from the hands of the Jews who wished to hurl Him down or to stone Him. And yet He is not said, on account of this, to be transfigured, but only on account of clarity, which pertains to the aspect of His Person.

SECOND ARTICLE [III, Q. 45, Art. 2]

Whether This Clarity Was the Clarity of Glory?

Objection 1: It would seem that this clarity was not the clarity of glory. For a gloss of Bede on Matt. 17:2, "He was transfigured before them," says: "In His mortal body He shows forth, not the state of immortality, but clarity like to that of future immortality." But the clarity of glory is the clarity of immortality. Therefore the clarity which Christ showed to His disciples was not the clarity of glory.

Obj. 2: Further, on Luke 9:27 "(That) shall not taste death unless [Vulg.: 'till'] they see the kingdom of God," Bede's gloss says: "That is, the glorification of the body in an imaginary vision of future beatitude." But the image of a thing is not the thing itself. Therefore this was not the clarity of beatitude.

Obj. 3: Further, the clarity of glory is only in a human body. But this clarity of the transfiguration was seen not only in Christ's body, but also in His garments, and in "the bright cloud" which "overshaded" the disciples. Therefore it seems that this was not the clarity of glory.

*On the contrary,* Jerome says on the words "He was transfigured before them" (Matt. 17:2): "He appeared to the Apostles such as He will appear on the day of judgment." And on Matt. 16:28, "Till they see the Son of Man coming in His kingdom," Chrysostom says: "Wishing to show with what kind of glory He is afterwards to come, so far as it was possible for them to learn it, He showed it to them in their present life, that they might not grieve even over the death of their Lord."

*I answer that,* The clarity which Christ assumed in His transfiguration was the clarity of glory as to its essence, but not as to its mode of being. For the clarity of the glorified body is derived from that of the soul, as Augustine says (Ep. ad Diosc. cxviii). And in like manner the clarity of Christ's body in His transfiguration was derived from His Godhead, as Damascene says (Orat. de Transfig.) and from the glory of His soul. That the glory of His soul did not overflow into His body from the first moment of Christ's conception was due to a certain Divine dispensation, that, as stated above (Q. 14, A. 1, ad 2), He might fulfil the mysteries of our redemption in a passible body. This did not, however, deprive Christ of His power of outpouring the glory of His soul into His body. And this He did, as to clarity, in His transfiguration, but otherwise than in a glorified body. For the clarity of the soul overflows into a glorified body, by way of a permanent quality affecting the body. Hence bodily refulgence is not miraculous in a glorified body. But in Christ's transfiguration clarity overflowed from His Godhead and from His soul into His body, not as an immanent quality affecting His very body, but rather after the manner of a transient passion, as when the air is lit up by the sun. Consequently the refulgence, which appeared in Christ's body then, was miraculous: just as was the fact of His walking on the waves of the sea. Hence Dionysius says (Ep. ad Cai. iv): "Christ excelled man in doing that which is proper to man: this is shown in His supernatural conception of a virgin and in the unstable waters bearing the weight of material and earthly feet."

Wherefore we must not say, as Hugh of St. Victor [*Innocent III, De Myst. Miss. iv] said, that Christ assumed the gift of clarity in the transfiguration, of agility in walking on the sea, and of subtlety in coming forth from the Virgin's closed womb: because the gifts are immanent qualities of a glorified body. *On the contrary,* whatever pertained to the gifts, that He had miraculously. The same is to be said, as to the soul, of the vision in which Paul saw God in a rapture, as we have stated in the Second Part (II-II, Q. 175, A. 3, ad 2).

Reply Obj. 1: The words quoted prove, not that the clarity of Christ was not that of glory, but that it was not the clarity of a glorified body, since Christ's body was not as yet immortal. And just as it was by dispensation that in Christ the glory of the soul should not overflow into the body so was it possible that by dispensation it might overflow as to the gift of clarity and not as to that of impassibility.

Reply Obj. 2: This clarity is said to have been imaginary, not as though it were not really the clarity of glory, but because it was a kind of image representing that perfection of glory, in virtue of which the body will be glorious.

Reply Obj. 3: Just as the clarity which was in Christ's body was a representation of His body's future clarity, so the clarity which was in His garments signified the future clarity of the saints, which will be surpassed by that of Christ, just as the brightness of the snow is surpassed by that of the sun. Hence Gregory says (Moral. xxxii) that Christ's garments became resplendent, "because in the height of heavenly clarity all the saints will cling to Him in the refulgence of righteousness. For His garments signify the righteous, because He will unite them to Himself," according to Isa. 49:18: "Thou shalt be clothed with all these as with an ornament."

The bright cloud signifies the glory of the Holy Ghost or the "power of the Father," as Origen says (Tract. iii in Matth.), by which in the glory to come the saints will be covered. Or, again, it may be said fittingly that it signifies the clarity of the world redeemed, which clarity will cover the saints as a tent. Hence when Peter proposed to make tents, "a bright cloud overshaded" the disciples.

THIRD ARTICLE [III, Q. 45, Art. 3]

Whether the Witnesses of the Transfiguration Were Fittingly Chosen?

Objection 1: It would seem that the witnesses of the transfiguration were unfittingly chosen. For everyone is a better witness of things that he knows. But at the time of Christ's transfiguration no one but the angels had as yet any knowledge from experience of the glory to come. Therefore the witnesses of the transfiguration should have been angels rather than men.

Obj. 2: Further, truth, not fiction, is becoming in a witness of the truth. Now, Moses and Elias were there, not really, but only in appearance; for a gloss on Luke 9:30, "They were Moses and Elias," says: "It must be observed that Moses and Elias were there neither in body nor in soul"; but that those bodies were formed "of some available matter. It is also credible that this was the result of the angelic ministries, through the angels impersonating them." Therefore it seems that they were unsuitable witnesses.

Obj. 3: Further, it is said (Acts 10:43) that "all the prophets give testimony" to Christ. Therefore not only Moses and Elias, but also all the prophets, should have been present as witnesses.

Obj. 4: Further, Christ's glory is promised as a reward to all the faithful (2 Cor. 3:18; Phil. 3:21), in whom He wished by His transfiguration to enkindle a desire of that glory. Therefore He should have taken not only Peter, James, and John, but all His disciples, to be witnesses of His transfiguration.

On the contrary is the authority of the Gospel.

*I answer that,* Christ wished to be transfigured in order to show men His glory, and to arouse men to a desire of it, as stated above (A. 1). Now men are brought to the glory of eternal beatitude by Christ--not only those who lived after Him, but also those who preceded Him; therefore, when He was approaching His Passion, both "the multitude that followed" and that "which went before, cried saying: 'Hosanna,'" as related Matt. 21:9, beseeching Him, as it were, to save them. Consequently it was fitting that witnesses should be present from among those who preceded Him--namely, Moses and Elias--and from those who followed after Him--namely, Peter, James, and John--that "in the mouth of two or three witnesses" this word might stand.

Reply Obj. 1: By His transfiguration Christ manifested to His disciples the glory of His body, which belongs to men only. It was therefore fitting that He should choose men and not angels as witnesses.

Reply Obj. 2: This gloss is said to be taken from a book entitled On the Marvels of Holy Scripture. It is not an authentic work, but is wrongly ascribed to St. Augustine; consequently we need not stand by it. For Jerome says on Matt. 17:3: "Observe that when the Scribes and Pharisees asked for a sign from heaven, He refused to give one; whereas here in order to increase the apostles' faith, He gives a sign from heaven, Elias coming down thence, whither he had ascended, and Moses arising from the nether world." This is not to be understood as though the soul of Moses was reunited to his body, but that his soul appeared through some assumed body, just as the angels do. But Elias appeared in his own body, not that he was brought down from the empyrean heaven, but from some place on high whither he was taken up in the fiery chariot.

Reply Obj. 3: As Chrysostom says on Matt. 17:3: "Moses and Elias are brought forward for many reasons." And, first of all, "because the multitude said He was Elias or Jeremias or one of the prophets, He brings the leaders of the prophets with Him; that hereby at least they might see the difference between the servants and their Lord." Another reason was " . . . that Moses gave the Law . . . while Elias . . . was jealous for the glory of God." Therefore by appearing together with Christ, they show how falsely the Jews "accused Him of transgressing the Law, and of blasphemously appropriating to Himself the glory of God." A third reason was "to show that He has power of death and life, and that He is the judge of the dead and the living; by bringing with Him Moses who had died, and Elias who still lived." A fourth reason was because, as Luke says (9:31), "they spoke" with Him "of His decease that He should accomplish in Jerusalem," i.e. of His Passion and death. Therefore, "in order to strengthen the hearts of His disciples with a view to this," He sets before them those who had exposed themselves to death for God's sake: since Moses braved death in opposing Pharaoh, and Elias in opposing Achab. A fifth reason was that "He wished His disciples to imitate the meekness of Moses and the zeal of Elias." Hilary adds a sixth reason--namely, in order to signify that He had been foretold by the Law, which Moses gave them, and by the prophets, of whom Elias was the principal.

Reply Obj. 4: Lofty mysteries should not be immediately explained to everyone, but should be handed down through superiors to others in their proper turn. Consequently, as Chrysostom says (on Matt. 17:3), "He took these three as being superior to the rest." For "Peter excelled in the love" he bore to Christ and in the power bestowed on him; John in the privilege of Christ's love for him on account of his virginity, and, again, on account of his being privileged to be an Evangelist; James on account of the privilege of martyrdom. Nevertheless He did not wish them to tell others what they had seen before His Resurrection; "lest," as Jerome says on Matt. 17:19, "such a wonderful thing should seem incredible to them; and lest, after hearing of so great glory, they should be scandalized at the Cross" that followed; or, again, "lest [the Cross] should be entirely hindered by the people" [*Bede, Hom. xviii; cf. Catena Aurea]; and "in order that they might then be witnesses of spiritual things when they should be filled with the Holy Ghost" [*Hilary, in Matth. xvii].

FOURTH ARTICLE [III, Q. 45, Art. 4]

Whether the Testimony of the Father's Voice, Saying, "This Is My Beloved Son," Was Fittingly Added?

Objection 1: It would seem that the testimony of the Father's voice, saying, "This is My beloved Son," was not fittingly added; for, as it is written (Job 33:14), "God speaketh once, and repeateth not the selfsame thing the second time." But the Father's voice had testified to this at the time of (Christ's) baptism. Therefore it was not fitting that He should bear witness to it a second time.

Obj. 2: Further, at the baptism the Holy Ghost appeared under the form of a dove at the same time as the Father's voice was heard. But this did not happen at the transfiguration. Therefore it seems that the testimony of the Father was made in an unfitting manner.

Obj. 3: Further, Christ began to teach after His baptism. Nevertheless, the Father's voice did not then command men to hear him. Therefore neither should it have so commanded at the transfiguration.

Obj. 4: Further, things should not be said to those who cannot bear them, according to John 16:12: "I have yet many things to say to you, but you cannot bear them now." But the disciples could not bear the Father's voice; for it is written (Matt. 17:6) that "the disciples hearing, fell upon their face, and were very much afraid." Therefore the Father's voice should not have been addressed to them.

On the contrary is the authority of the Gospel.

*I answer that,* The adoption of the sons of God is through a certain conformity of image to the natural Son of God. Now this takes place in two ways: first, by the grace of the wayfarer, which is imperfect conformity; secondly, by glory, which is perfect conformity, according to 1 John 3:2: "We are now the sons of God, and it hath not yet appeared what we shall be: we know that, when He shall appear, we shall be like to Him, because we shall see Him as He is." Since, therefore, it is in baptism that we acquire grace, while the clarity of the glory to come was foreshadowed in the transfiguration, therefore both in His baptism and in His transfiguration the natural sonship of Christ was fittingly made known by the testimony of the Father: because He alone with the Son and Holy Ghost is perfectly conscious of that perfect generation.

Reply Obj. 1: The words quoted are to be understood of God's eternal speaking, by which God the Father uttered the only-begotten and co-eternal Word. Nevertheless, it can be said that God uttered the same thing twice in a bodily voice, yet not for the same purpose, but in order to show the divers modes in which men can be partakers of the likeness of the eternal Sonship.

Reply Obj. 2: Just as in the Baptism, where the mystery of the first regeneration was proclaimed, the operation of the whole Trinity was made manifest, because the Son Incarnate was there, the Holy Ghost appeared under the form of a dove, and the Father made Himself known in the voice; so also in the transfiguration, which is the mystery of the second regeneration, the whole Trinity appears--the Father in the voice, the Son in the man, the Holy Ghost in the bright cloud; for just as in baptism He confers innocence, signified by the simplicity of the dove, so in the resurrection will He give His elect the clarity of glory and refreshment from all sorts of evil, which are signified by the bright cloud.

Reply Obj. 3: Christ came to give grace actually, and to promise glory by His words. Therefore it was fitting at the time of His transfiguration, and not at the time of His baptism, that men should be commanded to hear Him.

Reply Obj. 4: It was fitting that the disciples should be afraid and fall down on hearing the voice of the Father, to show that the glory which was then being revealed surpasses in excellence the sense and faculty of all mortal beings; according to Ex. 33:20: "Man shall not see Me and live." This is what Jerome says on Matt. 17:6: "Such is human frailty that it cannot bear to gaze on such great glory." But men are healed of this frailty by Christ when He brings them into glory. And this is signified by what He says to them: "Arise, and fear not."

# QUESTION 46

THE PASSION OF CHRIST (In Twelve Articles)

In proper sequence we have now to consider all that relates to Christ's leaving the world. In the first place, His Passion; secondly, His death; thirdly, His burial; and, fourthly, His descent into hell.

With regard to the Passion, there arises a threefold consideration: (1) The Passion itself; (2) the efficient cause of the Passion; (3) the fruits of the Passion.

Under the first heading there are twelve points of inquiry:

(1) Whether it was necessary for Christ to suffer for men's deliverance?

(2) Whether there was any other possible means of delivering men?

(3) Whether this was the more suitable means?

(4) Whether it was fitting for Christ to suffer on the cross?

(5) The extent of His sufferings;

(6) Whether the pain which He endured was the greatest?

(7) Whether His entire soul suffered?

(8) Whether His Passion hindered the joy of fruition?

(9) The time of the Passion;

(10) The place;

(11) Whether it was fitting for Him to be crucified with robbers?

(12) Whether Christ's Passion is to be attributed to the Godhead?

FIRST ARTICLE [III, Q. 46, Art. 1]

Whether It Was Necessary for Christ to Suffer for the Deliverance of the Human Race?

Objection 1: It would seem that it was not necessary for Christ to suffer for the deliverance of the human race. For the human race could not be delivered except by God, according to Isa. 45:21: "Am not I the Lord, and there is no God else besides Me? A just God and a Saviour, there is none besides Me." But no necessity can compel God, for this would be repugnant to His omnipotence. Therefore it was not necessary for Christ to suffer.

Obj. 2: Further, what is necessary is opposed to what is voluntary. But Christ suffered of His own will; for it is written (Isa. 53:7): "He was offered because it was His own will." Therefore it was not necessary for Him to suffer.

Obj. 3: Further, as is written (Ps. 24:10): "All the ways of the Lord are mercy and truth." But it does not seem necessary that He should suffer on the part of the Divine mercy, which, as it bestows gifts freely, so it appears to condone debts without satisfaction: nor, again, on the part of Divine justice, according to which man had deserved everlasting condemnation. Therefore it does not seem necessary that Christ should have suffered for man's deliverance.

Obj. 4: Further, the angelic nature is more excellent than the human, as appears from Dionysius (Div. Nom. iv). But Christ did not suffer to repair the angelic nature which had sinned. Therefore, apparently, neither was it necessary for Him to suffer for the salvation of the human race.

*On the contrary,* It is written (John 3:14): "As Moses lifted up the serpent in the desert, so must the Son of man be lifted up, that whosoever believeth in Him may not perish, but may have life everlasting."

*I answer that,* As the Philosopher teaches (Metaph. v), there are several acceptations of the word "necessary." In one way it means anything which of its nature cannot be otherwise; and in this way it is evident that it was not necessary either on the part of God or on the part of man for Christ to suffer. In another sense a thing may be necessary from some cause quite apart from itself; and should this be either an efficient or a moving cause then it brings about the necessity of compulsion; as, for instance, when a man cannot get away owing to the violence of someone else holding him. But if the external factor which induces necessity be an end, then it will be said to be necessary from presupposing such end--namely, when some particular end cannot exist at all, or not conveniently, except such end be presupposed. It was not necessary, then, for Christ to suffer from necessity of compulsion, either on God's part, who ruled that Christ should suffer, or on Christ's own part, who suffered voluntarily. Yet it was necessary from necessity of the end proposed; and this can be accepted in three ways. First of all, on our part, who have been delivered by His Passion, according to John (3:14): "The Son of man must be lifted up, that whosoever believeth in Him may not perish, but may have life everlasting." Secondly, on Christ's part, who merited the glory of being exalted, through the lowliness of His Passion: and to this must be referred Luke 24:26: "Ought not Christ to have suffered these things, and so to enter into His glory?" Thirdly, on God's part, whose determination regarding the Passion of Christ, foretold in the Scriptures and prefigured in the observances of the Old Testament, had to be fulfilled. And this is what St. Luke says (22:22): "The Son of man indeed goeth, according to that which is determined"; and (Luke 24:44, 46): "These are the words which I spoke to you while I was yet with you, that all things must needs be fulfilled which are written in the law of Moses, and in the prophets, and in the psalms concerning Me: for it is thus written, and thus it behooved Christ to suffer, and to rise again from the dead."

Reply Obj. 1: This argument is based on the necessity of compulsion on God's part.

Reply Obj. 2: This argument rests on the necessity of compulsion on the part of the man Christ.

Reply Obj. 3: That man should be delivered by Christ's Passion was in keeping with both His mercy and His justice. With His justice, because by His Passion Christ made satisfaction for the sin of the human race; and so man was set free by Christ's justice: and with His mercy, for since man of himself could not satisfy for the sin of all human nature, as was said above (Q. 1, A. 2), God gave him His Son to satisfy for him, according to Rom. 3:24, 25: "Being justified freely by His grace, through the redemption that is in Christ Jesus, whom God hath proposed to be a propitiation, through faith in His blood." And this came of more copious mercy than if He had forgiven sins without satisfaction. Hence it is said (Eph. 2:4): "God, who is rich in mercy, for His exceeding charity wherewith He loved us, even when we were dead in sins, hath quickened us together in Christ."

Reply Obj. 4: The sin of the angels was irreparable; not so the sin of the first man (I, Q. 64, A. 2).

SECOND ARTICLE [III, Q. 46, Art. 2]

Whether There Was Any Other Possible Way of Human Deliverance Besides the Passion of Christ?

Objection 1: It would seem that there was no other possible way of human deliverance besides Christ's Passion. For our Lord says (John 12:24):

"Amen, amen I say to you, unless the grain of wheat falling into the ground dieth, itself remaineth alone; but if it die, it bringeth forth much fruit." Upon this St. Augustine (Tract. li) observes that "Christ called Himself the seed." Consequently, unless He suffered death, He would not otherwise have produced the fruit of our redemption.

Obj. 2: Further, our Lord addresses the Father (Matt. 26:42): "My Father, if this chalice may not pass away but I must drink it, Thy will be done." But He spoke there of the chalice of the Passion. Therefore Christ's Passion could not pass away; hence Hilary says (Comm. 31 in Matth.): "Therefore the chalice cannot pass except He drink of it, because we cannot be restored except through His Passion."

Obj. 3: Further, God's justice required that Christ should satisfy by the Passion in order that man might be delivered from sin. But Christ cannot let His justice pass; for it is written (2 Tim. 2:13): "If we believe not, He continueth faithful, He cannot deny Himself." But He would deny Himself were He to deny His justice, since He is justice itself. It seems impossible, then, for man to be delivered otherwise than by Christ's Passion.

Obj. 4: Further, there can be no falsehood underlying faith. But the Fathers of old believed that Christ would suffer. Consequently, it seems that it had to be that Christ should suffer.

*On the contrary,* Augustine says (De Trin. xiii): "We assert that the way whereby God deigned to deliver us by the man Jesus Christ, who is mediator between God and man, is both good and befitting the Divine dignity; but let us also show that other possible means were not lacking on God's part, to whose power all things are equally subordinate."

*I answer that,* A thing may be said to be possible or impossible in two ways: first of all, simply and absolutely; or secondly, from supposition. Therefore, speaking simply and absolutely, it was possible for God to deliver mankind otherwise than by the Passion of Christ, because "no word shall be impossible with God" (Luke 1:37). Yet it was impossible if some supposition be made. For since it is impossible for God's foreknowledge to be deceived and His will or ordinance to be frustrated, then, supposing God's foreknowledge and ordinance regarding Christ's Passion, it was not possible at the same time for Christ not to suffer, and for mankind to be delivered otherwise than by Christ's Passion. And the same holds good of all things foreknown and preordained by God, as was laid down in the First Part (Q. 14, A. 13).

Reply Obj. 1: Our Lord is speaking there presupposing God's foreknowledge and predetermination, according to which it was resolved that the fruit of man's salvation should not follow unless Christ suffered.

Reply Obj. 2: In the same way we must understand what is here objected to in the second instance: "If this chalice may not pass away but I must drink of it"--that is to say, because Thou hast so ordained it--hence He adds: "Thy will be done."

Reply Obj. 3: Even this justice depends on the Divine will, requiring satisfaction for sin from the human race. But if He had willed to free man from sin without any satisfaction, He would not have acted against justice. For a judge, while preserving justice, cannot pardon fault without penalty, if he must visit fault committed against another--for instance, against another man, or against the State, or any Prince in higher authority. But God has no one higher than Himself, for He is the sovereign and common good of the whole universe. Consequently, if He forgive sin, which has the formality of fault in that it is committed against Himself, He wrongs no one: just as anyone else, overlooking a personal trespass, without satisfaction, acts mercifully and not unjustly. And so David exclaimed when he sought mercy: "To Thee only have I sinned" (Ps. 50:6), as if to say: "Thou canst pardon me without injustice."

Reply Obj. 4: Human faith, and even the Divine Scriptures upon which faith is based, are both based on the Divine foreknowledge and ordinance. And the same reason holds good of that necessity which comes of supposition, and of the necessity which arises of the Divine foreknowledge and will.

THIRD ARTICLE [III, Q. 46, Art. 3]

Whether There Was Any More Suitable Way of Delivering the Human Race Than by Christ's Passion?

Objection 1: It would seem that there was some other more suitable way of delivering the human race besides Christ's Passion. For nature in its operation imitates the Divine work, since it is moved and regulated by God. But nature never employs two agents where one will suffice. Therefore, since God could have liberated mankind solely by His Divine will, it does not seem fitting that Christ's Passion should have been added for the deliverance of the human race.

Obj. 2: Further, natural actions are more suitably performed than deeds of violence, because violence is "a severance or lapse from what is according to nature," as is said in De Coelo ii. But Christ's Passion brought about His death by violence. Therefore it would have been more appropriate had Christ died a natural death rather than suffer for man's deliverance.

Obj. 3: Further, it seems most fitting that whatsoever keeps something unjustly and by violence, should be deprived of it by some superior power; hence Isaias says (52:3): "You were sold gratis, and you shall be redeemed without money." But the devil possessed no right over man, whom he had deceived by guile, and whom he held subject in servitude by a sort of violence. Therefore it seems most suitable that Christ should have despoiled the devil solely by His power and without the Passion.

*On the contrary,* St. Augustine says (De Trin. xiii): "There was no other more suitable way of healing our misery" than by the Passion of Christ.

*I answer that,* Among means to an end that one is the more suitable whereby the various concurring means employed are themselves helpful to such end. But in this that man was delivered by Christ's Passion, many other things besides deliverance from sin concurred for man's salvation. In the first place, man knows thereby how much God loves him, and is thereby stirred to love Him in return, and herein lies the perfection of human salvation; hence the Apostle says (Rom. 5:8): "God commendeth His charity towards us; for when as yet we were sinners . . . Christ died for us." Secondly, because thereby He set us an example of obedience, humility, constancy, justice, and the other virtues displayed in the Passion, which are requisite for man's salvation. Hence it is written (1 Pet. 2:21): "Christ also suffered for us, leaving you an example that you should follow in His steps." Thirdly, because Christ by His Passion not only delivered man from sin, but also merited justifying grace for him and the glory of bliss, as shall be shown later (Q. 48, A. 1; Q. 49, AA. 1, 5). Fourthly, because by this man is all the more bound to refrain from sin, according to 1 Cor. 6:20: "You are bought with a great price: glorify and bear God in your body." Fifthly, because it redounded to man's greater dignity, that as man was overcome and deceived by the devil, so also it should be a man that should overthrow the devil; and as man deserved death, so a man by dying should vanquish death. Hence it is written (1 Cor. 15:57): "Thanks be to God who hath given us the victory through our Lord Jesus Christ." It was accordingly more fitting that we should be delivered by Christ's Passion than simply by God's good-will.

Reply Obj. 1: Even nature uses several means to one intent, in order to do something more fittingly: as two eyes for seeing; and the same can be observed in other matters.

Reply Obj. 2: As Chrysostom [*Athanasius, Orat. De Incarn. Verb.] says: "Christ had come in order to destroy death, not His own, (for since He is life itself, death could not be His), but men's death. Hence it was not by reason of His being bound to die that He laid His body aside, but because the death He endured was inflicted on Him by men. But even if His body had sickened and dissolved in the sight of all men, it was not befitting Him who healed the infirmities of others to have his own body afflicted with the same. And even had He laid His body aside without any sickness, and had then appeared, men would not have believed Him when He spoke of His resurrection. For how could Christ's victory over death appear, unless He endured it in the sight of all men, and so proved that death was vanquished by the incorruption of His body?"

Reply Obj. 3: Although the devil assailed man unjustly, nevertheless, on account of sin, man was justly left by God under the devil's bondage. And therefore it was fitting that through justice man should be delivered from the devil's bondage by Christ making satisfaction on his behalf in the Passion. This was also a fitting means of overthrowing the pride of the devil, "who is a deserter from justice, and covetous of sway"; in that Christ "should vanquish him and deliver man, not merely by the power of His Godhead, but likewise by the justice and lowliness of the Passion," as Augustine says (De Trin. xiii).

FOURTH ARTICLE [III, Q. 46, Art. 4]

Whether Christ Ought to Have Suffered on the Cross?

Objection 1: It would seem that Christ ought not to have suffered on the cross. For the truth ought to conform to the figure. But in all the sacrifices of the Old Testament which prefigured Christ the beasts were slain with a sword and afterwards consumed by fire. Therefore it seems that Christ ought not to have suffered on a cross, but rather by the sword or by fire.

Obj. 2: Further, Damascene says (De Fide Orth. iii) that Christ ought not to assume "dishonoring afflictions." But death on a cross was most dishonoring and ignominious; hence it is written (Wis. 2:20): "Let us condemn Him to a most shameful death." Therefore it seems that Christ ought not to have undergone the death of the cross.

Obj. 3: Further, it was said of Christ (Matt. 21:9): "Blessed is He that cometh in the name of the Lord." But death upon the cross was a death of malediction, as we read Deut. 21:23: "He is accursed of God that hangeth on a tree." Therefore it does not seem fitting for Christ to be crucified.

*On the contrary,* It is written (Phil. 2:8): "He became obedient unto death, even the death of the cross."

*I answer that,* It was most fitting that Christ should suffer the death of the cross.

First of all, as an example of virtue. For Augustine thus writes (QQ. lxxxiii, qu. 25): "God's Wisdom became man to give us an example in righteousness of living. But it is part of righteous living not to stand in fear of things which ought not to be feared. Now there are some men who, although they do not fear death in itself, are yet troubled over the manner of their death. In order, then, that no kind of death should trouble an upright man, the cross of this Man had to be set before him, because, among all kinds of death, none was more execrable, more fear-inspiring, than this."

Secondly, because this kind of death was especially suitable in order to atone for the sin of our first parent, which was the plucking of the apple from the forbidden tree against God's command. And so, to atone for that sin, it was fitting that Christ should suffer by being fastened to a tree, as if restoring what Adam had purloined; according to Ps. 68:5: "Then did I pay that which I took not away." Hence Augustine says in a sermon on the

Passion [*Cf. Serm. ci De Tempore]: "Adam despised the command, plucking the apple from the tree: but all that Adam lost, Christ found upon the cross."

The third reason is because, as Chrysostom says in a sermon on the Passion (De Cruce et Latrone i, ii): "He suffered upon a high rood and not under a roof, in order that the nature of the air might be purified: and the earth felt a like benefit, for it was cleansed by the flowing of the blood from His side." And on John 3:14: "The Son of man must be lifted up," Theophylact says: "When you hear that He was lifted up, understand His hanging on high, that He might sanctify the air who had sanctified the earth by walking upon it."

The fourth reason is, because, by dying on it, He prepares for us an ascent into heaven, as Chrysostom [*Athanasius, vide A, III, ad 2] says. Hence it is that He says (John 12:32): "If I be lifted up from the earth, I will draw all things to Myself."

The fifth reason is because it is befitting the universal salvation of the entire world. Hence Gregory of Nyssa observes (In Christ. Resurr., Orat. i) that "the shape of the cross extending out into four extremes from their central point of contact denotes the power and the providence diffused everywhere of Him who hung upon it." Chrysostom [*Athanasius, vide A. III, ad 2] also says that upon the cross "He dies with outstretched hands in order to draw with one hand the people of old, and with the other those who spring from the Gentiles."

The sixth reason is because of the various virtues denoted by this class of death. Hence Augustine in his book on the grace of the Old and New Testament (Ep. cxl) says: "Not without purpose did He choose this class of death, that He might be a teacher of that breadth, and height, and length, and depth," of which the Apostle speaks (Eph. 3:18): "For breadth is in the beam, which is fixed transversely above; this appertains to good works, since the hands are stretched out upon it. Length is the tree's extent from the beam to the ground; and there it is planted--that is, it stands and abides--which is the note of longanimity. Height is in that portion of the tree which remains over from the transverse beam upwards to the top, and this is at the head of the Crucified, because He is the supreme desire of souls of good hope. But that part of the tree which is hidden from view to hold it fixed, and from which the entire rood springs, denotes the depth of gratuitous grace." And, as Augustine says (Tract. cxix in Joan.): "The tree upon which were fixed the members of Him dying was even the chair of the Master teaching."

The seventh reason is because this kind of death responds to very many figures. For, as Augustine says in a sermon on the Passion (Serm. ci De Tempore), an ark of wood preserved the human race from the waters of the Deluge; at the exodus of God's people from Egypt, Moses with a rod divided the sea, overthrew Pharaoh and saved the people of God. the same Moses dipped his rod into the water, changing it from bitter to sweet; at the touch of a wooden rod a salutary spring gushed forth from a spiritual rock; likewise, in order to overcome Amalec, Moses stretched forth his arms with rod in hand; lastly, God's law is entrusted to the wooden Ark of the Covenant; all of which are like steps by which we mount to the wood of the cross.

Reply Obj. 1: The altar of holocausts, upon which the sacrifices of animals were immolated, was constructed of timbers, as is set forth Ex. 27; and in this respect the truth answers to the figure; but "it is not necessary for it to be likened in every respect, otherwise it would not be a likeness," but the reality, as Damascene says (De Fide Orth. iii). But, in particular, as Chrysostom [*Athanasius, vide A, III, ad 2] says: "His head is not cut off, as was done to John; nor was He sawn in twain, like Isaias, in order that His entire and indivisible body might obey death, and that there might be no excuse for them who want to divide the Church." While, instead of material fire, there was the spiritual fire of charity in Christ's holocaust.

Reply Obj. 2: Christ refused to undergo dishonorable sufferings which are allied with defects of knowledge, or of grace, or even of virtue, but not those injuries inflicted from without--nay, more, as is written Heb. 12:2: "He endured the cross, despising the shame."

Reply Obj. 3: As Augustine says (Contra Faust. xiv), sin is accursed, and, consequently, so is death, and mortality, which comes of sin. "But Christ's flesh was mortal, 'having the resemblance of the flesh of sin'"; and hence Moses calls it "accursed," just as the Apostle calls it "sin," saying (2 Cor. 5:21): "Him that knew no sin, for us He hath made sin"--namely, because of the penalty of sin. "Nor is there greater ignominy on that account, because he said: 'He is accursed of God.'" For, "unless God had hated sin, He would never have sent His Son to take upon Himself our death, and to destroy it. Acknowledge, then, that it was for us He took the curse upon Himself, whom you confess to have died for us." Hence it is written (Gal. 3:13): "Christ hath redeemed us from the curse of the law, being made a curse for us."

FIFTH ARTICLE [III, Q. 46, Art. 5]

Whether Christ Endured All Suffering?

Objection 1: It would seem that Christ did endure all sufferings, because Hilary (De Trin. x) says: "God's only-begotten Son testifies that He endured every kind of human sufferings in order to accomplish the sacrament of His death, when with bowed head He gave up the ghost." It seems, therefore, that He did endure all human sufferings.

Obj. 2: Further, it is written (Isa. 52:13): "Behold My servant shall understand, He shall be exalted and extolled, and shall be exceeding high; as many as have been astonished at Him [Vulg.: 'thee'], so shall His visage be inglorious among men, and His form among the sons of men." But Christ was exalted in that He had all grace and all knowledge, at which many were astonished in admiration thereof. Therefore it seems that He was "inglorious," by enduring every human suffering.

Obj. 3: Further, Christ's Passion was ordained for man's deliverance from sin, as stated above (A. 3). But Christ came to deliver men from every kind of sin. Therefore He ought to have endured every kind of suffering.

*On the contrary,* It is written (John 19:32): "The soldiers therefore came: and they broke the legs of the first, and of the other who was crucified with Him; but after they were come to Jesus, when they saw that He was already dead, they did not break His legs." Consequently, He did not endure every human suffering.

*I answer that,* Human sufferings may be considered under two aspects. First of all, specifically, and in this way it was not necessary for Christ to endure them all, since many are mutually exclusive, as burning and drowning; for we are dealing now with sufferings inflicted from without, since it was not beseeming for Him to endure those arising from within, such as bodily ailments, as already stated (Q. 14, A. 4). But, speaking generically, He did endure every human suffering. This admits of a threefold acceptance. First of all, on the part of men: for He endured something from Gentiles and from Jews; from men and from women, as is clear from the women servants who accused Peter. He suffered from the rulers, from their servants and from the mob, according to Ps. 2:1, 2: "Why have the Gentiles raged, and the people devised vain things? The kings of the earth stood up, and the princes met together, against the Lord and against His Christ." He suffered from friends and acquaintances, as is manifest from Judas betraying and Peter denying Him.

Secondly, the same is evident on the part of the sufferings which a man can endure. For Christ suffered from friends abandoning Him; in His reputation, from the blasphemies hurled at Him; in His honor and glory, from the mockeries and the insults heaped upon Him; in things, for He was despoiled of His garments; in His soul, from sadness, weariness, and fear; in His body, from wounds and scourgings.

Thirdly, it may be considered with regard to His bodily members. In His head He suffered from the crown of piercing thorns; in His hands and feet, from the fastening of the nails; on His face from the blows and spittle; and from the lashes over His entire body. Moreover, He suffered in all His bodily senses: in touch, by being scourged and nailed; in taste, by being given vinegar and gall to drink; in smell, by being fastened to the gibbet in a place reeking with the stench of corpses, "which is called Calvary"; in hearing, by being tormented with the cries of blasphemers and scorners; in sight, by beholding the tears of His Mother and of the disciple whom He loved.

Reply Obj. 1: Hilary's words are to be understood as to all classes of sufferings, but not as to their kinds.

Reply Obj. 2: The likeness is sustained, not as to the number of the sufferings and graces, but as to their greatness; for, as He was uplifted above others in gifts of graces, so was He lowered beneath others by the ignominy of His sufferings.

Reply Obj. 3: The very least one of Christ's sufferings was sufficient of itself to redeem the human race from all sins; but as to fittingness, it sufficed that He should endure all classes of sufferings, as stated above.

SIXTH ARTICLE [III, Q. 46, Art. 6]

Whether the Pain of Christ's Passion Was Greater Than All Other Pains?

Objection 1: It would seem that the pain of Christ's Passion was not greater than all other pains. For the sufferer's pain is increased by the sharpness and the duration of the suffering. But some of the martyrs endured sharper and more prolonged pains than Christ, as is seen in St. Lawrence, who was roasted upon a gridiron; and in St. Vincent, whose flesh was torn with iron pincers. Therefore it seems that the pain of the suffering Christ was not the greatest.

Obj. 2: Further, strength of soul mitigates pain, so much so that the Stoics held there was no sadness in the soul of a wise man; and Aristotle (Ethic. ii) holds that moral virtue fixes the mean in the passions. But Christ had most perfect strength of soul. Therefore it seems that the greatest pain did not exist in Christ.

Obj. 3: Further, the more sensitive the sufferer is, the more acute will the pain be. But the soul is more sensitive than the body, since the body feels in virtue of the soul; also, Adam in the state of innocence seems to have had a body more sensitive than Christ had, who assumed a human body with its natural defects. Consequently, it seems that the pain of a sufferer in purgatory, or in hell, or even Adam's pain, if he suffered at all, was greater than Christ's in the Passion.

Obj. 4: Further, the greater the good lost, the greater the pain. But by sinning the sinner loses a greater good than Christ did when suffering; since the life of grace is greater than the life of nature: also, Christ, who lost His life, but was to rise again after three days, seems to have lost less than those who lose their lives and abide in death. Therefore it seems that Christ's pain was not the greatest of all.

Obj. 5: Further, the victim's innocence lessens the sting of his sufferings. But Christ died innocent, according to Jer. 9:19: "I was as a meek lamb, that is carried to be a victim." Therefore it seems that the pain of Christ's Passion was not the greatest.

Obj. 6: Further, there was nothing superfluous in

Christ's conduct. But the slightest pain would have sufficed to secure man's salvation, because from His Divine Person it would have had infinite virtue. Therefore it would have been superfluous to choose the greatest of all pains.

*On the contrary,* It is written (Lam. 1:12) on behalf of Christ's Person: "O all ye that pass by the way attend, and see if there be any sorrow like unto My sorrow."

*I answer that,* As we have stated, when treating of the defects assumed by Christ (Q. 15, AA. 5, 6), there was true and sensible pain in the suffering Christ, which is caused by something hurtful to the body: also, there was internal pain, which is caused from the apprehension of something hurtful, and this is termed "sadness." And in Christ each of these was the greatest in this present life. This arose from four causes. First of all, from the sources of His pain. For the cause of the sensitive pain was the wounding of His body; and this wounding had its bitterness, both from the extent of the suffering already mentioned (A. 5) and from the kind of suffering, since the death of the crucified is most bitter, because they are pierced in nervous and highly sensitive parts--to wit, the hands and feet; moreover, the weight of the suspended body intensifies the agony, and besides this there is the duration of the suffering because they do not die at once like those slain by the sword. The cause of the interior pain was, first of all, all the sins of the human race, for which He made satisfaction by suffering; hence He ascribes them, so to speak, to Himself, saying (Ps. 21:2): "The words of my sins." Secondly, especially the fall of the Jews and of the others who sinned in His death chiefly of the apostles, who were scandalized at His Passion. Thirdly, the loss of His bodily life, which is naturally horrible to human nature.

The magnitude of His suffering may be considered, secondly, from the susceptibility of the sufferer as to both soul and body. For His body was endowed with a most perfect constitution, since it was fashioned miraculously by the operation of the Holy Ghost; just as some other things made by miracles are better than others, as Chrysostom says (Hom. xxii in Joan.) respecting the wine into which Christ changed the water at the wedding-feast. And, consequently, Christ's sense of touch, the sensitiveness of which is the reason for our feeling pain, was most acute. His soul likewise, from its interior powers, apprehended most vehemently all the causes of sadness.

Thirdly, the magnitude of Christ's suffering can be estimated from the singleness of His pain and sadness. In other sufferers the interior sadness is mitigated, and even the exterior suffering, from some consideration of reason, by some derivation or redundance from the higher powers into the lower; but it was not so with the suffering Christ, because "He permitted each one of His powers to exercise its proper function," as Damascene says (De Fide Orth. iii).

Fourthly, the magnitude of the pain of Christ's suffering can be reckoned by this, that the pain and sorrow were accepted voluntarily, to the end of men's deliverance from sin; and consequently He embraced the amount of pain proportionate to the magnitude of the fruit which resulted therefrom.

From all these causes weighed together, it follows that Christ's pain was the very greatest.

Reply Obj. 1: This argument follows from only one of the considerations adduced--namely, from the bodily injury, which is the cause of sensitive pain; but the torment of the suffering Christ is much more intensified from other causes, as above stated.

Reply Obj. 2: Moral virtue lessens interior sadness in one way, and outward sensitive pain in quite another; for it lessens interior sadness directly by fixing the mean, as being its proper matter, within limits. But, as was laid down in the Second Part (I-II, Q. 64, A. 2), moral virtue fixes the mean in the passions, not according to mathematical quantity, but according to quantity of proportion, so that the passion shall not go beyond the rule of reason. And since the Stoics held all sadness to be unprofitable, they accordingly believed it to be altogether discordant with reason, and consequently to be shunned altogether by a wise man. But in very truth some sadness is praiseworthy, as Augustine proves (De Civ. Dei xiv)--namely, when it flows from holy love, as, for instance, when a man is saddened over his own or others' sins. Furthermore, it is employed as a useful means of satisfying for sins, according to the saying of the Apostle (2 Cor. 7:10): "The sorrow that is according to God worketh penance, steadfast unto salvation." And so to atone for the sins of all men, Christ accepted sadness, the greatest in absolute quantity, yet not exceeding the rule of reason. But moral virtue does not lessen outward sensitive pain, because such pain is not subject to reason, but follows the nature of the body; yet it lessens it indirectly by redundance of the higher powers into the lower. But this did not happen in Christ's case, as stated above (cf. Q. 14, A. 1, ad 2; Q. 45, A. 2).

Reply Obj. 3: The pain of a suffering, separated soul belongs to the state of future condemnation, which exceeds every evil of this life, just as the glory of the saints surpasses every good of the present life. Accordingly, when we say that Christ's pain was the greatest, we make no comparison between His and the pain of a separated soul. But Adam's body could not suffer, except he sinned; so that he would become mortal, and passible. And, though actually suffering, it would have felt less pain than Christ's body, for the reasons already stated. From all this it is clear that even if Adam had suffered in the state of innocence, [though this was impossible] his pain would have been less than Christ's.

Reply Obj. 4: Christ grieved not only over the loss of His own bodily life, but also over the sins of all others. And this grief in Christ surpassed all grief of every contrite heart, both because it flowed from a greater wisdom and charity, by which the pang of contrition is intensified, and because He grieved at the one time for all sins, according to Isa. 53:4: "Surely He hath carried our sorrows." But such was the dignity of Christ's life in the body, especially on account of the Godhead united with it, that its loss, even for one hour, would be a matter of greater grief than the loss of another man's life for howsoever long a time. Hence the Philosopher says (Ethic. iii) that the man of virtue loves his life all the more in proportion as he knows it to be better; and yet he exposes it for virtue's sake. And in like fashion Christ laid down His most beloved life for the good of charity, according to Jer. 12:7: "I have given My dear soul into the hands of her enemies."

Reply Obj. 5: The sufferer's innocence does lessen numerically the pain of the suffering, since, when a guilty man suffers, he grieves not merely on account of the penalty, but also because of the crime, whereas the innocent man grieves only for the penalty: yet this pain is more intensified by reason of his innocence, in so far as he deems the hurt inflicted to be the more undeserved. Hence it is that even others are more deserving of blame if they do not compassionate him, according to Isa. 57:1: "The just perisheth, and no man layeth it to heart."

Reply Obj. 6: Christ willed to deliver the human race from sins not merely by His power, but also according to justice. And therefore He did not simply weigh what great virtue His suffering would have from union with the Godhead, but also how much, according to His human nature, His pain would avail for so great a satisfaction.

SEVENTH ARTICLE [III, Q. 46, Art. 7]

Whether Christ Suffered in His Whole Soul?

Objection 1: It would seem that Christ did not suffer in His whole soul. For the soul suffers indirectly when the body suffers, inasmuch as it is the "act of the body." But the soul is not, as to its every part, the "act of the body"; because the intellect is the act of no body, as is said De Anima iii. Therefore it seems that Christ did not suffer in His whole soul.

Obj. 2: Further, every power of the soul is passive in regard to its proper object. But the higher part of reason has for its object the eternal types, "to the consideration and consultation of which it directs itself," as Augustine says (De Trin. xii). But Christ could suffer no hurt from the eternal types, since they are nowise opposed to Him. Therefore it seems that He did not suffer in His whole soul.

Obj. 3: Further, a sensitive passion is said to be complete when it comes into contact with the reason. But there was none such in Christ, but only "pro-passions"; as Jerome remarks on Matt. 26:37. Hence Dionysius says in a letter to John the Evangelist that "He endured only mentally the sufferings inflicted upon Him." Consequently it does not seem that Christ suffered in His whole soul.

Obj. 4: Further, suffering causes pain: but there is no pain in the speculative intellect, because, as the Philosopher says (Topic. i), "there is no sadness in opposition to the pleasure which comes of consideration." Therefore it seems that Christ did not suffer in His whole soul.

*On the contrary,* It is written (Ps. 87:4) on behalf of Christ: "My soul is filled with evils": upon which the gloss adds: "Not with vices, but with woes, whereby the soul suffers with the flesh; or with evils, viz. of a perishing people, by compassionating them." But His soul would not have been filled with these evils except He had suffered in His whole soul. Therefore Christ suffered in His entire soul.

*I answer that,* A whole is so termed with respect to its parts. But the parts of a soul are its faculties. So, then, the whole soul is said to suffer in so far as it is afflicted as to its essence, or as to all its faculties. But it must be borne in mind that a faculty of the soul can suffer in two ways: first of all, by its own passion; and this comes of its being afflicted by its proper object; thus, sight may suffer from superabundance of the visible object. In another way a faculty suffers by a passion in the subject on which it is based; as sight suffers when the sense of touch in the eye is affected, upon which the sense of sight rests, as, for instance, when the eye is pricked, or is disaffected by heat.

So, then, we say that if the soul be considered with respect to its essence, it is evident that Christ's whole soul suffered. For the soul's whole essence is allied with the body, so that it is entire in the whole body and in its every part. Consequently, when the body suffered and was disposed to separate from the soul, the entire soul suffered. But if we consider the whole soul according to its faculties, speaking thus of the proper passions of the faculties, He suffered indeed as to all His lower powers; because in all the soul's lower powers, whose operations are but temporal, there was something to be found which was a source of woe to Christ, as is evident from what was said above (A. 6). But Christ's higher reason did not suffer thereby on the part of its object, which is God, who was the cause, not of grief, but rather of delight and joy, to the soul of Christ. Nevertheless, all the powers of Christ's soul did suffer according as any faculty is said to be affected as regards its subject, because all the faculties of Christ's soul were rooted in its essence, to which suffering extended when the body, whose act it is, suffered.

Reply Obj. 1: Although the intellect as a faculty is not the act of the body, still the soul's essence is the act of the body, and in it the intellective faculty is rooted, as was shown in the First Part, Q. 77, AA. 6, 8.

Reply Obj. 2: This argument proceeds from passion on the part of the proper object, according to which Christ's higher reason did not suffer.

Reply Obj. 3: Grief is then said to be a true passion, by which the soul is troubled, when the passion in the sensitive part causes reason to deflect from the rectitude of its act, so that it then follows the passion, and has no longer free-will with regard to it. In this way passion of the sensitive part did not extend to reason in Christ, but merely subjectively, as was stated above.

Reply Obj. 4: The speculative intellect can have no pain or sadness on the part of its object, which is truth considered absolutely, and which is its perfection: nevertheless, both grief and its cause can reach it in the way mentioned above.

EIGHTH ARTICLE [III, Q. 46, Art. 8]

Whether Christ's Entire Soul Enjoyed Blessed Fruition During the Passion?

Objection 1: It would seem that Christ's entire soul did not enjoy blessed fruition during the Passion. For it is not possible to be sad and glad at the one time, since sadness and gladness are contraries. But Christ's whole soul suffered grief during the Passion, as was stated above (A. 7). Therefore His whole soul could not enjoy fruition.

Obj. 2: Further, the Philosopher says (Ethic. vii) that, if sadness be vehement, it not only checks the contrary delight, but every delight; and conversely. But the grief of Christ's Passion was the greatest, as shown above (A. 6); and likewise the enjoyment of fruition is also the greatest, as was laid down in the first volume of the Second Part (I-II, Q. 34, A. 3). Consequently, it was not possible for Christ's whole soul to be suffering and rejoicing at the one time.

Obj. 3: Further, beatific "fruition" comes of the knowledge and love of Divine things, as Augustine says (Doctr. Christ. i). But all the soul's powers do not extend to the knowledge and love of God. Therefore Christ's whole soul did not enjoy fruition.

*On the contrary,* Damascene says (De Fide Orth. iii): Christ's Godhead "permitted His flesh to do and to suffer what was proper to it." In like fashion, since it belonged to Christ's soul, inasmuch as it was blessed, to enjoy fruition, His Passion did not impede fruition.

*I answer that,* As stated above (A. 7), the whole soul can be understood both according to its essence and according to all its faculties. If it be understood according to its essence, then His whole soul did enjoy fruition, inasmuch as it is the subject of the higher part of the soul, to which it belongs, to enjoy the Godhead: so that as passion, by reason of the essence, is attributed to the higher part of the soul, so, on the other hand, by reason of the superior part of the soul, fruition is attributed to the essence. But if we take the whole soul as comprising all its faculties, thus His entire soul did not enjoy fruition: not directly, indeed, because fruition is not the act of any one part of the soul; nor by any overflow of glory, because, since Christ was still upon earth, there was no overflowing of glory from the higher part into the lower, nor from the soul into the body. But since, *on the contrary,* the soul's higher part was not hindered in its proper acts by the lower, it follows that the higher part of His soul enjoyed fruition perfectly while Christ was suffering.

Reply Obj. 1: The joy of fruition is not opposed directly to the grief of the Passion, because they have not the same object. Now nothing prevents contraries from being in the same subject, but not according to the same. And so the joy of fruition can appertain to the higher part of reason by its proper act; but grief of the Passion according to the subject. Grief of the Passion belongs to the essence of the soul by reason of the body, whose form the soul is; whereas the joy of fruition (belongs to the soul) by reason of the faculty in which it is subjected.

Reply Obj. 2: The Philosopher's contention is true because of the overflow which takes place naturally of one faculty of the soul into another; but it was not so with Christ, as was said above.

Reply Obj. 3: Such argument holds good of the totality of the soul with regard to its faculties.

NINTH ARTICLE [III, Q. 46, Art. 9]

Whether Christ Suffered at a Suitable Time?

Objection 1: It would seem that Christ did not suffer at a suitable time. For Christ's Passion was prefigured by the sacrifice of the Paschal lamb: hence the Apostle says (1 Cor. 5:7): "Christ our Pasch is sacrificed." But the paschal lamb was slain "on the fourteenth day at eventide," as is stated in Ex. 12:6. Therefore it seems that Christ ought to have suffered then; which is manifestly false: for He was then celebrating the Pasch with His disciples, according to Mark's account (14:12): "On the first day of the unleavened bread, when they sacrificed the Pasch"; whereas it was on the following day that He suffered.

Obj. 2: Further, Christ's Passion is called His uplifting, according to John 3:14: "So must the Son of man be lifted up." And Christ is Himself called the Sun of Justice, as we read Mal. 4:2. Therefore it seems that He ought to have suffered at the sixth hour, when the sun is at its highest point, and yet the contrary appears from Mk. 15:25: "It was the third hour, and they crucified Him."

Obj. 3: Further, as the sun is at its highest point in each day at the sixth hour, so also it reaches its highest point in every year at the summer solstice. Therefore Christ ought to have suffered about the time of the summer solstice rather than about the vernal equinox.

Obj. 4: Further, the world was enlightened by Christ's presence in it, according to John 9:5: "As long as I am in the world I am the light of the world." Consequently it was fitting for man's salvation that Christ should have lived longer in the world, so that He should have suffered, not in young, but in old, age.

*On the contrary,* It is written (John 13:1): "Jesus, knowing that His hour was come for Him to pass out of this world to the Father"; and (John 2:4): "My hour is not yet come." Upon which texts Augustine observes: "When He had done as much as He deemed sufficient, then came His hour, not of necessity, but of will, not of condition, but of power." Therefore Christ died at an opportune time.

*I answer that,* As was observed above (A. 1), Christ's Passion was subject to His will. But His will was ruled by the Divine wisdom which "ordereth all things" conveniently and "sweetly" (Wis. 8:1). Consequently it must be said that Christ's Passion was enacted at an opportune time. Hence it is written in De Qq. Vet. et Nov. Test., qu. lv: "The Saviour did everything in its proper place and season."

Reply Obj. 1: Some hold that Christ did die on the fourteenth day of the moon, when the Jews sacrificed the Pasch: hence it is stated (John 18:28) that the Jews "went not into Pilate's hall" on the day of the Passion, "that they might not be defiled, but that they might eat the Pasch." Upon this Chrysostom observes (Hom. lxxxii in Joan.): "The Jews celebrated the Pasch then; but He celebrated the Pasch on the previous day, reserving His own slaying until the Friday, when the old Pasch was kept." And this appears to tally with the statement (John 13:1-5) that "before the festival day of the Pasch . . . when supper was done" . . . Christ washed "the feet of the disciples."

But Matthew's account (26:17) seems opposed to this; that "on the first day of the Azymes the disciples came to Jesus, saying: Where wilt Thou that we prepare for Thee to eat the Pasch?" From which, as Jerome says, "since the fourteenth day of the first month is called the day of the Azymes, when the lamb was slain, and when it was full moon," it is quite clear that Christ kept the supper on the fourteenth and died on the fifteenth. And this comes out more clearly from Mk. 14:12: "On the first day of the unleavened bread, when they sacrificed the Pasch," etc.; and from Luke 22:7: "The day of the unleavened bread came, on which it was necessary that the Pasch should be killed."

Consequently, then, others say that Christ ate the Pasch with His disciples on the proper day--that is, on the fourteenth day of the moon--"showing thereby that up to the last day He was not opposed to the law," as Chrysostom says (Hom. lxxxi in Matth.): but that the Jews, being busied in compassing Christ's death against the law, put off celebrating the Pasch until the following day. And on this account it is said of them that on the day of Christ's Passion they were unwilling to enter Pilate's hall, "that they might not be defiled, but that they might eat the Pasch."

But even this solution does not tally with Mark, who says: "On the first day of the unleavened bread, when they sacrificed the Pasch." Consequently Christ and the Jews celebrated the ancient Pasch at the one time. And as Bede says on Luke 22:7, 8: "Although Christ who is our Pasch was slain on the following day--that is, on the fifteenth day of the moon--nevertheless, on the night when the Lamb was sacrificed, delivering to the disciples to be celebrated, the mysteries of His body and blood, and being held and bound by the Jews, He hallowed the opening of His own immolation--that is, of His Passion."

But the words (John 13:1) "Before the festival day of the Pasch" are to be understood to refer to the fourteenth day of the moon, which then fell upon the Thursday: for the fifteenth day of the moon was the most solemn day of the Pasch with the Jews: and so the same day which John calls "before the festival day of the Pasch," on account of the natural distinction of days, Matthew calls the first day of the unleavened bread, because, according to the rite of the Jewish festivity, the solemnity began from the evening of the preceding day. When it is said, then, that they were going to eat the Pasch on the fifteenth day of the month, it is to be understood that the Pasch there is not called the Paschal lamb, which was sacrificed on the fourteenth day, but the Paschal food--that is, the unleavened bread--which had to be eaten by the clean. Hence Chrysostom in the same passage gives another explanation, that the Pasch can be taken as meaning the whole feast of the Jews, which lasted seven days.

Reply Obj. 2: As Augustine says (De Consensu Evang. iii): "'It was about the sixth hour' when the Lord was delivered up by Pilate to be crucified," as John relates. For it "was not quite the sixth hour, but about the sixth--that is, it was after the fifth, and when part of the sixth had been entered upon until the sixth hour was ended--that the darkness began, when Christ hung upon the cross. It is understood to have been the third hour when the Jews clamored for the Lord to be crucified: and it is most clearly shown that they crucified Him when they clamored out. Therefore, lest anyone might divert the thought of so great a crime from the Jews to the soldiers, he says: 'It was the third hour, and they crucified Him,' that they before all may be found to have crucified Him, who at the third hour clamored for His crucifixion. Although there are not wanting some persons who wish the Parasceve to be understood as the third hour, which John recalls, saying: 'It was the Parasceve, about the sixth hour.' For 'Parasceve' is interpreted 'preparation.' But the true Pasch, which was celebrated in the Lord's Passion, began to be prepared from the ninth hour of the night--namely, when the chief priests said: 'He is deserving of death.'" According to John, then, "the sixth hour of the Parasceve" lasts from that hour of the night down to Christ's crucifixion; while, according to Mark, it is the third hour of the day.

Still, there are some who contend that this discrepancy is due to the error of a Greek transcriber: since the characters employed by them to represent 3 and 6 are somewhat alike.

Reply Obj. 3: According to the author of De Qq. Vet. et Nov. Test., qu. lv, "our Lord willed to redeem and reform the world by His Passion, at the time of year at which He had created it--that is, at the equinox. It is then that day grows upon night; because by our Saviour's Passion we are brought from darkness to light." And since the perfect enlightening will come about at Christ's second coming, therefore the season of His second coming is compared (Matt. 24:32, 33) to the summer in these words: "When the branch thereof is now tender, and the leaves come forth, you know that summer is nigh: so you also, when you shall see all these things, know ye that it is nigh even at the doors." And then also shall be Christ's greatest exaltation.

Reply Obj. 4: Christ willed to suffer while yet young, for three reasons. First of all, to commend the more His love by giving up His life for us when He was in His most perfect state of life. Secondly, because it was not becoming for Him to show any decay of nature nor to be subject to disease, as stated above (Q. 14, A. 4). Thirdly, that by dying and rising at an early age Christ might exhibit beforehand in His own person the future condition of those who rise again. Hence it is written (Eph. 4:13): "Until we all meet into the unity of faith, and of the knowledge of the Son of God, unto a perfect man, unto the measure of the age of the fulness of Christ."

TENTH ARTICLE [III, Q. 46, Art. 10]

Whether Christ Suffered in a Suitable Place?

Objection 1: It would seem that Christ did not suffer in a suitable place. For Christ suffered according to His human nature, which was conceived in Nazareth and born in Bethlehem. Consequently it seems that He ought not to have suffered in Jerusalem, but in Nazareth or Bethlehem.

Obj. 2: Further, the reality ought to correspond with the figure. But Christ's Passion was prefigured by the sacrifices of the Old Law, and these were offered up in the Temple. Therefore it seems that Christ ought to have suffered in the Temple, and not outside the city gate.

Obj. 3: Further, the medicine should correspond with the disease. But Christ's Passion was the medicine against Adam's sin: and Adam was not buried in Jerusalem, but in Hebron; for it is written (Josh. 14:15): "The name of Hebron before was called Cariath-Arbe: Adam the greatest in the land of [Vulg.: 'among'] the Enacims was laid there."

*On the contrary,* It is written (Luke 13:33): "It cannot be that a prophet perish out of Jerusalem." Therefore it was fitting that He should die in Jerusalem.

*I answer that,* According to the author of De Qq. Vet. et Nov. Test., qu. lv, "the Saviour did everything in its proper place and season," because, as all things are in His hands, so are all places: and consequently, since Christ suffered at a suitable time, so did He in a suitable place.

Reply Obj. 1: Christ died most appropriately in Jerusalem. First of all, because Jerusalem was God's chosen place for the offering of sacrifices to Himself: and these figurative sacrifices foreshadowed Christ's Passion, which is a true sacrifice, according to Eph. 5:2: "He hath delivered Himself for us, an oblation and a sacrifice to God for an odor of sweetness." Hence Bede says in a Homily (xxiii): "When the Passion drew nigh, our Lord willed to draw nigh to the place of the Passion"--that is to say, to Jerusalem--whither He came five days before the Pasch; just as, according to the legal precept, the Paschal lamb was led to the place of immolation five days before the Pasch, which is the tenth day of the moon.

Secondly, because the virtue of His Passion was to be spread over the whole world, He wished to suffer in the center of the habitable world--that is, in Jerusalem. Accordingly it is written (Ps. 73:12): "But God is our King before ages: He hath wrought salvation in the midst of the earth"--that is, in Jerusalem, which is called "the navel of the earth" [*Cf. Jerome's comment on Ezech. 5:5].

Thirdly, because it was specially in keeping with His humility: that, as He chose the most shameful manner of death, so likewise it was part of His humility that He did not refuse to suffer in so celebrated a place. Hence Pope Leo says (Serm. I in Epiph.): "He who had taken upon Himself the form of a servant chose Bethlehem for His nativity and Jerusalem for His Passion."

Fourthly, He willed to suffer in Jerusalem, where the chief priests dwelt, to show that the wickedness of His slayers arose from the chiefs of the Jewish people. Hence it is written (Acts 4:27): "There assembled together in this city against Thy holy child Jesus whom Thou hast anointed, Herod, and Pontius Pilate, with the Gentiles and the people of Israel."

Reply Obj. 2: For three reasons Christ suffered outside the gate, and not in the Temple nor in the city. First of all, that the truth might correspond with the figure. For the calf and the goat which were offered in most solemn sacrifice for expiation on behalf of the entire multitude were burnt outside the camp, as commanded in Lev. 16:27. Hence it is written (Heb. 13:27): "For the bodies of those beasts, whose blood is brought into the holies by the high-priest for sin, are burned without the camp. Wherefore Jesus also, that He might sanctify the people by His own blood, suffered without the gate."

Secondly, to set us the example of shunning worldly conversation. Accordingly the passage continues: "Let us go forth therefore to Him without the camp, bearing His reproach."

Thirdly, as Chrysostom says in a sermon on the Passion (Hom. i De Cruce et Latrone): "The Lord was not willing to suffer under a roof, nor in the Jewish Temple, lest the Jews might take away the saving sacrifice, and lest you might think He was offered for that people only. Consequently, it was beyond the city and outside the walls, that you may learn it was a universal sacrifice, an oblation for the whole world, a cleansing for all."

Reply Obj. 3: According to Jerome, in his commentary on Matt. 27:33, "someone explained 'the place of Calvary' as being the place where Adam was buried; and that it was so called because the skull of the first man was buried there. A pleasing interpretation indeed, and one suited to catch the ear of the people, but, still, not the true one. For the spots where the condemned are beheaded are outside the city and beyond the gates, deriving thence the name of Calvary--that is, of the beheaded. Jesus, accordingly, was crucified there, that the standards of martyrdom might be uplifted over what was formerly the place of the condemned. But Adam was buried close by Hebron and Arbe, as we read in the book of Jesus Ben Nave." But Jesus was to be crucified in the common spot of the condemned rather than beside Adam's sepulchre, to make it manifest that Christ's cross was the remedy, not only for Adam's personal sin, but also for the sin of the entire world.

ELEVENTH ARTICLE [III, Q. 46, Art. 11]

Whether It Was Fitting for Christ to Be Crucified with Thieves?

Objection 1: It would seem unfitting for Christ to have been crucified with thieves, because it is written (2 Cor. 6:14): "What participation hath justice with injustice?" But for our sakes Christ "of God is made unto us justice" (1 Cor. 1:30); whereas iniquity applies to thieves. Therefore it was not fitting for Christ to be crucified with thieves.

Obj. 2: Further, on Matt. 26:35, "Though I should die with Thee, I will not deny Thee," Origen (Tract. xxxv in Matth.) observes: "It was not men's lot to die with Jesus, since He died for all." Again, on Luke 22:33, "I am ready to go with Thee, both into prison and death," Ambrose says: "Our Lord's Passion has followers, but not equals." It seems, then, much less fitting for Christ to suffer with thieves.

Obj. 3: Further, it is written (Matt. 27:44) that "the thieves who were crucified with Him reproached Him." But in Luke 22:42 it is stated that one of them who were crucified with Christ cried out to Him: "Lord, remember me when Thou shalt come into Thy kingdom." It seems, then, that besides the blasphemous thieves there was another man who did not blaspheme Him: and so the Evangelist's account does not seem to be accurate when it says that Christ was crucified with thieves.

*On the contrary,* It was foretold by Isaias (53:12): "And He was reputed with the wicked."

*I answer that,* Christ was crucified between thieves from one intention on the part of the Jews, and from quite another on the part of God's ordaining. As to the intention of the Jews, Chrysostom remarks (Hom. lxxxvii in Matth.) that they crucified the two thieves, one on either side, "that He might be made to share their guilt. But it did not happen so; because mention is never made of them; whereas His cross is honored everywhere. Kings lay aside their crowns to take up the cross: on their purple robes, on their diadems, on their weapons, on the consecrated table, everywhere the cross shines forth."

As to God's ordinance, Christ was crucified with thieves, because, as Jerome says on Matt. 27:33: "As Christ became accursed of the cross for us, so for our salvation He was crucified as a guilty one among the guilty." Secondly, as Pope Leo observes (Serm. iv de Passione): "Two thieves were crucified, one on His right hand and one on His left, to set forth by the very appearance of the gibbet that separation of all men which shall be made in His hour of judgment." And Augustine on John 7:36: "The very cross, if thou mark it well, was a judgment-seat: for the judge being set in the midst, the one who believed was delivered, the other who mocked Him was condemned. Already He has signified what He shall do to the quick and the dead; some He will set on His right, others on His left hand." Thirdly, according to Hilary (Comm. xxxiii in Matth.): "Two thieves are set, one upon His right and one upon His left, to show that all mankind is called to the sacrament of His Passion. But because of the cleavage between believers and unbelievers, the multitude is divided into right and left, those on the right being saved by the justification of faith." Fourthly, because, as Bede says on Mk. 15:27: "The thieves crucified with our Lord denote those who, believing in and confessing Christ, either endure the conflict of martyrdom or keep the institutes of stricter observance. But those who do the like for the sake of everlasting glory are denoted by the faith of the thief on the right; while others who do so for the sake of human applause copy the mind and behavior of the one on the left."

Reply Obj. 1: Just as Christ was not obliged to die, but willingly submitted to death so as to vanquish death by His power: so neither deserved He to be classed with thieves; but willed to be reputed with the ungodly that He might destroy ungodliness by His power. Accordingly, Chrysostom says (Hom. lxxxiv in Joan.) that "to convert the thief upon the cross, and lead him into paradise, was no less a wonder than to shake the rocks."

Reply Obj. 2: It was not fitting that anyone else should die with Christ from the same cause as Christ: hence Origen continues thus in the same passage: "All had been under sin, and all required that another should die for them, not they for others."

Reply Obj. 3: As Augustine says (De Consensu Evang. iii): We can understand Matthew "as putting the plural for the singular" when he said "the thieves reproached Him." Or it may be said, with Jerome, that "at first both blasphemed Him, but afterwards one believed in Him on witnessing the wonders."

TWELFTH ARTICLE [III, Q. 46, Art. 12]

Whether Christ's Passion Is to Be Attributed to His Godhead?

Objection 1: It would seem that Christ's Passion is to be attributed to His Godhead; for it is written (1 Cor. 2:8): "If they had known it, they would never have crucified the Lord of glory." But Christ is the Lord of glory in respect of His Godhead. Therefore Christ's Passion is attributed to Him in respect of His Godhead.

Obj. 2: Further, the principle of men's salvation is the Godhead Itself, according to Ps. 36:39: "But the salvation of the just is from the Lord." Consequently, if Christ's Passion did not appertain to His Godhead, it would seem that it could not produce fruit in us.

Obj. 3: Further, the Jews were punished for slaying Christ as for murdering God Himself; as is proved by the gravity of the punishment. Now this would not be so if the Passion were not attributed to the Godhead. Therefore Christ's Passion should be so attributed.

*On the contrary,* Athanasius says (Ep. ad Epict.): "The Word is impassible whose Nature is Divine." But what is impassible cannot suffer. Consequently, Christ's Passion did not concern His Godhead.

*I answer that,* As stated above (Q. 2, AA. 1, 2, 3, 6), the union of the human nature with the Divine was effected in the Person, in the hypostasis, in the suppositum, yet observing the distinction of natures; so that it is the same Person and hypostasis of the Divine and human natures, while each nature retains that which is proper to it. And therefore, as stated above (Q. 16, A. 4), the Passion is to be attributed to the suppositum of the Divine Nature, not because of the Divine Nature, which is impassible, but by reason of the human nature. Hence, in a Synodal Epistle of Cyril [*Act. Conc. Ephes., P. i, cap. 26] we read: "If any man does not confess that the Word of God suffered in the flesh and was crucified in the flesh, let him be anathema." Therefore Christ's Passion belongs to the suppositum of the Divine Nature by reason of the passible nature assumed, but not on account of the impassible Divine Nature.

Reply Obj. 1: The Lord of glory is said to be crucified, not as the Lord of glory, but as a man capable of suffering.

Reply Obj. 2: As is said in a sermon of the Council of Ephesus [*P. iii, cap. 10], "Christ's death being, as it were, God's death"--namely, by union in Person--"destroyed death"; since He who suffered "was both God and man. For God's Nature was not wounded, nor did It undergo any change by those sufferings."

Reply Obj. 3: As the passage quoted goes on to say: "The Jews did not crucify one who was simply a man; they inflicted their presumptions upon God. For suppose a prince to speak by word of mouth, and that his words are committed to writing on a parchment and sent out to the cities, and that some rebel tears up the document, he will be led forth to endure the death sentence, not for merely tearing up a document, but as destroying the imperial message. Let not the Jew, then, stand in security, as crucifying a mere man; since what he saw was as the parchment, but what was hidden under it was the imperial Word, the Son by nature, not the mere utterance of a tongue."

## QUESTION 47

OF THE EFFICIENT CAUSE OF CHRIST'S PASSION (In Six Articles)

We have now to consider the efficient cause of Christ's Passion, concerning which there are six points of inquiry:

(1) Whether Christ was slain by others, or by Himself?

(2) From what motive did He deliver Himself up to the Passion?

(3) Whether the Father delivered Him up to suffer?

(4) Whether it was fitting that He should suffer at the hands of the Gentiles, or rather of the Jews?

(5) Whether His slayers knew who He was?

(6) Of the sin of them who slew Christ.

FIRST ARTICLE [III, Q. 47, Art. 1]

Whether Christ Was Slain by Another or by Himself?

Objection 1: It would seem that Christ was not slain by another, but by Himself. For He says Himself (John 10:18): "No man taketh My life from Me, but I lay it down of Myself." But he is said to kill another who takes away his life. Consequently, Christ was not slain by others, but by Himself.

Obj. 2: Further, those slain by others sink gradually from exhausted nature, and this is strikingly apparent in the crucified: for, as Augustine says (De Trin. iv): "Those who were crucified were tormented with a lingering death." But this did not happen in Christ's case, since "crying out, with a loud voice, He yielded up the ghost" (Matt. 27:50). Therefore Christ was not slain by others, but by Himself.

Obj. 3: Further, those slain by others suffer a violent death, and hence die unwillingly, because violent is opposed to voluntary. But Augustine says (De Trin. iv): "Christ's spirit did not quit the flesh unwillingly, but because He willed it, when He willed it, and as He willed it." Consequently Christ was not slain by others, but by Himself.

*On the contrary,* It is written (Luke 18:33): "After they have scourged Him, they will put him to death."

*I answer that,* A thing may cause an effect in two ways: in the first instance by acting directly so as to produce the effect; and in this manner Christ's persecutors slew Him because they inflicted on Him what was a sufficient cause of death, and with the intention of slaying Him, and the effect followed, since death resulted from that cause. In another way someone causes an effect indirectly--that is, by not preventing it when he can do so; just as one person is said to drench another by not closing the window through which the shower is entering: and in this way Christ was the cause of His own Passion and death. For He could have prevented His Passion and death. Firstly, by holding His enemies in check, so that they would not have been eager to slay Him, or would have been powerless to do so. Secondly, because His spirit had the power of preserving His fleshly nature from the infliction of any injury; and Christ's soul had this power, because it was united in unity of person with the Divine Word, as Augustine says (De Trin. iv). Therefore, since Christ's soul did not repel the injury inflicted on His body, but willed His corporeal nature to succumb to such injury, He is said to have laid down His life, or to have died voluntarily.

Reply Obj. 1: When we hear the words, "No man taketh away My life from Me," we must understand "against My will": for that is properly said to be "taken away" which one takes from someone who is unwilling and unable to resist.

Reply Obj. 2: In order for Christ to show that the Passion inflicted by violence did not take away His life, He preserved the strength of His bodily nature, so that at the last moment He was able to cry out with a loud voice: and hence His death should be computed among His other miracles. Accordingly it is written (Mk. 15:39): "And the centurion who stood over against Him, seeing that crying out in this manner, He had given up the ghost, said: Indeed, this man was the Son of God." It was also a subject of wonder in Christ's death that He died sooner than the others who were tormented with the same suffering. Hence John says (19:32) that "they broke the legs of the first, and of the other that was crucified with Him," that they might die more speedily; "but after they were come to Jesus, when they saw that He was already dead, they did not break His legs." Mark also states (15:44) that "Pilate wondered that He should be already dead." For as of His own will His bodily nature kept its vigor to the end, so likewise, when He willed, He suddenly succumbed to the injury inflicted.

Reply Obj. 3: Christ at the same time suffered violence in order to die, and died, nevertheless, voluntarily; because violence was inflicted on His body, which, however, prevailed over His body only so far as He willed it.

SECOND ARTICLE [III, Q. 47, Art. 2]

Whether Christ Died Out of Obedience?

Objection 1: It would seem that Christ did not die out of obedience. For obedience is referred to a command. But we do not read that Christ was commanded to suffer. Therefore He did not suffer out of obedience.

Obj. 2: Further, a man is said to do from obedience what he does from necessity of precept. But Christ did not suffer necessarily, but voluntarily. Therefore He did not suffer out of obedience.

Obj. 3: Further, charity is a more excellent virtue than obedience. But we read that Christ suffered out of charity, according to Eph. 5:2: "Walk in love, as Christ also has loved us, and delivered Himself up for us." Therefore Christ's Passion ought to be ascribed rather to charity than to obedience.

*On the contrary,* It is written (Phil. 2:8): "He became obedient" to the Father "unto death."

*I answer that,* It was befitting that Christ should suffer out of obedience. First of all, because it was in keeping with human justification, that "as by the disobedience of one man, many were made sinners: so also by the obedience of one, many shall be made just," as is written Rom. 5:19. Secondly, it was suitable for reconciling man with God: hence it is written (Rom. 5:10): "We are reconciled to God by the death of His Son," in so far as Christ's death was a most acceptable sacrifice to God, according to Eph. 5:2: "He delivered Himself for us an oblation and a sacrifice to God for an odor of sweetness." Now obedience is preferred to all sacrifices. according to 1 Kings 15:22: "Obedience is better than sacrifices." Therefore it was fitting that the sacrifice of Christ's Passion and death should proceed from obedience. Thirdly, it was in keeping with His victory whereby He triumphed over death and its author; because a soldier cannot conquer unless he obey his captain. And so the Man-Christ secured the victory through being obedient to God, according to Prov. 21:28: "An obedient man shall speak of victory."

Reply Obj. 1: Christ received a command from the Father to suffer. For it is written (John 10:18): "I have power to lay down My life, and I have power to take it up again: (and) this commandment have I received of My Father"--namely, of laying down His life and of resuming it again. "From which," as Chrysostom says (Hom. lix in Joan.), it is not to be understood "that at first He awaited the command, and that He had need to be told, but He showed the proceeding to be a voluntary one, and destroyed suspicion of opposition" to the Father. Yet because the Old Law was ended by Christ's death, according to His dying words, "It is consummated" (John 19:30), it may be understood that by His suffering He fulfilled all the precepts of the Old Law. He fulfilled those of the moral order which are founded on the precepts of charity, inasmuch as He suffered both out of love of the Father, according to John 14:31: "That the world may know that I love the Father, and as the Father hath given Me commandment, so do I: arise, let us go hence"--namely, to the place of His Passion: and out of love of His neighbor, according to Gal. 2:20: "He loved me, and delivered Himself up for me." Christ likewise by His Passion fulfilled the ceremonial precepts of the Law, which are chiefly ordained for sacrifices and oblations, in so far as all the ancient sacrifices were figures of that true sacrifice which the dying Christ offered for us. Hence it is written (Col. 2:16, 17): "Let no man judge you in meat or drink, or in respect of a festival day, or of the new moon, or of the sabbaths, which are a shadow of things to come, but the body is Christ's," for the reason that Christ is compared to them as a body is to a shadow. Christ also by His Passion fulfilled the judicial precepts of the Law, which are chiefly ordained for making compensation to them who have suffered wrong, since, as is written Ps. 68:5: He "paid that which" He "took not away," suffering Himself to be fastened to a tree on account of the apple which man had plucked from the tree against God's command.

Reply Obj. 2: Although obedience implies necessity with regard to the thing commanded, nevertheless it implies free-will with regard to the fulfilling of the precept. And, indeed, such was Christ's obedience, for, although His Passion and death, considered in themselves, were repugnant to the natural will, yet Christ resolved to fulfill God's will with respect to the same, according to Ps. 39:9: "That I should do Thy will: O my God, I have desired it." Hence He said (Matt. 26:42): "If this chalice may not pass away, but I must drink it, Thy will be done."

Reply Obj. 3: For the same reason Christ suffered out of charity and out of obedience; because He fulfilled even the precepts of charity out of obedience only; and was obedient, out of love, to the Father's command.

THIRD ARTICLE [III, Q. 47, Art. 3]

Whether God the Father Delivered Up Christ to the Passion?

Objection 1: It would seem that God the Father did not deliver up Christ to the Passion. For it is a wicked and cruel act to hand over an innocent man to torment and death. But, as it is written (Deut. 32:4): "God is faithful, and without any iniquity." Therefore He did not hand over the innocent Christ to His Passion and death.

Obj. 2: Further, it is not likely that a man be given over to death by himself and by another also. But Christ gave Himself up for us, as it is written (Isa. 53:12): "He hath delivered His soul unto death." Consequently it does not appear that God the Father delivered Him up.

Obj. 3: Further, Judas is held to be guilty because he betrayed Christ to the Jews, according to John 6:71: "One of you is a devil," alluding to Judas, who was to betray Him. The Jews are likewise reviled for delivering Him up to Pilate; as we read in John 18:35: "Thy own nation, and the chief priests have delivered Thee up to me." Moreover, as is related in John 19:16: Pilate "delivered Him to them to be crucified"; and according to 2 Cor. 6:14: there is no "participation of justice with injustice." It seems, therefore, that God the Father did not deliver up Christ to His Passion.

*On the contrary,* It is written (Rom. 8:32): "God hath not spared His own Son, but delivered Him up for us all."

*I answer that,* As observed above (A. 2), Christ suffered voluntarily out of obedience to the Father. Hence in three respects God the Father did deliver up Christ to the Passion. In the first way, because by His eternal will He preordained Christ's Passion for the deliverance of the human race, according to the words of Isaias (53:6): "The Lord hath laid on Him the iniquities of us all"; and again (Isa. 53:10): "The Lord was pleased to bruise Him in infirmity." Secondly, inasmuch as, by the infusion of charity, He inspired Him with the will to suffer for us; hence we read in the same passage: "He was offered because it was His own will" (Isa. 53:7). Thirdly, by not shielding Him from the Passion, but abandoning Him to His persecutors: thus we read (Matt. 27:46) that Christ, while hanging upon the cross, cried out: "My God, My God, why hast Thou forsaken Me?" because, to wit, He left Him to the power of His persecutors, as Augustine says (Ep. cxl).

Reply Obj. 1: It is indeed a wicked and cruel act to hand over an innocent man to torment and to death against his will. Yet God the Father did not so deliver up Christ, but inspired Him with the will to suffer for us. God's "severity" (cf. Rom. 11:22) is thereby shown, for He would not remit sin without penalty: and the Apostle indicates this when (Rom. 8:32) he says: "God spared not even His own Son." Likewise His "goodness" (Rom. 11:22) shines forth, since by no penalty endured could man pay Him enough satisfaction: and the Apostle denotes this when he says: "He delivered Him up for us all": and, again (Rom. 3:25): "Whom"--that is to say, Christ--God "hath proposed to be a propitiation through faith in His blood."

Reply Obj. 2: Christ as God delivered Himself up to death by the same will and action as that by which the Father delivered Him up; but as man He gave Himself up by a will inspired of the Father. Consequently there is no contrariety in the Father delivering Him up and in Christ delivering Himself up.

Reply Obj. 3: The same act, for good or evil, is judged differently, accordingly as it proceeds from a different source. The Father delivered up Christ, and Christ surrendered Himself, from charity, and consequently we give praise to both: but Judas betrayed Christ from greed, the Jews from envy, and Pilate from worldly fear, for he stood in fear of Caesar; and these accordingly are held guilty.

FOURTH ARTICLE [III, Q. 47, Art. 4]

Whether It Was Fitting for Christ to Suffer at the Hands of the Gentiles?

Objection 1: It would seem unfitting that Christ should suffer at the hands of the Gentiles. For since men were to be freed from sin by Christ's death, it would seem fitting that very few should sin in His death. But the Jews sinned in His death, on whose behalf it is said (Matt. 21:38): "This is the heir; come, let us kill him." It seems fitting, therefore, that the Gentiles should not be implicated in the sin of Christ's slaying.

Obj. 2: Further, the truth should respond to the figure. Now it was not the Gentiles but the Jews who offered the figurative sacrifices of the Old Law. Therefore neither ought Christ's Passion, which was a true sacrifice, to be fulfilled at the hands of the Gentiles.

Obj. 3: Further, as related John 5:18, "the Jews sought to kill" Christ because "He did not only break the sabbath, but also said God was His Father, making Himself equal to God." But these things seemed to be only against the Law of the Jews: hence they themselves said (John 19:7): "According to the Law He ought to die because He made Himself the Son of God." It seems fitting, therefore, that Christ should suffer, at the hands not of the Gentiles, but of the Jews, and that what they said was untrue: "It is not lawful for us to put any man to death," since many sins are punishable with death according to the Law, as is evident from Lev. 20.

*On the contrary,* our Lord Himself says (Matt. 20:19): "They shall deliver Him to the Gentiles to be mocked, and scourged, and crucified."

*I answer that,* The effect of Christ's Passion was foreshown by the very manner of His death. For Christ's Passion wrought its effect of salvation first of all among the Jews, very many of whom were baptized in His death, as is evident from Acts 2:41 and Acts 4:4. Afterwards, by the preaching of Jews, Christ's Passion passed on to the Gentiles. Consequently it was fitting that Christ should begin His sufferings at the hands of the Jews, and, after they had delivered Him up, finish His Passion at the hands of the Gentiles.

Reply Obj. 1: In order to demonstrate the fulness of His love, on account of which He suffered, Christ upon the cross prayed for His persecutors. Therefore, that the fruits of His petition might accrue to Jews and Gentiles, Christ willed to suffer from both.

Reply Obj. 2: Christ's Passion was the offering of a sacrifice, inasmuch as He endured death of His own free-will out of charity: but in so far as He suffered from His persecutors it was not a sacrifice, but a most grievous sin.

Reply Obj. 3: As Augustine says (Tract. cxiv in Joan.): "The Jews said that 'it is not lawful for us to put any man to death,' because they understood that it was not lawful for them to put any man to death" owing to the sacredness of the feast-day, which they had already begun to celebrate. or, as Chrysostom observes (Hom. lxxxiii in Joan.), because they wanted Him to be slain, not as a transgressor of the Law, but as a public enemy, since He had made Himself out to be a king, of which it was not their place to judge. Or, again, because it was not lawful for them to crucify Him (as they wanted to), but to stone Him, as they did to Stephen. Better still is it to say that the power of putting to death was taken from them by the Romans, whose subjects they were.

FIFTH ARTICLE [III, Q. 47, Art. 5]

Whether Christ's Persecutors Knew Who He Was?

Objection 1: It would seem that Christ's persecutors did know who He was. For it is written (Matt. 21:38) that the husbandmen seeing the son said within themselves: "This is the heir; come, let us kill him." On this Jerome remarks: "Our Lord proves most manifestly by these words that the rulers of the Jews crucified the Son of God, not from ignorance, but out of envy: for they understood that it was He to whom the Father says by the Prophet: 'Ask of Me, and I will give Thee the Gentiles for Thy inheritance.'" It seems, therefore, that they knew Him to be Christ or the Son of God.

Obj. 2: Further, our Lord says (John 15:24): "But now they have both seen and hated both Me and My Father." Now what is seen is known manifestly. Therefore the Jews, knowing Christ, inflicted the Passion on Him out of hatred.

Obj. 3: Further, it is said in a sermon delivered in the Council of Ephesus (P. iii, cap. x): "Just as he who tears up the imperial message is doomed to die, as despising the prince's word; so the Jew, who crucified Him whom he had seen, will pay the penalty for daring to lay his hands on God the Word Himself." Now this would not be so had they not known Him to be the Son of God, because their ignorance would have excused them. Therefore it seems that the Jews in crucifying Christ knew Him to be the Son of God.

*On the contrary,* It is written (1 Cor. 2:8): "If they had known it, they would never have crucified the Lord of glory." And (Acts 3:17), Peter, addressing the Jews, says: "I know that you did it through ignorance, as did also your rulers." Likewise the Lord hanging upon the cross said: "Father, forgive them, for they know not what they do" (Luke 23:34).

*I answer that,* Among the Jews some were elders, and others of lesser degree. Now according to the author of De Qq. Nov. et Vet. Test., qu. lxvi, the elders, who were called "rulers, knew," as did also the devils, "that He was the Christ promised in the Law: for they saw all the signs in Him which the prophets said would come to pass: but they did not know the mystery of His Godhead." Consequently the Apostle says: "If they had known it, they would never have crucified the Lord of glory." It must, however, be understood that their ignorance did not excuse them from crime, because it was, as it were, affected ignorance. For they saw manifest signs of His Godhead; yet they perverted them out of hatred and envy of Christ; neither would they believe His words, whereby He avowed that He was the Son of God. Hence He Himself says of them (John 15:22): "If I had not come, and spoken to them, they would not have sin; but now they have no excuse for their sin." And afterwards He adds (John 15:24): "If I had not done among them the works that no other man hath done, they would not have sin." And so the expression employed by Job (21:14) can be accepted on their behalf: "(Who) said to God: depart from us, we desire not the knowledge of Thy ways."

But those of lesser degree--namely, the common folk--who had not grasped the mysteries of the Scriptures, did not fully comprehend that He was the Christ or the Son of God. For although some of them believed in Him, yet the multitude did not; and if they doubted sometimes whether He was the Christ, on account of the manifold signs and force of His teaching, as is stated John 7:31, 41, nevertheless they were deceived afterwards by their rulers, so that they did not believe Him to be the Son of God or the Christ. Hence Peter said to them: "I know that you did it through ignorance, as did also your rulers"--namely, because they were seduced by the rulers.

Reply Obj. 1: Those words are spoken by the husbandmen of the vineyard; and these signify the rulers of the people, who knew Him to be the heir, inasmuch as they knew Him to be the Christ promised in the Law, but the words of Ps. 2:8 seem to militate against this answer: "Ask of Me, and I will give Thee the Gentiles for Thy inheritance"; which are addressed to Him of whom it is said: "Thou art My Son, this day have I begotten Thee." If, then, they knew Him to be the one to whom the words were addressed: "Ask of Me, and I will give Thee the Gentiles for Thy inheritance," it follows that they knew Him to be the Son of God. Chrysostom, too, says upon the same passage that "they knew Him to be the Son of God." Bede likewise, commenting on the words, "For they know not what they do" (Luke 23:34), says: "It is to be observed that He does not pray for them who, understanding Him to be the Son of God, preferred to crucify Him rather than acknowledge Him." But to this it may be replied that they knew Him to be the Son of God, not from His Nature, but from the excellence of His singular grace.

Yet we may hold that they are said to have known also that He was verily the Son of God, in that they had evident signs thereof: yet out of hatred and envy, they refused credence to these signs, by which they might have known that He was the Son of God.

Reply Obj. 2: The words quoted are preceded by the following: "If I had not done among them the works that no other man hath done, they would not have sin"; and then follow the words: "But now they have both seen and hated both Me and My Father." Now all this shows that while they beheld Christ's marvelous works, it was owing to their hatred that they did not know Him to be the Son of God.

Reply Obj. 3: Affected ignorance does not excuse from guilt, but seems, rather, to aggravate it: for it shows that a man is so strongly attached to sin that he wishes to incur ignorance lest he avoid sinning. The Jews therefore sinned, as crucifiers not only of the Man-Christ, but also as of God.

SIXTH ARTICLE [III, Q. 47, Art. 6]

Whether the Sin of Those Who Crucified Christ Was Most Grievous?

Objection 1: It would seem that the sin of Christ's crucifiers was not the most grievous. Because the sin which has some excuse cannot be most grievous. But our Lord Himself excused the sin of His crucifiers when He said: "Father, forgive them: for they know not what they do" (Luke 23:34). Therefore theirs was not the most grievous sin.

Obj. 2: Further, our Lord said to Pilate (John 19:11): "He that hath delivered Me to thee hath the greater sin." But it was Pilate who caused Christ to be crucified by his minions. Therefore the sin of Judas the traitor seems to be greater than that of those who crucified Him.

Obj. 3: Further, according to the Philosopher (Ethic. v): "No one suffers injustice willingly"; and in the same place he adds: "Where no one suffers injustice, nobody works injustice." Consequently nobody wreaks injustice upon a willing subject. But Christ suffered willingly, as was shown above (AA. 1, 2). Therefore those who crucified Christ did Him no injustice; and hence their sin was not the most grievous.

*On the contrary,* Chrysostom, commenting on the words, "Fill ye up, then, the measure of your fathers" (Matt. 23:32), says: "In very truth they exceeded the measure of their fathers; for these latter slew men, but they crucified God."

*I answer that,* As stated above (A. 5), the rulers of the Jews knew that He was the Christ: and if there was any ignorance in them, it was affected ignorance, which could not excuse them. Therefore their sin was the most grievous, both on account of the kind of sin, as well as from the malice of their will. The Jews also of the common order sinned most grievously as to the kind of their sin: yet in one respect their crime was lessened by reason of their ignorance. Hence Bede, commenting on Luke 23:34, "Father, forgive them, for they know not what they do," says: "He prays for them who know not what they are doing, as having the zeal of God, but not according to knowledge." But the sin of the Gentiles, by whose hands He was crucified, was much more excusable, since they had no knowledge of the Law.

Reply Obj. 1: As stated above, the excuse made by our Lord is not to be referred to the rulers among the Jews, but to the common people.

Reply Obj. 2: Judas did not deliver up Christ to Pilate, but to the chief priests who gave Him up to Pilate, according to John 18:35: "Thy own nation and the chief priests have delivered Thee up to me." But the sin of all these was greater than that of Pilate, who slew Christ from fear of Caesar; and even greater than the sin of the soldiers who crucified Him at the governor's bidding, not out of cupidity like Judas, nor from envy and hate like the chief priests.

Reply Obj. 3: Christ, indeed willed His Passion just as the Father willed it; yet He did not will the unjust action of the Jews. Consequently Christ's slayers are not excused of their injustice. Nevertheless, whoever slays a man not only does a wrong to the one slain, but likewise to God and to the State; just as he who kills himself, as the Philosopher says (Ethic. v). Hence it was that David condemned to death the man who "did not fear to lay hands upon the Lord's anointed," even though he (Saul) had requested it, as related 2 Kings 1:5-14.

# QUESTION 48

OF THE EFFICIENCY OF CHRIST'S PASSION (In Six Articles)

We now have to consider Christ's Passion as to its effect; first of all, as to the manner in which it was brought about; and, secondly, as to the effect in itself. Under the first heading there are six points for inquiry:

(1) Whether Christ's Passion brought about our salvation by way of merit?

(2) Whether it was by way of atonement?

(3) Whether it was by way of sacrifice?

(4) Whether it was by way of redemption?

(5) Whether it is proper to Christ to be the Redeemer?

(6) Whether (the Passion) secured man's salvation efficiently?

FIRST ARTICLE [III, Q. 48, Art. 1]

Whether Christ's Passion Brought About Our Salvation by Way of Merit?

Objection 1: It would seem that Christ's Passion did not bring about our salvation by way of merit. For the sources of our sufferings are not within us. But no one merits or is praised except for that whose principle lies within him. Therefore Christ's Passion wrought nothing by way of merit.

Obj. 2: Further, from the beginning of His conception Christ merited for Himself and for us, as stated above (Q. 9, A. 4; Q. 34, A. 3). But it is superfluous to merit over again what has been merited before. Therefore by His Passion Christ did not merit our salvation.

Obj. 3: Further, the source of merit is charity. But Christ's charity was not made greater by the Passion than it was before. Therefore He did not merit our salvation by suffering more than He had already.

*On the contrary,* on the words of Phil. 2:9, "Therefore God exalted Him," etc., Augustine says (Tract. civ in Joan.): "The lowliness" of the Passion "merited glory; glory was the reward of lowliness." But He was glorified, not merely in Himself, but likewise in His faithful ones, as He says Himself (John 17:10). Therefore it appears that He merited the salvation of the faithful.

*I answer that,* As stated above (Q. 7, AA. 1, 9; Q. 8, AA. 1, 5), grace was bestowed upon Christ, not only as an individual, but inasmuch as He is the Head of the Church, so that it might overflow into His members; and therefore Christ's works are referred to Himself and to His members in the same way as the works of any other man in a state of grace are referred to himself. But it is evident that whosoever suffers for justice's sake, provided that he be in a state of grace, merits his salvation thereby, according to Matt. 5:10: "Blessed are they that suffer persecution for justice's sake." Consequently Christ by His Passion merited salvation, not only for Himself, but likewise for all His members.

Reply Obj. 1: Suffering, as such, is caused by an outward principle: but inasmuch as one bears it willingly, it has an inward principle.

Reply Obj. 2: From the beginning of His conception Christ merited our eternal salvation; but on our side there were some obstacles, whereby we were hindered from securing the effect of His preceding merits: consequently, in order to remove such hindrances, "it was necessary for Christ to suffer," as stated above (Q. 46, A. 3).

Reply Obj. 3: Christ's Passion has a special effect, which His preceding merits did not possess, not on account of greater charity, but because of the nature of the work, which was suitable for such an effect, as is clear from the arguments brought forward above all the fittingness of Christ's Passion (Q. 46, AA, 3, 4).

SECOND ARTICLE [III, Q. 48, Art. 2]

Whether Christ's Passion Brought About Our Salvation by Way of Atonement?

Objection 1: It would seem that Christ's Passion did not bring about our salvation by way of atonement. For it seems that to make the atonement devolves on him who commits the sin; as is clear in the other parts of penance, because he who has done the wrong must grieve over it and confess it. But Christ never sinned, according to 1 Pet. 2:22: "Who did no sin." Therefore He made no atonement by His personal suffering.

Obj. 2: Further, no atonement is made to another by committing a graver offense. But in Christ's Passion the gravest of all offenses was perpetrated, because those who slew Him sinned most grievously, as stated above (Q. 47, A. 6). Consequently it seems that atonement could not be made to God by Christ's Passion.

Obj. 3: Further, atonement implies equality with

the trespass, since it is an act of justice. But Christ's Passion does not appear equal to all the sins of the human race, because Christ did not suffer in His Godhead, but in His flesh, according to 1 Pet. 4:1: "Christ therefore having suffered in the flesh." Now the soul, which is the subject of sin, is of greater account than the flesh. Therefore Christ did not atone for our sins by His Passion.

*On the contrary,* It is written (Ps. 68:5) in Christ's person: "Then did I pay that which I took not away." But he has not paid who has not fully atoned. Therefore it appears that Christ by His suffering has fully atoned for our sins.

*I answer that,* He properly atones for an offense who offers something which the offended one loves equally, or even more than he detested the offense. But by suffering out of love and obedience, Christ gave more to God than was required to compensate for the offense of the whole human race. First of all, because of the exceeding charity from which He suffered; secondly, on account of the dignity of His life which He laid down in atonement, for it was the life of one who was God and man; thirdly, on account of the extent of the Passion, and the greatness of the grief endured, as stated above (Q. 46, A. 6). And therefore Christ's Passion was not only a sufficient but a superabundant atonement for the sins of the human race; according to 1 John 2:2: "He is the propitiation for our sins: and not for ours only, but also for those of the whole world."

Reply Obj. 1: The head and members are as one mystic person; and therefore Christ's satisfaction belongs to all the faithful as being His members. Also, in so far as any two men are one in charity, the one can atone for the other as shall be shown later (Suppl., Q. 13, A. 2). But the same reason does not hold good of confession and contrition, because atonement consists in an outward action, for which helps may be used, among which friends are to be computed.

Reply Obj. 2: Christ's love was greater than His slayers' malice: and therefore the value of His Passion in atoning surpassed the murderous guilt of those who crucified Him: so much so that Christ's suffering was sufficient and superabundant atonement for His murderer's crime.

Reply Obj. 3: The dignity of Christ's flesh is not to be estimated solely from the nature of flesh, but also from the Person assuming it--namely, inasmuch as it was God's flesh, the result of which was that it was of infinite worth.

THIRD ARTICLE [III, Q. 48, Art. 3]

Whether Christ's Passion Operated by Way of Sacrifice?

Objection 1: It would seem that Christ's Passion did not operate by way of sacrifice. For the truth should correspond with the figure. But human flesh was never offered up in the sacrifices of the Old Law, which were figures of Christ: nay, such sacrifices were reputed as impious, according to Ps. 105:38: "And they shed innocent blood: the blood of their sons and of their daughters, which they sacrificed to the idols of Chanaan." It seems therefore that Christ's Passion cannot be called a sacrifice.

Obj. 2: Further, Augustine says (De Civ. Dei x) that "a visible sacrifice is a sacrament--that is, a sacred sign--of an invisible sacrifice." Now Christ's Passion is not a sign, but rather the thing signified by other signs. Therefore it seems that Christ's Passion is not a sacrifice.

Obj. 3: Further, whoever offers sacrifice performs some sacred rite, as the very word "sacrifice" shows. But those men who slew Christ did not perform any sacred act, but rather wrought a great wrong. Therefore Christ's Passion was rather a malefice than a sacrifice.

*On the contrary,* The Apostle says (Eph. 5:2): "He delivered Himself up for us, an oblation and a sacrifice to God for an odor of sweetness."

*I answer that,* A sacrifice properly so called is something done for that honor which is properly due to God, in order to appease Him: and hence it is that Augustine says (De Civ. Dei x): "A true sacrifice is every good work done in order that we may cling to God in holy fellowship, yet referred to that consummation of happiness wherein we can be truly blessed." But, as is added in the same place, "Christ offered Himself up for us in the Passion": and this voluntary enduring of the Passion was most acceptable to God, as coming from charity. Therefore it is manifest that Christ's Passion was a true sacrifice. Moreover, as Augustine says farther on in the same book, "the primitive sacrifices of the holy Fathers were many and various signs of this true sacrifice, one being prefigured by many, in the same way as a single concept of thought is expressed in many words, in order to commend it without tediousness": and, as Augustine observe, (De Trin. iv), "since there are four things to be noted in every sacrifice--to wit, to whom it is offered, by whom it is offered, what is offered, and for whom it is offered--that the same one true Mediator reconciling us with God through the peace-sacrifice might continue to be one with Him to whom He offered it, might be one with them for whom He offered it, and might Himself be the offerer and what He offered."

Reply Obj. 1: Although the truth answers to the figure in some respects, yet it does not in all, since the truth must go beyond the figure. Therefore the figure of this sacrifice, in which Christ's flesh is offered, was flesh right fittingly, not the flesh of men, but of animals, as denoting Christ's. And this is a most perfect sacrifice. First of all, since being flesh of human nature, it is fittingly offered for men, and is partaken of by them under the Sacrament. Secondly, because being passible and mortal, it was fit for immolation. Thirdly, because, being sinless, it had virtue to cleanse from sins. Fourthly, because, being the offerer's own flesh, it was acceptable to God on account of His charity in offering up His own flesh. Hence it is that Augustine says (De Trin. iv): "What else could be so fittingly partaken of by men, or offered up for men, as human flesh? What else could be so appropriate for this immolation as mortal flesh? What else is there so clean for cleansing mortals as the flesh born in the womb without fleshly concupiscence, and coming from a virginal womb? What could be so favorably offered and accepted as the flesh of our sacrifice, which was made the body of our Priest?"

Reply Obj. 2: Augustine is speaking there of visible figurative sacrifices: and even Christ's Passion, although denoted by other figurative sacrifices, is yet a sign of something to be observed by us, according to 1 Pet. 4:1: "Christ therefore, having suffered in the flesh, be you also armed with the same thought: for he that hath suffered in the flesh hath ceased from sins: that now he may live the rest of his time in the flesh, not after the desires of men, but according to the will of God."

Reply Obj. 3: Christ's Passion was indeed a malefice on His slayers' part; but on His own it was the sacrifice of one suffering out of charity. Hence it is Christ who is said to have offered this sacrifice, and not the executioners.

FOURTH ARTICLE [III, Q. 48, Art. 3]

Whether Christ's Passion Brought About Our Salvation by Way of Redemption?

Objection 1: It would seem that Christ's Passion did not effect our salvation by way of redemption. For no one purchases or redeems what never ceased to belong to him. But men never ceased to belong to God according to Ps. 23:1: "The earth is the Lord's and the fulness thereof: the world and all they that dwell therein." Therefore it seems that Christ did not redeem us by His Passion.

Obj. 2: Further, as Augustine says (De Trin. xiii): "The devil had to be overthrown by Christ's justice." But justice requires that the man who has treacherously seized another's property shall be deprived of it, because deceit and cunning should not benefit anyone, as even human laws declare. Consequently, since the devil by treachery deceived and subjugated to himself man, who is God's creature, it seems that man ought not to be rescued from his power by way of redemption.

Obj. 3: Further, whoever buys or redeems an object pays the price to the holder. But it was not to the devil, who held us in bondage, that Christ paid His blood as the price of our redemption. Therefore Christ did not redeem us by His Passion.

*On the contrary,* It is written (1 Pet. 1:18): "You were not redeemed with corruptible things as gold or silver from your vain conversation of the tradition of your fathers: but with the precious blood of Christ, as of a lamb unspotted and undefiled." And (Gal. 3:13): "Christ hath redeemed us from the curse of the law, being made a curse for us." Now He is said to be a curse for us inasmuch as He suffered upon the tree, as stated above (Q. 46, A. 4). Therefore He did redeem us by His Passion.

*I answer that,* Man was held captive on account of sin in two ways: first of all, by the bondage of sin, because (John 8:34): "Whosoever committeth sin is the servant of sin"; and (2 Pet. 2:19): "By whom a man is overcome, of the same also he is the slave." Since, then, the devil had overcome man by inducing him to sin, man was subject to the devil's bondage. Secondly, as to the debt of punishment, to the payment of which man was held fast by God's justice: and this, too, is a kind of bondage, since it savors of bondage for a man to suffer what he does not wish, just as it is the free man's condition to apply himself to what he wills.

Since, then, Christ's Passion was a sufficient and a superabundant atonement for the sin and the debt of the human race, it was as a price at the cost of which we were freed from both obligations. For the atonement by which one satisfies for self or another is called the price, by which he ransoms himself or someone else from sin and its penalty, according to Dan. 4:24: "Redeem thou thy sins with alms." Now Christ made satisfaction, not by giving money or anything of the sort, but by bestowing what was of greatest price--Himself--for us. And therefore Christ's Passion is called our redemption.

Reply Obj. 1: Man is said to belong to God in two ways. First of all, in so far as he comes under God's power: in which way he never ceased to belong to God; according to Dan. 4:22: "The Most High ruleth over the kingdom of men, and giveth it to whomsoever he will." Secondly, by being united to Him in charity, according to Rom. 8:9: "If any man have not the Spirit of Christ, he is none of His." In the first way, then, man never ceased to belong to God, but in the second way he did cease because of sin. And therefore in so far as he was delivered from sin by the satisfaction of Christ's Passion, he is said to be redeemed by the Passion of Christ.

Reply Obj. 2: Man by sinning became the bondsman both of God and of the devil. Through guilt he had offended God, and put himself under the devil by consenting to him; consequently he did not become God's servant on account of his guilt, but rather, by withdrawing from God's service, he, by God's just permission, fell under the devil's servitude on account of the offense perpetrated. But as to the penalty, man was chiefly bound to God as his sovereign judge, and to the devil as his torturer, according to Matt. 5:25: "Lest perhaps the adversary deliver thee to the judge, and the judge deliver thee to the officer"--that is, "to the relentless avenging angel," as Chrysostom says (Hom. xi). Consequently, although, after deceiving man, the devil, so far as in him lay, held him unjustly in bondage as to both sin and penalty, still it was just that man should suffer it, God so permitting it as to the sin and ordaining it as to the penalty. And therefore justice required man's redemption with regard to God, but not with regard to the devil.

Reply Obj. 3: Because, with regard to God, redemption was necessary for man's deliverance, but not with regard to the devil, the price had to be paid not to the devil, but to God. And therefore Christ is said to have paid the price of our redemption--His own precious blood--not to the devil, but to God.

FIFTH ARTICLE [III, Q. 48, Art. 5]

Whether It Is Proper to Christ to Be the Redeemer?

Objection 1: It would seem that it is not proper to Christ to be the Redeemer, because it is written (Ps. 30:6): "Thou hast redeemed me, O Lord, the God of Truth." But to be the Lord God of Truth belongs to the entire Trinity. Therefore it is not proper to Christ.

Obj. 2: Further, he is said to redeem who pays the price of redemption. But God the Father gave His Son in redemption for our sins, as is written (Ps. 110:9): "The Lord hath sent redemption to His people," upon which the gloss adds, "that is, Christ, who gives redemption to captives." Therefore not only Christ, but the Father also, redeemed us.

Obj. 3: Further, not only Christ's Passion, but also that of other saints conduced to our salvation, according to Col. 1:24: "I now rejoice in my sufferings for you, and fill up those things that are wanting of the sufferings of Christ, in my flesh for His body, which is the Church." Therefore the title of Redeemer belongs not only to Christ, but also to the other saints.

*On the contrary,* It is written (Gal. 3:13): "Christ redeemed us from the curse of the Law, being made a curse for us." But only Christ was made a curse for us. Therefore only Christ ought to be called our Redeemer.

*I answer that,* For someone to redeem, two things are required--namely, the act of paying and the price paid. For if in redeeming something a man pays a price which is not his own, but another's, he is not said to be the chief redeemer, but rather the other is, whose price it is. Now Christ's blood or His bodily life, which "is in the blood," is the price of our redemption (Lev. 17:11, 14), and that life He paid. Hence both of these belong immediately to Christ as man; but to the Trinity as to the first and remote cause, to whom Christ's life belonged as to its first author, and from whom Christ received the inspiration of suffering for us. Consequently it is proper to Christ as man to be the Redeemer immediately; although the redemption may be ascribed to the whole Trinity as its first cause.

Reply Obj. 1: A gloss explains the text thus: "Thou, O Lord God of Truth, hast redeemed me in Christ, crying out, 'Lord, into Thy hands I commend my spirit.'" And so redemption belongs immediately to the Man-Christ, but principally to God.

Reply Obj. 2: The Man-Christ paid the price of our redemption immediately, but at the command of the Father as the original author.

Reply Obj. 3: The sufferings of the saints are beneficial to the Church, as by way, not of redemption, but of example and exhortation, according to 2 Cor. 1:6: "Whether we be in tribulation, it is for your exhortation and salvation."

SIXTH ARTICLE [III, Q. 48, Art. 6]

Whether Christ's Passion Brought About Our Salvation Efficiently?

Objection 1: It would seem that Christ's Passion did not bring about our salvation efficiently. For the efficient cause of our salvation is the greatness of the Divine power, according to Isa. 59:1: "Behold the hand of the Lord is not shortened that it cannot save." But "Christ was crucified through weakness," as it is written (2 Cor. 13:4). Therefore, Christ's Passion did not bring about our salvation efficiently.

Obj. 2: Further, no corporeal agency acts efficiently except by contact: hence even Christ cleansed the leper by touching him "in order to show that His flesh had saving power," as Chrysostom [*Theophylact, Enarr. in Luc.] says. But Christ's Passion could not touch all mankind. Therefore it could not efficiently bring about the salvation of all men.

Obj. 3: Further, it does not seem to be consistent for the same agent to operate by way of merit and by way of efficiency, since he who merits awaits the result from someone else. But it was by way of merit that Christ's Passion accomplished our salvation. Therefore it was not by way of efficiency.

*On the contrary,* It is written (1 Cor. 1:18) that "the word of the cross to them that are saved . . . is the power of God." But God's power brings about our salvation efficiently. Therefore Christ's Passion on the cross accomplished our salvation efficiently.

*I answer that,* There is a twofold efficient agency--namely, the principal and the instrumental. Now the principal efficient cause of man's salvation is God. But since Christ's humanity is the "instrument of the Godhead," as stated above (Q. 43, A. 2), therefore all Christ's actions and sufferings operate instrumentally in virtue of His Godhead for the salvation of men. Consequently, then, Christ's Passion accomplishes man's salvation efficiently.

Reply Obj. 1: Christ's Passion in relation to His flesh is consistent with the infirmity which He took upon Himself, but in relation to the Godhead it draws infinite might from It, according to 1 Cor. 1:25: "The weakness of God is stronger than men"; because Christ's weakness, inasmuch as He is God, has a might exceeding all human power.

Reply Obj. 2: Christ's Passion, although corporeal, has yet a spiritual effect from the Godhead united: and therefore it secures its efficacy by spiritual contact--namely, by faith and the sacraments of faith, as the Apostle says (Rom. 3:25): "Whom God hath proposed to be a propitiation, through faith in His blood."

Reply Obj. 3: Christ's Passion, according as it is compared with His Godhead, operates in an efficient manner: but in so far as it is compared with the will of Christ's soul it acts in a meritorious manner: considered as being within Christ's very flesh, it acts by way of satisfaction, inasmuch as we are liberated by it from the debt of punishment; while inasmuch as we are freed from the servitude of guilt, it acts by way of redemption: but in so far as we are reconciled with God it acts by way of sacrifice, as shall be shown farther on (Q. 49).

# QUESTION 49

OF THE EFFECTS OF CHRIST'S PASSION (In Six Articles)

We have now to consider what are the effects of Christ's Passion, concerning which there are six points of inquiry:

(1) Whether we were freed from sin by Christ's Passion?

(2) Whether we were thereby delivered from the power of the devil?

(3) Whether we were freed thereby from our debt of punishment?

(4) Whether we were thereby reconciled with God?

(5) Whether heaven's gate was opened to us thereby?

(6) Whether Christ derived exaltation from it?

FIRST ARTICLE [III, Q. 49, Art. 1]

Whether We Were Delivered from Sin Through Christ's Passion?

Objection 1: It would seem that we were not delivered from sin through Christ's Passion. For to deliver from sin belongs to God alone, according to Isa. 43:25: "I am He who blot out your iniquities for My own sake." But Christ did not suffer as God, but as man. Therefore Christ's Passion did not free us from sin.

Obj. 2: Further, what is corporeal does not act upon what is spiritual. But Christ's Passion is corporeal, whereas sin exists in the soul, which is a spiritual creature. Therefore Christ's Passion could not cleanse us from sin.

Obj. 3: Further, one cannot be purged from a sin not yet committed, but which shall be committed hereafter. Since, then, many sins have been committed since Christ's death, and are being committed daily, it seems that we were not delivered from sin by Christ's death.

Obj. 4: Further, given an efficient cause, nothing else is required for producing the effect. But other things besides are required for the forgiveness of sins, such as baptism and penance. Consequently it seems that Christ's Passion is not the sufficient cause of the forgiveness of sins.

Obj. 5: Further, it is written (Prov. 10:12): "Charity covereth all sins"; and (Prov. 15:27): "By mercy and faith, sins are purged away." But there are many other things of which we have faith, and which excite charity. Therefore Christ's Passion is not the proper cause of the forgiveness of sins.

*On the contrary,* It is written (Apoc. 1:5): "He loved us, and washed us from our sins in His own blood."

*I answer that,* Christ's Passion is the proper cause of the forgiveness of sins in three ways. First of all, by way of exciting our charity, because, as the Apostle says (Rom. 5:8): "God commendeth His charity towards us: because when as yet we were sinners, according to the time, Christ died for us." But it is by charity that we procure pardon of our sins, according to Luke 7:47: "Many sins are forgiven her because she hath loved much." Secondly, Christ's Passion causes forgiveness of sins by way of redemption. For since He is our head, then, by the Passion which He endured from love and obedience, He delivered us as His members from our sins, as by the price of His Passion: in the same way as if a man by the good industry of his hands were to redeem himself from a sin committed with his feet. For, just as the natural body is one though made up of diverse members, so the whole Church, Christ's mystic body, is reckoned as one person with its head, which is Christ. Thirdly, by way of efficiency, inasmuch as Christ's flesh, wherein He endured the Passion, is the instrument of the Godhead, so that His sufferings and actions operate with Divine power for expelling sin.

Reply Obj. 1: Although Christ did not suffer as God, nevertheless His flesh is the instrument of the Godhead; and hence it is that His Passion has a kind of Divine Power of casting out sin, as was said above.

Reply Obj. 2: Although Christ's Passion is corporeal, still it derives a kind of spiritual energy from the Godhead, to which the flesh is united as an instrument: and according to this power Christ's Passion is the cause of the forgiveness of sins.

Reply Obj. 3: Christ by His Passion delivered us from our sins causally--that is, by setting up the cause of our deliverance, from which cause all sins whatsoever, past, present, or to come, could be forgiven: just as if a doctor were to prepare a medicine by which all sicknesses can be cured even in future.

Reply Obj. 4: As stated above, since Christ's Passion preceded, as a kind of universal cause of the forgiveness of sins, it needs to be applied to each individual for the cleansing of personal sins. Now this is done by baptism and penance and the other sacraments, which derive their power from Christ's Passion, as shall be shown later (Q. 62, A. 5).

Reply Obj. 5: Christ's Passion is applied to us even through faith, that we may share in its fruits, according to Rom. 3:25: "Whom God hath proposed to be a propitiation, through faith in His blood." But the faith through which we are cleansed from sin is not lifeless faith, which can exist even with sin, but faith living through charity; that thus Christ's Passion may be applied to us, not only as to our minds, but also as to our hearts. And even in this way sins are forgiven through the power of the Passion of Christ.

SECOND ARTICLE [III, Q. 49, Art. 2]

Whether We Were Delivered from the Devil's Power Through Christ's Passion?

Objection 1: It would seem that we were not delivered from the power of the devil through Christ's Passion. For he has no power over others, who can do nothing to them without the sanction of another. But without the Divine permission the devil could never do hurt to any man, as is evident in the instance of Job (1, 2), where, by power received from God, the devil first injured him in his possessions, and afterwards in his body. In like manner it is stated (Matt. 8:31, 32) that the devils could not enter into the swine except with Christ's leave. Therefore the devil never had power over men: and hence we are not delivered from his power through Christ's Passion.

Obj. 2: Further, the devil exercises his power over men by tempting them and molesting their bodies. But even after the Passion he continues to do the same to men. Therefore we are not delivered from his power through Christ's Passion.

Obj. 3: Further, the might of Christ's Passion endures for ever, as, according to Heb. 10:14: "By one oblation He hath perfected for ever them that are sanctified." But deliverance from the devil's power is not found everywhere, since there are still idolaters in many regions of the world; nor will it endure for ever, because in the time of Antichrist he will be especially active in using his power to the hurt of men; because it is said of him (2 Thess. 2:9): "Whose coming is according to the working of Satan, in all power, and signs, and lying wonders, and in all seduction of iniquity." Consequently it seems that Christ's Passion is not the cause of the human race being delivered from the power of the devil.

*On the contrary,* our Lord said (John 12:31), when His Passion was drawing nigh: "Now shall the prince of this world be cast out; and I, if I be lifted up from the earth, will draw all things to Myself." Now He was lifted up from the earth by His Passion on the cross. Therefore by His Passion the devil was deprived of his power over man.

*I answer that,* There are three things to be considered regarding the power which the devil exercised over men previous to Christ's Passion. The first is on man's own part, who by his sin deserved to be delivered over to the devil's power, and was overcome by his tempting. Another point is on God's part, whom man had offended by sinning, and who with justice left man under the devil's power. The third is on the devil's part, who out of his most wicked will hindered man from securing his salvation.

As to the first point, by Christ's Passion man was delivered from the devil's power, in so far as the Passion is the cause of the forgiveness of sins, as stated above (A. 1). As to the second, it must be said that Christ's Passion freed us from the devil's power, inasmuch as it reconciled us with God, as shall be shown later (A. 4). But as to the third, Christ's Passion delivered us from the devil, inasmuch as in Christ's Passion he exceeded the limit of power assigned him by God, by conspiring to bring about Christ's death, Who, being sinless, did not deserve to die. Hence Augustine says (De Trin. xiii, cap. xiv): "The devil was vanquished by Christ's justice: because, while discovering in Him nothing deserving of death, nevertheless he slew Him. And it is certainly just that the debtors whom he held captive should be set at liberty since they believed in Him whom the devil slew, though He was no debtor."

Reply Obj. 1: The devil is said to have had such power over men not as though he were able to injure them without God's sanction, but because he was justly permitted to injure men whom by tempting he had induced to give consent.

Reply Obj. 2: God so permitting it, the devil can still tempt men's souls and harass their bodies: yet there is a remedy provided for man through Christ's Passion, whereby he can safeguard himself against the enemy's assaults, so as not to be dragged down into the destruction of everlasting death. And all who resisted the devil previous to the Passion were enabled to do so through faith in the Passion, although it was not yet accomplished. Yet in one respect no one was able to escape the devil's hands, i.e. so as not to descend into hell. But after Christ's Passion, men can defend themselves from this by its power.

Reply Obj. 3: God permits the devil to deceive men by certain persons, and in times and places, according to the hidden motive of His judgments; still, there is always a remedy provided through Christ's Passion, for defending themselves against the wicked snares of the demons, even in Antichrist's time. But if any man neglect to make use of this remedy, it detracts nothing from the efficacy of Christ's Passion.

THIRD ARTICLE [III, Q. 49, Art. 3]

Whether Men Were Freed from the Punishment of Sin Through Christ's Passion?

Objection 1: It would seem that men were not freed from the punishment of sin by Christ's Passion. For the chief punishment of sin is eternal damnation. But those damned in hell for their sins were not set free by Christ's Passion, because "in hell there is no redemption" [*Office of the Dead, Resp. vii]. It seems, therefore, that Christ's Passion did not deliver men from the punishment of sin.

Obj. 2: Further, no punishment should be imposed upon them who are delivered from the debt of punishment. But a satisfactory punishment is imposed upon penitents. Consequently, men were not freed from the debt of punishment by Christ's Passion.

Obj. 3: Further, death is a punishment of sin, according to Rom. 6:23: "The wages of sin is death." But men still die after Christ's Passion. Therefore it seems that we have not been delivered from the debt of punishment.

*On the contrary,* It is written (Isa. 53:4): "Surely He hath borne our iniquities and carried our sorrows."

*I answer that,* Through Christ's Passion we have been delivered from the debt of punishment in two ways. First of all, directly--namely, inasmuch as Christ's Passion was sufficient and superabundant satisfaction for the sins of the whole human race: but when sufficient satisfaction has been paid, then the debt of punishment is abolished. In another way--indirectly, that is to say--in so far as Christ's Passion is the cause of the forgiveness of sin, upon which the debt of punishment rests.

Reply Obj. 1: Christ's Passion works its effect in them to whom it is applied, through faith and charity and the sacraments of faith. And, consequently, the lost in hell cannot avail themselves of its effects, since they are not united to Christ in the aforesaid manner.

Reply Obj. 2: As stated above (A. 1, ad 4, 5), in order to secure the effects of Christ's Passion, we must be likened unto Him. Now we are likened unto Him sacramentally in Baptism, according to Rom. 6:4: "For we are buried together with Him by baptism into death." Hence no punishment of satisfaction is imposed upon men at their baptism, since they are fully delivered by Christ's satisfaction. But because, as it is written (1 Pet. 3:18), "Christ died" but "once for our sins," therefore a man cannot a second time be likened unto Christ's death by the sacrament of Baptism. Hence it is necessary that those who sin after Baptism be likened unto Christ suffering by some form of punishment or suffering which they endure in their own person; yet, by the co-operation of Christ's satisfaction, much lighter penalty suffices than one that is proportionate to the sin.

Reply Obj. 3: Christ's satisfaction works its effect in us inasmuch as we are incorporated with Him, as the members with their head, as stated above (A. 1). Now the members must be conformed to their head. Consequently, as Christ first had grace in His soul with bodily passibility, and through the Passion attained to the glory of immortality, so we likewise, who are His members, are freed by His Passion from all debt of punishment, yet so that we first receive in our souls "the spirit of adoption of sons," whereby our names are written down for the inheritance of immortal glory, while we yet have a passible and mortal body: but afterwards, "being made conformable" to the sufferings and death of Christ, we are brought into immortal glory, according to the saying of the Apostle (Rom. 8:17): "And if sons, heirs also: heirs indeed of God, and joint heirs with Christ; yet so if we suffer with Him, that we may be also glorified with Him."

FOURTH ARTICLE [III, Q. 49, Art. 4]

Whether We Were Reconciled to God Through Christ's Passion?

Objection 1: It would seem that we were not reconciled to God through Christ's Passion. For there is no need of reconciliation between friends. But God always loved us, according to Wis. 11:25: "Thou lovest all the things that are, and hatest none of the things which Thou hast made." Therefore Christ's Passion did not reconcile us to God.

Obj. 2: Further, the same thing cannot be cause and effect: hence grace, which is the cause of meriting, does not come under merit. But God's love is the cause of Christ's Passion, according to John 3:16: "God so loved the world, as to give His only-begotten Son." It does not appear, then, that we were reconciled to God through Christ's Passion, so that He began to love us anew.

Obj. 3: Further, Christ's Passion was completed by men slaying Him; and thereby they offended God grievously. Therefore Christ's Passion is rather the cause of wrath than of reconciliation to God.

*On the contrary,* The Apostle says (Rom. 5:10): "We are reconciled to God by the death of His Son."

*I answer that,* Christ's Passion is in two ways the cause of our reconciliation to God. In the first way, inasmuch as it takes away sin by which men became God's enemies, according to Wis. 14:9: "To God the wicked and his wickedness are hateful alike"; and Ps. 5:7: "Thou hatest all the workers of iniquity." In another way, inasmuch as it is a most acceptable sacrifice to God. Now it is the proper effect of sacrifice to appease God: just as man likewise overlooks an offense committed against him on account of some pleasing act of homage shown him. Hence it is written (1 Kings 26:19): "If the Lord stir thee up against me, let Him accept of sacrifice." And in like fashion Christ's voluntary suffering was such a good act that, because of its being found in human nature, God was appeased for every offense of the human race with regard to those who are made one with the crucified Christ in the aforesaid manner (A. 1, ad 4).

Reply Obj. 1: God loves all men as to their nature, which He Himself made; yet He hates them with respect to the crimes they commit against Him, according to Ecclus. 12:3: "The Highest hateth sinners."

Reply Obj. 2: Christ is not said to have reconciled us with God, as if God had begun anew to love us, since it is written (Jer. 31:3): "I have loved thee with an everlasting love"; but because the source of hatred was taken away by Christ's Passion, both through sin being washed away and through compensation being made in the shape of a more pleasing offering.

Reply Obj. 3: As Christ's slayers were men, so

also was the Christ slain. Now the charity of the suffering Christ surpassed the wickedness of His slayers. Accordingly Christ's Passion prevailed more in reconciling God to the whole human race than in provoking Him to wrath.

FIFTH ARTICLE [III, Q. 49, Art. 5]

Whether Christ Opened the Gate of Heaven to Us by His Passion?

Objection 1: It would seem that Christ did not open the gate of heaven to us by His Passion. For it is written (Prov. 11:18): "To him that soweth justice, there is a faithful reward." But the reward of justice is the entering into the kingdom of heaven. It seems, therefore, that the holy Fathers who wrought works of justice, obtained by faith the entering into the heavenly kingdom even without Christ's Passion. Consequently Christ's Passion is not the cause of the opening of the gate of the kingdom of heaven.

Obj. 2: Further, Elias was caught up to heaven previous to Christ's Passion (4 Kings 2). But the effect never precedes the cause. Therefore it seems that the opening of heaven's gate is not the result of Christ's Passion.

Obj. 3: Further, as it is written (Matt. 3:16), when Christ was baptized the heavens were opened to Him. But His baptism preceded the Passion. Consequently the opening of heaven is not the result of Christ's Passion.

Obj. 4: Further, it is written (Mic. 2:13): "For He shall go up that shall open the way before them." But to open the way to heaven seems to be nothing else than to throw open its gate. Therefore it seems that the gate of heaven was opened to us, not by Christ's Passion, but by His Ascension.

*On the contrary,* is the saying of the Apostle (Heb. 10:19): "We have [Vulg.: 'having a'] confidence in the entering into the Holies"--that is, of the heavenly places--"through the blood of Christ."

*I answer that,* The shutting of the gate is the obstacle which hinders men from entering in. But it is on account of sin that men were prevented from entering into the heavenly kingdom, since, according to Isa. 35:8: "It shall be called the holy way, and the unclean shall not pass over it." Now there is a twofold sin which prevents men from entering into the kingdom of heaven. The first is common to the whole race, for it is our first parents' sin, and by that sin heaven's entrance is closed to man. Hence we read in Gen. 3:24 that after our first parents' sin God "placed . . . cherubim and a flaming sword, turning every way, to keep the way of the tree of life." The other is the personal sin of each one of us, committed by our personal act.

Now by Christ's Passion we have been delivered not only from the common sin of the whole human race, both as to its guilt and as to the debt of punishment, for which He paid the penalty on our behalf; but, furthermore, from the personal sins of individuals, who share in His Passion by faith and charity and the sacraments of faith. Consequently, then the gate of heaven's kingdom is thrown open to us through Christ's Passion. This is precisely what the Apostle says (Heb. 9:11, 12): "Christ being come a high-priest of the good things to come . . . by His own blood entered once into the Holies, having obtained eternal redemption." And this is foreshadowed (Num. 35:25, 28), where it is said that the slayer* "shall abide there"--that is to say, in the city of refuge--"until the death of the high-priest, that is anointed with the holy oil: but after he is dead, then shall he return home." [*The Septuagint has 'slayer', the Vulgate, 'innocent'--i.e. the man who has slain 'without hatred and enmity'.]

Reply Obj. 1: The holy Fathers, by doing works of justice, merited to enter into the heavenly kingdom, through faith in Christ's Passion, according to Heb. 11:33: The saints "by faith conquered kingdoms, wrought justice," and each of them was thereby cleansed from sin, so far as the cleansing of the individual is concerned. Nevertheless the faith and righteousness of no one of them sufficed for removing the barrier arising from the guilt of the whole human race: but this was removed at the cost of Christ's blood. Consequently, before Christ's Passion no one could enter the kingdom of heaven by obtaining everlasting beatitude, which consists in the full enjoyment of God.

Reply Obj. 2: Elias was taken up into the atmospheric heaven, but not in to the empyrean heaven, which is the abode of the saints: and likewise Enoch was translated into the earthly paradise, where he is believed to live with Elias until the coming of Antichrist.

Reply Obj. 3: As was stated above (Q. 39, A. 5), the heavens were opened at Christ's baptism, not for Christ's sake, to whom heaven was ever open, but in order to signify that heaven is opened to the baptized, through Christ's baptism, which has its efficacy from His Passion.

Reply Obj. 4: Christ by His Passion merited for us the opening of the kingdom of heaven, and removed the obstacle; but by His ascension He, as it were, brought us to the possession of the heavenly kingdom. And consequently it is said that by ascending He "opened the way before them."

SIXTH ARTICLE [III, Q. 49, Art. 6]

Whether by His Passion Christ Merited to Be Exalted?

Objection 1: It seems that Christ did not merit to be exalted on account of His Passion. For eminence of rank belongs to God alone, just as knowledge of truth, according to Ps. 112:4: "The Lord is high above all nations, and His glory above the heavens." But Christ as man had the knowledge of all truth, not on account of any preceding merit, but from the very union of God and man, according to John 1:14: "We saw His glory . . . as it were of the only-Begotten of the Father, full of grace and of truth." Therefore neither had He exaltation from the merit of the Passion but from the union alone.

Obj. 2: Further, Christ merited for Himself from the first instant of His conception, as stated above (Q. 34, A. 3). But His love was no greater during the Passion than before. Therefore, since charity is the principle of merit, it seems that He did not merit exaltation from the Passion more than before.

Obj. 3: Further, the glory of the body comes from the glory of the soul, as Augustine says (Ep. ad Dioscor.). But by His Passion Christ did not merit exaltation as to the glory of His soul, because His soul was beatified from the first instant of His conception. Therefore neither did He merit exaltation, as to the glory of His body, from the Passion.

*On the contrary,* It is written (Phil. 2:8): "He became obedient unto death, even the death of the cross; for which cause God also exalted Him."

*I answer that,* Merit implies a certain equality of justice: hence the Apostle says (Rom. 4:4): "Now to him that worketh, the reward is reckoned according to debt." But when anyone by reason of his unjust will ascribes to himself something beyond his due, it is only just that he be deprived of something else which is his due; thus, "when a man steals a sheep he shall pay back four" (Ex. 22:1). And he is said to deserve it, inasmuch as his unjust will is chastised thereby. So likewise when any man through his just will has stripped himself of what he ought to have, he deserves that something further be granted to him as the reward of his just will. And hence it is written (Luke 14:11): "He that humbleth himself shall be exalted."

Now in His Passion Christ humbled Himself beneath His dignity in four respects. In the first place as to His Passion and death, to which He was not bound; secondly, as to the place, since His body was laid in a sepulchre and His soul in hell; thirdly, as to the shame and mockeries He endured; fourthly, as to His being delivered up to man's power, as He Himself said to Pilate (John 19:11): "Thou shouldst not have any power against Me, unless it were given thee from above." And, consequently, He merited a four-fold exaltation from His Passion. First of all, as to His glorious Resurrection: hence it is written (Ps. 138:1): "Thou hast known my sitting down"--that is, the lowliness of My Passion--"and My rising up." Secondly, as to His ascension into heaven: hence it is written (Eph. 4:9): "Now that He ascended, what is it, but because He also descended first into the lower parts of the earth? He that descended is the same also that ascended above all the heavens." Thirdly, as to the sitting on the right hand of the Father and the showing forth of His Godhead, according to Isa. 52:13: "He shall be exalted and extolled, and shall be exceeding high: as many have been astonished at him, so shall His visage be inglorious among men." Moreover (Phil. 2:8) it is written: "He humbled Himself, becoming obedient unto death, even to the death of the cross: for which cause also God hath exalted Him, and hath given Him a name which is above all names"--that is to say, so that He shall be hailed as God by all; and all shall pay Him homage as God. And this is expressed in what follows: "That in the name of Jesus every knee should bow, of those that are in heaven, on earth, and under the earth." Fourthly, as to His judiciary power: for it is written (Job 36:17): "Thy cause hath been judged as that of the wicked cause and judgment Thou shalt recover."

Reply Obj. 1: The source of meriting comes of the soul, while the body is the instrument of the meritorious work. And consequently the perfection of Christ's soul, which was the source of meriting, ought not to be acquired in Him by merit, like the perfection of the body, which was the subject of suffering, and was thereby the instrument of His merit.

Reply Obj. 2: Christ by His previous merits did merit exaltation on behalf of His soul, whose will was animated with charity and the other virtues; but in the Passion He merited His exaltation by way of recompense even on behalf of His body: since it is only just that the body, which from charity was subjected to the Passion, should receive recompense in glory.

Reply Obj. 3: It was owing to a special dispensation in Christ that before the Passion the glory of His soul did not shine out in His body, in order that He might procure His bodily glory with greater honor, when He had merited it by His Passion. But it was not beseeming for the glory of His soul to be postponed, since the soul was united immediately with the Word; hence it was beseeming that its glory should be filled by the Word Himself. But the body was united with the Word through the soul.

# QUESTION 50

OF THE DEATH OF CHRIST

We have now to consider the death of Christ; concerning which there are six subjects of inquiry:

(1) Whether it was fitting that Christ should die?

(2) Whether His death severed the union of Godhead and flesh?

(3) Whether His Godhead was separated from His soul?

(4) Whether Christ was a man during the three days of His death?

(5) Whether His was the same body, living and dead?

(6) Whether His death conduced in any way to our salvation?

FIRST ARTICLE [III, Q. 50, Art. 1]

Whether It Was Fitting That Christ Should Die?

Objection 1: It would seem that it was not fitting that Christ should die. For a first principle in any order is not affected by anything contrary to such order: thus fire, which is the principle of heat, can never become cold. But the Son of God is the fountain-head and principle of all life, according to Ps. 35:10: "With Thee is the fountain of life." Therefore it does not seem fitting for Christ to die.

Obj. 2: Further, death is a greater defect than sickness, because it is through sickness that one comes to die. But it was not beseeming for Christ to languish from sickness, as Chrysostom [*Athanasius, Orat. de Incarn. Verbi] says. Consequently, neither was it becoming for Christ to die.

Obj. 3: Further, our Lord said (John 10:10): "I am come that they may have life, and may have it more abundantly." But one opposite does not lead to another. Therefore it seems that neither was it fitting for Christ to die.

*On the contrary,* It is written, (John 11:50): "It is expedient that one man should die for the people . . . that the whole nation perish not": which words were spoken prophetically by Caiphas, as the Evangelist testifies.

*I answer that,* It was fitting for Christ to die. First of all to satisfy for the whole human race, which was sentenced to die on account of sin, according to Gen. 2:17: "In what day soever ye shall [Vulg.: 'thou shalt'] eat of it ye shall [Vulg.: 'thou shalt'] die the death." Now it is a fitting way of satisfying for another to submit oneself to the penalty deserved by that other. And so Christ resolved to die, that by dying He might atone for us, according to 1 Pet. 3:18: "Christ also died once for our sins." Secondly, in order to show the reality of the flesh assumed. For, as Eusebius says (Orat. de Laud. Constant. xv), "if, after dwelling among men Christ were suddenly to disappear from men's sight, as though shunning death, then by all men He would be likened to a phantom." Thirdly, that by dying He might deliver us from fearing death: hence it is written (Heb. 2:14, 15) that He communicated "to flesh and blood, that through death He might destroy him who had the empire of death and might deliver them who, through the fear of death, were all their lifetime subject to servitude." Fourthly, that by dying in the body to the likeness of sin--that is, to its penalty--He might set us the example of dying to sin spiritually. Hence it is written (Rom. 6:10): "For in that He died to sin, He died once, but in that He liveth, He liveth unto God: so do you also reckon that you are dead to sin, but alive unto God." Fifthly, that by rising from the dead, and manifesting His power whereby He overthrew death, He might instill into us the hope of rising from the dead. Hence the Apostle says (1 Cor. 15:12): "If Christ be preached that He rose again from the dead, how do some among you say, that there is no resurrection from the dead?"

Reply Obj. 1: Christ is the fountain of life, as God, and not as man: but He died as man, and not as God. Hence Augustine [*Vigilius Tapsensis] says against Felician: "Far be it from us to suppose that Christ so felt death that He lost His life inasmuch as He is life in Himself; for, were it so, the fountain of life would have run dry. Accordingly, He experienced death by sharing in our human feeling, which of His own accord He had taken upon Himself, but He did not lose the power of His Nature, through which He gives life to all things."

Reply Obj. 2: Christ did not suffer death which comes of sickness, lest He should seem to die of necessity from exhausted nature: but He endured death inflicted from without, to which He willingly surrendered Himself, that His death might be shown to be a voluntary one.

Reply Obj. 3: One opposite does not of itself lead to the other, yet it does so indirectly at times: thus cold sometimes is the indirect cause of heat: and in this way Christ by His death brought us back to life, when by His death He destroyed our death; just as he who bears another's punishment takes such punishment away.

SECOND ARTICLE [III, Q. 50, Art. 2]

Whether the Godhead Was Separated from the Flesh When Christ Died?

Objection 1: It would seem that the Godhead was separated from the flesh when Christ died. For as Matthew relates (27:46), when our Lord was hanging upon the cross He cried out: "My God, My God, why hast Thou forsaken Me?" which words Ambrose, commenting on Luke 23:46, explains as follows: "The man cried out when about to expire by being severed from the Godhead; for since the Godhead is immune from death, assuredly death could not be there, except life departed, for the Godhead is life." And so it seems that when Christ died, the Godhead was separated from His flesh.

Obj. 2: Further, extremes are severed when the mean is removed. But the soul was the mean through which the Godhead was united with the flesh, as stated above (Q. 6, A. 1). Therefore since the soul was severed from the flesh by death, it seems that, in consequence, His Godhead was also separated from it.

Obj. 3: Further, God's life-giving power is greater than that of the soul. But the body could not die unless the soul quitted it. Therefore, much less could it die unless the Godhead departed.

*On the contrary,* As stated above (Q. 16, AA. 4, 5), the attributes of human nature are predicated of the Son of God only by reason of the union. But what belongs to the body of Christ after death is predicated of the Son of God--namely, being buried: as is evident from the Creed, in which it is said that the Son of God "was conceived and born of a Virgin, suffered, died, and was buried." Therefore Christ's Godhead was not separated from the flesh when He died.

*I answer that,* What is bestowed through God's grace is never withdrawn except through fault. Hence it is written (Rom. 11:29): "The gifts and the calling of God are without repentance." But the grace of union whereby the Godhead was united to the flesh in Christ's Person, is greater than the grace of adoption whereby others are sanctified: also it is more enduring of itself, because this grace is ordained for personal union, whereas the grace of adoption is referred to a certain affective union. And yet we see that the grace of adoption is never lost without fault. Since, then there was no sin in Christ, it was impossible for the union of the Godhead with the flesh to be dissolved. Consequently, as before death Christ's flesh was united personally and hypostatically with the Word of God, it remained so after His death, so that the hypostasis of the Word of God was not different from that of Christ's flesh after death, as Damascene says (De Fide Orth. iii).

Reply Obj. 1: Such forsaking is not to be referred to the dissolving of the personal union, but to this, that God the Father gave Him up to the Passion: hence there "to forsake" means simply not to protect from persecutors. Or else He says there that He is forsaken, with reference to the prayer He had made: "Father, if it be possible, let this chalice pass away from Me," as Augustine explains it (De Gratia Novi Test.).

Reply Obj. 2: The Word of God is said to be united with the flesh through the medium of the soul, inasmuch as it is through the soul that the flesh belongs to human nature, which the Son of God intended to assume; but not as though the soul were the medium linking them together. But it is due to the soul that the flesh is human even after the soul has been separated from it--namely, inasmuch as by God's ordinance there remains in the dead flesh a certain relation to the resurrection. And therefore the union of the Godhead with the flesh is not taken away.

Reply Obj. 3: The soul formally possesses the life-giving energy, and therefore, while it is present, and united formally, the body must necessarily be a living one, whereas the Godhead has not the life-giving energy formally, but effectively; because It cannot be the form of the body: and therefore it is not necessary for the flesh to be living while the union of the Godhead with the flesh remains, since God does not act of necessity, but of His own will.

THIRD ARTICLE [III, Q. 50, Art. 3]

Whether in Christ's Death There Was a Severance Between His Godhead and His Soul?

Objection 1: It would seem that there was a severance in death between Christ's Godhead and His soul, because our Lord said (John 10:18): "No man taketh away My soul from Me: but I lay it down of Myself, and I have power to lay it down, and I have power to take it up again." But it does not appear that the body can set the soul aside, by separating the soul from itself, because the soul is not subject to the power of the body, but rather conversely: and so it appears that it belongs to Christ, as the Word of God, to lay down His soul: but this is to separate it from Himself. Consequently, by death His soul was severed from the Godhead.

Obj. 2: Further, Athanasius [*Vigilius Tapsensis, De Trin. vi; Bardenhewer assigns it to St. Athanasius: 45, iii. The full title is De Trinitate et Spiritu Sancto] says that he "is accursed who does not confess that the entire man, whom the Son of God took to Himself, after being assumed once more or delivered by Him, rose again from the dead on the third day." But the entire man could not be assumed again, unless the entire man was at one time separated from the Word of God: and the entire man is made of soul and body. Therefore there was a separation made at one time of the Godhead from both the body and the soul.

Obj. 3: Further, the Son of God is truly styled a man because of the union with the entire man. If then, when the union of the soul with the body was dissolved by death, the Word of God continued united with the soul, it would follow that the Son of God could be truly called a soul. But this is false, because since the soul is the form of the body, it would result in the Word of God being the form of the body; which is impossible. Therefore, in death the soul of Christ was separated from the Word of God.

Obj. 4: Further, the separated soul and body are not one hypostasis, but two. Therefore, if the Word of God remained united with Christ's soul and body, then, when they were severed by Christ's death, it seems to follow that the Word of God was two hypostases during such time as Christ was dead; which cannot be admitted. Therefore after Christ's death His soul did not continue to be united with the Word.

*On the contrary,* Damascene says (De Fide Orth. iii): "Although Christ died as man, and His holy soul was separated from His spotless body, nevertheless His Godhead remained unseparated from both--from the soul, I mean, and from the body."

*I answer that,* The soul is united with the Word of God more immediately and more primarily than the body is, because it is through the soul that the body is united with the Word of God, as stated above (Q. 6, A. 1). Since, then, the Word of God was not separated from the body at Christ's death, much less was He separated from the soul. Accordingly, since what regards the body severed from the soul is affirmed of the Son of God--namely, that "it was buried"--so is it said of Him in the Creed that "He descended into hell," because His soul when separated from the body did go down into hell.

Reply Obj. 1: Augustine (Tract. xlvii in Joan.), in commenting on the text of John, asks, since Christ is Word and soul and body, "whether He putteth down His soul, for that He is the Word? Or, for that He is a soul?" Or, again, "for that He is flesh?" And he says that, "should we say that the Word of God laid down His soul" . . . it would follow that "there was a time when that soul was severed from the Word"--which is untrue. "For death severed the body and soul . . . but that the soul was severed from the Word I do not affirm . . . But should we say that the soul laid itself down," it follows "that it is severed from itself: which is most absurd." It remains, therefore, that "the flesh itself layeth down its soul and taketh it again, not by its own power, but by the power of the Word dwelling in the flesh": because, as stated above (A. 2), the Godhead of the Word was not severed from the flesh in death.

Reply Obj. 2: In those words Athanasius never meant to say that the whole man was reassumed--that is, as to all his parts--as if the Word of God had laid aside the parts of human nature by His death; but that the totality of the assumed nature was restored once more in the resurrection by the resumed union of soul and body.

Reply Obj. 2: Through being united to human nature, the Word of God is not on that account called human nature: but He is called a man--that is, one having human nature. Now the soul and the body are essential parts of human nature. Hence it does not follow that the Word is a soul or a body through being united with both, but that He is one possessing a soul or a body.

Reply Obj. 4: As Damascene says (De Fide Orth. iii): "In Christ's death the soul was separated from the flesh: not one hypostasis divided into two: because both soul and body in the same respect had their existence from the beginning in the hypostasis of the Word; and in death, though severed from one another, each one continued to have the one same hypostasis of the Word. Wherefore the one hypostasis of the Word was the hypostasis of the Word, of the soul, and of the body. For neither soul nor body ever had an hypostasis of its own, besides the hypostasis of the Word: for there was always one hypostasis of the Word, and never two."

FOURTH ARTICLE [III, Q. 50, Art. 4]

Whether Christ Was a Man During the Three Days of His Death?

Objection 1: It would seem that Christ was a man during the three days of His death, because Augustine says (De Trin. iii): "Such was the assuming [of nature] as to make God to be man, and man to be God." But this assuming [of nature] did not cease at Christ's death. Therefore it seems that He did not cease to be a man in consequence of death.

Obj. 2: Further, the Philosopher says (Ethic. ix) that "each man is his intellect"; consequently, when we address the soul of Peter after his death we say: "Saint Peter, pray for us." But the Son of God after death was not separated from His intellectual soul. Therefore, during those three days the Son of God was a man.

Obj. 3: Further, every priest is a man. But during those three days of death Christ was a priest: otherwise what is said in Ps. 109:4 would not be true: "Thou art a priest for ever." Therefore Christ was a man during those three days.

*On the contrary,* When the higher [species] is removed, so is the lower. But the living or animated being is a higher species than animal and man, because an animal is a sensible animated substance. Now during those three days of death Christ's body was not living or animated. Therefore He was not a man.

*I answer that,* It is an article of faith that Christ was truly dead: hence it is an error against faith to assert anything whereby the truth of Christ's death is destroyed. Accordingly it is said in the Synodal epistle of Cyril [*Act. Conc. Ephes. P. I, cap. xxvi]: "If any man does not acknowledge that the Word of God suffered in the flesh, and was crucified in the flesh and tasted death in the flesh, let him be anathema." Now it belongs to the truth of the death of man or animal that by death the subject ceases to be man or animal; because the death of the man or animal results from the separation of the soul, which is the formal complement of the man or animal. Consequently, to say that Christ was a man during the three days of His death simply and without qualification, is erroneous. Yet it can be said that He was "a dead man" during those three days.

However, some writers have contended that Christ was a man during those three days, uttering words which are indeed erroneous, yet without intent of error in faith: as Hugh of Saint Victor, who (De Sacram. ii) contended that Christ, during the three days that followed His death, was a man, because he held that the soul is a man: but this is false, as was shown in the First Part (I, Q. 75, A. 4). Likewise the Master of the Sentences (iii, D, 22) held Christ to be a man during the three days of His death for quite another reason. For he believed the union of soul and flesh not to be essential to a man, and that for anything to be a man it suffices if it have a soul and body, whether united or separated: and that this is likewise false is clear both from what has been said in the First Part (I, Q. 75, A. 4), and from what has been said above regarding the mode of union (Q. 2, A. 5).

Reply Obj. 1: The Word of God assumed a united soul and body: and the result of this assumption was that God is man, and man is God. But this assumption did not cease by the separation of the Word from the soul or from the flesh; yet the union of soul and flesh ceased.

Reply Obj. 2: Man is said to be his own intellect, not because the intellect is the entire man, but because the intellect is the chief part of man, in which man's whole disposition lies virtually; just as the ruler of the city may be called the whole city, since its entire disposal is vested in him.

Reply Obj. 3: That a man is competent to be a priest is by reason of the soul, which is the subject of the character of order: hence a man does not lose his priestly order by death, and much less does Christ, who is the fount of the entire priesthood.

FIFTH ARTICLE [III, Q. 50, Art. 5]

Whether Christ's Was Identically the Same Body Living and Dead?

Objection 1: It would seem that Christ's was not identically the same body living and dead. For Christ truly died just as other men do. But the body of everyone else is not simply identically the same, dead and living, because there is an essential difference between them. Therefore neither is the body of Christ identically the same, dead and living.

Obj. 2: Further, according to the Philosopher (Metaph. v, text. 12), things specifically diverse are also numerically diverse. But Christ's body, living and dead, was specifically diverse: because the eye or flesh of the dead is only called so equivocally, as is evident from the Philosopher (De Anima ii, text. 9; Metaph. vii). Therefore Christ's body was not simply identically the same, living and dead.

Obj. 3: Further, death is a kind of corruption. But what is corrupted by substantial corruption after being corrupted, exists no longer, since corruption is change from being to non-being. Therefore, Christ's body, after it was dead, did not remain identically the same, because death is a substantial corruption.

*On the contrary,* Athanasius says (Epist. ad Epict.): "In that body which was circumcised and carried, which ate, and toiled, and was nailed on the tree, there was the impassible and incorporeal Word of God: the same was laid in the tomb." But Christ's living body was circumcised and nailed on the tree; and Christ's dead body was laid in the tomb. Therefore it was the same body living and dead.

*I answer that,* The expression "simply" can be taken in two senses. In the first instance by taking "simply" to be the same as "absolutely"; thus "that is said simply which is said without addition," as the Philosopher put it (Topic. ii): and in this way the dead and living body of Christ was simply identically the same: since a thing is said to be "simply" identically the same from the identity of the subject. But Christ's body living and dead was identical in its suppositum because alive and dead it had none other besides the Word of God, as was stated above (A. 2). And it is in this sense that Athanasius is speaking in the passage quoted.

In another way "simply" is the same as "altogether" or "totally": in which sense the body of Christ, dead and alive, was not "simply" the same identically, because it was not "totally" the same, since life is of the essence of a living body; for it is an essential and not an accidental predicate: hence it follows that a body which ceases to be living does not remain totally the same. Moreover, if it were to be said that Christ's dead body did continue "totally" the same, it would follow that it was not corrupted--I mean, by the corruption of death: which is the heresy of the Gaianites, as Isidore says (Etym. viii), and is to be found in the Decretals (xxiv, qu. iii). And Damascene says (De Fide Orth. iii) that "the term 'corruption' denotes two things: in one way it is the separation of the soul from the body and other things of the sort; in another way, the complete dissolving into elements. Consequently it is impious to say with Julian and Gaian that the Lord's body was incorruptible after the first manner of corruption before the resurrection: because Christ's body would not be consubstantial with us, nor truly dead, nor would we have been saved in very truth. But in the second way Christ's body was incorrupt."

Reply Obj. 1: The dead body of everyone else does not continue united to an abiding hypostasis, as Christ's dead body did; consequently the dead body of everyone else is not the same "simply," but only in some respect: because it is the same as to its matter, but not the same as to its form. But Christ's body remains the same simply, on account of the identity of the suppositum, as stated above.

Reply Obj. 2: Since a thing is said to be the same identically according to suppositum, but the same specifically according to form: wherever the suppositum subsists in only one nature, it follows of necessity that when the unity of species is taken away the unity of identity is also taken away. But the hypostasis of the Word of God subsists in two natures; and consequently, although in others the body does not remain the same according to the species of human nature, still it continues identically the same in Christ according to the suppositum of the Word of God.

Reply Obj. 3: Corruption and death do not belong to Christ by reason of the suppositum, from which suppositum follows the unity of identity; but by reason of the human nature, according to which is found the difference of death and of life in Christ's body.

SIXTH ARTICLE [III, Q. 50, Art. 6]

Whether Christ's Death Conduced in Any Way to Our Salvation?

Objection 1: It would seem that Christ's death did not conduce in any way to our salvation. For death is a sort of privation, since it is the privation of life. But privation has not any power of activity, because it is nothing positive. Therefore it could not work anything for our salvation.

Obj. 2: Further, Christ's Passion wrought our salvation by way of merit. But Christ's death could not operate in this way, because in death the body is separated from the soul, which is the principle of meriting. Consequently, Christ's death did not accomplish anything towards our salvation.

Obj. 3: Further, what is corporeal is not the cause of what is spiritual. But Christ's death was corporeal. Therefore it could not be the cause of our salvation, which is something spiritual.

*On the contrary,* Augustine says (De Trin. iv): "The one death of our Saviour," namely, that of the body, "saved us from our two deaths," that is, of the soul and the body.

*I answer that,* We may speak of Christ's death

in two ways, "in becoming" and "in fact." Death is said to be "in becoming" when anyone from natural or enforced suffering is tending towards death: and in this way it is the same thing to speak of Christ's death as of His Passion: so that in this sense Christ's death is the cause of our salvation, according to what has been already said of the Passion (Q. 48). But death is considered in fact, inasmuch as the separation of soul and body has already taken place: and it is in this sense that we are now speaking of Christ's death. In this way Christ's death cannot be the cause of our salvation by way of merit, but only by way of causality, that is to say, inasmuch as the Godhead was not separated from Christ's flesh by death; and therefore, whatever befell Christ's flesh, even when the soul was departed, was conducive to salvation in virtue of the Godhead united. But the effect of any cause is properly estimated according to its resemblance to the cause. Consequently, since death is a kind of privation of one's own life, the effect of Christ's death is considered in relation to the removal of the obstacles to our salvation: and these are the death of the soul and of the body. Hence Christ's death is said to have destroyed in us both the death of the soul, caused by sin, according to Rom. 4:25: "He was delivered up [namely unto death] for our sins": and the death of the body, consisting in the separation of the soul, according to 1 Cor. 15:54: "Death is swallowed up in victory."

Reply Obj. 1: Christ's death wrought our salvation from the power of the Godhead united, and not considered merely as His death.

Reply Obj. 2: Though Christ's death, considered "in fact" did not effect our salvation by way of merit, yet it did so by way of causality, as stated above.

Reply Obj. 3: Christ's death was indeed corporeal; but the body was the instrument of the Godhead united to Him, working by Its power, although dead.

## QUESTION 51

OF CHRIST'S BURIAL (In Four Articles)

We have now to consider Christ's burial, concerning which there are four points of inquiry:

(1) Whether it was fitting for Christ to be buried?

(2) Concerning the manner of His burial;

(3) Whether His body was decomposed in the tomb?

(4) Concerning the length of time He lay in the tomb.

FIRST ARTICLE [III, Q. 51, Art. 1]

Whether It Was Fitting for Christ to Be Buried?

Objection 1: It would seem unfitting for Christ to have been buried, because it is said of Him (Ps. 87:6): "He is [Vulg.: 'I am'] become as a man without help, free among the dead." But the bodies of the dead are enclosed in a tomb; which seems contrary to liberty. Therefore it does not seem fitting for Christ to have been buried.

Obj. 2: Further, nothing should be done to Christ except it was helpful to our salvation. But Christ's burial seems in no way to be conducive to our salvation. Therefore, it was not fitting for Him to be buried.

Obj. 3: Further, it seems out of place for God who is above the high heavens to be laid in the earth. But what befalls the dead body of Christ is attributed to God by reason of the union. Therefore it appears to be unbecoming for Christ to be buried.

*On the contrary,* our Lord said (Matt. 26:10) of the woman who anointed Him: "She has wrought a good work upon Me," and then He added (Matt. 26:12)--"for she, in pouring this ointment upon My body, hath done it for My burial."

*I answer that,* It was fitting for Christ to be buried. First of all, to establish the truth of His death; for no one is laid in the grave unless there be certainty of death. Hence we read (Mk. 15:44, 45), that Pilate by diligent inquiry assured himself of Christ's death before granting leave for His burial. Secondly, because by Christ's rising from the grave, to them who are in the grave, hope is given of rising again through Him, according to John 5:25, 28: "All that are in their graves shall hear the voice of the Son of God . . . and they that hear shall live." Thirdly, as an example to them who dying spiritually to their sins are hidden away "from the disturbance of men" (Ps. 30:21). Hence it is said (Col. 3:3): "You are dead, and your life is hid with Christ in God." Wherefore the baptized likewise who through Christ's death die to sins, are as it were buried with Christ by immersion, according to Rom. 6:4: "We are buried together with Christ by baptism into death."

Reply Obj. 1: Though buried, Christ proved Himself "free among the dead": since, although imprisoned in the tomb, He could not be hindered from going forth by rising again.

Reply Obj. 2: As Christ's death wrought our salvation, so likewise did His burial. Hence Jerome says (Super Marc. xiv): "By Christ's burial we rise again"; and on Isa. 53:9: "He shall give the ungodly for His burial," a gloss says: "He shall give to God and the Father the Gentiles who were without godliness, because He purchased them by His death and burial."

Reply Obj. 3: As is said in a discourse made at the Council of Ephesus [*P. iii, cap. 9], "Nothing that saves man is derogatory to God; showing Him to be not passible, but merciful": and in another discourse of the same Council [*P. iii, cap. 10]: "God does not repute anything as an injury which is an occasion of men's salvation. Thus thou shalt not deem God's Nature to be so vile, as though It may sometimes be subjected to injuries."

SECOND ARTICLE [III, Q. 51, Art. 2]

Whether Christ Was Buried in a Becoming Manner?

Objection 1: It would seem that Christ was buried in an unbecoming manner. For His burial should be in keeping with His death. But Christ underwent a most shameful death, according to Wis. 2:20: "Let us condemn Him to a most shameful death." It seems therefore unbecoming for honorable burial to be accorded to Christ, inasmuch as He was buried by men of position--namely, by Joseph of Arimathea, who was "a noble counselor," to use Mark's expression (Mk. 15:43), and by Nicodemus, who was "a ruler of the Jews," as John states (John 3:1).

Obj. 2: Further, nothing should be done to Christ which might set an example of wastefulness. But it seems to savor of waste that in order to bury Christ Nicodemus came "bringing a mixture of myrrh and aloes about a hundred pounds weight," as recorded by John (19:39), especially since a woman came beforehand to anoint His body for the burial, as Mark relates (Mk. 14:28). Consequently, this was not done becomingly with regard to Christ.

Obj. 3: Further, it is not becoming for anything done to be inconsistent with itself. But Christ's burial on the one hand was simple, because "Joseph wrapped His body in a clean linen cloth," as is related by Matthew (27:59), "but not with gold or gems, or silk," as Jerome observes: yet on the other hand there appears to have been some display, inasmuch as they buried Him with fragrant spices (John 19:40). Consequently, the manner of Christ's burial does not seem to have been seemly.

Obj. 4: Further, "What things soever were written," especially of Christ, "were written for our learning," according to Rom. 15:4. But some of the things written in the Gospels touching Christ's burial in no wise seem to pertain to our instruction--as that He was buried "in a garden . . . "in a tomb which was not His own," which was "new," and "hewed out in a rock." Therefore the manner of Christ's burial was not becoming.

*On the contrary,* It is written (Isa. 11:10): "And His sepulchre shall be glorious."

*I answer that,* The manner of Christ's burial is shown to be seemly in three respects. First, to confirm faith in His death and resurrection. Secondly, to commend the devotion of those who gave Him burial. Hence Augustine says (De Civ. Dei i): "The Gospel mentions as praiseworthy the deed of those who received His body from the cross, and with due care and reverence wrapped it up and buried it." Thirdly, as to the mystery whereby those are molded who "are buried together with Christ into death" (Rom. 6:4).

Reply Obj. 1: With regard to Christ's death, His patience and constancy in enduring death are commended, and all the more that His death was the more despicable: but in His honorable burial we can see the power of the dying Man, who, even in death, frustrated the intent of His murderers, and was buried with honor: and thereby is foreshadowed the devotion of the faithful who in the time to come were to serve the dead Christ.

Reply Obj. 2: On that expression of the Evangelist (John 19:40) that they buried Him "as the manner of the Jews is to bury," Augustine says (Tract. in Joan. cxx): "He admonishes us that in offices of this kind which are rendered to the dead, the custom of each nation should be observed." Now it was the custom of this people to anoint bodies with various spices in order the longer to preserve them from corruption [*Cf. Catena Aurea in Joan. xix]. Accordingly it is said in De Doctr. Christ. iii that "in all such things, it is not the use thereof, but the luxury of the user that is at fault"; and, farther on: "what in other persons is frequently criminal, in a divine or prophetic person is a sign of something great." For myrrh and aloes by their bitterness denote penance, by which man keeps Christ within himself without the corruption of sin; while the odor of the ointments expresses good report.

Reply Obj. 3: Myrrh and aloes were used on Christ's body in order that it might be preserved from corruption, and this seemed to imply a certain need (in the body): hence the example is set us that we may lawfully use precious things medicinally, from the need of preserving our body. But the wrapping up of the body was merely a question of becoming propriety. And we ought to content ourselves with simplicity in such things. Yet, as Jerome observes, by this act was denoted that "he swathes Jesus in clean linen, who receives Him with a pure soul." Hence, as Bede says on Mark 15:46: "The Church's custom has prevailed for the sacrifice of the altar to be offered not upon silk, nor upon dyed cloth, but on linen of the earth; as the Lord's body was buried in a clean winding-sheet."

Reply Obj. 4: Christ was buried "in a garden" to express that by His death and burial we are delivered from the death which we incur through Adam's sin committed in the garden of paradise. But for this "was our Lord buried in the grave of a stranger," as Augustine says in a sermon (ccxlviii), "because He died for the salvation of others; and a sepulchre is the abode of death." Also the extent of the poverty endured for us can be thereby estimated: since He who while living had no home, after death was laid to rest in another's tomb, and being naked was clothed by Joseph. But He is laid in a "new" sepulchre, as Jerome observes on Matt. 27:60, "lest after the resurrection it might be pretended that someone else had risen, while the other corpses remained. The new sepulchre can also denote Mary's virginal womb." And furthermore it may be understood that all of us are renewed by Christ's burial; death and corruption being destroyed. Moreover, He was buried in a monument "hewn out of a rock," as Jerome says on Matt. 27:64, "lest, if it had been constructed of many stones, they might say that He was stolen away by digging away the foundations of the tomb." Hence the "great stone" which was set shows that "the tomb could not be opened except by the help of many hands. Again, if He had been buried in the earth, they might have said: They dug up the soil and stole Him away," as Augustine observes [*Cf. Catena Aurea]. Hilary (Comment. in Matth. cap. xxxiii) gives the mystical interpretation, saying that "by the teaching of the apostles, Christ is borne into the stony heart of the gentile; for it is hewn out by the process of teaching, unpolished and new, untenanted and open to the entrance of the fear of God. And since naught besides Him must enter into our hearts, a great stone is rolled against the door." Furthermore, as Origen says (Tract. xxxv in Matth.): "It was not written by hazard: 'Joseph wrapped Christ's body in a clean winding-sheet, and placed it in a new monument,'" and that "'he rolled a great stone,' because all things around the body of Jesus are clean, and new, and exceeding great."

THIRD ARTICLE [III, Q. 51, Art. 3]

Whether Christ's Body Was Reduced to Dust in the Tomb?

Objection 1: It would seem that Christ's body was reduced to dust in the tomb. For just as man dies in punishment of his first parent's sin, so also does he return to dust, since it was said to the first man after his sin: "Dust thou art, and into dust thou shalt return" (Gen. 3:19). But Christ endured death in order to deliver us from death. Therefore His body ought to be made to return to dust, so as to free us from the same penalty.

Obj. 2: Further, Christ's body was of the same nature as ours. But directly after death our bodies begin to dissolve into dust, and are disposed towards putrefaction, because when the natural heat departs, there supervenes heat from without which causes corruption. Therefore it seems that the same thing happened to Christ's body.

Obj. 3: Further, as stated above (A. 1), Christ willed to be buried in order to furnish men with the hope of rising likewise from the grave. Consequently, He sought likewise to return to dust so as to give to them who have returned to dust the hope of rising from the dust.

*On the contrary,* It is written (Ps. 15:10): "Nor wilt Thou suffer Thy holy one to see corruption": and Damascene (De Fide Orth. iii) expounds this of the corruption which comes of dissolving into elements.

*I answer that,* It was not fitting for Christ's body to putrefy, or in any way be reduced to dust, since the putrefaction of any body comes of that body's infirmity of nature, which can no longer hold the body together. But as was said above (Q. 50, A. 1, ad 2), Christ's death ought not to come from weakness of nature, lest it might not be believed to be voluntary: and therefore He willed to die, not from sickness, but from suffering inflicted on Him, to which He gave Himself up willingly. And therefore, lest His death might be ascribed to infirmity of nature, Christ did not wish His body to putrefy in any way or dissolve no matter how; but for the manifestation of His Divine power He willed that His body should continue incorrupt. Hence Chrysostom says (Cont. Jud. et Gent. quod 'Christus sit Deus') that "with other men, especially with such as have wrought strenuously, their deeds shine forth in their lifetime; but as soon as they die, their deeds go with them. But it is quite the contrary with Christ: because previous to the cross all is sadness and weakness, but as soon as He is crucified, everything comes to light, in order that you may learn it was not an ordinary man that was crucified."

Reply Obj. 1: Since Christ was not subject to sin, neither was He prone to die or to return to dust. Yet of His own will He endured death for our salvation, for the reasons alleged above (Q. 51, A. 1). But had His body putrefied or dissolved, this fact would have been detrimental to man's salvation, for it would not have seemed credible that the Divine power was in Him. Hence it is on His behalf that it is written (Ps. 19:10): "What profit is there in my blood, whilst I go down to corruption?" as if He were to say: "If My body corrupt, the profit of the blood shed will be lost."

Reply Obj. 2: Christ's body was a subject of corruption according to the condition of its passible nature, but not as to the deserving cause of putrefaction, which is sin: but the Divine power preserved Christ's body from putrefying, just as it raised it up from death.

Reply Obj. 3: Christ rose from the tomb by Divine power, which is not narrowed within bounds. Consequently, His rising from the grave was a sufficient argument to prove that men are to be raised up by Divine power, not only from their graves, but also from any dust whatever.

FOURTH ARTICLE [III, Q. 51, Art. 4]

Whether Christ Was in the Tomb Only One Day and Two Nights?

Objection 1: It would seem that Christ was not in the tomb during only one day and two nights; because He said (Matt. 12:40): "As Jonas was in the whale's belly three days and three nights: so shall the Son of man be in the heart of the earth three days and three nights." But He was in the heart of the earth while He was in the grave. Therefore He was not in the tomb for only one day and two nights.

Obj. 2: Gregory says in a Paschal Homily (Hom. xxi): "As Samson carried off the gates of Gaza during the night, even so Christ rose in the night, taking away the gates of hell." But after rising He was not in the tomb. Therefore He was not two whole nights in the grave.

Obj. 3: Further, light prevailed over darkness by Christ's death. But night belongs to darkness, and day to light. Therefore it was more fitting for Christ's body to be in the tomb for two days and a night, rather than conversely.

*On the contrary,* Augustine says (De Trin. iv): "There were thirty-six hours from the evening of His burial to the dawn of the resurrection, that is, a whole night with a whole day, and a whole night."

*I answer that,* The very time during which Christ remained in the tomb shows forth the effect of His death. For it was said above (Q. 50, A. 6) that by Christ's death we were delivered from a twofold death, namely, from the death of the soul and of the body: and this is signified by the two nights during which He remained in the tomb. But since His death did not come of sin, but was endured from charity, it has not the semblance of night, but of day: consequently it is denoted by the whole day during which Christ was in the sepulchre. And so it was fitting for Christ to be in the sepulchre during one day and two nights.

Reply Obj. 1: Augustine says (De Consens. Evang. iii): "Some men, ignorant of Scriptural language, wished to compute as night those three hours, from the sixth to the ninth hour, during which the sun was darkened, and as day those other three hours during which it was restored to the earth, that is, from the ninth hour until its setting: for the coming night of the Sabbath follows, and if this be reckoned with its day, there will be already two nights and two days. Now after the Sabbath there follows the night of the first day of the Sabbath, that is, of the dawning Sunday, on which the Lord rose. Even so, the reckoning of the three days and three nights will not stand. It remains then to find the solution in the customary usage of speech of the Scriptures, whereby the whole is understood from the part": so that we are able to take a day and a night as one natural day. And so the first day is computed from its ending, during which Christ died and was buried on the Friday; while the second day is an entire day with twenty-four hours of night and day; while the night following belongs to the third day. "For as the primitive days were computed from light to night on account of man's future fall, so these days are computed from the darkness to the daylight on account of man's restoration" (De Trin. iv).

Reply Obj. 2: As Augustine says (De Trin. iv; cf. De Consens. Evang. iii), Christ rose with the dawn, when light appears in part, and still some part of the darkness of the night remains. Hence it is said of the women that "when it was yet dark" they came "to the sepulchre" (John 20:1). Therefore, in consequence of this darkness, Gregory says (Hom. xxi) that Christ rose in the middle of the night, not that night is divided into two equal parts, but during the night itself: for the expression "early" can be taken as partly night and partly day, from its fittingness with both.

Reply Obj. 3: The light prevailed so far in Christ's death (which is denoted by the one day) that it dispelled the darkness of the two nights, that is, of our twofold death, as stated above.

# QUESTION 52

OF CHRIST'S DESCENT INTO HELL (In Eight Articles)

We have now to consider Christ's descent into hell; concerning which there are eight points of inquiry:

(1) Whether it was fitting for Christ to descend into hell?

(2) Into which hell did He descend?

(3) Whether He was entirely in hell?

(4) Whether He made any stay there?

(5) Whether He delivered the Holy Fathers from hell?

(6) Whether He delivered the lost from hell?

(7) Whether He delivered the children who died in original sin?

(8) Whether He delivered men from Purgatory?

FIRST ARTICLE [III, Q. 52, Art. 1]

Whether It Was Fitting for Christ to Descend into Hell?

Objection 1: It would seem that it was not fitting for Christ to descend into hell, because Augustine says (Ep. ad Evod. cliv.): "Nor could I find anywhere in the Scriptures hell mentioned as something good." But Christ's soul did not descend into any evil place, for neither do the souls of the just. Therefore it does not seem fitting for Christ's soul to descend into hell.

Obj. 2: Further, it cannot belong to Christ to descend into hell according to His Divine Nature, which is altogether immovable; but only according to His assumed nature. But that which Christ did or suffered in His assumed nature is ordained for man's salvation: and to secure this it does not seem necessary for Christ to descend into hell, since He delivered us from both guilt and penalty by His Passion which He endured in this world, as stated above (Q. 49, AA. 1, 3). Consequently, it was not fitting that Christ should descend into hell.

Obj. 3: Further, by Christ's death His soul was separated from His body, and this was laid in the sepulchre, as stated above (Q. 51). But it seems that He descended into hell, not according to His soul only, because seemingly the soul, being incorporeal, cannot be a subject of local motion; for this belongs to bodies, as is proved in Phys. vi, text. 32; while descent implies corporeal motion. Therefore it was not fitting for Christ to descend into hell.

*On the contrary,* It is said in the Creed: "He descended into hell": and the Apostle says (Eph. 4:9): "Now that He ascended, what is it, but because He also descended first into the lower parts of the earth?" And a gloss adds: "that is--into hell."

*I answer that,* It was fitting for Christ to descend

into hell. First of all, because He came to bear our penalty in order to free us from penalty, according to Isa. 53:4: "Surely He hath borne our infirmities and carried our sorrows." But through sin man had incurred not only the death of the body, but also descent into hell. Consequently since it was fitting for Christ to die in order to deliver us from death, so it was fitting for Him to descend into hell in order to deliver us also from going down into hell. Hence it is written (Osee 13:14): "O death, I will be thy death; O hell, I will be thy bite." Secondly, because it was fitting when the devil was overthrown by the Passion that Christ should deliver the captives detained in hell, according to Zech. 9:11: "Thou also by the blood of Thy Testament hast sent forth Thy prisoners out of the pit." And it is written (Col. 2:15): "Despoiling the principalities and powers, He hath exposed them confidently." Thirdly, that as He showed forth His power on earth by living and dying, so also He might manifest it in hell, by visiting it and enlightening it. Accordingly it is written (Ps. 23:7): "Lift up your gates, O ye princes," which the gloss thus interprets: "that is--Ye princes of hell, take away your power, whereby hitherto you held men fast in hell"; and so "at the name of Jesus every knee should bow," not only "of them that are in heaven," but likewise "of them that are in hell," as is said in Phil. 2:10.

Reply Obj. 1: The name of hell stands for an evil of penalty, and not for an evil of guilt. Hence it was becoming that Christ should descend into hell, not as liable to punishment Himself, but to deliver them who were.

Reply Obj. 2: Christ's Passion was a kind of universal cause of men's salvation, both of the living and of the dead. But a general cause is applied to particular effects by means of something special. Hence, as the power of the Passion is applied to the living through the sacraments which make us like unto Christ's Passion, so likewise it is applied to the dead through His descent into hell. On which account it is written (Zech. 9:11) that "He sent forth prisoners out of the pit, in the blood of His testament," that is, by the power of His Passion.

Reply Obj. 3: Christ's soul descended into hell not by the same kind of motion as that whereby bodies are moved, but by that kind whereby the angels are moved, as was said in the First Part (Q. 53, A. 1).

SECOND ARTICLE [III, Q. 52, Art. 2]

Whether Christ Went Down into the Hell of the Lost?

Objection 1: It would seem that Christ went down into the hell of the lost, because it is said by the mouth of Divine Wisdom (Ecclus. 24:45): "I will penetrate to all the lower parts of the earth." But the hell of the lost is computed among the lower parts of the earth according to Ps. 62:10: "They shall go into the lower parts of the earth." Therefore Christ who is the Wisdom of God, went down even into the hell of the lost.

Obj. 2: Further, Peter says (Acts 2:24) that "God hath raised up Christ, having loosed the sorrows of hell, as it was impossible that He should be holden by it." But there are no sorrows in the hell of the Fathers, nor in the hell of the children, since they are not punished with sensible pain on account of any actual sin, but only with the pain of loss on account of original sin. Therefore Christ went down into the hell of the lost, or else into Purgatory, where men are tormented with sensible pain on account of actual sins.

Obj. 3: Further, it is written (1 Pet. 3:19) that "Christ coming in spirit preached to those spirits that were in prison, which had some time been incredulous": and this is understood of Christ's descent into hell, as Athanasius says (Ep. ad Epict.). For he says that "Christ's body was laid in the sepulchre when He went to preach to those spirits who were in bondage, as Peter said." But it is clear the unbelievers were in the hell of the lost. Therefore Christ went down into the hell of the lost.

Obj. 4: Further, Augustine says (Ep. ad Evod. clxiv): "If the sacred Scriptures had said that Christ came into Abraham's bosom, without naming hell or its woes, I wonder whether any person would dare to assert that He descended into hell. But since evident testimonies mention hell and its sorrows, there is no reason for believing that Christ went there except to deliver men from the same woes." But the place of woes is the hell of the lost. Therefore Christ descended into the hell of the lost.

Obj. 5: Further, as Augustine says in a sermon upon the Resurrection: Christ descending into hell "set free all the just who were held in the bonds of original sin." But among them was Job, who says of himself (Job 17:16): "All that I have shall go down into the deepest pit." Therefore Christ descended into the deepest pit.

*On the contrary,* Regarding the hell of the lost it is written (Job 10:21): "Before I go, and return no more, to a land that is dark and covered with the mist of death." Now there is no "fellowship of light with darkness," according to 2 Cor. 6:14. Therefore Christ, who is "the light," did not descend into the hell of the lost.

*I answer that,* A thing is said to be in a place in two ways. First of all, through its effect, and in this way Christ descended into each of the hells, but in different manner. For going down into the hell of the lost He wrought this effect, that by descending thither He put them to shame for their unbelief and wickedness: but to them who were detained in Purgatory He gave hope of attaining to glory: while upon the holy Fathers detained in hell solely on account of original sin, He shed the light of glory everlasting.

In another way a thing is said to be in a place through its essence: and in this way Christ's soul descended only into that part of hell wherein the just were detained. so that He visited them "in place," according to His soul, whom He visited "interiorly by grace," according to His Godhead. Accordingly, while remaining in one part of hell, He wrought this effect in a measure in every part of hell, just as while suffering in one part of the earth He delivered the whole world by His Passion.

Reply Obj. 1: Christ, who is the Wisdom of God, penetrated to all the lower parts of the earth, not passing through them locally with His soul, but by spreading the effects of His power in a measure to them all: yet so that He enlightened only the just: because the text quoted continues: "And I will enlighten all that hope in the Lord."

Reply Obj. 2: Sorrow is twofold: one is the suffering of pain which men endure for actual sin, according to Ps. 17:6: "The sorrows of hell encompassed me." Another sorrow comes of hoped-for glory being deferred, according to Prov. 13:12: "Hope that is deferred afflicteth the soul": and such was the sorrow which the holy Fathers suffered in hell, and Augustine refers to it in a sermon on the Passion, saying that "they besought Christ with tearful entreaty." Now by descending into hell Christ took away both sorrows, yet in different ways: for He did away with the sorrows of pains by preserving souls from them, just as a physician is said to free a man from sickness by warding it off by means of physic. Likewise He removed the sorrows caused by glory deferred, by bestowing glory.

Reply Obj. 3: These words of Peter are referred by some to Christ's descent into hell: and they explain it in this sense: "Christ preached to them who formerly were unbelievers, and who were shut up in prison"--that is, in hell--"in spirit"--that is, by His soul. Hence Damascene says (De Fide Orth. iii): "As He evangelized them who are upon the earth, so did He those who were in hell"; not in order to convert unbelievers unto belief, but to put them to shame for their unbelief, since preaching cannot be understood otherwise than as the open manifesting of His Godhead, which was laid bare before them in the lower regions by His descending in power into hell.

Augustine, however, furnishes a better exposition of the text in his Epistle to Evodius quoted above, namely, that the preaching is not to be referred to Christ's descent into hell, but to the operation of His Godhead, to which He gave effect from the beginning of the world. Consequently, the sense is, that "to those (spirits) that were in prison"--that is, living in the mortal body, which is, as it were, the soul's prison-house--"by the spirit" of His Godhead "He came and preached" by internal inspirations, and from without by the admonitions spoken by the righteous: to those, I say, He preached "which had been some time incredulous," i.e. not believing in the preaching of Noe, "when they waited for the patience of God," whereby the chastisement of the Deluge was put off: accordingly (Peter) adds: "In the days of Noe, when the Ark was being built."

Reply Obj. 4: The expression "Abraham's bosom" may be taken in two senses. First of all, as implying that restfulness, existing there, from sensible pain; so that in this sense it cannot be called hell, nor are there any sorrows there. In another way it can be taken as implying the privation of longed-for glory: in this sense it has the character of hell and sorrow. Consequently, that rest of the blessed is now called Abraham's bosom, yet it is not styled hell, nor are sorrows said to be now in Abraham's bosom.

Reply Obj. 5: As Gregory says (Moral. xiii): "Even the higher regions of hell he calls the deepest hell . . . For if relatively to the height of heaven this darksome air is infernal, then relatively to the height of this same air the earth lying beneath can be considered as infernal and deep. And again in comparison with the height of the same earth, those parts of hell which are higher than the other infernal mansions, may in this way be designated as the deepest hell."

THIRD ARTICLE [III, Q. 52, Art. 3]

Whether the Whole Christ Was in Hell?

Objection 1: It would seem that the whole Christ was not in hell. For Christ's body is one of His parts. But His body was not in hell. Therefore, the whole Christ was not in hell.

Obj. 2: Further, nothing can be termed whole when its parts are severed. But the soul and body, which are the parts of human nature, were separated at His death, as stated above (Q. 50, AA. 3, 4), and it was after death that He descended into hell. Therefore the whole (Christ) could not be in hell.

Obj. 3: Further, the whole of a thing is said to be in a place when no part of it is outside such place. But there were parts of Christ outside hell; for instance, His body was in the grave, and His Godhead everywhere. Therefore the whole Christ was not in hell.

*On the contrary,* Augustine says (De Symbolo iii): "The whole Son is with the Father, the whole Son in heaven, on earth, in the Virgin's womb, on the Cross, in hell, in paradise, into which He brought the robber."

*I answer that,* It is evident from what was said in the First Part (Q. 31, A. 2, ad 4), the masculine gender is referred to the hypostasis or person, while the neuter belongs to the nature. Now in the death of Christ, although the soul was separated from the body, yet neither was separated from the Person of the Son of God, as stated above (Q. 50, A. 2). Consequently, it must be affirmed that during the three days of Christ's death the whole Christ was in the tomb, because the whole Person was there through the body united with Him, and likewise He was entirely in hell, because the whole Person of Christ was there by reason of the soul united with Him, and the whole Christ was then everywhere by reason of the Divine Nature.

Reply Obj. 1: The body which was then in the

grave is not a part of the uncreated Person, but of the assumed nature. Consequently, the fact of Christ's body not being in hell does not prevent the whole Christ from being there: but proves that not everything appertaining to human nature was there.

Reply Obj. 2: The whole human nature is made up of the united soul and body; not so the Divine Person. Consequently when death severed the union of the soul with the body, the whole Christ remained, but His whole human nature did not remain.

Reply Obj. 3: Christ's Person is whole in each single place, but not wholly, because it is not circumscribed by any place: indeed, all places put together could not comprise His immensity; rather is it His immensity that embraces all things. But it happens in those things which are in a place corporeally and circumscriptively, that if a whole be in some place, then no part of it is outside that place. But this is not the case with God. Hence Augustine says (De Symbolo iii): "It is not according to times or places that we say that the whole Christ is everywhere, as if He were at one time whole in one place, at another time whole in another: but as being whole always and everywhere."

FOURTH ARTICLE [III, Q. 52, Art. 4]

Whether Christ Made Any Stay in Hell?

Objection 1: It would seem that Christ did not make any stay in hell. For Christ went down into hell to deliver men from thence. But He accomplished this deliverance at once by His descent, for, according to Ecclus. 11:23: "It is easy in the eyes of God on a sudden to make the poor man rich." Consequently He does not seem to have tarried in hell.

Obj. 2: Further, Augustine says in a sermon on the Passion (clx) that "of a sudden at our Lord and Saviour's bidding all 'the bars of iron were burst'" (Cf. Isa. 45:2). Hence on behalf of the angels accompanying Christ it is written (Ps. 23:7, 9): "Lift up your gates, O ye princes." Now Christ descended thither in order to break the bolts of hell. Therefore He did not make any stay in hell.

Obj. 3: Further, it is related (Luke 23:43) that our Lord while hanging on the cross said to the thief: "This day thou shalt be with Me in paradise": from which it is evident that Christ was in paradise on that very day. But He was not there with His body, for that was in the grave. Therefore He was there with the soul which had gone down into hell: and consequently it appears that He made no stay in hell.

*On the contrary,* Peter says (Acts 2:24): "Whom God hath raised up, having loosed the sorrows of hell, as it was impossible that He should be held by it." Therefore it seems that He remained in hell until the hour of the Resurrection.

*I answer that,* As Christ, in order to take our penalties upon Himself, willed His body to be laid in the tomb, so likewise He willed His soul to descend into hell. But the body lay in the tomb for a day and two nights, so as to demonstrate the truth of His death. Consequently, it is to be believed that His soul was in hell, in order that it might be brought back out of hell simultaneously with His body from the tomb.

Reply Obj. 1: When Christ descended into hell He delivered the saints who were there, not by leading them out at once from the confines of hell, but by enlightening them with the light of glory in hell itself. Nevertheless it was fitting that His soul should abide in hell as long as His body remained in the tomb.

Reply Obj. 2: By the expression "bars of hell" are understood the obstacles which kept the holy Fathers from quitting hell, through the guilt of our first parent's sin; and these bars Christ burst asunder by the power of His Passion on descending into hell: nevertheless He chose to remain in hell for some time, for the reason stated above.

Reply Obj. 3: Our Lord's expression is not to be understood of the earthly corporeal paradise, but of a spiritual one, in which all are said to be who enjoy the Divine glory. Accordingly, the thief descended locally into hell with Christ, because it was said to him: "This day thou shalt be with Me in paradise"; still as to reward he was in paradise, because he enjoyed Christ's Godhead just as the other saints did.

FIFTH ARTICLE [III, Q. 52, Art. 5]

Whether Christ Descending into Hell Delivered the Holy Fathers from Thence?

Objection 1: It would seem that Christ descending into hell did not deliver the holy Fathers from thence. For Augustine (Epist. ad Evod. clxiv) says: "I have not yet discovered what Christ descending into hell bestowed upon those righteous ones who were in Abraham's bosom, from whom I fail to see that He ever departed according to the beatific presence of His Godhead." But had He delivered them, He would have bestowed much upon them. Therefore it does not appear that Christ delivered the holy Fathers from hell.

Obj. 2: Further, no one is detained in hell except on account of sin. But during life the holy Fathers were justified from sin through faith in Christ. Consequently they did not need to be delivered from hell on Christ's descent thither.

Obj. 3: Further, if you remove the cause, you remove the effect. But that Christ went down into hell was due to sin which was taken away by the Passion, as stated above (Q. 49, A. 1). Consequently, the holy Fathers were not delivered on Christ's descent into hell.

*On the contrary,* Augustine says in the sermon on the Passion already quoted that when Christ descended into hell "He broke down the gate and 'iron bars' of hell, setting at liberty all the righteous who were held fast through original sin."

*I answer that,* As stated above (A. 4, ad 2), when Christ descended into hell He worked through the power of His Passion. But through Christ's Passion the human race was delivered not only from sin, but also from the debt of its penalty, as stated above (Q. 49, AA. 1, 3). Now men were held fast by the debt of punishment in two ways: first of all for actual sin which each had committed personally: secondly, for the sin of the whole human race, which each one in his origin contracts from our first parent, as stated in Rom. 5 of which sin the penalty is the death of the body as well as exclusion from glory, as is evident from Gen. 2 and 3: because God cast out man from paradise after sin, having beforehand threatened him with death should he sin. Consequently, when Christ descended into hell, by the power of His Passion He delivered the saints from the penalty whereby they were excluded from the life of glory, so as to be unable to see God in His Essence, wherein man's beatitude lies, as stated in the Second Part (I-II, Q. 3, A. 8). But the holy Fathers were detained in hell for the reason, that, owing to our first parent's sin, the approach to the life of glory was not opened. And so when Christ descended into hell He delivered the holy Fathers from thence. And this is what is written Zech. 9:11: "Thou also by the blood of Thy testament hast sent forth Thy prisoners out of the pit, wherein is no water." And (Col. 2:15) it is written that "despoiling the principalities and powers," i.e. "of hell, by taking out Isaac and Jacob, and the other just souls," "He led them," i.e. "He brought them far from this kingdom of darkness into heaven," as the gloss explains.

Reply Obj. 1: Augustine is speaking there against such as maintained that the righteous of old were subject to penal sufferings before Christ's descent into hell. Hence shortly before the passage quoted he says: "Some add that this benefit was also bestowed upon the saints of old, that on the Lord's coming into hell they were freed from their sufferings. But I fail to see how Abraham, into whose bosom the poor man was received, was ever in such sufferings." Consequently, when he afterwards adds that "he had not yet discovered what Christ's descent into hell had brought to the righteous of old," this must be understood as to their being freed from penal sufferings. Yet Christ bestowed something upon them as to their attaining glory: and in consequence He dispelled the suffering which they endured through their glory being delayed: still they had great joy from the very hope thereof, according to John 8:56: "Abraham your father rejoiced that he might see my day." And therefore he adds: "I fail to see that He ever departed, according to the beatific presence of His Godhead," that is, inasmuch as even before Christ's coming they were happy in hope, although not yet fully happy in fact.

Reply Obj. 2: The holy Fathers while yet living were delivered from original as well as actual sin through faith in Christ; also from the penalty of actual sins, but not from the penalty of original sin, whereby they were excluded from glory, since the price of man's redemption was not yet paid: just as the faithful are now delivered by baptism from the penalty of actual sins, and from the penalty of original sin as to exclusion from glory, yet still remain bound by the penalty of original sin as to the necessity of dying in the body because they are renewed in the spirit, but not yet in the flesh, according to Rom. 8:10: "The body indeed is dead, because of sin; but the spirit liveth, because of justification."

Reply Obj. 3: Directly Christ died His soul went down into hell, and bestowed the fruits of His Passion on the saints detained there; although they did not go out as long as Christ remained in hell, because His presence was part of the fulness of their glory.

SIXTH ARTICLE [III, Q. 52, Art. 6]

Whether Christ Delivered Any of the Lost from Hell?

Objection 1: It would seem that Christ did deliver some of the lost from hell, because it is written (Isa. 24:22): "And they shall be gathered together as in the gathering of one bundle into the pit, end they shall be shut up there in prison: and after many days they shall be visited." But there he is speaking of the lost, who "had adored the host of heaven," according to Jerome's commentary. Consequently it seems that even the lost were visited at Christ's descent into hell; and this seems to imply their deliverance.

Obj. 2: Further, on Zech. 9:11: "Thou also by the blood of Thy testament hast sent forth Thy prisoners out of the pit wherein is no water," the gloss observes: "Thou hast delivered them who were held bound in prisons, where no mercy refreshed them, which that rich man prayed for." But only the lost are shut up in merciless prisons. Therefore Christ did deliver some from the hell of the lost.

Obj. 3: Further, Christ's power was not less in hell than in this world, because He worked in every place by the power of His Godhead. But in this world He delivered some persons of every state. Therefore, in hell also, He delivered some from the state of the lost.

*On the contrary,* It is written (Osee 13:14): "O death, I will be thy death; O hell, I will be thy bite": upon which the gloss says: "By leading forth the elect, and leaving there the reprobate." But only the reprobate are in the hell of the lost. Therefore, by Christ's descent into hell none were delivered from the hell of the lost.

*I answer that,* As stated above (A. 5), when Christ descended into hell He worked by the power of His Passion. Consequently, His descent into hell brought the fruits of deliverance to them only who were united to His Passion through faith quickened by charity, whereby sins are taken away. Now those detained in the hell of the lost either had no faith in Christ's Passion, as infidels; or if they had faith, they had no conformity with the charity of the suffering Christ: hence they could not be cleansed from their sins. And on this account Christ's descent into hell brought them no deliverance from the debt of punishment in hell.

Reply Obj. 1: When Christ descended into hell, all who were in any part of hell were visited in some respect: some to their consolation and deliverance, others, namely, the lost, to their shame and confusion. Accordingly the passage continues: "And the moon shall blush, and the sun be put to shame," etc.

This can also be referred to the visitation which will come upon them in the Day of Judgment, not for their deliverance, but for their yet greater confusion, according to Sophon. i, 12: "I will visit upon the men that are settled on their lees."

Reply Obj. 2: When the gloss says "where no mercy refreshed them," this is to be understood of the refreshing of full deliverance, because the holy Fathers could not be delivered from this prison of hell before Christ's coming.

Reply Obj. 3: It was not due to any lack of power on Christ's part that some were not delivered from every state in hell, as out of every state among men in this world; but it was owing to the very different condition of each state. For, so long as men live here below, they can be converted to faith and charity, because in this life men are not confirmed either in good or in evil, as they are after quitting this life.

SEVENTH ARTICLE [III, Q. 52, Art. 7]

Whether the Children Who Died in Original Sin Were Delivered by Christ?

Objection 1: It would seem that the children who died in original sin were delivered from hell by Christ's descending thither. For, like the holy Fathers, the children were kept in hell simply because of original sin. But the holy Fathers were delivered from hell, as stated above (A. 5). Therefore the children were similarly delivered from hell by Christ.

Obj. 2: Further, the Apostle says (Rom. 5:15): "If by the offense of one, many died; much more the grace of God and the gift, by the grace of one man, Jesus Christ, hath abounded unto many." But the children who die with none but original sin are detained in hell owing to their first parent's sin. Therefore, much more were they delivered from hell through the grace of Christ.

Obj. 3: Further, as Baptism works in virtue of Christ's Passion, so also does Christ's descent into hell, as is clear from what has been said (A. 4, ad 2, AA. 5, 6). But through Baptism children are delivered from original sin and hell. Therefore, they were similarly delivered by Christ's descent into hell.

*On the contrary,* The Apostle says (Rom. 3:25): "God hath proposed Christ to be a propitiation, through faith in His blood." But the children who had died with only original sin were in no wise sharers of faith in Christ. Therefore, they did not receive the fruits of Christ's propitiation, so as to be delivered by Him from hell.

*I answer that,* As stated above (A. 6), Christ's descent into hell had its effect of deliverance on them only who through faith and charity were united to Christ's Passion, in virtue whereof Christ's descent into hell was one of deliverance. But the children who had died in original sin were in no way united to Christ's Passion by faith and love: for, not having the use of free will, they could have no faith of their own; nor were they cleansed from original sin either by their parents' faith or by any sacrament of faith. Consequently, Christ's descent into hell did not deliver the children from thence. And furthermore, the holy Fathers were delivered from hell by being admitted to the glory of the vision of God, to which no one can come except through grace; according to Rom. 6:23: "The grace of God is life everlasting." Therefore, since children dying in original sin had no grace, they were not delivered from hell.

Reply Obj. 1: The holy Fathers, although still held bound by the debt of original sin, in so far as it touches human nature, were nevertheless delivered from all stain of sin by faith in Christ: consequently, they were capable of that deliverance which Christ brought by descending into hell. But the same cannot be said of the children, as is evident from what was said above.

Reply Obj. 2: When the Apostle says that the grace of God "hath abounded unto many," the word "many" [*The Vulgate reads 'plures,' i.e. 'many more'] is to be taken, not comparatively, as if more were saved by Christ's grace than lost by Adam's sin: but absolutely, as if he said that the grace of the one Christ abounded unto many, just as Adam's sin was contracted by many. But as Adam's sin was contracted by those only who descended seminally from him according to the flesh, so Christ's grace reached those only who became His members by spiritual regeneration: which does not apply to children dying in original sin.

Reply Obj. 3: Baptism is applied to men in this life, in which man's state can be changed from sin into grace: but Christ's descent into hell was vouchsafed to the souls after this life when they are no longer capable of the said change. And consequently by baptism children are delivered from original sin and from hell, but not by Christ's descent into hell.

EIGHTH ARTICLE [III, Q. 52, Art. 8]

Whether Christ by His Descent into Hell Delivered Souls from Purgatory?

Objection 1: It would seem that Christ by His descent into hell delivered souls from Purgatory--for Augustine says (Ep. ad Evod. clxiv): "Because evident testimonies speak of hell and its pains, there is no reason for believing that the Saviour came thither except to rescue men from those same pains: but I still wish to know whether it was all whom He found there, or some whom He deemed worthy of such a benefit. Yet I do not doubt that Christ went into hell, and granted this favor to them who were suffering from its pains." But, as stated above (A. 6), He did not confer the benefit of deliverance upon the lost: and there are no others in a state of penal suffering except those in Purgatory. Consequently Christ delivered souls from Purgatory.

Obj. 2: Further, the very presence of Christ's soul had no less effect than His sacraments have. But souls are delivered from Purgatory by the sacraments, especially by the sacrament of the Eucharist, as shall be shown later (Suppl., Q. 71, A. 9). Therefore much more were souls delivered from Purgatory by the presence of Christ descending into hell.

Obj. 3: Further, as Augustine says (De Poenit. ix), those whom Christ healed in this life He healed completely. Also, our Lord says (John 7:23): "I have healed the whole man on the sabbath-day." But Christ delivered them who were in Purgatory from the punishment of the pain of loss, whereby they were excluded from glory. Therefore, He also delivered them from the punishment of Purgatory.

*On the contrary,* Gregory says (Moral. xiii): "Since our Creator and Redeemer, penetrating the bars of hell, brought out from thence the souls of the elect, He does not permit us to go thither, from whence He has already by descending set others free." But He permits us to go to Purgatory. Therefore, by descending into hell, He did not deliver souls from Purgatory.

*I answer that,* As we have stated more than once (A. 4, ad 2, AA. 5, 6, 7), Christ's descent into hell was one of deliverance in virtue of His Passion. Now Christ's Passion had a virtue which was neither temporal nor transitory, but everlasting, according to Heb. 10:14: "For by one oblation He hath perfected for ever them that are sanctified." And so it is evident that Christ's Passion had no greater efficacy then than it has now. Consequently, they who were such as those who are now in Purgatory, were not set free from Purgatory by Christ's descent into hell. But if any were found such as are now set free from Purgatory by virtue of Christ's Passion, then there was nothing to hinder them from being delivered from Purgatory by Christ's descent into hell.

Reply Obj. 1: From this passage of Augustine it cannot be concluded that all who were in Purgatory were delivered from it, but that such a benefit was bestowed upon some persons, that is to say, upon such as were already cleansed sufficiently, or who in life, by their faith and devotion towards Christ's death, so merited, that when He descended, they were delivered from the temporal punishment of Purgatory.

Reply Obj. 2: Christ's power operates in the sacraments by way of healing and expiation. Consequently, the sacrament of the Eucharist delivers men from Purgatory inasmuch as it is a satisfactory sacrifice for sin. But Christ's descent into hell was not satisfactory; yet it operated in virtue of the Passion, which was satisfactory, as stated above (Q. 48, A. 2), but satisfactory in general, since its virtue had to be applied to each individual by something specially personal (Q. 49, A. 1, ad 4, 5). Consequently, it does not follow of necessity that all were delivered from Purgatory by Christ's descent into hell.

Reply Obj. 3: Those defects from which Christ altogether delivered men in this world were purely personal, and concerned the individual; whereas exclusion from God's glory was a general defect and common to all human nature. Consequently, there was nothing to prevent those detained in Purgatory being delivered by Christ from their privation of glory, but not from the debt of punishment in Purgatory which pertains to personal defect. Just as on the other hand, the holy Fathers before Christ's coming were delivered from their personal defects, but not from the common defect, as was stated above (A. 7, ad 1; Q. 49, A. 5, ad 1).

# QUESTION 53

OF CHRIST'S RESURRECTION (In Four Articles)

We have now to consider those things that concern Christ's Exaltation; and we shall deal with (1) His Resurrection; (2) His Ascension; (3) His sitting at the right hand of God the Father; (4) His Judiciary Power. Under the first heading there is a fourfold consideration: (1) Christ's Resurrection in itself; (2) the quality of the Person rising; (3) the manifestation of the Resurrection; (4) its causality. Concerning the first there are four points of inquiry:

(1) The necessity of His Resurrection;

(2) The time of the Resurrection;

(3) Its order;

(4) Its cause.

FIRST ARTICLE [III, Q. 53, Art. 1]

Whether It Was Necessary for Christ to Rise Again?

Objection 1: It would seem that it was not necessary for Christ to rise again. For Damascene says (De Fide Orth. iv): "Resurrection is the rising again of an animate being, which was disintegrated and fallen." But Christ did not fall by sinning, nor was His body dissolved, as is manifest from what was stated above (Q. 51, A. 3). Therefore, it does not properly belong to Him to rise again.

Obj. 2: Further, whoever rises again is promoted to a higher state, since to rise is to be uplifted. But after death Christ's body continued to be united with the Godhead, hence it could not be uplifted to any higher condition. Therefore, it was not due to it to rise again.

Obj. 3: Further, all that befell Christ's humanity was ordained for our salvation. But Christ's Passion sufficed for our salvation, since by it we were loosed from guilt and punishment, as is clear from what was said above (Q. 49, A. 1, 3). Consequently, it was not necessary for Christ to rise again from the dead.

*On the contrary,* It is written (Luke 24:46): "It behooved Christ to suffer and to rise again from the dead."

*I answer that,* It behooved Christ to rise again, for five reasons. First of all; for the commendation of Divine Justice, to which it belongs to exalt them who humble themselves for God's sake, according to Luke 1:52: "He hath put down the mighty from their seat, and hath exalted the humble." Consequently, because Christ humbled Himself even to the death of the Cross, from love and obedience to God, it behooved Him to be uplifted by God to a glorious resurrection; hence it is said in His Person (Ps. 138:2): "Thou hast known," i.e. approved, "my sitting down," i.e. My humiliation and Passion, "and my rising up," i.e. My glorification in the resurrection; as the gloss expounds.

Secondly, for our instruction in the faith, since our belief in Christ's Godhead is confirmed by His rising again, because, according to 2 Cor. 13:4, "although He was crucified through weakness, yet He liveth by the power of God." And therefore it is written (1 Cor. 15:14): "If Christ be not risen again, then is our preaching vain, and our [Vulg.: 'your'] faith is also vain": and (Ps. 29:10): "What profit is there in my blood?" that is, in the shedding of My blood, "while I go down," as by various degrees of evils, "into corruption?" As though He were to answer: "None. 'For if I do not at once rise again but My body be corrupted, I shall preach to no one, I shall gain no one,'" as the gloss expounds.

Thirdly, for the raising of our hope, since through seeing Christ, who is our head, rise again, we hope that we likewise shall rise again. Hence it is written (1 Cor. 15:12): "Now if Christ be preached that He rose from the dead, how do some among you say, that there is no resurrection of the dead?" And (Job 19:25, 27): "I know," that is with certainty of faith, "that my Redeemer," i.e. Christ, "liveth," having risen from the dead; "and" therefore "in the last day I shall rise out of the earth . . . this my hope is laid up in my bosom."

Fourthly, to set in order the lives of the faithful: according to Rom. 6:4: "As Christ is risen from the dead by the glory of the Father, so we also may walk in newness of life": and further on; "Christ rising from the dead dieth now no more; so do you also reckon that you are dead to sin, but alive to God."

Fifthly, in order to complete the work of our salvation: because, just as for this reason did He endure evil things in dying that He might deliver us from evil, so was He glorified in rising again in order to advance us towards good things; according to Rom. 4:25: "He was delivered up for our sins, and rose again for our justification."

Reply Obj. 1: Although Christ did not fall by sin, yet He fell by death, because as sin is a fall from righteousness, so death is a fall from life: hence the words of Mic. 7:8 can be taken as though spoken by Christ: "Rejoice not thou, my enemy, over me, because I am fallen: I shall rise again." Likewise, although Christ's body was not disintegrated by returning to dust, yet the separation of His soul and body was a kind of disintegration.

Reply Obj. 2: The Godhead was united with Christ's flesh after death by personal union, but not by natural union; thus the soul is united with the body as its form, so as to constitute human nature. Consequently, by the union of the body and soul, the body was uplifted to a higher condition of nature, but not to a higher personal state.

Reply Obj. 3: Christ's Passion wrought our salvation, properly speaking, by removing evils; but the Resurrection did so as the beginning and exemplar of all good things.

SECOND ARTICLE [III, Q. 53, Art. 2]

Whether It Was Fitting for Christ to Rise Again on the Third Day?

Objection 1: It would seem unfitting that Christ should have risen again on the third day. For the members ought to be in conformity with their head. But we who are His members do not rise from death on the third day, since our rising is put off until the end of the world. Therefore, it seems that Christ, who is our head, should not have risen on the third day, but that His Resurrection ought to have been deferred until the end of the world.

Obj. 2: Further, Peter said (Acts 2:24) that "it was impossible for Christ to be held fast by hell" and death. Therefore it seems that Christ's rising ought not to have been deferred until the third day, but that He ought to have risen at once on the same day; especially since the gloss quoted above (A. 1) says that "there is no profit in the shedding of Christ's blood, if He did not rise at once."

Obj. 3: The day seems to start with the rising of the sun, the presence of which causes the day. But Christ rose before sunrise: for it is related (John 20:1) that "Mary Magdalen cometh early, when it was yet dark, unto the sepulchre": but Christ was already risen, for it goes on to say: "And she saw the stone taken away from the sepulchre." Therefore Christ did not rise on the third day.

*On the contrary,* It is written (Matt. 20:19): "They shall deliver Him to the Gentiles to be mocked, and scourged, and crucified, and the third day He shall rise again."

*I answer that,* As stated above (A. 1) Christ's Resurrection was necessary for the instruction of our faith. But our faith regards Christ's Godhead and humanity, for it is not enough to believe the one without the other, as is evident from what has been said (Q. 36, A. 4; cf. II-II, Q. 2, AA. 7, 8). Consequently, in order that our faith in the truth of His Godhead might be confirmed it was necessary that He should rise speedily, and that His Resurrection should not be deferred until the end of the world. But to confirm our faith regarding the truth of His humanity and death, it was needful that there should be some interval between His death and rising. For if He had risen directly after death, it might seem that His death was not genuine and consequently neither would His Resurrection be true. But to establish the truth of Christ's death, it was enough for His rising to be deferred until the third day, for within that time some signs of life always appear in one who appears to be dead whereas he is alive.

Furthermore, by His rising on the third day, the perfection of the number "three" is commended, which is "the number of everything," as having "beginning, middle, and end," as is said in De Coelo i. Again in the mystical sense we are taught that Christ by "His one death" (i.e. of the body) which was light, by reason of His righteousness, "destroyed our two deaths" (i.e. of soul and body), which are as darkness on account of sin; consequently, He remained in death for one day and two nights, as Augustine observes (De Trin. iv).

And thereby is also signified that a third epoch began with the Resurrection: for the first was before the Law; the second under the Law; and the third under grace. Moreover the third state of the saints began with the Resurrection of Christ: for, the first was under figures of the Law; the second under the truth of faith; while the third will be in the eternity of glory, which Christ inaugurated by rising again.

Reply Obj. 1: The head and members are likened in nature, but not in power; because the power of the head is more excellent than that of the members. Accordingly, to show forth the excellence of Christ's power, it was fitting that He should rise on the third day, while the resurrection of the rest is put off until the end of the world.

Reply Obj. 2: Detention implies a certain compulsion. But Christ was not held fast by any necessity of death, but was "free among the dead": and therefore He abode a while in death, not as one held fast, but of His own will, just so long as He deemed necessary for the instruction of our faith. And a task is said to be done "at once" which is performed within a short space of time.

Reply Obj. 3: As stated above (Q. 51, A. 4, ad 1, 2), Christ rose early when the day was beginning to dawn, to denote that by His Resurrection He brought us to the light of glory; just as He died when the day was drawing to its close, and nearing to darkness, in order to signify that by His death He would destroy the darkness of sin and its punishment. Nevertheless He is said to have risen on the third day, taking day as a natural day which contains twenty-four hours. And as Augustine says (De Trin. iv): "The night until the dawn, when the Lord's Resurrection was proclaimed, belongs to the third day. Because God, who made the light to shine forth from darkness, in order that by the grace of the New Testament and partaking of Christ's rising we might hear this--'once ye were darkness, but now light in the Lord'--insinuates in a measure to us that day draws its origin from night: for, as the first days are computed from light to darkness on account of man's coming fall, so these days are reckoned from darkness to light owing to man's restoration." And so it is evident that even if He had risen at midnight, He could be said to have risen on the third day, taking it as a natural day. But now that He rose early, it can be affirmed that He rose on the third day, even taking the artificial day which is caused by the sun's presence, because the sun had already begun to brighten the sky. Hence it is written (Mk. 16:2) that "the women come to the sepulchre, the sun being now risen"; which is not contrary to John's statement "when it was yet dark," as Augustine says (De Cons. Evang. iii), "because, as the day advances the more the light rises, the more are the remaining shadows dispelled." But when Mark says "'the sun being now risen,' it is not to be taken as if the sun were already apparent over the horizon, but as coming presently into those parts."

THIRD ARTICLE [III, Q. 53, Art. 3]

Whether Christ Was the First to Rise from the Dead?

Objection 1: It would seem that Christ was not the first to rise from the dead, because we read in the Old Testament of some persons raised to life by Elias and Eliseus, according to Heb. 11:35: "Women received their dead raised to life again": also Christ before His Passion raised three dead persons to life. Therefore Christ was not the first to rise from the dead.

Obj. 2: Further, among the other miracles which happened during the Passion, it is narrated (Matt. 27:52) that "the monuments were opened, and many bodies of the saints who had slept rose again." Therefore Christ was not the first to rise from the dead.

Obj. 3: Further, as Christ by His own rising is the cause of our resurrection, so by His grace He is the cause of our grace, according to John 1:16: "Of His fulness we all have received." But in point of time some others had grace previous to Christ--for instance all the fathers of the Old Testament. Therefore some others came to the resurrection of the body before Christ.

*On the contrary,* It is written (1 Cor. 15:20): "Christ is risen from the dead, the first fruits of them that sleep--because," says the gloss, "He rose first in point of time and dignity."

*I answer that,* Resurrection is a restoring from death to life. Now a man is snatched from death in two ways: first of all, from actual death, so that he begins in any way to live anew after being actually dead: in another way, so that he is not only rescued from death, but from the necessity, nay more, from the possibility of dying again. Such is a true and perfect resurrection, because so long as a man lives, subject to the necessity of dying, death has dominion over him in a measure, according to Rom. 8:10: "The body indeed is dead because of sin." Furthermore, what has the possibility of existence, is said to exist in some respect, that is, in potentiality. Thus it is evident that the resurrection, whereby one is rescued from actual death only, is but an imperfect one.

Consequently, speaking of perfect resurrection, Christ is the first of them who rise, because by rising He was the first to attain life utterly immortal, according to Rom. 6:9: "Christ rising from the dead dieth now no more." But by an imperfect resurrection, some others have risen before Christ, so as to be a kind of figure of His Resurrection.

And thus the answer to the first objection is clear: because both those raised from the dead in the old Testament, and those raised by Christ, so returned to life that they had to die again.

Reply Obj. 2: There are two opinions regarding them who rose with Christ. Some hold that they rose to life so as to die no more, because it would be a greater torment for them to die a second time than not to rise at all. According to this view, as Jerome observes on Matt. 27:52, 53, we must understand that "they had not risen before our Lord rose." Hence the Evangelist says that "coming out of the tombs after His Resurrection, they came into the holy city, and appeared to many." But Augustine (Ep. ad Evod. clxiv) while giving this opinion, says: "I know that it appears some, that by the death of Christ the Lord the same resurrection was bestowed upon the righteous as is promised to us in the end; and if they slept not again by laying aside their bodies, it remains to be seen how Christ can be understood to be 'the first-born of the dead,' if so many preceded Him unto that resurrection. Now if reply be made that this is said by anticipation, so that the monuments be understood to have been opened by the earthquake while Christ was still hanging on the cross, but that the bodies of the just did not rise then but after He had risen, the difficulty still arises--how is it that Peter asserts that it was predicted not of David but of Christ, that His body would not see corruption, since David's tomb was in their midst; and thus he did not convince them, if David's body was no longer there; for even if he had risen soon after his death, and his flesh had not seen corruption, his tomb might nevertheless remain. Now it seems hard that David from whose seed Christ is descended, was not in that rising of the just, if an eternal rising was conferred upon them. Also that saying in the Epistle to the Hebrews (11:40) regarding the ancient just would be hard to explain, 'that they should not be perfected without us,' if they were already established in that incorruption of the resurrection which is promised at the end when we shall be made perfect": so that Augustine would seem to think that they rose to die again. In this sense Jerome also in commenting on Matthew (27:52, 53) says: "As Lazarus rose, so also many of the bodies of the saints rose, that they might bear witness to the risen Christ." Nevertheless in a sermon for the Assumption [*Ep. ix ad Paul. et Eustoch.; among the supposititious works ascribed to St. Jerome] he seems to leave the matter doubtful. But Augustine's reasons seem to be much more cogent.

Reply Obj. 3: As everything preceding Christ's coming was preparatory for Christ, so is grace a disposition for glory. Consequently, it behooved all things appertaining to glory, whether they regard the soul, as the perfect fruition of God, or whether they regard the body, as the glorious resurrection, to be first in Christ as the author of glory: but that grace should be first in those that were ordained unto Christ.

FOURTH ARTICLE [III, Q. 53, Art. 4]

Whether Christ Was the Cause of His Own Resurrection?

Objection 1: It seems that Christ was not the cause of His own Resurrection. For whoever is raised up by another is not the cause of his own rising. But Christ was raised up by another, according to Acts 2:24: "Whom God hath raised up, having loosed the sorrows of hell": and Rom. 8:11: "He that raised up Jesus Christ from the dead, shall quicken also your mortal bodies." Therefore Christ is not the cause of His own Resurrection.

Obj. 2: Further, no one is said to merit, or ask from another, that of which he is himself the cause. But Christ by His Passion merited the Resurrection, as Augustine says (Tract. civ in Joan.): "The lowliness of the Passion is the meritorious cause of the glory of the Resurrection." Moreover He asked the Father that He might be raised up again, according to Ps. 40:11: "But thou, O Lord, have mercy on me, and raise me up again." Therefore He was not the cause of His rising again.

Obj. 3: Further, as Damascene proves (De Fide Orth. iv), it is not the soul that rises again, but the body, which is stricken by death. But the body could not unite the soul with itself, since the soul is nobler. Therefore what rose in Christ could not be the cause of His Resurrection.

*On the contrary,* Our Lord says (John 10:18): "No one taketh My soul from Me, but I lay it down, and I take it up again." But to rise is nothing else than to take the soul up again. Consequently, it appears that Christ rose again of His own power.

*I answer that,* As stated above (Q. 50, AA. 2, 3) in consequence of death Christ's Godhead was not separated from His soul, nor from His flesh. Consequently, both the soul and the flesh of the dead Christ can be considered in two respects: first, in respect of His Godhead; secondly, in respect of His created nature. Therefore, according to the virtue of the Godhead united to it, the body took back again the soul which it had laid aside, and the soul took back again the body which it had abandoned: and thus Christ rose by His own power. And this is precisely what is written (2 Cor. 13:4): "For although He was crucified through" our "weakness, yet He liveth by the power of God." But if we consider the body and soul of the dead Christ according to the power of created nature, they could not thus be reunited, but it was necessary for Christ to be raised up by God.

Reply Obj. 1: The Divine power is the same thing as the operation of the Father and the Son; accordingly these two things are mutually consequent, that Christ was raised up by the Divine power of the Father, and by His own power.

Reply Obj. 2: Christ by praying besought and merited His Resurrection, as man and not as God.

Reply Obj. 3: According to its created nature Christ's body is not more powerful than His soul; yet according to its Divine power it is more powerful. Again the soul by reason of the Godhead united to it is more powerful than the body in respect of its created nature. Consequently, it was by the Divine power that the body and soul mutually resumed each other, but not by the power of their created nature.

# QUESTION 54

OF THE QUALITY OF CHRIST RISING AGAIN (In Four Articles)

We have now to consider the quality of the rising Christ, which presents four points of inquiry:

(1) Whether Christ had a true body after His Resurrection?

(2) Whether He rose with His complete body?

(3) Whether His was a glorified body?

(4) Of the scars which showed in His body.

FIRST ARTICLE [III, Q. 54, Art. 1]

Whether Christ Had a True Body After His Resurrection?

Objection 1: It would seem that Christ did not have a true body after His Resurrection. For a true body cannot be in the same place at the same time with another body. But after the Resurrection Christ's body was with another at the same time in the same place: since He entered among the disciples "the doors being shut," as is related in John 20:26. Therefore it seems that Christ did not have a true body after His Resurrection.

Obj. 2: Further, a true body does not vanish from the beholder's sight unless perchance it be corrupted. But Christ's body "vanished out of the sight" of the disciples as they gazed upon Him, as is related in Luke 24:31. Therefore, it seems that Christ did not have a true body after His Resurrection.

Obj. 3: Further, every true body has its determinate shape. But Christ's body appeared before the disciples "in another shape," as is evident from Mk. 15:12. Therefore it seems that Christ did not possess a true body after His Resurrection.

*On the contrary,* It is written (Luke 24:37) that when Christ appeared to His disciples "they being troubled and frightened, supposed that they saw a spirit," as if He had not a true but an imaginary body: but to remove their fears He presently added: "Handle and see, for a spirit hath not flesh and bones, as you see Me to have." Consequently, He had not an imaginary but a true body.

*I answer that,* As Damascene says (De Fide Orth. iv): that is said to rise, which fell. But Christ's body fell by death; namely, inasmuch as the soul which was its formal perfection was separated from it. Hence, in order for it to be a true resurrection, it was necessary for the same body of Christ to be once more united with the same soul. And since the truth of the body's nature is from its form it follows that Christ's body after His Resurrection was a true body, and of the same nature as it was before. But had His been an imaginary body, then His Resurrection would not have been true, but apparent.

Reply Obj. 1: Christ's body after His Resurrection, not by miracle but from its glorified condition, as some say, entered in among the disciples while the doors were shut, thus existing with another body in the same place. But whether a glorified body can have this from some hidden property, so as to be with another body at the same time in the same place, will be discussed later (Suppl., Q. 83, A. 4) when the common resurrection will be dealt with. For the present let it suffice to say that it was not from any property within the body, but by virtue of the Godhead united to it, that this body, although a true one, entered in among the disciples while the doors were shut. Accordingly Augustine says in a sermon for Easter (ccxlvii) that some men argue in this fashion: "If it were a body; if what rose from the sepulchre were what hung upon the tree, how could it enter through closed doors?" And he answers: "If you understand how, it is no miracle: where reason fails, faith abounds." And (Tract. cxxi super Joan.) he says: "Closed doors were no obstacle to the substance of a Body wherein was the Godhead; for truly He could enter in by doors not open, in whose Birth His Mother's virginity remained inviolate." And Gregory says the same in a homily for the octave of Easter (xxvi in Evang.).

Reply Obj. 2: As stated above (Q. 53, A. 3), Christ rose to the immortal life of glory. But such is the disposition of a glorified body that it is spiritual, i.e. subject to the spirit, as the Apostle says (1 Cor. 15:44). Now in order for the body to be entirely subject to the spirit, it is necessary for the body's every action to be subject to the will of the spirit. Again, that an object be seen is due to the action of the visible object upon the sight, as the Philosopher shows (De Anima ii). Consequently, whoever has a glorified body has it in his power to be seen when he so wishes, and not to be seen when he does not wish it. Moreover Christ had this not only from the condition of His glorified body, but also from the power of His Godhead, by which power it may happen that even bodies not glorified are miraculously unseen: as was by a miracle bestowed on the blessed Bartholomew, that "if he wished he could be seen, and not be seen if he did not wish it" [*Apocryphal Historia Apost. viii, 2]. Christ, then, is said to have vanished from the eyes of the disciples, not as though He were corrupted or dissolved into invisible elements; but because He ceased, of His own will, to be seen by them, either while He was present or while He was departing by the gift of agility.

Reply Obj. 3: As Severianus [*Peter Chrysologus: Serm. lxxxii] says in a sermon for Easter: "Let no one suppose that Christ changed His features at the Resurrection." This is to be understood of the outline of His members; since there was nothing out of keeping or deformed in the body of Christ which was conceived of the Holy Ghost, that had to be righted at the Resurrection. Nevertheless He received the glory of clarity in the Resurrection: accordingly the same writer adds: "but the semblance is changed, when, ceasing to be mortal, it becomes immortal; so that it acquired the glory of countenance, without losing the substance of the countenance." Yet He did not come to those disciples in glorified appearance; but, as it lay in His power for His body to be seen or not, so it was within His power to present to the eyes of the beholders His form either glorified or not glorified, or partly glorified and partly not, or in any fashion whatsoever. Still it requires but a slight difference for anyone to seem to appear another shape.

SECOND ARTICLE [III, Q. 54, Art. 2]

Whether Christ's Body Rose Glorified?

[*Some editions give this article as the third, following the order of the introduction to the question. But it is evident from the first sentence of the body of A. 3 (A. 2 in the aforesaid editions), that the order of the Leonine edition is correct.]

Objection 1: It seems that Christ's body did not rise glorified. For glorified bodies shine, according to Matt. 13:43: "Then shall the just shine as the sun in the kingdom of their Father." But shining bodies are seen under the aspect of light, but not of color. Therefore, since Christ's body was beheld under the aspect of color, as it had been hitherto, it seems that it was not a glorified one.

Obj. 2: Further, a glorified body is incorruptible. But Christ's body seems not to have been incorruptible; because it was palpable, as He Himself says in Luke 24:39: "Handle, and see." Now Gregory says (Hom. in Evang. xxvi) that "what is handled must be corruptible, and that which is incorruptible cannot be handled." Consequently, Christ's body was not glorified.

Obj. 3: Further, a glorified body is not animal, but spiritual, as is clear from 1 Cor. 15. But after the Resurrection Christ's body seems to have been animal, since He ate and drank with His disciples, as we read in the closing chapters of Luke and John. Therefore, it seems that Christ's body was not glorified.

*On the contrary,* The Apostle says (Phil. 3:21): "He will reform the body of our lowness, made like to the body of His glory."

*I answer that,* Christ's was a glorified body in His Resurrection, and this is evident from three reasons. First of all, because His Resurrection was the exemplar and the cause of ours, as is stated in 1 Cor. 15:43. But in the resurrection the saints will have glorified bodies, as is written in the same place: "It is sown in dishonor, it shall rise in glory." Hence, since the cause is mightier than the effect, and the exemplar than the exemplate; much more glorious, then, was the body of Christ in His Resurrection. Secondly, because He merited the glory of His Resurrection by the lowliness of His Passion. Hence He said (John 12:27): "Now is My soul troubled," which refers to the Passion; and later He adds: "Father, glorify Thy name," whereby He asks for the glory of the Resurrection. Thirdly, because as stated above (Q. 34, A. 4), Christ's soul was glorified from the instant of His conception by perfect fruition of the Godhead. But, as stated above (Q. 14, A. 1, ad 2), it was owing to the Divine economy that the glory did not pass from His soul to His body, in order that by the Passion He might accomplish the mystery of our redemption. Consequently, when this mystery of Christ's Passion and death was finished, straightway the soul communicated its glory to the risen body in the Resurrection; and so that body was made glorious.

Reply Obj. 1: Whatever is received within a subject is received according to the subject's capacity. Therefore, since glory flows from the soul into the body, it follows that, as Augustine says (Ep. ad Dioscor. cxviii), the brightness or splendor of a glorified body is after the manner of natural color in the human body; just as variously colored glass derives its splendor from the sun's radiance, according to the mode of the color. But as it lies within the power of a glorified man whether his body be seen or not, as stated above (A. 1, ad 2), so is it in his power whether its splendor be seen or not. Accordingly it can be seen in its color without its brightness. And it was in this way that Christ's body appeared to the disciples after the Resurrection.

Reply Obj. 2: We say that a body can be handled not only because of its resistance, but also on account of its density. But from rarity and density follow weight and lightness, heat and cold, and similar contraries, which are the principles of corruption in elementary bodies. Consequently, a body that can be handled by human touch is naturally corruptible. But if there be a body that resists touch, and yet is not disposed according to the qualities mentioned, which are the proper objects of human touch, such as a heavenly body, then such body cannot be said to be handled. But Christ's body after the Resurrection was truly made up of elements, and had tangible qualities such as the nature of a human body requires, and therefore it could naturally be handled; and if it had nothing beyond the nature of a human body, it would likewise be corruptible. But it had something else which made it incorruptible, and this was not the nature of a heavenly body, as some maintain, and into which we shall make fuller inquiry later (Suppl., Q. 82, A. 1), but it was glory flowing from a beatified soul: because, as Augustine says (Ep. ad Dioscor. cxviii): "God made the soul of such powerful nature, that from its fullest beatitude the fulness of health overflows into the body, that is, the vigor of incorruption." And therefore Gregory says (Hom. in Evang. xxvi): "Christ's body is shown to be of the same nature, but of different glory, after the Resurrection."

Reply Obj. 3: As Augustine says (De Civ. Dei xiii): "After the Resurrection, our Saviour in spiritual but true flesh partook of meat with the disciples, not from need of food, but because it lay in His power." For as Bede says on Luke 24:41: "The thirsty earth sucks in the water, and the sun's burning ray absorbs it; the former from need, the latter by its power." Hence after the Resurrection He ate, "not as needing food, but in order thus to show the nature of His risen body." Nor does it follow that His was an animal body that stands in need of food.

THIRD ARTICLE [III, Q. 54, Art. 3]

Whether Christ's Body Rose Again Entire?

Objection 1: It would seem that Christ's body did not rise entire. For flesh and blood belong to the integrity of the body: whereas Christ seems not to have had both, for it is written (1 Cor. 15:50): "Flesh and blood can not possess the kingdom of God." But Christ rose in the glory of the kingdom of God. Therefore it seems that He did not have flesh and blood.

Obj. 2: Further, blood is one of the four humors. Consequently, if Christ had blood, with equal reason He also had the other humors, from which corruption is caused in animal bodies. It would follow, then, that Christ's body was corruptible, which is unseemly. Therefore Christ did not have flesh and blood.

Obj. 3: Further, the body of Christ which rose, ascended to heaven. But some of His blood is kept as relics in various churches. Therefore Christ's body did not rise with the integrity of all its parts.

*On the contrary,* our Lord said (Luke 24:39) while addressing His disciples after the Resurrection: "A spirit hath not flesh and bones as you see Me to have."

*I answer that,* As stated above (A. 2), Christ's body in the Resurrection was "of the same nature, but differed in glory." Accordingly, whatever goes with the nature of a human body, was entirely in the body of Christ when He rose again. Now it is clear that flesh, bones, blood, and other such things, are of the very nature of the human body. Consequently, all these things were in Christ's body when He rose again; and this also integrally, without any diminution; otherwise it would not have been a complete resurrection, if whatever was lost by death had not been restored. Hence our Lord assured His faithful ones by saying (Matt. 10:30): "The very hairs of your head are all numbered": and (Luke 21:18): "A hair of your head shall not perish."

But to say that Christ's body had neither flesh, nor bones, nor the other natural parts of a human body, belongs to the error of Eutyches, Bishop of Constantinople, who maintained that "our body in that glory of the resurrection will be impalpable, and more subtle than wind and air: and that our Lord, after the hearts of the disciples who handled Him were confirmed, brought back to subtlety whatever could be handled in Him" [*St. Gregory, Moral. in Job 14:56]. Now Gregory condemns this in the same book, because Christ's body was not changed after the Resurrection, according to Rom. 6:9: "Christ rising from the dead, dieth now no more." Accordingly, the very man who had said these things, himself retracted them at his death. For, if it be unbecoming for Christ to take a body of another nature in His conception, a heavenly one for instance, as Valentine asserted, it is much more unbecoming for Him at His Resurrection to resume a body of another nature, because in His Resurrection He resumed unto an everlasting life, the body which in His conception He had assumed to a mortal life.

Reply Obj. 1: Flesh and blood are not to be taken there for the nature of flesh and blood, but, either for the guilt of flesh and blood, as Gregory says [*St. Gregory, Moral. in Job 14:56], or else for the corruption of flesh and blood: because, as Augustine says (Ad Consent., De Resur. Carn.), "there will be neither corruption there, nor mortality of flesh and blood." Therefore flesh according to its substance possesses the kingdom of God, according to Luke 24:39: "A spirit hath not flesh and bones, as you see Me to have." But flesh, if understood as to its corruption, will not possess it; hence it is straightway added in the words of the Apostle: "Neither shall corruption possess incorruption."

Reply Obj. 2: As Augustine says in the same book: "Perchance by reason of the blood some keener critic will press us and say; If the blood was" in the body of Christ when He rose, "why not the rheum?" that is, the phlegm; "why not also the yellow gall?" that is, the gall proper; "and why not the black gall?" that is, the bile, "with which four humors the body is tempered, as medical science bears witness. But whatever anyone may add, let him take heed not to add corruption, lest he corrupt the health and purity of his own faith; because Divine power is equal to taking away such qualities as it wills from the visible and tractable body, while allowing others to remain, so that there be no defilement," i.e. of corruption, "though the features be there; motion without weariness, the power to eat, without need of food."

Reply Obj. 3: All the blood which flowed from Christ's body, belonging as it does to the integrity of human nature, rose again with His body: and the same reason holds good for all the particles which belong to the truth and integrity of human nature. But the blood preserved as relics in some churches did not flow from Christ's side, but is said to have flowed from some maltreated image of Christ.

FOURTH ARTICLE [III, Q. 54, Art. 4]

Whether Christ's Body Ought to Have Risen with Its Scars?

Objection 1: It would seem that Christ's body ought not to have risen with its scars. For it is written (1 Cor. 15:52): "The dead shall rise incorrupt." But scars and wounds imply corruption and defect. Therefore it was not fitting for Christ, the author of the resurrection, to rise again with scars.

Obj. 2: Further, Christ's body rose entire, as stated above (A. 3). But open scars are opposed to bodily integrity, since they interfere with the continuity of the tissue. It does not therefore seem fitting for the open wounds to remain in Christ's body; although the traces of the wounds might remain, which would satisfy the beholder; thus it was that Thomas believed, to whom it was said: "Because thou hast seen Me, Thomas, thou hast believed" (John 20:29).

Obj. 3: Further, Damascene says (De Fide Orth. iv) that "some things are truly said of Christ after the Resurrection, which He did not have from nature but from special dispensation, such as the scars, in order to make it sure that it was the body which had suffered that rose again." Now when the cause ceases, the effect ceases. Therefore it seems that when the disciples were assured of the Resurrection, He bore the scars no longer. But it ill became the unchangeableness of His glory that He should assume anything which was not to remain in Him for ever. Consequently, it seems that He ought not at His Resurrection to have resumed a body with scars.

*On the contrary,* Our Lord said to Thomas (John 20:27): "Put in thy finger hither, and see My hands; and bring hither thy hand, and put it into My side, and be not faithless but believing."

*I answer that,* It was fitting for Christ's soul at His Resurrection to resume the body with its scars. In the first place, for Christ's own glory. For Bede says on Luke 24:40 that He kept His scars not from inability to heal them, "but to wear them as an everlasting trophy of His victory." Hence Augustine says (De Civ. Dei xxii): "Perhaps in that kingdom we shall see on the bodies of the Martyrs the traces of the wounds which they bore for Christ's name: because it will not be a deformity, but a dignity in them; and a certain kind of beauty will shine in them, in the body, though not of the body." Secondly, to confirm the hearts of the disciples as to "the faith in His Resurrection" (Bede, on Luke 24:40). Thirdly, "that when He pleads for us with the Father, He may always show the manner of death He endured for us" (Bede, on Luke 24:40). Fourthly, "that He may convince those redeemed in His blood, how mercifully they have been helped, as He exposes before them the traces of the same death" (Bede, on Luke 24:40). Lastly, "that in the Judgment-day He may upbraid them with their just condemnation" (Bede, on Luke 24:40). Hence, as Augustine says (De Symb. ii): "Christ knew why He kept the scars in His body. For, as He showed them to Thomas who would not believe except he handled and saw them, so will He show His wounds to His enemies, so that He who is the Truth may convict them, saying: 'Behold the man whom you crucified; see the wounds you inflicted; recognize the side you pierced, since it was opened by you and for you, yet you would not enter.'"

Reply Obj. 1: The scars that remained in Christ's body belong neither to corruption nor defect, but to the greater increase of glory, inasmuch as they are the trophies of His power; and a special comeliness will appear in the places scarred by the wounds.

Reply Obj. 2: Although those openings of the wounds break the continuity of the tissue, still the greater beauty of glory compensates for all this, so that the body is not less entire, but more perfected. Thomas, however, not only saw, but handled the wounds, because as Pope Leo [*Cf. Append. Opp. August., Serm. clxii] says: "It sufficed for his personal faith for him to have seen what he saw; but it was on our behalf that he touched what he beheld."

Reply Obj. 3: Christ willed the scars of His wounds to remain on His body, not only to confirm the faith of His disciples, but for other reasons also. From these it seems that those scars will always remain on His body; because, as Augustine says (Ad Consent., De Resurr. Carn.): "I believe our Lord's body to be in heaven, such as it was when He ascended into heaven." And Gregory (Moral. xiv) says that "if aught could be changed in Christ's body after His Resurrection, contrary to Paul's truthful teaching, then the Lord after His Resurrection returned to death; and what fool would dare to say this, save he that denies the true resurrection of the flesh?" Accordingly, it is evident that the scars which Christ showed on His body after His Resurrection, have never since been removed from His body.

# QUESTION 55

OF THE MANIFESTATION OF THE RESURRECTION (In Six Articles)

We have now to consider the manifestation of the Resurrection: concerning which there are six points of inquiry:

(1) Whether Christ's Resurrection ought to have been manifested to all men or only to some special individuals?

(2) Whether it was fitting that they should see Him rise?

(3) Whether He ought to have lived with the disciples after the Resurrection?

(4) Whether it was fitting for Him to appeal to the disciples "in another shape"?

(5) Whether He ought to have demonstrated the Resurrection by proofs?

(6) Of the cogency of those proofs.

FIRST ARTICLE [III, Q. 55, Art. 1]

Whether Christ's Resurrection Ought to Have Been Manifested to All?

Objection 1: It would seem that Christ's Resurrection ought to have been manifested to all. For just as a public penalty is due for public sin, according to 1 Tim. 5:20: "Them that sin reprove before all," so is a public reward due for public merit. But, as Augustine says (Tract. civ in Joan.), "the glory of the Resurrection is the reward of the humility of the Passion." Therefore, since Christ's Passion was manifested to all while He suffered in public, it seems that the glory of the Resurrection ought to have been manifested to all.

Obj. 2: Further, as Christ's Passion is ordained for our salvation, so also is His Resurrection, according to Rom. 4:25: "He rose again for our justification." But what belongs to the public weal ought to be manifested to all. Therefore Christ's Resurrection ought to have been manifested to all, and not to some specially.

Obj. 3: Further, they to whom it was manifested were witnesses of the Resurrection: hence it is said (Acts 3:15): "Whom God hath raised from the dead, of which we are witnesses." Now they bore witness by preaching in public: and this is unbecoming in women, according to 1 Cor. 14:34: "Let women keep silence in the churches": and 1 Tim. 2:12: "I suffer not a woman to teach." Therefore, it does not seem becoming for Christ's Resurrection to be manifested first of all to the women and afterwards to mankind in general.

*On the contrary,* It is written (Acts 10:40): "Him God raised up the third day, and gave Him to be made manifest, not to all the people, but to witnesses preordained by God."

*I answer that,* Some things come to our knowledge by nature's common law, others by special favor of grace, as things divinely revealed. Now, as Dionysius says (Coel. Hier. iv), the divinely established law of such things is that they be revealed immediately by God to higher persons, through whom they are imparted to others, as is evident in the ordering of the heavenly spirits. But such things as concern future glory are beyond the common ken of mankind, according to Isa. 64:4: "The eye hath not seen, O God, besides Thee, what things Thou hast prepared for them that wait for Thee." Consequently, such things are not known by man except through Divine revelation, as the Apostle says (1 Cor. 2:10): "God hath revealed them to us by His spirit." Since, then, Christ rose by a glorious Resurrection, consequently His Resurrection was not manifested to everyone, but to some, by whose testimony it could be brought to the knowledge of others.

Reply Obj. 1: Christ's Passion was consummated in a body that still had a passible nature, which is known to all by general laws: consequently His Passion could be directly manifested to all. But the Resurrection was accomplished "through the glory of the Father," as the Apostle says (Rom. 6:4). Therefore it was manifested directly to some, but not to all.

But that a public penance is imposed upon public sinners, is to be understood of the punishment of this present life. And in like manner public merits should be rewarded in public, in order that others may be stirred to emulation. But the punishments and rewards of the future life are not publicly manifested to all, but to those specially who are preordained thereto by God.

Reply Obj. 2: Just as Christ's Resurrection is for the common salvation of all, so it came to the knowledge of all; yet not so that it was directly manifested to all, but only to some, through whose testimony it could be brought to the knowledge of all.

Reply Obj. 3: A woman is not to be allowed to teach publicly in church; but she may be permitted to give familiar instruction to some privately. And therefore as Ambrose says on Luke 24:22, "a woman is sent to them who are of her household," but not to the people to bear witness to the Resurrection. But Christ appeared to the woman first, for this reason, that as a woman was the first to bring the source of death to man, so she might be the first to announce the dawn of Christ's glorious Resurrection. Hence Cyril says on John 20:17: "Woman who formerly was the minister of death, is the first to see and proclaim the adorable mystery of the Resurrection: thus womankind has procured absolution from ignominy, and removal of the curse." Hereby, moreover, it is shown, so far as the state of glory is concerned, that the female sex shall suffer no hurt; but if women burn with greater charity, they shall also attain greater glory from the Divine vision: because the women whose love for our Lord was more persistent--so much so that "when even the disciples withdrew" from the sepulchre "they did not depart" [*Gregory, Hom. xxv in Evang.]--were the first to see Him rising in glory.

SECOND ARTICLE [III, Q. 55, Art. 2]

Whether It Was Fitting That the Disciples Should See Him Rise Again?

Objection 1: It would seem fitting that the disciples should have seen Him rise again, because it was their office to bear witness to the Resurrection, according to Acts 4:33: "With great power did the apostles give testimony to the Resurrection of Jesus Christ our Lord." But the surest witness of all is an eye-witness. Therefore it would have been fitting for them to see the very Resurrection of Christ.

Obj. 2: Further, in order to have the certainty of faith the disciples saw Christ ascend into heaven, according to Acts 1:9: "While they looked on, He was raised up." But it was also necessary for them to have faith in the Resurrection. Therefore it seems that Christ ought to have risen in sight of the disciples.

Obj. 3: Further, the raising of Lazarus was a sign of Christ's coming Resurrection. But the Lord raised up Lazarus in sight of the disciples. Consequently, it seems that Christ ought to have risen in sight of the disciples.

*On the contrary,* It is written (Mk. 16:9): The Lord "rising early the first day of the week, appeared first to Mary Magdalen." Now Mary Magdalen did not see Him rise; but, while searching for Him in the sepulchre, she heard from the angel: "He is risen, He is not here." Therefore no one saw Him rise again.

*I answer that,* As the Apostle says (Rom. 13:1): "Those things that are of God, are well ordered [Vulg.: 'Those that are, are ordained of God]." Now the divinely established order is this, that things above men's ken are revealed to them by angels, as Dionysius says (Coel. Hier. iv). But Christ on rising did not return to the familiar manner of life, but to a kind of immortal and God-like condition, according to Rom. 6:10: "For in that He liveth, He liveth unto God." And therefore it was fitting for Christ's Resurrection not to be witnessed by men directly, but to be proclaimed to them by angels. Accordingly, Hilary (Comment. Matth. cap. ult.) says: "An angel is therefore the first herald of the Resurrection, that it might be declared out of obedience to the Father's will."

Reply Obj. 1: The apostles were able to testify to the Resurrection even by sight, because from the testimony of their own eyes they saw Christ alive, whom they had known to be dead. But just as man comes from the hearing of faith to the beatific vision, so did men come to the sight of the risen Christ through the message already received from angels.

Reply Obj. 2: Christ's Ascension as to its term wherefrom, was not above men's common knowledge, but only as to its term whereunto. Consequently, the disciples were able to behold Christ's Ascension as to the term wherefrom, that is, according as He was uplifted from the earth; but they did not behold Him as to the term whereunto, because they did not see how He was received into heaven. But Christ's Resurrection transcended common knowledge as to the term wherefrom, according as His soul returned from hell and His body from the closed sepulchre; and likewise as to the term whereunto, according as He attained to the life of glory. Consequently, the Resurrection ought not to be accomplished so as to be seen by man.

Reply Obj. 3: Lazarus was raised so that he returned to the same life as before, which life is not beyond man's common ken. Consequently, there is no parity.

THIRD ARTICLE [III, Q. 55, Art. 3]

Whether Christ Ought to Have Lived Constantly with His Disciples After the Resurrection?

Objection 1: It would seem that Christ ought to have lived constantly with His Disciples, because He appeared to them after His Resurrection in order to confirm their faith in the Resurrection, and to bring them comfort in their disturbed state, according to John 20:20: "The disciples were glad when they saw the Lord." But they would have been more assured and consoled had He constantly shown them His presence. Therefore it seems that He ought to have lived constantly with them.

Obj. 2: Further, Christ rising from the dead did not at once ascend to heaven, but after forty days, as is narrated in Acts 1:3. But meanwhile He could have been in no more suitable place than where the disciples were met together. Therefore it seems that He ought to have lived with them continually.

Obj. 3: Further, as Augustine says (De Consens. Evang. iii), we read how Christ appeared five times on the very day of His Resurrection: first "to the women at the sepulchre; secondly to the same on the way from the sepulchre; thirdly to Peter; fourthly to the two disciples going to the town; fifthly to several of them in Jerusalem when Thomas was not present." Therefore it also seems that He ought to have appeared several times on the other days before the Ascension.

Obj. 4: Further, our Lord had said to them before the Passion (Matt. 26:32): "But after I shall be risen again, I will go before you into Galilee"; moreover an angel and our Lord Himself repeated the same to the women after the Resurrection: nevertheless He was seen by them in Jerusalem on the very day of the Resurrection, as stated above (Obj. 3); also on the eighth day, as we read in John 20:26. It seems, therefore, that He did not live with the disciples in a fitting way after the Resurrection.

*On the contrary,* It is written (John 20:26) that "after eight days" Christ appeared to the disciples. Therefore He did not live constantly with them.

*I answer that,* Concerning the Resurrection two things had to be manifested to the disciples, namely, the truth of the Resurrection, and the glory of Him who rose. Now in order to manifest the truth of the Resurrection, it sufficed for Him to appear several times before them, to speak familiarly to them, to eat and drink, and let them touch Him. But in order to manifest the glory of the risen Christ, He was not desirous of living with them constantly as He had done before, lest it might seem that He rose unto the same life as before. Hence (Luke 24:44) He said to them: "These are the words which I spoke to you, while I was yet with you." For He was there with them by His bodily presence, but hitherto He had been with them not merely by His bodily presence, but also in mortal semblance. Hence Bede in explaining those words of Luke, "while I was with you," says: "that is, while I was still in mortal flesh, in which you are yet: for He had then risen in the same flesh, but was not in the same state of mortality as they."

Reply Obj. 1: Christ's frequent appearing served to assure the disciples of the truth of the Resurrection; but continual intercourse might have led them into the error of believing that He had risen to the same life as was His before. Yet by His constant presence He promised them comfort in another life, according to John 16:22: "I will see you again, and your heart shall rejoice; and your joy no man shall take from you."

Reply Obj. 2: That Christ did not stay continually with the disciples was not because He deemed it more expedient for Him to be elsewhere: but because He judged it to be more suitable for the apostles' instruction that He should not abide continually with them, for the reason given above. But it is quite unknown in what places He was bodily present in the meantime, since Scripture is silent, and His dominion is in every place (Cf. Ps. 102:22).

Reply Obj. 3: He appeared oftener on the first day, because the disciples were to be admonished by many proofs to accept the faith in His Resurrection from the very outset: but after they had once accepted it, they had no further need of being instructed by so many apparitions. Accordingly one reads in the Gospel that after the first day He appeared again only five times. For, as Augustine says (De Consens. Evang. iii), after the first five apparitions "He came again a sixth time when Thomas saw Him; a seventh time was by the sea of Tiberias at the capture of the fishes; the eighth was on the mountain of Galilee, according to Mathew; the ninth occasion is expressed by Mark, 'at length when they were at table,' because no more were they going to eat with Him upon earth; the tenth was on the very day, when no longer upon the earth, but uplifted into the cloud, He was ascending into heaven. But, as John admits, not all things were written down. And He visited them frequently before He went up to heaven," in order to comfort them. Hence it is written (1 Cor. 15:6, 7) that "He was seen by more than five hundred brethren at once . . . after that He was seen by James"; of which apparitions no mention is made in the Gospels.

Reply Obj. 4: Chrysostom in explaining Matt. 26:32--"after I shall be risen again, I will go before you into Galilee," says (Hom. lxxxiii in Matth.), "He goes not to some far off region in order to appear to them, but among His own people, and in those very places" in which for the most part they had lived with Him; "in order that they might thereby believe that He who was crucified was the same as He who rose again." And on this account "He said that He would go into Galilee, that they might be delivered from fear of the Jews."

Consequently, as Ambrose says (Expos. in Luc.), "The Lord had sent word to the disciples that they were to see Him in Galilee; yet He showed Himself first to them when they were assembled together in the room out of fear. (Nor is there any breaking of a promise here, but rather a hastened fulfilling out of kindness)" [*Cf. Catena Aurea in Luc. xxiv, 36]: "afterwards, however, when their minds were comforted, they went into Galilee. Nor is there any reason to prevent us from supposing that there were few in the room, and many more on the mountain." For, as Eusebius [*Of Caesarea; Cf. Migne, P. G., xxii, 1003] says, "Two Evangelists, Luke and John, write that He appeared in Jerusalem to the eleven only; but the other two said that an angel and our Saviour commanded not merely the eleven, but all the disciples and brethren, to go into Galilee. Paul makes mention of them when he says (1 Cor. 15:6): 'Then He appeared to more then five hundred brethren at once.'" The truer solution, however, is this, that while they were in hiding in Jerusalem He appeared to them at first in order to comfort them; but in Galilee it was not secretly, nor once or twice, that He made Himself known to them with great power, "showing Himself to them alive after His Passion, by many proofs," as Luke says (Acts 1:3). Or as Augustine writes (De Consens. Evang. iii): "What was said by the angel and by our Lord--that He would 'go before them into Galilee,' must be taken prophetically. For if we take Galilee as meaning 'a passing,' we must understand that they were going to pass from the people of Israel to the Gentiles, who would not believe in the preaching of the apostles unless He prepared the way for them in men's hearts: and this is signified by the words 'He shall go before you into Galilee.' But if by Galilee we understand 'revelation,' we are to understand this as applying to Him not in the form of a servant, but in that form wherein He is equal to the Father, and which He has promised to them that love Him. Although He has gone before us in this sense, He has not abandoned us."

FOURTH ARTICLE [III, Q. 55, Art. 4]

Whether Christ Should Have Appeared to the Disciples "in Another Shape"?

Objection 1: It would seem that Christ ought not to have appeared to the disciples "in another shape." For a thing cannot appear in very truth other than it is. But there was only one shape in Christ. Therefore if He appeared under another, it was not a true but a false apparition. Now this is not at all fitting, because as Augustine says (QQ. lxxxiii, qu. 14): "If He deceives He is not the Truth; yet Christ is the Truth." Consequently, it seems that

Christ ought not to have appeared to the disciples "in another shape."

Obj. 2: Further, nothing can appear in another shape than the one it has, except the beholder's eyes be captivated by some illusions. But since such illusions are brought about by magical arts, they are unbecoming in Christ, according to what is written (2 Cor. 6:15): "What concord hath Christ with Belial?" Therefore it seems that Christ ought not to have appeared in another shape.

Obj. 3: Further, just as our faith receives its surety from Scripture, so were the disciples assured of their faith in the Resurrection by Christ appearing to them. But, as Augustine says in an Epistle to Jerome (xxviii), if but one untruth be admitted into the Sacred Scripture, the whole authority of the Scriptures is weakened. Consequently, if Christ appeared to the disciples, in but one apparition, otherwise than He was, then whatever they saw in Christ after the Resurrection will be of less import, which is not fitting. Therefore He ought not to have appeared in another shape.

*On the contrary,* It is written (Mk. 16:12): "After that He appeared in another shape to two of them walking, as they were going into the country."

*I answer that,* As stated above (AA. 1, 2), Christ's Resurrection was to be manifested to men in the same way as Divine things are revealed. But Divine things are revealed to men in various ways, according as they are variously disposed. For, those who have minds well disposed, perceive Divine things rightly, whereas those not so disposed perceive them with a certain confusion of doubt or error: "for, the sensual men perceiveth not those things that are of the Spirit of God," as is said in 1 Cor. 2:14. Consequently, after His Resurrection Christ appeared in His own shape to some who were well disposed to belief, while He appeared in another shape to them who seemed to be already growing tepid in their faith: hence these said (Luke 24:21): "We hoped that it was He that should have redeemed Israel." Hence Gregory says (Hom. xxiii in Evang.), that "He showed Himself to them in body such as He was in their minds: for, because He was as yet a stranger to faith in their hearts, He made pretense of going on farther," that is, as if He were a stranger.

Reply Obj. 1: As Augustine says (De Qq. Evang. ii), "not everything of which we make pretense is a falsehood; but when what we pretend has no meaning then is it a falsehood. But when our pretense has some signification, it is not a lie, but a figure of the truth; otherwise everything said figuratively by wise and holy men, or even by our Lord Himself, would be set down as a falsehood, because it is not customary to take such expressions in the literal sense. And deeds, like words, are feigned without falsehood, in order to denote something else." And so it happened here, as has been said.

Reply Obj. 2: As Augustine says (De Consens. Evang. iii): "Our Lord could change His flesh so that His shape really was other than they were accustomed to behold; for, before His Passion He was transfigured on the mountain, so that His face shone like the sun. But it did not happen thus now." For not without reason do we "understand this hindrance in their eyes to have been of Satan's doing, lest Jesus might be recognized." Hence Luke says (24:16) that "their eyes were held, that they should not know Him."

Reply Obj. 3: Such an argument would prove, if they had not been brought back from the sight of a strange shape to that of Christ's true countenance. For, as Augustine says (De Consens. Evang. iii): "The permission was granted by Christ," namely, that their eyes should be held fast in the aforesaid way, "until the Sacrament of the bread; that when they had shared in the unity of His body, the enemy's hindrance may be understood to have been taken away, so that Christ might be recognized." Hence he goes on to say that "'their eyes were opened, and they knew Him'; not that they were hitherto walking with their eyes shut; but there was something in them whereby they were not permitted to recognize what they saw. This could be caused by the darkness or by some kind of humor."

FIFTH ARTICLE [III, Q. 55, Art. 5]

Whether Christ Should Have Demonstrated the Truth of His Resurrection by Proofs?

Objection 1: It would seem that Christ should not have demonstrated the truth of His Resurrection by proofs. For Ambrose says (De Fide, ad Gratian. i): "Let there be no proofs where faith is required." But faith is required regarding the Resurrection. Therefore proofs are out of place there.

Obj. 2: Further, Gregory says (Hom. xxvi): "Faith has no merit where human reason supplies the test." But it was no part of Christ's office to void the merit of faith. Consequently, it was not for Him to confirm the Resurrection by proofs.

Obj. 3: Further, Christ came into the world in order that men might attain beatitude through Him, according to John 10:10: "I am come that they may have life, and may have it more abundantly." But supplying proofs seems to be a hindrance in the way of man's beatitude; because our Lord Himself said (John 20:29): "Blessed are they that have not seen, and have believed." Consequently, it seems that Christ ought not to manifest His Resurrection by any proofs.

*On the contrary,* It is related in Acts 1:3, that Christ appeared to His disciples "for forty days by many proofs, speaking of the Kingdom of God."

*I answer that,* The word "proof" is susceptible of a twofold meaning: sometimes it is employed to designate any sort "of reason in confirmation of what is a matter of doubt" [*Tully, Topic. ii]: and sometimes it means a sensible sign employed to manifest the truth; thus also Aristotle occasionally uses the term in his works [*Cf. Prior. Anal. ii; Rhetor. i]. Taking "proof" in the first sense, Christ did not demonstrate His Resurrection to the disciples by proofs, because such argumentative proof would have to be grounded on some principles: and if these were not known to the disciples, nothing would thereby be demonstrated to them, because nothing can be known from the unknown. And if such principles were known to them, they would not go beyond human reason, and consequently would not be efficacious for establishing faith in the Resurrection, which is beyond human reason, since principles must be assumed which are of the same order, according to 1 Poster. But it was from the authority of the Sacred Scriptures that He proved to them the truth of His Resurrection, which authority is the basis of faith, when He said: "All things must needs be fulfilled which are written in the Law, and in the prophets, and in the Psalms, concerning Me": as is set forth Luke 24:44.

But if the term "proof" be taken in the second sense, then Christ is said to have demonstrated His Resurrection by proofs, inasmuch as by most evident signs He showed that He was truly risen. Hence where our version has "by many proofs," the Greek text, instead of proof hastekmerion , i.e. "an evident sign affording positive proof" [*Cf. Prior. Anal. ii]. Now Christ showed these signs of the Resurrection to His disciples, for two reasons. First, because their hearts were not disposed so as to accept readily the faith in the Resurrection. Hence He says Himself (Luke 24:25): "O foolish and slow of heart to believe": and (Mk. 16:14): "He upbraided them with their incredulity and hardness of heart." Secondly, that their testimony might be rendered more efficacious through the signs shown them, according to 1 John 1:1, 3: "That which we have seen, and have heard, and our hands have handled . . . we declare."

Reply Obj. 1: Ambrose is speaking there of proofs drawn from human reason, which are useless for demonstrating things of faith, as was shown above.

Reply Obj. 2: The merit of faith arises from this, that at God's bidding man believes what he does not see. Accordingly, only that reason debars merit of faith which enables one to see by knowledge what is proposed for belief: and this is demonstrative argument. But Christ did not make use of any such argument for demonstrating His Resurrection.

Reply Obj. 3: As stated already (ad 2), the merit of beatitude, which comes of faith, is not entirely excluded except a man refuse to believe [whatever he does not see]. But for a man to believe from visible signs the things he does not see, does not entirely deprive him of faith nor of the merit of faith: just as Thomas, to whom it was said (John 20:29): "'Because thou hast seen Me, Thomas, thou hast believed,' saw one thing and believed another" [*Gregory, Hom. xxvi]: the wounds were what he saw, God was the object of His belief. But his is the more perfect faith who does not require such helps for belief. Hence, to put to shame the faith of some men, our Lord said (John 4:48): "Unless you see signs and wonders, you believe not." From this one can learn how they who are so ready to believe God, even without beholding signs, are blessed in comparison with them who do not believe except they see the like.

SIXTH ARTICLE [III, Q. 55, Art. 6]

Whether the Proofs Which Christ Made Use of Manifested Sufficiently the Truth of His Resurrection?

Objection 1: It would seem that the proofs which Christ made use of did not sufficiently manifest the truth of His Resurrection. For after the Resurrection Christ showed nothing to His disciples which angels appearing to men did not or could not show; because angels have frequently shown themselves to men under human aspect, have spoken and lived with them, and eaten with them, just as if they were truly men, as is evident from Genesis 18, of the angels whom Abraham entertained, and in the Book of Tobias, of the angel who "conducted" him "and brought" him back. Nevertheless, angels have not true bodies naturally united to them; which is required for a resurrection. Consequently, the signs which Christ showed His disciples were not sufficient for manifesting His Resurrection.

Obj. 2: Further, Christ rose again gloriously, that is, having a human nature with glory. But some of the things which Christ showed to His disciples seem contrary to human nature, as for instance, that "He vanished out of their sight," and entered in among them "when the doors were shut": and some other things seem contrary to glory, as for instance, that He ate and drank, and bore the scars of His wounds. Consequently, it seems that those proofs were neither sufficient nor fitting for establishing faith in the Resurrection.

Obj. 3: Further, after the Resurrection Christ's body was such that it ought not to be touched by mortal man; hence He said to Magdalen (John 20:17): "Do not touch Me; for I am not yet ascended to My Father." Consequently, it was not fitting for manifesting the truth of His Resurrection, that He should permit Himself to be handled by His disciples.

Obj. 4: Further, clarity seems to be the principal of the qualities of a glorified body: yet He gave no sign thereof in His Resurrection. Therefore it seems that those proofs were insufficient for showing the quality of Christ's Resurrection.

Obj. 5: [*This objection is wanting in the older codices, and in the text of the Leonine edition, which, however, gives it in a note as taken from one of the more recent codices of the Vatican.]

Further, the angels introduced as witnesses for the Resurrection seem insufficient from the want of agreement on the part of the Evangelists. Because in Matthew's account the angel is described as sitting upon the stone rolled back, while Mark states that he was seen after the women had entered the tomb; and again, whereas these mention one angel, John says that there were two sitting, and Luke says that there were two standing. Consequently, the arguments for the Resurrection do not seem to agree.

*On the contrary,* Christ, who is the Wisdom of God, "ordereth all things sweetly" and in a fitting manner, according to Wis. 8:1.

*I answer that,* Christ manifested His Resurrection in two ways: namely, by testimony; and by proof or sign: and each manifestation was sufficient in its own class. For in order to manifest His Resurrection He made use of a double testimony, neither of which can be rebutted. The first of these was the angels' testimony, who announced the Resurrection to the women, as is seen in all the Evangelists: the other was the testimony of the Scriptures, which He set before them to show the truth of the Resurrection, as is narrated in the last chapter of Luke.

Again, the proofs were sufficient for showing that the Resurrection was both true and glorious. That it was a true Resurrection He shows first on the part of the body; and this He shows in three respects; first of all, that it was a true and solid body, and not phantastic or rarefied, like the air. And He establishes this by offering His body to be handled; hence He says in the last chapter of Luke (39): "Handle and see; for a spirit hath not flesh and bones, as you see Me to have." Secondly, He shows that it was a human body, by presenting His true features for them to behold. Thirdly, He shows that it was identically the same body which He had before, by showing them the scars of the wounds; hence, as we read in the last chapter of Luke (39) he said to them: "See My hands and feet, that it is I Myself."

Secondly, He showed them the truth of His Resurrection on the part of His soul reunited with His body: and He showed this by the works of the threefold life. First of all, in the operations of the nutritive life, by eating and drinking with His disciples, as we read in the last chapter of Luke. Secondly, in the works of the sensitive life, by replying to His disciples' questions, and by greeting them when they were in His presence, showing thereby that He both saw and heard; thirdly, in the works of the intellective life by their conversing with Him, and discoursing on the Scriptures. And, in order that nothing might be wanting to make the manifestation complete, He also showed that He had the Divine Nature, by working the miracle of the draught of fishes, and further by ascending into heaven while they were beholding Him: because, according to John 3:13: "No man hath ascended into heaven, but He that descended from heaven, the Son of Man who is in heaven."

He also showed His disciples the glory of His Resurrection by entering in among them when the doors were closed: as Gregory says (Hom. xxvi in Evang.): "Our Lord allowed them to handle His flesh which He had brought through closed doors, to show that His body was of the same nature but of different glory." It likewise was part of the property of glory that "He vanished suddenly from their eyes," as related in the last chapter of Luke; because thereby it was shown that it lay in His power to be seen or not seen; and this belongs to a glorified body, as stated above (Q. 54, A. 1, ad 2, A. 2, ad 1).

Reply Obj. 1: Each separate argument would not suffice of itself for showing perfectly Christ's Resurrection, yet all taken collectively establish it completely, especially owing to the testimonies of the Scriptures, the sayings of the angels, and even Christ's own assertion supported by miracles. As to the angels who appeared, they did not say they were men, as Christ asserted that He was truly a man. Moreover, the manner of eating was different in Christ and the angels: for since the bodies assumed by the angels were neither living nor animated, there was no true eating, although the food was really masticated and passed into the interior of the assumed body: hence the angels said to Tobias (12:18, 19): "When I was with you . . . I seemed indeed to eat and drink with you; but I use an invisible meat." But since Christ's body was truly animated, His eating was genuine. For, as Augustine observes (De Civ. Dei xiii), "it is not the power but the need of eating that shall be taken away from the bodies of them who rise again." Hence Bede says on Luke 24:41: "Christ ate because He could, not because He needed."

Reply Obj. 2: As was observed above, some proofs were employed by Christ to prove the truth of His human nature, and others to show forth His glory in rising again. But the condition of human nature, as considered in itself, namely, as to its present state, is opposite to the condition of glory, as is said in 1 Cor. 15:43: "It is sown in weakness, it shall rise in power." Consequently, the proofs brought forward for showing the condition of glory, seem to be in opposition to nature, not absolutely, but according to the present state, and conversely. Hence Gregory says (Hom. xxvi in Evang.): "The Lord manifested two wonders, which are mutually contrary according to human reason, when after the Resurrection He showed His body as incorruptible and at the same time palpable."

Reply Obj. 3: As Augustine says (Tract. cxxi super Joan.), "these words of our Lord, 'Do not touch Me, for I am not yet ascended to My Father,'" show "that in that woman there is a figure of the Church of the Gentiles, which did not believe in Christ until He was ascended to the Father. Or Jesus would have men to believe in Him, i.e. to touch Him spiritually, as being Himself one with the Father. For to that man's innermost perceptions He is, in some sort, ascended unto the Father, who has become so far proficient in Him, as to recognize in Him the equal with the Father . . . whereas she as yet believed in Him but carnally, since she wept for Him as for a man." But when one reads elsewhere of Mary having touched Him, when with the other women, she "'came up and took hold of His feet,' that matters little," as Severianus says [*Chrysologus, Serm. lxxvi], "for, the first act relates to figure, the other to sex; the former is of Divine grace, the latter of human nature." Or as Chrysostom says (Hom. lxxxvi in Joan.): "This woman wanted to converse with Christ just as before the Passion, and out of joy was thinking of nothing great, although Christ's flesh had become much nobler by rising again." And therefore He said: "I have not yet ascended to My Father"; as if to say: "Do not suppose I am leading an earthly life; for if you see Me upon earth, it is because I have not yet ascended to My Father, but I am going to ascend shortly." Hence He goes on to say: "I ascend to My Father, and to your Father."

Reply Obj. 4: As Augustine says ad Orosium (Dial. lxv, Qq.): "Our Lord rose in clarified flesh; yet He did not wish to appear before the disciples in that condition of clarity, because their eyes could not gaze upon that brilliancy. For if before He died for us and rose again the disciples could not look upon Him when He was transfigured upon the mountain, how much less were they able to gaze upon Him when our Lord's flesh was glorified." It must also be borne in mind that after His Resurrection our Lord wished especially to show that He was the same as had died; which the manifestation of His brightness would have hindered considerably: because change of features shows more than anything else the difference in the person seen: and this is because sight specially judges of the common sensibles, among which is one and many, or the same and different. But before the Passion, lest His disciples might despise its weakness, Christ meant to show them the glory of His majesty; and this the brightness of the body specially indicates. Consequently, before the Passion He showed the disciples His glory by brightness, but after the Resurrection by other tokens.

Reply Obj. 5: As Augustine says (De Consens. Evang. iii): "We can understand one angel to have been seen by the women, according to both Matthew and Mark, if we take them as having entered the sepulchre, that is, into some sort of walled enclosure, and that there they saw an angel sitting upon the stone which was rolled back from the monument, as Matthew says; and that this is Mark's expression--'sitting on the right side'; afterwards when they scanned the spot where the Lord's body had lain, they beheld two angels, who were at first seated, as John says, and who afterwards rose so as to be seen standing, as Luke relates."

## QUESTION 56

OF THE CAUSALITY OF CHRIST'S RESURRECTION (In Two Articles)

We have now to consider the causality of Christ's Resurrection, concerning which there are two points of inquiry:

(1) Whether Christ's Resurrection is the cause of our resurrection?

(2) Whether it is the cause of our justification?

FIRST ARTICLE [III, Q. 56, Art. 1]

Whether Christ's Resurrection Is the Cause of the Resurrection of Our Bodies?

Objection 1: It would seem that Christ's Resurrection is not the cause of the resurrection of our bodies, because, given a sufficient cause, the effect must follow of necessity. If, then, Christ's Resurrection be the sufficient cause of the resurrection of our bodies, then all the dead should have risen again as soon as He rose.

Obj. 2: Further, Divine justice is the cause of the resurrection of the dead, so that the body may be rewarded or punished together with the soul, since they shared in merit or sin, as Dionysius says (Eccles. Hier. vii) and Damascene (De Fide Orth. iv). But God's justice must necessarily be accomplished, even if Christ had not risen. Therefore the dead would rise again even though Christ did not. Consequently Christ's Resurrection is not the cause of the resurrection of our bodies.

Obj. 3: Further, if Christ's Resurrection be the cause of the resurrection of our bodies, it would be either the exemplar, or the efficient, or the meritorious cause. Now it is not the exemplar cause; because it is God who will bring about the resurrection of our bodies, according to John 5:21: "The Father raiseth up the dead": and God has no need to look at any exemplar cause outside Himself. In like manner it is not the efficient cause; because an efficient cause acts only through contact, whether spiritual or corporeal. Now it is evident that Christ's Resurrection has no corporeal contact with the dead who shall rise again, owing to distance of time and place; and similarly it has no spiritual contact, which is through faith and charity, because even unbelievers and sinners shall rise again. Nor again is it the meritorious cause, because when Christ rose He was no longer a wayfarer, and consequently not in a state of merit. Therefore, Christ's Resurrection does not appear to be in any way the cause of ours.

Obj. 4: Further, since death is the privation of life, then to destroy death seems to be nothing else than to bring life back again; and this is resurrection. But "by dying, Christ destroyed our death" [*Preface of Mass in Paschal Time]. Consequently, Christ's death, not His Resurrection, is the cause of our resurrection.

*On the contrary,* on 1 Cor. 15:12: "Now if Christ be preached, that He rose again from the dead," the gloss says: "Who is the efficient cause of our resurrection."

*I answer that,* As stated in 2 Metaphysics, text 4: "Whatever is first in any order, is the cause of all that come after it." But Christ's Resurrection was the first in the order of our resurrection, as is evident from what was said above (Q. 53, A. 3). Hence Christ's Resurrection must be the cause of ours: and this is what the Apostle says (1 Cor. 15:20, 21): "Christ is risen from the dead, the first-fruits of them that sleep; for by a man came death, and by a man the resurrection of the dead."

And this is reasonable. Because the principle of human life-giving is the Word of God, of whom it is said (Ps. 35:10): "With Thee is the fountain of life": hence He Himself says (John 5:21): "As the Father raiseth up the dead, and giveth life; so the Son also giveth life to whom He will." Now the divinely established natural order is that every cause operates first upon what is nearest to it, and through it upon others which are more remote; just as fire first heats the nearest air, and through it it heats bodies that are further off: and God Himself first enlightens those substances which are closer to Him, and through them others that are more remote, as Dionysius says (Coel. Hier. xiii). Consequently, the Word of God first bestows immortal life upon that body which is naturally united with Himself, and through it works the resurrection in all other bodies.

Reply Obj. 1: As was stated above, Christ's Resurrection is the cause of ours through the power of the united Word, who operates according to His will. And consequently, it is not necessary for the effect to follow at once, but according as the Word of God disposes, namely, that first of all we be conformed to the suffering and dying Christ in this suffering and mortal life; and afterwards may come to share in the likeness of His Resurrection.

Reply Obj. 2: God's justice is the first cause of our resurrection, whereas Christ's Resurrection is the secondary, and as it were the instrumental cause. But although the power of the principal cause is not restricted to one instrument determinately, nevertheless since it works through this instrument, such instrument causes the effect. So, then, the Divine justice in itself is not tied down to Christ's Resurrection as a means of bringing about our resurrection: because God could deliver us in some other way than through Christ's Passion and Resurrection, as already stated (Q. 46, A. 2). But having once decreed to deliver us in this way, it is evident that Christ's Resurrection is the cause of ours.

Reply Obj. 3: Properly speaking, Christ's Resurrection is not the meritorious cause, but the efficient and exemplar cause of our resurrection. It is the efficient cause, inasmuch as Christ's humanity, according to which He rose again, is as it were the instrument of His Godhead, and works by Its power, as stated above (Q. 13, AA. 2, 3). And therefore, just as all other things which Christ did and endured in His humanity are profitable to our salvation through the power of the Godhead, as already stated (Q. 48, A. 6), so also is Christ's Resurrection the efficient cause of ours, through the Divine power whose office it is to quicken the dead; and this power by its presence is in touch with all places and times; and such virtual contact suffices for its efficiency. And since, as was stated above (ad 2), the primary cause of human resurrection is the Divine justice, from which Christ has "the power of passing judgment, because He is the Son of Man" (John 5:27); the efficient power of His Resurrection extends to the good and wicked alike, who are subject to His judgment.

But just as the Resurrection of Christ's body, through its personal union with the Word, is first in point of time, so also is it first in dignity and perfection; as the gloss says on 1 Cor. 15:20, 23. But whatever is most perfect is always the exemplar, which the less perfect copies according to its mode; consequently Christ's Resurrection is the exemplar of ours. And this is necessary, not on the part of Him who rose again, who needs no exemplar, but on the part of them who are raised up, who must be likened to that Resurrection, according to Phil. 3:21: "He will reform the body of our lowness, made like to the body of His glory." Now although the efficiency of Christ's Resurrection extends to the resurrection of the good and wicked alike, still its exemplarity extends properly only to the just, who are made conformable with His Sonship, according to Rom. 8:29.

Reply Obj. 4: Considered on the part of their efficiency, which is dependent on the Divine power, both Christ's death and His Resurrection are the cause both of the destruction of death and of the renewal of life: but considered as exemplar causes, Christ's death--by which He withdrew from mortal life--is the cause of the destruction of our death; while His Resurrection, whereby He inaugurated immortal life, is the cause of the repairing of our life. But Christ's Passion is furthermore a meritorious cause, as stated above (Q. 48, A. 1).

SECOND ARTICLE [III, Q. 56, Art. 2]

Whether Christ's Resurrection Is the Cause of the Resurrection of Souls?

Objection 1: It would seem that Christ's Resurrection is not the cause of the resurrection of souls, because Augustine says (Tract. xxiii super Joan.) that "bodies rise by His human dispensation, but souls rise by the Substance of God." But Christ's Resurrection does not belong to God's Substance, but to the dispensation of His humanity. Therefore, although Christ's Resurrection is the cause of bodies rising, nevertheless it does not seem to be the cause of the resurrection of souls.

Obj. 2: Further, a body does not act upon a spirit. But the Resurrection belongs to His body, which death laid low. Therefore His Resurrection is not the cause of the resurrection of souls.

Obj. 3: Further, since Christ's Resurrection is the cause why bodies rise again, the bodies of all men shall rise again, according to 1 Cor. 15:51: "We shall all indeed rise again." But the souls of all will not rise again, because according to Matt. 25:46: "some shall go into everlasting punishment." Therefore Christ's Resurrection is not the cause of the resurrection of souls.

Obj. 4: Further, the resurrection of souls comes of the forgiveness of sins. But this was effected by Christ's Passion, according to Apoc. 1:5: "He washed us from our sins in His own blood." Consequently, Christ's Passion even more than His Resurrection is the cause of the resurrection of souls.

*On the contrary,* The Apostle says (Rom. 4:25): "He rose again for our justification," which is nothing else than the resurrection of souls: and on Ps. 29:6: "In the evening weeping shall have place," the gloss says, "Christ's Resurrection is the cause of ours, both of the soul at present, and of the body in the future."

*I answer that,* As stated above, Christ's Resurrection works in virtue of the Godhead; now this virtue extends not only to the resurrection of bodies, but also to that of souls: for it comes of God that the soul lives by grace, and that the body lives by the soul. Consequently, Christ's Resurrection has instrumentally an effective power not only with regard to the resurrection of bodies, but also with respect to the resurrection of souls. In like fashion it is an exemplar cause with regard to the resurrection of souls, because even in our souls we must be conformed with the rising Christ: as the Apostle says (Rom. 6:4-11) "Christ is risen from the dead by the glory of the Father, so we also may walk in newness of life": and as He, "rising again from the dead, dieth now no more, so let us reckon that we (Vulg.: 'you')" are dead to sin, that we may "live together with Him."

Reply Obj. 1: Augustine says that the resurrection of souls is wrought by God's Substance, as to participation, because souls become good and just by sharing in the Divine goodness, but not by sharing in anything created. Accordingly, after saying that souls rise by the Divine Substance, he adds: the soul is beatified by a participation with God, and not by a participation with a holy soul. But our bodies are made glorious by sharing in the glory of Christ's body.

Reply Obj. 2: The efficacy of Christ's Resurrection reaches souls not from any special virtue of His risen body, but from the virtue of the Godhead personally united with it.

Reply Obj. 3: The resurrection of souls pertains to merit, which is the effect of justification; but the resurrection of bodies is ordained for punishment or reward, which are the effects of Him who judges. Now it belongs to Christ, not to justify all men, but to judge them: and therefore He raises up all as to their bodies, but not as to their souls.

Reply Obj. 4: Two things concur in the justification of souls, namely, forgiveness of sin and newness of life through grace. Consequently, as to efficacy, which comes of the Divine power, the Passion as well as the Resurrection of Christ is the cause of justification as to both the above. But as to exemplarity, properly speaking Christ's Passion and death are the cause of the forgiveness of guilt, by which forgiveness we die unto sin: whereas Christ's Resurrection is the cause of newness of life, which comes through grace or justice: consequently, the Apostle says (Rom. 4:25) that "He was delivered up," i.e. to death, "for our sins," i.e. to take them away, "and rose again for our justification." But Christ's Passion was also a meritorious cause, as stated above (A. 1, ad 4; Q. 48, A. 1).

# QUESTION 57

OF THE ASCENSION OF CHRIST (In Six Articles)

We have now to consider Christ's Ascension: concerning which there are six points of inquiry:

(1) Whether it belonged for Christ to ascend into heaven?

(2) According to which nature did it become Him to ascend?

(3) Whether He ascended by His own power?

(4) Whether He ascended above all the corporeal heavens?

(5) Whether He ascended above all spiritual creatures?

(6) Of the effect of the Ascension.

FIRST ARTICLE [III, Q. 57, Art. 1]

Whether It Was Fitting for Christ to Ascend into Heaven?

Objection 1: It would seem that it was not fitting for Christ to ascend into heaven. For the Philosopher says (De Coelo ii) that "things which are in a state of perfection possess their good without movement." But Christ was in a state of perfection, since He is the Sovereign Good in respect of His Divine Nature, and sovereignly glorified in respect of His human nature. Consequently, He has His good without movement. But ascension is movement. Therefore it was not fitting for Christ to ascend.

Obj. 2: Further, whatever is moved, is moved on account of something better. But it was no better thing for Christ to be in heaven than upon earth, because He gained nothing either in soul or in body by being in heaven. Therefore it seems that Christ should not have ascended into heaven.

Obj. 3: Further, the Son of God took human flesh for our salvation. But it would have been more beneficial for men if He had tarried always with us upon earth; thus He said to His disciples (Luke 17:22): "The days will come when you shall desire to see one day of the Son of man; and you shall not see it." Therefore it seems unfitting for Christ to have ascended into heaven.

Obj. 4: Further, as Gregory says (Moral. xiv), Christ's body was in no way changed after the Resurrection. But He did not ascend into heaven immediately after rising again, for He said after the Resurrection (John 20:17): "I am not yet ascended to My Father." Therefore it seems that neither should He have ascended after forty days.

*On the contrary,* Are the words of our Lord (John 20:17): "I ascend to My Father and to your Father."

*I answer that,* The place ought to be in keeping with what is contained therein. Now by His Resurrection Christ entered upon an immortal and incorruptible life. But whereas our dwelling-place is one of generation and corruption, the heavenly place is one of incorruption. And consequently it was not fitting that Christ should remain upon earth after the Resurrection; but it was fitting that He should ascend to heaven.

Reply Obj. 1: That which is best and possesses its good without movement is God Himself, because He is utterly unchangeable, according to Malachi 3:6: "I am the Lord, and I change not." But every creature is changeable in some respect, as is evident from Augustine (Gen. ad lit. viii). And since the nature assumed by the Son of God remained a creature, as is clear from what was said above (Q. 2, A. 7; Q. 16, AA. 8, 10; Q. 20, A. 1), it is not unbecoming if some movement be attributed to it.

Reply Obj. 2: By ascending into heaven Christ acquired no addition to His essential glory either in body or in soul: nevertheless He did acquire something as to the fittingness of place, which pertains to the well-being of glory: not that His body acquired anything from a heavenly body by way of perfection or preservation; but merely out of a certain fittingness. Now this in a measure belonged to His glory; and He had a certain kind of joy from such fittingness, not indeed that He then began to derive joy from it when He ascended into heaven, but that He rejoiced thereat in a new way, as at a thing completed. Hence, on Ps. 15:11: "At Thy right hand are delights even unto the end," the gloss says: "I shall delight in sitting nigh to Thee, when I shall be taken away from the sight of men."

Reply Obj. 3: Although Christ's bodily presence was withdrawn from the faithful by the Ascension, still the presence of His Godhead is ever with the faithful, as He Himself says (Matt. 28:20): "Behold, I am with you all days, even to the consummation of the world." For, "by ascending into heaven He did not abandon those whom He adopted," as Pope Leo says (De Resurrec., Serm. ii). But Christ's Ascension into heaven, whereby He withdrew His bodily presence from us, was more profitable for us than His bodily presence would have been.

First of all, in order to increase our faith, which is of things unseen. Hence our Lord said (John 26) that the Holy Ghost shall come and "convince the world . . . of justice," that is, of the justice "of those that believe," as Augustine says (Tract. xcv super Joan.): "For even to put the faithful beside the unbeliever is to put the unbeliever to shame"; wherefore he goes on to say (10): "'Because I go to the Father; and you shall see Me no longer'"--"For 'blessed are they that see not, yet believe.' Hence it is of our justice that the world is reproved: because 'you will believe in Me whom you shall not see.'"

Secondly, to uplift our hope: hence He says (John 14:3): "If I shall go, and prepare a place for you, I will come again, and will take you to Myself; that where I am, you also may be." For by placing in heaven the human nature which He assumed, Christ gave us the hope of going thither; since "wheresoever the body shall be, there shall the eagles also be gathered together," as is written in Matt. 24:28. Hence it is written likewise (Mic. 2:13): "He shall go up that shall open the way before them."

Thirdly, in order to direct the fervor of our charity to heavenly things. Hence the Apostle says (Col. 3:1, 2): "Seek the things that are above, where Christ is sitting at the right hand of God. Mind the things that are above, not the things that are upon the earth": for as is said (Matt. 6:21): "Where thy treasure is, there is thy heart also." And since the Holy Ghost is love drawing us up to heavenly things, therefore our Lord said to His disciples (John 16:7): "It is expedient to you that I go; for if I go not, the Paraclete will not come to you; but if I go, I will send Him to you." On which words Augustine says (Tract. xciv super Joan.): "Ye cannot receive the Spirit, so long as ye persist in knowing Christ according to the flesh. But when Christ withdrew in body, not only the Holy Ghost, but both Father and Son were present with them spiritually."

Reply Obj. 4: Although a heavenly place befitted Christ when He rose to immortal life, nevertheless He delayed the Ascension in order to confirm the truth of His Resurrection. Hence it is written (Acts 1:3), that "He showed Himself alive after His Passion, by many proofs, for forty days appearing to them": upon which the gloss says that "because He was dead for forty hours, during forty days He established the fact of His being alive again. Or the forty days may be understood as a figure of this world, wherein Christ dwells in His Church: inasmuch as man is made out of the four elements, and is cautioned not to transgress the Decalogue."

SECOND ARTICLE [III, Q. 57, Art. 2]

Whether Christ's Ascension into Heaven Belonged to Him According to His Divine Nature?

Objection 1: It would seem that Christ's Ascension into heaven belonged to Him according to His Divine Nature. For, it is written (Ps. 46:6): "God is ascended with jubilee": and (Deut. 33:26): "He that is mounted upon the heaven is thy helper." But these words were spoken of God even before Christ's Incarnation. Therefore it belongs to Christ to ascend into heaven as God.

Obj. 2: Further, it belongs to the same person to ascend into heaven as to descend from heaven, according to John 3:13: "No man hath ascended into heaven, but He that descended from heaven": and Eph. 4:10: "He that descended is the same also that ascended." But Christ came down from heaven not as man, but as God: because previously His Nature in heaven was not human, but Divine. Therefore it seems that Christ ascended into heaven as God.

Obj. 3: Further, by His Ascension Christ ascended to the Father. But it was not as man that He rose to equality with the Father; for in this respect He says: "He is greater than I," as is said in John 14:28. Therefore it seems that Christ ascended as God.

*On the contrary,* on Eph. 4:10: "That He ascended, what is it, but because He also descended," a gloss says: "It is clear that He descended and ascended according to His humanity."

*I answer that,* The expression "according to" can denote two things; the condition of the one who ascends, and the cause of his ascension. When taken to express the condition of the one ascending, the Ascension in no wise belongs to Christ according to the condition of His Divine Nature; both because there is nothing higher than the Divine Nature to which He can ascend; and because ascension is local motion, a thing not in keeping with the Divine Nature, which is immovable and outside all place. Yet the Ascension is in keeping with Christ according to His human nature, which is limited by place, and can be the subject of motion. In this sense, then, we can say that Christ ascended into heaven as man, but not as God.

But if the phrase "according to" denote the cause of the Ascension, since Christ ascended into heaven in virtue of His Godhead, and not in virtue of His human nature, then it must be said that Christ ascended into heaven not as man, but as God. Hence Augustine says in a sermon on the Ascension: "It was our doing that the Son of man hung upon the cross; but it was His own doing that He ascended."

Reply Obj. 1: These utterances were spoken prophetically of God who was one day to become incarnate. Still it can be said that although to ascend does not belong to the Divine Nature properly, yet it can metaphorically; as, for instance, it is said "to ascend in the heart of man" (cf. Ps. 83:6), when his heart submits and humbles itself before God: and in the same way God is said to ascend metaphorically with regard to every creature, since He subjects it to Himself.

Reply Obj. 2: He who ascended is the same as He who descended. For Augustine says (De Symb. iv): "Who is it that descends? The God-Man. Who is it that ascends? The self-same God-Man." Nevertheless a twofold descent is attributed to Christ; one, whereby He is said to have descended from heaven, which is attributed to the God-Man according as He is God: for He is not to be understood as having descended by any local movement, but as having "emptied Himself," since "when He was in the form of God He took the form of a servant." For just as He is said to be emptied, not by losing His fulness, but because He took our littleness upon Himself, so likewise He is said to have descended from heaven, not that He deserted heaven, but because He assumed human nature in unity of person.

And there is another descent whereby He descended "into the lower regions of the earth," as is written Eph. 4:9; and this is local descent: hence this belongs to Christ according to the condition of human nature.

Reply Obj. 3: Christ is said to ascend to the Father, inasmuch as He ascends to sit on the right hand of the Father; and this is befitting Christ in a measure according to His Divine Nature, and in a measure according to His human nature, as will be said later (Q. 58, A. 3).

THIRD ARTICLE [III, Q. 57, Art. 3]

Whether Christ Ascended by His Own Power?

Objection 1: It would seem that Christ did not ascend by His own power, because it is written (Mk. 16:19) that "the Lord Jesus, after He had spoken to them, was taken up to heaven"; and (Acts 1:9) that, "while they looked on, He was raised up, and a cloud received Him out of their sight." But what is taken up, and lifted up, appears to be moved by another. Consequently, it was not by His own power, but by another's that Christ was taken up into heaven.

Obj. 2: Further, Christ's was an earthly body, like to ours. But it is contrary to the nature of an earthly body to be borne upwards. Moreover, what is moved contrary to its nature is nowise moved by its own power. Therefore Christ did not ascend to heaven by His own power.

Obj. 3: Further, Christ's own power is Divine. But this motion does not seem to have been Divine, because, whereas the Divine power is infinite, such motion would be instantaneous; consequently, He would not have been uplifted to heaven "while" the disciples "looked on," as is stated in Acts 1:9. Therefore, it seems that Christ did not ascend to heaven by His own power.

*On the contrary,* It is written (Isa. 63:1): "This beautiful one in his robe, walking in the greatness of his strength." Also Gregory says in a Homily on the Ascension (xxix): "It is to be noted that we read of Elias having ascended in a chariot, that it might be shown that one who was mere man needed another's help. But we do not read of our Saviour being lifted up either in a chariot or by angels, because He who had made all things was taken up above all things by His own power."

*I answer that,* There is a twofold nature in Christ, to wit, the Divine and the human. Hence His own power can be accepted according to both. Likewise a twofold power can be accepted regarding His human nature: one is natural, flowing from the principles of nature; and it is quite evident that Christ did not ascend into heaven by such power as this. The other is the power of glory, which is in Christ's human nature; and it was according to this that He ascended to heaven.

Now there are some who endeavor to assign the cause of this power to the nature of the fifth essence. This, as they say, is light, which they make out to be of the composition of the human body, and by which they contend that contrary elements are reconciled; so that in the state of this mortality, elemental nature is predominant in human bodies: so that, according to the nature of this predominating element the human body is borne downwards by its own power: but in the condition of glory the heavenly nature will predominate, by whose tendency and power Christ's body and the bodies of the saints are lifted up to heaven. But we have already treated of this opinion in the First Part (Q. 76, A. 7), and shall deal with it more fully in treating of the general resurrection (Suppl., Q. 84, A. 1).

Setting this opinion aside, others assign as the cause of this power the glorified soul itself, from whose overflow the body will be glorified, as Augustine writes to Dioscorus (Ep. cxviii). For the glorified body will be so submissive to the glorified soul, that, as Augustine says (De Civ. Dei xxii), "wheresoever the spirit listeth, thither the body will be on the instant; nor will the spirit desire anything unbecoming to the soul or the body." Now it is befitting the glorified and immortal body for it to be in a heavenly place, as stated above (A. 1). Consequently, Christ's body ascended into heaven by the power of His soul willing it. But as the body is made glorious by participation with the soul, even so, as Augustine says (Tract. xxiii in Joan.), "the soul is beatified by participating in God." Consequently, the Divine power is the first source of the ascent into heaven. Therefore Christ ascended into heaven by His own power, first of all by His Divine power, and secondly by the power of His glorified soul moving His body at will.

Reply Obj. 1: As Christ is said to have risen by His own power, though He was raised to life by the power of the Father, since the Father's power is the same as the Son's; so also Christ ascended into heaven by His own power, and yet was raised up and taken up to heaven by the Father.

Reply Obj. 2: This argument proves that Christ did not ascend into heaven by His own power, i.e. that which is natural to human nature: yet He did ascend by His own power, i.e. His Divine power, as well as by His own power, i.e. the power of His beatified soul. And although to mount upwards is contrary to the nature of a human body in its present condition, in which the body is not entirely dominated by the soul, still it will not be unnatural or forced in a glorified body, whose entire nature is utterly under the control of the spirit.

Reply Obj. 3: Although the Divine power be infinite, and operate infinitely, so far as the worker is concerned, still the effect thereof is received in things according to their capacity, and as God disposes. Now a body is incapable of being moved locally in an instant, because it must be commensurate with space, according to the division of which time is reckoned, as is proved in Physics vi. Consequently, it is not necessary for a body moved by God to be moved instantaneously, but with such speed as God disposes.

FOURTH ARTICLE [III, Q. 57, Art. 4]

Whether Christ Ascended Above All the Heavens?

Objection 1: It would seem that Christ did not ascend above all the heavens, for it is written (Ps. 10:5): "The Lord is in His holy temple, the Lord's throne is in heaven." But what is in heaven is not above heaven. Therefore Christ did not ascend above all the heavens.

Obj. 2: [*This objection with its solution is omitted in the Leonine edition as not being in the original manuscript.]

Further, there is no place above the heavens, as is proved in De Coelo i. But every body must occupy a place. Therefore Christ's body did not ascend above all the heavens.

Obj. 3: Further, two bodies cannot occupy the same place. Since, then, there is no passing from place to place except through the middle space, it seems that Christ could not have ascended above all the heavens unless heaven were divided; which is impossible.

Obj. 4: Further, it is narrated (Acts 1:9) that "a cloud received Him out of their sight." But clouds cannot be uplifted beyond heaven. Consequently, Christ did not ascend above all the heavens.

Obj. 5: Further, we believe that Christ will dwell for ever in the place whither He has ascended. But what is against nature cannot last for ever, because what is according to nature is more prevalent and of more frequent occurrence. Therefore, since it is contrary to nature for an earthly body to be above heaven, it seems that Christ's body did not ascend above heaven.

*On the contrary,* It is written (Eph. 4:10): "He ascended above all the heavens that He might fill all things."

*I answer that,* The more fully anything corporeal shares in the Divine goodness, the higher its place in the corporeal order, which is order of place. Hence we see that the more formal bodies are naturally the higher, as is clear from the Philosopher (Phys. iv; De Coelo ii), since it is by its form that every body partakes of the Divine Essence, as is shown in Physics i. But through glory the body derives a greater share in the Divine goodness than any other natural body does through its natural form; while among other glorious bodies it is manifest that Christ's body shines with greater glory. Hence it was most fitting for it to be set above all bodies. Thus it is that on Eph. 4:8: "Ascending on high," the gloss says: "in place and dignity."

Reply Obj. 1: God's seat is said to be in heaven, not as though heaven contained Him, but rather because it is contained by Him. Hence it is not necessary for any part of heaven to be higher, but for Him to be above all the heavens; according to Ps. 8:2: "For Thy magnificence is elevated above the heavens, O God!"

Reply Obj. 2: [*Omitted in Leonine edition; see Obj.[2]]

A place implies the notion of containing; hence the first container has the formality of first place, and such is the first heaven. Therefore bodies need in themselves to be in a place, in so far as they are contained by a heavenly body. But glorified bodies, Christ's especially, do not stand in need of being so contained, because they draw nothing from the heavenly bodies, but from God through the soul. So there is nothing to prevent Christ's body from being beyond the containing radius of the heavenly bodies, and not in a containing place. Nor is there need for a vacuum to exist outside heaven, since there is no place there, nor is there any potentiality susceptive of a body, but the potentiality of reaching thither lies in Christ. So when Aristotle proves (De Coelo ii) that there is no body beyond heaven, this must be understood of bodies which are in a state of pure nature, as is seen from the proofs.

Reply Obj. 3: Although it is not of the nature of a body for it to be in the same place with another body, yet God can bring it about miraculously that a body be with another in the same place, as Christ did when He went forth from the Virgin's sealed womb, also when He entered among the disciples through closed doors, as Gregory says (Hom. xxvi). Therefore Christ's body can be in the same place with another body, not through some inherent property in the body, but through the assistance and operation of the Divine power.

Reply Obj. 4: That cloud afforded no support as a vehicle to the ascending Christ: but it appeared as a sign of the Godhead, just as God's glory appeared to Israel in a cloud over the Tabernacle (Ex. 40:32; Num. 9:15).

Reply Obj. 5: A glorified body has the power to be in heaven or above heaven, not from its natural principles, but from the beatified soul, from which it derives its glory: and just as the upward motion of a glorified body is not violent, so neither is its rest violent: consequently, there is nothing to prevent it from being everlasting.

FIFTH ARTICLE [III, Q. 57, Art. 5]

Whether Christ's Body Ascended Above Every Spiritual Creature?

Objection 1: It would seem that Christ's body did not ascend above every spiritual creature. For no fitting comparison can be made between things which have no common ratio. But place is not predicated in the same ratio of bodies and of spiritual creatures, as is evident from what was said in the First Part (Q. 8, A. 2, ad 1, 2; Q. 52, A. 1). Therefore it seems that Christ's body cannot be said to have ascended above every spiritual creature.

Obj. 2: Further, Augustine says (De Vera Relig. lv) that a spirit always takes precedence over a body. But the higher place is due to the higher things. Therefore it does not seem that Christ ascended above every spiritual creature.

Obj. 3: Further, in every place a body exists, since there is no such thing as a vacuum in nature. Therefore if no body obtains a higher place than a spirit in the order of natural bodies, then there will be no place above every spiritual creature. Consequently, Christ's body could not ascend above every spiritual creature.

*On the contrary,* It is written (Eph. 1:21): "God set Him above all principality, and Power, and every name that is named, not only in this world, but also in that which is to come."

*I answer that,* The more exalted place is due to the nobler subject, whether it be a place according to bodily contact, as regards bodies, or whether it be by way of spiritual contact, as regards spiritual substances; thus a heavenly place which is the highest of places is becomingly due to spiritual substances, since they are highest in the order of substances. But although Christ's body is beneath spiritual substances, if we weigh the conditions of its corporeal nature, nevertheless it surpasses all spiritual substances in dignity, when we call to mind its dignity of union whereby it is united personally with God. Consequently, owing to this very fittingness, a higher place is due to it above every spiritual creature. Hence Gregory says in a Homily on the Ascension (xxix in Evang.) that "He who had made all things, was by His own power raised up above all things."

Reply Obj. 1: Although a place is differently attributed to corporeal and spiritual substances, still in either case this remains in common, that the higher place is assigned to the worthier.

Reply Obj. 2: This argument holds good of Christ's body according to the conditions of its corporeal nature, but not according to its formality of union.

Reply Obj. 3: This comparison may be considered either on the part of the places; and thus there is no place so high as to exceed the dignity of a spiritual substance: in this sense the objection runs. Or it may be considered on the part of the dignity of the things to which a place is attributed: and in this way it is due to the body of Christ to be above spiritual creatures.

SIXTH ARTICLE [III, Q. 57, Art. 6]

Whether Christ's Ascension Is the Cause of Our Salvation?

Objection 1: It would seem that Christ's Ascension is not the cause of our salvation. For, Christ was the cause of our salvation in so far as He merited it.

But He merited nothing for us by His Ascension, because His Ascension belongs to the reward of His exaltation: and the same thing is not both merit and reward, just as neither are a road and its terminus the same. Therefore it seems that Christ's Ascension is not the cause of our salvation.

Obj. 2: Further, if Christ's Ascension be the cause of our salvation, it seems that this is principally due to the fact that His Ascension is the cause of ours. But this was bestowed upon us by His Passion, for it is written (Heb. 10:19): "We have [Vulg.: 'Having'] confidence in the entering into the holies by" His "blood." Therefore it seems that Christ's Ascension was not the cause of our salvation.

Obj. 3: Further, the salvation which Christ bestows is an everlasting one, according to Isa. 51:6: "My salvation shall be for ever." But Christ did not ascend into heaven to remain there eternally; for it is written (Acts 1:11): "He shall so come as you have seen Him going, into heaven." Besides, we read of Him showing Himself to many holy people on earth after He went up to heaven, to Paul, for instance (Acts 9). Consequently, it seems that Christ's Ascension is not the cause of our salvation.

*On the contrary,* He Himself said (John 16:7): "It is expedient to you that I go"; i.e. that I should leave you and ascend into heaven.

*I answer that,* Christ's Ascension is the cause of our salvation in two ways: first of all, on our part; secondly, on His.

On our part, in so far as by the Ascension our souls are uplifted to Him; because, as stated above (A. 1, ad 3), His Ascension fosters, first, faith; secondly, hope; thirdly, charity. Fourthly, our reverence for Him is thereby increased, since we no longer deem Him an earthly man, but the God of heaven; thus the Apostle says (2 Cor. 5:16): "If we have known Christ according to the flesh--'that is, as mortal, whereby we reputed Him as a mere man,'" as the gloss interprets the words--"but now we know Him so no longer."

On His part, in regard to those things which, in ascending, He did for our salvation. First, He prepared the way for our ascent into heaven, according to His own saying (John 14:2): "I go to prepare a place for you," and the words of Micheas (2:13), "He shall go up that shall open the way before them." For since He is our Head the members must follow whither the Head has gone: hence He said (John 14:3): "That where I am, you also may be." In sign whereof He took to heaven the souls of the saints delivered from hell, according to Ps. 67:19 (Cf. Eph. 4:8): "Ascending on high, He led captivity captive," because He took with Him to heaven those who had been held captives by the devil--to heaven, as to a place strange to human nature. captives in deed of a happy taking, since they were acquired by His victory.

Secondly, because as the high-priest under the Old Testament entered the holy place to stand before God for the people, so also Christ entered heaven "to make intercession for us," as is said in Heb. 7:25. Because the very showing of Himself in the human nature which He took with Him to heaven is a pleading for us, so that for the very reason that God so exalted human nature in Christ, He may take pity on them for whom the Son of God took human nature. Thirdly, that being established in His heavenly seat as God and Lord, He might send down gifts upon men, according to Eph. 4:10: "He ascended above all the heavens, that He might fill all things," that is, "with His gifts," according to the gloss.

Reply Obj. 1: Christ's Ascension is the cause of our salvation by way not of merit, but of efficiency, as was stated above regarding His Resurrection (Q. 56, A. 1, ad 3, 4).

Reply Obj. 2: Christ's Passion is the cause of our ascending to heaven, properly speaking, by removing the hindrance which is sin, and also by way of merit: whereas Christ's Ascension is the direct cause of our ascension, as by beginning it in Him who is our Head, with whom the members must be united.

Reply Obj. 3: Christ by once ascending into heaven acquired for Himself and for us in perpetuity the right and worthiness of a heavenly dwelling-place; which worthiness suffers in no way, if, from some special dispensation, He sometimes comes down in body to earth; either in order to show Himself to the whole world, as at the judgment; or else to show Himself particularly to some individual, e.g. in Paul's case, as we read in Acts 9. And lest any man may think that Christ was not bodily present when this occurred, the contrary is shown from what the Apostle says in 1 Cor. 14:8, to confirm faith in the Resurrection: "Last of all He was seen also by me, as by one born out of due time": which vision would not confirm the truth of the Resurrection except he had beheld Christ's very body.

# QUESTION 58

OF CHRIST'S SITTING AT THE RIGHT HAND OF THE FATHER (In Four Articles)

We have now to consider Christ's sitting at the right hand of the Father, concerning which there are four points of inquiry:

(1) Whether Christ is seated at the right hand of the Father?

(2) Whether this belongs to Him according to the Divine Nature?

(3) Whether it belongs to Him according to His human nature?

(4) Whether it is something proper to Christ?

FIRST ARTICLE [III, Q. 58, Art. 1]

Whether It Is Fitting That Christ Should Sit at the Right Hand of God the Father?

Objection 1: It would seem unfitting that Christ should sit at the right hand of God the Father. For right and left are differences of bodily position. But nothing corporeal can be applied to God, since "God is a spirit," as we read in John 4:24. Therefore it seems that Christ does not sit at the right hand of the Father.

Obj. 2: Further, if anyone sits at another's right hand, then the latter is seated on his left. Consequently, if Christ sits at the right hand of the Father, it follows that the Father is seated on the left of the Son; which is unseemly.

Obj. 3: Further, sitting and standing savor of opposition. But Stephen (Acts 7:55) said: "Behold, I see the heavens opened, and the Son of man standing on the right hand of God." Therefore it seems that Christ does not sit at the right hand of the Father.

*On the contrary,* It is written in the last chapter of Mark (16:19): "The Lord Jesus, after He had spoken to them, was taken up to heaven, and sitteth on the right hand of God."

*I answer that,* The word "sitting" may have a twofold meaning; namely, "abiding" as in Luke 24:49: "Sit [Douay: 'Stay'] you in the city": and royal or judiciary "power," as in Prov. 20:8: "The king, that sitteth on the throne of judgment, scattereth away all evil with his look." Now in either sense it belongs to Christ to sit at the Father's right hand. First of all inasmuch as He abides eternally unchangeable in the Father's bliss, which is termed His right hand, according to Ps. 15:11: "At Thy right hand are delights even to the end." Hence Augustine says (De Symb. i): "'Sitteth at the right hand of the Father': To sit means to dwell, just as we say of any man: 'He sat in that country for three years': Believe, then, that Christ dwells so at the right hand of the Father: for He is happy, and the Father's right hand is the name for His bliss." Secondly, Christ is said to sit at the right hand of the Father inasmuch as He reigns together with the Father, and has judiciary power from Him; just as he who sits at the king's right hand helps him in ruling and judging. Hence Augustine says (De Symb. ii): "By the expression 'right hand,' understand the power which this Man, chosen of God, received, that He might come to judge, who before had come to be judged."

Reply Obj. 1: As Damascene says (De Fide Orth. iv): "We do not speak of the Father's right hand as of a place, for how can a place be designated by His right hand, who Himself is beyond all place? Right and left belong to things definable by limit. But we style, as the Father's right hand, the glory and honor of the Godhead."

Reply Obj. 2: The argument holds good if sitting at the right hand be taken corporeally. Hence Augustine says (De Symb. i): "If we accept it in a carnal sense that Christ sits at the Father's right hand, then the Father will be on the left. But there"--that is, in eternal bliss, "it is all right hand, since no misery is there."

Reply Obj. 3: As Gregory says in a Homily on the Ascension (Hom. xxix in Evang.), "it is the judge's place to sit, while to stand is the place of the combatant or helper. Consequently, Stephen in his toil of combat saw Him standing whom He had as his helper. But Mark describes Him as seated after the Ascension, because after the glory of His Ascension He will at the end be seen as judge."

SECOND ARTICLE [III, Q. 58, Art. 2]

Whether It Belongs to Christ As God to Sit at the Right Hand of the Father?

Objection 1: It would seem that it does not belong to Christ as God to sit at the right hand of the Father. For, as God, Christ is the Father's right hand. But it does not appear to be the same thing to be the right hand of anyone and to sit on his right hand. Therefore, as God, Christ does not sit at the right hand of the Father.

Obj. 2: Further, in the last chapter of Mark (16:19) it is said that "the Lord Jesus was taken up into heaven, and sitteth on the right hand of God." But it was not as God that Christ was taken up to heaven. Therefore neither does He, as God, sit at the right hand of God.

Obj. 3: Further, Christ as God is the equal of the Father and of the Holy Ghost. Consequently, if Christ sits as God at the right hand of the Father, with equal reason the Holy Ghost sits at the right hand of the Father and of the Son, and the Father Himself on the right hand of the Son; which no one is found to say.

*On the contrary,* Damascene says (De Fide Orth. iv): that "what we style as the Father's right hand, is the glory and honor of the Godhead, wherein the Son of God existed before ages as God and as consubstantial with the Father."

*I answer that,* As may be gathered from what has been said (A. 1) three things can be understood under the expression "right hand." First of all, as Damascene takes it, "the glory of the Godhead": secondly, according to Augustine "the beatitude of the Father": thirdly, according to the same authority, "judiciary power." Now as we observed (A. 1) "sitting" denotes either abiding, or royal or judiciary dignity. Hence, to sit on the right hand of the Father is nothing else than to share in the glory of the Godhead with the Father, and to possess beatitude and judiciary power, and that unchangeably and royally. But this belongs to the Son as God. Hence it is manifest that Christ as God sits at the right hand of the Father; yet so that this preposition "at," which is a transitive one, implies merely personal distinction and order of origin, but not degree of nature or dignity, for there is no such thing in the Divine Persons, as was shown in the First Part (Q. 42, AA. 3, 4).

Reply Obj. 1: The Son of God is called the Father's "right hand" by appropriation, just as He is called the "Power" of the Father (1 Cor. 1:24). But "right hand of the Father," in its three meanings given above, is something common to the three Persons.

Reply Obj. 2: Christ as man is exalted to Divine honor; and this is signified in the aforesaid sitting; nevertheless such honor belongs to Him as God, not through any assumption, but through His origin from eternity.

Reply Obj. 3: In no way can it be said that the Father is seated at the right hand of the Son or of the Holy Ghost; because the Son and the Holy Ghost derive their origin from the Father, and not conversely. The Holy Ghost, however, can be said properly to sit at the right hand of the Father or of the Son, in the aforesaid sense, although by a kind of appropriation it is attributed to the Son, to whom equality is appropriated; thus Augustine says (De Doctr. Christ. i) that "in the Father there is unity, in the Son equality, in the Holy Ghost the connection of unity with equality."

THIRD ARTICLE [III, Q. 58, Art. 3]

Whether It Belongs to Christ As Man to Sit at the Right Hand of the Father?

Objection 1: It would seem that it does not belong to Christ as man to sit at the right hand of the Father, because, as Damascene says (De Fide Orth. iv): "What we call the Father's right hand is the glory and honor of the Godhead." But the glory and honor of the Godhead do not belong to Christ as man. Consequently, it seems that Christ as man does not sit at the right hand of the Father.

Obj. 2: Further, to sit on the ruler's right hand seems to exclude subjection, because one so sitting seems in a measure to be reigning with him. But Christ as man is "subject unto" the Father, as is said in 1 Cor. 15:28. Therefore it seems that Christ as man does not sit at the Father's right hand.

Obj. 3: Further, on Rom. 8:34: "Who is at the right hand of God," the gloss adds: "that is, equal to the Father in that honor, whereby God is the Father: or, on the right hand of the Father, that is, in the mightier gifts of God." And on Heb. 1:3: "sitteth on the right hand of the majesty on high," the gloss adds, "that is, in equality with the Father over all things, both in place and dignity." But equality with God does not belong to Christ as man; for in this respect Christ Himself says (John 14:28): "The Father is greater than I." Consequently, it appears unseemly for Christ as man to sit on the Father's right hand.

*On the contrary,* Augustine says (De Symb. ii): "By the expression 'right hand' understand the power which this Man, chosen of God, received, that He might come as judge, who before had come to be judged."

*I answer that,* As stated above (A. 2), by the expression "right hand" is understood either the glory of His Godhead, or His eternal beatitude, or His judicial and royal power. Now this preposition "at" signifies a kind of approach to the right hand; thus denoting something in common, and yet with a distinction, as already observed (De Symb. ii). And this can be in three ways: first of all, by something common in nature, and a distinction in person; and thus Christ as the Son of God, sits at the right hand of the Father, because He has the same Nature as the Father: hence these things belong to the Son essentially, just as to the Father; and this is to be in equality with the Father. Secondly, according to the grace of union, which, *on the contrary,* implies distinction of nature, and unity of person. According to this, Christ as man is the Son of God, and consequently sits at the Father's right hand; yet so that the expression "as" does not denote condition of nature, but unity of suppositum, as explained above (Q. 16, AA. 10, 11). Thirdly, the said approach can be understood according to habitual grace, which is more fully in Christ than in all other creatures, so much so that human nature in Christ is more blessed than all other creatures, and possesses over all other creatures royal and judiciary power.

So, then, if "as" denote condition of nature, then Christ, as God, sits "at the Father's right hand," that is, "in equality with the Father"; but as man, He sits "at the right hand of the Father," that is, "in the Father's mightier gifts beyond all other creatures," that is to say, "in greater beatitude," and "exercising judiciary power." But if "as" denote unity of person, thus again as man, He sits at the Father's right hand "as to equality of honor," inasmuch as with the same honor we venerate the Son of God with His assumed nature, as was said above (Q. 25, A. 1).

Reply Obj. 1: Christ's humanity according to the conditions of His nature has not the glory or honor of the Godhead, which it has nevertheless by reason of the Person with whom it is united. Hence Damascene adds in the passage quoted: "In which," that is, in the glory of the Godhead, "the Son of God existing before ages, as God and consubstantial with the Father, sits in His conglorified flesh; for, under one adoration the one hypostasis, together with His flesh, is adored by every creature."

Reply Obj. 2: Christ as man is subject to the Father, if "as" denote the condition of nature: in which respect it does not belong to Him as man to sit at the Father's right hand, by reason of their mutual equality. But it does thus belong to Him to sit at the right hand of the Father, according as is thereby denoted the excellence of beatitude and His judiciary power over every creature.

Reply Obj. 3: It does not belong to Christ's human nature to be in equality with the Father, but only to the Person who assumed it; but it does belong even to the assumed human nature to share in God's mightier gifts, in so far as it implies exaltation above other creatures.

FOURTH ARTICLE [III, Q. 58, Art. 4]

Whether It Is Proper to Christ to Sit at the Right Hand of the Father?

Objection 1: It would seem that it is not proper to Christ to sit at the right hand of the Father, because the Apostle says (Eph. 2:4, 6): "God . . . hath raised us up together, and hath made us sit together in the heavenly places through Christ Jesus." But to be raised up is not proper to Christ. Therefore for like reason neither is it proper to Him to sit "on the right hand" of God "on high" (Heb. 1:3).

Obj. 2: Further, as Augustine says (De Symb. i): "For Christ to sit at the right hand of the Father, is to dwell in His beatitude." But many more share in this. Therefore it does not appear to be proper to Christ to sit at the right hand of the Father.

Obj. 3: Further, Christ Himself says (Apoc. 3:21): "To him that shall overcome, I will give to sit with Me in My throne: as I also have overcome, and am set down with My Father in His throne." But it is by sitting on His Father's throne that Christ is seated at His right hand. Therefore others who overcome likewise, sit at the Father's right hand.

Obj. 4: Further, the Lord says (Matt. 20:23): "To sit on My right or left hand, is not Mine to give to you, but to them for whom it is prepared by My Father." But no purpose would be served by saying this, unless it was prepared for some. Consequently, to sit at the right hand is not proper to Christ.

*On the contrary,* It is written (Heb. 1:13): "To which of the angels said He at any time: Sit thou on My right hand, i.e. 'in My mightier gifts,'" or "'as my equal in the Godhead'"? [*The comment is from the gloss of Peter Lombard] as if to answer: "To none." But angels are higher than other creatures. Therefore, much less does it belong to anyone save Christ to sit at the Father's right hand.

*I answer that,* As stated above (A. 3), Christ is said to sit at the Father's right hand inasmuch as He is on equality with the Father in respect of His Divine Nature, while in respect of His humanity, He excels all creatures in the possession of Divine gifts. But each of these belongs exclusively to Christ. Consequently, it belongs to no one else, angel or man, but to Christ alone, to sit at the right hand of the Father.

Reply Obj. 1: Since Christ is our Head, then what was bestowed on Christ is bestowed on us through Him. And on this account, since He is already raised up, the Apostle says that God has, so to speak, "raised us up together with Him," still we ourselves are not raised up yet, but are to be raised up, according to Rom. 8:11: "He who raised up Jesus from the dead, shall quicken also your mortal bodies": and after the same manner of speech the Apostle adds that "He has made us to sit together with Him, in the heavenly places"; namely, for the very reason that Christ our Head sits there.

Reply Obj. 2: Since the right hand is the Divine beatitude, then "to sit on the right hand" does not mean simply to be in beatitude, but to possess beatitude with a kind of dominative power, as a property and part of one's nature. This belongs to Christ alone, and to no other creature. Yet it can be said that every saint in bliss is placed on God's right hand; hence it is written (Matt. 25:33): "He shall set the sheep on His right hand."

Reply Obj. 3: By the "throne" is meant the judiciary power which Christ has from the Father: and in this sense He is said "to sit in the Father's throne." But other saints have it from Christ; and in this respect they are said "to sit on Christ's throne"; according to Matt. 19:28: "You also shall sit upon twelve seats, judging the twelve tribes of Israel."

Reply Obj. 4: As Chrysostom says (Hom. lxv in Matth.), "that place," to wit, sitting at the right hand, "is closed not only to all men, but likewise to angels: for, Paul declares it to be the prerogative of Christ, saying: 'To which of the angels said He at any time: Sit on My right hand?'" Our Lord therefore "replied not as though some were going to sit there one day, but condescending to the supplication of the questioners; since more than others they sought this one thing alone, to stand nigh to Him." Still it can be said that the sons of Zebedee sought for higher excellence in sharing His judiciary power; hence they did not ask to sit on the Father's right hand or left, but on Christ's.

## QUESTION 59

OF CHRIST'S JUDICIARY POWER (In Six Articles)

We have now to consider Christ's judiciary power. Under this head there are six points of inquiry:

(1) Whether judiciary power is to be attributed to Christ?

(2) Whether it belongs to Him as man?

(3) Whether He acquired it by merits?

(4) Whether His judiciary power is universal with regard to all men?

(5) Whether besides the judgment that takes place now in time, we are to expect Him in the future general judgment?

(6) Whether His judiciary power extends likewise to the angels?

It will be more suitable to consider the execution of the Last Judgment when we treat of things pertaining to the end of the world [*See Suppl., QQ. 88, seqq.]. For the present it will be enough to touch on those points that concern Christ's dignity.

FIRST ARTICLE [III, Q. 59, Art. 1]

Whether Judiciary Power Is to Be Specially Attributed to Christ?

Objection 1: It would seem that judiciary power is not to be specially attributed to Christ. For judgment of others seems to belong to their lord; hence it is written (Rom. 14:4): "Who art thou that judgest another man's servant?" But, it belongs to the entire Trinity to be Lord over creatures. Therefore judiciary power ought not to be attributed specially to Christ.

Obj. 2: Further, it is written (Dan. 7:9): "The Ancient of days sat"; and further on (Dan. 7:10), "the judgment sat, and the books were opened." But the Ancient of days is understood to be the Father, because as Hilary says (De Trin. ii): "Eternity is in the Father." Consequently, judiciary power ought rather to be attributed to the Father than to Christ.

Obj. 3: Further, it seems to belong to the same person to judge as it does to convince. But it belongs to the Holy Ghost to convince: for our Lord says (John 16:8): "And when He is come," i.e. the Holy Ghost, "He will convince the world of sin, and of justice, and of judgment." Therefore judiciary power ought to be attributed to the Holy Ghost rather than to Christ.

*On the contrary,* It is said of Christ (Acts 10:42): "It is He who was appointed by God, to be judge of the living end of the dead."

*I answer that,* Three things are required for passing judgment: first, the power of coercing subjects; hence it is written (Ecclus. 7:6): "Seek not to be made a judge unless thou have strength enough to extirpate iniquities." The second thing required is upright zeal, so as to pass judgment not out of hatred or malice, but from love of justice, according to Prov. 3:12: "For whom the Lord loveth, He chasteneth: and as a father in the son He pleaseth Himself." Thirdly, wisdom is needed, upon which judgment is based, according to Ecclus. 10:1: "A wise judge shall judge his people." The first two are conditions for judging; but on the third the very rule of judgment is based, because the standard of judgment is the law of wisdom or truth, according to which the judgment is passed.

Now because the Son is Wisdom begotten, and Truth proceeding from the Father, and His perfect Image, consequently, judiciary power is properly attributed to the Son of God. Accordingly Augustine says (De Vera Relig. xxxi): "This is that unchangeable Truth, which is rightly styled the law of all arts, and the art of the Almighty Craftsman. But even as we and all rational souls judge aright of the things beneath us, so does He who alone is Truth itself pass judgment on us, when we cling to Him. But the Father judges Him not, for He is the Truth no less than Himself. Consequently, whatever the Father judges, He judges through It." Further on he concludes by saying: "Therefore the Father judges no man, but has given all judgment to the Son."

Reply Obj. 1: This argument proves that judiciary power is common to the entire Trinity, which is quite true: still by special appropriation such power is attributed to the Son, as stated above.

Reply Obj. 2: As Augustine says (De Trin. vi), eternity is attributed to the Father, because He is the Principle, which is implied in the idea of eternity. And in the same place Augustine says that the Son is the art of the Father. So, then, judiciary authority is attributed to the Father, inasmuch as He is the Principle of the Son, but the very rule of judgment is attributed to the Son who is the art and wisdom of the Father, so that as the Father does all things through the Son, inasmuch as the Son is His art, so He judges all things through the Son, inasmuch as the Son is His wisdom and truth. And this is implied by Daniel, when he says in the first passage that "the Ancient of days sat," and when he subsequently adds that the Son of Man "came even to the Ancient of days, who gave Him power, and glory, and a kingdom": and thereby we are given to understand that the authority for judging lies with the Father, from whom the Son received the power to judge.

Reply Obj. 3: As Augustine says (Tract. xcv in Joan.): "Christ said that the Holy Ghost shall convince the world of sin, as if to say 'He shall pour out charity upon your hearts.' For thus, when fear is driven away, you shall have freedom for convincing." Consequently, then, judgment is attributed to the Holy Ghost, not as regards the rule of judgment, but as regards man's desire to judge others aright.

SECOND ARTICLE [III, Q. 59, Art. 2]

Whether Judiciary Power Belongs to Christ As Man?

Objection 1: It would seem that judiciary power does not belong to Christ as man. For Augustine says (De Vera Relig. xxxi) that judgment is attributed to the Son inasmuch as He is the law of the first truth. But this is Christ's attribute as God. Consequently, judiciary power does not belong to Christ as man but as God.

Obj. 2: Further, it belongs to judiciary power to reward the good, just as to punish the wicked. But eternal beatitude, which is the reward of good works, is bestowed by God alone: thus Augustine says (Tract. xxiii super Joan.) that "the soul is made blessed by participation of God, and not by participation of a holy soul." Therefore it seems that judiciary power does not belong to Christ as man, but as God.

Obj. 3: Further, it belongs to Christ's judiciary power to judge secrets of hearts, according to 1 Cor. 4:5: "Judge not before the time; until the Lord come, who both will bring to light the hidden things of darkness, and will make manifest the counsels of the hearts." But this belongs exclusively to the Divine power, according to Jer. 17:9, 10: "The heart of man is perverse and unsearchable, who can know it? I am the Lord who search the heart, and prove the reins: who give to every one according to his way." Therefore judiciary power does not belong to Christ as man but as God.

*On the contrary,* It is said (John 5:27): "He hath given Him power to do judgment, because He is the Son of man."

*I answer that,* Chrysostom (Hom. xxxix in Joan.) seems to think that judiciary power belongs to Christ not as man, but only as God. Accordingly he thus explains the passage just quoted from John: "'He gave Him power to do judgment, because He is the Son of man: wonder not at this.' For He received judiciary power, not because He is man; but because He is the Son of the ineffable God, therefore is He judge. But since the expressions used were greater than those appertaining to man, He said in explanation: 'Wonder not at this, because He is the Son of man, for He is likewise the Son of God.'" And he proves this by the effect of the Resurrection: wherefore He adds: "Because the hour cometh when the dead in their graves shall hear the voice of the Son of God."

But it must be observed that although the primary authority of judging rests with God, nevertheless the power to judge is committed to men with regard to those subject to their jurisdiction. Hence it is written (Deut. 1:16): "Judge that which is just"; and further on (Deut. 1:17): "Because it is the judgment of God," that is to say, it is by His authority that you judge. Now it was said before (Q. 8, AA. 1, 4) that Christ even in His human nature is Head of the entire Church, and that God has "put all things under His feet." Consequently, it belongs to Him, even according to His human nature, to exercise judiciary power. On this account, it seems that the authority of Scripture quoted above must be interpreted thus: "He gave Him power to do judgment, because He is the Son of Man"; not on account of the condition of His nature, for thus all men would have this kind of power, as Chrysostom objects (Hom. xxxix in Joan.); but because this belongs to the grace of the Head, which Christ received in His human nature.

Now judiciary power belongs to Christ in this way according to His human nature on three accounts. First, because of His likeness and kinship with men; for, as God works through intermediary causes, as being closer to the effects, so He judges men through the Man Christ, that His judgment may be sweeter to men. Hence (Heb. 4:15) the Apostle says: "For we have not a high-priest, who cannot have compassion on our infirmities; but one tempted in all things like as we are, without sin. Let us go therefore with confidence to the throne of His grace." Secondly, because at the last judgment, as Augustine says (Tract. xix in Joan.), "there will be a resurrection of dead bodies, which God will raise up through the Son of Man"; just as by "the same Christ He raises souls," inasmuch as "He is the Son of God." Thirdly, because, as Augustine observes (De Verb. Dom., Serm. cxxvii): "It was but right that those who were to be judged should see their judge. But those to be judged were the good and the bad. It follows that the form of a servant should be shown in the judgment to both good and wicked, while the form of God should be kept for the good alone."

Reply Obj. 1: Judgment belongs to truth as its standard, while it belongs to the man imbued with truth, according as he is as it were one with truth, as a kind of law and "living justice" [*Aristotle, Ethic. v]. Hence Augustine quotes (De Verb. Dom., Serm. cxxvii) the saying of 1 Cor. 2:15: "The spiritual man judgeth all things." But beyond all creatures Christ's soul was more closely united with truth, and more full of truth; according to John 1:14: "We saw Him . . . full of grace and truth." And according to this it belongs principally to the soul of Christ to judge all things.

Reply Obj. 2: It belongs to God alone to bestow beatitude upon souls by a participation with Himself; but it is Christ's prerogative to bring them to such beatitude, inasmuch as He is their Head and the author of their salvation, according to Heb. 2:10: "Who had brought many children into glory, to perfect the author of their salvation by His Passion."

Reply Obj. 3: To know and judge the secrets of hearts, of itself belongs to God alone; but from the overflow of the Godhead into Christ's soul it belongs to Him also to know and to judge the secrets of hearts, as we stated above (Q. 10, A. 2), when dealing with the knowledge of Christ. Hence it is written (Rom. 2:16): "In the day when God shall judge the secrets of men by Jesus Christ."

THIRD ARTICLE [III, Q. 59, Art. 3]

Whether Christ Acquired His Judiciary Power by His Merits?

Objection 1: It would seem that Christ did not acquire His judiciary power by His merits. For judiciary power flows from the royal dignity: according to Prov. 20:8: "The king that sitteth on the throne of judgment, scattereth away all evil with his look." But it was without merits that Christ acquired royal power, for it is His due as God's Only-begotten Son: thus it is written (Luke 1:32): "The Lord God shall give unto Him the throne of David His father, and He shall reign in the house of Jacob for ever." Therefore Christ did not obtain judiciary power by His merits.

Obj. 2: Further, as stated above (A. 2), judiciary power is Christ's due inasmuch as He is our Head. But the grace of headship does not belong to Christ by reason of merit, but follows the personal union of the Divine and human natures: according to John 1:14, 16: "We saw His glory . . . as of the Only-Begotten of the Father, full of grace and truth . . . and of His fulness we all have received": and this pertains to the notion of headship. Consequently, it seems that Christ did not have judiciary power from merits.

Obj. 3: Further, the Apostle says (1 Cor. 2:15): "The spiritual man judgeth all things." But a man becomes spiritual through grace, which is not from merits; otherwise it is "no more grace," as is said in Rom. 11:6. Therefore it seems that judiciary power belongs neither to Christ nor to others from any merits, but from grace alone.

*On the contrary,* It is written (Job 36:17): "Thy cause hath been judged as that of the wicked, cause and judgment thou shalt recover." And Augustine says (Serm. cxxvii): "The Judge shall sit, who stood before a judge; He shall condemn the truly wicked, who Himself was falsely reputed wicked."

*I answer that,* There is nothing to hinder one

and the same thing from being due to some one from various causes: as the glory of the body in rising was due to Christ not only as befitting His Godhead and His soul's glory, but likewise "from the merit of the lowliness of His Passion" [*Cf. Augustine, Tract. civ in Joan.]. And in the same way it must be said that judiciary power belongs to the Man Christ on account of both His Divine personality, and the dignity of His headship, and the fulness of His habitual grace: and yet He obtained it from merit, so that, in accordance with the Divine justice, He should be judge who fought for God's justice, and conquered, and was unjustly condemned. Hence He Himself says (Apoc. 3:21): "I have overcome and am set down in My Father's throne [Vulg.: 'with My Father in His throne']." Now judiciary power is understood by "throne," according to Ps. 9:5: "Thou hast sat on the throne, who judgest justice."

Reply Obj. 1: This argument holds good of judiciary power according as it is due to Christ by reason of the union with the Word of God.

Reply Obj. 2: This argument is based on the ground of His grace as Head.

Reply Obj. 3: This argument holds good in regard to habitual grace, which perfects Christ's soul. But although judiciary power be Christ's due in these ways, it is not hindered from being His due from merit.

FOURTH ARTICLE [III, Q. 59, Art. 4]

Whether Judiciary Power Belongs to Christ with Respect to All Human Affairs?

Objection 1: It would seem that judiciary power concerning all human affairs does not belong to Christ. For as we read in Luke 12:13, 14, when one of the crowd said to Christ: "Speak to my brother that he divide the inheritance with me; He said to him: Man, who hath appointed Me judge, or divider over you?" Consequently, He does not exercise judgment over all human affairs.

Obj. 2: Further, no one exercises judgment except over his own subjects. But, according to Heb. 2:8, "we see not as yet all things subject to" Christ. Therefore it seems that Christ has not judgment over all human affairs.

Obj. 3: Further, Augustine says (De Civ. Dei xx) that it is part of Divine judgment for the good to be afflicted sometimes in this world, and sometimes to prosper, and in like manner the wicked. But the same was the case also before the Incarnation. Consequently, not all God's judgments regarding human affairs are included in Christ's judiciary power.

*On the contrary,* It is said (John 5:22): "The Father hath given all judgment to the Son."

*I answer that,* If we speak of Christ according to His Divine Nature, it is evident that every judgment of the Father belongs to the Son; for, as the Father does all things through His Word, so He judges all things through His Word.

But if we speak of Christ in His human nature, thus again is it evident that all things are subject to His judgment. This is made clear if we consider first of all the relationship subsisting between Christ's soul and the Word of God; for, if "the spiritual man judgeth all things," as is said in 1 Cor. 2:15, inasmuch as his soul clings to the Word of God, how much more Christ's soul, which is filled with the truth of the Word of God, passes judgment upon all things.

Secondly, the same appears from the merit of His death; because, according to Rom. 14:9: "To this end Christ died and rose again; that He might be Lord both of the dead and of the living." And therefore He has judgment over all men; and on this account the Apostle adds (Rom. 14:10): "We shall all stand before the judgment seat of Christ": and (Dan. 7:14) it is written that "He gave Him power, and glory, and a kingdom; and all peoples, tribes, and tongues shall serve Him."

Thirdly, the same thing is evident from comparison of human affairs with the end of human salvation. For, to whomsoever the substance is entrusted, the accessory is likewise committed. Now all human affairs are ordered for the end of beatitude, which is everlasting salvation, to which men are admitted, or from which they are excluded by Christ's judgment, as is evident from Matt. 25:31, 40. Consequently, it is manifest that all human affairs are included in Christ's judiciary power.

Reply Obj. 1: As was said above (A. 3, Obj. 1), judiciary power goes with royal dignity. Now Christ, although established king by God, did not wish while living on earth to govern temporarily an earthly kingdom; consequently He said (John 18:36): "My kingdom is not of this world." In like fashion He did not wish to exercise judiciary power over temporal concerns, since He came to raise men to Divine things. Hence Ambrose observes on this passage in Luke: "It is well that He who came down with a Divine purpose should hold Himself aloof from temporal concerns; nor does He deign to be a judge of quarrels and an arbiter of property, since He is judge of the quick and the dead, and the arbitrator of merits."

Reply Obj. 2: All things are subject to Christ in respect of that power, which He received from the Father, over all things, according to Matt. 28:18: "All power is given to Me in heaven and in earth." But as to the exercise of this power, all things are not yet subject to Him: this will come to pass in the future, when He shall fulfil His will regarding all things, by saving some and punishing others.

Reply Obj. 3: Judgments of this kind were exercised by Christ before His Incarnation, inasmuch as He is the Word of God: and the soul united with Him personally became a partaker of this power by the Incarnation.

FIFTH ARTICLE [III, Q. 59, Art. 5]

Whether After the Judgment That Takes Place in the Present Time, There Remains Yet Another General Judgment?

Objection 1: It would seem that after the Judgment that takes place in the present time, there does not remain another General Judgment. For a judgment serves no purpose after the final allotment of rewards and punishments. But rewards and punishments are allotted in this present time: for our Lord said to the thief on the cross (Luke 23:43): "This day thou shalt be with Me in paradise": and (Luke 16:22) it is said that "the rich man died and was buried in hell." Therefore it is useless to look forward to a final Judgment.

Obj. 2: Further, according to another (the Septuagint) version of Nahum 1:9, "God shall not judge the same thing a second time." But in the present time God judges both temporal and spiritual matters. Therefore, it does not seem that another final judgment is to be expected.

Obj. 3: Further, reward and punishment correspond with merit and demerit. But merit and demerit bear relation to the body only in so far as it is the instrument of the soul. Therefore reward or punishment is not due to the body save as the soul's instrument. Therefore no other Judgment is called for at the end (of the world) to requite man with reward or punishment in the body, besides that Judgment in which souls are now punished or rewarded.

*On the contrary,* It is said in John 12:48: "The word that I have spoken, the same shall judge you [Vulg.: 'him'] in the last day." Therefore there will be a Judgment at the last day besides that which takes place in the present time.

*I answer that,* Judgment cannot be passed perfectly upon any changeable subject before its consummation: just as judgment cannot be given perfectly regarding the quality of any action before its completion in itself and in its results: because many actions appear to be profitable, which in their effects prove to be hurtful. And in the same way perfect judgment cannot be passed upon any man before the close of his life, since he can be changed in many respects from good to evil, or conversely, or from good to better, or from evil to worse. Hence the Apostle says (Heb. 9:27): "It is appointed unto men once to die, and after this the Judgment."

But it must be observed that although man's temporal life in itself ends with death, still it continues dependent in a measure on what comes after it in the future. In one way, as it still lives on in men's memories, in which sometimes, contrary to the truth, good or evil reputations linger on. In another way in a man's children, who are so to speak something of their parent, according to Ecclus. 30:4: "His father is dead, and he is as if he were not dead, for he hath left one behind him that is like himself." And yet many good men have wicked sons, and conversely. Thirdly, as to the result of his actions: just as from the deceit of Arius and other false leaders unbelief continues to flourish down to the close of the world; and even until then faith will continue to derive its progress from the preaching of the apostles. In a fourth way, as to the body, which is sometimes buried with honor and sometimes left unburied, and finally falls to dust utterly. In a fifth way, as to the things upon which a man's heart is set, such as temporal concerns, for example, some of which quickly lapse, while others endure longer.

Now all these things are submitted to the verdict of the Divine Judgment; and consequently, a perfect and public Judgment cannot be made of all these things during the course of this present time. Wherefore, there must be a final Judgment at the last day, in which everything concerning every man in every respect shall be perfectly and publicly judged.

Reply Obj. 1: Some men have held the opinion that the souls of the saints shall not be rewarded in heaven, nor the souls of the lost punished in hell, until the Judgment-day. That this is false appears from the testimony of the Apostle (2 Cor. 5:8), where he says: "We are confident and have a good will to be absent rather from the body, and to be present with the Lord": that is, not to "walk by faith" but "by sight," as appears from the context. But this is to see God in His Essence, wherein consists "eternal life," as is clear from John 17:3. Hence it is manifest that the souls separated from bodies are in eternal life.

Consequently, it must be maintained that after death man enters into an unchangeable state as to all that concerns the soul: and therefore there is no need for postponing judgment as to the reward of the soul. But since there are some other things pertaining to a man which go on through the whole course of time, and which are not foreign to the Divine judgment, all these things must be brought to judgment at the end of time. For although in regard to such things a man neither merits nor demerits, still in a measure they accompany his reward or punishment. Consequently all these things must be weighed in the final judgment.

Reply Obj. 2: "God shall not judge twice the same thing," i.e. in the same respect; but it is not unseemly for God to judge twice according to different respects.

Reply Obj. 3: Although the reward or punishment of the body depends upon the reward or punishment of the soul, nevertheless, since the soul is changeable only accidentally, on account of the body, once it is separated from the body it enters into an unchangeable condition, and receives its judgment. But the body remains subject to change down to the close of time: and therefore it must receive its reward or punishment then, in the last Judgment.

SIXTH ARTICLE [III, Q. 59, Art. 6]

Whether Christ's Judiciary Power Extends to the Angels?

Objection 1: It would seem that Christ's judiciary power does not extend to the angels, because the good and wicked angels alike were judged in the beginning of the world, when some fell through sin while others were confirmed in bliss. But those already judged have no need of being judged again. Therefore Christ's judiciary power does not extend to the angels.

Obj. 2: Further, the same person cannot be both judge and judged. But the angels will come to judge with Christ, according to Matt. 25:31: "When the Son of Man shall come in His majesty, and all the angels with Him." Therefore it seems that the angels will not be judged by Christ.

Obj. 3: Further, the angels are higher than other creatures. If Christ, then, be judge not only of men but likewise of angels, then for the same reason He will be judge of all creatures; which seems to be false, since this belongs to God's providence: hence it is written (Job 34:13): "What other hath He appointed over the earth? or whom hath He set over the world which He made?" Therefore Christ is not the judge of the angels.

*On the contrary,* The Apostle says (1 Cor. 6:3): "Know you not that we shall judge angels?" But the saints judge only by Christ's authority. Therefore, much more does Christ possess judiciary power over the angels.

*I answer that,* The angels are subjects of Christ's judiciary power, not only with regard to His Divine Nature, as He is the Word of God, but also with regard to His human nature. And this is evident from three considerations. First of all, from the closeness of His assumed nature to God; because, according to Heb. 2:16: "For nowhere doth He take hold of the angels, but of the seed of Abraham He taketh hold." Consequently, Christ's soul is more filled with the truth of the Word of God than any angel: for which reason He also enlightens the angels, as Dionysius says (Coel. Hier. vii), and so He has power to judge them. Secondly, because by the lowliness of His Passion, human nature in Christ merited to be exalted above the angels; so that, as is said in Phil. 2:10: "In the name of Jesus every knee should bow, of those that are in heaven, on earth, and under the earth." And therefore Christ has judiciary power even over the good and wicked angels: in token whereof it is said in the Apocalypse (7:11) that "all the angels stood round about the throne." Thirdly, on account of what they do for men, of whom Christ is the Head in a special manner. Hence it is written (Heb. 1:14): "They are [Vulg.: 'Are they not'] all ministering spirits, sent to minister for them, who shall receive the inheritance of salvation (?)." But they are submitted to Christ's judgment, first, as regards the dispensing of those things which are done through them; which dispensing is likewise done by the Man Christ, to whom the angels ministered, as related (Matt. 4:11), and from whom the devils besought that they might be sent into the swine, according to Matt. 8:31. Secondly, as to other accidental rewards of the good angels, such as the joy which they have at the salvation of men, according to Luke 15:10: "There shall be joy before the angels of God upon one sinner doing penance": and furthermore as to the accidental punishments of the devils wherewith they are either tormented here, or are shut up in hell; and this also belongs to the Man Christ: hence it is written (Mk. 1:24) that the devil cried out: "What have we to do with thee, Jesus of Nazareth? art Thou come to destroy us?" Thirdly, as to the essential reward of the good angels, which is everlasting bliss; and as to the essential punishment of the wicked angels, which is everlasting damnation. But this was done by Christ from the beginning of the world, inasmuch as He is the Word of God.

Reply Obj. 1: This argument considers judgment as to the essential reward and chief punishment.

Reply Obj. 2: As Augustine says (De Vera Relig. xxxi): "Although the spiritual man judgeth all things, still he is judged by Truth Itself." Consequently, although the angels judge, as being spiritual creatures, still they are judged by Christ, inasmuch as He is the Truth.

Reply Obj. 3: Christ judges not only the angels, but also the administration of all creatures. For if, as Augustine says (De Trin. iii) the lower things are ruled by God through the higher, in a certain order, it must be said that all things are ruled by Christ's soul, which is above every creature. Hence the Apostle says (Heb. 2:5): "For God hath not subjected unto angels the world to come"--subject namely to Christ--"of whom we speak" [Douay: 'whereof we speak'] [*The words "subject namely to Christ" are from a gloss]. Nor does it follow that God set another over the earth; since one and the same Person is God and Man, our Lord Jesus Christ.

Let what has been said of the Mystery of His Incarnation suffice for the present.

TREATISE ON THE SACRAMENTS (QQ. 60-90)

# QUESTION 60

WHAT IS A SACRAMENT? (In Eight Articles)

After considering those things that concern the mystery of the incarnate Word, we must consider the sacraments of the Church which derive their efficacy from the Word incarnate Himself. First we shall consider the sacraments in general; secondly, we shall consider specially each sacrament.

Concerning the first our consideration will be fivefold: (1) What is a sacrament? (2) Of the necessity of the sacraments; (3) of the effects of the sacraments; (4) Of their cause; (5) Of their number.

Under the first heading there are eight points of inquiry:

(1) Whether a sacrament is a kind of sign?

(2) Whether every sign of a sacred thing is a sacrament?

(3) Whether a sacrament is a sign of one thing only, or of several?

(4) Whether a sacrament is a sign that is something sensible?

(5) Whether some determinate sensible thing is required for a sacrament?

(6) Whether signification expressed by words is necessary for a sacrament?

(7) Whether determinate words are required?

(8) Whether anything may be added to or subtracted from these words?

FIRST ARTICLE [III, Q. 60, Art. 1]

Whether a Sacrament Is a Kind of Sign?

Objection 1: It seems that a sacrament is not a kind of sign. For sacrament appears to be derived from "sacring" ( sacrando ); just as medicament, from medicando (healing). But this seems to be of the nature of a cause rather than of a sign. Therefore a sacrament is a kind of cause rather than a kind of sign.

Obj. 2: Further, sacrament seems to signify something hidden, according to Tob. 12:7: "It is good to hide the secret ( sacramentum ) of a king"; and Eph. 3:9: "What is the dispensation of the mystery ( sacramenti ) which hath been hidden from eternity in God." But that which is hidden, seems foreign to the nature of a sign; for "a sign is that which conveys something else to the mind, besides the species which it impresses on the senses," as Augustine explains (De Doctr. Christ. ii). Therefore it seems that a sacrament is not a kind of sign.

Obj. 3: Further, an oath is sometimes called a sacrament: for it is written in the Decretals (Caus. xxii, qu. 5): "Children who have not attained the use of reason must not be obliged to swear: and whoever has foresworn himself once, must no more be a witness, nor be allowed to take a sacrament," i.e. an oath. But an oath is not a kind of sign, therefore it seems that a sacrament is not a kind of sign.

*On the contrary,* Augustine says (De Civ. Dei x): "The visible sacrifice is the sacrament, i.e. the sacred sign, of the invisible sacrifice."

*I answer that,* All things that are ordained to one, even in different ways, can be denominated from it: thus, from health which is in an animal, not only is the animal said to be healthy through being the subject of health: but medicine also is said to be healthy through producing health; diet through preserving it; and urine, through being a sign of health. Consequently, a thing may be called a "sacrament," either from having a certain hidden sanctity, and in this sense a sacrament is a "sacred secret"; or from having some relationship to this sanctity, which relationship may be that of a cause, or of a sign or of any other relation. But now we are speaking of sacraments in a special sense, as implying the habitude of sign: and in this way a sacrament is a kind of sign.

Reply Obj. 1: Because medicine is an efficient cause of health, consequently whatever things are denominated from medicine are to be referred to some first active cause: so that a medicament implies a certain causality. But sanctity from which a sacrament is denominated, is not there taken as an efficient cause, but rather as a formal or a final cause. Therefore it does not follow that a sacrament need always imply causality.

Reply Obj. 2: This argument considers sacrament in the sense of a "sacred secret." Now not only God's but also the king's, secret, is said to be sacred and to be a sacrament: because according to the ancients, whatever it was unlawful to lay violent hands on was said to be holy or sacrosanct, such as the city walls, and persons of high rank. Consequently those secrets, whether Divine or human, which it is unlawful to violate by making them known to anybody whatever, are called "sacred secrets or sacraments."

Reply Obj. 3: Even an oath has a certain relation to sacred things, in so far as it consists in calling a sacred thing to witness. And in this sense it is called a sacrament: not in the sense in which we speak of sacraments now; the word "sacrament" being thus used not equivocally but analogically, i.e. by reason of a different relation to the one thing, viz. something sacred.

SECOND ARTICLE [III, Q. 60, Art. 2]

Whether Every Sign of a Holy Thing Is a Sacrament?

Objection 1: It seems that not every sign of a sacred thing is a sacrament. For all sensible creatures are signs of sacred things; according to Rom. 1:20: "The invisible things of God are clearly seen being understood by the things that are made." And yet all sensible things cannot be called sacraments. Therefore not every sign of a sacred thing is a sacrament.

Obj. 2: Further, whatever was done under the Old Law was a figure of Christ Who is the "Holy of Holies" (Dan. 9:24), according to 1 Cor. 10:11: "All (these) things happened to them in figure"; and Col. 2:17: "Which are a shadow of things to come, but the body is Christ's." And yet not all that was done by the Fathers of the Old Testament, not even all the ceremonies of the Law, were sacraments, but only in certain special cases, as stated in the Second Part (I-II, Q. 101, A. 4). Therefore it seems that not every sign of a sacred thing is a sacrament.

Obj. 3: Further, even in the New Testament many things are done in sign of some sacred thing; yet they are not called sacraments; such as sprinkling with holy water, the consecration of an altar, and such like. Therefore not every sign of a sacred thing is a sacrament.

*On the contrary,* A definition is convertible with the thing defined. Now some define a sacrament as being "the sign of a sacred thing"; moreover, this is clear from the passage quoted above (A. 1) from Augustine. Therefore it seems that every sign of a sacred thing is a sacrament.

*I answer that,* Signs are given to men, to whom it is proper to discover the unknown by means of the known. Consequently a sacrament properly so called is that which is the sign of some sacred thing pertaining to man; so that properly speaking a sacrament, as considered by us now, is defined as being the "sign of a holy thing so far as it makes men holy."

Reply Obj. 1: Sensible creatures signify something holy, viz. Divine wisdom and goodness inasmuch as these are holy in themselves; but not inasmuch as we are made holy by them. Therefore they cannot be called sacraments as we understand sacraments now.

Reply Obj. 2: Some things pertaining to the Old Testament signified the holiness of Christ considered as holy in Himself. Others signified His holiness considered as the cause of our holiness; thus the sacrifice of the Paschal Lamb signified Christ's Sacrifice whereby we are made holy: and such like are properly styled sacraments of the Old Law.

Reply Obj. 3: Names are given to things considered in reference to their end and state of completeness. Now a disposition is not an end, whereas perfection is. Consequently things that signify disposition to holiness are not called sacraments, and with regard to these the objection is verified: only those are called sacraments which signify the perfection of holiness in man.

THIRD ARTICLE [III, Q. 60, Art. 3]

Whether a Sacrament Is a Sign of One Thing Only?

Objection 1: It seems that a sacrament is a sign of one thing only. For that which signifies many things is an ambiguous sign, and consequently occasions deception: this is clearly seen in equivocal words. But all deception should be removed from the Christian religion, according to Col. 2:8: "Beware lest any man cheat you by philosophy and vain deceit." Therefore it seems that a sacrament is not a sign of several things.

Obj. 2: Further, as stated above (A. 2), a sacrament signifies a holy thing in so far as it makes man holy. But there is only one cause of man's holiness, viz. the blood of Christ; according to Heb. 13:12: "Jesus, that He might sanctify the people by His own blood, suffered without the gate." Therefore it seems that a sacrament does not signify several things.

Obj. 3: Further, it has been said above (A. 2, ad 3) that a sacrament signifies properly the very end of sanctification. Now the end of sanctification is eternal life, according to Rom. 6:22: "You have your fruit unto sanctification, and the end life everlasting." Therefore it seems that the sacraments signify one thing only, viz. eternal life.

*On the contrary,* In the Sacrament of the Altar, two things are signified, viz. Christ's true body, and Christ's mystical body; as Augustine says (Liber Sent. Prosper.).

*I answer that,* As stated above (A. 2) a sacrament properly speaking is that which is ordained to signify our sanctification. In which three things may be considered; viz. the very cause of our sanctification, which is Christ's passion; the form of our sanctification, which is grace and the virtues; and the ultimate end of our sanctification, which is eternal life. And all these are signified by the sacraments. Consequently a sacrament is a sign that is both a reminder of the past, i.e. the passion of Christ; and an indication of that which is effected in us by Christ's passion, i.e. grace; and a prognostic, that is, a foretelling of future glory.

Reply Obj. 1: Then is a sign ambiguous and the occasion of deception, when it signifies many things not ordained to one another. But when it signifies many things inasmuch as, through being mutually ordained, they form one thing, then the sign is not ambiguous but certain: thus this word "man" signifies the soul and body inasmuch as together they form the human nature. In this way a sacrament signifies the three things aforesaid, inasmuch as by being in a certain order they are one thing.

Reply Obj. 2: Since a sacrament signifies that which sanctifies, it must needs signify the effect, which is implied in the sanctifying cause as such.

Reply Obj. 3: It is enough for a sacrament that it signify that perfection which consists in the form, nor is it necessary that it should signify only that perfection which is the end.

FOURTH ARTICLE [III, Q. 60, Art. 4]

Whether a Sacrament Is Always Something Sensible?

Objection 1: It seems that a sacrament is not always something sensible. Because, according to the Philosopher (Prior. Anal. ii), every effect is a sign of its cause. But just as there are some sensible effects, so are there some intelligible effects; thus science is the effect of a demonstration. Therefore not every sign is sensible. Now all that is required for a sacrament is something that is a sign of some sacred thing, inasmuch as thereby man is sanctified, as stated above (A. 2). Therefore something sensible is not required for a sacrament.

Obj. 2: Further, sacraments belong to the kingdom of God and the Divine worship. But sensible things do not seem to belong to the Divine worship: for we are told (John 4:24) that "God is a spirit; and they that adore Him, must adore Him in spirit and in truth"; and (Rom. 14:17) that "the kingdom of God is not meat and drink." Therefore sensible things are not required for the sacraments.

Obj. 3: Further, Augustine says (De Lib. Arb. ii) that "sensible things are goods of least account, since without them man can live aright." But the sacraments are necessary for man's salvation, as we shall show farther on (Q. 61, A. 1): so that man cannot live aright without them. Therefore sensible things are not required for the sacraments.

*On the contrary,* Augustine says (Tract. lxxx super Joan.): "The word is added to the element and this becomes a sacrament"; and he is speaking there of water which is a sensible element. Therefore sensible things are required for the sacraments.

*I answer that,* Divine wisdom provides for each thing according to its mode; hence it is written (Wis. 8:1) that "she . . . ordereth all things sweetly": wherefore also we are told (Matt. 25:15) that she "gave to everyone according to his proper ability." Now it is part of man's nature to acquire knowledge of the intelligible from the sensible. But a sign is that by means of which one attains to the knowledge of something else. Consequently, since the sacred things which are signified by the sacraments, are the spiritual and intelligible goods by means of which man is sanctified, it follows that the sacramental signs consist in sensible things: just as in the Divine Scriptures spiritual things are set before us under the guise of things sensible. And hence it is that sensible things are required for the sacraments; as Dionysius also proves in his book on the heavenly hierarchy (Coel. Hier. i).

Reply Obj. 1: The name and definition of a thing is taken principally from that which belongs to a thing primarily and essentially: and not from that which belongs to it through something else. Now a sensible effect being the primary and direct object of man's knowledge (since all our knowledge springs from the senses) by its very nature leads to the knowledge of something else: whereas intelligible effects are not such as to be able to lead us to the knowledge of something else, except in so far as they are manifested by some other thing, i.e. by certain sensibles. It is for this reason that the name sign is given primarily and principally to things which are offered to the senses; hence Augustine says (De Doctr. Christ. ii) that a sign "is that which conveys something else to the mind, besides the species which it impresses on the senses." But intelligible effects do not partake of the nature of a sign except in so far as they are pointed out by certain signs. And in this way, too, certain things which are not sensible are termed sacraments as it were, in so far as they are signified by certain sensible things, of which we shall treat further on (Q. 63, A. 1, ad 2; A. 3, ad 2; Q. 73, A. 6; Q. 74, A. 1, ad 3).

Reply Obj. 2: Sensible things considered in their own nature do not belong to the worship or kingdom of God: but considered only as signs of spiritual things in which the kingdom of God consists.

Reply Obj. 3: Augustine speaks there of sensible things, considered in their nature; but not as employed to signify spiritual things, which are the highest goods.

FIFTH ARTICLE [III, Q. 60, Art. 5]

Whether Determinate Things Are Required for a Sacrament?

Objection 1: It seems that determinate things are not required for a sacrament. For sensible things are required in sacraments for the purpose of signification, as stated above (A. 4). But nothing hinders the same thing being signified by divers sensible things: thus in Holy Scripture God is signified metaphorically, sometimes by a stone (2 Kings 22:2; Zech. 3:9; 1 Cor. 10:4; Apoc. 4:3); sometimes by a lion (Isa. 31:4; Apoc. 5:5); sometimes by the sun (Isa. 60:19, 20; Mal. 4:2), or by something similar. Therefore it seems that divers things can be suitable to the same sacrament. Therefore determinate things are not required for the sacraments.

Obj. 2: Further, the health of the soul is more necessary than that of the body. But in bodily medicines, which are ordained to the health of the body, one thing can be substituted for another which happens to be wanting. Therefore much more in the sacraments, which are spiritual remedies ordained to the health of the soul, can one thing be substituted for another when this happens to be lacking.

Obj. 3: Further, it is not fitting that the salvation of men be restricted by the Divine Law: still less by the Law of Christ, Who came to save all. But in the state of the Law of nature determinate things were not required in the sacraments, but were put to that use through a vow, as appears from Gen. 28, where Jacob vowed that he would offer to God tithes and peace-offerings. Therefore it seems that man should not have been restricted, especially under the New Law, to the use of any determinate thing in the sacraments.

*On the contrary,* our Lord said (John 3:5): "Unless a man be born again of water and the Holy Ghost, he cannot enter into the kingdom of God."

*I answer that,* In the use of the sacraments two things may be considered, namely, the worship of God, and the sanctification of man: the former of which pertains to man as referred to God, and the latter pertains to God in reference to man. Now it is not for anyone to determine that which is in the power of another, but only that which is in his own power. Since, therefore, the sanctification of man is in the power of God Who sanctifies, it is not for man to decide what things should be used for his sanctification, but this should be determined by Divine institution. Therefore in the sacraments of the New Law, by which man is sanctified according to 1 Cor. 6:11, "You are washed, you are sanctified," we must use those things which are determined by Divine institution.

Reply Obj. 1: Though the same thing can be signified by divers signs, yet to determine which sign must be used belongs to the signifier. Now it is God Who signifies spiritual things to us by means of the sensible things in the sacraments, and of similitudes in the Scriptures. And consequently, just as the Holy Ghost decides by what similitudes spiritual things are to be signified in certain passages of

Scripture, so also must it be determined by Divine institution what things are to be employed for the purpose of signification in this or that sacrament.

Reply Obj. 2: Sensible things are endowed with natural powers conducive to the health of the body: and therefore if two of them have the same virtue, it matters not which we use. Yet they are ordained unto sanctification not through any power that they possess naturally, but only in virtue of the Divine institution. And therefore it was necessary that God should determine the sensible things to be employed in the sacraments.

Reply Obj. 3: As Augustine says (Contra Faust. xix), diverse sacraments suit different times; just as different times are signified by different parts of the verb, viz. present, past, and future. Consequently, just as under the state of the Law of nature man was moved by inward instinct and without any outward law, to worship God, so also the sensible things to be employed in the worship of God were determined by inward instinct. But later on it became necessary for a law to be given (to man) from without: both because the Law of nature had become obscured by man's sins; and in order to signify more expressly the grace of Christ, by which the human race is sanctified. And hence the need for those things to be determinate, of which men have to make use in the sacraments. Nor is the way of salvation narrowed thereby: because the things which need to be used in the sacraments, are either in everyone's possession or can be had with little trouble.

SIXTH ARTICLE [III, Q. 60, Art. 5]

Whether Words Are Required for the Signification of the Sacraments?

Objection 1: It seems that words are not required for the signification of the sacraments. For Augustine says (Contra Faust. xix): "What else is a corporeal sacrament but a kind of visible word?" Wherefore to add words to the sensible things in the sacraments seems to be the same as to add words to words. But this is superfluous. Therefore words are not required besides the sensible things in the sacraments.

Obj. 2: Further, a sacrament is some one thing, but it does not seem possible to make one thing of those that belong to different genera. Since, therefore, sensible things and words are of different genera, for sensible things are the product of nature, but words, of reason; it seems that in the sacraments, words are not required besides sensible things.

Obj. 3: Further, the sacraments of the New Law succeed those of the Old Law: since "the former were instituted when the latter were abolished," as Augustine says (Contra Faust. xix). But no form of words was required in the sacraments of the Old Law. Therefore neither is it required in those of the New Law.

*On the contrary,* The Apostle says (Eph. 5:25, 26): "Christ loved the Church, and delivered Himself up for it; that He might sanctify it, cleansing it by the laver of water in the word of life." And Augustine says (Tract. xxx in Joan.): "The word is added to the element, and this becomes a sacrament."

*I answer that,* The sacraments, as stated above (AA. 2, 3), are employed as signs for man's sanctification. Consequently they can be considered in three ways: and in each way it is fitting for words to be added to the sensible signs. For in the first place they can be considered in regard to the cause of sanctification, which is the Word incarnate: to Whom the sacraments have a certain conformity, in that the word is joined to the sensible sign, just as in the mystery of the Incarnation the Word of God is united to sensible flesh.

Secondly, sacraments may be considered on the part of man who is sanctified, and who is composed of soul and body: to whom the sacramental remedy is adjusted, since it touches the body through the sensible element, and the soul through faith in the words. Hence Augustine says (Tract. lxxx in Joan.) on John 15:3, "Now you are clean by reason of the word," etc.: "Whence hath water this so great virtue, to touch the body and wash the heart, but by the word doing it, not because it is spoken, but because it is believed?"

Thirdly, a sacrament may be considered on the part of the sacramental signification. Now Augustine says (De Doctr. Christ. ii) that "words are the principal signs used by men"; because words can be formed in various ways for the purpose of signifying various mental concepts, so that we are able to express our thoughts with greater distinctness by means of words. And therefore in order to insure the perfection of sacramental signification it was necessary to determine the signification of the sensible things by means of certain words. For water may signify both a cleansing by reason of its humidity, and refreshment by reason of its being cool: but when we say, "I baptize thee," it is clear that we use water in baptism in order to signify a spiritual cleansing.

Reply Obj. 1: The sensible elements of the sacraments are called words by way of a certain likeness, in so far as they partake of a certain significative power, which resides principally in the very words, as stated above. Consequently it is not a superfluous repetition to add words to the visible element in the sacraments; because one determines the other, as stated above.

Reply Obj. 2: Although words and other sensible things are not in the same genus, considered in their natures, yet have they something in common as to the thing signified by them: which is more perfectly done in words than in other things. Wherefore in the sacraments, words and things, like form and matter, combine in the formation of one thing, in so far as the signification of things is completed by means of words, as above stated. And under words are comprised also sensible actions, such as cleansing and anointing and such like: because they have a like signification with the things.

Reply Obj. 3: As Augustine says (Contra Faust. xix), the sacraments of things present should be different from sacraments of things to come. Now the sacraments of the Old Law foretold the coming of Christ. Consequently they did not signify Christ so clearly as the sacraments of the New Law, which flow from Christ Himself, and have a certain likeness to Him, as stated above. Nevertheless in the Old Law, certain words were used in things pertaining to the worship of God, both by the priests, who were the ministers of those sacraments, according to Num. 6:23, 24: "Thus shall you bless the children of Israel, and you shall say to them: The Lord bless thee," etc.; and by those who made use of those sacraments, according to Deut. 26:3: "I profess this day before the Lord thy God," etc.

SEVENTH ARTICLE [III, Q. 60, Art. 7]

Whether Determinate Words Are Required in the Sacraments?

Objection 1: It seems that determinate words are not required in the sacraments. For as the Philosopher says (Peri Herm. i), "words are not the same for all." But salvation, which is sought through the sacraments, is the same for all. Therefore determinate words are not required in the sacraments.

Obj. 2: Further, words are required in the sacraments forasmuch as they are the principal means of signification, as stated above (A. 6). But it happens that various words mean the same. Therefore determinate words are not required in the sacraments.

Obj. 3: Further, corruption of anything changes its species. But some corrupt the pronunciation of words, and yet it is not credible that the sacramental effect is hindered thereby; else unlettered men and stammerers, in conferring sacraments, would frequently do so invalidly. Therefore it seems that determinate words are not required in the sacraments.

*On the contrary,* our Lord used determinate words in consecrating the sacrament of the Eucharist, when He said (Matt. 26:26): "This is My Body." Likewise He commanded His disciples to baptize under a form of determinate words, saying (Matt. 28:19): "Go ye and teach all nations, baptizing them in the name of the Father, and of the Son, and of the Holy Ghost."

*I answer that,* As stated above (A. 6, ad 2), in the sacraments the words are as the form, and sensible things are as the matter. Now in all things composed of matter and form, the determining principle is on the part of the form, which is as it were the end and terminus of the matter. Consequently for the being of a thing the need of a determinate form is prior to the need of determinate matter: for determinate matter is needed that it may be adapted to the determinate form. Since, therefore, in the sacraments determinate sensible things are required, which are as the sacramental matter, much more is there need in them of a determinate form of words.

Reply Obj. 1: As Augustine says (Tract. lxxx super Joan.), the word operates in the sacraments "not because it is spoken," i.e. not by the outward sound of the voice, "but because it is believed" in accordance with the sense of the words which is held by faith. And this sense is indeed the same for all, though the same words as to their sound be not used by all. Consequently no matter in what language this sense is expressed, the sacrament is complete.

Reply Obj. 2: Although it happens in every language that various words signify the same thing, yet one of those words is that which those who speak that language use principally and more commonly to signify that particular thing: and this is the word which should be used for the sacramental signification. So also among sensible things, that one is used for the sacramental signification which is most commonly employed for the action by which the sacramental effect is signified: thus water is most commonly used by men for bodily cleansing, by which the spiritual cleansing is signified: and therefore water is employed as the matter of baptism.

Reply Obj. 3: If he who corrupts the pronunciation of the sacramental words--does so on purpose, he does not seem to intend to do what the Church intends: and thus the sacrament seems to be defective. But if he do this through error or a slip of the tongue, and if he so far mispronounce the words as to deprive them of sense, the sacrament seems to be defective. This would be the case especially if the mispronunciation be in the beginning of a word, for instance, if one were to say "in nomine matris" instead of "in nomine Patris." If, however, the sense of the words be not entirely lost by this mispronunciation, the sacrament is complete. This would be the case principally if the end of a word be mispronounced; for instance, if one were to say "patrias et filias." For although the words thus mispronounced have no appointed meaning, yet we allow them an accommodated meaning corresponding to the usual forms of speech. And so, although the sensible sound is changed, yet the sense remains the same.

What has been said about the various mispronunciations of words, either at the beginning or at the end, holds forasmuch as with us a change at the beginning of a word changes the meaning, whereas a change at the end generally speaking does not effect such a change: whereas with the Greeks the sense is changed also in the beginning of words in the conjugation of verbs.

Nevertheless the princip[al] point to observe is the extent of the corruption entailed by mispronunciation: for in either case it may be so little that it does not alter the sense of the words; or so great that it destroys it. But it is easier for the one to happen on the part of the beginning of the words, and the other at the end.

EIGHTH ARTICLE [III, Q. 60, Art. 8]

Whether It Is Lawful to Add Anything to the Words in Which the Sacramental Form Consists?

Objection 1: It seems that it is not lawful to add anything to the words in which the sacramental form consists. For these sacramental words are not of less importance than are the words of Holy Scripture. But it is not lawful to add anything to, or to take anything from, the words of Holy Scripture: for it is written (Deut. 4:2): "You shall not add to the word that I speak to you, neither shall you take away from it"; and (Apoc. 22:18, 19): "I testify to everyone that heareth the words of the prophecy of this book: if any man shall add to these things, God shall add to him the plagues written in this book. And if any man shall take away . . . God shall take away his part out of the book of life." Therefore it seems that neither is it lawful to add anything to, or to take anything from, the sacramental forms.

Obj. 2: Further, in the sacraments words are by way of form, as stated above (A. 6, ad 2; A. 7). But any addition or subtraction in forms changes the species, as also in numbers (Metaph. viii). Therefore it seems that if anything be added to or subtracted from a sacramental form, it will not be the same sacrament.

Obj. 3: Further, just as the sacramental form demands a certain number of words, so does it require that these words should be pronounced in a certain order and without interruption. If therefore, the sacrament is not rendered invalid by addition or subtraction of words, in like manner it seems that neither is it, if the words be pronounced in a different order or with interruptions.

*On the contrary,* Certain words are inserted by some in the sacramental forms, which are not inserted by others: thus the Latins baptize under this form: "I baptize thee in the name of the Father, and of the Son, and of the Holy Ghost"; whereas the Greeks use the following form: "The servant of God, N . . . is baptized in the name of the Father," etc. Yet both confer the sacrament validly. Therefore it is lawful to add something to, or to take something from, the sacramental forms.

*I answer that,* With regard to all the variations that may occur in the sacramental forms, two points seem to call for our attention. One is on the part of the person who says the words, and whose intention is essential to the sacrament, as will be explained further on (Q. 64, A. 8). Wherefore if he intends by such addition or suppression to perform a rite other from that which is recognized by the Church, it seems that the sacrament is invalid: because he seems not to intend to do what the Church does.

The other point to be considered is the meaning of the words. For since in the sacraments, the words produce an effect according to the sense which they convey, as stated above (A. 7, ad 1), we must see whether the change of words destroys the essential sense of the words: because then the sacrament is clearly rendered invalid. Now it is clear, if any substantial part of the sacramental form be suppressed, that the essential sense of the words is destroyed; and consequently the sacrament is invalid. Wherefore Didymus says (De Spir. Sanct. ii): "If anyone attempt to baptize in such a way as to omit one of the aforesaid names," i.e. of the Father, Son, and Holy Ghost, "his baptism will be invalid." But if that which is omitted be not a substantial part of the form, such an omission does not destroy the essential sense of the words, nor consequently the validity of the sacrament. Thus in the form of the Eucharist--"For this is My Body," the omission of the word "for" does not destroy the essential sense of the words, nor consequently cause the sacrament to be invalid; although perhaps he who makes the omission may sin from negligence or contempt.

Again, it is possible to add something that destroys the essential sense of the words: for instance, if one were to say: "I baptize thee in the name of the Father Who is greater, and of the Son Who is less," with which form the Arians baptized: and consequently such an addition makes the sacrament invalid. But if the addition be such as not to destroy the essential sense, the sacrament is not rendered invalid. Nor does it matter whether this addition be made at the beginning, in the middle, or at the end: For instance, if one were to say, "I baptize thee in the name of the Father Almighty, and of the only Begotten Son, and of the Holy Ghost, the Paraclete," the baptism would be valid; and in like manner if one were to say, "I baptize thee in the name of the Father, and of the Son, and of the Holy Ghost; and may the Blessed Virgin succour thee," the baptism would be valid.

Perhaps, however, if one were to say, "I baptize thee in the name of the Father, and of the Son, and of the Holy Ghost, and of the Blessed Virgin Mary," the baptism would be void; because it is written (1 Cor. 1:13): "Was Paul crucified for you or were you baptized in the name of Paul?" But this is true if the intention be to baptize in the name of the Blessed Virgin as in the name of the Trinity, by which baptism is consecrated: for such a sense would be contrary to faith, and would therefore render the sacrament invalid: whereas if the addition, "and in the name of the Blessed Virgin" be understood, not as if the name of the Blessed Virgin effected anything in baptism, but as intimating that her intercession may help the person baptized to preserve the baptismal grace, then the sacrament is not rendered void.

Reply Obj. 1: It is not lawful to add anything to the words of Holy Scripture as regards the sense; but many words are added by Doctors by way of explanation of the Holy Scriptures. Nevertheless, it is not lawful to add even words to Holy Scripture as though such words were a part thereof, for this would amount to forgery. It would amount to the same if anyone were to pretend that something is essential to a sacramental form, which is not so.

Reply Obj. 2: Words belong to a sacramental form by reason of the sense signified by them. Consequently any addition or suppression of words which does not add to or take from the essential sense, does not destroy the essence of the sacrament.

Reply Obj. 3: If the words are interrupted to such an extent that the intention of the speaker is interrupted, the sacramental sense is destroyed, and consequently, the validity of the sacrament. But this is not the case if the interruption of the speaker is so slight, that his intention and the sense of the words is not interrupted.

The same is to be said of a change in the order of the words. Because if this destroys the sense of the words, the sacrament is invalidated: as happens when a negation is made to precede or follow a word. But if the order is so changed that the sense of the words does not vary, the sacrament is not invalidated, according to the Philosopher's dictum: "Nouns and verbs mean the same though they be transposed" (Peri Herm. x).

## QUESTION 61

OF THE NECESSITY OF THE SACRAMENTS (In Four Articles)

We must now consider the necessity of the sacraments; concerning which there are four points of inquiry:

(1) Whether sacraments are necessary for man's salvation?

(2) Whether they were necessary in the state that preceded sin?

(3) Whether they were necessary in the state after sin and before Christ?

(4) Whether they were necessary after Christ's coming?

FIRST ARTICLE [III, Q. 61, Art. 1]

Whether Sacraments Are Necessary for Man's Salvation?

Objection 1: It seems that sacraments are not necessary for man's salvation. For the Apostle says (1 Tim. 4:8): "Bodily exercise is profitable to little." But the use of sacraments pertains to bodily exercise; because sacraments are perfected in the signification of sensible things and words, as stated above (Q. 60, A. 6). Therefore sacraments are not necessary for the salvation of man.

Obj. 2: Further, the Apostle was told (2 Cor. 12:9): "My grace is sufficient for thee." But it would not suffice if sacraments were necessary for salvation. Therefore sacraments are not necessary for man's salvation.

Obj. 3: Further, given a sufficient cause, nothing more seems to be required for the effect. But Christ's Passion is the sufficient cause of our salvation; for the Apostle says (Rom. 5:10): "If, when we were enemies, we were reconciled to God by the death of His Son: much more, being reconciled, shall we be saved by His life." Therefore sacraments are not necessary for man's salvation.

*On the contrary,* Augustine says (Contra Faust. xix): "It is impossible to keep men together in one religious denomination, whether true or false, except they be united by means of visible signs or sacraments." But it is necessary for salvation that men be united together in the name of the one true religion. Therefore sacraments are necessary for man's salvation.

*I answer that,* Sacraments are necessary unto man's salvation for three reasons. The first is taken from the condition of human nature which is such that it has to be led by things corporeal and sensible to things spiritual and intelligible. Now it belongs to Divine providence to provide for each one according as its condition requires. Divine wisdom, therefore, fittingly provides man with means of salvation, in the shape of corporeal and sensible signs that are called sacraments.

The second reason is taken from the state of man who in sinning subjected himself by his affections to corporeal things. Now the healing remedy should be given to a man so as to reach the part affected by disease. Consequently it was fitting that God should provide man with a spiritual medicine by means of certain corporeal signs; for if man were offered spiritual things without a veil, his mind being taken up with the material world would be unable to apply itself to them.

The third reason is taken from the fact that man is prone to direct his activity chiefly towards material things. Lest, therefore, it should be too hard for man to be drawn away entirely from bodily actions, bodily exercise was offered to him in the sacraments, by which he might be trained to avoid superstitious practices, consisting in the worship of demons, and all manner of harmful action, consisting in sinful deeds.

It follows, therefore, that through the institution of the sacraments man, consistently with his nature, is instructed through sensible things; he is humbled, through confessing that he is subject to corporeal things, seeing that he receives assistance through them: and he is even preserved from bodily hurt, by the healthy exercise of the sacraments.

Reply Obj. 1: Bodily exercise, as such, is not very profitable: but exercise taken in the use of the sacraments is not merely bodily, but to a certain extent spiritual, viz. in its signification and in its causality.

Reply Obj. 2: God's grace is a sufficient cause of man's salvation. But God gives grace to man in a way which is suitable to him. Hence it is that man needs the sacraments that he may obtain grace.

Reply Obj. 3: Christ's Passion is a sufficient cause of man's salvation. But it does not follow that the sacraments are not also necessary for that purpose: because they obtain their effect through the power of Christ's Passion; and Christ's Passion is, so to say, applied to man through the sacraments according to the Apostle (Rom. 6:3): "All we who are baptized in Christ Jesus, are baptized in His death."

SECOND ARTICLE [III, Q. 61, Art. 2]

Whether Before Sin Sacraments Were Necessary to Man?

Objection 1: It seems that before sin sacraments were necessary to man. For, as stated above (A. 1, ad 2) man needs sacraments that he may obtain grace. But man needed grace even in the state of innocence, as we stated in the First Part (Q. 95, A. 4; cf. I-II, Q. 109, A. 2; Q. 114, A. 2). Therefore sacraments were necessary in that state also.

Obj. 2: Further, sacraments are suitable to man by reason of the conditions of human nature, as stated above (A. 1). But man's nature is the same before and after sin. Therefore it seems that before sin, man needed the sacraments.

Obj. 3: Further, matrimony is a sacrament, according to Eph. 5:32: "This is a great sacrament; but I speak in Christ and in the Church." But matrimony was instituted before sin, as may be seen in Gen. 2. Therefore sacraments were necessary to man before sin.

*On the contrary,* None but the sick need remedies, according to Matt. 9:12: "They that are in health need not a physician." Now the sacraments are spiritual remedies for the healing of wounds inflicted by sin. Therefore they were not necessary before sin.

*I answer that,* Sacraments were not necessary in the state of innocence. This can be proved from the rectitude of that state, in which the higher (parts of man) ruled the lower, and nowise depended on them: for just as the mind was subject to God, so were the lower powers of the soul subject to the mind, and the body to the soul. And it would be contrary to this order if the soul were perfected either in knowledge or in grace, by anything corporeal; which happens in the sacraments. Therefore in the state of innocence man needed no sacraments, whether as remedies against sin or as means of perfecting the soul.

Reply Obj. 1: In the state of innocence man needed grace: not so that he needed to obtain grace by means of sensible signs, but in a spiritual and invisible manner.

Reply Obj. 2: Man's nature is the same before and after sin, but the state of his nature is not the same. Because after sin, the soul, even in its higher part, needs to receive something from corporeal things in order that it may be perfected: whereas man had no need of this in that state.

Reply Obj. 3: Matrimony was instituted in the state of innocence, not as a sacrament, but as a function of nature. Consequently, however, it foreshadowed something in relation to Christ and the Church: just as everything else foreshadowed Christ.

THIRD ARTICLE [III, Q. 61, Art. 3]

Whether There Should Have Been Sacraments After Sin, Before Christ?

Objection 1: It seems that there should have been no sacraments after sin, before Christ. For it has been stated that the Passion of Christ is applied to men through the sacraments: so that Christ's Passion is compared to the sacraments as cause to effect. But effect does not precede cause. Therefore there should have been no sacraments before Christ's coming.

Obj. 2: Further, sacraments should be suitable to the state of the human race, as Augustine declares (Contra Faust. xix). But the state of the human race underwent no change after sin until it was repaired by Christ. Neither, therefore, should the sacraments have been changed, so that besides the sacraments of the natural law, others should be instituted in the law of Moses.

Obj. 3: Further, the nearer a thing approaches to that which is perfect, the more like it should it be. Now the perfection of human salvation was accomplished by Christ; to Whom the sacraments of the Old Law were nearer than those that preceded the Law. Therefore they should have borne a greater likeness to the sacraments of Christ. And yet the contrary is the case, since it was foretold that the priesthood of Christ would be "according to the order of Melchisedech, and not . . . according to the order of Aaron" (Heb. 7:11). Therefore sacraments were unsuitably instituted before Christ.

*On the contrary,* Augustine says (Contra Faust. xix) that "the first sacraments which the Law commanded to be solemnized and observed were announcements of Christ's future coming." But it was necessary for man's salvation that Christ's coming should be announced beforehand. Therefore it was necessary that some sacraments should be instituted before Christ.

*I answer that,* Sacraments are necessary for man's salvation, in so far as they are sensible signs of invisible things whereby man is made holy. Now after sin no man can be made holy save through Christ, "Whom God hath proposed to be a propitiation, through faith in His blood, to the showing of His justice . . . that He Himself may be just, and the justifier of him who is of the faith of Jesus Christ" (Rom. 3:25, 26). Therefore before Christ's coming there was need for some visible signs whereby man might testify to his faith in the future coming of a Saviour. And these signs are called sacraments. It is therefore clear that some sacraments were necessary before Christ's coming.

Reply Obj. 1: Christ's Passion is the final cause of the old sacraments: for they were instituted in order to foreshadow it. Now the final cause precedes not in time, but in the intention of the agent. Consequently, there is no reason against the existence of sacraments before Christ's Passion.

Reply Obj. 2: The state of the human race after sin and before Christ can be considered from two points of view. First, from that of faith: and thus it was always one and the same: since men were made righteous, through faith in the future coming of Christ. Secondly, according as sin was more or less intense, and knowledge concerning Christ more or less explicit. For as time went on sin gained a greater hold on man, so much so that it clouded man's reason, the consequence being that the precepts of the natural law were insufficient to make man live aright, and it became necessary to have a written code of fixed laws, and together with these certain sacraments of faith. For it was necessary, as time went on, that the knowledge of faith should be more and more unfolded, since, as Gregory says (Hom. vi in Ezech.): "With the advance of time there was an advance in the knowledge of Divine things." Consequently in the old Law there was also a need for certain fixed sacraments significative of man's faith in the future coming of Christ: which sacraments are compared to those that preceded the Law, as something determinate to that which is indeterminate: inasmuch as before the Law it was not laid down precisely of what sacraments men were to make use: whereas this was prescribed by the Law; and this was necessary both on account of the overclouding of the natural law, and for the clearer signification of faith.

Reply Obj. 3: The sacrament of Melchisedech which preceded the Law is more like the Sacrament of the New Law in its matter: in so far as "he offered bread and wine" (Gen. 14:18), just as bread and wine are offered in the sacrifice of the New Testament. Nevertheless the sacraments of the Mosaic Law are more like the thing signified by the sacrament, i.e. the Passion of Christ: as clearly appears in the Paschal Lamb and such like. The reason of this was lest, if the sacraments retained the same appearance, it might seem to be the continuation of one and the same sacrament, where there was no interruption of time.

FOURTH ARTICLE [III, Q. 61, Art. 4]

Whether There Was Need for Any Sacraments After Christ Came?

Objection 1: It seems that there was no need for any sacraments after Christ came. For the figure should cease with the advent of the truth. But "grace and truth came by Jesus Christ" (John 1:17). Since, therefore, the sacraments are signs or figures of the truth, it seems that there was no need for any sacraments after Christ's Passion.

Obj. 2: Further, the sacraments consist in certain elements, as stated above (Q. 60, A. 4). But the Apostle says (Gal. 4:3, 4) that "when we were children we were serving under the elements of the world": but that now "when the fulness of time" has "come," we are no longer children. Therefore it seems that we should not serve God under the elements of this world, by making use of corporeal sacraments.

Obj. 3: Further, according to James 1:17 with God "there is no change, nor shadow of alteration." But it seems to argue some change in the Divine will that God should give man certain sacraments for his sanctification now during the time of grace, and other sacraments before Christ's coming. Therefore it seems that other sacraments should not have been instituted after Christ.

*On the contrary,* Augustine says (Contra Faust. xix) that the sacraments of the Old Law "were abolished because they were fulfilled; and others were instituted, fewer in number, but more efficacious, more profitable, and of easier accomplishment."

*I answer that,* As the ancient Fathers were saved through faith in Christ's future coming, so are we saved through faith in Christ's past birth and Passion. Now the sacraments are signs in protestation of the faith whereby man is justified; and signs should vary according as they signify the future, the past, or the present; for as Augustine says (Contra Faust. xix), "the same thing is variously pronounced as to be done and as having been done: for instance the word passurus (going to suffer) differs from passus (having suffered)." Therefore the sacraments of the New Law, that signify Christ in relation to the past, must needs differ from those of the Old Law, that foreshadowed the future.

Reply Obj. 1: As Dionysius says (Eccl. Hier. v), the state of the New Law. is between the state of the Old Law, whose figures are fulfilled in the New, and the state of glory, in which all truth will be openly and perfectly revealed. Wherefore then there will be no sacraments. But now, so long as we know "through a glass in a dark manner," (1 Cor. 13:12) we need sensible signs in order to reach spiritual things: and this is the province of the sacraments.

Reply Obj. 2: The Apostle calls the sacraments of the Old Law "weak and needy elements" (Gal. 4:9) because they neither contained nor caused grace. Hence the Apostle says that those who used these sacraments served God "under the elements of this world": for the very reason that these sacraments were nothing else than the elements of this world. But our sacraments both contain and cause grace: consequently the comparison does not hold.

Reply Obj. 3: Just as the head of the house is not proved to have a changeable mind, through issuing various commands to his household at various seasons, ordering things differently in winter and summer; so it does not follow that there is any change in God, because He instituted sacraments of one kind after Christ's coming, and of another kind at the time of the Law. Because the latter were suitable as foreshadowing grace; the former as signifying the presence of grace.

# QUESTION 62

OF THE SACRAMENTS' PRINCIPAL EFFECT, WHICH IS GRACE (In Six Articles)

We have now to consider the effect of the sacraments. First of their principal effect, which is grace; secondly, of their secondary effect, which is a character. Concerning the first there are six points of inquiry:

(1) Whether the sacraments of the New Law are the cause of grace?

(2) Whether sacramental grace confers anything in addition to the grace of the virtues and gifts?

(3) Whether the sacraments contain grace?

(4) Whether there is any power in them for the causing of grace?

(5) Whether the sacraments derive this power from Christ's Passion?

(6) Whether the sacraments of the Old Law caused grace?

FIRST ARTICLE [III, Q. 62, Art. 1]

Whether the Sacraments Are the Cause of Grace?

Objection 1: It seems that the sacraments are not the cause of grace. For it seems that the same thing is not both sign and cause: since the nature of sign appears to be more in keeping with an effect. But a sacrament is a sign of grace. Therefore it is not its cause.

Obj. 2: Further, nothing corporeal can act on a spiritual thing: since "the agent is more excellent than the patient," as Augustine says (Gen. ad lit. xii). But the subject of grace is the human mind, which is something spiritual. Therefore the sacraments cannot cause grace.

Obj. 3: Further, what is proper to God should not be ascribed to a creature. But it is proper to God to cause grace, according to Ps. 83:12: "The Lord will give grace and glory." Since, therefore, the sacraments consist in certain words and created things, it seems that they cannot cause grace.

*On the contrary,* Augustine says (Tract. lxxx in Joan.) that the baptismal water "touches the body and cleanses the heart." But the heart is not cleansed save through grace. Therefore it causes grace: and for like reason so do the other sacraments of the Church.

*I answer that,* We must needs say that in some way the sacraments of the New Law cause grace. For it is evident that through the sacraments of the New Law man is incorporated with Christ: thus the Apostle says of Baptism (Gal. 3:27): "As many of you as have been baptized in Christ have put on Christ." And man is made a member of Christ through grace alone.

Some, however, say that they are the cause of grace not by their own operation, but in so far as God causes grace in the soul when the sacraments are employed. And they give as an example a man who on presenting a leaden coin, receives, by the king's command, a hundred pounds: not as though the leaden coin, by any operation of its own, caused him to be given that sum of money; this being the effect of the mere will of the king. Hence Bernard says in a sermon on the Lord's Supper: "Just as a canon is invested by means of a book, an abbot by means of a crozier, a bishop by means of a ring, so by the various sacraments various kinds of grace are conferred." But if we examine the question properly, we shall see that according to the above mode the sacraments are mere signs. For the leaden coin is nothing but a sign of the king's command that this man should receive money. In like manner the book is a sign of the conferring of a canonry. Hence, according to this opinion the sacraments of the New Law would be mere signs of grace; whereas we have it on the authority of many saints that the sacraments of the New Law not only signify, but also cause grace.

We must therefore say otherwise, that an efficient cause is twofold, principal and instrumental. The principal cause works by the power of its form, to which form the effect is likened; just as fire by its own heat makes something hot. In this way none but God can cause grace: since grace is nothing else than a participated likeness of the Divine Nature, according to 2 Pet. 1:4: "He hath given us most great and precious promises; that we may be [Vulg.: 'you may be made'] partakers of the Divine Nature." But the instrumental cause works not by the power of its form, but only by the motion whereby it is moved by the principal agent: so that the effect is not likened to the instrument but to the principal agent: for instance, the couch is not like the axe, but like the art which is in the craftsman's mind. And it is thus that the sacraments of the New Law cause grace: for they are instituted by God to be employed for the purpose of conferring grace. Hence Augustine says (Contra Faust. xix): "All these things," viz. pertaining to the sacraments, "are done and pass away, but the power," viz. of God, "which works by them, remains ever." Now that is, properly speaking, an instrument by which someone works: wherefore it is written (Titus 3:5): "He saved us by the laver of regeneration."

Reply Obj. 1: The principal cause cannot properly be called a sign of its effect, even though the latter be hidden and the cause itself sensible and manifest. But an instrumental cause, if manifest, can be called a sign of a hidden effect, for this reason, that it is not merely a cause but also in a measure an effect in so far as it is moved by the principal agent. And in this sense the sacraments of the New Law are both cause and signs. Hence, too, is it that, to use the common expression, "they effect what they signify." From this it is clear that they perfectly fulfil the conditions of a sacrament; being ordained to something sacred, not only as a sign, but also as a cause.

Reply Obj. 2: An instrument has a twofold action; one is instrumental, in respect of which it works not by its own power but by the power of the principal agent: the other is its proper action, which belongs to it in respect of its proper form: thus it belongs to an axe to cut asunder by reason of its sharpness, but to make a couch, in so far as it is the instrument of an art. But it does not accomplish the instrumental action save by exercising its proper action: for it is by cutting that it makes a couch. In like manner the corporeal sacraments by their operation, which they exercise on the body that they touch, accomplish through the Divine institution an instrumental operation on the soul; for example, the water of baptism, in respect of its proper power, cleanses the body, and thereby, inasmuch as it is the instrument of the Divine power, cleanses the soul: since from soul and body one thing is made. And thus it is that Augustine says (Gen. ad lit. xii) that it "touches the body and cleanses the heart."

Reply Obj. 3: This argument considers that which causes grace as principal agent; for this belongs to God alone, as stated above.

SECOND ARTICLE [III, Q. 62, Art. 2]

Whether Sacramental Grace Confers Anything in Addition to the Grace of the Virtues and Gifts?

Objection 1: It seems that sacramental grace confers nothing in addition to the grace of the virtues and gifts. For the grace of the virtues and gifts perfects the soul sufficiently, both in its essence and in its powers; as is clear from what was said in the Second Part (I-II, Q. 110, AA. 3, 4). But grace is ordained to the perfecting of the soul. Therefore sacramental grace cannot confer anything in addition to the grace of the virtues and gifts.

Obj. 2: Further, the soul's defects are caused by sin. But all sins are sufficiently removed by the grace of the virtues and gifts: because there is no sin that is not contrary to some virtue. Since, therefore, sacramental grace is ordained to the removal of the soul's defects, it cannot confer anything in addition to the grace of the virtues and gifts.

Obj. 3: Further, every addition or subtraction of form varies the species (Metaph. viii). If, therefore, sacramental grace confers anything in addition to the grace of the virtues and gifts, it follows that it is called grace equivocally: and so we are none the wiser when it is said that the sacraments cause grace.

*On the contrary,* If sacramental grace confers nothing in addition to the grace of the virtues and gifts, it is useless to confer the sacraments on those who have the virtues and gifts. But there is nothing useless in God's works. Therefore it seems that sacramental grace confers something in addition to the grace of the virtues and gifts.

*I answer that,* As stated in the Second Part (I-II, Q. 110, AA. 3, 4), grace, considered in itself, perfects the essence of the soul, in so far as it is a certain participated likeness of the Divine Nature. And just as the soul's powers flow from its essence, so from grace there flow certain perfections into the powers of the soul, which are called virtues and gifts, whereby the powers are perfected in reference to their actions. Now the sacraments are ordained unto certain special effects which are necessary in the Christian life: thus Baptism is ordained unto a certain spiritual regeneration, by which man dies to vice and becomes a member of Christ: which effect is something special in addition to the actions of the soul's powers: and the same holds true of the other sacraments. Consequently just as the virtues and gifts confer, in addition to grace commonly so called, a certain special perfection ordained to the powers' proper actions, so does sacramental grace confer, over and above grace commonly so called, and in addition to the virtues and gifts, a certain Divine assistance in obtaining the end of the sacrament. It is thus that sacramental grace confers something in addition to the grace of the virtues and gifts.

Reply Obj. 1: The grace of the virtues and gifts perfects the essence and powers of the soul sufficiently as regards ordinary conduct: but as regards certain special effects which are necessary in a Christian life, sacramental grace is needed.

Reply Obj. 2: Vices and sins are sufficiently removed by virtues and gifts, as to present and future time, in so far as they prevent man from sinning. But in regard to past sins, the acts of which are transitory whereas their guilt remains, man is provided with a special remedy in the sacraments.

Reply Obj. 3: Sacramental grace is compared to grace commonly so called, as species to genus. Wherefore just as it is not equivocal to use the term "animal" in its generic sense, and as applied to a man, so neither is it equivocal to speak of grace commonly so called and of sacramental grace.

THIRD ARTICLE [III, Q. 62, Art. 3]

Whether the Sacraments of the New Law Contain Grace?

Objection 1: It seems that the sacraments of the New Law do not contain grace. For it seems that what is contained is in the container. But grace is not in the sacraments; neither as in a subject, because the subject of grace is not a body but a spirit; nor as in a vessel, for according toPhys. iv, "a vessel is a movable place," and an accident cannot be in a place. Therefore it seems that the sacraments of the New Law do not contain grace.

Obj. 2: Further, sacraments are instituted as means whereby men may obtain grace. But since grace is an accident it cannot pass from one subject to another. Therefore it would be of no account if grace were in the sacraments.

Obj. 3: Further, a spiritual thing is not contained by a corporeal, even if it be therein; for the soul is not contained by the body; rather does it contain the body. Since, therefore, grace is something spiritual, it seems that it cannot be contained in a corporeal sacrament.

*On the contrary,* Hugh of S. Victor says (De Sacram. i) that "a sacrament, through its being sanctified, contains an invisible grace."

*I answer that,* A thing is said to be in another in various ways; in two of which grace is said to be in the sacraments. First, as in its sign; for a sacrament is a sign of grace. Secondly, as in its cause; for, as stated above (A. 1) a sacrament of the New Law is an instrumental cause of grace. Wherefore grace is in a sacrament of the New Law, not as to its specific likeness, as an effect in its univocal cause; nor as to some proper and permanent form proportioned to such an effect, as effects in non-univocal causes, for instance, as things generated are in the sun; but as to a certain instrumental power transient and incomplete in its natural being, as will be explained later on (A. 4).

Reply Obj. 1: Grace is said to be in a sacrament not as in its subject; nor as in a vessel considered as a place, but understood as the instrument of some work to be done, according to Ezech. 9:1: "Everyone hath a destroying vessel [Douay: 'weapon'] in his hand."

Reply Obj. 2: Although an accident does not pass from one subject to another, nevertheless in a fashion it does pass from its cause into its subject through the instrument; not so that it be in each of these in the same way, but in each according to its respective nature.

Reply Obj. 3: If a spiritual thing exist perfectly in something, it contains it and is not contained by it. But, in a sacrament, grace has a passing and incomplete mode of being: and consequently it is not unfitting to say that the sacraments contain grace.

FOURTH ARTICLE [III, Q. 62, Art. 4]

Whether There Be in the Sacraments a Power of Causing Grace?

Objection 1: It seems that there is not in the sacraments a power of causing grace. For the power of causing grace is a spiritual power. But a spiritual power cannot be in a body; neither as proper to it, because power flows from a thing's essence and consequently cannot transcend it; nor as derived from something else, because that which is received into anything follows the mode of the recipient. Therefore in the sacraments there is no power of causing grace.

Obj. 2: Further, whatever exists is reducible to some kind of being and some degree of good. But there is no assignable kind of being to which such a power can belong; as anyone may see by running through them all. Nor is it reducible to some degree of good; for neither is it one of the goods of least account, since sacraments are necessary for salvation: nor is it an intermediate good, such as are the powers of the soul, which are natural powers; nor is it one of the greater goods, for it is neither grace nor a virtue of the mind. Therefore it seems that in the sacraments there is no power of causing grace.

Obj. 3: Further, if there be such a power in the sacraments, its presence there must be due to nothing less than a creative act of God. But it seems unbecoming that so excellent a being created by God should cease to exist as soon as the sacrament is complete. Therefore it seems that in the sacraments there is no power for causing grace.

Obj. 4: Further, the same thing cannot be in several. But several things concur in the completion of a sacrament, namely, words and things: while in one sacrament there can be but one power. Therefore it seems that there is no power of causing grace in the sacraments.

*On the contrary,* Augustine says (Tract. lxxx in Joan.): "Whence hath water so great power, that it touches the body and cleanses the heart?" And Bede says that "Our Lord conferred a power of regeneration on the waters by the contact of His most pure body."

*I answer that,* Those who hold that the sacraments do not cause grace save by a certain coincidence, deny the sacraments any power that is itself productive of the sacramental effect, and hold that the Divine power assists the sacraments and produces their effect. But if we hold that a sacrament is an instrumental cause of grace, we must needs allow that there is in the sacraments a certain instrumental power of bringing about the sacramental effects. Now such power is proportionate to the instrument: and consequently it stands in comparison to the complete and perfect power of anything, as the instrument to the principal agent. For an instrument, as stated above (A. 1), does not work save as moved by the principal agent, which works of itself. And therefore the power of the principal agent exists in nature completely and perfectly: whereas the instrumental power has a being that passes from one thing into another, and is incomplete; just as motion is an imperfect act passing from agent to patient.

Reply Obj. 1: A spiritual power cannot be in a corporeal subject, after the manner of a permanent and complete power, as the argument proves. But there is nothing to hinder an instrumental spiritual power from being in a body; in so far as a body can be moved by a particular spiritual substance so as to produce a particular spiritual effect; thus in the very voice which is perceived by the senses there is a certain spiritual power, inasmuch as it proceeds from a mental concept, of arousing the mind of the hearer. It is in this way that a spiritual power is in the sacraments, inasmuch as they are ordained by God unto the production of a spiritual effect.

Reply Obj. 2: Just as motion, through being an imperfect act, is not properly in a genus, but is reducible to a genus of perfect act, for instance, alteration to the genus of quality: so, instrumental power, properly speaking, is not in any genus, but is reducible to a genus and species of perfect act.

Reply Obj. 3: Just as an instrumental power accrues to an instrument through its being moved by the principal agent, so does a sacrament receive spiritual power from Christ's blessing and from the action of the minister in applying it to a sacramental use. Hence Augustine says in a sermon on the Epiphany (St. Maximus of Turin, Serm. xii): "Nor should you marvel, if we say that water, a corporeal substance, achieves the cleansing of the soul. It does indeed, and penetrates every secret hiding-place of the conscience. For subtle and clear as it is, the blessing of Christ makes it yet more subtle, so that it permeates into the very principles of life and searches the innermost recesses of the heart."

Reply Obj. 4: Just as the one same power of the principal agent is instrumentally in all the instruments that are ordained unto the production of an effect, forasmuch as they are one as being so ordained: so also the one same sacramental power is in both words and things, forasmuch as words and things combine to form one sacrament.

FIFTH ARTICLE [III, Q. 62, Art. 5]

Whether the Sacraments of the New Law Derive Their Power from Christ's Passion?

Objection 1: It seems that the sacraments of the New Law do not derive their power from Christ's Passion. For the power of the sacraments is in the causing of grace which is the principle of spiritual life in the soul. But as Augustine says (Tract. xix in Joan.): "The Word, as He was in the beginning with God, quickens souls; as He was made flesh, quickens bodies." Since, therefore, Christ's Passion pertains to the Word as made flesh, it seems that it cannot cause the power of the sacraments.

Obj. 2: Further, the power of the sacraments seems to depend on faith. for as Augustine says (Tract. lxxx in Joan.), the Divine Word perfects the sacrament "not because it is spoken, but because it is believed." But our faith regards not only Christ's Passion, but also the other mysteries of His humanity, and in a yet higher measure, His Godhead. Therefore it seems that the power of the sacraments is not due specially to Christ's Passion.

Obj. 3: Further, the sacraments are ordained unto man's justification, according to 1 Cor. 6:11: "You are washed . . . you are justified." Now justification is ascribed to the Resurrection, according to Rom. 4:25: "(Who) rose again for our justification." Therefore it seems that the sacraments derive their power from Christ's Resurrection rather than from His Passion.

*On the contrary,* on Rom. 5:14: "After the similitude of the transgression of Adam," etc., the gloss says: "From the side of Christ asleep on the Cross flowed the sacraments which brought salvation to the Church." Consequently, it seems that the sacraments derive their power from Christ's Passion.

*I answer that,* As stated above (A. 1) a sacrament in causing grace works after the manner of an instrument. Now an instrument is twofold; the one, separate, as a stick, for instance; the other, united, as a hand. Moreover, the separate instrument is moved by means of the united instrument, as a stick by the hand. Now the principal efficient cause of grace is God Himself, in comparison with Whom Christ's humanity is as a united instrument, whereas the sacrament is as a separate instrument. Consequently, the saving power must needs be derived by the sacraments from Christ's Godhead through His humanity.

Now sacramental grace seems to be ordained principally to two things: namely, to take away the defects consequent on past sins, in so far as they are transitory in act, but endure in guilt; and, further, to perfect the soul in things pertaining to Divine Worship in regard to the Christian Religion. But it is manifest from what has been stated above (Q. 48, AA. 1, 2, 6; Q. 49, AA. 1, 3) that Christ delivered us from our sins principally through His Passion, not only by way of efficiency and merit, but also by way of satisfaction. Likewise by His Passion He inaugurated the Rites of the Christian Religion by offering "Himself--an oblation and a sacrifice to God" (Eph. 5:2). Wherefore it is manifest that the sacraments of the Church derive their power specially from Christ's Passion, the virtue of which is in a manner united to us by our receiving the sacraments. It was in sign of this that from the side of Christ hanging on the Cross there flowed water and blood, the former of which belongs to Baptism, the latter to the Eucharist, which are the principal sacraments.

Reply Obj. 1: The Word, forasmuch as He was in the beginning with God, quickens souls as principal agent; but His flesh, and the mysteries accomplished therein, are as instrumental causes in the process of giving life to the soul: while in giving life to the body they act not only as instrumental causes, but also to a certain extent as exemplars, as we stated above (Q. 56, A. 1, ad 3).

Reply Obj. 2: Christ dwells in us "by faith" (Eph. 3:17). Consequently, by faith Christ's power is united to us. Now the power of blotting out sin belongs in a special way to His Passion. And therefore men are delivered from sin especially by faith in His Passion, according to Rom. 3:25: "Whom God hath proposed to be a propitiation through faith in His Blood." Therefore the power of the sacraments which is ordained unto the remission of sins is derived principally from faith in Christ's Passion.

Reply Obj. 3: Justification is ascribed to the Resurrection by reason of the term "whither," which is newness of life through grace. But it is ascribed to the Passion by reason of the term "whence," i.e. in regard to the forgiveness of sin.

SIXTH ARTICLE [III, Q. 62, Art. 6]

Whether the Sacraments of the Old Law Caused Grace?

Objection 1: It seems that the sacraments of the Old Law caused grace. For, as stated above (A. 5, ad 2) the sacraments of the New Law derive their efficacy from faith in Christ's Passion. But there was faith in Christ's Passion under the Old Law, as well as under the New, since we have "the same spirit of faith" (2 Cor. 4:13). Therefore just as the sacraments of the New Law confer grace, so did the sacraments of the Old Law.

Obj. 2: Further, there is no sanctification save by grace. But men were sanctified by the sacraments of the Old Law: for it is written (Lev. 8:31): "And when he," i.e. Moses, "had sanctified them," i.e. Aaron and his sons, "in their vestments," etc. Therefore it seems that the sacraments of the Old Law conferred grace.

Obj. 3: Further, Bede says in a homily on the Circumcision: "Under the Law circumcision provided the same health-giving balm against the wound of original sin, as baptism in the time of revealed grace." But Baptism confers grace now. Therefore circumcision conferred grace; and in like manner, the other sacraments of the Law; for just as Baptism is the door of the sacraments of the New Law, so was circumcision the door of the sacraments of the Old Law: hence the Apostle says (Gal. 5:3): "I testify to every man circumcising himself, that he is a debtor to the whole law."

*On the contrary,* It is written (Gal. 4:9): "Turn you again to the weak and needy elements?" i.e. "to the Law," says the gloss, "which is called weak, because it does not justify perfectly." But grace justifies perfectly. Therefore the sacraments of the old Law did not confer grace.

*I answer that,* It cannot be said that the sacraments of the Old Law conferred sanctifying grace of themselves, i.e. by their own power: since thus Christ's Passion would not have been necessary, according to Gal. 2:21: "If justice be by the Law, then Christ died in vain."

But neither can it be said that they derived the power of conferring sanctifying grace from Christ's Passion. For as it was stated above (A. 5), the power of Christ's Passion is united to us by faith and the sacraments, but in different ways; because the link that comes from faith is produced by an act of the soul; whereas the link that comes from the sacraments, is produced by making use of exterior things. Now nothing hinders that which is subsequent in point of time, from causing movement, even before it exists in reality, in so far as it pre-exists in an act of the soul: thus the end, which is subsequent in point of time, moves the agent in so far as it is apprehended and desired by him. On the other hand, what does not yet actually exist, does not cause movement if we consider the use of exterior things. Consequently, the efficient cause cannot in point of time come into existence after causing movement, as does the final cause. It is therefore clear that the sacraments of the New Law do reasonably derive the power of justification from Christ's Passion, which is the cause of man's righteousness; whereas the sacraments of the Old Law did not.

Nevertheless the Fathers of old were justified by faith in Christ's Passion, just as we are. And the sacraments of the old Law were a kind of protestation of that faith, inasmuch as they signified Christ's Passion and its effects. It is therefore manifest that the sacraments of the Old Law were not endowed with any power by which they conduced to the bestowal of justifying grace: and they merely signified faith by which men were justified.

Reply Obj. 1: The Fathers of old had faith in the future Passion of Christ, which, inasmuch as it was apprehended by the mind, was able to justify them. But we have faith in the past Passion of Christ, which is able to justify, also by the real use of sacramental things as stated above.

Reply Obj. 2: That sanctification was but a figure: for they were said to be sanctified forasmuch as they gave themselves up to the Divine worship according to the rite of the Old Law, which was wholly ordained to the foreshadowing of Christ's Passion.

Reply Obj. 3: There have been many opinions about Circumcision. For, according to some, Circumcision conferred no grace, but only remitted sin. But this is impossible; because man is not justified from sin save by grace, according to Rom. 3:24: "Being justified freely by His grace."

Wherefore others said that by Circumcision grace is conferred, as to the privative effects of sin, but not as to its positive effects. But this also appears to be false, because by Circumcision, children received the faculty of obtaining glory, which is the ultimate positive effect of grace. Moreover, as regards the order of the formal cause, positive effects are naturally prior to privative effects, though according to the order of the material cause, the reverse is the case: for a form does not exclude privation save by informing the subject.

Hence others say that Circumcision conferred grace also as regards a certain positive effect, i.e. by making man worthy of eternal life, but not so as to repress concupiscence which makes man prone to sin. And so at one time it seemed to me. But if the matter be considered carefully, this too appears to be untrue; because the very least grace is sufficient to resist any degree of concupiscence, and to merit eternal life.

And therefore it seems better to say that Circumcision was a sign of justifying faith: wherefore the Apostle says (Rom. 4:11) that Abraham "received the sign of Circumcision, a seal of the justice of faith." Consequently grace was conferred in Circumcision in so far as it was a sign of Christ's future Passion, as will be made clear further on (Q. 70, A. 4).

## QUESTION 63

OF THE OTHER EFFECT OF THE SACRAMENTS, WHICH IS A CHARACTER (In Six Articles)

We have now to consider the other effect of the sacraments, which is a character: and concerning this there are six points of inquiry:

(1) Whether by the sacraments a character is produced in the soul?

(2) What is this character?

(3) Of whom is this character?

(4) What is its subject?

(5) Is it indelible?

(6) Whether every sacrament imprints a character?

FIRST ARTICLE [III, Q. 63, Art. 1]

Whether a Sacrament Imprints a Character on the Soul?

Objection 1: It seems that a sacrament does not imprint a character on the soul. For the word "character" seems to signify some kind of distinctive sign. But Christ's members are distinguished from others by eternal predestination, which does not imply anything in the predestined, but only in God predestinating, as we have stated in the First Part (Q. 23, A. 2). For it is written (2 Tim. 2:19): "The sure foundation of God standeth firm, having this seal: The Lord knoweth who are His." Therefore the sacraments do not imprint a character on the soul.

Obj. 2: Further, a character is a distinctive sign. Now a sign, as Augustine says (De Doctr. Christ. ii) "is that which conveys something else to the mind, besides the species which it impresses on the senses." But nothing in the soul can impress a species on the senses. Therefore it seems that no character is imprinted on the soul by the sacraments.

Obj. 3: Further, just as the believer is distinguished from the unbeliever by the sacraments of the New Law, so was it under the Old Law. But the sacraments of the Old Law did not imprint a character; whence they are called "justices of the flesh" (Heb. 9:10) by the Apostle. Therefore neither seemingly do the sacraments of the New Law.

*On the contrary,* The Apostle says (2 Cor. 1:21, 22): "He . . . that hath anointed us is God; Who also hath sealed us, and given the pledge of the spirit in our hearts." But a character means nothing else than a kind of sealing. Therefore it seems that by the sacraments God imprints His character on us.

*I answer that,* As is clear from what has been already stated (Q. 62, A. 5) the sacraments of the New Law are ordained for a twofold purpose; namely, for a remedy against sins; and for the perfecting of the soul in things pertaining to the Divine worship according to the rite of the Christian life. Now whenever anyone is deputed to some definite purpose he is wont to receive some outward sign thereof; thus in olden times soldiers who enlisted in the ranks used to be marked with certain characters on the body, through being deputed to a bodily service. Since, therefore, by the sacraments men are deputed to a spiritual service pertaining to the worship of God, it follows that by their means the faithful receive a certain spiritual character. Wherefore Augustine says (Contra Parmen. ii): "If a deserter from the battle, through dread of the mark of enlistment on his body, throws himself on the emperor's clemency, and having besought and received mercy, return to the fight; is that character renewed, when the man has been set free and reprimanded? is it not rather acknowledged and approved? Are the Christian sacraments, by any chance, of a nature less lasting than this bodily mark?"

Reply Obj. 1: The faithful of Christ are destined to the reward of the glory that is to come, by the seal of Divine Predestination. But they are deputed to acts becoming the Church that is now, by a certain spiritual seal that is set on them, and is called a character.

Reply Obj. 2: The character imprinted on the soul is a kind of sign in so far as it is imprinted by a sensible sacrament: since we know that a certain one has received the baptismal character, through his being cleansed by the sensible water. Nevertheless from a kind of likeness, anything that assimilates one thing to another, or discriminates one thing from another, even though it be not sensible, can be called a character or a seal; thus the Apostle calls Christ "the figure" or charakter "of the substance of the Father" (Heb. 1:3).

Reply Obj. 3: As stated above (Q. 62, A. 6) the sacraments of the Old Law had not in themselves any spiritual power of producing a spiritual effect. Consequently in those sacraments there was no need of a spiritual character, and bodily circumcision sufficed, which the Apostle calls "a seal" (Rom. 4:11).

SECOND ARTICLE [III, Q. 63, Art. 2]

Whether a Character Is a Spiritual Power?

Objection 1: It seems that a character is not a spiritual power. For "character" seems to be the same thing as "figure"; hence (Heb. 1:3), where we read "figure of His substance," for "figure" the Greek has charakter . Now "figure" is in the fourth species of quality, and thus differs from power which is in the second species. Therefore character is not a spiritual power.

Obj. 2: Further, Dionysius says (Eccl. Hier. ii): "The Divine Beatitude admits him that seeks happiness to a share in Itself, and grants this share to him by conferring on him Its light as a kind of seal." Consequently, it seems that a character is a kind of light. Now light belongs rather to the third species of quality. Therefore a character is not a power, since this seems to belong to the second species.

Obj. 3: Further, character is defined by some thus: "A character is a holy sign of the communion of faith and of the holy ordination conferred by a hierarch." Now a sign is in the genus of relation, not of power. Therefore a character is not a spiritual power.

Obj. 4: Further, a power is in the nature of a cause and principle (Metaph. v). But a sign which is set down in the definition of a character is rather in the nature of an effect. Therefore a character is not a spiritual power.

*On the contrary,* The Philosopher says (Ethic. ii): "There are three things in the soul, power, habit, and passion." Now a character is not a passion: since a passion passes quickly, whereas a character is indelible, as will be made clear further on (A. 5). In like manner it is not a habit: because no habit is indifferent to acting well or ill: whereas a character is indifferent to either, since some use it well, some ill. Now this cannot occur with a habit: because no one abuses a habit of virtue, or uses well an evil habit. It remains, therefore, that a character is a power.

*I answer that,* As stated above (A. 1), the sacraments of the New Law produce a character, in so far as by them we are deputed to the worship of God according to the rite of the Christian religion. Wherefore Dionysius (Eccl. Hier. ii), after saying that God "by a kind of sign grants a share of Himself to those that approach Him," adds "by making them Godlike and communicators of Divine gifts." Now the worship of God consists either in receiving Divine gifts, or in bestowing them on others. And for both these purposes some power is needed; for to bestow something on others, active power is necessary; and in order to receive, we need a passive power. Consequently, a character signifies a certain spiritual power ordained unto things pertaining to the Divine worship.

But it must be observed that this spiritual power is instrumental: as we have stated above (Q. 62, A. 4) of the virtue which is in the sacraments. For to have a sacramental character belongs to God's ministers: and a minister is a kind of instrument, as the Philosopher says (Polit. i). Consequently, just as the virtue which is in the sacraments is not of itself in a genus, but is reducible to a genus, for the reason that it is of a transitory and incomplete nature: so also a character is not properly in a genus or species, but is reducible to the second species of quality.

Reply Obj. 1: Configuration is a certain boundary of quantity. Wherefore, properly speaking, it is only in corporeal things; and of spiritual things is said metaphorically. Now that which decides the genus or species of a thing must needs be predicated of it properly. Consequently, a character cannot be in the fourth species of quality, although some have held this to be the case.

Reply Obj. 2: The third species of quality contains only sensible passions or sensible qualities. Now a character is not a sensible light. Consequently, it is not in the third species of quality as some have maintained.

Reply Obj. 3: The relation signified by the word "sign" must needs have some foundation. Now the relation signified by this sign which is a character, cannot be founded immediately on the essence of the soul: because then it would belong to every soul naturally. Consequently, there must be something in the soul on which such a relation is founded. And it is in this that a character essentially consists. Therefore it need not be in the genus "relation" as some have held.

Reply Obj. 4: A character is in the nature of a sign in comparison to the sensible sacrament by which it is imprinted. But considered in itself, it is in the nature of a principle, in the way already explained.

THIRD ARTICLE [III, Q. 63, Art. 3]

Whether the Sacramental Character Is the Character of Christ?

Objection 1: It seems that the sacramental character is not the character of Christ. For it is written (Eph. 4:30): "Grieve not the Holy Spirit of God, whereby you are sealed." But a character consists essentially in something that seals. Therefore the sacramental character should be attributed to the Holy Ghost rather than to Christ.

Obj. 2: Further, a character has the nature of a sign. And it is a sign of the grace that is conferred by the sacrament. Now grace is poured forth into the soul by the whole Trinity; wherefore it is written (Ps. 83:12): "The Lord will give grace and glory." Therefore it seems that the sacramental character should not be attributed specially to Christ.

Obj. 3: Further, a man is marked with a character that he may be distinguishable from others. But the saints are distinguishable from others by charity, which, as Augustine says (De Trin. xv), "alone separates the children of the Kingdom from the children of perdition": wherefore also the children of perdition are said to have "the character of the beast" (Apoc. 13:16, 17). But charity is not attributed to Christ, but rather to the Holy Ghost according to Rom. 5:5: "The charity of God is poured forth in our hearts, by the Holy Ghost, Who is given to us"; or even to the Father, according to 2 Cor. 13:13: "The grace of our Lord Jesus Christ and the charity of God." Therefore it seems that the sacramental character should not be attributed to Christ.

*On the contrary,* Some define character thus: "A character is a distinctive mark printed in a man's rational soul by the eternal Character, whereby the created trinity is sealed with the likeness of the creating and re-creating Trinity, and distinguishing him from those who are not so enlikened, according to the state of faith." But the eternal Character is Christ Himself, according to Heb. 1:3: "Who being the brightness of His glory and the figure," or character, "of His substance." It seems, therefore, that the character should properly be attributed to Christ.

*I answer that,* As has been made clear above (A. 1), a character is properly a kind of seal, whereby something is marked, as being ordained to some particular end: thus a coin is marked for use in exchange of goods, and soldiers are marked with a character as being deputed to military service. Now the faithful are deputed to a twofold end. First and principally to the enjoyment of glory. And for this purpose they are marked with the seal of grace according to Ezech. 9:4: "Mark Thou upon the foreheads of the men that sigh and mourn"; and Apoc. 7:3: "Hurt not the earth, nor the sea, nor the trees, till we sign the servants of our God in their foreheads."

Secondly, each of the faithful is deputed to receive, or to bestow on others, things pertaining to the worship of God. And this, properly speaking, is the purpose of the sacramental character. Now the whole rite of the Christian religion is derived from Christ's priesthood. Consequently, it is clear that the sacramental character is specially the character of Christ, to Whose character the faithful are likened by reason of the sacramental characters, which are nothing else than certain participations of Christ's Priesthood, flowing from Christ Himself.

Reply Obj. 1: The Apostle speaks there of that sealing by which a man is assigned to future glory, and which is effected by grace. Now grace is attributed to the Holy Ghost, inasmuch as it is through love that God gives us something gratis, which is the very nature of grace: while the Holy Ghost is love. Wherefore it is written (1 Cor. 12:4): "There are diversities of graces, but the same Spirit."

Reply Obj. 2: The sacramental character is a thing as regards the exterior sacrament, and a sacrament in regard to the ultimate effect. Consequently, something can be attributed to a character in two ways. First, if the character be considered as a sacrament: and thus it is a sign of the invisible grace which is conferred in the sacrament. Secondly, if it be considered as a character. And thus it is a sign conferring on a man a likeness to some principal person in whom is vested the authority over that to which he is assigned: thus soldiers who are assigned to military service, are marked with their leader's sign, by which they are, in a fashion, likened to him. And in this way those who are deputed to the Christian worship, of which Christ is the author, receive a character by which they are likened to Christ. Consequently, properly speaking, this is Christ's character.

Reply Obj. 3: A character distinguishes one from another, in relation to some particular end, to which he, who receives the character is ordained: as has been stated concerning the military character (A. 1) by which a soldier of the king is distinguished from the enemy's soldier in relation to the battle. In like manner the character of the faithful is that by which the faithful of Christ are distinguished from the servants of the devil, either in relation to eternal life, or in relation to the worship of the Church that now is. Of these the former is the result of charity and grace, as the objection runs; while the latter results from the sacramental character. Wherefore the "character of the beast" may be understood by opposition, to mean either the obstinate malice for which some are assigned to eternal punishment, or the profession of an unlawful form of worship.

FOURTH ARTICLE [III, Q. 63, Art. 4]

Whether the Character Be Subjected in the Powers of the Soul?

Objection 1: It seems that the character is not subjected in the powers of the soul. For a character is said to be a disposition to grace. But grace is subjected in the essence of the soul as we have stated in the Second Part (I-II, Q. 110, A. 4). Therefore it seems that the character is in the essence of the soul and not in the powers.

Obj. 2: Further, a power of the soul does not seem to be the subject of anything save habit and disposition. But a character, as stated above (A. 2), is neither habit nor disposition, but rather a power: the subject of which is nothing else than the essence of the soul. Therefore it seems that the character is not subjected in a power of the soul, but rather in its essence.

Obj. 3: Further, the powers of the soul are divided into those of knowledge and those of appetite. But it cannot be said that a character is only in a cognitive power, nor, again, only in an appetitive power: since it is neither ordained to knowledge only, nor to desire only. Likewise, neither can it be said to be in both, because the same accident cannot be in several subjects. Therefore it seems that a character is not subjected in a power of the soul, but rather in the essence.

*On the contrary,* A character, according to its definition given above (A. 3), is imprinted in the rational soul "by way of an image." But the image of the Trinity in the soul is seen in the powers. Therefore a character is in the powers of the soul.

*I answer that,* As stated above (A. 3), a character is a kind of seal by which the soul is marked, so that it may receive, or bestow on others, things pertaining to Divine worship. Now the Divine worship consists in certain actions: and the powers of the soul are properly ordained to actions, just as the essence is ordained to existence. Therefore a character is subjected not in the essence of the soul, but in its power.

Reply Obj. 1: The subject is ascribed to an accident in respect of that to which the accident disposes it proximately, but not in respect of that to which it disposes it remotely or indirectly. Now a character disposes the soul directly and proximately to the fulfilling of things pertaining to Divine worship: and because such cannot be accomplished suitably without the help of grace, since, according to John 4:24, "they that adore" God "must adore Him in spirit and in truth," consequently, the Divine bounty bestows grace on those who receive the character, so that they may accomplish worthily the service to which they are deputed. Therefore the subject should be ascribed to a character in respect of those actions that pertain to the Divine worship, rather than in respect of grace.

Reply Obj. 2: The essence of the soul is the subject of the natural power, which flows from the principles of the essence. Now a character is not a power of this kind, but a spiritual power coming from without. Wherefore, just as the essence of the soul, from which man has his natural life, is perfected by grace from which the soul derives spiritual life; so the natural power of the soul is perfected by a spiritual power, which is a character. For habit and disposition belong to a power of the soul, since they are ordained to actions of which the powers are the principles. And in like manner whatever is ordained to action, should be attributed to a power.

Reply Obj. 3: As stated above, a character is ordained unto things pertaining to the Divine worship; which is a protestation of faith expressed by exterior signs. Consequently, a character needs to be in the soul's cognitive power, where also is faith.

FIFTH ARTICLE [III, Q. 63, Art. 5]

Whether a Character Can Be Blotted Out from the Soul?

Objection 1: It seems that a character can be blotted out from the soul. Because the more perfect an accident is, the more firmly does it adhere to its subject. But grace is more perfect than a character; because a character is ordained unto grace as to a further end. Now grace is lost through sin. Much more, therefore, is a character so lost.

Obj. 2: Further, by a character a man is deputed to the Divine worship, as stated above (AA. 3, 4). But some pass from the worship of God to a contrary worship by apostasy from the faith. It seems, therefore, that such lose the sacramental character.

Obj. 3: Further, when the end ceases, the means to the end should cease also: thus after the resurrection there will be no marriage, because begetting will cease, which is the purpose of marriage. Now the exterior worship to which a character is ordained, will not endure in heaven, where there will be no shadows, but all will be truth without a veil. Therefore the sacramental character does not last in the soul for ever: and consequently it can be blotted out.

*On the contrary,* Augustine says (Contra Parmen. ii): "The Christian sacraments are not less lasting than the bodily mark" of military service. But the character of military service is not repeated, but is "recognized and approved" in the man who obtains the emperor's forgiveness after offending him. Therefore neither can the sacramental character be blotted out.

*I answer that,* As stated above (A. 3), in a sacramental character Christ's faithful have a share in His Priesthood; in the sense that as Christ has the full power of a spiritual priesthood, so His faithful are likened to Him by sharing a certain spiritual power with regard to the sacraments and to things pertaining to the Divine worship. For this reason it is unbecoming that Christ should have a character: but His Priesthood is compared to a character, as that which is complete and perfect is compared to some participation of itself. Now Christ's Priesthood is eternal, according to Ps. 109:4: "Thou art a priest for ever, according to the order of Melchisedech." Consequently, every sanctification wrought by His Priesthood, is perpetual, enduring as long as the thing sanctified endures. This is clear even in inanimate things; for the consecration of a church or an altar lasts for ever unless they be destroyed. Since, therefore, the subject of a character is the soul as to its intellective part, where faith resides, as stated above (A. 4, ad 3); it is clear that, the intellect being perpetual and incorruptible, a character cannot be blotted out from the soul.

Reply Obj. 1: Both grace and character are in the soul, but in different ways. For grace is in the soul, as a form having complete existence therein: whereas a character is in the soul, as an instrumental power, as stated above (A. 2). Now a complete form is in its subject according to the condition of the subject. And since the soul as long as it is a wayfarer is changeable in respect of the free-will, it results that grace is in the soul in a changeable manner. But an instrumental power follows rather the condition of the principal agent: and consequently a character exists in the soul in an indelible manner, not from any perfection of its own, but from the perfection of Christ's Priesthood, from which the character flows like an instrumental power.

Reply Obj. 2: As Augustine says (Contra Parmen. ii), "even apostates are not deprived of their baptism, for when they repent and return to the fold they do not receive it again; whence we conclude that it cannot be lost." The reason of this is that a character is an instrumental power, as stated above (ad 1), and the nature of an instrument as such is to be moved by another, but not to move itself; this belongs to the will. Consequently, however much the will be moved in the contrary direction, the character is not removed, by reason of the immobility of the principal mover.

Reply Obj. 3: Although external worship does not last after this life, yet its end remains. Consequently, after this life the character remains, both in the good as adding to their glory, and in the wicked as increasing their shame: just as the character of the military service remains in the soldiers after the victory, as the boast of the conquerors, and the disgrace of the conquered.

SIXTH ARTICLE [III, Q. 63, Art. 6]

Whether a Character Is Imprinted by Each Sacrament of the New Law?

Objection 1: It seems that a character is imprinted by all the sacraments of the New Law: because each sacrament of the New Law makes man a participator in Christ's Priesthood. But the sacramental character is nothing but a participation in Christ's Priesthood, as already stated (AA. 3, 5). Therefore it seems that a character is imprinted by each sacrament of the New Law.

Obj. 2: Further, a character may be compared to the soul in which it is, as a consecration to that which is consecrated. But by each sacrament of the New Law man becomes the recipient of sanctifying grace, as stated above (Q. 62, A. 1). Therefore it seems that a character is imprinted by each sacrament of the New Law.

Obj. 3: Further, a character is both a reality and a sacrament. But in each sacrament of the New Law, there is something which is only a reality, and something which is only a sacrament, and something which is both reality and sacrament. Therefore a character is imprinted by each sacrament of the New Law.

*On the contrary,* Those sacraments in which a character is imprinted, are not reiterated, because a character is indelible, as stated above (A. 5): whereas some sacraments are reiterated, for instance, penance and matrimony. Therefore not all the sacraments imprint a character.

*I answer that,* As stated above (Q. 62, AA. 1, 5), the sacraments of the New Law are ordained for a twofold purpose, namely, as a remedy for sin, and for the Divine worship. Now all the sacraments, from the fact that they confer grace, have this in common, that they afford a remedy against sin: whereas not all the sacraments are directly ordained to the Divine worship. Thus it is clear that penance, whereby man is delivered from sin, does not afford man any advance in the Divine worship, but restores him to his former state.

Now a sacrament may belong to the Divine worship in three ways: first in regard to the thing done; secondly, in regard to the agent; thirdly, in regard to the recipient. In regard to the thing done, the Eucharist belongs to the Divine worship, for the Divine worship consists principally therein, so far as it is the sacrifice of the Church. And by this same sacrament a character is not imprinted on man; because it does not ordain man to any further sacramental action or benefit received, since rather is it "the end and consummation of all the sacraments," as Dionysius says (Eccl. Hier. iii). But it contains within itself Christ, in Whom there is not the character, but the very plenitude of the Priesthood.

But it is the sacrament of order that pertains to the sacramental agents: for it is by this sacrament that men are deputed to confer sacraments on others: while the sacrament of Baptism pertains to the recipients, since it confers on man the power to receive the other sacraments of the Church; whence it is called the "door of the sacraments." In a way Confirmation also is ordained for the same purpose, as we shall explain in its proper place (Q. 65, A. 3). Consequently, these three sacraments imprint a character, namely, Baptism, Confirmation, and order.

Reply Obj. 1: Every sacrament makes man a participator in Christ's Priesthood, from the fact that it confers on him some effect thereof. But every sacrament does not depute a man to do or receive something pertaining to the worship of the priesthood of Christ: while it is just this that is required for a sacrament to imprint a character.

Reply Obj. 2: Man is sanctified by each of the sacraments, since sanctity means immunity from sin, which is the effect of grace. But in a special way some sacraments, which imprint a character, bestow on man a certain consecration, thus deputing him to the Divine worship: just as inanimate things are said to be consecrated forasmuch as they are deputed to Divine worship.

Reply Obj. 3: Although a character is a reality and a sacrament, it does not follow that whatever is a reality and a sacrament, is also a character. With regard to the other sacraments we shall explain further on what is the reality and what is the sacrament.

## QUESTION 64

OF THE CAUSES OF THE SACRAMENTS (In Ten Articles)

In the next place we have to consider the causes of the sacraments, both as to authorship and as to ministration. Concerning which there are ten points of inquiry:

(1) Whether God alone works inwardly in the sacraments?

(2) Whether the institution of the sacraments is from God alone?

(3) Of the power which Christ exercised over the sacraments;

(4) Whether He could transmit that power to others?

(5) Whether the wicked can have the power of administering the sacraments?

(6) Whether the wicked sin in administering the sacraments?

(7) Whether the angels can be ministers of the sacraments?

(8) Whether the minister's intention is necessary in the sacraments?

(9) Whether right faith is required therein; so that it be impossible for an unbeliever to confer a sacrament?

(10) Whether a right intention is required therein?

FIRST ARTICLE [III, Q. 64, Art. 1]

Whether God Alone, or the Minister Also, Works Inwardly Unto the Sacramental Effect?

Objection 1: It seems that not God alone, but also the minister, works inwardly unto the sacramental effect. For the inward sacramental effect is to cleanse man from sin and enlighten him by grace. But it belongs to the ministers of the Church "to cleanse, enlighten and perfect," as Dionysius explains (Coel. Hier. v). Therefore it seems that the sacramental effect is the work not only of God, but also of the ministers of the Church.

Obj. 2: Further, certain prayers are offered up in conferring the sacraments. But the prayers of the righteous are more acceptable to God than those of any other, according to John 9:31: "If a man be a server of God, and doth His will, him He heareth." Therefore it stems that a man obtains a greater sacramental effect if he receive it from a good minister. Consequently, the interior effect is partly the work of the minister and not of God alone.

Obj. 3: Further, man is of greater account than an inanimate thing. But an inanimate thing contributes something to the interior effect: since "water touches the body and cleanses the soul," as Augustine says (Tract. lxxx in Joan.). Therefore the interior sacramental effect is partly the work of man and not of God alone.

*On the contrary,* It is written (Rom. 8:33): "God that justifieth." Since, then, the inward effect of all the sacraments is justification, it seems that God alone works the interior sacramental effect.

*I answer that,* There are two ways of producing an effect; first, as a principal agent; secondly, as an instrument. In the former way the interior sacramental effect is the work of God alone: first, because God alone can enter the soul wherein the sacramental effect takes place; and no agent can operate immediately where it is not: secondly, because grace which is an interior sacramental effect is from God alone, as we have established in the Second Part (I-II, Q. 112, A. 1); while the character which is the interior effect of certain sacraments, is an instrumental power which flows from the principal agent, which is God. In the second way, however, the interior sacramental effect can be the work of man, in so far as he works as a minister. For a minister is of the nature of an instrument, since the action of both is applied to something extrinsic, while the interior effect is produced through the power of the principal agent, which is God.

Reply Obj. 1: Cleansing in so far as it is attributed to the ministers of the Church is not a washing from sin: deacons are said to "cleanse," inasmuch as they remove the unclean from the body of the faithful, or prepare them by their pious admonitions for the reception of the sacraments. In like manner also priests are said to "enlighten" God's people, not indeed by giving them grace, but by conferring on them the sacraments of grace; as Dionysius explains (Coel. Hier. v).

Reply Obj. 2: The prayers which are said in giving the sacraments, are offered to God, not on the part of the individual, but on the part of the whole Church, whose prayers are acceptable to God, according to Matt. 18:19: "If two of you shall consent upon earth, concerning anything whatsoever they shall ask, it shall be done to them by My Father." Nor is there any reason why the devotion of a just man should not contribute to this effect. But that which is the sacramental effect is not impetrated by the prayer of the Church or of the minister, but through the merit of Christ's Passion, the power of which operates in the sacraments, as stated above (Q. 62, A. 5). Wherefore the sacramental effect is made no better by a better minister. And yet something in addition may be impetrated for the receiver of the sacrament through the devotion of the minister: but this is not the work of the minister, but the work of God Who hears the minister's prayer.

Reply Obj. 3: Inanimate things do not produce the sacramental effect, except instrumentally, as stated above. In like manner neither do men produce the sacramental effect, except ministerially, as also stated above.

SECOND ARTICLE [III, Q. 64, Art. 2]

Whether the Sacraments Are Instituted by God Alone?

Objection 1: It seems that the sacraments are not instituted by God alone. For those things which God has instituted are delivered to us in Holy Scripture. But in the sacraments certain things are done which are nowhere mentioned in Holy Scripture; for instance, the chrism with which men are confirmed, the oil with which priests are anointed, and many others, both words and actions, which we employ in the sacraments. Therefore the sacraments were not instituted by God alone.

Obj. 2: Further, a sacrament is a kind of sign. Now sensible things have their own natural signification. Nor can it be said that God takes pleasure in certain significations and not in others; because He approves of all that He made. Moreover, it seems to be peculiar to the demons to be enticed to something by means of signs; for Augustine says (De Civ. Dei xxi): "The demons are enticed . . . by means of creatures, which were created not by them but by God, by various means of attraction according to their various natures, not as an animal is enticed by food, but as a spirit is drawn by a sign." It seems, therefore, that there is no need for the sacraments to be instituted by God.

Obj. 3: Further, the apostles were God's vicegerents on earth: hence the Apostle says (2 Cor. 2:10): "For what I have pardoned, if I have pardoned anything, for your sakes have I done it in the person of Christ," i.e. as though Christ Himself had pardoned. Therefore it seems that the apostles and their successors can institute new sacraments.

*On the contrary,* The institutor of anything is he who gives it strength and power: as in the case of those who institute laws. But the power of a sacrament is from God alone, as we have shown above (A. 1; Q. 62, A. 1). Therefore God alone can institute a sacrament.

*I answer that,* As appears from what has been said above (A. 1; Q. 62, A. 1), the sacraments are instrumental causes of spiritual effects. Now an instrument has its power from the principal agent. But an agent in respect of a sacrament is twofold; viz. he who institutes the sacraments, and he who makes use of the sacrament instituted, by applying it for the production of the effect. Now the power of a sacrament cannot be from him who makes use of the sacrament: because he works but as a minister. Consequently, it follows that the power of the sacrament is from the institutor of the sacrament. Since, therefore, the power of the sacrament is from God alone, it follows that God alone can institute the sacraments.

Reply Obj. 1: Human institutions observed in the sacraments are not essential to the sacrament; but belong to the solemnity which is added to the sacraments in order to arouse devotion and reverence in the recipients. But those things that are essential to the sacrament, are instituted by Christ Himself, Who is God and man. And though they are not all handed down by the Scriptures, yet the Church holds them from the intimate tradition of the apostles, according to the saying of the Apostle (1 Cor. 11:34): "The rest I will set in order when I come."

Reply Obj. 2: From their very nature sensible things have a certain aptitude for the signifying of spiritual effects: but this aptitude is fixed by the Divine institution to some special signification. This is what Hugh of St. Victor means by saying (De Sacram. i) that "a sacrament owes its signification to its institution." Yet God chooses certain things rather than others for sacramental signification, not as though His choice were restricted to them, but in order that their signification be more suitable to them.

Reply Obj. 3: The apostles and their successors are God's vicars in governing the Church which is built on faith and the sacraments of faith. Wherefore, just as they may not institute another Church, so neither may they deliver another faith, nor institute other sacraments: *on the contrary,* the Church is said to be built up with the sacraments "which flowed from the side of Christ while hanging on the Cross."

THIRD ARTICLE [III, Q. 64, Art. 3]

Whether Christ As Man Had the Power of Producing the Inward Sacramental Effect?

Objection 1: It seems that Christ as man had the power of producing the interior sacramental effect. For John the Baptist said (John 1:33): "He, Who sent me to baptize in water, said to me: He upon Whom thou shalt see the Spirit descending and remaining upon Him, He it is that baptizeth with the Holy Ghost." But to baptize with the Holy Ghost is to confer inwardly the grace of the Holy Ghost. And the Holy Ghost descended upon Christ as man, not as God: for thus He Himself gives the Holy Ghost. Therefore it seems that Christ, as man, had the power of producing the inward sacramental effect.

Obj. 2: Further, our Lord said (Matt. 9:6): "That you may know that the Son of Man hath power on earth to forgive sins." But forgiveness of sins is an inward sacramental effect. Therefore it seems that Christ as man produces the inward sacramental effect.

Obj. 3: Further, the institution of the sacraments belongs to him who acts as principal agent in producing the inward sacramental effect. Now it is clear that Christ instituted the sacraments. Therefore it is He that produces the inward sacramental effect.

Obj. 4: Further, no one can confer the sacramental effect without conferring the sacrament, except he produce the sacramental effect by his own power. But Christ conferred the sacramental effect without conferring the sacrament; as in the case of Magdalen to whom He said: "Thy sins are forgiven Thee" (Luke 7:48). Therefore it seems that Christ, as man, produces the inward sacramental effect.

Obj. 5: Further, the principal agent in causing the inward effect is that in virtue of which the sacrament operates. But the sacraments derive their power from Christ's Passion and through the invocation of His Name; according to 1 Cor. 1:13: "Was Paul then crucified for you? or were you baptized in the name of Paul?" Therefore Christ, as man, produces the inward sacramental effect.

*On the contrary,* Augustine (Isidore, Etym. vi) says: "The Divine power in the sacraments works inwardly in producing their salutary effect." Now the Divine power is Christ's as God, not as man. Therefore Christ produces the inward sacramental effect, not as man but as God.

*I answer that,* Christ produces the inward sacramental effect, both as God and as man, but not in the same way. For, as God, He works in the sacraments by authority: but, as man, His operation conduces to the inward sacramental effects meritoriously and efficiently, but instrumentally. For it has been stated (Q. 48, AA. 1, 6; Q. 49, A. 1) that Christ's Passion which belongs to Him in respect of His human nature, is the cause of justification, both meritoriously and efficiently, not as the principal cause thereof, or by His own authority, but as an instrument, in so far as His humanity is the instrument of His Godhead, as stated above (Q. 13, AA. 2, 3; Q. 19, A. 1).

Nevertheless, since it is an instrument united to the Godhead in unity of Person, it has a certain headship and efficiency in regard to extrinsic instruments, which are the ministers of the Church and the sacraments themselves, as has been explained above (A. 1). Consequently, just as Christ, as God, has power of authority over the sacraments, so, as man, He has the power of ministry in chief, or power of excellence. And this consists in four things. First in this, that the merit and power of His Passion operates in the sacraments, as stated above (Q. 62, A. 5). And because the power of the Passion is communicated to us by faith, according to Rom. 3:25: "Whom God hath proposed to be a propitiation through faith in His blood," which faith we proclaim by calling on the name of Christ: therefore, secondly, Christ's power of excellence over the sacraments consists in this, that they are sanctified by the invocation of His name. And because the sacraments derive their power from their institution, hence, thirdly, the excellence of Christ's power consists in this, that He, Who gave them their power, could institute the sacraments. And since cause does not depend on effect, but rather conversely, it belongs to the excellence of Christ's power, that He could bestow the sacramental effect without conferring the exterior sacrament. Thus it is clear how to solve the objections; for the arguments on either side are true to a certain extent, as explained above.

FOURTH ARTICLE [III, Q. 64, Art. 4]

Whether Christ Could Communicate to Ministers the Power Which He Had in the Sacraments?

Objection 1: It seems that Christ could not communicate to ministers the power which He had in the sacraments. For as Augustine argues against Maximin, "if He could, but would not, He was jealous of His power." But jealousy was far from Christ Who had the fulness of charity. Since, therefore, Christ did not communicate His power to ministers, it seems that He could not.

Obj. 2: Further, on John 14:12: "Greater than these shall he do," Augustine says (Tract. lxxii): "I affirm this to be altogether greater," namely, for a man from being ungodly to be made righteous, "than to create heaven and earth." But Christ could not communicate to His disciples the power of creating heaven and earth: neither, therefore, could He give them the power of making the ungodly to be righteous. Since, therefore, the justification of the ungodly is effected by the power that Christ has in the sacraments, it seems that He could not communicate that power to ministers.

Obj. 3: Further, it belongs to Christ as Head of the Church that grace should flow from Him to others, according to John 1:16: "Of His fulness we all have received." But this could not be communicated to others; since then the Church would be deformed, having many heads. Therefore it seems that Christ could not communicate His power to ministers.

*On the contrary,* on John 1:31: "I knew Him not," Augustine says (Tract. v) that "he did not know that our Lord having the authority of baptizing . . . would keep it to Himself." But John would not have been in ignorance of this, if such a power were incommunicable. Therefore Christ could communicate His power to ministers.

*I answer that,* As stated above (A. 3), Christ had a twofold power in the sacraments. One was the power of authority, which belongs to Him as God: and this power He could not communicate to any creature; just as neither could He communicate the Divine Essence. The other was the power of excellence, which belongs to Him as man. This power He could communicate to ministers; namely, by giving them such a fulness of grace--that their merits would conduce to the sacramental effect--that by the invocation of their names, the sacraments would be sanctified--and that they themselves might institute sacraments, and by their mere will confer the sacramental effect without observing the sacramental rite. For a united instrument, the more powerful it is, is all the more able to lend its power to the separated instrument; as the hand can to a stick.

Reply Obj. 1: It was not through jealousy that Christ refrained from communicating to ministers His power of excellence, but for the good of the faithful; lest they should put their trust in men, and lest there should be various kinds of sacraments, giving rise to division in the Church; as may be seen in those who said: "I am of Paul, I am of Apollo, and I of Cephas" (1 Cor. 1:12).

Reply Obj. 2: This objection is true of the power of authority, which belongs to Christ as God. At the same time the power of excellence can be called authority in comparison to other ministers. Whence on 1 Cor. 1:13: "Is Christ divided?" the gloss says that "He could give power of authority in baptizing, to those to whom He gave the power of administering it."

Reply Obj. 3: It was in order to avoid the incongruity of many heads in the Church, that Christ was unwilling to communicate to ministers His power of excellence. If, however, He had done so, He would have been Head in chief; the others in subjection to Him.

FIFTH ARTICLE [III, Q. 64, Art. 5]

Whether the Sacraments Can Be Conferred by Evil Ministers?

Objection 1: It seems that the sacraments cannot be conferred by evil ministers. For the sacraments of the New Law are ordained for the purpose of cleansing from sin and for the bestowal of grace. Now evil men, being themselves unclean, cannot cleanse others from sin, according to Ecclus. 34:4: "Who [Vulg.: 'What'] can be made clean by the unclean?" Moreover, since they have not grace, it seems that they cannot give grace, for "no one gives what he has not." It seems, therefore, that the sacraments cannot be conferred by wicked men.

Obj. 2: Further, all the power of the sacraments is derived from Christ, as stated above (A. 3; Q. 62, A. 5). But evil men are cut off from Christ: because they have not charity, by which the members are united to their Head, according to 1 John 4:16: "He that abideth in charity, abideth in God, and God in him." Therefore it seems that the sacraments cannot be conferred by evil men.

Obj. 3: Further, if anything is wanting that is required for the sacraments, the sacrament is invalid; for instance, if the required matter or form be wanting. But the minister required for a sacrament is one who is without the stain of sin, according to Lev. 21:17, 18: "Whosoever of thy seed throughout their families, hath a blemish, he shall not offer bread to his God, neither shall he approach to minister to Him." Therefore it seems that if the minister be wicked, the sacrament has no effect.

*On the contrary,* Augustine says on John 1:33: "He upon Whom thou shalt see the Spirit," etc. (Tract. v in Joan.), that "John did not know that our Lord, having the authority of baptizing, would keep it to Himself, but that the ministry would certainly pass to both good and evil men . . . What is a bad minister to thee, where the Lord is good?"

*I answer that,* As stated above (A. 1), the ministers of the Church work instrumentally in the sacraments, because, in a way, a minister is of the nature of an instrument. But, as stated above (Q. 62, AA. 1, 4), an instrument acts not by reason of its own form, but by the power of the one who moves it. Consequently, whatever form or power an instrument has in addition to that which it has as an instrument, is accidental to it: for instance, that a physician's body, which is the instrument of his soul, wherein is his medical art, be healthy or sickly; or that a pipe, through which water passes, be of silver or lead. Therefore the ministers of the Church can confer the sacraments, though they be wicked.

Reply Obj. 1: The ministers of the Church do not by their own power cleanse from sin those who approach the sacraments, nor do they confer grace on them: it is Christ Who does this by His own power while He employs them as instruments. Consequently, those who approach the sacraments receive an effect whereby they are enlikened not to the ministers but to Christ.

Reply Obj. 2: Christ's members are united to their Head by charity, so that they may receive life from Him; for as it is written (1 John 3:14): "He that loveth not abideth in death." Now it is possible for a man to work with a lifeless instrument, and separated from him as to bodily union, provided it be united to him by some sort of motion: for a workman works in one way with his hand, in another with his axe. Consequently, it is thus that Christ works in the sacraments, both by wicked men as lifeless instruments, and by good men as living instruments.

Reply Obj. 3: A thing is required in a sacrament in two ways. First, as being essential to it: and if this be wanting, the sacrament is invalid; for instance, if the due form or matter be wanting. Secondly, a thing is required for a sacrament, by reason of a certain fitness. And in this way good ministers are required for a sacrament.

SIXTH ARTICLE [III, Q. 64, Art. 6]

Whether Wicked Men Sin in Administering the Sacraments?

Objection 1: It seems that wicked men do not sin in administering the sacraments. For just as men serve God in the sacraments, so do they serve Him in works of charity; whence it is written (Heb. 13:16): "Do not forget to do good and to impart, for by such sacrifices God's favor is obtained." But the wicked do not sin in serving God by works of charity: indeed, they should be persuaded to do so, according to Dan. 4:24: "Let my counsel be acceptable" to the king; "Redeem thou thy sins with alms." Therefore it seems that wicked men do not sin in administering the sacraments.

Obj. 2: Further, whoever co-operates with another in his sin, is also guilty of sin, according to Rom. 1:32: "He is [Vulg.: 'They are'] worthy of death; not only he that commits the sin, but also he who consents to them that do them." But if wicked ministers sin in administering sacraments, those who receive sacraments from them, co-operate in their sin. Therefore they would sin also; which seems unreasonable.

Obj. 3: Further, it seems that no one should act when in doubt, for thus man would be driven to despair, as being unable to avoid sin. But if the wicked were to sin in administering sacraments, they would be in a state of perplexity: since sometimes they would sin also if they did not administer sacraments; for instance, when by reason of their office it is their bounden duty to do so; for it is written (1 Cor. 9:16): "For a necessity lieth upon me: Woe is unto me if I preach not the gospel." Sometimes also on account of some danger; for instance, if a child in danger of death be brought to a sinner for baptism. Therefore it seems that the wicked do not sin in administering the sacraments.

*On the contrary,* Dionysius says (Eccl. Hier. i) that "it is wrong for the wicked even to touch the symbols," i.e. the sacramental signs. And he says in the epistle to Demophilus: "It seems presumptuous for such a man," i.e. a sinner, "to lay hands on priestly things; he is neither afraid nor ashamed, all unworthy that he is, to take part in Divine things, with the thought that God does not see what he sees in himself: he thinks, by false pretenses, to cheat Him Whom he calls his Father; he dares to utter, in the person of Christ, words polluted by his infamy, I will not call them prayers, over the Divine symbols."

*I answer that,* A sinful action consists in this, that a man "fails to act as he ought to," as the Philosopher explains (Ethic. ii). Now it has been said (A. 5, ad 3) that it is fitting for the ministers of sacraments to be righteous; because ministers should be like unto their Lord, according to Lev. 19:2: "Be ye holy, because I . . . am holy"; and Ecclus. 10:2: "As the judge of the people is himself, so also are his ministers." Consequently, there can be no doubt that the wicked sin by exercising the ministry of

God and the Church, by conferring the sacraments. And since this sin pertains to irreverence towards God and the contamination of holy things, as far as the man who sins is concerned, although holy things in themselves cannot be contaminated; it follows that such a sin is mortal in its genus.

Reply Obj. 1: Works of charity are not made holy by some process of consecration, but they belong to the holiness of righteousness, as being in a way parts of righteousness. Consequently, when a man shows himself as a minister of God, by doing works of charity, if he be righteous, he will be made yet holier; but if he be a sinner, he is thereby disposed to holiness. On the other hand, the sacraments are holy in themselves owing to their mystical consecration. Wherefore the holiness of righteousness is required in the minister, that he may be suitable for his ministry: for which reason he acts unbecomingly and sins, if while in a state of sin he attempts to fulfil that ministry.

Reply Obj. 2: He who approaches a sacrament, receives it from a minister of the Church, not because he is such and such a man, but because he is a minister of the Church. Consequently, as long as the latter is tolerated in the ministry, he that receives a sacrament from him, does not communicate in his sin, but communicates with the Church from whom he has his ministry. But if the Church, by degrading, excommunicating, or suspending him, does not tolerate him in the ministry, he that receives a sacrament from him sins, because he communicates in his sin.

Reply Obj. 3: A man who is in mortal sin is not perplexed simply, if by reason of his office it be his bounden duty to minister sacraments; because he can repent of his sin and so minister lawfully. But there is nothing unreasonable in his being perplexed, if we suppose that he wishes to remain in sin.

However, in a case of necessity when even a lay person might baptize, he would not sin in baptizing. For it is clear that then he does not exercise the ministry of the Church, but comes to the aid of one who is in need of his services. It is not so with the other sacraments, which are not so necessary as baptism, as we shall show further on (Q. 65, AA. 3, 4; Q. 62, A. 3).

SEVENTH ARTICLE [III, Q. 64, Art. 7]

Whether Angels Can Administer Sacraments?

Objection 1: It seems that angels can administer sacraments. Because a higher minister can do whatever the lower can; thus a priest can do whatever a deacon can: but not conversely. But angels are higher ministers in the hierarchical order than any men whatsoever, as Dionysius says (Coel. Hier. ix). Therefore, since men can be ministers of sacraments, it seems that much more can angels be.

Obj. 2: Further, in heaven holy men are likened to the angels (Matt. 22:30). But some holy men, when in heaven, can be ministers of the sacraments; since the sacramental character is indelible, as stated above (Q. 63, A. 5). Therefore it seems that angels too can be ministers of sacraments.

Obj. 3: Further, as stated above (Q. 8, A. 7), the devil is head of the wicked, and the wicked are his members. But sacraments can be administered by the wicked. Therefore it seems that they can be administered even by demons.

*On the contrary,* It is written (Heb. 5:1): "Every high priest taken from among men, is ordained for men in the things that appertain to God." But angels whether good or bad are not taken from among men. Therefore they are not ordained ministers in the things that appertain to God, i.e. in the sacraments.

*I answer that,* As stated above (A. 3; Q. 62, A. 5), the whole power of the sacraments flows from Christ's Passion, which belongs to Him as man. And Him in their very nature men, not angels, resemble; indeed, in respect of His Passion, He is described as being "a little lower than the angels" (Heb. 2:9). Consequently, it belongs to men, but not to angels, to dispense the sacraments and to take part in their administration.

But it must be observed that as God did not bind His power to the sacraments, so as to be unable to bestow the sacramental effect without conferring the sacrament; so neither did He bind His power to the ministers of the Church so as to be unable to give angels power to administer the sacraments. And since good angels are messengers of truth; if any sacramental rite were performed by good angels, it should be considered valid, because it ought to be evident that this is being done by the will of God: for instance, certain churches are said to have been consecrated by the ministry of the angels [*See Acta S.S., September 29]. But if demons, who are "lying spirits," were to perform a sacramental rite, it should be pronounced as invalid.

Reply Obj. 1: What men do in a less perfect manner, i.e. by sensible sacraments, which are proportionate to their nature, angels also do, as ministers of a higher degree, in a more perfect manner, i.e. invisibly--by cleansing, enlightening, and perfecting.

Reply Obj. 2: The saints in heaven resemble the angels as to their share of glory, but not as to the conditions of their nature: and consequently not in regard to the sacraments.

Reply Obj. 3: Wicked men do not owe their power of conferring sacraments to their being members of the devil. Consequently, it does not follow that a fortiori the devil, their head, can do so.

EIGHTH ARTICLE [III, Q. 64, Art. 8]

Whether the Minister's Intention Is Required for the Validity of a Sacrament?

Objection 1: It seems that the minister's intention is not required for the validity of a sacrament. For the minister of a sacrament works instrumentally. But the perfection of an action does not depend on the intention of the instrument, but on that of the principal agent. Therefore the minister's intention is not necessary for the perfecting of a sacrament.

Obj. 2: Further, one man's intention cannot be known to another. Therefore if the minister's intention were required for the validity of a sacrament, he who approaches a sacrament could not know whether he has received the sacrament. Consequently he could have no certainty in regard to salvation; the more that some sacraments are necessary for salvation, as we shall state further on (Q. 65, A. 4).

Obj. 3: Further, a man's intention cannot bear on that to which he does not attend. But sometimes ministers of sacraments do not attend to what they say or do, through thinking of something else. Therefore in this respect the sacrament would be invalid through want of intention.

*On the contrary,* What is unintentional happens by chance. But this cannot be said of the sacramental operation. Therefore the sacraments require the intention of the minister.

*I answer that,* When a thing is indifferent to many uses, it must needs be determined to one, if that one has to be effected. Now those things which are done in the sacraments, can be done with various intent; for instance, washing with water, which is done in baptism, may be ordained to bodily cleanliness, to the health of the body, to amusement, and many other similar things. Consequently, it needs to be determined to one purpose, i.e. the sacramental effect, by the intention of him who washes. And this intention is expressed by the words which are pronounced in the sacraments; for instance the words, "I baptize thee in the name of the Father," etc.

Reply Obj. 1: An inanimate instrument has no intention regarding the effect; but instead of the intention there is the motion whereby it is moved by the principal agent. But an animate instrument, such as a minister, is not only moved, but in a sense moves itself, in so far as by his will he moves his bodily members to act. Consequently, his intention is required, whereby he subjects himself to the principal agent; that is, it is necessary that he intend to do that which Christ and the Church do.

Reply Obj. 2: On this point there are two opinions. For some hold that the mental intention of the minister is necessary; in the absence of which the sacrament is invalid: and that this defect in the case of children who have not the intention of approaching the sacrament, is made good by Christ, Who baptizes inwardly: whereas in adults, who have that intention, this defect is made good by their faith and devotion.

This might be true enough of the ultimate effect, i.e. justification from sins; but as to that effect which is both real and sacramental, viz. the character, it does not appear possible for it to be made good by the devotion of the recipient, since a character is never imprinted save by a sacrament.

Consequently, others with better reason hold that the minister of a sacrament acts in the person of the whole Church, whose minister he is; while in the words uttered by him, the intention of the Church is expressed; and that this suffices for the validity of the sacrament, except the contrary be expressed on the part either of the minister or of the recipient of the sacrament.

Reply Obj. 3: Although he who thinks of something else, has no actual intention, yet he has habitual intention, which suffices for the validity of the sacrament; for instance if, when a priest goes to baptize someone, he intends to do to him what the Church does. Wherefore if subsequently during the exercise of the act his mind be distracted by other matters, the sacrament is valid in virtue of his original intention. Nevertheless, the minister of a sacrament should take great care to have actual intention. But this is not entirely in man's power, because when a man wishes to be very intent on something, he begins unintentionally to think of other things, according to Ps. 39:18: "My heart hath forsaken me."

NINTH ARTICLE [III, Q. 64, Art. 9]

Whether Faith Is Required of Necessity in the Minister of a Sacrament?

Objection 1: It seems that faith is required of necessity in the minister of a sacrament. For, as stated above (A. 8), the intention of the minister is necessary for the validity of a sacrament. But "faith directs in intention" as Augustine says against Julian (In Psalm xxxi, cf. Contra Julian iv). Therefore, if the minister is without the true faith, the sacrament is invalid.

Obj. 2: Further, if a minister of the Church has not the true faith, it seems that he is a heretic. But heretics, seemingly, cannot confer sacraments. For Cyprian says in an epistle against heretics (lxxiii): "Everything whatsoever heretics do, is carnal, void and counterfeit, so that nothing that they do should receive our approval." And Pope Leo says in his epistle to Leo Augustus (clvi): "It is a matter of notoriety that the light of all the heavenly sacraments is extinguished in the see of Alexandria, by an act of dire and senseless cruelty. The sacrifice is no longer offered, the chrism is no longer consecrated, all the mysteries of religion have fled at the touch of the parricide hands of ungodly men." Therefore a sacrament requires of necessity that the minister should have the true faith.

Obj. 3: Further, those who have not the true faith seem to be separated from the Church by excommunication: for it is written in the second canonical epistle of John (10): "If any man come to you, and bring not this doctrine, receive him not into the house, nor say to him; God speed you": and (Titus 3:10): "A man that is a heretic, after the first and second admonition avoid." But it seems that an excommunicate cannot confer a sacrament of the Church: since he is separated from the Church, to whose ministry the dispensation of the sacraments belongs. Therefore a sacrament requires of necessity that the minister should have the true faith.

*On the contrary,* Augustine says against the Donatist Petilian: "Remember that the evil lives of wicked men are not prejudicial to God's sacraments, by rendering them either invalid or less holy."

*I answer that,* As stated above (A. 5), since the minister works instrumentally in the sacraments, he acts not by his own but by Christ's power. Now just as charity belongs to a man's own power so also does faith. Wherefore, just as the validity of a sacrament does not require that the minister should have charity, and even sinners can confer sacraments, as stated above (A. 5); so neither is it necessary that he should have faith, and even an unbeliever can confer a true sacrament, provided that the other essentials be there.

Reply Obj. 1: It may happen that a man's faith is defective in regard to something else, and not in regard to the reality of the sacrament which he confers: for instance, he may believe that it is unlawful to swear in any case whatever, and yet he may believe that baptism is an efficient cause of salvation. And thus such unbelief does not hinder the intention of conferring the sacrament. But if his faith be defective in regard to the very sacrament that he confers, although he believe that no inward effect is caused by the thing done outwardly, yet he does know that the Catholic Church intends to confer a sacrament by that which is outwardly done. Wherefore, his unbelief notwithstanding, he can intend to do what the Church does, albeit he esteem it to be nothing. And such an intention suffices for a sacrament: because as stated above (A. 8, ad 2) the minister of a sacrament acts in the person of the Church by whose faith any defect in the minister's faith is made good.

Reply Obj. 2: Some heretics in conferring sacraments do not observe the form prescribed by the Church: and these confer neither the sacrament nor the reality of the sacrament. But some do observe the form prescribed by the Church: and these confer indeed the sacrament but not the reality. I say this in the supposition that they are outwardly cut off from the Church; because from the very fact that anyone receives the sacraments from them, he sins; and consequently is hindered from receiving the effect of the sacrament. Wherefore Augustine (Fulgentius, De Fide ad Pet.) says: "Be well assured and have no doubt whatever that those who are baptized outside the Church, unless they come back to the Church, will reap disaster from their Baptism." In this sense Pope Leo says that "the light of the sacraments was extinguished in the Church of Alexandria"; viz. in regard to the reality of the sacrament, not as to the sacrament itself.

Cyprian, however, thought that heretics do not confer even the sacrament: but in this respect we do not follow his opinion. Hence Augustine says (De unico Baptismo xiii): "Though the martyr Cyprian refused to recognize Baptism conferred by heretics or schismatics, yet so great are his merits, culminating in the crown of martyrdom, that the light of his charity dispels the darkness of his fault, and if anything needed pruning, the sickle of his passion cut it off."

Reply Obj. 3: The power of administering the sacraments belongs to the spiritual character which is indelible, as explained above (Q. 63, A. 3). Consequently, if a man be suspended by the Church, or excommunicated or degraded, he does not lose the power of conferring sacraments, but the permission to use this power. Wherefore he does indeed confer the sacrament, but he sins in so doing. He also sins that receives a sacrament from such a man: so that he does not receive the reality of the sacrament, unless ignorance excuses him.

TENTH ARTICLE [III, Q. 64, Art. 10]

Whether the Validity of a Sacrament Requires a Good Intention in the Minister?

Objection 1: It seems that the validity of a sacrament requires a good intention in the minister. For the minister's intention should be in conformity with the Church's intention, as explained above (A. 8, ad 1). But the intention of the Church is always good. Therefore the validity of a sacrament requires of necessity a good intention in the minister.

Obj. 2: Further, a perverse intention seems worse than a playful one. But a playful intention destroys a sacrament: for instance, if someone were to baptize anybody not seriously but in fun. Much more, therefore, does a perverse intention destroy a sacrament: for instance, if somebody were to baptize a man in order to kill him afterwards.

Obj. 3: Further, a perverse intention vitiates the whole work, according to Luke 11:34: "If thy eye be evil, thy" whole "body will be darksome." But the sacraments of Christ cannot be contaminated by evil men; as Augustine says against Petilian (Cont. Litt. Petil ii). Therefore it seems that, if the minister's intention is perverse, the sacrament is invalid.

*On the contrary,* A perverse intention belongs to the wickedness of the minister. But the wickedness of the minister does not annul the sacrament: neither, therefore, does his perverse intention.

*I answer that,* The minister's intention may be perverted in two ways. First in regard to the sacrament: for instance, when a man does not intend to confer a sacrament, but to make a mockery of it. Such a perverse intention takes away the truth of the sacrament, especially if it be manifested outwardly.

Secondly, the minister's intention may be perverted as to something that follows the sacrament: for instance, a priest may intend to baptize a woman so as to be able to abuse her; or to consecrate the Body of Christ, so as to use it for sorcery. And because that which comes first does not depend on that which follows, consequently such a perverse intention does not annul the sacrament; but the minister himself sins grievously in having such an intention.

Reply Obj. 1: The Church has a good intention both as to the validity of the sacrament and as to the use thereof: but it is the former intention that perfects the sacrament, while the latter conduces to the meritorious effect. Consequently, the minister who conforms his intention to the Church as to the former rectitude, but not as to the latter, perfects the sacrament indeed, but gains no merit for himself.

Reply Obj. 2: The intention of mimicry or fun excludes the first kind of right intention, necessary for the validity of a sacrament. Consequently, there is no comparison.

Reply Obj. 3: A perverse intention perverts the action of the one who has such an intention, not the action of another. Consequently, the perverse intention of the minister perverts the sacrament in so far as it is his action: not in so far as it is the action of Christ, Whose minister he is. It is just as if the servant [minister] of some man were to carry alms to the poor with a wicked intention, whereas his master had commanded him with a good intention to do so.

# QUESTION 65

OF THE NUMBER OF THE SACRAMENTS (In Four Articles)

We have now to consider the number of the sacraments: and concerning this there are four points of inquiry:

(1) Whether there are seven sacraments?

(2) The order of the sacraments among themselves;

(3) Their mutual comparison;

(4) Whether all the sacraments are necessary for salvation?

FIRST ARTICLE [III, Q. 65, Art. 1]

Whether There Should Be Seven Sacraments?

Objection 1: It seems that there ought not to be seven sacraments. For the sacraments derive their efficacy from the Divine power, and the power of Christ's Passion. But the Divine power is one, and Christ's Passion is one; since "by one oblation He hath perfected for ever them that are sanctified" (Heb. 10:14). Therefore there should be but one sacrament.

Obj. 2: Further, a sacrament is intended as a remedy for the defect caused by sin. Now this is twofold, punishment and guilt. Therefore two sacraments would be enough.

Obj. 3: Further, sacraments belong to the actions of the ecclesiastical hierarchy, as Dionysius explains (Eccl. Hier. v). But, as he says, there are three actions of the ecclesiastical hierarchy, namely, "to cleanse, to enlighten, to perfect." Therefore there should be no more than three sacraments.

Obj. 4: Further, Augustine says (Contra Faust. xix) that the "sacraments" of the New Law are "less numerous" than those of the Old Law. But in the Old Law there was no sacrament corresponding to Confirmation and Extreme Unction. Therefore these should not be counted among the sacraments of the New Law.

Obj. 5: Further, lust is not more grievous than other sins, as we have made clear in the Second Part (I-II, Q. 74, A. 5; II-II, Q. 154, A. 3). But there is no sacrament instituted as a remedy for other sins. Therefore neither should matrimony be instituted as a remedy for lust.

Obj. 6: On the other hand, It seems that there should be more than seven sacraments. For sacraments are a kind of sacred sign. But in the Church there are many sanctifications by sensible signs, such as Holy Water the Consecration of Altars, and such like. Therefore there are more than seven sacraments.

Obj. 7: Further, Hugh of St. Victor (De Sacram. i) says that the sacraments of the Old Law were oblations, tithes and sacrifices. But the Sacrifice of the Church is one sacrament, called the Eucharist. Therefore oblations also and tithes should be called sacraments.

Obj. 8: Further, there are three kinds of sin, original, mortal and venial. Now Baptism is intended as a remedy against original sin, and Penance against mortal sin. Therefore besides the seven sacraments, there should be another against venial sin.

*I answer that,* As stated above (Q. 62, A. 5; Q. 63, A. 1), the sacraments of the Church were instituted for a twofold purpose: namely, in order to perfect man in things pertaining to the worship of God according to the religion of Christian life, and to be a remedy against the defects caused by sin. And in either way it is becoming that there should be seven sacraments.

For spiritual life has a certain conformity with the life of the body: just as other corporeal things have a certain likeness to things spiritual. Now a man attains perfection in the corporeal life in two ways: first, in regard to his own person; secondly, in regard to the whole community of the society in which he lives, for man is by nature a social animal. With regard to himself man is perfected in the life of the body, in two ways; first, directly ( per se ), i.e. by acquiring some vital perfection; secondly, indirectly ( per accidens ), i.e. by the removal of hindrances to life, such as ailments, or the like. Now the life of the body is perfected directly, in three ways. First, by generation whereby a man begins to be and to live: and corresponding to this in the spiritual life there is Baptism, which is a spiritual regeneration, according to Titus 3:5: "By the laver of regeneration," etc. Secondly, by growth whereby a man is brought to perfect size and strength: and corresponding to this in the spiritual life there is Confirmation, in which the Holy Ghost is given to strengthen us. Wherefore the disciples who were already baptized were bidden thus: "Stay you in the city till you be endued with power from on high" (Luke 24:49). Thirdly, by nourishment, whereby life and strength are preserved to man; and corresponding to this in the spiritual life there is the Eucharist. Wherefore it is said (John 6:54): "Except you eat of the flesh of the Son of Man, and drink His blood, you shall not have life in you."

And this would be enough for man if he had an impassible life, both corporally and spiritually; but since man is liable at times to both corporal and spiritual infirmity, i.e. sin, hence man needs a cure from his infirmity; which cure is twofold. One is the healing, that restores health: and corresponding to this in the spiritual life there is Penance, according to Ps. 40:5: "Heal my soul, for I have sinned against Thee." The other is the restoration of former vigor by means of suitable diet and exercise: and corresponding to this in the spiritual life there is Extreme Unction, which removes the remainder of sin, and prepares man for final glory. Wherefore it is written (James 5:15): "And if he be in sins they shall be forgiven him."

In regard to the whole community, man is perfected in two ways. First, by receiving power to rule the community and to exercise public acts: and corresponding to this in the spiritual life there is the sacrament of order, according to the saying of Heb. 7:27, that priests offer sacrifices not for themselves only, but also for the people. Secondly in regard to natural propagation. This is accomplished by Matrimony both in the corporal and in the spiritual life: since it is not only a sacrament but also a function of nature.

We may likewise gather the number of the sacraments from their being instituted as a remedy against the defect caused by sin. For Baptism is intended as a remedy against the absence of spiritual life; Confirmation, against the infirmity of soul found in those of recent birth; the Eucharist, against the soul's proneness to sin; Penance, against actual sin committed after baptism; Extreme Unction, against the remainders of sins--of those sins, namely, which are not sufficiently removed by Penance, whether through negligence or through ignorance; order, against divisions in the community; Matrimony, as a remedy against concupiscence in the individual, and against the decrease in numbers that results from death.

Some, again, gather the number of sacraments from a certain adaptation to the virtues and to the defects and penal effects resulting from sin. They say that Baptism corresponds to Faith, and is ordained as a remedy against original sin; Extreme Unction, to Hope, being ordained against venial sin; the Eucharist, to Charity, being ordained against the penal effect which is malice; Order, to Prudence, being ordained against ignorance; Penance to Justice, being ordained against mortal sin; Matrimony, to Temperance, being ordained against concupiscence; Confirmation, to Fortitude, being ordained against infirmity.

Reply Obj. 1: The same principal agent uses various instruments unto various effects, in accordance with the thing to be done. In the same way the Divine power and the Passion of Christ work in us through the various sacraments as through various instruments.

Reply Obj. 2: Guilt and punishment are diversified both according to species, inasmuch as there are various species of guilt and punishment, and according to men's various states and habitudes. And in this respect it was necessary to have a number of sacraments, as explained above.

Reply Obj. 3: In hierarchical actions we must consider the agents, the recipients and the actions. The agents are the ministers of the Church; and to these the sacrament of order belongs. The recipients are those who approach the sacraments: and these are brought into being by Matrimony. The actions are "cleansing," "enlightening," and "perfecting." Mere cleansing, however, cannot be a sacrament of the New Law, which confers grace: yet it belongs to certain sacramentals, i.e. catechism and exorcism. But cleansing coupled with enlightening, according to Dionysius, belongs to Baptism; and, for him who falls back into sin, they belong secondarily to Penance and Extreme Unction. And perfecting, as regards power, which is, as it were, a formal perfection, belongs to Confirmation: while, as regards the attainment of the end, it belongs to the Eucharist.

Reply Obj. 4: In the sacrament of Confirmation we receive the fulness of the Holy Ghost in order to be strengthened; while in Extreme Unction man is prepared for the immediate attainment of glory; and neither of these two purposes was becoming to the Old Testament. Consequently, nothing in the old Law could correspond to these sacraments. Nevertheless, the sacraments of the old Law were more numerous, on account of the various kinds of sacrifices and ceremonies.

Reply Obj. 5: There was need for a special sacrament to be applied as a remedy against venereal concupiscence: first because by this concupiscence, not only the person but also the nature is defiled: secondly, by reason of its vehemence whereby it clouds the reason.

Reply Obj. 6: Holy Water and other consecrated things are not called sacraments, because they do not produce the sacramental effect, which is the receiving of grace. They are, however, a kind of disposition to the sacraments: either by removing obstacles, thus holy water is ordained against the snares of the demons, and against venial sins: or by making things suitable for the conferring of a sacrament; thus the altar and vessels are consecrated through reverence for the Eucharist.

Reply Obj. 7: Oblations and tithes, both the Law of nature and in the Law of Moses, ere ordained not only for the sustenance of the ministers and the poor, but also figuratively; and consequently they were sacraments. But now they remain no longer as figures, and therefore they are not sacraments.

Reply Obj. 8: The infusion of grace is not necessary for the blotting out of venial sin. Wherefore, since grace is infused in each of the sacraments of the New Law, none of them was instituted directly against venial sin. This is taken away by certain sacramentals, for instance, Holy Water and such like. Some, however, hold that Extreme Unction is ordained against venial sin. But of this we shall speak in its proper place (Suppl., Q. 30, A. 1).

SECOND ARTICLE [III, Q. 65, Art. 2]

Whether the Order of the Sacraments, As Given Above, Is Becoming?

Objection 1: It seems that the order of the sacraments as given above is unbecoming. For according to the Apostle (1 Cor. 15:46), "that was . . . first . . . which is natural, afterwards that which is spiritual." But man is begotten through Matrimony by a first and natural generation; while in Baptism he is regenerated as by a second and spiritual generation. Therefore Matrimony should precede Baptism.

Obj. 2: Further, through the sacrament of order man receives the power of agent in sacramental actions. But the agent precedes his action. Therefore order should precede Baptism and the other sacraments.

Obj. 3: Further, the Eucharist is a spiritual food; while Confirmation is compared to growth. But food causes, and consequently precedes, growth. Therefore the Eucharist precedes Confirmation.

Obj. 4: Further, Penance prepares man for the Eucharist. But a disposition precedes perfection. Therefore Penance should precede the Eucharist.

Obj. 5: Further, that which is nearer the last end comes after other things. But, of all the sacraments, Extreme Unction is nearest to the last end which is Happiness. Therefore it should be placed last among the sacraments.

*On the contrary,* The order of the sacraments, as given above, is commonly adopted by all.

*I answer that,* The reason of the order among the sacraments appears from what has been said above (A. 1). For just as unity precedes multitude, so those sacraments which are intended for the perfection of the individual, naturally precede those which are intended for the perfection of the multitude; and consequently the last place among the sacraments is given to order and Matrimony, which are intended for the perfection of the multitude: while Matrimony is placed after order, because it has less participation in the nature of the spiritual life, to which the sacraments are ordained. Moreover, among things ordained to the perfection of the individual, those naturally come first which are ordained directly to the perfection of the spiritual life, and afterwards, those which are ordained thereto indirectly, viz. by removing some supervening accidental cause of harm; such are Penance and Extreme Unction: while, of these, Extreme Unction is naturally placed last, for it preserves the healing which was begun by Penance.

Of the remaining three, it is clear that Baptism which is a spiritual regeneration, comes first; then Confirmation, which is ordained to the formal perfection of power; and after these the Eucharist which is ordained to final perfection.

Reply Obj. 1: Matrimony as ordained to natural life is a function of nature. But in so far as it has something spiritual it is a sacrament. And because it has the least amount of spirituality it is placed last.

Reply Obj. 2: For a thing to be an agent it must first of all be perfect in itself. Wherefore those sacraments by which a man is perfected in himself, are placed before the sacrament of order, in which a man is made a perfecter of others.

Reply Obj. 3: Nourishment both precedes growth, as its cause; and follows it, as maintaining the perfection of size and power in man. Consequently, the Eucharist can be placed before Confirmation, as Dionysius places it (Eccl. Hier. iii, iv), and can be placed after it, as the Master does (iv, 2, 8).

Reply Obj. 4: This argument would hold if Penance were required of necessity as a preparation to the Eucharist. But this is not true: for if anyone be without mortal sin, he does not need Penance in order to receive the Eucharist. Thus it is clear that Penance is an accidental preparation to the Eucharist, that is to say, sin being supposed. Wherefore it is written in the last chapter of the second Book of Paralipomenon (cf. 2 Paral 33:18): "Thou, O Lord of the righteous, didst not impose penance on righteous men." [*The words quoted are from the apocryphal Prayer of Manasses, which, before the Council of Trent, was to be found inserted in some Latin copies of the Bible.]

Reply Obj. 5: Extreme Unction, for this very reason, is given the last place among those sacraments which are ordained to the perfection of the individual.

THIRD ARTICLE [III, Q. 65, Art. 3]

Whether the Eucharist Is the Greatest of the Sacraments?

Objection 1: It seems that the Eucharist is not the principal of the sacraments. For the common good is of more account than the good of the individual (1 Ethic. ii). But Matrimony is ordained to the common good of the human race by means of generation: whereas the sacrament of the Eucharist is ordained to the private good of the recipient. Therefore it is not the greatest of the sacraments.

Obj. 2: Further, those sacraments, seemingly, are

greater, which are conferred by a greater minister. But the sacraments of Confirmation and order are conferred by a bishop only, who is a greater minister than a mere minister such as a priest, by whom the sacraments of the Eucharist is conferred. Therefore those sacraments are greater.

Obj. 3: Further, those sacraments are greater that have the greater power. But some of the sacraments imprint a character, viz. Baptism, Confirmation and order; whereas the Eucharist does not. Therefore those sacraments are greater.

Obj. 4: Further, that seems to be greater, on which others depend without its depending on them. But the Eucharist depends on Baptism: since no one can receive the Eucharist except he has been baptized. Therefore Baptism is greater than the Eucharist.

*On the contrary,* Dionysius says (Eccl. Hier. iii) that "No one receives hierarchical perfection save by the most God-like Eucharist." Therefore this sacrament is greater than all the others and perfects them.

*I answer that,* Absolutely speaking, the sacrament of the Eucharist is the greatest of all the sacraments: and this may be shown in three ways. First of all because it contains Christ Himself substantially: whereas the other sacraments contain a certain instrumental power which is a share of Christ's power, as we have shown above (Q. 62, A. 4, ad 3, A. 5). Now that which is essentially such is always of more account than that which is such by participation.

Secondly, this is made clear by considering the relation of the sacraments to one another. For all the other sacraments seem to be ordained to this one as to their end. For it is manifest that the sacrament of order is ordained to the consecration of the Eucharist: and the sacrament of Baptism to the reception of the Eucharist: while a man is perfected by Confirmation, so as not to fear to abstain from this sacrament. By Penance and Extreme Unction man is prepared to receive the Body of Christ worthily. And Matrimony at least in its signification, touches this sacrament; in so far as it signifies the union of Christ with the Church, of which union the Eucharist is a figure: hence the Apostle says (Eph. 5:32): "This is a great sacrament: but I speak in Christ and in the Church."

Thirdly, this is made clear by considering the rites of the sacraments. For nearly all the sacraments terminate in the Eucharist, as Dionysius says (Eccl. Hier. iii): thus those who have been ordained receive Holy Communion, as also do those who have been baptized, if they be adults.

The remaining sacraments may be compared to one another in several ways. For on the ground of necessity, Baptism is the greatest of the sacraments; while from the point of view of perfection, order comes first; while Confirmation holds a middle place. The sacraments of Penance and Extreme Unction are on a degree inferior to those mentioned above; because, as stated above (A. 2), they are ordained to the Christian life, not directly, but accidentally, as it were, that is to say, as remedies against supervening defects. And among these, Extreme Unction is compared to Penance, as Confirmation to Baptism; in such a way, that Penance is more necessary, whereas Extreme Unction is more perfect.

Reply Obj. 1: Matrimony is ordained to the common good as regards the body. But the common spiritual good of the whole Church is contained substantially in the sacrament itself of the Eucharist.

Reply Obj. 2: By order and Confirmation the faithful of Christ are deputed to certain special duties; and this can be done by the prince alone. Consequently the conferring of these sacraments belongs exclusively to a bishop, who is, as it were, a prince in the Church. But a man is not deputed to any duty by the sacrament of the Eucharist, rather is this sacrament the end of all duties, as stated above.

Reply Obj. 3: The sacramental character, as stated above (Q. 63, A. 3), is a kind of participation in Christ's priesthood. Wherefore the sacrament that unites man to Christ Himself, is greater than a sacrament that imprints Christ's character.

Reply Obj. 4: This argument proceeds on the ground of necessity. For thus Baptism, being of the greatest necessity, is the greatest of the sacraments, just as order and Confirmation have a certain excellence considered in their administration; and Matrimony by reason of its signification. For there is no reason why a thing should not be greater from a certain point of view which is not greater absolutely speaking.

FOURTH ARTICLE [III, Q. 65, Art. 4]

Whether All the Sacraments Are Necessary for Salvation?

Objection 1: It seems that all the sacraments are necessary for salvation. For what is not necessary seems to be superfluous. But no sacrament is superfluous, because "God does nothing without a purpose" (De Coelo et Mundo i). Therefore all the sacraments are necessary for salvation.

Obj. 2: Further, just as it is said of Baptism (John 3:5): "Unless a man be born again of water and the Holy Ghost, he cannot enter in to the kingdom of God," so of the Eucharist is it said (John 6:54): "Except you eat of the flesh of the Son of Man, and drink of His blood, you shall not have life in you." Therefore, just as Baptism is a necessary sacrament, so is the Eucharist.

Obj. 3: Further, a man can be saved without the sacrament of Baptism, provided that some unavoidable obstacle, and not his contempt for religion, debar him from the sacrament, as we shall state further on (Q. 68, A. 2). But contempt of religion in any sacrament is a hindrance to salvation. Therefore, in like manner, all the sacraments are necessary for salvation.

*On the contrary,* Children are saved by Baptism alone without the other sacraments.

*I answer that,* Necessity of end, of which we speak now, is twofold. First, a thing may be necessary so that without it the end cannot be attained; thus food is necessary for human life. And this is simple necessity of end. Secondly, a thing is said to be necessary, if, without it, the end cannot be attained so becomingly: thus a horse is necessary for a journey. But this is not simple necessity of end.

In the first way, three sacraments are necessary for salvation. Two of them are necessary to the individual; Baptism, simply and absolutely; Penance, in the case of mortal sin committed after Baptism; while the sacrament of order is necessary to the Church, since "where there is no governor the people shall fall" (Prov. 11:14).

But in the second way the other sacraments are necessary. For in a sense Confirmation perfects Baptism; Extreme Unction perfects Penance; while Matrimony, by multiplying them, preserves the numbers in the Church.

Reply Obj. 1: For a thing not to be superfluous it is enough if it be necessary either in the first or the second way. It is thus that the sacraments are necessary, as stated above.

Reply Obj. 2: These words of our Lord are to be understood of spiritual, and not of merely sacramental, eating, as Augustine explains (Tract. xxvi super Joan.).

Reply Obj. 3: Although contempt of any of the sacraments is a hindrance to salvation, yet it does not amount to contempt of the sacrament, if anyone does not trouble to receive a sacrament that is not necessary for salvation. Else those who do not receive orders, and those who do not contract Matrimony, would be guilty of contempt of those sacraments.

## QUESTION 66

OF THE SACRAMENT OF BAPTISM (In Twelve Articles)

We have now to consider each sacrament specially: (1) Baptism; (2) Confirmation; (3) the Eucharist; (4) Penance; (5) Extreme Unction; (6) Order; (7) Matrimony.

Concerning the first, our consideration will be twofold: (1) of Baptism itself; (2) of things preparatory to Baptism.

Concerning the first, four points arise for our consideration: (1) Things pertaining to the sacrament of Baptism; (2) The minister of this sacrament; (3) The recipients of this sacrament; (4) The effect of this sacrament.

Concerning the first there are twelve points of inquiry:

(1) What is Baptism? Is it a washing?

(2) Of the institution of this sacrament;

(3) Whether water be the proper matter of this sacrament?

(4) Whether plain water be required?

(5) Whether this be a suitable form of this sacrament: "I baptize thee in the name of the Father, and of the Son, and of the Holy Ghost"?

(6) Whether one could baptize with this form: "I baptize thee in the name of Christ?"

(7) Whether immersion is necessary for Baptism?

(8) Whether trine immersion is necessary?

(9) Whether Baptism can be reiterated?

(10) Of the Baptismal rite;

(11) Of the various kinds of Baptism;

(12) Of the comparison between various Baptisms.

FIRST ARTICLE [III, Q. 66, Art. 1]

Whether Baptism Is the Mere Washing?

Objection 1: It seems that Baptism is not the mere washing. For the washing of the body is something transitory: but Baptism is something permanent. Therefore Baptism is not the mere washing; but rather is it "the regeneration, the seal, the safeguarding, the enlightenment," as Damascene says (De Fide Orth. iv).

Obj. 2: Further, Hugh of St. Victor says (De Sacram. ii) that "Baptism is water sanctified by God's word for the blotting out of sins." But the washing itself is not water, but a certain use of water.

Obj. 3: Further, Augustine says (Tract. lxxx super Joan.): "The word is added to the element, and this becomes a sacrament." Now, the element is the water. Therefore Baptism is the water and not the washing.

*On the contrary,* It is written (Ecclus. 34:30): "He that washeth himself ( baptizatur ) after touching the dead, if he touch him again, what does his washing avail?" It seems, therefore, that Baptism is the washing or bathing.

*I answer that,* In the sacrament of Baptism, three things may be considered: namely, that which is sacrament only; that which is reality and sacrament; and that which is reality only. That which is sacrament only, is something visible and outward; the sign, namely, of the inward effect: for such is the very nature of a sacrament. And this outward something that can be perceived by the sense is both the water itself and its use, which is the washing. Hence some have thought that the water itself is the sacrament: which seems to be the meaning of the passage quoted from Hugh of St. Victor. For in the general definition of a sacrament he says that it is "a material element": and in defining Baptism he says it is "water."

But this is not true. For since the sacraments of the New Law effect a certain sanctification, there the sacrament is completed where the sanctification is completed. Now, the sanctification is not completed in water; but a certain sanctifying instrumental virtue, not permanent but transient, passes from the water, in which it is, into man who is the subject of true sanctification. Consequently the sacrament is not completed in the very water, but in applying the water to man, i.e. in the washing. Hence the Master (iv, 3) says that "Baptism is the outward washing of the body done together with the prescribed form of words."

The Baptismal character is both reality and sacrament: because it is something real signified by the outward washing; and a sacramental sign of the inward justification: and this last is the reality only, in this sacrament--namely, the reality signified and not signifying.

Reply Obj. 1: That which is both sacrament and reality--i.e. the character--and that which is reality only--i.e. the inward justification--remain: the character remains and is indelible, as stated above (Q. 63, A. 5); the justification remains, but can be lost. Consequently Damascene defined Baptism, not as to that which is done outwardly, and is the sacrament only; but as to that which is inward. Hence he sets down two things as pertaining to the character--namely, "seal" and "safeguarding"; inasmuch as the character which is called a seal, so far as itself is concerned, safeguards the soul in good. He also sets down two things as pertaining to the ultimate reality of the sacrament--namely, "regeneration" which refers to the fact that man by being baptized begins the new life of righteousness; and "enlightenment," which refers especially to faith, by which man receives spiritual life, according to Habac 2 (Heb. 10:38; cf. Habac 2:4): "But (My) just man liveth by faith"; and Baptism is a sort of protestation of faith; whence it is called the "Sacrament of Faith." Likewise Dionysius defined Baptism by its relation to the other sacraments, saying (Eccl. Hier. ii) that it is "the principle that forms the habits of the soul for the reception of those most holy words and sacraments"; and again by its relation to heavenly glory, which is the universal end of all the sacraments, when he adds, "preparing the way for us, whereby we mount to the repose of the heavenly kingdom"; and again as to the beginning of spiritual life, when he adds, "the conferring of our most sacred and Godlike regeneration."

Reply Obj. 2: As already stated, the opinion of Hugh of St. Victor on this question is not to be followed. Nevertheless the saying that "Baptism is water" may be verified in so far as water is the material principle of Baptism: and thus there would be "causal predication."

Reply Obj. 3: When the words are added, the element becomes a sacrament, not in the element itself, but in man, to whom the element is applied, by being used in washing him. Indeed, this is signified by those very words which are added to the element, when we say: "I baptize thee," etc.

SECOND ARTICLE [III, Q. 66, Art. 2]

Whether Baptism Was Instituted After Christ's Passion?

Objection 1: It seems that Baptism was instituted after Christ's Passion. For the cause precedes the effect. Now Christ's Passion operates in the sacraments of the New Law. Therefore Christ's Passion precedes the institution of the sacraments of the New Law: especially the sacrament of Baptism since the Apostle says (Rom. 6:3): "All we, who are baptized in Christ Jesus, are baptized in His death," etc.

Obj. 2: Further, the sacraments of the New Law derive their efficacy from the mandate of Christ. But Christ gave the disciples the mandate of Baptism after His Passion and Resurrection, when He said: "Going, teach ye all nations, baptizing them in the name of the Father," etc. (Matt. 28:19). Therefore it seems that Baptism was instituted after Christ's Passion.

Obj. 3: Further, Baptism is a necessary sacrament, as stated above (Q. 65, A. 4): wherefore, seemingly, it must have been binding on man as soon as it was instituted. But before Christ's Passion men were not bound to be baptized: for Circumcision was still in force, which was supplanted by Baptism. Therefore it seems that Baptism was not instituted before Christ's Passion.

*On the contrary,* Augustine says in a sermon on the Epiphany (Append. Serm., clxxxv): "As soon as Christ was plunged into the waters, the waters washed away the sins of all." But this was before Christ's Passion. Therefore Baptism was instituted before Christ's Passion.

*I answer that,* As stated above (Q. 62, A. 1), sacraments derive from their institution the power of conferring grace. Wherefore it seems that a sacrament is then instituted, when it receives the power of producing its effect. Now Baptism received this power when Christ was baptized. Consequently Baptism was truly instituted then, if we consider it as a sacrament. But the obligation of receiving this sacrament was proclaimed to mankind after the Passion and Resurrection. First, because Christ's Passion put an end to the figurative sacraments, which were supplanted by Baptism and the other sacraments of the New Law. Secondly, because by Baptism man is "made conformable" to Christ's Passion and Resurrection, in so far as he dies to sin and begins to live anew unto righteousness. Consequently it behooved Christ to suffer and to rise again, before proclaiming to man his obligation of conforming himself to Christ's Death and Resurrection.

Reply Obj. 1: Even before Christ's Passion, Baptism, inasmuch as it foreshadowed it, derived its efficacy therefrom; but not in the same way as the sacraments of the Old Law. For these were mere figures: whereas Baptism derived the power of justifying from Christ Himself, to Whose power the Passion itself owed its saving virtue.

Reply Obj. 2: It was not meet that men should be restricted to a number of figures by Christ, Who came to fulfil and replace the figure by His reality. Therefore before His Passion He did not make Baptism obligatory as soon as it was instituted; but wished men to become accustomed to its use; especially in regard to the Jews, to whom all things were figurative, as Augustine says (Contra Faust. iv). But after His Passion and Resurrection He made Baptism obligatory, not only on the Jews, but also on the Gentiles, when He gave the commandment: "Going, teach ye all nations."

Reply Obj. 3: Sacraments are not obligatory except when we are commanded to receive them. And this was not before the Passion, as stated above. For our Lord's words to Nicodemus (John 3:5), "Unless a man be born again of water and the Holy Ghost, he cannot enter into the kingdom of God, seem to refer to the future rather than to the present."

THIRD ARTICLE [III, Q. 66, Art. 3]

Whether Water Is the Proper Matter of Baptism?

Objection 1: It seems that water is not the proper matter of Baptism. For Baptism, according to Dionysius (Eccl. Hier. v) and Damascene (De Fide Orth. iv), has a power of enlightening. But enlightenment is a special characteristic of fire. Therefore Baptism should be conferred with fire rather than with water: and all the more since John the Baptist said when foretelling Christ's Baptism (Matt. 3:11): "He shall baptize you in the Holy Ghost and fire."

Obj. 2: Further, the washing away of sins is signified in Baptism. But many other things besides water are employed in washing, such as wine, oil, and such like. Therefore Baptism can be conferred with these also; and consequently water is not the proper matter of Baptism.

Obj. 3: Further, the sacraments of the Church flowed from the side of Christ hanging on the cross, as stated above (Q. 62, A. 5). But not only water flowed therefrom, but also blood. Therefore it seems that Baptism can also be conferred with blood. And this seems to be more in keeping with the effect of Baptism, because it is written (Apoc. 1:5): "(Who) washed us from our sins in His own blood."

Obj. 4: Further, as Augustine (cf. Master of the Sentences, iv, 3) and Bede (Exposit. in Luc. iii, 21) say, Christ, by "the touch of His most pure flesh, endowed the waters with a regenerating and cleansing virtue." But all waters are not connected with the waters of the Jordan which Christ touched with His flesh. Consequently it seems that Baptism cannot be conferred with any water; and therefore water, as such, is not the proper matter of Baptism.

Obj. 5: Further, if water, as such, were the proper matter of Baptism, there would be no need to do anything to the water before using it for Baptism. But in solemn Baptism the water which is used for baptizing, is exorcized and blessed. Therefore it seems that water, as such, is not the proper matter of Baptism.

*On the contrary,* our Lord said (John 3:5): "Unless a man be born again of water and the Holy Ghost, he cannot enter into the kingdom of God."

*I answer that,* By Divine institution water is the proper matter of Baptism; and with reason. First, by reason of the very nature of Baptism, which is a regeneration unto spiritual life. And this answers to the nature of water in a special degree; wherefore seeds, from which all living things, viz. plants and animals are generated, are moist and akin to water. For this reason certain philosophers held that water is the first principle of all things.

Secondly, in regard to the effects of Baptism, to which the properties of water correspond. For by reason of its moistness it cleanses; and hence it fittingly signifies and causes the cleansing from sins. By reason of its coolness it tempers superfluous heat: wherefore it fittingly mitigates the concupiscence of the fomes. By reason of its transparency, it is susceptive of light; hence its adaptability to Baptism as the "sacrament of Faith."

Thirdly, because it is suitable for the signification of the mysteries of Christ, by which we are justified. For, as Chrysostom says (Hom. xxv in Joan.) on John 3:5, "Unless a man be born again," etc., "When we dip our heads under the water as in a kind of tomb our old man is buried, and being submerged is hidden below, and thence he rises again renewed."

Fourthly, because by being so universal and abundant, it is a matter suitable to our need of this sacrament: for it can easily be obtained everywhere.

Reply Obj. 1: Fire enlightens actively. But he who is baptized does not become an enlightener, but is enlightened by faith, which "cometh by hearing" (Rom. 10:17). Consequently water is more suitable, than fire, for Baptism.

But when we find it said: "He shall baptize you in the Holy Ghost and fire," we may understand fire, as Jerome says (In Matth. ii), to mean the Holy Ghost, Who appeared above the disciples under the form of fiery tongues (Acts 2:3). Or we may understand it to mean tribulation, as Chrysostom says (Hom. iii in Matth.): because tribulation washes away sin, and tempers concupiscence. Or again, as Hilary says (Super Matth. ii) that "when we have been baptized in the Holy Ghost," we still have to be "perfected by the fire of the judgment."

Reply Obj. 2: Wine and oil are not so commonly used for washing, as water. Neither do they wash so efficiently: for whatever is washed with them, contracts a certain smell therefrom; which is not the case if water be used. Moreover, they are not so universal or so abundant as water.

Reply Obj. 3: Water flowed from Christ's side to wash us; blood, to redeem us. Wherefore blood belongs to the sacrament of the Eucharist, while water belongs to the sacrament of Baptism. Yet this latter sacrament derives its cleansing virtue from the power of Christ's blood.

Reply Obj. 4: Christ's power flowed into all waters, by reason of, not connection of place, but likeness of species, as Augustine says in a sermon on the Epiphany (Append. Serm. cxxxv): "The blessing that flowed from the Saviour's Baptism, like a mystic river, swelled the course of every stream, and filled the channels of every spring."

Reply Obj. 5: The blessing of the water is not essential to Baptism, but belongs to a certain solemnity, whereby the devotion of the faithful is aroused, and the cunning of the devil hindered from impeding the baptismal effect.

FOURTH ARTICLE [III, Q. 66, Art. 4]

Whether Plain Water Is Necessary for Baptism?

Objection 1: It seems that plain water is not necessary for Baptism. For the water which we have is not plain water; as appears especially in sea-water, in which there is a considerable proportion of the earthly element, as the Philosopher shows (Meteor. ii). Yet this water may be used for Baptism. Therefore plain and pure water is not necessary for Baptism.

Obj. 2: Further, in the solemn celebration of Baptism, chrism is poured into the water. But this seems to take away the purity and plainness of the water. Therefore pure and plain water is not necessary for Baptism.

Obj. 3: Further, the water that flowed from the side of Christ hanging on the cross was a figure of Baptism, as stated above (A. 3, ad 3). But that water, seemingly, was not pure, because the elements do not exist actually in a mixed body, such as Christ's. Therefore it seems that pure or plain water is not necessary for Baptism.

Obj. 4: Further, lye does not seem to be pure water, for it has the properties of heating and drying, which are contrary to those of water. Nevertheless it seems that lye can be used for Baptism; for the water of the Baths can be so used, which has filtered through a sulphurous vein, just as lye percolates through ashes. Therefore it seems that plain water is not necessary for Baptism.

Obj. 5: Further, rose-water is distilled from roses, just as chemical waters are distilled from certain bodies. But seemingly, such like waters may be used in Baptism; just as rain-water, which is distilled from vapors. Since, therefore, such waters are not pure and plain water, it seems that pure and plain water is not necessary for Baptism.

*On the contrary,* The proper matter of Baptism is water, as stated above (A. 3). But plain water alone has the nature of water. Therefore pure plain water is necessary for Baptism.

*I answer that,* Water may cease to be pure or plain water in two ways: first, by being mixed with another body; secondly, by alteration. And each of these may happen in a twofold manner; artificially and naturally. Now art fails in the operation of nature: because nature gives the substantial form, which art cannot give; for whatever form is given by art is accidental; except perchance when art applies a proper agent to its proper matter, as fire to a combustible; in which manner animals are produced from certain things by way of putrefaction.

Whatever artificial change, then, takes place in the water, whether by mixture or by alteration, the water's nature is not changed. Consequently such water can be used for Baptism: unless perhaps such a small quantity of water be mixed artificially with a body that the compound is something other than water; thus mud is earth rather than water, and diluted wine is wine rather than water.

But if the change be natural, sometimes it destroys the nature of the water; and this is when by a natural process water enters into the substance of a mixed body: thus water changed into the juice of the grape is wine, wherefore it has not the nature of water. Sometimes, however, there may be a natural change of the water, without destruction of species: and this, both by alteration, as we may see in the case of water heated by the sun; and by mixture, as when the water of a river has become muddy by being mixed with particles of earth.

We must therefore say that any water may be used for Baptism, no matter how much it may be changed, as long as the species of water is not destroyed; but if the species of water be destroyed, it cannot be used for Baptism.

Reply Obj. 1: The change in sea-water and in other waters which we have to hand, is not so great as to destroy the species of water. And therefore such waters may be used for Baptism.

Reply Obj. 2: Chrism does not destroy the nature of the water by being mixed with it: just as neither is water changed wherein meat and the like are boiled: except the substance boiled be so dissolved that the liquor be of a nature foreign to water; in this we may be guided by the specific gravity ( spissitudine ). If, however, from the liquor thus thickened plain water be strained, it can be used for Baptism: just as water strained from mud, although mud cannot be used for baptizing.

Reply Obj. 3: The water which flowed from the side of Christ hanging on the cross, was not the phlegmatic humor, as some have supposed. For a liquid of this kind cannot be used for Baptism, as neither can the blood of an animal, or wine, or any liquid extracted from plants. It was pure water gushing forth miraculously like the blood from a dead body, to prove the reality of our Lord's body, and confute the error of the Manichees: water, which is one of the four elements, showing Christ's body to be composed of the four elements; blood, proving that it was composed of the four humors.

Reply Obj. 4: Baptism may be conferred with lye and the waters of Sulphur Baths: because such like waters are not incorporated, artificially or naturally, with certain mixed bodies, and suffer only a certain alteration by passing through certain bodies.

Reply Obj. 5: Rose-water is a liquid distilled from roses: consequently it cannot be used for Baptism. For the same reason chemical waters cannot be used, as neither can wine. Nor does the comparison hold with rain-water, which for the most part is formed by the condensing of vapors, themselves formed from water, and contains a minimum of the liquid matter from mixed bodies; which liquid matter by the force of nature, which is stronger than art, is transformed in this process of condensation into real water, a result which cannot be produced artificially. Consequently rain-water retains no properties of any mixed body; which cannot be said of rose-water or chemical waters.

FIFTH ARTICLE [III, Q. 66, Art. 5]

Whether This Be a Suitable Form of Baptism: "I Baptize Thee in the Name of the Father, and of the Son, and of the Holy Ghost"?

Objection 1: It seems that this is not a suitable form of Baptism: "I baptize thee in the name of the Father, and of the Son, and of the Holy Ghost." For action should be ascribed to the principal agent rather than to the minister. Now the minister of a sacrament acts as an instrument, as stated above (Q. 64, A. 1); while the principal agent in Baptism is Christ, according to John 1:33, "He upon Whom thou shalt see the Spirit descending and remaining upon Him, He it is that baptizeth." It is therefore unbecoming for the minister to say, "I baptize thee": the more so thatEgo (I) is understood in the word baptizo (I baptize), so that it seems redundant.

Obj. 2: Further, there is no need for a man who does an action, to make mention of the action done; thus he who teaches, need not say, "I teach you." Now our Lord gave at the same time the precepts both of baptizing and of teaching, when He said (Matt. 28:19): "Going, teach ye all nations," etc. Therefore there is no need in the form of Baptism to mention the action of baptizing.

Obj. 3: Further, the person baptized sometimes does not understand the words; for instance, if he be deaf, or a child. But it is useless to address such a one; according to Ecclus. 32:6: "Where there is no hearing, pour not out words." Therefore it is unfitting to address the person baptized with these words: "I baptize thee."

Obj. 4: Further, it may happen that several are baptized by several at the same time; thus the apostles on one day baptized three thousand, and on another, five thousand (Acts 2, 4). Therefore the form of Baptism should not be limited to the singular number in the words, "I baptize thee": but one should be able to say, "We baptize you."

Obj. 5: Further, Baptism derives its power from Christ's Passion. But Baptism is sanctified by the form. Therefore it seems that Christ's Passion should be mentioned in the form of Baptism.

Obj. 6: Further, a name signifies a thing's property. But there are three Personal Properties of the Divine Persons, as stated in the First Part (Q. 32, A. 3). Therefore we should not say, "in the name," but "in the names of the Father, and of the Son, and of the Holy Ghost."

Obj. 7: Further, the Person of the Father is designated not only by the name Father, but also by that of "Unbegotten and Begetter"; and the Son by those of "Word," "Image," and "Begotten"; and the Holy Ghost by those of "Gift," "Love," and the "Proceeding One." Therefore it seems that Baptism is valid if conferred in these names.

*On the contrary,* our Lord said (Matt. 28:19): "Going . . . teach ye all nations, baptizing them in the name of the Father, and of the Son, and of the Holy Ghost."

*I answer that,* Baptism receives its consecration from its form, according to Eph. 5:26: "Cleansing it by the laver of water in the word of life." And Augustine says (De Unico Baptismo iv) that "Baptism is consecrated by the words of the Gospel." Consequently the cause of Baptism needs to be expressed in the baptismal form. Now this cause is twofold; the principal cause from which it derives its virtue, and this is the Blessed Trinity; and the instrumental cause, viz. the minister who confers the sacrament outwardly. Wherefore both causes should be expressed in the form of Baptism. Now the minister is designated by the words, "I baptize thee"; and the principal cause in the words, "in the name of the Father, and of the Son, and of the Holy Ghost." Therefore this is the suitable form of Baptism: "I baptize thee in the name of the Father, and of the Son, and of the Holy Ghost."

Reply Obj. 1: Action is attributed to an instrument as to the immediate agent; but to the principal agent inasmuch as the instrument acts in virtue thereof. Consequently it is fitting that in the baptismal form the minister should be mentioned as performing the act of baptizing, in the words, "I baptize thee"; indeed, our Lord attributed to the ministers the act of baptizing, when He said: "Baptizing them," etc. But the principal cause is indicated as conferring the sacrament by His own power, in the words, "in the name of the Father, and of the Son, and of the Holy Ghost": for Christ does not baptize without the Father and the Holy Ghost.

The Greeks, however, do not attribute the act of baptizing to the minister, in order to avoid the error of those who in the past ascribed the baptismal power to the baptizers, saying (1 Cor. 1:12): "I am of Paul . . . and I of Cephas." Wherefore they use the form: "May the servant of Christ, N . . ., be baptized, in the name of the Father," etc. And since the action performed by the minister is expressed with the invocation of the Trinity, the sacrament is validly conferred. As to the addition of "Ego" in our form, it is not essential; but it is added in order to lay greater stress on the intention.

Reply Obj. 2: Since a man may be washed with water for several reasons, the purpose for which it is done must be expressed by the words of the form.

And this is not done by saying: "In the name of the Father, and of the Son, and of the Holy Ghost"; because we are bound to do all things in that Name (Col. 3:17). Wherefore unless the act of baptizing be expressed, either as we do, or as the Greeks do, the sacrament is not valid; according to the decretal of Alexander III: "If anyone dip a child thrice in the water in the name of the Father, and of the Son, and of the Holy Ghost, Amen, without saying, I baptize thee in the name of the Father, and of the Son, and of the Holy Ghost, Amen, the child is not baptized."

Reply Obj. 3: The words which are uttered in the sacramental forms, are said not merely for the purpose of signification, but also for the purpose of efficiency, inasmuch as they derive efficacy from that Word, by Whom "all things were made." Consequently they are becomingly addressed not only to men, but also to insensible creatures; for instance, when we say: "I exorcize thee, creature salt" (Roman Ritual).

Reply Obj. 4: Several cannot baptize one at the same time: because an action is multiplied according to the number of the agents, if it be done perfectly by each. So that if two were to combine, of whom one were mute, and unable to utter the words, and the other were without hands, and unable to perform the action, they could not both baptize at the same time, one saying the words and the other performing the action.

On the other hand, in a case of necessity, several could be baptized at the same time; for no single one of them would receive more than one baptism. But it would be necessary, in that case, to say: "I baptize ye." Nor would this be a change of form, because "ye" is the same as "thee and thee." Whereas "we" does not mean "I and I," but "I and thou"; so that this would be a change of form.

Likewise it would be a change of form to say, "I baptize myself": consequently no one can baptize himself. For this reason did Christ choose to be baptized by John (Extra, De Baptismo et ejus effectu, cap. Debitum).

Reply Obj. 5: Although Christ's Passion is the principal cause as compared to the minister, yet it is an instrumental cause as compared to the Blessed Trinity. For this reason the Trinity is mentioned rather than Christ's Passion.

Reply Obj. 6: Although there are three personal names of the three Persons, there is but one essential name. Now the Divine power which works in Baptism, pertains to the Essence; and therefore we say, "in the name," and not, "in the names."

Reply Obj. 7: Just as water is used in Baptism, because it is more commonly employed in washing, so for the purpose of designating the three Persons, in the form of Baptism, those names are chosen, which are generally used, in a particular language, to signify the Persons. Nor is the sacrament valid if conferred in any other names.

SIXTH ARTICLE [III, Q. 66, Art. 6]

Whether Baptism Can Be Conferred in the Name of Christ?

Objection 1: It seems that Baptism can be conferred in the name of Christ. For just as there is "one Faith," so is there "one Baptism" (Eph. 4:5). But it is related (Acts 8:12) that "in the name of Jesus Christ they were baptized, both men and women." Therefore now also can Baptism be conferred in the name of Christ.

Obj. 2: Further, Ambrose says (De Spir. Sanct. i): "If you mention Christ, you designate both the Father by Whom He was anointed, and the Son Himself, Who was anointed, and the Holy Ghost with Whom He was anointed." But Baptism can be conferred in the name of the Trinity: therefore also in the name of Christ.

Obj. 3: Further, Pope Nicholas I, answering questions put to him by the Bulgars, said: "Those who have been baptized in the name of the Trinity, or only in the name of Christ, as we read in the Acts of the Apostles (it is all the same, as Blessed Ambrose saith), must not be rebaptized." But they would be baptized again if they had not been validly baptized with that form. Therefore Baptism can be celebrated in the name of Christ by using this form: "I baptize thee in the name of Christ."

*On the contrary,* Pope Pelagius II wrote to the Bishop Gaudentius: "If any people living in your Worship's neighborhood, avow that they have been baptized in the name of the Lord only, without any hesitation baptize them again in the name of the Blessed Trinity, when they come in quest of the Catholic Faith." Didymus, too, says (De Spir. Sanct.): "If indeed there be such a one with a mind so foreign to faith as to baptize while omitting one of the aforesaid names," viz. of the three Persons, "he baptizes invalidly."

*I answer that,* As stated above (Q. 64, A. 3), the sacraments derive their efficacy from Christ's institution. Consequently, if any of those things be omitted which Christ instituted in regard to a sacrament, it is invalid; save by special dispensation of Him Who did not bind His power to the sacraments. Now Christ commanded the sacrament of Baptism to be given with the invocation of the Trinity. And consequently whatever is lacking to the full invocation of the Trinity, destroys the integrity of Baptism.

Nor does it matter that in the name of one Person another is implied, as the name of the Son is implied in that of the Father, or that he who mentions the name of only one Person may believe aright in the Three; because just as a sacrament requires sensible matter, so does it require a sensible form. Hence, for the validity of the sacrament it is not enough to imply or to believe in the Trinity, unless the Trinity be expressed in sensible words. For this reason at Christ's Baptism, wherein was the source of the sanctification of our Baptism, the Trinity was present in sensible signs: viz. the Father in the voice, the Son in the human nature, the Holy Ghost in the dove.

Reply Obj. 1: It was by a special revelation from Christ that in the primitive Church the apostles baptized in the name of Christ; in order that the name of Christ, which was hateful to Jews and Gentiles, might become an object of veneration, in that the Holy Ghost was given in Baptism at the invocation of that Name.

Reply Obj. 2: Ambrose here gives this reason why exception could, without inconsistency, be allowed in the primitive Church; namely, because the whole Trinity is implied in the name of Christ, and therefore the form prescribed by Christ in the Gospel was observed in its integrity, at least implicitly.

Reply Obj. 3: Pope Nicolas confirms his words by quoting the two authorities given in the preceding objections: wherefore the answer to this is clear from the two solutions given above.

SEVENTH ARTICLE [III, Q. 66, Art. 7]

Whether Immersion in Water Is Necessary for Baptism?

Objection 1: It seems that immersion in water is necessary for Baptism. Because it is written (Eph. 4:5): "One faith, one baptism." But in many parts of the world the ordinary way of baptizing is by immersion. Therefore it seems that there can be no Baptism without immersion.

Obj. 2: Further, the Apostle says (Rom. 6:3, 4): "All we who are baptized in Christ Jesus, are baptized in His death: for we are buried together with Him, by Baptism into death." But this is done by immersion: for Chrysostom says on John 3:5: "Unless a man be born again of water and the Holy Ghost," etc.: "When we dip our heads under the water as in a kind of tomb, our old man is buried, and being submerged, is hidden below, and thence he rises again renewed." Therefore it seems that immersion is essential to Baptism.

Obj. 3: Further, if Baptism is valid without total immersion of the body, it would follow that it would be equally sufficient to pour water over any part of the body. But this seems unreasonable; since original sin, to remedy which is the principal purpose of Baptism, is not in only one part of the body. Therefore it seems that immersion is necessary for Baptism, and that mere sprinkling is not enough.

*On the contrary,* It is written (Heb. 10:22): "Let us draw near with a true heart in fulness of faith, having our hearts sprinkled from an evil conscience, and our bodies washed with clean water."

*I answer that,* In the sacrament of Baptism water is put to the use of a washing of the body, whereby to signify the inward washing away of sins. Now washing may be done with water not only by immersion, but also by sprinkling or pouring. And, therefore, although it is safer to baptize by immersion, because this is the more ordinary fashion, yet Baptism can be conferred by sprinkling or also by pouring, according to Ezech. 36:25: "I will pour upon you clean water," as also the Blessed Lawrence is related to have baptized. And this especially in cases of urgency: either because there is a great number to be baptized, as was clearly the case in Acts 2 and 4, where we read that on one day three thousand believed, and on another five thousand: or through there being but a small supply of water, or through feebleness of the minister, who cannot hold up the candidate for Baptism; or through feebleness of the candidate, whose life might be endangered by immersion. We must therefore conclude that immersion is not necessary for Baptism.

Reply Obj. 1: What is accidental to a thing does not diversify its essence. Now bodily washing with water is essential to Baptism: wherefore Baptism is called a "laver," according to Eph. 5:26: "Cleansing it by the laver of water in the word of life." But that the washing be done this or that way, is accidental to Baptism. And consequently such diversity does not destroy the oneness of Baptism.

Reply Obj. 2: Christ's burial is more clearly represented by immersion: wherefore this manner of baptizing is more frequently in use and more commendable. Yet in the other ways of baptizing it is represented after a fashion, albeit not so clearly; for no matter how the washing is done, the body of a man, or some part thereof, is put under water, just as Christ's body was put under the earth.

Reply Obj. 3: The principal part of the body, especially in relation to the exterior members, is the head, wherein all the senses, both interior and exterior, flourish. And therefore, if the whole body cannot be covered with water, because of the scarcity of water, or because of some other reason, it is necessary to pour water over the head, in which the principle of animal life is made manifest.

And although original sin is transmitted through the members that serve for procreation, yet those members are not to be sprinkled in preference to the head, because by Baptism the transmission of original sin to the offspring by the act of procreation is not deleted, but the soul is freed from the stain and debt of sin which it has contracted. Consequently that part of the body should be washed in preference, in which the works of the soul are made manifest.

Nevertheless in the Old Law the remedy against original sin was affixed to the member of procreation; because He through Whom original sin was to be removed, was yet to be born of the seed of Abraham, whose faith was signified by circumcision according to Rom. 4:11.

EIGHTH ARTICLE [III, Q. 66, Art. 8]

Whether Trine Immersion Is Essential to Baptism?

Objection 1: It seems that trine immersion is essential to Baptism. For Augustine says in a sermon on the Symbol, addressed to the Neophytes: "Rightly were you dipped three times, since you were baptized in the name of the Trinity. Rightly were you dipped three times, because you were baptized in the name of Jesus Christ, Who on the third day rose again from the dead. For that thrice repeated immersion reproduces the burial of the Lord by which you were buried with Christ in Baptism." Now both seem to be essential to Baptism, namely, that in Baptism the Trinity of Persons should be signified, and that we should be conformed to Christ's burial. Therefore it seems that trine immersion is essential to Baptism.

Obj. 2: Further, the sacraments derive their efficacy from Christ's mandate. But trine immersion was commanded by Christ: for Pope Pelagius II wrote to Bishop Gaudentius: "The Gospel precept given by our Lord God Himself, our Saviour Jesus Christ, admonishes us to confer the sacrament of Baptism to each one in the name of the Trinity and also with trine immersion." Therefore, just as it is essential to Baptism to call on the name of the Trinity, so is it essential to baptize by trine immersion.

Obj. 3: Further, if trine immersion be not essential to Baptism, it follows that the sacrament of Baptism is conferred at the first immersion; so that if a second or third immersion be added, it seems that Baptism is conferred a second or third time, which is absurd. Therefore one immersion does not suffice for the sacrament of Baptism, and trine immersion is essential thereto.

*On the contrary,* Gregory wrote to the Bishop Leander: "It cannot be in any way reprehensible to baptize an infant with either a trine or a single immersion: since the Trinity can be represented in the three immersions, and the unity of the Godhead in one immersion."

I answer that As stated above (A. 7, ad 1), washing with water is of itself required for Baptism, being essential to the sacrament: whereas the mode of washing is accidental to the sacrament. Consequently, as Gregory in the words above quoted explains, both single and trine immersion are lawful considered in themselves; since one immersion signifies the oneness of Christ's death and of the Godhead; while trine immersion signifies the three days of Christ's burial, and also the Trinity of Persons.

But for various reasons, according as the Church has ordained, one mode has been in practice, at one time, the other at another time. For since from the very earliest days of the Church some have had false notions concerning the Trinity, holding that Christ is a mere man, and that He is not called the "Son of God" or "God" except by reason of His merit, which was chiefly in His death; for this reason they did not baptize in the name of the Trinity, but in memory of Christ's death, and with one immersion. And this was condemned in the early Church. Wherefore in the Apostolic Canons (xlix) we read: "If any priest or bishop confer baptism not with the trine immersion in the one administration, but with one immersion, which baptism is said to be conferred by some in the death of the Lord, let him be deposed": for our Lord did not say, "Baptize ye in My death," but "In the name of the Father and of the Son, and of the Holy Ghost."

Later on, however, there arose the error of certain schismatics and heretics who rebaptized: as Augustine (Super. Joan., cf. De Haeres. lxix) relates of the Donatists. Wherefore, in detestation of their error, only one immersion was ordered to be made, by the (fourth) council of Toledo, in the acts of which we read: "In order to avoid the scandal of schism or the practice of heretical teaching let us hold to the single baptismal immersion."

But now that this motive has ceased, trine immersion is universally observed in Baptism: and consequently anyone baptizing otherwise would sin gravely, through not following the ritual of the Church. It would, however, be valid Baptism.

Reply Obj. 1: The Trinity acts as principal agent in Baptism. Now the likeness of the agent enters into the effect, in regard to the form and not in regard to the matter. Wherefore the Trinity is signified in Baptism by the words of the form. Nor is it essential for the Trinity to be signified by the manner in which the matter is used; although this is done to make the signification clearer.

In like manner Christ's death is sufficiently represented in the one immersion. And the three days of His burial were not necessary for our salvation, because even if He had been buried or dead for one day, this would have been enough to consummate our redemption: yet those three days were ordained unto the manifestation of the reality of His death, as stated above (Q. 53, A. 2). It is therefore clear that neither on the part of the Trinity, nor on the part of Christ's Passion, is the trine immersion essential to the sacrament.

Reply Obj. 2: Pope Pelagius understood the trine immersion to be ordained by Christ in its equivalent; in the sense that Christ commanded Baptism to be conferred "in the name of the Father, and of the Son, and of the Holy Ghost." Nor can we argue from the form to the use of the matter, as stated above (ad 1).

Reply Obj. 3: As stated above (Q. 64, A. 8), the intention is essential to Baptism. Consequently, one Baptism results from the intention of the Church's minister, who intends to confer one Baptism by a trine immersion. Wherefore Jerome says on Eph. 4:5, 6: "Though the Baptism," i.e. the immersion, "be thrice repeated, on account of the mystery of the Trinity, yet it is reputed as one Baptism."

If, however, the intention were to confer one Baptism at each immersion together with the repetition of the words of the form, it would be a sin, in itself, because it would be a repetition of Baptism.

NINTH ARTICLE [III, Q. 66, Art. 9]

Whether Baptism May Be Reiterated?

Objection 1: It seems that Baptism may be reiterated. For Baptism was instituted, seemingly, in order to wash away sins. But sins are reiterated. Therefore much more should Baptism be reiterated: because Christ's mercy surpasses man's guilt.

Obj. 2: Further, John the Baptist received special commendation from Christ, Who said of him (Matt. 11:11): "There hath not risen among them that are born of women, a greater than John the Baptist." But those whom John had baptized were baptized again, according to Acts 19:1-7, where it is stated that Paul rebaptized those who had received the Baptism of John. Much more, therefore, should those be rebaptized, who have been baptized by heretics or sinners.

Obj. 3: Further, it was decreed in the Council of Nicaea (Can. xix) that if "any of the Paulianists or Cataphrygians should be converted to the Catholic Church, they were to be baptized": and this seemingly should be said in regard to other heretics. Therefore those whom the heretics have baptized, should be baptized again.

Obj. 4: Further, Baptism is necessary for salvation. But sometimes there is a doubt about the baptism of those who really have been baptized. Therefore it seems that they should be baptized again.

Obj. 5: Further, the Eucharist is a more perfect sacrament than Baptism, as stated above (Q. 65, A. 3). But the sacrament of the Eucharist is reiterated. Much more reason, therefore, is there for Baptism to be reiterated.

*On the contrary,* It is written, (Eph. 4:5): "One faith, one Baptism."

*I answer that,* Baptism cannot be reiterated.

First, because Baptism is a spiritual regeneration; inasmuch as a man dies to the old life, and begins to lead the new life. Whence it is written (John 3:5): "Unless a man be born again of water and the Holy Ghost, He cannot see [Vulg.: 'enter into'] the kingdom of God." Now one man can be begotten but once. Wherefore Baptism cannot be reiterated, just as neither can carnal generation. Hence Augustine says on John 3:4: "'Can he enter a second time into his mother's womb and be born again': So thou," says he, "must understand the birth of the Spirit, as Nicodemus understood the birth of the flesh . . . . As there is no return to the womb, so neither is there to Baptism."

Secondly, because "we are baptized in Christ's death," by which we die unto sin and rise again unto "newness of life" (cf. Rom. 6:3, 4). Now "Christ died" but "once" (Rom. 6:10). Wherefore neither should Baptism be reiterated. For this reason (Heb. 6:6) is it said against some who wished to be baptized again: "Crucifying again to themselves the Son of God"; on which the gloss observes: "Christ's one death hallowed the one Baptism."

Thirdly, because Baptism imprints a character, which is indelible, and is conferred with a certain consecration. Wherefore, just as other consecrations are not reiterated in the Church, so neither is Baptism. This is the view expressed by Augustine, who says (Contra Epist. Parmen. ii) that "the military character is not renewed": and that "the sacrament of Christ is not less enduring than this bodily mark, since we see that not even apostates are deprived of Baptism, since when they repent and return they are not baptized anew."

Fourthly, because Baptism is conferred principally as a remedy against original sin. Wherefore, just as original sin is not renewed, so neither is Baptism reiterated, for as it is written (Rom. 5:18), "as by the offense of one, unto all men to condemnation, so also by the justice of one, unto all men to justification of life."

Reply Obj. 1: Baptism derives its efficacy from Christ's Passion, as stated above (A. 2, ad 1). Wherefore, just as subsequent sins do not cancel the virtue of Christ's Passion, so neither do they cancel Baptism, so as to call for its repetition. On the other hand the sin which hindered the effect of Baptism is blotted out on being submitted to Penance.

Reply Obj. 2: As Augustine says on John 1:33: "'And I knew Him not': Behold; after John had baptized, Baptism was administered; after a murderer has baptized, it is not administered: because John gave his own Baptism; the murderer, Christ's; for that sacrament is so sacred, that not even a murderer's administration contaminates it."

Reply Obj. 3: The Paulianists and Cataphrygians used not to baptize in the name of the Trinity. Wherefore Gregory, writing to the Bishop Quiricus, says: "Those heretics who are not baptized in the name of the Trinity, such as the Bonosians and Cataphrygians" (who were of the same mind as the Paulianists), "since the former believe not that Christ is God" (holding Him to be a mere man), "while the latter," i.e. the Cataphrygians, "are so perverse as to deem a mere man," viz. Montanus, "to be the Holy Ghost: all these are baptized when they come to holy Church, for the baptism which they received while in that state of error was no Baptism at all, not being conferred in the name of the Trinity." On the other hand, as set down in De Eccles. Dogm. xxii: "Those heretics who have been baptized in the confession of the name of the Trinity are to be received as already baptized when they come to the Catholic Faith."

Reply Obj. 4: According to the Decretal of Alexander III: "Those about whose Baptism there is a doubt are to be baptized with these words prefixed to the form: 'If thou art baptized, I do not rebaptize thee; but if thou art not baptized, I baptize thee,' etc.: for that does not appear to be repeated, which is not known to have been done."

Reply Obj. 5: Both sacraments, viz. Baptism and the Eucharist, are a representation of our Lord's death and Passion, but not in the same way. For Baptism is a commemoration of Christ's death in so far as man dies with Christ, that he may be born again into a new life. But the Eucharist is a commemoration of Christ's death, in so far as the suffering Christ Himself is offered to us as the Paschal banquet, according to 1 Cor. 5:7, 8: "Christ our pasch is sacrificed; therefore let us feast." And forasmuch as man is born once, whereas he eats many times, so is Baptism given once, but the Eucharist frequently.

TENTH ARTICLE [III, Q. 66, Art. 10]

Whether the Church Observes a Suitable Rite in Baptizing?

Objection 1: It seems that the Church observes an unsuitable rite in baptizing. For as Chrysostom (Chromatius, in Matth. 3:15) says: "The waters of Baptism would never avail to purge the sins of them that believe, had they not been hallowed by the touch of our Lord's body." Now this took place at Christ's Baptism, which is commemorated in the Feast of the Epiphany. Therefore solemn Baptism should be celebrated at the Feast of the Epiphany rather than on the eves of Easter and Whitsunday.

Obj. 2: Further, it seems that several matters should not be used in the same sacrament. But water is used for washing in Baptism. Therefore it is unfitting that the person baptized should be anointed thrice with holy oil first on the breast, and then between the shoulders, and a third time with chrism on the top of the head.

Obj. 3: Further, "in Christ Jesus . . . there is neither male nor female" (Gal. 3:23) . . . "neither Barbarian nor Scythian" (Col. 3:11), nor, in like manner, any other such like distinctions. Much less, therefore can a difference of clothing have any efficacy in the Faith of Christ. It is consequently unfitting to bestow a white garment on those who have been baptized.

Obj. 4: Further, Baptism can be celebrated without such like ceremonies. Therefore it seems that those mentioned above are superfluous; and consequently that they are unsuitably inserted by the Church in the baptismal rite.

*On the contrary,* The Church is ruled by the Holy Ghost, Who does nothing inordinate.

*I answer that,* In the sacrament of Baptism something is done which is essential to the sacrament, and something which belongs to a certain solemnity of the sacrament. Essential indeed, to the sacrament are both the form which designates the principal cause of the sacrament; and the minister who is the instrumental cause; and the use of the matter, namely, washing with water, which designates the principal sacramental effect. But all the other things which the Church observes in the baptismal rite, belong rather to a certain solemnity of the sacrament.

And these, indeed, are used in conjunction with the sacrament for three reasons. First, in order to arouse the devotion of the faithful, and their reverence for the sacrament. For if there were nothing done but a mere washing with water, without any solemnity, some might easily think it to be an ordinary washing.

Secondly, for the instruction of the faithful. Because simple and unlettered folk need to be taught by some sensible signs, for instance, pictures and the like. And in this way by means of the sacramental ceremonies they are either instructed, or urged to seek the signification of such like sensible signs. And consequently, since, besides the principal sacramental effect, other things should be known about Baptism, it was fitting that these also should be represented by some outward signs.

Thirdly, because the power of the devil is restrained, by prayers, blessings, and the like, from hindering the sacramental effect.

Reply Obj. 1: Christ was baptized on the Epiphany with the Baptism of John, as stated above (Q. 39, A. 2), with which baptism, indeed, the faithful are not baptized, rather are they baptized with Christ's Baptism. This has its efficacy from the Passion of Christ, according to Rom. 6:3: "We who are baptized in Christ Jesus, are baptized in His death"; and in the Holy Ghost, according to John 3:5: "Unless a man be born again of water and the Holy Ghost." Therefore it is that solemn Baptism is held in the Church, both on Easter Eve, when we commemorate our Lord's burial and resurrection; for which reason our Lord gave His disciples the commandment concerning Baptism as related by Matthew (28:19): and on Whitsun-eve, when the celebration of the Feast of the Holy Ghost begins; for which reason the apostles are said to have baptized three thousand on the very day of Pentecost when they had received the Holy Ghost.

Reply Obj. 2: The use of water in Baptism is part of the substance of the sacrament; but the use of oil or chrism is part of the solemnity. For the candidate is first of all anointed with Holy oil on the breast and between the shoulders, as "one who wrestles for God," to use Ambrose's expression (De Sacram. i): thus are prize-fighters wont to besmear themselves with oil. Or, as Innocent III says in a decretal on the Holy Unction: "The candidate is anointed on the breast, in order to receive the gift of the Holy Ghost, to cast off error and ignorance, and to acknowledge the true faith, since 'the just man liveth by faith'; while he is anointed between the shoulders, that he may be clothed with the grace of the Holy Ghost, lay aside indifference and sloth, and become active in good works; so that the sacrament of faith may purify the thoughts of his heart, and strengthen his shoulders for the burden of labor." But after Baptism, as Rabanus says (De Sacram. iii), "he is forthwith anointed on the head by the priest with Holy Chrism, who proceeds at once to offer up a prayer that the neophyte may have a share in Christ's kingdom, and be called a Christian after Christ." Or, as Ambrose says (De Sacram. iii), his head is anointed, because "the senses of a wise man are in his head" (Eccl 2:14): to wit, that he may "be ready to satisfy everyone that asketh" him to give "a reason of his faith" (cf. 1 Pet. 3:15; Innocent III, Decretal on Holy Unction).

Reply Obj. 3: This white garment is given, not as though it were unlawful for the neophyte to use others: but as a sign of the glorious resurrection, unto which men are born again by Baptism; and in order to designate the purity of life, to which he will be bound after being baptized, according to Rom. 6:4: "That we may walk in newness of life."

Reply Obj. 4: Although those things that belong to the solemnity of a sacrament are not essential to it, yet are they not superfluous, since they pertain to the sacrament's wellbeing, as stated above.

ELEVENTH ARTICLE [III, Q. 66, Art. 11]

Whether Three Kinds of Baptism Are Fittingly Described--viz. Baptism of Water, of Blood, and of the Spirit?

Objection 1: It seems that the three kinds of Baptism are not fittingly described as Baptism of Water, of Blood, and of the Spirit, i.e. of the Holy Ghost. Because the Apostle says (Eph. 4:5): "One Faith, one Baptism." Now there is but one Faith. Therefore there should not be three Baptisms.

Obj. 2: Further, Baptism is a sacrament, as we have made clear above (Q. 65, A. 1). Now none but Baptism of Water is a sacrament. Therefore we should not reckon two other Baptisms.

Obj. 3: Further, Damascene (De Fide Orth. iv) distinguishes several other kinds of Baptism. Therefore we should admit more than three Baptisms.

*On the contrary,* on Heb. 6:2, "Of the doctrine of Baptisms," the gloss says: "He uses the plural, because there is Baptism of Water, of Repentance, and of Blood."

*I answer that,* As stated above (Q. 62, A. 5), Baptism of Water has its efficacy from Christ's Passion, to which a man is conformed by Baptism, and also from the Holy Ghost, as first cause. Now although the effect depends on the first cause, the cause far surpasses the effect, nor does it depend on it. Consequently, a man may, without Baptism of Water, receive the sacramental effect from Christ's Passion, in so far as he is conformed to Christ by suffering for Him. Hence it is written (Apoc. 7:14): "These are they who are come out of great tribulation, and have washed their robes and have made them white in the blood of the Lamb." In like manner a man receives the effect of Baptism by the power of the Holy Ghost, not only without Baptism of Water, but also without Baptism of Blood: forasmuch as his heart is moved by the Holy Ghost to believe in and love God and to repent of his sins: wherefore this is also called Baptism of Repentance. Of this it is written (Isa. 4:4): "If the Lord shall wash away the filth of the daughters of Zion, and shall wash away the blood of Jerusalem out of the midst thereof, by the spirit of judgment, and by the spirit of burning." Thus, therefore, each of these other Baptisms is called Baptism, forasmuch as it takes the place of Baptism. Wherefore Augustine says (De Unico Baptismo Parvulorum iv): "The Blessed Cyprian argues with considerable reason from the thief to whom, though not baptized, it was said: 'Today shalt thou be with Me in Paradise' that suffering can take the place of Baptism. Having weighed this in my mind again and again, I perceive that not only can suffering for the name of Christ supply for what was lacking in Baptism, but even faith and conversion of heart, if perchance on account of the stress of the times the celebration of the mystery of Baptism is not practicable."

Reply Obj. 1: The other two Baptisms are included in the Baptism of Water, which derives its efficacy, both from Christ's Passion and from the Holy Ghost. Consequently for this reason the unity of Baptism is not destroyed.

Reply Obj. 2: As stated above (Q. 60, A. 1), a sacrament is a kind of sign. The other two, however, are like the Baptism of Water, not, indeed, in the nature of sign, but in the baptismal effect. Consequently they are not sacraments.

Reply Obj. 3: Damascene enumerates certain figurative Baptisms. For instance, "the Deluge" was a figure of our Baptism, in respect of the salvation of the faithful in the Church; since then "a few . . . souls were saved in the ark [Vulg.: 'by water']," according to 1 Pet. 3:20. He also mentions "the crossing of the Red Sea": which was a figure of our Baptism, in respect of our delivery from the bondage of sin; hence the Apostle says (1 Cor. 10:2) that "all . . . were baptized in the cloud and in the sea." And again he mentions "the various washings which were customary under the Old Law," which were figures of our Baptism, as to the cleansing from sins: also "the Baptism of John," which prepared the way for our Baptism.

TWELFTH ARTICLE [III, Q. 66, Art. 12]

Whether the Baptism of Blood Is the Most Excellent of These?

Objection 1: It seems that the Baptism of Blood is not the most excellent of these three. For the Baptism of Water impresses a character; which the Baptism of Blood cannot do. Therefore the Baptism of Blood is not more excellent than the Baptism of Water.

Obj. 2: Further, the Baptism of Blood is of no avail without the Baptism of the Spirit, which is by charity; for it is written (1 Cor. 13:3): "If I should deliver my body to be burned, and have not charity, it profiteth me nothing." But the Baptism of the Spirit avails without the Baptism of Blood; for not only the martyrs are saved. Therefore the Baptism of Blood is not the most excellent.

Obj. 3: Further, just as the Baptism of Water derives its efficacy from Christ's Passion, to which, as stated above (A. 11), the Baptism of Blood corresponds, so Christ's Passion derives its efficacy from the Holy Ghost, according to Heb. 9:14: "The Blood of Christ, Who by the Holy Ghost offered Himself unspotted unto God, shall cleanse our conscience from dead works," etc. Therefore the Baptism of the Spirit is more excellent than the Baptism of Blood. Therefore the Baptism of Blood is not the most excellent.

*On the contrary,* Augustine (Ad Fortunatum) speaking of the comparison between Baptisms says: "The newly baptized confesses his faith in the presence of the priest: the martyr in the presence of the persecutor. The former is sprinkled with water, after he has confessed; the latter with his blood. The former receives the Holy Ghost by the imposition of the bishop's hands; the latter is made the temple of the Holy Ghost."

*I answer that,* As stated above (A. 11), the shedding of blood for Christ's sake, and the inward operation of the Holy Ghost, are called baptisms, in so far as they produce the effect of the Baptism of Water. Now the Baptism of Water derives its efficacy from Christ's Passion and from the Holy Ghost, as already stated (A. 11). These two causes act in each of these three Baptisms; most excellently, however, in the Baptism of Blood. For Christ's Passion acts in the Baptism of Water by way of a figurative representation; in the Baptism of the Spirit or of Repentance, by way of desire; but in the Baptism of Blood, by way of imitating the (Divine) act. In like manner, too, the power of the Holy Ghost acts in the Baptism of Water through a certain hidden power; in the Baptism of Repentance by moving the heart; but in the Baptism of Blood by the highest degree of fervor of dilection and love, according to John 15:13: "Greater love than this no man hath that a man lay down his life for his friends."

Reply Obj. 1: A character is both reality and a sacrament. And we do not say that the Baptism of Blood is more excellent, considering the nature of a sacrament; but considering the sacramental effect.

Reply Obj. 2: The shedding of blood is not in the nature of a Baptism if it be without charity. Hence it is clear that the Baptism of Blood includes the Baptism of the Spirit, but not conversely. And from this it is proved to be more perfect.

Reply Obj. 3: The Baptism owes its pre-eminence not only to Christ's Passion, but also to the Holy Ghost, as stated above.

## QUESTION 67

OF THE MINISTERS BY WHOM THE SACRAMENT OF BAPTISM IS CONFERRED (In Eight Articles)

We have now to consider the ministers by whom the sacrament of Baptism is conferred. And concerning this there are eight points of inquiry:

(1) Whether it belongs to a deacon to baptize?

(2) Whether this belongs to a priest, or to a bishop only?

(3) Whether a layman can confer the sacrament of Baptism?

(4) Whether a woman can do this?

(5) Whether an unbaptized person can baptize?

(6) Whether several can at the same time baptize one and the same person?

(7) Whether it is essential that someone should raise the person baptized from the sacred font?

(8) Whether he who raises someone from the sacred font is bound to instruct him?

FIRST ARTICLE [III, Q. 67, Art. 1]

Whether It Is Part of a Deacon's Duty to Baptize?

Objection 1: It seems that it is part of a deacon's duty to baptize. Because the duties of preaching and of baptizing were enjoined by our Lord at the same time, according to Matt. 28:19: "Going . . . teach ye all nations, baptizing them," etc. But it is part of a deacon's duty to preach the gospel. Therefore it seems that it is also part of a deacon's duty to baptize.

Obj. 2: Further, according to Dionysius (Eccl. Hier. v) to "cleanse" is part of the deacon's duty. But cleansing from sins is effected specially by Baptism, according to Eph. 5:26: "Cleansing it by the laver of water in the word of life." Therefore it seems that it belongs to a deacon to baptize.

Obj. 3: Further, it is told of Blessed Laurence, who was a deacon, that he baptized many. Therefore it seems that it belongs to deacons to baptize.

*On the contrary,* Pope Gelasius I says (the passage is to be found in the Decrees, dist. 93): "We order the deacons to keep within their own province"; and further on: "Without bishop or priest they must not dare to baptize, except in cases of extreme urgency, when the aforesaid are a long way off."

*I answer that,* Just as the properties and duties of the heavenly orders are gathered from their names, as Dionysius says (Coel. Hier. vi), so can we gather, from the names of the ecclesiastical orders, what belongs to each order. Now "deacons" are so called from being "ministers"; because, to wit, it is not in the deacon's province to be the chief and official celebrant in conferring a sacrament, but to minister to others, his elders, in the sacramental dispensations. And so it does not belong to a deacon to confer the sacrament of Baptism officially as it were; but to assist and serve his elders in the bestowal of this and other sacraments. Hence Isidore says (Epist. ad Ludifred.): "It is a deacon's duty to assist and serve the priests, in all the rites of Christ's sacraments, viz. those of Baptism, of the Chrism, of the Paten and Chalice."

Reply Obj. 1: It is the deacon's duty to read the Gospel in church, and to preach it as one catechizing; hence Dionysius says (Eccl. Hier. v) that a deacon's office involves power over the unclean among whom he includes the catechumens. But to teach, i.e. to expound the Gospel, is the proper office of a bishop, whose action is "to perfect," as Dionysius teaches (Eccl. Hier. v); and "to perfect" is the same as "to teach." Consequently, it does not follow that the office of baptizing belongs to deacons.

Reply Obj. 2: As Dionysius says (Eccl. Hier. ii), Baptism has a power not only of "cleansing" but also of "enlightening." Consequently, it is outside the province of the deacon whose duty it is to cleanse only: viz. either by driving away the unclean, or by preparing them for the reception of a sacrament.

Reply Obj. 3: Because Baptism is a necessary sacrament, deacons are allowed to baptize in cases of urgency when their elders are not at hand; as appears from the authority of Gelasius quoted above. And it was thus that Blessed Laurence, being but a deacon, baptized.

SECOND ARTICLE [III, Q. 67, Art. 2]

Whether to Baptize Is Part of the Priestly Office, or Proper to That of Bishops?

Objection 1: It seems that to baptize is not part of the priestly office, but proper to that of bishops. Because, as stated above (A. 1, Obj. 1), the duties of teaching and baptizing are enjoined in the same precept (Matt. 28:19). But to teach, which is "to perfect," belongs to the office of bishop, as Dionysius declares (Eccl. Hier. v, vi). Therefore to baptize also belongs to the episcopal office.

Obj. 2: Further, by Baptism a man is admitted to the body of the Christian people: and to do this seems consistent with no other than the princely office. Now the bishops hold the position of princes in the Church, as the gloss observes on Luke 10:1: indeed, they even take the place of the apostles, of whom it is written (Ps. 44:17): "Thou shalt make them princes over all the earth." Therefore it seems that to baptize belongs exclusively to the office of bishops.

Obj. 3: Further, Isidore says (Epist. ad Ludifred.) that "it belongs to the bishop to consecrate churches, to anoint altars, to consecrate (conficere ) the chrism; he it is that confers the ecclesiastical orders, and blesses the consecrated virgins." But the sacrament of Baptism is greater than all these. Therefore much more reason is there why to baptize should belong exclusively to the episcopal office.

*On the contrary,* Isidore says (De Officiis. ii): "It is certain that Baptism was entrusted to priests alone."

*I answer that,* Priests are consecrated for the purpose of celebrating the sacrament of Christ's Body, as stated above (Q. 65, A. 3). Now that is the sacrament of ecclesiastical unity, according to the Apostle (1 Cor. 10:17): "We, being many, are one bread, one body, all that partake of one bread and one chalice." Moreover, by Baptism a man becomes a participator in ecclesiastical unity, wherefore also he receives the right to approach our Lord's Table. Consequently, just as it belongs to a priest to consecrate the Eucharist, which is the principal purpose of the priesthood, so it is the proper office of a priest to baptize: since it seems to belong to one and the same, to produce the whole and to dispose the part in the whole.

Reply Obj. 1: Our Lord enjoined on the apostles, whose place is taken by the bishops, both duties, namely, of teaching and of baptizing, but in different ways. Because Christ committed to them the duty of teaching, that they might exercise it themselves as being the most important duty of all: wherefore the apostles themselves said (Acts 6:2): "It is not reason that we should leave the word of God and serve tables." On the other hand, He entrusted the apostles with the office of baptizing, to be exercised vicariously; wherefore the Apostle says (1 Cor. 1:17): "Christ sent me not to baptize, but to preach the Gospel." And the reason for this was that the merit and wisdom of the minister have no bearing on the baptismal effect, as they have in teaching, as may be seen from what we have stated above (Q. 64, A. 1, ad 2; AA. 5, 9). A proof of this is found also in the fact that our Lord Himself did not baptize, but His disciples, as John relates (4:2). Nor does it follow from this that bishops cannot baptize; since what a lower power can do, that can also a higher power. Wherefore also the Apostle says (1 Cor. 1:14, 16) that he had baptized some.

Reply Obj. 2: In every commonwealth minor affairs are entrusted to lower officials, while greater affairs are restricted to higher officials; according to Ex. 18:22: "When any great matter soever shall fall out, let them refer it to thee, and let them judge the lesser matters only." Consequently it belongs to the lower officials of the state to decide matters concerning the lower orders; while to the highest it belongs to set in order those matters that regard the higher orders of the state. Now by Baptism a man attains only to the lowest rank among the Christian people: and consequently it belongs to the lesser officials of the Church to baptize, namely, the priests, who hold the place of the seventy-two disciples of Christ, as the gloss says in the passage quoted from Luke 10.

Reply Obj. 3: As stated above (Q. 65, A. 3), the sacrament of Baptism holds the first place in the order of necessity; but in the order of perfection there are other greater sacraments which are reserved to bishops.

THIRD ARTICLE [III, Q. 67, Art. 3]

Whether a Layman Can Baptize?

Objection 1: It seems that a layman cannot baptize. Because, as stated above (A. 2), to baptize belongs properly to the priestly order. But those things which belong to an order cannot be entrusted to one that is not ordained. Therefore it seems that a layman, who has no orders, cannot baptize.

Obj. 2: Further, it is a greater thing to baptize, than to perform the other sacramental rites of Baptism, such as to catechize, to exorcize, and to bless the baptismal water. But these things cannot be done by laymen, but only by priests. Therefore it seems that much less can laymen baptize.

Obj. 3: Further, just as Baptism is a necessary sacrament, so is Penance. But a layman cannot absolve in the tribunal of Penance. Neither, therefore, can he baptize.

*On the contrary,* Pope Gelasius I and Isidore say that "it is often permissible for Christian laymen to baptize, in cases of urgent necessity."

*I answer that,* It is due to the mercy of Him "Who will have all men to be saved" (1 Tim. 2:4) that in those things which are necessary for salvation, man can easily find the remedy. Now the most necessary among all the sacraments is Baptism, which is man's regeneration unto spiritual life: since for children there is no substitute, while adults cannot otherwise than by Baptism receive a full remission both of guilt and of its punishment. Consequently, lest man should have to go without so necessary a remedy, it was ordained, both that the matter of Baptism should be something common that is easily obtainable by all, i.e. water; and that the minister of Baptism should be anyone, even not in orders, lest from lack of being baptized, man should suffer loss of his salvation.

Reply Obj. 1: To baptize belongs to the priestly order by reason of a certain appropriateness and solemnity; but this is not essential to the sacrament. Consequently, if a layman were to baptize even outside a case of urgency; he would sin, yet he would confer the sacrament; nor would the person thus baptized have to be baptized again.

Reply Obj. 2: These sacramental rites of Baptism belong to the solemnity of, and are not essential to, Baptism. And therefore they neither should nor can be done by a layman, but only by a priest, whose office it is to baptize solemnly.

Reply Obj. 3: As stated above (Q. 65, AA. 3, 4), Penance is not so necessary as Baptism; since contrition can supply the defect of the priestly absolution which does not free from the whole punishment, nor again is it given to children. Therefore the comparison with Baptism does not stand, because its effect cannot be supplied by anything else.

FOURTH ARTICLE [III, Q. 67, Art. 4]

Whether a Woman Can Baptize?

Objection 1: It seems that a woman cannot baptize. For we read in the acts of the Council of Carthage (iv): "However learned and holy a woman may be, she must not presume to teach men in the church, or to baptize." But in no case is a woman allowed to teach in church, according to 1 Cor. 14:35: "It is a shame for a woman to speak in the church." Therefore it seems that neither is a woman in any circumstances permitted to baptize.

Obj. 2: Further, to baptize belongs to those having authority. wherefore baptism should be conferred by priests having charge of souls. But women are not qualified for this; according to 1 Tim. 2:12: "I suffer not a woman to teach, nor to use authority over man, but to be subject to him [Vulg.: 'but to be in silence']." Therefore a woman cannot baptize.

Obj. 3: Further, in the spiritual regeneration water seems to hold the place of the mother's womb, as Augustine says on John 3:4, "Can" a man "enter a second time into his mother's womb, and be born again?" While he who baptizes seems to hold rather the position of father. But this is unfitting for a woman. Therefore a woman cannot baptize.

*On the contrary,* Pope Urban II says (Decreta xxx): "In reply to the questions asked by your beatitude, we consider that the following answer should be given: that the baptism is valid when, in cases of necessity, a woman baptizes a child in the name of the Trinity."

*I answer that,* Christ is the chief Baptizer, according to John 1:33: "He upon Whom thou shalt see the Spirit descending and remaining upon Him, He it is that baptizeth." For it is written in Col. 3 (cf. Gal. 3:28), that in Christ there is neither male nor female. Consequently, just as a layman can baptize, as Christ's minister, so can a woman.

But since "the head of the woman is the man," and "the head of . . . man, is Christ" (1 Cor. 11:3), a woman should not baptize if a man be available for the purpose; just as neither should a layman in the presence of a cleric, nor a cleric in the presence of a priest. The last, however, can baptize in the presence of a bishop, because it is part of the priestly office.

Reply Obj. 1: Just as a woman is not suffered to teach in public, but is allowed to instruct and admonish privately; so she is not permitted to baptize publicly and solemnly, and yet she can baptize in a case of urgency.

Reply Obj. 2: When Baptism is celebrated solemnly and with due form, it should be conferred by a priest having charge of souls, or by one representing him. But this is not required in cases of urgency, when a woman may baptize.

Reply Obj. 3: In carnal generation male and female co-operate according to the power of their proper nature; wherefore the female cannot be the active, but only the passive, principle of generation. But in spiritual generation they do not act, either of them, by their proper power, but only instrumentally by the power of Christ. Consequently, on the same grounds either man or woman can baptize in a case of urgency.

If, however, a woman were to baptize without any urgency for so doing, there would be no need of rebaptism: as we have said in regard to laymen (A. 3, ad 1). But the baptizer herself would sin, as also those who took part with her therein, either by receiving Baptism from her, or by bringing someone to her to be baptized.

FIFTH ARTICLE [III, Q. 67, Art. 5]

Whether One That Is Not Baptized Can Confer the Sacrament of Baptism?

Objection 1: It seems that one that is not baptized cannot confer the sacrament of Baptism. For "none gives what he has not." But a non-baptized person has not the sacrament of Baptism. Therefore he cannot give it.

Obj. 2: Further, a man confers the sacrament of Baptism inasmuch as he is a minister of the Church. But one that is not baptized, belongs nowise to the Church, i.e. neither really nor sacramentally. Therefore he cannot confer the sacrament of Baptism.

Obj. 3: Further, it is more to confer a sacrament than to receive it. But one that is not baptized, cannot receive the other sacraments. Much less, therefore, can he confer any sacrament.

*On the contrary,* Isidore says: "The Roman Pontiff does not consider it to be the man who baptizes, but that the Holy Ghost confers the grace of Baptism, though he that baptizes be a pagan." But he who is baptized, is not called a pagan. Therefore he who is not baptized can confer the sacrament of Baptism.

*I answer that,* Augustine left this question without deciding it. For he says (Contra Ep. Parmen. ii): "This is indeed another question, whether even those can baptize who were never Christians; nor should anything be rashly asserted hereupon, without the authority of a sacred council such as suffices for so great a matter." But afterwards it was decided by the Church that the unbaptized, whether Jews or pagans, can confer the sacrament of Baptism, provided they baptize in the form of the Church. Wherefore Pope Nicolas I replies to the questions propounded by the Bulgars: "You say that many in your country have been baptized by someone, whether Christian or pagan you know not. If these were baptized in the name of the Trinity, they must not be rebaptized." But if the form of the Church be not observed, the sacrament of Baptism is not conferred. And thus is to be explained what Gregory II [*Gregory III] writes to Bishop Boniface: "Those whom you assert to have been baptized by pagans," namely, with a form not recognized by the Church, "we command you to rebaptize in the name of the Trinity." And the reason of this is that, just as on the part of the matter, as far as the essentials of the sacrament are concerned, any water will suffice, so, on the part of the minister, any man is competent. Consequently, an unbaptized person can baptize in a case of urgency. So that two unbaptized persons may baptize one another, one baptizing the other and being afterwards baptized by him: and each would receive not only the sacrament but also the reality of the sacrament. But if this were done outside a case of urgency, each would sin grievously, both the baptizer and the baptized, and thus the baptismal effect would be frustrated, although the sacrament itself would not be invalidated.

Reply Obj. 1: The man who baptizes offers but his outward ministration; whereas Christ it is Who baptizes inwardly, Who can use all men to whatever purpose He wills. Consequently, the unbaptized can baptize: because, as Pope Nicolas I says, "the Baptism is not theirs," i.e. the baptizers', "but His," i.e. Christ's.

Reply Obj. 2: He who is not baptized, though he belongs not to the Church either in reality or sacramentally, can nevertheless belong to her in intention and by similarity of action, namely, in so far as he intends to do what the Church does, and in baptizing observes the Church's form, and thus acts as the minister of Christ, Who did not confine His power to those that are baptized, as neither did He to the sacraments.

Reply Obj. 3: The other sacraments are not so necessary as Baptism. And therefore it is allowable that an unbaptized person should baptize rather than that he should receive other sacraments.

SIXTH ARTICLE [III, Q. 67, Art. 6]

Whether Several Can Baptize at the Same Time?

Objection 1: It seems that several can baptize at the same time. For unity is contained in multitude, but not vice versa. Wherefore it seems that many can do whatever one can but not vice versa: thus many draw a ship which one could draw. But one man can baptize. Therefore several, too, can baptize one at the same time.

Obj. 2: Further, it is more difficult for one agent to act on many things, than for many to act at the same time on one. But one man can baptize several at the same time. Much more, therefore, can many baptize one at the same time.

Obj. 3: Further, Baptism is a sacrament of the greatest necessity. Now in certain cases it seems necessary for several to baptize one at the same time; for instance, suppose a child to be in danger of death, and two persons present, one of whom is dumb, and the other without hands or arms; for then the mutilated person would have to pronounce the words, and the dumb person would have to perform the act of baptizing. Therefore it seems that several can baptize one at the same time.

*On the contrary,* Where there is one agent there is one action. If, therefore, several were to baptize one, it seems to follow that there would be several baptisms: and this is contrary to Eph. 4:5: "one Faith, one Baptism."

*I answer that,* The Sacrament of Baptism derives its power principally from its form, which the Apostle calls "the word of life" (Eph. 5:26). Consequently, if several were to baptize one at the same time, we must consider what form they would use. For were they to say: "We baptize thee in the name of the Father and of the Son and of the Holy Ghost," some maintain that the sacrament of Baptism would not be conferred, because the form of the Church would not be observed, i.e. "I baptize thee in the name of the Father and of the Son and of the Holy Ghost." But this reasoning is disproved by the form observed in the Greek Church. For they might say: "The servant of God, N . . ., is baptized in the name of the Father and of the Son and of the Holy Ghost," under which form the Greeks receive the sacrament of Baptism: and yet this form differs far more from the form that we use, than does this: "We baptize thee."

The point to be observed, however, is this, that by this form, "We baptize thee," the intention expressed is that several concur in conferring one Baptism: and this seems contrary to the notion of a minister; for a man does not baptize save as a minister of Christ, and as standing in His place; wherefore just as there is one Christ, so should there be one minister to represent Christ. Hence the Apostle says pointedly (Eph. 4:5): "one Lord, one Faith, one Baptism." Consequently, an intention which is in opposition to this seems to annul the sacrament of Baptism.

On the other hand, if each were to say: "I baptize thee in the name of the Father and of the Son and of the Holy Ghost," each would signify his intention as though he were conferring Baptism independently of the other. This might occur in the case where both were striving to baptize someone; and then it is clear that whichever pronounced the words first would confer the sacrament of Baptism; while the other, however great his right to baptize, if he presume to utter the words, would be liable to be punished as a rebaptizer. If, however, they were to pronounce the words absolutely at the same time, and dipped or sprinkled the man together, they should be punished for baptizing in an improper manner, but not for rebaptizing: because each would intend to baptize an unbaptized person, and each, so far as he is concerned, would baptize. Nor would they confer several sacraments: but the one Christ baptizing inwardly would confer one sacrament by means of both together.

Reply Obj. 1: This argument avails in those agents that act by their own power. But men do not baptize by their own, but by Christ's power, Who, since He is one, perfects His work by means of one minister.

Reply Obj. 2: In a case of necessity one could baptize several at the same time under this form: "I baptize ye": for instance, if they were threatened by a falling house, or by the sword or something of the kind, so as not to allow of the delay involved by baptizing them singly. Nor would this cause a change in the Church's form, since the plural is nothing but the singular doubled: especially as we find the plural expressed in Matt. 28:19: "Baptizing them," etc. Nor is there parity between the baptizer and the baptized; since Christ, the baptizer in chief, is one: while many are made one in Christ by Baptism.

Reply Obj. 3: As stated above (Q. 66, A. 1), the integrity of Baptism consists in the form of words and the use of the matter. Consequently, neither he who only pronounces the words, baptizes, nor he who dips. Wherefore if one pronounces the words and the other dips, no form of words can be fitting. For neither could he say: "I baptize thee": since he dips not, and therefore baptizes not. Nor could they say: "We baptize thee": since neither baptizes. For if of two men, one write one part of a book, and the other write the other, it would not be a proper form of speech to say: "We wrote this book," but the figure of synecdoche in which the whole is put for the part.

SEVENTH ARTICLE [III, Q. 67, Art. 7]

Whether in Baptism It Is Necessary for Someone to Raise the Baptized from the Sacred Font?

Objection 1: It seems that in Baptism it is not necessary for someone to raise the baptized from the sacred font. For our Baptism is consecrated by Christ's Baptism and is conformed thereto. But Christ when baptized was not raised by anyone from the font, but according to Matt. 3:16, "Jesus being baptized, forthwith came out of the water." Therefore it seems that neither when others are baptized should anyone raise the baptized from the sacred font.

Obj. 2: Further, Baptism is a spiritual regeneration, as stated above (A. 3). But in carnal generation nothing else is required but the active principle, i.e. the father, and the passive principle, i.e. the mother. Since, then, in Baptism he that baptizes takes the place of the father, while the very water of Baptism takes the place of the mother, as Augustine says in a sermon on the Epiphany (cxxxv); it seems that there is no further need for someone to raise the baptized from the sacred font.

Obj. 3: Further, nothing ridiculous should be observed in the sacraments of the Church. But it seems ridiculous that after being baptized, adults who can stand up of themselves and leave the sacred font, should be held up by another. Therefore there seems no need for anyone, especially in the Baptism of adults, to raise the baptized from the sacred font.

*On the contrary,* Dionysius says (Eccl. Hier. ii) that "the priests taking the baptized hand him over to his sponsor and guide."

*I answer that,* The spiritual regeneration, which takes place in Baptism, is in a certain manner likened to carnal generation: wherefore it is written (1 Pet. 2:2): "As new-born babes, endowed with reason desire milk [Vulg.: 'desire reasonable milk'] without guile." Now, in carnal generation the new-born child needs nourishment and guidance: wherefore, in spiritual generation also, someone is needed to undertake the office of nurse and tutor by forming and instructing one who is yet a novice in the Faith, concerning things pertaining to Christian faith and mode of life, which the clergy have not the leisure to do through being busy with watching over the people generally: because little children and novices need more than ordinary care. Consequently someone is needed to receive the baptized from the sacred font as though for the purpose of instructing and guiding them. It is to this that Dionysius refers (Eccl. Hier. xi) saying: "It occurred to our heavenly guides," i.e. the Apostles, "and they decided, that infants should be taken charge of thus: that the parents of the child should hand it over to some instructor versed in holy things, who would thenceforth take charge of the child, and be to it a spiritual father and a guide in the road of salvation."

Reply Obj. 1: Christ was baptized not that He might be regenerated, but that He might regenerate others: wherefore after His Baptism He needed no tutor like other children.

Reply Obj. 2: In carnal generation nothing is essential besides a father and a mother: yet to ease the latter in her travail, there is need for a midwife; and for the child to be suitably brought up there is need for a nurse and a tutor: while their place is taken in Baptism by him who raises the child from the sacred font. Consequently this is not essential to the sacrament, and in a case of necessity one alone can baptize with water.

Reply Obj. 3: It is not on account of bodily weakness that the baptized is raised from the sacred font by the godparent, but on account of spiritual weakness, as stated above.

EIGHTH ARTICLE [III, Q. 67, Art. 8]

Whether He Who Raises Anyone from the Sacred Font Is Bound to Instruct Him?

Objection 1: It seems that he who raises anyone from the sacred font is not bound to instruct him. For none but those who are themselves instructed can give instruction. But even the uneducated and ill-instructed are allowed to raise people from the sacred font. Therefore he who raises a baptized person from the font is not bound to instruct him.

Obj. 2: Further, a son is instructed by his father better than by a stranger: for, as the Philosopher says (Ethic. viii), a son receives from his father, "being, food, and education." If, therefore, godparents are bound to instruct their godchildren, it would be fitting for the carnal father, rather than another, to be the godparent of his own child. And yet this seems to be forbidden, as may be seen in the Decretals (xxx, qu. 1, Cap. Pervenit and Dictum est).

Obj. 3: Further, it is better for several to instruct than for one only. If, therefore, godparents are bound to instruct their godchildren, it would be better to have several godparents than only one. Yet this is forbidden in a decree of Pope Leo, who says: "A child should not have more than one godparent, be this a man or a woman."

*On the contrary,* Augustine says in a sermon for Easter (clxviii): "In the first place I admonish you, both men and women, who have raised children in Baptism, that ye stand before God as sureties for those whom you have been seen to raise from the sacred font."

*I answer that,* Every man is bound to fulfil those duties which he has undertaken to perform. Now it has been stated above (A. 7) that godparents take upon themselves the duties of a tutor. Consequently they are bound to watch over their godchildren when there is need for them to do so: for instance when and where children are brought up among unbelievers. But if they are brought up among Catholic Christians, the godparents may well be excused from this responsibility, since it may be presumed that the children will be carefully instructed by their parents. If, however, they perceive in any way that the contrary is the case, they would be bound, as far as they are able, to see to the spiritual welfare of their godchildren.

Reply Obj. 1: Where the danger is imminent, the godparent, as Dionysius says (Eccl. Hier. vii), should be someone "versed in holy things." But where the danger is not imminent, by reason of the children being brought up among Catholics, anyone is admitted to this position, because the things pertaining to the Christian rule of life and faith are known openly by all. Nevertheless an unbaptized person cannot be a godparent, as was decreed in the Council of Mainz, although an unbaptized person: because the person baptizing is essential to the sacrament, wherefore as the godparent is not, as stated above (A. 7, ad 2).

Reply Obj. 2: Just as spiritual generation is distinct from carnal generation, so is spiritual education distinct from that of the body; according to Heb. 12:9: "Moreover we have had fathers of our flesh for instructors, and we reverenced them: shall we not much more obey the Father of Spirits, and live?" Therefore the spiritual father should be distinct from the carnal father, unless necessity demanded otherwise.

Reply Obj. 3: Education would be full of confusion if there were more than one head instructor. Wherefore there should be one principal sponsor in Baptism: but others can be allowed as assistants.

## QUESTION 68

OF THOSE WHO RECEIVE BAPTISM (In Twelve Articles)

We have now to consider those who receive Baptism; concerning which there are twelve points of inquiry:

(1) Whether all are bound to receive Baptism?

(2) Whether a man can be saved without Baptism?

(3) Whether Baptism should be deferred?

(4) Whether sinners should be baptized?

(5) Whether works of satisfaction should be enjoined on sinners that have been baptized?

(6) Whether Confession of sins is necessary?

(7) Whether an intention is required on the part of the one baptized?

(8) Whether faith is necessary?

(9) Whether infants should be baptized?

(10) Whether the children of Jews should be baptized against the will of their parents?

(11) Whether anyone should be baptized in the mother's womb?

(12) Whether madmen and imbeciles should be baptized?

FIRST ARTICLE [III, Q. 68, Art. 1]

Whether All Are Bound to Receive Baptism?

Objection 1: It seems that not all are bound to receive Baptism. For Christ did not narrow man's road to salvation. But before Christ's coming men could be saved without Baptism: therefore also after Christ's coming.

Obj. 2: Further, Baptism seems to have been instituted principally as a remedy for original sin. Now, since a man who is baptized is without original sin, it seems that he cannot transmit it to his children. Therefore it seems that the children of those who have been baptized, should not themselves be baptized.

Obj. 3: Further, Baptism is given in order that a man may, through grace, be cleansed from sin. But those who are sanctified in the womb, obtain this without Baptism. Therefore they are not bound to receive Baptism.

*On the contrary,* It is written (John 3:5): "Unless a man be born again of water and the Holy Ghost, he cannot enter into the kingdom of God." Again it is stated in De Eccl. Dogm. xli, that "we believe the way of salvation to be open to those only who are baptized."

*I answer that,* Men are bound to that without which they cannot obtain salvation. Now it is manifest that no one can obtain salvation but through Christ; wherefore the Apostle says (Rom. 5:18): "As by the offense of one unto all men unto condemnation; so also by the justice of one, unto all men unto justification of life." But for this end is Baptism conferred on a man, that being regenerated thereby, he may be incorporated in Christ, by becoming His member: wherefore it is written (Gal. 3:27): "As many of you as have been baptized in Christ, have put on Christ." Consequently it is manifest that all are bound to be baptized: and that without Baptism there is no salvation for men.

Reply Obj. 1: At no time, not even before the coming of Christ, could men be saved unless they became members of Christ: because, as it is written (Acts 4:12), "there is no other name under heaven given to men, whereby we must be saved." But before Christ's coming, men were incorporated in Christ by faith in His future coming: of which faith circumcision was the "seal," as the Apostle calls it (Rom. 4:11): whereas before circumcision was instituted, men were incorporated in Christ by "faith alone," as Gregory says (Moral. iv), together with the offering of sacrifices, by means of which the Fathers of old made profession of their faith. Again, since Christ's coming, men are incorporated in Christ by faith; according to Eph. 3:17: "That Christ may dwell by faith in your hearts." But faith in a thing already present is manifested by a sign different from that by which it was manifested when that thing was yet in the future: just as we use other parts of the verb, to signify the present, the past, and the future. Consequently although the sacrament itself of Baptism was not always necessary for salvation, yet faith, of which Baptism is the sacrament, was always necessary.

Reply Obj. 2: As we have stated in the I-II, Q. 81, A. 3, ad 2, those who are baptized are renewed in spirit by Baptism, while their body remains subject to the oldness of sin, according to Rom. 8:10: "The body, indeed, is dead because of sin, but the spirit liveth because of justification." Wherefore Augustine (Contra Julian. vi) proves that "not everything that is in man is baptized." Now it is manifest that in carnal generation man does not beget in respect of his soul, but in respect of his body. Consequently the children of those who are baptized are born with original sin; wherefore they need to be baptized.

Reply Obj. 3: Those who are sanctified in the womb, receive indeed grace which cleanses them from original sin, but they do not therefore receive the character, by which they are conformed to Christ. Consequently, if any were to be sanctified in the womb now, they would need to be baptized, in order to be conformed to Christ's other members by receiving the character.

SECOND ARTICLE [III, Q. 68, Art. 2]

Whether a Man Can Be Saved Without Baptism?

Objection 1: It seems that no man can be saved without Baptism. For our Lord said (John 3:5): "Unless a man be born again of water and the Holy Ghost, he cannot enter the kingdom of God." But those alone are saved who enter God's kingdom. Therefore none can be saved without Baptism, by which a man is born again of water and the Holy Ghost.

Obj. 2: Further, in the book De Eccl. Dogm. xli, it is written: "We believe that no catechumen, though he die in his good works, will have eternal life, except he suffer martyrdom, which contains all the sacramental virtue of Baptism." But if it were possible for anyone to be saved without Baptism, this would be the case specially with catechumens who are credited with good works, for they seem to have the "faith that worketh by charity" (Gal. 5:6). Therefore it seems that none can be saved without Baptism.

Obj. 3: Further, as stated above (A. 1; Q. 65, A. 4), the sacrament of Baptism is necessary for salvation. Now that is necessary "without which something cannot be" (Metaph. v). Therefore it seems that none can obtain salvation without Baptism.

*On the contrary,* Augustine says (Super Levit. lxxxiv) that "some have received the invisible sanctification without visible sacraments, and to their profit; but though it is possible to have the visible sanctification, consisting in a visible sacrament, without the invisible sanctification, it will be to no profit." Since, therefore, the sacrament of Baptism pertains to the visible sanctification, it seems that a man can obtain salvation without the sacrament of Baptism, by means of the invisible sanctification.

*I answer that,* The sacrament of Baptism may be wanting to someone in two ways. First, both in reality and in desire; as is the case with those who neither are baptized, nor wished to be baptized: which clearly indicates contempt of the sacrament, in regard to those who have the use of the free-will. Consequently those to whom Baptism is wanting thus, cannot obtain salvation: since neither sacramentally nor mentally are they incorporated in Christ, through Whom alone can salvation be obtained.

Secondly, the sacrament of Baptism may be wanting to anyone in reality but not in desire: for instance, when a man wishes to be baptized, but by some ill-chance he is forestalled by death before receiving Baptism. And such a man can obtain salvation without being actually baptized, on account of his desire for Baptism, which desire is the outcome of "faith that worketh by charity," whereby God, Whose power is not tied to visible sacraments, sanctifies man inwardly. Hence Ambrose says of Valentinian, who died while yet a catechumen: "I lost him whom I was to regenerate: but he did not lose the grace he prayed for."

Reply Obj. 1: As it is written (1 Kings 16:7), "man seeth those things that appear, but the Lord beholdeth the heart." Now a man who desires to be "born again of water and the Holy Ghost" by Baptism, is regenerated in heart though not in body. Thus the Apostle says (Rom. 2:29) that "the circumcision is that of the heart, in the spirit, not in the letter; whose praise is not of men but of God."

Reply Obj. 2: No man obtains eternal life unless he be free from all guilt and debt of punishment. Now this plenary absolution is given when a man receives Baptism, or suffers martyrdom: for which reason is it stated that martyrdom "contains all the sacramental virtue of Baptism," i.e. as to the full deliverance from guilt and punishment. Suppose, therefore, a catechumen to have the desire for Baptism (else he could not be said to die in his good works, which cannot be without "faith that worketh by charity"), such a one, were he to die, would not forthwith come to eternal life, but would suffer punishment for his past sins, "but he himself shall be saved, yet so as by fire" as is stated 1 Cor. 3:15.

Reply Obj. 3: The sacrament of Baptism is said to be necessary for salvation in so far as man cannot be saved without, at least, Baptism of desire; "which, with God, counts for the deed" (Augustine, Enarr. in Ps. 57).

THIRD ARTICLE [III, Q. 68, Art. 3]

Whether Baptism Should Be Deferred?

Objection 1: It seems that Baptism should be deferred. For Pope Leo says (Epist. xvi): "Two seasons," i.e. Easter and Whitsuntide, "are fixed by the Roman Pontiff for the celebration of Baptism. Wherefore we admonish your Beatitude not to add any other days to this custom." Therefore it seems that Baptism should be conferred not at once, but delayed until the aforesaid seasons.

Obj. 2: Further, we read in the decrees of the Council of Agde (Can. xxxiv): "If Jews whose bad faith often 'returns to the vomit,' wish to submit to the Law of the Catholic Church, let them for eight months enter the porch of the church with the catechumens; and if they are found to come in good faith then at last they may deserve the grace of Baptism." Therefore men should not be baptized at once, and Baptism should be deferred for a certain fixed time.

Obj. 3: Further, as we read in Isa. 27:9, "this is all the fruit, that the sin . . . should be taken away." Now sin seems to be taken away, or at any rate lessened, if Baptism be deferred. First, because those who sin after Baptism, sin more grievously, according to Heb. 10:29: "How much more, do you think, he deserveth worse punishments, who hath . . . esteemed the blood of the testament," i.e. Baptism, "unclean, by which he was sanctified?" Secondly, because Baptism takes away past, but not future, sins: wherefore the more it is deferred, the more sins it takes away. Therefore it seems that Baptism should be deferred for a long time.

*On the contrary,* It is written (Ecclus. 5:8): "Delay not to be converted to the Lord, and defer it not from day to day." But the perfect conversion to God is of those who are regenerated in Christ by Baptism. Therefore Baptism should not be deferred from day to day.

*I answer that,* In this matter we must make a distinction and see whether those who are to be baptized are children or adults. For if they be children, Baptism should not be deferred. First, because in them we do not look for better instruction or fuller conversion. Secondly, because of the danger of death, for no other remedy is available for them besides the sacrament of Baptism.

On the other hand, adults have a remedy in the mere desire for Baptism, as stated above (A. 2). And therefore Baptism should not be conferred on adults as soon as they are converted, but it should be deferred until some fixed time. First, as a safeguard to the Church, lest she be deceived through baptizing those who come to her under false pretenses, according to 1 John 4:1: "Believe not every spirit, but try the spirits, if they be of God." And those who approach Baptism are put to this test, when their faith and morals are subjected to proof for a space of time. Secondly, this is needful as being useful for those who are baptized; for they require a certain space of time in order to be fully instructed in the faith, and to be drilled in those things that pertain to the Christian mode of life. Thirdly, a certain reverence for the sacrament demands a delay whereby men are admitted to Baptism at the principal festivities, viz. of Easter and Pentecost, the result being that they receive the sacrament with greater devotion.

There are, however, two reasons for forgoing this delay. First, when those who are to be baptized appear to be perfectly instructed in the faith and ready for Baptism; thus, Philip baptized the Eunuch at once (Acts 8); and Peter, Cornelius and those who were with him (Acts 10). Secondly, by reason of sickness or some kind of danger of death. Wherefore Pope Leo says (Epist. xvi): "Those who are threatened by death, sickness, siege, persecution, or shipwreck, should be baptized at any time." Yet if a man is forestalled by death, so as to have no time to receive the sacrament, while he awaits the season appointed by the Church, he is saved, yet "so as by fire," as stated above (A. 2, ad 2). Nevertheless he sins if he defer being baptized beyond the time appointed by the Church, except this be for an unavoidable cause and with the permission of the authorities of the Church. But even this sin, with his other sins, can be washed away by his subsequent contrition, which takes the place of Baptism, as stated above (Q. 66, A. 11).

Reply Obj. 1: This decree of Pope Leo, concerning the celebration of Baptism at two seasons, is to be understood "with the exception of the danger of death" (which is always to be feared in children) as stated above.

Reply Obj. 2: This decree concerning the Jews was for a safeguard to the Church, lest they corrupt the faith of simple people, if they be not fully converted. Nevertheless, as the same passage reads further on, "if within the appointed time they are threatened with danger of sickness, they should be baptized."

Reply Obj. 3: Baptism, by the grace which it bestows, removes not only past sins, but hinders the commission of future sins. Now this is the point to be considered--that men may not sin: it is a secondary consideration that their sins be less grievous, or that their sins be washed away, according to 1 John 2:1, 2: "My little children, these things I write to you, that you may not sin. But if any man sin, we have an advocate with the Father, Jesus Christ the just; and He is the propitiation for our sins."

FOURTH ARTICLE [III, Q. 68, Art. 4]

Whether Sinners Should Be Baptized?

Objection 1: It seems that sinners should be baptized. For it is written (Zech. 13:1): "In that day there shall be a fountain open to the House of David, and to the inhabitants of Jerusalem: for the washing of the sinner and of the unclean woman": and this is to be understood of the fountain of Baptism. Therefore it seems that the sacrament of Baptism should be offered even to sinners.

Obj. 2: Further, our Lord said (Matt. 9:12): "They that are in health need not a physician, but they that are ill." But they that are ill are sinners. Therefore since Baptism is the remedy of Christ the physician of our souls, it seems that this sacrament should be offered to sinners.

Obj. 3: Further, no assistance should be withdrawn from sinners. But sinners who have been baptized derive spiritual assistance from the very character of Baptism, since it is a disposition to grace. Therefore it seems that the sacrament of Baptism should be offered to sinners.

*On the contrary,* Augustine says (Serm. clxix): "He Who created thee without thee, will not justify thee without thee." But since a sinner's will is ill-disposed, he does not co-operate with God. Therefore it is useless to employ Baptism as a means of justification.

*I answer that,* A man may be said to be a sinner in two ways. First, on account of the stain and the debt of punishment incurred in the past: and on sinners in this sense the sacrament of Baptism should be conferred, since it is instituted specially for this purpose, that by it the uncleanness of sin may be washed away, according to Eph. 5:26: "Cleansing it by the laver of water in the word of life."

Secondly, a man may be called a sinner because he wills to sin and purposes to remain in sin: and on sinners in this sense the sacrament of Baptism should not be conferred. First, indeed, because by Baptism men are incorporated in Christ, according to Gal. 3:27: "As many of you as have been baptized in Christ, have put on Christ." Now so long as a man wills to sin, he cannot be united to Christ, according to 2 Cor. 6:14: "What participation hath justice with injustice?" Wherefore Augustine says in his book on Penance (Serm. cccli) that "no man who has the use of free-will can begin the new life, except he repent of his former life." Secondly, because there should be nothing useless in the works of Christ and of the Church. Now that is useless which does not reach the end to which it is ordained; and, on the other hand, no one having the will to sin can, at the same time, be cleansed from sin, which is the purpose of Baptism; for this would be to combine two contradictory things. Thirdly, because there should be no falsehood in the sacramental signs. Now a sign is false if it does not correspond with the thing signified. But the very fact that a man presents himself to be cleansed by Baptism, signifies that he prepares himself for the inward cleansing: while this cannot be the case with one who purposes to remain in sin. Therefore it is manifest that on such a man the sacrament of Baptism is not to be conferred.

Reply Obj. 1: The words quoted are to be understood of those sinners whose will is set on renouncing sin.

Reply Obj. 2: The physician of souls, i.e. Christ, works in two ways. First, inwardly, by Himself: and thus He prepares man's will so that it wills good and hates evil. Secondly, He works through ministers, by the outward application of the sacraments: and in this way His work consists in perfecting what was begun outwardly. Therefore the sacrament of Baptism is not to be conferred save on those in whom there appears some sign of their interior conversion: just as neither is bodily medicine given to a sick man, unless he show some sign of life.

Reply Obj. 3: Baptism is the sacrament of faith. Now dead faith does not suffice for salvation; nor is it the foundation, but living faith alone, "that worketh by charity" (Gal. 5:6), as Augustine says (De Fide et oper.). Neither, therefore, can the sacrament of Baptism give salvation to a man whose will is set on sinning, and hence expels the form of faith. Moreover, the impression of the baptismal character cannot dispose a man for grace as long as he retains the will to sin; for "God compels no man to be virtuous," as Damascene says (De Fide Orth. ii).

FIFTH ARTICLE [III, Q. 68, Art. 5]

Whether Works of Satisfaction Should Be Enjoined on Sinners That Have Been Baptized?

Objection 1: It seems that works of satisfaction should be enjoined on sinners that have been baptized. For God's justice seems to demand that a man should be punished for every sin of his, according to Eccles. 12:14: "All things that are done, God will bring into judgment." But works of satisfaction are enjoined on sinners in punishment of past sins. Therefore it seems that works of satisfaction should be enjoined on sinners that have been baptized.

Obj. 2: Further, by means of works of satisfaction sinners recently converted are drilled into righteousness, and are made to avoid the occasions of sin: "for satisfaction consists in extirpating the causes of vice, and closing the doors to sin" (De Eccl. Dogm. iv). But this is most necessary in the case of those who have been baptized recently. Therefore it seems that works of satisfaction should be enjoined on sinners.

Obj. 3: Further, man owes satisfaction to God not less than to his neighbor. But if those who were recently baptized have injured their neighbor, they should be told to make reparation to God by works of penance.

*On the contrary,* Ambrose commenting on Rom. 11:29: "The gifts and the calling of God are without repentance," says: "The grace of God requires neither sighs nor groans in Baptism, nor indeed any work at all, but faith alone; and remits all, gratis."

*I answer that,* As the Apostle says (Rom. 6:3, 4), "all we who are baptized in Christ Jesus, are baptized in His death: for we are buried together with Him, by Baptism unto death"; which is to say that by Baptism man is incorporated in the very death of Christ. Now it is manifest from what has been said above (Q. 48, AA. 2, 4; Q. 49, A. 3) that Christ's death satisfied sufficiently for sins, "not for ours only, but also for those of the whole world," according to 1 John 2:2. Consequently no kind of satisfaction should be enjoined on one who is being baptized, for any sins whatever: and this would be to dishonor the Passion and death of Christ, as being insufficient for the plenary satisfaction for the sins of those who were to be baptized.

Reply Obj. 1: As Augustine says in his book on Infant Baptism (De Pecc. Merit. et Remiss. i), "the effect of Baptism is to make those, who are baptized, to be incorporated in Christ as His members." Wherefore the very pains of Christ were satisfactory for the sins of those who were to be baptized; just as the pain of one member can be satisfactory for the sin of another member. Hence it is written (Isa. 53:4): "Surely He hath borne our infirmities and carried our sorrows."

Reply Obj. 2: Those who have been lately baptized should be drilled into righteousness, not by penal, but by "easy works, so as to advance to perfection by taking exercise, as infants by taking milk," as a gloss says on Ps. 130:2: "As a child that is weaned is towards his mother." For this reason did our Lord excuse His disciples from fasting when they were recently converted, as we read in Matt. 9:14, 15: and the same is written 1 Pet. 2:2: "As newborn babes desire . . . milk . . . that thereby you may grow unto salvation."

Reply Obj. 3: To restore what has been ill taken from one's neighbor, and to make satisfaction for wrong done to him, is to cease from sin: for the very fact of retaining what belongs to another and of not being reconciled to one's neighbor, is a sin. Wherefore those who are baptized should be enjoined to make satisfaction to their neighbor, as also to desist from sin. But they are not to be enjoined to suffer any punishment for past sins.

SIXTH ARTICLE [III, Q. 68, Art. 6]

Whether Sinners Who Are Going to Be Baptized Are Bound to Confess Their Sins?

Objection 1: It seems that sinners who are going to be baptized are bound to confess their sins. For it is written (Matt. 3:6) that many "were baptized" by John "in the Jordan confessing their sins." But Christ's Baptism is more perfect than John's. Therefore it seems that there is yet greater reason why they who are about to receive Christ's Baptism should confess their sins.

Obj. 2: Further, it is written (Prov. 28:13): "He that hideth his sins, shall not prosper; but he that shall confess and forsake them, shall obtain mercy." Now for this is a man baptized, that he may obtain mercy for his sins. Therefore those who are going to be baptized should confess their sins.

Obj. 3: Further, Penance is required before Baptism, according to Acts 2:38: "Do penance and be baptized every one of you." But confession is a part of Penance. Therefore it seems that confession of sins should take place before Baptism.

*On the contrary,* Confession of sins should be sorrowful: thus Augustine says (De Vera et Falsa Poenit. xiv): "All these circumstances should be taken into account and deplored." Now, as Ambrose says on Rom. 11:29, "the grace of God requires neither sighs nor groans in Baptism." Therefore confession of sins should not be required of those who are going to be baptized.

*I answer that,* Confession of sins is twofold. One is made inwardly to God: and such confession of sins is required before Baptism: in other words, man should call his sins to mind and sorrow for them; since "he cannot begin the new life, except he repent of his former life," as Augustine says in his book on Penance (Serm. cccli). The other is the outward confession of sins, which is made to a priest; and such confession is not required before Baptism. First, because this confession, since it is directed to the person of the minister, belongs to the sacrament of Penance, which is not required before Baptism, which is the door of all the sacraments. Secondly, because the reason why a man makes outward confession to a priest, is that the priest may absolve him from his sins, and bind him to works of satisfaction, which should not be enjoined on the baptized, as stated above (A. 5). Moreover those who are being baptized do not need to be released from their sins by the keys of the Church, since all are forgiven them in Baptism. Thirdly, because the very act of confession made to a man is penal, by reason of the shame it inflicts on the one confessing: whereas no exterior punishment is enjoined on a man who is being baptized.

Therefore no special confession of sins is required of those who are being baptized; but that general confession suffices which they make when in accordance with the Church's ritual they "renounce Satan and all his works." And in this sense a gloss explains Matt. 3:6, saying that in John's Baptism "those who are going to be baptized learn that they should confess their sins and promise to amend their life."

If, however, any persons about to be baptized, wish, out of devotion, to confess their sins, their confession should be heard; not for the purpose of enjoining them to do satisfaction, but in order to instruct them in the spiritual life as a remedy against their vicious habits.

Reply Obj. 1: Sins were not forgiven in John's Baptism, which, however, was the Baptism of Penance. Consequently it was fitting that those who went to receive that Baptism, should confess their sins, so that they should receive a penance in proportion to their sins. But Christ's Baptism is without outward penance, as Ambrose says (on Rom. 11:29); and therefore there is no comparison.

Reply Obj. 2: It is enough that the baptized make inward confession to God, and also an outward general confession, for them to "prosper and obtain mercy": and they need no special outward confession, as stated above.

Reply Obj. 3: Confession is a part of sacramental Penance, which is not required before Baptism, as stated above: but the inward virtue of Penance is required.

SEVENTH ARTICLE [III, Q. 68, Art. 7]

Whether the Intention of Receiving the Sacrament of Baptism Is Required on the Part of the One Baptized?

Objection 1: It seems that the intention of receiving the sacrament of Baptism is not required on the part of the one baptized. For the one baptized is, as it were, "patient" in the sacrament. But an intention is required not on the part of the patient but on the part of the agent. Therefore it seems that the intention of receiving Baptism is not required on the part of the one baptized.

Obj. 2: Further, if what is necessary for Baptism be omitted, the Baptism must be repeated; for instance, if the invocation of the Trinity be omitted, as stated above (Q. 66, A. 9, ad 3). But it does not seem that a man should be rebaptized through not having had the intention of receiving Baptism: else, since his intention cannot be proved, anyone might ask to be baptized again on account of his lack of intention. Therefore it seems that no intention is required on the part of the one baptized, in order that he receive the sacrament.

Obj. 3: Further, Baptism is given as a remedy for original sin. But original sin is contracted without the intention of the person born. Therefore, seemingly, Baptism requires no intention on the part of the person baptized.

*On the contrary,* According to the Church's ritual, those who are to be baptized ask of the Church that they may receive Baptism: and thus they express their intention of receiving the sacrament.

*I answer that,* By Baptism a man dies to the old life of sin, and begins a certain newness of life, according to Rom. 6:4: "We are buried together with" Christ "by Baptism into death; that, as Christ is risen from the dead . . . so we also may walk in newness of life." Consequently, just as, according to Augustine (Serm. cccli), he who has the use of free-will, must, in order to die to the old life, "will to repent of his former life"; so must he, of his own will, intend to lead a new life, the beginning of which is precisely the receiving of the sacrament. Therefore on the part of the one baptized, it is necessary for him to have the will or intention of receiving the sacrament.

Reply Obj. 1: When a man is justified by Baptism, his passiveness is not violent but voluntary: wherefore it is necessary for him to intend to receive that which is given him.

Reply Obj. 2: If an adult lack the intention of receiving the sacrament, he must be rebaptized. But if there be doubt about this, the form to be used should be: "If thou art not baptized, I baptize thee."

Reply Obj. 3: Baptism is a remedy not only against original, but also against actual sins, which are caused by our will and intention.

EIGHTH ARTICLE [III, Q. 68, Art. 8]

Whether Faith Is Required on the Part of the One Baptized?

Objection 1: It seems that faith is required on the part of the one baptized. For the sacrament of Baptism was instituted by Christ. But Christ, in giving the form of Baptism, makes faith to precede Baptism (Mk. 16:16): "He that believeth and is baptized, shall be saved." Therefore it seems that without faith there can be no sacrament of Baptism.

Obj. 2: Further, nothing useless is done in the sacraments of the Church. But according to the Church's ritual, the man who comes to be baptized is asked concerning his faith: "Dost thou believe in God the Father Almighty?" Therefore it seems that faith is required for Baptism.

Obj. 3: Further, the intention of receiving the sacrament is required for Baptism. But this cannot be without right faith, since Baptism is the sacrament of right faith: for thereby men "are incorporated in Christ," as Augustine says in his book on Infant Baptism (De Pecc. Merit. et Remiss. i); and this cannot be without right faith, according to Eph. 3:17: "That Christ may dwell by faith in your hearts." Therefore it seems that a man who has not right faith cannot receive the sacrament of Baptism.

Obj. 4: Further, unbelief is a most grievous sin, as we have shown in the Second Part (II-II, Q. 10, A. 3). But those who remain in sin should not be baptized: therefore neither should those who remain in unbelief.

*On the contrary,* Gregory writing to the bishop Quiricus says: "We have learned from the ancient tradition of the Fathers that when heretics, baptized in the name of the Trinity, come back to Holy Church, they are to be welcomed to her bosom, either with the anointing of chrism, or the imposition of hands, or the mere profession of faith." But such would not be the case if faith were necessary for a man to receive Baptism.

*I answer that,* As appears from what has been said above (Q. 63, A. 6; Q. 66, A. 9) Baptism produces a twofold effect in the soul, viz. the character and grace. Therefore in two ways may a thing be necessary for Baptism. First, as something without which grace, which is the ultimate effect of the sacrament, cannot be had. And thus right faith is necessary for Baptism, because, as it appears from Rom. 3:22, the justice of God is by faith of Jesus Christ.

Secondly, something is required of necessity for Baptism, because without it the baptismal character cannot be imprinted. And thus right faith is not necessary in the one baptized any more than in the one who baptizes: provided the other conditions are fulfilled which are essential to the sacrament. For the sacrament is not perfected by the righteousness of the minister or of the recipient of Baptism, but by the power of God.

Reply Obj. 1: Our Lord is speaking there of Baptism as bringing us to salvation by giving us sanctifying grace: which of course cannot be without right faith: wherefore He says pointedly: "He that believeth and is baptized, shall be saved."

Reply Obj. 2: The Church's intention in baptizing men is that they may be cleansed from sin, according to Isa. 27:9: "This is all the fruit, that the sin . . . should be taken away." And therefore, as far as she is concerned, she does not intend to give Baptism save to those who have right faith, without which there is no remission of sins. And for this reason she asks those who come to be baptized whether they believe. If, *on the contrary,* anyone, without right faith, receive Baptism outside the Church, he does not receive it unto salvation. Hence Augustine says (De Baptism. contr. Donat. iv): "From the Church being compared to Paradise we learn that men can receive her Baptism even outside her fold, but that elsewhere none can receive or keep the salvation of the blessed."

Reply Obj. 3: Even he who has not right faith on other points, can have right faith about the sacrament of Baptism: and so he is not hindered from having the intention of receiving that sacrament. Yet even if he think not aright concerning this sacrament, it is enough, for the receiving of the sacrament, that he should have a general intention of receiving Baptism, according as Christ instituted, and as the Church bestows it.

Reply Obj. 4: Just as the sacrament of Baptism is not to be conferred on a man who is unwilling to give up his other sins, so neither should it be given to one who is unwilling to renounce his unbelief. Yet each receives the sacrament if it be conferred on him, though not unto salvation.

NINTH ARTICLE [III, Q. 68, Art. 9]

Whether Children Should Be Baptized?

Objection 1: It seems that children should not be baptized. For the intention to receive the sacrament is required in one who is being baptized, as stated above (A. 7). But children cannot have such an intention, since they have not the use of free-will. Therefore it seems that they cannot receive the sacrament of Baptism.

Obj. 2: Further, Baptism is the sacrament of faith, as stated above (Q. 39, A. 5; Q. 66, A. 1, ad 1). But children have not faith, which demands an act of the will on the part of the believer, as Augustine says (Super Joan. xxvi). Nor can it be said that their salvation is implied in the faith of their parents; since the latter are sometimes unbelievers, and their unbelief would conduce rather to the damnation of their children. Therefore it seems that children cannot be baptized.

Obj. 3: Further, it is written (1 Pet. 3:21) that "Baptism saveth" men; "not the putting away of the filth of the flesh, but the examination of a good conscience towards God." But children have no conscience, either good or bad, since they have not the use of reason: nor can they be fittingly examined, since they understand not. Therefore children should not be baptized.

*On the contrary,* Dionysius says (Eccl. Hier. iii):

"Our heavenly guides," i.e. the Apostles, "approved of infants being admitted to Baptism."

*I answer that,* As the Apostle says (Rom. 5:17), "if by one man's offense death reigned through one," namely Adam, "much more they who receive abundance of grace, and of the gift, and of justice, shall reign in life through one, Jesus Christ." Now children contract original sin from the sin of Adam; which is made clear by the fact that they are under the ban of death, which "passed upon all" on account of the sin of the first man, as the Apostle says in the same passage (Rom. 5:12). Much more, therefore, can children receive grace through Christ, so as to reign in eternal life. But our Lord Himself said (John 3:5): "Unless a man be born again of water and the Holy Ghost, he cannot enter into the kingdom of God." Consequently it became necessary to baptize children, that, as in birth they incurred damnation through Adam so in a second birth they might obtain salvation through Christ. Moreover it was fitting that children should receive Baptism, in order that being reared from childhood in things pertaining to the Christian mode of life, they may the more easily persevere therein; according to Prov. 22:5: "A young man according to his way, even when he is old, he will not depart from it." This reason is also given by Dionysius (Eccl. Hier. iii).

Reply Obj. 1: The spiritual regeneration effected by Baptism is somewhat like carnal birth, in this respect, that as the child while in the mother's womb receives nourishment not independently, but through the nourishment of its mother, so also children before the use of reason, being as it were in the womb of their mother the Church, receive salvation not by their own act, but by the act of the Church. Hence Augustine says (De Pecc. Merit. et Remiss. i): "The Church, our mother, offers her maternal mouth for her children, that they may imbibe the sacred mysteries: for they cannot as yet with their own hearts believe unto justice, nor with their own mouths confess unto salvation . . . And if they are rightly said to believe, because in a certain fashion they make profession of faith by the words of their sponsors, why should they not also be said to repent, since by the words of those same sponsors they evidence their renunciation of the devil and this world?" For the same reason they can be said to intend, not by their own act of intention, since at times they struggle and cry; but by the act of those who bring them to be baptized.

Reply Obj. 2: As Augustine says, writing to Boniface (Cont. duas Ep. Pelag. i), "in the Church of our Saviour little children believe through others, just as they contracted from others those sins which are remitted in Baptism." Nor is it a hindrance to their salvation if their parents be unbelievers, because, as Augustine says, writing to the same Boniface (Ep. xcviii), "little children are offered that they may receive grace in their souls, not so much from the hands of those that carry them (yet from these too, if they be good and faithful) as from the whole company of the saints and the faithful. For they are rightly considered to be offered by those who are pleased at their being offered, and by whose charity they are united in communion with the Holy Ghost." And the unbelief of their own parents, even if after Baptism these strive to infect them with the worship of demons, hurts not the children. For as Augustine says (Cont. duas Ep. Pelag. i) "when once the child has been begotten by the will of others, he cannot subsequently be held by the bonds of another's sin so long as he consent not with his will, according to" Ezech. 18:4: "'As the soul of the Father, so also the soul of the son is mine; the soul that sinneth, the same shall die.' Yet he contracted from Adam that which was loosed by the grace of this sacrament, because as yet he was not endowed with a separate existence." But the faith of one, indeed of the whole Church, profits the child through the operation of the Holy Ghost, Who unites the Church together, and communicates the goods of one member to another.

Reply Obj. 3: Just as a child, when he is being baptized, believes not by himself but by others, so is he examined not by himself but through others, and these in answer confess the Church's faith in the child's stead, who is aggregated to this faith by the sacrament of faith. And the child acquires a good conscience in himself, not indeed as to the act, but as to the habit, by sanctifying grace.

TENTH ARTICLE [III, Q. 68, Art. 10]

Whether Children of Jews or Other Unbelievers Should Be Baptized Against the Will of Their Parents?

Objection 1: It seems that children of Jews or other unbelievers should be baptized against the will of their parents. For it is a matter of greater urgency to rescue a man from the danger of eternal death than from the danger of temporal death. But one ought to rescue a child that is threatened by the danger of temporal death, even if its parents through malice try to prevent its being rescued. Therefore much more reason is there for rescuing the children of unbelievers from the danger of eternal death, even against their parents' will.

Obj. 2: The children of slaves are themselves slaves, and in the power of their masters. But Jews and all other unbelievers are the slaves of kings and rulers. Therefore without any injustice rulers can have the children of Jews baptized, as well as those of other slaves who are unbelievers.

Obj. 3: Further, every man belongs more to God, from Whom he has his soul, than to his carnal father, from whom he has his body. Therefore it is not unjust if the children of unbelievers are taken away from their carnal parents, and consecrated to God by Baptism.

*On the contrary,* It is written in the Decretals (Dist. xlv), quoting the council of Toledo: "In regard to the Jews the holy synod commands that henceforward none of them be forced to believe: for such are not to be saved against their will, but willingly, that their righteousness may be without flaw."

*I answer that,* The children of unbelievers either have the use of reason or they have not. If they have, then they already begin to control their own actions, in things that are of Divine or natural law. And therefore of their own accord, and against the will of their parents, they can receive Baptism, just as they can contract marriage. Consequently such can lawfully be advised and persuaded to be baptized.

If, however, they have not yet the use of free-will, according to the natural law they are under the care of their parents as long as they cannot look after themselves. For which reason we say that even the children of the ancients "were saved through the faith of their parents." Wherefore it would be contrary to natural justice if such children were baptized against their parents' will; just as it would be if one having the use of reason were baptized against his will. Moreover under the circumstances it would be dangerous to baptize the children of unbelievers; for they would be liable to lapse into unbelief, by reason of their natural affection for their parents. Therefore it is not the custom of the Church to baptize the children of unbelievers against their parents' will.

Reply Obj. 1: It is not right to rescue a man from death of the body against the order of civil law: for instance, if a man be condemned to death by the judge who has tried him, none should use force in order to rescue him from death. Consequently, neither should anyone infringe the order of the natural law, in virtue of which a child is under the care of its father, in order to rescue it from the danger of eternal death.

Reply Obj. 2: Jews are slaves of rulers by civil slavery, which does not exclude the order of the natural and Divine law.

Reply Obj. 3: Man is ordained unto God through his reason, by which he can know God. Wherefore a child, before it has the use of reason, is ordained to God, by a natural order, through the reason of its parents, under whose care it naturally lies, and it is according to their ordering that things pertaining to God are to be done in respect of the child.

ELEVENTH ARTICLE [III, Q. 68, Art. 11]

Whether a Child Can Be Baptized While Yet in Its Mother's Womb?

Objection 1: It seems that a child can be baptized while yet in its mother's womb. For the gift of Christ is more efficacious unto salvation than Adam's sin unto condemnation, as the Apostle says (Rom. 5:15). But a child while yet in its mother's womb is under sentence of condemnation on account of Adam's sin. For much more reason, therefore, can it be saved through the gift of Christ, which is bestowed by means of Baptism. Therefore a child can be baptized while yet in its mother's womb.

Obj. 2: Further, a child, while yet in its mother's womb, seems to be part of its mother. Now, when the mother is baptized, whatever is in her and part of her, is baptized. Therefore it seems that when the mother is baptized, the child in her womb is baptized.

Obj. 3: Further, eternal death is a greater evil than death of the body. But of two evils the less should be chosen. If, therefore, the child in the mother's womb cannot be baptized, it would be better for the mother to be opened, and the child to be taken out by force and baptized, than that the child should be eternally damned through dying without Baptism.

Obj. 4: Further, it happens at times that some part of the child comes forth first, as we read in Gen. 38:27: "In the very delivery of the infants, one put forth a hand, whereon the midwife tied a scarlet thread, saying: This shall come forth the first. But he drawing back his hand, the other came forth." Now sometimes in such cases there is danger of death. Therefore it seems that that part should be baptized, while the child is yet in its mother's womb.

*On the contrary,* Augustine says (Ep. ad Dardan.): "No one can be born a second time unless he be born first." But Baptism is a spiritual regeneration. Therefore no one should be baptized before he is born from the womb.

*I answer that,* It is essential to Baptism that some part of the body of the person baptized be in some way washed with water, since Baptism is a kind of washing, as stated above (Q. 66, A. 1). But an infant's body, before being born from the womb, can nowise be washed with water; unless perchance it be said that the baptismal water, with which the mother's body is washed, reaches the child while yet in its mother's womb. But this is impossible: both because the child's soul, to the sanctification of which Baptism is ordained, is distinct from the soul of the mother; and because the body of the animated infant is already formed, and consequently distinct from the body of the mother. Therefore the Baptism which the mother receives does not overflow on to the child which is in her womb. Hence Augustine says (Cont. Julian. vi): "If what is conceived within a mother belonged to her body, so as to be considered a part thereof, we should not baptize an infant whose mother, through danger of death, was baptized while she bore it in her womb. Since, then, it," i.e. the infant, "is baptized, it certainly did not belong to the mother's body while it was in the womb." It follows, therefore, that a child can nowise be baptized while in its mother's womb.

Reply Obj. 1: Children while in the mother's womb have not yet come forth into the world to live among other men. Consequently they cannot be subject to the action of man, so as to receive the sacrament, at the hands of man, unto salvation. They can, however, be subject to the action of God, in Whose sight they live, so as, by a kind of privilege, to receive the grace of sanctification; as was the case with those who were sanctified in the womb.

Reply Obj. 2: An internal member of the mother is something of hers by continuity and material union of the part with the whole: whereas a child while in its mother's womb is something of hers through being joined with, and yet distinct from her. Wherefore there is no comparison.

Reply Obj. 3: We should "not do evil that there may come good" (Rom. 3:8). Therefore it is wrong to kill a mother that her child may be baptized. If, however, the mother die while the child lives yet in her womb, she should be opened that the child may be baptized.

Reply Obj. 4: Unless death be imminent, we should wait until the child has entirely come forth from the womb before baptizing it. If, however, the head, wherein the senses are rooted, appear first, it should be baptized, in cases of danger: nor should it be baptized again, if perfect birth should ensue. And seemingly the same should be done in cases of danger no matter what part of the body appear first. But as none of the exterior parts of the body belong to its integrity in the same degree as the head, some hold that since the matter is doubtful, whenever any other part of the body has been baptized, the child, when perfect birth has taken place, should be baptized with the form: "If thou art not baptized, I baptize thee," etc.

TWELFTH ARTICLE [III, Q. 68, Art. 12]

Whether Madmen and Imbeciles Should Be Baptized?

Objection 1: It seems that madmen and imbeciles should not be baptized. For in order to receive Baptism, the person baptized must have the intention, as stated above (A. 7). But since madmen and imbeciles lack the use of reason, they can have but a disorderly intention. Therefore they should not be baptized.

Obj. 2: Further, man excels irrational animals in that he has reason. But madmen and imbeciles lack the use of reason, indeed in some cases we do not expect them ever to have it, as we do in the case of children. It seems, therefore, that just as irrational animals are not baptized, so neither should madmen and imbeciles in those cases be baptized.

Obj. 3: Further, the use of reason is suspended in madmen and imbeciles more than it is in one who sleeps. But it is not customary to baptize people while they sleep. Therefore it should not be given to madmen and imbeciles.

*On the contrary,* Augustine says (Confess. iv) of his friend that "he was baptized when his recovery was despaired of": and yet Baptism was efficacious with him. Therefore Baptism should sometimes be given to those who lack the use of reason.

*I answer that,* In the matter of madmen and imbeciles a distinction is to be made. For some are so from birth, and have no lucid intervals, and show no signs of the use of reason. And with regard to these it seems that we should come to the same decision as with regard to children who are baptized in the Faith of the Church, as stated above (A. 9, ad 2).

But there are others who have fallen from a state of sanity into a state of insanity. And with regard to these we must be guided by their wishes as expressed by them when sane: so that, if then they manifested a desire to receive Baptism, it should be given to them when in a state of madness or imbecility, even though then they refuse. If, on the other hand, while sane they showed no desire to receive Baptism, they must not be baptized.

Again, there are some who, though mad or imbecile from birth, have, nevertheless, lucid intervals, in which they can make right use of reason. Wherefore, if then they express a desire for Baptism, they can be baptized though they be actually in a state of madness. And in this case the sacrament should be bestowed on them if there be fear of danger otherwise it is better to wait until the time when they are sane, so that they may receive the sacrament more devoutly. But if during the interval of lucidity they manifest no desire to receive Baptism, they should not be baptized while in a state of insanity.

Lastly there are others who, though not altogether sane, yet can use their reason so far as to think about their salvation, and understand the power of the sacrament. And these are to be treated the same as those who are sane, and who are baptized if they be willing, but not against their will.

Reply Obj. 1: Imbeciles who never had, and have not now, the use of reason, are baptized, according to the Church's intention, just as according to the Church's ritual, they believe and repent; as we have stated above of children (A. 9, ad Obj.). But those who have had the use of reason at some time, or have now, are baptized according to their own intention, which they have now, or had when they were sane.

Reply Obj. 2: Madmen and imbeciles lack the use of reason accidentally, i.e. through some impediment in a bodily organ; but not like irrational animals through want of a rational soul. Consequently the comparison does not hold.

Reply Obj. 3: A person should not be baptized while asleep, except he be threatened with the danger of death. In which case he should be baptized, if previously he has manifested a desire to receive Baptism, as we have stated in reference to imbeciles: thus Augustine relates of his friend that "he was baptized while unconscious," because he was in danger of death (Confess. iv).

# QUESTION 69

OF THE EFFECTS OF BAPTISM (In Ten Articles)

We must now consider the effects of Baptism, concerning which there are ten points of inquiry:

(1) Whether all sins are taken away by Baptism?

(2) Whether man is freed from all punishment by Baptism?

(3) Whether Baptism takes away the penalties of sin that belong to this life?

(4) Whether grace and virtues are bestowed on man by Baptism?

(5) Of the effects of virtue which are conferred by Baptism?

(6) Whether even children receive grace and virtues in Baptism?

(7) Whether Baptism opens the gates of the heavenly kingdom to those who are baptized?

(8) Whether Baptism produces an equal effect in all who are baptized?

(9) Whether insincerity hinders the effect of Baptism?

(10) Whether Baptism takes effect when the insincerity ceases?

FIRST ARTICLE [III, Q. 69, Art. 1]

Whether All Sins Are Taken Away by Baptism?

Objection 1: It seems that not all sins are taken away by Baptism. For Baptism is a spiritual regeneration, which corresponds to carnal generation. But by carnal generation man contracts none but original sin. Therefore none but original sin is taken away by Baptism.

Obj. 2: Further, Penance is a sufficient cause of the remission of actual sins. But penance is required in adults before Baptism, according to Acts 2:38: "Do penance and be baptized every one of you." Therefore Baptism has nothing to do with the remission of actual sins.

Obj. 3: Further, various diseases demand various remedies: because as Jerome says on Mk. 9:27, 28: "What is a cure for the heel is no cure for the eye." But original sin, which is taken away by Baptism, is generically distinct from actual sin. Therefore not all sins are taken away by Baptism.

*On the contrary,* It is written (Ezech. 36:25): "I will pour upon you clean water, and you shall be cleansed from all your filthiness."

*I answer that,* As the Apostle says (Rom. 6:3), "all we, who are baptized in Christ Jesus, are baptized in His death." And further on he concludes (Rom. 6:11): "So do you also reckon that you are dead to sin, but alive unto God in Christ Jesus our Lord." Hence it is clear that by Baptism man dies unto the oldness of sin, and begins to live unto the newness of grace. But every sin belongs to the primitive oldness. Consequently every sin is taken away by Baptism.

Reply Obj. 1: As the Apostle says (Rom. 5:15, 16), the sin of Adam was not so far-reaching as the gift of Christ, which is bestowed in Baptism: "for judgment was by one unto condemnation; but grace is of many offenses, unto justification." Wherefore Augustine says in his book on Infant Baptism (De Pecc. Merit. et Remiss. i), that "in carnal generation, original sin alone is contracted; but when we are born again of the Spirit, not only original sin but also wilful sin is forgiven."

Reply Obj. 2: No sin can be forgiven save by the power of Christ's Passion: hence the Apostle says (Heb. 9:22) that "without shedding of blood there is no remission." Consequently no movement of the human will suffices for the remission of sin, unless there be faith in Christ's Passion, and the purpose of participating in it, either by receiving Baptism, or by submitting to the keys of the Church. Therefore when an adult approaches Baptism, he does indeed receive the forgiveness of all his sins through his purpose of being baptized, but more perfectly through the actual reception of Baptism.

Reply Obj. 3: This argument is true of special remedies. But Baptism operates by the power of Christ's Passion, which is the universal remedy for all sins; and so by Baptism all sins are loosed.

SECOND ARTICLE [III, Q. 69, Art. 2]

Whether Man Is Freed by Baptism from All Debt of Punishment Due to Sin?

Objection 1: It seems that man is not freed by Baptism from all debt of punishment due to sin. For the Apostle says (Rom. 13:1): "Those things that are of God are well ordered [Vulg.: 'Those that are, are ordained of God']." But guilt is not set in order save by punishment, as Augustine says (Ep. cxl). Therefore Baptism does not take away the debt of punishment due to sins already committed.

Obj. 2: Further, the effect of a sacrament has a certain likeness to the sacrament itself; since the sacraments of the New Law "effect what they signify," as stated above (Q. 62, A. 1, ad 1). But the washing of Baptism has indeed a certain likeness with the cleansing from the stain of sin, but none, seemingly, with the remission of the debt of punishment. Therefore the debt of punishment is not taken away by Baptism.

Obj. 3: Further, when the debt of punishment has been remitted, a man no longer deserves to be punished, and so it would be unjust to punish him. If, therefore, the debt of punishment be remitted by Baptism, it would be unjust, after Baptism, to hang a thief who had committed murder before. Consequently the severity of human legislation would be relaxed on account of Baptism; which is undesirable. Therefore Baptism does not remit the debt of punishment.

*On the contrary,* Ambrose, commenting on Rom. 11:29, "The gifts and the calling of God ate without repentance," says: "The grace of God in Baptism remits all, gratis."

*I answer that,* As stated above (Q. 49, A. 3, ad 2; Q. 68, AA. 1, 4, 5) by Baptism a man is incorporated in the Passion and death of Christ, according to Rom. 6:8: "If we be dead with Christ, we believe that we shall live also together with Christ." Hence it is clear that the Passion of Christ is communicated to every baptized person, so that he is healed just as if he himself had suffered and died. Now Christ's Passion, as stated above (Q. 68, A. 5), is a sufficient satisfaction for all the sins of all men. Consequently he who is baptized, is freed from the debt of all punishment due to him for his sins, just as if he himself had offered sufficient satisfaction for all his sins.

Reply Obj. 1: Since the pains of Christ's Passion are communicated to the person baptized, inasmuch as he is made a member of Christ, just as if he himself had borne those pains, his sins are set in order by the pains of Christ's Passion.

Reply Obj. 2: Water not only cleanses but also refreshes. And thus by refreshing it signifies the remission of the debt of punishment, just as by cleansing it signifies the washing away of guilt.

Reply Obj. 3: In punishments inflicted by a human tribunal, we have to consider not only what punishment a man deserves in respect of God, but also to what extent he is indebted to men who are hurt and scandalized by another's sin. Consequently, although a murderer is freed by Baptism from his debt of punishment in respect of God, he remains, nevertheless, in debt to men; and it is right that they should be edified at his punishment, since they were scandalized at his sin. But the sovereign may remit the penalty to such like out of kindness.

THIRD ARTICLE [III, Q. 69, Art. 3]

Whether Baptism Should Take Away the Penalties of Sin That Belong to This Life?

Objection 1: It seems that Baptism should take away the penalties of sin that belong to this life. For as the Apostle says (Rom. 5:15), the gift of Christ is farther-reaching than the sin of Adam. But through Adam's sin, as the Apostle says (Rom. 5:12), "death entered into this world," and, consequently, all the other penalties of the present life. Much more, therefore, should man be freed from the penalties of the present life, by the gift of Christ which is received in Baptism.

Obj. 2: Further, Baptism takes away the guilt of both original and actual sin. Now it takes away the guilt of actual sin in such a way as to free man from all debt of punishment resulting therefrom. Therefore it also frees man from the penalties of the present life, which are a punishment of original sin.

Obj. 3: Further, if the cause be removed, the effect is removed. But the cause of these penalties is original sin, which is taken away by Baptism. Therefore such like penalties should not remain.

*On the contrary,* on Rom. 6:6, "that the body of sin may be destroyed," a gloss says: "The effect of Baptism is that the old man is crucified, and the body of sin destroyed, not as though the living flesh of man were delivered by the destruction of that concupiscence with which it has been bespattered from its birth; but that it may not hurt him, when dead, though it was in him when he was born." Therefore for the same reason neither are the other penalties taken away by Baptism.

*I answer that,* Baptism has the power to take away the penalties of the present life yet it does not take them away during the present life, but by its power they will be taken away from the just in the resurrection when "this mortal hath put on immortality" (1 Cor. 15:54). And this is reasonable. First, because, by Baptism, man is incorporated in Christ, and is made His member, as stated above (A. 3; Q. 68, A. 5). Consequently it is fitting that what takes place in the Head should take place also in the member incorporated. Now, from the very beginning of His conception Christ was "full of grace and truth," yet He had a passible body, which through His Passion and death was raised up to a life of glory. Wherefore a Christian receives grace in Baptism, as to his soul; but he retains a passible body, so that he may suffer for Christ therein: yet at length he will be raised up to a life of impassibility. Hence the Apostle says (Rom. 8:11): "He that raised up Jesus Christ from the dead, shall quicken also our [Vulg.: 'your'] mortal bodies, because of His Spirit that dwelleth in us [Vulg.: 'you']": and further on in the same chapter (Rom. 8:17): "Heirs indeed of God, and joint heirs with Christ: yet so, if we suffer with Him, that we may be also glorified with Him."

Secondly, this is suitable for our spiritual training: namely, in order that, by fighting against concupiscence and other defects to which he is subject, man may receive the crown of victory. Wherefore on Rom. 6:6, "that the body of sin may be destroyed," a gloss says: "If a man after Baptism live in the flesh, he has concupiscence to fight against, and to conquer by God's help." In sign of which it is written (Judges 3:1, 2): "These are the nations which the Lord left, that by them He might instruct Israel . . . that afterwards their children might learn to fight with their enemies, and to be trained up to war."

Thirdly, this was suitable, lest men might seek to be baptized for the sake of impassibility in the present life, and not for the sake of the glory of life eternal. Wherefore the Apostle says (1 Cor. 15:19): "If in this life only we have hope in Christ, we are of all men most miserable."

Reply Obj. 1: As a gloss says on Rom. 6:6, "that we may serve sin no longer--Like a man who, having captured a redoubtable enemy, slays him not forthwith, but suffers him to live for a little time in shame and suffering; so did Christ first of all fetter our punishment, but at a future time He will destroy it."

Reply Obj. 2: As the gloss says on the same passage (cf. ad 1), "the punishment of sin is twofold, the punishment of hell, and temporal punishment. Christ entirely abolished the punishment of hell, so that those who are baptized and truly repent, should not be subject to it. He did not, however, altogether abolish temporal punishment yet awhile; for hunger, thirst, and death still remain. But He overthrew its kingdom and power" in the sense that man should no longer be in fear of them: "and at length He will altogether exterminate it at the last day."

Reply Obj. 3: As we stated in the Second Part (I-II, Q. 81, A. 1; Q. 82, A. 1, ad 2), original sin spread in this way, that at first the person infected the nature, and afterwards the nature infected the person. Whereas Christ in reverse order at first repairs what regards the person, and afterwards will simultaneously repair what pertains to the nature in all men. Consequently by Baptism He takes away from man forthwith the guilt of original sin and the punishment of being deprived of the heavenly vision. But the penalties of the present life, such as death, hunger, thirst, and the like, pertain to the nature, from the principles of which they arise, inasmuch as it is deprived of original justice. Therefore these defects will not be taken away until the ultimate restoration of nature through the glorious resurrection.

FOURTH ARTICLE [III, Q. 69, Art. 4]

Whether Grace and Virtues Are Bestowed on Man by Baptism?

Objection 1: It seems that grace and virtues are not bestowed on man by Baptism. Because, as stated above (Q. 62, A. 1, ad 1), the sacraments of the New Law "effect what they signify." But the baptismal cleansing signifies the cleansing of the soul from guilt, and not the fashioning of the soul with grace and virtues. Therefore it seems that grace and virtues are not bestowed on man by Baptism.

Obj. 2: Further, one does not need to receive what one has already acquired. But some approach Baptism who have already grace and virtues: thus we read (Acts 10:1, 2): "There was a certain man in Cesarea, named Cornelius, a centurion of that which is called the Italian band, a religious man and fearing God"; who, nevertheless, was afterwards baptized by Peter. Therefore grace and virtues are not bestowed by Baptism.

Obj. 3: Further, virtue is a habit: which is defined as a "quality not easily removed, by which one may act easily and pleasurably." But after Baptism man retains proneness to evil which removes virtue; and experiences difficulty in doing good, in which the act of virtue consists. Therefore man does not acquire grace and virtue in Baptism.

*On the contrary,* The Apostle says (Titus 3:5, 6): "He saved us by the laver of regeneration," i.e. by Baptism, "and renovation of the Holy Ghost, Whom He hath poured forth upon us abundantly," i.e. "unto the remission of sins and the fulness of virtues," as a gloss expounds. Therefore the grace of the Holy Ghost and the fulness of virtues are given in Baptism.

*I answer that,* As Augustine says in the book on Infant Baptism (De Pecc. Merit. et Remiss. i) "the effect of Baptism is that the baptized are incorporated in Christ as His members." Now the fulness of grace and virtues flows from Christ the Head to all His members, according to John 1:16: "Of His fulness we all have received." Hence it is clear that man receives grace and virtues in Baptism.

Reply Obj. 1: As the baptismal water by its cleansing signifies the washing away of guilt, and by its refreshment the remission of punishment, so by its natural clearness it signifies the splendor of grace and virtues.

Reply Obj. 2: As stated above (A. 1, ad 2; Q. 68, A. 2) man receives the forgiveness of sins before Baptism in so far as he has Baptism of desire, explicitly or implicitly; and yet when he actually receives Baptism, he receives a fuller remission, as to the remission of the entire punishment. So also before Baptism Cornelius and others like him receive grace and virtues through their faith in Christ and their desire for Baptism, implicit or explicit: but afterwards when baptized, they receive a yet greater fulness of grace and virtues. Hence in Ps. 22:2, "He hath brought me up on the water of refreshment," a gloss says: "He has brought us up by an increase of virtue and good deeds in Baptism."

Reply Obj. 3: Difficulty in doing good and proneness to evil are in the baptized, not through their lacking the habits of the virtues, but through concupiscence which is not taken away in Baptism. But just as concupiscence is diminished by Baptism, so as not to enslave us, so also are both the aforesaid defects diminished, so that man be not overcome by them.

FIFTH ARTICLE [III, Q. 69, Art. 5]

Whether Certain Acts of the Virtues Are Fittingly Set Down As Effects of Baptism, to Wit--Incorporation in Christ, Enlightenment, and Fruitfulness?

Objection 1: It seems that certain acts of the virtues are unfittingly set down as effects of Baptism, to wit--"incorporation in Christ, enlightenment, and fruitfulness." For Baptism is not given to an adult, except he believe; according to Mk. 16:16: "He that believeth and is baptized, shall be saved." But it is by faith that man is incorporated in Christ, according to Eph. 3:17: "That Christ may dwell by faith in your hearts." Therefore no one is baptized except he be already incorporated in Christ. Therefore incorporation with Christ is not the effect of Baptism.

Obj. 2: Further, enlightenment is caused by teaching, according to Eph. 3:8, 9: "To me the least of all the saints, is given this grace . . . to enlighten all men," etc. But teaching by the catechism precedes Baptism. Therefore it is not the effect of Baptism.

Obj. 3: Further, fruitfulness pertains to active generation. But a man is regenerated spiritually by

Baptism. Therefore fruitfulness is not an effect of Baptism.

*On the contrary,* Augustine says in the book on Infant Baptism (De Pecc. Merit. et Remiss. i) that "the effect of Baptism is that the baptized are incorporated in Christ." And Dionysius (Eccl. Hier. ii) ascribes enlightenment to Baptism. And on Ps. 22:2, "He hath brought me up on the water of refreshment," a gloss says that "the sinner's soul, sterilized by drought, is made fruitful by Baptism."

*I answer that,* By Baptism man is born again unto the spiritual life, which is proper to the faithful of Christ, as the Apostle says (Gal. 2:20): "And that I live now in the flesh; I live in the faith of the Son of God." Now life is only in those members that are united to the head, from which they derive sense and movement. And therefore it follows of necessity that by Baptism man is incorporated in Christ, as one of His members. Again, just as the members derive sense and movement from the material head, so from their spiritual Head, i.e. Christ, do His members derive spiritual sense consisting in the knowledge of truth, and spiritual movement which results from the instinct of grace. Hence it is written (John 1:14, 16): "We have seen Him . . . full of grace and truth; and of His fulness we all have received." And it follows from this that the baptized are enlightened by Christ as to the knowledge of truth, and made fruitful by Him with the fruitfulness of good works by the infusion of grace.

Reply Obj. 1: Adults who already believe in Christ are incorporated in Him mentally. But afterwards, when they are baptized, they are incorporated in Him, corporally, as it were, i.e. by the visible sacrament; without the desire of which they could not have been incorporated in Him even mentally.

Reply Obj. 2: The teacher enlightens outwardly and ministerially by catechizing: but God enlightens the baptized inwardly, by preparing their hearts for the reception of the doctrines of truth, according to John 6:45: "It is written in the prophets . . . They shall all be taught of God."

Reply Obj. 3: The fruitfulness which I ascribed as an effect of Baptism is that by which man brings forth good works; not that by which he begets others in Christ, as the Apostle says (1 Cor. 4:15): "In Christ Jesus by the Gospel I have begotten you."

SIXTH ARTICLE [III, Q. 69, Art. 6]

Whether Children Receive Grace and Virtue in Baptism?

Objection 1: It seems that children do not receive grace and virtues in Baptism. For grace and virtues are not possessed without faith and charity. But faith, as Augustine says (Ep. xcviii), "depends on the will of the believer": and in like manner charity depends on the will of the lover. Now children have not the use of the will, and consequently they have neither faith nor charity. Therefore children do not receive grace and virtues in Baptism.

Obj. 2: Further, on John 14:12, "Greater than these shall he do," Augustine says that in order for the ungodly to be made righteous "Christ worketh in him, but not without him." But a child, through not having the use of free-will, does not co-operate with Christ unto its justification: indeed at times it does its best to resist. Therefore it is not justified by grace and virtues.

Obj. 3: Further, it is written (Rom. 4:5): "To him that worketh not, yet believing in Him that justifieth the ungodly, his faith is reputed to justice according to the purpose of the grace of God." But a child believeth not "in Him that justifieth the ungodly." Therefore a child receives neither sanctifying grace nor virtues.

Obj. 4: Further, what is done with a carnal intention does not seem to have a spiritual effect. But sometimes children are taken to Baptism with a carnal intention, to wit, that their bodies may be healed. Therefore they do not receive the spiritual effect consisting in grace and virtue.

*On the contrary,* Augustine says (Enchiridion lii): "When little children are baptized, they die to that sin which they contracted in birth: so that to them also may be applied the words: 'We are buried together with Him by Baptism unto death'": (and he continues thus) "'that as Christ is risen from the dead by the glory of the Father, so we also may walk in newness of life.'" Now newness of life is through grace and virtues. Therefore children receive grace and virtues in Baptism.

*I answer that,* Some of the early writers held that children do not receive grace and virtues in Baptism, but that they receive the imprint of the character of Christ, by the power of which they receive grace and virtue when they arrive at the perfect age. But this is evidently false, for two reasons. First, because children, like adults, are made members of Christ in Baptism; hence they must, of necessity, receive an influx of grace and virtues from the Head. Secondly, because, if this were true, children that die after Baptism, would not come to eternal life; since according to Rom. 6:23, "the grace of God is life everlasting." And consequently Baptism would not have profited them unto salvation.

Now the source of their error was that they did not recognize the distinction between habit and act. And so, seeing children to be incapable of acts of virtue, they thought that they had no virtues at all after Baptism. But this inability of children to act is not due to the absence of habits, but to an impediment on the part of the body: thus also when a man is asleep, though he may have the habits of virtue, yet is he hindered from virtuous acts through being asleep.

Reply Obj. 1: Faith and charity depend on man's will, yet so that the habits of these and other virtues require the power of the will which is in children; whereas acts of virtue require an act of the will, which is not in children. In this sense Augustine says in the book on Infant Baptism (Ep. xcviii): "The little child is made a believer, not as yet by that faith which depends on the will of the believer, but by the sacrament of faith itself," which causes the habit of faith.

Reply Obj. 2: As Augustine says in his book on Charity (Ep. Joan. ad Parth. iii), "no man is born of water and the Holy Ghost unwillingly which is to be understood not of little children but of adults." In like manner we are to understand as applying to adults, that man "without himself is not justified by Christ." Moreover, if little children who are about to be baptized resist as much as they can, "this is not imputed to them, since so little do they know what they do, that they seem not to do it at all": as Augustine says in a book on the Presence of God, addressed to Dardanus (Ep. clxxxvii).

Reply Obj. 3: As Augustine says (Serm. clxxvi): "Mother Church lends other feet to the little children that they may come; another heart that they may believe; another tongue that they may confess." So that children believe, not by their own act, but by the faith of the Church, which is applied to them: by the power of which faith, grace and virtues are bestowed on them.

Reply Obj. 4: The carnal intention of those who take children to be baptized does not hurt the latter, as neither does one's sin hurt another, unless he consent. Hence Augustine says in his letter to Boniface (Ep. xcviii): "Be not disturbed because some bring children to be baptized, not in the hope that they may be born again to eternal life by the spiritual grace, but because they think it to be a remedy whereby they may preserve or recover health. For they are not deprived of regeneration, through not being brought for this intention."

SEVENTH ARTICLE [III, Q. 69, Art. 7]

Whether the Effect of Baptism Is to Open the Gates of the Heavenly Kingdom?

Objection 1: It seems that it is not the effect of Baptism, to open the gates of the heavenly kingdom. For what is already opened needs no opening. But the gates of the heavenly kingdom were opened by Christ's Passion: hence it is written (Apoc. 4:1): "After these things I looked and behold (a great) door was opened in heaven." Therefore it is not the effect of Baptism, to open the gates of the heavenly kingdom.

Obj. 2: Further, Baptism has had its effects ever since it was instituted. But some were baptized with Christ's Baptism, before His Passion, according to John 3:22, 26: and if they had died then, the gates of the heavenly kingdom would not have been opened to them, since none entered therein before Christ, according to Mic. 2:13: "He went up [Vulg.: 'shall go up'] that shall open the way before them." Therefore it is not the effect of Baptism, to open the gates of the heavenly kingdom.

Obj. 3: Further, the baptized are still subject to death and the other penalties of the present life, as stated above (A. 3). But entrance to the heavenly kingdom is opened to none that are subject to punishment: as is clear in regard to those who are in purgatory. Therefore it is not the effect of Baptism, to open the gates of the heavenly kingdom.

*On the contrary,* on Luke 3:21, "Heaven was opened," the gloss of Bede says: "We see here the power of Baptism; from which when a man comes forth, the gates of the heavenly kingdom are opened unto him."

*I answer that,* To open the gates of the heavenly kingdom is to remove the obstacle that prevents one from entering therein. Now this obstacle is guilt and the debt of punishment. But it has been shown above (AA. 1, 2) that all guilt and also all debt of punishment are taken away by Baptism. It follows, therefore, that the effect of Baptism is to open the gates of the heavenly kingdom.

Reply Obj. 1: Baptism opens the gates of the heavenly kingdom to the baptized in so far as it incorporates them in the Passion of Christ, by applying its power to man.

Reply Obj. 2: When Christ's Passion was not as yet consummated actually but only in the faith of believers, Baptism proportionately caused the gates to be opened, not in fact but in hope. For the baptized who died then looked forward, with a sure hope, to enter the heavenly kingdom.

Reply Obj. 3: The baptized are subject to death and the penalties of the present life, not by reason of a personal debt of punishment but by reason of the state of their nature. And therefore this is no bar to their entrance to the heavenly kingdom, when death severs the soul from the body; since they have paid, as it were, the debt of nature.

EIGHTH ARTICLE [III, Q. 69, Art. 8]

Whether Baptism Has an Equal Effect in All?

Objection 1: It seems that Baptism has not an equal effect in all. For the effect of Baptism is to remove guilt. But in some it takes away more sins than in others; for in children it takes away only original sins, whereas in adults it takes away actual sins, in some many, in others few. Therefore Baptism has not an equal effect in all.

Obj. 2: Further, grace and virtues are bestowed on man by Baptism. But some, after Baptism, seem to have more grace and more perfect virtue than others who have been baptized. Therefore Baptism has not an equal effect in all.

Obj. 3: Further, nature is perfected by grace, as matter by form. But a form is received into matter according to its capacity. Therefore, since some of the baptized, even children, have greater capacity for natural gifts than others have, it seems that some receive greater grace than others.

Obj. 4: Further, in Baptism some receive not only spiritual, but also bodily health; thus Constantine was cleansed in Baptism from leprosy. But all the infirm do not receive bodily health in Baptism. Therefore it has not an equal effect in all.

*On the contrary,* It is written (Eph. 4:5): "One

Faith, one Baptism." But a uniform cause has a uniform effect. Therefore Baptism has an equal effect in all.

*I answer that,* The effect of Baptism is twofold, the essential effect, and the accidental. The essential effect of Baptism is that for which Baptism was instituted, namely, the begetting of men unto spiritual life. Therefore, since all children are equally disposed to Baptism, because they are baptized not in their own faith, but in that of the Church, they all receive an equal effect in Baptism. Whereas adults, who approach Baptism in their own faith, are not equally disposed to Baptism; for some approach thereto with greater, some with less, devotion. And therefore some receive a greater, some a smaller share of the grace of newness; just as from the same fire, he receives more heat who approaches nearest to it, although the fire, as far as it is concerned, sends forth its heat equally to all.

But the accidental effect of Baptism, is that to which Baptism is not ordained, but which the Divine power produces miraculously in Baptism: thus on Rom. 6:6, "that we may serve sin no longer," a gloss says: "this is not bestowed in Baptism, save by an ineffable miracle of the Creator, so that the law of sin, which is in our members, be absolutely destroyed." And such like effects are not equally received by all the baptized, even if they approach with equal devotion: but they are bestowed according to the ordering of Divine providence.

Reply Obj. 1: The least baptismal grace suffices to blot out all sins. Wherefore that in some more sins are loosed than in others is not due to the greater efficacy of Baptism, but to the condition of the recipient: for in each one it looses whatever it finds.

Reply Obj. 2: That greater or lesser grace appears in the baptized, may occur in two ways. First, because one receives greater grace in Baptism than another, on account of his greater devotion, as stated above. Secondly, because, though they receive equal grace, they do not make an equal use of it, but one applies himself more to advance therein, while another by his negligence baffles grace.

Reply Obj. 3: The various degrees of capacity in men arise, not from a variety in the mind which is renewed by Baptism (since all men, being of one species, are of one form), but from the diversity of bodies. But it is otherwise with the angels, who differ in species. And therefore gratuitous gifts are bestowed on the angels according to their diverse capacity for natural gifts, but not on men.

Reply Obj. 4: Bodily health is not the essential effect of Baptism, but a miraculous work of Divine providence.

NINTH ARTICLE [III, Q. 69, Art. 9]

Whether Insincerity Hinders the Effect of Baptism?

Objection 1: It seems that insincerity does not hinder the effect of Baptism. For the Apostle says (Gal. 3:27): "As many of you as have been baptized in Christ Jesus, have put on Christ." But all that receive the Baptism of Christ, are baptized in Christ. Therefore they all put on Christ: and this is to receive the effect of Baptism. Consequently insincerity does not hinder the effect of Baptism.

Obj. 2: Further, the Divine power which can change man's will to that which is better, works in Baptism. But the effect of the efficient cause cannot be hindered by that which can be removed by that cause. Therefore insincerity cannot hinder the effect of Baptism.

Obj. 3: Further, the effect of Baptism is grace, to which sin is in opposition. But many other sins are more grievous than insincerity, which are not said to hinder the effect of Baptism. Therefore neither does insincerity.

*On the contrary,* It is written (Wis. 1:5): "The Holy Spirit of discipline will flee from the deceitful." But the effect of Baptism is from the Holy Ghost. Therefore insincerity hinders the effect of Baptism.

*I answer that,* As Damascene says (De Fide Orth. ii), "God does not compel man to be righteous." Consequently in order that a man be justified by Baptism, his will must needs embrace both Baptism and the baptismal effect. Now, a man is said to be insincere by reason of his will being in contradiction with either Baptism or its effect. For, according to Augustine (De Bapt. cont. Donat. vii), a man is said to be insincere, in four ways: first, because he does not believe, whereas Baptism is the sacrament of Faith; secondly, through scorning the sacrament itself; thirdly, through observing a rite which differs from that prescribed by the Church in conferring the sacrament; fourthly, through approaching the sacrament without devotion. Wherefore it is manifest that insincerity hinders the effect of Baptism.

Reply Obj. 1: "To be baptized in Christ," may be taken in two ways. First, "in Christ," i.e. "in conformity with Christ." And thus whoever is baptized in Christ so as to be conformed to Him by Faith and Charity, puts on Christ by grace. Secondly, a man is said to be baptized in Christ, in so far as he receives Christ's sacrament. And thus all put on Christ, through being configured to Him by the character, but not through being conformed to Him by grace.

Reply Obj. 2: When God changes man's will from evil to good, man does not approach with insincerity. But God does not always do this. Nor is this the purpose of the sacrament, that an insincere man be made sincere; but that he who comes in sincerity, be justified.

Reply Obj. 3: A man is said to be insincere who makes a show of willing what he wills not. Now whoever approaches Baptism, by that very fact makes a show of having right faith in Christ, of veneration for this sacrament, and of wishing to conform to the Church, and to renounce sin. Consequently, to whatever sin a man wishes to cleave, if he approach Baptism, he approaches insincerely, which is the same as to approach without devotion. But this must be understood of mortal sin, which is in opposition to grace: but not of venial sin. Consequently, here insincerity includes, in a way, every sin.

TENTH ARTICLE [III, Q. 69, Art. 10]

Whether Baptism Produces Its Effect When the Insincerity Ceases?

Objection 1: It seems that Baptism does not produce its effect, when the insincerity ceases. For a dead work, which is void of charity, can never come to life. But he who approaches Baptism insincerely, receives the sacrament without charity. Therefore it can never come to life so as to bestow grace.

Obj. 2: Further, insincerity seems to be stronger than Baptism, because it hinders its effect. But the stronger is not removed by the weaker. Therefore the sin of insincerity cannot be taken away by Baptism which has been hindered by insincerity. And thus Baptism will not receive its full effect, which is the remission of all sins.

Obj. 3: Further, it may happen that a man approach Baptism insincerely, and afterwards commit a number of sins. And yet these sins will not be taken away by Baptism; because Baptism washes away past, not future, sins. Such a Baptism, therefore, will never have its effect, which is the remission of all sins.

*On the contrary,* Augustine says (De Bapt. cont. Donat. i): "Then does Baptism begin to have its salutary effect, when truthful confession takes the place of that insincerity which hindered sins from being washed away, so long as the heart persisted in malice and sacrilege."

*I answer that,* As stated above (Q. 66, A. 9), Baptism is a spiritual regeneration. Now when a thing is generated, it receives together with the form, the form's effect, unless there be an obstacle; and when this is removed, the form of the thing generated produces its effect: thus at the same time as a weighty body is generated, it has a downward movement, unless something prevent this; and when the obstacle is removed, it begins forthwith to move downwards. In like manner when a man is baptized, he receives the character, which is like a form; and he receives in consequence its proper effect, which is grace whereby all his sins are remitted. But this effect is sometimes hindered by insincerity. Wherefore, when this obstacle is removed by Penance, Baptism forthwith produces its effect.

Reply Obj. 1: The sacrament of Baptism is the work of God, not of man. Consequently, it is not dead in the man, who being insincere, is baptized without charity.

Reply Obj. 2: Insincerity is not removed by Baptism but by Penance: and when it is removed, Baptism takes away all guilt, and all debt of punishment due to sins, whether committed before Baptism, or even co-existent with Baptism. Hence Augustine says (De Bapt. cont. Donat. i): "Yesterday is blotted out, and whatever remains over and above, even the very last hour and moment preceding Baptism, the very moment of Baptism. But from that moment forward he is bound by his obligations." And so both Baptism and Penance concur in producing the effect of Baptism, but Baptism as the direct efficient cause, Penance as the indirect cause, i.e. as removing the obstacle.

Reply Obj. 3: The effect of Baptism is to take away not future, but present and past sins. And consequently, when the insincerity passes away, subsequent sins are indeed remitted, but by Penance, not by Baptism. Wherefore they are not remitted, like the sins which preceded Baptism, as to the whole debt of punishment.

## QUESTION 70

OF CIRCUMCISION (In Four Articles)

We have now to consider things that are preparatory to Baptism: and (1) that which preceded Baptism, viz. Circumcision, (2) those which accompany Baptism, viz. Catechism and Exorcism.

Concerning the first there are four points of inquiry:

(1) Whether circumcision was a preparation for, and a figure of, Baptism?

(2) Its institution;

(3) Its rite;

(4) Its effect.

FIRST ARTICLE [III, Q. 70, Art. 1]

Whether Circumcision Was a Preparation For, and a Figure of Baptism?

Objection 1: It seems that circumcision was not a preparation for, and a figure of Baptism. For every figure has some likeness to that which it foreshadows. But circumcision has no likeness to Baptism. Therefore it seems that it was not a preparation for, and a figure of Baptism.

Obj. 2: Further, the Apostle, speaking of the Fathers of old, says (1 Cor. 10:2), that "all were baptized in the cloud, and in the sea": but not that they were baptized in circumcision. Therefore the protecting pillar of a cloud, and the crossing of the Red Sea, rather than circumcision, were a preparation for, and a figure of Baptism.

Obj. 3: Further, it was stated above (Q. 38, AA. 1, 3) that the baptism of John was a preparation for Christ's. Consequently, if circumcision was a preparation for, and a figure of Christ's Baptism, it seems that John's baptism was superfluous: which is unseemly. Therefore circumcision was not a preparation for, and a figure of Baptism.

*On the contrary,* The Apostle says (Col. 2:11, 12): "You are circumcised with circumcision, not made by hand in despoiling the body of the flesh, but in the circumcision of Christ, buried with Him in Baptism."

*I answer that,* Baptism is called the Sacrament of

Faith; in so far, to wit, as in Baptism man makes a profession of faith, and by Baptism is aggregated to the congregation of the faithful. Now our faith is the same as that of the Fathers of old, according to the Apostle (2 Cor. 4:13): "Having the same spirit of faith . . . we . . . believe." But circumcision was a protestation of faith; wherefore by circumcision also men of old were aggregated to the body of the faithful. Consequently, it is manifest that circumcision was a preparation for Baptism and a figure thereof, forasmuch as "all things happened" to the Fathers of old "in figure" (1 Cor. 10:11); just as their faith regarded things to come.

Reply Obj. 1: Circumcision was like Baptism as to the spiritual effect of the latter. For just as circumcision removed a carnal pellicule, so Baptism despoils man of carnal behavior.

Reply Obj. 2: The protecting pillar of cloud and the crossing of the Red Sea were indeed figures of our Baptism, whereby we are born again of water, signified by the Red Sea; and of the Holy Ghost, signified by the pillar of cloud: yet man did not make, by means of these, a profession of faith, as by circumcision; so that these two things were figures but not sacraments. But circumcision was a sacrament, and a preparation for Baptism; although less clearly figurative of Baptism, as to externals, than the aforesaid. And for this reason the Apostle mentions them rather than circumcision.

Reply Obj. 3: John's baptism was a preparation for Christ's as to the act done: but circumcision, as to the profession of faith, which is required in Baptism, as stated above.

SECOND ARTICLE [III, Q. 70, Art. 2]

Whether Circumcision Was Instituted in a Fitting Manner?

Objection 1: It seems that circumcision was instituted in an unfitting manner. For as stated above (A. 1) a profession of faith was made in circumcision. But none could ever be delivered from the first man's sin, except by faith in Christ's Passion, according to Rom. 3:25: "Whom God hath proposed to be a propitiation, through faith in His blood." Therefore circumcision should have been instituted forthwith after the first man's sin, and not at the time of Abraham.

Obj. 2: Further, in circumcision man made profession of keeping the Old Law, just as in Baptism he makes profession of keeping the New Law; wherefore the Apostle says (Gal. 5:3): "I testify . . . to every man circumcising himself, that he is a debtor to do the whole Law." But the observance of the Law was not promulgated at the time of Abraham, but rather at the time of Moses. Therefore it was unfitting for circumcision to be instituted at the time of Abraham.

Obj. 3: Further, circumcision was a figure of, and a preparation for, Baptism. But Baptism is offered to all nations, according to Matt. 28:19: "Going . . . teach ye all nations, baptizing them." Therefore circumcision should have been instituted as binding, not the Jews only, but also all nations.

Obj. 4: Further, carnal circumcision should correspond to spiritual circumcision, as the shadow to the reality. But spiritual circumcision which is of Christ, regards indifferently both sexes, since "in Christ Jesus there is neither male nor female," as is written Col. 3 [*Gal. 3:28]. Therefore the institution of circumcision which concerns only males, was unfitting.

*On the contrary,* We read (Gen. 17) that circumcision was instituted by God, Whose "works are perfect" (Deut. 32:4).

*I answer that,* As stated above (A. 1) circumcision was a preparation for Baptism, inasmuch as it was a profession of faith in Christ, which we also profess in Baptism. Now among the Fathers of old, Abraham was the first to receive the promise of the future birth of Christ, when it was said to him: "In thy seed shall all the nations of the earth be blessed" (Gen. 22:18). Moreover, he was the first to cut himself off from the society of unbelievers, in accordance with the commandment of the Lord, Who said to him (Gen. 13:1): "Go forth out of thy country and from thy kindred." Therefore circumcision was fittingly instituted in the person of Abraham.

Reply Obj. 1: Immediately after the sin of our first parent, on account of the knowledge possessed by Adam, who was fully instructed about Divine things, both faith and natural reason flourished in man to such an extent, that there was no need for any signs of faith and salvation to be prescribed to him, but each one was wont to make protestation of his faith, by outward signs of his profession, according as he thought best. But about the time of Abraham faith was on the wane, many being given over to idolatry. Moreover, by the growth of carnal concupiscence natural reason was clouded even in regard to sins against nature. And therefore it was fitting that then, and not before, circumcision should be instituted, as a profession of faith and a remedy against carnal concupiscence.

Reply Obj. 2: The observance of the Law was not to be promulgated until the people were already gathered together: because the law is ordained to the public good, as we have stated in the Second Part (I-II, Q. 90, A. 2). Now it behooved the body of the faithful to be gathered together by a sensible sign, which is necessary in order that men be united together in any religion, as Augustine says (Contra Faust. xix). Consequently, it was necessary for circumcision to be instituted before the giving of the Law. Those Fathers, however, who lived before the Law, taught their families concerning Divine things by way of paternal admonition. Hence the Lord said of Abraham (Gen. 18:19): "I know that he will command his children, and his household after him to keep the way of the Lord."

Reply Obj. 3: Baptism contains in itself the perfection of salvation, to which God calls all men, according to 1 Tim. 2:4: "Who will have all men to be saved." Wherefore Baptism is offered to all nations. On the other hand circumcision did not contain the perfection of salvation, but signified it as to be achieved by Christ, Who was to be born of the Jewish nation. For this reason circumcision was given to that nation alone.

Reply Obj. 4: The institution of circumcision is as a sign of Abraham's faith, who believed that himself would be the father of Christ Who was promised to him: and for this reason it was suitable that it should be for males only. Again, original sin, against which circumcision was specially ordained, is contracted from the father, not from the mother, as was stated in the Second Part (I-II, Q. 81, A. 5). But Baptism contains the power of Christ, Who is the universal cause of salvation for all, and is "The Remission of all sins" (Post-Communion, Tuesday in Whitweek).

THIRD ARTICLE [III, Q. 70, Art. 3]

Whether the Rite of Circumcision Was Fitting?

Objection 1: It seems that the rite of circumcision was unfitting. For circumcision, as stated above (AA. 1, 2), was a profession of faith. But faith is in the apprehensive power, whose operations appear mostly in the head. Therefore the sign of circumcision should have been conferred on the head rather than on the virile member.

Obj. 2: Further, in the sacraments we make use of such things as are in more frequent use; for instance, water, which is used for washing, and bread, which we use for nourishment. But, in cutting, we use an iron knife more commonly than a stone knife. Therefore circumcision should not have been performed with a stone knife.

Obj. 3: Further, just as Baptism was instituted as a remedy against original sin, so also was circumcision, as Bede says (Hom. in Circum.). But now Baptism is not put off until the eighth day, lest children should be in danger of loss on account of original sin, if they should die before being baptized. On the other hand, sometimes Baptism is put off until after the eighth day. Therefore the eighth day should not have been fixed for circumcision, but this day should have been anticipated, just as sometimes it was deferred.

*On the contrary,* The aforesaid rite of circumcision is fixed by a gloss on Rom. 4:11: "And he received the sign of circumcision."

*I answer that,* As stated above (A. 2), circumcision was established, as a sign of faith, by God "of" Whose "wisdom there is no number" (Ps. 146:5). Now to determine suitable signs is a work of wisdom. Consequently, it must be allowed that the rite of circumcision was fitting.

Reply Obj. 1: It was fitting for circumcision to be performed on the virile member. First, because it was a sign of that faith whereby Abraham believed that Christ would be born of his seed. Secondly, because it was to be a remedy against original sin, which is contracted through the act of generation. Thirdly, because it was ordained as a remedy for carnal concupiscence, which thrives principally in those members, by reason of the abundance of venereal pleasure.

Reply Obj. 2: A stone knife was not essential to circumcision. Wherefore we do not find that an instrument of this description is required by any divine precept; nor did the Jews, as a rule, make use of such a knife for circumcision; indeed, neither do they now. Nevertheless, certain well-known circumcisions are related as having been performed with a stone knife, thus (Ex. 4:25) we read that "Sephora took a very sharp stone and circumcised the foreskin of her son," and (Joshua 5:2): "Make thee knives of stone, and circumcise the second time the children of Israel." Which signified that spiritual circumcision would be done by Christ, of Whom it is written (1 Cor. 10:4): "Now the rock was Christ."

Reply Obj. 3: The eighth day was fixed for circumcision: first, because of the mystery; since, Christ, by taking away from the elect, not only guilt but also all penalties, will perfect the spiritual circumcision, in the eighth age (which is the age of those that rise again), as it were, on the eighth day. Secondly, on account of the tenderness of the infant before the eighth day. Wherefore even in regard to other animals it is prescribed (Lev. 22:27): "When a bullock, or a sheep, or a goat, is brought forth, they shall be seven days under the udder of their dam: but the eighth day and thenceforth, they may be offered to the Lord."

Moreover, the eighth day was necessary for the fulfilment of the precept; so that, to wit, those who delayed beyond the eighth day, sinned, even though it were the sabbath, according to John 7:23: "(If) a man receives circumcision on the sabbath-day, that the Law of Moses may not be broken." But it was not necessary for the validity of the sacrament: because if anyone delayed beyond the eighth day, they could be circumcised afterwards.

Some also say that in imminent danger of death, it was allowable to anticipate the eighth day. But this cannot be proved either from the authority of Scripture or from the custom of the Jews. Wherefore it is better to say with Hugh of St. Victor (De Sacram. i) that the eighth day was never anticipated for any motive, however urgent. Hence on Prov. 4:3: "I was . . . an only son in the sight of my mother," a gloss says, that Bersabee's other baby boy did not count because through dying before the eighth day it received no name; and consequently neither was it circumcised.

FOURTH ARTICLE [III, Q. 70, Art. 4]

Whether Circumcision Bestowed Sanctifying Grace?

Objection 1: It seems that circumcision did not bestow sanctifying grace. For the Apostle says (Gal. 2:21): "If justice be by the Law, then Christ died in vain," i.e. without cause. But circumcision was an obligation imposed by the Law, according to Gal. 5:3: "I testify . . . to every man circumcising himself, that he is a debtor to do the whole law." Therefore, if justice be by circumcision, "Christ died in vain," i.e. without cause. But this cannot be allowed. Therefore circumcision did not confer grace whereby the sinner is made righteous.

Obj. 2: Further, before the institution of circumcision faith alone sufficed for justification; hence Gregory says (Moral. iv): "Faith alone did of old in behalf of infants that for which the water of Baptism avails with us." But faith has lost nothing of its strength through the commandment of circumcision. Therefore faith alone justified little ones, and not circumcision.

Obj. 3: Further, we read (Joshua 5:5, 6) that "the people that were born in the desert, during the forty years . . . were uncircumcised." If, therefore, original sin was taken away by circumcision, it seems that all who died in the desert, both little children and adults, were lost. And the same argument avails in regard to those who died before the eighth day, which was that of circumcision, which day could not be anticipated, as stated above (A. 3, ad 3).

Obj. 4: Further, nothing but sin closes the entrance to the heavenly kingdom. But before the Passion the entrance to the heavenly kingdom was closed to the circumcised. Therefore men were not justified from sin by circumcision.

Obj. 5: Further, original sin is not remitted without actual sin being remitted also: because "it is wicked to hope for half forgiveness from God," as Augustine says (De Vera et Falsa Poenit. ix). But we read nowhere of circumcision as remitting actual sin. Therefore neither did it remit original sin.

*On the contrary,* Augustine says, writing to Valerius in answer to Julian (De Nup. et Concup. ii): "From the time that circumcision was instituted among God's people, as 'a seal of the justice of the faith,' it availed little children unto sanctification by cleansing them from the original and bygone sin; just as Baptism also from the time of its institution began to avail unto the renewal of man."

*I answer that,* All are agreed in saying that original sin was remitted in circumcision. But some said that no grace was conferred, and that the only effect was to remit sin. The Master holds this opinion (Sent. iv, D, 1), and in a gloss on Rom. 4:11. But this is impossible, since guilt is not remitted except by grace, according to Rom. 3:2: "Being justified freely by His grace," etc.

Wherefore others said that grace was bestowed by circumcision, as to that effect which is the remission of guilt, but not as to its positive effects; lest they should be compelled to say that the grace bestowed in circumcision sufficed for the fulfilling of the precepts of the Law, and that, consequently, the coming of Christ was unnecessary. But neither can this opinion stand. First, because by circumcision children received the power of obtaining glory at the allotted time, which is the last positive effect of grace. Secondly, because, in the order of the formal cause, positive effects naturally precede those that denote privation, although it is the reverse in the order of the material cause: since a form does not remove a privation save by informing the subject.

Consequently, others said that grace was conferred in circumcision, also as a particular positive effect consisting in being made worthy of eternal life; but not as to all its effects, for it did not suffice for the repression of the concupiscence of the fomes, nor again for the fulfilment of the precepts of the Law. And this was my opinion at one time (Sent. iv, D, 1; Q. 2, A. 4). But if one consider the matter carefully, it is clear that this is not true. Because the least grace can resist any degree of concupiscence, and avoid every mortal sin, that is committed in transgressing the precepts of the Law; for the smallest degree of charity loves God more than cupidity loves "thousands of gold and silver" (Ps. 118:72).

We must say, therefore, that grace was bestowed in circumcision as to all the effects of grace, but not as in Baptism. Because in Baptism grace is bestowed by the very power of Baptism itself, which power Baptism has as the instrument of Christ's Passion already consummated. Whereas circumcision bestowed grace, inasmuch as it was a sign of faith in Christ's future Passion: so that the man who was circumcised, professed to embrace that faith; whether, being an adult, he made profession for himself, or, being a child, someone else made profession for him. Hence, too, the Apostle says (Rom. 4:11), that Abraham "received the sign of circumcision, a seal of the justice of the faith": because, to wit, justice was of faith signified: not of circumcision signifying. And since Baptism operates instrumentally by the power of Christ's Passion, whereas circumcision does not, therefore Baptism imprints a character that incorporates man in Christ, and bestows grace more copiously than does circumcision; since greater is the effect of a thing already present, than of the hope thereof.

Reply Obj. 1: This argument would prove if justice were of circumcision otherwise than through faith in Christ's Passion.

Reply Obj. 2: Just as before the institution of circumcision, faith in Christ to come justified both children and adults, so, too, after its institution. But before, there was no need of a sign expressive of this faith; because as yet believers had not begun to be united together apart from unbelievers for the worship of one God. It is probable, however, that parents who were believers offered up some prayers to God for their children, especially if these were in any danger. Or bestowed some blessing on them, as a "seal of faith"; just as the adults offered prayers and sacrifices for themselves.

Reply Obj. 3: There was an excuse for the people in the desert failing to fulfil the precept of circumcision, both because they knew not when the camp was removed, and because, as Damascene says (De Fide Orth. iv) they needed no distinctive sign while they dwelt apart from other nations. Nevertheless, as Augustine says (QQ. in Josue vi), those were guilty of disobedience who failed to obey through contempt.

It seems, however, that none of the uncircumcised died in the desert, for it is written (Ps. 104:37): "There was not among their tribes one that was feeble": and that those alone died in the desert, who had been circumcised in Egypt. If, however, some of the uncircumcised did die there, the same applies to them as to those who died before the institution of circumcision. And this applies also to those children who, at the time of the Law, died before the eighth day.

Reply Obj. 4: Original sin was taken away in circumcision, in regard to the person; but on the part of the entire nature, there remained the obstacle to the entrance of the kingdom of heaven, which obstacle was removed by Christ's Passion. Consequently, before Christ's Passion not even Baptism gave entrance to the kingdom. But were circumcision to avail after Christ's Passion, it would give entrance to the kingdom.

Reply Obj. 5: When adults were circumcised, they received remission not only of original, but also of actual sin: yet not so as to be delivered from all debt of punishment, as in Baptism, in which grace is conferred more copiously.

## QUESTION 71

OF THE PREPARATIONS THAT ACCOMPANY BAPTISM (In Four Articles)

We have now to consider the preparations that accompany Baptism: concerning which there are four points of inquiry:

(1) Whether catechism should precede Baptism?

(2) Whether exorcism should precede Baptism?

(3) Whether what is done in catechizing and exorcizing, effects anything, or is a mere sign?

(4) Whether those who are to be baptized should be catechized or exorcized by priests?

FIRST ARTICLE [III, Q. 71, Art. 1]

Whether Catechism Should Precede Baptism?

Objection 1: It seems that catechism should not precede Baptism. For by Baptism men are regenerated unto the spiritual life. But man begins to live before being taught. Therefore man should not be catechized, i.e. taught, before being baptized.

Obj. 2: Further, Baptism is given not only to adults, but also to children, who are not capable of being taught, since they have not the use of reason. Therefore it is absurd to catechize them.

Obj. 3: Further, a man, when catechized, confesses his faith. Now a child cannot confess its faith by itself, nor can anyone else in its stead; both because no one can bind another to do anything; and because one cannot know whether the child, having come to the right age, will give its assent to faith. Therefore catechism should not precede Baptism.

*On the contrary,* Rabanus says (De Instit. Cleric. i): "Before Baptism man should be prepared by catechism, in order that the catechumen may receive the rudiments of faith."

*I answer that,* As stated above (Q. 70, A. 1), Baptism is the Sacrament of Faith: since it is a profession of the Christian faith. Now in order that a man receive the faith, he must be instructed therein, according to Rom. 10:14: "How shall they believe Him, of Whom they have not heard? And how shall they hear without a preacher?" And therefore it is fitting that catechism should precede Baptism. Hence when our Lord bade His disciples to baptize, He made teaching to precede Baptism, saying: "Go ye . . . and teach all nations, baptizing them," etc.

Reply Obj. 1: The life of grace unto which a man is regenerated, presupposes the life of the rational nature, in which man is capable of receiving instruction.

Reply Obj. 2: Just as Mother Church, as stated above (Q. 69, A. 6, ad 3), lends children another's feet that they may come, and another's heart that they may believe, so, too, she lends them another's ears, that they may hear, and another's mind, that through others they may be taught. And therefore, as they are to be baptized, on the same grounds they are to be instructed.

Reply Obj. 3: He who answers in the child's stead: "I do believe," does not foretell that the child will believe when it comes to the right age, else he would say: "He will believe"; but in the child's stead he professes the Church's faith which is communicated to that child, the sacrament of which faith is bestowed on it, and to which faith he is bound by another. For there is nothing unfitting in a person being bound by another in things necessary for salvation. In like manner the sponsor, in answering for the child, promises to use his endeavors that the child may believe. This, however, would not be sufficient in the case of adults having the use of reason.

SECOND ARTICLE [III, Q. 71, Art. 2]

Whether Exorcism Should Precede Baptism?

Objection 1: It seems that exorcism should not precede Baptism. For exorcism is ordained against energumens or those who are possessed. But not all are such like. Therefore exorcism should not precede Baptism.

Obj. 2: Further, so long as man is a subject of sin, the devil has power over him, according to John 8:34: "Whosoever committeth sin is the servant of sin." But sin is taken away by Baptism. Therefore men should not be exorcized before Baptism.

Obj. 3: Further, Holy water was introduced in

order to ward off the power of the demons. Therefore exorcism was not needed as a further remedy.

*On the contrary,* Pope Celestine says (Epist. ad Episcop. Galliae): "Whether children or young people approach the sacrament of regeneration, they should not come to the fount of life before the unclean spirit has been expelled from them by the exorcisms and breathings of the clerics."

*I answer that,* Whoever purposes to do a work wisely, first removes the obstacles to his work; hence it is written (Jer. 4:3): "Break up anew your fallow ground and sow not upon thorns." Now the devil is the enemy of man's salvation, which man acquires by Baptism; and he has a certain power over man from the very fact that the latter is subject to original, or even actual, sin. Consequently it is fitting that before Baptism the demons should be cast out by exorcisms, lest they impede man's salvation. Which expulsion is signified by the (priest) breathing (upon the person to be baptized); while the blessing, with the imposition of hands, bars the way against the return of him who was cast out. Then the salt which is put in the mouth, and the anointing of the nose and ears with spittle, signify the receiving of doctrine, as to the ears; consent thereto as to the nose; and confession thereof, as to the mouth. And the anointing with oil signifies man's ability to fight against the demons.

Reply Obj. 1: The energumens are so-called from "laboring inwardly" under the outward operation of the devil. And though not all that approach Baptism are troubled by him in their bodies, yet all who are not baptized are subject to the power of the demons, at least on account of the guilt of original sin.

Reply Obj. 2: The power of the devil in so far as he hinders man from obtaining glory, is expelled from man by the baptismal ablution; but in so far as he hinders man from receiving the sacrament, his power is cast out by the exorcisms.

Reply Obj. 3: Holy water is used against the assaults of demons from without. But exorcisms are directed against those assaults of the demons which are from within. Hence those who are exorcized are called energumens, as it were "laboring inwardly."

Or we may say that just as Penance is given as a further remedy against sin, because Baptism is not repeated; so Holy Water is given as a further remedy against the assaults of demons, because the baptismal exorcisms are not given a second time.

THIRD ARTICLE [III, Q. 71, Art. 3]

Whether What Is Done in the Exorcism Effects Anything, or Is a Mere Sign?

Objection 1: It seems that what is done in the exorcism does not effect anything, but is a mere sign. For if a child die after the exorcisms, before being baptized, it is not saved. But the effects of what is done in the sacraments are ordained to the salvation of man; hence it is written (Mk. 16:16): "He that believeth and is baptized shall be saved." Therefore what is done in the exorcism effects nothing, but is a mere sign.

Obj. 2: Further, nothing is required for a sacrament of the New Law, but that it should be a sign and a cause, as stated above (Q. 62, A. 1). If, therefore, the things done in the exorcism effect anything, it seems that each of them is a sacrament.

Obj. 3: Further, just as the exorcism is ordained to Baptism, so if anything be effected in the exorcism, it is ordained to the effect of Baptism. But disposition must needs precede the perfect form: because form is not received save into matter already disposed. It would follow, therefore, that none could obtain the effect of Baptism unless he were previously exorcized; which is clearly false. Therefore what is done in the exorcisms has no effect.

Obj. 4: Further, just as some things are done in the exorcism before Baptism, so are some things done after Baptism; for instance, the priest anoints the baptized on the top of the head. But what is done after Baptism seems to have no effect; for, if it had, the effect of Baptism would be imperfect. Therefore neither have those things an effect, which are done in exorcism before Baptism.

*On the contrary,* Augustine says (De Symbolo I): "Little children are breathed upon and exorcized, in order to expel from them the devil's hostile power, which deceived man." But the Church does nothing in vain. Therefore the effect of these breathings is that the power of the devils is expelled.

*I answer that,* Some say that the things done in the exorcism have no effect, but are mere signs. But this is clearly false; since in exorcizing, the Church uses words of command to cast out the devil's power, for instance, when she says: "Therefore, accursed devil, go out from him," etc.

Therefore we must say that they have some effect, but, other than that of Baptism. For Baptism gives man grace unto the full remission of sins. But those things that are done in the exorcism remove the twofold impediment against the reception of saving grace. Of these, one is the outward impediment, so far as the demons strive to hinder man's salvation. And this impediment is removed by the breathings, whereby the demon's power is cast out, as appears from the passage quoted from Augustine, i.e. as to the devil not placing obstacles against the reception of the sacrament. Nevertheless, the demon's power over man remains as to the stain of sin, and the debt of punishment, until sin be washed away by Baptism. And in this sense Cyprian says (Epist. lxxvi): "Know that the devil's evil power remains until the pouring of the saving water: but in Baptism he loses it all."

The other impediment is within, forasmuch as, from having contracted original sin, man's sense is closed to the perception of the mysteries of salvation. Hence Rabanus says (De Instit. Cleric. i) that "by means of the typifying spittle and the touch of the priest, the Divine wisdom and power brings salvation to the catechumen, that his nostrils being opened he may perceive the odor of the knowledge of God, that his ears be opened to hear the commandments of God, that his senses be opened in his inmost heart to respond."

Reply Obj. 1: What is done in the exorcism does not take away the sin for which man is punished after death; but only the impediments against his receiving the remission of sin through the sacrament. Wherefore exorcism avails a man nothing after death if he has not been baptized.

Praepositivus, however, says that children who die after being exorcized but before being baptized are subjected to lesser darkness. But this does not seem to be true: because that darkness consists in privation of the vision of God, which cannot be greater or lesser.

Reply Obj. 2: It is essential to a sacrament to produce its principal effect, which is grace that remits sin, or supplies some defect in man. But those things that are done in the exorcism do not effect this; they merely remove these impediments. Consequently, they are not sacraments but sacramentals.

Reply Obj. 3: The disposition that suffices for receiving the baptismal grace is the faith and intention, either of the one baptized, if it be an adult, or of the Church, if it be a child. But these things that are done in the exorcism, are directed to the removal of the impediments. And therefore one may receive the effect of Baptism without them.

Yet they are not to be omitted save in a case of necessity. And then, if the danger pass, they should be supplied, that uniformity in Baptism may be observed. Nor are they supplied to no purpose after Baptism: because, just as the effect of Baptism may be hindered before it is received, so can it be hindered after it has been received.

Reply Obj. 4: Of those things that are done after Baptism in respect of the person baptized, something is done which is not a mere sign, but produces an effect, for instance, the anointing on the top of the head, the effect of which is the preservation of baptismal grace. And there is something which has no effect, but is a mere sign, for instance, the baptized are given a white garment to signify the newness of life.

FOURTH ARTICLE [III, Q. 71, Art. 4]

Whether It Belongs to a Priest to Catechize and Exorcize the Person to Be Baptized?

Objection 1: It seems that it does not belong to a priest to catechize and exorcize the person to be baptized. For it belongs to the office of ministers to operate on the unclean, as Dionysius says (Eccl. Hier. v). But catechumens who are instructed by catechism, and "energumens" who are cleansed by exorcism, are counted among the unclean, as Dionysius says in the same place. Therefore to catechize and to exorcize do not belong to the office of the priests, but rather to that of the ministers.

Obj. 2: Further, catechumens are instructed in the Faith by the Holy Scripture which is read in the church by ministers: for just as the Old Testament is recited by the Readers, so the New Testament is read by the Deacons and Subdeacons. And thus it belongs to the ministers to catechize. In like manner it belongs, seemingly, to the ministers to exorcize. For Isidore says (Epist. ad Ludifred.): "The exorcist should know the exorcisms by heart, and impose his hands on the energumens and catechumens during the exorcism." Therefore it belongs not to the priestly office to catechize and exorcize.

Obj. 3: Further, "to catechize" is the same as "to teach," and this is the same as "to perfect." Now this belongs to the office of a bishop, as Dionysius says (Eccl. Hier. v). Therefore it does not belong to the priestly office.

*On the contrary,* Pope Nicolas I says: "The catechizing of those who are to be baptized can be undertaken by the priests attached to each church." And Gregory says (Hom. xxix super Ezech.): "When priests place their hands on believers for the grace of exorcism, what else do they but cast out the devils?"

*I answer that,* The minister compared to the priest, is as a secondary and instrumental agent to the principal agent: as is implied in the very word "minister." Now the secondary agent does nothing without the principal agent in operating. And the more mighty the operation, so much the mightier instruments does the principal agent require. But the operation of the priest in conferring the sacrament itself is mightier than in those things that are preparatory to the sacrament. And so the highest ministers who are called deacons co-operate with the priest in bestowing the sacraments themselves: for Isidore says (Epist. ad Ludifred.) that "it belongs to the deacons to assist the priests in all things that are done in Christ's sacraments, in Baptism, to wit, in the Chrism, in the Paten and Chalice"; while the inferior ministers assist the priest in those things which are preparatory to the sacraments: the readers, for instance, in catechizing; the exorcists in exorcizing.

Reply Obj. 1: The minister's operation in regard to the unclean is ministerial and, as it were, instrumental, but the priest's is principal.

Reply Obj. 2: To readers and exorcists belongs the duty of catechizing and exorcizing, not, indeed, principally, but as ministers of the priest in these things.

Reply Obj. 3: Instruction is manifold. One leads to the embracing of the Faith; and is ascribed by Dionysius to bishops (Eccl. Hier. ii) and can be undertaken by any preacher, or even by any believer. Another is that by which a man is taught the rudiments of faith, and how to comport himself in receiving the sacraments: this belongs secondarily to the ministers, primarily to the priests. A third is instruction in the mode of Christian life: and this belongs to the sponsors. A fourth is the instruction in the profound mysteries of faith, and on the perfection of Christian life: this belongs to bishops ex officio, in virtue of their office.

## QUESTION 72

OF THE SACRAMENT OF CONFIRMATION
(In Twelve Articles)

We have now to consider the Sacrament of Confirmation. Concerning this there are twelve points of inquiry:

(1) Whether Confirmation is a sacrament?

(2) Its matter;

(3) Whether it is essential to the sacrament that the chrism should have been previously consecrated by a bishop?

(4) Its form;

(5) Whether it imprints a character?

(6) Whether the character of Confirmation presupposes the character of Baptism?

(7) Whether it bestows grace?

(8) Who is competent to receive this sacrament?

(9) In what part of the body?

(10) Whether someone is required to stand for the person to be confirmed?

(11) Whether this sacrament is given by bishops only?

(12) Of its rite.

FIRST ARTICLE [III, Q. 72, Art. 1]

Whether Confirmation Is a Sacrament?

Objection 1: It seems that Confirmation is not a sacrament. For sacraments derive their efficacy from the Divine institution, as stated above (Q. 64, A. 2). But we read nowhere of Confirmation being instituted by Christ. Therefore it is not a sacrament.

Obj. 2: Further, the sacraments of the New Law were foreshadowed in the Old Law; thus the Apostle says (1 Cor. 10:2-4), that "all in Moses were baptized, in the cloud and in the sea; and did all eat the same spiritual food, and all drank the same spiritual drink." But Confirmation was not foreshadowed in the old Testament. Therefore it is not a sacrament.

Obj. 3: Further, the sacraments are ordained unto man's salvation. But man can be saved without Confirmation: since children that are baptized, who die before being confirmed, are saved. Therefore Confirmation is not a sacrament.

Obj. 4: Further, by all the sacraments of the Church, man is conformed to Christ, Who is the Author of the sacraments. But man cannot be conformed to Christ by Confirmation, since we read nowhere of Christ being confirmed.

*On the contrary,* Pope Melchiades wrote to the bishops of Spain: "Concerning the point on which you sought to be informed, i.e. whether the imposition of the bishop's hand were a greater sacrament than Baptism, know that each is a great sacrament."

*I answer that,* The sacraments of the New Law are ordained unto special effects of grace: and therefore where there is a special effect of grace, there we find a special sacrament ordained for the purpose. But since sensible and material things bear a likeness to things spiritual and intelligible, from what occurs in the life of the body, we can perceive that which is special to the spiritual life. Now it is evident that in the life of the body a certain special perfection consists in man's attaining to the perfect age, and being able to perform the perfect actions of a man: hence the Apostle says (1 Cor. 13:11): "When I became a man, I put away the things of a child." And thence it is that besides the movement of generation whereby man receives life of the body, there is the movement of growth, whereby man is brought to the perfect age. So therefore does man receive spiritual life in Baptism, which is a spiritual regeneration: while in Confirmation man arrives at the perfect age, as it were, of the spiritual life. Hence Pope Melchiades says: "The Holy Ghost, Who comes down on the waters of Baptism bearing salvation in His flight, bestows at the font, the fulness of innocence; but in Confirmation He confers an increase of grace. In Baptism we are born again unto life; after Baptism we are strengthened." And therefore it is evident that Confirmation is a special sacrament.

Reply Obj. 1: Concerning the institution of this sacrament there are three opinions. Some (Alexander of Hales, Summa Theol. P. IV, Q. IX; St. Bonaventure, Sent. iv, D, 7) have maintained that this sacrament was instituted neither by Christ, nor by the apostles; but later in the course of time by one of the councils. Others (Pierre de Tarentaise, Sent. iv, D, 7) held that it was instituted by the apostles. But this cannot be admitted; since the institution of a new sacrament belongs to the power of excellence, which belongs to Christ alone.

And therefore we must say that Christ instituted this sacrament not by bestowing, but by promising it, according to John 16:7: "If I go not, the Paraclete will not come to you, but if I go, I will send Him to you." And this was because in this sacrament the fulness of the Holy Ghost is bestowed, which was not to be given before Christ's Resurrection and Ascension; according to John 7:39: "As yet the Spirit was not given, because Jesus was not yet glorified."

Reply Obj. 2: Confirmation is the sacrament of the fulness of grace: wherefore there could be nothing corresponding to it in the Old Law, since "the Law brought nothing to perfection" (Heb. 7:19).

Reply Obj. 3: As stated above (Q. 65, A. 4), all the sacraments are in some way necessary for salvation: but some, so that there is no salvation without them; some as conducing to the perfection of salvation; and thus it is that Confirmation is necessary for salvation: although salvation is possible without it, provided it be not omitted out of contempt.

Reply Obj. 4: Those who receive Confirmation, which is the sacrament of the fulness of grace, are conformed to Christ, inasmuch as from the very first instant of His conception He was "full of grace and truth" (John 1:14). This fulness was made known at His Baptism, when "the Holy Ghost descended in a bodily shape . . . upon Him" (Luke 3:22). Hence (Luke 4:1) it is written that "Jesus being full of the Holy Ghost, returned from the Jordan." Nor was it fitting to Christ's dignity, that He, Who is the Author of the sacraments, should receive the fulness of grace from a sacrament.

SECOND ARTICLE [III, Q. 72, Art. 2]

Whether Chrism Is a Fitting Matter for This Sacrament?

Objection 1: It seems that chrism is not a fitting matter for this sacrament. For this sacrament, as stated above (A. 1, ad 1), was instituted by Christ when He promised His disciples the Holy Ghost. But He sent them the Holy Ghost without their being anointed with chrism. Moreover, the apostles themselves bestowed this sacrament without chrism, by the mere imposition of hands: for it is written (Acts 8:17) that the apostles "laid their hands upon" those who were baptized, "and they received the Holy Ghost." Therefore chrism is not the matter of this sacrament: since the matter is essential to the sacrament.

Obj. 2: Further, Confirmation perfects, in a way, the sacrament of Baptism, as stated above (Q. 65, AA. 3, 4): and so it ought to be conformed to it as perfection to the thing perfected. But the matter, in Baptism, is a simple element, viz. water. Therefore chrism, which is made of oil and balm, is not a fitting matter for this sacrament.

Obj. 3: Further, oil is used as the matter of this sacrament for the purpose of anointing. But any oil will do for anointing: for instance, oil made from nuts, and from anything else. Therefore not only olive oil should be used for this sacrament.

Obj. 4: Further, it has been stated above (Q. 66, A. 3) that water is used as the matter of Baptism, because it is easily procured everywhere. But olive oil is not to be procured everywhere; and much less is balm. Therefore chrism, which is made of these, is not a fitting matter for this sacrament.

*On the contrary,* Gregory says (Registr. iv): "Let no priest dare to sign the baptized infants on the brow with the sacred chrism." Therefore chrism is the matter of this sacrament.

*I answer that,* Chrism is the fitting matter of this sacrament. For, as stated above (A. 1), in this sacrament the fulness of the Holy Ghost is given for the spiritual strength which belongs to the perfect age. Now when man comes to perfect age he begins at once to have intercourse with others; whereas until then he lives an individual life, as it were, confined to himself. Now the grace of the Holy Ghost is signified by oil; hence Christ is said to be "anointed with the oil of gladness" (Ps. 44:8), by reason of His being gifted with the fulness of the Holy Ghost. Consequently oil is a suitable matter of this sacrament. And balm is mixed with the oil, by reason of its fragrant odor, which spreads about: hence the Apostle says (2 Cor. 2:15): "We are the good odor of Christ," etc. And though many other things be fragrant, yet preference is given to balm, because it has a special odor of its own, and because it confers incorruptibility: hence it is written (Ecclus. 24:21): "My odor is as the purest balm."

Reply Obj. 1: Christ, by the power which He exercises in the sacraments, bestowed on the apostles the reality of this sacrament, i.e. the fulness of the Holy Ghost, without the sacrament itself, because they had received "the first fruits of the Spirit" (Rom. 8:23). Nevertheless, something of keeping with the matter of this sacrament was displayed to the apostles in a sensible manner when they received the Holy Ghost. For that the Holy Ghost came down upon them in a sensible manner under the form of fire, refers to the same signification as oil: except in so far as fire has an active power, while oil has a passive power, as being the matter and incentive of fire. And this was quite fitting: for it was through the apostles that the grace of the Holy Ghost was to flow forth to others. Again, the Holy Ghost came down on the apostles in the shape of a tongue. Which refers to the same signification as balm: except in so far as the tongue communicates with others by speech, but balm, by its odor. because, to wit, the apostles were filled with the Holy Ghost, as teachers of the Faith; but the rest of the believers, as doing that which gives edification to the faithful.

In like manner, too, when the apostles imposed their hands, and when they preached, the fulness of the Holy Ghost came down under visible signs on the faithful, just as, at the beginning, He came down on the apostles: hence Peter said (Acts 11:15): "When I had begun to speak, the Holy Ghost fell upon them, as upon us also in the beginning." Consequently there was no need for sacramental sensible matter, where God sent sensible signs miraculously.

However, the apostles commonly made use of chrism in bestowing the sacrament, when such like visible signs were lacking. For Dionysius says (Eccl. Hier. iv): "There is a certain perfecting operation which our guides," i.e. the apostles, "call the sacrifice of Chrism."

Reply Obj. 2: Baptism is bestowed that spiritual life may be received simply; wherefore simple matter is fitting to it. But this sacrament is given that we may receive the fulness of the Holy Ghost, Whose operations are manifold, according to Wis. 7:22, "In her is the" Holy "Spirit . . . one, manifold"; and 1 Cor. 12:4, "There are diversities of graces, but the same Spirit." Consequently a compound matter is appropriate to this sacrament.

Reply Obj. 3: These properties of oil, by reason of which it symbolizes the Holy Ghost, are to be found in olive oil rather than in any other oil. In fact, the olive-tree itself, through being an evergreen, signifies the refreshing and merciful operation of the Holy Ghost.

Moreover, this oil is called oil properly, and is very much in use, wherever it is to be had. And whatever other liquid is so called, derives its name from its likeness to this oil: nor are the latter commonly used, unless it be to supply the want of olive oil. Therefore it is that this oil alone is used for this and certain other sacraments.

Reply Obj. 4: Baptism is the sacrament of absolute necessity; and so its matter should be at hand everywhere. But it is enough that the matter of this sacrament, which is not of such great necessity, be easily sent to all parts of the world.

THIRD ARTICLE [III, Q. 72, Art. 3]

Whether It Is Essential to This Sacrament That the Chrism Which Is Its Matter Be Previously Consecrated by a Bishop?

Objection 1: It seems that it is not essential to this sacrament, that the chrism, which is its matter, be previously consecrated by a bishop. For Baptism which bestows full remission of sins is not less efficacious than this sacrament. But, though the baptismal water receives a kind of blessing before being used for Baptism; yet this is not essential to the sacrament: since in a case of necessity it can be dispensed with. Therefore neither is it essential to this sacrament that the chrism should be previously consecrated by a bishop.

Obj. 2: Further, the same should not be consecrated twice. But the sacramental matter is sanctified, in the very conferring of the sacrament, by the form of words wherein the sacrament is bestowed; hence Augustine says (Tract. lxxx in Joan.): "The word is added to the element, and this becomes a sacrament." Therefore the chrism should not be consecrated before this sacrament is given.

Obj. 3: Further, every consecration employed in the sacraments is ordained to the bestowal of grace. But the sensible matter composed of oil and balm is not receptive of grace. Therefore it should not be consecrated.

*On the contrary,* Pope Innocent I says (Ep. ad Decent.): "Priests, when baptizing, may anoint the baptized with chrism, previously consecrated by a bishop: but they must not sign the brow with the same oil; this belongs to the bishop alone, when he gives the Paraclete." Now this is done in this sacrament. Therefore it is necessary for this sacrament that its matter be previously consecrated by a bishop.

*I answer that,* The entire sanctification of the sacraments is derived from Christ, as stated above (Q. 64, A. 3). But it must be observed that Christ did use certain sacraments having a corporeal matter, viz. Baptism, and also the Eucharist. And consequently, from Christ's very act in using them, the matter of these sacraments received a certain aptitude to the perfection of the sacrament. Hence Chrysostom (Chromatius, In Matth. 3:15) says that "the waters of Baptism could never wash away the sins of believers, had they not been sanctified by contact with our Lord's body." And again, our Lord Himself "taking bread . . . blessed . . . and in like manner the chalice" (Matt. 26:26, 27; Luke 22:19, 20). For this reason there is no need for the matter of these sacraments to be blessed previously, since Christ's blessing is enough. And if any blessing be used, it belongs to the solemnity of the sacrament, not to its essence. But Christ did not make use of visible anointings, so as not to slight the invisible unction whereby He was "anointed above" His "fellows" (Ps. 44:8). And hence both chrism, and the holy oil, and the oil of the sick are blessed before being put to sacramental use. This suffices for the reply to the First Objection.

Reply Obj. 2: Each consecration of the chrism has not the same object. For just as an instrument derives instrumental power in two ways, viz. when it receives the form of an instrument, and when it is moved by the principal agent; so too the sacramental matter needs a twofold sanctification, by one of which it becomes fit matter for the sacrament, while by the other it is applied to the production of the effect.

Reply Obj. 3: Corporeal matter is receptive of grace, not so as to be the subject of grace, but only as the instrument of grace, as explained above (Q. 62, A. 3). And this sacramental matter is consecrated, either by Christ, or by a bishop, who, in the Church, impersonates Christ.

FOURTH ARTICLE [III, Q. 72, Art. 4]

Whether the Proper Form of This Sacrament Is: "I Sign Thee with the Sign of the Cross," Etc.?

Objection 1: It seems that the proper form of this sacrament is not: "I sign thee with the sign of the cross, I confirm thee with the chrism of salvation, in the name of the Father and of the Son and of the Holy Ghost. Amen." For the use of the sacraments is derived from Christ and the apostles. But neither did Christ institute this form, nor do we read of the apostles making use of it. Therefore it is not the proper form of this sacrament.

Obj. 2: Further, just as the sacrament is the same everywhere, so should the form be the same: because everything has unity, just as it has being, from its form. But this form is not used by all: for some say: "I confirm thee with the chrism of sanctification." Therefore the above is not the proper form of this sacrament.

Obj. 3: Further, this sacrament should be conformed to Baptism, as the perfect to the thing perfected, as stated above (A. 2, Obj. 2). But in the form of Baptism no mention is made of signing the character; nor again of the cross of Christ, though in Baptism man dies with Christ, as the Apostle says (Rom. 6:3-8); nor of the effect which is salvation, though Baptism is necessary for salvation. Again, in the baptismal form, only one action is included; and the person of the baptizer is expressed in the words: "I baptize thee, whereas the contrary is to be observed in the above form." Therefore this is not the proper form of this sacrament.

*On the contrary,* Is the authority of the Church, who always uses this form.

*I answer that,* The above form is appropriate to this sacrament. For just as the form of a natural thing gives it its species, so a sacramental form should contain whatever belongs to the species of the sacrament. Now as is evident from what has been already said (AA. 1, 2), in this sacrament the Holy Ghost is given for strength in the spiritual combat. Wherefore in this sacrament three things are necessary; and they are contained in the above form. The first of these is the cause conferring fulness of spiritual strength which cause is the Blessed Trinity: and this is expressed in the words, "In the name of the Father," etc. The second is the spiritual strength itself bestowed on man unto salvation by the sacrament of visible matter; and this is referred to in the words, "I confirm thee with the chrism of salvation." The third is the sign which is given to the combatant, as in a bodily combat: thus are soldiers marked with the sign of their leaders. And to this refer the words, "I sign thee with the sign of the cross," in which sign, to wit, our King triumphed (cf. Col. 2:15).

Reply Obj. 1: As stated above (A. 2, ad 1), sometimes the effect of this sacrament, i.e. the fulness of the Holy Ghost, was given through the ministry of the apostles, under certain visible signs, wrought miraculously by God, Who can bestow the sacramental effect, independently of the sacrament. In these cases there was no need for either the matter or the form of this sacrament. On the other hand, sometimes they bestowed this sacrament as ministers of the sacraments. And then, they used both matter and form according to Christ's command. For the apostles, in conferring the sacraments, observed many things which are not handed down in those Scriptures that are in general use. Hence Dionysius says at the end of his treatise on the Ecclesiastical Hierarchy (chap. vii): "It is not allowed to explain in writing the prayers which are used in the sacraments, and to publish their mystical meaning, or the power which, coming from God, gives them their efficacy; we learn these things by holy tradition without any display,"* i.e. secretly. [*The passage quoted in the text of the Summa differs slightly from the above, which is translated directly from the works of Dionysius.] Hence the Apostle, speaking of the celebration of the Eucharist, writes (1 Cor. 11:34): "The rest I will set in order, when I come."

Reply Obj. 2: Holiness is the cause of salvation. Therefore it comes to the same whether we say "chrism of salvation" or "of sanctification."

Reply Obj. 3: Baptism is the regeneration unto the spiritual life, whereby man lives in himself. And therefore in the baptismal form that action alone is expressed which refers to the man to be sanctified. But this sacrament is ordained not only to the sanctification of man in himself, but also to strengthen him in his outward combat. Consequently not only is mention made of interior sanctification, in the words, "I confirm thee with the chrism of salvation": but furthermore man is signed outwardly, as it were with the standard of the cross, unto the outward spiritual combat; and this is signified by the words, "I sign thee with the sign of the cross."

But in the very word "baptize," which signifies "to cleanse," we can understand both the matter, which is the cleansing water, and the effect, which is salvation. Whereas these are not understood by the word "confirm"; and consequently they had to be expressed.

Again, it has been said above (Q. 66, A. 5, ad 1) that the pronoun "I" is not necessary to the Baptismal form, because it is included in the first person of the verb. It is, however, included in order to express the intention. But this does not seem so necessary in Confirmation, which is conferred only by a minister of excellence, as we shall state later on (A. 11).

FIFTH ARTICLE [III, Q. 72, Art. 5]

Whether the Sacrament of Confirmation Imprints a Character?

Objection 1: It seems that the sacrament of Confirmation does not imprint a character. For a character means a distinctive sign. But a man is not distinguished from unbelievers by the sacrament of Confirmation, for this is the effect of Baptism; nor from the rest of the faithful, because this sacrament is ordained to the spiritual combat, which is enjoined to all the faithful. Therefore a character is not imprinted in this sacrament.

Obj. 2: Further, it was stated above (Q. 63, A. 2) that a character is a spiritual power. Now a power must be either active or passive. But the active power in the sacraments is conferred by the sacrament of order: while the passive or receptive power is conferred by the sacrament of Baptism. Therefore no character is imprinted by the sacrament of Confirmation.

Obj. 3: Further, in circumcision, which is a character of the body, no spiritual character is imprinted. But in this sacrament a character is imprinted on the body, when the sign of the cross is signed with chrism on man's brow. Therefore a spiritual character is not imprinted by this sacrament.

*On the contrary,* A character is imprinted in every sacrament that is not repeated. But this sacrament is not repeated: for Gregory II says (Ep. iv ad Bonifac.): "As to the man who was confirmed a second time by a bishop, such a repetition must be forbidden." Therefore a character is imprinted in Confirmation.

*I answer that,* As stated above (Q. 63, A. 2), a

character is a spiritual power ordained to certain sacred actions. Now it has been said above (A. 1; Q. 65, A. 1) that, just as Baptism is a spiritual regeneration unto Christian life, so also is Confirmation a certain spiritual growth bringing man to perfect spiritual age. But it is evident, from a comparison with the life of the body, that the action which is proper to man immediately after birth, is different from the action which is proper to him when he has come to perfect age. And therefore by the sacrament of Confirmation man is given a spiritual power in respect of sacred actions other than those in respect of which he receives power in Baptism. For in Baptism he receives power to do those things which pertain to his own salvation, forasmuch as he lives to himself: whereas in Confirmation he receives power to do those things which pertain to the spiritual combat with the enemies of the Faith. This is evident from the example of the apostles, who, before they received the fulness of the Holy Ghost, were in the "upper room . . . persevering . . . in prayer" (Acts 1:13, 14); whereas afterwards they went out and feared not to confess their faith in public, even in the face of the enemies of the Christian Faith. And therefore it is evident that a character is imprinted in the sacrament of Confirmation.

Reply Obj. 1: All have to wage the spiritual combat with our invisible enemies. But to fight against visible foes, viz. against the persecutors of the Faith, by confessing Christ's name, belongs to the confirmed, who have already come spiritually to the age of virility, according to 1 John 2:14: "I write unto you, young men, because you are strong, and the word of God abideth in you, and you have overcome the wicked one." And therefore the character of Confirmation is a distinctive sign, not between unbelievers and believers, but between those who are grown up spiritually and those of whom it is written: "As new-born babes" (1 Pet. 2:2).

Reply Obj. 2: All the sacraments are protestations of faith. Therefore just as he who is baptized receives the power of testifying to his faith by receiving the other sacraments; so he who is confirmed receives the power of publicly confessing his faith by words, as it were ex officio.

Reply Obj. 3: The sacraments of the Old Law are called "justice of the flesh" (Heb. 9:10) because, to wit, they wrought nothing inwardly. Consequently in circumcision a character was imprinted in the body only, but not in the soul. But in Confirmation, since it is a sacrament of the New Law, a spiritual character is imprinted at the same time, together with the bodily character.

SIXTH ARTICLE [III, Q. 72, Art. 6]

Whether the Character of Confirmation Presupposes of Necessity, the Baptismal Character?

Objection 1: It seems that the character of Confirmation does not presuppose, of necessity, the baptismal character. For the sacrament of Confirmation is ordained to the public confession of the Faith of Christ. But many, even before Baptism, have publicly confessed the Faith of Christ by shedding their blood for the Faith. Therefore the character of Confirmation does not presuppose the baptismal character.

Obj. 2: Further, it is not related of the apostles that they were baptized; especially, since it is written (John 4:2) that Christ "Himself did not baptize, but His disciples." Yet afterwards they were confirmed by the coming of the Holy Ghost. Therefore, in like manner, others can be confirmed before being baptized.

Obj. 3: Further, it is written (Acts 10:44-48) that "while Peter was yet speaking . . . the Holy Ghost fell on all them that heard the word . . . and [Vulg.: 'for'] they heard them speaking with tongues": and afterwards "he commanded them to be baptized." Therefore others with equal reason can be confirmed before being baptized.

*On the contrary,* Rabanus says (De Instit. Cleric. i): "Lastly the Paraclete is given to the baptized by the imposition of the high priest's hands, in order that the baptized may be strengthened by the Holy Ghost so as to publish his faith."

*I answer that,* The character of Confirmation, of necessity supposes the baptismal character: so that, in effect, if one who is not baptized were to be confirmed, he would receive nothing, but would have to be confirmed again after receiving Baptism. The reason of this is that, Confirmation is to Baptism as growth to birth, as is evident from what has been said above (A. 1; Q. 65, A. 1). Now it is clear that no one can be brought to perfect age unless he be first born: and in like manner, unless a man be first baptized, he cannot receive the sacrament of Confirmation.

Reply Obj. 1: The Divine power is not confined to the sacraments. Hence man can receive spiritual strength to confess the Faith of Christ publicly, without receiving the sacrament of Confirmation: just as he can also receive remission of sins without Baptism. Yet, just as none receive the effect of Baptism without the desire of Baptism; so none receive the effect of Confirmation, without the desire of Confirmation. And man can have this even before receiving Baptism.

Reply Obj. 2: As Augustine says (Ep. cclxv), from our Lord's words, "'He that is washed, needeth not but to wash his feet' (John 13:10), we gather that Peter and Christ's other disciples had been baptized, either with John's Baptism, as some think; or with Christ's, which is more credible. For He did not refuse to administer Baptism, so as to have servants by whom to baptize others."

Reply Obj. 3: Those who heard the preaching of Peter received the effect of Confirmation miraculously: but not the sacrament of Confirmation. Now it has been stated (ad 1) that the effect of Confirmation can be bestowed on man before Baptism, whereas the sacrament cannot. For just as the effect of Confirmation, which is spiritual strength, presupposes the effect of Baptism, which is justification, so the sacrament of Confirmation presupposes the sacrament of Baptism.

SEVENTH ARTICLE [III, Q. 72, Art. 7]

Whether Sanctifying Grace Is Bestowed in This Sacrament?

Objection 1: It seems that sanctifying grace is not bestowed in this sacrament. For sanctifying grace is ordained against sin. But this sacrament, as stated above (A. 6) is given only to the baptized, who are cleansed from sin. Therefore sanctifying grace is not bestowed in this sacrament.

Obj. 2: Further, sinners especially need sanctifying grace, by which alone can they be justified. If, therefore, sanctifying grace is bestowed in this sacrament, it seems that it should be given to those who are in sin. And yet this is not true.

Obj. 3: Further, there can only be one species of sanctifying grace, since it is ordained to one effect. But two forms of the same species cannot be in the same subject. Since, therefore, man receives sanctifying grace in Baptism, it seems that sanctifying grace is not bestowed in Confirmation, which is given to none but the baptized.

*On the contrary,* Pope Melchiades says (Ep. ad Episc. Hispan.): "The Holy Ghost bestows at the font the fulness of innocence; but in Confirmation He confers an increase of grace."

*I answer that,* In this sacrament, as stated above (AA. 1, 4), the Holy Ghost is given to the baptized for strength: just as He was given to the apostles on the day of Pentecost, as we read in Acts 2; and just as He was given to the baptized by the imposition of the apostles' hands, as related in Acts 8:17. Now it has been proved in the First Part (Q. 43, A. 3) that the Holy Ghost is not sent or given except with sanctifying grace. Consequently it is evident that sanctifying grace is bestowed in this sacrament.

Reply Obj. 1: Sanctifying grace does indeed take away sin; but it has other effects also, because it suffices to carry man through every step as far as eternal life. Hence to Paul was it said (2 Cor. 12:9): "My grace is sufficient for thee": and he says of himself (1 Cor. 15:10): "By the grace of God I am what I am." Therefore sanctifying grace is given not only for the remission of sin, but also for growth and stability in righteousness. And thus is it bestowed in this sacrament.

Reply Obj. 2: Further, as appears from its very name, this sacrament is given in order "to confirm" what it finds already there. And consequently it should not be given to those who are not in a state of grace. For this reason, just as it is not given to the unbaptized, so neither should it be given to the adult sinners, except they be restored by Penance. Wherefore was it decreed in the Council of Orleans (Can. iii) that "men should come to Confirmation fasting; and should be admonished to confess their sins first, so that being cleansed they may be able to receive the gift of the Holy Ghost." And then this sacrament perfects the effects of Penance, as of Baptism: because by the grace which he has received in this sacrament, the penitent will obtain fuller remission of his sin. And if any adult approach, being in a state of sin of which he is not conscious or for which he is not perfectly contrite, he will receive the remission of his sins through the grace bestowed in this sacrament.

Reply Obj. 3: As stated above (Q. 62, A. 2), the sacramental grace adds to the sanctifying grace taken in its wide sense, something that produces a special effect, and to which the sacrament is ordained. If, then, we consider, in its wide sense, the grace bestowed in this sacrament, it does not differ from that bestowed in Baptism, but increases what was already there. On the other hand, if we consider it as to that which is added over and above, then one differs in species from the other.

EIGHTH ARTICLE [III, Q. 72, Art. 8]

Whether This Sacrament Should Be Given to All?

Objection 1: It seems that this sacrament should not be given to all. For this sacrament is given in order to confer a certain excellence, as stated above (A. 11, ad 2). But all are not suited for that which belongs to excellence. Therefore this sacrament should not be given to all.

Obj. 2: Further, by this sacrament man advances spiritually to perfect age. But perfect age is inconsistent with childhood. Therefore at least it should not be given to children.

Obj. 3: Further, as Pope Melchiades says (Ep. ad Episc. Hispan.) "after Baptism we are strengthened for the combat." But women are incompetent to combat, by reason of the frailty of their sex. Therefore neither should women receive this sacrament.

Obj. 4: Further, Pope Melchiades says (Ep. ad Episc. Hispan.): "Although the benefit of Regeneration suffices for those who are on the point of death, yet the graces of Confirmation are necessary for those who are to conquer. Confirmation arms and strengthens those to whom the struggles and combats of this world are reserved. And he who comes to die, having kept unsullied the innocence he acquired in Baptism, is confirmed by death; for after death he can sin no more." Therefore this sacrament should not be given to those who are on the point of death: and so it should not be given to all.

*On the contrary,* It is written (Acts 2:2) that the Holy Ghost in coming, "filled the whole house," whereby the Church is signified; and afterwards it is added that "they were all filled with the Holy Ghost." But this sacrament is given that we may receive that fulness. Therefore it should be given to all who belong to the Church.

*I answer that,* As stated above (A. 1), man is spiritually advanced by this sacrament to perfect age. Now the intention of nature is that everyone born corporally, should come to perfect age: yet this is sometimes hindered by reason of the corruptibility of the body, which is forestalled by death. But much more is it God's intention to bring all things to perfection, since nature shares in this intention inasmuch as it reflects Him: hence it is written (Deut. 32:4): "The works of God are perfect." Now the soul, to which spiritual birth and perfect spiritual age belong, is immortal; and just as it can in old age attain to spiritual birth, so can it attain to perfect (spiritual) age in youth or childhood; because the various ages of the body do not affect the soul. Therefore this sacrament should be given to all.

Reply Obj. 1: This sacrament is given in order to confer a certain excellence, not indeed, like the sacrament of order, of one man over another, but of man in regard to himself: thus the same man, when arrived at maturity, excels himself as he was when a boy.

Reply Obj. 2: As stated above, the age of the body does not affect the soul. Consequently even in childhood man can attain to the perfection of spiritual age, of which it is written (Wis. 4:8): "Venerable old age is not that of long time, nor counted by the number of years." And hence it is that many children, by reason of the strength of the Holy Ghost which they had received, fought bravely for Christ even to the shedding of their blood.

Reply Obj. 3: As Chrysostom says (Hom. i De Machab.), "in earthly contests fitness of age, physique and rank are required; and consequently slaves, women, old men, and boys are debarred from taking part therein. But in the heavenly combats, the Stadium is open equally to all, to every age, and to either sex." Again, he says (Hom. de Militia Spirit.): "In God's eyes even women fight, for many a woman has waged the spiritual warfare with the courage of a man. For some have rivaled men in the courage with which they have suffered martyrdom; and some indeed have shown themselves stronger than men." Therefore this sacrament should be given to women.

Reply Obj. 4: As we have already observed, the soul, to which spiritual age belongs, is immortal. Wherefore this sacrament should be given to those on the point of death, that they may be seen to be perfect at the resurrection, according to Eph. 4:13: "Until we all meet into the unity of faith . . . unto the measure of the age of the fulness of Christ." And hence Hugh of St. Victor says (De Sacram. ii), "It would be altogether hazardous, if anyone happened to go forth from this life without being confirmed": not that such a one would be lost, except perhaps through contempt; but that this would be detrimental to his perfection. And therefore even children dying after Confirmation obtain greater glory, just as here below they receive more grace. The passage quoted is to be taken in the sense that, with regard to the dangers of the present combat, those who are on the point of death do not need this sacrament.

NINTH ARTICLE [III, Q. 72, Art. 9]

Whether This Sacrament Should Be Given to Man on the Forehead?

Objection 1: It seems that this sacrament should not be given to man on the forehead. For this sacrament perfects Baptism, as stated above (Q. 65, AA. 3, 4). But the sacrament of Baptism is given to man over his whole body. Therefore this sacrament should not be given on the forehead only.

Obj. 2: Further, this sacrament is given for spiritual strength, as stated above (AA. 1, 2, 4). But spiritual strength is situated principally in the heart. Therefore this sacrament should be given over the heart rather than on the forehead.

Obj. 3: Further, this sacrament is given to man that he may freely confess the faith of Christ. But "with the mouth, confession is made unto salvation," according to Rom. 10:10. Therefore this sacrament should be given about the mouth rather than on the forehead.

*On the contrary,* Rabanus says (De Instit. Cleric. i): "The baptized is signed by the priest with chrism on the top of the head, but by the bishop on the forehead."

*I answer that,* As stated above (AA. 1, 4), in this sacrament man receives the Holy Ghost for strength in the spiritual combat, that he may bravely confess the Faith of Christ even in face of the enemies of that Faith. Wherefore he is fittingly signed with the sign of the cross on the forehead, with chrism, for two reasons. First, because he is signed with the sign of the cross, as a soldier with the sign of his leader, which should be evident and manifest. Now, the forehead, which is hardly ever covered, is the most conspicuous part of the human body. Wherefore the confirmed is anointed with chrism on the forehead, that he may show publicly that he is a Christian: thus too the apostles after receiving the Holy Ghost showed themselves in public, whereas before they remained hidden in the upper room.

Secondly, because man is hindered from freely confessing Christ's name, by two things--by fear and by shame. Now both these things betray themselves principally on the forehead on account of the proximity of the imagination, and because the (vital) spirits mount directly from the heart to the forehead: hence "those who are ashamed, blush, and those who are afraid, pale" (Ethic. iv). And therefore man is signed with chrism, that neither fear nor shame may hinder him from confessing the name of Christ.

Reply Obj. 1: By baptism we are regenerated unto spiritual life, which belongs to the whole man. But in Confirmation we are strengthened for the combat; the sign of which should be borne on the forehead, as in a conspicuous place.

Reply Obj. 2: The principle of fortitude is in the heart, but its sign appears on the forehead: wherefore it is written (Ezech. 3:8): "Behold I have made . . . thy forehead harder than their foreheads." Hence the sacrament of the Eucharist, whereby man is confirmed in himself, belongs to the heart, according to Ps. 103:15: "That bread may strengthen man's heart." But the sacrament of Confirmation is required as a sign of fortitude against others; and for this reason it is given on the forehead.

Reply Obj. 3: This sacrament is given that we may confess freely: but not that we may confess simply, for this is also the effect of Baptism. And therefore it should not be given on the mouth, but on the forehead, where appear the signs of those passions which hinder free confession.

TENTH ARTICLE [III, Q. 72, Art. 10]

Whether He Who Is Confirmed Needs One to Stand* for Him? [*Literally, "to hold him"]

Objection 1: It seems that he who is confirmed needs no one to stand for him. For this sacrament is given not only to children but also to adults. But adults can stand for themselves. Therefore it is absurd that someone else should stand for them.

Obj. 2: Further, he that belongs already to the Church, has free access to the prince of the Church, i.e. the bishop. But this sacrament, as stated above (A. 6), is given only to one that is baptized, who is already a member of the Church. Therefore it seems that he should not be brought by another to the bishop in order to receive this sacrament.

Obj. 3: Further, this sacrament is given for spiritual strength, which has more vigor in men than in women, according to Prov. 31:10: "Who shall find a valiant woman?" Therefore at least a woman should not stand for a man in confirmation.

*On the contrary,* Are the following words of Pope Innocent, which are to be found in the Decretals (XXX, Q. 4): "If anyone raise the children of another's marriage from the sacred font, or stand for them in Confirmation," etc. Therefore, just as someone is required as sponsor of one who is baptized, so is someone required to stand for him who is to be confirmed.

*I answer that,* As stated above (AA. 1, 4, 9), this sacrament is given to man for strength in the spiritual combat. Now, just as one newly born requires someone to teach him things pertaining to ordinary conduct, according to Heb. 12:9: "We have had fathers of our flesh, for instructors, and we obeyed [Vulg.: 'reverenced']" them; so they who are chosen for the fight need instructors by whom they are informed of things concerning the conduct of the battle, and hence in earthly wars, generals and captains are appointed to the command of the others. For this reason he also who receives this sacrament, has someone to stand for him, who, as it were, has to instruct him concerning the fight.

Likewise, since this sacrament bestows on man the perfection of spiritual age, as stated above (AA. 2, 5), therefore he who approaches this sacrament is upheld by another, as being spiritually a weakling and a child.

Reply Obj. 1: Although he who is confirmed, be adult in body, nevertheless he is not yet spiritually adult.

Reply Obj. 2: Though he who is baptized is made a member of the Church, nevertheless he is not yet enrolled as a Christian soldier. And therefore he is brought to the bishop, as to the commander of the army, by one who is already enrolled as a Christian soldier. For one who is not yet confirmed should not stand for another in Confirmation.

Reply Obj. 3: According to Col. 3 *(Gal. 3:28), "in Christ Jesus there is neither male nor female." Consequently it matters not whether a man or a woman stand for one who is to be confirmed.

ELEVENTH ARTICLE [III, Q. 72, Art. 11]

Whether Only a Bishop Can Confer This Sacrament?

Objection 1: It seems that not only a bishop can confer this sacrament. For Gregory (Regist. iv), writing to Bishop Januarius, says: "We hear that some were scandalized because we forbade priests to anoint with chrism those who have been baptized. Yet in doing this we followed the ancient custom of our Church: but if this trouble some so very much we permit priests, where no bishop is to be had, to anoint the baptized on the forehead with chrism." But that which is essential to the sacraments should not be changed for the purpose of avoiding scandal. Therefore it seems that it is not essential to this sacrament that it be conferred by a bishop.

Obj. 2: Further, the sacrament of Baptism seems to be more efficacious than the sacrament of Confirmation: since it bestows full remission of sins, both as to guilt and as to punishment, whereas this sacrament does not. But a simple priest, in virtue of his office, can give the sacrament of Baptism: and in a case of necessity anyone, even without orders, can baptize. Therefore it is not essential to this sacrament that it be conferred by a bishop.

Obj. 3: Further, the top of the head, where according to medical men the reason is situated (i.e. the "particular reason," which is called the "cogitative faculty"), is more noble than the forehead, which is the site of the imagination. But a simple priest can anoint the baptized with chrism on the top of the head. Therefore much more can he anoint them with chrism on the forehead, which belongs to this sacrament.

*On the contrary,* Pope Eusebius (Ep. iii ad Ep. Tusc.) says: "The sacrament of the imposition of the hand should be held in great veneration, and can be given by none but the high priests. Nor is it related or known to have been conferred in apostolic times by others than the apostles themselves; nor can it ever be either licitly or validly performed by others than those who stand in their place. And if anyone presume to do otherwise, it must be considered null and void; nor will such a thing ever be counted among the sacraments of the Church." Therefore it is essential to this sacrament, which is called "the sacrament of the imposition of the hand," that it be given by a bishop.

*I answer that,* In every work the final completion is reserved to the supreme act or power; thus the preparation of the matter belongs to the lower craftsmen, the higher gives the form, but the highest of all is he to whom pertains the use, which is the end of things made by art; thus also the letter which is written by the clerk, is signed by his employer. Now the faithful of Christ are a Divine work, according to 1 Cor. 3:9: "You are God's building"; and they are also "an epistle," as it were, "written with the Spirit of God," according to 2 Cor. 3:2, 3. And this sacrament of Confirmation is, as it were, the final completion of the sacrament of Baptism; in the sense that by Baptism man is built up into a spiritual dwelling, and is written like a spiritual letter; whereas by the sacrament of Confirmation, like a house already built, he is consecrated as a temple of the Holy Ghost, and as a letter already written, is signed with the sign of the cross. Therefore the conferring of this sacrament is reserved to bishops, who possess supreme power in the Church: just as in the primitive Church, the fulness of the Holy Ghost was given by the apostles, in whose place the bishops stand (Acts 8). Hence Pope Urban I says: "All the faithful should, after Baptism, receive the Holy Ghost by the imposition of the bishop's hand, that they may become perfect Christians."

Reply Obj. 1: The Pope has the plenitude of power in the Church, in virtue of which he can commit to certain lower orders things that belong to the higher orders: thus he allows priests to confer minor orders, which belong to the episcopal power. And in virtue of this fulness of power the Pope, Blessed Gregory, allowed simple priests to confer this sacrament, so long as the scandal was ended.

Reply Obj. 2: The sacrament of Baptism is more efficacious than this sacrament as to the removal of evil, since it is a spiritual birth, that consists in change from non-being to being. But this sacrament is more efficacious for progress in good; since it is a spiritual growth from imperfect being to perfect being. And hence this sacrament is committed to a more worthy minister.

Reply Obj. 3: As Rabanus says (De Instit. Cleric. i), "the baptized is signed by the priest with chrism on the top of the head, but by the bishop on the forehead; that the former unction may symbolize the descent of the Holy Ghost on him, in order to consecrate a dwelling to God: and that the second also may teach us that the sevenfold grace of the same Holy Ghost descends on man with all fulness of sanctity, knowledge and virtue." Hence this unction is reserved to bishops, not on account of its being applied to a more worthy part of the body, but by reason of its having a more powerful effect.

TWELFTH ARTICLE [III, Q. 72, Art. 12]

Whether the Rite of This Sacrament Is Appropriate?

Objection 1: It seems that the rite of this sacrament is not appropriate. For the sacrament of Baptism is of greater necessity than this, as stated above (A. 2, ad 4; Q. 65, AA. 3, 4). But certain seasons are fixed for Baptism, viz. Easter and Pentecost. Therefore some fixed time of the year should be chosen for this sacrament.

Obj. 2: Further, just as this sacrament requires devotion both in the giver and in the receiver, so also does the sacrament of Baptism. But in the sacrament of Baptism it is not necessary that it should be received or given fasting. Therefore it seems unfitting for the Council of Orleans to declare that "those who come to Confirmation should be fasting"; and the Council of Meaux, "that bishops should not give the Holy Ghost with imposition of the hand except they be fasting."

Obj. 3: Further, chrism is a sign of the fulness of the Holy Ghost, as stated above (A. 2). But the fulness of the Holy Ghost was given to Christ's faithful on the day of Pentecost, as related in Acts 2:1. Therefore the chrism should be mixed and blessed on the day of Pentecost rather than on Maundy Thursday.

*On the contrary,* Is the use of the Church, who is governed by the Holy Ghost.

*I answer that,* Our Lord promised His faithful (Matt. 18:20) saying: "Where there are two or three gathered together in My name, there am I in the midst of them." And therefore we must hold firmly that the Church's ordinations are directed by the wisdom of Christ. And for this reason we must look upon it as certain that the rite observed by the Church, in this and the other sacraments, is appropriate.

Reply Obj. 1: As Pope Melchiades says (Ep. ad Epis. Hispan.), "these two sacraments," viz. Baptism and Confirmation, "are so closely connected that they can nowise be separated save by death intervening, nor can one be duly celebrated without the other." Consequently the same seasons are fixed for the solemn celebration of Baptism and of this sacrament. But since this sacrament is given only by bishops, who are not always present where priests are baptizing, it was necessary, as regards the common use, to defer the sacrament of Confirmation to other seasons also.

Reply Obj. 2: The sick and those in danger of death are exempt from this prohibition, as we read in the decree of the Council of Meaux. And therefore, on account of the multitude of the faithful, and on account of imminent dangers, it is allowed for this sacrament, which can be given by none but a bishop, to be given or received even by those who are not fasting: since one bishop, especially in a large diocese, would not suffice to confirm all, if he were confined to certain times. But where it can be done conveniently, it is more becoming that both giver and receiver should be fasting.

Reply Obj. 3: According to the acts of the Council of Pope Martin, "it was lawful at all times to prepare the chrism." But since solemn Baptism, for which chrism has to be used, is celebrated on Easter Eve, it was rightly decreed, that chrism should be consecrated by the bishop two days beforehand, that it may be sent to the various parts of the diocese. Moreover, this day is sufficiently appropriate to the blessing of sacramental matter, since thereon was the Eucharist instituted, to which, in a certain way, all the other sacraments are ordained, as stated above (Q. 65, A. 3).

# QUESTION 73

OF THE SACRAMENT OF THE EUCHARIST
(In Six Articles)

We have now to consider the sacrament of the Eucharist; and first of all we treat of the sacrament itself; secondly, of its matter; thirdly, of its form; fourthly, of its effects; fifthly, of the recipients of this sacrament; sixthly, of the minister; seventhly, of the rite.

Under the first heading there are six points of inquiry:

(1) Whether the Eucharist is a sacrament?
(2) Whether it is one or several sacraments?
(3) Whether it is necessary for salvation?
(4) Its names;
(5) Its institution;
(6) Its figures.

FIRST ARTICLE [III, Q. 73, Art. 1]

Whether the Eucharist Is a Sacrament?

Objection 1: It seems that the Eucharist is not a sacrament. For two sacraments ought not to be ordained for the same end, because every sacrament is efficacious in producing its effect. Therefore, since both Confirmation and the Eucharist are ordained for perfection, as Dionysius says (Eccl. Hier. iv), it seems that the Eucharist is not a sacrament, since Confirmation is one, as stated above (Q. 65, A. 1; Q. 72, A. 1).

Obj. 2: Further, in every sacrament of the New Law, that which comes visibly under our senses causes the invisible effect of the sacrament, just as cleansing with water causes the baptismal character and spiritual cleansing, as stated above (Q. 63, A. 6; Q. 66, AA. 1, 3, 7). But the species of bread and wine, which are the objects of our senses in this sacrament, neither produce Christ's true body, which is both reality and sacrament, nor His mystical body, which is the reality only in the Eucharist. Therefore, it seems that the Eucharist is not a sacrament of the New Law.

Obj. 3: Further, sacraments of the New Law, as having matter, are perfected by the use of the matter, as Baptism is by ablution, and Confirmation by signing with chrism. If, then, the Eucharist be a sacrament, it would be perfected by the use of the matter, and not by its consecration. But this is manifestly false, because the words spoken in the consecration of the matter are the form of this sacrament, as will be shown later on (Q. 78, A. 1). Therefore the Eucharist is not a sacrament.

*On the contrary,* It is said in the Collect [*Postcommunion "pro vivis et defunctis"]: "May this Thy Sacrament not make us deserving of punishment."

*I answer that,* The Church's sacraments are ordained for helping man in the spiritual life. But the spiritual life is analogous to the corporeal, since corporeal things bear a resemblance to spiritual. Now it is clear that just as generation is required for corporeal life, since thereby man receives life; and growth, whereby man is brought to maturity: so likewise food is required for the preservation of life. Consequently, just as for the spiritual life there had to be Baptism, which is spiritual generation; and Confirmation, which is spiritual growth: so there needed to be the sacrament of the Eucharist, which is spiritual food.

Reply Obj. 1: Perfection is twofold. The first lies within man himself; and he attains it by growth: such perfection belongs to Confirmation. The other is the perfection which comes to man from the addition of food, or clothing, or something of the kind; and such is the perfection befitting the Eucharist, which is the spiritual refreshment.

Reply Obj. 2: The water of Baptism does not cause any spiritual effect by reason of the water, but by reason of the power of the Holy Ghost, which power is in the water. Hence on John 5:4, "An angel of the Lord at certain times," etc., Chrysostom observes: "The water does not act simply as such upon the baptized, but when it receives the grace of the Holy Ghost, then it looses all sins." But the true body of Christ bears the same relation to the species of the bread and wine, as the power of the Holy Ghost does to the water of Baptism: hence the species of the bread and wine produce no effect except from the virtue of Christ's true body.

Reply Obj. 3: A sacrament is so termed because it contains something sacred. Now a thing can be styled sacred from two causes; either absolutely, or in relation to something else. The difference between the Eucharist and other sacraments having sensible matter is that whereas the Eucharist contains something which is sacred absolutely, namely, Christ's own body; the baptismal water contains something which is sacred in relation to something else, namely, the sanctifying power: and the same holds good of chrism and such like. Consequently, the sacrament of the Eucharist is completed in the very consecration of the matter, whereas the other sacraments are completed in the application of the matter for the sanctifying of the individual. And from this follows another difference. For, in the sacrament of the Eucharist, what is both reality and sacrament is in the matter itself, but what is reality only, namely, the grace bestowed, is in the recipient; whereas in Baptism both are in the recipient, namely, the character, which is both reality and sacrament, and the grace of pardon of sins, which is reality only. And the same holds good of the other sacraments.

SECOND ARTICLE [III, Q. 73, Art. 2]

Whether the Eucharist Is One Sacrament or Several?

Objection 1: It seems that the Eucharist is not one sacrament but several, because it is said in the Collect [*Postcommunion "pro vivis et defunctis"]: "May the sacraments which we have received purify us, O Lord": and this is said on account of our receiving the Eucharist. Consequently the Eucharist is not one sacrament but several.

Obj. 2: Further, it is impossible for genera to be multiplied without the species being multiplied: thus it is impossible for one man to be many animals. But, as stated above (Q. 60, A. 1), sign is the genus of sacrament. Since, then, there are more signs than one, to wit, bread and wine, it seems to follow that here must be more sacraments than one.

Obj. 3: Further, this sacrament is perfected in the consecration of the matter, as stated above (A. 1, ad 3). But in this sacrament there is a double consecration of the matter. Therefore, it is a twofold sacrament.

*On the contrary,* The Apostle says (1 Cor. 10:17): "For we, being many, are one bread, one body, all that partake of one bread": from which it is clear that the Eucharist is the sacrament of the Church's unity. But a sacrament bears the likeness of the reality whereof it is the sacrament. Therefore the Eucharist is one sacrament.

*I answer that,* As stated in Metaph. v, a thing is said to be one, not only from being indivisible, or continuous, but also when it is complete; thus we speak of one house, and one man. A thing is one in perfection, when it is complete through the presence of all that is needed for its end; as a man is complete by having all the members required for the operation of his soul, and a house by having all the parts needful for dwelling therein. And so this sacrament is said to be one. Because it is ordained for spiritual refreshment, which is conformed to corporeal refreshment. Now there are two things required for corporeal refreshment, namely, food, which is dry sustenance, and drink, which is wet sustenance. Consequently, two things concur for the integrity of this sacrament, to wit, spiritual food and spiritual drink, according to John: "My flesh is meat indeed, and My blood is drink indeed." Therefore, this sacrament is materially many, but formally and perfectively one.

Reply Obj. 1: The same Collect at first employs the plural: "May the sacraments which we have received purify us"; and afterwards the singular number: "May this sacrament of Thine not make us worthy of punishment": so as to show that this sacrament is in a measure several, yet simply one.

Reply Obj. 2: The bread and wine are materially several signs, yet formally and perfectively one, inasmuch as one refreshment is prepared therefrom.

Reply Obj. 3: From the double consecration of the matter no more can be gathered than that the sacrament is several materially, as stated above.

THIRD ARTICLE [III, Q. 73, Art. 3]

Whether the Eucharist Is Necessary for Salvation?

Objection 1: It seems that this sacrament is necessary for salvation. For our Lord said (John 6:54): "Except you eat the flesh of the Son of Man, and drink His blood, you shall not have life in you." But Christ's flesh is eaten and His blood drunk in this sacrament. Therefore, without this sacrament man cannot have the health of spiritual life.

Obj. 2: Further, this sacrament is a kind of spiritual food. But bodily food is requisite for bodily health. Therefore, also is this sacrament, for spiritual health.

Obj. 3: Further, as Baptism is the sacrament of our Lord's Passion, without which there is no salvation, so also is the Eucharist. For the Apostle says (1 Cor. 11:26): "For as often as you shall eat this bread, and drink the chalice, you shall show the death of the Lord, until He come." Consequently, as Baptism is necessary for salvation, so also is this sacrament.

*On the contrary,* Augustine writes (Ad Bonifac. contra Pelag. I): "Nor are you to suppose that children cannot possess life, who are deprived of the body and blood of Christ."

*I answer that,* Two things have to be considered in this sacrament, namely, the sacrament itself, and what is contained in it. Now it was stated above (A. 1, Obj. 2) that the reality of the sacrament is the unity of the mystical body, without which there can be no salvation; for there is no entering into salvation outside the Church, just as in the time of the deluge there was none outside the Ark, which denotes the Church, according to 1 Pet. 3:20, 21. And it has been said above (Q. 68, A. 2), that before receiving a sacrament, the reality of the sacrament can be had through the very desire of receiving the sacrament. Accordingly, before actual reception of this sacrament, a man can obtain salvation through the desire of receiving it, just as he can before Baptism through the desire of Baptism, as stated above (Q. 68, A. 2). Yet there is a difference in two respects. First of all, because Baptism is the beginning of the spiritual life, and the door of the sacraments; whereas the Eucharist is, as it were, the consummation of the spiritual life, and the end of all the sacraments, as was observed above (Q. 63, A. 6): for by the hallowings of all the sacraments preparation is made for receiving or consecrating the Eucharist. Consequently, the reception of Baptism is necessary for starting the spiritual life, while the receiving of the Eucharist is requisite for its consummation; by partaking not indeed actually, but in desire, as an end is possessed in desire and intention. Another difference is because by Baptism a man is ordained to the Eucharist, and therefore from the fact of children being baptized, they are destined by the Church to the Eucharist; and just as they believe through the Church's faith, so they desire the Eucharist through the Church's intention, and, as a result, receive its reality. But they are not disposed for Baptism by any previous sacrament, and consequently before receiving Baptism, in no way have they Baptism in desire; but adults alone have: consequently, they cannot have the reality of the sacrament without receiving the sacrament itself. Therefore this sacrament is not necessary for salvation in the same way as Baptism is.

Reply Obj. 1: As Augustine says, explaining John 6:54, "This food and this drink," namely, of His flesh and blood: "He would have us understand the fellowship of His body and members, which is the Church in His predestinated, and called, and justified, and glorified, His holy and believing ones." Hence, as he says in his Epistle to Boniface (Pseudo-Beda, in 1 Cor. 10:17): "No one should entertain the slightest doubt, that then every one of the faithful becomes a partaker of the body and blood of Christ, when in Baptism he is made a member of Christ's body; nor is he deprived of his share in that body and chalice even though he depart from this world in the unity of Christ's body, before he eats that bread and drinks of that chalice."

Reply Obj. 2: The difference between corporeal and spiritual food lies in this, that the former is changed into the substance of the person nourished, and consequently it cannot avail for supporting life except it be partaken of; but spiritual food changes man into itself, according to that saying of Augustine (Confess. vii), that he heard the voice of Christ as it were saying to him: "Nor shalt thou change Me into thyself, as food of thy flesh, but thou shalt be changed into Me." But one can be changed into Christ, and be incorporated in Him by mental desire, even without receiving this sacrament. And consequently the comparison does not hold.

Reply Obj. 3: Baptism is the sacrament of Christ's death and Passion, according as a man is born anew in Christ in virtue of His Passion; but the Eucharist is the sacrament of Christ's Passion according as a man is made perfect in union with Christ Who suffered. Hence, as Baptism is called the sacrament of Faith, which is the foundation of the spiritual life, so the Eucharist is termed the sacrament of Charity, which is "the bond of perfection" (Col. 3:14).

FOURTH ARTICLE [III, Q. 73, Art. 4]

Whether This Sacrament Is Suitably Called by Various Names?

Objection 1: It seems that this sacrament is not suitably called by various names. For names should correspond with things. But this sacrament is one, as stated above (A. 2). Therefore, it ought not to be called by various names.

Obj. 2: Further, a species is not properly denominated by what is common to the whole genus. But the Eucharist is a sacrament of the New Law; and it is common to all the sacraments for grace to be conferred by them, which the name "Eucharist" denotes, for it is the same thing as "good grace." Furthermore, all the sacraments bring us help on our journey through this present life, which is the notion conveyed by "Viaticum." Again something sacred is done in all the sacraments, which belongs to the notion of "Sacrifice"; and the faithful intercommunicate through all the sacraments, which this Greek word Synaxis and the Latin Communio express. Therefore, these names are not suitably adapted to this sacrament.

Obj. 3: Further, a host [*From Latin hostia, a victim] seems to be the same as a sacrifice. Therefore, as it is not properly called a sacrifice, so neither is it properly termed a "Host."

*On the contrary,* is the use of these expressions by the faithful.

*I answer that,* This sacrament has a threefold significance. One with regard to the past, inasmuch as it is commemorative of our Lord's Passion, which was a true sacrifice, as stated above (Q. 48, A. 3), and in this respect it is called a "Sacrifice."

With regard to the present it has another meaning, namely, that of Ecclesiastical unity, in which men are aggregated through this Sacrament; and in this respect it is called "Communion" or Synaxis . For Damascene says (De Fide Orth. iv) that "it is called Communion because we communicate with Christ through it, both because we partake of His flesh and Godhead, and because we communicate with and are united to one another through it."

With regard to the future it has a third meaning, inasmuch as this sacrament foreshadows the Divine fruition, which shall come to pass in heaven; and according to this it is called "Viaticum," because it supplies the way of winning thither. And in this respect it is also called the "Eucharist," that is, "good grace," because "the grace of God is life everlasting" (Rom. 6:23); or because it really contains Christ, Who is "full of grace."

In Greek, moreover, it is called Metalepsis , i.e. "Assumption," because, as Damascene says (De Fide Orth. iv), "we thereby assume the Godhead of the Son."

Reply Obj. 1: There is nothing to hinder the same thing from being called by several names, according to its various properties or effects.

Reply Obj. 2: What is common to all the sacraments is attributed antonomastically to this one on account of its excellence.

Reply Obj. 3: This sacrament is called a "Sacrifice" inasmuch as it represents the Passion of Christ; but it is termed a "Host" inasmuch as it contains Christ, Who is "a host (Douay: 'sacrifice') . . . of sweetness" (Eph. 5:2).

FIFTH ARTICLE [III, Q. 73, Art. 5]

Whether the Institution of This Sacrament Was Appropriate?

Objection 1: It seems that the institution of this sacrament was not appropriate, because as the Philosopher says (De Gener. ii): "We are nourished by the things from whence we spring." But by Baptism, which is spiritual regeneration, we receive our spiritual being, as Dionysius says (Eccl. Hier. ii). Therefore we are also nourished by Baptism. Consequently there was no need to institute this sacrament as spiritual nourishment.

Obj. 2: Further, men are united with Christ through this sacrament as the members with the head. But Christ is the Head of all men, even of those who have existed from the beginning of the world, as stated above (Q. 8, AA. 3, 6). Therefore the institution of this sacrament should not have been postponed till the Lord's supper.

Obj. 3: Further, this sacrament is called the memorial of our Lord's Passion, according to Matt. 26 (Luke 22:19): "Do this for a commemoration of Me." But a commemoration is of things past. Therefore, this sacrament should not have been instituted before Christ's Passion.

Obj. 4: Further, a man is prepared by Baptism for the Eucharist, which ought to be given only to the baptized. But Baptism was instituted by Christ after His Passion and Resurrection, as is evident from Matt. 28:19. Therefore, this sacrament was not suitably instituted before Christ's Passion.

*On the contrary,* This sacrament was instituted by Christ, of Whom it is said (Mk. 7:37) that "He did all things well."

*I answer that,* This sacrament was appropriately instituted at the supper, when Christ conversed with His disciples for the last time. First of all, because of what is contained in the sacrament: for Christ is Himself contained in the Eucharist sacramentally. Consequently, when Christ was going to leave His disciples in His proper species, He left Himself with them under the sacramental species; as the Emperor's image is set up to be reverenced in his absence. Hence Eusebius says: "Since He was going to withdraw His assumed body from their eyes, and bear it away to the stars, it was needful that on the day of the supper He should consecrate the sacrament of His body and blood for our sakes, in order that what was once offered up for our ransom should be fittingly worshiped in a mystery."

Secondly, because without faith in the Passion there could never be any salvation, according to Rom. 3:25: "Whom God hath proposed to be a propitiation, through faith in His blood." It was necessary accordingly that there should be at all times among men something to show forth our Lord's Passion; the chief sacrament of which in the old Law was the Paschal Lamb. Hence the Apostle says (1 Cor. 5:7): "Christ our Pasch is sacrificed." But its successor under the New Testament is the sacrament of the Eucharist, which is a remembrance of the Passion now past, just as the other was figurative of the Passion to come. And so it was fitting that when the hour of the Passion was come, Christ should institute a new Sacrament after celebrating the old, as Pope Leo I says (Serm. lviii).

Thirdly, because last words, chiefly such as are spoken by departing friends, are committed most deeply to memory; since then especially affection for friends is more enkindled, and the things which affect us most are impressed the deepest in the soul. Consequently, since, as Pope Alexander I says, "among sacrifices there can be none greater than the body and blood of Christ, nor any more powerful oblation"; our Lord instituted this sacrament at His last parting with His disciples, in order that it might be held in the greater veneration. And this is what Augustine says (Respons. ad Januar. i): "In order to commend more earnestly the death of this mystery, our Saviour willed this last act to be fixed in the hearts and memories of the disciples whom He was about to quit for the Passion."

Reply Obj. 1: We are nourished from the same things of which we are made, but they do not come to us in the same way; for those out of which we are made come to us through generation, while the same, as nourishing us, come to us through being eaten. Hence, as we are new-born in Christ through Baptism, so through the Eucharist we eat Christ.

Reply Obj. 2: The Eucharist is the perfect sacrament of our Lord's Passion, as containing Christ crucified; consequently it could not be instituted before the Incarnation; but then there was room for only such sacraments as were prefigurative of the Lord's Passion.

Reply Obj. 3: This sacrament was instituted during the supper, so as in the future to be a memorial of our Lord's Passion as accomplished. Hence He said expressively: "As often as ye shall do these things" [*Cf. Canon of the Mass], speaking of the future.

Reply Obj. 4: The institution responds to the order of intention. But the sacrament of the Eucharist, although after Baptism in the receiving, is yet previous to it in intention; and therefore it behooved to be instituted first. Or else it can be said that Baptism was already instituted in Christ's Baptism; hence some were already baptized with Christ's Baptism, as we read in John 3:22.

SIXTH ARTICLE [III, Q. 73, Art. 6]

Whether the Paschal Lamb Was the Chief Figure of This Sacrament?

Objection 1: It seems that the Paschal Lamb was not the chief figure of this sacrament, because (Ps. 109:4) Christ is called "a priest according to the order of Melchisedech," since Melchisedech bore the figure of Christ's sacrifice, in offering bread and wine. But the expression of likeness causes one thing to be named from another. Therefore, it seems that Melchisedech's offering was the principal figure of this sacrament.

Obj. 2: Further, the passage of the Red Sea was a figure of Baptism, according to 1 Cor. 10:2: "All . . . were baptized in the cloud and in the sea." But the immolation of the Paschal Lamb was previous to the passage of the Red Sea, and the Manna came after it, just as the Eucharist follows Baptism. Therefore the Manna is a more expressive figure of this sacrament than the Paschal Lamb.

Obj. 3: Further, the principal power of this sacrament is that it brings us into the kingdom of heaven, being a kind of "viaticum." But this was chiefly prefigured in the sacrament of expiation when the "high-priest entered once a year into the Holy of Holies with blood," as the Apostle proves in Heb. 9. Consequently, it seems that that sacrifice was a more significant figure of this sacrament than was the Paschal Lamb.

*On the contrary,* The Apostle says (1 Cor. 5:7, 8): "Christ our Pasch is sacrificed; therefore let us feast . . . with the unleavened bread of sincerity and truth."

*I answer that,* We can consider three things in this sacrament: namely, that which is sacrament only, and this is the bread and wine; that which is both reality and sacrament, to wit, Christ's true body; and lastly that which is reality only, namely, the effect of this sacrament. Consequently, in relation to what is sacrament only, the chief figure of this sacrament was the oblation of Melchisedech, who offered up bread and wine. In relation to Christ crucified, Who is contained in this sacrament, its figures were all the sacrifices of the Old Testament, especially the sacrifice of expiation, which was the most solemn of all. While with regard to its effect, the chief figure was the Manna, "having in it the sweetness of every taste" (Wis. 16:20), just as the grace of this sacrament refreshes the soul in all respects.

The Paschal Lamb foreshadowed this sacrament in these three ways. First of all, because it was eaten with unleavened loaves, according to Ex. 12:8: "They shall eat flesh . . . and unleavened bread." As to the second because it was immolated by the entire multitude of the children of Israel on the fourteenth day of the moon; and this was a figure of the Passion of Christ, Who is called the Lamb on account of His innocence. As to the effect, because by the blood of the Paschal Lamb the children of Israel were preserved from the destroying Angel, and brought from the Egyptian captivity; and in this respect the Paschal Lamb is the chief figure of this sacrament, because it represents it in every respect.

From this the answer to the Objections is manifest.

## QUESTION 74

OF THE MATTER OF THIS SACRAMENT (In Eight Articles)

We have now to consider the matter of this sacrament: and first of all as to its species; secondly, the change of the bread and wine into the body of Christ; thirdly, the manner in which Christ's body exists in this sacrament; fourthly, the accidents of bread and wine which continue in this sacrament.

Under the first heading there are eight points for inquiry:

(1) Whether bread and wine are the matter of this sacrament?

(2) Whether a determinate quantity of the same is required for the matter of this sacrament?

(3) Whether the matter of this sacrament is wheaten bread?

(4) Whether it is unleavened or fermented bread?

(5) Whether the matter of this sacrament is wine from the grape?

(6) Whether water should be mixed with it?

(7) Whether water is of necessity for this sacrament?

(8) Of the quantity of the water added.

FIRST ARTICLE [III, Q. 74, Art. 1]

Whether the Matter of This Sacrament Is Bread and Wine?

Objection 1: It seems that the matter of this sacrament is not bread and wine. Because this sacrament ought to represent Christ's Passion more fully than did the sacraments of the Old Law. But the flesh of animals, which was the matter of the sacraments under the Old Law, shows forth Christ's Passion more fully than bread and wine. Therefore the matter of this sacrament ought rather to be the flesh of animals than bread and wine.

Obj. 2: Further, this sacrament is to be celebrated in every place. But in many lands bread is not to be found, and in many places wine is not to be found. Therefore bread and wine are not a suitable matter for this sacrament.

Obj. 3: Further, this sacrament is for both hale and weak. But to some weak persons wine is hurtful. Therefore it seems that wine ought not to be the matter of this sacrament.

*On the contrary,* Pope Alexander I says (Ep. ad omnes orth. i): "In oblations of the sacraments only bread and wine mixed with water are to be offered."

*I answer that,* Some have fallen into various errors about the matter of this sacrament. Some, known as the Artotyrytae, as Augustine says (De Haeres. xxviii), "offer bread and cheese in this sacrament, contending that oblations were celebrated by men in the first ages, from fruits of the earth and sheep." Others, called Cataphrygae and Pepuziani, "are reputed to have made their Eucharistic bread with infants' blood drawn from tiny punctures over the entire body, and mixed with flour." Others, styled Aquarii, under guise of sobriety, offer nothing but water in this sacrament.

Now all these and similar errors are excluded by the fact that Christ instituted this sacrament under the species of bread and wine, as is evident from Matt. 26. Consequently, bread and wine are the proper matter of this sacrament. And the reasonableness of this is seen first, in the use of this sacrament, which is eating: for, as water is used in the sacrament of Baptism for the purpose of spiritual cleansing, since bodily cleansing is commonly done with water; so bread and wine, wherewith men are commonly fed, are employed in this sacrament for the use of spiritual eating.

Secondly, in relation to Christ's Passion, in which the blood was separated from the body. And therefore in this sacrament, which is the memorial of our Lord's Passion, the bread is received apart as the sacrament of the body, and the wine as the sacrament of the blood.

Thirdly, as to the effect, considered in each of the partakers. For, as Ambrose (Mag. Sent. iv, D, xi) says on 1 Cor. 11:20, this sacrament "avails for the defense of soul and body"; and therefore "Christ's body is offered" under the species of bread "for the health of the body, and the blood" under the species of wine "for the health of the soul," according to Lev. 17:14: "The life of the animal [Vulg.: 'of all flesh'] is in the blood."

Fourthly, as to the effect with regard to the whole Church, which is made up of many believers, just "as bread is composed of many grains, and wine flows from many grapes," as the gloss observes on 1 Cor. 10:17: "We being many are . . . one body," etc.

Reply Obj. 1: Although the flesh of slaughtered animals represents the Passion more forcibly, nevertheless it is less suitable for the common use of this sacrament, and for denoting the unity of the Church.

Reply Obj. 2: Although wheat and wine are not produced in every country, yet they can easily be conveyed to every land, that is, as much as is needful for the use of this sacrament: at the same time one is not to be consecrated when the other is lacking, because it would not be a complete sacrament.

Reply Obj. 3: Wine taken in small quantity cannot do the sick much harm: yet if there be fear of harm, it is not necessary for all who take Christ's body to partake also of His blood, as will be stated later (Q. 80, A. 12).

SECOND ARTICLE [III, Q. 74, Art. 2]

Whether a Determinate Quantity of Bread and Wine Is Required for the Matter of This Sacrament?

Objection 1: It seems that a determinate quantity of bread and wine is required for the matter of this sacrament. Because the effects of grace are no less set in order than those of nature. But, "there is a limit set by nature upon all existing things, and a reckoning of size and development" (De Anima ii). Consequently, in this sacrament, which is called "Eucharist," that is, "a good grace," a determinate quantity of the bread and wine is required.

Obj. 2: Further, Christ gave no power to the ministers of the Church regarding matters which involve derision of the faith and of His sacraments, according to 2 Cor. 10:8: "Of our power which the Lord hath given us unto edification, and not for your destruction." But it would lead to mockery of this sacrament if the priest were to wish to consecrate all the bread which is sold in the market and all the wine in the cellar. Therefore he cannot do this.

Obj. 3: Further, if anyone be baptized in the sea, the entire sea-water is not sanctified by the form of baptism, but only the water wherewith the body of the baptized is cleansed. Therefore, neither in this sacrament can a superfluous quantity of bread be consecrated.

*On the contrary,* Much is opposed to little, and great to small. But there is no quantity, however small, of the bread and wine which cannot be consecrated. Therefore, neither is there any quantity, however great, which cannot be consecrated.

*I answer that,* Some have maintained that the priest could not consecrate an immense quantity of bread and wine, for instance, all the bread in the market or all the wine in a cask. But this does not appear to be true, because in all things containing matter, the reason for the determination of the matter is drawn from its disposition to an end, just as the matter of a saw is iron, so as to adapt it for cutting. But the end of this sacrament is the use of the faithful. Consequently, the quantity of the matter of this sacrament must be determined by comparison with the use of the faithful. But this cannot be determined by comparison with the use of the faithful who are actually present; otherwise the parish priest having few parishioners could not consecrate many hosts. It remains, then, for the matter of this sacrament to be determined in reference to the number of the faithful absolutely. But the number of the faithful is not a determinate one. Hence it cannot be said that the quantity of the matter of this sacrament is restricted.

Reply Obj. 1: The matter of every natural object has its determinate quantity by comparison with its determinate form. But the number of the faithful, for whose use this sacrament is ordained, is not a determinate one. Consequently there is no comparison.

Reply Obj. 2: The power of the Church's ministers is ordained for two purposes: first for the proper effect, and secondly for the end of the effect. But the second does not take away the first. Hence, if the priest intends to consecrate the body of Christ for an evil purpose, for instance, to make mockery of it, or to administer poison through it, he commits sin by his evil intention, nevertheless, on account of the power committed to him, he accomplishes the sacrament.

Reply Obj. 3: The sacrament of Baptism is perfected in the use of the matter: and therefore no more of the water is hallowed than what is used. But this sacrament is wrought in the consecration of the matter. Consequently there is no parallel.

THIRD ARTICLE [III, Q. 74, Art. 3]

Whether Wheaten Bread Is Required for the Matter of This Sacrament?

Objection 1: It seems that wheaten bread is not requisite for the matter of this sacrament, because this sacrament is a reminder of our Lord's Passion. But barley bread seems to be more in keeping with the Passion than wheaten bread, as being more bitter, and because Christ used it to feed the multitudes upon the mountain, as narrated in John 6. Therefore wheaten bread is not the proper matter of this sacrament.

Obj. 2: Further, in natural things the shape is a sign of species. But some cereals resemble wheat, such as spelt and maize, from which in some localities bread is made for the use of this sacrament. Therefore wheaten bread is not the proper matter of this sacrament.

Obj. 3: Further, mixing dissolves species. But wheaten flour is hardly to be found unmixed with some other species of grain, except in the instance of specially selected grain. Therefore it does not seem that wheaten bread is the proper matter for this sacrament.

Obj. 4: Further, what is corrupted appears to be of another species. But some make the sacrament from bread which is corrupted, and which no longer seems to be wheaten bread. Therefore, it seems that such bread is not the proper matter of this sacrament.

*On the contrary,* Christ is contained in this sacrament, and He compares Himself to a grain of wheat, saying (John 12:24): "Unless the grain of wheat falling into the ground die, itself remaineth alone." Therefore bread from corn, i.e. wheaten bread, is the matter of this sacrament.

*I answer that,* As stated above (A. 1), for the use of the sacraments such matter is adopted as is commonly made use of among men. Now among other breads wheaten bread is more commonly used by men; since other breads seem to be employed when this fails. And consequently Christ is believed to have instituted this sacrament under this species of bread. Moreover this bread strengthens man, and so it denotes more suitably the effect of this sacrament. Consequently, the proper matter for this sacrament is wheaten bread.

Reply Obj. 1: Barley bread serves to denote the hardness of the Old Law; both on account of the hardness of the bread, and because, as Augustine says (Q. 83): "The flour within the barley, wrapped up as it is within a most tenacious fibre, denotes either the Law itself, which was given in such manner as to be vested in bodily sacraments; or else it denotes the people themselves, who were not yet despoiled of carnal desires, which clung to their hearts like fibre." But this sacrament belongs to Christ's "sweet yoke," and to the truth already manifested, and to a spiritual people. Consequently barley bread would not be a suitable matter for this sacrament.

Reply Obj. 2: A begetter begets a thing like to itself in species, yet there is some unlikeness as to the accidents, owing either to the matter, or to weakness within the generative power. And therefore, if there be any cereals which can be grown from the seed of the wheat (as wild wheat from wheat seed grown in bad ground), the bread made from such grain can be the matter of this sacrament: and this does not obtain either in barley, or in spelt, or even in maize, which is of all grains the one most resembling the wheat grain. But the resemblance as to shape in such seems to denote closeness of species rather than identity; just as the resemblance in shape between the dog and the wolf goes to show that they are allied but not of the same species. Hence from such grains, which cannot in any way be generated from wheat grain, bread cannot be made such as to be the proper matter of this sacrament.

Reply Obj. 3: A moderate mixing does not alter the species, because that little is as it were absorbed by the greater. Consequently, then, if a small quantity of another grain be mixed with a much greater quantity of wheat, bread may be made therefrom so as to be the proper matter of this sacrament; but if the mixing be notable, for instance, half and half; or nearly so, then such mixing alters the species; consequently, bread made therefrom will not be the proper matter of this sacrament.

Reply Obj. 4: Sometimes there is such corruption of the bread that the species of bread is lost, as when the continuity of its parts is destroyed, and the taste, color, and other accidents are changed; hence the body of Christ may not be made from such matter. But sometimes there is not such corruption as to alter the species, but merely disposition towards corruption, which a slight change in the savor betrays, and from such bread the body of Christ may be made: but he who does so, sins from irreverence towards the sacrament. And because starch comes of corrupted wheat, it does not seem as if the body of Christ could be made of the bread made therefrom, although some hold the contrary.

FOURTH ARTICLE [III, Q. 74, Art. 4]

Whether This Sacrament Ought to Be Made of Unleavened Bread?

Objection 1: It seems that this sacrament ought not to be made of unleavened bread. Because in this sacrament we ought to imitate Christ's institution. But Christ appears to have instituted this sacrament in fermented bread, because, as we have read in Ex. 12, the Jews, according to the Law, began to use unleavened bread on the day of the Passover which is celebrated on the fourteenth day of the moon; and Christ instituted this sacrament at the supper which He celebrated "before the festival day of the Pasch" (John 13:1, 4). Therefore we ought likewise to celebrate this sacrament with fermented bread.

Obj. 2: Further, legal observances ought not to be continued in the time of grace. But the use of unleavened bread was a ceremony of the Law, as is clear from Ex. 12. Therefore we ought not to use unfermented bread in this sacrament of grace.

Obj. 3: Further, as stated above (Q. 65, A. 1; Q. 73, A. 3), the Eucharist is the sacrament of charity just as Baptism is the sacrament of faith. But the fervor of charity is signified by fermented bread, as is declared by the gloss on Matt. 13:33: "The kingdom of heaven is like unto leaven," etc. Therefore this sacrament ought to be made of leavened bread.

Obj. 4: Further, leavened or unleavened are mere accidents of bread, which do not vary the species. But in the matter for the sacrament of Baptism no difference is observed regarding the variation of the accidents, as to whether it be salt or fresh, warm or cold water. Therefore neither ought any distinction to be observed, as to whether the bread be unleavened or leavened.

*On the contrary,* According to the Decretals (Extra, De Celebr. Miss.), a priest is punished "for presuming to celebrate, using fermented bread and a wooden cup."

*I answer that,* Two things may be considered touching the matter of this sacrament, namely, what is necessary, and what is suitable. It is necessary that the bread be wheaten, without which the sacrament is not valid, as stated above (A. 3). It is not, however, necessary for the sacrament that the bread be unleavened or leavened, since it can be celebrated in either.

But it is suitable that every priest observe the rite of his Church in the celebration of the sacrament. Now in this matter there are various customs of the Churches: for, Gregory says: "The Roman Church offers unleavened bread, because our Lord took flesh without union of sexes: but the Greek Churches offer leavened bread, because the Word of the Father was clothed with flesh; as leaven is mixed with the flour." Hence, as a priest sins by celebrating with fermented bread in the Latin Church, so a Greek priest celebrating with unfermented bread in a church of the Greeks would also sin, as perverting the rite of his Church. Nevertheless the custom of celebrating with unleavened bread is more reasonable. First, on account of Christ's institution: for He instituted this sacrament "on the first day of the Azymes" (Matt. 26:17; Mk. 14:12; Luke 22:7), on which day there ought to be nothing fermented in the houses of the Jews, as is stated in Ex. 12:15, 19. Secondly, because bread is properly the sacrament of Christ's body, which was conceived without corruption, rather than of His Godhead, as will be seen later (Q. 76, A. 1, ad 1). Thirdly, because this is more in keeping with the sincerity of the faithful, which is required in the use of this sacrament, according to 1 Cor. 5:7: "Christ our Pasch is sacrificed: therefore let us feast . . . with the unleavened bread of sincerity and truth."

However, this custom of the Greeks is not unreasonable both on account of its signification, to which Gregory refers, and in detestation of the heresy of the Nazarenes, who mixed up legal observances with the Gospel.

Reply Obj. 1: As we read in Ex. 12, the paschal solemnity began on the evening of the fourteenth day of the moon. So, then, after immolating the Paschal Lamb, Christ instituted this sacrament: hence this day is said by John to precede the day of the Pasch, while the other three Evangelists call it "the first day of the Azymes," when fermented bread was not found in the houses of the Jews, as stated above. Fuller mention was made of this in the treatise on our Lord's Passion (Q. 46, A. 9, ad 1).

Reply Obj. 2: Those who celebrate the sacrament with unleavened bread do not intend to follow the ceremonial of the Law, but to conform to Christ's institution; so they are not Judaizing; otherwise those celebrating in fermented bread would be Judaizing, because the Jews offered up fermented bread for the first-fruits.

Reply Obj. 3: Leaven denotes charity on account of one single effect, because it makes the bread more savory and larger; but it also signifies corruption from its very nature.

Reply Obj. 4: Since whatever is fermented partakes of corruption, this sacrament may not be made from corrupt bread, as stated above (A. 3, ad 4); consequently, there is a wider difference between unleavened and leavened bread than between warm and cold baptismal water: because there might be such corruption of fermented bread that it could not be validly used for the sacrament.

FIFTH ARTICLE [III, Q. 74, Art. 5]

Whether Wine of the Grape Is the Proper Matter of This Sacrament?

Objection 1: It seems that wine of the grape is not the proper matter of this sacrament. Because, as water is the matter of Baptism, so is wine the matter of this sacrament. But Baptism can be conferred with any kind of water. Therefore this sacrament can be celebrated in any kind of wine, such as of pomegranates, or of mulberries; since vines do not grow in some countries.

Obj. 2: Further, vinegar is a kind of wine drawn from the grape, as Isidore says (Etym. xx). But this sacrament cannot be celebrated with vinegar. Therefore, it seems that wine from the grape is not the proper matter of this sacrament.

Obj. 3: Further, just as the clarified wine is drawn from grapes, so also are the juice of unripe grapes and must. But it does not appear that this sacrament may be made from such, according to what we read in the Sixth Council (Trull., Can. 28): "We have learned that in some churches the priests add grapes to the sacrifice of the oblation; and so they dispense both together to the people. Consequently we give order that no priest shall do this in future." And Pope Julius I rebukes some priests "who offer wine pressed from the grape in the sacrament of the Lord's chalice." Consequently, it seems that wine from the grape is not the proper matter of this sacrament.

*On the contrary,* As our Lord compared Himself to the grain of wheat, so also He compared Himself to the vine, saying (John 15:1): "I am the true vine." But only bread from wheat is the matter of this sacrament, as stated above (A. 3). Therefore, only wine from the grape is the proper matter of this sacrament.

*I answer that,* This sacrament can only be performed with wine from the grape. First of all on account of Christ's institution, since He instituted this sacrament in wine from the grape, as is evident from His own words, in instituting this sacrament (Matt. 26:29): "I will not drink from henceforth of this fruit of the vine." Secondly, because, as stated above (A. 3), that is adopted as the matter of the sacraments which is properly and universally considered as such. Now that is properly called wine, which is drawn from the grape, whereas other liquors are called wine from resemblance to the wine of the grape. Thirdly, because the wine from the grape is more in keeping with the effect of this sacrament, which is spiritual; because it is written (Ps. 103:15): "That wine may cheer the heart of man."

Reply Obj. 1: Such liquors are called wine, not properly but only from their resemblance thereto. But genuine wine can be conveyed to such countries wherein the grape-vine does not flourish, in a quantity sufficient for this sacrament.

Reply Obj. 2: Wine becomes vinegar by corruption; hence there is no returning from vinegar to wine, as is said in Metaph. viii. And consequently, just as this sacrament may not be made from bread which is utterly corrupt, so neither can it be made from vinegar. It can, however, be made from wine which is turning sour, just as from bread turning corrupt, although he who does so sins, as stated above (A. 3).

Reply Obj. 3: The juice of unripe grapes is at the stage of incomplete generation, and therefore it has not yet the species of wine: on which account it may not be used for this sacrament. Must, however, has already the species of wine, for its sweetness [*"Aut dulcis musti Vulcano decoquit humorem"; Virgil, Georg. i, 295] indicates fermentation which is "the result of its natural heat" (Meteor. iv); consequently this sacrament can be made from must. Nevertheless entire grapes ought not to be mixed with this sacrament, because then there would be something else besides wine. It is furthermore forbidden to offer must in the chalice, as soon as it has been squeezed from the grape, since this is unbecoming owing to the impurity of the must. But in case of necessity it may be done: for it is said by the same Pope Julius, in the passage quoted in the argument: "If necessary, let the grape be pressed into the chalice."

SIXTH ARTICLE [III, Q. 74, Art. 6]

Whether Water Should Be Mixed with the Wine?

Objection 1: It seems that water ought not to be mixed with the wine, since Christ's sacrifice was foreshadowed by that of Melchisedech, who (Gen. 14:18) is related to have offered up bread and wine only. Consequently it seems that water should not be added in this sacrament.

Obj. 2: Further, the various sacraments have their respective matters. But water is the matter of Baptism. Therefore it should not be employed as the matter of this sacrament.

Obj. 3: Further, bread and wine are the matter of this sacrament. But nothing is added to the bread. Therefore neither should anything be added to the wine.

*On the contrary,* Pope Alexander I writes (Ep. 1 ad omnes orth.): "In the sacramental oblations which in mass are offered to the Lord, only bread and wine mixed with water are to be offered in sacrifice."

*I answer that,* Water ought to be mingled with the wine which is offered in this sacrament. First of all on account of its institution: for it is believed with probability that our Lord instituted this sacrament in wine tempered with water according to the custom of that country: hence it is written (Prov. 9:5): "Drink the wine which I have mixed for you." Secondly, because it harmonizes with the representation of our Lord's Passion: hence Pope Alexander I says (Ep. 1 ad omnes orth.): "In the Lord's chalice neither wine only nor water only ought to be offered, but both mixed because we read that both flowed from His side in the Passion." Thirdly, because this is adapted for signifying the effect of this sacrament, since as Pope Julius says (Concil. Bracarens iii, Can. 1): "We see that the people are signified by the water, but Christ's blood by the wine. Therefore when water is mixed with the wine in the chalice, the people is made one with Christ." Fourthly, because this is appropriate to the fourth effect of this sacrament, which is the entering into everlasting life: hence Ambrose says (De Sacram. v): "The water flows into the chalice, and springs forth unto everlasting life."

Reply Obj. 1: As Ambrose says (De Sacram. v), just as Christ's sacrifice is denoted by the offering of Melchisedech, so likewise it is signified by the water which flowed from the rock in the desert, according to 1 Cor. 10:4: "But they drank of the spiritual rock which came after them."

Reply Obj. 2: In Baptism water is used for the purpose of ablution: but in this sacrament it is used by way of refreshment, according to Ps. 22:3: "He hath brought me up on the water of refreshment."

Reply Obj. 3: Bread is made of water and flour; and therefore, since water is mixed with the wine, neither is without water.

SEVENTH ARTICLE [III, Q. 74, Art. 7]

Whether the Mixing with Water Is Essential to This Sacrament?

Objection 1: It seems that the mixing with water is essential to this sacrament. Because Cyprian says to Cecilius (Ep. lxiii): "Thus the Lord's chalice is not water only and wine only, but both must be mixed together: in the same way as neither the Lord's body be of flour only, except both," i.e. the flour and the water "be united as one." But the admixture of water with the flour is necessary for this sacrament. Consequently, for the like reason, so is the mixing of water with the wine.

Obj. 2: Further, at our Lord's Passion, of which this is the memorial, water as well as blood flowed from His side. But wine, which is the sacrament of the blood, is necessary for this sacrament. For the same reason, therefore, so is water.

Obj. 3: Further, if water were not essential to this sacrament, it would not matter in the least what kind of water was used; and so water distilled from roses, or any other kind might be employed; which is contrary to the usage of the Church. Consequently water is essential to this sacrament.

*On the contrary,* Cyprian says (Ep. lxiii): "If any of our predecessors, out of ignorance or simplicity, has not kept this usage," i.e. of mixing water with the wine, "one may pardon his simplicity"; which would not be the case if water were essential to the sacrament, as the wine or the bread. Therefore the mingling of water with the wine is not essential to the sacrament.

*I answer that,* Judgment concerning a sign is to be drawn from the thing signified. Now the adding of water to the wine is for the purpose of signifying the sharing of this sacrament by the faithful, in this respect that by the mixing of the water with the wine is signified the union of the people with Christ, as stated (A. 6). Moreover, the flowing of water from the side of Christ hanging on the cross refers to the same, because by the water is denoted the cleansing from sins, which was the effect of Christ's Passion. Now it was observed above (Q. 73, A. 1, ad 3), that this sacrament is completed in the consecration of the matter: while the usage of the faithful is not essential to the sacrament, but only a consequence thereof. Consequently, then, the adding of water is not essential to the sacrament.

Reply Obj. 1: Cyprian's expression is to be taken in the same sense in which we say that a thing cannot be, which cannot be suitably. And so the comparison refers to what ought to be done, not to what is essential to be done; since water is of the essence of bread, but not of the essence of wine.

Reply Obj. 2: The shedding of the blood belonged directly to Christ's Passion: for it is natural for blood to flow from a wounded human body. But the flowing of the water was not necessary for the Passion; but merely to show its effect, which is to wash away sins, and to refresh us from the heat of concupiscence. And therefore the water is not offered apart from the wine in this sacrament, as the wine is offered apart from the bread; but the water is offered mixed with the wine to show that the wine belongs of itself to this sacrament, as of its very essence; but the water as something added to the wine.

Reply Obj. 3: Since the mixing of water with the wine is not necessary for the sacrament, it does not matter, as to the essence of the sacrament, what kind of water is added to the wine, whether natural water, or artificial, as rose-water, although, as to the propriety of the sacrament, he would sin who mixes any other than natural and true water, because true water flowed from the side of Christ hanging on the cross, and not phlegm, as some have said, in order to show that Christ's body was truly composed of the four elements; as by the flowing blood, it was shown to be composed of the four humors, as Pope Innocent III says in a certain Decree. But because the mixing of water with flour is essential to this sacrament, as making the composition of bread, if rose-water, or any other liquor besides true water, be mixed with the flour, the sacrament would not be valid, because it would not be true bread.

EIGHTH ARTICLE [III, Q. 74, Art. 8]

Whether Water Should Be Added in Great Quantity?

Objection 1: It seems that water ought to be added in great quantity, because as blood flowed sensibly from Christ's side, so did water: hence it is written (John 19:35): "He that saw it, hath given testimony." But water could not be sensibly present in this sacrament except it were used in great quantity. Consequently it seems that water ought to be added in great quantity.

Obj. 2: Further, a little water mixed with much wine is corrupted. But what is corrupted no longer exists. Therefore, it is the same thing to add a little water in this sacrament as to add none. But it is not lawful to add none. Therefore, neither is it lawful to add a little.

Obj. 3: Further, if it sufficed to add a little, then as a consequence it would suffice to throw one drop of water into an entire cask. But this seems ridiculous. Therefore it does not suffice for a small quantity to be added.

*On the contrary,* It is said in the Decretals (Extra, De Celeb. Miss.): "The pernicious abuse has prevailed in your country of adding water in greater quantity than the wine, in the sacrifice, where according to the reasonable custom of the entire Church more wine than water ought to be employed."

*I answer that,* There is a threefold opinion regarding the water added to the wine, as Pope Innocent III says in a certain Decretal. For some say that the water remains by itself when the wine is changed into blood: but such an opinion cannot stand, because in the sacrament of the altar after the consecration there is nothing else save the body and the blood of Christ. Because, as Ambrose says in De Officiis (De Mysteriis ix): "Before the blessing it is another species that is named, after the blessing the Body is signified; otherwise it would not be adored with adoration of latria." And therefore others have said that as the wine is changed into blood, so the water is changed into the water which flowed from Christ's side. But this cannot be maintained reasonably, because according to this the water would be consecrated apart from the wine, as the wine is from the bread.

And therefore as he (Innocent III, Decretals, Extra, De Celeb. Miss.) says, the more probable opinion is that which holds that the water is changed into wine, and the wine into blood. Now, this could not be done unless so little water was used that it would be changed into wine. Consequently, it is always safer to add little water, especially if the wine be weak, because the sacrament could not be celebrated if there were such addition of water as to destroy the species of the wine. Hence Pope Julius I reprehends some who "keep throughout the year a linen cloth steeped in must, and at the time of sacrifice wash a part of it with water, and so make the offering."

Reply Obj. 1: For the signification of this sacrament it suffices for the water to be appreciable by sense when it is mixed with the wine: but it is not necessary for it to be sensible after the mingling.

Reply Obj. 2: If no water were added, the signification would be utterly excluded: but when the water is changed into wine, it is signified that the people is incorporated with Christ.

Reply Obj. 3: If water were added to a cask, it would not suffice for the signification of this sacrament, but the water must be added to the wine at the actual celebration of the sacrament.

## QUESTION 75

OF THE CHANGE OF BREAD AND WINE INTO THE BODY AND BLOOD OF CHRIST (In Eight Articles)

We have to consider the change of the bread and wine into the body and blood of Christ; under which head there are eight points of inquiry:

(1) Whether the substance of bread and wine remain in this sacrament after the consecration?*

(2) Whether it is annihilated?

(3) Whether it is changed into the body and blood of Christ?

(4) Whether the accidents remain after the change?

(5) Whether the substantial form remains there?

(6) Whether this change is instantaneous?

(7) Whether it is more miraculous than any other change?

(8) By what words it may be suitably expressed?

[*The titles of the Articles here given were taken by St. Thomas from his Commentary on the Sentences (Sent. iv, D, 90). However, in writing the Articles he introduced a new point of inquiry, that of the First Article; and substituted another division of the matter under discussion, as may be seen by referring to the titles of the various Articles. Most editions have ignored St. Thomas's original division, and give the one to which he subsequently adhered.]

FIRST ARTICLE [III, Q. 75, Art. 1]

Whether the Body of Christ Be in This Sacrament in Very Truth, or Merely As in a Figure or Sign?

Objection 1: It seems that the body of Christ is not in this sacrament in very truth, but only as in a figure, or sign. For it is written (John 6:54) that when our Lord had uttered these words: "Except you eat the flesh of the Son of Man, and drink His blood," etc., "Many of His disciples on hearing it said: 'this is a hard saying'": to whom He rejoined: "It is the spirit that quickeneth; the flesh profiteth nothing": as if He were to say, according to Augustine's exposition on Ps. 4 [*On Ps. 98:9]: "Give a spiritual meaning to what I have said. You are not to eat this body which you see, nor to drink the blood which they who crucify Me are to spill. It is a mystery that I put before you: in its spiritual sense it will quicken you; but the flesh profiteth nothing."

Obj. 2: Further, our Lord said (Matt. 28:20): "Behold I am with you all days even to the consummation of the world." Now in explaining this, Augustine makes this observation (Tract. xxx in Joan.): "The Lord is on high until the world be ended; nevertheless the truth of the Lord is here with us; for the body, in which He rose again, must be in one place; but His truth is spread abroad everywhere." Therefore, the body of Christ is not in this sacrament in very truth, but only as in a sign.

Obj. 3: Further, no body can be in several places at the one time. For this does not even belong to an angel; since for the same reason it could be everywhere. But Christ's is a true body, and it is in heaven. Consequently, it seems that it is not in very truth in the sacrament of the altar, but only as in a sign.

Obj. 4: Further, the Church's sacraments are ordained for the profit of the faithful. But according to Gregory in a certain Homily (xxviii in Evang.), the ruler is rebuked "for demanding Christ's bodily presence." Moreover the apostles were prevented from receiving the Holy Ghost because they were attached to His bodily presence, as Augustine says on John 16:7: "Except I go, the Paraclete will not come to you" (Tract. xciv in Joan.). Therefore Christ is not in the sacrament of the altar according to His bodily presence.

*On the contrary,* Hilary says (De Trin. viii): "There is no room for doubt regarding the truth of

Christ's body and blood; for now by our Lord's own declaring and by our faith His flesh is truly food, and His blood is truly drink." And Ambrose says (De Sacram. vi): "As the Lord Jesus Christ is God's true Son so is it Christ's true flesh which we take, and His true blood which we drink."

*I answer that,* The presence of Christ's true body and blood in this sacrament cannot be detected by sense, nor understanding, but by faith alone, which rests upon Divine authority. Hence, on Luke 22:19: "This is My body which shall be delivered up for you," Cyril says: "Doubt not whether this be true; but take rather the Saviour's words with faith; for since He is the Truth, He lieth not."

Now this is suitable, first for the perfection of the New Law. For, the sacrifices of the Old Law contained only in figure that true sacrifice of Christ's Passion, according to Heb. 10:1: "For the law having a shadow of the good things to come, not the very image of the things." And therefore it was necessary that the sacrifice of the New Law instituted by Christ should have something more, namely, that it should contain Christ Himself crucified, not merely in signification or figure, but also in very truth. And therefore this sacrament which contains Christ Himself, as Dionysius says (Eccl. Hier. iii), is perfective of all the other sacraments, in which Christ's virtue is participated.

Secondly, this belongs to Christ's love, out of which for our salvation He assumed a true body of our nature. And because it is the special feature of friendship to live together with friends, as the Philosopher says (Ethic. ix), He promises us His bodily presence as a reward, saying (Matt. 24:28): "Where the body is, there shall the eagles be gathered together." Yet meanwhile in our pilgrimage He does not deprive us of His bodily presence; but unites us with Himself in this sacrament through the truth of His body and blood. Hence (John 6:57) he says: "He that eateth My flesh, and drinketh My blood, abideth in Me, and I in him." Hence this sacrament is the sign of supreme charity, and the uplifter of our hope, from such familiar union of Christ with us.

Thirdly, it belongs to the perfection of faith, which concerns His humanity just as it does His Godhead, according to John 14:1: "You believe in God, believe also in Me." And since faith is of things unseen, as Christ shows us His Godhead invisibly, so also in this sacrament He shows us His flesh in an invisible manner.

Some men accordingly, not paying heed to these things, have contended that Christ's body and blood are not in this sacrament except as in a sign, a thing to be rejected as heretical, since it is contrary to Christ's words. Hence Berengarius, who had been the first deviser of this heresy, was afterwards forced to withdraw his error, and to acknowledge the truth of the faith.

Reply Obj. 1: From this authority the aforesaid heretics have taken occasion to err from evilly understanding Augustine's words. For when Augustine says: "You are not to eat this body which you see," he means not to exclude the truth of Christ's body, but that it was not to be eaten in this species in which it was seen by them. And by the words: "It is a mystery that I put before you; in its spiritual sense it will quicken you," he intends not that the body of Christ is in this sacrament merely according to mystical signification, but "spiritually," that is, invisibly, and by the power of the spirit. Hence (Tract. xxvii), expounding John 6:64: "the flesh profiteth nothing," he says: "Yea, but as they understood it, for they understood that the flesh was to be eaten as it is divided piecemeal in a dead body, or as sold in the shambles, not as it is quickened by the spirit . . . Let the spirit draw nigh to the flesh . . . then the flesh profiteth very much: for if the flesh profiteth nothing, the Word had not been made flesh, that It might dwell among us."

Reply Obj. 2: That saying of Augustine and all others like it are to be understood of Christ's body as it is beheld in its proper species; according as our Lord Himself says (Matt. 26:11): "But Me you have not always." Nevertheless He is invisibly under the species of this sacrament, wherever this sacrament is performed.

Reply Obj. 3: Christ's body is not in this sacrament in the same way as a body is in a place, which by its dimensions is commensurate with the place; but in a special manner which is proper to this sacrament. Hence we say that Christ's body is upon many altars, not as in different places, but "sacramentally": and thereby we do not understand that Christ is there only as in a sign, although a sacrament is a kind of sign; but that Christ's body is here after a fashion proper to this sacrament, as stated above.

Reply Obj. 4: This argument holds good of Christ's bodily presence, as He is present after the manner of a body, that is, as it is in its visible appearance, but not as it is spiritually, that is, invisibly, after the manner and by the virtue of the spirit. Hence Augustine (Tract. xxvii in Joan.) says: "If thou hast understood" Christ's words spiritually concerning His flesh, "they are spirit and life to thee; if thou hast understood them carnally, they are also spirit and life, but not to thee."

SECOND ARTICLE [III, Q. 75, Art. 2]

Whether in This Sacrament the Substance of the Bread and Wine Remains After the Consecration?

Objection 1: It seems that the substance of the bread and wine does remain in this sacrament after the consecration: because Damascene says (De Fide Orth. iv): "Since it is customary for men to eat bread and drink wine, God has wedded his Godhead to them, and made them His body and blood": and further on: "The bread of communication is not simple bread, but is united to the Godhead." But wedding together belongs to things actually existing. Therefore the bread and wine are at the same time, in this sacrament, with the body and the blood of Christ.

Obj. 2: Further, there ought to be conformity between the sacraments. But in the other sacraments the substance of the matter remains, like the substance of water in Baptism, and the substance of chrism in Confirmation. Therefore the substance of the bread and wine remains also in this sacrament.

Obj. 3: Further, bread and wine are made use of in this sacrament, inasmuch as they denote ecclesiastical unity, as "one bread is made from many grains and wine from many grapes," as Augustine says in his book on the Creed (Tract. xxvi in Joan.). But this belongs to the substance of bread and wine. Therefore, the substance of the bread and wine remains in this sacrament.

*On the contrary,* Ambrose says (De Sacram. iv): "Although the figure of the bread and wine be seen, still, after the Consecration, they are to be believed to be nothing else than the body end blood of Christ."

*I answer that,* Some have held that the substance of the bread and wine remains in this sacrament after the consecration. But this opinion cannot stand: first of all, because by such an opinion the truth of this sacrament is destroyed, to which it belongs that Christ's true body exists in this sacrament; which indeed was not there before the consecration. Now a thing cannot be in any place, where it was not previously, except by change of place, or by the conversion of another thing into itself; just as fire begins anew to be in some house, either because it is carried thither, or because it is generated there. Now it is evident that Christ's body does not begin to be present in this sacrament by local motion. First of all, because it would follow that it would cease to be in heaven: for what is moved locally does not come anew to some place unless it quit the former one. Secondly, because every body moved locally passes through all intermediary spaces, which cannot be said here. Thirdly, because it is not possible for one movement of the same body moved locally to be terminated in different places at the one time, whereas the body of Christ under this sacrament begins at the one time to be in several places. And consequently it remains that Christ's body cannot begin to be anew in this sacrament except by change of the substance of bread into itself. But what is changed into another thing, no longer remains after such change. Hence the conclusion is that, saving the truth of this sacrament, the substance of the bread cannot remain after the consecration.

Secondly, because this position is contrary to the form of this sacrament, in which it is said: "This is My body," which would not be true if the substance of the bread were to remain there; for the substance of bread never is the body of Christ. Rather should one say in that case: "Here is My body."

Thirdly, because it would be opposed to the veneration of this sacrament, if any substance were there, which could not be adored with adoration of latria.

Fourthly, because it is contrary to the rite of the Church, according to which it is not lawful to take the body of Christ after bodily food, while it is nevertheless lawful to take one consecrated host after another. Hence this opinion is to be avoided as heretical.

Reply Obj. 1: God "wedded His Godhead," i.e. His Divine power, to the bread and wine, not that these may remain in this sacrament, but in order that He may make from them His body and blood.

Reply Obj. 2: Christ is not really present in the other sacraments, as in this; and therefore the substance of the matter remains in the other sacraments, but not in this.

Reply Obj. 3: The species which remain in this sacrament, as shall be said later (A. 5), suffice for its signification; because the nature of the substance is known by its accidents.

THIRD ARTICLE [III, Q. 75, Art. 3]

Whether the Substance of the Bread or Wine Is Annihilated After the Consecration of This Sacrament, or Dissolved into Their Original Matter?

Objection 1: It seems that the substance of the bread is annihilated after the consecration of this sacrament, or dissolved into its original matter. For whatever is corporeal must be somewhere. But the substance of bread, which is something corporeal, does not remain, in this sacrament, as stated above (A. 2); nor can we assign any place where it may be. Consequently it is nothing after the consecration. Therefore, it is either annihilated, or dissolved into its original matter.

Obj. 2: Further, what is the term wherefrom in every change exists no longer, except in the potentiality of matter; e.g. when air is changed into fire, the form of the air remains only in the potentiality of matter; and in like fashion when what is white becomes black. But in this sacrament the substance of the bread or of the wine is the term wherefrom, while the body or the blood of Christ is the term "whereunto": for Ambrose says in De Officiis (De Myster. ix): "Before the blessing it is called another species, after the blessing the body of Christ is signified." Therefore, when the consecration takes place, the substance of the bread or wine no longer remains, unless perchance dissolved into its (original) matter.

Obj. 3: Further, one of two contradictories must be true. But this proposition is false: "After the consecration the substance of the bread or wine is something." Consequently, this is true: "The substance of the bread or wine is nothing."

*On the contrary,* Augustine says (Q. 83): "God is not the cause of tending to nothing." But this sacrament is wrought by Divine power. Therefore, in this sacrament the substance of the bread or wine is not annihilated.

*I answer that,* Because the substance of the bread and wine does not remain in this sacrament, some, deeming that it is impossible for the substance of the bread and wine to be changed into Christ's flesh and blood, have maintained that by the consecration, the substance of the bread and wine is either dissolved into the original matter, or that it is annihilated.

Now the original matter into which mixed bodies can be dissolved is the four elements. For dissolution cannot be made into primary matter, so that a subject can exist without a form, since matter cannot exist without a form. But since after the consecration nothing remains under the sacramental species except the body and the blood of Christ, it will be necessary to say that the elements into which the substance of the bread and wine is dissolved, depart from thence by local motion, which would be perceived by the senses. In like manner also the substance of the bread or wine remains until the last instant of the consecration; but in the last instant of the consecration there is already present there the substance of the body or blood of Christ, just as the form is already present in the last instant of generation. Hence no instant can be assigned in which the original matter can be there. For it cannot be said that the substance of the bread or wine is dissolved gradually into the original matter, or that it successively quits the species, for if this began to be done in the last instant of its consecration, then at the one time under part of the host there would be the body of Christ together with the substance of bread, which is contrary to what has been said above (A. 2). But if this begin to come to pass before the consecration, there will then be a time in which under one part of the host there will be neither the substance of bread nor the body of Christ, which is not fitting. They seem indeed to have taken this into careful consideration, wherefore they formulated their proposition with an alternative viz. that (the substance) may be annihilated. But even this cannot stand, because no way can be assigned whereby Christ's true body can begin to be in this sacrament, except by the change of the substance of bread into it, which change is excluded the moment we admit either annihilation of the substance of the bread, or dissolution into the original matter. Likewise no cause can be assigned for such dissolution or annihilation, since the effect of the sacrament is signified by the form: "This is My body." Hence it is clear that the aforesaid opinion is false.

Reply Obj. 1: The substance of the bread or wine, after the consecration, remains neither under the sacramental species, nor elsewhere; yet it does not follow that it is annihilated; for it is changed into the body of Christ; just as if the air, from which fire is generated, be not there or elsewhere, it does not follow that it is annihilated.

Reply Obj. 2: The form, which is the term wherefrom, is not changed into another form; but one form succeeds another in the subject; and therefore the first form remains only in the potentiality of matter. But here the substance of the bread is changed into the body of Christ, as stated above. Hence the conclusion does not follow.

Reply Obj. 3: Although after the consecration this proposition is false: "The substance of the bread is something," still that into which the substance of the bread is changed, is something, and consequently the substance of the bread is not annihilated.

FOURTH ARTICLE [III, Q. 75, Art. 4]

Whether Bread Can Be Converted into the Body of Christ?

Objection 1: It seems that bread cannot be converted into the body of Christ. For conversion is a kind of change. But in every change there must be some subject, which from being previously in potentiality is now in act. because as is said in Phys. iii: "motion is the act of a thing existing in potentiality." But no subject can be assigned for the substance of the bread and of the body of Christ, because it is of the very nature of substance for it "not to be in a subject," as it is said in Praedic. iii. Therefore it is not possible for the whole substance of the bread to be converted into the body of Christ.

Obj. 2: Further, the form of the thing into which another is converted, begins anew to inhere in the matter of the thing converted into it: as when air is changed into fire not already existing, the form of fire begins anew to be in the matter of the air; and in like manner when food is converted into non-pre-existing man, the form of the man begins to be anew in the matter of the food. Therefore, if bread be changed into the body of Christ, the form of Christ's body must necessarily begin to be in the matter of the bread, which is false. Consequently, the bread is not changed into the substance of Christ's body.

Obj. 3: Further, when two things are diverse, one never becomes the other, as whiteness never becomes blackness, as is stated in Phys. i. But since two contrary forms are of themselves diverse, as being the principles of formal difference, so two signate matters are of themselves diverse, as being the principles of material distinction. Consequently, it is not possible for this matter of bread to become this matter whereby Christ's body is individuated, and so it is not possible for this substance of bread to be changed into the substance of Christ's body.

*On the contrary,* Eusebius Emesenus says: "To thee it ought neither to be a novelty nor an impossibility that earthly and mortal things be changed into the substance of Christ."

*I answer that,* As stated above (A. 2), since Christ's true body is in this sacrament, and since it does not begin to be there by local motion, nor is it contained therein as in a place, as is evident from what was stated above (A. 1, ad 2), it must be said then that it begins to be there by conversion of the substance of bread into itself.

Yet this change is not like natural changes, but is entirely supernatural, and effected by God's power alone. Hence Ambrose says [(De Sacram. iv): "See how Christ's word changes nature's laws, as He wills: a man is not wont to be born save of man and woman: see therefore that against the established law and order a man is born of a Virgin": and] [*The passage in the brackets is not in the Leonine edition] (De Myster. iv): "It is clear that a Virgin begot beyond the order of nature: and what we make is the body from the Virgin. Why, then, do you look for nature's order in Christ's body, since the Lord Jesus was Himself brought forth of a Virgin beyond nature?" Chrysostom likewise (Hom. xlvii), commenting on John 6:64: "The words which I have spoken to you," namely, of this sacrament, "are spirit and life," says: i.e. "spiritual, having nothing carnal, nor natural consequence; but they are rent from all such necessity which exists upon earth, and from the laws here established."

For it is evident that every agent acts according as it is in act. But every created agent is limited in its act, as being of a determinate genus and species: and consequently the action of every created agent bears upon some determinate act. Now the determination of every thing in actual existence comes from its form. Consequently, no natural or created agent can act except by changing the form in something; and on this account every change made according to nature's laws is a formal change. But God is infinite act, as stated in the First Part (Q. 7, A. 1; Q. 26, A. 2); hence His action extends to the whole nature of being. Therefore He can work not only formal conversion, so that diverse forms succeed each other in the same subject; but also the change of all being, so that, to wit, the whole substance of one thing be changed into the whole substance of another. And this is done by Divine power in this sacrament; for the whole substance of the bread is changed into the whole substance of Christ's body, and the whole substance of the wine into the whole substance of Christ's blood. Hence this is not a formal, but a substantial conversion; nor is it a kind of natural movement: but, with a name of its own, it can be called "transubstantiation."

Reply Obj. 1: This objection holds good in respect of formal change, because it belongs to a form to be in matter or in a subject; but it does not hold good in respect of the change of the entire substance. Hence, since this substantial change implies a certain order of substances, one of which is changed into the other, it is in both substances as in a subject, just as order and number.

Reply Obj. 2: This argument also is true of formal conversion or change, because, as stated above (ad 1), a form must be in some matter or subject. But this is not so in a change of the entire substance; for in this case no subject is possible.

Reply Obj. 3: Form cannot be changed into form, nor matter into matter by the power of any finite agent. Such a change, however, can be made by the power of an infinite agent, which has control over all being, because the nature of being is common to both forms and to both matters; and whatever there is of being in the one, the author of being can change into whatever there is of being in the other, withdrawing that whereby it was distinguished from the other.

FIFTH ARTICLE [III, Q. 75, Art. 5]

Whether the Accidents of the Bread and Wine Remain in This Sacrament After the Change?

Objection 1: It seems that the accidents of the bread and wine do not remain in this sacrament. For when that which comes first is removed, that which follows is also taken away. But substance is naturally before accident, as is proved in Metaph. vii. Since, then, after consecration, the substance of the bread does not remain in this sacrament, it seems that its accidents cannot remain.

Obj. 2: Further, there ought not to be any deception in a sacrament of truth. But we judge of substance by accidents. It seems, then, that human judgment is deceived, if, while the accidents remain, the substance of the bread does not. Consequently this is unbecoming to this sacrament.

Obj. 3: Further, although our faith is not subject to reason, still it is not contrary to reason, but above it, as was said in the beginning of this work (I, Q. 1, A. 6, ad 2; A. 8). But our reason has its origin in the senses. Therefore our faith ought not to be contrary to the senses, as it is when sense judges that to be bread which faith believes to be the substance of Christ's body. Therefore it is not befitting this sacrament for the accidents of bread to remain subject to the senses, and for the substance of bread not to remain.

Obj. 4: Further, what remains after the change has taken place seems to be the subject of change. If therefore the accidents of the bread remain after the change has been effected, it seems that the accidents are the subject of the change. But this is impossible; for "an accident cannot have an accident" (Metaph. iii). Therefore the accidents of the bread and wine ought not to remain in this sacrament.

*On the contrary,* Augustine says in his book on the Sentences of Prosper (Lanfranc, De Corp. et Sang. Dom. xiii): "Under the species which we behold, of bread and wine, we honor invisible things, i.e. flesh and blood."

*I answer that,* It is evident to sense that all the accidents of the bread and wine remain after the consecration. And this is reasonably done by Divine providence. First of all, because it is not customary, but horrible, for men to eat human flesh, and to drink blood. And therefore Christ's flesh and blood are set before us to be partaken of under the species of those things which are the more commonly used by men, namely, bread and wine. Secondly, lest this sacrament might be derided by unbelievers, if we were to eat our Lord under His own species. Thirdly, that while we receive our Lord's body and blood invisibly, this may redound to the merit of faith.

Reply Obj. 1: As is said in the book De Causis, an effect depends more on the first cause than on the second. And therefore by God's power, which is the first cause of all things, it is possible for that which follows to remain, while that which is first is taken away.

Reply Obj. 2: There is no deception in this sacrament; for the accidents which are discerned by the senses are truly present. But the intellect, whose proper object is substance as is said in De Anima iii, is preserved by faith from deception.

And this serves as answer to the third argument; because faith is not contrary to the senses, but concerns things to which sense does not reach.

Reply Obj. 4: This change has not properly a subject, as was stated above (A. 4, ad 1); nevertheless the accidents which remain have some resemblance of a subject.

SIXTH ARTICLE [III, Q. 75, Art. 6]

Whether the Substantial Form of the Bread Remains in This Sacrament After the Consecration?

Objection 1: It seems that the substantial form of the bread remains in this sacrament after the consecration. For it has been said (A. 5) that the accidents remain after the consecration. But since bread is an artificial thing, its form is an accident. Therefore it remains after the consecration.

Obj. 2: Further, the form of Christ's body is His soul: for it is said in De Anima ii, that the soul "is the act of a physical body which has life in potentiality". But it cannot be said that the substantial form of the bread is changed into the soul. Therefore it appears that it remains after the consecration.

Obj. 3: Further, the proper operation of a things follows its substantial form. But what remains in this sacrament, nourishes, and performs every operation which bread would do were it present. Therefore the substantial form of the bread remains in this sacrament after the consecration.

*On the contrary,* The substantial form of bread is of the substance of bread. But the substance of the bread is changed into the body of Christ, as stated above (AA. 2, 3, 4). Therefore the substantial form of the bread does not remain.

*I answer that,* Some have contended that after the consecration not only do the accidents of the bread remain, but also its substantial form. But this cannot be. First of all, because if the substantial form of the bread were to remain, nothing of the bread would be changed into the body of Christ, excepting the matter; and so it would follow that it would be changed, not into the whole body of Christ, but into its matter, which is repugnant to the form of the sacrament, wherein it is said: "This is My body."

Secondly, because if the substantial form of the bread were to remain, it would remain either in matter, or separated from matter. The first cannot be, for if it were to remain in the matter of the bread, then the whole substance of the bread would remain, which is against what was said above (A. 2). Nor could it remain in any other matter, because the proper form exists only in its proper matter. But if it were to remain separate from matter, it would then be an actually intelligible form, and also an intelligence; for all forms separated from matter are such.

Thirdly, it would be unbefitting this sacrament: because the accidents of the bread remain in this sacrament, in order that the body of Christ may be seen under them, and not under its proper species, as stated above (A. 5).

And therefore it must be said that the substantial form of the bread does not remain.

Reply Obj. 1: There is nothing to prevent art from making a thing whose form is not an accident, but a substantial form; as frogs and serpents can be produced by art: for art produces such forms not by its own power, but by the power of natural energies. And in this way it produces the substantial forms of bread, by the power of fire baking the matter made up of flour and water.

Reply Obj. 2: The soul is the form of the body, giving it the whole order of perfect being, i.e. being, corporeal being, and animated being, and so on. Therefore the form of the bread is changed into the form of Christ's body, according as the latter gives corporeal being, but not according as it bestows animated being.

Reply Obj. 3: Some of the operations of bread follow it by reason of the accidents, such as to affect the senses, and such operations are found in the species of the bread after the consecration on account of the accidents which remain. But some other operations follow the bread either by reason of the matter, such as that it is changed into something else, or else by reason of the substantial form, such as an operation consequent upon its species, for instance, that it "strengthens man's heart" (Ps. 103:15); and such operations are found in this sacrament, not on account of the form or matter remaining, but because they are bestowed miraculously upon the accidents themselves, as will be said later (Q. 77, A. 3, ad 2, 3; AA. 5, 6).

SEVENTH ARTICLE [III, Q. 75, Art. 7]

Whether This Change Is Wrought Instantaneously?

Objection 1: It seems that this change is not wrought instantaneously, but successively. For in this change there is first the substance of bread, and afterwards the substance of Christ's body. Neither, then, is in the same instant, but in two instants. But there is a mid-time between every two instants. Therefore this change must take place according to the succession of time, which is between the last instant in which the bread is there, and the first instant in which the body of Christ is present.

Obj. 2: Further, in every change something is in becoming and something is in being. But these two things do not exist at the one time for, what is in becoming, is not yet, whereas what is in being, already is. Consequently, there is a before and an after in such change: and so necessarily the change cannot be instantaneous, but successive.

Obj. 3: Further, Ambrose says (De Sacram. iv) that this sacrament "is made by the words of Christ." But Christ's words are pronounced successively. Therefore the change takes place successively.

*On the contrary,* This change is effected by a power which is infinite, to which it belongs to operate in an instant.

*I answer that,* A change may be instantaneous from a threefold reason. First on the part of the form, which is the terminus of the change. For, if it be a form that receives more and less, it is acquired by its subject successively, such as health; and therefore because a substantial form does not receive more and less, it follows that its introduction into matter is instantaneous.

Secondly on the part of the subject, which sometimes is prepared successively for receiving the form; thus water is heated successively. When, however, the subject itself is in the ultimate disposition for receiving the form, it receives it suddenly, as a transparent body is illuminated suddenly. Thirdly on the part of the agent, which possesses infinite power: wherefore it can instantly dispose the matter for the form. Thus it is written (Mk. 7:34) that when Christ had said, "'Ephpheta,' which is 'Be thou opened,' immediately his ears were opened, and the string of his tongue was loosed."

For these three reasons this conversion is instantaneous. First, because the substance of Christ's body which is the term of this conversion, does not receive more or less. Secondly, because in this conversion there is no subject to be disposed successively. Thirdly, because it is effected by God's infinite power.

Reply Obj. 1: Some [*Cf. Albert the Great, Sent. iv, D, 11; St. Bonaventure, Sent., iv, D, 11] do not grant simply that there is a mid-time between every two instants. For they say that this is true of two instants referring to the same movement, but not if they refer to different things. Hence between the instant that marks the close of rest, and another which marks the beginning of movement, there is no mid-time. But in this they are mistaken, because the unity of time and of instant, or even their plurality, is not taken according to movements of any sort, but according to the first movement of the heavens, which is the measure of all movement and rest.

Accordingly others grant this of the time which measures movement depending on the movement of the heavens. But there are some movements which are not dependent on the movement of the heavens, nor measured by it, as was said in the First Part (Q. 53, A. 3) concerning the movements of the angels. Hence between two instants responding to those movements there is no mid-time. But this is not to the point, because although the change in question has no relation of itself to the movement of the heavens, still it follows the pronouncing of the words, which (pronouncing) must necessarily be measured by the movement of the heavens. And therefore there must of necessity be a mid-time between every two signate instants in connection with that change.

Some say therefore that the instant in which the bread was last, and the instant in which the body of Christ is first, are indeed two in comparison with the things measured, but are one comparatively to the time measuring; as when two lines touch, there are two points on the part of the two lines, but one point on the part of the place containing them. But here there is no likeness, because instant and time is not the intrinsic measure of particular movements, as a line and point are of a body, but only the extrinsic measure, as place is to bodies.

Hence others say that it is the same instant in fact, but another according to reason. But according to this it would follow that things really opposite would exist together; for diversity of reason does not change a thing objectively.

And therefore it must be said that this change, as stated above, is wrought by Christ's words which are spoken by the priest, so that the last instant of pronouncing the words is the first instant in which Christ's body is in the sacrament; and that the substance of the bread is there during the whole preceding time. Of this time no instant is to be taken as proximately preceding the last one, because time is not made up of successive instants, as is proved in Phys. vi. And therefore a first instant can be assigned in which Christ's body is present; but a last instant cannot be assigned in which the substance of bread is there, but a last time can be assigned. And the same holds good in natural changes, as is evident from the Philosopher (Phys. viii).

Reply Obj. 2: In instantaneous changes a thing is "in becoming," and is "in being" simultaneously; just as becoming illuminated and to be actually illuminated are simultaneous: for in such, a thing is said to be "in being" according as it now is; but to be "in becoming," according as it was not before.

Reply Obj. 3: As stated above (ad 1), this change comes about in the last instant of the pronouncing of the words. For then the meaning of the words is finished, which meaning is efficacious in the forms of the sacraments. And therefore it does not follow that this change is successive.

EIGHTH ARTICLE [III, Q. 75, Art. 8]

Whether This Proposition Is False: "The Body of Christ Is Made Out of Bread"?

Objection 1: It seems that this proposition is

false: "The body of Christ is made out of bread." For everything out of which another is made, is that which is made the other; but not conversely: for we say that a black thing is made out of a white thing, and that a white thing is made black: and although we may say that a man becomes black still we do not say that a black thing is made out of a man, as is shown in Phys. i. If it be true, then, that Christ's body is made out of bread, it will be true to say that bread is made the body of Christ. But this seems to be false, because the bread is not the subject of the making, but rather its term. Therefore, it is not said truly that Christ's body is made out of bread.

Obj. 2: Further, the term of becoming is something that is, or something that is made. But this proposition is never true: "The bread is the body of Christ"; or "The bread is made the body of Christ"; or again, "The bread will be the body of Christ." Therefore it seems that not even this is true: "The body of Christ is made out of bread."

Obj. 3: Further, everything out of which another is made is converted into that which is made from it. But this proposition seems to be false: "The bread is converted into the body of Christ," because such conversion seems to be more miraculous than the creation of the world, in which it is not said that non-being is converted into being. Therefore it seems that this proposition likewise is false: "The body of Christ is made out of bread."

Obj. 4: Further, that out of which something is made, can be that thing. But this proposition is false: "Bread can be the body of Christ." Therefore this is likewise false: "The body of Christ is made out of bread."

*On the contrary,* Ambrose says (De Sacram. iv): "When the consecration takes place, the body of Christ is made out of the bread."

*I answer that,* This conversion of bread into the body of Christ has something in common with creation, and with natural transmutation, and in some respect differs from both. For the order of the terms is common to these three; that is, that after one thing there is another (for, in creation there is being after non-being; in this sacrament, Christ's body after the substance of bread; in natural transmutation white after black, or fire after air); and that the aforesaid terms are not coexistent.

Now the conversion, of which we are speaking, has this in common with creation, that in neither of them is there any common subject belonging to either of the extremes; the contrary of which appears in every natural transmutation.

Again, this conversion has something in common with natural transmutation in two respects, although not in the same fashion. First of all because in both, one of the extremes passes into the other, as bread into Christ's body, and air into fire; whereas non-being is not converted into being. But this comes to pass differently on the one side and on the other; for in this sacrament the whole substance of the bread passes into the whole body of Christ; whereas in natural transmutation the matter of the one receives the form of the other, the previous form being laid aside. Secondly, they have this in common, that on both sides something remains the same; whereas this does not happen in creation: yet differently; for the same matter or subject remains in natural transmutation; whereas in this sacrament the same accidents remain.

From these observations we can gather the various ways of speaking in such matters. For, because in no one of the aforesaid three things are the extremes coexistent, therefore in none of them can one extreme be predicated of the other by the substantive verb of the present tense: for we do not say, "Non-being is being" or, "Bread is the body of Christ," or, "Air is fire," or, "White is black." Yet because of the relationship of the extremes in all of them we can use the preposition ex (out of), which denotes order; for we can truly and properly say that "being is made out of non-being," and "out of bread, the body of Christ," and "out of air, fire," and "out of white, black." But because in creation one of the extremes does not pass into the other, we cannot use the word "conversion" in creation, so as to say that "non-being is converted into being": we can, however, use the word in this sacrament, just as in natural transmutation. But since in this sacrament the whole substance is converted into the whole substance, on that account this conversion is properly termed transubstantiation.

Again, since there is no subject of this conversion, the things which are true in natural conversion by reason of the subject, are not to be granted in this conversion. And in the first place indeed it is evident that potentiality to the opposite follows a subject, by reason whereof we say that "a white thing can be black," or that "air can be fire"; although the latter is not so proper as the former: for the subject of whiteness, in which there is potentiality to blackness, is the whole substance of the white thing; since whiteness is not a part thereof; whereas the subject of the form of air is part thereof: hence when it is said, "Air can be fire," it is verified by synecdoche by reason of the part. But in this conversion, and similarly in creation, because there is no subject, it is not said that one extreme can be the other, as that "non-being can be being," or that "bread can be the body of Christ": and for the same reason it cannot be properly said that "being is made of ( de ) non-being," or that "the body of Christ is made of bread," because this preposition "of" ( de ) denotes a consubstantial cause, which consubstantiality of the extremes in natural transmutations is considered according to something common in the subject. And for the same reason it is not granted that "bread will be the body of Christ," or that it "may become the body of Christ," just as it is not granted in creation that "non-being will be being," or that "non-being may become being," because this manner of speaking is verified in natural transmutations by reason of the subject: for instance, when we say that "a white thing becomes black," or "a white thing will be black."

Nevertheless, since in this sacrament, after the change, something remains the same, namely, the accidents of the bread, as stated above (A. 5), some of these expressions may be admitted by way of similitude, namely, that "bread is the body of Christ," or, "bread will be the body of Christ," or "the body of Christ is made of bread"; provided that by the word "bread" is not understood the substance of bread, but in general "that which is contained under the species of bread," under which species there is first contained the substance of bread, and afterwards the body of Christ.

Reply Obj. 1: That out of which something else is made, sometimes implies together with the subject, one of the extremes of the transmutation, as when it is said "a black thing is made out of a white one"; but sometimes it implies only the opposite or the extreme, as when it is said--"out of morning comes the day." And so it is not granted that the latter becomes the former, that is, "that morning becomes the day." So likewise in the matter in hand, although it may be said properly that "the body of Christ is made out of bread," yet it is not said properly that "bread becomes the body of Christ," except by similitude, as was said above.

Reply Obj. 2: That out of which another is made, will sometimes be that other because of the subject which is implied. And therefore, since there is no subject of this change, the comparison does not hold.

Reply Obj. 3: In this change there are many more difficulties than in creation, in which there is but this one difficulty, that something is made out of nothing; yet this belongs to the proper mode of production of the first cause, which presupposes nothing else. But in this conversion not only is it difficult for this whole to be changed into that whole, so that nothing of the former may remain (which does not belong to the common mode of production of a cause), but furthermore it has this difficulty that the accidents remain while the substance is destroyed, and many other difficulties of which we shall treat hereafter (Q. 77). Nevertheless the word "conversion" is admitted in this sacrament, but not in creation, as stated above.

Reply Obj. 4: As was observed above, potentiality belongs to the subject, whereas there is no subject in this conversion. And therefore it is not granted that bread can be the body of Christ: for this conversion does not come about by the passive potentiality of the creature, but solely by the active power of the Creator.

## QUESTION 76

OF THE WAY IN WHICH CHRIST IS IN THIS SACRAMENT (In Eight Articles)

We have now to consider the manner in which Christ exists in this sacrament; and under this head there are eight points of inquiry:

(1) Whether the whole Christ is under this sacrament?

(2) Whether the entire Christ is under each species of the sacrament?

(3) Whether the entire Christ is under every part of the species?

(4) Whether all the dimensions of Christ's body are in this sacrament?

(5) Whether the body of Christ is in this sacrament locally?

(6) Whether after the consecration, the body of Christ is moved when the host or chalice is moved?

(7) Whether Christ's body, as it is in this sacrament, can be seen by the eye?

(8) Whether the true body of Christ remains in this sacrament when He is seen under the appearance of a child or of flesh?

FIRST ARTICLE [III, Q. 76, Art. 1]

Whether the Whole Christ Is Contained Under This Sacrament?

Objection 1: It seems that the whole Christ is not contained under this sacrament, because Christ begins to be in this sacrament by conversion of the bread and wine. But it is evident that the bread and wine cannot be changed either into the Godhead or into the soul of Christ. Since therefore Christ exists in three substances, namely, the Godhead, soul and body, as shown above (Q. 2, A. 5; Q. 5, AA. 1, 3), it seems that the entire Christ is not under this sacrament.

Obj. 2: Further, Christ is in this sacrament, forasmuch as it is ordained to the refection of the faithful, which consists in food and drink, as stated above (Q. 74, A. 1). But our Lord said (John 6:56): "My flesh is meat indeed, and My blood is drink indeed." Therefore, only the flesh and blood of Christ are contained in this sacrament. But there are many other parts of Christ's body, for instance, the nerves, bones, and such like. Therefore the entire Christ is not contained under this sacrament.

Obj. 3: Further, a body of greater quantity cannot be contained under the measure of a lesser. But the measure of the bread and wine is much smaller than the measure of Christ's body. Therefore it is impossible that the entire Christ be contained under this sacrament.

*On the contrary,* Ambrose says (De Officiis): "Christ is in this sacrament."

*I answer that,* It is absolutely necessary to confess according to Catholic faith that the entire Christ is in this sacrament. Yet we must know that there is something of Christ in this sacrament in a twofold manner: first, as it were, by the power of the sacrament; secondly, from natural concomitance. By the power of the sacrament, there is under the species of this sacrament that into which the pre-existing substance of the bread and wine is changed, as expressed by the words of the form, which are effective in this as in the other sacraments; for instance, by the words: "This is My body," or, "This is My blood." But from natural concomitance there is also in this sacrament that which is really united with that thing wherein the aforesaid conversion is terminated. For if any two things be really united, then wherever the one is really, there must the other also be: since things really united together are only distinguished by an operation of the mind.

Reply Obj. 1: Because the change of the bread and wine is not terminated at the Godhead or the soul of Christ, it follows as a consequence that the Godhead or the soul of Christ is in this sacrament not by the power of the sacrament, but from real concomitance. For since the Godhead never set aside the assumed body, wherever the body of Christ is, there, of necessity, must the Godhead be; and therefore it is necessary for the Godhead to be in this sacrament concomitantly with His body. Hence we read in the profession of faith at Ephesus (P. I., chap. xxvi): "We are made partakers of the body and blood of Christ, not as taking common flesh, nor as of a holy man united to the Word in dignity, but the truly life-giving flesh of the Word Himself."

On the other hand, His soul was truly separated from His body, as stated above (Q. 50, A. 5). And therefore had this sacrament been celebrated during those three days when He was dead, the soul of Christ would not have been there, neither by the power of the sacrament, nor from real concomitance. But since "Christ rising from the dead dieth now no more" (Rom. 6:9), His soul is always really united with His body. And therefore in this sacrament the body indeed of Christ is present by the power of the sacrament, but His soul from real concomitance.

Reply Obj. 2: By the power of the sacrament there is contained under it, as to the species of the bread, not only the flesh, but the entire body of Christ, that is, the bones the nerves, and the like. And this is apparent from the form of this sacrament, wherein it is not said: "This is My flesh," but "This is My body." Accordingly, when our Lord said (John 6:56): "My flesh is meat indeed," there the word flesh is put for the entire body, because according to human custom it seems to be more adapted for eating, as men commonly are fed on the flesh of animals, but not on the bones or the like.

Reply Obj. 3: As has been already stated (Q. 75, A. 5), after the consecration of the bread into the body of Christ, or of the wine into His blood, the accidents of both remain. From which it is evident that the dimensions of the bread or wine are not changed into the dimensions of the body of Christ, but substance into substance. And so the substance of Christ's body or blood is under this sacrament by the power of the sacrament, but not the dimensions of Christ's body or blood. Hence it is clear that the body of Christ is in this sacrament by way of substance,and not by way of quantity. But the proper totality of substance is contained indifferently in a small or large quantity; as the whole nature of air in a great or small amount of air, and the whole nature of a man in a big or small individual. Wherefore, after the consecration, the whole substance of Christ's body and blood is contained in this sacrament, just as the whole substance of the bread and wine was contained there before the consecration.

SECOND ARTICLE [III, Q. 76, Art. 2]

Whether the Whole Christ Is Contained Under Each Species of This Sacrament?

Objection 1: It seems that the whole Christ is not contained under both species of this sacrament. For this sacrament is ordained for the salvation of the faithful, not by virtue of the species, but by virtue of what is contained under the species, because the species were there even before the consecration, from which comes the power of this sacrament. If nothing, then, be contained under one species, but what is contained under the other, and if the whole Christ be contained under both, it seems that one of them is superfluous in this sacrament.

Obj. 2: Further, it was stated above (A. 1, ad 1) that all the other parts of the body, such as the bones, nerves, and the like, are comprised under the name of flesh. But the blood is one of the parts of the human body, as Aristotle proves (De Anima Histor. i). If, then, Christ's blood be contained under the species of bread, just as the other parts of the body are contained there, the blood ought not to be consecrated apart, just as no other part of the body is consecrated separately.

Obj. 3: Further, what is once in being cannot be again in becoming. But Christ's body has already begun to be in this sacrament by the consecration of the bread. Therefore, it cannot begin again to be there by the consecration of the wine; and so Christ's body will not be contained under the species of the wine, and accordingly neither the entire Christ. Therefore the whole Christ is not contained under each species.

*On the contrary,* The gloss on 1 Cor. 11:25, commenting on the word "Chalice," says that "under each species," namely, of the bread and wine, "the same is received"; and thus it seems that Christ is entire under each species.

*I answer that,* After what we have said above (A. 1), it must be held most certainly that the whole Christ is under each sacramental species yet not alike in each. For the body of Christ is indeed present under the species of bread by the power of the sacrament, while the blood is there from real concomitance, as stated above (A. 1, ad 1) in regard to the soul and Godhead of Christ; and under the species of wine the blood is present by the power of the sacrament, and His body by real concomitance, as is also His soul and Godhead: because now Christ's blood is not separated from His body, as it was at the time of His Passion and death. Hence if this sacrament had been celebrated then, the body of Christ would have been under the species of the bread, but without the blood; and, under the species of the wine, the blood would have been present without the body, as it was then, in fact.

Reply Obj. 1: Although the whole Christ is under each species, yet it is so not without purpose. For in the first place this serves to represent Christ's Passion, in which the blood was separated from the body; hence in the form for the consecration of the blood mention is made of its shedding. Secondly, it is in keeping with the use of this sacrament, that Christ's body be shown apart to the faithful as food, and the blood as drink. Thirdly, it is in keeping with its effect, in which sense it was stated above (Q. 74, A. 1) that "the body is offered for the salvation of the body, and the blood for the salvation of the soul."

Reply Obj. 2: In Christ's Passion, of which this is the memorial, the other parts of the body were not separated from one another, as the blood was, but the body remained entire, according to Ex. 12:46: "You shall not break a bone thereof." And therefore in this sacrament the blood is consecrated apart from the body, but no other part is consecrated separately from the rest.

Reply Obj. 3: As stated above, the body of Christ is not under the species of wine by the power of the sacrament, but by real concomitance: and therefore by the consecration of the wine the body of Christ is not there of itself, but concomitantly.

THIRD ARTICLE [III, Q. 76, Art. 3]

Whether Christ Is Entire Under Every Part of the Species of the Bread and Wine?

Objection 1: It seems that Christ is not entire under every part of the species of bread and wine. Because those species can be divided infinitely. If therefore Christ be entirely under every part of the said species, it would follow that He is in this sacrament an infinite number of times: which is unreasonable; because the infinite is repugnant not only to nature, but likewise to grace.

Obj. 2: Further, since Christ's is an organic body, it has parts determinately distant. For a determinate distance of the individual parts from each other is of the very nature of an organic body, as that of eye from eye, and eye from ear. But this could not be so, if Christ were entire under every part of the species; for every part would have to be under every other part, and so where one part would be, there another part would be. It cannot be then that the entire Christ is under every part of the host or of the wine contained in the chalice.

Obj. 3: Further, Christ's body always retains the true nature of a body, nor is it ever changed into a spirit. Now it is the nature of a body for it to be "quantity having position" (Predic. iv). But it belongs to the nature of this quantity that the various parts exist in various parts of place. Therefore, apparently it is impossible for the entire Christ to be under every part of the species.

*On the contrary,* Augustine says in a sermon (Gregory, Sacramentarium): "Each receives Christ the Lord, Who is entire under every morsel, nor is He less in each portion, but bestows Himself entire under each."

*I answer that,* As was observed above (A. 1, ad 3), because the substance of Christ's body is in this sacrament by the power of the sacrament, while dimensive quantity is there by reason of real concomitance, consequently Christ's body is in this sacrament substantively, that is, in the way in which substance is under dimensions, but not after the manner of dimensions, which means, not in the way in which the dimensive quantity of a body is under the dimensive quantity of place.

Now it is evident that the whole nature of a substance is under every part of the dimensions under which it is contained; just as the entire nature of air is under every part of air, and the entire nature of bread under every part of bread; and this indifferently, whether the dimensions be actually divided (as when the air is divided or the bread cut), or whether they be actually undivided, but potentially divisible. And therefore it is manifest that the entire Christ is under every part of the species of the bread, even while the host remains entire, and not merely when it is broken, as some say, giving the example of an image which appears in a mirror, which appears as one in the unbroken mirror, whereas when the mirror is broken, there is an image in each part of the broken mirror: for the comparison is not perfect, because the multiplying of such images results in the broken mirror on account of the various reflections in the various parts of the mirror; but here there is only one consecration, whereby Christ's body is in this sacrament.

Reply Obj. 1: Number follows division, and therefore so long as quantity remains actually undivided, neither is the substance of any thing several times under its proper dimensions, nor is Christ's body several times under the dimensions of the bread; and consequently not an infinite number of times, but just as many times as it is divided into parts.

Reply Obj. 2: The determinate distance of parts in an organic body is based upon its dimensive quantity; but the nature of substance precedes even dimensive quantity. And since the conversion of the substance of the bread is terminated at the substance of the body of Christ, and since according to the manner of substance the body of Christ is properly and directly in this sacrament; such distance of parts is indeed in Christ's true body, which, however, is not compared to this sacrament according to such distance, but according to the manner of its substance, as stated above (A. 1, ad 3).

Reply Obj. 3: This argument is based on the nature of a body, arising from dimensive quantity. But it was said above (ad 2) that Christ's body is compared with this sacrament not by reason of dimensive quantity, but by reason of its substance, as already stated.

FOURTH ARTICLE [III, Q. 76, Art. 4]

Whether the Whole Dimensive Quantity of Christ's Body Is in This Sacrament?

Objection 1: It seems that the whole dimensive quantity of Christ's body is not in this sacrament. For it was said (A. 3) that Christ's entire body is contained under every part of the consecrated host. But no dimensive quantity is contained entirely in any whole, and in its every part. Therefore it is impossible for the entire dimensive quantity of Christ's body to be there.

Obj. 2: Further, it is impossible for two dimensive quantities to be together, even though one be separate from its subject, and the other in a natural body, as is clear from the Philosopher (Metaph. iii). But the dimensive quantity of the bread remains in this sacrament, as is evident to our senses. Consequently, the dimensive quantity of Christ's body is not there.

Obj. 3: Further, if two unequal dimensive quantities be set side by side, the greater will overlap the lesser. But the dimensive quantity of Christ's body is considerably larger than the dimensive quantity of the consecrated host according to every dimension. Therefore, if the dimensive quantity of Christ's body be in this sacrament together with the dimensive quantity of the host, the dimensive quantity of Christ's body is extended beyond the quantity of the host, which nevertheless is not without the substance of Christ's body. Therefore, the substance of Christ's body will be in this sacrament even outside the species of the bread, which is unreasonable, since the substance of Christ's body is in this sacrament, only by the consecration of the bread, as stated above (A. 2). Consequently, it is impossible for the whole dimensive quantity of Christ's body to be in this sacrament.

*On the contrary,* The existence of the dimensive quantity of any body cannot be separated from the existence of its substance. But in this sacrament the entire substance of Christ's body is present, as stated above (AA. 1, 3). Therefore the entire dimensive quantity of Christ's body is in this sacrament.

*I answer that,* As stated above (A. 1), any part of Christ is in this sacrament in two ways: in one way, by the power of the sacrament; in another, from real concomitance. By the power of the sacrament the dimensive quantity of Christ's body is not in this sacrament; for, by the power of the sacrament that is present in this sacrament, whereat the conversion is terminated. But the conversion which takes place in this sacrament is terminated directly at the substance of Christ's body, and not at its dimensions; which is evident from the fact that the dimensive quantity of the bread remains after the consecration, while only the substance of the bread passes away.

Nevertheless, since the substance of Christ's body is not really deprived of its dimensive quantity and its other accidents, hence it comes that by reason of real concomitance the whole dimensive quantity of Christ's body and all its other accidents are in this sacrament.

Reply Obj. 1: The manner of being of every thing is determined by what belongs to it of itself, and not according to what is coupled accidentally with it: thus an object is present to the sight, according as it is white, and not according as it is sweet, although the same object may be both white and sweet; hence sweetness is in the sight after the manner of whiteness, and not after that of sweetness. Since, then, the substance of Christ's body is present on the altar by the power of this sacrament, while its dimensive quantity is there concomitantly and as it were accidentally, therefore the dimensive quantity of Christ's body is in this sacrament, not according to its proper manner (namely, that the whole is in the whole, and the individual parts in individual parts), but after the manner of substance, whose nature is for the whole to be in the whole, and the whole in every part.

Reply Obj. 2: Two dimensive quantities cannot naturally be in the same subject at the same time, so that each be there according to the proper manner of dimensive quantity. But in this sacrament the dimensive quantity of the bread is there after its proper manner, that is, according to commensuration: not so the dimensive quantity of Christ's body, for that is there after the manner of substance, as stated above (ad 1).

Reply Obj. 3: The dimensive quantity of Christ's body is in this sacrament not by way of commensuration, which is proper to quantity, and to which it belongs for the greater to be extended beyond the lesser; but in the way mentioned above (ad 1, 2).

FIFTH ARTICLE [III, Q. 76, Art. 5]

Whether Christ's Body Is in This Sacrament As in a Place?

Objection 1: It seems that Christ's body is in this sacrament as in a place. Because, to be in a place definitively or circumscriptively belongs to being in a place. But Christ's body seems to be definitively in this sacrament, because it is so present where the species of the bread and wine are, that it is nowhere else upon the altar: likewise it seems to be there circumscriptively, because it is so contained under the species of the consecrated host, that it neither exceeds it nor is exceeded by it. Therefore Christ's body is in this sacrament as in a place.

Obj. 2: Further, the place of the bread and wine is not empty, because nature abhors a vacuum; nor is the substance of the bread there, as stated above (Q. 75, A. 2); but only the body of Christ is there. Consequently the body of Christ fills that place. But whatever fills a place is there locally. Therefore the body of Christ is in this sacrament locally.

Obj. 3: Further, as stated above (A. 4), the body of Christ is in this sacrament with its dimensive quantity, and with all its accidents. But to be in a place is an accident of a body; hence "where" is numbered among the nine kinds of accidents. Therefore Christ's body is in this sacrament locally.

*On the contrary,* The place and the object placed must be equal, as is clear from the Philosopher (Phys. iv). But the place, where this sacrament is, is much less than the body of Christ. Therefore Christ's body is not in this sacrament as in a place.

*I answer that,* As stated above (A. 1, ad 3; A. 3), Christ's body is in this sacrament not after the proper manner of dimensive quantity, but rather after the manner of substance. But every body occupying a place is in the place according to the manner of dimensive quantity, namely, inasmuch as it is commensurate with the place according to its dimensive quantity. Hence it remains that Christ's body is not in this sacrament as in a place, but after the manner of substance, that is to say, in that way in which substance is contained by dimensions; because the substance of Christ's body succeeds the substance of bread in this sacrament: hence as the substance of bread was not locally under its dimensions, but after the manner of substance, so neither is the substance of Christ's body. Nevertheless the substance of Christ's body is not the subject of those dimensions, as was the substance of the bread: and therefore the substance of the bread was there locally by reason of its dimensions, because it was compared with that place through the medium of its own dimensions; but the substance of Christ's body is compared with that place through the medium of foreign dimensions, so that, *on the contrary,* the proper dimensions of Christ's body are compared with that place through the medium of substance; which is contrary to the notion of a located body.

Hence in no way is Christ's body locally in this sacrament.

Reply Obj. 1: Christ's body is not in this sacrament definitively, because then it would be only on the particular altar where this sacrament is performed: whereas it is in heaven under its own species, and on many other altars under the sacramental species. Likewise it is evident that it is not in this sacrament circumscriptively, because it is not there according to the commensuration of its own quantity, as stated above. But that it is not outside the superficies of the sacrament, nor on any other part of the altar, is due not to its being there definitively or circumscriptively, but to its being there by consecration and conversion of the bread and wine, as stated above (A. 1; Q. 15, A. 2, sqq.).

Reply Obj. 2: The place in which Christ's body is, is not empty; nor yet is it properly filled with the substance of Christ's body, which is not there locally, as stated above; but it is filled with the sacramental species, which have to fill the place either because of the nature of dimensions, or at least miraculously, as they also subsist miraculously after the fashion of substance.

Reply Obj. 3: As stated above (A. 4), the accidents of Christ's body are in this sacrament by real concomitance. And therefore those accidents of Christ's body which are intrinsic to it are in this sacrament. But to be in a place is an accident when compared with the extrinsic container. And therefore it is not necessary for Christ to be in this sacrament as in a place.

SIXTH ARTICLE [III, Q. 76, Art. 6]

Whether Christ's Body Is in This Sacrament Movably?

Objection 1: It seems that Christ's body is movably in this sacrament, because the Philosopher says (Topic. ii) that "when we are moved, the things within us are moved": and this is true even of the soul's spiritual substance. "But Christ is in this sacrament," as shown above (Q. 74, A. 1). Therefore He is moved when it is moved.

Obj. 2: Further, the truth ought to correspond with the figure. But, according to the commandment (Ex. 12:10), concerning the Paschal Lamb, a figure of this sacrament, "there remained nothing until the morning." Neither, therefore, if this sacrament be reserved until morning, will Christ's body be there; and so it is not immovably in this sacrament.

Obj. 3: Further, if Christ's body were to remain under this sacrament even until the morrow, for the same reason it will remain there during all coming time; for it cannot be said that it ceases to be there when the species pass, because the existence of Christ's body is not dependent on those species. Yet Christ does not remain in this sacrament for all coming time. It seems, then, that straightway on the morrow, or after a short time, He ceases to be under this sacrament. And so it seems that Christ is in this sacrament movably.

*On the contrary,* it is impossible for the same thing to be in motion and at rest, else contradictories would be verified of the same subject. But Christ's body is at rest in heaven. Therefore it is not movably in this sacrament.

*I answer that,* When any thing is one, as to subject, and manifold in being, there is nothing to hinder it from being moved in one respect, and yet to remain at rest in another just as it is one thing for a body to be white, and another thing, to be large; hence it can be moved as to its whiteness, and yet continue unmoved as to its magnitude. But in Christ, being in Himself and being under the sacrament are not the same thing, because when we say that He is under this sacrament, we express a kind of relationship to this sacrament. According to this being, then, Christ is not moved locally of Himself, but only accidentally, because Christ is not in this sacrament as in a place, as stated above (A. 5). But what is not in a place, is not moved of itself locally, but only according to the motion of the subject in which it is.

In the same way neither is it moved of itself according to the being which it has in this sacrament, by any other change whatever, as for instance, that it ceases to be under this sacrament: because whatever possesses unfailing existence of itself, cannot be the principle of failing; but when something else fails, then it ceases to be in it; just as God, Whose existence is unfailing and immortal, ceases to be in some corruptible creature because such corruptible creature ceases to exist. And in this way, since Christ has unfailing and incorruptible being, He ceases to be under this sacrament, not because He ceases to be, nor yet by local movement of His own, as is clear from what has been said, but only by the fact that the sacramental species cease to exist.

Hence it is clear that Christ, strictly speaking is immovably in this sacrament.

Reply Obj. 1: This argument deals with accidental movement, whereby things within us are moved together with us. But with things which can of themselves be in a place, like bodies, it is otherwise than with things which cannot of themselves be in a place, such as forms and spiritual substances. And to this mode can be reduced what we say of Christ, being moved accidentally, according to the existence which He has in this sacrament, in which He is not present as in a place.

Reply Obj. 2: It was this argument which seems to have convinced those who held that Christ's body does not remain under this sacrament if it be reserved until the morrow. It is against these that Cyril says (Ep. lxxxiii): "Some are so foolish as to say that the mystical blessing departs from the sacrament, if any of its fragments remain until the next day: for Christ's consecrated body is not changed, and the power of the blessing, and the life-giving grace is perpetually in it." Thus are all other consecrations irremovable so long as the consecrated things endure; on which account they are not repeated. And although the truth corresponds with the figure, still the figure cannot equal it.

Reply Obj. 3: The body of Christ remains in this sacrament not only until the morrow, but also in the future, so long as the sacramental species remain: and when they cease, Christ's body ceases to be under them, not because it depends on them, but because the relationship of Christ's body to those species is taken away, in the same way as God ceases to be the Lord of a creature which ceases to exist.

SEVENTH ARTICLE [III, Q. 76, Art. 7]

Whether the Body of Christ, As It Is in This Sacrament, Can Be Seen by Any Eye, at Least by a Glorified One?

Objection 1: It seems that the body of Christ, as it is in this sacrament, can be seen by the eye, at least by a glorified one. For our eyes are hindered from beholding Christ's body in this sacrament, on account of the sacramental species veiling it. But the glorified eye cannot be hindered by anything from seeing bodies as they are. Therefore, the glorified eye can see Christ's body as it is in this sacrament.

Obj. 2: Further, the glorified bodies of the saints will be "made like to the body" of Christ's "glory," according to Phil. 3:21. But Christ's eye beholds Himself as He is in this sacrament. Therefore, for the same reason, every other glorified eye can see Him.

Obj. 3: Further, in the resurrection the saints will be equal to the angels, according to Luke 20:36. But the angels see the body of Christ as it is in this sacrament, for even the devils are found to pay reverence thereto, and to fear it. Therefore, for like reason, the glorified eye can see Christ as He is in this sacrament.

*On the contrary,* As long as a thing remains the same, it cannot at the same time be seen by the same eye under diverse species. But the glorified eye sees Christ always, as He is in His own species, according to Isa. 33:17: "(His eyes) shall see the king in his beauty." It seems, then, that it does not see Christ, as He is under the species of this sacrament.

*I answer that,* The eye is of two kinds, namely, the bodily eye properly so-called, and the intellectual eye, so-called by similitude. But Christ's body as it is in this sacrament cannot be seen by any bodily eye. First of all, because a body which is visible brings about an alteration in the medium, through its accidents. Now the accidents of Christ's body are in this sacrament by means of the substance; so that the accidents of Christ's body have no immediate relationship either to this sacrament or to adjacent bodies; consequently they do not act on the medium so as to be seen by any corporeal eye. Secondly, because, as stated above (A. 1, ad 3; A. 3), Christ's body is substantially present in this sacrament. But substance, as such, is not visible to the bodily eye, nor does it come under any one of the senses, nor under the imagination, but solely under the intellect, whose object is "what a thing is" (De Anima iii). And therefore, properly speaking, Christ's body, according to the mode of being which it has in this sacrament, is perceptible neither by the sense nor by the imagination, but only by the intellect, which is called the spiritual eye.

Moreover it is perceived differently by different intellects. For since the way in which Christ is in this sacrament is entirely supernatural, it is visible in itself to a supernatural, i.e. the Divine, intellect, and consequently to a beatified intellect, of angel or of man, which, through the participated glory of the Divine intellect, sees all supernatural things in the vision of the Divine Essence. But it can be seen by a wayfarer through faith alone, like other supernatural things. And not even the angelic intellect of its own natural power is capable of beholding it; consequently the devils cannot by their intellect perceive Christ in this sacrament, except through faith, to which they do not pay willing assent; yet they are convinced of it from the evidence of signs, according to James 2:19: "The devils believe, and tremble."

Reply Obj. 1: Our bodily eye, on account of the sacramental species, is hindered from beholding the body of Christ underlying them, not merely as by way of veil (just as we are hindered from seeing what is covered with any corporeal veil), but also because Christ's body bears a relation to the medium surrounding this sacrament, not through its own accidents, but through the sacramental species.

Reply Obj. 2: Christ's own bodily eye sees Himself existing under the sacrament, yet it cannot see the way in which it exists under the sacrament, because that belongs to the intellect. But it is not the same with any other glorified eye, because Christ's eye is under this sacrament, in which no other glorified eye is conformed to it.

Reply Obj. 3: No angel, good or bad, can see anything with a bodily eye, but only with the mental eye. Hence there is no parallel reason, as is evident from what was said above.

EIGHTH ARTICLE [III, Q. 76, Art. 8]

Whether Christ's Body Is Truly There When Flesh or a Child Appears Miraculously in This Sacrament?

Objection 1: It seems that Christ's body is not truly there when flesh or a child appears miraculously in this sacrament. Because His body ceases to be under this sacrament when the sacramental species cease to be present, as stated above (A. 6). But when flesh or a child appears, the sacramental species cease to be present. Therefore Christ's body is not truly there.

Obj. 2: Further, wherever Christ's body is, it is there either under its own species, or under those of the sacrament. But when such apparitions occur, it is evident that Christ is not present under His own species, because the entire Christ is contained in this sacrament, and He remains entire under the form in which He ascended to heaven: yet what appears miraculously in this sacrament is sometimes seen as a small particle of flesh, or at times as a small child. Now it is evident that He is not there under the sacramental species, which is that of bread or wine. Consequently, it seems that Christ's body is not there in any way.

Obj. 3: Further, Christ's body begins to be in this sacrament by consecration and conversion, as was said above (Q. 75, AA. 2, 3, 4). But the flesh and blood which appear by miracle are not consecrated, nor are they converted into Christ's true body and blood. Therefore the body or the blood of Christ is not under those species.

*On the contrary,* When such apparition takes place, the same reverence is shown to it as was shown at first, which would not be done if Christ were not truly there, to Whom we show reverence of latria. Therefore, when such apparition occurs, Christ is under the sacrament.

*I answer that,* Such apparition comes about in two ways, when occasionally in this sacrament flesh, or blood, or a child, is seen. Sometimes it happens on the part of the beholders, whose eyes are so affected as if they outwardly saw flesh, or blood, or a child, while no change takes place in the sacrament. And this seems to happen when to one person it is seen under the species of flesh or of a child, while to others it is seen as before under the species of bread; or when to the same individual it appears for an hour under the appearance of flesh or a child, and afterwards under the appearance of bread. Nor is there any deception there, as occurs in the feats of magicians, because such species is divinely formed in the eye in order to represent some truth, namely, for the purpose of showing that Christ's body is truly under this sacrament; just as Christ without deception appeared to the disciples who were going to Emmaus. For Augustine says (De Qq. Evang. ii) that "when our pretense is referred to some significance, it is not a lie, but a figure of the truth." And since in this way no change is made in the sacrament, it is manifest that, when such apparition occurs, Christ does not cease to be under this sacrament.

But it sometimes happens that such apparition comes about not merely by a change wrought in the beholders, but by an appearance which really exists outwardly. And this indeed is seen to happen when it is beheld by everyone under such an appearance, and it remains so not for an hour, but for a considerable time; and, in this case some think that it is the proper species of Christ's body. Nor does it matter that sometimes Christ's entire body is not seen there, but part of His flesh, or else that it is not seen in youthful guise, but in the semblance of a child, because it lies within the power of a glorified body for it to be seen by a non-glorified eye either entirely or in part, and under its own semblance or in strange guise, as will be said later (Suppl., Q. 85, AA. 2, 3).

But this seems unlikely. First of all, because Christ's body under its proper species can be seen only in one place, wherein it is definitively contained. Hence since it is seen in its proper species, and is adored in heaven, it is not seen under its proper species in this sacrament. Secondly, because a glorified body, which appears at will, disappears when it wills after the apparition; thus it is related (Luke 24:31) that our Lord "vanished out of sight" of the disciples. But that which appears under the likeness of flesh in this sacrament, continues for a long time; indeed, one reads of its being sometimes enclosed, and, by order of many bishops, preserved in a pyx, which it would be wicked to think of Christ under His proper semblance.

Consequently, it remains to be said, that, while the dimensions remain the same as before, there is a miraculous change wrought in the other accidents, such as shape, color, and the rest, so that flesh, or blood, or a child, is seen. And, as was said already, this is not deception, because it is done "to represent the truth," namely, to show by this miraculous apparition that Christ's body and blood are truly in this sacrament. And thus it is clear that as the dimensions remain, which are the foundation of the other accidents, as we shall see later on (Q. 77, A. 2), the body of Christ truly remains in this sacrament.

Reply Obj. 1: When such apparition takes place, the sacramental species sometimes continue entire in themselves; and sometimes only as to that which is principal, as was said above.

Reply Obj. 2: As stated above, during such apparitions Christ's proper semblance is not seen, but a species miraculously formed either in the eyes of the beholders, or in the sacramental dimensions themselves, as was said above.

Reply Obj. 3: The dimensions of the consecrated bread and wine continue, while a miraculous change is wrought in the other accidents, as stated above.

## QUESTION 77

OF THE ACCIDENTS WHICH REMAIN IN THIS SACRAMENT (In Eight Articles)

We must now consider the accidents which remain in this sacrament; under which head there are eight points of inquiry:

(1) Whether the accidents which remain are without a subject?

(2) Whether dimensive quantity is the subject of the other accidents?

(3) Whether such accidents can affect an extrinsic body?

(4) Whether they can be corrupted?

(5) Whether anything can be generated from them?

(6) Whether they can nourish?

(7) Of the breaking of the consecrated bread?

(8) Whether anything can be mixed with the consecrated wine?

FIRST ARTICLE [III, Q. 77, Art. 1]

Whether the Accidents Remain in This Sacrament Without a Subject?

Objection 1: It seems that the accidents do not remain in this sacrament without a subject, because there ought not to be anything disorderly or deceitful in this sacrament of truth. But for accidents to be without a subject is contrary to the order which God established in nature; and furthermore it seems to savor of deceit, since accidents are naturally the signs of the nature of the subject. Therefore the accidents are not without a subject in this sacrament.

Obj. 2: Further, not even by miracle can the definition of a thing be severed from it, or the definition of another thing be applied to it; for instance, that, while man remains a man, he can be an irrational animal. For it would follow that contradictories can exist at the one time: for the "definition of a thing is what its name expresses," as is said in Metaph. iv. But it belongs to the definition of an accident for it to be in a subject, while the definition of substance is that it must subsist of itself, and not in another. Therefore it cannot come to pass, even by miracle, that the accidents exist without a subject in this sacrament.

Obj. 3: Further, an accident is individuated by its subject. If therefore the accidents remain in this sacrament without a subject, they will not be individual, but general, which is clearly false, because thus they would not be sensible, but merely intelligible.

Obj. 4: Further, the accidents after the consecration of this sacrament do not obtain any composition. But before the consecration they were not composed either of matter and form, nor of existence ( quo est ) and essence ( quod est ). Therefore, even after consecration they are not composite in either of these ways. But this is unreasonable, for thus they would be simpler than angels, whereas at the same time these accidents are perceptible to the senses. Therefore, in this sacrament the accidents do not remain without a subject.

*On the contrary,* Gregory says in an Easter Homily (Lanfranc, De Corp. et Sang. Dom. xx) that "the sacramental species are the names of those things which were there before, namely, of the bread and wine." Therefore since the substance of the bread and the wine does not remain, it seems that these species remain without a subject.

*I answer that,* The species of the bread and wine, which are perceived by our senses to remain in this sacrament after consecration, are not subjected in the substance of the bread and wine, for that does not remain, as stated above (Q. 75, A. 2); nor in the substantial form, for that does not remain (Q. 75, A. 6), and if it did remain, "it could not be a subject," as Boethius declares (De Trin. i). Furthermore it is manifest that these accidents are not subjected in the substance of Christ's body and blood, because the substance of the human body cannot in any way be affected by such accidents; nor is it possible for Christ's glorious and impassible body to be altered so as to receive these qualities.

Now there are some who say that they are in the surrounding atmosphere as in a subject. But even this cannot be: in the first place, because atmosphere is not susceptive of such accidents. Secondly, because these accidents are not where the atmosphere is, nay more, the atmosphere is displaced by the motion of these species. Thirdly, because accidents do not pass from subject to subject, so that the same identical accident which was first in one subject be afterwards in another; because an accident is individuated by the subject; hence it cannot come to pass for an accident remaining identically the same to be at one time in one subject, and at another time in another. Fourthly, since the atmosphere is not deprived of its own accidents, it would have at the one time its own accidents and others foreign to it. Nor can it be maintained that this is done miraculously in virtue of the consecration, because the words of consecration do not signify this, and they effect only what they signify.

Therefore it follows that the accidents continue in this sacrament without a subject. This can be done by Divine power: for since an effect depends more upon the first cause than on the second, God Who is the first cause both of substance and accident, can by His unlimited power preserve an accident in existence when the substance is withdrawn whereby it was preserved in existence as by its proper cause, just as without natural causes He can produce other effects of natural causes, even as He formed a human body in the Virgin's womb, "without the seed of man" (Hymn for Christmas, First Vespers).

Reply Obj. 1: There is nothing to hinder the common law of nature from ordaining a thing, the contrary of which is nevertheless ordained by a special privilege of grace, as is evident in the raising of the dead, and in the restoring of sight to the blind: even thus in human affairs, to some individuals some things are granted by special privilege which are outside the common law. And so, even though it be according to the common law of nature for an accident to be in a subject, still for a special reason, according to the order of grace, the accidents exist in this sacrament without a subject, on account of the reasons given above (Q. 75, A. 5).

Reply Obj. 2: Since being is not a genus, then being cannot be of itself the essence of either substance or accident. Consequently, the definition of substance is not--"a being of itself without a subject," nor is the definition of accident--"a being in a subject"; but it belongs to the quiddity or essence of substance "to have existence not in a subject"; while it belongs to the quiddity or essence of accident "to have existence in a subject." But in this sacrament it is not in virtue of their essence that accidents are not in a subject, but through the Divine power sustaining them; and consequently they do not cease to be accidents, because neither is the definition of accident withdrawn from them, nor does the definition of substance apply to them.

Reply Obj. 3: These accidents acquired individual being in the substance of the bread and wine; and when this substance is changed into the body and blood of Christ, they remain in that individuated being which they possessed before, hence they are individual and sensible.

Reply Obj. 4: These accidents had no being of their own nor other accidents, so long as the substance of the bread and wine remained; but their subjects had such being through them, just as snow is white through whiteness. But after the consecration the accidents which remain have being; hence they are compounded of existence and essence, as was said of the angels, in the First Part (Q. 50, A. 2, ad 3); and besides they have composition of quantitative parts.

SECOND ARTICLE [III, Q. 77, Art. 2]

Whether in This Sacrament the Dimensive Quantity of the Bread or Wine Is the Subject of the Other Accidents?

Objection 1: It seems that in this sacrament the dimensive quantity of the bread or wine is not the subject of the other accidents. For accident is not the subject of accident; because no form can be a subject, since to be a subject is a property of matter. But dimensive quantity is an accident. Therefore dimensive quantity cannot be the subject of the other accidents.

Obj. 2: Further, just as quantity is individuated by substance, so also are the other accidents. If, then, the dimensive quantity of the bread or wine remains individuated according to the being it had before, in which it is preserved, for like reason the other accidents remain individuated according to the existence which they had before in the substance. Therefore they are not in dimensive quantity as in a subject, since every accident is individuated by its own subject.

Obj. 3: Further, among the other accidents that remain, of the bread and wine, the senses perceive also rarity and density, which cannot be in dimensive quantity existing outside matter; because a thing is rare which has little matter under great dimensions, while a thing is dense which has much matter under small dimensions, as is said in Phys. iv. It does not seem, then, that dimensive quantity can be the subject of the accidents which remain in this sacrament.

Obj. 4: Further, quantity abstract from matter seems to be mathematical quantity, which is not the subject of sensible qualities. Since, then, the remaining accidents in this sacrament are sensible, it seems that in this sacrament they cannot be subjected in the dimensive quantity of the bread and wine that remains after consecration.

*On the contrary,* Qualities are divisible only accidentally, that is, by reason of the subject. But the qualities remaining in this sacrament are divided by the division of dimensive quantity, as is evident through our senses. Therefore, dimensive quantity is the subject of the accidents which remain in this sacrament.

*I answer that,* It is necessary to say that the other accidents which remain in this sacrament are subjected in the dimensive quantity of the bread and wine that remains: first of all, because something having quantity and color and affected by other accidents is perceived by the senses; nor is sense deceived in such. Secondly, because the first disposition of matter is dimensive quantity, hence Plato also assigned "great" and "small" as the first differences of matter (Aristotle, Metaph. iv). And because the first subject is matter, the consequence is that all other accidents are related to their subject through the medium of dimensive quantity; just as the first subject of color is said to be the surface, on which account some have maintained that dimensions are the substances of bodies, as is said in Metaph. iii. And since, when the subject is withdrawn, the accidents remain according to the being which they had before, it follows that all accidents remain founded upon dimensive quantity.

Thirdly, because, since the subject is the principle of individuation of the accidents, it is necessary for what is admitted as the subject of some accidents to be somehow the principle of individuation: for it is of the very notion of an individual that it cannot be in several; and this happens in two ways. First, because it is not natural to it to be in any one; and in this way immaterial separated forms, subsisting of themselves, are also individuals of themselves. Secondly, because a form, be it substantial or accidental, is naturally in someone indeed, not in several, as this whiteness, which is in this body. As to the first, matter is the principle of individuation of all inherent forms, because, since these forms, considered in themselves, are naturally in something as in a subject, from the very fact that one of them is received in matter, which is not in another, it follows that neither can the form itself thus existing be in another. As to the second, it must be maintained that the principle of individuation is dimensive quantity. For that something is naturally in another one solely, is due to the fact that that other is undivided in itself, and distinct from all others. But it is on account of quantity that substance can be divided, as is said in Phys. i. And therefore dimensive quantity itself is a particular principle of individuation in forms of this kind, namely, inasmuch as forms numerically distinct are in different parts of the matter. Hence also dimensive quantity has of itself a kind of individuation, so that we can imagine several lines of the same species, differing in position, which is included in the notion of this quantity; for it belongs to dimension for it to be "quantity having position" (Aristotle, Categor. iv), and therefore dimensive quantity can be the subject of the other accidents, rather than the other way about.

Reply Obj. 1: One accident cannot of itself be the subject of another, because it does not exist of itself. But inasmuch as an accident is received in another thing, one is said to be the subject of the other, inasmuch as one is received in a subject through another, as the surface is said to be the subject of color. Hence when God makes an accident to exist of itself, it can also be of itself the subject of another.

Reply Obj. 2: The other accidents, even as they were in the substance of the bread, were individuated by means of dimensive quantity, as stated above. And therefore dimensive quantity is the subject of the other accidents remaining in this sacrament, rather than conversely.

Reply Obj. 3: Rarity and density are particular qualities accompanying bodies, by reason of their having much or little matter under dimensions; just as all other accidents likewise follow from the principles of substance. And consequently, as the accidents are preserved by Divine power when the substance is withdrawn, so, when matter is withdrawn, the qualities which go with matter, such as rarity and density, are preserved by Divine power.

Reply Obj. 4: Mathematical quantity abstracts not from intelligible matter, but from sensible matter, as is said in Metaph. vii. But matter is termed sensible because it underlies sensible qualities. And therefore it is manifest that the dimensive quantity, which remains in this sacrament without a subject, is not mathematical quantity.

THIRD ARTICLE [III, Q. 77, Art. 3]

Whether the Species Remaining in This Sacrament Can Change External Objects?

Objection 1: It seems that the species which remain in this sacrament cannot affect external objects. For it is proved in Phys. vii, that forms which are in matter are produced by forms that are in matter, but not from forms which are without matter, because like makes like. But the sacramental species are species without matter, since they remain without a subject, as is evident from what was said above (A. 1). Therefore they cannot affect other matter by producing any form in it.

Obj. 2: Further, when the action of the principal agent ceases, then the action of the instrument must cease, as when the carpenter rests, the hammer is moved no longer. But all accidental forms act instrumentally in virtue of the substantial form as the principal agent. Therefore, since the substantial form of the bread and wine does not remain in this sacrament, as was shown above (Q. 75, A. 6), it seems that the accidental forms which remain cannot act so as to change external matter.

Obj. 3: Further, nothing acts outside its species, because an effect cannot surpass its cause. But all the sacramental species are accidents. Therefore they cannot change external matter, at least as to a substantial form.

*On the contrary,* If they could not change external bodies, they could not be felt; for a thing is felt from the senses being changed by a sensible thing, as is said in De Anima ii.

*I answer that,* Because everything acts in so far as it is an actual being, the consequence is that everything stands in the same relation to action as it does to being. Therefore, because, according to what was said above (A. 1), it is an effect of the Divine power that the sacramental species continue in the being which they had when the substance of the bread and wine was present, it follows that they continue in their action. Consequently they retain every action which they had while the substance of the bread and wine remained, now that the substance of the bread and wine has passed into the body and blood of Christ. Hence there is no doubt but that they can change external bodies.

Reply Obj. 1: The sacramental species, although they are forms existing without matter, still retain the same being which they had before in matter, and therefore as to their being they are like forms which are in matter.

Reply Obj. 2: The action of an accidental form depends upon the action of a substantial form in the same way as the being of accident depends upon the being of substance; and therefore, as it is an effect of Divine power that the sacramental species exist without substance, so is it an effect of Divine power that they can act without a substantial form, because every action of a substantial or accidental form depends upon God as the first agent.

Reply Obj. 3: The change which terminates in a substantial form is not effected by a substantial form directly, but by means of the active and passive qualities, which act in virtue of the substantial form. But by Divine power this instrumental energy is retained in the sacramental species, just as it was before: and consequently their action can be directed to a substantial form instrumentally, just in the same way as anything can act outside its species, not as by its own power, but by the power of the chief agent.

FOURTH ARTICLE [III, Q. 77, Art. 4]

Whether the Sacramental Species Can Be Corrupted?

Objection 1: It seems that the sacramental species cannot be corrupted, because corruption comes of the separation of the form from the matter. But the matter of the bread does not remain in this sacrament, as is clear from what was said above (Q. 75, A. 2). Therefore these species cannot be corrupted.

Obj. 2: Further, no form is corrupted except accidentally, that is, when its subject is corrupted; hence self-subsisting forms are incorruptible, as is seen in spiritual substances. But the sacramental species are forms without a subject. Therefore they cannot be corrupted.

Obj. 3: Further, if they be corrupted, it will either be naturally or miraculously. But they cannot be corrupted naturally, because no subject of corruption can be assigned as remaining after the corruption has taken place. Neither can they be corrupted miraculously, because the miracles which occur in this sacrament take place in virtue of the consecration, whereby the sacramental species are preserved: and the same thing is not the cause of preservation and of corruption. Therefore, in no way can the sacramental species be corrupted.

*On the contrary,* We perceive by our senses that the consecrated hosts become putrefied and corrupted.

*I answer that,* Corruption is "movement from being into non-being" (Aristotle, Phys. v). Now it has been stated (A. 3) that the sacramental species retain the same being as they had before when the substance of the bread was present. Consequently, as the being of those accidents could be corrupted while the substance of the bread and wine was present, so likewise they can be corrupted now that the substance has passed away.

But such accidents could have been previously corrupted in two ways: in one way, of themselves; in another way, accidentally. They could be corrupted of themselves, as by alteration of the qualities, and increase or decrease of the quantity, not in the way in which increase or decrease is found only in animated bodies, such as the substances of the bread and wine are not, but by addition or division; for, as is said inMetaph. iii, one dimension is dissolved by division, and two dimensions result; while *on the contrary,* by addition, two dimensions become one. And in this way such accidents can be corrupted manifestly after consecration, because the dimensive quantity which remains can receive division and addition; and since it is the subject of sensible qualities, as stated above (A. 1), it can likewise be the subject of their alteration, for instance, if the color or the savor of the bread or wine be altered.

An accident can be corrupted in another way, through the corruption of its subject, and in this way also they can be corrupted after consecration; for although the subject does not remain, still the being which they had in the subject does remain, which being is proper, and suited to the subject. And therefore such being can be corrupted by a contrary agent, as the substance of the bread or wine was subject to corruption, and, moreover, was not corrupted except by a preceding alteration regarding the accidents.

Nevertheless, a distinction must be made between each of the aforesaid corruptions; because, when the body and the blood of Christ succeed in this sacrament to the substance of the bread and wine, if there be such change on the part of the accidents as would not have sufficed for the corruption of the bread and wine, then the body and blood of Christ do not cease to be under this sacrament on account of such change, whether the change be on the part of the quality, as for instance, when the color or the savor of the bread or wine is slightly modified; or on the part of the quantity, as when the bread or the wine is divided into such parts as to keep in them the nature of bread or of wine. But if the change be so great that the substance of the bread or wine would have been corrupted, then Christ's body and blood do not remain under this sacrament; and this either on the part of the qualities, as when the color, savor, and other qualities of the bread and wine are so altered as to be incompatible with the nature of bread or of wine; or else on the part of the quantity, as, for instance, if the bread be reduced to fine particles, or the wine divided into such tiny drops that the species of bread or wine no longer remain.

Reply Obj. 1: Since it belongs essentially to corruption to take away the being of a thing, in so far as the being of some form is in matter, it results that by corruption the form is separated from the matter. But if such being were not in matter, yet like such being as is in matter, it could be taken away by corruption, even where there is no matter; as takes place in this sacrament, as is evident from what was said above.

Reply Obj. 2: Although the sacramental species are forms not in matter, yet they have the being which they had in matter.

Reply Obj. 3: This corruption of species is not miraculous, but natural; nevertheless, it presupposes the miracle which is wrought in the consecration, namely, that those sacramental species retain without a subject, the same being as they had in a subject; just as a blind man, to whom sight is given miraculously, sees naturally.

FIFTH ARTICLE [III, Q. 77, Art. 5]

Whether Anything Can Be Generated from the Sacramental Species?

Objection 1: It seems that nothing can be generated from the sacramental species: because, whatever is generated, is generated out of some matter: for nothing is generated out of nothing, although by creation something is made out of nothing. But there is no matter underlying the sacramental species except that of Christ's body, and that body is incorruptible. Therefore it seems that nothing can be generated from the sacramental species.

Obj. 2: Further, things which are not of the same genus cannot spring from one another: thus a line is not made of whiteness. But accident and substance differ generically. Therefore, since the sacramental species are accidents, it seems that no substance can be generated from them.

Obj. 3: Further, if any corporeal substance be generated from them, such substance will not be without accident. Therefore, if any corporeal substance be generated from the sacramental species, then substance and accident would be generated from accident, namely, two things from one, which is impossible. Consequently, it is impossible for any corporeal substance to be generated out of the sacramental species.

*On the contrary,* The senses are witness that something is generated out of the sacramental species, either ashes, if they be burned, worms if they putrefy, or dust if they be crushed.

*I answer that,* Since "the corruption of one thing is the generation of another" (De Gener. i), something must be generated necessarily from the sacramental species if they be corrupted, as stated above (A. 4); for they are not corrupted in such a way that they disappear altogether, as if reduced to nothing; *on the contrary,* something sensible manifestly succeeds to them.

Nevertheless, it is difficult to see how anything can be generated from them. For it is quite evident that nothing is generated out of the body and blood of Christ which are truly there, because these are incorruptible. But if the substance, or even the matter, of the bread and wine were to remain in this sacrament, then, as some have maintained, it would be easy to account for this sensible object which succeeds to them. But that supposition is false, as was stated above (Q. 75, AA. 2, 4, 8).

Hence it is that others have said that the things generated have not sprung from the sacramental species, but from the surrounding atmosphere. But this can be shown in many ways to be impossible. In the first place, because when a thing is generated from another, the latter at first appears changed and corrupted; whereas no alteration or corruption appeared previously in the adjacent atmosphere; hence the worms or ashes are not generated therefrom. Secondly, because the nature of the atmosphere is not such as to permit of such things being generated by such alterations. Thirdly, because it is possible for many consecrated hosts to be burned or putrefied; nor would it be possible for an earthen body, large enough to be generated from the atmosphere, unless a great and, in fact, exceedingly sensible condensation of the atmosphere took place. Fourthly, because the same thing can happen to the solid bodies surrounding them, such as iron or stone, which remain entire after the generation of the aforesaid things. Hence this opinion cannot stand, because it is opposed to what is manifest to our senses.

And therefore others have said that the substance of the bread and wine returns during the corruption of the species, and so from the returning substance of the bread and wine, ashes or worms or something of the kind are generated. But this explanation seems an impossible one. First of all, because if the substance of the bread and wine be converted into the body and blood of Christ, as was shown above (Q. 75, AA. 2, 4), the substance of the bread and wine cannot return, except the body and blood of Christ be again changed back into the substance of bread and wine, which is impossible: thus if air be turned into fire, the air cannot return without the fire being again changed into air. But if the substance of bread or wine be annihilated, it cannot return again, because what lapses into nothing does not return numerically the same. Unless perchance it be said that the said substance returns, because God creates anew another new substance to replace the first. Secondly, this seems to be impossible, because no time can be assigned when the substance of the bread returns. For, from what was said above (A. 4; Q. 76, A. 6, ad 3), it is evident that while the species of the bread and wine remain, there remain also the body and blood of Christ, which are not present together with the substance of the bread and wine in this sacrament, according to what was stated above (Q. 75, A. 2). Hence the substance of the bread and wine cannot return while the sacramental species remain; nor, again, when these species pass away; because then the substance of the bread and wine would be without their proper accidents, which is impossible. Unless perchance it be said that in the last instant of the corruption of the species there returns (not, indeed, the substance of bread and wine, because it is in that very instant that they have the being of the substance generated from the species, but) the matter of the bread and wine; which, matter, properly speaking, would be more correctly described as created anew, than as returning. And in this sense the aforesaid position might be held.

However, since it does not seem reasonable to say that anything takes place miraculously in this sacrament, except in virtue of the consecration itself, which does not imply either creation or return of matter, it seems better to say that in the actual consecration it is miraculously bestowed on the dimensive quantity of the bread and wine to be the subject of subsequent forms. Now this is proper to matter; and therefore as a consequence everything which goes with matter is bestowed on dimensive quantity; and therefore everything which could be generated from the matter of bread or wine, if it were present, can be generated from the aforesaid dimensive quantity of the bread or wine, not, indeed, by a new miracle, but by virtue of the miracle which has already taken place.

Reply Obj. 1: Although no matter is there out of which a thing may be generated, nevertheless dimensive quantity supplies the place of matter, as stated above.

Reply Obj. 2: Those sacramental species are indeed accidents, yet they have the act and power of substance, as stated above (A. 3).

Reply Obj. 3: The dimensive quantity of the bread and wine retains its own nature, and receives miraculously the power and property of substance; and therefore it can pass to both, that is, into substance and dimension.

SIXTH ARTICLE [III, Q. 77, Art. 6]

Whether the Sacramental Species Can Nourish?

Objection 1: It seems that the sacramental species cannot nourish, because, as Ambrose says (De Sacram. v), "it is not this bread that enters into our body, but the bread of everlasting life, which supports the substance of our soul." But whatever nourishes enters into the body. Therefore this bread does not nourish: and the same reason holds good of the wine.

Obj. 2: Further, as is said in De Gener. ii, "We are nourished by the very things of which we are made." But the sacramental species are accidents, whereas man is not made of accidents, because accident is not a part of substance. Therefore it seems that the sacramental species cannot nourish.

Obj. 3: Further, the Philosopher says (De Anima ii) that "food nourishes according as it is a substance, but it gives increase by reason of its quantity." But the sacramental species are not a substance. Consequently they cannot nourish.

*On the contrary,* The Apostle speaking of this sacrament says (1 Cor. 11:21): "One, indeed, is hungry, and another is drunk": upon which the gloss observes that "he alludes to those who after the celebration of the sacred mystery, and after the consecration of the bread and wine, claimed their oblations, and not sharing them with others, took the whole, so as even to become intoxicated thereby." But this could not happen if the sacramental species did not nourish. Therefore the sacramental species do nourish.

*I answer that,* This question presents no difficulty, now that we have solved the preceding question. Because, as stated in De Anima ii, food nourishes by being converted into the substance of the individual nourished. Now it has been stated (A. 5) that the sacramental species can be converted into a substance generated from them. And they can be converted into the human body for the same reason as they can into ashes or worms. Consequently, it is evident that they nourish.

But the senses witness to the untruth of what some maintain; viz. that the species do not nourish as though they were changed into the human body, but merely refresh and hearten by acting upon the senses (as a man is heartened by the odor of meat, and intoxicated by the fumes of wine). Because such refreshment does not suffice long for a man, whose body needs repair owing to constant waste: and yet a man could be supported for long if he were to take hosts and consecrated wine in great quantity.

In like manner the statement advanced by others cannot stand, who hold that the sacramental species nourish owing to the remaining substantial form of the bread and wine: both because the form does not remain, as stated above (Q. 75, A. 6): and because to nourish is the act not of a form but rather of matter, which takes the form of the one nourished, while the form of the nourishment passes away: hence it is said inDe Anima ii that nourishment is at first unlike, but at the end is like.

Reply Obj. 1: After the consecration bread can be said to be in this sacrament in two ways. First, as to the species, which retain the name of the previous substance, as Gregory says in an Easter Homily (Lanfranc, De Corp. et Sang. Dom. xx). Secondly, Christ's very body can be called bread, since it is the mystical bread "coming down from heaven." Consequently, Ambrose uses the word "bread" in this second meaning, when he says that "this bread does not pass into the body," because, to wit, Christ's body is not changed into man's body, but nourishes his soul. But he is not speaking of bread taken in the first acceptation.

Reply Obj. 2: Although the sacramental species are not those things out of which the human body is made, yet they are changed into those things stated above.

Reply Obj. 3: Although the sacramental species are not a substance, still they have the virtue of a substance, as stated above.

SEVENTH ARTICLE [III, Q. 77, Art. 7]

Whether the Sacramental Species Are Broken in This Sacrament?

Objection 1: It seems that the sacramental species are not broken in this sacrament, because the Philosopher says in Meteor. iv that bodies are breakable owing to a certain disposition of the pores; a thing which cannot be attributed to the sacramental species. Therefore the sacramental species cannot be broken.

Obj. 2: Further, breaking is followed by sound. But the sacramental species emit no sound: because the Philosopher says (De Anima ii), that what emits sound is a hard body, having a smooth surface. Therefore the sacramental species are not broken.

Obj. 3: Further, breaking and mastication are seemingly of the same object. But it is Christ's true body that is eaten, according to John 6:57: "He that eateth My flesh, and drinketh My blood." Therefore it is Christ's body that is broken and masticated: and hence it is said in the confession of Berengarius: "I agree with the Holy Catholic Church, and with heart and lips I profess, that the bread and wine which are placed on the altar, are the true body and blood of Christ after consecration, and are truly handled and broken by the priest's hands, broken and crushed by the teeth of believers." Consequently, the breaking ought not to be ascribed to the sacramental species.

*On the contrary,* Breaking arises from the division of that which has quantity. But nothing having quantity except the sacramental species is broken here, because neither Christ's body is broken, as being incorruptible, nor is the substance of the bread, because it no longer remains. Therefore the sacramental species are broken.

*I answer that,* Many opinions prevailed of old on this matter. Some held that in this sacrament there was no breaking at all in reality, but merely in the eyes of the beholders. But this contention cannot stand, because in this sacrament of truth the sense is not deceived with regard to its proper object of judgment, and one of these objects is breaking, whereby from one thing arise many: and these are common sensibles, as is stated in De Anima ii.

Others accordingly have said that there was indeed a genuine breaking, but without any subject. But this again contradicts our senses; because a quantitative body is seen in this sacrament, which formerly was one, and is now divided into many, and this must be the subject of the breaking.

But it cannot be said that Christ's true body is broken. First of all, because it is incorruptible and impassible: secondly, because it is entire under every part, as was shown above (Q. 76, A. 3), which is contrary to the nature of a thing broken.

It remains, then, that the breaking is in the dimensive quantity of the bread, as in a subject, just as the other accidents. And as the sacramental species are the sacrament of Christ's true body, so is the breaking of these species the sacrament of our Lord's Passion, which was in Christ's true body.

Reply Obj. 1: As rarity and density remain under the sacramental species, as stated above (A. 2, ad 3), so likewise porousness remains, and in consequence breakableness.

Reply Obj. 2: Hardness results from density; therefore, as density remains under the sacramental species, hardness remains there too, and the capability of sound as a consequence.

Reply Obj. 3: What is eaten under its own species, is also broken and masticated under its own species; but Christ's body is eaten not under its proper, but under the sacramental species. Hence in explaining John 6:64, "The flesh profiteth nothing," Augustine (Tract. xxvii in Joan.) says that this is to be taken as referring to those who understood carnally: "for they understood the flesh, thus, as it is divided piecemeal, in a dead body, or as sold in the shambles." Consequently, Christ's very body is not broken, except according to its sacramental species. And the confession made by Berengarius is to be understood in this sense, that the breaking and the crushing with the teeth is to be referred to the sacramental species, under which the body of Christ truly is.

EIGHTH ARTICLE [III, Q. 77, Art. 8]

Whether Any Liquid Can Be Mingled with the Consecrated Wine?

Objection 1: It seems that no liquid can be mingled with the consecrated wine, because everything mingled with another partakes of its quality. But no liquid can share in the quality of the sacramental species, because those accidents are without a subject, as stated above (A. 1). Therefore it seems that no liquid can be mingled with the sacramental species of the wine.

Obj. 2: Further, if any kind of liquid be mixed with those species, then some one thing must be the result. But no one thing can result from the liquid, which is a substance, and the sacramental species, which are accidents; nor from the liquid and Christ's blood, which owing to its incorruptibility suffers neither increase nor decrease. Therefore no liquid can be mixed with the consecrated wine.

Obj. 3: Further, if any liquid be mixed with the consecrated wine, then that also would appear to be consecrated; just as water added to holy-water becomes holy. But the consecrated wine is truly Christ's blood. Therefore the liquid added would likewise be Christ's blood otherwise than by consecration, which is unbecoming. Therefore no liquid can be mingled with the consecrated wine.

Obj. 4: Further, if one of two things be entirely corrupted, there is no mixture (De Gener. i). But if we mix any liquid, it seems that the entire species of the sacramental wine is corrupted, so that the blood of Christ ceases to be beneath it; both because great and little are difference of quantity, and alter it, as white and black cause a difference of color; and because the liquid mixed, as having no obstacle, seems to permeate the whole, and so Christ's blood ceases to be there, since it is not there with any other substance. Consequently, no liquid can be mixed with the consecrated wine.

*On the contrary,* It is evident to our senses that another liquid can be mixed with the wine after it is consecrated, just as before.

*I answer that,* The truth of this question is evident from what has been said already. For it was said above (A. 3; A. 5, ad 2) that the species remaining in this sacrament, as they acquire the manner of being of substance in virtue of the consecration, so likewise do they obtain the mode of acting and of being acted upon, so that they can do or receive whatever their substance could do or receive, were it there present. But it is evident that if the substance of wine were there present, then some other liquid could be mingled with it.

Nevertheless there would be a different effect of such mixing both according to the form and according to the quantity of the liquid. For if sufficient liquid were mixed so as to spread itself all through the wine, then the whole would be a mixed substance. Now what is made up of things mixed is neither of them, but each passes into a third resulting from both: hence it would result that the former wine would remain no longer. But if the liquid added were of another species, for instance, if water were mixed, the species of the wine would be dissolved, and there would be a liquid of another species. But if liquid of the same species were added, of instance, wine with wine, the same species would remain, but the wine would not be the same numerically, as the diversity of the accidents shows: for instance, if one wine were white and the other red.

But if the liquid added were of such minute quantity that it could not permeate the whole, the entire wine would not be mixed, but only part of it, which would not remain the same numerically owing to the blending of extraneous matter: still it would remain the same specifically, not only if a little liquid of the same species were mixed with it, but even if it were of another species, since a drop of water blended with much wine passes into the species of wine (De Gener. i).

Now it is evident that the body and blood of Christ abide in this sacrament so long as the species remain numerically the same, as stated above (A. 4; Q. 76, A. 6, ad 3); because it is this bread and this wine which is consecrated. Hence, if the liquid of any kind whatsoever added be so much in quantity as to permeate the whole of the consecrated wine, and be mixed with it throughout, the result would be something numerically distinct, and the blood of Christ will remain there no longer. But if the quantity of the liquid added be so slight as not to permeate throughout, but to reach only a part of the species, Christ's blood will cease to be under that part of the consecrated wine, yet will remain under the rest.

Reply Obj. 1: Pope Innocent III in a Decretal writes thus: "The very accidents appear to affect the wine that is added, because, if water is added, it takes the savor of the wine. The result is, then, that the accidents change the subject, just as subject changes accidents; for nature yields to miracle, and power works beyond custom." But this must not be understood as if the same identical accident, which was in the wine previous to consecration, is afterwards in the wine that is added; but such change is the result of action; because the remaining accidents of the wine retain the action of substance, as stated above, and so they act upon the liquid added, by changing it.

Reply Obj. 2: The liquid added to the consecrated wine is in no way mixed with the substance of Christ's blood. Nevertheless it is mixed with the sacramental species, yet so that after such mixing the aforesaid species are corrupted entirely or in part, after the way mentioned above (A. 5), whereby something can be generated from those species. And if they be entirely corrupted, there remains no further question, because the whole will be uniform. But if they be corrupted in part, there will be one dimension according to the continuity of quantity, but not one according to the mode of being, because one part thereof will be without a subject while the other is in a subject; as in a body that is made up of two metals, there will be one body quantitatively, but not one as to the species of the matter.

Reply Obj. 3: As Pope Innocent says in the aforesaid Decretal, "if after the consecration other wine be put in the chalice, it is not changed into the blood, nor is it mingled with the blood, but, mixed with the accidents of the previous wine, it is diffused throughout the body which underlies them, yet without wetting what surrounds it." Now this is to be understood when there is not sufficient mixing of extraneous liquid to cause the blood of Christ to cease to be under the whole; because a thing is said to be "diffused throughout," not because it touches the body of Christ according to its proper dimensions, but according to the sacramental dimensions, under which it is contained. Now it is not the same with holy water, because the blessing works no change in the substance of the water, as the consecration of the wine does.

Reply Obj. 4: Some have held that however slight be the mixing of extraneous liquid, the substance of Christ's blood ceases to be under the whole, and for the reason given above (Obj. 4); which, however, is not a cogent one; because "more" or "less" diversify dimensive quantity, not as to its essence, but as to the determination of its measure. In like manner the liquid added can be so small as on that account to be hindered from permeating the whole, and not simply by the dimensions; which, although they are present without a subject, still they are opposed to another liquid, just as substance would be if it were present, according to what was said at the beginning of the article.

# QUESTION 78

OF THE FORM OF THIS SACRAMENT (In Six Articles)

We must now consider the form of this sacrament; concerning which there are six points of inquiry:

(1) What is the form of this sacrament?

(2) Whether the form for the consecration of the bread is appropriate?

(3) Whether the form for the consecration of the blood is appropriate?

(4) Of the power of each form?

(5) Of the truth of the expression?

(6) Of the comparison of the one form with the other?

FIRST ARTICLE [III, Q. 78, Art. 1]

Whether This Is the Form of This Sacrament: "This Is My Body," and "This Is the Chalice of My Blood"?

Objection 1: It seems that this is not the form of this sacrament: "This is My body," and, "This is the chalice of My blood." Because those words seem to belong to the form of this sacrament, wherewith Christ consecrated His body and blood. But Christ first blessed the bread which He took, and said afterwards: "Take ye and eat; this is My body" (Matt. 26:26). Therefore the whole of this seems to belong to the form of this sacrament: and the same reason holds good of the words which go with the consecration of the blood.

Obj. 2: Further, Eusebius Emissenus (Pseudo-Hieron: Ep. xxix; Pseudo-Isid.: Hom. iv) says: "The invisible Priest changes visible creatures into His own body, saying: 'Take ye and eat; this is My body.'" Therefore, the whole of this seems to belong to the form of this sacrament: and the same hold good of the works appertaining to the blood.

Obj. 3: Further, in the form of Baptism both the minister and his act are expressed, when it is said, "I baptize thee." But in the words set forth above there is no mention made either of the minister or of his act. Therefore the form of the sacrament is not a suitable one.

Obj. 4: Further, the form of the sacrament suffices for its perfection; hence the sacrament of Baptism can be performed sometimes by pronouncing the words of the form only, omitting all the others. Therefore, if the aforesaid words be the form of this sacrament, it would seem as if this sacrament could be performed sometimes by uttering those words alone, while leaving out all the others which are said in the mass; yet this seems to be false, because, were the other words to be passed over, the said words would be taken as spoken in the person of the priest saying them, whereas the bread and wine are not changed into his body and blood. Consequently, the aforesaid words are not the form of this sacrament.

*On the contrary,* Ambrose says (De Sacram. iv): "The consecration is accomplished by the words and expressions of the Lord Jesus. Because, by all the other words spoken, praise is rendered to God, prayer is put up for the people, for kings, and others; but when the time comes for perfecting the sacrament, the priest uses no longer his own words, but the words of Christ. Therefore, it is Christ's words that perfect this sacrament."

*I answer that,* This sacrament differs from the other sacraments in two respects. First of all, in this, that this sacrament is accomplished by the consecration of the matter, while the rest are perfected in the use of the consecrated matter. Secondly, because in the other sacraments the consecration of the matter consists only in a blessing, from which the matter consecrated derives instrumentally a spiritual power, which through the priest who is an animated instrument, can pass on to inanimate instruments. But in this sacrament the consecration of the matter consists in the miraculous change of the substance, which can only be done by God; hence the minister in performing this sacrament has no other act save the pronouncing of the words. And because the form should suit the thing, therefore the form of this sacrament differs from the forms of the other sacraments in two respects. First, because the form of the other sacraments implies the use of the matter, as for instance, baptizing, or signing; but the form of this sacrament implies merely the consecration of the matter, which consists in transubstantiation, as when it is said, "This is My body," or, "This is the chalice of My blood." Secondly, because the forms of the other sacraments are pronounced in the person of the minister, whether by way of exercising an act, as when it is said, "I baptize thee," or "I confirm thee," etc.; or by way of command, as when it is said in the sacrament of order, "Take the power," etc.; or by way of entreaty, as when in the sacrament of Extreme Unction it is said, "By this anointing and our intercession," etc. But the form of this sacrament is pronounced as if Christ were speaking in person, so that it is given to be understood that the minister does nothing in perfecting this sacrament, except to pronounce the words of Christ.

Reply Obj. 1: There are many opinions on this matter. Some have said that Christ, Who had power of excellence in the sacraments, performed this sacrament without using any form of words, and that afterwards He pronounced the words under which others were to consecrate thereafter. And the words of Pope Innocent III seem to convey the same sense (De Sacr. Alt. Myst. iv), where he says: "In good sooth it can be said that Christ accomplished this sacrament by His Divine power, and subsequently expressed the form under which those who came after were to consecrate." But in opposition to this view are the words of the Gospel in which it is said that Christ "blessed," and this blessing was effected by certain words. Accordingly those words of Innocent are to be considered as expressing an opinion, rather than determining the point.

Others, again, have said that the blessing was effected by other words not known to us. But this statement cannot stand, because the blessing of the consecration is now performed by reciting the things which were then accomplished; hence, if the consecration was not performed then by these words, neither would it be now.

Accordingly, others have maintained that this blessing was effected by the same words as are used now; but that Christ spoke them twice, at first secretly, in order to consecrate, and afterwards openly, to instruct others. But even this will not hold good, because the priest in consecrating uses these words, not as spoken in secret, but as openly pronounced. Accordingly, since these words have no power except from Christ pronouncing them, it seems that Christ also consecrated by pronouncing them openly.

And therefore others said that the Evangelists did not always follow the precise order in their narrative as that in which things actually happened, as is seen from Augustine (De Consens. Evang. ii). Hence it is to be understood that the order of what took place can be expressed thus: "Taking the bread He blessed it, saying: This is My body, and then He broke it, and gave it to His disciples." But the same sense can be had even without changing the words of the Gospel; because the participle "saying" implies sequence of the words uttered with what goes before. And it is not necessary for the sequence to be understood only with respect to the last word spoken, as if Christ had just then pronounced those words, when He gave it to His disciples; but the sequence can be understood with regard to all that had gone before; so that the sense is: "While He was blessing, and breaking, and giving it to His disciples, He spoke the words, 'Take ye,'" etc.

Reply Obj. 2: In these words, "Take ye and eat," the use of the consecrated, matter is indicated, which is not of the necessity of this sacrament, as stated above (Q. 74, A. 7). And therefore not even these words belong to the substance of the form. Nevertheless, because the use of the consecrated matter belongs to a certain perfection of the sacrament, in the same way as operation is not the first but the second perfection of a thing, consequently, the whole perfection of this sacrament is expressed by all those words: and it was in this way that Eusebius understood that the sacrament was accomplished by those words, as to its first and second perfection.

Reply Obj. 3: In the sacrament of Baptism the minister exercises an act regarding the use of the matter, which is of the essence of the sacrament: such is not the case in this sacrament; hence there is no parallel.

Reply Obj. 4: Some have contended that this sacrament cannot be accomplished by uttering the aforesaid words, while leaving out the rest, especially the words in the Canon of the Mass. But that this is false can be seen both from Ambrose's words quoted above, as well as from the fact that the Canon of the Mass is not the same in all places or times, but various portions have been introduced by various people.

Accordingly it must be held that if the priest were to pronounce only the aforesaid words with the intention of consecrating this sacrament, this sacrament would be valid because the intention would cause these words to be understood as spoken in the person of Christ, even though the words were pronounced without those that precede. The priest, however, would sin gravely in consecrating the sacrament thus, as he would not be observing the rite of the Church. Nor does the comparison with Baptism prove anything; for it is a sacrament of necessity: whereas the lack of this sacrament can be supplied by the spiritual partaking thereof, as Augustine says (cf. Q. 73, A. 3, ad 1).

SECOND ARTICLE [III, Q. 78, Art. 2]

Whether This Is the Proper Form for the Consecration of the Bread: "This Is My Body"?

Objection 1: It seems that this is not the proper form of this sacrament: "This is My body." For the effect of a sacrament ought to be expressed in its form. But the effect of the consecration of the bread is the change of the substance of the bread into the body of Christ, and this is better expressed by the word "becomes" than by "is." Therefore, in the form of the consecration we ought to say: "This becomes My body."

Obj. 2: Further, Ambrose says (De Sacram. iv), "Christ's words consecrate this sacrament. What word of Christ? This word, whereby all things are made. The Lord commanded, and the heavens and earth were made." Therefore, it would be a more proper form of this sacrament if the imperative mood were employed, so as to say: "Be this My body."

Obj. 3: Further, that which is changed is implied in the subject of this phrase, just as the term of the change is implied in the predicate. But just as that into which the change is made is something determinate, for the change is into nothing else but the body of Christ, so also that which is converted is determinate, since only bread is converted into the body of Christ. Therefore, as a noun is inserted on the part of the predicate, so also should a noun be inserted in the subject, so that it be said: "This bread is My body."

Obj. 4: Further, just as the term of the change is determinate in nature, because it is a body, so also is it determinate in person. Consequently, in order to determine the person, it ought to be said: "This is the body of Christ."

Obj. 5: Further, nothing ought to be inserted in the form except what is substantial to it. Consequently, the conjunction "for" is improperly added in some books, since it does not belong to the substance of the form.

*On the contrary,* our Lord used this form in consecrating, as is evident from Matt. 26:26.

*I answer that,* This is the proper form for the consecration of the bread. For it was said (A. 1) that this consecration consists in changing the substance of bread into the body of Christ. Now the form of a sacrament ought to denote what is done in the sacrament. Consequently the form for the consecration of the bread ought to signify the actual conversion of the bread into the body of Christ. And herein are three things to be considered: namely, the actual conversion, the term whence, and the term whereunto.

Now the conversion can be considered in two ways: first, in becoming, secondly, in being. But the conversion ought not to be signified in this form as in becoming, but as in being. First, because such conversion is not successive, as was said above (Q. 75, A. 7), but instantaneous; and in such changes the becoming is nothing else than the being. Secondly, because the sacramental forms bear the same relation to the signification of the sacramental effect as artificial forms to the representation of the effect of art. Now an artificial form is the likeness of the ultimate effect, on which the artist's intention is fixed; just as the art-form in the builder's mind is principally the form of the house constructed, and secondarily of the constructing. Accordingly, in this form also the conversion ought to be expressed as in being, to which the intention is referred.

And since the conversion is expressed in this form as in being, it is necessary for the extremes of the conversion to be signified as they exist in the fact of conversion. But then the term whereunto has the proper nature of its own substance; whereas the term whence does not remain in its own substance, but only as to the accidents whereby it comes under the senses, and can be determined in relation to the senses. Hence the term whence of the conversion is conveniently expressed by the demonstrative pronoun, relative to the sensible accidents which continue; but the term whereunto is expressed by the noun signifying the nature of the thing which terminates the conversion, and this is Christ's entire body, and not merely His flesh; as was said above (Q. 76, A. 1, ad 2). Hence this form is most appropriate: "This is My body."

Reply Obj. 1: The ultimate effect of this conversion is not a becoming but a being, as stated above, and consequently prominence should be given to this in the form.

Reply Obj. 2: God's word operated in the creation of things, and it is the same which operates in this consecration, yet each in different fashion: because here it operates effectively and sacramentally, that is, in virtue of its signification. And consequently the last effect of the consecration must needs be signified in this sentence by a substantive verb of the indicative mood and present time. But in the creation of things it worked merely effectively, and such efficiency is due to the command of His wisdom; and therefore in the creation of things the Lord's word is expressed by a verb in the imperative mood, as in Gen. 1:3: "Let there be light, and light was made."

Reply Obj. 3: The term whence does not retain the nature of its substance in the being of the conversion, as the term whereunto does. Therefore there is no parallel.

Reply Obj. 4: The pronoun "My," which implicitly points to the chief person, i.e. the person of the speaker, sufficiently indicates Christ's person, in Whose person these words are uttered, as stated above (A. 1).

Reply Obj. 5: The conjunction "for" is set in this form according to the custom of the Roman Church, who derived it from Peter the Apostle; and this on account of the sequence with the words preceding: and therefore it is not part of the form, just as the words preceding the form are not.

THIRD ARTICLE [III, Q. 78, Art. 3]

Whether This Is the Proper Form for the Consecration of the Wine: "This Is the Chalice of My Blood," Etc.?

Objection 1: It seems that this is not the proper form for the consecration of the wine. "This is the chalice of My blood, of the New and Eternal Testament, the Mystery of Faith, which shall be shed for you and for many unto the forgiveness of sins." For as the bread is changed by the power of consecration into Christ's body, so is the wine changed into Christ's blood, as is clear from what was said above (Q. 76, AA. 1, 2, 3). But in the form of the consecration of the bread, the body of Christ is expressly mentioned, without any addition. Therefore in this form the blood of Christ is improperly expressed in the oblique case, and the chalice in the nominative, when it is said: "This is the chalice of My blood."

Obj. 2: Further, the words spoken in the consecration of the bread are not more efficacious than those spoken in the consecration of the wine, since both are Christ's words. But directly the words are spoken--"This is My body," there is perfect consecration of the bread. Therefore, directly these other words are uttered--"This is the chalice of My blood," there is perfect consecration of the blood; and so the words which follow do not appeal to be of the substance of the form, especially since they refer to the properties of this sacrament.

Obj. 3: Further, the New Testament seems to be an internal inspiration, as is evident from the Apostle quoting the words of Jeremias (31:31): "I will perfect unto the house of Israel a New Testament . . . I will give My laws into their mind" (Heb. 8:8). But a sacrament is an outward visible act. Therefore, in the form of the sacrament the words "of the New Testament" are improperly added.

Obj. 4: Further, a thing is said to be new which is near the beginning of its existence. But what is eternal has no beginning of its existence. Therefore it is incorrect to say "of the New and Eternal," because it seems to savor of a contradiction.

Obj. 5: Further, occasions of error ought to be withheld from men, according to Isa. 57:14: "Take away the stumbling blocks out of the way of My people." But some have fallen into error in thinking that Christ's body and blood are only mystically present in this sacrament. Therefore it is out of place to add "the mystery of faith."

Obj. 6: Further, it was said above (Q. 73, A. 3, ad 3), that as Baptism is the sacrament of faith, so is the Eucharist the sacrament of charity. Consequently, in this form the word "charity" ought rather to be used than "faith."

Obj. 7: Further, the whole of this sacrament, both as to body and blood, is a memorial of our Lord's Passion, according to 1 Cor. 11:26: "As often as you shall eat this bread and drink the chalice, you shall show the death of the Lord." Consequently, mention ought to be made of Christ's Passion and its fruit rather in the form of the consecration of the blood, than in the form of the consecration of the body, especially since our Lord said: "This is My body, which shall be delivered up for you" (Luke 22:19).

Obj. 8: Further, as was already observed (Q. 48, A. 2; Q. 49, A. 3), Christ's Passion sufficed for all; while as to its efficacy it was profitable for many. Therefore it ought to be said: "Which shall be shed for all," or else "for many," without adding, "for you."

Objection 9: Further, the words whereby this sacrament is consecrated draw their efficacy from Christ's institution. But no Evangelist narrates that Christ spoke all these words. Therefore this is not an appropriate form for the consecration of the wine.

*On the contrary,* The Church, instructed by the apostles, uses this form.

*I answer that,* There is a twofold opinion regarding this form. Some have maintained that the words "This is the chalice of My blood" alone belong to the substance of this form, but not those words which follow. Now this seems incorrect, because the words which follow them are determinations of the predicate, that is, of Christ's blood. consequently they belong to the integrity of the expression.

And on this account others say more accurately that all the words which follow are of the substance of the form down to the words, "As often as ye shall do this," which belong to the use of this sacrament, and consequently do not belong to the substance of the form. Hence it is that the priest pronounces all these words, under the same rite and manner, namely, holding the chalice in his hands. Moreover, in Luke 22:20, the words that follow are interposed with the preceding words: "This is the chalice, the new testament in My blood."

Consequently it must be said that all the aforesaid words belong to the substance of the form; but that by the first words, "This is the chalice of My blood," the change of the wine into blood is denoted, as explained above (A. 2) in the form for the consecration of the bread; but by the words which come after is shown the power of the blood shed in the Passion, which power works in this sacrament, and is ordained for three purposes. First and principally for securing our eternal heritage, according to Heb. 10:19: "Having confidence in the entering into the holies by the blood of Christ"; and in order to denote this, we say, "of the New and Eternal Testament." Secondly, for justifying by grace, which is by faith according to Rom. 3:25, 26: "Whom God hath proposed to be a propitiation, through faith in His blood . . . that He Himself may be just, and the justifier of him who is of the faith of Jesus Christ": and on this account we add, "The Mystery of Faith." Thirdly, for removing sins which are the impediments to both of these things, according to Heb. 9:14: "The blood of Christ . . . shall cleanse our conscience from dead works," that is, from sins; and on this account, we say, "which shall be shed for you and for many unto the forgiveness of sins."

Reply Obj. 1: The expression "This is the chalice of My blood" is a figure of speech, which can be understood in two ways. First, as a figure of metonymy; because the container is put for the contained, so that the meaning is: "This is My blood contained in the chalice"; of which mention is now made, because Christ's blood is consecrated in this sacrament, inasmuch as it is the drink of the faithful, which is not implied under the notion of blood; consequently this had to be denoted by the vessel adapted for such usage.

Secondly, it can be taken by way of metaphor, so

that Christ's Passion is understood by the chalice by way of comparison, because, like a cup, it inebriates, according to Lam. 3:15: "He hath filled me with bitterness, he hath inebriated me with wormwood": hence our Lord Himself spoke of His Passion as a chalice, when He said (Matt. 26:39): "Let this chalice pass away from Me": so that the meaning is: "This is the chalice of My Passion." This is denoted by the blood being consecrated apart from the body; because it was by the Passion that the blood was separated from the body.

Reply Obj. 2: As was said above (ad 1; Q. 76, A. 2, ad 1), the blood consecrated apart expressly represents Christ's Passion, and therefore mention is made of the fruits of the Passion in the consecration of the blood rather than in that of the body, since the body is the subject of the Passion. This is also pointed out in our Lord's saying, "which shall be delivered up for you," as if to say, "which shall undergo the Passion for you."

Reply Obj. 3: A testament is the disposal of a heritage. But God disposed of a heavenly heritage to men, to be bestowed through the virtue of the blood of Jesus Christ; because, according to Heb. 9:16: "Where there is a testament the death of the testator must of necessity come in." Now Christ's blood was exhibited to men in two ways. First of all in figure, and this belongs to the Old Testament; consequently the Apostle concludes (Heb. 9:16): "Whereupon neither was the first indeed dedicated without blood," which is evident from this, that as related in Ex. 24:7, 8, "when every" commandment of the law "had been read" by Moses, "he sprinkled all the people" saying: "This is the blood of the testament which the Lord hath enjoined unto you."

Secondly, it was shown in very truth; and this belongs to the New Testament. This is what the Apostle premises when he says (Rom. 9:15): "Therefore He is the Mediator of the New Testament, that by means of His death . . . they that are called may receive the promise of eternal inheritance." Consequently, we say here, "The blood of the New Testament," because it is shown now not in figure but in truth; and therefore we add, "which shall be shed for you." But the internal inspiration has its origin in the power of this blood, according as we are justified by Christ's Passion.

Reply Obj. 4: This Testament is a "new one" by reason of its showing forth: yet it is called "eternal" both on account of God's eternal pre-ordination, as well as on account of the eternal heritage which is prepared by this testament. Moreover, Christ's Person is eternal, in Whose blood this testament is appointed.

Reply Obj. 5: The word "mystery" is inserted, not in order to exclude reality, but to show that the reality is hidden, because Christ's blood is in this sacrament in a hidden manner, and His Passion was dimly foreshadowed in the Old Testament.

Reply Obj. 6: It is called the "Sacrament of Faith," as being an object of faith: because by faith alone do we hold the presence of Christ's blood in this sacrament. Moreover Christ's Passion justifies by faith. Baptism is called the "Sacrament of Faith" because it is a profession of faith. This is called the "Sacrament of Charity," as being figurative and effective thereof.

Reply Obj. 7: As stated above (ad 2), the blood consecrated apart represents Christ's blood more expressively; and therefore mention is made of Christ's Passion and its fruits, in the consecration of the blood rather than in that of the body.

Reply Obj. 8: The blood of Christ's Passion has its efficacy not merely in the elect among the Jews, to whom the blood of the Old Testament was exhibited, but also in the Gentiles; nor only in priests who consecrate this sacrament, and in those others who partake of it; but likewise in those for whom it is offered. And therefore He says expressly, "for you," the Jews, "and for many," namely the Gentiles; or, "for you" who eat of it, and "for many," for whom it is offered.

Reply Obj. 9: The Evangelists did not intend to hand down the forms of the sacraments, which in the primitive Church had to be kept concealed, as Dionysius observes at the close of his book on the ecclesiastical hierarchy; their object was to write the story of Christ. Nevertheless nearly all these words can be culled from various passages of the Scriptures. Because the words, "This is the chalice," are found in Luke 22:20, and 1 Cor. 11:25, while Matthew says in chapter 26:28: "This is My blood of the New Testament, which shall be shed for many unto the remission of sins." The words added, namely, "eternal" and "mystery of faith," were handed down to the Church by the apostles, who received them from our Lord, according to 1 Cor. 11:23: "I have received of the Lord that which also I delivered unto you."

FOURTH ARTICLE [III, Q. 78, Art. 4]

Whether in the Aforesaid Words of the Forms There Be Any Created Power Which Causes the Consecration?

Objection 1: It seems that in the aforesaid words of the forms there is no created power which causes the consecration. Because Damascene says (De Fide Orth. iv): "The change of the bread into Christ's body is caused solely by the power of the Holy Ghost." But the power of the Holy Ghost is uncreated. Therefore this sacrament is not caused by any created power of those words.

Obj. 2: Further, miraculous works are wrought not by any created power, but solely by Divine power, as was stated in the First Part (Q. 110, A. 4). But the change of the bread and wine into Christ's body and blood is a work not less miraculous than the creation of things, or than the formation of Christ's body in the womb of a virgin: which things could not be done by any created power. Therefore, neither is this sacrament consecrated by any created power of the aforesaid words.

Obj. 3: Further, the aforesaid words are not simple, but composed of many; nor are they uttered simultaneously, but successively. But, as stated above (Q. 75, A. 7), this change is wrought instantaneously. Hence it must be done by a simple power. Therefore it is not effected by the power of those words.

*On the contrary,* Ambrose says (De Sacram. iv): "If there be such might in the word of the Lord Jesus that things non-existent came into being, how much more efficacious is it to make things existing to continue, and to be changed into something else? And so, what was bread before consecration is now the body of Christ after consecration, because Christ's word changes a creature into something different."

*I answer that,* Some have maintained that neither in the above words is there any created power for causing the transubstantiation, nor in the other forms of the sacraments, or even in the sacraments themselves, for producing the sacramental effects. This, as was shown above (Q. 62, A. 1), is both contrary to the teachings of the saints, and detracts from the dignity of the sacraments of the New Law. Hence, since this sacrament is of greater worth than the others, as stated above (Q. 65, A. 3), the result is that there is in the words of the form of this sacrament a created power which causes the change to be wrought in it: instrumental, however, as in the other sacraments, as stated above (Q. 62, AA. 3, 4). For since these words are uttered in the person of Christ, it is from His command that they receive their instrumental power from Him, just as His other deeds and sayings derive their salutary power instrumentally, as was observed above (Q. 48, A. 6; Q. 56, A. 1, ad 3).

Reply Obj. 1: When the bread is said to be changed into Christ's body solely by the power of the Holy Ghost, the instrumental power which lies in the form of this sacrament is not excluded: just as when we say that the smith alone makes a knife we do not deny the power of the hammer.

Reply Obj. 2: No creature can work miracles as the chief agent. Yet it can do so instrumentally, just as the touch of Christ's hand healed the leper. And in this fashion Christ's words change the bread into His body. But in Christ's conception, whereby His body was fashioned, it was impossible for anything derived from His body to have the instrumental power of forming that very body. Likewise in creation there was no term wherein the instrumental action of a creature could be received. Consequently there is no comparison.

Reply Obj. 3: The aforesaid words, which work the consecration, operate sacramentally. Consequently, the converting power latent under the forms of these sacraments follows the meaning, which is terminated in the uttering of the last word. And therefore the aforesaid words have this power in the last instant of their being uttered, taken in conjunction with those uttered before. And this power is simple by reason of the thing signified, although there be composition in the words uttered outwardly.

FIFTH ARTICLE [III, Q. 78, Art. 5]

Whether the Aforesaid Expressions Are True?

Objection 1: It seems that the aforesaid expressions are not true. Because when we say: "This is My body," the word "this" designates a substance. But according to what was said above (AA. 1, 4, ad 3; Q. 75, AA. 2, 7), when the pronoun "this" is spoken, the substance of the bread is still there, because the transubstantiation takes place in the last instant of pronouncing the words. But it is false to say: "Bread is Christ's body." Consequently this expression, "This is My body," is false.

Obj. 2: Further, the pronoun "this" appeals to the senses. But the sensible species in this sacrament are neither Christ's body nor even its accidents. Therefore this expression, "This is My body," cannot be true.

Obj. 3: Further, as was observed above (A. 4, ad 3), these words, by their signification, effect the change of the bread into the body of Christ. But an effective cause is understood as preceding its effect. Therefore the meaning of these words is understood as preceding the change of the bread into the body of Christ. But previous to the change this expression, "This is My body," is false. Therefore the expression is to be judged as false simply; and the same reason holds good of the other phrase: "This is the chalice of My blood," etc.

*On the contrary,* These words are pronounced in the person of Christ, Who says of Himself (John 14:6): "I am the truth."

*I answer that,* There have been many opinions on this point. Some have said that in this expression, "This is My body," the word "this" implies demonstration as conceived, and not as exercised, because the whole phrase is taken materially, since it is uttered by a way of narration: for the priest relates that Christ said: "This is My body."

But such a view cannot hold good, because then these words would not be applied to the corporeal matter present, and consequently the sacrament would not be valid: for Augustine says (Tract. lxxx in Joan.): "The word is added to the element, and this becomes a sacrament." Moreover this solution ignores entirely the difficulty which this question presents: for there is still the objection in regard to the first uttering of these words by Christ; since it is evident that then they were employed, not materially, but significatively. And therefore it must be said that even when spoken by the priest they are taken significatively, and not merely materially. Nor does it matter that the priest pronounces them by way of recital, as though they were spoken by Christ, because owing to Christ's infinite power, just as through contact with His flesh the regenerative power entered not only into the waters which came into contact with Christ, but into all waters throughout the whole world and during all future ages, so likewise from Christ's uttering these words they derived their consecrating power, by whatever priest they be uttered, as if Christ present were saying them.

And therefore others have said that in this phrase the word "this" appeals, not to the senses, but to the intellect; so that the meaning is, "This is My body"--i.e. "The thing signified by 'this' is My body." But neither can this stand, because, since in the sacraments the effect is that which is signified, from such a form it would not result that Christ's body was in very truth in this sacrament, but merely as in a sign, which is heretical, as stated above (Q. 85, A. 1).

Consequently, others have said that the word "this" appeals to the senses; not at the precise instant of its being uttered, but merely at the last instant thereof; as when a man says, "Now I am silent," this adverb "now" points to the instant immediately following the speech: because the sense is: "Directly these words are spoken I am silent." But neither can this hold good, because in that case the meaning of the sentence would be: "My body is My body," which the above phrase does not effect, because this was so even before the utterance of the words: hence neither does the aforesaid sentence mean this.

Consequently, then, it remains to be said, as stated above (A. 4), that this sentence possesses the power of effecting the conversion of the bread into the body of Christ. And therefore it is compared to other sentences, which have power only of signifying and not of producing, as the concept of the practical intellect, which is productive of the thing, is compared to the concept of our speculative intellect which is drawn from things, because "words are signs of concepts," as the Philosopher says (Peri Herm. i). And therefore as the concept of the practical intellect does not presuppose the thing understood, but makes it, so the truth of this expression does not presuppose the thing signified, but makes it; for such is the relation of God's word to the things made by the Word. Now this change takes place not successively, but in an instant, as stated above (Q. 77, A. 7). Consequently one must understand the aforesaid expression with reference to the last instant of the words being spoken, yet not so that the subject may be understood to have stood for that which is the term of the conversion; viz. that the body of Christ is the body of Christ; nor again that the subject be understood to stand for that which it was before the conversion, namely, the bread, but for that which is commonly related to both, i.e. that which is contained in general under those species. For these words do not make the body of Christ to be the body of Christ, nor do they make the bread to be the body of Christ; but what was contained under those species, and was formerly bread, they make to be the body of Christ. And therefore expressly our Lord did not say: "This bread is My body," which would be the meaning of the second opinion; nor "This My body is My body," which would be the meaning of the third opinion: but in general: "This is My body," assigning no noun on the part of the subject, but only a pronoun, which signifies substance in common, without quality, that is, without a determinate form.

Reply Obj. 1: The term "this" points to a substance, yet without determining its proper nature, as stated above.

Reply Obj. 2: The pronoun "this" does not indicate the accidents, but the substance underlying the accidents, which at first was bread, and is afterwards the body of Christ, which body, although not informed by those accidents, is yet contained under them.

Reply Obj. 3: The meaning of this expression is, in the order of nature, understood before the thing signified, just as a cause is naturally prior to the effect; but not in order of time, because this cause has its effect with it at the same time, and this suffices for the truth of the expression.

SIXTH ARTICLE [III, Q. 78, Art. 6]

Whether the Form of the Consecration of the Bread Accomplishes Its Effect Before the Form of the Consecration of the Wine Be Completed?

Objection 1: It seems that the form of the consecration of the bread does not accomplish its effect until the form for the consecration of the wine be completed. For, as Christ's body begins to be in this sacrament by the consecration of the bread, so does His blood come to be there by the consecration of the wine. If, then, the words for consecrating the bread were to produce their effect before the consecration of the wine, it would follow that Christ's body would be present in this sacrament without the blood, which is improper.

Obj. 2: Further, one sacrament has one completion: hence although there be three immersions in Baptism, yet the first immersion does not produce its effect until the third be completed. But all this sacrament is one, as stated above (Q. 73, A. 2). Therefore the words whereby the bread is consecrated do not bring about their effect without the sacramental words whereby the wine is consecrated.

Obj. 3: Further, there are several words in the form for consecrating the bread, the first of which do not secure their effect until the last be uttered, as stated above (A. 4, ad 3). Therefore, for the same reason, neither do the words for the consecration of Christ's body produce their effect, until the words for consecrating Christ's blood are spoken.

*On the contrary,* Directly the words are uttered for consecrating the bread, the consecrated host is shown to the people to be adored, which would not be done if Christ's body were not there, for that would be an act of idolatry. Therefore the consecrating words of the bread produce their effect before the words are spoken for consecrating the wine.

*I answer that,* Some of the earlier doctors said that these two forms, namely, for consecrating the bread and the wine, await each other's action, so that the first does not produce its effect until the second be uttered.

But this cannot stand, because, as stated above (A. 5, ad 3), for the truth of this phrase, "This is My body," wherein the verb is in the present tense, it is required for the thing signified to be present simultaneously in time with the signification of the expression used; otherwise, if the thing signified had to be awaited for afterwards, a verb of the future tense would be employed, and not one of the present tense, so that we should not say, "This is My body," but "This will be My body." But the signification of this speech is complete directly those words are spoken. And therefore the thing signified must be present instantaneously, and such is the effect of this sacrament; otherwise it would not be a true speech. Moreover, this opinion is against the rite of the Church, which forthwith adores the body of Christ after the words are uttered.

Hence it must be said that the first form does not await the second in its action, but has its effect on the instant.

Reply Obj. 1: It is on this account that they who maintained the above opinion seem to have erred. Hence it must be understood that directly the consecration of the bread is complete, the body of Christ is indeed present by the power of the sacrament, and the blood by real concomitance; but afterwards by the consecration of the wine, conversely, the blood of Christ is there by the power of the sacrament, and the body by real concomitance, so that the entire Christ is under either species, as stated above (Q. 76, A. 2).

Reply Obj. 2: This sacrament is one in perfection, as stated above (Q. 73, A. 2), namely, inasmuch as it is made up of two things, that is, of food and drink, each of which of itself has its own perfection; but the three immersions of Baptism are ordained to one simple effect, and therefore there is no resemblance.

Reply Obj. 3: The various words in the form for consecrating the bread constitute the truth of one speech, but the words of the different forms do not, and consequently there is no parallel.

# QUESTION 79

OF THE EFFECTS OF THIS SACRAMENT (In Eight Articles)

We must now consider the effects of this sacrament, and under this head there are eight points of inquiry:

(1) Whether this sacrament bestows grace?

(2) Whether the attaining of glory is an effect of this sacrament?

(3) Whether the forgiveness of mortal sin is an effect of this sacrament?

(4) Whether venial sin is forgiven by this sacrament?

(5) Whether the entire punishment due for sin is forgiven by this sacrament?

(6) Whether this sacrament preserves man from future sins?

(7) Whether this sacrament benefits others besides the recipients?

(8) Of the obstacles to the effect of this sacrament.

FIRST ARTICLE [III, Q. 79, Art. 1]

Whether Grace Is Bestowed Through This Sacrament?

Objection 1: It seems that grace is not bestowed through this sacrament. For this sacrament is spiritual nourishment. But nourishment is only given to the living. Therefore since the spiritual life is the effect of grace, this sacrament belongs only to one in the state of grace. Therefore grace is not bestowed through this sacrament for it to be had in the first instance. In like manner neither is it given so as grace may be increased, because spiritual growth belongs to the sacrament of Confirmation, as stated above (Q. 72, A. 1). Consequently, grace is not bestowed through this sacrament.

Obj. 2: Further, this sacrament is given as a spiritual refreshment. But spiritual refreshment seems to belong to the use of grace rather than to its bestowal. Therefore it seems that grace is not given through this sacrament.

Obj. 3: Further, as was said above (Q. 74, A. 1), "Christ's body is offered up in this sacrament for the salvation of the body, and His blood for that of the soul." Now it is not the body which is the subject of grace, but the soul, as was shown in the Second Part (I-II, Q. 110, A. 4). Therefore grace is not bestowed through this sacrament, at least so far as the body is concerned.

*On the contrary,* Our Lord says (John 6:52): "The bread which I will give, is My flesh for the life of the world." But the spiritual life is the effect of grace. Therefore grace is bestowed through this sacrament.

*I answer that,* The effect of this sacrament ought to be considered, first of all and principally, from what is contained in this sacrament, which is Christ; Who, just as by coming into the world, He visibly bestowed the life of grace upon the world, according to John 1:17: "Grace and truth came by Jesus Christ," so also, by coming sacramentally into man causes the life of grace, according to John 6:58: "He that eateth Me, the same also shall live by Me." Hence Cyril says on Luke 22:19: "God's life-giving Word by uniting Himself with His own flesh, made it to be productive of life. For it was becoming that He should be united somehow with bodies through His sacred flesh and precious blood, which we receive in a life-giving blessing in the bread and wine."

Secondly, it is considered on the part of what is represented by this sacrament, which is Christ's Passion, as stated above (Q. 74, A. 1; Q. 76, A. 2, ad 1). And therefore this sacrament works in man the effect which Christ's Passion wrought in the world. Hence, Chrysostom says on the words, "Immediately there came out blood and water" (John 19:34): "Since the sacred mysteries derive their origin from thence, when you draw nigh to the awe-inspiring chalice, so approach as if you were going to drink from Christ's own side." Hence our Lord Himself says (Matt. 26:28): "This is My blood . . . which shall be shed for many unto the remission of sins."

Thirdly, the effect of this sacrament is considered from the way in which this sacrament is given; for it is given by way of food and drink. And therefore this sacrament does for the spiritual life all that material food does for the bodily life, namely, by sustaining, giving increase, restoring, and giving delight. Accordingly, Ambrose says (De Sacram. v): "This is the bread of everlasting life, which supports the substance of our soul." And Chrysostom says (Hom. xlvi in Joan.): "When we desire it, He lets us feel Him, and eat Him, and embrace Him." And hence our Lord says (John 6:56): "My flesh is meat indeed, and My blood is drink indeed."

Fourthly, the effect of this sacrament is considered from the species under which it is given. Hence Augustine says (Tract. xxvi in Joan.): "Our Lord betokened His body and blood in things which out of many units are made into some one whole: for out of many grains is one thing made," viz. bread; "and many grapes flow into one thing," viz. wine. And therefore he observes elsewhere (Tract. xxvi in Joan.): "O sacrament of piety, O sign of unity, O bond of charity!"

And since Christ and His Passion are the cause of grace, and since spiritual refreshment, and charity cannot be without grace, it is clear from all that has been set forth that this sacrament bestows grace.

Reply Obj. 1: This sacrament has of itself the power of bestowing grace; nor does anyone possess grace before receiving this sacrament except from some desire thereof; from his own desire, as in the case of the adult, or from the Church's desire in the case of children, as stated above (Q. 73, A. 3). Hence it is due to the efficacy of its power, that even from desire thereof a man procures grace whereby he is enabled to lead the spiritual life. It remains, then, that when the sacrament itself is really received, grace is increased, and the spiritual life perfected: yet in different fashion from the sacrament of Confirmation, in which grace is increased and perfected for resisting the outward assaults of Christ's enemies. But by this sacrament grace receives increase, and the spiritual life is perfected, so that man may stand perfect in himself by union with God.

Reply Obj. 2: This sacrament confers grace spiritually together with the virtue of charity. Hence Damascene (De Fide Orth. iv) compares this sacrament to the burning coal which Isaias saw (Isa. 6:6): "For a live ember is not simply wood, but wood united to fire; so also the bread of communion is not simple bread but bread united with the Godhead." But as Gregory observes in a Homily for Pentecost, "God's love is never idle; for, wherever it is it does great works." And consequently through this sacrament, as far as its power is concerned, not only is the habit of grace and of virtue bestowed, but it is furthermore aroused to act, according to 2 Cor. 5:14: "The charity of Christ presseth us." Hence it is that the soul is spiritually nourished through the power of this sacrament, by being spiritually gladdened, and as it were inebriated with the sweetness of the Divine goodness, according to Cant 5:1: "Eat, O friends, and drink, and be inebriated, my dearly beloved."

Reply Obj. 3: Because the sacraments operate according to the similitude by which they signify, therefore by way of assimilation it is said that in this sacrament "the body is offered for the salvation of the body, and the blood for the salvation of the soul," although each works for the salvation of both, since the entire Christ is under each, as stated above (Q. 76, A. 2). And although the body is not the immediate subject of grace, still the effect of grace flows into the body while in the present life we present "our [Vulg.: 'your'] members" as "instruments of justice unto God" (Rom. 6:13), and in the life to come our body will share in the incorruption and the glory of the soul.

SECOND ARTICLE [III, Q. 79, Art. 2]

Whether the Attaining of Glory Is an Effect of This Sacrament?

Objection 1: It seems that the attaining of glory is not an effect of this sacrament. For an effect is proportioned to its cause. But this sacrament belongs to "wayfarers" ( viatoribus ), and hence it is termed "Viaticum." Since, then, wayfarers are not yet capable of glory, it seems that this sacrament does not cause the attaining of glory.

Obj. 2: Further, given sufficient cause, the effect follows. But many take this sacrament who will never come to glory, as Augustine declares (De Civ. Dei xxi). Consequently, this sacrament is not the cause of attaining unto glory.

Obj. 3: Further, the greater is not brought about by the lesser, for nothing acts outside its species. But it is the lesser thing to receive Christ under a strange species, which happens in this sacrament, than to enjoy Him in His own species, which belongs to glory. Therefore this sacrament does not cause the attaining of glory.

*On the contrary,* It is written (John 6:52): "If any man eat of this bread, he shall live for ever." But eternal life is the life of glory. Therefore the attaining of glory is an effect of this sacrament.

*I answer that,* In this sacrament we may consider both that from which it derives its effect, namely, Christ contained in it, as also His Passion represented by it; and that through which it works its effect, namely, the use of the sacrament, and its species.

Now as to both of these it belongs to this sacrament to cause the attaining of eternal life. Because it was by His Passion that Christ opened to us the approach to eternal life, according to Heb. 9:15: "He is the Mediator of the New Testament; that by means of His death . . . they that are called may receive the promise of eternal inheritance." Accordingly in the form of this sacrament it is said: "This is the chalice of My blood, of the New and Eternal Testament."

In like manner the refreshment of spiritual food and the unity denoted by the species of the bread and wine are to be had in the present life, although imperfectly, but perfectly in the state of glory. Hence Augustine says on the words, "My flesh is meat indeed" (John 6:56): "Seeing that in meat and drink, men aim at this, that they hunger not nor thirst, this verily nought doth afford save only this meat and drink which maketh them who partake thereof to be immortal and incorruptible, in the fellowship of the saints, where shall be peace, and unity, full and perfect."

Reply Obj. 1: As Christ's Passion, in virtue whereof this sacrament is accomplished, is indeed the sufficient cause of glory, yet not so that we are thereby forthwith admitted to glory, but we must first "suffer with Him in order that we may also be glorified" afterwards "with Him" (Rom. 8:17), so this sacrament does not at once admit us to glory, but bestows on us the power of coming unto glory. And therefore it is called "Viaticum," a figure whereof we read in 3 Kings 19:8: "Elias ate and drank, and walked in the strength of that food forty days and forty nights unto the mount of God, Horeb."

Reply Obj. 2: Just as Christ's Passion has not its effect in them who are not disposed towards it as they should be, so also they do not come to glory through this sacrament who receive it unworthily. Hence Augustine (Tract. xxvi in Joan.), expounding the same passage, observes: "The sacrament is one thing, the power of the sacrament another. Many receive it from the altar . . . and by receiving" . . . die . . . Eat, then, spiritually the heavenly "bread, bring innocence to the altar." It is no wonder, then, if those who do not keep innocence, do not secure the effect of this sacrament.

Reply Obj. 3: That Christ is received under another species belongs to the nature of a sacrament, which acts instrumentally. But there is nothing to prevent an instrumental cause from producing a more mighty effect, as is evident from what was said above (Q. 77, A. 3, ad 3).

THIRD ARTICLE [III, Q. 79, Art. 3]

Whether the Forgiveness of Mortal Sin Is an Effect of This Sacrament?

Objection 1: It seems that the forgiveness of mortal sin is an effect of this sacrament. For it is said in one of the Collects (Postcommunion, Pro vivis et defunctis): "May this sacrament be a cleansing from crimes." But mortal sins are called crimes. Therefore mortal sins are blotted out by this sacrament.

Obj. 2: Further, this sacrament, like Baptism, works by the power of Christ's Passion. But mortal sins are forgiven by Baptism, as stated above (Q. 69, A. 1). Therefore they are forgiven likewise by this sacrament, especially since in the form of this sacrament it is said: "Which shall be shed for many unto the forgiveness of sins."

Obj. 3: Further, grace is bestowed through this sacrament, as stated above (A. 1). But by grace a man is justified from mortal sins, according to Rom. 3:24: "Being justified freely by His grace." Therefore mortal sins are forgiven by this sacrament.

*On the contrary,* It is written (1 Cor. 11:29): "He that eateth and drinketh unworthily, eateth and drinketh judgment to himself": and a gloss of the same passage makes the following commentary: "He eats and drinks unworthily who is in the state of sin, or who handles (the sacrament) irreverently; and such a one eats and drinks judgment, i.e. damnation, unto himself." Therefore, he that is in mortal sin, by taking the sacrament heaps sin upon sin, rather than obtains forgiveness of his sin.

*I answer that,* The power of this sacrament can be considered in two ways. First of all, in itself: and thus this sacrament has from Christ's Passion the power of forgiving all sins, since the Passion is the fount and cause of the forgiveness of sins.

Secondly, it can be considered in comparison with the recipient of the sacrament, in so far as there is, or is not, found in him an obstacle to receiving the fruit of this sacrament. Now whoever is conscious of mortal sin, has within him an obstacle to receiving the effect of this sacrament; since he is not a proper recipient of this sacrament, both because he is not alive spiritually, and so he ought not to eat the spiritual nourishment, since nourishment is confined to the living; and because he cannot be united with Christ, which is the effect of this sacrament, as long as he retains an attachment towards mortal sin. Consequently, as is said in the book De Eccles. Dogm.: "If the soul leans towards sin, it is burdened rather than purified from partaking of the Eucharist." Hence, in him who is conscious of mortal sin, this sacrament does not cause the forgiveness of sin.

Nevertheless this sacrament can effect the forgiveness of sin in two ways. First of all, by being received, not actually, but in desire; as when a man is first justified from sin. Secondly, when received by one in mortal sin of which he is not conscious, and for which he has no attachment; since possibly he was not sufficiently contrite at first, but by approaching this sacrament devoutly and reverently he obtains the grace of charity, which will perfect his contrition and bring forgiveness of sin.

Reply Obj. 1: We ask that this sacrament may be the "cleansing of crimes," or of those sins of which we are unconscious, according to Ps. 18:13: "Lord, cleanse me from my hidden sins"; or that our contrition may be perfected for the forgiveness of our sins; or that strength be bestowed on us to avoid sin.

Reply Obj. 2: Baptism is spiritual generation, which is a transition from spiritual non-being into spiritual being, and is given by way of ablution. Consequently, in both respects he who is conscious of mortal sin does not improperly approach Baptism. But in this sacrament man receives Christ within himself by way of spiritual nourishment, which is unbecoming to one that lies dead in his sins. Therefore the comparison does not hold good.

Reply Obj. 3: Grace is the sufficient cause of the forgiveness of mortal sin; yet it does not forgive sin except when it is first bestowed on the sinner. But it is not given so in this sacrament. Hence the argument does not prove.

FOURTH ARTICLE [III, Q. 79, Art. 4]

Whether Venial Sins Are Forgiven Through This Sacrament?

Objection 1: It seems that venial sins are not forgiven by this sacrament, because this is the "sacrament of charity," as Augustine says (Tract. xxvi in Joan.). But venial sins are not contrary to charity, as was shown in the Second Part (I-II, Q. 88, AA. 1, 2; II-II, Q. 24, A. 10). Therefore, since contrary is taken away by its contrary, it seems that venial sins are not forgiven by this sacrament.

Obj. 2: Further, if venial sins be forgiven by this sacrament, then all of them are forgiven for the same reason as one is. But it does not appear that all are forgiven, because thus one might frequently be without any venial sin, against what is said in 1 John 1:8: "If we say that we have no sin, we deceive ourselves." Therefore no venial sin is forgiven by this sacrament.

Obj. 3: Further, contraries mutually exclude each other. But venial sins do not forbid the receiving of this sacrament: because Augustine says on the words, "If any man eat of it he shall [Vulg.: 'may'] not die for ever" (John 6:50): "Bring innocence to the altar: your sins, though they be daily . . . let them not be deadly." Therefore neither are venial sins taken away by this sacrament.

*On the contrary,* Innocent III says (De S. Alt. Myst. iv) that this sacrament "blots out venial sins, and wards off mortal sins."

*I answer that,* Two things may be considered in this sacrament, to wit, the sacrament itself, and the reality of the sacrament: and it appears from both that this sacrament has the power of forgiving venial sins. For this sacrament is received under the form of nourishing food. Now nourishment from food is requisite for the body to make good the daily waste caused by the action of natural heat. But something is also lost daily of our spirituality from the heat of concupiscence through venial sins, which lessen the fervor of charity, as was shown in the Second Part (II-II, Q. 24, A. 10). And therefore it belongs to this sacrament to forgive venial sins. Hence Ambrose says (De Sacram. v) that this daily bread is taken "as a remedy against daily infirmity."

The reality of this sacrament is charity, not only as to its habit, but also as to its act, which is kindled in this sacrament; and by this means venial sins are forgiven. Consequently, it is manifest that venial sins are forgiven by the power of this sacrament.

Reply Obj. 1: Venial sins, although not opposed to the habit of charity, are nevertheless opposed to the fervor of its act, which act is kindled by this sacrament; by reason of which act venial sins are blotted out.

Reply Obj. 1: The passage quoted is not to be understood as if a man could not at some time be without all guilt of venial sin: but that the just do not pass through this life without committing venial sins.

Reply Obj. 3: The power of charity, to which this sacrament belongs, is greater than that of venial sins: because charity by its act takes away venial sins, which nevertheless cannot entirely hinder the act of charity. And the same holds good of this sacrament.

FIFTH ARTICLE [III, Q. 79, Art. 5]

Whether the Entire Punishment Due to Sin Is Forgiven Through This Sacrament?

Objection 1: It seems that the entire punishment due to sin is forgiven through this sacrament. For through this sacrament man receives the effect of Christ's Passion within himself as stated above (AA. 1, 2), just as he does through Baptism. But through Baptism man receives forgiveness of all punishment, through the virtue of Christ's Passion, which satisfied sufficiently for all sins, as was explained above (Q. 69, A. 2). Therefore it seems the whole debt of punishment is forgiven through this sacrament.

Obj. 2: Further, Pope Alexander I says (Ep. ad omnes orth.): "No sacrifice can be greater than the body and the blood of Christ." But man satisfied for his sins by the sacrifices of the old Law: for it is written (Lev. 4, 5): "If a man shall sin, let him offer" (so and so) "for his sin, and it shall be forgiven him." Therefore this sacrament avails much more for the forgiveness of all punishment.

Obj. 3: Further, it is certain that some part of the debt of punishment is forgiven by this sacrament; for which reason it is sometimes enjoined upon a man, by way of satisfaction, to have masses said for himself. But if one part of the punishment is forgiven, for the same reason is the other forgiven: owing to Christ's infinite power contained in this sacrament. Consequently, it seems that the whole punishment can be taken away by this sacrament.

*On the contrary,* In that case no other punishment would have to be enjoined; just as none is imposed upon the newly baptized.

*I answer that,* This sacrament is both a sacrifice and a sacrament. it has the nature of a sacrifice inasmuch as it is offered up; and it has the nature of a sacrament inasmuch as it is received. And therefore it has the effect of a sacrament in the recipient, and the effect of a sacrifice in the offerer, or in them for whom it is offered.

If, then, it be considered as a sacrament, it produces its effect in two ways: first of all directly through the power of the sacrament; secondly as by a kind of concomitance, as was said above regarding what is contained in the sacrament (Q. 76, AA. 1, 2). Through the power of the sacrament it produces directly that effect for which it was instituted. Now it was instituted not for satisfaction, but for nourishing spiritually through union between Christ and His members, as nourishment is united with the person nourished. But because this union is the effect of charity, from the fervor of which man obtains forgiveness, not only of guilt but also of punishment, hence it is that as a consequence, and by concomitance with the chief effect, man obtains forgiveness of the punishment, not indeed of the entire punishment, but according to the measure of his devotion and fervor.

But in so far as it is a sacrifice, it has a satisfactory power. Yet in satisfaction, the affection of the offerer is weighed rather than the quantity of the offering. Hence our Lord says (Mk. 12:43: cf. Luke 21:4) of the widow who offered "two mites" that she "cast in more than all." Therefore, although this offering suffices of its own quantity to satisfy for all punishment, yet it becomes satisfactory for them for whom it is offered, or even for the offerers, according to the measure of their devotion, and not for the whole punishment.

Reply Obj. 1: The sacrament of Baptism is directly ordained for the remission of punishment and guilt: not so the Eucharist, because Baptism is given to man as dying with Christ, whereas the Eucharist is given as by way of nourishing and perfecting him through Christ. Consequently there is no parallel.

Reply Obj. 2: Those other sacrifices and oblations did not effect the forgiveness of the whole punishment, neither as to the quantity of the thing offered, as this sacrament does, nor as to personal devotion; from which it comes to pass that even here the whole punishment is not taken away.

Reply Obj. 3: If part of the punishment and not the whole be taken away by this sacrament, it is due to a defect not on the part of Christ's power, but on the part of man's devotion.

SIXTH ARTICLE [III, Q. 79, Art. 6]

Whether Man Is Preserved by This Sacrament from Future Sins?

Objection 1: It seems that man is not preserved by this sacrament from future sins. For there are many that receive this sacrament worthily, who afterwards fall into sin. Now this would not happen if this sacrament were to preserve them from future sins. Consequently, it is not an effect of this sacrament to preserve from future sins.

Obj. 2: Further, the Eucharist is the sacrament of charity, as stated above (A. 4). But charity does not seem to preserve from future sins, because it can be lost through sin after one has possessed it, as was stated in the Second Part (II-II, Q. 24, A. 11). Therefore it seems that this sacrament does not preserve man from sin.

Obj. 3: Further, the origin of sin within us is "the law of sin, which is in our members," as declared by the Apostle (Rom. 7:23). But the lessening of the fomes, which is the law of sin, is set down as an effect not of this sacrament, but rather of Baptism. Therefore preservation from sin is not an effect of this sacrament.

*On the contrary,* our Lord said (John 6:50): "This is the bread which cometh down from heaven; that if any man eat of it, he may not die": which manifestly is not to be understood of the death of the body. Therefore it is to be understood that this sacrament preserves from spiritual death, which is through sin.

*I answer that,* Sin is the spiritual death of the soul. Hence man is preserved from future sin in the same way as the body is preserved from future death of the body: and this happens in two ways. First of all, in so far as man's nature is strengthened inwardly against inner decay, and so by means of food and medicine he is preserved from death. Secondly, by being guarded against outward assaults; and thus he is protected by means of arms by which he defends his body.

Now this sacrament preserves man from sin in both of these ways. For, first of all, by uniting man with Christ through grace, it strengthens his spiritual life, as spiritual food and spiritual medicine, according to Ps. 103:5: "(That) bread strengthens [Vulg.: 'may strengthen'] man's heart." Augustine likewise says (Tract. xxvi in Joan.): "Approach without fear; it is bread, not poison." Secondly, inasmuch as it is a sign of Christ's Passion, whereby the devils are conquered, it repels all the assaults of demons. Hence Chrysostom says (Hom. xlvi in Joan.): "Like lions breathing forth fire, thus do we depart from that table, being made terrible to the devil."

Reply Obj. 1: The effect of this sacrament is received according to man's condition: such is the case with every active cause in that its effect is received in matter according to the condition of the matter. But such is the condition of man on earth that his free-will can be bent to good or evil. Hence, although this sacrament of itself has the power of preserving from sin, yet it does not take away from man the possibility of sinning.

Reply Obj. 2: Even charity of itself keeps man from sin, according to Rom. 13:10: "The love of our neighbor worketh no evil": but it is due to the mutability of free-will that a man sins after possessing charity, just as after receiving this sacrament.

Reply Obj. 3: Although this sacrament is not ordained directly to lessen the fomes, yet it does lessen it as a consequence, inasmuch as it increases charity, because, as Augustine says (Q. 83), "the increase of charity is the lessening of concupiscence." But it directly strengthens man's heart in good; whereby he is also preserved from sin.

SEVENTH ARTICLE [III, Q. 79, Art. 7]

Whether This Sacrament Benefit Others Besides the Recipients?

Objection 1: It seems that this sacrament benefits only the recipients. For this sacrament is of the same genus as the other sacraments, being one of those into which that genus is divided. But the other sacraments only benefit the recipients; thus the baptized person alone receives effect of Baptism. Therefore, neither does this sacrament benefit others than the recipients.

Obj. 2: Further, the effects of this sacrament are the attainment of grace and glory, and the forgiveness of sin, at least of venial sin. If therefore this sacrament were to produce its effects in others besides the recipients, a man might happen to acquire grace and glory and forgiveness of sin without doing or receiving anything himself, through another receiving or offering this sacrament.

Obj. 3: Further, when the cause is multiplied, the effect is likewise multiplied. If therefore this sacrament benefit others besides the recipients, it would follow that it benefits a man more if he receive this sacrament through many hosts being consecrated in one mass, whereas this is not the Church's custom: for instance, that many receive communion for the salvation of one individual. Consequently, it does not seem that this sacrament benefits anyone but the recipient.

*On the contrary,* Prayer is made for many others during the celebration of this sacrament; which would serve no purpose were the sacrament not beneficial to others. Therefore, this sacrament is beneficial not merely to them who receive it.

*I answer that,* As stated above (A. 3), this sacrament is not only a sacrament, but also a sacrifice. For, it has the nature of a sacrifice inasmuch as in this sacrament Christ's Passion is represented, whereby Christ "offered Himself a Victim to God" (Eph. 5:2), and it has the nature of a sacrament inasmuch as invisible grace is bestowed in this sacrament under a visible species. So, then, this sacrament benefits recipients by way both of sacrament and of sacrifice, because it is offered for all who partake of it. For it is said in the Canon of the Mass: "May as many of us as, by participation at this Altar, shall receive the most sacred body and blood of Thy Son, be filled with all heavenly benediction and grace."

But to others who do not receive it, it is beneficial by way of sacrifice, inasmuch as it is offered for their salvation. Hence it is said in the Canon of the Mass: "Be mindful, O Lord, of Thy servants, men and women . . . for whom we offer, or who offer up to Thee, this sacrifice of praise for themselves and for all their own, for the redemption of their souls, for the hope of their safety and salvation." And our Lord expressed both ways, saying (Matt. 26:28, with Luke 22:20): "Which for you," i.e. who receive it, "and for many," i.e. others, "shall be shed unto remission of sins."

Reply Obj. 1: This sacrament has this in addition to the others, that it is a sacrifice: and therefore the comparison fails.

Reply Obj. 2: As Christ's Passion benefits all, for the forgiveness of sin and the attaining of grace and glory, whereas it produces no effect except in those who are united with Christ's Passion through faith and charity, so likewise this sacrifice, which is the memorial of our Lord's Passion, has no effect except in those who are united with this sacrament through faith and charity. Hence Augustine says to Renatus (De Anima et ejus origine i): "Who may offer Christ's body except for them who are Christ's members?" Hence in the Canon of the Mass no prayer is made for them who are outside the pale of the Church. But it benefits them who are members, more or less, according to the measure of their devotion.

Reply Obj. 3: Receiving is of the very nature of the sacrament, but offering belongs to the nature of sacrifice: consequently, when one or even several receive the body of Christ, no help accrues to others. In like fashion even when the priest consecrates several hosts in one mass, the effect of this sacrament is not increased, since there is only one sacrifice; because there is no more power in several hosts than in one, since there is only one Christ present under all the hosts and under one. Hence, neither will any one receive greater effect from the sacrament by taking many consecrated hosts in one mass. But the oblation of the sacrifice is multiplied in several masses, and therefore the effect of the sacrifice and of the sacrament is multiplied.

EIGHTH ARTICLE [III, Q. 79, Art. 8]

Whether the Effect of This Sacrament Is Hindered by Venial Sin?

Objection 1: It seems that the effect of this sacrament is not hindered by venial sin. For Augustine (Tract. xxvi in Joan.), commenting on John 6:52, "If any man eat of this bread," etc., says: "Eat the heavenly bread spiritually; bring innocence to the altar; your sins, though they be daily, let them not be deadly." From this it is evident that venial sins, which are called daily sins, do not prevent spiritual eating. But they who eat spiritually, receive the effect of this sacrament. Therefore, venial sins do not hinder the effect of this sacrament.

Obj. 2: Further, this sacrament is not less powerful than Baptism. But, as stated above (Q. 69, AA. 9, 10), only pretense checks the effect of Baptism, and venial sins do not belong to pretense; because according to Wis. 1:5: "the Holy Spirit of discipline will flee from the deceitful," yet He is not put to flight by venial sins. Therefore neither do venial sins hinder the effect of this sacrament.

Obj. 3: Further, nothing which is removed by the action of any cause, can hinder the effect of such cause. But venial sins are taken away by this sacrament. Therefore, they do not hinder its effect.

*On the contrary,* Damascene says (De Fide Orth. iv): "The fire of that desire which is within us, being kindled by the burning coal," i.e. this sacrament, "will consume our sins, and enlighten our hearts, so that we shall be inflamed and made godlike." But the fire of our desire or love is hindered by venial sins, which hinder the fervor of charity, as was shown in the Second Part (I-II, Q. 81, A. 4; II-II, Q. 24, A. 10). Therefore venial sins hinder the effect of this sacrament.

*I answer that,* Venial sins can be taken in two ways: first of all as past, secondly as in the act of being committed. Venial sins taken in the first way do not in any way hinder the effect of this sacrament. For it can come to pass that after many venial sins a man may approach devoutly to this sacrament and fully secure its effect. Considered in the second way venial sins do not utterly hinder the effect of this sacrament, but merely in part. For, it has been stated above (A. 1), that the effect of this sacrament is not only the obtaining of habitual grace or charity, but also a certain actual refreshment of spiritual sweetness: which is indeed hindered if anyone approach to this sacrament with mind distracted through venial sins; but the increase of habitual grace or of charity is not taken away.

Reply Obj. 1: He that approaches this sacrament with actual venial sin, eats spiritually indeed, in habit but not in act: and therefore he shares in the habitual effect of the sacrament, but not in its actual effect.

Reply Obj. 2: Baptism is not ordained, as this sacrament is, for the fervor of charity as its actual effect. Because Baptism is spiritual regeneration, through which the first perfection is acquired, which is a habit or form; but this sacrament is spiritual eating, which has actual delight.

Reply Obj. 3: This argument deals with past venial sins, which are taken away by this sacrament.

## QUESTION 80

OF THE USE OR RECEIVING OF THIS SACRAMENT IN GENERAL (In Twelve Articles)

We have now to consider the use or receiving of this sacrament, first of all in general; secondly, how Christ used this sacrament.

Under the first heading there are twelve points of inquiry:

(1) Whether there are two ways of eating this sacrament, namely, sacramentally and spiritually?

(2) Whether it belongs to man alone to eat this sacrament spiritually?

(3) Whether it belongs to the just man only to eat it sacramentally?

(4) Whether the sinner sins in eating it sacramentally?

(5) Of the degree of this sin;

(6) Whether this sacrament should be refused to the sinner that approaches it?

(7) Whether nocturnal pollution prevents man from receiving this sacrament?

(8) Whether it is to be received only when one is fasting?

(9) Whether it is to be given to them who lack the use of reason?

(10) Whether it is to be received daily?

(11) Whether it is lawful to refrain from it altogether?

(12) Whether it is lawful to receive the body without the blood?

FIRST ARTICLE [III, Q. 80, Art. 1]

Whether There Are Two Ways to Be Distinguished of Eating Christ's Body?

Objection 1: It seems that two ways ought not to be distinguished of eating Christ's body, namely, sacramentally and spiritually. For, as Baptism is spiritual regeneration, according to John 3:5: "Unless a man be born again of water and the Holy Ghost," etc., so also this sacrament is spiritual food: hence our Lord, speaking of this sacrament, says (John 6:64): "The words that I have spoken to you are spirit and life." But there are no two distinct ways of receiving Baptism, namely, sacramentally and spiritually. Therefore neither ought this distinction to be made regarding this sacrament.

Obj. 2: Further, when two things are so related that one is on account of the other, they should not be put in contradistinction to one another, because the one derives its species from the other. But sacramental eating is ordained for spiritual eating as its end. Therefore sacramental eating ought not to be divided in contrast with spiritual eating.

Obj. 3: Further, things which cannot exist without one another ought not to be divided in contrast with each other. But it seems that no one can eat spiritually without eating sacramentally; otherwise the fathers of old would have eaten this sacrament spiritually. Moreover, sacramental eating would be to no purpose, if the spiritual eating could be had without it. Therefore it is not right to distinguish a twofold eating, namely, sacramental and spiritual.

*On the contrary,* The gloss says on 1 Cor. 11:29: "He that eateth and drinketh unworthily," etc.: "We hold that there are two ways of eating, the one sacramental, and the other spiritual."

*I answer that,* There are two things to be considered in the receiving of this sacrament, namely, the sacrament itself, and its fruits, and we have already spoken of both (QQ. 73, 79). The perfect way, then, of receiving this sacrament is when one takes it so as to partake of its effect. Now, as was stated above (Q. 79, AA. 3, 8), it sometimes happens that a man is hindered from receiving the effect of this sacrament; and such receiving of this sacrament is an imperfect one. Therefore, as the perfect is divided against the imperfect, so sacramental eating, whereby the sacrament only is received without its effect, is divided against spiritual eating, by which one receives the effect of this sacrament, whereby a man is spiritually united with Christ through faith and charity.

Reply Obj. 1: The same distinction is made regarding Baptism and the other sacraments: for, some receive the sacrament only, while others receive the sacrament and the reality of the sacrament. However, there is a difference, because, since the other sacraments are accomplished in the use of the matter, the receiving of the sacrament is the actual perfection of the sacrament; whereas this sacrament is accomplished in the consecration of the matter: and consequently both uses follow the sacrament. On the other hand, in Baptism and in the other sacraments that imprint a character, they who receive the sacrament receive some spiritual effect, that is, the character. which is not the case in this sacrament. And therefore, in this sacrament, rather than in Baptism, the sacramental use is distinguished from the spiritual use.

Reply Obj. 2: That sacramental eating which is also a spiritual eating is not divided in contrast with spiritual eating, but is included under it; but that sacramental eating which does not secure the effect, is divided in contrast with spiritual eating; just as the imperfect, which does not attain the perfection of its species, is divided in contrast with the perfect.

Reply Obj. 3: As stated above (Q. 73, A. 3), the effect of the sacrament can be secured by every man if he receive it in desire, though not in reality. Consequently, just as some are baptized with the Baptism of desire, through their desire of baptism, before being baptized in the Baptism of water; so likewise some eat this sacrament spiritually ere they receive it sacramentally. Now this happens in two ways. First of all, from desire of receiving the sacrament itself, and thus are said to be baptized, and to eat spiritually, and not sacramentally, they who desire to receive these sacraments since they have been instituted. Secondly, by a figure: thus the Apostle says (1 Cor. 10:2), that the fathers of old were "baptized in the cloud and in the sea," and that "they did eat . . . spiritual food, and . . . drank . . . spiritual drink." Nevertheless sacramental eating is not without avail, because the actual receiving of the sacrament produces more fully the effect of the sacrament than does the desire thereof, as stated above of Baptism (Q. 69, A. 4, ad 2).

SECOND ARTICLE [III, Q. 80, Art. 2]

Whether It Belongs to Man Alone to Eat This Sacrament Spiritually?

Objection 1: It seems that it does not belong to man alone to eat this sacrament spiritually, but likewise to angels. Because on Ps. 77:25: "Man ate the bread of angels," the gloss says: "that is, the body of Christ, Who is truly the food of angels." But it would not be so unless the angels were to eat Christ spiritually. Therefore the angels eat Christ spiritually.

Obj. 2: Further, Augustine (Tract. xxvi in Joan.) says: By "this meat and drink, He would have us to understand the fellowship of His body and members, which is the Church in His predestinated ones." But not only men, but also the holy angels belong to that fellowship. Therefore the holy angels eat of it spiritually.

Obj. 3: Further, Augustine in his book De Verbis Domini (Serm. cxlii) says: "Christ is to be eaten spiritually, as He Himself declares: 'He that eateth My flesh and drinketh My blood, abideth in Me, and I in him.'" But this belongs not only to men, but also to the holy angels, in whom Christ dwells by charity, and they in Him. Consequently, it seems that to eat Christ spiritually is not for men only, but also for the angels.

*On the contrary,* Augustine (Tract. xxvi in Joan.) says: "Eat the bread" of the altar "spiritually; take innocence to the altar." But angels do not approach the altar as for the purpose of taking something therefrom. Therefore the angels do not eat spiritually.

*I answer that,* Christ Himself is contained in this sacrament, not under His proper species, but under the sacramental species. Consequently there are two ways of eating spiritually. First, as Christ Himself exists under His proper species, and in this way the angels eat Christ spiritually inasmuch as they are united with Him in the enjoyment of perfect charity, and in clear vision (and this is the bread we hope for in heaven), and not by faith, as we are united with Him here.

In another way one may eat Christ spiritually, as He is under the sacramental species, inasmuch as a man believes in Christ, while desiring to receive this sacrament; and this is not merely to eat Christ spiritually, but likewise to eat this sacrament; which does not fall to the lot of the angels. And therefore although the angels feed on Christ spiritually, yet it does not belong to them to eat this sacrament spiritually.

Reply Obj. 1: The receiving of Christ under this sacrament is ordained to the enjoyment of heaven, as to its end, in the same way as the angels enjoy it; and since the means are gauged by the end, hence it is that such eating of Christ whereby we receive Him under this sacrament, is, as it were, derived from that eating whereby the angels enjoy Christ in heaven. Consequently, man is said to eat the "bread of angels," because it belongs to the angels to do so firstly and principally, since they enjoy Him in his proper species; and secondly it belongs to men, who receive Christ under this sacrament.

Reply Obj. 2: Both men and angels belong to the fellowship of His mystical body; men by faith, and angels by manifest vision. But the sacraments are proportioned to faith, through which the truth is seen "through a glass" and "in a dark manner." And therefore, properly speaking, it does not belong to angels, but to men, to eat this sacrament spiritually.

Reply Obj. 3: Christ dwells in men through faith, according to their present state, but He is in the blessed angels by manifest vision. Consequently the comparison does not hold, as stated above (ad 2).

THIRD ARTICLE [III, Q. 80, Art. 3]

Whether the Just Man Alone May Eat Christ Sacramentally?

Objection 1: It seems that none but the just man may eat Christ sacramentally. For Augustine says in his book De Remedio Penitentiae (cf. Tract. in Joan. xxv, n. 12; xxvi, n. 1): "Why make ready tooth and belly? Believe, and thou hast eaten . . . For to believe in Him, this it is, to eat the living bread." But the sinner does not believe in Him; because he has not living faith, to which it belongs to believe "in God," as stated above in the Second Part (II-II, Q. 2, A. 2; Q. 4, A. 5). Therefore the sinner cannot eat this sacrament, which is the living bread.

Obj. 2: Further, this sacrament is specially called "the sacrament of charity," as stated above (Q. 78, A. 3, ad 6). But as unbelievers lack faith, so all sinners lack charity. Now unbelievers do not seem to be capable of eating this sacrament, since in the sacramental form it is called the "Mystery of Faith." Therefore, for like reason, the sinner cannot eat Christ's body sacramentally.

Obj. 3: Further, the sinner is more abominable before God than the irrational creature: for it is said of the sinner (Ps. 48:21): "Man when he was in honor did not understand; he hath been compared to senseless beasts, and made like to them." But an irrational animal, such as a mouse or a dog, cannot receive this sacrament, just as it cannot receive the sacrament of Baptism. Therefore it seems that for the like reason neither may sinners eat this sacrament.

*On the contrary,* Augustine (Tract. xxvi in Joan.), commenting on the words, "that if any man eat of it he may not die," says: "Many receive from the altar, and by receiving die: whence the Apostle saith, 'eateth and drinketh judgment to himself.'" But only sinners die by receiving. Therefore sinners eat the body of Christ sacramentally, and not the just only.

*I answer that,* In the past, some have erred upon this point, saying that Christ's body is not received sacramentally by sinners; but that directly the body is touched by the lips of sinners, it ceases to be under the sacramental species.

But this is erroneous; because it detracts from the truth of this sacrament, to which truth it belongs that so long as the species last, Christ's body does not cease to be under them, as stated above (Q. 76, A. 6, ad 3; Q. 77, A. 8). But the species last so long as the substance of the bread would remain, if it were there, as was stated above (Q. 77, A. 4). Now it is clear that the substance of bread taken by a sinner does not at once cease to be, but it continues until digested by natural heat: hence Christ's body remains just as long under the sacramental species when taken by sinners. Hence it must be said that the sinner, and not merely the just, can eat Christ's body.

Reply Obj. 1: Such words and similar expressions are to be understood of spiritual eating, which does not belong to sinners. Consequently, it is from such expressions being misunderstood that the above error seems to have arisen, through ignorance of the distinction between corporeal and spiritual eating.

Reply Obj. 2: Should even an unbeliever receive the sacramental species, he would receive Christ's body under the sacrament: hence he would eat Christ sacramentally, if the word "sacramentally" qualify the verb on the part of the thing eaten. But if it qualify the verb on the part of the one eating, then, properly speaking, he does not eat sacramentally, because he uses what he takes, not as a sacrament, but as simple food. Unless perchance the unbeliever were to intend to receive what the Church bestows; without having proper faith regarding the other articles, or regarding this sacrament.

Reply Obj. 3: Even though a mouse or a dog were to eat the consecrated host, the substance of Christ's body would not cease to be under the species, so long as those species remain, and that is, so long as the substance of bread would have remained; just as if it were to be cast into the mire. Nor does this turn to any indignity regarding Christ's body, since He willed to be crucified by sinners without detracting from His dignity; especially since the mouse or dog does not touch Christ's body in its proper species, but only as to its sacramental species. Some, however, have said that Christ's body would cease to be there, directly it were touched by a mouse or a dog; but this again detracts from the truth of the sacrament, as stated above. None the less it must not be said that the irrational animal eats the body of Christ sacramentally; since it is incapable of using it as a sacrament. Hence it eats Christ's body accidentally, and not sacramentally, just as if anyone not knowing a host to be consecrated were to consume it. And since no genus is divided by an accidental difference, therefore this manner of eating Christ's body is not set down as a third way besides sacramental and spiritual eating.

FOURTH ARTICLE [III, Q. 80, Art. 4]

Whether the Sinner Sins in Receiving Christ's Body Sacramentally?

Objection 1: It seems that the sinner does not sin in receiving Christ's body sacramentally, because Christ has no greater dignity under the sacramental species than under His own. But sinners did not sin when they touched Christ's body under its proper species; nay, rather they obtained forgiveness of their sins, as we read in Luke 7 of the woman who was a sinner; while it is written (Matt. 14:36) that "as many as touched the hem of His garment were healed." Therefore, they do not sin, but rather obtain salvation, by receiving the body of Christ.

Obj. 2: Further, this sacrament, like the others, is a spiritual medicine. But medicine is given to the sick for their recovery, according to Matt. 9:12: "They that are in health need not a physician." Now they that are spiritually sick or infirm are sinners. Therefore this sacrament can be received by them without sin.

Obj. 3: Further, this sacrament is one of our greatest gifts, since it contains Christ. But according to Augustine (De Lib. Arb. ii), the greatest gifts are those "which no one can abuse." Now no one sins except by abusing something. Therefore no sinner sins by receiving this sacrament.

Obj. 4: Further, as this sacrament is perceived by taste and touch, so also is it by sight. Consequently, if the sinner sins by receiving the sacrament, it seems that he would sin by beholding it, which is manifestly untrue, since the Church exposes this sacrament to be seen and adored by all. Therefore the sinner does not sin by eating this sacrament.

Obj. 5: Further, it happens sometimes that the sinner is unconscious of his sin. Yet such a one does not seem to sin by receiving the body of Christ, for according to this all who receive it would sin, as exposing themselves to danger, since the Apostle says (1 Cor. 4:4): "I am not conscious to myself of anything, yet I am not hereby justified." Therefore, the sinner, if he receive this sacrament, does not appear to be guilty of sin.

*On the contrary,* The Apostle says (1 Cor. 11:29): "He that eateth and drinketh unworthily, eateth and drinketh judgment to himself." Now the gloss says on this passage: "He eats and drinks unworthily who is in sin, or who handles it irreverently." Therefore, if anyone, while in mortal sin, receives this sacrament, he purchases damnation, by sinning mortally.

*I answer that,* In this sacrament, as in the others, that which is a sacrament is a sign of the reality of the sacrament. Now there is a twofold reality of this sacrament, as stated above (Q. 73, A. 6): one which is signified and contained, namely, Christ Himself; while the other is signified but not contained, namely, Christ's mystical body, which is the fellowship of the saints. Therefore, whoever receives this sacrament, expresses thereby that he is made one with Christ, and incorporated in His members; and this is done by living faith, which no one has who is in mortal sin. And therefore it is manifest that whoever receives this sacrament while in mortal sin, is guilty of lying to this sacrament, and consequently of sacrilege, because he profanes the sacrament: and therefore he sins mortally.

Reply Obj. 1: When Christ appeared under His proper species, He did not give Himself to be touched by men as a sign of spiritual union with Himself, as He gives Himself to be received in this sacrament. And therefore sinners in touching Him under His proper species did not incur the sin of lying to Godlike things, as sinners do in receiving this sacrament.

Furthermore, Christ still bore the likeness of the body of sin; consequently He fittingly allowed Himself to be touched by sinners. But as soon as the body of sin was taken away by the glory of the Resurrection, he forbade the woman to touch Him, for her faith in Him was defective, according to John 20:17: "Do not touch Me, for I am not yet ascended to My Father," i.e. "in your heart," as Augustine explains (Tract. cxxi in Joan.). And therefore sinners, who lack living faith regarding Christ are not allowed to touch this sacrament.

Reply Obj. 2: Every medicine does not suit every stage of sickness; because the tonic given to those who are recovering from fever would be hurtful to them if given while yet in their feverish condition. So likewise Baptism and Penance are as purgative medicines, given to take away the fever of sin; whereas this sacrament is a medicine given to strengthen, and it ought not to be given except to them who are quit of sin.

Reply Obj. 3: By the greatest gifts Augustine understands the soul's virtues, "which no one uses to evil purpose," as though they were principles of evil. Nevertheless sometimes a man makes a bad use of them, as objects of an evil use, as is seen in those who are proud of their virtues. So likewise this sacrament, so far as the sacrament is concerned, is not the principle of an evil use, but the object thereof. Hence Augustine says (Tract. lxii in Joan.): "Many receive Christ's body unworthily; whence we are taught what need there is to beware of receiving a good thing evilly . . . For behold, of a good thing, received evilly, evil is wrought": just as on the other hand, in the Apostle's case, "good was wrought through evil well received," namely, by bearing patiently the sting of Satan.

Reply Obj. 4: Christ's body is not received by being seen, but only its sacrament, because sight does not penetrate to the substance of Christ's body, but only to the sacramental species, as stated above (Q. 76, A. 7). But he who eats, receives not only the sacramental species, but likewise Christ Himself Who is under them. Consequently, no one is forbidden to behold Christ's body, when once he has received Christ's sacrament, namely, Baptism: whereas the non-baptized are not to be allowed even to see this sacrament, as is clear from Dionysius (Eccl. Hier. vii). But only those are to be allowed to share in the eating who are united with Christ not merely sacramentally, but likewise really.

Reply Obj. 5: The fact of a man being unconscious of his sin can come about in two ways. First of all through his own fault, either because through ignorance of the law (which ignorance does not excuse him), he thinks something not to be sinful which is a sin, as for example if one guilty of fornication were to deem simple fornication not to be a mortal sin; or because he neglects to examine his conscience, which is opposed to what the Apostle says (1 Cor. 11:28): "Let a man prove himself, and so let him eat of that bread, and drink of the chalice." And in this way nevertheless the sinner who receives Christ's body commits sin, although unconscious thereof, because the very ignorance is a sin on his part.

Secondly, it may happen without fault on his part, as, for instance, when he has sorrowed over his sin, but is not sufficiently contrite: and in such a case he does not sin in receiving the body of Christ, because a man cannot know for certain whether he is truly contrite. It suffices, however, if he find in himself the marks of contrition, for instance, if he "grieve over past sins," and "propose to avoid them in the future" [*Cf. Rule of Augustine]. But if he be ignorant that what he did was a sinful act, through ignorance of the fact, which excuses, for instance, if a man approach a woman whom he believed to be his wife whereas she was not, he is not to be called a sinner on that account; in the same way if he has utterly forgotten his sin, general contrition suffices for blotting it out, as will be said hereafter (Suppl., Q. 2, A. 3, ad 2); hence he is no longer to be called a sinner.

FIFTH ARTICLE [III, Q. 80, Art. 5]

Whether to Approach This Sacrament with Consciousness of Sin Is the Gravest of All Sins?

Objection 1: It seems that to approach this sacrament with consciousness of sin is the gravest of all sins; because the Apostle says (1 Cor. 11:27): "Whosoever shall eat this bread, or drink the chalice of the Lord unworthily, shall be guilty of the body and of the blood of the Lord": upon which the gloss observes: "He shall be punished as though he slew Christ." But the sin of them who slew Christ seems to have been most grave. Therefore this sin, whereby a man approaches Christ's table with consciousness of sin, appears to be the gravest.

Obj. 2: Further, Jerome says in an Epistle (xlix): "What hast thou to do with women, thou that speakest familiarly with God at the altar?" [*The remaining part of the quotation is not from St. Jerome]. Say, priest, say, cleric, how dost thou kiss the Son of God with the same lips wherewith thou hast kissed the daughter of a harlot? "Judas, thou betrayest the Son of Man with a kiss!" And thus it appears that the fornicator approaching Christ's table sins as Judas did, whose sin was most grave. But there are many other sins which are graver than fornication, especially the sin of unbelief. Therefore the sin of every sinner approaching Christ's table is the gravest of all.

Obj. 3: Further, spiritual uncleanness is more abominable to God than corporeal. But if anyone was to cast Christ's body into mud or a cess-pool, his sin would be reputed a most grave one. Therefore, he sins more deeply by receiving it with sin, which is spiritual uncleanness, upon his soul.

*On the contrary,* Augustine says on the words, "If I had not come, and had not spoken to them, they would be without sin" (Tract. lxxxix in Joan.), that this is to be understood of the sin of unbelief, "in which all sins are comprised," and so the greatest of all sins appears to be, not this, but rather the sin of unbelief.

*I answer that,* As stated in the Second Part (I-II, Q. 73, AA. 3, 6; II-II, Q. 73, A. 3), one sin can be said to be graver than another in two ways: first of all essentially, secondly accidentally. Essentially, in regard to its species, which is taken from its object: and so a sin is greater according as that against which it is committed is greater. And since Christ's Godhead is greater than His humanity, and His humanity greater than the sacraments of His humanity, hence it is that those are the gravest sins which are committed against the Godhead, such as unbelief and blasphemy. The second degree of gravity is held by those sins which are committed against His humanity: hence it is written (Matt. 12:32): "Whosoever shall speak a word against the Son of Man, it shall be forgiven him; but he that shall speak against the Holy Ghost, it shall not be forgiven him, neither in this world nor in the world to come." In the third place come sins committed against the sacraments, which belong to Christ's humanity; and after these are the other sins committed against mere creatures.

Accidentally, one sin can be graver than another on the sinner's part. For example, the sin which is the result of ignorance or of weakness is lighter than one arising from contempt, or from sure knowledge; and the same reason holds good of other circumstances. And according to this, the above sin can be graver in some, as happens in them who from actual contempt and with consciousness of sin approach this sacrament: but in others it is less grave; for instance, in those who from fear of their sin being discovered, approach this sacrament with consciousness of sin.

So, then, it is evident that this sin is specifically graver than many others, yet it is not the greatest of all.

Reply Obj. 1: The sin of the unworthy recipient is compared to the sin of them who slew Christ, by way of similitude, because each is committed against Christ's body; but not according to the degree of the crime. Because the sin of Christ's slayers was much graver, first of all, because their sin was against Christ's body in its own species, while this sin is against it under sacramental species; secondly, because their sin came of the intent of injuring Christ, while this does not.

Reply Obj. 2: The sin of the fornicator receiving Christ's body is likened to Judas kissing Christ, as to the resemblance of the sin, because each outrages Christ with the sign of friendship. but not as to the extent of the sin, as was observed above (ad 1). And this resemblance in crime applies no less to other sinners than to fornicators: because by other mortal sins, sinners act against the charity of Christ, of which this sacrament is the sign, and all the more according as their sins are graver. But in a measure the sin of fornication makes one more unfit for receiving this sacrament, because thereby especially the spirit becomes enslaved by the flesh, which is a hindrance to the fervor of love required for this sacrament.

However, the hindrance to charity itself weighs more than the hindrance to its fervor. Hence the sin of unbelief, which fundamentally severs a man from the unity of the Church, simply speaking, makes him to be utterly unfit for receiving this sacrament; because it is the sacrament of the Church's unity, as stated above (Q. 61, A. 2). Hence the unbeliever who receives this sacrament sins more grievously than the believer who is in sin; and shows greater contempt towards Christ Who is in the sacrament, especially if he does not believe Christ to be truly in this sacrament; because, so far as lies in him, he lessens the holiness of the sacrament, and the power of Christ acting in it, and this is to despise the sacrament in itself. But the believer who receives the sacrament with consciousness of sin, by receiving it unworthily despises the sacrament, not in itself, but in its use. Hence the Apostle (1 Cor. 11:29) in assigning the cause of this sin, says, "not discerning the body of the Lord," that is, not distinguishing it from other food: and this is what he does who disbelieves Christ's presence in this sacrament.

Reply Obj. 3: The man who would throw this sacrament into the mire would be guilty of more heinous sin than another approaching the sacrament fully conscious of mortal sin. First of all, because he would intend to outrage the sacrament, whereas the sinner receiving Christ's body unworthily has no such intent; secondly, because the sinner is capable of grace; hence he is more capable of receiving this sacrament than any irrational creature. Hence he would make a most revolting use of this sacrament who would throw it to dogs to eat, or fling it in the mire to be trodden upon.

SIXTH ARTICLE [III, Q. 80, Art. 6]

Whether the Priest Ought to Deny the Body of Christ to the Sinner Seeking It?

Objection 1: It seems that the priest should deny the body of Christ to the sinner seeking it. For Christ's precept is not to be set aside for the sake of avoiding scandal or on account of infamy to anyone. But (Matt. 7:6) our Lord gave this command: "Give not that which is holy to dogs." Now it is especially casting holy things to dogs to give this sacrament to sinners. Therefore, neither on account of avoiding scandal or infamy should this sacrament be administered to the sinner who asks for it.

Obj. 2: Further, one must choose the lesser of two evils. But it seems to be the lesser evil if the sinner incur infamy; or if an unconsecrated host be given to him; than for him to sin mortally by receiving the body of Christ. Consequently, it seems that the course to be adopted is either that the sinner seeking the body of Christ be exposed to infamy, or that an unconsecrated host be given to him.

Obj. 3: Further, the body of Christ is sometimes given to those suspected of crime in order to put them to proof. Because we read in the Decretals: "It often happens that thefts are perpetrated in monasteries of monks; wherefore we command that when the brethren have to exonerate themselves of such acts, that the abbot shall celebrate Mass, or someone else deputed by him, in the presence of the community; and so, when the Mass is over, all shall communicate under these words: 'May the body of Christ prove thee today.'" And further on: "If any evil deed be imputed to a bishop or priest, for each charge he must say Mass and communicate, and show that he is innocent of each act imputed." But secret sinners must not be disclosed, for, once the blush of shame is set aside, they will indulge the more in sin, as Augustine says (De Verbis. Dom.; cf. Serm. lxxxii). Consequently, Christ's body is not to be given to occult sinners, even if they ask for it.

*On the contrary,* on Ps. 21:30: "All the fat ones of the earth have eaten and have adored," Augustine says: "Let not the dispenser hinder the fat ones of the earth," i.e. sinners, "from eating at the table of the Lord."

*I answer that,* A distinction must be made among sinners: some are secret; others are notorious, either from evidence of the fact, as public usurers, or public robbers, or from being denounced as evil men by some ecclesiastical or civil tribunal. Therefore Holy Communion ought not to be given to open sinners when they ask for it. Hence Cyprian writes to someone (Ep. lxi): "You were so kind as to consider that I ought to be consulted regarding actors, and that magician who continues to practice his disgraceful arts among you; as to whether I thought that Holy Communion ought to be given to such with the other Christians. I think that it is beseeming neither the Divine majesty, nor Christian discipline, for the Church's modesty and honor to be defiled by such shameful and infamous contagion."

But if they be not open sinners, but occult, the Holy Communion should not be denied them if they ask for it. For since every Christian, from the fact that he is baptized, is admitted to the Lord's table, he may not be robbed of his right, except from some open cause. Hence on 1 Cor. 5:11, "If he who is called a brother among you," etc., Augustine's gloss remarks: "We cannot inhibit any person from Communion, except he has openly confessed, or has been named and convicted by some ecclesiastical or lay tribunal." Nevertheless a priest who has knowledge of the crime can privately warn the secret sinner, or warn all openly in public, from approaching the Lord's table, until they have repented of their sins and have been reconciled to the Church; because after repentance and reconciliation, Communion must not be refused even to public sinners, especially in the hour of death. Hence in the (3rd) Council of Carthage (Can. xxxv) we read: "Reconciliation is not to be denied to stage-players or actors, or others of the sort, or to apostates, after their conversion to God."

Reply Obj. 1: Holy things are forbidden to be given to dogs, that is, to notorious sinners: whereas hidden deeds may not be published, but are to be left to the Divine judgment.

Reply Obj. 2: Although it is worse for the secret sinner to sin mortally in taking the body of Christ, rather than be defamed, nevertheless for the priest administering the body of Christ it is worse to commit mortal sin by unjustly defaming the hidden sinner than that the sinner should sin mortally; because no one ought to commit mortal sin in order to keep another out of mortal sin. Hence Augustine says (Quaest. super Gen. 42): "It is a most dangerous exchange, for us to do evil lest another perpetrate a greater evil." But the secret sinner ought rather to prefer infamy than approach the Lord's table unworthily.

Yet by no means should an unconsecrated host be given in place of a consecrated one; because the priest by so doing, so far as he is concerned, makes others, either the bystanders or the communicant, commit idolatry by believing that it is a consecrated host; because, as Augustine says on Ps. 98:5: "Let no one eat Christ's flesh, except he first adore it." Hence in the Decretals (Extra, De Celeb. Miss., Ch. De Homine) it is said: "Although he who reputes himself unworthy of the Sacrament, through consciousness of his sin, sins gravely, if he receive; still he seems to offend more deeply who deceitfully has presumed to simulate it."

Reply Obj. 3: Those decrees were abolished by contrary enactments of Roman Pontiffs: because Pope Stephen V writes as follows: "The Sacred Canons do not allow of a confession being extorted from any person by trial made by burning iron or boiling water; it belongs to our government to judge of public crimes committed, and that by means of confession made spontaneously, or by proof of witnesses: but private and unknown crimes are to be left to Him Who alone knows the hearts of the sons of men." And the same is found in the Decretals (Extra, De Purgationibus, Ch. Ex tuarum). Because in all such practices there seems to be a tempting of God; hence such things cannot be done without sin. And it would seem graver still if anyone were to incur judgment of death through this sacrament, which was instituted as a means of salvation. Consequently, the body of Christ should never be given to anyone suspected of crime, as by way of examination.

SEVENTH ARTICLE [III, Q. 80, Art. 7]

Whether the Seminal Loss That Occurs During Sleep Hinders Anyone from Receiving This Sacrament?

Objection 1: It seems that seminal loss does not hinder anyone from receiving the body of Christ: because no one is prevented from receiving the body of Christ except on account of sin. But seminal loss happens without sin: for Augustine says (Gen. ad lit. xii) that "the same image that comes into the mind of a speaker may present itself to the mind of the sleeper, so that the latter be unable to distinguish the image from the reality, and is moved carnally and with the result that usually follows such motions; and there is as little sin in this as there is in speaking and therefore thinking about such things." Consequently these motions do not prevent one from receiving this sacrament.

Obj. 2: Further, Gregory says in a Letter to Augustine, Bishop of the English (Regist. xi): "Those who pay the debt of marriage not from lust, but from desire to have children, should be left to their own judgment, as to whether they should enter the church and receive the mystery of our Lord's body, after such intercourse: because they ought not to be forbidden from receiving it, since they have passed through the fire unscorched."

From this it is evident that seminal loss even of one awake, if it be without sin, is no hindrance to receiving the body of Christ. Consequently, much less is it in the case of one asleep.

Obj. 3: Further, these movements of the flesh seem to bring with them only bodily uncleanness. But there are other bodily defilements which according to the Law forbade entrance into the holy places, yet which under the New Law do not prevent receiving this sacrament: as, for instance, in the case of a woman after child-birth, or in her periods, or suffering from issue of blood, as Gregory writes to Augustine, Bishop of the English (Regist. xi). Therefore it seems that neither do these movements of the flesh hinder a man from receiving this sacrament.

Obj. 4: Further, venial sin is no hindrance to receiving the sacrament, nor is mortal sin after repentance. But even supposing that seminal loss arises from some foregoing sin, whether of intemperance, or of bad thoughts, for the most part such sin is venial; and if occasionally it be mortal, a man may repent of it by morning and confess it. Consequently, it seems that he ought not to be prevented from receiving this sacrament.

Obj. 5: Further, a sin against the Fifth Commandment is greater than a sin against the Sixth. But if a man dream that he has broken the Fifth or Seventh or any other Commandment, he is not on that account debarred from receiving this sacrament. Therefore it seems that much less should he be debarred through defilement resulting from a dream against the Sixth Commandment.

*On the contrary,* It is written (Lev. 15:16): "The man from whom the seed of copulation goeth out . . . shall be unclean until evening." But for the unclean there is no approaching to the sacraments. Therefore, it seems that owing to such defilement of the flesh a man is debarred from taking this which is the greatest of the sacraments.

*I answer that,* There are two things to be weighed regarding the aforesaid movements: one on account of which they necessarily prevent a man from receiving this sacrament; the other, on account of which they do so, not of necessity, but from a sense of propriety.

Mortal sin alone necessarily prevents anyone from partaking of this sacrament: and although these movements during sleep, considered in themselves, cannot be a mortal sin, nevertheless, owing to their cause, they [sometimes] have mortal sin connected with them; which cause, therefore, must be investigated. Sometimes they are due to an external spiritual cause, viz. the deception of the demons, who can stir up phantasms, as was stated in the First Part (I, Q. 111, A. 3), through the apparition of which, these movements occasionally follow. Sometimes they are due to an internal spiritual cause, such as previous thoughts. At other times they arise from some internal corporeal cause, as from abundance or weakness of nature, or even from surfeit of meat or drink. Now every one of these three causes can be without sin at all, or else with venial sin, or with mortal sin. If it be without sin, or with venial sin, it does not necessarily prevent the receiving of this sacrament, so as to make a man guilty of the body and blood of the Lord: but should it be with mortal sin, it prevents it of necessity.

For such illusions on the part of demons sometimes come from one's not striving to receive fervently; and this can be either a mortal or a venial sin. At other times it is due to malice alone on the part of the demons who wish to keep men from receiving this sacrament. So we read in the Conferences of the Fathers (Cassian, Collat. xxii) that when a certain one always suffered thus on those feast-days on which he had to receive Communion, his superiors, discovering that there was no fault on his part, ruled that he was not to refrain from communicating on that account, and the demoniacal illusion ceased.

In like fashion previous evil thoughts can sometimes be without any sin whatever, as when one has to think of such things on account of lecturing or debating; and if it be done without concupiscence and delectation, the thoughts will not be unclean but honest; and yet defilement can come of such thoughts, as is clear from the authority of Augustine (Obj. 1). At other times such thoughts come of concupiscence and delectation, and should there be consent, it will be a mortal sin: otherwise it will be a venial sin.

In the same way too the corporeal cause can be without sin, as when it arises from bodily debility, and hence some individuals suffer seminal loss without sin even in their wakeful hours; or it can come from the abundance of nature: for, just as blood can flow without sin, so also can the semen which is superfluity of the blood, according to the Philosopher (De Gener. Animal. i). But occasionally it is with sin, as when it is due to excess of food or drink. And this also can be either venial or mortal sin; although more frequently the sin is mortal in the case of evil thoughts on account of the proneness to consent, rather than in the case of consumption of food and drink. Hence Gregory, writing to Augustine, Bishop of the English (Regist. xi), says that one ought to refrain from Communion when this arises from evil thoughts, but not when it arises from excess of food or drink, especially if necessity call for Communion. So, then, one must judge from its cause whether such bodily defilement of necessity hinders the receiving of this sacrament.

At the same time a sense of decency forbids Communion on two accounts. The first of these is always verified, viz. the bodily defilement, with which, out of reverence for the sacrament, it is unbecoming to approach the altar (and hence those who wish to touch any sacred object, wash their hands): except perchance such uncleanness be perpetual or of long standing, such as leprosy or issue of blood, or anything else of the kind. The other reason is the mental distraction which follows after the aforesaid movements, especially when they take place with unclean imaginings. Now this obstacle, which arises from a sense of decency, can be set aside owing to any necessity, as Gregory says (Regist. xi): "As when perchance either a festival day calls for it, or necessity compels one to exercise the ministry because there is no other priest at hand."

Reply Obj. 1: A person is hindered necessarily, only by mortal sin, from receiving this sacrament: but from a sense of decency one may be hindered through other causes, as stated above.

Reply Obj. 2: Conjugal intercourse, if it be without sin, (for instance, if it be done for the sake of begetting offspring, or of paying the marriage debt), does not prevent the receiving of this sacrament for any other reason than do those movements in question which happen without sin, as stated above; namely, on account of the defilement to the body and distraction to the mind. On this account Jerome expresses himself in the following terms in his commentary on Matthew (Epist. xxviii, among St. Jerome's works): "If the loaves of Proposition might not be eaten by them who had known their wives carnally, how much less may this bread which has come down from heaven be defiled and touched by them who shortly before have been in conjugal embraces? It is not that we condemn marriages, but that at the time when we are going to eat the flesh of the Lamb, we ought not to indulge in carnal acts." But since this is to be understood in the sense of decency, and not of necessity, Gregory says that such a person "is to be left to his own judgment." "But if," as Gregory says (Regist. xi), "it be not desire of begetting offspring, but lust that prevails," then such a one should be forbidden to approach this sacrament.

Reply Obj. 3: As Gregory says in his Letter quoted above to Augustine, Bishop of the English, in the Old Testament some persons were termed polluted figuratively, which the people of the New Law understand spiritually. Hence such bodily uncleannesses, if perpetual or of long standing, do not hinder the receiving of this saving sacrament, as they prevented approaching those figurative sacraments; but if they pass speedily, like the uncleanness of the aforesaid movements, then from a sense of fittingness they hinder the receiving of this sacrament during the day on which it happens. Hence it is written (Deut. 23:10): "If there be among you any man, that is defiled in a dream by night, he shall go forth out of the camp; and he shall not return before he be washed with water in the evening."

Reply Obj. 4: Although the stain of guilt be taken away by contrition and confession nevertheless the bodily defilement is not taken away, nor the mental distraction which follows therefrom.

Reply Obj. 5: To dream of homicide brings no bodily uncleanness, nor such distraction of mind as fornication, on account of its intense delectation; still if the dream of homicide comes of a cause sinful in itself, especially if it be mortal sin, then owing to its cause it hinders the receiving of this sacrament.

EIGHTH ARTICLE [III, Q. 80, Art. 8]

Whether Food or Drink Taken Beforehand Hinders the Receiving of This Sacrament?

Objection 1: It seems that food or drink taken beforehand does not hinder the receiving of this sacrament. For this sacrament was instituted by our Lord at the supper. But when the supper was ended our Lord gave the sacrament to His disciples, as is evident from Luke 22:20, and from 1 Cor. 11:25. Therefore it seems that we ought to take this sacrament after receiving other food.

Obj. 2: Further, it is written (1 Cor. 11:33): "When you come together to eat," namely, the Lord's body, "wait for one another; if any man be hungry, let him eat at home": and thus it seems that after eating at home a man may eat Christ's body in the Church.

Obj. 3: Further, we read in the (3rd) Council of Carthage (Can. xxix): "Let the sacraments of the altar be celebrated only by men who are fasting, with the exception of the anniversary day on which the Lord's Supper is celebrated." Therefore, at least on that day, one may receive the body of Christ after partaking of other food.

Obj. 4: Further, the taking of water or medicine, or of any other food or drink in very slight quantity, or of the remains of food continuing in the mouth, neither breaks the Church's fast, nor takes away the sobriety required for reverently receiving this sacrament. Consequently, one is not prevented by the above things from receiving this sacrament.

Obj. 5: Further, some eat and drink late at night, and possibly after passing a sleepless night receive the sacred mysteries in the morning when the food is not digested. But it would savor more of moderation if a man were to eat a little in the morning and afterwards receive this sacrament about the ninth hour, since also there is occasionally a longer interval of time. Consequently, it seems that such taking of food beforehand does not keep one from this sacrament.

Obj. 6: Further, there is no less reverence due to this sacrament after receiving it, than before. But one may take food and drink after receiving the sacrament. Therefore one may do so before receiving it.

*On the contrary,* Augustine says (Resp. ad Januar., Ep. liv): "It has pleased the Holy Ghost that, out of honor for this great sacrament, the Lord's body should enter the mouth of a Christian before other foods."

*I answer that,* A thing may prevent the receiving of this sacrament in two ways: first of all in itself, like mortal sin, which is repugnant to what is signified by this sacrament, as stated above (A. 4): secondly, on account of the Church's prohibition; and thus a man is prevented from taking this sacrament after receiving food or drink, for three reasons. First, as Augustine says (Resp. ad Januar., Ep. liv), "out of respect for this sacrament," so that it may enter into a mouth not yet contaminated by any food or drink. Secondly, because of its signification, i.e. to give us to understand that Christ, Who is the reality of this sacrament, and His charity, ought to be first of all established in our hearts, according to Matt. 6:33: "Seek first the kingdom of God." Thirdly, on account of the danger of vomiting and intemperance, which sometimes arise from over-indulging in food, as the Apostle says (1 Cor. 11:21): "One, indeed, is hungry, and another is drunk."

Nevertheless the sick are exempted from this

general rule, for they should be given Communion at once, even after food, should there be any doubt as to their danger, lest they die without Communion, because necessity has no law. Hence it is said in the Canon de Consecratione: "Let the priest at once take Communion to the sick person, lest he die without Communion."

Reply Obj. 1: As Augustine says in the same book, "the fact that our Lord gave this sacrament after taking food is no reason why the brethren should assemble after dinner or supper in order to partake of it, or receive it at meal-time, as did those whom the Apostle reproves and corrects. For our Saviour, in order the more strongly to commend the depth of this mystery, wished to fix it closely in the hearts and memories of the disciples; and on that account He gave no command for it to be received in that order, leaving this to the apostles, to whom He was about to entrust the government of the churches."

Reply Obj. 2: The text quoted is thus paraphrased by the gloss: "If any man be hungry and loath to await the rest, let him partake of his food at home, that is, let him fill himself with earthly bread, without partaking of the Eucharist afterwards."

Reply Obj. 3: The wording of this decree is in accordance with the former custom observed by some of receiving the body of Christ on that day after breaking their fast, so as to represent the Lord's supper. But this is now abrogated, because as Augustine says (Resp. ad Januar., Ep. liv), it is customary throughout the whole world for Christ's body to be received before breaking the fast.

Reply Obj. 4: As stated in the Second Part (II-II, Q. 147, A. 6, ad 2), there are two kinds of fast. First, there is the natural fast, which implies privation of everything taken before-hand by way of food or drink: and such fast is required for this sacrament for the reasons given above. And therefore it is never lawful to take this sacrament after taking water, or other food or drink, or even medicine, no matter how small the quantity be. Nor does it matter whether it nourishes or not, whether it be taken by itself or with other things, provided it be taken by way of food or drink. But the remains of food left in the mouth, if swallowed accidentally, do not hinder receiving this sacrament, because they are swallowed not by way of food but by way of saliva. The same holds good of the unavoidable remains of the water or wine wherewith the mouth is rinsed, provided they be not swallowed in great quantity, but mixed with saliva.

Secondly, there is the fast of the Church, instituted for afflicting the body: and this fast is not hindered by the things mentioned (in the objection), because they do not give much nourishment, but are taken rather as an alterative.

Reply Obj. 5: That this sacrament ought to enter into the mouth of a Christian before any other food must not be understood absolutely of all time, otherwise he who had once eaten or drunk could never afterwards take this sacrament: but it must be understood of the same day; and although the beginning of the day varies according to different systems of reckoning (for some begin their day at noon, some at sunset, others at midnight, and others at sunrise), the Roman Church begins it at midnight. Consequently, if any person takes anything by way of food or drink after midnight, he may not receive this sacrament on that day; but he can do so if the food was taken before midnight. Nor does it matter, so far as the precept is concerned, whether he has slept after taking food or drink, or whether he has digested it; but it does matter as to the mental disturbance which one suffers from want of sleep or from indigestion, for, if the mind be much disturbed, one becomes unfit for receiving this sacrament.

Reply Obj. 6: The greatest devotion is called for at the moment of receiving this sacrament, because it is then that the effect of the sacrament is bestowed, and such devotion is hindered more by what goes before it than by what comes after it. And therefore it was ordained that men should fast before receiving the sacrament rather than after. Nevertheless there ought to be some interval between receiving this sacrament and taking other food. Consequently, both the Postcommunion prayer of thanksgiving is said in the Mass, and the communicants say their own private prayers.

However, according to the ancient Canons, the following ordination was made by Pope Clement I, (Ep. ii), "If the Lord's portion be eaten in the morning, the ministers who have taken it shall fast until the sixth hour, and if they take it at the third or fourth hour, they shall fast until evening." For in olden times, the priest celebrated Mass less frequently, and with greater preparation: but now, because the sacred mysteries have to be celebrated oftener, the same could not be easily observed, and so it has been abrogated by contrary custom.

NINTH ARTICLE [III, Q. 80, Art. 9]

Whether Those Who Have Not the Use of Reason Ought to Receive This Sacrament?

Objection 1: It seems that those who have not the use of reason ought not to receive this sacrament. For it is required that man should approach this sacrament with devotion and previous self-examination, according to 1 Cor. 11:28: "Let a man prove himself, and so let him eat of that bread, and drink of the chalice." But this is not possible for those who are devoid of reason. Therefore this sacrament should not be given to them.

Obj. 2: Further, among those who have not the use of reason are the possessed, who are called energumens. But such persons are kept from even beholding this sacrament, according to Dionysius (Eccl. Hier. iii). Therefore this sacrament ought not to be given to those who have not the use of reason.

Obj. 3: Further, among those that lack the use of reason are children, the most innocent of all. But this sacrament is not given to children. Therefore much less should it be given to others deprived of the use of reason.

*On the contrary,* We read in the First Council of Orange, (Canon 13); and the same is to be found in the Decretals (xxvi, 6): "All things that pertain to piety are to be given to the insane": and consequently, since this is the "sacrament of piety," it must be given to them.

*I answer that,* Men are said to be devoid of reason in two ways. First, when they are feeble-minded, as a man who sees dimly is said not to see: and since such persons can conceive some devotion towards this sacrament, it is not to be denied them.

In another way men are said not to possess fully the use of reason. Either, then, they never had the use of reason, and have remained so from birth; and in that case this sacrament is not to be given to them, because in no way has there been any preceding devotion towards the sacrament: or else, they were not always devoid of reason, and then, if when they formerly had their wits they showed devotion towards this sacrament, it ought to be given to them in the hour of death; unless danger be feared of vomiting or spitting it out. Hence we read in the acts of the Fourth Council of Carthage (Canon 76). and the same is to be found in the Decretals (xxvi, 6): "If a sick man ask to receive the sacrament of Penance; and if, when the priest who has been sent for comes to him, he be so weak as to be unable to speak, or becomes delirious, let them, who heard him ask, bear witness, and let him receive the sacrament of Penance. then if it be thought that he is going to die shortly, let him be reconciled by imposition of hands, and let the Eucharist be placed in his mouth."

Reply Obj. 1: Those lacking the use of reason can have devotion towards the sacrament; actual devotion in some cases, and past in others.

Reply Obj. 2: Dionysius is speaking there of energumens who are not yet baptized, in whom the devil's power is not yet extinct, since it thrives in them through the presence of original sin. But as to baptized persons who are vexed in body by unclean spirits, the same reason holds good of them as of others who are demented. Hence Cassian says (Collat. vii): "We do not remember the most Holy Communion to have ever been denied by our elders to them who are vexed by unclean spirits."

Reply Obj. 3: The same reason holds good of newly born children as of the insane who never have had the use of reason: consequently, the sacred mysteries are not to be given to them. Although certain Greeks do the contrary, because Dionysius says (Eccl. Hier. ii) that Holy Communion is to be given to them who are baptized; not understanding that Dionysius is speaking there of the Baptism of adults. Nor do they suffer any loss of life from the fact of our Lord saying (John 6:54), "Except you eat the flesh of the Son of Man, and drink His blood, you shall not have life in you"; because, as Augustine writes to Boniface (Pseudo-Beda, Comment. in 1 Cor. 10:17), "then every one of the faithful becomes a partaker," i.e. spiritually, "of the body and blood of the Lord, when he is made a member of Christ's body in Baptism." But when children once begin to have some use of reason so as to be able to conceive some devotion for the sacrament, then it can be given to them.

TENTH ARTICLE [III, Q. 80, Art. 10]

Whether It Is Lawful to Receive This Sacrament Daily?

Objection 1: It does not appear to be lawful to receive this sacrament daily, because, as Baptism shows forth our Lord's Passion, so also does this sacrament. Now one may not be baptized several times, but only once, because "Christ died once" only "for our sins," according to 1 Pet. 3:18. Therefore, it seems unlawful to receive this sacrament daily.

Obj. 2: Further, the reality ought to answer to the figure. But the Paschal Lamb, which was the chief figure of this sacrament, as was said above (Q. 73, A. 9) was eaten only once in the year; while the Church once a year commemorates Christ's Passion, of which this sacrament is the memorial. It seems, then, that it is lawful to receive this sacrament not daily, but only once in the year.

Obj. 3: Further, the greatest reverence is due to this sacrament as containing Christ. But it is a token of reverence to refrain from receiving this sacrament; hence the Centurion is praised for saying (Matt. 8:8), "Lord, I am not worthy that Thou shouldst enter under my roof"; also Peter, for saying (Luke 5:8), "Depart from me, for I am a sinful man, O Lord." Therefore, it is not praiseworthy for a man to receive this sacrament daily.

Obj. 4: Further, if it were a praiseworthy custom to receive this sacrament frequently, then the oftener it were taken the more praise-worthy it would be. But there would be greater frequency if one were to receive it several times daily; and yet this is not the custom of the Church. Consequently, it does not seem praiseworthy to receive it daily.

Obj. 5: Further, the Church by her statutes intends to promote the welfare of the faithful. But the Church's statute only requires Communion once a year; hence it is enacted (Extra, De Poenit. et Remiss. xii): "Let every person of either sex devoutly receive the sacrament of the Eucharist at least at Easter; unless by the advice of his parish priest, and for some reasonable cause, he considers he ought to refrain from receiving for a time." Consequently, it is not praiseworthy to receive this sacrament daily.

*On the contrary,* Augustine says (De Verb. Dom., Serm. xxviii): "This is our daily bread; take it daily, that it may profit thee daily."

*I answer that,* There are two things to be considered regarding the use of this sacrament. The first is on the part of the sacrament itself, the virtue of which gives health to men; and consequently it is profitable to receive it daily so as to receive its fruits daily. Hence Ambrose says (De Sacram. iv): "If, whenever Christ's blood is shed, it is shed for the forgiveness of sins, I who sin often, should receive it often: I need a frequent remedy." The second thing to be considered is on the part of the recipient, who is required to approach this sacrament with great reverence and devotion. Consequently, if anyone finds that he has these dispositions every day, he will do well to receive it daily. Hence, Augustine after saying, "Receive daily, that it may profit thee daily," adds: "So live, as to deserve to receive it daily." But because many persons are lacking in this devotion, on account of the many drawbacks both spiritual and corporal from which they suffer, it is not expedient for all to approach this sacrament every day; but they should do so as often as they find themselves properly disposed. Hence it is said in De Eccles. Dogmat. liii: "I neither praise nor blame daily reception of the Eucharist."

Reply Obj. 1: In the sacrament of Baptism a man is conformed to Christ's death, by receiving His character within him. And therefore, as Christ died but once, so a man ought to be baptized but once. But a man does not receive Christ's character in this sacrament; He receives Christ Himself, Whose virtue endures for ever. Hence it is written (Heb. 10:14): "By one oblation He hath perfected for ever them that are sanctified." Consequently, since man has daily need of Christ's health-giving virtue, he may commendably receive this sacrament every day.

And since Baptism is above all a spiritual regeneration, therefore, as a man is born naturally but once, so ought he by Baptism to be reborn spiritually but once, as Augustine says (Tract. xi in Joan.), commenting on John 3:4, "How can a man be born again, when he is grown old?" But this sacrament is spiritual food; hence, just as bodily food is taken every day, so is it a good thing to receive this sacrament every day. Hence it is that our Lord (Luke 11:3), teaches us to pray, "Give us this day our daily bread": in explaining which words Augustine observes (De Verb. Dom., Serm. xxviii): "If you receive it," i.e. this sacrament, every day, "every day is today for thee, and Christ rises again every day in thee, for when Christ riseth it is today."

Reply Obj. 2: The Paschal Lamb was the figure of this sacrament chiefly as to Christ's Passion represented therein; and therefore it was partaken of once a year only, since Christ died but once. And on this account the Church celebrates once a year the remembrance of Christ's Passion. But in this sacrament the memorial of His Passion is given by way of food which is partaken of daily; and therefore in this respect it is represented by the manna which was given daily to the people in the desert.

Reply Obj. 3: Reverence for this sacrament consists in fear associated with love; consequently reverential fear of God is called filial fear, as was said in the Second Part (I-II, Q. 67, A. 4, ad 2; II-II, Q. 19, AA. 9, 11, 12); because the desire of receiving arises from love, while the humility of reverence springs from fear. Consequently, each of these belongs to the reverence due to this sacrament; both as to receiving it daily, and as to refraining from it sometimes. Hence Augustine says (Ep. liv): "If one says that the Eucharist should not be received daily, while another maintains the contrary, let each one do as according to his devotion he thinketh right; for Zaccheus and the Centurion did not contradict one another while the one received the Lord with joy, whereas the other said: 'Lord I am not worthy that Thou shouldst enter under my roof'; since both honored our Saviour, though not in the same way." But love and hope, whereunto the Scriptures constantly urge us, are preferable to fear. Hence, too, when Peter had said, "Depart from me, for I am a sinful man, O Lord," Jesus answered: "Fear not."

Reply Obj. 4: Because our Lord said (Luke 11:3), "Give us this day our daily bread," we are not on that account to communicate several times daily, for, by one daily communion the unity of Christ's Passion is set forth.

Reply Obj. 5: Various statutes have emanated according to the various ages of the Church. In the primitive Church, when the devotion of the Christian faith was more flourishing, it was enacted that the faithful should communicate daily: hence Pope Anaclete says (Ep. i): "When the consecration is finished, let all communicate who do not wish to cut themselves off from the Church; for so the apostles have ordained, and the holy Roman Church holds." Later on, when the fervor of faith relaxed, Pope Fabian (Third Council of Tours, Canon 1) gave permission "that all should communicate, if not more frequently, at least three times in the year, namely, at Easter, Pentecost, and Christmas." Pope Soter likewise (Second Council of Chalon, Canon xlvii) declares that Communion should be received "on Holy Thursday," as is set forth in the Decretals (De Consecratione, dist. 2). Later on, when "iniquity abounded and charity grew cold" (Matt. 24:12), Pope Innocent III commanded that the faithful should communicate "at least once a year," namely, "at Easter." However, in De Eccles. Dogmat. xxiii, the faithful are counseled "to communicate on all Sundays."

ELEVENTH ARTICLE [III, Q. 80, Art. 11]

Whether It Is Lawful to Abstain Altogether from Communion?

Objection 1: It seems to be lawful to abstain altogether from Communion. Because the Centurion is praised for saying (Matt. 8:8): "Lord, I am not worthy that Thou shouldst enter under my roof"; and he who deems that he ought to refrain entirely from Communion can be compared to the Centurion, as stated above (A. 10, ad 3). Therefore, since we do not read of Christ entering his house, it seems to be lawful for any individual to abstain from Communion his whole life long.

Obj. 2: Further, it is lawful for anyone to refrain from what is not of necessity for salvation. But this sacrament is not of necessity for salvation, as was stated above (Q. 73, A. 3). Therefore it is permissible to abstain from Communion altogether.

Obj. 3: Further, sinners are not bound to go to Communion: hence Pope Fabian (Third Council of Tours, Canon 1) after saying, "Let all communicate thrice each year," adds: "Except those who are hindered by grievous crimes." Consequently, if those who are not in the state of sin are bound to go to Communion, it seems that sinners are better off than good people, which is unfitting. Therefore, it seems lawful even for the godly to refrain from Communion.

*On the contrary,* Our Lord said (John 6:54): "Except ye eat the flesh of the Son of Man, and drink His blood, you shall not have life in you."

*I answer that,* As stated above (A. 1), there are two ways of receiving this sacrament namely, spiritually and sacramentally. Now it is clear that all are bound to eat it at least spiritually, because this is to be incorporated in Christ, as was said above (Q. 73, A. 3, ad 1). Now spiritual eating comprises the desire or yearning for receiving this sacrament, as was said above (A. 1, ad 3, A. 2). Therefore, a man cannot be saved without desiring to receive this sacrament.

Now a desire would be vain except it were fulfilled when opportunity presented itself. Consequently, it is evident that a man is bound to receive this sacrament, not only by virtue of the Church's precept, but also by virtue of the Lord's command (Luke 22:19): "Do this in memory of Me." But by the precept of the Church there are fixed times for fulfilling Christ's command.

Reply Obj. 1: As Gregory says: "He is truly humble, who is not obstinate in rejecting what is commanded for his good." Consequently, humility is not praiseworthy if anyone abstains altogether from Communion against the precept of Christ and the Church. Again the Centurion was not commanded to receive Christ into his house.

Reply Obj. 2: This sacrament is said not to be as necessary as Baptism, with regard to children, who can be saved without the Eucharist, but not without the sacrament of Baptism: both, however, are of necessity with regard to adults.

Reply Obj. 3: Sinners suffer great loss in being kept back from receiving this sacrament, so that they are not better off on that account; and although while continuing in their sins they are not on that account excused from transgressing the precept, nevertheless, as Pope Innocent III says, penitents, "who refrain on the advice of their priest," are excused.

TWELFTH ARTICLE [III, Q. 80, Art. 12]

Whether It Is Lawful to Receive the Body of Christ Without the Blood?

Objection 1: It seems unlawful to receive the body of Christ without the blood. For Pope Gelasius says (cf. De Consecr. ii): "We have learned that some persons after taking only a portion of the sacred body, abstain from the chalice of the sacred blood. I know not for what superstitious motive they do this: therefore let them either receive the entire sacrament, or let them be withheld from the sacrament altogether." Therefore it is not lawful to receive the body of Christ without His blood.

Obj. 2: Further, the eating of the body and the drinking of the blood are required for the perfection of this sacrament, as stated above (Q. 73, A. 2; Q. 76, A. 2, ad 1). Consequently, if the body be taken without the blood, it will be an imperfect sacrament, which seems to savor of sacrilege; hence Pope Gelasius adds (cf. De Consecr. ii), "because the dividing of one and the same mystery cannot happen without a great sacrilege."

Obj. 3: Further, this sacrament is celebrated in memory of our Lord's Passion, as stated above (Q. 73, AA. 4, 5; Q. 74, A. 1), and is received for the health of soul. But the Passion is expressed in the blood rather than in the body; moreover, as stated above (Q. 74, A. 1), the blood is offered for the health of the soul. Consequently, one ought to refrain from receiving the body rather than the blood. Therefore, such as approach this sacrament ought not to take Christ's body without His blood.

*On the contrary,* It is the custom of many churches for the body of Christ to be given to the communicant without His blood.

*I answer that,* Two points should be observed regarding the use of this sacrament, one on the part of the sacrament, the other on the part of the recipients; on the part of the sacrament it is proper for both the body and the blood to be received, since the perfection of the sacrament lies in both, and consequently, since it is the priest's duty both to consecrate and finish the sacrament, he ought on no account to receive Christ's body without the blood.

But on the part of the recipient the greatest reverence and caution are called for, lest anything happen which is unworthy of so great a mystery. Now this could especially happen in receiving the blood, for, if incautiously handled, it might easily be spilt. And because the multitude of the Christian people increased, in which there are old, young, and children, some of whom have not enough discretion to observe due caution in using this sacrament, on that account it is a prudent custom in some churches for the blood not to be offered to the reception of the people, but to be received by the priest alone.

Reply Obj. 1: Pope Gelasius is speaking of priests, who, as they consecrate the entire sacrament, ought to communicate in the entire sacrament. For, as we read in the (Twelfth) Council of Toledo, "What kind of a sacrifice is that, wherein not even the sacrificer is known to have a share?"

Reply Obj. 2: The perfection of this sacrament does not lie in the use of the faithful, but in the consecration of the matter. And hence there is nothing derogatory to the perfection of this sacrament; if the people receive the body without the blood, provided that the priest who consecrates receive both.

Reply Obj. 3: Our Lord's Passion is represented in the very consecration of this sacrament, in which the body ought not to be consecrated without the blood. But the body can be received by the people without the blood: nor is this detrimental to the sacrament. Because the priest both offers and consumes the blood on behalf of all; and Christ is fully contained under either species, as was shown above (Q. 76, A. 2).

## QUESTION 81

OF THE USE WHICH CHRIST MADE OF THIS SACRAMENT AT ITS INSTITUTION (In Four Articles)

We have now to consider the use which Christ made of this sacrament at its institution; under which heading there are four points of inquiry:

(1) Whether Christ received His own body and blood?

(2) Whether He gave it to Judas?

(3) What kind of body did He receive or give, namely, was it passible or impassible?

(4) What would have been the condition of Christ's body under this sacrament, if it had been reserved or consecrated during the three days He lay dead?

FIRST ARTICLE [III, Q. 81, Art. 1]

Whether Christ Received His Own Body and Blood?

Objection 1: It seems that Christ did not receive His own body and blood, because nothing ought to be asserted of either Christ's doings or sayings, which is not handed down by the authority of Sacred Scripture. But it is not narrated in the gospels that He ate His own body or drank His own blood. Therefore we must not assert this as a fact.

Obj. 2: Further, nothing can be within itself except perchance by reason of its parts, for instance, as one part is in another, as is stated inPhys. iv. But what is eaten and drunk is in the eater and drinker. Therefore, since the entire Christ is under each species of the sacrament, it seems impossible for Him to have received this sacrament.

Obj. 3: Further, the receiving of this sacrament is twofold, namely, spiritual and sacramental. But the spiritual was unsuitable for Christ, as He derived no benefit from the sacrament; and in consequence so was the sacramental, since it is imperfect without the spiritual, as was observed above (Q. 80, A. 1). Consequently, in no way did Christ partake of this sacrament.

*On the contrary,* Jerome says (Ad Hedib., Ep. xxx), "The Lord Jesus Christ, Himself the guest and banquet, is both the partaker and what is eaten."

*I answer that,* Some have said that Christ during the supper gave His body and blood to His disciples, but did not partake of it Himself. But this seems improbable. Because Christ Himself was the first to fulfill what He required others to observe: hence He willed first to be baptized when imposing Baptism upon others: as we read in Acts 1:1: "Jesus began to do and to teach." Hence He first of all took His own body and blood, and afterwards gave it to be taken by the disciples. And hence the gloss upon Ruth 3:7, "When he had eaten and drunk, says: Christ ate and drank at the supper, when He gave to the disciples the sacrament of His body and blood. Hence, 'because the children partook [*Vulg.: 'are partakers' (Heb. 2:14)] of His flesh and blood, He also hath been partaker in the same.'"

Reply Obj. 1: We read in the Gospels how Christ "took the bread . . . and the chalice"; but it is not to be understood that He took them merely into His hands, as some say, but that He took them in the same way as He gave them to others to take. Hence when He said to the disciples, "Take ye and eat," and again, "Take ye and drink," it is to be understood that He Himself, in taking it, both ate and drank. Hence some have composed this rhyme:

"The King at supper sits, The twelve as guests He greets, Clasping Himself in His hands, The food Himself now eats."

Reply Obj. 2: As was said above (Q. 76, A. 5), Christ as contained under this sacrament stands in relation to place, not according to His own dimensions, but according to the dimensions of the sacramental species; so that Christ is Himself in every place where those species are. And because the species were able to be both in the hands and the mouth of Christ, the entire Christ could be in both His hands and mouth. Now this could not come to pass were His relation to place to be according to His proper dimensions.

Reply Obj. 3: As was stated above (Q. 79, A. 1, ad 2), the effect of this sacrament is not merely an increase of habitual grace, but furthermore a certain actual delectation of spiritual sweetness. But although grace was not increased in Christ through His receiving this sacrament, yet He had a certain spiritual delectation from the new institution of this sacrament. Hence He Himself said (Luke 22:15): "With desire I have desired to eat this Pasch with you," which words Eusebius explains of the new mystery of the New Testament, which He gave to the disciples. And therefore He ate it both spiritually and sacramentally, inasmuch as He received His own body under the sacrament which sacrament of His own body He both understood and prepared; yet differently from others who partake of it both sacramentally and spiritually, for these receive an increase of grace, and they have need of the sacramental signs for perceiving its truth.

SECOND ARTICLE [III, Q. 81, Art. 2]

Whether Christ Gave His Body to Judas?

Objection 1: It seems that Christ did not give His body to Judas. Because, as we read (Matt. 26:29), our Lord, after giving His body and blood to the disciples, said to them: "I will not drink from henceforth of this fruit of the vine, until that day when I shall drink it with you new in the kingdom of My Father." From this it appears that those to whom He had given His body and blood were to drink of it again with Him. But Judas did not drink of it afterwards with Him. Therefore he did not receive Christ's body and blood with the other disciples.

Obj. 2: Further, what the Lord commanded, He Himself fulfilled, as is said in Acts 1:1: "Jesus began to do and to teach." But He gave the command (Matt. 7:6): "Give not that which is holy to dogs." Therefore, knowing Judas to be a sinner, seemingly He did not give him His body and blood.

Obj. 3: Further, it is distinctly related (John 13:26) that Christ gave dipped bread to Judas. Consequently, if He gave His body to him, it appears that He gave it him in the morsel, especially since we read (John 13:26) that "after the morsel, Satan entered into him." And on this passage Augustine says (Tract. lxii in Joan.): "From this we learn how we should beware of receiving a good thing in an evil way . . . For if he be 'chastised' who does 'not discern,' i.e. distinguish, the body of the Lord from other meats, how must he be 'condemned' who, feigning himself a friend, comes to His table a foe?" But (Judas) did not receive our Lord's body with the dipped morsel; thus Augustine commenting on John 13:26, "When He had dipped the bread, He gave it to Judas, the son of Simon the Iscariot [Vulg.: 'to Judas Iscariot, the son of Simon']," says (Tract. lxii in Joan.): "Judas did not receive Christ's body then, as some think who read carelessly." Therefore it seems that Judas did not receive the body of Christ.

*On the contrary,* Chrysostom says (Hom. lxxxii in Matth.): "Judas was not converted while partaking of the sacred mysteries: hence on both sides his crime becomes the more heinous, both because imbued with such a purpose he approached the mysteries, and because he became none the better for approaching, neither from fear, nor from the benefit received, nor from the honor conferred on him."

*I answer that,* Hilary, in commenting on Matt. 26:17, held that Christ did not give His body and blood to Judas. And this would have been quite proper, if the malice of Judas be considered. But since Christ was to serve us as a pattern of justice, it was not in keeping with His teaching authority to sever Judas, a hidden sinner, from Communion with the others without an accuser and evident proof; lest the Church's prelates might have an example for doing the like, and lest Judas himself being exasperated might take occasion of sinning. Therefore, it remains to be said that Judas received our Lord's body and blood with the other disciples, as Dionysius says (Eccl. Hier. iii), and Augustine (Tract. lxii in Joan.).

Reply Obj. 1: This is Hilary's argument, to show that Judas did not receive Christ's body. But it is not cogent; because Christ is speaking to the disciples, from whose company Judas separated himself: and it was not Christ that excluded him. Therefore Christ for His part drinks the wine even with Judas in the kingdom of God; but Judas himself repudiated this banquet.

Reply Obj. 2: The wickedness of Judas was known to Christ as God; but it was unknown to Him, after the manner in which men know it. Consequently, Christ did not repel Judas from Communion; so as to furnish an example that such secret sinners are not to be repelled by other priests.

Reply Obj. 3: Without any doubt Judas did not receive Christ's body in the dipped bread; he received mere bread. Yet as Augustine observes (Tract. lxii in Joan.), "perchance the feigning of Judas is denoted by the dipping of the bread; just as some things are dipped to be dyed. If, however, the dipping signifies here anything good" (for instance, the sweetness of the Divine goodness, since bread is rendered more savory by being dipped), "then, not undeservedly, did condemnation follow his ingratitude for that same good." And owing to that ingratitude, "what is good became evil to him, as happens to them who receive Christ's body unworthily."

And as Augustine says (Tract. lxii in Joan.), "it must be understood that our Lord had already distributed the sacrament of His body and blood to all His disciples, among whom was Judas also, as Luke narrates: and after that, we came to this, where, according to the relation of John, our Lord, by dipping and handing the morsel, does most openly declare His betrayer."

THIRD ARTICLE [III, Q. 81, Art. 3]

Whether Christ Received and Gave to the Disciples His Impassible Body?

Objection 1: It seems that Christ both received and gave to the disciples His impassible body. Because on Matt. 17:2, "He was transfigured before them," the gloss says: "He gave to the disciples at the supper that body which He had through nature, but neither mortal nor passible." And again, on Lev. 2:5, "if thy oblation be from the frying-pan," the gloss says: "The Cross mightier than all things made Christ's flesh fit for being eaten, which before the Passion did not seem so suited." But Christ gave His body as suited for eating. Therefore He gave it just as it was after the Passion, that is, impassible and immortal.

Obj. 2: Further, every passible body suffers by contact and by being eaten. Consequently, if Christ's body was passible, it would have suffered both from contact and from being eaten by the disciples.

Obj. 3: Further, the sacramental words now spoken by the priest in the person of Christ are not more powerful than when uttered by Christ Himself. But now by virtue of the sacramental words it is Christ's impassible and immortal body which is consecrated upon the altar. Therefore, much more so was it then.

*On the contrary,* As Innocent III says (De Sacr. Alt. Myst. iv), "He bestowed on the disciples His body such as it was." But then He had a passible and a mortal body. Therefore, He gave a passible and mortal body to the disciples.

*I answer that,* Hugh of Saint Victor (Innocent III, De Sacr. Alt. Myst. iv), maintained, that before the Passion, Christ assumed at various times the four properties of a glorified body--namely, subtlety in His birth, when He came forth from the closed womb of the Virgin; agility, when He walked dryshod upon the sea; clarity, in the Transfiguration; and impassibility at the Last Supper, when He gave His body to the disciples to be eaten. And according to this He gave His body in an impassible and immortal condition to His disciples.

But whatever may be the case touching the other qualities, concerning which we have already stated what should be held (Q. 28, A. 2, ad 3; Q. 45, A. 2), nevertheless the above opinion regarding impassibility is inadmissible. For it is manifest that the same body of Christ which was then seen by the disciples in its own species, was received by them under the sacramental species. But as seen in its own species it was not impassible; nay more, it was ready for the Passion. Therefore, neither was Christ's body impassible when given under the sacramental species.

Yet there was present in the sacrament, in an impassible manner, that which was passible of itself; just as that was there invisibly which of itself was visible. For as sight requires that the body seen be in contact with the adjacent medium of sight, so does passion require contact of the suffering body with the active agents. But Christ's body, according as it is under the sacrament, as stated above (A. 1, ad 2; Q. 76, A. 5), is not compared with its surroundings through the intermediary of its own dimensions, whereby bodies touch each other, but through the dimensions of the bread and wine; consequently, it is those species which are acted upon and are seen, but not Christ's own body.

Reply Obj. 1: Christ is said not to have given His mortal and passible body at the supper, because He did not give it in mortal and passible fashion. But the Cross made His flesh adapted for eating, inasmuch as this sacrament represents Christ's Passion.

Reply Obj. 2: This argument would hold, if Christ's body, as it was passible, were also present in a passible manner in this sacrament.

Reply Obj. 3: As stated above (Q. 76, A. 4), the accidents of Christ's body are in this sacrament by real concomitance, but not by the power of the sacrament, whereby the substance of Christ's body comes to be there. And therefore the power of the sacramental words extends to this, that the body, i.e. Christ's, is under this sacrament, whatever accidents really exist in it.

FOURTH ARTICLE [III, Q. 81, Art. 4]

Whether, If This Sacrament Had Been Reserved in a Pyx, or Consecrated at the Moment of Christ's Death by One of the Apostles, Christ Himself Would Have Died There?

Objection 1: It seems that if this sacrament had been reserved in a pyx at the moment of Christ's death, or had then been consecrated by one of the apostles, that Christ would not have died there. For Christ's death happened through His Passion. But even then He was in this sacrament in an impassible manner. Therefore, He could not die in this sacrament.

Obj. 2: Further, on the death of Christ, His blood was separated from the body. But His flesh and blood are together in this sacrament. Therefore He could not die in this sacrament.

Obj. 3: Further, death ensues from the separation of the soul from the body. But both the body and the soul of Christ are contained in this sacrament. Therefore Christ could not die in this sacrament.

*On the contrary,* The same Christ Who was upon the cross would have been in this sacrament. But He died upon the cross. Therefore, if this sacrament had been reserved, He would have died therein.

*I answer that,* Christ's body is substantially the same in this sacrament, as in its proper species, but not after the same fashion; because in its proper species it comes in contact with surrounding bodies by its own dimensions: but it does not do so as it is in this sacrament, as stated above (A. 3). And therefore, all that belongs to Christ, as He is in Himself, can be attributed to Him both in His proper species, and as He exists in the sacrament; such as to live, to die, to grieve, to be animate or inanimate, and the like; while all that belongs to Him in relation to outward bodies, can be attributed to Him as He exists in His proper species, but not as He is in this sacrament; such as to be mocked, to be spat upon, to be crucified, to be scourged, and the rest. Hence some have composed this verse:

"Our Lord can grieve beneath the sacramental veils
But cannot feel the piercing of the thorns and nails."

Reply Obj. 1: As was stated above, suffering belongs to a body that suffers in respect of some extrinsic body. And therefore Christ, as in this sacrament, cannot suffer; yet He can die.

Reply Obj. 2: As was said above (Q. 76, A. 2), in virtue of the consecration, the body of Christ is under the species of bread, while His blood is under the species of wine. But now that His blood is not really separated from His body; by real concomitance, both His blood is present with the body under the species of the bread, and His body together with the blood under the species of the wine. But at the time when Christ suffered, when His blood was really separated from His body, if this sacrament had been consecrated, then the body only would have been present under the species of the bread, and the blood only under the species of the wine.

Reply Obj. 3: As was observed above (Q. 76, A. 1, ad 1), Christ's soul is in this sacrament by real concomitance; because it is not without the body: but it is not there in virtue of the consecration. And therefore, if this sacrament had been consecrated then, or reserved, when His soul was really separated from His body, Christ's soul would not have been under this sacrament, not from any defect in the form of the words, but owing to the different dispositions of the thing contained.

# QUESTION 82

OF THE MINISTER OF THIS SACRAMENT (In Ten Articles)

We now proceed to consider the minister of this sacrament: under which head there are ten points for our inquiry:

(1) Whether it belongs to a priest alone to consecrate this sacrament?

(2) Whether several priests can at the same time consecrate the same host?

(3) Whether it belongs to the priest alone to dispense this sacrament?

(4) Whether it is lawful for the priest consecrating to refrain from communicating?

(5) Whether a priest in sin can perform this sacrament?

(6) Whether the Mass of a wicked priest is of less value than that of a good one?

(7) Whether those who are heretics, schismatics, or excommunicated, can perform this sacrament?

(8) Whether degraded priests can do so?

(9) Whether communicants receiving at their hands are guilty of sinning?

(10) Whether a priest may lawfully refrain altogether from celebrating?

[*This is the order observed by St. Thomas in writing the Articles; but in writing this prologue, he placed Article 10 immediately after Article 4 (Cf. Leonine edition).]

FIRST ARTICLE [III, Q. 82, Art. 1]

Whether the Consecration of This Sacrament Belongs to a Priest Alone?

Objection 1: It seems that the consecration of this sacrament does not belong exclusively to a priest. Because it was said above (Q. 78, A. 4) that this sacrament is consecrated in virtue of the words, which are the form of this sacrament. But those words are not changed, whether spoken by a priest or by anyone else. Therefore, it seems that not only a priest, but anyone else, can consecrate this sacrament.

Obj. 2: Further, the priest performs this sacrament in the person of Christ. But a devout layman is united with Christ through charity. Therefore, it seems that even a layman can perform this sacrament. Hence Chrysostom (Opus imperfectum in Matth., Hom. xliii) says that "every holy man is a priest."

Obj. 3: Further, as Baptism is ordained for the salvation of mankind, so also is this sacrament, as is clear from what was said above (Q. 74, A. 1; Q. 79, A. 2). But a layman can also baptize, as was stated above (Q. 67, A. 3). Consequently, the consecration of this sacrament is not proper to a priest.

Obj. 4: Further, this sacrament is completed in the consecration of the matter. But the consecration of other matters such as the chrism, the holy oil, and blessed oil, belongs exclusively to a bishop; yet their consecration does not equal the dignity of the consecration of the Eucharist, in which the entire Christ is contained. Therefore it belongs, not to a priest, but only to a bishop, to perform this sacrament.

*On the contrary,* Isidore says in an Epistle to Ludifred (Decretals, dist. 25): "It belongs to a priest to consecrate this sacrament of the Lord's body and blood upon God's altar."

*I answer that,* As stated above (Q. 78, AA. 1, 4), such is the dignity of this sacrament that it is performed only as in the person of Christ. Now whoever performs any act in another's stead, must do so by the power bestowed by such a one. But as the power of receiving this sacrament is conceded by Christ to the baptized person, so likewise the power of consecrating this sacrament on Christ's behalf is bestowed upon the priest at his ordination: for thereby he is put upon a level with them to whom the Lord said (Luke 22:19): "Do this for a commemoration of Me." Therefore, it must be said that it belongs to priests to accomplish this sacrament.

Reply Obj. 1: The sacramental power is in several things, and not merely in one: thus the power of Baptism lies both in the words and in the water. Accordingly the consecrating power is not merely in the words, but likewise in the power delivered to the priest in his consecration and ordination, when the bishop says to him: "Receive the power of offering up the Sacrifice in the Church for the living as well as for the dead." For instrumental power lies in several instruments through which the chief agent acts.

Reply Obj. 2: A devout layman is united with Christ by spiritual union through faith and charity, but not by sacramental power: consequently he has a spiritual priesthood for offering spiritual sacrifices, of which it is said (Ps. 1:19): "A sacrifice to

God is an afflicted spirit"; and (Rom. 12:1): "Present your bodies a living sacrifice." Hence, too, it is written (1 Pet. 2:5): "A holy priesthood, to offer up spiritual sacrifices."

Reply Obj. 3: The receiving of this sacrament is not of such necessity as the receiving of Baptism, as is evident from what was said above (Q. 65, AA. 3, 4; Q. 80, A. 11, ad 2). And therefore, although a layman can baptize in case of necessity, he cannot perform this sacrament.

Reply Obj. 4: The bishop receives power to act on Christ's behalf upon His mystical body, that is, upon the Church; but the priest receives no such power in his consecration, although he may have it by commission from the bishop. Consequently all such things as do not belong to the mystical body are not reserved to the bishop, such as the consecration of this sacrament. But it belongs to the bishop to deliver, not only to the people, but likewise to priests, such things as serve them in the fulfillment of their respective duties. And because the blessing of the chrism, and of the holy oil, and of the oil of the sick, and other consecrated things, such as altars, churches, vestments, and sacred vessels, makes such things fit for use in performing the sacraments which belong to the priestly duty, therefore such consecrations are reserved to the bishop as the head of the whole ecclesiastical order.

SECOND ARTICLE [III, Q. 82, Art. 2]

Whether Several Priests Can Consecrate One and the Same Host?

Objection 1: It seems that several priests cannot consecrate one and the same host. For it was said above (Q. 67, A. 6), that several cannot at the same time baptize one individual. But the power of a priest consecrating is not less than that of a man baptizing. Therefore, several priests cannot consecrate one host at the same time.

Obj. 2: Further, what can be done by one, is superfluously done by several. But there ought to be nothing superfluous in the sacraments. Since, then, one is sufficient for consecrating, it seems that several cannot consecrate one host.

Obj. 3: Further, as Augustine says (Tract. xxvi in Joan.), this is "the sacrament of unity." But multitude seems to be opposed to unity. Therefore it seems inconsistent with the sacrament for several priests to consecrate the same host.

*On the contrary,* It is the custom of some Churches for priests newly ordained to co-celebrate with the bishop ordaining them.

*I answer that,* As stated above (A. 1), when a priest is ordained he is placed on a level with those who received consecrating power from our Lord at the Supper. And therefore, according to the custom of some Churches, as the apostles supped when Christ supped, so the newly ordained co-celebrate with the ordaining bishop. Nor is the consecration, on that account, repeated over the same host, because as Innocent III says (De Sacr. Alt. Myst. iv), the intention of all should be directed to the same instant of the consecration.

Reply Obj. 1: We do not read of Christ baptizing with the apostles when He committed to them the duty of baptizing; consequently there is no parallel.

Reply Obj. 2: If each individual priest were acting in his own power, then other celebrants would be superfluous, since one would be sufficient. But whereas the priest does not consecrate except as in Christ's stead; and since many are "one in Christ" (Gal. 3:28); consequently it does not matter whether this sacrament be consecrated by one or by many, except that the rite of the Church must be observed.

Reply Obj. 3: The Eucharist is the sacrament of ecclesiastical unity, which is brought about by many being "one in Christ."

THIRD ARTICLE [III, Q. 82, Art. 3]

Whether Dispensing of This Sacrament Belongs to a Priest Alone?

Objection 1: It seems that the dispensing of this sacrament does not belong to a priest alone. For Christ's blood belongs to this sacrament no less than His body. But Christ's blood is dispensed by deacons: hence the blessed Lawrence said to the blessed Sixtus (Office of St. Lawrence, Resp. at Matins): "Try whether you have chosen a fit minister, to whom you have entrusted the dispensing of the Lord's blood." Therefore, with equal reason the dispensing of Christ's body does not belong to priests only.

Obj. 2: Further, priests are the appointed ministers of the sacraments. But this sacrament is completed in the consecration of the matter, and not in the use, to which the dispensing belongs. Therefore it seems that it does not belong to a priest to dispense the Lord's body.

Obj. 3: Further, Dionysius says (Eccl. Hier. iii, iv) that this sacrament, like chrism, has the power of perfecting. But it belongs, not to priests, but to bishops, to sign with the chrism. Therefore likewise, to dispense this sacrament belongs to the bishop and not to the priest.

*On the contrary,* It is written (De Consecr., dist. 12): "It has come to our knowledge that some priests deliver the Lord's body to a layman or to a woman to carry it to the sick: The synod therefore forbids such presumption to continue; and let the priest himself communicate the sick."

*I answer that,* The dispensing of Christ's body belongs to the priest for three reasons. First, because, as was said above (A. 1), he consecrates as in the person of Christ. But as Christ consecrated His body at the supper, so also He gave it to others to be partaken of by them. Accordingly, as the consecration of Christ's body belongs to the priest, so likewise does the dispensing belong to him. Secondly, because the priest is the appointed intermediary between God and the people; hence as it belongs to him to offer the people's gifts to God, so it belongs to him to deliver consecrated gifts to the people. Thirdly, because out of reverence towards this sacrament, nothing touches it, but what is consecrated; hence the corporal and the chalice are consecrated, and likewise the priest's hands, for touching this sacrament. Hence it is not lawful for anyone else to touch it except from necessity, for instance, if it were to fall upon the ground, or else in some other case of urgency.

Reply Obj. 1: The deacon, as being nigh to the priestly order, has a certain share in the latter's duties, so that he may dispense the blood; but not the body, except in case of necessity, at the bidding of a bishop or of a priest. First of all, because Christ's blood is contained in a vessel, hence there is no need for it to be touched by the dispenser, as Christ's body is touched. Secondly, because the blood denotes the redemption derived by the people from Christ; hence it is that water is mixed with the blood, which water denotes the people. And because deacons are between priest and people, the dispensing of the blood is in the competency of deacons, rather than the dispensing of the body.

Reply Obj. 2: For the reason given above, it belongs to the same person to dispense and to consecrate this sacrament.

Reply Obj. 3: As the deacon, in a measure, shares in the priest's "power of enlightening" (Eccl. Hier. v), inasmuch as he dispenses the blood, so the priest shares in the "perfective dispensing" (Eccl. Hier. v) of the bishop, inasmuch as he dispenses this sacrament whereby man is perfected in himself by union with Christ. But other perfections whereby a man is perfected in relation to others, are reserved to the bishop.

FOURTH ARTICLE [III, Q. 82, Art. 4]

Whether the Priest Who Consecrates Is Bound to Receive This Sacrament?

Objection 1: It seems that the priest who consecrates is not bound to receive this sacrament. Because, in the other consecrations, he who consecrates the matter does not use it, just as the bishop consecrating the chrism is not anointed therewith. But this sacrament consists in the consecration of the matter. Therefore, the priest performing this sacrament need not use the same, but may lawfully refrain from receiving it.

Obj. 2: Further, in the other sacraments the minister does not give the sacrament to himself: for no one can baptize himself, as stated above (Q. 66, A. 5, ad 4). But as Baptism is dispensed in due order, so also is this sacrament. Therefore the priest who consecrates this sacrament ought not to receive it at his own hands.

Obj. 3: Further, it sometimes happens that Christ's body appears upon the altar under the guise of flesh, and the blood under the guise of blood; which are unsuited for food and drink: hence, as was said above (Q. 75, A. 5), it is on that account that they are given under another species, lest they beget revulsion in the communicants. Therefore the priest who consecrates is not always bound to receive this sacrament.

*On the contrary,* We read in the acts of the (Twelfth) Council of Toledo (Can. v), and again (De Consecr., dist. 2): "It must be strictly observed that as often as the priest sacrifices the body and blood of our Lord Jesus Christ upon the altar, he must himself be a partaker of Christ's body and blood."

*I answer that,* As stated above (Q. 79, AA. 5, 7), the Eucharist is not only a sacrament, but also a sacrifice. Now whoever offers sacrifice must be a sharer in the sacrifice, because the outward sacrifice he offers is a sign of the inner sacrifice whereby he offers himself to God, as Augustine says (De Civ. Dei x). Hence by partaking of the sacrifice he shows that the inner one is likewise his. In the same way also, by dispensing the sacrifice to the people he shows that he is the dispenser of Divine gifts, of which he ought himself to be the first to partake, as Dionysius says (Eccl. Hier. iii). Consequently, he ought to receive before dispensing it to the people. Accordingly we read in the chapter mentioned above (Twelfth Council of Toledo, Can. v): "What kind of sacrifice is that wherein not even the sacrificer is known to have a share?" But it is by partaking of the sacrifice that he has a share in it, as the Apostle says (1 Cor. 10:18): "Are not they that eat of the sacrifices, partakers of the altar?" Therefore it is necessary for the priest, as often as he consecrates, to receive this sacrament in its integrity.

Reply Obj. 1: The consecration of chrism or of anything else is not a sacrifice, as the consecration of the Eucharist is: consequently there is no parallel.

Reply Obj. 2: The sacrament of Baptism is accomplished in the use of the matter, and consequently no one can baptize himself, because the same person cannot be active and passive in a sacrament. Hence neither in this sacrament does the priest consecrate himself, but he consecrates the bread and wine, in which consecration the sacrament is completed. But the use thereof follows the sacrament, and therefore there is no parallel.

Reply Obj. 3: If Christ's body appears miraculously upon the altar under the guise of flesh, or the blood under the guise of blood, it is not to be received. For Jerome says upon Leviticus (cf. De Consecr., dist. 2): "It is lawful to eat of this sacrifice which is wonderfully performed in memory of Christ: but it is not lawful for anyone to eat of that one which Christ offered on the altar of the cross." Nor does the priest transgress on that account, because miraculous events are not subject to human laws. Nevertheless the priest would be well advised to consecrate again and receive the Lord's body and blood.

FIFTH ARTICLE [III, Q. 82, Art. 5]

Whether a Wicked Priest Can Consecrate the Eucharist?

Objection 1: It seems that a wicked priest cannot consecrate the Eucharist. For Jerome, commenting on Sophon. iii, 4, says: "The priests who perform the Eucharist, and who distribute our Lord's blood to the people, act wickedly against Christ's law, in deeming that the Eucharist is consecrated by a prayer rather than by a good life; and that only the solemn prayer is requisite, and not the priest's merits: of whom it is said: 'Let not the priest, in whatever defilement he may be, approach to offer oblations to the Lord'" (Lev. 21:21, Septuagint). But the sinful priest, being defiled, has neither the life nor the merits befitting this sacrament. Therefore a sinful priest cannot consecrate the Eucharist.

Obj. 2: Further, Damascene says (De Fide Orth. iv) that "the bread and wine are changed supernaturally into the body and blood of our Lord, by the coming of the Holy Ghost." But Pope Gelasius I says (Ep. ad Elphid., cf. Decret. i, q. 1): "How shall the Holy Spirit, when invoked, come for the consecration of the Divine Mystery, if the priest invoking him be proved full of guilty deeds?" Consequently, the Eucharist cannot be consecrated by a wicked priest.

Obj. 3: Further, this sacrament is consecrated by the priest's blessing. But a sinful priest's blessing is not efficacious for consecrating this sacrament, since it is written (Malachi 2:2): "I will curse your blessings." Again, Dionysius says in his Epistle (viii) to the monk Demophilus: "He who is not enlightened has completely fallen away from the priestly order; and I wonder that such a man dare to employ his hands in priestly actions, and in the person of Christ to utter, over the Divine symbols, his unclean infamies, for I will not call them prayers."

*On the contrary,* Augustine (Paschasius) says (De Corp. Dom. xii): "Within the Catholic Church, in the mystery of the Lord's body and blood, nothing greater is done by a good priest, nothing less by an evil priest, because it is not by the merits of the consecrator that the sacrament is accomplished, but by the Creator's word, and by the power of the Holy Spirit."

*I answer that,* As was said above (AA. 1, 3), the priest consecrates this sacrament not by his own power, but as the minister of Christ, in Whose person he consecrates this sacrament. But from the fact of being wicked he does not cease to be Christ's minister; because our Lord has good and wicked ministers or servants. Hence (Matt. 24:45) our Lord says: "Who, thinkest thou, is a faithful and wise servant?" and afterwards He adds: "But if that evil servant shall say in his heart," etc. And the Apostle (1 Cor. 4:1) says: "Let a man so account of us as of the ministers of Christ"; and afterwards he adds: "I am not conscious to myself of anything; yet am I not hereby justified." He was therefore certain that he was Christ's minister; yet he was not certain that he was a just man. Consequently, a man can be Christ's minister even though he be not one of the just. And this belongs to Christ's excellence, Whom, as the true God, things both good and evil serve, since they are ordained by His providence for His glory. Hence it is evident that priests, even though they be not godly, but sinners, can consecrate the Eucharist.

Reply Obj. 1: In those words Jerome is condemning the error of priests who believed they could consecrate the Eucharist worthily, from the mere fact of being priests, even though they were sinners; and Jerome condemns this from the fact that persons defiled are forbidden to approach the altar; but this does not prevent the sacrifice, which they offer, from being a true sacrifice, if they do approach.

Reply Obj. 2: Previous to the words quoted, Pope Gelasius expresses himself as follows: "That most holy rite, which contains the Catholic discipline, claims for itself such reverence that no one may dare to approach it except with clean conscience." From this it is evident that his meaning is that the priest who is a sinner ought not to approach this sacrament. Hence when he resumes, "How shall the Holy Spirit come when summoned," it must be understood that He comes, not through the priest's merits, but through the power of Christ, Whose words the priest utters.

Reply Obj. 3: As the same action can be evil, inasmuch as it is done with a bad intention of the servant; and good from the good intention of the master; so the blessing of a sinful priest, inasmuch as he acts unworthily is deserving of a curse, and is reputed an infamy and a blasphemy, and not a prayer; whereas, inasmuch as it is pronounced in the person of Christ, it is holy and efficacious. Hence it is said with significance: "I will curse your blessings."

SIXTH ARTICLE [III, Q. 82, Art. 6]

Whether the Mass of a Sinful Priest Is of Less Worth Than the Mass of a Good Priest?

Objection 1: It seems that the mass of a sinful priest is not of less worth than that of a good priest. For Pope Gregory says in the Register: "Alas, into what a great snare they fall who believe that the Divine and hidden mysteries can be sanctified more by some than by others; since it is the one and the same Holy Ghost Who hallows those mysteries in a hidden and invisible manner." But these hidden mysteries are celebrated in the mass. Therefore the mass of a sinful priest is not of less value than the mass of a good priest.

Obj. 2: Further, as Baptism is conferred by a minister through the power of Christ Who baptizes, so likewise this sacrament is consecrated in the person of Christ. But Baptism is no better when conferred by a better priest, as was said above (Q. 64, A. 1, ad 2). Therefore neither is a mass the better, which is celebrated by a better priest.

Obj. 3: Further, as the merits of priests differ in the point of being good and better, so they likewise differ in the point of being good and bad. Consequently, if the mass of a better priest be itself better, it follows that the mass of a bad priest must be bad. Now this is unreasonable, because the malice of the ministers cannot affect Christ's mysteries, as Augustine says in his work on Baptism (Contra Donat. xii). Therefore neither is the mass of a better priest the better.

*On the contrary,* It is stated in Decretal i, q. 1: "The worthier the priest, the sooner is he heard in the needs for which he prays."

*I answer that,* There are two things to be considered in the mass. namely, the sacrament itself, which is the chief thing; and the prayers which are offered up in the mass for the quick and the dead. So far as the mass itself is concerned, the mass of a wicked priest is not of less value than that of a good priest, because the same sacrifice is offered by both.

Again, the prayer put up in the mass can be considered in two respects: first of all, in so far as it has its efficacy from the devotion of the priest interceding, and in this respect there is no doubt but that the mass of the better priest is the more fruitful. In another respect, inasmuch as the prayer is said by the priest in the mass in the place of the entire Church, of which the priest is the minister; and this ministry remains even in sinful men, as was said above (A. 5) in regard to Christ's ministry. Hence, in this respect the prayer even of the sinful priest is fruitful, not only that which he utters in the mass, but likewise all those he recites in the ecclesiastical offices, wherein he takes the place of the Church. on the other hand, his private prayers are not fruitful, according to Prov. 28:9: "He that turneth away his ears from hearing the law, his prayer shall be an abomination."

Reply Obj. 1: Gregory is speaking there of the holiness of the Divine sacrament.

Reply Obj. 2: In the sacrament of Baptism solemn prayers are not made for all the faithful, as in the mass; therefore there is no parallel in this respect. There is, however, a resemblance as to the effect of the sacrament.

Reply Obj. 3: By reason of the power of the Holy Ghost, Who communicates to each one the blessings of Christ's members on account of their being united in charity, the private blessing in the mass of a good priest is fruitful to others. But the private evil of one man cannot hurt another, except the latter, in some way, consent, as Augustine says (Contra Parmen. ii).

SEVENTH ARTICLE [III, Q. 82, Art. 7]

Whether Heretics, Schismatics, and Excommunicated Persons Can Consecrate?

Objection 1: It seems that heretics, schismatics, and excommunicated persons are not able to consecrate the Eucharist. For Augustine says (Liber sentent. Prosperi xv) that "there is no such thing as a true sacrifice outside the Catholic Church": and Pope Leo I says (Ep. lxxx; cf. Decretal i, q. 1): Elsewhere "(i.e. than in the Church which is Christ's body) there is neither valid priesthood nor true sacrifice." But heretics, schismatics, and excommunicated persons are severed from the Church. Therefore they are unable to offer a true sacrifice.

Obj. 2: Further (Decretal, caus. i, q. 1), Innocent I is quoted as saying: "Because we receive the laity of the Arians and other pestilential persons, if they seem to repent, it does not follow that their clergy have the dignity of the priesthood or of any other ministerial office, for we allow them to confer nothing save Baptism." But none can consecrate the Eucharist, unless he have the dignity of the priesthood. Therefore heretics and the like cannot consecrate the Eucharist.

Obj. 3: Further, it does not seem feasible for one outside the Church to act on behalf of the Church. But when the priest consecrates the Eucharist, he does so in the person of the entire Church, as is evident from the fact of his putting up all prayers in the person of the Church. Therefore, it seems that those who are outside the Church, such as those who are heretics, schismatics, and excommunicate, are not able to consecrate the Eucharist.

*On the contrary,* Augustine says (Contra Parmen. ii): "Just as Baptism remains in them," i.e. in heretics, schismatics, and those who are excommunicate, "so do their orders remain intact." Now, by the power of his ordination, a priest can consecrate the Eucharist. Therefore, it seems that heretics, schismatics, and those who are excommunicate, can consecrate the Eucharist, since their orders remain entire.

*I answer that,* Some have contended that heretics, schismatics, and the excommunicate, who are outside the pale of the Church, cannot perform this sacrament. But herein they are deceived, because, as Augustine says (Contra Parmen. ii), "it is one thing to lack something utterly, and another to have it improperly"; and in like fashion, "it is one thing not to bestow, and quite another to bestow, but not rightly." Accordingly, such as, being within the Church, received the power of consecrating the Eucharist through being ordained to the priesthood, have such power rightly indeed; but they use it improperly if afterwards they be separated from the Church by heresy, schism, or excommunication. But such as are ordained while separated from the Church, have neither the power rightly, nor do they use it rightly. But that in both cases they have the power, is clear from what Augustine says (Contra Parmen. ii), that when they return to the unity of the Church, they are not re-ordained, but are received in their orders. And since the consecration of the Eucharist is an act which follows the power of order, such persons as are separated from the Church by heresy, schism, or excommunication, can indeed consecrate the Eucharist, which on being consecrated by them contains Christ's true body and blood; but they act wrongly, and sin by doing so; and in consequence they do not receive the fruit of the sacrifice, which is a spiritual sacrifice.

Reply Obj. 1: Such and similar authorities are to be understood in this sense, that the sacrifice is offered wrongly outside the Church. Hence outside the Church there can be no spiritual sacrifice that is a true sacrifice with the truth of its fruit, although it be a true sacrifice with the truth of the sacrament; thus it was stated above (Q. 80, A. 3), that the sinner receives Christ's body sacramentally, but not spiritually.

Reply Obj. 2: Baptism alone is allowed to be conferred by heretics, and schismatics, because they can lawfully baptize in case of necessity; but in no case can they lawfully consecrate the Eucharist, or confer the other sacraments.

Reply Obj. 3: The priest, in reciting the prayers of the mass, speaks instead of the Church, in whose unity he remains; but in consecrating the sacrament he speaks as in the person of Christ, Whose place he holds by the power of his orders. Consequently, if a priest severed from the unity of the Church celebrates mass, not having lost the power of order, he consecrates Christ's true body and blood; but because he is severed from the unity of the Church, his prayers have no efficacy.

EIGHTH ARTICLE [III, Q. 82, Art. 8]

Whether a Degraded Priest Can Consecrate This Sacrament?

Objection 1: It seems that a degraded priest cannot consecrate this sacrament. For no one can perform this sacrament except he have the power of consecrating. But the priest "who has been degraded has no power of consecrating, although he has the power of baptizing" (App. Gratiani). Therefore it seems that a degraded priest cannot consecrate the Eucharist.

Obj. 2: Further, he who gives can take away. But the bishop in ordaining gives to the priest the power of consecrating. Therefore he can take it away by degrading him.

Obj. 3: Further, the priest, by degradation, loses either the power of consecrating, or the use of such power. But he does not lose merely the use, for thus the degraded one would lose no more than one excommunicated, who also lacks the use. Therefore it seems that he loses the power to consecrate, and in consequence that he cannot perform this sacrament.

*On the contrary,* Augustine (Contra Parmen. ii) proves that "apostates" from the faith "are not deprived of their Baptism," from the fact that "it is not restored to them when they return repentant; and therefore it is deemed that it cannot be lost." But in like fashion, if the degraded man be restored, he has not to be ordained over again. Consequently, he has not lost the power of consecrating, and so the degraded priest can perform this sacrament.

*I answer that,* The power of consecrating the Eucharist belongs to the character of the priestly order. But every character is indelible, because it is given with a kind of consecration, as was said above (Q. 63, A. 5), just as the consecrations of all other things are perpetual, and cannot be lost or repeated. Hence it is clear that the power of consecrating is not lost by degradation. For, again, Augustine says (Contra Parmen. ii): "Both are sacraments," namely Baptism and order, "and both are given to a man with a kind of consecration; the former, when he is baptized; the latter when he is ordained; and therefore it is not lawful for Catholics to repeat either of them." And thus it is evident that the degraded priest can perform this sacrament.

Reply Obj. 1: That Canon is speaking, not as by way of assertion, but by way of inquiry, as can be gleaned from the context.

Reply Obj. 2: The bishop gives the priestly power of order, not as though coming from himself, but instrumentally, as God's minister, and its effect cannot be taken away by man, according to Matt. 19:6: "What God hath joined together, let no man put asunder." And therefore the bishop cannot take this power away, just as neither can he who baptizes take away the baptismal character.

Reply Obj. 3: Excommunication is medicinal. And therefore the ministry of the priestly power is not taken away from the excommunicate, as it were, perpetually, but only for a time, that they may mend; but the exercise is withdrawn from the degraded, as though condemned perpetually.

NINTH ARTICLE [III, Q. 82, Art. 9]

Whether It Is Permissible to Receive Communion from Heretical, Excommunicate, or Sinful Priests, and to Hear Mass Said by Them?

Objection 1: It seems that one may lawfully receive Communion from heretical, excommunicate, or even sinful priests, and to hear mass said by them. Because, as Augustine says (Contra Petilian. iii), "we should not avoid God's sacraments, whether they be given by a good man or by a wicked one." But priests, even if they be sinful, or heretics, or excommunicate, perform a valid sacrament. Therefore it seems that one ought not to refrain from receiving Communion at their hands, or from hearing their mass.

Obj. 2: Further, Christ's true body is figurative of His mystical body, as was said above (Q. 67, A. 2). But Christ's true body is consecrated by the priests mentioned above. Therefore it seems that whoever belongs to His mystical body can communicate in their sacrifices.

Obj. 3: Further, there are many sins graver than fornication. But it is not forbidden to hear the masses of priests who sin otherwise. Therefore, it ought not to be forbidden to hear the masses of priests guilty of this sin.

*On the contrary,* The Canon says (Dist. 32): "Let no one hear the mass of a priest whom he knows without doubt to have a concubine." Moreover, Gregory says (Dial. iii) that "the faithless father sent an Arian bishop to his son, for him to receive sacrilegiously the consecrated Communion at his hands. But, when the Arian bishop arrived, God's devoted servant rebuked him, as was right for him to do."

*I answer that,* As was said above (AA. 5, 7), heretical, schismatical, excommunicate, or even sinful priests, although they have the power to consecrate the Eucharist, yet they do not make a proper use of it; *on the contrary,* they sin by using it. But whoever communicates with another who is in sin, becomes a sharer in his sin. Hence we read in John's Second Canonical Epistle (11) that "He that saith unto him, God speed you, communicateth with his wicked works." Consequently, it is not lawful to receive Communion from them, or to assist at their mass.

Still there is a difference among the above, because heretics, schismatics, and excommunicates, have been forbidden, by the Church's sentence, to perform the Eucharistic rite. And therefore whoever hears their mass or receives the sacraments from them, commits sin. But not all who are sinners are debarred by the Church's sentence from using this power: and so, although suspended by the Divine sentence, yet they are not suspended in regard to others by any ecclesiastical sentence: consequently, until the Church's sentence is pronounced, it is lawful to receive Communion at their hands, and to hear their mass. Hence on 1 Cor. 5:11, "with such a one not so much as to eat," Augustine's gloss runs thus: "In saying this he was unwilling for a man to be judged by his fellow man on arbitrary suspicion, or even by usurped extraordinary judgment, but rather by God's law, according to the Church's ordering, whether he confess of his own accord, or whether he be accused and convicted."

Reply Obj. 1: By refusing to hear the masses of such priests, or to receive Communion from them, we are not shunning God's sacraments; *on the contrary,* by so doing we are giving them honor (hence a host consecrated by such priests is to be adored, and if it be reserved, it can be consumed by a lawful priest): but what we shun is the sin of the unworthy ministers.

Reply Obj. 2: The unity of the mystical body is the fruit of the true body received. But those who receive or minister unworthily, are deprived of the fruit, as was said above (A. 7; Q. 80, A. 4). And therefore, those who belong to the unity of the Faith are not to receive the sacrament from their dispensing.

Reply Obj. 3: Although fornication is not graver than other sins, yet men are more prone to it, owing to fleshly concupiscence. Consequently, this sin is specially inhibited to priests by the Church, lest anyone hear the mass of one living in concubinage. However, this is to be understood of one who is notorious, either from being convicted and sentenced, or from having acknowledged his guilt in legal form, or from it being impossible to conceal his guilt by any subterfuge.

TENTH ARTICLE [III, Q. 82, Art. 10]

Whether It Is Lawful for a Priest to Refrain Entirely from Consecrating the Eucharist?

Objection 1: It seems to be lawful for a priest to refrain entirely from consecrating the Eucharist. Because, as it is the priest's office to consecrate the Eucharist, so it is likewise to baptize and administer the other sacraments. But the priest is not bound to act as a minister of the other sacraments, unless he has undertaken the care of souls. Therefore, it seems that likewise he is not bound to consecrate the Eucharist except he be charged with the care of souls.

Obj. 2: Further, no one is bound to do what is unlawful for him to do; otherwise he would be in two minds. But it is not lawful for the priest who is in a state of sin, or excommunicate, to consecrate the Eucharist, as was said above (A. 7). Therefore it seems that such men are not bound to celebrate, and so neither are the others; otherwise they would be gainers by their fault.

Obj. 3: Further, the priestly dignity is not lost by subsequent weakness: because Pope Gelasius I says (cf. Decretal, Dist. 55): "As the canonical precepts do not permit them who are feeble in body to approach the priesthood, so if anyone be disabled when once in that state, he cannot lose that he received at the time he was well." But it sometimes happens that those who are already ordained as priests incur defects whereby they are hindered from celebrating, such as leprosy or epilepsy, or the like. Consequently, it does not appear that priests are bound to celebrate.

*On the contrary,* Ambrose says in one of his Orations (xxxiii): "It is a grave matter if we do not approach Thy altar with clean heart and pure hands; but it is graver still if while shunning sins we also fail to offer our sacrifice."

*I answer that,* Some have said that a priest may lawfully refrain altogether from consecrating, except he be bound to do so, and to give the sacraments to the people, by reason of his being entrusted with the care of souls.

But this is said quite unreasonably, because everyone is bound to use the grace entrusted to him, when opportunity serves, according to 2 Cor. 6:1: "We exhort you that you receive not the grace of God in vain." But the opportunity of offering sacrifice is considered not merely in relation to the faithful of Christ to whom the sacraments must be administered, but chiefly with regard to God to Whom the sacrifice of this sacrament is offered by consecrating. Hence, it is not lawful for the priest, even though he has not the care of souls, to refrain altogether from celebrating; and he seems to be bound to celebrate at least on the chief festivals, and especially on those days on which the faithful usually communicate. And hence it is that (2 Macc. 4:14) it is said against some priests that they "were not now occupied about the offices of the altar . . . despising the temple and neglecting the sacrifices."

Reply Obj. 1: The other sacraments are accomplished in being used by the faithful, and therefore he alone is bound to administer them who has undertaken the care of souls. But this sacrament is performed in the consecration of the Eucharist, whereby a sacrifice is offered to God, to which the priest is bound from the order he has received.

Reply Obj. 2: The sinful priest, if deprived by the Church's sentence from exercising his order, simply or for a time, is rendered incapable of offering sacrifice; consequently, the obligation lapses. But if not deprived of the power of celebrating, the obligation is not removed; nor is he in two minds, because he can repent of his sin and then celebrate.

Reply Obj. 3: Weakness or sickness contracted by a priest after his ordination does not deprive him of his orders; but hinders him from exercising them, as to the consecration of the Eucharist: sometimes by making it impossible to exercise them, as, for example, if he lose his sight, or his fingers, or the use of speech; and sometimes on account of danger, as in the case of one suffering from epilepsy, or indeed any disease of the mind; and sometimes, on account of loathsomeness, as is evident in the case of a leper, who ought not to celebrate in public: he can, however, say mass privately, unless the leprosy has gone so far that it has rendered him incapable owing to the wasting away of his limbs.

## QUESTION 83

OF THE RITE OF THIS SACRAMENT (In Six Articles)

We have now to consider the Rite of this sacrament, under which head there are six points of inquiry:

(1) Whether Christ is sacrificed in the celebration of this mystery?

(2) Of the time of celebrating;

(3) Of the place and other matters relating to the equipment for this celebration;

(4) Of the words uttered in celebrating this mystery;

(5) Of the actions performed in celebrating this mystery.

(6) Of the defects which occur in the celebration of this sacrament.

FIRST ARTICLE [III, Q. 83, Art. 1]

Whether Christ Is Sacrificed in This Sacrament?

Objection 1: It seems that Christ is not sacrificed in the celebration of this sacrament. For it is written (Heb. 10:14) that "Christ by one oblation hath perfected for ever them that are sanctified." But that oblation was His oblation. Therefore Christ is not sacrificed in the celebration of this sacrament.

Obj. 2: Further, Christ's sacrifice was made upon the cross, whereon "He delivered Himself for us, an oblation and a sacrifice to God for an odor of sweetness," as is said in Eph. 5:2. But Christ is not crucified in the celebration of this mystery. Therefore, neither is He sacrificed.

Obj. 3: Further, as Augustine says (De Trin. iv), in Christ's sacrifice the priest and the victim are one and the same. But in the celebration of this sacrament the priest and the victim are not the same. Therefore, the celebration of this sacrament is not a sacrifice of Christ.

*On the contrary,* Augustine says in the Liber Sentent. Prosp. (cf. Ep. xcviii): "Christ was sacrificed once in Himself, and yet He is sacrificed daily in the Sacrament."

*I answer that,* The celebration of this sacrament is called a sacrifice for two reasons. First, because, as Augustine says (Ad Simplician. ii), "the images of things are called by the names of the things whereof they are the images; as when we look upon a picture or a fresco, we say, 'This is Cicero and that is Sallust.'" But, as was said above (Q. 79, A. 1), the celebration of this sacrament is an image representing Christ's Passion, which is His true sacrifice. Accordingly the celebration of this sacrament is called Christ's sacrifice. Hence it is that Ambrose, in commenting on Heb. 10:1, says: "In Christ was offered up a sacrifice capable of giving eternal salvation; what then do we do? Do we not offer it up every day in memory of His death?" Secondly it is called a sacrifice, in respect of the effect of His Passion: because, to wit, by this sacrament, we are made partakers of the fruit of our Lord's Passion. Hence in one of the Sunday Secrets (Ninth Sunday after Pentecost) we say: "Whenever the commemoration of this sacrifice is celebrated, the work of our redemption is enacted." Consequently, according to the first reason, it is true to say that Christ was sacrificed, even in the figures of the Old Testament: hence it is stated in the Apocalypse (13:8): "Whose names are not written in the Book of Life of the Lamb, which was slain from the beginning of the world." But according to the second reason, it is proper to this sacrament for Christ to be sacrificed in its celebration.

Reply Obj. 1: As Ambrose says (commenting on Heb. 10:1), "there is but one victim," namely that which Christ offered, and which we offer, "and not many victims, because Christ was offered but once: and this latter sacrifice is the pattern of the former. For, just as what is offered everywhere is one body, and not many bodies, so also is it but one sacrifice."

Reply Obj. 2: As the celebration of this sacrament is an image representing Christ's Passion, so the altar is representative of the cross itself, upon which Christ was sacrificed in His proper species.

Reply Obj. 3: For the same reason (cf. Reply Obj. 2) the priest also bears Christ's image, in Whose person and by Whose power he pronounces the words of consecration, as is evident from what was said above (Q. 82, AA. 1, 3). And so, in a measure, the priest and victim are one and the same.

SECOND ARTICLE [III, Q. 83, Art. 2]

Whether the Time for Celebrating This Mystery Has Been Properly Determined?

Objection 1: It seems that the time for celebrating this mystery has not been properly determined. For as was observed above (A. 1), this sacrament is representative of our Lord's Passion. But the commemoration of our Lord's Passion takes place in the Church once in the year: because Augustine says (Enarr. ii in Ps. 21): "Is not Christ slain as often as the Pasch is celebrated? Nevertheless, the anniversary remembrance represents what took place in by-gone days; and so it does not cause us to be stirred as if we saw our Lord hanging upon the cross." Therefore this sacrament ought to be celebrated but once a year.

Obj. 2: Further, Christ's Passion is commemorated in the Church on the Friday before Easter, and not on Christmas Day. Consequently, since this sacrament is commemorative of our Lord's Passion, it seems unsuitable for this sacrament to be celebrated thrice on Christmas Day, and to be entirely omitted on Good Friday.

Obj. 3: Further, in the celebration of this sacrament the Church ought to imitate Christ's institution. But it was in the evening that Christ consecrated this sacrament. Therefore it seems that this sacrament ought to be celebrated at that time of day.

Obj. 4: Further, as is set down in the Decretals (De Consecr., dist. i), Pope Leo I wrote to Dioscorus, Bishop of Alexandria, that "it is permissible to celebrate mass in the first part of the day." But the day begins at midnight, as was said above (Q. 80, A. 8, ad 5). Therefore it seems that after midnight it is lawful to celebrate.

Obj. 5: Further, in one of the Sunday Secrets (Ninth Sunday after Pentecost) we say: "Grant us, Lord, we beseech Thee, to frequent these mysteries." But there will be greater frequency if the priest celebrates several times a day. Therefore it seems that the priest ought not to be hindered from celebrating several times daily.

On the contrary is the custom which the Church observes according to the statutes of the Canons.

*I answer that,* As stated above (A. 1), in the celebration of this mystery, we must take into consideration the representation of our Lord's Passion, and the participation of its fruits; and the time suitable for the celebration of this mystery ought to be determined by each of these considerations. Now since, owing to our daily defects, we stand in daily need of the fruits of our Lord's Passion, this sacrament is offered regularly every day in the Church. Hence our Lord teaches us to pray (Luke 11:3): "Give us this day our daily bread": in explanation of which words Augustine says (De Verb. Dom. xxviii): "If it be a daily bread, why do you take it once a year, as the Greeks have the custom in the east? Receive it daily that it may benefit you every day."

But since our Lord's Passion was celebrated from the third to the ninth hour, therefore this sacrament is solemnly celebrated by the Church in that part of the day.

Reply Obj. 1: Christ's Passion is recalled in this sacrament, inasmuch as its effect flows out to the faithful; but at Passion-tide Christ's Passion is recalled inasmuch as it was wrought in Him Who is our Head. This took place but once; whereas the faithful receive daily the fruits of His Passion: consequently, the former is commemorated but once in the year, whereas the latter takes place every day, both that we may partake of its fruit and in order that we may have a perpetual memorial.

Reply Obj. 2: The figure ceases on the advent of the reality. But this sacrament is a figure and a representation of our Lord's Passion, as stated above. And therefore on the day on which our Lord's Passion is recalled as it was really accomplished, this sacrament is not consecrated. Nevertheless, lest the Church be deprived on that day of the fruit of the Passion offered to us by this sacrament, the body of Christ consecrated the day before is reserved to be consumed on that day; but the blood is not reserved, on account of danger, and because the blood is more specially the image of our Lord's Passion, as stated above (Q. 78, A. 3, ad 2). Nor is it true, as some affirm, that the wine is changed into blood when the particle of Christ's body is dropped into it. Because this cannot be done otherwise than by consecration under the due form of words.

On Christmas Day, however, several masses are said on account of Christ's threefold nativity. Of these the first is His eternal birth, which is hidden in our regard, and therefore one mass is sung in the night, in the "Introit" of which we say: "The Lord said unto Me: Thou art My Son, this day have I begotten Thee." The second is His nativity in time, and the spiritual birth, whereby Christ rises "as the day-star in our [Vulg.: 'your'] hearts" (2 Pet. 1:19), and on this account the mass is sung at dawn, and in the "Introit" we say: "The light will shine on us today." The third is Christ's temporal and bodily birth, according as He went forth from the virginal womb, becoming visible to us through being clothed with flesh: and on that account the third mass is sung in broad daylight, in the "Introit" of which we say: "A child is born to us." Nevertheless, on the other hand, it can be said that His eternal generation, of itself, is in the full light, and on this account in the gospel of the third mass mention is made of His eternal birth. But regarding His birth in the body, He was literally born during the night, as a sign that He came to the darknesses of our infirmity; hence also in the midnight mass we say the gospel of Christ's nativity in the flesh.

Likewise on other days upon which many of God's benefits have to be recalled or besought, several masses are celebrated on one day, as for instance, one for the feast, and another for a fast or for the dead.

Reply Obj. 3: As already observed (Q. 73, A. 5), Christ wished to give this sacrament last of all, in order that it might make a deeper impression on the hearts of the disciples; and therefore it was after supper, at the close of day, that He consecrated this sacrament and gave it to His disciples. But we celebrate at the hour when our Lord suffered, i.e. either, as on feast-days, at the hour of Terce, when He was crucified by the tongues of the Jews (Mk. 15:25), and when the Holy Ghost descended upon the disciples (Acts 2:15); or, as when no feast is kept, at the hour of Sext, when He was crucified at the hands of the soldiers (John 19:14), or, as on fasting days, at None, when crying out with a loud voice He gave up the ghost (Matt. 27:46, 50).

Nevertheless the mass can be postponed, especially when Holy orders have to be conferred, and still more on Holy Saturday; both on account of the length of the office, and also because orders belong to the Sunday, as is set forth in the Decretals (dist. 75).

Masses, however, can be celebrated "in the first part of the day," owing to any necessity; as is stated De Consecr., dist. 1.

Reply Obj. 4: As a rule mass ought to be said in the day and not in the night, because Christ is present in this sacrament, Who says (John 9:4, 5): "I must work the works of Him that sent Me, whilst it is day: because the night cometh when no man can work; as long as I am in the world, I am the light of the world." Yet this should be done in such a manner that the beginning of the day is not to be taken from midnight; nor from sunrise, that is, when the substance of the sun appears above the earth; but when the dawn begins to show: because then the sun is said to be risen when the brightness of his beams appears. Accordingly it is written (Mk. 16:1) that "the women came to the tomb, the sun being now risen"; though, as John relates (John 20:1), "while it was yet dark they came to the tomb." It is in this way that Augustine explains this difference (De Consens. Evang. iii).

Exception is made on the night of Christmas eve, when mass is celebrated, because our Lord was born in the night (De Consecr., dist. 1). And in like manner it is celebrated on Holy Saturday towards the beginning of the night, since our Lord rose in the night, that is, "when it was yet dark, before the sun's rising was manifest."

Reply Obj. 5: As is set down in the decree (De Consecr., dist. 1), in virtue of a decree of Pope Alexander II, "it is enough for a priest to celebrate one mass each day, because Christ suffered once and redeemed the whole world; and very happy is he who can worthily celebrate one mass. But there are some who say one mass for the dead, and another of the day, if need be. But I do not deem that those escape condemnation who presume to celebrate several masses daily, either for the sake of money, or to gain flattery from the laity." And Pope Innocent III says (Extra, De Celebr. Miss., chap. Consuluisti) that "except on the day of our Lord's birth, unless necessity urges, it suffices for a priest to celebrate only one mass each day."

THIRD ARTICLE [III, Q. 83, Art. 3]

Whether This Sacrament Ought to Be Celebrated in a House and with Sacred Vessels?

Objection 1: It seems that this sacrament ought not to be celebrated in a house and with sacred vessels. For this sacrament is a representation of our Lord's Passion. But Christ did not suffer in a house, but outside the city gate, according to Heb. 1:12: "Jesus, that He might sanctify the people by His own blood, suffered without the gate." Therefore, it seems that this sacrament ought not to be celebrated in a house, but rather in the open air.

Obj. 2: Further, in the celebration of this sacrament the Church ought to imitate the custom of Christ and the apostles. But the house wherein Christ first wrought this sacrament was not consecrated, but merely an ordinary supper-room prepared by the master of the house, as related in Luke 22:11, 12. Moreover, we read (Acts 2:46) that "the apostles were continuing daily with one accord in the temple; and, breaking bread from house to house, they took their meat with gladness." Consequently, there is no need for houses, in which this sacrament is celebrated, to be consecrated.

Obj. 3: Further, nothing that is to no purpose ought to be done in the Church, which is governed by the Holy Ghost. But it seems useless to consecrate a church, or an altar, or such like inanimate things, since they are not capable of receiving grace or spiritual virtue. Therefore it is unbecoming for such consecrations to be performed in the Church.

Obj. 4: Further, only Divine works ought to be recalled with solemnity, according to Ps. 91:5: "I shall rejoice in the works of Thy hands." Now the consecration of a church or altar, is the work of a man; as is also the consecration of the chalice, and of the ministers, and of other such things. But these latter consecrations are not commemorated in the Church. Therefore neither ought the consecration of a church or of an altar to be commemorated with solemnity.

Obj. 5: Further, the truth ought to correspond with the figure. But in the Old Testament, which was a figure of the New, the altar was not made of hewn stones: for, it is written (Ex. 20:24): "You shall make an altar of earth unto Me . . . and if thou make an altar of stone unto Me, thou shalt not build it of hewn stones." Again, the altar is commanded to be made of "setim-wood," covered "with brass" (Ex. 27:1, 2), or "with gold" (Ex. 25). Consequently, it seems unfitting for the Church to make exclusive use of altars made of stone.

Obj. 6: Further, the chalice with the paten represents Christ's tomb, which was "hewn in a rock," as is narrated in the Gospels. Consequently, the chalice ought to be of stone, and not of gold or of silver or tin.

Obj. 7: Further, just as gold is the most precious among the materials of the altar vessels, so are cloths of silk the most precious among other cloths. Consequently, since the chalice is of gold, the altar cloths ought to be made of silk and not of linen.

Obj. 8: Further, the dispensing and ordering of the sacraments belong to the Church's ministers, just as the ordering of temporal affairs is subject to the ruling of secular princes; hence the Apostle says (1 Cor. 4:1): "Let a man so esteem us as the ministers of Christ and the dispensers of the mysteries of God." But if anything be done against the ordinances of princes it is deemed void. Therefore, if the various items mentioned above are suitably commanded by the Church's prelates, it seems that the body of Christ could not be consecrated unless they be observed; and so it appears to follow that Christ's words are not sufficient of themselves for consecrating this sacrament: which is contrary to the fact. Consequently, it does not seem fitting for such ordinances to be made touching the celebration of this sacrament.

*On the contrary,* The Church's ordinances are Christ's own ordinances; since He said (Matt. 18:20): "Wherever two or three are gathered together in My name, there am I in the midst of them."

*I answer that,* There are two things to be considered regarding the equipment of this sacrament: one of these belongs to the representation of the events connected with our Lord's Passion; while the other is connected with the reverence due to the sacrament, in which Christ is contained verily, and not in figure only.

Hence we consecrate those things which we make use of in this sacrament; both that we may show our reverence for the sacrament, and in order to represent the holiness which is the effect of the Passion of Christ, according to Heb. 13:12: "Jesus, that He might sanctify the people by His own blood," etc.

Reply Obj. 1: This sacrament ought as a rule to be celebrated in a house, whereby the Church is signified, according to 1 Tim. 3:15: "That thou mayest know how thou oughtest to behave thyself in the house of God, which is the Church of the living God." Because "outside the Church there is no place for the true sacrifice," as Augustine says (Liber Sentent. Prosp. xv). And because the Church was not to be confined within the territories of the Jewish people, but was to be established throughout the whole world, therefore Christ's Passion was not celebrated within the city of the Jews, but in the open country, that so the whole world might serve as a house for Christ's Passion. Nevertheless, as is said in De Consecr., dist. 1, "if a church be not to hand, we permit travelers to celebrate mass in the open air, or in a tent, if there be a consecrated altar-table to hand, and the other requisites belonging to the sacred function."

Reply Obj. 2: The house in which this sacrament is celebrated denotes the Church, and is termed a church; and so it is fittingly consecrated, both to represent the holiness which the Church acquired from the Passion, as well as to denote the holiness required of them who have to receive this sacrament. By the altar Christ Himself is signified, of Whom the Apostle says (Heb. 13:15): "Through Him we offer a sacrifice of praise to God." Hence the consecration of the altar signifies Christ's holiness, of which it was said (Luke 1:35): "The Holy one born of thee shall be called the Son of God." Hence we read in De Consecr., dist. 1: "It has seemed pleasing for the altars to be consecrated not merely with the anointing of chrism, but likewise with the priestly blessing."

And therefore, as a rule, it is not lawful to celebrate this sacrament except in a consecrated house. Hence it is enacted (De Consecr., dist. 1): "Let no priest presume to say mass except in places consecrated by the bishop." And furthermore because pagans and other unbelievers are not members of the Church, therefore we read (De Consecr., dist. 1): "It is not lawful to bless a church in which the bodies of unbelievers are buried, but if it seem suitable for consecration, then, after removing the corpses and tearing down the walls or beams, let it be rebuilt. If, however, it has been already consecrated, and the faithful lie in it, it is lawful to celebrate mass therein." Nevertheless in a case of necessity this sacrament can be performed in houses which have not been consecrated, or which have been profaned; but with the bishop's consent. Hence we read in the same distinction: "We deem that masses are not to be celebrated everywhere, but in places consecrated by the bishop, or where he gives permission." But not without a portable altar consecrated by the bishop: hence in the same distinction we read: "We permit that, if the churches be devastated or burned, masses may be celebrated in chapels, with a consecrated altar." For because Christ's holiness is the fount of all the Church's holiness, therefore in necessity a consecrated altar suffices for performing this sacrament. And on this account a church is never consecrated without consecrating the altar. Yet sometimes an altar is consecrated apart from the church, with the relics of the saints, "whose lives are hidden with Christ in God" (Col. 3:3). Accordingly under the same distinction we read: "It is our pleasure that altars, in which no relics of saints are found enclosed, be thrown down, if possible, by the bishops presiding over such places."

Reply Obj. 3: The church, altar, and other like inanimate things are consecrated, not because they are capable of receiving grace, but because they acquire special spiritual virtue from the consecration, whereby they are rendered fit for the Divine worship, so that man derives devotion therefrom, making him more fitted for Divine functions, unless this be hindered by want of reverence. Hence it is written (2 Macc. 3:38): "There is undoubtedly in that place a certain power of God; for He that hath His dwelling in the heavens is the visitor, and the protector of that place."

Hence it is that such places are cleansed and exorcised before being consecrated, that the enemy's power may be driven forth. And for the same reason churches defiled by shedding of blood or seed are reconciled: because some machination of the enemy is apparent on account of the sin committed there. And for this reason we read in the same distinction: "Wherever you find churches of the Arians, consecrate them as Catholic churches without delay by means of devout prayers and rites." Hence, too, it is that some say with probability, that by entering a consecrated church one obtains forgiveness of venial sins, just as one does by the sprinkling of holy water; alleging the words of Ps. 84:2, 3: "Lord, Thou hast blessed Thy land . . . Thou hast forgiven the iniquity of Thy people." And therefore, in consequence of the virtue acquired by a church's consecration, the consecration is never repeated. Accordingly we find in the same distinction the following words quoted from the Council of Nicaea: "Churches which have once been consecrated, must not be consecrated again, except they be devastated by fire, or defiled by shedding of blood or of anyone's seed; because, just as a child once baptized in the name of the Father, and of the Son, and of the Holy Ghost, ought not to be baptized again, so neither ought a place, once dedicated to God, to be consecrated again, except owing to the causes mentioned above; provided that the consecrators held faith in the Holy Trinity": in fact, those outside the Church cannot consecrate. But, as we read in the same distinction: "Churches or altars of doubtful consecration are to be consecrated anew."

And since they acquire special spiritual virtue from their consecration, we find it laid down in the same distinction that "the beams of a dedicated church ought not to be used for any other purpose, except it be for some other church, or else they are to be burned, or put to the use of brethren in some monastery: but on no account are they to be discarded for works of the laity." We read there, too, that "the altar covering, chair, candlesticks, and veil, are to be burned when warn out; and their ashes are to be placed in the baptistery, or in the walls, or else cast into the trenches beneath the flag-stones, so as not to be defiled by the feet of those that enter."

Reply Obj. 4: Since the consecration of the altar signifies Christ's holiness, and the consecration of a house the holiness of the entire Church, therefore the consecration of a church or of an altar is more fittingly commemorated. And on this account the solemnity of a church dedication is observed for eight days, in order to signify the happy resurrection of Christ and of the Church's members. Nor is the consecration of a church or altar man's doing only, since it has a spiritual virtue. Hence in the same distinction (De Consecr.) it is said: "The solemnities of the dedication of churches are to be solemnly celebrated each year: and that dedications are to be kept up for eight days, you will find in the third book of Kings" (8:66).

Reply Obj. 5: As we read in De Consecr., dist. 1, "altars, if not of stone, are not to be consecrated with the anointing of chrism." And this is in keeping with the signification of this sacrament; both because the altar signifies Christ, for in 1 Cor. 10:3, it is written, "But the rock was Christ": and because Christ's body was laid in a stone sepulchre. This is also in keeping with the use of the sacrament. Because stone is solid, and may be found everywhere, which was not necessary in the old Law, when the altar was made in one place. As to the commandment to make the altar of earth, or of unhewn stones, this was given in order to remove idolatry.

Reply Obj. 6: As is laid down in the same distinction, "formerly the priests did not use golden but wooden chalices; but Pope Zephyrinus ordered the mass to be said with glass patens; and subsequently Pope Urban had everything made of silver." Afterwards it was decided that "the Lord's chalice with the paten should be made entirely of gold, or of silver or at least of tin. But it is not to be made of brass, or copper, because the action of the wine thereon produces verdigris, and provokes vomiting. But no one is to presume to sing mass with a chalice of wood or of glass," because as the wood is porous, the consecrated blood would remain in it; while glass is brittle and there might arise danger of breakage; and the same applies to stone. Consequently, out of reverence for the sacrament, it was enacted that the chalice should be made of the aforesaid materials.

Reply Obj. 7: Where it could be done without danger, the Church gave order for that thing to be used which more expressively represents Christ's Passion. But there was not so much danger regarding the body which is placed on the corporal, as there is with the blood contained in the chalice. And consequently, although the chalice is not made of stone, yet the corporal is made of linen, since Christ's body was wrapped therein. Hence we read in an Epistle of Pope Silvester, quoted in the same distinction: "By a unanimous decree we command that no one shall presume to celebrate the sacrifice of the altar upon a cloth of silk, or dyed material, but upon linen consecrated by the bishop; as Christ's body was buried in a clean linen winding-sheet." Moreover, linen material is becoming, owing to its cleanness, to denote purity of conscience, and, owing to the manifold labor with which it is prepared, to denote Christ's Passion.

Reply Obj. 8: The dispensing of the sacraments belongs to the Church's ministers; but their consecration is from God Himself. Consequently, the Church's ministers can make no ordinances regarding the form of the consecration, and the manner of celebrating. And therefore, if the priest pronounces the words of consecration over the proper matter with the intention of consecrating, then, without every one of the things mentioned above--namely, without house, and altar, consecrated chalice and corporal, and the other things instituted by the Church--he consecrates Christ's body in very truth; yet he is guilty of grave sin, in not following the rite of the Church.

FOURTH ARTICLE [III, Q. 83, Art. 4]

Whether the Words Spoken in This Sacrament Are Properly Framed?

Objection 1: It seems that the words spoken in this sacrament are not properly framed. For, as Ambrose says (De Sacram. iv), this sacrament is consecrated with Christ's own words. Therefore no other words besides Christ's should be spoken in this sacrament.

Obj. 2: Further, Christ's words and deeds are made known to us through the Gospel. But in consecrating this sacrament words are used which are not set down in the Gospels: for we do not read in the Gospel, of Christ lifting up His eyes to heaven while consecrating this sacrament: and similarly it is said in the Gospel: "Take ye and eat" ( comedite ) without the addition of the word "all," whereas in celebrating this sacrament we say: "Lifting up His eyes to heaven," and again, "Take ye and eat ( manducate ) of this." Therefore such words as these are out of place when spoken in the celebration of this sacrament.

Obj. 3: Further, all the other sacraments are ordained for the salvation of all the faithful. But in the celebration of the other sacraments there is no common prayer put up for the salvation of all the faithful and of the departed. Consequently it is unbecoming in this sacrament.

Obj. 4: Further, Baptism especially is called the sacrament of faith. Consequently, the truths which belong to instruction in the faith ought rather to be given regarding Baptism than regarding this sacrament, such as the doctrine of the apostles and of the Gospels.

Obj. 5: Further, devotion on the part of the faithful is required in every sacrament. Consequently, the devotion of the faithful ought not to be stirred up in this sacrament more than in the others by Divine praises and by admonitions, such as, "Lift up your hearts."

Obj. 6: Further, the minister of this sacrament is the priest, as stated above (Q. 82, A. 1). Consequently, all the words spoken in this sacrament ought to be uttered by the priest, and not some by the ministers, and some by the choir.

Obj. 7: Further, the Divine power works this sacrament unfailingly. Therefore it is to no purpose that the priest asks for the perfecting of this sacrament, saying: "Which oblation do thou, O God, in all," etc.

Obj. 8: Further, the sacrifice of the New Law is much more excellent than the sacrifice of the fathers of old. Therefore, it is unfitting for the priest to pray that this sacrifice may be as acceptable as the sacrifice of Abel, Abraham, and Melchisedech.

Objection 9: Further, just as Christ's body does not begin to be in this sacrament by change of place, as stated above (Q. 75, A. 2), so likewise neither does it cease to be there. Consequently, it is improper for the priest to ask: "Bid these things be borne by the hands of thy holy angel unto Thine altar on high."

*On the contrary,* We find it stated in De Consecr., dist. 1, that "James, the brother of the Lord according to the flesh, and Basil, bishop of Caesarea, edited the rite of celebrating the mass": and from their authority it is manifest that whatever words are employed in this matter, are chosen becomingly.

*I answer that,* Since the whole mystery of our salvation is comprised in this sacrament, therefore is it performed with greater solemnity than the other sacraments. And since it is written (Eccles. 4:17): "Keep thy foot when thou goest into the house of God"; and (Ecclus. 18:23): "Before prayer prepare thy soul," therefore the celebration of this mystery is preceded by a certain preparation in order that we may perform worthily that which follows after. The first part of this preparation is Divine praise, and consists in the "Introit": according to Ps. 49:23: "The sacrifice of praise shall glorify me; and there is the way by which I will show him the salvation of God": and this is taken for the most part from the Psalms, or, at least, is sung with a Psalm, because, as Dionysius says (Eccl. Hier. iii): "The Psalms comprise by way of praise whatever is contained in Sacred Scripture."

The second part contains a reference to our present misery, by reason of which we pray for mercy, saying: "Lord, have mercy on us," thrice for the Person of the Father, and "Christ, have mercy on us," thrice for the Person of the Son, and "Lord, have mercy on us," thrice for the Person of the Holy Ghost; against the threefold misery of ignorance, sin, and punishment; or else to express the "circuminsession" of all the Divine Persons.

The third part commemorates the heavenly glory, to the possession of which, after this life of misery, we are tending, in the words, "Glory be to God on high," which are sung on festival days, on which the heavenly glory is commemorated, but are omitted in those sorrowful offices which commemorate our unhappy state.

The fourth part contains the prayer which the priest makes for the people, that they may be made worthy of such great mysteries.

There precedes, in the second place, the instruction of the faithful, because this sacrament is "a mystery of faith," as stated above (Q. 78, A. 3, ad 5). Now this instruction is given "dispositively," when the Lectors and Sub-deacons read aloud in the church the teachings of the prophets and apostles: after this "lesson," the choir sing the "Gradual," which signifies progress in life; then the "Alleluia" is intoned, and this denotes spiritual joy; or in mournful offices the "Tract", expressive of spiritual sighing; for all these things ought to result from the aforesaid teaching. But the people are instructed "perfectly" by Christ's teaching contained in the Gospel, which is read by the higher ministers, that is, by the Deacons. And because we believe Christ as the Divine truth, according to John 8:46, "If I tell you the truth, why do you not believe Me?" after the Gospel has been read, the "Creed" is sung in which the people show that they assent by faith to Christ's doctrine. And it is sung on those festivals of which mention is made therein, as on the festivals of Christ, of the Blessed Virgin, and of the apostles, who laid the foundations of this faith, and on other such days.

So then, after the people have been prepared and instructed, the next step is to proceed to the celebration of the mystery, which is both offered as a sacrifice, and consecrated and received as a sacrament: since first we have the oblation; then the consecration of the matter offered; and thirdly, its reception.

In regard to the oblation, two things are done, namely, the people's praise in singing the "offertory," expressing the joy of the offerers, and the priest's prayer asking for the people's oblation to be made acceptable to God. Hence David said (1 Para 29:17): "In the simplicity of my heart, I have . . . offered all these things: and I have seen with great joy Thy people which are here present, offer Thee their offerings": and then he makes the following prayer: "O Lord God . . . keep . . . this will."

Then, regarding the consecration, performed by supernatural power, the people are first of all excited to devotion in the "Preface," hence they are admonished "to lift up their hearts to the Lord," and therefore when the "Preface" is ended the people devoutly praise Christ's Godhead, saying with the angels: "Holy, Holy, Holy"; and His humanity, saying with the children: "Blessed is he that cometh." In the next place the priest makes a "commemoration," first of those for whom this sacrifice is offered, namely, for the whole Church, and "for those set in high places" (1 Tim. 2:2), and, in a special manner, of them "who offer, or for whom the mass is offered." Secondly, he commemorates the saints, invoking their patronage for those mentioned above, when he says: "Communicating with, and honoring the memory," etc. Thirdly, he concludes the petition when he says: "Wherefore that this oblation," etc., in order that the oblation may be salutary to them for whom it is offered.

Then he comes to the consecration itself. Here he asks first of all for the effect of the consecration, when he says: "Which oblation do Thou, O God," etc. Secondly, he performs the consecration using our Saviour's words, when he says: "Who the day before," etc. Thirdly, he makes excuse for his presumption in obeying Christ's command, saying: "Wherefore, calling to mind," etc. Fourthly, he asks that the sacrifice accomplished may find favor with God, when he says: "Look down upon them with a propitious," etc. Fifthly, he begs for the effect of this sacrifice and sacrament, first for the partakers, saying: "We humbly beseech Thee"; then for the dead, who can no longer receive it, saying: "Be mindful also, O Lord," etc.; thirdly, for the priests themselves who offer, saying: "And to us sinners," etc.

Then follows the act of receiving the sacrament. First of all, the people are prepared for Communion; first, by the common prayer of the congregation, which is the Lord's Prayer, in which we ask for our daily bread to be given us; and also by private prayer, which the priest puts up specially for the people, when he says: "Deliver us, we beseech Thee, O Lord," etc. Secondly, the people are prepared by the "Pax" which is given with the words, "Lamb of God," etc., because this is the sacrament of unity and peace, as stated above (Q. 73, A. 4; Q. 79, A. 1). But in masses for the dead, in which the sacrifice is offered not for present peace, but for the repose of the dead, the "Pax" is omitted.

Then follows the reception of the sacrament, the priest receiving first, and afterwards giving it to others, because, as Dionysius says (Eccl. Hier. iii), he who gives Divine things to others, ought first to partake thereof himself.

Finally, the whole celebration of mass ends with the thanksgiving, the people rejoicing for having received the mystery (and this is the meaning of the singing after the Communion); and the priest returning thanks by prayer, as Christ, at the close of the supper with His disciples, "said a hymn" (Matt. 26:30).

Reply Obj. 1: The consecration is accomplished by Christ's words only; but the other words must be added to dispose the people for receiving it, as stated above.

Reply Obj. 2: As is stated in the last chapter of John (verse 25), our Lord said and did many things which are not written down by the Evangelists; and among them is the uplifting of His eyes to heaven at the supper; nevertheless the Roman Church had it by tradition from the apostles. For it seems reasonable that He Who lifted up His eyes to the Father in raising Lazarus to life, as related in John 11:41, and in the prayer which He made for the disciples (John 17:1), had more reason to do so in instituting this sacrament, as being of greater import.

The use of the word manducate instead of comedite makes no difference in the meaning, nor does the expression signify, especially since those words are no part of the form, as stated above (Q. 78, A. 1, ad 2, 4).

The additional word "all" is understood in the Gospels, although not expressed, because He had said (John 6:54): "Except you eat the flesh of the Son of Man . . . you shall not have life in you."

Reply Obj. 3: The Eucharist is the sacrament of the unity of the whole Church: and therefore in this sacrament, more than in the others, mention ought to be made of all that belongs to the salvation of the entire Church.

Reply Obj. 4: There is a twofold instruction in the Faith: the first is for those receiving it for the first time, that is to say, for catechumens, and such instruction is given in connection with Baptism. The other is the instruction of the faithful who take part in this sacrament; and such instruction is given in connection with this sacrament. Nevertheless catechumens and unbelievers are not excluded therefrom. Hence in De Consecr., dist. 1, it is laid down: "Let the bishop hinder no one from entering the church, and hearing the word of God, be they Gentiles, heretics, or Jews, until the mass of the Catechumens begins," in which the instruction regarding the Faith is contained.

Reply Obj. 5: Greater devotion is required in this sacrament than in the others, for the reason that the entire Christ is contained therein. Moreover, this sacrament requires a more general devotion, i.e. on the part of the whole people, since for them it is offered; and not merely on the part of the recipients, as in the other sacraments. Hence Cyprian observes (De Orat. Domin. 31), "The priest, in saying the Preface, disposes the souls of the brethren by saying, 'Lift up your hearts,' and when the people answer--'We have lifted them up to the Lord,' let them remember that they are to think of nothing else but God."

Reply Obj. 6: As was said above (ad 3), those things are mentioned in this sacrament which belong to the entire Church; and consequently some things which refer to the people are sung by the choir, and same of these words are all sung by the choir, as though inspiring the entire people with them; and there are other words which the priest begins and the people take up, the priest then acting as in the person of God; to show that the things they denote have come to the people through Divine revelation, such as faith and heavenly glory; and therefore the priest intones the "Creed" and the "Gloria in excelsis Deo." Other words are uttered by the ministers, such as the doctrine of the Old and New Testament, as a sign that this doctrine was announced to the peoples through ministers sent by God. And there are other words which the priest alone recites, namely, such as belong to his personal office, "that he may offer up gifts and prayers for the people" (Heb. 5:1). Some of these, however, he says aloud, namely, such as are common to priest and people alike, such as the "common prayers"; other words, however, belong to the priest alone, such as the oblation and the consecration; consequently, the prayers that are said in connection with these have to be said by the priest in secret. Nevertheless, in both he calls the people to attention by saying: "The Lord be with you," and he waits for them to assent by saying "Amen." And therefore before the secret prayers he says aloud, "The Lord be with you," and he concludes, "For ever and ever." Or the priest secretly pronounces some of the words as a token that regarding Christ's Passion the disciples acknowledged Him only in secret.

Reply Obj. 7: The efficacy of the sacramental words can be hindered by the priest's intention. Nor is there anything unbecoming in our asking of God for what we know He will do, just as Christ (John 17:1, 5) asked for His glorification.

But the priest does not seem to pray there for the consecration to be fulfilled, but that it may be fruitful in our regard, hence he says expressively: "That it may become to us the body and the blood." Again, the words preceding these have that meaning, when he says: "Vouchsafe to make this oblation blessed," i.e. according to Augustine (Paschasius, De Corp. et Sang. Dom. xii), "that we may receive a blessing," namely, through grace; "enrolled,' i.e. that we may be enrolled in heaven; 'ratified,' i.e. that we may be incorporated in Christ; 'reasonable,' i.e. that we may be stripped of our animal sense; 'acceptable,' i.e. that we who in ourselves are displeasing, may, by its means, be made acceptable to His only Son."

Reply Obj. 8: Although this sacrament is of itself preferable to all ancient sacrifices, yet the sacrifices of the men of old were most acceptable to God on account of their devotion. Consequently the priest asks that this sacrifice may be accepted by God through the devotion of the offerers, just as the former sacrifices were accepted by Him.

Reply Obj. 9: The priest does not pray that the sacramental species may be borne up to heaven; nor that Christ's true body may be borne thither, for it does not cease to be there; but he offers this prayer for Christ's mystical body, which is signified in this sacrament, that the angel standing by at the Divine mysteries may present to God the prayers of both priest and people, according to Apoc. 8:4: "And the smoke of the incense of the prayers of the saints ascended up before God, from the hand of the angel." But God's "altar on high" means either the Church triumphant, unto which we pray to be translated, or else God Himself, in Whom we ask to share; because it is said of this altar (Ex. 20:26): "Thou shalt not go up by steps unto My altar, i.e. thou shalt make no steps towards the Trinity." Or else by the angel we are to understand Christ Himself, Who is the "Angel of great counsel" (Isa. 9:6: Septuagint), Who unites His mystical body with God the Father and the Church triumphant.

And from this the mass derives its name ( missa ); because the priest sends ( mittit ) his prayers up to God through the angel, as the people do through the priest, or else because Christ is the victim sent ( missa ) to us: accordingly the deacon on festival days "dismisses" the people at the end of the mass, by saying: "Ite, missa est," that is, the victim has been sent ( missa est ) to God through the angel, so that it may be accepted by God.

FIFTH ARTICLE [III, Q. 83, Art. 5]

Whether the Actions Performed in Celebrating This Sacrament Are Becoming?

Objection 1: It seems that the actions performed in celebrating this mystery are not becoming. For, as is evident from its form, this sacrament belongs to the New Testament. But under the New Testament the ceremonies of the old are not to be observed, such as that the priests and ministers were purified with water when they drew nigh to offer up the sacrifice: for we read (Ex. 30:19, 20): "Aaron and his sons shall wash their hands and feet . . . when they are going into the tabernacle of the testimony . . . and when they are to come to the altar." Therefore it is not fitting that the priest should wash his hands when celebrating mass.

Obj. 2: Further, (Ex. 30:7), the Lord commanded Aaron to "burn sweet-smelling incense" upon the altar which was "before the propitiatory": and the same action was part of the ceremonies of the Old Law. Therefore it is not fitting for the priest to use incense during mass.

Obj. 3: Further, the ceremonies performed in the sacraments of the Church ought not to be repeated. Consequently it is not proper for the priest to repeat the sign of the cross many times over this sacrament.

Obj. 4: Further, the Apostle says (Heb. 7:7): "And without all contradiction, that which is less, is blessed by the better." But Christ, Who is in this sacrament after the consecration, is much greater than the priest. Therefore quite unseemingly the priest, after the consecration, blesses this sacrament, by signing it with the cross.

Obj. 5: Further, nothing which appears ridiculous ought to be done in one of the Church's sacraments. But it seems ridiculous to perform gestures, e.g. for the priest to stretch out his arms at times, to join his hands, to join together his fingers, and to bow down. Consequently, such things ought not to be done in this sacrament.

Obj. 6: Further, it seems ridiculous for the priest to turn round frequently towards the people, and often to greet the people. Consequently, such things ought not to be done in the celebration of this sacrament.

Obj. 7: Further, the Apostle (1 Cor. 13) deems it improper for Christ to be divided. But Christ is in this sacrament after the consecration. Therefore it is not proper for the priest to divide the host.

Obj. 8: Further, the ceremonies performed in this sacrament represent Christ's Passion. But during the Passion Christ's body was divided in the places of the five wounds. Therefore Christ's body ought to be broken into five parts rather than into three.

Objection 9: Further, Christ's entire body is consecrated in this sacrament apart from the blood. Consequently, it is not proper for a particle of the body to be mixed with the blood.

Objection 10: Further, just as, in this sacrament, Christ's body is set before us as food, so is His blood, as drink. But in receiving Christ's body no other bodily food is added in the celebration of the mass. Therefore, it is out of place for the priest, after taking Christ's blood, to receive other wine which is not consecrated.

Objection 11: Further, the truth ought to be conformable with the figure. But regarding the Paschal Lamb, which was a figure of this sacrament, it was commanded that nothing of it should "remain until the morning." It is improper therefore for consecrated hosts to be reserved, and not consumed at once.

Objection 12: Further, the priest addresses in the plural number those who are hearing mass, when he says, "The Lord be with you": and, "Let us return thanks." But it is out of keeping to address one individual in the plural number, especially an inferior. Consequently it seems unfitting for a priest to say mass with only a single server present. Therefore in the celebration of this sacrament it seems that some of the things done are out of place.

*On the contrary,* The custom of the Church stands for these things: and the Church cannot err, since she is taught by the Holy Ghost.

*I answer that,* As was said above (Q. 60, A. 6), there is a twofold manner of signification in the sacraments, by words, and by actions, in order that the signification may thus be more perfect. Now, in the celebration of this sacrament words are used to signify things pertaining to Christ's Passion, which is represented in this sacrament; or again, pertaining to Christ's mystical body, which is signified therein; and again, things pertaining to the use of this sacrament, which use ought to be devout and reverent. Consequently, in the celebration of this mystery some things are done in order to represent Christ's Passion, or the disposing of His mystical body, and some others are done which pertain to the devotion and reverence due to this sacrament.

Reply Obj. 1: The washing of the hands is done in the celebration of mass out of reverence for this sacrament; and this for two reasons: first, because we are not wont to handle precious objects except the hands be washed; hence it seems indecent for anyone to approach so great a sacrament with hands that are, even literally, unclean. Secondly, on account of its signification, because, as Dionysius says (Eccl. Hier. iii), the washing of the extremities of the limbs denotes cleansing from even the smallest sins, according to John 13:10: "He that is washed needeth not but to wash his feet." And such cleansing is required of him who approaches this sacrament; and this is denoted by the confession which is made before the "Introit" of the mass. Moreover, this was signified by the washing of the priests under the Old Law, as Dionysius says (Eccl. Hier. iii). However, the Church observes this ceremony, not because it was prescribed under the Old Law, but because it is becoming in itself, and therefore instituted by the Church. Hence it is not observed in the same way as it was then: because the washing of the feet is omitted, and the washing of the hands is observed; for this can be done more readily, and suffices for denoting perfect cleansing. For, since the hand is the "organ of organs" (De Anima iii), all works are attributed to the hands: hence it is said in Ps. 25:6: "I will wash my hands among the innocent."

Reply Obj. 2: We use incense, not as commanded by a ceremonial precept of the Law, but as prescribed by the Church; accordingly we do not use it in the same fashion as it was ordered under the Old Law. It has reference to two things: first, to the reverence due to this sacrament, i.e. in order by its good odor, to remove any disagreeable smell that may be about the place; secondly, it serves to show the effect of grace, wherewith Christ was filled as with a good odor, according to Gen. 27:27: "Behold, the odor of my son is like the odor of a ripe field"; and from Christ it spreads to the faithful by the work of His ministers, according to 2 Cor. 2:14: "He manifesteth the odor of his knowledge by us in every place"; and therefore when the altar which represents Christ, has been incensed on every side, then all are incensed in their proper order.

Reply Obj. 3: The priest, in celebrating the mass, makes use of the sign of the cross to signify Christ's Passion which was ended upon the cross. Now, Christ's Passion was accomplished in certain stages. First of all there was Christ's betrayal, which was the work of God, of Judas, and of the Jews; and this is signified by the triple sign of the cross at the words, "These gifts, these presents, these holy unspotted sacrifices."

Secondly, there was the selling of Christ. Now he was sold to the Priests, to the Scribes, and to the Pharisees: and to signify this the threefold sign of the cross is repeated, at the words, "blessed, enrolled, ratified." Or again, to signify the price for which He was sold, viz. thirty pence. And a double cross is added at the words--"that it may become to us the Body and the Blood," etc., to signify the person of Judas the seller, and of Christ Who was sold.

Thirdly, there was the foreshadowing of the Passion at the last supper. To denote this, in the third place, two crosses are made, one in consecrating the body, the other in consecrating the blood; each time while saying, "He blessed."

Fourthly, there was Christ's Passion itself. And so in order to represent His five wounds, in the fourth place, there is a fivefold signing of the cross at the words, "a pure Victim, a holy Victim, a spotless Victim, the holy bread of eternal life, and the cup of everlasting salvation."

Fifthly, the outstretching of Christ's body, and the shedding of the blood, and the fruits of the Passion, are signified by the triple signing of the cross at the words, "as many as shall receive the body and blood, may be filled with every blessing," etc.

Sixthly, Christ's threefold prayer upon the cross is represented; one for His persecutors when He said, "Father, forgive them"; the second for deliverance from death, when He cried, "My God, My God, why hast Thou forsaken Me?" the third referring to His entrance into glory, when He said, "Father, into Thy hands I commend My spirit"; and in order to denote these there is a triple signing with the cross made at the words, "Thou dost sanctify, quicken, bless."

Seventhly, the three hours during which He hung upon the cross, that is, from the sixth to the ninth hour, are represented; in signification of which we make once more a triple sign of the cross at the words, "Through Him, and with Him, and in Him."

Eighthly, the separation of His soul from the body is signified by the two subsequent crosses made over the chalice.

Ninthly, the resurrection on the third day is represented by the three crosses made at the words--"May the peace of the Lord be ever with you."

In short, we may say that the consecration of this sacrament, and the acceptance of this sacrifice, and its fruits, proceed from the virtue of the cross of Christ, and therefore wherever mention is made of these, the priest makes use of the sign of the cross.

Reply Obj. 4: After the consecration, the priest makes the sign of the cross, not for the purpose of blessing and consecrating, but only for calling to mind the virtue of the cross, and the manner of Christ's suffering, as is evident from what has been said (ad 3).

Reply Obj. 5: The actions performed by the priest in mass are not ridiculous gestures, since they are done so as to represent something else. The priest in extending his arms signifies the outstretching of Christ's arms upon the cross. He also lifts up his hands as he prays, to point out that his prayer is directed to God for the people, according to Lam. 3:41: "Let us lift up our hearts with our hands to the Lord in the heavens": and Ex. 17:11: "And when Moses lifted up his hands Israel overcame." That at times he joins his hands, and bows down, praying earnestly and humbly, denotes the humility and obedience of Christ, out of which He suffered. He closes his fingers, i.e. the thumb and first finger, after the consecration, because, with them, he had touched the consecrated body of Christ; so that if any particle cling to the fingers, it may not be scattered: and this belongs to the reverence for this sacrament.

Reply Obj. 6: Five times does the priest turn round towards the people, to denote that our Lord manifested Himself five times on the day of His Resurrection, as stated above in the treatise on Christ's Resurrection (Q. 55, A. 3, Obj. 3). But the priest greets the people seven times, namely, five times, by turning round to the people, and twice without turning round, namely, when he says, "The Lord be with you" before the "Preface," and again when he says, "May the peace of the Lord be ever with you": and this is to denote the sevenfold grace of the Holy Ghost. But a bishop, when he celebrates on festival days, in his first greeting says, "Peace be to you," which was our Lord's greeting after Resurrection, Whose person the bishop chiefly represents.

Reply Obj. 7: The breaking of the host denotes three things: first, the rending of Christ's body, which took place in the Passion; secondly, the distinction of His mystical body according to its various states; and thirdly, the distribution of the graces which flow from Christ's Passion, as Dionysius observes (Eccl. Hier. iii). Hence this breaking does not imply severance in Christ.

Reply Obj. 8: As Pope Sergius says, and it is to be found in the Decretals (De Consecr., dist. ii), "the Lord's body is threefold; the part offered and put into the chalice signifies Christ's risen body," namely, Christ Himself, and the Blessed Virgin, and the other saints, if there be any, who are already in glory with their bodies. "The part consumed denotes those still walking upon earth," because while living upon earth they are united together by this sacrament; and are bruised by the passions, just as the bread eaten is bruised by the teeth. "The part reserved on the altar till the close of the mass, is His body hidden in the sepulchre, because the bodies of the saints will be in their graves until the end of the world": though their souls are either in purgatory, or in heaven. However, this rite of reserving one part on the altar till the close of the mass is no longer observed, on account of the danger; nevertheless, the same meaning of the parts continues, which some persons have expressed in verse, thus:

"The host being rent-- What is dipped, means the blest; What is dry, means the living; What is kept, those at rest."

Others, however, say that the part put into the chalice denotes those still living in this world, while the part kept outside the chalice denotes those fully blessed both in soul and body; while the part consumed means the others.

Reply Obj. 9: Two things can be signified by the chalice: first, the Passion itself, which is represented in this sacrament, and according to this, by the part put into the chalice are denoted those who are still sharers of Christ's sufferings; secondly, the enjoyment of the Blessed can be signified, which is likewise foreshadowed in this sacrament; and therefore those whose bodies are already in full beatitude, are denoted by the part put into the chalice. And it is to be observed that the part put into the chalice ought not to be given to the people to supplement the communion, because Christ gave dipped bread only to Judas the betrayer.

Reply Obj. 10: Wine, by reason of its humidity, is capable of washing, consequently it is received in order to rinse the mouth after receiving this sacrament, lest any particles remain: and this belongs to reverence for the sacrament. Hence (Extra, De Celebratione missae, chap. Ex parte), it is said: "The priest should always cleanse his mouth with wine after receiving the entire sacrament of Eucharist: except when he has to celebrate another mass on the same day, lest from taking the ablution-wine he be prevented from celebrating again"; and it is for the same reason that wine is poured over the fingers with which he had touched the body of Christ.

Reply Obj. 11: The truth ought to be conformable with the figure, in some respect: namely, because a part of the host consecrated, of which the priest and ministers or even the people communicate, ought not to be reserved until the day following. Hence, as is laid down (De Consecr., dist. ii), Pope Clement I ordered that "as many hosts are to be offered on the altar as shall suffice for the people; should any be left over, they are not to be reserved until the morrow, but let the clergy carefully consume them with fear and trembling." Nevertheless, since this sacrament is to be received daily, whereas the Paschal Lamb was not, it is therefore necessary for other hosts to be reserved for the sick. Hence we read in the same distinction: "Let the priest always have the Eucharist ready, so that, when anyone fall sick, he may take Communion to him at once, lest he die without it."

Reply Obj. 12: Several persons ought to be present at the solemn celebration of the mass. Hence Pope Soter says (De Consecr., dist. 1): "It has also been ordained, that no priest is to presume to celebrate solemn mass, unless two others be present answering him, while he himself makes the third; because when he says in the plural, 'The Lord be with you,' and again in the Secrets, 'Pray ye for me,' it is most becoming that they should answer his greeting." Hence it is for the sake of greater solemnity that we find it decreed (De Consecr. dist. 1) that a bishop is to solemnize mass with several assistants. Nevertheless, in private masses it suffices to have one server, who takes the place of the whole Catholic people, on whose behalf he makes answer in the plural to the priest.

SIXTH ARTICLE [III, Q. 83, Art. 6]

Whether the Defects Occurring During the Celebration of This Sacrament Can Be Sufficiently Met by Observing the Church's Statutes?

Objection 1: It seems that the defects occurring during the celebration of this sacrament cannot be sufficiently met by observing the statutes of the Church. For it sometimes happens that before or after the consecration the priest dies or goes mad, or is hindered by some other infirmity from receiving the sacrament and completing the mass. Consequently it seems impossible to observe the Church's statute, whereby the priest consecrating must communicate of his own sacrifice.

Obj. 2: Further, it sometimes happens that, before the consecration, the priest remembers that he has eaten or drunk something, or that he is in mortal sin, or under excommunication, which he did not remember previously. Therefore, in such a dilemma a man must necessarily commit mortal sin by acting against the Church's statute, whether he receives or not.

Obj. 3: Further, it sometimes happens that a fly or a spider, or some other poisonous creature falls into the chalice after the consecration. Or even that the priest comes to know that poison has been put in by some evilly disposed person in order to kill him. Now in this instance, if he takes it, he appears to sin by killing himself, or by tempting God: also in like manner if he does not take it, he sins by acting against the Church's statute. Consequently, he seems to be perplexed, and under necessity of sinning, which is not becoming.

Obj. 4: Further, it sometimes happens from the server's want of heed that water is not added to the chalice, or even the wine overlooked, and that the priest discovers this. Therefore he seems to be perplexed likewise in this case, whether he receives the body without the blood, thus making the sacrifice to be incomplete, or whether he receives neither the body nor the blood.

Obj. 5: Further, it sometimes happens that the priest cannot remember having said the words of consecration, or other words which are uttered in the celebration of this sacrament. In this case he seems to sin, whether he repeats the words over the same matter, which words possibly he has said before, or whether he uses bread and wine which are not consecrated, as if they were consecrated.

Obj. 6: Further, it sometimes comes to pass owing to the cold that the host will slip from the priest's hands into the chalice, either before or after the breaking. In this case then the priest will not be able to comply with the Church's rite, either as to the breaking, or else as to this, that only a third part is put into the chalice.

Obj. 7: Further, sometimes, too, it happens, owing to the priest's want of care, that Christ's blood is spilled, or that he vomits the sacrament received, or that the consecrated hosts are kept so long that they become corrupt, or that they are nibbled by mice, or lost in any manner whatsoever; in which cases it does not seem possible for due reverence to be shown towards this sacrament, as the Church's ordinances require. It does not seem then that such defects or dangers can be met by keeping to the Church's statutes.

*On the contrary,* Just as God does not command an impossibility, so neither does the Church.

*I answer that,* Dangers or defects happening to this sacrament can be met in two ways: first, by preventing any such mishaps from occurring: secondly, by dealing with them in such a way, that what may have happened amiss is put right, either by employing a remedy, or at least by repentance on his part who has acted negligently regarding this sacrament.

Reply Obj. 1: If the priest be stricken by death or grave sickness before the consecration of our Lord's body and blood, there is no need for it to be completed by another. But if this happens after the consecration is begun, for instance, when the body has been consecrated and before the consecration of the blood, or even after both have been consecrated, then the celebration of the mass ought to be finished by someone else. Hence, as is laid down (Decretal vii, q. 1), we read the following decree of the (Seventh) Council of Toledo: "We consider it to be fitting that when the sacred mysteries are consecrated by priests during the time of mass, if any sickness supervenes, in consequence of which they cannot finish the mystery begun, let it be free for the bishop or another priest to finish the consecration of the office thus begun. For nothing else is suitable for completing the mysteries commenced, unless the consecration be completed either by the priest who began it, or by the one who follows him: because they cannot be completed except they be performed in perfect order. For since we are all one in Christ, the change of persons makes no difference, since unity of faith insures the happy issue of the mystery. Yet let not the course we propose for cases of natural debility, be presumptuously abused: and let no minister or priest presume ever to leave the Divine offices unfinished, unless he be absolutely prevented from continuing. If anyone shall have rashly presumed to do so, he will incur sentence of excommunication."

Reply Obj. 2: Where difficulty arises, the less dangerous course should always be followed. But the greatest danger regarding this sacrament lies in whatever may prevent its completion, because this is a heinous sacrilege; while that danger is of less account which regards the condition of the receiver. Consequently, if after the consecration has been begun the priest remembers that he has eaten or drunk anything, he ought nevertheless to complete the sacrifice and receive the sacrament. Likewise, if he recalls a sin committed, he ought to make an act of contrition, with the firm purpose of confessing and making satisfaction for it: and thus he will not receive the sacrament unworthily, but with profit. The same applies if he calls to mind that he is under some excommunication; for he ought to make the resolution of humbly seeking absolution; and so he will receive absolution from the invisible High

Priest Jesus Christ for his act of completing the Divine mysteries.

But if he calls to mind any of the above facts previous to the consecration, I should deem it safer for him to interrupt the mass begun, especially if he has broken his fast, or is under excommunication, unless grave scandal were to be feared.

Reply Obj. 3: If a fly or a spider falls into the chalice before consecration, or if it be discovered that the wine is poisoned, it ought to be poured out, and after purifying the chalice, fresh wine should be served for consecration. But if anything of the sort happen after the consecration, the insect should be caught carefully and washed thoroughly, then burned, and the "ablution," together with the ashes, thrown into the sacrarium. If it be discovered that the wine has been poisoned, the priest should neither receive it nor administer it to others on any account, lest the life-giving chalice become one of death, but it ought to be kept in a suitable vessel with the relics: and in order that the sacrament may not remain incomplete, he ought to put other wine into the chalice, resume the mass from the consecration of the blood, and complete the sacrifice.

Reply Obj. 4: If before the consecration of the blood, and after the consecration of the body the priest detect that either the wine or the water is absent, then he ought at once to add them and consecrate. But if after the words of consecration he discover that the water is absent, he ought notwithstanding to proceed straight on, because the addition of the water is not necessary for the sacrament, as stated above (Q. 74, A. 7): nevertheless the person responsible for the neglect ought to be punished. And on no account should water be mixed with the consecrated wine, because corruption of the sacrament would ensue in part, as was said above (Q. 77, A. 8). But if after the words of consecration the priest perceive that no wine has been put in the chalice, and if he detect it before receiving the body, then rejecting the water, he ought to pour in wine with water, and begin over again the consecrating words of the blood. But if he notice it after receiving the body, he ought to procure another host which must be consecrated together with the blood; and I say so for this reason, because if he were to say only the words of consecration of the blood, the proper order of consecrating would not be observed; and, as is laid down by the Council of Toledo, quoted above (ad 1), sacrifices cannot be perfect, except they be performed in perfect order. But if he were to begin from the consecration of the blood, and were to repeat all the words which follow, it would not suffice, unless there was a consecrated host present, since in those words there are things to be said and done not only regarding the blood, but also regarding the body; and at the close he ought once more to receive the consecrated host and blood, even if he had already taken the water which was in the chalice, because the precept of the completing this sacrament is of greater weight than the precept of receiving the sacrament while fasting, as stated above (Q. 80, A. 8).

Reply Obj. 5: Although the priest may not recollect having said some of the words he ought to say, he ought not to be disturbed mentally on that account; for a man who utters many words cannot recall to mind all that he has said; unless perchance in uttering them he adverts to something connected with the consecration; for so it is impressed on the memory. Hence, if a man pays attention to what he is saying, but without adverting to the fact that he is saying these particular words, he remembers soon after that he has said them; for, a thing is presented to the memory under the formality of the past (De Mem. et Remin. i).

But if it seem to the priest that he has probably omitted some of the words that are not necessary for the sacrament, I think that he ought not to repeat them on that account, changing the order of the sacrifice, but that he ought to proceed: but if he is certain that he has left out any of those that are necessary for the sacrament, namely, the form of the consecration, since the form of the consecration is necessary for the sacrament, just as the matter is, it seems that the same thing ought to be done as was stated above (ad 4) with regard to defect in the matter, namely, that he should begin again with the form of the consecration, and repeat the other things in order, lest the order of the sacrifice be altered.

Reply Obj. 6: The breaking of the consecrated host, and the putting of only one part into the chalice, regards the mystical body, just as the mixing with water signifies the people, and therefore the omission of either of them causes no such imperfection in the sacrifice, as calls for repetition regarding the celebration of this sacrament.

Reply Obj. 7: According to the decree, De Consecr., dist. ii, quoting a decree of Pope Pius I, "If from neglect any of the blood falls upon a board which is fixed to the ground, let it be taken up with the tongue, and let the board be scraped. But if it be not a board, let the ground be scraped, and the scrapings burned, and the ashes buried inside the altar and let the priest do penance for forty days. But if a drop fall from the chalice on to the altar, let the minister suck up the drop, and do penance during three days; if it falls upon the altar cloth and penetrates to the second altar cloth, let him do four days' penance; if it penetrates to the third, let him do nine days' penance; if to the fourth, let him do twenty days' penance; and let the altar linens which the drop touched be washed three times by the priest, holding the chalice below, then let the water be taken and put away nigh to the altar." It might even be drunk by the minister, unless it might be rejected from nausea. Some persons go further, and cut out that part of the linen, which they burn, putting the ashes in the altar or down the sacrarium. And the Decretal continues with a quotation from the Penitential of Bede the Priest: "If, owing to drunkenness or gluttony, anyone vomits up the Eucharist, let him do forty days' penance, if he be a layman; but let clerics or monks, deacons and priests, do seventy days' penance; and let a bishop do ninety days'. But if they vomit from sickness, let them do penance for seven days." And in the same distinction, we read a decree of the (Fourth) Council of Arles: "They who do not keep proper custody over the sacrament, if a mouse or other animal consume it, must do forty days' penance: he who loses it in a church, or if a part fall and be not found, shall do thirty days' penance." And the priest seems to deserve the same penance, who from neglect allows the hosts to putrefy. And on those days the one doing penance ought to fast, and abstain from Communion. However, after weighing the circumstances of the fact and of the person, the said penances may be lessened or increased. But it must be observed that wherever the species are found to be entire, they must be preserved reverently, or consumed; because Christ's body is there so long as the species last, as stated above (Q. 77, AA. 4, 5). But if it can be done conveniently, the things in which they are found are to be burned, and the ashes put in the sacrarium, as was said of the scrapings of the altar-table, here above.

# QUESTION 84

OF THE SACRAMENT OF PENANCE (In Ten Articles)

We must now consider the Sacrament of Penance. We shall consider (1)Penance itself; (2) Its effect; (3) Its Parts; (4) The recipients of this sacrament; (5) The power of the ministers, which pertains to the keys; (6) The solemnization of this sacrament.

The first of these considerations will be twofold: (1) Penance as a sacrament; (2) Penance as a virtue.

Under the first head there are ten points of inquiry:

(1) Whether Penance is a sacrament?

(2) Of its proper matter;

(3) Of its form;

(4) Whether imposition of hands is necessary for this sacrament?

(5) Whether this sacrament is necessary for salvation?

(6) Of its relation to the other sacraments;

(7) Of its institution;

(8) Of its duration;

(9) Of its continuance;

(10) Whether it can be repeated?

FIRST ARTICLE [III, Q. 84, Art. 1]

Whether Penance Is a Sacrament?

Objection 1: It would seem that Penance is not a sacrament. For Gregory [*Cf. Isidore, Etym. vi, ch. 19] says: "The sacraments are Baptism, Chrism, and the Body and Blood of Christ; which are called sacraments because under the veil of corporeal things the Divine power works out salvation in a hidden manner." But this does not happen in Penance, because therein corporeal things are not employed that, under them, the power of God may work our salvation. Therefore Penance is not a sacrament.

Obj. 2: Further, the sacraments of the Church are shown forth by the ministers of Christ, according to 1 Cor. 4:1: "Let a man so account of us as of the ministers of Christ, and the dispensers of the mysteries of God." But Penance is not conferred by the ministers of Christ, but is inspired inwardly into man by God, according to Jer. 31:19: "After Thou didst convert me, I did penance." Therefore it seems that Penance is not a sacrament.

Obj. 3: Further, in the sacraments of which we have already spoken above, there is something that is sacrament only, something that is both reality and sacrament, and something that is reality only, as is clear from what has been stated (Q. 66, A. 1). But this does not apply to Penance. Therefore Penance is not a sacrament.

*On the contrary,* As Baptism is conferred that we may be cleansed from sin, so also is Penance: wherefore Peter said to Simon Magus (Acts 8:22): "Do penance . . . from this thy wickedness." But Baptism is a sacrament as stated above (Q. 66, A. 1). Therefore for the same reason Penance is also a sacrament.

*I answer that,* As Gregory says [*Isidore, Etym. vi, ch. 19], "a sacrament consists in a solemn act, whereby something is so done that we understand it to signify the holiness which it confers." Now it is evident that in Penance something is done so that something holy is signified both on the part of the penitent sinner, and on the part of the priest absolving, because the penitent sinner, by deed and word, shows his heart to have renounced sin, and in like manner the priest, by his deed and word with regard to the penitent, signifies the work of God Who forgives his sins. Therefore it is evident that Penance, as practiced in the Church, is a sacrament.

Reply Obj. 1: By corporeal things taken in a wide sense we may understand also external sensible actions, which are to this sacrament what water is to Baptism, or chrism to Confirmation. But it is to be observed that in those sacraments, whereby an exceptional grace surpassing altogether the proportion of a human act, is conferred, some corporeal matter is employed externally, e.g. in Baptism, which confers full remission of all sins, both as to guilt and as to punishment, and in Confirmation, wherein the fulness of the Holy Ghost is bestowed, and in Extreme Unction, which confers perfect spiritual health derived from the virtue of Christ as from an extrinsic principle. Wherefore, such human acts as are in these sacraments, are not the essential matter of the sacrament, but are dispositions thereto. On the other hand, in those sacraments whose effect corresponds to that of some human act, the sensible human act itself takes the place of matter, as in the case of Penance and Matrimony, even as in bodily medicines, some are applied externally, such as plasters and drugs, while others are acts of the person who seeks to be cured, such as certain exercises.

Reply Obj. 2: In those sacraments which have a corporeal matter, this matter needs to be applied by a minister of the Church, who stands in the place of Christ, which denotes that the excellence of the power which operates in the sacraments is from Christ. But in the sacrament of Penance, as stated above (ad 1), human actions take the place of matter, and these actions proceed from internal inspiration, wherefore the matter is not applied by the minister, but by God working inwardly; while the minister furnishes the complement of the sacrament, when he absolves the penitent.

Reply Obj. 3: In Penance also, there is something which is sacrament only, viz. the acts performed outwardly both by the repentant sinner, and by the priest in giving absolution; that which is reality and sacrament is the sinner's inward repentance; while that which is reality, and not sacrament, is the forgiveness of sin. The first of these taken altogether is the cause of the second; and the first and second together are the cause of the third.

SECOND ARTICLE [III, Q. 84, Art. 2]

Whether Sins Are the Proper Matter of This Sacrament?

Objection 1: It would seem that sins are not the proper matter of this sacrament. Because, in the other sacraments, the matter is hallowed by the utterance of certain words, and being thus hallowed produces the sacramental effect. Now sins cannot be hallowed, for they are opposed to the effect of the sacrament, viz. grace which blots out sin. Therefore sins are not the proper matter of this sacrament.

Obj. 2: Further, Augustine says in his book De Poenitentia [Cf. Serm. cccli]: "No one can begin a new life, unless he repent of the old." Now not only sins but also the penalties of the present life belong to the old life. Therefore sins are not the proper matter of Penance.

Obj. 3: Further, sin is either original, mortal or venial. Now the sacrament of Penance is not ordained against original sin, for this is taken away by Baptism, [nor against mortal sin, for this is taken away by the sinner's confession]*, nor against venial sin, which is taken away by the beating of the breast and the sprinkling of holy water and the like. Therefore sins are not the proper matter of Penance. [*The words in brackets are omitted in the Leonine edition].

*On the contrary,* The Apostle says (2 Cor. 12:21): "(Who) have not done penance for the uncleanness and fornication and lasciviousness, that they have committed."

*I answer that,* Matter is twofold, viz. proximate and remote: thus the proximate matter of a statue is a metal, while the remote matter is water. Now it has been stated (A. 1, ad 1, ad 2), that the proximate matter of this sacrament consists in the acts of the penitent, the matter of which acts are the sins over which he grieves, which he confesses, and for which he satisfies. Hence it follows that sins are the remote matter of Penance, as a matter, not for approval, but for detestation, and destruction.

Reply Obj. 1: This argument considers the proximate matter of a sacrament.

Reply Obj. 2: The old life that was subject to death is the object of Penance, not as regards the punishment, but as regards the guilt connected with it.

Reply Obj. 3: Penance regards every kind of sin in a way, but not each in the same way. Because Penance regards actual mortal sin properly and chiefly; properly, since, properly speaking, we are said to repent of what we have done of our own will; chiefly, since this sacrament was instituted chiefly for the blotting out of mortal sin. Penance regards venial sins, properly speaking indeed, in so far as they are committed of our own will, but this was not the chief purpose of its institution. But as to original sin, Penance regards it neither chiefly, since Baptism, and not Penance, is ordained against original sin, nor properly, because original sin is not done of our own will, except in so far as Adam's will is looked upon as ours, in which sense the Apostle says (Rom. 5:12): "In whom all have sinned." Nevertheless, Penance may be said to regard original sin, if we take it in a wide sense for any detestation of something past: in which sense Augustine uses the term in his book De Poenitentia(Serm. cccli).

THIRD ARTICLE [III, Q. 84, Art. 3]

Whether the Form of This Sacrament Is: "I Absolve Thee"?

Objection 1: It would seem that the form of this sacrament is not: "I absolve thee." Because the forms of the sacraments are received from Christ's institution and the Church's custom. But we do not read that Christ instituted this form. Nor is it in common use; in fact in certain absolutions which are given publicly in church (e.g. at Prime and Compline and on Maundy Thursday), absolution is given not in the indicative form by saying: "I absolve thee," but in the deprecatory form, by saying: "May Almighty God have mercy on you," or: "May Almighty God grant you absolution and forgiveness." Therefore the form of this sacrament is not: "I absolve thee."

Obj. 2: Further, Pope Leo says (Ep. cviii) that God's forgiveness cannot be obtained without the priestly supplications: and he is speaking there of God's forgiveness granted to the penitent. Therefore the form of this sacrament should be deprecatory.

Obj. 3: Further, to absolve from sin is the same as to remit sin. But God alone remits sin, for He alone cleanses man inwardly from sin, as Augustine says (Contra Donatist. v, 21). Therefore it seems that God alone absolves from sin. Therefore the priest should say not: "I absolve thee," as neither does he say: "I remit thy sins."

Obj. 4: Further, just as our Lord gave His disciples the power to absolve from sins, so also did He give them the power "to heal infirmities," "to cast out devils," and "to cure diseases" (Matt. 10:1; Luke 9:1). Now the apostles, in healing the sick, did not use the words: "I heal thee," but: "The Lord Jesus Christ heal [Vulg.: 'heals'] thee," as Peter said to the palsied man (Acts 9:34). Therefore since priests have the power which Christ gave His apostles, it seems that they should not use the form: "I absolve thee," but: "May Christ absolve thee."

Obj. 5: Further, some explain this form by stating that when they say: "I absolve thee," they mean "I declare you to be absolved." But neither can this be done by a priest unless it be revealed to him by God, wherefore, as we read in Matt. 16:19 before it was said to Peter: "Whatsoever thou shalt bind upon earth," etc., it was said to him (Matt. 16:17): "Blessed art thou Simon Bar-Jona: because flesh and blood have not revealed it to thee, but My Father Who is in heaven." Therefore it seems presumptuous for a priest, who has received no revelation on the matter, to say: "I absolve thee," even if this be explained to mean: "I declare thee absolved."

*On the contrary,* As our Lord said to His disciples (Matt. 28:19): "Going . . . teach ye all nations, baptizing them," etc., so did He say to Peter (Matt. 16:19): "Whatsoever thou shalt loose on earth," etc. Now the priest, relying on the authority of those words of Christ, says: "I baptize thee." Therefore on the same authority he should say in this sacrament: "I absolve thee."

*I answer that,* The perfection of a thing is ascribed to its form. Now it has been stated above (A. 1, ad 2) that this sacrament is perfected by that which is done by the priest. Wherefore the part taken by the penitent, whether it consist of words or deeds, must needs be the matter of this sacrament, while the part taken by the priest, takes the place of the form.

Now since the sacraments of the New Law accomplish what they signify, as stated above (Q. 62, A. 1, ad 1), it behooves the sacramental form to signify the sacramental effect in a manner that is in keeping with the matter. Hence the form of Baptism is: "I baptize thee," and the form of Confirmation is: "I sign thee with the sign of the cross, and I confirm thee with the chrism of salvation," because these sacraments are perfected in the use of their matter: while in the sacrament of the Eucharist, which consists in the very consecration of the matter, the reality of the consecration is expressed in the words: "This is My Body."

Now this sacrament, namely the sacrament of Penance, consists not in the consecration of a matter, nor in the use of a hallowed matter, but rather in the removal of a certain matter, viz. sin, in so far as sins are said to be the matter of Penance, as explained above (A. 2). This removal is expressed by the priest saying: "I absolve thee": because sins are fetters, according to Prov. 5:22. "His own iniquities catch the wicked, and he is fast bound with the ropes of his own sins." Wherefore it is evident that this is the most fitting form of this sacrament: "I absolve thee."

Reply Obj. 1: This form is taken from Christ's very words which He addressed to Peter (Matt. 16:19): "Whatsoever thou shalt loose on earth," etc., and such is the form employed by the Church in sacramental absolution. But such absolutions as are given in public are not sacramental, but are prayers for the remission of venial sins. Wherefore in giving sacramental absolution it would not suffice to say: "May Almighty God have mercy on thee," or: "May God grant thee absolution and forgiveness," because by such words the priest does not signify the giving of absolution, but prays that it may be given. Nevertheless the above prayer is said before the sacramental absolution is given, lest the sacramental effect be hindered on the part of the penitent, whose acts are as matter in this sacrament, but not in Baptism or Confirmation.

Reply Obj. 2: The words of Leo are to be understood of the prayer that precedes the absolution, and do not exclude the fact that the priest pronounces absolution.

Reply Obj. 3: God alone absolves from sin and forgives sins authoritatively; yet priests do both ministerially, because the words of the priest in this sacrament work as instruments of the Divine power, as in the other sacraments: because it is the Divine power that works inwardly in all the sacramental signs, be they things or words, as shown above (Q. 62, A. 4; Q. 64, AA. 1, 2). Wherefore our Lord expressed both: for He said to Peter (Matt. 16:19): "Whatsoever thou shalt loose on earth," etc., and to His disciples (John 20:23): "Whose sins you shall forgive, they are forgiven them." Yet the priest says: "I absolve thee," rather than: "I forgive thee thy sins," because it is more in keeping with the words of our Lord, by expressing the power of the keys whereby priests absolve. Nevertheless, since the priest absolves ministerially, something is suitably added in reference to the supreme authority of God, by the priest saying: "I absolve thee in the name of the Father, and of the Son, and of the Holy Ghost," or by the power of Christ's Passion, or by the authority of God. However, as this is not defined by the words of Christ, as it is for Baptism, this addition is left to the discretion of the priest.

Reply Obj. 4: Power was given to the apostles, not that they themselves might heal the sick, but that the sick might be healed at the prayer of the apostles: whereas power was given to them to work instrumentally or ministerially in the sacraments; wherefore they could express their own agency in the sacramental forms rather than in the healing of infirmities. Nevertheless in the latter case they did not always use the deprecatory form, but sometimes employed the indicative or imperative: thus we read (Acts 3:6) that Peter said to the lame man: "What I have, I give thee: In the name of Jesus Christ of Nazareth, arise and walk."

Reply Obj. 5: It is true in a sense that the words, "I absolve thee" mean "I declare thee absolved," but this explanation is incomplete. Because the sacraments of the New Law not only signify, but effect what they signify. Wherefore, just as the priest in baptizing anyone, declares by deed and word that the person is washed inwardly, and this not only significatively but also effectively, so also when he says: "I absolve thee," he declares the man to be absolved not only significatively but also effectively. And yet he does not speak as of something uncertain, because just as the other sacraments of the New Law have, of themselves, a sure effect through the power of Christ's Passion, which effect, nevertheless, may be impeded on the part of the recipient, so is it with this sacrament. Hence Augustine says (De Adult. Conjug. ii): "There is nothing disgraceful or onerous in the reconciliation of husband and wife, when adultery committed has been washed away, since there is no doubt that remission of sins is granted through the keys of the kingdom of heaven." Consequently there is no need for a special revelation to be made to the priest, but the general revelation of faith suffices, through which sins are forgiven. Hence the revelation of faith is said to have been made to Peter.

It would be a more complete explanation to say that the words, "I absolve thee" mean: "I grant thee the sacrament of absolution."

FOURTH ARTICLE [III, Q. 84, Art. 4]

Whether the Imposition of the Priest's Hands Is Necessary for This Sacrament?

Objection 1: It would seem that the imposition of the priest's hands is necessary for this sacrament. For it is written (Mk. 16:18): "They shall lay hands upon the sick, and they shall recover." Now sinners are sick spiritually, and obtain recovery through this sacrament. Therefore an imposition of hands should be made in this sacrament.

Obj. 2: Further, in this sacrament man regains the Holy Ghost Whom he had lost, wherefore it is said in the person of the penitent (Ps. 1:14): "Restore unto me the joy of Thy salvation, and strengthen me with a perfect spirit." Now the Holy Ghost is given by the imposition of hands; for we read (Acts 8:17) that the apostles "laid their hands upon them, and they received the Holy Ghost"; and (Matt. 19:13) that "little children were presented" to our Lord, "that He should impose hands upon them." Therefore an imposition of hands should be made in this sacrament.

Obj. 3: Further, the priest's words are not more efficacious in this than in the other sacraments. But in the other sacraments the words of the minister do not suffice, unless he perform some action: thus, in Baptism, the priest while saying: "I baptize thee," has to perform a bodily washing. Therefore, also while saying: "I absolve thee," the priest should perform some action in regard to the penitent, by laying hands on him.

*On the contrary,* When our Lord said to Peter (Matt. 16:19): "Whatsoever thou shalt loose on earth," etc., He made no mention of an imposition of hands; nor did He when He said to all the apostles (John 20:13): "Whose sins you shall forgive, they are forgiven them." Therefore no imposition of hands is required for this sacrament.

*I answer that,* In the sacraments of the Church the imposition of hands is made, to signify some abundant effect of grace, through those on whom the hands are laid being, as it were, united to the ministers in whom grace should be plentiful. Wherefore an imposition of hands is made in the sacrament of Confirmation, wherein the fulness of the Holy Ghost is conferred; and in the sacrament of order, wherein is bestowed a certain excellence of power over the Divine mysteries; hence it is written (2 Tim. 1:6): "Stir up the grace of God which is in thee, by the imposition of my hands."

Now the sacrament of Penance is ordained, not that man may receive some abundance of grace, but that his sins may be taken away; and therefore no imposition of hands is required for this sacrament, as neither is there for Baptism, wherein nevertheless a fuller remission of sins is bestowed.

Reply Obj. 1: That imposition of hands is not sacramental, but is intended for the working of miracles, namely, that by the contact of a sanctified man's hand, even bodily infirmity might be removed; even as we read of our Lord (Mk. 6:5) that He cured the sick, "laying His hands upon them," and (Matt. 8:3) that He cleansed a leper by touching him.

Reply Obj. 2: It is not every reception of the Holy Ghost that requires an imposition of hands, since even in Baptism man receives the Holy Ghost, without any imposition of hands: it is at the reception of the fulness of the Holy Ghost which belongs to Confirmation that an imposition of hands is required.

Reply Obj. 3: In those sacraments which are perfected in the use of the matter, the minister has to perform some bodily action on the recipient of the sacrament, e.g. in Baptism, Confirmation, and Extreme Unction; whereas this sacrament does not consist in the use of matter employed outwardly, the matter being supplied by the part taken by the penitent: wherefore, just as in the Eucharist the priest perfects the sacrament by merely pronouncing the words over the matter, so the mere words which the priest while absolving pronounces over the penitent perfect the sacrament of absolution. If, indeed, any bodily act were necessary on the part of the priest, the sign of the cross, which is employed in the Eucharist, would not be less becoming than the imposition of hands, in token that sins are forgiven through the blood of Christ crucified; and yet this is not essential to this sacrament as neither is it to the Eucharist.

FIFTH ARTICLE [III, Q. 84, Art. 5]

Whether This Sacrament Is Necessary for Salvation?

Objection 1: It would seem that this sacrament is not necessary for salvation. Because on Ps. 125:5, "They that sow in tears," etc., the gloss says: "Be not sorrowful, if thou hast a good will, of which peace is the meed." But sorrow is essential to Penance, according to 2 Cor. 7:10: "The sorrow that is according to God worketh penance steadfast unto salvation." Therefore a good will without Penance suffices for salvation.

Obj. 2: Further, it is written (Prov. 10:12): "Charity covereth all sins," and further on (Prov. 15:27): "By mercy and faith sins are purged away." But this sacrament is for nothing else but the purging of sins. Therefore if one has charity, faith, and mercy, one can obtain salvation, without the sacrament of Penance.

Obj. 3: Further, the sacraments of the Church take their origin from the institution of Christ. But according to John 8 Christ absolved the adulterous woman without Penance. Therefore it seems that Penance is not necessary for salvation.

*On the contrary,* our Lord said (Luke 13:3): "Unless you shall do penance, you shall all likewise perish."

*I answer that,* A thing is necessary for salvation in two ways: first, absolutely; secondly, on a supposition. A thing is absolutely necessary for salvation, if no one can obtain salvation without it, as, for example, the grace of Christ, and the sacrament of Baptism, whereby a man is born again in Christ. The sacrament of Penance is necessary on a supposition, for it is necessary, not for all, but for those who are in sin. For it is written (2 Paral. 37 [*The prayer of Manasses, among the Apocrypha]), "Thou, Lord, God of the righteous, hast not appointed repentance to the righteous, to Abraham, Isaac and Jacob, nor to those who sinned not against Thee." But "sin, when it is completed, begetteth death" (James 1:15). Consequently it is necessary for the sinner's salvation that sin be taken away from him; which cannot be done without the sacrament of Penance, wherein the power of Christ's Passion operates through the priest's absolution and the acts of the penitent, who co-operates with grace unto the destruction of his sin. For as Augustine says (Tract. lxxii in Joan. [*Implicitly in the passage referred to, but explicitly Serm. xv de verb. Apost.]), "He Who created thee without thee, will not justify thee without thee." Therefore it is evident that after sin the sacrament of Penance is necessary for salvation, even as bodily medicine after man has contracted a dangerous disease.

Reply Obj. 1: This gloss should apparently be understood as referring to the man who has a good will unimpaired by sin, for such a man has no cause for sorrow: but as soon as the good will is forfeited through sin, it cannot be restored without that sorrow whereby a man sorrows for his past sin, and which belongs to Penance.

Reply Obj. 2: As soon as a man falls into sin, charity, faith, and mercy do not deliver him from sin, without Penance. Because charity demands that a man should grieve for the offense committed against his friend, and that he should be anxious to make satisfaction to his friend; faith requires that he should seek to be justified from his sins through the power of Christ's Passion which operates in the sacraments of the Church; and well-ordered pity necessitates that man should succor himself by repenting of the pitiful condition into which sin has brought him, according to Prov. 14:34: "Sin maketh nations miserable"; wherefore it is written (Ecclus. 30:24): "Have pity on thy own soul, pleasing God."

Reply Obj. 3: It was due to His power of excellence, which He alone had, as stated above (Q. 64, A. 3), that Christ bestowed on the adulterous woman the effect of the sacrament of Penance, viz. the forgiveness of sins, without the sacrament of Penance, although not without internal repentance, which He operated in her by grace.

SIXTH ARTICLE [III, Q. 84, Art. 6]

Whether Penance Is a Second Plank After Shipwreck?

Objection 1: It would seem that Penance is not a second plank after shipwreck. Because on Isa. 3:9, "They have proclaimed abroad their sin as Sodom," a gloss says: "The second plank after shipwreck is to hide one's sins." Now Penance does not hide sins, but reveals them. Therefore Penance is not a second plank.

Obj. 2: Further, in a building the foundation takes the first, not the second place. Now in the spiritual edifice, Penance is the foundation, according to Heb. 6:1: "Not laying again the foundation of Penance from dead works"; wherefore it precedes even Baptism, according to Acts 2:38: "Do penance, and be baptized every one of you." Therefore Penance should not be called a second plank.

Obj. 3: Further, all the sacraments are planks, i.e. helps against sin. Now Penance holds, not the second but the fourth, place among the sacraments, as is clear from what has been said above (Q. 65, AA. 1, 2). Therefore Penance should not be called a second plank after shipwreck.

*On the contrary,* Jerome says (Ep. cxxx) that "Penance is a second plank after shipwreck."

*I answer that,* That which is of itself precedes naturally that which is accidental, as substance precedes accident. Now some sacraments are, of themselves, ordained to man's salvation, e.g. Baptism, which is the spiritual birth, Confirmation which is the spiritual growth, the Eucharist which is the spiritual food; whereas Penance is ordained to man's salvation accidentally as it were, and on something being supposed, viz. sin: for unless man were to sin actually, he would not stand in need of Penance and yet he would need Baptism, Confirmation, and the Eucharist; even as in the life of the body, man would need no medical treatment, unless he were ill, and yet life, birth, growth, and food are, of themselves, necessary to man.

Consequently Penance holds the second place with regard to the state of integrity which is bestowed and safeguarded by the aforesaid sacraments, so that it is called metaphorically "a second plank after shipwreck." For just as the first help for those who cross the sea is to be safeguarded in a whole ship, while the second help when the ship is wrecked, is to cling to a plank; so too the first help in this life's ocean is that man safeguard his integrity, while the second help is, if he lose his integrity through sin, that he regain it by means of Penance.

Reply Obj. 1: To hide one's sins may happen in two ways: first, in the very act of sinning. Now it is worse to sin in public than in private, both because a public sinner seems to sin more from contempt, and because by sinning he gives scandal to others. Consequently in sin it is a kind of remedy to sin secretly, and it is in this sense that the gloss says that "to hide one's sins is a second plank after shipwreck"; not that it takes away sin, as Penance does, but because it makes the sin less grievous. Secondly, one hides one's sin previously committed, by neglecting to confess it: this is opposed to Penance, and to hide one's sins thus is not a second plank, but is the reverse, since it is written (Prov. 28:13): "He that hideth his sins shall not prosper."

Reply Obj. 2: Penance cannot be called the foundation of the spiritual edifice simply, i.e. in the first building thereof; but it is the foundation in the second building which is accomplished by destroying sin, because man, on his return to God, needs Penance first. However, the Apostle is speaking there of the foundation of spiritual doctrine. Moreover, the penance which precedes Baptism is not the sacrament of Penance.

Reply Obj. 3: The three sacraments which precede Penance refer to the ship in its integrity, i.e. to man's state of integrity, with regard to which Penance is called a second plank.

SEVENTH ARTICLE [III, Q. 84, Art. 7]

Whether This Sacrament Was Suitably Instituted in the New Law?

Objection 1: It would seem that this sacrament was unsuitably instituted in the New Law. Because those things which belong to the natural law need not to be instituted. Now it belongs to the natural law that one should repent of the evil one has done: for it is impossible to love good without grieving for its contrary. Therefore Penance was unsuitably instituted in the New Law.

Obj. 2: Further, that which existed in the Old Law had not to be instituted in the New. Now there was Penance in the old Law wherefore the Lord complains (Jer. 8:6) saying: "There is none that doth penance for his sin, saying: What have I done?" Therefore Penance should not have been instituted in the New Law.

Obj. 3: Further, Penance comes after Baptism, since it is a second plank, as stated above (A. 6). Now it seems that our Lord instituted Penance before Baptism, because we read that at the beginning of His preaching He said (Matt. 4:17): "Do penance, for the kingdom of heaven is at hand." Therefore this sacrament was not suitably instituted in the New Law.

Obj. 4: Further, the sacraments of the New Law were instituted by Christ, by Whose power they work, as stated above (Q. 62, A. 5; Q. 64, A. 1). But Christ does not seem to have instituted this sacrament, since He made no use of it, as of the other sacraments which He instituted. Therefore this sacrament was unsuitably instituted in the New Law.

*On the contrary,* our Lord said (Luke 24:46, 47): "It behooved Christ to suffer, and to rise again from the dead the third day: and that penance and remission of sins should be preached in His name unto all nations."

*I answer that,* As stated above (A. 1, ad 1, ad 2), in this sacrament the acts of the penitent are as matter, while the part taken by the priest, who works as Christ's minister, is the formal and completive element of the sacrament. Now in the other sacraments the matter pre-exists, being provided by nature, as water, or by art, as bread: but that such and such a matter be employed for a sacrament requires to be decided by the institution; while the sacrament derives its form and power entirely from the institution of Christ, from Whose Passion the power of the sacraments proceeds.

Accordingly the matter of this sacrament pre-exists, being provided by nature; since it is by a natural principle of reason that man is moved to repent of the evil he has done: yet it is due to Divine institution that man does penance in this or that way. Wherefore at the outset of His preaching, our Lord admonished men, not only to repent, but also to "do penance," thus pointing to the particular manner of actions required for this sacrament. As to the part to be taken by the ministers, this was fixed by our Lord when He said to Peter (Matt. 16:19): "To thee will I give the keys of the kingdom of heaven," etc.; but it was after His resurrection that He made known the efficacy of this sacrament and the source of its power, when He said (Luke 24:47) that "penance and remission of sins should be preached in His name unto all nations," after speaking of His Passion and resurrection. Because it is from the power of the name of Jesus Christ suffering and rising again that this sacrament is efficacious unto the remission of sins.

It is therefore evident that this sacrament was suitably instituted in the New Law.

Reply Obj. 1: It is a natural law that one should repent of the evil one has done, by grieving for having done it, and by seeking a remedy for one's grief in some way or other, and also that one should show some signs of grief, even as the Ninevites did, as we read in John 3. And yet even in their case there was also something of faith which they had received through Jonas' preaching, inasmuch as they did these things in the hope that they would receive pardon from God, according as we read (John 3:9): "Who can tell if God will turn and forgive, and will turn away from His fierce anger, and we shall not perish?" But just as other matters which are of the natural law were fixed in detail by the institution of the Divine law, as we have stated in the Second Part (I-II, Q. 91, A. 4; I-II, Q. 95, A. 2; Q. 99), so was it with Penance.

Reply Obj. 2: Things which are of the natural law were determined in various ways in the Old and in the New Law, in keeping with the imperfection of the Old, and the perfection of the New. Wherefore Penance was fixed in a certain way in the Old Law--with regard to sorrow, that it should be in the heart rather than in external signs, according to Joel 2:13: "Rend your hearts and not your garments"; and with regard to seeking a remedy for sorrow, that they should in some way confess their sins, at least in general, to God's ministers. Wherefore the Lord said (Lev. 5:17, 18): "If anyone sin through ignorance . . . he shall offer of the flocks a ram without blemish to the priest, according to the measure and estimation of the sin, and the priest shall pray for him, because he did it ignorantly, and it shall be forgiven him"; since by the very fact of making an offering for his sin, a man, in a fashion, confessed his sin to the priest. And accordingly it is written (Prov. 28:13): "He that hideth his sins, shall not prosper: but he that shall confess, and forsake them, shall obtain mercy." Not yet, however, was the power of the keys instituted, which is derived from Christ's Passion, and consequently it was not yet ordained that a man should grieve for his sin, with the purpose of submitting himself by confession and satisfaction to the keys of the Church, in the hope of receiving forgiveness through the power of Christ's Passion.

Reply Obj. 3: If we note carefully what our Lord said about the necessity of Baptism (John 3:3, seqq.), we shall see that this was said before His words about the necessity of Penance (Matt. 4:17); because He spoke to Nicodemus about Baptism before the imprisonment of John, of whom it is related afterwards (John 3:23, 24) that he baptized, whereas His words about Penance were said after John was cast into prison.

If, however, He had admonished men to do penance before admonishing them to be baptized, this would be because also before Baptism some kind of penance is required, according to the words of Peter (Acts 2:38): "Do penance, and be baptized, every one of you."

Reply Obj. 4: Christ did not use the Baptism which He instituted, but was baptized with the baptism of John, as stated above (Q. 39, AA. 1, 2). Nor did He use it actively by administering it Himself, because He "did not baptize" as a rule, "but His disciples" did, as related in John 4:2, although it is to be believed that He baptized His disciples, as Augustine asserts (Ep. cclxv, ad Seleuc.). But with regard to His institution of this sacrament it was nowise fitting that He should use it, neither by repenting Himself, in Whom there was no sin, nor by administering the sacrament to others, since, in order to show His mercy and power, He was wont to confer the effect of this sacrament without the sacrament itself, as stated above (A. 5, ad 3). On the other hand, He both received and gave to others the sacrament of the Eucharist, both in order to commend the excellence of that sacrament, and because that sacrament is a memorial of His Passion, in which Christ is both priest and victim.

EIGHTH ARTICLE [III, Q. 84, Art. 8]

Whether Penance Should Last Till the End of Life?

Objection 1: It would seem that Penance should not last till the end of life. Because Penance is ordained for the blotting out of sin. Now the penitent receives forgiveness of his sins at once, according to Ezech. 18:21: "If the wicked do penance for all his sins which he hath committed . . . he shall live and shall not die." Therefore there is no need for Penance to be further prolonged.

Obj. 2: Further, Penance belongs to the state of beginners. But man ought to advance from that state to the state of the proficient, and, from this, on to the state of the perfect. Therefore man need not do Penance till the end of his life.

Obj. 3: Further, man is bound to observe the laws of the Church in this as in the other sacraments. But the duration of repentance is fixed by the canons, so that, to wit, for such and such a sin one is bound to do penance for so many years. Therefore it seems that Penance should not be prolonged till the end of life.

*On the contrary,* Augustine says in his book, De Poenitentia [*De vera et falsa Poenitentia, the authorship of which is unknown]: "What remains for us to do, save to sorrow ever in this life? For when sorrow ceases, repentance fails; and if repentance fails, what becomes of pardon?"

*I answer that,* Penance is twofold, internal and

external. Internal penance is that whereby one grieves for a sin one has committed, and this penance should last until the end of life. Because man should always be displeased at having sinned, for if he were to be pleased thereat, he would for this very reason fall into sin and lose the fruit of pardon. Now displeasure causes sorrow in one who is susceptible to sorrow, as man is in this life; but after this life the saints are not susceptible to sorrow, wherefore they will be displeased at, without sorrowing for, their past sins, according to Isa. 65:16. "The former distresses are forgotten."

External penance is that whereby a man shows external signs of sorrow, confesses his sins verbally to the priest who absolves him, and makes satisfaction for his sins according to the judgment of the priest. Such penance need not last until the end of life, but only for a fixed time according to the measure of the sin.

Reply Obj. 1: True penance not only removes past sins, but also preserves man from future sins. Consequently, although a man receives forgiveness of past sins in the first instant of his true penance, nevertheless he must persevere in his penance, lest he fall again into sin.

Reply Obj. 2: To do penance both internal and external belongs to the state of beginners, of those, to wit, who are making a fresh start from the state of sin. But there is room for internal penance even in the proficient and the perfect, according to Ps. 83:7: "In his heart he hath disposed to ascend by steps, in the vale of tears." Wherefore Paul says (1 Cor. 15:9): "I . . . am not worthy to be called an apostle because I persecuted the Church of God."

Reply Obj. 3: These durations of time are fixed for penitents as regards the exercise of external penance.

NINTH ARTICLE [III, Q. 84, Art. 9]

Whether Penance Can Be Continuous?

Objection 1: It would seem that penance cannot be continuous. For it is written (Jer. 31:16): "Let thy voice cease from weeping, and thy eyes from tears." But this would be impossible if penance were continuous, for it consists in weeping and tears. Therefore penance cannot be continuous.

Obj. 2: Further, man ought to rejoice at every good work, according to Ps. 99:1: "Serve ye the Lord with gladness." Now to do penance is a good work. Therefore man should rejoice at it. But man cannot rejoice and grieve at the same time, as the Philosopher declares (Ethic. ix, 4). Therefore a penitent cannot grieve continually for his past sins, which is essential to penance. Therefore penance cannot be continuous.

Obj. 3: Further, the Apostle says (2 Cor. 2:7): "Comfort him," viz. the penitent, "lest perhaps such an one be swallowed up with overmuch sorrow." But comfort dispels grief, which is essential to penance. Therefore penance need not be continuous.

*On the contrary,* Augustine says in his book on Penance [*De vera et falsa Poenitentia, the authorship of which is unknown]: "In doing penance grief should be continual."

*I answer that,* One is said to repent in two ways, actually and habitually. It is impossible for a man continually to repent actually, for the acts, whether internal or external, of a penitent must needs be interrupted by sleep and other things which the body needs. Secondly, a man is said to repent habitually. And thus he should repent continually, both by never doing anything contrary to penance, so as to destroy the habitual disposition of the penitent, and by being resolved that his past sins should always be displeasing to him.

Reply Obj. 1: Weeping and tears belong to the act of external penance, and this act needs neither to be continuous, nor to last until the end of life, as stated above (A. 8): wherefore it is significantly added: "For there is a reward for thy work." Now the reward of the penitent's work is the full remission of sin both as to guilt and as to punishment; and after receiving this reward there is no need for man to proceed to acts of external penance. This, however, does not prevent penance being continual, as explained above.

Reply Obj. 2: Of sorrow and joy we may speak in two ways: first, as being passions of the sensitive appetite; and thus they can nowise be together, since they are altogether contrary to one another, either on the part of the object (as when they have the same object), or at least on the part of the movement, for joy is with expansion [*Cf. I-II, Q. 33, A. 1] of the heart, whereas sorrow is with contraction; and it is in this sense that the Philosopher speaks in Ethic. ix. Secondly, we may speak of joy and sorrow as being simple acts of the will, to which something is pleasing or displeasing. Accordingly, they cannot be contrary to one another, except on the part of the object, as when they concern the same object in the same respect, in which way joy and sorrow cannot be simultaneous, because the same thing in the same respect cannot be pleasing and displeasing. If, on the other hand, joy and sorrow, understood thus, be not of the same object in the same respect, but either of different objects, or of the same object in different respects, in that case joy and sorrow are not contrary to one another, so that nothing hinders a man from being joyful and sorrowful at the same time--for instance, if we see a good man suffer, we both rejoice at his goodness and at the same time grieve for his suffering. In this way a man may be displeased at having sinned, and be pleased at his displeasure together with his hope for pardon, so that his very sorrow is a matter of joy. Hence Augustine says [*De vera et falsa Poenitentia, the authorship of which is unknown]: "The penitent should ever grieve and rejoice at his grief."

If, however, sorrow were altogether incompatible with joy, this would prevent the continuance, not of habitual penance, but only of actual penance.

Reply Obj. 3: According to the Philosopher (Ethic. ii, 3, 6, 7, 9) it belongs to virtue to establish the mean in the passions. Now the sorrow which, in the sensitive appetite of the penitent, arises from the displeasure of his will, is a passion; wherefore it should be moderated according to virtue, and if it be excessive it is sinful, because it leads to despair, as the Apostle teaches (2 Cor. 2:7), saying: "Lest such an one be swallowed up with overmuch sorrow." Accordingly comfort, of which the Apostle speaks, moderates sorrow but does not destroy it altogether.

TENTH ARTICLE [III, Q. 84, Art. 10]

Whether the Sacrament of Penance May Be Repeated?

Objection 1: It would seem that the sacrament of Penance should not be repeated. For the Apostle says (Heb. 6:4, seqq.): "It is impossible for those, who were once illuminated, have tasted also the heavenly gift, and were made partakers of the Holy Ghost . . . and are fallen away, to be renewed again to penance." Now whosoever have done penance, have been illuminated, and have received the gift of the Holy Ghost. Therefore whosoever sin after doing penance, cannot do penance again.

Obj. 2: Further, Ambrose says (De Poenit. ii): "Some are to be found who think they ought often to do penance, who take liberties with Christ: for if they were truly penitent, they would not think of doing penance over again, since there is but one Penance even as there is but one Baptism." Now Baptism is not repeated. Neither, therefore, is Penance to be repeated.

Obj. 3: Further, the miracles whereby our Lord healed bodily diseases, signify the healing of spiritual diseases, whereby men are delivered from sins. Now we do not read that our Lord restored the sight to any blind man twice, or that He cleansed any leper twice, or twice raised any dead man to life. Therefore it seems that He does not twice grant pardon to any sinner.

Obj. 4: Further, Gregory says (Hom. xxxiv in Evang.): "Penance consists in deploring past sins, and in not committing again those we have deplored": and Isidore says (De Summo Bono ii): "He is a mocker and no penitent who still does what he has repented of." If, therefore, a man is truly penitent, he will not sin again. Therefore Penance cannot be repeated.

Obj. 5: Further, just as Baptism derives its efficacy from the Passion of Christ, so does Penance. Now Baptism is not repeated, on account of the unity of Christ's Passion and death. Therefore in like manner Penance is not repeated.

Obj. 6: Further, Ambrose says on Ps. 118:58, "I entreated Thy face," etc., that "facility of obtaining pardon is an incentive to sin." If, therefore, God frequently grants pardon through Penance, it seems that He affords man an incentive to sin, and thus He seems to take pleasure in sin, which is contrary to His goodness. Therefore Penance cannot be repeated.

*On the contrary,* Man is induced to be merciful by the example of Divine mercy, according to Luke 6:36: "Be ye . . . merciful, as your Father also is merciful." Now our Lord commanded His disciples to be merciful by frequently pardoning their brethren who had sinned against them; wherefore, as related in Matt. 18:21, when Peter asked: "How often shall my brother off end against me, and I forgive him? till seven times?" Jesus answered: "I say not to thee, till seven times, but till seventy times seven times." Therefore also God over and over again, through Penance, grants pardon to sinners, especially as He teaches us to pray (Matt. 6:12): "Forgive us our trespasses, as we forgive them that trespass against us."

*I answer that,* As regards Penance, some have erred, saying that a man cannot obtain pardon of his sins through Penance a second time. Some of these, viz. the Novatians, went so far as to say that he who sins after the first Penance which is done in Baptism, cannot be restored again through Penance. There were also other heretics who, as Augustine relates in De Poenitentia [*De vera et falsa Poenitentia, the authorship of which is unknown], said that, after Baptism, Penance is useful, not many times, but only once.

These errors seem to have arisen from a twofold source: first from not knowing the nature of true Penance. For since true Penance requires charity, without which sins are not taken away, they thought that charity once possessed could not be lost, and that, consequently, Penance, if true, could never be removed by sin, so that it should be necessary to repeat it. But this was refuted in the Second Part (II, Q. 24, A. 11), where it was shown that on account of free-will charity, once possessed, can be lost, and that, consequently, after true Penance, a man can sin mortally.--Secondly, they erred in their estimation of the gravity of sin. For they deemed a sin committed by a man after he had received pardon, to be so grave that it could not be forgiven. In this they erred not only with regard to sin which, even after a sin has been forgiven, can be either more or less grievous than the first, which was forgiven, but much more did they err against the infinity of Divine mercy, which surpasses any number and magnitude of sins, according to Ps. 50:1, 2: "Have mercy on me, O God, according to Thy great mercy: and according to the multitude of Thy tender mercies, blot out my iniquity." Wherefore the words of Cain were reprehensible, when he said (Gen. 4:13): "My iniquity is greater than that I may deserve pardon." And so God's mercy, through Penance, grants pardon to sinners without any end, wherefore it is written (2 Paralip. 37 [*Prayer of Manasses, among the Apocrypha. St. Thomas is evidently quoting from memory, and omits the words in brackets.]): "Thy merciful promise is unmeasurable and unsearchable . . . (and Thou repentest) for the evil brought upon man." It is therefore evident that Penance can be repeated many times.

Reply Obj. 1: Some of the Jews thought that a man could be washed several times in the laver of Baptism, because among them the Law prescribed certain washing-places where they were wont to cleanse themselves repeatedly from their uncleannesses. In order to disprove this the Apostle wrote to the Hebrews that "it is impossible for those who were once illuminated," viz. through Baptism, "to be renewed again to penance," viz. through Baptism, which is "the laver of regeneration, and renovation of the Holy Ghost," as stated in Titus 3:5: and he declares the reason to be that by Baptism man dies with Christ, wherefore he adds (Heb. 6:6): "Crucifying again to themselves the Son of God."

Reply Obj. 2: Ambrose is speaking of solemn Penance, which is not repeated in the Church, as we shall state further on (Suppl., Q. 28, A. 2).

Reply Obj. 3: As Augustine says [*De vera et falsa Poenitentia, the authorship of which is unknown], "Our Lord gave sight to many blind men at various times, and strength to many infirm, thereby showing, in these different men, that the same sins are repeatedly forgiven, at one time healing a man from leprosy and afterwards from blindness. For this reason He healed so many stricken with fever, so many feeble in body, so many lame, blind, and withered, that the sinner might not despair; for this reason He is not described as healing anyone but once, that every one might fear to link himself with sin; for this reason He declares Himself to be the physician welcomed not of the hale, but of the unhealthy. What sort of a physician is he who knows not how to heal a recurring disease? For if a man ail a hundred times it is for the physician to heal him a hundred times: and if he failed where others succeed, he would be a poor physician in comparison with them."

Reply Obj. 4: Penance is to deplore past sins, and, while deploring them, not to commit again, either by act or by intention, those which we have to deplore. Because a man is a mocker and not a penitent, who, while doing penance, does what he repents having done, or intends to do again what he did before, or even commits actually the same or another kind of sin. But if a man sin afterwards either by act or intention, this does not destroy the fact that his former penance was real, because the reality of a former act is never destroyed by a subsequent contrary act: for even as he truly ran who afterwards sits, so he truly repented who subsequently sins.

Reply Obj. 5: Baptism derives its power from Christ's Passion, as a spiritual regeneration, with a spiritual death, of a previous life. Now "it is appointed unto man once to die" (Heb. 9:27), and to be born once, wherefore man should be baptized but once. On the other hand, Penance derives its power from Christ's Passion, as a spiritual medicine, which can be repeated frequently.

Reply Obj. 6: According to Augustine (De vera et falsa Poenitentia, the authorship of which is unknown), "it is evident that sins displease God exceedingly, for He is always ready to destroy them, lest what He created should perish, and what He loved be lost," viz. by despair.

## QUESTION 85

OF PENANCE AS A VIRTUE (In Six Articles)

We must now consider penance as a virtue, under which head there are six points of inquiry:

(1) Whether penance is a virtue?
(2) Whether it is a special virtue?
(3) To what species of virtue does it belong?
(4) Of its subject;
(5) Of its cause;
(6) Of its relation to the other virtues.

FIRST ARTICLE [III, Q. 85, Art. 1]

Whether Penance Is a Virtue?

Objection 1: It would seem that penance is not a virtue. For penance is a sacrament numbered among the other sacraments, as was shown above (Q. 84, A. 1; Q. 65, A. 1). Now no other sacrament is a virtue. Therefore neither is penance a virtue.

Obj. 2: Further, according to the Philosopher (Ethic. iv, 9), "shame is not a virtue," both because it is a passion accompanied by a bodily alteration, and because it is not the disposition of a perfect thing, since it is about an evil act, so that it has no place in a virtuous man. Now, in like manner, penance is a passion accompanied by a bodily alteration, viz. tears, according to Gregory, who says (Hom. xxxiv in Evang.) that "penance consists in deploring past sins": moreover it is about evil deeds, viz. sins, which have no place in a virtuous man. Therefore penance is not a virtue.

Obj. 3: Further, according to the Philosopher (Ethic. iv, 3), "no virtuous man is foolish." But it seems foolish to deplore what has been done in the past, since it cannot be otherwise, and yet this is what we understand by penance. Therefore penance is not a virtue.

*On the contrary,* The precepts of the Law are about acts of virtue, because "a lawgiver intends to make the citizens virtuous" (Ethic. ii, 1). But there is a precept about penance in the Divine law, according to Matt. 4:17: "Do penance," etc. Therefore penance is a virtue.

*I answer that,* As stated above (Obj. 2; Q. 84, A. 10, ad 4), to repent is to deplore something one has done. Now it has been stated above (Q. 84, A. 9) that sorrow or sadness is twofold. First, it denotes a passion of the sensitive appetite, and in this sense penance is not a virtue, but a passion. Secondly, it denotes an act of the will, and in this way it implies choice, and if this be right, it must, of necessity, be an act of virtue. For it is stated in Ethic. ii, 6 that virtue is a habit of choosing according to right reason. Now it belongs to right reason than one should grieve for a proper object of grief as one ought to grieve, and for an end for which one ought to grieve. And this is observed in the penance of which we are speaking now; since the penitent assumes a moderated grief for his past sins, with the intention of removing them. Hence it is evident that the penance of which we are speaking now, is either a virtue or the act of a virtue.

Reply Obj. 1: As stated above (Q. 84, A. 1, ad 1; AA. 2, 3), in the sacrament of Penance, human acts take the place of matter, which is not the case in Baptism and Confirmation. Wherefore, since virtue is a principle of an act, penance is either a virtue or accompanies a virtue, rather than Baptism or Confirmation.

Reply Obj. 2: Penance, considered as a passion, is not a virtue, as stated above, and it is thus that it is accompanied by a bodily alteration. On the other hand, it is a virtue, according as it includes a right choice on the part of the will; which, however, applies to penance rather than to shame. Because shame regards the evil deed as present, whereas penance regards the evil deed as past. Now it is contrary to the perfection of virtue that one should have an evil deed actually present, of which one ought to be ashamed; whereas it is not contrary to the perfection of virtue that we should have previously committed evil deeds, of which it behooves us to repent, since a man from being wicked becomes virtuous.

Reply Obj. 3: It would indeed be foolish to grieve for what has already been done, with the intention of trying to make it not done. But the penitent does not intend this: for his sorrow is displeasure or disapproval with regard to the past deed, with the intention of removing its result, viz. the anger of God and the debt of punishment: and this is not foolish.

SECOND ARTICLE [III, Q. 85, Art. 2]

Whether Penance Is a Special Virtue?

Objection 1: It would seem that penance is not a special virtue. For it seems that to rejoice at the good one has done, and to grieve for the evil one has done are acts of the same nature. But joy for the good one has done is not a special virtue, but is a praiseworthy emotion proceeding from charity, as Augustine states (De Civ. Dei xiv, 7, 8, 9): wherefore the Apostle says (1 Cor. 13:6) that charity "rejoiceth not at iniquity, but rejoiceth with the truth." Therefore, in like manner, neither is penance, which is sorrow for past sins, a special virtue, but an emotion resulting from charity.

Obj. 2: Further, every special virtue has its special matter, because habits are distinguished by their acts, and acts by their objects. But penance has no special matter, because its matter is past sins in any matter whatever. Therefore penance is not a special virtue.

Obj. 3: Further, nothing is removed except by its contrary. But penance removes all sins. Therefore it is contrary to all sins, and consequently is not a special virtue.

*On the contrary,* The Law has a special precept about penance, as stated above (Q. 84, AA. 5, 7).

*I answer that,* As stated in the Second Part (I-II, Q. 54, A. 1, ad 1, A. 2), habits are specifically distinguished according to the species of their acts, so that whenever an act has a special reason for being praiseworthy, there must needs be a special habit. Now it is evident that there is a special reason for praising the act of penance, because it aims at the destruction of past sin, considered as an offense against God, which does not apply to any other virtue. We must therefore conclude that penance is a special virtue.

Reply Obj. 1: An act springs from charity in two ways: first as being elicited by charity, and a like virtuous act requires no other virtue than charity, e.g. to love the good, to rejoice therein, and to grieve for what is opposed to it. Secondly, an act springs from charity, being, so to speak, commanded by charity; and thus, since charity commands all the virtues, inasmuch as it directs them to its own end, an act springing from charity may belong even to another special virtue. Accordingly, if in the act of the penitent we consider the mere displeasure in the past sin, it belongs to charity immediately, in the same way as joy for past good acts; but the intention to aim at the destruction of past sin requires a special virtue subordinate to charity.

Reply Obj. 2: In point of fact, penance has indeed a general matter, inasmuch as it regards all sins; but it does so under a special aspect, inasmuch as they can be remedied by an act of man in co-operating with God for his justification.

Reply Obj. 3: Every special virtue removes formally the habit of the opposite vice, just as whiteness removes blackness from the same subject: but penance removes every sin effectively, inasmuch as it works for the destruction of sins, according as they are pardonable through the grace of God if man co-operate therewith. Wherefore it does not follow that it is a general virtue.

THIRD ARTICLE [III, Q. 85, Art. 3]

Whether the Virtue of Penance Is a Species of Justice?

Objection 1: It would seem that the virtue of penance is not a species of justice. For justice is not a theological but a moral virtue, as was shown in the Second Part (II-II, Q. 62, A. 3). But penance seems to be a theological virtue, since God is its object, for it makes satisfaction to God, to Whom, moreover, it reconciles the sinner. Therefore it seems that penance is not a species of justice.

Obj. 2: Further, since justice is a moral virtue it observes the mean. Now penance does not observe the mean, but rather goes to the extreme, according to Jer. 6:26: "Make thee mourning as for an only son, a bitter lamentation." Therefore penance is not a species of justice.

Obj. 3: Further, there are two species of justice, as stated in Ethic. v, 4, viz. "distributive" and "commutative." But penance does not seem to be contained under either of them. Therefore it seems that penance is not a species of justice.

Obj. 4: Further, a gloss on Luke 6:21, "Blessed are ye that weep now," says: "It is prudence that teaches us the unhappiness of earthly things and the happiness of heavenly things." But weeping is an act of penance. Therefore penance is a species of prudence rather than of justice.

*On the contrary,* Augustine says in De Poenitentia [*De vera et falsa Poenitentia, the authorship of which is unknown]: "Penance is the vengeance of the sorrowful, ever punishing in them what they are sorry for having done." But to take vengeance is an act of justice, wherefore Tully says (De Inv. Rhet. ii) that one kind of justice is called vindictive. Therefore it seems that penance is a species of justice.

*I answer that,* As stated above (A. 1, ad 2) penance is a special virtue not merely because it sorrows for evil done (since charity would suffice for that), but also because the penitent grieves for the sin he has committed, inasmuch as it is an offense against God, and purposes to amend. Now amendment for an offense committed against anyone is not made by merely ceasing to offend, but it is necessary to make some kind of compensation, which obtains in offenses committed against another, just as retribution does, only that compensation is on the part of the offender, as when he makes satisfaction, whereas retribution is on the part of the person offended against. Each of these belongs to the matter of justice, because each is a kind of commutation. Wherefore it is evident that penance, as a virtue, is a part of justice.

It must be observed, however, that according to the Philosopher (Ethic. v, 6) a thing is said to be just in two ways, simply and relatively. A thing is just simply when it is between equals, since justice is a kind of equality, and he calls this the politic or civil just, because all citizens are equal, in the point of being immediately under the ruler, retaining their freedom. But a thing is just relatively when it is between parties of whom one is subject to the other, as a servant under his master, a son under his father, a wife under her husband. It is this kind of just that we consider in penance. Wherefore the penitent has recourse to God with a purpose of amendment, as a servant to his master, according to Ps. 122:2: "Behold, as the eyes of servants are on the hands of their masters . . . so are our eyes unto the Lord our God, until He have mercy on us"; and as a son to his father, according to Luke 15:21: "Father, I have sinned against heaven and before thee"; and as a wife to her husband, according to Jer. 3:1: "Thou hast prostituted thyself to many lovers; nevertheless return to Me, saith the Lord."

Reply Obj. 1: As stated in Ethic. v, 1, justice is a virtue towards another person, and the matter of justice is not so much the person to whom justice is due as the thing which is the subject of distribution or commutation. Hence the matter of penance is not God, but human acts, whereby God is offended or appeased; whereas God is as one to whom justice is due. Wherefore it is evident that penance is not a theological virtue, because God is not its matter or object.

Reply Obj. 2: The mean of justice is the equality that is established between those between whom justice is, as stated in Ethic. v. But in certain cases perfect equality cannot be established, on account of the excellence of one, as between father and son, God and man, as the Philosopher states (Ethic. viii, 14), wherefore in such cases, he that falls short of the other must do whatever he can. Yet this will not be sufficient simply, but only according to the acceptance of the higher one; and this is what is meant by ascribing excess to penance.

Reply Obj. 3: As there is a kind of commutation in favors, when, to wit, a man gives thanks for a favor received, so also is there commutation in the matter of offenses, when, on account of an offense committed against another, a man is either punished against his will, which pertains to vindictive justice, or makes amends of his own accord, which belongs to penance, which regards the person of the sinner, just as vindictive justice regards the person of the judge. Therefore it is evident that both are comprised under commutative justice.

Reply Obj. 4: Although penance is directly a species of justice, yet, in a fashion, it comprises things pertaining to all the virtues; for inasmuch as there is a justice of man towards God, it must have a share in matter pertaining to the theological virtues, the object of which is God. Consequently penance comprises faith in Christ's Passion, whereby we are cleansed of our sins, hope for pardon, and hatred of vice, which pertains to charity. Inasmuch as it is a moral virtue, it has a share of prudence, which directs all the moral virtues: but from the very nature of justice, it has not only something belonging to justice, but also something belonging to temperance and fortitude, inasmuch as those things which cause pleasure, and which pertain to temperance, and those which cause terror, which fortitude moderates, are objects of commutative justice. Accordingly it belongs to justice both to abstain from pleasure, which belongs to temperance, and to bear with hardships, which belongs to fortitude.

FOURTH ARTICLE [III, Q. 85, Art. 4]

Whether the Will Is Properly the Subject of Penance?

Objection 1: It would seem that the subject of penance is not properly the will. For penance is a species of sorrow. But sorrow is in the concupiscible part, even as joy is. Therefore penance is in the concupiscible faculty.

Obj. 2: Further, penance is a kind of vengeance, as Augustine states in De Poenitentia [*De vera et falsa Poenitentia, the authorship of which is unknown]. But vengeance seems to regard the irascible faculty, since anger is the desire for vengeance. Therefore it seems that penance is in the irascible part.

Obj. 3: Further, the past is the proper object of the memory, according to the Philosopher (De Memoria i). Now penance regards the past, as stated above (A. 1, ad 2, ad 3). Therefore penance is subjected in the memory.

Obj. 4: Further, nothing acts where it is not. Now penance removes sin from all the powers of the soul. Therefore penance is in every power of the soul, and not only in the will.

*On the contrary,* Penance is a kind of sacrifice, according to Ps. 50:19: "A sacrifice to God is an afflicted spirit." But to offer a sacrifice is an act of the will, according to Ps. 53:8: "I will freely sacrifice to Thee." Therefore penance is in the will.

*I answer that,* We can speak of penance in two ways: first, in so far as it is a passion, and thus, since it is a kind of sorrow, it is in the concupiscible part as its subject; secondly, in so far as it is a virtue, and thus, as stated above (A. 3), it is a species of justice. Now justice, as stated in the Second Part (I-II, Q. 56, A. 6), is subjected in the rational appetite which is the will. Therefore it is evident that penance, in so far as it is a virtue, is subjected in the will, and its proper act is the purpose of amending what was committed against God.

Reply Obj. 1: This argument considers penance as a passion.

Reply Obj. 2: To desire vengeance on another, through passion, belongs to the irascible appetite, but to desire or take vengeance on oneself or on another, through reason, belongs to the will.

Reply Obj. 3: The memory is a power that apprehends the past. But penance belongs not to the apprehensive but to the appetitive power, which presupposes an act of the apprehension. Wherefore penance is not in the memory, but presupposes it.

Reply Obj. 4: The will, as stated above (I, Q. 82, A. 4; I-II, Q. 9, A. 1), moves all the other powers of the soul; so that it is not unreasonable for penance to be subjected in the will, and to produce an effect in each power of the soul.

FIFTH ARTICLE [III, Q. 85, Art. 5]

Whether Penance Originates from Fear?

Objection 1: It would seem that penance does not originate from fear. For penance originates in displeasure at sin. But this belongs to charity, as stated above (A. 3). Therefore penance originates from love rather than fear.

Obj. 2: Further, men are induced to do penance, through the expectation of the heavenly kingdom, according to Matt. 3:2 and Matt. 4:17: "Do penance, for the kingdom of heaven is at hand." Now the kingdom of heaven is the object of hope. Therefore penance results from hope rather than from fear.

Obj. 3: Further, fear is an internal act of man. But penance does not seem to arise in us through any work of man, but through the operation of God, according to Jer. 31:19: "After Thou didst convert me I did penance." Therefore penance does not result from fear.

*On the contrary,* It is written (Isa. 26:17): "As a woman with child, when she draweth near the time of her delivery, is in pain, and crieth out in her pangs, so ere we become," by penance, to wit; and according to another [*The Septuagint] version the text continues: "Through fear of Thee, O Lord, we have conceived, and been as it were in labor, and have brought forth the spirit of salvation," i.e. of salutary penance, as is clear from what precedes. Therefore penance results from fear.

*I answer that,* We may speak of penance in two ways: first, as to the habit, and then it is infused by God immediately without our operating as principal agents, but not without our co-operating dispositively by certain acts. Secondly, we may speak of penance, with regard to the acts whereby in penance we co-operate with God operating, the first principle [*Cf. I-II, Q. 113] of which acts is the operation of God in turning the heart, according to Lam. 5:21: "Convert us, O Lord, to Thee, and we shall be converted"; the second, an act of faith; the third, a movement of servile fear, whereby a man is withdrawn from sin through fear of punishment; the fourth, a movement of hope, whereby a man makes a purpose of amendment, in the hope of obtaining pardon; the fifth, a movement of charity, whereby sin is displeasing to man for its own sake and no longer for the sake of the punishment; the sixth, a movement of filial fear whereby a man, of his own accord, offers to make amends to God through fear of Him.

Accordingly it is evident that the act of penance results from servile fear as from the first movement of the appetite in this direction and from filial fear as from its immediate and proper principle.

Reply Obj. 1: Sin begins to displease a man, especially a sinner, on account of the punishments which servile fear regards, before it displeases him on account of its being an offense against God, or on account of its wickedness, which pertains to charity.

Reply Obj. 2: When the kingdom of heaven is said to be at hand, we are to understand that the king is on his way, not only to reward but also to punish. Wherefore John the Baptist said (Matt. 3:7): "Ye brood of vipers, who hath showed you to flee from the wrath to come?"

Reply Obj. 3: Even the movement of fear proceeds from God's act in turning the heart; wherefore it is written (Deut. 5:29): "Who shall give them to have such a mind, to fear Me?" And so the fact that penance results from fear does not hinder its resulting from the act of God in turning the heart.

SIXTH ARTICLE [III, Q. 85, Art. 6]

Whether Penance Is the First of the Virtues?

Objection 1: It would seem that penance is the first of the virtues. Because, on Matt. 3:2, "Do penance," etc., a gloss says: "The first virtue is to destroy the old man, and hate sin by means of penance."

Obj. 2: Further, withdrawal from one extreme seems to precede approach to the other. Now all the other virtues seem to regard approach to a term, because they all direct man to do good; whereas penance seems to direct him to withdraw from evil. Therefore it seems that penance precedes all the other virtues.

Obj. 3: Further, before penance, there is sin in the soul. Now no virtue is compatible with sin in the soul. Therefore no virtue precedes penance, which is itself the first of all and opens the door to the others by expelling sin.

*On the contrary,* Penance results from faith, hope, and charity, as already stated (AA. 2, 5). Therefore penance is not the first of the virtues.

*I answer that,* In speaking of the virtues, we do not consider the order of time with regard to the habits, because, since the virtues are connected with one another, as stated in the Second Part (I-II, Q. 65, A. 1), they all begin at the same time to be in the soul; but one is said to precede the other in the order of nature, which order depends on the order of their acts, in so far as the act of one virtue presupposes the act of another. Accordingly, then, one must say that, even in the order of time, certain praiseworthy acts can precede the act and the habit of penance, e.g. acts of dead faith and hope, and an act of servile fear; while the act and habit of charity are, in point of time, simultaneous with the act and habit of penance, and with the habits of the other virtues. For, as was stated in the Second Part (I-II, Q. 113, AA. 7, 8), in the justification of the ungodly, the movement of the free-will towards God, which is an act of faith quickened by charity, and the movement of the free-will towards sin, which is the act of penance, are simultaneous. Yet of these two acts, the former naturally precedes the latter, because the act of the virtue of penance is directed against sin, through love of God; where the first-mentioned act is the reason and cause of the second.

Consequently penance is not simply the first of the virtues, either in the order of time, or in the order of nature, because, in the order of nature, the theological virtues precede it simply. Nevertheless, in a certain respect, it is the first of the other virtues in the order of time, as regards its act, because this act is the first in the justification of the ungodly; whereas in the order of nature, the other virtues seem to precede, as that which is natural precedes that which is accidental; because the other virtues seem to be necessary for man's good, by reason of their very nature, whereas penance is only necessary if something, viz. sin, be presupposed, as stated above (Q. 55, A. 2), when we spoke of the relation of the sacrament of penance to the other sacraments aforesaid.

Reply Obj. 1: This gloss is to be taken as meaning that the act of penance is the first in point of time, in comparison with the acts of the other virtues.

Reply Obj. 2: In successive movements withdrawal from one extreme precedes approach to the other, in point of time; and also in the order of nature, if we consider the subject, i.e. the order of the material cause; but if we consider the order of the efficient and final causes, approach to the end is first, for it is this that the efficient cause intends first of all: and it is this order which we consider chiefly in the acts of the soul, as stated in Phys. ii.

Reply Obj. 3: Penance opens the door to the other virtues, because it expels sin by the virtues of faith, hope and charity, which precede it in the order of nature; yet it so opens the door to them that they enter at the same time as it: because, in the justification of the ungodly, at the same time as the free-will is moved towards God and against sin, the sin is pardoned and grace infused, and with grace all the virtues, as stated in the I-II, Q. 65, AA. 3, 5.

# QUESTION 86

OF THE EFFECT OF PENANCE, AS REGARDS THE PARDON OF MORTAL SIN (In Six Articles)

We must now consider the effect of Penance; and (1) as regards the pardon of mortal sins; (2) as regards the pardon of venial sins; (3) as regards the return of sins which have been pardoned; (4) as regards the recovery of the virtues.

Under the first head there are six points of inquiry:

(1) Whether all mortal sins are taken away by Penance?

(2) Whether they can be taken away without Penance?

(3) Whether one can be taken away without the other?

(4) Whether Penance takes away the guilt while the debt remains?

(5) Whether any remnants of sin remain?

(6) Whether the removal of sin is the effect of Penance as a virtue, or as a sacrament?

FIRST ARTICLE [III, Q. 86, Art. 1]

Whether All Sins Are Taken Away by Penance?

Objection 1: It would seem that not all sins are taken away by Penance. For the Apostle says (Heb. 12:17) that Esau "found no place of repentance, although with tears he had sought it," which a gloss explains as meaning that "he found no place of pardon and blessing through Penance": and it is related (2 Macc. 9:13) of Antiochus, that "this wicked man prayed to the Lord, of Whom he was not to obtain mercy." Therefore it does not seem that all sins are taken away by Penance.

Obj. 2: Further, Augustine says (De Serm. Dom. in Monte i) that "so great is the stain of that sin (namely, when a man, after coming to the knowledge of God through the grace of Christ, resists fraternal charity, and by the brands of envy combats grace itself) that he is unable to humble himself in prayer, although he is forced by his wicked conscience to acknowledge and confess his sin." Therefore not every sin can be taken away by Penance.

Obj. 3: Further, our Lord said (Matt. 12:32): "He that shall speak against the Holy Ghost, it shall not be forgiven him, neither in this world nor in the world to come." Therefore not every sin can be pardoned through Penance.

*On the contrary,* It is written (Ezech. 18:22): "I will not remember" any more "all his iniquities that he hath done."

*I answer that,* The fact that a sin cannot be taken away by Penance may happen in two ways: first, because of the impossibility of repenting of sin; secondly, because of Penance being unable to blot out a sin. In the first way the sins of the demons and of men who are lost, cannot be blotted out by Penance, because their will is confirmed in evil, so that sin cannot displease them as to its guilt, but only as to the punishment which they suffer, by reason of which they have a kind of repentance, which yet is fruitless, according to Wis. 5:3: "Repenting, and groaning for anguish of spirit." Consequently such Penance brings no hope of pardon, but only despair. Nevertheless no sin of a wayfarer can be such as that, because his will is flexible to good and evil. Wherefore to say that in this life there is any sin of which one cannot repent, is erroneous, first, because this would destroy free-will, secondly, because this would be derogatory to the power of grace, whereby the heart of any sinner whatsoever can be moved to repent, according to Prov. 21:1: "The heart of the king is in the hand of the Lord: whithersoever He will He shall turn it."

It is also erroneous to say that any sin cannot be pardoned through true Penance. First, because this is contrary to Divine mercy, of which it is written (Joel 2:13) that God is "gracious and merciful, patient, and rich in mercy, and ready to repent of the evil"; for, in a manner, God would be overcome by man, if man wished a sin to be blotted out, which God were unwilling to blot out. Secondly, because this would be derogatory to the power of Christ's Passion, through which Penance produces its effect, as do the other sacraments, since it is written (1 John 2:2): "He is the propitiation for our sins, and not for ours only, but also for those of the whole world."

Therefore we must say simply that, in this life, every sin can be blotted out by true Penance.

Reply Obj. 1: Esau did not truly repent. This is evident from his saying (Gen. 27:41): "The days will come of the mourning of my father, and I will kill my brother Jacob." Likewise neither did Antiochus repent truly; since he grieved for his past sin, not because he had offended God thereby, but on account of the sickness which he suffered in his body.

Reply Obj. 2: These words of Augustine should be understood thus: "So great is the stain of that sin, that man is unable to humble himself in prayer," i.e. it is not easy for him to do so; in which sense we say that a man cannot be healed, when it is difficult to heal him. Yet this is possible by the power of God's grace, which sometimes turns men even "into the depths of the sea" (Ps. 67:23).

Reply Obj. 3: The word or blasphemy spoken against the Holy Ghost is final impenitence, as Augustine states (De Verb. Dom. xi), which is altogether unpardonable, because after this life is ended, there is no pardon of sins. Or, if by the blasphemy against the Holy Ghost, we understand sin committed through certain malice, this means either that the blasphemy itself against the Holy Ghost is unpardonable, i.e. not easily pardonable, or that such a sin does not contain in itself any motive for pardon, or that for such a sin a man is punished both in this and in the next world, as we explained in the Second Part (III, Q. 14, A. 3).

SECOND ARTICLE [III, Q. 86, Art. 2]

Whether Sin Can Be Pardoned Without Penance?

Objection 1: It would seem that sin can be pardoned without Penance. For the power of God is no less with regard to adults than with regard to children. But He pardons the sins of children without Penance. Therefore He also pardons adults without penance.

Obj. 2: Further, God did not bind His power to the sacraments. But Penance is a sacrament. Therefore by God's power sin can be pardoned without Penance.

Obj. 3: Further, God's mercy is greater than man's. Now man sometimes forgives another for offending him, without his repenting: wherefore our Lord commanded us (Matt. 5:44): "Love your enemies, do good to them that hate you." Much more, therefore, does God pardon men for offending him, without their repenting.

*On the contrary,* The Lord said (Jer. 18:8): "If that nation . . . shall repent of their evil" which they have done, "I also will repent of the evil that I have thought to do them," so that, on the other hand, if man "do not penance," it seems that God will not pardon him his sin.

*I answer that,* It is impossible for a mortal actual sin to be pardoned without penance, if we speak of penance as a virtue. For, as sin is an offense against God, He pardons sin in the same way as he pardons an offense committed against Him. Now an offense is directly opposed to grace, since one man is said to be offended with another, because he excludes him from his grace. Now, as stated in the Second Part (I-II, Q.

110, A. 1), the difference between the grace of God and the grace of man, is that the latter does not cause, but presupposes true or apparent goodness in him who is graced, whereas the grace of God causes goodness in the man who is graced, because the good-will of God, which is denoted by the word "grace," is the cause of all created good. Hence it is possible for a man to pardon an offense, for which he is offended with someone, without any change in the latter's will; but it is impossible that God pardon a man for an offense, without his will being changed. Now the offense of mortal sin is due to man's will being turned away from God, through being turned to some mutable good. Consequently, for the pardon of this offense against God, it is necessary for man's will to be so changed as to turn to God and to renounce having turned to something else in the aforesaid manner, together with a purpose of amendment; all of which belongs to the nature of penance as a virtue. Therefore it is impossible for a sin to be pardoned anyone without penance as a virtue.

But the sacrament of Penance, as stated above (Q. 88, A. 3), is perfected by the priestly office of binding and loosing, without which God can forgive sins, even as Christ pardoned the adulterous woman, as related in John 8, and the woman that was a sinner, as related in Luke vii, whose sins, however, He did not forgive without the virtue of penance: for as Gregory states (Hom. xxxiii in Evang.), "He drew inwardly by grace," i.e. by penance, "her whom He received outwardly by His mercy."

Reply Obj. 1: In children there is none but original sin, which consists, not in an actual disorder of the will, but in a habitual disorder of nature, as explained in the Second Part (I-II, Q. 82, A. 1), and so in them the forgiveness of sin is accompanied by a habitual change resulting from the infusion of grace and virtues, but not by an actual change. On the other hand, in the case of an adult, in whom there are actual sins, which consist in an actual disorder of the will, there is no remission of sins, even in Baptism, without an actual change of the will, which is the effect of Penance.

Reply Obj. 2: This argument takes Penance as a sacrament.

Reply Obj. 3: God's mercy is more powerful than man's, in that it moves man's will to repent, which man's mercy cannot do.

THIRD ARTICLE [III, Q. 86, Art. 3]

Whether by Penance One Sin Can Be Pardoned Without Another?

Objection 1: It would seem that by Penance one sin can be pardoned without another. For it is written (Amos 4:7): "I caused it to rain upon one city, and caused it not to rain upon another city; one piece was rained upon: and the piece whereupon I rained not, withered." These words are expounded by Gregory, who says (Hom. x super Ezech.): "When a man who hates his neighbor, breaks himself of other vices, rain falls on one part of the city, leaving the other part withered, for there are some men who, when they prune some vices, become much more rooted in others." Therefore one sin can be forgiven by Penance, without another.

Obj. 2: Further, Ambrose in commenting on Ps. 118, "Blessed are the undefiled in the way," after expounding verse 136 ("My eyes have sent forth springs of water"), says that "the first consolation is that God is mindful to have mercy; and the second, that He punishes, for although faith be wanting, punishment makes satisfaction and raises us up." Therefore a man can be raised up from one sin, while the sin of unbelief remains.

Obj. 3: Further, when several things are not necessarily together, one can be removed without the other. Now it was stated in the Second Part (I-II, Q. 73, A. 1) that sins are not connected together, so that one sin can be without another. Therefore also one sin can be taken away by Penance without another being taken away.

Obj. 4: Further, sins are the debts, for which we pray for pardon when we say in the Lord's Prayer: "Forgive us our trespasses," etc. Now man sometimes forgives one debt without forgiving another. Therefore God also, by Penance, forgives one sin without another.

Obj. 5: Further, man's sins are forgiven him through the love of God, according to Jer. 31:3: "I have loved thee with an everlasting love, therefore have I drawn thee, taking pity on thee." Now there is nothing to hinder God from loving a man in one respect, while being offended with him in another, even as He loves the sinner as regards his nature, while hating him for his sin. Therefore it seems possible for God, by Penance, to pardon one sin without another.

*On the contrary,* Augustine says in De Poenitentia [*De vera et falsa Poenitentia, the authorship of which is unknown]: "There are many who repent having sinned, but not completely; for they except certain things which give them pleasure, forgetting that our Lord delivered from the devil the man who was both dumb and deaf, whereby He shows us that we are never healed unless it be from all sins."

*I answer that,* It is impossible for Penance to take one sin away without another. First because sin is taken away by grace removing the offense against God. Wherefore it was stated in the Second Part (I-II, Q. 109, A. 7; Q. 113, A. 2) that without grace no sin can be forgiven. Now every mortal sin is opposed to grace and excludes it. Therefore it is impossible for one sin to be pardoned without another. Secondly, because, as shown above (A. 2) mortal sin cannot be forgiven without true Penance, to which it belongs to renounce sin, by reason of its being against God, which is common to all mortal sins: and where the same reason applies, the result will be the same. Consequently a man cannot be truly penitent, if he repent of one sin and not of another. For if one particular sin were displeasing to him, because it is against the love of God above all things (which motive is necessary for true repentance), it follows that he would repent of all. Whence it follows that it is impossible for one sin to be pardoned through Penance, without another. Thirdly, because this would be contrary to the perfection of God's mercy, since His works are perfect, as stated in Deut. 32:4; wherefore whomsoever He pardons, He pardons altogether. Hence Augustine says [*De vera et falsa Poenitentia, the authorship of which is unknown], that "it is irreverent and heretical to expect half a pardon from Him Who is just and justice itself."

Reply Obj. 1: These words of Gregory do not refer to the forgiveness of the guilt, but to the cessation from act, because sometimes a man who has been wont to commit several kinds of sin, renounces one and not the other; which is indeed due to God's assistance, but does not reach to the pardon of the sin.

Reply Obj. 2: In this saying of Ambrose "faith" cannot denote the faith whereby we believe in Christ, because, as Augustine says on John 15:22, "If I had not come, and spoken to them, they would not have sin" (viz. unbelief): "for this is the sin which contains all others": but it stands for consciousness, because sometimes a man receives pardon for a sin of which he is not conscious, through the punishment which he bears patiently.

Reply Obj. 3: Although sins are not connected in so far as they turn towards a mutable good, yet they are connected in so far as they turn away from the immutable Good, which applies to all mortal sins in common; and it is thus that they have the character of an offense which needs to be removed by Penance.

Reply Obj. 4: Debt as regards external things, e.g. money, is not opposed to friendship through which the debt is pardoned; hence one debt can be condoned without another. On the other hand, the debt of sin is opposed to friendship, and so one sin or offense is not pardoned without another; for it would seem absurd for anyone to ask even a man to forgive him one offense and not another.

Reply Obj. 5: The love whereby God loves man's nature, does not ordain man to the good of glory from which man is excluded by any mortal sin; but the love of grace, whereby mortal sin is forgiven, ordains man to eternal life, according to Rom. 6:23: "The grace of God (is) life everlasting." Hence there is no comparison.

FOURTH ARTICLE [III, Q. 86, Art. 4]

Whether the Debt of Punishment Remains After the Guilt Has Been Forgiven Through Penance?

Objection 1: It would seem that no debt of punishment remains after the guilt has been forgiven through Penance. For when the cause is removed, the effect is removed. But the guilt is the cause of the debt of punishment: since a man deserves to be punished because he has been guilty of a sin. Therefore when the sin has been forgiven, no debt of punishment can remain.

Obj. 2: Further, according to the Apostle (Rom. 5) the gift of Christ is more effective than the sin of Adam. Now, by sinning, man incurs at the same time guilt and the debt of punishment. Much more therefore, by the gift of grace, is the guilt forgiven and at the same time the debt of punishment remitted.

Obj. 3: Further, the forgiveness of sins is effected in Penance through the power of Christ's Passion, according to Rom. 3:25: "Whom God hath proposed to be a propitiation, through faith in His Blood . . . for the remission of former sins." Now Christ's Passion made satisfaction sufficient for all sins, as stated above (QQ. 48, 49, 79, A. 5). Therefore after the guilt has been pardoned, no debt of punishment remains.

*On the contrary,* It is related (2 Kings 12:13) that when David penitent had said to Nathan: "I have sinned against the Lord," Nathan said to him: "The Lord also hath taken away thy sin, thou shalt not die. Nevertheless . . . the child that is born to thee shall surely die," which was to punish him for the sin he had committed, as stated in the same place. Therefore a debt of some punishment remains after the guilt has been forgiven.

*I answer that,* As stated in the Second Part (I-II, Q. 87, A. 4), in mortal sin there are two things, namely, a turning from the immutable Good, and an inordinate turning to mutable good. Accordingly, in so far as mortal sin turns away from the immutable Good, it induces a debt of eternal punishment, so that whosoever sins against the eternal Good should be punished eternally. Again, in so far as mortal sin turns inordinately to a mutable good, it gives rise to a debt of some punishment, because the disorder of guilt is not brought back to the order of justice, except by punishment: since it is just that he who has been too indulgent to his will, should suffer something against his will, for thus will equality be restored. Hence it is written (Apoc. 18:7): "As much as she hath glorified herself, and lived in delicacies, so much torment and sorrow give ye to her."

Since, however, the turning to mutable good is finite, sin does not, in this respect, induce a debt of eternal punishment. Wherefore, if man turns inordinately to a mutable good, without turning from God, as happens in venial sins, he incurs a debt, not of eternal but of temporal punishment. Consequently when guilt is pardoned through grace, the soul ceases to be turned away from God, through being united to God by grace: so that at the same time, the debt of punishment is taken away, albeit a debt of some temporal punishment may yet remain.

Reply Obj. 1: Mortal sin both turns away from God and turns to a created good. But, as stated in the Second Part (I-II, Q. 71, A. 6), the turning away from God is as its form while the turning to created good is as its matter. Now if the formal element of anything be removed, the species is taken away: thus, if you take away rational, you take away the human species. Consequently mortal sin is said to be pardoned from the very fact that, by means of grace, the aversion of the mind from God is taken away together with the debt of eternal punishment: and yet the material element remains, viz. the inordinate turning to a created good, for which a debt of temporal punishment is due.

Reply Obj. 2: As stated in the Second Part (I-II, Q. 109, AA. 7, 8; Q. 111, A. 2), it belongs to grace to operate in man by justifying him from sin, and to co-operate with man that his work may be rightly done. Consequently the forgiveness of guilt and of the debt of eternal punishment belongs to operating grace, while the remission of the debt of temporal punishment belongs to co-operating grace, in so far as man, by bearing punishment patiently with the help of Divine grace, is released also from the debt of temporal punishment. Consequently just as the effect of operating grace precedes the effect of co-operating grace, so too, the remission of guilt and of eternal punishment precedes the complete release from temporal punishment, since both are from grace, but the former, from grace alone, the latter, from grace and free-will.

Reply Obj. 3: Christ's Passion is of itself sufficient to remove all debt of punishment, not only eternal, but also temporal; and man is released from the debt of punishment according to the measure of his share in the power of Christ's Passion. Now in Baptism man shares the Power of Christ's Passion fully, since by water and the Spirit of Christ, he dies with Him to sin, and is born again in Him to a new life, so that, in Baptism, man receives the remission of all debt of punishment. In Penance, on the other hand, man shares in the power of Christ's Passion according to the measure of his own acts, which are the matter of Penance, as water is of Baptism, as stated above (Q. 84, AA. 1, 3). Wherefore the entire debt of punishment is not remitted at once after the first act of Penance, by which act the guilt is remitted, but only when all the acts of Penance have been completed.

FIFTH ARTICLE [III, Q. 86, Art. 5]

Whether the Remnants of Sin Are Removed When a Mortal Sin Is Forgiven?

Objection 1: It would seem that all the remnants of sin are removed when a mortal sin is forgiven. For Augustine says in De Poenitentia [*De vera et falsa Poenitentia, the authorship of which is unknown]: "Our Lord never healed anyone without delivering him wholly; for He wholly healed the man on the Sabbath, since He delivered his body from all disease, and his soul from all taint." Now the remnants of sin belong to the disease of sin. Therefore it does not seem possible for any remnants of sin to remain when the guilt has been pardoned.

Obj. 2: Further, according to Dionysius (Div. Nom. iv), "good is more efficacious than evil, since evil does not act save in virtue of some good." Now, by sinning, man incurs the taint of sin all at once. Much more, therefore, by repenting, is he delivered also from all remnants of sin.

Obj. 3: Further, God's work is more efficacious than man's. Now by the exercise of good human works the remnants of contrary sins are removed. Much more, therefore, are they taken away by the remission of guilt, which is a work of God.

*On the contrary,* We read (Mk. 8) that the blind man whom our Lord enlightened, was restored first of all to imperfect sight, wherefore he said (Mk. 8:24): "I see men, as it were trees, walking"; and afterwards he was restored perfectly, "so that he saw all things clearly." Now the enlightenment of the blind man signifies the delivery of the sinner. Therefore after the first remission of sin, whereby the sinner is restored to spiritual sight, there still remain in him some remnants of his past sin.

*I answer that,* Mortal sin, in so far as it turns inordinately to a mutable good, produces in the soul a certain disposition, or even a habit, if the acts be repeated frequently. Now it has been said above (A. 4) that the guilt of mortal sin is pardoned through grace removing the aversion of the mind from God. Nevertheless when that which is on the part of the aversion has been taken away by grace, that which is on the part of the inordinate turning to a mutable good can remain, since this may happen to be without the other, as stated above (A. 4). Consequently, there is no reason why, after the guilt has been forgiven, the dispositions caused by preceding acts should not remain, which are called the remnants of sin. Yet they remain weakened and diminished, so as not to domineer over man, and they are after the manner of dispositions rather than of habits, like the fomes which remains after Baptism.

Reply Obj. 1: God heals the whole man perfectly; but sometimes suddenly, as Peter's mother-in-law was restored at once to perfect health, so that "rising she ministered to them" (Luke 4:39), and sometimes by degrees, as we said above (Q. 44, A. 3, ad 2) about the blind man who was restored to sight (Matt. 8). And so too, He sometimes turns the heart of man with such power, that it receives at once perfect spiritual health, not only the guilt being pardoned, but all remnants of sin being removed as was the case with Magdalen (Luke 7); whereas at other times He sometimes first pardons the guilt by operating grace, and afterwards, by co-operating grace, removes the remnants of sin by degrees.

Reply Obj. 2: Sin too, sometimes induces at once a weak disposition, such as is the result of one act, and sometimes a stronger disposition, the result of many acts.

Reply Obj. 3: One human act does not remove all the remnants of sin, because, as stated in the Predicaments (Categor. viii) "a vicious man by doing good works will make but little progress so as to be any better, but if he continue in good practice, he will end in being good as to acquired virtue." But God's grace does this much more effectively, whether by one or by several acts.

SIXTH ARTICLE [III, Q. 86, Art. 6]

Whether the Forgiveness of Guilt Is an Effect of Penance?

Objection 1: It would seem that the forgiveness of guilt is not an effect of penance as a virtue. For penance is said to be a virtue, in so far as it is a principle of a human action. But human action does nothing towards the remission of guilt, since this is an effect of operating grace. Therefore the forgiveness of guilt is not an effect of penance as a virtue.

Obj. 2: Further, certain other virtues are more excellent than penance. But the forgiveness of sin is not said to be the effect of any other virtue. Neither, therefore, is it the effect of penance as a virtue.

Obj. 3: Further, there is no forgiveness of sin except through the power of Christ's Passion, according to Heb. 9:22: "Without shedding of blood there is no remission." Now Penance, as a sacrament, produces its effect through the power of Christ's Passion, even as the other sacraments do, as was shown above (Q. 62, AA. 4, 5). Therefore the forgiveness of sin is the effect of Penance, not as a virtue, but as a sacrament.

*On the contrary,* Properly speaking, the cause of a thing is that without which it cannot be, since every defect depends on its cause. Now forgiveness of sin can come from God without the sacrament of Penance, but not without the virtue of penance, as stated above (Q. 84, A. 5, ad 3; Q. 85, A. 2); so that, even before the sacraments of the New Law were instituted, God pardoned the sins of the penitent. Therefore the forgiveness of sin is chiefly the effect of penance as a virtue.

*I answer that,* Penance is a virtue in so far as it is a principle of certain human acts. Now the human acts, which are performed by the sinner, are the material element in the sacrament of Penance. Moreover every sacrament produces its effect, in virtue not only of its form, but also of its matter; because both these together make the one sacrament, as stated above (Q. 60, A. 6, ad 2, A. 7). Hence in Baptism forgiveness of sin is effected, in virtue not only of the form (but also of the matter, viz. water, albeit chiefly in virtue of the form) [*The words in brackets are omitted in the Leonine edition] from which the water receives its power--and, similarly, the forgiveness of sin is the effect of Penance, chiefly by the power of the keys, which is vested in the ministers, who furnish the formal part of the sacrament, as stated above (Q. 84, A. 3), and secondarily by the instrumentality of those acts of the penitent which pertain to the virtue of penance, but only in so far as such acts are, in some way, subordinate to the keys of the Church. Accordingly it is evident that the forgiveness of sin is the effect of penance as a virtue, but still more of Penance as a sacrament.

Reply Obj. 1: The effect of operating grace is the justification of the ungodly (as stated in the Second Part, I-II, Q. 113), wherein there is, as was there stated (AA. 1, 2, 3), not only infusion of grace and forgiveness of sin, but also a movement of the free-will towards God, which is an act of faith quickened by charity, and a movement of the free-will against sin, which is the act of penance. Yet these human acts are there as the effects of operating grace, and are produced at the same time as the forgiveness of sin. Consequently the forgiveness of sin does not take place without an act of the virtue of penance, although it is the effect of operating grace.

Reply Obj. 2: In the justification of the ungodly there is not only an act of penance, but also an act of faith, as stated above (ad 1: I-II, Q. 113, A. 4). Wherefore the forgiveness of sin is accounted the effect not only of the virtue of penance, but also, and that chiefly, of faith and charity.

Reply Obj. 3: The act of the virtue of penance is subordinate to Christ's Passion both by faith, and by its relation to the keys of the Church; and so, in both ways, it causes the forgiveness of sin, by the power of Christ's Passion.

To the argument advanced in the contrary sense we reply that the act of the virtue of penance is necessary for the forgiveness of sin, through being an inseparable effect of grace, whereby chiefly is sin pardoned, and which produces its effect in all the sacraments. Consequently it only follows that grace is a higher cause of the forgiveness of sin than the sacrament of Penance. Moreover, it must be observed that, under the Old Law and the law of nature, there was a sacrament of Penance after a fashion, as stated above (Q. 84, A. 7, ad 2).

## QUESTION 87

OF THE REMISSION OF VENIAL SIN (In Four Articles)

We must now consider the forgiveness of venial sins, under which head there are four points of inquiry:

(1) Whether venial sin can be forgiven without Penance?

(2) Whether it can be forgiven without the infusion of grace?

(3) Whether venial sins are forgiven by the sprinkling of holy water, a bishop's blessing, the beating of the breast, the Lord's Prayer, and the like?

(4) Whether a venial sin can be taken away without a mortal sin?

FIRST ARTICLE [III, Q. 87, Art. 1]

Whether Venial Sin Can Be Forgiven Without Penance?

Objection 1: It would seem that venial sin can be forgiven without penance. For, as stated above

(Q. 84, A. 10, ad 4), it is essential to true penance that man should not only sorrow for his past sins, but also that he should purpose to avoid them for the future. Now venial sins are forgiven without any such purpose, for it is certain that man cannot lead the present life without committing venial sins. Therefore venial sins can be forgiven without penance.

Obj. 2: Further, there is no penance without actual displeasure at one's sins. But venial sins can be taken away without any actual displeasure at them, as would be the case if a man were to be killed in his sleep, for Christ's sake, since he would go to heaven at once, which would not happen if his venial sins remained. Therefore venial sins can be forgiven without penance.

Obj. 3: Further, venial sins are contrary to the fervor of charity, as stated in the Second Part (II-II, Q. 24, A. 10). Now one contrary is removed by another. Therefore forgiveness of venial sins is caused by the fervor of charity, which may be without actual displeasure at venial sin.

*On the contrary,* Augustine says in De Poenitentia [*De vera et falsa Poenitentia, the authorship of which is unknown], that "there is a penance which is done for venial sins in the Church every day" which would be useless if venial sins could be forgiven without Penance.

*I answer that,* Forgiveness of sin, as stated above (Q. 86, A. 2), is effected by man being united to God from Whom sin separates him in some way. Now this separation is made complete by mortal sin, and incomplete by venial sin: because, by mortal sin, the mind through acting against charity is altogether turned away from God; whereas by venial sin man's affections are clogged, so that they are slow in tending towards God. Consequently both kinds of sin are taken away by penance, because by both of them man's will is disordered through turning inordinately to a created good; for just as mortal sin cannot be forgiven so long as the will is attached to sin, so neither can venial sin, because while the cause remains, the effect remains.

Yet a more perfect penance is requisite for the forgiveness of mortal sin, namely that man should detest actually the mortal sin which he committed, so far as lies in his power, that is to say, he should endeavor to remember each single mortal sin, in order to detest each one. But this is, not required for the forgiveness of venial sins; although it does not suffice to have habitual displeasure, which is included in the habit of charity or of penance as a virtue, since then venial sin would be incompatible with charity, which is evidently untrue. Consequently it is necessary to have a certain virtual displeasure, so that, for instance, a man's affections so tend to God and Divine things, that whatever might happen to him to hamper that tendency would be displeasing to him, and would grieve him, were he to commit it, even though he were not to think of it actually: and this is not sufficient for the remission of mortal sin, except as regards those sins which he fails to remember after a careful examination.

Reply Obj. 1: When man is in a state of grace, he can avoid all mortal sins, and each single one; and he can avoid each single venial sin, but not all, as was explained in the Second Part (I-II, Q. 74, A. 8, ad 2; Q. 109, A. 8). Consequently penance for mortal sins requires man to purpose abstaining from mortal sins, all and each; whereas penance for venial sins requires man to purpose abstaining from each, but not from all, because the weakness of this life does not allow of this. Nevertheless he needs to have the purpose of taking steps to commit fewer venial sins, else he would be in danger of falling back, if he gave up the desire of going forward, or of removing the obstacles to spiritual progress, such as venial sins are.

Reply Obj. 2: Death for Christ's sake, as stated above (Q. 66, A. 11), obtains the power of Baptism, wherefore it washes away all sin, both venial and mortal, unless it find the will attached to sin.

Reply Obj. 3: The fervor of charity implies virtual displeasure at venial sins, as stated above (Q. 79, A. 4).

SECOND ARTICLE [III, Q. 87, Art. 2]

Whether Infusion of Grace Is Necessary for the Remission of Venial Sins?

Objection 1: It would seem that infusion of grace is necessary for the remission of venial sins. Because an effect is not produced without its proper cause. Now the proper cause of the remission of sins is grace; for man's sins are not forgiven through his own merits; wherefore it is written (Eph. 2:4, 5): "God, Who is rich in mercy, for His exceeding charity, wherewith He loved us, even when we were dead in sins, hath quickened us together in Christ, by Whose grace you are saved." Therefore venial sins are not forgiven without infusion of grace.

Obj. 2: Further, venial sins are not forgiven without Penance. Now grace is infused, in Penance as in the other sacraments of the New Law. Therefore venial sins are not forgiven without infusion of grace.

Obj. 3: Further, venial sin produces a stain on the soul. Now a stain is not removed save by grace which is the spiritual beauty of the soul. Therefore it seems that venial sins are not forgiven without infusion of grace.

*On the contrary,* The advent of venial sin neither destroys nor diminishes grace, as stated in the Second Part (II-II, Q. 24, A. 10). Therefore, in like manner, an infusion of grace is not necessary in order to remove venial sin.

*I answer that,* Each thing is removed by its contrary. But venial sin is not contrary to habitual grace or charity, but hampers its act, through man being too much attached to a created good, albeit not in opposition to God, as stated in the Second Part (I-II, Q. 88, A. 1; II-II, Q. 24, A. 10). Therefore, in order that venial sin be removed, it is not necessary that habitual grace be infused, but a movement of grace or charity suffices for its forgiveness.

Nevertheless, since in those who have the use of free-will (in whom alone can there be venial sins), there can be no infusion of grace without an actual movement of the free-will towards God and against sin, consequently whenever grace is infused anew, venial sins are forgiven.

Reply Obj. 1: Even the forgiveness of venial sins is an effect of grace, in virtue of the act which grace produces anew, but not through any habit infused anew into the soul.

Reply Obj. 2: Venial sin is never forgiven without some act, explicit or implicit, of the virtue of penance, as stated above (A. 1): it can, however, be forgiven without the sacrament of Penance, which is formally perfected by the priestly absolution, as stated above (Q. 87, A. 2). Hence it does not follow that infusion of grace is required for the forgiveness of venial sin, for although this infusion takes place in every sacrament, it does not occur in every act of virtue.

Reply Obj. 3: Just as there are two kinds of bodily stain, one consisting in the privation of something required for beauty, e.g. the right color or the due proportion of members, and another by the introduction of some hindrance to beauty, e.g. mud or dust; so too, a stain is put on the soul, in one way, by the privation of the beauty of grace through mortal sin, in another, by the inordinate inclination of the affections to some temporal thing, and this is the result of venial sin. Consequently, an infusion of grace is necessary for the removal of mortal sin, but in order to remove venial sin, it is necessary to have a movement proceeding from grace, removing the inordinate attachment to the temporal thing.

THIRD ARTICLE [III, Q. 87, Art. 3]

Whether Venial Sins Are Removed by the Sprinkling of Holy Water and the Like?

Objection 1: It would seem that venial sins are not removed by the sprinkling of holy water, a bishop's blessing, and the like. For venial sins are not forgiven without Penance, as stated above (A. 1). But Penance suffices by itself for the remission of venial sins. Therefore the above have nothing to do with the remission of venial sins.

Obj. 2: Further, each of the above bears the same relation to one venial sin as to all. If therefore, by means of one of them, some venial sin is remitted, it follows that in like manner all are remitted, so that by beating his breast once, or by being sprinkled once with holy water, a man would be delivered from all his venial sins, which seems unreasonable.

Obj. 3: Further, venial sins occasion a debt of some punishment, albeit temporal; for it is written (1 Cor. 3:12, 15) of him that builds up "wood, hay, stubble" that "he shall be saved, yet so as by fire." Now the above things whereby venial sins are said to be taken away, contain either no punishment at all, or very little. Therefore they do not suffice for the full remission of venial sins.

*On the contrary,* Augustine says in De Poenitentia [*Hom. 30 inter 1; Ep. cclxv] that "for our slight sins we strike our breasts, and say: Forgive us our trespasses," and so it seems that striking one's breast, and the Lord's Prayer cause the remission of venial sins: and the same seems to apply to the other things.

*I answer that,* As stated above (A. 2), no infusion of fresh grace is required for the forgiveness of a venial sin, but it is enough to have an act proceeding from grace, in detestation of that venial sin, either explicit or at least implicit, as when one is moved fervently to God. Hence, for three reasons, certain things cause the remission of venial sins: first, because they imply the infusion of grace, since the infusion of grace removes venial sins, as stated above (A. 2); and so, by the Eucharist, Extreme Unction, and by all the sacraments of the New Law without exception, wherein grace is conferred, venial sins are remitted. Secondly, because they imply a movement of detestation for sin, and in this way the general confession [*i.e. the recital of the Confiteor or of an act of contrition], the beating of one's breast, and the Lord's Prayer conduce to the remission of venial sins, for we ask in the Lord's Prayer: "Forgive us our trespasses." Thirdly, because they include a movement of reverence for God and Divine things; and in this way a bishop's blessing, the sprinkling of holy water, any sacramental anointing, a prayer said in a dedicated church, and anything else of the kind, conduce to the remission of venial sins.

Reply Obj. 1: All these things cause the remission of venial sins, in so far as they incline the soul to the movement of penance, viz., the implicit or explicit detestation of one's sins.

Reply Obj. 2: All these things, so far as they are concerned, conduce to the remission of all venial sins: but the remission may be hindered as regards certain venial sins, to which the mind is still actually attached, even as insincerity sometimes impedes the effect of Baptism.

Reply Obj. 3: By the above things, venial sins are indeed taken away as regards the guilt, both because those things are a kind of satisfaction, and through the virtue of charity whose movement is aroused by such things.

Yet it does not always happen that, by means of each one, the whole guilt of punishment is taken away, because, in that case, whoever was entirely free from mortal sin, would go straight to heaven if sprinkled with holy water: but the debt of punishment is remitted by means of the above, according to the movement of fervor towards God, which fervor is aroused by such things, sometimes more, sometimes less.

FOURTH ARTICLE [III, Q. 87, Art. 4]

Whether Venial Sin Can Be Taken Away Without Mortal Sin?

Objection 1: It would seem that venial sin can

be taken away without mortal sin. For, on John 8:7: "He that is without sin among you, let him first cast a stone at her," a gloss says that "all those men were in a state of mortal sin: for venial offenses were forgiven them through the legal ceremonies." Therefore venial sin can be taken away without mortal sin.

Obj. 2: Further, no infusion of grace is required for the remission of venial sin, but it is required for the forgiveness of mortal sin. Therefore venial sin can be taken away without mortal sin.

Obj. 3: Further, a venial sin differs from a mortal sin more than from another venial sin. But one venial sin can be pardoned without another, as stated above (A. 3, ad 2; Q. 87, A. 3). Therefore a venial sin can be taken away without a mortal sin.

*On the contrary,* It is written (Matt. 5:26): "Amen I say to thee, thou shalt not go out from thence," viz., from the prison, into which a man is cast for mortal sin, "till thou repay the last farthing," by which venial sin is denoted. Therefore a venial sin is not forgiven without mortal sin.

*I answer that,* As stated above (Q. 87, A. 3), there is no remission of any sin whatever except by the power of grace, because, as the Apostle declares (Rom. 4:8), it is owing to God's grace that He does not impute sin to a man, which a gloss on that passage expounds as referring to venial sin. Now he that is in a state of mortal sin is without the grace of God. Therefore no venial sin is forgiven him.

Reply Obj. 1: Venial offenses, in the passage quoted, denote the irregularities or uncleannesses which men contracted in accordance with the Law.

Reply Obj. 2: Although no new infusion of habitual grace is requisite for the remission of venial sin, yet it is necessary to exercise some act of grace, which cannot be in one who is a subject of mortal sin.

Reply Obj. 3: Venial sin does not preclude every act of grace whereby all venial sins can be removed; whereas mortal sin excludes altogether the habit of grace, without which no sin, either mortal or venial, is remitted. Hence the comparison fails.

## QUESTION 88

OF THE RETURN OF SINS WHICH HAVE BEEN TAKEN AWAY BY PENANCE (In Four Articles)

We must now consider the return of sins which have been taken away by Penance: under which head there are four points of inquiry:

(1) Whether sins which have been taken away by Penance return simply through a subsequent sin?

(2) Whether more specially as regards certain sins they return, in a way, on account of ingratitude?

(3) Whether the debt of punishment remains the same for sins thus returned?

(4) Whether this ingratitude, on account of which sins return, is a special sin?

FIRST ARTICLE [III, Q. 88, Art. 1]

Whether Sins Once Forgiven Return Through a Subsequent Sin?

Objection 1: It would seem that sins once forgiven return through a subsequent sin. For Augustine says (De Bapt. contra Donat. i, 12): "Our Lord teaches most explicitly in the Gospel that sins which have been forgiven return, when fraternal charity ceases, in the example of the servant from whom his master exacted the payment of the debt already forgiven, because he had refused to forgive the debt of his fellow-servant." Now fraternal charity is destroyed through each mortal sin. Therefore sins already taken away through Penance, return through each subsequent mortal sin.

Obj. 2: Further, on Luke 11:24, "I will return into my house, whence I came out," Bede says: "This verse should make us tremble, we should not endeavor to explain it away lest through carelessness we give place to the sin which we thought to have been taken away, and become its slave once more." Now this would not be so unless it returned. Therefore a sin returns after once being taken away by Penance.

Obj. 3: Further, the Lord said (Ezech. 18:24): "If the just man turn himself away from his justice, and do iniquity . . . all his justices which he hath done, shall not be remembered." Now among the other "justices" which he had done, is also his previous penance, since it was said above (Q. 85, A. 3) that penance is a part of justice. Therefore when one who has done penance, sins, his previous penance, whereby he received forgiveness of his sins, is not imputed to him. Therefore his sins return.

Obj. 4: Further, past sins are covered by grace, as the Apostle declares (Rom. 4:7) where he quotes Ps. 31:1: "Blessed are they whose iniquities are forgiven, and whose sins are covered." But a subsequent mortal sin takes away grace. Therefore the sins committed previously, become uncovered: and so, seemingly, they return.

*On the contrary,* The Apostle says (Rom. 11:29): "The gifts and the calling of God are without repentance." Now the penitent's sins are taken away by a gift of God. Therefore the sins which have been taken away do not return through a subsequent sin, as though God repented His gift of forgiveness.

Moreover, Augustine says (Lib. Resp. Prosperi i [*Cf. Prosper, Responsiones ad Capitula Gallorum ii]): "When he that turns away from Christ, comes to the end of this life a stranger to grace, whither does he go, except to perdition? Yet he does not fall back into that which had been forgiven, nor will he be condemned for original sin."

*I answer that,* As stated above (Q. 86, A. 4), mortal sin contains two things, aversion from God and adherence to a created good. Now, in mortal sin, whatever attaches to the aversion, is, considered in itself, common to all mortal sins, since man turns away from God by every mortal sin, so that, in consequence, the stain resulting from the privation of grace, and the debt of everlasting punishment are common to all mortal sins. This is what is meant by what is written (James 2:10): "Whosoever . . . shall offend in one point, is become guilty of all." On the other hand, as regards their adherence they are different from, and sometimes contrary to one another. Hence it is evident, that on the part of the adherence, a subsequent mortal sin does not cause the return of mortal sins previously dispelled, else it would follow that by a sin of wastefulness a man would be brought back to the habit or disposition of avarice previously dispelled, so that one contrary would be the cause of another, which is impossible. But if in mortal sins we consider that which attaches to the aversion absolutely, then a subsequent mortal sin [causes the return of that which was comprised in the mortal sins before they were pardoned, in so far as the subsequent mortal sin] [*The words in brackets are omitted in the Leonine edition.] deprives man of grace, and makes him deserving of everlasting punishment, just as he was before. Nevertheless, since the aversion of mortal sin is [in a way, caused by the adherence, those things which attach to the aversion are*] diversified somewhat in relation to various adherences, as it were to various causes, so that there will be a different aversion, a different stain, a different debt of punishment, according to the different acts of mortal sin from which they arise; hence the question is moved whether the stain and the debt of eternal punishment, as caused by acts of sins previously pardoned, return through a subsequent mortal sin.

Accordingly some have maintained that they return simply even in this way. But this is impossible, because what God has done cannot be undone by the work of man. Now the pardon of the previous sins was a work of Divine mercy, so that it cannot be undone by man's subsequent sin, according to Rom. 3:3: "Shall their unbelief make the faith of God without effect?"

Wherefore others who maintained the possibility of sins returning, said that God pardons the sins of a penitent who will afterwards sin again, not according to His foreknowledge, but only according to His present justice: since He foresees that He will punish such a man eternally for his sins, and yet, by His grace, He makes him righteous for the present. But this cannot stand: because if a cause be placed absolutely, its effect is placed absolutely; so that if the remission of sins were effected by grace and the sacraments of grace, not absolutely but under some condition dependent on some future event, it would follow that grace and the sacraments of grace are not the sufficient causes of the remission of sins, which is erroneous, as being derogatory to God's grace.

Consequently it is in no way possible for the stain of past sins and the debt of punishment incurred thereby, to return, as caused by those acts. Yet it may happen that a subsequent sinful act virtually contains the debt of punishment due to the previous sin, in so far as when a man sins a second time, for this very reason he seems to sin more grievously than before, as stated in Rom. 2:5: "According to thy hardness and impenitent heart, thou treasurest up to thyself wrath against the day of wrath," from the mere fact, namely, that God's goodness, which waits for us to repent, is despised. And so much the more is God's goodness despised, if the first sin is committed a second time after having been forgiven, as it is a greater favor for the sin to be forgiven than for the sinner to be endured.

Accordingly the sin which follows repentance brings back, in a sense, the debt of punishment due to the sins previously forgiven, not as caused by those sins already forgiven but as caused by this last sin being committed, on account of its being aggravated in view of those previous sins. This means that those sins return, not simply, but in a restricted sense, viz., in so far as they are virtually contained in the subsequent sin.

Reply Obj. 1: This saying of Augustine seems to refer to the return of sins as to the debt of eternal punishment considered in itself, namely, that he who sins after doing penance incurs a debt of eternal punishment, just as before, but not altogether for the same reason. Wherefore Augustine, after saying (Lib. Resp. Prosperi i [*Cf. Prosper, Responsiones ad Capitula Gallorum ii]) that "he does not fall back into that which was forgiven, nor will he be condemned for original sin," adds: "Nevertheless, for these last sins he will be condemned to the same death, which he deserved to suffer for the former," because he incurs the punishment of eternal death which he deserved for his previous sins.

Reply Obj. 2: By these words Bede means that the guilt already forgiven enslaves man, not by the return of his former debt of punishment, but by the repetition of his act.

Reply Obj. 3: The effect of a subsequent sin is that the former "justices" are not remembered, in so far as they were deserving of eternal life, but not in so far as they were a hindrance to sin. Consequently if a man sins mortally after making restitution, he does not become guilty as though he had not paid back what he owed; and much less is penance previously done forgotten as to the pardon of the guilt, since this is the work of God rather than of man.

Reply Obj. 4: Grace removes the stain and the debt of eternal punishment simply; but it covers the past sinful acts, lest, on their account, God deprive man of grace, and judge him deserving of eternal punishment; and what grace has once done, endures for ever.

SECOND ARTICLE [III, Q. 88, Art. 2]

Whether Sins That Have Been Forgiven, Return

Through Ingratitude Which Is Shown Especially in Four Kinds of Sin?

Objection 1: It would seem that sins do not return through ingratitude, which is shown especially in four kinds of sin, viz., hatred of one's neighbor, apostasy from faith, contempt of confession and regret for past repentance, and which have been expressed in the following verse:

"Fratres odit, apostata fit, spernitque, fateri, Poenituisse piget, pristina culpa redit."

For the more grievous the sin committed against God after one has received the grace of pardon, the greater the ingratitude. But there are sins more grievous than these, such as blasphemy against God, and the sin against the Holy Ghost. Therefore it seems that sins already pardoned do not return through ingratitude as manifested in these sins, any more than as shown in other sins.

Obj. 2: Further, Rabanus says: "God delivered the wicked servant to the torturers, until he should pay the whole debt, because a man will be deemed punishable not only for the sins he commits after Baptism, but also for original sin which was taken away when he was baptized." Now venial sins are reckoned among our debts, since we pray in their regard: "Forgive us our trespasses ( debita )." Therefore they too return through ingratitude; and, in like manner seemingly, sins already pardoned return through venial sins, and not only through those sins mentioned above.

Obj. 3: Further, ingratitude is all the greater, according as one sins after receiving a greater favor. Now innocence whereby one avoids sin is a Divine favor, for Augustine says (Confess. ii): "Whatever sins I have avoided committing, I owe it to Thy grace." Now innocence is a greater gift, than even the forgiveness of all sins. Therefore the first sin committed after innocence is no less an ingratitude to God, than a sin committed after repentance, so that seemingly ingratitude in respect of the aforesaid sins is not the chief cause of sins returning.

*On the contrary,* Gregory says (Moral. xviii [*Cf. Dial. iv]): "It is evident from the words of the Gospel that if we do not forgive from our hearts the offenses committed against us, we become once more accountable for what we rejoiced in as forgiven through Penance": so that ingratitude implied in the hatred of one's brother is a special cause of the return of sins already forgiven: and the same seems to apply to the others.

*I answer that,* As stated above (A. 1), sins pardoned through Penance are said to return, in so far as their debt of punishment, by reason of ingratitude, is virtually contained in the subsequent sin. Now one may be guilty of ingratitude in two ways: first by doing something against the favor received, and, in this way, man is ungrateful to God in every mortal sin whereby he offends God Who forgave his sins, so that by every subsequent mortal sin, the sins previously pardoned return, on account of the ingratitude. Secondly, one is guilty of ingratitude, by doing something not only against the favor itself, but also against the form of the favor received. If this form be considered on the part of the benefactor, it is the remission of something due to him; wherefore he who does not forgive his brother when he asks pardon, and persists in his hatred, acts against this form. If, however, this form be taken in regard to the penitent who receives this favor, we find on his part a twofold movement of the free-will. The first is the movement of the free-will towards God, and is an act of faith quickened by charity; and against this a man acts by apostatizing from the faith. The second is a movement of the free-will against sin, and is the act of penance. This act consists first, as we have stated above (Q. 85, AA. 2, 5) in man's detestation of his past sins; and against this a man acts when he regrets having done penance. Secondly, the act of penance consists in the penitent purposing to subject himself to the keys of the Church by confession, according to Ps. 31:5: "I said: I will confess against myself my injustice to the Lord: and Thou hast forgiven the wickedness of my sin": and against this a man acts when he scorns to confess as he had purposed to do.

Accordingly it is said that the ingratitude of sinners is a special cause of the return of sins previously forgiven.

Reply Obj. 1: This is not said of these sins as though they were more grievous than others, but because they are more directly opposed to the favor of the forgiveness of sin.

Reply Obj. 2: Even venial sins and original sin return in the way explained above, just as mortal sins do, in so far as the favor conferred by God in forgiving those sins is despised. A man does not, however, incur ingratitude by committing a venial sin, because by sinning venially man does not act against God, but apart from Him, wherefore venial sins nowise cause the return of sins already forgiven.

Reply Obj. 3: A favor can be weighed in two ways. First by the quantity of the favor itself, and in this way innocence is a greater favor from God than penance, which is called the second plank after shipwreck (cf. Q. 84, A. 6). Secondly, a favor may be weighed with regard to the recipient, who is less worthy, wherefore a greater favor is bestowed on him, so that he is the more ungrateful if he scorns it. In this way the favor of the pardon of sins is greater when bestowed on one who is altogether unworthy, so that the ingratitude which follows is all the greater.

THIRD ARTICLE [III, Q. 88, Art. 3]

Whether the Debt of Punishment That Arises Through Ingratitude in Respect of a Subsequent Sin Is As Great As That of the Sins Previously Pardoned?

Objection 1: It would seem that the debt of punishment arising through ingratitude in respect of a subsequent sin is as great as that of the sins previously pardoned. Because the greatness of the favor of the pardon of sins is according to the greatness of the sin pardoned, and so too, in consequence, is the greatness of the ingratitude whereby this favor is scorned. But the greatness of the consequent debt of punishment is in accord with the greatness of the ingratitude. Therefore the debt of punishment arising through ingratitude in respect of a subsequent sin is as great as the debt of punishment due for all the previous sins.

Obj. 2: Further, it is a greater sin to offend God than to offend man. But a slave who is freed by his master returns to the same state of slavery from which he was freed, or even to a worse state. Much more therefore he that sins against God after being freed from sin, returns to the debt of as great a punishment as he had incurred before.

Obj. 3: Further, it is written (Matt. 18:34) that "his lord being angry, delivered him" (whose sins returned to him on account of his ingratitude) "to the torturers, until he paid all the debt." But this would not be so unless the debt of punishment incurred through ingratitude were as great as that incurred through all previous sins. Therefore an equal debt of punishment returns through ingratitude.

*On the contrary,* It is written (Deut. 25:2): "According to the measure of the sin shall the measure also of the stripes be," whence it is evident that a great debt of punishment does not arise from a slight sin. But sometimes a subsequent mortal sin is much less grievous than any one of those previously pardoned. Therefore the debt of punishment incurred through subsequent sins is not equal to that of sins previously forgiven.

*I answer that,* Some have maintained that the debt of punishment incurred through ingratitude in respect of a subsequent sin is equal to that of the sins previously pardoned, in addition to the debt proper to this subsequent sin. But there is no need for this, because, as stated above (A. 1), the debt of punishment incurred by previous sins does not return on account of a subsequent sin, as resulting from the acts of the subsequent sin. Wherefore the amount of the debt that returns must be according to the gravity of the subsequent sin.

It is possible, however, for the gravity of the subsequent sin to equal the gravity of all previous sins. But it need not always be so, whether we speak of the gravity which a sin has from its species (since the subsequent sin may be one of simple fornication, while the previous sins were adulteries, murders, or sacrileges); or of the gravity which it incurs through the ingratitude connected with it. For it is not necessary that the measure of ingratitude should be exactly equal to the measure of the favor received, which latter is measured according to the greatness of the sins previously pardoned. Because it may happen that in respect of the same favor, one man is very ungrateful, either on account of the intensity of his scorn for the favor received, or on account of the gravity of the offense committed against the benefactor, while another man is slightly ungrateful, either because his scorn is less intense, or because his offense against the benefactor is less grave. But the measure of ingratitude is proportionately equal to the measure of the favor received: for supposing an equal contempt of the favor, or an equal offense against the benefactor, the ingratitude will be so much the greater, as the favor received is greater.

Hence it is evident that the debt of punishment incurred by a subsequent sin need not always be equal to that of previous sins; but it must be in proportion thereto, so that the more numerous or the greater the sins previously pardoned, the greater must be the debt of punishment incurred by any subsequent mortal sin whatever.

Reply Obj. 1: The favor of the pardon of sins takes its absolute quantity from the quantity of the sins previously pardoned: but the sin of ingratitude does not take its absolute quantity from the measure of the favor bestowed, but from the measure of the contempt or of the offense, as stated above: and so the objection does not prove.

Reply Obj. 2: A slave who has been given his freedom is not brought back to his previous state of slavery for any kind of ingratitude, but only when this is grave.

Reply Obj. 3: He whose forgiven sins return to him on account of subsequent ingratitude, incurs the debt for all, in so far as the measure of his previous sins is contained proportionally in his subsequent ingratitude, but not absolutely, as stated above.

FOURTH ARTICLE [III, Q. 88, Art. 4]

Whether the Ingratitude Whereby a Subsequent Sin Causes the Return of Previous Sins, Is a Special Sin?

Objection 1: It would seem that the ingratitude, whereby a subsequent sin causes the return of sins previously forgiven, is a special sin. For the giving of thanks belongs to counterpassion which is a necessary condition of justice, as the Philosopher shows (Ethic. v, 5). But justice is a special virtue. Therefore this ingratitude is a special sin.

Obj. 2: Further, Tully says (De Inv. Rhet. ii) that thanksgiving is a special virtue. But ingratitude is opposed to thanksgiving. Therefore ingratitude is a special sin.

Obj. 3: Further, a special effect proceeds from a special cause. Now ingratitude has a special effect, viz. the return, after a fashion, of sins already forgiven. Therefore ingratitude is a special sin.

*On the contrary,* That which is a sequel to every sin is not a special sin. Now by any mortal sin whatever, a man becomes ungrateful to God, as evidenced from what has been said (A. 1). Therefore ingratitude is not a special sin.

*I answer that,* The ingratitude of the sinner is sometimes a special sin; and sometimes it is not, but a circumstance arising from all mortal sins in common committed against God. For a sin takes its species according to the sinner's intention, wherefore the Philosopher says (Ethic. v, 2) that "he who commits adultery in order to steal is a thief rather than an adulterer."

If, therefore, a sinner commits a sin in contempt of God and of the favor received from Him, that sin is drawn to the species of ingratitude, and in this way a sinner's ingratitude is a special sin. If, however, a man, while intending to commit a sin, e.g. murder or adultery, is not withheld from it on account of its implying contempt of God, his ingratitude will not be a special sin, but will be drawn to the species of the other sin, as a circumstance thereof. And, as Augustine observes (De Nat. et Grat. xxix), not every sin implies contempt of God in His commandments. Therefore it is evident that the sinner's ingratitude is sometimes a special sin, sometimes not.

This suffices for the Replies to the Objections: for the first (three) objections prove that ingratitude is in itself a special sin; while the last objection proves that ingratitude, as included in every sin, is not a special sin.

# QUESTION 89

OF THE RECOVERY OF VIRTUE BY MEANS OF PENANCE (In Six Articles)

We must now consider the recovery of virtues by means of Penance, under which head there are six points of inquiry:

(1) Whether virtues are restored through Penance?

(2) Whether they are restored in equal measure?

(3) Whether equal dignity is restored to the penitent?

(4) Whether works of virtue are deadened by subsequent sin?

(5) Whether works deadened by sin revive through Penance?

(6) Whether dead works, i.e. works that are done without charity, are quickened by Penance?

FIRST ARTICLE [III, Q. 89, Art. 1]

Whether the Virtues Are Restored Through Penance?

Objection 1: It would seem that the virtues are not restored through penance. Because lost virtue cannot be restored by penance, unless penance be the cause of virtue. But, since penance is itself a virtue, it cannot be the cause of all the virtues, and all the more, since some virtues naturally precede penance, viz., faith, hope, and charity, as stated above (Q. 85, A. 6). Therefore the virtues are not restored through penance.

Obj. 2: Further, Penance consists in certain acts of the penitent. But the gratuitous virtues are not caused through any act of ours: for Augustine says (De Lib. Arb. ii, 18: In Ps. 118) that "God forms the virtues in us without us." Therefore it seems that the virtues are not restored through Penance.

Obj. 3: Further, he that has virtue performs works of virtue with ease and pleasure: wherefore the Philosopher says (Ethic. i, 8) that "a man is not just if he does not rejoice in just deeds." Now many penitents find difficulty in performing deeds of virtue. Therefore the virtues are not restored through Penance.

*On the contrary,* We read (Luke 15:22) that the father commanded his penitent son to be clothed in "the first robe," which, according to Ambrose (Expos. in Luc. vii), is the "mantle of wisdom," from which all the virtues flow together, according to Wis. 8:7: "She teacheth temperance, and prudence, and justice, and fortitude, which are such things as men can have nothing more profitable in life." Therefore all the virtues are restored through Penance.

*I answer that,* Sins are pardoned through Penance, as stated above (Q. 86, A. 1). But there can be no remission of sins except through the infusion of grace. Wherefore it follows that grace is infused into man through Penance. Now all the gratuitous virtues flow from grace, even as all the powers result from the essence of the soul; as stated in the Second Part (I-II, Q. 110, A. 4, ad 1). Therefore all the virtues are restored through Penance.

Reply Obj. 1: Penance restores the virtues in the same way as it causes grace, as stated above (Q. 86, A. 1). Now it is a cause of grace, in so far as it is a sacrament, because, in so far as it is a virtue, it is rather an effect of grace. Consequently it does not follow that penance, as a virtue, needs to be the cause of all the other virtues, but that the habit of penance together with the habits of the other virtues is caused through the sacrament of Penance.

Reply Obj. 2: In the sacrament of Penance human acts stand as matter, while the formal power of this sacrament is derived from the power of the keys. Consequently the power of the keys causes grace and virtue effectively indeed, but instrumentally; and the first act of the penitent, viz., contrition, stands as ultimate disposition to the reception of grace, while the subsequent acts of Penance proceed from the grace and virtues which are already there.

Reply Obj. 3: As stated above (Q. 86, A. 5), sometimes after the first act of Penance, which is contrition, certain remnants of sin remain, viz. dispositions caused by previous acts, the result being that the penitent finds difficulty in doing deeds of virtue. Nevertheless, so far as the inclination itself of charity and of the other virtues is concerned, the penitent performs works of virtue with pleasure and ease, even as a virtuous man may accidentally find it hard to do an act of virtue, on account of sleepiness or some indisposition of the body.

SECOND ARTICLE [III, Q. 89, Art. 2]

Whether, After Penance, Man Rises Again to Equal Virtue?

Objection 1: It would seem that, after Penance, man rises again to equal virtue. For the Apostle says (Rom. 8:28): "To them that love God all things work together unto good," whereupon a gloss of Augustine says that "this is so true that, if any such man goes astray and wanders from the path, God makes even this conduce to his good." But this would not be true if he rose again to lesser virtue. Therefore it seems that a penitent never rises again to lesser virtue.

Obj. 2: Further, Ambrose says [*Cf. Hypognosticon iii, an anonymous work falsely ascribed to St. Augustine] that "Penance is a very good thing, for it restores every defect to a state of perfection." But this would not be true unless virtues were recovered in equal measure. Therefore equal virtue is always recovered through Penance.

Obj. 3: Further, on Gen. 1:5: "There was evening and morning, one day," a gloss says: "The evening light is that from which we fall; the morning light is that to which we rise again." Now the morning light is greater than the evening light. Therefore a man rises to greater grace or charity than that which he had before; which is confirmed by the Apostle's words (Rom. 5:20): "Where sin abounded, grace did more abound."

*On the contrary,* Charity whether proficient or perfect is greater than incipient charity. But sometimes a man falls from proficient charity, and rises again to incipient charity. Therefore man always rises again to less virtue.

*I answer that,* As stated above (Q. 86, A. 6, ad 3; Q. 89, A. 1, ad 2), the movement of the free-will, in the justification of the ungodly, is the ultimate disposition to grace; so that in the same instant there is infusion of grace together with the aforesaid movement of the free-will, as stated in the Second Part (I-II, Q. 113, AA. 5, 7), which movement includes an act of penance, as stated above (Q. 86, A. 2). But it is evident that forms which admit of being more or less, become intense or remiss, according to the different dispositions of the subject, as stated in the Second Part (I-II, Q. 52, AA. 1, 2; Q. 66, A. 1). Hence it is that, in Penance, according to the degree of intensity or remissness in the movement of the free-will, the penitent receives greater or lesser grace. Now the intensity of the penitent's movement may be proportionate sometimes to a greater grace than that from which man fell by sinning, sometimes to an equal grace, sometimes to a lesser. Wherefore the penitent sometimes arises to a greater grace than that which he had before, sometimes to an equal, sometimes to a lesser grace: and the same applies to the virtues, which flow from grace.

Reply Obj. 1: The very fact of falling away from the love of God by sin, does not work unto the good of all those who love God, which is evident in the case of those who fall and never rise again, or who rise and fall yet again; but only to the good of "such as according to His purpose are called to be saints," viz. the predestined, who, however often they may fall, yet rise again finally. Consequently good comes of their falling, not that they always rise again to greater grace, but that they rise to more abiding grace, not indeed on the part of grace itself, because the greater the grace, the more abiding it is, but on the part of man, who, the more careful and humble he is, abides the more steadfastly in grace. Hence the same gloss adds that "their fall conduces to their good, because they rise more humble and more enlightened."

Reply Obj. 2: Penance, considered in itself, has the power to bring all defects back to perfection, and even to advance man to a higher state; but this is sometimes hindered on the part of man, whose movement towards God and in detestation of sin is too remiss, just as in Baptism adults receive a greater or a lesser grace, according to the various ways in which they prepare themselves.

Reply Obj. 3: This comparison of the two graces to the evening and morning light is made on account of a likeness of order, since the darkness of night follows after the evening light, and the light of day after the light of morning, but not on account of a likeness of greater or lesser quantity. Again, this saying of the Apostle refers to the grace of Christ, which abounds more than any number of man's sins. Nor is it true of all, that the more their sins abound, the more abundant grace they receive, if we measure habitual grace by the quantity. Grace is, however, more abundant, as regards the very notion of grace, because to him who sins more a more gratuitous favor is vouchsafed by his pardon; although sometimes those whose sins abound, abound also in sorrow, so that they receive a more abundant habit of grace and virtue, as was the case with Magdalen.

To the argument advanced in the contrary sense it must be replied that in one and the same man proficient grace is greater than incipient grace, but this is not necessarily the case in different men, for one begins with a greater grace than another has in the state of proficiency: thus Gregory says (Dial. ii, 1): "Let all, both now and hereafter, acknowledge how perfectly the boy Benedict turned to the life of grace from the very beginning."

THIRD ARTICLE [III, Q. 89, Art. 3]

Whether, by Penance, Man Is Restored to His Former Dignity?

Objection 1: It would seem that man is not restored by Penance to his former dignity: because a gloss on Amos 5:2, "The virgin of Israel is cast down," observes: "It is not said that she cannot rise up, but that the virgin of Israel shall not rise; because the sheep that has once strayed, although the shepherd bring it back on his shoulder, has not the same glory as if it had never strayed." Therefore man does not, through Penance, recover his former dignity.

Obj. 2: Further, Jerome says: "Whoever fail to preserve the dignity of the sacred order, must be content with saving their souls; for it is a difficult thing to return to their former degree." Again, Pope Innocent I says (Ep. vi ad Agapit.) that "the canons framed at the council of Nicaea exclude penitents from even the lowest orders of clerics." Therefore man does not, through Penance, recover his former dignity.

Obj. 3: Further, before sinning a man can advance to a higher sacred order. But this is not permitted to a penitent after his sin, for it is written (Ezech. 44:10, 13): "The Levites that went away . . . from Me . . . shall never [Vulg.: 'not'] come near to Me, to do the office of priest": and as laid down in the Decretals (Dist. 1, ch. 52), and taken from the council of Lerida: "If those who serve at the Holy Altar fall suddenly into some deplorable weakness of the flesh, and by God's mercy do proper penance, let them return to their duties, yet so as not to receive further promotion." Therefore Penance does not restore man to his former dignity.

*On the contrary,* As we read in the same Distinction, Gregory writing to Secundinus (Regist. vii) says: "We consider that when a man has made proper satisfaction, he may return to his honorable position": and moreover we read in the acts of the council of Agde: "Contumacious clerics, so far as their position allows, should be corrected by their bishops, so that when Penance has reformed them, they may recover their degree and dignity."

*I answer that,* By sin, man loses a twofold dignity, one in respect of God, the other in respect of the Church. In respect of God he again loses a twofold dignity. One is his principal dignity, whereby he was counted among the children of God, and this he recovers by Penance, which is signified (Luke 15) in the prodigal son, for when he repented, his father commanded that the first garment should be restored to him, together with a ring and shoes. The other is his secondary dignity, viz. innocence, of which, as we read in the same chapter, the elder son boasted saying (Luke 15:29): "Behold, for so many years do I serve thee, and I have never transgressed thy commandments": and this dignity the penitent cannot recover. Nevertheless he recovers something greater sometimes; because as Gregory says (Hom. de centum Ovibus, 34 in Evang.), "those who acknowledge themselves to have strayed away from God, make up for their past losses, by subsequent gains: so that there is more joy in heaven on their account, even as in battle, the commanding officer thinks more of the soldier who, after running away, returns and bravely attacks the foe, than of one who has never turned his back, but has done nothing brave."

By sin man loses his ecclesiastical dignity, because thereby he becomes unworthy of those things which appertain to the exercise of the ecclesiastical dignity. This he is debarred from recovering: first, because he fails to repent; wherefore Isidore wrote to the bishop Masso, and as we read in the Distinction quoted above (Obj. 3): "The canons order those to be restored to their former degree, who by repentance have made satisfaction for their sins, or have made worthy confession of them. On the other hand, those who do not mend their corrupt and wicked ways are neither allowed to exercise their order, nor received to the grace of communion."

Secondly, because he does penance negligently, wherefore it is written in the same Distinction (Obj. 3): "We can be sure that those who show no signs of humble compunction, or of earnest prayer, who avoid fasting or study, would exercise their former duties with great negligence if they were restored to them."

Thirdly, if he has committed a sin to which an irregularity is attached; wherefore it is said in the same Distinction (Obj. 3), quoting the council of Pope Martin [*Martin, bishop of Braga]: "If a man marry a widow or the relict of another, he must not be admitted to the ranks of the clergy: and if he has succeeded in creeping in, he must be turned out. In like manner, if anyone after Baptism be guilty of homicide, whether by deed, or by command, or by counsel, or in self-defense." But this is in consequence not of sin, but of irregularity.

Fourthly, on account of scandal, wherefore it is said in the same Distinction (Obj. 3): "Those who have been publicly convicted or caught in the act of perjury, robbery, fornication, and of such like crimes, according to the prescription of the sacred canons must be deprived of the exercise of their respective orders, because it is a scandal to God's people that such persons should be placed over them. But those who commit such sins occultly and confess them secretly to a priest, may be retained in the exercise of their respective orders, with the assurance of God's merciful forgiveness, provided they be careful to expiate their sins by fasts and alms, vigils and holy deeds." The same is expressed (Extra, De Qual. Ordinand.): "If the aforesaid crimes are not proved by a judicial process, or in some other way made notorious, those who are guilty of them must not be hindered, after they have done penance, from exercising the orders they have received, or from receiving further orders, except in cases of homicide."

Reply Obj. 1: The same is to be said of the recovery of virginity as of the recovery of innocence which belongs to man's secondary dignity in the sight of God.

Reply Obj. 2: In these words Jerome does not say that it is impossible, but that it is difficult, for man to recover his former dignity after having sinned, because this is allowed to none but those who repent perfectly, as stated above. To those canonical statutes, which seem to forbid this, Augustine replies in his letter to Boniface (Ep. clxxxv): "If the law of the Church forbids anyone, after doing penance for a crime, to become a cleric, or to return to his clerical duties, or to retain them the intention was not to deprive him of the hope of pardon, but to preserve the rigor of discipline; else we should have to deny the keys given to the Church, of which it was said: 'Whatsoever you shall loose on earth shall be loosed in heaven.'" And further on he adds: "For holy David did penance for his deadly crimes, and yet he retained his dignity; and Blessed Peter by shedding most bitter tears did indeed repent him of having denied his Lord, and yet he remained an apostle. Nevertheless we must not deem the care of later teachers excessive, who without endangering a man's salvation, exacted more from his humility, having, in my opinion, found by experience, that some assumed a pretended repentance through hankering after honors and power."

Reply Obj. 3: This statute is to be understood as applying to those who do public penance, for these cannot be promoted to a higher order. For Peter, after his denial, was made shepherd of Christ's sheep, as appears from John 21:21, where Chrysostom comments as follows: "After his denial and repentance Peter gives proof of greater confidence in Christ: for whereas, at the supper, he durst not ask Him, but deputed John to ask in his stead, afterwards he was placed at the head of his brethren, and not only did not depute another to ask for him, what concerned him, but henceforth asks the Master instead of John."

FOURTH ARTICLE [III, Q. 89, Art. 4]

Whether Virtuous Deeds Done in Charity Can Be Deadened?

Objection 1: It would seem that virtuous deeds done in charity cannot be deadened. For that which is not cannot be changed. But to be deadened is to be changed from life to death. Since therefore virtuous deeds, after being done, are no more, it seems that they cannot afterwards be deadened.

Obj. 2: Further, by virtuous deeds done in charity, man merits eternal life. But to take away the reward from one who has merited it is an injustice, which cannot be ascribed to God. Therefore it is not possible for virtuous deeds done in charity to be deadened by a subsequent sin.

Obj. 3: Further, the strong is not corrupted by the weak. Now works of charity are stronger than any sins, because, as it is written (Prov. 10:12), "charity covereth all sins." Therefore it seems that deeds done in charity cannot be deadened by a subsequent mortal sin.

*On the contrary,* It is written (Ezech. 18:24): "If the just man turn himself away from his justice . . . all his justices which he hath done shall not be remembered."

*I answer that,* A living thing, by dying, ceases to have vital operations: for which reason, by a kind of metaphor, a thing is said to be deadened when it is hindered from producing its proper effect or operation.

Now the effect of virtuous works, which are done in charity, is to bring man to eternal life; and this is hindered by a subsequent mortal sin, inasmuch as it takes away grace. Wherefore deeds done in charity are said to be deadened by a subsequent mortal sin.

Reply Obj. 1: Just as sinful deeds pass as to the act but remain as to guilt, so deeds done in charity, after passing, as to the act, remain as to merit, in so far as they are acceptable to God. It is in this respect that they are deadened, inasmuch as man is hindered from receiving his reward.

Reply Obj. 2: There is no injustice in withdrawing the reward from him who has deserved it, if he has made himself unworthy by his subsequent fault, since at times a man justly forfeits through his own fault, even that which he has already received.

Reply Obj. 3: It is not on account of the strength of sinful deeds that deeds, previously done in charity, are deadened, but on account of the freedom of the will which can be turned away from good to evil.

FIFTH ARTICLE [III, Q. 86, Art. 5]

Whether Deeds Deadened by Sin, Are Revived by Penance?

Objection 1: It would seem that deeds deadened by sin are not revived by Penance. Because just as past sins are remitted by subsequent Penance, so are deeds previously done in charity, deadened by subsequent sin. But sins remitted by Penance do not return, as stated above (Q. 88, AA. 1, 2). Therefore it seems that neither are dead deeds revived by charity.

Obj. 2: Further, deeds are said to be deadened by comparison with animals who die, as stated above (A. 4). But a dead animal cannot be revived. Therefore neither can dead works be revived by Penance.

Obj. 3: Further, deeds done in charity are deserving of glory according to the quantity of grace or charity. But sometimes man arises through Penance to lesser grace or charity. Therefore he does not receive glory according to the merit of his previous works; so that it seems that deeds deadened by sin are not revived.

*On the contrary,* on Joel 2:25, "I will restore to you the years, which the locust . . . hath eaten," a gloss says: "I will not suffer to perish the fruit which you lost when your soul was disturbed." But this fruit is the merit of good works which was lost through sin. Therefore meritorious deeds done before are revived by Penance.

*I answer that,* Some have said that meritorious works deadened by subsequent sin are not revived by the ensuing Penance, because they deemed such works to have passed away, so that they could not be revived. But that is no reason why they should not be revived: because they are conducive to eternal life (wherein their life consists) not only as actually existing, but also after they cease to exist actually, and as abiding in the Divine acceptance. Now, they abide thus, so far as they are concerned, even after they have been deadened by sin, because those works, according as they were done, will ever be acceptable to God and give joy to the saints, according to Apoc. 3:11: "Hold fast that which thou hast, that no man take thy crown." That they fail in their efficacy to bring the man, who did them, to eternal life, is due to the impediment of the supervening sin whereby he is become unworthy of eternal life. But this impediment is removed by Penance, inasmuch as sins are taken away thereby. Hence it follows that deeds previously deadened, recover, through Penance, their efficacy in bringing him, who did them, to eternal life, and, in other words, they are revived. It is therefore evident that deadened works are revived by Penance.

Reply Obj. 1: The very works themselves of sin are removed by Penance, so that, by God's mercy, no further stain or debt of punishment is incurred on their account: on the other hand, works done in charity are not removed by God, since they abide in His acceptance, but they are hindered on the part of the man who does them; wherefore if this hindrance, on the part of the man who does those works, be removed, God on His side fulfills what those works deserved.

Reply Obj. 2: Deeds done in charity are not in themselves deadened, as explained above, but only with regard to a supervening impediment on the part of the man who does them. On the other hand, an animal dies in itself, through being deprived of the principle of life: so that the comparison fails.

Reply Obj. 3: He who, through Penance, arises to lesser charity, will receive the essential reward according to the degree of charity in which he is found. Yet he will have greater joy for the works he had done in his former charity, than for those which he did in his subsequent charity: and this joy belongs to the accidental reward.

SIXTH ARTICLE [III, Q. 89, Art. 6]

Whether the Effect of Subsequent Penance Is to Quicken Even Dead Works?

Objection 1: It would seem that the effect of subsequent Penance is to quicken even dead works, those, namely, that were not done in charity. For it seems more difficult to bring to life that which has been deadened, since this is never done naturally, than to quicken that which never had life, since certain living things are engendered naturally from things without life. Now deadened works are revived by Penance, as stated above (A. 5). Much more, therefore, are dead works revived.

Obj. 2: Further, if the cause be removed, the effect is removed. But the cause of the lack of life in works generically good done without charity, was the lack of charity and grace, which lack is removed by Penance. Therefore dead works are quickened by charity.

Obj. 3: Further, Jerome in commenting on Agg. i, 6: "You have sowed much," says: "If at any time you find a sinner, among his many evil deeds, doing that which is right, God is not so unjust as to forget the few good deeds on account of his many evil deeds." Now this seems to be the case chiefly when past evil deeds are removed by Penance. Therefore it seems that through Penance, God rewards the former deeds done in the state of sin, which implies that they are quickened.

*On the contrary,* The Apostle says (1 Cor. 13:3): "If I should distribute all my goods to feed the poor, and if I should deliver my body to be burned, and have not charity, it profiteth me nothing." But this would not be true, if, at least by subsequent Penance, they were quickened. Therefore Penance does not quicken works which before were dead.

*I answer that,* A work is said to be dead in two ways: first, effectively, because, to wit, it is a cause of death, in which sense sinful works are said to be dead, according to Heb. 9:14: "The blood of Christ . . . shall cleanse our conscience from dead works." These dead works are not quickened but removed by Penance, according to Heb. 6:1: "Not laying again the foundation of Penance from dead works." Secondly, works are said to be dead privatively, because, to wit, they lack spiritual life, which is founded on charity, whereby the soul is united to God, the result being that it is quickened as the body by the soul: in which sense too, faith, if it lack charity, is said to be dead, according to James 2:20: "Faith without works is dead." In this way also, all works that are generically good, are said to be dead, if they be done without charity, inasmuch as they fail to proceed from the principle of life; even as we might call the sound of a harp, a dead voice. Accordingly, the difference of life and death in works is in relation to the principle from which they proceed. But works cannot proceed a second time from a principle, because they are transitory, and the same identical deed cannot be resumed. Therefore it is impossible for dead works to be quickened by Penance.

Reply Obj. 1: In the physical order things whether dead or deadened lack the principle of life. But works are said to be deadened, not in relation to the principle whence they proceeded, but in relation to an extrinsic impediment; while they are said to be dead in relation to a principle. Consequently there is no comparison.

Reply Obj. 2: Works generically good done without charity are said to be dead on account of the lack of grace and charity, as principles. Now the subsequent Penance does not supply that want, so as to make them proceed from such a principle. Hence the argument does not prove.

Reply Obj. 3: God remembers the good deeds a man does when in a state of sin, not by rewarding them in eternal life, which is due only to living works, i.e. those done from charity, but by a temporal reward: thus Gregory declares (Hom. de Divite et Lazaro, 41 in Evang.) that "unless that rich man had done some good deed, and had received his reward in this world, Abraham would certainly not have said to him: 'Thou didst receive good things in thy lifetime.'" Or again, this may mean that he will be judged less severely: wherefore Augustine says (De Patientia xxvi): "We cannot say that it would be better for the schismatic that by denying Christ he should suffer none of those things which he suffered by confessing Him; but we must believe that he will be judged with less severity, than if by denying Christ, he had suffered none of those things. Thus the words of the Apostle, 'If I should deliver my body to be burned and have not charity, it profiteth me nothing,' refer to the obtaining of the kingdom of heaven, and do not exclude the possibility of being sentenced with less severity at the last judgment."

# QUESTION 90

OF THE PARTS OF PENANCE, IN GENERAL (In Four Articles)

We must now consider the parts of Penance: (1) in general; (2) each one in particular.

Under the first head there are four points of inquiry:

(1) Whether Penance has any parts?
(2) Of the number of its parts;
(3) What kind of parts are they?
(4) Of its division into subjective parts.

FIRST ARTICLE [III, Q. 90, Art. 1]

Whether Penance Should Be Assigned Any Parts?

Objection 1: It would seem that parts should not be assigned to Penance. For it is the Divine power that works our salvation most secretly in the sacraments. Now the Divine power is one and simple. Therefore Penance, being a sacrament, should have no parts assigned to it.

Obj. 2: Further, Penance is both a virtue and a sacrament. Now no parts are assigned to it as a virtue, since virtue is a habit, which is a simple quality of the mind. In like manner, it seems that parts should not be assigned to Penance as a sacrament, because no parts are assigned to Baptism and the other sacraments. Therefore no parts at all should be assigned to Penance.

Obj. 3: Further, the matter of Penance is sin, as stated above (Q. 84, A. 2). But no parts are assigned to sin. Neither, therefore, should parts be assigned to Penance.

*On the contrary,* The parts of a thing are those out of which the whole is composed. Now the perfection of Penance is composed of several things, viz. contrition, confession, and satisfaction. Therefore Penance has parts.

*I answer that,* The parts of a thing are those into which the whole is divided materially, for the parts of a thing are to the whole, what matter is to the form; wherefore the parts are reckoned as a kind of material cause, and the whole as a kind of formal cause (Phys. ii). Accordingly wherever, on the part of matter, we find a kind of plurality, there we shall find a reason for assigning parts.

Now it has been stated above (Q. 84, AA. 2, 3), that, in the sacrament of Penance, human actions stand as matter: and so, since several actions are requisite for the perfection of Penance, viz., contrition, confession, and satisfaction, as we shall show further on (A. 2), it follows that the sacrament of Penance has parts.

Reply Obj. 1: Every sacrament is something simple by reason of the Divine power, which operates therein: but the Divine power is so great that it can operate both through one and through many, and by reason of these many, parts may be assigned to a particular sacrament.

Reply Obj. 2: Parts are not assigned to penance as a virtue: because the human acts of which there are several in penance, are related to the habit of virtue, not as its parts, but as its effects. It follows, therefore, that parts are assigned to Penance as a sacrament, to which the human acts are related as matter: whereas in the other sacraments the matter does not consist of human acts, but of some one external thing, either simple, as water or oil, or compound, as chrism, and so parts are not assigned to the other sacraments.

Reply Obj. 3: Sins are the remote matter of Penance, inasmuch, to wit, as they are the matter or object of the human acts, which are the proper matter of Penance as a sacrament.

SECOND ARTICLE [III, Q. 90, Art. 2]

Whether Contrition, Confession, and Satisfaction Are Fittingly Assigned As Parts of Penance?

Objection 1: It would seem that contrition, confession, and satisfaction are not fittingly assigned as parts of Penance. For contrition is in the heart, and so belongs to interior penance; while confession consists of words, and satisfaction in deeds; so that the two latter belong to interior penance. Now interior penance is not a sacrament, but only exterior penance which is perceptible by the senses. Therefore these three parts are not fittingly assigned to the sacrament of Penance.

Obj. 2: Further, grace is conferred in the sacraments of the New Law, as stated above (Q. 62, AA. 1, 3). But no grace is conferred in satisfaction. Therefore satisfaction is not part of a sacrament.

Obj. 3: Further, the fruit of a thing is not the same as its part. But satisfaction is a fruit of penance, according to Luke 3:8: "Bring forth . . . fruits worthy of penance." Therefore it is not a part of Penance.

Obj. 4: Further, Penance is ordained against sin. But sin can be completed merely in the thought by consent, as stated in the Second Part (I-II, Q. 72, A. 7): therefore Penance can also. Therefore confession in word and satisfaction in deed should not be reckoned as parts of Penance.

*On the contrary,* It seems that yet more parts should be assigned to Penance. For not only is the body assigned as a part of man, as being the matter, but also the soul, which is his form. But the aforesaid three, being the acts of the penitent, stand as matter, while the priestly absolution stands as form. Therefore the priestly absolution should be assigned as a fourth part of Penance.

*I answer that,* A part is twofold, essential and quantitative. The essential parts are naturally the form and the matter, and logically the genus and the difference. In this way, each sacrament is divided into matter and form as its essential parts. Hence it has been said above (Q. 60, AA. 5, 6) that sacraments consist of things and words. But since quantity is on the part of matter, quantitative parts are parts of matter: and, in this way, as stated above (A. 1), parts are assigned specially to the sacrament of Penance, as regards the acts of the penitent, which are the matter of this sacrament.

Now it has been said above (Q. 85, A. 3, ad 3) that an offense is atoned otherwise in Penance than in vindictive justice. Because, in vindictive justice the atonement is made according to the judge's decision, and not according to the discretion of the offender or of the person offended; whereas, in Penance, the offense is atoned according to the will of the sinner, and the judgment of God against Whom the sin was committed, because in the latter case we seek not only the restoration of the equality of justice, as in vindictive justice, but also and still more the reconciliation of friendship, which is accomplished by the offender making atonement according to the will of the person offended. Accordingly the first requisite on the part of the penitent is the will to atone, and this is done by contrition; the second is that he submit to the judgment of the priest standing in God's place, and this is done in confession; and the third is that he atone according to the decision of God's minister, and this is done in satisfaction: and so contrition, confession, and satisfaction are assigned as parts of Penance.

Reply Obj. 1: Contrition, as to its essence, is in the heart, and belongs to interior penance; yet, virtually, it belongs to exterior penance, inasmuch as it implies the purpose of confessing and making satisfaction.

Reply Obj. 2: Satisfaction confers grace, in so far as it is in man's purpose, and it increases grace, according as it is accomplished, just as Baptism does in adults, as stated above (Q. 68, A. 2; Q. 69, A. 8).

Reply Obj. 3: Satisfaction is a part of Penance as a sacrament, and a fruit of penance as a virtue.

Reply Obj. 4: More things are required for good, "which proceeds from a cause that is entire," than for evil, "which results from each single defect," as Dionysius states (Div. Nom. iv). And thus, although sin is completed in the consent of the heart, yet the perfection of Penance requires contrition of the heart, together with confession in word and satisfaction in deed.

The Reply to the Fifth Objection is clear from what has been said.

THIRD ARTICLE [III, Q. 90, Art. 3]

Whether These Three Are Integral Parts of Penance?

Objection 1: It would seem that these three are not integral parts of Penance. For, as stated above (Q. 84, A. 3), Penance is ordained against sin. But sins of thought, word, and deed are the subjective and not integral parts of sin, because sin is predicated of each one of them. Therefore in Penance also, contrition in thought, confession in word, and satisfaction in deed are not integral parts.

Obj. 2: Further, no integral part includes within itself another that is condivided with it. But contrition includes both confession and satisfaction in the purpose of amendment. Therefore they are not integral parts.

Obj. 3: Further, a whole is composed of its integral parts, taken at the same time and equally, just as a line is made up of its parts. But such is not the case here. Therefore these are not integral parts of Penance.

*On the contrary,* Integral parts are those by which the perfection of the whole is integrated. But the perfection of Penance is integrated by these three. Therefore they are integral parts of Penance.

*I answer that,* Some have said that these three are subjective parts of Penance. But this is impossible, because the entire power of the whole is present in each subjective part at the same time and equally, just as the entire power of an animal, as such, is assured to each animal species, all of which species divide the animal genus at the same time and equally: which does not apply to the point in question. Wherefore others have said that these are potential parts: yet neither can this be true, since the whole is present, as to the entire essence, in each potential part, just as the entire essence of the soul is present in each of its powers: which does not apply to the case in point. Therefore it follows that these three are integral parts of Penance, the nature of which is that the whole is not present in each of the parts, either as to its entire power, or as to its entire essence, but that it is present to all of them together at the same time.

Reply Obj. 1: Sin forasmuch as it is an evil, can be completed in one single point, as stated above (A. 2, ad 4); and so the sin which is completed in thought alone, is a special kind of sin. Another species is the sin that is completed in thought and word: and yet a third species is the sin that is completed in thought, word, and deed; and the quasi-integral parts of this last sin, are that which is in thought, that which is in word, and that which is in deed. Wherefore these three are the integral parts of Penance, which is completed in them.

Reply Obj. 2: One integral part can include the whole, though not as to its essence: because the foundation, in a way, contains virtually the whole building. In this way contrition includes virtually the whole of Penance.

Reply Obj. 3: All integral parts have a certain relation of order to one another: but some are only related as to position, whether in sequence as the parts of an army, or by contact, as the parts of a heap, or by being fitted together, as the parts of a house, or by continuation, as the parts of a line; while some are related, in addition, as to power, as the parts of an animal, the first of which is the heart, the others in a certain order being dependent on one another: and thirdly some are related in the order of time: as the parts of time and movement. Accordingly the parts of Penance are related to one another in the order of power and time, since they are actions, but not in the order of position, since they do not occupy a place.

FOURTH ARTICLE [III, Q. 90, Art. 4]

Whether Penance Is Fittingly Divided into Penance Before Baptism, Penance for Mortal Sins, and Penance for Venial Sins?

Objection 1: It would seem that penance is unfittingly divided into penance before Baptism, penance for mortal, and penance for venial sins. For Penance is the second plank after shipwreck, as stated above (Q. 84, A. 6), while Baptism is the first. Therefore that which precedes Baptism should not be called a species of penance.

Obj. 2: Further, that which can destroy the greater, can destroy the lesser. Now mortal sin is greater than venial; and penance which regards mortal sins regards also venial sins. Therefore they should not be considered as different species of penance.

Obj. 3: Further, just as after Baptism man commits venial and mortal sins, so does he before Baptism. If therefore penance for venial sins is distinct from penance for mortal sins after Baptism, in like manner they should be distinguished before Baptism. Therefore penance is not fittingly divided into these species.

*On the contrary,* Augustine says in De Poenitentia [*Cf. Hom. 30 inter 1] that these three are species of Penance.

*I answer that,* This is a division of penance as a virtue. Now it must be observed that every virtue acts in accordance with the time being, as also in keeping with other due circumstances, wherefore the virtue of penance has its act at this time, according to the requirements of the New Law.

Now it belongs to penance to detest one's past sins, and to purpose, at the same time, to change one's life for the better, which is the end, so to speak, of penance. And since moral matters take their species from the end, as stated in the Second Part (I-II, Q. 1, A. 3; Q. 18, AA. 4, 6), it is reasonable to distinguish various species of penance, according to the various changes intended by the penitent.

Accordingly there is a threefold change intended by the penitent. The first is by regeneration unto a new life, and this belongs to that penance which precedes Baptism. The second is by reforming one's past life after it has been already destroyed, and this belongs to penance for mortal sins committed after Baptism. The third is by changing to a more perfect operation of life, and this belongs to penance for venial sins, which are remitted through a fervent act of charity, as stated above (Q. 87, AA. 2, 3).

Reply Obj. 1: The penance which precedes Baptism is not a sacrament, but an act of virtue disposing one to that sacrament.

Reply Obj. 2: The penance which washes away mortal sins, washes away venial sins also, but the converse does not hold. Wherefore these two species of penance are related to one another as perfect and imperfect.

Reply Obj. 3: Before Baptism there are no venial sins without mortal sins. And since a venial sin cannot be remitted without mortal sin, as stated above (Q. 87, A. 4), before Baptism, penance for mortal sins is not distinct from penance for venial sins.

---

The End